❷返信メールの表現

1. 早速返事をいただきありがとう.
2. 8月7日のメールをありがとう.
3. 新住所を知らせてくれてありがとう.
4. お便りをいただくうれしいです.
5. すぐに返事をしなくてごめんなさい.
6. それはいいですねぇ. よろこんでパーティー[会]に出席します.
7. その日は先約があるのでごめんなさい. また次の機会にでも.

Thank you for your prompt reply.
Thank you for your Aug. 7th e-mail.
Thank you for letting me know your new address.
Nice [Glad] to hear from you.
I'm sorry I didn't write back earlier [sooner].
That sounds great. I'll be glad to attend the party [meeting].
Sorry, I have a previous engagement on that day. Maybe next time.

❸最後に付け加える表現

1. すぐにお会いできますように.
2. 近々お会いできますように.
3. (気軽に)メールをください.
4. 気軽にメールを送ってください.
5. 連絡をとり合いましょう.
6. 助けていただきありがとう.
7. ご協力に感謝します.
8. わざわざ時間を作ってもらってありが〔とう〕
9. 落ち着いたらまたメールを送ります.
10. またご連絡します.
11. すぐに返事をいただければと思います〔.〕
12. どうかできるだけ早く返事をください.
13. すぐにお便りをいただけるのを楽しみにしています.
14. あなたからもっとたくさんお便りをもらえるのを楽しみにしています.
15. この次のメールではご家族のことをもっと教えてください.
16. 追伸. 緊急の場合に備えて, 私の携帯電話の番号は090-4567-XXXXです.

Hope to see you soon.
Hope we can get together in the near future.
Drop me a line.
Feel free to e-mail me.
Let's keep in touch.
Thank you for your assistance [help]. / I 〔appreciate your assistance [help]〕.
〔...〕
〔Please〕 respond ASAP [at your earliest 〔convenience〕].
Look(ing) forward to hearing from you soon.
I'll be looking forward to more messages from you.
Tell me more about your family in your next e-mail.
P.S. In case of emergency, my cellular phone number is 090-4567-XXXX.

略語とスマイリー(顔文字)

((略語))			((スマイリー))	
AFAIK	As Far As I Know	私が知っている限り	:-)	にこっ(笑顔)
ASAP	As Soon As Possible	至急	;-)	ウインク
BTW	By The Way	ところで	:-(	悲しい
FWIW	For What It's Worth	真偽のほどは分からないが	:-0	びっくりした
FYI	For Your Information	ご参考までに		
IMHO	In My Humble Opinion	私個人の意見では		
LOL	Laughing Out Loud	爆笑して		
TIA	Thanks In Advance	よろしく		

＊スマイリーは, 日本では(^o^)など縦位置のものが一般的ですが, 英文Eメールではふつう横倒しの顔が使われます.

FAVORITE
JAPANESE-ENGLISH DICTIONARY

フェイバリット
和英辞典

CD付 2色刷

編集委員
浅野 博　緒方孝文　牧野 勤

TOKYO SHOSEKI

はしがき

英語学習者のみなさんへ

みなさんが英語を学ばれる目的はさまざまだと思いますが、「自分の思うことを英語で自由に表してみたい」というのは、だれもが抱いている望みであろうと思います。言いたいことがあるのに思うように言えないというのは、日本語でも感じることがあるわけですが、外国語ではだれもが感じる大きな障害です。そこで、手っ取り早い方法として、和英辞典に頼ることになりますが、それでも思うようにいかないであきらめてしまうか、努力しながらも不満に思っている人が多いのではないでしょうか。

そこで、和英辞典の特徴と主な使い方を述べておきますので、よく読んで、まずできるところから実践するようにしてください。

和英辞典の特徴

辞典というものは、便利なものではありますが、完全なものではありません。それは、英英辞典でも英和辞典でも同じです。それは二十巻にもなる百科事典でも同じでしょう。しかし、辞典や事典が全く無くなってしまったらやはり困ります。したがって、大切なことは、自分の目的に合わせた上手な利用法を工夫することです。そのために参考になることを以下に述べることにします。

和英辞典の大きな目的は、日本語の単語や表現を英語ではどう表すかを示すことです。しかし、厄介な問題が少なくとも2つあります。

(1) 単語でも完全には一致しない

日本語＝英語のように対応するものはほとんどありません。それは違う言語ではやむを得ないことです。もちろん単語によって程度の差はあります。例えば、イヌ＝dog というのはこれ以外に言いようのないもので、1対1で対応できるように見えます。それでも、文法的には冠詞とか複数形の問題が生じます。また、日本人と英米人では、この動物に抱く文化的なイメージが違う場合があります。人間の仲間としての飼い犬のイメージでは、日本人もかなり欧米人のそれに近づいてきましたが、悪いイメージの表現には差があるのが普通です。例えば、英和辞典に lead a dog's life は「みじめな生活を送る」とあります。これを直訳して「イヌの生活を送る」としても、日本語として意味があいまいで、よくわからないものになります。日本語の少し古い言い方に「犬死にする」がありますが、「(無謀なあだ討ちを試みて返り討ちになるように) 無駄な死に方をする」ということです。ところが、英語にも die a dog's death というのがあるので、同じかと思うと「悲惨な死に方をする」ということで、かなり差があります。このように、単語として1対1になるものも、表現となると一致しないことが多くありますから注意してください。

(2) 類似表現を応用する

日本語は急速に多様化しています。日本語と一口に言っても、地域差、年齢差などによって違いがあるのは昔からですが、現在は、わずかな年数で変わる流行語、若者ことば、俗語など実に多様化しています。そうしたものを採用することは、辞典には非常に難しいことです。したがって、みなさんには、英語によるコミュニケーションの基本を考えて和英辞典を利用してもらいたいと思います。その「基本」とは、まず「伝えたい内容」を考えて、それをとにかく平易な英語で伝えることを心がけることです。例えば、「(あなたのファッション) めっちゃいけてる」と言いたいとすると、このままの表現を和英辞典に求めてもまず無理です。また、英語でこうした流行語的なニュアンスを出すこともむりですから、表したいことを「とてもすばらしい」とか「すごくかっこいい」などと言い換えてみれば、英語に直しやすくなります。そして、Your fashion is really wonderful. とか You look great [terrific] in that dress. とか言えれば十分に意図は達成されます。また、こういう表現ならば、英和辞典にも和英辞典にも見つかります。和英辞典に見つからない語句、表現は、別の日本語に言い換える工夫をしてみてください。

さらに応用する工夫を

和英辞典を利用しても,「ぴったりと一致する例文がない」という不満を感じる人は少なくありません。しかし, 単語でもそうですから, ましてやすべての例文を辞典に求めることはできないでしょう. したがって, 解決策としては, 求めるのに近い例文を見つけて, それを応用することが必要です.

例えば,「私たちは意見がばらばらだった」と言い表したいとします. この辞典で「いけん・意見」を引いてみると, [意見が・は] という項があって,「意見」が主語になる場合の例があることがすぐわかります. その中で, 一番近いのは「私の意見は君のとはまるで違う」でしょう. その英文は My opinion is totally different from yours. ですから, とりあえず Our opinions were totally different. とか Each of us had a very different opinion. と言えば, 趣旨は十分伝わります. いちいち「ばらばら」をどう表そうかと考えなくても,「まったく違う」でよいことになります.

英語のインプットを多く

英語が上達する最初の条件は, なるべく大量の英文に触れて, 耳と目からのインプットを多くすることです. それをしないで, 必要になると和英辞典で引いた単語を並べるような方法で英文を作っても通じるようなものになりません. また, 生の英文に触れる場合は, 誰がどういう人にどういう場面で使っている英語なのかということを徐々に注意するようにしてください. やがて, これはかなり乱暴で下品な表現だとか, 大変にかしこまった堅い表現ということがわかってくるでしょう. そうなれば, 日本語を英語に訳す場合も, そうしたニュアンスにふさわしい英文を応用することができるようになります. 初めからあまり欲張らずに, 基本的な表現で, 正しく意図を表現できるようになることを目指してください.

本辞典協力者への謝辞とお願い

本辞典は, 別記のように多くの協力者を得ることによって編集することができました. そのほかにも, 多くの先生方から貴重なご助言や情報をいただきました. また, 参考にさせていただいた文献もたくさんあります. いちいちお名前を挙げませんが, ここに心から感謝申し上げます.

また, 東京書籍(株)英語辞典編集部, および日本アイアール(株)の方々にたいへんお世話になりました.

なお今後も, ご利用いただく方々からのご指摘によって, よりすぐれた辞典とすべく改善に努力いたすつもりでおります. ご意見などをお寄せくださるようお願いいたします.

2001年9月

編集委員代表　　浅野　博

編集委員

浅野　博　　緒方孝文　　牧野　勤

校閲協力

Tom Baker	Donald C. Boone
Gregory D. Cottrell	Russell L. Fauss
Tom Gally	J.B. Jones
Mark Schreiber	Rachel A. Vigil
奥村秀樹	小林ひろみ

執筆・校正

浅田幸善　　伊東武彦　　鵜飼桂名
緒方孝文　　奥村秀樹　　佐々木大介
武富直人　　遠峯伸一郎　中和彩子
根本貴行　　西川健誠　　星野あゆみ
横堀仁志　　森　聡美
Tom Gally （短歌・俳句英訳）

調査・校正協力	浅見奈央　　佐古典子　　生川千佳 西根恵子　　堀　光恵　　堀　百恵
イラスト	伊藤照雄
装丁	道吉　剛　　稲葉克彦
編集協力	日本アイアール株式会社

解説図

- **見出し語と漢字表記**

  最重要語・重要語・一般語の3種類があります。
  ⇨「2. 見出し語」

- **動詞の自他**

  自他で自動詞, 他動詞の区別を示しました。
  ⇨「4. 訳語」(動詞)

- **不規則動詞**

  不規則な変化をする動詞には*を付けました。
  ⇨「4. 訳語」(動詞)

- **注記**

  注意点は(❖)の中に記しました。

- **発想指示**

  英語的な発想の助けとなるように, 英語に近づけて書き直した日本語です。
  ⇨「5. 用例」(発想指示)

- **用例の一部の強調**

  日本語は太字で, 英語をイタリック体で対応する箇所を強調しています。
  ⇨「5. 用例」(強調)

- **会話用例**

  会話形式の用例には💬を付けています。
  ⇨「5. 用例」(会話用例)

いりょう² 医療 medical care [treatment] U
——医療の medical /彼女は何度も医療援助を要請した She made repeated requests for *medical aid*.
|医療過誤〖法律〗malpractice / 医療器械[器具] medical appliances, medical instruments / 医療機関 medical institution / 医療制度 health care system / 医療費 medical expenses / 医療保険 health [medical-care] insurance

いれる 入れる

❶ 中に入れる　　　　　put ... in [into] ~
❷ 学校などに行かせる　send
❸ 採用する・収容する　employ; accommodate
❹ 含める　　　　　　　include
❺ スイッチをつける　　turn [switch] on

❶【中に入れる】put* ... in [into] ~; (注ぐ) pour 他; (挿入する) insert 他; (入れておく) keep* ... in ~; (入れてやる) let* ... in (~)
牛乳を冷蔵庫に入れなさい *Put* the milk *in* the refrigerator.
彼はその本をポケットに入れた He *put* the book *into* his pocket.
彼女はコーヒーを1杯いれてくれた She *poured* [*made*] me a cup of coffee. (❖pour は「すでにできているコーヒーを注ぐ」, make は「コーヒーを作る」の意味)
カードキーをここに入れるとドアのロックが解除されます *Insert* the card key here and the door will be unlocked.
お気に入りのアクセサリーはその箱に入れてある I *keep* my favorite accessories *in* that box.
ドアをあけて猫を中に入れてやりなさい Open the door and *let* the cat *in*.
◆次の手紙に私の写真を入れて送ります(→同封します) I'll *enclose* a photo of myself *in* the next letter. / 彼女は茶色のコンタクトレンズを入れていた She *wore* brown contact lenses. / カメラにフィルムを入れるときに失敗してしまった I *loaded* the film *into* the camera the wrong way. / この仕事のデータをすべてコンピュータに入れてある We *have input* all of the data about this job *into* the computer. / おふろに水を入れてちょうだい *Run* the bathwater.
💬「紅茶にミルクと砂糖をお入れしますか」「ミルクだけお願いします」"Would you like some milk and sugar in your tea?" "Just milk, please."
❷【学校などに行かせる】send* 他
両親は弟を全寮制の学校に入れた My parents *sent* my brother *to* a boarding school.
◆少年犯罪者は更生施設に入れられる Juvenile offenders *are taken* to rehabilitation facilities.
❸【採用する・収容する】(採用する) employ 他; (収容する) accommodate 他
新しいスタッフをもう何人か入れる必要がある We need to *employ* a few more people as staff.
その会議室は100人程度までは入れられる The conference room *can accommodate* about a hundred people.
◆コンサートはすでに始まっていて休憩時間まで中に入れてもらえなかった(→中に入れなかった) The concert had started already, and I couldn't *get in* until the intermission.
❹【含める】include 他; (数える) count 他
家賃は管理費を入れて7万5千円です The rent is 75,000 yen *including* (the) upkeep.

- **名詞の CU**

  C は数えられる名詞(可算名詞)で U は数えられない名詞(不可算名詞)です。
  ⇨「4. 訳語」(名詞)

- **副見出し語**

  ⇨「2. 見出し語」(副見出し語)

- **複合語**

  ⇨「3. 複合語」

- **訳語一覧**

  多義語の場合は, 代表的な訳語をまとめて挙げています。
  ⇨「4. 訳語」(訳語一覧)

- **訳語**

  ⇨「4. 訳語」

- **用例**

  訳語を使った用例を最初に並べ, 訳語を使っていない用例を◆に続けて後に並べています。
  ⇨「5. 用例」

この辞典について

1. 主な特長

1. 「使いやすい」(user-friendly) 和英辞典をめざしてこの辞典を編集しました.
2. 見出し語は,日常生活で必要となる基本語彙を中心に,コンピュータ,インターネット関連の新語や時事用語,また口語表現などを積極的に取り入れました.
3. 訳語の羅列を避け,日本語と英語の意味のずれが分かるように説明を加えました.日本固有の事物など,適切な訳語がない場合には説明的な英語を載せました.
4. 日本語のニュアンスができるだけ伝わり,かつ自然な英語になるよう,日本語に精通している英語のネイティブスピーカーが繰り返し英文をチェックしました.
5. 囲みや特別ページなど,英語の学習者にとって役に立つ情報をいろいろな角度から盛り込みました.

2. 見出し語

収録語数 見出し語約32,000語,複合語を入れると約45,000語になります.

配列
1. 見出し語は五十音順に並べました.
2. 同じかなが続くときは,以下の順序にしました.
   (a) 接頭語,接尾語はこの順序でそれ以外の語の後に並べました.
      さい オ → さい- 最- → -さい -歳
   (b) 清音→濁音→半濁音の順に並べました.
      ヘヤ → ベヤ → ペヤ
   (c) 直音→促音の順に並べました.
      しつけ 躾 → しっけ 湿気
   (d) 直音→拗音の順に並べました.
      きやく 規約 → きゃく 客
   (e) 音引きは直前の文字に含まれる母音とみなし,該当する位置に並べました.
      みずうみ 湖 → ミズーリ → みすえる 見据える
   (f) カタカナ→ひらがなの順に並べました.
      アンプ → あんぷ 暗譜
3. 読みが同じで,かなの表記が一致する場合は,原則として使用頻度の高いものから並べ,右肩に数字を付けて区別しました.
   あい^1 愛 → あい^2 藍

重要度 重要度に応じて次の3つのランクに分類しました.
1. 赤で印刷した2行取り見出し語　　最重要語 (約1,000語)
2. 赤で印刷した1行取り見出し語　　重要語　 (約2,000語)
3. 黒で印刷した1行取り見出し語　　一般語　 (約29,000語)

副見出し語 見出し語の品詞と異なる品詞の訳語を載せる場合,見出し語と用法が大きく異なる訳語を載せる場合は,——の後に副見出し語を立てました.主に見出し語がサ変動詞や形容動詞の語幹の場合です.また,日本語と英語の対応が分かりにくい場合は,必要に応じて英語の品詞を示しました.

あさね 朝寝　**——朝寝する** sleep* late in the morning

あいだ 間
❶【時間】—— 前 (…の間) for, during; (…のうちに) in, within; (2つの時点の間) between —— 腰 (…する・している間) while

日本文化に関係する見出し語	日本文化に関係する事物で米英では一般的ではない事物を表す見出し語には，⛰を付け，原則として日本語名のローマ字表記をイタリック体で示し，説明的な訳を併記しました．説明的な訳が長くなる場合は，囲みを設け，日本語と英語で詳しく説明しました．ただし，日本語起源の語でも，英語化していると思われるものは，イタリック体にしませんでした．⇒「日本の事物紹介一覧」p.XIV

あがりゆ 上がり湯 ⛰ *agariyu*, hot water outside the bathtub for rinsing off after having taken a bath

和製英語	日本で英語らしく作った語である和製英語など，英語に訳す際に注意が必要な見出し語には⚠を付けました．

エアコン ⚠ air conditioner ⓒ

都道府県名	都道府県名を見出し語として立項し，囲みの中でその都道府県を紹介する際の一例を日本語と英語で示しました．
文法用語	高校生が英語を学ぶ際に必要となる文法用語を見出し語として立項し，囲みの中に簡単な解説を載せました．⇒「文法用語一覧」p.XV

3．複合語

見出し語が名詞の場合，他の名詞などと結合してできた複合語は‖の後に並べました．その際，まず見出し語で始まる複合語を五十音順に並べ，その後，それ以外の複合語を五十音順に並べました．ただし，句や文の中で示したほうがいい複合語に関しては，用例の中で取り上げました．

4．訳語

並べ方	訳語は使用頻度の高いものから並べ，コンマ (,) で区切りました．ただし，意味や使い方が異なるものについては，セミコロン (；) を使って区別し，かっこ内にその違いを示しました．また，意味が大きく異なるものは，❶❷❸で区分し，使用頻度の高いものから並べました．

い² 意 （意味） meaning ⓤⓒ, sense ⓒ; （意志） will ⓤⓒ, intention ⓤⓒ

あう² 合う
❶【適合する】fit* 自他, suit 他

使い方	訳語の使い方についての注意点，訳語の解説は，(❖) の中に記しました．

あおしんごう 青信号 green light ⓒ (❖この場合の「青」に blue は使えない)

使い分け	訳語の使い分けについて注意が必要なものは，以下のように訳語を並べ，ニュアンスの違いを説明しました．

え¹ 絵

picture ©; painting ©; drawing ©; illustration ©
painting: 絵の具で描いたもの．
drawing: 鉛筆・クレヨンなどで描いたもの．
illustration: 挿絵．
picture: 以上すべてを含む．

語法	意味や用法についての日本語と英語の大きなずれ，注意が必要な英語の語法については，「語法」の囲みでそれを説明しました．

いか¹ 以下

[語法]
「…以下」は，厳密に数量をいう場合は，…の数を含むが，比較的あいまいに「…より少ない」という意味で用いる場合も多い．英語で表現するとき，どちらに当たるのかよく見きわめて使い分けるようにする．

名詞	1．訳語が名詞の場合は，複数の語からなる説明的な訳語を除いて，©Uでその名詞が可算名詞であるか，不可算名詞であるかを示しました．ただし，用例で成句の一部として使われる場合は，その使われ方が©Uと一致しないことがあります． 2．不規則な変化をする名詞には複数形を示しました．
動詞	1．訳語が動詞の場合は，句動詞を除いて，⾃他で自動詞，他動詞の区別を示しました．ただし，訳語として用いられる文脈での区別なので，必ずしもその動詞のすべての用法を示しているわけではありません． 2．不規則な変化をする動詞には，be 動詞を除き，右肩にアステリスク（*）を付けました．ただし，その動詞がその訳語の並びの中で2回以上登場する場合は，2回目以降の動詞には省略しました．⇨巻末「主な不規則動詞変化表」p.1803
発音記号	発音の仕方に注意が必要な訳語については，直後に［ ］に入れて発音記号を示しました．発音は原則として米発音のみとしました．⇨「発音記号表」p.XVI
訳語一覧	見出し語が多義語の場合は，各意味の代表的な訳語を見出し語のすぐ下に示して，訳語を一覧できるようにしました．

あがる¹ 上がる

❶ 昇る・上昇する	go up, rise
❷ 値段・地位・程度	improve; increase, rise, go up; reach
❸ 終了する	stop, finish, end
❹ 平静を失う	get [become] nervous
❺ 声・火	rise
❻ 訪ねる	visit
❼ 食べる・飲む	have; eat; drink

つづり	原則として米つづりで統一しましたが，重要な英語には英つづりも併記しました．

5. 用例

並べ方
1. 訳語が挙げられている場合，訳語を使った用例を最初に並べ，訳語を使っていない用例を◆に続けて後に並べました．
2. どちらの用例も，原則として句用例→文用例の順に並べました．
3. 最重要語と重要語の場合，見やすさを考え，訳語を使った文用例は行頭始まりを原則としました．
4. 用例を追い込む場合は，太いスラッシュ（**/**）を用例間に入れました．
5. 1つの日本語に対して英語の訳が複数並ぶ場合は，句用例ではセミコロン（;）を，文用例では細いスラッシュ（/）を用例間に入れました．

助詞分け
見出し語が名詞の場合，用例が多く並ぶときは，〖意見が・は〗，〖意見を・に〗のように助詞との結び付きによって用例を分類しました．

強調
1. 求める用例にすばやく行き着けるように，見出し語部分の日本語を太字にしました．ただし，その語と他の語との結びつきが強い場合は，それらの語句全体を太字にしました．
2. 日本語の太字部分に対応する英語部分をイタリック体で示し，日本語と英語の対応する部分が分かるようにしました．ただし，この対応はあくまで一応の目安です．

発想指示
日本語と英語の文の構造が著しくかけ離れている場合は，英語的な発想の助けとなるように，英語に近づけて書き直した日本語を（→ ）の中に示しました．

構文指示
動詞の文型など重要な英語の構文は，その用例の直前に示しました．
【signal＋(to) 名＋that 節】彼は私に電車が来ると合図した He *signaled* (*to*) me *that* the train was coming.

会話用例
複数の人による会話形式の用例は，最初に🗨を付けて会話用例であることが分かるようにしました．
🗨「けさは何時に**起きた**の」「7時ちょっと過ぎくらい」 "What time *did* you *get up* this morning?" "A little past seven."

慣用表現・ことわざ
日本語の慣用表現・ことわざは，それぞれ 慣用表現 ことわざ のラベルを付けました．
慣用表現 その計画は絵に描いたもちだ The project is *pie in the sky*.
ことわざ 鉄は熱いうちに打て Strike while the iron is hot.

短歌・俳句
短歌 俳句 の後に，高校の国語の教科書に掲載されている代表的な短歌・俳句とその英訳を載せました．一部歴史的仮名づかいを採用していますが，和英辞典であることを考慮し，難しい漢字はできるだけ避けました．英語の音節の数は原則として短歌・俳句の音節の数と合わせました．⇨「短歌・俳句一覧」p.XV

6. 英作文ノート

「英作文ノート」という囲みを設け，英作文の際に注意しなければならない事柄を具体

的な例を挙げて説明しました．⇨「英作文ノート一覧」p.XIII

7. コミュニケーションスキル

英語でのコミュニケーションに役立つ表現を行為別にまとめました．
⇨「コミュニケーションスキル一覧」p.XIII

8. 関連語

見出し語に関連した語を 関連語 を付けて示しました．多くの語を示す場合は，「…のいろいろ」という形式の囲みを設け，その中で示しました．
⇨「『いろいろ』囲み一覧」p.XIII

9. コロケーション

基本的な語のコロケーション（語と語の慣用的な結び付き）が分かるように次のような囲みを設けました．

> **コロケーション** -color-
> 〘形容詞＋～〙明るい～ a bright [brilliant] color / 鮮やかな～ a fresh [lively] color / 薄い～ a light [pale] color / 落ち着いた[地味な]～ a quiet color / くすんだ～ a dull color / 暗い～ a dark color / けばけばしい～ a tawdry [gaudy] color / 濃い～ a rich color / はでな～ a loud color / ぼやけた～ a faint color / 柔らかい～ a soft [delicate] color

10. 主な記号　　＊があるものは2.と5.に詳しい説明があります．

名 名詞	代 代名詞	動 動詞	形 形容詞	副 副詞
前 前置詞	助 助動詞	冠 冠詞	接 接続詞	間 間投詞

《米》米国用法　《英》英国用法

( )	補足的な説明・省略可能	[ ]	発音記号・言い換え
〔 〕	専門語などの百科表示	❖	語法注記
∥	訳語などと用例との区切り	/	用例間の区切り
⇨	…を見よ	×	間違いの例
◆	訳語を用いない用例＊	🅲	会話用例＊
🗻	日本の事物に関するもの＊	⚠	和製英語＊

《公式的》	堅い文章や改まったスピーチなどで使う言葉
《口語的》	親しい人どうしの会話やEメール・手紙などで使う言葉
《俗語》	《口語的》よりもさらにくだけた表現で，やや下品な言葉
《卑語》	非常に下品で，人前で使うべきでない言葉
《文語》	堅い文章や文学作品などで使われる言葉
《古風》	今日(こんにち)では，やや古めかしい響きをもつようになった言葉
《小児語》	幼い子供が使う言葉

その他，《軽蔑的》，《戯言的》，《婉曲的》など，語のニュアンスを具体的に示しました．

11. 特別ページ

●テーマ別表現集

6つのテーマについて、会話やスピーチで役立つ表現を収録しました。

→「テーマ別表現集一覧」p.XIII

●場面・状況別会話

実際の英会話にすぐに使える表現、モデル会話を場面・状況別に収録しました。
→ p.1681

12. 囲み等一覧

●コミュニケーションスキル一覧

あいさつ …… 3	聞き返す …… 371	同情 …… 1042
あいづち …… 7	希望・願望 …… 391	励ます …… 1205
謝る …… 53	義務 …… 394	不満 …… 1332
意見 …… 93	許可 …… 417	ほめる …… 1399
意図 …… 126	賛成・反対 …… 603	意見・判断の保留 …… 1400
依頼 …… 136	紹介 …… 697	道を尋ねる …… 1457
確認 …… 293	推量 …… 749	命令 …… 1491
感謝 …… 353	説明 …… 809	呼びかける …… 1583
感情 …… 354	提案・勧誘 …… 999	

●テーマ別表現集一覧

高齢化と介護 …… 522	スキーとスノーボード …… 755	性 …… 781
サッカー …… 589	相撲 …… 775	野球 …… 1530

●英作文ノート一覧

握手には2つの手が必要！ …… 18	「アメリカン」は好きですか？ …… 525
「夜」は明けない？ …… 21	「…歳の」の英語は？ …… 566
「足」の意味に注意！ …… 25	**He is sure ...** の後は？ …… 629
和製英語に注意！ …… 44	10代後半は「ハイティーン」？ …… 672
apologize の使い方 …… 52	「～をご紹介します」の英語は？ …… 696
「…いくらで」は定冠詞 …… 90	**like** の後は単数，複数？ …… 753
類推は危険！ …… 102	**prefer** のとる前置詞は？ …… 753
the の有無に注意！ …… 119	赤道の上か下か？ …… 800
遅すぎるのは「今」！ …… 131	「幸せそうに」の英語は？ …… 837
目的語に注意！ …… 142	**each other** と前置詞 …… 878
「疑わない」なら **that**! …… 158	注文は書店にするものだけど… …… 944
「…しないうちに」の訳し方 …… 159	**lead** では通じない！ …… 961
「…から」≠ **from** …… 167	「次のとおり」は決まった表現 …… 967
「運が…」は **a, an** を付けない …… 176	**convenient** は主語に注意 …… 976
「永久に忘れません」の訳し方 …… 180	釣りは川でするもの …… 991
「道を教える」の場合は **tell** …… 221	「どう」≠ **how** …… 1035
過去は ~ing，未来は **to** 不定詞 …… 240	「どれくらい」に要注意！ …… 1092
abroad に **to** はいらない …… 266	**often** と **a, an** …… 1127
「買ってやる」では **to** は不用 …… 276	**resemble** に **to** はいらない …… 1149
現在完了の文では **since** …… 334	「はい」だけど **No** …… 1191
「感動する」＝「感動させられる」 …… 359	「梅雨に入る」の英語は？ …… 1197
「マナー」≠ **manner** …… 409	**necessary** の主語は？ …… 1275
3人兄弟は **two** か **three** か …… 412	「何百万人もの…」の英語は？ …… 1286
「黒い目」は **dark eyes** …… 459	**almost** は形容詞ではない …… 1396
「健康診断を受ける」は何ていう？ …… 490	サンドイッチ語順 …… 1472
「交通が激しい」は何という？ …… 514	「…より」必ずしも **than** ならず …… 1587

●「いろいろ」囲み一覧

「歩く」のいろいろ …… 60	写真のいろいろ …… 661
医者のいろいろ …… 98	祝日のいろいろ …… 680
いすのいろいろ …… 100	チーズのいろいろ …… 927
犬のいろいろ …… 128	猫のいろいろ …… 1161
役職名のいろいろ …… 268	部のいろいろ …… 1299
科目のいろいろ …… 332	保険のいろいろ …… 1386
化粧品のいろいろ …… 475	星座のいろいろ …… 1388
国旗の呼称のいろいろ …… 543	陸上競技のいろいろ …… 1604
酒のいろいろ …… 582	惑星のいろいろ …… 1645

●日本の事物紹介一覧

項目	ページ
赤ちょうちん	12
生け花	92
いなり寿司	127
浮世絵	151
うどん	166
梅干し	170
運動会	178
干支(えと)	185
絵馬	186
演歌	188
縁側	189
お色直し	195
お好み焼き	217
押し入れ	221
お歳暮	225
おせち	225
お茶漬け	229
お中元	230
おでん	232
お年玉	234
おにぎり	237
おはらい	238
おみくじ	241
おみこし	241
お宮参り	242
折り紙	252
温泉	257
書き初め	285
かっぱ	319
門松	322
歌舞伎	327
カラオケ	335
空手	337
カルチャーセンター	340
着物	396
灸(きゅう)	400
弓道	405
狂言	409
ゲートボール	472
げた	476
結婚式	479
元号	491
剣道	496
碁	500
こいのぼり	501
高校野球	508
ゴールデンウイーク	526
こけし	532
こたつ	541
こんにゃく	563
コンパ	563
座敷	584
刺身	585
茶道	592
三三九度	601
地蔵(菩薩(ぼさつ))	632
七五三	637
七福神	637
しめ縄	657
尺八	660
三味線	663
じゃんけん	664
修学旅行	667
柔道	674
塾	679
正月	698
将棋	699
障子	702
焼酎(しょうちゅう)	706
しょうゆ	712
書道	720
除夜の鐘	721
しり取り	724
しるこ	726
新幹線	729
神社	733
神道	738
吸い物	748
すき焼き	754
すごろく	761
寿司	762
墨絵	772
相撲	774
赤飯	800
節句	803
切腹	808
節分	808
禅	813
線香	816
扇子(せん)	819
銭湯	824
千羽鶴	825
惣菜	834
雑煮	839
そうめん	839
草履	840
そば	851
鯛	858
大安	859
大福	872
たくあん	882
たこ焼き	885
畳	893
七夕(祭り)	902
足袋(たび)	906
だるま	915
短歌	919
茶(日本茶)	936
ちんどん屋	956
梅雨(つゆ)	989
出前	1018
てるてる坊主	1022
天狗(てんぐ)	1026
てんぷら	1030
豆腐	1047
床の間	1063
仲人(なこうど)	1109
納豆	1112
忍者	1151
年賀(年賀状)	1170
能	1175
のり	1184
のれん	1187
俳句	1193
はし	1208
パチンコ	1217
はっぴ	1223
初もうで	1223
花見	1229
はり	1239
はんこ	1247
彼岸(ひがん)	1260
ひな祭り	1282
びょうぶ	1291
ふすま	1319
ふとん	1328
振りそで	1338
ふろしき	1344
文楽	1350
忘年会	1379
盆	1402
漫画	1440
漫才	1441
まんじゅう	1441
見合い	1445
みそ	1455
みつ豆	1460
名刺	1488
もち	1509
厄年	1532
ようかん	1568
落語	1596
浪人	1634
和歌	1641
わび	1650

●短歌・俳句一覧

赤い椿 河東碧梧桐(へきごとう)	983 (ツバキ)	熟田津(にぎたづ)に 額田王(ぬかたのおおきみ)	612 (潮)
秋来ぬと 藤原敏行	305 (風)	初しぐれ 松尾芭蕉	597 (猿)
秋の田の 天智天皇	990 (露)	花の色は 小野小町	1226 (花)
秋深き 松尾芭蕉	1075 (隣)	春過ぎて 持統天皇	1241 (春)
荒海や 松尾芭蕉	48 (天の川)	万緑の 中村草田男	1188 (歯)
幾山河 若山牧水	906 (旅)	久方の 紀友則	1260 (光)
牛飼いが 伊藤左千夫	155 (牛)	ピストルが 山口誓子	1270 (ピストル)
海に出て 山口誓子	169 (海)	向日葵(ひまわり)は 前田夕暮	1285 (ヒマワリ)
奥山に 猿丸大夫	1522 (紅葉)	吹くからに 文屋康秀	54 (あらし)
柿くへば 正岡子規	284 (柿)	古池や 松尾芭蕉	232 (音)
かささぎの 中納言家持	658 (霜)	ふるさとの 石川啄木(たくぼく)	1341 (ふるさと)
かたつむり 飯田龍太	311 (カタツムリ)	降る雪や 中村草田男	1339 (降る)
瓶(かめ)にさす 正岡子規	332 (かめ)	牡丹(ぼたん)散りて 与謝蕪村	1391 (ぼたん)
谺(こだま)して 杉田久女	541 (こだま)	また電話 俵万智	1032 (電話)
「この味が」 俵万智	597 (サラダ)	街をゆき 木下利玄	1449 (ミカン)
金色(こんじき)の 与謝野晶子	113 (イチョウ)	マッチ擦る 寺山修司	1429 (マッチ)
寂しさに 良寛(りょうかん)法師	1549 (夕暮れ)	みづうみの 島木赤彦	1453 (湖)
五月雨(さみだれ)を 松尾芭蕉	594 (五月雨)	見渡せば 藤原定家	15 (秋)
「寒いね」と 俵万智	594 (寒い)	名月を 小林一茶	1488 (名月)
閑かさや 松尾芭蕉	811 (セミ)	瘦蛙(やせがえる) 小林一茶	279 (蛙(かえる))
死に近き 斎藤茂吉	607 (死)	山里は 源宗于朝臣	1334 (冬)
白鳥は 若山牧水	10 (青)	山路来て 松尾芭蕉	773 (すみれ)
雀(すずめ)の子 小林一茶	764 (雀)	やれ打つな 小林一茶	1198 (ハエ)
大海の 源実朝	1118 (波)	やは肌の 与謝野晶子	1214 (肌)
田子の浦に 山部赤人	1556 (雪)	雪とけて 小林一茶	547 (子供)
旅に病んで 松尾芭蕉	1561 (夢)	ゆく秋の 佐佐木信綱	450 (雲)
月天心 与謝蕪村	966 (月)	世の中に 在原業平(ありわらのなりひら)	581 (桜)
友がみな 石川啄木(たくぼく)	1081 (友)	ラグビーの 寺山修司	1597 (ラグビー)
菜の花や 与謝蕪村	1116 (菜の花)	分け行つても 種田山頭火	1541 (山)

●文法用語一覧

受身	152	形式主語	468	助動詞	720	付加疑問文	1306
格	288	形容詞	471	所有代名詞	721	副詞	1311
過去完了(形)	299	現在完了(形)	491	数	750	不定詞	1326
過去分詞	299	現在分詞	492	数詞	750	不定代名詞	1327
仮定法	321	5文型	551	接続詞	806	部分否定	1330
関係代名詞	350	固有名詞	555	前置詞	822	分詞構文	1347
関係副詞	350	再帰代名詞	567	代名詞	873	補語	1387
感嘆文	358	最上級	571	他動詞	901	名詞	1489
間投詞	359	指示代名詞	626	動名詞	1048	目的語	1506
疑問代名詞	396	時制の一致	631	人称代名詞	1151	話法	1651
強調構文	413	自動詞	647	比較級	1259		
句動詞	446	集合名詞	670	非制限用法	1270		

●主な図版一覧

家	78	腰	536	天気図	1025	ひげ	1265
居間	132	財布	574	泣く	1107	ひざ	1267
上	147	サッカー	589	なべ	1116	びん	1296
縁側	189	皿	596	庭	1149	振る	1339
オートバイ	205	下	633	葉	1188	帽子	1376
階	262	下着	635	はさみ	1207	前	1412
かぎ	284	自転車	646	バスケットボール	1212	目	1484
木	365	自動車	647	花	1225	山	1540
着る	424	図形	759	針	1239	横	1576
空港	434	たんす	922	バレーボール	1242	笑う	1652
靴	444	テニス	1016	ワンメイク(スキーとスノーボード)			755

発音記号表

母音			子音			
発音記号	つづり字例		発音記号	つづり字例		
[iː]	eat sea	people	[p]	pen	spend	stop
[i]	big sit	winter	[b]	bed	black	cab
[e]	egg sell	head	[t]	table	tea	hat
[æ]	cap sad	happy	[d]	desk	dog	bed
[ɑː]	father calm	garage	[k]	key	cool	sick
[ɑ]	not Tom	college	[g]	good	give	bag
[ɔː]	all call	saw	[f]	fox	fish	life
[ʌ]	sun bus	love	[v]	voice	very	move
[ə]	ago away	bottom	[θ]	three	thin	both
[uː]	pool blue	lose	[ð]	they	mother	breathe
[u]	book sugar	put	[s]	six	nice	miss
[ei]	age say	rain	[z]	zero	cousin	nose
[ai]	ice side	buy	[ʃ]	ship	sheep	wash
[ɔi]	oil point	enjoy	[ʒ]	vision	usually	measure
[au]	out town	now	[h]	hat	hill	home
[ou]	old note	boat	[r]	rich	read	try
[əːr]	bird earth	third	[l]	love	long	color
[iər]	hear ear	deer	[tʃ]	chair	choose	teach
[eər]	hair bear	care	[dʒ]	joy	just	large
[uər]	tour poor	moor	[m]	milk	meet	come
			[n]	name	pencil	ten
			[ŋ]	long	king	singer
			[w]	wall	want	win
			[j]	young	yes	year

1. 各記号は右側の単語の下線部分の発音を示しています.
2. 発音記号 [r] が [*r*] のような斜字体になっているのは，この音が発音される場合と，発音されない場合の両方があることを示しています.

   [*r*]　bird [báːrd]　　→　[báːrd] または [báːd]

   [*r*] 以外にも次のような斜字体の例があります.

   [*d*]　handbag [hǽn*d*bæg]　→　[hǽndbæg] または [hǽnbæg]

   [*h*]　white [*h*wáit]　→　[hwáit] または [wáit]

   [*j*]　duty [d*j*úːti]　→　[djúːti] または [dúːti]

3. アクセントの置かれる位置は，seaside [síːsàid] や overcome [òuvərkám] のように，第1（最も強い）アクセントを [´]，第2（次に強い）アクセントを [`] で示しました.

あ

ああ¹ ❶【感嘆】oh, ah; wow(❖wow は比較的強い驚き, 喜びなどを表す)

> 語法
> (1) oh, ah ともに, 驚き・喜び・悲しみ・嘆き・賞賛などの感情を表すが, oh のほうが一般的で, 意味の範囲が広い. 応答などにも用いる ∥ ああ, どうしよう Oh [Ah], what should I do?
> (2) 欧米では, 感嘆を表す句の中に慣習的に神の名を使うことが多い. また乱用を避けるため, god の婉曲的な表現として gosh, goodness, Heavens などを用いることもある ∥ ああ大変! *Oh, (my) God!*
> (3) いずれも後にふつう(!)か(,)を伴う.

ああ, おもしろかった *Oh, it was funny.* / ああ, スペインに行きたいなあ *Oh, I want to go to Spain!* / ああ, びっくりした *Ah* [*Wow*; *Oh, boy*]*! What a surprise!*
◆ああ, 思い出した *Now,* I remember.
❷【応答・返答】(理解・同意) oh; (肯定) yes, 《口語的》yeah, aha(❖「なるほど, ははあ」という満足感を表す) ∥ ああ, ところで, お母さんはお元気ですか *Oh, by the way,* how's your mother? / ああ, そうかい *Oh, yeah?*
💬「彼女の恋人ってどんな人」「ああ, なかなかりっぱな人だよ」"What's her boyfriend like?" *"Oh,* he's really something."
💬「彼はぐあいが悪くて来られないのです」「ああ, そうですか」"He can't come because he is sick." *"Oh,* I see."

ああ² ああなるとは思わなかった *That* is not what I had expected. / 彼女, ああいうふうにかっこつけてるだけさ She is just showing off *that way.* / *That's her way* of showing off. / ああいう感じのかばんが欲しいな I want a bag *like that.*

アーカンソー Arkansas [ɑ́ːrkənsɔ̀ː](❖米国中南部の州;《略語》Ark.,《郵便》AR)

アーケード arcade Ⓒ ∥ アーケード街 a shopping arcade

アース ⚠️《米》ground Ⓒ Ⓤ,《英》earth Ⓒ Ⓤ ── アースする《米》ground 他,《英》earth 他 ∥ 洗濯機のアースをつける *ground* a washing machine

アーチ arch Ⓒ ── アーチ形の arched ∥ アーチ形のまゆ *arched* eyebrows

アーチェリー archery Ⓤ ∥ アーチェリーをする do [practice] *archery* ◆アーチェリーの選手 an archer

アーメン amen(❖キリスト教で祈りの最後に唱える言葉)

アーモンド almond [ɑ́ːmənd] Ⓒ ∥ アーモンドを散りばめたケーキ a cake studded [sprinkled] with *almonds*

アール (面積の単位) are Ⓒ (《略語》a.) (❖フランス語から)

アールエイチ Rh (因子) the Rhesus [Rh] factor
◆Rhプラス[マイナス]の血液型 a *Rhesus positive* [*negative*] blood type

ああん はい, ああんして Now, say *"ah."* (❖患者などに口を大きくあけるように言う言葉)

ああんああん その少年は道端でああんああんと(→大声で)泣いていた The boy was crying *loudly* on the roadside.

あい¹ 愛 love Ⓒ Ⓤ (また a ～); affection Ⓒ Ⓤ; devotion Ⓤ; attachment Ⓒ Ⓤ; (キリスト教の) charity Ⓤ
➡ あいじょう, あいする, 場面・状況別会話 p.1692

> love: 愛を表す最も一般的な語. 異性だけではなく, 家族・友人・国・事物などに対しても用いる.
> affection: 親の子に対する愛情など, 穏やかで永続的な愛情を表す.
> devotion: 比較的長期にわたる献身的な愛情を表す.
> attachment: 人・物に対する愛着を表す.

〖～(の)愛〗
永遠の愛 eternal [abiding] *love* / 親の愛 parental *affection* / 神への愛 the *love* of God (❖「神の愛」の意味にもなる) / 真実の愛 true *love* / 報われない愛 unrequited *love* / 母の子供への愛 the *love* of a mother for her child
〖愛を・に〗
人の愛を得る win [gain] a person's *affection(s)* / (手紙の結びで)愛をこめて, ニックより Lots of *love*, Nick
愛に国境はない *Love* has no borders.
母親の愛に代わるものはない There is no substitute for a mother's *love*.
彼女は彼への愛に身をこがしている She is consumed with *love* for him.
〖愛の〗
愛のきずな a bond of *love* / 愛の告白 declaration of one's *love* / 愛のしるし a token of one's *love*
彼は私に愛の言葉をささやいた He whispered words of *love* to me.
◆愛のない結婚 a *loveless* marriage / 人に愛の手を差し伸べる give *a helping hand* to a person / 愛のこもった手紙 an *affectionate* letter
〖愛が・は〗
彼が病気の間中, 妻の愛が彼を支えた His wife's *love* sustained him throughout his illness.
彼女は愛が世界を救えると堅く信じている She has a firm belief that *love* can save the world.
お金では買えない Money can't buy *love*.
私たちの愛は永遠に続くだろう Our *love* will last forever.
彼らの愛はすぐにさめるだろう Their *love* for each other will soon cool.

あい² 藍 (染料) indigo Ⓤ; (色) indigo Ⓤ,

indigo-blue [U] ―藍色の indigo-blue
[ことわざ] 青は藍より出でて藍より青し The scholar may surpass his [her] master. (→弟子が師匠をしのぐことがある)

あいあいがさ 相合傘 相合傘で歩く *walk together under one umbrella*; *share an umbrella* / 相合傘の二人 a couple *sharing one umbrella*

アイアン (ゴルフクラブ) iron [C] ‖7番アイアン *a seven-iron*

あいいれない 相容れない (両立しない) be incompatible with ...; (矛盾する) be inconsistent with ... ‖その考えは私たちの考え方と全く相いれないものだ The concept *is* quite *incompatible with* our way of thinking.

あいうち 相打ち (剣道で)両者の面は相打ちになった The two *hit each other's men* [helmets] *simultaneously* with their *shinai* [bamboo swords].

アイエムエフ IMF (❖ the *I*nternational *M*onetary *F*und (国際通貨基金)の略語)

あいえんか 愛煙家 heavy [habitual] smoker [C]

アイオーシー IOC (❖ the *I*nternational *O*lympic *C*ommittee (国際オリンピック委員会)の略語)

アイオワ Iowa (❖米国中西部の州; 《略語》Ia., 《郵便》IA)

あいかぎ 合い鍵 duplicate key [C]; (マスターキー) master key [C], skeleton key [C], passkey [C] ‖合いかぎを作る make *a duplicate key*

あいかわらず 相変わらず (いつものように) (as ...) as ever, (as ...) as usual; (いまだに) still; (いつも) always ‖彼女は相変わらず上品だ She is *as* elegant *as ever*. / 彼は相変わらず近所の人といざこざを起こしている He's *always* having trouble with his neighbors.
💬「彼女は元気?」「相変わらず忙しそうだよ」 "How's she doing?" "She looks busy *as usual*."
💬「最近どう」「相変わらずさ」 "What's up?" "*Not much*."

あいがん[1] 哀願 《公式的》entreaty [C] [U] ―哀願する implore [他], 《公式的》entreat [他] ‖哀願するような目で with an *imploring* look

あいがん[2] 愛玩 ―愛玩用の pet ‖愛玩動物 pet animals

あいぎ 合い着 (春ごろに着る服) spring clothing [U]; (秋ごろに着る服) fall clothing [U]

あいきどう 合気道 🗻 aikido [aikíːdou] [U], a type of Japanese traditional martial art of self-defense

アイキュー IQ (❖*i*ntelligence *q*uotient (知能指数)の略語) ‖彼女のIQは120です She has *an IQ* of 120.

あいきょう 愛敬・愛嬌 charm [U] ―あいきょうのある charming, cute, winning ‖もって生まれた機知とあいきょう natural wit and *charm* / わざとあいきょうを振りまく turn on *the charm*

あいくるしい 愛くるしい cute, lovely ‖愛くるしい赤ん坊 a *cute* [a *lovely*, an *adorable*] baby

あいけん 愛犬 *one's* (pet) dog ‖愛犬家 a dog lover, a lover of dogs

あいこ これでおあいこだ Now we're *even*. / That makes us *even*.

あいご 愛護 ‖動物愛護協会 a humane society / 動物愛護週間 Animal Protection Week / 動物愛護団体 an animal-rights organization

あいこう 愛好 (特に一時的な) 《口語的》fancy [C] 《通例単数形》, fondness [U] ―愛好する love [他] (❖受身にはできない) ◆クラシック音楽は彼の愛好するものの一つだ Classical music is one of his *great loves*. (❖この love は名詞) / 彼女はマンドリン愛好会に入っている She is in *the* mandolin *club*.
‖愛好家[者] a lover, a fan

あいこうしん 愛校心 school spirit [U], love for *one's* school ‖愛校心をかきたてる whip up *school spirit*

あいこく 愛国 ―愛国的な patriotic ‖愛国心を育てる make (*a person*) feel *patriotic*
‖愛国者 a patriot / 愛国心 patriotism

あいことば 合い言葉 (味方どうしの合図) password [C]; (スローガン) slogan [C]

アイコン 〖コンピュータ〗icon [C]

あいさい 愛妻 *one's* dearly-beloved wife
‖愛妻家 a devoted husband

あいさつ 挨拶

❶【出会い・別れなどのあいさつ】greeting [C] [U], 《公式的》compliments, 《公式的》salute [C] [U]; (あいさつの言葉) greetings, salutation [C]
―あいさつする greet [他], 《公式的》salute [他] [自] ➔ [コミュニケーションスキル] p.3
あいさつを交わす exchange *greetings* / あいさつをする[返す] give [return] *a salute* / 心のこもったあいさつ a hearty *greeting* / (手紙などの)時候のあいさつ *seasonal greetings* used in correspondence
彼女に「やあ」と言ったのに, あいさつを返さなかった I said "Hello" to her, but she didn't return *my greeting*.
園児たちは大きな声であいさつした The kindergarten pupils cried (out) *a greeting*.
彼女は「こんにちは」と彼にあいさつした She *greeted* him with "Hello!"
◆陽子, こちらに来て高田さんにごあいさつしなさい Come here, Yoko, and *say hello to* Ms. Takada.

❷【会合などでのあいさつ】speech [C], address [C] (❖address は特に公式な場での演説に用いる)
―あいさつする give* [make*] a speech [an address]
委員長が開会のあいさつをした The chairperson *gave an* opening *speech*.
◆ひと言ごあいさつを申し上げます Let me say [Allow me to say] *a few words*.

❸【その他】
私に何のあいさつもなく(→私の許可なしで)彼は私のコンピュータを使った He used my computer *without my permission*.
おいに就職の世話をしてやったのにひと言のあいさ

あいさつ

コミュニケーションスキル —あいさつ—

①親しい人とどこかで会ったとき

(A) **Good morning**, Mr. Brown. It's a beautiful day, isn't it?
おはようございます、ブラウンさん、いいお天気ですね。

(B) **Hello [Hi]**, John. How are you (doing)?
やあ、こんにちは、ジョン。元気かい?

(C) **How's everything (going)? / How's it going?**
調子はどうだい。

(D) **What's up? / What's new? / How are things?**
何か変わったことあった?

(E) **How's school [business]?**
学校[仕事]はどうだい。

(F) **I haven't seen you for a long time. / It's been a long time since we last saw each other.**
久しぶりだね。

②別れるとき

(G) **See you (again).**
じゃあ、またお会いするまで。

(H) **Bye (for now).**
じゃあ、さよなら。

(I) **I'm afraid I must go [be going] now.**
そろそろ行かなきゃ。

☞ (A)は時間に応じて、**Good afternoon.**(午後の場合)や **Good evening.**(夕方から夜)のように使い分ける。ただし改まった場合を除き、これらの代わりに Hello. や Hi. を使うほうが多い。

☞ (B)は親しい人に声をかける最も一般的な言い方。Hi. は Hello. よりくだけた語。

☞ 相手の近況を尋ねる場合は、(C)～(E)のようにいう。家族どうしのつきあいがあるなら、How's your family?(ご家族はお元気ですか)も便利な表現。

☞ (F)は久しぶりにだれかと会ったときに使える表現。場合によっては、**I haven't seen you for ages. / Long time no see.**(ずいぶん長いこと会わなかったね)のようにもいえる。

☞ (G), (H)は別れるときのあいさつで最も一般的な表現。次にいつ会うかがはっきりしているときは、**See you tomorrow [next week].**(またあした[来週])のようにいう。また、親しい間柄では、あした会うというのがはっきりしている場合でも See you. や Bye. だけで終わることも多い。

☞ (I)は自分の都合で話を切り上げたいときに使う。I'm afraid を付けることで、「すみませんが」という気持ちを表す。類似表現に I'm afraid I must **say goodbye [be leaving] now.** がある。

③相手から声をかけられたときの答え方

(A) Hi, John. How are you (doing)?
-**Just fine,**「**thank you [thanks]. How are you?**
やあ、こんにちは、ジョン。元気かい―元気だよ。君は?

(B) How's everything?
-**Pretty good. [OK. / So-so.] And you?**
調子はどうだい。―とてもいいよ。[いいよ。;まあまあだよ。] で、君は?

(C) What's up, Ken?
-**Nothing much [(in) particular].**
何か変わったことあったかい、ケン?―特に何も。

(D) I haven't seen you for a long time.
-**Yes, it's been quite a while. How have you been?**
久しぶり。―本当に久しぶりだね。元気だった?

(E) See you tomorrow.
-**See you.**
じゃあ、またあした。―またね。

(F) Bye for now.
-**Bye.**
じゃあ、さよなら。―じゃあね。

(G) I look forward to seeing you again. Goodbye.
-**(It was) nice seeing you. Bye.**
またお会いしましょう。さようなら。―お会いできてうれしかったです。それじゃ。

☞ (A)や(B)のように声をかけられたときは、Fine. や So-so. などの短い言葉で答え、相手の状況も尋ねてあげるのがマナー。最初の How are you (doing)? は are を強く発音し(doing が入るときは doing を強く)。とてもフランクな表現になる)、応答したほうが相手に問い返すときは、How are yóu? と you を強めていう。So-so.(まあまあね)は体調のほか、勉強や仕事の進みぐあいにも使える便利な表現。

☞ (C)の What's up? は状況によっては、「どうしたの」(=What's the matter?)の意味にもなる。

☞ (D)の聞き返しで、How are you? ではなく How have you been? と現在完了時制で尋ねることで、(今までどうでしたか)というニュアンスが出る。Yes. の後に例えば Almost five years.(もう5年になるかな)のように具体的に答えることも可能。

☞ (E), (F)では See you. の後に **I'll call you later.**(後で電話するよ)のように言葉を添えることもある。

☞ 午前中か午後早くだれかと会ったときは、別れ際に **Have a nice day!**(どうぞよい一日を)、また週末を迎える前の金曜日には **Have a nice weekend!**(どうぞよい週末を)のように声をかける。言われたほうは **Thank you. (The) same to you.** と答えるのがマナー。また学生、同僚などの間で、おどけて **T.G.I.F.!**(<Thank God it's Friday!)(うれしいね、花金だ!)ということもある。

☞ (G)の look forward to *do*ing を使った表現は、(E)や(F)より改まった表現。家に遊びに来る人に対して電話などで、**We're looking forward to seeing you.** のようにいうと「お待ちしています」の意味になる。

つもない(→礼を言わない) I found my nephew a job, but he *has never thanked me*.
‖あいさつ状 a greeting card; (通知状) a notice

あいじ 愛児 *one's* dear [beloved] child

アイシー IC (❖integrated circuit(集積回路)の略語)

あいしゃ¹ 愛車 *one's* (own) car

あいしゃ² 愛社 ‖愛社精神 loyalty for *one's* company

アイシャドー eye shadow ⓒⓊ ‖アイシャドーをつける[つけている]「put on [wear] *eye shadow*

あいしゅう 哀愁 melancholy Ⓤ, 《文語》pathos Ⓤ, sadness Ⓤ /哀愁を帯びた melancholy, 《公式的》melancholic ‖哀愁を帯びた表情をしている have a *melancholic* expression

あいしょう¹ 相性 彼女とはどうも相性が悪い I just *don't get along with* her. / *The chemistry is just not there* between her and me. / 星占いによると彼との相性はとてもいい My horoscope says that he and I will *make a good couple*.

あいしょう² 愛称 nickname ⓒ, pet name ⓒ ‖ビルはウィリアムの愛称です Bill is *a nickname for* William.
◆彼女はビッキーという愛称で呼ばれていた She was nicknamed Vicky.

あいじょう 愛情 love Ⓤ (またa～), affection ⓒⓊ, devotion Ⓤ, attachment ⓒⓊ ──愛情深い affectionate ⇨ あい(愛), あいする

愛情のあかしとして as *a pledge of love* / 愛情のこもった手紙 an *affectionate* letter / 人の愛情にこたえる return a person's *love* / 人に愛情を注ぐ shower a person *with love*

彼は親の愛情に飢えている He's *starved for the love* of his parents.

子供に対する母親の愛情ほど強い愛はない There is no *love* stronger than a mother's *love for* her child.

犬は愛情や世話にこたえる Dogs respond to *love* and care.

彼は自分の生徒たちに深い愛情をいだいていた He had a deep *love for* his students.

◆愛情のない夫婦 a *loveless* couple / 彼女は愛情をこめてその花を育てた She raised the flower *with tender loving care*.

あいしょうか 愛唱歌 *one's* favorite song

あいじん 愛人 (女性からみた男性の) lover 《通例 one's～》, (口語的) man ⓒ; (男性からみた女性の) girl ⓒ《通例 one's～》, love ⓒ《通例 one's～》, mistress ⓒ

アイス (氷)ice Ⓤ; (アイスクリーム)ice cream Ⓤⓒ ⇨ アイスクリーム ‖アイスピック an ice pick / アイスペール an ice bucket / アイスボックス an icebox

あいず 合図 sign ⓒ, motion ⓒ; signal ⓒ; cue ⓒ ──合図する sign ⓔ, motion ⓔ, make* a sign; signal ⓔ, give* a signal

sign, motion: 身ぶり・手ぶりによる合図.
signal: 身ぶりによる合図のほか, 特に約束事として決められた意味をもつものや, 音や光による合図.
cue: 主に舞台・撮影などの合図.

先生からの合図で at [on] *a sign from* the teacher / 助けを求めて合図する *signal for* help

老人はもっとそばに来るよう私に手で合図した The old man *motioned* (to) me with his hand *to* come closer.

僕が手をたたいたらスタートの合図だよ When I clap my hands, that's *your cue to* start.

彼女は子供たちにおしゃべりをやめるよう合図した She *made a sign to* the children *to* stop talking.

【signal [sign]＋(to [for]) 名(人)＋to *do*】 トムはウェーターに水を持ってくるよう合図した Tom *signaled* (to) the waiter *to* bring him water.

【signal＋(to) 名＋that節】 彼は私に電車が来ると合図した He *signaled* (to) me *that* the train was coming.

◆笛の合図に(→笛が鳴るとすぐに)子供たちはプールに飛び込んだ As soon as the whistle was blown, the children jumped into the swimming pool. / 私は彼に後についてくるよう合図した I *beckoned* him *to* follow me. / 彼は入るように私に目で合図した(→ウインクした) He *winked at* me *to* enter. / その船は合図の旗をかかげた The ship raised a *signal flag*.

アイスキャンディー ⚠(米)《商標名》Popsicle ⓒ, 《英》ice lolly ⓒ (❖×ice candy とはいわない)

アイスクリーム ice cream Ⓤⓒ(❖《英》では単に ice ともいう) ‖アイスクリームを3つください Three *ice creams*, please. ◆シングル[ダブル]のアイスクリーム《米》a single-[double-]*scoop*

🄮 「何のアイスクリームにする」「ラムレーズンにしようかな」"What flavor of *ice cream* are you going to have?" "Well, I think I'll have rum raisin."
‖アイスクリーム店 an ice-cream parlor / バニラアイスクリーム vanilla ice cream

アイスコーヒー ice(d) coffee Ⓤⓒ

アイススケート ice skating Ⓤ ── アイススケートをする ice-skate ⓔ (❖単に skate ともいう) ‖アイススケート靴 ice skates ⓒ / アイススケート場 an ice rink (❖単に rink ともいう)

アイスティー ice(d) tea Ⓤⓒ

アイスホッケー ice hockey Ⓤ (❖《米》では単に hockey ともいう)

アイスランド Iceland (❖公式名 the Republic of Iceland) ──アイスランド人 Icelander ⓒ ──アイスランド語 Icelandic Ⓤ ── アイスランド(人[語])の Icelandic

アイスリンク an ice rink

あいする 愛する (愛している)love ⓔ(❖通例進行形にはできない); (恋している) be in love ──愛すべき lovable ⇨ あい(愛)

愛すべき性格 a *lovable* character / 平和を愛する国民 a peace-*loving* people

私たちは子供たちを深く愛している We *love* our children deeply. /
クマのプーさんは世界中の多くの人々に愛されている Winnie the Pooh *is loved* by many people around the world. /
彼らは深く愛し合っている They *are* madly *in love with each other*.

あいせき 相席 ━━相席する share a table ∥ こちらの女性とご相席願えますか Would you mind *sharing a table with* this lady?

あいそ 愛想 愛想のいい声で in a *pleasant* voice / お愛想 *pleasantries* / お愛想を言う (→へつらう) *flatter* / 愛想笑いをする put on *a fake smile* / あの店員はいつも愛想がいい That salesclerk is always *pleasant* [*friendly*]. / 彼は愛想よくあいさつした He greeted me *affably*. / 妹は愛想のない(→そっけない)返事をした My sister gave me a *curt* [*blunt*] reply. / 彼女にはほとほと愛想が尽きた I'm completely *disgusted with* her.

∥愛想笑い a put-on smile
⇨ぶあいそう

あいぞう 愛憎 love and hatred

アイソトープ (同位元素) isotope ⓒ

あいだ 間

❶【時間】━━前(…の間) for, during; (…のうちに) in, within; (2つの時点の間) between ━━圈(…する・している間) while

語法
(1)「…の間」の「…」に期間を表す名詞がくる場合, その日本語に当たる英語が the, this, my などで限定されないときは for を用い, 限定されるときは during を用いる. ただし the past ..., the last ... などには during, for ともに用いられる ∥ 私たちは1週間の間そのホテルに滞在した We stayed at the hotel *for* a week. / 夏休みの間何度か海に行った I went to the sea a couple of times *during* the summer vacation.
(2)「…のうちに」「…以内に」のように期限を表す場合は, in または within を用いる. within のほうが, その意味が強調される.
(3)「…から〜の間」のように2つの時点を表す場合は, between を用いる.
(4)「私の留守の間」は,「私が留守にしている間」のように「…している間」と言い換えることができる. このような場合, 前置詞ではなく, 接続詞 while を用いて表すこともできる. 一般に接続詞を用いるほうが口語的になる ∥ 私の留守の間 *during* my absence; (→私が留守にしている間) *while* I'm [I was] absent (❖この場合, 口語では absent ではなく, out または away のほうがふつう)

かぜをひいたのか, この2, 3日の間, のどが痛い I might have a cold. I've had a sore throat *for* the past two or three days. /
数週間の間, 雨が降っていない There hasn't been any rain *for* several weeks. /
今年は冬の間に雪が降らなかった We didn't have any snow *during* the winter this year. /
1週間の間にこの本を読まなければならない I have to read this book *in* [*within*] a week. /
体育館は7月10日から20日までの間使用できない You can't use the gym *between* July 10 *and* 20. / You can't use the gym *from* July 10 *until* [*till, to,* (米)*through*] 20. /
トムが日本にいる間にいっしょに旅行をしたかったが, 残念ながらできなかった I wanted to travel with Tom *while* he was in Japan, but unfortunately I couldn't. /
当分の間, 新しいパソコンを買うつもりはありません I don't plan to buy a new computer *for a while*. /
長い間待ったけど, 隆志は現れなかった I waited (*for*) *a long time*, but Takashi never showed up.

◆しばらくの間お待ちください Please wait *a moment*. / 兄は夏休みの間ずっとアルバイトをした My brother worked part time all *through* (*the*) *summer vacation*. / 夜の間ずっと工事の音がうるさくて, よく眠れなかった There was loud noise from the construction work *all night*, so I couldn't sleep very well. / 弟が小さい間は, 家族で旅行することはほとんどなかった Our family almost never took any trips *when* my (younger) brother was little. / 家に着くまでの間, どうか雨が降ってきませんように I hope it doesn't rain *until* we get home. / その間中ずっと真希は新しい恋人の話ばかりしていた Maki just talked about her new boyfriend *the whole time*.

💬「夏休みの間にどこかへ行った?」「お盆の間は父のいなかの島根に行っていたけど, それ以外は家にいたよ」"Did you go anywhere *during* summer vacation?" "*During Bon* I went to my father's hometown in Shimane. Otherwise, I just stayed home."

❷【空間】 between
ロッカーと壁の間に100円玉が落ちている A 100-yen coin is *between* the locker *and* the wall. /
由香と真弓の間にいるのはだれですか Who's that *between* Yuka *and* Mayumi? /
図書館で本を借りたら, ページの間に手紙がはさまっていた When I borrowed a book from the library, I found a letter *between* the pages. /
駅までの間のどこかにコンビニがないかな I wonder if there's a convenience store *between* here *and* the station. /
その観光船は小島の間を縫って進みます The tour boat goes *between* some small islands. /
30センチくらいずつ間をあけていすを並べてください Line up the chairs with spaces of about thirty centimeters *between* them.

◆木立の間を吹く風の音が心地よい The sound of wind *through* the trees is calming. /
ここから2キロの間急な上り坂が続きます The steep uphill slope continues *for* the next

two kilometers. / すみません，間をもっと詰めて座ってください Excuse me. Could you please sit *closer together*?
❸【関係】(主に2つ・2人の間) between; (3つ・3人以上の間) among
最近2人の間はうまくいっていないみたいだ Things don't seem to be going well *between* (*the two of*) *them* recently.
2つの事件の間には何か関係がありそうだ There seems to be a connection *between* the two incidents.
私たちの間ではこのアニメのキャラクターが今はやっています This cartoon character is popular *among* us now.
そのクッキーをあなたたちの間で分けてください Divide those cookies *among* you.

あいたいする 相対する (向かい合う) face each other; (対立する) conflict Ⓐ, oppose

あいだがら 間柄 (関係) relationship Ⓤ, relations; (交際上の仲) terms ‖彼女と彼とはどういう間柄ですか What is her *relationship to* him? / 彼とは親しい間柄だ I'm *on good terms with* him.

アイダホ Idaho (❖米国北西部の州; 《略語》Id., Ida, 〔郵地〕ID)

あいち 愛知

愛知県は，日本でも有数の大都市である名古屋を含み，人口は全国で第4位を占めています。世界的に有名な自動車メーカーであるトヨタ自動車の本社は，この会社に由来する豊田市にあります。また瀬戸・常滑を中心に窯業も盛んで，「瀬戸物」といえば陶磁器の通称にもなっています。
Aichi Prefecture includes Nagoya (one of the biggest cities in Japan), and has the fourth biggest population in the country. Toyota, a world-famous automaker, has its head office in a city named Toyota after the company. The ceramics industry, which is centered in Seto and Tokoname, is also famous. "Setomono" (literally meaning "ceramics produced in Seto") has become a synonym for ceramics.

あいちゃく 愛着 attachment Ⓒ Ⓤ; (愛情) a passion, love Ⓤ (また〜) ‖彼女はこの古い家に深い愛着がある She *is* deeply *attached to* this old house. / このレコードには愛着がある This record *is dear to* my heart.

あいちょう¹ 哀調 pathos Ⓤ ◆哀調を帯びたメロディー a *sad* melody

あいちょう² 愛鳥 ‖愛鳥家 a bird lover / 愛鳥週間 Bird Week

あいつ guy Ⓒ, fellow Ⓒ ‖全くあいつらときたら Those *guys*! ◆あいつに思い知らせてやる I'll show *him*. / あいつは何者だ Who is *that person*? / あいつなら反対するに決まってる Of course *he* would object!

あいついで 相次いで (次々に) one after another; (連続して) in succession ‖貴重な遺品が相次いで発見された Remains of great significance were discovered *one after another*.

あいつぐ 相次ぐ (連続する) successive (❖比較変化なし) ‖相次ぐ自動車事故 *successive* car accidents

あいづち 相槌 ‖私は彼女の言葉に相づちを打った I *nodded at* her words.
⇨ コミュニケーションスキル p.7

あいて 相手
❶【組になる相手】(結婚・仕事などの) partner Ⓒ; (結婚の) match Ⓒ; (デートの) 《米》date Ⓒ, 《口語的》steady Ⓒ; (対等の相手方) counterpart Ⓒ
貿易相手国 a trading *partner*
ダンスの相手がいない I haven't got *a partner to* dance with.
リサは彼にぴったりの相手です Lisa is *a perfect match for* him.
❷【敵対者・ライバル】(試合・議論などの) opponent Ⓒ, rival Ⓒ; (好敵手) match Ⓒ (また〜); (競争相手) competitor Ⓒ, competition Ⓤ
相手を打ち破る defeat *one's opponent* / 競争相手の一歩先を行く keep [stay] one jump ahead *of a rival* / 売り上げで競争相手を上回る outstrip *a rival* in sales
そのボクサーは対戦相手をダウンさせた The boxer knocked *his opponent* down.
将棋に関しては僕では彼の相手にならない I'm *no match for* him in *shogi*. (→彼は僕よりはるかにうまい) He *is* much better than me [I] in *shogi*.
◆ 3人の候補者を相手に闘う *run against* three other candidates / 相手にとって不足のない敵 a *worthy enemy* / 彼は思わぬ相手に破れた He was beaten by *a dark horse*.
❸【行為の対象】(❖特定の語を用いるのではなく，状況によって訳し分けることが多い)
人の相手をする *keep* a person *company*
(電話で)相手の方がお出になりました Your *party* is on the line.
だれか話し相手が欲しい I need *someone to talk to*.
テニスの相手をしてくれない？ Will you play tennis *with me*?
その通りには外国人相手の店がたくさんある There are many shops *for foreigners* on that street.
あんなやつ相手にするな(→ほうっておけ) *Leave* him *alone*. / (→気にかけるな) *Don't bother with* him.
彼はだれにもまともに相手にしてもらえない He *isn't taken* seriously by anybody.
質問する相手を間違えてるよ You are asking *the wrong person*.
彼は有名な女優の相手役に抜擢(ばってき)された He was chosen to *play opposite* a famous actress.
相手の身になってごらん Put yourself *in his* [*her*] *shoes*.

アイディア idea Ⓒ ‖あふれ出るアイディア a flow *of ideas* / あるアイディアが頭に浮かんだ An *idea* popped into my mind. / I hit on

あいとう

コミュニケーションスキル —あいづち—

①相手の話を聞きあいづちを入れる

(A) This is my first visit to Japan.
 −Oh, **really**? I hope you'll enjoy your stay.
日本へ来たのは今回が初めてなんです。—ほう，そうですか。ご滞在をどうぞお楽しみください。

(B) I met Susie yesterday.
 −Oh, **did you**? How was she getting along?
きのうスージーに会ったよ。—おや，そうですか。彼女はどんな様子でしたか。

(C) What do you think of this picture? A masterpiece, isn't it?
 −**Well, um** … I'm afraid it's beyond most people.
君, この絵をどう思う。傑作だろ。—ううん，さあどうかな…だれにも理解できないんじゃないかな。

(D) Do you know a store that sells maps?
 −**Let me see [Let's see]** … I think there's a bookstore next to the station.
地図を売っている店, 知らない? —ちょっと待ってね…駅前に本屋があったはずだけど。

☞ (A) の really? は上昇調で発音し,「本当ですか」という軽い驚きを伝える表現. **Not really!** を下降調で発音すると,「まさか」の意味になる.

☞ (B) は相手の言葉の最初の部分をそのまま Did you (meet Susie yesterday)? の疑問形にしたもの. 現在形なら Do you?, また三人称単数なら Does he [she]? のようになる.

☞ 相手に何かを尋ねられたときに, 即座に返事ができないときは, (C), (D) のような言いよどみの表現を用いると便利. (D) の Let me see. は「ちょっと待って」の意味.

②驚き・感嘆の気持ちを表す

(A) Have you got everything?
 −**Oh! [Dear me!]** I forgot my camera!
忘れ物はないかい. —あっ, カメラを忘れちゃった!

(B) I'll bake a cake for your birthday.
 −**Wow! (That's) great!** I can't wait (for it).
あなたの誕生日にケーキを焼いてあげる. —うわあ, それはすごい! 待ちきれないよ.

☞ Oh!, Wow!, (That's) great! はどれも驚きや喜びを表す最も一般的な語で, 男女の別なく用いられる. あまり過剰にならない程度に使うのがよい. (A) で Oh! の代わりに Dear me! を用いるのは主に女性. 激しい驚きや恐怖を言い表すには, **Oh, my God! / Oh God! / My God!** がよく用いられるが, God(神) という直接な言葉を避けるため, 遠回し語として **Gosh, Gee, Goodness** などが使われることがある.

③相手の言葉に対する理解や疑問を伝える

(A) He had lived in Kobe for five years.
 −**I see.** That explains why he knows so much about the city.
彼は神戸に5年間住んでいたんだよ。—なるほど. だから彼は神戸に詳しいわけですね.

(B) It was just a joke. I just wanted to cheer her up.
 −OK. **I know how you feel.**
ただの冗談だったんだよ. 彼女を元気づけたかっただけなんだ. —ああ, 気持ちは分かってるよ.

(C) I'm sure he won't say yes to your proposal.
 −**Why? / How come?**
彼は君の提案には賛成しないと思うよ—どうして.

(D) I hear Sara is going to move to Chicago.
 −**No kidding! / You must be kidding!**
サラがシカゴに引っ越すらしいよ. —冗談だろう!

(E) He is going out with Hiroko.
 −**I can't believe it! / Incredible!**
彼は寛子とつきあっているんだ. —まさか! / 信じられない!

☞ 相手の言っていることを理解できたことを伝えるには, (A) の I see. のほか, **I understand.** や **I got it.** もよく使われる. (B) の I know how you feel. は「私には君の気持ちは分かる」という意味.

☞ (C) の How come? は口語で, 特に驚いて理由を尋ねるときによく使われる. why を用いた表現と異なる点は語順で, Why won't he say yes to my proposal? に対して How come he won't say yes to my proposal? と How come 以下が主語+述語動詞になる.

☞ (D) の No kidding! と You must be kidding! は,「まさか!」とか「うそお!」に相当. あまり深刻な意味ではなく, 軽い疑いを表す言葉. **No joke [joking]!, You must be joking!** などともいう.

---

an *idea.* / それはいいアイディアだ That's *a good idea.*

コロケーション –idea–
【形容詞+〜】使い古された〜 a formulaic idea / 陳腐な〜 a stale [shopworn] idea / 斬新(ざんしん)な〜 a fresh idea
【動詞+〜】〜を思いつく come up with an idea / 〜を出す present an idea / 〜を盗む pick an idea

‖アイディア商品 novelties / アイディアマン an idea man

あいてどる 相手取る 国を相手取って訴訟を起こす bring an action [a claim] *against* the nation

アイテム item Ⓒ

アイデンティティー identity ⓤⒸ

あいとう 哀悼 (悔やみ) condolence ⓤⒸ (しばしば複数形〜s) ‖彼らは犠牲者の遺族に哀悼の意を表した They *expressed their condolences*

to the families of the victims.

あいどく 愛読 探偵小説の愛読者 *a great reader of detective stories* / 私はこの本を愛読している(→私の愛読書の一つだ) This book *is one of my favorites.* / 母は大江健三郎の作品を愛読している(→好きだ) My mother *likes* Oe Kenzaburo's books.
‖愛読書 *one's favorite book [books]*

アイドル idol ◯ ‖アイドル歌手 a pop idol [star] (◆通例 ×idol singer とはいわない)

あいにく (不幸にも) unfortunately, unhappily, unluckily; (残念ながら) I'm afraid ... / あいにく美術館は閉まっていた *Unfortunately,* the art museum was closed. / ちょうど出かけようとしたときに, あいにく雨が降ってきた Just when I was going out, *unfortunately* it started to rain.
◆ハイキングにはあいにくの天気だった The weather was *unfavorable for* hiking.
💬「コンサートには来られますか」「あいにくその日は先約があってだめなんですよ」"Can you come to our concert?" "*I'm afraid* not. I've got a previous engagement on that day."

アイヌ (アイヌ人) Ainu ◯ ──アイヌの Ainu ◯ ‖アイヌ語 Ainu

あいのり 相乗り car pool ◯ (◆米国で, 通学・通勤などの自動車の相乗り); (オートバイなどの) ride pillion ◯ ◆自転車に相乗りする *ride on* a bicycle *together*; *ride double* on a bicycle

アイバンク eye bank ◯ ‖アイバンクに登録している I am registered with *an eye bank.*

あいはんする 相反する conflict (with ...) ──相反した (矛盾した) contradictory; (入れない感情の) ambivalent ‖相反する意見 *conflicting* opinions / 彼は父親に対して尊敬と軽蔑(けいべつ)という相反する感情をもっている He has *ambivalent* feelings of respect and contempt toward [about] his father.

あいぶ 愛撫 caress ◯ ──愛撫する caress 他, fondle 他; (口語的)pet 他

あいべや 相部屋 彼女とはそのユースホステルで相部屋だった I *shared a room* with her in the youth hostel.

あいぼう 相棒 partner ◯, companion ◯; (通例男の)(口語的)buddy ◯; (仲間) mate ◯ / 彼にとって, 自分の犬はたいへんよい相棒である His dog is such *a good partner [companion] to* him.

アイボリー (象牙(ぞうげ)色) ivory ◯.

あいま 合い間 interval ◯; (勉強・仕事などの) break ◯ ◆授業の合い間に数学の宿題を終わらせた I finished the math homework *between* classes.

あいまい 曖昧 ──あいまいな (2つ以上の意味にとれる) ambiguous; (漠然とした) vague; (態度をはっきりさせない) noncommittal; (不鮮明(ふせんめい)の) obscure
あいまいな言い方 *a vague [an ambiguous]* expression / あいまいな返事をする give a *vague* reply
彼のあいまいな態度にいやけがさしたので, 別れることにした I got tired of his *noncommittal*

behavior, so I decided to break up with him.
3年も前のことなので, 記憶がかなりあいまいだ It happened three years ago, so my memory is quite *vague.*
あの人の言うことはいつもあいまい模糊(も)としている Everything he says is *vague.*

あいまって 相まって その彫刻は周りの自然とあいまって(→いっしょになって)人々を感動させずにおかない The sculpture *together with* the surrounding nature surely moves people.

あいよう 愛用 私の愛用の(→お気に入りの)英和辞典 my *favorite* English-Japanese dictionary / 私はこのシャンプーを愛用している(→いつも使っている) I *use* this shampoo *regularly.*

あいよく 愛欲 sexual desire ◯ ◯; (強い性欲) lust ◯ ◯

あいらしい 愛らしい (かわいらしい) sweet, cute, pretty; (天使のような) angelic

アイルランド Ireland ──アイルランド人 (男性) Irishman ◯; (女性) Irishwoman ◯; 《集合的》the Irish ──アイルランド語 Irish ◯ ──アイルランド(人[語])の Irish

アイロン iron ◯ ──アイロンをかける iron 他他, press 他 ‖アイロンがけのいらないシャツ a *non-iron* shirt / シャツにアイロンをかける *iron [press]* a shirt / しわをアイロンで伸ばす *iron out* the wrinkles
‖アイロン台 an ironing board / スチームアイロン a steam iron

あう¹ 会う・遭う

❶【人と会う】 meet* 他自, see* 他; (偶然に会う) encounter 他, (口語的)run* into *a person*

<語法>
「人と会う」の意味では, meet も see も使える場合が多い. しかし, see は「見かける」だけの意味で使う場合があるが, meet は「会って話す」のニュアンスが強い.「初めて会う」「約束して会う」の意味では meet を使う.

私はけさ電車の中で山田先生に会った I *met [saw]* Ms. Yamada on the train this morning.
きょうの放課後, いつもの所で会わない? Do you want to *meet* at the usual place after school today? (*see* は使えない)
今度の日曜日, 文化祭のことで水島さんに会うつもりです I plan to *meet [see]* Mr. Mizushima this Sunday regarding the Culture Festival.
ここが彼と初めて会った場所です This is (the place) where I first *met* my boyfriend.
このごろ彼女にあまり会っていない I *haven't seen* her much recently.
その人には一度も会ったことがありません I've *never met* him [her].
きょう健と図書館で会う約束をしていたのに, 約束をすっぽかされた Ken and I had agreed to *meet* at the library today, but he broke

his promise.
きのう駅でばったり旧友に会った I encountered [ran into] an old friend of mine at the station yesterday.
またお会いできるといいですね I hope to see you again. / I hope (that) I can see you again.
あなたに会いたくてたまらない I really want to see you.

🍀「いつ会いましょうか」「あすはどうですか」 "When shall we meet?" "How about tomorrow?"

🍀「また近々会えるかな」「たぶんね」 "Do you think we can meet again soon?" "Probably."

🍀「やあ, 久しぶり」「この前会ったのはいつだったっけ」 "Hi! I haven't seen you for a long time!" "When was the last time we saw each other?"

❷【知り合いになる】
お会いできてうれしいです Nice to meet you. / (I'm) glad to meet you. / (I'm) pleased to meet you. / It's nice meeting you. (❖初めて会った人にはではなく meet を用いる, 最後の表現は「会えてよかった」の意味で別れ際にも用いる)

❸【遭遇する・経験する】experience 他, encounter 他, run* into …; (事故などに) have* 他
火災にあう experience [have] a fire
交通事故にあわないように気をつけよう Be careful not to have a traffic accident.

◆にわか雨にあう be caught in a shower / 不意打ちにあう be caught off guard / 猛反対にあう be fiercely opposed / 私はどんなつらい目にあってもがんばれる自信がある I'm confident that I can hold on no matter what happens (to me).

慣用表現 「会うは別れの始め」といいますが, みなさんともうお別れしなければなりません It is said that we meet only to part, and now it is time for us to say good-bye.

あう² 合う

❶【適合する】fit* 自 他, suit 他
この靴は小さすぎて私の足に合わない These shoes are too small. They don't fit (me). (❖「私の足」に合わせて my feet を英文に入れる必要はない)
このジャケットは体にぴったり合っている This jacket fits just right.
その役はその俳優には合わないだろう The role wouldn't fit that actor.
このかぎは合っていない This key doesn't fit (the lock). / This key doesn't work.
この地方の気候は喘息(ぜんそく)の人に合っているらしい The climate in this region seems to suit [be good for] people with asthma.
日本の食べ物があなたのお口に合うといいのですが I hope Japanese food will suit you. / I hope you will like Japanese food.

❷【調和する】go* (well) with …, match 他
その赤いブラウス, スカートに合ってるね The red blouse goes well with the skirt.
ピザにはコーラが合う Cola goes well with pizza.
このカーテンは壁紙の色と合わない This curtain doesn't match the color of the wallpaper.
このドラムは曲調にあまり合ってない This drumming doesn't go very well with this song.

◆彼の服装はあまり私の趣味に合わない His clothes are not much to my liking. / I don't like his clothes very much.

❸【一致する・正しい】agree 自, match 自, correspond 自, coincide 自
彼らはそこへどうやって行くかについては意見が合わなかった They didn't agree (about) how to get there. (❖wh- 節[句]を伴うと前置詞が省略されることがある)
あなたの言っていることは, 全然事実と合ってない What you're saying does not agree at all with reality.
私の考えはほかの人たちの考えと合わない My ideas don't correspond [agree] with those of the others.
何度やっても計算が合わない I've calculated it again and again, but the results don't match.
私たちは服の好みが合う Our tastes in clothes coincide. / We have the same tastes in clothes.

◆この計算は合っていないと思う I don't think this calculation is right. / あの時計は合っていますか Is that clock right? / 答え合わせをしたら答えが合っていなかった I checked the answer and it was wrong. / 僕と目が合うと彼女はにっこりほほえんだ When her eyes met mine, she gave me a smile.

慣用表現 あのバッテリーは呼吸が合っている That pitcher and catcher are a good combination. / 私と彼とはどうも反(そ)りが合わない He and I never agree (with each other). / このアルバイトは割に合わない This part-time job is not worth it.

-あう －合う

語法 「互いに」の意味では each other, one another を用いるが, 状況に応じて他の表現も使う.

2 人は助け合って燃えているビルから脱出した The two of them helped each other escape from the burning building. / 治と和男の 2 人と宿題の見せ合いをした Osamu, Kazuo and I showed our homework to one another.

アウト 〖野球・テニス・ゴルフ〗out C ——アウトで out / 4回の表ワンアウトで with one out in the top of the fourth / 彼はサードゴロでアウトになった He grounded out to third. / 審判はバッターアウトを宣告した The umpire called the batter out. / 彼は三塁に盗塁を試みたがアウトになった He was out [caught] stealing third (base).

アウトコース 〖野球〗outside C (↔inside);

アウトサイダー

(陸上の) outside track ◆彼はアウトコースの球を投げた He pitched the batter *outside*.

アウトサイダー (よそ者) outsider

アウトドア ―アウトドアの outdoor (↔indoor) ∥アウトドア用品の専門店 the store that sells only *outdoor* items

アウトバーン autobahn [áutobɑːn] (❖ドイツ・オーストリア・スイスの高速道路)

アウトプット 〔コンピュータ〕(出力) output ∥アウトプットする output*

アウトライン (輪郭・概略) outline; (要旨・概略) summary ∥この計画のアウトラインがつかめない I can't understand *the outline* of this project.

アウトロー (無法者)《古風》outlaw

あえぐ 喘ぐ ❶【息を切らす】pant, gasp, puff ∥私たちは山頂までの急な坂道をあえぎながら登った We *panted* as we climbed the steep slope to the top of the mountain.
❷【苦しむ】suffer ∥世界には貧困にあえぐ人々がいる There are people in this world who *are suffering from* poverty. ◆その打者は打撃不振にあえいでいる The batter *has been troubled* by a batting slump.

あえて 敢えて (あえて…する) dare to *do* ∥彼女はあえて反論しなかった She *didn't dare to* argue with him. ◆私はあえてみなさんにこの計画の見直しを提案したいと思います I would like to (*go so far as to*) propose to you that this plan be revised. ∥彼はなぜのどしゃ降りの雨の中をあえて出かけたのか Why did he go out *in spite of* this pouring rain? ∥言いにくいけれどあえて言えば、あなたの作文は推敲(すいこう)が必要だ I hate to tell you this, *but* your composition needs to be revised. ∥そんな高価な物をあえて買おうとは思わない I would *never* consider buying such an expensive thing. ∥病気を押してまであえて出かける必要はない You don't have to go out when you're sick.

あえもの 和え物 flavored side dish

あえる 和える (野菜などを) toss ∥ゆでたインゲンを練りごまであえる *toss* boiled beans with sesame paste

あえん 亜鉛 〔化学〕zinc (❖元素記号は Zn) ◆亜鉛メッキされた鉄板 a *galvanized* iron plate

あお 青 blue; (緑) green ――青い blue; (緑の) green; (顔色が) pale (❖日本語では「青信号」「青葉」などというが、英語では blue ではなく green を用いる)
淡い青 light *blue* ∥ 濃い青 dark *blue* ∥ 青いリンゴ a *green* apple ∥ 青い鳥 a *blue bird*; (→比喩的に) *the bluebird of happiness*
信号が青になるまで待ちなさい Wait till the signal turns *green*./ (→青信号を待ちなさい) Wait for the *green* light.
その女の子は金髪で青い目をしていた The girl had blond hair and *blue* eyes.
彼女は体が弱くて、いつも青い顔をしている (→顔色が悪い) She's not in very good shape. Her *face* is always *pale*.
野原先生はその知らせを聞いて青くなった Ms. Nohara *turned pale* when she heard the news.
🍀「顔色が青いけど大丈夫?」「うん、大丈夫。でもちょっとかぜをひいたのかもしれない」"You look *pale*. Are you okay?" "Yeah, I'm fine. I may have caught a little cold, though."

∥青あざ a bruise ∥ 青色申告 a blue tax return (form) ∥ 青かび green mold [《英》mould] ∥ 青信号 ⇨ あおしんごう ∥ 青竹 green bamboo ∥ 青葉 ⇨ あおば

短歌 白鳥は哀(かな)しからずや空の青海のあをにも染まずただよふ (若山牧水)
The white bird is sad.
Beneath the blue of heaven,
above the blue waves,
she floats alone, always white:
never blue like sea and sky.

あおあお 青々 ―青々とした (草などに覆われた) green; (よく茂った) lush; (深い青色の) (deep) blue ∥青々とした牧草地 *green* pasture ∥ 青々とした草木がどこまでも広がっていた *Lush* grass and trees spread out endlessly.

あおいきといき 青息吐息 不景気でどこの会社も青息吐息だ (→困難なときだ) Every company *is having a difficult time* because of the recession.

あおぐ¹ 仰ぐ ❶【上を見る】look up ∥星空を仰ぐ *look up* at the starry sky
❷【敬う】look up ∥人々は彼女を師と仰いだ People *looked up* to her *as* their teacher.
❸【教えなどを求める】ask, seek* ∥医者の指示を仰ぐ *ask for* a doctor's advice

あおぐ² 扇ぐ (扇子(せんす)などで) fan ∥あおいで火をおこす *fan* the fire into flames ∥ 生徒たちはノートであおいでいた The students *were fanning* themselves with their notebooks.

あおくさい 青臭い (未熟な) inexperienced, raw, 《口語的》green; (子供じみた) immature ∥彼は若くてまだ青臭い新人だ He is a young and *green* newcomer [rookie].
◆彼女はとても青臭い野菜ジュースを毎日飲んでる Every day she drinks vegetable juice which *smells very green*.

あおざめる 青ざめる (青くなる) turn pale [white] ∥彼はその知らせを聞いて青ざめた He *turned pale* at the news. ◆青ざめた顔 a *pale* face ∥ 女の人の顔は恐怖で青ざめていた Her face was *white* with terror.

あおじゃしん 青写真 (設計図などの複写・計画案) blueprint ∥平和のための青写真を作る make [draw] *a blueprint* for peace

あおじろい 青白い pale; (病的な) pallid ∥青白く光る星 *pale* twinkling stars ∥ 父は病み上がりで、まだ青白い顔をしている My father is recovering from an illness. His face still looks *pale*.

あおしんごう 青信号 green light (❖この場合の「青」に blue は使えない) ∥青信号になったら渡りなさい You can cross the street on

[with] *the green light.* / 私の計画に上司が青信号を出した My boss *gave the green light to* my idea.

あおすじ 青筋 (blue) vein [C] ∥彼は額に青筋を立てて怒った He was so angry that *his veins stood out* on his forehead.

あおぞら 青空 a [the] blue sky ∥私たちは青空の下で昼食をとった We had lunch under *the blue sky*.
‖青空市 an open-air market / 青空教室 an open-air class / 青空コンサート an open-air concert

あおたがい 青田買い 青田買いをする(→水田の稲を成熟前に先買いする) *buy unripe rice at the rice field*; (→卒業前の学生の採用を決定する) *recruit future employees from students before they graduate from college or high school*

あおにさい 青二才 inexperienced young man [C], 《口語的》greenhorn [C]
◆彼はまだ青二才だ He is still「*a greenhorn* [*green, wet behind the ears*].

あおのり 青海苔 dried green seaweed [U]

あおば 青葉 (緑の葉) fresh green leaves ∥青葉の季節がやってきた The season of *fresh green leaves* has come.

あおむく 仰向く (顔を上に向ける) turn *one's* face up [upward]; (上を向く) look up [upward]

あおむけ 仰向け あおむけに倒れる「turn over [fall down] *on one's back* / 彼女は弟をあおむけに寝かせた She laid her little brother *on his back*.

あおむし 青虫 green caterpillar [C]

あおもの 青物 (野菜類) vegetables; (青野菜) greens ➾ やさい ‖青物市場 a vegetable market

あおもり 青森

> 青森県は本州の最北端に位置しています. その寒冷な気候はリンゴ栽培に適しており, 全国一の生産量を誇っています. また"ねぶた祭"でも有名です. この県の南西部から秋田県にかけて広がる白神山地には, 世界最大級のブナの原生林が保存されており, 世界遺産に登録されています. Aomori Prefecture is located in the northernmost part of Honshu. Its cold weather is suitable for growing apples, and it ranks first in apple production in the country. Also it is famous for the Nebuta Festival. The Shirakami Mountains, ranging from the southwestern part of this prefecture to Akita, have been registered in the World Nature Legacy as having the world's largest virgin beech tree forest.

あおり 煽り その会社は円高のあおりを受けて倒産した The company went bankrupt *because of* the strong yen.

あおる 煽る (風が) blow* [他], toss [他]; (けしかける) stir up ∥強風にあおられてそのグライダーはバランスを失った The glider *was tossed* by a strong wind and lost its balance. / そのような発言は反日感情をあおるだろう Such remarks will *stir up* anti-Japanese feelings.

あか[1] 赤 red [U]; (深紅色) crimson [U]; (緋(ひ)色) scarlet [U] (❖scarlet は crimson より明るい赤色) ──赤い red; crimson; scarlet ∥濃い赤 dark [deep] *red* / 薄い赤 light [pale] *red* / 赤と白の塗料を混ぜる mix *red* paint with white (paint)
木の葉の色が緑から赤に変わった The (color of the) leaves changed from green to *red*.
君には赤がよく似合う *Red* looks good on you.
彼女が横に座ったので彼は赤くなった He「*turned red* [(→赤面した) *blushed*] when she sat beside him.
赤ペンで誤りを直してください Correct errors with *a red pen*.
◆赤っ恥をかいた It was *a total embarrassment*.
‖赤い羽根募金 the Red Feather fund-raising drive / 赤ワイン red wine
[慣用表現] 彼は赤の他人です He is *a complete* [*total*] *stranger* to me.

あか[2] 垢 (汚れ) dirt [U], grime [U]; (湯あか) fur [U], scale [U] ∥あかを落とす wash off *the dirt* / あの男性は体中あかだらけだった That man's body was covered with *dirt*.
◆手あかのついた本 a *well-thumbed* book

あかあか(と) 赤々(と) brightly ∥炭火が赤々と燃えている The charcoal is burning *brightly*. ◆赤々と燃える火 a *bright* fire

あかがい 赤貝 ark shell [C]

あがき 足掻き (もがき) struggle [C] ➾ わるあがき

あかぎれ chap [C] ◆あかぎれの手 *chapped* hands / 彼女の手はあかぎれが切れている Her hands *are chapped*.

あかげ 赤毛 red hair [U]; (赤褐色の) ginger hair [U] ──赤毛の red-headed ∥赤毛の人 a person with *red* [*ginger*] *hair*; 《口語的》a redhead (❖後の表現は特に女性についていう)

あかし 証 (証拠) proof [U], a tribute ∥ブランドンはスティーブに友情のあかしを求めた Brandon demanded *proof* of friendship from [×to] Steve.
◆私は身のあかしを立てた(→身の潔白を証明した) I proved *my innocence*.

あかじ 赤字 ❶【欠損】deficit [C], 《英》overspend [C], the red ∥100万円の赤字を出す[埋める] have [make up] *a deficit* of one million yen / 今月わが家は赤字だ Our household budget *is in the red* this month. / 増大する貿易赤字が経済に大きな負担をかけている The expanding *trade deficit* is putting an enormous strain on the economy.
❷【文字】(英文字など) red letters; (漢字など) red characters; (印字など) red print [U], red type [U] ◆赤字を入れる *make corrections in red ink*
‖赤字経営 operating in the red / 赤字国債 deficit bonds / 赤字予算 a deficit budget

アカシア acacia [əkéiʃə]

あかしお 赤潮 red tide ‖赤潮が魚介類に大被害を与えた The red tide caused great harm to fish and shellfish.

あかしんごう 赤信号 red light ‖赤信号で止まる stop at a red light ｜ 赤信号を無視する run a red light ｜ 雨不足で飲み水の供給に赤信号がともった The supply of drinking water is in danger because of the drought.

あかす 明かす ❶【明らかにする】(暴露する) reveal, disclose; (話す) tell* ‖真相を明かす reveal [disclose] the truth ｜ 君にだけ秘密を明かそう I'll tell my secret only to you. ◆身分を明かす identify oneself ｜ 種を明かす give away the trick ｜ 彼女は本心を明かそうとはしなかった She wouldn't show her true feelings. ｜ 名前を明かさないという条件で彼はその病院に多額の寄付をした He gave a large sum of money to the hospital on condition that it would remain anonymous.

❷【夜を過ごす】spend*; (眠らずに) stay up ‖私たちは駅の待合室で一夜を明かした We spent the night in the waiting room at the station. ｜ 友人と朝まで語り明かした I stayed up all night talking with a friend.

慣用表現 何とかしてあいつの鼻をあかしてやりたい I want to get the better of him somehow.

あかちゃん 赤ちゃん baby,《公式的》infant (❈itで受けることもあるが、性別が分かる場合は he, she で受ける)

《～(の)赤ちゃん》
1歳と3か月の赤ちゃん a fifteen-month old baby (❈英米では赤ちゃんの年齢は1歳を過ぎても月数を用いることが多い) ｜ 男[女]の赤ちゃん a baby boy [girl] (❈×a boy [girl] baby とはいわない) ｜ かわいい赤ちゃん a cute baby ｜ 生まれたばかりの赤ちゃん a new-born baby ｜ イルカの赤ちゃん a baby dolphin

《赤ちゃんが・は》
彼女のおなかには赤ちゃんがいる She is expecting a baby.
彼女に先月赤ちゃんが生まれた She had a baby last month.
赤ちゃんは男の子ですか、女の子ですか Is the baby a he or a she?
赤ちゃんは母親のおっぱいを吸った The baby sucked at its mother's breast.

《赤ちゃんを・に》
赤ちゃんを母乳で育てる nourish a baby with its mother's milk
彼らは赤ちゃんを大輔と名づけた They named their baby Daisuke.
彼女は赤ちゃんに1日8回ミルクをやる She feeds her baby eight times a day.

《その他》
赤ちゃんのお守りをする take care of a baby; (→ベビーシッターとして) baby-sit
彼は私を赤ちゃん扱いする He treats me like a baby.
‖赤ちゃん言葉 baby talk

あかちょうちん 赤ちょうちん 赤ちょうちんとは典型的な日本の居酒屋を指しますが、店の入り口によく店名の入った赤いちょうちんがぶら下がっていることからそのような総称となっています。
Akachochin, literally "red lantern," is a typical Japanese-style drinking place. At the entrance is often hung a signature red lantern, which has become synonymous with taverns.

あかつき 暁 ❶【夜明け】dawn, daybreak, daylight ‖暁の空 a dawn sky ❷【物事が実現したそのとき】この計画が成功した暁には盛大なパーティーを開こう Once this project is a success, let's have a big party.

あがったり 上がったり この長雨で私たちの商売は上がったりだ Because of the long spell of rainy weather, our business has been slack.

あかつち 赤土 (赤い粘土) red clay, red earth

アカデミー academy (しばしば Academy) ‖アカデミー賞 an Academy Award, an Oscar

アカデミック (学問的な) academic ‖彼女はその都市のアカデミックな雰囲気が気に入っています She likes the academic atmosphere of the city.

あかてん 赤点 (落第点) failing grade; (不可) F ◆failure ‖化学のテストは赤点だった I got an F on my chemistry test.

あかとんぼ 赤蜻蛉 red dragonfly

あかぬけ 垢抜け ——あか抜けた (上品な・洗練された) refined, polished; (教養がある) sophisticated; (しゃれた) stylish, chic, smart; (都会風の) urbane (↔rustic) ——あか抜けない unrefined; unsophisticated ‖彼女の作法はとてもあか抜けている She has very refined manners. ｜ 都会に移ってからマイクはあか抜けてきた Since Mike moved to the city he has become more sophisticated.

あかね 茜 (茜色) madder

あかふだ 赤札 (特価品・見切り品) a red tag indicating a specially priced item, "sale" tag; (売約済みの札) "sold" tag

あかぼう 赤帽 ❶【赤い帽子】red cap ❷【駅・空港などの】porter,《米口語的》red-cap

あかみ¹ 赤身 (脂肪のない肉) lean (↔fat); (牛肉・羊肉などの) red meat ‖赤身の肉 lean meat; the lean (of meat)

あかみ² 赤味 redness ——赤みがかった reddish ‖傷跡の赤みがまだ消えない The redness of my scar still remains. ｜ ブレンダは赤みがかった茶色い髪をしている Brenda has reddish-brown hair. ◆彼女のほほにようやく赤みがさしてきた Finally the color started to return to her cheeks.

あがめる 崇める (神などを崇拝する) worship; (尊敬する) respect ‖彼らは自分たちの先祖を神のようにあがめる They worship their ancestors as gods.

あからがお 赤ら顔 ruddy face ‖赤ら顔の

男 a man *with a ruddy face*; a *ruddy-faced man*

あからさま 他人の欠点をあからさまに言う state *frankly* another person's faults / 不快感をあからさまに顔に出す show *one's* displeasure *openly* (on *one's* face)

あからめる 赤らめる （恥ずかしさから）blush 自; （興奮などで）flush 自 ∥彼女は彼の冗談に顔を赤らめた She *blushed* at his joke.

あかり 明かり （光）light Ⓤ; （照明）light Ⓒ, lamp Ⓒ

> 語法 天井についている照明は light(s)という場合が多い. 机, 床などに置いてある照明は light とも lamp ともいう. lamp は比較的小さく, 電球が1個程度しかないものを指す場合が多い.

薄明かり dim *light* / ランプの明かりで by [in] *the light* of a lamp

彼女は部屋の明かりをつけた［消した］ She turned on [off] *the light* in her room.

明かりを消すにはこのスイッチを押しなさい Flick this switch to turn *the light* off.

こんなに暗い明かりで勉強したら目を痛めるでしょう You'll strain your eyes if you study in this dim *light*.

この店の明かりはいつも暗くしてある *The lights* in this store are always turned down.

明かりが点滅しているのが見えた We could see *a light* blinking.

ドアの下から明かりがもれていた I could see *light* under the door.

トイレの明かりがつけっぱなしだった *The light* in the bathroom was on.

◆月明かりの中の散歩 a walk in *the moonlight* / ろうそくの明かりが揺らめいた *The candlelight* flickered.

あがり 上がり ❶【上昇】increase Ⓒ Ⓤ, rise Ⓒ ∥土地の値上がり *an increase* in land prices

❷【完了・できばえ】（完了）end Ⓒ, finish Ⓤ; （できばえ）result Ⓒ Ⓤ, quality Ⓤ ∥これで上がりだ！ That's *the end*!

◆一丁上がり！ *One order is ready*! ❖これは「注文の品が用意できた」の意味だが, 英語には日本語のような決まり文句はない.

❸【利益】profit Ⓒ Ⓤ ∥この季節は店の上がりも多い The store's *profits* are good at this time of year.

-あがり -上がり ❶【直後】（…の後に）after ∥私は雨上がりの空を見上げた I looked up at the sky *after the rain.* / 姉はふろ上がりにストレッチを欠かさない My sister always has a stretch *after a bath.*

◆病み上がり（→病気から回復したばかり）なのだから無理しなくてもいいよ Since you *have just recovered from an illness*, you don't have to work so hard.

❷【出身】（元…．前…）ex- ❖名詞の前に付ける. ただし軽蔑的なニュアンスはない ∥役人上がりの an *ex*-government official / 大統領は軍人上がりだ The President is an *ex*-serviceman.

あがりおり 上がり下り 階段を上がり下りする go [walk] *up and down* the stairs

あがりこむ 上がり込む （入り込む）come* [go*, step, walk] in（❖目的語をとるときは into ...）, enter 他 ∥彼は彼女の家に上がり込んで長時間彼女と話した He *went into* her house and talked to her for a long time.

あがりさがり 上がり下がり rise and fall ──上がり下がりする rise* and fall*, fluctuate 自 ∥この季節は気温の上がり下がりが激しい In this season, the temperature *rises and falls drastically.* / 近年円相場の上がり下がりが激しい In recent years, the value of the yen *has been fluctuating sharply*.

あがりゆ 上がり湯 *agariyu*, hot water outside the bathtub for rinsing off after having taken a bath

あがる¹ 上がる

❶ 昇る・上昇する	go up, rise
❷ 値段・地位・程度	improve; increase, rise, go up; reach
❸ 終了する	stop, finish, end
❹ 平静を失う	get [become] nervous
❺ 声・火	rise
❻ 訪れる	visit
❼ 食べる・飲む	have; eat; drink

❶【昇る・上昇する】go* up, rise* 自; （ふろなどから出る）get* out of ...

階段[はしご]を上がる *go up* the stairs [ladder] / 舞台に上がる *go up on* (the) stage

エレベーターで最上階まで上がった I *went up to* the top floor in the elevator.

屋根に上がると海が見える If you *go up on* the roof, you can see the ocean.

幕がゆっくりと上がった The curtain *rose* [*went up*] slowly.

火口付近から煙が上がっていた Smoke *was rising* from around the crater.

急いでプールから上がりなさい Hurry up and *get out of* the pool.

父はふろから上がると必ずビールを飲む My dad always drinks some beer when he *gets out of* the bath.

◆（船乗りが）陸に上がる *go on shore* / 寝違えたのか, 肩が痛くて腕が上がらない Maybe I slept wrong. My shoulder hurts so much (that) I *can't lift* my arm.

❷【値段・地位・程度】（よくなる）improve 自; （上昇する）increase 自, rise* 自, go* up; （あるレベルに達する）reach 他

社会的地位が上がる *rise* in society; *achieve* a higher position

高2になってから英語の成績が上がった My English *grades have improved* since I moved up to the 11th grade.

きょうは気温が30度まで上がるらしい The temperature is supposed to「*go up to* [*reach*] 30 degrees today.

水位は2メートルまで上がった The water *reached* a level of two meters.

あがる

ガソリンの値段が上がった Gas *prices have gone up [increased]*. / 列車のスピードが徐々に上がった The speed of the train *increased* gradually. / ここ数日、円は上がったり下がったりしている The yen *has been rising and falling* for the past few days. / 物価は上がる傾向にある Prices tend to *increase*.

◆彼は経営するアパートから毎月40万円上がる He *gets* 400,000 yen a month from the apartment house he owns. / 妹は来年中学校に上がる My sister *will enter* junior high school next year. / 消費税が上がった The consumption tax *has been raised*. / 新しい経済政策の効果があった(→効果が証明された) The new economic policy *proved effective*.

❣「ひとり暮らしを始めてから料理の腕は上がった?」「全然．いつも外食だもん」"*Has your cooking improved* since you started living by yourself?" "Not at all. I always eat out."

❸【終了する】stop 自他, finish 自他, end 自他

雨が上がった It *stopped raining*. / やっと作文が書き上がった I *finished writing* the composition at last. / ◆今回の旅行は思ったよりも安く上がった This trip *cost less* than I had expected. / バッテリーが上がっている(→切れている) The battery *is dead* [《英》*flat*].

❹【平静を失う】get* [become*] nervous

あがってしまって、自分が何を言っているのか分からなくなった I *got so nervous* (that) I didn't know what I was saying. / 試験であがらないようにするおまじないを知っていますか Do you know any tricks for *not getting nervous* during tests?

❺【声・火】rise* 自

その歌手が舞台に登場すると大歓声があがった Cheers *rose* from the audience when the singer appeared on stage. / 町の中心部から火の手が上がった Flames *rose* from the center of the town.

❻【訪ねる】visit

あした先生のお宅にあいさつに上がるつもりです I'*m visiting* our teacher's home tomorrow to say hello.

❼【食べる・飲む】have* 他; (食べる) eat* 他; (飲む) drink* 他

うちの畑でとれたスイカです．どうぞおあがりください We grew these watermelons on our farm. Please *have* one.

❽【すっかり…する】

語法 「あがる」は動詞に付いて「すっかり…する」の意味を加える．「晴れ上がる」clear up のように動詞に副詞 up を付けて表すことができる語もあるが，必ずしも「あがる」と up が一対一に対応するわけではない． ➡ できあがる

あがる² 挙がる 彼は次の総理大臣として名前が挙がっている His name *has been raised* [*mentioned*] as the possible next Prime Minister. / その事件を立証するたくさんの証拠が挙がっている A lot of evidence *has been found* to prove the case. / ついに犯人が挙がった(→つかまった) Finally the criminal *was caught*. / 先生の質問に、いっせいに手が挙がった(→みんなが手を挙げた) Everyone *raised their hands* in response to the teacher's question.

あがる³ 揚がる てんぷらが揚がったら夕食にしよう We can start dinner as soon as the tempura *is finished*. / たこ、たこ、あがれ、天まであがれ *Go up*, kite. *Fly up* to the sky. (❖英語では慣用表現ではない) / 夜空に数千発の花火があがった Several thousand *fireworks* [*rockets*] *lit up* the night sky.

あかるい 明るい

❶【光が十分ある】light, bright ──明るく brightly, bright

明るい部屋 a *bright* [*sunny*] room (❖sunny は日光で明るい場合のみ用いる)

もっと明るい所で本を読みなさい Read the book in a *brighter* place. / 明るいうちに帰らなきゃ I have to go home 「*while it's still light* [(→暗くなる前に)*before (it gets) dark*]. / 夏の間その国では夜10時を回ってもまだ明るい In that country, it's still *light* after 10 p.m. during the summertime. / 2匹の小犬が明るい日差しの中でじゃれ合っていた Two puppies were playing in the *bright* sunlight. / 太陽は明るく輝いていた The sun was shining *bright* [*brightly*]. / 外がだんだん明るくなってきた It's getting *light* outside.

◆朝の6時ごろ空が明るくなる The sky *lightens* about 6 o'clock in the morning. / テレビでアニメを見るときは必ず部屋を明るくしましょう Make sure there is enough *light* in the room when watching cartoons on TV.

❷【性格・気分・雰囲気が】bright; (陽気な) cheerful, sunny ──明るく brightly; cheerfully

明るい笑顔 a *bright* smile / 明るい性格 a *cheerful* personality; a *sunny* disposition / 明るい家庭 a *cheerful* [*happy*] family

第一に彼女は正直で．それに明るい For one thing, she's honest, and for another she's *cheerful*.

◆最近クラスの雰囲気が明るくなったように思う The atmosphere in the class seems to *have brightened up* recently. / その知らせは彼女の表情を明るくした The news *brightened* her expression.

❸【色が澄んでいる】bright

明るい色 a *bright* [*brilliant*] color

ここはもっと明るい青を使ったほうがいい You should use a *brighter* blue here.

◆明るい色の服 *brightly* colored clothing

❹【希望がもてる】bright, promising

明るい未来 a *bright* future / 次の10年間について明るい見通し a *bright* outlook for the next decade

今年の経済情勢の見通しはあまり明るくない The outlook for the economy this year isn't very *bright*.

❺【公明正大な】
明るい政治 *clean* politics

❻【よく知っている】know* a lot, be knowledgeable, be familiar with ...

村井教授はインドネシアの事情に明るい Prof. Murai *knows a lot about* conditions in Indonesia.

◆私はこのあたりの地理に明るくない I *don't know much about* where things are around here.

あかるさ 明るさ ❶【光の輝き・鮮やかさ】brightness ⓤ (↔darkness), light ⓤ ∥ノブを回すとライトの明るさを調節できます You can control *the brightness* of the lights by turning the knob.

❷【快活・陽気】cheerfulness ⓤ ∥私の性格の長所は明るさだけだ The only good point of my personality is *my cheerfulness*.

❸【目・顔などの輝き】light ⓤ ∥彼の顔に明るさが戻った *The light* came back to his face.

あかるみ 今年に入ってすぐ彼の汚職事件が明るみに出た His corruption 「*came to light* [*was brought to light*] at the beginning of this year.

あかんたい 亜寒帯 (北極に近い) the subarctic zone;(南極に近い) the subantarctic zone

あかんべ pulling down *one's* lower eyelid with the index finger ◆その男の子は私に向かってあかんべをした The boy *stuck* [*put*] *his tongue out* at me.(❖英米では,人に向かって舌を出すと軽蔑・拒否などのしぐさになる)

あかんぼう 赤ん坊 baby ⓒ ⇨あかちゃん

あき¹ 秋

fall ⓤ, autumn ⓤ(❖《米》では通常 fall を用い,autumn は詩などで,または形容詞的用法で用いる。《英》では autumn がふつう)

米国では学校は秋に始まる School begins *in* (*the*) *fall* [*autumn*] in America.

彼らは2000年の秋に結婚した They got married *in the fall* [*autumn*] *of* 2000.

その歌手は今年の秋に来日する予定です The singer will come to Japan *this fall* [*autumn*].

山々は秋の色に染まっている The hills are full of *fall* [*autumn*] colors.

語法
(1) ふつう「秋に」というときは in fall でも in the fall でもよい。ただし,「…年の秋」という場合は the を付けることが多い。
(2) last, next, this などを伴う場合は前置詞は不要 ∥彼らは昨年の秋,大阪に引っ越した They moved to Osaka *last fall*.
(3) 形容詞的にも用いる ∥秋の天気 *fall* weather / 秋の果物 *autumn* fruit

∥秋風 an autumn wind [breeze] / 秋口 the beginning of autumn / 秋雨 an autumn rain / 秋空 the fall [autumn] sky / 秋晴れ a clear fall [autumn] day / 初秋 early fall [autumn] / 晩秋 late fall [autumn]

慣用表現 彼らの愛情に秋風が吹き始めた(→熱が冷めてきた)Their love *began to cool down*. / 秋の日は釣瓶(つるべ)落とし Dusk comes suddenly in fall [autumn]. / 秋の夜長 the long nights of fall [autumn] / 読書[スポーツ, 芸術, 食欲]の秋 Fall [Autumn] *is the best season for reading* [*sports, appreciating art, eating*].(❖欧米にはこのような考え方はない)

短歌 見渡せば花も紅葉(もみじ)もなかりけり浦の苫屋(とまや)の秋の夕暮(藤原定家)
Wherever I look
I see no cherry blossoms
and no crimson leaves —
only a thatched cottage and
the autumn shore at evening.

あき² 空き vacancy ⓒ;(仕事などの)opening ⓒ ∥このアパートには今空きがない There are no *vacancies* [*vacant rooms*] now in this apartment house. / 次回のツアーにまだ空きがありますか Does the next tour still have any *vacancies*?

◆505便に空きはありますか Does flight 505 have any *vacant seats*? / この雑誌にその記事を載せる空きはない There is no *space* for the article in this magazine.

∥空き時間 free time / 空き地 a vacant lot / 空き箱 an empty box / 空きびん an empty bottle / 空き家 an empty house

あき³ 飽き 飽きのこないデザインの家具 furniture of a *conservative* design / 父の科学技術の話には本当に飽きがきた I'm really *getting* 「*bored with* [*tired of*] my dad's stories about science and technology.

あきあき 飽き飽き ──飽き飽きする be fed up with …, be (sick and) tired of … ∥勉強しなさいという母の口癖には飽き飽きしている I'm (*sick and*) *tired of* Mom always telling me to study.

◆あいつのだじゃれにはもう飽き飽きした I've *had enough of* his stupid jokes.

あきかん 空き缶 empty can ⓒ,《英》empty tin ⓒ ∥窓から空き缶を捨てるな Don't throw *empty cans* out of the window.

あきす 空き巣(盗みを働くこと)theft ⓒⓤ, stealing ⓤ;(盗みを働く人)thief ⓒ (複 thieves) ∥私たちは留守中に空き巣に入られた(→留守中に空き巣が私たちの家に入った)*A thief sneaked into our house* while we were out. / *Our house was broken into* while we were out.

あきた 秋田

北京・ニューヨークとほぼ同じ緯度にある秋田県は,雄大な山々や神秘的な湖などの自然美に恵まれており,県内に4つの国立・国定公園があります。郷土色豊かな伝統行事も多く,特に「かまくら」「なまはげ」は有名です。また秋田には美人が多いともいわれ,秋田美人といわれています。

Akita Prefecture shares the same latitude with Beijing and New York. It's blessed with natural beauty like magnificent mountains and mysterious lakes, and it has four national and seminational parks. There are also many traditional festivals unique to this prefecture. The Kamakura and Namahage festivals in winter are especially well known. Also it is said that there are many beautiful women in Akita. They are called *Akita Bijin*.

あきたりない 飽き足りない（満足できない）be not satisfied with ...;（飽きない）be not tired of ... *∥*あんなにビデオゲームで遊んだのに, 弟はまだ飽き足りないらしい Even though my brother has been playing the video game a long time, he *doesn't seem tired of* it yet.

あきち 空き地（1区画の）vacant [empty] lot ⓤ,（何もない土地）vacant land [ground] ⓤ *∥*子供たちが空き地で遊んでいる Children are playing in *a vacant lot*.

あきっぽい 飽きっぽい, fickle *∥*彼は飽きっぽい性格で, 何をやっても長続きしない He has a *fickle* personality. He never sticks to anything for very long.

あきない 商い, business ⓤ, trade ⓤ ⇨ しょうばい

あきなう 商う（品物を扱う）deal* in ...;（売る）sell* ⓗ ⓤ,（品物を売買する）trade in ... *∥*兄は輸入雑貨を商っている My brother *deals in* imported goods.

あきびん 空き瓶 empty bottle

あきや 空き家（人の住んでいない家）vacant [unoccupied] house ⓤ *∥*その建物の隣に空き家がある There is *a vacant house* next to the building. ◆あの家はまだ空き家のままだ That house still stands *vacant* [*unoccupied*].

あきらか 明らか ――明らかな clear, obvious, apparent ――明らかに clearly, obviously ――明らかになる become* clear, turn out, emerge ⓔ, appear ⓔ

【明らか（な）】
明らかな誤り an *obvious* mistake / 明らかな証拠 *clear* evidence / 明らかな徴候 a *clear* signal

彼がうそをついているのはだれが見ても明らかだった It was *apparent* to everyone that he was lying.

彼の失敗はだれの目にも明らかだった His failure was *apparent* to all.

【明らかに】
明らかにあなたが間違っている *Clearly* you're wrong. / It's *clear* that you are wrong.

◆彼らは明らかに気分を害したようだった They looked *decidedly* offended.

【明らかになる】
問題がだんだん明らかになってきた The problem *became* increasingly *clear*.

運転手は酔っていたことが明らかになった It *turned out* [*emerged*] that the driver had been drunk.

いずれ真実は明らかになる The truth *will appear* [*come out*] sooner or later.

慣用表現 そんなことは火を見るよりも明らかだ It's *as plain as day*. /（口語的）It's *as plain as the nose on your face*.

あきらめ 諦め resignation ⓤ *∥*チーム全体があきらめムードに包まれていた The entire team had fallen into a mood of *resignation*. ◆姉はあきらめがいい[悪い] My sister *knows* [*doesn't know*] *when to give up*. / 何事もあきらめが肝心だ *It's important to accept whatever happens*.

あきらめる 諦める give* up
夢をあきらめてはいけない Don't *give up* your dreams.

あきらめるのはまだ早い It's too soon to *give up*.

彼は教師になることをすっかりあきらめた He *gave up* any idea of becoming a teacher.

彼を説得するのはあきらめた I *gave up* trying to persuade him.

彼女は別れたいと言っているのだから, あなたも潔くあきらめたらどう Since she says she wants to break up, you should just *give her up* and be done with it.

数学ができず大学進学をなかばあきらめかけていたのに, 合格通知が届いた I couldn't do the math and *had almost given up* going to college, but then I received a notice that I had passed.

あきる 飽きる be [get*] tired of ...;（いやになる）（口語的）be [get] sick of ...,《口語的》be fed up with ...

漫画を読むのに飽きたので, 散歩に出かけた I *got tired of* reading comics, so I went out for a walk.

あの映画は何度見ても飽きない I *never get tired of* that movie no matter how many times I see it.

よく飽きないで同じ曲を何度も聴けるね How can you listen to the same song again and again *without getting tired of* it?

オーストラリアでは飽きるほどステーキを食べた In Australia I ate steak until I *was sick of* it.

子供たちは一日中プールにいて飽きることを知らない The kids can spend all day in the pool *without getting tired of* it.

彼の自慢話はもう聞き飽きた I'*m fed up with* his bragging.

アキレスけん アキレス腱〖解剖〗Achilles(') tendon ⓒ;（唯一の弱点）Achilles(') heel ⓒ *∥*彼は走っていてアキレス腱を切った He tore *his Achilles tendon* while he was running.

あきれる 呆れる（驚く）be amazed;（仰天する）be astonished (at ...);（うんざりする）be disgusted (with ...) *∥*彼のずうずうしさにはあきれてものも言えない I'm so *amazed at* his impudence *that I don't know what to say*. / 母は髪を金髪に染めてきた兄を見てあきれた顔をした My mom *looked astonished* when

my brother came home with his hair dyed blond.
◆1年も部屋の掃除をしていないなんて, あきれた人だね You haven't cleaned your room for a year? How *disgusting*! / あきれた！アメリカの首都を知らないの？ *You're kidding* [*I'm dumbfounded*]! You don't even know the capital of the United States?

🖉「彼, 自分のことをどこかの大会社の御曹司（ぎっし）だって言ってたよ」「御曹司が聞いてあきれるよ」"He said his family owns some big company." "What *an obvious lie*!"

あく¹ 開く
(ドアなどが) open 圓; (幕が) rise* 圓
そのドアは外側に[内側に]あく The door *opens* outward [inward].
あの天窓はあくのですか Does that skylight *open*?
予定より20分遅れて幕があいた The curtain *rose* 20 minutes later than the scheduled time.
◆このかぎではドアがあかないよ This key *doesn't open* [*unlock*] the door. (❖この openは「…をあける」の意味の他動詞) / ふたがなかなかあかない The lid won't「*come off* [*open*]. 銀行は何時から何時まであいていますか When *is* the bank *open*? (❖この openは「あいている」の意味の形容詞) / What are the bank's hours? / ひよこの目はもうあいていた The chick's eyes *were* already *open*.

🖉「デパートは何時にあきますか」「10時にあいて, 7時に閉まります」"When does the department store *open*?" "It *opens* at ten and closes at seven."

慣用表現 あいた口がふさがらない *I'm speechless*.

あく² 空く
❶【場所・中身が】be empty; (部屋・場所などが) be vacant
更衣室が空いたら, 急いで着替えをすませよう When the changing room *is empty* [*free*], let's hurry up and change.
このクッキーの箱, 空いたらちょうだいね Let me have this cookie box when it *is empty*.
席が空いたので, 座ろう The seats *are empty* [*vacant*] now. Let's sit down.
◆あのテーブルは空いているみたいだよ It looks like *no one's sitting* at that table. / 今晩空いている部屋はありませんか Do you have any *vacancies* tonight?

🖉「この席, 空いていますか」「はい[いいえ]」 "Is anyone sitting here?" "No, no one is. [Yes, someone is.]" / "Is this seat taken?" "No, it isn't. [Yes, it is.]"

❷【すき間ができる】have* 「a gap [gaps]
このつり橋は板と板の間がすいているので気をつけてください This rope bridge *has gaps* between the boards. Be careful.
◆この英語の文章では, 段落と段落の間が1行空いている This English text has an *extra* line between paragraphs.

❸【使えるようになる】
このパソコン, 空いたら教えてください When *you are done with* this computer, please let me know.
◆公衆電話がなかなか空かなくていらいらした I got annoyed because the pay phones *were being used* for a long time.

❹【時間が】be free
きょうの午後, 空いてる？ *Are you free* this afternoon?
◆手が空いたら, 部屋の掃除を手伝って When *you're not busy* [*When you have time*], help me clean the room.

❺【地位などが】be open
生徒会の書記の席が空いたままになっている The post of secretary of the Student Council *is still open*.

あく³ 悪
(邪悪) evil ⓊU (↔good) (❖「害悪」の意味では ⓒC), wickedness ⓊU; (悪徳) vice ⓊU (↔virtue); (不正) wrong ⓊU (↔right) / 悪の権化 the personification of *evil* / 必要悪 *a necessary evil* / 悪の巣 a nest of *vice* / あの男の子は善と悪の区別がつかない That boy can't tell the difference between good and *evil*.

あく⁴ 灰汁
(灰の) lye ⓊU; (野菜などの) bitterness ⓊU, bad [harsh] taste ⓊU; (料理で出る) scum ⓊU ∥ゼンマイのあくを抜く remove the royal fern's *bitterness* ◆彼はあくが強い He *has a strong personality*.

アクアラング
《商標名》aqualung ⓒC, scuba ⓒC

あくい 悪意
malice ⓊU, ill will ⓊU ∥その少年は悪意に満ちた目で私をにらんだ The boy looked at me with eyes full of *malice*. / 私は彼に全く悪意をいだいていない I bear no *malice* to him. ◆悪意のないうそ a *white* lie / 別に悪意があってそう言ったわけではない I didn't mean any *harm* when I said that. / 人の忠告を悪意にとってはいけないよ Don't *be resentful about* others' advice.

あくうん 悪運
悪運が強い have the devil's (own) luck; have the luck of the devil / 先月は悪運続きだった I had a run of *bad luck* last month.

あくえいきょう 悪影響
bad influence ⓒC ∥暴力シーンの多い映画は若い人たちに悪影響を及ぼす Movies with too much violence have *a bad influence on* young people.
◆喫煙は健康に悪影響を及ぼすことがあります Smoking can *be bad for* your health.

あくかんじょう 悪感情
ill will ⓊU, bad [ill] feeling ⓊU, hard feelings ∥悪感情をいだく bear *ill will* / 彼らの間には悪感情が残った Some *bad feeling* remained between them. / They still bore *ill will* for each other.

あくじ 悪事
evil act ⓒC, bad thing ⓒC ∥悪事を働く commit *an evil act* ◆彼は何か悪事をたくらんでいるに違いない He must be plotting *something bad*.

ことわざ 悪事千里を走る Bad news travels fast. (→悪い知らせはすぐに伝わる)

あくしつ 悪質 ——悪質な(悪意のある) wicked, malicious; (不正な)《口語的》crooked ∥悪質な犯罪 a *wicked* crime ∥悪質なコンピュータウイルス a *malicious* computer virus ∥悪質な業者 a *crooked* businessman [company]

アクシデント accident ⓒ, happening ⓒ

あくしゅ 握手 handshake ⓒ ——握手する shake* hands ∥力強い握手 a firm *handshake* ∥私は彼と握手した I *shook hands with* him. / I *shook* his *hand.* / I *shook* him *by the hand.* ∥彼は握手で私を迎えた He greeted me with a *handshake*.
◆固い握手を交わす clasp hands ∥私は彼に握手を求めた I *offered* him *my hand*.

> **英作文ノート** 握手には2つの手が必要！
> 私は知事と握手した
> →×I shook *hand* with the governor.
> →○I shook *hands* with the governor.
> ★握手は双方2つの手でするもので,「両者の手」という意味で必ず複数形 hands を用いる。似た例に make friends with …「…と友達になる」, change trains「電車を乗り換える」などがある．

あくしゅう¹ 悪臭 bad smell ⓒ, stench ⓒ, stink ⓒ ∥悪臭の元を断つ cut off the source of *a bad smell* ∥腐った魚の悪臭が鼻をついた I smelled the *stench* of rotten fish.
◆どぶの水が悪臭を放っている The water in the ditch *stinks* [*is letting off a stink*].

あくしゅう² 悪習 (個人の) bad habit ⓒ; (社会・団体の) bad custom ⓒ; (しきたり) bad habitual practice ⓒ ∥たばこをぽい捨てする悪習を改める stop [kick, give up] *the bad habit* of dropping cigarette butts anywhere

あくしゅみ 悪趣味 bad [poor, vulgar] taste Ⓤ ——悪趣味な vulgar, kitsch, 《口語的》tacky, sick ∥悪趣味な冗談 a *sick* joke ∥彼が着ているシャツは悪趣味だ The shirt that he is wearing is *tacky*.

あくじゅんかん 悪循環 vicious circle ⓒ (↔virtuous circle), spiral ⓒ ∥悪循環を断ち切る break *the vicious circle*

アクション (演技・動作) action ⓒⓊ ∥アクション映画 an *action* film; (→アクションに満ちた映画) an *action*-packed film ∥アクション！ *Action*!《撮影の合図》

あくせい¹ 悪性 ——悪性の【医学】malignant (↔benign); (伝染性の) virulent ∥悪性腫瘍(しゅよう) a *malignant* tumor; a *malignancy*
◆悪性の(→ひどい)かぜをひいた I've got a *bad* cold.

あくせい² 悪政 misrule ⓒ; (失政)《公式的》maladministration Ⓤ ∥その国の悪政はようやく終わった The *misrule* of the country has finally ended.

あくせく (忙しく) busily ∥母は一日中あくせく働いている My mother is working *busily* all day long. ◆そんなにあくせく働くことはない You don't have to *keep your nose to the grindstone*.《※ keep *one's* nose to the grindstone は口語で「あくせく働く」の意味の慣用句》

アクセサリー ⚠ ❶【装身具】《集合的》jewelry, 《英》jewellery [dʒúːəlri] Ⓤ

> 英語の accessory は帽子・かばん・時計・傘なども含み，主に指輪・イヤリングなどの装飾品を指す日本語の「アクセサリー」とは意味が異なるので注意．

アクセサリーをつける[つけている]'put on [wear] *jewelry*
❷【付属品】accessories ∥自動車のアクセサリー auto *accessories*

アクセス 〔コンピュータ〕access Ⓤ ——アクセスする access ⓗ ∥アクセス時間 *access* time ∥インターネットにアクセスする *access* the Internet

アクセル ⚠ (自動車の) accelerator ⓒ,《米》gas pedal ⓒ ∥アクセルを踏む press (down) *the accelerator*;《米口語的》step on *the gas*

あくせん 悪銭 ことわざ Easy come, easy go. (→得やすいものは失いやすい); Ill gotten, ill spent. (→不当に得られたものは不当に使われる)

あくせんくとう 悪戦苦闘 英語の小説を読むのに悪戦苦闘した I *struggled hard to* read a novel in English.

アクセント ❶【強勢】accent ⓒⓊ, stress Ⓤ ∥アクセント記号[符号] an *accent* (mark) ∥第1アクセント primary *accent* [*stress*] ∥第2アクセント secondary *accent* [*stress*] ∥第1音節にアクセントをつけてはいけません Don't place *the accent* on the first syllable.
❷【強調】accent ⓒⓊ ∥このドレスはウエストラインにアクセントをおいている This dress gives *an accent* to your waistline. / This dress *accents* your waistline.

あくそうきゅう 悪送球 bad throw ⓒ ∥キャッチャーが三塁に悪送球をした The catcher made a *bad throw* to third.

あくたい 悪態 curse ⓒ, abuse Ⓤ ——悪態をつく curse ⓗ, swear* ⓗ, call (*a person*) names ∥彼は先生に悪態をついた He *cursed at* the teacher.

アクティブ (活発な) active

あくてんこう 悪天候 bad [rough] weather Ⓤ ∥悪天候のため東京への到着が遅れた(→悪天候が到着を遅らせた) *Bad weather* delayed our arrival in Tokyo.

あくどい (色などが) gaudy; (卑劣な) nasty ∥あくどい化粧 *gaudy* makeup ∥あくどい商売 *nasty* business

あくとう 悪党 villain ⓒ, scoundrel ⓒ
◆この悪党め You *bastard*! / You *devil*!

あくどう 悪童 (いたずらっ子) naughty [mischievous] child ⓒ

あくとく 悪徳 vice Ⓤ (↔virtue) ∥悪徳業者 a dishonest dealer ∥悪徳商法 dishonest business

あくにん 悪人 bad [wicked] person ⓒ; (極悪人) monster ⓒ

あくび 欠伸 yawn ⓒ ∥あくびをかみ殺す(→抑える) stifle [suppress] *a yawn* ∥彼は授業中大きなあくびをした He gave *a* big *yawn* during the class. ◆彼女の演説は非常に退屈で多

あげしお

くの人があくびをしていた Her speech was so boring that a lot of people *yawned*.(❖この yawn は動詞) / 私の弟はあくびをしておやすみと言った My little brother *yawned good night*.(❖yawn には「あくびをしながら…と言う」の意味もある)

あくひつ 悪筆 bad [poor] handwriting ⓤ, bad [poor] penmanship ⓤ /彼はひどい悪筆だ He has very *bad [poor] handwriting*. / His *handwriting* is very *poor*.

あくひょう 悪評 bad reputation ⓒ,《公式的》infamy ⓤ;(不評) disrepute ⓤ /悪評を買う *get a bad reputation*

あくびょうどう 悪平等 false equality ⓤ

あくぶん 悪文 (よくない文体) bad style ⓒ;(つたない文章) poor writing ⓤ
◆彼の小論文は悪文で私は全く理解できなかった His essay was so *poorly written* that I couldn't understand it at all.

あくへい 悪弊 (組織・社会などの)《公式的》malady ⓒ

あくへき 悪癖 bad habit ⓒ /悪癖に陥る fall [get] into *a bad habit*

あくま 悪魔 devil ⓒ; (魔王) Satan, the Devil; (悪霊) demon ⓒ /悪魔を崇拝する worship *the Devil*
‖悪魔払い an exorcism

あくまで(も) (全く) completely, definitely; (最後まで) to the end [last] /私はあくまでも生徒会長に立候補するつもりだ I *definitely* intend to run for Student Council President. ◆彼はあくまでも自分の無実を主張した He *insisted on* his innocence. / これはあくまでも下書きなので、そのつもりでお読みください This is *only* a rough draft. Please keep that in mind when you read it.

あくむ 悪夢 bad dream ⓒ, nightmare ⓒⓤ(❖nightmare は比喩的にも用いる) /その事故の後、私は悪夢を見るようになった I have had *nightmares* since the accident. ◆悪夢のような出来事 a *nightmarish* incident

-あぐむ 兄はだれに一票を投じようかと考えあぐんでいる My brother *really doesn't know* who to vote for. / そのチームは強かったので、攻めあぐんだ(→思うように攻められなかった) The team was tough, and we *were unable to make any headway* against it.

あくめい 悪名 (悪い評判) bad reputation ⓒ
──悪名高い infamous, notorious

あくやく 悪役 villain ⓒ,《俗語》heavy ⓒ /悪役を演じる play *the villain [heavy]*

あくゆう 悪友 (悪い仲間) bad companion ⓒ (❖×bad friend とはいわない);(集合的)bad company ⓤ /彼はまだ悪友とつきあっている He still keeps *bad company*. / 悪友のために彼は道を誤った He was misled by *bad companions*.

あくよう 悪用 abuse [əbjúːs] ⓤⓒ, (誤用) misapplication ⓤⓒ, misuse [mìsjúːs] ⓒⓤ ㊥;──悪用する (権利・地位などを) abuse [əbjúːz] ㊥; misapply ㊥ (❖通例受身で), misuse [mìsjúːz] ㊥ /特権[権威]の悪用 *an abuse of* privilege [authority]
◆その同窓会名簿は悪用された The alumni directory *was used for illicit purposes*.

あぐら あぐらをかいて座る sit *cross-legged*(❖「いすに足を組んで座る」は sit with *one's* legs crossed on the chair) /栄光の上にあぐらをかいている *rest [sit] on one's laurels*

あくりょう 悪霊 evil spirit ⓒ /彼は悪霊に取りつかれていると信じ込んでいる He believes that he is possessed by [with] *an evil spirit*.

あくりょく 握力 grip ⓤ《また a~》, a hold /握力が強い[弱い] have *a strong [weak] grip*
‖握力計 a hand dynamometer

アクリル ――アクリル(性)の acrylic /アクリル樹脂 *acrylic* resin / アクリル繊維 *acrylic* fiber / アクリルペイント *acrylic* (paint)

あくる 明くる (次の) the next, the following(❖the following は the next よりも文語的) /あくる朝[年] *the next [following]* morning [year] / 私のいとこは日曜日に到着し、あくる日出発した My cousin arrived here on Sunday, and left *the next* day.

あくろ 悪路 bad [rough] road ⓒ

アクロバット (曲芸) acrobatics; (曲芸師) acrobat ⓒ /アクロバットの acrobatic / アクロバット飛行 *acrobatic* flight; *stunt* flying / 空中のアクロバット aerial *acrobatics*

-あけ -明け 夏休み明けに生物学のテストがある We'll have the biology test *after the summer vacation*. / やっと梅雨明けだ(→梅雨が終わった) Finally *the rainy season is over*.

あげ 揚げ ⇨あぶらあげ

あげあし 揚げ足 彼はいつも私の言ったことの揚げ足を取る He always *trips* me *up about* what I say [(→失言をとらえる) *catches* me *up on* slips of the tongue].
‖揚げ足取り《口語的》nitpicking

あげおろし 上げ下ろし 荷の上げ下ろしに5時間近くかかってしまった It took nearly five hours to *load and unload* the cargo.

あけがた 明け方 (夜明け) dawn ⓤⓒ, daybreak ⓤ /明け方に雨が降り始めた The rain started *at dawn [with the dawn]*. / 明け方に地震があった The earthquake hit *at dawn*.

あげく 挙句・揚句 さんざん迷ったあげく、結局そのかばんは買わなかった *After* thinking it over, I ended up not buying the bag. / お母さんったら、財布を落として機嫌が悪くって、あげくの果てには私たちにまで当たり散らすんだもの My mom got into such a bad mood after she lost her wallet that she *ended up* getting mad at us, too.

あけくれ 明け暮れ 夏休みはバイトに明け暮れした I *did nothing but* a part-time job during the summer vacation.

あけくれる 明け暮れる 読書に明け暮れる *spend all one's time* reading; read *day in, day out*

あげしお 上げ潮 ❶【満潮】the flood tide (↔the ebb tide), the incoming [rising]

あ

tide
❷【風潮・時勢】tide [C]《通例単数形》 ‖上げ潮に乗る(→時勢に順応する) go [swim] with *the tide* [*flow*]

あけすけ 明け透け **—あけすけな** (あからさまな) open, frank; (遠慮のない) outspoken, candid **—あけすけに** openly, frankly; outspokenly, candidly ‖ 彼女はあけすけに政府の政策を非難した She *openly* attacked the government's policy.

あげぞこ 上げ底 (にせの底) false bottom [C]; (底上げされた) raised bottom [C] ‖そのチョコレートの箱は上げ底だ That box of chocolate has *a false* [*raised*] *bottom*.

あけっぱなし 開けっ放し ドアはあけっぱなしにしておいてください Please *leave* [*keep*] the door *open*. / ジャムのびんのふたがあけっぱなしになっていたよ The jam jar *was left open*.

あけっぴろげ 開けっ広げ **—あけっぴろげな** (率直な) open, frank; (あからさまな) unconcealed

あげて 挙げて 私たちは甲子園球場で全力を挙げて戦いました We played [fought] *as hard as we could* at Koshien Stadium. / 国を挙げて応援したが, 日本チームは1勝もできなかった *The whole country* was rooting for them, but the Japanese team didn't win a single victory.

あけのみょうじょう 明けの明星 the morning star; (金星) Venus

あげはちょう 揚羽蝶 swallowtail (butterfly) [C]

あけはなす 開け放す ドアはあけ放してあった (→広くあいていた) The door *was wide open*.

あけぼの 曙 (明け方) dawn [U] [C], daybreak [U] ‖文明の曙 *the dawn* of civilization

あげもの 揚げ物 deep-fried food [C]; (揚げ物の料理) deep-fried dish [thing] [C] ◆昼食に魚の揚げ物と新鮮なサラダを食べた I had *deep-fried* fish and fresh salad for lunch.

あける[1] 開ける

(開く) open [他]; (あけておく) leave* [keep*] ... open; (かぎを) unlock [他]; (包み・荷物などを) unpack [他], unwrap [他]

カーテンをあける *open* [*draw*] the curtain(s) / ドアのかぎをあける *unlock* the door / ドアをほんの少しあける *open* a door a crack

口を大きくあけて *Open your mouth wide*.

あまりに眠くて目をあけていられない I'm so sleepy (that) I can hardly *keep* my eyes *open*.

窓をあけて新鮮な空気を入れましょうか Shall I *open* the window and let in some fresh air?

窓をあけたままにしておいてください Please *leave* the windows *open*.

彼は門をあけて私たちを通してくれた He *opened* the gate and let us through.

彼は財布をあけて1,000円札を数枚取り出した He *opened* his wallet and took out several 1,000-yen bills.

教科書の45ページをあけなさい *Open* your textbook to [《英》at] page 45.

お母さん, 人の机の引き出しを勝手にあけないでよ Mom, *don't* just *open* other people's desk drawers without asking.

◆私は湯気に当てて手紙をあけた I steamed the letter *open*. (❖この open は形容詞) / びんのふたをあけてもらえませんか Could you please「*take* the lid *off* [*unscrew* the lid *from*] the bottle? / 蛇口をあけてくれませんか Will you *turn* the tap *on*, please?

[慣用表現] 選挙はふたをあけてみないと分からないよ We won't know how the election turned out *until the results are in*.

あける[2] 空ける

❶【中身・容器・場所を】(容器を) empty [他]; (飲み干す) drink* up; (部屋・家などを) leave* [自] [他]; (留守にする) be away

バケツの水をあける *empty* a bucket of water

持ち物検査でかばんの中身をあけるように言われた At the baggage inspection, I was told to *empty* my bags.

父は一晩で1升びんを2本あけたらしい It looks like Dad *drank up* two bottles of sake in one night.

家をあけている間友人に飼い犬を預けた I left my dog with a friend while I *was away*.

この部屋をこれから使うので, ちょっとあけてもらえますか We will be using this room. Could you please *leave*?

◆おみこしが通るので道をあけてください A portable shrine will be passing through. Please *clear* the way.

❷【穴・すき間を】(きりで) drill [他]; (空間を) make* [他]

ここにきりで穴をあけなさい *Drill* a hole here.

机と壁の間にすき間をあけてください *Make* a space between the desk and the wall.

◆余白をあける *leave* a margin / 1行ずつあけて英文を書きなさい Write English sentences *on every other line*. / 彼女は耳にピアスの穴をあけている She *has pierced ears*. / キツツキがその木をつついて穴をあけた A woodpecker *pecked a hole* in the tree. / 彼はシャツに穴をあけてしまった He *tore a hole* in his shirt.

❸【使えるようにする】leave* [他], keep* [他]

転校生のためにこの机はあけておこう Let's *keep* this desk for a transfer student.

この席は予約のお客様のためにあけております This seat [table] *is being kept* for a customer who made a reservation.

❹【時間を】

来週の週末はあけてある I'm *keeping* next weekend *free*.

彼はその日一日彼女のためにあけておいた He *reserved* the whole day for her./ He *kept* the entire day *open* for her.

あける[3] 明ける ❶【夜が】break* [自]; (空が白む) dawn [自] ‖夜が明けた The day *broke*./ Morning came.

◆夜が明けて(→夜明けに)鳥たちが鳴き始めた

Birds began to chirp *at daybreak*.

> [英作文ノート]「夜」は明けない?
> もうすぐ夜が明ける
> →×(The) *night* will break soon.
> →○(The) *day* will break soon.
> ★日本語の「夜」につられて night を用いないこと. break は, ここでは自動詞「始まる」の意味.

❷【年が】begin* [自], start [自] //年が明けたら平安神宮に初もうでに行こう Let's visit the Heian Shrine *after the New Year begins*.
◆明けましておめでとうございます *Happy New Year*!

❸【終わる】end [自], be over //梅雨が明けた The rainy season「*has ended* [*is over*]. (❖×was over とはいわない)

[慣用表現]明けても暮れても受験勉強では体がもたないよ You're going to get exhausted studying for exams *day in, day out*. / 明けても暮れても彼のことばかり思っている I think about him *all the time*.

あげる[1] 上げる

❶ 高い位置へ	put up, raise
❷ 程度・価値	raise; turn up
❸ 声・音	
❹ 与える	give

❶【高い位置へ】put* up, raise [他]
ブラインドを上げる *raise* [*draw up*, *open*] the blinds
このたんすは2階に上げてください Please *put* this bureau *up* on the second floor.
よく見えないので, それをもっと高く上げてください We can't see very well. Please *raise* that higher.
パイロットは機首を上げた The pilot *raised* [*brought up*] the airplane's nose.
彼女は雑誌から目を上げた She *raised her eyes* from the magazine.
◆気球を上げる *fly* a balloon / しぶきを上げて泳ぐ *splash* while swimming / 手を上げろ! *Hands up*!/ *Hold your hands up*! / このかばんを網棚に上げてもらえませんか Could you *put* this bag *on* the rack? / うつむいていないで, 顔を上げて答えなさい Stop hanging your head. *Look up* (at me) and answer the question. / いつまでも寝てないで, 起きてふとんを上げたら(→ふとんを片づけたら)どう Instead of lying around all day, how about getting up and *putting away your futon*? / あの山は今も噴煙を上げている That volcano *is* still *emitting smoke*. / 佐藤君は髪をかき上げるのが癖(くせ)だ Sato has a habit of *brushing* his hair *back* (with his hand).

❷【程度・価値】(程度・料金などを) raise [他]; (音量・温度などを) turn up
(オーブンなどの)温度を上げる *turn up* the heat [temperature] / 値段を上げる *raise* prices / 音量を上げる *turn up* the sound [volume] / 水準を上げる *raise* a standard
おこづかいを上げてほしいと母に訴えた I asked my mother to *raise* my allowance.
◆高度を上げる *gain* height [altitude] / 勉強の能率を上げるにはどうしたらいいかを考えた I thought about how I could study *more efficiently*. / もうけることだけを考えるのではなく, 品質を上げる努力もしてほしい You shouldn't think only about making profits. You should also try to *improve* product quality. / 彼女は高速道路に入るとスピードを上げた She「*speeded up* [*picked up speed*] after getting on the expressway. / 私たちは仕事のペースを上げなければならない We *must quicken* the pace of our work. / We *must work more quickly*.

❸【声・音】
驚いて悲鳴をあげる *cry out* in surprise
彼女はその衝撃的なニュースを聞いて大声をあげた She *exclaimed loudly* at the shocking news.
負傷した男性はうめき声をあげた The injured man *groaned*.

❹【与える】give* [他]
弟の誕生日にプレゼントをあげた I *gave* my brother a present on his birthday.
このお年玉, お嬢さんにあげてください Please *give* this *otoshidama* [New Year's gift money] *to* your daughter.
これ, よかったら君にあげるよ If you want, I'*ll give* it *to* you.

❺【終える・すます】
今度のパーティーは, 1人2,000円で上げたいと思っている We're planning to *keep the cost* of the next party *at* 2,000 yen per person.
仕事を早く上げないと締め切りに間に合わない If we don't work faster, we won't finish on time.

❻【供える】
神棚にお神酒(みき)をあげる *place* sacred wine *on* a Shinto altar / 仏壇に線香をあげる *light* incense *on* a Buddhist altar

❼【…してあげる】
もう遅いから, 家まで車で送ってあげるよ It's late. I'*ll drive* you home.
妹の夏休みの宿題を手伝ってあげた I *helped* my sister with her summer vacation homework.
交差点で目の不自由な人の手を引いてあげた At the intersection I *guided* a blind [visually impaired] person by hand.
💬「夕ごはんできた?」「もう少し待って. できたら呼んであげるから」"Is dinner ready?" "In a few minutes. I'*ll call* you when it's ready."

❽【…し終える】
この本は一晩で読み上げた I *read* this entire book in one night. / I *finished reading* this book in one night.
クリスマスまでにはこのセーターを編み上げたいと思っている I want to *finish knitting* this sweater by Christmas.

❾【その他】
大きな利益をあげる *make a* big *profit*

その映像を見て私はあげそう(→吐きそう)になった I felt like *throwing up* [*vomiting*] when I saw the picture.

あげる² 挙げる

❶【手を】raise 働, put* up
賛成の人は手を挙げてください All who agree, please *raise* your hands.

❷【例・名前などを】mention 働, name 働, give* 働, offer 働
大統領選に4人の名前が挙げられています Four names *have been mentioned* in the race for President.
コーチは次の試合の先発ピッチャーとして島田君の名前を挙げた The coach *named* Shimada as starting pitcher for the next game.
これまで読んだ本の中で最も感銘を受けた本を1冊挙げてください Of all the books that you have read, please *name* the one that made the biggest impression on you.
例を挙げてください Please *give an example*.
彼女が犯人だというなら,証拠を挙げる必要がある If you say that she committed the crime, then you have to *offer* some evidence.
◆次に挙げることわざを知っていますか Do you know the *following* proverb?

❸【式を】have* 働, hold* 働
二人は11月に式を挙げる They are going to *have the wedding ceremony* in November.

❹【全力を】
決勝戦では全力を挙げて戦った We played *as hard as we could* in the finals.

❺【犯人を】
早く殺人事件の犯人を挙げてもらわないと,夜もおちおち眠れない If they don't *arrest* the murderer soon, I won't be able to sleep at night.

あげる³ 揚げる

❶【油で】(たっぷりの油で) deep-fry 働, fry ... in deep fat, fry 働 (❖fry は「油・バターなどでいためる」の意味でも用いる) ‖てんぷらを揚げよう Let's *fry* some tempura. ‖ エビを油で揚げなさい *Deep-fry* some shrimp in oil. ‖ このコロッケは揚げたてだよ These croquettes *were just fried*. ‖ とり肉に衣をつけて揚げてください Dip the chicken in the batter and *deep-fry* it.

❷【高い位置へ】たこをあげる *fly* a kite ‖ 帆をあげる *raise* [*hoist*] the sails ‖ 花火をあげる *set* [*shoot*] *off* fireworks

❸【陸に】港で船荷を揚げる *unload* cargo at a port ‖ 台風が接近しているので,漁師は漁船を陸にあげた A typhoon is coming, so the fishermen *have pulled* their boats *onto* shore.

あけわたす 明け渡す

(家などを)(公式的)vacate 働;(敵などに)surrender 働;(屈服して)(公式的)yield 働 働 ‖ 私は次の水曜日までに部屋を明け渡さなければならない I have to *vacate* my room by next Wednesday. ‖ フランスは決してこの領土を明け渡さないだろう France would never *surrender* [*yield*] this territory.

あご 顎

□ (❖複数形 jaws は上下のあごと歯を含めた口部を指す);(下あごの先) chin □ ‖ 上[下]あご *the upper* [*lower*] *jaw* ‖ 二重あご *a double chin* ‖ あごがはずれる *dislocate one's jaw* ‖ あごの骨を折る *break one's jaw* ‖ あごを引く *draw in one's chin* ‖ そのボクサーはあごに軽く一発くらった The boxer received a light blow to *the jaw*.
‖あごひげ ⇒ あごひげ
慣用表現 あの先輩はいつも人をあごで使う That older student always *bosses* people *around*. ‖ 彼はゴール寸前であごを出して,ダウンしてしまった He *had nothing left* and collapsed just before the finish line.

アコーディオン accordion □, piano accordion □,《口語的》squeezebox □ ‖ アコーディオンを弾く play *the accordion*
‖アコーディオンカーテン[ドア] a folding door, an accordion door (❖通例英語では×accordion curtain とはいわない) ‖ アコーディオンプリーツ accordion pleats

あこがれ 憧れ longing □ □, yearning □ □;(あこがれの対象) idol □;(夢) dream □ ‖ 名声への強いあこがれをいだく have *a great longing* [*yearning*] *for fame* ‖ 彼は多くのサッカーファンにとってあこがれの的(፨)だ He's *the idol* of many soccer fans.
◆彼の新しい車は男の子みんなのあこがれ(→羨望(蛇))の的だった His new car was *the envy* of all the boys.

あこがれる 憧れる long for ..., have* a longing for ...;(夢見る) dream* of ...;(切望する) yearn for [after] ...;(人にあこがれる) adore 働
私はいなかの生活にとてもあこがれている I have *a great longing for* life in the country. ‖ I really *want to* live in the country.
小学生のころ,プロのサッカー選手にあこがれていた When I was in elementary school, I *dreamed of* becoming a professional soccer player.
山下さんは南の島のさんさんと照りつける太陽にあこがれている Mr. Yamashita *dreams of* the sun shining brightly on southern [tropical] islands.
生徒たちはその新しい英語の先生にあこがれている The students *adore* the new English teacher.

あごひげ 顎鬚 beard □ (❖首の部分も含む) ⇒ ひげ 図版 ◆あごひげのある男 a *bearded* man

あごひも 顎紐 (ヘルメットなどの) chinstrap □ (❖アメリカの一般的の帽子にはふつうあごひもはない) ‖ ヘルメットをかぶるときはあごひもをかけるのを忘れないで When you wear a helmet, don't forget to fasten *the chinstrap*.

あさ¹ 朝

morning □ □ (❖morning は日の出から正午または昼までを指す場合と,朝12時から正午までを指す場合がある) ——朝の morning (❖morning は名詞だが,形容詞的にも用いる)

あざける

語法
(1) morning は, 特定の朝を指して用いられることが多いので, the morning となることが多いが,「すばらしい朝」a lovely morning のように形容詞で修飾する場合は, 不定冠詞が付くことがある.
(2)「朝に」は in the morning というが, 特定の日・曜日の朝をいうときは, on を用いる // 1月1日の朝に *on the morning of January 1* / 月曜日の朝は交通量が多い Traffic is heavy *on Monday morning*.(❖この場合は無冠詞)
(3) ただし, early, late などを伴う場合は, in を用いる // 1月1日の朝早くに *in the early morning* of January 1; *early in the morning* on January 1
(4) morning は, one, this, tomorrow, next, every, all などを付けて副詞的に用いることができる // あすの朝早く起きなければならない I have to get up early *tomorrow morning*. / 彼は毎朝30分ジョギングする He jogs for 30 minutes *every morning*. / 私はきのうの朝グレイ氏に会った I met Mr. Grey *yesterday morning*.
(5) 次のような副詞的な表現では, 通例冠詞を付けない // 朝から晩まで *from morning till [to] night* / 朝までよく眠った I slept well *till morning*.

朝の散歩 a *morning* walk
平日は朝早く起きます I get up *early in the morning* on weekdays.
最近朝の6時ごろ空が明るくなる These days the sky lightens up about 6 o'clock *in the morning*.
私は毎朝シャワーを浴びる I take a shower *every morning*.
健太のことを朝からずっと待っています I have been waiting for Kenta *since (this) morning*.
私はいつも日曜の朝に洗濯をする I usually do the washing *on Sunday morning*.
あすの朝7時に起こしてください Please wake me up at seven *tomorrow morning*.
朝一番に彼に電話するよ I'll call him *first thing in the morning*.
その朝目がさめると雪が降っていた When I woke up *that morning*, it was snowing.
私は試験に合格するために朝から晩まで一生懸命勉強した I studied hard *from morning till night* to pass the exam.
朝の集会が体育館で開かれた The *morning* assembly was held in the gym.
私は朝に強い(→朝型だ) I'm a *morning person*.
◆その店は毎日朝9時から夕方6時まであいています The store is open from *9 a.m.* to [till] 6 p.m. every day. / 朝から晩まで(→一日中)好きなことだけをして過ごすことができたらなあ I wish I could do just what I want to do *all day* (long).
🅔「朝はいつもちゃんと食べてる?」「時間がなくてほとんど食べないんだ」"Do you have break-

fast regularly?" "No, I rarely have time for breakfast."

あさ² 麻 hemp ⓤ; (亜麻の繊維) flax ⓤ; (麻・リネン製品) linen ⓤ //(また複数形 ~s)

あざ 痣 bruise ⓒ; (殴られてできた目の周りの) black eye ⓒ (❖日本人などの「黒い目(瞳)」は例 dark eyes または brown eyes という); (生まれつきの) birthmark ⓒ //机にすねをぶつけてひどいあざができた I hit my shin against the desk and got a bad *bruise*.

あさい 浅い

❶【深さが】shallow(↔deep); (平らな) flat
浅い皿 a *shallow* [*flat*] dish / 浅い川 a *shallow* river
このプールはこちら側は深いが, 向こう側は浅い This swimming pool is deep on this end and *shallow* on that end.
◆このなべはシチューを作るには浅すぎる This pan *isn't deep enough* [*is too shallow*] to make stew.

❷【程度が】(傷が) slight; (眠りが) light; (考えなどが) shallow, superficial
浅い傷 a *slight* cut [*scratch*] / 眠りの浅い人 a *light* sleeper
彼の考えは浅い His thinking is *shallow*.
私はこの分野については浅い知識しかありません I have only *superficial* knowledge about this subject. / I *don't know much* about this subject.
◆私は英語の教師としてはまだ経験が浅い I *don't have much experience* as an English teacher yet. / 弟のけがは出血量のわりには傷が浅くて安心した I was relieved that my brother's cut *wasn't* as *deep* as it seemed from the bleeding.

❸【時間が】short
歴史の浅い学校 a school with *a short history*
友子はテニスを始めてからまだ日が浅い It's only been *a short time* since Tomoko started playing tennis. / Tomoko started playing tennis only *recently*.

❹【色が】
浅い(→薄い)緑 *light* [*pale*] green

あさいち 朝市 morning market ⓒ; (屋外の) open-air market ⓒ //この町では毎朝朝市が立つ This town has *an open-air market* every morning.

あさいと 麻糸 hemp thread ⓤⓒ

あさがえり 朝帰り 朝帰りする come (back) home in the morning

あさがお 朝顔 morning glory ⓒⓤ

あさがた¹ 朝方 きょうの朝方 this *early morning* / 彼女は朝方に出発した She left「*early in the morning* [*in the early morning*].

あさがた² 朝型 (朝型の人) morning person ⓒ(↔night person)

あさぎり 朝霧 morning mist [haze] ⓒⓤ

あさぐろい 浅黒い dark(↔fair), swarthy; (日焼けした) brown

あざける 嘲る (ばかにする) make* fun of ..., ridicule ⓦ; (やじる) jeer ⓦ //おまえに

あさごはん

他人の失敗をあざける資格があるのか Do you think you have the right to *make fun of* other people's failures?

あさごはん 朝御飯 breakfast ⓒⓊ
⇨ちょうしょく

あせ 浅瀬 shoal ⓒ, the shallows; (歩いて渡れる所) ford ⓒ; (早瀬) riffle ⓒ ∥私たちは小川の浅瀬を歩いて渡った We walked across *the shoal* of a stream. ◆その船は浅瀬に乗り上げた The boat *went [ran] aground*.

あさって 明後日 the day after tomorrow ∥あさってまでに宿題を終わらせなくてはいけない I have to finish my homework by *the day after tomorrow*. ◆あさっての朝[晩] the morning [evening] *after next*

あさっぱら 朝っぱら 父は朝っぱらから飲み始めた My father started drinking *bright and early*.

あさつゆ 朝露 morning dew Ⓤ

あさね 朝寝 ——朝寝する sleep* late in the morning ◆週末はいつも朝寝する(→遅く起きる) I always *get up late* on weekends.

あさねぼう 朝寝坊 late riser ⓒ ——朝寝坊する (遅く起きる) get* up late; (いつもより長く眠っている) sleep* in; (うっかり寝過ごす) oversleep* ⓘ ∥けさ朝寝坊して授業に遅れてしまった I *overslept* this morning, and was late for class.

あさはか 浅はか ——あさはかな (考えなどが浅い) shallow; (愚かな) stupid, foolish ∥そんなあさはかな考えは捨てなさい Stop thinking such *shallow* thoughts. / あんな甘い言葉にだまされるなんて, 我ながらあさはかだった I have to admit I was *stupid* to be tricked by that smooth talk.

あさばん 朝晩 morning and evening ∥朝晩冷え込むようになった *The mornings and evenings* are getting cooler. /「毎朝毎晩」の意味では通例複数形

あさひ (朝の太陽) the morning sun; (昇る太陽) the rising sun ∥水面が朝日を反射してきらめいていた The surface of the water shone in *the morning sun*. / 朝日を浴びながら私は海岸沿いを歩いていた I was getting *the morning sun* while I was walking along the seashore.

あさましい 浅ましい (恥ずべき) shameful; (卑劣な) mean; (情けない) miserable ∥弟のこづかいを巻き上げるなんて, おまえはなんてあさましいやつだ It's *shameful* of you to cheat your brother out of his allowance.

あざみ 薊 thistle [θísl] ⓒ

あざむく 欺く deceive ⓘ, cheat ⓘ ⇨だます

あさめし 朝飯 breakfast ⓒⓊ
🅒「この宿題を全部一晩でできるの?」「こんなの朝飯前だよ」"Can you do all this homework in one night?" "(It's) *no sweat*. / *It's a cinch*./ *It's a piece of cake*."

あさもや 朝靄 morning mist [haze] ⓒⓊ (❖hazeのほうが濃い) ∥その湖は朝もやに包まれていた The lake was covered in a veil of *morning mist*.

あざやか 鮮やか ❶【鮮明な】——鮮やかな (明るい) bright, brilliant; (生々しい) vivid ——鮮やかに brightly, brilliantly; vividly ∥鮮やかな緑色 *bright [brilliant, vivid]* green / 紅葉が夕日に照らされてひときわ鮮やかに見えた The autumn leaves glowed especially *brightly* in the evening sun. / この写真を見ると, そのときの情景が鮮やかによみがえる When I look at this picture, I remember *vividly* how things were then.
◆色鮮やかな花 *colorful* flowers

❷【みごとな】——鮮やかな splendid; (うまい) skillful ——鮮やかに skillfully ∥彼女のハンドルさばきは鮮やかだった She handled the steering wheel *skillfully*. / She drove *with finesse*. / そのスケート選手はトリプルアクセルを鮮やかに決めた The skater *skillfully* completed the triple axel.

あさやけ 朝焼け the glow of dawn

あさゆう 朝夕 morning and evening ⇨あさばん

あざらし 海豹 seal ⓒ ◆アザラシの毛皮 *sealskin*

あさり 浅蜊 Japanese littleneck (clam) ⓒ; (二枚貝の総称) clam ⓒ ∥アサリをとる dig for *clams*

あさる 漁る ❶【探し求める】hunt ⓘ; (廃棄された物の中から) scavenge ⓘ ∥母はバーゲンセールで安物をあさるのが好きだ My mother likes to *hunt for* bargains at sales. / 野良犬が残飯をあさっていた The stray dog *was scavenging for* leftover food.

❷【やたらに…する】ブランド品を買いあさる *hunt around for* brand-name products

あされん 朝練 姉がバレーの朝練があるので6時半にはうちを出る My sister leaves home at 6:30 for *morning* volleyball *practice*.

あざわらう 嘲笑う scoff ⓘ, laugh ⓘ; (冷笑する) sneer ⓘ; (ばかにする) ridicule ⓘ, mock ⓘ ∥面と向かって人をあざ笑う *laugh in a person's face*

あし¹ 足・脚

❶【体の】leg ⓒ (❖通例足首から上の部分をいうが, 足全体を指すこともある); (くるぶしより下) foot ⓒ (複 feet); (犬・猫などの) paw ⓒ (❖かぎつめ(claw)のある動物の足); (馬・牛などの) hoof ⓒ (複 hooves, ~s) (❖ひづめのある動物の足); (タコなどの) arm ⓒ, tentacle ⓒ
【~(の)足】
素足 bare feet / 大根足 *fat legs* / 靴ずれした足 *a sore foot*
【足が・は】
足が太い have fat [thick] *legs* / 足が細い have slender *legs* / 足がつる get [have] (a) cramp in *one's leg*
足がしびれてしまった My *legs* have gone to sleep.
長い距離を歩いて足が痛い My *legs* ache because of the long walk.
一日中立ちっぱなしで足がむくんだ My *feet* are swollen from standing all day long.
クモは足が8本ある Spiders have eight *legs*.

〖足を・に〗
足を開く spread *one's legs* / 足を組んで座る sit *with one's legs crossed* / 足を引きずる drag *one's feet* [*heels*]
彼はスキーをしていて足を折った He broke *his leg* while skiing.
けさ電車の中で足を踏まれた Somebody stepped on *my foot* on the train this morning.
彼女はショッピングの後喫茶店に入って足を休めた She went to a coffee shop to *rest her legs* after shopping.
彼は左足にけがをした He got injured *in the left leg*.
◆足を滑らせる lose *one's footing*

〖その他〗
◆足の甲 *one's instep* / 足の裏 *one's sole* /
足の指で鉛筆をはさむことができますか Can you pick up a pencil with *your toes*? / 目をつむって片足で立ってごらん Try to *stand on one foot* with your eyes closed.

英作文ノート 「足」の意味に注意！
彼女は足が長い
→ ×She has long *feet*.
→ ○She has long *legs*.
★「足が長い」というときの「足」はももから下の部分を指しているので, feet ではなく, legs を用いる.「彼は足が大きい」は He has big *feet*. という.

❷【物の】（机・いすなどの）leg ©；（グラスの）stem ©
脚の長いグラス a glass *with a long stem*
このテーブルの脚は折りたたむことができる *The legs* of this table can be folded.

❸【歩行・訪問】
彼は足が速い（→速く走る）He *runs fast*.
彼女は足を速めた She *quickened her pace*.
彼に大声で呼びかけたが, 彼は足を止めなかった I shouted at him, but he just *kept going*.
ニューヨーク滞在中, その美術館に何度か足を運んだ When I was in New York, I *visited* the art museum several times.
せっかく岡山まで来たんだから, 足を伸ばして倉敷まで行ってみようよ Since we've come all the way to Okayama, let's *go on to* Kurashiki, too.
姉は大学から帰るとその足で出かけた My sister came home from college and then went *right back* out *again*.

❹【交通手段】
大雪のため首都圏の電車が止まり, 多くの人々の足が奪われた The heavy snowfall stopped the trains in the Tokyo area, and many people *were left without transportation*.

慣用表現 岸壁の上に立つと足がすくんだ *My legs froze* when I stood on the cliff. / 彼女とデートの約束をしてからは, 足が地につかない思いだ I've been *walking on air* ever since I made a date with her. / 犯人は残した指紋から足がついた They *tracked down* the criminal from the fingerprints he left. / 今回のパーティーでは5,000円も足が出た The party *ran over (the) budget* by 5,000 yen. / 最近図書館から足が遠のいている I *haven't been going to* the library *as much as I used to*. / 歩きっぱなしで足が棒になった I walked so much (that) *my legs became really stiff*. / この本で紹介したレストランはすべて私が足で調べたものです I *went and ate at all the restaurants* I introduced in this book. / 兄の部屋はたくさんの本で足の踏み場もない My brother's room has so many books (that) *there's no place to stand*. / 彼は悪徳な商売から足を洗った He 「*gave up* [*quit*]」 his dishonest business. / 野手のたび重なるエラーがピッチャーの足を引っぱった The fielders' repeated errors *heavily burdened* the pitcher. / 彼女は私の恩人なのだから, 足を向けて寝られるはずがない I'm so indebted to her that *I would never do anything to harm her*.

あし² 葦 reed © © ╱人間は考える葦である Man is *a* thinking *reed*. (✿数学者・哲学者パスカルの言葉)

あじ¹ 味

❶【食べ物】taste ⓤ（また a ～）；（香りを伴った）flavor,《英》flavour ⓤ © ──味がする taste ⓘ (✿進行形にはできない)

〖〜(の)味〗
みつの味 a taste [*flavor*] of honey / バナナ味のアイスクリーム ice cream *with a banana flavor*; banana-flavored ice cream
このチーズはガーリック味だ This cheese *tastes of* [*like*] garlic.
◆トマト味のソース *tomato-based* sauce / おふくろの味 *one's mom's cooking* / 隠し味にしょうゆを少し加えた I've added a little bit of soy sauce *as a secret ingredient*.

〖味が〗
このケーキは味がいい[よくない] This cake *tastes good* [*bad*].
このシチューは味が濃い[薄い] This stew has *a strong* [*weak*] *flavor*.
牛乳の味が変だ The milk *tastes strange*.
これは苦い味がする This *has a bitter taste*. / This *tastes* bitter.
かぜをひいていて何も味が分からない I have a cold, so I *can't taste* anything.
塩を少々加えると味がよくなるよ It'll *taste better* if you add a little salt.
💬「それってどんな味がするの」「ヨーグルトみたいな味だよ」 "What does it *taste like*?" "It *tastes* like yogurt."

〖味を〗
調味料を入れて, もっと味をつけたほうがいい You should add some seasoning to give it some more *flavor*.
スープの味を見てから塩を加えなさい *Taste* the soup before you add salt.

❷【おもしろみ・趣】interest ⓤ（また an ～）, character ⓤ ©
あの悪役はなかなか味のある俳優だ The actor playing the villain has a lot of *charac-*

ter.
◆味もそっけもない文章 a *dull* composition / これはなかなか味のある字だね This calligraphy is quite *interesting*. / こんな趣向を凝らすなんて,あなたもなかなか味なことをするじゃないか You're pretty *clever* to come up with a plan like this.
❸《ぐあい・調子》
書き味のいい(→よく書ける)ボールペン a ballpoint pen that *writes well* / 切れ味のいい(→よく切れる)ナイフ a knife that *cuts well*
❹《経験》
彼は貧乏の味を知らない He's *never experienced* poverty.
慣用表現 彼らはその映画がヒットしたことに味を占めて(→ヒットしたので)続編を作った *Because the movie was a great success, they made a sequel.*

あじ² 鯵 horse mackerel ⓒ《◆「肉」の意味では》a dried, filleted *horse mackerel* with its head and tail still on / アジのたたき *horse mackerel*, green onions, and ginger salad

アジア Asia [éiʒə] ―アジア人 Asian [éiʒən] ⓒ ―アジア(人)の Asian / 日本はアジアの東にある Japan is located in the east of *Asia*.
‖アジア大陸 Asia, the Asian Continent / 小アジア Asia Minor

あしあと 足跡 footprint ⓒ, trace ⓒ ⓤ;《通った跡》tracks /《クマの足跡》a bear's *tracks*; bear *tracks* / 強盗の足跡が柔らかい地面に残っていた The burglar's *footprints* remained in the soft soil.

あしおと 足音 footstep ⓒ, step ⓒ, tread ⓤ《また a 〜》/足音で彼だと分かる I recognize his *step*. / だれもいないはずの部屋で足音がした There was (*the sound of*) *footsteps* in a room that's supposed to be empty.
◆足音を忍ばせて歩く walk *quietly*
慣用表現 この地方にもやっと春の足音が聞こえてきた *The signs of spring* have finally come to this area, too.

あしか 海驢 sea lion

あしがかり 足掛かり foothold ⓒ, footing ⓒ;《建築用の》scaffold ⓒ / そのがけには何の足がかりもないように見える It seems there are no *footholds* on the cliff.
◆彼女はその映画出演を足がかりに大女優へと成長した Her performance in the movie led to her becoming a major movie star.

あしかけ 足掛け こちらに引っ越してきてから,足掛け5年(→約5年)になります It has been *about* five years since I moved here.

あしかせ 足枷 fetters《手かせ・足かせ》manacles,《重荷》burden ⓒ / その囚人たちは手かせと足かせをはめられていた The prisoners were wearing *manacles*.
◆子供が彼の足かせになっている(→自由を束縛されている) He *is shackled with* a child.

あしからず 悪しからず あなたといっしょに行けませんがあしからず(→申しわけないがいっしょに行けません) I'm sorry, *but* I can't come with you. / パーティーには行けないのでしからずご了承ください(→お許しください) *Please forgive me* for not coming to your party.

あしきり 足切り その試験で400点に満たない学生は足切りされる The students with a score of less than 400 points in that exam *will be weeded out*.

あしくび 足首 ankle ⓒ / 足首をねんざする sprain [twist] *one's ankle* / 看護婦は足首に包帯を巻いてくれた The nurse wound the bandage around *my ankle*.

あしげ 足蹴 ―足げにする《ける》kick ⓗ,《ひどい仕打ちをする》treat *a person* very badly

あじけない 味気無い,《退屈な》boring, dull;《食物・音楽などが》bland;《おもしろみ・風味がない》insipid / 味気ないワイン *insipid* wine / 味気ない生活から抜け出す escape from a *boring* life

あしこし 足腰 足腰が立たなくなる become unable to stand [get] up / 私は足腰(→下半身)を鍛えるために毎日運動をしている I do exercises every day to 「build up [strengthen] *the lower part of my body*. / 祖父は年々足腰(→体[足])が弱っている My grandfather's 「*body* is [*legs* are] getting weaker year by year.

あじさい 紫陽花 hydrangea [haidréindʒə] ⓒ

アシスタント assistant ⓒ / アシスタントディレクター an *assistant* director / 浩は月曜日から金曜日まで私のアシスタントを務める Hiroshi works as *an assistant to* me from Monday to [through] Friday.

あした 明日 tomorrow ⇨あす / それはあしたやるよ,約束する I'll do it *tomorrow*, I promise. / じゃあまたあしたね See you *tomorrow*. / あしたは休みだよ,知らなかったのかい We have a day off *tomorrow*, didn't you know?
ことわざ あしたはあしたの風が吹く *Tomorrow is another day*.

あしだい 足代《運賃》fare ⓒ ⓤ,《米》carfare ⓤ

あじつけ 味付け seasoning ⓤ ―味つけする《塩・コショウなどで》season ⓗ, flavor ⓗ /ニンニクで料理を味つけする *flavor* a dish with garlic / 彼女は魚に塩とコショウで味つけした She *seasoned* the fish with salt and pepper. / このスープの味つけは濃すぎる *The seasoning* in the soup is too heavy.
‖味つけのり seasoned *nori*, a kind of edible seaweed

あしでまとい 足手まとい drag ⓒ;《精神的な重荷》burden ⓒ / 彼は私たちの足手まといになるだけだ He's such *a drag* [*burden*] on us.

アジト《隠れ家》hideout ⓒ, safe house ⓒ

あしどめ 足止め・足留め 列車事故のため私たちは駅で足止めを食った We *were* 「*held up* [*stranded*] at the station because of the train accident.

あしどり 足取り ❶《歩く様子》step ⓒ, pace ⓒ《また a 〜》/ 軽い[重い]足取りで歩く walk with *a light* [*heavy*] step

あずかる

❷【犯人などの】trace ⓒⓊ ∥その犯人の足取りはまだつかめていないそうだ I heard there is yet no *trace* of the criminal.

あじな 味な 彼はなかなか味な(→しゃれた)ことを言った He said rather *smart* things.

あしなみ 足並み step ⓒ, pace Ⓤ ∥(また〜)∥足並みをそろえて歩く walk *in step* / 新チームの選手の足並みがそろうには時間がかかるろう It will take the new team's members some time to *get in step*. (❖上記例のような場合stepは無冠詞)

あしならし 足慣らし 100メートル走に出場する前に、軽く足慣らしをしなさい Have a quick *warm-up* before the 100-meter dash.

あしば 足場 (建築用の) scaffold ⓒ, scaffolding Ⓤ; (足がかり) footing ⓒ, foothold ⓒ ∥建築現場に足場を組む put up「a *scaffold* [*scaffolding*] on a building site / 事業の足場を固める gain [secure] a firm *foothold* [*footing*] in business
◆雨のせいで足場が悪い(→地面がぬかるんでいる) *The ground* is muddy because of rain.

あしばや 足早 彼女は足早に(→急いで)去っていった She walked away *fast* [*quickly*].

あしぶみ 足踏み ─足踏みする (踏み鳴らす) stamp 🔊 ∥彼女は体を温めるために足踏みをしながらバスを待っていた She waited for a bus, *stamping her feet* to keep warm.
◆交渉は完全な足踏み状態である The negotiations are at *a complete standstill*.
∥足踏み式ポンプ a foot pump

あしもと 足元・足下 足元注意《掲示》Watch *your step*! / 道が滑りやすくなっているので足元に気をつけてください *The road* is slippery so watch *your step*. / 酔っ払いは足元がふらついていた The drunk walked with *a tottering step*. / The drunk staggered as he walked. / 子猫が足元でじゃれている A kitten is playing *at my feet*. / その赤ちゃんはだいぶ足元がしっかりしてきた The baby is walking steadier.
慣用表現 会社は経営不振で足元に火がついている The company *is in a critical business condition*. / あなたの数学の成績に比べたら私のなんか足元にも及びません My achievements in math *do not compare to* yours. / I'm no *match for* you in math. / 人の足元を見る(→弱みにつけ込む)ようなまねをするな Don't *take advantage of* another's weakness.

あしらう ❶【扱う】treat 🔊 ∥彼は彼女を冷たくあしらった He *treated* her coldly.
◆人を鼻であしらう 《口語的》*turn up one's nose at* a person; (→軽蔑して) *treat* a person *with scorn* [*contempt*]
❷【取り合わせる】(料理に付け合わせを添える) garnish 🔊, (飾る) decorate 🔊 ∥母は食卓の上に花をあしらった My mother *decorated* a table with flowers.

アジる (…を要求して[…に反対して]扇動する) agitate for [against] ...

あじわい 味わい、taste ⓊⒸ, (趣・風情) flavor, 《英》flavour ⓊⒸ ∥この本はとても味わい深い言葉で書かれている I found a very *tasteful* phrase from the book.

あじわう 味わう ❶【賞味する・鑑賞する】taste 🔊; (じっくり味わう) savor 🔊; (鑑賞する) appreciate 🔊 ∥ワインを味わう *savor* the flavors of wine / 詩を味わって読む *enjoy reading* poetry; *savor* poetry / もっと味わって食べたらどう Why don't you *savor* the taste of the food? / 私にとって旅の最大の楽しみはその土地の名物を味わうことだ My greatest pleasure in traveling is to *taste* local specialties.
❷【経験する】experience 🔊, taste 🔊 ∥敗北を味わう *taste* defeat

あす 明日 tomorrow ⇨ あした ∥あすの天気 *tomorrow*'s weather; weather for *tomorrow* / きょうできることをあすに延ばすな Never put off till *tomorrow* what you can do today.
慣用表現 人のことを笑ってなんかいられない。あすはわが身かもしれない You should not laugh at others because *it could also happen to you*.
ことわざ あすの百よりきょうの五十 A bird in the hand is worth two in the bush. (→手中の1羽はやぶの中の2羽に値する)

あずかり 預かり これは佐藤さんからの預かり物です Ms. Sato left this *in my care* [*charge*].
∥預かり証(手荷物の) a check / 手荷物預かり所(駅などの)《米》a baggage room,《英》a left luggage office; (ホテル・劇場などの) a cloakroom

あずかる¹ 預かる
❶【保管する】keep*🔊; (世話をする) look after ..., take* care of ...
かばんを預かっててね。すぐ戻るから Please *keep* my bag for me. I'll be back soon.
荷物を預かってもらえませんか Will you *look after* my baggage? / May I leave my baggage with you?
休暇中は猫を近所の人に預かってもらおう I'll ask my neighbor to「*take care of* [*look after*]」my cat during my vacation.
◆かばんをお預かりしましょうか Can I take your bag?
❷【任される】
留守を預かる be left to「*look after* [*take care of*]」things at home
医者は患者の命を預かっている(→責任がある) The doctor *is responsible for* the lives of his patients.
父がうちのサッカーチームを預かっている(→担当している) My father *is in charge of* this soccer team. / (→監督・コーチである)My father *is the manager* [*coach*] of this soccer team.

あずかる² 与かる ❶【関係する】(関係する) have* something to do with ...; (参加する) take* part in ..., participate in ...
◆そんなことは私のあずかり知るところではない(→関係ない) I *have nothing to do with* such a thing.
❷【目上の人から受ける】おほめにあずかり身に余る光栄です To receive such praise is a

greater honor than I deserve.
🗣「ご紹介します. 東京大学教授で世界的に有名な心理学者の岡氏です」「ただ今ご紹介にあずかりました岡和雄です」"I'd like to introduce Mr. Oka. He's a professor at Tokyo University, and a world-famous psychologist." "Thank you, Mr. X, *for introducing me*. I am Oka Kazuo." (✦ X に紹介者の名前を入れる)

あずき 小豆 adzuki bean ◯ ‖あずき色（赤褐色）russet;（黒みがかった赤）blackish red

あずけいれる 預け入れる deposit ⊕

あずける 預ける
❶ 《物・人を》 leave*⊕;（クロークなどに）《米》check ⊕;（委託する）trust ⊕
家をあけている間友人に飼い犬を預けた I *left* my dog *with* a friend while I was away.
二人は子供を両親に預けて海外旅行に出かけた The couple *left* their child *with* his grandparents while they traveled abroad.
貴重品はフロントに預けたほうがいいよ You should *leave* your valuables *with* the front desk.
彼にお金を預けた I *trusted* him *with* my money. / I *trusted* my money to him.
◆彼女は仕事があったので託児所に子供を預けた She *put* her child *in* a day-care center because she had a job.
❷ 《銀行に》 deposit ⊕, bank ⊕
もらったお年玉はすべて銀行に預けた I *deposited* all my New Year's gift money in [into] the bank.
◆彼女は郵便局に300万預けている She *has* three million yen *on deposit* with the post office.

アステリスク asterisk [ǽstərisk] ◯ (✦星印の記号(*))

アスパラガス asparagus ⓤ (✦数えるときは a spear of … とする)

アスピリン aspirin ⓤ;（錠剤）aspirin (tablet) ◯

アスファルト asphalt [ǽsfɔːlt] ⓤ, 《米》blacktop ⓤ ✦ blacktop は「アスファルトの舗装道路」の意味でも用いる. ‖アスファルトの道路 an *asphalt* road

アスベスト asbestos ⓤ

あずまや（木陰の休憩所）《文語》bower [báuər] ◯;（公園などの休憩所）summerhouse ◯;（木やつるで囲まれた）arbor ◯

アスレチック（運動競技）athletics ‖アスレチッククラブ an *athletic* club (✦ health club, fitness club ともいう)

あせ 汗 sweat [swét] ⓤ (✦「汗をかいている状態」は a sweat);（公式的）perspiration ⓤ (✦ sweat の婉曲的表現. 人についてのみ用いる)
──汗をかく sweat*⊕,（公式的）perspire ⊕
《汗が》
からいものを食べると汗が出る Hot, spicy food makes you *sweat*.
駅の階段を駆け上がって電車に乗ったとたん汗が吹き出した I ran up the stairs in the station and got on the train, and suddenly I *began to sweat heavily*.
汗が目に入って痛い *Sweat* ran into my eye and it hurts.
《汗を》
彼は額に汗をかいていた He *had sweat* on his forehead.
シャワーを浴びて汗を流したい I want to take a shower and *wash off the sweat*.
彼女はリストバンドで汗をぬぐった She *wiped the sweat* with her wrist band.
人は寝ている間にコップ1杯分の汗をかくといわれている It is said that humans *lose as much as a glass of water as sweat* while sleeping.
《その他》
大汗をかく《口語的》*sweat like a pig* / 汗にまみれたシャツ a shirt *soaked in sweat*
私は汗っかきだ I *sweat easily [heavily]*.
リハーサルを終えたダンサーたちは全員汗びっしょりだった The dancers *were dripping sweat* after the rehearsal.
慣用表現 この辞書は彼らの汗と涙の結晶だ This dictionary is *the fruit of their sweat and tears*. / 選手たちの額を玉のような汗が流れていた *Beads of sweat* were running down the players' foreheads. / きょうの試合は手に汗握る試合だった Today's match *was really exciting*. / これは私が額に汗して稼いだお金です I *sweated to earn* this money. / 冷や汗をかく break out in *a cold sweat*

あぜ 畦 ⇨ あぜみち

アセアン ASEAN [ǽsiæn] (✦ Association of Southeast Asian Nations (東南アジア諸国連合)の略語)

あせくさい 汗臭い sweaty ‖その汗臭いシャツをどかしてよ Put away these *sweaty* shirts! / 汗臭いぞ. シャワーを浴びてこい You *smell sweaty*. Go take a shower.

アセスメント（査定・評価）assessment ⓤ ‖環境アセスメント environmental *assessment*

あせだく 汗だく 彼は汗だくだった He *was sweating heavily*. / His body *was covered with sweat*. / 彼女は汗だくになって働いた She *was drenched in sweat* from working.

あせばむ 汗ばむ 彼の額は汗ばんでいた His forehead was *slightly wet with sweat*. / きょうは汗ばむ陽気だ (→暑くて汗でじっとりする日だ) It's a hot and *sweaty* day.

あせみず 汗水 少年は汗水たらして働いていた The boy was working hard and *dripping with sweat*. / これは母が汗水たらして稼いだお金だ This is the money earned *by the sweat of* my mother's *brow*.

あぜみち 畦道 a footpath between rice fields

あせみどろ 汗みどろ sweaty and dirty ‖試合の後, 部員たちはみんな汗みどろだった After the game, all the players were *sweaty and dirty*.

あせも heat rash ⓤ, prickly heat ⓤ ‖首の周りにあせもができた I've got "*heat rash [prickly heat]*" around my neck.

あせる¹ 焦る （いらいらする）become* [get*] impatient; （あわてる）be in a panic, panic 自; （急ぐ）hurry 自 ∥パソコンが立ち上がらないのであせってしまった I *became impatient* because I couldn't boot my computer.
◆時間は十分あるからあせらなくていいよ We have plenty of time. *Don't be in such a hurry.* / あせった．もうちょっとで車にひかれるところだった Gosh, *it was close!* I was almost hit by a car! / 締め切りが近づいているのであせっている I *feel pressed for time* because the deadline is coming up.
💬「早くしろよ」「そんなにあせるなよ」"Hurry up!" "*Don't be impatient.*"

あせる² 褪せる （色・情熱などが）fade 自他; （変色する）discolor 自他 ∥色あせたジーンズ faded [washed-out] jeans / この壁紙は色あせない This wallpaper *won't fade* [*discolor*]. / 彼女のケンへの情熱はすでに色あせてしまった Her passion for Ken *has already faded*.

あぜん 唖然 その話を聞いて彼女はあ然とした She *was dumbfounded* [*speechless*] *at* hearing the story.

あそこ （そこ）there; （向こう）over there; （あの場所）that place

┌─────────────────────────────┐
│ 語法   │
│ (1)日本語の「あそこ」は，自分からも相手からも離れた場所をいうが，there は相手の近くの場所もいう． │
│ (2)over there のほうが there よりも遠くを指すことが多い． │
│ (3)over there 以外にも，位置によって down there（下方; 町の中心より離れて），in there（中に），out there（外に），up there（上に; 町の中心方向に）などが用いられる． │
└─────────────────────────────┘

あそこに電話ボックスがあるよ There's a telephone booth *over there.* / あそこにいる女性は有名なピアニストだ The woman *over there* is a famous pianist. / （電話で）あそこで会いましょう Let's meet *at that place.*
◆彼はあそこまでやることはなかったと思う He went a bit too far in doing *that*. / あそこが初めて彼に会った喫茶店です *That's* the coffee shop where I first met him.
💬「あそこにいる子はだれ」「健二だよ」"Who's that boy *over there*?" "He's Kenji."

あそばせる 遊ばせる 子供たちを砂場で遊ばせた I *sent* the children *to play* in the sandbox. / この高価な機械を遊ばせておく余裕は我々にはない We can't afford to have this expensive machine *lying idle*.

あそび 遊び
❶【遊戯】play Ⓤ; （ゲーム）game Ⓒ ──遊びをする play 自他 ⇨あそぶ
ままごとをする a *play house* / 火遊びをする（→火を使って遊ぶ）*play with matches*; （→危険なことをする）*play with fire*
遊びと勉強のけじめをつけなさい You should separate *play* and study.
宿題を全部片づけたら遊びに行ってよろしい You may *go out and play* when you have finished your homework.
彼は遊び盛りの年ごろだ He's at the age of *wanting to play a lot*.
おいは泥んこ遊びに夢中だった My nephew was lost [absorbed] in *playing in the mud*.
❷【娯楽・楽しみ】pleasure Ⓤ Ⓒ, amusement Ⓒ; （気晴らし）pastime Ⓒ
今度は仕事ではなく遊びでここに来たい I'd like to come here again *for pleasure*, not on business.
母はたまに遊びでピアノを弾いている My mother plays the piano once in a while *for her own amusement*.
◆ほんの遊びのつもりでダンスを習い始めたんです I *wasn't so serious* when I started dancing lessons. / 遊び半分で柔道をやっているとけがをするよ You'll hurt yourself if you do judo *half-heartedly*.
❸【訪問】
ぜひ遊びにいらしてください Be sure to *come (and) see* us.
近いうちに遊びに行くよ I'll *come (and) see* you pretty soon.
隣の猫が時々うちに遊びに来る Our neighbor's cat *visits* us occasionally.
❹【部品などの】play Ⓤ
このハンドルは遊びが少なすぎる[多すぎる] There's too little [much] *play* in this steering wheel.
∥遊び相手(仲間) a companion; （特に子供の）a playmate / 遊び時間 playtime / 遊び道具 a plaything; （おもちゃ）a toy / 遊び人（遊んで暮らす金持ちの男）a playboy / 遊び場 a playground / 遊び部屋 a playroom / 言葉遊び wordplay

あそびほうける 遊び呆ける 息子はたとえ宿題がたくさんあっても遊びほうけている（→遊んでばかりいる）My son *does nothing but play* even when he has a lot of homework.

あそびまわる 遊び回る play around; （はしゃぎ回る）romp 自, frolic 自

あそぶ 遊ぶ
❶【遊戯をする・楽しむ】play 自他; （楽しむ）have* fun, enjoy *oneself*
犬子と遊ぶ *play* with a puppy / トランプをして遊ぶ *play* cards / 外で遊ぶ *play* outside / 家の中で遊ぶ *play* 「in the house [inside]
子供たちは一日中公園で遊んだ The children *played* in the park all day (long).
妹は人形で遊んでいる My sister *is playing* with the dolls.
通りで遊んではいけません *Don't play* in the street.
最近は忙しくて遊ぶ暇がない I've been so busy these days that I *have no time to enjoy myself*.
◆兄はよく渋谷で遊んでから帰宅する My brother often *spends time* in Shibuya before coming home. / 僕らは中学時代よくいっしょに遊んでいた We used to *run around* to-

あだ

gether when we were in junior high. / あの俳優は若いころ相当遊んだといううわさだ That actor is said to *have spent a reckless youth.*

❷「何して遊ぼうか」「先週買ったゲーム、持ってきたんだ。それやろうよ」"What shall we *play* with?" "I've brought a new game I bought last week. Let's play it."

❷〖何もしないでいる〗(怠ける) idle away
遊んでばかりはいられないぞ You can't *just idle away* your time.
◆一生遊んで(=働かずに)暮らせたらいいのになぁ I wish I could live *without working* all my life.

❸〖使われていない〗⇨ あそばせる
遊んでいるパソコンがあったら貸してください Please lend me your *extra* computer.

慣用表現 よく学びよく遊べ ⇨ まなぶ

あだ 仇 恩をあだで返す(→善に悪で報いる)ようなまねをするな Don't *return my good with evil.*/(→えさを与える手をかむな)Don't *bite the hand that feeds you.*/あなたを助けようと思ってしたことがかえって(→傷つけた)あだになってしまいました I intended to help you, but *ended up hurting* you.

アダージョ 〖音楽〗adagio Ⓒ (複 ~s) ——アダージョの adagio

あたい 値・価 (価値) value Ⓤ; (数値) value Ⓒ ——値する deserve 他, be worthy of … ∥注目に値する結果 a result *worthy of note* / 次の連立方程式の x, y の値を求めなさい What are *the values* of x and y in these simultaneous equations? / 君の努力は賞賛に値する Your efforts *deserve* [*are worthy of*] *praise.*

あたえる 与える

❶〖一般的に〗give* 他; (贈る) present 他; (供給する) provide 他, supply 他; (許可などを) allow 他; (権利・許可・金品を) 《公式的》grant 他; (授与する) award 他

【give＋名(人)＋名】≒【give＋名＋to 名(人)】彼女は息子にこづかいを与えた She *gave* her son *an allowance.*/ She *gave* an allowance *to* her son.
もう一度チャンスを与えてください *Give* me another [a second] *chance.*
成績優秀者には奨学金が与えられる Those who achieve excellent grades *will be given* scholarships.
彼女はあなたに許可を与えてくれましたか Did she *give* you *permission*?
与えられた時間内にすべての問いに答えることはできなかった I couldn't answer all the questions *in the given time.*
彼女はできるだけ面接官にいい印象を与えようとした She tried to *give* the interviewer as good an impression as possible.

【provide＋名＋for 名(人)】≒【provide＋名(人)＋with 名】彼らは難民に食料と水を与えた They *provided* food and water *for* the refugees. / They *provided* the refugees *with* food and water.

国会議員には様々な特権が与えられている Diet members *are allowed* various *privileges.*
彼らは彼の研究に多額の金を与えた They *granted* him a large sum of money for his study.
彼女の作品には審査員特別賞が与えられた She *was awarded* a special judges' prize for her work.
◆動物にえさを与えないでください Please *do not feed* the animals. / 彼は最終決定を下す権限を与えられた He *was authorized to* make the final decision.

❷〖割り当てる〗assign [əsáin] 他
生徒一人一人に役割が与えられた Each student *was assigned* a role.
◆僕は与えられた課題をこなすので精一杯だった It was all I could do to do *the assignments.*

❸〖影響を及ぼす〗
暴風雨はその地域に大きな被害を与えた The storm *caused* [*did*] extensive *damage* to the area.
増税が私たちの生活にかなり影響を与えた The tax increase *affected* our lives greatly.
その女優のファッションは若い女性に大きな影響を与えている The actress' fashion *has a great influence on* young girls. (❖affect は直接的影響の場合をいう。間接的影響の場合は通例 influence を用いる)

あたかも as if [though] … (❖as if [though]の後では、通例仮定法が用いられる。ただし、口語では直説法を用いることも多い) ——前 (just) like … ⇨ まるで ∥ 調理場はあたかも戦場のようだった The kitchen was *just like* a battlefield.

あたたかい 暖かい・温かい

❶〖温度が〗(心地よい温度の) warm; (気候が温暖な) mild; (熱い・暑い) hot ——暖かく・温かく warmly
暖か、湿った空気 *warm,* moist air / 暖かい色調 a *warm* tone
彼女は温かいミルクを頼んだ She asked for *hot* milk. (❖飲食物の場合は通例 hot)
パリがこんなに暖かいなんて思わなかったよ How was I to know (that) it would be this *warm* in Paris?
冷たい外気が入ってきて室内の暖かい空気と混ざり合った Cold air from outside mixed with the *warm* air in the room.
暖かくして寝ていなさい Keep *warm* in bed.
ようやく暖かくなってきた It finally began to *get warmer.*
そこでは暖かいコートが必要だ You need a *warm* coat there.
山では暖かい格好をしたほうがいいですよ You should *dress warmly* in the mountains.

❷〖心が〗warm; (親切な) kind, warm-hearted; (心からの) cordial ——温かく warmly; (愛情をこめて) fondly
子供の成長を温かく見守る watch *fondly* as a child grows up
彼は心の温かい人だ He is a *warm-hearted*

person.
彼女は私が落ち込んでいたとき温かい言葉をかけてくれた She gave me *warm* [*kind*] *words* when I was feeling down.
私は新しい学校で温かい歓迎を受けた The new school gave me a *warm* welcome. (◆I received a warm welcome at the new school.ともいえるが，前の表現のほうがふつう)
慣用表現 今ふところが暖かい I'm *flush with cash* now.

あたたかさ 暖かさ・温かさ warmth ⓤ /私たちは彼女の心の温かさに感動した We were touched by *the warmth* of her heart.
◆もう12月だというのに10月並みの暖かさだ For December, it's as *warm* as October.

あたたかみ 暖かみ・温かみ（温度・心の）warmth ⓤ

あたたまる 暖まる・温まる get* [become*] warm(er), warm up; (火などで) warm *oneself* /ストーブをつけても部屋がなかなか暖まらなかった I turned on the heater, but the room wouldn't *warm up*./ おふろに入って温まりなさい Take a bath and *warm yourself* [*yourselves*]. ◆心温まる贈り物 a *heart-warming* gift / 彼女の話を聞いて心が温まりました Her story *warmed* my heart.

あたためる 暖める・温める ❶【温度を上げる】warm ⓣ, heat ⓣ /彼らが来る前に部屋を暖めておこう We'll *warm* [*heat*] (*up*) the room before they come./ コーヒーを温めて飲んだ I *warmed* [*heated*] *up* some coffee and drank it. ◆そのパイは温めて出しなさい Serve the pie *hot*.
❷【だいじに持つ】長い間温めてきた計画を彼女に話すつもりだ I'm going to tell her about the plan I *have been nursing* for a long time./ 同窓会で旧交を温めた We *renewed our friendship* at the class reunion.

アタック ――アタックする（攻撃を仕掛ける）attack ⓣ; (難問などにいどむ) challenge ⓣ; (試みる) try ⓣ /彼らは危険を承知で冬山にアタックした（→冬山登山を試みた）They *tried to climb* mountain in the winter though they knew it was dangerous.
◆今週末彼女にアタックする（→つきあってもらえるかと聞く）つもりなんだ I'll try to *ask* her *to go out with me* this weekend.

語法
「彼女にアタックする」は，好意を持っている女性に「交際を申し込む」の意味だが，英語で attack her というと「彼女に暴力的行為を加える」という意味になる．

アタッシェケース attaché [ǽtəʃéi] case ⓒ
アタッチメント（付属品）attachment ⓒ
あだな あだ名 nickname ⓒ /人にあだ名をつける give a *nickname* to a person / みな私を「アリス」というあだ名で呼んだ Everybody called me by *my nickname* "Alice."/ 彼は走るのがとても遅いから彼のあだ名は「カメ」だ Since he runs so slowly, his *nickname* is "Turtle."
◆彼は「シューレス・ジョー」というあだ名で呼ばれた He *was nicknamed* "Shoeless Joe."

あたふた（急いで）hurriedly, in a hurry, hastily, in haste /彼女はあたふたと部屋を出ていった She left the room *hurriedly*.
◆彼女は身分証明書をなくしてあたふたした She *panicked* when she lost her I.D.

アダプター〔電気〕adapter, adaptor ⓒ

あたま 頭

語法
(1) 日本語の「頭」と英語の head はどちらも，「首から上の部分」を指す場合と「額および頭髪部分」を指す場合とがあるが，head は「頭」だけではなく「顔」「首」の訳語としても用いられることがある / 窓から顔を出す put [stick] *one's head* out of the window / 首を振る shake *one's head*
(2)「頭」を含んだ日本語の表現でも head 以外の語を用いて訳す場合がある．

❶【首から上の部分】head ⓒ
頭を低くする lower *one's head*
彼は僕より頭1つ分背が高い He is taller than me [I] *by a head*./ He is *a head* taller than me [I].
蛇が頭をもたげている The snake's *head* is raised.
◆選手たちは監督に軽く頭を下げた The players *bowed* slightly to the manager.
❷【額および頭髪部分】head ⓒ
頭をかく scratch *one's head*（◆英米では困惑や不満，または考えまいとしていることを表す） / 犬の頭をなでる pat a dog *on the head*; pat a dog's *head* / 頭を強打する hit *one's head* (*very*) *hard* / 頭のてっぺんからつま先まで *from head to toe* [*foot*]; *from top to bottom*/ はげ頭 a bald *head*
かぜで頭が痛い My *head aches* with a cold./ I *have a headache* from a cold.
頭が重い My *head feels heavy*./ I *feel heavy in the head*.
あいつが先に僕の頭をたたいたんだ He *hit me on the head* first.
ボールがそのバッターの頭に当たった The ball *caught* the batter *on the head*.
ぼうっとしていて柱に頭をぶつけてしまった I absent-mindedly *hit my head against* a pillar.
❸【頭髪】《集合的》hair ⓤ
頭を刈ってもらう have *one's hair* cut; have a *haircut* / 頭を洗う wash *one's hair*
その老人は白髪頭だった The old man had gray *hair*.
彼はぼさぼさの頭をしている He has *a mop of hair*.
◆頭を丸める shave *one's head*
❹【思考力・考え方】（知力）brain ⓒ ⓤ, head ⓒ; (記憶力・理性) mind ⓤ
〖頭が・は〗
頭がいい[悪い] have *a good* [*bad*] *head* [*brain*] / 彼は頭があまりよくない He *doesn't have much of a brain*.
◆父は頭がかたい（→頑固だ）My father is

stubborn. / 祖母は頭が柔らかい My grandmother *is flexible in her thinking*. / 彼女は頭が切れる She *is very bright* [*smart, clever*]. / だんだん頭がこんがらかってきた I'*m getting confused*. / 姉は結婚式のことで頭がいっぱいだ My sister *is* 「*full of* [*preoccupied with*]」 her wedding ceremony.

《頭に》
あるアイディアが頭に浮かんだ An idea *came into my mind*.
そのことを頭に入れておいてください *Keep that in mind*.

《頭の》
彼は頭の回転が速い[鈍い] He *has a quick* [*slow*] *mind*.
試験が始まったとたん私の頭の中は真っ白になった *My mind went blank* as soon as the exam began.
◆彼は頭のよい生徒だ He is an *intelligent* student.

《頭を》
頭を使いなさい *Use your head* [*brain*].
彼女はその問題に頭を悩ませた She *racked her brains* over the problem.
なかなか頭を切り替えられない I can't *change my mind* [*thinking, opinion*] easily.

《その他》
彼女のことが頭から離れない I *can't get her out of my mind*.

❺【上の部分】(上端) head ⓒ; (先端) tip ⓒ
くぎの頭 *the head of* a nail / 鼻の頭 *the tip of one's nose*
◆富士山が頭を雲の上に出している The *peak* [*summit*] of Mt. Fuji is sticking out of the clouds.

❻【最初】beginning ⓒ《通例単数形》
来月の頭に at *the beginning of* the next month
兄は頭から私の話を聞こうとしない My brother won't listen to me *from the beginning*.

❼【人数】head ⓒ
食事には1人頭5,000円かかった The meal cost 5,000 yen *per* [*a*] *head*.

慣用表現 あの人には頭が上がらない I *can't oppose* that person. / 数学の試験のことを考えると頭が痛い Math tests *are a headache*. / Math tests *give me a headache*. / 頭隠して尻隠さず *bury one's head in the sand* / あの人には頭が下がる思いだ I think [feel] I should *take my hat off* to that person. / 彼はだれに対しても頭が低い He *is* always *humble*. / He *humbles himself* to everyone. / あの人たちは頭が古い Their thinking *is* 「*out of date* [*old-fashioned*]. / あいつの言うことはいちいち頭にくる Every word he says *makes me angry*. / 悪天候続きで農家の人々は頭を抱えている Farmers *are tearing their hair out* over the continuing bad weather. / どうして私が彼に頭を下げなければならないの Why do I *have to apologize* to him? / この問題はちょっと頭をひねったくらいでは解けない Solving this problem requires *more than a little thought*. / This problem cannot be solved *with only a little thought*. / 頭を冷やせよ *Cool down* [*off*].

あたまうち 頭打ち 米の価格が頭打ちになった(→天井値に達した) Rice prices *have reached their ceiling*. / その会社では50歳で給料が頭打ちになる Salary *reaches the upper limit* at the age of 50 in that company.

あたまかず 頭数 the number of people, head ⓒ / 頭数を数える count *heads* [*the number of people*] ◆頭数をそろえる make up *the number* / ラグビーをするのに頭数が1人足りない We're one person short (of the required *number*) to play rugby.

あたまきん 頭金 (手付金) deposit ⓒ; (分割払いなどの) down payment ⓒ / 頭金として1万円払う pay 10,000 yen as *a down payment*; pay 10,000 yen *down* / 新しいパソコンの頭金を支払った I made *a down payment* on a new PC.

あたまごなしに 頭ごなしに 彼は自分の息子をいつも頭ごなしに(→弁明する機会すら与えず)にしかる He always scolds his son *without giving him even a chance to explain*.

あたまだし 頭出し このビデオは頭出しができる This VCR can *skip to the beginning of programs* on a tape.

あたまでっかち 頭でっかち (頭部が大きすぎる) top-heavy; (理論だけで実践の伴わない) armchair /頭でっかちの建物 a *top-heavy* building / 頭でっかちの理論家 an *armchair theorist*

あたまわり 頭割り 収益を頭割りする「*share in* [*split*] the profits *equally* / 勘定は頭割りにしよう Let's *split* the bill *equally*.

あたらしい 新しい

new (↔old); (新鮮な) fresh; (新品の) brand-new; (ニュースなどが最新の) the latest, 《口語的》hot; (現代風の) modern —— 新しく newly

新しい理論 a *new theory* / 新しい年[世紀] a *new year* [*century*] / 新しい考え a *new* [*fresh*] *idea* / 新しい(→最新の)ニュース *the latest news*; *fresh news*; 《口語的》*hot news* / 新しい風(→新たな政治勢力) a *new political force* / 新しくオープンしたディスカウント店 a *newly opened* discount store

うわあっ,新しい自転車買ったの? Wow! You've got a *new* bike?

新しいコンピュータが学校に入った *New* computers have been put in at our school.

ロンドンでの新しい生活にもすぐ慣れるでしょう You will soon *adjust* (yourself) *to* your *new* life in London.

ノートがもうすぐ終わりそうだ. 新しいのを買わなきゃ My notebook is running out. I have to buy a *new one*.

妹は真新しい制服を着てうれしそうだった My sister looked happy in her *brand-new* school uniform.

彼のノーベル賞受賞はまだ我々の記憶に新しい His winning of the Nobel prize is still *fresh in our minds*.

雪の上にはまだ新しいウサギの足跡がついていた There were *fresh* tracks of a rabbit in the snow.
祖父は昔から新しい物が好きだったらしい My grandfather seems to have been fond of *modern* things.
気分を変えるために壁紙を新しくした I put up *new* wallpaper to change my mood.
野菜は新しければ新しいほどおいしい *The fresher* the vegetables, the more delicious (they are). / (→新鮮な野菜が最もおいしい) *Fresh* vegetables are the most delicious.

💬「新しい英語の先生が来るんだよ」「厳しくないといいなあ」 "We are going to have a *new* English teacher." "I hope he's not demanding."

💬「新しい学校はどう」「快適だよ. もう友達もいっぱいできたし」 "How's your *new* school?" "It's fine. I've already got a lot of friends."

💬「ねえ, 変わった靴はいてるね」「この形が今いちばん新しいんだよ」 "Hey, you've got unusual shoes on!" "These are of *the latest* style."

あたらずさわらず 当たらず障らず ⇨ あたりさわり

あたらない 当たらない それは驚くに当たらない That is *hardly* surprising. / That's *nothing to be* surprised at.

あたり¹ 辺り
❶【近所・そば】
私はこのあたりは不案内です I'm a stranger in *this neighborhood*. / I'm not familiar with *this neighborhood*.
以前このあたりは森だった Formerly *this neighborhood* was a forest.
私の住んでいるあたりはとても静かだ It's very quiet in *my neighborhood*.
あたりを見渡したが公衆電話は見当たらなかった I *looked around*, but couldn't find a public phone.
そのときあたりに人影はなかった There was no one *around* then.
あたり一面に美しい花が咲いていた There were beautiful flowers *all around* (the place).
彼は以前中野あたりに住んでいたそうだ I hear he used to live *in the* Nakano *area*.

💬「すみません. このあたりにコンビニはありませんか」「その角を曲がった所にありますよ」 "Excuse me, but is there a convenience store *around* [*near*] *here*?" "It's around the corner."

❷【およそ】
来週あたり(→来週のいつか)は桜も満開だろう The cherry blossoms will be in full bloom *sometime next week*.
きょうの授業はこのあたりで終わりにしましょう Let's knock off the lesson *here* for today.

慣用表現 その男はあたりかまわず大声をあげて話した The man spoke in a loud voice *without any regard for other people around him*.

あたり² 当たり ❶【的中・成功】当たり！ *You're* [*That's*] *right*! / (→的(🎯)に)*You hit it*! / (→クイズなどで)*You guessed right*! / その映画はアメリカで当たりだった The movie was *a big hit* [*success*] in America.

💬「何かいいことあったの」「当たり！ 英語のテストで100点取ったの」 "Did something good happen to you?" "*You guessed right*! I got 100 on the English exam."

❷【打球・ぶつかること】いい当たりだったが, 三塁手の真正面だった He *hit* the ball well [*hard*], but it went right to the third baseman. / ガードレールにぶつかったときの当たりは強かったが, バンパーがへこんだだけだった My car *hit* the guardrail hard, but only the bumper dented. ⇨ たいあたり

❸【感じ】彼女は当たりが柔らかい She has mild *manners*. / 当たりがあったらリールを巻け Reel in when you feel *a bite*. ⇨ くちあたり, ひとあたり

❹【身体的害】食あたり *food poisoning* / 熱いお湯に長くつかっていると湯あたりする(→くらくらする)よ You will *feel dizzy* from soaking in a hot bath too long.

慣用表現 ボールの当たりどころが悪かったので, 彼は左腕を骨折した He broke his left arm because the ball *hit the weak part* of it.

-あたり -当たり per, a (❖perは商業英語などで用いられ, 日常的にはaが用いられる) / 1時間あたり2,000円 2,000 yen *per* [*an*] hour / 食事には1人あたり100ドルかかった The meal cost 100 dollars *per* [*a*] person [head].
◆バレル[ダース]あたり *by the* barrel [dozen] (❖byの後は通例《the+単位を表す名詞》)

あたりさわり 当たり障り 彼らは当たりさわりのない(→害のない)会話をした They had a *harmless* talk. / その政治家は当たりさわりのない(→どっちつかずの)返事をした The politician gave a *noncommittal* answer.

あたりちらす 当たり散らす 《口語的》take* it out on *a person*, take *one's* anger out on *a person* / スワローズが負けたので, 彼は家族に当たり散らした When the Swallows lost the game, he *took it out on* his family.

あたりどし 当たり年 映画の当たり年 *a good year* for films / 今年はブドウの当たり年だった We've had *a good crop* of grapes this year.

あたりはずれ 当たり外れ 天気予報には当たりはずれがある(→いつも正しいとは限らない) The weather forecast [report] is not always right.

あたりまえ 当たり前 ——形(当然な) natural; (ふつうの) ordinary, usual; (ありふれた) common, commonplace ——副(もちろん) of course / 人に助けてもらったらお礼を言うのが当たり前だ It's *natural* to say thank you when you are given help. / 女優といっても, 彼女はふだんはごく当たり前の女性だ She may be an actress, but in everyday life she's just an *ordinary* [*average*] woman. /

あたる

海外旅行は今やごく当たり前のことである Traveling abroad is *commonplace* nowadays.
◆ゆうべ2時間しか寝ていないんじゃ、眠くなるのは当たり前だ *No wonder* you feel sleepy after getting only two hours of sleep last night.
🗨「私のことまだ怒ってる？」「当たり前だろ」"Are you still angry with [at] me?" "*Of course* I am."

あたる 当たる

❶ぶつかる	hit, strike
❷的中する	guess right; prove right
❸くじなどに	win
❹指名される	be called on
❺光・風などを受ける	be exposed
❻相当する	be; be equivalent [equal] to ...
❼体の害になる	disagree with ...; be poisoned

❶【ぶつかる】hit* 働, strike* 働 ⊕
的(ﾏﾄ)に当たる *hit* the mark [target]
ボールが彼の頭に当たった The ball *hit* [*struck*] him on the head.
シャベルが何か硬いものに当たった My shovel *struck* against something hard.

❷【的中する】(正しく言い当てる) guess right; (予言・予想などが) prove* right
彼女の推測は当たった She *guessed right*.(◆「はずれる」は guess wrong)
きょうの天気予報は当たったね Today's weather forecast *proved right*.(◆「はずれる」は prove wrong)
◆勘が当たった My intuition *was right*./ あの占い師はよく当たるという評判です That fortune teller is said to *be trustworthy*./ 私の答えが当たった I *answered correctly*./ My answer *was correct*.
🗨「占いは当たったの？」「いいえ．占い師の占いがすべて当たるとは限らないよ」"Did the fortune-telling *come true*?" "No. Not all fortune tellers' predictions do."

❸【くじなどに】(賞金・賞品を当てる) win* 働
どうか1等賞が当たりますように I hope I'll *win* the first prize.
宝くじに当たったんだって？ 信じられない！ You've *won* the lottery? That's too good to be true!
くじで何が当たったと思う？ パリ旅行よ！ Guess what I *won* in the lottery. A trip to Paris!

❹【指名される】be called on
英語の時間に2回も当たっちゃったよ I *was called on* twice in English class.

❺【光・風などを受ける】(さらされる) be exposed; (日光を) get* sunshine [sun]; (暖をとる) warm *oneself*
こたつにあたる *warm oneself at* a kotatsu
ここはよく日が当たる This place *gets* a lot of *sunshine*./ This place *is sunny*.

この部屋は西日が当たる This room *gets the afternoon sun*.
もっと近くに来てストーブにあたったら Why don't you come closer and *warm yourself by the heater*?
◆夜風にあたる *expose one's body to the night breeze*./ 午後は私の部屋には日が当たらない In the afternoon my room *is in shadows*./ 通りの日の当たる側を歩いた I walked on the *sunny* side of the street.

❻【相当する】(…である) be; (等しい) be equivalent [equal] to ...; (一致する) correspond to ...; (日時が) fall* on [upon] ...
明は私のいとこに当たる Akira *is* my cousin.
あっちがちょうど北の方向に当たる That direction *is* dead north.
1 升は約1.8リットルに当たる One *sho is equivalent [equal] to* approximately 1.8 liters.
私の誕生日は今年は月曜日に当たる My birthday *falls on* a Monday this year.
◆退学処分に当たる行為 an act that *merits* expulsion from school
🗨「『伝統』に当たる英語は何ですか」「tradition かなぁ」"What *is* the English word *for* 'dento'?" "It's 'tradition,' maybe."

❼【体の害になる】(食べ物が合わない) disagree with ...; (中毒症状を起こす) be poisoned
カキにあたった The oysters *disagreed with* me./ I *got food poisoning* from the oysters.

❽【調べる・さぐる】
ちゃんと辞書にあたってスペルを確かめたほうがいいよ It's best to *check* the dictionary for the correct spelling./ It's best to *look up* the word in the dictionary for the correct spelling.
英語の原文にあたりなさい Please *check* [*refer to*] the original English text.
本人にあたって聞いてみろ Ask her [him] *in person*./ Ask her [him] *directly*.

❾【成功する】
この商売はきっと当たるよ I'm sure this business will *be a success*.

❿【担当する】
総勢2,000人の警官がそのパレードの警備に当たった A total of 2,000 police officers *were on guard* at the parade.
彼と彼の家族は自宅で祖母の介護に当たった He and his family *nursed* [*cared for*] his grandmother at home.

⓫【その他】
人につらくあたる *treat* a person *harshly* [*badly*]
ほかの店をあたってごらん *Try* another shop.
機械のご使用にあたっては説明書をよくお読みください Please carefully read the instructions *for* operating the machine.
慣用表現 ためらってないで，当たって砕けろ(→最善を尽くせ)，だよ Don't hesitate. *Do your best*! [*Go for broke*!] / 当たらずさわらずの返事 a *noncommittal* reply / 当たり散らす あたりちらす

アダルト （大人・成人） adult ⓒ ‖アダルトビデオ an adult [a porno] video

あちこち
あちこち捜したが，かぎは見つからなかった I searched for the key *here and there*, but I couldn't find it.
私は彼女をあちこち案内した I showed her *around*.
部屋のあちこちにたくさんの本が散らかっていた Many books were scattered *around* the room.
ヨーロッパをあちこち旅行した I traveled *around* Europe.
その町のあちこちにまだ戦争のつめ跡が見られる Traces of war can still be seen *all over* the town.
町のあちこちを歩き回った I went to *various places* in the town.

あちら
❶【場所・方向】 （そこ） there; （向こう） over there; （方向） that way; (あの場所) that place ⇨ あそこ ‖あちらへ行こう Let's go *there*. / 出口はあちらです The exit is *over there*. / あちらに着いたら必ずメールをください Please make sure to send me an e-mail when you get *there*. / あちらではもう雪が降っているらしい I hear it is already snowing *there*.
❷【人・物】 that ‖あちらがベーカーさんです *That* is Mr. Baker. / あちらのかばんを見せてください Please show me *that* bag.
慣用表現 あちらを立てればこちらが立たぬ(→すべての人を満足させることはできない) *You can't please everyone.*

あちらこちら
あちらこちらに美しいチューリップが咲いている Beautiful tulips are flowering *here and there*. ⇨ あちこち

あっ
（驚き） oh, ah ‖あっ ，そうか *Oh*, I see. / あっ ，財布忘れてきちゃった(→持ってこなかった) *Oh!* I didn't bring my purse. / 世間をあっと言わせる *cause a sensation* / あっ，痛い *Ouch!*
🅔 「カメラ持ってきた？」「あっ，忘れちゃった」 "Did you bring your camera?" "*Oh!* I forgot [left] it!"

あつあつ
熱々 （飲み物などが） piping hot
◆慎吾と敬子は熱々の仲だ(→深く愛し合っている) Shingo and Keiko *are madly in love with each other*.

あつい 厚い
❶【物が】 thick (↔thin) ――厚く thick, thickly
厚い氷 *thick* ice / 厚い雲 *thick* [(→濃い) *dense*, (→重苦しい) *heavy*] clouds / 厚い本 a *thick* [*fat*] book / 厚い唇 *thick* [*full*] lips / ジャムを厚く塗る spread the jam *thick* [*thickly*] / 肉を厚く切ってください Will you cut the meat *thick* [*thickly*]?
◆そのチームは選手の層が厚い That team has a *good* [*deep*] bench. / 彼女はいつも化粧が厚い She always wears *heavy* make-up.
❷【心が】 （温かい） warm; （親切な） kind

私たちは厚いもてなしを受けた We received a *warm* welcome.
◆彼女は情に厚い人だ She is a *warm-hearted* person. / ご親切厚く御礼申し上げます *I am very grateful to you* for your kindness. / *Thank you very much* for your kindness. / *I really appreciate* your kindness.
慣用表現 彼は面(ﾂﾗ)の皮が厚い He *has a thick skin* [*hide*].

あつい² 暑い
hot (↔cold); （少し暑い） warm
ある暑い日に on a hot *day* / うだるように暑い *sweltering* [*boiling*] (*hot*) / 焼けるように暑い *scorching* [*burning, roasting*] (*hot*)
きょうはかなり[少し]暑い It's quite [somewhat] *hot* today.
東京の夏はとても暑い It gets very *hot* in summer in Tokyo.
米は暑くて湿気の多い国で最もよく育つ Rice grows (the) best in *hot and humid* countries.
今は暑い盛りだから食品の保存には特に気をつけなさい You should be very careful in preserving foods because it's *the hottest season of the year*.
◆庭の高い木々が暑い日差しをさえぎっていた The tall trees in the garden blocked *the blazing sun*. / 今年の夏は蒸し暑い日が多かった We had many *sultry* days this summer. / 湿気が多いより暑いほうがまだいい *Heat* is preferable to humidity.
🅔 「この部屋，ちょっと暑くない？」「そうだね．エアコン入れようか」 "It's *rather warm* in here, isn't it?" "It is. Shall I turn on the air conditioner?"

あつい³ 熱い
❶【物が】 hot (↔cold); （熱した） heated
熱い紅茶を1杯いただけますか Would you give me a (cup of) *hot* tea?
熱いふろに入りたい I want to take a *hot* bath.
熱いコーヒーを1杯飲めば体が温まりますよ A cup of *hot* coffee will warm you up.
◆額が熱で熱い My forehead *burns* with fever.
❷【心が】 （真剣な） intent; （激しい） intense
人々は熱いまなざしで彼女を見た People looked at her with an *intent* gaze.
彼は私に祖国に対する熱い思いを語った He told me of his *intense* love for his own country.
◆あの二人はお熱い仲だ Those two are *madly in love with each other*.
ことわざ 鉄は熱いうちに打て ⇨ てつ

あっか¹ 悪化 deterioration Ⓤ ――悪化する deteriorate ⓘ, worsen ⓘ, get* [become*] worse ‖事態はますます悪化している Things *are getting worse and worse*. / 彼の容態は今度の旅行で悪化した His condition *worsened* on this trip.

あっか² 悪貨 bad money Ⓤ

[あ]

[慣用表現] 悪貨は良貨を駆逐する *Bad money drives out good.*

あつかい 扱い ❶【物・問題の】(操作) operation [U]; (取り扱い) handling [U] ◆この機械の扱いに慣れるには少し時間がかかる It takes a while to get used to *operating* this machine. / 彼はパソコンの扱い方に詳しい He is acquainted with *how to operate* a personal computer. / カメラの扱いには注意して Be careful *with* the camera. / これはいまだに扱いの難しい問題だ This remains a *touchy* subject.

❷【人の】(処遇) treatment [U] ∥特別扱い special *treatment* / 非人間的な扱い inhumane *treatment* ◆姉はいつも私を子供扱いする My sister always *treats* me *as* [*like*] *a child.* / 彼女は部下の扱い方がうまい She's good at *managing* her staff.

あつかう 扱う

❶【物を】handle [他]; (操作する) operate [他]

この箱は丁寧に扱ってください *Handle* this package carefully [with care].

パソコンを乱暴に扱うな Don't *handle* [*run*] the personal computer roughly.

❷【問題などを】handle [他]; (処理する) deal* with ...; (論じる)《公式的》treat [他]

そのテレビ番組は環境問題を扱っていた The TV program *dealt with* the environmental problem.

あなたはその問題をどのように扱うつもりですか How do you propose to *deal with* the matter?

彼の意見をそんなに軽く扱ってはいけない Don't *treat* his opinions so lightly.

◆すべての新聞が彼についての記事を大きく扱った All the papers *featured* the story about him.

❸【人を】(接する) treat [他], deal* with ...; (操る) manage [他]

人を丁重に扱う *treat* a person *politely* [*with kid gloves*] / 人をひどく扱う *treat* a person *badly* [《口語的》*like a dog*]

すべての生徒は平等に扱われるべきだ Every student should *be treated equally*.

彼は扱いにくい人だ He's *a difficult person to deal with.*

彼女は子供たちを扱うのがうまい She's good at *managing* children.

◆彼女は軽く扱われるべき人物でない She is not a person to *be trifled with.*

❹【商品を】handle [他], deal* in ...

どんな商品を扱っていますか What sorts of merchandise do you *handle*?

この会社は主に絹製品を扱っている This company *deals* chiefly *in* silk goods.

◆その店ではイギリスからの輸入品を専門に扱っている That shop *specializes in* imports from Britain.

[会話] 「すみません, この本置いてますか」「申しわけございませんが, 当店では外国の本は扱っておりません」"Excuse me, but do you have this book?" "I'm sorry, but we *don't deal in* foreign books."

あつかましい 厚かましい brazen; (生意気な)《公式的》impudent; (恥知らずの) shameless ∥厚かましい態度 a *brazen* [an *impudent*] attitude / なんて厚かましい How *impudent*! / What *a nerve*!

あつがみ 厚紙 (厚手の紙) thick paper [U]; (ボール紙) cardboard [U]; (紙を何枚もはり合わせた厚紙) pasteboard [U] ∥厚紙1枚 a piece [sheet] of *cardboard* [*thick paper, pasteboard*]

あつがり 暑がり 私はとても暑がりだ(→暑さに敏感だ) I'*m* very *sensitive* [*susceptible*] *to heat.*

あつがる 暑がる 子供たちは暑がっている(→暑いと不満を言っている) My children *are complaining about the heat.* / 窓が全部閉まっていたので部屋にいたみんなが暑がった(→暑く感じた) Everybody in the room *felt the heat* because all windows were shut.

あっかん[1] 圧巻 (最高の部分) the best part; (ハイライト) highlight [C]; (見せ場) climax [C] ∥主人公の女性が恋人を捨てたシーンが圧巻(→見せ場)だった The scene where the heroine left her lover was *the climax*.

あっかん[2] 悪漢 villain [vílən] [C]; (小説・映画などの)《口語的》baddy, baddie [C] ∥悪漢小説 a picaresque novel

あつぎ 厚着 ━厚着する (動作) put* on warm clothes, bundle up; (状態) be heavily dressed, wear* heavy clothes ∥外は雪が降っているから厚着をしていったほうがいいよ It is snowing outside, so maybe you should *put on warm clothes.*

◆そんなに厚着して暑くないの? Aren't you feeling hot *in* such *heavy clothes*?

あつくるしい 暑苦しい (蒸し暑い) sultry, 《口語的》muggy, stuffy, close and hot ∥ゆうべは暑苦しくてよく眠れなかった *It was* so *muggy* last night I couldn't sleep well. / この部屋は暑苦しい This room *is close and hot.* ◆勇は暑苦しい格好をしている Isamu *is overdressed for the* (*hot*) *weather.*

あっけ 呆気 彼女のはでな服を見てあっけにとられてしまった(→驚いて口もきけなくなった) I *was dumbfounded* by her loud dress. / 私たちは父がものすごい勢いで食べるのを見てあっけにとられた We *were astonished* to see our father stuffing himself with food.

あつげしょう 厚化粧 あの女優はいつも厚化粧だ That actress always *wears heavy make-up.*

あっけない 呆気ない あっけない(→期待はずれの)幕切れ a *disappointing* ending / あっけなく(→あまりにも簡単に)敗れる lose *too easily* / その映画の結末はあっけないものだった The movie ended in *disappointment.* / 休暇はあっけなく(→あまりにも早く)終わった The vacation ended *all too soon.*

あっけらかん(と) 彼はへまをやらかしてもあっけらかんと(→何事もなかったかのように)していた He behaved *as if nothing had happened* when he made a blunder. / 彼女はあっけ

らかんとした人だ She is an *easy-going* person.

あっこう 悪口 abuse ◆彼女は夫に向かって悪口雑言(ぞうごん)を並べたてた She hit her husband with *a torrent of curses*.

あつさ¹ 厚さ thickness ‖氷の厚さ *the thickness* of the ice ◆厚さ7センチの壁 a seven-centimeter-*thick* wall; a wall seven centimeters *thick* / この辞書は厚さが5センチある This dictionary is five centimeters *thick*.

🔊「板の厚さはどれくらいですか」「3センチくらいです」 "How *thick* is the board?" "It's about three centimeters *thick*."

あつさ² 暑さ heat ‖うだるような暑さ sweltering [boiling, oppressive] *heat* / 焼けつくような暑さ scorching [burning] *heat* / 猛烈な暑さ intense *heat* / 暑さに弱い be sensitive to *heat* / この山荘にいると夏の暑さを忘れることができる In this mountain cottage you can forget the *heat* of summer. / この暑さに耐えられない I can't stand this *heat*. / この暑さで完全にばてしまった This *heat* has done me in completely. / 暑さ厳しき折からご自愛ください I hope you will watch out for yourself in this *heat*. (◈英語の手紙では、このような結びの言葉を用いない)

◆きょうは今年いちばんの暑さだ This is the *hottest* day of the year.

慣用表現 暑さ寒さも彼岸まで *Extremes of temperature last only till the equinox*.

あつさ³ 熱さ heat; (温度) temperature ‖お湯の熱さを計る measure *the temperature* of the hot water

あっさく 圧搾 compression, pressure ―圧搾する compress, press ‖圧搾機 a compressor / 圧搾空気 compressed air

あっさり ❶【簡単に】 easily, readily ‖彼はあっさり自分の誤りを認めた He admitted his fault *readily*.

❷【しつこくない】 (食べ物が) plain; (消化のよい) light; (性格がざっくばらんな) frank ‖あっさりした食べ物 *plain* food / あっさりした(→消化のよい)ものが食べたい I want to have a *light* meal. / 彼女はとてもあっさりした性格です She is a very *frank* person.

あっしゅく 圧縮 compression ―圧縮する (圧力を加えて) compress; (文章などを) condense ‖空気を圧縮する *compress* air / ファイルを圧縮して送ってください *Compress* the file and send it to me.
‖圧縮ガス compressed gas / 圧縮機 a compressor / 圧縮空気 compressed air

あっしょう 圧勝 overwhelming victory; (選挙の) landslide (victory) ―圧勝する overwhelm ‖僕らは決勝戦で中央高校に圧勝した We *overwhelmed* Chuo High School team in the final. / 彼らはその試合で相手チームに圧勝した They *won an overwhelming victory* over their opponent in the game. / 選挙は保守党の圧勝に終わった The election ended in *a landslide victory* for the conservative party.

あっせい 圧政 tyranny, despotism ‖圧政に苦しむ groan under *tyranny [despotism]* ◆圧政を敷く *rule with a rod of iron*

あっせん 斡旋 (はからい) (公式的) good offices; (世話) help, assistance ‖彼らは私の友達のあっせんで家を買った They purchased a house「*through the assistance* [*with the help*] of a friend of mine.

◆人に就職のあっせんをする *help* a person (*to*) *find a job*

あつぞこぐつ 厚底靴 platform shoes ‖いつ厚底靴がはやりだしたのかしら I wonder when *platform shoes* came into fashion.

あっち ❶【方向】 over there, there; (あちらへ) that way, in that direction ⇨あちら ‖出口はあっちです The exit is *over there*. / 彼らはあっちへ行きました They went *in that direction*. / 郵便局はあっちです The post office is *that way*. / (→反対方向です) The post office is *the other way*. ◆あっちへ行け Get lost!/ Get out (of here)!/ Go away!

🔊「この荷物はどこへ置きましょうか」「あっちの隅においてください」 "Where should I put this baggage?" "Please put it in the corner *over there*."

❷【人・物を指して】 that ⇨あれ¹ ‖こっちよりあっちのほうがいいです I'd prefer *that* one to this one. / I like *that* better than this. (◈複数のものを指す場合は those を用いる)

あつで 厚手 ―厚手の thick, heavy ⇨あつい(厚い) ‖厚手の布 *thick* cloth / 厚手のコート a *heavy* [*thick*] coat

あっと そのニュースは世間をあっと言わせた The news *startled* [*astonished*] the world. / あっという間に(→一瞬)の出来事だった It happened in *a flash* [*an instant*]. / 夏休みはあっという間に(→速く)過ぎた My summer vacation went *all too quickly*.

あっとう 圧倒 ―圧倒する overwhelm
―圧倒的(な) overwhelming ―圧倒的に overwhelmingly

圧倒的な勝利を得る win *an overwhelming victory*

きのうわが大学チームは他大学を圧倒して優勝した Our university team *overwhelmed* the other teams and won the championship yesterday.

今川軍は織田軍に圧倒された The Imagawa troops *were overwhelmed* by the Oda troops.

私たちはグランドキャニオンの景観に圧倒された We *were overwhelmed* by the sight of the Grand Canyon.

その法案は圧倒的多数で可決された The bill passed *by an overwhelming majority*.

◆わが家は圧倒的に(→家族のほとんどが)西武ファンだ *Most of* our family are Lions fans.

アットホーム ⚠ ―アットホームな (家庭的な) homey; (居心地のよい) cozy ‖アットホームな雰囲気 a *homey* atmosphere (◈× *at home atmosphere* とはいわない)

アットランダム ⇨アトランダム

アッパーカット uppercut ‖人にアッパーカ

あっぱく

ットを浴びせる hit a person *with an uppercut*; *uppercut* a person / 彼はあごにアッパーカットを食らってダウンした He was downed by *an uppercut* to the jaw.

あっぱく 圧迫（圧力）pressure ⓊⒸ;（抑圧）oppression ⓊⒸ;（抑制）suppression ⓊⒸ;（ストレス）stress ⓊⒸ ―圧迫する pressure ⓗ; oppress ⓗ; suppress ⓗ /圧迫を受ける be subjected to *pressure* / 胸に圧迫感がある have *a feeling of pressure* on the chest

あっぱれ 天晴れ ―あっぱれな（賞賛に値する）admirable, praiseworthy;（みごとな）splendid /あっぱれな行い *admirable* [*praiseworthy*] conduct ◆あっぱれ! *Bravo!*/ *Well done!*/ 君は敵ながらあっぱれだ（→君の優秀さは認めねばならない）I *have to hand it to* you.

アップ ❶【上にあがること】パソコンの売り上げが去年に比べアップした Sales of PCs *are up* over last year. / 社長は社員に賃金のアップを約束した The president promised the employees *increased* wages.
❷【撮影】顔のアップは撮らないで Please don't take *a (facial) close-up*.
❸【髪型】髪をアップにしている wear *one's* hair *up*

あっぷあっぷ あっぷあっぷする（→おぼれて死にそうになる）be almost [nearly] drowned; almost [nearly] drown

アップツーデート ―アップツーデートな（最新の）up-to-date（❖名詞の後で用いる場合は up to date とすることがある）/アップツーデートな話題 an *up-to-date* topic

アップリケ appliqué Ⓒ（❖フランス語から）/アップリケのついたスカート an *appliqué* skirt

アップルパイ apple pie Ⓒ

あつまり 集まり ❶【集会】meeting Ⓒ;（非公式でうちとけた）gathering Ⓒ;（特定の目的をもった）assembly Ⓒ /あしたクラブの集まりがある Our club has *a meeting* tomorrow. ◆きょうは集まり（→出席）がいいね[悪いね] There is *a good* [*poor*] *attendance* today.
❷【集合体】（人・物の）group Ⓒ（❖〖英〗では単数形で複数扱いになることがある）;（塊）body Ⓒ, mass Ⓒ /雲は小さな水滴の集まりだ Clouds are *masses* of droplets of water.

あつまる 集まる

❶【人が】gather ⓗ, get* [come*] together;（群がる）flock ⓗ, crowd ⓗ;（ある目的のために）assemble ⓗ;（会合する）meet* ⓗ
みなさん, 集まってください *Gather round*, everybody.
100人を超える学生が集まった More than 100 students *gathered*.
ファンがその選手の周りに集まった The fans *gathered* [*crowded*] around the player.
その大道芸を見ようと群衆が集まってきた A crowd *gathered* to see the street performance.
何千という観光客がその広場に集まる Thousands of tourists *flock* to the square.
多くの人々が増税反対のデモをするために公園に集まった A lot of people *assembled* in the park to demonstrate against higher taxes.
全部員が週1回ここに集まる All the members *meet* here once a week.
❷【物が】
お金はいくら集まりましたか How much money *was collected*?
神保町にはたくさんの古本屋が集まっている（→密集している）Secondhand bookstores *stand close together* in Jimbocho.
多くの豪華なホテルがこの新しく開発された地域に集まっている（→集中している）Many gorgeous hotels *are concentrated* in this newly developed area.
この種の虫は光に集まる習性がある This kind of insect has a habit of *swarming* to light.
❸【関心などが】
国民の関心がその殺人事件に集まった（→殺人事件が国民の関心を引きつけた）The murder case *has attracted* the interest of the nation.

あつみ 厚み（厚さ）thickness Ⓤ;（比喩的な意味で）depth Ⓤ ―厚みのある heavy, thick ⇒ あつさ（厚さ）/厚みのある生地 thick cloth / 彼の知識には厚みがない His knowledge is lacking in *depth*.

あつめる 集める

❶【物・人を】gather ⓗ;（ある目的をもって）collect ⓗ;（資金などを）raise ⓗ;（呼び寄せる）call together
情報を集める *collect* [*gather*] information / 証拠を集める *collect* [*gather*] evidence / 署名を集める *collect* petition signatures / 善意でお金を集める *raise* money for charity
少年は部屋のあちこちに散らばったおもちゃを集めた The boy *gathered* (*up*) the toys that were scattered around the room.
彼は外国の切手を集めている He *collects* foreign stamps.
1人500円ずつ集めたいと思います I'd like to *collect* 500 yen from each of you.
国会議員たちは次の選挙に向けて資金を集めている Diet members *are raising* funds for the next election.
体育館にみんなを集めてよ *Call* [*Get*] *together* all the members at the gym.
❷【関心などを】attract ⓗ
オゾン層の破壊がかなりの注目を集めている The depletion of the ozone layer *has attracted* considerable attention.
彼の発見は世界中の関心を集めている His discovery *has attracted* interest all over the world.
◆彼女はどこへ行ってもみんなの注目を集める Wherever she goes, she *draws* people's *attention*.

あつらえ 誂え ―あつらえの（服・靴などが）custom-made /ズボンは別あつらえにした（→別に仕立てる）ほうがよさそうですね It looks as though you should have your slacks *custom-made*.

あつらえむき 誂え向き このワンピースはパーテ

ィーにはおあつらえ向きだ(→適している) This dress is *just right* for a party. / ハイキングにはおあつらえ向きの(→理想的な)天気だ It's *ideal* weather for hiking. / 彼はその仕事におあつらえ向きの(→ぴったりの)人物だ He is (*just*) the *right* person for the job. / The job is *suitable* for him.

あつらえる 誂える order [他] ➩ちゅうもん
◆私はあの店で礼服をあつらえた I *placed an order for* a formal suit with that shop.

あつりょく 圧力 pressure [C] [U]
この物体が空気から受けている圧力を計算しなさい Calculate *the pressure* applied by air on this object.
急に実験が中止になるとは，政府から圧力がかかったのだろうか Was the experiment canceled suddenly because of *pressure* from the government?
我々はいかなる政治的圧力にも屈しない We will not give in to any *political pressure*.
‖圧力計 a pressure gauge / 圧力団体 a lobby, a pressure group / 圧力なべ a pressure cooker

あつれき 軋轢 (摩擦) friction [C] [U]; (不和) discord [C] [U]; (争い) conflict [C] [U] ‖貿易に対する様々な制限により，両国間にあつれきが生じている Various restrictions on trade have caused *friction* between the two countries.

あて 当て ❶【考え・見当】これからどこか行く当てがあるの？ Do you have *a destination* in mind? / 私は繁華街を当てもなくさまよっていた I just *wandered around* the entertainment district. / この時間なら彼は家にいるだろうと思ったのだが当てがはずれた I thought he would be home now, but I *was wrong*.
❷【頼りにすること】私は彼の協力を当てにしていた I *was counting on* his cooperation. / あまり当てにされても困る Don't *count on* me too much. / 彼女はあまり当てにならない You *can't rely on* her. / 私は天気予報を当てにしていない I never *rely on* weather forecasts. / 人の財布を当てにするのはよしてくれ Stop *depending on* me for money.
💬「困ったことがあったらいつでも電話してくれ」「ありがとう．当てにしてるよ」"If you have any problems, call me any time." "Thank you. I know I can *rely on* you."
❸【当て物】pad [C] ‖ひざ当て knee *pads*

-あて -宛 彼女あての手紙 a letter *for* [*addressed to*] her / 編集局あてに手紙を書く write *to* the editorial office / 私は息子あてに小包を送った I sent a package *to* my son. / 私あてにファックスが来ていますか Are there any faxes *for* me?

あてがう 宛がう 私にあてがわれた部屋は狭くて汚かった The room *assigned* to me was small and dirty. / 彼にはこの仕事をあてがっておこう Let's *give* this job to him.

あてこすり 当て擦り (不快なことを遠回しに言うこと) insinuation [U], 《口語的》dig [C]; (いやみ) sarcasm [U], sarcastic remark [C] ―当てこする insinuate [他], 《口語的》dig* at ..., have* [take*] a dig at ...; (ほのめかす) hint [他], imply [他] ‖彼に対して当てこすりを言う *have* [*take*] *a dig at* him ◆彼女の言葉は明らかに私への当てこすりだった What she said *was* obviously *meant* for me.

あてこむ 当て込む (当てにする) count on ...; (期待する) expect [他]; (希望を持つ) hope [他] [自] ‖私たちは彼の助けを当てこんでいた We *counted on* his help.
◆クリスマスの売り上げを当てこんでおもちゃをたくさん仕入れた We stocked many toys *in expectation of* sales at Christmas.

あてさき 宛先 address [C] ‖あて先不明で手紙が戻ってきた My letter was returned because it had *the* wrong *address*.

あてじ 当て字 (音だけで当てた字) phonetic equivalent [C]; (勝手に使う代用漢字) false substitute character [C]

あてずいりょう 当て推量 wild guess [C], guesswork [U], 《口語的》shot [C] ―当て推量をする guess [他] [自], make* a shot (at ...) ‖当て推量で *by guesswork*; *at a guess* / 当て推量で答えてはいけない Don't *guess at the answer*.

あてずっぽう 当てずっぽう (でたらめな推測) wild guess [C]; (やみくもに答えること) a shot in the dark ‖当てずっぽうに答えたら意外にも当たっていた I *made a wild guess*, and to my surprise it turned out to be right.

あてつけ 当て付け 《口語的》dig [C], snide remark [C]; (言動) 《公式的》insinuation [U] [C] ‖人に当てつけを言う make *insinuations* against a person; make *snide remarks* about a person / 私には当てつけがましく聞こえる It sounds *like a dig* at me.
◆その冗談は私への当てつけだった(→実は私に向けられていた) That joke *was actually directed* at me.

あてつける 当て付ける あの二人にはすっかり当てつけられてしまった(→仲のよさを見せつけた) The couple *showed off* just *how much they loved each other*.

あてどなく あてどなくさまよう wander *aimlessly*

あてな 宛名 address [C] ‖私は封筒にあて名を書いた I wrote *the address* on the envelope. ◆その手紙のあて名は父になっていた The letter *was addressed to* my father. / この手紙はあて名が間違っている This letter *is incorrectly addressed*. / 封筒のあて名ははっきり書いてください Please *address* the envelope *clearly*.

あてにげ 当て逃げ 当て逃げ事故の被害者 the victim of *a hit-and-run accident*

アテネ Athens [ǽθinz] (❖ギリシャの首都)

アデノイド 〖医学〗adenoids

あてはずれ 当て外れ (期待はずれ) disappointment [C] ‖あのチームの敗退はとんだ当てはずれだった The defeat of that team was quite *a disappointment* to me.
◆彼の小説は全くの当てはずれだった His novel *was* completely *disappointing*. / I *was*

completely *disappointed by* his novel.

あてはまる 当てはまる（適合する）apply ⾃；(該当する) be true of ... ／『この規則はすべての場合に当てはまるというものではない This rule doesn't *apply* to all situations. ／ アメリカ人は陽気だというが、それは彼には当てはまらない They say that Americans are cheerful, but that's *not true of* him.

あてはめる 当てはめる（適用する）apply ⾃ ／この問題にその法則を当てはめてみるとどうなるだろうか What happens if you try *applying* the rule to this problem?

あでやか 艶やか ──あでやかな（魅惑的な）fascinating, charming; (上品な・優雅な) elegant; (華麗な・華やかな) gorgeous ／あでやかに着飾った魅力的な女の子たち attractive girls in *gorgeous* dress ／ 彼女の着物姿はあでやかだった She looked *charming* [*fascinating*] in a kimono.

あてられる 当てられる 私は彼らの毒気にあてられたように感じた I felt I *was the target of* their spite. ／ 新婚夫婦の家に行くというのはあてられに行くようなものだ If you visit newlyweds, you're just asking to *be embarrassed*. (❖be embarrassed は「きまりの悪い」の意味)

あてる¹ 当てる

❶【ぶつける・命中させる】hit* ⾃, strike* ⾃ ドッジボールで僕は太郎にボールを当てた I threw the ball at Taro and *hit* him in dodge ball.

ここからあの的(蛍)に1発で当ててみせるよ I'll *hit* that target from here in one shot.

◆彼の球は速すぎて当てるのが精一杯だった His pitches were so fast that all I could do was try to *make contact*.

❷【推測する】guess ⾃ ⾃

私が何を考えているか当ててごらん Try to *guess* what I'm thinking.

彼女は私の年齢を言い当てた She *guessed* my age *right*. ／ (口語的) She *made a good shot at* my age.

◆10問中7問当てればなかなかのものだ Seven *right answers* out of ten isn't bad.

🔴「来週旅行に行くんだって？ どこに行くの」「どこか当ててみて」"I hear you're going on a trip next week. Where are you going?" "*Guess* where."

❸【じかに触れさせる】(さらす) expose ⾃

この植物はあまり日光に当てないほうがいい This plant shouldn't *be exposed* to too much sun.

◆洗濯物は風に当てて乾かすのがいちばんだ The best way to dry laundry is to *hang* it *out* in the wind.

❹【密着させる・あてがう】(置く) put* ⾃, place ⾃; (手に持って) hold* ⾃

母は私のおでこに手を当てて熱があるかどうかみた My mother *put her hand on* my forehead to see if I had a fever.

やけどをしたら患部にしばらく氷を当てておきなさい When you get burned, you should *hold* some ice *on* the affected area for a while.

◆自分が何をしたのか胸に手を当てて(→じっくり) 考えてみなさい Think *carefully* about what you have done. ／ 定規を当ててその机の高さを測ってみた I measured the exact height of the desk *with a ruler*. ／ 彼はジーパンのひざに継ぎを当ててもらった He had patches *put on* the knees of his jeans.

❺【賞を得る・利益を得る】

妹がくじでハワイ旅行を当てた My sister *won* a trip to Hawaii in the lottery.

彼はその商売でひと山当てた He *made a fortune* out of the business.

父は競馬で大穴を当てた My father *hit a long shot* at the horse races.

❻【指名する】(名前を言う) call on ...

宿題をやってこなかった日に限って先生に当てられる The teacher *calls on* me only on days when I haven't done my homework.

あてる² 充てる（取っておく）put* [set*] ... aside; (費やす・使う) spend* ⾃, use ⾃; (割り当てる) allocate ⾃, (公式的)allot ⾃; (仕事・部屋などを) assign ⾃; (時間などを) devote ⾃ ／そのお金を生活費にあてる *use* the money for *one's living expenses* ／ 夜を読書の時間にあてる *devote* evening hours to reading books ／ 私はボーナスをヨーロッパ旅行にあてるつもりだ I'm going to *put* the bonus *aside* for my trip to Europe. ／ 私は毎日1時間をバイオリンの練習にあてている I *spend* an hour practicing the violin every day. ／ 政府は2億円を洪水の被災者救済にあてた The government *allocated* 200 million yen for the relief of the victims of the flood.

あてる³ 宛てる（手紙などを）address ⾃ ／山田先生にあてた手紙 a letter *addressed to* Mr. Yamada

アデレード Adelaide (❖オーストラリアの都市)

あと¹ 後

❶【時間の推移】(…の後で) after; (…して、それから) and (then)

私は彼が帰った後, 友達に電話をかけた *After* he went home, I called a friend of mine.

そのけんかの後はしばらく彼と話をしなかった *After* that quarrel, I didn't talk to him for a while.

運動の後の水は最高だ Nothing beats water *after* exercise.

私は東京で1泊した後, ニューヨークへ飛んだ I stayed overnight at [in] Tokyo *and then* flew to New York.

❷【以後・将来】later

その仕事は後に回してもいいですか Can I put that work off until *later*?

後になって後悔しても知らないよ It's not my fault if you regret it *later*.

じゃ、また後で See you *later*.

ごはんは後にする、とにかく今はふろに入りたいんだ I'll eat *later*. Right now I want to

take a bath.
◆満員です。この後の(→次の)バスをご利用ください This bus is full. Please take *the next* one.
❸【追加】(追加の) another; (さらに) more
あと1日たてば夏休みだ One *more* day and it's summer vacation.
月末までにあと5冊本を読まなければならない I have to read「five *more* books [*another* five books]」by the end of the month.
◆ロンドンとパリと, あとベルリンにも行ってみたい I want to visit London, Paris, *and* Berlin *as well*.
❹【後ろ】(最後) end ◯; (背中) back ◯
私は切符を買うのに列の後についた I stood at *the end* of the line for buying tickets.
その小説は後の方になるにつれてさらに退屈になってきた The novel got more boring toward *the end*.
◆その店員は万引きの後を追いかけた The shop clerk *ran after* the shoplifter. / 彼は高校卒業と同時に故郷を後にした(→去った) He *left* his hometown as soon as he graduated from high school. / 私たちは案内人の後について城の中に入っていった We *followed* the guide into the castle.
❺【残り】 the rest
きょうはこれで帰ろうと思うんだけど, 後をお願いしてもいいかい I'm going home now. Can I ask you to handle *the rest*?
後は想像におまかせします I'll leave *the rest* to your imagination.
◆両親をいっぺんになくして後に残された子供たちが不憫(ふびん)だ I really feel sorry for those children who lost both their parents at one time.
慣用表現 2度目の失敗をして, 彼にはもう後がなかった After failing twice, 「he *was washed up* [*there was nothing more* he could do]」. / 料理が後から後から出てきて食べきれなかった Food *kept coming and coming* until I couldn't eat anymore. / もう後には引けない(→引き返せない) *There's no turning back* now. / そうまで言われては後に引けない(→やるしかない) If that's how it is, then we *have to do it*. / 後は野となれ山となれ *If we get through this, then the rest won't matter.* / あのときの恋人とのけんかがまだ後を引いている That quarrel with my boyfriend still *affects* our relationship. / ピーナッツは後を引くね It's hard to stop eating peanuts.

あと² 跡 mark ◯; (押しつけてできた) print ◯; (痕跡(こんせき)) trace ◯ ◯; (傷跡) scar ◯; (跡) site ◯
たんすを引っぱったら床に跡がついてしまった When I pulled out the dresser, it left *marks* on the floor.
彼のわき腹には手術の跡が残っていた He had *a scar* from surgery on his side.
私たちは取りこわされた工場の跡を訪れた We visited *the site* of a factory that had been torn down.

◆彼女の英語には進歩の跡が見られる Her English shows *signs* of improvement. / 何者かが私たちの跡をつけているようだった Someone seemed to *be tailing* us. / 彼は亡父の跡を継いで畑仕事に精を出している *Following in* his late father's *footsteps*, he now works hard on the farm.
慣用表現 その歌手が死んだとき, 何人かの若者が跡を追うように自殺をはかった When the singer died, several young people tried to kill themselves *in sympathy*. / このパソコンは人気があるので, 客の注文が跡を絶たないらしい This computer has been very popular. *There* seems to *have been no letup* in orders from customers. / 密入国者が跡を絶たない *There is no end* to illegal immigrants.

あとあし 後足 hind leg ◯ (↔fore leg) /馬は後足で立ち上がった The horse stood on *its hind legs*. / 犬は後足で立って歩いた The dog walked on *its hind legs*.
慣用表現 後足で砂をかける(→去り際に迷惑をかける) *do something spiteful on leaving*

あとあじ 後味 aftertaste ◯ /このワインは後味がさわやかだ This wine has *a refreshing aftertaste*.
◆先日けんかをしたときの後味の悪さが急に思い出された I suddenly remembered *the bad feeling after* the quarrel the other day.

あとあと 後々 (将来) the future /後々面倒が起こらないよう気をつけたほうがいいよ You should be careful not to get into trouble *in the future*. / 彼は後々のことを考えて(→将来のために)貯金している He is saving up for *the future*.

あとおし 後押し push ◯; (支持・支援) support ◯, backing ◯; (後援者) supporter ◯, backer ◯ ──後押しする push ◯; (支持する) support ◉, back up /荷車を後押しする *push* a cart *from behind* / 彼女は彼の事業を後押しした She *supported* his business. / 有力者の後押しがなかったら(→有力な後援者がいなかったら), 彼は選挙に当選しなかっただろう Without influential *backers*, he would not have won the election.

あとがき 後書き (本文に対する) postscript ◯ ◯《略語》P.S.; (著者以外の) afterword ◯

あとかた 跡形 trace ◯ ◯; (公式的) vestige ◯ /跡形もなく without (*a*) *trace* ◆地震の後, 私の家は跡形もなかった Nothing remained of my house after the earthquake. / その部屋に展示されていたピカソの絵は跡形もなく消えていた The painting by Picasso which had been exhibited in the room *disappeared into thin air*.

あとかたづけ 後片付け ──後片づけをする (掃除する) clean up; (整頓(せいとん)する) put* ... in order, straighten up; (食器などの後片づけをする) clear ◉; (食器を洗う) wash [do*] the dishes /パーティーの後で会場の後片づけをする *put* the hall back *in order* after the party / 私は夕食の後片づけをした I *cleared the table* after dinner.

あとがま 後釜（後任）successor ⓒ ◆彼が後藤さんの後がまに座った He *succeeded* Mr. Goto.

あとくされ 後腐れ 後腐れのないようにする leave no seeds of *future trouble* / 私たちは後腐れのないように割り勘にした We had separate checks to avoid *trouble in the future*.

あどけない（無邪気な）innocent; (子供らしい) childlike / あどけない表情 an *innocent* look / 彼女にはまだあどけないところがあった There was still something *childlike* about her.

あとさき 後先 彼は後先（→結果を）考えずに家を飛び出した He ran out of the house *without thinking about the consequences*. / 話が後先になりましたが（→これを先に言うべきだったが）… *I should have said this first*, but …

あとしまつ 後始末 ❶【解決・清算する】settlement Ⓤ ⓒ ──後始末をする settle ⑯, wind* [wáind] up, deal* with … / けんかの後始末をつける *settle* a quarrel / 私はその問題の後始末を頼まれた I was asked to *settle* the matter.

❷【整頓(とん)する】──後始末をする put* … in order, clean up ⇒ あとかたづけ / 遊んだら後始末をしなさい *Put* your room back *in order* after playing.

あとずさり 後退り ──後ずさりする (退く) draw* back; (一歩後退する) step back; (後方へ移動する) move back; (しりごみする) back away, 《文語》shrink* ⑯ / 彼女は驚いて後ずさりした She *drew back* in surprise. / その女の子は後ずさりして犬から離れた The girl *backed away* from the dog.

あとぜめ 後攻め うちのチームが後攻めだ（→先に守る）Our team *fields first*.

あとち 跡地 取りこわされたビルの跡地 *the site* of a demolished building

あとぢえ 後知恵 hindsight Ⓤ / 後知恵ながら、違ったやり方をするべきだった *Hindsight* now tells me that I should have done it differently.

ことわざ げすの後知恵 ⇒ げす

あとつぎ 跡継ぎ 社長の跡継ぎ *the successor* to the president ⇒ あととり

あととり 跡取り heir [éər] ⓒ, heiress [érəs] ⓒ; inheritor ⓒ; successor ⓒ

| heir, heiress: 特に血縁関係・遺言により法律的に決まる相続人を指す。
| inheritor: 財産・肩書きなどを受け継ぐ人を指す。血縁の有無は特に問わない。
| successor: ある人の地位・仕事などを後継者として引き継ぐ人を指す。

彼は大きな病院の跡取り息子だ He is *the son and heir to* a big hospital.

あとのまつり 後の祭り いまさら悔やんでも後の祭りだ（→遅すぎる）It's *too late* to worry [fret] about it now.

アドバイザー（助言者）adviser, advisor ⓒ

アドバイス（忠告・助言）advice [ədváis] Ⓤ ──アドバイスする advise [ədváiz] ⑯ ⑯

あとばらい 後払い（延期された支払い）deferred payment Ⓤ; (着払い) cash [collect] on delivery, C.O.D. / カーペットの代金は後払いで結構です You can have the carpet sent to you C.O.D. [*cash on delivery*].

アドバルーン a large balloon with an advertising streamer, advertising balloon ⓒ

アトピー atopy Ⓤ (❖ 英語の atopy は日本語の「アトピー」ほど一般的ではない)
◆アトピー性皮膚炎 *atopic* dermatitis

あとまわし 後回し 難しい問題を後回しにする *leave* the difficult problems *until later* / その件は後回しにしよう（→後で取り上げよう）Let's *take up* the matter *later*.

あとめ 跡目 (家督・財産) the headship of a family, the family property; (後継者) successor ⓒ ◆兄が父の跡目を継いだ My brother *succeeded* my father.
‖跡目相続 succession to (the headship of) a house

あともどり 後戻り ──後戻りする (戻る) go* back; (引き返す) turn back / 新しいやり方に行き詰まって結局昔の状態に後戻りした We got stuck trying the new method, so we ended up *going back to* the old system. / 結婚式の日取りが決まっていよいよ後戻りできなくなったと感じた When we set the date for our wedding, I felt that now there was no *turning back*.

アトラクション（余興）entertainment ⓒ; (呼び物) attraction ⓒ; (呼び物に添える出し物) sideshow ⓒ; (実演) stage show ⓒ

アトランダム ──アトランダムに at random / 当選番号をアトランダムに選ぶ select the winning numbers *at random*

アトリエ（画家・写真家などの仕事場）atelier [ætəljéi] ⓒ (❖ フランス語から), studio [stjúːdiòu] ⓒ (複 〜s)

アドリブ（即興のせりふ・演奏など）ad lib ──アドリブの[で] ad-lib / アドリブで演技をする perform *ad-lib* / 彼はアドリブで話した He spoke *ad-lib*.

アドレス（住所）address ⓒ;【コンピュータ】address ⓒ;【ゴルフ】address Ⓤ ‖アドレス帳 an address book / メールアドレス an e-mail address

アドレナリン adrenaline Ⓤ

あな 穴

❶【開口部】hole ⓒ, opening ⓒ (❖ どちらも底のあるなしにかかわらず用いることができる)

母はよく庭に穴を掘って生ごみを埋めていた My mother used to *dig holes* in the yard to bury garbage.

子供のころはよくふすまに穴をあけて怒られたものだ When I was a child, I often used to get scolded for *making holes* in the sliding doors.

はき古したズボンにとうとう穴があいた My old, worn-out pants finally *got a hole* in them.

左官屋さんに壁の穴をふさいでもらった I had a plasterer *fill the hole* in the wall.

ひもを通すためにプラスチック板にきりで穴をあけた I *made a hole* in the plastic sheet with an awl so that I could pass a string through it.

◆針の穴 *the eye of a needle* / 鼻の穴 *a nostril* / その道路は穴ぼこだらけだった The road was full of *potholes*.

❷【欠員・不足】

私は彼女があけた穴(→失敗)をどうやって埋めようかと考えた I tried to find a way to make up for her *mistake*.

私の手違いで経理に大きな穴をあけてしまった My mistake led to *a* big accounting *loss*.

その女優は30年間，一度も舞台に穴をあけたことがない The actress *has never missed* a stage performance for 30 years.

彼の議論には穴が多い There are a lot of *holes* in his arguments.

ゴールキーパーがこのチームの穴だ(→うまいゴールキーパーがいない) This team *has no good* goalkeepers.

❸【番狂わせの勝負】

彼は競馬ではいつも穴をねらう He always goes for *the long shot* on horse races.

兄はそのレースで大穴を当てた My brother *made a killing* at the race.

[慣用表現] みんなに秘密を知られてしまって，穴があったら入りたい Everyone found out my secret. *I wish I had a hole to crawl into.* / そんなに穴のあくほど私を見ないでちょうだい Stop *staring* at me like that.

アナーキスト (無政府主義者) anarchist [C]

あなうめ 穴埋め (当座の間に合わせ) stopgap [C] **──穴埋めする** (空所を埋める) fill in; (損失を補う) make* up for ..., make good ‖損失の穴埋めをする *make up for* the loss / 忘れてごめん，今度穴埋めするよ I'm sorry I forgot. I'*ll make up for* it next time. ‖穴埋め記事 a filler / 穴埋め問題 a fill-in-the-blanks question

アナウンサー announcer [C], newscaster [C], 《英》newsreader [C], broadcaster [C]

アナウンス announcement [C][U] **──アナウンスする** announce [他] ‖列車到着のアナウンス *a* train arrival *announcement* / 事故のため電車が遅れているというアナウンスがあった It *was announced* (that) the trains were delayed due to an accident.

あながち 宇宙旅行もあながち夢ではない(→完全に夢というわけではない) Space travel is not *altogether* a dream. / 弱いチームだからといってあながち負けるとはいえない(→必ずしも負けるとは限らない) The weaker team does not *necessarily* lose.

あなぐま 穴熊 〔動物〕 badger [C]

あなご 穴子 〔魚〕 conger (eel) [C]

あなた 貴方 (あなたは・あなたが) you; (あなたの) your; (あなたに・あなたを) you; (あなたのもの) yours; (あなた自身) yourself

[語法]
(1) 日本語の「あなた」はふつう目上の人に対しては使わないが，英語の you は年上・年下，地位の上下，男女に関係なく使うことができる．つまり日本語の「あなた」「君」「おまえ」など二人称の語は英語ではすべて you になる．
(2) 夫婦間，恋人間での呼びかけには，(my) dear, darling, honey などを使うが，名前で呼び合うことも多い．

あなづり 穴釣り 父は湖で穴釣りをしていた My father *was fishing in the ice* on the lake.

あなどる 侮る (見下す) look down on ...; (軽蔑(けいべつ)する) despise [他]; (軽視する) make* light of ...; (過小評価する) underestimate [他] ‖小学生だからといって彼女を侮ってはいけない You shouldn't *make light of* her because she is an elementary school pupil. / クラスメートの多くは彼の実力を侮っているようだ Most of the classmates seem to *underestimate* his abilities. ◆侮りがたい(→手強い)ライバル a *formidable* rival

あなば 穴場 釣りの穴場 *a good out-of-the-way* fishing *spot* / 友達においしいレストランの穴場を教えてもらった My friend told me about *a good little-known restaurant*.

アナリスト analyst [C] ‖証券アナリスト *a* security *analyst*

アナログ analog, analogue [C] (↔digital) **──アナログ(式)の** analog, analogue ‖アナログ時計 an analog watch [clock]

あに 兄 brother [C]

[語法]
特別の場合を除き，英語では「兄／弟」「姉／妹」を区別せず，単に brother, sister という．区別するときは，「兄」は an older [《英》elder] brother または a big brother,「弟」は a younger brother または a little [kid] brother とする．「姉」は an older [《英》elder] sister または a big sister,「妹」は a younger sister または a little [kid] sister とする．「兄さん」「姉さん」という呼びかけには本人の名前を用いる．

私のいちばん上の兄 my *oldest* [*eldest*] *brother* / 実の兄 *one's real brother* / 義理の兄 *one's brother-in-law*

アニマル animal [C]

アニメ ⚠(アニメーション) (animated) cartoon [C] (❖animated cartoon が正式な言い方); (動画製作) animation [U] **──アニメの** animated ➩ [場面・状況別会話] p.1706 ‖アニメを制作する produce *animated cartoons* ‖アニメ映画 an animated film / アニメキャラクター a cartoon character / アニメ作家 an animator

あによめ 兄嫁 *one's* older brother's wife; (義理の姉) *one's* sister-in-law (複 sisters-in-law, ～s)

あね 姉 sister [C]; older [elder, big] sister [C] (❖older [elder, big] は，特に年が上であることを明示する場合以外省略される) ➩ あに ‖私のいちばん上の姉 my *oldest* [*eldest*] *sister* / 実の姉 *one's real sister* / 義理の姉 *one's sister-in-law*

あねったい 亜熱帯 the subtropical zone [region], the subtropics **──亜熱帯の** subtropical, semitropical

あねむこ 姉婿 *one's* older sister's hus-

アネモネ 【植物】anemone [ənémənìː]

あの (そばにいない人・手元にないものを指して) that; (お互いに了解しているものを指して) the

語法
(1) 特に質問をする場合や相手の注意を促す場合など、初めて話題にのぼってお互いが了解していないものには、ふつう that (複数のときは those)を用いる // (離れた所にある家を指して) あの家を見てごらん Look at *that* house. / (遠くにいる人を指して) あの男の人たちはだれ？ Who are *those* men?
(2) 何度か話題にのぼっていてお互いに了解しているものには、ふつう the を用いる. 代名詞で表せる場合は代名詞を使う // 先頃あげたあの本、ちょっと貸してくれないかな May I borrow *the* book I gave you last week? / 「きのう順子から電話があったよ」「あれ、あの人 (→彼女は) 今どこにいるんだっけ」"I had a phone call from Junko yesterday." "Oh, where is *she* now?"
(3) 話題には直接のぼっていないがお互いが了解しているものには、that (複数のときは those) を用いても the を用いてもよいが、that のほうが「あの」という指示の意味が強くなる. しばしば嫌悪や驚きの感情にうったえる表現となる // またあの言い訳をしようっていうんじゃないだろうね You aren't going to give me *that* same old excuse, are you? / またあの広司が遅刻だ *That* Hiroshi is late again.

あの(う) (呼びかけ) excuse me, hello, hey, hi, 《米口語的に》say; (言葉に詰まったとき) er, 《米》uh, 《口語的に》you know; (相手の言葉を受けて) well /あの、ちょっとお聞きしたいんですが *Excuse me*, may I ask you a question? / あのう、お願いがあるんだけど *Hey*, can I ask you a favor?
💬「あなたたち2人は本当に仲がいいですね」「あの、実は、僕たち兄弟なんです」"You two are really good friends." "*Well*, actually, we are brothers."

あのてこのて あの手この手 そのセールスマンはあの手この手で新製品を売ろうとした That salesperson tried *every possible means* to sell the new product.

あのとき あの時 then, (at) that time /あのときはすごく緊張していたのでうまく話せなかった I couldn't speak well because I was very nervous *then*. / あのとき見た映画が忘れられない I can't forget the movie I saw *(at) that time*.

あのね (呼びかけ) hey, hi, 《米口語的》say, 《英口語的》I say; (注意を促して) listen, look (here) /あのね、お母さん、見せたいものがあるんだけど *Hey*, Mom, I want to show you something. / あのね、あしたは私の誕生日なの *Listen*, tomorrow is my birthday.

あのへん あの辺 (あのあたり) around there; (あの近くに) near there
💬「僕の眼鏡見なかった？」「あのへんにあったと思うよ」"Did you see my glasses?" "They were *around there*, I guess."

あのよ あの世 (この世に対して) the next world [life] /祖母はあの世へ行ってしまった My grandmother *went to the next world* [*went to Heaven, passed away*]. (💡 die の婉曲的な言い方. ほかに go to *one's* final rest, leave this world などともいう)

あのよう あの様 あのようにはとてもできない I can't possibly do it *like that*. / あのようなきれいな服を着てみたい I want to wear a beautiful dress *like that*.

アノラック (フード付きの防水・防寒着) 《米》parka □, 《英》anorak □

アパート ⚠ (1世帯分の部屋) 《米》apartment □, 《英》flat □; (建物全体) apartment house [building] □, 《英》a block of flats

英作文ノート 和製英語に注意！
彼女はこのあたりのアパートに住んでいる
→ ×She lives in an *apart* near here.
→ ○She lives in an *apartment* near here.
★ カタカナ語を英訳するときは注意しなければならない.

家具付きアパートを借りる rent *a furnished apartment* [*flat*] / 新婚夫婦にアパートを賃貸しする lease *an apartment* to newlyweds / アパートの上階の部屋 *an* upstairs *apartment* / 5階建てのアパート *a* five-story *apartment house* [*building*] / この近くでよいアパートを探している He is looking for *a good apartment* near here. / アパートの部屋代についてはすぐ話がついた We soon agreed on a rent for *the apartment*. / 私は2部屋あるアパートに住んでいます I live in *a two-room apartment*. / 私たちは同じ階のアパートに住んでいる We live on the same floor of *the apartment house*.

アバウト ⚠ アバウトな (→大ざっぱな) 計画を立てる make a *rough* plan

あばく 暴く (悪事などを) expose 📖; (陰謀などを) uncover 📖; (秘密・情報などを) disclose 📖, reveal 📖; (明るみに出す) bring* ... to light; (正体を) unmask 📖; (墓などを) violate 📖, open 📖 /陰謀 [スキャンダル] をあばく *expose* a plot [scandal] / あばかれた陰謀 an *uncovered* plot / その報告書は彼が犯罪者だったことをあばいている The report *discloses* that he was a criminal. / 太郎は友人に秘密をあばかれた Taro's secret *was revealed* by his friend.

あばた 痘痕 pockmark □, pit □ ◆あばた面(ゔ) a *pockmarked* [*pocked, pitted*] face
ことわざ あばたもえくぼ Love is blind. (→恋は盲目)

あばらぼね 肋骨 rib □ (💡1本はa rib, 全体はthe ribs) /彼はその事故であばら骨を3本折った He broke three *ribs* in the accident.

あばらや 荒家・荒屋 (掘っ立て小屋) hut □, shack □, hovel □; (荒れ果てた) tumble-down [dilapidated] house □; (自分の家を謙遜(な)して) *one's* humble abode [cottage]

アパルトヘイト apartheid [əpάːrteit] □ (💡ア

フリカーンス語で「隔離」の意味. 南アフリカ共和国がかつてとっていた有色人種差別政策)

あばれもの 暴れ者 ⇒あばれんぼう

あばれる 暴れる (乱暴にふるまう) act violently [rough, wild]; (もがく) struggle ⾃ /馬が突然暴れ始めた The horse suddenly *started acting rough.* / その小さな男の子は母親から逃げ出そうと暴れた The little boy *struggled* to get away from his mother.
◆酔っ払いが駅のホームで暴れていた A drunk *was being unruly* on the station platform. / 暴れたい(→大騒ぎしたい)なら外に行きなさい If you want to *run around,* go outside. / 君には新天地で大いに暴れてきて(→活躍して)もらいたい I hope you *will do your best* in your new location.

アパレル (商品用の衣料) apparel [əpǽrəl] ⓤ / アパレル産業 *apparel* industry

あばれんぼう 暴れん坊 rough [wild] fellow ⓒ; (口語的) rowdy ⓒ, (米口語的) roughneck ⓒ

アピール (呼びかけ) appeal ⓤⓒ; (権力・権威者への請願) petition ⓒ ━━アピールする appeal ⾃ⓒ; petition ⾃他 / 審判にアピールする *appeal* [*make an appeal*] to the referee / 平和へのアピール *an appeal* for peace / セックスアピール sex *appeal* / この小説は若者に全然アピールしない This novel *does not appeal* to young people at all.

あびせる 浴びせる 彼女は怒りのあまり彼の顔に水を浴びせかけた She was so angry (that) she *splashed* water in his face. / 民衆はうそをついた大統領に非難を浴びせた The people *showered* their lying president *with* criticism. / 彼は彼女に矢つぎばやに質問を浴びせた He *peppered* her *with* questions.

あひる 家鴨 (総称・雌) duck ⓒ; (雄) drake ⓒ;(子) duckling ⓒ / アヒルががあがあ鳴いている *Ducks* are quacking.

あびる 浴びる
❶【水や光を全身に受ける】(水を) bathe ⾃; (さらされる) be exposed
川では象の群れが水を浴びていた A herd of elephants *was bathing* in the river.
私の祖父は広島で放射能を浴びていた My grandfather *was exposed to* radiation in Hiroshima.
◆きょうは汗をかいたからごはんの前にひとふろ浴びるよ I got sweaty today, so I'll *take a quick bath* before dinner. / そのヒマワリは日の光を浴びてどんどん成長した The sunflower grew quickly *in the sunlight.*
❷【比喩的な意味で】
彼の演奏は満場のかっさいを浴びた His performance *received applause* from the full house.
政府の政策は痛烈な批判を浴びた The government's policy *was sharply criticized.*
彼女の小説は直木賞を取っていちやく脚光を浴びた(→有名になった) Her novel suddenly *became famous* after it won the Naoki prize.
父はかつて浴びるように酒を飲んだと言った My father said that he used to drink *like a fish.*

あぶ 虻 gadfly ⓒ; (大型の) horsefly ⓒ ⇒あぶはちとらず

あぶく 泡 bubble ⓒ (しばしば複数形 ~s); (bubbleの集まり) foam ⓤ, froth ⓤ /あぶくをたてる blow *bubbles*

あぶくぜに あぶく銭 (楽に稼いだ金) easy [unearned] money ⓤ; (不正利得) ill-gotten gains; (ぼろもうけした金) fast [quick] buck ⓒ

アフターケア (退院後・出獄後などの指導) aftercare ⓤ, follow-up care ⓤ; (保証期間中のサービス) (repair) service ⓤⓒ /❖英語のaftercareには,「品物販売後の修理や手入れなどのサービス」という意味はない) /この病院はアフターケアが充実している This hospital gives good *aftercare.*

アフターサービス ⚠ (販売後のサービス) after-sales service ⓤ; ❖×after-service とはいわない; (自動車・機械などの修理・点検) service ⓤⓒ; (修理サービス) repair service ⓤ; (顧客サービス) customer service ⓤ

あぶない 危ない

❶【安全が保証されない】dangerous; perilous; risky; hazardous
dangerous: 危険を引き起こす可能性があるもの全般に使える.
perilous: 命にかかわるような差し迫った大きな危険を表すややかたい語.
risky: 行為・状況が場合によって危険なものになるという意味で用いる.
hazardous: 健康などに対して害を及ぼす危険をはらんでいることを表す.

傘をさして自転車に乗るのはとても危ない It's very *dangerous* to ride a bicycle holding an umbrella.
素人が株に手を出すなんて危ないからやめなさい Don't get involved in buying stock, because it's too *risky* for lay people.
◆危ない! *Watch out!* / *Look out!* / 彼の運転は危ない He drives *dangerously.* / 彼は一度危ない目にあってみたらいいんだ He should find out sometime what real *danger* is like. / あの会社は危ないともっぱらのうわさだ It's widely rumored that the company *is in danger of failing.* / その患者は危ない状態を脱した The patient is out of *danger.* / 危なかった！もうちょっとで彼に気づかれるところだった *It was close!* He almost found it out.

❷【悪いことが起こりそうで信用できない】
正確な値段は知らないが１万円だと危ないかもしれない(→足りないかもしれない) I don't know the exact price, but 10,000 yen might *not be enough.*
台所をのぞくと息子が危ない手つきで料理していた I peeked into the kitchen and saw my son cooking *awkwardly.*
主力選手のけがで優勝が危なくなってきた Due to the main player's injury, the team *might not* win the championship.
彼が時間に間に合うかどうか危ないものだ(→疑問

あぶなく

に思う) I *doubt* he will make it on time.
❸【常軌を逸した】
彼の目つきって何だか危ないよね He looks *like a weirdo*, doesn't he?
慣用表現 彼らは危ない橋を渡ってやくざと裏で取引をした They *crossed over the line* and did business secretly with the yakuza.

あぶなく 危なく (もう少しで) almost, nearly ➡あやうく *║私は危なく偽物をつかまされるところだった* I was *almost* fooled into buying a fake.

あぶなげ 危なげ 彼のすることには危なげがない Everything he does *is safe*. *║*横綱は危なげない相撲で小結を押し出した The *yokozuna easily* pushed the *komusubi* out of the ring.

あぶなっかしい 危なっかしい (危険な) dangerous; (不安定な) precarious, unsteady; (不器用な) awkward, clumsy; (安全でない) unsafe *║*危なっかしい足取りで歩く walk with *unsteady* steps
◆彼女は危なっかしい手つきではさみで紙を切っている She is *awkwardly* cutting the paper with scissors. *║* 彼の運転は危なっかしい He's an *unskillful* [a *bad*] driver.

アブノーマル ──アブノーマルな abnormal (↔normal) *║*アブノーマルな性格 an *abnormal* character

あぶはちとらず 虻蜂取らず 一度に2つの外国語を勉強するなんて, あぶはち取らずになってしまうよ If you study two foreign languages at a time, you'll *never master either of them*.

あぶら¹ 油

(総称) oil Ⓤ; (動植物油) fat Ⓤ; (どろりとした油) grease Ⓤ (✦いずれも種類を表すときは Ⓒ)
チャーハンは油を入れすぎるとおいしくできない Fried rice won't taste good if you use too much *oil*.
彼はてんぷらを揚げる前に油の温度をチェックした He checked the *oil* temperature before frying the tempura.
フライパンに油をひいて目玉焼きを作った I *put some oil* in the frying pan and fried some eggs.
タンカーが座礁して海に油が流れ出した The tanker ran aground and spilled *oil* into the ocean.
洗い物をする前に油汚れを紙でぬぐった I wiped *the grease* off the dishes with paper before washing them.
換気扇の掃除をしているうちに油まみれになってしまった I *got all covered with grease* while cleaning the ventilating fan.
◆兄は家中の扉に油を差して回った My (older) brother went around *oiling* all the doors in the house.
*║*オリーブ油 olive oil *║* ごま油 sesame oil *║* サラダ油 salad oil *║* パーム油 palm oil *║* ベニバナ油 safflower oil
慣用表現 彼らは喫茶店で油を売っていた They *shot the breeze* in a coffee shop. *║* 授業をサボったのがばれて先生にさんざん油をしぼられた The teacher really *chewed me out* when she found out that I had cut class. *║* 彼女にそんなことを言ったら火に油を注ぐようなものだ If you say that to her, it's like *pouring gasoline on a fire*. *║* あの兄弟は水と油だ Those brothers *are like oil and water*.

あぶら² 脂 (油脂) fat Ⓤ Ⓒ; (脂状のもの) grease Ⓤ ◆彼は脂っこい食べ物が好きだ He likes *greasy* food. *║* 彼女はダイエット中だって脂身の多い肉を食べなかった She said she was on a diet, so she didn't eat any *fatty* meat. *║* 私は脂性だ I have *oily skin*.
慣用表現 彼は作家として今がいちばん脂の乗っている時期だ He's *in top form* as a writer now.

あぶらあげ 油揚げ 🍱 *abura-age*, (deep-)fried bean curd *║*油揚げ1枚 a piece of *fried bean curd*
慣用表現 とびに油揚げをさらわれる ➡ とび

あぶらあせ 脂汗 greasy [oily] sweat Ⓤ Ⓒ *║*脂汗をかく break out with *a greasy* [*an oily*] *sweat*

あぶらえ 油絵 oil painting Ⓤ Ⓒ, oil Ⓒ, a painting in oils ◆油絵を描く *paint in oils* *║*油絵画家 an oil painter *║* 油絵の具 oil paints, oil colors, oils

あぶらぎる 脂ぎる become* greasy ──脂ぎった greasy *║*脂ぎった顔 a *greasy* face

あぶらむし 油虫 (アリマキ) plant louse Ⓒ, aphid Ⓒ; (ゴキブリ) cockroach Ⓒ

アフリカ Africa (略語)Afr.) ──アフリカの African *║*アフリカ系アメリカ人 an *African American*
*║*アフリカ大陸 the African Continent

アプリケーションソフト【コンピュータ】application Ⓒ, application(s) software Ⓤ, application(s) program Ⓒ

あぶる 炙る (肉・魚などを) roast ⊕Ⓒ,《米》broil ⊕Ⓒ,《英》grill ⊕Ⓒ; (かりかりにする) crisp ⊕Ⓒ; (暖める) warm ⊕Ⓒ *║*肉を火であぶる *roast* meat over a fire *║* のりを弱火であぶる *crisp* dried seaweed over a slow fire

あふれる 溢れる

❶【入りきらずにこぼれる】(液体・人などが) overflow ⊜Ⓒ; (液体が) run* over; (こぼれる) spill* ⊜Ⓒ; (川などが氾濫(はんらん)する) flood ⊜Ⓒ
その店は客が中に入りきらずに道路にまであふれていた The store's customers couldn't all get in, so they *overflowed* [*spilled out*] into the road.
蛇口を閉めるのを忘れていたせいでふろの水が床にあふれていた I forgot to turn off the faucet, so the bath water *ran over* onto the floor.
コーラを勢いよく注いだらコップから泡があふれた I poured the cola quickly, and the foam *overflowed* from the glass.
大雨で川があふれた The river *was flooded* by the heavy rain.

❷【満ちている】be filled with ..., be full of ...
彼女はあふれんばかりの涙をたたえて彼に窮状を

訴えた Her eyes *were filled with* tears as she appealed to him in despair.
行楽地はどこも親子連れであふれていた All the resorts *were full of* parents with children.
その町は活気にあふれていた The town *was full of* activity.

あぶれる 不況のせいで仕事にあぶれる若者が増えてきている(→不況が仕事のない若者を増やしてきている) The recession has left more and more young people *unemployed.*

アフロアメリカン African-American [C], Afro-American [C] ━アフロアメリカンの African-American, Afro-American

アプローチ (接近すること) approach [C]; (ゴルフ) approach shot [C] ━アプローチする approach [他] ∥別の観点からその問題にアプローチする *approach* the problem from a different angle

あべこべ 順序があべこべだ The order is *backward.* / 彼は駅とはあべこべの方向に歩いていった / He walked the *opposite* direction from the station. / 彼が言うのとはあべこべに彼女は実に気さくな人だった *Unlike* what he said, she was actually easy to get along with.

アベック ⚠couple [C] (❖「恋人の二人連れ」を強調するなら a couple on a date. 日本語はフランス語の avec から) ∥遊園地は若いアベックでいっぱいだった The amusement park was crowded with many young *couples.*

アペリティフ (食前酒) apéritif [C] (❖フランス語から)

アベレージ (平均) average [C] ∥バッティングアベレージ *a* batting *average*

あへん 阿片 opium [U] ∥アヘン中毒 *opium* addiction / アヘン戦争 the *Opium* War

アポイント(メント) (面会の約束) appointment [C] ∥アポイントを取ってある have *an appointment* / 佐藤さんとアポイントを取りたいのですが I'd like to make *an appointment* with Mr. Sato.

あほう 阿呆 fool [C], silly person [C]

あほうどり albatross [C] (複 ~, ~es)

アボカド avocado [C] (複 ~s, ~es)

アポストロフィ apostrophe [C] ➾ [巻末付録] (句読法)

あま¹ 尼 (一般の) nun [C]; (ローマカトリックの) sister [C] (❖呼びかけにも用いる); (キリスト教以外の) priestess [C]; (仏教の) Buddhist nun [C] ∥尼になる become *a nun*; enter a convent
∥尼寺 a convent

あま² 海女 🖼 an *ama*, a woman who works diving for shellfish, seaweed or pearls

あまあし 雨脚・雨足 雨脚が激しくなってきた It has started to *rain* harder.

あまい 甘い

❶【味・においが】sweet
このジュースは甘い This juice *is sweet.*
彼女は甘い物が好きだ She *likes sweet things.* / She *has a sweet tooth.*
この桃は甘い香りがする This peach *smells sweet.*
◆その飲み薬は子供向けに甘くしてある That medicine *is sweetened* for children. / この漬物, ちょっと甘かったかしら(→少し塩味が足りないようだ) Maybe these pickles *need a little more salt.*
❷【心地よい】sweet; honeyed (❖特に人をだます意図があるときに用いる)
私はその歌手の甘い歌声に聞きほれた I was enchanted by the singer's *sweet* voice.
彼女は彼の甘い言葉にだまされた She was deceived by his *honeyed* words.
◆彼は甘いマスクで若い女性の間で人気がある He's popular among young women because of *his good looks.*
❸【楽観的な】optimistic
君の見通しは甘いんじゃないかと思うよ I'm afraid your forecast *is* too *optimistic.*
◆彼は判断が甘かった He *was slack* in judgment. / 彼らを甘く見ないほうがいい(→過小評価しないほうがいい) You *shouldn't underestimate* them.
❹【厳しくない】generous, indulgent
彼女の評価は思ったより甘かった Her evaluation *was* more *generous* than I expected.
彼は自分の娘には甘い He *is indulgent to* his daughter.
❺【きちんとしていない】
このねじは甘く(→ゆるく)なってきている This screw has become *loose.*
この写真は少しピントが甘かったようだ This photograph seems a bit *out of focus.*
[慣用表現] ひとりで甘い汁を吸おうとしたって, そうはいかないぞ I won't let you *take the lion's share.*

あまえ 甘え dependence [U] ◆君には甘えがある(→他人に頼りすぎている) You *are too dependent on* others.

あまえび 甘海老 shrimp [C]

あまえる 甘える behave like a spoiled child; (動物が) fawn [自] ◆甘えないでよ Don't *act spoiled.* / その子は甘えた声で母親を呼んだ The child *whined* for his mother. / これ以上親に甘えることはできない I can't *depend on* my parents' help anymore. / ではお言葉に甘えさせていただきます Thank you very much. *I will accept your offer.*

あまえんぼう 甘えん坊 (甘やかされた子供) spoiled [pampered] child [C]; (甘えてねだる子供) wheedling child [C]; (お母さん子) mama's child [C] ◆彼は本当に甘えん坊だ He is *a* really *pampered boy.* / 末娘は甘えん坊でしょうがない(→とても甘やかされている) My youngest daughter *is quite spoiled.*

あまがえる 雨蛙 tree [green] frog [C]

あまがさ 雨傘 umbrella [C] ➾かさ(傘)

あまからい 甘辛い salty-sweet

あまぐ 雨具 (雨着) rainwear [U]; (装備) rain gear [U]; (用具) rain things ◆雨具を持ってくるのを忘れないようにしなさい Don't for-

あまくだり

get to bring *an umbrella* with you. (◆「雨具」と英語でいう場合，umbrella や raincoat などと具体的にいうのがふつう．)
関連語 傘 an umbrella / 折りたたみ傘 a folding umbrella / レインコート a raincoat / 長靴 rain boots

あまくだり 天下り その役人は民間企業に天下りした(→仕事を得るためにコネを使った) The government official *used influence to take up a job* in a private company.

あまくち 甘口 ——甘口の (酒などが) sweet (↔dry); (カレーが) mild (↔hot) ∥甘口のワイン *sweet* wine / 甘口のカレー *mild* curry

あまぐつ 雨靴 (一般的に) rain boots; (ゴム長靴)《米》rubber [《英》wellington] boots

あまぐも 雨雲 rain cloud Ⓒ, 【気象】nimbus Ⓒ Ⓤ (複 ~es, nimbi) ∥雨雲が低く垂れこめている *Rain clouds* are hanging low.

あまぐり 甘栗 sweet roasted [broiled] chestnut Ⓒ

あまごい 雨乞い praying for rain ——雨乞い(を)する pray for rain

あまざけ 甘酒 amazake, sweet low-alcohol drink made from fermented rice or sake lees

あまざらし 雨曝し ——雨ざらしの weather-beaten, weathered ∥雨ざらしの木材 *weather-beaten* timber ◆自転車が雨ざらしになっている The bicycle *is exposed to rain*.

あまじお 甘塩 ——甘塩の lightly salted ∥甘塩のサケ *lightly salted* salmon

あます 余す 大会まで余すところ1週間となった We have only one *more* week until the tournament. / この小説には彼の人となりが余すところなく描かれている This novel depicts his character *completely [in every detail]*.

あまずっぱい 甘酸っぱい (果物などが) sweet and sour; (ほろ苦い) bittersweet ∥甘ずっぱい思い出 *bittersweet* memories / このアンズジャムは甘ずっぱい This apricot jam *tastes sweet and sour*.

あまだれ 雨垂れ raindrop Ⓒ ∥雨だれの音が聞こえる We can hear the patter of *raindrops*.

アマチュア amateur Ⓒ (↔professional) ——アマチュアの amateur ∥アマチュアオーケストラ an *amateur* orchestra / アマチュアスポーツ *amateur* sports / アマチュア無線家 an *amateur* radio operator; a (radio) ham / アマチュア選手 an *amateur* player ◆アマチュア精神 *amateurism*

あまったるい 甘ったるい (ひどく甘い) too sweet, sugary; (感傷的な) sugary ∥このおしるこは甘ったるい This *oshiruko is too sweet* for me. / 彼女はいつも甘ったるい声で話す She always talks in a *sugary* voice.

あまったれ 甘ったれ (甘えん坊) spoiled [pampered] child Ⓒ ∥弟は本当に甘ったれだ My brother *is a really spoiled boy*.

あまったれる 甘ったれる 彼は高校生にもなるのにいまだに甘ったれたところがある He still *has a spoiled streak* though he is a high school student. / 甘ったれるな! Stop cod-

dling *yourself*!

あまど 雨戸 sliding storm window Ⓒ; (よろい戸) shutter Ⓒ ◆欧米のふつうの家には日本のような雨戸はない．ただし雨戸に類似した rain shutter, storm shutter を使用している地方もある) ∥雨戸をあける[閉める] open [close] *the shutters*

あまどい 雨樋 a gutter (at the eaves), trough Ⓒ ∥雨どいをつける install *gutters*

あまとう 甘党 兄は甘党だ(=甘いものが好きだ) My brother *has a sweet tooth*. / My brother *likes sweet things*.

あまなっとう 甘納豆 amanatto, sugared beans, sugar-glazed beans

あまねく 遍く (広く) widely, extensively; (一般に) generally; (普遍的に) universally ◆それはあまねく人の知るところだ It is a matter of *common* knowledge.

あまのがわ 天の川 the Milky Way; (銀河) the Galaxy
俳句 荒海や佐渡によこたふ天の川(松尾芭蕉)
Look! The stormy sea.
And lying above Sado
is the Milky Way.

あまのじゃく 天の邪鬼 (つむじ曲がりの人) contrary person Ⓒ, perverse person Ⓒ; (ひねくれ者) gadfly Ⓒ; (性質) perversity Ⓤ, perverseness Ⓤ ∥彼はあまのじゃくで，何かにつけ私に反対する He is *a perverse person* and he opposes me in everything.

あまみ 甘味 sweetness Ⓤ ◆スープに甘みをつける add *a sweet flavor to* soup; *sweeten* soup / このメロンは甘みが足りない This melon *isn't sweet enough*.

あまみず 雨水 rainwater Ⓤ ∥バケツに雨水をためる store *rainwater* in a bucket

あまもよう 雨模様 (雨のきざし) a sign of rain; (雨天) rainy skies ◆雨模様だ *It looks rainy*.

あまもり 雨漏り a leak in the roof ——雨漏りする leak 圓 ∥屋根の雨漏りがひどい The roof *leaks badly*. / The roof has *a bad leak*. ◆雨漏りするので父は屋根を直した My father fixed the *leaky* roof.

あまやかす 甘やかす (甘やかしてだめにする) spoil* 他, pamper 他; (好きなようにさせる) indulge 他 ∥末っ子は甘やかされる傾向がある The youngest tend to *get spoiled*. / 弟は甘やかされて育った My brother *was pampered* as he grew up. / 最近の親は子供を甘やかしすぎる Parents today *indulge* their children too much.

あまやどり 雨宿り ——雨宿りする shelter [take* shelter] from the rain ∥私たちは木の下で雨宿りをした We *took shelter from the rain* under a tree.

あまり[1]
❶【あまり…でない】(程度) not very …, not … much, not too …; (回数) not … often, rarely, seldom; (数) not … many; (量) not … much
私はあまり上手に英語を話せない I *don't speak* English *very* well.

最近あまり彼女に会っていない I *haven't* seen her *much* recently.

その問題にはあまり深入りしたくない I *don't* want to pursue the matter *too* far.

彼はあまり知られていないがすばらしい歌手だ He's *not very* well known, but he's a great singer.

私はあまり本を読まない I *rarely* read books.

🔵「何か食べたい？」「いや、あんまり」"Do you want to eat something?" "*Not really*."

❷【あまり…すぎる】too;（そんなに）so

我々は成功のためにあまりに高い代償を払った We paid *too* high a price for success.

その話はあまりにうますぎて本当だとは思えない That's *too* good to be true.

最初からあまりがんばりすぎるなよ Don't work *too* hard from the beginning.

あまり騒ぐと先生に怒られるぞ The teacher will get angry if you make *so* much noise.

あまりにも腹が立ったので彼を殴りそうになった I got *so* angry (that) I almost hit him.

あまりにも不愉快だったので電話をがちゃんと切った I was *so* annoyed (that) I just slammed down the phone.

❸【…の[という]あまり】

彼女は緊張のあまり（→とても緊張したので）何も話さなかった She was *so* tense *that* she *couldn't* say anything.

その子は恐怖のあまり（→恐怖のために）泣きだした The child began to cry *in fear*.

彼は勝ちを急ぐあまりに無謀な走塁をした He was in *such* a hurry to win *that* he ran the bases recklessly.

あまり² 余り（残ったもの）the rest, the remainder;〖数学〗remainder ◯ ∥余りはみんなで分けてください Share *the rest* with everyone. / 20を6で割ると3，余りは2だ Twenty divided by six is three「*remainder two* [with *a remainder* of two].

◆この学校には400人余りの（→400人と少しの）生徒がいます There are 400-*odd* [*just over* 400] students in this school. / 彼は宴会の余り物を家に持って帰った He brought back *the leftovers* from the party.

あまりある 君の苦労は察するに余りある（→十分に察することができないほどだ）I *can't* appreciate your efforts *enough*. / You've worked *harder than I can imagine*. / 彼女の明るい性格は短所を補って余りある Her cheerful character *more than* compensates for her shortcomings.

アマリリス〖植物〗amaryllis ◯

あまる 余る

❶【残る】remain ⓐ, be left over;〖数学〗leave* ⓜ

今月のおこづかいはまだ700円余っている I still have 700 yen「*left over* [*remaining*] from my allowance this month.

給食のパンが余っていた Bread *was left over* from the school lunch.

テストは簡単だったので30分も余ってしまった The test was easy, so I *had* 30 minutes *left over* at the end.

17を7で割ると3が余る Seventeen divided by seven *leaves* a remainder of three.

◆この学校はパソコンが余っている（→多すぎる）のではないか Aren't there *too many* personal computers at this school?

❷【限界を超えている】

この本は難しすぎて私の手に余る（→理解を超えている）This book is *too hard* for me *to* understand.

身に余る光栄です The honor is *more than I deserve*.

彼のふるまいは目に余る（→黙って見ていられないほどひどい）His behavior *is unbearable*.

彼は勢い余ってころんだ He *lost control of his momentum* and fell down.

あまんじる 甘んじる 父は薄給に甘んじていた My father「*didn't complain about* [*was resigned to*] his low salary. / 彼らは屈辱的な条件を甘んじて受けた They *accepted* the humiliating conditions *without protest*. / これからも現状に甘んじることなく努力しなさい Don't just *accept things as they are*. Keep on working to improve.

あみ 網 net ◯;（焼き網）grill ◯ ∥網を打つ cast「*throw* *a net* / 網を張る draw *a net* / 網にイルカがかかって大問題になった It became a big problem when dolphins got caught in *the nets*. / 子供のころはよく網を持ってバッタを捕りにいったものです When I was a child, I would often go out with *a net* in order to catch grasshoppers. / 彼らは法の網をかいくぐって商売していた They did business by slipping through *the net of the law*.

◆警察は連続殺人犯をつかまえるために捜査の網を広げた The police widened *the dragnet* to capture the serial killer.

∥網タイツ fishnet stockings / 地引き網 a dragnet / トロール網 a trawl net

あみあげぐつ 編み上げ靴 lace-ups, lace(-up) boots

あみき 編み機 knitting machine ◯

あみだ 阿弥陀 子供たちはみんな帽子をあみだにかぶっていた All the children wore their hats *pushed back*. / だれが買い出しに行くかあみだくじを引いて決めよう Let's *draw lots* to decide who's going shopping.

あみだす 編み出す（考え出す）think* out, work out;（発明する）invent ⓜ;（考案する）devise ⓜ ∥私たちはついにこの難問を解く方法を編み出した We finally *thought out* a way to solve this difficult problem. / 彼女は英単語をたくさん暗記できる方法を編み出した She *worked out* how to memorize many English words.

あみだな 網棚 rack ◯,《主に英》luggage rack ◯ ∥網棚に荷物を載せる put baggage on *a rack* / 学校に着いてから電車の網棚にかばんを置き忘れたのに気づいた After getting to school, I found that I had left my schoolbag on *the rack* of the train.

あみど 網戸（扉・戸）screen door ◯;（窓）window screen ◯ ∥私は網戸を取りはずして洗

った I took away *the window screens* and washed them.
アミノさん アミノ酸〔化学〕amino acid ⓒ
あみのめ 網の目 a mesh (of a net) ◆鉄道が網の目のように全国に広がっている *A network of railroads* covers the whole country.
あみばり 編み針 (かぎ針) crochet hook ⓒ; (棒針) knitting needle ⓒ
あみぼう 編み棒 knitting needle ⓒ
あみめ¹ 網目 a mesh (of a net) /網目の細かいふるい a sieve with *a fine mesh*
あみめ² 編み目 stitch ⓒ /編み目の細かい[粗い]セーター a sweater with tight [loose] *stitches*
あみもの 編み物 (編むこと) knitting ⓤ, crochet ⓤ; (編んだもの) knitted goods ── 編み物をする knit* ⓐⓒ, crochet ⓐⓒ /私は最近編み物に凝っている *Knitting* is my latest enthusiasm./ あの女の子は編み物が上手だ That girl *can knit* well.
あむ 編む (編み針で) knit* ⓐⓒ; (髪などを)《米》braid ⓐ /母さんは私にセーターを編んでくれた Mom *knitted* me a sweater. / 妹は長い髪をゆるく編んでいる My sister *braids* her long hair loosely.
アムステルダム Amsterdam (❖オランダの首都)

あめ¹ 雨

❶【空から降ってくる水】rain ⓤ (❖雨の状態を表す形容詞を伴う場合は ⓒ, また it を主語として「雨が降る」の意味の動詞としても用いられる)
雨が降りそうだ It looks like *rain*.
雨が降りだした *It* started to *rain*.
きょうは激しい雨が降っている *It's raining* hard today.
3日間雨が降り続いている *It* has been *raining* for three days.
ようやく雨が上がった(→降りやんだ) *It* finally stopped *raining*.
家に帰る途中で雨にあった I was caught in the *rain* on the way home.
(天気予報で)あすは雨になるでしょう *It will rain* tomorrow.
◆遠足は雨で中止になった The excursion *was rained out*./ 今年の6月は雨の日が多かった We had a lot of *rainy days* in June this year.

[語法] It will rain.「雨が降るだろう」といえるのはふつう天気予報など何らかの情報に基づいて確実に雨が降るだろうと予想するときだけである。空模様などを見て漠然と降りそうだと予想するときは It looks like rain. または It's (probably) going to rain. のようにいう。

❷【雨のように降ってくるもの】a rain of ..., a shower of ...
質問の雨 *a shower of* questions
その地区には弾丸の雨が降り注いだ *A shower* [*hail*] *of* bullets poured onto that area.
‖大雨 a heavy [hard] rain / 霧雨 (a) drizzle / 豪雨 a torrential rain, a downpour / 小雨 a light [little] rain / にわか雨 a (sudden) shower

慣用表現 雨が降ろうとやりが降ろうと(→何が起ころうと)僕はあした出発するよ *Come rain or shine*, I'm leaving tomorrow./ 雨降って地固まる *After rain comes fair weather.*/ *After a storm comes a calm.*

あめ² 飴 (砂糖菓子)《主に米》candy ⓤ ⓒ, drop ⓒ /のどあめ a cough drop / あめをなめる suck (on) *a candy*

慣用表現 彼はあめとむちとを巧みに使い分けた He skillfully used both *the carrot and the stick*. (❖英語では"ニンジンとむち"という)

あめあがり 雨上がり 雨上がりの澄んだ空 a clear sky *after the rain* / 雨上がりで道がぬかるんでいた *After the rain lifted*, the road was muddy.
あめいろ 飴色 amber color ⓒ; (褐色) brown ⓤ /タマネギをあめ色になるまでいためてください Fry the onions until they are *brown*.
アメーバ〔生物〕amoeba [əmíːbə](複 〜s, amoebae) /アメーバ性赤痢 *amoebic* dysentery / アメーバ運動 *amoeboid* movement
あめおとこ 雨男 a man whose presence seems to cause rain ◆彼は雨男だ(→彼といっしょにいるときはいつも雨が降る) *Whenever I am with* him, *it rains*.
あめおんな 雨女 a woman whose presence seems to cause rain
アメジスト amethyst
アメダス AMeDAS (❖*Automated Meteorological Data Acquisition System* (自動気象観測システム)の略語)
あめつづき ここ1週間ずっと雨続きだ *It has been raining for a week.* / 雨続きでいやになる This *long rain* is getting me down.
あめもよう 雨模様 ⇒あまもよう
アメリカ (アメリカ合衆国) the United States (of America)《単数扱い》(❖しばしば the U.S.A. または the U.S. と略される。米国外にいる米国人は自国を指して通例 the States という。米国内では the United States または America という); (アメリカ大陸) America ── アメリカ人 American ⓒ ── アメリカ(人)の American
私はアメリカに行ったことがない I've never been to *the U.S.*
彼女はアメリカ人だ She is *American*.
彼はアメリカ人の女性と結婚した He married an *American* woman.
バーボンはアメリカのウイスキーだ Bourbon is *American* whiskey.
‖アメリカインディアン a Native American, an American Indian / アメリカ英語 American English / アメリカ国旗 the American national flag; (星条旗) the Stars and Stripes / アメリカ政府 the U.S. government / アメリカ独立戦争 the Revolutionary War, the American Revolution, the War of American Independence / アメリカ文学 American literature / 北[中央, 南] アメリカ North [Central, South] America

/ ラテンアメリカ Latin America

アメリカンフットボール《米》football [U], 《英》American football [U] (❖football は米国ではアメリカンフットボールを指すが, 英国ではサッカーまたはラグビーのことをいう)

あめんぼ water strider [C]

あや 文·綾 それはちょっとした言葉のあやだよ That's just *a figure of speech*.

あやうい 危うい 医者は彼の命は危ういと言った The doctor said he was *in critical condition*. / 私たちは危ういところを助かった We had a *narrow* escape. ➩ あぶない

あやうく 危うく (もう少しで) almost, nearly; (かろうじて) narrowly, barely ∥彼はスピードを出しすぎて危うく事故を起こすところだった He drove so fast (that) he *almost* caused a traffic accident. / 彼女は彼の作り話に危うくだまされるところだった She was *nearly* taken in by his story.

あやかる 娘を祖母にあやかって(→ちなんで)洋子と名づけた I named my daughter Yoko *after* my grandmother.

「彼, 懸賞で50万円当たったんだって」「すごいな! あやかりたいよ(→彼と同じくらい幸福になりたい)」 "I hear he won a prize and got 500,000 yen." "Wow! *I wish I were as lucky as* him [he]."

あやしい 怪しい

❶【疑わしい】(疑いを起こさせる) suspicious; (信頼できない) doubtful; (不確かな) uncertain; (変な) strange

怪しい男を見かけませんでしたか Didn't you see a *suspicious* man?

こんなに親切にしてくれるなんて怪しいなあ There's something *suspicious* about how nice you are to me.

彼の書く日本語には怪しい(→おかしな)ものが少なくない There's a lot of *strange* Japanese in his writing.

◆雲行きが怪しくなってきた The clouds look *threatening*. / 彼女は私に本を持ってきてくれると言ったが, 怪しいものだ(→信用できない) She said she would bring the book for me, but I *don't trust* her. / あの二人は最近どうも怪しい(→何かが進行しているように見える) *Something seems to be going on* between those two recently.

❷【不思議な】

怪しい魅力 *bewitching* attractiveness

その水晶玉は怪しい光を放っていた The crystal ball shone *uncannily*.

❸【下手な·ぎこちない】poor, clumsy

彼の中国語はかなり怪しい His Chinese *is* rather *poor*.

あやしげ 怪しげ ―怪しげな (疑わしい) suspicious-looking, doubtful; (いかがわしい) shady; (うさんくさい) fishy ∥怪しげな話 a *fishy* story / 怪しげな男が家の周りをうろついている A *suspicious-looking* man is wandering around near my house.

あやしむ 怪しむ suspect [他], doubt [他] ∥そんなことをしてると泥棒ではないかと怪しまれるよ You *will be suspected* of being a thief for doing such a thing.

あやす (小さな子を揺すって) cradle [他]; (寝かしつける) lull [他]; (機嫌をとる) humor, 《英》humour [他] ∥泣いている赤ん坊を抱いてあやす *cradle* a crying baby in *one's* arms

あやつりにんぎょう 操り人形 marionette [C], puppet [C] (❖puppet は比喩的な意味でも使う) ∥その大統領は彼らの操り人形だ The president is their *puppet*.

あやつる 操る (人形などを) handle [他]; (人·機械などを) manipulate [他] ∥それらの人形を上手に操るようになるまで3年はかかる It takes at least three years to be able to *handle* those puppets skillfully. / 彼は裏でだれかに操られているんじゃないかと思う I think he's *being manipulated* by somebody behind the scenes.

◆彼は5か国語を自在に操るという評判だ They say he *has a good command of* five languages. / 彼女は2本のバトンを巧みに操った She *twirled* two batons *skillfully*.

あやとり 綾取り cat's cradle [U] ∥あや取りをする play *cat's cradle*

あやぶむ 危ぶむ (疑う) doubt [他]; (悪い結果を恐れる) fear [他]; (心配する) worry [自] ∥彼女がその試験に合格するのを危ぶむ人はいなかった Nobody *doubted* her passing the exam.

◆財政改革関連の法案のいくつかは今国会での成立が危ぶまれている Several of the financial reform bills *are unlikely to* pass the current Diet.

あやふや ―あやふやな (確かではない) uncertain, shaky,《口語的》iffy; (あいまいな) vague ∥記憶があやふやなものではっきりとは言えませんが, 彼女はその場にいたと思います My memory is *shaky* [*vague*] so I can't say for certain, but I think that she was there. / 国民は彼のあやふやな答弁を激しく非難した The people sharply criticized his *vague* testimony.

あやまち 過ち (誤り) mistake [C]; (過失) fault [C] (❖「過失の責任」の意味では [U]); (ふとした軽い) lapse [C] ∥過ちを犯す make *a mistake* / 彼は同じ過ちを繰り返した He made *the* same *mistake* again. / 私は自分の過ちを認めて謝罪した I admitted my *mistake* and apologized. / 彼は1度きりの過ちだと言っていたが, 私は彼が3度は泥酔したことを覚えている He said that it was *his* only *lapse*, but I remember him being dead drunk three times. ◆二人きりで旅行に行くだなんて, 過ちでもあったらどうするの If just the two of you go traveling together, what happens *if things go wrong*?

あやまって 誤って (別のものと間違えて) by mistake; (うっかり) by accident; (偶然) accidentally ➩ あやまる(誤る) ∥その子供は誤って池に落ちた The child fell into the pond *by accident*. / 彼女は誤って針で親指を刺した She *accidentally* pricked her thumb with a needle.

あやまり 誤り error [C][U], mistake [C] (❖error のほうがかたい語) ∥誤りを犯す make *a mis-*

あやまる

take / 彼は私の文章の誤りを正してくれた He corrected *the errors* in my writing. / 誤りを指摘するだけでは問題を解決したことにはならない Only identifying *the mistakes* will not solve the problem.

あやまる¹ 誤る mistake* ⓣ, make* a mistake ――誤った（間違った）wrong
誤った考え a *wrong* idea / 選択を誤る make a *wrong* choice
どうもあなたの住所を誤って覚えていたようです I'm afraid I'd *mistaken* your address.
◆運転を誤る *mishandle* one's car / 判断を誤る *misjudge* / 身を誤る *take the wrong path in life* / 今回は監督が人選を誤ったのではないか I think the coach *chose the wrong players* this time. / 彼はギャンブルを知って道を踏み外した He *went bad* after he started gambling. / この薬品は扱いを誤ると爆発するので注意して運んでください This chemical will explode if it *is handled improperly*. Please transport it carefully.

あやまる² 謝る apologize ⓘ, make* an apology ⇒ コミュニケーションスキル p.53

> 英作文ノート **apologize の使い方**
> 彼は私の本をなくしたことを私に謝った
> →×He *apologized* me for losing my book.
> →×He *apologized* to me that he lost my book.
> →○He *apologized* to me for losing my book.
> ★apologize は自動詞で〈apologize to + 人 + for + 行為など〉の語順となる。that 節を用いることはできない。状況から明らかな場合は、to ... または for ... の部分を省略することがある。

彼のふるまいについて君に謝らなければならない I must *apologize to* you *for* his behavior.
お母さんに謝りなさい *Apologize to* your mother.
謝ってすむんだったら警察なんかいらないよ There'd be no need for the police if *apologizing* was enough.
◆気分を害されたのでしたら謝ります *I'm sorry* if I made you feel bad.

あやめ 菖蒲 iris ⓒ

あゆ 鮎 ayu ⓒ, sweetfish ⓒ / アユ漁が解禁になった The *ayu* season has opened.

あゆみ 歩み 非常にゆっくりとした歩みではあったが彼らは着実に進歩していった They were making progress, though at *a very slow pace*. / 彼らは会社の歩み（→歴史）を1冊の本にまとめた They compiled a book about *the history* of the company.

あゆみより 歩み寄り 《妥協》compromise ⓤⓒ;《相互の譲歩》《公式的》mutual concession ⓤⓒ / 労働者と経営者の間に歩み寄りのきざしが見える There are signs of *compromise* between the labor and management. / 両国はお互いの歩み寄りによって紛争を解決した The two countries settled the dispute *by mutual concessions*.

あゆみよる 歩み寄る ❶【近寄る】walk [step] up / 先生は居眠りしている生徒の方に歩み寄った The teacher *walked up* to the student dozing off.
❷【譲歩する】《妥協する》compromise ⓘ;《折り合う》meet* *a person* halfway / 与党と野党はその条件で歩み寄った The ruling party *compromised with* the opposition party on the terms. / 両者はお互いに歩み寄り訴訟を解決した Both sides *met each other halfway* to settle the lawsuit.

あゆむ 歩む 苦難の道を歩む take *a* thorny path / 私が歩んできた道 the path I *have followed* ⇒ あるく

あら¹ あら、こんなところに隠れていたんだ So this is where you were hiding! / あら、まさか会えるなんて驚きね Wow, what a surprise running into you! / あら、もうおしまい？ Huh? Is that the end? / あら、あれは何かしら Look! What's that?

あら² 粗《欠点》fault ⓒ;《不備》flaw ⓒ;《欠陥》defect ⓒ / 彼はいつも人のあら探しばかりしている He *is always finding fault with* others. / この報告書にはあらが目立つ There are many *flaws* in this report.

アラーム alarm

あらあらしい 荒々しい（乱暴な）rough, violent / 彼の口調はいつになく荒々しかった His tone *was* unusually *rough*.

あらい¹ 荒い（乱暴な）rough, violent;（波が）rough / あいつは人使いが荒いから気をつけろよ Be careful with him. He treats people *rough* [*roughly*]. / 波が荒い The waves *are rough*. ◆彼は気性が荒くてすぐ人に八つ当たりする He has a *terrible* temper and often takes it out on other people. / 彼は興奮して息づかいが荒くなった He became excited and *began to pant*. / 祖父は金づかいの荒い人だった My grandfather「*was a spendthrift* [*squandered his money*]. 慣用表現 その会社の社長は「世界中の人にこの商品を知ってもらいたい」と鼻息が荒かった The company's president declared *enthusiastically*, "I want people throughout the world to know this product."

あらい² 粗い（ざらざらした）rough;（きめが）coarse / この布地は手ざわりが粗い This fabric feels *rough*. / このざるでは目が粗すぎてふるいの代わりには使えない This strainer *is too coarse* to be used as a sifter.
◆私はそのプラスチックの表面をサンドペーパーで粗く削った I scraped the surface of the plastic *roughly* with sandpaper.

あらい³ 洗い washing ⓤ / 下洗い preliminary *washing*
‖洗い場（浴室の）space to wash *oneself* before getting into a bathtub

あらいあげる 洗い上げる 真っ白に洗い上げる *wash to* a very bright white / 身辺を洗い上げる *make a thorough investigation of a person*

あらいおとす 洗い落とす wash out [off];（すすぎ落とす）rinse off / 手の汚れを洗い落と

あらいもの

コミュニケーションスキル —謝る—
①相手に謝る

(A) **Excuse me. [I'm sorry. / Sorry. / Pardon me.]**
ごめんなさい [すみません].

(B) **I'm very [really, terribly, awfully] sorry.**
本当にごめんなさい.

(C) **I apologize.**
本当に申しわけありません.

(D) **Excuse me for a moment.**
ちょっと失礼します.

(E) **I'm sorry** I'm late.
遅れてすみません.

(F) **I'm sorry to** trouble [bother] you so often.
たびたびお手数をかけて申しわけありません.

(G) **I'm sorry to** have kept you waiting so long.
長いことお待たせしてすみません.

(H) **I'm sorry to interrupt you,** but you're wanted on the phone.
お話中失礼ですが, あなたにお電話です.

☞ 英米では, 通りを歩いていてだれかと肩が触れたり, 人の前を横切ったりするような場合にも, Excuse me. のようにいうのがマナー. (A) の I'm sorry. および Sorry. は自分に非があることをわびる最も一般的な表現. (B) のように very, really などを sorry の前に添えると, さらに丁寧なわび方となる.

☞ (C) の I apologize. は (A) や (B) よりずっと改まった言い方で, 「おわびします」の響きがある.

☞ 日本語の「すみません」と英語の Excuse me. や I'm sorry. との違いに注意. 店で店員を呼んだり, 道を尋ねるために人を呼び止めるような場合は, Excuse me. を用い, I'm sorry. は使わない. また, 日本人は「ありがとう」と礼を述べるつもりで, よく「すみません」というが, これは英語の Thank you. に相当する. レストランでウェーターを呼ぶとき, 日本人は「すみません」とよくいうが, 英語では手を上げて Waiter! と声をかける.

☞ 席をちょっとはずしたりするような場合は, (D) を用いる.

☞ わびる理由がはっきりしている場合は, (E) 〜 (G) のように, I'm sorry の後にその具体的な理由をつけていう.

☞ (H) は相手がしていること(ほかの人と話し中など)を中断させる必要がある場合の決まった言い方.

②謝罪に対する応答

(A) Oh, excuse me.
 —**That's** 「**all right [okay]**.
あ, すみません. —大丈夫ですよ.

(B) Oh, I'm sorry. It was my fault.
 —**No,** it was **mine**. I should have been more careful.
あ, ごめんなさい. 私が悪かったのです. —いいえ, 私のほうこそ. もっと注意していればよかったのです.

(C) I'm sorry I'm late. Traffic was heavy.
 —**No problem. [Never mind.]** These things happen.
遅れてすみません. 道が込んでまして. —いいんですよ [気にしないでください]. よくあることです.

(D) I'm terribly sorry I didn't call you.
 —Oh, **it's nothing. Just forget it**.
電話しなくて本当にごめんなさい.
—そんなこと何でもありません. 忘れてください.

(E) Excuse me for a moment. I have to make a call.
 —**Certainly.**
ちょっと失礼して, 電話をしてきます. —どうぞ.

☞ Excuse me. あるいは I'm sorry. と相手が謝った場合, (A) の That's 「all right [okay]. が最もよく使われる. **That's quite all right.** のようにもいう. (C) の Never mind. もよく使われる.

☞ It's [It was] my fault. は「私が悪かったのです」と自分の非を認める表現で my を強く言う. 相手がこのように謝ってきた場合か, 明らかに相手が悪い場合は, That's 「all right [okay]. あるいは Never mind. のように答える. 自分にも落ち度があった場合は, (B) のように「私のほうこそ」と答える.

☞ 特に相手が自分の失敗などを気にしているような場合は, (D) のようにいってあげるとよい.

☞ (E) では相手が席をはずす許可を求めているので, Certainly. または **Sure. Please go ahead.** (もちろんですとも. どうぞ) のように答える.

す wash the dirt *off* one's hands

あらいぐま 洗い熊 【動物】 raccoon ⓒ

あらいざらい 洗いざらい 彼は自分の犯した罪を洗いざらい白状した He made a *full* confession of his crimes.

あらいざらし 洗いざらし ━洗いざらしの washed-out, faded 〃彼はいつも洗いざらしのジーンズをはいている He always wears *washed-out* jeans.

あらいだす 洗い出す 計画の問題点を洗い出す *bring* the problem of the plan *to light* / 警察は全力で事件の背後関係を洗い出した (→ 明らかにした) The police did their best to *illuminate* the background of the case.

あらいたて 洗い立て 洗いたてのシャツは着心地がいい I feel comfortable in this *freshly washed* shirt.

あらいなおす 洗い直す (もう一度洗う) wash ... again; (再検討する) reconsider ㊥ 〃汚れが落ちていなかったので靴下を洗い直した Since the stain didn't come out, I *washed* the socks *again*./ その計画は全面的に洗い直す必要がある We need to *reconsider* the whole plan thoroughly.

あらいながす 洗い流す wash away [off]; (すすいで流す) rinse out 〃シャンプーを洗い流す *rinse* the shampoo *out* of *one's* hair / 私は車についた泥を洗い流した I *washed* the mud *off* my car.

あらいもの 洗い物 (食器) the dishes; (洗濯

物) wash 🔴🟡，《集合的》laundry [lɔ́:ndri] 🔴 / 洗い物をする do *the dishes* ◆洗い物がたまっている(→洗うべき皿[服]がたくさんある) I have a lot of *dishes [clothes] to wash*.

あらう　洗う

wash 🔴🟡；(きれいにする) clean 🔴🟡；(ごしごしと) scrub 🔴🟡；(シャンプーで) shampoo 🔴 / 顔を洗っていらっしゃい *Wash* your face. / ごはんの前には手を洗いなさい *Wash your hands* before you eat. / 湯ぶねにつかる前に体を洗いなさい *Wash yourself [your body]* before you soak in the bathtub. / 姉は毎晩髪を洗う My sister *shampoos her hair* every night. / ◆その少女の歌に心が洗われるような気がした I felt as if *my spirit had been cleansed* by the girl's song. / 彼の身元を洗っておいてくれ (→調査しておけ) *Investigate* his identity. / 慣用表現 彼はギャンブルから足を洗った He *put his gambling days behind him*.

あらうみ　荒海　rough sea

あらかじめ　予め　in advance, beforehand ⇨まえもって //出かけるんだったらあらかじめ言っておいてくれ When you go out, let me know *in advance*.

あらかせぎ　荒稼ぎ　──荒稼ぎする (短期間で大もうけする) make* a killing；(大金を稼ぐ) earn a lot of money / 彼は最近市場で荒稼ぎしている He's *been making a killing* on the market recently.

あらかた　夏休みの宿題はあらかた(→ほとんど)終わった I've *almost* finished the [my] homework for summer vacation.

アラカルト　きょうはアラカルトで頼もうよ(→メニューを見ながら注文しよう) Let's order *à la carte* today.(❖日本語のアラカルトは一品料理という意味の名詞としても使えるが、フランス語の *à la carte* は「メニューを見ながら(食べるものを決める)」という意味の形容詞・副詞)

あらくれもの　荒くれ者　(乱暴者) rough [tough] guy 🟡，《米口語的》roughneck 🟡

あらけずり　粗削り　──粗削りな (大ざっぱな) rough, crude；(洗練されていない) unrefined, unsophisticated

あらさがし　粗探し　(口語的) nitpicking 🔴；(批評) criticism 🔴 ──あら探しをする (欠点を探す) find* fault with ...；(批評する) criticize 🔴🟡 // 彼は他人のあら探しをするような人間ではない He is above *finding fault with* others.

あらし　嵐　storm 🟡 ──あらしの stormy // あらしの日に on a *stormy* day / あらしのような拍手 *a storm of* applause / あらしの前の静けさ the calm before *the storm* / 今夜はあらしになりそうだ We're going to have *a storm* tonight. / あらしは去った *The storm is over*. / その船は海であらしにあって沈没した The ship sank in *a storm* at sea.

短歌 吹くからに秋の草木のしをるればむべ山風をあらしといふらむ (文屋康秀) When it starts to blow

the grass and leaves of autumn
shrivel and expire.
No wonder they say the wind
gusts and blasts, rages and roars.

あらしまわる　荒らし回る　彼らはついに村々を荒らし回っていた(→村々で盗みを働いていた)泥棒を捕らえた At last they caught the thief who *had been stealing* in the villages.

あらす　荒す　(損害を与える) damage 🔴，(台なしにする) spoil* 🔴🟡；(泥棒が部屋などを) ransack 🔴 //イノシシに畑が荒らされた The fields *were damaged* by wild boars. / 机の引き出しには荒らされた痕跡(跡)があった A drawer of my desk showed traces of *having been ransacked*. ◆人の縄張りを荒らすな(→私の縄張りにくるな) *Keep out of* my territory./ *Keep off* my turf.

アラスカ　Alaska (❖米国北西部の州；(略語) Alas.；(郵便)AK)

あらすじ　粗筋　(小説などの筋) plot 🟡，story 🟡 //その映画のあらすじを言わないで Don't tell me *the plot* of the movie.

あらそい　争い　(もめごと) trouble 🟡 (また複数形～s)；(けんか) fight 🟡；(不和) discord 🟡 //争いの種 an apple of *discord*; a bone of *contention* / あの夫婦の間には争いが絶えない(→いつももめごとがある) That couple is always having *troubles*. / 彼は権力争いに巻き込まれた He got involved in *a power game*. / 縄張り争いをしているんじゃないぞ There is no time to *fight for [over] turf*. / わがチームは早くも優勝争いから脱落した Our team has already dropped out of *the race for the championship*.

あらそう　争う

fight* 🔴🟡；(競争する) compete 🟡；(闘争する) struggle 🟡

彼は自分の弟と議長のいすを争った He *fought* his own brother for the post of chairperson.

彼らは建物の所有権をめぐって裁判で争っている They *are fighting* in the court over the ownership of the building.

◆彼は校内でも一、二を争う大食漢だ(→最もたくさん食べる人の一人だ) He has *one of the biggest* appetites in the school. / その商品が発売になるや彼らは先を争って飛びついた As soon as the products were released, they *scrambled* to get them. / 事態は一刻を争う(→むだにできる時間はない) *There's no time to lose.* / 気がついたら父さんと同じことをしていた。血は争えないね(→この父にしてこの息子あり) I found myself acting like my dad. *Like father, like son.*

あらた　新た　──新たな (新しい) new, fresh；(もう一つの) another ──新たに (新しく) newly //新たな生活を始める start *a new life* / 事件は新たな局面を迎えた The case has entered *a new phase*. / 新たな証拠がいくつかあがってきた *Some fresh evidence has come up*. / 彼らはこの紛争が新たな世界大戦を引き起こすことを懸念している

あらだてる 事を荒立てないように（→事態を悪くしないように）してくれよ Please *don't make matters worse*.

あらたまる 改まる（変わる）change ⓘ;（新しくなる）be renewed;（改善される）get better, improve ⓘ ——改まった（形式ばった）formal;（堅苦しい）stiff;（丁寧な）polite 〃彼の素行はいっこうに改まる気配がない There is no hint that his behavior has started to *improve*. / そんなに改まっちゃってどうしたの You're looking so *stiff*. What happened?

あらためて 改めて（もう一度）again;（別のときに）another time 〃では、改めて質問しますが、あなたは自分が悪いとは思っていないのですね Then I ask you *again*: you don't think you're wrong, right? / 詳しくはまた改めてご連絡します I'll give you the details *another time*. ◆改めて（→特に）言うことはありません I have nothing *in particular* to say. / その問題についてはまた日を改めて（→別の日に）お話しましょう Let's talk about the matter *another day*.

あらためる 改める（変える）change ⓘ;（部分的に変える）alter ⓘ;（修正する）revise ⓘ;（改正する）reform ⓘ;（改善する）improve ⓘ 〃規則を改める *revise* rules
君のその悪い習慣は改めたほうがいい You had better *change* those bad habits of yours.
その一件があってから私は彼に対する態度を改めた That incident made me *revise* [(→よくした)*improve*] my attitude to him.
◆服装を改める *dress oneself properly* / 乗車券を改める *check* (passenger) tickets

あらっぽい 荒っぽい、粗っぽい ——荒っぽく roughly 〃荒っぽい手段をとる take *rough* measures / グラスを荒っぽく扱わないでよ Don't handle the glasses *roughly*.
◆荒っぽい性格 a *violent* disposition / 荒っぽいまねはするな Don't use *violence*.

あらて 新手 新手の（→新しい種類の）詐欺に引っかかった I was swindled in *a new kind of* fraud. / ようやく追っ手を逃れたと思ったところに新手（→新たな追っ手）が現れた When I thought I had escaped from my pursuers at last, *more of them* appeared.

あらなみ 荒波 rough waves [seas] ◆人生の荒波にもまれて彼も丸くなった（→人生の苦労が彼を円熟させた）*The hardships* of life have matured and mellowed him.

あらぬ 有らぬ あらぬ（→事実無根の）うわさを立てられて迷惑している I'm annoyed with *groundless* rumors.

アラバマ Alabama（◆米国南東部の州;《略語》Ala., 《郵便》AL）

アラビア Arabia ——アラビア人 Arab ⓘ ——アラビア語 Arabic ⓤ ——アラビアの Arabian ——アラビア語の Arabic ǁアラビア数字 Arabic numerals

あらびき 粗びき 粗びきのソーセージ a sausage of *coarsely ground meat* / コショウを粗びきにする grind pepper *coarsely*

アラブ Arab ——アラブ語 Arab ——アラブの Arabian ——アラブ人の Arab ǁアラブ諸国 *Arab* countries / アラブ世界 the *Arab* world

あらまし （概略）outline ⓒ, sketch ⓒ ǁ事件のあらましを述べる give *an outline* of the case

あらゆる （すべての）all;（どれひとつとっても）every（◆数えられる名詞の単数形に付ける）ǁかつて天文学はあらゆる科学の手本だった Astronomy was once a model for *all other* sciences. / 彼は目的を達するためにあらゆる手段を尽くした He employed *every* possible means to achieve his purpose.

あららげる 荒らげる 彼は声を荒らげて（→さらに大きな声で）息子をしかった He scolded his son *in an increasingly loud voice*.

あらりえき 荒利益 gross margin ⓒ

あらりょうじ 荒療治 この会社を建て直すには荒療治（→思いきった方策）が必要だ *Drastic measures* should be taken to rebuild the company.

あられ 霰 ❶【雪あられ・氷あられ】hail ⓤ（また a ～）ǁ突然あられが降り始めた Suddenly *the hail* began to fall. / 通りには銃弾が雨あられと降り注いだ There was *a hail of* bullets in the streets.
❷【あられもち】grilled [fried] bits of rice cake

あられもない 彼女はあられもない格好で現れた She showed up *scantily dressed*.

あらわ 露 肌をあらわにする *bare one's skin* / その一件で二人の対立があらわになった（→その一件が対立を明らかにした）The incident *has revealed* the conflict between the two. / 彼は感情をあらわにした（→見せた）He *showed* emotion.

あらわざ 荒技 daring move ⓒ

あらわす¹ 表す

（見せる）show*;（表現する）express ⓘ;（象徴する）represent ⓘ;（意味する）stand* ⓘ 〃彼は支持者に感謝の意を表した He *showed* his appreciation to his supporters.
私は言いたいことをうまく言葉で表せなくてもどかしい思いをした I felt irritated because I *couldn't express* myself in right words.
この絵は戦争の悲惨さを表している This picture *represents* the misery of the war.
UNは国連を表す UN *stands for* the United Nations.
〖慣用表現〗名は体を表す *The name of a thing shows what it is*.

あらわす² 現す （姿を見せる）appear ⓘ, 《口語的》show* up;（あらわにする）reveal ⓘ;（見せる）show 〃正体を現す *reveal one's* true self / 講演者が姿を現すと講堂はとたんに静かになった As the lecturer *appeared*, the

auditorium became silent all at once.
慣用表現 その新人はめきめきと頭角を現してきた The freshman *has come to the fore remarkably*. / その詐欺師はついに馬脚を現した The swindler *has finally betrayed his true nature*.

あらわす³ 著す (本などを書く) write* 働; (出版する) publish 働 ‖彼は生涯に5冊の本を著した He *wrote* five books in his lifetime.

あらわれ 表れ (表現) expression C U; (しるし) sign C ‖彼が相手の健闘をたたえたのはスポーツマン精神の表れだ It is *a sign* of his sportsmanship that he has praised his opponent's good play.

あらわれる¹ 現れる

appear 働, come* *a person's* way; (隠れていたものが) come out, emerge 働; (約束の時間に来る) show* up, turn up

昨夜あの山の上に UFO が現れたそうだ They say a UFO *appeared* above that mountain last night.

星占いには魅力的な男性が現れるかもって書いてあるよ The horoscope says an attractive man may *come my way*.

茂みの中から急に人影が現れた A figure suddenly 「*came out* [*emerged*] *from* the bushes.

彼は時間に正確なので, ぼちぼち現れてもいい時間なんだが He's punctual and it is about time for him to *show* [*turn*] *up*.

◆ようやく薬の効き目が現れてきた(→効き始めた) The drug *is* finally *starting to* work.

あらわれる² 表れる (反映する) reflect 働; (見せる) show* 働; (表現する) express 働

彼女の表情には本当の気持ちが表れていた Her expressions *reflected* how she really felt.

彼のすぐれた才能は5歳のとき描いた絵にすでに表れていた His drawing at the age of five already *showed* his great gift.

あらんかぎり 有らん限り 私たちはあらん限りの力で(→全力で)その岩を押した We pushed the rock *with all our strength*. / 彼らはあらん限りの声を上げて助けを求めた They shouted for help *at the top of their voices* [*lungs*].

あり 蟻 ant C ‖シロアリ a termite
慣用表現 コンサート会場周辺の警備は厳重でアリのはい出る隙(ホサ)もなかった(→だれも気づかれずには出入りできないほどだった) The security around the concert hall was so tight that *no one could enter or exit without being noticed*.

アリア 〔音楽〕 aria C

ありあまる 有り余る 金はありあまるほどあったが, 彼は満ち足りていなかった Even though he had *more than enough* money, he was not satisfied. / 君にはありあまる才能がある You surely have *plenty of* talents.

ありあり(と) (鮮明に) vividly; (はっきりと) clearly ‖そのときの情景は今でもありありと思い浮かべられる I still remember the scene *vividly*. / 生徒たちの顔には不満の色がありありと浮かんでいた Dissatisfaction was *clearly* seen on the students' faces.

ありあわせ 有り合わせ (料理) pot luck U
◆ゆうべはあり合わせのもので食事をすませた We had *whatever we could find* for dinner last night. / あり合わせのものばかりですが(→特別なものは何もありませんが), どうぞ召し上がれ This is *nothing special* but enjoy!

アリーナ arena C ‖アイスアリーナ an ice arena, a skating arena

ありうる 有り得る (十中八九そうだ) probable; (可能性がある) possible

🅔 「彼, また1等賞を取ったんだって」「ああ, ありうる, ありうる(→全然驚くことではない)」"I hear he won the first prize again." "Oh, that's *no surprise*."

🅔 「あの二人が結婚するって本当かな」「まあ, ありうる話ではあるね」"Is it true those two will get married?" "Well, it is *possible*."

ありえない 有り得ない impossible ‖彼女が歌手になったって? そんなことありえないよ She has become a singer? That's *impossible*!
◆学校に腕時計を忘れてきたなんてありえない. 帰りの電車ではちゃんとしていたんだから I *can't have left* my watch at school. I had it on the train home.

ありか 必死で捜したがついにかぎのありかは分からずじまいだった I looked everywhere for the key, but could never find *where it was*.

ありかた 在り方 教育のあり方 *the ideal method of education* / 政治のあり方が問われているというのに政治家はそれをよく理解していない *The way politics should be conducted* is in question but the politicians don't understand that.

ありがたい 有り難い

ちょっと手を貸していただけると非常にありがたいのですが(→感謝します) I'd *be most grateful to* you if you could lend me a helping hand.

お気持ちはありがたいのですが(→好意には感謝しますが), 先約があるもので *Thank you for* your kindness, but I have another commitment.

命が助かっただけでもありがたいと思いなさい(→喜びなさい) You should *be glad* that your life has been spared at least.

ありがたいことに(→幸運にも)だれも私が失敗したことに気づいていないようだ *Luckily* no one seems to notice that I have failed.

彼は私のことをありがたくない(→歓迎できない) 客だと思っているようだ He seems to regard me as an *unwelcome* guest.

記念品をくれるというのでありがたく(→感謝して) ちょうだいした They offered me some commemorative goods and I accepted them *with thanks*.

彼の説教をありがたがる(→よいと思う)人の気持ちが分からない I can't understand the feeling of the people who *think highly of* his sermons.

💬「少し手伝おうか」「ありがたい(→助かるなあ). 頼むよ」 "Want some help?" *"Thank God! Please."* (❖Want some help?は do you want some help?の略)

ありがたみ 有り難み 今どきの若者は金のありがたみ(→価値)を知らなさすぎる Young people don't know *the value* of money too little these days.

ありがためいわく 有り難迷惑 彼は自分の手助けがありがた迷惑になるということを分かっていない He doesn't know that his well-intentioned aid turns out to be *a nuisance*.

ありがち 有りがち ありがちな(→よく尋ねられる)質問 *frequently* asked questions / この手の間違いは若者にありがちだ These kinds of mistakes *are typical of* youth.

💬「暑い日ってついアイスクリームを買いたくなるよ」「うん、ありがちだ(→みんなそうしがちだ)」"I often feel like buying some ice cream on hot days." "Yeah, *so does everyone*."

ありがとう 有り難う
Thank you., Thanks.

語法
(1)「ありがとう」の最も一般的な言い方は、Thank you. で、だれに対しても用いることができる。会話では、特に親しい間柄でThanks. をよく用いる。感謝の気持ちを強調したいときは、Thank you very [so] much. (Thank you so much.は女性が好んで用いる)、Thanks a lot.などという.
(2)「…を[…してくれて]ありがとう」というときは、後にfor を付けて Thank you for …. とする / お手紙ありがとう *Thank you for* your letter. / 手伝ってくれてありがとう *Thanks for* helping me.
(3)「どういたしまして」と答えるときは、You're welcome., Not at all., Sure., That's all right.などという.
➡どういたしまして

お招きくださってありがとうございます *Thank you very much for* inviting me. / *It is very kind of you to* invite me.

傘を貸してくれてありがとう *Thank you for* lending me your umbrella. / *It is kind of you to* lend me your umbrella.

本当にどうもありがとう *Thank you very much* indeed. (❖×Thank you indeed.とはいわない)

◆どうもありがとう *I owe you one.* (❖援助に対するお礼、「あなたには借りができた」の意味) / ご助力いただき本当にありがとうございます I really *appreciate* your help.

💬「コーヒー飲む？」「いいね. ありがとう」"Do you want a cup of coffee?" "Sure. *Thanks.*"

💬「手伝っていただいて本当にありがとうございます」「いえいえ、どういたしまして」*"Thank you very much for* your help." "You're quite welcome."

💬「少々お待ちください——すみません、そのCDの在庫はないようです」「そうですか. じゃ、ほかを当たってみます. ありがとう」"Hold on please —— Sorry, we don't have that CD in stock." "Oh, OK. I'll try somewhere else. *Thanks anyway [just the same].*" (❖自分の要求などが、相手が努力してもかなえられなかったときの言い方)

💬「誕生日おめでとう. はい、プレゼント」「わあ、どうもありがとう」"Happy birthday! This is for you." "Oh, *thank you so much.*"

💬「遠いところを来てくれてありがとう」「こちらこそ、お招きいただいてありがとう」*"Thank you for* coming all the way to see us." *"Thank you for* inviting me." (❖後のThank youはyouにアクセントを置く)

ありがね 有り金 彼は有り金すべてを(→自分の金をすべて)その事業につぎ込んだ He invested *all his money* in the business.

ありきたり 在り来たり ありきたりの(一般的な) common; (ふつうの) ordinary; (陳腐な) commonplace; (飽きるほどなじんだ) tired (old) / コンピュータは最近ありきたりのものになってきている Computers are getting *commonplace* nowadays. / 彼はありきたりのジョークを飛ばした He told a *tired old* joke.

ありさま 有り様 (状態) state ⓒ; (状況) condition ⓒ / 世の中のありさま *the state* of the world / 今のありさまでは成功はおぼつかない In *the present state*, we're not likely to succeed. ◆彼らはかわいそうなほどひどいありさまだった They were in *a sorry plight*.

ありじごく 蟻地獄 ant lion (larva) ⓒ ◆あり地獄に落ちる(→苦しい状況に陥る) fall into *a pit of agony*

ありそう ——ありそうな (十中八九そうだ) probable, likely (❖probable よりは確信の度合いが低い); (もっともらしい) plausible / いかにもありそうな話 a *plausible* story / 彼がイギリスに行くなんてことはまずありそうもない It's *not probable* that he will go to Britain at all. ◆きょうは何かよいことがありそうな気がした I had a kind of feeling that something good *would happen* today.

アリゾナ Arizona (❖米国南西部の州; 《略語》Ariz., 〔郵便〕AZ)

ありやき 有田焼 (有田の磁器) *Arita* porcelain Ⓤ ⓒ

ありつく (手に入れる) get* ⓔ; (見つける) find* ⓔ ◆きのうはなかなか昼飯にありつけなかった(→遅くなるまで昼食がとれなかった) Yesterday I *couldn't have* lunch until late.

ありったけ 彼は何とか彼女の気を引こうとありったけの知恵をしぼった He racked his brains *for any way* to attract her.

ありとあらゆる (すべての) every; (種々雑多な) miscellaneous / ありとあらゆる方法を試したがどれもうまくいかなかった I tried *every* method *under the sun*, but nothing worked. / その店にはありとあらゆる商品があった The shop was full of *miscellaneous* goods.

ありのまま 私は警官にありのままの事実を話した I told the *bare* facts to the policeman. / 思ったことをありのままに(→率直に)話せる友

達が欲しい I want friends that I can *frankly* speak my mind to. / 彼はありのままの自分(=本当は自分はどんな人なのか)をさらけ出すことを怖がっている He's afraid to expose *what he really is.*

アリバイ 〔法律〕alibi ◎ //アリバイをでっちあげる fake *an alibi* / 私には確固としたアリバイがある I have *a cast-iron alibi.* / 彼のアリバイは完璧(%)すぎてどうも怪しい(→完全には信じられない) His *alibi* is so perfect that I can't fully believe it. / 彼女のアリバイはあっさり崩れた Her *alibi* fell apart easily.

ありふれた (一般的な) common; (陳腐な) commonplace; (ふつうの) ordinary; (いつもの) usual; (日常的な) everyday //ありふれた日常のひとこま a slice of *everyday* life / 「鈴木」というのは日本ではとてもありふれた名字だ The surname "Suzuki" *is* very *common* in Japan.

ありもしない 彼はありもしない話をして(→作り話で)みんなを怖がらせた He frightened everyone with *a story that* [*was pure fiction* [*he had made up*].

ありゅう 亜流 (人) imitator ©; (物) poor imitation ©

ありゅうさんガス 亜硫酸ガス sulfur dioxide Ⓤ

ある¹ 在る・有る

❶ 存在する	there is [are] ...; be
❷ 所有する	have; possess, own
❸ 起こる・行われる	happen; be held
❹ 数量がある	be

❶【存在する】(不特定の物・人が) there is [are] ... (❖is [are]は, 後に続く名詞(句)の数・時制に応じて変わる); (特定の物・人が) be ⓐ; (建物などが立っている) stand* ⓐ; (横にして置かれている) lie* ⓐ; (位置する) be ⓐ, be located; (含む) contain ⓐ

語法
(1) 会話では, there is [are]は, there's [ðərz], there're [ðərə]となることが多い.
(2) 通例 there is [are]には, 初めて話題になるものが続く. そのため, a, an, some, anyなどが付いた名詞(句)や何も付かない数えられない名詞(句)はくるが, 通例 the, my, this, that, Tom'sなどが付いた特定の物・人を表す名詞(句)はこない. 日本語から考えると, 「…が[は]〜にある」の表現では, 助詞「が」は初めて話題になるものを示し, 助詞「は」はすでに話題になっているものを示すことが多いので, 「…が〜にある」の場合には there is [are]が使えるが, 「…は〜にある」の場合は使えないということができる. ただし, いつもそうなるとは限らないので, 文の意味をよく考えて英語に訳す必要がある. // 引き出しの中には(1通の)手紙があった There was *a letter* in the drawer. / その手紙は引き出しの中にあった *The letter was* in the drawer. / びんの中にはミルクが入っている There's *some milk* in the bottle.

(3) thereの後には, be動詞以外の自動詞がくることがある // それについてはまだいくつか疑問点がある(→残っている) There still *remain* some doubts about it.

冷蔵庫の中にメロンがある (→1つ) *There's* a melon in the fridge. / (→複数) *There're* melons in the fridge.

メロンは冷蔵庫の中にある The melon *is* in the fridge. / The melons *are* in the fridge. (❖ × There「is the melon [are the melons] in the fridge.とはいわない)

私の日記帳は机の上にあった My diary *was* [*was lying*] on the desk.

この家には部屋が5つある *There're* five rooms in this house. / (→この家は5つの部屋をもっている) This house *has* five rooms.

学校の近くに桜並木がある *There's* a row of cherry trees near our school.

私たちの学校は町の中心にあります Our school *is* [*stands*] in the center of the town.

札幌は北海道にあります Sapporo *is* [*is located*] in Hokkaido.

まだ十分時間がある(→残っている) *There is* plenty of time *left*.

彼が当選するチャンスはありそうにない *There seems to be* no chance of his being elected.(❖to beは省略可能)

◆そこの角(%)を左に曲がると, 右手に郵便局があります Turn left at that corner, and *you'll find* the post office on the right. / 彼女は彼についてあることないこと言い触らしていた She gossiped about him *recklessly.*

💬「きょうの新聞どこにあるの」「目の前にあるでしょ」"*Where's* today's newspaper?" "It's right in front of you."

💬「箱の中には何がありますか」「赤いボールが2つあります」"What's in the box?" "*There're* two red balls."

❷【所有する】(一般に物を) have* ⓐ; (土地・財産など)《公式的》possess ⓐ, own ⓐ

お金は十分ある I *have* enough money.

彼女は絵の才能がある She *has* a talent for drawing.

彼には莫大(%)な資産がある He *possesses* a large fortune.

彼女には大きな農場がある She *owns* a big farm.

◆私たちは次の世代のために緑の地球を守る責任がある We *are responsible for* keeping the earth green for the next generation.

💬「君の家にはパソコン, ある?」「あるよ. ノートパソコンだよ」"Do you *have* a personal computer at home?" "Yes, I *do*. It's a notebook computer."

❸【起こる・行われる】happen ⓐ, occur ⓐ; (行われる) be held

何があった What *happened*?

その事件は第二次世界大戦中にあった The event *happened* [*occurred*] during World War II.

10月に文化祭がある Our school festival will

be held in October. / We will have a school festival in October.
◆きょうは授業が6時間ある I have six classes today. / きのう大きな地震があった We had [There was] a big earthquake yesterday. / きのう近くのデパートで火事があった There was a fire [A fire broke out] in the nearby department store yesterday.

❹【数量がある】(高さ・長さなどが) be 🗎

この橋は長さが3,000メートルある This bridge is 3,000 meters long [in length].

あの相撲取りは体重が200キロある The sumo wrestler's weight is 200 kilograms. / The sumo wrestler weighs 200 kilograms.

あのビルは高さが100メートル以上ある That building is more than 100 meters high [tall].

🍎「身長はどのくらいあるの」「175センチあります」 "How tall are you?" "I'm 175 centimeters (tall)."

🍎「このチーズの重さはどのくらいありますか」「およそ2キロです」 "How much [What] does this cheese weigh?" "It's about two kilograms."

🍎「ここからその公園まではどのくらいありますか」「1キロくらいだから、歩いて15分です」 "How far is it from here to the park?" "About one kilometer. It's a 15-minute walk."

❺【…したことがある】(経験) have done

フランスへ行く前に何度もエスカルゴを食べたことがあった I had eaten escargots many times before I went to France.

🍎「中国へ行ったことがありますか」「ええ、2度」 "Have you (ever) been to China?" "Yes, twice."

❻【…することが[も]ある】

日曜日は図書館へ行くこともある(→時に図書館へ行く)が、たいていはうちにいる I sometimes go to the library on Sunday, but I usually stay at home.

火山の噴火で津波が起こることがある A volcanic eruption can start a tsunami.

❼【…してある】(完了・結果) have done

パーティーのことはサラに話してある I've told Sarah about the party.

あなたの切符はもう買ってある I've already bought a ticket for you.

◆この紙に何か書いてあるぞ(→書かれている) Something is written on this paper.

❽【…である】(断定) be 🗎 ⇒-です

彼女は世界的に有名な映画俳優である She is a world-famous movie star.

ある² 或る

certain; some; one; a, an

certain: 話し手には分かっているがはっきりとは言いたくない場合に用いる.

some: 数えられる名詞の単数形または数えられない名詞の前に付けて、通例話し手が特定できないものを表すのに用いる.

one: 過去の不特定の時点を表すのに用いる.

a, an: 数えられる名詞の単数形に付けて、通例話し手が特定できないものを表すのに用いる.

ある理由で私はそのパーティーに参加しなかった For a certain reason, I didn't join in the party.

ある意味で彼女は正しいのかもしれない She may be right in a (certain) sense.

ある程度コンピュータのことは知っている I know computers to some [a certain] extent.

8月のある朝、電車の中で斎藤先生にお会いした One morning in August, I met Mr. Saito on a train.

あるいは (もしかしたら) perhaps; (または) or ∥あるいは君のやり方が正しかったのかもしれないが、私は後悔しないよ Perhaps your way was right, but I don't regret it.

🍎「彼が行くべきだよ」「あるいは君か、ね」 "He must go." "Or you, maybe."

あるかせる 歩かせる 〖野球〗(四球を与える) walk ⑭ ∥ 石井は先頭打者を歩かせた Ishii walked the leadoff batter. ◆彼はいやがる私を無理やり歩かせた He compelled me to walk while I was not willing to.

あるがまま 事故現場はあるがままにしておきなさい Leave the scene of the accident as it is. ⇒ありのまま

アルカリ 〖化学〗alkali [ǽlkəlài] ⓒ Ⓤ (↔acid)
——アルカリ性の alkaline

あるきまわる 歩き回る walk around; (ぶらぶらさまよう) wander ⑭ ∥ 部屋の中でうろうろ歩き回るのはやめてちょうだい Stop walking around the room. / 私は街をぶらぶら歩き回った I wandered around the streets.

あるく 歩く

walk 🗎 ⑭; (徒歩で行く) go* [come*] on foot

私は学校へ歩いて行く I walk to school.

彼は雨の中を歩いて家に帰った He walked home in the rain.

彼は歩くのがとても速いのでついて行けない He walks so fast that I can't keep up with him.

真弓とジョンが腕を組んで[並んで]歩いていた Mayumi and John were walking「arm in arm [side by side].

浜辺を少し歩きませんか Shall we walk along the beach?

ここから駅までは歩いて10分かかります It takes 10 minutes to walk from here to the station.

一日中歩きどおしだったのでとても疲れた I had been walking all day and felt so tired.

渋滞がひどくて歩いたほうがましなくらいだった The traffic was so heavy (that) we might as well have walked.

歩くことは体によい Walking is good for your health.

彼は学校へ歩いて行ける所に住んでいる He lives within walking distance of school.

彼はフォアボールで一塁に歩いた He was walked to first base.

◆バス停から歩いて3分以内の所にコンビニが5軒もある There are as many as five convenience stores *within three minutes' walk* of the bus stop. / 長い距離を歩いて足が痛い My legs feel sore from *the long walk*. / 彼女はいつも赤いハンドバッグを持ち歩いている She always *carries* a red handbag. / ちょっとそのへんを歩いてきます I'm going to *take a walk* around here.

🔑「駅まで歩く，それともバスに乗る？」「歩こう」"Shall we *go* to the station *on foot* or by bus?" "Let's *walk*." (◆「バスで」by bus,「電車で」by train などとは対比して「歩いて」というときは on foot を用いる)

--- 「歩く」のいろいろ ---

足を引きずって歩く walk with a limp / いばって歩く swagger / 大またで歩く stride / 重い足取りで歩く walk with a heavy foot [tread] / 軽い足取りで歩く walk with a light foot [tread] / さまよい歩く wander / つま先で歩く tiptoe / とぼとぼ歩く trudge, plod / ぶらぶら歩く stroll / よちよち歩く toddle

アルコール alcohol [ǽlkəhɔːl] ⓤ (◆特にエチルアルコールを指すことが多い); (酒類一般) alcoholic drinks [beverages] / エチル [メチル] アルコール ethyl [methyl] *alcohol* / 消毒用アルコール rubbing *alcohol* / 彼は医者にアルコールを止められている(→医者に酒を飲むなと言われている) He has been told by his doctor that he mustn't drink any *alcoholic beverages*. ◆彼はアルコールに強い[弱い] He can [can't] hold *his liquor*. / 一般に日本酒のほうがワインよりもアルコール度数が高いものだ(→強いものだ) Generally speaking, sake is *stronger* than wine. / 毎年4月または何人かの新入生が急性アルコール中毒で病院に運ばれる Every April several freshmen are brought into the hospital because of *alcohol poisoning*.

あるじ 主 (一般に) master ⓒ; (客に対して) host ⓒ (◆女性形は hostess); (持ち主) owner ⓒ

アルゼンチン Argentina (◆公式名 the Argentine Republic) ――アルゼンチン人 Argentine ⓒ ――アルゼンチン(人)の Argentine

アルちゅう アル中 (中毒患者) alcoholic ⓒ; (中毒症) alcoholism ⓤ

アルツハイマーびょう アルツハイマー病〔医学〕Alzheimer's disease ⓒ (◆老年期に発生する痴呆(ちほう)症)

アルト〔音楽〕 alto ⓤⓒ (複 ～s)

アルバイト ⚠ (非常勤の仕事) part-time job ⓒ; (非常勤労働者) part-time worker ⓒ, part-timer ⓒ (◆日本語はドイツ語の Arbeit から); アルバイトをする work part-time, do* a part-time job

⇒ 場面・状況別会話 p.1688

私はコンビニでアルバイトをしている I *work part-time* at a convenience store. / 本屋のアルバイトを探している I'm looking for *a part-time job* at a bookstore. / 彼女はアルバイトをしながら歌手になる勉強をしている She *works part-time* while training to be a singer. / きょうアルバイトの面接に行ってきた I went to an interview for *a part-time job* today. ◆彼はアルバイトで子供たちに英語を教えている He teaches English to children *on the side*.

‖アルバイト学生 a working student

アルパカ〔動物〕alpaca ⓒ (◆「アルパカの毛織物」の意味では ⓤ)

アルバム album ⓒ この写真を全部アルバムにはりたいんだけれど，手伝ってくれない？ I want to stick all these photos in *my album*. Can you help me? / 彼は，私の好きなロックバンドが今新しいアルバムに取りかかっていることを教えてくれた He told me that my favorite rock band was now at work on *a new album*.

‖卒業記念アルバム《米》a yearbook

アルピニスト (登山家) alpinist ⓒ, mountaineer ⓒ

アルファ alpha ⓒ (◆ギリシャ文字の第1字)

‖アルファ星 an alpha star / アルファ線 alpha rays / アルファ波 alpha wave(s)

アルファベット alphabet ⓒ ロシア語のアルファベットはわかりません I don't know *the Russian alphabet*. ◆ここの本をタイトルのアルファベット順に並べなさい Put these books *in alphabetical order* by title.

アルプス the Alps 《複数扱い》 ――アルプスの Alpine ‖日本アルプス *the Japan Alps*

あるべき それが家族のあるべき姿だ That's *the way* a family *should be*.

アルペン ――アルペンの alpine [ǽlpaɪn] ‖アルペンスキー *alpine* skiing

アルペンきょうぎ アルペン競技 alpine events (◆それぞれの種目は an alpine event)

関連語 女子回転 women's slalom / 男子大回転 men's giant slalom / スーパー大回転 super giant slalom / 滑降 downhill / 複合 combined

あるまじき 君の態度は紳士としてあるまじき態度だ Your behavior is *inappropriate for* a gentleman.

アルマジロ〔動物〕armadillo ⓒ (複 ～s)

アルミ ‖アルミ合金 an aluminum alloy / アルミサッシ an aluminum sash / アルミ箔(はく)[ホイル] aluminum foil, tinfoil

アルミニウム〔化学〕《米》aluminum ⓤ, 《英》aluminium ⓒ (◆元素記号 Al)

あれ¹

(あの物・あの人・あのこと) that (複 those) (◆日本語の「あれ」は，話し手からも聞き手からも遠く離れた物・人・事を指すが，英語の that は聞き手に近いものにも指す); (あのこと) then

あれを見てごらん Look at *that*. / あれよりこれのほうがいい I like this (one) better than *that*. / あれは30年前のことだった *That* was 30 years ago.

健にはあれ以来一度も会っていない I haven't seen Ken at all *since then*.

あれからどうなったのですか What happened *after that*?

💬「あれは何ですか」「銭湯です」 "What's *that*?" "It's a public bath."

💬「あれはだれですか」「トムです」 "Who's *that*?" "It's Tom."

あれ² (何かに気がついて) oh; (悪いことなどを思い出して) my; (相手の注意を喚起するために) look, listen ⇒ おや²

💬「あれ, あそこにいる譲二じゃない？」「あれ, 本当だ」 "*Look*, isn't that boy over there Joji?" "*Oh*, yes, it's him."

💬「ねえ, 自転車って英語でどう言うんだっけ」「ええと…あれ, 何て言ったっけ」 "Hey, how should we say '*jitensha*' in English?" "Well …, *my*, how should we say it?"

あれから あの2人, あれから(→あの後)どこへ行ったんだろう I wonder where the two of them went *after that*. / あれから(→あのとき以来)ずっとこの街に住んでいたんですよ I've been living in this town *ever since that time*.

あれきり あれきり(→あれ以来)彼を見かけていない. He's never been seen *since*.

あれくるう 荒れ狂う あらしのせいで海は荒れ狂っていた The sea *was wild* with the storm.

あれこれ そんなにあれこれ(→たくさん)言わなくてもいいよ You don't have to say so *much*. / あれこれ(→すべてのことを)考えたんだけど, やっぱりきょうは行くことにするよ *All things considered*, I've decided to go today.

あれしょう 荒れ性 (肌が乾燥しやすい人) a person who suffers from dry skin

あれた 荒れた (天候・海などが) wild; (場所が) rough; (手・皮膚がひび割れた) chapped ⇒ あれる

あれだけ 彼はあれだけ勉強してきたんだから試験に合格するはずだ He ought to pass the exam because he's been working *so hard*. / あれだけの才能がありながら, 彼はまだマイナーリーグにいる With all *that* talent, he is still in the Minor leagues.

あれち 荒れ地 (使われていない土地) wasteland ⓒⓤ, wastes; (荒野) wilderness ⓒ; (不毛の地) barren land ⓒ

あれで 彼はあれでよくプロだなんて言えたもんだね(→いったいどうしたらプロだなんて言えるのか) How on earth can he say he is a professional? (→he を強く読むことで「あの彼が」という強調の意味を表現できる)

あれの 荒れ野 wilderness ⓒ

あれはてる 荒れ果てる go* to ruin, fall* into disrepair ──荒れ果てた (すっかり台なしにされた) devastated, ruined ⇒ あれる

あれほうだい 荒れ放題 その庭は荒れ放題だった(→全く手入れがされていなかった) The garden *was totally neglected*.

あれほど あれほど言ったのに I told you *so*! / あれほどタフな男が失恋くらいで休むもんかね Such a strong guy wouldn't be absent because of a broken heart.

あれもよう 荒れ模様 きょうの東京はかなりの荒れ模様だ(→かなり天気が悪い) The weather *is fairly bad* in Tokyo today. / 会議は荒れ模様だ The meeting *seems to get stormy*.

あれやこれや あれやこれやできのうは2時まで寝られなかった *With this or that*, I didn't manage to go to bed until 2 a.m. last night.

あれよあれよ あれよあれよという間に(→驚いてただ見ている間に)彼はその本を持っていってしまった He took the book away *while we watched in blank amazement*. / (→見ている前で) He took the book away *right before our eyes*.

あれる 荒れる

❶【天候・海】be stormy; (海が) be rough

荒れた海 a rough [stormy, wild] sea

台風が近づいているのであすは(天気が)荒れるだろう It will *be stormy* tomorrow because a typhoon is approaching.

❷【肌】get* [become*] rough; (ひび・あか切れになる) chap ⓘ

荒れた肌 rough skin

私は冬になると手が荒れる My hands *get rough [chapped]* in winter.

◆荒れた唇 chapped lips

❸【生活・機嫌】

彼の生活は荒れている He is leading a *wild life*.

真由美はきょう荒れている Mayumi *is in a bad temper [mood]* today.

❹【家・土地】

その家が荒れていた The house *was dilapidated [ruined, in ruins]*.

この村の畑は荒れている(→草が生い茂っている) The fields *are overgrown* (with weeds) in this village.

❺【状態】

国会はその法案をめぐって大荒れに荒れた(→収拾がつかなくなった) The Diet *got out of control* over the bill.

アレルギー allergy [ǽlərdʒi] ⓒ ──アレルギーの allergic [ələ́rdʒik] ‖私は卵アレルギーだ I'm *allergic* to eggs.

◆父はコンピュータアレルギーだ(→大嫌いだ) My father *hates* computers.

‖アレルギー性疾患 an allergic disease / アレルギー性鼻炎 an allergic coryza / アレルギー反応 an allergic reaction

アレンジ (編曲) arrangement ⓤ (◆編曲された作品は ⓒ) ──アレンジする arrange ⓘ ‖オーケストラ用にアレンジした曲 *an* orchestral *arrangement* / この歌のアレンジはだれがやったんだい Who *arranged* this song?

アロエ 【植物】 aloe ⓒ

アロハシャツ Hawaiian [aloha] shirt ⓒ

あわ 泡 (ひと粒の泡) bubble ⓒ (通例複数形 ~s); (bubble が集まってできたもの) foam ⓤ, froth ⓤ; (ついだビールの) head ⓒ; (せっけんの) lather ⓤ (また a ~)

◆彼は口から泡を吹いて倒れた He *foamed* at the mouth and fell to the ground.

あわ

[慣用表現] 彼らは警官を見ると泡を食って(→あわてて)逃げ出した They ｢*hurried away* [*quickly ran away*]｣ at the sight of policemen. / 私のミスで計画は水の泡になってしまった(→煙になって消えた) Our plan *went up in smoke* due to his failure.

あわ² 粟 (雑穀) millet Ⓤ

あわい 淡い (色が明るい) light; (色が白っぽい) pale; (色が柔らかい) soft; (わずかな) faint ∥彼女の部屋は淡いパステル調だった Her room was decorated in *soft pastel colors*. / 彼の返事によって私のごく淡い期待も打ち砕かれた His reply dashed my *faintest* hope.
◆私はその先生に淡い恋心(→わずかな恋心)をいだいていた I felt *a touch of* affection for the teacher.

あわさる 合わさる この合板は3枚の板が合わさってできている This plywood is made of three boards *put together*.

あわせて 合わせて altogether, in total, in all ∥合わせて5,000円になります That'll be 5,000 yen *altogether*.
◆この小説は3冊合わせて1,000ページになる This novel contains 1,000 pages *in a total of* three volumes.

あわせもつ 合わせ持つ・併せ持つ だれもが長所と短所を合わせもっている Everyone *has* strengths *and* weaknesses.

あわせる¹ 合わせる・併せる

❶【1つにする】put* together; (協力する) work together; (結合する) combine ㊥; join ㊥

その選手ははかの選手全員の得点を合わせた点数より多く得点した The player scored more points than the rest of the team *put together*.
私は手を合わせて祈りました I *put* my hands *together* in prayer.
みんなで力を合わせればなんとかなるよ It will all work out somehow if we *work together*.
世界平和のため我々は力を合わせなければならない We *must work together* in the interest(s) of world peace.
2つの村を合わせて1つの町にした They *combined* [*joined*] two villages into a town.

❷【合計する】add ㊥㊥

私と弟のお金を合わせると10万円になる My money and my brother's *add up to* 100,000 yen.
◆2クラス合わせるとちょうど80人だ The *total* head count of the two classes is just 80. / みんなのお金を合わせても3,000円にしかならない We have only 3,000 yen *altogether* [*in all*].

❸【一致させる】(調整する) set* ㊥, adjust ㊥; (適応させる) adapt ㊥, fit* ㊥; (調和させる) match ㊥; (照合する) check ㊥

時計を時報に合わせる *set* a clock by a time signal / カーペットに合わせてカーテンの色を選ぶ pick out the color of a curtain to *match* the carpet

目覚まし時計を6時に合わせた I *set* my alarm clock for 6 o'clock.
生活のしかたを周囲の状況に合わせたらどうだい Why don't you *adapt* your way of life to circumstances?
私は文男の予定に合わせて試合の日を決めた I arranged the date of the game to *fit* Fumio's schedule.
さあ, 自分の答えを解答と合わせなさい Now, *check* your answers against the answer sheet.
◆カメラのピントを合わせる *focus one's* camera / 彼女は話を合わせるのがうまい She *joins conversations* smoothly. / 私は違う局にラジオを合わせた I *tuned* the radio to a different station. / 彼女はギターの伴奏に合わせて歌った She sang *to the accompaniment* of a guitar.

[慣用表現] 両親に合わせる顔がない How can I *face* my parents?

あわせる² 会わせる 彼女は入院中の友達に会わせてくれるように頼んだ She asked that she *be allowed to visit* her friend in the hospital. / 男が入ってきて店長に会わせろと言った A man came in and *demanded to see* the manager.

あわただしい 慌ただしい (大急ぎの) hasty, hurried ――あわただしく hastily, hurriedly ――あわただしさ haste Ⓤ∥彼らは5分で昼食を終えるとあわただしく出ていった They finished lunch in five minutes and left *hastily*. / 都会の生活のあわただしさに慣れすぎいなか暮らしが退屈に感じるものだ When you get used to *the haste* of urban life, you're likely to think country life dull.

あわだつ 泡立つ (ぶくぶくと) bubble ㊥; (細かな泡が) foam ㊥; (せっけんが) lather ㊥

あわだてき 泡立て器 beater Ⓒ, whisk Ⓒ ∥卵の泡立て器 *an egg beater*

あわだてる 泡立てる beat* ㊥; (ホイップする) whip ㊥

あわふためく 慌てふためく go* into a panic ⇒あわてる ∥彼らはその音にあわてふためいて逃げていった They *went into a panic* at the sound and ran away.

あわてもの 慌て者 (おっちょこちょい) scatterbrain Ⓒ; (せっかちな人) hasty person Ⓒ; (そこつ者) careless person Ⓒ

あわてる 慌てる (動転する) be upset; (混乱する) go* into a panic; (急いでする) hurry ㊥㊥, rush ㊥

彼はその事故の知らせにひどくあわてた He *was* very *upset* at the news of the accident.
あわてて結論を出すことはないよ You don't have to *rush* to a conclusion.
Y2K問題を心配した人々はあわてて食料などの生活必需品を買いだめした Worried about the Y2K computer bug, people *went into a panic* and stocked up on food and other supplies.
父が倒れたと聞いてあわてて病院に向かった I *hurried* to the hospital since I heard my father had fallen ill.

◆彼は何があってもあわてないタイプだ(→落ち着いている) He's a guy who *keeps his composure* no matter what may happen.

🖋「あした試験だって。どうしよう」「あわてるなって。君なら大丈夫」 "They say we'll have a test tomorrow. What'll we do?" "*Take it easy!* You'll get through it."

あわび 鮑 abalone ⓒ

あわや あわや橋から転落というところで彼は身を立て直した At the moment he *nearly* fell from the bridge, he recovered his balance.

あわゆき 淡雪・泡雪 light snow Ⓤ

あわよくば あわよくばひともうけできるかと思っていたが、実際は損をしただけだった I thought *if I were lucky* I could earn some money, but in fact I only lost my money.

あわれ 哀れ (同情) pity Ⓤ, compassion Ⓤ; (みじめさ) misery Ⓤ ──哀れな (かわいそうな) poor; (同情を誘う) pitiful; (みじめな) miserable ∥彼の話は聴衆の哀れを誘った His story brought *pity* to the audience. / この絵のよさが分からないとは哀れなやつめ What a *poor* fellow who can't appreciate this good painting! / 彼にはこんな哀れな姿(→みじめな状況)を見せられないよ I don't want to reveal my *miserable* situation to him.

◆難破船の乗組員たちは哀れ海のもくずと消えた *Sadly* [*Regrettably*], the crew of the wrecked ship sank to the bottom of the ocean.

あわれみ 哀れみ (同情) pity Ⓤ, compassion Ⓤ ∥そのかわいそうな犬を見て彼女の心に哀れみの情がわいた *Pity* stirred in her heart when she saw the poor dog.

◆哀れみを請う beg for *a person's sympathy* / そんな哀れみの目で見るのはよしてちょうだい Don't look at me so *pitifully*.

あわれむ 哀れむ feel* pity for ... / 自分を哀れんでいる暇があったら勉強しなさい Study rather than *feel pity for* yourself.

◆彼らは酒を飲むしか能がないなんて哀れむべきことさ How *miserable* [*sorrowful*] it is that they can do nothing but drink!

あん¹ 案 (計画) plan ⓒ; (考え) idea ⓒ; (提案) proposal ⓒ ∥君の案は今度の会議にかけてみるよ I'll submit your *plan* at the next meeting. / 何かよい案はありませんか Do you have any good *ideas*? / 先方がきのうこんな案を出してくれたんですが、どうでしょう They made this *proposal* yesterday. What do you think of it?

[慣用表現] 案に相違して(→予想に反して)彼らはその問題をすんなりと解いてしまった *Contrary to all expectations*, they easily solved the problem.

あん² 餡 (sweet) bean paste Ⓤ ∥あんパン a bun with a red-bean-paste filling

あんい 安易 ──安易な easy ──安易に easily; (軽く) lightly ∥安易な解決策 an *easy* solution / 私は事態を安易に考えすぎていたようだ I think I took the matters too *lightly*.

あんうん 暗雲 (黒い雲) dark clouds ◆日本の不況が世界経済に暗雲を投げかけた The recession in Japan *cast a cloud over* the world economy.

あんか 行火 foot warmer ⓒ ∥電気あんか an electric *foot warmer*

アンカー (リレーなどの) anchor ⓒ, anchor runner [swimmer] ⓒ

アンカーマン (ニュースキャスター) anchorperson ⓒ; (男性の) anchorman ⓒ; (女性の) anchorwoman ⓒ

あんがい 案外 (思いがけなく) unexpectedly; (驚いたことに) surprisingly ∥彼は大男だと聞いていたのに案外(→予想外に)小さくてびっくりした As I was told he was a big guy, I was surprised to find him *unexpectedly* small. / 彼は案外(→君が思っているより)若いんだよ He is younger *than you may think*. / 彼女は園芸家として有名だが、登山の趣味があるということは案外(→あまり)知られていない She's famous as a gardener, but it is *less* known that she also likes climbing.

アンカラ Ankara (❖トルコの首都)

アンカレッジ Anchorage (❖米国の都市)

あんき 暗記 memorization Ⓤ ──暗記する learn* [know*] ... by heart (❖暗記して覚えているというときは know を用いる)、memorize ⓘ ∥彼は友達全員の電話番号を暗記している He *knows* all his friends' telephone numbers *by heart*. / 英語は暗記物だというのは(→暗記で英語をマスターできるというのは)、部分的には正しいかもしれない It may be partially true that you can master English by *memorizing* it.

◆彼女は公式を丸暗記した She *learned* the formulas *by rote*. / 僕は暗記は苦手だ(→記憶力が悪い) I have *a bad memory*.

あんぎゃ 行脚 (巡礼の旅) pilgrimage ⓒ

◆彼は遺跡を訪ねて全国を行脚した He *went on a nationwide tour* visiting ruins.

アングラ ⚠ (地下の・前衛的な) underground (❖名詞の前で用いる)

あんぐり 彼女は私の姿を見てあんぐりと口をあけた *Her jaw dropped* when she saw me.

アングル (カメラの角度) angle ⓒ ∥彼のカメラアングルはよい(→よい角度から写真を撮る) He takes pictures from good *angles*.

アングロサクソン アングロサクソン人 Anglo-Saxon ⓒ ──アングロサクソン(人)の Anglo-Saxon

アンケート (質問状) questionnaire ⓒ; (質問) question ⓒ; (調査) survey ⓒ (❖日本語はフランス語の enquête から) ∥お帰りの際にはアンケートにご記入ください Please fill out *the questionnaire* when you leave. / (電話などで)アンケートにご協力いただけませんか Would you mind if I asked you a few *questions*? / この件について街頭でアンケートをとってみました We carried out *a survey* of this matter on the streets.

あんけん 案件 (項目) item ⓒ; (問題) matter ⓒ; (訴訟) case ⓒ

あんこ 餡こ ⇒あん(餡)

あ

あんごう 暗号 cipher [C][U], code [U][C] ∥彼らは3日で暗号の解読に成功した They succeeded in deciphering *the code* in three days. ◆暗号化された電子メール an *encrypted* e-mail

アンコール encore [C] (❖フランス語から) ∥彼はアンコールにこたえて昔のヒット曲を1曲歌った He sang one of his old hits as *an encore.*

あんこく 暗黒 (暗やみ) darkness [U] ‖暗黒街 the underworld / 暗黒時代(特にヨーロッパ中世の) the Dark Ages

アンゴラ (毛・毛織物) angora [U] ‖アンゴラウサギ an angora (rabbit)

あんさつ 暗殺 assassination [U][C] ━暗殺する assassinate [他], hit* [他] ∥ケネディ暗殺事件 *the assassination* of Kennedy / 彼は何者かによって暗殺された He *was assassinated* by someone.
‖暗殺者 an assassin, a hit man

あんざん¹ 安産 easy delivery [C] ∥安産だといいね I hope you*'ll have an easy delivery.*

あんざん² 暗算 mental arithmetic [calculation] [U] ━暗算する do* mental arithmetic ◆私はおつりを暗算した I *added up* the change *in my mind.*

アンサンブル ensemble [ɑːnsáːmbl] [C] (❖フランス語から)

あんじ 暗示 suggestion [U][C], hint [C] ━暗示する suggest [他], hint [他] ∥彼は暗示にかかりやすい He's easily influenced by *suggestion.*/ He's very suggestible.
‖自己暗示〘心理〙autosuggestion

あんしつ 暗室 (写真現像用の) darkroom [C]

あんじゅう 安住 彼女はようやく安住の地(→平和に暮らせる場所)を見つけた She finally found *the place where she could live peacefully.*

あんしょう¹ 暗唱 recitation [U][C] ━暗唱する recite [他] ∥彼は芭蕉の句をいくつか暗唱した He *recited* some of the haiku of Basho.

あんしょう² 暗礁 (underwater) reef [C], (underwater) rocks; (計画などの行き詰まり) deadlock [C][U] ∥船が暗礁に乗り上げた The ship ran into *an underwater reef.* / 計画は暗礁に乗り上げた The plan ended in (*a*) *deadlock.*

あんしょうばんごう 暗証番号 (キャッシュカードの) personal identification number [C] (《略語》PIN)

あんじる 案じる (心配する) worry [自]; (考え出す) think* out ∥彼の身を案じていたところに入院の知らせが入った I *was worrying about* him when I heard the news that he entered the hospital. / 事態を改善させるために一計を案じた I *thought out* a plan to improve the situation.

あんしん 安心

relief [U]《また a ～》; (信頼感) confidence [U]; (心の安らぎ) peace of mind ━安心する be relieved; (気が楽になる) feel* at ease

彼なら絶対安心だ(→彼には全幅の信頼を寄せている) I *have every confidence in* him.

私は彼が無事に帰ってきたのを見て安心した I *was relieved* to see him come back safe and sound.

家に帰ってきたら何だか安心した Somehow I *felt at ease* when I got home.

◆たまには電話でもしてお母さんを安心させて(→無事を知らせて)あげなさい You should call your mother once in a while so that she knows you're okay. / だれも君の分は取らないから安心して(→心配しないで)食べなさい *Don't worry*, nobody will take your food. Go ahead and eat. / お嬢さんの面倒はちゃんとみますからご安心ください *Rest assured that* we'll take good care of your daughter. / ここなら坊やの手も届かないから安心(→安全)です This place should *be safe* as your boy can't reach it. / 彼らは安心して(→平和に)暮らせる町作りに励んだ They worked hard to improve the conditions in the town so that they would be able to *live in peace.*
‖安心感 a sense of security

あんず 杏 apricot [C]

あんずる 案ずる ⇨あんじる
[ことわざ] 案ずるより産むがやすし It is often easier to do something than to worry about it.(→物事は心配するより実際にやってみるほうが簡単なことがよくある)

あんせい 安静 (休養) rest [U][C] ∥私は絶対安静を命じられた I was ordered to take *a complete rest.* ◆しばらく安静にしていればすぐによくなりますよ If you *rest quietly* for a while, you'll get better soon.

あんぜん 安全

safety [U]; security [U] (❖security は主に「危害から守られている状態」を指す) ━安全な safe; secure ━安全に safely; securely

身の安全を保証する assure [guarantee] *a person's safety* / 安全策をとる play (it) *safe*

大切な書類は安全な場所にしまっておきなさい Keep important documents in a *safe* place.

消防士が人々をより安全な所へ導いた The fire fighters led the people to a *safer* place.

安全のためヘルメットをかぶってください Please wear helmets *for your safety.*

彼の財産は銀行に安全に保管されている His fortune is kept *safely* in the bank.

ここなら安全だろう We'll be *safe* here.

この水は飲んでも安全です This water is *safe* for drinking.

その都市は洪水があっても安全だと思われていた The city was believed to be *secure* in case of a flood.

彼らは計画の安全性を我々に保証した They assured us of *the safety* of their plan.

それは国家の安全保障にかかわる問題だ That's an issue of *national security.*

‖安全運転 safe driving(❖×safety driving とはいわない); 《掲示》Drive Safely / 安全かみそり a safety razor / 安全ガラス safety glass / 安全装置 a safety device; (機械・銃などの) a safety (catch) / 安全第一《掲示》Safety First / 安全地帯 (歩行者のための) a traffic island, a safety island [zone] / 安全ピン a safety pin / 安全ベルト a safety belt, a seat belt / 安全弁 a safety valve / 安全保障条約 a security treaty [pact] / (国連)安全保障理事会 the (U.N.) Security Council / 家内安全 household safety / 交通安全 traffic [road] safety / 交通安全週間 a Traffic Safety Week, 《英》a Road Safety Week

あんそくび 安息日 the Sabbath(❖ユダヤ教・キリスト教などで労働や活動を禁じた曜日)

あんだ 安打 【野球】hit ◎ ∥ 内野安打を打つ get *an infield hit* / 彼はきのうのゲームで7安打を許した He allowed seven *hits* yesterday. ◆僕はきょう4打数3安打だった I *hit* [*went*] *three-for-four* today.

アンダー 彼は第1ラウンドを5アンダーで終えた He finished the first round at five *under par*.

アンダーウエア（下着類）《集合的》underwear ⓤ

アンダーシャツ《米》undershirt ⓒ,《英》vest ⓒ

アンダースロー ⚠【野球】submarine ⓒ;【ソフトボール】underhand throw ⓒ(❖×under throw とはいわない) ◆アンダースローのピッチャー a *submarine* pitcher; a submariner

アンダーライン underline ⓒ ∥ 重要な単語にはアンダーラインが引いてある Important words *are underlined*.

あんたい 安泰 今回の成功で彼の社内での地位も安泰だろう(→成功が地位を確かなものにするだろう) This success would make his position in the company *secure*.

あんたん 暗澹 日本の将来を思うと暗澹たる気持ちになる I *get deeply depressed* when I think about the future of Japan.

アンダンテ 【音楽】andante ⓒ(❖イタリア語から)

あんち 安置 霊安室に遺体を安置する *place* a (dead) body in the mortuary

アンチ- anti- ◆うちの父さんはアンチ巨人だ My father *loves to hate* the Giants. / My father *roots against* the Giants.
∥ アンチテーゼ an antithesis

あんちゅうもさく 暗中模索 私はまだ暗中模索の状態だ(→どうすればよいかはよく分からないが, すべきことを探しているところだ) I'm still *trying to find what to do, though I don't know exactly how I can find it.*

あんちょく 安直 ─安直な (いいかげんな) sloppy, (楽な) easy, (安い) cheap ∥ その政治家の安直な答弁に支持者は失望した The politician's supporters were dismayed by his *sloppy* answers.

あんちょこ crib notes

アンチョビー 【魚】anchovy ⓒ

アンツーカー アンツーカーのトラック an *En-Tout-Cas* [*all-weather*] track(❖En-Tout-Cas は商標名. all-weather は「全天候用の」の意味)

あんてい 安定
stability ⓤ; steadiness ⓤ ─安定した stable; steady
| stable: しばしば変わりやすかったものが, 今は落ち着いて安定している.
| steady: 急に変化したりせずずっと安定している.

彼らは財政改革のためには政治的な安定が必要だと訴えた They claimed that *political stability* was essential to financial reform.
彼は安定した仕事を見つけたいと思っていた He wanted to find himself a *steady* job.
患者の容態は今は安定している The patient's condition *is stable* now.
ダイヤモンドが硬いのは結晶構造が安定していて結合力が強いためである Diamonds are hard because of their *stable* crystal structure and strong bonds.
その仕事についてから, 彼の生活は安定した His livelihood *became stable* after he got the job.
◆政府は物価を安定させるための手段を探している The government is seeking the way to *stabilize* prices. / このところ天気が安定している The weather *has settled* recently.
∥ 安定感 a sense of stability / 安定剤 【化学】a stabilizer / 安定多数 a stable majority / 精神安定剤 a tranquilizer

アンティーク (骨董(こっとう)品) antique ⓒ

アンテナ《米》antenna ⓒ,《英》aerial ⓒ ∥ 室内アンテナ *an indoor antenna* / アンテナを設置する install *an antenna*

あんてん 暗転 (ステージの) blackout ⓒ
◆事態が暗転した(→悪くなった) The situation *got worse*.

あんど 安堵 relief ⓤ(《また a ～》) ∥ 彼はほっと安堵の息をついた He breathed *a sigh of relief*.

あんな 何であんな態度をとったんだ What was the reason for *such* an attitude? / あんな騒音が音楽といわれているなんて信じられないよ I can't believe (that) *that* noise is called music! / あんな場所に行っちゃいけません You shouldn't go to *that kind of* place. / あんなやつ(→彼のような男)を信用したのが間違いだったよ I made a mistake in trusting *a man like him*.

あんない 案内

❶【場所・道など】guidance ⓤ; (案内する人) guide ⓒ, conductor ⓒ ─案内する guide ⓥ; lead* ⓥ; show* ⓥ; usher ⓥ
| guide: 旅行者などに対し説明を加えたりしながら案内する.
| lead: 先に立って導く.
| show: 部屋・席などへ連れて行き, そこにとどまらせる. around を伴う場合は「案内して回る」の意味.
| usher: 仕事として人を座席などへ連れていく.

この町には不慣れなので案内が必要だ We are strangers in this town, and so we need

あんない

a guide.
彼女が私たちを彼の部屋に案内してくれた She led [*showed, ushered*] us to his room. / She *showed* us the way to his room.
私が街をご案内しましょう I'll show you *around* the city.
彼を中にご案内(→お通し)してください *Show* him *in*, please.
彼女は私たちをバッキンガム宮殿に案内してくれた She *showed* us Buckingham Palace.
◆ガイドが美術館を案内してくれた The guide *conducted* us *around* the museum. / そのドキュメンタリー番組の案内役をダン・ラザーが務めた The documentary was introduced by Dan Rather.

❷【知らせ】information ⓤ, notice ⓒⓤ ──案内する inform ⓗ, notify ⓗ
新規開店したレストランの案内を受けた I got *information about* [*notice of*] their newly opened restaurant. / They *informed* [*notified*] me *of* their newly opened restaurant.

◆ご案内申し上げます *Attention, please!* / *May I have your attention, please?* ✤場内放送などの最初の言葉

❸【招待】invitation ⓤ; (案内状) invitation (card) ⓒ ──案内する invite ⓗ
開店記念パーティーへご案内申し上げます *You are cordially invited to* the party to celebrate the opening of our new shop.

‖案内係 an information desk clerk; (公共施設などの) an attendant; (劇場などの) an usher / 案内広告(新聞・雑誌上の) a classified ad / 案内書 a guide, a guidebook, a handbook / 案内所 an information desk, an information office (✤掲示ではしばしば information) / 案内状 an invitation (card) / 案内図 a (guide) map

あんなに 彼女はなぜあんなに早く帰ってしまったのだろう I wonder why she left *so* early. / 彼があんなに強情だとは思ってもみなかった I've never imagined that he could be *that* obstinate. / あんなに食べたんだからおなかをこわしたって当然よ *With all the dishes you have eaten*, it serves you right if you have an upset stomach.

あんに 暗に 彼は暗に金をよこせと言った He *indirectly* demanded my money. / 彼は私の提案を暗に彼を批判しているものと受け止めたようだった He seemed to interpret my suggestion as an *implicit* criticism of him.

あんのじょう 案の定(予想どおり)《米口語的》sure enough, as (might have been) expected [feared] (✤feared は「恐れていたとおりの意味で用いる」) / 彼は怠けていたので, 案の定試験に落ちた He had been lazy, and *sure enough* he failed the examination.

あんば 鞍馬(体操用具)《米》side horse ⓒ, 《英》pommel horse ⓒ; (競技)《米》the side horse, 《英》the pommel horse

あんばい 塩梅 テストのあんばいはどうだい *How* is your exam? / いいあんばいに(→幸運にも)雨が降ってきた *Luckily* it started to rain.

アンパイア (野球などの審判) umpire ⓒ

アンバランス ⚠ imbalance ⓒⓤ (✤英語の unbalance は「動揺させる」の意味の動詞として使われることが多い) ──アンバランスな imbalanced, unbalanced

あんぴ 安否 (無事であること) safety ⓤ / 彼は息子の安否を心配している He's worrying about his son's *safety*.

アンプ (増幅器) amplifier ⓒ, 《口語的》amp ⓒ

あんぷ 暗譜 モーツァルトを暗譜で演奏する play Mozart *from memory*

アンペア 〔電気〕ampere ⓒ, 《口語的》amp ⓒ (✤電流の強さの単位; 《略語》A, a) / この機械には5アンペアのヒューズが必要だ This machine needs a five-*amp* fuse.
‖アンペア数〔電気〕(an) amperage

あんぽじょうやく 安保条約(安全保障条約) security treaty [pact] ⓒ / 日米安保条約 the U.S.-Japan [Japan-U.S.] *Security Treaty* (✤米国ではふつう U.S.-Japan のように U.S.を先にいう)

あんま 按摩(行為) massage ⓤ; (男性のあんま師) masseur [mæsə́ːr] ⓒ; (女性のあんま師) masseuse [mæsúːz] ⓒ

あんまく 暗幕 blackout curtain ⓒ

あんまり 私を置いていくなんてあんまりだ It's *too much* for you to leave me behind. / あんまりむちゃをするんじゃないよ Don't be *so* reckless. ⇨あまり¹

あんみん 安眠 sound sleep ⓒ / 安眠を妨げる disturb *a person's sound sleep*
◆ゆうべは安眠できなかった I couldn't sleep *soundly* last night.

あんもく 暗黙 ──暗黙の(無言の) tacit, unspoken ‖暗黙の同意 a *tacit* agreement / 彼らの間には暗黙の了解があったようだ They seemed to share *an unspoken understanding*.

アンモナイト ammonite ⓒ ‖アンモナイトの化石 a fossilized *ammonite*

アンモニア 〔化学〕ammonia ⓤ

あんやく 暗躍 禁酒法の時代にはマフィアが暗躍した(→舞台裏で活躍した) The Mafia *was active behind the scenes* in the Prohibition era.

あんゆ 暗喩 〔修辞〕metaphor ⓒⓤ

あんよ (足) tootsies

あんらく 安楽 comfort ⓤ, easiness ⓤ ──安楽な comfortable, easy ‖安楽な生活を送る lead an *easy* life
‖安楽いす an easy chair / 安楽死 euthanasia, (a) mercy killing

い

イ 〘音楽〙A ‖ *イ長調[短調]* で in (the key of) *A* major [minor]

い¹ 胃 stomach ―胃の gastric (※名詞の前で用いる) ‖ *丈夫な胃* an iron *stomach* / (食べ物が)胃にもたれる sit heavy in *a person's stomach* / 胃の検査を受ける have one's *stomach* examined / 胃が痛い My *stomach* hurts. / I have *a stomachache*. / 最近どうも胃の調子が悪い I've been suffering from *stomach* trouble(s) lately. / この薬は胃にやさしい This medicine is gentle on your *stomach*. / チョコレートの食べすぎで胃がおかしくなった Too much chocolate upset *my stomach*. ◆胃にもたれる食事 a *heavy* meal ⇒いえき, いえん (胃炎), いかいよう, いカメラ, いがん, いけいれん, いつう

い² 意 (意味) meaning, sense; (意志) will, intention
慣用表現 彼は人に何を言われようが意に介さない (→気にしない) He *doesn't care* what other people say about him. / 彼女の意にかなう服はその店にはなかった(→どの服も彼女は気に入らなかった) She didn't *like* any of the dresses at that store. / その新しいプロジェクトは社長の意に添うものではなかった The new project didn't *comply with* the president's wishes. / 親のコネで就職するのは彼の意に反している(→親のコネで就職したくない) He *doesn't want* to get a job through his parents' connections. / その結果は意に満たないものだった The result was *unsatisfactory*. / 人を自分の意のままに動かす *twist* a person *around one's little finger*; *have* a person *wrapped around one's little finger* / 妹はいつも意のままに(→好きなように)ふるまう My sister always behaves just *as she pleases [likes]*. / 母は私の意をくんで(→私の気持ちを考慮して)その話には触れなかった My mother didn't mention it *out of consideration for my feelings*. / 彼女は意を決して立ち上がった She *made up her mind* and stood up. / 彼は味方がたくさんいると知って意を強くした(→勇気づけられた) He *was encouraged* to learn that many people were on his side. / 彼は彼らの援助に深く感謝の意を表した He *showed* deep *appreciation* for their help.

い³ 井 (井戸) well
慣用表現 確かに彼はこの町では有名だが, 井の中の蛙(かわず)にすぎない Certainly he is a big name in this town, but he's *just a big fish in a small pond*.

い⁴ 異 (異議) objection ‖ 異を差しはさむ raise *an objection* ◆私の意見に異を唱える者は彼以外にはいなかった Nobody *objected to* my opinion except (for) him.

い⁵ 亥 (十二支の第12番目) the (Wild) Boar ⇒えと

い⁶ 医 (医学) medicine

-い -位 (順位) place; (位階) rank (※共に省略することが多い) ‖ 第1 [第2]位に in first [second] *place* / 小数第2位 the second decimal *place* ◆1位になる win (*the*) *first prize* / 2位に終わる come off *second-best* (※「優勝を逃す, 負ける」の意味) ◆あのボクシング選手は現在世界1位にランクされている That boxer is currently ranked *first* in the world.

いあつ 威圧 (公式的)coercion ―威圧する (公式的)coerce (※しばしば受身で); (おどしつける) overawe (※通例受身で) ―威圧的な (公式的)coercive; (いばり散らす) domineering; (尊大な) imperious ‖ 人に対して威圧的な態度をとる take a *coercive* attitude toward a person / 彼女は厳粛な雰囲気に威圧されているようだった She seemed *overawed* by the solemn atmosphere.

いあわせる 居合わせる ‖ 私はたまたまそこに居合わせた I *happened to be* there. / 居合わせた人はみなその歌を歌った All those *present* sang the song together.

いあん 慰安 comfort, consolation, (公式的)solace ‖ 慰安婦 (集合的)comfort women, women forced into prostitution by the Japanese military during World War II / 慰安旅行 a recreational trip

いい

❶ すぐれている		good, nice, fine
❷ (道徳的に)正しい		right, good
❸ 適当だ		good, right
❹ 好ましい		good
❺ 十分だ		enough

❶ 【すぐれている】 good (↔bad), nice, fine
いいカメラを持っていますね You have a *good* camera.
吉田先生はいい先生だ Mr. Yoshida is a *good* teacher.
いいことを思いついたぞ I've got a *good* idea.
他人のいいところを見るように努めなさい Try to find *good* points in others.
数学の試験でいい点を取った I got a *good* grade on the math test.
あなたは発音がとてもいいですね You've got really *good* pronunciation.
◆性能のいい車 a *high-performance* car / 彼は頭がいい He's *smart* [*clever, bright*]. (※ bright は主に子供や生徒に用いる) / 姉は学校の成績がいい My sister is doing *well* at school. / 腕のいい弁護士に相談しなさい You should consult a *competent* lawyer. / 彼女はいつも質のいい洋服を着ている She always wears *high-quality* clothes.

🅔「ぐあいはもういいの?」「おかげさんでね」 "Are you *all right* now?" "Yeah,

❷【(道徳的に)正しい】right (↔wrong), good

私はいいと思うことをしたまでだ I only did what I thought was *right*.

やっていいことと悪いことの区別もつかないのか Can't you even tell *right* from wrong?

やり方はこれでいいのかしら Am I doing it *right*?

人を傷つけないためにうそをつくのはいいことですか Is it *right* to tell a lie in order not to hurt people?

◆いい子にしてなさい(→行儀よくしなさい) *Behave* yourself. / 自分だけいい子になろうとするな Don't pretend to be *innocent*.

🍡「いいお天気になったね」「私の日ごろの行いがいいからよ」 "What a beautiful day!" "That's because I've been a *good* girl."

❸【適当だ】good, right

このかばんは小旅行にちょうどいい This bag is just the *right* size for a short trip.

この靴は私にちょうどいい(→ぴったり合う) These shoes *fit* me just *right*.

彼はちょうどいいときに現れた He appeared at just the *right* time.

息子も早くいい人を見つけて結婚してくれるといいんだけど I hope my son will find *the right woman* and get married soon.

🍡「店を手伝ってくれる人を探しているんだが」「それならいい人を知ってます」 "We are looking for someone who could work in our shop." "I know the *right* person for that job."

❹【好ましい】good, nice, fine; (快い) pleasant; (有効な) effective

何かいいことでもあったのですか Did something *good* happen?

彼女はいい友達だ She is a *good* friend of mine.

山口君はいいやつだ Yamaguchi is a *nice* guy.

いいお天気ですね It's a *nice* [*beautiful*] day, isn't it?

部屋中にラベンダーのいい香りがした The room was filled with a [the] *pleasant* smell of lavender.

歩くことは健康にいい Walking is *good* for your health.

英語を話ういい機会だからぜひ行くべきだ That's a *good* chance to speak English and you've got to go.

アトピーにいいとされる方法はすべて試してみた I've tried everything that is regarded *effective* for soothing atopic dermatitis.

だれの人生にもいいときもあれば悪いときもある There are *good* times and bad times in everybody's life.

海外赴任といえば聞こえはいいが，彼の場合は事実上の左遷(さん)だ Being transferred to a branch office overseas sounds *nice*, but in his case it's actually a demotion.

◆彼女はいちばんいい服を着て出かけた She put on her *best* clothes and went out. /

納豆は体にいい食べ物(→健康食品)だ Natto is a *health* food. / このタオルは手ざわりがいい(→柔らかい) This towel is *nice and soft* to the touch. / その歌手はいい声をしている That singer has a *beautiful* voice. / 日本では赤と白の組み合わせは縁起がいいとされている The combination of red and white is supposed to be *lucky* in Japan. / 彼女と結婚できるなんてあいつも運のいい男だ He is such a *lucky* man to marry her. / 彼女は彼をいいように利用している She always takes *advantage* of him. / 彼にはいいようにさせておけ Let him do *as he likes* [*pleases*]. / あいつのどこがいいんだ(→好きなのか) What do you *like* about him? / どうしたらいいのか分からない I don't know *what to do*.

🍡「今度新しくオープンしたお店に行ってみない?」「いいね」 "Why don't we go to the shop that just opened?" "*Sounds great*."

🍡「何か食べたい物ある」「ピザがいいな」 "Do you want to eat anything in particular?" "I'd like some pizza."

🍡「飼うなら犬と猫，どっちがいい」「犬がいいな」 "Which *would* you like to have, a dog or a cat?" "I'd like a dog."

🍡「何曜日が都合がいいですか」「木曜以外ならいつでも」 "Which day of the week would be *convenient* for you?" "Any day except Thursday."

❺【十分だ】enough; (準備のできた) ready

準備はいいかい Are you *ready*?

お説教はもういい! I've had *enough* of your lectures!

おまえはもっと分別があっていい年だ You are *old enough* to know better.

彼一人の都合で日程を変えるなんてわがままもいいとこだ We've heard *enough* of his selfish demands to change the schedule just for him.

◆これでいいですか Will this *do*? / いい年をしていまだに親の世話になっているのか Are you still financially dependent on your parents *at your age*? / そのボタンを押すだけでいい You *only have to* push that button. / トーストは1枚でいいです I'll take just one slice of toast. / 彼女はそろそろ家に着いてもいいころだ It is *about time* she got home. / その本は難しくて進むのは1日にいいとこ(→多くて)10ページだ That book is so difficult that I can only read 10 pages a day *at most*.

🍡「もういいかい」「まあだだよ」 "*Ready*?" "No, not yet!" (✿アメリカの隠れん坊では鬼が "Ready or not, here I come!" (さあ行くぞ)" と言って捜し始める)

🍡「タマネギはあとどのくらいいためるの」「そのくらいでいいよ」 "How much longer do I have to fry the onions?" "That's *enough*."

❻【不要だ】

私のコーヒーには砂糖はいいからミルクを多めに入れてください I'd like plenty of cream in my coffee, but *no* sugar.

🍡「写真代払うよ。いくらだった」「いいよ。いくら

もかかってないから」"I'll pay for the photo. How much was it?" "Oh, *don't worry*. It was nothing."

🍀「紅茶もっと飲む?」「いや,もういい」"Want some more tea?" "*No, thanks*."

🍀「卵が安いけど,買う?」「卵はいいよ.うちにまだたくさんあるから」"The eggs are cheap. Shall we buy some?" "*Better not*. We've still got plenty at home."

❼【(さしつかえない)(…してもよい) may *do*, can *do*; (…しなくてよい) do not have [need] to *do*; (かまわない) do not mind [care]; (間に合う) will do

家に帰ってもいいですか *May* I go home?

もう目をあけていいよ Now you *can* open your eyes.

話したくなければ話さなくていい You *don't have to* talk if you don't want to.

イタリアンパセリがなければふつうのパセリでいい If you can't find Italian parsley, regular (parsley) *will do*.

◆そのミーティングは出ても出なくてもいい *It doesn't matter* if you attend the meeting or not. / 自分の部屋の掃除くらいはしてもいいじゃないの? Can't you even clean your own room? / You might at least clean your own room. / ちょっといいですか(→少し時間はありますか) Have you got a minute?

🍀「本当にごめんなさい」「いいわよ」"I'm terribly sorry." "That's *all right*."

🍀「窓をあけてもいいですか」「ええ,どうぞ」"*Do you mind if I* open the window?" "No. Please go ahead." (❖Do you mind if …?は「…してもいいですか」という許可を求める表現. mind 自体は「いやがる」という意味なので,「いいですよ」は "No, not at all." "No, of course not." のように否定で答える)

🍀「あともうちょっとだよ.がんばれ」「いいから先に行って」"Come on! We're almost there!" "Oh, don't wait for me."

🍀「こんな高価な物いただけません」「いいから,いいから.とっておいて」"I can't take such an expensive thing." "Oh, please accept it."

❽【…した[する]ほうがいい】should *do*; (…すべき) had better *do* ⇒ ほう(方)

語法

had better は should よりも強制の意味が強く,時にはおどしが含まれることがある.目上の人に対してはあまり用いないほうがよい.should は「…したほうがいい」という最も一般的な表現.口語では had better の had を省略することも多い.

彼には本当のことを話したほうがいい You *should* tell him the truth.

すぐ医者に診(ミ)てもらったほうがいい You'*d better* go (and) see a doctor at once.

◆出かけるよりうちにいたほうがいい I *prefer* staying at home *to* going out. / 彼女に謝るくらいなら死んだほうがいい I *would rather* die *than* apologize to her.

❾【悪いことを反対にいう】

あんまりいい気になるなよ(→自分に自信をもちすぎるな) Don't *be* so *sure of* yourself.

こんな大きなテーブルをもらったところでいい迷惑だ It's a real *nuisance* to be given such a huge table like this.

🍀「彼女,自分は悪くないって言い張るんだよ」「いい性格してるよね」"She insists that she did nothing wrong." "What *a brazen hypocrite*!"

🍀「あいつ彼女にふられたんだぜ」「いい気味だ」"His girlfriend turned him down." "(It) *serves him right*!"

❿【その他】

君みたいないい若者がそんなことを言ってちゃだめだ (Such) *a young man* like you shouldn't say things like that.

午後には雨がやむといいのだが I *hope* it "will stop [stops] raining in the afternoon.

数学なんてこの世になければいいのに I *wish* mathematics didn't exist! (❖現在の事実に反する願望を表す場合は wish を使った仮定法過去の形を用いる)

彼女が事実上の指導者といってもいいくらいだ She *could be* called the actual leader.

彼の絵のほとんどはいい値がついていた Most of his paintings were *highly priced*.

その仕事はいい金になるだろう That business would be *highly profitable*.

彼がお人よしなのをいいことに(→利用して)彼女はいつも彼に仕事を押しつける She *takes advantage of* his passivity to foist a lot of her work (off) onto him.

そんな虫のいい話が通ると思っているのか You're asking a lot. Do you believe that's acceptable?

着いたらうちに電話するのよ.いい? Call home when you get there. *OK*?

いいかい,このことはみんなにはないしょだよ *Listen*, this is just between us.

いいぞ!その調子だ Way to go!/ Go for it! (❖Go for itは何かをやっている途中で励ますのに用いる.成しとげた場合は Way to go!を用いる)

🍀「宝くじで1万円当たっちゃった」「いいなあ」"I won 10,000 yen in the lottery." "*Lucky you*!"

⇒ よい(良い)

いいあい 言い合い (口論) quarrel Ⓒ, argument Ⓒ /私はささいなことでよく姉と言い合いをする I often have *quarrels* with my sister over trivial matters.

いいあう 言い合う (口論する) quarrel Ⓘ, argue Ⓘ /弟たちはどの番組を見るかで言い合っていた My brothers *were quarreling with each other* over which program to watch. ◆彼らは冗談を言い合った They *told each other* jokes. / 私たちはその映画について感想を言い合った We *exchanged* our opinions about [《口語的》*compared notes* on] the movie.

いいあてる 言い当てる (正しく推測する) guess Ⓘ Ⓒ, guess … right /彼女は私の年齢を言い当てた She *guessed* my age *right*.

いいあやまる 言い誤る 彼はその歌手がドイツ人だと言ったが、それは単に言い誤っただけだ He said the singer was a German, but that was just *a slip of the tongue*.

いいあらそい 言い争い、argument ⓒ, quarrel ⓒ; (つまらないことで) squabble ⓒ
◆お願いだから言い争いはやめて Stop *arguing*, for goodness sake! / 彼らはいつも言い争いをしている They *are* always *quarrelling with* each other.

いいあらそう 言い争う argue ⓘ, quarrel ⓘ, have* an argument [a quarrel] //彼は勘定のことでウェーターと言い争った He *argued with* the waiter about the bill. / 健二は父親と自分の将来のことについて言い争った Kenji *had a quarrel with* his father about his future. ◆あなたと奥さんがいつも言い争っていたというのは本当ですか Is it true that you and your wife *were* always *fighting*?

いいあらわす 言い表す (表現する) express ⓘ; (言葉にする) put* ... into words //私がどれほどあなたに感謝しているか言葉では言い表せません Words can't *express* how grateful I am to you. ◆彼女の美しさは言葉では言い表せない Her beauty *is beyond description*.

いいえ

❶【返答】no; (否定の問いに対して) yes

【語法】
日本語では、問いの文そのものに対して「いいえ」という返事をするのに対し、英語では問いの文にかかわらず、答える内容が肯定であればyes,否定であればnoを用いる。例えば「犬を好きではないですか」という問いに対し「(いいえ)好きです」と答えたい場合、答える内容は「好きだ」という肯定文なので英語ではyesという.

「はい」か「いいえ」で答えてください Please answer yes or *no*.

🍒「コーヒーをもう少しいかがですか」「いいえ,結構です」 "Would you like some more coffee?" "*No*, thank you."

🍒「田中さんはご在宅ですか」「いいえ、今、外出中です」 "Is Mr. Tanaka at home?" "*No*, he is out now."

🍒「スポーツは好きですか」「いいえ、特に好きというほどではありません」 "Do you like sports?" "*Not* especially."

🍒「すぐやらなければいけませんか」「いいえ,その必要はありません」 "Must I do it now?" "*No*, you don't have to."

🍒「たばこはお吸いになりますか」「いいえ、吸いません」 "Do you smoke?" "*No*, I don't."

🍒「こちらの方向に回すんですか」「いいえ、その逆です」 "Do you turn it this way?" "*No*, it's the other way round."

🍒「和食が好きではないのですか」「いいえ、そんなことはありませんよ」 "Don't you like Japanese food?" "*Yes*, I like it."

🍒「きのう送ったメールはそちらに届いていませんね」「いいえ、届きましたよ」 "You haven't received the e-mail I sent yesterday, have you?" "*Yes*, I have."

❷【反論】no; (否定文に対して) yes

🍒「ニューヨークは物価が高そうだな」「いいえ、そうでもないですよ」 "Living costs must be very high in New York." "*No*, not really."

🍒「英語はあまり得意じゃないんです」「いいえ、そんなことはありませんよ」 "I'm not good at English." "*Yes*, you are!"

🍒「お母さん、洋子が私の傘をどこかに忘れてきたのよ」「いいえ、私はちゃんと持って帰ったってば」 "Mom, Yoko left my umbrella somewhere." "*I didn't*! I brought it back with me, I swear!"

❸【感謝・謝罪に対する返答】

🍒「いろいろお世話になりました」「いいえ、どういたしまして」 "Thank you very much for your help." "You're welcome. / Not at all."

🍒「お手間をとらせて申しわけありません」「いいえ、どういたしまして」 "I'm sorry I'm causing [to cause] you trouble." "Oh, don't worry."

🍒「あっ、ごめんなさい」「いいえ、大丈夫ですよ」 "Oh, excuse me." "That's OK [all right]."

🍒「何もおかまいできませんで」「いいえ、こちらこそ急におじゃましまして」 "I'm sorry I wasn't a better host [hostess]." "Well, I dropped in on you unannounced."

いいかえす 言い返す (口答えをする) talk [answer] back; (反論する) retort ⓘ ⓘ //彼は自分は無実だと言い返した "I'm innocent," he *retorted*. / He *retorted that* he was innocent.

いいかえる 言い換える (ほかの言葉で言う) say* [put*] (...) in other words, say [put] (...) in another way; (分かりやすく言い直す) paraphrase ⓘ ⓘ, reword ⓘ, translate ⓘ ⓘ //専門語を平易な言葉に言い換える *translate* technical terms into simple language
◆言い換えれば全員にその責任があるということだ *In other words* everyone is responsible for that.

いいがかり 言い掛かり 私がそのかぎをなくしたなんて言いがかりだ(→誤って非難している) You *are falsely accusing* me of having lost the key. / その男は私がわざとぶつかったと言いがかりをつけてきた(→けんかを吹っ掛けようとした) The man *tried to pick a fight*, saying I intentionally bumped into him.

いいかける 言い掛ける 今、何を言いかけていたんですか What *were* you *going to say*? / 彼女は何かを言いかけたが最後まで言わなかった She *began to say* something, but didn't finish it.

いいかげん いい加減

❶【適度】
ぬるすぎず熱すぎずちょうどいいいいかげんのふろだ The bath water is neither tepid nor too hot, but *just about the right temperature*.

❷【大ざっぱ・無責任】—— いいかげんな (無責

任な) irresponsible; (信用できない) unreliable; (疑わしい) dubious, 《口語的》fishy; (あいまいな) vague, noncommittal; (いいかげんな) half-hearted; (おざなりな) casual (❖名詞の前で用いる); (雑な) sloppy, slipshod
——いいかげんに (適当に) any old how, 《口語的》anyhow; (真剣でなく) half-heartedly; (雑に) sloppily

彼女は私の質問に対していいかげんな返事しかしなかった She only gave a *vague* [*noncommittal*] answer to my question.

あんないいかげんな人にはこの仕事を任せられない We can't leave this job to such an *irresponsible* person.

僕はその講演をいいかげんにしか聞いていなかった I was only listening to the lecture *half-heartedly*.

◆いいかげんな (→でたらめな) 話 a *fish* story (❖a fishy story は「人を欺く話」の意味) / そういうことをいいかげんにやってはいけません You shouldn't *play at* things like that. / その問題はいいかげんに扱っていいものではない That issue is not something to *be trifled with*.

❸ (だいぶ・かなり) pretty, quite

いいかげん疲れちゃったよ、休まない？ I'm *pretty* tired. Why don't we have a break?

子供たちはこのゲームにもいいかげん飽きていた The children were *quite* bored with the game.

◆彼のぐちを聞かされるのはいいかげんうんざりだ I'm *sick and tired of* [*fed up with*] hearing his complaints.

❹ (そのくらい・ほどほど)

「冗談もいいかげんにしろ」と彼は叫んだ "*Stop joking!*" he shouted.

いいかげんにしろ！ (→もう十分だ) *That's enough!*; *Enough is enough!*; *That will do!* / (→その話はやめろ) *Knock it off!*; *Give me a break!*

いいかた　言い方　one's way [manner] of speaking, how to speak [say]; (表現) expression ⓒ / あいまいな言い方 loose *expressions* / おまえはものの言い方を知らない You don't know how to *speak* properly. ◆漠然とした言い方をする *speak* in general terms / 彼の言い方は気に入らないが彼の意見はもっともだと思う I agree with him even though I don't like the *way he said* it. / ものの言い方に気をつけなさい Watch your *words*. / 父親に向かってその言い方は何だ How dare you *speak* to your father that way?

いいかねる　言い兼ねる　彼がそんなひどいことを言ったの？ あの人なら言いかねないね Did he say that? That's just the sort of awful thing he *would say*. / その問題については何とも言いかねる I *cannot comment on* that problem.

いいかわす　言い交わす　(語り合う) have* a talk (with ...); (約束をする) promise ⓘ ⓣ; (結婚の約束をする) get* engaged / 彼らは言い交わした仲だ (→婚約している) They *are engaged*.

いいき　いい気　代表選手に選ばれたからといっていい気になるな (→うぬぼれるな) Don't *be conceited* just because you made the team. (❖make the team は「代表選手に選ばれる」の意味) / 仕事を人に押しつけて旅行に行くなんて彼女もいい気なもんだ (→彼女は旅行に行くとき人の気持ちも考えず仕事を私に押しつけた) She *thoughtlessly* left her work with me when she went on vacation. / あなたが無断で車を使ったことを聞いたらお父さんはきっといい気はしないよ Your father *won't be too pleased* to hear that you used his car without permission.

いいきかせる　言い聞かせる　自分のせいじゃないと彼は自分に言い聞かせた He *told* himself (that) it wasn't his fault. / 兄はあいつには近づくなと僕に言い聞かせた My brother tried to *persuade* me *to* stay away from him.

いいきみ　いい気味　いい気味だ (→当然の報いだ) (It) *serves you right!* (❖第三者に対していう場合は you を him, her などに変える)

🅔「あいつ、彼女にふられたんだって」「いい気味だ (→ふられて当然だ)」 "I hear his girlfriend left him." "He *deserves* it."

いいきる　言い切る　(きっぱりと言う) declare ⓘ, assert ⓘ / 美恵はピカソを超える画家はいないと言い切った Mie *declared that* Picasso was the best artist ever. / 彼はそこにいたと思うが、絶対にそうだとは言い切れない I think he was there, but I *can't swear to* it.

いいぐさ　言い種・言い草　世話になった人に対してなんて言いぐさなんだ What *a thing to say* to someone who has done so much for you! / 彼の言いぐさ (→彼の言ったこと) が気に食わなかった I didn't like *what he said*.

イーグル　(ゴルフ) eagle ⓒ; (ワシ) eagle ⓒ

いいくるめる　言いくるめる　(おだてて…させようとする) coax *a person to do*; (おだてて…させる) coax [talk] *a person* into *doing* / 彼は両親を言いくるめて旅行の代金を出してもらった He *coaxed* his parents *into* giving him money for the trip.

いいこ　いい子　good boy [girl] ⓒ / いい子だからおとなしくしてるのよ Be a good boy [girl] and behave yourself. / 自分だけいい子になろうとするな Don't pretend to be *innocent*.

いいこと　頭痛をいいことに (→口実に) 体育の授業を休んだ I skipped P.E. class *on the pretext of* a headache. / いいことを教えてあげよう You know *something* [*what*]? (❖情報を提供するときなどに用いる) / 運のいいことに列車はまだ出発していなかった *Luckily* (*for me*), the train hadn't left yet.

イーシー　EC (❖European Community (ヨーロッパ [欧州] 共同体) の略語)

イージーオーダー　⚠ イージーオーダーのスーツ a *tailored* suit (❖英語では「既製品の」を off-the-rack または ready-made, 「仕立ての、あつらえた」を made to order または custom-made, tailor-made という)

いいしぶる　言い渋る　(言うのをためらう) hesitate to say; (いやいや言う) be reluctant to say / その生徒は遅刻の理由を言い渋った The pupil *hesitated to say* why he was late.

いいしれぬ 言い知れぬ （言葉にできない）inexpressible; （説明できない）indescribable ∥ そのニュースを聞いて言い知れぬ不安に襲われた I was filled with *inexpressible* anxiety at the news.

いいすぎ 言い過ぎ サッカーはブラジルの国技と言っても言いすぎではない It's not *too much to say* that soccer is the national sport of Brazil.
🅔「政治家はみなうそつきだ」「それは言いすぎだよ」"Politicians are all liars." "You've gone *too far*."

イースター （復活祭）Easter; （復活祭の日）Easter Sunday [Day]

いいすてる 言い捨てる 彼は「二度と来るもんか」と言い捨てて去っていった His *parting shot* was "I'll never come back again."（❖parting shot は「捨てぜりふ」の意味）

イースト yeast ⓤⓒ; （イースト菌）yeast fungus ⓒ

イーゼル （画架）easel ⓒ

いいせん いい線
🅔「どう、似合う」「わりといい線いってるよ」"How do I look?" "Pretty *cool*."

いいそこなう 言い損なう 彼はその発言は言いそこなっただけだと言った He said that remark was only *a slip of the tongue*. ∥ あわてていて肝心なことを言いそこなった In my hurry, I *forgot to say* the most important thing.

いいそびれる 言いそびれる 花を贈ってくれた友人たちにお礼を言いそびれた I *missed the chance to* thank my friends for the flowers.

いいだしっぺ 言い出しっ屁 君が言いだしっぺなんだから先に行けよ You go first, because you *brought* it *up*.（❖you brought it up の you を強く発音する） ∥ それってだれが言いだしっぺなの（→だれが最初に言ったか） Who was *the first to say* that?

いいたす 言い足す add 他 ∥ 何か言い足すことはありませんか Do you have anything to *add*? ∥ 「彼のせいじゃないよ」と健は言い足した "It's not his fault," Ken *added*.

いいだす 言い出す （提案する）suggest 他, propose 他; （話題を持ち出す）bring* up ∥ パーティーをやろうってだれが言いだしたの Who *suggested* holding a party? ∥ それを言いだしたのはそっちだろう You *brought* it *up*. / You *said* it *first*.（❖共に You を強く発音する）
◆姉は言いだしたら聞かない（→いったん主張し始めたら決して譲らない） Once my sister *starts insisting on* something, she never gives in. ∥ 彼はいつも突然見当違いのことを言いだす（→話が脱線する） He always *goes* [*flies*] *off on* [*at*] *a tangent*.

いいたてる 言い立てる （指摘する）point out; （主張する）insist 他, assert 他 ∥ 人の欠点を言いたててばかりいると嫌われるよ（→人々は君を嫌うだろう）People will dislike you if you keep *pointing out* their faults.
◆つまらないことをいちいち言いたてるんじゃない Don't *quibble over* trifles.

いいちがい 言い違い a slip of the tongue
⇨いいあやまる

いいつかる 言い付かる この手紙をあなたに渡すよう言いつかっております I've been *told* to hand this letter to you.

いいつくす 言い尽くす 言いたいことはすべて言い尽くした I *said everything* I wanted to say. ∥ オーロラの神秘的な美しさは言葉では言い尽くせない The mysterious beauty of the northern lights *is beyond words* [*description*].

いいつくろう 言い繕う （言い訳をする）make* an excuse; （隠す）cover up; （誤り・失敗を）explain away ∥ 彼女は自分のしでかした大失敗を言いつくろった She *made an excuse for* the terrible mistake she had made.

いいつけ 言い付け （命令）order ⓒ, 《公式的/古風》bidding ⓤ ∥ 言いつけに背(そむ)く disobey *the order* / 人の言いつけどおりにする do a person's *bidding* ◆言いつけを守る（→従順な）生徒 an *obedient* pupil

いいつける 言い付ける （告げ口する）《口語的》tell* on ...（❖on の後は「告げ口される人」がくる）, report 他; （命令する）tell* 他, order 他 ∥ 先生に言いつけてやる I'll *tell on* you to our teacher. ∥ 料理長は見習いに皿洗いを言いつけた The chef *told* the apprentice *to* wash the dishes. ◆何でもお言いつけください I am at your service.

いいつたえ 言い伝え （伝説）legend ⓒⓤ ∥ 言い伝えによると according to (a) *legend* / その湖には人魚がすむという言い伝えがある The *legend* says that a mermaid lives in that lake.

いいつたえる 言い伝える hand down ∥ その話はわが校で昔から言い伝えられてきた The story *has been handed down* from the past in our school.

いいとおす 言い通す persist 自 ∥ 彼は何も知らないと言い通した He *persisted in saying* that he didn't know anything.

いいなおす 言い直す （訂正する）correct *oneself*; （言葉を換えて言う）put* it the other way, reword ∥ 司会者はタイトルを間違えたがすぐに言い直した The MC announced the title wrong, but *corrected himself* immediately.

いいなずけ 許嫁・許婚 （男性）one's fiancé; （女性）one's fiancée（❖発音は共に [fiːɑnséi]）

いいならわし 言い習わし （習慣）tradition ⓤ; （言い回し）(common) saying

いいなり 言いなり 人の言いなりになっている be (like) *putty in a person's hands* ∥ 彼はいつも母親の言いなりだ He is always *at his mother's beck and call*. / He is always *under his mother's thumb*. ∥ 人の言いなりになってはいけません You shouldn't *dance to* other people's *tune*.

いいにくい 言いにくい 言いにくいことだが（→言いたくないが）彼はキャプテンには向いていないと思う I *hate to say it, but* I don't think he is fit to be (a) captain. ∥ 彼女は言いにく

そうに(→ためらいながら)上司に退職を申し出た She *hesitantly* told her boss that she wanted to leave her job. / 外国人の名前は言いにくい(→発音しにくい)ものが多い Many foreign names are *hard to pronounce*.

いいね 言い値 (売り手が指定される価格) asking price ⓒ ◆彼らはこの絵をこちらの言い値で買ってくれた They bought the painting *at the price we asked*.

いいのがれ 言い逃れ (言い訳) excuse ⓒⓊ; (言葉を濁すこと) evasion Ⓤⓒ ── 言い逃れる excuse *oneself*, explain away; give* an evasive answer /それは単に言い逃れにすぎない That's just *an excuse*. / もう言い逃れはできないぞ(→言い訳を聞くつもりはない) I'm not going to listen to any of *your excuses*. / 彼は何とか言い逃れようとした He tried to *explain away*.

いいのこす 言い残す 両親は犬の世話をするよう言い残して旅行に行った My parents *told* me *to* look after our dog and went on a trip. / 何か言い残したことはありませんか Don't you *have anything else to say?*

いいはる 言い張る (頑固に主張する) insist ⓘⓣ; (固執する) persist ⓘ; (断言する) assert ⓣ /彼は自分は無罪だと言い張った He *insisted that* he was innocent./ He *insisted on* his innocence./ He *insisted on* his being innocent. / ひとりではそこに行くなと言ったが、彼女は行くと言い張った I told her not to go there alone, but she *persisted*.

いいふくめる 言い含める そのことは彼女によく言い含めておきなさい(→前もって説明しなさい) *Explain* it to her *beforehand*.

いいふらす 言い触らす (広める) spread* ⓣ, (口語的)put* about [around] /そんなデマ(→根拠のないうわさ)を言い触らしたのはだれだ Who *spread* such a groundless rumor? ◆彼は私についてのうそを言い触らして回っている He *is going around telling* lies about me. / 彼女には言っちゃだめだよ。すぐ言い触らすんだから Don't tell it to her, because she is such *a scandalmonger*. (❖ scandalmonger は「悪口などを言い触らす人」の意味)

いいふるす 言い古す 言い古された表現 a *hackneyed* expression; a *cliché*

いいぶん 言い分 *one's* say; (主張) *one's* claim /こちらの言い分も聞いてくれませんか Won't you let me have *my say?* ◆双方の言い分を聞く hear *both sides* / 学生の言い分(→主張)が通って学園祭をやることになった The administration accepted the students' *argument* for holding a school festival. / 何か言い分がありますか Do you have *anything to say?* / 健二の言い分も聞いてみようよ Let's hear *what* Kenji *has to say.* / 彼女の言い分は正しいと思う I guess (that) *he's* right.

イーブン イーブンの (互角・対等の) even, equal /これでお互い条件はイーブンだ(→同じ立場だ) Now we are *on equal terms* with each other.

‖イーブンパー〚ゴルフ〛even par

いいまかす 言い負かす 最近では15歳の娘が私を言い負かすこともある My 15-year-old daughter sometimes *beats* me *in arguments* these days.

いいまちがい 言い間違い a *slip of the tongue* ⇨ いいあやまる ‖言い間違いをする make *a slip of the tongue*

いいまわし 言い回し (表現) expression ⓒ, a turn of phrase ‖うまい言い回し(→的(㊥)を射た表現) an apt *expression* / 彼は言い回しがうまい He has *a good turn of phrase*. ◆日本語特有の言い回し a uniquely Japanese *figure of speech*

いいめ いい目 アフリカ旅行で彼はあまりいい目にはあわなかった(→どちらかというとついていなかった) He *was rather unlucky* during his trip to Africa.

イーメール Eメール e(-)mail Ⓤ ⓒ, E-mail Ⓤⓒ (❖electronic *mail* の略語)
⇨ メール, 前・後見返し

イーユー EU ❖ European Union (ヨーロッパ[欧州]連合)の略語)

いいよう 言い様 もっとほかに言いようがあるだろう(→もっと感じよく言うこともできただろうに) You *could have said* it *more nicely*. / 私は彼の態度に言いようのない怒りを覚えた *Inexplicable* anger arose in me at his attitude. / 君の発想はばかげているとしか言いようがない Your idea is *perfectly* absurd. / 私は言いようのない喜びを感じた I felt *indescribably* happy.

💬「独創的といえなくもない」「ものは言いようだね」"It could be called original." "You know *how to put things*."

慣用表現 ものも言いようで角(㊥)が立つ(→言い方ひとつで他人を怒らせることがある) *Your manner of speaking alone may offend other people.*

いいよどむ 言い淀む 彼女はスピーチの最後で言いよどんだ(→言葉に詰まった) She *got stuck on a word* at the end of her speech.

いいよる 言い寄る (近づく) approach ⓣ, make* approaches [advances] to *a person*; (異性に) (口語的) make* a pass at *a person* /その俳優はあるスーパーモデルに言い寄ったらしい They say the actor *was making a pass at* a supermodel. / 彼女は言い寄る男の子をみんなはねつけてしまう She shuns every boy that *approaches* her.

いいわけ 言い訳 excuse ⓒⓊ; (失敗の) (口語的) alibi ⓒ; (口実) (口語的) out ⓒ (通例単数形) ── 言い訳 (を)する make* an excuse, excuse *oneself*
言い訳無用 None of your *excuses!*
それは言い訳にならない That's no *excuse.*
もっとましな言い訳は思いつかないの？ Can't you invent *a better excuse?*
彼は花びんをこわしたことのうまい言い訳を思いついた He thought up *a good excuse* for breaking the vase.
彼は遅くなった言い訳をした He *excused himself for* being late.
彼は電車が遅れたんだと言い訳した He *made the excuse that* the train had been de-

またあのいつもの言い訳をするつもりじゃないでしょうね You aren't going to give me that same old *excuse*, are you?
◆言い訳なんか聞きたくない．すぐ金を返してくれ I don't want any 「*ifs, ands or buts* [(英)*ifs and buts*]. I want my money back now! (❖"ifs, ands or buts"は「If や But で始まる言い訳や不平」の意味) / どんな言い訳をするつもりなの What have you got to *say for yourself*?

コロケーション -excuse-

【形容詞＋～】ありがちな～ a common excuse / うまい～ a good [an acceptable] excuse / 下手な～ a poor [bad, feeble] excuse / 説得力のない～ a weak excuse / 陳腐な～ a ready-made excuse / 手の込んだ～ an elaborate excuse / もっともな～ a legitimate excuse / もっともらしい～ a plausible excuse

---

いいわすれる 言い忘れる forget* to say [tell] /そうそう，言い忘れるところだった Oh, I almost *forget to tell* you. / 言い忘れてたんだけどその CD 持ってるから貸してあげてもいいよ I *forgot to tell* you, but I've got that CD, so I can lend it to you.

いいわたす 言い渡す (判決などを宣告する) sentence 他; (公式的) pronounce 他 自; impose 他; (命令する) tell* 他, order 他 /法廷は彼に終身刑を言い渡した The court *pronounced* [*imposed*] a life sentence *on* him. / 会社は彼に3か月の自宅待機を言い渡した The company *told* him *that* he would have to be laid off for three months. / 医者は父に禁酒を言い渡した The doctor *ordered* my father to stop drinking.
◆裁判官は彼に懲役２年執行猶予(ﾕｳﾖ)５年を言い渡した The judge *gave* him a two-year sentence, suspended for five years.

いいん¹ 委員 committee member ⓒ, a member of the committee; (委員全体) committee ⓒ /(学級での係) monitor ⓒ /図書委員 *a library monitor* / 編集委員 *a member of the editorial board*
明子は学園祭の実行委員に選ばれた Akiko was chosen to be *a member of the executive committee* of the school festival.
すべての委員はその会議に出席しなければならない All *committee members* must be present at the conference.
◆僕たちは剛を学級委員に推薦した We put forward Tsuyoshi for *class representative*. (❖ class representative は「クラスの代表者」の意味) / 専門家の委員たちがその問題に関して討論した *A panel of experts* had a discussion about the issue.

いいん² 医院 (開業医の個人診療所) (米)(doctor's) office ⓒ, (英) surgery ⓒ; (単科の診療所) clinic ⓒ /平井医院 Dr. Hirai's *office* [*surgery*]

いいんかい 委員会 committee ⓒ; commission ⓒ (しばしば Commission); board ⓒ; panel ⓒ (❖いずれも特に〈英〉では単数形で複数扱いになることがある)

committee: 代表として選出されたメンバーによる委員会.
commission: 公式に任命されて構成される委員会.
board: 短期間で組織・解散せず，恒常的に設置される委員会.
panel: 専門家で組織された委員会.

委員会のメンバーである be on *the committee* [*panel*] / 委員会を設ける form [organize, set up] *a committee* / 委員会の決定 a *committee* decision / 委員会の答申 the findings of *the committee* / 委員会は来月会合を開きます *The committee* will meet next month. / この委員会は5人の教員で構成されている This *committee* 「is made up of [consists of] five teachers.
‖運営委員会 a steering committee / 教育委員会 a board of education / 原子力委員会 the Atomic Energy Commission / 国際オリンピック委員会 (略語)IOC) the International Olympic Committee ((略語)IOC) / 執行[実行]委員会 an executive committee / 小委員会 a subcommittee / 常任委員会 a standing committee / 審査委員会 a jury / 調査委員会(事故などの) (米)an inquest, (英)a court of inquiry / 特別委員会 a special committee / 予算委員会 a budget committee

いいんちょう 委員長 chairperson ⓒ; (男性の) chairman ⓒ; (女性の) chairwoman ⓒ; (委員長の職) chairmanship ⓒⓊ /委員長の役職は会員が交替で務める The *chairmanship* of the committee rotates among its members.
🅔「君が学級委員長に選ばれたよ」「まさか」"You were elected *class president*." "Never!"
‖副委員長 a vice-chairman

いう 言う

❶ 話す・述べる　say, speak, talk, tell
❷ 表現する　express; describe
❸ 呼ぶ　call
❹ 意味する　mean
❺ 主張する　insist; claim
❻ 言及する　mention, refer to ...
❼ 命令する　tell, order

❶【話す・述べる】 say* 他 自, speak* 自 他, talk 自 他, tell* 他 自; (意見を言う) remark 他 自

語法
「大げさに言う」exaggerate,「お世辞を言う」flatter,「小声で言う」whisper など, 日本語では2語以上でいう場合でも，英語では1語で表せる場合が多い．

一般的に言えば *generally speaking* / 率直に言えば *to speak frankly; frankly (speaking)*; *to be frank (with you); to be plain with you* / 実を言うと *to tell (you) the truth* / 控えめに言っても *to say the least (of it)*; to put it *mildly*

それ以上言わなくてもいい *Enough said.*/ *Say no more.*

言いたいのはそれだけですか *Is that all you want to say?*

彼女は実際に何と言ったのですか *What did she actually say?*

彼の言っていることは事実と符合しない *What he says doesn't agree with the facts.*

医者はその子は大丈夫だと言った *The doctor said the child was all right.*

彼女は何も言わずにどんどん歩いていった *She walked along without saying anything.*

それについて言うべきことは何も[あまり]ない *There is nothing [not much] to be said about that.*

きょうの新聞では犯人が逮捕されたといっている *Today's paper says the suspect has been arrested.*

本当のことを言ってくれ *Tell me the truth.*

そのことはだれにも言わないでね *Don't tell it to anybody.*

何か私に言うことはない？ *Don't you have something to tell me?*

これは使っちゃだめって何度言ったら分かるの *How many times do I have to tell you not to use this?*

言っていることがよく分かりません *I don't know what you are talking about.*

だから言わんこっちゃない(→そう言ったじゃないか) *I told you so!*

よく言うよ(→人のことは言えないじゃないか) *Look who's talking!*

◆簡潔に言えば *to be brief; in brief; to make [cut] a long story short; in short* / 厳密に言えば *to be accurate [precise, exact]* / 正直に言えば *to be honest (with you); in all honesty* / ひと言で言えば *in a [one] word; (put it) in a nutshell* / もう一度言ってください (*I beg your*) *pardon?* / *Come again?* / *Sorry?* / *Excuse me?* / 全く君の言うとおりだ *You are absolutely right.* / 彼は私たちにその問題について意見を言った *He gave us his opinion about the problem.*

🅒「それだけですか」「はい、今言えるのはそれだけです」"*Is that all?*" "*Yes. That's all I can say at this moment.*"

🅒「遊園地はなんか飽きちゃった」「そんなこと言わないで行こうよ」"*I've kind of lost interest in going to amusement parks.*" "*Oh, come on, let's go.*"

❷【表現する】express ㊥, 《口語的》put* ㊥; (描写する) describe ㊥

私がどんなにうれしかったかとても言葉では言えない *Words cannot express just how happy I was.*

彼女は彼のことを思いやりがあると言うが、私に言わせれば優柔不断なだけだ *She describes him as considerate, but I would say he is just indecisive.*

◆私の母はよく言えば大らか、悪く言えば大ざっぱな人だ *To say it nicely, my mother is unconcerned: to say it bluntly, she is care-less.* / 彼は言ってみればチームの牽引(けんいん)車のような人だ *He is the locomotive of our team, so to speak.*

🅒「それってどんな味」「うーん、何て言ったらいいかな、今まで食べたことないような味だよ」"*What does it taste like?*" "*Well, how should I say this – it's the most distinctive taste I've ever experienced.*"

❸【呼ぶ】call ㊥

うちの犬の名前はイブといいます *Our dog is called Eve.*

私がうそつきだっていうの？ *Are you calling me a liar?*

その一連の島々は太平洋の真珠の首飾りといわれている *That chain of the islands is called "the pearl necklace of the Pacific."*

◆その本のタイトルは何といいますか *What's the title of the book?*

🅒「しょうゆは英語で何というのですか」"*soy sauce*で" "*How do you say* [*What do you call*] '*shoyu*' *in English?*" "*We call it 'soy sauce'.*"

❹【意味する】mean* ㊥

私は本気で言っているのです *I mean it.* / *I mean what I say.*

何が言いたいんだ(→どういう意味で言っているのか) *What do you mean by that?*

すべて彼のせいだと言いたいのですか *Do you mean that it's all his fault?*

🅒「努力してもむだだと言いたいわけ？」「そんなつもりで言ったんじゃない」"*You mean that all my efforts are useless?*" "*I didn't mean that!*"

❺【主張する】(言い張る) insist ㊥ ㊤; (断言する) claim ㊥, assert ㊥, declare ㊥

どうしてもというならご一緒しましょう *I'll come with you if you insist.*

彼はそこへ行くと言って聞かなかった *He insisted on going there.*

被疑者はその自白は強要されたものだと言った *The suspect insisted that he was forced into confessing.*

その政治家は自分は事件とはいっさい関係がないと言った *The politician claimed that he had nothing to do with that case.*

その地域に住む何人かの人々がUFOを見たと言っている *Several people in the area assert that they have seen UFOs.*

彼女は仕事を辞めるつもりはないときっぱり言った *She declared she was never going to quit the job.*

❻【言及する】mention ㊥, refer to ...

彼はその男性の名前を言いましたか *Did he mention that man's name?*

彼女はその事故については言わなかった *She didn't mention the accident.*

【mention (+to 名(人))+that 節】私があなたに頼んだということは彼女に言わないでください *Please don't mention to her that I asked you.*

◆この間君の言っていた映画を見てきたよ *I went to see the movie you were talking*

❼【命令する】tell*, order; (忠告する) advise

言われたとおりにしろ Do *as you are told*.

医者は私にもっと運動するように言った My doctor *told* me *to* do more exercise.

◆生徒が言うことを聞かないからといって暴力を振るうのは言語道断だ You can never use violent discipline only because the students *are disobedient*. / 親の言うことを聞くべきだ You should listen to *your parents' advice*. / 彼にここで会おうと言われた He *said* to meet him here. (❖口語的表現) / ここではうるさくしないよう子供たちに言って聞かせなければならない We will have to *persuade* the kids not to make so much noise here.

❡「学校にまた遅刻しちゃった」「ほらね，だから早く家を出なさいと言ってるでしょ」"I was late for school again." "You see! I'm always *telling* you *to* leave the house early."

❽【うわさする】say*, talk

人の言うところではそのおばあさんは身寄りがないということだった *People said that* the old woman had no family.

世間に何を言われようと気にするな Don't worry about *what people say about you*.

その劇作家は筆が遅いとよくいわれている *It is often said that* the playwright is a slow writer.

❾【頼む】ask

彼女は私に披露宴でスピーチをしてほしいと言った She *asked* me *to* make a speech at the wedding reception.

私は母に猫の面倒をちゃんと見てくれるよう言っておいた I *asked* my mother *to* look after my cat.

◆どうかしろなんて急に言われても困る *That's all a bit too sudden for me to* do anything about it.

❿【提案する】suggest

彼は入院している先生のお見舞いに行こうと言った He *suggested* going to see our teacher in the hospital.

父は私にもう一度やってみるように言った My father *suggested that* I (should) try again. (❖should を用いるのは主に《英》)

彼女は夫にたまには外食しようと言った She *suggested to* her husband *that* they go out to dinner for a change.

⓫【認める】admit, acknowledge; (否認する) deny; (告白する) confess

彼女は自分が間違っていたと言った She *admitted* she was wrong.

窓ガラスを割ったのは僕じゃないとその少年は言った The boy *denied* breaking the window.

正直に言いなさい．彼が好きなんでしょう Come on! *Confess*! You like him, don't you?

⓬【文句を言う】complain, make* a complaint; (騒ぎたてる) make a noise [fuss], fuss

彼女はいつも上司の不平を言っている She *is always complaining about* her boss.

彼はスープがぬるいとウエートレスに文句を言った He *complained to* the waitress *that* the soup was not hot.

⓭【音を立てる】

風で窓ががたがたいっている The windows *are rattling* in the wind.

その古いドアはあけるときいきいいった The old door *squeaked* as I opened it.

⓮【…という】

彼女は礼文島という小さな島で生まれ育った She was born and brought up on a small island *called* Rebun-to.

スミスさんという方がお目にかかりたいそうです A man *named* Mr. Smith [*A Mr. Smith*] is asking to see you.

明子から30分ほど遅れるという電話があった Akiko *called and said* she would be about half an hour late.

その投手がメジャーへ移籍するといううわさが流れている There is *a rumor* spreading *that* the pitcher is going to be transferred to a Major League team.

⓯【その他】

この年になると体が言うことをきかない I'm so old that *my body has stopped listening to me*.

彼は言わずと知れたサッカーの名選手だった *As everyone knows*, he was a great soccer player.

そのバイオリン奏者は日本は言うに及ばず世界中で有名だ The violinist is famous *not only* in Japan *but also* abroad.

彼女は自分はスターだと言わんばかりにふるまった She behaved *as if to say* she was a star.

言っていいことと悪いことがあるだろう (→言うべきではないことがある) *There are some things you shouldn't say*.

家の壁という壁に彼女の写真がはってあった I found her photos on *every wall* of the house.

今の仕事にこれといって不満があるわけではない I have nothing to complain about in my current job.

「隣の芝生は青い」とはよく言われることだ *People often say*, "The grass is always greener on the other side of the fence."

言わせてもらうけど，言わせてもらうけど，私はそれを自分の目で見たんだ *I'm telling you*, I saw it with my own eyes.

最後まで言わせて *Let me finish talking*.

カラオケといえばこの前の土曜日に4時間歌ったよ *Speaking of* karaoke, we spent four hours singing last Saturday.

考え直せなんて彼には言うだけむだだ You really can't make him change his mind.

慣用表現 言わぬが花 *It's better left unsaid*. / 金がものを言う ➡ かね

ことわざ 言うは易(やす)く行うは難(かた)し *Easier said than done*.

いうことなし 言うことなし 今回の結果については言うことなしだ (→完全に満足している) I'm *perfectly satisfied with* the result this time. / 見かけも性格もよくてお金持ちなんて言うことなしじゃないか Good-looking, good personality, and he's rich too – *what more could you want?*

いうなれば 言うなれば（いわば）*so to speak, as it were* (✲挿入的に用いる) 《フリッターは言うなれば洋風のてんぷらです Fritters are Western-style tempura, *so to speak*.

いうにいわれぬ 言うに言われぬ 《彼にも言うに言われぬ事情があったんだろう He must have had a reason he *couldn't tell (to)* anybody. / 母は言うに言われぬ苦労をして私を育ててくれた My mother went through *indescribable* [*unspeakable*] hardships to bring me up.

いうにおよばず 言うに及ばず *not to mention* 《その歌は10代の若者は言うに及ばず中年のサラリーマンにも人気がある That song is popular among middle-aged workers, *not to mention* teenagers.

いうまでもない 言うまでもない 《正直が最良の策であることは言うまでもない *Needless to say*, honesty is the best policy. / バランスのとれた食事が大切なのは言うまでもない *It goes without saying that* well-balanced diet is important. / 彼女は英語は言うまでもなくスペイン語とフランス語も話せる She can speak Spanish and French, *not to speak of* English. / 言うまでもなく彼は現在最も魅力的な俳優の一人である *Obviously*, he is one of the most attractive actors today. / ダンスは言うまでもなく歌うのも苦手だ I'm not good at singing, *let alone* dancing. (✲let alone は通例否定文の後に置き「…などとんでもない」の意味)

いえ 家

❶ [家屋・自宅] house ⓒ (複 ~s), home ⓒ ― 家に[で・へ] home

⇨ 図版 p.78, 場面・状況別会話 p.1724

> [語法] house は建物としての家, home は生活の場としての家を指し, 後者には「暖かい場所」というイメージがある. ただし《米》では home を建物の意味で用いることも多い.

〖～(の)家〗
木造の家 a wooden *house* / 鉄筋コンクリートの家 a「reinforced concrete [ferroconcrete] *house* / れんが造りの家 a *house* made of bricks / 赤い屋根の家 a red-roofed *house* / 2階建ての家 a two-storied [two-story] *house* / 一戸建ての家 a detached *house* / ジョン・レノンがかつて住んでいた家 the former *home* of John Lennon

〖家が・は〗
その火災で数百戸の家が焼け落ちた Hundreds of *houses* (were) burnt to ashes in the fire.
その家は奇妙な外観をしている The *house* has a strange appearance.
彼の家は通りから引っ込んだ所にある His *house* stands back from the street.

この家は修理の必要がある This *house* needs repairing. / This *house* needs to be repaired.

〖家の〗
家の改築 *house* conversion / 家の土台を造る lay the foundation(s) of *a house*
彼は自分の家の設計に有名な建築家を雇った He engaged a famous architect to design his *house*.
家の近くに大きな公園がある There is a big park *near my house*.
家の中が散らかっていてごめんなさい Please excuse the messy *house*.
この家の家賃は月15万円です This *house* rents [lets] for 150,000 yen a month.
◆彼はあなたの家の近くに住んでいるそうですよ I hear he lives *somewhere your way*.

〖家を〗
古くなった家を修理してもらう have *an old house* fixed up
彼女はいつもより早く家を出た She left *home* earlier than usual.
父は遺言で私に家を残してくれた My father left me *the house* in his will.
地震で2万人以上の人が家を失った More than 20,000 people lost *their homes* in the quake.
◆家を恋しがる be homesick / 家をあけている間友人に飼い犬を預けた I left my dog with a friend *while I was away*. / その候補者は支持を求めて各家を回った The candidate *paid house-to-house calls* asking for support.

〖家に・で〗
家に帰りなさい Go (back) *home*.
あすは家にいますか Will you be (*at*) *home* tomorrow?
この天気の中を出かけるよりはむしろ家にいたい I would rather stay *home* than go out in this weather.
彼女は今ごろはもう家に着いているだろう She should be *home* by now.
慎吾はガールフレンドを家に招待した Shingo invited his girlfriend to *his house*.
彼女は子供をひとりで家に残してきたことを後悔した She regretted leaving her child alone *at home*.
この週末でバーベキューをする予定だ We are going to have a barbecue *at our home* this weekend.
◆彼女は夏休みの間私の家に滞在した She stayed *with us* during summer vacation. / 祖母は家にいるのが好きだ My grandmother is *a homebody*.

〖その他〗
家から駅まで歩いて15分かかる It takes 15 minutes to walk *from my house* to the station.
赤ん坊がいるので彼女はなかなか家から出られない She is tied to *her home* because of her baby.
家まで送ります I'll see you *home*.
車で家まで送るよ I'll drive you *home*. / I'll give you a lift [ride] *home*.

彼女の悲鳴が家中に響いた Her scream echoed *throughout the house*.

コロケーション -house-
【動詞+〜】〜を建てる build [《口語的》put up] a house / 〜を改装する remodel a house / 〜を下見する view a house / 〜を貸す《米》rent [《英》let] a house / 〜を賃借りする take a lease on a house / 〜に侵入する break into a house / 〜に放火する set a house on fire

❷【家庭・家族】(家族) family Ⓒ, house Ⓒ; (家計) household Ⓒ
家を捨てる abandon *one's family* / 家を切り盛りする manage *a house* [*household*]
おじの家は大家族だ My uncle has *a large family*.
私は彼の家とは遠縁に当たる I'm distantly connected with *his family*.
彼は家のことは奥さんに任せっきりだ He leaves all *responsibility for the house* to his wife.
家の者が心配しているかもしれないので帰ります I've got to go now, because *my family* might be worrying about me.
◆私は10年以上ブーンさんの家とは仲よくしている I have been friends with *the Boones* for over 10 years.

❸【家系】family Ⓒ
彼は裕福な家の出だ He *comes from a wealthy family*.
彼の家は代々米屋をやっている His *family* has owned a rice shop for generations.
うちでは姉が家(→家業)を継いだ My sister 「succeeded to [took over] *our family business*.
◆金持ちの家に生まれる be born with a silver spoon in *one's* mouth

いえい 遺影 (故人の写真) a memorial photo(graph) [picture] of a deceased person
いえがら 家柄 よい家柄の出の女性 a woman from *a good family* / 由緒ある家柄 *a family* of ancient lineage / 彼は高貴な家柄の出だ He comes from *a noble stock*.
いえき 胃液 gastric juice Ⓤ Ⓒ
いえじ 家路 家路につく set off *for home*; make *one's way home* / 激しい雨の中、家路を急いだ She *hurried home* through the driving rain. / 私たちはしばらく散策してから家路についた We walked around for a while and then turned *homeward*.
イエス (肯定の返事) yes Ⓒ //イエスかノーで答えてください Just answer 「*yes or no* [with *a yes or a no*]. / その申し出に彼女はイエスと言わなかった She didn't say *yes* to the offer.
‖イエスマン a yes-man
いえで 家出 ——家出する run* away (from home) //彼は15歳のとき家出した He *ran away from home* when he was 15.
‖家出少年[少女] a runaway boy [girl] / 家出人 a runaway, a missing person
いえども 彼は格下といえども侮(あなど)れない相手だ *Though* he is ranked lower than me, he is a formidable opponent. / 最近は子供といえどもかなりストレスに悩まされている *Even* children are under a lot of stress these days.
💬「宝くじにでも当たったの?」「当たらずといえども遠からずってとこかな」"You won the lottery or something?" "*Not exactly, but you are pretty close.*"
いえなみ 家並み その通りに面して瀟洒(しょうしゃ)な家並みが続いている *A row of elegant houses* faces the street.
いえもと 家元 (an) *iemoto*, the head of a school //彼の父親は日本舞踊の家元だ His father is *the head of a school* of traditional

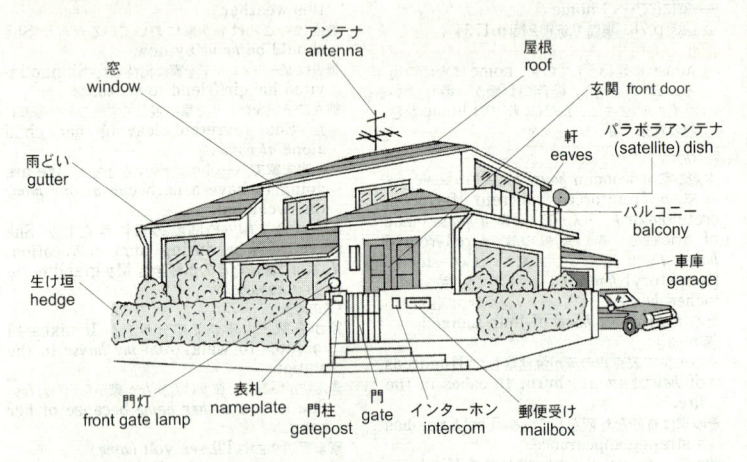

家 house

- 窓 window
- 雨どい gutter
- 生け垣 hedge
- 門灯 front gate lamp
- 表札 nameplate
- 門柱 gatepost
- 門 gate
- インターホン intercom
- 郵便受け mailbox
- アンテナ antenna
- 屋根 roof
- 玄関 front door
- 軒 eaves
- パラボラアンテナ (satellite) dish
- バルコニー balcony
- 車庫 garage

Japanese dancing.
‖家元制度 the system of licensing the teaching of a traditional Japanese art
イエローカード yellow card

いえん¹ 以遠 高尾に遠に向かう電車は終了していた There were no more trains running *beyond* Takao.

いえん² 胃炎 〔医学〕 gastritis [gæstráitəs]

いおう 硫黄 〔化学〕 sulfur, (英)sulphur (❖元素記号S) ‖硫黄の刺激臭 the pungent smell of *sulfur* / マッチをすると硫黄のにおいがする When you strike a match, it smells of *sulfur*.

いおり 庵 (隠者のすみか) hermitage

イオン 〔化学〕 ion [áiən] ‖陽[陰]イオン positive [negative] *ions*
‖イオン化傾向 ionization tendency / イオン化装置 an ionizer / イオン圏 the ionosphere

いか¹ 以下
【語法】
「…以下」は，厳密に数量をいう場合は，…の数を含むが，比較的あいまいに「…より少ない」という意味で用いる場合も多い．英語で表現するとき，どちらに当たるのかをよく見きわめて使い分けるようにする．

❶【…を含みそれより下】 ... or less; (数が) ... or fewer; (…を超えない) ... and [or] under [below], not more than ...

5歳以下の子供の入場は無料です Children *aged five and under* [*below*] are admitted free.
私はそれを2,000円かそれ以下で手に入れたい I want to get it *for 2,000 yen or less*.
その試験に合格するのは毎年だいたい100人以下です *Not more than* 100 examinees pass the exam every year.
◆小学生以下は半額です Preschoolers *and elementary school students* are half price. / 姉は1日の食事を1,600キロカロリー以下に抑えている My sister *limits* her meals *to* 1,600 calories a day.

❷【…を含まずそれより下・…未満】(程度・数量などが) below, under, less than ...; (数が) fewer than ...
ゆうべは気温が0度以下に下がった The temperature fell *below zero* [*freezing*] last night.
小学生のころは身長は平均以下だった My height was *below average* when I was in elementary school.
その店は在庫品を原価以下で売りさばいた The store sold off the stock *below cost*.

❸【…をはじめその他一同】
リーダー以下(→リーダーを含めて)20名の団体 a group of 20, *including the leader* / 社長以下受付係に至るまで *from the president* down to the receptionists

❹【…に続くもの・下記】 the following
以下は休み中に読むべき本のリストです *The following* is the list of books to be read during the vacation.

◆結論は以下のとおり The conclusion is *as follows*. / 以下の説明に従ってください Follow *the instructions below*. / 以下次号に続く *To be continued*. / 15ページ以下を参照 See *p. 15 ff*. (❖ ff. は (and the) following (pages [lines])の意味のラテン語を略したもの)

いか² 医科 medical department ‖医科大学 a medical college [school]

いか³ 烏賊 (ヤリイカ) squid (複～, ～s); (コウイカ) cuttlefish (複～, ～es) ‖イカには足が10本ある A *squid* [*cuttlefish*] has 10 arms. (❖イカの「足」は arm)

いが 毬 (クリなどの) bur, burr ; (とげ) prickle

いがい¹ 意外 ――意外な (予期しない) unexpected, undreamed-of; (驚くべき) surprising ――意外に unexpectedly; surprisingly, to *one's* surprise

意外な結果 an *unexpected* result / その映画の意外な結末 *the surprising end* of the movie
かなり意外だったが彼女は我々の申し出に同意した She rather *unexpectedly* agreed to our proposal.
意外なことに道路はそれほど込んでいなかった *To our surprise*, the traffic was not that heavy.
◆その試験は意外に(→予想していたよりも)やさしかった The exam was easier *than I had expected*. / イタリアがフランスに敗れたのは意外だ I'm *surprised that* Italy was beaten by France. / 着いてみると意外なことが私たちを待ちかまえていた A *surprise* awaited us on our arrival.

💬 「彼女，実はスポーツウーマンなんだよ」「へえ，意外だな」"She is really a sportswoman." "That's *surprising*."
💬 「あの映画がグランプリなんだって」「別に意外じゃないよ」"You know what? That movie won the Grand Prix!" "I'm *not surprised*."

いがい² 遺骸 (遺体) (dead) body , corpse

-いがい -以外
❶【…を除いて】 except (for), but

【語法】
[except (for)とbut] (1) except のほうがbutよりも「除外されるもの」を強調する ‖ ジム以外はみんな来た(→「ジムだけ」が来なかった) Everybody *except* Jim came. / ジム以外はみんな来た(→ジムを除けば「全員来た」) Everybody *but* Jim came.
(2) but は通例 all や anything, everybody などの any-, every- で始まる語とともに用いる ‖ 彼はニンジン以外は全部食べた He ate *everything but* carrots.

[except と except for] (1) 文頭にくるときは except for を用いる ‖ ジム以外はみんなここにいます *Except for* [×Except] Jim, we are all here.
(2) 後ろに (原形) 不定詞，前置詞句, that [wh-]節がくるときは except を用いる ‖ 待つ以外に私にできることは何もなかった

There was nothing I could do *except* wait. / この道路は週末以外はそれほど込まない Traffic is not that heavy on this road *except* on weekends.

動物は虫類以外はみんな好きだ I like all animals *except* (*for*) reptiles.
亜美以外はみんな遅刻した *Except for* Ami, everyone was late.
この仕事以外のことなら何でもします I will do anything *but* this job.
私たち以外だれも本当のことを知らない No one knows the truth *except for* us.
彼は忙しいか疲れているとき以外，決してタクシーを使わない He never takes a taxi *except* when he is busy or tired.
その双子の姉妹は1人の左ほおにほくろがある以外はうりふたつだった The twin sisters looked exactly the same *except* that one had a mole on the left cheek.
💬「君のうちに行ってもいい？」「月曜と木曜以外ならいつでも」"Can I come to your place?" "Anytime *except* Mondays and Thursdays."
❷【…に加えて…のほかに】(…に加えて) besides, in addition to ..., as well as ...; (…のほかに) other than ..., outside, 《主に米・口語的》outside of ..., beyond
話を聞く以外に彼に何をしてやれるというのですか What can I do for him *besides* listen to him? (❖動詞とともに用いる場合，besides の後は動詞の原形)
私たちの先生は英語以外にフランス語も話せる Our teacher can speak French *as well as* English.
ホットケーキ以外の物は作れないのかい Can't you cook anything *other than* hot cakes?
隣人だという以外，彼とは何の関係もない He is my neighbor, but *beyond* that I have nothing to do with him.
私以外にそのことに気づいた人はいなかった Nobody noticed it *outside of* me.
彼は自分の専門以外のことは何ひとつ知らない He doesn't know anything *outside* his field.
◆それ以外に手がなかった There was *no other* way. / 信頼できるのは君以外にいない(→君は僕が信頼できる唯一の人だ) You are the only person I can rely on.

いがいが のどのいがいが *a scratchy feeling* in *one's* throat

いかいよう 胃潰瘍 stomach [gastric] ulcer [C]

いかが 如何
❶【様子を尋ねる】how
💬「ご機嫌いかがですか」「元気です．どうも」"*How* are you (doing)?" "Fine, thanks. And you?"
💬「ご家族はいかがお過ごしですか」「とても元気です」"*How* is your family coming along?" "Very well, thank you."
💬「お寿司(ᵗ)はいかがですか」「とてもおいしいです」"*How* do you like sushi?" "It's excellent."
💬「けさはご気分はいかがですか」「おかげさまで．いいですよ」"*How* are you feeling this morning?" "I'm feeling fine, thank you."
💬「旅行はいかがでしたか」「とても楽しかったですよ」"*How* was your trip?" "We enjoyed it very much."
💬「では，今度の木曜はいかがですか」「すみません，ほかの約束があるんです」"*How about* next Thursday?" "Sorry, but I've got another appointment."
❷【勧める】
💬「お茶はいかがですか」「はい，いただきます」"*Would you like* a cup of tea?" "Yes, please."
💬「もう少しいかが」「いいえ，結構です」"*Would you like* some more?" "No, thank you."
💬「ごはんのお代わりはいかがですか」「もう十分いただきました」"*Would you like* a second helping of rice?" "I've had quite enough, thank you."
💬「アイスクリームはいかが」「ええ，ぜひ」"*Would you care for* ice cream?" "Sure, why not?"
💬「お飲み物はいかがなさいますか」「オレンジジュースのS(サイズ)1つ」"*What about* something to drink?" "A small orange juice."
💬「今晩夕食をいっしょにいかがですか」「ごめんなさい，また今度ね」"*Do you suppose* we could have dinner tonight?" "Sorry, some other time."

いかがわしい (怪しげな) dubious; (人が怪しげな) suspicious; (後ろ暗い) shady; (わいせつな) obscene ‖いかがわしい雑誌 an *obscene* magazine / そのアパートにはいかがわしい人物が出入りしていた A *suspicious* person was going in and out of that apartment. / 彼はいかがわしい商売にかかわっているらしい He is said to be involved in *shady* business.
◆いかがわしい(→評判の悪い)場所 a *disreputable* place

いかく 威嚇 threat [C] ―威嚇する threaten [他] ―威嚇的な threatening ‖その犬は私に威嚇のポーズをとった The dog assumed a *threatening* posture against me.
◆警官は逃走する容疑者に対して威嚇射撃をした The police officer fired *a warning shot* at the fleeing suspect.

いがく 医学 medicine [U], medical science [U] ―医学の medical (❖名詞の前で用いる) ―医学的に medically ‖ヒポクラテスは医学の父と呼ばれている Hippocrates is called the father of *medicine*. / 彼は難病に苦しむ人々を救おうと医学を学んだ He studied *medicine* to save people suffering from incurable diseases.
‖医学界 medical circles / 医学者 a medical scientist / 医学書 a medical book / 医学生 a medical student, 《口語的》a medic / 医学博士 Doctor of Medicine (《略語》MD) /

医学部 the faculty of medicine, (a) medical school / 医学用語 a medical term / 漢方医学 Chinese medicine / 外科医学 surgery / 精神医学 psychiatry / 東洋医学 oriental [Eastern] medicine / 内科医学 internal medicine / 法医学 forensic medicine / 放射線医学 radiology / 予防医学 preventive medicine / 臨床医学 clinical medicine

いがぐりあたま 毬栗頭 その男の子はいがぐり頭をしていた The boy had *close-cropped hair*.

いかさま (偽物) fake ⓒ, sham ⓒ; (不正・いんちき) (口語的) take-in ⓒ ——いかさまの (偽の) fake, sham, phony, bogus ◆いかさまの(→鉛などを詰めた)さいころ a *loaded* dice / トランプでいかさまをする *cheat at* cards ‖いかさま師 a swindler, 《口語的》a fraud

いかす¹ 生かす・活かす

❶【生かしておく】keep* ... alive, let* ... live

やつを生かしてはおけない I can't *let* him *live*.

もし脳死になったとしたら生命維持装置で生かされたくはない If I became brain dead, I wouldn't want to *be kept alive* by a life-support machine.

❷【活用する】(使う) use ⊕, make* use of ..., take* advantage of ...; (最大限に利用する) make the most [best use] of ...

将来は英語を生かせる仕事がしたい In the future, I'd like to get a job in which I *can use* my English.

才能を生かせばきっと成功しますよ *Use* your ability and you will succeed.

君は自分の経験を最大限生かすべきだ You should *make the most of* your experience.

◆日本料理は素材の持ち味を生かす(→本来の味を引き出す)料理だ Japanese cuisine *brings out* the natural flavor of each ingredient. / チャンスを生かすも殺すも自分しだいだ It's up to you *whether you take your chance or not*.

いかす² (かっこいい)《米口語的》cool, (口語的) funky ‖いかす男 a *cool* guy / そのブーツ, なかなかいかしてるじゃない Those boots are pretty *cool*.

いかすい 胃下垂【医学】gastroptosis [gæstrɑptóusis] ⓤ

いかだ 筏 raft ⓒ ‖丸太のいかだ *a raft* of logs / いかだで川下りをした We went down the river on *a raft*.

いがた 鋳型 mold ⓒ, cast ⓒ ‖金属を鋳型に流し込む pour metal into *a mold* [*cast*]

子供たちを鋳型にはめるような画一的な教育は見直されてきている Uniform education that *molds* children *into one and the same type* has been gradually phased out.

いかつい (厳しい表情の) stern, grim; (ごつい顔の) rugged [rʌ́gid], craggy; (角張った) square ‖いかつい顔立ち *rugged* features / いかつい肩 *square* shoulders / その警備員はいかつい顔をして門の前に立っていた The guard *was grim-faced* as he stood in front of the gate.

いかなる 如何なる 彼はいかなる種類の援助も受けようとしなかった He would not accept help in *any shape or form*. / いかなる不正も根絶しなければならない *Any sort of* corruption must be rooted out. / 彼はいかなる犠牲を払っても彼女と結婚したかった He wanted to marry her *at「any cost* [*all costs*]」

いかに 如何に (どのように・どの程度) how; (どんなに…でも) however (✤形容詞・副詞の直前に用いる), no matter how ‖問題はお父さんをいかにして説得するかだね The question is *how* you should persuade your father. / 細部がいかに精密に描かれているか注目してください Note *how* precisely the details are drawn. / 彼はいったん決めたらいかに困難であろうとやりとげる Once he makes up his mind, he will accomplish it *however* difficult it may be.

いかにも 如何にも (まさに) just, exactly; (さも…のように) as if ... ‖それはいかにも節子らしい話だ That sounds *just like* Setsuko. / 僕たちの先生はいかにも大学生というふうに見える Our teacher looks *just like* a college student. / 彼はいかにも目撃したかのようにその事故について話した He told about the accident *as if* he had witnessed it. ◆慈善事業に寄付するなんていかにも彼女らしかった It was *typical* of her to make a contribution to charity. / 彼はいかにも丈夫そうだが, 実はそうでもない He *does* look strong and healthy, but really he is not that strong.

💬 「彼, バンドでギターやってるんだよ」「いかにもって感じだね(→簡単に想像がつく)」"He plays guitar in a band." "That's *easy to guess*."

いかばかり 如何ばかり 彼女の喜びはいかばかりだろうか I can well imagine just *how* happy she is.

いがみあう いがみ合う (反目する) feud ⓘ; (口論する) quarrel ⓘ ‖両家は昔からいがみ合っている The two families *have been feuding with* each other for a long time.

◆2つの派閥のいがみ合い the *strife* between two factions / あの2人はいつもいがみ合っている Those two *are* always *at each other's throats*.

いかめしい 厳めしい (表情などが) stern; (厳粛な) grave; (堂々とした) impressive ‖いかめしい顔つき a *stern* look / いかめしい門構えの家 a house with an *impressive* gate

いカメラ 胃カメラ gastrocamera ⓒ (✤gastrocameraは日本で開発・命名されたもので, 欧米ではあまり一般的でない)

◆胃カメラの検査を受ける have *an endoscopic examination of one's stomach*(✤*endoscopic*は「内視鏡による」の意味)

いかもの 如何物 (偽物) fake ⓒ, sham ⓒ, bogus [phony] article ⓒ ◆私はその店でいかものをつかまされた Some *bogus stuff* was fobbed off on me at that store. / その作家はいかもの食いだったといわれている That writ-

...er is said to have had *bizarre tastes in food*.

いがらっぽい のどがいがらっぽい I've got a *scratchy* throat.

いかり¹ 怒り anger ⓤ; (激しい) rage ⓤ, fury ⓤ, outrage

激しい怒り a storm of *anger* / 突然の怒り a flush of *anger* / 怒りのはけ口 an outlet for one's *anger*

私は怒りがこみ上げてくるのを感じた I felt *the anger* rising in me.

彼の怒りは今にも爆発しそうだった He was simmering with *rage*.

怒りはやがて悲しみに変わった *Anger* soon resolved itself into sorrow.

彼女は夫に怒りをぶちまけた She vented *her anger* on her husband.

彼の顔は怒りで真っ赤になった His face turned red *with anger*.

怒りにまかせて彼女はその手紙を破った She tore the letter into pieces *in a fit of anger*.

彼は怒りにかられた *Anger* spurred him on.

彼女は怒りのあまり言葉を失っていた She was speechless *with rage*.

慣用表現 怒り心頭に発する (→急に怒りが高まる) fly into a rage

コロケーション -anger-
【動詞+～】～を顔に出す show one's anger / ～を抑える control [suppress] one's anger / ～を爆発させる explode in anger / ～を静める calm a person's anger / ～を口に出す voice one's anger / ～を買う arouse a person's anger

いかり² 錨・碇 anchor ⓒ (◆「いかりを下ろす [上げる]」などの慣用的な表現にはふつう冠詞を付けない) / いかりを下ろす cast [drop] *anchor* / いかりを上げる weigh *anchor* ◆彼らは桟橋の近くにいかりを下ろした They *anchored* the boat near the pier. (◆この anchor は動詞)

いかりくるう 怒り狂う be furiously angry

いかる 怒る ❶【怒る】get* angry ◆僕が停学になって父は烈火のごとく怒った My dad *hit the roof* when I was suspended from school.
❷【角張る】肩をいからせる square one's shoulders

いかれる ❶【頭の狂った】彼は完全にいかれている He *is good and crazy*. (◆good and ... は「完全に」の意味) / He must *be gone off his head*.
❷【故障した】エンジンがどうもいかれた (→故障した) ようだ It looks like the engine *broke down*. / 定期券の磁気がいかれてしまった The magnetic strip of my commuter pass *has been damaged*.
❸【夢中になった】彼はその女の子にすっかりいかれている He *is crazy about* that girl.

いかん¹ 如何 天候のいかんにかかわらず *irrespective of the weather* / 契約が更新されるかどうかは今季の成績いかんによる Whether you get your contract renewed or not depends on *how well you have played this season*.

慣用表現 いかんせん (→あいにく) 風が強くて庭でのバーベキューは無理だ *Unfortunately*, there's too much wind to have a barbecue in the garden. / それはいかんともしがたい *This can't be helped*. / (→私たちにできることは何もない) *There's nothing we can do about* it.

いかん² 遺憾 regret ⓤⓒ ――遺憾な regrettable; (嘆かわしい) (公式的に) deplorable; (不満な) unsatisfactory ⇨いかんなく / 遺憾の意を表する express one's *regret* / 控訴が棄却されたのはまことに遺憾です We feel it is deeply *regrettable* that the suit was dismissed.
◆遺憾ながら大統領の訪日は延期になりました *Regrettably*, the President's visit to Japan was postponed. / 子供向けのテレビ番組にはまだまだ遺憾な点が多い The selection of TV programs for children *leaves a lot to be desired*.

いかん³ 移管 transfer ⓤ ――移管する (管轄を移す) transfer ⓗ

いがん 胃癌 stomach cancer ⓤⓒ, (a) cancer of the stomach ‖医者は彼に胃癌の手術をした The doctor operated on him for *stomach cancer*.

いがんたいしょく 依願退職 (辞職) resignation ⓤ ❖resignation には「自分から (退職する)」の意味が含まれる) ――依願退職する (辞職する) resign [rizáin] ⓗ

いかんなく 遺憾なく (十分に) fully, satisfactorily, to the full / 実力を遺憾なく発揮する show [display] one's ability *to the full*

いき¹ 息

❶【呼吸】breath [bréθ] ⓤ (また a ～); (息をすること) breathing ⓤ ――息をする breathe [bríːð] ⓘ ⓗ
《息が》
息ができない！ I can't *breathe*!
吐く息が白い (→息が見える) We can see *our breath*.
走ると息がぜいぜいする Running leaves me puffing for *breath*.
煙が部屋に広がるにつれて息が苦しくなった As the smoke filled the room, *it became hard to breathe*.
◆ショックで息が止まりそうになる *gasp in [with] shock* / もちがのどに詰まって息ができなくなった I *choked on mochi*. / えり元がきつくて息が詰まりそうだ This tight collar *is choking* me.
《息を》
深く息を吸ってから吐いてください Take a deep *breath* and then *breathe out*.
どれくらい息を止めていられるかい How long can you *hold your breath*?
亜紀は息を切らして教室に駆け込んできた Aki burst into the classroom, 「*out of breath* [*breathless*]*.
彼は大きく息を吸い込んで水中に潜った *With a deep intake of breath* he dove into the water.

私は息をつくために立ち止まった I stopped to 「*get my breath (back)* [*catch my breath*]. /
私たちは怖くて息を潜めていた We *held our breath* in fear.
◆ 息を切らせて階段を上がる go *panting* up the stairs / その力士は息を切らせて取組後のインタビューに答えた The sumo wrestler *panted out* his words at the post-fight interview. / 彼女は指に息を吹きかけて暖めた She *blew on* her fingers to warm them.
《その他》
小鳥はついに息絶えた The bird *breathed its last*.
助け出されたとき彼は息も絶え絶えだった He *was barely breathing* when rescued.

❷【慣用表現】
【息が合う】2人のダンサーは息がぴったり合っていた The two dancers *performed in perfect harmony*.
【息がある】がれきの下で発見された老人はまだ息があった(→生きていた) The old man found under the rubble *was still alive*.
【息がかかる】彼には専務の息がかかっている(→支援を受けている) He *has the backing of* the executive director.
【息が切れる】あまりがんばりすぎると息が切れる(→続かなくなる) Don't work too hard, or you *won't be able to go on*.
【息が詰まる】その職場は何となく息が詰まりそうな雰囲気だった The atmosphere of that office was kind of *stifling*.
【息が長い】彼は息の長い(→人気の続く)歌手になりたいと思っている He wants to be a singer with *enduring popularity*.
【息の根を止める】あいつの息の根を止めてやる(→殺してやる) I'll *kill* him. / I'll *finish* him *off*.
【息を凝らす】観客は息を凝らしてフリーキックを見守った The spectators watched the free kick *with bated breath*.
【息を殺す】私たちは息を殺してセミが脱皮するのを見守った We *held our breath* and watched the cicada cast off its shell.
【息をつく】ピアノの発表会の準備で母は息つく暇もないほど(→非常に)忙しい My mother is *too* busy preparing for the piano recital. / その映画は息もつかせぬアクションの連続だ That's an action-packed movie that *will take your breath away*.
【息をのむ】私は彼のひどいけがに思わず息をのんだ I *gasped* with surprise at his serious injury. / 山頂からの美しい眺めに彼は息をのんだ The beautiful scenery from the peak *took my breath away*.
【息をはずませる】「駅からずっと走ってきたんだ」と彼は息をはずませて言った "I've run all the way from the station," he 「*panted* [*said panting*].
【息を引き取る】彼女の祖父は昨夜遅く息を引き取った Her grandfather 「*passed away* [《文語》*breathed his last*] late last night.
【息を潜める】僕は息を潜めて木の陰に隠れていた I was hiding in a tree *with bated breath*.

【息を吹き返す】その会社は新しい技術の導入によって息を吹き返した(→復興した) The company *has revived* with the introduction of (a) new technology. / その子供は人工呼吸を受けて息を吹き返した The child *revived* after being given artificial respiration.
⇨いきぎれ, いきぐるしい, いきせきかる, いきづまる(息詰まる)

いき² 生き 生きのいい若者 a *cheerful and lively* young person / その店の魚は生きがいい They sell *fresh* fish at that store.
‖生き餌 live bait / 生き地獄 (a) hell, (a) living death / 生き字引 / 生きじびき / 生き証人 a living witness / 生き血 ⇨いきち
[慣用表現] 生き恥をさらす ⇨いきはじ

いき³ 行き 行きは新幹線で帰りは飛行機にした I *went* by Shinkansen [bullet train], and came back by plane. / 私は学校の行き帰りによく彼女を見かけた I often saw her *on my way to and from* school. / 濃霧のため羽田行きは全便に遅れが出ています Due to the dense fog, all flights *for* [*into*] Haneda have been delayed. / 仙台行きの最終の飛行機に乗った I took the last plane (bound) *for* Sendai. / 父はニューヨーク行きを延期した My father postponed *going to* New York.

いき⁴ 粋 ―いき は (洗練された) smart, sophisticated; (しゃれた) fashionable, stylish; (服が) chic [ʃiːk] ‖いきなレストラン a *smart* restaurant / 彼女はいつもいきな着こなしをしている She always wears *chic* clothes. ◆ 彼のいきなはからいで僕は彼女と2人きりになることができた Thanks to his *kind help*, I was able to be alone with her.

いき⁵ 域 (水準) level ◻ / 将棋で彼の域に達するには相当な努力が必要だ It would take a lot of effort to *reach* his *level* at shogi. / 彼女の歌唱技術は今や完成の域に達した Her singing technique has now reached *perfection*. / 君の話は推測の域を出ない What you have said is only *a guess*. / 彼のギターはプロの域に達している His guitar technique is no less than (that of a) *professional*.

いき⁶ 意気 (意気込み) spirit ◻ (また a～); (士気) morale ◻, spirits ‖意気消沈する be *in low spirits* / その知らせに僕らの意気はあがった Our *spirits soared* at the news. / 熱烈な応援に選手たちの意気もあがった The enthusiastic cheer *encouraged the spirits of* the players. / 私は彼と意気投合した I found a *kindred spirit* in him.
◆ 私は試験に合格して意気揚々と帰ってきた I found out I passed the exam and came home *riding high*. / 立候補者は意気盛んに演説をして回った The candidate went on the campaign trail *enthusiastically*.
🅔「次こそは成功させるよ」「その意気だ」"I'll make it next time." "*That's the spirit.*"

いき⁷ 遺棄 (放棄) abandonment ◻, dereliction ◻; (被扶養者の)【法律】desertion ◻ ◻
◆ 彼に対する死体遺棄の容疑は晴れた He has been cleared of *abandoning* the body.

いぎ¹ 異議 (反対意見) objection ◻ ◻; (抗議)

いぎ

protest ⓤ /異議あり! *Objection!* / 異議なし! *No objection!* / (法廷で)異議を認めます[認めません] *Objection* sustained [overruled, denied]. / 彼女は我々の決定に異議を唱えた She *raised an objection* to our decision. / 異議はないと考えていいですか Am I to understand that you have *no objection*?

いぎ² 意義 (重要性) **significance** ⓤ, **importance** ⓤ; (意味) **meaning**, **sense** ⓤ; (目的・趣旨) **intent** ⓤ, **point** ⓤ /オリンピックは参加することに意義がある The *meaning* of the Olympic games lies in participating. / 意義のある人生を送る lead a *meaningful* [*worthwhile*] life / それについて議論するのは大いに意義のあることだ It's very *important to* talk about that.

いぎ³ 威儀 (威厳) **dignity** ⓤ; (重々しさ) **solemnity** ⓤ ◆参列者は威儀を正して式典に臨んだ Those present participated in the ceremony *in a dignified manner*.

いきあう 行き会う (出会う) **come* across ...**, **run* into ...** /通りで昔の友人に行き会った I *came across* an old friend on the street.

いきあたりばったり 行き当たりばったり
——行き当たりばったりの (無計画な) **haphazard**; (運まかせの) **hit-or-miss** ——行き当たりばったりに (無計画に) **haphazardly**; (無作為に) **at random** /あの店の経営は行き当たりばったりだ The management of that shop is *haphazard*. / 野党はその政策を行き当たりばったりだと非難した The opposition party criticized the policy as *haphazard*.
◆行き当たりばったりの旅 a *rambling* mode of travel
🅔「どこに泊まるの」「ううん、行き当たりばったりで探すよ(→運を信じるよ)」 "Where are you going to stay?" "I don't know. I'll *trust my luck*."

いきあたる 行き当たる 私たちは森で道に迷ったが、最後には正しい道に行き当たった We got lost in the woods but finally *struck* the right path.

いきいき 生き生き 生き生きとした表情 a *fresh* complexion / 生き生きとした描写 a *vivid* description / きょうは生き生きしてるね You look *fresh* today. / この絵はあの有名な戦いを生き生きと描写している This painting *vividly* represents that famous battle. / 本当に好きなことをやっているときに人は生き生きするものだ People are *at their best* when doing what they really like.

いきうつし 生き写し (よく似た人) **double** ⓒ, (口語的) the **spitting image** /その俳優はまさにジェームズ・ディーンの生き写しだ The actor is *the spitting image* of James Dean.
◆彼は父親に生き写しだ He is *the living image* of his father. / あなたはお母さんに生き写しですね You *look exactly like* your mother.

いきうま 生き馬 |慣用表現| 彼は生き馬の目を抜くようなコンピュータソフトの業界で働いている He works in the *dog-eat-dog* world of computer software.

いきうめ 生き埋め 地震による多くの建物の倒壊で数百人が生き埋めになった Many buildings collapsed in the earthquake and several hundred people *were buried alive*.

いきおい　勢い

❶【力】(強さ・力) **force** ⓤ, **power** ⓤ; (速さ) **speed** ⓤ; (活力) **energy** ⓤ, **vigor** ⓤ

激しい風の勢いでたくさんの木がなぎ倒された The great *force* of the wind has blown down a lot of trees.
あらしはだんだん勢いを増して[弱めて]きている The storm is gradually 「growing in [losing]」 *force*.
◆勢いを増す[失う] gain [lose] *impetus* / その産業にかつての勢いはない That industry *is a mere shadow of* its *former self*. / レースの終盤で彼は勢いを盛り返した He *rallied* toward the end of the race. / 津波がすさまじい勢いで村を襲った The tsunami hit the village with great *violence*. / その会社は日の出の勢いで(→急速に)発展している The company has been growing *very rapidly*. / 火は勢いよく燃え上がった The fire *blazed up*. / ホースから勢いよく水が吹き出した Water *shot out* from the hose.
🅔「その仕事、引き受けたの?」「うん、なんか彼の勢いに押されちゃって」 "Did you take the job?" "Yes, I *was* kind of *overwhelmed by* his *energy*."

❷【はずみ】**momentum** ⓤ
勢いがつく *gather* [*gain*] *momentum*
彼はジャンプ台から勢いをつけてプールに飛び込んだ He *gathered momentum* and jumped into the swimming pool.
ライバルチームが試合に出ないということで僕らは勢いをそがれてしまった We *lost some momentum* because our rivals dropped out of the tournament.
力士は勢い余って土俵の外に飛び出した(→自分自身の力が力士の体を外に出させた) His own *momentum* drove the wrestler out of the ring.
◆小野のゴールでチームは勢いづいた Ono's goal *put* the team *in high spirits*. / 彼は酔った勢いで(→酒の影響で大胆になって)彼女に好きだと言ってしまった *Emboldened by alcohol*, he told her that he loved her.

❸【成り行き】(当然) **naturally**, **as a matter of course**; (結果として) **consequently**
そんな恐ろしい事件の後ではいきおい懐疑的にならざるをえない *As a matter of course*, people get skeptical after such an awful incident.
|慣用表現| 14歳の少女は破竹の勢いでトーナメントを勝ち進んだ The 14-year-old girl *swept away* the competition in the tournament.

いきおいこむ 勢い込む 少年は勢い込んでたった今見てきたことを話した The boy talked *enthusiastically* about what he had just seen.

いきがい 生きがい 彼にとっては子供たちが生きがいだ His children are *his life*. / He lives

for his children. / あなたの生きがいは何ですか What do you *live for*? / What's your *reason for living*? / 生きがいのある(→生きる価値のある)人生を送りたいと思う I want to lead a life *worth living*. / 子供が生まれて新たな生きがいを感じるようになった After my baby was born, I had a new *will to live*.

いきかう 行き交う 行き交う人々を眺めながらコーヒーを飲んだ I had a cup of coffee watching people「*coming and going* [*walking to and fro*].

いきかえり 行き帰り 私は学校の行き帰りに彼女を見かけた I saw her *on my way to and from* school. / そこへの行き帰りだけで半日かかった It took me half a day just to *go there and back*.

いきかえる 生き返る come* (back) to life, revive ⓔ, be revived ∥水の中で茎を少し切ればその花は生き返るよ Trim the stem in water, and the flower *will revive*. ◆冷たいシャワーを浴びて生き返ったような気がした I felt *refreshed* after taking a cold shower. / イエス・キリストははりつけになった後,生き返ったとされている Jesus Christ is said to *have risen from the dead* after the crucifixion.

いきがかり 行き掛かり 行きがかり上しかたなく彼女を家まで送った I walked her home *because of the circumstances*.

いきがけ 行き掛け 駅への行きがけに郵便局に寄った I stopped by the post office *on my way to* the station.

いきかた¹ 生き方 lifestyle ⓒ, a way of life [living] ∥昔ながらの生き方 *a traditional way of life* / その経験は私の生き方を一変させた That experience changed *the whole mode of my life*.

いきかた² 行き方 その女性は私に市役所への行き方を教えてくれた The woman told me *how to get to* the city hall. / 駅への行き方は2つあります There are two *ways* [*routes*] to the station.

いきがる 粋がる (気取る) put* on airs ∥いきがるなよ! Don't *put on airs*!

いきき 行き来 この道は車の行き来が激しい *The traffic* is heavy on this street. / 母は家と病院の間を1日に何度も行き来した My mother *went back and forth* between the house and the hospital many times a day. / 磯野家と山田家はよく行き来する間柄だ The Isono's and the Yamada's often *visit with each other*. / 彼とは行き来がなくなってもう10年以上になる(→10年以上前に連絡をとらなくなった) I lost *contact* with him more than 10 years ago.

いきぎれ 息切れ —息切れする get* out of breath, lose* *one's* breath ∥最寄駅の階段を上がっただけで息切れする Recently I *get out of breath* just from going up the stairs in the station. ◆あまりがんばりすぎると途中で息切れするよ Don't work too hard, or you'll *run out of steam*.

いきぐるしい 息苦しい (息の詰まりそうな) choking, stifling,《口語的》suffocating; (風通しの悪い) stuffy; (緊張した) tense ∥この部屋は息苦しい This room *is stuffy*. / 7月の京都は息苦しいほどの暑さだった The heat of July in Kyoto was almost *suffocating*. ◆ネクタイを締めると息苦しいからいやだ I don't like wearing ties because they *choke* me.

いきごみ 意気込み (熱意) enthusiasm ⓤ, spirit ⓤ; (決意) determination ⓤ ∥君には意気込みが全く感じられない I can't see any *enthusiasm* in you. / 最初の意気込みはどこへやら(→非常な熱意をもって始めたが),彼女はあっさりバレエをやめてしまった She started off taking ballet lessons with great *enthusiasm*, but soon she quit it. / 彼は記者に次回のオリンピックにかける意気込みを語った He told *his determination* to be in the next Olympic Games to the reporter.

いきごむ 意気込む 彼女は本場の英語を身につけると意気込んでアメリカに出発した She set off for America *with great expectations* of studying living English. / 彼はそのコンテストで1等賞を取ると意気込んでいる He *is eager to get* (the) first prize in the contest.

いきさき 行き先 destination ⓒ ∥行き先くらいちゃんと言っていきなさい You've got to at least tell me *your destination* before leaving. / 母は私に行き先を告げずに出かけた My mother went out without telling me *where she was going*.

🄔(タクシーで)「お客さん,行き先は?」「東京駅までお願いします」*"Where to*, sir [ma'am]?" "To Tokyo Station, please."

🄔「田中さん,あしたから休暇で海外だって」「へえ,行き先は?」"Ms. Tanaka is going abroad on vacation tomorrow." "Do you know *where*?"

いきさつ どういういきさつで彼女と知り合ったのですか *How* did you get to know her? / 事のいきさつは後で話すよ I'll explain *the details* of the event later. / いきさつは知らないどそんなに落ち込まないで *I don't know what's got you down*, but please don't feel so bad.

いきざま 生きざま りっぱな生きざま *an* admirable *life*

いきじびき 生き字引 walking dictionary ⓒ

いきすぎ 行き過ぎ 警察は調査にいきすぎがあったことを認めた The police admitted that their investigation *had gone too far*. / 学校が生徒の前髪の長さまで指定するのはいきすぎだ The school *is exceeding its authority* to designate even the length of the students' bangs.

いきすぎる 行き過ぎる (通り過ぎる) go* past ∥本に熱中していて家の前を行き過ぎてしまった I was absorbed in reading, and *went past* my house. ◆有名人に対するいきすぎた報道はプライバシーの侵害だ *Too much* media exposure is an invasion of privacy.

🄔「ABCホールってこんなに遠かったっけ?」「行き過ぎちゃったのかな」"Was ABC Hall this far?" "I'm afraid *we've gone past*

いきせききる 息せき切る 彼は息せき切って走ってきた He came up running, *out of breath*.

いきた 生きた live [láiv], living ∥生きた化石 a *living* fossil / 静岡の親戚(炒)から生きたイセエビが送られてきた Our relative in Shizuoka sent us some *live* lobsters. / 彼は2年のアメリカ生活で生きた英語を身につけた He mastered *living* English while he stayed in America for two years.

◆恐ろしくて生きた心地がしなかった(→死ぬほど怖かった) I *was scared to death*.

🔑「おどり食いって何ですか」「魚を生きたまま食べるんだよ」 "What's *odorigui*?" "You eat some kinds of fish *alive*."

いきだおれ 行き倒れ 行き倒れになる collapse and die by the roadside

いきち 生き血 (生きた動物の血) the blood of a living animal, 《文語》lifeblood ∥その政策は社会的弱者の生き血をすするようなものだ That policy is like *sucking the lifeblood out of* the disadvantaged.

いきちがい 行き違い 私の手紙はあなたのと行き違いになったようだ My letter seems to *have crossed* yours. / 彼は以前その会社と何か行き違い(→誤解)があったらしい It seems that he had some kind of *trouble* with that company before.

🔑「ついさっきまゆみが迎えに行ったよ」「ほんと？行き違いになっちゃったんだ」 "Mayumi went to see you just now!" "Really? We must *have passed each other on the way*."

いきづかい 息遣い (呼吸) breathing Ⓤ
◆彼は荒い息づかいをしていた He *was breathing* hard [heavily].

いきつぎ 息継ぎ 私はクロールで息継ぎができない I can't *take a breath* when I'm swimming the crawl.

いきつく 行き着く (着く) arrive ⓐ; (予定外の場所に) (口語的)fetch up; (行き当たる) hit* ⓐ ∥さんざん歩いているうちに小さな村に行き着いた We *fetched up* at a small village after walking quite a long time.

◆彼は行き着くところまで行ってしまった He's passed *the point of no return*.

いきづく 息づく (生きている) be alive ∥相撲の世界には今も昔ながらの伝統が息づいている The old traditions *are* still *alive* in the world of sumo.

いきつけ 行きつけ ――行きつけの(お気に入りの) favorite ∥行きつけの場所 one's *favorite* spot;《口語的》a stamping ground

いきづまり¹ 行き詰まり ⇒ゆきづまり

いきづまる¹ 行き詰まる ⇒ゆきづまる

いきづまる² 息詰まる (息をのむような) breathtaking; (興奮させる) exciting, thrilling; (重苦しい) oppressive ∥息詰まるような沈黙 *oppressive* silence / 決勝戦は息詰まるような熱戦だった The final was a very *exciting* [*thrilling*] game.

いきどおり 憤り (怒り) anger Ⓤ, resentment Ⓤ Ⓒ; (不正などに対する) indignation Ⓤ ∥大統領はテロに対する憤りをあらわにした The President openly showed *his indignation* toward terrorism.

◆ほとんどの国民は官僚の不正に憤りを感じている Most people *feel indignant at* the corruption of the bureaucrats.

いきどおる 憤る (憤慨している) be indignant ∥地域の住民は不法なごみの投棄に憤っている The locals *are indignant* at the illegal dumping of waste.

いきとどく 行き届く 手入れの行き届いた庭 a *well-kept* garden ∥そのレストランはサービスが行き届いているという評判だ That restaurant has a reputation for *good service*. / 彼の踊りは指先まで神経が行き届いている When dancing, he *pays full attention to* his whole body, right down to his fingertips.

いきどまり 行き止まり (袋小路) dead end Ⓒ, blind alley [lane] ◆この通りは300メートル先で行き止まりです This street *ends* 300 meters ahead.

いきながらえる 生き長らえる (生きる) live ⓐ; (生き残る) survive ⓐ ∥彼女は癌(ﾞ)を克服して90歳まで生き長らえた She got over cancer and *lived to* be 90.

いきなり (突然) suddenly; (だしぬけに) abruptly; (予告なしに) without notice ∥路地からいきなり子供が飛び出してきた A child *suddenly* ran out of the alley. / 父はいきなり中国への転勤を命じられた My father was transferred to China *without notice*. / 前を歩いていた男性がいきなり立ち止まったのでぶつかってしまった The man walking in front of me stopped *abruptly*, so I bumped into him.

いきぬき 息抜き (ひと休み) rest Ⓤ Ⓒ,《口語的》breather Ⓒ; (気晴らし) relaxation Ⓤ Ⓒ ∥たまには息抜きも必要だ You should take *a rest* once in a while.

◆彼は息抜きに(→リラックスするために)よくジャズを聴く He often listens to jazz *to relax*.

いきぬく 生き抜く それは動乱の時代を生き抜いた1人の女性の物語だ That's a story about a woman who *survived* [*lived through*] turbulent times.

いきのこり 生き残り (生存・存続) survival Ⓤ; (生存者) survivor Ⓒ ∥その会社は生き残りをかけてリストラに踏み切った The company started to reduce the personnel, struggling *for survival*.

いきのこる 生き残る survive ⓐ ⓗ ∥我々の会社が生き残るためにはこのプロジェクトを成功させることが絶対に必要だ The success of this project is a must for our company *to survive*. / その事故で奇跡的に4人の乗客が生き残った Four passengers miraculously *survived* the accident.

いきのびる 生き延びる survive ⓐ ⓗ, live out ∥彼は20日間海上を漂流したがらのように生き延びたかを話した He described how he *had survived* for 20 days adrift on the sea. / あの動物たちが生き延びられればいいのだが I wish those animals could *survive*.

いきはじ 生き恥 生き恥をさらすくらいなら死んだほうがましだ I would sooner die than *live in shame*.

いきまく 息巻く (激しく言う) say* furiously; (いばる) boast [他], brag [他] ‖やつはけんかで負けたことがないと息巻いた He *boasted* [*bragged*] *that* he had never been beaten in a fight.

いきむ 息む (下腹に力を入れる) strain *one's* abdomen; (トイレで) strain *oneself*; (分娩(ぶんべん)で) bear* down

いきもの 生き物 living thing [C], (living) being [C], 《集合的》life [U]; (動物・鳥・昆虫などの) creature [C] ‖太陽はすべての生き物に必要である The sun is necessary for all *living things*. / 言葉は生き物だ Words are *living things*. / 水中には様々な生き物がすんでいる Various *creatures* live under water.

いきょう[1] 異教 (異なった宗教) different religion [C]; (異端) heresy [U] ――異教の (キリスト教・ユダヤ教・イスラム教のいずれでもない) pagan, 《古風》heathen; (異端の) heretical ‖異教徒 a pagan, 《古風》a heathen, a heretic

いきょう[2] 異郷・異境 (異国の地) foreign land [country] [C] ‖その作家は祖国を追われ異郷で病に倒れた The writer was exiled from his country and fell ill *in a foreign land*.

いぎょう 偉業 great achievement [C], great work [U]; (功績) feat [C] ‖彼はプルースト全集の翻訳という偉業を成しとげた He achieved *the great work* of translating the complete works of Proust. / ワクチンによる予防法の発見は医学史に残る偉業だ The discovery of vaccination was *a great achievement* in medical history.

いきょく 医局 medical office [C] ‖医局員 a member of the medical staff / 医局長 the chief of the medical staff

イギリス (Great) Britain, the United Kingdom (《略語》the U.K.); England ――イギリス人 《集合的》the British ――イギリスの British; English

[語法]
(1) イギリスの正式名称は「グレートブリテンおよび北部アイルランド連合王国」(the United Kingdom of Great Britain and Northern Ireland)という.
(2) イギリスはグレートブリテン島のイングランド(England), スコットランド(Scotland), ウェールズ(Wales)と北部アイルランド(Northern Ireland)から成る連合王国であり, その一部である England を全体の国名として用いるのは避けたほうがよい.
(3) 同様に English(man[woman])もイングランド人を指すので「イギリス人」という場合は British を用いる.

彼は先月イギリスへ出発した He left for *Britain* last month.

『オアシス』はイギリスのロックグループだ "Oasis" is a *British* rock group.

その男の人にはイギリスなまりがあった The man had *a British accent*.

‖イギリス英語 British English / イギリス海峡 the English Channel (❖単に the Channel ともいう) / イギリス連邦 the Commonwealth of Nations

いきりたつ いきり立つ いきり立った群衆は警官隊に向かって石を投げつけた The *enraged* crowd threw stones at the police.

いきる 生きる

❶【生存する】live [自] [他] (↔die); (生きている) be alive (↔be dead), be living ⇒いきた

私たちは酸素なしでは生きられない We *cannot live* without oxygen.

まさか生きて帰れるとは思わなかった I never thought that I would come back *alive*.

もし君のお父さんがまだ生きていたならどう言うだろう What would your father say if he *were* still *alive*?

その作家は17世紀に生きた人だ The writer *lived* in the 17th century.

祖父は90歳まで生きた (→生きて90歳になった) My grandfather *lived* to be 90.

短い命ではあったが彼は精一杯生きた He *lived his life to the full*, though it was short.

コアラはユーカリの葉を食べて生きている Koalas *live* on eucalyptus leaves. (❖live on ... は「…を常食にしている」の意味)

マザーテレサは多くの人の心の中に今も生き続けている Mother Teresa still *lives on* in many people's minds. (❖この on は「続けて」の意味の副詞)

マーゴ・フォンテーンはバレエひとすじに生きた Margot Fonteyn *lived* solely for ballet.

走っているときには生きているという実感がわいてくる I feel really *alive* when I'm running.

◆それは生きるか死ぬかの問題だ That's a matter of *life and death*. / 水がなければどんな生物も生きられない If it were not for water, there *would be no life*. / 生きるべきか死ぬべきか, それが問題だ *To be or not to be*, that is the question. (❖『ハムレット』の中の言葉) / 生きているうちに(→死ぬ前に)スカイダイビングをやってみたい I'd like to try skydiving *before I die*. / その絵の中の人物はまるで生きているように見える The person in that painting looks so *lifelike*.

❷【生活する】live [自] [他]

彼は彼女なしで生きるなんて想像できなかった He couldn't imagine himself *living* without her.

世界には生きるために働かなければならない子供たちがいる There are children in the world who have to work in order to *live*.

◆これからどうやって生きていくつもりなんだ How are you going to *make a living* from now on? / プロのミュージシャンとして生きていくのは簡単なことではない It's not easy to *make a living* as a professional musician.

いきわかれ

❸ [有効である]

あの約束はまだ生きていますか Is that promise still *effective*?

19世紀の法律がいまだに生きているのには驚いた I was surprised to find some laws from 19th century are still *valid*.

❹ [効果が発揮される]

シンプルな衣装のほうが彼女の個性が生きる(→長所を引き出す) A simple outfit will *bring out* the best in her looks.

合唱部にいた経験が今になって生きてきた My experience in the chorus club has turned out to be *useful* now.

いきわかれ 生き別れ
彼女は子供のころ生き別れになった(→引き離された)母親を捜している She is looking for her mother who she *was parted from* in childhood.

いきわたる 行き渡る
全員に行き渡るだけの皿がありますか Are there *enough* plates for everyone? / 生徒数が多すぎると教師の注意が全員に行き渡らない(→全員に注意を払うことができない) If the number of students is too large, the teacher *won't be able to pay attention* to everyone.

いく¹ 行く

❶ 目的地に向かって進む go, come
❷ 事が運ぶ・進展する
❸ …しに行く

❶ [目的地に向かって進む] go* 圓; (相手のいる所・相手と同方向へ) come* 圓; (到着する) get* 圓; (訪れる) visit 他

語法
(1) go は話し手の方でも聞き手の方でもない「ほかの場所へ行く」ことを表し、「聞き手の方へ行く」ことには come を用いる. 話し手と聞き手がいっしょに行く場合、行く場所に重点をおくなら go, 聞き手が話し手とともに行くという点に注目するなら come を使う ∥ 私はあす大阪に行きます I'm *going* to Osaka tomorrow. / きょうの午後あなたの家に行ってもいいですか May I *come* to your house this afternoon? / 映画に行くんだけど、君もいっしょに行かない? I'm *going* to a movie. Won't you *come* with me?

(2)「学校へ行く(→学校へ勉強しに行く)」など、単にその建物や場所へ行くことではなく、それ本来の目的のために行くということを表す場合は冠詞を付けない ∥ 私はバスで学校へ行きます I *go to school* by bus.

歯医者に行く *go* to the dentist('s) / 上の階[2階]へ行く *go* upstairs

先月私は家族と北海道に行った I *went to* Hokkaido with my family last month.

きょう銀行に行かなければならない I must *go to* the bank today.

彼女はどこへ行ってもみんなの注目を集める Wherever she *goes*, she draws people's attention.

どこでも好きな所に行きなさい You *may go* anywhere you like.

彼はどっちの方向に行きましたか Which way did he *go*?

どこの高校に行っていますか What high school do you *go to*?

君はもう行ってよろしい You may *go* now.

あっちへ行って! *Go* away!

さあ行こう Let's *go*.

そろそろ行きましょうか Shall we *go* now?

もう行かなくては I have to *go* now.

先に行って. すぐ追いつくから *Go* ahead. I'll catch up soon.

あすの午後あなたの家へ行ってもいいですか May I *come to* your place tomorrow afternoon?

駅へはどう行けばいいですか How can I *get to* the station?

彼女はあちこちの店に行ってたくさんのみやげ物を買った She *visited* this shop and that, and bought a lot of souvenirs.

この道をまっすぐ行けば千駄ヶ谷の駅に出ます *Go* along this street, and you'll come to Sendagaya Station.

彼女はイギリスに行ってしまった She's gone to Britain. (❖have [has] gone は「行ってしまってここにはいない」の意味)

◆友人を見送りに空港まで行ってきたところです I*'ve been* to the airport to see my friend off. / 外国にはまだ行ったことがない I*'ve never been* abroad. / 彼女は仕事でニューヨークに行っている She *is* in New York on business. / 男は通路を行ったり来たりした The man *walked up and down* the aisle. / 彼は学校に行く途中で交通事故にあった He had a traffic accident *on his way to* school.

🗨「ごはんですよ」「今行きます」 "Dinner's ready." "*Coming*!/ I'm *coming*!" (❖×I'm going. とはいわない)

🗨「どこ行ってたの」「コンビニ」 "Where *have* you *been*?" "To the convenience store."

🗨「私もいっしょに行っていいですか」「もちろん」 "May I *come* with you?" "Sure."

🗨「来週香港へ行くんだ」「何しに」 "I'm *going to* Hong Kong next week." "What for?"

🗨「カナダへ行ったことがありますか」「ええ. 昨年の夏に行きました」 "*Have you ever been to* Canada?" "Yes. I *went* there last summer."

🗨「バス、ちょうど行っちゃったみたい」「じゃあタクシーで行こう(→タクシーを使おう)か」 "It looks like the bus *has* just *left*." "Then, shall we *take* a taxi?"

🗨「三大テノールのコンサートはどうだった」「最高だったよ. 君も行けばよかったのに」 "How was the Three Tenors concert?" "Absolutely wonderful. You really *should have gone*."

❷ [事が運ぶ・進展する]

物事はなかなか計画どおりにはいかないものだ Things *don't* always *go* as you have planned.

今のところすべてうまくいっています Every-

thing *is going well* so far.
彼女は義母とあまりうまくいっていない She *isn't getting along well* with her mother-in-law.
完璧(%%)とはいかないがこのケーキはなかなかうまく焼けた This cake is nicely done, though it *might not be* perfect.
その説明はどうも納得がいかない I'm *not satisfied with* the explanation.
彼女はわが道を行く人だ She *has her own way* in everything she does.
後で連絡がいくと思います You'll *be informed* soon.
彼は若く見えるが実はけっこう年がいっている He looks young but actually he *is* pretty *old*.

❸【…しに行く】

> (1)「…しに行く」は go+*doing* で表せることが多い ∥キャンプに行く *go camping* / 踊りに行く *go dancing*
> (2)「(場所)へ…しに行く」というときの前置詞に注意する. 英語では「〜で…すること」を「…しに行く」というような塊(%%)でとらえるため,「〜へ」の部分を×to …とはしない ∥デパートに買い物に行く *go shopping at* [×to] a department store / 川に泳ぎに行く *go swimming in* [×to] a river
> (3) 口語的な表現に go (and) *do*, come (and) *do* があるが, これは go [come] を原形で用いる場合にしか使えない. それ以外では go [come] *to do* のようにする ∥牛乳を買いに行ってちょうだい *Go (and) get* some milk for me. / きのういとこのところへ遊びに行った I *went to see* my cousin yesterday.

映画を見に行く *go to (see)* a movie; *go to the movies* / ドライブに行く *go for a drive*
父と私はたまに釣りに行く My father and I *go fishing* once in a while.
渋谷へ買い物に行った I *went shopping in* Shibuya.
今年の冬は北海道にスキーをしに行くつもりだ I'm *going skiing in* Hokkaido this winter.
今度の日曜日にピクニックに行こう Let's *go on a picnic* next Sunday.
ちょっと散歩に行きませんか Shall we *go for a little walk*?
きょうの午後なら手伝いに行けます I *can come and help* you this afternoon.
彼に会いに行けなくて残念です I regret that I can't *come to see* him.

いく² 逝く ぼっくり逝く *die* suddenly / また1人映画界の巨匠が逝った Another great master of the film world *passed away*.

いく- 幾- ⇒いくつ, いくら ∥幾人かの人 *some* [*several*] people / その問題を解決するには幾通りかの方法がある There are *some* ways to solve the problem. / 幾千万の星が夜空にまたたいている *Hundreds and* [*of*] *thousands of* stars twinkle in the sky. / 幾久しくお幸せに May you have a *long*, happy life to-

gether. / I wish you happiness *for ever*.

イグアナ 〖動物〗iguana ⓒ

いくえいかい 育英会 scholarship foundation [association] ⓒ ∥日本育英会 *the* Japan *Scholarship Foundation*

いくえいしきん 育英資金 scholarship fund ⓒ

いくえにも 幾重にも 幾重にも重なる山並みが雲の動きによって色を変えた *Row upon row* of mountains changed color beneath the moving clouds. / 幾重にもおわび申し上げます I am *extremely* sorry. / I beg you *a thousand* apologies.(❖後の表現は非常に丁寧だが, 皮肉に受け取られることもある)

いぐさ 藺草 rush ⓒ

いくじ¹ 育児 育児に追われる be busy 「with *the care of* [*raising*] *one's baby*」/ 父親も育児に参加するべきだ Fathers should take their share of *caring for their babies*. / 彼女は育児ノイローゼになった She became *neurotic from the pressure of raising her child*.
∥育児休暇 child-care leave; (母親の) maternity leave; (父親の) paternity leave / 育児室 a nursery / 育児書 a book on child care

いくじ² 意気地 弟はまるで意気地がない My little brother is really *chicken-hearted*.
∥意気地なし a coward, 《口語的》 a chicken

いくせい 育成 (訓練) training ⓤ; (養成・進化) cultivation ⓤ ──育成する (訓練する) train ⓣ; (教育する) educate ⓣ; (栽培する) grow* ⓣ ∥彼は現役を引退し後進の育成にあたっている He retired as a player and now he *is training* the younger generation.

いくた 幾多 ──幾多の (多くの) many, much; (非常に多くの) a great number of … ∥彼らは人生で幾多の困難を切り抜けてきた They have passed through *much* hardship in their lives.

いくつ 幾つ

❶【何個】how many
いくつ欲しいの *How many* do you want?
お皿はあといくつ足りないの *How many* more plates do you need?
◆いくつでも(→好きなだけ)お取りください You can take *as many as you want*. / 3に7を足すといくつになりますか *What* do you get if you add three to [and] seven? / 5の2乗はいくつですか *What* is the square of five?

❷【何歳】how old
あなたのお父さんはおいくつになられましたか May I ask *how old* your father is?
◆彼はいくつになっても変わらない He hasn't *ever* changed.

🅒「坊ちゃんはおいくつですか」「3歳です」 "*How old* is your son?" "He's three."

いくつか 幾つか some; a few; several

> 漠然とした数を表す最も一般的な語が some で, かなり広い範囲の数を表す. 日本語であえて「いくつか」とはいわない場合でも, その意味が含まれていれば英語では付けることが多い. a

few は「数は少ないがある」ことを強調するが，a を付けない場合は「ほとんど…ない」という否定の意味が強くなる．several は名詞の前に用い，3以上で many より少ない漠然とした数を表す．ほかに「2, 3の」の意味では a couple of ... なども用いられる．

この計画にはいくつかの欠点がある There are *some* faults in this plan.
我々はその2つの犯罪にいくつかの類似点を発見した We have found *some* similarity between the two crimes.
彼は例をいくつか挙げて自分の考えを説明した He illustrated his idea with *some* examples.
私は自分用にいくつか買った I've bought myself *some*.
ここにあるクッションをいくつか借りてもいいですか Can I borrow *some* [*any*] of the cushions here? (◆貸してもらえると期待している場合は some, 借りられるかどうか分からない場合は any を用いる)
彼はいくつかの薬品を調合した He compounded *several* drugs.
リンゴのいくつかには虫が食った穴があいていた *Several* of the apples had worm holes.
先生，いくつか質問していいですか Sir [Ma'am], may I ask *a few* questions?
この法則はいくつかの例外を除けばすべてに当てはまる This rule applies to all except for *a few* isolated cases.

いくつも 幾つも (多数) many, a lot of ‖ 彼女はいくつも帽子を持っている She has *many* [*a lot of*] hats.

いくど 幾度 how many times, how often ⇒なんど(何度) ◆彼女に幾度となく手紙を出したが返事は1通も来なかった I wrote to her *so many times*, but never got a single letter back.

いくどうおん 異口同音 人々は異口同音に「その名前は口にするな」と言った Everyone said *in chorus*, "Don't mention that name." / 彼らは異口同音に慎太郎の手腕をほめた *With one voice* they praised Shintaro for his ability.

いくにち 幾日 その地方では幾日も雨が降り続いた It kept raining *for days* in that region.

イグニッション (点火装置) the ignition ‖ イグニッションキー an ignition key

いくぶん 幾分 (少し) a little, rather; (やや) somewhat; (多少) more or less; (ある程度) in some measure, in part, to some degree [extent] ‖ きょうは幾分涼しい It is *somewhat* cool today. / 空は幾分曇っていた The sky was *rather* overcast. / 予報によると今年の梅雨明けは例年より幾分早まる見込みだ The weather forecast says the rainy season will end *a little* earlier this year than usual.

いくもう 育毛 hair restoration Ⓤ ‖ 育毛剤 (a) hair-restorer

イクラ ⚠ (サケの卵) salmon roe Ⓤ (◆日本語はロシア語の ikra から)

いくら 幾ら

❶【金額】how much
(値段は)いくらですか *How much*?
このパソコンはいくらですか *How much* is this PC?
この牛肉は1キロいくらですか *How much* per kilo is this beef?
この小包を日本へ送るのにいくらかかりますか *How much* does it cost to send this package to Japan?
彼女があなたにいくら借金をしているか私は知らない I don't know *how much* she owes you.
このアパートの家賃はいくらですか *How much* is the rent for this apartment?
全部でおいくらですか *How much* does it cost all together? / What does the lot come to?
参考までに，それにいくら支払ったのですか Just out of interest, *how much* did you pay for it?
◆東京までの運賃はいくらですか *What's the fare* to Tokyo? / このカメラの値段はいくらですか *What's the price* of this camera? (◆× How much is the price of ...? とはいわない) / 収入は手取り[税込み]でいくらですか *What do you earn* after [before] tax?
🅔「今いくらお金持ってるの」「あんまり持ってない」 "*How much* money do you have with you?" "Not much."
🅔「お金かかりそうだね」「いや，いくらもかからないよ」 "It must be expensive." "No, not really."

英作文ノート 「…いくらで」は定冠詞
その市場では魚はキロいくらで売っている
→×They sell fish by *a* kilogram at the market.
→○They sell fish by *the* kilogram at the market.
★単位を表す「1キロいくらで」とか「1日いくらで」「1ダースいくらで」は, by the kilogram, by the day, by the dozen のように by the＋単位で表現する． by a ... とはいわないので注意．

❷【どんなに…しても】
彼女をいくらほめても足りない You *cannot* admire her *enough*.
車を運転するときにはいくら注意してもしすぎることはない You *cannot* be *too* careful when driving (a car).
彼はいくら必死にやっても毎回失敗してしまう *No matter how* hard he tries, he always fails.
あなたのご協力にはいくら感謝しても足りません No thanks can repay you for your help.
靖子は好きな歌手の話をいくらしても飽きない Yasuko *never* tires of talking about her favorite singer.
キノコはノーカロリーだからいくら食べても太らない Mushrooms have no calories, so you

can eat them *as much as* you want without getting fat.
いくら何でもそれはひどい *Whatever the reason is*, that's terrible.
いくらかかってもかまわない (→出費は問題ではない) *Expense [Money] is no object*.

いくらか 幾らか (少し) *some, a bit, a little*; (やや) *somewhat*
彼女は容子にいくらかお金を貸した She lent *some* money to Yoko.
私には予備の資金がいくらかある I have *some* funds kept in reserve.
バンパーが衝撃をいくらか吸収してくれた The car bumper absorbed *some* of the impact.
彼はいくらか疲れているように見えた He looked *somewhat* tired.
私もいくらか払います I'll pay for *some* of it, too.
◆その人物はその事件といくらか関係がある That person *has something to do with* the incident.

いくらでも 幾らでも いくらでも好きなだけ取っていいよ You can take *as much [many] as* you like. (❖数えられないものには much, 数えられるものには many を用いる) / そういう話はいくらでもある There are *great many* cases like that. / 金ならいくらでも出す I'll pay *however much* is necessary. / (寄付を集めて) 金額はいくらでも結構です *Any* sum is acceptable.

いくらも 幾らも お金はもういくらも残っていなかった I had *only a little* money left. / 彼はいくらも進まないうちに休もうと言いだした He said he wanted to rest before we had gotten *very far*. / 中古のギターならいくらもしないだろう A secondhand guitar will *not cost* you *much*.

いけ 池 pond ⓒ /学校の裏手にある池 *a pond* at the back of the school / 池でボートをこぐ row a boat on *a pond* / 池に模型の船を浮かべる float a model ship on *a pond* / ボールは転がって池に落ちた The ball rolled into *the pond*.

いけい 畏敬 (尊敬と恐れの気持ち) awe Ⓤ /その山は村の人々に畏敬の念をいだかせた That mountain inspired *awe* in the people of the village.

いけいれん 胃痙攣 stomach cramps

いけがき 生け垣 hedge ⓒ /生け垣を刈り込む trim *a hedge* / 彼は庭に生け垣をめぐらした He planted *a hedge* around the garden.

いけす 生け簀 (料理店などの) a water tank to keep fish alive until they are cooked; (養魚場) fishpond ⓒ

いけすかない いけ好かない (感じが悪い) disagreeable, unpleasant ◆あいつはどうもいけ好かない (→何となく嫌いだ) Somehow, [I don't know why, but] I *don't like* him.

いけどり 生け捕り 畑を荒らしていた猿を数匹生け捕りにした We *caught* some monkeys (*alive*) which were eating crops in the field.

いけない

❶ 必要　　　must *do*; have to *do*
❷ 禁止　　　cannot *do*, must not *do*
❸ よくない　bad; wrong

❶【必要】must *do*; have* to *do*; have got to *do*; need (to) *do*; should *do*, ought to *do*

> must: 命令的で,「…しなければならない」の意味. ほかに選択はない.
> have to:「…することが必要」,または「…しなければいけない」.
> have got to: have to の強調形. 必要性が大きい, または緊急である.
> need (to):「…することが必要だ」という意味.
> should, ought to: should と ought to はほぼ同じで,「…するほうがいい」の意味.

君たちは互いに助け合わなければいけない You *must* help each other.
人の気持ちを考えなければいけない You *must* consider other people's feelings.
試験前にこの単語を全部覚えなければいけない I *must* learn all these words before the exam.
この本全部読まなければいけないの？ そんなの無理だよ Do I *have to* read all these books? That's impossible.
それは君が我慢しなきゃいけないことだ That's something you *have to* put up with.
きょうは8時までに家に帰らなくてはいけない I've *got to* be home by eight this evening.
靴を磨かないといけない I *need to* polish my shoes.
このジーパンは洗濯しないといけない This pair of jeans *needs* a wash.
弟によいお手本を示さなければいけないよ You *should* set your brother a good example.

❷【禁止】(…してはいけない) cannot *do*, must not *do*; (…するべきでない) should not *do*

ここでたばこを吸ってはいけない You *can't* smoke in here.
現実から目を背けてはいけない You *shouldn't* turn away from the reality.
◆ドアをあけっぱなしにしてはいけない *Don't* leave the door open. / この川で泳いではいけない Swimming *is not allowed* in this river. / 芝生に入ってはいけません *Keep off* the grass. / ここに自転車を置いてはいけないことになっています You *are not supposed to* leave your bicycles here. / だれも許可なくその部屋に入ってはいけない *No* person *may* enter the room without permission. / すべきこととしてはいけないことを教えよう I'll tell you what to do and *what not to do*.

❸【よくない】(悪い) bad; (誤った) wrong; (いたずらな) naughty
いけない子ね You *naughty* boy!
この髪型のどこがいけないの What's *wrong*

with my hairstyle?
何かいけないこと言った？ Did I say something *wrong*?
◆いけない！ おふろの水、止めるの忘れてた Oh no! I forgot to turn off the tap for the bath! / いけないのは君の優柔不断なところです *The problem* with you is your indecisiveness.

🅴「かぜをこじらせたようだ」「そいつはいけないね」 "My cold is getting worse." "*That's too bad*."

❹【用心・懸念】
雨が降るといけないから（→降った場合に備えて）傘を持っていきなさい Take an umbrella with you, (just) *in case* it rains.

かぜをひくといけないので上着を持っていった I took a jacket with me *for fear of* catching a cold.

ご両親が心配するといけないから（→心配しないように）電話しておきなさい Call your parents *so that* they *won't* be worried about you.

いけにえ 生け贄 sacrifice ◯ *//*神々へ生けにえをささげる offer [make] *a sacrifice* to the gods ◆古代の人々はいろいろな動物を神々への生けにえにしていた Ancient people *sacrificed* various animals to their gods.

いけばな 生け花・活け花 🔲 *ikebana*, flower arrangement *//*彼女は高校に入ったときから生け花をやっている She has been practicing *flower arrangement* since she entered high school.

> 初期仏教でささげ物として使われていた花にその起源をもつ生け花は、15世紀に発展を遂げました。いくつかの流派があり、それぞれが独自のスタイルをもっていますが、最初に3本の木花で三角形を作る、という規則は共通しています。
> *Ikebana*, Japanese flower arrangement, with its origin in the early Buddhist flower offerings, developed in the 15th century. There are several schools and each has its own style. But there are certain rules common to all the schools like starting by forming a triangle with three main flowers.

いける¹ 生ける・活ける ❶【花を生ける】 arrange ⓣ *//*この花を生けてくれませんか Will you *arrange* these flowers?

❷【生きている】 生きとし生けるもの all *living creatures* / 妻が自分のもとを去ってから彼は生ける屍(しかばね)のようになってしまった After his wife left him, he was just *a shell of his former self*.

いける² 行ける ❶【行くことができる】 車で［歩いて］行ける距離 (a) *driving [walking] distance* / その競技場へはバスで行ける You *can get* to the stadium *by bus*. / The stadium is *accessible by* bus. → いく（行く）

❷【味がよい】 good, delicious *//*こいつはいける This *is good [delicious]*. / このワインはけっこういける This wine *tastes* pretty *good*. / This wine *isn't bad*. ❖ 積極的にほめる意味で「悪くない」という言い方をすることもある）

◆そのインド料理店はなかなかいけるよ That Indian restaurant is quite *a find*. ❖ find は「掘り出し物」の意味）

❸【酒が飲める】
🅴「いける口ですか（→たくさん飲みますか）」「ほんのつきあい程度です」 "Do you *drink much*?" "Oh, I'm just a social drinker."

❹【その他】 彼はフランス語もいける（→話せる） He *can* also *speak* French.

いけん¹ 意見

❶【考え】 opinion ◯; view ◯; idea ◯; thought ◯; comment ◯
→ コミュニケーションスキル p.93

> opinion: 特定の話題に対する自分の考えや判断を指す.
> view: 物事に対する個人的な見解, ものの見方.
> idea: 話題に対しての反応ではなく, 自発的に心の中に浮かぶ考え.
> thought: 「考え」一般を表す語.
> comment: 文章あるいは口頭での論評.

《～(の)意見》
それはあなたの個人的な意見ですか Is that your *personal opinion*?
これは私の専門家としての意見です This is my *professional opinion*.
彼も同じ意見のようだ He seems to have *the same opinion*.
私の意見では彼はその仕事には向いていないと思う *In my opinion*, he isn't fit for that job.
我々は外部の意見も求めるべきだ We should ask for *an outside opinion*.

《意見が・は》
この件に関してあなたのご意見はいかがですか What is your *opinion* about [on] this matter?
私の意見は君のとはまるで違う My *opinion* is totally different from yours.
その候補者に対する彼らの意見は正反対のものである Their *views on* the candidate are totally opposite.
あなたの意見は見当はずれだ Your *comment* is beside the point.
彼は自分の意見が通らず残念そうだった He appeared to be sorry that his *idea* was turned down.
この問題では専門家の間で意見が大きく分かれる On this subject, there is much difference of *opinion* among experts.
◆駅で会うのがいちばんよいということでみんなの意見が一致した We all *agreed that* it was best to meet at the station. / そこへどうやって行くかについては意見が合わなかった We *didn't agree (on [about])* how to get there.

《意見を・に》
自分の意見に固執する stick [hold] to *one's opinion*
同僚は私の意見に賛成だと答えた My colleague answered that he「shared my *opinion* [agreed with me].
市議会は祭りに関して市民の意見を求めた The

コミュニケーションスキル —意見—
①意見を求める表現

(A) **What do you think about [of] ...?**
…をどう思いますか.
(B) **How do you feel about ...?**
…をどう思いますか.
(C) **What's your opinion about [on] ...? [Tell me what you think about ...?]**
…についてのあなたのご意見[お考え]はどうですか.
(D) **Give me your frank opinion about ....**
…について率直なご意見をお聞かせください.
(E) **Does anybody have comments on** this matter?
この問題についてどなたかご意見はありませんか.
(F) **Does anybody have a different opinion? How [What] about you,** Mr. Kato?
どなたか違った意見はありませんか. 加藤さんどうですか.
(G) **Do you have any idea** who sent this letter to us?
この手紙をだれが送ってきたのか, 思い当たることはありませんか.
(H) **How do you like** the way he speaks?
彼の言い方はどうですか.

☞ 相手の考えを尋ねる場合, (A) ~ (C) が最も基本的な表現. (A) は What で始めることに注意. (D) は特に率直な意見を遠慮なく述べてほしいときに用いる.

☞ (F) の How [What] about you? は, 司会者などがその場にいる人を次々と指名していくような場合によく用いる.

☞ (G) の Do you have any idea ...? は, idea の後に what, who, where などの疑問詞で始まる間接疑問を置いて, 「…か知っているか」と尋ねる表現になる.

☞ (H) の How do you like ...? は特定のものについて, 相手の好みや印象を尋ねる表現. だが論理的な場面でも使われる. 例えば (H) のような問いに次のように答えることがある.
I don't like it, because he looks arrogant, and he's too wordy. 嫌いだね. 態度が横柄だし, 口数が多すぎるから.

②意見を述べる表現

(A) What do you think about [of] our new mascot?
 -**I think** it's very attractive and it'll be a hit with young people.
わが社の新しいマスコットをどう思いますか. —たいへん魅力的で, 若者にうけると思いますよ.
(B) How do you feel about this plan?
 -Well, **I think** it's okay, but we need to look into it in more detail.
この計画をどう思う. —ううん, いいと思うけど, もっと細かく検討する必要があるね.
(C) So what's your opinion?
 -**In my opinion**, it would cost too much to change the whole system.
で, 君の意見は? —私の意見としては, システム全体を変えるのはコストがかかりすぎると思うね.
(D) How do you like my new hat?
 -**Oh, it looks very nice and matches your dress.**
私の新しい帽子どうかしら. —いや, とてもすてきで, ドレスに合っているよ.
(E) Do you have any comment?
 -**No, I'd rather not say anything about it.**
何かコメントはありますか. —いや, 遠慮しておきます.

☞ 意見や考え方を求められた場合, I think ... と答えるのが最も常識的だが, ほかに (C) の **In my opinion, I feel ...** (…と感じる), **My idea is that ...** (私の考えでは…だ) などが用いられる. このような表現はあまり繰り返すとくどいので, 発言の最初だけでよい.

☞ (D) How do you like ...? に対する答え方で, 日本人は I like it. だけで終わることが多いが, それだけで終わらせずに, できるだけ理由を付け加えたほうがよい.

☞ (E) はあえて意見やコメントを差し控えたい場合に用いる表現.

city council appealed to the citizens for *opinions* about the festival.
あなたの友人に自分の意見を押しつけてはいけない Don't force your *opinions* on your friends.
委員は長い討論を通して意見をまとめた The committee members formed *an opinion* through lengthy discussions.
母は教育に関して確固とした意見をもっている My mother has strong *opinions* about education.
空欄に意見を書いてください Write your *comment* in the blank spaces.
どうぞ自由に意見を述べてください Please express your *opinion* freely.
君はこの件に関して意見を翻(ひるがえ)すべきではない You should not reverse your *opinion* in this matter.
私は自分の意見を変える気はない I won't shift my *opinion* [ground].
その問題をめぐって私たちは活発に意見を交わした We had a lively exchange of *opinions* with each other on that problem.
◆環境問題についてどういう意見をもっていますか *What do you think about* environmental problems?

コロケーション -opinion-
《形容詞＋～》 一般的な～ a prevailing opinion / 客観的な～ an objective opinion / 好意的～ a favorable opinion / 公平な～ a fair opinion / 少数～ a minority opinion / 率直な～ an honest opinion / 断固とした～ a decided

opinion / 批判的～ a critical opinion / 賛成～ a supporting opinion / 反対～ an opposing opinion

❷【忠告】advice ⓤ (❖数えるときは a piece of ... とする) ──意見する advise 他自; (教え諭す) reason 自
あいつに意見しようとしてもむだだ It is no use trying to *reason with* him.
今回は君の意見に従うよ I'll take your *advice* this time.
◆小島先生は演劇部のご意見番(→アドバイザー)だ Ms. Kojima is *the advisor* of the drama club.
‖意見広告 opinion advertisement; (コラム形式の) an advertorial / 意見書 a written opinion

いけん² 違憲 ──違憲の unconstitutional / 最高裁判所はその法律が違憲であるとの判決を下した The Supreme Court ruled that the bill was *unconstitutional*.
‖違憲立法審査 a constitutional review

いげん 威厳 dignity ⓤ /威厳を保つ maintain [keep] *one's dignity* / 彼には威厳というものがない He lacks *dignity*. / 威厳のある門構えの家 a house with an *imposing gate* / あの老婦人は威厳がある That elderly woman *is dignified*. / 年をとるにつれて彼はより威厳が増していった The older he grew, the more *dignified* he became.

いご¹ 以後
❶【これから先・今後】after this, from now on, (主に米) in the future
以後気をつけます I'll be more careful 「*from now on* [*in the future*].
以後10年間保険料は据(す)え置きです The insurance premium will be frozen for 10 years *after this*.
❷【…以後】after, since ➪ いこう(以降), いらい(以来)
4月1日以後 on or after April 1 (❖4月1日を含む. 単に after April 1 とすると厳密には4月1日を含まない)
それ以後彼からは何の連絡もない I haven't heard from him *since then*.

いご² 囲碁 ➪ ご(碁)

いこい 憩い この公園は市民の憩いの場だ This park is *a place of recreation* for the people. / この番組を見て憩いのひとときをお過ごしください / ゆったりくつろいで番組を楽しんでください) Sit back, *relax* and enjoy the program.

いこう¹ 意向 (意図) intention ⓤ ⓒ; (願望) wish ⓒ /人の意向を尋ねる ask a person's *intention* / できるだけご意向に添えるよう努力します We'll try our best to comply with *your wishes*. / 住民の意向に反してダムの建設計画が進められている Plans for constructing a dam are in the works against the people's *wishes*. ◆大統領は辞任する意向だと報じられている It is reported that the President *intends* to resign.

いこう² 以降 after ➪ いご(以後) ‖写真は水曜日以降に取りに来てください Come pick up your photos *after* Wednesday. / 9月以降めっきり涼しくなった *After* September it suddenly became cool.
◆あしたの朝電話して. でも9時以降にね(→ 9時前には電話しないで) Call me tomorrow morning, but *not before* nine.

いこう³ 威光 父親の威光(→影響力)をかさに着て under the influence of one's father / その指揮者は威光を放っていた The conductor *had an aura of authority*.

いこう⁴ 移行 (転換) changeover ⓒ 《通例単数形》, shift ⓒ; (推移・変遷) transition ⓒ; (権利・責任などの) handover ⓒ ──移行する change over ‖現在新しい医療制度への移行が進んでいる *The transition* to a new health care system is now in progress. / 市場経済への移行によって様々な問題が生じた *The changeover* to a market economy caused a lot of problems.
‖移行措置 transitional measures

いこう⁵ 遺稿 死後20年たってからその作家の遺稿が発見された Some of the writer's *unpublished manuscripts* were found 20 years after his death.

いこう⁶ 憩う (くつろぐ) relax 他自; (休息する) rest 他自

イコール 5プラス3イコール8 Five plus [and] three *makes* [*equals*, *is* (*equal to*)] eight. / ひとりっ子イコールわがままとは限らない Being an only child does not necessarily *mean* he [she] is spoiled.

いこく 異国 foreign country ⓒ ◆長崎は異国情緒のある町だ Nagasaki is an *exotic* city.

いごこち 居心地 その小さなホテルは居心地がよい That little hotel *has a cozy atmosphere*. / 親戚(しんせき)の家に下宿したがあまり居心地のいいものではなかった I boarded with my relatives, but I found it a little *uncomfortable*. / 居心地はどうだった How was the atmosphere? / お偉方に囲まれ彼は居心地が悪そうだった He was *like a fish out of water*, surrounded by big shots.

いこじ 意固地 ──いこじな (かたくなな) obstinate; (強情な) stubborn ‖いこじな態度をとる adopt a *stubborn* attitude / 彼女はいこじになっていて彼に口をきかない She is too *stubborn* to talk to him.
◆父は私が芸能界に入るのをいこじなまでに反対した My father *persistently* objected to my entering show business.

いこつ 遺骨 (火葬後の) a person's ashes ‖遺骨を拾う gather a person's ashes

イコン (聖画像) icon [áikən]

いこん 遺恨 (うらみ) grudge ⓒ ‖遺恨試合 a *grudge* fight [match] / 人に遺恨をいだく bear [hold] *a grudge* against a person

いざ いざというときには(→非常の際には)ここに連絡しなさい Call this number *in an emergency*. / いざというときのために非常持ち出し袋を用意しています He keeps a bag stuffed with emergency supplies to be taken out *in case of emergency*. / 彼はいざというときの切り札を持っている He *has a* [*another*] *card up his sleeve*. (✿ have ... up one's sleeve は「いざというときのために…を隠し持っている」の意味) / いざ出発というときになって彼女は行かないと言いだした *When it was time to go*, she said she wasn't going. / それは簡単そうに見えるがいざ自分でやってみると難しい It looks easy, but *when it comes to doing it myself*, it proves difficult. / 彼はいざというときに頼りになる人 He is someone you can count on *when the crunch comes.* / ほかの人はいざ知らず、私は行きません *I don't know* about the others, but I won't go. / 子供ならいざ知らず(→子供なら許されるだろうが)、分別のある大人がこんなことをするなんて Children would be excused in doing this, but it doesn't apply to a mature person.

いさい¹ 委細 (詳細) details, particulars / (広告などで)委細面談 *Particulars to be arranged personally.* ◆彼はその計画を委細かまわず(→予想される困難を考慮せずに)推し進めた He pushed forward with his plan *without taking into consideration the difficulties he would encounter.*

いさい² 異彩 彼の作品は出品作の中でひときわ異彩を放っていた His work *stood out* among the exhibits.

いさかい 諍い (ささいな口げんか) quarrel ⓒ, (口語的)tiff ⓒ; (争い事) trouble Ⓤ (また複数形 ~s) / そのいさかいは誤解から始まった The *quarrel* started from a misunderstanding.

いざかや 居酒屋 tavern ⓒ

いさぎよい 潔い, (快い) graceful; (勇敢な) brave; (正々堂々とした) sportsmanlike ――潔く with good grace; (未練なく) without reluctance / 彼は最後まで潔い態度を貫いた He kept *brave* attitude to the very end. / 彼らは潔く負けを認めた They admitted their defeat *with good grace.* / 今回だめだったら潔くあきらめるよ If I don't make it this time, I'll give up *without reluctance.* ◆その大臣は潔く国の責任を認め被害者に謝罪した The minister *had the grace to* admit the government's guilt and apologize to the victims. / 彼はどんなときでも言い訳するのを潔しとしない He *is too proud to* make excuses under any circumstance. / 潔くないぞ *Don't be a bad sport.*

いさく 遺作 *one's posthumous work(s)* ◆その美術館には先日亡くなった画家の遺作が展示されている *The posthumously discovered works* of the painter who died recently are displayed in the museum. / 『イル・ポスティーノ』がその俳優の遺作となった *Il Postino* became the actor's *last work.*

いざこざ (もめごと) trouble Ⓤ (また複数形 ~s); (口論) quarrel ⓒ / 彼が警察とのいざこざを起こしたのはこれが初めてではない This is not the first time he's been in *trouble* with the police. ◆その家は近所の人々といざこざが絶えなかった The family *were* always *quarreling with* their neighbors.

いささか (少し) a little, slightly; (幾分) somewhat; (かなり) pretty, rather / 彼が現れたのにはいささか驚いた I was *a little* surprised at his appearance. / 小さなおいっ子の相手をしていささかくたびれた I got *pretty* tired from looking after my little nephew. / 被告はその判決にいささかもひるむ様子がなかった The accused didn't show *the slightest* shock to hear the judgement.

いざなう 誘う ⇨ さそう

いさましい 勇ましい brave, courageous; (大胆な) bold ――勇ましく bravely, courageously / 勇ましい兵士 a *brave* soldier / 上司に食ってかかるとは彼女も勇ましいね It's *bold* of her to challenge her boss.

いさみあし 勇み足 (相撲で) stepping out of the ring accidentally ◆調子に乗って勇み足にならないように(→いきすぎないように)しなさい Be careful not to get carried away and *go too far*.

いさめる 諫める remonstrate ⓔ / 彼は上司をいさめて危険な投資をやめさせた He *remonstrated with* his boss against making risky investments.

いさん 遺産 inheritance ⓒ 《通例単数形》; legacy ⓒ; bequest ⓒ; heritage Ⓤ

| inheritance: 相続財産. |
| legacy: 遺言によって譲られるもの. |
| bequest: 自発的に寄付・寄贈するもの. |
| heritage: 特に伝統・言語・建築など文化的な遺産に用いる. |

文化遺産 cultural *heritage* / 歴史的な遺産 historical *heritage* / 遺産を相続する come into *an inheritance* / 彼の莫大な遺産をめぐって親族間で遺産争いが起こった His family and relatives quarreled over his enormous *inheritance*.

◆彼女はめいに多額の遺産(→財産)を残した She left her niece *a great fortune*.

‖遺産相続 inheritance, succession to property / 遺産相続人 an inheritor, an heir [éər] / 世界遺産 world heritage

いし¹ 石

stone ⓒ Ⓤ; rock ⓒ Ⓤ; pebble ⓒ; (宝石) gemstone ⓒ

| stone: 「石, 小石」を表す最も一般的な語. |
| rock: stone よりやや大きいもの. 《米》では stone と同義にも用いる. |
| pebble: 小ぶりで丸い石. |

石を投げるな Don't throw *stones*.
その壁は石でできている The wall is made of *stone*.
その男の子は石につまずいて転んだ The boy stumbled [tripped] on [over] *a stone* and fell.
私はぬれた石を踏んで滑った I slipped on *a* wet *stone*.
この石を動かすのはひと仕事だ Moving this *stone* is a real labor.
石は川の流れで角(<small>かど</small>)が取れて丸くなっている The

いし

stones have been worn smooth by the flow of the river.
◆石だらけの荒れ地 *stony* wastes
∥石うす a grindstone / 石けり遊び hopscotch / 石畳 a stone pavement / 石塀 a stone wall / 石うす a millstone / 軽石 pumice / 巨石(有史以前の) a megalith / 敷石(舗装用) a paving stone / 誕生石 (a) birthstone / 砥石(とぃし) a grindstone, a whetstone / 飛び石 a steppingstone / 墓石 a gravestone, a tombstone / 火打ち石 (a) flint / 御影(みかげ)石 granite
[慣用表現] 石にかじりついてでもやり通せ Carry it through *at any cost.* / 石の上にも三年 *Perseverance will always win in the end.* (◆「忍耐が最後には勝つ」の意味). / 話題がその事件に及ぶと彼女は石のように押し黙った When we came to talk about the incident, she *fell silent.* / 転がる石には苔(こけ)がつかない *A rolling stone gathers no moss.* (◆転々と落ち着かない人は成功しない、または、常に活動的にしていればさびつくことがない、の2つの解釈がある)

いし² 意志 will / 強い[弱い]意志 a strong [weak] *will* / 自由意志 free *will* / 意志に反して against *one's will* / 彼女は自分の意志で出ていった She left of her own *will.* / 彼は意志薄弱だ He has *a weak will.* / ◆彼に辞任の意志はない He *won't* resign. / ウィンストン・チャーチルは意志強固な性格の持ち主だった Winston Churchill had a *determined* character.

いし³ 意思(意図) intention; (考え) mind ∥意思表示をする express one's *intentions* / 外国人との意思の疎通 *communication* with foreign people / 彼は手話で意思を伝えた He *made himself understood* by means of sign language. / 彼女の留学の意思は堅い She's *determined* to study abroad.
∥意思決定 decision-making

いし⁴ 医師 doctor / 医師の診断を仰ぐ ask for a *doctor's diagnosis*
∥医師会 a medical association / 医師国家試験 the National Examination for Medical Practitioners / 医師団 a team of doctors / 医師法 the Medical Practitioners' Law / 医師免許 a medical license

いし⁵ 遺志 彼は父親の遺志(→亡父の願い)を継いで医者になった He carried out his *late* father's *wish* and became a doctor. / 故人の遺志(→最後の願い)により葬儀は行われなかった A funeral was not held according to *the last wishes* of the deceased.

いじ¹ 意地
❶【誇り・気骨】(誇り) pride; (気骨) spirit
彼女にも女の意地がある She has *her pride* as a woman.
決勝に進んで、世界に我々の意地を見せよう We've got to make it to the finals and show the world that we've got (*the*) *spirit.*
❷【気立て・性根】⇒ いじきたない、いじわる
彼女のことを黙ってるなんて意地が悪いよ *It's mean of* you not *to* tell her about it.
彼は金には意地汚い He *is greedy* for money.
レポーターはその俳優に意地の悪い質問をした The reporter asked the actor an *embarrassing* question.
そんな意地汚い食べ方はやめなさい Don't eat so *greedily.*
❸【強情】
1点だけ彼が意地を通した(→譲らなかった)ことがある There is one point on which he *stuck to his guns.*
そんなつまらないことで意地をはるな *Don't be obstinate* about such trifles.
私が家業を継がないと言うと母は意地になって反対した When I told my mother I wanted to leave the family business, she *obstinately* opposed it.
あんなやつ、意地でも(→絶対に)口をきくもんか I'll *never ever* talk to him.

いじ² 維持 maintenance; (家屋・土地などの) upkeep; (保存) preservation ─ 維持する maintain; (保つ) hold*, keep*; (保持する) preserve
平和維持活動 a peace-*keeping* operation / 健康を維持する *keep* fit / 秩序を維持する *keep* [*maintain, preserve*] order / 世界平和を維持する *keep* [*maintain, preserve*] world peace
秩序と安全の維持が我々の最優先事項だ The *maintenance* of good order and safety is our first priority.
現状を維持するだけでも大変だ It's even difficult only to *maintain* the present condition.
その車の維持費は年間50万円以上かかる It costs upward of 500,000 yen a year to *maintain* the car.
∥生命維持装置 a life-support machine

いじ³ 遺児 交通遺児のための募金が行われた A fund-raising campaign was held for *children orphaned* by traffic accidents.

いしあたま 石頭 うちの父は本当に石頭(→頑固)で耳にピアスの穴をあけるのを許してくれない My father *is* really *hardheaded* and won't let me have my ears pierced.

いじいじ 彼はいつもいじいじしている He *is* always *hesitant* [*timid*].

いしがき 石垣 stone wall

いしかわ 石川

石川県は日本列島のほぼ中央に位置し、日本海に面しています。三大庭園に数えられる兼六園、三大名山の一つとされる白山など観光名所も多く、全国から多くの観光客が訪れています。また、輪島塗り・九谷焼・加賀友禅に代表される伝統工芸は、今なお大切に受け継がれています。
Ishikawa Prefecture is located in central Japan and faces the Japan Sea. The Kenrokuen Garden, one of Japan's three greatest gardens, and Mt. Hakusan, one of Japan's three major mountains, are among the popular destinations for tourists from all over the

country. Various traditional handicrafts have been well preserved, the most typical of which are Wajima lacquerware, Kutani porcelain and Kaga yuzen, or colorfully dyed silk fabrics.

いしき 意識

❶【知覚・感覚があること】(知覚) consciousness [U]《また a ～》; (正気) *one's* senses
意識を失う lose *consciousness*
彼が意識を取り戻す見込みはほとんどない There is little hope of his *recovering consciousness.*/ There is little hope that he will *recover consciousness.*
◆医師が来たときには彼はほとんど意識がなかった He was barely *conscious* when the doctor arrived. / そのボクサーは相手を殴って意識不明にした The boxer knocked his opponent *unconscious.* / 被害者は意識不明の重体です The victim *is in a coma.* / 私は暑さで意識がもうろうとしていた I *was dazed* by the heat.

❷【認識・自覚】awareness [U]《また an ～》; (自覚) consciousness [U]《また a ～》, sense [U]《また a ～》
罪の意識が全くない have no *sense of guilt*
◆政治意識の高い人 a politically *aware* [*conscious*] person / 彼女はちょっと自意識過剰だよね She *is* a little *too self-conscious*, isn't she? / あんまりカメラを意識しないで自然にしてて Don't「*look at* [*pay attention to*] the camera. Just act naturally. / 君は他人を意識しすぎだ You *are too aware of* other people. / いつごろから彼を意識するようになったの When did you *become interested in* him? / 彼は明らかに意識的に私を避けている Obviously he avoids me *on purpose.*

[会]「芸能人ってテレビに出るようになってからどんどんきれいになるね」「やっぱり見られてるって意識があるからだよ」"You know, TV personalities get more and more charming after they start appearing on TV." "That's because they *know* they're being watched."

いじきたない 意地汚い greedy //その一件で彼は金に意地汚いということが暴露された The case uncovered the fact that he is *greedy for* money. ◆残ってる物全部食うなんてあいつも意地汚いやつだなあ He is such *a glutton* that he ate up everything that was left. (❖glutton は「大食い」の意味)

いじくる (手でさわる) finger [他]; (もてあそぶ) play with ..., toy with ... ➩いじる

いしけり 石蹴り hopscotch [U] //石けりをする play *hopscotch*

いじける あまり失敗を責めたてると彼もいじけてしまうよ If you keep blaming him for the mistakes, he will become *timid.* / 彼女は昔からずっと美人の姉と比べられていじけていた(→劣等感をもっていた) She *has had a sense of inferiority* for a long time, being compared with her beautiful sister.

いしころ 石ころ stone [C], 《米》rock [C]; (小さくて丸い) pebble [C]

いしずえ 礎 (礎石) foundation stone [C], cornerstone [C]; (基礎・土台) foundation [C]
◆東京オリンピックは日本の高度成長の礎となった The Tokyo Olympics *played a seminal role* in the rapid economic growth of Japan.

いしだたみ 石畳 (石畳の道) stone pavement [C] ◆パリの多くの通りは石畳である Many streets in Paris *are paved with stone.*

いしだん 石段 stone step [C] //ずっと使われて石段はすり減っている *The stone steps* are being worn away by continuous use.

いしつ 異質 ━異質な different //異質な文化と出会う encounter a *different* culture
◆人は一般的に異質なものに対しては潜在的な恐怖をもつ Generally, people have subconscious fear of *the unfamiliar.*

いじっぱり 意地っ張り ━意地っぱりの (頑固な) stubborn; (主張を押し通す) obstinate //彼女は父親に似てかなりの意地っぱりだ She is pretty *stubborn* just like her father.

いしつぶつ 遺失物 lost article [C], 《英》lost property [U] ‖遺失物取扱所 《米》the lost and found, 《英》the lost property (office)

いしばし 石橋 stone bridge [C]
[慣用表現] 彼は石橋をたたいて渡るような(→非常に慎重な)男だ He is an *extremely cautious* man.

いじめ 苛め bullying [U]; (からかい) teasing ➩ [場面・状況別会話] p.1744 //いじめを許してはいけない *Bullying* should not be allowed.
◆弱い者いじめをするな Don't *play the bully.* / 彼女は小学校のときいじめにあった She *was bullied* in elementary school.

いじめっこ 苛めっ子 bully [C]

いじめられっこ 苛められっ子 bullied child [C]

いじめる 苛める

(弱い者を) bully [他]; (からかう) tease [他] [自], 《口語的》pick on *a person*, bait [他]; (つらくあたる) be hard on *a person*
妹をいじめちゃいけません Don't「*pick on* [*tease*] your little sister.
私は子供のころよくいじめられた I *was* often *bullied* when I was a child.
彼らは彼がいじめられるのを黙って見ていた They saw him *being bullied*, but did nothing.
彼は新入社員なんだからあんまりいじめるなよ Don't *be* too *hard on* him, because he is new to the job.
◆浦島太郎は子供たちにいじめられていたカメを助けた *Urashima-taro* saved the turtle which *had been ill-treated* by children.

いしゃ 医者

doctor [C] (❖《英》では surgeon(外科医)を含めずに physician(内科医)だけを指す場合が多い); (内科医) 《主に米》physician [C] (❖《英》では doctor がふつう); (外科医) surgeon [C] ➩ [場面・状況別会話] p.1694
医者を呼ぶ call *a doctor* (in) / 医者を呼びにや

る send for *a doctor* / 医者にかかる see [consult] *a doctor* / かかりつけの医者 *a family doctor* / 腕のいい医者 *a skillful doctor* / 医者の忠告で on *a doctor's* advice / お医者さんごっこをする pretend to be *a doctor*
すぐに医者に診(み)てもらったほうがいい You should go (and) see *a doctor* at once.
彼はよい医者を紹介してくれた He recommended *a good doctor*.
医者は私に長期の休養をとることを勧めた The *doctor* advised me to take a long rest.
それについては医者と相談したほうがいい You ought to consult *your doctor* about it.
順子は医者になるために勉強している Junko is studying to be *a doctor*.
◆医者を開業する practice *medicine*

---**医者のいろいろ**---
眼科医 an ophthalmologist / 産科医 an obstetrician / 産婦人科医 an obsterician and gynecologist((略語)OB/GYN) / 歯科医 a dentist,(公式的)a dental surgeon / 小児科医 a pediatrician / 整形外科医 an orthopedist / 整骨医 an osteopath / 精神科医 a psychiatrist / 精神分析医 a psychoanalyst / 精神療法医 a psychotherapist / 脳外科医 a brain surgeon / 婦人科医 a gynecologist

いしやきいも 石焼き芋 sweet potatoes baked in hot pebbles
いしゃりょう 慰謝料 (離婚の) alimony ⓤ; (賠償) compensation ⓤ, (compensatory) damages ‖慰謝料を支払う pay *alimony* [*compensation*] / 慰謝料を受け取る receive *alimony* [*compensation*] / 彼女は不当解雇に対する慰謝料として500万円を請求した She demanded five million yen as *compensation* for her unfair dismissal.
いしゅ 異種 different kind ⓒ ──異種の different, (公式的)heterogeneous
いしゅう 異臭 (いやなにおい) nasty smell ⓒ; (強烈な悪臭) stench ⓒ / 腐った牛乳が異臭を放っている The rotten milk is giving off *a nasty smell*. ◆異臭がした It *smelled bad* [(口語的) *stank*]. / 新宿駅の構内でちょっとした異臭騒ぎがあった There was a little *fuss over a strange smell* on the grounds of Shinjuku Station.
いじゅう 移住 (外国への) emigration ⓤⓒ; (外国からの) immigration ⓤⓒ ──移住する (外国へ) emigrate ⓘ; (外国から) immigrate ⓘ ‖彼の家族は彼が5歳のときにドイツからアメリカに移住した His family *immigrated to* the United States *from* Germany when he was five. / 彼の祖父は若いころペルーへ移住した His grandfather *emigrated to* Peru early in his life. ◆東南アジア諸国からオーストラリアに移住する人が増えている There is an increasing number of *immigrants* to Australia from Southeast Asian countries.
‖移住者 (外国への) an emigrant; (外国からの) an immigrant / 移住地 a settlement
いしゅく¹ 畏縮 彼女は舞台で失敗を恐れるあまり畏縮してしまった She was so afraid of making mistakes on the stage that she *held back too much*. / 相手がいくら偉い人だからといって畏縮することはない Don't *be overawed* by others no matter how important they are.
いしゅく² 萎縮 ──萎縮する〔医学〕(筋肉などが) atrophy ⓘ ‖筋萎縮症 muscular dystrophy
いしょ 遺書 (遺言書) will ⓒ /彼は遺書を残さなかった He didn't leave *a will*.
◆自殺した男の机の引き出しには3通の遺書があった(→3通の手紙を残していた) The man had left three *letters* in a drawer of his desk before he killed himself.
いしょう¹ 衣装 (ある時代・民族・職業などに特有の衣服) costume ⓒ ⓤ; (衣服の総称) clothes /舞台衣装 *a stage costume* / 民族衣装 *a folk* [*national*] *costume* / 彼女は衣装持ちだ She *has a lot of clothes*. / (❖wardrobe は「持ち衣装全体」の意味) / キルトはスコットランドの伝統的な衣装だ The kilt is *a traditional costume of* Scotland. ◆日本の結婚式では貸し衣装を借りるのが一般的だ In Japan, most people *rent dresses* for their wedding.
ことわざ 馬子にも衣装 Fine feathers make fine birds. (→美しい羽毛が鳥をりっぱに見せる)
いしょう² 意匠 (デザイン) design ⓤⓒ
◆意匠を凝らしたイタリア製の家具 *elaborately designed* Italian furniture
‖意匠登録 registration of a design, copyright on a design

いじょう¹ 以上
❶【それより上】more than …; (…を超えて) over, above; (…かそれより上) not less than …, nothing less than …

語法
日本語の「…以上」はふつう…の数を含むが, more than, over, above はすべて後に続く数を含まない。たとえば more than five は「5 より上」を表し, 5 そのものは含まないので, 厳密にいえば日本語の「5以上」とは異なる. 正確に表したい場合は five or [and] over, five or [and] more のようにいう.

平均以上で[の] *above* (the) average / 30歳以上の人 people (of) 30 *and above* [*over, older*]
彼らは結婚して20年以上になる They've been married for *over* 20 years.
彼はこれまでに100冊以上の本を書いている He has written *more than* 100 books so far.
この報告書は60ページ以上もある This report is *over* 60 pages long.
500人以上の人がパーティーに参加した *More than* 500 attended the party.
1時間以上もバスを待っている I've been waiting for the bus for *more than* an hour.
きのう私は12時間以上寝た I slept *over* 12 hours yesterday.
彼女は必要以上に物を欲しがる She wants *more than is necessary*.

彼女の講演は思っていた以上に専門的だった Her lecture was *more* technical *than I had expected.*
◆もうこれ以上決定を先延ばしにはできませんよ You can't put off making a decision *any longer.* / これ以上何も言うな Enough said!/ Say no *more*!/ Leave it at that!/ もうこれ以上お金を浪費してはいけない Don't waste *any more* money. / これ以上言うことはありません I have nothing *further* to say. / 彼らは収入以上の暮らしをしている They are living *beyond* their means. / 彼は正規の就業時間以上は働かない He never works *outside* regular working hours. / そのテレビ番組への反響は予想以上だった The response to the TV program *surpassed* all expectations. / 私は彼にそれ以上近寄るなと叫んだ I shouted at him not to come *any closer.*

❷【すでに述べたこと】the above,《公式的》the foregoing ——以上の above,《公式的》foregoing

以上はすべて料金に含まれます *The above* are all included in the fee.

以上の説明について何か質問はありますか Does anybody have questions about the *foregoing* explanation?

◆この件について言うことは何もない. 以上 I have nothing to say about this. *Period.*(❖話の終わりに断定的に用いる) / 以上です That's all. / 以上できょうの会議を終了します Now today's meeting is finished.

❸【…するからには】(…だから) since; (一度…したからには) once; (…となった今) now (that)...

本体がこわれてしまっている以上, どうすることもできません We can do nothing about it, *since* the body itself has broken down.

始めた以上は最後までやり通せ *Once* you have started, you've got to carry it through.

大学を卒業した以上, 親からは独立したい *Now that* I've graduated from college, I want to be independent of my parents.

いじょう² 異常 abnormality ◯ⓤ; (心身の) disorder ◯ⓤ ——異常な (正常でない) abnormal (↔normal); (ふつうでない) unusual; (並はずれた) extraordinary ——異常に abnormally; unusually; extraordinarily

異常な人間 an *abnormal* person / 異常な体験 an *unusual* experience / 異常に暑い夏 an *unusually* hot summer / 異常な行動をする behave *extraordinarily*

その写真の男性は異常なほど太っていた The man in the photo looked *extraordinarily* fat.

◆イナゴの異常発生 *a plague* of locusts / 飛行機が離陸しようとしたとき, 異常な音を聞いた When the plane was about to take off, I heard a *strange* sound. / すべて異常はないようだ Everything seems to be *in order.* / 彼は精神に異常をきたしている He *is* mentally *disturbed.*

🅔「それは食べすぎだよ」「最近異常に食欲があるんだよね」"You are eating like a pig!" "I get *awfully* hungry these days."

‖異常気象 abnormal [extraordinary] weather / 異常心理学 abnormal psychology / 異常接近 a near miss

いじょう³ 異状 (故障) trouble ⓤ; (心身の) disorder ⓤⓒ/脳の異状 *a brain disorder*

◆精密検査の結果, 特に異状は認められなかった The complete medical examination proved that there was nothing *wrong.* / その弁当を食べた人のうち約20人が異状を訴えた About twenty people who ate the same box lunch complained that there was *something wrong* with their stomach.

🅔「特に変わったことはないか」「異状なしです」"Is there anything unusual?" "*Nothing* (*wrong*), sir."

いじょう⁴ 委譲 (任務・権限などの) delegation ⓤ, devolution ⓤ ——委譲する delegate ⓗ, devolve ⓗ

いしょく¹ 衣食 food and clothing (❖語順が日本語と逆になることに注意) ➾いしょくじゅう ことわざ 衣食足りて礼節を知る Well-fed, well-bred. (→食欲が満たされれば行儀がよくなる)

いしょく² 委嘱 (任務などの委託) commission ⓤ ——委嘱する (委託する) commission ⓗ; (信じて任せる) entrust ⓗ/環境省はその検査を民間の会社に委嘱した The Ministry of the Environment *commissioned* a private company to do the examination.

いしょく³ 異色 ——異色の (独特の) unique /それは映画祭に出品された映画の中でもかなり異色の作品だ That's quite *unique* among all the films entered in the cinema festival. ◆歌舞伎役者とバレエダンサーという異色コンビ(→興味深いコンビ)による舞台を見に行った I went to see a stage performance by *an interesting duo* of a Kabuki actor and a ballet dancer.

いしょく⁴ 移植 transplant ⓤⓒ; (臓器などの) transplantation ⓤ ——移植する transplant ⓗ/臓器移植 an organ *transplant* / その少女はアメリカで心臓移植手術を受けた The girl had a heart *transplant* operation in America. / 芽が出てきたらもっと大きなプランターに移植しなさい When the seeds sprout, you should *transplant* them into a bigger planter.

‖移植ごて a trowel / 移植片 an implant

いしょくじゅう 衣食住 food, clothing and shelter(❖英語では「食・衣・住」の順); (生活に最低限必要なもの) basic necessities /難民に衣食住を与える provide refugees with *food, clothing and shelter*

いじらしい 小さな女の子が弟の世話をしていてじらしかった(→弟の世話をしているのを見て感動した) I *was moved* to see a little girl taking care of her little brother.

いじる ❶【手でさわる】(指でさわる) finger ⓗ; (もてあそぶ) fiddle ⓘ, monkey ⓘ; (手をつけて) /彼女は落ち着かない様子で髪の毛をいじっていた She *was fingering* her hair nervously. / 私がいない間にコンピュータ

をいじらないでくれ Don't *fiddle with* my computer while I'm out. / 素人は配線を下手にいじらないほうがいい An amateur should not *tamper with* the wiring.
❷【興味本位でする】父は庭いじりが趣味だ My father's hobby is *gardening*.

いしわた 石綿 (アスベスト) asbestos ◎

いじわる 意地悪 (意地悪な人) nasty person ◎,《口語的》meanie ◎ ――意地悪な mean, nasty; (悪意のある) malicious, spiteful ――意地悪く meanly, nastily; maliciously, spitefully ∥意地悪く笑う give a *nasty* grin / どうしてあなたは私にそんなに意地悪なの Why are you so *mean* to him? / 妹に意地悪をしちゃいけません Don't be *nasty* to your sister. / 彼にそのことを教えないなんて意地悪だよ It would be *spiteful* of you to keep it secret from him. ◆彼女は記者の意地悪な質問もうまくかわした She skillfully dodged the reporter's *embarrassing* question. / 意地悪されたら先生に報告することがだいじです It is important for you to tell your teacher when you *are bullied.*

いしん¹ 威信 (名声・信望) prestige ◎; (威厳) dignity ◎ ∥そのスキャンダルは大統領の威信を失墜させた That scandal damaged *the prestige* of the President. / 警察は威信の回復に努めている The police are trying to regain *prestige.*

いしん² 維新 (明治維新) the (Meiji) Restoration

いじん 偉人 great man [woman] ◎; (傑出した人) giant ◎ ∥偉人伝 the lives [biographies] of *great men and women*

いしんでんしん 以心伝心 direct communication from mind to mind ◆彼らは以心伝心の間柄だ (→彼らの間にはテレパシーのようなものがあるようだ) There seems to exist a sort of *telepathy* between them.

いす 椅子

❶【腰かけ】(背もたれのある 1 人用いす) chair ◎; (ソファー) sofa ◎, couch ◎; (背もたれのないいす) stool ◎
いすに座る sit in [on] *a chair* (✿in の場合は深々と腰かけるという含みがある) / いすを引き寄せる draw [pull] up *a chair* / いすを丸く [1列に] 並べる arrange *chairs*「in a circle [in a row]
このいすは背の高さに応じて調節できる This *chair* can be adjusted for your height.
もう少しでいすから転げ落ちるところだった I almost fell off *my chair*.
このいすの脚は少しぐらぐらする The legs of this *chair* aren't very firm.
丸いすはすべて床に固定されていた All *the stools* were attached [fixed] to the floor.
彼はいすから立ち上がって私を迎えてくれた He rose from *his chair* and greeted me.

---いすのいろいろ---
安楽いす an easy chair / 折りたたみいす a folding chair; (キャンプ用) a campstool / 回転いす a swivel chair / 車いす a wheelchair / ソファーベッド a divan bed / デッキチェア a deck chair, 《米》a beach chair / ピアノスツール a piano stool / ひじかけいす an armchair / ベンチ a bench / 補助いす an occasional chair / ロッキングチェア a rocking chair, a rocker

❷【地位・ポジション】post
彼は社長のいすをめぐって自分の弟と争った He fought his own brother for *the post* of president.
∥いす取りゲーム musical chairs

いずみ 泉 (自然の) spring ◎; (人工の) fountain ◎ ∥トレビの泉 the Trevi *Fountain* / 知恵の泉 *a fountain* of wisdom

イスラエル Israel [ízriəl] (✿公式名 the State of Israel) ――イスラエル人 Israeli [izréili] ◎ ――イスラエル(人)の Israeli

イスラム Islam [izlάːm] (✿イスラム教およびイスラム圏・イスラム教徒全体を指す) ――イスラムの Islamic [izlǽmik] ∥イスラム教 Islam / イスラム教原理主義 Islamic Fundamentalism / イスラム教国 《集合的》Islam / イスラム教徒 (1 人) a Muslim; 《集合的に》Islam

いずれ

❶【そのうち】(近いうちに) soon; (やがて) eventually; (遅かれ早かれ) sooner or later; (結局) in the end
事件のいきさつはいずれ明らかになるだろう The whole story of the event will unfold *soon*.
彼はいずれ父親の事業を継ぐことになる He will *eventually* take over his father's business.
◆いずれ近いうちにおじゃまします I'll come (and) see you *one of these days*.

❷【とにかく】
いずれにせよ今では遅すぎる It's too late now, *anyhow.*
いずれにしてもそこへは行くつもりだ I'm going there *anyway.*
いずれにしても電話をください Give me a call *in any case.*

❸【どれ・どちら】(一方の) either; (両方の) both; (すべての) all
クレジットカードと小切手のいずれかで払うことができる You can pay with *either* a credit card *or* a check.
新幹線, 車のいずれで行っても 3 時間はかかる It'll take three hours by *either* Shinkansen *or* car.
このおもちゃはいずれも手作りです *All* of these toys are hand-made.
彼ら 2 人はいずれも早稲田大学の出身だ They *both* graduated from Waseda University.
◆その 3 人姉妹はいずれ劣らぬ (→同じように) 美人ぞろいだ Those three sisters are *equally* pretty. / AからEのうち, いずれか 1 つを選び丸をつけなさい Choose one out of A

いすわる 居座る (地位などに) remain in the position; (動かない) stay on 〃彼はできるだけ長いこと議長の座に居座るつもりらしい He is trying to *remain in the position* of chairperson as long as possible. ◆太平洋高気圧が日本上空に居座っている A high-pressure system off the Pacific [The Pacific anticyclone] *is lingering* over Japan.

いせい¹ 威勢 威勢のいい掛け声とともにみこしが近づいてきていた A *mikoshi* was coming near with *lively* [*energetic*] shouts. / さっきまで威勢のいいことを言ってたくせにもう疲れたの? You *were boasting* until a moment ago and now you are saying you're tired?

いせい² 異性 the opposite sex 〃初めて異性を意識したのはいつですか When did you become conscious of *the opposite sex*?
◆彼女には異性の(→男性の)友達がたくさんいる She has a lot of *male* friends. (❖「女性の」は female)

いせい³ 以西 (…より西) west of …; (…とそれより西) … and westward

いせいしゃ 為政者 (政治家) statesman ⓒ; (統治者) ruler ⓒ

いせえび 伊勢蝦 (spiny) lobster ⓒ

いせき¹ 移籍 transfer Ⓤ ⓒ ──移籍する transfer ⓐ 〃何人かの選手が日本のチームから外国のチームに移籍した A few players *transferred* from a Japanese team to a foreign one.
‖移籍料 a transfer fee

いせき² 遺跡 (廃墟(訳)) ruins, remains; (史跡) monument ⓒ 〃古代ローマの遺跡 ancient Roman *ruins* / 有史以前の遺跡 prehistoric *monuments* / トロイの遺跡はまずシュリーマンによって発掘された The *Remains* of Troy were first excavated by Schliemann.

いせつ 異説 (異なった意見) different opinion [view] ⓒ 〃それについては異説を唱える学者が大勢いる Many scholars give *different opinions* about it.

いせん 緯線 latitude line ⓒ

いぜん¹ 以前 ──以前に before (↔after); (かつて) once, formerly; (前もって) previously ──以前の former (❖名詞の前で用いる) ➔かつて
1964年以前に *before* 1964 / ルネサンス以前の絵画 paintings *before* the Renaissance
以前どこかでお会いしましたよね I remember that I met you somewhere *before*.
以前うちではダックスフントを飼っていた We *once* had a dachshund in our family.
以前にも似たような症状を経験しましたか Have you experienced similar symptoms *before*?
彼は以前より記憶力が落ちている He has a worse memory than *before*.
オーストラリアには以前に3回行ったことがある I've been to Australia three times *before*.
彼の報告は以前言っていたことと一致しない His report disagrees with what he said *previously*.
現実的には産休後に以前の役職に戻れる女性はほとんどいない The reality is that few women can return to their *former* post after maternity leave.
◆この会社の以前の社長 a *one-time* president of this company / 父は以前ほど酒を飲まなくなった My father drinks less *than he used to*. / 彼はもう以前の彼ではない He is not *what he used to be*. / 彼はいい点数を取ったので以前にも増して勉強に励んだ His good marks encouraged him to study *even harder*. / 人を殴るなんてモラル以前の問題だ Hitting other people is *beneath consideration as* a moral issue.

いぜん² 依然 (まだ) still 〃その地域は依然フランスの支配を受けている The area is *still* under French rule. / その問題は依然として棚上げ状態だ That issue is *still* pending.

いそ 磯 (海岸) (sea)shore ⓒ; (浜辺) beach ⓒ 〃磯伝いに along *the beach*
◆いその香り the smell of *the sea* / 何人かの子供たちがいそ遊びをしていた Some children *were playing in the tide pool*.
‖磯釣り surf-casting

いそいそ(と) 姉は真新しいワンピースを着ていそいそと(→楽しそうに)デートに出かけた My sister went out *cheerfully* for a date in a brand-new dress.

いそいで 急いで in a hurry, in haste; (あわただしく) in a rush; (速く) quickly, rapidly ➔いそぐ 〃そんなに急いで行くことはなかったのに You needn't have gone *in such a hurry*.

いそう 移送 ──移送する transfer ⓐ 〃患者は近くの大学病院に移送された The patient *was transferred to* a university hospital nearby.

いそうろう 居候 私は半年間, 東京の姉のところに居候した I *lived* [*mooched*] *off* my sister in Tokyo for six months. (❖ live off は「…のやっかいになる」の意味)

いそがしい 忙しい

busy; (従事して) engaged (❖名詞の前では用いない) ──忙しく busily
忙しい人[日] a *busy* person [day]
悪いけど忙しいんです Excuse me, but I'm *busy*.
彼は忙しすぎるといつも不平ばかり言っている He's always complaining that he's *too busy*.
ハチは巣箱の周りをぶんぶんいいながら忙しく働いていた The bees were working *busily*, humming around the hive.
彼女はきょう一日中忙しく飛び回った She *was as busy as a bee* all day today. (❖ be as busy as a bee は「ミツバチのように忙しく動き回る」の意味)
本日はお忙しい中ご来場いただきまことにありがとうございます We'd like to thank you for taking the time *out of your busy*

いそがせる

schedule to be with us today.

【be busy+(in) doing】(❖in は通例省略される) 彼女は荷造りで忙しかった She *was busy (in) packing*. / 先生はテストの採点で忙しかった The teacher *was busy scoring* papers.

【be busy+with[at] 名】彼は仕事で忙しかった He *was busy with [at] work*. / 8月の終わりにはたいていの子供たちは夏休みの宿題で忙しくなる Most children *get busy with* their summer homework at the end of August.

◆彼女はいつも5人の子供の世話で忙しい She *is* always *occupied with* her five children. / 彼にとって悲しみを忘れるいちばんの方法は忙しく(→一生懸命)働くことだった The best remedy for his grief was *hard work*.

💬「ちょっと手伝って」「ごめん, 今忙しくて手が離せないの」 "Can you give me a hand?" "Sorry, I'm *tied up* at the moment."

💬「旅行はどうだった」「楽しかったけど, ちょっと忙しかったな」 "How was the trip?" "It was enjoyable, but a little *hectic*."

いそがせる 急がせる hurry ⊕, hasten ⊕ ❖いそぐ / 先生はバスに間に合うように私たちを急がせた The teacher *hurried* us along to catch the bus.

いそぎ 急ぎ 急ぎの注文 a *rush* order / 急ぎの用があるのでゆっくりしていられません I have *urgent* business, so I can't stay long. / 大急ぎでしたらいっぱい忘れ物をしてしまった I prepared *in such a hurry* that I forgot to bring a lot of things. / 雨が降り始めたので僕たちは急ぎ足で駅に向かった It started to rain, so we *hurried* to the station.

いそぎんちゃく 磯巾着 sea anemone ⓒ

いそぐ 急ぐ

hurry ⊕,《公式的》hasten [héisən] ⊕

彼らは学校へ急いだ They *hurried* to school. 急げ! *Hurry up*! / *Quick*! / *Shake a leg*!

急ぐ必要がないから自分のペースで続けなさい You *don't have to hurry*. Just keep on going at your own pace.

彼女は大雨の中, 家路を急いだ She *hurried* home in the heavy rain.

急いで下りてらっしゃい, ケン. 8時ですよ *Hurry* down, Ken. It's 8 o'clock.

急がないとバスに乗り遅れるよ *Hurry up, or [otherwise]* you'll miss the bus.

彼女は急いで謝った She *hastened* to apologize.

この仕事を急いでしなければならない I have to *hurry (up)* this job.

けが人を急いで病院に運んだ They *hurried* the injured to the hospital.

彼に会いたい一心で彼女は駅に急いだ(→彼に会いたい気持ちが彼女を駅へ急がせた) Her impatience to see him *hurried* her to the station.

◆急いでいたので, 私たちは駅まで走った *Being in a hurry*, we ran to the station. / 私たちは全く急いでいません We're *in no hurry*. /

彼は時計を見ると急いで部屋を出ていった *The moment* he saw the clock, he *hurriedly* left the room. / 急いで昼食をとりましょう Let's have a *quick* lunch. / 我々は先を急ぐ救急車に道をあけた We made way for the *speeding ambulance*. / 結論を急ぐな Don't *jump to conclusions*.

ことわざ 急がば回れ Haste makes waste.(→あわてるとむだが生まれる); Slow and [but] steady wins the race.(→遅くても着実なほうが最後には勝つ) / 善は急げ ➡ぜん(善)

いぞく 遺族 the bereaved (family) (❖bereaved は「肉親(または友人)を亡くした」の意味) / 遺族は悲しみに包まれていた Sorrow surrounded *the bereaved family*.

◆その飛行機事故の遺族によって慰霊碑が建てられた A monument was put up by *the families of those killed* in the crash.

‖遺族年金 a pension for the bereaved

いぞん¹ 依存 (頼ること) dependence ⓤ (↔independence); (信頼) reliance ⓤ ——依存する depend ⓘ / その国は食糧や医薬品を外国からの援助に依存している That country *depends [is dependent]* on foreign aid for food and medicine. ◆世界の国々はますます互いに依存するようになってきている All countries are getting more and more *interdependent*.(❖「相互依存」は interdependence)

> [英作文ノート] 類推は危険!
> その学生は生活費を両親に依存している
> →×The student is dependent *of* his parents for living costs.
> →○The student is dependent *on* his parents for living costs.
> ★be independent of ...「…から独立している」からの類推で, 前置詞を of にしないように注意.

いぞん² 異存 objection ⓒ / その決定に異存はありません I have no *objection* to the decision.

いた 板 board ⓒ,《集合的》boarding ⓤ; (厚板材) plank ⓒ; (金属などの薄板) plate ⓒ

板に穴をあける poke a hole in *a board*

彼は素手で板を2つにたたき割った He split *the board* in two with a karate chop.

その板は厚みが3センチほどあった That *board* was about three centimeters thick.

◆板張りの床 a *wooden* floor

‖板ガラス plate glass / 板切れ a piece of wood / 板チョコ a chocolate bar, a bar of chocolate / 板塀 a board fence / 合板 plywood / スキー板(1組) (a pair of) skis / 洗濯板 a washboard / 羽子板 a battledore / ブリキ板 tinplate / まな板 a cutting [chopping] board

慣用表現 純は学校の制服が板についてきた(→自然に見えてきた) Jun *is starting to look natural* in her school uniform. / 彼女の保母さんぶりもだんだん板についてきたようだ(→彼女は保母であることに慣れ始めている) She's *beginning to feel at home* as a kindergarten teacher. / 彼は自分の母親と妻との間で板ばさみになって

いる He *is caught in the crossfire* between his mother and his wife.

いたい¹ 痛い

❶【物理的な痛み】—— 形 painful; (ひりひりする) sore —— 動 hurt* 自, ache 自, have* a pain [an ache] ▷いたむ(痛む)

かぜで頭が痛い My head *aches* from a cold.

畳に座っていたので足が痛い My legs *ache* from sitting on *tatami*.

背中が痛い I *have an ache* in my back. / I've *got a backache*.

のどが痛い I have a *sore* throat.

働きすぎで体中が痛かった I *felt sore* all over after working too much.

クラゲに刺されるとそんなに痛いとは知らなかった I didn't know that the sting of a jellyfish was so *painful*.

◆痛そうなふりをして in mock *pain* / 頭[歯]が痛い I *have a headache* [*toothache*]. / (つかまれて)腕が痛いよ You *are hurting* my arm. / 頭が痛くて死にそうだ My head *is killing* me. / 彼女は痛くて金切り声をあげた She screamed *in* [*with*] *pain*.

❢「痛っ！」「ごめん．大丈夫？」 "*Ouch!*" "I'm sorry. Are you OK?"(❖"Ouch!"は突然痛みを感じたときに発する声．発音は /áutʃ/)

❢「ついにピアスの穴，あけたよ」「痛くなかった？」 "I finally got my ears pierced!" "Didn't it *hurt*?"

❢「足の裏のマッサージに行かない？」「いやだよ，痛そうじゃないか(→痛みに耐えられそうにない)」 "Shall we go and have a massage on the soles of our feet?" "Oh, no! I wouldn't be able to bear *the pain*."

❷【弱点】

耳の痛い話 *a home truth* / 頭の痛い問題 a *vexing* [*troublesome*] *problem*

彼の批判は痛いところをついていた His criticism came [hit] *close to home*.

きっと彼の言葉が彼女の痛いところをついたんだろう His words must *have touched a* 「*sore spot* [*nerve*] with her.

次の2試合に私たちのチームの主力選手が出られないのは痛い It *hurts* our team that our star player can't play for the next two games.

慣用表現 彼女の気持ちが痛いほど分かった I *strongly* sympathized with her. / I felt *deeply* for her. / 今度またここへ来たら痛い目にあうぞ You'll *be in trouble* if you come back here again. / 彼がどんなことを言ったって痛くもかゆくもない He can say whatever he wants to say, because *it won't hurt me at all*. / 私は痛くもない腹を探られた I *was unfairly suspected*.

いたい² 遺体 (dead) body C, (公式的) remains //身元不明の遺体 *an* unidentified *body* / 事故現場から3人の遺体が収容された Three *bodies* were recovered from the scene of the accident. ◆遺体解剖の結果，死因は心不全と断定された The autopsy showed that the cause of the death was heart failure.

‖遺体安置所 a morgue

いだい¹ —— 偉大な great //偉大な発明 a *great* invention / モーツァルトは18世紀の最も偉大な音楽家の一人だ Mozart is one of *the greatest* musicians of the 18th century. / 英国は多くの偉大な詩人を生んできた Britain has produced many *great* poets.

いだい² 医大 medical school C, a school of medicine ‖医大生 a medical student

いたいけ (無邪気な) innocent; (年端もいかない)《文語》tender(❖名詞の前で用いる) //いたいけな子供たちがその惨事に巻き込まれた The terrible accident snuffed out the lives of *innocent* children.

いたいたしい 痛々しい (痛ましい) painful; (哀れを誘う) pitiful //彼女の手首の傷跡が痛々しかった It was *painful* to see the wound on her wrist. ◆一人息子を亡くした父親は痛々しいほどにやつれていた The father who lost his only son looked *painfully* gaunt.

いたガラス 板ガラス (上質で厚い) plate glass U; (薄い) sheet glass U

いたがる 痛がる 彼女は相当痛がっているから足の骨が折れているかもしれない She *is in* such *great pain* that she might have broken her leg.

いたく 委託 (信用して任せること) trust U; (任務) commission U; (商品の委託販売) consignment U —— 委託する consign 他; (仕事などを) entrust 他 //業務を委託する *entrust one's* business / 彼女は中古の洋服の委託販売を始めた She started *selling* secondhand clothes *on consignment*. / その会社は東京都の委託を受けて清掃作業を行っている The company is doing the cleaning *on commission from* the Tokyo Metropolitan Government.

‖委託金 trust fund, money in trust

いだく 抱く 大望をいだいた若者 *an ambitious* young man / 少年よ，大志をいだけ Boys, *be ambitious*! / 多くの国民は政治に対して不信感をいだいている A lot of people *have* no trust in politics. / 犯人は被害者に対して大変なうらみをいだいていたと思われる The murderer seems *to have borne* intense hatred against the victim.

いたけだか 居丈高 彼は急に居丈高になった(→高圧的な態度をとった) He suddenly changed to *a high-handed attitude*.

いたしかゆし 痛し痒し ハワイ旅行が当たったはいいが，仕事を休んで行ったため収入が減り，痛しかゆしだった When I won a free trip to Hawaii, it was *a mixed blessing* because I had to take off unpaid days from work to go.

いたす 致す

語法 「いたす」は目上の人に対して「(私が)…する」という改まった言い方で，英語で特に決まった訳語はない．文全体を丁寧な表現にしたり，「(私に)…させてください」という言い方で表せるが，特に丁寧にいう必要がない場合も多い．

いたずら

お支払いはお早めにお願いいたします We would be grateful for prompt payment of the fee. / ステーキの焼きかげんはどのようにいたしましょうか How would you like your steak? / 切符を拝見いたします May I see your ticket?

💬「手伝っていただいて本当にありがとうございます」「どういたしまして」"Thank you very much for your help." "You're welcome." ➡ どういたしまして

いたずら¹ 悪戯

❶【悪ふざけ】(子供のたわいない) mischief Ⓤ; (悪意のない) trick Ⓒ; (かつぐこと) hoax Ⓒ; (悪ふざけ) practical joke Ⓒ, prank Ⓒ —— いたずらな mischievous; (わんぱくな) naughty, impish

悪質ないたずら a mean prank / いたずらっ子 a mischievous child
子供はいたずら好きなものだ Kids are fond of mischief.
彼は子供のころ私によくいたずらをしたものだった He used to play tricks on me in his childhood.
あの子にいたずらさせないように何か手を打たなきゃ We've got to do something to keep that child out of mischief.
私に対してもう二度とそんないたずらはしないで Don't pull a trick like that on me again.
おまえたち、またいたずらをたくらんでるな You are up to your old tricks, aren't you boys?
ビル爆破の予告電話はいたずらだったと判明した The telephone warning that the building would be blown up turned out to be a hoax.
このいたずら坊主め You naughty boy! / You little rascal!
◆運命のいたずら a twist of fate; the tricks of fortune; an irony / 彼女はいたずらっぽく笑った She smiled at me archly. / She gave me an arch smile. / この電話機にはいたずら電話防止の機能がある This telephone can prevent prank [obscene] calls. / "prank call は「わいせつな電話」の意味) / 彼女のノートにはたくさんいたずら書きがあった There were a lot of doodles on her notebook. (✎ doodle は「考え事などをしながら描く無意味な絵や図形」の意味) / お父さんのパソコンをいたずらしちゃだめよ Don't play with your father's computer.

💬「この絵、20万円だって」「これが？ まるで子供のいたずら書きじゃないか」"Look! This painting is 200,000 yen!" "This one? It looks no better than childish graffiti to me!"

💬「どうしてこんなことをしたんだ」「初めはいたずら半分だったんです」"Why did you do such a thing?" "I did it just for fun at first."

❷【みだらな行為】(女性・子供などに対する) molestation Ⓤ
数名の女性患者にいたずらをしたとして歯科医師が逮捕された A dentist was arrested for the molestation of some female patients.

いたずら² 徒ら ——いたずらに (むだに) in vain, to no purpose, uselessly; (無為に) idly / 兄はいたずらに努力を重ねたが、結局弁護士にはなれなかった My brother continued all his efforts to become a lawyer, but in vain.

◆私は大学時代、いたずらに時を過ごしてしまった (→時間をむだにした) と後悔している I regret that I wasted [idled away] my time while in college. / 彼はいつもいたずらに (→不必要に) みんなの不安をあおるようなことを言う He always tells scary stories that make everyone unnecessarily cautious.

いただき 頂 (山の) mountaintop Ⓒ, summit Ⓒ; (先のとがった) peak Ⓒ; (てっぺん) top Ⓒ / その山の頂は雪で覆われていた The mountaintop [top of the mountain] was covered with snow.

いただきます

クリスチャンの中には食前 (または食後) の祈りをする家庭もあるが、日本語の「いただきます」に当たる英語の決まり文句はない。あえて訳すなら Let's eat. (食べましょう) などでもよいでしょうか。英米人の家庭に招かれて "Please help yourself." (どうぞお召し上がりください) などと勧められたら "Thank you." といって食べ始めればよい。➡ ごちそうさま

いただく 頂く・戴く

❶ もらう　　　have; receive
❷ 食べる・飲む　have; eat; drink
❸ …してもらう

❶【もらう】(得る) have* ㉻; (受け取る) receive ㉻; (選び取る) take* ㉻
パンフレットをもう1部いただけますか Can I have another brochure?
きのうお手紙をいただきました I received your letter yesterday.
こんな高価な物はいただけません I can't have such an expensive thing.
◆少しお時間をいただけませんか Could you spare me a few minutes? / このペンはいただけるのですか Can I keep this pen? / 金曜までにお返事をいただきたいと思います Please let us know your answer by Friday. / それをどうすべきか助言をいただきたいのですが Could you give me some advice on how to do it? / このゲームはいただきだ！ I win this game.

💬「とてもお似合いですよ」「これいただくわ」"It looks really good on you." "I'll take this."

💬「だれかこの本いりませんか」「いただけるのなら (→だれもいらないのなら)」"Does anybody want to keep this book?" "I'd like to, if nobody wants it."

❷【食べる・飲む】have* ㉻; (食べる) eat* ㉻; (飲む) drink* ㉻
みんなでケーキをいただきましょう Every-

body, let's *have* some cake.

朝はヨーグルトだけいただきます I *eat* only yogurt for breakfast.

コーヒーの代わりにハーブティーをいただきます I'll *have* herbal tea instead of coffee.

◆私はコーヒーはブラックでいただきます I'd *like* my coffee black.

💬「クッキーはいかがですか」「はい、いただきます」 "Would you like some cookies?" "Yes, *please*." (❖いらないときは No, thank you. などと答える)

💬「肉をもう1切れいかがですか」「もう十分いただきました。ありがとう」 "Would you like another slice of meat?" "I've *had* quite enough, thank you."

❸【…してもらう】

私と席を替わっていただけませんか *Would you* change seats with me?

写真を撮っていただけませんか *Would you* *mind* taking a photo of us?

タクシーを呼んでいただけませんか *Could you* call me a cab?

車で迎えに来ていただけますでしょうか *I wonder* [*I was wondering, I'm wondering*] *if* you could pick me up. (❖進行形を用いるとさらに丁寧になる)

推薦状を書いていただけるとありがたいのですが *I would very much appreciate it if you could* write me a letter of recommendation.

ここにお名前を書いていただけますか *Would you take the trouble to* sign your name here?

気をつかっていただいて恐縮です *I'm very grateful to* you *for* your consideration.

おたばこはご遠慮いただきたいのですが *Could you possibly* refrain from smoking?

(電話で)少々お待ちいただけますか *May I* put you on hold?

失礼ながら自己紹介させていただきます *Allow me to* introduce myself.

喜んでお手伝いさせていただきます *I'll be pleased to* help you out. / *I'd be only too glad to* help you.

❹【上にのせる】

雪をいただいた山 a mountain *capped* [*crowned*] with snow; a snow-*capped* mountain / 英国の王冠をいただく *wear* the *crown* of England

❺【その他】

彼女の踊りはよかったけどあの衣装はいただけない(→好きではない) Her dancing was great, but I *didn't like* the costume.

いたたまれない 多大な迷惑をかけたことを思うといたたまれない(→逃げ出したい)気がした When I thought of having caused so much trouble, I felt like *running away*. / 遺族の悲しみを思うといたたまれない気持ちでいっぱいです I *can't bear* to think of the sorrow of the bereaved family.

いたち 鼬 weasel ⓒ

慣用表現 殺虫剤が強力になればなるほど害虫の耐性が強くなる。まさにいたちごっこだ(→悪循環だ) The more effective a pesticide becomes, the more resistant the harmful insects get. *It's a vicious circle*.

いたチョコ 板チョコ a bar of chocolate, chocolate bar ⓒ

いたって 至って (とても) very, awfully; (きわめて) extremely, absolutely /両親はいたって元気です My parents are in *very* good health. / 彼女はいたって質素な暮らしをしていた She lived an *extremely* simple life.

いたで 痛手 (心の傷) scar ⓒ, (公式的) wound ⓒ; (損害) damage ⓤ, loss ⓒ /事件が起こった地域の住民は精神的に大きな痛手を負った The incident left *a* deep *scar* in the community. / その学校の閉鎖は地域にとって大きな痛手だった The closing of the school was *a great loss* to the community.

◆心に痛手を負った人々を慰めるのに動物療法は有効だ Animal therapy is effective for soothing *the bruised psyche*.

いたのま 板の間 (床) wooden floor ⓒ; (部屋) a room with a wooden floor

いたばさみ 板挟み 義理と人情の板ばさみになる *be caught between* obligations and emotions / 友達2人がけんかして私は板ばさみだった Two of my friends had a quarrel and I *was caught in a dilemma*.

いたぶる (いじめる) bully 他; (ゆする) extort 他 /私は彼が下級生をいたぶっているのを見た I saw him *bullying* a lower grade student.

いたまえ 板前 a cook (in a Japanese restaurant) /板前の修業をする get training to become *a cook* of Japanese food

いたましい 痛ましい (哀れな) pitiful, pathetic; (つらい) painful; (悲劇的な) tragic; (むごい) cruel /破壊された都市の痛ましい光景 the *pathetic* sights of the destroyed city / その少女は痛ましい事故で両親を亡くした The girl lost her parents in a *tragic* accident.

いたみ¹ 痛み pain ⓤⓒ; ache [éik] ⓒⓤ (❖しばしば複合語を作る)

pain:「痛み」を表す一般的な語。特に急激で鋭い痛みということが多い。

ache: ふつう体の内部から起こる継続的な痛みを指す。

彼は傷の痛みにじっと耐えた He bore *the pain* of his wound.

痛みはいつまでも続くように思われた *The pain* seemed endless.

この薬は痛みをやわらげる This drug eases *the pain*.

その薬のおかげで痛みが消えた The medicine freed me from *the pain*.

子供は痛みに悲鳴をあげた The child gave a cry of *pain*.

患者は痛みでうめいた The patient moaned with *pain*.

足の痛みはすぐに治まるでしょう *The pain* in your leg will soon pass.

痛みは2, 3日は続くだろう *The pain* will persist for a couple of days.

いたみ

背中に激しい痛みを感じた I felt *a sharp pain* in my back.
心の痛みはなかなか消えない The 「*mental pain* [*pain inside*]」won't disappear easily.

> コロケーション -pain-
> 《形容詞＋～》 きりきりするような～ piercing pain / 刺すような～ stabbing pain / しつこい～ obstinate pain / 鋭い～ acute pain / 耐えがたい～ intolerable pain / 断続的な～ continual pain / 鈍い～ dull pain / ひどい～ dreadful pain / 慢性的な～ chronic pain / 焼けつくような～ searing pain
> 《～＋動詞》 ～に耐える endure pain / ～を取り除く［やわらげる］ kill [relieve] pain

‖痛み止め a painkiller,《公式的》a palliative

いたみ² 傷み（損傷）damage Ⓤ；(日常的な使用による消耗) wear and tear；(果実などの) bruise Ⓒ ◆このラジオは傷みがひどくて修理できない This radio *is damaged* beyond repair.

いたむ¹ 痛む
❶【体が】ache [éik] ⊕, hurt* ⊕, have* [feel*] a pain
けがした腕が痛む My injured arm *hurts*.
ひどく頭が痛む My head *aches* terribly.
彼は左足が痛むので，けんけんをして歩いた He was hopping along because his left leg *hurt*.
(医師が) どこが痛むのですか Where does it *hurt*?
◆食事の後に胃が痛む I *get stomachache* after eating meals. / 右肩に痛むところがある I have a *painful* place on my right shoulder.
❷【心が】
虐待を受けた子供たちを思うと心が痛む My heart *aches* [《口語的／比喩的》*bleeds*] *for* those abused children.
良心が痛むからそんなことはできません I can't do such a thing, otherwise my conscience will *bother* me.
そのニュースを聞いて胸が痛んだ The news *made me sad*. / I *felt sorry to* hear the news.

いたむ² 傷む
❶【食べ物が腐る】spoil* ⊕, go* bad；(傷がつく) get* bruised
梅雨時は食べ物が傷みやすい Food 「*goes bad* [*spoils*]」easily during the rainy season.
彼が持ってきた桃のいくつかは傷んでいた Some of the peaches he brought *were bruised*.
◆傷んでいない果物 *unblemished* fruit / この肉は少し傷んでいる This meat *is* a bit *spoiled* [《英》*off*].
❷【破損する】(損なわせる) damage ⊕
パーマとヘアダイで私の髪はかなり傷んでいる My hair *is* rather *damaged from* having it permed and dyed.
その橋はだいぶ傷んでいるので修理が必要です That bridge *is damaged* badly and needs repairing.
◆その家は長年ほうっておかれすっかり傷んでいた The house *had decayed* over (the) years of neglect. / この私のジャケットは着古して相当傷んでいる This jacket of mine is very much the worse for wear.

いたむ³ 悼む mourn ⊕ ⊛,《公式的》deplore ⊕ (◆進行形にはできない)；(嘆く) lament ⊕ / 私たちは愛する友の死を悼んだ We *mourned* the death of our beloved friend.

いためつける 痛め付ける 彼は昔の悪い仲間たちにさんざん痛めつけられた He *was beaten up* by members of his old gang. / 貴重なサンゴが空港の建設で痛めつけられてしまうだろう Precious coral would *be badly damaged* by building the airport.

いためる¹ 炒める fry ⊕ ⊛；(ソテーする) sauté [soutéi] ⊕ ‖タマネギをあめ色になるまでいためます *Fry* onions until brown. (❖料理の本などにある説明文)

🅔「料理はしますか」「簡単な野菜いためぐらいなら」"Do you cook?" "I only do simple cooking, like *stir-frying vegetables*." (❖stir-fryは特に中華料理で「肉・野菜などをかき混ぜながら強火でいためること」を指す)

いためる² 痛める hurt* ⊕, injure ⊕ ‖彼女は階段から落ちて背中を痛めた She *hurt* her back when she fell down the stairs.

◆彼女がおなかを痛めた（→血の実の）子供 *natural* child / 少女は子犬の死に小さな胸を痛めた The death of the puppy *made* the girl *sad*. / お母さんはおまえのことで心を痛めている（→心配している）Your mother *is worried about* you. / 彼らは資金繰りに頭を痛めている（→苦労している）ようだ They seem to *have difficulty* raising funds.

いたらない 至らない （不注意な）careless / 私が至らないばかりにご迷惑をおかけしました I apologize for causing you trouble. I was *careless*.

◆至らぬ点もあるかと思いますが（→経験は浅いですが）どうぞよろしくお願いします Although *I'm not that experienced*, I hope I can do a good job. (❖このように謙遜(ｹﾝｿﾝ)する言い方は英語にないため，そのまま訳すと誤解される場合が多く，あえて言う必要はない)

いたり 至り 会長よりお祝いの言葉をいただき光栄の至りです It is *my greatest honor* to be congratulated by the president.

イタリア Italy (❖公式名 the Republic of Italy) ──イタリア人 Italian Ⓒ ──イタリア語 Italian Ⓤ ──イタリア(人[語])の Italian

イタリック （斜字体）italics ──イタリックの italic ➡巻末付録（句読法）‖イタリック体 *italic* letters [type] / 書名は通例イタリックで印刷されている The titles of books are usually printed *in italics*.

いたる 至る ❶【達する】(道などが) lead* ⊕ (◆たどり着く) (◆進行形にはできない) ‖戦争に至る一連の出来事 the sequence of events *leading up to* a war / 中山道は木曽を経て京都に至る Nakasendo *leads to* Kyoto via Kiso. / 我々はその件に関して合意に至っていない We *haven't reached* an agreement on that issue. ◆死に至る病気 a *fatal* disease; a *terminal* illness ╱ 最終結論に至る *come to* a final conclusion

❷【及ぶ】現在に至るまで彼の記録は破られていない His record *hasn't yet* been broken. ╱ 東北地方から九州に至る広い範囲で大雨のおそれがあります There is a danger of heavy rain over a large area *extending from* Tohoku *to* Kyushu. ╱ さいわい大事には至らなかった Fortunately, *it didn't get serious*.

❸【…の結果になる】（終わる）result in ..., end in ... ╱彼はそのけがが元で足を切断するに至った His injury *resulted in* the amputation of his leg.

⇨いたらない, いたり

いたるところ 至る所（どこでも）everywhere;（一面に）all over ╱世界中至る所で日本の製品を目にすることができる Japanese products can be found *everywhere* [*anywhere*] in the world. ╱ あたりを見回すと花が至る所にあった I looked around and found flowers *all over* the field.

◆その建物は至る所塗り直されていた The building was repainted *throughout*.

いたれりつくせり 至れり尽くせり 両親は至れり尽くせりのツアーでハワイに行った My parents traveled in Hawaii on a *well-organized* package tour.

🄮「サービスはどうだった」「至れり尽くせりだったよ」"How was the service?" "*Absolutely perfect*!"

いたわり 労わり 彼は他人に対するいたわりの気持ちに欠けている He lacks *consideration for* others.

いたわる 労わる（だいじにする）take* good care of ...;（親切にする）be* kind ╱もう年なんだから自分の体をいたわるべきだ Now that you are getting old, you should *take good care of* yourself. ╱ お年寄りをいたわろう Let's *be kind to* old people.

いたん 異端 heresy Ⓤ Ⓒ ━━異端の heretical ╱ダーウィンの進化論も最初は異端視された Darwinism *was* first *regarded as heresy*.

◆彼は昔、映画界の異端児と呼ばれていた He was once called *an enfant terrible* [ɑːnfɑ̃n terɪ́ːbl] in the world of cinema.

‖異端者 a heretic

いち¹ 一

one;（1番目）the first

3分の1 *one* third

1足す1は2 *One* plus [and] *one* equal(s) [make(s), is, are] two.

私はスペイン語で1から10まで数えられる I can count *from one to* ten in Spanish.

試合は2対1で負けてしまった We lost the game two to *one*.

◆きのう子猫が1匹うちの庭に迷い込んできた *A* kitten strayed into our garden yesterday. ╱ コンピュータの知識にかけては彼はクラスで1番だ When it comes to computer knowledge, he *is second to none in the class*. ╱ 彼は数年前ソムリエのコンテストで世界一の栄冠に輝いた He won *the world championship* in the sommelier competition several years ago.

慣用表現 彼女は一を聞いて十を知る（→理解が早い）人だ She is *very quick to understand*. ╱ いちかばちかやってみよう I'll *take a chance* [*give it a try*], *and sink or swim*. ╱ 彼女は私がアメリカにいる間から十まで（→すべて）面倒を見てくれた She was attentive to *my every need* while I was in America. ╱ もう一度一から（→始めから）やり直そう Let's *start again from the beginning*. ╱ Let's *make a new start*. ╱ 父は一教師にすぎない My father is *only* [*just*] a teacher. ╱ 私のいとこは県で一, 二を争う秀才だ My cousin is really smart, *one of the best* students in the prefecture. ╱ うまくなるためには一にも二にも練習だ If you want to get any better, *all you can do* is practice. ╱ 母は一も二もなく（→ためらうことなく）賛成した My mother agreed *without hesitation*. ╱ 彼は一も二もなく（→すげなく）その申し出を断った He *flatly* turned down the offer.

いち² 位置

❶【場所】position Ⓒ;（決められた）place Ⓒ;（所在地）location Ⓒ ━━位置する be located

選手はみなそれぞれの位置についた All the players took up their *positions* on the field.

彼らは星の位置から方向が分かる They can tell directions by *the position* of the stars.

その船は船の位置を私たちに知らせてきた The boat signaled her *position* to us.

読んだ後は本を所定の位置に戻してください Put the books back *in place* after reading them.

鹿児島は九州の南の方に位置している Kagoshima *is located* in the southern part of Kyushu.

◆太陽はまだ低い位置にあった The sun *was* still low in the sky. ╱ 位置について, 用意, ドン！ *On your mark*! *Get set*! *Go*!

❷【地位・順位】（地位）position Ⓒ;（順位）（米）place Ⓒ,《英》position Ⓒ

重要な位置を占める hold *an* important *position*

小林はトップと3打差の4位という位置につけている Kobayashi is now in fourth *place*, three shots behind the leader.

◆彼は世界で最高峰に位置づけられるトランペット奏者だ He is one of the *top-ranking* trumpet players in the world.

いち³ 市（市場）market Ⓒ;（見本市）fair Ⓒ ╱国際見本市 an international trade fair ╱ のみの市 a flea market ╱ 私たちの町では毎月10日に市が立つ The 10th is (the) *market day* in our city. ◆がらくた市 a rummage [《英》jumble] *sale*

関連語 バザー a bazaar ╱ 展示会 an exposition

いちいち 一々 父は私の着るものにいちいち（→いつも）けちをつける My father is *always* criticizing what I wear. / 短縮ダイヤルを使えば番号をいちいち(→毎回)押さなくてもよい If you use the speed dial, you don't have to push numbers *all the time*.

いちいん¹ 一因 (原因の一つ) contributing [contributory] factor ⓒ; (原因) cause ⓒ ◆失業率の増加は社会不安を引き起こす一因となる The increase in the unemployment rate is *a contributing factor to* social unrest.

いちいん² 一員 member ⓒ ／ 社会[家族]の一員 *a member* of society [a family] ◆彼はサッカーのイタリア代表チームの一員になった He *made* the Italian national soccer team.

いちえん 一円 関東一円(→至る所)に大雨洪水注意報が出ています There is a flood warning *throughout* [*all over*] the Kanto area [region, district].

いちおう 一応
彼のことは好きではないが、一応(→それでも)助けてやった I don't like him, but I helped him *all* [*just*] *the same*.
彼女はそのことを知っているはずだが一応(→念のため)確認しておこう I think she knows it, but I'll ask her *just to make sure*.
ホテルの部屋には自炊に必要なものが一応(→基本的な用具が)そろっている The hotel rooms are equipped with *basic* utensils for cooking.
一応(→万一に備えて)水着も持っていこう I'm going to bring my swimsuit along *just in case*.
その交渉は一応の(→仮の)合意に達した The negotiation has produced a *tentative* agreement.
ウィンドウズなら一応(→ある程度)使えます I can use Windows *to some extent*.
これでも一応社会人です But *at least* I'm a working adult.
❷「日曜の練習には出るの?」「うん、一応ね」 "Are you going to come to (the) practice on Sunday?" "Yeah, *I think so*."

いちがいに 一概に 安物は品質が劣るとは一概には言えない Inexpensive things are *not necessarily* of lower quality.
❷「踊りは小さいときからやってないとプロにはなれないね」「一概にそうとも言えないよ」 "You've got to start at an early age to be a professional dancer." "That's *not always* true."

いちがつ 一月 January Ⓤⓒ (略語)Jan.)
語法
「1月に」というとき前置詞はinを用い、「1月…日に」というときはonを用いる。

1月1日 *January* 1; the first of *January*(❖January 1 [1st]は(the) first と読む. the を付けるのは《主に英》) / 1月に in *January* / 1月15日に on *January* 15; on the 15th of *January*
1月は雪が多かった In *January*, we had a lot of snow.
湾岸戦争は1991年1月に始まった The Gulf War started in *January* of 1991.

いちかばちか 一か八か いちかばちかやってみろ *Take a chance* [*gamble*] on it. / いちかばちかやってみよう *Let's take a chance*./ *Sink or swim*, I'll try./ Let's *go for broke*.

いちがん 一丸 地域の人々は一丸となって暴力団追放に取り組んだ The local people *united to* get rid of the mobsters.

いちがんレフ 一眼レフ (カメラ) single-lens reflex camera ⓒ /(略語)SLR.

いちぎてき 一義的 彼は一義的な(→あいまいでない)表現を使った He used an *unequivocal* expression.

いちぐん¹ 一軍 その選手はひざのけがを克服し一軍に復帰した The player got over his injury in the knee and came back to *the first team*.

いちぐん² 一群 カラスの一群 *a flock* of crows / オオカミの一群 *a pack* of wolves / 牛の一群 *a herd* of cattle / イルカの一群 *a school* of dolphins ⇒ むれ

いちげい 一芸 何か一芸に秀でていればその大学を受験することができる You can apply to that university if you have some *special talent*.

いちげき 一撃 (こぶしなどによる) blow ⓒ; (武器などによる) stroke ⓒ /(とどめを刺すような)強烈な一撃 *a knockout blow* / 一撃で *at a blow* [*stroke*]; *in one blow* [*stroke*] / そのボクサーは相手のあごに強烈な一撃を食らわせた That boxer gave his opponent *a hard blow to* the jaw.

いちげんか 一元化 行政の窓口を一元化する *unify* government offices

いちご 苺 strawberry ⓒ /来週の日曜日にイチゴ狩りに行きます We'll go *picking strawberries* next Sunday.
∥イチゴジャム strawberry jam
関連語 ブラックベリー a blackberry / ブルーベリー a blueberry / ラズベリー a raspberry

いちごいちえ 一期一会 一期一会(→一生に一度だけの機会)の出会いを大切にしなければならない You should realize the importance of meeting people because each time might be *a once-in-a-lifetime event*.

いちころ いちころでやられてしまった I was knocked out *with one punch*.

いちごん 一言 一言のもとに(→きっぱりと)断る "turn down [refuse] *flatly*" / 学生たちはその講義を一言一句聞きもらすまいと真剣に聞いていた The students were listening attentively so as not to miss *a single word* of the lecture.

いちざ 一座 (同席している人々) all those present, everyone present [there]; (芸人などの) troupe ⓒ; (劇団) company ⓒ /一座の人々はどっと笑いだした Everyone present [*there*] burst into laughter.

いちじ¹ 一時
❶【あのとき・かつて】 once, at one time
僕は一時タイ料理を作るのに凝っていた I *once* went in for Thai cooking.
その町は一時炭鉱の町として栄えた That town *once* prospered on coal.

◆彼女はアナウンサーだが一時女優としても活躍した She is an announcer and *one-time* actress.

💬「何とか間に合いそうだ」「やれやれ，一時はどうなることか(→終えられないか)と心配したよ」"I'm sure I can make it now." "Thank God! I was really worried you might not be able to finish it."

❷【そのときだけ】⇨いちじてき

その屋根は一時しのぎの補修をしているだけだから長くはもたないだろう Since the roof is only *temporarily* repaired, it won't last long.

◆彼は一時逃れの言い訳を並べた He came up with *makeshift* excuses. / He made excuses to *buy time*. / 僕が大道芸人になりたいというのは一時の気まぐれじゃない I want to be a street performer, and that's not a *passing* fancy. / 3万円あればとりあえず一時しのぎになるだろう Thirty thousand yen *will do for the time being*.

❸【しばらくの間】for a while [time]

患者は一時危険な状態だった The patient was in a critical condition *for a time*.

◆生産を一時停止する *suspend* production / 天気予報によると曇り一時雨ということだ The weather forecast says it will be cloudy with *intermittent rain*. / 臨時ニュースのため番組が一時中断された A flash news item *interrupted* the program.

‖一時預り所 (駅などの)《米》a baggage room, 《英》a left luggage office; (ホテル・劇場などの)《米》a checkroom,《英》a cloakroom / 一時金 (1度だけの手当) a one-time allowance / 一時停止《掲示》Stop; Halt / 一時払い payment in full [a lump sum]

いちじ² 一次 一次の (最初の)(the) first / 第一次世界大戦 *The First* War; World War I (❖Ⅰは one と読む)

‖一次関数 linear function / 一次産業 primary industry / 一次試験 a preliminary examination / 一次方程式 linear equation / 一次予選 the first preliminary

いちじ³ 一事 彼は一事が万事ああいう調子だ He is *always* like that. / He does *everything* that way.

いちじいっく 一字一句 一字一句訳そうとしないで文全体の意味を考えなさい Try to get the meaning of the sentence before translating it *word for word*.

いちじく 無花果 (実) fig Ⓒ; (木) fig tree Ⓒ

いちじつ 一日 慣用表現 コンピュータの操作については私より彼に一日の長がある(→彼は私より少し進んでいる)He *is a little ahead of* me in operating a computer. / 彼女は夫の帰国を一日千秋の思いで待った(→待ちこがれた)She waited *impatiently* for her husband to return home.

いちじてき 一時的 ──一時的な (仮の) temporary, provisional; (つかの間の) passing (❖名詞の前で用いる),《公式的》transitory ──時的に temporarily 《少し熱が出るかもしれないが，一時的なものだから心配いらない You might get a slight fever, but don't worry because that's only *temporary*. / 彼は今陶芸に凝っているが，それは一時的な興味にすぎない He is crazy about pottery now, but that's only a *passing* interest.

◆この部屋のすべての家具を一時的に隣の部屋に移しておいた We moved all the furniture in this room to the next room *for a while*.

いちじゅん 一巡 警備員は夜間にビルの中を一巡する Security guards *make the rounds* of the building during the night. / 東山高校は3回に打者一巡の猛攻で8点取った The Higashiyama High School team scored eight points by *running through the entire batting order* in the third inning.

いちじるしい 著しい (際立った) remarkable, striking ──著しく remarkably, strikingly 《その2国間には経済力に著しい格差がある There is a *striking* gap in economic power between those two countries. / 日本人の体格はここ数十年で著しく向上した The Japanese physique has *remarkably* improved in the past few decades.

◆1990年代の半ば日本では著しい米不足が起こった In the mid-1990s there was a *serious* rice shortage in Japan.

いちず 一途 ──いちずな (ひたむきな) single-minded; (真剣な) sincere ──いちずに single-mindedly; sincerely 《彼はプロ野球の選手になろうといちずに努力した He made a *sincere* effort to be a professional baseball player. ◆彼女はいちずに彼のことを愛した She loved him *wholeheartedly*.

いちぞく 一族 (一家族) one's [a] (whole) family; (親族全体) one's [the] relatives; (氏族) clan Ⓒ / 織田一族 the Oda *clan* / 彼の一族は名門だ He is from *a* distinguished *family*. / 祖母の介護について話し合うため一族が集まった *All the relatives* got together to talk about the issue of Grandma's care.

いちぞん 一存 そのご質問に私の一存ではお答えできません(→答える権限がない) I don't have the authority to answer your question (*on my own*).

いちだい 一代 (一生) one's lifetime 《父は一代で今の財産を築いた Starting from nothing, my father has built up a fortune in *his lifetime*.

いちたいいち 一対一 一対一の対応 *one-to-one* correspondence / 一対一で(→2人だけで)話そう Let's talk, *just two of us*. / 彼は自分の息子と一対一で向き合う必要がある He needs to have a *face-to-face* talk with his son.

いちだいじ 一大事 それは一大事だ *Good heavens!/ Heavens!* / 彼らがうちとの契約を取り消したりしたら一大事だ(→どうしよう)*What if* they cancel the contract with us?

💬「もし彼の入国ビザが下りなかったら？」「それこそ一大事だよ」"What if he can't get an entry visa?" "That would be *serious*."

いちだん¹ 一団 group Ⓒ; (行動を共にする) party Ⓒ, team Ⓒ / 一団となって in a *group*

いちだん

[body] / 外国人旅行者の一団 a group of foreign visitors
◆車は歩道を歩いていた生徒の一団につっ込んだ The car ran into a troop of schoolchildren walking on the sidewalk.

いちだん² 一段（階段の）step ◎; (はしごの) rung ◎ ── **いちだんと** (いっそう) still, even (✤共に比較級を強める) /私は駅の階段を1段おきに駆け上がった I ran up the stairs in the station *two steps at a time*. / あすは寒さがいちだんと厳しくなるようだ It will be *even [still] colder* tomorrow.
◆彼は女性社員を一段低く見ている He *looks down on* female employees. / 君はバレーボールがいちだんと上達したね You have made *further* progress in volleyball.

いちだんらく 一段落 私たちの仕事も一段落ついた We *have finished the first stage* of the project.

いちど 一度

❶【1回】once, one time ⇒いちどに
一生に一度 *once in a lifetime* / 1か月に1度 *once* a month / 一度ならず *more than once*
北海道へは1度だけ行ったことがある I have only been to Hokkaido *once*.
◆年に1度の祭り *an annual festival* / 一度でいいから好きなだけ買い物をしてみたい *If only I could shop to my heart's content!* / サッカー・ワールドカップは4年に1度開催される The World Cup soccer tournament is held (*once*) *every four years*. / 彼は一度こうと決めたら決して考えを曲げない *Once* he has made up his mind, he never changes it. (✤この once は接続詞) / 一度(→いずれ)うちに遊びに来てください Come see us at home *sometime*. / 彼女に約束をすっぽかされたのは一度や二度ではない She has broken appointments with me *many times*.
❷「一度(→以前)どこかでお会いしましたよね」「そうですか」"I think I've met you somewhere *before*." "Oh, really?"

❷【一度も…ない】never, not … ever
私はまだ一度も外国へ行ったことがない I have *never* been abroad.
そのような言葉は一度も聞いたことがないと思います I *don't* think I've *ever* heard any such word.

❸【もう一度】(once) again, once more, one more time
もう一度やってごらん Try (it) *again*.
死ぬ前にもう一度ギリシャを訪れたい I want to visit Greece *once more* before I die.
もう一度だけ僕と会ってもらえませんか Would you please meet me just *one more time*?
もう一度言ってください Could you please say that *again*? / I beg your *pardon*? / *Pardon* (me)?
◆もう一度チャンスをください Give me *another* [*a second*] chance.

いちどう 一同 (みんな) all; (だれも) everyone, everybody / 出席者一同 *all* those present / 一同を代表して on [(米) in] behalf

of *all* / あなたにお会いできるのを一同楽しみにしています We are *all* looking forward to seeing you.

いちどく 一読 その小説は一読の価値がある That novel is worth *reading*. / 一読しただけではその記事は分かりにくい The article is hard to understand at *first reading*.

いちどに 一度に（いっぺんに）at a time; (同時に) at once, at the same time / 一度にそんなにたくさんのケーキは食べられない I can't eat so much cake *at a time*. / 私は一度に2つのことはできない I can't do two things *at once*. / クリスマスと誕生日が一度に来たみたいだ This is like having Christmas and my birthday *at the same time*!

いちなん 一難 [慣用表現] 一難去ってまた一難 *One misfortune followed another*.

いちにち 一日 a [one] day (✤特に「1日」を強調したいときは one day とする)

1日おきに *every other* [*second*] *day*; *every two days* / 1日休みをとる take *a day* off
1日は24時間ある There are 24 hours in *a day*.
郵便は1日2回配達される The mail is delivered twice *a day*.
札幌行きは1日7便あります There are seven departures *a day* for Sapporo.
彼はかぜで一日中寝込んでいた He stayed in bed *all day* (*long*) because of a cold.
きょうはとてもいい一日だった I had *a very good day* today.
1日は雨に降られたが, それ以外はとてもよい旅だった We had rain on *one day*, but otherwise it was a very good trip.
彼はその日まる1日彼女のためにあけておいた He reserved *the whole day* for her.
一日としてその事件のことを忘れたことはなかった *Not a single day* went by when I didn't think about the case.
これは一日二日で終わる仕事ではない This job can't be done *in a day or two*.
日一日と寒さが厳しくなってきました It's getting colder *day by day*.
彼は決定を一日一日と延ばした He put off making a decision *from day to day*.
◆この問題の一日も早い解決を望みます I hope for the resolution of this problem *as soon as possible*.
[慣用表現] 一日一善 *Do your good deed for the day*. / ローマは一日にして成らず ⇒ローマ

いちにん 一任 一任する (任せる) leave*⑩; (委任する) entrust ⑩ / あなたに一任します I'll leave it *to you*. / 彼女は次回のイベントの企画を一任されている She *has been entrusted with* planning the next event.

いちにんしょう 一人称 《文法》the first person / その小説は一人称で語られている That novel is written in *the first person*.

いちにんまえ 一人前 一图（1人分の量）a [one] portion, a [one] serving ── 圖（1人につき）each, per person [head] / (レストランで)てんぷらの盛り合わせを1人前お願いします *One* (*serving* [*order*] of) assorted tempura, please. / その店ではしゃぶしゃぶが1人前3,000円で食べ放題だ That restaurant offers an "all-you-can-eat" special of *shabu-shabu* for 3,000 yen *each* [*per person*]. / このレストランは1人前の量がけっこう多い *The portions* [*servings*] at this restaurant are fairly large.

◆彼女はもう一人前の(→大人の)女性だ She *has* already *grown up* into a woman. / 彼は一人前のシェフになって帰国した He returned home as a *full-fledged* cook. / こいつ,子供のくせに口だけは一人前の(→大人のような)ことをきく) This kid is talking *like an adult*!

いちねん¹ 一年 a [one] year
一年中 *all (the) year round; year-round* / 1年おきに *every other* [*second*] *year; every two years*

その会社は1年で売り上げを2倍にした The company doubled its sales *in a year*.
このパスポートはあと1年有効です This passport is good *for another year*.
このCDプレーヤーは機械の故障について1年間の保証付きだ This CD player is guaranteed *for one year* against mechanical failure.
私たちが結婚してちょうど1年たちました It has been *a year* to the day since we got married.
この地方では2月は1年でいちばん寒い月である February is the coldest month of *the year* in this area.

🅔「日本に来てどのくらいですか」「1年半です」"How long have you been here in Japan?" "*A year and a half*."

いちねん² 一念 その少年は母親に会いたい一念ではるばるアルゼンチンへ行った That boy went all the way to Argentina out of *a burning desire to* see his mother. / 彼は一念発起して(→堅く決心して)自分の会社を設立した He *made a firm decision* [(→思いきって) *took the plunge*] and started his own business.

いちねんせい 一年生 ❶【学年】first-year student ◎; (高校・大学の) 《米》freshman ◎ (❖【英】では大学にのみ用いる。また《米》では小学校1年から高校3年までを通して数えるため,高校1年生は 10th-grader ともいう); (小学校の) 《米》first-grader ◎; (中学校の) 《米》seventh-grader ◎ / 弟は小学校の1年生だ My brother is *a first-grader* [*in the first grade*].

🅔「君は何年生ですか」「高校1年生です」"What grade are you in?" "I'm *in the 10th grade*."

❷【植物】―― 一年生の annual ◆稲は一年生植物だ Rice plants are *annuals*.

いちば 市場 market ◎; (主に米) mart ◎; (市が開かれる広場) marketplace ◎ / 魚[青物]市場 *a fish* [*vegetable*] *market* / やみ市場 *a black market* / 市場に買い物に行く go to (*the*) *market* / 市場に露店を出す *run a market stall*

いちはやく 逸早く (素早く) quickly, promptly; (ただちに) immediately, at once

◆ABCテレビの記者がいち早く事故現場に駆けつけた A reporter from ABC was *quick to* get to the scene of the accident.

いちばん 一番

❶【順番】the first (place) (《略語》1st) (↔last), number one, No. 1 ―― 1番の the first ―― 1番に first

1番の歌詞 *the first* verse (of a song)
だれがそのレースで1番にゴールするだろうか I wonder who will finish [come in] *first* in the race.
1番線から快速高尾行き,発車します A rapid train for Takao is leaving from Platform [《米》Track] (*No.*) *1*.
頂上への一番乗りは僕たちだった We were *the first* to get to the summit.
花と聞いて一番に思い浮かべるのはやっぱりバラだ When it comes to flowers, I always think of roses *first*.
あすの朝一番にお電話します I'll call you *first thing tomorrow morning*.
◆美香は音楽ではクラスで1番だった Mika *led* the class in music.

❷【最も】(❖通例,形容詞・副詞の最上級を用いて表す)

私のいちばん上の姉 my *eldest* sister
健は僕のいちばんの親友だ Ken is my *best* friend.
クラスの男子の中ではだれがいちばん背が高いですか Who is *the tallest* of all the boys in your class?
数学は私のいちばん苦手[好き]な科目だ Mathematics is my *weakest* [*favorite*] subject. (❖favorite は1語で「いちばん好きな」という意味なので most は不要)
いちばん近い病院へはどう行けばいいですか How do I get to *the nearest* hospital?
眠気ざましにはコーヒーがいちばんだ Coffee works *best* to keep me awake.
京都への訪問で何がいちばん印象に残りましたか What impressed you *most* on your visit to Kyoto?
私がいちばんいやなのは高い所に上がることだ *The last thing* (that) I want to do is go up to a high place.
彼女がいちばん勉強しないが,いつもいい点を取る She studies *the least*, but always gets good marks.
彼のいちばんの気がかりは病気の母のことだった His *main* concern was his sick mother.
彼女がいちばん恐れていたことが現実となった Her *worst* fears were realized.
この冬いちばんといっていいような大雪だ This is one of *the heaviest* snows this winter.
25ページのいちばん上に聖書からの引用があります *At the top* of page 25 is a quotation from the Bible.

🅔「どんな音楽が好きですか」「ジャズがいちばん好きです」"What kind of music do you like?" "I like jazz *best*."

いちぶ

|| 1番打者 the lead-off batter / 一番星 the first star of the evening / 一番列車 the first train

慣用表現 彼女は開口一番,「離婚することになったの」と言った The first thing she said was "I'm getting divorced."

いちぶ 一部
❶【一部分】(a) part, a portion ── 一部の some; (部分的な) partial

これらは彼の膨大な著作のうちのほんの一部です These copies are only *part of* his extensive works.

この交換留学制度では費用の一部をその財団が負担する The foundation will bear *a portion of* the expenses for this exchange program.

一部の人たちはその重要性に気づいている *Some* people have realized its significance.

その仕事が遅れた原因の一部は僕にある I accept *my portion of* the blame for the delay in the work.

◆その人形は一部のマニアの間では絶大な人気がある That doll is extremely popular among *a small population of* maniacs. / That doll has *a cult following*. / 教師が一部の(→特定の)生徒をひいきにしてはいけない A teacher shouldn't favor *certain* pupils.

❷【1冊】a copy

これらのブックレットは1部200円です These booklets are 200 yen per *copy*. (❖per の後の名詞には a [an]を付けない)

いちぶしじゅう 一部始終 その事故の一部始終を話してください Please give me *the full details* of the accident. / 彼女は一部始終を知っている She knows *the whole story*.

いちぶぶん 一部分 (a) part ⇨ いちぶ

いちべつ 一瞥 (ちらりと見ること) a glance, a look ── 一瞥する glance ❺, cast* a glance ‖彼女は僕に一瞥もくれずにわきを通り過ぎた She walked by without even *glancing* at me. / 彼は一瞥しただけでその本をテーブルの上に放り投げた He only *cast a glance [glanced] at* the book and then threw it on the table.

いちぼう 一望 丘の上の城からはリスボンの町を一望することができる The castle on the hill *overlooks* the city of Lisbon. / 展望台からは周囲の島々が一望のもとに見渡せた The observatory *commanded a nice view* of surrounding islands.

いちまい 一枚 (紙・板・ガラスなど) a sheet; (パン・肉・ハムなど) a slice; (一片) a piece

語法
皿(plate), 硬貨(coin)など数えられる名詞にはふつうに a [an]か one を付ければよい. また日本語で「…枚」と数えるものでも, 英語では異なる数え方をすることがあるので注意が必要.

パン1枚 *a slice [piece] of* bread / 板ガラス1枚 *a sheet of* glass / 1枚の布 *a piece of* cloth / 新聞紙1枚 *a piece of* newspaper / 1枚の紙 *a sheet [piece, leaf] of* paper (❖一定の大きさ・型をもつ紙には a sheet, 大きさ・型が定まらないものには a piece を用いる. またルーズリーフなどの用紙は a leaf という)

◆パンツ1枚 *a pair of* briefs / レタスの葉1枚 *a lettuce leaf* / お皿をもう1枚お願いします Can I have *another* plate, please?

慣用表現 僕よりも彼女のほうが一枚うわてだった She was *a cut above* me. / She *had a slight edge on* me. / その件に関しては彼が一枚かんでいるにちがいない I'm sure he 「*has a hand [is involved] in* that situation.

いちまいいわ 一枚岩 monolith ⓒ ◆わが社の一枚岩の団結を誇りに思っている I'm proud of our *strongly solidified* company.

いちまつ 一抹 一抹の寂しさ *a touch [hint] of* loneliness / 妹の将来に一抹の不安を感じている I feel *somewhat [a little, rather]* uneasy about my sister's future.

いちみ 一味 (犯罪者・悪者の) gang ⓒ, ring ⓒ, mob ⓒ ‖スパイの一味 a spy *ring* / 警察は隠れ家まで一味の後をつけていた The police trailed *the gang* to their hideout.

いちみゃく 一脈 彼らは一脈相通ずるところがある They *have something in common*.

いちめい¹ 一命 a [one's] life ◆彼はその事故で重傷を負ったが, さいわい一命は取り留めた He was badly injured in that accident, but narrowly *escaped death*.

いちめい² 一名 (1人) a [one] person ‖1名様限り *one person* only / 入会金は1名につき2,500円になります The membership fee will be 2,500 yen *per person*. (❖per の後の名詞には a [an]を付けない)

いちめん 一面 ❶【側面・半面】a [one] side, an [one] aspect ‖君には一面しか見ていない You are looking at only *one side [aspect]* of the issue. / 彼女はふだんは現実的だが一面ロマンチストのところもある She is usually realistic but does have a romantic *side*. / 彼の性格の意外な一面が分かった An unexpected *aspect* of his character was revealed.

❷【そのあたり全体】一面火の海だった *The whole place* was enveloped in flames. / 空は一面どんよりと曇っていた The sky was overcast. / あたり一面に空き缶が散乱していた There were empty cans *all over the place*. / 牧場は一面緑に覆われていた The pasture was covered with green.

❸【新聞の第1ページ】the front page ‖皇太子の結婚が新聞の一面トップを飾った The marriage of the prince made *the front page*.

いちもうさく 一毛作 single cropping ⓤ

いちもうだじん 一網打尽 警察はその一帯の麻薬密売グループを一網打尽にした The police *rounded up* the area's drug dealers.

いちもく 一目 みんな彼には一目置いている Everyone *views* him *with respect*. / 彼女はだんだん同僚の間で一目置かれるようになった She gradually *gained the respect of* her colleagues.

いちもくさん 一目散 少年たちは先生がやってくるのを見て一目散に逃げ出した The boys 「*ran away at full speed [took to their heels]*

when they saw their teacher coming.

いちもくりょうぜん 一目瞭然 彼が彼女のことを好きなのは一目瞭然だ It's quite obvious that he likes her. / 彼が間違っていることは一目瞭然だった It was clear at a glance that he was wrong.

いちもん¹ 一文 一文無しになる 《口語的》go broke / 彼は一文無しだった He didn't have a penny. / 彼は一文無しだった He was penniless. / 彼は一文無しだった He was (flat) broke. / おまえの金なんてびた一文受け取るもんか I won't take one red cent from you. / それは一文の値打ちもない It's not worth a cent [penny].

いちもん² 一門 （家族）family ⓒ; （氏族）clan ⓒ; （宗派）sect ⓒ; （学問・芸術などの流派）school ⓒ

いちや 一夜 一夜の宿を求める ask for a night's lodging / 彼は一夜にして有名になった He became famous overnight. / 人々は体育館で不安な一夜を過ごした People spent an uneasy night in the gym.

いちやく 一躍 （突然）suddenly 《彼はこの前のテストでいちやくトップにおどり出た He suddenly jumped to the top in the last exam.
◆そのアイドルはCMに出ていちやく（→一夜にして）売れっ子になった The pop idol became popular overnight after appearing in some TV commercials.

いちゃつく ほかの女性といちゃついたりしたら別れるからね I'll leave you if you ever flirt with other women. / 人前でいちゃつくカップルを見るのは好きじゃない I don't like seeing couples making out in public.

いちやづけ 一夜漬け 一夜漬けのキュウリ cucumbers pickled overnight / 歴史のテストのために一夜漬けをした I crammed overnight for the history exam. / 一夜漬け（→一晩での勉強）ではいい点絶対に取れないよ You're never going to get good scores by studying just one night.

いちゃもん おれにいちゃもんをつける気か Are you trying to pick a fight with me?

いちゅう 意中 意中を明かす open up one's mind [heart] / 意中の人（→心当たりの人）はだれなの Who's on your mind? / （→好きな人）Who are you in love with? / スポーツ紙によると彼のチームは横浜らしい A sports newspaper says the team he has in mind is Yokohama.

いちょう¹ 胃腸 one's stomach （◆正確にはthe stomach and intestines だが，一般的にstomachで通じる），《口語的》insides 《きょうは胃腸の調子が悪い I've got an upset stomach today. ◆彼女は胃腸が弱い[丈夫だ] She has weak [good] digestion.
‖胃腸炎〔医学〕gastroenteritis / 胃腸薬 stomach medicine, 〔消化剤〕digestive

いちょう² 銀杏 ginkgo [gíŋkou] ⓒ（複 ～es, ~s）（◆gingkoともつづる）《イチョウ並木 a line of ginkgo trees
短歌 金色（こがね）のちひさき鳥のかたちして銀杏ちる夕日の岡に （与謝野晶子）
In fluttering form

like many small golden birds
they drift slowly down
from the maidenhair branches
upon the hill at sunset.

いちよう 一様 試合には負けたが彼らの表情は一様に満足そうだった Though they lost the game, they *all* looked content. / その村の女性たちは一様に黒っぽいスカートをはいていた The women in that village *uniformly* wore dark skirts.

いちよく 一翼 情報産業の一翼をになう play *a role* [*part*] *in* the information industry

いちらん 一覧 （一覧表）list ⓒ, table ⓒ; （カタログ）catalog ⓒ ——一覧する（ざっと目を通す）glance ⓐ 《参考文献一覧 *a list* of references; a bibliography / 彼は私の報告書を一覧した He *glanced* [*skimmed*] *through* my report.

いちらんせい 一卵性 ‖一卵性双生児 identical twins; （一卵性双生児の1人）an identical twin

いちり 一理 彼の言うことにも一理ある（→理にかなっている）*There's a certain logic* in what he says.

いちりつ 一律 送料は全国一律300円です The postage is 300 yen *to anywhere in the country*. / そのカードで売り場の全商品が一律5パーセント引きになる *All* items on the floor will be five percent off with that card. / それらの問題は一律には論じられない We cannot discuss *all* of those problems *in the same manner*.

いちりゅう 一流 ——一流の （一級の）first-class, first-rate; （高級な）exclusive; （主要な）leading; （最高の）top, best
一流ホテル a *first-class* [*first-rate, five-star*] hotel （◆*five-star*（5つ星）はホテルなどの格が最高級であることを示す） / 一流レストラン an *exclusive* restaurant / 一流会社 a *leading* company
彼のおじは当代一流の指揮者の一人だ His uncle is one of the *top* [*best*] conductors today.
◆一流のシェフ a *master* [*cordon bleu*] chef / この英会話学校の講師はみな一流大学卒のネイティブだ All teachers of this English conversation school are native speakers from *prestigious* [*top-notch*] colleges.
慣用表現 それは彼一流の（→独特の）ほめ言葉だ That's *his peculiar way* of praise.

いちりょうじつ 一両日 一両日中にご連絡します I'll contact you *in a day or two*.

いちりん 一輪 （花）a (single) flower; （車輪）a (single) wheel
◆花びんにバラを一輪さしてあった *A (single)* rose was put in the vase.
‖一輪ざし a small flower vase / 一輪車 a unicycle, a monocycle; （手押し車）a wheelbarrow, a barrow

いちるい 一塁 first (base) ‖一塁を守る play *first* (*base*) / 一塁に出る 「get to [make, reach] *first* (*base*)
‖一塁側スタンド the right field stands / 一

塁手 a first baseman

いちれい 一例 an example ‖これはゴシック建築の典型的な一例です This is *a* typical *example* of Gothic architecture. ◆一例を挙げると… *For example [instance]* …

いちれつ 一列 a line, (英) a queue [kjúː]; (座席などの) a row; (横列) a rank; (縦列) a file ‖1列に並んで in *a line* [*queue*] / 彼女はいすを1列に並べた She arranged the chairs *in a row*. ◆人々は1列に並んで食糧の配給を待っていた People *lined up* to receive their food rations.

いちれん 一連 ── 一連の (ひも状の) a string of ..., a rope of ...; (ひと続きの) a chain of ..., a series of ..., a sequence of ..., a set of ...

| a chain of: 1つの出来事が次の出来事を誘発する場合.
| a series of: 特に順序に関係なくひとつながりの出来事が起こる場合.
| a sequence of: 特定の順番に物事が起こる場合.
| a set of: 順序に関係なく, たまたま1つの結果を産することになる偶然の出来事を総称する場合.

1連の真珠のネックレス *a string* [*rope*] *of* pearls / 一連のテロ行為 *a series of* terrorist acts / 東欧で起こった一連の出来事 *a chain of* events that took place in Eastern Europe

いちろ 一路 彼らは一路(→まっすぐに)帰国の途についた They headed *straight* for home.

いちろう 一浪 僕は一浪して今年和歌山大学に入った(→高校卒業後1年間受験勉強してから和歌山大学に合格できた) I spent a year after high school studying for entrance exams before I made it into Wakayama University.

いつ

when; (何時に) what time; (今からどれくらい早く) how soon ⇨いつまで, いつも

1学期はいつ終わりますか *When* does the first term finish?
いつニューヨークから帰ってきたのですか *When* did you get back from New York?
お子さんはいつ生まれる予定ですか *When* is your baby due?
彼の到着予定がいつか知らせてください Please inform me *when* he will be arriving.
その番組はいつ始まるの *What time* does that program begin?
注文した本はいつ届きますか *How soon* will I get the book I ordered?
いつ私がうそをついたっていうの *When* have I told a lie? (✿ ふつう when は現在完了形とともには用いないが, この例のように反語的に強調して用いることがある)

◆一休さんっていつの時代の人なの *Which* period did Ikkyu live in? / いったいいつの間にこれを全部やったのですか *Whenever did you find time* to do all this? (✿ whenever は when の強調形で「いったいいつ」の意味) / このつぼはいつごろのものだと思いますか *How old* do you think this pot is? / いつ訪ねても彼女は君を歓迎してくれるだろう *Whenever* you (may) visit her, she'll welcome you. / 先週のいつだったか渋谷で彼女を見かけた I remember seeing her in Shibuya *sometime* last week. / スピルバーグの映画はいつ見ても興奮させられる I *always* find it exciting to watch Spielberg's movies.

🗨 「誕生日はいつですか」「5月27日です」 "*When* is your birthday?" "It's (on) May 27."

🗨 「いつ会いましょうか」「あすはどうですか」 "*When* shall we meet?" "How about tomorrow?"

🗨 「彼はいつ戻りますか」「全く分かりません」 "*When* do you think he will come back?" "I've got no idea."

いつう 胃痛 (腹痛) stomachache ⒞⒰ ‖ 緊張からくる胃痛 *a stomachache* caused by tension / 胃痛がする I have (a) *stomachache*.

いつか¹

❶ 【未来】 someday, sometime (✿ some day [time] と2語にもつづる), one day; (やがて) in time; (いずれ) eventually, sooner or later

こんな恐ろしい病気はいつかこの世からなくなってほしい I hope *someday* the world will be rid of these awful diseases.
君の夢はいつか実現するだろう Your dream will come true *someday*.
いつかまた会いましょう *One day* we'll meet again.
来週のいつか彼に会いに行くつもりだ I'm going to see him *sometime* next week.
不規則な生活を続けているといつか病気になるよ If you go on keeping irregular hours, *sooner or later* you'll get sick.
◆それはまたいつか別のときに話そう Let's talk about it *some other time*. / 彼が目的を達成する日がいつかきっと来るだろう The day *will* come when he achieves his goal.

🗨 「映画でも見に行かない?」「ごめん, またいつかね」 "Shall we go to movies or something?" "Sorry, *some other time*."

❷ 【過去】 (かつて) once; (以前に) before; (過去のあるとき) sometime in the past

そのレストランにはいつか行ったような気がする I think I've been to that restaurant *once*.
いつかどこかでお会いしましたね I've seen you somewhere *before*.

いつか² 五日 5日間 for *five days* / 7月5日 July (*the*) *fifth*

いっか¹ 一家 (家族) a [one's] family ‖ 一家の大黒柱 the breadwinner in *a family* / 坂本さんの家は音楽一家だ The Sakamotos are a musical *family*. / 彼のうちは冬休みに一家そろってハワイに行くそうだ I hear *his whole family* is going to Hawaii during winter vacation. / 西洋人はクリスマスを一家団らんで過ごすことが多い Western people usually spend Christmas *with their families*. / これは天皇ご一家がお泊まりになったホテルです This is the hotel where *the* Imperial *family* stayed.

‖一家心中 a family suicide

いっか² 一過 午後には台風一過の青空が広がった *The typhoon passed*, and the blue sky appeared in the afternoon. / ワインブームは一過性のものではない The popularity of wine is not just *temporary*.

いっかい¹ 一階 (米)the first floor, (英)the ground floor (❖(英)では the first floor は2階の意味になるので注意); (2階建ての家の) downstairs ➡ かい(階) /受付窓口は1階にあります The reception window is *on the first floor*.

いっかい² 一回 (1度) once, one time /週[月]に1回 *once* a week [month] / もう1回やってごらん Try it *once again* [*more*]. / そこには1回しか行ったことがある I have only been there *once*. / もう1回見せてもらえますか Can I see it *one more time*?

◆ (ゲームなどで) 1回200円 200 yen *a try* / (野球で) 1回の表[裏] the top [bottom] of *the first inning* / 彼女は1回で司法試験に合格した She passed the National Bar Examination *on her first attempt*.

‖1回生(大学の) a freshman / 1回戦 the first game; (トーナメントの) the first round

いっかく 一角 (片隅) a corner; (1つの角) an angle /校庭の一角に大きな桜の木がある There is a tall cherry tree in *the corner* of the school grounds.

◆ 氷山の一角(→先端) *the tip* of the iceberg / 山林の一角にごみが大量に違法投棄されている Huge amounts of garbage have been unlawfully dumped in *part* of the forest.

‖一角獣 a unicorn

いっかくせんきん 一攫千金 彼はいつも一攫千金を夢見ている He is always dreaming of *making a fortune at one stroke*.

いっかつ 一括 一括購入する buy *in bulk* / 一括払いで支払う pay *in one lump sum* / 生命保険料を一括で(→全額一度に)払うと割安になる You can save money if you pay life insurance premiums *up front and in full*. / これらの問題を一括して処理することはできない You can't deal with these problems *all at once*.

‖一括協定 a package deal / 一括法案 an omnibus bill

いつかは someday; (いずれは) eventually, sooner or later ‖一生懸命努力すればいつかは成功するだろう If you try hard, you will *eventually* succeed.

いつから (いつ) when; (すでにどのくらい長く) how long /新しい法律が効力を発するのはいつからですか When does the new law take effect? / いつから長野にお住まいですか How *long* have you been living in Nagano?

🟥 「いつから柔道を始めたの」「去年[5年前]からです」"*How long* have you been practicing judo?" "Since last year. [(For) five years.]"

🟥 「いつから彼とつきあってるの」「1か月くらい前から」"*Since when* have you been going out with him?" "Since about a month ago." (❖Since when …?にはしばしば驚き・非難の気持ちが含まれる)

いっかん¹ 一巻 (2巻以上から成る本の1冊) a volume (《略語》vol.) /第1巻 *Vol. I* (❖volume one と読む); *Book One*

慣用表現 今コンピュータがハングアップしたらそれこそ一巻の終わりだ If the computer freezes now, it *will be the end of the world*.

いっかん² 一貫 首尾一貫した方針 a *consistent* policy / 被告は終始一貫して無罪を主張していた The accused insisted on his innocence *from start to finish*. / その政治家は言うこととすることが一貫していない That politician *says one thing and does another*. / 彼の話は一貫性に欠けている What he says lacks *consistency*.

‖一貫作業 a continuous [nonstop] operation

いっかん³ 一環 来月授業の一環として博物館へ行きます We are going to a museum as *a part of* the course next month.

いっき 一気 一気に (ひと息に) in one breath, in one draft; (休まずに) at a stretch ➡ いっきのみ /グラスの水を一気に飲む drink a glass of water *in one draft*

◆ 一気に本を読み終える read a book *in one sitting* (❖in one sitting は「最後まで席を立たずに」の意味) / 彼女は駅の階段を一気に駆け上がった She sprinted up the stairs in the station *without stopping*.

いっきいちゆう 一喜一憂 家族はみな彼の病状に一喜一憂していた All his family were watching over his condition, *happily and anxiously by turns*.

いっきうち 一騎打ち a single combat, a one-on-one struggle /最終レースでは山田と林の一騎打ちになった The last race turned out to be *a「one-on-one struggle [head-to-head confrontation]* between Yamada and Hayashi.

いっきのみ 一気飲み 一気飲みする chug 自他, (米口語的)chug-a-lug 自他 (❖「一気、一気」という掛け声は"Chug it, chug it, go, go, go!"のようにいう) /彼はビールを一気飲みした He *chugged* (a) beer.

いっきゅう 一級 (最上級) the first (grade) ── (最高級の) first-rate, first-class; (すばらしい) excellent /これは一級品のワインだ This is a *first-class* wine.

◆ 第1級殺人 *first-degree* murder

いっきょ 一挙 ── 一挙に (一気に) at a stroke, in one stroke; (きっぱりと) once and for all /重要な証人が現れて事件は一挙に解決した A key witness was found, and the case was cleared up *once and for all*.

慣用表現 監督は彼女の一挙一動を見守っていた The director was watching her *every move*. / それは一挙両得だ That *will kill two birds with one stone*. (❖英語は「一石二鳥だ」の意味のことわざ)

いつく 居着く (定住する) settle (down) /その公園にはたくさんの野良猫が居着いている Many stray cats *have settled down* in the

いっく

park. ◆兄は少しも家に居着かない My brother almost *never stays* at home.

いっく 一句　彼は庭の梅の木を見ながら一句ひねった He composed *a haiku* while looking at an *ume* [a plum] tree in the garden.

いつくしむ 慈しむ　彼女は養子として迎え入れた2人の子供を慈しみ育てた She raised two adopted children *with tender loving care*.

いっけん 一見　——图（ちょっと見ること）a [one] glance, a look——副 at a glance, at first sight [glance]; (外見上は) seemingly, apparently　/一見して彼のしわざと分かった I could tell *at a glance* that he had done it. / 一見したところ彼らはうまくいっているようだった *At first sight* they appeared to be getting along very well. / 一見したところでは彼女はその知らせに動揺していなかった She was *seemingly* undisturbed by that news.
◆あの映画は一見の価値がある That movie *is worth seeing*.
ことわざ 百聞は一見にしかず ⇒ ひゃくぶん

いっけんや 一軒屋・一軒家　(孤立した家) an isolated [a solitary] house; (一戸建ての家) a house, 《主に英》a detached house (◆house はふつう「一戸建ての家」を指すので特に説明は不要) / 彼は森の奥の一軒家に住んでいる He lives in *an isolated house* deep in the forest.

いっこ 一個　レタス1個 *a head of* lettuce / せっけん1個 *a cake* [*bar*] *of* soap / チーズケーキ1個 *a piece of* cheesecake / 1個ちょうだい Give me *one*. / このザクロは1個300円です These pomegranates are 300 yen *a piece*. / 彼は棚に並んだグラスを1個1個手に取って見た He picked up and looked at the glasses on the shelf *one by one*. ⇒ -こ(-個)

いっこう 一行　a party, a company; (随行員) a suite [swíːt], an entourage; (護衛) an escort (◆以上すべて1つの集団とみなす場合は単数扱い, 個々に重点をおく場合は複数扱い) / 一行は京都へ向かった *The party* has left for Kyoto. / 総理とその一行はモスクワに向けてきょうの午後羽田を出発する The Prime Minister and his *entourage* will leave Haneda for Moscow this afternoon.

いっこうに 一向に　雨はいっこうに降る気配がない It isn't *at all* likely to rain. / 私はいっこうにかまいません It doesn't matter to me *at all*. / I *don't* care about it *a bit*.
◆様々な薬を試したが彼女の病状はいっこうによくならなかった She tried every medicine but her condition *didn't get any better*.
🅔「勝手に和食を用意しましたが, よろしかったですか」「いっこうにかまいません」"We've prepared a Japanese meal without asking you. Is it OK?" "*That's fine with [by] me*."

いっこく 一刻　(少しの間) a moment,《口語的》a minute; (一瞬) an instant　/ 刻一刻と出発の時間が迫ってきた The departure time is getting closer (and closer) *moment by moment*. / 事は一刻を争う There's *not a moment* [*minute*] *to be lost*. / This is an urgent situation.
◆一刻もむだにはできないぞ We've got no *time* to lose. / 一刻の猶予（⁽ゆうよ⁾）も許されない状況だ The situation *doesn't permit any delay*. / 一刻も早く戻ってきてください Please come back *as soon as possible* [*you can*].

いっこだて 一戸建て　a house; (一家族の家) a single-family house (◆house はふつう「一戸建ての家」を指すので特に説明は不要)

いっさい 一切　（すべて）all, everything ——一切の all
私たちは彼に一切を任せた We left *everything* to him.
一切の費用はこちらで負担します We'll take care of *all* the expenses.
彼はギャンブルで一切合切をすってしまった He lost *everything he owned* gambling.
◆容疑者は一切を白状した The suspect proceeded to make a *full* confession. / 彼はアルコールはいっさい飲まない He *never* drinks alcohol. / その事件に関する一切の質問にはお答えできません I can't answer *any* questions concerning the issue. / 私たちの組織は政府の干渉をいっさい受けない Our organization *is free from any* interference by the government.

いつざい 逸材　その選手は10年に1人の逸材だといわれている The player is said to be one of *the best of* the decade.

いっさくじつ 一昨日　the day before yesterday ⇒ おととい

いっさくねん 一昨年　the year before last ⇒ おととし

いっさくばん 一昨晩　(おとといの夜) the night [evening] before last

いっさんかたんそ 一酸化炭素【化学】carbon monoxide 🇺 ‖一酸化炭素中毒 carbon monoxide poisoning

いっし¹ 一糸　ニュース映像では子供たちが一糸乱れず行進していた Children were marching *in perfect order* in the news film. / そのビーチでは人々は一糸まとわぬ姿で海水浴を楽しんでいる People enjoy swimming *stark naked* on that beach.

いっし² 一矢　どうせ負けると分かっていてもせめて一矢を報いたい I know we're going to lose, but I want to *make* at least *a little rally*.

いつしか 季節はいつしか秋になっていた The season had changed to fall *before I knew it*.

いっしき 一式　a set; (道具などの) a kit　/工具一式 *a set of* tools; a tool *kit* / 裁縫道具一式 *a sewing kit* / 家具一式 *a set of* furniture

いっしゅ 一種　(1つの種類) a kind [sort]; (1つの型) a type; (変種) a variety　/鯨は哺乳類の一種だ A whale is a *kind* of mammal. / その部屋には一種奇妙な雰囲気が漂っている There's *a kind* [*sort*] *of* strange atmosphere in the room. ◆あの人には一種独特の雰囲気がある There's *something unique* about that person.

いっしゅう¹ 一周（ひと回り）a [one] round;（競技用トラックの）a [one] lap
◆1周400メートルのトラック a track 400 meters *around* / 島を車で[歩いて]1周してみよう Let's *drive* [*walk*] *around the island.* / 世界一周旅行ができたらなあ I wish I could *travel around the world.* / 私たちは北海道一周旅行をした We made [took] *a tour* of Hokkaido.

いっしゅう² 一蹴 彼の申し出はその場で一蹴された（→きっぱりと拒絶された）His offer *was flatly turned down* on the spot. / ラグビーの試合で私たちは彼らを一蹴した（→簡単に勝った）We *beat* them *easily* in the rugby game. /《米口語的》We *mopped the floor with* them in the rugby game.

いっしゅうかん 一週間 a week（❖ふつう日曜から土曜までを指すが、特定の日から7日間の意味にも用いる）∥出発の日が1週間繰り上げになった The date of departure has been advanced by *a week*. / これを1週間かそこらで仕上げなければならない I have to get this done in *a week* or so. / 試験は1週間にわたった The examinations extended over *a week.* / 好天はあと1週間続くでしょう Clear weather will continue *for another week.* / 彼女はまる1週間休暇をとった She took *the whole week* off.

いっしゅうき 一周忌 the first anniversary of *a person's* death

いっしゅうねん 一周年 私たちは結婚1周年を祝った We celebrated *our first* wedding *anniversary.*

いっしゅん 一瞬 a moment ∥喜びの一瞬 a glad *moment* / ほんの一瞬（の間）for *a fleeting moment*; for *a split second* / 一瞬静まり返った後、割れんばかりの拍手が起こった After *a moment* of silence there was a storm of applause. / 彼らは一瞬の隙(╲)に逃げ出した They ran away *in an opportune moment.*
◆一瞬の気のゆるみ a lapse of concentration（❖lapseは「ふとした軽い過失」の意味）/ レーザーは一瞬にしてバーコードを読み取る Lasers can read information from bar codes *in a flash.* / 一瞬の出来事だった It happened *in an instant.*

いっしょ 一緒

❶【共に】—いっしょに together;（…といっしょに）(along [together]) with ...

僕らは小さいころよくいっしょに遊んでいた We used to run around *together* when we were small.

友人は私に職員室にいっしょに行ってくれと頼んだ My friend asked me to go to the teachers' office *with* him.

カレーはふつうごはんかナンといっしょに出される Curry is usually served *with* rice or naan.

結婚というのは単に2人がいっしょに暮らすということではない Marriage is not simply a matter of two people living *together.*

僕は弟とその部屋をいっしょに使っている I share the room *with* my brother.

私は彼に手作りのカードといっしょにチョコをあげた I gave him chocolate (*along*) *with* my handmade card.

◆ではまた夕食のときにご一緒します I'll *join you* later for dinner. / 今晩夕食をいっしょにいかがですか Do you suppose *we* could have dinner tonight?

💬「映画の券が2枚あるんだ、いっしょに行かない？」「喜んで」"I've got two movie tickets. Won't you come *with* me?" "Sure."

💬「ご一緒していただけますか」「いいですとも」"Do you mind going *with* me?" "Not in the least. / I certainly don't."

💬「どんな人がタイプ」「いっしょにいて楽しい人」"What's your type?" "Someone who is fun to be *with.*"

❷【同じ】the same

私たちは小学校がいっしょだった（→同じ小学校に通った）We went to *the same* elementary school.

僕の意見は君のといっしょだ I've got *the same* opinion *as* you.

◆彼女は10年前といっしょだ（→10年前から少しも変わっていない）She *hasn't changed a bit* since 10 years ago.

💬「そのかばん、いいね」「ありがとう。この靴といっしょに買ったの」"I like your bag." "Thanks. I bought it *at the same time* I bought these shoes."

❸【「いっしょにする[なる]」の形で】

調味料とスパイスは全部いっしょにして（→混ぜ合わせて）からなべに加えなさい Mix all the seasoning and spices *together* before putting them into the pan.

同情と愛情をいっしょにしては（→混同しては）いけない Don't confuse pity *with* love.

学校へ行く途中で先生と偶然いっしょになった I *ran across* my teacher on the [my] *way* to school.

彼といっしょになる（→結婚する）気はあるの？ Do you have any intention of *marrying* him?

💬「サングラスかけるとやくざみたいだよ」「（彼らと）いっしょにしないでくれ」"The sunglasses make you look like a *yakuza.*" "*Don't put me in the same class* as them."

いっしょう 一生（生涯）a [*one's*] life;（一生の間）a [*one's*] lifetime

彼は一生独身を通した He remained single *all* [*throughout*] *his life.*

彼は一生その村を出ることはなかった（→その村にずっと住んでいた）He lived in that village *till the end of his life.*

そんな大金、一生かかってもたまらないよ It would take more than *my lifetime* to save up that much money.

こんな一生に一度のチャンスを逃したら後悔するぞ If you miss *the chance of a lifetime,* you'll be sorry for it.

彼女の一生は波乱万丈だった Her *life* was full of ups and downs.

その修道女は貧しい人々のために一生をささげた The nun devoted *her life* to the poor.
- 一生のお願いです It's the only favor that *I'll ever ask you of.* / ご恩は一生忘れません I'll never forget your kindness *as long as I live.* / シンデレラはその後一生幸せに暮らしました Cinderella lived happily *ever after.* / 貧しい人々に仕えることが彼女の一生の仕事だった Her *lifework* was to serve the poor people. / その画家は1枚の絵も売れないまま一生を終えた The artist *died* before he could sell a single painting.

慣用表現 彼は交通事故で九死に一生を得た He *barely escaped being killed* in the traffic accident. / He *had a narrow escape from death* in the traffic accident.

いっしょう² 一笑 彼は私の悩みを一笑に付した He *laughed off* my personal problem.

いっしょうけんめい 一生懸命 (熱心に) very hard
期末試験に向けてみんな一生懸命勉強している Everybody is studying *very hard* for the final exams.
- 一生懸命働くことが成功へのかぎだ *Hard work* is the key to success. / 一生懸命がんばります *I'll do my best*.

いっしょく 一色 町は祝賀ムード一色だった The whole city was in a mood of celebration. / 見渡すかぎり雪で白一色だった As far as the eye could see, *everything was white with snow*.

いっしょくそくはつ 一触即発 その2国間は一触即発の状態だ There's a potential *explosive [touch-and-go, hair-trigger]* situation between the two countries.

いっしょくた 一緒くた 私はほかの地方から来た人々といっしょくたにされた I *was lumped together with* people from other districts.

いっしん¹ 一心 彼女は息子の無事を一心に祈った She prayed *fervently* for her son's safety. / 彼に会いたい一心で彼女は駅に急いだ *Her impatience* to see him hurried her to the station. / 彼と私は一心同体だ He and I are *one in mind and body.* / 子供たちは一心不乱にそのゲームをやっていた The children *were absorbed in* playing the game.

いっしん² 一身 その選手は国民の期待を一身に背負ってオリンピックに出場した The athlete participated in the Olympics *with the nation's expectations on his shoulders.* / 少女は両親の愛情を一身に受けて育った The girl grew up *bathed in the love and affection of her parents.* / その教授は一身上の都合により辞職した The professor resigned from his university *for personal [private] reasons.*

いっしん³ 一新 新しい町へ引っ越して気分が一新した I *feel refreshed* by my move to a new city. / そのデパートでは従業員の制服を一新した The department store *has renewed* the uniform of their employees.

いっしん⁴ 一審 a first trial / その男は一審で有罪判決が下った The man was found guilty in *the first trial*.

いっしんいったい 一進一退 日本の景気は一進一退を繰り返している Japan's economy *has been seesawing*.

いっしんきょう 一神教 (唯一神を信じる宗教) monotheism Ⓤ (↔polytheism) ー 一神教の monotheistic

いっしんとう 一親等 the first degree of relationship [kinship] → しんとう(親等)

いっすい 一睡 ゆうべは一睡もできなかった I *didn't「get a wink of sleep [sleep a wink]* last night. / 彼女は一睡もせずに母親の看病をした She *stayed up all night* taking care of her sick mother.

いっする 逸する 一生にまたとないような好機を逸してしまった I *missed [lost] the chance of a lifetime.* / 彼女にお礼を言うつもりだったが機を逸してしまった I was going to thank her, but I *missed the opportunity*.

慣用表現 常軌を逸したふるまい *eccentric behavior*

いっすん 一寸 一寸先さえ見えなかった We couldn't see *an inch ahead* of us. / それは一寸たりとも動かさないように Do not move it *even an inch*.

慣用表現 一寸先はやみ (→何が起こるかだれも知らない) *Nobody knows what the future holds.*

ことわざ 一寸の光陰軽んずべからず *Nothing is as precious as time.* (→時間ほど貴重なものはない) / 一寸の虫にも五分の魂 *Even a worm will turn.* (→反撃する)

いっせい¹ 一斉 ー いっせいに (同時に) (all) at once, at the same time; (いっしょに) all together
花はいっせいに咲き始めた The flowers began to bloom *all at once*.
記者たちは彼に対していっせいに質問を浴びせかけた All the reporters showered him with questions *at the same time*.
赤ちゃんたちがいっせいに泣きだした The babies started to cry *all together*.
- 彼女の友人たちはいっせいに私を非難した All her friends criticized me *in chorus*.
‖ 一斉検挙 a wholesale arrest, (口語的) a roundup / 一斉射撃 a volley, a fusillade

いっせい² 一世 エリザベス1世 Elizabeth *I* (❖Iは the First と読む) / ロサンゼルスに住む日系1世 *an issei [a first-generation Japanese-American]* living in Los Angeles / この音楽は10年ほど前に一世を風靡(ふうび)した This kind of music *was all the rage* about ten years ago.

いっせいちだい 一世一代 一世一代の賭(か)けをする take the chance of *one's life*

いっせき 一石 その出来事は政界に一石を投じた (→議論を喚起した) The incident *aroused a controversy in* political circles.

いっせき 一席 新しいメンバーを迎えたので一席設けよう (→パーティーをしよう) と思います We are thinking of *giving a party* to welcome our new members.

いっせきにちょう 一石二鳥 古い洋服を処分できてお金も入るなんて一石二鳥だ You can get rid of the old clothes and even get money for them. That's a real chance to *kill two birds with one stone*.

いっせつ¹ 一説 一説によると黒幕はある大物の政治家らしい *Some say* [*Another story is*] *that* a big shot in politics is operating behind the scenes.

いっせつ² 一節 『マザーグース』の一節を引用する quote *a passage* from *Mother Goose*

いっせん¹ 一戦 (闘争) a battle, a fight; (試合) a game, a match ∥この一戦に勝てばチームは上部リーグに昇格する If the team wins this *game*, it will go to the upper division of the league. ◆彼らは育児に関して一戦交えていた(→議論していた) They *were arguing about* how a child should be raised.

いっせん² 一線 一線を越える(→限度を超える) *go beyond the limit* ∥ 彼女は仕事とプライベートにはっきりと一線を画している She keeps her private life clearly *separate from* her work. ∥ 彼が一線を退いてから2年たった It's been two years since he *stepped down*.

いっそ そんなことをするくらいならいっそ死んだほうがましだ I *would rather* die *than* do such a thing. / I'll die *first before* doing such a thing. ∥ あまり修理代がかかるようならいっそのことビデオを買い替えよう If the repair costs a lot, why don't we *just* buy a new VCR.

いっそう¹ 一層 **even, still**(❖共に比較級を強める); **all the more**(❖原因・理由を表す語句とともに用いる)

12月になったらいっそう寒さが増すだろう It'll become *even* [*still*] colder when December comes around.

私はいっそう勉強に励んだ I studied *even* [*still*] harder.

◆君になお一層の努力が必要だ You should make a *greater* effort. / 花嫁姿の彼女はいっそう美しく見えた She looked *more* beautiful *than ever* in her bridal dress.

いっそう² 一掃 —— 一掃する **sweep*** **(away), wipe out, clear (away)**; (犯罪を) **clean up** ∥その委員会は省内の不正を一掃するために組織された The commission was organized in order to *wipe out* corruption in the Ministry. / 彼は走者一掃のスリーベースを放った He hit a triple and *cleared the bases*. ◆在庫一掃セール a *clearance* sale

いっそくとび 一足飛び 彼女の父はベルボーイから一足飛びにそのホテルの総支配人になった Her father *leapfrogged* from bellboy to general manager of the hotel.

いつぞや いつぞやどこかでお会いしましたね I've seen you *before*, haven't I? / いつぞやはすてきな花束をありがとうございました Thank you for the lovely flowers that you gave me *the other day*.

いったい¹ 一体
❶【ひとまとまり】
カヌーに乗って川を下るうち自然と一体になった気がした I felt like I *was part of* nature while canoeing down the river.
うちのチームにもようやく一体感が生まれてきた Our team finally has begun to feel *a sense of unity*.
そのテレビはビデオと一体型だ The television *is equipped with* a VCR.

❷[一体全体] **on earth, in the world**(❖疑問詞の直後に置いて意味を強める); **for Christ's [God's, heaven's, Pete's] sake**

【語法】上記以外にも疑問文を強める語に the deuce, the devil, the hell などがあり、いずれも疑問詞の直後に置く。さらに however, whatever, whoever なども強調形の疑問詞として用いられる(❖how ever, what ever のように2語にもつづる)。また会話では単に語勢を強めるだけでニュアンスが伝わる場合も多い。

いったいだれがそんなうわさを広めたのか Who *on earth* has spread such a rumor?
君はいったい何を言っているんだね What *in the world* are you saying?
いったい何が起こっているんだ What's going on here, *for God's sake*?
彼らをいったいどこへ連れていったのですか *Wherever* [*Where ever*] did you take them?
いったい何をしたい気なんだ *Whatever* are you trying to do?
君はいったい自分を何様だと思っているんだ Who *the hell* do you think you are?
◆それはいったいどういう意味なんだ What do you mean by that? / いったいどうなっているのだろう What's it all coming to?

【英作文ノート】the の有無に注意!
いったいどうして彼は学校をやめたのか
→×Why *on the earth* did he quit school?
→○Why *on earth* did he quit school?
→○Why *in the world* did he quit school?
★「一体全体」の意味では world には the が付くが、earth には the が付かない。似たような表現でも the の有無には注意.

いったい² 一帯 この蛇は八重山諸島一帯に生息している This kind of snake inhabits *the whole area* of the Yaeyama Islands. ∥ 今夜は北陸地方一帯に大雪のおそれがある There is a possibility of heavy snow *all over* the Hokuriku district.

いったいぜんたい 一体全体 **on earth, in the world,** 《俗語》**the hell**(❖いずれも疑問詞の直後に置く) ⇨いったい❷ ∥一体全体どうして君がここにいるんだ(→ここで何をしているのか) What *on earth* are you doing here?

いつだつ 逸脱 **deviation** ⓊⒸ —— 逸脱する **deviate** ⓘ ∥それは当初の計画から逸脱している It *deviates from* the original plan.

いったりきたり 行ったり来たり 私は家と学校を行ったり来たりしなければならなかった I had to *go back and forth* between home and school. ∥ 彼は部屋の中を行ったり来たりしていた He *was pacing* the room *to and*

fro.

いったん¹ 一旦 once /弟はいったん泣き始めるとお菓子をもらうまで泣きやまない Once my little brother starts crying, he won't stop until he gets some candy.
◆いったんうちに帰ってからまた来ます I'll go home *first* and come back again. / 彼はいったんはその仕事を引き受けたが断った He *first* agreed to take on the job, but then took back his words.

いったん² 一端 この責任の一端は私たちにある We are *partly responsible* for this. /この手紙の発見により真実の一端が明らかになるだろう The discovery of this letter will provide *some sidelights* on the truth.

いっち 一致

(意見・話などの) agreement ⓤ,《公式的》accord ⓤ;(好み・出来事などの偶然の)coincidence ⓒⓤ ―― 一致する agree ⓐⓘ; accord ⓐ; coincide ⓐ(❖いずれも進行形にはできない)
時制の一致 verb tense *agreement* / 奇妙な偶然の一致 a funny *coincidence*

私たちの意見は完全に一致している We *are in complete agreement*.

彼らはその点に関して意見が一致した They *agreed on* that point.

私は姉と服装の趣味が一致する My taste in clothing *coincides with* my sister's.

君の報告は以前言っていたことと一致しない Your report *doesn't agree [disagrees] with* what you said before.

彼女の供述は目撃者の証言と一致しない Her version *does not accord with* the witness' statements.

◆言行を一致させる *fit* the action *to* the words; *reconcile* the action with the words / 凶器に残された指紋は彼のと一致した The fingerprints on the weapon *matched* his. / その提案は満場一致で可決された The proposal was accepted *by a unanimous vote*. / 彼らは一致協力してその問題に取り組んだ They made a united *effort* to solve the problem. / 労働者は一致団結して経営側と交渉した The workers *united together* to negotiate with the management.

いっちゃく 一着 (1 位) first place; (上下そろいの衣服) a suit (of clothes) /彼女は200メートル走で1着になった She *won first place* [came in *first*] in the 200-meter dash. / 彼はその洋服屋でスーツを1着あつらえた He ordered *a suit* in that tailor's.

いっちゅうや 一昼夜 all day and night, a whole day and night

いっちょう 一丁 豆腐1丁 *a block of* tofu / (ゲームなどで) 最後にもう一丁やるか Do you want to play *one* last *time*?

いっちょういっせき 一朝一夕 それは一朝一夕に(→すぐに)解決するような問題ではない That's not the kind of issue which would be solved *instantly*.

いっちょういったん 一長一短 どの提案も一長一短あって決めるのが難しい It's hard to decide because every suggestion has *both advantages and disadvantages*.

いっちょうら 一張羅 (いちばん上等な服) one's best clothes [suit]; (晴れ着) one's Sunday best

いっちょくせん 一直線 (1本の直線) a straight line ―― 一直線に (まっすぐ) straight /その道は西に向かって一直線に続いていた The road stretched out *straight* west.

いつつ 五つ five ⓒⓤ ⇨ご(五) /5つ星のホテル a *five-star* hotel
‖5つ子 quintuplets;(5つ子の1人)a quintuplet(❖口語では《米》quint,《英》quin ともいう)

いっつい 一対 a pair /一対のひな人形 *a pair of* hina dolls / 彼らは好一対の夫婦だ They make *a fine pair*.

いって 一手 ❶《方法・手段》way ⓤ;(将棋・チェスなどの指し手) move ⓒ ◆一手先を読む think *one step ahead*

❷《独占》彼女はその仕事を一手に引き受けた She *undertook* the job *single-handedly*. / その会社は日本でそのおもちゃを一手に販売している The company *is the exclusive dealer* of the toy in Japan.

慣用表現 彼は押しの一手で彼女をくどいたらしい They say his *persistence* finally won her heart.

いってい 一定 ―― 一定の (不変の) constant; (限定された) definite, certain(❖名詞の前で用いる);(規則的な) fixed; (規則的な) regular ‖(❖通例名詞の前で用いる);(一様の) uniform, steady /一定の間隔で at *regular intervals* / 一定の収入がある have a *regular [fixed] income* / それらの薬品の使用には一定の基準が設けられている There is a *definite* standard in using the chemicals. / 私たちは一定の速度で走った We ran at a *steady rate [speed]*. ◆倉庫の中は摂氏17度で一定に保たれている The temperature is *constantly* kept at 17℃ in the warehouse. / 一定の手続きを踏まなければならない You must follow a *specific* procedure.

いってき 一滴 (ひとしずく) a drop /1滴ずつ *drop by drop* / 彼は酒は一滴も飲まない He *never touches a drop*. / He *doesn't drink at all*.

いってきます 行って来ます

日本語の「行ってきます」「行ってらっしゃい」に当たる決まった英語のあいさつは特にない. 学校や仕事などいつもの決まった場所に出かけるときはふつう I'm going now.(行ってきます)のようにいうことが多く,ほかの場所に出かけるときは行き先を付けて I'm going to Tom's.(トムの家に行ってきます)などという. または簡単に Bye(-bye).(じゃあね)などですませることも多い.

いってつ 一徹 彼は頑固一徹な男だ He is such a *stubborn* [an *obstinate*, an *inflexible*] man.

いってみれば 言ってみれば　結婚とは言ってみれば大きな賭(か)けだ Marriage is a big gamble *in a way*.

いつでも　(どんなときでも) (at) any time,《主に米》anytime, whenever; (常に) always
いつでも力になるよ I'm *always* ready to help.
私の部屋はいつでも好きなときに使っていいですよ You can use my room「*(at) any time* [*whenever*] you like.
困ったときはいつでも相談しなさい Come to me *whenever* [*anytime*] you are in trouble.

いってらっしゃい 行ってらっしゃい

> 日本語の「行ってきます」「行ってらっしゃい」に当たる決まった英語のあいさつは特にない. 状況に応じて Have fun!(楽しんできなさい), Have a nice day!(よい一日を), Good luck!(幸運を祈ってる)などといったり, 単に Bye.(じゃあね), See you later.(じゃあまた)のようなあいさつですませることが多い.

いってん¹　一転　笑っていた彼女の顔が一転して泣き顔になった Her smiling face *suddenly changed* into a crying face. / その出来事で形勢は一転した The situation *switched completely* because of the incident. / 引っ越して心機一転, 一からやり直すつもりだ I'm moving out to *turn over a new leaf*. (❖turn over a new leaf は「生活を一新する」の意味の比喩的表現)

いってん²　一点　私たちのチームは１点差でその試合に勝った Our team won the game *by one point*. / 彼は空の一点を見つめていた He was gazing *at a point* in the sky. / 私はこの一点に関してだけは譲れない I cannot concede on this particular *point*. / 彼女の言葉に一点の曇りもない(→ほんの少しの疑いもない) *There's not a shadow* [*speck*] *of doubt* in what she said.

いってん³　一天　the (whole) sky / 一天にわかにかき曇った(→空が急に雲に覆われた) The sky suddenly became overcast.

いってんばり　一点張り　彼はそれに関して知らぬ存ぜぬの一点張りだった(→かたくなに知らないと言い続けた) He *stubbornly kept on saying* that he knew nothing about it.

いっと　一途　その産業は衰退の一途をたどっている The industry *is*「*in terminal decline* [*steadily declining*].

いっとう　一等　(１等賞) (the) first prize; (１位) first place / 彼は英語スピーチコンテストで１等賞を取った He won [got] (*the*) *first prize* in the English speech contest. / 彼らは800メートルリレーで１等になった They「*won first place* [*came in first*] in the 800-meter relay. ◆広尾といえば東京の一等地の一つだ Hiroo is one of *the best and most expensive places* in Tokyo.
∥一等航海士 a first officer [mate] / 一等親 the first degree of relationship [kinship] / 一等星 a star of the first magnitude

いっとうりょうだん　一刀両断　彼は一刀両断に(→速やかに決断を下しあっという間に)その難問を解決した He *made a quick decision* and solved that difficult problem *immediately*.

いっとき　一時　民子のことは一時も忘れなかった I never *once* forgot Tamiko.

いつと（は）**なしに**　彼女はいつとはなしに父親を避けるようになった She began to avoid her father *without realizing it at first*.
➪いつのまにか

いつなんどき　いつ何時　いつ何時自分の会社が倒産するかもしれないご時世だ The times are so unstable that your company might go bankrupt *at any time* [*moment*].

いつになく　彼女はいつになく機嫌が悪そうだから近寄るな She is in an *unusually* bad mood now, so stay away from her. / 妹はきょうはいつになく素直だ My sister is *being* obedient today. (❖進行形を使うと「ふだんと違って」の意味が加わる)

いつのまにか　いつの間にか　いつの間にか試合は終わっていた The game was over *before we noticed it*. / 彼はいつの間にかいなくなっていた(→だれも彼が去るのに気づかなかった) Nobody noticed him leaving. / いつの間にか数年が過ぎていた The years *had slipped by* [*past*].

いっぱ　一派　(集団) a group; (党派) a party; (学派・流派) a school; (分派・宗派) a sect ∥佐藤氏とその一派が新党を旗揚げした Mr. Sato and his *group* started a new party.

いっぱい 一杯

| ❶ 容器に満ちる分量 | a cup of ... |
| ❷ たくさん・あふれるほど | full; a lot of ... |

❶【容器に満ちる分量】(カップ１杯の) a cup of ...; (グラス１杯の) a glass of ...; (茶わん１杯の) a bowl of ...

> ほかにも a bucket of (バケツ１杯), a basket of (かご１杯) など容器によって様々な言い方がある. また正確に「…１杯分の量」を表すには a tablespoonful [teaspoonful] of (大さじ[茶さじ]１杯), a cupful of (カップ１杯など) -ful を付けて用いる.

水[牛乳] １杯 *a glass of* water [milk]
ごはんをもう１杯いかがですか Would you like *another bowl of* rice?
「コーヒーでも１杯どうですか」「いただきます」"How about *a cup of* coffee?" "That sounds nice."
🅒「もう１杯いかが」「ええ, いただきます[いえ, 結構です]」"Would you like *another cup?*" "Yes, please [No, thank you]."

❷【たくさん・あふれるほど】full; (たくさんの) a lot of ..., lots of ...
水のいっぱい入ったバケツ a bucket *full of* water
彼はいつも元気いっぱいだ He *is* always *full of energy* [*vigor*].
口の中をいっぱいにしたままでしゃべるな Don't

speak with your mouth *full*.
きょうはやることがいっぱいある I've got *lots of things to do* today.
◆腕いっぱいのバラ *an armful of* roses / びんをいっぱいにする *fill* a bottle / そのグラスは水が縁でいっぱいに入っていた The glass *was filled to the brim with* water. / 私の心は感謝の気持ちでいっぱいになった My heart *was filled with* gratitude. / 席は予約でいっぱいです The seats are *fully* reserved. / その新しい店は買い物客でいっぱいだ The new store *is crowded with* shoppers. / 日光が部屋いっぱいに差し込んだ The room *was flooded with* sunlight. / 彼は間近に迫った演奏会のことで頭がいっぱいだ He *is completely preoccupied with* the coming concert. / 今週はスケジュールがいっぱいだ I've got *a very busy timetable* this week.

🔈「お代わりはいかが」「もうおなかいっぱいです」 "Would you like another helping?" "No, thank you. I'm *full*."

❸【限界・ぎりぎり】
車を壁際いっぱいに寄せる park *right against* a wall
この仕事は3月いっぱいはかかるだろう This work will take *until the end of* March.
彼はバットを力一杯振った He swung the bat *with all his strength*.
精一杯やってみますが、何も保証はできませんよ I'*ll do my best*, but I can't promise anything.
私はそのパーティーで目一杯楽しんだ I enjoyed myself *to the max* at the party.

🔈「手伝ってもらえない？」「ごめん、手一杯なんだ」 "Won't you help me?" "Sorry, I can't. *My hands are full*."

❹【酒を飲むこと】a drink
一杯飲みに行こう Let's go and *have [take] a drink*.
彼が一杯おごってくれた He treated me to *a drink*.
私たちは一杯やりながら仕事の話をした We talked about work over *a drink*.

❺【その他】
あいつにはまんまと一杯食わされた(→だまされた) I *was* completely *taken in* by him.

いっぱいいっぱい 一杯一杯 これでいっぱいいっぱいだ(→これ以上はできない) I *can't do any more*./ (→最善を尽くした)I did 「*my best* [*the best I could*].

いっぱく 一泊 ━━ 1泊の overnight ━━ 1泊する stay overnight ∥私たちは軽井沢へ1泊旅行をした We made *an overnight trip* to Karuizawa. / 彼は友人の家に1泊した He *stayed overnight* at his friend's house.
◆そのホテルは1泊2食付きで1人2万円だ The hotel charges 20,000 yen a person *per night including two meals*.

いっぱし 一端 ━━ いっぱしの (有能な) competent, able, capable ∥彼はいっぱしの実業家だ He is a *competent* [*an able*] businessman. ◆彼はまだ13歳なのにいっぱしの(→大人のような)口をきく Though he is only 13, he

already talks *like an adult*.

いっぱつ 一発 的(まと)をめがけて銃を一発撃つ fire *a shot* at the target / 私はあごに一発食らった I got [took] *a blow* to the jaw. / ホームランを一発かっとばせ Hit [Blast] *a home run*! / 一発勝負だ(→勝負は1回だけだ) This is *the one and only match* [*game*].

いっぱん 一般
(世間一般) the (general) public ━━ 一般的な general; (ふつうの) common, popular, ordinary ━━ 一般的に generally, in general; commonly
一般的傾向 a *general* tendency
彼の音楽は世間一般には受け入れられなかった His music was not accepted by *the general public*.
この寺は一般に公開されていますか Is this temple open *to the public*?
その映画は今週の土曜日から一般公開される That movie *will be in general release* this Saturday.
彼女は経済学の専門家として一般的に認められている She is *generally* acknowledged to be an expert in economics.
一般的に言って日本人は野球が好きだ *Generally speaking*, Japanese people like baseball.
一般に女性は男性より長生きする *In general*, women live longer than men.
◆一般的な高校生 an *average* high school student / 一般的な意見 a *prevailing* opinion / その病院は資金を一般の寄付に頼っている The hospital is dependent on *public charity* for funds. / これだけの事例では一般化することはできない We can't *generalize* from these few incidents.
∥一般開業医 a general practitioner ((略語)) GP) / 一般会計 the general account / 一般教育科目(大学の) ((主に米)) liberal arts, ((英)) liberal studies / 一般教養 general knowledge / 一般市民 a civilian / 一般事務 paperwork / 一般大衆 ordinary [common] people, the general public / 一般病棟 a general ward / 一般論 a generalization, generalities

いっぴき 一匹 猫が1匹うちの庭に迷い込んできた *A* cat strayed into our garden.
∥一匹狼 (おおかみ) a lone wolf, ((口語的)) a loner; a maverick (◆「異端児」のニュアンスがある)

いっぴつ 一筆 (短信) a note, a line ∥あちらに到着したら一筆書いて送ります I'll drop you *a note* [*line*] when I get there.
◆広樹は両親に一筆したためた Hiroki *wrote a letter* to his parents.

いっぴん 逸品 (すぐれた品) excellent item [article] ⓒ; (傑作) masterpiece ⓒ; (珍品) rare item [article], rarity ⓒ

いっぴんりょうり 一品料理 à la carte [àːləkάːrt]dish ⓒ (◆à la carte は according to the menu という意味のフランス語で、メニューから1品ずつ好きな料理を選んで注文すること)

いっぷいっせい 一夫一婦制 monogamy

◻

いっぷう 一風 彼は一風変わったところがある There's something *odd* [*eccentric*] about him.

いっぷく 一服 ❶【たばこ】a smoke —— 一服する have* a smoke ∥彼は一服するために外に出た He went out for *a smoke*.
❷【休憩】a rest, a break —— 一服する take* a rest [break] ∥このへんで一服しようか Shall we *take a break* now?
❸【薬】(1回分の薬) a dose ∥この薬を毎食後に一服飲んでください You have to take *a dose* of this medicine after each meal.

いっぷたさいせい 一夫多妻制 polygamy ◻

いっぺん¹ 一遍 (1度) once, one time —— 一遍に at a [one] time; (同時に・すぐに) at once ➡いちど ∥バンジージャンプを一遍だけやってみたい I want to try bungee jumping just *once*. / 私はいっぺんに2つのことはできない I can't do two things *at a time*.
◆通り一遍の知識 *superficial* knowledge / 彼女はどんなに複雑な公式もいっぺんで覚えてしまう She can memorize any formula *immediately* no matter how complicated it is.

いっぺん² 一変 経済情勢が一変した The economic situation *has changed completely*. / その事故は姉の生き方を一変させた The accident *changed the whole mode of* my sister's life.

いっぺん³ 一片 a piece ∥1片の紙切れ *a piece of* paper ◆空には一片の雲もなかった There was not *a* cloud in the sky. / 彼には一片の良心もない He doesn't have *a bit of* conscience.

いっぺんとう 一辺倒 彼はジーンズ一辺倒だ(→いつもジーンズをはいている) He *always* wears jeans.

いっぽ 一歩 a [one] step ∥1歩前に出る[後ろに下がる] take *one step* forward [backward] / これ以上一歩も歩けません I can't walk *a step* farther. / これは平和に向けての大きな一歩だ This is *a big step* toward peace. / 彼女は一歩一歩目標に向かって進んでいる She is advancing *step by step* toward her goal. / 一瞬間違えたら大惨事になるところだった *One wrong step* would have led to a terrible accident.
◆彼は破産の一歩手前だ He *is on the brink of* (financial) ruin. / 私はジャーナリストとしての第一歩を踏み出した My career as a journalist *has just begun*. / 彼女の焼くケーキは売っているケーキに一歩もひけをとらない Her homemade cakes *are no less delicious than* the cakes sold at shops. / この点に関しては一歩も譲れません I *can never budge an inch* on this point.

いっぽう¹ 一方
❶【片側】(1つの側) one side; (片方) one; (もう片方) the other(❖one と the other はしばしば対で用いる)
ロープのもう一方の端 *the other* end of the rope
船が急に一方に傾いた The boat suddenly leaned [listed] *to one side*.
この本の装丁は2種類あり、一方は廉価版でもう一方は革装だ This book comes in two editions, *one* cheap and *the other* bound in leather.
都会での生活は刺激的であるが、一方でストレスも多い *On the one hand*, city life is exciting, *but on the other* (*hand*), it can be stressful.(❖on the one hand ..., on the other hand ～ は「一方では…, 他方では～」の意味. また on the other hand はふつう接続詞またはセミコロンとともに用いる)
多くの点でこの製品のほうがもう一方のものよりすぐれている In many ways this product is better than *the other*.
2つのテーマのうちどちらか一方を選んで作文をしなければならない We have to write an essay on *either one* of these two topics.
◆仕事のない人がいる一方で働きすぎで病気になる人もいる Some people work too much, *while* others get sick from overwork. / この道路は一方通行だ This is a *one-way* street.

❷【一方的】—— 一方的な (勝負などが) one-sided; (関係などが) one-way; (当事者のうち一方のみの) unilateral —— 一方的に unilaterally
一方的な試合 a *one-sided* game / 一方的な勝利 *one-sided* victory / 一方的な決定 a *unilateral* decision
それは君の一方的な意見にすぎない That's only your *one-sided* view.
彼らは一方的に休戦を宣言した They declared a *unilateral* cease-fire.
◆彼女は一方的に彼に別れを告げた She *selfishly* ended the relationship with him.

❸【…するばかり】
こういう仕事をしていると目は悪くなる一方だ My eyesight *keeps getting worse* due to this kind of work.
日本では出生率は減る一方だ The birth rate *has been steadily decreasing* in Japan.

いっぽう² 一報 東京に着いたらご一報ください *Let me know* when you arrive in Tokyo. / 航空機墜落事故の第一報が入ってきたのは午前4時だった *The first report* of the plane crash came in at 4 a.m.

いっぽん 一本
❶【物】
チョーク1本 a [one] piece of chalk / 赤ワイン1本 a [one] bottle of red (wine) / (酒を)一本つける heat a bottle of sake
絵筆を1本買った I bought a [one] paintbrush.
❷【柔道など】
一本取る gain a point(❖柔道では clinch an *ippon* ともいう)
❸【その他】
🕭「早くしないといつもの電車に遅れるわよ」「いい, 1本遅らす」 "Hurry up, or you'll miss the (usual) train." "It's OK. I'll take *the* next *one*."
∥一本勝負 a one-game match

いっぽんか

[慣用表現] 彼女は一本気な人だ She is a *single-minded* person. / 彼は一本立ちして(→独立して)日本料理店を開いた He *became an entrepreneur* and opened a Japanese restaurant. / その先生の話は一本調子で聞いていて眠くなった The teacher spoke *in a boring monotone* which made me sleepy. / これは一本取られた(→君の勝ちだ) *You win.* / *You beat me.* / *You got me there.* / 私は志望校を一本にしぼった I decided which school to apply to. / 私は中央大学一本やりで受験します I'll take the entrance examination of Chuo University *only*.

いっぽんか 一本化 (統一・統合) unification ⓤ ── 一本化する (一つにする) unify ⓗ, put* together

いつまで 彼はいつまで町にいるのですか *How long* is he going to stay in town? / その仕事はいつまでに(→いつ)終えなければならないのですか *When* do you have to finish the job? / 彼女はいったいいつまで黙秘を続けるつもりだろう(→いつ沈黙を破るのだろう) *When* is she going to break her silence? / いつまで待っても彼女は来なかった I *waited* for her *forever* but she never showed up.

いつまでも (永遠に) forever (and ever); (ずっと) always // 私たちの愛はいつまでも続こう Our love will last *forever.* / あなたが私のためにしてくれたことはいつまでも忘れません(→ずっと覚えている) I'll 「*always* remember [(決して忘れない) *never* forget] what you did for me. ◆痛みはいつまでも続くように思われた The pain seemed *endless.* / そして彼らはいつまでも幸せに暮らしましたとさ And they lived happily *ever after.* (❖おとぎ話の結びに使われる)

いつも

❶【常に・いつでも】 always, all the time
彼はいつも「あきらめるな」と言っていた He *always* said, "Never give up."
この時間の電車はいつも込んでいる The trains are *always* packed at this time of the day.
金持ちがいつも幸せだとは限らない The rich are *not always* happy.
その家の庭はいつもきれいに手入れされている The garden of that house is neatly kept *all the time.*
◆買い物に行くといつもお金を使いすぎてしまう *Whenever* [*Every time*] I go shopping, I spend too much money. / おばは家に来るときはいつも何か持ってきてくれる My aunt *never fails to* bring us some presents when she visits us. / 首相にはいつも護衛がついている The prime minister is *constantly* attended by bodyguards. / 彼女の誕生日をいつも忘れてしまう I *keep forgetting* her birthday. / 彼女はいつも私に協力を惜しまない She *never begrudges* me cooperation.

🅔「君はいつも学校に遅刻してくるね」「いつもじゃないよ」 "You're *always* late for school." "*Not always.*"

🅔「どっちの味方なんだ」「僕はいつもあなたの味方ですよ」 "Whose side are you on?" "I'm *always on your side.*"

❷【ふつう・ふだん】 usually ── いつもの usual
私はいつもバスで学校に行く I *usually* go to school by bus.
彼女はいつもより早く[遅く]家を出た She left home earlier [later] *than usual.*
いつもの場所で5時に会おう Let's meet at five at the *usual* place.
いつものでいいですか Will you have *your usual?* (❖the [*one's*] usual で「いつもの[お決まりの]物」の意味)
いつものように彼は11時に床についた *As usual,* he went to bed at 11.
きょうはいつもの(の君)と違うね You don't look 「*your usual self* [*yourself*] today.
◆彼らはいつものやり方で彼女にごちそうをした They treated her in their *accustomed* way. / 彼女はいつもの席に着いた She took her *habitual* seat. / 彼は夕食がすむといつも部屋に引きこもる *Each* night after dinner, he withdraws into his room.

いづらい 居辛い 彼女は継母とそりが合わず家にいづらくなった She didn't get along with her stepmother and *felt uncomfortable* living with her in the same house.

いつわ 逸話 (秘話) anecdote ⓒ; (話) story ⓒ // その作家にはおもしろい逸話がいくつかある There are some interesting *anecdotes* about that writer.

いつわり 偽り (うそ) lie ⓒ (↔truth); (うそをつくこと) lying ⓤ; (虚偽) (公式的) untruth ⓒⓤ ── 偽りの (うその) false, (公式的)untruthful // 偽りの報告書 *a false* report
◆自分ではやりたくないというのが偽りのない気持ちです To be honest, I wouldn't want to do it myself. / これから私が言うことにいっさいうそ偽りはありません I'm going to tell you *nothing but the truth.*

いつわる 偽る (うそを言う) lie ⓗ, tell* a lie; (ふりをする) pretend ⓗ, feign ⓗ; (気持ちなどを) disguise ⓗ; (だます) deceive ⓗ
真実を偽る *disguise* the fact
彼女は年齢を偽っていた She *had lied* about her age.
私は病気だと偽って会合を欠席した I 「*pretended to* be sick [*feigned* illness] and didn't attend the meeting.
◆彼は自分を外科医と偽った He *passed himself off as a surgeon.* / 彼女は名前を偽って働いていた She worked *under a false name.*

イディオム (慣用句) idiom ⓒ
イデオロギー ideology ⓒ ── イデオロギー(上)の ideological
いてざ 射手座 〖天文・占星〗 Sagittarius (❖「射手座の人」の意味では ⓒ)
いでたち 出で立ち 彼女はパーティーにはでなでたちで現れた She showed up for the party in *her fancy outfit.*
いてつく 凍て付く (凍りつく) freeze* ⓗ
◆12月の小樽は凍てつくような寒さだった It

was *freezing* cold in Otaru in December. (❖この freezing は副詞的に用いられた形容詞)

いてもたっても 居ても立っても 彼の事故のことを聞いても立ってもいられなかった(→じっと座っていられなかった) I *couldn't sit still* after hearing about his accident.

いてん 移転 (引っ越し) move ©; (建物などの) relocation ⓤ; (譲渡) transfer © ——**移転する** move ⓐ ∥首都の移転 the *relocation* of the (nation's) capital / 事務所は新宿から早稲田に移転した The office *moved from* Shinjuku *to* Waseda.

∥移転先 one's new address / 移転通知 a change-of-address notice / 移転登記 registration of a transfer

いでん 遺伝 heredity ⓤ ——**遺伝する** (受け継ぐ) inherit ⓗ ——**遺伝(性)の** hereditary ∥彼女の頑固なところは父親の遺伝だ She *inherited* her stubbornness *from* her father.

∥遺伝学 genetics / 遺伝学者 a geneticist / 遺伝形質 hereditary traits / 隔世遺伝 atavism / 優性遺伝 dominant inheritance / 劣性遺伝 recessive inheritance

いでんし 遺伝子 gene © ——**遺伝子の** genetic ∥遺伝子銀行 a gene bank / 遺伝子組み替え recombination / 遺伝子組み替え食品 genetically modified food / 遺伝子工学 genetic engineering / 遺伝子操作 genetic manipulation / 遺伝子治療 gene therapy

いと¹ 糸

thread ⓤ, (編み物用) yarn ⓤ, (釣り糸) (fishing) line ©

クモの糸 a spider's *thread*

糸が切れた[からまった] The *thread* broke [got tangled].

針と糸を貸してください Can I borrow a needle and *thread*?

老人は日がな一日桟橋に座って糸を垂れていた The old man sat all day casting *a line* from the pier.

◆針に糸を通してもらえますか Could you *thread* [*run a thread through*] a needle for me?

∥糸巻き 《米》a spool, 《英》a reel / 糸ようじ dental floss / 生糸 raw silk / 絹糸 silk thread / 毛糸 woolen yarn / ミシン糸 sewing thread / 木綿糸 cotton thread

慣用表現 私とあなたは赤い糸で結ばれている(→いっしょになる運命だ) You and I *are destined to be together*. / だれかが陰で糸を引いているにちがいない Someone must *be pulling strings behind the scenes*.

いと² 意図 intention ⓤ ©, 《公式的》intent ⓤ ©; (目的) purpose © ——**意図する** intend ⓗ ——**意図的な** intentional ——**意図的に** intentionally; purposely, on purpose ⇨ コミュニケーションスキル p.126 ∥意図したとおりの結果 an *intended* result / あなたの意図がどこにあるか全く分からない I have no idea what 「your real *purpose* is [you

want]. / その事故は意図的なものだった The accident was *intentional*. / 彼を意図的に無視したんじゃなくて単に気がつかなかったんだ I didn't ignore him *intentionally*, but I just didn't recognize him.

いど¹ 井戸 well © ∥井戸を掘る dig [sink] *a well* / 井戸がかれてしまった The *well* has run dry. ◆彼女は近所の主婦たちとしょっちゅう井戸端会議をする She is always engaged in *idle chatter* with the housewives in her neighborhood. (❖英語にも water-cooler chat という似た言葉がある)

∥井戸水 well water

いど² 緯度 latitude ⓤ ∥パリは札幌とほぼ同じ緯度にある Paris is on [at] about *the* same *latitude* as Sapporo.

∥緯度線 a parallel

関連語 経度 longitude / 南緯 the south latitudes / 北緯 the north latitudes

いとう¹ 以東 (…より東) east of ...; (…よりも東) ... and eastward

いとう² 厭う 彼は雨にぬれるのもいとわずテントの片づけを手伝ってくれた He *didn't mind* getting wet and helped taking down the tent.

いどう¹ 移動 movement ⓤ © ——**移動する** move ⓗ ⓐ

机を移動するのを手伝ってくれ Help me *move* the desk, will you?

すぐに車を移動させてください Please *move* your car right away.

◆荷物を移動していただけますか Would you mind *shifting* your baggage? / その探険隊は1日に約50キロ移動している The expedition *travels* about fifty kilometers a day.

∥移動性高気圧 a migratory anticyclone / 移動電話 a cellular [cell] phone, a mobile (phone) / 移動図書館 a bookmobile, 《英》a mobile library / 移動病院 a mobile hospital

いどう² 異動 (人員の配置替え) change ©, transfer © ∥彼女は海外支店への異動を願い出た She asked for *a transfer* to an overseas branch. / 鈴木さんは東京からニューヨークに異動になった Mr. Suzuki *was transferred from* Tokyo *to* New York.

∥人事異動 personnel changes

いとおしむ わが子をいとおしむ *feel affection for one's child*

いときりば 糸切り歯 (犬歯) canine tooth ©

いとぐち 糸口 (手がかり) clue ©; (かぎ) key © ∥その事件はまだ解決の糸口さえ見つかっていない Not even *a clue* to the incident has been found yet. / 彼らは交渉の行き詰まりを打開する糸口を見いだした They found *a key* to break the deadlock over the negotiation. ◆彼らはお互いに会話の糸口をつかめずにいる They are unable to find *a common topic* of conversation.

いとこ 従兄弟・従姉妹 (first) cousin © ∥またいとこ(→はとこ) *a second cousin* / 彼は父方のいとこです He is *my cousin* on my fa-

コミュニケーションスキル —意図—

[…するつもりだ…しようと思う]

(A) be going to *do*
(B) intend to *do*
(C) plan to *do*
(D) be thinking of *doing*
(E) mean (to) *do*

☞ 意図を表すとき口語で最もふつうの言い方は(A)で，(B)は意図を強調するとき，(C)は計画中，(D)は考慮中であることを強調しようとするときに用いる．また(E)も意図を強調した表現だが，(B)よりは弱い．

☞ I will ... も一人称の意志や意図を表すが，あらかじめ予定されていない意図を表すことが多い．

"I have a lot of work to do today."
"I'll help you."（「きょうはすることがたくさんある」「お手伝いしますよ」）

① be going to *do*

What **are** you **going to** do this weekend?
今週末は何をするつもりなの．

I'm **going to** see a movie with my boyfriend on Sunday.
日曜日に彼と映画を見に行こうと思っているの．

I'm not 「**going to** [**gonna**] be there. (❖gonna ... はくだけた言い方)
私はそこへ行くつもりもない．

I **was going to** have a big party last night.
きのうの夜盛大なパーティを開くつもりだった．(❖「が，結果的に開か[け]なかった」を含意している)

I **wasn't going to** tell you about it. (❖「が，結果的に話してしまった」を含意している)

② intend to *do* など

She says that she **intends to** be a doctor in the future.
彼女は将来医者になるつもりだと言っている．

I didn't **intend to** hurt you. / I had no **intention of** hurting you.
私はあなたを傷つけるつもりはなかった．(❖「が，結果的に傷つけてしまった」を含意)

I **had intended to** go out (for) shopping today.
きょうは買い物に出かけるつもりだった．(❖「が，結果的に出かけなかった」を含意)

My **intention is to** make a trip around the world.
私は世界一周旅行をするつもりだ．(→私の意志は世界一周旅行をすることだ)

③ plan to *do* / be thinking of *doing*

Where **are** you **planning to** go this summer?
今年の夏はどこへ行くつもりなの．

I'm **thinking of** going to Germany if I can.
できたらドイツに行きたいんだけど．

☞ [plan to *do* / be thinking of *doing*] はどうしようかとまだ計画中・考慮中である気持ちを表す．

④ mean (to) *do*

I've been **meaning to** thank you.
ずっとありがとうと言おうと思っていました．

I didn't **mean to** offend you.
あなたの気持ちを傷つけるつもりで言ったわけじゃないんだ．

---

ther's side.

いどころ 居所（住所）address ◎；（行方）whereabouts《単数または複数扱い》
◆ だれか彼の居所を知りませんか Does anybody know *where he is*?
[慣用表現] 彼女はきょうは朝から虫の居所が悪い（→ 機嫌が悪い）She *has been in a bad mood* since this morning.

いとしい 愛しい（親愛な）dear；（最愛の）dearest, beloved ∥ いとしいわが子 *one's dear* child

いとしご 愛し子 *one's* beloved [dearest] child

いとなみ 営み（やるべき仕事）work ⓤ ∥ 自然の営み *the work* of nature ◆動物たちは冬の営みに忙しそうだ The animals look very busy *preparing for* winter. / 彼女は日々の営みの中に喜びを見いだした She found pleasures everywhere in *her daily life*.

いとなむ 営む（経営する）run* ⓣ, manage ⓣ；（挙行する）hold* ⓣ ∥ 実家は花屋を営んでいます My family *runs* a flower shop. / ここで彼の3回忌の法要が営まれた The memorial service for the second anniversary of his death *was held* here.

◆ 弁護士[医師]を営む *practice law* [*medicine*] / 自営業を営む *do business on one's own* / 社会生活を営む *have* a social life

いとのこ 糸鋸 coping saw ◎；（電動糸のこ）jigsaw ◎

いとま 暇 彼女のしでかした失敗は枚挙にいとまがない（→数えきれない）She has made *too many* blunders *to count*. ➪ おいとま

いとまき 糸巻き（米）spool ◎,（英）reel ◎；（ミシンなどの）bobbin ◎

いどむ 挑む challenge ⓣ ∥ 茂樹は私にテニスで勝負をいどんできた Shigeki *challenged* me *to* a game of tennis. / その選手はアジア大会で世界記録にいどみます The athlete is going to *challenge himself to* set a new world record. ◆彼は先月アフリカの最高峰にいどんだ He *took on* the highest peak in Africa last month.

いとめ 糸目 [慣用表現] 彼女は焼き物に関しては金に糸目をつけない She *spends money extravagantly* on pottery. / *Money is no object* when she is buying pottery.

いとめる 射止める（射殺する）shoot* ⓣ, dead；（獲得する）win* ⓣ, gain ⓣ, get* ⓣ ∥ どうやって彼女のハートを射止めたの How did you *win* her heart?

いとも その子供はいとも簡単に九九を覚えてしまった The child learned the multiplication tables *so easily*. / 彼女はその問題をいとも簡単に解いたんだ She solved the problem, *just like that*. (※指をぱちんと鳴らしながら「これくらいたやすく」という意味で使う)

いな 否 問題は私たちが彼を信頼できるか否かだ The point is *whether* we can trust him *or not*.

いない 居ない 僕には父がいない I have *no* father. / 今うちにはだれもいない *Nobody's* (at) *home* now. / だれかいない？ Is anybody there?

-いない -以内 (時間・距離などが) within; (…未満) less than; (…以下) in ... or less
2週間以内に本を返却してください You are expected to return the books *within* two weeks.
私の家は駅から歩いて10分以内の所にある My house is *within* 10 minutes' walk from the station.
ご注文を受けてから30分以内にお届けします We guarantee to deliver your order *within* 30 minutes.
材料費は全部で1万円以内に収まった We could buy all the ingredients for *less than* 10,000 yen.
それを400字以内に要約しなさい Summarize it *in* 400 characters *or less*.
◆3分以内に戻ります I'll be back *in* three minutes.

いないいないばあ いないいないばあをする play *peekaboo*

いなおる 居直る (座り直す) sit* up / 彼は突然居直った(→開き直った) He suddenly *took a defiant attitude*.
‖居直り強盗 a burglar who turns violent

いなか 田舎
❶【都会に対して】the country, the countryside (※the countryside は美しい田園風景のイメージがある); (都市に対して・地方) the provinces, 《口語的/軽蔑的》the sticks ――いなかの country; (いなか風の) rustic; (都会から離れた) rural; (いなかくさい) provincial
いなかに住む live in *the country* / いなかの人々 *country* folk
彼はいなかの出身だ He comes from a *rural* area.
私はいなかの生活にとてもあこがれている I have a great longing for life in *the country*.
自然の美しさは都会に住む人々をいなかに引きつける The beauty of nature attracts city dwellers to *the countryside*.
‖いなかなまり a rural [rustic, provincial] accent / いなか町 a country town / いなか者 a provincial, a rustic (※共にやや軽蔑的な表現), 《米口語的/軽蔑的》a hick, a bumpkin
❷【故郷】one's home [hometown]; (出生地) one's birthplace
いなかの両親がリンゴを箱いっぱい送ってくれた My parents back *home* sent me a box full of apples.
正月休みはいなかに帰ります I'm going *home* for the New Year holidays.
🅔「いなかはどちらですか」「山形です」"Where's *your hometown*?" "It's Yamagata."

いながらにして 居ながらにして インターネットのおかげで家にいながらにしてあらゆる情報を得ることができる Thanks to the Internet, we can get any kind of information *at home*.

いなくなる 居なくなる このあたりの蛍はすっかりいなくなった Fireflies *have* completely *disappeared* from this neighborhood.

いなご 蝗 locust

いなさく 稲作 (稲の栽培) rice growing Ⓤ, cultivation of rice; (稲の作柄) rice crop Ⓒ / 9月の台風は稲作に大きな被害をもたらした The typhoon in September caused extensive damage to *the rice crop*. ◆アジアでは広く稲作が行われている(→米が栽培されている) *Rice* is widely *grown* in Asia.

いなずま 稲妻 lightning (◆1回の稲妻は a flash of lightning) / 稲妻のような速さで as quick as *lightning*; with *lightning* speed / 空に稲妻が走った *Lightning* flashed across the sky. / There was *a flash of lightning* in the sky.

いなせ はっぴを着たいなせな若い衆 *dashing* young men in *happi*

いななく (馬が) neigh [néi] Ⓘ, whinny Ⓘ; (ロバが) bray Ⓘ

いなびかり 稲光 lightning Ⓤ ⇨いなずま

いなほ 稲穂 an ear of rice

いなめない 否めない undeniable ‖歴史についての否めない事実 *undeniable* truth about history / 彼が傲慢(ごう)だということは否めない It's *undeniable* [There's *no denying*] that he is arrogant.

いなや 否や 夕food を食べ始めるやいなや電話のベルが鳴った The telephone rang「*as soon as* [*the moment, the minute*] I began to eat dinner.

いならぶ 居並ぶ 居並ぶモデルの中でも彼女はひときわ美しかった Her beauty was outstanding among *all* the models.

いなり 稲荷 🈁 an *inari*, a shrine for the deity of grain

いなりずし 稲荷寿司 🈁

味つけをした油揚げ(揚げた豆腐)の中に寿司を詰めたものです。「いなり」とは穀物の神を祭った神社を指し、その神の使者であるキツネの好物が油揚げとされたことからこの名がつきました。*Inarizushi* is sushi packed in sweetened *abura-age*, fried tofu. *Inari* means a shrine dedicated to the deity of grain, and foxes were believed to be the deity's messengers. As they loved *abura-age*, this kind of sushi came to be called *inarizushi*.

いなん 以南 (…より南) south of ...; (…とそれより南) ..., and southward

イニシアチブ (主導権) initiative Ⓒ Ⓤ ‖イニシアチブをとる take *the initiative*

い

イニシャル initial [C]; (模様としての) monogram [C] ∥私のイニシャルはN.I.です My *initials* are N.I. ◆イニシャル入りの財布 a *monogrammed* wallet

いにん 委任 commission [U] **──委任する** (仕事などを) entrust [他]; (人に任せる) leave* [他] ∥その寺の再建はABC社に委任された *The commission* to rebuild the temple *was given* to ABC Company. / 彼は自分の息子に店の運営を委任した He *entrusted* management of the shop *to* his son. / He *entrusted* his son *with* management of the shop. ◆全権を委任する *give a person* plenary powers
‖委任状 a letter of attorney; 〔法律〕(a) power of attorney / 委任統治 (a) mandate / 委任投票 a proxy vote

イニング 〔野球〕inning [C]

いぬ[1] 犬

❶【動物】dog [C], 《小児語》doggie [C]; (子犬) puppy [C], pup [C]
うちでは犬を2匹飼っている We have [keep] two *dogs*.
犬をつないでおきなさい Hold *the dog* on a leash [《英》lead].
妹は自分の犬に芸を教えている My sister teaches her *dog* tricks.
犬の散歩は私の役目だ I「take *our dog* for a walk [walk *our dog*].
ゆうべ隣の犬がうるさくほえていた The neighbor's *dog* was barking noisily last night.
彼女の犬に手をかまれた Her *dog* bit me on the hand.
❷【スパイ】spy [C]; (警察の) 《米俗語》stool pigeon [C], 《英俗語》nark [C]
‖犬小屋 a kennel, a doghouse / 犬ぞり a sled, 《英》a sledge / 犬猫病院 a pet clinic [hospital] / 警察犬 a police dog / 野良犬 a stray dog / 番犬 a guard dog, 《米》a watchdog / 牧羊犬 a sheepdog / 盲導犬 a guide dog, a Seeing Eye dog / 猟犬 a hound, a hunting dog
[慣用表現] ほえる犬はめったにかまない ➩ほえる
[ことわざ] 犬も歩けば棒に当たる Once a dog walks, it surely hits a stick.; Expect the unexpected. (→予期せぬことが起こると思え) / 夫婦げんかは犬も食わない ➩ふうふ

> **-犬のいろいろ-**
> 秋田犬 Akita / ウェルシュコーギー Welsh corgi / ゴールデンレトリーバー golden retriever / コッカースパニエル cocker spaniel / シーズー Shih Tzu / シェパード German shepherd / シベリアンハスキー Siberian husky / スコッチテリア Scottish terrier / セントバーナード St. Bernard / ダックスフント dachshund / ダルメシアン Dalmatian / チャウチャウ chow chow / チワワ Chihuahua / ドーベルマン Doberman pinscher / パグ pug / ビーグル beagle / プードル poodle / ブルテリア bull terrier / ブルドッグ bulldog / ボクサー boxer / ポメラニアン Pomeranian / ヨークシャテリア Yorkshire terrier / ラブラドールレトリーバー Labrador retriever

いぬ[2] 戌 (十二支の第11番目) the Dog ➩えと

イヌイット Inuit [C] (複 ~, ~s)

いぬかき 犬掻き dog(-)paddle [U], doggie(-)paddle [U] ∥犬かきをする swim (*the*) *dog* [*doggie*] *paddle*

いぬじに 犬死に 彼は犬死にした (→無意味に死んだ) He *died* 「*in vain* [*for nothing, to no purpose*]. / (→みじめな死に方をした) He *died* 「*a dog's death* [*like a dog*].

いね 稲 rice [U], rice plant [C] ∥稲を刈る reap [harvest] *rice* / 9月には稲刈りが始まる *The rice harvest* starts in September.
‖稲こき rice threshing / 稲作 ➩いなさく / 稲田 a rice [paddy] field

いねむり 居眠り (うたた寝) doze [C], 《口語的》snooze [C]; (昼寝) nap [C] **──居眠りする** doze (off), 《口語的》snooze [自]; (こっくりする) 《口語的》nod (off) ∥授業がとてもつまらなかったので居眠りをしてしまった I *dozed off* because the class was so boring. / その老人は暖炉のそばで居眠りしていた The old man *was nodding* (*off*) by the fire.
◆その事故の原因はドライバーの居眠り運転だった The accident was caused because the driver *fell asleep at the wheel*.

いのこり 居残り (罰としての放課後の) detention [U] [C] ◆彼は河野先生にしばしば居残りをさせられていた He *was* often *kept* [*forced to stay*] *after school* by Mr. Kono.

いのこる 居残る (放課後に) stay after school; (残業する) work overtime

いのしし 猪 wild boar [C]; (イノシシの肉) boar [U]

いのち 命

life [U] (↔death); (個人の) life [C] (複 lives)
〖命が・は〗
その救助活動の成否に何百もの命がかかっている Hundreds of *lives* are at stake in the rescue operation.
◆彼の命はもう長くない His *days* are numbered. / 息子の命が惜しかったら金を持ってこい (→金を持ってこい, さもないとおまえの息子は死ぬ) Bring some money or your son will be dead. / それを見たときは命が縮まる思いだった (→死ぬほど怖かった) When I saw it, I *was scared to death*.
〖命を・に〗
命をかける risk [hazard] *one's life*
彼らは国のために命をささげた They laid down *their lives* for their country.
多くの若者が戦争で命を落とした Many young *lives* were lost in the war.
彼はその赤ん坊の命を救った He saved the baby's *life*.
医者は彼女の命に別状はないと言った The doctor said her *life* was in no danger.
彼女は我々の計画に命を吹き込んだ She

breathed *life* into our project.
◆それは命にかかわる傷(→致命傷)になりかねない It might be a *mortal* [*deadly, fatal*] injury. / 彼は自らの命を絶った He 「*committed suicide* [*killed himself*].
《その他》
君は命の恩人だ You *really saved my life*.
子供たちは私たち夫婦の命です Our children are 「our *life* [the breath of *life*].
私たちは命がけでそれをやらなければならない We have to do it *at the risk of our own lives*.
ありがたいことに命拾いしたよ Thank God! *My life has been spared*.(❖ほかは被害を受けたが自分は助かった場合に用いる)
◆倒れたときに頭部を強打したことが彼の命取りとなった Hitting his head hard against the floor when he fell turned out to be *fatal* to him. / 彼のミスが私たちの計画にとって命取りになった His mistake was *fatal* to our plan. / 命知らずの(→向こう見ずな)ドライバーが年々増えている The number of *reckless* drivers is increasing each year.
∥命綱 a lifeline
慣用表現 命からがら逃れる have *a narrow escape*;《口語的》get away *by the skin of one's teeth* / 何日か休みをとって命の洗濯をしなくちゃ(→元気を取り戻さなくちゃ) I need to take a couple days' off and *refresh myself*.
ことわざ 命あっての物種(もの) While there is life, there is hope.(→生きているかぎり希望はある)

イノベーション (革新) innovation ⓤ

いのり 祈り prayer ⓤⓒ;(祈禱(きとう)) devotions;(食前・食後の) grace ⓤⓒ //神に祈りをささげる offer 「*a prayer* [*devotions*] to God; *pray to God* / 私たちの祈りは聞き届けられた(→かなえられた) Our *prayers* were answered [heard].

いのる 祈る pray ⓐⓗ;(願う) wish ⓗⓐ
彼女はひざまずいて祈った She *prayed* on her (bended) knees. / She knelt down *in prayer*.
【pray+to 名/for 名】死者たちの冥福(めいふく)を祈る *pray for* the souls of the dead / 私は彼らが無事戻るよう神に祈った I *prayed to* God *for* their safe return.
【pray+that 節】あなたが早く回復するようにと毎晩祈っています Every night I *pray that* you will recover soon.
幸運を祈ります I *wish* you (best of) good luck.(❖会話では単に Good luck., Best of luck.などという)
ご多幸をお祈りします I *wish* you all happiness in your life.(❖手紙の結びには With best wishes.を用いる)
◆祖父の健康を祈って乾杯した We *drank to* our grandfather's health. / あなたの試験合格を心からお祈りします I sincerely *hope* (that) you will pass the exam.

いはい 位牌 ━━ an *ihai*, a memorial tablet kept on a Buddhist family altar

いはしょ 居場所 one's whereabouts《単数または複数扱い》/ 近親者が彼の居場所を教えてくれた His close relative told me 「*his whereabouts* [*where he was*]. ◆ここには私の居場所がない気がする Somehow I feel like I *don't belong here*.

いはつ 遺髪 (形見としての故人の髪) a lock of a deceased person's hair as a keepsake

いばら 茨 (植物のとげ) thorn ⓒ;(とげのある植物) thorn ⓒⓤ
慣用表現 栄光へたどり着くためにはいばらの道を歩まねばならない You have to tread *a thorny path* to glory.

いばらき 茨城

茨城県は、その地理的条件を生かした農業・漁業のほか、最先端の工業や原子力など、様々な分野で発展を遂げてきました。徳川幕府ゆかりの地である水戸は、三大庭園の一つである偕楽園と、日本一の生産量を誇る納豆で有名です。
Ibaraki Prefecture has made progress in various fields, from agriculture and fishery (thanks to its favorable geography) to advanced technology and nuclear power. Mito, which had much to do with the Tokugawa clan, is now well-known for Kairakuen Garden (one of Japan's three greatest gardens). It is also the country's biggest producer of *natto*.

いばる 威張る (自慢する) boast ⓐⓗ, brag ⓐⓗ;(偉そうにふるまう) swagger ⓐ; いばった (横柄な) haughty, arrogant; (高圧的な) overbearing;(うぬぼれの強い) proud; (ボス面をする)《口語的》bossy //彼女は試験で満点を取ったと言っていばっていた(→自慢していた) She *was boasting* [*bragging*] that she got a perfect score in the exam. / その政治家はひどくいばった口調で話すので多くの人に嫌われていた The politician talked in so *haughty* [*arrogant*] a manner that many people disliked him. / あの子がクラスでいちばんいばっている That boy [girl] is *the bossiest* in the class.

いはん 違反 violation ⓒⓤ;(契約などの不履行) breach ⓒⓤ;(違反行為) offense,《英》offence ⓒ (通例単数形) ━━違反する break*ⓗ, violate ⓗ; breach ⓗ
法律 [規則] 違反 *a violation* of the law [rules] / 契約違反 (*a*) *breach* of contract
交通 [駐車] 違反で１万円取られた I was fined 10,000 yen for *a* traffic [parking] *violation* [one].
あなたの行動は法律に違反していた Your action *violated* [*was against*] the law.
◆彼はスピード違反で罰金を科せられた He was fined *for speeding*.
∥違反切符 (交通違反の) a ticket / 違反者 a violator, an offender

いびき snore ⓒ ◆父はいつも大きないびきをかく My father always *snores* so loudly.

いびつ 歪 ━━いびつな (形・性格の) warped ⇨ゆがむ //その戸はいびつになっていてあけにくい The door is *warped*, so it's not easy to open it. ◆このいびつな花びんを見てよ Just

いひょう 意表 意表をついた彼の行動にだれもが絶句した His action was so *surprising* that everyone was at a loss for words. / 彼女の言葉に私たちは意表をつかれた We *were surprised* to hear what she said. / Her words *took us by surprise*.

いびる (人をいじめる) give* *a person* a hard time; (人につらくあたる) be hard on *a person* ⇨いじめる

いひん 遺品 an article of the deceased [departed] ◆この指輪は母の遺品です(→母はこの指輪を私に残した) My mother *left* me this ring.

いふ 畏怖 awe ◉; (恐怖) fear ◉◉ ‖神に畏怖の念をいだいている be [stand] in *awe* of God ◆私たちはその山の壮麗さに畏怖の念をいだいた We *were awed* by the magnificence of the mountain.

イブ Eve ‖クリスマスイブ Christmas *Eve*

いふう 威風 彼は威風堂々とした男だ He is a man [*with majesty* [*of dignity*]]. / その城は丘の上に威風堂々とそびえている The castle stands on a hill *majestically*.

いぶかしい 訝しい (不確かである) doubtful; (疑わしい) suspicious ‖私が「おはよう」と声をかけると、その女の子はいぶかしげな顔でこちらを見た The girl [*gave me a doubtful look* [*looked at me doubtfully*]] when I said "Good morning" to her.

いぶかる 訝る 私は彼の証言をいぶかっている I *doubt* his testimony.

いぶき 息吹 breath ◉ ‖そよ風に春の息吹が感じられる We can feel *the breath of spring* in the breeze. ◆新時代の息吹(→予感)が感じられるかい Do you feel *the winds of change* for the new generation?

いふきょうだい[しまい] 異父兄弟[姉妹] half brother [sister] ◉ (✿異母兄弟[姉妹]と同語を用いる)

いふく 衣服 clothes [klóuz], (衣類)《集合的》clothing ◉ (✿clothes より意味が広い。数えるときは an article [a piece, an item] of ... とする); (服装) dress ◉ (✿男女を問わない) ‖[場面・状況別会話] p.1726 ‖警察は手がかりがないかと彼の衣服を改めた(→調べた) The police searched his *clothes* for some clues.

いぶくろ 胃袋 stomach ◉ ⇨い(胃)

いぶす 燻す 部屋から蚊をいぶし出す *repel* mosquitoes from the room *with smoke* / 彼はその芝居でいぶし銀の演技を見せた He made a *low-keyed but steady* performance in the play.

いぶつ¹ 異物 foreign matter [substance] ◉, foreign body ◉ ‖スーパーで売られていた食品のいくつかに異物が混入されていた Some *foreign substance* had been added to some foods sold at the supermarket.

◆トイレ内に異物を捨てないでください Do not throw *foreign articles* in the toilet.

いぶつ² 遺物 relic ◉; (古い建物などの) survivor ◉ ‖中世の遺物 *survivors* from the Middle Ages ◆彼の著作はすでに過去の遺物と化している(→時代遅れになった) His work is already *out of date*.

イブニング(ドレス) evening dress ◉

いぶんか 異文化 foreign [different] culture ◉ ‖異文化に接するときはカルチャーショックを経験する People experience culture shock when coming into contact with *a foreign [different] culture*. ◆異文化間コミュニケーション *intercultural* communication

いぶんし 異分子 foreign [alien] element ◉; (部外者) outsider ◉ ‖異分子を排除する eliminate *foreign [alien] elements* / 彼はその党内の異分子とみなされている He is regarded as *an outsider* in the party.

いへん 異変 暖冬異変(→異常に暖かい冬) *unusually warm winter* / 天候の異変 *unusual [abnormal] weather* / 今、教育の世界には異変が起きつつある *Something* is happening in the world of education now.

イベント event ◉ ‖メーンイベント *the main event* / 今年もこのホールでは数々のイベントが予定されている Various *events* are due to take place in this hall this year, too.

いぼ 疣 wart ◉ ‖いぼ痔(ぢ)《口語的》 blind piles

いほう 違法 illegality ◉ ‖ただし個々の違法行為は ◉ ―― 違法な illegal, unlawful ‖違法行為 an *illegal* act / 違法駐車 *illegal* parking / スピードの出しすぎは違法だ Speeding is *illegal*.

いほうじん 異邦人 foreigner ◉

いぼきょうだい[しまい] 異母兄弟[姉妹] half brother [sister] ◉ (✿異父兄弟[姉妹]と同語を用いる)

いほく 以北 (...より北) north of ...; (...とそれより北) ... and northward

いま¹ 今

❶【現在】now, at present, at the moment; (このごろ) nowadays, these days; (今日) today ―― 今の present; (今日の) of today

《今(は・が)は》

今何時ですか What time is it (*now*)?(✿状況から明らかなので、特に now という必要はない)

オーストラリアは今夏だ It is summer *now* in Australia.

今仕事中だから後で電話します I'm at work *now*, so I'll call you later.

イチゴは今が旬(しゅん)だ Strawberries are *now* in season.

今はとにかく少し眠りたい All I want to do *now* is (to) have some sleep.

今言えるのはそれだけです That's all I can say *at present*.

これが今いちばんいいオートバイだ This is the best-value motorcycle going *at the moment*.

◆今はけんかをしているときではない *This* is no time for quarreling. / 今はホテル住まいをしています I'm *currently* living in a hotel.

🔤「今何してるの」「テレビ見てる」 "What are

you doing (*now*)?" "I'm watching TV."
《今から》
今から10年後には僕らはどうなっているだろう What will become of us 10 years *from now*?
今から準備をすれば十分間に合うよ If you get started *now*, you'll have plenty of time for preparation.
◆今から話すことはほかの人には黙っていてね Don't tell anybody what I'm going to tell you.

英作文ノート 遅すぎるのは「今」！
今からでは遅すぎる
→×It's too late *from now*.
→○It's too late *now*.
★日本語の「から」につられて from now としないこと. from now (on)は「今後は」の意味で, Try harder from now on.(今後はもっとがんばりなさい)のように使う.

《今の》
今の子供たちは様々なストレスにさらされている Children *of today* suffer from various kinds of stress.
◆今の大統領 the *current* President / 今の段階で結果を予想してもしかたがない It would be meaningless to estimate the result *at this stage*. / 私は今のままのあなたでいてほしい I want you to stay *just the way you are*. / 今のうちに(→手遅れになる前に)虫歯を治したほうがいいよ You should treat your bad teeth *before it is too late*.

《今では・今でも》
今ではあらゆる仕事にコンピュータが欠かせない *Nowadays* computers are indispensable for any kind of work.
◆この劇場は今では使われていない This theater is *no longer* used. / 彼は今でも彼女のことを愛している He *still* loves her.

《その他》
今こそ君の夢を実現するときだ *Now* is the time to realize your dream.
もう時間がないぞ. 今しかないんだ We have little time left. It's now or never.
今までの努力が水の泡になってしまった All my efforts *up till* [*to*] *now* just turned out to be nothing.
◆彼はいつも今はやりの服を着ている He is always dressed in *the current fashion*. / ナイチンゲールの功績は昔も今も高く評価されている Nightingale's achievements *were and are* highly regarded.
👂「彼女, 会社を辞めるって騒いでるよ」「今に始まったことじゃないでしょ」 "She's threatening to quit her job." "*That's nothing new*."

❷【近い未来・過去】(今すぐ) at once, immediately, 《口語的》right away [now]; (たった今) just, just now(❖justは単独で通例現在完了形とともに用いるが, just nowは過去形とともに用いる)

私たちは今すぐ出発したほうがいい We had better start *at once*.

今すぐここから出ていけ Get out of here *right now* [*this minute*]!
彼は朝食をたった今すませたところだ He finished his breakfast *just now*.
彼は今着いたところです He has *just* arrived. / 《口語的》He *just* arrived.
◆今コーヒーを入れますから I am *just* making you coffee. (❖この just は「今ちょうど」の意味で, 進行形または be about [going] to とともに用いる)
👂「夕食ができたよ」「今行くよ」 "Dinner is ready." "*Coming*!/ *I'm coming*!"(❖×I'm going.とはいわない)
慣用表現 今泣いたからすがもう笑った *You were crying a moment ago, and now you are all smiles*. / 今にして思えばその出来事がきっかけで2人の関係は悪化したのだ *Looking back on it now*, the incident led to the break between the two. / 今の今まで彼の話を信じきっていた I didn't suspect the least bit of his story *up until now*. / タランティーノは今をときめく映画監督の一人だ Tarantino is one of the most brilliant movie directors (*of*) *today*.

いま² 居間 living room ⓒ, 《主に英》sitting room ⓒ ➡ 図鑑 p.132

いまいち 今いち あのホテルのサービスはいまいちだった(→あまりよくなかった) The service of that hotel was *not quite good*. / このデザートはいまいち物足りない(→もう少し何か欲しい) This dessert needs *a little bit* more of something.

いまいましい disgusting, irritating, annoying 〖あいつは本当にいまいましいやつだ He's such a *disgusting* fellow. ◆このいまいましいコンピュータ, 動かないんだ This *stupid* computer doesn't work. / ええい, いまいましい. コードがからまってほどけないぞ *Damn it*! I can't get these cords untangled.

いまかいまか 今か今か 私たちは彼の到着を今か今かと待っていた We were waiting *impatiently* for his arrival.

いまごろ 今頃 now, this time; (今ごろまでには) by now 〖弘樹君は今ごろ何をしているのかな I wonder what Hiroki is doing *now*. / 彼は今ごろはもう家に帰っているはずだ He should have been home *by now*. / 去年の今ごろはもう雪が降っていた It was already snowing around *this time* last year.

いまさら 今更 いまさら謝ったってもう遅いよ It's too late to say you're sorry *now*. / それを見ていまさらのように(→今初めてそれを見たかのように)彼は驚いた He was surprised as if he saw it *now for the first time*. / いまさらその件に関して説明するまでもないだろう I don't think you'll need any more explanation on the matter.

いましがた 今し方 just(❖現在完了形とともに用いるが, 口語では過去形とともに用いることもある), just now(❖現在完了形の文では用いない), a moment ago 〖彼は今しがた部屋を出ていった He left the room *just now*. / He has *just* left the room. / 《口語的》He *just*

イマジネーション

left the room. / 洋一は今しがた仕事を終えました Yoichi finished work *a moment ago*.

イマジネーション (想像力) imagination ◎ ◻ //彼女はイマジネーションが豊かだ She is full of *imagination*.

いまじぶん 今時分 今時分(→こんな時間に)だれだろう I wonder who it is *at this time of the day*?

いましめ 戒め (警告) warning ◻; (教訓) lesson ◻ //彼の失敗を戒めにしよう Let his failure be *a warning [lesson]* to us.

いましめる 戒める (公式的) admonish 🖲; (警告する) warn 🖲; (しかる) scold 🖲 //父親は息子の怠惰を戒めた The father *scolded [admonished]* his son *for being lazy*. / 彼は私に二度と同じ過ちを繰り返さないよう戒めた He *warned* me *against* making the same mistake again.

いまだ(に) 未だ(に) still; (否定文で) yet; (いまだかつて…ない) never //その風習はいまだに日本に残っている The custom is *still* found in Japan. / その町にはいまだに内戦の傷跡が残っている The town *still* bears the scars of the civil war. / 彼は彼女のことがいまだに忘れられない He can't really get rid of her *yet*. / 私はいまだかつて幽霊を見たことがない I've *never* seen a ghost (*before*).
◆ その事件はいまだに解決されていない The case *remains* unsolved.

いまでこそ 今でこそ 彼は今でこそ大会社の社長だがひと昔前は借金を抱えて大変だった He's the president of a big company *now*, but he was hard up with debt a while ago.

いまどき 今時 今どきの若い人 the young people *of today*; *today's* young people / そんな考えは今どきはやらない That kind of idea is out of fashion *nowadays [these days]*. / 進んで親の手伝いをするなんて今どき珍しい子 How rare it is for us *nowadays [these days]* to see a child help his [her] parents willingly like he [she] does!

いまなお 今尚 その女優の美貌(ぼう)は今なお健在だ The actress has preserved her beauty *to this day*.

いまに 今に (近いうちに) soon, before long; (いつか) someday, in time, in the future //そんなことばかり言っていると今に後悔する If you keep saying such things, *soon* you're going to be sorry. / そんなに落ち込むなよ. 今に彼も分かるさ Don't be so depressed. He'll understand it *someday*.
◆ 今に見ていろ (会話) *Just you wait.* / まあ今に分かるさ (会話) You'll see. ❖「自分の言い分の正しさが分かるだろう」の意味

いまにも 今にも (at) any moment, (at) any minute, any minute now; (今にも…しそうで) ready to *do* //今にも雨が降りだしそうだ It can begin raining *(at) any moment*. / その葉は今にも落ちそうだ That leaf looks *ready to fall*. ◆ 彼女は今にも倒れそうなほど真っ青だった She was so pale that she was *fit to faint*.

いまのところ 今のところ (現在は) at present, at the moment, now; (差し当たって) for now, for the present; (今までのところ) so far //今のところ順調にいっている Things are going well *at present*. / (会話) *So far*, so good. / 今のところは2人で間に合っている Two people are enough *for the present*. / 今のところ最初の2章を読んだだけで

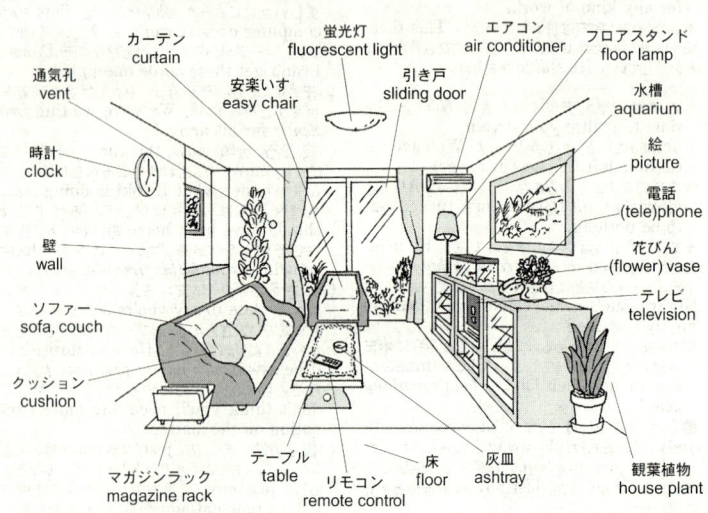

居間 living room

- カーテン curtain
- 蛍光灯 fluorescent light
- エアコン air conditioner
- フロアスタンド floor lamp
- 通気孔 vent
- 安楽いす easy chair
- 引き戸 sliding door
- 水槽 aquarium
- 時計 clock
- 絵 picture
- 電話 (tele)phone
- 壁 wall
- 花びん (flower) vase
- ソファー sofa, couch
- テレビ television
- クッション cushion
- マガジンラック magazine rack
- テーブル table
- リモコン remote control
- 床 floor
- 灰皿 ashtray
- 観葉植物 house plant

す I've only read the first two chapters *so far*.

いまひとつ 今一つ 彼女はいまひとつ(→少々)社交性に欠ける She's *a little* lacking in sociability. / 彼の話にはいまひとつ説得力がない His speech is *not quite* persuasive.

いまふう 今風 ——今風の modern ∥今風の建物 a *modern* building

いままで 今まで (今までずっと) until [till, up to] now; (今までのところ) so far; (今までに) ever; (一度も…ない) never ∥今までで最高のスコア the best score *ever* / いったい今までどこへ行っていたんだ Where on earth have you been *until now* [*all this while*]? / そのなぞは今までのところ解明されていない The mystery has been left unsolved *up until now*. / 今までのところミスは見つかっていない We haven't found any mistakes *so far*. / この映画は今まで見た中で最高だ This is the best movie (that) I've *ever* seen. / こんな寒さは今まで経験したことがありません I've *never* experienced cold weather like this.
◆今までどおり仲よくしよう Let's be friends *like we have been*.

いまや 今や 今や町中が彼女の話でもちきりだ She is *now* the talk of the town. / 彼は今や遅しと友達を待っている He's waiting for his friend *impatiently*. / 海外旅行は今や特別なことではない Traveling abroad is nothing special *nowadays*.

いまわしい 忌まわしい (恐ろしい) horrible, awful; (むかつくような) disgusting ∥いまわしい光景 a *horrible* scene

いみ 意味

meaning Ⓤ Ⓒ, sense Ⓒ; (言外の意味) implication Ⓒ, connotation Ⓒ; (意義) significance Ⓤ; (趣旨) 《公式的》the import ——意味する mean* 他 (✦進行形にはできない); (暗に) imply, connote 他

〖意味が·は〗
私はこの単語の意味が分からない I don't know *the meaning* of this word.
天皇の沖縄訪問には象徴的な意味があった The Emperor's visit to Okinawa had symbolic *significance*.
行間に本当の意味が隠されている *The* actual *import* is hidden between the lines.
名声や富は私にはたいした意味はない Fame and wealth do not *mean* much to me.
勉強は継続してやらなければ意味がない It [*doesn't mean anything* [*is meaningless*] to study unless you continue.

〖意味を〗
彼女はその単語の意味を辞書で調べた She consulted the dictionary for *the meaning* of the word. / She looked up the word in the dictionary.
君の言っていることは全く意味をなさない What you are saying *doesn't make* any *sense*.
私は彼女の言葉の意味をとり違えていた I mistook what she had *meant*.

〖意味する〗
英語の book は日本語で「本」を意味する The English word "book" *means* "hon" in Japanese.
あの標識は徐行を意味しています That sign *means* that you must go slow.

〖その他〗
それはどういう意味で言っているのですか What do you *mean* by that?
僕はそんな意味で言ったんじゃありません I didn't *mean* that.
ある意味では彼らは一つ穴のむじなだ *In a sense* [*way*], they are all part of the same gang.
その2つの単語に意味の違いはありますか Is there any difference in *meaning* between the two words?
◆彼女は意味深なことを言った She said something *meaningful*. / 彼は僕を見て意味ありげに笑った He gave me a *meaningful* smile. / 厳密な意味では(→厳密に言えば)その2匹の犬は種類が違う *Strictly speaking*, those two dogs are of different kinds.
🅔「e-mail の e ってどういう意味ですか」「『電子の』という意味です」"What's *the meaning* of the 'e' in 'e-mail'? / What does the 'e' in 'e-mail' *mean*?" "'Electronic.'/ It *means* 'electronic.'"
∥意味論 semantics

> **コロケーション** -meaning-
> 〖形容詞＋~〗あいまいな~ an obscure meaning / 隠れた~ an inner meaning / 二重の~ a double meaning / 深い~ a profound meaning / 本来の~ the original meaning / 明確な~ a clear meaning / 文字どおりの~ a literal meaning

いみあい 意味合い その言葉には様々な意味合いがある The word has many different *shades of meaning*. / その風習は宗教的な意味合いが強い The custom has strong religious *meaning*.

いみきらう 忌み嫌う 彼女はその男を忌み嫌っていた She *just hated* that man. / She *avoided* the man *like the plague*.

イミテーション (模造品) imitation Ⓒ ——イミテーションの imitation ∥イミテーションパール an *imitation* pearl

いみょう 異名 (あだ名) nickname Ⓒ; (別名) another name ◆その選手は「巨人キラー」という異名をとっている The player *has been nicknamed* "the Giants-killer."

いみん 移民 (他国からの) immigrant Ⓒ; (他国への) emigrant Ⓒ ——移民する (他国から) immigrate 自; (他国へ) emigrate 自 ∥移民たちはその港で船を降りた *The immigrants* got off the boat at the port.
∥移民局 the Immigration Office / 移民法 immigration laws

いむしつ 医務室 (学校などの) dispensary Ⓒ; (医師の診察室) doctor's office Ⓒ

イメージ image Ⓒ
企業イメージ a corporate *image*

そのワンピースは彼女のイメージにぴったりだ That dress perfectly fits her *image*.

最近彼女, イメージが変わったと思わないか Don't you think that *her image* has changed recently?

その大学はイメージアップした The college *has improved its image*.

そのうわさで彼はイメージダウンした The rumor [*gave* him *a bad image* [*damaged his image*]. (❖×image up, image down とはいわない)

◆彼についてはあまりいいイメージ(→印象)をもっていない I don't have *a very good* [*positive*] *impression* of him. / 彼女は髪を短くしてすっかりイメージチェンジした She *looks completely different* with her hair cut short.

‖イメージトレーニング positive imaging

いも 芋 (サツマイモ) sweet potato ⓒ; (ジャガイモ) potato ⓒ; (サトイモ) taro (複 ~s)

子供たちは大喜びで芋掘りをした The kids enjoyed digging (*sweet*) *potatoes*.

慣用表現 イモっぽい(→いなかくさい)やつ *a bumpkin* / ディズニーランドはいつも芋を洗うような人出だ(→人でいっぱいだ) Disneyland *is* always *crammed with people*.

いもうと 妹

(younger [little, 《米口語》kid]) sister ⓒ (❖英語では「姉」「妹」の区別をしないことが多く, sister 1語で「姉妹」を表す. また little sister は成人した妹には使わない)

私には13歳になる妹がいます I have *a* (*younger* [*little*]) *sister* who is 13.

彼女は私の義理の妹です She is my *sister-in-law*.

いもづる 芋蔓 麻薬の密輸グループは芋づる式に(→次々に)逮捕された The drug smugglers were arrested *one after another*.

いもの 鋳物 casting ⓒ, molding ⓒ ‖鋳物工場 a foundry

いもむし 芋虫 caterpillar ⓒ

いもり newt ⓒ

いもん 慰問 被災地を慰問する *visit* a disaster area *to console* [*comfort, cheer up*] the people there

いや ❶【否定】no; (否定疑問文に対して) yes

私の祖父は70歳…いや, 71歳です My grandfather is 70 — *no*, he is 71.

いやとは言わせませんよ I won't take *no* for an answer.

◆私は, いや彼らでさえそれを解けなかった I couldn't solve it *nor could they*. / 彼は私に2,000円, いや違った, 3,000円貸してくれた He lent me 2,000 — *I mean* 3,000 yen.

🗨「お茶をもう1杯いかがですか」「いや, 結構です」"Would you like another cup of tea?" "*No*, thanks."

🗨「彼女に電話しなかったの?」「いや, したよ」"Didn't you call her?" "*Yes*, I did."

🗨「僕はだれがやったか知らないよ」「いや, 知っているはずだ」"I don't know who did it."
"Of course you do."

❷【その他】
いやあ疲れたなあ *Oh*, I'm so tired.

🗨「どうして仕事辞めちゃったの」「いや, いろいろあってね」"How come you quit the job?" "*Well*, that's a long story."

いや² 嫌 (不愉快な) unpleasant, disagreeable; (むかつくような) disgusting, nasty ——いやだ (嫌う) hate 働, dislike 働 ⇨いやに

〖いやな〗
何かいやなことでもあったの Did anything *unpleasant* happen?

あいつは本当にいやなやつだ He's really a *nasty* piece of work.

◆いやなにおい *a foul* smell / 仕事を頼むと彼は露骨にいやな顔をした He didn't hide *his annoyance* when I asked him to do some work. / 彼女はいやな顔ひとつせず掃除を手伝ってくれた She helped me clean without showing the slightest sign of *reluctance*. / 何となくいやな(→悪いことが起こる)予感がする Somehow I feel something *bad* will happen.

〖いやだ〗
こんな寒い日に出かけるのはいやだ I *hate* going out on such a cold day.

コンピュータは見るのもいやだ I just *hate* computers, and don't even want to see them.

◆毎日残業の生活はもういやだ I'*m sick and tired of* working overtime every day.

〖その他〗
◆もう私のことがいやになったんでしょう? You *don't love* me anymore, do you? / いやでも我慢すべきだよ You should put up with it *whether you like it or not*. / 私は彼の無神経さをいやというほど知っている I'm *painfully aware of his insensitivity*. / 足をいやというほどたんすの角(🈂)にぶつけた I hit my leg *hard* against the corner of the chest. / どうしてもいやなら行かなくていいよ You don't have to go *if* you really *don't want to*.

🗨「代わりにそこに行ってくれない?」「絶対いや」"Will you please go there instead of me?" "*No way*!"

🗨「学校で傷害事件ですって」「いやな世の中になったわね」"I hear there was an assault at a school." "The world has become such an *unpleasant* place to live in."

いやいや 嫌々 いやいややるくらいなら手伝ってくれなくていい I don't want you to help me if you *are so unwilling to* do it. / 弟は両親の言葉にいやいや従った My brother *reluctantly* obeyed our parents' order.

いやおうなし 否応なし 私はいやおうなしに掃除を手伝わされた I had to help clean *whether I liked it or not*. / 彼らはいやおうなしに国を捨てなければならなかった They *were forced to* leave their country.

いやがうえにも いやが上にも 有名ロックバンドが登場すると学園祭はいやが上にも(→いっそう)盛り上がった As the famous rock band came onto the stage, the school festival livened up *even more.*

いやがおうでも 否が応でも いやがおうでも(→何があっても)この仕事を年内に終えなければならない We must finish this work by the end of this year *at any rate.*

いやがらせ 嫌がらせ 人にいやがらせをする *harass* a person / 性的いやがらせを受ける suffer *sexual harassment*; be *sexually harassed* / 私は一晩中いやがらせの電話に悩まされた *The annoying phone calls* bothered me all night long.

いやがる 嫌がる (嫌う) hate [他], dislike [他]; (気が進まない) be reluctant [unwilling] to *do* ‖多くの子供たちは歯医者に行くのをいやがる Many children *hate* to go to the dentist's. / その少年はみんながいやがる仕事を進んでやる The boy voluntarily takes the jobs which everyone else *is reluctant to* take. ◆私は映画に行きたかったが彼はいやがった I wanted to go to a movie but he *objected.*

いやく[1] 医薬 国連は難民に食料と医薬品を援助した The U. N. aided refugees with food and *medicine* [*medical supplies*].

いやく[2] 意訳 free [loose] translation [U] [C] ◆君の翻訳は意訳しすぎだ Your translation is *too free.*

いやく[3] 違約 (契約違反) (a) breach of contract ━違約する break* a contract ‖違約金 penalty for default [breach of contract] / 違約条項(契約書の) a penalty clause

いやけ 嫌気 のらりくらりとした彼の態度にいやけがさしてきた I'*m getting sick and tired of* his ambiguous attitude.

いやしい 卑しい (貪欲(どんよく)な) greedy; (下品な) vulgar; (身分の低い) humble, low; (みすぼらしい) shabby ‖いやしい言葉づかい *vulgar* language / 彼は金にいやしい He is *greedy for* money.

いやしくも いやしくも子の親ならそんなことはできるはずがない No parent could do such a thing. / いやしくもスポーツマンならベストを尽くせ If you are a sportsman *at all*, you've got to try your best.

いやしむ 卑しむ (さげすむ) despise [他] ◆いやしむべき行動 a *despicable* conduct

いやす 癒す (人・傷などを) heal [他]; (病気・けがを) cure [他]; (渇きを) quench [他]; (満足させる) satisfy [他] ‖失恋の痛手をいやすには時間が必要だ It takes a while to *heal* a broken heart. / 彼は雨水でのどの渇きをいやした He *quenched* his thirst with rainwater. ◆時がすべてをいやしてくれる(→時は偉大な治療者だ) Time is *a* great *healer.*

いやに (非常に) awfully, terribly ‖きのうはいやに寒かった It was *awfully* cold yesterday. ◆きょうの兄はいやに機嫌がいい My brother looks *very* happy today.

[会]「けさはいやに早起きね, どうしたの」「目覚ましを間違ってセットしたんだ」 "What made you get up *so* early this morning?" "I set the alarm clock for the wrong time."

いやはや いやはやそれはお気の毒に *Oh*, that's [it's] too bad. / ここで君に会うとはいやはや驚きだ It's *really* surprising to see you here.

イヤホン earphone [C]《通例複数形 ～s》 ‖イヤホンで音楽を聴く listen to the music with *earphones*

いやみ 嫌味 人にいやみを言う *make a dig at* a person / 「ご協力ありがとう」と彼はいやみたっぷりに言った "Thanks so much for your help," he said *sarcastically* [*snidely*]. / 彼女にはいやみが通じなかった She didn't get *my irony.*

いやらしい 嫌らしい (卑わいな) obscene; (好色な) lustful; (わいせつな) indecent,《口語的》dirty; (不快にさせる) disgusting, nasty ‖いやらしいジョーク *dirty* jokes / 時々いやらしいいたずら電話がかかってくる Sometimes I get *obscene* phone calls. / あいつ, 先生の前だといい子ぶるんだよ. いやらしい性格だよな He pretends to be a good student in the teachers' presence — he's *disgusting* [(→狡猾(こうかつ)だ) *cunning*], isn't he? ◆彼はいやらしい目つきでその女性を見た He looked at the woman *with lust* in his eyes.

イヤリング earring [C]《通例複数形 ～s》

いよいよ

❶【ますます】

12月に入って寒さもいよいよ厳しくなってきた It began to get *colder and colder* in December.

祖父は年をとるにつれ, いよいよ頑固になった My grandfather became *more and more* stubborn as he got older.

❷【ついに・とうとう】at last, finally

いよいよその時がやってきた The time has come *at last.*

あすはいよいよ川田大の合格発表の日だ *Finally*, the results of the entrance examination will be announced at Kawada University tomorrow.

◆彼が総裁選に出馬という話はいよいよ現実味を帯びてきた The rumor of his running for the party's presidency is *quite likely to* be true.

❸【切迫した状態】

いよいよというときに彼女は彼との婚約を解消した She broke (off) her engagement to him *at the last moment.*

彼はいよいよという段になるまで何もしない He doesn't do anything *until he gets pressed for time.*

いよいよとなったらここに電話して助けてもらいなさい *When the time comes*, call this number for help.

いよう[1] 異様 ━異様な (奇怪な) grotesque; (風変わりな) strange, weird; (巨大な) monstrous ━異様に grotesquely ‖その生き物は異様な姿をしている The creature has a *grotesque* shape. / 私は昨夜異様な物音で目がさめた I woke up last night because of a *strange* sound.

いよう[2] 威容・偉容 そのホテルは威容を誇っていた(→外観が堂々としていた) The hotel stood

[コミュニケーションスキル] ―依頼―

①依頼するときの表現

(A) Close the door, **please.**
ドアを閉めてくれる？
(B) **Can [Will] you** carry the baggage?
その荷物を運んでもらえるかい.
(C) **Could [Would] you** give me a hand?
手を貸していただけますか.
(D) **Do you think you could possibly** pick me up tomorrow morning?
あす車で迎えに来ていただけますでしょうか.
(E) **Would you mind** waiting for a moment?
少しお待ちいただけますでしょうか.

☞(A)から(E)に行くにつれて，くだけた言い方から丁寧な表現になる. ほかに**I'd like you to come with me.**(いっしょに来てほしいのですが)のような表現もある.

☞依頼するときの切り出し方には，**Could you do me a favor and ...?** や **May I ask you a favor?** (どちらも「お願いがあるのですが」の意味)という表現がよく使われる.

Could you do me a favor and check my speech draft? お願いがあるのですが，私のスピーチの原稿に目を通していただけますか.

☞Could you ...? などの依頼の文の前か後に，**If you don't mind** を付けると，「さしつかえなければ」という控えめなニュアンスを添えることができる.

If you don't mind, could you take a picture of us? さしつかえなければ，私たちの写真を撮ってもらえますか.

②依頼に応じるときの表現

(A) Will you open the window?
–Sure. / All right.
窓をあけてくれない？ ―いいよ.
(B) Can you check my English?
–OK. / All right.
私の英語をチェックしてくれる？ ―いいですよ.
(C) Could you drive me home?
–Yes, of course. / Sure.
車で家まで送ってくれますか―もちろんいいですよ. /いいですよ.
(D) Could you lend your support to the project?
–It would be a pleasure. / With pleasure.
その計画に援助いただけますか―ええ，喜んで.
(E) Would you mind getting together again tomorrow?
–No, not at all. / Of course not.
あすまた会ってもらえますか―ええ，かまいませんよ.

☞(A)(B)(C)がふつう. (D)は丁寧な表現. (E)の Would you mind ...? に対する応答のしかたには注意. どうしても断る場合は次のようになる.

"Do you mind my smoking here?"
"Sorry I do."
「ここでたばこを吸ってよいですか」「すみませんが吸わないでください」

☞(A)から(D)までの断る表現としては，**I'm sorry, (but) I can't., I wish I could, but I can't., I'm afraid not.** などがある.

Could you come here this afternoon?
–I'm sorry, (but) I can't. I have a previous engagement. 午後こちらへ来ていただけますか―すみません. 先約がありまして.

---

with *majestic appearance.*

いよく 意欲 will [U][C], readiness [U]《またa～》, zeal [U], zest [U]《またa～》;(動機づけ) motivation [U];(勤労意欲) morale [U] ―意欲的な ambitious, motivated;(熱心な) eager ―意欲的に ambitiously;(熱心に) eagerly, enthusiastically

創作意欲 *zeal for* creating / 意欲的な生徒 an *ambitious* student

生きる意欲を失うな Never lose *the will* to live.

彼には働く意欲が欠けている He lacks *motivation* to work.

彼はボランティア活動に意欲的に取り組んでいる He is *eagerly* [*enthusiastically*] engaged in the volunteer activities.

◆意欲をそそる仕事 a *challenging* job / 子供たちに学習意欲を起こさせる *motivate* children *to* study hard

‖意欲作 an ambitious work

いらい 依頼

❶【頼むこと】request [C] ―依頼する ask ⑩,《公式的》request ⑩

➾ [コミュニケーションスキル]

医療援助の依頼を受ける receive *a request for* medical aid / その会社の依頼によって at the company's *request*; at *the request* of the company

彼らの依頼はきっぱりと断った I firmly turned down their *request*.

【ask [request]+名(人)+to *do*】その弁護士に自分の弁護を依頼した I *asked* [*requested*] the lawyer *to* plead for me.

【ask [request]+that 節】彼はその作家に小説の執筆を依頼した He *asked* [*requested*] *that* the writer (should) write a novel. (❖that 節中で should を用いるのは主に《英》)

[コロケーション] -request-
〖形容詞+～〗口頭の～ an oral request / 正式な～ a formal request / 非公式な～ an informal [unofficial] request / 文書による～ a written request
〖動詞+～〗～する make a request / ～に応じる grant a request / ～を断る deny [reject] a request

❷【依存すること】

息子は依頼心が強すぎるようだ My son seems to be too dependent on others.

‖依頼状 a letter of request / 依頼人(弁護士

などに) a client, 《集合的》a practice / 依頼料(弁護士などの)《法律》a retainer

いらい² 以来 since (※現在または話題の時点まで及んでいる動作・状態の起点を表す) ➡ -から
それ以来 *since* then
1889年の建造以来その塔にはたくさんの人が訪れている The tower has been visited by many people *since* it was built in 1889.
昨年の事故以来, 彼は入退院を繰り返している He has been in and out of hospitals *since* last year's car accident.
それ以来彼の姿を見かけた者はいない Nobody has seen him (*ever*) *since*.
◆卒業以来彼らには全然会っていない I haven't seen them *after* the graduation.

いらいら (いらだち) irritation Ⓤ, annoyance Ⓤ ──**いらいらする** get* irritated, get annoyed ∥なかなかバスがやってこないのでいらいらした I *got irritated* because the bus kept me waiting for a long time. / 彼が私のことに干渉するので本当にいらいらした I *got* really *annoyed with* him *for* interfering in my affairs. ∥この女の子にはいらいらさせられる This girl is *irritating* [*annoying*]. / お父さん, 何をいらいらしているの What's *eating* you, Dad? / その音は私をいらいらさせる The noise *irritates* [*annoys*] me./ The noise *gets on* my nerves. / きょうの彼女は相当いらいらしてるから近づかないほうがいい She *is* very *touchy* today, so you should stay away from her.
💬「まだ彼から電話がないの?」「いらいらしても始まらないよ(→落ち着いて. 待つしかないのだから)」"Hasn't he called yet?" "Calm down. There's nothing we can do but wait."

イラスト Ⓐillustration Ⓒ (※英語の illustration は物事をより分かりやすく説明するために用いるものすべてを表すため, 必ずしも絵とは限らない) ∥カラフルなイラストが入った本 a book with colorful *illustrations* / 直子はイラストが得意です Naoko is good at *drawing*.

イラストレーター illustrator

いらだたしい 苛立たしい (いらいらさせる) irritating, annoying ∥電車が遅れているのに何の説明もないというのはいらだたしい It's *irritating* when a train gets delayed without any explanation. ◆自分の犯したミスにとてもいらだたしかった I *was* so *irritated* with myself for the mistake.

いらだち 苛立ち irritation Ⓤ; (じれったさ) impatience Ⓤ ∥彼はいらだちを隠しきれなかった He failed to disguise *his impatience*.

いらだつ 苛立つ (いらいらする) get* irritated [annoyed] ∥私たちは彼の怠慢さにいらだった We *got irritated with* his laziness. / 彼はその騒音にかなりいらだってきている He's *getting* so *annoyed* with that noise.
◆大臣はその質問にややいらだって答えた The minister answered the question *with* a touch of *irritation*.

いらっしゃい (店で) いらっしゃいませ May [Can] I help you? / What can I do for you? / (家などで) いらっしゃい(→ようこそ) Welcome! / (→お入りなさい) Come (on) in!

いらっしゃる

【語法】「いらっしゃる」は「来る」「行く」「いる」などの敬語だが, 英語にはそれに当たる訳語はない. また, 多くの場合, 日本語ほど丁寧な表現を用いなくても特に失礼に当たらない.

よくいらっしゃいました It was very nice of you to *come*. / 次に京都へいらっしゃる折にはぜひうちにお立ち寄りください Next time you *visit* Kyoto, please drop in on us. / パーティーへはいらっしゃるのですか *Are* you *going to* the party? / この3日間どちらにいらっしゃったのですか Where *were* you for the last three days? / ご兄弟はいらっしゃいますか Do you *have* any brothers or sisters? / (電話で)正人さんはいらっしゃいますか May I speak to Masato? / *Is* Masato there? / 失礼ですが, ケントさんでいらっしゃいますか Excuse me, but *are* you Mr. Kent?

いられない ぐずぐずしてはいられない There's no time to lose. / 君を好きにならずにいられない I *can't help* falling in love with you. / 入試に合格したからといってのんびりしてばかりはいられないよ You *can't afford to* sit back and relax just because you passed the entrance exam.

いり 入り 日の入り sunset / 寒の[土用の]入り *the beginning* [*first day*] of midwinter [midsummer] / 大入り(満員) *a full house* / いい映画だったが入りはよくなかった Though that was a good movie, it flopped at the box office.

-いり -入り クリーム[砂糖]入りのコーヒー coffee *with* cream [sugar] / 挿絵入りの本 an *illustrated* book / 12個入りのチョコレート 1箱 a pack of 12 [a dozen] chocolates / 芸能界入りする *go into* show business / 中年の仲間入りをする *reach* middle age / いよいよ君も大人の仲間入り(→一人前の大人)だ Now you *are a full-fledged adult*.

いりえ 入り江 inlet Ⓒ; (湾) bay Ⓒ, cove Ⓒ

いりぐち 入り口 entrance Ⓒ (↔exit)(※(英)では掲示に Way In も用いる); (戸口) door Ⓒ, doorway Ⓒ; (門) gate Ⓒ / 正面入り口 *the* front *entrance* / 駅の入り口はどこですか Where is *the entrance* to the station? / 公園の入り口で待ってるよ I'll be waiting for you at *the* park *gate*.
◆洞穴の入り口 *the mouth* of a cave

いりくむ 入り組む 入り組んだ問題 a *complicated* [*complex*] problem / 裏道は迷路のように入り組んでいた The alleys were *intricate* like a maze. / 状況はかなり入り組んでいる We've got pretty *intricate* circumstances.

イリジウム 《化学》iridium Ⓤ (※元素記号 Ir)

いりたまご 煎り卵 scrambled eggs

イリノイ Illinois (※米国中西部の州; (略語) Ill.; (郵便) IL)

いりびたる 入り浸る 彼らは最近ゲームセンターに入り浸っている They *hang around* the

いりまじる 入り交じる　私は不安と期待の入り交じった気持ちでアメリカでの生活を始めた I started my life in America with *mixed* feelings of anxiety and hope.

いりみだれる 入り乱れる　そのデッドボールをきっかけに敵味方入り乱れての大乱闘になった When the batter was hit by a pitch, the game turned into a *confused* brawl.

いりゅう 慰留　私たちは彼に職にとどまるよう慰留したが，彼は決心を変えなかった We *tried to persuade* him to stay [remain] in office, but he didn't change his mind.

いりゅうひん 遺留品　犯行現場では遺留品がほとんど見つからなかった Few things were left behind at the scene of the crime.

いりょう¹ 衣料　《集合的》clothing ⓤ；(衣服) clothes [klóuz], wear ⓤ (✦ wear はしばしば複合語を作る．また商業的に用いることが多い)
⇨ ふく(服) / 冬物衣料 winter *clothes* / 婦人用衣料 ladies' *wear*
∥衣料品店 a clothing store

いりょう² 医療　medical care [treatment] ⓤ ―医療の medical／彼女は何度も医療援助を要請した She made repeated requests for *medical aid*.
∥医療過誤《法律》malpractice／医療器械[器具] medical appliances, medical instruments／医療機関 medical institution／医療制度 health care system／医療費 medical expenses／医療保険 health [medical-care] insurance

いりよう 入り用　いくら[何が]ご入り用ですか How much [What] do you *need*?

いりょく 威力　power ⓤ；(権威) authority ⓤ／その小さな爆弾は車1台を吹き飛ばすほどの威力がある The *power* of that little bomb is strong enough to blow away a car.
◆そのタイヤは凍結した道でその威力を発揮する The tire will prove its *traction* to the full on frozen roads.

いる¹ 居る

❶存在する	there is [are] …; be
❷住む・暮らす	live
❸持っている	have

❶【存在する】(不特定の人・動物が) there is [are] … (✦ is [are]は…にくる名詞(句)の人称・数・時制に応じて変わる); (特定の人・動物が) be ⓘ; (とどまる) stay ⓘ; (実在する) exist ⓘ

語法
(1)通例日本語では，「いる」は人・動物など生物の存在を表し，「ある」は無生物の存在を表すが，英語の there is [are], be は，どちらの場合にも用いる／テーブルの上に猫が1匹いる *There is* a cat on the table.／テーブルの上にリンゴが1個ある *There is* an apple on the table.
(2)会話では，there is [are]は，there's [ðərz], there're [ðərə]となることが多い．
(3)例文 there is [are] …の…には，初めて話題になるものがくる．そのため，a, an, some, any, many などが付いた名詞(句)や何も付かない数えられない名詞(句)はくるが，ふつう the, my, this, that, Tom's などが付いた特定の物・人を表す名詞(句)はこない．
(4)日本語から考えると，「…が[は]～にいる」の表現では，助詞「が」は初めて話題になるものを示し，助詞「は」はすでに話題になっているものを示すことが多いので，「…が～にいる」の場合には there is [are]が使えるが，「…は～にいる」の場合には使えないことがある．ただし，この区別がいつも明確であるとは限らないので，文の意味をよく考えて英語に訳す必要がある／校庭にはたくさんの生徒がいた There were *many students* in the schoolyard.／その少年はゲームセンターにいた *The boy* was in the video arcade.
(5)ただし，探していたものを見つけた場合，驚きを表す場合，注意を喚起する場合などには，the, my などが there is [are] …の…にくることがある／うちの赤ちゃん，あそこの砂場にいるわ There's *my baby* in the sandbox!／私たちの先生がテレビに出ている！ There's *our teacher* on TV!

【there is [are]＋名＋副】教室には何人かの生徒がいる *There are* some students in the classroom.／この写真の中には男性が1人，女性が1人，赤ん坊が1人いる *There's* a man, a woman and a baby in this photograph. (✦口語では，be 動詞の後に複数のものが続く場合でもしばしば there is の短縮形 there's が用いられる)／放課後部室にはだれもいなかった *There was nobody* in the club room after school.／電車の中で急病人が出たとき，たまたま医者が乗り合わせていた *There* happened to *be* a doctor on the train when one of the passengers was suddenly taken ill.

【be＋副】父は出張で今は大阪にいる My father *is* in Osaka on a business trip now.／こんなときに彼がいてくれたらなあ I wish he *were* [《口語的》*was*] around at times like this.

しばらくここにいてね．すぐ戻るから Please *stay* here for a while. I'll be back soon.

幽霊って本当にいると思う？ Do you believe ghosts really *exist*?

🗨「あしたはどこかへ出かける？」「一日中うちにいるよ」"Are you going out tomorrow?" "I'*ll be* [stay] home all day."

🗨「母さんはどこ」「隣の家にいるよ」"Where's Mother?" "She's (in the house) next door."

🗨「だれかそこにいるの」「僕だよ」"Who's there?" "It's me."

🗨「この問題を解ける人はいないの？」「私がやってみます」"Can't anyone solve this problem?" "I'll try it."

❷【住む・暮らす】live ⓘ; (生息する) inhabit ⓗ／この鳥は熱帯地方にいる This bird *lives in* [*inhabits*] the tropics.／彼女はニューヨークにいる She *is* (*living*) in

New York. (❖live の進行形は一時的に住んでいることを強調する)

◆昔々ある所に勇敢な王子様がいました Once upon a time *there was* [*lived*] a brave prince.

❸【持っている】have*㊥

私には兄弟も姉妹もいない I *don't have* any brothers and sisters.

彼には奥さんがいる He *has* a wife./ (→結婚している) He is married.

🍀「何かペットはいる(→飼っている)？」「ええ．犬が２匹います」 "Do you *have* any pets?" "Yes, I do. I *have* two dogs."

❹【…ている】

泣いている赤ちゃん a *crying* baby

このことはみんなにないしょにしててね Please *keep* this *secret* from everybody.

そのビデオはこわれている The VCR *is broken*.

彼女のことは昔からよく知っています I *have known* her very well for a long time.

ちょうど彼に電話をかけようとしていたところに彼から電話がかかってきた I *was just about to* call him when he gave me a call.

➪ -していた, -している

❺【いられない】

彼は彼女が困っているのを見て黙って(→助けずに)いられなかった He *couldn't but* help her when he saw her in trouble.

ぐずぐずしてはいられない We have no time to lose.

➪いられない

いる² 要る

(必要とする) need㊥; (欲しい) want㊥; (時間・金銭・労力などが) take*㊥; (費用・労力などが) cost*㊥ ➪ひつよう

外国語を習得するにはかなりの忍耐がいる You *need* a lot of patience to master a foreign language.

この川を泳いで渡るのには大変な勇気がいる It *takes* a lot of courage to swim across this river.

コンピュータのプログラムを組むのはかなりの時間と労力がいる Making a computer program *costs* much time and effort.

いるだけ持っていきなさい You can take *as much as you want*.

何も心配はいらないよ You *don't need* to worry./ There's nothing to worry about.

◆おつりはいらないよ(→君がとっておいて) Keep the change.

🍀「お母さん，本を買うのにお金がいるんだけど」「いくらいるの」 "Mom, I *need* some money to buy a book." "How much do you *need*?"

🍀「だれかこのセーターいらない？」「いる」 "Does anybody *want* this sweater?" "I do."

いる³ 射る (矢を) shoot*㊥; (当てる) hit*㊥　弓で矢を射る *shoot* an arrow from a bow

慣用表現 彼女の質問は的(まと)を射ていた Her question *was very much to the point*.

いる⁴ 炒る・煎る (豆などを) roast　//コーヒー豆をこんがりといる *roast* coffee beans /　ゴマをいる *roast* [*toast*] sesame seeds

いるい 衣類 《集合的》clothing Ⓤ; (衣服) clothes; (持ち合わせ) a wardrobe　//ふく(服) //夏物衣類 summer *clothing* / 被害者への食料と衣類の支給 the supply of food and *clothing* for the victims

いるか 海豚 dolphin

いるす 居留守　だれか訪ねてきたが，居留守を使った(→留守のふりをした) Someone *was at the door*, but I *pretended to be out*.

イルミネーション illumination ◆クリスマスのため通りにはイルミネーションが施されていた The street *was illuminated* for Christmas.

-いれ -入れ (自転車の)空気入れ a bicycle pump /　くず入れ 《米》a trash can, 《英》a dustbin /　札入れ a wallet, 《米》a billfold /　筆入れ a pencil case

いれい¹ 異例 (例外) exception Ⓒ　——異例の (例外の) exceptional; (前例のない) unprecedented; (ふつうでない) unusual　//異例の昇進 an *exceptional* promotion

いれい² 慰霊　//慰霊祭 a memorial service / 慰霊碑 a memorial

いれかえ 入れ替え・入れ換え　その映画館は入れ替え制だ(→上映と上映の間に劇場を空にする) They clear the theater between shows. / 今度の週末には夏物と冬物の入れ替えをしないといけない I have to *replace* the summer clothing in my closet *with* winter clothing this weekend.

いれかえる 入れ替える・入れ換える　彼は無断で私のデータを入れ替えてしまった He *replaced* my data without notice. / 窓をあけて空気を入れ替えよう(→新鮮な空気を入れよう) Let's open the windows and *let* some fresh air *in*. /　これからは心を入れ替えてまじめに働きます I'll *turn over a new leaf* and work hard from now on.

いれかわり 入れ替わり　週末には入れ替わり立ち替わり(→次々と)訪問客がやってくる We have visitors *one after another* on weekends.

いれかわる 入れ替わる　その高校のほとんどの教職員が入れ替わった Most of the teachers in the high school *were replaced*.

イレギュラー イレギュラーバウンド *an irregularly bouncing ball* /　そのボールはイレギュラーして柵(さく)を越えた The ball *bounced* [*bounded*] *irregularly* over the fence.

いれずみ 入れ墨 tattoo Ⓒ (複 ~s)　彼女は肩にチョウの入れ墨をしている She *has a tattoo* of a butterfly [*has a butterfly tattooed*] on her shoulder.

いれぢえ 入れ知恵　入れ知恵をする *put an idea into a person's head* /　いったいだれの入れ知恵なんだ Who *put it into your head*?

いれちがい 入れ違い　弟と入れ違いに母が帰ってきた(→弟が出かけたちょうどその時ノ母が帰ってきた) Just as my brother went out, moth-

[い]

er came home.

いれば 入れ歯 false [artificial] tooth [C]; (総入れ歯) dentures // 入れ歯をする[はずす]「put in [take out] *false teeth* / 祖父は総入れ歯だ My grandfather wears「*a full set of false teeth* [*dentures*].

いれもの 入れ物 container [C], case [C]

いれる 入れる

❶ 中に入れる	put ... in [into] 〜
❷ 学校などに行かせる	send
❸ 採用する・収容する	employ; accommodate
❹ 含める	include
❺ スイッチをつける	turn [switch] on

❶【中に入れる】put* ... in [into] 〜; (注ぐ) pour [他]; (挿入する) insert [他]; (入れておく) keep* ... in 〜; (入れてやる) let* ... in (〜)

牛乳を冷蔵庫に入れなさい *Put* the milk *in* the refrigerator.

彼はその本をポケットに入れた He *put* the book *into* his pocket.

彼女はコーヒーを1杯いれてくれた She *poured* [*made*] me a cup of coffee. (❖pour は「すでにできているコーヒーを注ぐ」, make は「コーヒーを作る」の意味)

カードキーをここに入れるとドアのロックが解除されます *Insert* the card key here and the door will be unlocked.

お気に入りのアクセサリーはその箱に入れてある I *keep* my favorite accessories *in* that box.

ドアをあけて猫を中に入れてやりなさい Open the door and *let* the cat *in*.

◆次の手紙に私の写真を入れて送ります(→同封します) I'll *enclose* a photo of myself *in* the next letter. / 彼女は茶色のコンタクトレンズを入れていた She *wore* brown contact lenses. / カメラにフィルムを入れるときに失敗してしまった I *loaded* the film *into* the camera the wrong way. / この仕事のデータはすべてコンピュータに入れてある We *have input* all of the data about this job *into* the computer. / おふろに水を入れてちょうだい *Run* the bathwater.

💬「紅茶にミルクと砂糖をお入れしますか」「ミルクだけお願いします」"Would you like some milk and sugar in your tea?" "Just milk, please."

❷【学校などに行かせる】send* [他]

両親は弟を全寮制の学校に入れた My parents *sent* my brother *to* a boarding school.

◆少年犯罪者は更生施設に入れられる Juvenile offenders *are taken to* rehabilitation facilities.

❸【採用する・収容する】(採用する) employ [他]; (収容する) accommodate [他]

新しいスタッフをもう何人か入れる必要がある We need to *employ* a few more people as staff.

その会議室は100人程度までは入れられる The conference room *can accommodate* about a hundred people.

◆コンサートはすでに始まっていて休憩時間まで中に入れてもらえなかった(→中に入れなかった) The concert had started already, and I couldn't *get in* until the intermission.

❹【含める】include [他]; (数える) count [他]

家賃は管理費を入れて7万5千円です The rent is 75,000 yen *including* (the) upkeep.

出席者の数に自分を入れるのを忘れていた I forgot to *count* myself in the number of the attendees.

◆私も仲間に入れてもらえる? Can I *join* you? / 新しい学校で彼女はなかなかクラスの仲間に入れてもらえなかった She *wasn't accepted* by her classmates in the new school for a while.

❺【スイッチをつける】turn [switch] on (↔turn [switch] off)

暖房を入れてもらえますか Will you *turn* the heater *on*?

炊飯器のスイッチを入れるのを忘れていた I forgot to *switch on* the rice cooker.

❻【その他】

就職してから彼女は毎月家に3万円入れている(→両親に払っている) She *has been paying* her parents 30,000 yen a month since she started working.

私の部屋にやっとエアコンを入れてもらった I finally got an air-conditioner *installed* in my room.

選挙でだれに入れるか決めましたか Have you decided yet who to *vote for*?

それは計算に入れてあります I *have taken* that *into account*.

この学校は英語教育に力を入れている This school *puts emphasis on* English education.

お耳に入れておきたい(→あなたに話したい)ことがあるのですが I have something *to tell you*.

大和さんには後で電話を入れておきます I'll *call* Ms. Yamato later.

いろ 色

❶【色】color, 《英》colour [C][U]

[語法]
日本語で「黄色, 茶色」などというとき, 英語では特に後ろに color を付けず, それぞれ yellow, brown でよい. また「…の(ような)色をした」という場合は-colored を付けて表すことができる // 明るい色の brightly-colored / さび色の rust-colored

洗ったら色がにじんでしまった *The color* ran when I washed it.

君のかばんは形も色も私のと似ている Your bag is similar to mine both in shape and *color*.

葉の色が緑から赤に変わった *The color* of the leaves changed from green to red.

あなたにははっきりした色がとても似合う Clear *colors* suit you very well.

◆雄のクジャクには色鮮やかな羽がある The peacock has *colorful* feathers. / この壁紙は色があせますか Will this wallpaper *fade*? / 彼女はその絵にクレヨンで色をつけ始めた She began *coloring* the picture with crayons. / 色物は白い物と分けて洗濯したほうがいい You'd better wash *the colored clothes* separately from the whites.

💬「これの色違いはありますか」「はい、グレーと青があります」"Do you have this in *a different color*?" "Yes, we have it in gray and blue."

💬「何色のTシャツにする」「私はどれでもいいから適当に選んで」"*Which color* of T-shirt shall we buy?" "I don't care which. You pick one."

┌─────────────────────────────────┐
│ コロケーション　-color-
│ 〖形容詞＋～〗明るい～ a bright [brilliant] color / 鮮やかな～ a fresh [lively] color / 薄い～ a light [pale] color / 落ち着いた[地味な]～ a quiet color / くすんだ～ a dull color / 暗い～ a dark color / けばけばしい～ a tawdry [gaudy] color / 濃い～ a rich color / はでな～ a loud color / ぼやけた～ a faint color / 柔らかい～ a soft [delicate] color
└─────────────────────────────────┘

❷【肌の色】
色白[色黒]の肌 (a) *fair* [*dark*] *skin*
この口紅の色は私の肌の色に合わない This shade of lipstick doesn't match my *complexion*. (❖complexion は特に「顔の色」をいう)

❸【表情・様子】
彼の目にちらっと喜びの色が浮かんだ His eyes gleamed with pleasure.
彼女は最近疲労の色が濃い She *seems* to be suffering from fatigue recently.
被告には全く反省の色が見えなかった The accused showed no *signs* of regret.
妹は突然目の色を変えて(→狂ったように)勉強しだした My sister suddenly started to study *like mad*.

❹【色情・恋愛】(情事) love affair ⓒ
◆彼は色におぼれている He indulges in *sensual pleasures*.

❺【その他】
💬「全部で10万でどうですか」「もう少し色をつけてもらえませんかね」"How about 100,000 yen for all?" "Could you *give* [*make*] *me a better offer*?"

∥色盲 color blindness / 寒色 cool colors / 原色 primary colors / 多色 multicolor / 単色 monochrome / 暖色 warm colors / 中間色 neutral colors / 補色 complementary colors

いろあい　色合い　(色調) shade ⓒ, tone ⓒ ∥ この着物の赤の色合いはとてもすてきだ This kimono is *a good shade of* red. / 彼の映画には教訓的な色合いがある His films have *a moralistic tone*. ◆彼女は柔らかい色合いの服を好むようだ *Soft-colored* clothes seem to meet her taste.

いろあせる　色褪せる　fade ⓘ ⇒ あせる(褪せる) ∥年々思い出は色あせていく Memories *fade away* year by year. ◆色あせたジーンズ *washed-out* jeans / この色あせたカーテン替えたほうがいいんじゃない I think we should change these *faded* [*discolored*] curtains.

いろいろ　色々　—いろいろな various; (多種の) a variety of ..., all kinds [sorts] of ...; (種々の) different
いろいろな理由で for *various* reasons
庭はいろいろな植物と花でいっぱいだった The garden was blooming with *various* plants and flowers.
その店はいろいろな種類のワインを置いている The shop stocks *a large variety of* wines.
辞書にもピンからキリまでいろいろある There are *all kinds of* dictionaries, good and bad. / There are dictionaries and then there are dictionaries.
私は昔ピアノやバレエなどいろいろな習い事をしていた I used to take *many different* lessons, such as piano and ballet.
◆この方法はいろいろと応用できる This method is of *wide* application. / いろいろ考えた末に彼女は決意した She made up her mind after *much* thought. / この絵は私にいろいろなことを連想させる This picture suggests *a lot of* things to me.

💬「いろいろとありがとうございました」「どういたしまして」"Thank you *for everything*." "Not at all."

💬「どうして彼と別れちゃったの」「いろいろあってね」"How come you broke up with him?" "Well, *that's a long story*."

いろう　慰労　その会社は箱根のホテルで従業員の慰労会を開いた The company held an employee *banquet* at a hotel in Hakone *in appreciation of their services*.
∥慰労金(ボーナス) a bonus

いろえんぴつ　色鉛筆　color [colored] pencil ⓒ
いろおとこ　色男　(ハンサムな男) handsome man ⓒ, 《俗語》hunk ⓒ
いろがみ　色紙　colored paper ⓤ
いろぐろ　色黒　—色黒の dark (-skinned)
いろけ　色気　(性的魅力) sex appeal ⓤ; (興味・関心) interest ⓤ 《また an ～》 ∥彼女はいつも色気のない格好ばかりしている She always wears clothes with *no sex appeal*. / 彼はそのプロジェクトに色気を見せている He *seems to have interest in* that project.
◆君の彼女はとても色気があると思うよ I think your girlfriend is very *sexy*. / 彼女をデートに誘ったが、色気のない(→そっけない)返事をされた When I asked for date, she gave me a *blunt* [*curt*] answer. / 弟は色気づいてきたように見える(→性に関心をもち始めた) My little brother seems to *be interested in sex* recently. / 妹はまだまだ色気(→恋愛)より食い気だ My little sister is still more interested in food than (in) *romance*.

いろじろ　色白　—色白の fair (-skinned) /

いろずり

彼女は色白だ She has a *fair* skin.

いろずり 色刷り この漫画本の何ページかは色刷りだ Some pages of this comic book *are printed in color*.

いろづく 色付く 木の葉が色づき始めている The tree leaves *are turning red*.

いろっぽい 色っぽい (セクシーな) sexy; (誘惑するような) seductive ∥色っぽいポーズ a *sexy* pose / その女性は色っぽい目つきで彼を見た The woman gave him a *seductive* look.

いろつや 色艶 (顔色) complexion ◎ ∥彼女は顔の色つやがよい She has a good *complexion*.

いろどり 彩り そのシェフの作る料理は彩りが豊かなことで有名だ The chef's cooking is famous for richness *in color*. / 美しい着物に身を包んだ女性たちがそのパーティーに彩りを添えた The women dressed in beautiful kimono added *color* to the party.

いろとりどり 色とりどり 色とりどりの果物 *colorful* fruits / クリスマスツリーが色とりどりの電球で飾られている The Christmas tree is ornamented with *multi-colored* lights.

いろどる 彩る (色をつける) color, (英) colour ◎ ∥日光の山々は紅葉に美しく彩られていた The mountains in Nikko *were colored* beautifully with red and yellow leaves.

いろなおし 色直し ⇨ おいろなおし

いろは 私は料理のいろはも知らない I don't even have *basic knowledge* of cooking. / I don't even know *the ABC's* of cooking.

いろめ 色目 彼女はいつもクラスの男子に色目を使っている She *is* always *making eyes at* boys in the class.

いろめがね 色眼鏡 彼は僕たちのことを色眼鏡で見ている He *is prejudiced* [*biased*] *against* us.

いろよい 色好い 取引先からあまり色よい返事は返ってこなかった We didn't receive a *favorable* answer from our client.

いろり 囲炉裏 🖼 an *irori*, an open hearth set into a floor

いろわけ 色分け 都道府県の地図を4つの色で色分けした I *painted* the prefectures on the map *in four colors*.

いろん 異論 (異なる意見) different opinion ◎; (反対) objection ◎ ∥この点では全く異論はありません I have no *objection* on this score. / その計画について異論を唱える者がいる Someone 「*raised an objection* [*objected*] *to* the plan. / それが問題解決の最善の方法だということに異論はない I *don't dispute* that it is the best way to solve the problem.

いわ 岩 rock ◎ ◎
その小さな船は岩にぶつかってばらばらになった The small boat broke up on *the rocks*.
∥岩棚 a (rock) ledge / 岩登り rock climbing / 岩場 a rocky tract / 岩肌 a rock surface / 岩ぶろ a natural-stone bathtub / 岩山 a rocky mountain

いわい 祝い (祝うこと) celebration ◎ ◎, congratulation ◎; (祝いの品) present ◎, gift ◎; (祝いの言葉) congratulations ―

祝いの《公式的》celebratory, congratulatory
父は誕生日のお祝いにマウンテンバイクを買ってくれた My father bought me a mountain bike 「as my birthday *present* [for my birthday].
私たちは彼女の結婚祝いに絵を贈った We sent her a painting as *a wedding gift*.
心からお祝い申し上げます I wish to offer you *my* sincere *congratulations*.
彼は彼女の卒業に際しお祝いの言葉を贈った He sent her *his congratulations* on her graduation.
●「9月に結婚するの」「それはおめでとう。じゃお祝いしなきゃ」"I'm getting married in September." "Oh, *congratulations*! That calls for *celebration*."

いわう 祝う (物事を) celebrate ◎ ◎; (人を) congratulate ◎
クリスマスを祝う *celebrate* Christmas
両親は結婚20周年を祝った My parents *celebrated* their 20th wedding anniversary.
みんなが私たちの婚約を祝ってくれた Everyone *congratulated* us *on* our engagement.
◆アイルランド人は聖パトリックの日を祝う Irish people *observe* St. Patrick's Day. / 私たちは彼女の昇進を祝って乾杯した We *toasted* her promotion.

> **英作文ノート** 目的語に注意！
> 私たちは彼の就職を祝った
> → ×We *celebrated that he succeeded* in getting a job.
> → ○We *celebrated his success* in getting a job.
> → ○We *congratulated him on his success* in getting a job.
> ★celebrateは「人以外」の名詞を目的語とするが、that節は用いない。congratulateは「人」を目的語にし、「…に祝いの言葉を述べる」という意味で用いる。

いわかん 違和感 新しいクラスにはまだ違和感を覚える I still *feel out of place* in my new class. / この花びんは和室に置くには違和感がある This vase *doesn't fit in* a Japanese-style room.

いわく 曰く いわくつきの人物 a person *with a past* / ことわざにいわく「早起きは三文の得」だ A proverb *says* "The early bird catches the worm." / 彼が最近早く帰るのには何かいわく (→理由) がありそうだ Recently he has been going home early, but there must be some *reason for* that.

いわし 鰯 sardine ◎ (複 ～, ～s)
∥いわし雲 fleecy clouds, cirrocumulus
〔慣用表現〕いわしの頭も信心から *You can make a god* [*religion*] *out of anything*. (→何でも神[宗教]にすることができる)

いわずもがな 言わずもがな そんなことは言わずもがなだ (→言わないほうがよい) *It's better to leave it unsaid*. / You shouldn't say it. / 大人は言わずもがな (→言うまでもなく) 小学生

でもが携帯電話を持っている Even schoolchildren have their own cell phones, *to say nothing of* adults. / 彼女はイタリア語と中国語が話せる。英語は言わずもがなだ She can speak Italian and Chinese, *not to mention* English.

いわて 岩手

> 全国第2位の面積をもつ岩手県は、本州の北部、太平洋側に位置しており、天然のリアス式海岸や南部富士と呼ばれる岩手山など、美しい自然に恵まれています。この県の出身者には宮沢賢治、石川啄木といった有名な詩人がおり、また民話の宝庫としても知られています。
> Iwate Prefecture is the second largest prefecture in area. It is located in the north of Honshu, facing the Pacific Ocean. The prefecture is blessed with beautiful nature, such as a long, natural sawtooth coastline and Mt. Iwate, also known as Nambu-Fuji. Among the celebrities from this prefecture are Miyazawa Kenji and Ishikawa Takuboku, both of whom were famous poets. It is also well known as a center of folklore.

いわば 言わば so to speak, as it were(※文中または文末で用いる); (ある意味では) in a sense, in a way; (実質的には) virtually, practically / 彼はいわば私の父のようなものだ He is my father, *as it were*.

いわゆる 所謂 what is called, what we [you, they] call; so-called (※自分はそうは思わないが、という皮肉をこめて用いることが多い) / 日本のいわゆる開放市場 Japan's *so-called* open market / 彼はいわゆる優等生とはタイプが違う He is different from *what is called* an honor student.

いわれ 謂れ ❶ 【理由】 reason □; (原因) cause □ / 私がそれをしなければならないいわれはない There is no *reason* why I should do that. ◆いわれのない差別 *groundless [unjustified]* discrimination / 君に怠け者呼ばわりされるいわれはない You have no *right* to call me lazybones.
❷ 【由来】 story □; (言い伝え) history □; (起源) origin □ □ / この岩には何かいわれがあるのですか Does this rock have any *story*? / 私たちはその神社のいわれを調べた We traced *the history [origin]* of the shrine.

いん¹ 印 (印章・はんこ) seal □; (スタンプ) stamp □ / ゴム印 a rubber *stamp* / 日付印 a date *stamp*

いん² 韻 rhyme [ráim] □ / 韻を踏んで in *rhyme* ◆stream は dream と韻を踏んでいる "Stream" *rhymes with* "dream." / "Stream" *is a rhyme for* "dream." (※後の表現の rhyme は「韻を踏む語」の意味) ‖脚韻 rhyme / 頭韻 alliteration

いんうつ 陰鬱 ―陰鬱な gloomy; (憂鬱な) melancholy; (気落ちしたような) depressing; (気落ちした) depressed / 陰鬱な空模様 a *gloomy* weather / 彼は陰鬱な表情をし

ていた He looked *depressed*.

いんえい 陰影 (影) shadow □; (日陰の部分) shade □ ◆絵に陰影をつける *shade* a painting [drawing] / 陰影に富んだ描写 a description rich in *nuance(s)*

インカ Inca / インカ帝国 the Inca Empire / インカ文明 the Inca civilization

いんか 引火 ignition □ ―引火する catch* fire, 《公式的》ignite 《ガソリンにたばこの火が引火した The gasoline 「*caught fire from* [*was ignited by*] a cigarette.
◆この素材は引火しやすい This material is *highly flammable*.

いんが 因果 (原因と結果) cause and effect; (運命) destiny □, fate □ / これも因果とあきらめた I resigned myself to *my fate*.
◆因果な(→望まれない)商売 an *unwished-for* business / この2つの事件の因果関係はまだ解明されていない The *causal relationship* between these two incidents has not yet been clarified. / 何の因果でこんな目にあわなきゃいけないんだろう Why on earth is this happening to me?
慣用表現 因果応報 *As you sow, so shall you reap.* (→自分でまいた種は自分で刈り取れ)

いんがし 印画紙 photographic paper

いんかん 印鑑 (印章・はんこ) seal □ (※欧米では印鑑を使う習慣はなく、通例署名ですませる) / 印鑑を登録する have *one's personal seal* registered
‖印鑑証明 a certificate of seal impression

いんき 陰気 ―陰気な gloomy; (非常に陰気な) dismal / 陰気な声 a *gloomy* voice / 暗くて陰気くさい場所 dark, *dismal* places / 彼は陰気な性格だ He has a *gloomy* disposition. / そんなに陰気な顔をしてどうしたの You look so *gloomy*. What's the matter with you?

いんきょ 隠居 (退職後の生活・余生) retirement □; (退職した人) retired person □; (老人) old man □ ―隠居する retire □, go* into retirement ◆父は隣のご隠居と将棋を指している My father is playing *shogi* with *our old neighbor*.

いんきょく 陰極 【電気】negative pole □

いんぎん 慇懃 ―いんぎんな polite, courteous ―いんぎんに politely, courteously / 彼はいんぎん無礼に(→丁重なうわべが彼の横柄さを隠している) A facade of politeness hides his disrespect.

インク ink □; (カートリッジ) (ink-)cartridge □ / インクのしみ an *ink* blot / スペアインク a spare *ink-cartridge* / この万年筆はインクが切れている This fountain pen has run out of *ink*.
‖インク消し an ink eraser / インクスタンド an inkstand / インクつぼ an ink pot

イングランド England ―イングランド人 English □, 《集合的》the English ―イングランド(人)の English → イギリス

いんけい 陰茎 penis □ (複 penes, ~es)

いんけん 陰険 ―陰険な (悪賢い) sly; (狡猾(25)な) cunning, crafty, tricky; (邪悪な) wicked, sinister ‖陰険なやり方 crafty means / 陰で僕の悪口を言うなんて陰険なやつだ It was *sly* of him to speak about me behind my back. ◆彼女は陰険な目つきで私を見た She gave me a look of *veiled malice*.

いんげん 隠元 (サヤインゲン) green bean [C], 《米》string bean [C]; (インゲンマメ) kidney bean [C]

いんこ 〘鳥〙parakeet [C]

いんご 隠語 secret language [U]; (仲間内での) cant [U], 《公式的》argot [ɑ́ːrgou] [C][U]

インコース ⚠(野球) inside [C]; (陸上競技) inside track [C] ―インコースの[に] inside ‖ インコースを走る run on *the inside track* / インコース低めの直球 a low *inside* fastball / 彼はインコースに球を投げた He pitched the ball *inside*.

インサイド inside [C]

いんさつ 印刷 print [U]; (印刷術) printing [U]; (印刷の業務) press [U] ―印刷する print [他][自]

カラー印刷 color *printing* / 印刷に回される go to *press*

このパンフレットは印刷が不鮮明だ *The print* in this brochure is not clear. / This brochure *is* not clearly *printed*.

その広告はカラーで印刷されている The advertisement *is printed* in color.

この機械は絵や文字を高速で印刷する This machine *prints* pictures and words very fast.

年賀状のあて名はいつもワープロで印刷している I always use my word processor to *print out* addresses on New Year's cards.

◆印刷ミス *a misprint*; *a typographical error*

‖印刷機 a printer, a press, a printing press [machine] / 印刷所 a printing [print] shop / 印刷物 〘郵便〙printed matter; (広告・宣伝用の) 《口語的》literature; (1枚刷りの) a leaflet / 印刷屋 a printer / オフセット印刷 (an) offset (printing) / 活版印刷 metal type printing

いんさん 陰惨 ―陰惨な (ぞっとするような) horrible, ghastly ‖陰惨な光景 a *horrible* sight / 陰惨な殺人事件 a *horrible* murder case

いんし[1] 印紙 (証紙) stamp [C] ‖収入印紙 *a revenue stamp* / 領収書に印紙をはる put *a stamp* on a receipt

‖印紙税 property transfer tax

いんし[2] 因子 (原因となる要素) factor [C] ‖遺伝因子 *a* genetic *factor* / Rh因子 *the* Rh *factor*

いんじ 印字 ―印字する print [他], type [他]

いんしつ 陰湿 陰湿ないじめ *sneaky* psychological bullying / 彼は陰湿な手口で相手を陥れた He framed his counterpart in a *dirty, underhanded* way.

いんしゅ 飲酒 drinking [U] ‖飲酒は肝臓障害を引き起こすことがある *Drinking* can cause liver problems. ◆飲酒運転をする *drink and drive*

‖飲酒運転 drunk(en) driving, 《米》〘法律〙DWI (❖*d*riving *w*hile *i*ntoxicated の略語) / 飲酒癖 a drinking habit

いんしゅう 因習・因襲 (しきたり) convention [C]; (古い習慣) old custom [tradition] [C] ‖因習に従う follow *conventions* / 因習にとらわれている be a slave to *old customs*

インシュリン 〘生化学〙insulin [U] ‖インシュリン注射 an *insulin* injection

いんしょう 印象

impression [C][U] ―印象的な impressive

人にいい[悪い]印象を与える make *a* good [bad] *impression* on a person

私は彼がまだ親離れしていないという印象を受けた I got *the impression* that he was still dependent on his parents.

その音楽のリズムはとても単純だが印象的だ The rhythm of the music is very simple but *impressive*.

◆新しい秘書は上司に好印象を与えた The new secretary *impressed* the boss *favorably*. / 彼の性格について私は彼女とは違った印象をもっている I *feel* differently than she does about his personality. / 彼女は美人だがどちらかといえば印象が薄い She is beautiful, but rather *unimpressive*.

[e]「今回の展覧会で特に印象に残った作品は何ですか」「ゴッホの『ひまわり』です」 "What *impressed* you most in this exhibition?" "Van Gogh's *Sunflowers*."

[e]「彼女の第一印象はどうだった」「内気な感じがしたな」 "What was *your first impression* of her? / What did you think of her?" "Well, she looked kind of shy to me."

‖印象主義 Impressionism / 印象派(芸術家) an Impressionist

いんしょく 飲食 eating and drinking (❖語順に注意) ―飲食する eat* and drink* ‖館内での飲食を禁ず *Eating and drinking* are not allowed in this hall.

‖飲食店 a restaurant, an eatery / 飲食物 food and drink; (軽いもの) refreshments

いんすう 因数 〘数学〙factor [C]

いんすうぶんかい 因数分解 factorization [U] ―因数分解する 《米》factor [他], factorize [他]

インスタント ‖インスタントカメラ an instant camera / インスタントコーヒー instant coffee / インスタント食品 instant food(s) / インスタントラーメン instant ramen

インストール パソコンにソフトをインストールする *install* software in a PC

インストラクター instructor [C] ‖ダイビングのインストラクター *a* diving *instructor*

インスピレーション inspiration [U][C] ‖そのときふとインスピレーションがわいた I had *a* sudden *inspiration* then.

◆彼は自然からインスピレーションを受けて曲を作る He writes music *inspired* by nature.

いんせい 陰性 ―陰性の negative (↔positive) ‖検査の結果は陰性だった The result of the test was *negative*.

いんぜい 印税 royalty [C] ∥本の印税で生活する live on *the royalties* from *one's* books
いんせき[1] 引責 監督はチームの成績不振のため引責辞任した The manager *took responsibility for* the poor performance of his team *and resigned.*
いんせき[2] 姻戚 (結婚による親戚(しんせき))《口語的》*one's* in-law ◆彼はその有名人と姻戚関係にある He *is related to* the celebrity's family *by marriage.*
いんせき[3] 隕石 meteorite [C]
いんそつ 引率 ━引率する (連れていく) take* [他]; (案内する) lead* [他] ∥5人の保母が公園へ園児を引率した Five kindergarten teachers *took* the children to the park.
‖引率者 a leader
インターチェンジ interchange [C]
インターナショナル (国際的な) international
インターネット the Internet, the Net ∥インターネットにアクセスする access *the Internet* / インターネット上にホームページを開設する put up a Web site on *the Internet*
➩ [場面・状況別会話] p.1700
インターハイ ⚠(高校総体) inter-high school athletic meet [C] ∥わが校のサッカー部はインターハイの決勝まで進んだ Our school's soccer team went on to the final of *the inter-high school athletic meet.*
インターバル (間隔・中休み) interval [C]; (劇場などの休憩時間) intermission [C] (❖《英》では interval ともいう)
インターフェロン 〔生化学〕interferon [U]
インターホン ⚠intercom [C] (❖*intercom*munication system の略語. 英語の interphone は「(社内などの)内部電話」の意味) ∥インターホンで話す talk over *the intercom*
インターン 《米》intern [C], 《英》houseman [C]; (インターンの地位・期間) internship [U]
いんたい 引退 retirement [U] [C] ━引退する retire [自] ∥彼の引退が公式に発表された His *retirement* has been officially announced. / 前大統領は政界から引退した The former president *retired from* politics.
インタビュアー interviewer [C] (↔interviewee)
インタビュー interview [C] ━インタビューする interview [他], hold* an interview ∥街頭インタビュー *a* man-in-the-street *interview* / 大統領との単独インタビュー *an* exclusive *interview with* the President / テレビのインタビューでその女優は新興宗教団体とのかかわりを否定した In *a* television *interview* the actress denied any relations with the cult.
インチ inch [C] (❖長さの単位. 1/12フィート, 2.54cm; 《略語》in.; 数字の後に″を付けて表す) ∥28インチのカラーテレビ a 28-*inch* color television
いんちき (詐欺) fraud [U]; (偽物) fake [C] ━いんちきの (偽の) fake, phony, 《米》bogus; (うその) false; (うさんくさい) fishy ∥そのうわさはどうもいんちきくさい There is something *fishy* about the rumor. ◆賭(か)け事でいんちきをする *cheat* at gambling
いんちょう 院長 (病院の) the director (of a hospital); (学院などの) the principal, the president (of a school)
インディアナ Indiana (❖米国中西部の州; 《略語》Ind., 〔郵便〕IN)
インディアン ⚠ Native American [C] (❖(American) Indian は蔑称とみなされるほか, Indian には「インド人」の意味もあるので注意が必要) ◆インディアン居留区 an *Indian* reservation
インデックス (索引) index [C] (複 ~es, indices) ∥インデックスカード an *index* card
インテリ (知識人) intellectual [C]; (教育のある人) educated person [C], 《しばしば軽蔑的》highbrow [C]; (総称) the intelligentsia (❖日本語はロシア語の intelligentsiya から) ∥インテリが好みそうな本 a book which *intellectuals* would like to read / インテリぶらないでよ Don't fancy yourself as *an intellectual.* ◆彼女のうちはインテリの一家だ Her family members are all *highly educated.*
インテリア ⚠(室内装飾) interior decoration [design] [U] (❖英語の interior は「内部(の)」「室内(の)」の意味) ∥彼女は今和風のインテリアに凝っている She is into Japanese-style *interior decoration* now.
‖インテリアデザイナー an interior designer [decorator]
インテリジェントビル ⚠intelligent [computerized office] building [C]
インド India ━インド人 Indian [C] ━インド(人)の Indian ‖インド洋 the Indian Ocean
インドア indoor (↔outdoor) ∥インドアテニス[スポーツ] *indoor* tennis [sports]
インドシナ Indochina ‖インドシナ半島 Indochina
イントネーション intonation [U] [C] ∥上がり[下がり]調子のイントネーション *a* rising [falling] *intonation*
インドネシア Indonesia (❖公式名 the Republic of Indonesia) ━インドネシア人 Indonesian [C] ━インドネシア語 Indonesian [U] ━インドネシア(人[語])の Indonesian
イントロ (序奏) 《口語的》intro [C] (複 ~s); (導入) introduction [U] [C] ∥8小節のイントロ *an* eight-bar *intro*
いんとん 隠遁 retirement [U]; (人目を避けること) seclusion [U] ━隠遁する live in seclusion, seclude *oneself* from others ◆隠遁生活を送る live *a secluded life*
いんない 院内 ‖院内感染 an in-hospital infection
いんにく 印肉 stamp pad [C]
いんねん 因縁 (関係) relation [U] [C]; (つながり) connection [U] [C]; (運命) fate [U] [C] ∥彼女とは浅からぬ因縁がある I have *a* close *connection* [*relation*] with her. / 因縁と思ってあきらめた I surrendered to *my fate.*
◆ここで会ったのも何かの因縁でしょう(→ここで会

インパクト

うよう運命づけられていた) We must *have been destined to* meet here. / 男が私がぶつかったと因縁をつけてきた(→けんかをふっかけた) The man *picked a fight with* me, saying I had bumped into him.

インパクト (衝撃) impact Ⓒ ◆彼女の演技には強烈なインパクト(→印象)があった Her performance left *a strong impression* on me.

いんぶ 陰部 (婉曲的)the private parts, the pubic region; (生殖器) genitals

インフォーマル (形式ばらない) informal

インフォームドコンセント (患者の同意を得て治療すること) informed consent Ⓤ

インフォメーション (情報) information Ⓤ (❖数えるときはa piece of ... とする); (案内所) information Ⓒ /インフォメーションセンター an *information* center / ツーリストインフォメーション a tourist *information*

インプット (入力) input Ⓤ Ⓒ ――インプットする input* ⓥ /コンピュータにデータをインプットする *input* data *into* a computer

インフルエンザ (公式的)influenza Ⓤ, (口語的) flu Ⓤ /インフルエンザの予防接種 a *flu* shot / 弟はインフルエンザにかかった My brother has caught *the flu*. / 今インフルエンザがはやっている *Flu* is spreading [raging] now.

インフレ(―ション) inflation Ⓤ (↔deflation) ――インフレの inflationary /インフレ対策 an *anti-inflation* measure / 悪性インフレ an *inflationary* spiral / インフレ傾向 an *inflationary* trend / インフレを抑止する control *inflation* / インフレが深刻な問題になってきている *Inflation* has become a serious problem.

いんぶん 韻文 (散文に対して) verse Ⓤ; (詩) poetry Ⓤ

いんぼう 陰謀 plot Ⓒ, intrigue Ⓤ Ⓒ; (共謀) conspiracy Ⓤ Ⓒ /政府に対して陰謀を企てる hatch [form] *a plot* against the government; *plot* against the government / 彼らは大統領暗殺の陰謀をあばいた They exposed *a plot* to assassinate the President. / 彼女は彼らの陰謀に巻き込まれた She got involved in their *conspiracy*.

インポ(テンツ) (男性の性的不能) impotence Ⓤ (❖日本語はドイツ語のImpotenzから) ――インポの impotent

いんめつ 隠滅 ‖証拠隠滅 concealment of evidence

いんもう 陰毛 pubic hair Ⓤ

いんゆ 隠喩 [修辞]metaphor Ⓒ ――隠喩のmetaphorical

いんよう¹ 引用 quotation Ⓤ Ⓒ, quote Ⓒ; (自説を補強するための) citation Ⓤ Ⓒ ――引用する quote ⓦ ⓥ; cite ⓦ /シェークスピアからの引用句 a *phrase* (*quoted*) *from* Shakespeare / 『論語』の一節を引用する *quote* [*cite*] a line *from The Analects of Confucius* / 10ページのいちばん上にキーツからの引用があります At the top of page 10 is *a quotation from* Keats.

‖引用符 quotation marks, 《口語的》quotes / 引用文 a quotation, a citation, 《口語的》a quote

いんよう² 飲用 飲用水 *drinking water* / この水は飲用には適しません This water isn't *drinkable* [*safe to drink*].

いんりつ 韻律 (詩の) meter Ⓤ Ⓒ; (リズム) rhythm Ⓤ Ⓒ ――韻律の metrical ‖韻律学 prosody

いんりょう 飲料 drink Ⓒ Ⓤ; (公式的) beverage Ⓒ (❖水・薬以外の飲み物を指す) /今年の夏は炭酸飲料の売れ行きがいい *Carbonated drinks* are selling well this summer.

‖飲料水 drinking water / アルコール飲料 alcoholic drinks [beverages] / 清涼飲料 soft drinks, cooling beverages

いんりょく 引力 (物体間の力) gravitation Ⓤ; (地球の重力) gravity Ⓤ; (引き合う力) attraction Ⓒ ――引力の gravitational (❖名詞の前で用いる) ‖万有引力の法則 the law of *gravitation* [*gravity*] / 月の引力は地球に作用する The moon's *gravity* exerts an influence on the earth.

‖万有引力 universal gravity

いんれき 陰暦 the lunar calendar /陰暦の12月 December by *the lunar calendar*

う

う¹ 鵜 cormorant ◎ ‖鵜飼い cormorant fishing
<慣用表現> 刑事は鵜の目鷹(たか)の目で(→とても注意深く)犯罪の証拠を探した The detective looked for evidence of the crime *very carefully*.

う² 卯 (十二支の第4番目) the Rabbit ⇒ えと

ウイークエンド weekend ◎ (❖通例土・日を指すが、金曜の夜を含むこともある)

ウイークデー weekday ◎ (❖通例土・日を除く曜日) ‖その店はウイークデーは夜9時までいている The shop is open until 9 p.m. on *weekdays*.

ウイークポイント (欠点) weak point ◎
◆彼のウイークポイント(→彼が苦手なもの)を教えてよ Tell me *something he's not good at*.

ウィーン Vienna [vié nə] (❖オーストリアの首都)

ういういしい 初々しい (無邪気で純真な) innocent, charmingly naive; (入りたての) fresh

ウイスキー whiskey, whisky ◎ ◎ (❖通例米国・アイルランド産は whiskey, スコットランド産は whisky とつづる) ‖バーボンウイスキー bourbon *whiskey* / ウイスキーの水[ソーダ]割り *whiskey* and water [soda]

ウィスコンシン Wisconsin (❖米国中北部の州;《略記》Wis., Wisc.,《郵便》WI)

ウイット wit ◎ ‖彼の小説はウイットに富んでいる His novels *are「full of wit [witty]*.

ういてんぺん 有為転変 有為転変の世の中だ (→この世のすべてのものは変化する) Everything in the world must change.

ウイニング ‖ウイニングショット a winning shot / ウイニングボール a winning ball / ウイニングラン《米》a victory lap,《英》a lap of honour (❖×winning run とはいわない)

ウイルス [医学] virus [vái ərəs] ◎ ‖コンピュータウイルス *a computer virus* / エイズウイルス *the HIV virus*
‖ウイルス性肝炎 viral hepatitis

ウインカー turn signal ◎,《米》blinkers,《英》winkers ‖ウインカーを出す flash *a turn signal*

ウインク wink ◎ ——ウインクする wink ⾃ ‖彼は私に大きくウインクしてみせた He gave me *a big wink*.

ウインタースポーツ winter sports

ウインドー (商品を陳列する場所) (show)window ◎; (コンピュータの) window ◎ ‖ウインドーに飾ってあるコートはいくらですか How much is the coat in *the window*?
◆ウインドーショッピングをする go *window-shopping*; window-shop

ウインドサーフィン windsurfing ◎ ‖ウインドサーフィンをする go *windsurfing*

ウインドブレーカー《米》windbreaker ◎,《英》windcheater ◎

ウインナ (ソーセージ) Vienna sausage ◎,《米》wiener ◎,《米》weenie ◎ ‖ウインナコーヒー Viennese coffee

ウーマンリブ women's liberation [lib] ◎

ウール wool [wúl] ◎ ——ウールの woolen,《英》woollen(❖名詞の前で用いる) ‖ウールのスカーフ a *woolen* scarf

ウーロンちゃ 烏龍茶 oolong tea ◎

うぅん (ためらい・不同意などを表す) hum [hʌ́m]; (言うべき言葉を探して) um [ʌ́m], er [ə́ːr], well; (苦痛のうめき声) oof; (おいしい物の話で) yum
💬「ねえ、トムのことどう思う」「うぅん、まあまあだけどかっこいいっていうほどじゃないよね」"Hey, what do you think of Tom?" "*Well, er,* he's OK, but not really good-looking."

うえ¹ 上

❶ 高い所	top; on, over, above; up, upward; upper
❷ 年齢	older, elder
❸ 地位・能力	upper, higher; better, superior

❶【高い所】——図 top ◎ ——前 (表面に接して) on (↔off); (真上に) over (↔under); (離れて上方に) above (↔below) ——副 up (↔down); (上の方向に) upward (↔downward) ——形 (上の部分の) upper

<語法>
(1)「上」はある物よりも「高い」位置にあることを表すが、on は物の表面に接していることを表す。そのため、on は, on the table「テーブルの上に」のように、「接して上にある」場合だけではなく、on the wall「壁に」や on the ceiling「天井に」などのように、物の上部以外の面に接している場合にも用いられる。
(2) above は、物に接触しないで、上方の位置にあることを表す。over は、真上を覆っている感じを表す。

[図: ランプが on the ceiling、絵が above [over] the table、on the wall、花瓶が on the table、テーブルの上のものが over the table]

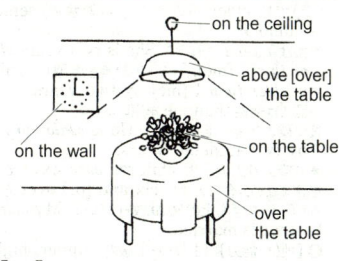

〖上に〗
テーブルの上に花びんを置いてちょうだい Put

the vase *on* the table.
彼は机の上に両足をのせて座っていた He was sitting with his feet *on* the desk.
この川の上には橋がかけられる A bridge will be built *over* this river.
ジャージの上に制服を着るのはみっともない You look ridiculous wearing your uniform *over* your gym clothes.
塔はほかの建物の上に高くそびえている The tower soars *above* the other buildings.
〖上の〗
山の上の小屋 a cabin *on the top of* the mountain / スクリーンの上の画像 an image *on* the screen / 机の上の手紙 a letter *on* the desk / 上の階 the *upper* floor / 上の歯 the *upper* teeth
名前を紙の上の方に書きなさい Sign your name *at the top of* the paper.
その少女はバースデーケーキの上のろうそくを吹き消した The girl blew out the candles *on* her birthday cake.
◆上の部屋 an *upstairs* room / 彼女は上の階へスーツケースを運んだ She carried her suitcase *upstairs*.
〖上で〗
氷の上で滑って転ぶ slip *on* the ice / 上で述べたとおり as (is) mentioned *above*
彼女の視線はその写真の上でとまった Her eyes came to rest *on* the photo.
◆赤ん坊が母親のひざの上で眠っていた The baby was sleeping *in* her mother's lap.
〖上を〗
上を見てごらん Look *up*.
ホバークラフトは波の上を滑るように進んだ The hovercraft skimmed *over* the waves.
見上げると私たちの上を飛行機が飛んでいた When we looked up, an airplane was flying *over* us.
〖その他〗
上から4行目の文 the sentence in the fourth line *from the top* / 上からのぞき込む peep *from above*
知らない人が私を上から下までじろじろ見た A stranger looked me *up and down*.
💬「彼の帽子はどこ」「テーブルの上よ」"Where's his hat?" "It's *on* the table."
❷【年齢】older (↔younger), elder(❖どちらも old の比較級. elder は通例名詞の前で用いる. 《米》では older がふつう); (先輩の) senior (↔junior)
彼女は私より2つ上です She is two years *older than* I [me]. / (→年齢差を強調して) She is *older than* I [me] by two years. (❖口語では通例 than me を用いる)
彼は僕より学年で2つ上だ He is *senior to* me by two academic years.
◆6歳より上の子供 children *over* six (❖6歳を含まない. 含むときは six and [or] over とする) / いちばん上の兄は結婚している My *oldest* brother is married.
❸【地位・能力】(上位の・上級の) upper, higher; (すぐれた) better, superior
上のクラス an *upper* [a *higher*] class
テニスでは僕のほうがあいつより上だ I'm a *better* tennis player [I play tennis *better*] *than* he [him].
これはあのパソコンよりも性能の点ではるかに上だ This computer is far [vastly] *superior to* that one in power.
◆彼女はその警察官よりも階級が上だ She is *above* the police officer in rank. / She ranks *above* the police officer.
❹【…の面で】
敵の軍隊は数の上で優勢であった The enemy forces were superior *in number*.
暦の上ではもう夏だ *The calendar says* it is already summer.
パソコンを購入する上で何を考慮したらいいですか What should I consider *if* I buy a computer?
❺【結果】
合意のうえで *by mutual consent* / 酔ったうえでのけんか a *drunken* fight
よく考えたうえでご返事ください Please answer me *after you consider it carefully*.
❻【追加】
彼ったらジュースを2本飲んだうえに牛乳も飲んだのよ *Besides* [*In addition to*] two bottles of juice, he drank some milk.
[慣用表現] どんな分野でも上には上があるものだ *There's always someone above you* in any field. / きのうわが家は上を下への大騒ぎだった Our home was in *utter confusion* yesterday. / 上を見ればきりがないよ *Don't be too ambitious*.

うえ[2] 飢え (空腹) hunger [U]; (飢餓) starvation [U] (❖hunger よりも「苦しみ, 死ぬ」という感じが強い)
◆世界中の飢えに苦しむ子供たちを救うため多くのアーチストが団結した Many artists united to help the *starving* children of [in] the world.

ウエーター waiter [C] (❖呼びかけにも用いる)
◆アルバイトでウエーターをしています I *wait* (*on*) *tables* part-time.

ウエート weight [U][C]; (重点) emphasis [C][U] (複 emphases) ‖君はもうちょっと勉強にウエートをおいたほうがいい You should *put* a little more *emphasis* on your studies.

ウエートリフティング weight lifting [U]

ウエートレス waitress [C] (❖呼びかけにも用いる)

ウエーブ wave [C] ‖スタンドではウエーブが始まった People in the stands began to do *the wave*. ◆姉は美容院でウエーブをかけた My sister ｢*had her hair waved* [*got a wave*] at a beauty salon. / 彼女の髪にはウエーブがかかっている She has *wavy* hair.

ウェールズ Wales ―ウェールズ人 Welshman [C]; (女性) Welshwoman [C]; (集合的) the Welsh ―ウェールズ語 Welsh [U] ―ウェールズ(人[語])の Welsh

うえかえ 植え替え transplant [U][C] ―植え替える transplant [他]; (移す) move [他]

うえき 植木 (鉢植え) potted plant [C]
◆父は今庭で植木の手入れをしています My fa-

ther *is gardening* in the yard now.
‖植木ばさみ gardening shears / 植木鉢 a (plant) pot / 植木屋(人) a gardener; (店) a nursery

うえこみ 植え込み (生け垣) hedge [C]; (低木の)《集合的》shrubbery [C][U]

うえじに 飢え死に starvation [U] ―飢え死にする die of hunger, starve (to death)

ウエスタン western [C]《しばしばWestern》(❖19世紀の米国西部のカウボーイや開拓者などを描いた映画・小説など) ‖カントリー(アンド)ウエスタン country and western / マカロニウエスタン a spaghetti western

ウエスト waist [C]; (胴回り) waistline [C] ∥このドレスはウエストがゆるすぎる This dress is too loose in [around] *the waist*. / ウエストを細くしたい I want to *reduce my waistline*.
‖ウエストポーチ《米》a waist pack, a bum bag

ウエストバージニア West Virginia (❖米国東部の州;《略語》W.Va.,〖郵便〗WV)

ウエストボール ⚠(野球で) wasted pitch [C]

うえつける 植え付ける (植物を) plant [他] (❖比喩的にも用いる); (印象・思想などを) implant [他] ◆監督は選手たちに勝負への執念を植えつけた The manager *implanted* into the players the persistence needed to win the game.

ウエット ⚠ ―ウエットな (感傷的な) sentimental (❖英語の wet は「気の弱い, 意気地がない」の意味) ∥ウエットな性格の人 a *sentimental* person
‖ウエットスーツ a wet suit / ウエットティッシュ a towelette

ウエディング wedding [C] ‖ウエディングケーキ a wedding cake / ウエディングドレス a wedding dress / ウエディングマーチ a wedding march

ウェリントン Wellington (❖ニュージーランドの首都)

うえる[1] 植える plant [他] ∥裏庭にトマトを植えた We *planted* tomatoes in the back garden. ◆おばの家の庭にはいろいろな花が植えてある *There are* a lot of flowers in my aunt's garden.

うえる[2] 飢える be [go*] hungry; (ひどく) starve [自] ∥私も飢えている子供たちのために何かをしたい I, too, want to do something to help the *starving* children. / 彼は親の愛情に飢えている He *is hungry for* parental affection.

ウエルターきゅう ウエルター級 (ボクシングなどの階級) welterweight class [C]
◆ウエルター級の選手 *a welterweight*

ウエルダン ―ウエルダンの (肉などが十分焼けた) well-done
💬「ステーキの焼き方はどうなさいますか」「ウエルダンでお願いします」"How would you like your steak?" "*Well-done.*"

うお 魚 fish [C] (複 ~, ~es) ➾ うおざ
‖魚市場 a fish market
[ことわざ] 魚心あれば水心 (You) scratch my back and I'll scratch yours. (→私の背中をかいてくれたらあなたの背中をかいてあげよう)

うおうさおう 右往左往 ゆうべは大きなネズミが出たといって家中が右往左往した (→あちこち走り回って大騒ぎになった) We saw a big rat in the house last night, and we all *ran this way and that* and got into a real mess.

ウォークマン 《商標名》Walkman [C]; (携帯用ヘッドホンステレオ) personal stereo [C] ∥ウォークマンで音楽を聴く listen to music on *a Walkman*

ウオーターフロント waterfront [C]

ウオーミングアップ ⚠(スポーツなどの) warm-up [C] ―ウオーミングアップする (スポーツなどで) warm up ∥選手たちはウオーミングアップを始めた The players began *warming up*.

ウォールがい ウォール街 Wall Street (❖ニューヨーク市の金融業の中心地)

うおがし 魚河岸 (waterfront) fish market [C]

うおざ 魚座〖天文・占星〗Pisces [U] (❖「魚座の人」の意味では [C])

ウオツカ vodka [vɑ́dkə] [U]

うおのめ 魚の目 (足の裏の) corn [C]

ウォン (韓国の通貨単位) won [U]

うかい 迂回《主に米》detour [C] ―迂回する (遠回りをする) detour [自], make* [take*] a detour ∥道路工事中のため迂回します We'll *make a detour* to avoid the road work.
‖迂回路 a detour, a roundabout route

うがい gargling [U], gargle [C] ―うがいする gargle [自] ∥外から帰ったらうがいをしなさい *Gargle* when you come home.
‖うがい薬 (a) gargle

うかうか うかうかしていると(→怠けていると)彼に追い抜かされるよ Don't *be lazy*, or he'll get ahead of you.

うかがい 伺い この件に関しては上役にお伺いを立てておいたほうがいい You should *feel out* your boss on this matter. / 彼はご機嫌伺いにおばのところへ立ち寄った He dropped in on his aunt to *pay his respects*.

うかがう[1] 伺う

❶【訪問する】visit [他]; (正式に) call [自]; (相手のところに行く) come* [自]
ご自宅に伺ってもよろしいですか May I *visit* your house?
何もなければあす伺います If nothing prevents us, we'*ll come* and see you tomorrow.

❷【尋ねる】ask [他]
お年を伺ってもよろしいですか Would it be all right if I *ask* your age?
◆ひとつ伺いたいのですが Excuse me, but *I have a question*.

❸【聞く】hear* [他][自]
おうわさはかねがね伺っております I'*ve heard* a lot about you.
◆ご用件を伺います *May I help you?* / ご病気だと伺っていたんですが(そうではなかったんですね) I *was given to understand* that you were ill.

[う]

うかがう[2] **窺う**
❶【様子を見る】(観察する) study [他]; (のぞき見る) peep [自]
ドアのすき間から中をうかがう *peep* through the door
彼は両親の顔色ばかりうかがっている He *is* always *studying* his parents' faces.
❷【機会を待つ】
あいつはただパーティーを抜け出そうと機会をうかがっているだけだよ He's only *waiting his chance* to escape from the party.
❸【察知される】
彼の話し方には育ちのよさがうかがわれる His way of speaking *suggests* that he's been well brought up.

うかされる 浮かされる 彼はまる3日間も高熱に浮かされている He *has been delirious with a high fever* for three full days.

うかす 浮かす 食費を浮かす *cut down one's food expenses* / 彼女は少し腰を浮かせて座布団を敷いた She *rose slightly* and slid a cushion in.

うかつ 迂闊 ―うかつな (不注意な) careless; (考えなしの) thoughtless ∥教科書を忘れてくるとはうかつだったね It was *careless* of you to have left your textbook behind.
◆うかつにも彼女にそれを言ってしまった I *thoughtlessly* told it to her.

うがった 穿った (洞察力のある) penetrating ∥うがった見方をする provide *penetrating* insight

うかばれる 浮かばれる 犯人もようやくつかまって，これで彼も浮かばれるだろう Now that the criminal was caught at last, he would *rest in peace*. / 3か月の努力が水の泡では彼女も浮かばれまい (→全然満足できないだろう) She *won't be satisfied at all* if her three-month effort is in vain.

うかびあがる 浮かび上がる (水面などに) rise* [自]; (姿などが) emerge [自] ∥水面に浮かび上がる *rise* [*come up*] *to* the surface / 捜査開始の1か月後容疑者の名が浮かび上がってきた A suspect *emerged* one month after the start of the investigation.

うかぶ 浮かぶ

❶【水面・空中に】float [自]
この種の木は水に浮かばない This type of wood *doesn't float* (on water).
青空に白い雲が浮かんでいた White clouds *were floating* in the blue sky.
◆湖に浮かんでいたモーターボートが急に動き始めた A motorboat *on* the lake suddenly started to move.
❷【心の中に】occur [自] (❖受身にはできない), strike* [他] (❖進行形にはできない), come* to ...; (ぱっと) flash [自]
その本を読んでいるうちに妙な考えが頭に浮かんだ As I read the book, some strange thoughts *occurred to* me.
突然名案が浮かんだ A good idea suddenly *struck* [*flashed into*] my mind.
彼の名前がなかなか浮かんでこなかった His name *didn't come to my mind* easily.
◆おい，いい考えが浮かんだぞ Say, I'*ve got* an idea! / その話を聞いて最初に頭に浮かんだのが彼女のことだった (→その話は彼女のことを思い出させた) The story *reminded me of* her first.
❸【表面化する】appear [自]
富士山の姿が朝もやの中に浮かんできた Mt. Fuji *appeared* through the morning mist.
彼女の顔にようやくほほえみが浮かんだ Finally a smile *appeared* on her face.
◆少女の目に涙が浮かんだ Tears「*came to* [*welled up in*] the girl's eyes.

うかべる **浮かべる**
❶【水面・空中に】float [他]
池に模型の船を浮かべる *float* a model ship on a pond
❷【心の中に】(想像する) imagine [他]; (思い出す) recall [他], remember [他] [自]
寂しくなったときには故郷の風景を心に浮かべた When I felt lonely, I *recalled* the scenes of my hometown.
❸【表面化させる】wear* [他]
その子は口元にほほえみを浮かべていた The child *wore* a smile on her lips.
◆彼女は目に涙を浮かべてさよならと言った She said goodbye *with tears in her eyes*.

うかる 受かる pass [自] [他] ∥試験に受かる *pass* an examination / 受かったの？ そりゃすごい You *passed*? That's great.

うかれる 浮かれる 彼女とデートする約束を取りつけたくらいでそんなに浮かれないで (→興奮しないで) よ *Don't get* so *excited* just because she agreed to go on a date with you.

うき[1] 雨季・雨期 rainy [wet] season [C] ∥この地方にははっきりとした雨季がある This region has *a* distinct *rainy season*.

うき[2] 浮き (釣りの) float [C]

うきあがる 浮き上がる come* up to the surface; (潜水艦などが) surface [自]; (周囲とずれている) be not in harmony with ... ∥彼，ひとりで浮き上がっているみたいね Only he *doesn't* seem to *be in harmony with* them.

うきあしだつ 浮き足立つ そんなことに浮き足立って (→心配して) いては成功はおぼつかないぞ You won't succeed if such a thing can *make you nervous*.

うきうき 浮き浮き 弟はあしたから修学旅行に行くのでうきうきしている My brother *is happy* since he is going on a school trip tomorrow.

うきしずみ 浮き沈み ups and downs, highs and lows ∥人生の浮き沈み *the ups and downs* of life ◆浮き沈みの激しい人生を送る live a *checkered* life

うきたつ 浮き立つ 翌日は学校が休みだと思うと心が浮き立った (→元気づけられた) I *cheered up* at the thought that there was no school the next day.

うきでる 浮き出る 夜空に月がくっきりと浮き出て見えた The moon *stood out* in sharp contrast *against* the night sky.

うけつぐ

うきぶくろ 浮き袋 (水泳の) float ◎; (救命具) life preserver ◎; (魚の) (air) bladder ◎

うきぼり 浮き彫り relief ⓤ◎ ‖彼は木で美しい浮き彫りを彫った He carved *a fine relief* out of wood. ◆その小説は現代に生きる女性たちの姿を浮き彫りにしている The novel *brings out* how present-day women live.

うきめ 憂き目 その政党は前回の選挙で敗北の憂き目にあった That political party *suffered a defeat* in the last election.

うきよ 浮き世 (この世) the [this] world; (人生) life ⓤ ‖気の毒だけどね、それも浮き世の習いというものさ That's too bad, but, you know, that's *life*. ◆あの人にはちょっと浮き世離れしたところがある (=隠者のような生活をしている) He's kind of *living the life of hermit*.

うきよえ 浮世絵

1680年ごろから1850年代ごろの間に栄えた木版画のことで、その時代の庶民の暮らしぶりが描かれています。また、役者や美しい女性の肖像も浮世絵のテーマの一つです。浮世絵の独特なスタイルは海外の多くの画家にも影響を与えています。*Ukiyo-e* is a kind of woodcut print which flourished from about the 1680s to the 1850s. It depicts the everyday life of common people, and portraits of actors and beautiful women are also among its themes. Many foreign artists have been influenced by this unique style.

うきわ 浮き輪 inner tube ◎; (救命具) life preserver ◎

うく 浮く
❶【浮かぶ】float ⓘ
氷は水に浮く Ice *floats* on water.
◆一瞬体が宙に浮いたような気がした I had the feeling that I *was tossed in the air* for a moment.
❷【金などが】
友達の家に泊めてもらったのでホテル代が浮いた (→節約できた) I stayed at my friend's house, so I could *save* (on) *hotel expenses*.
❸【周囲から遊離する】
パーティーにジーンズで行ったらすっかり浮いてしまった (→場違いに感じさせられた) Going to the party with jeans on, I was made to *feel completely out of place*.
慣用表現 彼女には浮いたうわさの一つもない (→ゴシップとは無縁だ) She has nothing to do with gossip. / 彼は浮かぬ顔で教室に入ってきた He came into the classroom *with a long face*. / 不況のせいで計画が宙に浮いてしまった The recession caused the plan to be *suspended*. / 彼女は浮くようなお世辞を言った Her flattery was *disgusting* to me.

うぐいす 鶯 (Japanese) bush warbler ◎
‖うぐいす色 dark brownish green

ウクレレ 〖音楽〗ukulele [jùːkəléili] ◎

うけ 受け (人気) popularity ⓤ◎; (評判) reputation ⓤ◎ 《また a ~》 ‖彼は先生のうけがいい He *has a good reputation* among his teachers. ◆そのTVコマーシャルは若い世代のうけをねらっている That TV commercial is designed to *appeal to* the younger generation.

うけあう 請け合う (保証する) assure ⓗ, guarantee ⓗ ‖彼のことなら請け合いますよ I (can) *assure you of* his nature. / 商品を1週間以内に配送することを請け合います I *guarantee* to deliver the goods within a week.

うけいれ 受け入れ 彼らは外国人選手の受け入れに好意的だ They're in favor of *accepting* players from foreign countries.

うけいれる 受け入れる (意識的に) accept ⓗ; (受ける) receive ⓗ; (クラブなどの会員として) admit ⓗ; (いやなこと・つらいことを) face up to ... ‖彼らは妥協案をしぶしぶ受け入れた They *accepted* the compromise reluctantly. / 私たちの学校は3人のアメリカ人を交換留学生として受け入れた Our school *received* [*admitted*] three Americans as exchange students. / 私はなかなかその事故のことを受け入れられなかった I couldn't *face up to* the accident readily.

うけうり 受け売り 彼の意見は本多先生の受け売りにすぎない He's just *parroting* what Mr. Honda said.

うけおい 請負 (契約) contract ◎ⓤ ‖請負で *by contract* / その仕事は請負に出した We put the work out to *contract*.
‖請負人 a contractor

うけおう 請け負う (契約する) contract ⓗ; (引き受ける) 《公式的》undertake* ⓗ ‖仕事を請け負う *undertake* a task / その会社はそのビルの新築工事を請け負った The company *contracted* to build a new building.

うけぐち 受け口 (物を受ける) pocket ◎; (口の) a mouth with a protruding lower jaw

うけこたえ 受け答え 彼女の娘はまだ小さいのに受け答えがしっかりしている (→きちんと応答する) Her daughter *responds* well though she's just a little child.

うけざら 受け皿 (カップなどの) saucer ◎ ‖受け皿付きのカップ a cup and *saucer*
◆うちの社長は希望退職者の受け皿 (→受け入れてくれる会社) を探している Our president is looking for *firms to accept* the members who are going to take voluntary retirement from our company.

うけたまわる 承る だれかご用を承っておりますか *Is anyone serving you?* / ご注文を承ります *May I take your order?* / ご用命確かに承りました We *will* certainly *attend to* your request.

うけつぐ 受け継ぐ (財産・性格などを) inherit ⓗ (❖通例進行形にできない); (仕事などを) succeed to ...; (引き継ぐ) take* over ‖父の事業を受け継ぐ *succeed to* [*take over*] one's father's business / 彼女は両親のすぐれた音楽的才能を受け継いでいる She *has inherited* her great musical talent from her parents.
◆これらの伝統工芸は代々受け継がれてきたもの

うけつけ

です These traditional arts *have been handed down* for generations.

うけつけ 受付 (場所) reception [information] desk ⓒ (◆掲示では Information); (係) receptionist ⓒ /受付で予約があるか尋ねられた *The receptionist* asked me if I had a reservation. / I was asked at *the desk* if I had a reservation. ◆応募の受付は9月からです(→9月に受付を開始します) We'll start *accepting* the applications in September.
‖受付期間 application period / 受付番号 a receipt number

うけつける 受け付ける (受諾する) accept ⓣ, take* ⓣ; (受け取る) receive ⓣ /期日を過ぎた応募は受け付けません We won't *accept* the applications after the deadline. / 彼はどんな忠告も全く受け付けなかった He *had* never *taken* any kind of advice.

◆きょうはだるいから、からい料理は胃が受け付けないんじゃないかな I'm feeling very weak. I don't think I *can stomach* spicy food today. (◆この stomach は「…を食べても気持ち悪くならない」という意味の動詞)

うけとめる 受け止める (ボールなどを) catch* ⓣ; (事態などを) take* ⓣ /彼は速球をやすやすと受け止めた He *caught* the fastball easily. / 君はもう少し事態を深刻に受け止めるべきだ You should *take* it a bit more seriously.

うけとり 受取 (領収証) receipt ⓒ /おそれありますが受取にサイン願います Excuse me, but sign this *receipt*, please. ◆小包の受け取りを拒否する *refuse to receive [accept] a parcel*
‖受取勘定 receivables / 受取人 a recipient

うけとる 受け取る
❶【手に入れる】 receive ⓣ, get* ⓣ; (喜んで) accept ⓣ, take* ⓣ
たくさんの郵便物を受け取る *receive [get] a lot of mail* / わいろを受け取る *take [accept] bribes*
彼女は心から感謝してそのプレゼントを受け取った She *accepted* the present with hearty thanks.
❷【理解・解釈する】 (受け止める) take* ⓣ (◆通例進行形にはできない); (解釈する) interpret ⓣ
彼は私が言うことをいつも悪く受け取る He always *takes* my words badly.
私は彼女がうなずいたのを同意と受け取った I *interpreted* her nod as consent.
君のことをけなしたつもりはなかったんだけど、どうも逆に受け取られたようだね I didn't intend to speak ill of you, but you seem to *have taken* it to the contrary.

うけながす 受け流す 彼の言うことなんて適当に受け流しておけばいいよ(→まじめに受け取る必要はない) You *don't* have to *take* his words *seriously*.

うけみ 受け身・受身 (消極性) passivity ⓤ; (柔道などの) *ukemi*, a protective way of falling in martial arts; 〖文法〗 (受動態) the passive voice ──受け身の (消極的な) passive // (柔道などで) 受け身をとる do [take] *ukemi* / 最近彼はどうも受け身になりがちだ He seems to have become *passive* nowadays.

受身は、態(voice)の一つの形で、受動態ともいう。ふつう主語がある動作・作用を受けることを表し、英語では〈be＋過去分詞〉の形で表される。反対に、主語が動作・作用を及ぼす場合の動詞の形は、能動態(active voice)という // *English is used* in many areas of the world. 英語は世界の多くの地域で使われている / The elevators *are now being checked*. エレベーターは今点検中だ(→点検されているところだ) / Radium *was discovered* by the Curies. ラジウムはキュリー夫妻によって発見された

うけもち 受け持ち 僕たちの受け持ちの先生は山田先生です Mrs. Yamada is our *class [homeroom]* teacher.

うけもつ 受け持つ take* [be in] charge of …; (教える) teach* ⓣ /高橋先生は4年生のクラスを受け持っている Mr. Takahashi *is in charge of* the fourth grade class. / 来年は新入生のクラスを受け持つことになりそうだ I'll *be teaching* a freshman class next year.

うける 受ける

❶ 受け止める　　　　catch
❷ 受け取る　　　　　receive, get
❸ 受諾する　　　　　accept
❹ 教育・試験・手術などを　receive, get, take
❺ 被害などを　　　　suffer

❶【受け止める】 (ボールなどを) catch* ⓣ
手でボールを受ける *catch a ball with one's hand(s)*
ダイヤは太陽の光を受けてきらきらと輝いた The diamond *caught* the sunlight and sparkled. / The diamond sparkled *in* the sunlight.

❷【受け取る・与えられる】 receive ⓣ, get* ⓣ

「…を受ける」を「(他人から)…される」という受身の文と考えて、〈be＋過去分詞〉で表すことも多い // 彼女はその絵で表彰を受けた(→表彰された) She *received an award* for the painting. / She *was awarded a prize* for the painting. / 私は新しい学校で温かい歓迎を受けた(→温かく歓迎された) I *received* a warm welcome at the new school. / I *was* warmly *welcomed* at the new school.

彼の家族は生活保護を受けている His family *is receiving [on]* welfare.
私たちはパーティーへの招待を受けた We *received* an invitation to a party. / We *were invited to* a party.
そのテストに合格した学生だけが奨学金を受けることができる Only those students who pass the exam can *get* scholarships.

◆許可を受けずに学校を早退することはできません You can't leave school before classes are over *without permission*. / あすは8時までに

登校するようにと指示を受けた We *were told to be at school by eight tomorrow morning.* / 不勉強だと先生からおしかりを受けた I *was reproached by my teacher for being lazy.* / 姉は違法駐車で注意を受けた My sister *was given a warning* for illegal parking. / 僕は他人から影響を受けやすい I'm *easily influenced* by other people. / 私は日本に生を受けた I *was born* in Japan. / その電話を受けたのは僕の母です It *was my mother who answered the phone.*

❸【受諾する・応じる】accept 他
注文を受ける accept [take] an order (❖ accept は「大きな契約などを受ける」, take は「レストランなどでオーダーを受ける」の意味)
私は喜んで彼の申し出を受けた I gladly *accepted* his offer.
とても残念ですがあなたのお誘いを受けることはできません Much to my regret, I am unable to *accept* your invitation.

❹【教育・試験・手術などを】(教育・試験などを) receive 他, get* 他, take* 他;(手術などを) undergo* 他;(裁判を) stand* 他
大学教育を受ける人の数が増えている The number of people who *receive [get] a college education* is increasing.
私は広告代理店の面接を受けた I *got an interview* with an advertising agency.
彼女は週3回音楽のレッスンを受けている She *takes [gets] music lessons* three times a week.
私は来月, 大学の入学試験を受ける I *will take [sit (for)] the university's entrance examination* next month.
彼女は心臓の手術を受けた She *underwent an operation* on her heart.
私はきのう健康診断を受けた I *underwent a medical checkup* yesterday.
彼は汚職容疑で裁判を受けている He *is standing trial* for bribery.
◆彼はアメリカで教育を受けた He *was educated* in America. / 彼女は看護の訓練を受けた She *was trained* in nursing.

❺【被害などを】suffer 他
自動車産業は大損害を受けた The automobile industry *suffered heavy losses.*
彼はつかまって拷問を受けた He *was caught* and *suffered torture.*
◆激しい爆撃でその町は大きな被害を受けた The town *was badly damaged* by the heavy bombing. / 囚人たちは幾多の残虐行為を受けた The prisoners *were subjected to* many cruelties. / 遅霜のため, 苗の多くが被害を受けた(→遅霜が被害を与えた) A late frost *damaged* many of the seedlings.

❻【感じ・ショックなどを】
彼はいい人そうだという印象を受けた I *got [had] the impression* that he was a good-natured person.
大統領が暗殺されたというニュースにショックを受けた I *was shocked* by the news that the President had been assassinated.
子供のころ僕はエジソンの伝記を読んで刺激を受けた Edison's biography *stimulated* [*inspired*] *me* when I was a boy.
彼女の優しさに私は感銘を受けた I *was struck* by her kindness.

❼【罰を】receive 他, take* 他
彼はうそをついたために罰を受けた He *received punishment* for telling lies. / He *was punished* for telling lies.
◆その殺人犯は死刑の判決を受けた The murderer *was sentenced to* death. / 彼は自分の犯した罪の報いを受けた He *paid for* his crime.

❽【言葉の意味を】
あいつの言うことなんか真に受けるなよ Don't *take* him *at his word.* / Don't *take* what he says so *seriously.*

❾【好評を得る】
この小説は若い読者にうけるでしょうか Will this novel *appeal to* young readers?
彼女の歌は10代の若者にたいへんうけている Her songs are very *popular with [among]* teenagers.
私の冗談が大いにうけた My joke *got [raised] a big laugh.*

うけわたし 受け渡し (配達) delivery Ⓤ // 商品の受け渡し *the delivery* of goods

うごうのしゅう 烏合の衆 (無秩序な群衆) disorderly crowd Ⓤ ◆あの政党はまさに烏合の衆だ(→指導者を欠いてどうすればよいかわからない人の集まりだ) That political party is just *like a flock of sheep without a shepherd.*

うごかす 動かす

❶ 物の位置を　　　move; shift
❷ 体・物の部分を　move; exercise
❸ 機械などを　　　work, operate, run

❶【物の位置を】move 他;(少し) shift 他
テーブルをもう少し右へ動かしてください Please *move [shift] the table* a little to the right.
家の前に止めてあった車を駐車場へ動かした I *moved the car* parked in front of the house to the parking lot.
◆冷蔵庫は重くてとてもひとりで動かせるものではなかった The refrigerator was so heavy that I *couldn't budge* it by myself. (❖ budge は通例否定文で用いる)

❷【体・物の部分を】(運動する) exercise 自;(揺り動かす) sway 他自;(軽く揺り動かす) stir 他;(ぶらぶらさせる) swing* 他;(くねらす) wriggle 他
手を動かす *move one's hands*
健康のためにも毎日体を動かすべきだ You should *exercise* every day for (your) health.
風が木の葉を動かした The wind *stirred* the leaves.
ホール内の人々は音楽に合わせて体を左右に動かしていた People in the hall *swayed* (their bodies) to the music.

うごき

その少年はテーブルの下で足をぶらぶら動かしていた The boy *was swinging* his legs under the table.
◆隣部屋の物音を聞いて犬は耳をぴくっと動かした The dog *twitched* its ears at the sound in the next room.

❸【機械などを】(操作する) work 他, operate 他, run* 他;(使う) use 他

この機械の動かし方(→操作のしかた)を教えてください. Please tell me *how to work* [*operate, run*] this machine. /(→使い方)Please tell me *how to use* this machine.

❹【人・会社などを】

彼がこの会社を動かしている(→指揮をとっている) He *takes* [*holds*] *control of* this company. /(→経営している)He *manages* this company.

あのチームの監督は選手の動かし方がうまい The manager of that team is good at *managing* [*controlling*] his players.

❺【事実・世界などを変える】

彼がその犯罪を犯したのは動かしがたい(→否定できない)事実だ It is an *undeniable* [(→議論の余地のない) *indisputable*] fact that he committed the crime.

あの男はいずれ世界を動かす(→変える)ような大人物になるだろう That man is going to be great enough to *change* the world.

❻【心・考えなどを】

僕は田中先生の話に大いに心を動かされた(→感動した) I *was* deeply *affected* [*moved, touched*] *by* Mr. Tanaka's speech.

彼女はテレビの言うことに動かされやすい(→影響されやすい) She *is* easily *affected* [*influenced*] *by* what is said on TV.

私に対する彼の真剣な態度が私の心を動かした(→考えを変えさせた) His serious attitude toward me *made me change my mind*.

うごき 動き

❶【動くこと】movement 他他; a move; motion 他他

movement: 人や物の特定の動き.
move: 何らかの目的を伴う個々の動き.
motion: 特に動く過程, 動き方に関心がある場合に用いる.

私は彼女の唇のかすかな動きに気づいた I noticed *a* slight *movement* of her lips.

彼は彼女の一つ一つの動きに魅せられていた He was attracted to her every *move*.

我々はこの惑星の動きを観測した We observed *the motion* of the planet.

◆牛は動きがのろい A cow *moves* slowly. / 両足とも泥にはまって動きがとれなかった Both my feet *were stuck fast* in the mud. / 中田は素早い動きで相手ディフェンダーをかわした Nakata faked out the defender on the opposing team with *a* swift *dodge*.

❷【動向・変化】(動向・風潮) movement 他他, trend 他;(変化) change 他他;(進展) development 他他

現在の世界経済の動き *the* current world economic *trend*

男女平等に向けての動きが高まっている There is *a* growing *movement* toward equality between men and women.

警察は一味の動きをひそかに監視している The police have been spying on the gang's *movements* [*activities*].

その政党内部で大きな動きがあった There was *a big change* within the party.

捜査に新たな動きが見られた There were some new *developments* in the investigation.

⇨みうごき

うごく 動く

❶ 位置が	move; run
❷ 機械が働く	work, go
❸ 人・組織が働く	act
❹ 変化する	change
❺ 考え・心が	be moved

❶【位置が】move 自;(列車・バスなどが運行する) run* 自

飛行機はゆっくり動き始めた The plane *began to move* slowly.

ネズミはかごの中を動き回っていた The mouse *was moving around* in the cage.

冷蔵庫を移動させようとしたが, ちっとも動かなかった I tried to move the refrigerator, but it *wouldn't move* [*budge*].

動くな, さもないと撃つぞ Don't *move* [*Freeze, Don't make a move*], or I'll shoot!

大雪のため電車は動いていない Trains *are not running* because of the heavy snow.

◆寝違えて首が動かない I slept wrong and now I *can't move my neck*. (❖この move は他動詞) / メリーゴーランドの馬は上下に動く The horses of a merry-go-round *go* up and down. / 彼ははしごを動かないように押さえた He *held* the ladder *steady*. / 交通渋滞で動けなかった We *were stuck* in a traffic jam. / 私が切符を買う間そこを動かないでね *Stay put* while I buy the tickets.

❷【機械が働く】(正常に機能する) work 自, go* 自;(作動する) operate 自, run* 自

僕のパソコンが動かないんだ My PC *doesn't work*.

この機械がどのように動くのか調べなければならない I must find out how this machine *operates*.

この車は電気で動く This car *runs* on electricity.

◆オルゴールはぜんまいで動く A music box *is driven* by a spring. / このラジコンカーは電池で動いている This radio-controlled model car *is powered* by batteries.

❸【人・組織が働く】(実行する) act 自

生徒たちは先生の指示どおりに動いた The students *acted* as their teacher told them. / The students *did* what their teacher told them to.

◆事件解決のために警察は今すぐ動くべきだ The police should *take action* immediately to solve the crime.

❹【変化する】change 圁;（状況などで変わる）vary 圁;（物価などが変動する）fluctuate 圁

世の中は日々動いている The world *is changing* from day to day.

野菜の値段は季節によって多少動く The prices of vegetables *vary* [*fluctuate*] a little with the seasons.

◆その男が犯人だという動かぬ証拠がある There is *indisputable* [*certain*, *undeniable*] evidence that he committed the crime. / 彼のチームの勝利は動くまい（→確実だ）*It is certain that* his team will win the game.

❺【考え・心が】（感動する）be moved, be touched

彼女は金なんかで動かないよ She *won't be moved* [*influenced*] by money.

そのテレビ番組を見て心が動いた I *was moved* [*touched*] by the TV program.

◆この件に関して私の考えは動かない I *am immovable* on this issue. / 彼の申し出に心が動いた（→心が引かれた）が、結局ından His offer *seemed attractive*, but in the end, I didn't accept it.

うさぎ 兎 rabbit ⓒ;（野ウサギ）hare ⓒ // うさぎ跳びをする *rabbit-hop*
‖ウサギ小屋 a rabbit hutch（❖「狭い家」の意味で比喩的にも用いる）

うさばらし 憂さ晴らし うさばらしにカラオケに行かない? Why don't we go to karaoke to *let off* some *steam*?

うさんくさい 胡散臭い suspicious,《口語的》fishy // うさんくさい商売 *fishy* business

うし[1] 牛《集合的》cattle《複数扱い》;（雌牛・乳牛）cow ⓒ;（去勢されていない雄牛）bull ⓒ;（去勢雄牛）ox ⓒ（複 oxen）;（子牛）calf [kǽf] ⓒ（複 calves）

80頭の牛 80 head of *cattle*（❖「…頭」と数える場合の head は単複同形）
‖牛飼い a cattle herder,《古風》a cowherd;（カウボーイ）a cowhand, a cowboy / 牛小屋 a cowshed / 狂牛病 mad cow disease, BSE / 闘牛 a bullfight / 肉牛 beef cattle / 乳牛 a (milk) cow

短歌 牛飼いが歌詠(よ)む時に世の中の新しき歌大いにおこる（伊藤左千夫）
When even this cowherd recites
the poems he has made,
the world is filled
with new poems
for a new world.

うし[2] 丑（十二支の第2番目）the Ox ➡えと

うじ 蛆 maggot ⓒ

うじうじ うじうじしていないで（→恥ずかしがらないで）彼に電話でもしてみたらどう Don't be too *shy*. Why don't you call him?

うしなう　失う

lose* ⦿

毎年約1万もの人の命が交通事故で失われている About ten thousand lives *are lost* in traffic accidents every year.

僕らが失うものなんて何もない We've got nothing to *lose*.

長引く不況のせいでおじが職を失った My uncle *lost* his job because of the continuing recession.

総選挙で1人の閣僚が議席を失った A minister *lost* his seat in the general election.

子供たちはすぐそのおもちゃへの興味を失った The children soon *lost* their interest in the toy.

人は健康を失って初めてその大切さに気づく It is not until we *lose* our health that we realize its importance. / We don't realize the importance of health till we *lose* it.

どんなときでも平常心を失わないで *Don't lose* [*Keep*] your calm no matter what happens.

◆反撃の機会を失ってしまった We *missed* the chance to fight back. / 床の血痕(こん)を見ると彼は気を失った He *fainted* at the sight of blood on the floor.

うじゃうじゃ ケーキにはアリがうじゃうじゃ群がっていた The cake was covered in *a swarm of* ants.

うしろ　後ろ

── 图 back ⓒ《通例 the ～》, rear ⓒ《通例 the ～》── 前 behind, at the back of …（↔in front of …）,《米》(in) back of …
── 形 in front (↔front)（❖名詞の前で用いる）
── 副 back,《米》in back, backward

上体を後ろに反(そ)らす lean *back* [*backward*]

後ろの席に座りなさい Sit in *the back* [*rear*] (*seat*).

和子の後ろにいるのはだれですか Who's *behind* [*in back of*] Kazuko?

私の後ろに1列に並んでください Please line up *behind* me.

彼女はカーテンの後ろに隠れた She hid *behind* the curtain.

彼はその選手に後ろからタックルしたためにイエローカードを食らった He received a yellow card for tackling the player *from behind*.

後ろを見ろよ、あの犬、まだついてくる Look *back* [*behind*]. The dog is still following us.

◆突然彼は後ろを振り返った Suddenly he *turned around*.

うしろあし 後ろ足（動物の）back [hind] leg ⓒ // 後ろ足で立つ stand on *one's hind legs*

うしろがみ 後ろ髪 私は後ろ髪を引かれる思いでその場を立ち去った *Feeling so sorry*, I left there.

うしろぐらい 後ろ暗い shady // 彼はどうも後ろ暗い取り引きにかかわっている He seems to be involved in a *shady* business.

うしろすがた 後ろ姿 彼の後ろ姿は父親にそっくりだ He resembles his father very closely *from the back*.

うしろだて 後ろ楯（支援）backup ⓤ, support ⓤ;（後援者）supporter ⓒ, patron ⓒ // 彼らの後ろ盾がなかったらこの計画はきっと失敗していただろう Without their *support*, this plan would surely have failed.

うしろまえ 後ろ前 君のセーター, 後ろ前だよ Your sweater is on *backward(s)*.

うしろむき 後ろ向き 彼は腕をばたばたさせて後ろ向きにプールに落ちた He flapped his arms as he fell *backward* into the pool. / 君の意見は後ろ向きすぎる Your opinion is too *retrogressive*.

うしろめたい 後ろめたい あんな誠実な女の子にうそをつくのはどうも後ろめたい *I'm feeling a bit guilty* about telling a lie to such a genuine girl. / 私は何も後ろめたいこと(→話せないようなこと)はしていない I didn't do anything that I *can't tell you (about)*.

うしろゆび 後ろ指 彼は自分が後ろ指をさされていることに気づいていない He doesn't know they *are criticizing* him *behind his back*.

うす 臼 (つきうす) an *usu*, a kind of large, heavy, strong mortar used to make rice dumplings or to crush grains (❖ *mortar* は香辛料などをすりつぶす小さなすり鉢); (ひきうす) mill

うず 渦 (水流の) whirlpool; (回転の速い) whirl; (通例単数形); (大きくて危険な) vortex (複 ～es, vortices)

◆その川は河口付近で渦を巻いている The river *whirls* near its mouth.

うすあかり 薄明かり (主に日没後の) twilight; (ぼんやりとした光) the dim light

うすあじ 薄味 病気の父のために料理は薄味にした I *lightly seasoned* the food for my sick dad.

うすい 薄い

❶ 厚みがない	thin; sheer
❷ 色が	light, pale
❸ 飲食物が	weak; thin
❹ 密度・濃度が低い	thin

❶【厚みがない】thin (↔thick); (透(す)き通るほど薄い) sheer ――薄く thin, thinly

薄い本 a *thin* book / ナイロンの薄いストッキング a pair of *sheer* nylon stockings / 薄く切ったレモン *thinly* sliced lemon; (→そのレモン1枚)a *thin* slice of lemon

この紙は非常に薄いのですぐに破れてしまう This paper is so *thin* that it tears easily.

薄いシャツ1枚しか着ていなかったので外は少し寒かった I only had a *thin* shirt on, so I felt a little cold outside.

パンを厚く切りましょうか, 薄く切りましょうか Shall I slice the bread thick or *thin*?

❷【色が】light, pale

薄い色 a *light* [*pale*] color / 薄い青 *light* [*pale*] blue

❸【飲食物が】(飲み物が) weak (↔strong); (スープなどが) thin (↔thick)

私は薄いコーヒー[紅茶]が好きです I like *weak* coffee [tea].

このスープちょっと薄くない? Don't you think this soup is just a little *thin*?

◆この店の料理は味が薄すぎる The dishes this restaurant serves taste *bland* [*insipid*]. / The dishes this restaurant serves are *too lightly seasoned*.

❹【密度・濃度が低い】thin

僕の父は頭のてっぺんが薄くなってきている My father *is getting thin* on top. / My father's hair *is thinning*.

山頂に近づくにつれて空気は薄くなっていった The air *got thinner* as we approached the summit.

空には薄い雲が出ていた There were *thin* clouds in the sky.

◆私の母は化粧が薄い My mother 「*puts on* [*wears*] *little* makeup.

❺【少ない・程度が低い】

利益の薄い商売 business which yields *little* [*thin*] profits

残念ながらわがチームの勝利の望みは非常に薄い Unfortunately, there is only a *slim* hope that our team will *win* the game.

彼は最近影が薄い(→目立たない) He *keeps a low profile* these days. / (→元気がない) He's *lacking in vigor* these days.

うすうす 薄々 祖父は自分が癌(がん)だとうすうす感づいていたようだ Granddad seemed to have a *vague* idea that he had cancer.

うずうず 君と話がしたくてうずうずしていたんだよ I've *been itching* to have a talk with you.

うすかわ 薄皮 thin skin

うすぎ 薄着 薄着をする *dress lightly*

うすぎたない 薄汚い (みすぼらしい) shabby; (くすんだ) dingy; (汚れた) dirty / 薄汚い外套 a *dirty* coat

うすきみわるい 薄気味悪い weird; (不気味で恐ろしい) eerie; (お化けの出そうな) spooky

うすぎり 薄切り 薄切りのハム *sliced* ham / トマトを薄切りにする cut a tomato into *thin slices*

うずく 疼く (鈍痛がする) ache [éik]; 冬になると肩の古傷がうずく My old shoulder injury *aches* in winter.

◆かつて裏切った友人のことを聞くたびに良心がうずく It always *pricks my conscience* to hear of a friend I once betrayed.

うずくまる 蹲る (かがむ) crouch; (しゃがむ) squat /彼女はおなかが痛くなってそこにうずくまった She had a stomachache and *crouched down* there.

うすぐもり 薄曇り (天気予報で)あすは薄曇りでしょう It'll be *slightly cloudy* tomorrow.

うすぐらい 薄暗い (明かりの乏しい) dim; (照明が弱い) dimly-lit; (暗くて陰険な感じのする) gloomy /そんな薄暗い部屋でテレビを見るな Don't watch TV in such a *dimly-lit* room. / 私は父の薄暗い書斎に忍び込んでみた I tried sneaking into my dad's *gloomy* study.

◆空が薄暗くなってきた The sky *is getting* [*turning*] *dark*.

うすくらがり 薄暗がり 薄暗がりの中から人影が現れた A figure emerged from *the gloom*.

うすげしょう 薄化粧 彼女はきょうは薄化粧だ

She is wearing *little* [*light*] *makeup* today. / 一夜明けると富士山は薄化粧していた(→うっすらと雪に覆われていた) Mt. Fuji *was lightly coated with snow* overnight.

うすごおり 薄氷 ゆうべは寒かったので水たまりに薄氷が張っている It was cold last night, so puddles have *a thin layer of ice*.

ウスターソース Worcester(shire) sauce ⓤ

うずたかい 堆い 彼の机の上には雑誌がうずたかく積み上げられていた There were *huge stacks of* magazines on his desk.

うすっぺら 薄っぺら ━━**薄っぺらな**(薄い) thin;(薄くてぺらぺらの) flimsy;(浅薄な) shallow;(表面的な) superficial 〖薄っぺらな知識 *shallow* knowledge / そんな薄っぺらな服を着ているとかぜをひきますよ You'll get a cold with such a *flimsy* dress on. / あんな薄っぺらな人間に僕の絵のよさが分かるものか Such a *superficial* man can never appreciate my paintings.

うすで 薄手 ━━**薄手の** thin;(服などが薄くて涼しい) light 〖薄手の生地 *thin* cloth / 薄手のセーター a *light* sweater

うすのろ 薄のろ (動作ののろい人)(米口語的)slowpoke ⓒ, (英口語的)slow coach ⓒ;(間抜け)《口語的》dimwit ⓒ

うすび 薄日 雨があがって雲間から薄日がさしてきた The rain has stopped and *soft sunlight* is coming through the cloudy sky.

うずまき 渦巻き whirl ⓒ《通例単数形》;(勢いのよい水の) whirlpool ⓒ;(小さい) eddy ⓒ;(大きくて危険な) vortex ⓒ(複 〜es, vortices);(大きい) maelstrom ⓒ

うずまく 渦巻く(水・空気などが) whirl ⓘ ◆学園祭が中止になって学生の間に不満が渦巻いている(→とめどなく沸き上がっている) *There is no end to the rising* dissatisfaction among the students over the cancellation of the school festival.

うずまる 埋まる (沈む) sink* ⓘ;(埋められる) be buried ⇒ うまる, うもれる

うすめ 薄目 薄目をあける open *one's eyes slightly* / 薄めのコーヒー *weak* coffee

うすめる 薄める dilute ⓣ;(どろっとしたものを) thin ⓣ;(水で薄める) water down 〖薄めたスープ *thinned* soup / この濃縮ジュースは水で薄めて飲むものです You should 「*dilute this concentrated juice with water* [*water this concentrated juice down*].

うずめる 埋める bury ⓣ;(いっぱいにする) fill ⓣ, pack into ... 〖彼はまくらに顔を埋めて泣いた He *buried* his face in the pillow and sobbed. / 5万人の観客がスタンドを埋めていた Fifty thousand spectators *filled* [*packed into*] the stadium.

うずもれる 埋もれる 砂漠に埋もれた遺跡 ruins *buried* under a desert ⇒ うもれる

うすよごれる 薄汚れる 弟が薄汚れた子犬を拾ってきた My little brother brought a *dirty* puppy home.

うずら 鶉 quail ⓒ(複 〜s, 〜)〖ウズラの卵 a *quail's* egg

うすらぐ 薄らぐ (弱くなっていく) subside ⓘ;(消えていく) fade ⓘ;(楽になる) ease 〖歳月とともに事故の記憶も薄らいでいった The memories of the accident *faded away* as time went by. ◆ 4月になってようやく寒さも薄らいできた(→少し暖かくなった) April came and finally *it got a bit warmer*.

うすらさむい 薄ら寒い (肌寒い) chilly

うすれる 薄れる (弱くなっていく) subside ⓘ;(消えていく) fade ⓘ 〖その歌手への私の関心は薄れていった My interest in the singer gradually *subsided*. ◆そのゲームの目新しさはすぐに薄れてしまった The novelty of the game soon *wore off*.

うすわらい 薄笑い その知らせを聞くと彼は薄笑いを浮かべた He *curled his lip* at the news.

うせつ 右折 right turn ⓒ ━━**右折する** turn (to the) right 〖右折禁止《掲示》*No Right Turn*

うせる 失せる disappear ⓘ ◆とっととうせろ! *Get out of here!*/ *Get lost!*/ *Out of my sight!*/ すっかりその仕事をやる気がうせた I totally *lost* motivation to do that job.

うそ 嘘 lie ⓒ(❖日本語の「うそ」よりはるかに強い非難・軽蔑の意味を含む。相手の冗談めいた言葉に対し「うそでしょう」と言うような場合には, You're kidding.などを用いる);(たわいない)《口語的》fib ⓒ;(作り話)《口語的》story ⓒ ━━**うその**(虚偽の) false, untrue

真っ赤なうそ *a downright lie* / 露骨なうそ *a bald-faced* [*barefaced*] *lie* / 見えすいたうそ *an obvious* [*a palpable, a transparent*] *lie* / 悪意のないうそ *a white lie* / うそ八百 *a pack* [*tissue, web*] *of lies* / 人のうそを見破る *detect a person's lie*

彼は決してうそをつかない He never tells *a lie*.
彼女にうそをついて悪かったと思っている I feel guilty about *telling* 「*her a lie* [*a lie to her*].
その証人はうその証言をした The witness made *a false* statement. / The witness told *a falsehood*.
うそをつくんじゃありません, ジョン Don't *tell stories*, John.(❖この表現は子供に対して用いられる)
◆うそ泣きをする *pretend to cry* / 彼女の本にはうその(→事実でない)記述がある Her book has some descriptions *which are not true*. / 昨夜の高熱がうそのように, すっかり元気になった Now that 「*I'm feeling better* [*I've recovered*], I can't believe I was suffering a high fever last night. / あのチームが優勝したなんてうそのような話だ(→信じられない) It is *incredible* [*unbelievable*] that their team won the championship.

🅔 「ねえ, 宝くじで1,000万円当たったよ」「うそでしょう!」"Hey, I won 10 million yen in a lottery!" "*No kidding!*/ *You're kidding* (*me*)!/ *You must be kidding* (*me*)!/ *Come off it!*"

‖うそ発見器 a lie detector,《公式的》a polygraph

ことわざ うそから出たまこと A lie turned into the truth as a result. / うそも方便 The

うそつき

end justifies the means.(→目的は手段を正当化する)

うそつき 嘘つき (非難されるべき) liar ⓒ; (悪意のない)(口語的)fibber ⓒ; (二枚舌)(口語的)double-dealer ⓒ ∥新しいおもちゃを買ってくれるって言ったじゃないか。うそつき！ You said you'd buy me a new toy. You *liar*!
ことわざ うそつきは泥棒の始まり A person who will lie will steal.(→うそは盗みにつながる); Show me a liar and I'll show you a thief.(→私に彼がうそつきであることを証明してくれれば,彼が泥棒であることを証明しよう)

うそぶく (自慢する) boast 自他 ∥彼はけんかで負けたことがないとうそぶいた He *boasted* that he had never lost a fight.

うた 歌 song ⓒ; (詩) poem ⓒ, (集合的)poetry ⓤ; (子供向けの詩) rhyme ⓒ; (日本の短歌) tanka (poem)
→ 場面・状況別会話 p.1702
恋の歌 a love *song* ∥ 悲しい歌 a sad *song* ∥ 歌を歌う sing a *song* ∥ 田園の風景を歌に詠む make [compose] a *tanka* about a country scene
◆この歌手,ルックスはなかなかだけど歌は下手だ This singer is fairly good-looking but *sings* quite badly.
∥歌番組 a musical show

うたいて 歌い手 singer ⓒ (❖プロに限らない)

うたいもんく 謳い文句 catchphrase ⓒ, catchword ⓒ

うたう¹ 歌う
sing* 自他; (鼻歌で) hum 自他
→ 場面・状況別会話 p.1712
低音で歌う *sing* low ∥ コーラスで歌う *sing* in chorus ∥ ピアノの伴奏に合わせて歌う *sing* to the accompaniment of a piano
では,日本の歌を歌います Now, I'll *sing* a Japanese song.
彼女は子守歌を歌って赤ん坊を寝かしつけた She *sang* the baby to sleep.(❖この sleep は名詞)
彼女は鼻歌を歌いながらやってきた She came *humming* to herself.

うたう² 謳う (宣言する) declare 他, pronounce 他; (述べる) state 他 ∥減税をうたっておきながらあの首相は何もしなかった That prime minister *declared* that he would lower the taxes but did nothing.
◆うちの高校は野球では強豪とうたわれている(→野球が強いと評判だ) Our high school *has a reputation for* being strong in baseball.

うたがい 疑い (疑念) doubt ⓒ ⓤ; (嫌疑) suspicion ⓤ ⓒ
彼女が有罪になるのは疑いの余地がない She'll be found guilty *beyond a shadow of a doubt*.
彼らは私を疑いの目で見た They looked on me *with suspicion*.
10年にも及ぶ裁判の末にその男性にかけられた疑いは晴れた After a 10-year trial, the man was cleared of *the suspicion*.
疑いを招くような行動は慎みたまえ You should refrain from doing anything that *invites people's suspicions*.
◆彼は誘拐の疑いで警察に指名手配されている He's wanted by the police *for* kidnapping. ∥ 私の上役には収賄の疑いがかけられている My boss *is suspected of* accepting bribes. ∥ この実験が成功するのは疑いない This experiment will succeed *undoubtedly*.

うたがいぶかい 疑い深い, suspicious; (懐疑的な) skeptical ∥私はどうも疑い深いたちでしてね I sort of have a *suspicious* nature.

うたがう 疑う
(不確かに思う) doubt 他; (容疑があると思う) suspect 他
君を疑っているわけではないが,だれかがそれを持ち出したのは確かだ I'm not *doubting* you but someone certainly removed it.
警察は彼が偽証しているのではないかと疑っているようだ The police seem to *suspect* him *of* giving false evidence.
【doubt+if 節／whether 節】そんなことをしたら,僕は君の良心を疑う If you did so, I would *doubt if* you have a conscience.
◆私は自分の目を疑った(→信じられなかった) I *couldn't believe my eyes*. ∥ 私はこれが最善の方法だと信じて疑わない(→強く信じている) I *do believe* this is the best way. ∥ 彼女が勉強家であることに疑う余地はない There's no doubt she's a hard-working student.

> 英作文ノート 「疑わない」なら **that**!
> 私は彼がその試験に合格することを信じて疑わない
> →×*I don't doubt if* [*whether*] he will pass the exam.
> →○*I don't doubt that* he will pass the exam.
> ★ doubt は,肯定文では doubt whether [if] ... の形を用いることができるが,否定文・疑問文では doubt の後の接続詞は if や whether ではなく that を用いる。なお,口語では「信じて疑わない」=「強く信じる」と考えて I do believe that he will ... ということも多い。

うたがわしい 疑わしい (うそのように思われる) doubtful; (確かではない) dubious (❖名詞の前では用いない) ∥彼の論文が事実に基づいているかどうかは疑わしい It is *doubtful* whether his thesis is based on fact. ∥ この計画がうまくいくかどうかは疑わしいと思う We're *dubious* about the success of this plan.
◆彼のアリバイには疑わしいところはない His alibi *is above suspicion*.
慣用表現 彼の説明に納得したわけではないが,疑わしきは罰せずだ I'm not fully contented with his explanations but *give him the benefit of the doubt*.

うたたね うたた寝 (口語的)snooze ⓒ, doze ⓒ; (特に日中の) nap ⓒ ∥彼は昼食の後よくうたた寝している He often *takes a snooze* after lunch.

うだつがあがらない うだつが上がらない
彼ももうベテランのはずなのに, うだつが上がらない(→ほとんど出世していない)ね He *has seldom received promotion* though he's very experienced.

うだるような うだるような暑さ *boiling* [*sweltering*] heat

うたれる 打たれる (感動する) be moved, be touched; (感銘を受ける) be impressed; (強い感情に襲われる) be struck //私は彼の小説に心打たれた I *was touched by* his novel. / ナイアガラの滝を見て私たちは畏敬(ぃ)の念に打たれた We *were struck with* awe at the sight of Niagara Falls.

うち¹ 内

❶【内部・内面】──图 inside ⓒ (↔outside) ──形 inside ──副 inside; (屋内に) indoors
そのドアは内からはあかない The door doesn't open from *the inside*.
窓が閉まっていたので熱気が内にこもっていた *The inside* was stuffy with hot air, because the windows had been closed.
明かりを消したので内も外も真っ暗だ I turned off the light, so it's dark *inside* [*indoors*] and out.
◆手の内を見せる show *one's hand*; lay *one's cards* on the table / 胸の内を明かす open *one's heart* / 彼は情熱を内に秘めている He has passion *in* him.

❷【期間内】──前 (…以内に) within; (…の間に) during ──接 while
2, 3日のうちにまた電話するよ I'll call you again *within a few days*. ❖in を用いると「2, 3日したら」の意味になる
朝のうちは晴れていたが, 今は曇っている It was sunny *during* the morning but it's cloudy now.
夏休みのうちに海外旅行がしたい I want to travel overseas *during* [*over*] the summer vacation.
若いうちにたくさん本を読むべきです You should read a lot of books *while* you're young.
◆明るいうちに(→暗くなる前に)帰ろう Let's go home *before dark*.

> 英作文ノート 「…しないうちに」の訳し方
> 暗くならないうちに花に水をやりなさい
> →✕Water the flowers *while it doesn't get dark*.
> →〇Water the flowers *before it gets dark*.
> ★「…しないうちに」は,「…する前に」の意味なので before を用いる.

❸【範囲内】(…の中で) of, in (❖通例 of の後は複数名詞, in の後は単数名詞); (…の中から) out of …; (…の間で) among, between (❖通例 among は 3 つ以上のものの間, between は 2 つのものの間を表す)
あなたたちのうちでいちばん年下はだれですか Which *of* you is the youngest?
彼女は私たちのクラスのうちでいちばん走るのが速い She runs (the) fastest *in* our class. / She is the fastest runner *in* our class.
この 3 つのうちから 1 つを選んでください Choose one (*out*) *of* these three.
この本は仲間うちでは人気がある This book is popular *among my friends*.
◆子供にとっては遊びも勉強のうちだ Playing is *part of* learning for children. / こんなのはけんかのうちには入らない This *doesn't count as* an argument.

❹【所属団体】
うちのチームはチームワークがとれていない *Our* team's teamwork is not good. / *Our* team lacks teamwork.

うち² 家

(建物) house (複 ～s [háuziz]); (家庭) home ⓤⓒ
うちの前に青い車が止まっていた A blue car was parked in front of *our house*.
うちに電話しなくちゃ I must call *home*.
きょうはうち, だれもいないんだ There's no one *at home* today.
大学に受かったらうちを出なさいよ You must leave *home* when you enter the university.
◆うちでは(→私の家族は)テレビをあまり見ません *My family* doesn't watch much TV. / うちは 5 人家族です *We* are a family of five. / たまにはうちに泊まりにおいでよ Come and stay overnight with *us* occasionally. / うちの人ったらすごいやきもち焼きなんですよ I must say *my man* is very jealous. / うちらはそんなこと言わないよ *We* don't say so.

うちあい 打ち合い・撃ち合い (テニスなどの) rally ⓒ; (銃などの) gunfight ⓒ

うちあげ 打ち上げ (ロケットなどの) blast-off ⓤⓒ, lift-off ⓤⓒ; (宴会) party ⓒ //打ち上げ10秒前! Ten seconds to *blast-off*! / 学園祭も終わったことだし打ち上げをしようよ The school festival is over; let's have *a party* to toast it.
‖打ち上げパーティー a celebration party / 打ち上げ花火 a (sky)rocket

うちあけばなし 打ち明け話 彼女の打ち明け話を聞かされて気が重くなった I got depressed as she let me in on her *innermost secrets*.

うちあける 打ち明ける (心を開く) open *one's heart*; (秘密を教える) confide 他; (白状する) confess 他自 //秘密を打ち明ける *confide one's secret* / あのわんぱく坊主が蛇が怖いと打ち明けた That naughty boy *confessed* that he was afraid of snakes. / 彼には悩みを打ち明けられる友達がいない He has no friend he can *open his heart to*.
◆真実を打ち明ける(→話す)べきだったのに You ought to have *told* the truth.

うちあげる 打ち上げる ❶【空中に】(ロケットなどを) launch 他, blast off; (花火などを) set* [let*] off; (野球で凡フライを) pop up //スペースシャトルはこの木曜に打ち上げられる The space shuttle *will be launched* this Thursday. / 多摩川で花火が打ち上げられた

Fireworks *were set off* on the Tama river.

❷【海岸に】wash up (❖通例受身で); (船などを) strand [他] //海岸には山のようなごみが打ち上げられていた A pile of garbage *was washed up* on the beach.

うちあわせ 打ち合わせ (会議) meeting [C]; (取り決め) arrangement [C][U] //打ち合わせはすみましたか Have you finished *the meeting*? ◆打ち合わせどおりにやってくれよ Do *as arranged.*

うちあわせる 打ち合わせる arrange [他] [自], make* an arrangement //卒業式の音楽について彼女と打ち合わせておくのを忘れないでね Don't forget to *arrange* with her about the music for the graduation ceremony. / この件については田島さんと打ち合わせておいたほうがいいね You should *make an arrangement* with Mr. Tajima about this matter.

うちいわい 内祝い (身内での祝い事) private [family] celebration [C]; (贈り物) a gift given on the occasion of a private [family] celebration

うちうち 内々 結婚式は内々で(→家族や親しい友達だけで)すませようと思っています We're going to celebrate our wedding *with only our families and close friends.*

うちおとす 撃ち落とす shoot* down //鳥を撃ち落とす *shoot down* birds

うちかえす 打ち返す (テニスで) return [他]; (殴り返す) hit* back

うちかつ 打ち勝つ (克服する) overcome* [他], get* over ..., conquer [他]; (野球で) outhit* [他] //困難[敵]に打ち勝つ *overcome* 「a difficulty [*one's* enemy] / 病に打ち勝つ *conquer* disease

うちがわ 内側 the inside ━内側の inside, inner (❖比較変化なし. 名詞の前で用いる) ━内側に[で] within, inside (❖within より口語的で比較的小さく囲まれた場所について用いる) //その部屋は内側からかぎがかかっている The room is locked from *the inside.* / 白線の内側にお立ちください Please stay *within* the white line.

うちき 内気 ━内気な (恥ずかしがる) shy, bashful; (臆病(おくびょう)で話をしない) timid //彼は内気すぎて初めて会ったときにはろくに話もできなかった He was so *shy* that we talked of almost nothing when we first met.

うちきる 打ち切る (止める) stop [他]; (突然止める) break* off; (話・会などを終わらせる) close [他] //交渉を打ち切る *break off* the negotiation / 母を怒らせたらこづかいを打ち切られてしまった As I made Mom angry, my pocket money *has been stopped.* / この話は打ち切りだ The matter *is closed.*

うちきん 内金 (手付金) partial payment [C], deposit [C] ◆内金として1万円払います I will pay you 10,000 yen *in advance.*

うちくだく 打ち砕く (粉々に砕く) smash [他]; (希望などを) dash [他], shatter [他] //最後の望みも打ち砕かれた My last hope *has been dashed.*

うちけし 打ち消し 〔文法〕negative [C]

うちけす 打ち消す (否定する) deny [他] //その政治家は疑惑を打ち消していたが結局罪を犯していたことが分かった The statesman *had denied* involvement in the scandal, but in the end he turned out to be guilty.

うちこむ 打ち込む ❶【打って入れる】drive* [他]; (金づちで) hammer [他] //地面にくいを打ち込む *drive* a stake *into* the ground / くさびをしっかり打ち込む *drive* a wedge home ◆ベーブ・ルースは観客席へ本塁打を打ち込んだ Babe Ruth *sent* a ball *into* the stands for a home run.

❷【没頭する】devote [dedicate] *oneself* to ... //彼は昼夜を分かたず研究に打ち込んだ He *devoted himself to* his study day and night.

❸【入力する】〔コンピュータ〕input* [他], type in //あすまでにこのデータを打ち込んでおいてくれ *Input* these data by tomorrow.

うちじに 討ち死に 討ち死にする *be killed in a battle*

うちだす 打ち出す (考えなどを示す)《公式的》put* forth; (プリンターに) print out //データをプリンターで打ち出す *print out* the data / 首相はその問題に対する解決策を打ち出した The prime minister *put forth* the solution to the problem.

うちたてる 打ち立てる 世界新記録を打ち立てる *set* [*establish*] a new world record

うちつける 打ち付ける (ぶつける) bang [他]; (くぎで留める) nail [他]; (風雨が) beat* [自] //彼は壁に頭を打ちつけていらだちを表した He *banged* his head against a wall to show his irritation. / その木箱のふたはくぎで打ちつけてあった The cover of the wooden box *was nailed down.*

うちでし 内弟子 (徒弟) apprentice [C]

うちとける 打ち解ける (心を開く) open up, come* out of *one's* shell //彼はなかなかうちとけない He *doesn't open up* easily. ◆彼らはすぐにうちとけた(→友達になった) They soon *made friends with* each other.

うちどころ 打ち所 転んだときにどうも打ちどころが悪かったみたいだ I must *have had a bad fall.*

[慣用表現] 彼のスピーチはすばらしかった. 非の打ちどころがないよ His speech was superb. *It cannot be faulted.*

うちとる 打ち取る 松坂は4番バッターを三振に打ち取った Matsuzaka *struck out* the clean-up hitter.

うちぬく 打ち抜く・撃ち抜く (貫通する) penetrate [他], pierce [他]; (弾が) shoot* through ... //弾は彼の頭を撃ち抜いた The bullet *penetrated* [*pierced*] his head./ (→彼は頭を撃ち抜かれた) He *was shot through* the head.

うちのめす 打ちのめす overwhelm [他] (❖通例受身で); (殴ってひどく傷つける) beat* up; (気絶させる) knock out //事故の知らせに彼女は打ちのめされた She *was overwhelmed* by the news of the accident. / 彼はやくざにさ

んざん打ちのめされた He *was beaten up* terribly by some *yakuza*.
うちのり 内法 (内側の寸法) inner measurement ⓒ; (内側の直径) inner diameter ⓒ
うちひしがれる 打ちひしがれる (感情に押しつぶされる) be overwhelmed, be overcome ∥彼女は両親の死に打ちひしがれていた She *was overwhelmed with grief* when her parents died.
うちべんけい 内弁慶 彼は内弁慶だ(→うちではいばるが外では臆病(おくびょう)だ) He's *bossy at home but meek outside*. (✦英語には He's a lion at home and a mouse abroad. (うちではライオンだが外ではネズミだ)という表現がある)
うちポケット 内ポケット inner [inside] pocket ⓒ
うちまく 内幕 (内部の情報) inside information ⓒ; (秘密) secret ⓒ ∥君にはあの会社の内幕を探ってきてもらいたい I'd like you to investigate *the inside information of the company*. / 彼はその事件の内幕を暴露した He *divulged the secrets* of the event.
うちまた 内股 (歩き方) a pigeon-toed walk ◆彼は内またた He *is pigeon-toed*.
うちみ 打ち身 bruise [brúːz] ⓒ, 【医学】contusion ⓒⓊ
うちみず 打ち水 暑さをやわらげようと庭に打ち水をした I *watered* the garden to cool down.
うちやぶる 打ち破る (負かす) beat* ⓗ, defeat ⓗ; (こわす) break* ⓗ; (粉々にこわす) shatter ⓗ ∥敵を打ち破る *beat* [*defeat*] *one's enemy* / ドアを打ち破る *break down* a door / 古い慣習を打ち破る *break* (*down*) an old custom / 窓を打ち破る *shatter* a window

うちゅう 宇宙

space Ⓤ; (大気圏外) outer space Ⓤ; (秩序ある体系としての) the cosmos; (森羅万象) the universe ── 宇宙の space, cosmic

宇宙に行く go into *space* / 宇宙のかなた deep *space* / 宇宙の神秘 the secrets of *the universe*

∥宇宙開発 space development / 宇宙開発事業団 the National Space Development Agency / 宇宙科学 space science / 宇宙科学者 a space scientist / 宇宙空間 outer space / 宇宙産業 space industry / 宇宙時代 the Space Age, the space age / 宇宙食 space food / 宇宙人 an alien, an extraterrestrial (✦E.T.と略すこともある) / 宇宙ステーション a space station / 宇宙生物学 space biology / 宇宙船 a spaceship, a (space)craft, a space vehicle / 宇宙線 cosmic rays / 宇宙船地球号 spaceship earth / 宇宙探査 space exploration / 宇宙探査船 a space probe / 宇宙飛行 a space flight / 宇宙飛行士 an astronaut / 宇宙服 a spacesuit / 宇宙兵器 a space weapon / 宇宙遊泳 a space walk / 宇宙旅行 space travel / 宇宙ロケット a space rocket / 宇宙論 cosmology / 航空宇宙産業 aerospace / 小宇宙 a microcosm / 大宇宙 the macrocosm

うちょうてん 有頂天 入試に受かったので私は有頂天になっていた As I passed the entrance exam, I *felt on top of the world*.
うちよせる 打ち寄せる wash ⓗⓘ; (穏やかにひたひたと) lap ⓗⓘ; (連続的に) beat* ⓘ (✦常に副詞・前置詞句を伴う); (波が砕ける) break* ⓘ ∥波が岸辺に打ち寄せていた The waves *were washing* [*lapping*] (against) the shore. / (→ 激しく) The waves *were pounding* against the shore. / 波が岩に打ち寄せていた Waves *were beating* [*breaking*] against the rock.
うちわ¹ 内輪 これは内輪の話だよ This is just *between you and me*. / 彼の小説は内輪うけしかしなかった(→友人にしか評価されなかった) His novel *was appreciated* only *by his friends*. / 彼らは内輪もめばかりしている They *always quarrel among themselves*. / 内輪の恥をさらすようなことはしないでくれ Don't *wash our dirty linen in public*. (✦「汚れた下着を人前で洗うな」の意味) / 内輪の問題(→家庭の問題)に首をつっ込まないでほしい You shouldn't poke your nose into *our family's affairs*.
うちわ² 団扇 (round) fan ⓒ
[慣用表現] 宝くじが当たったおじは左うちわで暮らしている An uncle of mine *is on easy street* as he won a lottery.
うちわけ 内訳 breakdown ⓒ; (明細) details

うつ¹ 打つ

❶ たたく・ぶつ　　　　　　strike; hit; beat
❷ 水・網を
❸ うどん・そばなどを
❹ 感銘・感動を与える　　　　strike, impress
❺ 電報を　　　　　　　　　telegraph

❶ [たたく・ぶつ・ぶつける]【公式的】strike* ⓗⓘ; hit* ⓗⓘ; beat* ⓗⓘ; knock ⓘⓗ; bang ⓘ; slap ⓘ

> strike: 強い一撃を,いきなり与えることをいうかたい語.
> hit: ねらいを定めてたたく,または一撃を与えること.
> beat: 連続して打つこと.
> knock: しばしば偶然の結果として打つこと.また,ドアなどをたたくこと.
> bang: 大きな音を立てて打つこと.
> slap: 平手でびしゃっと打つこと.

彼はラケットでボールを打った He *struck* [*hit*] the ball with a racket.
連中はバットで彼を打った They *struck* [*hit*, *beat*] him with bats.
彼はきょうの試合でホームランを2本打った He *hit* two home runs in today's game. (✦「ヒットを打つ」は get a hit)
彼女はハンマーでくぎを打った She *hit* a nail with a hammer.
時計が3時を打った The clock *struck* three.
彼女は心臓が速く打つのを感じた She felt her heart *beating* fast.
転んだ拍子に床に頭を打った I *knocked*

[banged, hit] my head on the floor when I fell.
その母親は息子の顔をぴしゃりと打った The mother *slapped* 「her son in the face [her son's face].
◆手紙をタイプで打つ *type* a letter / (野球で)僕が1番を打つ I'm the first to *bat.* / 取れないようにしっかりとくぎを打ってください *Nail* it *down* so it won't come off.
❷【水・網を】
川に網を打つ *cast* [*throw*] a net in the river
涼を求めて庭に水を打った We *sprinkled* water on the garden to make us feel cool.
❸【うどん・そばなどを】
うどんを打つ *make udon* noodles (from dough)
❹【感銘・感動を与える】(感銘・強い印象を与える) strike* [他], impress [他]; (感動・同情させる) touch [他], 《公式的》move [他]
彼女の優しさに打たれた I *was struck* [*impressed, touched, moved*] by her kindness.
❺【電報を】telegraph [他][自], 《米》wire [他][自]
彼は息子にすぐに家に帰れと電報を打った He *telegraphed* [*wired*] his son to come home at once.
◆私たちは彼らに祝電を打った We *sent* them *our congratulations by wire.*
❻【注射を】
医者がインフルエンザ予防の注射を打ってくれた The doctor *gave* me an injection against the flu.
❼【印・点・番号などを】(点を) dot [他]; (番号を) number [他]
i に点を打つのを忘れないで Don't forget to *dot* the "i."
我々の商品には通し番号が打たれている Our products *are* serially *numbered.*
❽【その他】
巧妙な手を打つ *make* an excellent move / ばくちを打つ *gamble*
あの子にいたずらさせないように何か手を打ってくださいよ *Do something* to keep that child out of mischief.
赤ん坊は時々寝返りを打った The baby sometimes *turned* (*over*) *in bed.*
[会]「1万でどうです」「分かった, 1万で手を打とう」"How about 10,000?" "OK, *let's call it* 10,000."
[慣用表現] 打てば響くような返事 a *quick* [*prompt*] reply / この出来事が私と彼との交際にピリオドを打った This event *put a period to* my relationship with him. / 水を打ったようにしんとしている You could hear a pin drop. (❖「ピンの落ちる音でも聞こえる」の意味)

うつ² 撃つ shoot* [他][自], fire [他][自]
ピストルで撃つ *shoot* with a pistol / ライフル銃を撃つ *fire* a rifle
動くな, 撃つぞ Freeze [Halt, Hold it], or *I'll shoot!*
猟師はクマを撃った The hunter *shot* a bear.

うつ³ 討つ (かたきを) avenge [他], revenge [他] (❖avenge は正義の罰を加える意味で, revenge は個人的なうらみを晴らす意味だが, 現在はほとんど区別なく用いられる); (襲う) assault [他]; (殺す) kill [他] ∥きっと君のかたきは討ってやる *I'll avenge* you. / 彼は殺された父のかたきを討った He *avenged* [*got revenge for*] his father's murder.

うつ⁴ 鬱 (鬱病)〖医学〗depression [U]

うつうつ 鬱々 鬱々とした日々が続いた(→何日もひどく憂鬱(ゆう)だった) I was *deeply depressed* for days.

うっかり (不注意で) carelessly; (軽率に) thoughtlessly; (ぼんやりして) absent-mindedly ∥彼はうっかり秘密をもらしてしまった He *carelessly* told the secret. ◆彼女との待ち合わせを忘れるなんて君もうっかりしているね It's *careless* of you to forget an appointment with her. / 彼はうっかりミスが多すぎる He makes too many *careless mistakes.*
[会]「ねえ, あの本持ってきてくれた?」「あっ, ごめん. うっかりしていた(→忘れていた)よ」"Hey, did you bring me the book?" "Oh, I'm sorry. I *forgot.*"

うつくしい 美しい

beautiful (↔ugly); pretty; lovely; good-looking; handsome; (華麗な) glorious; (甘美な) sweet; (場所などが絵のように) picturesque [pìktʃərésk]

> beautiful: 美しいことをいう最も一般的な語. 女性・物・場所などに用いる.
> pretty: 若い女性や物・場所のかわいらしいこと.
> lovely: 女性・物・場所などが上品で心の温かみを感じさせること.
> good-looking: 容姿のよいことを意味し, 男女どちらにも用いる.
> handsome: 男性の容姿のよいことをいい, 主に書き言葉. 女性に対しても用いるがその場合は知性・りりしさを備えたという意味.

美しい友情 a *beautiful* friendship
彼女はなんて美しい女性だろう What a *beautiful* [*lovely*] lady she is!
あちらこちらに美しいチューリップが咲いている *Beautiful* [*Pretty, Lovely*] tulips are flowering here and there.
あんなふうな美しい家に住んでみたいな I wish I had a *beautiful* house like that one.
今までこんなに美しい光景を見たことがない I have never seen such a *beautiful* [*lovely, glorious, picturesque*] sight.
彼女の美しい声が好きだ I like her *beautiful* [*lovely, sweet*] voice.
◆彼女は本当に美しい She is *a* real *beauty.* / 彼は心の美しい男性だ He is a *kind-hearted* man. / He has *a heart of gold.* / 彼女の髪は美しくウエーブして肩にかかっている Her hair waves *beautifully* over her shoulders.

うつくしさ 美しさ beauty [U]; (清らかさ) purity [U] ∥自然の美しさは都会に住む人々をいなかに引きつける *The beauty* of nature attracts city dwellers to the countryside.

うつし 写し (手書き・機械による) copy [C]; (正副2通のうちの副) duplicate [C]; (複写) photocopy ⓒ /この論文の写しをとってください Please make *a copy* of this thesis.

うつす¹ 移す

❶【移動させる】move ⓗ; shift ⓗ; transfer ⓗ

> move: 移動させるという意味で最も一般的な語.
> shift: 特に少しだけずらすことを意味する.
> transfer: 別の場所, 地位などに移し替えることを意味する.

あすの会議に備えてその机をこっちへ移してください *Move* the desks here for tomorrow's meeting.

彼女は重心を右足に移した She *shifted* her weight to the right foot.

お茶はポットに移しておいたよ I've *transferred* the tea into the pot.

本籍を東京から沖縄に移した I *transferred* my family register from Tokyo to Okinawa.(✤英米には戸籍制度がない)

❷【病気などを】give* ⓗ; (感染させる) infect ⓗ

君にかぜをうつされちゃったみたいだ I'm afraid you *gave* me a cold.

❸【実現させる】

準備が整いしだい計画を実行に移そう We'll carry *out* the plan as soon as we get ready.

うつす² 映す (映画などを) project ⓗ; (反射する) reflect ⓗ

スライドを映しながら説明しましょう I'll explain *by* [*while*] *projecting* some slides.

湖が美しい夕日を映していた The lake *reflected* the beautiful sunset.

◆ 私は自分の姿を鏡に映してみた(→鏡に映る自分を見た) I just looked at myself in the mirror.

うつす³ 写す (複写する) copy ⓗ ⓘ, make* a copy; (写真を撮る) take* ⓗ

君のノートを写したいんだけど May I *copy* your notebook?

すみません, 写真を写していただけますか Excuse me, could you *take* our picture?

旅先で写した写真を見せてあげるよ I'll show you some pictures that I *took* on the trip.

うっすら ─うっすらと (わずかに) slightly, lightly; (薄く) thinly; (まばらに) sparsely; (かすかに) vaguely, faintly /父のあごにはうっすらとひげが生えている Father's beard grows *sparsely* on the chin./ 富士山はうっすらと雪化粧していた Mt. Fuji was *lightly* covered with snow. ◆ 子供のころのことはもううっすらとしか覚えていない I have a *vague* memory of my childhood now.

うっせき 鬱積 鬱積された不満 one's pent-up discontent / 人々の心中に堕落した政治家への怒りが鬱積している People *are smoldering with* anger against the corrupt politicians.

うっそう 鬱蒼 私はうっそうとした森の中を歩いた I walked in the *dense* [*thick*] forest.

うったえ 訴え (訴訟) suit ⓗ ⓘ; (世論などへの) appeal ⓗ ⓘ; (声高な主張) cry ⓗ /住民の訴えは棄却された The inhabitants' *suit* was dismissed./ 有権者の訴えに耳を貸さない政治家なんて役に立たない Politicians who won't listen to *the appeals* of the voters are useless.

うったえる 訴える

❶【訴訟を起こす・告発する】sue ⓗ; charge ⓗ; accuse ⓗ

> sue: 特に賠償金などを求めて訴訟を起こすことを指す.
> charge: 警察などが告発するという意味.
> accuse: 人を非難することに重点が置かれ, 必ずしも公的機関に訴えることを意味しない.

彼は殺人罪で訴えられた He was 「*charged with* [*accused of*] murder.

【sue＋名＋for 名】(✤sue A for B は「Bのかどで A を訴える」と「B を求めて A を訴える」という2つの意味がある) 彼はその会社を契約違反で訴えた He *sued* the company *for* breach of contract./ 彼らは損害賠償を求めて会社を訴えた They *sued* the company *for* damages.

◆ 彼は詐欺で訴えられた He *was taken to court for* fraud./ その歌手はある雑誌を名誉毀損(きそん)で訴えた The singer *brought an action* [*a suit*] *against* a magazine *for* libel.

❷【不平・苦情などを言う】(不平・苦情などを) complain ⓘ, (援助などを) appeal ⓘ, make* an appeal

彼は腹痛を訴えた He *complained of* a stomachache.

彼女は店長に値段が高すぎると訴えた She *complained* to the shopkeeper that the price was too high.

生徒たちは学校に校則の改正を訴えた The students *appealed to* the school *for* modification of the school rules.

◆ その少年は訴えるような目で私の方を見た The boy gave me an *appealing* look.

❸【その力を頼りにする】(よくない手段に) resort to ...

彼は武力に訴えることに反対している He is opposed to *resorting to* force.

◆ 権力に訴える have resort to authority

❹【人の心に】appeal ⓘ (✤進行形にはできない); (感動させる) move ⓗ, touch ⓗ

感情[理性・良心]に訴える *appeal to* emotions [reason, conscience]

この小説は若い読者に強く訴えるものがあった This novel *appealed* strongly *to* young readers.

うっちゃり 〔相撲〕 an *utchari*, a technique for toppling over the opponent outside at the edge of the ring [*dohyo*]

うっちゃる (ほうっておく) leave* ⓗ; (無視する) neglect ⓗ /あの子ったら宿題をうっちゃって(→そのままにして)いったいどこへ行ったんだろう Where on earth did he go, *leaving* the assignment?

うつつ 現 (現実) reality ⓘ

[慣用表現] うちの兄は映画にうつつを抜かしている(→映画中毒だ) My brother *is addicted to* movies. / 彼は街で知り合った若い女性にうつつを抜かしている(→夢中になっている) He *is crazy about* a girl he met on the street.

うつて 打つ手 それに関しては打つ手がない *There's nothing we can do* about it.

うってかわる 打って変わる 前日までの荒天とは打って変わって(→対照的に)運動会の当日は好天に恵まれた It cleared up the very day of the athletic meet *in contrast to* the rough weather we'd had till the day before.

うってつけ ―うってつけの (まさにそのための) very (❖名詞の前で用いる); (完璧(かんぺき)な) perfect; (理想的な) ideal ∥佐藤さんはその仕事にうってつけの人物だ Mr. Sato is the *very* person for the job. / その役を演じるのにうってつけの男を見つけた I found the *perfect* man to play the part.

うっとうしい (憂鬱(ゆううつ)な) gloomy; (いらいらさせられる) annoying ∥うっとうしい天気が続いています We have a series of *gloomy* weather. ◆日曜日なのに仕事をしなくちゃならないなんて, うっとうしいなあ It's *a nuisance* that I have to work even on Sunday.

うっとり 彼はその音楽にうっとりと聴きほれた He *was fascinated to* listen to the music. / 彼女はうっとりとした表情で彼を見ていた She looked at him *with an enchanted look on her face*. / 私はその絵の美しさにうっとりしていた I *was enchanted with* the beauty of the picture.

うつびょう 鬱病 depression [U] [C] ―鬱病の depressed ∥鬱病になる *get depressed*; *suffer from depression*
‖鬱病患者 a depressive

うつぶせ 俯せ そのベッドの上にうつぶせに寝てください Lie on the bed「*on your face* [*face down*], please.

うっぷん 鬱憤 (欲求不満) (pent-up) frustration [U]; (腹立ち) anger [U], 《公式的》 spleen [U] ∥人に当たり散らしてうっぷんを晴らすのはよくない It's wrong to「*vent your frustration* [*let off steam*] by taking out your anger on others.

ウツボ 〔魚〕moray [C]

うつむく 俯く (下を向く) look down; (うなだれる) hang* *one's* head ∥彼は先生にしかられてうつむいてしまった He *hung his head* because he was scolded by his teacher.
◆彼女はうつむきかげんに歩く(→やや前かがみになる) She *bends a bit* while walking.

うつらうつら うつらうつらしているところに電話が鳴った I *was*「*half asleep* [*dozing*] when the phone rang. ➩ うとうと

うつり 映り 彼は写真映りがよい He is *photogenic*. / 彼はテレビ映りが悪い He is *not telegenic*. / このテレビは映りが悪い This television *doesn't have a clear picture*.

うつりかわり 移り変わり (変化) change [C] [U] ∥彼は季節の移り変わりにむとんちゃくだ He doesn't care about *the change* of seasons.
◆このところ政局の移り変わりが激しい The political situation *is changing* a lot these days.

うつりかわる 移り変わる change [自], come* and go* ∥生活様式は時代とともに移り変わる Lifestyles *change* with the times.

うつりぎ 移り気 ―移り気な (浮気な) fickle; (気まぐれな) capricious ∥移り気な男 a *fickle* man / 彼女は移り気な性格で何事もやりとげられない She has a *capricious* nature and can't finish anything.

うつる¹ 移る

❶【移動する】(移動する・引っ越す) move [自], 《主に英・公式的》remove [自]; (転任・転校・移籍する) transfer [自]
新居へ移るのはいつですか When *are* you *moving* into your new house?
窓側の席に移ってもいいですか May I *move* to the window seat?
その選手はジャイアンツからスワローズへ移った That player *transferred* from the Giants to the Swallows.
◆私の兄は大阪支社から東京本社に移った(→転勤させられた) My brother *was transferred* from the Osaka branch to the head office in Tokyo.

❷【変わる】change [自], turn [自]; (進む) move on, go* on; (時が) go by, pass [自]; (知らぬ間に) drift [自]
話題はサッカーに移った Our talk *changed* [*turned, drifted*] to soccer.
次の議題に移りましょう Shall we *move* [*go*] *on* to the next topic? / Shall we *proceed* to the next topic?
彼女の興味はロックからジャズに移った Her interest *has turned* from rock to jazz.
時が移り, 私はそのうわさを忘れてしまった As time *went by*, I forgot about the rumor.

❸【感染・伝染する】―[動] (人が病気になる) catch* [他] ―[形] (病気が伝染する) infectious, contagious (❖infectious は特に空気感染, contagious は接触感染するもの), 《口語的》 catching (❖名詞の前では用いない)
父のかぜがうつった I *caught* a cold from my father.
コレラは人にうつる Cholera is *infectious* [*catching*].
◆インフルエンザは人にうつりやすい(→簡単に広がる) Flu *spreads* easily.

❹【その他】
石油ストーブの炎がカーテンに移った The flame of the oil heater *spread* to the curtain.
靴の色が白い靴下に移ってしまった The color of the shoes *rubbed off onto* my white socks.
ほかの食べ物ににおいが移らないようにラップをしなさい Put it in plastic wrap so that the other foods *don't pick up* its smell.
警察は事件解決に向けて早速行動に移った(→行動をとった) The police *took action* immediately to solve the case.
情が移る前にその子犬を誰かにあげなさい Give the puppy away to somebody before

you become attached to it.

うつる² 映る
❶【反射する】be reflected
湖には満月が映っていた The full moon *was reflected* in the lake.

❷【映像が現れる】
カーテンに自分の影が映っていた My shadow *appeared against* the curtain.
テレビが映らないよ(→作動しない) This TV *doesn't work*.
このテレビはいくつか映らないチャンネルがある This TV *doesn't get* several channels.

❸【見える】
大都会に引っ越してきた当初は目に映るものがみんな新鮮だった Everything I *saw* was new when I moved to the metropolis.
私の目には彼の行いは利己的に映った(→私には思われた) It *seemed* to me that his deed was selfish.

うつる³ 写る
君が写っているのはこの写真だけですか Is this the only photo you *are in*?
この写真はきれいに写っている This picture *has come [turned] out* well. / その写真にはUFOのような物が写っていた There was something like a UFO in the picture.

うつろ ──うつろな (空虚な) hollow; (無関心な) blank; (ぼんやりした) vacant / うつろな表情 a *vacant* look / 何だか目がうつろだよ Your eyes are somewhat *hollow*.

うつろう 移ろう (変わる) change ⓐ

うつわ 器 (入れ物) container ⓒ; (皿) dish ⓒ ◆大きな器の人 a *competent* person / あいつは総理大臣の器じゃない(→総理大臣に適した男ではない) He's not *the man for* a prime minister.

うで 腕
❶【人などの】arm ⓒ (❖通例肩から手首までを指すが、手首より先(hand)を含むこともある。また、ひじから手首までの前腕は forearm, 肩からひじまでの上腕は upper arm という); (クレーンなどの) boom ⓒ ⓓ

《腕を》
腕を曲げる[伸ばす, 上げる, 下げる] bend [stretch, raise, lower] one's arm(s)
彼は私の腕をつかんだ He caught [seized] me *by the arm*. / He caught [seized] my *arm*.
彼は腕を組んで座っていた He was sitting *with his arms folded*.
僕たちは腕を組んで通りを歩いた We walked *arm in arm* along the street.
◆彼女は腕をまくって(→そでをまくり上げて)食器を洗い始めた She *rolled up her sleeves* and began to wash the dishes.

《腕が・は》
兄の腕はとても太い My brother's *arms* are very thick.
彼は肩幅が広く腕が長い He has broad shoulders and long *arms*.
きのうから左の腕が痛い I have had a pain in *my left arm* since yesterday.

《腕に・の》
彼は右腕に傷跡がある He has a scar on *his right arm*.
彼女はバッグを腕にかけた She slung her bag over *her arm*.
彼女はぬいぐるみのクマを両腕に抱きしめた She held her teddy bear in *her arms*.
彼女は事故で腕の骨を折った She broke (a bone in) *her arm* in the accident.

❷【技量】(技術) skill ⓤ ⓒ; (能力) ability ⓤ ⓒ
彼はしばらく会わないうちにすっかりギターの腕をあげた He greatly *improved his skill in* playing the guitar since I last saw him a while ago.
この店の成功は君の料理の腕しだいだ This restaurant's success depends on your cooking *skills*.
ここが腕の見せどころだ This is *a chance to show my skill*.
◆彼は腕のよい職人になるでしょう He will make a *good* craftsman. / その歯医者は無愛想だが腕は確かだ Though the dentist is unsociable, he is *skillful*. / 最近ボウリングの腕が落ちてしまった I've gotten rusty in bowling these days. / そのコンテストでは素人の料理人たちが腕を競い合った Amateur cooks *competed with each other* in the competition.

慣用表現 将棋だったら腕に覚えがある(→自信がある) I *am confident of my skill* in playing shogi. / これは私が腕によりをかけて作ったカレーです I *put all my cooking skills* into making this special curry. / その中華料理店では中国人シェフが腕をふるっている Chinese chefs *show off their cooking skills* in the Chinese restaurant. / 彼女はレッスンを受けてバイオリンの腕を磨いた She *polished up [improved]* her violin playing by taking lessons.

うできき 腕利き ──腕利きの skilled, skillful / 腕利きの弁護士 a *skilled* lawyer

うでぐみ 腕組み 彼は腕組みをして考え込んでいた He was deep in thought *with his arms folded*. (❖「腕組みをする」という動作は fold one's arms という)

うでくらべ 腕比べ・腕競べ 私は兄とテニスの腕比べをした I *competed with* my brother in tennis.

うでずく 腕ずく 彼らは私の財布を腕ずくで(→暴力を振るって)奪った They robbed me of the purse *by using force*.

うでずもう 腕相撲 arm wrestling ⓤ ◆友人と腕相撲をした I *arm-wrestled (with)* my friend.

うでたてふせ 腕立て伏せ 《米》push-up ⓒ, 《英》press-up ⓒ / 腕立てふせを50回する do 50 *push-ups*

うでだめし 腕試し 私は腕試しに TOEIC の試験を受けてみた(→試験で能力を確かめてみた) I *tried my hand [skill]* at the TOEIC exam.

うでっぷし 腕っ節 彼は腕っぷしが強い He is *muscular [strong]*. / あいつは腕っぷしの強さが自慢だ He's proud of *his (physical)*

うでどけい 腕時計 watch, wristwatch ‖腕時計をする put on *a watch* / デジタルの腕時計 *a digital watch* / クォーツ式腕時計 *a watch* with a quartz movement

うでまえ 腕前 (技能) skill, hand; (スポーツの) technique ‖彼女はみんなにスキーの腕前を披露した She showed everybody *her* skiing *technique*.
◆サッカーについては彼はかなりの腕前だ(→上手だ) He's fairly *good at* soccer.

うでまくら 腕まくら 彼は腕まくらをしてテレビを見ていた He was watching TV, *resting his head on his arm*.

うでまくり 腕まくり 私は腕まくりをして片付けに取りかかった I *rolled up my sleeves* and started cleaning up.

うでわ 腕輪 bracelet

うてん 雨天 遠足は雨天決行します We *carry out* the school excursion *even if it rains*. / 祭りは雨天順延の予定です *If it rains,* the festival is to *be postponed till the first fine day*. / 試合は雨天中止になりました The game was *rained out*.

うど 慣用表現 あいつはうどの大木だ(→大きいだけで役に立たない) He's *large but good for nothing*.

うとい 疎い (よく知らない) know* little of …; (無知である) be ignorant of … ‖彼女は機械にはうとい She *knows little of* machines. / 彼は世事にうとすぎる He's *too ignorant of the world*. ◆このあたりの地理にはうといんです I'm *a stranger* around here.
ことわざ 去る者は日々にうとし ⇒さる(去る)

うとうと うとうとしているところに話しかけられた I *was half asleep* when I was talked to. / 祖父は暖炉のそばに座ってうとうとしていた Granddad sat *nodding off* by the fireplace.

うとましい 疎ましい (好みに合わない) disagreeable; (不快な) unpleasant
◆彼はだんだん彼女がうとましくなってきた He gradually began to *feel annoyed* by her.

うどん udon (noodles)
‖うどん粉(小麦粉) wheat flour / 手打ちうどん handmade [homemade] noodles

うどんは小麦粉を練って延ばしたものを細長く切っためんの一種です。しょうゆ・みりんなどで味つけしただし汁で食べます。うどんにのせる様々な具によってそれぞれ独特の名前がありますが、どのうどんにもネギやトウガラシの薬味を添えるのが一般的です。
Udon is a kind of noodle made from dough that is kneaded, rolled out, and sliced into long strips. *Udon* is served in a soup flavored with soy sauce and *mirin* (sweet sake). It is full of variety in its flavor and toppings, each of which have special names. But common to any kind of *udon* is the use of Japanese leek (or green onions) and red pepper as condiments.

うとんじる 疎んじる (避ける) avoid; (近寄らない) stay away from …; (無視する) neglect ‖彼はとても無作法でみんなからうとんじられていた He was so rude that everyone *avoided* [*stayed away from*] him. / 彼は上司にうとんじられていた He *was* rather *neglected* by his boss.

うながす 促す 環境問題に対する自覚を促す *promote* awareness of environmental problems / 夏子はみなに促されて舞台の前に出た *Urged* by everyone, Natsuko stepped forward on the stage. / 彼らは植物の成長を促す(→助ける)薬の開発に成功した They succeeded to develop a chemical to *help* plants grow faster. / 交通事故が増えてきているため警察は市民に注意を促した The police *called* citizens' *attention* to the increasing traffic accidents.

うなぎ 鰻 eel (複 ～, ～s) ‖ウナギのかば焼き *a spitchcocked* [split and grilled] *eel* (seasoned with sugar and soy sauce) (❖ spitchcock は「(ウナギなど)を裂いて直火(じか)で焼く」の意味)
‖ウナギ屋 an eel restaurant / 電気ウナギ an electric eel
慣用表現 僕のいる寮の部屋はうなぎの寝床だ My dorm room is *long and narrow*. / 当時東京の地価はうなぎ登りだった The land prices in Tokyo *were soaring* [*skyrocketing*] then.

うなされる ずいぶんうなされていたけど、悪い夢でも見たのかい You *groaned much while* (*you were*) *asleep*; did you have some kind of a nightmare?

うなじ 項 the nape of *one's* neck

うなじゅう う重 (an) *unaju*, barbecued eel on rice served in a lacquered lunchbox

うなずく 頷く nod ‖全員が彼女に賛成してうなずいた Everyone *nodded* in agreement with her. / そういう事情だったのであれば、君がこの話を断ったのもうなずける Under such circumstances, I *can understand* why you have rejected the offer.

うなだれる (恥ずかしさ・罪悪感などで) hang* *one's* head ‖彼はうなだれて何も言わなかった He *hung his head* and didn't say anything.

うなり 唸り (人の) groan, moan; (犬などの) growl [grául]; (とどろき) roar ‖負傷した男性はうなり声をあげた The injured man gave *a groan* [*moan*]. / 犬は低いうなり声をあげた The dog gave a low *growl*. / 機械はうなりをあげて動き始めた The machine began to work with *a roar*.

うなる 唸る (人が) groan, moan; (犬などが) growl; (とどろく) roar ‖患者は痛くてうなっていた The patient *was groaning* [*moaning*] with pain. / 犬が僕に向かってうなった A dog *growled* [*snarled*] at me. (❖snarl は「歯をむいてうなる」の意味) / キーを回すとエンジンがうなった The engine *roared* as I turned the key. / 木々の間を抜けて風のうなる音が聞こえる I can hear the wind *moaning* through the trees.

◆その芝居は観客をうならせた（→感動させた）The play *impressed* the audience.

慣用表現 彼には金がうなるほどある He has *a whole lot of* money./ He is *rolling in* money./ He has money *to burn*.

うに 海胆・雲丹 sea urchin C

うぬぼれ 自惚れ （過大評価）conceit U; （高慢）pride U; （見え・虚栄心）vanity U ∥彼はうぬぼれの強いやつだ He is *full of conceit*./ He is a *conceited* guy./ うぬぼれがあるのか彼女は現実を判断できない *Her pride* blinds her to reality.

うぬぼれる 自惚れる be conceited; （鼻にかける）be vain; （自慢する）be proud; （その気になる）flatter *oneself* ∥うぬぼれるな Don't *be conceited*./ Don't *think too highly of yourself*./ 彼は自分の容姿(ᆢ)にうぬぼれている He *is very vain about* his looks./ 彼らは自分たちの成功にうぬぼれている They *are too proud of* their success./ 彼女は自分は大女優だとうぬぼれている She *flatters herself* that she is a great actress.

うね 畝 （畑の）ridge C; （編み物などの）rib U ∥畝織り[模様] ribbing

うねうね ──うねうねした（道・川などが）winding ──うねうねする wind* [wáind] ⦿ ∥うねうねした道[川] a *winding* road [river]/ 小道は森の中をうねうねと続いていた The path *wound* through the forest.

うねり （波などの）a [the] swell, roll C; （丘などの）undulation C U ∥（波の）大きなうねり *a* heavy *swell*

うねる （道・川などが）wind* [wáind] ⦿, meander ⦿; （波・海などが）roll ⦿, swell* ⦿; （土地などが）《公式的》undulate ⦿, roll ⦿ ∥ゆるやかにうねる丘 gently *undulating* [*rolling*] hills / 波はうねって岸へ打ち寄せていた Waves *were rolling* onto the shore./ 川はその都市の中をうねりながら流れていた The river *wound* [*meandered*] through the city.

うのはな 卯の花 《植物》deutzia U; （おから）okara, a by-product of making tofu

うのみ 鵜呑み 彼は彼女の話をうのみにした He *swallowed* her story./ 新聞に書いてあることをうのみにしてはいけない Don't *blindly believe* what newspapers say.

うのめたかのめ 鵜の目鷹の目 その記者は鵜の目鷹の目で新聞のネタを探している The journalist is *on the lookout for* news stories.

うは 右派 the right, the right wing 《単数または複数扱い》; （党員）rightist C

うば 乳母 nanny C

うばいあう 奪い合う scramble ⦿ ⦿ ∥よい席を奪い合う *scramble* to get good seats / 選手たちは激しくボールを奪い合った Players *scrambled* heatedly *for* possession of the ball.

うばいかえす 奪い返す get* back; （軍事的に）retake* ⦿, recapture ⦿

うばいとる 奪い取る seize ⦿; （だまして）cheat ⦿ ∥警官は犯人から凶器を奪い取った The police officer *seized* the weapon from the criminal.

うばう 奪う

❶ [盗み取る] （強奪する）rob ⦿; （盗む）steal* ⦿ ⦿; （ひったくる）snatch ⦿

その男は老婦人から財布を奪った The man *robbed* an old lady *of* her purse.

私はきのうかばんを奪われた I *was robbed of* my bag yesterday.

> 英作文ノート 「…から」≠ **from**
> 彼らはその学生から時計を奪った
> →×They *robbed* his watch *from* the student.
> →○They *robbed* the student *of* his watch.
> ★「人・場所から物を奪う」は《rob＋人・場所＋of＋物》となり、前置詞fromは用いない。なお、robは力ずくで奪うという意味だが、stealはこっそり盗むという意味で、They stole his watch. （彼らは彼の時計を盗んだ）のように使う。

❷ [取り上げる] take* ⦿, deprive ⦿; （財産などを）《公式的》dispossess ⦿; （人命を）claim ⦿, kill ⦿

独裁者は市民から政治的権利を奪った The dictator *deprived* citizens *of* their political rights.

警官は強盗からナイフを奪った The police officer *took* the knife *away from* the robber.

その戦争は多くの人命を奪った The war *took* a heavy toll of lives.

◆鉄道のストライキで多くの通勤客の足が奪われた The rail strike *inconvenienced* many commuters.

❸ [心・注意を] （魅了する）fascinate ⦿, absorb ⦿, take* ⦿; （引きつける）attract ⦿

彼女の美しさに彼は心を奪われた He *was fascinated* by her beauty./ Her beauty *fascinated* him.

彼らはその絵の美しい色使いに目を奪われた The beautiful color of the painting *attracted their attention*.

うばぐるま 乳母車 《米》baby carriage [buggy] C, 《英》pram C; （折りたたみの）《米》stroller C

うぶ 初 ──うぶな （世間知らずの）naive; （純真な）innocent; （経験がない）inexperienced ∥彼はうぶだったので、だまされていることに気づかなかった He was too *naive* to realize that they were deceiving him.

うぶげ 産毛 down U, 《口語的》fuzz U

うぶごえ 産声 the first cry (of a new born baby) ∥産声をあげる give *one's* first *cry*; (→生まれる) be born

うぶゆ 産湯 the first bath (of a new born baby) ∥赤ん坊に産湯を使わせる give a newborn baby *his* [*her*] *first bath*

うま¹ 馬 （一般的な総称）horse C; （雌馬）mare C; （雄の子馬）colt C; （雌の子馬）filly C; （幼馬）foal C; （小型の馬）pony C

馬に乗る ride [get on, mount] *a horse* (❖ get on, mount は「馬にまたがる動作」をいう) /

うま

馬から降りる「get off [dismount] *a horse*／馬から落ちる fall off *a horse*／馬にくらをつける put a saddle on *a horse*／馬を調教する train *a horse*
その馬が鼻の差で優勝した The *horse* won by a nose.
‖馬小屋 stables／馬面 a horseface／当て馬(候補) a stalking horse／穴馬 a dark horse／競走馬 a racehorse／種馬 a stallion, (集合的)stud
慣用表現 彼は仕事で生き馬の目を抜くような競争を強(し)いられている He has been forced into a *dog-eat-dog* competition in his work. (❖ dog-eat-dog は「すさまじく争う」「仲間うちで殺し合う」という意味)／彼らはうまが合うようだ They seem to *be on good terms with* each other.／私は彼女とはどうもうまが合わない Somehow I *can't get along well with* her.／そんなどこの馬の骨とも知れないやつとはつきあうな Don't go around with somebody *you don't really know about*.
ことわざ 今の彼に何を言っても馬の耳に念仏だ No matter what you say to him now, *it's like talking to a wall*.

うま² 午 (十二支の第7番目) the Horse ⇒ え と

うまい 旨い

❶【味がよい】delicious; good, nice; tasty
  delicious: 味がとてもよいことを表す. 通例疑問文・否定文には用いない.
  good, nice: 口語では最もよく使われる一般的な語.
  tasty: 「味わい深い」というニュアンスの語. 甘い物にはあまり用いない.
何かうまいものを食べよう Let's eat something *delicious*.
湯上がりに飲む冷たい牛乳はうまい Cold milk *tastes good* after a bath.
台所からパンの焼けるうまそうなにおいがしてきた There came *a delicious smell* of baking bread from the kitchen.

❷【上手な・すばらしい】good, clever, skillful; (抜け目ない) cunning
彼女は運転がうまい She is a *good* driver.
僕は文章を書くのはうまくないんだ I'm not *good at* writing.
うまいことを言うね That's a *clever* way of saying it.
彼女は小さな子供の扱いがうまい She *is skillful with* small children.／She *has a way with* small children.
◆口のうまい販売員 a *smooth* salesperson／うまいぞ！ *Well done*!(❖賞賛の言葉)／スージーは教えるのがうまい Susie teaches *well*.

❸【自分に都合のよい】good; (もうかる) profitable
それはうまい考えだ That's a *good* idea.
そんなうまい商売はないかなあ I want to get into some *profitable* business.
それは話がうますぎる It's *too good to be true*.
◆うまいぐあいに(→さいわい)列車はまだ発車していなかった *Luckily (for me)*, the train hadn't left yet.
慣用表現 ひとりでうまい汁を吸おうったってだめだぞ You can't *take all the credit* for yourself.

うまく

❶【上手に】well; (巧みに) skillfully; (手ぎわよく) neatly
この表現はうまく英語に訳せない This expression doesn't translate *well* into English.
彼はうまくそのトラブルを逆手にとった He *skillfully* turned the trouble to his advantage.
◆野球がもっとうまくなりたい I want to get *better at* playing baseball.／何て言ったらいいのかな, うまく言えないや How should I say it? I can't think of any *good* expressions.／その学生は英語を話すのが目に見えてうまくなった The student *made* noticeable *progress in* speaking English.
🅒「英語を話すのがうまくなりたい」「練習すればもっとうまくなりますよ」"I want to speak English *well*." "You'll speak it *better* if you practice."

❷【順調に】well; (首尾よく) successfully; (運よく) luckily
万事うまくいった Everything worked out *well*.
学校ではうまくいってるの？ Is everything going *well* at school?
交渉はうまくまとまった The negotiations concluded *successfully*.
◆運転免許の試験はうまくいった(→どうだった)？ *How* did you make out on your driving test?／正直言って, 彼とはあまりうまくやっていけない To be frank, I find it difficult to *get along with* him.／うまくいってよかったね I'm glad you *made it*.／交渉はうまくいかなかった The talks *didn't get [go] anywhere*.／彼は従業員とうまくやっているHe *is on good terms with* his employees.

うまとび 馬跳び leapfrog ⓤ ‖馬跳びをする play *leapfrog*

うまのり 馬乗り 警備員は強盗の上に馬乗りになった The guard *sat astride* the robber.

うまみ 旨み good flavor [taste] ⓤ ‖それぞれの素材のうまみを引き出す bring out *the good flavor* [*taste*] *of* each ingredient
◆うまみのある(→もうかる)商売 a *profitable* business／円高はわが社にとってうまみがあった The strong yen *was advantageous to* our company.

うまや 厩舎・厩 stable ⓒ (しばしば複数形 ~s) (❖複数形 stables は時に単数扱い)

うまる 埋まる (埋もれる) be buried; (いっぱいになる) be filled ‖この山のどこかに宝が埋まっている Treasure *is buried* somewhere on this mountain.／コンサートホールは音楽ファンで埋まった The concert hall *was* 「*filled with* [*full of*]" music lovers.
◆道が雪で埋まっている The road *is covered with* snow.／どの席も埋まっていた Every

うまれ 生まれ birth ⓤ, origin ⓤ《また複数形〜s》/高貴な生まれの人 a person of noble birth ◆インド生まれの英国人 a British national born in India / 彼は生まれはキューバだった He originally came from Cuba. / 彼は生まれも育ちもニューヨークだ He was born and raised in New York.

🍀「彼は何月生まれですか」「7月です」 "In which month was he born?" "In July."

‖生まれ故郷 one's native town, one's hometown

うまれかわり 生まれ変わり 私はこの子は祖父の生まれ変わりだと思う I believe that this child is the reincarnation of my grandfather.

うまれかわる 生まれ変わる be born again, be reborn ‖生まれ変わるとしたら何になりたいですか If you were to be born again, what would you like to be?
◆そのことがあってから彼は生まれ変わったように（→別人のように）まじめに働きだした After that, he came to work earnestly as if he were a different person.

うまれそだつ 生まれ育つ 私は海辺の小さな村で生まれ育った I was born and raised [brought up, bred, reared] in a small village by the sea.

うまれつき 生まれつき naturally, by nature, by birth ――生まれつきの native, innate, natural（⊖通例名詞の前で用いる）‖彼女は生まれつき髪がカールしている Her hair curls naturally. ◆彼は生まれつき頭がよい He was born smart.

うまれながら 生まれながら 彼は生まれながらのリーダーだ He is a born leader. / 人はみな生まれながらにして平等である（→平等に造られている）All men are created equal.

うまれる 生まれる

❶【子が】be born

僕は1985年11月18日に生まれた I was born on November 18, 1985.

彼は青森で生まれ秋田で育った He was born in Aomori and raised in Akita.

私は日本人の父とフランス人の母の間に生まれた I was born of a Japanese father and a French mother.

ポチに子犬が4匹生まれた Four puppies were born to Pochi.

彼女はドイツ人として生まれたが、後にアメリカ国籍を取った She was born German, but later became an American citizen.

◆生まれたばかりの赤ん坊 a new-born [new born, newborn] baby / 彼女に先月赤ちゃんが生まれた She had a baby last month. / お子さんはいつ生まれる予定ですか When is your baby due? / 彼はもう一度自分の生まれた土地を訪れたいと思っていた He wished to visit his birthplace once again. / その赤ん坊は生まれたとき3,200グラムあった The baby weighed 3,200 grams at birth. / 彼は生まれて初めて海を見た He saw an ocean for the first time in his life. / 私は生まれてこのかた日本を出たことがない I've never been out of Japan in all my life. / 彼は生まれながらの音楽家だ He is a born musician.

❷【物事が生じる】

1960年代にアフリカでは多くの国が生まれた A lot of countries came into existence in Africa in the 1960's.

スピードスケートで2つの公認世界記録が生まれた Two official world records have been set [made] in speed skating.

石油不足のために社会不安が生まれた The oil shortage caused the social unrest.

ハーバード大学は1636年に生まれた Harvard University was established [founded] in 1636.

うみ¹ 海

the sea, the ocean; (ある状態の) sea ⓒ

穏やかな海 the peaceful ocean / 血の海 a sea of blood / 海で泳ぐ swim in the sea [ocean] / 海に泳ぎに行く go swimming in the sea

海が荒れている[ないでいる] The sea is rough [calm].

そのホテルは海に面しています The hotel looks toward the ocean.

地球の4分の3は海で覆われている Three quarters of the earth is covered by (the) sea.

一面はまたたく間に火の海と化した The whole place turned into a sea of flame in no time.

◆船が激しく揺れて私は海に投げ出された The boat rolled badly and I was pitched into the water.

‖海の家(仮設の) a beach house; (常設の) a clubhouse / 海の男(漁師) a fisherman; (船乗り) a sailor / 海の幸 sea food, the fruits of the sea / 海の日 Marine Day

慣用表現 彼はまた海のものとも山のものともつかない（→どうなるか見当がつかない）Nobody knows what he will turn out to be.

俳句 海に出て木枯帰るところなし(山口誓子) Blowing out to sea
with no home to go home to —
the chill winter wind

うみ² 膿 pus ⓤ ◆うみの出ている傷口 a running sore

うみ³ 生み・産み 生みの母親 one's birth [biological] mother ⇒うみのおや, うみのくるしみ

うみがめ 海亀 〖動物〗(sea) turtle ⓒ

うみせんやません 海千山千 あいつは海千山千の男（→キツネのようにずる賢い人）だ He's a sly [crafty] old fox.

うみだす 生み出す・産み出す create ⊖ ⊖, produce ⊖ ⊖ ‖その小説家は最新作で新しいヒーローを生み出した The novelist created a new hero in her latest book. / 新しい勉強法はよい結果を生み出した The new method of learning produced [brought about] positive results.

うみたて 生み立て・産み立て 生みたての卵 a fresh [new-laid] egg

うみつける 産みつける (鳥・昆虫が卵を) lay* [他], (魚・カエルなどが卵を) spawn [他]
うみなり 海鳴り a roar of the sea ◆遠くの海鳴り the distant *murmur of the sea*
うみねこ 海猫 black-tailed gull [C]
うみのおや 生みの親・産みの親 (実父・実母) *one's* natural [birth, biological] parent; (創始者・創設者) founder [C], father [C]
◆エジソンは電球の生みの親だ(→発明した) Edison *invented* the electric light bulb.
[慣用表現] 生みの親より育ての親 *Foster parents are often closer to children than natural parents.*
うみのくるしみ 生みの苦しみ・産みの苦しみ (出産の) the labor of childbirth, labor pains; (事業などの) growing pains
うみびらき 海開き the opening of an ocean beach to swimmers, the beginning of the swimming season
うみべ 海辺 (波打ち際) beach [C], the seashore(❖単に shore ともいう); (海辺の保養地) the seaside //彼女は海辺で貝殻を売っている She sells seashells *on the seashore.* (❖英語の早口言葉)

うむ[1] 生む・産む

❶【子供を】give* birth to ...; (分娩(ぶんべん)する)《公式的》be delivered of ...; (動物が) breed* [自]; (卵を) lay* [他] [自]; (魚・カエルなどが) spawn [他] [自]
先日姉が3つ子を産んだ My sister「*gave birth to* [*had*] triplets the other day.
その鶏はけさ卵を産んだ The hen *laid* an egg this morning.
❷【作り出す】produce [他] [自]; (引き起こす) cause [他]; (主に悪いことを) give* rise to ...
英国は多くの偉大な詩人を生んできた Britain *has produced* many great poets.
スピードの出しすぎが多くの交通事故を生んでいる Speeding *causes* many traffic accidents.
◆誤解を生むおそれのある記事 a *misleading* article / マルクスの思想が共産主義を生んだ Marx's ideas *gave birth to* communism.
[ことわざ] 案ずるより産むがやすし ➩ あんずる

うむ[2] 有無 受付係は私に予約の有無を尋ねた The receptionist asked me「*whether* I had a reservation (*or not*) [*if* I had a reservation]. / 私は妹を有無を言わせず(→無理やり)歯医者に連れていった I took my sister to the dentist *by force.*
うむ[3] 膿む (傷口などが) fester [自]
うむ[4] 倦む (飽きる) get* tired (of ...) ◆彼はうまずたゆまず研究を続けた He *persevered with* [*in*] his studies.
うめ 梅 an *ume*, Japanese apricot [C] (❖口語では plum で代用することも多い) //梅の木[花] an *ume* tree [blossom]
うめあわせ 埋め合わせ compensation [U]
◆先週欠勤した分の埋め合わせをちゃんとしてね *Be sure to make up for* the time you were absent last week. / いろいろとありがとう. 必ずこの埋め合わせはするよ Thanks a lot. I'll be sure to *return the favor.*
うめあわせる 埋め合わせる (償う) make* up for ..., compensate for ..., 《公式的》repair [他] //自分が引き起こした損害を埋め合わせるためなら何でもします I'd do anything to *repair* the damage I've done.
うめきごえ 呻き声 groan [C], moan [C] //うめき声をあげる give [let out] *a groan*
うめく 呻く groan [自], moan [自] //患者は痛みでうめいた The patient *moaned* with pain.
うめくさ 埋め草 (新聞などの) filler [C]
うめこむ 埋め込む embed [他] (❖通例受身で); (身体に) implant [他]
うめしゅ 梅酒 *ume* [plum] liquor [U], *ume* [plum] wine [U]
うめたて 埋め立て reclamation [U] //埋め立て工事 *reclamation work*
‖埋め立て地 reclaimed land
うめたてる 埋め立てる reclaim [他] //海を埋め立てて空港を建設する *reclaim* land *from* the sea and construct an airport
うめぼし 梅干し 🗻

梅干しは梅の実を塩漬けにし, 天日で干したものです. 日本では昔から健康によい食品とされてきましたが, 初めて食べる人はそのすっぱさに驚くかもしれません. 梅干しはごはんに付け合わせるだけではなく, 様々な料理にも使われます.
An *umeboshi* is an *ume* pickled in salt and dried in the sun. They have been considered a health food in Japan since ancient times, but those who taste them for the first time may find them surprisingly sour. *Umeboshi* are used in various dishes as well as being served with rice.

うめる[1] 埋める (土の中に) bury [他]; (穴・すき間などを) fill [他]; (補う) make* up for ...
地中に宝物を埋める *bury* treasure in the ground / 溝を埋める *fill up* a ditch / 赤字を埋める *make up for* the deficit
適当な単語で空欄を埋めなさい *Fill in* the blanks with the appropriate words.
この欠員を埋める人が見つからなかった No one was found to *fill* this vacant post.
うめる[2] ふろをうめる *add some cold water* to a bath
うもう 羽毛 feather [C]; (綿毛) down [U] //羽毛ぶとん a *down* quilt
うもれる 埋もれる be buried //このあたりには貴重な宝が埋もれているといわれている It is said that a valuable treasure *is buried* around here.
◆埋もれた(→隠れた)才能 a *hidden* talent / 道路は雪に埋もれていた The road *was covered with* snow. / 彼は今の地位に埋もれさせておくのはもったいない人物だ He is really a somebody and deserves a higher position than his present one.
うやうやしい 恭しい respectful, 《公式的》reverent //遺影に向かってうやうやしく一礼する「make a *respectful* bow [bow *respectfully*] toward the photograph of a deceased person

うやまう 敬う respect ㊇, honor, 《英》honour ㊇ 自 ; (崇拝する) worship ㊇ 自 ／両親は老人を敬うようにと私をしつけた My parents taught me to *respect* the old [elderly] people.
うやむや うやむや(→あいまいな) 返事をする give a *vague* answer ／ この件はうやむやにすべきではない We'd better not *leave* the matter *undecided* [*unsettled, unresolved*, 《口語的》*up in the air*].
うようよ 田んぼにオタマジャクシがうようよしている There's *a swarm of* tadpoles in the rice paddies. ／ その森には蚊がうようよいる The woods *are teeming with* mosquitoes.
うよきょくせつ 紆余曲折 その結論が出るまでには紆余曲折があった There had been *a lot of twists and turns* before we reached the conclusion.
うよく 右翼 the right (wing); (野球の) right field ㊇ ‖右翼手 a right fielder ／ 右翼団体 a rightist organization

うら 裏

❶ 裏側・裏面　　the back
❷ 後ろ・背後　　the back, the rear
❸ 隠れた面
❹ 野球　　　　the bottom (half)

❶【裏側・裏面】the back; (反対側) the reverse (side), the other side; (表とされる側に対して逆の側) the wrong side; (裏張り・裏地) lining ㊄ ㊂
硬貨の裏 *the reverse* (*side*) of a coin ／ 布地の裏 *the wrong side* of the cloth ／ 月の裏側 *the other side* of the moon
封筒の裏に名前を書いた I wrote my name on *the back* of an envelope.
◆足の裏 *a sole* ／ 上着の裏(→内側)に私の名前がししゅうしてある My name is embroidered on *the inside* of my jacket. ／ このコートは裏がウール地だ(→裏打ちされている) This overcoat is *lined* with wool. ／ 表か裏か？ Heads or *tails*? (❖硬貨を投げて勝負などを決めるときにいう言葉) ／ 裏へ続く 《米》*Over* ／ 《英》*P.T.O.* (❖Please turn over. の略語)
❷【後ろ・背後】the back, the rear ——裏の back, rear (❖いずれも名詞の前で用いる)
その家の裏にある小さな庭 a small garden「*at the back of* [*behind*, 《米》*in back of*] the house ／ 学校の裏にある池 a pond *at* [*in*] *the rear of* the school
裏(→裏口)に回ってください Please go around to *the back door*.
◆彼らは裏に庭のある家を持っている They have a house with a garden *in back*.
❸【隠れた面】
彼の言葉には裏の(→隠された)意味があった His words carried a *hidden* meaning.
私は裏で何が行われているか知らない I don't know what is going on *backstage*.
◆どんな事柄にも裏と表がある *There are two sides* to everything.

❹【野球】the bottom (half)
9回裏ツーアウト満塁だ The bases are loaded, with two outs, in *the bottom of* the ninth.

慣用表現 裏には裏がある(→複雑な事情がある) *There are wheels within wheels*. ／ 彼は賢いといわれているが, 裏を返せば(→実際には)ずるいだけだ He is said to be clever, but *the truth is that* he is only cunning. ／ 相手の裏をかく *outwit* [《口語的》*outsmart*] one's opponent(s) ／ 彼の供述の裏をとって(→正確であることを確かめて)くれ Please *verify* his statement.

うらうち 裏打ち (補強用の) backing ㊄ ㊂ ——裏打ちする (衣服などを) line ㊇, back ㊇ (❖しばしば受身で) ◆彼には経験に裏打ちされた実力がある(→経験が彼の実力を証明している) His experience *has proven* his ability.
うらおもて 裏表 (両面) both sides ◆トレーナーが裏表だよ You're wearing your sweatshirt *inside out*. ／ 彼は裏表のない[ある]人だ He is a *sincere* [*two-faced*] man.
うらがえし 裏返し 私はセーターを裏返しに着ていた I was wearing my sweater *inside out*. ／ 彼があなたに厳しいのは愛情の裏返しだ His strict attitude to you is *the flip side* of his love.
うらがえす 裏返す (向きを逆にする) reverse ㊇; (ひっくり返す) turn over
◆ジーンズは裏返しで洗います I *turn* the jeans *inside out* before washing.
うらがき 裏書き (小切手などの) endorsement ㊂ ——裏書きする endorse ㊇, (証明する) confirm ㊇, prove* ㊇
うらかた 裏方 (劇場の) stagehand ㊂, sceneshifter ㊂
うらがね 裏金 (政治運動の) slush fund ㊄
うらがわ 裏側 the reverse ⇨うら
うらぎり 裏切り betrayal ㊄ ㊂, treachery ㊄ ㊂ ‖裏切り者 a traitor, a betrayer, 《口語的》a rat
うらぎる 裏切る (人を) betray ㊇; (恋人・配偶者を) cheat on ..., 《口語的》two-time ㊇; (希望・期待を) disappoint ㊇, fail ㊇
人の信頼を裏切る *betray* a person's trust
ユダはイエスを裏切った Judas *betrayed* Jesus.
期待を裏切ってごめんなさい I'm sorry to *disappoint* your expectations.
うらぐち 裏口 back door ㊂ ‖裏口から入る enter through *the back door* ◆大学へ裏口入学する *get into* a university *through the back door*; *buy one's way into* a university (❖後者は「お金を使って…に入る」の意味)
うらこうさく 裏工作 dirty tricks
うらごえ 裏声 【音楽】falsetto ㊂ ㊄ (複 ~s)
◆裏声で歌う sing *falsetto*
うらごし 裏漉し straining ㊄; (道具) strainer ㊂ ——裏ごしする strain ㊇
うらさく 裏作 second cropping ㊂
うらさびしい うら寂しい うら寂しい漁村 a *somehow forlorn* village
うらじ 裏地 (服などの) liner ㊂, lining ㊄ ㊂
うらづけ 裏付け その理論には事実の裏付けがな

うらづける 裏付ける (支える) support 働, back up; (証明する) prove* 働働; (確証する) 《公式的》corroborate 働 ‖ その証拠によって彼女の主張が裏付けられた Her claims *were supported* [*backed up*, *confirmed*] by the evidence. / その報告が彼の正当性を裏付けた The report *proved him* (to be) *right*.

うらて 裏手 the back ‖ その建物の裏手には美しい庭がある There's a beautiful garden *at the back of* the building.

うらどおり 裏通り back street ©, alleyway ©

うらない 占い fortune-telling ⓤ
→ 場面・状況別会話 p.1714
‖ 占い師 a fortune-teller

うらなう 占う tell* *a person's* fortune; (予測する) predict 働 ‖ あなたのことをトランプ [星占い] で占ってあげる I'll *tell your fortune* 「*with cards* [*by the stars*].
◆手相を占う *read a person's hand* [*palm*] ‖ 私は占い師に恋愛運を占ってもらった I went to a fortune-teller to *learn* about my future love life. / この知事選挙は政局の行方を占ううえで重要な選挙だ This election for governor will be important for *determining* the political trends.

ウラニウム 〖化学〗uranium ⓤ (❖元素記号 U)

うらにわ 裏庭 backyard © (❖〚米〛では芝が植えられていることが多いが, 〚英〛では通例舗装され塀で囲まれている)

うらばなし 裏話 inside story ©

うらはら 裏腹 ‖ 我々の期待とはうらはら(→反対)に, 彼は決勝で負けた *Contrary to* our expectations, he lost in the finals. / 彼の行動と言葉はうらはらだ(→一致しない) His deeds *are inconsistent with* his words.

うらばんぐみ 裏番組 ‖ 私はクイズ番組が見たかったが, 妹は裏番組の相撲を見ると言って聞かなかった I wanted to watch a quiz show, but my sister insisted on watching a sumo tournament *on another channel*.

うらびょうし 裏表紙 back cover ©

うらぶれる うらぶれた表情 [通り] a *forlorn* look [*street*] / うらぶれた生活を送る live *in misery*; 《口語的》lead *a dog's life*

うらまち 裏町 the back streets

うらみ 恨み grudge ©, ill feeling ⓤ, spite ⓤ ‖ (…に)うらみをいだく have *a grudge* (*against* …) / うらみを買う incur *a person's ill feeling* / うらみを晴らす pay back *the ill feeling*

うらみち 裏道 (建物や塀ではさまれた) alley ©, back lane [street] ©

うらむ 恨む have* [bear*, hold*] a grudge against *a person*, have ill feeling against *a person*; (悪く思う) think* ill of … ‖ 彼は私をうらんでいるようだ He seems to *bear a grudge against* me. / He seems to *bear me a grudge*.
◆うらみっこなしだよ *No hard feelings.*

うらめ 裏目 ‖ 私のしたことはすべて自分にとって裏目に出た Everything I did *worked against* me. / 彼が計画したことはすべて裏目に出た All the things he had planned *backfired* (*on him*). (❖*backfire* は「計画などが期待と逆の結果になる」の意味)

うらめしい 恨めしい ‖ その子供は母親をうらめしそうに(→とがめるように)見た The child looked at his mother *reproachfully*. / The child gave his mother a *reproachful* look. / 中学のときにきちんと英語の勉強をしていなかったことがうらめしい(→とても後悔している) I *bitterly regret* that I didn't study English hard when I was in junior high school.

うらもん 裏門 back gate ©

うらやま 裏山 a mountain behind *one's* house

うらやましい 羨ましい (うらやましがる) envious; (うらやましがらせる) enviable ‖ 洋子がうらやましそうな顔をしているよ Yoko looks *envious*. / あなたの才能がうらやましい I am *envious of* your ability. / I *envy* (*you for*) your ability.
◆彼が懸賞に当たったと聞いて同級生たちはみんなうらやましがった His classmates all *envied* him to hear that he won the prize. / みんながうらやましそうに僕の腕時計を見た Everybody looked at my watch *enviously* [*with envy*]. / 彼の成功をうらやましいとは全然思わなかった I felt no *envy* at his success.

うらやむ 羨む envy 働, be envious of …, feel* envy of …; (嫉妬(ʂっ)する) be jealous of … (❖嫌悪感など否定的な含みを伴う) ‖ 同僚たちは彼の成功をうらやんだ His colleagues *envied* (him) his success. / 彼女は姉の美しさをうらやんでいる She *is jealous of* her sister's beauty.
◆彼女は人のうらやむような給料をもらっている She gets an *enviable* salary.

うららか うららかな春の日に on a *beautiful* [*lovely*] spring day

うらわざ 裏技
🅔「ここをクリックすると自動保存されるんだ」「へえ, そんな裏技があるとは知らなかった」"If you click here, it will be saved automatically." "Wow! I didn't know about that *secret trick*."

ウラン 〖化学〗uranium ⓤ (❖元素記号 U)

うり¹ 瓜 (マクワウリ) melon ©
慣用表現 孝子は母親とうりふたつだ Takako *looks just like* her mother. / Takako is her mother's *double*.

うり² 売り ‖ 彼らは家を売りに出した They *put up* their house *for sale*. / あの家は売りに出ています That house *is for sale*. / 交渉のうまいのが彼女の最大の売り(→武器)だ Her negotiating skills are her best *weapon*.

うりあげ 売り上げ・売上 sales; (収益) pro-

ceeds //総売り上げ gross *sales* / 売り上げの増加[減少] an increase [a drop] in *sales* / 今月の売上高は先月より多かった This month's *sales* were larger than last month. / パソコンの売り上げが去年に比べアップ[ダウン]している *Sales* of PCs are up [down] over last year.
‖売上金 takings / 売上伝票 a sales slip / 売上目標 a sales target

うりあるく 売り歩く peddle [他], hawk [他]

うりおしみ 売り惜しみ 米の売り惜しみをする *be unwilling to sell* rice

うりきれ 売り切れ 売り切れ《掲示》*Sold Out* / 申しわけありませんが売り切れです I'm sorry, but we'*ve sold out.*

うりきれる 売り切れる (切符などが) sell* out //その店のパンは昼前には売り切れるほど人気がある The bakery's bread is so popular that it *sells out* before noon.

うりこ 売り子 salesperson [C], 《米》salesclerk [C], 《英》shop assistant [C]; (列車・競技場などの) 《米》butcher [C]; (駅の) vendor [C]

うりことば 売り言葉 売り言葉に買い言葉で, 私は彼をののしった I cursed him *tit for tat.*

うりこみ 売り込み (本・映画などの) 《口語的》plug [C] ◆彼らは新商品の売り込みに奔走している They are making every effort to *sell* the new product.

うりこむ 売り込む (自分を) 《口語的》sell* *oneself*, push *oneself* forward; (商品などを) 《口語的》push [他]
◆新人女優を売り込む *promote* a new actress / この種の車をアメリカに売り込む(→市場を見つける)のは難しい It's difficult to *find a market* in America for this type of car.

うりさばく 売り捌く 在庫品を売りさばく *sell off* goods in stock

うりだし 売り出し 大売り出し《掲示》(*Bargain*) *Sale* (❖bargain を付けないほうがふつう) / 歳末大売り出し *a* year-end *sale* / 彼の最新の CD は今売り出し中である His latest CD *is* now *on sale.* / 彼は今売り出し中の(→人気を得つつある)若手俳優だ He is a young actor *who is gaining popularity.*

うりだす 売り出す (品物を) put* ... on sale [the market]; (名を広める) gain [win*] popularity //その CD-ROM はもうすぐ売り出される The CD-ROM *will be put on sale* soon. / 彼は最近, 役者として売り出している These days, he *is gaining* [*winning*] *popularity* as an actor. ◆２区画の土地が売り出されていた Two plots of land *were for sale.*

うりつくす 売り尽くす sell* off *one's* stock

うりつける 売り付ける palm [fob] ... off, palm [fob] *a person* off with ... //彼は私に古い家具を売りつけた He *palmed* the old furniture *off on* me.

うりて 売り手 seller [C] ‖売り手市場 a seller's [sellers'] market

うりとばす 売り飛ばす sell* off //彼は切手集めに飽きてコレクションを売りとばしてしまった He *sold off* his collection of stamps because he lost interest in it.

うりぬし 売り主 seller [C] (↔buyer); (不動産などの)〖法律〗vendor [C]

うりね 売値 selling price [C]

うりば 売り場 (デパートの) department [C] (《略語》dep., dept., dpt.); (カウンター) counter [C]; (売店・スタンド) stand [C] //靴売り場 *a counter* for shoes / 紳士服売り場 *the* men's clothing *department*
◆切符売り場 *a box office*; *a* ticket *office* [*counter*] / そのデパートは売り場面積が日本一だ The department store has *the* biggest *retail space* in Japan.

うりはらう 売り払う 家を売り払う(→処分する) *dispose of* a house / 彼は読まなくなった漫画を売り払った(→すべて売った) He *sold all* his comic books that he no longer read.

うりもの 売り物 売り物の車 a car *for sale* / 売り物にならない *be unsalable* [*not salable*]; *be unfit for sale* / この本は売り物ではない This book *is* not *for* [*on*] *sale.* / ネギとコンニャクが下仁田の売り物(→名物)だ Leeks and *konnyaku* are *famous* [*special*] *products* of Shimonita.

うりや 売り家 a house for sale

うりょう 雨量 rainfall [U] ◆ゆうべは１時間の雨量が50ミリを超えた We had more than 50 millimeters of *rain* an hour last night.
‖雨量計 a rain gauge

うりわたす 売り渡す (売る) sell* [他]; (裏切る) 《口語的》sell *a person* down the river

うる[1] 売る

❶【品物を】sell* [他] [自]
高く[安く]売る *sell* at a high [low] price
その店はいろいろな物を売っている They *sell* a lot of things at the store. / The store *sells* a lot of things.
(店員に向かって)辞書は売っていますか Do you *sell* dictionaries?
その店では香水をグラム単位で売っている They *sell* perfume *by the gram* at that shop.
この本, 君に1,000円で売ってあげるよ I'*ll sell* 「you this book [this book to you] *for* 1,000 yen.
革製品が魅力的な値段で売られている Leather goods *are sold* at attractive prices.
◆このコーヒーカップは４つの色[サイズ]が売られている This coffee cup *comes in* four colors [sizes]. / その店はありとあらゆる商品を売っている The shop *is full of* miscellaneous goods. / 彼はその雑誌に車を売る広告を出した He advertised his car *for sale* in the magazine.
[会話]「そのノートいいなあ」「駅前の店で売ってるよ」 "I like your notebook." "You *can buy* [*get*] one at the shop in front of the station."

❷【名前などを】
彼の慈善行為は名を売るためのものだった In order to *become famous*, he held charitable events.
生徒会長に立候補するなら, 今から顔を売っておい

う

たほうがいいぞ If you run for the student council president, you should *get publicity* from now on.

❸【その他】

おまえ，けんかを売る気か Are you *picking a fight* [*quarrel*] *with* me?

その政治家は金のために祖国を売った(→裏切った) The politician *betrayed* [*sold out*] his country for money.

うる[2] 得る ➾ える

うるうどし 閏年 leap year [U] [C]

うるおい 潤い (ほどよい湿り気) moisture [U]
◆潤いのある肌 *moist* skin / 潤いのある[ない]生活を送る lead a *full* [*dull*] life / 潤いのある声 a *sweet* voice

うるおう 潤う (湿る) be moistened; (利益・恩恵を受ける) benefit [profit] from ... ‖その町は自動車産業で潤っている The town *benefits* [*profits*] *from* the automobile industry.

うるおす 潤す (湿らす) moisten [他], wet* [他]; (利益・恩恵を与える) benefit [他], profit [他]
◆水でのどを潤す(→渇きをいやす) *satisfy* [*quench*] *one's thirst* with water

ウルグアイラウンド the Uruguay Round (❖GATT 加盟国による多角的貿易交渉)

うるさい

❶【騒々しい】noisy

うるさい男の子たち *noisy* boys

彼女は隣のピアノの音がうるさいとぶつぶつ言っていた She was muttering about her neighbor's *noisy* piano playing.

◆うるさい(→静かにしろ)！ (*Be*) *quiet*!/ (→黙れ) *Shut up*! / テレビがうるさいぞ The television is too *loud*. / あんなにうるさくては眠れないよ With all that *noise*, I can't get to sleep.

❷【うっとうしい・迷惑な】annoying; (しつこい) persistent

うるさく質問する人 a *persistent* questioner

蚊がうるさい These mosquitoes「*are annoying* [*are annoying me*]. (❖後の表現の annoying は動詞 annoy の現在分詞)

◆人のうるさい目のない所で away from *prying* eyes / 彼女は人形を買ってくれとうるさくせがんだ She kept *bothering* me to buy a doll. / うるさいな．何回もだめって言ったでしょ *Enough of that*. I've said no a thousand times.

❸【口やかましい】(好みなどが) particular, picky; (厳しい) strict

彼は家具の好みがとてもうるさい He is very *particular about* furniture.

戸田先生は私たちの服装にとてもうるさい Mrs. Toda is very *strict* about our clothes.

◆時間にうるさい人 *a stickler for* punctuality

うるさがる 難しい質問でうるさがらせる *bother* [*annoy, trouble*] *a person* with difficult questions / 私はみんなにうるさがられた(→やっかい者扱いされた) I *was treated as* [*like*] *a nuisance* by everybody.

うるし 漆 lacquer [U] ◆漆塗りのはし *lacquered* chopsticks
‖漆細工 lacquerware

ウルトラ- ultra- [ʌ́ltrə-] ◆彼はウルトラ級の高校生投手だ He is an *outstanding* pitcher for a high school student.

うるむ 潤む be wet [moist] ‖彼の目は涙で潤んでいた His eyes *were wet* [*moist*] with tears.
◆啓子は目を潤ませながらさよならを言った Keiko said goodbye *with tears in her eyes*.

うるわしい 麗しい 見目麗しい女性 a *beautiful* lady / その小説には若者たちの麗しい友情が描かれている The *heartwarming* friendship of young people is described in the novel.

うれい 憂い・愁い (心配) anxiety [U], worry [U]; (恐れ) fear [C] [U]; (悲しみ) sorrow [U], grief [U] ‖うれいを帯びた表情が彼の顔に浮かんだ A look of *sorrow* passed over his face.
[ことわざ] 備えあればうれいなし ➾ そなえ

うれえる 憂える (心配する) be anxious, be concerned ‖彼は病気がちな子供の将来を憂えている He *is anxious about* the future of his sickly child.

うれくち 売れ口 (販路・需要) market [U] [C], outlet [C]

うれしい 嬉しい

glad, happy, joyful

うれしい知らせ *joyful* [*glad, good*] news

またお会いできてうれしいです I'm *happy* [*glad*] to see you again./ It's *good* to see you again.

口では言えないほどうれしかった I just can't tell you how *glad* [*happy*] I was.

彼女は結婚式でとてもうれしそうだった She looked *happy* [*joyful*] at her wedding.

◆盗まれた財布が戻ってきて彼はうれしかった He *was pleased at* the return of his stolen wallet. / 無事に帰国されてうれしく思います I *am delighted* (that) you have come home safely. / 皿洗いを手伝ってくれるとうれしいんだけど I *wish* you would help me do the dishes. / たいへんうれしいことに私たちのチームがそのトーナメントで優勝した *To our* great *joy* [*delight*], our team won the tournament.

うれしがらせる 嬉しがらせる please [他], delight [他]

うれしさ 嬉しさ joy [U], delight [U] ‖彼はうれしさを隠しきれなかった He couldn't suppress *his joy*.

うれしなき 嬉し泣き うれし泣きをする *cry for* [*with*] *joy*; *weep for* [*with*] *joy*

うれしなみだ 嬉し涙 tears of joy

うれすじ 売れ筋 売れ筋の商品 a *good* seller / 今このお店でいちばんの売れ筋は何ですか What *sells best* in this store now?

ウレタン urethane [U] ‖ウレタンフォーム urethane foam

うれっこ 売れっ子 売れっ子の女優 a *popular* [*sought-after*] actress

うれのこり　売れ残り
今年は冷夏のせいでエアコンの売れ残りがたくさん出た Because of the cool summer, a lot of air conditioners 「*were left* [*remained*] *unsold* this year. / 将来売れ残りにはなりたくない I don't want to *miss the chance to get married* in the future.

うれゆき　売れ行き
sale ⓒ / 今月の売れ行き（→売り上げ）はいつもよりよかった[悪かった] This month's *sales* were larger [smaller] than usual. / エアコンの売れ行きは季節によって変わる *Sales* of air-conditioners vary with the seasons.
◆その辞書の売れ行きはどうですか How *is* the dictionary *selling*? / この車は売れ行きがよい[悪い] This car *sells well* [*badly*].

うれる¹　売れる
❶ 【商品が】 sell*⊕, be sold
このCDはよく売れる This CD 「*sells well* [*is a good seller*]」.
彼のアルバムは1週間で100万枚売れた His album *sold* a million copies in a week.
その家は10万ドルで売れた The house *was sold for* 100,000 dollars.
そのTシャツは飛ぶように売れた The T-shirt *sold like hot cakes*.
◆この家はかなりの高値で売れた This house *fetched* a very high price. (❖ fetch は「…の値になる」の意味)

❷ 【名が】
売れない作家 an *unsuccessful* writer
日本でいちばん売れている(→人気のある)ミュージシャンはだれですか Who is the most *popular* musician in Japan?
彼は世界的に名の売れた(→有名な)デザイナーだ He is a *world-famous* designer.

うれる²　熟れる
ripen ⊕ / カキは秋に熟れる Persimmons *ripen* in (the) fall.
◆熟れたトマト *ripe* tomatoes

うろうろ　うろうろする
hang* around [《英》about], wander ⊕⊕, loiter ⊕ / 当てもなくうろうろする *wander about* aimlessly
◆彼はうろうろ歩き回った He was walking *to and fro*.

うろおぼえ　うろ覚え
彼はトーマス何とかという名前だったと思うが, うろ覚えだ His name is Thomas something or other, but I *can't remember exactly*. / あの人のことはうろ覚えにしか覚えていない I have only a dim [faint] *memory* of that man.

うろこ　鱗
(魚・蛇などの) scales
∥うろこ雲 a cirrocumulus
慣用表現 目からうろこが落ちる ➪ め(目)

うろたえる
panic ⊕, lose* *one's head*, be upset / 何があっても決してうろたえるな Never *panic* [*lose your head*] whatever happens.

うろちょろ
君に目の前をうろちょろされては集中できないよ I can't concentrate with you *hovering* over me.

うろつく
hang* around [《英》about], mill ⊕ / 繁華街をうろつく *hang around* downtown

うわあご　上顎
upper jaw ⓒ

うわがき　上書き
（手紙などのあて先） address ⓒ ——上書きする〔コンピュータ〕overwrite*⊕

うわき　浮気
flirtation ⓒ, affair ⓒ ——浮気する 《口語的》cheat ⊕, fool around [about], play around [about] / 浮気しないでね Don't *cheat on* me. / 彼はどうも浮気をしているようだ He seems to *be having an affair*.
∥浮気者 a flirt

うわぎ　上着
coat ⓒ, jacket ⓒ; (下着に対して) outerwear ⓤ / 私は上着にブラシをかけた I gave *my jacket* a brush.

うわぐすり　釉薬
glaze ⓒ

うわくちびる　上唇
upper lip ⓒ

うわごと
delirious utterance ⓒ ◆彼女は一晩中熱に浮かされてうわごとを言っていた She was delirious with a fever and *raved* all night.

うわさ　噂
rumor, 《英》rumour ⓤⓒ, 《口語的》talk ⓤ, report ⓒⓤ; (私生活などの) gossip ⓤⓒ
〖うわさは〗
そのうわさは根も葉もないものだと分かった The *rumor* turned out (to be) totally groundless.
そのうわさはたちまち近所の人たちの間に広まった The *rumor* spread [got around] rapidly among the neighbors.
〖うわさを〗
うわさを(きっぱり)否定する deny *a rumor* (firmly); give a (firm) denial to *a rumor*
だれかが変なうわさを広めているようだ Somebody seems to be spreading [putting out] *a strange rumor*.
インフレのうわさを非常によく耳にする There is a lot of *talk* about inflation.
◆彼女たちは喫茶店で友達のうわさをしていた They *were gossiping* about their friends in a coffee shop.
〖うわさに〗
あの二人は町のうわさになっている That couple *is the talk of* the town.
うわさによると来月新しい先生が来るんだって *I heard a rumor that* a new teacher is coming next month.
◆高橋氏のことはうわさには聞いているが面識はない I *know* Mr. Takahashi *by reputation*, but I have never met him.
〖その他〗
渡辺氏が結婚するといううわさだ There's a *rumor* [*It is rumored, Rumor has it*] that Mr. Watanabe is getting married.
◆みんな彼女のうわさでもちきりだ Her name is *on everyone's lips*. / ちょうど君のことをうわさしていたところだよ We were just *talking* about you.
慣用表現 うわさをすれば影だ. ほらトムが来た *Speak of the devil*, here comes Tom.
ことわざ 人のうわさも七十五日 *A rumor will last only for 75 days.*; A wonder lasts but nine days. (→驚くべきことも9日しか続か

うわずる 上擦る (声が) crack ◉ ✦ 彼は緊張のあまり声がうわずっていた He was so nervous that he *spoke with a high-pitched voice*.

うわつく 浮つく 浮ついた(→軽薄な)態度 a *frivolous* attitude / 浮ついた気持ちでいてはいけない Don't take it so *lightly*. / Be more serious.

うわっつら 上っ面 (外見) appearance ⓤⓒ; (表面) surface ⓒ ⇒うわべ ‖上っ面のみを論じる《口語的》scratch *the surface*

うわっぱり 上っ張り smock ⓒ, overall ⓒ

うわづみ 上積み 退職金を上積みする *raise* the amount of retirement benefits

うわて 上手 …より一枚うわてである《口語的》be *a cut above* ... / 彼は私よりうわてだ He is *more than a match for* me. / He is *superior to* me.
‖上手投げ(野球の) an overhand throw; (相撲の) an overarm throw

うわぬり 上塗り coating ⓤⓒ, overlay ⓒ
◆そんなことを言ったら恥の上塗りになるぞ Saying such a thing will *add to* your shame.

うわのせ 上乗せ 彼らは合意した価格にさらに5万円上乗せしてきた They *put* [*added*] another 50,000 yen *on* the agreed price.

うわのそら 上の空 absent-mindedness ⓤ, abstraction ⓤ ──うわの空の absent-minded, distrait
◆彼は私の話をただうわの空で聞いていた He was listening to me only *absent-mindedly*.

うわばき 上履き indoor shoes

うわべ 上辺 (表面) surface ⓒ; (外見) appearance ⓤⓒ ‖うわべを飾る keep up *appearances* / うわべを取りつくろうために for *appearance*'s sake; for the sake of *appearance* / うわべで判断してはいけない Don't judge *by appearances*. / 彼はうわべはやさしく見えた He seemed kind *on the surface*.
◆うわべだけの知識 a *superficial* knowledge / 私は彼のうわべの礼儀正しさにだまされなかった I saw through his *seeming* politeness.

うわまえ 上前 《口語的》kickback ⓤⓒ ‖上前をはねる pocket *a kickback*

うわまわる 上回る exceed ⓣ, be above / 彼の知能は平均をはるかに上回っている His intelligence is far *above* average. / 1人あたりの所得で日本は英国を上回っている Japan *exceeds* the U.K. in per capita income.
◆今年は予想を上回る雨量があった We had *more* rain this year *than expected*.

うわむき 上向き upturn ⓒ ◆景気は上向きになってきた Business is looking [*picking*] *up*.

うわむく 上向く 専門家は今年の後半には景気が上向く(→回復する)だろうと語った The expert said the economy would *improve* [*get better*] later this year.

うわめづかい 上目使い …を上目づかいに見る cast *an upturned glance at* ...; look at ... *with upturned eyes*

うわやく 上役 《口語的》*one's* boss, *one's* superior

うん¹ (肯定) yes, 《口語的》yeah; uh-huh [ʌhʌ́] (✿相づちを打ったり同意するときに用いる)
彼女がうんと言うことはまずないだろう It is highly improbable that she will say *yes*.
◆うんとうなずく(→賛意を示す) nod *one's approval* / うんともすんとも言わない(→答えない) give no answer / うん, 分かった OK. I have it now. / うん, いい考えが浮かんだぞ Say, I've got an idea! / 彼にうんと言って(→同意して)もらえた? Did you 「get his *OK* [win his *consent*]?

🔊 「用意できた?」「うん, できたよ」 "Are you ready?" "*Yes*, I am."

🔊 「気に入った?」「うん」 "Did you like it?" "*Yeah*."

🔊 「寒くない?」「うん, 寒くないよ」 "Aren't you cold?" "*No*, I'm not." (✿日本語では「うん」になるが、英語では答える内容が否定のときは常にNo.で答える)

🔊 「お願いしてもいいかしら」「うん, いいよ. 何?」 "Will you do me a favor?" "*Sure*. What is it?"

うん² 運 luck ⓤ, fortune ⓤ; (偶然) chance ⓤⓒ ⇒うんめい

【英作文ノート】「運が…」は **a, an** を付けない
彼女は運がいい
→×She *has a good luck*.
→○She *has good luck*.
★luckは抽象名詞で、形容詞が付いても a[an]を付けない. 「彼女は運が悪い」なら She has bad [hard, tough] luck. となる.「彼女は運がいい[悪い]」は She is lucky [unlucky]. / She is fortunate [unfortunate]. / She's in [out of] luck. ともいう.「今週は不運続きだ」なら I've had bad luck all week. となる.

ギャンブル[商売]運 luck 「at gambling [in business]」/ 運を試す try *one's luck* / 運が尽きる run out of *luck* / 悪運続き a run of *bad luck*

運が悪かったね Tough [*Hard*] *luck*!
運に任せてやってみよう Let's *take a chance*.
私は運がない Luck is [*goes*] *against* me.
運が私に味方した *Luck* was on my side.
ほんの少し運がよければ彼は成功していただろう *With* a little bit of *luck*, he would have succeeded.
勝負は時の運だ Victory is a matter of *chance*.
彼は運よく試験に合格した He had *the good fortune* to pass the test. / *Fortunately* he passed the test.
傘をなくしたとは運が悪いですね It was *hard* [*tough*] *luck* losing your umbrella.
あの事故を起こしてしまったのが運のつきだった Causing that accident was just my *worst luck*.
◆運よく座席が2つとれた We were *lucky* to get two seats. / *Luckily* we got two seats. / 運悪くそこにいたんだ I was in the wrong place *at the wrong time*. (✿事件・事故などに

巻き込まれたときにいう)

うんえい 運営 management Ⓤ, administration Ⓤ ──運営する manage 他, administer 他, run* 自他 ‖事業を運営する run [manage] a business / 学校運営 school administration ‖ 生徒会が文化祭を運営した The student council *ran* the school festival.

‖運営委員会 a steering committee / 運営資金 operating [working] funds / 運営費 operating [running] costs

うんが 運河 canal Ⓒ, watercourse Ⓒ, waterway Ⓒ ‖スエズ運河 the Suez Canal

うんきゅう 運休 suspension Ⓤ ──運休する (一時停止する) be suspended; (取り消す) be canceled [英) cancelled] ‖台風のため飛行機は運休している Flights *are suspended* because of the typhoon.

うんこ stools, 《米口語的》poop Ⓤ, 《卑語》shit Ⓤ《また a ～》‖犬のうんこ dog *poop* / うんこがしたくなった I need to take *poop*.

うんこう 運行・運航 (列車・バスなどの) service Ⓤ Ⓒ, run Ⓒ, (飛行機の) flight Ⓒ, (天体の) movement Ⓤ ‖駅から私の学校までバスが運行しています There is (a) bus *service available* from the station to my school. / The buses *run* from the station to my school. / 濃霧のため羽田行きは全便運航に遅れが出ています Due to the dense fog, all *flights* for [to] Haneda *have been delayed*.

うんざり ──うんざりする get* fed up, get sick (and tired); (退屈する) get bored ‖もうこの仕事にはうんざりだ I'm fed up with this job. / 彼の言い訳を聞くのはうんざりだ I'm *sick (and tired) of* hearing his excuses. / 彼は毎日同じことをするのにうんざりしてきていた He *was getting bored of* doing the same thing every day. ◆彼女はうんざりした顔でテーブルを片づけていた She was clearing the table *with a bored look*.

うんせい 運勢 fortune Ⓤ ‖人の運勢を占う tell a person's *fortune*

うんそう 運送 transportation Ⓤ, 《公式的》carriage Ⓤ; (長距離貨物) freight Ⓤ (◆《米》では陸上または空輸,《英》では水上運送に用いられる)──運送する transport 他

‖運送会社 a transportation company / 運送業 (旅客の) transportation business; (荷物の) carrier business / 運送業者 a carrier; (引っ越しなどの) a mover / 運送料 transportation charge

うんだめし 運試し ‖運試しにそのコンテストに応募してみた I entered the contest to *try my luck*.

うんち 《卑語》 shit Ⓤ,《米口語的／小児語》poop Ⓤ Ⓒ

うんちく 蘊蓄 ‖彼は講演で日本文化に関するうんちくを傾けた He *drew on vast reserves of knowledge of* Japanese culture in his lecture.

うんちん 運賃 (旅客の) fare Ⓒ, (貨物の) freight rates ‖片道の運賃 a「one way [《英》single] *fare* / 往復の運賃 a「round trip [《英》return] *fare* / 割引運賃 a reduced *fare* ‖ 来月, バス運賃の値上げが予定されている *Bus fares* are to be raised next month. / 子供運賃は大人運賃の半額です The children's *fare* is half the adults'.

‖運賃後払い fare to collect / 運賃精算所 a fare adjustment office / 運賃表 a fare table / 運賃前払い fare prepaid / 航空運賃 an airfare

うんでいのさ 雲泥の差 ‖実際に見るのと聞くのとでは雲泥の差がある There's *a big difference between* hearing about something *and* actually seeing it.

うんてん 運転

(自動車などの) driving Ⓤ; (機械の操作) operation Ⓤ ──運転する (自動車を) drive* 他 自; (車・機械を) run* 他; (機械を操作する) operate 他

機械を運転する *operate* [*run*] a machine / クレーンを運転する *operate* [*use*] a crane

彼女は運転がうまい She *drives* well. / She is *good at driving*. / She is *a good driver*.

気をつけて運転しなさい *Drive* carefully.

父は飲酒運転をして警察につかまった My father was caught by the police for *drunken driving*.

エスカレーターは今運転中だ The escalator *is in operation* now.

◆彼が運転している間は安心だった I felt safe while he *was at [behind] the wheel*. / 眠くなったので彼に運転を代わってもらった I got sleepy and let him *take [get behind] the wheel*. / 日曜日には臨時列車が運転されます Extra trains *run [are run]* on Sundays.

‖運転資金 working funds [capital] / 運転手 (自動車の) a driver; (お抱え運転手) a chauffeur (◆女性形 chauffeuse); (電車の) a motorman; (機械の) an operator / 運転席 a driver's seat; (電車・トラック・バスの) a cab / 運転免許証 《米》a driver's license, 《英》a driving licence / 安全運転 safe driving (◆×safety driving とはいわない) / 試運転 ⇨しうんてん

うんと ‖うんと食べる eat *much* / 若いうちにうんと本を読むべきです You should read *a lot of* books while you're young. / 先生にうんとしかられた I was scolded *severely* by my teacher.

うんどう 運動

❶【身体を動かすこと】 exercise Ⓤ Ⓒ, workout Ⓒ; (スポーツ) sport Ⓒ Ⓤ ──運動する exercise 自, get* [take*, do*] exercise, work out

激しい運動 hard [vigorous, violent] *exercise* / 軽い運動 light [gentle] *exercise*

君は適度な運動をするべきだ You should get some moderate *exercise*.

毎日運動していると病気になりにくくなる *Exercising* every day lessens the chance of getting sick.

運動しすぎると危険なこともあるというのは彼らに

は驚きだった They were astonished that *too much exercise* might be dangerous.
私は運動不足で太った I've put on weight due to *lack of exercise*.
父は毎日1時間ほど運動をしている My father *works out* every day for about an hour.
◆運動神経がいい[悪い]（→反射神経がいい[鈍い]）have quick [slow] *reflexes* / 彼はレースの前に準備運動をした He *warmed up* before the race. / 彼は毎日犬を運動させる He *exercises* his dog every day.

❷【活動・働きかけ】（社会的・政治的な）movement ◎；（特定の目的などの）campaign ◎；（募金などの）drive ◎ ――運動する campaign ⓥ

反戦運動を行う carry on *an antiwar movement* / 市長の辞任を求める運動をする *campaign [agitate]* for the mayor's resignation

彼は環境運動にかかわっていた He was associated with *the environmental movement*.
その作家はかつて学生運動の中心人物だった The writer was once the leader of *the student movement*.
彼は独立のために戦う運動を指導した He led *the movement* to fight for independence.
彼は大統領選の選挙運動を指揮した He conducted the president's *election campaign*.
◆コカイン追放運動 a fight against cocaine

❸【物体の】motion ◎，movement ◎◎
運動の法則 the laws [principle] of *motion* / ブラウン運動 Brownian *motion [movement]* / エレベーターの上下運動 up-and-down *movement* of the elevator

‖運動員（社会的・政治的な）a campaigner；（選挙の）a canvasser / 運動着 sportswear / 運動靴（スニーカー）gym shoes，（主に米）sneakers，（英）plimsolls / 運動場（競技場）an athletic field；（学校の）a playground / 運動選手 an athlete / 運動部 an athletic club / 禁煙運動 an antismoking campaign / 草の根運動 a grassroots movement / 市民運動 a citizens movement / 女性（解放）運動 the women's movement / 政治運動 a political campaign [movement] / 反核運動 an antinuclear movement / 労働運動 a labor movement

うんどうかい 運動会 🏁 field [《英》sports] day ◎；（競技会）athletic meet ◎

運動会は毎年学校・会社・その他の団体によって開かれる競技大会のことです。運動会は体育の日のころによく開催されます。様々なレースや綱引きなどの競争のほか、だれもが参加できる楽しいゲームもあります。
Undokai is a term referring to a field day held every year by schools, companies and other organizations. It is usually held in the fall, often around Sports-Health Day (the second Monday of October). There are various races and competitive events such as tug-of-war. Other events are just for fun, so everyone can participate.

うんともすんとも ⇨うん¹
うんぬん 云々 and so forth [on], et cetera [et sétərə]（❖英語の and so forth [on]にあたるラテン語。通例 etc.と書く）⇨など
◆結果を云々しても（→批判しても）しかたがない It is no use *criticizing* the result.

うんぱん 運搬 conveyance ◎；（輸送）《米》transportation ◎，《英》transport ◎，《公式的》carriage ◎ ――運搬する carry ⓥ，convey ⓥ；（輸送する）transport ⓥ ⇨ゆそう（輸送）/ 家具をトラックで運搬する *transport* furniture by truck
‖運搬車 a carriage

うんめい 運命

fate ◎◎（しばしば Fate），（避けがたい）destiny ◎◎，（避けがたい悲惨な）doom ◎◎《通例単数形》；fortune ⓥ（❖幸運の意味合いが強い）；（巡り合わせ）one's lot

自らの運命を開く work out *one's* own *destiny* / 運命のいたずらで by *a twist [an irony] of fate* / 人と運命を共にする throw in *one's lot* with a person / 人の運命を決定づける seal a person's *fate*

だれも自分の運命は分からない No one knows his or her *fate*.
運命は私の思いどおりにならなかった *Fate* was against me.
運命と思ってあきらめた I've resigned myself to *fate*.
その出来事は彼の運命を左右した The event affected his *fate [destiny]*.
運命の女神があなたにほほえみますように May *Fortune* smile on you.
◆運命的な出会いをする have *a fateful encounter* / 私たちはみんな運命を共にしている We are all *in the same boat*. / その女王は数奇な運命をたどった The queen *was fated to follow* a turbulent *path through life*. / 私たちは二度と会うことのない運命にあった We *were destined* never to meet again. / 彼女は俳優になるよう運命づけられていた She *was destined for* an acting career. / ついに運命の瞬間がやってきた At last *the fateful moment* has come.
‖運命論 fatalism

うんゆ 運輸（輸送）《米》transportation ◎，《英》transport ◎ ⇨ゆそう（輸送）
‖運輸会社 a transportation [an express] company / 運輸省 the Ministry of Transport（❖2001年国土交通省に統合）⇨こくどこうつうしょう

うんよう 運用 use ◎ ――運用する use ⓥ ⇨かつよう /「資金の運用 *the use* of funds
◆その会社は資金の運用を誤った The company *misused* the funds.

え

え¹ 絵
picture ◯; painting ◯; drawing ◯; illustration ◯
|painting: 絵の具で描いたもの.
|drawing: 鉛筆・クレヨンなどで描いたもの.
|illustration: 挿絵.
|picture: 以上すべてを含む.

油絵 *an oil painting* / モネの絵 *a painting by Monet* / 花の絵を描く draw [paint] *a picture of a flower*
彼女は絵を描くのが下手[上手]だ She is poor [good] at *painting pictures*.
この絵をどこにかけましょうか Where should I hang this *picture*?
彼の絵は市立美術館で展示された His *paintings* were displayed in the city art museum.
子供たちはその山の絵を描いた The children painted (*pictures* of) the mountain.
◆彼は絵の才能(→絵を描く才能)がある He has a talent for *drawing*.
‖絵空事 *a pipe dream* / 絵札 *a face card* 慣用表現 その計画は絵に描いたもちだ The project is *pie in the sky*. / 彼は勤勉を絵に描いたような人だ He is *the incarnation of diligence*. / He is *diligence itself*. / この風景は絵になる This scene *will make a very good picture*. / 彼は何をやらせても絵になる He *looks good* no matter what he does. / 絵のように美しい情景 *a picturesque* scene

え² 柄
handle ◯ ‖ナイフの柄 *the handle* of a knife / ほうきの柄 *a broom handle*

エアコン ⚠ air conditioner ◯ ◆エアコンのきいた部屋 an *air-conditioned* room

エアターミナル air terminal

エアバス airbus ◯

エアバッグ airbag ◯

エアポケット air pocket ◯ ‖エアポケットに入る hit *an air pocket*

エアメール (航空便) airmail, air mail ◯; (郵便物) airmail letter [parcel]◯ / 手紙をエアメールで送る send a letter *by airmail*; *airmail* a letter(◆後の表現の airmailは「エアメールで送る」の意味の動詞)

エアロビクス aerobics [eəróubɪks] ◯ (単数または複数扱い) / 週に2回エアロビクスをします I *do aerobics* twice a week.

えい¹ 少年はボールをえいっと(→カー杯)投げた The boy threw the ball「(*at*) *full strength* [*as hard as he could*].

えい² 鱝 ray ◯

えいえいじてん 英英辞典 English-English dictionary ◯ (◆英米などでは特に断らなくても、an English dictionary で「英英辞典」を指す)

エイエルティー ALT (✦ *Assistant Language Teacher* (外国語指導助手)の略語)
⇒ 場面・状況別会話 p.1746

えいえん 永遠 eternity ◯; (不滅) immortality ◯ ――永遠の eternal, everlasting; immortal ――永遠に eternally, forever ‖永遠の愛を誓う pledge *eternal love* / 永遠の真理 *eternal truth* / 私たちの愛は永遠に続くだろう Our love will「*last forever* [*never die*]. / 彼は永遠の眠りについた He has gone to *his eternal rest*.

えいが 映画
(個々の作品) movie ◯, film ◯, 《公式的》motion picture ◯; (総称) the movies, the cinema ⇒ 場面・状況別会話 p.1704

《〜映画》
アクション映画 *an* action *movie* [*film*] / アニメ映画 *an* animated *movie* [*film*] (✦《米》では「日本のアニメ映画」のことを anime という) / 記録映画 *a* documentary *film*; a documentary / 白黒映画 *a* black-and-white *movie* [*film*] / 成人映画 *an* adult *movie* [*film*] / 戦争映画 *a* war *movie* [*film*] / 短編映画 *a short film* / テレビ映画 *a* TV *movie* / B級映画 *a* B *movie* / ホラー映画 *a* horror *movie* / ポルノ映画 *a* porn(ographic) *movie* / 無声映画 *a* silent *movie* [*film*] / トム・ハンクス主演の映画 *a movie* starring [featuring] Tom Hanks
◆2本立ての映画 *a double feature*

《映画を》
映画を見に行く go to *the movies* / 映画を上映する show *a movie* / 映画を監督する direct *a movie* / 映画を撮影する shoot (*a film*) / 映画を制作する produce [make] *a movie*
僕はその映画をテレビで見た I watched the *movie* on TV. (◆ふつう映画館で見るときは see, テレビで見るときは watch を用いる)

《映画が/は》
今度の土曜日にいよいよその映画が封切りになる The *film* will finally open [be released] next Saturday.
その映画はスタジオで[ロケで]撮影された The *movie* was filmed「in the studio [on location]」.

《映画に》
その俳優はたくさんの映画に出ている The actor appears *in* a lot of *movies*.

《その他》
その小説は映画化された The novel *was made into a film*.
映画の上映に先立って主演女優の舞台あいさつがあった The leading actress appeared on the stage to say a few words before *the showing* (*of the movie*) started.
● 「チャップリンの映画を見たことがありますか」「はい、『モダン・タイムス』を見ました」 "Have you ever seen any Charlie Chaplin *movies*?" "Yes. I've seen *Modern Times*."
● 「オリオン座では今何の映画をやってるの」「タイ

[え]

トルは忘れたけど, 確か古いフランス映画だったと思う」 "*What's on* [*showing, playing*] at the Orion?" "I forgot the title, but I think it was *an old French movie*."

[会]「映画のチケットが2枚あるんだけど, いっしょに行かない?」「ごめん. その映画, もう見ちゃったんだ」 "I've got two *movie tickets*. Would you like to go with me?" "Sorry, but I've seen that *movie* already."

‖映画音楽 screen music / 映画界 the movies, the film world / 映画会社 a movie [film] company / 映画館《米》a movie theater [house], 《英》a cinema / 映画監督 a (movie) director / 映画祭 a film festival / 映画撮影所 a movie studio / 映画産業 the movie industry, the movie business / 映画スター a film [movie] star / 映画制作 filmmaking, film production / 映画俳優 (男性) a movie actor; (女性) a movie actress / 映画ファン a movie fan, a moviegoer, 《口語的》a movie buff

[関連語] 字幕 subtitles / 吹き替え dubbing / 洋画 a foreign film / 邦画 a Japanese film / ロードショー a road show / 試写会 a preview / 配給会社 a distributing company

えいかいわ 英会話 English conversation [U]

英会話を習いたい I want to take lessons in *English conversation*.

◆彼は英会話が得意[苦手]だ He is good [poor] at *conversational English*.

‖英会話学校 an English language school / 英会話教室 an English conversation class

えいかく 鋭角 acute angle [C]

えいかん 栄冠 crown [C] ◆わがチームは栄冠に輝いた Our team *was crowned with victory*. / Our team *won the championship*.

えいきゅう 永久 eternity [U]; (不変) permanence [U] ―永久的な eternal; permanent ―永久に forever, for good (❖ for good のほうが口語的), eternally; permanently

彼は永久に帰ってこないように思われた He seemed to have gone *for good*.

これは永久になぞのままだろう This will remain a mystery *forever*.

◆この製品には永久保証がついている This product comes with *a lifetime guarantee*.

> [英作文ノート]「永久に忘れません」の訳し方
> このことは永久に忘れません
> →×I will *not forget* this *forever*.
> →○I will *never forget* this *all my life*.
> →○I will *remember* this *forever*.
> ★not ... forever は部分否定になり, 上の例だと「このことを永久に忘れないわけではありません」となってしまう.

‖永久歯 a permanent tooth / 永久磁石 a permanent magnet

えいきょう 影響

influence [U][C]; (効果) effect [C][U]; (強烈な) impact [C] ―影響する influence [他]; (直接的に) affect [他]

中国ではまだ孔子の影響が残っている *The influence* of Confucius is still alive in China.

増税が我々の生活にかなりの影響を及ぼした The tax increase *affected* our lives greatly.

人々は環境に大いに影響される People *are* greatly *influenced* by their environment.

風の変化が試合に大きく影響している The shift in wind *is having a* big *effect on* the game.

彼女は彼に悪い影響を与えている She *is a* bad *influence on* him. (❖この influence は「影響を及ぼす人・物」の意味)

喫煙は健康に悪影響を及ぼす Smoking has *a bad* [*harmful*] *effect on* your health.

若い世代の人々は外国からの影響を受けやすい The younger generation is easily affected by foreign *influences*.

彼の影響でバイオリンを始めました Due to his *influence*, I took up the violin./ He *influenced* me to take up the violin.

彼はいまだ政界に強い影響力をもっている He still exerts *a* strong *influence on* the political world.

◆大雪の影響で飛行機の出発が延びた The flights were postponed *because of* the heavy snow.

えいぎょう 営業 (業務) business [U]; (販売) sales ―営業する do* business, operate [自] ‖新しい営業方針を採用する adopt new *business policies* / 営業時間中にご連絡ください Contact us during *business hours*. / 彼は営業マンだ(→営業部で働いている) He *works in sales* [*the sales department*]. / 彼女は営業成績がよい She has *a* good *sales record*. / 円高のためにその会社は営業不振に陥った The company went into *a business slump* due to the strong yen.

◆営業中《掲示》*Open*; *Yes, We Are Open* / 当社は9時から5時まで営業いたします Our office *is open* from nine to five. / 営業担当者をよこしてください We would like you to send around *your salesperson*. / その店は年中無休, 24時間営業だ The shop is *open 24 hours a day*, seven days a week.

‖営業案内 a business guide / 営業所 an office; (支店) a branch (office) / 営業戦略 marketing strategy / 営業停止(営業免許の停止) the suspension of *one's* business license / 営業部 a sales department [division] / 営業部長 a sales director / 営業妨害 obstruction of *a person's* business

えいご 英語

English [U], the English language (❖ English よりもかたい表現)

〚英語が・は〛

あなたは英語が話せますか Do you speak *English*? (❖ Can you speak English? も用いるが, あからさまに相手の英語能力を問うことになる可能性があるので注意が必要)

彼女は英語が(→英語を話すのが)うまい[下手だ] She is good [poor] at *English*./ She is a

good [poor] speaker of *English*. / She speaks good [poor] *English*.
僕はもっと英語がうまくなりたい I want to improve *my English*.
彼の英語は分からなかった I didn't understand his *English*.
ロンドンで私の英語は全然通じなかった(→英語で私のいうことを理解してもらえなかった) I couldn't make myself understood in *English* in London.
〖英語を〗
彼は英語らしい英語を話す He speaks idiomatic *English*.
私はもう5年以上英語を習っているのに全然しゃべれない I can't speak *English* at all even though I've been studying it for more than five years.
〖英語の〗
英語の(→英語で書かれた)本 a book (*written*) *in English* / 英語の話し言葉[書き言葉] spoken [written] *English*
彼は英語のテストでよい成績を取った He did well on *the English test* [*exam*].
週に何時間英語の授業がありますか How many *English classes* do you have a week?
父は高校で英語の先生をしている My father is *an English teacher* [*teaches English*] at a high school.
ここに英語の分かる人はいますか Is there *anyone who speaks English* here?
〖英語で〗
その質問に彼女は英語で答えた She answered the question *in English*.
🅔「「はさみ」は英語で何といいますか」「scissors です」 "How do you say 'hasami' *in English*? / What is *the English* (*word*) *for* 'hasami'?" "Scissors."
〖その他〗
通じる英語 communicative *English*
彼女にはすばらしい英語力がある She has *a good command of English*.
兄は英語学を専攻している My brother is majoring in *English*.
∥英語教育 the teaching of English / 英語国民 English-speaking people / アメリカ英語 American English / イギリス英語 British English / オーストラリア英語 Australian English / 時事英語 media [news] English / 商業英語 business English / 標準英語 standard English

えいこう 栄光 glory ⓤ ∥過去の栄光 departed *glory* / (過去の)栄光の日々 *glory days* / …に栄光をもたらす bring *glory* to …

えいこく 英国 (Great) Britain; England(❖ 厳密には Britain の一部だが、これで英国を代表させることがある) ──英国の British; English ⇨ イギリス ∥英国人は紅茶を飲むのが好きだ *English people* like to drink tea. / 彼は米国人だと思っていたのだが、実際は英国人だった I assumed that he was American, but actually he was *British*.

えいこせいすい 栄枯盛衰 rise and fall
【慣用表現】栄枯盛衰は世の習い(→人生には浮き沈みがある) *Life has its ups and downs*.

えいさい 英才 (bright) talent ⓤ; (人) gifted [talented] person ⓒ ∥英才教育 special education for gifted children

えいさくぶん 英作文 English composition ⓤⓒ ∥英作文を書く write *an English composition* [*essay*] ◆私は英作文(→日本語から英語に直すこと)が苦手だ I'm not good at *Japanese-to-English translation*.

えいし 英詩 (総称) English poetry ⓤ; (個々の作品) English poem ⓒ

えいじ 英字 English letter ⓒ ∥英字新聞 an English-language newspaper

えいしゃ 映写 projection ⓤ ──映写する project ⓗ ∥映写機 a (motion-picture) projector / 映写技師 a projectionist / 映写室 a projection room / 映写幕 a screen

えいじゅう 永住 ──永住する settle ⓘ ∥彼はスイスに永住するつもりだ He is planning to *settle down* in Switzerland. ◆彼女はアメリカ人と結婚して、永住権を得た She married an American and got *a green card*. (❖ green card は米国の永住権を表す通称)

エイズ 〔医学〕 AIDS ⓤ (❖ Acquired *I*mmunodeficiency [*I*mmune *D*eficiency] *S*yndrome(後天性免疫不全症候群)の略語) ∥エイズに感染している have *AIDS*; be infected with *AIDS* / エイズに苦しむ人々を支援する support people suffering from *AIDS*
∥エイズウイルス the AIDS virus, HIV / エイズ患者 an AIDS patient [victim], a person with AIDS(《略語》PWA) / エイズ感染者 an HIV-positive person, an HIV carrier / エイズ治療薬 a cure for AIDS

えいせい¹ 衛生 (衛生設備の状態) sanitation ⓤ; (衛生状態) hygiene [háidʒiːn] ⓤ ──衛生的な sanitary(❖名詞の前で用いる); hygienic ∥衛生状態が悪い地域 areas where *hygiene* is poor / 彼らは衛生観念が発達している They are highly conscious of *hygiene*. / 特に夏場は衛生に気をつけなくてはいけません You have to be careful about *sanitation*, especially in summer. ◆不衛生な環境 an *unsanitary* [*unhygienic*] environment
∥衛生試験場 a hygienic laboratory / 環境衛生 environmental sanitation / 公衆衛生 public health / 歯科衛生士 a (dental) hygienist / 精神衛生 mental health [hygiene]

えいせい² 衛星 (惑星の衛星) satellite ⓒ, moon ⓒ; (人工衛星) (artificial) satellite ⓒ ∥月は地球の衛星である The moon is *a satellite* of the earth. / この番組はロンドンから衛星生中継でお送りしています We're bringing this program to you *live by satellite* from London. / 人工衛星が軌道からはずれてしまった[軌道に乗った] *The satellite* has "gone out of [been put in] orbit." / これらのテレビ番組は衛星中継で伝えられている These TV programs *are transmitted by satellite*. / このアパートではテレビ衛星放送が入る We can get *satellite* TV in this apartment. (❖ TV をbroadcasts にするとラジオの衛星放送の意味も含

‖衛星国 a satellite state / 衛星都市 a satellite city / 気象衛星 a weather satellite / 軍事衛星 a military satellite / スパイ衛星 a spy satellite / 通信衛星 a communications satellite

えいせいちゅうりつ 永世中立 permanent neutrality ◎ ‖永世中立国 a permanently neutral country

えいぞう 映像 image ◎, picture ◎ ‖映像を送る transmit *images* / うちのテレビは映像があまり鮮明ではない Our TV doesn't have *a very sharp [clear] picture*.

◆首相の外遊のニュース映像 *a news film of the prime minister's trip abroad*

えいぞく 永続 ――永続的な lasting, enduring, permanent ‖永続する last long / 永続的な平和 *lasting* peace

えいだん 英断 英断を下す(→賢明な決断を下す) make *a wise decision*; (→思いきった措置をとる) take「*a decisive step [drastic action]*

えいち 英知 wisdom ◎ ◆その辞典の編纂(へんさん)に多くの英知が集められた A lot of *intellectuals* were assembled to compile the dictionary.

エイチアイブイ [医学] HIV ◎ (❖**human immunodeficiency virus**(ヒト免疫不全ウイルス)の略語) ‖HIVに感染している be infected with *HIV* / HIV抗体陽性である be *HIV positive*

えいてん 栄転 promotion ◎ ――栄転する be promoted ‖彼女は本社の営業部長に栄転した She *was promoted to* sales director at the headquarters.

えいびん 鋭敏 ――鋭敏な sharp; (感覚などが) acute, keen ‖鋭敏なジャーナリスト an *acute* journalist / 鋭敏な頭脳 *keen* intellect / 鋭敏な嗅覚(きゅうかく) a *keen* sense of smell

えいぶん 英文 (英語) English ◎; (英語の文) English sentence [text] ◎

◆英文の手紙 an *English* letter; a letter (written) in *English* ‖英文科 an English department / 英文和訳 a translation from English to Japanese

えいぶんがく 英文学 English literature ◎

えいぶんぽう 英文法 English grammar ◎

えいへい 衛兵 guardsman ◎, guard ◎

えいべい 英米 Britain and America, America and Britain ――英米の British and American, American and British, Anglo-American ‖英米人 the British and Americans

えいみん 永眠 ――永眠する pass away (❖die の婉曲的な言い方)

えいやく 英訳 English translation ◎

◆次の日本語を英訳しなさい *Put [Translate]* the following Japanese *into English*.

えいゆう 英雄 (男性) hero ◎; (女性) heroine ◎ ――英雄的な heroic ‖英雄的な行い *heroic deed* / 人を英雄視する *regard* a person *as a hero* ‖リンカーンはアメリカの英雄だ Lincoln is *an* American *hero*. / 彼らは死去した国民的英雄をたたえて彼の大好きだった歌を歌った They sang his favorite song as a tribute to *the* deceased *national hero*.

えいよ 栄誉 honor, (英)honour ◎, glory ◎ ‖栄誉に輝く be covered in [with] *glory*; be honored / 優勝の栄誉をたたえて校歌が演奏された The school song was played *in honor of* winning the championship.

‖国民栄誉賞 the People's Honor Award

えいよう 栄養 (栄養物) nourishment ◎; (栄養摂取) nutrition ◎

栄養と休養を十分にとることが大切だ It's important to take sufficient *nutrition* and rest.

このスープは栄養満点だ This soup is *full of nourishment*. / This soup is *very nourishing*.

◆栄養のある食べ物 *nourishing [nutritious]* food / 栄養バランスのよい食事 a *well-balanced diet* / 栄養のいい[よくない]赤ん坊 a *well [badly] nourished* baby / 彼は栄養が足りない He *is undernourished*.

‖栄養価 nutritional [food] value / 栄養学 nutrition / 栄養強化食品 enriched food / 栄養剤 a nutrient / 栄養士 a dietician / 栄養失調 malnutrition / 栄養素 a nutrient / 栄養不良 undernourishment

えいり¹ 営利 profit ◎ ‖営利目的の *profit-making* / 営利目的で for *profit*

‖営利事業 a commercial enterprise / 営利主義 commercialism / 営利団体 a commercial organization / 非営利組織 a nonprofit organization((略語)NPO)

えいり² 鋭利 ――鋭利な sharp ‖それは鋭利な物で刺した傷跡だった The stab wounds were caused by a *sharp* object.

エイリアン (異星人) alien ◎; (地球外生物) extraterrestrial ◎ ((略語)E.T.)

えいりんしょ 営林署 district forestry office ◎

えいわじてん 英和辞典 English-Japanese dictionary ◎

ええ ❶[返答・相づち] (肯定の答え) Yes, Yeah (❖くだけた言い方); (否定文に対する答え) No; (相づち) Uh-huh [əhʌ́] ◎

🅔「彼は越後大学に入学したんだよね」「ええ, そうです」"He entered Echigo University, didn't he?" "*Yes*, he did."

🅔「窓をあけましょうか」「ええ, お願いします」"Shall I open the window?" "*Yes*, please."

🅔「電話を借りてもいいですか」「ええ, どうぞ」"May I use your telephone?" "*Sure*."

❷[驚き・疑問]

🅔「彼女, ハワイ旅行が当たったんだって」「ええっ, 本当?」"I hear she won a trip to Hawaii!" "*Really*?"

🅔「来週また数学のテストがあるらしいよ」「ええっ, きのうやったばかりなのに?」"Do you know we'll have another math exam next week?" "*What*? We just had one yesterday!"

エーエム (ラジオの) AM ◎ (❖**amplitude modulation**(振幅変調)の略語)

エーカー acre [C] (❖約4,047m²; 《略語》A., a., ac.) ∥その牧場は10エーカーの広さだ The pasture has an area of 10 *acres*.

エージェンシー (代理店・代理業) agency [C]

エージェント (代理人・代理業者) agent [C]

エース ace [C] ∥ハートのエース *the ace* of hearts / うちのチームのエースピッチャー *the ace* [*number one*] pitcher on our team

エーテル ether [íːθər] [U]

エーデルワイス 〔植物〕edelweiss [C]

ええと Let me see., Let's see. (❖何かを思い出したり, 捜している場合); OK, O.K. (❖別の話題に移ったり, 間をおいたりする場合); Well (❖考えるために間をおく場合) ∥ええと…, そうだね, 金曜日なら都合がつくよ *Let me see*. … Yes, I'm available on Friday.

💬「そこへはどう行けばいいですか」「ええと, …」"How can I get there?" "*Let me see*. …"

💬「私の辞書がどこにあるか知りませんか」「ええと, ここにあります」"Do you know where my dictionary is?" "*Um*, here it is."

エーブイ AV ⚠ AV機器 *audiovisual equipment* (❖AVは *a*udio*v*isual (視聴覚の) の略語だが英語ではあまり省略形を用いない) / その女優はAV (→アダルトビデオ) に出ていた The actress used to appear in *adult videos*. (❖この意味のAVは和製略語)

エープリルフール ⚠April Fool's Day (❖英語の April Fool はエープリルフールにだまされた人, またはそのうそやいたずらを指す) ∥エープリルフールの冗談に引っかかる fall for an *April Fool's Day* joke

エール yell [jél] [C] ∥エールを交換する exchange *yells* ◆エールを送る (→励まし[支援]のメッセージを送る) give *an encouraging* [*a supportive*] *message*; (→人を励ます) encourage *a person*

えがお 笑顔 smile [C] ∥明るい笑顔 *a* sunny *smile* / 彼の笑顔を見て彼が試験に合格したことが分かった His *smile* told me (that) he had passed the exam. / 彼女は笑顔で我々を出迎えた She greeted us *with a smile*.

えかき 絵描き painter [C], artist [C]

えがく 描く

❶【絵にする】(絵の具で) paint [他]; (鉛筆・ペン・クレヨンなどで) draw* [他]; (心に描く) imagine [他], picture [他]

子供たちはその山の絵を描いた The children *painted* the mountain.

悪魔が黒猫として描かれていた Devils *were drawn* as black cats.

彼は宇宙飛行士になった自分の姿を心に描いた He *pictured* himself as an astronaut.

❷【描写する】(示す) show* [他]; (描写する) portray [他], 《公式的》depict [他]; (表現する) describe [他], represent [他]

その絵は日本の庶民の暮らしを描いている The painting *portrays* [*depicts*] the lives of ordinary people in Japan.

この小説は彼女を天使のように描いている This novel *represents* her as an angel.

◆その本は中国人の生活を生き生きと描いている The book *gives* us *a good picture of* how Chinese people live. / あの飛行機は円を描きながら飛んでいる That plane is flying *in a circle*.

えがたい 得難い (貴重な) invaluable ∥得がたい経験 an *invaluable* experience

えき[1] 駅

station [C] (❖鉄道の駅であることを明示するには, railroad station や train station を用いる)

東京駅 Tokyo *Station* (❖駅名は無冠詞) / 地下鉄の駅 *a* subway *station* / 駅までバスで行く take a bus to *the station*

駅へはどう行けばいいですか How can I get to *the station*?

駅に着いたら電話をください Give me a call when you arrive at *the station*.

この道路は駅前で大通りと交差している This road crosses the main street *in front of the station*.

午前中にご到着ですか, それなら駅へ迎えに行けます Are you arriving in the morning? If so, I can meet you at *the station*.

急行列車はこの駅を通過します Express trains pass through this *station*.

次の駅で降ります[乗り換えます] We「get off [change trains] at *the next station*.

💬「ここから最寄りの駅まで歩いてどれくらいですか」「だいたい5分くらいです」"How long does it take to walk from here to *the nearest station*?" "About five minutes."

💬「すごい雨だよ」「お母さんに頼んで駅まで送ってもらおうか」"It's raining really hard." "Shall we ask Mom to drive us to *the station*?"

💬「京都まで駅はあといくつありますか」「3つです」"How many *stations* [*stops*] are there between here and Kyoto?" "There are three."

‖駅員 a station employee; (駅全体の職員) the station staff / 駅長 a stationmaster / 駅長室 the stationmaster's office / 駅ビル a station building with a shopping complex / 駅弁 ➔ えきべん

えき[2] 液 liquid [U] [C]

えき[3] 益 (利益) profit [U]; (効用) use [U] ∥彼らとけんかしても何の益もない It's no *use* arguing with them.

えきか 液化 liquefaction [U] ━液化する liquefy [自] [他] ‖液化石油ガス liquefied petroleum gas (《略語》LPG) / 液化天然ガス liquefied natural gas (《略語》LNG)

エキサイト ━エキサイトする get* excited ∥そのボクサーは試合前からかなりエキサイトしていた The boxer *had* already *gotten excited* before the match started.

エキシビション (展覧会) exhibition [èksibíʃən] [C]

えきしゃ 易者 fortune-teller [C]

えきしょう 液晶 liquid crystal [U] ‖液晶画面 a liquid crystal screen / 液晶テレビ a liquid crystal display [an LCD] TV

えきじょうか 液状化 liquefaction [U] ‖液状

化現象 a liquefaction phenomenon
エキス ⚠ (抽出物) extract / レモンのエキス lemon extract
エキストラ extra
エキスパート (専門家) expert
エキスパンダー expander
エキスポ (博覧会) expo (しばしば Expo) (複 ~s)
エキセントリック ――エキセントリックな (風変わりな) eccentric
エキゾチック ――エキゾチックな (異国風の) exotic [igzátik]
えきたい 液体 liquid, fluid (❖ fluid は液体 (liquid) と気体 (gas) の総称だが, ふつうは液体を指す) / 無色透明の液体 a colorless and transparent liquid / 液体洗剤 a liquid detergent / 液体燃料 liquid fuel
えきちゅう 益虫 beneficial insect
えきちょう 益鳥 beneficial bird
えきでん 駅伝 an ekiden, a long-distance relay race over public roads
えきびょう 疫病 plague, epidemic / 疫病の蔓延(まんえん)を防ぐ contain an epidemic
えきべん 駅弁 a box lunch sold at a station (for a train trip)
エキュ ECU, ecu [eikú:] (❖ European Currency Unit (欧州通貨単位) の略語)
エクスタシー ecstasy
エクスプレス (急行) express
エグゼクティブ (上級管理職) executive
えくぼ dimple / 彼女は笑うとえくぼができる Dimples appear on her face when she smiles.
えぐる 抉る scrape, gouge ◆ 胸にえぐるような痛みを感じる feel a sharp pain in the chest / 問題の核心をえぐる get to the core of a problem
エクレア éclair (❖ フランス語から)
えげつない その会社はえげつない商売をすることで悪名高い The company is notorious for its unscrupulous way of business.
エゴ (自我) ego (複 ~s) ; (エゴイズム) selfishness, egoism ◆ 彼はエゴの塊(かたまり)だ He is very selfish.
エゴイスト (利己主義者) selfish [self-centered] person ――エゴイストの selfish, self-centered
エコー echo ; (音響効果) echo effect / (カラオケの) エコーをきかす turn on the echo effect
エコノミークラス economy class, (米) coach (class) / エコノミークラスの航空券 an economy class air ticket ◆ エコノミークラスで旅行する travel economy [by coach]
エコノミスト (経済学者) economist
えこひいき 教師は生徒をえこひいきしてはいけない A teacher should not favor one student over another. / その先生はえこひいきをしない The teacher is not partial to anybody.
エコロジー (生態学) ecology

えさ 餌 (釣り針・わななどにつけるえさ) bait ; (動物飼育用のえさ) feed ; (食べ物) food / 魚はえさに食いついた The fish snapped at the bait.
◆ 釣り針にえさをつける bait a hook / この鳥のえさは何ですか What does this bird feed on? (❖ feed on ... は「(動物が)…を常食とする」の意味) / 鳥にえさをやらないでください Do not feed the birds.
えじき 餌食 prey / 彼はペテン師のえじきとなった He fell prey to a swindler.
エジプト Egypt [íːdʒipt] (❖ 公式名 the Arab Republic of Egypt) ――エジプト人 Egyptian [idʒípʃən] ――エジプト(人)の Egyptian
えしゃく 会釈 bow, nod ――会釈する nod / 彼女はすれ違いざまに先生に会釈をした She nodded to the teacher as she passed him. / 社長は私に親しげに会釈をしてくれた The president gave me a friendly nod.
エジンバラ Edinburgh (❖ 英国の都市)
エスエフ SF (❖ science fiction (空想科学小説) の略語) ; sci-fi [sáifái] / SF映画 an SF movie / SF作家[小説] an SF writer [novel]
エスエル SL ⚠ steam locomotive (❖ SL は和製略語)
エスオーエス SOS / SOSを発信する send an SOS
エスカレーター escalator / 上り[下り]のエスカレーター an up [a down] escalator / エスカレーターに乗る take an escalator / エスカレーターで上[下]に行く go up [down] on an escalator / この学校はエスカレーター式で (→入学試験を受けずに) 大学に行ける The students at this school can go on to the university without taking entrance exams.
エスカレート ――エスカレートする escalate / 紛争はその事件をきっかけにエスカレートしていった As a result of that incident, the conflict escalated further.
エスキモー Eskimo (複 ~s, ~) (❖ 軽蔑的な響きをもつため, イヌイット (Inuit) を使うことが多い) ――エスキモーの Eskimo
◆ エスキモー語 Eskimo
エスコート ――エスコートする (付き添う) escort
エスサイズ Sサイズ small, S ⇒ サイズ
エスじ S字 ――S字の S-shaped
エステティシャン (a)esthetician (❖ 英米ではあまりなじみのある言葉ではない)
エステティックサロン ⚠ beauty-treatment clinic (❖ ×(a)esthetic salon とはいわない)
エスニック ――エスニックの ethnic / エスニック料理 ethnic food [cooking, dishes]
エスプリ wit (❖ 日本語はフランス語の esprit から) ◆ エスプリのきいた冗談 a witty joke
エスペラント Esperanto
えせ (偽の) pseudo- [sjú:dou] ; (自称) would-be / えせ文化人 a pseudo-intellec-

えだ 枝 branch ◎; (大枝) bough [báu] ◎; (小枝) twig ◎; (花・葉・果実などをつけた小枝) spray ◎ ∥木の枝を切る cut *a branch* from a tree / 枝ぶりのいい木 (→形のいい枝をもった木) a tree *with shapely branches* / チンパンジーが枝から枝へとぶら下がって移動していた A chimpanzee was swinging *from branch to branch*. ◆丸の内線は中野坂上で枝分かれしている The Marunouchi Line *splits* at Nakanosakaue.

えたい 得体 得体のしれない人物 a *dubious* character

えだげ 枝毛 split end ◎

えだまめ 枝豆 green soybean ◎

エチケット etiquette ◎; (行儀作法) manners ∥エチケットを守る observe *the rules of etiquette* / それはエチケットに反する That is against *etiquette*.

エチルアルコール ethyl alcohol ◎

えつ 悦 父は念願のゴルフクラブを手に入れてひとり悦に入っている My father looks *extremely happy* to get the golf club he had long wanted to buy.

えっ (聞き返し) What?, You what?, Pardon (me)?, 《英》Eh? (❖What?はややぞんざいな言い方); (驚き) What!, Oh? ∥えっ、何ですって *Pardon*? What did you say? / えっ、水がないって？ *What*! No water?
🔹「ほら、メグが手を振っているよ」「えっ、(彼女は)どこにいるの」 "Look! Meg is waving to us." "*Oh*? Where is she?"

えっきょう 越境 ──越境する cross the border ◆越境入学する (→学区外の学校に入る) enter a school outside *one's* school district

エックスせん X線 X-rays ∥X線検査 an X-ray examination / X線写真 an X-ray / X線療法 X-ray therapy

えづけ 餌付け ──餌付けする get* an animal to feed on the food you give it ◆そのイルカたちは餌付けされている (→人間にえさをもらう) Those dolphins *have accepted food from humans*.

えっけん 越権 そんなことをするのは彼の越権行為だ He overstepped (the boundaries of) *his authority* by doing that.

エッジ (端) edge ◎ ∥スキー板のエッジを研(と)ぐ sharpen *the edge of the skis*

エッセー essay ◎ ∥君のエッセーはとてもよく書けている Your *essay* is very well written.

エッセンス (本質) essence ◎ ∥禅のエッセンスが詰まった本 a book that contains *the essence of Zen*

エッチ エッチ (いやらしい) dirty (❖英語にはこの「エッチ」に当たる決まった表現はない) ∥エッチな冗談 a *dirty* joke / エッチなおやじ a *dirty* old man ◆彼とエッチする (→セックスする) have *sex* with *one's* boyfriend

エッチング etching ◎ (❖個々の作品は ◎)

えっとう 越冬 ──越冬する winter ◉, spend* the winter ∥越冬隊 a wintering party

エッフェルとう エッフェル塔 the Eiffel [áifəl] Tower

えっぺい 閲兵 review ◎ ◎ ──閲兵する review ◉

えつらん 閲覧 reading ◎ ──閲覧する read* ◉ ∥その図書館ではアメリカの主な雑誌が閲覧できる You can read the major American magazines at the library.
∥閲覧室 a reading room

エディター (編集者・ファイル編集ソフト) editor ◎

えてして 得てして 私たちは自分の過ちでもえてして他人を責めがちだ We *are apt to* blame others for our own faults.

エデン ∥エデンの園《聖書》the Garden of Eden, Eden, Paradise

えと 干支 △ *eto*, the (twelve) signs of the Chinese zodiac ◆今年の干支は申(ﾋﾞ)です This is the Year of the Monkey (according to Chinese astrology).

> 干支は、12種類の動物で象徴される中国式十二宮のことで、実在する動物に加え、想像上の動物とされる「辰(ﾂ)」が含まれています。西洋の十二宮が月を示すのに対し、干支は年を示します。
> *Eto* refers to the Chinese zodiac signs symbolized by twelve animals including a mythical animal, the dragon *tatsu*. While the Western zodiac signs indicate the months, *eto* represents years.

えど 江戸 Edo ∥江戸時代 the Edo period / 江戸幕府 the Edo shogunate

えとく 会得 ──会得する (十分理解する) understand* ◉, grasp ◉; (覚えて身につける) learn* ◉; (熟達する) master ◉ ∥道具の使い方を会得する *learn* how to use a tool

エトセトラ etc., et cetera

えどっこ 江戸っ子 △ an *Edokko*, a person born and bred in Tokyo

エナメル enamel ◎ ∥エナメル革 patent leather / エナメル質(歯の) enamel

えにっき 絵日記 picture diary ◎

エヌジー NG ⚠ NGシーン an outtake (❖NGは no good の和製略語)

エネルギー ⚠ energy [énərdʒi] ◎ (❖日本語はドイツ語の Energie から) ∥仕事にエネルギーを注ぐ put *one's energy* into *one's* work / エネルギーを節約する save *energy* / 太陽エネルギーを電力に変える convert *solar energy* into electricity / エネルギー消費が大幅に減少した *The consumption of energy* has decreased substantially. / エネルギー資源の大半を海外に仰いでいる The great bulk of *energy resources* comes from abroad.
∥エネルギー危機 an energy crisis / エネルギー源 a source of energy / エネルギー問題 an energy problem / 位置エネルギー potential energy / 運動エネルギー kinetic energy / 核エネルギー nuclear energy / 代替エネルギー alternative energy

エネルギッシュ ⚠ ──エネルギッシュな energetic [ènərdʒétik] (❖日本語はドイツ語の energisch から) ──エネルギッシュに energetically 〖エネルギッシュな人 an *energetic* person; a person *with a lot of energy*

えのぐ 絵の具 colors, paints(※水彩・油絵どちらにも用いられる); (水彩用) watercolors; (油彩用) oil colors 〖絵の具で絵を描く paint *in colors*
‖絵の具箱 a paint box

えはがき 絵葉書 picture postcard ⓒ
⇨巻末付録 (手紙・はがきの書き方)

えび 海老・蝦 (小エビ) shrimp ⓒ (複 ～s, ～); (車エビ) prawn ⓒ; (イセエビ) (spiny) lobster ⓒ 〖エビフライ a fried prawn
ことわざ エビで鯛(ﾀｲ)を釣る throw a shrimp to catch a sea bream; (→少しの努力で大きな利益を得る) get a large profit with a little effort

エピソード (逸話) anecdote ⓒ; (話) story ⓒ; (挿話) episode ⓒ 〖…にまつわる興味深いエピソード an interesting *story* about ...

えびちゃ 海老茶 maroon ⓤ ──えび茶の maroon, reddish brown

えひめ 愛媛

四国の北西部に位置する愛媛県は、北は瀬戸内海、西は宇和海に面しており、温暖な気候を利用したミカン栽培は全国的にも有名です。県都である松山は、日本最古の歴史をもつ道後温泉をはじめ、夏目漱石の小説『坊ちゃん』の舞台としても有名です。

Ehime Prefecture is located in northwestern Shikoku, facing the Seto Inland Sea to the north and the Uwa Sea to the west. Thanks to its mild climate, the cultivation of mandarin oranges has flourished in this prefecture and has gained a nationwide reputation. The capital of the prefecture, Matsuyama, is well known for the Dogo Onsen, the oldest hot spring in Japan, and also as the scene of a famous novel written by Natsume Soseki, *Botchan*.

エピローグ (結末) epilogue ⓤ

エフエム FM ⓤ (※ *f*requency *m*odulation (周波数変調)の略語) 〖FM放送局 an *FM* station

えふで 絵筆 brush ⓒ, paintbrush ⓒ

エフビーアイ FBI (※ the *F*ederal *B*ureau of *I*nvestigation ((米国) 連邦捜査局)の略語)

エプロン apron ⓒ 〖エプロンをつける[つけている] "put on [wear] *an apron*

エフワン F1, Formula One 〖F1ドライバー an F1 driver / F1レース Formula One racing

エベレスト Mt. Everest

えほん 絵本 picture book ⓒ ◆飛び出す絵本 *a pop-up book*
‖絵本作家 a picture-book writer

えま 絵馬 🔼

絵馬とは願い事をするとき、あるいは願い事がかなったときに神社や寺に奉納する板絵のことです。昔は神の乗り物とされていた馬が奉納されて

いましたが、やがて馬の絵を描いた絵馬が用いられるようになりました。今(ｲﾏ)では馬だけではなく、十二支の動物やかなり斬新(ｻﾝｼﾝ)の絵も描かれています。

An ema, a wooden tablet with a picture on it, is offered at shrines or temples when one prays for something or the prayers are answered. In ancient times horses were offered because they were believed to be the mount of the gods. Eventually the horse was replaced by an *ema* with a picture of a horse. Now you can find various motifs for *ema* including the 12 animals of the zodiac and some quite original themes.

えみ 笑み smile ⓒ ◆彼女は満面に笑みをたたえていた She was all *smiles*. / 彼は満面の笑みを浮かべて私たちを出迎えた He greeted us *with a big smile*.

エムサイズ Mサイズ medium ⓒⓤ, M ⓒⓤ
⇨サイズ

エムブイピー MVP (※ *m*ost *v*aluable *p*layer (最優秀選手)の略)

エメラルド emerald ⓒ 〖エメラルド色 emerald / エメラルドグリーン emerald green

えもいわれぬ えも言われぬ indescribable
〖えもいわれぬ美しい風景 a scene of *indescribable* beauty

えもの 獲物 (狩猟の)《集合的》game ⓤ; (しとめた) kill ⓒ《通例単数形》; (1回の猟[漁]での捕獲量) catch ⓒ, bag ⓒ; (えじき) prey ⓤ 〖野生の獲物を狩る hunt wild *game* / ライオンが獲物にそっと忍び寄った A lion stalked *its prey*. ◆きょうは獲物が多いぞ We *bagged a lot* today. / オオカミはふつう群れで獲物を狩る Wolves usually *hunt* in packs.

えら 鰓 gill [gíl] ⓒ《通例複数形～s》◆彼はえらが張っている (→四角いあごをしている) He *has a square jaw*.
‖えら呼吸 breathing through gills

エラー error ⓒ ──エラーする make* an error 〖捕手のエラーでうちに1点入った We got a run through the catcher's *error*.

えらい 偉い

❶〖りっぱだ〗(偉大な) great; (著名な) distinguished
偉い芸術家 a *great* artist / 偉い学者 a *distinguished* scholar
◆いっさい陰口を言わないのが彼女の偉いところだ (→陰口を言わないという点で彼女を尊敬する) I *admire* her for never talking about people behind their backs. / 彼は自分のことを偉いと思っている He thinks he's *somebody*. (※この somebody は「ひとかどの人物」の意味)

🅔「彼、毎日うちに帰ると両親の店の手伝いをしてるんだって」「偉いねえ」 "I hear he helps at his parents' shop every day after he gets home." "*Good for him*!"

🅔「だれか忘れるかもしれないと思って、余分に持ってきたよ」「直ちゃん、偉い！」 "I thought

somebody might forget, so I've brought some extra." "You're great, Nao-chan!"

❷【地位が高い】(有力な) important, big
偉い人 a *big* name [person]
彼はえらそうなことばかり言っている He's always talking *big*.

❸【重大な・はなはだしい】
えらいことになったぞ We're *in big trouble* now.
えらい(→とてもひどい)目にあった A *terrible* thing happened to me.
彼はえらく(→とても)ご機嫌ななめだった He was *very* angry.
彼らは僕のことがえらく(→とても)気に入ったようだ They seemed to like me *very much*.

えらぶ 選ぶ

choose* 働; select 働, pick 働 (❖select よりも口語的); (選出する) elect 働; (好む) prefer 働 (❖進行形にはできない)
好きなのを選んでください *Choose* the one you like.
私は母の誕生日のお祝いにこのスカーフを選びました I *chose* this scarf as my mother's birthday present.
花の種類が多すぎてどれを選べばいいのか分からない There's such a large variety of flowers that I don't know *which one to choose*.
リストの中からどれか1冊選んでレポートを書きなさい *Pick* one book from the list and write a paper on it.
メインディッシュは次の5種類の中から選んでください Please *choose* a main dish *from among* the following five courses.
彼ら2人のどちらかなんて私には選べない I just *can't choose between* the two of them.
桑田君は生徒会長に選ばれた Kuwata *was elected* president of the student council. (❖役職者が1人のときは無冠詞)
彼は柔道のオリンピック代表選手に選ばれた He *was picked for* the Olympic judo team.
僕だったらあっちよりこっちのほうを選ぶ I would *prefer* this *to* that.
◆第2外国語にはスペイン語を選んだ I *took* Spanish as my second foreign language. / 私は恥じながら生きるより死を選ぶ I *would rather* die *than* live in shame.

🗨 「彼女へのプレゼントの選びにつきあってくれないか」「いいよ」 "Could you come and help me *choose* a present for my girlfriend?" "OK."

🗨 「彼女,最近よくテレビに出てるね」「CMのオーディションで2万人の中から選ばれたんだって」 "She often appears on TV these days." "I know. They say she *was selected* from among 20,000 applicants in an audition for a commercial."

えり 襟 collar 🄲; (上着のえりの折り返し) lapel 🄲
/えりを立てる turn up *one's* collar / コートのえりを立てて with *the collar of one's* overcoat turned up / 彼女は上着のえりにブローチをつけていた She had a brooch on *the lapel* of her jacket.
|慣用表現| えりを正して話を聞く *straighten up* and *pay attention* / えりを正す(→態度を改める) *shape up*; *improve one's behavior*

えりあし 襟足 the nape (of *one's* neck)

エリート ⚠(集合的) the elite (❖日本語の「エリート」は個人を指すことが多いが,英語の elite は集団を意味する) /彼の兄は東大出のエリートです His brother is one of *the elite*, being a graduate of the University of Tokyo.
‖エリート意識 elitism / エリートコース the fast track, the beaten track of career success / エリート社員 an elite employee

えりくび 襟首 the nape [scruff] (of *one's* neck) /人のえり首をつかむ hold a person by *the scruff of the neck*

えりごのみ 選り好み 弟は食べ物のえり好みが激しい My brother is very *particular* [*choosy*, *picky*] *about* his food. (❖choosy, picky は particular よりもくだけた表現で, picky は非難をこめて用いられることが多い)

えりすぐり 選りすぐり ━━えりすぐりの select, picked /日本チームはえりすぐりのメンバーでアジア大会に臨んだ *Select* members of the Japanese team participated in the Asian tournament.

えりすぐる 選りすぐる select 働

えりぬき 選り抜き えり抜きの選手たち the *very best* players

えりまき 襟巻 scarf 🄲, 《古風》muffler 🄲 /えり巻きをしている wear *a scarf* (around the neck) / えり巻きをはずす take off *a scarf*

えりわける 選り分ける sort out

える 得る

get* 働; acquire 働; win* 働; gain 働; obtain 働; earn 働
- get: 最も一般的な語.
- acquire: get よりも, 努力して, または時間をかけてというニュアンスをもつ.
- win: 賞品・勝利・名誉などを勝ち取る.
- gain: 地位・名声・待遇などを獲得する.
- obtain: 努力・依頼などによって獲得するという意味の改まった表現.
- earn: 名声・信用・金などを得る.

どうやってその情報を得たのですか How did you *get* the information?
早退するには先生の許可を得なければならない You must *get* your teacher's permission to leave school before the classes are over.
彼はようやくアメリカの永住権を得た He finally *acquired* a green card.
その考えは多くの人の支持を得た The idea *gained* support from a lot of people.
彼女はピアニストとして国際的な評価を得ている She *has gained* an international reputation as a pianist.
彼は悲しい話で我々の同情を得ようとした He *tried to gain* our sympathy by telling a

[え]

sad story.
達成感というものは努力をして初めて得られるものだ A sense of fulfillment *can be obtained* only after you've worked hard to achieve something.
お金を得るためには働かねばならない We must work to *earn* money.
◆得るものの多い(→実り豊かな)経験 a *rewarding* [*fruitful*] experience / 私はその経験から多くのものを得た(→多くのことを学んだ) I *learned* a lot from that experience.

エルエスアイ LSI(❖*l*arge-*s*cale *i*ntegrated circuit(大規模集積回路)の略語)

エルエル LL ⚠ LL教室 *a language laboratory*(❖LLは和製略語. 英語では language lab と略す) / LLサイズのTシャツ an *extra-large* T-shirt(❖XLと略す)

エルサイズ Lサイズ large [C][U], L [C][U]
➾サイズ

エルサレム Jerusalem(❖イスラエルの首都. ただし国際的には認められていない)

エルディーケー LDK ⚠ 3LDKのマンション a *three-bedroom* apartment (*with a kitchen and a living and dining room*)(❖英語では a three-bedroom apartment だけがふつう. LDK は living, dining, kitchen の頭文字をとった和製略語. 英語では用いない)

エルニーニョ El Niño [U][C] (❖スペイン語から)

エルピーガス LPガス LPG [U] (❖*l*iquefied *p*etroleum *g*as(液化石油ガス)の略語)

エレガント ―エレガントな elegant

エレキギター electric guitar [C]

エレクトーン electronic [electric] organ [C]
(❖「エレクトーン」は商標名)

エレクトロニクス (電子工学) electronics《単数扱い》

エレベーター elevator [C], 《英》 lift [C] ‖下り[上り]のエレベーター *a* down [*an* up] *elevator* / 自動運転のエレベーター *a* self-service *elevator* / エレベーターで上る[下りる] go up [down] in *an elevator* / エレベーターに乗る[を降りる] ride [get off] *an elevator* / 5階までエレベーターに乗る take *the elevator* to the fifth floor / エレベーターが下りてきた *The elevator* came down.

エロス (神話) Eros(❖ギリシャ神話の恋愛の神); (性愛) eros [U]

エロチック ―エロチックな erotic, sexually exciting

エロぼん エロ本 dirty magazine [C]; (ポルノ)《口語的》 porn [U]

えん[1] 縁 (血縁などの関係) relation [U]; (結びつき) connection [C]; (機会) chance [C]
その人とは縁もゆかりもない(→何の関係もない) I *have no relation with* that man./ I *have nothing to do with* that man.
縁あってその先生のもとで言語学の研究をすることになった I've *got a chance* to study linguistics under that professor.
また縁があったらお会いしましょう(→再び会える機会があるといいですね) I hope we'll get another *chance* to meet.
◆(親が)親子の縁を切る *disown one's child* / 彼女とは縁を切った I *am through with* my girlfriend. / ブランド物にはあまり縁がない(→興味がない) I *have little interest* in brand-name items. / 彼女は気立てはいいのにどうも縁遠い(→結婚する可能性が少ない) She is a nice person, but somehow *there's not much prospect of her getting married.* / ポルトガルは日本と縁の深い国だ Portugal has had *a close relationship* with Japan. / その女優はベルギー王室と縁続きにあった The actress *was related to* the Belgian royal family. / ここでお会いしたのも何かの縁(→うれしい偶然)でしょう I met you here *by a happy coincidence.*
[ことわざ] 金の切れ目が縁の切れ目 ➾かね(金)

えん[2] 円
❶【円形】 circle [C] ➾ずけい [図版]
円を描いて飛ぶ fly in *a circle*
コンパスで円を描いた I drew *a circle* with the compass.
❷【通貨単位】 yen [C] (複〜)
100マルクは円に換算していくらですか How much is 100 marks *in yen*?
車を100万円で買った I bought the car for one million *yen.*
日本円を米ドルに両替できますか Can I exchange *Japanese yen* for American dollars?
円がドルに対して下がった[上がった] *The yen* has fallen [risen] against the dollar.
‖円借款 yen credit / 円相場 the exchange rate of the yen

えん[3] 宴 banquet [C]; (祝宴) feast [C] ‖宴を張る give [hold] *a banquet* ◆宴もたけなわだ *The party is in full swing.*

えんいん 遠因 (遠い原因) remote causes

えんえい 遠泳 long-distance swim [C] ―遠泳する have* a long-distance swim

えんえき 演繹 deduction [U] ―演繹的な deductive ―演繹する deduce [他]
‖演繹法 the deductive method, deduction

えんえん 延々 延々と続く車の列 a *continuous* line of cars / 延々2時間も待つ wait for two *long* hours / 会議は延々と何時間も続いた The meeting *dragged on* for hours. / サハラ砂漠が延々と続いていた The Sahara continued *forever.*

えんか[1] 演歌 🗻 (an) *enka*, a sentimental Japanese ballad
‖演歌歌手 an *enka* singer

明治時代の民権思想を庶民に分かりやすく伝えるために演説を歌にしたのが演歌の始まりでした. その後どんどん形を変えてきた演歌は, 今日(こんにち)ではもっぱら別れなど男女間の出来事をテーマにした情緒的なものになっています. 特に中高年の人々に人気があり, カラオケでは好んで歌われています.
Enka, which traces back to the Meiji period (1868-1912), was a kind of speech set to music as a means of easily spreading the new ideas of people's rights. It underwent a big transforma-

tion through the years to become the *enka* of today. Modern lyrics are more emotional, focusing upon problems between men and women, such as the sorrow of parting. *Enka* is popular especially among people middle-age and older, and it is often sung in karaoke places.

えんか² 塩化 ‖塩化水素 hydrogen chloride / 塩化ナトリウム sodium chloride / 塩化ビニール vinyl chloride / 塩化物 a chloride

えんかい¹ 沿海 coast ⓒ
‖沿海漁業 coastal fishery / 沿海地方 a coastal area

えんかい² 宴会 party ⓒ; (正式の) banquet ⓒ; (祝宴) feast ⓒ (❖日本での「飲み会」の意味では drinking party を使う) ‖宴会を開く hold *a party*
‖宴会場 a banquet hall

えんがい 煙害 damage caused by smoke

えんかく 沿革 history ⓒ ‖この会社の沿革 *the history* of this company

えんかくそうさ 遠隔操作 remote control ⓤ ‖遠隔操作で by *remote control*

えんかつ 円滑 ―円滑な smooth ―円滑に smoothly ‖円滑に進む go *smoothly*

えんがわ 縁側 🏠 an engawa; porch ⓒ, veranda(h) ⓒ (❖通例建物の1階の側面にあり, 床が地面より少し高くなっていて屋根がついている)

engawa　porch, veranda(h)

縁側は畳の部屋の外に設けられた板敷きの廊下のような空間で, 部屋との間には障子があります。縁側は家屋と庭を結ぶ役割を果たすほか, 家族や近所の人々とおしゃべりを楽しんだりする空間でもあります。しかし, 広い土地を確保するのが困難な現代では, 縁側を持つことも難しくなってきています。
An *engawa* is a wooden-floored porch along the outside of *tatami* rooms. It is separated from the rooms by *shoji* (sliding paper doors). It connects the house to the garden and provides a place to chat with family or neighbors. Nowadays, however, it is getting difficult to obtain enough space for *engawa* because the land available to one family is very small.

えんがん 沿岸 coast ⓒ ―沿岸の coastal ‖太平洋沿岸 the Pacific Coast; the coast of the Pacific Ocean / 船は沿岸を航行した The ship sailed along *the coast*.
‖沿岸漁業 coastal fishery / 沿岸地域 a coastal area

えんき 延期 postponement ⓤⓒ ―延期する postpone 🖋, put* off (❖put off のほうが口語的)
会議を次の金曜に延期することにした We decided to *postpone* [*put off*] the meeting till next Friday.
雨なら, 運動会は2日間延期になります If it rains, the athletic meet *will be put off* for two days.

えんぎ¹ 演技 performance ⓒ, acting ⓤ
すぐれた[お粗末な]演技 an artistic [a miserable] *performance*
彼らの演技は私たちの期待どおりだった Their *performance* lived [came] up to our expectations.
メリル・ストリープの演技力には定評がある Meryl Streep has a reputation for *her acting*.
◆スケートの自由演技 free skating / 彼は演技がうまい He *is a good actor*. / 彼女の怒りは本物で, 演技ではなかった Her anger was real. It wasn't *an act*.

えんぎ² 縁起 13は縁起の悪い数字だと信じられている Thirteen is believed to be an *unlucky* number. / 塩をこぼすことは縁起が悪いとされる To spill salt is thought to *bring bad luck*. / 縁起でもないことを言わないでくれ Don't say such a *sinister* thing. / うちの祖母は縁起をかつぐ(→迷信深い) My grandmother *is superstitious*. / その選手は縁起をかついで以前優勝したときにつけていたのと同じ靴を履いた *For good luck* the runner put on the same shoes he had worn the last time he won.
‖縁起物 a good luck charm

えんきょく 婉曲 ―婉曲(的)な euphemistic ◆彼女は婉曲に(→遠回しに)ビルのプロポーズを断った She turned down Bill's proposal of marriage *in a roundabout way*.
‖婉曲語法 euphemism / 婉曲表現 a euphemism, a euphemistic expression

えんきょり 遠距離 ―遠距離の long-distance ‖遠距離通勤 commuting a long distance / 遠距離列車 a long-distance train / 遠距離恋愛 a long-distance relationship

えんきん 遠近 ‖遠近感 a sense of perspective / 遠近法 perspective / 遠近両用眼鏡 bifocals, bifocal glasses / 遠近両用レンズ a bifocal lens

えんぐみ 縁組み (結婚) marriage ⓒ; (養子縁組み) adoption ⓤ

えんぐん 援軍 reinforcements ‖援軍を送る send [bring up] *reinforcements* / 援軍を要請する request *reinforcements*

えんけい 円形 ―円形の circular, round ‖円形劇場 an amphitheater / 円形脱毛症 a bald spot

えんげい 園芸 gardening ⓤ ◆彼女は園芸に凝っている She *is a keen gardener*.
‖園芸家 a gardener / 園芸学 horticulture

／園芸植物 a garden plant ／園芸用具 gardening tools ／園芸用手袋 gardening gloves

えんげい² 演芸 entertainment ⓤ,《米》vaudeville [vɔ́ːdəvìl] ⓤ,《英》variety ⓤ ‖演芸会 a show, a variety (show) ／演芸場 a vaudeville theater

エンゲージリング ⚠ engagement ring ⓒ (❖×engage ring とはいわない)

えんげき 演劇 play ⓒ (❖drama より一般的な語), drama ⓒⓤ ❖総称としては ⓤ, 個々の作品は ⓒ —演劇の theatrical ‖初めて劇場へ行って演劇に対する新しい関心が芽生えた My first visit to a theater awakened a new interest in *drama*. ／この演劇が日本で上演されたことはない This *play* has never been performed in Japan.
◆彼の夢は演劇の世界で働くことである His dream is to do theater work.
‖演劇界 the theater, the theatrical world ／演劇部 a drama club

エンゲルけいすう エンゲル係数 Engel's coefficient ⓒ (❖ 米 米ではほどなじみがない)
◆わが家のエンゲル係数は高い (→収入の多くを食費に使う) We *spend much of our income on food*.

えんこ¹ —えんこする break* down ‖通勤途中車がえんこした My car *broke down* on my way to work.

えんこ² 縁故 (血縁) relation ⓤ; (つて) connections ‖縁故を頼って下宿先を見つける use one's *connections* to find a place to live ／彼はこの会社に縁故採用された He *got a job with this company because of his connections*.

えんご 援護 (支援) support ⓤ, help ⓤ; (軍隊) cover ⓤ —援護する (支援する) support ⓤ, help ⓤ; (援護射撃する) cover ⓗ ‖洪水の被災者を援護する *help* the flood victims
‖援護射撃 covering fire

えんざい 冤罪 false charge [accusation] ⓒ ‖彼は殺人の冤罪を晴らした He cleared himself of *a false accusation* of murder.

えんさん 塩酸 hydrochloric acid ⓤ

えんし 遠視 farsightedness ⓤ,《英》longsightedness ⓤ —遠視の farsighted,《英》longsighted ‖遠視である be *farsighted*; have *far sight*

えんじ¹ 園児 kindergarten [nursery school] ⓒ child ⓒ (❖ kindergarten は幼稚園, nursery school は保育園)

えんじ² 臙脂 dark red ⓤ

エンジェル エンゼル

エンジニア engineer [èndʒɪníər] ⓒ

えんしゅう¹ 円周 circumference ⓒⓤ ‖円周 40センチ 40 centimeters in *circumference* ‖円周率 pi [pái], the ratio of the circumference of a circle to its diameter

えんしゅう² 演習 (大学のゼミナール) seminar ⓒ; (軍事演習) exercise ⓒ (しばしば複数形〜s); (大演習) maneuvers ‖合同軍事演習 joint military *exercises* ／演習中で on maneuvers

えんじゅく 円熟 (成熟) maturity ⓤ; (円満) mellowness ⓤ —円熟する mature ⓗ; mellow ⓗ ‖彼の歌は円熟の域に達している He has reached *maturity* as a singer. ／いろいろ経験して彼女も人間的に円熟した She *has matured* through a lot of experience.

えんしゅつ 演出 direction ⓤ —演出する direct ⓗ ‖芝居を演出する *direct* a play ‖演出家 a director ／演出効果 a stage effect

えんしょ 炎暑 intense [great] summer heat ⓤ

えんじょ 援助

help, assistance ⓤ; (公的な) aid ⓤ —援助する help ⓗ, assist ⓗ; aid ⓗ ‖援助を申し出る offer *help* ／困っている人たちを援助する *help* the needy ／援助を増やす [減らす] increase [reduce] *aid* ／困っている国を援助する *give aid to* needy nations ／援助の手を差し延べる offer *a helping hand*
彼は父親に援助を求めた He asked his father for *help*.
彼らは政府の援助を受けて日本に留学している They have come to Japan to study *with government help*.
‖援助交際 (金をもらってするデート) compensated dating; (10代の少女の売春) teenage prostitution ／医療援助 medical aid ／軍事援助 military aid ／経済援助 economic aid ／財政援助 financial aid [assistance] ／対外援助 overseas aid

エンジョイ 彼女はアメリカでの生活をエンジョイしている She is「*having a good time* [*enjoying her life*] in America.

えんしょう¹ 炎症 inflammation ⓤⓒ, irritation ⓤ ‖炎症を起こさせる cause *inflammation* ◆傷口が炎症を起こしている The wound *is inflamed*.

えんしょう² 延焼 —延焼する (広がる) spread* ⓗ ‖延焼を食い止める stop a fire from *spreading* ／火はあっという間に近所に延焼した The fire rapidly *spread* to the neighboring houses.

えんじょう 炎上 —炎上する blaze ⓗ, go* up in flames

えんじる 演じる play ⓗ, perform ⓗ 主役 [わき役] を演じる *play*「the leading [a supporting] role
トム・ハンクスは『アポロ13号』で宇宙飛行士 (の役) を演じた Tom Hanks *played* (the part of) an astronaut in *Apollo 13*.
日本は国際舞台で重要な役割を演じている Japan *is playing* an important role [part] on the international scene.
◆彼女はよい妻を演じてきた (→ふりをしてきた) She *has been pretending to be* a good wife.

エンジン engine ⓒ ‖エンジンをかける [止める] start [stop] *an engine* ／エンジンブレーキをかける *brake* with *the engine* ／エンジンは順調に動いている The *engine* is running smoothly now. ／101便はエンジントラブルの

ため出発が遅れます Flight 101 will be delayed due to *engine trouble*.
◆けさ車のエンジンがどうしてもかからなかった My car wouldn't start this morning.
慣用表現 エンジンがかかってきた(→本調子になってきた) I'm hitting my stride.

えんじん 円陣 circle C ‖円陣を組む form *a circle* ‖円陣を組んで座る sit in *a circle*

えんしんぶんりき 遠心分離器 centrifugal separator C

えんしんりょく 遠心力 centrifugal force U

えんすい 円錐 cone C ——円すいの conical ⇨ずけい〔図版〕

えんずい 延髄 medulla oblongata C

エンスト ⚠ stall C, engine failure U C (❖「エンスト」は和製英語である「エンジンストップ」を略したもの) ◆私の車はよくエンストを起こす My car often *stalls*. / 私の車がエンストした My car's engine *gave out*.

えんせい¹ 遠征 expedition C ——遠征する make* an expedition; tour 他 ‖遠征中の[で] on *tour*
‖遠征試合 an away game / 遠征隊 an expeditionary force

えんせい² 厭世 ——厭世的な pessimistic
‖厭世主義 pessimism

えんぜつ 演説 speech C, address C (❖ speechより改まった語) ——演説する give* [make*] a speech
その政治家は民主主義について演説をした The politician *gave a speech on* democracy.
‖基調演説 a keynote speech / 就任演説 an inaugural speech / 選挙演説 a campaign speech

エンゼル (天使) angel C ‖エンゼルフィッシュ an angelfish

えんせん 沿線 沿線の住人 people living *along* [*near, on*] *the line* / 私は東西線沿線に住んでいます I live *near* [*on*] *the Tozai line.*

えんそ 塩素《化学》chlorine U (❖ 元素記号 Cl) ◆飲み水を塩素で消毒する treat drinking water *with chlorine*

えんそう 演奏 performance C ——演奏する play 他 自, perform 他 自 (❖ perform はやや改まった語)
生演奏 a live *performance* / ピアノを演奏する *play* the piano
演奏中にプログラムをかさかさせないようにしなさい Be careful not to rustle your programs *during the performances.*
彼はトランペットで「星条旗よ永遠なれ」を演奏した He *played* The Stars and Stripes Forever on a trumpet.
有名なピアニストが今夜テレビで演奏する A famous pianist *will play* on TV tonight.
‖演奏会 a concert / 演奏者 a player, a performer

えんそく 遠足 excursion C, outing C ‖遠足に出かける go on *an excursion* / 子供たちは学校の遠足で動物園に行った The children went to the zoo on *a school excursion*.

エンターテイナー (芸能人) entertainer

エンターテインメント (娯楽) entertainment U C

えんだい¹ 遠大 ——遠大な (将来まで見通した) farsighted; (広範囲の) far-reaching; (壮大な) grand, ambitious ‖遠大な事業 a *far-sighted* [*an ambitious*] project / 彼は私に遠大な計画を語った He told me his *grand* plan.

えんだい² 演題 subject C, topic C ‖その講演の演題は次期選挙だった The *topic* of the lecture was the next election.

えんだか 円高 appreciation of the yen; (強い円) a [the] stronger yen ‖その店では円高差益還元セールをやっている They are having a sale in order to *pass the benefits of the stronger yen on to* consumers.
◆最近は円高ドル安だ Recently *the yen has strengthened against the dollar.* / きょうは急激な円高が進んでいる The yen has been *gaining strength* rapidly today.

えんだん¹ 演壇 platform C, podium C (複 ~s, podia), rostrum C (複 ~s, rostra) ‖演壇に立つ[上る]「stand on [climb on to] *the platform*

えんだん² 縁談 an offer of marriage (through a matchmaker) ◆縁談をまとめる arrange *a marriage* / 姉に縁談が持ち上がった My sister has been offered *a marriage*.

えんちゃく 延着 ——延着する arrive late, be delayed

えんちゅう 円柱 pillar C, column C; (図形) cylinder C ⇨ずけい〔図版〕

えんちょう¹ 延長 extension U C ——延長する extend 他, lengthen 他; (時間を長引かせる) prolong 他
夏期休暇の延長 an extension of one's summer holidays / 線[地下鉄]を延長する *extend* a line [subway]
家族はそのスキー場の滞在を1週間延長した The family *extended* their stay at the ski resort by a week.
修学旅行は授業の延長だ A school trip is *an extension* of regular classes.
◆(野球の)延長戦に入る go into 「*extra innings* [*an extra inning*] / 我々は賃貸契約の期限を半年延長した We *renewed* our lease for another six months.

えんちょう² 園長 幼稚園[動物園]の園長 *the director of* a kindergarten [zoo]

エンディング (終わり) ending

えんてん 炎天 炎天下で働く work *under the scorching sun*

えんとう 円筒 cylinder C ——円筒形の cylindrical, round

えんどう¹ 沿道 (街筋) route C; (路傍) roadside C ‖沿道は大声で声援を送る人たちで埋め尽くされていた The route was crowded with people cheering loudly.

えんどう² 豌豆 pea C ‖エンドウの皮をむく shell *peas*

えんどおい 縁遠い 父はコンピュータには縁遠い My father *has little interest in* computers. ⇨ えん(縁)

えんとつ 煙突 chimney C; (工場・汽船など

の) smokestack [C]; (機関車・汽船などの) funnel [C] ‖煙突を掃除する sweep *a chimney*

エンドラン hit-and-run play [C]

エントリー (参加登録) entry [U] [C] ─エントリーする enter [他] [自] ‖10人がその競技にエントリーした Ten competitors「*entered* [*signed up for*] the race.

えんにち 縁日 festival (day) [C], feast (day) [C] ‖縁日にはたくさんの出店が出る A lot of stands appear on *festival days*.

えんのした 縁の下 (床の下の空間) the space under the floor, crawlspace [C]
[慣用表現] 彼[彼女]は縁の下の力持ちだ He [She] has been *an unsung hero* [*heroine*]. (❖an unsung hero [heroine]は「(詩歌で)たたえられることのない英雄」の意味)

えんばん 円盤 disk [C]; (円盤投げ用) discus [C] ‖円盤を投げる throw *the discus* ◆空飛ぶ円盤 *a flying saucer*; *a UFO*
‖円盤投げ(競技) the discus throw

えんぴつ 鉛筆 pencil [C] ‖鉛筆で書く write「*with a pencil* [*in pencil*] / 先のとがった鉛筆 a sharp *pencil* (❖「シャープペンシル」は a mechanical pencil) / 消しゴム付きの鉛筆 *a pencil* with an eraser on the end / 鉛筆の芯(しん) the lead of *a pencil* / ナイフで鉛筆を削った I sharpened *the pencil* with a knife.
‖鉛筆入れ a pencil case / 鉛筆削り a pencil sharpener / 赤鉛筆 a red pencil / 色鉛筆 a colored pencil

えんびふく 燕尾服 tailcoat [C], tails

えんぶきょく 円舞曲 waltz [C]

えんぶん 塩分 salt [U] ‖塩分控えめの食事 a *low-salt* diet / 病気を防ぎたければ塩分を減らしなさい Eat less *salt* if you want to avoid illness.

えんぽう 遠方 distance [C], distant place [C] ─遠方の faraway (❖名詞の前で用いる) ‖遠方に島影が見えた We could see an island *in the distance*. ◆遠方からめいが私を訪ねてきた My niece *came a long way* to visit me.

えんま 閻魔 *Emma*, the king of Hell

えんまく 煙幕 smoke screen [C] ‖彼は煙幕を張って本心を明かそうとはしなかった He *put up a smoke screen* to hide his real intentions.

えんまちょう 閻魔帳 teacher's grade book [C]

えんまん 円満 ─円満な happy, peaceful; (性格が) amiable ─円満に peacefully ‖円満な家庭 a *happy* home / 円満な人柄 an *amiable* personality / 夫婦円満 a *happy* marriage ◆円満な性質 a *mild* disposition / 彼らのいさかいは円満に解決した Their differences were settled *amicably*.

えんむすび 縁結び 彼女が私たち二人にとっての縁結びの神様だった She was *the cupid* who brought us together.

えんめい 延命 prolongation of life ◆延命効果のある薬 a drug that helps to *prolong life*
‖延命装置 life-sustaining [life-support] equipment / 延命措置 life-sustaining treatment

えんやす 円安 depreciation of the yen; (弱い円) a [the] weaker yen
◆ここしばらく円安ドル高が続いている *The yen has been weak against the dollar* for some time. / 円安が進んでいる *The yen keeps weakening*.

えんゆうかい 園遊会 garden party [C], 《米》lawn party [C]

えんよう 遠洋 ‖遠洋漁業 fishing in distant oceans, deep-sea fishing / 遠洋航海 ocean voyage

えんりょ 遠慮

❶【控えめ】reserve [U] ─遠慮する (ためらう) hesitate [自]; (控えめだ) be reserved
何でも遠慮なく質問してください *Don't hesitate to* ask me any questions.
彼は遠慮深い He *is reserved*.
君の弱点は他人に遠慮しすぎることだ Your weak point is that you *are too reserved* towards others.
◆彼女には何でも遠慮なく話せる I can tell her anything *without reservation*. / 彼は遠慮がちに金を貸してほしいと頼んできた He *hesitantly* asked me to lend him some money. / 遠慮なく言わせてもらえば，君は集中力に欠けるときがある Let me be quite *blunt* (with you); you sometimes lack concentration. / この問題についての遠慮のない意見をいただきたいと思います We'd like to have your *candid* opinion on this issue. / 遠慮なくケーキを召し上がってください Please *help yourself to* the cake. / いつでも遠慮なく電話をしてください *Feel free to* call me any time.
[e]「こちらにコーヒーを用意してありますので，どうぞご遠慮なく」「ありがとう」 "Please *feel free to help yourself to* coffee here." "Thank you."
[e]「ちょっとおじゃましてもいいかしら」「遠慮しないで(→かしこまらずに)入って」 "May I have some of your time?" "Sure. Come on in. *Don't stand on ceremony*."

❷【差し控えること】
おたばこ[携帯電話の使用]はご遠慮ください Please *refrain from* smoking [using cellular phones].
ご好意はありがたいのですが，体調が悪いので遠慮させていただきます Thank you for your kind offer, but I'll have to *decline* it because I'm not feeling very well. (❖decline は「…を丁寧に断る」の意味)
[e]「飲み物はいかがですか」「いや，遠慮しておきます」 "Will you have a drink?" "No, thanks. *I'd rather not*."
[慣用表現] 彼らは彼の最新作を遠慮会釈なくけなした They criticized his latest work *mercilessly*.

えんろ 遠路 遠路はるばるおいでくださりありがとうございます Thank you for coming「*all this way* [*such a long way*].

お

お 尾 tail [C]; (キツネなどの) brush [C] //その犬は尾を振って僕の後をついてきた The dog followed me wagging *its tail.*

[慣用表現] 彼は前回の失敗がまだ尾を引いている(→影響を与えている)ようだ It seems that his failure last time *still affects him.*

お- 御- (❖丁寧さを表す接頭辞の「お-」に当たる表現は英語にはない. 英語で丁寧にいう場合は please や助動詞を用いる) //こちらにお名前をご記入願います Please fill in your name here. / 少しお待ちいただけますか Would you wait (for) a moment?

おあいそ お愛想 人にお愛想を言う *pay* a person *compliments* / おあいそ(→勘定)お願いします *Check* [《英》*Bill*], please!

おあいにくさま お生憎様 (皮肉をこめて) おあいにくさま! *Too bad*!/ *Sorry for that*!

💬「第 4 レースの『デザートローズ』に 1 万円かけたぞ」「おあいにくさま. そいつかぜひいてるよ」"I bet 10,000 yen on *Desert Rose* in the fourth race." "*Tough luck*. He has (the) flu."

オアシス oasis [ouéisis] [C] (複 oases) (❖比喩的に「憩いの場」の意味も含む) //その美術館は都会の真ん中にあるオアシスだ That art museum is *an oasis* in the center of the city.

おあずけ お預け うちの犬は「お手」と「お預け」ができる Our dog can "shake hands" and "*eat on cue*." (❖実際に犬に向かっていう言葉は "Wait!" "Don't eat it!" など) / 父の入院で旅行はしばらくお預けになった(→延期された) Because my father was hospitalized, our trip *was put off* for a while.

おあつらえむき お誂え向き この辞書は初めて英語を学ぶ人におあつらえ向きだ This is an *ideal* dictionary for first-time students of English. / 彼女はその仕事におあつらえ向きだ She *is suited for* [*to*] the job.

おい[1] (ぞんざいな呼びかけ) hey; (話の初めや注意を引くとき) say, 《英》I say; (相手の注意を促して) look (here); (あいさつの呼びかけ) hi, hello; (説得・挑戦などを表して) come on //おい, 黙れよ *Hey*, shut up. / おい, いい考えが浮かんだぞ *Say*, I've got an idea! / おい, 落ち着けよ *Come on*, take it easy.

おい[2] 老い (老齢) old age [U] ◆老いの一徹(→老人の頑固さ) the stubbornness of *an old man* / 海では老いも若きも楽しそうに泳いでいる *Both young and old* are having a good time swimming in the sea.

おい[3] 甥 nephew [C] //私のおいは今年小学校に上がる My *nephew* enters elementary school this year.

おいあげる 追い上げる (迫る) gain on ...; (追いつく) catch* up (with ...) //彼はレースの終盤でトップを走る選手を追い上げていった He *began gaining on* the leading runner in the last stage of the race.

おいうち 追い討ち·追い撃ち 父親の会社が倒産し, 追い討ちをかけるように次々と不幸が彼を襲った After his father's company went bankrupt, a run of misfortunes came on him *as though to compound his misery.*

おいえげい お家芸 (専門) specialty [C] //商品を何でも小さくするというのが日本企業のお家芸だ Miniaturizing all types of products is *a specialty* of Japanese companies.

◆体操はかつて日本のお家芸(→日本選手の得意なスポーツ)だった Gymnastics used to be a sport which Japanese athletes *were really good at.*

おいおい[1] 追い追い (しだいに) gradually; (少しずつ) little by little; (やがて) in (due) time //新しい学校にもおいおい慣れてくるでしょう You will *gradually* get used to the new school. / そのことに関してはおいおい話します I'll tell you about it *in due time.*

おいおい[2] 飼っていた犬が死んだと聞いて, 彼はおいおい泣いた He *cried his eyes* [*heart*] *out* to hear his dog had died.

おいおとす 追い落とす 彼は部長を追い落としてその地位を得た He *pushed aside* the manager and got the position.

おいかえす 追い返す (追い払う) turn [send*] away //しつこいセールスマンを追い返す *turn* [*send*] a persistent salesman *away*

おいかける 追い掛ける (後を追う) run* [go*] after ..., chase [他] //彼がフリスビーを投げると犬はそれを全速力で追いかけた When he threw a frisbee, the dog *ran after* it at full speed. / 店員は泥棒を追いかけたが途中で見失った The salesclerk *chased* the thief but then lost sight of him. / パパラッチとはゴシップをねらって有名人を追いかけるカメラマンのことだ Paparazzi are the photographers who *go after* celebrity gossip.

おいかぜ 追い風 fair [favorable, following] wind [C], tailwind [C] ◆風は追い風だ The wind *is favorable.* / 好調な経済が追い風となって与党が圧勝した The strong economy *contributed to* the ruling party's landslide victory.

おいこし 追い越し //追い越し禁止《掲示》《米》No Passing, 《英》No Overtaking / 追い越し禁止区域 a no-passing zone / 追い越し車線 the passing [fast] lane

おいこす 追い越す pass [自] [他]; (追いつき追い越す) overtake* [他]; (先に出る) get* ahead of ...; (勝る) surpass [他]; (能力などで上回る) outstrip [他] //白い車が猛スピードで私たちを追い越していった A white car *passed* us at high speed. / 彼は英語では兄を追い越した He *got ahead of* his brother in English.

◆彼女は母親の背を追い越した She *grew taller than* her mother.

おいこみ 追い込み ゴール近くになりランナーは

最後の追い込みをかけた The runner *put on a final spurt* before the finish line. / 受験勉強もいよいよ追い込みの段階に入った Studying for the entrance examination is now in *the final stage*.

おいこむ 追い込む drive* [他]; (困難な立場に) drive [put*] *a person* into a corner ∥牧羊犬は手ぎわよく羊を囲いに追い込んだ The sheepdog *drove* the sheep *into* the enclosure skillfully. / 大統領はそのスキャンダルによって窮地に追い込まれた The scandal *drove* the President *into a corner*. / The President *had his back to the wall* because of the scandal. ◆あなたが断ったので彼は難しい立場に追い込まれた Your refusal *put* him *in* a difficult position.

おいさき 老い先 老い先短い(→何年も生きることはない)母に親孝行がしたい I want to take good care of my mother, *who doesn't have many years to live*.

おいしい 《口語的》good; (味のよい) tasty; (とてもおいしい) delicious; (食欲をそそる) appetizing

おなかがすいているときは何を食べてもおいしい Anything tastes *good* when you are hungry.

スープが少しぬるかったことを除けば料理はおいしかった The food *was good* except (that) the soup was a little bit cold.

パスタのおいしいお店知ってるんだけど, 今度行かない? I know a *good* pasta restaurant. Do you want to go sometime?

空気がおいしい The air smells *good*.

焼きたてのパンはとてもおいしそうなにおいがする Bread fresh from the oven smells *delicious* [*appetizing*].

テーブルにはおいしそうな料理が並んでいた The table was spread with *delicious-looking* dishes.

台所からおいしそうなにおいがしてきた There came an *appetizing* smell from the kitchen.

◆彼は私の作る料理をいつもおいしそうに食べてくれる He always eats what I prepare for him *with great relish*. / その仕事はかなりおいしい That job *is* pretty *juicy*. (❖juicy は「楽に稼げる」という意味の口語的な表現)

💬「バニラアイスに熱々のコーヒーをかけるのよ」「うん, おいしそう」"You pour hot coffee over vanilla ice cream." "Umm, *yum*!" (❖Yum! [jʌ́m]はおいしいものの話をするときに用いる感嘆詞)

おいしげる 生い茂る 空き地には雑草が生い茂っている The vacant lot *is overgrown with* weeds. / 公園の周りには木が生い茂っていた Trees *grew thickly* around the park.

おいすがる 追い縋る その男の子は母親が仕事に出かけようとすると追いすがって泣いた As his mother left for work, the boy *ran after* her crying. / その野球選手はしつこく追いすがる報道陣にうんざりしている The baseball player is sick of the reporters who *keep hounding* him.

おいそれと (即座に) immediately, at once; (簡単に) easily, just like that ∥その仕事はおいそれとは引き受けられない I can't take that job *just like that*. ◆そんな大金, おいそれと払えるもんじゃない I can't pay that much money *at the drop of a hat*. (❖at the drop of a hat は「即座に」の意味)

おいだし 追い出し 追い出しコンパ a *farewell* [*send-off*] party

おいだす 追い出す (追い払う) drive* out; (放り出す) throw* out; (追放する) expel [他], kick out ∥私は窓をあけてハチを部屋から追い出した I opened the window to *drive* a bee *out of* the room. / 夜遅くにうるさくしてるとアパートを追い出されるよ You'*ll be kicked out of* the apartment if you keep being noisy late at night. / 彼は素行不良で学生寮から追い出された He *was expelled from* the school dorm for his bad behavior.

おいたち 生い立ち (子供時代) *one's* childhood, *one's* early life ∥彼は私に自分の生い立ちを語った He told me about *his early life*. / その歌手の不幸な生い立ちはよく知られている The story of the singer's unhappy *childhood* is well-known.

おいたて 追い立て 家賃を滞納していたので, 家主から追いたてを食った(→立ち退き通知を受けた) As I hadn't paid my rent, I *was given notice to move out* by the landlord.

おいたてる 追い立てる 彼女は息子を学校へ追いたてた She *hurried* her son *off* to school. / 僕はいつも時間に追いたてられているような気がする I feel like I'*m* always *pressed for* time.

おいちらす 追い散らす (追い払う) drive* away; (散り散りにする) scatter [他] ∥彼は物見高いやじ馬を追い散らした He *drove away* a crowd of curious onlookers.

おいつく 追い付く catch* up with ..., overtake* [他] ∥彼があんまり速く走ったので私たちは追いつけなかった He ran so fast that we *couldn't catch up with* him. / 私は彼にバス停で追いついた I *overtook* him at the bus stop. ◆そのゲームソフトは生産が需要に追いつかないほどの人気だ That computer game software is so popular that the production *is far from enough to meet* the demands.

[慣用表現] アジア諸国は日本に追いつけ追い越せと経済力の強化に努めている Asian countries are trying to *catch up with and get ahead of* Japan's economic power.

おいつめる 追い詰める (窮地に追い込む) drive* [put*] ... into a corner; (追跡して) track [run*] down ∥警察は犯人を袋小路に追いつめた The police *ran down* the criminal in a blind alley. / 彼はかなり追いつめられているらしい It seems he's really 「*been driven into a corner* [*got his back to the wall*].

おいて 於いて (位置・場所) at, in; (関して) in, on ∥自分の責任において *at one's* own risk / 大体において *in* principle / 自分に忠

実であることは人生において大切なことだ Being true to yourself is important *in* life. / アメリカはマルチメディアの開発において世界をリードしている The U.S. leads the world *in* the development of multimedia technology.

おいで お出で 今度の日曜にうちにおいでよ *Come over to* my place next Sunday. / もしこちらにおいでになることがあれば，ぜひお立ち寄りください If you ever *come* this way, be sure to come and see us. / (電話などで)中井さんはおいでですか *Is* Mr. Nakai *in*? / その犬はまるでおいでおいでをするかのように前足を動かした The dog moved his paw as if he *were beckoning*. / 公園に遊びに行っておいで *Go* and play in the park.

おいてきぼり 置いてきぼり 友達はみんな先に行ってしまい，僕は置いてきぼりを食った All my friends had gone on ahead, and I *was left behind*.

おいとま

🗣「そろそろおいとましなきゃ」「まだいいじゃないですか」"*I must be going now.*" "Don't leave so soon."

おいぬく 追い抜く (追い越す) pass [他], overtake* [他] ‖赤い車が私たちの車を追い抜いた A red car *overtook* ours. / 彼は3人の走者を追い抜いて先頭に立った He *passed* [*outstripped*] three runners and went into the lead.

おいはぎ 追剝ぎ (強盗) robber [C]

おいはらう 追い払う chase [他] [自], drive* away [out, off]; (放り出す) cast* out; (取り除く) get* rid of ... ‖彼はごみの集積所に集まるカラスを追い払った He *drove away* the crows flocking around the dump. / 力士は悪霊を追い払うためにしこを踏む Sumo wrestlers stamp their feet to *drive out* evil spirits. / 私は頭に浮かぶいやな想像を追い払おうとした I tried to *get rid of* the unpleasant idea that came into my mind.

おいぼれ 老いぼれ dotage [C]

おいぼれる 老いぼれる (もうろくする) become* [go*] senile

おいまわす 追い回す chase (after ...), run* after ...; (つきまとう) follow ... about [around] ‖あいつはいつも女の子を追い回している He *is* always *chasing* (*after*) girls.

◆家事に追い回される毎日だ(→毎日家事で忙しい) I'*m busy with* housework every day.

おいめ 負い目 私は彼女に負い目がある I *am indebted to* her. (❖ be indebted to ... は「…に恩を受けている」の意味)

おいもとめる 追い求める (追求する) pursue [他], seek* (after ...) ‖真実を追い求める *pursue* the truth / 幸福を追い求める *seek* (*after*) happiness / 彼は理想ばかり追い求めている He *is* always *pursuing* his ideals.

おいやる 追いやる (追い払う・せきたてる) drive* [他] ‖その不祥事で彼は辞任に追いやられた That scandal *drove* him *to* resign.

◆そのほうきは部屋の片隅に追いやられていた(→ほうっておかれていた) The broom *had been left neglected* in a corner of the room.

オイル oil [U] ‖オリーブオイル olive *oil* / (車の)オイルを交換してください Will you change *the* motor *oil*? / 背中にオイルを塗ってくれる? Rub some *oil* on my back, will you? ‖オイルクロス oilcloth / オイルショック an oil crisis (❖ ×oil shock とはいわない) / オイルダラー oil dollars, petrodollars / オイルフェンス a boom (to contain an oil spill) (❖ ×oil fence とはいわない)

おいる 老いる grow* [get*, become*] old, age [自] ◆老いた母 *one's aged* mother

[慣用表現] 彼は老いてますます盛んだ(→元気だ) He *is still hale and hearty in his old age*.

[ことわざ] 老いては子に従え When you are old, you should follow your children's advice.

おいろなおし お色直し 🗻

> 結婚披露宴の途中で花嫁が衣装を替えることをお色直しといいます．着物から洋装のドレスに着替えることが多いようです．ふつう花嫁が行いますが，最近では花婿もお色直しをすることがあります．
>
> *Oironaoshi* is the practice of a bride changing dresses during a wedding reception. In many cases, brides change from a kimono to a Western-style dress. It is usually brides who practice *oironaoshi*, but recently some bridegrooms also have come to follow the practice.

おう[1] 追う

❶【追いかける】go* after ..., run* after ...; (ついていく) follow [他]; (追跡する) chase [他]; (追い求める) pursue [他]

理想を追う *pursue one's* ideals / 流行を追う *follow* (the) fashion

警察が彼女を追っている The police *are chasing* her. / The police *are after* her.

子ガモたちは母ガモの後を追ってどこへでもついていく Ducklings 「*go after* [*follow*] their mother wherever she goes.

その赤ちゃんはずっと目で母親を追っていた The baby's eyes *kept following* its mother.

そのハンターは獲物を追って森の奥深くまで入っていった The hunter went deep into the forest *pursuing* his prey.

◆追いつ追われつの接戦 a *seesaw* game / 警察は行方不明の女性の足取りを追っている The police *are trying to find some trace* of the missing woman. / 彼は警察に追われている He *is wanted* by the police. / 目先の利益ばかり追わず(→固執せず)もっと長期的に考えよう Let's think on a long-term basis instead of just *sticking to* our immediate interests.

❷【追放する】(国から) exile [他]; (地位・職などから) oust [他] (❖ 共に通例受身で用いる)

その作家は国を追われた The writer *was exiled from* his country.

彼は監督の地位を追われた He *was ousted from* his post as a manager.

❸【せかす】

おう

彼はいつも仕事に追われている He *is* always *busy* [*pressed*] *with* his job.
姉は育児に追われso暇もままならない My sister *is* so *busy* taking care of her baby that she doesn't have time to go out.

❹【順に進む】
追って通知があるまで *until further notice*
彼女は日を追うごとに元気になっていった Her health improved *day by day*.
順を追って説明します I'll explain it *in order*.

おう² 負う

❶【背負う】 carry ... on *one's* back ⇒せおう
◆馬に荷を負わせる *burden* a horse *with* a load

❷【身に受ける】(責任などを) assume 他, take* 他
後のことについては私が全責任を負います I *will assume* [*take*] *full responsibility* for what follows.
駐車場内での事故・盗難に関してはいっさい責任を負いません We *assume no responsibility* for any accidents or thefts in the parking lot.
◆私たちは納税の義務を負っている We *have an obligation* to pay our taxes. / We *are obliged* to pay our taxes. / 責めを負うべきは彼のほうだ It is she who *is to blame*. / この仕事はだんだん私の手に負えなくなってきた This work *is getting out of hand*.

❸【傷などを】 get* [be] injured
10人の通行人がその爆発で重傷を負った Ten passers-by *were* [*got*] *seriously injured* by the blast.
◆一生の傷を負う *be scarred for life* / 私は背中にひどい打撲傷を負った I *got* a bad *bruise* on my back. / 彼はその事故で軽いやけどを負った He *suffered* minor burns in the accident. / 彼女は地震でかすり傷ひとつ負わずに生き延びた She survived the quake *without a scratch*.

❹【恩恵を受ける】
この交換留学制度はボランティアの協力に負うところが大きい This exchange program *owes a great deal to* volunteers' cooperation.

おう³ 王 king ©(❖特定の王を指す場合は大文字. 名前とともに用いる場合は無冠詞); (君主) monarch © /アーサー王伝説 the legend of *King* Arthur / ライオンは百獣の王と呼ばれている The lion is called *the king of beasts*.
‖三冠王 the Triple Crown / 石油王 an oil tycoon [magnate] / ホームラン王 the home-run king

おうい 王位 the crown, the throne ‖王位継承者 the heir to *the throne* / 王位につく「come to [ascend] *the throne*; be crowned / 王位についている be on *the throne*; wear *the crown* / 王位を継ぐ succeed to *the crown*

おういん 押印 ——押印する put* *one's* seal (on ...)

おうえん 応援
(声援) cheering ⓤ, cheer ©; (支持) support ⓤ; (助け) help ⓤ, aid ⓤ ——応援する cheer 自他, (米口語的)root for ...; support 他; (米) 観客のほとんどは地元のチームを応援した Most of the spectators *cheered* (*for*) the home team.
友達がたくさん応援に駆けつけてくれた A lot of my friends came to *support* me.
人手が足りなかったので私たちは彼らに応援を頼んだ Because we were short-handed, we *asked* them *for help*.
◆私たちはホークスを応援している We're *supporters of* the Hawks.
🖉「オランダとイタリア, どっちを応援してるの」「もちろんオランダ」 "Which team *are* you *supporting*, Holland or France?" "Holland, of course."
‖応援演説 a campaign speech / 応援歌 a fight song, 《米》a rooters' song, 《英》a supporters' song / 応援団 a cheering party [group] / 応援団員 a member of the cheering party; (女子の) a cheerleader / 応援(団)席 a cheering section / 応援団長 the head of a cheering party

おうおうにして 往々にして (時々) occasionally, sometimes; (しばしば) often, frequently ‖フランス人は往々にして英語のHを落として発音する As is *often* the case with French people, they drop the 'h' sound in English. / そういうことは往々にして起こるものだ That type of thing happens *occasionally*.

おうか 謳歌 彼らは今まさに青春を謳歌している They *are singing the joys of* youth now.

おうかくまく 横隔膜 〔解剖〕 diaphragm [dáiəfræm] ©

おうかん 王冠 crown ©; (びんの) bottle cap ©

おうぎ 扇 (folding) fan © ◆扇形の葉 a *fan-shaped* leaf ‖扇形〔数学〕a sector

おうきゅう¹ 応急 ——応急の (緊急の) emergency; (一時的な) temporary ‖応急措置をとる take an *emergency* [a *temporary*, a *stopgap*] measure ◆彼はこわれた本箱を応急修理した He *patched up* the broken bookcase.
‖応急手当 first aid

おうきゅう² 王宮 royal palace ©

おうけ 彼女は王家の出だ She is from *a royal family*.

おうけん 王権 sovereignty ⓤ, sovereign power [authority] ⓤ‖王権神授説 (a) divine right

おうこう 横行 アフリカではいまだに密猟が横行している Poaching still *prevails* in Africa.

おうこうきぞく 王侯貴族 the royalty and aristocracy [nobility] (❖集合的に用いる)

おうこく 王国 kingdom ©; (君主国) monarchy © ‖デンマーク王国 the *Kingdom* of Denmark
◆静岡はサッカー王国(→サッカー指向の県)だ Shizuoka is *a soccer-oriented prefecture*. / Shizuoka is *the home of soccer dynasty*.

おうごん 黄金 gold ⓤ ——黄金の gold,

golden ‖黄金の左腕 a *golden* left arm ‖黄金郷 El Dorado / 黄金時代 a *golden age* / 黄金律《聖書》the *golden rule*

おうざ 王座（王座）throne ⓒ; (首位) the championship ‖前回の全米オープンでは弱冠20歳の青年が王座についた A young man of only 20 *won the championship* in the last U.S. open.

おうさま 王様 king ⓒ ⇒おう(王)

おうし 雄牛・牡牛（去勢されていない）bull ⓒ;（去勢した）ox ⓒ(複 oxen) ⇒おうしざ

おうじ 王子 prince ⓒ(❖王女は princess) ‖エドワード王子 *Prince* Edward

おうしざ 牡牛座《天文・占星》Taurus Ⓤ(❖「牡牛座の人」の意味では ⓒ)

おうしつ 王室（王家）royal family ⓒ(❖英国王室は the Royal Family) ‖王室に入る(＝王家の一員になる) become a member of *a royal family*

おうじゃ 王者（王）king ⓒ, (競技などの) champion ⓒ ――王者の royal,《公式的》regal, kingly ‖彼には王者の風格が漂っている He has *a kingly air* about him.

おうしゅう¹ 応酬 やじの応酬(→やり取り) *an exchange* of heckling / 交渉は決裂し最後は非難の応酬に終わった The negotiations broke down and ended in *mutual recrimination*.

おうしゅう² 押収 seizure Ⓤⓒ;（没収）confiscation Ⓤⓒ ――押収する seize ⓟ, confiscate ⓟ ‖それらの密輸品は税関で押収された Those smuggled goods *were seized* at customs. / 警察は家宅捜査をして証拠物件を押収した The police searched the house and *seized [confiscated]* the evidence.

おうしゅう³ 欧州（ヨーロッパ）Europe ――欧州の European ‖欧州議会 the European Parliament / 欧州通貨制度 the European Monetary System《略語》EMS / 欧州通貨単位 the European Currency Unit《略語》ECU [eikúː] / 欧州連合 the European Union《略語》EU

おうじょ 王女 princess ⓒ（❖王子は prince）‖アン王女 *Princess* Anne / 第1王女 *a princess* royal

おうじょう 往生 めいで電車の中で大泣きされて往生した(→困った) I *was at a loss* when my niece cried at the top of her lungs on the train. / あいつは往生際が悪い(→負けてぐずぐず言う人だ) He's *a bad [poor] loser*. / 濃霧のために私の乗った飛行機はロンドンで立ち往生した My plane *was stuck* in London due to dense fog. ⇒だいおうじょう

おうしょくじんしゅ 黄色人種 Mongoloid ⓒ, the Mongolian races;（アジア人）Asians;(❖the yellow races は差別的な言い方とされる)

おうじる 応じる
❶【答える】answer ⓟⓒ, reply ⓟⓒ, respond to …
質問にはいつでも応じます I'm always ready to *answer* your questions.
彼らは我々のボランティアを募る呼びかけに笑顔で応じてくれた They *responded to* our call for volunteers with a smile.

❷【受諾する】(受け入れる) accept ⓟ;（同意する) agree to …;（承諾する)《公式的》comply with …
彼女はその式への招待に応じた She *accepted* the invitation to the ceremony.
チャンピオンは彼の挑戦に応じなかった The champion *didn't accept* [*take up*] his challenge.
犯人は人質を解放することに応じた The criminal *agreed to* release the hostages.
彼はこちらの要求に快く応じてくれた He was willing to *comply with* our request.
◆価格は相談に応じます The price *is negotiable*. / その選手はファンからサインを求められて快く応じた When asked for an autograph by his fan, the player gave one willingly.

❸【要求を満たす】(見合う) meet* ⓟ;（満足させる) satisfy ⓟ
すべての要求に応じることはできません It's impossible to *meet* [*satisfy*] every demand.

❹【…に応じて】
このいすは背の高さに応じて調節できる This chair can be adjusted *to your height*.
壁紙は好みに応じて変えられる You can change the wallpaper *to your taste*.
彼は必要に応じてきちんとした服装をする He dresses formally *when necessary*.
その歌手は求めに応じて何曲か歌った The singer sang some numbers *by request*.
収入に応じて税金を払わなければならない You must pay tax *according to* your income level.

おうしん 往診（医者の側から）house call ⓒ;（患者の側から）doctor's visit ⓒ ――往診する make* a house call, visit ⓟ ‖医者はある老人を往診した The doctor *visited* an old man. / 先生はただ今往診に出かけております The doctor is out on *a house call*.
‖往診料 a doctor's visiting fee

おうせい¹ 旺盛 弟は食欲旺盛だ My brother *has a good appetite*. / 太郎はいつでも元気旺盛だ Taro *is always full of energy* [*vigor*]. / 子供は好奇心が旺盛だ Children *are very curious about everything*. / 彼女は知識欲が旺盛だ She *has a great desire to learn*.

おうせい² 王政（君主政治）monarchy Ⓤ
‖王政主義者 a royalist / 王政復古 the Restoration

おうせい³ 王制（王・女王の政治）royal rule [government] Ⓤ

おうせつ 応接 reception ⓒ ‖応接係 a receptionist / 応接室（会社などの）a reception room / 応接間 a drawing room(❖英米の一般的な家庭ではふつう来客をもてなすため、特に応接間を設けることはまれ)

おうせん 応戦 ――応戦する（反撃する）counter ⓟ, fight* back ‖彼らは敵の攻撃に必死になって応戦した They desperately *fought back against* the enemy's attack.

おうぞく 王族《集合的》royalty ⓤ;（王室）royal family ⓒ

おうたい 応対〔応接する〕receive ⑭;（客に対して）attend ⓐ, serve ⓐ, wait on *a person*;（電話などに対して）answer ⑭ / 彼は訪問客の応対に忙しそうだった He looked busy *receiving* visitors. / 私の代わりに応対に出てちょうだい *Answer* the door for me, please. / 彼は電話の応対が横着だ（→横柄に応対する）He *answers* phone calls arrogantly. ◆応対のうまい［下手な］人 a person *with good [poor] people skills*（❂「人あしらいのうまい［下手な］」の意味で用いられる文句）/ そのレストランは客への応対がよい They *give good service* at that restaurant.

おうたい² 横隊 rank ⓒ（❂縦隊は file）/ 2列横隊で *in double ranks*

おうだん¹ 横断 crossing ⓒ ⓤ ——横断する cross ⑭, go* across ... / 海峡横断 *a channel crossing* / 道路を横断するときは気をつけなさい Be careful (in) *crossing* the road. ◆僕は車でシドニーからパースにかけて大陸横断の旅をした I made a *transcontinental* trip from Sydney to Perth by car. / 彼は水泳による大西洋横断に成功した He succeeded in *swimming across the Atlantic*.

‖横断禁止《掲示》No Crossing（❂No Xingとも書く）/ 横断歩道《米》a crosswalk,《英》a zebra [pedestrian] crossing / 横断幕 a banner / 横断面 a cross section / 大陸横断鉄道 a transcontinental railroad [railway]

おうだん² 黄疸〔医学〕jaundice [dʒíːndəs] ⓤ

おうちゃく 横着 ——横着な（怠惰な）lazy;（ずうずうしい）impudent ‖横着しないでちゃんと歯を磨きなさい *Don't be lazy* and brush your teeth. ◆私はけさ横着してふとんをしまわなかった *Out of laziness* I didn't put away the futon this morning.

おうちょう 王朝 dynasty ⓒ / ロマノフ王朝 *the Romanov dynasty*

おうて 王手 check ⓤ, checkmate ⓤ / 王手! *Check!* / 王手をかける *put the King in check; check the opponent's king*

◆スワローズが優勝に王手をかけた（→優勝まであと1勝となった）Now the Swallows *have just one more win to go*.

おうてん 横転 ——横転する turn over (on its side) / 列車は脱線した後横転し、多数の乗客が負傷した The train *turned over* after leaving the track, and many passengers were injured.

おうと 嘔吐 vomiting ⓤ ——嘔吐する vomit ⓐ ⑭,（口語的）throw* up / その光景を見て私は嘔吐をもよおした The scene made me *feel like throwing up*.

おうとう 応答 answer ⓒ, reply ⓒ, response ⓤ ⓒ（❂後の語はど形式ばった表現）——応答する answer ⑭, reply ⓐ, respond ⓐ / ただちに応答せよ *Respond [Answer] immediately.* / ドアをノックしたが応答はなかった I knocked on the door, but there was no *answer [response]*. ◆（無線で）応答願います *Do you read me?*

‖質疑応答 questions and answers, Q & A

おうどう 王道 ことわざ 学問に王道なし ➩がくもん

おうとつ 凹凸 凹凸の激しい道 a *very rough [bumpy, rugged]* road / 凹凸のあるほうを上にしてください Turn the *rough* side up.

‖凹凸レンズ a concave-convex lens

おうねん 往年 ——往年の（かつての）former, one-time ◆往年の名女優 a *formerly [once]* famous actress

おうひ 王妃 queen (consort) ⓒ / 王妃マリー・アントワネット *Queen* Marie Antoinette

おうふく 往復

——往復する go* to ... and back, make* a round trip / 往復の（切符・料金が）《米》round-trip,《英》return

東京と静岡の間を往復する *make a round trip* between Tokyo and Shizuoka

駅まで往復すると30分はかかる It takes at least half an hour to *go to the station and back*.

東京から名古屋までの往復（切符）を2枚ください Two *round-trip [《英》return] tickets* from Tokyo to Nagoya, please.

◆その村へのバスの便は1日に3往復しかない There are only three *buses* a day to the village. / 駅からホテルまでは送迎バスが定期的に往復している There is *a regular shuttle bus service* from the station to the hotel.（❂shuttle serviceは「（交通機関の）折り返し運行」の意味）

▶「最近どう」「すごく忙しくて毎日会社と家の往復だよ」 "How's it going?" "I'm so busy that I just *shuttle* between home and the office every day."

‖往復書簡 correspondence / 往復はがき a postcard with a prepaid reply attached（❂英米にはない）/ 往復料金《米》a round-trip fare,《英》a double [return] fare

おうぶん¹ 応分 応分の（→資力に応じた）寄付をする contribute *according to one's means*

おうぶん² 欧文（ヨーロッパ諸国の言語で書かれた文章）European writing /（ローマ字）Roman letter /, Roman alphabet

おうへい 横柄 ——横柄な（傲慢な）arrogant;（地位などを鼻にかけた）haughty;（生意気な）insolent ——横柄に arrogantly; haughtily; insolently / 横柄な態度 an *arrogant [a haughty]* manner / あの政治家はいつも横柄な物言いをする That politician always speaks in an *arrogant* way.

おうべい 欧米（ヨーロッパとアメリカ）Europe and America;（西洋）the West ——欧米の European and American, European-American; Western / 明治時代になると日本には多くの欧米文化が取り入れられた In the Meiji era, many *Western cultures* were introduced to Japan.

‖欧米化 westernization / 欧米諸国 European and American countries, Western countries / 欧米人 Europeans and Americans, Westerners

おうぼ 応募 (申し込み) application [C][U]; (コンテストなどへの) entry [C][U] **―応募する** apply for ...; enter [他] //事務所には応募が殺到した The office was swamped with *applications.* / その仕事に応募するには修士の学位と推薦状が必要だ In order to *apply for* that job, you need a master's degree and a letter of recommendation. / 私の姉はよく新聞や雑誌の懸賞に応募する My sister often *enters* contests in newspapers and magazines. ◆彼女は500人の応募者の中から選ばれた She was selected from 500 *applicants*.
‖応募手続 application procedure / 応募用紙 an application form

おうぼう 横暴 **―横暴な** (暴君のような) tyrannical; (高圧的な) oppressive, high-handed //横暴なやり方 a *high-handed* manner / 彼の横暴な態度には我慢できない I can't put up with his *tyrannical* attitude.

おうむ 鸚鵡 parrot [C]
[慣用表現] その子供は私の言ったことをおうむ返しに言った The child *repeated* [*parroted*] my words. (❖parrot には「相手をばかにしてまねる」というニュアンスがある)

おうよう[1] 応用 (適用) application [U] **―応用する** apply [他] (❖進行形にはできない) //科学上の発見を日常生活に応用する *apply* scientific discoveries *to* daily life / この方法はいろいろと応用できる[応用がきく] This method *has* wide *application*. ◆僕は数学の応用問題が苦手だ I'm not good at solving *story* [*applied*] *problems* in math.
‖応用化学 applied chemistry / 応用言語学 applied linguistics / 応用物理学 applied physics

おうよう[2] 鷹揚 **―鷹揚な** (寛大な) generous; (大らかな) easy, easy-going; (心の広い) broad-minded //彼は鷹揚な人だ He is an *easy-going* type of man. ◆あの俳優はいつも鷹揚に構えている(→堂々としている) That actor always *assumes a grand manner*.

おうらい 往来 (行き来) traffic [U], 《口語的》comings and goings; (道路) street [C] //往来の喧騒(けんそう) the buzz [hum] of *traffic*
◆小さな犬が往来の激しい道路に迷い込んだ A little dog strayed into the *busy* street.

おうりつ 王立 **―王立の** royal

おうりょう 横領 embezzlement [U] **―横領する** embezzle [他][自] //公金横領の罪に問われる be accused of *embezzling public money* / あの女性は横領罪で逮捕された That woman was arrested for *embezzlement*. / 彼は会社の金を1,000万円横領した He *embezzled* 10 million yen from his company.

おうレンズ 凹レンズ concave lens [C]

おえつ 嗚咽 sobbing [U], sob [C] **―おえつする** (むせび泣く) sob [自][他] //彼女はおえつをこらえながら愛犬の死について話した She told me about her pet dog's death, trying not to *sob*.

おえらがた お偉方 《口語的》 big shot [C], bigwig [C]; (要人) VIP, V.I.P. [víːàipíː] [C] (❖*v*ery *i*mportant *p*erson の略語); (権威者) authority [C] //政界のお偉方 political *big shots* [*bigwigs*]

おえる 終える
❶【終了する】 end [他], close [他]; (仕上げる) finish [他]; (完璧(かんぺき)に) complete [他]; (締めくくる) conclude [他]; (やり終える) 《口語的》get* through with ...
一生を終える *end* [*finish*] *one's* days
彼女が歌い終えると, 聴衆から割れんばかりの拍手が起こった The audience burst into applause when she *finished singing*. (❖ ×finished to sing とはいわない)
彼女はシェークスピアの一節を引用してスピーチを終えた She *concluded* her speech by quoting a passage from Shakespeare.
私はやっと宿題を終えた At last I *got through with* my homework.
その仕事を終えるのに彼らにはあと10分しか時間が残されていなかった They had only 10 more minutes to *complete* the task.
◆私はこの小説を読み終えた I'*m done with* this novel.
❷【修了する】 (課程を) finish [他], complete [他]; (卒業する) graduate [自]
大学を終える *graduate from* a university
彼は来年学業を終える He *will finish* school next year.

おお (感嘆・驚きなどを表して) Oh!; (承諾・応答を表して) Yes!, Yeah!

おお- 大- (大きさ・数量・程度などが大きい) big; large; great

> [語法]
> big は形・数量・規模などの点で大きいことを表す口語的な語. 特に感覚的に大きいと感じる場合に用いる. large は特に広さ・数量が大きいときに用いられる客観的な語. great は big や large よりも賞賛・驚きなどの感情を伴う.

大地震 a *big* earthquake / 大海原 the *great* ocean / 大うそつき a *big* liar / 大おば a *great*-aunt; a *grandaunt* / 大人数 a *large* [*great*] number of people

おおあじ 大味 **―大味の** (味のない) bland, tasteless //この店の料理はどれも大味だ All the dishes in this restaurant are *bland*.

おおあたり 大当たり (大ヒット) big [smash] hit [C], 《口語的》smash [C]; (大成功) great success [C] //そのミュージカルは大当たりだった The musical was *a great success*.
◆私は福引で大当たりした I *hit the jackpot* in the lottery. (❖hit the jackpot は「(くじなどで)大金を得る」の意味) / 『タイタニック』は90年代後半に大当たりした映画だ *Titanic* was a *blockbuster* movie in the late 90s.

おおあな 大穴 (大きな穴) big hole [C] ◆大穴をあける(→多額の欠損を引き起こす) *cause a great loss* / 彼は競馬ではいつも大穴(→穴馬)をねらう He always *goes for a dark horse* at races.

おおあめ 大雨 heavy rain [C][U]; (どしゃ降り) downpour [C] //大雨のため野球の試合は中止となった The baseball game was canceled because of *heavy rain*. ◆きのうは大雨だった *It*

おおあらし

rained heavily yesterday.
‖大雨洪水注意報 a rain and flood warning

おおあらし 大嵐（激しいあらし）heavy [severe] storm,《公式的》tempest◎

おおあれ 大荒れ　低気圧の接近に伴って海や山では大荒れになりそうです With low atmospheric pressure approaching, *a heavy storm will rage* in the mountains and oceans. / 彼の発言をめぐって会議は大荒れとなった His statement *threw* the conference *into an uproar*. / 彼女，大荒れだから（→機嫌が悪いから）近づかないほうがいいよ You'd better stay away from her because she's *in such a bad mood*.

おおあわて 大慌て　突然の豪雨に大あわてで洗濯物を取り込んだ I *rushed* to bring in the laundry when it suddenly started pouring.

おおい¹ 多い

❶【数・量が】a lot of ..., lots of ..., plenty of ...; (数が) many, a number of ...; (量が) much

> 語法
> 口語では a lot of, lots of が最も一般的で，数えられる名詞・数えられない名詞のいずれにも用いることができる．また plenty of には「十分に・たっぷりある」というニュアンスがある．疑問文や否定文ではふつう数えられる名詞には many，数えられない名詞には much を用いる．より形式ばった表現には，数えられる名詞に用いる a great many，数えられない名詞に用いる a great deal of, a large amount of などがある．

今年は雪が多い There has been *a lot of* snow this year. / We've had *a lot of* snow this year.
ニューヨークには訪ねたい場所がとても多い There are *a good number of* places to visit in New York.
このあたりは韓国料理の店が多い There are *many* Korean restaurants around here.
彼は苦労が多かった He suffered *many* hardships.
宿題が多すぎて休み中どこにも遊びに行けなかった I couldn't go anywhere during the vacation because I had *too much* homework.
◆彼らには共通点が多い They have *a lot* in common. / 牛乳にはカルシウムが多い Milk is *rich in* calcium. / 横浜は大阪よりも人口が多い Yokohama has a *larger* population than Osaka City. / 彼女のワードローブには黒い服が多い Her wardrobe is *full of* black clothes. / アメリカでの食事の量は日本よりかなり多い The portions are *much bigger* in America than in Japan. / 留学で実り多い年を過ごした I had a *fruitful* year studying abroad. / 私のクラスは男子より女子が多い Girls *outnumber* boys in my class.
🔊「僕らは全員で8人だったよね」「あれ，1人多いよ」"There are supposed to be eight of us, right?" "Wait, *there's one too many*."

❷【頻度が】
彼は遅刻することが多い He is *often* late.
最近人の名前が思い出せないことが多い Recently I *often* have trouble (in) recalling people's names.
このあたりは交通事故が多い Traffic accidents are *frequent* in this area.

おおい² 覆い，cover◎, covering◎ ‖家具に覆いをかける put *a cover* on [over] the furniture ◆銅像の覆いを取る *unveil* a statue / 皿の覆いを取る *uncover* a dish

おおい³ hey, hello;（遠くにいる人への呼びかけ）yoo-hoo [júːhúː] ‖おおい，何やってんだ Hey, what are you doing? / おおい，聞こえるか Hey, can you hear me?

おおいかくす 覆い隠す　僕がちょっとからかうと，彼女は恥ずかしそうに両手で顔を覆い隠した She shyly *covered* her face *with* her hands when I made fun of her. / 彼らはこれまでその秘密を覆い隠してきた They have *covered up [concealed]* the secret.

おおいかぶさる 覆いかぶさる　その細い道に覆いかぶさるようにササの葉が茂っていた Bamboo *spread* its willowy leaves *over* the narrow path.

おおいそぎ 大急ぎ ─大急ぎの urgent, pressing ─大急ぎで（あわてて）in a great hurry;（急いで）hurriedly ‖私は大急ぎで宿題を終わらせて外へ遊びに行った I did my homework *hurriedly* and went out to play. / 彼は大急ぎで昼食をとった He ate lunch *in a great hurry*.
◆母が倒れたと聞いて彼は大急ぎで家に帰った He *rushed* home, hearing his mother had collapsed. / みんなが来る前に大急ぎで部屋の掃除をしなくては I've got to clean my room *very quickly* before they come.

おおいた 大分

> 大分県は九州の北東部に位置し，北で瀬戸内海に面しています．全面積の7割以上を占める山地は，霧島・白山両火山帯の一部を構成しています．そのため温泉が豊富で，数では全国第1位を誇り，特に別府・湯布院は全国的に有名です．
> Oita Prefecture is located in northeastern Kyushu, facing the Seto Inland Sea to the north. A mountainous region covers more than 70 percent of the prefecture and is part of both the Kirishima and Hakusan Volcanic Zones. This gives the prefecture the largest number of hot springs in the country. Beppu and Yufuin are especially famous nationwide.

おおいに 大いに（非常に）very, very much,《公式的》greatly (◆通例よい意味をもつ動詞・分詞・形容詞とともに用いる);（高度に）highly ‖その夜私たちはパーティーで大いに楽しんだ That night we enjoyed ourselves *very much* at the party. / その俳優が舞台に上がると会場は大いに沸き返った The audience got *very* excited by the actor's appearance on the stage. / 我々は彼のジョークを聞いて大いに笑った We were *greatly* amused at his jokes.

◆彼の心ない言葉で彼女のプライドは大いに(→深く)傷ついた Her pride was *deeply* hurt by his insensitive words. / そのチームが優勝する可能性は大いにある There is a *strong* possibility that the team will win the championship.

おおいばり 大威張り ━大いばりする boast [自] [他], 《口語的》brag [自] [他] ∥彼は東大に受かったと言って大いばりだった He *boasted of* having passed the entrance exam for the University of Tokyo.

おおいり 大入り (劇場) full [packed] house [C]; (観客) large audience [C] ∥大相撲は連日大入り満員だ A grand sumo tournament has *a large audience* day after day.

◆映画館は大入り満員だった The movie theater *was packed to capacity.* / コンサートは大入りだった There was *large attendance* at the concert.

‖大入り袋 a full-house bonus [souvenir] / 大入り満員 a full house

おおう 覆う

cover [他], blanket [他] (❖通例受身で); (ベールをかぶせるように) veil [他]; (すっぽりと) envelop [他], wrap [他]

その小さな村はすっぽりと雪に覆われていた The small village *was covered with* [*in*] snow.

その競技場の壁面はツタで覆われている The walls of the stadium *are covered with* vines.

歩道は落ち葉で覆われていた The sidewalk *was blanketed with* fallen leaves.

富士山の頂上は雲に覆われている The top of Mt. Fuji *is wrapped in* clouds.

◆雪に覆われた峰々 *snow-covered* peaks / チョコレートで覆ったケーキ a *chocolate-covered* cake / ペンギンの赤ちゃんの体はふわふわした羽毛に覆われている Baby penguins *are feathered with* down. / それは目を覆いたくなるような(→見ていられないような)恐ろしい光景だった It was such a horrible scene that I *could hardly look at it.*

おおうつし 大写し close-up [klóusʌ̀p] [C] ∥…を大写しにする take *a close-up* of ... ◆テレビで容疑者の顔が大写しにされた Television cameras *zoomed in* on the suspect's face.

おおうりだし 大売り出し sale [C]; (特別の) special sale [C]; (在庫一掃の) clearance sale [C] ∥夏物大売り出し *a* summer *sale* / 歳末大売り出し *a* big [great] year-end *sale* / あのデパートでは今在庫一掃の大売り出しをやっている That department store is having *a clearance sale* now.

オーエー OA office automation [U] (❖英語ではふつうOAとはしない) ‖OA機器 office (automation) equipment (❖机・いすなどを含むすべての備品を指してこう呼ぶことが多い)

オーエル OL ⚠(女性会社員) female office worker [C]; (勤め人一般) office worker [C], clerk [C] (❖OL (office lady)は和製英語. 英語では男女の区別なく office worker, clerk を用いるのが一般的) ∥お昼どきにはこの店はOLやサラリーマンでにぎわう At lunchtime this restaurant gets crowded with *office workers.*

おおおとこ 大男 large [tall, big] man [C]; (巨人) giant [C] ◆雲つくような大男 *a towering man*

おおがかり 大掛かり ━大がかりな (大規模な) large-scale; (野心的な) ambitious ∥大がかりな公共事業 *large-scale* public works ◆その殺人事件の大がかりな捜査が行われた The investigation of the murder was made *on a large scale.*

おおかぜ 大風 gale [C], strong wind [C] ∥台風の影響で一晩中大風が吹き荒れていた There were *gales* all night because of the typhoon.

おおかた 大方 ❶【ほとんど】almost, nearly ━大方の most ∥大方の人は彼の提案に賛成した *Most* people agreed to his proposal. / 庭の草むしりもおおかた終わった I *almost* finished pulling the weeds out in the garden.

❷【世間一般】generally ━大方の general ∥大方の予想に反して, 彼が最優秀男優賞を受賞した *Contrary to what was generally expected*, he won the Best Actor Award.

❸【おそらく】probably; (ことによると) perhaps ◆おおかたそんなことだろうと思っていたよ I thought *as much.*

おおがた 大型・大形 ━大型の large-size(d); (大規模の) large-scale; (大きい) large, big, great ∥大型新人 a *great* rookie / 大型冷蔵庫 a *large* [*large-sized, full-sized*] refrigerator / 大型トラックと乗用車が正面衝突した A *large* truck and a car collided head-on. / 大型台風のため停電になった The *large-scale* [*big*] typhoon cut all the electricity. ◆大型バス *a coach*

おおかみ 狼 wolf [C] (複 wolves) ∥オオカミの一群 a pack of *wolves* / あいつは狼だから近づかないほうがいい He is *a wolf in sheep's clothing.* You'd better keep away from him. (❖a wolf in sheep's clothingは「羊の皮を着たオオカミ」の意味)

‖一匹狼 a lone wolf, 《口語的》a loner, a maverick (❖「異端児」のニュアンスがある)

おおがら 大柄 大柄な女性 a *large* woman / 大柄な模様のワンピース a dress *with large patterns*; a *large-patterned* dress

おおかれすくなかれ 多かれ少なかれ more or less; (ある程度) to some extent ∥子供は多かれ少なかれ親の影響を受ける Children are *more or less* influenced by their parents.

おおきい[な] 大きい[な]

❶【サイズ・数量など】big (↔small, little); large (↔small); great; huge; (音量が) loud

| big: 形・数量・規模などの点で大きいことを表

おおきく

す口語的な語．特に感覚的に大きいと感じる場合に用いる．
large: 特に広さ・数量などに用いられる客観的な語であるが，時に主観的感情も含む．
great: big, large よりも賞賛・驚きなどの感情を伴い「(並はずれて) 大きい，巨大な」というニュアンスがある．
huge: 「ばかでかい」というやや誇張したニュアンスで用いることが多い．

5 より大きな数字 a number *bigger than* five
家の近くに大きな公園がある There is a *big* [*large*] park near my house.
彼はわきに大きな包みを抱えていた He was carrying a *big* [*large*] package under his arm.
鯨は現存する最も大きな動物だ Whales are *the biggest* animals in existence today.
バルセロナはマドリッドに次いでスペインで 2 番目に大きな都市だ Barcelona is *the second biggest* city in Spain after Madrid.
このジーンズをもっと大きいのと取り替えたいのですが I would like to exchange these jeans for *bigger ones*.
大きな波が防波堤に打ちつけた The *huge* waves crashed against the breakwater.
そんなに大きな声を出さないでよ Don't speak in such a *loud* voice.
◆大きい順に *in order of size* / 妹のほうが私より大きい My sister *is taller than* me. / もう少し大きな声で話していただけますか Would you speak *a bit louder*, please?

❷【程度・規模】big, great; (重大な) serious, severe

別の大きな問題が持ち上がった Another *big* problem reared its head.
ワールドカップは世界中に大きな興奮を引き起こした The World Cup caused *great* excitement all over the world.
バレーボールをするときには彼の背の高さは大きな強みだ His height is a *great* advantage when he plays volleyball.
暴風雨はその地域に大きな被害をもたらした The storm did *great* [*serious*, *severe*] damage to the district.
彼の死は私たちにとって大きなショックだった His death was a *great* shock to us.
オゾン層の破壊は人間の健康にとって大きな脅威だ The destruction of the ozone layer is a *serious* menace to human health.

◆大きなスケールの人だ He is *a man of high caliber*. / 事故は 2 つの大きな通りが交差する地点で起こった The accident occurred at the junction of two *main* streets. / 喫煙は肺癌(ﾊﾟｲｶﾞﾝ)の大きな原因だ Smoking is a *major* cause of lung cancer. / 彼女は 3 つ上の姉に大きな影響を受けている She is *strongly* influenced by her sister who is three years older than her. / 彼女があきらめると思っているならそれは大きな間違いだ You've *completely misunderstood* if you think she will give up.

❸【その他】

彼の子供たちはもう大きい(→大人だ) His children *are grown up* now.
この試合に勝ったことは大きい Our victory in this game *is important*.
プレゼントの包みをあけると子供たちは大きな歓声をあげた The children *cried out with joy* when they opened the presents.
彼は大きなことばかり言っている He's *always 「talking big* [*boasting*]*.
社長の息子はたいして仕事もしないくせに会社で大きな顔をしている(→いばっている) The president's son *puts on airs* in the office even though he doesn't really do anything.
大きなお世話だ！ *That's none of your business!*

おおきく 大きく

❶【大きく…する】

口を大きくあけて Open your mouth *wide*.
風の変化がこの試合に大きく影響している The shift in wind is having a *big* effect on this game.
この問題は専門家の間で意見が大きく分かれる On this subject, there is *much* difference of opinion among experts.
すべての新聞が彼の死の記事を大きく扱った All the papers *featured* the story of his death.
海外での経験が彼を大きく成長させた His experiences abroad matured him *considerably*.

❷【大きくする】(広げる) enlarge ㊥, expand ㊥

あのデパートは最近店を大きくした That department store *has been enlarged* lately.
その会社は事業を大きくした The company *expanded* its business.
◆テレビの音を大きくしてください *Turn up* (the volume on) the TV.

❸【大きくなる】become* big; (成長する) grow* (up)

彼がその発言をしてから問題はさらに大きくなった The problem *became* even *bigger* after he made the remark.
大きくなったら保母さんになりたい I want to be a nursery school teacher *when I grow up*.
◆騒音はますます大きくなった The noise *became* even *louder*. / 彼はきのう宝くじに当たって気が大きくなっている He won the lottery yesterday, so he's *feeling generous* now.

おおきさ 大きさ size Ⓤ Ⓒ

ふつうの大きさのテーブル a table of standard *size* / ピンポン玉ほどの大きさの卵 an egg about *the size* of a ping-pong ball
その絵はどれくらいの大きさですか What is *the size* of the painting? / How *large* is the painting?
私は彼女の家の大きさに驚いた I was amazed at *the size* of her house.
このビデオカメラは従来の物の約半分の大きさだ This video camera is about *half 「the size* of [*as big as*]*」 old ones.

◆ニンジンをひと口大の大きさに切る cut a carrot into *bite-sized pieces* / このホールは1,000人を収容できる大きさがある This hall *is large enough* to hold 1,000 people. / このベッドの大きさは幅150センチに長さ250センチです *The measurements* of this bed are 150 by 250 centimeters.

おおきな 大きな ⇨ おおきい[な]

おおきめ 大きめ 大きめの(→ゆったりした)セーター a *loose* sweater / もう少し大きめのコートはありますか Do you have a little *larger* coat?

オーきゃく O脚 bowlegs ◆彼女はO脚だ She's *bowlegged*.

おおく 多く a lot; many; much (❖many は数えられる名詞, much は数えられない名詞, a lot はどちらにも用いる) ──多くの a lot of ..., lots of ...; (多数の) many; (多量の) much; (大部分の) most ⇨ おおい(多い)

その経験を通して私は多くのことを学んだ I learned *a lot* through the experience.

かなり多くの小説が毎年日本語に翻訳されている *A good many* novels are translated into Japanese every year.

聴衆の多くはティーンエージャーだった *Many of* the audience were teenagers.

パーティーに来た人は多くはなかった *Not many* people came to the party. (❖Many people didn't come to the party.は「多くの人がパーティーに来なかった」の意味)

子供にあまり多くを期待するな Don't expect *too much* of your child.

彼はそのことについてあまり多くを語らなかった He didn't say *much* about it.

◆僕が1日に読めるのは多くて10ページだ I can read 10 pages a day *at most*.

オーク oak ◎Ū ∥オーク製のテーブル an *oak* table

おおぐい 大食い (よく食べる人) glutton ◎, big eater ◎ ◆彼はやせているが実は大食いだ (→よく食べる) He is thin, but actually he *eats a lot*.

オークション (競売) auction ◎Ū ∥オークションで売る[買う] sell [buy] at *auction* / この絵は来月オークションにかけられる The painting *will be* [*put up for auction* [*auctioned off*] next month.

おおぐち 大口 ❶【大きな口】彼女は大口をあけて笑っている She is laughing *with her mouth wide open*.

❷【大量】大口の買い物 a *large* purchase / ABC社から大口の注文が入った We got a *big* order from the ABC Company.

慣用表現 彼はよく大口をたたくのでみんなに嫌われている He is disliked by everyone because he often *brags* [*talks big*].

おおぐまざ 大熊座 the Great Bear, Ursa Major

おおくらしょう 大蔵省 the Ministry of Finance, the Finance Ministry (❖2001年財務省に改称) ⇨ ざいむしょう

オーケー OK, O.K., okay (❖以上いずれも名詞, 動詞, 形容詞としても用いられる), all right ∥万事オーケーだ Everything is *OK*. / この件に関しては先生からオーケーをもらっています I got *an OK* on this matter from my teacher. / 彼は私たちの案にオーケーしてくれた He *OK'd* our plan.

🗨 「新聞持ってきてくれる?」「オーケー」 "Will you bring me a newspaper?" "*OK.*/ *All right.*"

おおげさ 大袈裟 ──大げさな exaggerated ──大げさに exaggeratedly ∥彼女は大げさに身ぶりを交えて事の一部始終を語った She told me the whole story with *exaggerated* gestures. / 週刊誌は事実を大げさにする傾向がある Weeklies tend to *exaggerate* the facts. / 彼女の話はいつも大げさだ She always *exaggerates* stories.

オーケストラ (管弦楽団) orchestra ◎ (❖構成員に重点をおく場合には時に複数扱い); (交響楽団) symphony orchestra ◎ ∥オーケストラの指揮をとる conduct [lead] *an orchestra* ◆オーケストラの演奏会 an *orchestral* concert ∥オーケストラボックス an orchestra pit

おおごえ 大声 loud voice ◎ ∥大声で in *a loud voice* ◆彼は苦痛で大声をあげた He *cried out* with pain. / その話を聞くとみな大声で笑った Everyone laughed *loudly* to hear the story. / 彼は通りの向こうから大声で私を呼んだ She *called out* to me from the other side of the street. / 男は大声で助けを求めた The man *screamed* for help.

おおごしょ 大御所 leading figure ◎, (公式的) doyen [dɔ́iən] ◎ (❖女性形は doyenne) ∥文壇の大御所 *a leading figure* in the literary world ◆財界の大御所 *a tycoon* in the financial world

おおごと 大事 このことが学校に知られたら大事だ If the school administration finds this out, we'll *be in trouble*. / 大事にならないうちに手を打つべきだ You should do something *before it gets serious*.

おおさか 大阪

大阪府は面積が全国で2番目に小さく, 同時に人口が全国で2番目に多い府です. 昔から交通・貿易・商業の中心として栄え, 京都とともに『上方文化』として知られる独特の文化をはぐくんできました. その文化は今も受け継がれており, いろいろな面でよく東京と比較されます.

Osaka Prefecture has the second largest population in the country, as well as the second smallest area. It has been the center of transportation, trade and commerce since ancient times, and together with Kyoto it has cultivated a unique culture known as "kamigata culture." The culture has been well preserved, and Osaka is often compared with Tokyo in various aspects.

おおざけのみ 大酒飲み heavy [hard] drinker ◎, (軽蔑的) drunkard ◎ ◆彼は大酒飲みだ (→たくさん酒を飲む) He *drinks plenty*.

おおさじ 大匙 tablespoon ◎; (大さじ1杯分)

おおざっぱ

tablespoonful ©（複 ～s, tablespoonsful）《略語》tbs., tbsp.）∥次にしょうゆを大さじ2杯加えます Next, add two *tablespoons* [*tablespoonfuls*] of soy sauce.

おおざっぱ 大雑把 ――大ざっぱな（概略の）rough; (いいかげんな) sloppy, careless ――大ざっぱに roughly ∥大ざっぱに見積もって10万円くらいでしょう A *rough* estimate comes to about a hundred thousand yen. / 大ざっぱに言うとそこには100人ほどの人がいた There were a hundred people there, *roughly speaking*.

おおさわぎ 大騒ぎ 《口語的》fuss Ⓤ; (混乱) confusion Ⓤ ――大騒ぎする fuss ⓐ, make* a fuss; (歓声をあげる) whoop ⓐ; (どんちゃん騒ぎをする) whoop it up ∥何を大騒ぎしているんだい What *are* you *fussing about*? / 彼女の誕生パーティーで大騒ぎをした We *whooped it up* at her birthday party. / ある議員の不祥事で国会は大騒ぎとなった The Diet was thrown into *confusion* over a Diet member's scandal.

おおしい 雄々しい (男らしい) manly; (勇敢な) brave ――雄々しく manfully; bravely

オージー OG ⚠ (卒業生) graduate Ⓒ; (女の卒業生)《主に米》alumna Ⓒ（複 alumnae ），《英》old girl Ⓒ(❖OGは和製略語) ⇨オービー

おおすじ 大筋 (概略) outline Ⓒ ∥事件の大筋 *the outline* of an incident ◆話の大筋をつかむ get *a rough idea* of the story / 大筋において私はあなたに同意します *In principle* [*generally*] I agree with you. / 被告は容疑を大筋で認めた The accused admitted to *most of* the charges.

オーストラリア Australia (❖公式名 the Commonwealth of Australia) ――オーストラリア人 Australian Ⓒ,《俗語》Aussie Ⓒ ――オーストラリア(人)の Australian,《俗語》Aussie

オーストリア Austria(❖公式名 the Republic of Austria) ――オーストリア人 Austrian Ⓒ ――オーストリア(人)の Austrian

おおずもう 大相撲 grand sumo tournament Ⓒ ⇨すもう ∥きょうの結びの一番は大相撲(→熱戦)だった Today's final match was *an exciting fight* [*a long-drawn-out bout*]. ∥大相撲春場所 the Spring Sumo Tournament

おおぜい 大勢 (たくさんの人) many [a lot of] people, a great [large] number of people; (群集) a (large) crowd
大勢の人がパレード見物に集まった A *crowd of people* gathered to see the parade.
そのパーティーには大勢の人が招待された A *lot of people* were invited to the party.
大勢の人が座り込みの抗議に加わった A *large* [*great*] *number of people* joined the sit-in protest.
大勢の人がデパートの中にどっと入っていった *The crowd* swarmed into the department store.
大勢の前で話すのは苦手だ I don't like speaking *in front of a large crowd*.

◆大勢の家族を養う support a *large* family

おおぜき 大関 🔰 (an) *ozeki*, a sumo wrestler of the second highest rank

おおそうじ 大掃除 general (house) cleaning Ⓤ, spring cleaning Ⓤ(また a～) ◆うちでは年末に必ず大掃除をする We always *clean the whole house* at the end of the year.

おおぞら 大空 鳥が大空に羽ばたいていった A bird flew up into *the sky*.

オーソリティー (権威・大家) authority Ⓒ; (専門家) expert Ⓒ ∥彼は経済学のオーソリティーだ He is *an authority on* economics.

おおぞん 大損 heavy [big, great] loss Ⓒ ∥競馬で大損をした I suffered *a heavy loss* at the horse races.

オーダー (注文・順序) order Ⓒ ――オーダーする order ⓗ ∥バッティングオーダー the batting order / メールオーダー (通信販売) mail order / ラストオーダー last order

オーダーメード ⚠ ――オーダーメードの made-to-order, custom-made; (服が) tailor-made (❖「オーダーメード」は和製英語) ∥オーダーメードの服 a *made-to-order* [*tailor-made, custom-made*] dress

◆このスーツはオーダーメードです I *had* this suit *made to order*.

おおだい 大台 (到達の水準) level Ⓒ, mark Ⓒ ∥世界の人口は60億人の大台に乗った The world's population topped *the six billion mark*. / そのCDの売り上げは100万枚の大台を突破した The CD sales exceeded [passed] *the one million mark*.

おおだすかり 大助かり 彼に家まで車で送ってもらって大助かりだった He was「*very helpful* [*a great help*] to me in driving me home.

おおちがい 大違い big [great] difference Ⓒ; (大きな間違い) big mistake Ⓒ ∥実際に見るのと聞くのとでは大違いだ There's a big *difference* between hearing about something and actually seeing it.

◆結果は私が考えていたのとは大違いだった The result *was quite* [*completely*] *different from* what I had expected.

おおっぴら 大っぴら ――おおっぴらに (公に) openly, publicly; (自由に) freely ∥二十歳(はたち)になったらおおっぴらにたばこが吸える I can smoke *openly* when I become 20.

◆この件はまだおおっぴらにはできない We cannot make this matter *public* yet.

おおつぶ 大粒 大粒の雨 *big drops* of rain / 彼女の目から大粒の涙がこぼれ落ちた *Large tears* dropped from her eyes. / 彼の額には大粒の汗がにじんでいた *Large beads of sweat* stood out on his forehead.

おおづめ 大詰め (終わり) end Ⓒ; (結末) close Ⓒ; (芝居の) finale Ⓒ ∥2国間の交渉は大詰めに近づいた The negotiations between the two countries drew to *an end* [*a close*]. ◆捜査もいよいよ大詰めを迎えた The investigation *reached the final stages* at last.

おおて 大手 (主要な会社) big [major] company ©, major corporation ©; (大企業) big enterprise © ‖父は大手商社に勤めています My father works for *a major trading company.* / 私鉄大手8社の従業員は賃上げを要求してストに入った The employees of *the eight biggest* private railroad *companies* went on strike for higher wages.

◆コンピュータ業界の最大手 the largest [biggest] company in the computer industry

おおで 大手 大手を振って(→意気揚々と)家に帰る go home *in triumph* / その男は私たちの前に大手を広げて立ちはだかった The man stood in front of us *with arms outstretched.*

オーディオ audio [stereo] system ©; (装置全体) audio [stereo] equipment ⓤ; (構成部分) stereo component © ‖オーディオ機器 audio-visual equipment / オーディオテープ an audio tape / オーディオマニア an audiophile

オーディション audition © ‖彼女はそのCMモデルのオーディションに合格した She passed *the audition* to be the model in the commercial. / 私はテレビドラマの主役のオーディションを受けた I *had an audition [auditioned]* for the leading role in a TV drama.

オーデコロン (eau de cologne) [(òu də kəlóun)] ⓤ (❖フランス語から) ‖オーデコロンをつける put on (*eau de cologne*)

おおどうぐ 大道具 (stage) set ©; (舞台背景) scenery ⓤ ‖大道具方 a scenesifter

おおどおり 大通り main [(英)high] street ©, avenue ©, boulevard © ‖この道路は駅前で大通りと交差している This road crosses *the main street* in front of the station. / その衝突事故で大通りは通行止めになった The crash obstructed *the main street.*

オートキャンプ ⚠ car camping © (❖「オートキャンプ」は和製英語)

オートバイ ⚠ motorcycle ©, (英) motorbike © (❖「オートバイ」は和製英語. また motorbike は(米)では小型オートバイの意味) ⇒ 図版 ‖彼はオートバイで海まで行った He went to the sea *on a motorcycle [by motorcycle].*

オートフォーカス (自動焦点合わせ) autofocus © ‖オートフォーカスのカメラ an *autofocus* camera ◆このカメラはオートフォーカスだ This camera *focuses automatically.*

オードブル (前菜) hors d'oeuvre [ɔ́ːr dɜ́ːrv] © (複 ~s, ~) (❖フランス語から)

オートマチック ―オートマチックの (自動の) automatic ‖オートマチック車 *an automatic (car)* (❖正式には a car with an automatic transmission)

オートミール oatmeal ⓤ ‖オートミールのクッキー an *oatmeal* cookie

オートメーション automation ⓤ ◆この製品の製造過程は完全にオートメーション化されている The process of making these products *is fully automated.*

オートレース (自動車の) car [automobile] race ©; (オートバイの) motorcycle race © (❖「オートレース」は和製英語)

オートロック ⚠ ―オートロックの self-locking (❖「オートロック」は和製英語) ‖この部屋のドアはオートロックになっています The door of this room is *self-locking.*

オーナー owner © ‖ホテルのオーナー *a hotel owner* / プロ野球チームのオーナー *the owner*

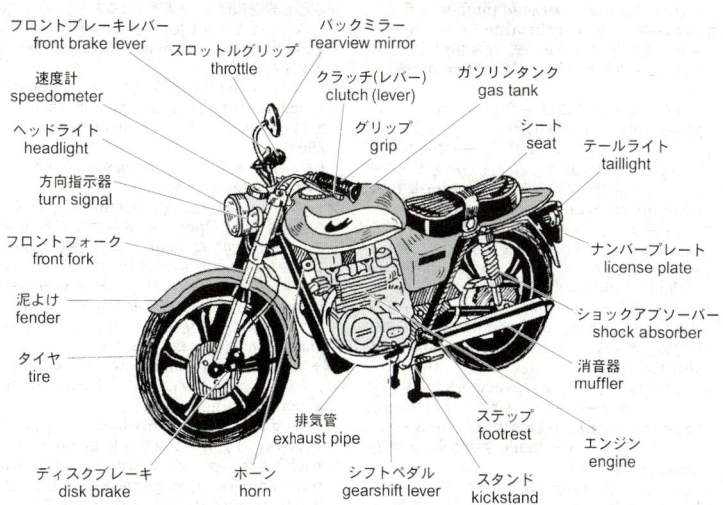

フロントブレーキレバー front brake lever
バックミラー rearview mirror
スロットルグリップ throttle
速度計 speedometer
クラッチ(レバー) clutch (lever)
ガソリンタンク gas tank
ヘッドライト headlight
グリップ grip
シート seat
テールライト taillight
方向指示器 turn signal
フロントフォーク front fork
ナンバープレート license plate
泥よけ fender
ショックアブソーバー shock absorber
タイヤ tire
消音器 muffler
排気管 exhaust pipe
ステップ footrest
エンジン engine
ディスクブレーキ disk brake
ホーン horn
シフトペダル gearshift lever
スタンド kickstand

オートバイ motorcycle

お

of a professional baseball team
◆オーナードライバー drivers who own their cars(❖×owner-driver とはいわない)
おおなた 大なた big hatchet [C] ◆市は来年度の予算に大なたを振るった(→思いきって削った) The city *made a drastic cut* in the budget for the next fiscal year. / The city *let the ax fall* on next year's budget.
オーバー ⚠
❶【誇張】 ―オーバーな exaggerated //オーバーな演技 *exaggerated* acting / それはちょっとオーバーだよ That's a little *exaggerated.* ◆彼はいつもオーバーな言い方をする He *is* always *exaggerating* things.
❷【超過】 ―オーバーする exceed [他], go* over [beyond] ... //予算をオーバーする *exceed* the budget / 志願者の人数は定員をはるかにオーバーした The number of applicants far *exceeded* the prescribed number.
❸【コート】 overcoat [C], coat [C] //オーバーを着る[脱ぐ]「put on [take off] *an overcoat*
オーバーコート overcoat [C]
オーバースロー ⚠(野球) overhand [overarm] throw [C] (❖英語の overthrow は「暴投」の意味) ◆彼はオーバースローのピッチャーだ He pitches *overarm.*
オーバータイム ⚠ オーバータイムをとられた(→バスケットボールで) We were penalized for「*violating the three-second rule* [(→バレーボールで) *touching the ball too many times in succession*].
オーバーネット ⚠ (バレーボールで)オーバーネットをとられた We were penalized for *reaching over the net.*
オーバーハンド overhand [C] ◆オーバーハンドのピッチャー an *overhand* pitcher
オーバーヒート overheating [U] ―オーバーヒートする overheat [自] //車のエンジンがオーバーヒートした My car's engine *overheated.*
オーバーヘッドプロジェクター overhead projector [C] (《略語》OHP)
オーバーホール overhaul [C] ―オーバーホールする overhaul [他] //そろそろ車をオーバーホールに出さなくてはならない It's high time I *had* my car's engine *overhauled.*
オーバーラップ ―オーバーラップする overlap [自] [他] //その光景が子供のころの記憶とオーバーラップした The scene *overlapped with* my childhood memory.
オーバーラン overrun [C] ―オーバーランする overrun* [他], overshoot* [他] //飛行機は滑走路をオーバーランした The airplane *overshot* the runway.
オーバーワーク (過労) overwork [U] ◆彼女はこのところオーバーワークぎみだ She seems to *be overworking* recently. / 彼はオーバーワークで倒れた He made himself sick *by working too hard.*
おおはば 大幅 ―大幅な (大きい) big, large; (金額などが) substantial; (急激な) sharp; (思いきった) drastic ―大幅に greatly; sharply
予定を大幅に変更する make *drastic* changes in a plan
旧型のコンピュータが大幅に値下げされている Old model computers have been *sharply* reduced in price.
医療政策における大幅な予算削減が発表された A *sharp* cut in the budget for medical services has been announced.
彼は部長に昇進して収入が大幅にアップした He got a *substantial* pay raise after being promoted to division head.
◆濃霧で飛行機が大幅に遅れた The flight was delayed *quite a while* due to dense fog.
おおばんぶるまい 大盤振る舞い 正月は家に友人を呼んで大盤ぶるまいをした On New Year's Day I invited my friends to my house and *gave a big feast.*
オービー OB ⚠❶【卒業生】 graduate [C]; (男子の卒業生) 《米》alumnus [C] (複 alumni), 《英》old boy [C] (❖OB は和製略語) //うちの会社には慶応大学のOBが多い There are many *graduates* of Keio University in my company. ◆バスケット部のOB *a former member* of the basketball club
❷【ゴルフの】 out of bounds
オープニング opening [C] ‖オープニングセレモニー an opening ceremony
おおぶね 大船 [慣用表現]大船に乗った気でいなさい(→信頼して安心してください) You may *rely on me and put yourself at ease.* / (→すべて任せてください) *Leave everything to me.*
おおぶり 大振り (大きく振ること) big swing [C] ―大ぶりの (大型の) large(-sized) //大ぶりの器(うつわ) a *large(-sized)* bowl
おおぶろしき 大風呂敷 [慣用表現]彼はすぐに大ぶろしきを広げる(→大げさなことを言う)ので内心みんなうんざりしていた We all were disgusted with him inside because he always *talks big.*
オーブン oven [ʌ́vən] [C] //オーブンでケーキを焼く bake a cake in *an oven* / オーブンは200度に温めておきます Preheat *the oven* to 200℃.
‖オーブントースター a toaster oven (❖×oven toaster とはいわない)
オープン (開始すること) opening [C]; (公開選手権試合) the Open ―オープンする open [自] ―オープンな open //新しい劇場のオープン *the opening of* a new theater / 新しいデパートがきのうオープンした A new department store *opened* yesterday. / 全米オープンではラフターが優勝した Rafter won the championship in *the U.S. Open.*
◆オープンな人 a *frank* person / 彼女とだったら何でもオープンに話せる I can tell her about anything *openly.*
‖オープンカー a convertible (❖×open car とはいわない) / オープンサンド an open sandwich / オープン戦 a pre-season exhibition game (❖×open game とはいわない. また英語の opening game は「開幕戦」の意味)
オーボエ oboe [óubou] [C] ‖オーボエ奏者 an oboist

おおぼら 大ぼら 彼は大ぼらを吹いてばかりいる He *is always boasting [talking big]*.
おおまか 大まか ──大まかな rough; (一般的な) general ──大まかに roughly 〃大まかな概算 a *rough* estimate / 大まかな計画 a *rough* plan ◆彼はヨーロッパ旅行の計画を大まかに説明した He *outlined* his plan to travel through Europe. / その2つは大まかに言って(→基本的に)同じ物 Those two are *basically* the same.
おおまじめ 大真面目 彼はその荒唐無稽(ｹｲ)な計画に大まじめに取り組んでいる He is struggling with the ridiculous plan *very earnestly*.
おおまた 大股 long stride ◎ ◆彼は怒って大またで去っていった He *strode off* angrily.
おおまちがい 大間違い 何でも思いどおりになると思ったら大間違いだぞ If you think you can have your own way in everything, *you are dead wrong*.
おおまわり 大回り (スキー・スケートなどの)大回りターン a *wide* turn
おおみえ 大見得 (役者が)大みえを切る(→ポーズをとる) strike a pose / 彼は数学のテストで満点を取るとおおみえを切った(→大げさに宣言した) He *pompously declared* (that) he would get a perfect score on the math exam.
おおみず 大水 (洪水) flood ◎ 〃大水で橋が流された *The flood* washed away the bridge.
おおみそか 大晦日 the last day of the year; (その日の夜) New Year's Eve 〃大みそかには家族全員集まって, そばを食べたりテレビを見たりする On *New Year's Eve* the whole family gets together, eating *soba* and watching TV.
オーム 〔電気〕ohm ◎ (◆電気抵抗の単位; (記号)Ω) 〃オームの法則 Ohm's law
おおむかし 大昔 ancient times; (先史時代) prehistoric times; (原始時代) primitive ages 〃日本人は大昔から米を食べてきた The Japanese have lived on rice *since ancient times*. ◆恐竜は大昔に地球上から姿を消した Dinosaurs vanished from the face of the earth *a long time ago*.
おおむぎ 大麦 barley ◎
おおむね (全般的に) on the whole; (ほとんど) almost 〃この絵はおおむね完成している I have *almost* finished this picture. / 計画はおおむね順調にいっている *On the whole* the plan has been carried out satisfactorily.
おおめ¹ 大目 今回だけは大目に見て(→見逃して)やろう I'll *overlook* it this time only.
おおめ² 多め 万一に備えてお金は少し多めに持っていなさい You should have *extra* money with you just in case. / お昼がかなり多めだったからまだおなかはすいていません I'm not hungry yet because I had a *rather big* lunch.
おおめだま 大目玉 (ひどくしかること) (good) scolding ◎ 〃窓ガラスを割って父親に大目玉を食らった After breaking a windowpane I *got a good scolding* from my father.
おおもじ 大文字 capital letter ◎, capital ◎ ──大文字の capital 〃固有名詞はふつう大文字で始まる Proper nouns usually begin with *capitals*.
おおもと 大本 (土台) foundation ◎; (基礎) basis ◎ (複 bases); (根底) root ◎
おおもの 大物 important figure ◎, (口語的) big name [shot] ◎ ──大物の big, great 〃経済界の大物たち *the big names* in the economic world / うちのチームにはこれだけの大物選手がそろっているんだから負けるわけにはいかない With so many *great players* on our team, we simply cannot lose. / 彼女は初めての釣りで大物を釣った She got *a big fish* in her first try at fishing.
◆この子は将来きっと大物になる(→成功する)だろう This kid will surely *make it big* in the future.
おおもり 大盛り 大盛りのカレーライス a *jumbo-sized* curry and rice / チャーハンの大盛り1つお願いします I'll have *a large serving of* fried rice.
おおや 大家 (男性) landlord ◎; (女性) landlady ◎

おおやけ 公 ──公の (公式の) official (↔unofficial); (公共の) public (↔private)
公の発表によると失業率は4パーセントだ The unemployment rate is four percent according to an *official* announcement.
その事実は彼女の死後に公にされた The fact *was made public* after her death.
◆彼女が公の場で(→人前で)涙を見せたことは一度もない She has never shed tears *in public*. / 彼女は死刑制度を支持すると公の場で表明した She's *on record as saying* she favors the death penalty. (❖be on record は「記録されている」の意味)
おおやすうり 大安売り (big) sale ◎
おおゆき 大雪 heavy snow ◎; (降雪量) heavy snowfall ◎ 〃昨夜は大雪だった We had a *heavy snow* last night. / It snowed *heavily* last night. / 大雪のために電車が遅れた The trains were delayed as a result of *a heavy snowfall*.
おおよそ roughly; (約) approximately, about ──おおよその rough; approximate 〃だれがそんなことをしたのかおおよその見当はつく I can make a *rough* guess who did that. / 私はこの絵のおおよその価値しか知らない I only know the *approximate* value of the picture.
オーライ all right, OK, O.K., okay 〃バック, オーライ *All right*. Come on back.
おおらか 大らか ──大らかな (心が広い) broad-minded; (寛大な) generous; (あくせくしない) easygoing 〃彼はとても大らかなのでみんなに好かれている He is so *broad-minded* that he is liked by everyone.
オーラル 〃オーラルコミュニケーション oral communication / オーラルメソッド an oral method (❖外国語教授法の一つ)
オール¹ (船のかい) oar ◎ 〃彼はオール(でボート)をこぐのが速い He「*pulls on the oars* [*rows a boat*] fast.

オール² 彼女の１学期の成績はオールＡだった She got *straight A's* in the first term.

オールウエザーコート (全天候型コート) all-weather court ⓒ

オールスター ‖オールスターキャスト an all-star cast ⓒ / オールスターゲーム an all-star game

オールドミス ⚠ old maid ⓒ (❖「オールドミス」は和製英語)

オールナイト オールナイトの映画館 an *all-night* movie theater / オールナイトの店 an *all-night* store / 私たちはオールナイトでカラオケを楽しんだ We enjoyed karaoke *all night (long)*.

オールバック ⚠ 兄は髪をオールバックにしている My brother *wears* [*combs*] *his hair straight back*. (❖「オールバック」は和製英語)

オールマイティー ⚠ 彼はスポーツにかけてはオールマイティーだ When it comes to sports, he's *really good at anything*.

オールラウンド —オールラウンドの《米》all-around,《英》all-round ‖オールラウンドプレーヤー an all-around player

オーロラ aurora [ɔrɔ́ːrə] (複～s, aurorae) (❖北極付近のものを the northern lights, 南極付近のものを the southern lights ともいう)

おおわざ 大技 bold [daring] move

おおわらい 大笑い good [hearty] laugh ⓒ, a roar of laughter ‖その話を聞いて大笑いした I「*had a good laugh* [*laughed heartily*] at the story. / そのテレビ番組を見て私たちは大笑いした The TV program *gave* us *a good laugh*.

おおわらわ 大わらわ きのうは文化祭の準備におおわらわだった(→とても忙しかった) We were very busy preparing for the school festival yesterday. / きょうは一日中おおわらわだった I had a *hectic* day today.

おか 丘 hill ⓒ; (小さい丘) hillock ⓒ ‖丘のふもと the bottom of *a hill* / 急勾配(こうばい)の丘 a steep *hill* / うちの学校の校舎は丘の中腹にある Our school building is on「*the side of a hill* [*a hillside*].

おかあさん お母さん (母親) mother ⓒ; (呼びかけ) 《米口語的》Mom(my), 《英口語的》Mum(my)

> **語法**
> 家族の間では mother を固有名詞のように扱い, 書くときは冠詞を付けず大文字で書き始めるのがふつう. 他人に母親のことをいう場合は my mother を用いる. 子供の母親に対する呼びかけは Mom, Mum が最も一般的. Mommy, Mummy は主に幼児が用いる.

お母さんによろしくお伝えください Please give my (best) regards to *your mother*.

お母さん, 金井さんから電話だよ *Mom*, a phone call from Mr. Kanai!

💬 「お母さんはどこ」「台所にいるよ」"Where's *Mom*?" "She's in the kitchen."

💬 「お母さんはいらっしゃる？」「いえ, 母は出かけております」"Is *your mother* home?" "No, she's gone now."

おかえし お返し (返礼) return ⓒ ⓤ; (おつり) change ⓤ ‖お返しに in return / 9,000円のお返しです Here's *your change* of 9,000 yen. / 別にお返しを期待しているわけじゃない I'm not expecting anything *in return*. / いつか必ずこのお返しはしてやる I'll be sure to *pay you back* for this.

おかえりなさい お帰りなさい

> 英語には日本語の「お帰りなさい」に相当する決まった言い方はない. Hi!, Hello! などのあいさつの言葉を用いたり, How was your day? などと聞いたりする. また旅先から戻ってきた人などに対しては Welcome home [back]!, Glad to see you back! などと言う.

おかかえ お抱え —お抱えの (個人的な) personal; (弁護士など) retained ‖彼にはお抱えの秘書がいる He has *his own personal* secretary.
‖お抱え運転手 a chauffeur [ʃoufə́ːr] / お抱え弁護士 a retained lawyer

おがくず おが屑 sawdust

おかげ お陰 —おかげで thanks to … (❖皮肉で悪い意味にも用いる); (理由で) because of …, due to …, owing to …

通りがかりの人たちが手伝ってくれたおかげでコンタクトレンズが見つかった I found my contact lens, *thanks to* the help of some passers-by.

私が早稲田大学に合格したのは家庭教師の先生のおかげです *It's all thanks to* my tutor that I made it into Waseda University.

その事件のおかげで地元の夏祭りが中止になった *Owing to* the incident, the local summer festival was canceled.

◆ 私が今日(ǎ)あるのは母のおかげです I *owe* what I am now *to* my mother. / いつものバスに乗り遅れたおかげで事故にあわずにすんだ *Because* I missed the (usual) bus, I escaped the accident. / コンピュータのおかげでその仕事は短時間で終わった(→コンピュータは私たちがその仕事を短時間で終えられるようにしてくれた) The computer *enabled* us *to* finish the work in a short time.

💬 「けさのご気分はいかがですか」「おかげさまで, いいですよ」"How are you feeling this morning?" "I'm feeling fine, *thank you*."

💬 「募金活動のほうはどうでしたか」「おかげさまでたくさん集まりました」"How did the fund-raising campaign go?" "*Fortunately*, a lot of people gave us donations."

💬 「お母様のぐあいはいかがですか」「おかげさまで, すっかりよくなりました」"How's your mother?" "*Thank you for asking*. She's very well now." (❖ Thank you for asking. は相手の気づかいに対して感謝の意を表す言い方)

おかしい・おかしな

❶【こっけいな】funny; amusing; comical; ridiculous

> funny 「おかしい」を表す最も一般的な語. 笑い声をあげるようなおかしさを指す.

amusing: funny よりも「おかしさ」の度合いは低く，くすっと笑うような感じのおかしさをいうことが多い．
comical: 人の笑いを誘うような「おかしさ」を指す．
ridiculous:「ばかげている」の意味．

何がそんなにおかしいの What's so *funny*?

この本すごくおかしいから，ちょっと読んでみて This book *is* really *amusing* and you should have a look at it.

◆だれもが私の話を信じたのは本当におかしかった *To my amusement*, everyone believed my story. / 彼の女装がおかしくて思わず吹き出してしまった I burst into laughter at the *hilarious* sight of him in women's clothes. (✿hilariousは「笑い転げるほどおかしい」の意味)

🔊「あの映画見た？」「見たよ．めちゃくちゃおかしかった」"Did you see that movie?" "I did. It *was* really *funny*!"

❷【妙な・ふつうでない】(奇妙な) strange, odd, funny;（変な）(口語的) weird;（いつもと違う）unusual;（ばかげている）ridiculous

それはおかしい That's *strange*.

ゆうべすごくおかしな夢を見た I had the *strangest* dream last night.

その服にその靴はちょっとおかしいよ Those shoes *look* a little *odd* with that dress.

彼女が遅刻するなんておかしいよ It's *unusual* for her to be late.

君が弁償しなくちゃいけないなんておかしいよ It's *ridiculous* that you should have to pay for the loss.

◆プリンターの調子がおかしい There's *something wrong* with the printer. / 彼の申し出を受けないなんておかしいですか Am I being *unreasonable* in not accepting his offer? / あいつは少し頭がおかしいよ He *is not* (quite) 「*right in the head* [*in his right mind*]." / 彼はもういつ来てもおかしくない He'll be coming at any minute.

🔊「ドアにかぎがかかってるよ」「おかしいな，ついさっきまであいてたのに」"The door's locked." "*That's weird*. It was open a minute ago."

🔊「(私の服装は)おかしくない？」「うん，とても似合ってるよ」"*Do I look all right*?" "Yes, you look wonderful."

❸【怪しい】suspicious

彼の報告におかしな点があるはずがない There can't be anything *suspicious* in his report.

おかしさ (楽しさ) amusement Ⓤ；(こっけいさ) funniness Ⓤ ◆彼女はおかしさ(→笑いたい衝動)をこらえながらそのことを話してくれた She told me about it suppressing *her impulse* [*urge*] *to laugh*.

おかしらつき 尾頭付き (まるごとの魚) a fish with its head and tail ◆祝い事にはよくタイの尾頭付きが出される Grilled sea bream *with its head and tail still on* are often served on happy occasions.

おかす¹ 犯す (罪を) commit Ⓤ；(法律を) violate Ⓤ；(間違いを) make* Ⓤ；(女性を) rape Ⓤ

過ちを犯す *commit* [*make*] an error / 校則を犯す *violate* [*break*] the school regulations

とんでもない間違いを犯してしまった I *made* an enormous mistake.

彼は犯罪[罪，不正]を犯した He *committed* a crime [a sin, an injustice].

殺人を犯したのはその警官だった It was the police officer that *committed* the murder.

◆あの男は殺人の罪を犯している That man *is guilty of* murder. / 彼は何の罪を犯していないことが分かった He was found *innocent of any crime*.

おかす² 侵す (侵害する) violate Ⓤ, (公式的) infringe Ⓤ；(侵略する) invade Ⓤ

国籍不明の航空機が日本の領空を侵した An unidentified aircraft *violated* Japan's territorial airspace.

君に私のプライバシーを侵す権利はない You have no right to *violate* my privacy.

基本的人権を侵してはならない Basic human rights *must not be infringed*.

おかす³ 冒す ❶【危険を冒す】run* [take*] a risk, risk Ⓤ

私は全財産を失うような危険を冒したくない I *don't want to run the risk of* losing all my money.

彼は命の危険を冒すほどばかではない He is not such a fool as to *risk his life*.

◆その母親は命の危険を冒してわが子を助けようとした The mother tried to save her child *at the risk of her life*. / 彼らは危険を冒して荒れた海に乗り出した They *ventured out* into the stormy sea.

❷【病気が人を冒す】(病気などが) affect Ⓤ, attack Ⓤ

彼の肺は癌(ガン)に冒されていた His lungs *were affected* by cancer.

HIVウイルスは体の免疫機能を冒す The HIV virus *attacks* the body's immune system.

おかず 今晩のおかずは何ですか What's for *dinner* this evening? / テーブルにはたくさんのおかずが並んでいた There were many kinds of *food* on the table.

> 英米には主食，副食という考え方がないため「おかず」に相当する英語はなく，dishes served with rice などと説明的に訳すしかない．side dish は「主要な料理ではないもの」という意味で，日本でいう「おかず」と同じでない．

おかっぱ お河童 bob Ⓒ, bobbed hair Ⓤ ◆おかっぱの女の子 a girl with *bobbed hair* / 妹は髪をおかっぱにしている My sister *wears* [*has*] *her hair in a bob*.

おかどちがい お門違い ──お門違いの (間違いの) wrong；(適切ではない) irrelevant ◆彼女に文句を言うなんてお門違いだよ It *is wrong* for you to complain to her.

おかぶ お株 明子は数学ではいつもクラスのトップだが，今回ばかりは由紀にお株を奪われた(→由紀が明子を負かした) Akiko is usually ranked first in her class in math, but this time Yuki *beat her at her own game*.

おかまい お構い 彼らは周りの迷惑もおかまいなしに騒いでいた They were being noisy *without any regard for* whether they bothered other people.

💬「コーヒー、いれますね」「どうぞおかまいなく」 "I'll make you some coffee." "*Don't go to any trouble*."

💬「じゃそろそろ失礼します」「何のおかまいもできませんが、夕食でも食べていってください」 "I must be going now." "*We're not having anything special*, but please stay and have dinner with us."

おがみたおす 拝み倒す 彼は両親を拝み倒してお金を借りた(→貸してくれるよう頼み込んだ) He *begged* his parents *relentlessly* to lend him money.

おがむ 拝む (あがめる) worship 他; (祈る) pray 自 // ひざまずいて拝む *pray* on *one's knees* / 祖母は毎朝神棚を拝む My grandmother *worships* at the Shinto altar every morning. / 私は本堂の前で手を合わせて拝んだ I *prayed* in front of the main temple with joined hands. ◆ 初日の出を拝む *watch* the sunrise on New Year's Day

おかやま 岡山

> 日本で最も有名な昔話の一つ、「桃太郎」のふるさとである岡山県は、日本の西部、中国地方の中心に位置し、瀬戸内海に面しています。温暖な気候に恵まれたこの県では果樹栽培が盛んで、桃やブドウは全国でも有数の生産量を誇っています。
>
> Okayama Prefecture is the home of "Momotaro," one of the most famous Japanese folktales. It is located in the central Chugoku region in western Honshu and faces onto the Seto Inland Sea. Thanks to its mild climate, fruit cultivation has flourished in this prefecture. Okayama is one of Japan's top producers of peaches and grapes.

オカリナ ocarina C (✦イタリア語から)

オカルト (超自然的なもの) the occult

おがわ 小川 brook C, (米) creek C, stream C (✦この順で大きくなる) // 小川のせせらぎの音 the murmur of *a little brook* / 小川のそばに大きな果樹園が見えます You can see a large orchard beside *the stream*.

おかわり お代わり (食事の) a second [another] helping; (飲み物の) (口語的) refill C // デザートのお代わりをする have *a second helping* of dessert / その店ではコーヒーはただでお代わりができる You can ask for coffee *refills* for free at the restaurant.

💬「ごはんのお代わりはいかが」「いただきます[もう結構です]」 "Would you like *another helping* of rice?" "Yes, please. [No, thank you.]"

おかん 悪寒 chill C // きのうから悪寒がする I've been feeling [having] *chills* since yesterday.

おかんむり 彼は朝からおかんむりだ(→機嫌が悪い) He's *been in a bad mood* since this morning.

おき 沖 船は海岸の5キロ沖に停泊した(→いかりを下ろした) The ship dropped anchor five kilometers *off* the coast. / 漁船は沖に出た The fishing boat put out to *the open sea*. / 沖にヨットが浮かんでいるのが見える I can see sailboats floating *offshore*. / その船は日本海沖で遭難した The ship was wrecked *off the coast* in the Sea of Japan.

-おき -置き 1日おきに花に水をやる water flowers *every other* [*second*] *day* / ごみを2日おきに出す take out the garbage 「*every three days* [*every third day*] / 薬を8時間おきに飲む take medicines *every eight hours* / 列車は5分おきに出ています Trains run 「*every five minutes* [*at five-minute intervals*]. / 街路樹は5メートルおきに植わっている The trees lining on the street are planted 「*at intervals of five meters* [*every five meters, five meters apart*].

おきあい 沖合い、沖合いで *off the coast* // 沖合漁業 offshore fishing

おきあがる 起き上がる (起床する) get* up (✦「立ち上がる」「地面から起き上がる」の意味もある); (立ち上がる) stand* up; (公式的) rise* 自; (体を起こす) sit* up; (転んで) pick *oneself* up // その子供は転んだがすぐ起き上がった The child fell down but 「*picked himself up* [*got up*] immediately. / 祖母はやっとベッドに起き上がれるようになった My grandmother *could* finally *sit up* in bed.

おきかえる 置き換える (並べ換える) rearrange 他; (取り替える) replace 他 // 父は私の机を窓側に置き換えてくれた My father *rearranged* my desk to face the window. ◆XをYに置き換える *substitute* Y *for* X

おきざり 置き去り ——置き去りにする (後へ残す) leave* ... *behind*; (見捨てる) desert 他, abandon 他 // 母親が赤ちゃんを橋の下に置き去りにするという事件があった There was an incident in which a mother *abandoned* her baby under a bridge. / みんな私を置き去りにして行ってしまった Everyone had gone *leaving* me *behind*.

オキシダント (photochemical) oxidant C // オキシダント濃度 the level of oxidants

オキシドール peroxide U, hydrogen peroxide solution U

おきっぱなし 置きっぱなし テーブルの上に財布を置きっぱなしにするなんて泥棒に取ってくれと言っているようなものだ *Leaving* your wallet on the table is an open invitation to thieves.

おきて 掟 (規則) rule C; (公の統制規則) regulation C; (法) law C // おきてを破る break *the law* / おきてに従う obey [keep, observe] *the law* / ジャングルのおきて *the law* of the jungle

おきてがみ 置き手紙 (書き置き) note C; (伝言) message C // 私は母に置き手紙をして外出した I left a note [*message*] for my mother and went out.

おきどけい 置き時計 (一般的に) clock C (✦

携帯用時計は watch)；（卓上の）table [desk] clock [C]

おぎなう 補う （埋め合わせをする）make* up (for ...), compensate [他] [自]；（補足する）supplement [他]

損失[赤字]を補う *make up* a loss [deficit] / 残業して収入を補う *supplement one's* income by working overtime

彼は猛勉強によって知識の不足を補わなければならなかった He had to *make up for* his lack of knowledge by hard study.

彼女の今回の手柄は前回の失敗を補って余りある Her success this time *more than compensates for* her mistake last time.

◆足りない栄養素を補うための食品が多く発売されている There are many kinds of *supplementary* foods on sale now. / 適当な語を補って文を完成させなさい Complete the sentences *with* suitable words.

おきなわ 沖縄

沖縄県は九州の南方，東シナ海に点在する多くの島々から成り，日本で唯一の亜熱帯気候です．古くは琉球(りゅうきゅう)と呼ばれ，中国をはじめアジア諸国との交易も盛んでした．その独特の文化・風習に加えて美しい自然に恵まれ，日本だけでなく海外からも多くの観光客が訪れています．
Okinawa Prefecture consists of many islands dotting the East China Sea. It is south of Kyushu and is the only prefecture with a subtropical climate. It used to be called Ryukyu, and it had active trade with other Asian countries, especially China. Okinawa attracts tourists not only from all over the country but also from abroad because of its unique culture and rich natural beauty.

おきにいり お気に入り favorite [C] ―お気に入りの favorite ∥私のお気に入りの辞書 my *favorite* dictionary / 彼はお気に入りのCDをかけた He put on *his favorite* CD. / どのチームがお気に入りですか Which team is *your favorite*? ◆あいつは先生のお気に入りだ He's the teacher's *pet*.(❖pet はしばしば軽蔑的な意味で用いられる)

おきぬけ 起き抜け 起き抜けに(→朝一番に)新聞を取りに行く go (and) get a newspaper *first thing in the morning* / 起き抜けに(→起きてすぐ)冷たい水で顔を洗った I washed my face in cold water *as soon as I got up*.

おきば 置き場 place [C]；（物置・車庫）shed [C]；（空間・余地）room [U] ∥自転車置き場 *a place for* parking bicycles; *a* bicycle *shed* / 道具置き場 *a* tool *shed*

◆私の部屋は狭くてソファーの置き場がない There is no *space* [*room*] for a sofa in my small room. / 恥ずかしくて身の置き場がない(→どうしていいか分からない) I *don't know what to do with myself* out of shame.

おきびき 置き引き （人）baggage thief [C] (❖日本語の「置き引き」に当たる英語はない)

◆友達は空港で置き引きにあった(→目を離したすきに荷物を盗まれた) My friend *had his baggage stolen* at the airport *while he wasn't looking*.

おきまり お決まり ―お決まりの（いつもの）usual；（習慣の）customary；（型にはまった）stereotyped, conventional ∥お決まりの文句 a *conventional* phrase / それは彼女のお決まりの言い訳だ That's her *usual* excuse.

おきみやげ 置き土産 （別れの際の贈り物）parting present [gift] [C]；（形見）keepsake [C] ◆彼女は膨大な残務処理を置きみやげに会社を辞めた She quit her job *leaving* a lot of paperwork undone.

おきもの 置物 （飾り物）ornament [C]；（名目だけの人）figurehead [C] ∥陶器の置物 *a* china [ceramic] *ornament* / その女性党首は単なる置物と思われていた The chairwoman of the political party was regarded as *a figurehead*.

おきゅう お灸 moxa cautery [U], moxibustion [U] ◆足にお灸をすえる *cauterize one's* leg *with moxa*

[慣用表現] 学校をサボったのがばれて両親にお灸をすえられた When my parents found out I had skipped school, they *told* me *off*.

おぎり お義理 父はお義理でそのゴルフコンペに参加した My father participated in the golf competition *out of social obligation*.

おきる 起きる

❶起床する	get up
❷目をさます	wake (up)
❸寝ないでいる	stay up
❹起き上がる	
❺生じる	happen, occur

❶【起床する】get* up, rise* [自]

私はいつも6時に起きます I usually *get up* at six.

彼は9時になってようやく起きた He *didn't get up until* 9 o'clock.

その村の人々は日の出とともに起きて働く The people in the village *rise* with the sun and start working.

◆私は朝起きたらまず最初にコップ1杯の水を飲む I drink a glass of water *the first thing in the morning*.

[会]「けさは何時に起きたの」「7時ちょっと過ぎくらい」 "What time *did* you *get up* this morning?" "A little past seven."

[会]「早く起きなさい．もう8時を回ってるわよ」「うん，あと5分だけ」 "*Get out of bed*! It's past eight now." "Just five more minutes ...."

[会]「もう寝るの？」「うん，あした早く起きなきゃいけないから」 "Are you going to bed already?" "Yeah, I've got to *get up* early tomorrow."

❷【目をさます】wake* (up), awake* [自]，《公式的》waken [自]

ほら，起きて！ *Wake up*!

僕が起きたときにはもう家族は全員出かけていた

おきわすれる

By the time I *woke up*, all the family had already gone out.

◆赤ちゃんが起きるといけないから(→赤ちゃんを起こさないように)静かにしてちょうだい Be quiet so that we won't *wake* the baby.

🔴「まゆみはもう起きてるかな」「まだ寝ぼけてる(→半分眠っている)みたい」"*Is* Mayumi *up* now?" "Not quite. Looks like she's half asleep."

❸【寝ないでいる】stay up, sit* up, be up

遅くまで起きていると朝早く起きられませんよ If you *stay up late*, you won't be able to get up early in the morning.

ゆうべは試験勉強をしていて遅くまで起きていた I *sat up late* last night preparing for the exam.

僕の兄はいつも2時ごろまで起きている My brother usually *stays up* until 2 o'clock.

◆彼は父親が帰ってくるまで起きていようとした He tried to *stay awake* until his father came home.

🔴「目の下にくまができてるよ」「ワールドカップを見てずっと起きてたんだ」"You've got dark rings under your eyes." "I *was up* all night watching the World Cup."

❹【起き上がる】

あすには起きられるでしょう You'll be able to *leave your bed* tomorrow.

🔴「おばあちゃん、入院してるんだって?」「うん、でももう起きて歩けるようになったよ」"I hear your grandma is in the hospital." "Yes, but now she's *up and around*."

❺【生じる】(予期せぬことが) happen 🅑, occur 🅘 ✿ occur is happen よりやや改まった語; (突然) break* out

事故は起きるものだ Accidents will *happen*.

そこで起きたことはなぞのままだ What *happened* there remains a mystery.

そのレストランでゆうべぼやが起きた A small fire *broke out* in that restaurant last night.

また別の問題が起きるのは避けられなかった It was inevitable that another problem would *occur*.

◆その事故は人為的なミスによって起きた(→引き起こされた) The accident *was caused by* human error. / この急カーブではよく事故が起きる This sharp curve *is the scene of many accidents*. / 休みが長いとなかなか宿題に取りかかる気が起きない When the vacation is long, I just *don't feel like* starting on the homework.

🔴「いったい何を騒いでるの」「大変なことが起きたのよ」"What's the fuss all about?" "Something incredible *has happened*!"

おきわすれる 置き忘れる(置いてくる) leave* (... behind) 〘私はかばんをどこかに置き忘れてしまった I *have left* my bag somewhere.

🔴「私の傘はどうしたの」「ごめん、電車に置き忘れちゃった」"What have you done with my umbrella?" "I'm sorry. I *left* it on the train."

おく¹ 置く

❶ある場所・状態に置く put; place
❷後に残す・放置する leave
❸設置する set up, place
❹住まわせる keep, have
❺品物を扱う have, carry

❶【ある場所・状態に置く】put* 🅐; place 🅘; lay* 🅐; set* 🅐

> put: 「置く」の一般的な語. 必ずしもはっきりした目的はない.
> place: 意図した場所に置く.
> lay: 平らになるように置く.
> set: 特定の場所に注意を払って置く.

第2音節にアクセントを置く *put* [*place*] the accent on the second syllable

眼鏡をどこへ置いたか忘れてしまった I've forgotten where I *put* my glasses.

彼は雑誌をわきに置いた He *laid* the magazine aside.

彼女は生けた花をテーブルに置いた She *set* her flower arrangement on the table.

先生は英文法に重点をおいた The teacher *put* [*placed*, *laid*] an emphasis on English grammar.

◆彼女はやっと自分が置かれている状況に気づいた She finally awoke to the situation *she was in*.

🔴「きょうの新聞、どこに置いたの」「テーブルの上」"Where *did* you *put* today's paper?" "On the table."

🔴「デスクトップのコンピュータならわりと安く買えるよ」「でも、置く場所がないからなあ」"If it's a desk-top computer, you can buy one at a rather reasonable price." "Well, *there's no room for* that."

❷【後に残す・放置する】(後に残す) leave* 🅐

チップを置いていく *leave* a tip

荷物は玄関に置いてください *Leave* your baggage in the hall, please.

彼は家族を日本に置いてひとりイギリスへ向かった He headed for England, *leaving* his family in Japan.

食事中に席を立つときはナプキンをいすの上に置きなさい If you leave the table during the meal, *leave* your napkin on the chair.

🔴「早くしないと置いていくよ」「待って、すぐ行くから」"Hurry up, or *I'll leave you*." "Wait, I'm coming!"

❸【設置する】set* up, place 🅘, locate 🅘 (✿ 用例仮名を)

その会社は福岡・大阪・名古屋・札幌に支社を置いている The company's branches *are located* in Fukuoka, Osaka, Nagoya and Sapporo.

◆IOCの本部はジュネーブに置かれている The headquarters of IOC *is in* Geneva. / その国は国連の監視下に置かれている The country *is under* U.N. *observation*.

❹【住まわせる】(雇っている) keep*

have* ㉺; (下宿人を) take* in 使用人を置く keep a servant

◆おばの家では学生の下宿人を3人置いている (→部屋を貸している) My aunt *rents* rooms *out to* three students.

❺ (品物を扱う) (商品として持つ) have* ㉺, carry ㉺; (売る) sell* ㉺

その店はいろいろな種類のワインを置いている The shop *carries* a large variety of wines.

💬「すみません,『ニューズウイーク』は置いていますか」「はい, こちらのラックにございます」"Excuse me. Do you *have* Newsweek?" "Yes, they're on the rack here."

❻【隔てる】➡ -おき

💬「彼とは完全に別れたの?」「ううん, でもしばらく距離をおこうと思って」"Are you completely finished with him?" "No, but I think it's better to *keep away from him* for a while."

❼【…しておく】

この辞書をいつも手元に置いておくとよい You should always *keep* this dictionary at hand.

洗い物は後でやるからそのままにしておいて I'll do the dishes later, so just *leave* them.

換気のためにドアはしばらくあけておきなさい *Leave* the door *open* for a while for ventilation.

💬「彼女はただの友達だよ」「まあ, そういうことにしておこう」"She's just a friend." "Well, *we can say so if you insist*."

💬「何か持っていこうか」「食事は用意しておくから飲み物を持ってきて」"Shall I bring something?" "*I'll prepare* food, so bring some drinks."

💬「ねえ, 元気出してよ」「ひとりにしておいて」"Come on, cheer up!" "*Leave me alone*."

❽【その他】

彼は信用のおける人だ He is a *reliable* person.

彼女をおいてリーダーはいない *No one else but* her should be the leader.

そんなことしたらただじゃおかないぞ If you do that, *I'll make you sorry (for it)*.

おく² 奥 (後ろ) the back; (深い所) the depths ‖彼女の寝室は家の奥の方にある Her bedroom is *at the back of* the house. ◆彼は奥の部屋からスキー板を出してきた He took out a pair of skis from *the back room*. / もう少し奥に詰めてもらえませんか Could you please *move back [in]* a little? / あいつは心の奥では何を考えているのか分からない I don't know what he has *deep in his mind*. / この通りのいちばん奥にある家がうちです The house *at the end of* this street is mine.

慣用表現 フラメンコは奥の深い芸術だ Flamenco is an art *of great depth*.

おく³ 億 a [one] hundred million ‖その選手の年俸は5億円だ The player earns five *hundred million* yen a year. ◆何億年も昔 *hundreds of millions of years ago* / 10億ドル a *billion* / 負債は数十億ドルに達している The debts run into *billions* of dollars.

おくがい 屋外 the outdoors (単数扱い), the open air ──屋外の outdoor, open-air, outside (❖いずれも名詞の前で用いる) ──屋外で outdoors, in the open air, outside ‖屋外のカフェ an *outdoor* café / 屋外プール an *outdoor* pool / 屋外競技 *outdoor* sports

おくさま 奥様 (妻) one's wife (複 wives); (呼びかけ) madam, ma'am (❖女性に対する丁寧な呼びかけ) ‖奥様によろしくお伝えください Please give my best (regards) to *your wife*. / 奥様, こちらなどはいかがでしょう Would you like this one, *ma'am*?

◆岡本さんの奥様 *Mrs*. Okamoto

おくさん 奥さん (妻) one's wife (複 wives); (呼びかけ) ma'am ‖彼が奥さんと離婚するなんて思ってもみなかった I never dreamed that he would divorce *his wife*. / 奥さんは元気ですか How is *your wife*?

◆横山さんの奥さんはお花の先生だ *Mrs*. Yokoyama is a flower arrangement instructor.

おくじょう 屋上 roof ⓒ; (特に屋根と区別して) rooftop ⓒ ‖屋上庭園 a *roof [rooftop]* garden / ヘリコプターをビルの屋上に着陸させる land a helicopter on *the roof* of the building / そのデパートの屋上には遊園地がある There is an amusement park on *the roof* of that department store.

おくする 臆する 彼女はおくすることなく意見を述べた She expressed her opinion *without hesitation*.

おくそく 憶測 guess ⓒ, 《公式的》conjecture ⓒⓊ, 《公式的》speculation Ⓤⓒ ──臆測する guess ㉺, conjecture ㉺, speculate ㉺ ‖その作家のなぞの死について様々な憶測が飛び交っていた There was a lot of *speculation* going around about the author's mysterious death. / その事件についての彼の臆測は当たっていた His *conjecture [speculation]* about the event was right. / 憶測でものを言うのはやめたほうがいい You should stop saying things that are only *speculation*.

おくそこ 奥底 (底) the bottom; (深い所) the depths ‖彼女は心の奥底からその子供たちを愛している She loves those children *from the bottom of her heart*.

オクターブ 〚音楽〛octave [ǽktiv] ⓒ ‖1オクターブ下げて歌う sing *an octave* lower

おくち 奥地 (内陸部) the interior; (沿岸に対して) the hinterlands; (森林などの) the backwoods ‖彼はその島の奥地を探検した He explored *the interior* of the island.

◆彼らはコンゴの奥地へ向かった They traveled *to the heart* of the Congo.

おくづけ 奥付 publisher's inscription ⓒ, publisher's emblem ⓒ

おくて 奥手 彼は兄と違っておくてだ Unlike his brother, he is *a late bloomer*.

おくない 屋内 ──屋内の indoor (❖名詞の前

で用いる)　━屋内で indoors //屋内プール an *indoor* swimming pool / 屋内テニスコート an *indoor* tennis court / 雨が降りだしたので屋内で昼食を食べた It began to rain, so we ate lunch *indoors*.
‖屋内運動場 a gymnasium,《口語的》a gym

おくに お国 お国自慢をする「*talk proudly* [*boast*] *about one's hometown* / お国なまりで話す speak with *a regional accent* / お国(→出身)はどちらですか Where do you come from?/ Where are you from? / 祭りのときに訪れるとその場所のお国ぶりがいちばんよく分かる It's easiest to see *the local flavor* of a place if you visit during a festival.

おくのて 奥の手 (最後の手段) last resort [C]; (最後・最善の手) *one's* last [best] card; (切り札) trump (card) [C] //奥の手を出す play *one's best card* ◆奥の手を用意している have *a* [*another*] *card* up *one's* sleeve (❖原義は「トランプの札をそでの下に隠し持つ」の意味) / 私たちにはまだ奥の手がある We still *have an ace in the hole*.

おくば 奥歯 back tooth [C]; (臼歯) molar (tooth) [C] //奥歯を抜いてもらう have *a molar* pulled (out)
[慣用表現] 奥歯に物がはさまったような言い方をするな(→率直に言え) *Speak* [*Talk*] *frankly*./ (→遠回しに言うな) *Don't beat around* [*about*] *the bush*.

おくびょう 臆病 ━臆病な (気の小さい) timid, chickenhearted; (卑怯な) cowardly ━臆病に timidly //うちの犬は臆病でちょっとした物音にもびくつく Our dog *is timid* and easily frightened by the slightest sound.
💬「彼がスピーチすることになってたのに来なかったんだよ」「急に臆病風に吹かれでもしたのかな」 "He was supposed to make a speech, but he never showed up." "Well, he might *have lost his nerve*."
‖臆病者 a coward,《俗語》a chicken

おくふかい 奥深い deep; (比喩的に) profound //その泉は森の奥深い所にある The spring is *deep* in the forest. / そのときは先生の言葉の奥深い意味が分からなかった I didn't understand the *profound* meaning of my teacher's words then.

おくまった 奥まった secluded //マンションの奥まった1室 a *secluded* room of an apartment ◆彼の家は商店街から少し奥まった所にある His house stands *a little back* from the shopping district.

おくまる 奥まる be deep; (奥に伸びている) extend far back

おくまん 億万 ‖億万長者 a billionaire, a multimillionaire

おくめん 臆面 彼は臆面もなく(→恥ずかしげもなく)金を貸してくれと言ってきた He asked me to lend him money *unabashedly*.

おくやみ お悔やみ condolence [U] (❖「お悔やみの言葉」の意味では condolences) //お悔やみを述べる offer [send] *one's condolences* / お悔やみ状 *a letter of condolence* / 心からお悔やみ申し上げます Please accept *my* deepest *condolences*. ◆お父様のご逝去を深くお悔やみ申し上げます Let me express *my* deep *regret* over your father's death.

おくゆかしい 奥床しい (洗練された) refined; (優雅な) elegant, graceful; (慎み深い) modest; (控えめな) reserved //奥ゆかしい態度 *modest* behavior / 彼女はいつも元気がいいが実はとても奥ゆかしい女性だ She always looks cheerful, but in fact she is very *reserved*.

おくゆき 奥行き depth [U][C]; (長さ) length [C]; (広さ) extent [U] //舞台の奥行きは12メートルだ The stage is 12 meters「*in depth* [*deep*].
◆奥行きのある学識 *profound* knowledge

オクラ 〔植物〕okra [U]

おくらいり お蔵入り その映画は2年間お蔵入りになっていた The movie *had been put in storage* for two years.

おくらせる 遅らせる delay [他]; (延期する) postpone [他], put* off; (時計を) put back //時計を1時間遅らせる *put* a watch *back* one hour / 彼らは出発を1週間遅らせることにした They decided to *delay* starting for a week. / これ以上計画の実行を遅らせることはできない We can no longer *put off* carrying out the plan.
◆電車を1本遅らせる *let* one train *go by*

オクラホマ Oklahoma(❖米国中南部の州;《略語》Okla.,〔郵便〕OK)

おくりおおかみ 送り狼 あいつは送り狼かもしれないから気をつけろ He might be *a wolf in sheep's clothing*, so be careful when he sees you home. (❖a wolf in sheep's clothing は「親切を装った危険人物」の意味)

おくりかえす 送り返す send* back; (戻す) return [他] //こわれていたので品物をすぐに送り返した I *sent* the item *back* immediately because it was broken.
◆彼らは本国に飛行機で送り返された They *were flown back* to their home country.

おくりがな 送り仮名 🖼 *okurigana*, the ending of a verb, adverb or adjective written in *kana*

おくりこむ 送り込む (送る) send* [他]; (派遣する) dispatch [他] //スパイを送り込む *send out* a spy / 視察団を現地に送り込む *dispatch* an inspecting party to the spot

おくりさき 送り先 (届け先) destination [C]; (受取人) addressee [C], receiver [C] //送り先を書くのを忘れないように Don't forget to write *the destination*.

おくりじょう 送り状 invoice [C] //送り状を荷造り明細書と照合する check *the invoice* against the packing list / 貴社の送り状を受け取りました We have received your *invoice*.

おくりだす 送り出す (外へ) send* off; (物を) send out; (玄関まで送る) see* ... out //子供を学校に送り出してから家事をします I do housework after *sending* my children *off to* school. ◆あの大学は毎年多くの卒業生を一流

企業に送り出している That university *places* many graduates *with* leading companies every year.

おくりとどける 送り届ける 彼は私を家まで送り届けてから自宅へ帰った He went home after *seeing* me *home*.

おくりバント 送りバント sacrifice bunt ◎ ∥打者は送りバントで走者を二塁に進めた The batter advanced the runner to second *with a sacrifice bunt*./ The batter *sacrificed* the runner to second.

おくりむかえ 送り迎え 彼女は毎日子供たちを学校まで送り迎えしている She *takes* her children *to and from* school every day.

おくりもの 贈り物 gift ◎, present ◎ (❖親しい個人間での日常的な贈り物は present を用いる. gift はやや改まった語)

誕生日の贈り物 *a* birthday *present*

すてきな贈り物をありがとう Thank you for *the* lovely *present*.

私たちの感謝のしるしとしてこのささやかな贈り物をお受け取りください Please accept this small *gift* as a token of our gratitude.

彼は彼女にちょっとした贈り物をすることを思いついた It occurred to him that he would send *a* little *present* to her.

おくる¹ 送る

❶【物を】send* ⓜ (↔receive); (輸送する) ship ⓜ

手紙を航空便で送る *send* a letter airmail / 合図を送る *send* [*give*] a signal

最新カタログを送ってください Please *send* me your latest catalog.

彼は両親に金を送ってくれと手紙を書いた He wrote a letter to his parents, asking them to *send* him money.

私は彼女の結婚にお祝いの言葉を送った I *sent* her my congratulations on her marriage.

【send+名(人)+名】≒【send+名+to 名(人)】

彼は私たち全員にクリスマスカードを送ってくれた He *sent* each of us Christmas cards./ He *sent* Christmas cards *to* each of us.

◆電子メールを送る *e-mail*; *send an e-mail* / ファックスを送る *fax*; *send a fax* / 人に盛大な拍手を送る *give* a person *a* big hand / フォワードにロングパスを送る *make a long pass* to the forward / その発表に拍手が送られた The announcement *was greeted with cheers*. / 私は5人に招待状を送った I *mailed* an invitation to five people. (❖mail は「郵便で送る」の意味)

🅮「この荷物, アメリカまで船便で送ったらどのくらいかかるかな」「2, 3か月はかかるよ, きっと」"I wonder how long it would take to America if I *send* this by ship?" "At least a couple of months, I guess."

❷【人を】(見送る) see* off; (付き添う) see ⓜ; (家まで) see ... home; (車で) drive* ⓜ; (玄関まで) see out

◆車で家まで送ってもらえませんか Would you *give* me a ride [*lift*] *home*?

🅮「ねえ, お母さんは?」「おばあちゃんを羽田空港まで送りに行ってる」"Where's Mom?" "She *went to see* Grandma *off* at Haneda Airport."

🅮「方向が同じだし, 家まで送ろうか」「そうしてもらえるとありがたい」"I'm going the same way, so shall I *see you home*?" "Yes, that would be nice."

🅮「家に帰る途中です」「じゃ, お宅まで車で送らせてください」"I'm on my way home." "Then, *let me drive you* home."

❸【過ごす】(時を過ごす) pass ⓜ, spend* ⓜ; (生活を) lead* ⓜ, live ⓜ (❖共に後ろに a ... life を伴う)

幸せな[静かな, 多忙な]生活を送る *lead* a happy [quiet, busy] life

◆彼女は不幸な子供時代を送った She *had* an unhappy childhood.

おくる² 贈る (あげる) give* ⓜ; (贈呈する) present ⓜ; (授与する) award ⓜ

プレゼントを贈る *give* a present / わいろを贈る *give* [*offer*] bribes

彼女は母親に珍しい種類のカーネーションを贈った She *gave* her mother a rare variety of carnation.

日本ではバレンタインデーにチョコレートを贈る習慣がある It is a custom in Japan to *give* chocolate on Valentine's Day.

大統領がじきじきに賞を贈ることになっている The president himself is going to *present* the prizes.

彼の写真に対して1等賞が贈られた They *awarded* him the first prize for his photograph.

おくれ 遅れ・後れ delay ◎ⓜ ∥その遅れは私たちの計画には致命的だった The *delay* was fatal to our plan.

◆遅れを取り戻す make up for *lost time* / 知恵遅れの子 a *slow* child; a *developmentally disabled* child / 列車は10分遅れて駅に着いた The train arrived at the station *10 minutes late* [*behind schedule*]. / そのプロジェクトの進行に遅れが出ている The project *has fallen behind schedule*. / 弟は勉強の遅れを取り戻そうとがんばっている My brother is trying hard to *catch up on* his studies. / 私は最初から彼女に遅れをとってしまった I *fell* [*got, lagged*] *behind* her from the start.

おくればせながら 遅ればせながら 遅ればせながら次のことをお知らせいたします(→知らせるのが遅れてすみません) *I'm sorry to be late* in informing you about the following. / 遅ればせながらお誕生日おめでとう *I know I'm late, but* happy birthday *anyway*.

おくれる 遅れる・後れる

❶【予定時間・約束に】be late, be delayed

早く起きなさい! 学校に遅れますよ Get up, or you'*ll be late for* school!

次の電車は5分ほど遅れる模様です The next train will *be delayed* by five minutes.

◆渋滞のため彼らは1時間遅れて到着した Due to the traffic jam, they arrived *an hour*

お

late.
[会話]「珍しいね，君が遅刻するなんて」「すみません．バスが遅れたんです」"It's unusual for you to be late." "Sorry, the bus *was late.*"
❷【遅れをとる】fall* behind；（遅れている）be behind
1週間学校を休んでいたのでクラスのみんなに遅れてしまった Because I was absent from school for a week, I *fell behind* my classmates.
私たちの車はエンジンがトラブルを起こしてほかの車からずいぶん遅れた Our car had engine trouble and *fell* far *behind* the other cars.
彼女は流行に遅れないようにと必死だ She's trying hard *not to fall behind* the fashion.
◆時代に遅れないためにはその雑誌を読むといい You should read that magazine to *keep up with the times.*
❸【時計が】lose* [他]；（遅れている）be slow（↔be fast）
この時計は5分遅れている This clock *is* five minutes *slow.*
私の時計は1日に10秒遅れる My watch *loses* 10 seconds a day.
◆ロサンゼルスはニューヨークより3時間遅れている Los Angeles *is* three hours *behind* New York.

おけ 桶（大きな）tub [C]；（手おけ）bucket [C]，《主に米》pail [C]

おける 於ける 社会における女性の役割 women's role *in* society / 彼は日本における農業の重要性を強調した He emphasized the importance of agriculture *in* Japan.

おこがましい（厚かましい）《公式的》impudent；（ずうずうしい）presumptuous；（生意気な）impertinent ‖私がこんなことを言うのもおこがましいのですが，… It may be *impertinent* of me to say this, but .... / 先生にあんなことを言うなんて彼はおこがましいやつだ It is *presumptuous* of him to say such a thing to the teacher.

おこさま お子様 ‖お子様ランチ a kid's special [plate]

おこす[1] 起こす

❶目をさまさせる	wake up
❷立たせる	raise
❸引き起こす	cause
❹始める	start

❶【目をさまさせる】wake* up, awaken [他]；（呼んで）call [他]
あすの朝7時に私を起こしてください Please *wake* me *up* at seven tomorrow morning.
けさは母親からの電話で起こされた The phone call from my mother *woke* me *up* this morning.
もし8時までに降りてこなかったら起こしに来てね If I don't come down by eight, please *come to* [*and*] *wake* me *up.*
◆起こさないでください *Do not disturb.*
[会話]「ごめん，起こしちゃった？」「ううん，もう起きてたよ」"Sorry, did I *wake* you *up*?" "No, I've been awake."
❷【立たせる】raise [他]；（体を起こす）sit* up
看護婦は彼がベッドで体を起こすのを手伝った The nurse helped him *sit up* in bed.
◆彼は倒れた私の自転車を起こしてくれた He *lifted up* my bicycle which had fallen over.
❸【引き起こす】cause [他]；（もたらす）bring* about
熟練した運転手でも事故を起こすことがある Even an experienced driver may *cause* an accident.
◆奇跡を起こす *achieve* a miracle / もめごとを起こす *make* trouble / 政府に対して反乱を起こす *rebel* against the government / 彼女は必ずといっていいほど問題を起こす She *is* nearly always *a problem.*
❹【始める】start [他]，begin* [他]；（設立する）set* up
父は私が事業を起こすのを援助してくれた My father helped me *start* my own business.
◆人を相手取って訴訟を起こす *bring* an action against a person / 彼はゼロから自分の会社を起こした He *built* his business from scratch. / 彼らは会社に対して損害賠償の訴えを起こした They *sued* the company for damages.
❺【生じさせる】
電気を起こす *generate* electricity / かんしゃくを起こす *lose one's temper* / 心臓発作を起こす *suffer* a heart attack
行動を起こす時が来た The time is ripe for action.
彼は子供たちに学習意欲を起こさせた He *motivated* his children *to* study.
[慣用表現] 寝た子を起こすな *Let sleeping dogs lie.*（→眠っている犬はそのままにしておけ）

おこす[2] 興す（産業などの発展を助ける）promote [他]；（再建する）restore [他]；（復興させる）revive [他] ‖産業を興す *promote* industry
◆村おこし *local trade promotion*

おごそか 厳か ―厳かな（厳粛な）solemn [sάləm]（❖名詞の前で用いる）；（荘重な）grave；（威厳のある）stately ―厳かに solemnly; gravely ‖厳かな誓い a *solemn* vow / 卒業式は厳かに執(と)り行われた The graduation ceremony was performed *in a solemn atmosphere.*

おこたる 怠る neglect [他] ‖職務を怠る *neglect one's* duties / 植物に水をやるのを怠ってしまった I *neglected to* water my plants.
◆自分の責務を怠るな *Never forget* your duties. / 注意を怠って（→不注意になって）はいけない Don't *be careless.* / 彼は毎朝のジョギングを決して怠らない He *never fails to* jog every morning.

おこない 行い（行為）act [C]，《公式的》deed [C]；（ふるまい）behavior [U]，《公式的》conduct [U]（❖behaviorは「人に対する態度」，conductは「道徳面から見たふるまい」を指す）

親切な行い an act of kindness / 行いを改める improve one's behavior; mend one's ways
子供たちがまねするかもしれないから行いを慎みなさい Be careful of your conduct since children might follow your ways.

🅔「ああ、せっかくの旅行なのに雪が降るなんて」「日ごろの行いが悪いんだよ」"Gee, we're going on a trip and it's snowing!" "That's because you're always misbehaving!"

コロケーション	-conduct-
〖形容詞＋～〗正しい～ proper conduct / ばかげた[恥ずべき]～ silly [shameful] conduct / よい[悪い]～ good [bad] conduct / りっぱな～ honorable conduct

おこなう 行う

(する) do* 🅐, perform 🅐 (❖do よりややかたい語); (実行する) carry out; (式などを催す) hold* 🅐; (試験などを行う) give* 🅐
実験を行う do [make] an experiment / 手術を行う perform an operation / 入学式を行う hold an entrance ceremony / 英語の授業を行う give an English lesson
来週、試験を行います I'll give you an exam next week.
吉村教授はその遺跡の調査を行っている Professor Yoshimura has been carrying out the investigation into the ruins.
◆試合を行う play a game / 恩赦を行う grant [give] a pardon / 新聞各社が首相の支持率に関する世論調査を行った Newspapers conducted a poll to find out the approval rating of the Prime Minister.

ことわざ 言うは易(ﾔｽ)く行うは難(ｶﾀ)し ➪いう

おこなわれる 行われる (開催される) take* place, be held ➪ おこなう / 卒業式は3月25日に行われた The graduation ceremony was held on March 25.
◆天候に関係なく試合は行われます The game will be played regardless of the weather. / この検査は定期的に行われている This test is run at fixed intervals.

おこのみやき お好み焼き 🏠

お好み焼きは、水で溶いた小麦粉に野菜・肉・魚介類などを混ぜ、鉄板の上で丸く焼いたものです。大阪や広島を中心に、西日本で人気があります。「お好み」(好きなように)の名が示すとおり、好みに合わせて様々な具を加えることができます。Okonomiyaki is made by mixing flour and water with vegetables, meat, or seafood and cooking the mixture in a round shape on an iron plate. It is popular in western Japan, especially in Osaka and Hiroshima. As the name okonomi- means "what you like," you can add anything you like.

おこらせる 怒らせる make* a person angry; (感情を害する) offend 🅐 (❖しばしば受身で) / 君を怒らせるつもりはなかったんだ I didn't mean to offend you.

おこり 起こり (起源) origin ⓒ; (始まり) the beginning; (原因) cause ⓒ / 民主主義の起こり the beginning of democracy / 平仮名の起こりは漢字にある Hiragana has its origin in Chinese characters. ◆事の起こりはこうなんです This is how it happened.

おごり 奢り ❶【ごちそうすること】treat ⓒ / これは私のおごりです This is my treat. ◆飲み物は僕のおごりだ The drinks are on me.
❷【ぜいたく】luxury ⓤ / おごりを極める live in luxury

おこりっぽい 怒りっぽい (気が短い) quick-[hot-, short-]tempered; (すぐ腹を立てる) irritable; (気難しい) touchy ◆怒りっぽい男 a man with hot [quick] temper / 彼は本当に怒りっぽい He has a really quick temper.

おこりんぼう 怒りん坊 (怒りっぽい人) hot-[quick-, short-]tempered person ⓒ
◆ほんとに怒りん坊なんだから You are really hot-tempered.

おこる¹ 怒る

get* [be] angry, 《口語的》get [be] mad; (かんしゃくを起こす) lose* one's temper; (しかる) scold 🅐
彼はつまらないことですぐ怒る He easily gets angry over trivial things.
当然ながら彼は怒っているようだった He looked angry, of course.
君のお母さんが怒るのも無理はない It is natural that your mother gets angry.
彼女が怒るのを見たことがない I have never known her to lose her temper.
彼はしょっちゅう遅刻して先生に怒られている(→先生は彼を怒っている) The teacher is always scolding him for being late.

【be angry＋with 名(人)＋(for 名 [doing])】
彼女は私のことをあまり手紙をよこさないといって怒っている She is angry with me for not writing to her often.

【be angry＋that 節】彼女が約束を守らなかったと彼は怒っていた He was angry that she didn't keep her promise.

◆怒った顔 an angry face / 犬を怒らせる provoke a dog / 彼女は怒ってドアをバタンと閉めた She slammed the door angrily. / そのことが知れたらお母さんはかんかんに怒るだろう Your mother will be furious when she finds it out. (❖furious は「激怒して」の意味)

🅔「彼女、僕のこと相当怒っているだろうな」「大丈夫だよ、ちゃんと謝れば許してくれるさ」"She must be really angry with me." "It should be OK. She'll forgive you if you say you're sorry with all your heart."

🅔「何をそんなに怒ってるの」「お姉ちゃんが私のシャンプー、勝手に使ったのよ」"What are you so angry about?" "My stupid sister used my shampoo without asking me." (❖stupid を付けるとより怒っていることを表す。ただしかなり乱暴な表現)

🅔「まだ私のこと、怒ってる？」「いや、もういいよ」

"Are you still *angry* with me?" "No, not anymore."

🔄 「彼、怒ったのなんのって」「そりゃそうでしょうね」 "He *got* more than *angry*." "I can easily imagine that."

おこる² 起こる

❶【発生する】(偶然に) happen 圓; (予期しないことが) occur 圓; (突発的に) break* out
事故はいつ何時起こるか分からない(=いつでも起こりうる) An accident can *happen* at any time.
何か変わったことが起こったら知らせてください Please let me know if anything unusual *happens*.
彼女に何が起こったのだろう What *has happened* to her? / What *has become* of her?
事故は2つの大きな通りの交差する地点で起こった The accident *occurred* at the junction of the two main streets.
湾岸戦争は1991年に起こった The Gulf War *broke out* in 1991.
◆ここでいったい何が起こっているのですか What's *going on* here? / 聴衆から割れんばかりの拍手が起こった Thunderous applause *burst* from the audience.

❷【起因する】(始まる) start from ...; (結果として) result from ...; (引き起こされる) be caused
その乱闘は初めはささいな言い争いから起こった The brawl *started from* a little quarrel.
貧血は鉄分不足で起こる Anemia *is caused by* lack of iron.
この種の病気は不衛生な環境のために起こる This kind of disease *results from* an unsanitary environment.
◆その戦争は宗教的対立から起こった The war *grew out of* a religious conflict.

おこる³ 興る (生まれる) come* into existence [being]; (生じる) rise* 圓, develop 圓 // そのころ朝鮮半島に新しい国が興った A new country then *came into existence* on the Korean Peninsula.

おごる² 奢る (ごちそうする) treat 他 圓, give* *a person* a treat; (買ってやる) buy* 他 // 今回は僕がおごるよ I'll *treat* you this time. / 今度は私がおごる番です It's my turn to *treat*. / 彼がコーヒーを1杯おごってくれた He *treated* me to a cup of coffee. / お昼をおごらせてください Let me *buy* you lunch.
◆夕食は僕がおごる Dinner *is on me*.

おごる² 驕る (慢心する) be proud ◆おごった性格 *proud* nature

慣用表現 おごれる者は久しからず *Pride goes before a fall*. (→おごりの後には没落が来る)

おさえ 押さえ・抑え その学生たちは先生の抑えがきかない Those students *are out of* the teacher's *control*.

おさえつける 押さえ付ける・抑え付ける press 他; (抑圧する) suppress 他 // その国の人々は支配者に押さえつけられていた The people of the country *were suppressed* by the ruler.
◆父は言うことを聞かない弟を押さえつけた My father *reined in* my disobedient brother.

おさえる¹ 押さえる

❶【押しつける】hold* 他; (圧迫する) press 他; (押さえつける) hold [press] down
ドアを押さえていてもらえますか Would you please *hold* the door open?
止血するにはまず傷口を布で押さえるとよい You should first *press* a piece of cloth to the wound in order to stop bleeding.

🔄 「おい、はしごが動かないように押さえててくれ」「こう？」 "Hey, *hold* the ladder steady for me, will you?" "Like this?"

❷【捕らえる】(つかまえる) catch* 他; (手に入れる) get* 他, obtain 他; (確保する) secure 他
その国会議員は収賄の現場を押さえられた The Diet member *was caught* just as he was receiving the bribe.
警察は容疑者の犯行を証明する動かぬ証拠を押さえた The police *got* [*obtained, secured*] firm evidence that the suspect had committed the crime.
◆要点を押さえて(→明確に)説明しなさい Explain the main points *clearly*.

おさえる² 抑える

❶【感情をこらえる】(抑制する) control 他, restrain 他; (我慢する) suppress 他, hold* [keep*] back
感情を抑える *control one's* feelings; *control oneself* / 怒り[笑い, 涙]を抑える *restrain one's* anger [laughter, tears]
私は何とか怒りを抑えた I managed to *hold back* my anger.
彼の傲慢(ごうまん)な態度に僕は怒りを抑えることができなかった I couldn't *suppress* my anger at his arrogant behavior.
◆私は涙を抑えることができなかった I *couldn't help crying*. / I *couldn't help but cry*. / 彼女は彼についていきたいという抑えがたい衝動にかられた She felt an *irresistible* impulse to follow him.

🔄 「もう彼女とは絶対口きかないからね」「まあ抑えて。何があったの」 "I swear I'll never talk to her again!" "Hey, *calm down*. What happened?"

❷【増加・悪化を食い止める】(抑制する) control 他; (低く抑える) keep* [hold*] down; (制限する) limit
インフレを抑える *control* inflation / 出費を抑える *limit* expenditures
◆痛みを抑える *kill* pain / 費用を最小限に抑えなければならない We have to *keep* the cost *to a minimum*. / 木村は相手チームを1安打[2点]に抑えた Kimura *held* the opponent to "one hit [two runs]". / 物価の急激な高騰とは対照的に我々の賃金は低く抑えられている In contrast to the sharp rise in prices, our wages *are being held* at a low level.

❸【鎮圧する】put* down, suppress 他
暴動を抑える *put down* a riot
◆万里の長城は外敵の侵攻を抑える(→防ぐ)ために築かれた The Great Wall of China was

おさがり お下がり hand-me-downs ── お下がりの hand-me-down ∥小さいころ私はいつも姉のお下がりを着ていた I used to wear my big sister's *hand-me-downs*.

おさき お先 お先にどうぞ *After you, please.* / *Go ahead.* / お先に失礼します(→先に行く) *Excuse me for going first.* / (→先に帰る) *I must be going now.*
慣用表現 お先真っ暗だ(→希望がもてない) *There's no hope for the future.*

おさげ お下げ pigtail ⓒ; (三つ編み)《米》braid ⓒ,《英》plait ⓒ ∥髪をお下げにしている wear *one's* hair in *braids* / 母にお下げを結ってもらった I had my hair done in *braids* by my mother. ◆彼女は髪をお下げにした She *let her hair down*.

おさつ お札 paper money ⓤ,《米》bill ⓒ,《英》note ⓒ

おさと お里 食べ方ひとつでお里が知れる(→育ちが分かる)ものだ The way you eat *reveals your background*.

おさない 幼い (年が少ない) small, little, very young; (幼稚な) childish; (未熟な) immature ∥彼は幼い子供の扱いがとても上手だ He is very skillful with *small* children. / 私は幼いころ仙台に住んでいた I lived in Sendai when I was *small*. / あなたの考え方はまだ幼い Your way of thinking *is* still *immature*.
◆彼女の話し方は幼い She speaks *childishly*.

おさなごころ 幼心 その友達のひと言は幼心にも(→小さな子供だったとき)ひどく傷ついた *Though I was a small child*, I was deeply hurt by my friend's words.

おさななじみ 幼なじみ childhood friend ⓒ ∥幼なじみが大阪に引っ越してしまった My *childhood friend* moved to Osaka.
◆私たちは幼なじみだ We *have known* [*been friends with*] *each other from childhood*.

おさなり お座なり ──おさなりの (通りいっぺんの)《公式的》perfunctory ──おさなりに《公式的》perfunctorily ∥おざなりのあいさつ a *perfunctory* greeting / おざなりな返事をする give a *perfunctory* reply

おさまる¹ 収まる

❶【入る】fit* into ...
みやげを買いすぎてスーツケースに収まらなくなった I bought so many souvenirs that they *didn't fit into* my suitcase.
◆今月の娯楽費は予算内に収まらなかった This month's entertainment expenses *went over budget*.

❷【静まる】(風などが) subside ⓘ, die down,《公式的》abate ⓘ; (過ぎる) go* ⓘ; (やむ) stop ⓘ; (暴動などが) be put down
騒ぎが収まるまで外に出ないほうがいい You had better stay home until the disturbance *subsides*.
先週始まった円相場の急落もようやく収まった The sudden fall of yen which started last week *has* finally *stopped*.
彼に対する怒りはなかなか収まらなかった My anger toward him didn't *die down* easily.
彼はあらしが収まるまで安心することができなかった He could not rest till the storm finally *died down* [*abated*].

❸【解決する】be settled
ストが収まった The strike *was settled*.
◆彼のユーモアにあふれた言葉でその場は丸く収まった(→みんなをなごませた)His humorous words *put everyone there at ease*.

❹【落ち着く】
彼はついに社長の座に収まった He finally *achieved* the post of president.

❺【その他】
あの二人は元のさやに収まった They *were back together again*.

おさまる² 納まる
お礼をさせていただかないと私の気持ちが納まりません Let me offer you some reward. Otherwise *I won't feel right*.
彼女が仕事を辞めて家庭の主婦に納まるとは考えにくい It's hard to imagine her *becoming a housewife and giving up her job*.
慣用表現 あんなひどい仕打ちを受けては腹の虫が納まらない I *can't take* that bad treatment *lying down*.

おさまる³ 治まる

❶【痛みなどが】(やわらぐ) ease ⓘ; (なくなる) go* ⓘ
薬を飲んだら少しずつ痛みが治まってきた The pain gradually *eased* after taking the medicine. / The medicine gradually *eased* the pain.
💡「かぜはどう」「頭痛は治まったんだけど,せきがひどいんだ」"How's your cold?" "Well, my headache *is gone*, but I've got a bad cough."

❷【国・世の中が】be settled, settle down; (平和である) be at peace

おさむい お寒い お寒いギャグ a *poor* [*bad*] gag / 日本の危機管理対策の現状はお寒いかぎりだ(→望まれるものとはほど遠い)Japan's crisis management policy *leaves much to be desired*.

おさめる¹ 収める

❶【得る】
勝利を収める win [*gain*] a victory
そのミュージカルは大成功を収めた The musical *was a great success*.
彼は莫大(ばくだい)な富を手中に収めた He *came into possession* of great fortune.
わが校は全国合唱コンクールで優秀な成績を収めた Our school *achieved* brilliant results at a national chorus competition.

❷【中に入れる】
この本にはその作家の初期の作品も収められている The writer's earliest works *are* also *included* in this book.
正倉院には宝物が多数収められている A lot of treasures *are stored* in Shosoin.
私はその美しい日の出をカメラに収めた I *took a*

photo of the beautiful sunrise.

1か月の食費は3万円以内に収めるようにしている I try to *keep* my food expenses (*to*) *within* 30,000 yen a month.

❸【解決する】(話し合いなどで) settle ⓣ; (力ずくで) suppress ⓣ, put* down

彼が争議を丸く収めてくれた He *settled* the dispute peacefully.

おさめる² 納める

❶【納入する】pay* ⓣ

税金を納める *pay* taxes

授業料は分割で納めることもできます You can *pay* your (school) fees in installments.

❷【受け取る】accept ⓣ

ささやかですが感謝のしるしにお納めください *Please accept* this small token of my gratitude.

おさめる³ 治める

rule ⓣ ⓘ; govern ⓣ; administer ⓣ; reign over ...

| rule: 権力を行使して支配する.
| govern: 行政を行う.
| administer: 行政の運営をする.
| reign over: 王・女王が君臨する(必ずしも権力は行使しない).

国を治める *administer* a country

その国は女王が治めていた The Queen *reigned over* the country.

昔は天皇が日本を治めていた In the old days Japan *was ruled by* the Emperor.

おさめる⁴ 修める

(勉強する) study ⓣ; (修了する) complete ⓣ; (知識などを習得する) acquire ⓣ, master ⓣ ∥姉は大学で仏文学を修めた My sister *studied* French literature in college.

おさらい (復習) review ⓒ; (練習) exercise ⓒ; (劇・音楽などの) rehearsal ⓒ ∥では先週のおさらいから始めましょう Now, let's start with *a review* of last week's lesson.

おさん お産 (出産) childbirth ⓤ; (分娩) delivery ⓒ; (陣痛) labor ⓤ ∥お産が軽い[重い] have *an easy* [*a difficult*] *delivery* / 昔はお産で亡くなる女性も少なくなかった In the old days there were quite a few women who died *in childbirth*. ◆お産をする give birth; have a baby ∥ 姉はお産が近い My sister *is near her* (*baby's*) *due date*.

おし 押し (ポンプを)ひと押しするとちょうど適量のシャンプーが出る You'll get the right amount of shampoo *with just one push.* / とにかく押しの一手で行くしかない All we can do is *push forward*. / そのセールスマンはとても押しが強い That salesman *is very pushy* [*aggressive*].

おじ 伯父・叔父 uncle ⓒ

大おじ *a great-uncle*; *a grand*(*-*)*uncle*

おじが私たちを駅で迎えてくれた We were met by *our uncle* at the station.

おじがこのアパートの保証人になってくれている *My uncle* is my sponsor for (the lease on) this apartment.

おしあい 押し合い 電車に乗ろうとみな押し合いへし合いしている People *are pushing and shoving* to get on a train.

おしあける 押し開ける push [throw*] open; (無理に) force open ∥彼女は無理やりドアを押しあけた She *forced* 「*the door open* [*open the door*].

おしあげる 押し上げる push up ∥窓を押し上げる *push* the window *up*

おしあてる 押し当てる 壁に耳を押し当てる *press one's* ear *against* [*to*] the wall / 彼女は額にハンカチを押し当てた She *held* a handkerchief *to* her forehead.

おしい 惜しい

❶【もったいない】

そのかばんは捨てるには惜しい(→よすぎる) That bag *is too good* to be thrown away.

彼女は娘のバレエレッスンには惜しげもなく金を使った(→金を使うのをいとわなかった) She *didn't mind* spending money on her daughter's ballet lessons.

何もお金が惜しくて反対しているのではない I'm *not objecting just because* I *don't want to pay the money.*

🍏「このへんの服,もう着ないから処分しようかな」「それは惜しい! フリーマーケットに出せば?」"I never wear these clothes any more. I think I'll throw them away." "*That's a shame*! Why don't you sell them at a flea market?"

❷【残念だ】

日本は惜しいところで優勝を逃してしまった Japan failed to win the championship *by a narrow margin.*

惜しいことに父からもらった時計をなくした *Unfortunately* I lost the watch I got from my father.

惜しいなあ,あと1分あったら逆転できたのに *That's too bad*! We could have won an upset victory with just one more minute.

本当に惜しい人を亡くしました(→彼[彼女]の死は私たちにとって大きな損失です) His [Her] death is a great loss to us.

🍏「『薔薇(ℓ̈)』って漢字で書ける?」「こうかな?」「惜しい!」"Can you write 'rose' in Chinese characters?" "Something like this?" "*That's close*!"

❸【捨てがたい】

息子の命が惜しければ警察には知らせるな *If you want to see your son alive*, don't report this to the police.

だれでも自分の命は惜しいものだ Life *is dear to* everybody.

おじいさん¹ お祖父さん grandfather ⓒ, 《口語的》grandpa ⓒ, 《口語的》gran(d)dad ⓒ, 《口語的》gran(d)daddy ⓒ (❖「おじいちゃん」というニュアンスの語)

おじいさんはお元気ですか How's *your grandfather*?

あなたのおじいさんはとても若々しいですね Your *grandfather* is very youthful.

おじいさん² お爺さん (年をとった男性) old [elderly] man ⓒ; (呼びかけ) Mister, Sir ∥バスの中でおじいさんに席を譲った I gave my

seat to *an old man* in the bus.

おしいる 押し入る (泥棒などが) break* into ...; (力ずくで侵入する) enter ... by force //その店に押し入ったのは彼らだ、間違いない They're the ones that *broke into* the shop, I'm sure.

おしいれ 押し入れ

押し入れは作りつけのクローゼットで、ふすまで開け閉めします。昼間寝具をしまったり、またふだんあまり使わない物や季節はずれの衣服などを収納する場所です。
An *oshiire* is a built-in closet with sliding paper doors called *fusuma*. It is used to store bedding during the day as well as out-of-season clothes and other things that are not necessary all the time.

おしうり 押し売り (強引な売り込み) hard sell ⓤ《また a ~》; (強引に売る人) high-pressure salesperson ⓒ ◆親切の押し売り *unwanted* kindness / 押し売りお断り《掲示》*No Soliciting* (❖solicit は「(人に)せがむ」の意味)

おしえ 教え (教義) teachings; (教授) instruction ⓤ; (助言) advice ⓤ; (格言)《公式的》precept ⓒ //キリストの教え *the teachings* of Christ / 彼はいつでも親の教えを守っている He always follows his parents' *advice* [*precepts*]. / 吉田教授に法律の教えを受けた I received *instruction* in law from Professor Yoshida. ◆聖書には神の教えが書かれている The Bible contains the *Word of God*.

おしえご 教え子 one's pupil, one's student //うちには父の昔の教え子がよく遊びに来る My father's former *students* often come to my house.

おしえこむ 教え込む teach* ⓣ; (しつける) train ⓣ; (繰り返し教える) drill ⓣ,《公式的》inculcate ⓣ //犬に芸を教え込む *teach* [*train*] a dog to do tricks / 小さいとき母に礼儀作法を教え込まれた When I was a child, I *was inculcated with* good manners by my mother.

おしえる 教える

❶【教授する】(知識・技術などを体得させる) teach* ⓣⓘ; (指導する) instruct ⓣ; (特に個人的に教授する) give* lessons

父は高校で数学を教えています My father *teaches* mathematics at a high school.

彼女は子供たちに英語を教えて生計を立てている She earns [makes] her living by *teaching* English to children.

この大学ではドイツ語は教えていません German *is not taught* at this university.

ベーカー先生は教えるのがとてもうまい Mr. Baker *teaches* very well. / Mr. Baker is a very good teacher.

彼女は新入社員にコンピュータの使い方を教えている She *instructs* the new employees on how to use the computer.

【teach＋名(人)＋名】≒【teach＋名＋to 名(人)】

彼女は子供たちに音楽を教えた She *taught* her children music. / She *taught* music *to* her children.

◆猫に芸を教えるのは難しい It's difficult to *train* cats to do tricks. / その監督には多くのことを教えられた // その監督から多くのことを学んだ I *learned* a lot from the coach.

❢「だれか着付けを教えてくれないかなあ」「知子のお母さんに頼んでみたら？」"I wonder if there's anybody who can *give* me *lessons in* dressing in (a) kimono." "Why don't you ask Tomoko's mother?"

❷【告げる・示す】tell* ❹, show* ❹

英作文ノート 「道を教える」の場合は **tell**

その美術館へ行く道を教えてくれませんか
→ ×Would you *teach* me the way to the art museum?
→ ○Would you *tell* me the way to the art museum?
→ ○Could you *tell* me how to get to the art museum?

★道を「教える」場合は tell を用いる。teach は学科や技術などの指導のときに用いる。Would you *show* me the way to ...? ともいうが、実際に連れていくか、地図を書いて教える場合に用いる。

彼が何と言ったか正確に教えてください Could you *tell* me exactly what he said?

本当のことを教えてくれてありがとう It was very generous of you to *tell* the truth.

その歯医者は私に正しい歯の磨き方を教えてくれた The dentist *showed* me how to brush my teeth properly.

◆そのことを教えてくださってありがとうございます It's nice of you to *let* me *know* that. / 彼女は理由を教えてほしいと私に迫った She *pressed me for* a reason. / 電話番号を教えてくれますか Will you *give* me your phone number?

❢「それから彼女は何て言ったの」「教えないよ」"What did she say then?" "*I'm not telling you!*"

おしかえす 押し返す push [press] back //電車の中で隣の人が押してくるので、私も押し返してやった In the train, the man next to me pushed against me, so I *pushed him back*.

おしかける 押し掛ける ❶【訪ねる】visit ⓣ; (招かれずに) invite *oneself* //近いうちに新居に押しかけるよ I'll *visit* you at your new home one of these days. ◆突然こんなふうに押しかけてしまってごめんなさい I'm sorry to *descend on* you like this. (❖descend on [upon] は「…を不意に訪ねる」の意味)

❷【殺到する】crowd ⓘ, throng ⓘ //大勢の人々が連日そのアウトレットモールに押しかけている A Lot of people *crowd into* [*throng to*] the outlet mall every day. ◆テレビレポーターたちがその俳優の自宅に押しかけた TV reporters *rushed to* the actor's home.

おじぎ お辞儀 bow [báu] ⓒ ──おじぎする bow ⓘ, make* a bow (❖bow は「尊敬・崇拝」の気持ちを表す重々しいおじぎのことで、日本

おしきせ

人のあいさつとしてのおじぎとはニュアンスが異なる) 軽くおじぎする *a bow slightly*; *make a slight bow* / 商人は王様に深々とおじぎをした The merchant 「*made a* deep *bow* [*bowed deeply*] *to* the king. / 人に会ったときおじぎをするのが日本人の慣習だ It is a custom of [for, with] the Japanese to *bow* when they meet someone.

おしきせ お仕着せ 学校のお仕着せの(→強制された)行事は好きではない I don't like school events *which are forced on us*.

おじぎそう おじぎ草 〔植物〕sensitive plant Ⓒ

おしきる 押し切る 彼らは両親の反対を押し切って(→反対にもかかわらず)結婚した They got married *in spite of* their parents' disapproval. / 与党は数の力で押し切ってその法案を通した The ruling party *had a strong enough majority* to pass the bill.

おしくも 惜しくも (残念なことに) to *one's regret, regrettably, unfortunately* / 私たちの母校は惜しくも準決勝で敗退した *Unfortunately* our old school was defeated in the semifinal. / 彼女の絵は惜しくも入選を逃した *To our regret*, her painting did not win a prize.

おしくらまんじゅう 押しくら饅頭 毎日押しくらまんじゅうで会社に来るのはうんざりだ I'm tired of coming to work every day *in a sardine can*. (❖sardine can は「イワシの缶詰」のこと。比喩的に「ぎゅうぎゅう詰め」の電車やバスを指す)

おじけづく 怖じ気づく その話を聞いておじけづいて(→恐怖心にとらわれて)しまった Listening to the story, I *was seized with fear*. / 弟は面接が始まる前からおじけづいている My brother *gets cold feet* even before the interview starts.

おしげもなく 惜しげもなく (気前よく) generously; (ふんだんに) freely; (進んで) willingly; (湯水のように) like water / 彼は金を惜しげもなく使う He spends money *like water*.

おしこむ 押し込む push ... into ~; (無理やり) force ... into ~ / 僕はその本をジーパンのポケットに押し込んだ I *pushed* the book *into* the pocket of my jeans. / 彼女は自分の服をすべてスーツケースの中に押し込んだ She *forced* all her clothes *into* her suitcase.

◆祖母は私の手の中にお金を押し込んだ My grandmother *pressed* some money *into* my hand. / 彼らは1つの小部屋に押し込まれた They *were crowded into* one small room. / たくさんの人々が小さなバスに押し込まれた Many people *were crammed into* the small bus. / 彼はシャツのすそをズボンの中に押し込んだ He *tucked* his shirt *into* his pants.

おしこめる 押し込める (押し込む) cram ... into ~; (閉じ込める・監禁する) shut* up; (かぎをかけて) lock up / 私たちは狭い部屋に押し込められた We *were crammed into* a small room.

おしころす 押し殺す 押し殺した声 a *hushed* voice / 笑いを押し殺す *suppress one's laughter*

おじさん (おじ) uncle Ⓒ; (中年の男性) man Ⓒ (複 men), gentleman Ⓒ; (呼びかけ) Sir, 《口語的》Mister ⇒おじ / 明おじさんはよく釣りに連れていってくれる *Uncle* Akira often takes me fishing. / おじさん、何か落ちましたよ You dropped something, *Sir*. / 毎朝駅で背の高いおじさんを見かける I see a tall *man* at the station every morning.

おしすすめる 推し進める (進行させる) go* ahead with ...; (どんどん進める) push ahead with ...; (突き進む) push forward / 政府はその経済政策を推し進めている The government *pushes ahead with* its economic policy.

おしたおす 押し倒す push down; (強い力で倒す) bring* down; (風が) blow* down / 人々がどっと群がって彼は押し倒された A surge of people *pushed* him *down*.

おしだし 押し出し 大関が押し出しで横綱を破った The *ozeki* won by *pushing* the *yokozuna out of the ring*. / 8回表に押し出しで1点入った There was *a forced run* in the top of the eighth inning.

おしだす 押し出す push out; (力ずくで) force out; (しぼって) squeeze [press] out / チューブから絵の具を押し出す *squeeze* paint *out of* a tube

◆その党は消費税率引き下げを前面に押し出して選挙に臨んだ(→その党のいちばんの公約は消費税率引き下げだった) The party's *biggest election promise* was a reduction of the consumption tax.

おしだまる 押し黙る keep* [remain] silent / 白熱した議論の間、彼はずっと押し黙っていた He *kept silent* during the heated discussion.

おしつけがましい 押し付けがましい pushy / 彼の押しつけがましいところが好きになれない I don't like his *pushy* ways.

おしつける 押し付ける (圧迫する) push [press] ... against ...; (強制する) force ... on, thrust* ⓤ, impose ⓤ / あなたの友人に自分の意見を押しつけてはいけない Don't *force* your opinions *on* your friends. / 母は私に自分のやり方を押しつけた My mother *imposed* her ways *on* me. / その仕事は彼に押しつけられた The task *was thrust upon* him.

◆彼は私を壁に押しつけた He *pinned* me *against* the wall.

おしっこ 《小児語》weewee Ⓤ (また a ~) (❖wee-wee は Ⓤ (また a ~), wee Ⓤ (また a ~), 《口語的》pee Ⓤ (また a ~) ——おしっこする weewee ⓘ, 《口語的》pee ⓘ, take* [have*] a pee, do* a weewee / お母さん、おしっこ Mom, I gotta (go) *pee*.

◆弟がおしっこをもらしてしまった My brother *wet his pants*.

おしつぶす 押し潰す crush ⓤ; (ぺしゃんこにする) squash ⓤ; (粉々に砕く) smash ⓤ / 持っていた花が満員電車の中で押しつぶされた The flowers I was carrying *got squashed* in the crowded train. ◆彼らはみな不安に押しつぶされそうな思いだった All of them *were oppressed by* [*with*] worry. / 雪の重みで押しつぶされた家もあった Some houses *collapsed* under the weight of snow.

おしつまる 押し詰まる 今年も押し詰まってきた(→年の終わりに近づいている) We *are approaching* [*getting close to, drawing near*] *the end* of the year.

おしとおす 押し通す (言い張る) insist on …; (固執する) persist in …, stick* to … ∥彼はあくまでも自分の意見を押し通そうとした He *insisted on* his opinion.
◆妹はいつもわがままを押し通す My sister *has* always *had her own way*.

おしどり mandarin duck [C] ∥おしどり夫婦(幸せな夫婦) a happily-married couple, (a couple of) lovebirds(❖ボタンインコのこと. 雌雄の仲がよいことから)

おしながす 押し流す (流し去る) wash away; (運び去る) carry away; (一挙に運び去る) sweep* away ∥時代の波に押し流される *be carried away* by the current of the times / 川の増水で多くの家が押し流された Many houses *were washed away* by the rise of the river.

おしのける 押しのける (わきへ) push [press] … aside; (ひじで) elbow [他]; (肩で) shoulder [他]
◆彼らは私を押しのけていった They *pushed past* [*by*] me. / 彼女は群衆を押しのけて進んだ She *thrust her way through* the crowd.

おしのび お忍び ―お忍びで incognito ∥王女がお忍びで街に出るところからその映画は始まる The movie starts with the princess going into town *incognito*.

おしはかる 推し量る guess [他], suppose [他]
➾すいりょう(推量)

おしばな 押し花 pressed flower [C]
◆押し花を作る *press flowers*

おしべ 雄蕊 stamen [C] (複 ~s, stamina)

おしボタン 押しボタン (push) button [C]
◆押しボタン式横断歩道 a *push-button* crossing

おしぼり お絞り 🗻 an *oshibori*, a rolled hand towel served either steaming hot or refreshingly cold (❖おしぼりを出す習慣は英米にはない)

おしまい きょうはこれでおしまいにしましょう *That's all for today.* / もし彼女に本当のことがばれたらおしまいだ If she finds out the truth, I'*ll be finished*. / おれはもうおしまいだ *It's all over* [*up*] *with* me.
💬「作り方はすごく簡単よ. お湯を入れて混ぜるだけ」「それでおしまい?」 "How to make it is really simple. Just pour in hot water and stir." "*Is that it?*"

おしまくる 押しまくる (どんどん押す) push and push; (押し続ける) keep* pushing

おしまれる 惜しまれる その歌手はみなに惜しまれながら引退した The singer retired *to everyone's regret*.

おしみない 惜しみない その女性は子供たちにお菓子を惜しみなく与えた The woman gave children sweets *freely*. / だれもが両チームに惜しみない拍手を送った Everyone gave *lavish* applause to the both teams.

おしむ 惜しむ
❶【しぶる】spare [他], grudge [他] (❖共に通例否定文・疑問文で用いる)
私は外国切手を集めるのに出費を惜しまない I *spare no* expense in collecting foreign stamps.
彼女は労を惜しむことなく私の計画を支えてくれた She *spared no pains* in supporting my plan.
客を歓迎するためには費用を惜しまないと彼は言った He said that *no* expense *was spared* to welcome the guests.
彼女はいつも私に協力を惜しまない She *never grudges* me her cooperation.
◆時間を惜しまない *be generous with one's time* / 君のためなら協力は惜しまないからいつでも言ってくれ I'*m willing to* help you, so just ask me any time.
❷【残念に思う】regret [他]
人々はその女優の早すぎる死を惜しんだ People *regretted* the early death of the actress.
◆彼はホストファミリーとの別れを惜しんだ He *spent a while taking sad leave* of his host family.
❸【だいじにする】
彼は食事の時間も惜しんで(→ほとんど食事の時間をとらず)そのミステリーを読みふけった He was really into reading the mystery and *hardly took time to eat*.
僕は寸暇を惜しんで勉強した I *gave every spare moment to* studying.

おしめ 《米》diaper [C], 《英口語的》nappy [C]
◆赤ちゃんのおしめを替える *change* a baby (❖change には「(赤ん坊の)おしめを取り替える」の意味がある)

おしもおされもしない 押しも押されもしない 彼は押しも押されもしない(→名声が定まった)球界の大スターだ He is an *established* star in the baseball world.

おしもどす 押し戻す push [press] back
◆彼女は僕のプレゼントをテーブルの向こうから押し戻した She *pushed* my present across the table *to* me.

おしもんどう 押し問答 ―押し問答する bandy words with …; (やかましく口論する) wrangle [自]; (口論する) quarrel [自] ∥その店で店員と客が押し問答をしていた At the store, a clerk and a shopper *were wrangling*.

おしゃか お釈迦 携帯電話をトイレに落としておしゃかにしてしまった I dropped my cell phone in the toilet and *ruined* it.

おしゃぶり 《米》pacifier [C], 《英》dummy [C]

おしゃべり (雑談) chat [C][U]; (むだ話) chatter [U], 《口語的》chitchat [U]; (おしゃべりな人) talkative person [C], talker [C], 《口語的》bigmouth [C], 《口語的》chatterbox [C] ―おしゃべりする (雑談する) chat [自]; (ぺちゃくちゃと) chatter [自] ∥女の子たちは映画スターについ

べちゃくちゃおしゃべりしていた The girls *were chattering* about film stars. / 彼女はおしゃべりだから秘密にしておきたいことは話さないほうがいいよ You'd better not tell her what you want to keep secret, because she's such a 「*great talker* [*terrible gossip*].
◆おしゃべりはやめて早く寝なさい Stop *talking* and go to sleep.

おしゃま 3歳のめいはおしゃまだ My three-year-old niece is *a little lady*.

おじゃま お邪魔 来週おじゃまします(→会いに行きます) *I'll come to see you* next week. / おじゃましました(→時間を割いてくれてありがとう) *Thank you for your time.* / (→時間をとらせてすみません) *I'm sorry to take up your time.* (❖後者は(「相手の)時間をとって申しわけない」という日本的な発想の表現. 英米では前者を用いるのがふつう) / おじゃましてすみません *I'm sorry* [*I hate*] *to bother you.* (❖人に話しかけるときの決まり文句) / おじゃましてすみませんが、電話をお借りできますか (*I'm*) *sorry to disturb you*, but can I use your phone? / おじゃましてよろしいですか *Could I interrupt* (*you*)? / おじゃまでなければよいのですが *I hope I'm not disturbing you.*

💬「すみません、おじゃまします」「どうぞ」"Hello. *May I come in?*" "Yes, of course."

おしやる 押しやる ギターは部屋の隅に押しやられていた The guitar *sat neglected* in a corner of the room.

おしゃれ お洒落 ――おしゃれな (流行に敏感な) fashionable; (洗練された) refined, fine; (上品な、センスのよい) stylish, tasteful; (しゃれた) smart ‖おしゃれなレストラン a *stylish* restaurant / 父はおしゃれな服がとても好きだ My father has a great fancy for *smart* clothes.
◆姉はおしゃれだ(=いい服を着ることが好きだ) My sister *likes to dress nicely.* / (→着る物や身なりに気を配る) My sister *is careful about her dress and appearance.* / 静香はおしゃれをしてやってきた Shizuka came *all dressed up.*

おじゃん 期限は来週の月曜だって？ 週末がおじゃんだ The deadline is next Monday? *There* [*Bang*] *goes* my weekend!

おしょう 和尚 Buddhist priest ⓒ; (住職) the chief bonze [priest] of a temple

おじょうさん お嬢さん (娘) *a person's daughter*; (呼びかけ) young lady, Miss(❖名前の分からない若い女性や女性店員などに対して用いる) ‖「お嬢さん、お手伝いしましょうか Can I help you, *Miss?* / 僕の記憶が正しければ、彼のお嬢さんはうちの息子と同い年だ If I remember right(ly), his *daughter* is as old as my son. ◆その女優はお嬢さん育ちで(→甘やかされて育ったため)いっさい家事をしたことがなかった The actress *had been indulged as a child* and had never done any housework.
‖お嬢さん学校 a school for daughters from upper-class families

おしょく 汚職 corruption ⓤ, (主に米)graft ⓤ; (贈収賄) bribery ⓤ; (汚職事件) scandal ⓒ ‖政治汚職の摘発 the exposure of political *corruption* / この汚職事件は大衆の政治不信を招いた This *scandal* generated public distrust in politics. / 政府内には汚職が蔓延(誤)している The government is rife with *corruption.* / 彼はその本の中で前大統領がその汚職にかかわっていたと書いた He wrote in the book that the former president was implicated in the *scandal.*

おしよせる 押し寄せる (群がる) crowd ⓘ ⓣ, throng ⓘ ⓣ; (大挙して) flock ⓘ; (波のように) surge ⓘ ‖押し寄せる波 *surging* waves / 人々は出口に押し寄せた People *thronged* toward the exit. / 成田空港にはその俳優のファンが大勢押し寄せた A lot of the actor's fans *flocked* to Narita Airport.
◆へんぴな南の島々にも時代の波が押し寄せてきている The trend of the times *has reached* even remote tropical islands.

おしろい 白粉 (face) powder ⓤ ‖おしろいをつける put on *powder*; *powder one's face*

オシログラフ oscillograph ⓒ

オシロスコープ oscilloscope ⓒ

おしわける 押し分ける (押しのける) push [elbow, force] *one's* way through ...; (引き離す) push apart ‖人込みを押し分けてホームにたどり着いた I *pushed my way through* a crowd to get to the platform. / 私は人の波を押し分けて進まなければならなかった I had to *force my way through* the crowd.

おす¹ 押す

❶【力を加える】push ⓘ ⓣ (↔pull); (押しつける) press ⓘ ⓣ; (乱暴に) shove [ʃʌv] ⓘ ⓣ; (強く・急に) thrust* ⓘ ⓣ

押さないで *Don't push*!

彼はその重いドアを押してあけた He *pushed* the heavy door *open*.

このボタンを押すとスチュワーデスが来てくれます If you *press* this button, a flight attendant will come and help you.

自転車がパンクしたので押して帰らなければならなかった The tire of my bicycle went flat, so I had to *push* it home.

💬「すみません、シャッター押して(→写真を撮って)もらえます？」「はい、ここを押すだけですか」"Excuse me, but could you *take a picture* for us?" "Sure. Just *press* here?"

❷【印を】stamp ⓣ

図書館員は本に日付を押した The librarian *stamped* the date in the book.
◆切手に消印を押す *cancel* a stamp / ここに印を押してください *Put* the seal here. / きょうはタイムカードを押すのを忘れていた I forgot to *punch* my time card today.

❸【その他】

彼は病気を押してチームの応援に行った He went to cheer on [for] his team *in spite of his illness.*

今のところアントラーズが押しぎみに試合を進めている The Antlers are playing *on the offensive* so far.

彼らは親の反対を押して結婚した They got

married *against* their parents' wishes.

おす² 推す ❶【推量する】suppose ㉰, guess ㉰ ‖結果は推して知るべしだ(→容易に想像できる) *You can easily imagine* the consequences.

❷【推薦する】recommend ㉰ ‖彼は満場一致で議長に推された He *was recommended for* the post of chairperson unanimously.

おす³ 雄 male ◎ (↔female), 《口語的》he ‖―雄の male ‖君のうちの犬は雄ですか, 雌ですか Is your dog 「*male* or *female* [*a he* or *a she*]?

おすい 汚水 (汚染された水) polluted water ◎; (汚れた水) filthy water ◎; (廃水・排水) waste water ◎; (下水) sewage [súːidʒ] ◎ ‖その工場は川に汚水を垂れ流しにしていた The factory had discharged *polluted water* into the river.

‖汚水処理 sewage disposal / 汚水処理場 a sewage disposal [treatment] plant

おずおず 彼はおずおずとその部屋に入っていった He *timidly* entered the room.

オスカー (オスカー像) Oscar ◎; (アカデミー賞) Academy Award ◎

おすすめ お勧め そのレストランは私のおすすめです That restaurant is the one I *would recommend*.

💬「おすすめ料理は何ですか」「うちのビーフシチューはお客様に人気がありますよ」"What's *the specialty of the house*? / What would you recommend?" "Our beef stew is very popular with our customers."

おすそわけ お裾分け いなかからブドウをたくさん送ってきたので近所の人におすそ分けした My family back home sent me a lot of grapes, so I *shared* them *with* my neighbors.

おすなおすな 押すな押すな スタジアムは押すな押すなの混雑だった The stadium *was jammed* [*packed*] *with people*. / 新しいスーパーは押すな押すなの大盛況だ The new supermarket *is doing a roaring* [*flourishing*] *business*.

おすみつき お墨付き (正式な許可) 《口語的》official go-ahead ◎, 《口語的》green light ◎; (認可のしるし) the seal of approval; (正式な保証) official guarantee ◎ ‖教室を使ってもよいという先生のお墨付きをもらった We got *an official go-ahead* from our teacher for the use of the classroom.

オセアニア Oceania [òuʃiǽniə]

おせいぼ お歳暮 (an) *oseibo*, a year-end gift [present] ‖おじのお歳暮に商品券を送った I sent gift certificates to my uncle as *a year-end gift*.

12月の中旬頃, 会社あるいは個人間で世話になった相手に贈り物をすることをお歳暮といいます (夏に贈るものはお中元).
Around mid-December, companies and individuals send gifts to those who have helped them. These gifts are called *oseibo*. (Summer gifts are called *ochugen*.)

おせじ お世辞 flattery ◎; (社交的賛辞) compliment ◎ ‖心にもないお世辞を言う make *an* insincere [empty] *compliment* / お世辞じゃなくて本当にそう思います This is not *flattery*. I really mean it. / お世辞を言ったって何も出ないよ *Compliments* won't do you any good. ◆彼はいつも上司にお世辞を言っている He *is* always *flattering* his boss. / 彼はお世辞にもハンサムとはいえない I can't say *even in courtesy* that he's handsome.

💬「あんまりきれいになったんで見違えたよ」「お世辞が上手ですね」"You've become so beautiful that I didn't recognize you at first." "*I'm flattered!* / *You flatter me!*"

おせち お節

おせちとは新年の三が日に食べる特別な料理で, ふつう重箱と呼ばれる華やかな絵柄が描かれた箱に盛られます. 保存のきくものばかりなので, 三が日の間料理をする必要がありません. また, それぞれの料理には新しい年における健康や繁栄への願いがこめられています.
Osechi are the special foods served on the first three days of the New Year. They are usually stored in ornate lacquered boxes called *jubako*. Because the foods are preserved, people do not have to bother to cook during the three days. Each dish has a symbolism significant to the New Year, such as wishing for good health and prosperity.

おせっかい お節介 ―おせっかいな (世話をやきたがる) meddlesome; (差し出がましい) officious; (詮索(穿)好きな) nosy ‖おせっかいな人 a *nosy* person

◆人のおせっかいをやくのはやめなさい Don't *meddle in* other people's affairs. / 余計なおせっかいだ Mind your own business.
‖おせっかいやき 《口語的》a busybody

オセロ (ゲーム) 《商標名》Othello [əθélou] ‖オセロをやろう Let's have a game of *Othello*.

おせん 汚染 pollution ◎, contamination ◎ (◆pollution は一般的に「汚染された状態」を表し, contamination は「特定の物質によって汚染されている」というニュアンスがある) ――汚染する pollute ㉰, contaminate ㉰

汚染された川 a *polluted* river

彼らは大気[水質]汚染の原因を調査した They investigated causes of *air* [*water*] *pollution*.

その病気は水銀汚染によってもたらされた The illness was caused by mercury *contamination*.

◆その都市は全河川から汚染をなくす事業に熱心に取り組んでいる The city is involved in a project to *decontaminate* all its rivers.

‖汚染物質 a contaminant, (a) pollutant / 汚染防止 pollution control / 環境汚染 environmental pollution / 放射能汚染 radioactive contamination

おぜんだて　お膳立て　(準備) preparations, arrangements ∥パーティーのおぜん立てはすっかり整った *The arrangements* for the party are complete.

おそい　遅い

❶【時刻・時間が】late (↔early) ―― 遅く late (↔early)
遅い朝食をとる have a *late* breakfast
遅くなってすみません I'm sorry *I'm late*.
彼は遅くなった言い訳をした He excused himself for *being late*.
レポートは遅くても2月末までに提出しなさい Hand in your papers by the end of February *at the latest*.
午後遅くまでかかってやっと掃除が終わった I finally finished cleaning *late in the afternoon*.
彼は朝早くから夜遅くまで働いている He works from early in the morning *until late at night*.
日曜日には遅くまで寝ていたい I like to sleep *late* on Sundays.
🔴「遅かったね(→やっと来たね)」「ごめん、電車に乗り遅れたんだ」*"You are here at last!"* "Sorry, I missed a train."
🔴「お母さん、啓子のうちに行ってきます」「あまり遅くならないようにね」"Mom, I'm going to Keiko's." "OK. Don't be *late*."
🔴「もう遅いので失礼します」「よかったら夕食を食べていってください」*"It's getting late*, and I think I must be going now." "Why don't you stay for dinner?"
🔴「ああ、もっと勉強しておけばよかった」「いまさら後悔しても遅いよ」"I really should have studied more." "It's *too late* to be sorry now."

❷【速度が】slow (↔fast, quick) ―― 遅く slowly (↔fast, quickly, rapidly)
私は食べるのが遅い I'm a *slow* eater. / I eat *slowly*.
彼は理解の遅い生徒たちにも根気強く教えた He taught even *slow* students with great patience.
警察は暴徒に対して行動を起こすのが遅かった The police *were slow* to take action against the rioters.
何かを待っているときは時間がたつのが遅く感じられる Time seems to pass *slowly* when you are waiting for something.

おそう　襲う

❶【人・動物などが】(襲撃する) attack 🔵 🔴, make* an attack; (激しく) assault 🔵
彼女は背後から襲われた She *was attacked* from behind.
番犬は泥棒に激しく襲いかかった The watchdog made a violent *attack* on the thief.
◆その老人はクマに襲われた The old man *was set upon* by a bear. ∥ ボニーとクライドは銀行を襲った Bonnie and Clyde *robbed* [*held up*] the bank.

❷【災害・病気・恐怖などが】(不意に) strike* 🔵; (打撃を与える) hit* 🔵; (感情が) seize 🔵 (❖通例受身で); (病気・害虫が) attack 🔵
大きな地震が夜明けにその都市を襲った A big earthquake *hit* [*struck*] the city at daybreak.
台風が本州を襲った A typhoon *hit* [*struck*] the mainland of Japan.
私は突然恐怖に襲われた Suddenly I *was seized by* terror.
中世のヨーロッパをペストが襲った The plague *attacked* Medieval Europe.

おそうまれ　遅生まれ 📅　遅生まれの人(→4月2日から12月31日までの間に生まれた人) a person *born between April 2 and December 31*

おそかれはやかれ　遅かれ早かれ sooner or later (❖語順に注意); (いつか) someday, sometime; (結局) after all, in the end, eventually ∥遅かれ早かれ真実は明らかになるだろう The truth will out *sooner or later*.

おそくとも　遅くとも at (the) latest ∥遅くともあすまでには仕事を終わらせます I'll finish the work by tomorrow *at the latest*.

おそざき　遅咲き ―― 遅咲きの late-blooming[-blossoming] ∥遅咲きの梅 a *late-blooming*[*-blossoming*] ume tree

おそじも　遅霜 spring [late] frost 🔵 ∥遅霜のため、苗の多くが被害を受けた A *late frost* injured many of the seedlings.

おそなえ　お供え　(供えるもの) offering 🔵; (鏡もち) mochi [rice paste] offering 🔵 ―― お供えする offer 🔴, make* an offering ∥祖母は神棚にお供えをした My grandmother *offered something* at the Shinto altar.

おそばん　遅番　(午後の) afternoon shift 🔵; (夜間の) night shift 🔵 ∥きょうは遅番だ I am *on the afternoon shift* today.

おそまきながら　遅まきながら 遅まきながら私はドイツ語の勉強を始めた *Belatedly* [*Though a little too late*], I started studying German.

おそましい　(恐ろしい) horrifying ∥おそましい光景 a *horrifying* sight
◆それは聞くだけでもおそましい話だった Just hearing the story *gave me the creeps*.

おそまつ　お粗末 ―― お粗末な poor, miserable ∥お粗末な演技 a *poor* [*miserable*] performance / その映画はお粗末だった That movie *was of poor quality*.
🔴「ごちそうさま」「お粗末さまでした」"That was delicious." "Oh, *it was nothing special*."

おそらく　恐らく

probably, likely, perhaps, maybe, possibly (❖この順に確実性は低くなる。(米)では maybe、(英)では perhaps がよく用いられる) ➡ たぶん
それはおそらく彼らの希望を十分満たすだろう It will *probably* answer to their request.
彼はおそらく家にいるだろう He is (very) *likely* at home.
◆おそらく彼の名は歴史に残るだろう *Presumably* his name will go down in history. ∥おそらく彼女は米国に帰ったのだろう *For all I know*, she could be back in the U.S. / 彼

女は今ごろはおそらく家に着いているだろう She *should* be home by now.

🅔「彼, あした来るかな」「おそらくね」 "Will he come tomorrow?" "*Maybe*."

おそるおそる 恐る恐る (臆病に) timidly; (こわごわ) fearfully ∥彼女はおそるおそるドアをノックした She *timidly* knocked the door.

おそるべき 恐るべき (恐ろしい) terrible, terrifying; (驚くべき) marvelous, amazing ∥恐るべき事実 a *terrifying* fact / その国では恐るべき犯罪が行われていた A *terrible* crime had been committed in that country. / 彼は恐るべきスピードで仕事をこなした He did the work at a *marvelous* speed.

おそれ¹ 恐れ (恐怖) fear 🅤🅒; ∥無知は恐れをもたらす Ignorance causes *fear*. / 彼女は以前男性に対して恐れをいだいていた She used to have a *fear* of men. ◆恐れを知らない冒険家 a *fearless* adventurer / 彼らは目の前に立ちはだかる氷の壁に恐れをなして引き返した They turned back, *intimidated* by the soaring ice wall in front of them.

おそれ² 虞 (心配・懸念) fear 🅤🅒; (危険) danger 🅤🅒, risk 🅒🅤 ∥ここで地震が起こるおそれは大いにある[あまりない] There is great [not much] *risk* of an earthquake here. ◆絶滅のおそれのある鳥 an *endangered* species of bird / 誤解を生むおそれのある記事 a *misleading* article / あすは北陸全域で大雪のおそれ(→可能性)があります There's *a possibility* of heavy snow tomorrow all over the Hokuriku district. / 妊婦による喫煙は胎児に悪影響を及ぼすおそれがある Smoking by pregnant women *can* have a bad effect on babies.

おそれいる 恐れ入る ∥おそれ入りますがこちらにお名前とご住所をお書きいただけますか *Excuse me, but* may I have your name and address here？ / お忙しいところおいでいただいておそれ入ります(→ありがとうございます) *Thank you very much for* coming in spite of your busy schedule. / 彼女の厚かましさにはほんと入った(→あきれかえった) I *was really floored* by her impudence. / おそれ入りました *My hat is off to you*! / *I take my hat off to you*! (✍帽子を脱ぐことから「降参する」の意)

おそれおおい 恐れ多い ∥恐れ多くも陛下からお言葉を賜った His Majesty the Emperor *very graciously* spoke to me.

おそれおののく 恐れ戦く (恐怖で震える) tremble [shudder] with fear ◆彼らはその予言を聞いて恐れおののいた They *were terrified at* the prophecy.

おそれる 恐れる (怖がる) be afraid of ..., fear 🅣; (これから起こることに対して) dread 🅣 ∥彼は人前で話すことを恐れている He *dreads* speaking in public.

【be afraid of + 名】動物は火を恐れる Animals *are afraid of* fire. / 彼女は病気の再発を恐れていた She *was afraid of* a recurrence of the disease.

【be afraid + of *doing*】失敗を恐れるな Don't *be afraid of* making mistakes.

◆彼女がいちばん恐れていたことが現実となった Her *worst fears* were realized. / 無知だと思われるのを恐れて私はそれをすべて知っているかのようなふりをした I acted as if I knew it all *for fear that* I would be thought ignorant. / 私は小さいころ父を恐れていた I *was scared of* my father when I was small.

おそろい お揃い ∥双子の女の子はおそろいの服を着ていた The twin girls were wearing *matching* dresses.

🅔「みなさん, おそろいでどちらへ」「箱根へ行ってきます」 "Where are you *all* going?" "To Hakone."

おそろしい 恐ろしい

❶[怖い] terrible; (恐怖・嫌悪感を与える) dreadful; (ぞっとするような) horrible, awful

恐ろしい事故 a *terrible* [*dreadful, horrible*] accident

恐ろしい光景を見て私は背筋が寒くなった The *terrible* sight sent shivers up and down my spine.

こんな恐ろしい病気はいつかこの世からなくなってほしい I hope someday the world will be rid of these *awful* diseases.

なんて恐ろしいことを言うの What a *horrible* thing to say!

◆平気でうそをつける自分が恐ろしい I'm *alarmed* by my own skill as a liar. / 恐ろしくて口がきけなかった I *was too frightened* to speak.

❷[ものすごい]

きのうはおそろしく暑かった It was *terribly* hot yesterday.

🅔「映画はどうだった」「おそろしく退屈だった」 "How was the movie?" "It was *awfully* boring."

おそろしさ 恐ろしさ fear 🅤, terror 🅤 ∥子供は恐ろしさのあまり泣きだした The child began to cry *in* [*with*] *terror*.

おそわる 教わる (教えられる) be taught; (習って身につける) learn* 🅣; (継続して授業などを受ける) take* lessons ∥祖母に料理を教わった I *learned* how to cook from my grandmother. / My grandmother *taught* me how to cook. / 私は矢島先生に英語を教わった I *was taught* English by Mr. Yajima.

オゾン [化学] ozone [óuzoun] 🅤 ∥オゾン層の破壊は人間の健康にとって大きな脅威だ The destruction of *the ozone layer* is a serious menace to human health.

∥オゾンホール an ozone hole

おたおた おたおたするな *Don't get* [*be*] *upset*! / *Take it easy*! ∥彼女は彼が事故にあったと聞いておたおたするばかりだった She *got into a state* when she was told that he had an accident.

おたがい お互い ——お互いに each other, one another; (相互に) mutually ∥私たちはお互いに意見を出し合った We exchanged

おたがいさま　お互い様　困ったときはお互いさまだ（→もし私が困っていたらあなたも私に同じことをするだろう） You'd do the same for me (if I were in trouble). / 忙しいのはお互いさまだ（→あなたが忙しいというのなら私もだ） If you are busy, so am I.

💬「君のその格好, かなり変だよ」「お互いさまじゃないか」 "You look pretty strange in those clothes." "Look who's talking!"

おたかくとまる　お高くとまる
💬「彼女, お高くとまってるよね」「ほんと, 何様のつもりかしら」 "She's stuck up, isn't she?" "I know. I wonder who she thinks she is."

オタク　nerd 🄲, geek 🄲 (❖非社交的で「ださい」人という, やや軽蔑的な表現. ゲーム業界などでは日本語のotakuをそのまま用いることもある); (…狂) freak 🄲, maniac 🄲 // コンピュータオタク a computer nerd

おたく　お宅（相手の家） your home [house], (《口語的》your place; (相手) you / もしかすると今度の週末お宅に伺うかもしれません Perhaps I'll call on you next weekend.
◆駅でお宅のお嬢さんを見かけました I saw your daughter at the station.
💬「お宅に伺ってもよろしいですか」「もちろん」 "May I visit your house?" "By all means."

おたずねもの　お尋ね者　wanted person 🄲; (指名手配の犯人) wanted criminal 🄲; (容疑者) suspect 🄲 / 彼はお尋ね者の身だ He is wanted by the police.

おたちだい　お立ち台　(舞台・ステージ) stage 🄲; (演壇) platform 🄲

おだて　(お世辞) flattery Ⓤ // そんなおだてには乗らないわよ I won't fall for flattery like that.
◆私はおだてに乗って彼の宿題を引き受けてしまった I was flattered into doing his homework. / 姉はおだてに乗りやすい My sister is easily flattered.

おだてる　(お世辞を言う) flatter 🄳; (うまい言葉でだます) wheedle 🄳 / 彼女は彼をおだてて皿洗いをさせた She flattered him into washing the dishes.
◆おだてったってむだだよ Flattery won't get you anywhere.

おたふくかぜ　お多福風邪　〔医学〕(the) mumps (単数扱い)

おだぶつ　お陀仏　もしここからだれかに突き落とされたらおだぶつだ（→ 死ぬ） If someone pushes me down from here, I'll be a dead man.

おたま　お玉　(soup) ladle 🄲 // みそ汁をお玉ですくってわんによそう ladle miso soup into a bowl

おたまじゃくし　お玉杓子　(カエルの子) tadpole 🄲, 《米》polliwog 🄲; (音符) (musical) note 🄲; (お玉) (soup) ladle 🄲 // オタマジャクシはカエルになる A tadpole grows into a frog.

おだやか　穏やか　——穏やかな calm; gentle; mild; quiet; peaceful　——穏やかに calm-ly; gently; mildly; quietly; peacefully

calm:「荒れていない・静かな・冷静な」の意味で, 主に天候・海などについていう.
gentle:「天候・人柄などに用い,「優しい」というニュアンスがある.
mild:「厳しくない・控えめな」の意味で, 気候や人柄・態度などについていう.
quiet:「静かな・落ち着いた」の意味で, 人柄・海・日などについていう.
peaceful:「平和な・平穏な」の意味で, 主に海・日・生活などに用いる.

穏やかな海 a calm sea / 穏やかな物腰 a gentle manner
きょうは穏やかな1日だった It was a peaceful day today.
穏やかに話し合おう Let's talk quietly.
彼が望んでいたのはつましく穏やかな生活だった What he wanted was a simple, quiet life.
穏やかな風が部屋を通り抜けた A gentle breeze wafted through the room.
別れた彼女が新しい恋人と歩いているのを見て心中穏やかではなかった I wasn't calm inside to see my ex-girlfriend walking with her new boyfriend.

💬「こうなったら裁判に訴えるしかないよ」「どうしたの, 穏やかじゃないね」 "All we can do now is go to court." "What's the matter? You look pretty upset."

おち　落ち　(手落ち) omission 🄲; (笑い話の) punch line 🄲 // この住所録にはいくつか落ちがある There are some omissions in this address book. / 彼らの漫才は落ちがよく分からなかった I didn't get the punch line of their comic dialogue.　◆この洗剤は落ちがいい（→よく汚れを落とす） This detergent washes dirt out well. / そんなやり方では失敗するのが落ちだろう That way is bound to end in failure.

おちあう　落ち合う　meet* 🄳 // 2つの川が落ち合う地点 the spot where the two rivers meet / 私たちは2時に公園の前で落ち合うことにした We decided to meet in front of the park at two.

おちいる　陥る　(病気などに) fall* into …; (好ましくない状態に) be thrown into … // 患者は一時昏睡(ౠ)状態に陥った The patient fell into a coma for a while. / 政府は財政難に陥った The government was thrown into financial difficulties.
◆自己嫌悪に陥る be sunk in self-hatred

おちおち　病気の祖母が心配で夜もおちおち眠れない I'm so anxious about my sick grandmother that I can't sleep well.

おちこぼれ　落ちこぼれ　(中途退学者) dropout 🄲　◆彼は小学校のときクラスの落ちこぼれだったそうだ I hear he dropped behind in his studies when he was in elementary school.

おちこむ　落ち込む　(落ちる) fall* into …; (陥没する) fall [cave] in; (下がる) drop 🄳; (気分が滅入る) be depressed // その子供は小さな穴に落ち込んだ The child fell into a small hole. / 地震で道路の一部が落ち込んだ Part of the road *fell* [*caved*] *in* because of the earthquake. / その町の人口は 3 万人に落ち込んだ The population of the town *dropped to 30,000*. / 彼は財布を落としてすっかり落ち込んでいる He *is very depressed* because he has lost his wallet.

おちつき 落ち着き ❶【平静さ】calmness ⓤ, composure ⓤ;（沈着）one's presence of mind ∥その話を聞いても彼女は落ち着きを失わなかった She kept *her presence of mind* when she heard the story. / 彼はやっと落ち着きを取り戻した At last, he recovered *his「presence of mind* [*composure*]*.
◆彼の妹は年のわりには落ち着きがある（→冷静沈着だ） His sister *is calm* [*self-possessed*] for her age. / 隣に座っている男の子は落ち着きがない（→そわそわしている） The boy sitting next to me *is restless*.
❷【安定】このはしごは落ち着きが悪い This ladder *is unsteady*.

おちつきはらう 落ち着き払う （冷静にしている）keep* cool, be composed ∥彼はいつでも落ち着きをはらっている He always *keeps cool*.
◆彼女は記者の厳しい質問にも落ち着きをはらっているように見えた She appeared *cool, calm and collected* in spite of the reporters' harsh questions.

おちつく 落ち着く
❶【気持ちなどが静まる】calm down, calm [compose] *oneself*;（くつろぐ）relax ⓘ
落ち着いて！ *Calm down*! / *Take it easy*! / *Don't get so excited*!
状況もようやく落ち着いた The situation finally *calmed down*.
◆落ち着いた色 a *quiet* color / 落ち着いた感じのネクタイを締める wear a *quiet* necktie / 温かいコーヒーを飲むと落ち着くよ A cup of hot coffee *will relax you*. / 彼女は人前に出て落ち着かなかった（→緊張した） She *felt nervous* in company. / 彼は落ち着いた（→静かな）声で答えた He replied with [in] a *calm* voice. / そんなに広い部屋ではどうも私は落ち着かない（→くつろげない） I *don't feel at ease* in such a large room. / 彼女は危険に直面しても落ち着いていた（→冷静だった） She *stayed calm* in the face of danger. / 弟の帰りが遅いので母は落ち着かない様子だった（→不安そうだった） My mother looked *anxious* because my brother was late.
❷【新しい職・生活などに】settle ⓘ
兄は結婚してからずいぶん落ち着いた My brother *has* quite *settled down* since he got married.
新居に落ち着いたら電話してください Please call me when you *have settled into* your new house.
彼も新しい仕事に落ち着いたころだろう He should *have settled into* his new job by now.
❸【安定する】settle down, stabilize ⓘ, be stabilized
その国の物価は最近落ち着いている The prices in the country *have been stabilized* these days.
腹痛もだいぶ落ち着きました My stomach-ache *has* almost *settled down*.
◆今週は天気が落ち着かない（→変わりやすい） The weather *has been changeable* this week.
❹【結論などに達する】（終わる）end up;（…ということになる）come* to …
そのことはまた来週話し合うということで落ち着いた We *came to* a decision to discuss it again next week.

おちつける 落ち着ける 気を落ち着けなさい *Calm down* [*yourself*]. / 私は心を落ち着けてからスピーチを始めた I *calmed myself* and started to make a speech.

おちど 落ち度 fault ⓒ ∥それは彼の落ち度ではない It is not his *fault*. / He is not to blame for it. / 彼女は自分の落ち度を認めた She admitted her *fault* [*error*].

おちば 落ち葉 fallen leaf ⓒ;（枯れた葉）dead leaf ⓒ ∥落ち葉をかき集めなさい Rake *the dead leaves* together. / 彼は裏庭からすべての落ち葉を掃（は）いて除いた He swept all *the fallen leaves* off [from] the backyard.
◆一面の黄色い落ち葉 a blanket of yellow *leaves*

おちぶれる 落ちぶれる 彼は昔はぜいたくな暮らしをしていたが、今ではすっかり落ちぶれてしまった Though he was leading a luxurious life before, he *has come down in the world*.

おちぼ 落ち穂 gleanings

おちめ 落ち目 あのタレントももう落ち目だね（→人気がなくなってきた） That TV personality *is losing his popularity*. / That TV personality's *popularity is declining*. / 彼も落ち目だ（→運がなくなってきた） He *is down on his luck*.

おちゃ お茶 ❶【茶】tea ⓤ ∥濃い［薄い］お茶 strong [weak] *tea* / お茶の葉 *tea* leaves / お茶を飲む have *a cup of tea* / お茶をいれる［つぐ］make [pour] *tea* / （会社で）お茶くみをする serve *tea* at the office

💬「お茶をもう 1 杯いただけますか」「いいですよ」 "Can I have another cup of *tea*?" "Sure."

💬「ああ疲れた．そろそろお茶にしようか」「うん，いいね」 "I'm so tired. Let's take *a tea* [*coffee*] *break*, shall we?" "Good idea."

❷【茶道】私は週に 1 回お茶を習っています I take *tea ceremony* lessons once a week.

慣用表現 そんなことは彼にとってはお茶の子さいさいだ（→とても簡単だ） That's *a piece of cake* for him. / 記者の質問に対してその政治家はお茶を濁した The politician *gave an evasive answer* to the reporter's question.

→ **ちゃ**

おちゃづけ お茶漬け

お茶漬けとは茶わんに盛ったごはんに熱い緑茶を注いで食べるものをいい，ふつうはサケ・梅干し・のりなどの具をのせて食べる．
Hot green tea poured onto a bowl of rice is called *ochazuke*. It usually has

toppings like salmon, pickled plum or *nori*.

おちゅうげん お中元

夏の盛りのころ、会社あるいは個人間で世話になった相手に贈り物をすることをお中元といいます。元来日本には、盆に先祖の供養に用いる供物を親戚(しんせき)や近所の人々に配る習慣があり、それが世俗化して宗教的な意味合いがなくなったものが現在のお中元です。
At midsummer, gifts are exchanged between companies or individuals. These gifts are called *ochugen*. This practice traces back to the custom of sharing with relatives and neighbors one's offerings to the souls of family ancestors during *bon* (the Buddhist souls' day festival). Nowadays, however, it is secularized and has lost its religious meaning.

おちょうしもの お調子者 クラスのお調子者 a class *clown*. / お調子者なんだから(→おだてに乗りやすい) You *are easily flattered*. / 彼はお調子者だ(→調子に乗って自制を失う) He *easily gets carried away*.

おちょこ お猪口 small sake cup
慣用表現 風がきつくて傘がおちょこになった My umbrella *was blown inside out* by a high wind.

おちょぼぐち おちょぼ口 真希はおちょぼ口をしている Maki has *a cute little mouth*. / その子はおちょぼ口をしてみせた(→唇をすぼめた) The child *puckered* (*up*) *his lips*.

おちる 落ちる

❶【落下する・低い方へ移動する】fall*; (突然) drop
彼女が階段から落ちてけがをした She *fell down* the stairs and got injured.
その少年は足を滑らせて川に落ちてしまった The boy slipped and *fell into* the river.
ニュートンはリンゴが木から落ちるのを見て引力の法則を発見した Newton discovered the law of gravity, watching an apple *fall from* a tree.
ガラスびんが床に落ちて粉々になった The glass bottle *fell* (*down*) *to* the floor and shattered.
◆何か落ちましたよ You *dropped* something. / 冬は日が落ちるのが早い The sun 「*goes down* [*sets*]」 quickly in winter. / 本の重みで棚が落ちた The shelf 「*gave way* [*collapsed*]」 under the weight of the books. / 道にお金が落ちていた I found some money *lying* in the street. / 先日その木に雷が落ちた The tree *was struck* by lightning last month. / 彼の打ったボールは池に落ちた The ball he shot *landed* in the pond. / 雨のしずくが屋根からぽたぽた落ちている Raindrops *are dripping* from the roof.

❷【程度が下がる・衰える】fall*, drop, go* [come*] down
数学の成績が落ちた My math grades *went down*.
今年はデパート各社で売り上げが落ちている Sales *have fallen off* this year in every department store.
◆その選手は20キロ地点を過ぎたころからスピードが落ちてきた The runner began to *drop* [*reduce*] his speed after passing the 20 kilometer mark. / その一件で彼の信用は落ちてしまった That affair *ruined* his reputation. / その歌手は今では人気が落ちた The singer *is no longer popular*. / The singer *has lost his* [*her*] *popularity*. / 彼は以前より記憶力が落ちている He *has a worse memory* than before. / 価格が安いからといって必ずしも品質が落ちるとは限らない Low prices don't necessarily mean that the products *are of low quality*. / 彼が加わるとすぐに話が落ちる(→卑わいな話になる) When he joins in, *the conversation* soon *turns dirty*.

❸【落第する】fail
僕は英検1級の一次試験は通ったが、二次で落ちてしまった I *passed* the first screening of the first-grade STEP test, but *failed in* the second.
弟は自動車の実技試験に2度落ちた My brother *failed* his driving test twice.

❹【取れる】(しみ・汚れなどが) come* off, be removed
シャツのしみはいくら洗っても落ちなかった Though I washed my shirt over and over, the stain *wouldn't come off*.
◆水に落ちにくいマスカラ *waterproof* mascara / ジーパンは洗濯するうちにだんだん色が落ちる The color of the jeans gradually *fades* after washing.

❺【抜ける】(抜けている) be missing, be left out, be omitted
名簿から彼女の名前が落ちていた Her name *was missing* from the list. / Her name *was not on* the list.

❻【最終的にある状態になる】
彼はひとめで彼女と恋に落ちた He *fell in love* with her at first sight.
彼は深い眠りに落ちた He *fell into a* deep *sleep*.
そのシャガールの絵は10万ドルでアメリカ人の手に落ちた(→落札した) The Chagall 「*went to* [*was knocked down to*]」 an American at 100,000 dollars.
慣用表現 彼は問うに落ちず、語るに落ちた(→問いただされても答えなかったのに、思わず自分から本当のことを言ってしまった) Though he *never answered when questioned*, he *let the truth slip* later.

おちんちん《小児語》peter, weenie

おつ 乙 ❶【第2番目】甲と乙(→前者と後者) the former and *the latter*; the one and *the other* / その2チームは甲乙つけがたい好チームだ Those two teams are both good, and *it's hard to decide which one is better*.

❷【しゃれた】おつなことを言いますね That was *well-put*. / *Well-put*! / この料理はおつな

味だ This dish tastes *nice*.

おつかい お使い, errand ⓒ 〃子供を文房具屋までお使いに行かせた I *sent* my child *on an errand* to a stationery shop. / ちょっとお使いに行ってきてくれる? Would you *go on an errand*?

おっかない 家に帰るとお母さんがおっかない顔をして家の前に立っていた When I got home, my mother was standing in front of the house with a *fierce* look.

おっかなびっくり (こわごわ) timidly, gingerly; (びくびくして) nervously 〃私はおっかなびっくりドアをあけた I opened the door *timidly*. / その子はおっかなびっくり寝ている犬のそばを通り過ぎた The child passed by the sleeping dog *nervously*.

おつかれさま お疲れ様

> 日本語の「お疲れさま」に当たる英語の決まったあいさつはない。仕事を終えて帰るときはGoodbye!やSee you tomorrow!という別れのあいさつがそれに当たり、家庭で帰宅した夫や妻に対して言う言葉としては How was your day? などが相当する。

おつき お付き (付き人・世話人) attendant ⓒ; (護衛) escort ⓒ, entourage [ɑ̀ntuːráːʒ] ⓒ (❖entourage は「護衛団」の意味); (側近) aide ⓒ 〃国王とお付きの者たち the King and *his attendants*

おっくう 億劫 疲れるとしゃべるのもおっくうになる(→しゃべる気がしない) I *don't feel like* talking to anyone when I am tired. / 毎日日記をつけるのはおっくうだ(→面倒だ) It's *a lot of trouble* to write in my diary every day.

おつげ お告げ (神託) oracle ⓒ, divine message ⓒ

おっしゃる 何とおっしゃいましたか *I beg your pardon?* / *What did you say?* / おっしゃることは分かりますが、それは無理だと思います I understand what you *say*, but I think it is impossible. / おっしゃるとおりです You're (quite) *right*. / You *said it*.

おっす おっす, 元気? *Hi!* How are you doing? (❖(米)では What's up? をあいさつ代わりに使う)

おっちょこちょい (うっかり者)《口語的》scatterbrain ⓒ 〃政彦はおっちょこちょいでよく計算間違いをする Masahiko is such *a scatterbrain* that he often makes mistakes in calculation.

おって¹ 追って later (on), afterward 〃そのことについては追って連絡します I'll let you know about it *later*.

おって² 追っ手 pursuer ⓒ, chaser ⓒ 〃彼は何とか追っ手をまいた He somehow dodged *his pursuer*. / 彼女は友人を追っ手からかくまってやった She sheltered her friend from *her pursuers*.

おっと¹ 夫 husband ⓒ,《口語的》hubby ⓒ 〃最愛の夫 one's *beloved husband* / 内縁の夫 one's *common-law husband* / 前の夫 one's *ex-husband* / 妻のしりに敷かれた夫 a henpecked *husband* / 彼女にはアメリカ人の夫がいる She has *an* American *husband*. / 彼は彼女にとってよい夫になるでしょう He will make her *a nice husband*.

おっと² oops [úːps]; (驚いたり失敗したときなどに用いる), whoops, oh 〃おっと, 危ない *Oh*, look [watch] *out!* / おっと, もう少しで転ぶところだった *Oops!* I nearly [almost] fell down. / おっと, 失礼 *Oh*, pardon me.

おっとせい (fur) seal ⓒ

おっとり おっとりした(→穏やかな)女性 a *gentle* woman / 彼女はおっとりしている(→のんきだ) She *is very easygoing*. / 彼はいつもおっとりと構えている(→落ち着いている) He always remains *calm*.

おっぱい 赤ちゃんにおっぱいを飲ませる *give* a baby *the breast*; *nurse* a baby / 赤ん坊は母親のおっぱいを飲んでいた The baby was sucking [nursing] at its mother's *breast*. / あの子いいおっぱいしてるな That girl has nice *breasts*.

おつり お釣り change ⓤ 〃おつりはいりません Keep *the change*. / はい, おつりです Here's *the change*. / 30円のおつりです That makes 30 yen *change*. / 5,000円でおつりはありますか Do you have *change* for 5,000 yen?

おてあげ お手上げ 数学はお手上げだ I'm *hopeless* at mathematics. / もうお手上げだ(→どうにもできることは何もない) *There is nothing I can do*. / (→もうどうしようもない) *I can't help it*. / お手上げです(→降参だ)。答えを教えてください *I give up*. Please tell me the answer.

おてあらい お手洗い bathroom ⓒ, toilet ⓒ; (デパート・劇場など) rest room ⓒ 〃すみません, お手洗いはどこですか Excuse me, but where is *the rest room*? / Where can I wash my hands? (❖後の表現は遠回しな言い方) / お手洗いをお借りしていいですか May I use *your bathroom*?

おでかけ お出掛け 今夜はお出かけですか *Are you going out* tonight? / またお出かけください(→来てください) Please *come* again.

おでき 〔医学〕boil ⓒ, (吹き出物) rash ⓒ 〃首の後ろにおできができた I've got *a boil* on the back of my neck.

おでこ forehead [fɔ́ːrəd] ⓒ, brow [bráu] ⓒ (❖brow はまゆまで含むこともある) 〃彼はおでこが広い He has *a broad forehead*. / 父はおでこにしわを寄せた My father wrinkled *his brow*.

おてだま お手玉 (an) *otedama*, (a) beanbag 〃お手玉をして遊ぶ *juggle* (with) *beanbags*

おてつき お手付き あっ, 今お手つきしたでしょう Hey, you just *touched the wrong card*, didn't you?

おてつだいさん お手伝いさん (家政婦) housekeeper ⓒ, helper ⓒ, (house)maid ⓒ

おてのもの お手の物 (長所) one's strong point; (得意な) one's *forte*, one's specialty 〃裁縫はお手の物だ Sewing is *my spe-*

おてもり お手盛り 議員たちはお手盛りの昇給を決めた The members of the Diet decided to raise *their own* salary.

おてやわらかに お手柔らかに どうかお手柔らかに願います (Please) *go easy on* me. / (→厳しくしないでください) (Please) *don't be too hard on* me.

おてん (公式的) stain ⓒ, blot ⓒ, blemish ⓒ; (欠点) flaw ⓒ ∥その事件は彼の経歴に大きな汚点を残した The incident left *a great stain* [*blot*] *on* his career.

おでん

「おでん」は「お田楽」の略称で、現在のおでんになったのは明治時代になってからです。今日(にち)のおでんといえば、しょうゆ味のスープで大根・こんにゃく・ちくわ・卵などを煮込んだ料理のことをいいます。寒い季節になると、コンビニエンスストアや屋台でもよく見かけるようになります。

Oden is an abbreviated form of *odengaku*. It was in the Meiji period (1868-1912) when the *oden* of today came on the scene. In this dish, various ingredients such as *daikon* (radish), *konnyaku* (firm vegetable gelatin), *chikuwa* (fish-paste roll) and eggs are cooked in soy sauce-seasoned broth. As the weather becomes colder, *oden* can easily be found in convenience stores and at stands on street corners.

おてんきや お天気屋 彼はお天気屋だから、また気が変わるかもしれない He may change his mind because he is so *moody*.

おてんば お転婆 tomboy ⓒ ∥子供のころはおてんばでした I was *a tomboy* when I was a child.

おと 音

sound Ⓤ ⓒ; (騒音・雑音) noise Ⓤ ⓒ; (信号音) tone ⓒ

電話の音で目をさました I woke up to *the sound* [*ringing*] of the telephone.

私たちはその音にびっくりした The *sound* startled us.

飛行機が離陸しようとしたとき異常な音を聞いた The plane was about to take off, when I heard *a strange sound*.

食事中に音を立てるのは行儀が悪い It is bad manners to *make noise* at table.

彼女は音を立てないようにゆっくりと階段を上った She went up the stairs slowly so that she *wouldn't make any noise*.

車の音がうるさくて眠れなかった I couldn't go to sleep because of *the noise* of the traffic.

音の速さは1秒に約340メートルだ *Sound* travels about 340 meters a second.

◆ラジオの音を小さくしてください Please *turn down* the radio. / このCDプレーヤー、音が出ないよ This CD player *doesn't work*. / ドアが閉まる音がした I *heard* the door close. / 岩に打ち寄せる波の音が聞こえた I *heard* the wash of waves against the rocks. / オーケストラのメンバーは今音合わせをやっている The members of the orchestra *are* now *tuning* their instruments.

🅔「何か音がしなかった?」「別に何も聞こえなかったけど」"*Didn't* you *hear* something?" "No, I didn't."

俳句 古池や蛙(かわず)飛びこむ水の音(松尾芭蕉)
It's just an old pond.
A frog jumps in. Then it's just
the sound of water.

おとうさん お父さん (父親) father ⓒ; (呼びかけ) Dad, 《小児語》Daddy

語法

家族の間では father を固有名詞のように扱い、書くときは冠詞を付けず大文字で書き始める。他人に父親のことをいう場合は my father を用いる。子供の父親に対する呼びかけで一般的なのは Dad. やや古い言い方には Pa, Papa, Pop などもある。

お父さんはご在宅ですか Is *your father* in?
お父さん、これ見て *Daddy*, look at this.
そうだ、お父さんに聞いてみよう Oh! I'm going to ask *Dad* about it.

おとうと 弟 brother ⓒ

語法

特別の場合を除き、英語では「兄」「弟」を区別せず単に brother という。区別するときは、「兄」は an older [《英》elder] brother または a big brother、「弟」は a younger brother または a little [kid] brother とする。「兄さん」という呼びかけには本人の名前を用いる。

義理の弟 a brother-in-law

(紹介して) 弟です This is *my younger brother*.

僕は弟と部屋をいっしょに使っている I share a room with *my brother*.

彼は私にとって弟のような存在だ He is like *a brother* to me.

おとおし お通し appetizer ⓒ

おどおど おどおどしている be timid [nervous] / その男は人前に出てもおどおどした様子はなかった The boy wasn't *shy or timid* in front of other people.

おどかす 脅かし threat ⓒ 《通例単数形》; menace ⓒ; (脅迫) intimidation Ⓤ, extortion Ⓤ; (恐喝) blackmail Ⓤ ⇨ おどし

おどかす 脅かす (びっくりさせる) frighten ⓗ, 《口語的》scare ⓗ; (急に) startle ⓗ ∥脅かさないでくれ *You scared me!* / 彼は野良猫を脅かして庭から追い払った He *frightened* stray cats *out of* his garden.

おとぎ ∥おとぎの国 a fairyland / おとぎ話 a fairy tale [story]; (子供向けの話) a children's story

おどけ 戯け (ふざけ・戯れ) fun Ⓤ; (冗談) joke ⓒ ∥おどけ者(冗談を言う人) a joker; (道化師) a clown

おどける 戯ける clown (around), play the fool ∥彼は子供たちを笑わせようとおどけてみせた He *played the fool* to make the children laugh. ◆その役者はおどけた演技で人気を集めている The actor is very popular because of his *funny* performance.

おとこ 男
man ⓒ (複 men); guy ⓒ; gentleman ⓒ; male ⓒ; (恋人) boyfriend ⓒ

[語法]
man は成人男性を指す最も一般的な語. guy はくだけた言い方で, gentleman は丁寧に接するときに用いる. male は生物学的な性別を強調し, 口語で人に用いると失礼になることがある.

男と女 *men* and women / 背の高い[低い]男の人 a tall [short] *man*
男らしくしなさい Be *a man*.
彼女はいつも男のような格好をしている She is always dressed *like a man*.
妹に男ができたらしい My sister seems to have *a boyfriend*.
おまえももう一人前の男だ You've grown up to be *a man*.
これは男と男の約束だ This is a promise between one *man* and another.
彼女は男運が悪い She has no luck *with men*.
あいついい男だ He's such *a nice guy*.
◆男の赤ちゃん *a baby boy* / 男の学生[店員] a *male* student [clerk]
🔊「鈴木先生と話してる男の人, だれか知ってる?」「新しい英語の先生だよ」"Do you know who's that *man* talking with Mr. Suzuki?" "He's a new teacher of English."

[慣用表現] ここであきらめたら男がすたる(→面目がつぶれる) I'll *lose face (as a man)* if I give up now. / 男に二言はない *Men shouldn't take back their words.* / 彼は男の中の男だ He is *a man among men.* / 彼はその一件で男を上げた(→評判を上げた) He *earned a good reputation* because of the incident.

[ことわざ] 男は度胸, 女はあいきょう *Bravery is for men, charm for women.*

おとこぎらい 男嫌い 姉は男嫌いだ My sister *hates men*.

おとこごころ 男心 彼女のあどけない笑顔は彼の男心をくすぐった Her innocent smile played on his *male instincts*.

[慣用表現] 男心と秋の空 *A man's heart is as changeable as the autumn sky.* (→男の気持ちは秋の空のように変わりやすい)

おとこざかり 男盛り あの俳優は今男盛りだ That actor *is* now *in the prime of life [manhood]*.

おとこしゃかい 男社会 man's world ⓒ; (男性優位の社会) male-dominated society ⓒ; (男中心の社会) male-oriented world ⓒ / 日本はまだまだ男社会だ Japan is still a *male-dominated society*.

おとこじょたい 男所帯 all-male household ⓒ; (男やもめの) widower's household ⓒ; (独身者の) bachelor's household ⓒ

おとこで 男手 (男の働き手) male help ⓤ; (男の人) man ⓒ / 男手が足りません We don't have enough *male help*.
◆このピアノを運ぶのに男手が必要だ We need *the help of a man* to carry this piano. / 彼は男手ひとつで子供を育てた He raised his children *all by himself*.

おとこともだち 男友達 male friend ⓒ (◆boyfriend はふつう「恋人」の意味)

おとこなき 男泣き 父は親友の死を聞いて男泣きした My father *wept bitterly* to hear his best friend's death.

おとこのこ 男の子 (少年) boy ⓒ (◆通例17, 18歳ごろまでを指す); (男の赤ちゃん) baby boy ⓒ; (息子) son ⓒ; (若い男性) young man ⓒ / 行儀のよい男の子 a well-behaved *boy* / 5歳の男の子 a *boy* of five / その3歳の男の子はもう時計が読める The three-year-old *boy* can already tell time. ◆赤ちゃんは男の子ですか, 女の子ですか Is the baby *he* or *she*?

おとこまえ 男前 handsome [good-looking] man ⓒ ◆彼は頭がよくて男前だ He is smart and *handsome* [*good-looking*].

おとこまさり 男勝り ──男勝りの (男性のような) masculine,《軽蔑的》mannish
◆佐藤さんは男勝りの仕事ぶりだ(→佐藤さんの熱心な仕事ぶりを見るとどんな男も恥じ入る) Every man would *be put to shame* when they see how intensely Ms. Sato works.

おとこもの 男物 (男性用衣料品) menswear ⓤ, men's wear ⓤ ◆男物の時計 a *man's* watch

おとこやく 男役 male part [role] ⓒ / 男役を演じる play *a male part*

おとこやもめ 男やもめ widower ⓒ / 彼は5年前から男やもめだ He has been *a widower* for five years.

おとこらしい 男らしい manly, masculine / 男らしい態度 a *manly* attitude / 彼はハンサムで男らしい人だった He was good-looking and *manly*.
◆男らしくしなさい Be [Act *like*] *a man*. / 彼女は彼の男らしさにすっかり心を奪われた She was quite taken by his *manliness*.

おとさた 音沙汰 その後, 彼女からは何の音さたもない I *haven't heard from* her since then. / 3年間音さたのなかった彼が突然電話をかけてきた He suddenly called me *after three years' silence*.

おどし 脅し threat ⓤⓒ ⇒おどす / 彼は私を殺すと繰り返しおどしをかけてきた He repeated *his threat* to kill me.
◆おどし文句 *threatening words*

おとしあな 落とし穴 pitfall ⓒ; (わな・謀略) trap ⓒ / 落とし穴を掘る dig *a pitfall* / 人に落とし穴を仕掛ける set [lay] *a trap* for a person

おとしいれる 陥れる (わなにかける) trap ⑯, set* [lay*] a trap (for ...); (窮地に追い込む) drive* ⑯, throw* ⑯; (ぬれぎぬを着せる) frame* ⑯ / 人を陥れて契約書にサインさせる *trap* a person *into* signing the contract / その手紙が私を窮地に陥れた That letter *threw* me *into* a real crisis.

おとしご 落とし子 大勢の孤児たちは戦争の落とし子だ A great number of orphans appeared in *the aftermath of the war*.

おとしだま お年玉 (an) *otoshidama*, New Year's gift money, a New Year's (money) gift ‖祖父がお年玉に1万円くれた My grandfather gave me 10,000 yen as *a New Year's gift*.
‖お年玉付き年賀はがき a lottery New Year's card

> お年玉とは新年に両親や親戚(<small>しんせき</small>)、あるいは近所の人から子供たちがもらうお金のことをいいます。*Otoshidama* is New Year's gift money given to children by parents, close relatives or neighbors.

おとしぬし 落とし主 1週間たってもその定期券の落とし主は現れなかった The person who *had lost* the commuter pass didn't show up after a week.

おとしもの 落とし物 lost article ◆落とし物の財布は交番に届けなければならない A *lost* [*found*] wallet should be taken to the police box. / 谷先生、これ落とし物です Ms. Tani, 「I found this [someone lost this].

おとす 落とす

❶ 上から下へ　　drop
❷ なくす　　　　lose
❸ 取り除く　　　get [take] out, remove
❹ 程度を下げる　lower; lose
❺ 落第する　　　fail

❶【上から下へ】drop
ちょっと！財布を落としましたよ Hey! You *dropped* your wallet!
彼女は花びんを落として割ってしまった She *dropped* the vase and broke it.
◆公園の木々はすっかり葉を落としていた The trees in the park *were stripped* bare *of leaves*.

❷【なくす】lose*
電車の中で切符を落としてしまった I've *lost* [*dropped*] my ticket on the train.
1人の警官がその事件で命を落とした A police officer *lost his life* in the incident.
❥「どのへんでコンタクトを落としたのですか」「こ のあたりだと思うんですが」"Whereabouts did you *lose* your contact lens?" "I think it was somewhere around here."

❸【取り除く】get* [take*] out, remove;（洗い落とす）wash out [off]
このカーテンの汚れは落とせますか Can you *get* this dirt *out of* the curtain?
うちに帰ってまずするのは化粧を落とすことです The first thing I do when I get home is to *remove* my makeup.
このシャツの汚れは落とせる You can *wash* this stain *out of* the shirt.
◆車に乗る前に靴の泥を落としなさい *Wipe* the mud *off* your shoes before getting into the car.

❹【程度を下げる】lower;（信頼などを）

lose*
スピードを落とす *lower* the speed / 声を落とす *lower one's voice* / 信用を落とす *lose credit*
夏までに3キロ落としたい I'd like to *lose three kilograms* by summer.
◆照明を落とす *dim* the lights / 彼は交差点でスピードを落とした He *slowed down* at the intersection.

❺【落第する】fail
数学は通ったが英語を落とした I passed (in) math but *failed (in)* English.
試験官は最終試験で受験者の3分の1を落とした The examiners *failed* one third of the examinees on the final exam.

❻【抜かす】leave* out;（見落とす・聞き落とす）miss out
その名簿から彼の名前を落としてしまった I've *left* his name *out of* the list.

❼【その他】
CDからお気に入りの曲をMDに落とした（→ダビングした）I *copied* the songs I like from the CD onto an MD.
気を落とすな Don't *lose heart*! / Don't *be discouraged*.
次の試合を落とすわけにはいかない We can't afford to *lose* the next game.
浩二はその知らせを聞くとがっくり肩を落とした（→落胆した）Koji *got depressed* when he heard the news.
書籍代は必要経費で落とせる（→控除される経費として請求できる）The cost of books *can be claimed* as a deductible expense.
彼はどんな女の子でも落とせるとうそぶいている He boasts that he *can win* any girl's *heart*.

おどす 脅す threaten,《公式的》menace;（怖がらせる）frighten, scare, terrify /彼は彼女を銃でおどした He *threatened* her with a gun. / 彼は殺すぞと言っておどしてきた He *threatened to* kill me. / He *threatened that* he would kill me. / 私は不良にナイフでおどされた I *was menaced* by a delinquent with a knife. / 強盗は彼女をおどして金庫をあけさせた The burglar *scared* her *into* opening the safe.

おとずれ 訪れ 春の訪れは近い Spring *is drawing near*. / Spring *is near* [*close*] *at hand*. / 桜のつぼみは春の訪れを告げる Cherry buds are a signal that spring *is coming*.

おとずれる 訪れる visit;（場所を）call at ...;（人を）call on [in] ...（❖call in は《主に英》）;（到来する）come* /‖義父の招待で、彼は神戸を訪れた At his father-in-law's invitation, he *visited* Kobe. / 帰りに恵子のところ[恵子の家]を訪れた I *called*「*on* Keiko [*at Keiko's house*] on my way home. / そのうちチャンスが訪れるかもしれないからあきらめてはいけない The chance may yet *come*, so you shouldn't give up.

おととい 一昨日 the day before yesterday（❖《米》では副詞的に用いるとき the が省略される）/‖それは私がおととい彼女から聞いたのと同じ

うわさだ It's the same rumor as I heard from her *(the) day before yesterday*. ◆おとい来やがれ! *Never come here again!*

おととし 一昨年 the year before last
◆その協定はおととし廃止された The agreement was voided *two years ago*.

おとな 大人
adult ©(❖一般に, 《米》では21歳以上, 《英》では18歳以上を指す)(→child); grown-up ©(❖子供が大人を指しているの場合が多い); (男の) man ©(複 men); (女の) woman ©(複 women) (→an adult, grown-up
大人1枚, 子供2枚ください One *adult* (ticket) and two children, please.
大人の言うことがいつも正しいとは限らない What *adults* say is not always right.
私はもう子供じゃない, 大人だ I'm not a boy [girl] but *a man* [*woman*]!
息子はようやく大人の味が分かるようになってきた My son has finally started to enjoy *adult food*.
◆もっと大人になりなさい *Grow up!* / その少女は時折大人びた表情を見せる The girl sometimes looks quite *womanly*.
🄲「大人になったら何になりたい」「サッカー選手になりたい」"What do you want to be when you *grow up*?" "I want to be a soccer player."

おとなげない 大人気ない (子供っぽい) childish /大人げないことをする[言う] Don't be *childish*./ (→年相応にふるまえ) Act your age.
◆彼があんなに大人げないとは思っていなかった (→もっと分別のある年だと思っていた) I thought he was old enough to know better.

おとなしい (温和な・落ち着いた) gentle, mild, quiet; (従順な) obedient; (行儀がよい) well-behaved; (動物が人になれた) tame; (色・柄が落ち着いた) quiet, plain ― おとなしく obediently; quietly //彼は生まれつきおとなしい He *is gentle* by nature. / 彼らは子供たちがおとなしくしているように気をつけていた They were trying to keep their children *quiet*. / エレン, おとなしく待っててね Ellen, wait for me *quietly*. / 怖がらないで, この犬はおとなしいから Don't be afraid. This dog *is tame*.
◆おとなしくしなさい (→いい子にしろ) Be *a good boy* [*girl*]. / (→静かにしろ) Be *quiet*! / その女の子は家ではおとなしい (→行儀がよい) The girl *behaves well* at home.

おとなっぽい 大人っぽい, 大人っぽくふるまう act *in a grown-up way* / 彼女はいつも大人っぽい格好をしている She is always dressed *in a mature way*.

おとめ 乙女 (young) girl ©, 《文語》maiden ©, 《文語》virgin ©
◆あなたは乙女心が分かっていない You don't understand *how young girls feel*.

おとめざ 乙女座 【天文・占星】Virgo ♉(❖「乙女座の人」の意味では ©), the Virgin

おとも お供 (付き人・世話人) attendant ©

―お供する accompany ⓿, come* with ..., go* with ... //おばの海外旅行に私がお供することになった I'm going to *accompany* my aunt on a trip abroad.
🄲「私もお供していいですか」「もちろんです」"May I *come with* you?" "No problem at all."

おとり decoy ©; (誘い寄せるもの) bait Ⓤ(《またa ～》, lure ©/…をおとりに使う use ... as *a decoy* / おとりに引っかかる(→えさに食いつく) rise to *the bait*
∥おとり捜査 a sting (operation)

おどり 踊り dance ©; (踊ること) dancing Ⓤ/彼女は毎週金曜日に踊りを習っている She takes *dance* [*dancing*] lessons every Friday. / 彼は踊りがうまい He is good at *dancing*. / 踊りに行こう Let's go *dancing*. (❖×go for dancing とはいわない)

おどりあがる 躍り上がる jump ⓿, leap* ⓿/彼はその知らせを聞くとおどり上がって喜んだ He *jumped* [*leaped*] *for joy* when he heard the news.

おどりぐい 踊り食い 🍱 *odorigui*, eating small fish alive

おどりこ 踊り子 dancer ©

おどりでる 躍り出る 壇上におどり出る(→突然現れる) *appear suddenly* on the stage / ひのき舞台におどり出る(→脚光を浴びる) *burst into the spotlight* [*limelight*] / 幹男はついにレースの先頭におどり出た Mikio finally *gained* [*took*] *the lead* in the race.

おどりば 踊り場 (階段の) landing ©

おとる 劣る be inferior
彼の英語の語彙(ご)力は彼女よりかなり劣っている His English vocabulary *is* much *inferior to* hers.
このグラスは質の点ではそちらのより劣る This glass *is* 「*inferior* in quality *to* that one [*worse* in quality *than* that one].
◆彼は母親に劣らず(→と同じくらい)絵がうまい He is *as* good at painting *as* his mother. / 彼女は自分の兄に勝るとも劣らず勇気がある She is *not less brave than* her elder brother. / 彼女は数学ではクラスのだれにも劣らない She *is second to none* in math in her class.

おどる¹ 踊る
❶【踊りをする】 dance ⓿ ⓿
音楽に合わせて踊る *dance to* the music / 2人一組になって踊る *dance in pairs* / バレエを踊る *dance* ballet / ワルツを踊る *dance* the waltz; waltz
僕と踊っていただけますか Will you *dance* with me?
❷【操られて行動する】
彼はあの男に踊らされている(→あの男が彼を思いのままに操っている) That man *has* [*keeps*] him *on a string*.

おどる² 躍る 私たちは胸をおどらせてトムを待った We waited for Tom *with our hearts thumping*. / 久しぶりに彼女に会えると思うと心がおどる My heart *leaps* at the thought of seeing her for the first time in a long

おとろえ

おとろえ 衰え decline ⓊUNKNOWN《また a ~》 ∥体力の衰え decline in one's strength / その産業は衰えを見せる一方だ The industry is in terminal *decline*.
◆最近記憶力の衰えが激しい Recently his memory *has begun to fail rapidly*.

おとろえる 衰える get* [become*] weak, weaken ⓘ; (健康などが) fail ⓘ; (風などが) die down; (衰弱する・低下する) decline ⓘ
最近父は体力がめっきり衰えた Recently my father *has gotten weak* considerably.
彼女は視力が衰えてきている Her eyesight *is failing [going]*.
台風の勢力は衰えてきている The typhoon *is dying down*.
彼は人気が衰えてきている His popularity *is declining* [*on the decline*]. / He *is losing* popularity.
◆火の勢いは一向に衰えなかった The fire *showed no signs of abating*.

おどろかす 驚かす (びっくりさせる) surprise ⓘ, astonish ⓘ, amaze ⓘ; (怖がらせる) scare ⓘ, frighten ⓘ; (衝撃を与える) shock ⓘ ∥君にはいつも驚かされる You always *surprise* me. / 暗やみで圭介を驚かせた I *scared* Keisuke in the dark. / 巨大なコンサートホールを作るという市長の計画はみんなを驚かせた The mayor's plan to build a huge concert hall *shocked* everyone.

おどろき 驚き surprise Ⓤ, astonishment Ⓤ; (精神的な打撃) shock Ⓤ; (驚嘆) wonder Ⓤ, amazement Ⓤ (✤具体的な「驚くべきこと」の意味ではいずれも Ⓒ) ∥驚きの表情が彼の顔に浮かんだ A look of *surprise* [A *surprised* expression] passed over his face. / その災害で死者が出なかったとは驚きだ It is「a wonder [*surprising*, *amazing*]」that nobody was killed in the disaster.

おどろく 驚く

be surprised; (びっくり仰天する) be amazed, be astonished; (不思議に思う) wonder ⓘ ⓘ (✤進行形にはできない)

【語法】
surprise, amaze, astonish は「物・事」を主語にして「…が〜を驚かせる」と能動態でも表せる ∥ 彼はその事件に驚いた He *was surprised at [by]* the event. (→その事件は彼を驚かせた) The event *surprised* him.

【be surprised+at [by] 名】私たちはその結果に驚いた We *were surprised at [by]* the result.

【be surprised+to *do*】彼女は彼が絵のコンテストで1位になったと知って驚いた She *was surprised to* know he had won (the) first prize in the contest with his painting.

【be surprised+that 節】私は彼が来なかったことに驚いてはいない I'm not surprised *that* he didn't come.
これまでの人生でこんなに驚いたことはない I've *never been* so *surprised* in my life.
彼女につきあっている人がいるからって何も驚くことはない That she has a boyfriend is *nothing to be surprised about*.
私は彼女の突然の転校に(→彼女が突然転校したことに)驚いた I *was amazed that* she changed her school abruptly.
彼が環境問題に無関心なのには驚いた I *wondered at* his indifference to the environmental problems.
◆驚くほどたくさんの人々 an *amazing* number of people / 最近の携帯電話は驚くほど機能が充実している Cell phones these days have an *amazingly* wide choice of functions. / 驚いたことに,だれもその問題を解けなかった To my surprise [*Surprisingly*], no one could solve the problem. / 私は驚いて振り返った I looked back *in surprise*.

💬 「やあ,裕美.久しぶりだね」「あ,驚いた! いつ坊主頭にしたの」"Hi, Yumi. Long time no see." "*Oh, my God*! When did you have your head shaved?"

おどろくべき 驚くべき (意外な) surprising, astonishing; (驚嘆すべき) amazing, marvelous; (目をみはる) remarkable ∥驚くべきペースで at an *astonishing* rate / 科学の驚くべき進歩 *remarkable* advances in science / 日本は戦後驚くべき発展をとげた Japan made *surprising* progress after the war.
◆彼は驚くべき音楽の才能を発揮し始めた He began to show *remarkable* ability in music.

おないどし 同い年 君と僕は同い年です You and I [me] are *the same age*. / You are *as old as* I (am). / You are the same age as I (am). (✤口語ではI (am) の代わりに me を用いることが多い)

おなか stomach Ⓒ, 《口語的》 belly Ⓒ ∥空腹でおなかが鳴っている My *stomach* is growling with hunger. / おなかが痛い My *stomach* aches. / I have a pain *in my stomach*. / I have a stomachache. / おなかのぐあいがよくない I have an upset *stomach*. / I feel sick to *my stomach*.
◆おなかがすいた I'm hungry. / もうおなかいっぱいだ I'm full now. / I've had enough.

おながざる 尾長猿 〖動物〗guenon Ⓒ

おながれ お流れ 雨で きょうの試合はお流れになった Today's game *was called off* because of rain.

おなさけ お情け 先生のお情けで何とか卒業できた My teacher felt *sympathy* for me, so I was able to graduate.

おなじ 同じ

❶【同一の・同様の】the same; (全く同じ) identical
アパートの同じ階 *the same* story of the apartment building
私たちは同じ学校に通っていて,同じクラスです We go to *the same* school and are in *the same* class.
私は彼女と誕生日が同じだ My birthday is *the*

same as hers.

私はあなたのと[あなたが買ったのと]同じ辞書を買いました I bought *the same* dictionary *as yours [that you did]*.

これは数年前私たちが泊まったのと同じ部屋だ This is *the same* [*identical*] room (that) we stayed in several years ago.

私にはこの2つの歌は同じに聞こえる To me the two songs sound *the same* [*identical*].

この問題についての私の考えは彼女と同じだ My view on this problem *is identical to* hers.

◆こんなマニュアルあってもなくても同じだ This manual *doesn't make any difference.* /

これらの犬はみな同じ種類です These dogs are all *of a kind.* / 同じような話を聞いたことがある I've heard *similar* stories. / 同じ英語でもオーストラリア英語はアメリカ英語とずいぶん違う *Although they are both English*, Australian English is quite different from American English.

🍎「コーヒーをお願いします」「私も同じ」 "Coffee, please." "*Same* here."

❷【数・量・程度など】 the same, equal

私たちのクラスの男子の数は女子の数と同じだ The number of boys in our class is *the same as* that of girls.

その2つの時計は値段が同じだった Those two watches were *the same* price.

この木はあの木と同じ樹齢だ This tree is *the same* age *as* that one.

その2つの箱は重さがほぼ同じだ The two boxes *are* roughly *equal* in weight.

正方形は4つの同じ長さの辺をもつ A square has four *equal* sides.

❸【同じように・同じく】 (同程度に) equally; (同様に) likewise; (〜と同じくらい…) as … as 〜; (〜だけでなく…もまた) … as well as 〜; (…もまた) … as well

2人の女の子は同じくらい背が高い The two girls are *equally* tall.

山田先生は私たちに同じようにするよう言った Ms. Yamada told us to do *likewise*.

私は彼と同じくらい多くの本を持っている I have *as* many books *as* he (does). (❖×I have books as many as he. とはいわない)

この山は富士山と同じくらいの高さがある This mountain is (*as*) high *as* Mt. Fuji (is).

デビッドはキャシーと同じくらい日本語がうまい David can speak Japanese *as well as* Cathy (does).

彼は英語を上手に話すが, 私だって同じくらい(上手に)話せる He speaks English well, and I speak it just *as well*.

❹【どうせ】

同じ買うなら高性能のパソコンを買いたい I want to buy a high-performance PC *if* I buy one.

ことわざ 同じ穴のむじな They are badgers living in the same den.; They are birds of a feather. (→同じ羽をした鳥に)

おなじく 同じく 彼女は娘たちと同じくらい活動的だ She is *no less* active *than* her daughters.

🍎「僕はこの映画はいいと思わないな」「同じく(いいと思わない)」 "I don't think this is a good movie." "*Me neither*."

おなじみ お馴染み 〔おなじみの〕 familiar, well-known /おなじみの顔 *familiar* faces / おなじみのメロディーが耳にとまった A *familiar* tune met my ear.

オナニー ⚠masturbation Ⓤ (❖日本語はドイツ語の Onanie から) ◆オナニーをする *masturbate*

おなら (米)gas Ⓤ, (英)wind Ⓤ, (卑語)fart Ⓒ /おならをする *pass gas*; *break wind*; *fart*

おに 鬼 (童話・民話などの) ogre Ⓒ; (悪魔・悪霊) demon Ⓒ, devil Ⓒ, fiend Ⓒ; (鬼ごっこの鬼) it Ⓤ

仕事の鬼 a *demon* for work / サッカーの鬼 a soccer *fiend*

桃太郎は鬼退治に鬼が島へ行きました Momotaro went to Onigashima to wipe *the ogres* out.

(鬼ごっこで)僕が最初に鬼になるよ I'll be *it* first.

◆鬼コーチのしごきに耐える endure the training of *a tough coach* / 鬼は外, 福は内! *Bad luck out, good luck in!*

🍎「鬼はだれ」「僕だよ」 "Who's *it*?" "I am."

慣用表現 彼は鬼の首でも取ったかのように(→勝ち誇って)間違いを指摘した He pointed out some mistakes *triumphantly* [*in triumph*]. / 私は心を鬼にして彼の頼みを断った I *hardened my heart* and declined his request.

ことわざ 彼はいい体格をしているから練習すれば鬼に金棒だ He has a good build, and practice will double his advantage. (❖*double one's advantage* は「…の優位を倍増する」の意味) / 鬼のいぬ間の洗濯 When [While] the cat is away, the mice will play. (→猫がいないとネズミが遊ぶ) / あの山田がかぜで休んだとは, まさに鬼のかく乱だ That Yamada is absent because of a cold. So he's *mortal* after all. (❖*be mortal after all* は「結局不死身ではない」の意味) / 鬼の目にも涙 Even a cold-hearted person can sometimes be moved to tears. (→冷たい人でさえ時には感動して涙を流すことがある) / 来年のことを言うと鬼が笑う ➾ らいねん / 渡る世間に鬼はない ➾ わたる(渡る)

オニオン onion Ⓒ /オニオンスープ onion soup

おにぎり お握り

おにぎりはごはんを三角, 丸, または俵形に手で握ったものです. 中には梅干し・おかか・サケなどを詰め, 最後にのりで巻きます. 最近ではてんぷらや肉, または野菜が入ったおにぎりも人気があります. ひと昔前まではおにぎりは家庭で作るものでしたが, 今ではコンビニエンスストアなどで手軽に買えるようになりました.

Onigiri are rice balls made by hand in triangular, round or cylindrical shapes. They are stuffed with foods like pickled plums, dried shaved bonito or broiled salmon and then wrapped in *nori*. Now, *onigiri* with ingredients such as tempura, meat, or vegetables are also popular. In the past *onigiri* were made at home, but now it is possible to buy them anywhere — at convenience stores for example.

おにごっこ 鬼ごっこ tag ◻ ∥鬼ごっこをする play *tag*

おにもつ お荷物 みんなのお荷物になりたくない I don't want to be *a burden* to everyone.

おね 尾根 ridge ◻ ∥尾根づたいに along *the ridge*

おねがい お願い, request ◻, wish ◻ ⇒ ねがい ◆お願いがあるのですが May I ask a favor (of you)? / May I ask you a favor? / 一生のお願い(→二度と何かをお願いしたりしません). 友達と旅行に行かせて Please let me go on a trip with my friends. *I'll never ask you for anything again*!

💬「手伝いましょうか」「すみません, お願いします」 "Would you like some help?" "Oh, *please*. Thank you."

おねしょ bed(-)wetting ◻ ─おねしょする wet *the [one's] bed*

おの 斧, 《主に英》axe ◻; (手おの) hatchet ◻

おのおの 各々・各 ◻ each ∥生徒はおのおの自分のリコーダーを持っています *Each* student has their [his] own recorder. (❖each は単数扱い. 代名詞で受けるときは his を用いるのがふつうだったが, 最近は their を用いることが多い) ∥おのおのが1つずつリンゴをもらった We were *each* given an apple.

◆どの国民にもおのおのの性格がある Every nation has its *own* character.

おのずから 自ずから (自然に) naturally ◆彼の行動がおのずから物語っている His action speaks *for itself*. / 心配しなくてもそれはおのずから解決します Don't worry. That will work *itself* out.

おのぼりさん お上りさん (いなかからの観光客) rustic tourist ◻; (いなか者) (country) bumpkin ◻

おのれ 己 oneself ∥己を知る know *oneself* / 己に克(ﾖ)つ(→自制する) control *oneself* / 己に忠実であることは人生において大切なことだ Being true to *oneself* is important in life.

おば 伯母・叔母 aunt ◻
彼女は母方のおばです She is *my aunt* on my mother's side.
僕にはドイツに住むおばがいる I have *an aunt* living in Germany.

おばあさん¹ お祖母さん grandmother ◻, 《口語的》 grandma ◻, granny, grannie ◻ (❖「おばあちゃん」というニュアンスの語)
母方[父方]のおばあさん *one's* maternal [paternal] *grandmother*
彼のおばあさんは還暦を迎えた His *grandmother* has reached the age of 60.
おばあさん, 肩もんであげようか Shall I massage your shoulders, *Grandma*?

おばあさん² お婆さん (年をとった女性) old woman [lady] ◻; (呼びかけ) Ma'am

オパール opal ◻

オハイオ Ohio (❖米国北東部の州;《略語》O., 〔郵便〕OH)

おばけ お化け (幽霊) ghost ◻, spirit ◻; (怪物) monster ◻ ⇒ 場面・状況別会話 p.1722 ∥子供たちはハロウィーンの日にお化けに変装した On Halloween the children dressed up as *monsters*. ◆お化けかぼちゃ a *monstrous* [《米口語的》 humongous] pumpkin / そのホテルにはお化けが出るらしい The hotel is said to *be haunted*.
∥お化け屋敷 a haunted house

おはこ 十八番 (得意・専門)《米》specialty,《英》speciality ◻ ∥イタリア料理が私のおはこだ Italian cooking is my *specialty*.

おばさん (おば) aunt ◻; (中年の女性) lady ◻, woman ◻ (複 women); (呼びかけ) madam, ma'am ◆おば ∥掃除のおばさん *a cleaning lady [woman]* / 雅子おばさんは大阪に住んでいる *Aunt Masako* lives in Osaka.

◆鈴木のおばさん *Mrs. Suzuki*

おはじき お弾き 🖼 *ohajiki*, small discs used in a children's game similar to marbles (❖英米にもおはじきに似たビー玉遊び(*marbles*)がある)

おはな お花 (華道・生け花) flower arranging [arrangement] ◻

おばな 雄花 〔植物〕 male flower ◻

おはなばたけ お花畑 a field of flowers

おはよう お早う Good morning. (❖午前中のあいさつ. 口語では単に Morning. ともいう)

> 語法
> (1) Good morning. は夜中の0時から正午まで使う. そのため, 時刻によっては日本語の「こんにちは」に当たることもある.
> (2) Good morning. の後にふつう相手の名前を言う.
> (3) 親しい間柄では Hello. や Hi. を用いることが多い. Hello. や Hi. は一日中, 時間に関係なく使える.

💬「金子先生, おはようございます」「おはよう, 知子」 "*Good morning*, Mrs. Kaneko." "*Good morning*, Tomoko."

おはらい お祓い 🖼

おはらいとは, 一般的に神社で行う厄(ﾔｸ)払い, また邪悪なものや悪霊, 不浄を清めることを指します. 特に多くの災難に見舞われるとされる厄年(ﾔｸどし)には多くの人が神社で厄をはらってもらいます. また葬式から帰ると, 玄関先あるいは直接体に塩をひとつまみ振りかけて清める習慣があります. さらに, 店の入り口に塩を置いて厄よけをすることもあります.
Oharai is the exorcism, usually held at shrines, or purification of vicious spirits, bad luck and uncleanliness. Especially during *yakudoshi* (critical or unlucky years when one is supposed to be exposed to many misfortunes), many people get purified at shrines. Another kind of *oharai* is the custom

of sprinkling a pinch of salt over the doorstep of the house or over yourself when you come back from a funeral. Some people put salt in front of the entrance to their business to keep out misfortune.

おはらいばこ お払い箱 彼は勤務態度が悪かったのでお払い箱になった They *gave* him *the ax* [*boot*] for his bad attitude toward work. (◆give a person the ax [boot]は「人を解雇する」という意味の口語的な表現)

おび 帯 (和服の) an *obi*, a broad sash around the waist of a kimono; (ベルト) belt ⓒ; (飾り帯) sash ⓒ; (書籍の) narrow book wrapper ‖帯を締める tie [fasten] an *obi* / 帯を解く undo [untie] an *obi* ‖帯留め an *obi* clip [fastener] / 黒帯 (柔道などの) a black belt

ことわざ 帯に短したすきに長し The cloth is too short for an *obi* and too long for a sash.; It's good for neither one nor the other. (→一方にも他方にも役に立たない)

おびえる 脅える be frightened, be scared ‖その子はトラのほえる声におびえた The child *was frightened by* [*at*] the tiger's roar.
◆おびえた表情 a *scared* look / 暴力におびえながら暮らす live *under threat* of violence / 彼はおびえている子供をぎゅっと抱きしめた He hugged the *frightened* child to him.

おびきだす おびき出す lure away ‖犯人を隠れ家からおびき出す *lure* a criminal *away* from a hideout

おびきよせる おびき寄せる lure ⓣ ‖敵をわなにおびき寄せる *lure* an enemy *into* a trap

おびただしい 路上にはおびただしい数の人がいた There was a *large* crowd of people on the street. / 毎年、交通事故でおびただしい数の犠牲者が出る A *large number of* people are killed in traffic accidents every year.

おひつじざ 牡羊座〖天文・占星〗Aries ⓤ (◆「牡羊座の人」の意味では ⓒ)

おひとよし お人好し (だまされやすい人)〘口語的〙sucker ⓒ ――お人よしの good-natured; (だまされやすい) simple, gullible ‖彼はお人よしだ He is a *good-natured* person. / (→簡単にだまされる) He *is easily cheated*. / 彼は彼女の言うことを全部信じてしまうほどのお人よしだ He's *simple* enough to believe everything she says.

おひなさま お雛様 [△] (*hina*) doll ⓒ, Girls' Festival doll ⓒ

オピニオンリーダー opinion leader

おびふう 帯封 wrapper

おびやかす 脅かす (おどす) threaten ⓣ,〘公式的〙menace ⓣ; (驚かす) frighten ⓣ ‖核兵器は人類の平和を脅かしている Nuclear weapons *are threatening* human beings' peace.

おひゃくど お百度 私は許しを請うために彼のところへお百度を踏んだ (→何度も何度も訪ねた) I *visited* him *over and over* (*again*) to ask his pardon.
‖お百度参り *ohyakudomairi*, walking back and forth in front of a shrine or a temple 100 times in prayer

おひらき お開き 会合をお開きにする *break up* a meeting / 会は11時でお開きになった The party *broke up* at 11.

おびる 帯びる ❶【含む】赤みを帯びた葉 a *reddish* leaf / 丸みを帯びた形状 a *rounded* form / 哀愁を帯びた曲 a *sorrowful* tune / 酒気帯び運転 driving *under the influence of alcohol* / 彼のノーベル賞受賞が現実味を帯びてきた His winning of a Nobel prize *is becoming a reality*.
❷【任務などを受ける】その使節団は重要な任務を帯びていた The delegation *was charged with* an important mission.

おひれ 尾ひれ タブロイド紙は事実に尾ひれをつける (→大げさに言う) 傾向がある Tabloid papers tend to *exaggerate* the fact.

オフ CDプレーヤーのスイッチをオフにする turn [switch] the CD player *off*
‖シーズンオフ the *off-season*

オフィシャル (公式の) official ‖オフィシャルゲーム an official game / オフィシャルルール an official rule / オフィシャルレコード an official record

オフィス (事務所) office ⓒ ‖オフィスオートメーション office automation / オフィス街 a business area / オフィスビル《米》an office building,《英》an office block

オフェンス (攻撃) offense,《英》offence ⓤ

おふくろ mother ⓒ,《米口語的》mom,《英口語的》mum ⓒ ‖おふくろの味が恋しい I miss *my mother's cooking*. / うちはおふくろが厳しくて *Our mother* is strict with us.

オブザーバー (傍聴者) observer ⓒ ‖その会議でのオブザーバー *an observer* at the conference

オフサイド〖スポーツ〗offside ⓤ ◆オフサイドの反則をする be *offside*

おぶさる 負ぶさる (背負われる) be carried on *a person's* back ◆女の子は母親の背中に負ぶさって泣いていた The little girl was crying *on* her mother's *back*.

オフシーズン the off-season ――オフシーズンで[に] off-season, out of season

オブジェ objet d'art [ɔːbʒei dάːr] ⓒ (複 objets d'art) (◆フランス語から)

オプション option ⓒ ――オプションの optional ‖ほかにはどんなオプションがありますか What are other *options*? / サンルーフはオプションです A sunroof is *an option* [*optional*].
関連語 オプショナルツアー an optional tour

おふせ お布施 offering ⓒ

オフセット ‖オフセット印刷 offset (printing)

おぶつ 汚物 filth ⓤ, 〘口語的〙muck ⓤ; (排泄(⤴)物) excrement ⓤ ‖汚物入れ (トイレの) a sanitary container

オプティミズム (楽天主義) optimism ⓤ

オブラート △ a digestible wrapper for

オフライン

medications or sweets(💠 日本語はオランダ語の oblaat から)

オフライン【コンピュータ】off(-)line ‖オフライン処理 off-line processing / オフラインミーティング an off-line meeting

おふる お古 hand-me-downs ‖兄のお古を着る wear one's brother's *hand-me-downs* ◆お古のギター a *hand-me-down* guitar

オフレコ ⚠ ──オフレコの(記録にとどめないい) off the record, off-the-record ‖オフレコの発言 an *off-the-record* remark

オフロード ──オフロードの off-road ‖オフロード用の車 an *off-road* vehicle ◆オフロードバイク a dirt bike

おべっか flattery Ⓤ ──おべっかを使う flatter 働他, 《口語的》butter up, suck up to *a person* ‖彼はいつも上司におべっかを使っている He *is* always *flattering* [*buttering up, sucking up to*] his boss.
‖おべっか使い a flatterer

オペック OPEC [óupek] (💠 *Organization of Petroleum Exporting Countries* (石油輸出国機構)の略語)

オペラ (歌劇) opera ⒸⓊ ‖オペラ歌手 an opera singer / オペラグラス opera glasses

オペレーションセンター operation center [《英》centre] Ⓒ

オペレーター (機械・バスなどの) operator Ⓒ; (コンピュータの) keyboarder Ⓒ, computer operator Ⓒ

オペレッタ (軽歌劇) operetta ⒸⓊ

おべんちゃら flattery Ⓤ ➡ おせじ

おぼえ 覚え
❶【記憶・経験】
(…にとって)見覚え[聞き覚え]がある look [sound] familiar (to …)
先月のいつだったか彼に会った覚えがある I *remember* seeing him sometime last month.
この歌に聞き覚えはありますか Do you *recognize* this song?
君にそんなことを言われる覚えはない(→君にそんなことを言う権利はない) You have no right to say such a thing to me.
彼はわいろとは身に覚えがない(→関係ない)と言い切った He asserted that he *had nothing to do with* the bribe.

> **英作文ノート** 過去は ～ing, 未来は to 不定詞
> 私は以前どこかで彼女に会った覚えがある
> →×I *remember* to see her somewhere before.
> →○I *remember* seeing her somewhere before.
> ★〈remember＋動名詞〉は「…したことを覚えている」,〈remember＋to 不定詞〉は「これから…することを覚えている」の意味になる.

❷【記憶力・習得】
彼女はもの覚えが遅い[早い] She *is* a slow [quick] *learner*.
人の顔に関しては覚えがいい[悪い] I *have* a good [bad] *memory* for faces.
❸【自信】

彼は将棋なら腕に覚えがある He *is confident of his skill* in *shogi*.

おぼえがき 覚え書き (メモ) note Ⓒ; (外交上の) memorandum Ⓒ (複 ～s, memoranda)

おぼえる　覚える

❶【記憶する】(暗記する) memorize 働他, learn* … by heart; (覚えている) remember 働他 自 (💠 通例進行形にはできない); (心に留めておくよう) bear* [keep*] … in mind
英単語を覚える *memorize* English words; *learn* English words *by heart*
彼の電話番号を忘れてしまった. 覚えてる？ I've forgotten his phone number. Do you *remember* it?
【remember＋doing】ここで遊んだこと覚えてるかい Do you *remember playing* here?
【remember＋that節】彼女とは以前どこかで会ったのを覚えている I *remember that* I met her somewhere before.
この教訓を覚えておきなさい Bear [Keep] this lesson *in mind*.
覚えてろよ! *I'll remember this!* (💠 英語では「(自分が)覚えておくからな」という)
◆私は名前を覚えるのが苦手です I *have a poor memory for* names.
❷【習得する】learn* 働他
弟はもう九九を覚えた My brother *has already learned* his multiplication tables.
彼女はコンピュータの使い方を覚えたがっている She is eager to *learn* how to use the computer.
🅒「いつ英語を覚えたのですか」「ロンドンで暮らしていたときです」"When did you *learn* English?" "(I picked it up) when I lived in London."
❸【感じる】feel* 自
突然空腹を覚えた I suddenly *felt* hungry.
◆厳しい自然に生きる動物たちの姿に感動を覚えた I *was moved* [*impressed*] *by* the animals surviving in severe natural conditions.

オホーツクかい オホーツク海 the Sea of Okhotsk [oukátsk]

おぼしい 思しい 私は犯人とおぼしき男を見た I saw a man who *seemed* [*appeared*] *to be* the criminal. (💠 appear は主に視覚による判断を示す. seem は五感のいずれでもよい)

おぼつかない ❶【疑わしい】doubtful, uncertain ‖その計画が実行されるかどうかおぼつかない It *is doubtful* whether the plan will be carried out. ‖彼の成功はおぼつかないと思う I see *little hope* of his success.
❷【頼りない】unsteady ‖彼は2週間前に退院はしたがまだ足元がおぼつかない He left the hospital two weeks ago, but *is still unsteady* on his feet.
◆酔っ払った男性がおぼつかない足取りで通りを横切った A drunken man *staggered* [*walked unsteadily*] across the street.

おぼっちゃん お坊ちゃん ➡ ぼっちゃん

おぼれる 溺れる
❶【水中で】(おぼれて死ぬ) drown 自, drowned; (おぼれて死にそうになる) nearly

[almost] drown, be nearly [almost] drowned

日本語の「おぼれる」は必ずしも「死ぬ」ことを意味しないが，英語のdrown, be drownedは「おぼれて死ぬ」ことを意味する // 私は海でおぼれたが，監視員に助けられた I *nearly [almost] drowned*, but was saved by a lifeguard. (❖ ×I drowned in the sea, but … とはいわない)

おぼれている人 a *drowning* man / おぼれて死んだ人 a *drowned* man

見ろ！ 子供がおぼれているぞ！ Look! A kid *is drowning*.

彼女はもう少しでおぼれて死ぬところだった She came near (to) *drowning*.

その犬は子供がおぼれているところを助けた The dog saved a child from *drowning*.

❷【夢中になる】(ふける) indulge in …; (癖(s)がつく) take* to …

彼は酒におぼれている He *indulges in* drinking.

ことわざ おぼれる者はわらをもつかむ A drowning man will catch [clutch] at a straw.

おぼろげ 朧気 — **おぼろげな** dim, vague // おぼろげな記憶 a *dim* memory ◆遠くに島がおぼろげに見える I can see an island *vaguely* in the distance. / あの男の子のことはおぼろげに覚えています I 「*dimly* remember [have a *dim* memory of] that boy.

おぼろづき 朧月 hazy [misty, pale] moon C

おぼん お盆 🗾 the Bon festival ⇨ ぼん²

おまいり お参り 神社にお参りする *visit* a shrine *and pray*

おまえ お前 you ⇨ あなた

おまけ (景品) giveaway C, 《主に米・口語的に》 freebie C, free gift C; (割引) discount C U // 少しおまけしてくれませんか Can you give [do, allow] me a little *discount*, please?

◆これ，おまけ（→ただ）です This is *for nothing*. / 今予約するとホテルでのフリードリンクがおまけにつきます If you book now, a free drink at the hotel *will be thrown in*.

おまけに what is more, besides, moreover; (さらに悪いことに) what is worse, to make matters worse // 彼はハンサムでおまけに性格がよい He's handsome, *(and) what's more*, he's good-natured. / そんな遅い時間に出かけるわけにはいかないし，おまけにきょうは娘が病気なのです I can't go out at such a late hour. *Besides*, my daughter is sick today. / 道に迷い，おまけに日も暮れてきていた We got lost *and 「what was worse [to make matters worse]*, it was getting dark.

おませ 姉はおませな子供だった My sister was a *precocious* child. / 子供のときたいがい女の子のほうが男の子よりおませだ Generally, girls are more *grown-up* than boys at an early age.

おまちどおさま お待ちどおさま お待ちどおさまでした(→待たせてすみません) I'm sorry to have kept you waiting. / (→物を差し出して) Here you are.

おまつりきぶん お祭り気分 年末年始はお祭り気分で勉強に身が入らなかった I was in *a festive mood* around New Year's, so I didn't feel like studying.

おまつりさわぎ お祭り騒ぎ festivities, 《文語》merrymaking U ◆彼がオリンピックで金メダルを取って地元はお祭り騒ぎだった When he got a gold medal in the Olympics, his hometown *was filled with excitement*.

おまもり お守り charm C, amulet C, talisman C // 入試合格祈願のお守り a *good-luck charm* for entrance exams / お守りを身につける wear *a charm*

おまる (病人用) bedpan C; (幼児用) potty C

おまわりさん お巡りさん police officer C; (男の) policeman C; (女の) policewoman C; (呼びかけ) officer C // すみません，お巡りさん，どこへ行けばタクシーがつかまりますか Excuse me, *officer*, where can I get a taxi?

おみくじ お神籤 🗾

多くの神社や寺では，くじを引いて運勢を占うことができますが，これをおみくじといいます。細長い紙切れに，全体運のほか結婚・学業・旅行などいろいろなことについての短いアドバイスが書かれています。凶が出たときは，運が上向くことを願って近くにある木に結びつけます。
Fortunetelling by drawing lots is available at many shrines and temples. This is called *"omikuji."* On a strip of paper, brief advice is given for various aspects of life such as marriage, schooling and travel, as well as fortune in general. If you get a bad fortune, you tie the *omikuji* to a nearby tree hoping your fortune will get better.

おみこし お神輿 🗾

神道のご神体をのせる輿(こし)をおみこしといいます。祭りのときには，そろいのはっぴを着た人々が「わっしょい，わっしょい」の掛け声とともにおみこしをかついで町内を練り歩きます。
An *omikoshi* is a portable Shinto shrine containing a deity. During festivals, people in matching *happi* coats carry the *omikoshi* along the streets, shouting *"Wasshoi, wasshoi."*

おみそれ お見それ あなたがこんなにテニスが上手だとは，おみそれしました I've never guessed you were so good at tennis. I *guessed wrong*.

オミット — **オミットする** (省く) omit ⊕

おみやげ お土産 (記念品) souvenir C; (贈り物) gift C, present C // オランダのおみやげといえば木靴が有名だ Wooden shoes are *a* popular *souvenir* of Holland. / 免税店で母へのおみやげを買った I bought *a present* for my mother at a duty-free shop.

◆鈴木のおばさんはうちに来るときはいつも何かおみやげを持ってきてくれる Mrs. Suzuki brings

おみやまいり

something for us every time she visits our home.
🅔「はい、おみやげ」「わあ、ありがとう！」 *"This is for you." "Oh, thanks!"*

おみやまいり お宮参り

生まれた赤ん坊を初めて神社に連れて行き、その子供のすこやかな成長をお願いすることをお宮参りといいます。生後どのくらいたってから行うかは地方によってまちまちですが、生後1か月ほどで行うことが多いです。
Omiyamairi is the practice of taking a newborn baby to a Shinto shrine for the first time to pray for its healthy growth. The age of the baby varies from region to region, but in many regions people take their babies to a shrine when they are one month old.

おむすび お結び ── an *omusubi*, a rice ball ⇨ おにぎり

おむつ 《米》diaper ◯,《英口語的》nappy ◯ ⇨ おしめ ∥紙おむつ *a disposable diaper* / おむつを取り替える *change a person's diaper* / うちの息子はまだおむつが取れない My son is still in *diapers*.
∥おむつかぶれ *diaper* [*nappy*] *rash*

オムニバス 《選集》omnibus ◯

オムレツ omelet, 《英》omelette ◯

おめい 汚名 《悪評》bad name [reputation] ◯,《公式的》infamy ◯,《不名誉》disgrace ◯,《公式的》dishonor,《英》dishonour ◯ / 汚名を返上する overturn *one's bad reputation* ◆彼は臆病(おくびょう)者の汚名を着せられた He *was branded* [*labeled*] (*as*) *a coward*.

おめおめと おめおめと負けを認めるわけにはいかない I can't bear the shame of admitting defeat. / 約束を破っておきながら、よくおめおめとそんなことが言えたものだ You broke your promise. *How dare* you say such a thing!

オメガ omega ◯ (⚙ギリシャ文字の第24字)

おめかし ──おめかしする 《着飾る》dress up;《化粧する》make* up /きょうはずいぶんおめかししてるじゃない You *are all dressed up* today.

おめだま お目玉 母からお目玉を食った I *got a* (*good*) *scolding* [*talking-to*, *telling-off*] from my mother.

おめでた 彼女はおめでただそうだ I hear *she's expecting* [*going to have*] *a baby*. / おめでた (→出産)はいつですか When is *the happy* [*blessed*] *event*?

おめでたい ❶【祝うべき】happy, joyful /阿部さんの家ではおめでたいことが続いた One *happy* event followed another in Mr. Abe's family.

❷【ばか正直な】simple, silly, naive ∥彼女の言うことをすべて信じるなんて君もおめでたいね How *simple* of you to believe everything she said!

おめでとう

ご卒業おめでとうございます I *congratulate you on your graduation*.

誕生日おめでとう *Happy birthday* (*to you*)! / *Many happy returns* (*of the day*)!
明けましておめでとう (*A*) *Happy New Year*! (⚙返答は Same [The same] to you.)
🅔「結婚おめでとう」「どうもありがとう」 *"Congratulations on your marriage!" "Thank you very much."*

> (1)合格・昇進など努力して得た成功や入学・卒業・婚約・結婚に対しては Congratulations! を用いるのが一般的。
> (2)日本語の「おめでとう」はあらゆる場合に用いられる祝いの言葉だが、英語の Congratulations! は新年・クリスマス・誕生日のあいさつには用いない。

おめにかかる お目にかかる 初めてお目にかかります *How do you do*?

おめみえ お目見得 ──お目見えする come* out; (初出演・初登場) make* *one's* debut [first appearance] /スカラ座にお目見えする *make one's debut* at the Scala ◆フォードの新型車があすお目見えする(→展示される) New-model Fords *will be on display* tomorrow.

おもい¹ 思い

❶【考え】thought ◯◯(⚙「考えること」の意味では ◯, 具体的な「考え」の意味では ◯)
自分の思いを作文に書いた I wrote my *thought* in my composition.
それをどうやろうかと彼は思いをめぐらした He spent some *thought* on how to do it.
◆私は中学時代に思いをはせた(→思い起こした) I *recollected* my junior high school days. / 彼が来るなんて思いもよらなかった(→想像できなかった) I *never dreamed* that he would come.

❷【望み】(夢) dream ◯; (願い) wish ◯
いつか君の思いはかなうだろう Some day *your dream* will come true.
◆思いのままに(→好きなように)ふるまって許されるのは子供だけだ Only kids are forgiven after behaving *as they like*.

❸【気持ち・経験】(気持ち) feeling ◯; (経験) experience ◯
修学旅行では楽しい思いをした I had *a good experience* during the school trip.
◆私はみじめな思いをした I *felt* miserable. /
思いを新たにして新年を迎えた I greeted the New Year *feeling* refreshed. / 彼女は自分の子供たちにつらい思いをさせたくなかった She didn't want her children to have *a hard time*.

❹【愛情】love ◯
私は彼に思いを打ち明けた I declared *my love* to him. / I told him that I loved him.
彼女はひそかに広昭に思いを寄せている She *is secretly in love with* Hiroaki.

❺【大切にすること】
彼は母親思いだ He *cares a lot for* his mother. / He's *very kind to* his mother.

おもい² 重い

❶【荷物・体重など】heavy (↔light)

この石は重すぎて簡単には動かせない This stone is *too heavy* to move easily.
重い荷物を持ち上げたときぎっくり腰になった When I lifted the *heavy* baggage, I strained my back.
隆志のほうが誠よりも5キロ重い Takashi is five kilograms *heavier* than Makoto.
❷【程度】(問題・状況などが) serious, heavy
—重く seriously, heavily
重い病気 a *serious* illness [disease] / 重い犯罪 a *serious* offense
重い税金が貧しい人たちを苦しめた The *heavy* taxes oppressed the poor.
この仕事への責任が彼に重くのしかかっている Responsibility for this work is pressing *heavily* on him.
事態を重く見た政府は閣僚会議を開いた The government took the situation *seriously* and held a Cabinet meeting.
❸【気持ち】(気落ちした) depressed, 《口語的》blue; (沈んだ) heavy
重い気持ちで with a *heavy* heart
私は試験のことで気が重かった I *was depressed about* [*over*] the exam.
❹【人・動作】heavy
重い足取りで歩く walk *with a heavy foot*; walk *heavily*
きょうは頭が重い My head feels *heavy* today.
[慣用表現] 亜紀は重い腰を上げて(→いやいや)その仕事に取りかかった Aki *reluctantly* started to do the work. / 彼女は口が重い She *speaks reservedly*. (❖reservedly は「控えめに」の意味)

おもいあがり 思い上がり (うぬぼれ) conceit [U]; (傲慢(ごうまん)) arrogance [U]

おもいあがる 思い上がる 思い上がるのもいいかげんにしろ Don't *be conceited*./ Don't *think too highly of yourself*. / 彼女の思い上がった態度には抵抗を感じる Her *arrogant* [*conceited*] attitude puts me off.

おもいあたる 思い当たる どうして彼が私に腹を立てていたのか, 全く思い当たる節がない I *don't have* the slightest [faintest, foggiest] *idea* why he was angry with me. / そうそう, そう言われれば思い当たるところがある Oh, yes, that *reminds* me of something.

おもいあまる 思い余る 思いあまって(→何と言えばいいのか分からず), 彼は彼女を抱きしめた *Not knowing what to say*, he gave her a hug. / 信次は思いあまって(→解決策が分からず途方にくれて)仕事を途中で投げ出してしまった Shinji was *at a loss how to find a solution* and gave up on his work halfway.

おもいいれ 思い入れ このかばんには思い入れがあってどうしても手放せない I simply can't part with this bag because it has *sentimental value* for me.

おもいうかぶ 思い浮かぶ よい考えが思い浮かんだ A good idea *occurred to* me./ I *hit on* a good idea. / 彼女に確かに一度会っているのだが顔が思い浮かばない I did meet her once but I *can't* ｢*picture* her [*remember* her face].

おもいうかべる 思い浮かべる この絵を見ると母を思い浮かべる This painting *recalls* my mother to me. / 私は今でもその事件をはっきりと思い浮かべることができる I still *have a* clear *picture of* the incident. / 沖縄といえばすぐ青い海を思い浮かべる Okinawa always *reminds* me *of* the blue sea.

おもいえがく 思い描く 私は東京での新生活を思い描いた I *imagined* a new life in Tokyo. / 彼女はその小屋をすてきな山荘だと思い描いていた She *had visualized* the hut as a lovely lodge.

おもいおこす 思い起こす recall [他], recollect [他][自], remember [他][自] ➡おもいだす

おもいおもい 思い思い 思い思いの考えを述べる(→自由に述べる) express *one's* opinion *freely* / みんな思い思いの所で弁当を食べた Everybody ate lunch *where they liked*. / 卒業後祐子と真弓は思い思いの道に(→別々の道に)進んだ After graduation, Yuko and Mayumi went *their separate ways*.

おもいかえす 思い返す (振り返る) look back, reflect [自]; (考えを変える) change *one's* mind ∥思い返せば学生時代はたくさんのいい友達に恵まれていた *Looking back on* my school days, I realize I was lucky to have a lot of good friends.

おもいがけず 思いがけず unexpectedly ∥なつかしい友達から思いがけず電話があった My dear old friend telephoned me *unexpectedly*. ◆思いがけず空港で旧友と会った I *ran* [*bumped*] *into* an old friend of mine at the airport.

おもいがけない 思いがけない unexpected ∥思いがけない客 an *unexpected* visitor / 彼の思いがけない質問に驚いて私は言葉に窮した Surprised by his *unexpected* question, I was at a loss for words.

おもいきった 思い切った (大胆な) daring, bold; (抜本的な) drastic ∥思いきった行動 *drastic* action / 彼の提案に反対するとは君も思いきったことをするね You are *bold* enough to be against his proposal. / 彼は何か思いきった対策がとられるべきだと主張した He urged that some *drastic* measures should be taken.

おもいきって 思い切って 思いきって彼女に話しかけてみたらどう Why don't you *find the courage to* talk to her? / 1人の学生だけが思いきって彼に議論をいどんだ Only one student *dared to* argue with him. / 私たちは彼に思いきって真実を伝えたがむだだった We *ventured to* tell him the truth, but it was useless.

おもいきり 思い切り 思いきり遊ぶ play *to one's heart's content* / 思いきり泣く have *a good* cry / 彼はその男を思いきりけった He gave the man *a good* kick./ He kicked the man *as hard as possible*. / 紀子は思いきりがいい[悪い](→決断が早い[遅い]) Noriko *is quick* [*slow*] *to decide*.

おもいこみ 思い込み (先入観) prejudice [C]

[U] ◆彼は思い込みが激しい(→いったん考えをもったらそれに固執する) Once he gets an idea into his head, he *really clings to it*.

おもいこむ 思い込む (決めてかかる) assume [他]; (信じる) believe [他]; (当然…だと思う) take* (it) for granted (that ...) ∥彼のことを米国人だと思い込んでいたが, 実際は英国人だった I *assumed that* he was American, but actually he was British. / 当時人々は太陽が地球の周りを回っていると思い込んでいた In those days people *believed* the sun went around the earth. / 私は彼女をてっきり男の子だと思い込んでいた I just *took it for granted* she was a boy.

◆いったん思い込んだら彼女はやりとげるだろう Once she *makes up her mind*, she'll carry it out [through].

おもいしらせる 思い知らせる 今回の試験で彼との実力の差を思い知らされた The exams this time *made me realize* there was a big difference between his ability and mine. / あいつに思い知らせてやる I'*ll show* him!

おもいしる 思い知る 彼らは間もなく世論の力を思い知る(→痛感する)だろう They will *feel* the force of public opinion soon. / 自分が全く間違っていたことを思い知った I *realized that* I was totally wrong.

おもいすごし 思い過ごし 君の思い過ごしだよ It is *only* your *imagination*. / 私の心配は思い過ごしだった My fears proved (to be) *groundless*.

おもいだしわらい 思い出し笑い
💬「何思い出し笑いしてるの」「いや, 別に」"*What made you smile?*" "Oh, nothing."
(❖「思い出し笑い」に当たる英語は特になく, 「何があなたを笑わせたのか」のようにいう)

おもいだす 思い出す

remember [他][自]; 《公式的》recollect [他][自], recall [他]; (思い出させる) remind [他]

remember: 「思い出す」の一般的な語. 意識的に思い出す場合と自然に思い出される場合の両方に用いる.
recollect, recall: 共に意識的に思い出すことを意味するややかたい語.
remind: remind *a person* of [about] ... の形で用いて, 「人に…を思い起こさせる」の意味.

あなたのことを思い出してはみんなでよく話をしています We often *remember* you and talk about you.

ああ, 思い出した Now, I *remember*. (❖この場合, ×I remembered., ×I've remembered. とはいわない)

【remember＋that 節】彼はその本を喫茶店に忘れてきたことを思い出した He *remembered* (*that*) he had left the book at the coffee shop.

【remember＋wh-節】そのとき何が起こったのか思い出してみて Try to *remember what* happened then. / どこにそのかぎを置いたか思い出せなかった I *couldn't remember where* I had put the key.

彼の名前がどうしても思い出せない I *can't* possibly *remember* his name.

彼女は事件のあった夜, 銀行の近くで白い車が止まっていたことを思い出した She *recalled* seeing a white car parked near the bank on the night of the incident.

思い出せるかぎりでは彼の名前は矢野といったと思います As far as I *can recollect*, his name was Yano.

【remind＋名(人)＋of 名】この曲を聞くと中学生のころを思い出す This song *reminds* me *of* my junior high school days.

それで思い出した That *reminds* me. (❖ ×That reminded me. とはいわない)

◆私は彼女の名前を思い出すことができなかった I couldn't *call* [*bring*] her name *to mind*.

💬「英語でスピーチをしたんだって?」「思い出させないでよ」"You gave a speech in English, right?" "*Don't remind* me!"

おもいたつ 思い立つ 彼女は突然思い立ってベリーダンスを習い始めた Suddenly she *had the idea* of learning belly dancing, and started it immediately.

[ことわざ] 思い立ったが吉日 The day you decide to do something is the best day to start it.; Never put off till tomorrow what you can do today. (→きょうできることをあすに延ばすな)

おもいちがい 思い違い mistake [C], misunderstanding [C][U] ∥彼の意見は我々に対する思い違いに基づいている His opinion is based on *a misunderstanding* about us.

◆すみません, 思い違いをしていました I'm sorry, but *I was mistaken* [*wrong*]. / 思い違いをなさっていると思います. そのような名前の者はここには住んでおりません You must *be mistaken*—no one of that name lives here.

おもいつき 思い付き idea [C], notion [C]; (考え) thought [C] ∥それはいい思いつきだ That's *a* good *idea*.

◆ほんの思いつきだけどあの公園でお昼を食べない? *It just came to my mind*, but why don't we have lunch in that park? / 思いつきでものを言うなよ(→よく考えたことだけを言え) Say only what you've (already) thought over. / (→考えずにものを言うな) Don't speak without thinking.

おもいつく 思い付く think* of ..., hit* on [upon] ..., strike* on [upon] ... ∥思いつくことを何でも言ってください Whatever you *think of*, let us know. / この問題を解決するいいアイディアが何も思いつかない I *can't think of* any good idea to solve this problem.

◆いい考えを思いついた I *have* a good idea. / 彼は新しい店について独創的な案を思いついた An ingenious plan for a new shop *came to* him. / もっとましな言い訳は思いつかないの? Can't you *invent* a better excuse?

おもいつめる 思い詰める (心配する) worry [自][他]; (深刻に考える) take* ... seriously; (考え込む) brood [自] ∥そんなに思い詰めるな Don't *worry about it* so much. / Take it easy. / 彼は何事に関しても思い詰める性格だ

He *takes* everything *seriously*. ◆彼女は思い詰めた様子でベンチに座っている She was sitting on the bench *with a worried look*.

おもいで 思い出 memory ⓒ, recollection ⓒⓤ, (公式的) remembrance ⓒⓤ, reminiscence ⓤⓒ (❖いずれもしばしば複数形で用いられる)

幼年時代の幸せな思い出 happy *memories* of one's childhood / 思い出にふける be lost in *memories*

その歌を聞いていると苦い思い出がよみがえった Listening to the song, bitter *memories* flooded over me. / The song brought back bitter *memories*.

この教室には楽しい思い出がたくさんあります This classroom is full of sweet *memories* for me.

彼女の思い出がいまだに私の心に残っている *Memories* of her still remain in my heart.

アメリカ旅行の思い出にそれをとってある I keep it as *a remembrance* [*memento*, *reminder*] of my trip to America.

富士登山は海外からの留学生たちにとっていい思い出になるだろう It will be *a good memory* for the students from abroad to climb Mt. Fuji.

◆思い出深い経験 a *memorable* experience / 若いころの思い出の品 a *souvenir* of *one's* youth

> **コロケーション** -memory-
> 【形容詞＋〜】楽しい〜 a happy [sweet, fond] memory / 悲しい〜 a sad memory / 大切な〜 a precious [treasured] memory / 苦い〜 a bitter memory / よい〜 a pleasant memory / いやな〜 an unpleasant memory

おもいではなし 思い出話 reminiscences

◆祖父が私たちに若いころの思い出話をしてくれた My grandfather used to *reminisce to* us about his youth.

おもいどおり 思い通り どうか僕の思いどおりにやらせてください Please let me do it *the way I like*. / Please let me go my *own way*. / 我々の思いどおりに事が進んだ Things went *as we wished*. / 彼女は何でも自分の思いどおりにしないと気がすまない She must have everything *in her own way*.

おもいとどまる 思いとどまる (断念する) give* up; (考え直す) change *one's* mind ∥ 私たちは資金不足のためその計画を思いとどまった We *gave up* the plan for lack of funds. / 彼を思いとどまらせるには相当の説得が必要だろう It'll take a lot of persuasion to *make* him *change his mind*.

◆私は辞表を出そうとしたが思いとどまった I was going to hand in my resignation, but I *held* it *back*.

おもいなおす 思い直す (再考する) reconsider ⓔ; (考えを変える) change *one's* mind; (考え直してやめる) think* better of ... ∥ 彼に本当のことを話すつもりだったが思い直してやめた I was going to tell him the truth but *thought better of* it.

おもいなやむ 思い悩む be worried, worry ⓔ ∥ 僕がどんなに思い悩んだか君には分からないだろう You have no idea how *worried I was*.

おもいのこす 思い残す 僕たちはベストを尽くしたので思い残すこと(→後悔)はありません We did our best, so we have nothing to *regret*.

おもいのほか 思いの外 試験の結果は思いのほかよかった The exam results were *unexpectedly* good. / 彼女のけがは思いのほかひどかった(→だれもそれほどひどいとは予想しなかった) *Nobody expected that* her injury would be so serious. / 思いのほか早く到着した We arrived sooner *than we had expected*.

おもいめぐらす 思い巡らす (あれこれ考える) think* this way and that, consider ⓔ, reflect on ... ∥ 彼はどう答えようか思いめぐらしている He *is considering* how to respond. / 彼の言葉について思いめぐらした I *reflected on* his words.

おもいもよらない 思いも寄らない 私は全く思いもよらない人からデートを申し込まれた I was asked to go out on a date by a most *unlikely* person. / 彼女が詩を書くなんて思いもよらなかった I've *never imagined* her writing poems.

おもいやられる 思いやられる 彼の行く末が思いやられる I *can't help worrying about* his future.

おもいやり 思いやり (配慮) consideration ⓤ, thoughtfulness ⓤ; (親切) kindness ⓤ, tenderness ⓤ; (心の温かさ) warmth ⓤ; (同情) sympathy ⓤ ∥ 他人への思いやりを見せる show *consideration* for others / 彼の忠告は思いやりの現れだ His advice is indicative 「of *his kindness* [(that) he is *kind*]. / 彼は思いやりに欠ける He is lacking in *warmth*.

◆思いやりのある手紙 a *sympathetic* letter / 圭子は人に思いやりがある Keiko is 「*kind to* [*considerate of*] others. / そんなことを言うなんて君も思いやりのない人だ It's *inconsiderate* of you to say such a thing.

おもいやる 思いやる consider ⓔ, think* of ... ∥ 人の気持ちも思いやらなきゃいけない You must *consider* other people's feelings. / 息子のことを思いやってくださってありがとうございました It was very good of you to *think of* my son.

おもいわずらう 思い煩う be worried, worry ⓔ ∥ 仕事のことを思いわずらって，とうとう彼の神経は参ってしまった The *constant worries* of his job finally broke him down.

おもう 思う

❶ 考える	think
❷ 見なす	regard ... as 〜, look upon ... as 〜
❸ 信じる	believe
❹ 疑問に思う	doubt; suspect
❺ 想像する・予期する	imagine; expect

おもう

❻ 希望する　want, hope, wish
❼ 意図する　be going to do
❽ 感じる　feel
❾ 心配する・気にする　mind

❶【考える】think* 他自
あすは雪が降ると思う I think (that) it will snow tomorrow. (◆think の後の接続詞 that は省略されることが多い)
彼女はそれに反対しないと思う I don't think [suppose] she will oppose that. (◆英語では「…しないと思う」を「…するとは思わない」というのがふつう)
このつぼはいつごろのものだと思いますか How old do you think this pot is? (◆×Do you think how old this …?とはいわない)
どっちを買うほうがいいと思う？ Which do you think I should buy? (◆×Do you think which I …?とはいわない)
太郎と次郎ではどちらが走るのが速いと思いますか Who do you think can run faster, Taro or Jiro? (◆×Which do you think …?, ×Do you think who can …?とはいわない)
我思う，ゆえに我あり I think, therefore I am. (◆哲学者デカルトの言葉)

🅡「それ，いい考えだと思うな」「私もそう思うわ」"I think that's quite an idea." "I think so, too." (◆so は that 節の代用。「いや，そう思わない」は No, I don't think so.という)

🅡「秋の京都がいちばん美しいと思う。あなたはどう思う」「私もそう思う」"I think Kyoto is the most beautiful in fall. How about you? [What's your opinion?]" "Me too."

🅡「この映画はいいとは思わないね」「私も（いいとは思わない）」"I don't think this is a good movie." "Me neither./ Neither do I."

🅡「彼はこのプレゼントを気に入るかな」「うん，喜ぶと思うよ」"Will he like this present?" "Yes, he'll be happy, I think." (◆I think は文末や挿入句的にも用いる)

【語法】
「…をどう思いますか」は, What do you think of [about] …?といい, ×How do you think of [about] …?とはいわない. 好き嫌いなどを聞くときには, How do you like …?などという. この場合は, ×What do you like …?とはいわない // このような音楽をどう思いますか What do you think of this kind of music? / 日本の着物をどう思いますか How do you like Japanese kimonos?

❷【みなす】（…を～とみなす）regard [look upon] … as ～, consider … (as [to be]) ～
彼らは彼を賢いと思っている They regard [look upon] him as clever.
彼が犯人だとは思わないよ I don't consider him (as) the criminal.

❸【信じる】（信じる）believe 他自（◆通例進行形にはできない）；（確信している）be sure
彼がその手紙を書いたと思われている He is believed to have written the letter.
神様はいると思いますか Do you believe in God?
彼女はたくさん運動をするのがよいと思っている She believes in getting plenty of exercise.
マイクには3人の子供がいると思いますよ Mike has, I believe, three children.
きっとブルズが勝つと思う I'm sure the Bulls will win.

❹【疑問に思う】（…でないと思う）doubt 他；（どうも…らしいと思う）suspect 他（◆進行形にはできない）；（…かしらと思う）wonder 他
あの話，本当じゃないんじゃないかと思っていた I doubted if that story was true.
彼らは彼の首に残っている跡から考えて殺人だと思った They suspected murder, judging by the marks on his neck.
いったい彼らは何をしているのだろうと思った I wondered what they might be doing.

❺【想像する・予期する】imagine 他（◆進行形にはできない），（口語的）dream* of [about] …; (推測する) guess 他（推定する）suppose 他（◆通例進行形にはできない）；（予期する）expect 他, think* 他；（悪いことを）be afraid
彼って思ってたとおりいい人ね He is just as nice as I imagined [expected].
優勝するなんて夢にも思わなかった I didn't even dream of getting first prize.
あなたがきょうらっしゃるとは思っていなかった I didn't expect you to come today.
その店ではクレジットカードが使えるものと思っていた I thought I could pay by credit card at the store.
この問題は私には解けないと思います I'm afraid I can't solve this problem.

❻【希望する】want 他, hope 他, wish 他
アンは歌手になりたいと思っている Ann wants [hopes, wishes] to be a singer.
あなたがこの曲を気に入ってくれればと思います I hope you'll like this music. (◆wish は実現不可能あるいは可能性の乏しい願望を表すので，この場合は不適切)
またお会いできるとよいと思っていたのですが I had hoped to see you again. / I had hoped that I would see you again. (◆実現しなかったことを表すのに had hoped を用いる)
私は時々空を飛べたらいいのにと思う I sometimes wish I could fly.
◆なれるかどうか分かりませんが，オリンピック選手になりたいと思います I don't know if I can, but I would like to be an Olympic athlete.

❼【意図する】be going to do, intend to do; (計画する) plan to do
私は今年の夏オーストラリアでホームステイしようと思っている I'm going [planning] to stay with an Australian family this summer.
父は私に家業を継がせようと思っている My father intends me to follow in the family business.
◆もう二度とそこへは行くまいと思った（→決めた）I decided I would never go there again.

❽【感じる】feel* 🔄 🔁
何か変だと思ったらセーターを後ろ前に着ていた I *felt* something was wrong, and then I noticed I was wearing the sweater backward.
ひとりで家にいたが少しも寂しいと思わなかった I *didn't feel* lonely at all when I was alone at home.

❾【心配する・気にする】mind 🔁
彼の批判は別に何とも思わなかった I *didn't mind* his comments.

❿【その他】
彼は時々祖国のことを思う (→思い出す) He sometimes *recalls* his native country.
私は時々あなたといっしょに遊んだころのことを思う (→思い出す) I sometimes *remember* the (good) old days when we played together.
まだ彼のことを思っているの (→愛しているの)? Do you still *love* him? / *Are* you still *in love with* him?
親は子を思うものだ It's natural for parents to *care about* their children.
思えば, 子供のころはよく遊んだね I *remember* we played a lot when we were kids.
その演説では彼はユーモラスに話すかと思えばまじめに話したりもした In that speech, he was humorous and serious *by turns*.

おもうぞんぶん 思う存分 思う存分 泣く have a *good* cry / 思う存分スキーを楽しんだ I enjoyed skiing *to my heart's content*. / 思う存分食べた I ate *as much as I liked*. / I ate *my fill*.

おもうつぼ 思う壺 かんしゃくを起こしたりしたら, (まさに) やつらの思うつぼだ If you lose your temper, you'll *play* (right) *into their hands*. / それこそやつの思うつぼだ That's *just what he wants you to do*.

おもうに 思うに
🗣「思うに彼は何か問題を抱えているな」「かもね」"I *think* he has a problem." "Maybe."

おもおもしい 重々しい, (厳粛な) grave, solemn; (威厳のある) dignified; (真剣な) serious; (重苦しい) heavy /重々しい口調で in a *solemn* [*grave*] tone / 会場には重々しい雰囲気が漂っていた There was a *solemn* air in the hall. ◆彼は重々しくうなずいた He nodded *gravely*.

おもかげ 面影 彼には昔の面影が全くない (→すっかり変わった) He is quite different from *what he used to be*. / He is not *what he used to be*. / 息子には私の父の面影がある My son *has some resemblance to* my father. / (→私の父を思い出させる) My son *reminds me of* my father.

おもかじ 面舵 starboard Ⓤ

おもき 重き 先生は英文法に重きをおいている The teacher *puts emphasis on* English grammar. / 彼の意見は決議の際に重きをなした His opinion *weighed heavily* in the decision.

おもく 重く ⇨おもい(重い)

おもくるしい 重苦しい (空・空気などが) heavy; (雰囲気などが) oppressive; (めいらせる) depressing; (陰気な) gloomy; (息の詰まる) stifling //重苦しい沈黙が続いた There was a long *heavy* silence. / 彼が失業して以来, 家の中は重苦しい雰囲気に包まれている There has been a *gloomy* atmosphere in his house since he lost his job.

おもさ 重さ weight Ⓤ Ⓒ ((略語))wt. //責任の重さ *the weight* of responsibility / その棚は本の重さを支えきれなかった The shelf couldn't sustain *the weight* of the books.
🗣「この荷物の重さはどのくらいですか」「約3キロです」"What's *the weight* of this baggage? / How much does this baggage *weigh*?" "It's about three kilograms. / It weighs about three kilograms."

おもし 重し weight Ⓒ //紙の上に重しを置く put *a weight* on a piece of paper

おもしろい 面白い

❶興味深い	interesting
❷楽しい	amusing
❸こっけいな	funny
❹わくわくさせる	exciting

❶【興味深い】interesting; (魅力的な) fascinating
おもしろい本 an *interesting* book
彼はモンゴルでのおもしろい体験を話してくれた He told me about an *interesting* experience he had in Mongolia.
これは私が今まで見た中で最もおもしろい映画だ This is the most *interesting* movie that I've ever seen.
アムステルダムはおもしろい町だ Amsterdam is a *fascinating* city.
最近英語がおもしろい Recently I find English *interesting*.
◆数学がおもしろくなくなってきた I'm losing *interest in* math. / おもしろいことに都会に行きたがる人もいれば, 反対に離れたがる人もいる *Interestingly enough*, some want to move into town while others want to leave.
🗣「旅行は楽しかった?」「うん, とっても, 特に長崎がおもしろかった」"Did you enjoy the trip?" "Yes, very much. Especially Nagasaki *was interesting*."

❷【楽しい】amusing, enjoyable; (演劇などが) entertaining
おもしろいゲーム an *amusing* game
彼の話はとてもおもしろかった His story *was* highly *amusing*.
◆パーティーはとてもおもしろかった I *had a lot of fun* at the party. / そのパソコンはおもしろいように (→よく) 売れているらしい I hear the PC is selling *very well*. / あいつばかりもててておもしろくない It's *a real drag* that he's the only one who's popular with girls.

❸【こっけいな】funny; (ユーモアのある) humorous, 《英》humourous
おもしろい話 a *funny* story
彼はいつもおもしろい冗談を言う He often

おもしろがる

makes a *funny* joke.
次郎はおもしろいやつだ Jiro is a *funny* fellow.
❹【わくわくさせる】exciting
🄮「おもしろい試合だったね」「あんな試合見たの初めてだよ」"It was an *exciting* game, wasn't it?" "I've never watched such a game before."

おもしろがる 面白がる be amused; (興味を示す) show* [express] interest 〃みんなビルの話をおもしろがった All of us *were amused at* Bill's story.
◆彼の言ったことなんか気にするな, おもしろがって言っただけだから Don't mind what he said.「He said it only *in fun*. [He *was* only *kidding*.]

おもしろさ 面白さ 彼は英語を学ぶおもしろさに目ざめた He woke to *the pleasure of* studying English.

おもしろはんぶん 面白半分 面白半分にそんなことをするな Don't do such a thing *just for fun*.

おもしろみ 面白み おもしろみのない人(→退屈な人) *a bore* / おもしろみのない(→単調な)仕事 a *monotonous* job / 彼の講義には何のおもしろみも感じられなかった(→私の関心をそそらなかった) His lecture didn't *interest* me at all.

おもたい 重たい ⇨ おもい(重い)

おもだった 主だった 委員会の主だったメンバー the *leading* members of a council / そのアパートには主だった電化製品はすでに備わっている *Major* electric appliances have already been installed in the apartment. ⇨ おもな

おもちゃ 玩具 toy Ⓒ
おもちゃの車 a toy car
弟はおもちゃで遊んでいた My brother was playing with *his toys*.
おもちゃ売り場はこの下の階にあります *The toy counter* is on the floor below this one.
◆電話をおもちゃにしてはいけません Don't play [toy] *with* the telephone.
‖おもちゃ箱 a toy box / おもちゃ屋(店) a toy store

おもて 表

❶【表面】face Ⓒ; (前面・正面) the front; (硬貨などの) head Ⓒ (↔tail) ── 表の *front* (❖名詞の前で用いる)
封筒の表 the *face* [*front*] of an envelope / 表のドアにかぎをかける lock the *front* door
そのビルは工事中なので, 表からは入れない The building is under construction and you cannot enter from *the front*.
彼女は表を上にしてカードを置いた She put the cards down *face up*. (❖「表を下にして」は face down)
コインを投げて決めよう, 表か裏か? Let's toss for it. *Heads* or tails?
◆彼は感情を決して表に出さない He *never shows his feelings*.
❷【戸外】outside

表で遊ぶ play *outside*
表はまだ暗い It's still dark *outside*.
表へ出ろ Come *outside*!
❸【野球】the top (half)
スワローズは8回表に5点を入れた The Swallows scored five runs in *the top of* the eighth.

おもてざた 表沙汰 事実が表ざたになれば君の立場は苦しくなるだろう You'll find yourself in a difficult situation, if the facts *become* [*are made*] *public*.

おもてだつ 表立つ 表立った(→目に見える)変化 a *visible* change / 表立って(→公然と)彼を非難する者はいなかった No one criticized him *publicly* [*in public*].

おもてむき 表向き その会社は表向きは順調に見えたが, 実際は経営難に陥っていた *To* [*By*] *all appearances* everything was fine, but actually the company was in financial difficulties. / 表向きには合意に達したが, まだ解決すべき課題は多い *Officially* they reached an agreement, but still there are a lot of problems to be solved.

おもな 主な (最も主要な) chief, principal; (中心的な) main; (指導的な) leading (❖いずれも名詞の前で用いる)
日本の主な工業都市 *chief* industrial cities in Japan / その劇の主な登場人物 the *principal* characters in the play / 日本の主な輸出品 the *main* exports of Japan / その委員会の主なメンバー the *leading* members of the committee
ドイツの主な都市を訪ねた I visited the *main* [*principal*] cities in Germany.

おもなが 面長 面長の顔 an *oval* face (❖long face は「浮かぬ顔」の意味)

おもに¹ 主に (中心的に) mainly, chiefly; (たいてい) mostly
そのチームのレギュラーは主に2年生だ The regulars of the team are *mainly* second year students.
私はヨーロッパを, 主にフランスを旅行しました I traveled around Europe, *mainly* France.
この会社は主に絹製品を扱っている This company deals *chiefly* in silk goods.
その店の客は主に学生だ The customers at the shop are *mostly* students.

おもに² 重荷 (heavy) burden Ⓒ, (heavy) load Ⓒ 〃重荷をかつぐ shoulder *a heavy burden*; carry [bear] *a heavy load* on *one's* shoulders / あのロープはそんな重荷に耐えられますか Will that rope hold such *a heavy load*? / 母親の病気がずっと彼女の心の重荷になっていた Her mother's illness has been *a burden* [*load*] on her mind.

おもねる その候補者は大衆におもねって(→喜ばせようと)減税を公約した The candidate promised tax cuts to *please* the public.

おもみ 重み weight Ⓤ; (重要性) importance Ⓤ 〃雪の重みでたくさんの枝が音を立てて折れた Many branches snapped under *the weight* of the snow. / 長年の経験が彼の言葉

に重みを与えている His years of experience gives *weight* to his words.

おもむき 趣 (魅力) charm [U] [C]; (味わい) taste [U]《また a ～》, flavor, 《英》flavour [U] [C]; (雰囲気) atmosphere [U] [C] //1960年代の趣の音楽 music with *a* 1960s' *flavor* / その通りは趣がある The street has *a charm* [*an atmosphere*] of its own.
◆その町は訪れるたびに趣を異にする The town *looks different* every time I visit.

おもむく 赴く (行く) go* [自]; (出発する) leave* [自] [他] //戦地におもむく *go to* the front
◆心のおもむくままにまかせる *give free play to one's* heart

おもむろに (ゆっくり) slowly; (落ち着いて) quietly //おもむろに立ち上がる stand up *slowly* / 彼はおもむろに身分証明書を取り出して警官に見せた He *slowly* took out his ID card and showed it to the police officer.

おもや 母屋・母家 the main house

おもらし お漏らし おもらしをする *wet oneself* [*one's pants*] / あの赤ちゃんはおもらししていないかい Isn't that baby *wet*?

おもり[1] 重り (はかりの) weight [C]; (釣り糸・魚網の) sinker [C] //釣り糸におもりをつける put *a sinker* on a fishing line; weight a fishing line

おもり[2] お守り baby-sitting [U] ◆きょうは姉の赤ちゃんのお守りをしなければいけない I have to「*look after* [*baby-sit*] my sister's baby.

おもわく 思惑 (期待) expectation [U] [C]; (予測・計算) calculation [U] [C]; (投機) speculation [U] [C] //株の思わく買いをする buy stocks as *a speculation* / 残念ながら，事は彼らの思わくどおりに運ばなかった Unfortunately, things *didn't meet* [*come*] *up to* their *expectations*./ Unfortunately, things *fell short of* their *expectations*.
◆世間の思わくなどあまり気にすべきでない You shouldn't be concerned much about what other people think of you.

おもわしい 思わしい (満足のいく) satisfactory; (好ましい) good; (健康で) well //結果は思わしくなかった The results *were not satisfactory*. / 患者の容態はあまり思わしくない The patient *is not doing* very *well*.

おもわず 思わず (我知らず) in spite of *oneself*; (無意識に) unconsciously, involuntarily

腹が立って思わず彼をどなってしまった I got angry and shouted at him *in spite of myself*.

彼女は体重計の数字を見て思わずため息をついた She sighed *involuntarily* when she saw the number indicated on the scale.

◆ごめん，思わず口がすべったんだ I'm sorry. It was just a slip of the tongue. / そのコマーシャルを見て思わず笑ってしまった I *couldn't help laughing at* the commercial. / 私はスヌーピーグッズを見つけると思わず買ってしまう When I come across an item with Snoopy on it, I just *can't resist* buying it.

おもわせぶり 思わせ振り 思わせぶりな言葉[表情] a *suggestive* remark [look] / 彼は彼女に思わせぶりな(→意味ありげな)視線を送った He gave her a *significant* glance.

おもわせる 思わせる それらの絵はマグリットの手法を思わせた Those pictures *were suggestive* [*reminiscent*] *of* the style of Magritte.

おもわぬ 思わぬ (予期せぬ) unexpected, unforeseen; (偶然の) accidental //思わぬ結果 *unexpected* [*unforeseen*] effects / 思わぬ事故にあう have an *unexpected* accident

おもわれる 思われる seem [自], appear [自] (❖appearは主に外見による判断を表す) //痛みはいつまでも続くように思われた The pain *seemed* endless. / 彼に考えを変えさせるのは不可能だと思われる It *seems* impossible to make him change his mind. / 彼女はジムを知っていると思われる She *appears to* know Jim./ It *appears that* she knows Jim.
◆彼がその手紙を書いたと思われている He *is believed to* have written the letter.

おもんじる 重んじる (尊重する) respect [他], 《公式的》esteem [他]; (高く評価する) value [他], think* much [highly] of ..., make* much of ... //何よりも真実を重んじる *value* truth above anything else / 古い伝統を重んじる *respect* old traditions

おや[1] 親

❶【生むもの・育てるもの】(両親) *one's* parents; (女親または男親) parent [C]
親鳥 a *parent* [*mother*, *father*] bird / 育ての親 *a* foster *parent* / 実の親 *a* natural *parent* / 理解のある親 *an* understanding *parent*

親の言うことには従うべきだ You should obey *your parents*.

私はまだ親のすねをかじっている(→親に頼っている) I still *depend* [*live*] *on my parents*.

制服を着てたばこを買いに来るなんて親の顔が見てみたい He came to buy cigarettes in his school uniform. *What kind of parents would raise a son like this?*

◆彼女は親の愛情に飢えている She has a hunger for *parental affection*.

❷【ゲームの】(トランプなどの) dealer [C]; (賭博(とばく)の胴元) banker [C]
◆(トランプで)親はだれですか Whose deal is it?
[ことわざ] 親の心子知らず Children do not know how dearly their parents love them. (→子供は親がどれほど自分のことを愛しているか知らない) / この親にしてこの子あり Like father, like son./ Like mother, like daughter.

おや[2] Oh!, My!, Dear (me)! (❖軽い驚きを表す. dearは女性が使うことが多い) //おや，あそこにいるの真由美だよ *Oh*, that's Mayumi over there. / おや，なんて散らかっているの *My*! What a mess!
◆おや，君本当にそう思うのかい *Well*, do you really think so? / 彼の話におや(→何かおかしい)と思った I thought *there was something strange* about what he had told me.
[会]「きのう田中に会ったよ」「おや，本当？」“I

おやおや

saw Tanaka yesterday." "*Oh, really*?"

おやおや おやおや, びしょぬれじゃないの *Oh, dear*! You are all wet! / おやおや, またお会いしましたね *Well, well*! Nice to see you again!

おやがいしゃ 親会社 parent company ◯; (持株会社) holding company ◯

おやかた 親方 (職場を統率する人) boss ◯, chief ◯ (◆男女の別なく用いられる); (相撲部屋の) stable master ◯; (職人の) master ◯
◆大工の親方 a *master* carpenter

おやがわり 親代わり 両親が亡くなって以来, 兄が私たちの親代わりをしてきた My brother has been *like a parent* to us ever since our parents died.

おやこ 親子 parent and child (◆状況に応じて father and son (父と息子), mother and daughter (母と娘) などと具体的にいうこともある) / 親子関係 the relations [relationship] between *parents and children* / 親子のきずな the ties between *parent and child* / 彼らは親子 (→父と娘) です They are *father and daughter*.
◆彼女とその夫とは親子ほど (→父親であってもおかしくないほど) 年が離れている Her husband is *old enough to be her father*. / 彼は息子と親子の縁を切った (→勘当した) He *disowned* his son. / 映画館は親子連れ (→多くの家族) でにぎわった The movie theater was crowded with *families*.
‖親子電話 a party line (telephone) / 親子丼(どん) a bowl of rice with chicken and eggs on it

おやこうこう 親孝行 礼子はとても親孝行だ Reiko *is very kind to her parents*. / Reiko is a very good daughter.
|慣用表現|親孝行したいときには親はなし *By the time you realize how much you owe to your parents, they are gone*.

おやごころ 親心 ご両親が君に厳しくするのも親心からだ Your parents are strict on [with] you out of *parental love*.

おやじ 親父 (父親) one's father, 《口語的》 one's dad, 《俗語》 the [one's] old man; (年配の男性) old man ◯

おやしお 親潮 (千島海流) the Okhotsk [oukátsk] [Kurile] Current

おやしらず 親知らず wisdom tooth ◯

おやすい お安い 山田君, こんな美人とデートなんてお安くないね Yamada, you're doing all right, going on a date with such a pretty girl.

おやすみ お休み good night
人におやすみを言う say *good night* to a person / 人におやすみのキスをする kiss a person *good night*
おやすみ, サラ *Good night*, Sarah. / (→ぐっすり眠りなさい) Sleep tight, Sarah.
◆よくおやすみになれ (→眠り) ましたか Did you *sleep* well?

おやつ お八つ (間食) snack ◯; (軽食・茶菓) refreshments ◆おやつの時間 《米》 a *coffee break*; 《英》 a *tea break*

おやばか 親馬鹿 彼は息子の写真を撮るのに毎日フィルム1本使うという親ばかぶりを発揮している He's such *a doting father* that he uses a full roll of film every day taking photos of his son.

おやばなれ 親離れ 親離れできない子供 a child who *is still dependent on his [her] parents*

おやふこう 親不孝 僕は今まで親不孝をしてきた (→悪い息子だった) I've been *a bad son*.

おやぶん 親分 (統率者) boss ◯; (暴力団の) gang leader ◯ / 彼は親分肌のところがある (→仲間の面倒見がいい) He is *like a boss* in taking good care of his friends. / (→頼られるのが好き) He likes to be depended [counted] on by other people.
◆彼は親分気取りだ He *is very bossy*.

おやま 女形 [アクセント記号] an *oyama*, an actor who plays a female role in kabuki

おやまあ ⇒おや², まあ

おやもと 親元 彼は18のときに親元を離れ東京でひとり暮らしを始めた He *left home* at the age of 18 and started living alone in Tokyo.

おやゆずり 親譲り 彼女の音楽の才能は親譲りだ Her musical talent is 「*inherited from her parents* [*in her blood*].

おやゆび 親指 (手の) thumb [θÁm] ◯; (足の) big toe ◯

おゆ お湯 ⇒ゆ

およぎ 泳ぎ (泳ぐこと・水泳) swimming ◯; (ひと泳ぎ) a swim / ひと泳ぎする have *a swim* / プールへ泳ぎに行こう Let's go *swimming* in the pool. / Let's go for *a swim* in the pool. / ジャックは泳ぎがうまい Jack is good at *swimming*. / (→すぐれた泳ぎ手だ) Jack is a good swimmer.

およぐ 泳ぐ
❶【水中を】 swim* 自他, 《英》 bathe 自他
クロール [平泳ぎ, 背泳ぎ] で泳ぐ swim [do] (the) crawl [breaststroke, backstroke] / プールで泳ぐ swim [*have a swim*] in the pool / 川を泳いで渡る swim (*across*) a river
彼は3キロ泳げる He *can swim* three kilometers.
私はよく川に泳ぎに行った I used to *go swimming* [*for a swim*] in the river. (◆×to the river とはいわない)
見たことのない魚が湖を泳いでいた A strange fish *was swimming around* in the lake.
❣「泳げる？」「全然だめ」 "Can you *swim*?" "I can't swim 「*at all* [*a stroke*]."
❷【比喩的に】
世の中を巧みに泳ぐ *get along* skillfully [craftily] in the world
警察は差し当たり容疑者を泳がせておくことにした The police decided to have the suspect *remain at large* for the moment.

およそ
❶【約】 about, 《口語的》 around; (概算で) approximately (◆ややかたい語); (大ざっぱに言って) roughly ──およその approximate; rough ⇒やく(約)
およその見積もり a *rough* estimate

私の体重はおよそ60キロです I weigh *about* sixty kilos.
週末にはおよそ１万人の人がこの遊園地を訪れます *Roughly* ten thousand people visit this amusement park each weekend.
その学校にはおよそ500人の生徒がいる The school has *approximately* five hundred pupils.
◆１マイルはおよそ1.6キロメートルに等しい One mile is *almost* equal to 1.6 kilometers.
❷【概略】(一般的に) in general, generally (speaking) ―およその approximate, rough
およその見当 an *approximate* [a *rough*] idea
およそ女性は男性より長生きするものだ *In general*, women live longer than men.
❸【全く】quite; (完璧(かんぺき)に) completely, totally
そんなのはおよそばかげた考えだ Such an idea is *quite* absurd.

およばずながら 及ばずながら 及ばずながらお手伝いします(→できるかぎりのことをします) I'll do *what little I can* to help you. / I'll do my best to help you.

およばない 及ばない
❶【できない・かなわない】
彼の跳躍は学校記録に及ばなかった(→届かなかった) His jump *fell short of* the school record.
テニスではあいつの足元にも及ばないよ I'*m no match for* him in tennis at all.
私の絵が入賞するなんて思いも及びませんでした It *never occurred to me* that my painting would win a prize.
❷【必要がない】
彼に電話をするには及ばないよ You *don't have* [*need*] *to* call him. / You *needn't* call him.
[ことわざ] 過ぎたるはなお及ばざるがごとし ⇒すぎる

およばれ お呼ばれ 今夜は久保さんの家へ夕食にお呼ばれだ I'*m invited to* dinner at Mr. Kubo's house this evening.

および[1] 及び and (❖3語以上並べる場合，コンマで区切って最後の語の直前にだけ and を置くことが多い．and の前のコンマは省略可能) ‖ベルギー，オランダおよびルクセンブルク Belgium, Holland(,) *and* Luxembourg

および[2] お呼び 田中部長，お呼びでございますか Did you *call* me, Ms. Tanaka? / 楽譜も読めないやつなんかお呼びじゃないよ We *don't need* anybody who can't read music.

およびごし 及び腰 ―及び腰の (おどおどした) timid; (優柔不断の) indecisive; (意志の弱い) weak

およぶ 及ぶ
❶【達する】reach [他] [自]; (伸びる) extend [自]; (ある範囲にわたる) cover [他], range [自]; (広がる) spread* [自]; (総計…になる) amount to ... (❖いずれも状態を表す動詞なので進行形にはできない)
工事費は10億円に及んだ The construction costs *reached* [*amounted to*] one billion yen.
台風による被害は全国に及んだ The damage from the typhoon *extended* all over the country.
会議は深夜に及んだ The meeting *extended* [*lasted*] till late at night.
彼の演説は様々な話題に及んだ His speech *ranged over* various topics.
◆力の及ぶかぎりお手伝いします I'll *do my best* to help you.
❷【匹敵する】match [他], equal [他], be equal to ... ⇒およばない
このエッセーはあなたが最初に書いたものには及ばない This essay *doesn't match* the first one you wrote.
数学で彼に及ぶ者はいない No one *equals* [*is equal to*] him in math.
❸【行為に至る】
彼は綿密な計算のうえで犯行に及んだ He *committed* his [the] crime after careful calculation.
❹【…するには及ばない】⇒およばない
💬「車で送ってくださってどうもありがとうございました」「お礼には及びませんよ」"Thank you so much for driving me home." "*You're welcome.*/ *Don't mention it.*"
❺【その他】
この期(ご)に及んでじたばたしてもしようがない There's no use making a fuss *at this stage of the game.*

およぼす 及ぼす (影響などを) exercise [他]; (害を) do* [他]; (力を行使する) exert [他]; (影響を) influence [他]
喫煙は非喫煙者の健康にとても悪い影響を及ぼすおそれがある Smoking can *do* great mischief to non-smokers' health.
彼はいまだ政界に強い影響を及ぼしている He still *exerts* a strong influence on the political world.
天候は植物の生育に影響を及ぼす Weather *influences* the growth of plants.

オラトリオ 〔音楽〕oratorio [C] (複 ~s)

オランウータン 〔動物〕orangutan(g) [C]

オランダ the Netherlands, Holland (❖公式名(the Kingdom of the Netherlands) ―オランダ人 (男性) Dutchman [C]; (女性) Dutchwoman [C]; (総称) the Dutch ―オランダ語 Dutch [U] ―オランダ(人[語])の Dutch

おり[1] 折 (場合) occasion [C]; (機会) chance [C], opportunity [C] ‖母は折に触れて自分の小さいころの話を私たちにしてくれた *On occasion* [*Occasionally*] Mother would tell us about her childhood. / 私の町へいらっしゃる折にはぜひお知らせください If you get *a chance* to come to my town, please let me know.
◆折を見て彼に聞いてみます I'll ask him「*at the right time* [*at his convenience*]. / 次に京都へいらっしゃる折にはぜひ私たちのところへお立ち寄りください Next *time* you visit Kyoto, please drop in on us. / こちらから電話しようとした折も折，彼から電話がかかってきた I *was just about to* call him *when* he called me.

おり² 澱 (かす) dregs, sediment

おり³ 檻 cage; (動物園などの大きな鳥小屋) aviary; (小動物用の) hutch, coop; (家畜用の) pen; (監房) (prison) cell

おり⁴ 織り (織り方) weave ‖平織り *a plain weave*

おりあい 折り合い (妥協) compromise; (仲) relationship ‖我々はどうにか折り合いをつけた We managed to reach *a compromise*. ◆彼女は近所の人と折り合いがよくないようだ She doesn't seem to *be getting along well with* her neighbors. / 彼は従業員との折り合いがよい[悪い] He *is on good [bad] terms with* his employees.

おりあう 折り合う (妥協する) compromise; (合意・同意する) reach [come*] to] (an) agreement ‖我々は価格の点で彼らと折り合わなかった We couldn't *reach an agreement with* them on the price.

おりあしく 折悪しく unfortunately, unluckily ‖折あしく私が電話したとき彼女はいなかった *Unfortunately* [*Unluckily*], she was out when I phoned.

おりいって 折り入って ‖折り入って頼みたいことがあるのですが May I ask *a special* favor of you?

オリーブ (植物) olive; (色) olive (green) ‖——オリーブ(色)の olive ‖オリーブ油 olive oil

オリエンテーション orientation ‖オリエンテーションを受ける [行う] receive [hold] *an orientation* / 新入生対象のオリエンテーションに参加する participate in *an orientation* for new students

オリエンテーリング orienteering

オリエント the Orient ‖オリエント急行 the Orient Express

おりおり 折々 ‖その公園では四季折々の花を楽しむことができる You can enjoy flowers of *the season* in the park.

オリオン (オリオン座) Orion [əráiən] ‖オリオン座の3つ星 *Orion's* Belt

おりかえし 折り返し ❶【衣服の】(えりの) lapel; (ズボンの)《主に米》cuff,《英》turn-up

❷【引き返すこと】東西線は事故のため中野-大手町間で折り返し運転をしている The Tozai Line *is running only between* Nakano *and* Otemachi due to the accident.

❸【すぐに】折り返しこちらからお電話します I'll call you back *immediately*.

‖折り返し(地)点 the turning point, the turn

おりかえす 折り返す (すそ・そでなどを) fold up [back], turn up; (引き返す) turn back ‖ズボンのすそを折り返す *turn up* the trousers; *fold up* the bottom of the trousers / 我々は町のはずれまで行って折り返した We went to the edge of the town and then *turned back*.

おりかさなる 折り重なる ‖人々は折り重なって倒れた People fell down *on top of one another* [*one upon another*].

おりかさねる 折り重ねる ‖新聞を折り重ねる (→折って積み上げる) *fold and pile* [*stack*] *up* the newspapers

おりがみ 折り紙 ❶【遊び】origami (◆origami は英語化しているが, 通じない場合は the art of folding square pieces of colored paper などと説明する) ◆折り紙でツルを折る fold *a piece of paper* into a crane

日本の伝統的な遊びの一つである折り紙は, 色紙を折って動物や花などを形作る芸術です. 小さなツルをたくさん糸でつなげたものを千羽鶴といい, 病気の人を元気づけるために贈られます. Origami, a traditional Japanese pastime, is the art of folding square pieces of colored paper to form figures such as animals and flowers. *Sembazuru*, which is a string of many small *origami* cranes, is often given to a sick person in order to bolster his or her spirits.

❷【保証】本物であると折り紙付きの(→保証された) 絵 a painting *certified* to be genuine / 彼女の医師としての腕前は折り紙付きだ(→頼れる) She is a *reliable* [*dependable*] doctor.

おりから 折から ‖折から(→出かけようとしたちょうどそのとき)の雨でピクニックは取りやめになった The picnic was called off because it began to rain *when we were about to go*. / 寒い折から, お体どうぞおだいじに Take good care of yourself *in this cold weather*.

おりこみ 折り込み (雑誌・新聞の) insert, fold(-)out ‖折り込み広告 an (advertising) insert, an insertion

おりこむ¹ 折り込む ‖新聞にちらしを折り込む *insert* bills in newspapers

おりこむ² 織り込む (糸を) weave*, interweave* ‖金糸を織り込んだ布 cloth with gold thread *woven in* ◆彼は話にユーモアを織り込んだ He *incorporated* [*wove*] some humor *into* the book.

オリジナリティー (独創性) originality ‖彼の絵はオリジナリティーに欠ける His paintings lack *originality*.

オリジナル (原作・原画) original ‖——オリジナルの original

◆そのアイディアは彼のオリジナルではない The idea was not *originally* his.

おりたたみ 折り畳み ‖——折りたたみの folding, foldaway, fold-up (◆いずれも名詞の前で用いる) ‖折りたたみ式ベッド a *folding* [*foldaway, fold-up*] bed

◆折りたたみナイフ a *clasp* knife / 折りたたみ傘 a collapsible umbrella

おりたたむ 折り畳む fold ‖新聞紙を折りたたむ *fold up* a piece of newspaper / そのいすは平らに折りたためる The chair *folds up* flat. / 毛布を2つに折りたたむ *double* a blanket; *fold* a blanket *in two*

おりづめ 折り詰め ‖折り詰めの弁当 a (Japanese) box lunch

おりづる 折り鶴 folded paper crane

おりまげる 折り曲げる (物・体の部分を)

bend* 他 自; (紙・布などを) fold 他, turn back [down] /針金を折り曲げてハンガーを作った I *bent* the wire to make a hanger. / この書類は折り曲げないでください Please do not *fold* these papers. / 彼は上体を折り曲げるようにして洞窟(どうくつ)へ入っていった He *bent down* and went into the cave.

おりめ 折り目 (布地・紙などの) fold C; (ズボンの) crease C; (衣服のひだ) pleat C /折り目に沿って布を切る cut the cloth along *the fold* ◆ ズボンに折り目をつける *crease* the trousers

慣用表現 彼女は折り目正しい人だ(→礼儀正しい) She *behaves properly*. / She *is well-mannered*.

おりもの¹ 織物 fabric C U, textile C, (woven) cloth U /綿[絹, 毛]織物 cotton [silk, woolen] *fabrics*

‖織物業 the textile industry

おりもの² 下り物 〖生理〗 vaginal discharge C U

おりよく 折よく 雨の中を歩いていたら折よく(→偶然)母の車が通りかかった I was walking in the rain when my mother's car *happened to* come by.

おりる 降りる・下りる

❶【上から下への移動】 go* [come*] down, get* down, climb down, 《公式的》descend 自 他

山を下りる go [come, climb] *down* a mountain / はしごを下りる climb [get] *down* a ladder / 谷に下りる道 a path *descending* into the valley

エレベーターが下りてきた The elevator *came down*.

子供たちが夕食のために(上の階から)下りてきた The children *came down* (the stairs) to dinner.

◆ 丘の斜面を滑り下りる *slide down* a hillside / 幕が下りた The curtain *fell*. / その店はここ2, 3日シャッターが下りたままだ The shop *has been closed with its shutters down* for the last few days.

❷【乗り物から】(バス・電車などから) get* off; (タクシーなどから) get out

バス[電車, 飛行機, 船, 自転車]から降りる *get off* a bus [a train, an airplane, a boat, a bicycle] / 車から降りる *get out of* a car

武道館へ行くんだったら九段下駅で降りるといいよ You should *get off* at Kudanshita Station to go to Budokan.

◆ (混雑した電車で)降ります(→降ろしてくれ) *Let me out*. / その車から男性が降りてきた A man *came out of* the car.

❸【退く】(辞職する) resign 自 他, quit* 自 他; (放棄する) give* up

彼は事故の責任をとって職を降りた He took responsibility for the accident and *resigned (from)* his post.

彼女はジュリエットの役を降りた She *gave up* the part of Juliet.

◆ そういう条件なら私を除外して(→受ける) In that case, *count me out*.

❹【その他】

年金が下りる(→受ける) *receive* a pension

間もなく学校から許可が下りる(→得られる)だろう We'll soon *get permission* from school.

カーテンをあけると窓に霜が降りていた I opened the curtain and found *there was frost* on the window.

オリンピック the Olympics, the Olympic Games, 《公式的》the Olympiad /冬季オリンピック *the* Winter *Olympics*; *the* Winter *Olympic Games* / オリンピックの金メダリスト an *Olympic* gold medalist / オリンピックは4年に一度開かれます *The Olympic Games* are held every four years.

‖オリンピック競技場 an Olympic Stadium / オリンピック選手 an Olympian, an Olympic athlete / オリンピック村 an Olympic village / 国際オリンピック委員会 the International Olympic Committee(《略語》IOC)

おる¹ 折る

❶【折り曲げる】(たたむ) fold 他 自; (曲げる) bend* 他 自; (折り返す) turn back

1枚の紙を2つに折る *fold* a sheet of paper double [in two, in half] / ひざを折る *bend one's knees* / ページの隅を折る *turn back* the corner of a page / 折り紙でカエルを折る *fold* a piece of paper *into* a frog

彼女は手紙を折って封筒に入れた She *folded* the letter and put it in the envelope.

◆ 指を折って数える count *on one's fingers*

❷【曲げて切り離す】break* 他; (ぽきっと折る) snap 他

枝を折る *snap* a twig *off*

彼はスキーをしていて脚を折った He *broke [fractured]* his leg while skiing.

慣用表現 話の腰を折って申しわけありませんが、1つ質問があります I'm sorry to 「*interrupt you [cut you short]*, but I'd like to ask a question. / その作家は筆を折った The writer *gave up writing*. / 先生は私のためにいろいろと骨を折ってくれた The teacher *went to a lot of trouble* for me.

おる² 織る weave* 他 自 /敷き物を織る *weave* a rug / 機(はた)を織る *weave on [at]* a loom

オルガスムス △orgasm [ɔ́ːrɡæzm] C U (◆日本語はドイツ語の Orgasmus から) /オルガスムスに達する reach *orgasm*; have *an orgasm*

オルガン (pipe) organ C; (足踏み式の) harmonium C; (電子オルガン) electronic organ C ‖オルガン奏者 an organist

オルゴール △(米)music box C, (英)musical box C (◆日本語はオランダ語の orgel から) /オルゴールを鳴らす play *a music box*

おれ 俺 I ➡ わたし(私)

おれい お礼 thanks; (お礼の言葉) thank-you C; (感謝の気持ち) gratitude U; (報酬) reward C /お礼の手紙 a *thank-you* letter / お礼のしるし a token of *one's gratitude* / お礼の気持ちを表す express *one's thanks [gratitude]* / ぜひひと言お礼を言わせてください Just let me say a word of *thanks*.

◆あなたには何とお礼を言っていいか分かりません I don't know how to *thank* you. / 手伝ったお礼に彼がこの本をくれた He gave me this book *in return for* my help.

オレゴン Oregon (※米国北西部の州;《略語》Ore., Oreg.,《郵便》OR)

おれせんグラフ 折れ線グラフ (line) graph ◎

おれる 折れる
❶【物が】(こわれる) break* 圓, be broken; (ぽきりと) snap 圓
医者は指の骨が折れていると言った The doctor said my finger *was broken*.
枝は彼の体重を支えきれずぽきっと折れた The branch couldn't bear his weight and *snapped*.
◆この卓球台は2つに折れる This ping-pong table *can be folded* in two.
❷【譲歩する】give* in,《公式的》yield 圓
彼は彼女のしつこい要求に折れた He *gave in* [*yielded*] to her persistent demands.
❸【道】turn 圓 他
その車は角(変)を左に折れた The car *turned* (*to*) the left at the corner.
道は右に折れている The road *turns to* the right.

オレンジ orange ◎◎; (色) orange ◎ ∥オレンジをしぼる[の皮をむく] squeeze [peel] *an orange* / オレンジひと切れ a piece of *orange* / オレンジジュース1杯 a glass of *orange juice*

おろおろ 夫の事故の知らせに彼女はおろおろするばかりだった She was *beside herself* when she heard about her husband's accident. / 炎から逃れようと人々はおろおろと逃げ惑うばかりだった People could do nothing but run around *in confusion* to escape the flames. / 授業中に突然指されて彼女はしばらくおろおろした When she was called suddenly on in class, she *floundered* [*got confused*] for a few seconds.

おろか 愚か ──愚かな stupid, foolish, silly ──愚かに(も) stupidly, foolishly ∥そんなことを言うなんて君は愚かだったね It *was stupid* [*foolish*] of you to say such a thing. / 愚かにも答案用紙に名前を書き忘れてしまった *Foolishly*, I forgot to write my name on the answer sheet. ◆愚かにも彼女の言葉を信じてしまった I *was fool enough* to believe what she said to me.
∥愚か者 a fool, an idiot

-おろか 彼女は英語はおろか日本語さえ正しくしゃべれない She can't even speak proper Japanese, *to say nothing of* English. / 車はおろかテレビを買う金すらない I don't even have enough money to buy a TV, *[let alone* [*much less*] a car.

おろし¹ 卸し (卸し売り) wholesale ◎ ◆…を卸しで買う[売る] buy [sell] ... *wholesale*; buy [sell] ... *at a wholesale price*
∥卸売業者 a wholesaler / 卸売店 a wholesale store / 卸業 the wholesale trade / 卸値 a wholesale price

おろし² 下ろし ∥おろし金 a grater / 大根おろし grated *daikon*

おろす¹ 降ろす・下ろす

❶【上から下へ】get* [take*, bring*] down; (下に置く) put* down; (引き下ろす) pull down, lower 他
ブラインドを下ろす「take down [pull down] the window shade / (船の)帆を下ろす *lower the sails* / 荷物を網棚から下ろす *take* [*get*] *one's* baggage *down* from the rack
かばんを下ろしてベンチに腰を下ろした I *put* my bag *down* and *sat down* on a bench.
彼が2階からソファーを下ろすのを手伝った I helped him *bring* a sofa *down* from upstairs.
◆なべを火から下ろす *take* a pot *off* the fire / 彼女の髪は下ろすと腰まで届いた When she *let* her hair *down*, it reached her waist.
❷【乗り物などから】drop 他; (人を) let* off; (積み荷を) unload 他 圓
船の荷を降ろす *unload* a ship
僕は彼に東京駅で降ろしてくれと頼んだ I asked him to *let* [*drop*] me *off* at Tokyo Station.
運転手はトラックから大きな箱を降ろした The driver *unloaded* a large box from the truck.
❸【退かせる】(降格する) demote 他; (解任する) relieve 他; (はずす) take* *a person off* ...
議長の座から降ろされる be *relieved* of *one's* post as chairperson
彼は職務怠慢で支配人の職を降ろされた He *was demoted from* the post of manager because of neglect of duty.
◆その女優は主役を降ろされた The actress *was removed* [*dropped*] *from* the leading role.
❹【貯金などを】withdraw* 他, draw* out
銀行(口座)から5万円下ろす *withdraw* 50,000 yen from the bank (account)
❺【新品の品物を】
スーツを下ろす wear *one's new* suit
彼女は下ろしたての靴を履いて出かけた She went out in her *brand-new* shoes.
❻【その他】
魚をおろす *fillet* a fish / 大根をおろす *grate* a *daikon* radish / 根を下ろす *take* root
彼女は20歳のときに子供をおろした She *had an abortion* at the age of 20.
庭の木の枝を下ろした I *trimmed off* the branches of trees in my garden.

おろす² 卸す wholesale 他 圓, sell* ... wholesale ∥小売店に靴を卸す *wholesale* shoes to retail stores

おろそか 疎か 勉強をおろそかにする *neglect one's studies* / 避難訓練をおろそかにしていたため多くの犠牲者が出た There were heavy casualties because they *had been neglectful* [*negligent*] of fire drills.

おわかれかい お別れ会 farewell party ◎

おわせる 負わせる ❶【荷物】burden 他 ∥馬

に荷を負わせる *burden* a horse *with* a load
❷【傷】hurt* [他], injure [他], wound [他] (❖hurt のほうが injure より軽いけが. wound は刃物や銃などによるけがをいう) ∥彼は運転を誤り通行人に大けがを負わせてしまった He lost control of the car and seriously *injured* a pedestrian.
❸【責任など】(失敗などの責任を) blame [他]; (仕事・義務などを)《公式的》charge [他], impose [他] ∥人に義務を負わせる *impose* an obligation *on* a person; *place* a person *under* an obligation / 彼らはその失敗の責任を私に負わせた They *blamed* the failure *on* me./ They *laid* [*put*] the blame for the failure *on* me.

おわび お詫び apology [C] ―おわびする apologize [自] ∥本当におわびの言葉もございません I really don't know how to *apologize*.
◆私の過ちをおわびします *I'm sorry for* my mistake.

おわらい お笑い (物笑いの種) joke [C]《通例単数形》, 《口語的》a laugh, laughing-stock [C] ∥とんだお笑いぐさだ *That's a joke* [*laugh*]!/ *What a joke* [*laugh*]!
‖お笑いタレント a (TV) comedian / お笑い番組 a (TV) comedy show

おわり 終わり end [C], 《公式的》the [a] close; (映画・物語などの結末) ending [C]; (最後) the last; (結び) conclusion [U][C]
〖終わりが〗
何事にも終わりがある All things must have *an end.*/ Nothing lasts forever.
この仕事は終わりが全く見えない(→いつ終わるか全然分からない) I don't have the slightest idea when this job will come to *an end.*
この映画は終わりがおもしろい This movie has *an* interesting *ending.*
〖終わりに〗
今月の終わりに入試の合格発表がある The results of the entrance exam will be announced *at the end of* this month.
パーティーも終わりに近づいたころようやく彼が現れた He finally showed up when the party was drawing to *a close.*
式の終わりに全員で賛美歌を歌った *At the conclusion* of the ceremony, we all sang a hymn together.
◆きょうはこのへんで終わりにしましょう *So much for today.*/ *Let's call it a day.*
〖終わりを〗
そのけがが元で彼の野球選手生命は終わりを告げた The injury put *an end* to his career as a baseball player.
〖終わりまで〗
初めから終わりまで from beginning *to end*
◆終わりまで言わせてください *Let* me *finish* (*talking*). / その本を一気に終わりまで読んだ I read the book *through* without a break. / 私は映画の初めから終わりまで泣いていた I wept *throughout* the entire movie.
〖その他〗
講演の終わりごろ私は眠ってしまった *Toward the end* of the lecture, I fell asleep.
◆私たちの仲ももう終わりね It's *all over* between us./ We *are through.* / おれはもう終わりだ(→万事休すだ) It's *all over with* me./ I'*m done for.*/ I'*m doomed.*
[慣用表現] 終わりよければすべてよし *All is well that ends well.*

おわる 終わる

❶【終了・完了】end [自], finish [自], be over (❖be over は終わった状態をいう); (話・会などが) close [自]
学校は3時半に終わります Our school day *ends* at 3:30.
2学期はいつ終わるのですか When does the second term *finish*?
やっと夏が終わった Summer *is over* at last.
◆今年ももうすぐ終わる This year *is coming to an end* soon. / 仕事はほとんど終わった The job *is* nearly *done.* / 8回終わって我々がリードしている We're ahead *after* the eighth inning. / まだ仕事が[君との話は]終わってない I *am* not *finished with* 「the work [you] yet. / 私の話が終わる(→話を終える)まで静かにしてください Please keep quiet until I'*ve finished* my speech. / 部屋の掃除は終わったの? *Have* you *finished* cleaning your room? / 彼は10分で宿題を終わらせた He *finished* his homework in 10 minutes. / もう忘れろ. すっかり終わったことなんだから Just forget it. It's all *in the past.* / さあ, 終わったぞ There! It's *all done*!
❷【…に[で]終わる】end [result] in …
彼の計画は失敗に終わった His plan *ended* [*resulted*] *in* failure.
◆それは未解決のままで終わった It *remained* unsolved. / その計画は夢に終わった *Nothing came of* the plan.
❸【…(し)終わる】finish *doing*
話し終わる *finish talking*
食べ終わったらテーブルを片づけなさい Clear the table *after* you *finish eating.*

オン CDプレーヤーのスイッチをオンにする *turn* [*switch*] the CD player *on* / 17番コースで2オンした I *reached the green* on the 17th hole *in two strokes.*

おん[1] 恩

(好意) kindness [U], favor [U]; (恩義) obligation [C]
人に恩を返す repay *an obligation* on a person
ご恩は決して忘れません I will never forget *your kindness.*
いつか彼の恩に報いなければならない I must *repay* him *for* his *favor* some day.
◆鈴木先生にはとても恩を感じています I *owe* a great deal *to* Mr. Suzuki./ I *am indebted to* Mr. Suzuki. / あんなに面倒を見てやったのに, 彼は恩をあだで返してきた Though I had looked after him a lot, he 「*returned evil for good* [*bit the hand that fed him*].
[会]「じゃあ, ノートをとっておいてあげるよ」「ありが

とう. 恩に着るよ」"Then, I'll take notes for you." "Thanks. *I'll be grateful to you*."

おん² 音 sound ◎;〖音声〗(言語音) phone ◎; (漢字の読み方) the pronunciation of *kanji* based on Chinese

おんいき 音域 range ◎ ∥マライア・キャリーの音域は7オクターブといわれている Mariah Carey is said to have *a range* of seven octaves.

オンエア 彼らの新番組がオンエア中である Their new program is *on the air*./ Their new program is *being broadcast*.

おんかい 音階〖音楽〗(musical) scale ◎ ∥長[短]音階 the major [minor] *scale* / 全[半]音階 the diatonic [chromatic] *scale*

おんがえし 恩返し 彼らに恩返しをしなければならない I have to *return* [*repay*] their kindness. / 私は命の恩人に恩返ししたいと思った I wanted to *do something for* the person who saved my life *to show my gratitude*.

おんがく 音楽

music ◎ ──音楽の musical
⇨ 場面・状況別会話 p.1702
音楽の先生 a *music* teacher / 音楽を聴く[鑑賞する]「listen to [appreciate] *music*
私は音楽の時間(→授業)が大好きです I like *music* class very much.
みんな音楽に合わせて歌った Everyone sang *to the music*.
彼にはすばらしい音楽の才能がある He has great *musical* talent.
🗨「どんな音楽が好きですか」「ジャズがいちばん好きです」"What kind of *music* do you like?" "I like jazz best."
∥音楽家 a musician / 音楽会 a concert; (独奏[独唱]会) a recital / 音楽学校 a music school, a conservatory / 音楽教育 music(al) education / 音楽祭 a music festival / 音楽室 a music room / 音楽番組 a music program / 音楽評論家 a music critic / クラシック音楽 classical music / ポピュラー音楽 pop(ular) music / 民族音楽 ethnic music

おんかん 音感 a sense of pitch ∥絶対音感 absolute [perfect] pitch

おんぎ 恩義 debt ◎◎, obligation ◎
◆私は優子の援助に対し恩義を感じている I *feel indebted to* Yuko for her help.

おんきせがましい 恩着せがましい 彼女は僕に対していつも恩着せがましい態度をとる She always takes a *patronizing* attitude toward me. / (→恩義を感じることを期待する)She expects me to feel indebted to her for anything she does for me.

おんきゅう 恩給 pension ◎ ∥恩給で生活をする live on a *pension*
∥恩給受給者 a pensioner

おんきょう 音響 sound ◎◎; (すさまじい音) crash ◎ ∥その建物は大音響とともに崩れた The building collapsed *with a great crash*.
◆このコンサートホールは音響(効果)がすばらしい This concert hall has good *acoustics*./ The *acoustics* of this concert hall are good.
∥音響音声学 acoustic phonetics / 音響学 acoustics / 音響効果 sound effects

おんけい 恩恵 (利益) benefit ◎◎ ∥その国の人々は充実した福祉の恩恵を受けている People 「*get the benefit of* [*are blessed with*] comprehensive welfare in that country.

おんけつどうぶつ 温血動物 warm-blooded animal

おんけん 穏健 ──穏健な moderate, 《公式的》temperate; (中道の) middle-of-the-road ∥穏健な人物 a *temperate* person / 彼の政治的見解は穏健である His political views are *moderate* [*middle-of-the-road*].
∥穏健派(個人) a moderate (person); (団体) the moderates

おんこう 温厚 ──温厚な gentle, mild(-mannered), good-tempered, (穏やかな) good-natured ∥彼女は温厚な人柄でめったに怒ることはない She is a *mild-mannered* person and rarely gets angry.

おんさ 音叉〖音楽〗tuning fork ◎

オンザロック ⚠ on the rocks (❖ × on the rock とはいわない) ∥ウイスキーのオンザロックを飲む drink whiskey *on the rocks*

おんし 恩師 one's (former) teacher(s)

おんしつ¹ 温室 greenhouse ◎; (大きいもの) hothouse ◎, 《主に英》glasshouse ◎ ∥温室でサボテンを育てる grow cactuses in a *greenhouse* ◆温室栽培した花 flowers *grown under glass*
∥温室効果〖気象〗the greenhouse effect / 温室栽培 greenhouse [hothouse] cultivation / 温室植物 a greenhouse [hothouse] plant
慣用表現 彼女は温室育ちだ(→過保護に育てられた) She *was brought up overprotected*./ She *was a hothouse child*.

おんしつ² 音質 the quality of sound; (楽器・声の音色) timbre [tǽmbər] ◎◎

おんしゃ 恩赦 pardon ◎; (特に政治犯に対して) amnesty ◎◎ ∥人に恩赦を行う grant [give] a person *a pardon*

おんしょう 温床 (苗床) hotbed ◎; (悪などの) hotbed ◎ 〖通例単数形〗, nest ◎, breeding ground ◎ ∥悪の温床 a hotbed [nest] of vice / 犯罪の温床 a breeding ground for crime

おんじょう 温情 (思いやり) kindness ◎; (情け) mercy ◎◎ ──温情ある (思いやりのある) kind; (温かい心の) warm; (情け深い) merciful ∥裁判官は温情を示し彼を減刑した The judge, *showing mercy*, reduced his sentence.
◆彼女は温情あふれる人柄だ She is a *kind-hearted* [*warm-hearted*] person.

おんしらず 恩知らず ──恩知らずな ungrateful ∥ありがとうのひと言も言わずに立ち去るなんてあいつは恩知らずだ He is very *ungrateful* to have left without any single word of thanks.

おんしん 音信　彼女とは去年の冬から音信不通だ I haven't heard (any news) *from* her since last winter. / その後ぱったり彼からの音信が途絶えた(→一通も手紙を受け取っていない) I haven't received *a single letter* from him since then.

おんじん 恩人　林さんは私の恩人だ(→林さんに負うところが大きい) I *owe* Mr. Hayashi *very much*. / 君は命の恩人だ You really *saved my life*. / I *owe* my life to you.

オンス ounce [áuns] ⓒ (《略語》oz.)

おんすいプール 温水プール　heated (swimming) pool ⓒ

おんせい 音声　sound Ⓤ; (声) voice Ⓤ ⓒ ‖テレビの音声を大きく[小さく]する turn *the sound* up [down] on the TV
‖音声学 phonetics / 音声合成 speech [voice] synthesis / 音声多重放送 multiplex broadcasting / 音声認識 voice recognition

おんせつ 音節 [音声] syllable ⓒ ‖"window" という単語には２つ音節があります The word "window" has two *syllables*.

おんせん 温泉　hot spring ⓒ; (温泉地) spa ⓒ; (温泉宿) hot-spring resort ⓒ
温泉に行ってのんびりする go to *a hot spring* and relax
‖温泉宿 an inn at a hot-spring resort / 温泉療法 a hot-spring cure

> 日本には最新設備を備えた大型の健康ランドのようなものから，昔ながらのひなびた風情のあるまで，数多くの温泉があります．湯治のために長期間滞在することは今にはまれになりましたが，現在でも最もリラックスできる旅行地として老若男女を問わずとても人気があります．
> There are various types of hot-spring resorts in Japan, from large spa-type facilities with the latest equipment to old traditional hot springs with rustic charm. These days it has become rare for people to stay for a long time at hot-spring resorts to take a hot-spring cure, but hot springs are still very popular among people of all generations as the most relaxing place to go.

おんそく 音速　the speed of sound ‖その飛行機は音速の２倍の速さで飛ぶ The plane flies at twice *the speed of sound*. / The plane flies at Mach 2.
◆音速を超える break *the sound* [*sonic*] *barrier*
‖超音速 supersonic speed

おんぞん 温存　——温存する　(とっておく) save ⓗ; (保つ) keep* ⓗ ‖試合に備えて力を温存しておくんだ I *am saving* my energy *for* the competition. / 後々のために我々は切り札を温存している We *are keeping* our strongest card for later.

おんたい 温帯　the Temperate Zone (しばしば the temperate zone) ‖温帯植物 the flora of the Temperate Zone / 温帯低気圧 an extratropical cyclone

おんだん 温暖　——温暖な　temperate, mild; (暖かい) warm ‖温暖な気候 a *temperate* [*mild, warm*] climate
◆地球温暖化 global *warming*
‖温暖前線 a warm front

おんち 音痴　——音痴の tone-deaf ‖彼は音痴だ He is *tone-deaf*. / (→調子っぱずれに歌う) He sings *out of tune*.
◆私は方向[味]音痴だ I *have no sense of* direction [taste].

おんちゅう 御中　西田商会御中　Messrs. Nishida & Co. (❖Messrs. [mésərz] は Mr. の複数形で人名の入った社名に用いる) / ABC社人事課御中 The [*To the*] personnel department, ABC Company

おんちょう¹ 音調　(音の高さ) pitch ⓒ; (音の調子) tone ⓒ; (音の抑揚) intonation Ⓤ ⓒ; (音の強弱) accent Ⓤ ⓒ

おんちょう² 恩寵 grace Ⓤ ‖神の恩寵により by *the grace* of God

おんてい 音程　interval ⓒ ◆僕のギターの音程が狂っている My guitar *is*「*out of tune* [*not in tune*]. / 彼の歌は音程がはずれているね He is singing *off-key*.

おんど¹ 温度 temperature Ⓤ ⓒ
体感温度 sensible *temperature* / 高い[低い]温度 a high [low] *temperature* / 部屋の温度を上げる[下げる] raise [lower] *the temperature* of the room
温度が20度まで上がった[下がった] The *temperature* rose [fell] to 20 degrees.

おんど² 音頭　ダニエルが音頭をとってパーティーが催された Daniel *took the lead* in holding the party. / 原さんが新婚夫婦への乾杯の音頭をとった Mr. Hara *proposed a toast* to the newly married couple.

おんとう 穏当　——穏当な　(理にかなった) reasonable; (穏健な) moderate; (妥当な) proper, appropriate ‖彼の見方は穏当さを欠いていた His point of view was not *reasonable* [*moderate*] enough.
◆穏当な(→受け入れられる)結果だったといえよう You could say it was an *acceptable* result.

おんどく 音読　——音読する read* aloud, read out ‖その物語を音読する *read* the story *aloud* [*out*]

おんどけい 温度計　thermometer ⓒ ‖温度計は摂氏18度を指している *The thermometer* reads [stands at] 18℃.

おんどり 雄鳥・雄鶏 (雄の鶏) rooster ⓒ, 《主に英》cock ⓒ (❖cock は俗語で「ペニス」を意味するので《米》では rooster を用いるほうがよい); (雄の鳥一般) male bird

おんな 女

woman ⓒ (複 women); lady ⓒ; girl ⓒ; female ⓒ; (恋人) girlfriend ⓒ

> 類語
> woman は成人女性を指す最も一般的な語. lady は丁寧に接するときに用いる. girl は一般に若い女性を指す. female は生物学的な性別を強調し，口語で人に用いると失礼になることがある.

おんなおや 女親 female parent ◎, mother ◎

正雄兄ちゃん，女の人から電話だよ Masao, you have a call from *a woman*.

彼に女ができたらしい He seems to have *a girlfriend*.

◆彼は女のような高い声で話す He speaks in a high *feminine* voice.

📢「ご兄弟は？」「女ばかり 3 人です」 "Do you have any brothers and sisters?" "Three of us are all *girls*."

おんながた 女形 ➡おやま

おんなぎらい 女嫌い woman-hater ◎

おんなごころ 女心 君は女心（→女性の心理）を分かっていない You don't understand *the psychology of a woman*.

ことわざ 女心と秋の空 A women's mind is as changeable as the wind.（→女心は風のように変わりやすいものだ）

おんなざかり 女盛り 彼女はまさに今女盛りだ She is「*in the prime* [*at the peak*] *of womanhood*」right now.

おんなしゅじん 女主人（特に使用人を置いた家の）（古風）mistress ◎;（旅館・宿屋の）landlady ◎;（接待する人）hostess ◎

おんなたらし 女たらし womanizer ◎;（女のしりを追いかける男）skirt-chaser ◎, woman-chaser ◎

おんなで 女手 あの人は女手ひとつで（→自分ひとりで）子供を育て上げた She brought up her children all「*on her own* [*by herself*]」.

おんなともだち 女友達 female friend ◎;（女性によっては）《主に米》girlfriend ◎

おんなのこ 女の子（女の子供）girl ◎;（若い未婚女性）(young) lady ◎;（娘）daughter ◎;（女の赤ん坊）baby girl ◎ ‖12 歳の女の子 a 12-year-old *girl* / うちのいちばん上の女の子はこの 3 月に大学を出ました Our eldest *daughter* graduated from the university last March.

◆赤ちゃんは男の子ですか，女の子ですか Is the baby he or *she*?

おんなもの 女物（女性用衣料品）ladies' [women's] wear ⓤ ◆女物の靴 *ladies'* [*women's*] shoes

おんならしい 女らしい feminine ‖彼女がそんな女らしい服を着るのは珍しい It is unusual for her to wear such *feminine* clothes.

◆彼女もすっかり女らしくなった（→一人前の女性に成長した）She *has grown up into a woman*. / あの人には女らしさが欠けている She lacks (in) *femininity*.

おんねん 怨念 死者の怨念 a dead person's malice

おんのじ 御の字 半日働いて 5,000 円もらえれば御の字だ Five thousand yen for a half-day job is *more than enough*.

おんぱ 音波 sound [sonic] wave ◎ ‖超音波 an ultrasonic (sound) wave, ultrasound

オンパレード そのデザイナーの春物コレクションはピンクの服のオンパレードだった There were pink clothes *on parade* in the designer's spring collection.

おんびん 穏便 ―穏便な（平和的な）peaceful;（穏やかな）quiet ―穏便に peacefully; quietly;（寛容に）leniently ‖その件はぜひ穏便にすませたい We want to settle the matter *peacefully*. / We want to reach a *peaceful* settlement of the matter. / 彼のことは穏便に取り計らっていただきたい I'd like you to treat him *leniently*.

おんぷ 負んぶ piggyback ride ◎ ‖パパ，おんぶして Give me *a piggyback ride*, Daddy!

◆その母親は赤ちゃんをおんぶしていた The mother *was carrying* her baby *on her back*.

慣用表現 彼は何から何まで親におんぶにだっこだ He *depends on* his parents *for everything*. / He *is totally dependent on* his parents.

おんぷ 音符 (musical) note ◎ ‖全 [4 分，8 分] 音符 *a whole* [*a quarter*, *an eighth*] *note*

おんぷう 温風 a current of warm air ‖温風暖房機 a convector (heater)

オンブズマン（行政監察官）ombudsman [ámbudzmən] ◎（◆スウェーデン語から）

おんぼろ ―おんぼろの battered;（車などが）（口語的）beat(en)-up（◆名詞の前で用いる）;（服などが）ragged [rǽgid],（口語的）raggedy [rǽgədi];（服・家などが）shabby ‖おんぼろ車 a *battered* old car / おんぼろのジーンズ *ragged* jeans / おんぼろ小屋 a *shabby* shack

おんやく 音訳 transliteration ◎ⓤ

おんよみ 音読み a Chinese-style reading of a *kanji*

オンライン online ‖オンラインシステム an *online* system / オンライン情報サービス an *online* information service

おんりょう 音量 volume [váljəm] ⓤ, sound ⓤ ◆ラジオの音量を上げる［下げる］ *turn up* [*down*] the radio

おんわ 温和 ―温和な（気候などが）mild, temperate;（性格などが）gentle ‖温和な気候 a *mild* [*temperate*] climate / 彼はとても温和な人柄で，だれからも好かれている He is such a *gentle* person that everyone likes him.

か

か¹ 可（成績）C ©（複 ～s, ～'s），D ©（複 ～s, ～'s）（❖一般に米国の学校では成績を A (Excellent), B (Good), C (Average), D (Below Average), F (Failure)で表し，「可」はだいたい C か D に当たる）/ ドイツ語の成績は可だった I got *a C* in German.
◆未経験者可（→経験不要）No experience necessary. / この試験は辞書持ち込み可です You *can* use a dictionary for this exam.
慣用表現 可もなく不可もなくといったところだ It's *neither good nor bad*./ It's *so-so*.

か² 科 ❶【専門・学科】（大学・病院など）department ©《しばしば Department》；（課程）course © / 内[外]科「internal medicine [surgery] *department* / 商業[普通]科 commercial [general] *course* / 彼は英文科を志望している He wants to study in *the* English *department*.
❷【分類】【生物】family © / トラはネコ科に属する The tiger belongs to *the* cat *family*.

か³ 蚊 mosquito ©（複 ～es, ～s）/ ゆうべ蚊にひどく食われた I was badly bitten by *mosquitoes* last night. / 蚊に刺されたところがかゆくてだめだ Don't scratch *your mosquito bites*.
‖蚊取り線香 a mosquito coil / 蚊帳(ｶﾔ) a mosquito net
慣用表現 蚊の鳴くような声で *in a very faint voice*

か⁴ 課（会社・官庁などの）section ©, division ©（❖division のほうが section よりも大きい）；（組織の）department ©；(教科書の) lesson © / 会計課 *the* accounts *section*; *the* accounting *department* / 第5課 *Lesson* Five

-か¹

❶【疑問を表す終助詞】
🔴「これはあなたの辞書ですか」「はい，そうです[いいえ，違います]」"*Is this* your dictionary?" "Yes, it is. [No, it isn't.]"

語法
英語で疑問文を作るときは次のようにする．ただし会話では，肯定文の語尾を上げて発音するだけで疑問の意味を表す場合もある．
(1) be動詞を含む文…《be 動詞＋主語＋～？》の語順 / この自転車はあなたのですか *Is this bicycle* yours? / 武士は今家にいますか *Is Takeshi* (at) home now?
(2) 助動詞を含む文…《助動詞＋主語＋動詞＋～？》の語順 / 入ってもいいですか *May I come* in? / ドアをあけてもらえませんか *Would you open* the door? / 京都に行ったことはありますか *Have you* ever *been* to Kyoto?
(3) 一般動詞の文…《Do [Does, Did]＋主語＋動詞(の原形)＋～？》の語順 / 兄弟はいますか *Do you have* any brothers? / ゆうべ私に電話をくれましたか *Did you call me last night*?
(4) 疑問詞を含む文…ふつう疑問詞を文頭に置く / あの男の人はだれですか *Who* is that man? / あなたはどれが好きですか *Which one* do you like?
(5) 間接疑問文…主節の後ろに従属節の疑問文を平叙文の語順に直して置く / これが何か分かりますか Do you know *what this is*? / 私は彼女がどこに住んでいるのか知りません I don't know *where she lives*.

❷【不確かなこと・あいまいさ】
いつかまた遊びに来てください Please come and see me again *sometime*.
その CD-ROM は5,000円かそこらで買える You can buy that CD-ROM for [at] *around* 5,000 yen.
コーヒーか何かいかがですか Would you like coffee *or something*?
その歌手はまだ18歳かそこらだ That singer is only 18 *or so*.
泣いていたのか彼女の目は真っ赤だった Her eyes were all red, *maybe* [*perhaps*] because she had been crying.
どういうわけかきょうは気分がすぐれない *I don't know why*, but I don't feel well today.
はたして彼女の話は本当だろうか *I wonder if* her story is true.

❸【依頼・提案】
窓をあけてもらえませんか *Will you* open the window?
駅へ行く道を教えていただけませんか *Could you* tell me the way to the station?
ここで一服しませんか *Shall we* take a break now? / *Let's* take a break now.
水を1杯もらえますか A glass of water, *please*.
オーストラリアで日本語を教えてみませんか *Why don't you* try teaching Japanese in Australia?

❹【反語・非難・命令】
だれがそんなこと気にするものか *Who cares*? (❖「だれも気にしない」という意味合い)
そんなばかなことを言うやつがあるか *Don't talk such nonsense*!
きょうは早く起きろと言ったじゃないか *I told you* to get up early today!
ドアにはかぎをかけておくんだぞ，いいか Make sure the door is locked. *All right*? [*OK*?, *You got that*?, *Got it*?]
静かにしないか *Be quiet*!

❺【驚き・感動】
もう2月か，時間のたつのは早いなあ It's February *already*. Time really flies.
何だ，知っていたのか Oh. You knew it?
そうか，ポチのしわざだったのか *Oh, I see*. Pochi did it!
🔴「ここがグランドキャニオンか」「すごいね，地球の

歴史を見てるって感じ」"So, this is the Grand Canyon." "Amazing! I feel like I'm seeing the history of the earth!"

❻ [(…か~のどちらか)]
(either) ... or ~; (…かどうか) whether ... (or not).

7月か8月に旅行に行くつもりだ I'm going to travel in (either) July or August.

それは電子メールかファックスでお送りします I'll send it to you either by e-mail or by fax.

彼女に本当のことを言うべきかどうか迷っている I can't decide whether to tell her the truth or not.

-か² ―化 工業化 industrialization / 経営の合理化 the streamlining of management / 高齢化社会 an aging society

が¹ 我 self Ⓤ, ego ⒸⓊ (複～s) ◆彼は我が強い(→自分勝手だ) He is selfish./ (→自己主張が強い) He is self-assertive.(❖(米)では必ずしも否定的なニュアンスはない) / 彼女は何にでも我を通したがる(→思いどおりにしたがる) She wants to have everything her own way. / そんなに我をはるな Don't be so obstinate.

が² 蛾 moth Ⓒ

-が
❶ [主語・目的語を表す]

語法
(1) 日本語では，その文で(または会話で)初めて現れるものに対して「…が」を，すでに話題になったものに対して「…は」を用いることが多い．英語では前者に不定冠詞，後者に定冠詞を付けて表すことができる // 猫が庭に迷い込んできた．その猫はとても人なつっこかった A cat strayed into the garden. The cat really liked people.
(2) 特に主語を強調するために「…が」を用いる文脈の場合，英語ではその語を強く発音したり，語順を変えたりして強調を表す // そっちが先にこれを始めたんだ It's you who started this. (❖It's ... that [who, which] ~ は強調構文と呼ばれ，... の部分の語句が強調される)
(3) 天候・時間・距離などを表す文では通例 it を主語にする // 雨が降り始めた It began to rain.

外国人が道で私に話しかけてきた A foreigner spoke to me on the street.

庭のバラが咲き始めた The roses in our garden came into bloom.

キリンは首が長い Giraffes have long necks.

彼は英語とドイツ語が話せる He can speak English and German.

💬「コーヒーと紅茶，どっちがいい?」「紅茶がいいな」 "Which would you like, coffee or tea?" "Tea, please."

❷ [しかし・けれども] but; (それでも) still, yet; (…だけれども) though, although

あちこち捜したがその本は見つからなかった I'd looked everywhere, but I couldn't find the book.

あなたの気持ちも分かるが私にはどうすることもできない I understand how you feel, but there's nothing I can do for you.

彼女はやせているが実はよく食べる Though she's thin, she eats a lot.

❸ [そして] and

先週彼に会ったが，君によろしくとのことだった I met him last week, and he asked me to say hello to you.

僕には姉が2人いるが，今は2人とも外国に住んでいる I have two sisters, and both of them now live abroad.

❹ [(…しようが…であろうが)]
人に何を言われようが私は気にしない I don't care what others say.

雨が降ろうが降るまいがあすの試合は行われる Tomorrow's game will be played [whether it rains or not (come) rain or shine].

❺ [願望・控えめな気持ち]
お願いがあるのですが May I ask you a favor?

このシャツを大きいのと取り替えたいのですが I would like to exchange this shirt for a bigger one.

何とか最終電車に間に合うといいのだが I hope I can catch the last train.

彼も来られたらよかったんだが I wish he could come.

💬「いらっしゃいませ」「あの，結婚式用の服を探しているんですが」 "May I help you?" "Yes, I'm looking for a dress to wear to a wedding."

カー car Ⓒ ‖カーステレオ a car stereo / カーフェリー a car ferry / カーポート a car port, a carport / カー用品 auto accessories / カーラジオ a car radio

かあかあ (カラスの鳴き声) caw ⇒ なく(鳴く), croak

があがあ (アヒルなどの鳴き声) quack Ⓒ; (鳥の鳴き声) squawk Ⓒ ⇒ なく(鳴く) ◆があがあ言うのはやめてくれ Stop nagging me.

カーキ khaki ――カーキ色の khaki

かあさん 母さん mother Ⓒ ⇒ おかあさん

カースト (インドの世襲的階級) caste Ⓒ Ⓤ

ガーゼ ⚠ gauze [gɔ́ːz] Ⓤ (❖日本語はドイツ語のGaze から)

カーソル [コンピュータ] cursor Ⓒ / マウスを使ってカーソルを動かしてみてください Try to move the cursor with the mouse.

カーディガン cardigan Ⓒ

ガーデニング gardening Ⓤ

カーテン curtain Ⓒ; (厚手の) drapes ‖レースのカーテンをつるす hang [put up] lace curtains / 彼女は窓のカーテンを引いた She drew the curtains over the window. (❖draw は「カーテンをあける・閉める」の両方に用いられるので，明確にする場合には open, close を用いる)

‖カーテンコール a curtain call / カーテンリング a [curtain] ring / カーテンレール a curtain rail / カーテンロッド a curtain rod

カート cart Ⓒ ‖ゴルフカート a golf cart

カード ❶【紙片】card ⓒ /(トランプの)カードを配る deal *cards* / 今度は君がカードを引く番だよ Now it's your turn to draw *a card*.
🔄「現金でお支払いになりますか」「いえ、カードでお願いします」"Will you be paying in cash?" "No, I'll *charge it*."
❷【試合】card ⓒ /きょうの第3試合に好カードが組まれている Today's third game is *a drawing card*.
‖カード式公衆電話 a card phone / 会員カード a membership card / キャッシュカード (銀行の) a bank card / クリスマスカード a Christmas card / クレジットカード a credit card, 《口語的》plastic money / バースデーカード a birthday card

ガード¹ ⚠（陸橋）《主に米》overpass ⓒ,《主に英》flyover ⓒ ◆ガード下の焼き鳥屋 a *yakitori* stand *beneath the underpass*

ガード²（防御）guard Ⓤ ◆そのチームはガードが固い The team has *a strong defense*. / 彼女はガードが固い It is hard to make *an approach* to her.

ガードマン ⚠(security) guard ⓒ (◆「ガードマン」は和製英語。英語の guardsman は「兵士」の意味)

カートリッジ cartridge ⓒ

ガードル girdle ⓒ

ガードレール guardrail ⓒ,《主に英》crash barrier ⓒ

カートン carton ⓒ /たばこ1カートン *a carton* of cigarettes

カーナビゲーション car navigation system ⓒ

カーニバル carnival ⓒⓊ

カーネーション carnation ⓒ

カーブ（道などの）curve ⓒ, bend ⓒ;（野球の）curve(ball) ⓒ ──カーブする curve ⊜ⓘ, bend* ⊜ /その道路はカーブが多い The road has many *curves* [*twists*]. / 道は急カーブしている The road *curves* [*bends*] *sharply*. / その車は猛スピードでカーブを曲がった The car *took the curve* at high speed. / 金田はカーブを投げた Kaneda pitched *a curve*.
‖ヘアピンカーブ a hairpin bend

カーペット carpet ⓒ (◆通例、部屋全体に敷き詰めたものを指す。部分的な敷物・マットは rug という)

ガーベラ【植物】gerbera ⓒ

カーラー curler ⓒ, roller ⓒ /髪にカーラーを巻く put *curlers* in *one's* hair

ガーリック garlic Ⓤ

カーリング【スポーツ】curling Ⓤ

カール curl ⓒ ──カールする curl ⊜ⓘ /髪の毛をカールしてもらう have *one's* hair *curled* / 彼女の髪のカールは生まれつきだ Her hair *curls* naturally.

ガールスカウト（組織）《米》the Girl Scouts,《英》the Girl Guides;（団員）girl scout [guide] ⓒ

ガールフレンド girlfriend ⓒ (◆英語の girlfriend はふつう決まった恋人を指す。単なる女性の友達の場合は woman friend, female friend などという)

かい¹ 会

❶【集まり】meeting ⓒ; gathering ⓒ; conference ⓒ; convention ⓒ; party ⓒ; meet ⓒ

> meeting:「話し合いのための会合」を意味する最も一般的な語.
> gathering: 非公式でうちとけた集まりを指す. 口語では get-together ともいう.
> conference: 専門的な問題について討議する会議を指す.
> convention: 各国の代表が集まるような大規模な会議を指す.
> party: 社交的な集まりを指す.
> meet:《主に米》で運動競技の会に用いる.《英》では meeting ともいう.

送別[歓迎]会 a farewell [welcome] *party* /運よくその会に間に合った Fortunately I was in time for the *meeting*.

> 〖コロケーション〗 –meeting–
> 《動詞＋～》~に出席する attend a meeting / ~を欠席する absent *oneself* from a meeting / ~を延期する「put off [postpone] a meeting / ~を招集する call a meeting / ~を催す hold [have] a meeting

❷【組織・団体】（協会・同好会）association ⓒ, society ⓒ;（小規模の）club ⓒ, circle ⓒ /会を結成する set up *an association* / 会に入会する[を脱退する] join [leave] *a club*

かい² 回

❶【回数】time ⓒ (◆3回以上は three times のようにいうが, 1回は once, 2回は twice というのがふつう)
4, 5回 four or five *times*
彼は週に5回も図書館に行く He goes to the library as often as five *times* a week.
年に1, 2回は旅行に行きたいものだ I'd like to go on a trip *once or twice* a year.
◆3回勝負 a *three-game* match / 年1回の健康診断 a *yearly* checkup / もう一回やってごらん Try it (*once*) *again*. / 僕は毎晩腕立てふせを20回やっている I do *20* push-ups every night. / 彼女は3回目の挑戦で司法試験に合格した She passed the bar exam on her *third try*.
🔄「フランスには何回行ったことがあるの」「2回です」"*How many times* have you been to France?" "I've been there *twice*."

❷【野球の試合】inning ⓒ
9回の表[裏]に in the top [bottom] of *the ninth inning*
やった！8回が終わってリードしているぞ Boy! We're ahead after *the eighth inning*.
その試合は回を重ねるごとに白熱してきた The game got more exciting with each *inning*.

かい³ 階（建物のそれぞれの）floor ⓒ;（建物全体の）story,《英》storey ⓒ

> 〖語法〗
> 《米》では1階を the first floor と呼び, 以後

2階，3階，…を the second floor, the third floor, …と呼ぶのに対し，《英》では1階を the ground floor と呼び，以後 the first floor, the second floor, …と呼ぶため《米》の数え方と1階ずつずれる．

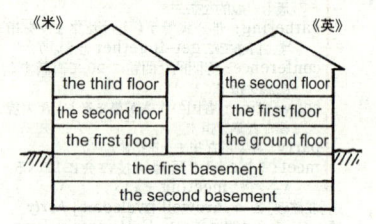

《米》	《英》
the third floor	the second floor
the second floor	the first floor
the first floor	the ground floor
the first basement	
the second basement	

最上階 *the top floor*
その会社はこのビルの2階にある The office is on *the second floor* of this building. / 彼女は僕と同じ階に住んでいる She lives on *the same floor* as me. / あの家は3階建てだ That house is *three stories high*. / 駐車場は地下2階にある Parking is *on the second basement level*. / この箱を2階に運ぶのを手伝ってくれませんか Could you help me carry this box *upstairs*? / 彼女は上[下]の階へスーツケースを運んだ She carried her suitcase *up* [*down*] *the stairs*. / スチュワートさん一家はうちの上の階に住んでいる The Stewarts live *above* us.

かい⁴ 甲斐（報い）reward ©⓾ ◆やりがいのある仕事 a *challenging* job / 苦労のかいがあった My efforts *were rewarded* [*paid off*]. / 努力のかいがあって（→努力のおかげで）入試に合格した *Thanks to* hard work, I passed the entrance examination. / この本は読みがいがある（→読む価値がある）This book *is worth reading*. / It *is worthwhile reading* this book. / 彼女は手厚い看護のかいもなく死んだ *Though* she was nursed tenderly, she died. / 彼には忠告してもかいがなかった My advice *was useless* to him.

●「森さんはどんな人ですか」「誠実で頼りがいのある人です」 "What's Mr. Mori like?" "He's an honest, *reliable* person."

かい⁵ 下位 lower position ©⓾, lower rank ©⓾ ◆そのチームはこれまで毎年下位に低迷していた So far the team *has ranked low* every year.
‖下位概念〖論理〗a subordinate concept / 下位区分 subdivision / 下位打線〖野球〗the bottom of the batting order
⇒さいかい（最下位）

かい⁶ 貝 shellfish ©⓾（複～s）;（二枚貝）clam ©;（貝殻）shell © / 貝ボタン a *shell* button
[慣用表現] 彼女は貝のように口を閉ざした She *shut up like a clam*. / She *clammed up*.

かい⁷ 買い（買うこと）buying ⓾ / 売り買い *buying* and selling（❖語順に注意）

●「このジャケットが9,800円だって」「それは絶対買いだよ(→とても安いから買うべきだ)」"Look! This jacket costs only 9,800 yen!" "That's *a real bargain*! You've got to buy it."

かい⁸ 櫂（カヌー用）paddle ©;（ボート用の）oar © / かいをこぐ pull *an oar*

かい⁹ 解 solution ©⓾ ◆方程式の解を求める(→方程式を解く) *solve* the equation

-かい¹ -界 the world, circle ©（しばしば複数形～s）/ 学界 the academic *world* / 財界 financial *circles* / スポーツ界 the sports *world*; *the world* of sports / 芸能界 the *world* of show business
◆映画界 *the screen* / 植物[動物, 鉱物]界 *the plant [animal, mineral] kingdom*

-かい² -海 日本海 *the Sea* of Japan / 東シナ海 *the East China Sea* / エーゲ海 *the Aegean Sea*

がい 害（人に対する）harm ⓾;（物に対する）damage ⓾ ⇒がいする / 害をもたらす cause *harm* [*damage*] / 害を被る suffer *harm* [*damage*] / この薬品は人体に直接的な害はない This chemical causes no direct *damage* to the human body. ◆過剰な運動は体に害になることがある Too much exercise can *be harmful to* your health.
[慣用表現] 喫煙は百害あって一利なしだとよくいわれる It is often said that smoking *does no good but much harm*.

-がい¹ -外 時間外労働 *overtime* work / あいつが昇進するなんて全くの問題外だ His promotion *is completely out of the question*. / トムは予想外の大成功を収めて私たちを喜ばせた To our delight, Tom has succeeded *beyond our expectations*. / 彼は自分の専門外のことは何ひとつ知らない He doesn't know anything *outside his field*.

-がい² -街 住宅街 a residential *area* / 商店街 a shopping *arcade* / 学生街 a student *quarter* / ビジネス街 a business *park* / ウォール街 Wall *Street* / その都市の中心街 *the central part* of the city

かいあく 改悪 法律を改悪する *revise* the law *for the worse*

がいあく 害悪（悪）evil ©⓾, poison ©⓾;（悪影響）bad influence ⓾ / この名作も当時は世に害悪を流すものとみなされた This masterpiece was thought to have [be] *a bad influence* on society in those days.

かいあげる 買い上げる（買い占める）buy* up / 彼は店にあるバラをすべて買い上げた He *bought up* all the roses in the shop.
◆政府は余った米を買い上げた The government *bought* the excess (of) rice. / 現金でお買い上げの物はすべて25パーセント割引します We can give you a 25 percent discount on all cash *purchases*.

かいあさる 買い漁る 佐藤教授は研究に必要な本を買いあさった Professor Sato *bought* books for his study *one after another*. / 彼女は香港で安い化粧品を買いあさった She *hunted for* low-priced cosmetics in Hong

Kong.
がいあつ 外圧 foreign pressure ⓤ 〃外圧に屈する yield to *foreign pressure*
かいいき 海域 sea area ⓒ, waters ◆周辺の海域 the surrounding *sea*
かいいぬ 飼い犬 one's (house [pet]) dog / 家をあけている間友人に飼い犬を預けた I left *my dog* with a friend while I was away.
慣用表現 飼い犬に手をかまれる (→信用していた者に裏切られる) be betrayed by a person whom one has trusted
かいいれる 買い入れる buy*, purchase (buy よりも改まった語。大きな物・高価な物の購入の場合に用いる) / その図書館は漱石全集を買い入れた The library *purchased* Soseki's complete works.
かいいん 会員 member ⓒ, 《集合的》membership ⓤ (また a 〜) (❖会員数や会員資格も表す) 〃会員のみ《掲示》*Members* Only / そのクラブの会員になる become *a member* of the club / クラブの会員資格を取る[失う] obtain [lose] *membership* in a club / このクラブは会員が少ない[多い] This club has *a* small [large] *membership*. / 当会ではただ今会員を募集しています We are now accepting applications for *membership*.
‖会員権 membership / 会員証 a membership card / 会員制 a membership system / 会員名簿 a list of members, a membership roster, the rolls (of the club) / 終身会員 a life member / 準会員 an associate member / 正会員 a (regular) member / 非会員 a non-member
かいうん 海運 海運業 the shipping [maritime] trade / 海運国 a maritime [seafaring] nation
かいえん¹ 開演 開演は午後 2 時です The curtain *rises* at two in the afternoon. / たいていの劇場は 7 時半開演です Most theaters have *a* 7:30 *curtain*. / Most performances *begin* at 7:30.
かいえん² 開園 動物園は朝 9 時に開園する The zoo *opens* at nine in the morning.
かいおうせい 海王星 《天文》Neptune
かいおき 買い置き (在庫) stock ⓒ 〃買い置きの缶詰 *a back stock* of canned food
🔴「おふろの電球が切れちゃった」「確か買い置きがあったわよ」"The light bulb in the bathroom has burned out." "I think we have *a stock* of bulbs."
かいか¹ 階下 the downstairs ―階下へ[で] downstairs ―階下の downstairs (❖名詞の前で用いる) 〃トムは電話に出るために階下へ駆け下りた Tom ran *downstairs* to answer the telephone.
かいか² 開花 flower ⓤ, bloom ⓤ; (才能などの) the flowering ―開花する bloom; (木などが) blossom / 今年はバラの開花が遅かった This year our roses *came into flower* late. ◆彼の才能は晩年になって開花した His talent *flowered* during his later years.
‖開花期 blossoming [flowering] time / 開花予想 the forecast of the blossom

かいか³ 開架 ―開架式の open shelf, open stack
かいが 絵画 (一般に) picture ⓒ; (絵の具などで描いた絵) painting ⓒ; (鉛筆・クレヨンなどによる線画) drawing ⓒ 〃彼女の興味はロマン派の絵画に集中している Her interest is centered on Romantic *paintings*.
がいか 外貨 foreign currency ⓒⓤ 〃外貨を獲得する gain *foreign currency*
‖外貨準備高 foreign currency reserves / 外貨保有高 foreign currency holdings / 外貨預金 foreign currency deposit
ガイガーカウンター (放射能測定器) Geiger counter ⓒ
かいかい 開会 the opening (of a meeting) ―開会する open, call (the meeting) to order / 開会の辞を述べる give *an opening address* / ここに会議の開会を宣言します I now declare this meeting *open*. ◆国会は現在開会中(→会期中)だ The Diet *is* now "*in session* [*sitting*]*.
‖開会式 an opening ceremony
かいがい 海外 (外国) foreign countries ―海外の oversea, foreign ―海外へ[に] abroad, overseas ⇨ がいこく
海外への留学生 a student *overseas* / 海外からの留学生 an *overseas* student; a student *from abroad*
一度は海外へ行ってみたい I want to go *abroad* once.
私たちは時々海外で公演します We sometimes perform *abroad*.
彼は海外留学を考えている He is considering "*going abroad to study* [*studying abroad*]*.
彼女は以前より海外出張が多くなった She *goes abroad on business* more than she used to.
海外旅行をすると自分の国のことがよく分かる When you *travel abroad* [*overseas*], you get a better understanding of your own country.
‖海外居住者 a resident in a foreign country / 海外市場 an overseas market / 海外事情 foreign affairs / 海外支店 an overseas branch / 海外駐在員 an overseas representative / 海外ニュース foreign [world] news, news from abroad
がいかい¹ 外海 the open sea; (公海) the high seas; (大洋) the ocean
がいかい² 外界 the outside world
かいがいしい 甲斐甲斐しい (勤勉な) diligent; (てきぱきとした) brisk ―かいがいしく diligently; briskly
かいかく 改革 reform ⓤⓒ; (特に宗教の) reformation ⓤⓒ ―改革する reform
政治改革に着手する initiate political *reform*
政府は教育制度を改革しようとしている The government is trying to *reform* the educational system.
‖改革案 a reform plan / 行政改革 an administrative reform / 宗教改革 a religious reformation (❖16世紀ヨーロッパで起こった「宗教改革」は the Reformation) / 税制改

革 a tax reform
がいかく 外角 (数学の) exterior angle ©; (野球の) the outside
◆外角に投げる pitch *outside* / 外角高めの直球 a ball high and *outside*
がいかくだんたい 外郭団体 affiliated organization ©
かいかつ 快活 ——快活な cheerful ——快活に cheerfully ‖彼女は快活なのでみんなから好かれていた She was so *cheerful* that everyone liked her.
かいかつ 概括 (概括されたもの) summary ©; (概括すること) generalization ©∪ ——概括する summarize ⨁⨀, sum up ‖最後の章では, すべての議論を概括することにします In the last chapter we'll *sum up* all the arguments.
かいかぶる 買い被る (過大評価する) overestimate ⨁, overrate ⨁ ‖あなたは彼の力を買いかぶっているのだ I think you *overestimated* his ability.
◆買いかぶらないでください *Don't give me more credit than I deserve.*
かいがら 貝殻 shell ©∪, seashell ©∪ ‖浜辺で貝殻を拾う gather *seashells* on the beach
‖貝殻細工 shellwork
かいかん¹ 快感 pleasure ©∪ ‖快感を覚える feel *pleasure*; feel *good*
◆彼は勝利の快感に酔いしれていた He *was elated at* the victory.
かいかん² 会館 hall © ‖ 学生会館 a students' hall / 市民会館 a city hall
かいかん³ 開館 図書館は月曜日を除く毎日開館しています The library *is open* every day except Mondays.
‖開館時間 (あいている時間) opening hours; (あく時間) opening time

かいがん 海岸 the coast; the (sea)shore; the seaside; the beach

> coast: 陸側から見た沿岸のこと. 地図・天気予報などでよく用いられる.
> (sea)shore: 海辺の土地, 特に海から見た岸のこと.
> seaside: 保養地・行楽地としての海岸.
> beach: 砂浜・なぎさのこと.

フランスの南海岸 the south coast of France
海岸に沿って松林がある There is a pine wood along *the seashore.*
その村は美しい海岸で名高い The village is famous for *its* beautiful *beach.*
‖海岸線 a coastline / 海岸通り a seafront (street)
がいかん¹ 外観 appearance ∪©, look ©; (建物の) exterior © ‖その家は奇妙な外観をしている The house has *a strange appearance.* / The house *looks* strange. / そのホテルの外観が気に入った I was pleased with *the look* of the hotel.
がいかん² 概観 survey ©, overview ©
——概観する survey ⨁ ‖本書の目的はシュールレアリズムの歴史を概観することである The aim of this book is (to give) *a historical overview* of Surrealism.

かいき¹ 会期 session © ‖会期中である *be in session* / 議会の会期は延長されるだろう The parliamentary *session* will be extended.
かいき² 怪奇 ——怪奇な (不可解な) mysterious; (外見が) grotesque ‖複雑怪奇な殺人事件 a *very complicated and mysterious* murder
‖怪奇映画 a horror movie / 怪奇小説 a mystery
かいき³ 皆既 ‖皆既日[月]食 a total eclipse of the sun [moon]
-かいき -回忌 祖父の三[七]回忌 the second [sixth] *anniversary of* my grandfather's *death* (◆満2年目の法要を三回忌, 満6年目を七回忌と呼ぶので英語とは数がずれる)

かいぎ¹ 会議

meeting ©; council ©; conference ©
> meeting: あらゆる会議に用いられる最も一般的な語.
> council: 助言・審議をする小規模で私的な会議.
> conference: 専門的な問題について公に協議する大規模な会議.

この議論は次の会議に持ち越すことにしましょう Let's carry this discussion over to *our* next *meeting.*
会議では環境破壊の問題が取り上げられた The problem of environmental destruction was brought up at *the conference.*
その会議の目的は世界経済のより緊密な統合にある The aim of the *conference* is the closer integration of the world's economy.
🔴「鈴木さんをお願いします」「申しわけありませんがただ今会議中です」"May I talk to Mr. Suzuki?" "I'm sorry, but he's *in a meeting* now."

[コロケーション] -meeting-
【動詞+〜】 〜に出席する attend a meeting / 〜を延期する「put off [postpone] a meeting / 〜を終了する close a meeting / 〜を休会にする adjourn a meeting / 〜を中止する「call off [cancel] a meeting / 〜を始める begin a meeting / 〜を開く hold [have] a meeting / 〜を予定する arrange a meeting / 〜を招集する call a meeting

‖会議室 a conference room / 会議録 minutes / 円卓会議 a round-table conference / 家族会議 a family council / 緊急会議 an emergency [urgent] meeting / 軍縮会議 a disarmament conference / 国際会議 an international conference / 重役会議 a meeting of the board of directors / 首脳会議 a summit, a top-level meeting / 職員会議 (教員の) a teachers' meeting / テレビ会議 a teleconference / 本会議 (国会などの) a plenary session
かいぎ² 懐疑 ——懐疑的な skeptical ‖私はこの実験の成功には懐疑的だ I「*am skeptical about* [*doubt*] the success of this experiment.

‖懐疑主義 skepticism / 懐疑論者 a skeptic
がいき 外気 (open) air ◫ ‖外気に触れる be exposed to the (open) air
‖外気圏 the exosphere
かいきいわい 快気祝い そのレストランで祖母の快気祝いをした We had a party at that restaurant to *celebrate* our grandmother's *recovery from her illness*.
かいきせん 回帰線 tropic ◫ ‖北回帰線 the Tropic of Cancer / 南回帰線 the Tropic of Capricorn
かいぎゃく 諧謔 wit ◫, humor ◫ ◆諧謔を弄(ろう)する make *a witty remark*
かいきゅう 階級 class ◫; (地位・身分) rank ◫◫ ‖階級が上がる advance in *rank* / 労働者[支配]階級に属する belong to the *working* [*ruling*] *class* / 田島選手は2階級制覇を成しげた Ms. Tajima won the championships in two *classes*.
‖階級意識 class consciousness / 階級社会 a class(-based) society / 階級制度 the class system / 階級闘争 class struggle [conflict] / 上流[下層]階級 the upper [lower] class(es) / 知識階級 the intelligentsia / 中流階級 the middle class / 特権階級 the privileged classes
かいきょ 快挙 その映画はアカデミー賞9部門受賞という快挙を成しとげた The film accomplished *the splendid achievement* of winning nine Academy Awards.
かいきょう¹ 海峡 strait ◫ 《しばしば複数形～s》; channel ◫ 《❖strait よりも広い》 ‖津軽海峡 the Tsugaru *Straits* / イギリス海峡 the (English) *Channel* / ドーバー海峡を渡る cross the *Strait(s) of Dover* / 海峡横断フェリー the *cross-channel* ferries
かいきょう² 回教 (イスラム教) Islam ◫
‖回教寺院 a mosque / 回教徒 a Muslim
かいぎょう¹ 開業 ──開業する (商店を) set* up a shop, open up; (医者・弁護士が) practice ◫◉ ‖彼は20年間ここで歯医者を開業している He *has been practicing* as a dentist here for 20 years.
‖開業医 《公式的》a general practitioner 《略語》GP
かいぎょう² 改行 ──改行する begin* a new line [paragraph] ◆改行キー the *return* (key)
がいきょう 概況 (全体の状況) general conditions ‖天気概況 the general weather *conditions* ◆概況報告書 *a fact sheet*
かいきょく 開局 ──開局する start up ‖新しいテレビ局が来年開局する予定だ A new TV station is due to *start up* next year.
かいきる 買い切る (全部買う) buy* up ‖彼は店にある在庫の品を買い切った He *bought up* all the stock in the store.
◆その会社は内野席を買い切った(→全席を予約した) The company *reserved* all the seats in the infield stands.
かいきん¹ 解禁 (通商などの) the lifting of the ban [embargo] (on ...); (狩猟の) the opening of the hunting [fishing] season
◆今月の初めにアユ釣りが解禁になった The *ayu* (fishing) *season opened* at the beginning of this month.
かいきん² 皆勤 perfect attendance ◫ ‖皆勤賞 a prize for perfect attendance
かいきんシャツ 開襟シャツ open-necked [open-collar] shirt ◫
かいぐい 買い食い 彼らはいつも学校の帰りに買い食いをする They always *buy* snacks and *eat them* on the way home from school.
かいくぐる (すり抜ける) slip through ...; (うまくかわす) dodge ◫◉ ‖テロリストは捜査網をかいくぐって逃げた The terrorists *slipped through* the dragnet.
かいぐん 海軍 the navy 《単数または複数扱い》; (上陸部隊) the naval force ──海軍の naval ‖海軍に入隊する join *the navy*
‖海軍基地 a naval base / 海軍軍人 a navy man, a sailor / 海軍士官 a naval officer

かいけい 会計
❶【金銭の出し入れ】accounts; (経理) accounting ◫
一般[特別]会計 general [special] *accounts*
きのうのうちの会社で会計監査が行われた Our *accounts were audited* [*examined*] yesterday.
❷【勘定】(勘定書) bill ◫, 《米》check ◫
会計をすませる(→勘定を支払う) pay *the bill*
(レストランで)会計をお願いします *Check* [*Bill*], please.
‖会計課 the accounting department [section] / 会計係 an accountant; (ホテルなどの) a cashier / 会計学 accounting / 会計監査 an audit / 会計検査院 the Board of Audit / 会計士 an accountant / 会計年度 a fiscal [《英》financial] year / 会計報告 a financial report

かいけつ 解決

solution ◫, 《公式的》resolution ◫; (紛争などの) settlement ◫ ──解決する solve ◫◉, 《公式的》resolve ◫◉; settle ◫◉
問題を解決する *solve* a problem / 国際紛争を解決する *settle* international disputes / 解決方法を見つける work out *a solution*
この問題の一日も早い解決を望んでいます I hope for *the* quickest possible *resolution* to this problem.
後悔したところで何の解決にもならない Regrets won't lead to any *solution*.
その事件は未解決のままだ The case remains 「*to be solved* [*unsolved*]」.
彼らのいさかいは円満に解決した Their differences *were settled* amicably.
この問題は簡単には解決できない There's no magic *solution* for this problem.
◆心配しなくてもそれは自然に解決しますよ Don't worry. That *will work itself out*.
住民からの情報が事件解決につながった The information from the local people helped *clear up* the case.
かいけつびょう 壊血病 〔医学〕scurvy ◫
かいけん¹ 会見 interview ◫ ──会見する

かいけん

have* an interview ∥外交官は大臣と大使館で会見した The diplomat *had an interview with* the minister at the embassy. ∥大統領は記者会見をした The president gave 「*an interview to the press* [*a press conference*]. ◆米国の国務長官は日本の外相と会談した The U.S. Secretary of State *met* his Japanese counterpart.

かいけん² 改憲 (憲法の改正) amendment to the constitution

かいげん 改元 the official naming of a new era

がいけん 外見 (外観・見た目) appearance ⓤ; (外側) the outside, the exterior ∥外見で人を判断すべきではない You shouldn't judge people *by their appearance*. ◆彼は外見からすると30代半ばくらいだ He *looks like* he's in his mid-30s. ∥ 僕と兄は外見は似ているが性格は全く違う I resemble my brother *in looks* but not in character at all.

かいげんれい 戒厳令 martial law ⓤ ∥その町には今戒厳令が敷かれている The city is under *martial law* now.

かいこ¹ 解雇 dismissal ⓒⓤ, discharge ⓒ; (一時的な) layoff ⓒ ─解雇する dismiss ⊕, discharge ⊕; (一時的に) lay* off ⇨ ひ ◆彼はその職を解雇された He *was dismissed* from the position.
∥解雇通知 a dismissal notice,《米口語的》a pink slip ∥ 不当解雇 unfair dismissal

かいこ² 回顧 ─回顧する look back ⇨ おもいだす ∥回顧展 a retrospective exhibition ∥ 回顧録 reminiscences,《公式的》memoirs

かいこ³ 蚕 silkworm ⓒ

かいこ⁴ 懐古 retrospection ⓤ; (懐古の情) nostalgia ⓤ ─懐古的な nostalgic ◆彼には懐古趣味がある He *likes to look back on his good old days*.

かいご 介護 care ⓤ, nursing ⓤ ─介護する nurse ⊕, care for ... 高齢化と介護 p.522 ∥今日《公》介護を必要としている人は少なくない Today there are not a few people *with special needs*.
∥介護施設 nursing facilities ∥ 介護保険 long-term care insurance ∥ 在宅介護 residential care ∥ 老人介護 care for the elderly [aged]

かいこう¹ 開口 開口一番, 彼は「頼みがあるんだ」と言った *The first thing he said* was "Do me a favor."

かいこう² 開校 ─開校する found a school ◆私たちの学校は1900年に開校した Our school *was founded* in 1900.
∥開校記念日 School Foundation Day

かいこう³ 開港 ─開港する open a port

かいこう⁴ 開講 2003年4月開講予定 The course *will start* in April of 2003.

かいこう⁵ 海溝 trench ⓒ ∥日本海溝 *the* Japan *Trench*

かいごう 会合 meeting ⓒ ⇨ かい(会) ∥会合を開く hold *a meeting* ◆我々は定期的に会合をもっている We *meet* regularly.

がいこう 外交 (外交術) diplomacy ⓤ ─外交の diplomatic; (対外的な) foreign ∥外交関係を結ぶ establish *diplomatic relations* ∥ その国は近隣諸国との外交を絶った The country broke off *diplomatic relations* with its neighbors. ∥ 彼は外交問題に詳しい He is an expert on *diplomatic affairs*. ∥ 彼女はその問題の解決に外交的手腕を発揮した She displayed *her diplomatic skill* in settling the issue.
∥外交員(販売員) a salesperson, a salesman, a saleswoman ∥ 外交官 a diplomat ∥ 外交辞令(お世辞) a compliment, flattery ∥ 外交政策 diplomatic policy ∥ 外交団 the diplomatic corps [kɔ́ːr] ∥ 外交ルート diplomatic channels ∥ ドル外交 dollar diplomacy ∥ 武力外交 gunboat diplomacy

がいこうてき 外向的 ─外交的な extroverted (↔introverted), outgoing ◆彼女は外向的(な人)だ She *is an extrovert*.

かいこく¹ 戒告 reprimand ⓒⓤ ◆戒告処分を受ける *be reprimanded*

かいこく² 開国 1850年代, 日本は欧米諸国に対して開国した In the 1850's, Japan *opened its borders* to Europeans and Americans.

がいこく 外国

foreign country ⓒ ─外国の foreign ─外国に[で] abroad, overseas ⇨ かいがい

> 英作文ノート **abroad に to はいらない**
> 私は近い将来外国へ行きたい
> →×I want to *go to abroad* in the near future.
> →○I want to *go abroad* in the near future.
> ★abroad は「外国へ」という意味の副詞なので, go abroad といい, go abroad to とはいわない. 「外国へ行く」は, 「go to [visit] another country ともいう.

私の父はよく外国へ行く My father often goes *abroad*.

あなたは外国へ行ったことがありますか Have you ever been *abroad* [*to a foreign country*]?

生徒たちは学習する外国語を選択することができる The students have a choice of *foreign languages* to study.

彼は外国なまりの日本語を話す He speaks Japanese *with a foreign accent*.

このバッグは外国製だ This bag is *of foreign make*.

◆外国人を雇用する hire *foreigners*
∥外国為替 foreign exchange ∥ 外国為替市場 a foreign exchange market ∥ 外国為替相場 a foreign exchange rate ∥ 外国航路 an outward voyage ∥ 外国語学校 a school of foreign languages ∥ 外国人登録 alien registration ∥ 外国人登録法 the Alien Registration Law ∥ 外国人労働者 a foreign worker ∥ 外国製品 foreign products ∥ 外国貿易 foreign trade [commerce]

がいこつ 骸骨 skeleton ◆彼女は骸骨のようにやせ細っていた She *was* all skin and bones.

かいこむ 買い込む 私たちは地震に備えて非常食を買い込んだ We *bought* a lot of emergency provisions in case of an earthquake.

かいごろし 飼い殺し 会社で飼い殺しになる(→解雇されずにつまらない仕事を与えられる)くらいなら辞めるべきだ If they *keep giving you meaningless tasks instead of dismissing you*, you should leave the company.

かいこん 開墾 ――開墾する (耕す) cultivate 他; (じゃまな物を取り払う) clear 他 ◆彼らはその土地の大部分を開墾した They *brought* most of the land *under cultivation*.

かいさい 開催 ――開催する hold* 他; (開会する) open 他 ‖次のサミットはどこで開催されるのですか Where will the next summit meeting *be held*? / 私たちの学校の文化祭は今, 開催中です Our school festival *is now open*. / 長野は1998年冬季オリンピックの開催地だった Nagano *played host to* the 1998 Winter Olympic Games.
‖開催国 a host country / 開催都市 a host city

かいざい 介在 intervention C U ――介在する intervene 自, lie* [stand*] between …

がいさい 外債 (負債の) foreign [external] debt C U; (債権の) foreign bond C

かいさつ 改札 (切符を調べること) the inspection of tickets; (改札口) ticket gate C ‖自動改札を通る go through *an automatic ticket gate*
🅔 「待ち合わせはどこにしようか」「高円寺の改札を出た所は?」 "Where should we meet?" "How about *by the gate* at Koenji Station?"
‖改札係 a ticket collector

かいさん 解散 (集会などの) breakup C; (組織・議会などの) dissolution U ――解散する break* up, part 自; dissolve 他
駅で解散します We *will part* at the station.
その人気ロックグループは先月解散した The popular rock group *broke up* last month.
警官たちはデモを解散させた The police *broke up* the demonstration.
総理大臣は国会を解散する権限をもっている The Prime Minister has the power to *dissolve* the Diet.
‖解散権 the right to dissolve

がいさん 概算 (概算した量・額) estimate C, approximation C U; (概算すること) estimation C ――概算する estimate 他 自 ‖旅行の費用は概算で5万円です The cost of the journey *is estimated* at 50,000 yen. / ざっと概算しても300人の学生が彼の授業に出席していた *At a rough estimate*, about three hundred students attended his lecture.
‖概算価格 an approximate price

かいさんぶつ 海産物 marine products, seafood U

かいし 開始 beginning C, start C, 《公式的》commencement C U ――開始する begin* 自他, start 自他; (会などを) open 他 自
大雪のために試合の開始がかなり遅れた The *start* of the game was greatly delayed by the heavy snow.
警察はその事件の調査を開始した The police *began* [*started*] to investigate the incident.
私たちは昼食後討議を開始した We *opened* our discussion after lunch.

かいじ 海事 maritime affairs ‖海事法 maritime law

がいし 外資 foreign capital U ‖外資の流入 an inward flow of *foreign capital*
◆姉は外資系の銀行で働いている My sister works for *a foreign-affiliated bank*.

がいして 概して (一般的に) in general, generally (speaking); (全体的に見て) on the whole (❖すべて文頭で用いることが多い) ➡ふつう(普通), たいてい ‖概してこの地方は雨が多い *In general*, we have much rain in this region. / 女の子は概して甘い物が好きだ *Generally speaking*, girls love sweets. / 新商品の売れ行きは概して順調だ *On the whole*, the new products are selling well.

かいしめる 買い占める buy* up; (商品・株などを) corner 他

かいしゃ 会社

company C ((略語) Co., co.); firm C; corporation C ((略語) Corp., corp.); office C
  company:「会社」を表す最も一般的な語.
  firm: company と同様に日常的な語. 2人以上から成る合資会社を指す.
  corporation: 法人化された会社を指す, ややかたい語.
  office:「会社に行く」などという場合の「会社」に用いる.

《会社が・は》
この会社は主に絹製品を扱っている This *company* deals chiefly in silk goods.
うちの会社は来春5人採用する予定だ Our *company* is going to employ five people next spring.
多くの会社が不況で倒産した A lot of *companies* went bankrupt because of the recession.

《会社に・へ》
私は新橋にある会社に勤めています I work for *a company* in Shimbashi.
彼はふだん6時まで会社にいる He usually stays at [in] *the office* until 6 o'clock.
僕がこの会社に入ってからもう7年になる Seven years have already passed since I started working for this *company*.
🅔 「お母さんは?」「もう会社へ行ったわよ」 "Where's Mom?" "She's gone to *the office*."

《会社の》
会社の旅行で箱根に行った I went to Hakone on a *company* trip.

がいしゃ

父は会社の人とゴルフに行った My father went golfing with *some people from his office*.
会社のほうに電話をかけてください Call me at *the office*.
彼女はその会社の25パーセントの株を所有している She holds 25 percent of the *company's* stock.

【会社を】
父は昨年会社を辞めた My father left *the company* last year.

◆彼は会社を首になった He was fired from *his job*. / 会社を辞めようかと思っているんだ I'm thinking of quitting *the job*.

┌─ コロケーション ─ -company- ─┐
【動詞＋～】 ～に勤める work for a company / ～に就職する be hired by a company; get employment in a company / ～を経営する manage [run] a company / ～を設立する「set up [establish, form] a company / ～を(定年)退職する retire from one's company
└────────────────────┘

‖会社員 an office worker, a company employee / 会社人間 a corporate person / 会社法 corporate law / 会社訪問 a visit to a company for collecting information about employment / 親会社 a parent company / 関連会社 an affiliated [associated] company / 航空会社 an airline company / 子会社 a subsidiary company / 証券会社 a securities company / 貿易会社 a trading company / 保険会社 an insurance company / 民間会社 a private company / 旅行会社 a travel agency

┌─ 役職名のいろいろ ─┐
取締役会長 chairman [chairwoman, chairperson] (of the board of directors) / 取締役社長 president / 取締役副社長 vice-president / 代表取締役 representative director / 専務取締役 senior managing director / 常務取締役 managing director / 取締役 director / 監査役 auditor / 顧問 advisor / 部長 department manager / 課長 section manager / 係長 subsection chief
└────────────────────┘

がいしゃ 外車 foreign car ⓒ; (輸入車) imported car ⓒ

かいしゃく 解釈 interpretation ⓊⒸ; (説明) explanation ⒸⓊ ──解釈する interpret 他; (説明する) explain 他; (受け取る) take* 他 ‖この文はいろいろに解釈できる This sentence *can be interpreted* in various ways. / 私は彼女の沈黙を承諾と解釈した I *took* her silence *as* approval.

◆彼は私の説明を誤って解釈した He *misinterpreted* my explanation.

かいしゅう¹ 回収 collection Ⓤ ──回収する (集める) collect 他; (取り戻す) get* back; (不良品などを) recall 他, call in ‖家庭ごみは週に1度回収される Household rubbish *is collected* once a week. / その会社は不良品の回収を余儀なくされた The company had to *recall* sub-standard products. ◆兵士たちの遺体の回収は不可能だった *The recovery* of the soldiers' remains was impossible.

かいしゅう² 改修 (修理) repair ⒸⓊ; (改善) improvement ⒸⓊ ──改修する repair 他; improve 他 ‖彼は家を改修する仕事をしている His job is *doing* home *improvements*. / 台風で講堂の屋根を改修しなければならなくなった They had to *repair* the roof of the hall after the typhoon.

◆美術館は改修工事のために閉まっている The museum is closed for *renovation*.

かいしゅう³ 改宗 conversion ⓊⒸ ──改宗する convert 他 ‖晩年、彼はキリスト教に改宗した In the latter years of his life, he *was converted to* Christianity.

‖改宗者 a convert

かいしゅう⁴ 会衆 (集合的) attendance ⒸⓊ, audience ⒸⓊ; (教会の) 《集合的》congregation ⒸⓊ ‖ローマ法王は会衆一同に祝福を与えた The Pope blessed *the congregation*.

かいじゅう¹ 怪獣 monster ⒸⓊ ‖怪獣映画 a monster movie

かいじゅう² 懐柔 ──懐柔する placate 他; (うまいことを言ってなだめる) conciliate 他

◆懐柔策をとる take *conciliatory measures*

がいしゅつ 外出 ──外出する go* out
彼女は毎週金曜日の晩に外出する She *goes out* every Friday evening.
医者は私にしばらく外出を控えるようにと言った The doctor told me not to *go out* for a while.

◆その老人はめったに外出しない The old man seldom *leaves his house*. / 彼女は外出先から電話をかけてきた She called me from (*the place*) *where she was*.

🅔「優子さんはご在宅ですか」「いいえ、今、外出中です」 "Is Yuko there?" "No, she *is out* now."

かいしょ 楷書 ▲ *kaisho*, the block-style Japanese script

かいじょ 解除 cancellation Ⓤ ──解除する (警報など) cancel 他; (制限・禁止など) lift 他 ‖今しがた暴風警報は解除された The storm warning *was canceled* a short time ago. / その国は経済制裁の解除を求め続けている The country keeps calling for *the lifting* of (the) economic sanctions.

◆ストを解除する *call off* a strike / 契約を解除する *terminate one's* contract

‖武装解除 disarmament

かいしょう¹ 解消 ──解消する break* up, dissolve 他 ‖(政党の) 連合は間もなく解消するだろう I think the coalition will soon *break up*.

◆彼らは婚約を解消した They *have broken off* their engagement. / ストレス解消には泳ぐのがいちばんだ Swimming is the best way to *get rid of stress*. / 父は二日酔いは寝て解消するしかないと言う My father says if you have a hangover, it's best to *sleep it off*. / 交通渋滞を解消するために(→改善策として)新し

い道路が作られた A new road was built *as a remedy for* the traffic jams. / 彼らは結婚生活を解消した They *put an end to* their marriage.

かいしょう² 甲斐性 彼はかい性がある(→よい稼ぎ手だ) He is *a good provider*. / 彼は何をしても長続きしない，全くかい性なし(→役立たず)だ He soon loses interest in everything. He is such *a good-for-nothing guy*.

かいしょう³ 快勝 きのう日本チームはペルーに快勝した The Japan team *gained a clear-cut victory* over Peru yesterday.

かいしょう⁴ 改称 その通りは「並木通り」と改称された The street *was renamed* "Namiki-dori."

かいじょう¹ 会場 (❖英語には「会が催される場一般」を指す言葉がないため，会館や敷地・ホールなど，会が催される個々の場を指す語を用いる) / 議長は会場の静粛を求めた The chairperson called *the meeting* to order. / コンサート会場は若者でいっぱいだった *The* concert *hall* was crowded with young people. / 次回の万博の会場はどこですか(→どこで開催されるか) Where will the next 「World's Fair [Expo]」 *be held*?

かいじょう² 海上 ―海上で[に] at sea, on the sea, afloat(❖at the sea は「海辺で」の意味) / 海上を航行する sail *on the sea*

◆台風は午後には東の海上に抜けるでしょう The typhoon will *be over the eastern sea* this afternoon.

‖海上自衛隊 the Maritime Defense Force / 海上封鎖 a naval blockade / 海上保安庁 the Coast Guard / 海上輸送 marine transport

かいじょう³ 開場 opening Ⓤ ―**開場する** open ⊕ / 『午後6時開場 Doors *open* at 6:00 p.m. / 早朝から開場を待つ人の長い列ができた People waiting for *the opening* formed a long line early in the morning.

かいじょう⁴ 階上 the upstairs (単数扱い) ―**階上へ[に，で]** upstairs ―**階上の** upstairs / 階上の部屋 the *upstairs* room; the room *above*

がいしょう¹ 外相 (外務大臣) the foreign minister, the minister of foreign affairs

がいしょう² 外傷 external injury Ⓤ Ⓒ; external wound Ⓒ (❖injury は事故などによるもの，wound は凶器による意図的なものに用いる)

‖心的外傷 (a) trauma

がいしょう³ 外商 ‖外商部 the direct sales department

かいしょく 会食 あすは取引先との会食がある We are going to *dine with* our business connections.

がいしょく 外食 ―外食する eat* out / 毎日外食するのにはすっかり飽きてしまった I'm tired of *eating out* every day.

‖外食産業 the food service industry

かいしん¹ 会心 この彫刻は彼女の会心の作(→最高の作品の一つ)だ This statue is *one of her best works*. / 彼はその知らせに会心の笑みを浮かべた His face wore *a smile of satisfaction* at the news.

かいしん² 回診 (doctor's) rounds, visit Ⓒ ―**回診する** visit ⊕ / 田中先生は今回診中です Dr. Tanaka *is out on his rounds* now.

かいしん³ 改心 reformation Ⓤ Ⓒ ―**改心する** reform ⊕ / 彼は今ではすっかり改心している He *has* completely *reformed*.

かいしん⁴ 改新 reform Ⓒ / 『大化の改新 the Taika *Reform*

がいしん 外信 (外国からの通信や情報) foreign news Ⓤ ‖外信部 the foreign news department [desk]

がいじん 外人 foreigner Ⓒ, alien Ⓒ (❖いずれも「よそ者」といった排他的な響きがあるので，visitor あるいは国籍を使うほうが好ましい) / 彼女は外人と結婚したらしい I hear she got married to *a foreigner*.

かいず 海図 (marine) chart Ⓒ ◆彼は海図にない島に漂着した He was washed up on the shore of an *uncharted* island.

かいすい 海水 seawater Ⓤ, saltwater Ⓤ ◆その沿岸付近の海水の温度は夏でも低い The water along that coast is cold even in summer.

‖海水魚 a saltwater fish / 海水パンツ swimming trunks / 海水浴 swimming in the sea / 海水浴客 a swimmer / 海水浴場 a beach (resort), a seaside resort

かいすう 回数 the number of times / 『先生は彼が欠席した回数を数えた The teacher counted up 「*the number of times* [*how many times*]」 he had been absent.

‖回数券 (一片) a commuter coupon ticket

がいすう 概数 (およその数) approximate number Ⓒ; (端数のない数) round figures [numbers] ―**概数で** in round figures [numbers]

かいする¹ 介する 私はジョンを介してその話を聞きました I heard the news *through* John. / 彼は通訳を介してゲストと話をした He spoke with the guest *through* an interpreter. / 私はあなたがどこへ行こうが意に介さない I *don't mind* where you go.

かいする² 解する (理解する) understand* ⊕; (受け取る) take* ⊕; (鑑賞する) appreciate ⊕ / 彼はいつでも私の言葉を悪く解する He always *takes* what I say badly. / 彼はユーモアを解さない He *doesn't appreciate* [*have a sense of*] humor.

がいする 害する (傷つける) injure ⊕, hurt* ⊕; damage ⊕ (❖injure, hurt は人の感情や身体，damage は人の健康や事物を害する場合に用いる) / 彼の思いやりのなさが彼女の感情を害した His thoughtlessness *injured* her feelings. / 喫煙により健康が害されることがある Smoking can *damage* your health.

◆君は彼女の感情[気分]を害してしまったことに気づいているのか Are you aware of *having offended* her?

かいせい¹ 快晴 ―快晴の (晴れた) fine; (雲のない) clear ―**快晴の空** *a clear sky* / 幸いにも文化祭当日は快晴に恵まれた Fortunately the weather was *fine* on the day of the school festival.

かいせい² 改正 (全面的な) revision ⓊⒸ; (法律などの) amendment ⓊⒸ **——改正する** revise 他; amend 他 ∥JRのダイヤはこの3月に改正される The JR timetable *will be revised* this March.

かいせい³ 改姓 **——改姓する** change *one's* family name

かいせき 解析 〖幾何〗analysis ⓊⒸ (複 analyses) ∥解析幾何学 analytical geometry

かいせつ 解説 (説明) explanation ⒸⓊ; (論評) comment Ⓒ, commentary ⒸⓊ **——解説する** explain; comment 自
ニュース解説 news *commentary*
彼は最近の選挙での新政党の勝利について解説した He *commented on* the success of the new party in the recent election.
この美術館ではそれぞれの絵に詳しい解説が施されている In this museum, each painting is given *a detailed explanation*.
◆エイズに関する解説記事 *an interpretive article* on AIDS ∥ 解説は元日本代表チームの監督、岡田さんです *The commentator* is the former manager of the national team, Mr. Okada.
∥解説者 a commentator; (ニュースの) a newscaster; (特に政治に関する) a pundit / 解説書(説明書) a manual

かいせつ² 開設 establishment Ⓤ; (創設) foundation Ⓤ **——開設する** open 他, establish 他, set* up ∥区役所のビルの中にスポーツセンターが開設された A sports center *was established* in the ward office building. / インターネット上にホームページを開設しました I *opened* a home page on the Internet.

がいせつ 概説 survey Ⓒ ∥現代中国映画概説 *a survey* of modern Chinese movies

かいせん¹ 回線 〖電気〗circuit Ⓒ, line Ⓒ ∥ (電話の) 共同回線 a party *line* / 回線のぐあいが悪くて突然電話が切れた A defect in *the circuit* caused the telephone to be cut off suddenly. ∥何百件もの電話がかかってきて2時間近く電話回線はパンク状態だった Hundreds of calls jammed *the switchboard* for almost two hours.

かいせん² 改選 reelection ⒸⓊ **——改選する** reelect 他 ∥国会議員の半数を改選する *re-elect* half the members of the Diet

かいせん³ 開戦 the outbreak of war ◆その事件の翌年、日中戦争が開戦した The year following that incident, the Sino–Japanese war *began*.

かいせん⁴ 海戦 naval [sea] battle Ⓒ

かいぜん 改善 improvement Ⓒ **——改善する** improve 他, better 他, make* ... better
政府の経済政策にはまだまだ改善の余地がある There's much room for *improvement* in the government's economic policy.
これからもサービスの改善に努めて参ります We'll keep on making efforts to *improve* the quality of service.
◆教育制度の改善 *reform* of the educational system

かいせん¹ 外線 (電話の) outside line [call] Ⓒ ∥外線のかけ方を教えてください Please tell me how to make *outside* calls.

がいせん² 凱旋 **——凱旋する** return in triumph ∥優勝チームが母校に凱旋した The winning team *returned* to their school *in triumph*.
∥凱旋門 a triumphal arch

がいぜんせい 蓋然性 probability ⓊⒸ

かいそ¹ 改組 reorganization Ⓤ; (内閣の) reshuffle Ⓒ **——改組する** reorganize 他; reshuffle Ⓒ

かいそ² 開祖 (宗派などの) founder Ⓒ

かいそう¹ 回想 《公式的》 recollection Ⓤ, reminiscence Ⓤ **——回想する** recollect 他, recall 他; (過去を振り返る) look back ∥回想にふける indulge in *reminiscences* / 私は学生時代を回想した I *looked back on* my school days.
◆老人はいすに座り昔のことを回想していた The old man was sitting in the chair *musing over* memories of the past. (❖ muse over ...は「(思い出などに)浸る」の意味)
∥回想シーン (a) flashback / 回想録《公式的》a memoir, reminiscences

かいそう² 回送 **——回送する** (手紙を転送する) forward 他, send* on ∥手紙はこちらの住所に回送してください Please *forward* the letter to this address.
◆3番線に停車中の列車は回送電車です The train at Platform 3 is *out-of-service*.

かいそう³ 改装 refurbishment ⓊⒸ **——改装する** refurbish 他, remodel 他 ∥その喫茶店は店内を改装中だ They *are refurbishing* the inside of the cafe.

> 日本語では家や部屋の改装を「リフォーム」というが、英語の reform は「制度を改善する」「人を改心させる」という意味の語で、「(建物などの)改装」という意味では用いない.

かいそう⁴ 階層 (地位・身分) rank ⒸⓊ; (社会的・経済的) class Ⓒ, a walk of life ∥その集会にはあらゆる階層の人々が参加していた People of all *ranks and classes* attended the assembly.

かいそう⁵ 会葬 **——会葬する** (葬儀に出席する) attend a funeral ◆会葬者全員が黙祷(もくとう)をささげた All of *the mourners* prayed in silence.

かいそう⁶ 海草・海藻 seaweed ⓊⒸ

かいぞう 改造 remodeling Ⓤ; (内閣の) reshuffle Ⓒ **——改造する** (形を変える) remodel 他; (別の物にする) convert 他; (一部を変える) alter 他; (内閣を) reshuffle 他 ∥部屋を仕事場に改造する *convert* a room *into* a studio / 近いうちに内閣改造があるかもしれない There could be another *cabinet reshuffle* in the near future. ◆彼は自転車をレース用に改造した He *modified* his bike for racing.

がいそう 外装 (建物などの外側) the exterior; (自動車などの) trim ⓊⒸ ∥外装工事 exterior work

かいぞえ 介添え（花嫁の）bridesmaid ⓒ;（花婿の）best man ⓒ;（手伝う人）helper ⓒ

かいそく¹ 快速 快速はこの駅には止まらない Rapid-service trains pass this station.
‖快速艇 a speedboat / 快速球 a fastball, a fireball

かいそく² 会則 rule ⓒ, regulation ⓒ ‖当会の会則を遵守(ﾞｼ)すること You must obey the rules of this society.

かいぞく 海賊 pirate ⓒ ‖海賊船 a pirate (ship) / 海賊版 a pirated edition

かいたい 解体（建物の取りこわし）demolition ⓤ ⓒ;（機械などの分解）dismantlement ⓤ ——解体する（取りこわす）demolish ⓗ, take* [pull] down;（分解する）take [pull] ... apart, dismantle ⓗ ⓔ ‖古い病院の解体工事が始まった They began to *demolish* the old hospital. / 仮設住宅は解体されたうえで移送される The temporary dwellings will be transported after they *are taken apart*. ◆車を解体する *scrap* a car / その政治団体は戦後間もなく解体された The political group *was disbanded* soon after the war.

かいたく 開拓 reclamation ⓤ;（開墾(ｺﾝ)）cultivation ⓤ ——開拓する reclaim ⓗ; cultivate ⓗ;（開発する）open ⓗ ‖原野を開拓する *cultivate* the wilds / 新しい市場を開拓する *open up* a new market ◆彼は引っ越すとすぐに近くのレストランを開拓し始めた As soon as he moved, he began to *try* the restaurants around his new place.
‖開拓事業 reclamation work / 開拓者 a pioneer;（入植者）a settler / 開拓者精神 frontier spirit / 開拓地 reclaimed land

かいだく 快諾 転載について出版社の快諾を得た The publishers gave *their ready consent* to the reproduction.

かいだし 買い出し 僕たちは近所のスーパーに食料の買い出しに出かけた We went to a nearby supermarket to *buy* food.

かいだす 掻い出す（船から水を）bail out

かいたたく 買い叩く（口語的）beat* down（❖目的語には「人」「値段」いずれもくる）‖この家を売っても買いたたかれるに決まっている The price of this house will probably *be beaten down*.

かいだめ 買い溜め ——買いだめする stock up with [on] ...

がいため 外為（外国為替）foreign exchange ⓤ ‖外為法 the Foreign Exchange and Foreign Trade Control Law

かいだん¹ 階段（屋外の）steps;（屋内の）stairs;（ひと続きの）flight ⓒ;（手すりなどを含む）staircase
彼は老人が階段を上がるのを助けた He assisted the old man up the stairs.
階段から落ちて背中を痛めた I hurt my back when I fell down the stairs.
私はアパートの急な階段を駆け上がった I ran up the steep steps of the apartment house.
‖非常階段 emergency stairs, a fire escape / らせん階段 a spiral staircase

かいだん² 会談 talks ——会談する hold* talks, talk ⓗ,（公式的）confer ⓗ
和平会談は成功しなかった The peace talks were not successful.
首相はワシントンで大統領と会談する予定だ The Prime Minister will *hold talks with* the President in Washington.
‖首脳会談 summit talks [meeting]

かいだん³ 怪談 ghost story ⓒ

ガイダンス（指導）guidance ⓤ;（新入生などに対する案内･説明）orientation ⓤ ‖就職ガイダンス employment counseling

かいちく 改築 reconstruction ⓤ, rebuilding ⓤ ——改築する reconstruct ⓗ, rebuild* ⓗ ‖家の改築のための資金を確保する collect funds for *reconstruction* of a house / 私たちは改築の費用をざっと計算した We reckoned the cost of *rebuilding*.

かいちゅう 海中 海中の undersea（❖名詞の前で用いる）◆海中に飛びこむ jump *into the sea*
‖海中公園 an undersea park / 海中探検 an undersea exploration / 海中トンネル a submarine tunnel

がいちゅう 害虫 harmful insect ⓒ;（総称）vermin ⓤ《複数扱い》‖害虫を駆除する get rid of *harmful insects*

かいちゅうでんとう 懐中電灯《米》flashlight ⓒ,《主に英》torch

かいちゅうどけい 懐中時計 pocket watch ⓒ

かいちょう¹ 会長（会の責任者）chairperson ⓒ;（組織のトップ）president ⓒ ‖日本サッカー協会会長 the president of the Football Association of Japan

かいちょう² 快調 きょうは心身ともに快調だ I'm *in good condition* [shape] both mentally and physically today. / 彼の新しい事業は快調な滑り出しを見せた His new business started off *smoothly*.

がいちょう 害鳥 harmful bird ⓒ;（総称）vermin ⓤ《複数扱い》

かいつう 開通 ——開通する open ⓗ ⓔ ‖海峡横断トンネルが開通した The cross-channel tunnel *was opened*. ◆日本で電話が開通したのは1889年だった Telephone service in Japan *started* in 1889.
‖開通式 an opening ceremony

かいづか 貝塚 shell mound ⓒ;〔考古学〕kitchen midden ⓒ

かいつけ 買い付け（購入）purchase ⓤ ◆店のオーナーはイタリアに商品の買いつけに行っている The owner of the shop has gone to Italy to *purchase* goods to sell.

かいつける 買い付ける（買う）buy* ⓗ, purchase ⓗ ‖業者はインドで大量の綿を買いつけた The dealer *purchased* a lot of cotton in India.

かいつまむ sum up ‖彼は事件の経緯をかいつまんで話した He *summed up* the course of the case. / 要点をかいつまんで（→手短に）話してくれ Tell me the points *briefly*.

かいて 買い手 buyer ⓒ ‖売り手と買い手 the

かいてい

seller and *the buyer* / 車の買い手は見つかりましたか Have you found *a buyer* for your car? ◆この家はすでに買い手がついている This house *is* already *under offer*.
‖買い手市場 a buyer's market

かいてい¹ 改定 revision ⓤ ⓒ ──改定する revise ⓗ ‖運賃の改定 *a revision* of fares

かいてい² 改訂 revision ⓤ ⓒ ──改訂する revise ⓗ ‖地図帳は毎年改訂が必要だ Atlases need to *be revised* every year.
‖改訂版 a revised edition

かいてい³ 海底 the bottom of the sea; (海底の表面) the seabed ‖海底に沈む sink to *the bottom of the sea* ◆海底トンネルを掘る dig *an undersea tunnel*
‖海底火山 a submarine volcano / 海底ケーブル a submarine cable / 海底地震 a submarine earthquake / 海底油田 a submarine oil field

かいてい⁴ 開廷 ──開廷する open [convene] a court ◆現在ちょうど開廷中である The court is now *sitting*.

かいてき 快適 ──快適な comfortable; (気持ちのよい) pleasant ──快適に comfortably ‖快適に暮らす live *comfortably* [*in comfort*] / この車は乗り心地が快適だ This car *is comfortable* to ride in. / 私は快適な空の旅を楽しんだ I enjoyed a *pleasant* flight.
🖉「新しい職場はどう」「快適だよ」"How's your new office?" "It's *fine*."

がいてき 外敵 foreign enemy

かいてん¹ 回転 turn ⓒ; revolution ⓤ ⓒ; rotation ⓤ ⓒ; spin ⓤ ⓒ ──回転する turn ⓗ; revolve ⓗ; rotate ⓗ; spin* ⓗ

　turn: 一般的に「回転する」の意味.
　revolve: 地球の公転のように, ある点を中心に回る.
　rotate: 地球の自転のように, その物自体の軸を中心に回る.
　spin: こまのように軸を中心に速く回る.

大観覧車はぐるぐると回転し続けていた The Ferris wheel kept *turning* around and around.
そのフィギュアスケートの選手は4回転ジャンプができる The figure skater can do *four quick spins*.
車輪は車軸を中心に回転する A wheel *revolves* on its axle.
◆あの少年は頭の回転が速い(→賢い) That boy *is bright* [*smart*]. / この寿司(し)屋は客の回転がいい This sushi shop *has a good flow of customers*.
‖回転いす a swivel chair / 回転競技(スキーの) a slalom / 回転資金 revolving fund / 回転ドア a revolving door / 回転木馬 a merry-go-round

かいてん² 開店 ──開店する open ⓗ ‖開店と同時にバーゲン目当ての客がどっとなだれ込んだ As soon as *the store opened*, the bargain hunters charged in. ◆うちの店は開店休業状態だ(→店はあいているが客が来ない) Our shop *is open, but has no customers*.

がいでん 外電 foreign telegram ⓒ, foreign news ⓤ ◆外電によると… An *overseas report* says ….

ガイド (人) guide ⓒ; (本) guidebook ⓒ ‖ガイドが美術館を案内してくれた The guide conducted us around the museum.
‖ガイドライン a guideline

かいとう¹ 解答 answer ⓒ; solution ⓒ (❖一般には solution は複雑で難解な問題を扱う場合に用いられる. またテストなどでは answer は解答案, solution は正答を指す) ──解答する answer ⓗ; solve ⓗ
彼らは私の解答が正しいと認めた They conceded that my *answer* was correct.
この問題の解答は28ページにあります The *solution* to this question is on page 28.
‖解答者 a panelist / 解答集 answers / 解答用紙 an answer sheet / 解答欄 the space for answers

かいとう² 回答 (返答) answer ⓒ, reply ⓒ ‖明確な回答 *a definite answer* / 彼は私の依頼にすぐ回答をくれた He made *an immediate reply* to my request.
‖回答者(アンケートなどの) a respondent

かいとう³ 解凍 ──解凍する defrost ⓗ, thaw ⓗ ‖この肉を解凍するにはしばらく時間がかかる It'll take a while to *defrost* [*thaw (out)*] this meat.
◆圧縮されたファイルを解凍する uncompress [expand] a compressed file

かいどう 街道 highway ⓒ ‖水戸街道 *the* Mito *Highway* / 表街道と裏街道 *highways and byways*
慣用表現 彼は出世街道を走っている He *is climbing the ladder of success*.

がいとう¹ 該当 ──該当する (条件に当てはまる) fall* [come*] under …; (相当する) correspond ⓗ ‖第6条がそれに該当する It *falls under* Article Six. / Article Six *is applicable* to it. ◆大賞は該当者なしだった The judges *withheld the Grand Prize because none of the entries deserved it*.

がいとう² 街頭 the street ‖街頭でちらしを配る give out handbills *on the street* / 彼は街頭演説を行った He *made a speech on the street*.
‖街頭インタビュー a man-in-the-street interview / 街頭デモ a street demonstration / 街頭募金 street fund raising

がいとう³ 街灯 street lamp ⓒ, street light ⓒ ‖街灯に灯がともった The street lights were turned on.

がいとう⁴ 外套 (オーバー) overcoat ⓒ

かいどく¹ 買い得 bargain ⓒ, good buy ⓒ ‖このネックレスは本当に買い得だ This necklace is *a real bargain*.

かいどく² 解読 ──解読する (暗号・文字を) decipher ⓗ; (暗号を) crack ⓗ, break* ⓗ, decode ⓗ ‖敵側の暗号を解読する *crack* [*break*] the enemy's code

がいどく 害毒 (社会に対する) poison ⓤ

かいとる 買い取る buy* ⓗ ‖その店では中古のコンピュータを買い取ってくれる The store *buys* used computers.

かいならす 飼い馴らす tame [他]; (家畜化する) domesticate [他] //彼は野生の猿を飼い馴らした He *tamed* wild monkeys.

かいなん 海難 (海上での災難) sea disaster [C]; (難破) shipwreck [U][C] //何百人もの人々がその海難で命を落とした Hundreds of people died in the *sea disaster*.
‖海難救助 a sea rescue, a salvage

かいにゅう 介入 intervention [U][C] ━介入する intervene [自], step in //通貨市場への政府の介入 government *intervention* in the currency markets / その紛争の解決に国連が介入しなければならないかもしれない The UN may have to *step in* to settle the dispute.
‖軍事介入 armed intervention

かいにん 解任 dismissal [C][U] ━解任する dismiss [他], discharge [他], remove [他] //彼は職務を解任された He *was discharged from* his job.

かいぬし 飼い主 owner [C], master [C] //この子犬の飼い主を探しています We are looking for *the owner* of this puppy.
◆飼い主のいない猫 an *ownerless* cat

かいねこ 飼い猫 *one's* (house [pet]) cat

がいねん 概念 idea [C], concept [C]; (考え方) conception [C][U] //既成概念 *established ideas* / 美の概念を規定するのは難しい It is difficult to define *the concept* of beauty.
‖概念芸術 conceptual art

かいば 飼い葉 (家畜の飼料) fodder [U], forage [U] ‖かいばおけ a crib

がいはく 外泊 ━外泊する stay out overnight [all night] //彼は無断外泊をした He *stayed out all night* without permission.
◆今夜は友達のうちに外泊する予定だ I'm going to *stay at* a friend's house tonight.

かいばしら 貝柱 (ホタテの) scallop [U]; (二枚貝一般の) adductor muscle [C]

かいはつ 開発 development [U][C]; (営利目的の) exploitation [U] ━開発する develop [他]; exploit [他]
新薬を開発する *develop* a new medicine / 天然資源を開発する *exploit* natural resources / 宇宙開発計画 a space *development* plan
この機械は我々が新たに開発した製品です This machine is *a* new *development* of ours.
多くのホテルがこの新しく開発された地域に集まっている Many hotels are concentrated in this newly *developed* area.
‖開発援助 development assistance / 開発業者 a developer / 開発途上国 a developing country / 都市再開発 urban renewal

かいばつ 海抜 (高度) altitude [U][C] ◆その山は海抜5,030メートルです The mountain is 5,030 meters *above sea level*.

かいひ[1] 会費 (membership) fee [C]; (分担金) dues //会費を集める collect *fees* / クラブの会員は全員毎月500円の会費を払うことになっている Every member of the club is supposed to pay *a* monthly *fee* of 500 yen. / 僕はまだ会費を払っていない I haven't paid *my dues* yet. ◆そのパーティーは会費制で行われた We *had to pay for our share* of the party.
‖月[年]会費 a monthly [an annual] fee

かいひ[2] 回避 avoidance [U]; (責任・義務などの) evasion [U][C] ━回避する avoid [他]; evade [他] //責任を回避する *avoid* [*evade*] responsibility / 我々は何があっても戦争だけは回避しなければならない We must *avoid* war at all costs.
◆危険を回避する *keep from* danger / 航空3社のストは回避される模様だ It is likely that the strike at the three airline companies will *be called off*.

がいひ 外皮 (皮一般) skin [C][U]; (果物・穀物・種子などの) hull [C]; (果物の硬い皮) rind [U][C]

かいびかえ 買い控え 消費税率が上がった直後は消費者の買い控えが目立った Right after the consumption tax rate was raised, people *refrained from big purchases*.

かいひょう 開票 ballot [vote] counting [U] ━開票する count the votes [ballots] //投票は即日開票されることになっている *The ballots* are to *be counted* on the day of the election. / 開票結果はあすの朝には発表されるだろう *The result of the vote counting* will be announced tomorrow morning.
‖開票所 a ballot [vote] counting office / 開票速報 up-to-the-minute (election) returns

かいひん 海浜 ‖海浜公園 a seaside park

がいぶ 外部 the outside, the exterior //建物の外部から侵入するのは不可能だ It is impossible to break into the building from *the outside*. ◆情報を外部にもらす *leak* information / 犯人はそのとき刑務所にいて外部との連絡は絶たれていた The criminal was in prison then and had no way to communicate with *the outside world*.

かいふう 開封 手紙を開封する *open* a letter

かいふく 回復

❶【病気が治る】recovery [U] ━回復する recover [自], get* well [better]; (よくなる) improve [自]
その患者は回復が早い[遅い] The patient *is recovering quickly* [*slowly*].
彼の病気はなかなか回復のきざしが見えない His illness *doesn't seem to be getting any better*.
彼女のめざましい回復に医者も驚いているようだった Even the doctor looked surprised at her rapid *recovery*.
祖父は手術の後少しずつ回復に向かっている My grandfather *is getting better* little by little after the operation.
彼女が回復する見込みはありますか Is there any hope that she *will recover*?
◆その少年はようやく健康を回復した The boy finally *regained* his health.

❷【元のよい状態に戻る】recovery [U]; (復旧) restoration [U] ━回復する recover [自][他]; (よくなる) improve [自], become* [get*] better; (復旧させる) restore [他]
法と秩序の回復 *the restoration* of law and order / 意識を回復する *recover* conscious-

かいぶつ

ness
天気は回復した The weather 「*became better [improved]*」.
専門家は今年の後半には景気が回復するだろうと語った The expert said the economy would *improve* later this year.
◆名誉を回復する *regain one's* honor

かいぶつ 怪物 monster ⓒ ‖彼はその湖で怪物を見たと言い張っている He claims that he saw *a monster* in the lake.

がいぶん 外聞 彼は恥も外聞もなく(→他人がどう思うか気にせず)泣きわめいた He wailed *without caring what other people might think*.

かいへい 開閉 ──開閉する open and shut* ‖ドアは自動的に開閉した The door *opened and shut* automatically.

かいへいたい 海兵隊 (米国の) the Marine Corps [kɔ́ːr], the Marines; (英国の) the Royal Marines ‖海兵隊員 a marine

かいほう¹ 解放 release ⓤ; (束縛・専制などからの) liberation ⓤ (❖口語では短縮して lib ともいう) ──解放する (自由にする) release ㊛, free ㊛, set* free; (束縛・専制などから) liberate ㊛
彼らは人質の解放に応じた They agreed to *release [free]* the hostages.
その薬のおかげで痛みから解放された The medicine 「*freed me from [relieved me of]* the pain.
◆やっとテスト勉強から解放された I'm finally *through with* studying for tests. / 彼は退職して解放感を味わった Retirement gave him *a feeling of freedom*.
‖女性解放運動 women's liberation [lib] / 奴隷解放宣言 the Emancipation Proclamation / パレスチナ解放機構 the Palestine Liberation Organization ((略語)) PLO

かいほう² 開放 ──開放する (あける) open ㊛; (あけたままにする) leave* ... open ‖日本はもっと市場を開放すべきだと思う I think that Japan should *open* its markets to a greater extent. / 開放厳禁 Don't leave the door *open*. ◆開放的な空間 *open* space / この庭園は一般に開放されている This garden *is open* to the public. (❖この open は形容詞)
‖開放市場 an *open* market / 開放政策 an open-door policy

かいほう³ 介抱 ──介抱する (付き添う) attend ㊛; (看護する) nurse ㊛; (面倒を見る) look after ..., take* care of ... ‖ゆうべはだれが彼を介抱したんですか Who *looked after* him last night?

かいほう⁴ 会報 bulletin ⓒ; (学会などの) transactions; (団体組織の) newsletter ⓒ

かいほう⁵ 快方 彼の健康状態は快方に向かった His condition *took a turn for the better*.

かいほう⁶ 解法 (解答) solution ⓒ

かいぼう 解剖 dissection ⓤⓒ, anatomy ⓒⓤ ──解剖する dissect ㊛, anatomize ㊛ ‖きのう生物の時間にカエルの解剖をした We *dissected* a frog in biology class yesterday.
◆死体解剖の結果, 彼女は毒殺されたことが分かった The autopsy [*postmortem*] showed that she was poisoned.
‖解剖学 anatomy / 解剖図 an anatomical chart / 司法解剖 a legal postmortem / 生体解剖 vivisection

かいまく 開幕 (始まること) opening ⓤ ──開幕する open ㊛; (始まる) start ㊛, begin* ㊛ ‖オリンピックはあす開幕する The Olympic Games *will start* tomorrow.
◆そのチームは開幕戦から勝ち続けている(→負け知らずである) The team has been undefeated since (they won) *the first game*. / 開幕は午後7時です *The curtain rises* at 7 p.m.
‖開幕試合 an opening game, an opener

かいまみる 垣間見る (ちらっと見る) catch* a glimpse ‖人込みの中に彼女の姿がかいま見えた I *caught a glimpse of* her among the crowd. ◆その言葉に彼の苦悩の一端をかいま見た気がした His words suggested that he was worrying.

かいむ 皆無 (無・ゼロ) nothing ⓤ ‖彼の経済学に関する知識はほとんど皆無だった He knew almost *nothing* about economics.
◆我々が負ける可能性は皆無だ There is *no* fear of our losing *whatsoever*.

がいむ 外務 foreign affairs ‖外務省 the Ministry of Foreign Affairs / 外務大臣 the Foreign Minister, the Minister of Foreign Affairs

かいめい¹ 改名 ──改名する rename ㊛ ‖その競走馬はラッキーボーイと改名された The racehorse *was renamed* "Lucky Boy."

かいめい² 解明 ──解明する (解く) solve ㊛; (明らかにする) clarify ㊛ ‖そのなぞは今までのところ解明されていない The mystery *has* not *been solved* as yet.
◆原因を解明する *identify* the cause / その問題はより一層の解明が必要である The issue needs further *clarification*.

かいめつ 壊滅 ruin ⓤ, destruction ⓤ ──壊滅する be destroyed completely, be ruined ‖警察はその組織を壊滅状態に追い込んだ The police made the organization fall into *ruin*. ◆その大地震で町は壊滅した The earthquake *completely destroyed* the city. / 暴風雨はその地方の農作物に壊滅的な被害をもたらした The storm did *devastating damage* to the region's crops.

かいめん¹ 海面 (海抜の標準) sea level ⓤ; (海の表面) the surface of the sea ‖このあたりは海面より1メートル低い This area is one meter below *sea level*.

かいめん² 海綿 sponge ⓒⓤ ‖海綿動物 a sponge

がいめん 外面 the outside (↔the inside), the exterior (↔the interior) ‖その建物の外面はガラス張りだった The building had *a* glass *exterior*.

かいもく 皆目 この問題の解き方は皆目見当がつかない I don't have 「*any* idea *at all* [the *faintest* idea]」 how to solve this problem.

かいもどす 買い戻す buy* back, redeem ㊛

かいもの 買い物 shopping ⓤ; (買った物)

purchase ◯,《口語的》buy ◯
→ 場面・状況別会話 p.1682
私はよく彼女の買い物を手伝う I often help her do *the shopping*.
この辞書はいい買い物(→買い得品)だった This dictionary was a「*good buy* [*bargain*]」
家はほとんどの人にとって生涯で最も高価な買い物だ A house is *the* most expensive *purchase* for most people.
◆スーパーへ買い物に行く go shopping at a supermarket (❖×to a supermarket とはいわない) / 私は買い物中に偶然旧友に会った I came across an old friend of mine *while shopping*. / 旅行の最終日にはあちこち買い物をして回った We *shopped around* on the last day of our trip. / その新しい店は買い物客でいっぱいだ The new store is crowded with *shoppers*.
🅔「週末に買い物に行かない?」「うん.ちょうど新しい服を買おうと思っていたところなんだ」"Do you want to *go shopping* this weekend?" "Sure. I was just thinking of buying some new clothes."
‖買い物かご a shopping basket / 買い物袋《米》a shopping bag, 《英》a carrier bag

がいや 外野〔野球〕the outfield /外野フライを打つ hit *a fly ball to the outfield* / 彼は外野を守っている He plays *the outfield*.
‖外野手 an outfielder / 外野席 bleachers

かいやく 解約 (契約の)cancellation ◯ ── 解約する (契約を)cancel ⊕; (銀行口座を)close ⊕ /彼は保険を解約した He *canceled* the insurance. / 私はその銀行の口座を解約した I *closed* my account at the bank.
‖解約金 cancellation fee

がいゆう 外遊 travel [trip] abroad ◯ ── 外遊する travel abroad /首相の外遊の映像が届いた We received news footage of the Prime Minister's *travels abroad*.

かいよう¹ 海洋 the sea, the ocean ‖海洋汚染 sea contamination / 海洋学 oceanography / 海洋性気候 an oceanic climate / 海洋生物学 marine biology

かいよう² 潰瘍〔医学〕ulcer [Ʌlsər] ◯ /彼は心労のあまり胃潰瘍になった He got *a stomach ulcer* from too much worry.

がいよう¹ 概要 (要約) summary ◯, brief ◯; (あらまし) outline ◯

がいよう² 外洋 (外海) the open sea; (公海) the high seas ◆外洋航行の定期船 an *ocean liner*

がいようやく 外用薬 a medicine for external use [application] (❖薬のラベルには"For external use only"などと書かれている)

かいらい 傀儡 (操り人形) puppet ◯ ‖かいらい国家 a puppet state / かいらい政権 a puppet government

がいらい 外来 外来の文化 a *foreign* culture / 「パン」という言葉はポルトガル語からの外来語です The word "pan"「*is borrowed* [is *a loanword*] from Portuguese.
‖外来患者 an outpatient / 外来種 introduced species

かいらく 快楽 pleasure ⓤ◯, joy ⓤ◯ ‖快楽にふける indulge *oneself* in pleasure
‖快楽主義 Epicureanism,〔哲学〕hedonism / 快楽主義者 an epicurean, a hedonist,《英》a sybarite

かいらん 回覧 ──回覧する circulate ⊕, pass around /これを回覧してください Please *pass* this *around*. / 数人がすでにその草稿を回覧していた A few people *have* already *circulated* the draft.
‖回覧版 a circular (notice)

かいり 海里 nautical [sea] mile ◯

かいりき 怪力 彼は怪力の持ち主だった He was a man of *extraordinary strength*.

かいりつ 戒律 (宗教の戒律) religious precept ◯ ‖仏教の戒律を守る observe (the) Buddhist (*religious*) precepts

がいりゃく 概略 (要約) summary ◯; (あらまし) outline ◯ ‖『日本史』[事件]の概略 *an outline* of 「Japanese history [the case]」/ この報告書の概略を2ページにまとめてくれませんか Will you write *a two-page summary* of this report? / その会合で話し合ったことの概略をお話ししましょう I'll give you *an outline* of what was discussed at the meeting. ◆彼らはダム建設計画の概略を説明した They *outlined* their proposal for building a dam.

かいりゅう 海流 ocean current ◯ ‖日本海流 the Japan *Current*

かいりょう 改良 improvement ⓤ◯ ──改良する improve ⊕, better ⊕ ‖このソフトはよくなっているがまだ改良の余地がある This software has gotten better, but there's still room *for improvement*. / 全体としてはよい計画だが細部についてはまだ改良の必要がある Overall the plan is good, but the details still need to *be improved*. / 彼女はランの品種改良に成功した She succeeded in *improving* a variety of orchid. ◆この新しい車にはいくつかの改良が加えられている This new car has several added *refinements*.

カイロ Cairo (❖エジプトの首都)

かいろ¹ 回路〔電気〕circuit ◯ ◆電気回路の故障 an *electrical* fault
‖集積回路 an integrated circuit

かいろ² 海路 sea route ◯ ◆彼は海路宮崎に向かった He headed for Miyazaki *by sea*.
ことわざ 待てば海路の日和あり It is a long lane that has no turning.(→曲がり角のない道はない); Everything comes to those who wait.(→待っていれば何でもやってくる)

かいろ³ 懐炉 a *kairo*, a pocket warmer

がいろ 街路 street ◯; (大通り) avenue ◯ ‖その街路の両側には桜の木が並んでいる Cherry trees line both sides of the *street*.
‖街路樹 a street tree

かいろう 回廊 (廊下) corridor ◯; (修道院などの中庭を囲む廊下) cloister ◯

カイロプラクティック chiropractic (therapy) ⓤ

がいろん 概論 (手引き・入門) introduction ◯; (概観) survey ◯; (概略) outline ◯ ‖フラ

ンス文学概論 a survey of French literature

かいわ 会話 conversation ⓊⒸ; (対話・対談) dialog ⓊⒸ
日常会話 everyday *conversation*
きょうは英会話の授業があった I had an English *conversation* class today.
彼らの会話はよどみなく続いた Their *conversation* flowed freely.
私は彼女と短い会話を交わした I had *a* short *conversation* with her.
この映画には会話はところどころにしかない *Dialog* is sparse in this movie.
会話のじゃまをするな Don't interrupt *our conversation*.
◆会話体の英語 *colloquial* English

かいわい 界隈 neighborhood Ⓤ, areaⒸ ‖
この界わいには学生がたくさん住んでいる A lot of students live in this *neighborhood*.

かいん 下院 (一般の) the Lower House; (米国の) the House of Representatives, the House; (英国の) the House of Commons, the Commons ‖下院議員《米》a Representative, a Member of Congress, 《英》 a Member of Parliament ╱ 下院議長 the Speaker

かう¹ 買う

❶【物を買う】 buy* ⓗ (↔sell),《公式的》purchase ⓗ,《口語的》get* ⓗ

> 英作文ノート 「買ってやる」では to は不用
> 彼の父は彼に車を買ってやった
> →×His father bought a car *to* him.
> →○His father bought him a car.
> →○His father bought a car *for* him.
> ★give などの類推から前置詞を to にしないこと. buy は,《buy＋名(人)＋名》または《buy＋名＋for 名(人)》の構文をとる. この動詞の仲間には, build「建ててやる」, cook「料理してやる」, make「作ってやる」などがある.

父は私に時計を買ってくれた My father *bought* me a watch./ My father *bought* a watch *for* me.
私はその本を2,000円で買った I *bought* the book for 2,000 yen./ (→その本に2,000円払った) I *paid* 2,000 yen for the book.
彼はその車を安く買った He *bought* the car cheap.
僕はそのスーツを値札の40パーセント引きで買った I *bought* the suit at 40 percent off the marked price.
彼はこのチケットを彼女から買った He *bought* this ticket from [off] her.
そのパソコンをクレジットで買った I *bought* the personal computer on credit.
私たちには車を買うだけの金があった There was enough money for us to *buy* a car. / We had enough money to *buy* a car.
悟は自分用に靴を1足買った Satoru *bought* himself a pair of shoes.
中古車なら50万しないで買えると思うよ I believe you *can get* a used car for under 500,000 yen.
当時私には高価な物を買う余裕はなかった At that time I could not afford to *buy* expensive things.
僕のラケットを貸してあげるよ, そうすれば買わなくてすむだろ I'll lend you my racket. It'll save you from *buying* one.
私はあなたが買ったのと同じ辞書を買った I *bought* the same dictionary「as yours [that you did].
博物館はそのつぼを1,000万円で買った The museum *purchased* the pot for 10 million yen.
◆彼は私の絵を10万円で買おうと言った He *offered* 100,000 yen *for* my painting.

🅔 「ほんとにいい天気だねえ」「そうだ, サンドイッチでも買って外で食べようよ」"What a beautiful day!" "I tell you what, let's *buy* some sandwiches and eat outside."

🅔 「このバッグすごくいいけど, 8万だって」「とてもじゃないけど買えないよね」"I really love this bag, but it's 80,000 yen!" "There's no way we can *afford* it."

🅔 「ちょっとコンビニに行ってくる」「じゃあ, ついでにおしょうゆ買ってきて」"I'm going to a convenience store." "Then *get* a bottle of soy sauce for me, will you?"

❷【招く】
怒りを買う make a person angry; arouse a person's anger
パーティーでの君の態度はひんしゅくを買っていた Your attitude *was frowned on* [*upon*] at the party.
彼の成功は同僚のねたみを買った His success *inspired* [*aroused*] envy in his colleagues.

❸【評価する】
(高く評価する) think* highly of ..., have* a high opinion of ..., put* a high value on [upon] ...
彼は上司に能力を高く買われている His boss「*has a high opinion of* [*highly appreciates*] his ability.
私たちはその歯医者の腕を高く買っています We *think highly of* the dentist's skills.
◆私は彼女の人柄を買って雇った I hired her *because of* her good personality.

❹【引き受ける】
売られたけんかは買うしかない I just *can't ignore* it if someone tries to pick a fight with me.
彼女はサッカー部のマネージャーを買って出た She *offered* to be the manager of the soccer club.

かう² 飼う (所有する) have* ⓗ; (世話をする) keep* ⓗ; (家畜を飼育する) raise ⓗ
このマンションではペットは飼えない We can't *keep* a pet in this condominium.
山田さんは牧場で羊を飼っている Mr. Yamada *raises* sheep on his farm.

🅔 「何かペットを飼っていますか」「はい, 猫を2匹飼ってます」"Do you *have* any pets?" "Yes, I *have* two cats."

カウボーイ cowboy [C] ‖カウボーイハット a cowboy hat

ガウン gown [C]; (部屋着) 《米》bathrobe [C]; 《主に英》dressing gown [C]

カウンセラー counselor [C] ∥カウンセラーに相談する consult *a counselor*

カウンセリング counseling [U] ∥医師のカウンセリングを受ける receive *counseling* from a doctor

カウンター (銀行・商店などの) counter [C]; (スーパーのレジ) checkout [C]; (酒場の) bar [C]; (空港の) check-in counter [desk] [C]; (計数器) counter [C] ∥寿司(す)屋のカウンター席に座る sit at *the counter* in a sushi bar

‖カウンターアタック〖サッカー〗a counter-attack / カウンターパンチ〖ボクシング〗a counterpunch

カウント 〖野球・ボクシング〗count [C] ∥カウントはワンストライクワンボールだ *The count* is one ball and one strike. (❖日本語ではストライクを先にいうが, 英語ではボールを先にいう)

‖カウントダウン a countdown

かえ 替え spare [C]; (詰め替え品) refill [C]; (服の) change [C] ∥かみそりの替え刃 *spare* razor *blades* / 替えの服を持っていく必要がある You need to take *a change* of clothes.

かえうた 替え歌 parody [C]

かえす[1] 返す

return [他], give* back (❖give back のほうが口語的); (お金を) pay* back; (手渡しで) hand back; (元の位置へ) put* back

借金を返す *pay back one's* debt (❖銀行からの借金の場合は*one's* loan) / 恩をあだで返す *return* evil for good / ほほえみを返す *return* a smile

彼はありがとうと言って彼女にノートを返した He *returned* her notebook with his thanks.

この本は図書館に返さないといけない I have to *return* this book *to* the library.

この CD を江利に返さなくては I must *hand* this CD *back to* Eri.

読み終わったらその本は棚に返しておきなさい *Put* the book *back* on the shelf when you're through.

彼女に「やあ」と言ったのに, あいさつを返さなかった "Hello," I said to her, but she didn't *return my greeting*. (❖この return は「(相手の行為)に応じる」の意味)

◆恩を返す *repay* an obligation / ボールを打ち返す *hit* a ball *back* / 返す言葉もなかった I didn't know 「how to *answer* [what to *say*]. / お言葉を返すようですが, 私はその計画には反対です *I'm sorry to contradict you*, but I object to the plan.

💬「この本, 貸してもらえない?」「いいよ. でも月末までには返してね」"Can you lend me this book?" "Sure, but *give* it *back* by the end of the month."

💬「先週貸した500円いつ返してくれる」「来週まで待ってよ. 必ず返すから」"When will you *pay* me *back* the 500 yen I lent you last week?" "Please wait until next week. Then I'll *pay* you *back* for sure."

かえす[2] 帰す (許可して) let* *a person* go back; (帰宅させる) let *a person* go home, send* *a person* home ∥先生はクラスの全生徒を家へ帰した The teacher *let* all his [her] students *go home*.

◆釣った魚を川に帰した I *released* the fish I had caught *back into* the river.

かえす[3] 孵す hatch [他] ∥人工的に卵をかえす *hatch* eggs artificially

-かえす -返す ボールを打ち返す *hit* a ball *back* / 私はその本を読み返した I *reread* the book. / 彼らは駅に引き返した They *turned back* to the station.

かえすがえす 返す返す 彼に会えなかったのは返す返すも(→非常に)残念だ It's a *great* pity (that) I failed to see him.

かえだま 替え玉 substitute [C], double [C]; (競技などの替え玉選手) 《米》ringer [C] ∥替え玉受験をする *illegally use* a *substitute for one at an exam*

かえって 却って (その代わりに) instead; (…よりむしろ) rather than …; (結局) after all; (実のところ) actually

恵美子を手伝うつもりが, かえって迷惑をかけてしまった I wanted to help Emiko, but *instead* I caused her more trouble.

彼をなだめようとしたが, かえって火に油を注ぐ結果となった I tried to appease him but *instead* added fuel to the fire.

選手本人よりもかえって観客のほうが緊張しているようだった The spectators seemed to be nervous *rather than* the player himself.

雨が降っていたが, 彼らにはかえって都合がよかった It was raining, but *actually* it was convenient for them.

◆家具の中には古いほうがかえってよいものもある Some furniture is *all the better for* being old. / 私は教師だが, かえって生徒たちからいろいろなことを教えられた I am a teacher, but I've learned a lot from my students *as things turns out*. / トレーニングのしすぎでかえって健康を害してしまった Training too hard did *more* harm *than* good to my health. / 彼のことを忘れようとすればするほど, かえって思いは強まるばかりだった *The harder* I *tried to* forget him, *the more* my love for him grew. / 彼は難しい仕事があるとかえってがんばる He *thrives on* hard work.

かえで 楓 maple (tree) [C]

かえり 帰り return [U][C]; (帰り道) the way home

カナダからのお帰りを首を長くして待っています I'll be waiting for *your return* from Canada.

帰りに本屋へ寄っていこう Let's drop into the bookstore *on the way home*.

帰りのバスはすいていた The bus wasn't crowded *on my way home*.

◆生徒たちは帰りじたくを始めた Students began *preparing to go home*.

💬「何で毎日こんなに帰りが遅いの」「文化祭の準備

かえりがけ

で忙しいんだよ」"Why do you *come home* so late every day?" "I'm busy preparing for the school festival."

かえりがけ 帰りがけ 彼は帰りがけに(→帰宅途中)本屋に立ち寄った He dropped in at a bookstore *on his way home*.

かえりざく 返り咲く make* a comeback, come* back ∥彼は政界への返り咲きを果たした He *made a comeback* in politics.
◆その曲はヒットチャートの１位に返り咲いた The song *regained* the number one spot [position] on the charts.

かえりみる¹ 顧みる (昔を) look back on [upon, to] ...; (気にかける) take* notice of ...; (思いやる) have* [show*] regard for ... ∥学生時代をかえりみる *look back on one's* school days / 彼は母親の忠告をほとんど [全く]かえりみなかった He *took* little [no] *notice of* his mother's advice. / 彼は他人の気持ちなどほとんどかえりみない He *has* [*shows*] little *regard for* the feelings of others.
◆彼は身の危険をかえりみず激流の中に飛び込んだ He dove into the raging stream *with no thought for* his own safety.

かえりみる² 省みる (反省する) reflect ⾃

かえる¹ 帰る

come* [go*, get*, be] back; (家・故郷・本国へ) come [go, get] home, return ⾃; (出発する) leave* 他⾃, go ⾃

語法
come back [home]は話者のいる所に, また go back [home]は話者のいる所から別の所に「帰る」ことを意味し, get back [home]はそのいずれの場合にも用いられる. また be backは「帰っている状態」を表す.

まっすぐ家に帰る *go right home* / (文明社会を離れて)自然に帰る *go* [*get*] *back to* nature
私が家に帰るまで夕食を待ってもらえる? Can you hold dinner until I *get home*?
かばん預かってて. すぐ帰ってくるから Please keep my bag for me. I'll *be back* soon.
ご両親はいつヨーロッパから帰られたのですか When did your parents *return* from Europe?
鳥は夕方巣に帰る Birds *return to* their nests toward evening.
帰りたい人は帰ってもよろしい Those who wish to *leave* may do so.
彼女はなぜあんなに早く帰ってしまったのだろう I wonder why she *left* so early.
もうお帰りにならなくてはいけないのですか Do you have to *go* [*leave*] so soon?
◆帰れ(→出て行け)! *Get out (of here)*! / 帰ったよ I'*m home*! / (電話などで)彼は何時に帰りますか What time *is* he *expected* (*back*)? / 彼は永久に帰ってこないように思われた He seemed to *have gone* for good. / 自転車のタイヤがパンクしたので歩いて帰らなければならなかった My bike got a flat tire, so I had to *walk home*. / これが家に帰るいちばんの近道だ This is the shortest way *home*.

☏「家に帰るところです」「じゃ, お宅まで車で送らせてください」"I'm *on my way home*." "Then, let me drive you home."

☏「今晩は何時ごろ帰ってくるの」「遅くなるよ, たぶん11時ぐらい」"What time will you *come back* tonight?" "I'll *be back* late, perhaps about 11 o'clock."

かえる² 変える

(全体的に) change 他; (一部を) alter 他; (変更・修正する) modify 他; (形状・性能・性質を) transform 他, turn 他
髪型[職]を変える *change one's* hairstyle [job] / チャンネルを変える *change* channels / 太陽エネルギーを電力に変える *change* [*turn*] solar energy *into* electricity
話題を変えましょう Let's *change* the subject.
彼はその映画を見て環境問題に対する考え方を変えた He *changed* his opinion about the environmental problems after he watched the film.
その経験が彼女を強い人間に変えた That experience *changed* [*turned*] her *into* a strong person.
この出来事はこの国の歴史を大きく変えることになった This event was to *change* the country's history in a drastic way.
◆気分を変えるために部屋の模様替えをする rearrange *one's* room *for a change of pace* / このランプは明るさを変えることができる The brightness of this lamp *is variable*. / そのレストランは毎週メニューを変える The restaurant *varies* the menu every week. / 彼女は声を変えて電話した She *disguised* her voice on the phone.

かえる³ 代[替, 換]える

(取り替える) replace 他; (代用する) substitute 他⾃; (交換する) exchange 他; (同種のものと交換する) change 他
今回はバターに代えてオリーブオイルを使った I *substituted* olive oil *for* butter this time. / I used olive oil *instead of* butter this time.
母親の愛に代えられるものはない Nothing can *replace* [*take the place of*] a mother's love.
トラベラーズチェックをポンド[現金]に替えたいのですが I'd like to *exchange* [*change*] my traveler's checks *for* pounds [cash].
うちでは古い電話機を新しいコードレスに替えた We *have replaced* our old phone *with* a new cordless one.
電池を換える必要がある The battery should *be changed* [*replaced*].
◆ゴールキーパーを中村に代えたほうがいいな We should *put* Nakamura *in* as the (new) goalkeeper [*change* the goalkeeper *to* Nakamura].

かえる⁴ 返る return ⾃; (戻される) be returned
盗まれた自転車が私のところに返ってきた My

stolen bike *was returned to* me.
生きとし生けるものは土に返る All living things *return to* the soil.
◆ 正気[我]に返る *come to oneself* / なくした財布が返ってきて彼はうれしかった He was pleased at *the return of* his lost wallet.

かえる⁵ 孵る *hatch* ⑪ /ひながかえった The chickens *hatched*.

かえる⁶ 蛙 *frog* ⓒ, (ヒキガエル) *toad* ⓒ
[ことわざ] 蛙の子は蛙 *Like father, like son.* (→この父にしてこの子あり) / 蛙の面(つら)に水 *Like water off a duck's back.* (→アヒルの背中に水をかけるようなものだ)
[俳句] 痩(や)蛙まけるな一茶是(これ)に有り (小林一茶) Skinny little frog! Don't let the world beat you down. Issa is here, too.

かえん 火炎 /火炎びん *a Molotov cocktail*, 《英》*a petrol bomb* / 火炎放射器 *a flame-thrower*

かお 顔

❶【体の部位】(顔面) *face* ⓒ; (頭部) *head* ⓒ (❖*face* は *head* に含まれ, *head* の前面を指す)
〖~顔〗
ほっそりした顔 *a thin face* / うりざね顔 *an oval face* / ぽっちゃり顔 *a plump face* / 日焼けした顔 *a suntanned face*
美樹は丸顔だ Miki has *a round face*.
〖顔が・は〗
熱で顔がほてった My *face* was flushed with heat.
彼の顔は怒りで真っ赤になった His *face* flushed red with anger. (❖「恥ずかしさで赤くなる」場合は動詞に blush を用いる)
〖顔から・に・も〗
彼女の顔から血の気がうせた The blood drained *from* her *face*.
彼の言葉を聞いて彼女の顔に笑みが浮かんだ His words brought a smile *to* her *face*.
◆ もうおまえなんか顔も見たくない I *can't stand the very sight* of you any longer.
〖顔を〗
顔を洗う wash *one's face* / 人の顔を殴る *hit a person in the face* / 両手で顔を覆う *cover one's face* with both hands
その少女はかわいらしい顔をしている The girl has *a pretty face*.
彼は寒さで青い顔をしている He is blue in *the face* with (the) cold.
父の顔をまともに見ることができなかった I couldn't look my father *in the face*.
彼は苦痛に顔をゆがめた His *face* was contorted with pain.
女の人が窓から顔を出して助けを求めて叫んだ A woman stuck her *head* out of the window and cried for help.
◆ 私が声をかけると彼女は本から顔を上げた As I called her, she *looked up* from the book. / 二人は顔を見合わせた The two *looked at each other*. / タケノコが顔を出し始めた Bamboo shoots started to *come out*.

❷【表情】*face* ⓒ, *look* ⓒ, *expression* ⓒ

〖~顔〗
うれしそうな[悲しげな]顔 *a happy [long] face* / 浮かぬ顔 *a gloomy face [expression]* / 無表情な顔 *a blank [an impassive] face* / わけ知り顔でうなずく nod 「*with a knowing look* [*knowingly*]
◆ 彼女はいやな顔ひとつせず残業を引き受けてくれた She *uncomplainingly* agreed to work overtime.
〖顔に〗
彼は感情が顔に出やすい He shows his feelings easily (*on his face*).
彼は怒りを顔に出さなかった His *face* didn't show his anger. / He didn't show his anger on *his face*.
🅔「何で分かるの」「顔に書いてあるよ」"How do you know that?" "*It's written on your face*."
〖顔を〗
彼女は驚いた顔をしていた Her *face* showed surprise. / She *looked* surprised.
彼女はその手紙を読むと顔を曇らせた Her *face clouded* (*over*) when she read the letter.
彼女の父は彼女のはでな服装を見て顔をしかめた Her father *made a face* when he saw her gaudy clothes.
◆ 恵子は会っても知らん顔をする Even when Keiko sees me, she *pretends not to recognize me*. / 彼らは私の意見にいやな顔をした They *frowned on* [*upon*] my opinion. / 彼は平気な顔をしてるが, 内心はとても怖いんだ He 「*looks calm* [*puts on a brave face*], but he is really scared inside.
〖顔で〗
新入生たちはみな晴れやかな顔で入学式に臨んだ Every new student attended the entrance ceremony *with a bright face*.

❸【慣用表現】
【合わせる顔】こんな成績では家に帰って両親に合わせる顔がない I'*m ashamed to go home and look* my parents *in the face* because I got such a bad grade.
【大きな顔をする】そのクラブでは新入りの彼がいちばん大きな顔をしている Though he is a newcomer, he *acts as if he were the biggest* in the club.
【顔が売れている】その政治家は地元では顔が売れている The politician *is influential* in his home district.
【顔がきく】彼はその方面では顔がきく(→影響力がある)らしい I hear that he *has influence* in the field.
【顔がつぶれる】君がそんなことをすると私の顔がつぶれる I'*ll lose face* if you do such a thing.
【顔が広い】彼女は顔が広い She *knows a lot of people*.
【顔から火が出る】顔から火が出る思いだった I *flushed* [*blushed*] *with embarrassment*.
【顔だ】黒田さんはこのへんでは顔だ(→よく知られている) Mr. Kuroda *is well known* in this neighborhood.
【顔に泥を塗る】おまえは自分の父親の顔に泥を塗る(→恥をかかせる)つもりか Are you going to

bring shame on your father?
【顔に似合わず】彼は顔に似合わず小心者だ He is a timid man *despite of his appearance*.
【顔を売る】彼女は単に顔を売るのが目的でその役目を引き受けた She took on the role only to *make herself popular*.
【顔をそろえる】その試合には大物選手がずらりと顔をそろえた Major players *showed up* at the game.
【顔を出す】彼女はパーティーに顔を出した She *put in an appearance* at the party.
【顔を立てる】この場は彼の顔を立てて黙っていよう In this case I'll keep silent to *allow* him *to save face*.
【顔を見せる】近ごろ彼はこの店に顔を見せなくなった He *hasn't shown up* in this store lately.

かおあわせ 顔合わせ きのう新入社員の顔合わせがあった The new staff *were introduced to one another* yesterday.
‖初顔合わせ(対戦) the first match

かおいろ 顔色 color [C][U], complexion [C] ‖顔色を変える change *color* / 顔色がよい have *a* high *color* / 健康そうな顔色をしている have *a* healthy *complexion* ◆顔色が悪いけど大丈夫ですか You *look pale*. Are you OK? / 彼はとても顔色がよくなっている He *looks* a good deal *better*. / その子はいつも母親の顔色をうかがっている The child *is* always *watching* his [her] mother's *mood*.

かおく 家屋 house [C], building [C] ‖その地震で多数の家屋が倒壊した Many *houses* collapsed in the quake.

かおじゃしん 顔写真 a photograph of *a person's* face, ID photo [C]; (犯人の) 《口語的》 mug shot [C]

カオス (混沌(こんとん)) chaos [kéiɑs] [U]

かおだち 顔立ち features, looks ‖男性的な顔立ち masculine *looks* / 少女はとても整った顔立ちをしている The girl has very regular *features*. ◆彼は顔立ちが整っている He is *handsome*.

かおつき 顔つき features, look [C], expression [C] ‖考え事をしている[思慮深い]顔つき *a* thoughtful *expression* / 満足した顔つきで with *a* satisfied *look* / 彼は背が高く，やせ型で特徴のない顔つきをしている He is a tall, thin man, with plain *features*.
◆みんな真剣な顔つきをしていた Everybody *looked* serious.

かおなじみ 顔なじみ familiar face [C]
◆彼とはその飲み屋で顔なじみだ I *often meet* him at the bar.

かおぶれ 顔ぶれ line-up [C] ◆いつもの顔ぶれが集まった *The usual people* gathered.

かおまけ 顔負け 彼はプロ選手顔負けの速球を投げる(→彼の速球はプロ選手を恥じ入らせる) His fastball *puts* the professional players *to shame*.

かおみしり 顔見知り acquaintance [U]《また an ～》 ‖彼女とはそのパーティーで顔見知りになった I *made her acquaintance* at the party.
◆私は彼と顔見知りだ I *know* him *by sight*.

かおむけ 顔向け 彼も息子がそんなことをしたのでは世間に顔向けできまい He'*ll be ashamed to look people in the face* after his son did such a thing.

かおやく 顔役 (影響力の持ち主) influential man [C]; (ボス) 《口語的》 boss [C]

かおり 香り・薫り (よい香り) fragrance [U][C]; (コーヒーなどの) aroma [U][C]; (ほのかな香気) scent [U][C]; (におい一般) smell [C] (❖修飾語が付かないといやなにおいを意味することが多い) 香水のかすかな香り *a* faint *fragrance* of perfume / 香り豊かなコーヒー豆 coffee beans *full of aroma*
ラベンダーはいい香りがする Lavender has *a* sweet *smell*./ Lavender *smells* sweet.
そのバラの香りは彼の古い記憶を呼び起こした *The scent* of the roses awoke old memories in him.

かおる 香る・薫る smell* [自] ‖甘く香る *smell* sweet

がか 画家 painter [C] ‖日本画家 *a painter* in the Japanese style

かかあでんか かかあ天下 彼の家はかかあ天下だ(→彼はしりに敷かれている) He *is henpecked*. / His wife *wears the pants* in his family.

かがい 課外 ‖課外活動 extracurricular activities / 課外授業 an extracurricular lesson; (補習) a supplementary lesson

かがいしゃ 加害者 (暴行の) 《公式的》 assailant [C]; (殺人の) murderer [C] ‖彼女は加害者の顔をはっきりと覚えていた She remembered *her assailant's* face vividly.

かかえこむ 抱え込む 彼女は人形を腕にしっかり抱え込んで放そうとしなかった She *held* a doll tightly in her arms, and wouldn't let it go. / 彼は深刻な問題を抱え込んだ He *has been landed with* serious problems.

かかえる 抱える hold* ... in *one's* arms
彼は大きな袋を両手に抱えている He *is holding* a big bag *in his arms*. (❖「運んでいる」の意味を出すなら He is carrying ... とする)
◆彼女はノートパソコンを小わきにかかえてやってきた She came *with* a notebook computer *under her arm*. / 彼の秘書はそのとき様々な仕事を抱えていた His secretary *had* many different jobs to do then. / その会社は多くの従業員を抱えている The company *has* a lot of employees. / 私たちは世界が抱えている問題を直視しなければならない We must look squarely at the problems *of* the world. / 彼らはその非行少年に頭を抱えている(→悩んでいる) They *are worried about* the bad boy. / 私たちは彼の冗談に腹を抱えて笑った We *roared with laughter* at his joke.

カカオ cacao [C] (複 ～s)

かかく 価格 price [C]
原油価格の急落 an abrupt drop in oil *prices*
この店の商品の価格は多少低めに設定されている *The prices* of the goods in this store are set a little lower than average.
この価格帯の車を探しています I'm looking for a car within this *price range*.
‖価格協定 price-fixing / 価格統制 price

controls / 価格破壊 price slashing / 卸売価格 a wholesale price / 小売価格 a retail price / 市場価格 (a) market value / 消費者価格 a consumer price / 適正価格 (a) fair value / 末端価格 (麻薬などの) a street value / 割引価格 a reduced price

かがく¹ 科学 science ⓤ ⓒ ──科学の scientific
大気汚染に関する科学的データ the *scientific* data on air pollution
科学は20世紀にめざましい発展を遂げた *Science* has made remarkable progress in the 20th century.
◆彼は科学に通じている He *is scientifically literate*.
∥科学技術 science and technology / 科学技術庁 the Science and Technology Agency(❖2001年文部科学省に統合) / 科学者 a scientist / 科学博物館 a science museum / 応用科学 (an) applied science / 行動科学 (a) behavioral science / 自然科学 (a) natural science / 社会科学 (a) social science / 情報科学 (an) information science / 生命科学 life sciences

かがく² 化学 chemistry ⓤ ──化学の chemical (❖通例名詞の前で用いる)
化学の実験をする conduct *chemistry* experiments
∥化学記号 a chemical symbol / 化学工学 chemical engineering / 化学工業 (a) chemical industry / 化学式 a chemical formula / 化学者 a chemist / 化学製品 a chemical product / 化学繊維(合成繊維) (a) synthetic fiber / 化学洗剤 (a) chemical cleansing agent / 化学調味料 (a) chemical seasoning / 化学反応 a chemical reaction / 化学肥料 (a) fertilizer / 化学兵器 a chemical weapon / 化学変化 (a) chemical change / 化学方程式 a chemical equation / 化学薬品 a chemical

ががく 雅楽 *gagaku*, traditional music of the Japanese Imperial Court

かかげる 掲げる (旗などを) fly* ⓣ; (主張などを) put* up; (つるすように) hang* ⓣ
白旗を掲げる *fly* [*show*] the white flag
その党は社会福祉をテーマに掲げている The political party *puts up* social welfare as its theme.
中華料理店の大きな看板が門の上に掲げられている The big sign of the Chinese restaurant *is hung* on its gate.

かかし 案山子 scarecrow ⓒ

かかす 欠かす
隆は毎朝欠かさずラジオ体操をする Takashi *never misses* the radio exercise program every morning.
彼は欠かさず礼拝に行く He goes to church *regularly*.
ワインは肉料理には欠かせない Wine *is a necessary accompaniment* to meat dishes.
外国語を学ぶうえである程度の文法は欠かせない Some grammar *is a must* for learning a foreign language.

見知らぬ土地での車の運転に地図は欠かせない A map *is indispensable* for driving in a strange land.

かかと 踵 heel ⓒ ∥この靴のかかとは少しすり減っている The *heels* of these shoes have seen some hard wear. ◆かかとの高い[低い]靴を履く wear *high-heeled* [*flat*] shoes

かがみ¹ 鏡 mirror ⓒ; (姿見) looking glass ⓒ ∥彼女は鏡を見た(→鏡の中の自分自身を見た) She looked at herself in the *mirror*.
◆湖面は鏡のようになめらかだった The surface of the lake was (as) smooth as *glass*.
∥手鏡 a hand mirror

かがみ² 鑑 paragon ⓒ, model ⓒ ◆彼は生徒のかがみだ He is a *model* [*an ideal*] student.

かがむ 屈む stoop ⓘ; (体を前に曲げる) bend* ⓘ, lean* ⓘ; (しゃがむ) crouch ⓘ ∥彼はかがんで少女にキスをした He *bent over* the girl and kissed her. / 戸口が低いのでかがんで通ってください The doorway is low, so please *stoop* [*bend*] *down* to go through. ∥少年はかがんでボールを拾った The boy *leaned over* to pick up the ball.

かがめる 屈める bend* ⓣ, stoop ⓘ ∥彼女は身をかがめて歩いた She *bent* as she walked. / 彼は硬貨を拾おうと身をかがめた He *stooped* to pick up the coin.
◆彼は植え込みの後ろに腰をかがめた He *crouched down* behind a bush.

かがやかしい 輝かしい bright, brilliant; (栄光ある) glorious ∥輝かしい功績 a *brilliant* accomplishment / わが国は輝かしい歴史をもつ Our country has a *glorious* past.

かがやかす 輝かす 彼女は大きなダイヤモンドに目を輝かせた She *gazed* at the big diamond *with bright eyes*. / 彼女は誕生日プレゼントに顔を輝かせた She *beamed at* her birthday present.

かがやき 輝き brightness ⓤ, brilliance ⓤ, glitter ⓤ, sparkle ⓤⓒ; (目の) twinkle ⓒ《通例単数形》∥ダイヤモンドの輝き the *brilliance* of a diamond ∥彼女の目には幸せそうな輝きがあった She had *a* happy *twinkle* in her eyes.

かがやく 輝く shine* ⓘ; glitter ⓘ; sparkle ⓘ; twinkle ⓘ; light* ⓘ
　shine: 光を放つ, また反射して明るく見える.
　glitter: 光を反射して断続的にぴかぴか光る.
　sparkle: 宝石・目などが輝く.
　twinkle: 目が喜び・楽しみなどで輝く.
　light: 顔・目などが晴れ晴れとする.

太陽が明るく輝いていた The sun *was shining* brightly.
彼女の顔は喜びに輝いていた Her face *was shining with happiness*.
星が冬の夜空に輝いていた Stars *glittered* in the winter sky.
ダイヤモンドは太陽の光を受けてきらきら輝いた The diamond *sparkled* in the sunlight.
子供たちはそのプレゼントを見て目を輝かせた The children's *eyes sparkled* when they saw the present.
その知らせを聞いて彼女の表情がぱっと輝いた

Her face *lit up* when she heard the news.

かかり 係 charge ◻; (公共施設などの案内係) attendant ◻ ∥僕は黒板を消す係です I am *in charge of* erasing the blackboard. / 係の人はどこですか Where is *the person in charge*? ◆受付係は私に予約をしているかどうか尋ねた The receptionist asked me whether [if] I had a reservation.

-がかり それは10年がかりの大事業だった The big enterprise *took* as long as 10 years. / 3人がかりでピアノを運んだ It *took* three people to carry the piano.

かかりあい 掛かり合い ⇨ かかわり
かかりあう 掛かり合う ⇨ かかわる
かかりいん 係員 the person in charge
かかりきり 彼女は一日中子供の世話にかかりきりだった(→とても忙しかった) She *was very busy* taking care of her child all day. / この3か月間, 彼はその本の翻訳にかかりきりだ He *has devoted all his time to* translating the book for three months.

かかりちょう 係長 subsection chief ◻ (❖英語にはこの日本語に相当する決まった語がない)

かかりつけ 掛かり付け かかりつけの医者 one's *regular* doctor; the *family* doctor
かがりび 篝火 bonfire ◻ ∥かがり火をたく make [build] *a bonfire*

かかる¹ 掛かる

❶ぶら下がる	hang
❷覆われる・かぶる	be covered with ...; be splashed with ...
❸時間や費用を要する	take
❹作動する	
❺電話が	
❻付加される	
❼つかまる・捕らえられる	be caught
❽始める	begin
❾扱われる	see

❶【ぶら下がる・宙づりになる】hang* ⓔ
タペストリーが壁にかかっていた Tapestries *hung* on the wall.
彼のジャケットはすべて洋服だんすにかかっている All his jackets *hang* in the wardrobe.
彼女の髪は腰までかかっていた Her hair *hung* down to her waist.
空に満月がかかっていた The full moon *hung* [was] in the sky.

❷【覆われる・かぶる・置かれる】(…に覆われる) be covered with ...; (…がはねかかる) be splashed with ...; (置かれている) be on ...
山にはうっすらと霧がかかっていた The mountain *was covered with* a thin mist.
車がそばを通り過ぎたときに私のスカートに泥がかかった My skirt *was splashed with* mud as a car passed by me.
なべが火にかかっている The pan *is on* the stove [fire].
◆ビニールのかかった漫画本 a comic book *sealed in plastic*

❸【時間や費用などを要する】(時間が) take* ⓔ; (費用が) cost* ⓔ
家から駅まで歩いて15分かかる It takes 15 minutes *to* walk from my house to the station.
東京から福岡まで飛行機で行くのにいくらお金がかかるだろう How much does *it cost to* fly from Tokyo to Fukuoka?
その計画の唯一の欠点は非常に金がかかることだ The plan's only weakness is that *it will cost* a lot.
◆この機械はその仕事にかかる時間を半分にすることができる This machine can halve the time *needed for* the work. / いくらかかってもかまわない(→出費は問題ではない) *Expense* is no object. / 妹は手がかかりすぎる(→時間と世話を要する) My sister *claims* too much of my time and attention. / 電車で約50分かかる It's about a 50-minute trip by train. / 宿題を終わらせるのに一晩かかった I *spent* the whole night finishing my homework.

❹【作動する】(かぎが) lock ⓔ, be locked; (音楽が) be played; (エンジンなどが) start ⓔ
ドアはカチッといってかぎがかかった The door *locked* with a click.
彼はドアをあけようとしたがかぎがかかっていた He tried the door, but it *was locked*.
ラジオで私のリクエストした曲がかかった The song I requested *was played* on the radio.
なぜエンジンがかからないのだろう Why *won't* the engine *start*?
◆CDが大きな音でかかっている A CD *is playing* loudly.

❺【電話が】
ゆうべあなたから電話がかかるのを待ってたのに I was expecting your *call* last night.
食事中に私に電話がかかってきた There was a *telephone call* during the meal.
5回目でようやく電話がかかった(→つながった) The phone call finally *connected* [*got through*] on the fifth try.

❻【付加される】
ウエーブのかかった金髪 *wavy* blond hair
私の息子に嫌疑がかかった Suspicion *fell on* my son.
彼に殺人の容疑がかかった He *was suspected* of murder.
たばこには重い税金がかかっている Heavy *taxes are imposed on* tobacco. / Tobacco *is heavily taxed*.
そのチームはプレッシャーのかかった試合を制した The team won the *high-pressure* game.

❼【つかまる・捕らえられる】be caught
ウサギがわなにかかった A rabbit *was caught* in the trap.
◆きのうはちっとも魚がかからなかった(→魚がえさに食いつかなかった) The fish *didn't bite* yesterday.

❽【始める・攻める】(始める) begin* ⓔ; (攻る) attack ⓔ
仕事にかかる前に考えをよくまとめなさい Col-

lect your thoughts before you *begin* your work.
◆私は彼の言ったことは本当だと決めてかかった I *assumed* the truth of his statement. / さあかかってこい Now, *come on*!
❾【扱われる】(医者などに診(ん)てもらう) see*, consult; (人に会う) see
私はここ数年, 医者にかかっていない I've *not seen* a doctor for these past few years.
きょうの午後お目にかかりたいのですが I'd like to *see* you this afternoon.
◆その問題は現在審議にかかっている The matter *is under deliberation* now. / 彼の手にかかるとただの木材がすばらしい工芸品に変わってしまう *Under his craftsmanship* mere wood is changed into splendid artifacts. / ついに彼は敵の手にかかった(→敵に殺された) At last he *was killed* by the enemy.
❿【その他】
暗示にかかる *be influenced by a person's suggestion*
そんなことをしたら彼女に迷惑がかかってしまう Doing such a thing will *put* her *out*.
彼女はいつも鼻にかかった声で話す She always speaks in a *nasal* tone.

かかる² 架かる 空に美しいにじがかかっていた A beautiful rainbow *spanned* the sky. / その川にかかっている橋がこわれた The bridge *over [across]* the river was damaged. / 江戸川に新しく橋がかかった A new bridge *was built* over the Edo River. / 列車はトンネルにかかった The train *reached* the tunnel.

かかる³ 罹る get*, catch*, 《口語的》come* down with ...; (苦しむ) suffer from ... / 彼は心臓病にかかっている He *is suffering from* heart disease. / 彼はマラリアにかかった He *came down with* malaria.
◆彼女は癌にかかっているらしい She seems to *have* cancer. / 私の子供たちは流感にかかっている My children *are ill with* influenza.

かかる⁴ 懸かる (依存する) depend; (心配する) be anxious ‖彼の成功は彼らが助けてくれるかどうかにかかっている His success *depends on* whether they will help him or not. / あしたの試合のことが気にかかって眠れない I *am so anxious about* tomorrow's game that I can hardly sleep.

-かかる 彼は僕に殴りかかった He *swung his fist at* me. / ライオンは突然シカに飛びかかった The lion *made a sudden spring at* the deer. / 番犬は泥棒に激しく襲いかかった The watchdog *made a* violent *attack on [against]* the thief. / 上着の第2ボタンが取れかかっている The second button of your jacket *is coming off*. / 彼のボートは湖で沈みかかっていた His boat *was sinking* in the lake. / この犬たちはおぼれかかった人を救助するよう訓練されています These dogs are trained to rescue *drowning* people. / 私はたまたま学校の前を通りかかった I *happened to pass by* the school.

かがる darn, hemstitch, hem; (つくろう) mend

-がかる 黄色がかった赤 red *with a dash of* yellow; *yellowish* red / やや灰色がかった黒い髪 dark hair *tinged with* gray / 芝居がかった身ぶり a *dramatic* [*theatrical*] gesture

かがわ 香川
全国で最も面積の小さい県である香川県は, 四国の北東に位置し, 瀬戸内海に面しています. 気候は温暖で雨が少なく, しばしば水不足に悩まされてきました. この県には名所旧跡が数多くありますが, 特に「こんぴらさん」の愛称で知られる金毘羅(ら)宮は海の守護神として有名で, 多くの参拝者が訪れています.
Kagawa Prefecture, which has the smallest land area in the country, is located in northeastern Shikoku, facing the Seto Inland Sea. The climate is mild with little rain, and the prefecture has often suffered water shortages. Among many famous places of scenic beauty and historical interest is Kotohira Shrine, better known as "Kompirasan." It is dedicated to the guardian god of the sea, and it attracts many visitors.

かかわらず 拘らず
❶【…にもかかわらず】in spite of ..., despite, though, although

語法
(1) **[in spite of と despite]** 共に後ろに名詞・動名詞を伴う. despite のほうがかたい語だが, 新聞などでは好まれる.
(2) **[though と although]** though のほうがくだけた語. 共に後ろに節を伴う. ただし, though は形容詞や副詞を接続することができる. また though 節の主語と主節の主語が同じ場合, though 節の《主語＋be 動詞》は省略が可能 ‖ 彼女は病気だったにもかかわらず学校へ行った *Though* (she was) sick, she went to school.

雪にもかかわらず試合は行われた The game was played *in spite of* snow.
老齢にもかかわらず祖父はその山に登った *Despite* his advanced age, my grandfather climbed the mountain.
とても疲れていたにもかかわらず彼女は眠れなかった *Though* she was very tired, she couldn't go to sleep.
◆全く不利な状況にもかかわらず彼女は成功した She succeeded *against* all (the) odds. / それにもかかわらず彼は計画を実行した *Notwithstanding* [*Nevertheless*], he carried out the plan. / 私の忠告にもかかわらず彼女は同じ間違いを犯した *After all* my advice, she made the same mistake.

❷【…に関係なく】regardless of ..., irrespective of ...
水泳は年齢・性別にかかわらずだれでも楽しめる Any person can enjoy swimming *regardless of age or sex*.
そのイベントは天候のいかんにかかわらず行われ

る The event will be held *irrespective of the weather*.
◆好むと好まざるとにかかわらずパーティーに出席しなければならない You must go to the party *whether you like it or not*.

かかわり 係わり・関わり 彼はこの会社と何らかのかかわりがある He *has something to do with* this firm. / それは私にはかかわりのないことだ That's [It's] *not my problem*. / おまえにはかかわりのないことだ That's *none of your business*. / 彼とかかわりをもたないほうがいいよ You'd *be better off having nothing to do with* him. ⇨かんけい

かかわりあう 係わり合う・関わり合う その問題にはかかわり合いたくない I don't want to *get involved in* that matter.

かかわる 係わる・関わる (関係する) associate [concern] *oneself* with ...; (影響する) affect ⊕
彼は労働運動にかかわっていた He *associated himself with* the labor movement.
そんなことにかかわっている暇はない I have no time to *concern myself with* such matters.
彼の決断は私たちの将来にかかわる His decision *will affect* our future.
それは学校の名誉にかかわる It *will affect the honor* of our school.
◆彼女はほかの学生たちとはなるべくかかわらない(→距離をおく)ようにしている She tries to *keep herself apart* from other students.

かかん 果敢 ─果敢な bold, daring ◆彼は困難に果敢に立ち向かった He *daringly* faced the difficulties.

かき¹ 下記 下記の問いに答えよ Answer the 「*following* questions [questions *below*]. / 出席者は下記のとおりです The attendees are *as follows*.

かき² 夏期・夏季 summer Ⓤ Ⓒ, summertime Ⓤ ‖夏期休暇 (米) summer vacation, (英) summer holidays / 夏期講座 a summer course / 夏期講習 (a) summer school, a summer seminar

かき³ 柿 Japanese persimmon Ⓒ
[俳句] 柿くへば鐘が鳴るなり法隆寺(正岡子規)
Chewing a persimmon,
I hear the temple bell toll
from Horyuji.

かき⁴ 火気 火気厳禁 (掲示) *Flammable* (❖ flammable は「可燃性の」の意味)

かき⁵ 牡蠣 oyster Ⓒ ‖生ガキ a raw *oyster* / カキフライ fried oysters

かぎ¹ 鍵
key Ⓒ; (錠) lock Ⓒ; (掛け金) latch Ⓒ; (ダイヤル式の) combination lock Ⓒ
かぎをかぎ穴に差し込む insert *a key* into *a keyhole* / 合いかぎを作る make *a duplicate of a key*
彼はかぎを家中捜し回った He looked for the *key* all over the house.
一生懸命働くことが成功へのかぎだ Hard work is *the key to success*.

その計画がうまくいくかどうかのかぎを握っているのは健だった It was Ken who *held the key* to the success of the plan.
◆外出するときはドアにちゃんとかぎをかけなさい See that you *lock* the door when you go out. / 2階の窓にかぎがかかっているか確かめてください Please make sure that the windows upstairs *are locked*. / どうやって彼はドアのかぎをあけたのだろう How did he *unlock* the door?

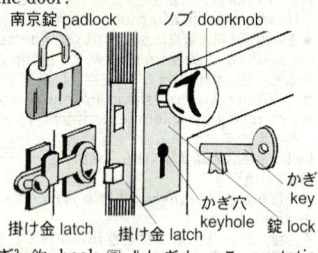

南京錠 padlock ノブ doorknob
かぎ key
かぎ穴 keyhole 錠 lock
掛け金 latch 掛け金 latch

かぎ² 鉤 hook Ⓒ ‖かぎかっこ quotation marks / かぎ鼻 a hooked nose / かぎホック a hook and eye

かきあげ 掻き揚げ 🍳 *kakiage*, mixed shrimp, scallop and vegetables battered and deep-fried

かきあげる 書き上げる finish writing ‖彼はその小説をたった2週間で書き上げた He *finished writing* the novel in no more than two weeks.

かきあつめる 掻き集める rake ⊕, scrape together [up] ‖落ち葉をかき集めなさい *Rake* the fallen leaves (into a pile). / 彼は新たな政党を結成するために資金をかき集めた He *scraped together* enough money to organize his new political party.

かきあらためる 書き改める (書き直す) rewrite* ⊕; (改作する) adapt ‖彼はその小説を子供向けに書き改めた He *rewrote* [*adapted*] the novel for children.

かきあらわす 書き表す (表現する) express ⊕ ‖彼は気持ちを詩に書き表した He *expressed* his feeling in a poem.

かきいれどき 書き入れ時 the busiest season ◆12月は商店の書き入れ時だ December is *the busiest month* for shops.

かきいれる 書き入れる write* in, fill in ⇨かきこむ(書き込む), きにゅう ‖ここに名前を書き入れなさい *Write in* your name here.

かきうつす 書き写す copy ⊕, transcribe ⊕ ‖彼はその本から一節を手帳に書き写した He *copied* a passage from the book into his notebook.

かきおき 書き置き note Ⓒ, written message Ⓒ ‖書き置きを残しておいていただけますか Would you leave me *a note*?

かきおとす 書き落とす (書き忘れる) omit ⊕ (❖ わざと抜かす場合にもいう), forget* to write, leave* out ‖だいじなことを書き落としていました I *forgot to write* [*omitted*] an important thing.

かきおろし 書き下ろし 彼はテレビ用の新しい脚本を書き下ろした He *wrote* a new play *especially for* television.

かきかえる 書き換える (名義を) transfer [他]; (更新する) renew [他] ∥運転免許を書き換える *renew one's* driving license / 彼は土地の所有権を息子の名義に書き換えた He *transferred* ownership of the land to his son.

かきかた 書き方 ❶【書く方法】how to write ∥君は手紙の書き方を学んだほうがいい You should learn *how to write* a letter.
❷【習字】《公式的》penmanship [U]

かきくわえる 書き加える add [他] ∥私はリストに彼女の名前を書き加えた I *added* her name to the list.

かきけす 掻き消す drown [他] (❖しばしば out を伴う); (突然姿を消す) disappear suddenly, vanish [自] ∥観衆のかっさいで彼の言葉がかき消されてしまった The cheers from the audience *drowned out* his words.

かきごおり かき氷 🗻 *kakigori*, shaved ice flavored with syrup

かきことば 書き言葉 written language [C]
◆書き言葉の英語 *written* English

かきこみ 書き込み note [C] ∥だれかが下の余白に書き込みをした Someone wrote [made] *notes* on the bottom margin. ◆その本にはたくさんの書き込み(→いたずら書き)があった There were a lot of *doodles* in the book.

かきこむ[1] 書き込む fill in [out], write* in ∥彼が書き込むように名前の欄をあけておいてください Please leave the name blank for him to *fill in*. / 書類に必要事項はもう書き込んである I *have* already *filled in* [*out*] the document. (❖fill in は「空欄に書く」, fill out は「必要事項を記入する」の意味)

かきこむ[2] 掻き込む 《口語的》gobble [他], bolt [他] ∥彼は朝食をかき込むとあわてて出かけていった He *bolted down* his breakfast and left hurriedly.

かきしるす 書き記す write* down
⇨ かきとめる, かく(書く)

かきそえる 書き添える add [他] ⇨ かきくわえる

かきそこなう 書き損なう 名前を書きそこなう *make a mistake in writing one's* name
⇨ かきまちがえる

かきぞめ 書き初め 🗻

> 書き初めは年初めの書道の儀式で, 新年に向けて気持ちを新しくし, また字がうまくなりますようにとの願いをこめて, ふつう1月2日に行われます. 主に子供たちや書道愛好家が参加しますが, 大勢が集まって神社で行われることもあります.
> *Kakizome* is a calligraphy ritual at the beginning of the year, usually done on January 2. The purpose is to refresh the spirit and to wish for improved handwriting in the new year. This ceremony is most common among children and calligraphy enthusiasts, and it is sometimes done in a large group at shrines.

がきだいしょう 餓鬼大将 the boss of the kids (in the neighborhood); (いじめっ子) bully [C]

かきだし 書き出し the beginning (of a story) ◆手紙の書きだし *the opening lines* of a letter / その小説は次のような書きだしで始まる The novel begins like this.

かきたす 書き足す add [他] ⇨ かきくわえる

かきだす[1] 書き出す (一覧表を作る) make* a list; (要点などを抜粋する) extract [他] ∥店で買うものを書き出しておこう I'll *make a list of* things to buy at the shop. / 彼はその本から好きな文句を書き出した He *extracted* his favorite passages from the book.

かきだす[2] 掻き出す 暖炉から灰をかき出す *scrape* ash *out* of the fireplace

かぎだす 嗅ぎ出す scent [他], smell* [他]

かきたてる[1] 書き立てる write* up, 《口語的》splash [他] ∥週刊誌はこぞってその政治スキャンダルについて書きたてた All the weekly magazines *wrote up* stories of the political scandal.

かきたてる[2] 掻き立てる arouse [他], excite [他], stir [他] ∥彼の話は私たちの好奇心をかきたてた His story *aroused* our curiosity. / その童話が少女の想像力をかきたてた The fairy tale *stirred* the girl's imagination.

かきちらす 書き散らす (なぐり書きする) scribble [他], scrawl [他] ∥部屋には書き散らされたメモが残っていた Some *scribbled* notes were left in the room.

かきつけ 書き付け (覚え書) note [C]; (他人に対しての) memo [C] (複 ～s)

かきつける 書き付ける write* down
⇨ かきとめる

かぎつける 嗅ぎ付ける (危険・獲物などを) smell* [他], sniff [他] (❖共にしばしば out を伴う); (秘密などを) 《口語的》nose out ∥猟犬は獲物をかぎつけて走りだした The hound started to run, *sniffing out* his prey.
◆新聞記者はスキャンダルをかぎつける鋭い勘をもっている Newspaper reporters have *a nose for* scandal. / 彼らが私たちの秘密をかぎつけなければいいが I hope they don't *get wind of* our secret.

かぎっこ 鍵っ子 latchkey child [C]

かぎって 限って その日に限って子供たちは会館に入ることを許される The hall allows children in *only* on that day. / 彼に限ってそんなうそをつくはずがない He is *the last person to* tell such a lie. / うちの子に限ってそんないかがわしい場所に出入りしているはずがない Our child *would never* hang around such a sleazy place. / 急いでいるときに限ってプリンターが故障する *Just when* we're in a hurry, the printer breaks down.

かきつばた 杜若 〖植物〗iris [C] [áiəris]

かきとめ 書留 registered mail [U] ―書留にする register [他] ∥この手紙を書留にしたいのですが I'd like to *have* this letter *registered*. / この小包を書留で送ってください Please send this package by *registered mail*.

‖書留速達 registered special delivery
かきとめる 書き留める write* [take*, put*] down; (メモする) note [他], take notes of ...; (記録する) record [他], mark down ‖要点を書き留める *take notes of* the main points / 忘れないうちにその考えを書き留めておきなさい *Write down* that idea before you forget it. / 警官は彼の住所と電話番号を書き留めた The policeman *put down* his address and telephone number.
かきとり 書き取り dictation [U] [C] (❖口述を書き取ることを指す) ‖英語の書き取りテスト *an* English *dictation test*
◆きょうは漢字の書き取りのテストがある We have a test in *writing Kanji* today.
かきとる 書き取る 彼は私が言ったことをすべて書き取った He *wrote down* everything I said. / 先生は文章を生徒に書き取らせた The teacher *dictated* a passage to the class.
かきなおす 書き直す (書き換える) rewrite* [他]; (もう一度書く) write* ... over (again); (清書する) write out ‖彼はその原稿を数回書き直した He *rewrote* the manuscript several times. / 彼女はそれを書き直させられた She was made to *write* it *over again*.
かきながす 書き流す (すらすら書く) write* off, dash off
かきなぐる 書きなぐる scribble [他], scrawl [他] ‖その紙切れには彼女の住所が書きなぐってあった Her address *was scribbled* on the piece of paper.
かきならす 掻き鳴らす strum [他] [自] ‖ギターをかき鳴らす *strum* (*on*) a guitar
かきね 垣根 (柵(さく)) fence [C]; (生け垣) hedge [C] ‖私の家は垣根で囲まれている My house is enclosed by *a hedge*.
かきのこす 書き残す (書いて残す) leave* [他]; (書かずにおく) leave ... unwritten ‖遺書を書き残す *leave* a will / その作家は話の最後の部分を書き残したまま死んでしまった The author died *leaving* the final part of the story *unwritten*.
かぎばり 鉤針 crochet [krouʃéi] needle [hook] [C] ◆かぎ針編みの帽子 a *crocheted* cap
かきまぜる 掻き混ぜる (泡立てる) beat* [他]; (かき回して混ぜる) stir [他] ‖小麦粉と卵をボールに入れ, いっしょによくかき混ぜます Put the flour and eggs into a bowl and *beat* them together well.
◆ビーカーの液体を少しかき混ぜた I *gave* a few *stirs* to the liquid in the beaker.
かきまちがえる 書き間違える うっかりしていてあて先を書き間違えてしまった(→間違ったあて名を書いた) I was absent-minded and *wrote the wrong* address.
かきまわす 掻き回す (かき混ぜる) stir [他]; (捜して引っかき回す) rummage [自] ‖私はスプーンでコーヒーをかき回した I *stirred* my coffee with a spoon. / 彼は書類を捜してかばんの中をかき回した He *rummaged* in his bag for some papers.
◆彼は会議をかき回した(→混乱させた) He *threw* the meeting *into disorder*.
かきみだす 掻き乱す (人の心を) disturb [他], agitate [他]; (混乱させる) confuse [他], throw* ... into confusion ‖その事件に村の平和はかき乱された The event *disturbed* the peace of the village.
かきむしる 掻きむしる (髪を) tear* [他]; (つめで引っかく) scratch [他] ‖髪をかきむしる *tear one's* hair / 彼は混乱して頭をかきむしった He became confused and *scratched* his head. / 戦争の犠牲者のことを考えると胸をかきむしられる思いだった The thought of the victims of the war *tore my heart out*.
かきもの 書き物 writing [U] ‖書き物机 a *writing* desk / 彼は毎日たくさんの書き物をする He does a lot of *writing* every day.
かきゅう[1] 下級 ―下級の (階層・価値が) lower; (地位・品質が) inferior; (役職・年齢が) junior ◆健治は下級生の面倒見がいい Kenji takes good care of *the underclassmen*.
‖下級裁判所 a lower court
かきゅう[2] 火急 ―火急の (緊急の) urgent, pressing ‖火急の用事を思い出した I remembered some *urgent* business.
かきょう[1] 佳境 the most interesting part, climax [C] ‖彼の話もいよいよ佳境に入ってきた His story was reaching *the climax* [*most interesting part*].
かきょう[2] 華僑 overseas Chinese [C]
かぎょう[1] 家業 family business [U] ‖私は息子に家業を継がせたい I want my son to follow in *the family business*.
かぎょう[2] 稼業 *one's* business, *one's* occupation ◆サラリーマン稼業(→サラリーマンであること)は考えていたほど楽ではない *Being a salaried worker* is not so easy as I imagined.
かきょく 歌曲 song [C]; (ドイツ歌曲) lied [líːd] [C] (複 lieder [líːdər])
-かぎらない -限らない
頭のよい男の子がだれでも女の子にもてるとは限らない *Not all* smart boys are popular with girls.
金持ちが必ずしも幸せだとは限らない The rich are *not always* happy.
若いからといって彼女が未熟だとは限らない Just because she is young(, that) *doesn't necessarily* mean she is inexperienced.
ある場合に当てはまることが別の場合にも当てはまるとは限らない(→当てはまらないかもしれない) What is true of one case *may not* be true of another.
その傾向は若者だけに限らない The trend is *not limited* to young people.
➜かぎる
かぎられた 限られた (有限の) limited; (制限された) restricted ➜かぎる ‖限られた資源 *limited* resources
かぎり 限り limit [C]; (終わり) end [C] ―限りある finite [fáinait], limited ―限りない (無限の) limitless, boundless; (終わりのない) endless, infinite [ínfinət]
限りなく広がる宇宙 the *boundless* universe
天然資源には限りがある There is *a limit* to

natural resources.
彼の欲望には限りがない His desire knows no *end*.
私たちは限りある資源を有効に活用しなければならない We must make good use of *limited* resources.
◆このサービスは20歳未満の方に限り有効です This service is available *only* to people under 20. / 観衆は選手たちに声を限りに声援を送った The crowd cheered the players *at the top of their lungs*. / 彼らは力の限り戦った They fought *with all their strength*.

-かぎり 限り
生きているかぎりあなたのことは決して忘れません I'll never forget you *as long as I live*.
見渡すかぎり銀世界だった *As far as the eye could see*, the world was white with snow.
私に関するかぎり何も申し上げることはありません *As far as I am concerned*, I have nothing to say.
君が謝らないかぎり智子は君のことを許さないだろう Tomoko will not forgive you *unless* you apologize to her.
私の知るかぎりこの劇が日本で上演されたことはない *To the best of my knowledge*, this play has never been performed in Japan.
そんなことは私が記憶するかぎりでは起っていない Nothing like that has happened *within my memory*.
その大学は今年限りで(→来年)移転する The university will move *next year*.
この券は本日限り有効です This ticket is good *only* (*for*) today.
彼の決心はいつでもその場限りだ(→続かない) His resolutions *never last*.
自宅のおふろが温泉だなんてうらやましいかぎりです I *really envy you* (*for*) your hot spring bath at home.
➭できるかぎり

かぎりない 限りない boundless, limitless
➭かぎり

かぎる 限る
❶【制限する】limit 他; restrict 他; confine 他
limit: 程度・範囲などの限界点を定めること.
restrict: 境界線・限界区域を決めて，それを越えるのを禁止すること.
confine: 人間などを範囲内に無理に閉じ込めること.
座席数は限られている The number of seats *is limited*.
水泳は夏だけとは限らない Swimming *is not limited* to the summer.
◆入場は招待客に限ります Admission is by invitation *only*.
❷【いちばんよい】
汗をかいた後はシャワーに限る A shower is (*the*) *best* after you've been sweating.
寿司(を)を食べるならその店に限る It's *the only place* for eating sushi.
❸【必ずしも…ない】
多数決が最もよいとは限らない Majority rule is *not always* best.

➭-かぎらない

かきわける 掻き分ける 彼らは群衆をかき分けて進んだ They *plowed* [*opened a way*, *forced a passage*] *through* the crowd.

かぎわける 嗅ぎ分ける smell* out
➭かぎつける，かぐ(嗅ぐ)

かきん 家禽 (集合的) poultry (複数扱い), fowl ⓒ (複 ~，~s) (❖特に食用のめんどり (hen)を指す)

かく¹ 書く

write* 他 自
手紙を書く *write* a letter / 雑誌に小説を書く *write* a novel for a magazine
その本は簡単な英語で書かれている That book *is written* in simple English.
名前をペンで書いてください Please *write* your name with a pen.
彼女はそのケーキの作り方を詳しく書いた She *wrote out* the recipe for the cake.
何か書く物をお持ちですか Do you have something to *write* with?
あなたの詩はよく書けていると思う I think your poem *is well written*.
◆日記を書く(→つづ続ける) *keep* a diary / その単語をどう書くのか教えてください Please tell me how to *spell* that word. / 星占いには魅力的な男性が現れるって書いてあるわ The horoscope *says* an attractive man will come my way. / 到着したら一筆書いて送ります I'll *drop* you *a note* when I arrive. / 彼女はきれいな字を書く Her *handwriting* is neat.
💬「新聞に何て書いてある」「強い台風が来るらしいよ」"What does the paper *say*?" "It *says* that a strong typhoon is coming."

かく² 描く
(線画を) draw* 他; (絵の具で) paint 他 自
➭えがく
子供たちはクレヨンで絵を描いていた The children *were drawing* with crayons.
彼は肖像画を描くようにその画家に頼んだ He asked the artist to *paint* his picture.
簡単な地図をかいてください Please *draw* a rough map.

かく³ 掻く (つめなどで) scratch 他 自; (熊手(ネネ)で) rake 他 自; (雪を) (米) shovel 他 //背中がかゆい，ちょっとかいて My back itches. Can you *scratch* it? / 猫が体をかいている The cat *is scratching* itself. / 彼は答えに詰まって頭をかいた He was at a loss for the answer and *scratched his head*. (❖scratch *one's* head は「てれ」ではなく「当惑」のしぐさ)

かく⁴ 欠く lack 他 自, want 他 自; (瀬戸物の縁などを) chip 他 //彼の態度は誠実さを欠いている His attitude *was lacking* [*wanting*] *in* sincerity. ◆水は私たちの生活には欠くことができない Water *is essential* to (our) life. (→水なしでは生きていけない)We *can't* live *without* water. / この茶わんは縁を欠いている There is *a chip* on the lip of this rice bowl.

かく⁵ 核 nucleus ⓒ (複 nuclei, ~es) ——核の nuclear, atomic ➭場面・状況別会話

か

p.1740 ∥日本への核(→核兵器)の持ち込みは禁じられている The introduction of *nuclear weapons* into Japan is banned.

◆非核三原則 the three *nonnuclear* principles / 反戦運動の核となる人物 a *key* [*central*, *leading*] figure in the antiwar movement / 「ノーモア・ヒロシマ」は有名な反核スローガンである "No more Hiroshimas" is a famous *antinuclear* slogan.

‖核エネルギー nuclear energy / 核家族 a nuclear family / 核軍縮 nuclear disarmament / 核シェルター a nuclear shelter / 核実験 a nuclear test / 核戦争 a nuclear war / 核弾頭 a nuclear warhead / 核燃料 nuclear fuel / 核廃棄物 nuclear waste(s) / 核爆弾 a nuclear bomb / 核爆発 a nuclear explosion / 核反応 (a) nuclear reaction / 核武装 nuclear armament / 核分裂〔物理〕nuclear fission / 核兵器 a nuclear weapon / 核保有国 a nuclear power / 核ミサイル a nuclear missile / 核融合〔物理〕nuclear fusion / 核抑止力 a nuclear deterrent (❖以上の複合語では,「核家族」を除いて nuclear の代わりに atomic を用いることができる)

かく⁶ 格 ❶【レベル】彼女は1人だけ格が違った (→別格だ) She *was in a class of her own.* / 我々と彼らのチームとでは格が違う Our team *is not comparable with* theirs. / Our team and theirs *are not in the same league.*

❷【語と語の関係】〔文法〕case [C] [U]

> 格とは,他の語との関係を示す代名詞・名詞の語形変化のことである.英語には主格(nominative case),所有格(possessive case),目的格(objective case)がある.代名詞の場合は,主格 I,所有格 my,目的格 me のように変化するが,名詞は主格と目的格が同じ形で,所有格だけが -'s または -s' の形をとる.
> ➔にんしょうだいめいし

かく⁷ 角 angle [C] ➔かくど ◆内角[外角]低めの球 a low *inside* [*outside*] pitch; a ball low on *the inside* [*outside*]

‖鋭角 an acute angle / 外角 an exterior angle / 直角 a right angle / 鈍角 an obtuse angle / 内角 an interior angle

かく- 各- (それぞれの) each; (どの…も) every ∥国連の各加盟国 *each* member of the United Nations / その銀行員はリストの各項目を調べた The bank clerk checked *each* item on the list. ◆スズメは日本の各地でふつうに見られる Sparrows are common *throughout* Japan.

かぐ¹ 家具 furniture [U]

> [語法]
> furniture は移動可能な机・戸棚・じゅうたんなど家具全体を指し,数えるときは a piece of ...(家具1点),two pieces of ...(家具2点)のようにいう.

家具一式 a set of *furniture* / 輸入家具 imported *furniture*

ヒノキは家具を作るのによい材料です Japanese cypress is a good material for making *furniture.*

◆家具付きの部屋 a *furnished* room / 彼の部屋には家具がほとんどなかった His room was barely *furnished.*

かぐ² 嗅ぐ smell* [他]; (鼻を鳴らして) sniff [他] ∥そのにおいをかいでごらん Try *smelling* that. / その肉がまだ大丈夫か,においをかいでみて *Smell* the meat to see if it is still OK. / クロが何かをかいでいるよ Kuro *is sniffing at* something.

がく¹ 学 ―学のある educated ∥彼は相当に学のある人のようだった He seemed to be a highly *educated* person.

[ことわざ] 少年老いやすく学成りがたし Art is long, life is short. (→学芸は長く,人生は短い)

がく² 萼 a cup (of a flower),〔植物〕calyx [C] (複 ~es, calyces)

がく³ 額 ❶【金額】sum [C], amount [C] ➔きんがく ∥その腕時計を買うにはある程度の額のお金が必要だ You need *a* certain *amount* of money to buy the watch.

❷【額縁】frame [C] ∥この額に入れると絵が引き立ちます This *frame* shows the painting to good advantage. ◆私は母の写真を額に入れた I *framed* the picture of my mother.

かくあげ 格上げ (昇格) promotion [C] [U] ◆須藤氏は支配人に格上げされた Mr. Sudo *was promoted* to manager. (❖地位を表す名詞は無冠詞)

がくい 学位 (academic) degree [C] ∥彼は2年前に文学修士の学位を取った Two years ago, he got *the degree* of Master of Arts. / この仕事に応募するには博士の学位と推薦状が必要です In order to apply for this job, you need *a* 「*doctor's degree* [*doctorate*] and a letter of recommendation.

‖学位論文 (博士論文) a doctoral dissertation; (修士論文) a master's thesis

かくいつ 画一 (規格化) standardization [U]; (一様) uniformity [U]; (統制) regimentation [U] ◆最近,画一的な教育が多くの問題を引き起こしている Recently, *uniform* education has been causing many problems.

がくいん 学院 academy [C], school [C]

かくう 架空 ―架空の (想像上の) imaginary; (作り事の) fictitious ∥架空の動物 an *imaginary* animal / このドラマの登場人物はすべて架空のものです All the characters in this drama are *fictitious.*

かくえき 各駅 この電車は急行ですか,それとも各駅ですか Is this an express or a *local* train? / この列車は各駅停車ですか Does this train stop *at every station*?

がくえん 学園 school [C] ‖学園祭 a school festival / 学園紛争 campus unrest

かくかい 各界 各界(→様々な分野)の名士 celebrities from *various fields*

がくがい 学外 この公開講座は主に学外の人々を対象にしている This extension course is mainly targeted at people from *outside the university.*

かくかく かくかくしかじかの理由で for *such and such* reasons

がくがく ひざが恐怖でがくがくした My knees *trembled* [*shook*] with fear. / 歩きすぎで足ががくがくした My legs *got shaky* from walking too much.

かくがり 角刈り crew cut [C], 《米口語的》 flattop [C] ‖頭を角刈りにする have *one's* hair cut in *a crew cut*

かくぎ 閣議 cabinet meeting [C] ‖緊急閣議 an urgent [emergency] cabinet meeting / 定例閣議 a regular cabinet meeting / 臨時閣議 an extraordinary [a special] cabinet meeting

がくぎょう 学業 studies [C]; (学校の勉強) schoolwork [U] ‖学業に精を出す concentrate on *one's studies*; study hard / 私は学業には熱が入らなかった My heart wasn't in *my studies*. ◆彼は来年学業を終える He will finish *school* next year.
‖学業成績 an academic record

がくげい 学芸 ‖学芸員 a curator / 学芸会 (劇中心の) a drama festival; (音楽中心の) a music festival / 学芸欄 a culture page [column]

かくげつ 隔月 every two months, every other month ◆隔月刊の雑誌 a *bimonthly* magazine

かくげん 格言 proverb [C], saying [C]; (処世訓) maxim [C]

かくご 覚悟 ―覚悟する (用意ができている) be ready, be prepared; (決心する) make* up *one's* mind
覚悟はいいかい *Are* you *ready*?
何が起ころうと覚悟はできている I'*m ready* [*prepared*] *for* anything.
覚悟を決めて水の中に飛び込んだ I *made up my mind* and jumped into the water.
◆彼らは職を失う覚悟で(→危険を冒して)やった They *risked* losing their jobs. / 危険を覚悟でやらないと成功できませんよ You cannot succeed without *taking risks*. / 彼は負けを覚悟で(→負けるかもしれないが)チャンピオンに挑戦した He has challenged the champion, *though* he *might* be beaten.

かくさ 格差 (相違) difference [C], 《公式的》 disparity [U] [C]; (隔たり) gap [C] ‖男女間の賃金格差が広がった[縮まった] *The disparity* in pay between men and women has widened [narrowed].

かくざい 角材 (rectangular) lumber [U]

がくさいてき 学際的 ―学際的な interdisciplinary ‖学際的研究 *interdisciplinary* studies

かくさく 画策 ―画策する scheme [他] [自]; (企てる) plot [他] ‖彼らは政府の転覆を画策した They *plotted* to overthrow the government. / 彼はその会社の乗っ取りを画策していた He *was scheming* to take over the company.

かくさげ 格下げ demotion [U] [C] ―格下げする downgrade [他], demote [他] ‖彼は平社員に格下げになった He *was demoted* to the rank and file.

かくざとう 角砂糖 lump [cube] sugar [U] (❖数えるときは a lump [cube] of ... とする) ‖コーヒーに角砂糖をいくつ入れますか How many *lumps* (*of sugar*) in your coffee?

かくさん[1] 拡散 (光・気体・液体などの) diffusion [U]; (蔓延(まんえん)) proliferation [U] 《また a ～》 ‖核兵器不拡散条約 the Nuclear Non-Proliferation Treaty (《略語》 NPT)

かくさん[2] 核酸 〔生化学〕 nucleic acid [C]

かくじ 各自 each ➾おのおの, それぞれ ‖学生は各自個室を持っている *Each* student has a separate room. / 学生たちは各自課題を抱えている The students *each* have their own assignments. ◆各自で辞典を買いなさい *Every one of you* should buy a dictionary.

がくし[1] 学士 (称号) bachelor [C]; (人) college [university] graduate [C] ‖学士号を取る get *a bachelor's degree* / 文学士 *a Bachelor* of Arts
‖学士院 an academy

がくし[2] 学資 school expenses

かくしあじ 隠し味 secret ingredient [C] ‖隠し味に塩をひとつまみ加える add a pinch of salt as *a secret ingredient*

かくしカメラ 隠しカメラ hidden camera [C]

かくしき 格式 formality [U] [C] ―格式ばった formal ‖格式ばった儀式 a *formal* ceremony / 彼は細かいところまで格式にこだわる He observes *formalities* even about minor things. ◆格式の高い家 a family *high in social standing*

がくしき 学識 (学問) learning [U]; (知識) knowledge [U] 《また a ～》 ‖学識のある人 a person *of knowledge*; a *learned* person (❖learned は [lə́ːrnid] と発音する)
◆彼は学識者というにはほど遠い He is far from being *a scholar*.
‖学識経験者 a person with profound knowledge and experience

かくしげい 隠し芸 宴会で隠し芸を披露する display *one's hidden talent*(*s*) at a party

かくしごと 隠し事 (秘密) secret [C] ◆彼は私に何か隠し事をしている He's *keeping* something *from* me. / 私に隠し事をしてもだめだ You can't *hide* anything *from* me.

かくしだて 隠し立て 彼女は隠しだてをしない人だ She is *an open book*.

かくしつ 確執 (長期にわたる反目) feud [fjúːd] [C]; (根強い不和) deep-rooted discord [U]

かくじつ[1] 確実 ―確実な sure, certain; (信頼できる) reliable ―確実に surely, certainly ➾かならず, たしか

[語法]
sure と certain はほぼ同じ意味だが, sure は「きっと…だ」という話者の主観的な確信を表すのに対し, certain は客観的な根拠に基づく確かさを表す. また sure は ×It is sure to [that] ...とはできないことに注意 ‖ 彼女が試験に合格するのは確実だ It is *certain* that she will pass the exam. / She is *sure* to pass the exam.

病気の確実な治療法 a *certain* cure for a dis-

かくじつ ease
恵子がキャプテンに選ばれるのは確実だろう I'm *sure* (that) Keiko will be elected captain.
大介が彼女と結婚するのは確実だ It's *a sure thing* that Daisuke will marry her.
◆その発見は彼の名声を確実なものにした The discovery *ensured* his fame. / 事態は確実によくなりつつある Things are getting *steadily* better. / ここまでのことは確実に証明されている This much has been *definitely* proved.

かくじつ² 隔日 (1日おき) every other day

かくしどり 隠し撮り 彼らは密会の現場を隠し撮りされた Their secret meeting *was photographed secretly*.

かくしマイク 隠しマイク hidden microphone ⓒ,《俗語》bug ⓒ

がくしゃ 学者 scholar ⓒ; (学のある人) a man of learning ǁ彼女は著名な学者だ She is *a well-known scholar*. ◆祖父は学者肌の男だった My grandfather was a *scholarly* man. / 彼は言語学者だ He is *a linguist*.

かくしゅ 各種 (種々の) various, several kinds of ... ǁテーブルの上には食材が各種取りそろえられていた There were *various* ingredients for cooking on the table.
ǁ各種学校 (一般に) a college, a school; (職業訓練学校) a vocational school

かくしゅう 隔週 ―隔週で[に] every other week, biweekly ǁ隔週土曜は休みです We have a day off *every other Saturday*.

かくじゅう 拡充 expansion ⓤ ―拡充する expand ⓐ ⓑ

がくしゅう 学習 (勉強すること) study ⓤ; (修得すること) learning ⓤ ―学習する study ⓐ ⓑ; learn* ⓐ ⓑ
その先生は私に学習意欲を起こさせた The teacher motivated me to *study* hard.
◆この辞書は英語学習者にとって特に価値がある This dictionary is especially valuable to *learners* of English.
ǁ学習参考書 a study aid / 学習指導要領 course guidelines / 学習塾 a cram school

がくじゅつ 学術 (学問) learning ⓤ; (科学) science ⓤ ⓒ ―学術的な learned [lə́ːrnid], academic, scientific ǁ学術書 an academic [a scientific, a learned] book / 学術調査 a scientific [an academic] investigation / 学術用語 a term,《集合的》nomenclature [nóumənklèitfər]

かくしょう 確証 conclusive [hard] evidence ⓤ, positive proof ⓒ ǁ私はそのとき彼がそこにいたという確証をつかんだ I got *conclusive evidence* that he was there then.

がくしょう 楽章 movement ⓒ ǁこの交響曲は4楽章から成る There are four *movements* in this symphony.

がくしょく 学食 school cafeteria ⓒ

かくしん 確信 (信念) belief ⓤ, conviction ⓒ ⓤ (❖belief よりかたい語); (自信) confidence ⓤ ―確信する be sure [certain] (❖sure は話者の主観的な確信を表す), be convinced
僕たちは勝利を確信していた We *were sure* [*of winning* [*that* we would win].
彼が無実だということにあまり確信がもてない I'*m not* quite *sure that* he is innocent.

かくしん² 革新 (改革) reform ⓤ ⓒ; (新しいものの導入) innovation ⓤ ⓒ ―革新的な reformist; (進歩的な) progressive ǁ革新思想 progressive ideas / 革新政党 a reformist party / 技術革新 technological innovation

かくしん³ 核心 (中心) the heart, the core; (要点) the point ǁ問題の核心に触れる get [come] to *the heart* of the matter / 彼の質問は核心をついていた His question got to *the point*.

かくじん 各人 (一人一人) each (person); (みんな) everyone, everybody ǁ各人各様のやり方がある *Each person* has his or her own way of doing things.

かくす 隠す

hide* ⓐ, conceal ⓐ (❖conceal は故意に何かを隠すという意味であるのに対し、hide は必ずしも故意ではない); (覆い隠す) cover ⓐ; (秘密にしておく) keep* ... secret; (物事・感情などを) disguise ⓐ
感情を隠す *hide one's* feelings / 事実を隠す *disguise* the fact / 手で顔を隠す *cover one's* face with *one's* hands

彼はその箱を毛布の下に隠した He *hid* the box under the blanket.

彼女の言葉には隠された意味があった Her words carried a *hidden* meaning.

彼らはやぶの奥深くへ身を隠した They *hid* themselves deep in the thicket.

警察がその資料を隠していた事実が明らかになった The fact was made public that the police *had concealed* the documents.

彼女は恥ずかしさを笑いで隠した She laughed to *cover* her shame.

私は結婚したことを同僚に隠していた I *kept* my marriage *secret from* my colleagues.

◆何を隠そう(→実を言うと)、その手紙を書いたのはこの私だ *To tell the truth*, it was I who wrote the letter.

かくすい 角錐〔数学〕pyramid ⓒ ǁ三角すい *a triangular pyramid* / 四角すい *a quadrangular pyramid*

かくすう 画数 the number of strokes in a Chinese character

かくする 画する (しるす) mark ⓐ ǁその理論は一時代を画した The theory *marked* the beginning of a new epoch. ◆時代を画する発明 an *epoch-making* invention / 彼の作品は印象派の絵画とは一線を画している *There's a clear demarcation line* between his works and Impressionist paintings.

かくせい 隔世 ǁ隔世遺伝 a throwback,《公式的》atavism

がくせい 学生

student ⓒ (❖《米》では中学・高校・大学すべての学生に用いられるため、明確にしたい場合は a high school student, a college student の

ように表す.《英》ではふつう大学生を指す)
学部[大学院]の学生 an undergraduate [a graduate] student
原さんは山形大学の学生だ Mr. Hara is *a student* at Yamagata University.(❖×a student of とはしない)
この奨学金は外国人学生を対象とする This scholarship is designed for foreign *students*.
二人は学生結婚だ They got married when *they were students.*

コロケーション –student–
【形容詞＋～】勤勉な～ a diligent student / 勉強をしない～ an idle [a lazy] student / 優秀な～ an excellent student / ずば抜けて優秀な～ an exceptional [outstanding] student / 平均的な～ an average student

‖学生運動 a student movement / 学生課 a student affairs section / 学生会館 a student union / 学生時代 one's school days / 学生自治会 a student [《英》students'] union / 学生証 a student ID card / 学生食堂 a school cafeteria / 学生生活 student life / 学生服 a school uniform / 学生部長 a dean of students / 学生寮 a student dormitory, a dorm / 学生割引 a student discount

かくせいき 拡声器 loudspeaker ⓒ
かくせいざい 覚醒剤 stimulant (drug) ⓒ,《口語的》speed ⓤ
かくせいそうち 拡声装置 public-address system ⓒ(《略認》PA)
かくぜつ 隔絶 ここは文明社会から隔絶された別世界だ This place is another world, *isolated from* civilization.
がくせつ 学説 (教義・教え) doctrine ⓒⓤ;(理論) theory ⓒⓤ
がくぜん 愕然 be shocked ‖私は『彼女』が実は男だと知ってがく然とした I *was shocked* to learn that "she" was a guy.
がくそく 学則 school regulations [rules] ⇨ こうそく(校則)

かくだい 拡大 (展開) expansion ⓤ;(延長) extension ⓤⓒ;(レンズなどによる) magnification ⓤ;(紛争などの激化) escalation ⓒⓤ
——拡大する expand ⾃他; extend ⾃他; magnify 他; escalate ⾃
米国はアジア諸国との貿易を拡大している The U.S. *is expanding* its trade with Asian countries.
その出版社は映画製作にまで事業を拡大している The publisher *is expanding* [*branching out*] into producing films.
このレンズを使えば文字を3倍に拡大できます With this lens, you *can magnify* the size of the letters (by) three times.
学内問題が社会問題にまで拡大した The problem at the school *escalated* into a social problem.
‖拡大鏡 a magnifying glass, a magnifier / 拡大コピー an enlarged photocopy

がくたい 楽隊 band ⓒ
かくだん 格段 コンピュータの性能はここ数年で格段に進歩した The performance of computers has progressed *remarkably* in the past few years. / あなたと私とでは体力に格段の差がある There is a *big* difference in physical stamina between you and me.
がくだん 楽団 (musical) band ⓒ(❖主に軽音楽・吹奏楽の楽団を指す);(管弦楽団) orchestra ⓒ / 交響楽団 a symphony *orchestra*
‖楽団員 a bandsman
かくち 各地 世界各地を旅する travel *around the world* / アメリカ文化は世界各地に浸透している American culture has spread *all over the world*.
かくちょう¹ 拡張 (膨張) expansion ⓤ;(伸張) extension ⓤ;(幅を広げる) widening ⓤ
——拡張する expand ⾃他; extend ⾃他; widen ⾃他 / 軍備を拡張する expand armaments / 道路を拡張する *widen* a road / その団体は空港の拡張に反対している The group is opposing *the expansion* of the airport.
かくちょう² 格調 この本の序文は格調高い文体で書かれている The preface of this book is written in an *elegant* [*elevated*] style.
がくちょう 学長《米》president ⓒ,《英》principal ⓒ, chancellor ⓒ(《米》では一部の大学の学長を,《英》では実務のない名誉学長を指す)
かくづけ 格付け ——格付けする rank 他⾃ / このワインには最高級の格付けがされている This wine *ranks* highest of all. ◆格付けの高い[低い]金融機関 a financial institution with high [low] *ratings* / その会社は債券に対する格付けを行っている The company *rates* bonds.
‖格付け機関 a credit rating agency

かくてい 確定 ——確定する settle 他; fix 他
——確定的な (明確な) definite;(最終的な) final;(決定した) fixed
旅行の日程が確定した Our itinerary *has been fixed* [*settled*].
彼の当選はまだ確定していない It isn't *definite* yet whether he has won the election.
◆警察は事故の原因の確定を急いでいる The police are hurrying to *determine* the cause of the accident. / 有罪が確定するまでは無罪とみなされます You are presumed innocent until *proven* guilty.
‖確定申告 a final income tax return
カクテル cocktail ⓒ ‖彼女は客にカクテルを作ってあげた She made mixed *a cocktail* for her guest.
‖カクテルパーティー a cocktail party
かくど 角度 angle ⓒ / 角度を広げる[狭(⾃)める] increase [decrease] *an angle* / 角度を測る measure *an angle* / 急角度で at *a sharp angle* / ボールを25度の角度で投げる throw a ball at a 25°*angle*(❖25°は twenty-five degree と読む) / その角度は5度3分8秒で The *angle* is 5°3'8''.(❖5°3'8'' は five degrees, three minutes, and eight seconds と読む) / この事件は様々な角度から検討する必要がある We need to investigate this case

かくとう

from different *angles* [*points of view*].

かくとう 格闘 ──格闘する fight* 自 他, grapple 自, struggle 自, wrestle 自 他 / 孝は山のような宿題と格闘している最中だった Takashi was in the middle of *grappling with* a pile of homework.
‖格闘技 a combative sport

がくどう 学童 schoolchild C ‖学童保育 after-school care

かくとく 獲得 ──獲得する acquire 他, get* 他, gain 他, 《公式的》obtain 他; (賞などを) win* 他 / 過半数を獲得する *gain* [*get, win*] a majority / 議席を獲得する *win* a seat in parliament / 彼女はコンテストで1等賞を獲得した She *won* (the) first prize in the contest.
◆その国では共産党が政権を獲得した The Communist Party *came to* [*into*] *power* in the country.

がくない 学内 彼女は学内のスピーチコンテストで優勝した She won the *intramural* speech contest.

かくにん 確認 confirmation U, (身元の) identification U ──確認する make* sure, confirm 他; identify 他; (調べる) check 自 他 ⇨ みかくにん, コミュニケーションスキル p.293 / ホテル[飛行機]の予約を確認する *confirm* the hotel [plane] reservations / 先生は全員そろったかどうかを確認した The teacher *made sure* that everybody was there. / 乗客の無事が確認された The safety of the passengers *has been confirmed*. / 死体の身元が確認された They *identified* the dead body. / その本が出版されているかどうか確認してみます I'll *check* to see if the book is in print.
◆道路を渡るときは左右を確認しなさい *Look both ways* before you cross the road.

かくねん 隔年 every other year ‖この調査は隔年で行われている This research is carried out *every other year*.

がくねん 学年 (学校の年度) school [academic] year C; (学年)《米》grade C,《英》form C

語法
《米》ではふつう学年を小学校から通して数えるため，日本の中学校の第1学年，第2学年，第3学年はそれぞれ the seventh grade, the eighth grade, the ninth grade に当たる。また高校は4年制の場合，a freshman, a sophomore, a junior, a senior という呼び方もする。ただし，日本の学校の学年には year を用いて the first year of high school (高校1年) のように表すこともできる。

アメリカでは学年は9月に始まり6月に終わる In America *the school year* begins in September and ends in June. / 妹は私よりも2つ下の学年です My sister is two *grades* below me at school. / 彼と私は同じ学年です He and I are in *the* same *grade*. / 学年末試験 year-end examinations, final examinations

かくのうこ 格納庫 (飛行機の) hangar C

がくは 学派 school C ‖フロイト学派 the Freudian *school*

がくばつ 学閥 (軽蔑的) academic clique C

かくばった 角張った square; (やせて骨ばった) angular

かくはん 攪拌 ──攪拌する stir 他 ⇨ かきまぜる ‖攪拌器 a mixer

がくひ 学費 school expenses; (授業料) tuition U, school fees ‖学費は年々上がっている *Tuition* is going up every year.

がくふ 楽譜 (musical) score C; (1枚刷りの) sheet music U ‖楽譜を覚えたかい? そろそろ楽譜なしでやろうよ Have you memorized *the score*? Now let's play without it. ◆私は全く楽譜が読めない I can't read *music* at all.

がくぶ 学部《米》college C U, school C, faculty C

英米ではそれぞれの大学の慣習により学部の呼び方は様々で，日本のように統一されているわけではない。《米》では総合大学の学部を college または school と呼ぶ場合が多い。さらに「学科」には department を用いるのが一般的である。

私たちの大学には10の学部がある Our university has 10 *colleges*.
‖学部学生 an undergraduate (student), 《口語的》an undergrad / 医学部 the college of medicine / 教育学部 the college of education / 経済学部 the college of economics / 工学部 the college of engineering / 歯学部 the college of dentistry / 商学部 the college of commerce / 農学部 the college of agriculture / 文学部 the college of literature / 法学部 the college of law / 理学部 the college of science

がくふう 学風 (学校の伝統的な気風) (school) tradition C U ‖この大学は堅実な学風で知られている This university is known for its strong *traditions*.

がくぶち 額縁 (picture) frame C

かくへいき 核兵器 nuclear weapon C, 《口語的》nuke C ‖核兵器全面禁止を訴える appeal for a total ban on *nuclear weapons* / 核兵器反対! No *nukes*!
‖戦略核兵器 strategic nuclear weapons

かくべつ 格別 彼の作るカレーは格別だ(→特においしい) The curry he makes *tastes especially good.* / きのうは格別(→いつになく)寒かった It was *unusually* cold yesterday. / 本年度の当社の総売り上げは良好ですが，格別すぐれているわけでもありません Our gross sales this year are good but not *exceptional*. / その老人の言葉には格別の味わいがあった(→私に深い感銘を与えた) The old man's words *deeply impressed* me.

かくほ 確保 ──確保する secure 他 ‖花見の場所を確保するのも楽ではない It's pretty hard to *secure* a place to view the cherry blossoms. ◆彼らは乗客の安全確保を最優先した They gave highest priority to *the safe-*

コミュニケーションスキル —確認—

①相手の話の内容や不明な点を確認するとき

(A) **You mean [Do you mean, Are you saying] we can't use this computer without entering a password?**
パスワードを入れないとこのコンピュータは使えないということですか.

(B) **What you are saying is that …?**
あなたが言われているのは…ということですね?

(C) **What do you mean by the word "…"? / In what sense are you using the word "…"?**
…という単語をあなたはどのような意味で使っているのですか.

☞ 相手の話の内容を確認する表現としては, (A), (B) が一般的.
☞ (C)はある特定の語句の意味を確認する言い方. 同じ意味で **I don't understand the meaning of the word "…"** とも表現する.

②相手が自分の話の内容を理解しているかどうか確認するとき

(A) **Do you understand? / Do you see what I mean?**
私の言っていることが分かりますか.

(B) **Are you following [Do you follow] me?**
私の言っていることが分かりますか.

(C) **Are you with me?**
私の言っていることが分かりますか.

(D) **Do I make myself clear? / Is that clear (enough)?**
私の言っていることがお分かりですか.

☞ 相手が自分の話の内容を理解しているかどうかを確認したいときは(A)が最も一般的. 同じ意味で **You know what I mean?, Do you get it?, You got it?** なども口語でよく使われる.
☞ (D)は状況や言い方によっては威圧的な響きをもつ. ある程度の時間をかけて説明した後の確認として使われる表現だが, **Do I make myself understood?** や **Have I made myself clear?** のようにもいう.

---

ty of the passengers. / 図書館の席, 確保しておいてね *Save* me *a seat* at the library.

がくぼう 学帽 school cap ⓒ

かくほうめん 各方面 その発見は各方面(→様々な分野)で話題になっている That discovery is talked about *in many fields*.

かくまう 匿う harbor ⓗ, shelter ⓗ ‖彼が私をかくまってくれた He *sheltered* [*offered shelter to*] me.

かくまく 角膜 〔眼科〕cornea [kɔ́ːrniə] ⓒ ‖角膜移植 a corneal transplant

かくめい 革命 revolution ⓤ ⓒ ——革命的な revolutionary
革命を起こす start [raise] *a revolution*
その国で突然, 革命が起こった *A revolution* 「broke out [occurred] unexpectedly in the country.
彼の考えはその当時全く革命的なものだった His idea was positively *revolutionary* for those days.
その発見は癌(ガン)の治療に革命をもたらした The discovery brought about *a revolution* in cancer treatment.
‖革命家 a revolutionary / 革命軍 a revolutionary army / 革命政府 a revolutionary government / 価格革命 price revolution / 産業革命 the Industrial Revolution / 農業革命 the agricultural revolution / 反革命 (a) counterrevolution / フランス革命 the French Revolution / 武力革命 an armed revolution / 文化大革命 the Cultural Revolution / ロシア革命 the Russian Revolution

がくめい 学名 〈集合的〉nomenclature [nóumənklèitfər] ⓤ, scientific name

がくめん 額面 face value ⓒ ⓤ ‖額面割れ a drop below par
慣用表現 彼の話を額面どおりに受け取るべきではなかった I shouldn't *have taken* his story *at face value*.

がくもん 学問 learning ⓤ; (個々の学問) subject ⓒ, study ⓒ ——学問の・学問的な academic ⇨ がく(学), がくしき
学問のある人 a person of *learning* / 学問の自由 *academic* freedom
私は学問的な話には興味がなかった I wasn't interested in *academic* subjects.
◆彼は若いころ学問に励んだ He *studied hard* when he was young.
ことわざ 学問に王道なし There is no royal road to learning.

がくや 楽屋 dressing room ⓒ, greenroom ⓒ

かくやく 確約 assurance, definite promise ⓤ ‖確約を得る receive *an assurance*; get *a definite promise* / 確約はできません I can't give you *a definite promise*.

かくやす 格安 (買い得品) bargain ⓒ ‖格安の値段で at *a bargain price* / 私のグレーのジャケットは格安だった My gray jacket was *a real bargain*.

がくゆう 学友 fellow student ⓒ, schoolmate ⓒ

がくようひん 学用品 school supplies; (文房具) stationery ⓤ

かぐら 神楽 *kagura*, sacred music and dance performed at shrines during Shinto rites

かくらん 攪乱 ——攪乱する throw* … into confusion ‖彼は巧みに敵を攪乱した He skillfully *threw* the enemy *into confusion*.

がくらん 学らん a school uniform with a stand-up collar

かくり 隔離 ——隔離する isolate ⓗ; (伝染予防のために) quarantine ⓗ (◆通例受身で) ‖彼は数日間, 別の病室に隔離された He *was isolated* [*quarantined*] in another (hospital) room for a few days.
‖隔離病棟 an isolation ward

かくりつ¹ 確立 ——確立する establish ⓗ ‖日

本はその国と友好関係を確立した Japan *established* friendly relations with the country. / 彼はピアニストとしての名声を確立した He *established* his fame as a pianist.

かくりつ² 確率 probability ◯ //この計画は成功する確率が高い[低い] This project has a high [low] *probability* of success. / そのくじの1等に当選する確率は300万分の1だ The *probability* of winning the first prize in the lottery is one in three million.

かくりょう 閣僚 cabinet minister ◯, a member of the cabinet

がくりょく 学力 academic competence ◯, scholastic ability ◯ //この大学に入るには高い学力が必要だ Entering this university requires high *scholastic ability*.
‖学力テスト an achievement test

がくれい 学齢 school age ◯ ◆学齢期の子供の数は年々減っている The number of *school-age* children is decreasing year by year.

かくれが 隠れ家 hiding place ◯; (犯罪者などの) hideout ◯, hideaway ◯ //警察は隠れ家まで一味の後をつけていった The police trailed the gang to *their hideout*.

がくれき 学歴 one's educational [academic] background //彼女はどんな学歴の人ですか What is her *academic* [*educational*] *background*? / 日本では学歴がものを言うと信じている親がいまだに多い In Japan quite a few parents still believe that *one's educational background* counts for a lot.
◆彼は高い学歴の持ち主だ(→よい大学を出た) He graduated from a top university. / 彼女は自分の学歴を鼻にかけたりしない She makes no pretense to *being educated*.
‖学歴社会 a society which puts too much value on a person's academic background / 学歴主義 diplomaism

かくれみの 隠れ蓑 (悪事などを隠す手段) cover ◯◯, cloak ◯, 《口語的》front ◯ //彼は公務を隠れみのに非合法な活動をしていた His official business was *a cover for* illegal activities.

かくれる 隠れる

hide* ⓣⓘ; (見えなくなる) disappear ⓘ //隠れた(→隠された)才能 a *hidden* talent / 戸の後ろにだれか隠れている Someone *is hiding* behind the door. / 典子の家はビルの陰に隠れている Noriko's house *is hidden* by the building. / 男の子はテーブルの下に隠れた The boy *hid* (*himself*) underneath the table.
◆彼は親に隠れて賭(か)け事をやっている He gambles *without* his parents' *knowledge*. / 彼は山に隠れ住んでいるらしい They say he *lives in seclusion* in the mountain. / 実は昔その歌手の隠れファンだったんだ In fact, I was once *a secret admirer* of that singer.

かくれんぼ(う) 隠れん坊 hide-and-seek ◯ //隠れん坊をする play *hide-and-seek*

かくろん 各論 details //各論に入る get down to the *details* [*particulars*]

がくわり 学割 student discount ◯

がくん 英語の成績ががくんと(→急激に)下がった My English grade *suddenly* got worse. / バスががくんと止まった The bus stopped *with a jerk*. (❖jerk は「突然の激しい動き」の意味)

かけ¹ 掛け 掛けで…を買う[売る] buy [sell] … *on credit* ➾つけ

かけ² 賭け bet ◯, gambling ◯ //人と賭けをする make *a bet* with a person / 賭けに応じる take *a bet* / 僕の言うとおりにすれば賭けに勝つよ Take my tip and you'll win *the bet*. ◆7対2の賭け率で with *the odds* at 7 to 2 / 私は酒もたばこも賭け事もやらない I don't drink, smoke, or *gamble*.
‖賭け金 stakes, a bet

-かけ -掛け 洋服かけ a clothes *hanger* / 帽子かけ a hat *rack*; (スタンド式の) a hat *tree* / テーブルの上には食べかけのリンゴが残されていた There was a *half-eaten* apple on the table. / 彼女は手紙を書きかけのまま放ってある She has left the letter *unfinished*.

かげ¹ 陰

(日陰) shade ◯

> 語法 shade は光がさえぎられてできる暗い所や光のあたらない所をいい, shadow は光が物にあたってできるその物の形をした影をいう.

あの木の陰で休もう Let's take a rest in *the shade* of that tree.
このシャツは陰干しにしてください Please dry this shirt in *the shade*.
◆彼はドアの陰から私を呼んだ He called me from *behind* the door. / 陰で人の悪口を言うのは卑怯(ひきょう)だ It's unfair to say bad things about others *behind their backs*. / 彼は政界の陰の実力者だといわれている He is said to be a「*behind-the-scenes power* [*gray eminence*] of the political world.
慣用表現 あの少女にはどことなく陰がある There *is an air of gloom* about that girl. / この事件はだれかが陰で糸を引いているにちがいない Someone must *be pulling wires* [*strings*] in this case. / 彼は陰になり日なたになり私をかばってくれた He protected me *publicly and privately*.
ことわざ 寄らば大樹の陰 If you need shelter, you should choose a big tree.

かげ² 影

shadow ◯ (❖比喩的な意味にも用いられる); (シルエット) silhouette ◯; (水面・鏡などに映ったもの) reflection ◯ ➾かげ(陰)
幽霊には影がない Ghosts don't have [cast] *shadows*.
その大木は長い影を落としていた That big tree threw *a long shadow* across the field.
息子の病気は彼らの家庭に暗い影を落とした Their son's illness cast *a dark shadow* [*cloud*] over their home.

窓に映った自分の影を見て彼は驚いた He was astonished to see his own *reflection* in the window.
◆私はぼんやりとした影が窓の所に立っているのを見た I saw *a dim shape* standing at the window. / 湖に山の影が映っていた The mountain *was reflected* in the lake.
💬「僕がここにいるのがなぜ分かったの」「カーテンに影が映ったもの」"How did you know I was here?" "Because *your silhouette* appeared against [on] the curtain."
慣用表現 うわさをすれば影 ⇒うわさ / 彼は優秀な弟のせいでいつも影が薄かった He *was always overshadowed* by his brilliant younger brother. / 影の内閣 *a shadow cabinet* / 工事現場を訪れてみると母校はすでに影も形もなかった When I visited the construction site, I saw that my school *had already disappeared without a trace.* / 学校でのいじめは最近影を潜(ひそ)めている(→収まったように見える) Recently bullying in schools *seems to have subsided.* / 彼は年老いて見る影もなくなった Since he got old, he's *become a shadow of his former self.*

がけ 崖 cliff ⓒ, precipice ⓒ ‖崖をよじ登る climb (up) *the cliff* ◆A社は破産するかどうかのがけっぷちに立っている Company A is *on the verge* of bankruptcy.

-がけ -掛け 10人がけのロングシート a bench *for 10 persons* / 帰りがけに(→帰る途中で)本屋に寄った I dropped in at the bookstore *on my way home.*

かけあう 掛け合う (交渉する) negotiate ⓘ ‖おまえを雇ってくれるよう私が会社にかけあってやろう I'll *negotiate with* the company about hiring you. ◆波打ち際で子供たちは水のかけ合いをしていた Children *were splashing* water *on each other* on the beach.

かけあがる 駆け上がる run* up ‖階段を駆け上がる *run up* the stairs

かけあし 駆け足 run ⓒ; (馬の) gallop ⓤ (また a ~) ‖駆け足をする run* ⓘ ‖その場で駆け足をする *run* in place / 彼らは駆け足でグラウンドを1周した They *ran* around the playground. ◆本校の歩みを駆け足で(→簡単に)ご紹介します We'll show a *brief* history of our school. / 秋は駆け足で近づいてきている Fall is approaching *quickly.*

かけあわせる 掛け合わせる (動植物を交配する) cross ⓘ; (掛け算をする) multiply ⓘ

かけい¹ 家系 (family) line ⓒ, 《公式的》lineage [línɪdʒ] ⓤⓒ ‖王の家系 *a line* of kings ◆彼の家系は王室にさかのぼる His *ancestry* can be traced back to the royal family. ‖家系図 a family tree

かけい² 家計 family budget ⓒ, household economy ⓒ ‖私が英語を教えて得る収入は家計の足しになっている The money I get from teaching English supplements *the family budget.*
◆彼は家族に不自由させることなく家計を支えた He *maintained his family* in comfort. / 今は家計が苦しい We *are badly off* now.
‖家計簿 a household account book

かげえ 影絵 shadow picture ⓒ; (シルエット) silhouette ⓒ

かけおち 駆け落ち elopement ⓒ ⓤ, runaway marriage ⓒ ──駆け落ちする run* away, elope ⓘ

かけおりる 駆け下りる run* down

かけがえのない 掛け替えのない (取り替えのきかない) irreplaceable; (貴重な) valuable, precious ‖生命ほどかけがえのないものはない Nothing is as *valuable* as life. / 私たちはその事故でかけがえのない友人を亡くした We lost an *irreplaceable* friend in the accident.

かけがね 掛け金 latch ⓒ ‖掛け金をはずす open [undo] *a latch* / 掛け金をかける close *a latch*

かげき¹ 過激 ──過激な (考えなどが偏った) extreme; (考えなどが急進的な) radical; (感情・言葉などが) violent ‖過激な思想 a *radical* idea / 過激派グループ a *radical* group / 過激な発言は慎んだほうがいいよ You shouldn't make any *violent* remarks.

かげき² 歌劇 (オペラ) opera ⓤⓒ ‖歌劇歌手 an opera singer / 歌劇場 an opera house / 歌劇団 an opera company

かけきん 掛け金 (保険の) premium ⓒ

がけくずれ 崖崩れ landslide ⓒ

かげぐち 陰口 backbiting ⓤ ◆彼はいつも人の陰口ばかりたたいている He always 「*speaks ill of* [《口語的》*bad-mouths*] other people *behind their backs.*

かけごえ 掛け声 call ⓒ; (大声) shout ⓒ ‖ハトは手品師の掛け声とともに消えた The pigeon vanished at the magician's *shout.*
◆私たちは勲に「がんばれ」と掛け声をかけた We *called* to Isao, "Come on!"
慣用表現 その改革案は掛け声だけに終わった(→何の役にも立たなかった) The reform plan *came to nothing.*

かけごと 賭け事 gambling ⓤ ──賭け事をする gamble ⓘ ⇒かけ(賭け)

かけこむ 駆け込む run* [rush, dash] into ...; (保護を求めて) seek* [take*] refuge in [at] ... ‖突然激しい雨が降りだしたので彼女は家の中に駆け込んだ It suddenly began to rain hard, so she *ran into* her house. ◆駆け込み乗車をする「dash onto [rush aboard] a train just before the doors close

かけざん 掛け算 multiplication ⓤ ──掛け算をする multiply ⓘⓘ

かけじく 掛け軸 (hanging) scroll ⓒ

かけず 掛け図 (地図) wall map ⓒ; (図表) wall chart ⓒ

かけすて 掛け捨て この保険は掛け捨てだ This insurance *pays nothing on its expiration.*

かけずりまわる 駆けずり回る run* about; (忙しい) be busy ⇒かけまわる

かけそば 掛け蕎麦 ▲ *kakesoba*, buckwheat noodles eaten in hot broth

かけだし 駆け出し (初心者) beginner ⓒ, novice ⓒ ‖駆け出しの新聞記者 a *novice* news-

かけだす paperman; a *cub* reporter / その有名な俳優は私たちに駆けだしのころのおもしろい話をしてくれた The famous actor told us funny stories about *his early days*.

かけだす 駆け出す (外に走って出る) run* [dash] out; (走り始める) start running, begin* to run /家に戻ると犬が小屋から駆け出してきた When I came home, my dog *dashed out* of his house. / 警官が現れるとその男は突然駆けだした When a police officer appeared, the man suddenly *began to run*.

かけちがえる 掛け違える ほら,ボタンをかけ違えてるよ Hey, you've *buttoned up the wrong way*.

かけつ 可決 approval ──可決する approve, pass, adopt, carry (※通例受身で) /その修正案は満場一致で可決された The amendment *was passed* [*approved*] unanimously. / その決議案は10票差で可決された The resolution *was carried* [*adopted*] by 10 votes.

-かげつ 箇月 この犬は生後2か月です This dog is two *months* old.

かけつける 駆け付ける 消防車が現場に駆けつけた Some fire engines *rushed to* the scene. / 全国からボランティアが支援に駆けつけた (→集まった) Volunteers from all over the country *rallied* to help.

かけっこ 駆けっこ race /子供たちが通りで駆けっこをしていた Children *were running races* on the street.

かけて 今晩からあすの朝にかけて雪になるでしょう It will snow from tonight *till* [*to*] tomorrow morning. / ギターの腕前にかけてはだれも彼にかなわない Nobody can rival him *when it comes to* playing the guitar. (※when it comes to ... は「…の話[こと]になると」の意味) / 将棋にかけては裕史の右に出る者はいない (→いちばんの将棋指しだ) Hiroshi is the best *shogi* player.

かけどけい 掛け時計 wall clock

かけなおす 掛け直す (再び電話する) call again; (折り返し電話する) call back /10分後にこちらからかけ直します I'll call you *back* in 10 minutes.

かげながら 陰ながら 陰ながらご成功をお祈りします I pray that you will succeed. (※英語には「陰ながら」に当たる決まった表現はなく,単に「ご成功をお祈りします」というしかない)

かけぬける 駆け抜ける run* through ... / 彼は通りを全速力で駆け抜けた He *ran* full speed *through* the street.

かけね 掛け値 掛け値なしの (→正味の)値段 a *net* price / 掛け値なしにこの絵には相当の価値がある It's *no exaggeration to say that* this painting has great value.

かけのぼる 駆け上る run* up ⇒かけあがる

かけはし 掛け橋 bridge /彼らのボランティア活動は両国間のかけ橋になった Their volunteer work acted as *a bridge* between the two countries.

かけはなれる 掛け離れる (真実などと非常に異なる) be far from ...; (2者に非常に異なる) be quite different from ... /彼の言ったことは真実からかけ離れたものだった What he said *was*「*far from*「*wide of*」*the truth.* / 君の考え方と僕の考え方は非常にかけ離れている Your way of thinking and mine *are*「*quite different from each other* [*worlds apart*].

かけひき 駆け引き bargaining; (外交上の) diplomacy /彼には相当に駆け引きがうまい He's pretty sharp at *bargaining*.

かけぶとん 掛け布団 quilt; (かける物の総称) cover (※欧米では毛布(blanket)をかけるのが一般的で,寒いときにはその上に quilt などを重ねる)

かげぼうし 影法師 shadow

かけまわる 駆け回る run* around [about] / 子供たちが運動場を駆け回っている Children *are running around* in the playground.
◆彼は一日中資金集めに駆け回っていた He *was busy* raising funds all day.

かげむしゃ 影武者 (代役・替え玉) a person's double

かけめぐる 駆け巡る run* through ... /その曲が私の頭の中をぐるぐると駆けめぐっていた The tune kept *running through* my head.

かけもち 掛け持ち 彼は2つの大学をかけもちで (→2つの異なる大学で) 教えている He teaches at two different universities.

かけよる 駆け寄る run* up /多くのファンがその選手に駆け寄った Many fans *ran up to* the player.

かけら 欠けら (broken) piece, fragment; (木・瀬戸物などの) chip /割れたガラスのかけら *a piece* of broken glass
◆彼には勇気のかけらもない He doesn't have *a scrap* of courage. / 彼女の言葉には誠実さのかけらもなかった There was not *an iota* of honesty in her words.

かげり 陰り decline ◆景気にかげりが見え始めたのはそのころだった It was then that the economy began to *slip*.

かける¹ 掛ける・架ける

❶つるす	hang
❷置く・浴びせる	cover; put; splash; sprinkle
❸座る	sit (down)
❹作動させる	start; play
❺かぎを	lock
❻電話する	call, phone
❼橋などを	
❽時間・費用を費やす	spend
❾掛け算をする	multiply

❶【つるす】hang* この絵はどこにかけましょうか Where should I *hang* this picture?
制服をハンガーにかけておきなさい *Hang* your uniform on a hanger.
◆彼女はバッグを肩にかけて部屋を出ていった She *slung* her bag over her shoulder and

went out of the room.

❷【置く・浴びせる】（覆う）cover 🈩;（置く）put* 🈩;（浴びせる）splash 🈩;（粉末を振りかける）sprinkle 🈩

今晩は冷えるから毛布を2枚かけよう It's cold tonight. I'll cover myself with two blankets.

やかんを火にかけて Put the kettle on the stove.

誤って彼の服に水をかけてしまった I splashed water on his clothes by mistake.

彼女はイチゴに砂糖をかけた She sprinkled 「sugar on the strawberries [the strawberries with sugar]. (❖もっと細かい粉状のもの(きな粉・粉砂糖など)をかけるには dust を用いる)

◆肩にショールをかける drape a shawl around one's shoulders / 肉をはかりにかける weigh meat on the scales / プレゼントの箱にリボンをかけてもらった I had the box containing the present tied with ribbon. / 彼女はサラダにレモンじょうゆをかけた She poured some lemon juice and soy sauce over [on] the salad.

❸【座る】sit* (down), take* [have*] a seat

このいすにおかけください Please sit down on [in] this chair. (❖on はひじかけのないいすに, in はひじかけのあるいすに座ることを表す)

❹【作動させる】（エンジンを）start 🈩;（CD・音楽などを）play 🈩

僕はエンジンを何度もかけ直してみた I tried again and again to 「start (up) the engine [get the engine going].

彼は家に帰ると早速買ってきたばかりの CD をかけた He played the CD he had just bought as soon as he got home.

この番組ではみなさんからのリクエスト曲をおかけします We play your requests on this show.

◆彼は急にブレーキをかけた He braked [put on the brakes] suddenly. / 目覚まし時計を6時にかけた I've set the alarm clock for six.

❺【かぎを】lock 🈩

玄関のかぎをかけ忘れた I forgot to lock the front door.

❻【電話する】call 🈩🈔, phone 🈩🈔

ごめんね, ゆうべ電話をかけられなくて I'm sorry I couldn't call you last night.

(間違い電話に対して)何番におかけですか What number are you calling?

◆この番号にかければ私に連絡がつきます You can reach me at [on] this number.

❼【橋などを】

川に橋をかける build [construct] a bridge across a river

彼は軒(のき)にはしごをかけた He put [set] (up) a ladder against the eaves.

❽【時間・費用を費やす】spend* 🈩

守はパソコンにかなりの金額をかけている Mamoru spends a large amount of money on his computer.

観光にまる1日かけるのはもったいない It's a waste to spend a whole day sightseeing.

◆言葉は時間をかけて少しずつ変わっていく Languages gradually change over time.

❾【掛け算をする】multiply 🈩

10に2をかける multiply 10 by 2

◆2かける3は6 Two times three equals six.

❿【ぞうきん・ブラシなどを】

床にぞうきんをかける wipe the floor with a cloth / 床にモップをかける mop the floor / シャツにアイロンをかける iron a shirt

彼女は髪[靴]にブラシをかけている She is brushing her hair [shoes].

⓫【苦労・負担を与える】（苦労させる）trouble 🈩;（負担を与える）burden 🈩

彼女に私自身の悩み事で負担をかけたくない I wouldn't like to burden her with my own troubles.

◆あなたに迷惑をかけたくないんです I don't want to cause you trouble. / ご不便をおかけして申しわけありません I'm sorry for the inconvenience.

⓬【作用を期待して働きかける】

彼女は「この試合は勝てる」と繰り返し, 自分を暗示にかけた She repeated "I can win this game" to herself and made herself believe it.

彼らは実行委員会に圧力をかけてそのイベントを中止させようとした They put pressure on the executive committee to cancel the event.

魔女は彼にのろいをかけた The witch 「put a curse on [cursed] him.

⓭【手続きに付す】put*

その男を裁判にかける put the man on trial

彼の家は競売にかけられた His house was put up for auction.

◆その問題を取り上げて投票にかけることにした We decided to bring the matter up for a vote.

⓮【話しかける】speak* to ...

卒業式で, 先生は私たち一人一人に声をかけてくれた Our teacher spoke to each of us at the graduation ceremony.

◆私は彼女に何の慰めの言葉もかけられなかった I could give her no words of comfort.

⓯【心にとめる】care 🈔, worry 🈔 (❖くよくよ思い悩むというニュアンスが強い)

私は服装は気にかけません I don't care [bother] about my clothes.

母は留学中の姉のことを気にかけている My mother is worrying about my sister who is studying abroad.

⓰【その他】

クマをわなにかける trap a bear / シャツのボタンをかける button (up) one's shirt / 神にかけて誓う swear in the name of God

私は事故に備えて自動車保険をかけた I insured my car against accidents.

あんなやつに情けをかける必要はない You don't have to show 「sympathy for [kindness to, mercy to] a man like that.

持っている切手をすべてお目にかけましょう I'll

show you all the stamps I have. / 私たちは最終走者に望みをかけた We set our hopes on the anchor runner.

かける² 欠ける (不足する) lack ⓘ, want ⓘ, be lacking [wanting]; (瀬戸物の縁など) ∥彼の話し方は迫力に欠けていた His delivery lacked punch. / 彼は誠実さに欠けている He is wanting [lacking] sincerity. / 湯のみの縁が欠けている The rim of the teacup is chipped [broken off]. ◆君の論文は最後の数ページが欠けていた Your paper had the last few pages missing. / 月が欠けていく The moon is waning. / メンバーが1人欠けている We are one member short.

かける³ 賭ける・懸ける bet* ⓘⓘ, stake ⓘ ∥彼はその馬に5万円賭けた He bet 50,000 yen on that horse. / スワローズが優勝するのに僕は1,000円賭けよう I'll bet you 1,000 yen that the Swallows will win the pennant. / 彼女が来ないほうに賭けるよ I'll bet that she doesn't come. / 彼は公約の実現に政治生命を賭けた He staked his political career on the fulfillment of his pledge. ◆私たちは命をかけてでもそれをしなければならない We have to do it at the risk of our own lives. / 彼は優勝をかけて兄と競争しなければならなかった He had to compete with his brother for the championship.

かける⁴ 駆ける run* ⓘ ∥私は急いで公園に駆けていった I ran quickly to the park. ◆野生の馬の群れが川の方へ駆けていった The herd of wild horses galloped toward the river.

かける⁵ 書ける ∥このペンはよく書ける This pen writes well. / あなたの作文はとてもよく書けている Your composition is very well written.

-かける -掛ける やりかけの(→終わっていない)仕事 an unfinished job / 何千人もの人々が餓死しかけている Thousands of people are starving. / ろうそくは消えかけていた The candle was about to go out. / 夕飯を食べかけたら(→始めたら)由里から電話がかかってきた Just when I started eating dinner, I got a call from Yuri. / 僕はこの川でおぼれかけた(→もう少しでおぼれそうになった)ことがある Once I almost drowned in this river. / 私は空港で見知らぬ人に話しかけられた I was spoken to by a stranger at the airport.

かげる 陰る (暗くなる) get* dark ∥急に日が陰ってきた Suddenly it got dark.

かげろう 陽炎 heat haze ⓘ

かげん¹ 加減
❶【程合い・ほどよくすること】
ふろの温度をかげんする adjust the temperature of bath water / ステーキの焼きかげんはどのようにいたしますか How would you like your steak? / 自分のばかさかげんにはほとほといやになった I was really disgusted with「how stupid I was [my stupidity]. / このステーキの焼きかげんはちょうどよい This steak is cooked just right. / ねえ，スープの味かげんを見てくれない？ Say, could you taste the soup?
❷【体の調子】
▶「おかげんはどうですか」「ずいぶんよくなりました」 "How are you doing?" "I'm feeling much better."
❸【…ぎみ】
彼女はいつもうつむきかげんで歩いている She is always walking with her head slightly drooping.

かげん² 下限 lower limit ⓒ

かこ 過去
❶【過ぎ去った時間】the past
過去を振り返る look back on the past / 過去のことを悔やんでも始まらない There's no point in regretting the past. / タイプライターは過去のものになった Typewriters have become a thing of the past. ◆私は過去3年間，旅行をしていない I haven't taken a trip for the past three years.
❷【経歴】past ⓒ《また a ～》(❖「後ろめたい，いかがわしい過去」の意味にもなる)
彼女は自分の過去が明らかにされるのではないかと心配していた She was afraid that her past might be revealed. / 彼はいかがわしい過去のある男だ He is a man with a past.
❸【文法上の時制】the past (tense)
∥過去形《文法》the past tense (form)

かご 籠 (編みかご) basket ⓒ; (鳥かご) cage ⓒ ∥買い物かご a shopping basket ◆彼女がクリをかごいっぱい持ってきてくれた She brought us a basketful of chestnuts.

かこい 囲い fence ⓒ, enclosure ⓒ ∥池に囲いをしなくちゃ I'd better put up a fence around the pond.

かこう¹ 下降 ――下降する (力などが衰える) decline ⓘ; (低い位置に移動する) descend ⓘ ∥日本での出生率がここ数年，下降線をたどっている The birthrate in Japan has declined over the past few years. ◆そのグループの人気は早くも下降気味だ The popularity of the group is waning rapidly.

かこう² 加工 ――加工する process ⓘ ∥おじの工場ではチーズを加工している My uncle's factory processes cheese. ◆防水加工の繊維 a waterproof fabric / この金属は加工しやすい This metal is easily worked.
∥加工食品 processed food(s)

かこう³ 囲う enclose ⓘ, surround ⓘ, circle ⓘ ∥美穂の家は周りを生け垣で囲ってある Miho's house is enclosed with a hedge. ◆彼は女を囲っているという話だ They say that he keeps a woman.

かこう⁴ 火口 crater ⓒ ∥火口湖 a crater lake

かこう⁵ 河口 the mouth of a river

かごう 化合 combination ⓒ ――化合する

combine 〔他〕〔自〕, unite 〔自〕 //水素は酸素と化合して水になる Hydrogen *combines* [*unites*] *with* oxygen and turns into water.
◆有機化合物 organic *compounds*
かこうがん 花崗岩 granite [grǽnit] ⓤ
かこかんりょう(けい) 過去完了(形)〔文法〕the past perfect

> 完了形の一つで,《had＋過去分詞》の形で表される.過去のある時点を基準にしてそれより前に起こった出来事との時間的関係を表現するのに用いられる.現在完了と同じく,「完了[結果]」「経験」「継続」などを表す. ⇒げんざいかんりょう. // The last train *had* already *left* the station when I arrived. 私が駅に着いたときには,終電はすでに出てしまっていた / She *had lived* in Shanghai before she came to Japan. 彼女は日本に来る前は上海に住んでいた

かこく 過酷・苛酷 ―過酷な (厳しい) severe;(無慈悲な) pitiless, merciless //苛酷な仕打ち a *pitiless* [*merciless*] *treatment* / 彼らは過酷な労働条件を強(し)いられた They were forced to endure *severe* working conditions. ◆その２匹の犬は過酷な生活環境に耐えた The two dogs endured *harsh* living conditions.
かごしま 鹿児島

> 鹿児島県は九州の南端,つまり日本本土の最南端に位置しています.有名な桜島をはじめ,いくつかの大きな火山があり,温泉の数は全国第２位です.また農業・畜産が盛んで,黒豚やサツマイモは特に有名です.さらに,老木の杉の「縄文杉」で有名な屋久島は世界遺産に指定されています.
> Kagoshima Prefecture is located in the southernmost part of Kyushu, in other words, at the southern edge of mainland Japan. In this prefecture there are some big volcanoes like the famous Sakurajima, and the number of hot springs is the second largest in the country. Agriculture and animal husbandry are the main industries here, and Kagoshima Berkshire swine and sweet potatoes are especially well known. Furthermore, Yakushima Island, famous for a very old cedar *Jomon-sugi*, has been designated as a world natural heritage site.

かこつける 彼は病気にかこつけてミーティングを欠席した He absented himself from the meeting *on the pretext of* being sick.
かこぶんし 過去分詞〔文法〕the past participle

(1)過去分詞は,動詞の原形に-(e)dを付けて作る規則的なもと,それ以外の方法で作る不規則なものとがある. ⇒巻末付録 (不規則動詞変化表)
(2)過去分詞は形容詞的な働きをする.通例,他動詞の過去分詞は受身的な意味を,自動詞の過去分詞は能動的な意味をもつ // *damaged*

goods (＝goods that *were damaged* 傷つけられた商品) 傷物の商品 / an *escaped* prisoner (＝a prisoner who *escaped* 脱走した囚人) 脱走犯
(3)過去分詞は《動詞＋過去分詞》の形で用いたり, see, hearなどの感覚動詞とともに用いることができる. // The store remained *closed* all day. その店は一日中閉まったままだった / She heard her name *called*. 彼女は自分の名前が呼ばれるのを聞いた
(4)過去分詞は,受身・完了形・分詞構文でも用いられる. ⇒うけみ,かこかんりょう(けい),げんざいかんりょう(けい),ぶんしこうぶん

かこみ 囲み fence ⓒ, enclosure ⓒ //囲みを破る break through *the fence* [*enclosure*]
‖囲み記事 a box
かこむ 囲む enclose 〔他〕, surround 〔他〕 //皇居はお堀に囲まれている The Imperial Palace *is surrounded* by moats.
◆テーブルを囲んで座りましょう Let's sit *around* the table. / 正しい答えを丸で囲みなさい *Circle* the correct answer. / その歌手はファンに囲まれていた The singer *was encircled* by his fans.
かこん 禍根 この出来事は将来に禍根を残すだろう This incident will be *a source of trouble* in the future.
かごん 過言 今やイタリア料理の第一人者と言っても過言ではない It is no exaggeration to say that he is the leading authority in the field of Italian cooking now.
かさ¹ 傘 (雨傘) umbrella ⓒ;(日傘) sunshade ⓒ, parasol ⓒ
傘をさす[たたむ] open [close] *an umbrella* / 折りたたみ傘 *a folding umbrella*
彼女は私に傘を差し出してくれた She held out *an umbrella* to me.
私の傘に入りませんか Won't you come under *my umbrella*?
傘を忘れないようにしなさい Don't leave *your umbrella*.
‖傘立て an umbrella stand
慣用表現 日本はアメリカの核の傘の下にいるとされている It is regarded that Japan is under *the nuclear umbrella* of the U.S.
かさ² 笠 (電灯などの) shade ⓒ;(竹の) bamboo hat ⓒ;(スゲの) sedge hat ⓒ;(キノコの) cap ⓒ
慣用表現 彼は父親の威光をかさに着て(→利用して)いばり散らしている He *takes advantage of* his father's influence to act bossy.
かさ³ 嵩 bulk ⓤ, volume ⓤ ◆あらしの後,川は３メートル水かさを増した The river *rose* three meters after the storm.
かざあな 風穴 彼らが停滞ぎみのこの業界に風穴をあけた(→新風を吹き込んだ) They *breathed a new life into* this stagnating industry.
かさい 火災 fire ⓒ //火災の予防策を講じる take precautions against *fire* / その船で火災が起きた *A fire* broke out on the ship. / その火災で数百戸の家が焼け落ちた The *fire* destroyed hundreds of houses.

‖火災訓練 a fire drill / 火災報知器 a fire alarm / 火災保険 fire insurance

かざい 家財 household goods [effects], 〘法律〙movables

かさかさ 手がかさかさだわ My hands are *dry and rough.* / 黄色くなった葉が冷たい風にかさかさと音を立てた The yellow leaves *rustled* in the cold wind.

がさがさ ➔かさかさ

かざかみ 風上 帆船は風上に向かって進んだ The sailboat went *windward* [*upwind*]. / チーターは風上のガゼルをねらっている The cheetah is eyeing the gazelle *upwind* of it.

[慣用表現]学生の風上にも置けない(→学生と呼ばれる価値がない)やつだ He *isn't worthy of being called* a student.

かさく 佳作 fine work [C] ‖選外佳作 an honorable mention

かざぐるま 風車 《米》 pinwheel [C], 《英》 windmill [C]

かざしも 風下 火山灰は風下の町を襲った The ash hit the town *downwind* of the volcano.

かざす (日光をさえぎる) shade [他] ‖彼女は手をかざして空を見上げた She looked up to the sky *shading her eyes with her hand.*

◆彼は暖炉に手をかざした He *warmed his hands over* the fireplace.

がさつ ―がさつな boorish, rough ‖彼はがさつだが心の優しい人だ He's *boorish*, but his heart is gentle.

かさなりあう 重なり合う overlap [自] ‖その2つの研究は部分的に重なり合う Those two pieces of research *overlap* to some extent.

かさなる 重なる be piled (up); (日時が) fall* on ...

クリスマスが日曜日と重なった Christmas *fell on* (a) Sunday.

◆箱が重なっている *There's a pile* of boxes. / 子犬たちは重なるようにして寝ていた The puppies were sleeping *in a heap.* / 悪いことは重なるものだ Misfortunes *come one after another.* / 小さな事件が重なってついには戦争の勃発(ぼっ)につながった *A series of* small incidents led up to the outbreak of war.

かさねがさね 重ね重ね 重ね重ねの不幸 *a series of* misfortunes / 重ね重ねお礼申し上げます Thank you *very much.*

かさねぎ 重ね着 シャツの上にセーターを重ね着する *wear* a sweater *over* a shirt / 厚く重ね着をして出かけた I went out *with* thick *layers of clothes on.*

かさねる 重ねる (積む) pile (up); (きちんと積む) stack (up); (繰り返す) repeat [他] [自]

そんなにお皿を重ねちゃいけません *Don't stack* (*up*) that many dishes.

◆失敗を重ねる *go through* failures *one after another* / 靴下を2枚重ねてはく *put on* a pair of socks *over another* / 楽器には月日を重ねるごとに音がよくなっていくものもある Some musical instruments come to sound better and better *as years go by.* / 彼らは議論を重ねた末，やっと合意に達した After *much* discussion they finally came to an agreement.

かさばる 嵩ばる おみやげで荷物がかさばった My baggage *got bulky with* presents.

かさぶた scab [C] ‖傷がかさぶたになった *A scab* has formed over the cut.

かざみ 風見 weather vane [C] ‖風見鶏 a weathercock

かさむ 嵩む 今月は予想以上に出費がかさんだ The expenses *increased* more than I had expected this month. / フランスに行った帰りは荷物がかさんで大変だった I had much trouble with *bulky* baggage when I came back from France.

かざむき 風向き the direction of the wind

◆風向きが南に変わった *The wind* turned to the south. / そのシュートで試合の風向きが変わった(→形勢が悪くなった) The shot made *the situation* of the game worse for us.

かざり 飾り decoration [U] [C], ornament [C] [U] ‖クリスマスの飾り Christmas *decorations* / 彼女は髪に飾りをつけていた She wore *an ornament* in her hair. / 七夕の日，笹(ささ)に飾りをつけた We put up *decorations* [*ornaments*] of bamboo grass on the day of *Tanabata.* / この古いポストは飾りで実際には使えません This old mailbox is just *an ornament* ―― you can't use it. ◆レースの飾りがついたブラウス a blouse *ornamented* with lace / 私は彼の飾りのない文が好きだ I like his *simple* style of writing.

‖飾り棚 a display cabinet / 飾りボタン a fancy button

かざりけ 飾り気 彼は飾りけのない人だ He is an *unaffected* [a *frank*] person.

かざりつけ 飾り付け decoration [U] ‖私たちはみんなでパーティーの飾りつけをした We put up *the* party *decorations* together.

◆ショーウインドーにはクリスマスの飾りつけがされていた *The* Christmas *display* was set out in the shop windows.

かざりつける 飾り付ける decorate [他] ‖ケーキは一面飾りつけられていた The cake *was decorated* all over.

かざる 飾る (装飾する) decorate [他], ornament [他] (❖しばしば受身で), 《公式的》adorn [他]; (陳列する) display [他]

テーブルは美しい花で飾られていた The table *was decorated* [*ornamented, adorned*] *with* beautiful flowers.

あなたの家ではひな人形を飾りますか Does your family *display* [*set out*] *hina* dolls?

◆飾らない笑顔 an *open* smile / うわべを飾る *keep up* appearances / 飾らずに話す speak *plainly* / KO勝利を飾る *win* by (a) knockout / ひろ子は華やかなデビューを飾った Hiroko *made* a brilliant debut. / 皇太子のご結婚が新聞の一面を飾った The marriage of the prince *made* the front page. / あそこに飾ってある靴を見せてください Please show me the shoes *on display* over there. / 彼

女はかわいらしい花で髪を飾った She *dressed* her hair *with* a little flower.

かさん 加算 addition ―加算する add 働 ‖この料金に消費税が加算されます A consumption tax *will be added* to this charge.

かざん 火山 volcano [valkéinou] ⓒ (複 ～es, ～s) ‖その火山は3年前に噴火した The *volcano* erupted three years ago.
‖火山活動 volcanic activity ／ 火山岩 lava ／ 火山帯 a volcanic zone ／ 火山灰 volcanic ash ／ 海底火山 a submarine volcano ／ 活火山 an active volcano ／ 休火山 a dormant volcano ／ 死火山 an extinct volcano 関連語 火砕流 a pyroclastic flow ／ 噴火 (an) eruption ／ 噴火口 a crater ／ マグマ magma

かさんめいし 可算名詞〖文法〗 countable noun ⓒ ⇒ めいし(名詞) ‖不可算名詞 an uncountable noun

かし¹ 菓子 (公式的) confection ⓒ; (砂糖菓子)(米)candy ⓤⓒ, (英)sweets; (ケーキ)cake ⓤⓒ ❖大きなケーキをまるごと1つをいう場合はⓒ, 切り分けたものを指す場合や, 漠然とした意味で用いるときはⓤ; (パイ・タルトなど) pastry ⓒ; (クッキー)(主に米)cookie ⓒ, (主に英)biscuit ⓒ
お菓子はいかがですか Will you have some *sweets*?
‖菓子パン (a) sweet bread ／ 菓子屋(米)a candy [(英)sweet] shop ／ 洋菓子 Western confectionery ／ 和菓子 (traditional) Japanese confectionery

かし² 貸し 貸し間あり〖掲示〗 *Rooms* 「*for Rent* [(英)*to Let*] ／ 田代君に2,000円貸しがある I *loaned* Tashiro 2,000 yen. ／ 彼にはこの前宿題を手伝ってやったという貸しがある I helped him do his homework the other day, and so he must feel *indebted to me* for it.
‖貸し衣装 a rental costume ／ 貸し金庫 a safe-deposit box ／ 貸し自転車 a rental bicycle ／ 貸し賃 (a) rent ／ 貸しビデオ a rental video ／ 貸しビル a building with rental office spaces ／ 貸し別荘 a rental cottage ／ 貸し部屋 a rental room ／ 貸し家(米)a house「for rent [(英)to let]

かし³ 華氏 Fahrenheit [fǽrənhàit] (《略語》F) ⇒ せっし ‖氷は華氏32度でできる Ice forms at 32°*F*.
‖華氏温度計 a Fahrenheit thermometer

かし⁴ 歌詞 the words (of a song); (流行歌などの) lyrics ‖CDの歌詞カード (→印刷された歌詞) *the printed lyrics of the songs* on the CD ／ 私は『ムーンリバー』の歌詞が好きだ I like *the words of* Moon River.

かし⁵ 樫 oak ❖カシワ, ナラなども指す)

かし⁶ 仮死 その子犬は仮死状態で生まれた The puppy was born *half-dead*.

かし⁷ 河岸 (魚市場) fish market

かじ¹ 火事 fire ⓒⓤ
火事だ! *Fire*!
ゆうべ3丁目で火事があった There was *a fire* [*A fire* broke out] in 3-chome last night.
彼の家は昨夜の火事で全焼した His house burnt down in *the fire* last night.
その大火事で町は焼けて灰になった The *big fire* reduced the town to ashes.
隣の家が火事だ! The house next door is *on fire*!
消防車は火事の現場に急行した The fire engine rushed to *the scene of the fire*.
◆その火事で6名の死者が出た Six people died in the *blaze*.
🗨「その女性は火事のときに, 重い金庫と子供2人を抱えて外に飛び出したそうだよ」「まさに火事場のばか力(→いざというときには, 思っている以上の力を出すことができる)ってやつだね」"I heard that she rushed out of her house holding her heavy safe and her two children when the house was *on fire*." "People say *you can exert much more strength than you think you have in an emergency*."
‖火事場泥棒 a looter at a fire ／ 山火事 a forest fire

かじ² 家事 housework ⓤ; (定期的な雑用) household chore ⓒ ‖男の人が家事をして何が悪いの What's wrong with men doing *housework*? ／ 両親は家事を分担している My parents share *the household chores*.
◆私は母の家事を手伝った I helped my mother with *the housekeeping*.

かじ³ 舵 rudder ⓤ, helm ⓤ (❖helmは「支配」という比喩的な意味でも用いる) ‖彼が会社経営のかじをとっている He *is at the helm of* the company. ／ おもかじ!《号令》*Starboard*! ／ とりかじ!《号令》*Port*! ／ このボートはかじがとりやすい This boat *steers* easily.
‖かじとり ⇒ かじとり

がし 餓死 starvation ⓤ ―餓死する die of hunger, starve to death ‖その国で多くの人が餓死した Many people「*starved to death* [*died of hunger*] in that country.

カシオペヤざ カシオペヤ座 Cassiopeia

かじかむ 手がかじかんじゃった My hands *are numb with* cold.

かしかり 貸し借り これで貸し借りなしだ(→五分五分だ) Now we're *even*. ／ That makes us *even*.

かじきまぐろ 梶木鮪〖魚〗(マカジキ) marlin ⓒ (複 ～, ～s); (メカジキ) swordfish ⓒ (複 ～, ～s)

かしきり 貸し切り charter ⓤ ◆そのレストランはきょうは一日貸し切りだ That restaurant *is reserved* all day today.
‖貸し切りバス a chartered bus

かしげる 傾げる tilt 働 ‖首をかしげる *tilt one's head*

かしこ ⇒ けいぐ

かしこい 賢い wise; clever; smart; intelligent

> wise: 知識や経験によって物事を正しく判断できる賢さ.
> clever: 頭がよく機敏なことを表し,「ずる賢い」という意味もある.

smart: 飲み込みがよく抜け目がない賢さ. intelligent: 知的な頭のよさをいう.

うちの犬はとても賢い Our dog is very *clever*. / そこに気がつくとは君もなかなか賢い It's very *wise* [*clever*] of you to notice that. / また同じ失敗をしたのか. もっと賢くなれよ You made the same mistake again. You have to be *smarter* than that.

◆あなたは賢い選択をした You made a *good choice*.

かしこまる 畏まる stand* on ceremony ‖ そんなにかしこまるなよ Don't stand on *ceremony* so much.

◆かしこまった話はこれくらいにしておきましょう Now let's stop talking *so formally*.

🔴「戻るまでここで待っていてください」「かしこまりました」"Wait here till I come back." "Yes, sir [ma'am]."

🔴「それ, プレゼント用に包んでもらえますか」「かしこまりました」"Can you gift-wrap it, please?" "Certainly."

かしだおれ 貸し倒れ〘商業〙bad debt C

かしだし 貸し出し lending U, loan U (❖「貸付金」の意味では U) ◆図書の貸し出し期間は2週間です(→2週間借りられる) You can *borrow* books *for two weeks*. / 図書館でタイ料理の本を探したが貸し出し中だった I looked for a Thai cook book in the library, but it *was out*.

かしだす 貸し出す lend* out; (有料で) rent ➡かす(貸す)

かしつ 過失 (失敗) mistake C, error C U (❖mistake よりかたい語); (落ち度) fault C; (必要な注意を怠ること)〘法律〙negligence U ‖ 重大な過失を犯す make *a* serious *mistake*; commit *a* serious *fault* / 過失を認める avow *one's mistakes* / 人を過失で告発する accuse a person of *negligence*

‖過失致死罪 accidental [involuntary] manslaughter [homicide]

かじつ 果実 fruit U C ‖果実酒 (a fruit) wine

かしつき 加湿器 humidifier C

かしつけ 貸し付け loan C U ‖1年間で返済する貸付金 *a loan* payable in a year

‖貸付信託 a loan trust

かしつける 貸し付ける loan C

かじとり 舵取り (かじ手) helmsman C, steersman C; (レース艇の) coxswain C

カジノ casino C (複 〜s)

カシミヤ cashmere U

かしゃ 貨車 (米) freight car C, 《英》(goods) wagon C

かじや 鍛冶屋 smith C, blacksmith C

かしゃく 呵責 彼にうそをついたことについて良心の呵責を感じている I *feel guilty* [*the pricks of conscience*] *about* telling him a lie.

➡りょうしん(良心)

かしゅ 歌手 singer C ‖アイドル歌手 a pop idol [star] (❖×idol singer とはいわない) / オペラ歌手 an opera singer / 新人歌手 a budding singer / 流行歌手 a pop singer

かじゅ 果樹 fruit tree C ‖果樹園 (柑橘(かんきつ)類 などの) a grove; (柑橘類以外の) an orchard; (ブドウ園) a vineyard

カジュアル ─カジュアルな casual ‖カジュアルウエア 〘集合的〙casual wear

かしゅう 歌集 (歌を集めた本) songbook C; (和歌を集めた本) a collection [an anthology] of waka

かじゅう¹ 果汁 fruit juice U C (❖juice は果汁100パーセントのものに限って用いる)

◆果汁入りのジュース a *fruit drink*

かじゅう² 加重 スキーで左にターンする際には右足に加重します Put your *weight on* your right foot when you turn left in skiing.

がしゅう 画集 a collection of paintings

かしょ 箇所 (場所) place C; (点) point C; (部分) part C (❖英語では日本語の「〜か所」に当たる語を特に必要としない場合も少なくない) ‖訂正すべき箇所には印をつけてください Will you mark *the parts* to correct?

◆彼の作文には何か所か(→いくつかの)間違いがあった There were *several* mistakes in his composition. / この CD には1か所(→1つ)傷がある There is a scratch on this CD.

かじょう¹ 過剰 excess U (また an 〜); (余剰) surplus U C ─過剰な excessive ‖父は過剰な健康崇拝に取りつかれているようだ My father's worship of health is *excessive*.

◆彼には自意識過剰なところがある There is an air of *self-consciousness* about him. / 彼女は自信過剰だ She is *overconfident*.

‖過剰防衛 excessive self-defense / 人口過剰 overpopulation / 生産過剰 overproduction

かじょう² 箇条 (項目) item C; (条項) article C, clause C ‖12か条から成る条約 a treaty which consists of 12 *articles*

◆授業の要点を箇条書きにした I *itemized* the points of the lesson.

がしょう¹ 画商 picture [art] dealer C

がしょう² 賀正 Happy New Year!, New Year's Greetings (❖かしこまって書く場合は"I wish you a happy new year."のようにする)

がじょう 賀状 New Year's card C

かしょうひょうか 過小評価 underestimate C, underestimation C ─過小評価する underestimate 他, underrate 他

かしょうりょく 歌唱力 one's singing ability

かしょく 過食 overeating U ‖過食症〘医学〙bulimia

かしら 頭 (頭部) head C; (長) chief C, principal C, head C

-かしら (自問) I wonder ...; (希望) I hope ...; (依頼) Will you ...? (❖日本語の「〜かしら」には女性的な響きがあるが, これらの英語にはそのようなニュアンスはない)

父の日のプレゼントは何にしようかしら I *wonder* what I should give for Father's Day.

だれか手伝ってくれないかしら I *hope* somebody will help me.

◆彼はあなたのことが好きじゃないかしら I *imagine* (*that*) he likes you.

🔴「一つ頼んでいいかしら」「いいよ, 何?」"Will

かず

you do me a favor? / *Can I* ask a favor?" "Sure. What is it?"

🅔「午後には晴れるといいですね」「でも降るんじゃないかしら」"I hope it will be fine in the afternoon." "But *I'm afraid* it'll rain."

🅔「今夜は外食するというのはどうかしら」「それもいいね」"*Maybe* we *could* eat out tonight. / *What do you say* to eating out tonight?" "That's one possibility."

かしらもじ 頭文字 initial (letter) ⓒ

かじりつく (かみつく) bite* into ...; (固執する) cling* [stick*] to ... ∥ライオンはその肉にかじりついた The lion *bit into* the meat.
◆石にかじりついてでも(→どんな犠牲を払っても)この仕事はやりとげる I will complete this job *at any cost*. / 彼は一日中机にかじりついて(→机の前に座って)試験勉強をしていた He *sat at his desk* all day preparing for the exam.

かじる bite* ⓗ; (少しずつ) nibble ⊜ ⓗ; (硬い物を) gnaw [nɔ́ː] ⊜ ⓗ; (ぽりぽりと) crunch ⊜ ⓗ ∥リンゴをかじる *bite* an apple / 犬が骨をかじっている A dog *is gnawing* [*crunching*] *on* a bone. / 彼はせんべいをかじりながらテレビを見ていた He was watching TV *crunching* rice crackers. ◆親のすねをかじる *sponge off one's parents* / フランス語を少々かじる *learn a bit of* French

かしん¹ 過信 彼は自分の実力を過信していた He *was overconfident of* his own ability. / 現代人は情報を過信する(→無批判に信じる)傾向がある Modern people are likely to *believe* information *blindly*.

かしん² 家臣 (封建時代の) vassal ⓒ

かじん 歌人 poet ⓒ

かす¹ 貸す

(無料で) lend* ⓗ (↔ borrow); (有料で) rent (out) (◆rent には「借りる」の意味もあるので、明確にするためによく out を用いる)

> 語法
> lend は無料で移動可能な物を貸し出すときに用いるが, rent (out) は物を一定期間, 一定の金額で有料で貸すときに用いる. 例えば, 友達に車を貸すときは通例 lend a car だが, レンタカー会社が貸す[から借りる]ときは rent a car となる. 家・土地・部屋などの賃貸には rent や lease を用いる.

自転車貸します《掲示》*Rent* a Cycle
自転車を貸していただけませんか Will you *lend* me your bicycle? / (→借りてもいいですか) May I *borrow* your bicycle?
ちょっとペンを貸してもらえますか Could you just *lend* me your pen, please?
君はだれにお金を貸したの Who did you *lend* your money to?
あそこでボートを貸してくれるよ They *will rent out* a boat over there.
◆電話を貸してください(→使ってもいいですか) May I *use* your phone? / (広告で)即金で貸します. 電話は1234-5678 Dial 1234-5678 for a quick *loan*.

🅔「お金を貸してくれない? あした返すからさ」「うん, 場合によるね. いくらいるの」"Can you *lend* me some money? I'll pay you back tomorrow." "Well, it depends. How much do you need?"

[慣用表現] ちょっと顔を貸してくれよ *Can you come with me* for a minute? / 知恵を貸してください(→助言をください) Could you *give* me *some advice*? / もしあなたが手を貸してくれなかったら成功していなかっただろう I couldn't have succeeded if you *hadn't helped* me. / 彼女は彼の言うことに耳を貸そうとしなかった She *turned a deaf ear to* what he said.

かす² 課す impose ⓗ, put* ⓗ ∥政府は外国製品に対し新たな税を課した The government *has imposed* a new tax *on* foreign products. / 彼女は新人を教育するという仕事を課されている She *has been given* the job of training newcomers.

かす³ 化す change [turn] into ... ∥一面は血の海と化した The whole place *turned into* a pool of blood. ◆彼女は復讐(ふくしゅう)の鬼と化した(→復讐に取りつかれた) She *became obsessed with* revenge.

かす⁴ 科す fine ⓗ ∥スピード違反で2万円の罰金を科せられた I *was fined* 20,000 yen *for* speeding.

かす⁵ 滓 dregs ∥おまえは人間のかすだ You are *the dregs* of humanity.
◆マッチの燃えかす a *dead* match

かず 数

number ⓒ; (数字) figure ⓒ ➡ [巻末付録] (数と数式)

大きい数 *a high* [*large*] *number* / 小さい数 *a low* [*small*] *number* / 5けたの数 *five-digit number*; five *figures* (◆「2［3］けたの数」は double [triple] figures である)

私は箱の中の卵の数を数えた I *counted the* (*number of*) eggs in the box.
この町の家の数は800軒です *The number of* houses in this town is 800.
ボールの数が合わない *The number of* balls is not right.
数えているうちにカードの数が分からなくなった I *lost count of the number of* cards while counting.
◆何事も上達したければ数をこなすことだ You should *try as many times as possible* if you want to be good at it. / *The more you try, the better you will be at it.* / すごい数の人が列を作って待っているのを見てびっくりした It surprised me to see *so many* people waiting in line.

‖基[序]数 a cardinal [an ordinal] number / 偶[奇]数 an even [odd] number / 単[複]数形 the singular [a plural] form

[慣用表現] 数ある辞書の中でこれを選んだ理由は何ですか What was the reason you chose this from *all the many* other dictionaries? / その戦争の犠牲になった人は数知れない *Innumerable* [*Countless*] people fell victim to the war. / 与党は数にものを言わせてその議案

を通過させた The ruling party passed the bill *by force of numbers*. / 車の事故は数の上では減ってきている Car accidents have been decreasing *in number*. / 彼の苦労に比べれば私の苦労などものの数ではない(→何でもない) My efforts *are nothing compared to* his.

ガス
❶【気体】gas Ⓤ
ガスをつける[消す] turn on [off] *the gas*
ガスがもれてるよ! *Gas* is leaking!
この部屋はガス臭い This room smells of *gas*. / I smell *gas* in this room.
犯人はガス自殺した The criminal *killed himself with gas*.
◆有害なガスで大気を汚染する pollute the air with toxic *fumes*
❷【ガソリン】gasoline Ⓤ, gas Ⓤ,《英》petrol Ⓤ
車はガス欠で動かなかった The car wouldn't move because it *was out of gas*.
❸【体内の】
豆を食べるとおなかにガスがたまる Beans give you *gas*.
❹【霧】fog ⒸⓊ ⇨きり(霧)
‖ガス会社 a gas company / ガス管 a gas pipe / ガス警報器 a gas alarm / ガスこんろ a gas stove / ガス室 a gas chamber / ガスストーブ a gas heater [《英》fire] / ガス中毒 gas poisoning / ガス爆発 a gas explosion / ガスボンベ a gas cylinder / ガスマスク a gas mask / ガスもれ a gas leak / ガス湯沸かし器 a gas water heater / ガスライター a gas lighter / ガスレンジ a gas range / 催涙ガス tear gas / 毒ガス poison gas / 都市ガス city gas / 排気ガス exhaust (gas) / プロパンガス propane (gas) / フロンガス a chlorofluorocarbon

かすか ─かすかな (音・色・光などが) faint; (形・記憶などが) dim; (わずかな) slight ─ (形・記憶などが) faintly; dimly; slightly
かすかな物音 a *faint* sound
窓から富士山がかすかに見える I can see Mt. Fuji *dimly* through the window.
あの少年のことはかすかに覚えています I「*dimly* remember [have a *dim* memory of] that boy.
私は彼女の唇がかすかに動いたのに気づいた I noticed a *slight* movement of her lips.

かずかず 数々 ─数々の (多くの) many ⇨ おおく *この2人の選手は数々の名勝負を繰り広げてきた These two players have played *many* exciting games.
◆この公園には数々の楽しい思い出がある This park *is full of* sweet memories for me.

カスタード custard Ⓤ ‖カスタード入りのパイ a pie with a *custard* filling
‖カスタードプリン custard pudding

カスタネット castanets

カステラ ⚠ sponge cake ⒸⓊ (❖日本語はポルトガル語の Castella から)

かずのこ 数の子 (=ニシンの卵) herring roe Ⓤ

かすみ 霞 haze ⒸⓊ, mist ⒸⓊ ‖山にはかすみがかかっていた A *haze* hung over the mountain. ◆この目薬は疲れ目による目のかすみに効く This eyewash is effective against *blurry vision* due to eye strain.
[慣用表現] 君も仕事を探さなきゃ, かすみを食って生きていけないんだから You should find a job. You can't *live on air*.

かすみそう 霞草 〔植物〕 baby's [babies'] breath Ⓒ

かすむ 霞む (目が) be dim; (視界が) be hazy ‖彼の目は涙でかすんでいた His eyes *were dim* with tears. / 遠くに山がかすんで見えた We had a *hazy* view of the mountains in the distance.
◆わき役がよすぎて主役がかすんでしまった(→陰に隠れた) The leading actor *was overshadowed* by the fine supporting actor.

かすめる 掠める ❶【盗む】steal* ⓣ ‖その少年はおもちゃ屋からプラモデルをかすめた The boy *stole* a plastic model from the toy store.
❷【すれすれの所を通る】graze ⓣ; (ボールなどが) brush by …; (表面すれすれを) skim ⓣ ‖ボールが彼の頭をかすめた The ball *brushed by* his head. / (→当たりそうだった) The ball *almost hit* his head as it flew by. / 台風は本州をかすめて太平洋に抜けた The typhoon *grazed* the mainland of Japan and passed into the Pacific.
❸【不安などが】一抹の不安が彼女の心をかすめた A bit of fear *flashed through* her mind.

かすりきず 掠り傷 scratch Ⓒ ‖ほんのかすり傷だ It's only [just] *a scratch*. / 彼女は地震でかすり傷ひとつ負わずに無事だった She survived the quake without *a scratch*.

かする¹ 掠る graze ⓣ ⇨かすめる ‖運よく相手の車をかすっただけだった Luckily, I just *grazed* [*shaved*] the other car.

かする² 化する ⇨かす(化す)
かする³ 科する ⇨かす(科す)
かする⁴ 課する ⇨かす(課す)

かすれる 掠れる (声が) become* husky ‖ きのう歌いすぎて声がかすれた My voice *has become husky* from too much singing yesterday. ◆このペン, だんだんかすれてきた This pen is starting to *skip*.

かぜ¹ 風
wind ⒸⓊ (❖形容詞を伴わないときは通例 the を付ける); (そよ風) breeze ⒸⓊ; (強風) gale Ⓒ; (すき間風) draft Ⓒ
涼しい風 a cool *breeze* / 一陣の風 a gust of *wind* / 風力8の風 a force-eight *gale*
天気予報によると, あすは南風が吹くようだ The weather forecast says *the wind* will blow from the south tomorrow.
きのうは風が強かった There was *a strong wind* yesterday.
風が激しくなってきた[弱まってきた] *The wind* is「*getting up* [*dropping*].
風がやんだ *The wind* has stopped.
風はたいしてなかった There was not much (of a) *breeze*.
◆彼の自転車はさっそうと風を切って走った He

went *briskly* on his bicycle.

‖追い風 a tailwind / 季節風 a seasonal wind / 逆風 an adverse wind / 潮風 a sea breeze / 順風 a fair [following] wind / 台風 a typhoon / つむじ風 a whirlwind / 暴風雨 a storm / 向かい風 a headwind

慣用表現 風が吹けば桶屋(おけや)がもうかる(→物事は意外なところに影響を及ぼすことがある) *Things sometimes bring about most unexpected consequences.* / 彼がアメリカの大学に入学したと風の便りに聞いた I heard from someone [*A little bird told me*] (*that*) he entered a university in the U.S. / おごってくれるなんてどういう風の吹き回し？(→何が私におごる気にさせたの？) Whatever made you treat me? / あの店は売れ行き上々で不景気などどこ吹く風だ(→不景気と無縁だ) That store is doing good business and *is untouched by* the depression.

ことわざ あしたはあしたの風が吹く ⇒あした

関連語 木枯らし a wintry wind / 竜巻 a tornado, a cyclone / 春一番 the first spring gale

短歌 秋来ぬと目にはさやかに見えねども風の音にぞおどろかれぬる(藤原敏行)
Has autumn arrived?
My eyes are still uncertain,
for I see no signs.
But the rustle of the breeze
thrills me with the sound of fall.

かぜ² 風邪 cold C U; (流感)《公式的》influenza C U; 《口語的》flu U
かぜをひく catch [get] (*a*) *cold* / かぜをひいている have *a cold* / ひどい[軽い]かぜ a bad [slight] *cold* / かぜをひきやすい susceptible to *colds* / かぜをひき直す catch another *cold*
由美はかぜで3日間学校を休んでいる Yumi has been absent from school for three days *because of* a cold.
彼女は弟からかぜをうつされた She got *a cold* from her brother.
今年のかぜはしつこい This year's *colds* are stubborn [hard to shake off].
かぜをこじらせるといけないから出かけちゃだめよ Don't go out. It'll make *your cold* worse.
学校でかぜがはやっている The flu is「spreading [going around] in our school.
かぜは万病の元 A cold can develop into all kinds of diseases.

💬「今夜のパーティー、来る？」「いや、やめとく。かぜぎみなんだ」"Are you coming to the party tonight?" "I don't think so. I have *a touch of a cold*."

‖かぜ薬 cold medicine / かぜ声(しわがれ声) a hoarse voice; (鼻声) a nasal voice / 夏かぜ a summer cold / のどかぜ a sore throat / 鼻かぜ a head cold (✿ ×a nose cold とはいわない)

関連語 くしゃみ a sneeze / せき a cough / 鼻詰まり the sniffles / 鼻水 snivel

かぜあたり 風当たり その政治家に対する風当たりは相当に強い The politician *is being severely criticized.*

かせい¹ 加勢 ―加勢する help 他, aid 他
彼はいつでも弱い者に加勢する He always *aids* those who are weak.

かせい² 火星 Mars ‖火星人 a Martian

かせい³ 仮性 ‖仮性近視 mild shortsightedness

かぜい 課税 taxation U ―課税する tax 他 ‖たばこは課税の対象となっている Cigarettes are subject to *taxation.*

‖課税所得 taxable income / 累進課税 progressive taxation

かせいか 家政科 home economics department C

かせいソーダ 苛性ソーダ caustic soda U

かせいふ 家政婦 housekeeper C ‖住み込みの家政婦 a resident *housekeeper*

かせき 化石 fossil [fásəl] C ‖ティラノサウルスの化石 a tyrannosaur *fossil* / 生きた化石 a living *fossil* / 化石を発掘する turn up *a fossil*

‖化石燃料 a fossil fuel

かせぎ 稼ぎ earnings; (収入) income C U
◆うちでは姉がいちばん稼ぎがいい My sister *earns* (the) most *money* in our family.
‖稼ぎ手 an earner

かせぐ 稼ぐ earn 他, make* money
生活費を稼ぐ *earn one's* living
アルバイトをしてお金を稼ぐつもりだ I'm going to work part-time and *earn* [*make*] money.
彼は月にどのくらい稼いでいるの How much does he *earn* a month?

慣用表現 彼はぐあいが悪いと言って時間を稼ごうとした He *tried to gain time* by saying he wasn't well. / 彼は先生の点数を稼ごう(→先生に気に入られよう)と、学級委員長に立候補した He ran for class president in order to *find favor with* the teacher.

かせつ¹ 仮説 hypothesis [haipάθəsis] C (複 hypotheses) ‖仮説を立てる form *a hypothesis*

かせつ² 仮設 ―仮設の (一時的な) temporary ‖仮設住宅 a temporary dwelling

かせつ³ 架設 (橋の) construction U

カセット cassette C ‖カセットテープ a cassette tape / カセットテープレコーダー a cassette tape recorder / カセットデッキ a cassette deck / カセットプレーヤー a cassette player

かぜとおし 風通し (通気) ventilation U
◆風通しのいい部屋 a *well-ventilated* [an *airy*] room / 風通しの悪い部屋 a *poorly-ventilated* [*stuffy*] room / 窓をあけて風通しをよくしなさい Open the window and *make the room airy.*

かせん¹ 下線 underline C ◆覚えるべき表現に下線を引いた I *underlined* the expressions I had to remember. / 下線部を英訳しなさい Translate *the underlined part* into English.

かせん² 河川 river C ‖河川改修工事 river improvement work / 河川敷 a riverbed

かせん³ 寡占 oligopoly ‖寡占市場 an oligopolistic market

がぜん 俄然 (急に) suddenly ‖彼の得点で我々のチームはがぜん有利になった His gaining a point *suddenly* gave our team the advantage.

かそ 過疎 depopulation ◆過疎地域 a「*sparsely populated* [*depopulated*] area / 農村では急速に過疎化が進んでいる The rural population *has been* rapidly *decreasing*.

かそう 下層 ‖下層雲 lower clouds / 下層階級 (the) lower class

かそう² 火葬 cremation ─火葬する cremate ‖火葬場《米》a crematory,《主に英》a crematorium

かそう³ 仮装 ─仮装する (変装する) disguise ‖定雄はスーパーマンの仮装をした Sadao「*disguised himself* [*was dressed*] *as* Superman.
‖仮装行列 a「fancy dress [costume] parade / 仮装舞踏会 a fancy dress ball

かそう⁴ 仮想 ─仮想の (想像上の) imaginary ⇨そうてい(想定) ‖仮想現実 virtual reality / 仮想敵国 a potential adversary

がぞう 画像 picture / 鮮明な[ぼやけた]画像 a clear [blurred] *picture* ◆デジタルカメラで写真を撮りパソコンでその画像処理を行った I took pictures with a digital camera and *processed* their *images* on a PC.

かぞえあげる 数え上げる count,《公式的》enumerate ‖裁判長は彼らの犯した犯罪の数を数え上げた The presiding judge *enumerated* the many crimes they committed. / 言語学についての研究論文など数え上げたらきりがない(→多すぎて数えられない) The papers on linguistics *are too many to count*.

かぞえうた 数え歌 counting song

かぞえる 数える

count,《公式的》number
そのままで10数えろ Stay as you are and *count* (to) 10.
その子は英語で1から100まで数えられる The child *can count* from one to a hundred in English.
その子は指を折って10まで数えた The child *counted* (*up*) *to* 10 on his fingers. (◆英米人は指を順に折って数えるのではなく、握った手の指を順に立てて数える)
彼は財布の中のお金を数えた He *counted* the money in the wallet.
彼は日本で十指に数えられる建築家だ He is *counted among* the top 10 architects in Japan.
この地震の被災者は10万人を数えた The victims of this earthquake *numbered* a hundred thousand.
◆10数える間 for *a count of* 10 / 私はおつりを数え間違えた I *miscounted* the change. / 子供たちはクリスマスを指折り数えて待っていた Children *were looking forward to* Christmas. / 彼は数えきれないほどのファンレターをもらった He received *countless* fan letters. / それを本当に理解している人は数えるほどしかいないそうだ I hear *only a handful of* people really understand it.

かそく 加速 acceleration ─加速する accelerate, speed* up ‖車を加速する *accelerate* a car
‖加速器 an accelerator / 加速度〖物理〗acceleration

かぞく 家族

a [one's] family (◆夫婦とその子供とから成るものを基本とするが、時にその夫婦の親や親戚(½½)も含む),《口語的》one's folks (◆《米》では特に当人の両親をいう)

<u>語法</u>
(1) family は、家族を1つの単位とみなす場合は単数扱い、家族の構成員に重点をおく場合、特に《英》では複数扱いになることがある ‖うちの家族はみな相撲のファンだ《英》My *family are* all sumo fans.
(2) 家族の構成員の多い少ないは large, small で表す ‖彼の家族は大家族です He has *a* large *family*. (◆×He has many families.とはしない. families は「複数の家族(家庭)」の意味)
(3) folks は複数扱い.

(子供が見てもさしつかえない)家族向けテレビ番組 a *family* TV show
ご家族は何人ですか How many people are there in *your family*? / How large is *your family*?
うちは5人家族です There are five people in my *family*. / We are *a family* of five.
彼の収入は家族を養っていくのには十分だ His income is adequate to support [feed, keep] *his family*.
この地区には6家族が住んでいます Six *families* live in this area.
夏休みに私は家族と北海道に行きました I went to Hokkaido with *my family* during the summer vacation.
彼らは私を家族の一員として迎え入れてくれた They welcomed me as「*a member of their family* [*their family* member].
この前の日曜日、動物園は家族連れでいっぱいだった The zoo was crowded with *families* last Sunday.
ご家族のみなさんによろしくお伝えください Please「give my best regards [say hello] to *your family*.
◆家族的な雰囲気のある民宿 a family-run inn filled with a *homey* [《主に英》*homely*] atmosphere
💬「ご家族のみなさんはお元気でいらっしゃいますか」「おかげさまで元気です」"How is [《英》are] *your family*? / How are *your folks*?" "They're fine, thank you."
‖家族会議 a family meeting / 家族計画 family planning / 家族制度 the family system / 家族手当 a family allowance / 核家族 a nuclear family

ガソリン 《米》gasoline Ⓤ,《米口語的》gas Ⓤ,《英》petrol Ⓤ ∥ハイオク[レギュラー, 無鉛]ガソリン high-octane [regular, unleaded] *gasoline* / ガソリンが切れた I've run out of *gas*. / 彼の車はガソリンを食う His car *consumes a lot of gas*. / His car *is a gas guzzler*. (❖ gas guzzler は米口語的表現で「ガソリンを食う車」の意味) / ガソリンを満タンにしてください Fill it [her] up, please.
∥ガソリンスタンド a filling [service,《米》gas,《英》petrol] station,《英》a garage (❖「ガソリンスタンド」は和製英語)

かた¹ 肩

a [*one's*] shoulder (❖日本語の「肩」よりもより広い範囲を意味し, 肩甲骨なども含む. 両肩を含む上背部全体は shoulders と複数形でいう)

【～(の)肩】
その力士は右の肩を脱きゅうした The sumo wrestler dislocated *his* right *shoulder*.
父はなで[いかり]肩をしている My father has *sloping* [*square*] *shoulders*.
◆シャツの肩にしみができてしまった I got stain on *the shoulder* of my shirt.

【肩が】
私は肩が凝っている I have stiff *shoulders*. / My *shoulders* feel stiff. / I have a stiff neck.

【肩を・に】
彼は肩に傷跡がある He has a scar on *his shoulder*.
彼女の髪は肩にかかっている Her hair falls [comes] to *her shoulders*.
彼は肩にダンボール箱をかついでいた He was carrying [bearing] a cardboard box on *his shoulder*.
そのチームの最終走者が肩にたすきをかけた The last runner of the team put the sash on over *his shoulder*.
彼女は私の肩をポンとたたいた She tapped [patted] me on *the shoulder*.
彼は彼女の肩を抱いた He put his arm around her *shoulders*.
ジョーンズさんは肩をすくめた Mr. Jones *shrugged his shoulders*.
僕らは肩を並べて通りを歩いた We walked along the street 「*shoulder to shoulder* [*side by side*]. / We walked *abreast* along the street.

【肩の】
◆さあ深呼吸をして肩の力を抜きなさい(→リラックスしなさい) Now take a deep breath and *relax*. / 肩のいい(→強い·腕をもった)キャッチャーだ He is a catcher *with a strong arm*.

【その他】
牛の肩肉 *a shoulder* of beef
男は彼女が肩からさげていたバッグを奪った The man snatched the bag *hanging from* her *shoulder*.
◆肩で息をする *breathe hard* [*heavily*]; (→息苦しくてあえぐ) *gasp for breath* / 彼は私を肩で押しのけた He *shouldered* me *away* [*aside*].

∥肩パッド shoulder pads / 肩幅 ⇨かたはば / 四十[五十]肩 a frozen shoulder

〔慣用表現〕彼らはその団体に肩入れした They *supported* [*aided*] the group. / 彼は肩で風を切って通りを歩いていた (→いばって・歩いていた) He *was swaggering* along the street. / このクラブの未来は君たちの肩にかかっている The future of this club *is on* [*rests upon*] your *shoulders*. / 肩の凝らない音楽 *light music* / 娘が仕事を見つけ私たちも肩の荷が下りた It took a load off our *mind(s)* that our daughter has got a job. / 彼女は不合格の知らせを聞いてがっくりと肩を落とした Her *shoulders drooped* [She *lowered her shoulders*] in disappointment when she was informed that she hadn't passed the exam. / ギターに関しては彼に肩を並べる者はいない He *is second to none* at the guitar. / (→彼と同じくらいうまく弾ける人はいない) *No one* can play the guitar *as well as* he *can*. / 君は彼の肩を持つ (→味方をする)のか Do you mean you take 「*his side* [*sides with* him]?

かた² 型・形

❶ 鋳型・型紙   mold; pattern
❷ 形   shape
❸ 型式   model; type; style
❹ 慣例   convention; pattern

❶【鋳型・型紙】(鋳型) mold,《英》mould Ⓒ; (型紙) pattern Ⓒ
溶けた鉛を型に流し込む pour molten lead into *a mold* / ドレス用の型紙 *a dress pattern* / ドレス用の型をとる cut out *a pattern* for a dress
◆歯の型をとる take *an impression* of a *person's* teeth
❷【形】shape Ⓒ Ⓤ ⇨ かたち
そのジャケットはすぐに型崩れした The jacket soon 「*lost its shape* [(→伸びて型が崩れた) *stretched out of shape*].
◆卵形の顔 an *oval* face / 扇形の皿 a *fan-shaped* dish
❸【型式】(自動車などの) model Ⓒ; (タイプ) type Ⓒ; (流行のスタイル) style Ⓒ Ⓤ
初期型のラジオ *an early model* of a radio
僕の車は1998年型だ My car is *a 1998 model*.
当社の新型車は燃料節減型です Our *new model* is a real fuel-saver!
私はこの型のベッドが欲しい I want this *type* of bed.
彼女は最新型の服に身を包んでいた She was dressed in *the latest style*.
❹【慣例】convention Ⓤ Ⓒ; (行動などの様式) pattern Ⓒ
彼女はクラシック音楽の型を破った演奏をする Her performance breaks with *the conventions* of classical music.
◆彼は結婚生活に関して型にはまった考え方をする He has a *conventional* [*stereotyped, stereotypical*] view on marriage. (❖「型にはまらない」は unconventional を用いる)

❺【武道などで手本となる動き】
空手の型をいくつか習ったことがある I have learned some karate *forms*.
∥自由形 freestyle

かた³ 片 国際紛争に片をつける(→解決する) *settle* international disputes / その事件はまだ片がついていない(→解決されていない) The case *remains to be solved*. / 妻のほうが娘を引き取るということで片がついた(→話が決まった) They *have settled* that the wife will take care of their daughter.

かた⁴ 過多 excess Ⓤ(また an ～) ∥供給過多 an excess of supply, an excessive supply, (an) oversupply / 人口過多 overpopulation

かた⁵ 潟 (砂州などで外海から切り離された海域) lagoon Ⓒ

-かた 方 ❶【人】あのかた(→男性)が川野さんです That *gentleman* is Mr. Kawano. / (→女性) That *lady* is Miss [Mrs., Ms.] Kawano. / あの帽子をかぶったかたはどなたですか Who is that *gentleman* [*lady*] with a hat? / 次のかた、どうぞ *Next*, please.
⇒ひと

❷【方法】way Ⓒ,《公式的》manner Ⓒ《通例単数形》; (やり方) how to *do*; (体系的な) method Ⓒ / 野菜の育て方に関する本 the book on *how to grow* vegetables / 僕は彼女の話し方が好きだ I like her *way* [*manner*] *of talking*. / 私は彼女の話し方が好きだ I like *the way* she talks. / コンピュータの使い方を教えてもらえますか Could you show me *how* [*the way*] *to use* the computer?

❸【血筋】side Ⓒ / 彼は父[母]方のいとこです He's my cousin *on my father's* [*mother's*] *side*.

❹【気付】c/o (❀(in) care of ... の略語) ∥林春男様方山田麻里子様 Miss Yamada Mariko, *c/o* Mr. Hayashi Haruo (❀郵便局留めにする場合は、あて名の上方か左下隅に c/o Postmaster と書く)

がた がたのきている戸 a rickety door / 私の車はかなりがたがきている My car is a *battered* old one. / (→古いのでしばしば故障する) My car is so old that I often have trouble with it. / 私は胃にがたがきている My stomach *is worn out*.

-がた -型 ハート型のクッキー *heart-shaped* cookies / 最新型のコンピュータ the *latest model* computer / 髪型を変える change one's *hairstyle* / 血液型はB型です My *blood type* is B.

かたあし 片足 one leg —片足の one-legged ∥片足で立つ stand on *one leg*; stand on *one foot*

かたい 固い・堅い・硬い

❶ 容易に形を変えない	hard; firm; solid; stiff; tough
❷ 結合が強い	tight; firm; stiff
❸ 融通のきかない	strict; serious; stubborn; formal
❹ 意志が強い	firm; strong
❺ 緊張した	nervous; stiff
❻ 堅実な・確かな	sound; certain, sure

❶【容易に形を変えない】hard; firm; solid; stiff; tough

hard: 最も一般的な語. 容易に曲げたり砕いたり切ったりできないこと.
firm: クッションなど、物の引き締まった硬さをいう.
solid: 中が詰まっていて頑丈であること.
stiff: 曲げたり動かしたりしにくいこと.
tough: 特に肉などの食べ物について用いる.

硬いベッド a *hard* [*firm*] bed / 硬いいす a *hard* [*stiff*] chair / 硬いブラシ a *stiff* brush
シャベルが何か硬いものに当たった My shovel struck against something *hard*.
その木は岩のように硬くて削ることができなかった The wood was as *hard* as rock, so I couldn't carve it.
ビルは硬い地盤の上に建っている The building stands on *solid* [*firm*] ground.
私は体が硬い My body is *stiff*.
このステーキ、すごく硬いよ This steak is very *tough*.

❷【結合が強い】(きつい) tight; (力をこめた) firm; (動かしにくい) stiff
固い握手 a *firm* handshake / 固い(→きつくしまった)ふた a *tight* [*stiff*] lid
結び目が固すぎてほどけない The knot is *too tight* to untie.

❸【融通のきかない・きまじめな】(厳格な) strict; (まじめな) serious; (頑固な) stubborn, obstinate; (形式ばった) formal
内容のかたい本 a *serious* book / そうかたいことを言わないで Don't be so *strict* [*serious*].
この表現はかたすぎる This expression is *too formal*.

❹【意志が強い】(揺るぎない) firm; (強固な) strong ⇒つよい
堅い信念 a *firm* [*strong*] belief / 堅い友情 a *strong* friendship
彼の辞職の決意は堅い His determination to resign is *firm*.

❺【緊張した】nervous; (こわばった) stiff
硬い表情 a *nervous* [*stiff*] look
初めての主役ですっかり硬くなってしまった I *got nervous* because it was my first time playing the leading role.

❻【堅実な・確かな】(堅実な) sound; (確かな) certain, sure ⇒かくじつ(確実)
堅い商売 a *sound* business
中森氏の当選は堅いね(→きっと当選する) I'm *certain* [*sure*] *that* Mr. Nakamori will be elected. / Mr. Nakamori is *certain* [*sure*] *to* be elected.

◆そのチームは守りが堅い The team is *strong* on defense.

慣用表現 頭のかたい大人たちには困ってしまう I'm fed up with those *inflexible* [*obstinate*] adults. / 彼女は口がかたい(→秘密を守る) She can *keep a secret*. / She is *discreet*.

かだい[1] 課題 (問題) problem Ⓒ; (争点) issue Ⓒ; (仕事) task Ⓒ; (題目) subject Ⓒ; (宿題) 《主に米》assignment Ⓒ, homework Ⓤ //我々の当面の課題 our present [immediate] *problem* / この会議での中心課題 *the* main *issue* of this conference / 貿易障壁を減らすことが日本の緊急課題の一つだ To reduce trade barriers is one of Japan's urgent *tasks.* / 論文の課題を与えられた I was given *the subject* of the thesis.

かだい[2] 過大 評論家たちは彼を過大評価している Critics *are overestimating* [*overrating*] him. / 人々は彼の優勝に過大な期待を寄せていた People expected *too much* of him to win the championship.

-がたい -難い 忘れがたいヨーロッパ旅行 an *unforgettable* [a *memorable*] trip to Europe / 彼が不合格だったなんて信じがたいことだ It is *hard* [*difficult*] *to believe* that he couldn't pass the exam./ It is *unbelievable* [*incredible*] that he couldn't pass the exam. / 彼は理解しがたい He is *hard to understand.* / 1週間後には私の寂しさは耐えがたいほどになった After a week my loneliness became *unbearable.*

かたいじ 片意地 そう片意地をはらずに僕たちのグループに入ったらどうだい *Don't be* so *obstinate* and join our group.

かたいっぽう 片一方 片一方しかないイヤリングがこんなにたまってしまった I have all these earrings that are only *one of a pair*.

かたいなか 片田舎 out-of-the-way place Ⓒ, the remote countryside ➩ いなか

かたいれ 肩入れ 君, やけに彼女に肩入れするね You really *give* her *a lot of support*, don't you?

かたうで 片腕 (一方の腕) one arm; (信頼のおける補佐役) *one's* right-hand man //社長の片腕となって働く work as the president's *right-hand man*

がたおち がた落ち 先日の失言で, その政治家の評判はがた落ちだ The politician's reputation *has declined sharply* because of the improper remark he made the other day. / 今学期の彼女の成績はがた落ちだった Her grades *went down terribly* in this term.

かたおもい 片思い one-sided love Ⓤ, unrequited love Ⓤ ◆彼は彼女に片思いしていた He loved her although she didn't love him./ (→彼の彼女への愛は報われなかった) His love for her was not requited [returned].

かたおや 片親 片親の家庭 a *one-parent* [*single-parent*] family / 片親の子 a child *with only one parent*; (→父のいない子供) a *fatherless* child; (→母のいない子供) a *motherless* child

かたがき 肩書き (職場での地位) position Ⓒ, title Ⓒ; (学位) degree Ⓒ //父の肩書きは人事部長だ My father holds *the position* [*title*] of personnel manager.
◆彼の肩書きはピアニスト兼作曲家だ He is both a pianist and a composer.

かたかけ 肩掛け (ショール) shawl Ⓒ; (ストール) stole Ⓒ

かたかた 大きなトラックが通ると僕の部屋の窓はカタカタいう The windows of my room *rattle slightly* every time a big truck goes by.

かたがた あすお礼かたがたごあいさつに伺いたいのですが I'd like to visit you tomorrow to thank you in person.

がたがた ❶【音】列車の車輪のガタガタいう音 *the rattle* of train wheels / 風で窓がガタガタいっている The windows *are rattling* in the wind./ The wind *is rattling* the window. / バスは山道をガタガタ走った The bus *rattled* along the mountain road.
❷【揺れ・震え】彼女は恐怖でがたがた震えていた She *was trembling* [*shivering, shaking*] with fear.
❸【不安定】がたがたの戸 a *rickety* [*wobbly*] door / 古くてがたがたの車 a *battered* old car / 舗装されていないがたがたの道 an *bumpy*, unpaved road / 経営ががたがたの(→金策に行き詰まった)会社 a *financially doomed* company
慣用表現 がたがた言うんじゃない(→文句を言うのをやめろ) *Stop complaining* [*grumbling*].

かたかな 片仮名 *katakana*, one of the two Japanese syllabaries, which is used mainly for loanwords and foreign names (❖syllabary [síləbèri] は「字音表」の意味)

かたがわ 片側 one side //通りの片側には桜並木が続いていた There was a line of cherry trees along *one side* of the street. ◆片側2車線の道路 a road with two lanes (going) *each way* / この通りは事故のため片側通行となっている Traffic is restricted to *one lane* of this street because of an accident.

かたがわり 肩代わり (引き受ける) shoulder ㊀, take* on ... //私は友人の借金を肩代わりした I *shouldered* my friend's debts./ (→友人の代わりに払った) I *paid back* my friend's debts *for* him [her].

かたき 敵 (敵) enemy Ⓒ; (ライバル) rival Ⓒ //彼は僕を目のかたきにしているようだ He seems to *regard* me *as his enemy.* / 彼女は私の恋がたき[商売がたき]だ She is my「*rival in love* [*business rival*]. ◆彼は彼女のかたきを討とうと決意した He decided to *avenge* [*revenge, take revenge for*] her.
‖かたき役(映画などの) a villain

かたぎ 気質 彼は職人かたぎの人だ He is a man *with the traditional craftsman's spirit* [*temperament*]. / うちの祖父は昔かたぎだ(→古い考え方をする) My grandfather *thinks in an old-fashioned way.*

かたく 固く・堅く・硬く
❶【物体】hard —硬くする[なる] harden ㊀㊁ ➩ かたい
バターを冷蔵庫に入れて硬くした I *hardened* the butter by keeping it in the fridge.
もちは日がたつと硬くなる *Mochi becomes* [*gets*] *hard* as days go by./ *Mochi hard-*

ens as days go by.
♦卵を硬くゆでる make a *hard-boiled* egg; *hard-boil* an egg
❷【きつく】tight(ly); (しっかりと) firm(ly), fast
ぞうきん，もっと固くしぼって Please wring out the washcloth more *tightly*.
ドアは固く閉ざされていた The door was shut *fast*.
♦ジャムの(びんの)ふたを固くしめる *tighten* the lid on a jam jar
❸【まじめに】seriously; (厳格に) strictly; (断固として) firmly
そんなにかたく考える必要はないよ You don't need to take it so *seriously*.
この博物館内での写真撮影はかたく禁じられている Photography is *strictly* forbidden in this museum.
ビルは自分が正しいと堅く信じている Bill *firmly* believes he is right.
♦私は一生懸命勉強しようと堅く決心した I *made a firm decision to* study hard.
❹【緊張して】
そんなに硬く構える必要はないよ You don't have to be so *nervous* [*tense*].
彼女は彼に話しかけられると身を硬くした She *stiffened* as he spoke to her.

かたくそうさく 家宅捜索 警察は家宅捜索を要求した The police demanded that *the house (should) be searched*.
‖家宅捜索令状【法律】a search warrant

かたくな 頑な 彼女はその件についてはかたくなに口を閉ざした She *stubbornly* kept her mouth shut about the matter.

かたくりこ 片栗粉 (ジャガイモから採るでんぷん) potato starch

かたくるしい 堅苦しい (形式ばった) formal; (融通のきかない) rigid ──堅苦しく (まじめに) seriously; (厳格に) strictly ‖彼女の文章は堅苦しい She writes in a *formal* style. / 堅苦しいあいさつは抜きにしましょう Let's skip the *formal* greetings. / そんなに堅苦しく考えることはないよ You don't need to take it so *seriously*. / 僕は堅苦しいのは苦手だ I can't stand *formalities*.

かたぐるま 肩車 その少年は父親に肩車をしてもらった The boy *rode on* his father's *shoulders*. / The father *carried* his son *on his shoulders*.

かたごし 肩越し 彼女は私を肩越しに見た She looked at me *over her shoulder*. / 僕は前の人が読んでいる雑誌を肩越しにのぞき込んだ I looked into the magazine, which the man in front of me was reading, *over his shoulder*.

かたこと 片言 私は片言のスペイン語しか話せない I can speak only *a little* Spanish. / うちの赤ん坊が片言を話し始めた Our baby has begun to utter *some words*.

かたこり 肩凝り 肩こりがする have *stiff shoulders*; have *a stiff neck*

かたさ 固さ・堅さ・硬さ (物の) hardness Ⓤ; (決心などの) firmness Ⓤ; (堅苦しさ) stiff-

ness Ⓤ; (頑固さ) stubbornness Ⓤ ⇨かたい ‖ダイヤモンドの硬さ *the hardness of* diamond / 彼の演技には緊張による硬さがある There's *stiffness* in his performance caused by tension.

かたず 固唾 観衆はかたずをのんで決勝戦を見守った The spectators *held their breath* as they watched the final game.

かたすかし 肩透かし 彼女に結婚を申し込もうとしたが肩すかしを食わされた (→彼女はその話題を避けた) I tried to ask her to marry me, but she *evaded* the topic. / 彼女は来ると言っていたが姿を見せなかったので肩すかしを食わされた感じだ (→がっかりした) She said she would come, so I *feel disappointed* that she didn't turn up.

かたすみ 片隅 corner Ⓒ, nook Ⓒ ‖部屋の片隅に本が積んである There is a pile of books in *the corner* of the room. / ページの片隅を折る *make a dog-ear*; *dog-ear* a page

かたたたき 肩叩き 祖母の肩たたきをした I *massaged* my grandmother's *shoulders*. / 彼女は会社で肩たたきされている She'*s been asked to retire* from the company *in a roundabout way*.

かたち 形
❶【物の姿】shape Ⓒ Ⓤ, form Ⓒ Ⓤ
それはどんな形ですか What *shape* [*form*] is it?
それは丸い形をしている It has *a* round *shape* [*form*].
この石は形がいいね This stone has *a good shape* [*form*]./ This stone *is well shaped*. (❖「形が悪い」は a bad shape [form], ill shaped を用いる)
そのチョコレートは三日月の形に作られていた The chocolate was made in *the shape* [*form*] of a crescent.
あなたのかばんは形も色も私のと似ている Your bag is similar to mine both in *shape* [*form*] and color.
その帽子は洗濯したら形が崩れてしまった The cap lost *its shape* [*form*] after it was washed.
♦この花は星のような形をしている This flower *is shaped like* a star.
❷【整った状態】
彼女の理論はだんだんまとまった形になっている Her theory is beginning to take *shape*.
彼のアイディアは新商品という形で実現した His idea came in *the form* of a new product.
❸【表面的な形式】form Ⓤ ⇨けいしき
形より中身のほうが大切だ Substance is more important than *form*.
♦形だけのあいさつ *a formal greeting* / 私たちの軍隊は形だけの抵抗にあった Our troops encountered only *token* resistance. / 形ばかりのお礼ですがお受け取りください Please accept this *small* gift as a token of our gratitude.

かたちづくる 形作る その星座は4つの星で形

作られている The constellation *is made up of* four stars. / 人の性格は幼いころに形作られる A person's character *is formed* in childhood.

かたづく 片付く ❶【部屋などが】麻理の部屋はきちんと片づいていた Mari's room was「*in good order* [*neat and tidy*]」

❷【問題・仕事などが】(解決する) be settled; (終шего) be finished / やっとその問題が片づいた The problem *has been settled* at last. / 私の仕事は5時前に片づいた My work *was finished* before five.

◆遊びに行くのは宿題が片づいてからにしなさい You can go out to play only after you *have finished* your homework.

❸【嫁に行く】(→結婚した) Our daughter *has* finally *gotten married*.

がたつく このいすはがたついている This chair *is shaky* [*wobbly*].

かたづける 片付ける
❶【部屋・物を】(整頓(ﾄﾝ)する) put* ... in order, tidy ㊥; (しまう) put away; (取り除く) remove ㊥; (きれいにする) clear ㊥, clean up

部屋を片づけなさい *Put* your room *in order*. / *Tidy* (*up*) your room. / *Straighten* (*up*) your room.

守, おもちゃは片づけたの? *Have* you *put* your toys *away*, Mamoru?

ウエートレスはテーブルから皿を片づけた The waitress *removed* [*cleared* (*away*)] the dishes from the table.

(食後に)テーブル(の上)を片づけた I *cleared* the table.

私たちは祭りが行われた公園をきれいに片づけた We *cleaned up* the park where the festival had been held.

◆家をきれいに片づけましょう Let's *get* the house *straight*.

❷【仕事・問題などを】(終わらせる) finish ㊥; (解決する) settle ㊥; (解明する) solve ㊥

夕食前に宿題を片づけてしまおう I'm going to *finish* my homework before supper.

まずその問題から片づけよう Let's *settle* the problem first.

◆じゃま者は片づけろ(→殺せ) *Get rid of* [*Eliminate*] the troublemakers.

かたっぱしから 片っ端から 家にある本は片っ端から(→次々に)読んだ I read all the books in my house *one after another*.

かたつむり 蝸牛 snail ◎ /カタツムリの殻 a snail shell

俳句 かたつむり甲斐も信濃も雨のなか(飯田龍太)
The snails on the ground
in Kai and in Shinano,
gliding in the rain

かたて 片手 one hand /彼は片手に花束, もう一方の手にケーキの箱を持ってやってきた He came with a bunch of flowers in *one hand* and a box of cake in the other. / 応募者は片手で数えられるほどしかいなかった I could count the applicants *on one hand*.

かたてま 片手間 彼女は料理の片手間に弟の宿題を見てやった *While* cooking, she *intermittently* helped her brother do his homework. / 彼は商店経営の片手間に油絵を描いている *While* he runs a store, he does oil painting *in his spare time*.

かたどおり 型通り ──型どおりの (型にはまった) conventional; (形式的な) formal; (紋切り型の) stereotypical /型どおりのあいさつ a *conventional* [*formal*] greeting

かたとき 片時 moment ◎ /よちよち歩きを始めた子供からは片時も目が離せない You can't take your eyes off your toddler *even for a moment*. / (→常に監視していなければならない) You have to keep your eye on your toddler *all the time*.

◆彼は彼女の写真を片時も離さない(→常に携帯している) He *always* carries her picture with him.

かたどる 象る モミジの葉をかたどった皿 a dish *in the shape of* a maple leaf; a dish *shaped like* a maple leaf

かたな 刀 sword [sɔːrd] ◎; (短刀) dagger ◎; (軍刀) saber ◎ /刀を抜く[納める] draw [sheathe] *a sword* / 刀をさす put on *a sword*; (→さしている) wear *a sword* / 刀を振り回す whirl *a sword*

かたなし 形無し 腕っぷしの強い彼も口げんかでは彼女にかたなしだった Even a physically strong man like him *couldn't do anything* to her in a quarrel.

かたならし 肩ならし ⇒ ウオーミングアップ
かたはし 片端 キュウリの片端は切り落としてください Cut off *one end* of the cucumber.

かたはば 肩幅 the breadth of *one's* shoulders ◆うちの父は肩幅が広い[狭い] My father has broad [narrow] *shoulders*.

かたひじ 肩肘 ⇒ 肩ひじ張らず気楽にいきましょうよ *Don't get* so *formal* [*uptight*] and just take it easy.

かたぶつ 堅物 strait-laced person ◎
かたほう 片方 (対になる2つの物の一方) one (❖もう一方は the other) ⇒ いっぽう(一方) / 靴下が片方なくなっちゃった *One of the socks is missing*. / もう片方の(→もう一方の)スリッパはどこにあるの Where is *the other* slipper? / Where is *the mate* to this slipper?

◆このテーブルは片方(→片側)に傾いている This table is tilting to *one side*.

かたぼう 片棒 慣用表現 強盗事件の片棒をかつぐ *be* (*a*) *party to* a robbery; (→共犯者になる) *be* 「*a partner* [*an accomplice*] *in* a robbery; (→加わる) *take part in* a robbery

かたまり 塊 ❶【固まったもの】(大きな) mass ◎; (小さくて硬い) lump ◎; (パン・チーズ・肉・木材の) chunk ◎; (平らな面がある木・石などの) block ◎ /ひと塊のバター[石炭] *a lump of* butter [coal] / 岩[雪, 雲]の塊 *a mass of* rock [snow, clouds] / 氷の塊 *a block of ice* / ひと塊のパン *a chunk* [*loaf*] *of* bread

❷【集合体】group ◎ (❖(英)では単数形で複数扱いになることがある); (同じ種類の人・動物・物などの) cluster ◎ /彼らはひと塊になって走っ

ていた They were running *in a group* [*cluster*]. ◆うそのかたまり *a pack* [*tissue, web*] of lies / ジェフは自信の塊だ Jeff *is full of* confidence.

かたまる 固まる

❶【物が】become* hard, harden 自; (ゼリー・セメントなどが) set* 自
粘土が固まってきた The clay *has ⌈become hard* [*hardened*].
冷蔵庫のゼリーが固まったら食べてもいいわよ You may have the Jell-O in the refrigerator when it *sets*.

❷【確固としたものになる】
やっと町を去る決意が固まった I finally *made up my mind* to leave town.
クラスの意見がまだ固まらない(→形にならない) The opinion of our class *has not taken shape* yet.
現場から指紋が発見され,その男が犯人であるという証拠が固まった The finger prints found at the scene of the crime *have made an unshakable case* that the man was the criminal.

❸【集まる】
私たちは先生の周りに固まった We *gathered* around our teacher.
留学しても日本人ばかりで固まっていては意味がない There's no point in studying abroad if you only *hang around* with other Japanese.
春になるとこのへんにはチューリップが固まって咲く Tulips come out *in clusters* around here in spring.

かたみ¹ 形見 keepsake ⓒ, memento ⓒ (複 ~(e)s) //祖父は形見としてこの帽子をくれた My grandfather gave me this cap as *a keepsake*. / 亡くなった父の形見分けをした The *mementos* of our late father were distributed among us.

かたみ² 肩身 肩身が狭いして肩身が狭い思いだ(→恥ずかしい) I *feel ashamed* that I'm the only one who failed. / (→ひけ目を感じる) I *feel small* because I'm the only one who failed.

かたみち 片道 東京までの片道切符をください *A one-way* [《英》*single*] *ticket* to Tokyo, please. / 家から学校までは片道1時間かかる It takes an hour from my home to my school.

かたむき 傾き slant ⓒ《通例単数形》, tilt ⓒ; (勾配) slope ⓒ(また a ~) //20度の傾き *a slope* [*an inclination*] of 20 degrees / 柱の傾き *the tilt* of the pillar
◆この部屋は床の傾きがひどい This room has a terribly *slanting* floor.

かたむく 傾く

❶【斜めになる】 slant 自, incline 自; (垂直なものが) lean* 自; (水平なものが) slope 自; (一方が持ち上がって) tilt 自
傾いた筆跡 *slanting* [*sloping*] handwriting
ピサの斜塔は傾いている The Tower of Pisa *leans* to one side.

この部屋の床は入り口の方へわずかに傾いている The floor of this room *slopes* slightly down to the entrance.
◆強風でボートが傾いた The boat *listed* in the strong wind.

❷【傾向を帯びる】 lean* 自, be inclined
彼の意見[社会主義]に傾く lean toward ⌈*his opinion* [*socialism*]
その候補者に投票しようという気持ちに傾いている I'm *inclined* ⌈*toward* voting [*to* vote] for the candidate.

❸【衰える】 decline 自
年がたつにつれてその産業は傾いていった The industry *declined* as years went by.

❹【日・月が】
日は西に傾いていた The sun *was ⌈going down* [*sinking, setting*] in the west.

かたむける 傾ける

❶【物を】 lean* 他, incline 他 (✦通例進行形にはできない); (一方を持ち上げて) tilt 他, tip 他
頭を前[後ろ]に傾ける lean [*incline*] one's head forward [*backward*] / 机を傾ける *tilt* [*tip*] a desk

❷【集中する】 (専念する) devote *oneself*; (耳を) listen 自
彼は英語教育に全力を傾けた He *devoted himself* [*all his energy*] *to* English teaching.
僕たちはエミリーの話にじっと耳を傾けた We *listened* attentively to Emily.

かため 片目 one eye ⇨め(目) //彼は片目が見えない He is blind in *one eye*. / 片目を閉じてごらん Close *one eye*.

かためる 固める

❶【物を】 harden 他, make* ... hard; (土などを) firm 他 ⇨かたまる
溶けた鉄を冷やして固めた I *hardened* the melted steel by cooling it. / I made the melted steel *hard* by cooling it.
僕たちは土を踏みしめて固めた We *firmed* the soil by stomping [treading] on it.
◆ゼリーを冷蔵庫で固める *let* the Jell-O *set* in the refrigerator / 土手をコンクリートで固める *concrete* the river bank

❷【確かなものにする】(強める) strengthen 他; (地位などを) consolidate 他
守備を固める *strengthen* the defense
この参考書で英文解釈の基礎を固めたい I want to *strengthen* my basic skills in the interpretation of English by using this study aid.
◆防具で身を固める *put on* protective gear / 彼はその大学へ行く決意を固めた He ⌈*made up his mind* [*made a firm decision*] to go to the university.

慣用表現 結婚して身を固める marry and *settle down* / 彼の言ったことはすべてうそで固めた話だった What he told us was totally *a pack* [*tissue*] *of lies*.

かたやぶり 型破り ——型破りな (ふつうでない) unusual; (因習にとらわれない) unconventional //型破りな発想 an *unconventional* idea / 母の育児方法は当時としては型破りだった

The way my mother brought up her children was *unconventional* in those days.

かたよる 片寄る・偏る ――偏った (偏見がある) biased, prejudiced; (不公平な) partial, unfair; (情報などが) slanted
偏った報道 a *biased* [*partial, slanted*] report 彼の考えはかなり偏っている His point of view *is* quite *biased* [*partial*].
◆偏った食事は健康によくない It's not good for your health to have a *poorly-balanced* diet. / 台風の進路は予想より東に偏っている The course of the typhoon *has deviated* east from the predicted one.

かたりあう 語り合う 私たちは将来について語り合った We *talked with* each other about our future.

かたりぐさ 語り草 彼女の名演は今でも語り草となっている Her excellent performance *is* still *talked about*.

かたりつたえる 語り伝える その地方に語り伝えられた物語 a tale *that has been passed down* in this region

かたりて 語り手 narrator ©

かたる 語る (話す) talk 自 他; speak* 自 他; (伝える) tell* 自 他; (物語る) narrate 他
私は真実を語った I *told* [*spoke*] the truth.
その老人は私たちに戦争について語った The old man *told* us *about* the war.
僕らは一晩語り明かした We *talked the night away*. / We *talked all night*.
この話は世代から世代へと語り継がれるだろう This story will *be told* from generation to generation.
この歌はミシシッピ川について語っている This song *tells of* [*about*] the Mississippi River.
彼女の目が本心を語っていた Her eyes *told* what she really thought.
◆専門家は今年の後半には景気が回復するだろうと語った The expert *said* the economy would improve later this year.
慣用表現 彼はまさに語るに落ちるで, 極秘の計画をしゃべってしまった (→彼はあんなにしゃべるべきでなかった. 彼は極秘の計画をうっかりもらしてしまった) He shouldn't *have talked* that much —— he accidentally revealed the secret plan.

カタルシス catharsis [kəθάːrsis] ⓤ Ⓒ (複 catharses)

カタログ catalog, 《英》 catalogue © / カタログ販売 a *catalog* sale / 貴社製ステレオの最新カタログを送ってください Please send me *the* latest *catalog* of your stereos.

かたわら 傍ら ❶【すぐそば】 ――かたわらに ――前 by, beside; (端に) at the side of ...
――副 by; (わきに) aside / ビル群のかたわらに1本の木が立っている There is a tree standing *by* [*beside*] the cluster of buildings. / 道のかたわらに車を止めた I stopped the car *at the side of* the road. / 私はかたわらによけて車を通した I stepped *aside* to let a car pass through. ◆名前を呼ぶとその犬はかたわらに寄ってきた The dog came *near* when I

called his name.
❷【…する一方で】 彼は学校で勉強するかたわら家の商売も手伝っている *While* studying at school, he helps his parents run a store.

かたわれ 片割れ 銀行強盗の片割れ (→ 2 人以上の中の 1 人) がけさつかまった One of the bank robbers was arrested this morning. / (→もう 1 人) *The other* bank robber was arrested this morning.

かたん 荷担・加担 ――荷担する (悪事に) be (a) party; (一枚加わる) have* a hand; (参加する) take* part / この事件には彼が荷担したと思われる He seems to *have been* (a) *party to* this case.

かだん 花壇 (flower) bed © / 母は花壇にヒマワリの種をまいた My mother sowed sunflower seeds *in the flower bed*.

がたん 彼女の数学の成績はがたんと (→急激に) 落ちた Her math grade fell *sharply* [(→突然) *suddenly*]. / バスががたんと止まった The bus *jerked to a stop*.

かち¹ 価値
value ⓤ Ⓒ, worth ⓤ

> 語法 個々の状況に応じた有用性の意味では value, 本質的な価値の意味では worth を用いる傾向があるが, どちらもほとんど同じ意味で用いることが多い. worth はやや文語的.

――価値のある valuable, worthwhile, worthy; (価値がある) be worth
価値が高い [低い] *be of* great [*little*] *value* / 歴史的価値がある建物 a building of historic *value* [*worth*] / 価値のある一品 a *valuable* [*worthwhile, worthy*] article
人間の価値は外見では分からない We can't judge people's *worth* by their appearance.
彼が持っていた CD は 10 年もたてばかなり価値が出ると思う I guess the CD that he had will increase a lot in *value* in 10 years.
私にはこの彫刻の価値が分からない I can't understand *the value of* this sculpture.
難しいかもしれないが, やってみる価値はあると思う It may be hard, but I think it *is worth* a try.
この古い切手は優に 1 万円の価値がある This old stamp *is well worth* 10,000 yen.
あの皿はそんなに高いお金を払うだけの価値はない That dish *isn't worth* that much money.
私のダイヤモンドはどれくらいの価値がありますか What [How much] *is* my diamond *worth*?
その映画は一見の価値がある The movie *is worth seeing*. / It is worth your while to see the movie.
私たちは互いに価値観が全く違う We are quite different from each other in *the sense of values*.
その車は人気俳優が使用したことで付加価値がついた Used by a popular actor, the car has

got *an added value.*
◆ 彼にとって社会的地位は何の価値もない Social status *has no meaning* for him. / その本の内容は専門的すぎて私には利用価値がない The contents of the book are highly specialized and *are (of) no use* to me.
‖価値判断 *a value judgment* / 市場価値 *market value*

かち² 勝ち 大関は勝ちを意識しすぎていて, 体がよく動いていない The *ozeki* isn't moving smoothly because he cares too much about *winning*. / 試合は9対7でスワローズの勝ちだった The Swallows *won* the game 9 to 7. / 君の勝ちだ You *win*. / You've *won*.（❖後者は勝敗の決した後で, また, 前者は会話で「君の言うとおりだ, 私が折れるよ」の意味で用いる）/ 結局チャンピオンは挑戦者に勝ちを譲った（→挑戦者に勝たせた）The champion *let* the challenger *win* after all.
逆転勝ち a come-from-behind win
慣用表現 早い者勝ち *First come, first served.*

-がち 彼女は他人のことに干渉しがちだ She *tends* [*is inclined, is apt, is liable*] *to* meddle with other people's affairs. / 彼は病気がちだ He *is liable* to sickness. / 彼女は勉強をサボりがちだ（→しばしば怠ける）She *often* neglects her studies. / それはありがちだね It *is not unusual.*

かちあう かち合う (行事などが) clash ⊜ / 田中さんの結婚式と鈴木さんの結婚式がかち合ってしまった Mr. Tanaka's wedding *clashed with* Mr. Suzuki's wedding. / (→日取りが重なった) Mr. Tanaka's wedding *falls on the same day as* Mr. Suzuki's wedding. / クラスの男女間で意見が食い合った (→意見の衝突があった) *There was a conflict* of opinions between boys and girls in the class.

かちかち ❶【音】時計のカチカチいう音が聞こえる I can hear 「*the tick* of the clock [the clock *ticking*].
❷【硬さ】バケツの水がかちかちに凍っていた The water in the bucket was frozen *solid*. / もちがかちかちになった The *mochi has gotten hard*. / ステージ上では緊張してかちかちになってしまった I was so nervous that I *froze up* on the stage.

がちがち 緊張してがちがちになる *freeze out* of nervousness / 寒さで歯がかちがち鳴った My teeth *chattered* with the cold.

かちき 勝ち気 僕の妹は勝ち気な性格で, どんなときでも人に負けるのが嫌いだ My little sister is *strong-minded* [(→頑固な) *unyielding*, (→競争心の強い) *competitive*] and never wants to lose to anyone in any case.

かちく 家畜 domestic(ated) animal ⓒ, (集合的) livestock ⓤ (単数または複数扱い) (❖単に stock ともいう); (家畜牛)(集合的) cattle / 家畜を飼う raise [keep] *livestock* [*cattle*]
‖家畜小屋 a livestock shed, 《米》a barn

かちこす 勝ち越す 私たちは5試合を3勝2敗で勝ち越した We *ended* five matches with three wins and two loses. / 彼は6回表に勝ち越しのホームランを打った He hit a home run in the top of the sixth inning *to take the lead against* the opponent.

かちとる 勝ち取る (賞品・勝利・名声などを) win* ⊕; (努力して名声・人気などを) gain ⊕; (達成する) achieve ⊕ / 勝利[金メダル]を勝ち取る *win* a victory [gold medal] / 平等を勝ち取る *achieve* [*gain, win*] equality

かちぬき 勝ち抜き ‖勝ち抜き戦 (トーナメント) a tournament

かちぬく 勝ち抜く わがチームは厳しい予選を勝ち抜いてきた Our team *has gotten through* the severe preliminary matches.

かちのこる 勝ち残る 彼らは決勝まで勝ち残った (→勝ち進んだ) They *advanced* [*got through*] to the finals.

かちほこる 勝ち誇る be triumphant, (公式的) be exultant [ɪgzʌ́ltənt] / 彼女は勝ちほこった顔をした She looked *triumphant*. ◆ 彼は勝ちほこって両手を上げた He raised his hands *triumphantly* [*in triumph*].

かちぼし 勝ち星 win ⓒ / その力士は今場所5つの勝ち星をあげた The sumo wrestler had five *wins* in this tournament.

かちまけ 勝ち負け 勝ち負けはあまり気にするな Don't worry so much whether you will *win or lose*.

かちめ 勝ち目 (a) chance (of winning); (可能性) odds / この勝負, 挑戦者に十分勝ち目がある[全く勝ち目がない] The challenger 「*has a good chance* [*doesn't even have a slim chance*] *of winning* this match. / 我々に勝ち目がある[ない] The odds are 「*in our favor* [*against us*].

かちゃかちゃ 台所からお皿のかちゃかちゃいう音が聞こえる I can hear *the clink* of dishes from the kitchen.

がちゃがちゃ ドアの取っ手をがちゃがちゃ回したがかぎがかかっていてあかなかった I turned the doorknob with *a clatter* [*rattle*], but it was locked and didn't open. / 皿をがちゃがちゃわせるな Don't *clatter* the dishes.

がちゃん テーブルから皿が落ちてがちゃんと割れてしまった The dish dropped from the table and 「*broke with a crash* [*crashed onto the floor*]. / あまりに不愉快だったので電話をがちゃんと切った I was so annoyed I just *slammed* the phone *down*.

かちゅう¹ 火中 火中に身を投じる plunge into *the flames*
慣用表現 火中の栗(くり)を拾う (→他人のために危険を冒す) *take risks for a person*

かちゅう² 渦中 彼女は事件の渦中に巻き込まれた She *got tangled* [*caught*] *up in* the case.

かちょう 課長 section manager [chief] ⓒ, the manager [chief, head] of a section
‖課長代理 an acting [a deputy] section manager [chief] / 課長補佐 an assistant section manager [chief]

がちょう 鵞鳥 goose ⓒ (複 geese) (❖雌だけを指す場合もある); (雄) gander ⓒ; (ひな) gosling ⓒ / ガチョウががあがあ鳴いている The geese are honking.

かちり　かちりとドアのかぎをかける lock the door with *a click* / (コンピュータの)マウスのボタンをかちりと押す *click* the button on a (computer) mouse

かちん　(乾杯して)グラスをかちんと鳴らす *clink glasses* / あいつの言葉にはかちんときた His words *got on my nerves.* / I *was offended* by his words.

カツ　cutlet 回 (❖通例子羊や子牛の薄切り肉をいう) ‖ トン[チキン]カツ *a breaded and deep fried flat piece of pork [chicken]*

かつ¹　勝つ

❶【勝負に】(競技・競争などに) win* 自他; (負かす) beat* 他, defeat 他

試合に勝つ *win* a game / 賭(ゕ)けに勝つ *win* a bet / 議論に勝つ *win* an argument / 訴訟に勝つ *win* a suit / 対戦相手に勝つ *beat* [*defeat*] one's opponent

ホークスはライオンズに 7 対 6 で勝った The Hawks "*won over* [*won* the game against, *beat*] the Lions (by) 7 to 6. (❖ ×win the Lions とはいわない)

勝ったぞ！これであいこだ *I win!* We're even now.

競技会でだれが勝つかはだれにも分からない. Nobody knows who will *win* the contest.

◆我々のチームは 3 点勝っている Our team *is up* [*leading, ahead*] by three points. / 彼には勝てないよ I'm *no match for him.* / He's *more than a match for* me.

ことわざ 勝てば官軍 Might is [makes] right. (→力は正義である)

❷【克服する】overcome* 他 自, get* over …; (耐える) resist 他 自

悪習[困難, 逆境]に勝つ *overcome* "bad habits [a difficulty, adversity]

彼女は誘惑に勝てずその箱をあけてしまった She couldn't *resist* [*overcome*] the temptation to open the box.

❸【ある要素が強い】

この配色は赤が勝ちすぎている Red is too *conspicuous* in this color scheme.

かつ²　且つ　必要かつ十分な条件 a necessary *and* sufficient condition / 話をするときには, ゆっくりかつ明瞭(ゕ゙)に話しなさい When you speak, speak slowly *and* clearly. / 彼は学業優秀であり, なおかつスポーツも万能だ (→学業だけでなくスポーツも) He is *not only* doing well in classes *but (also)* good at any kinds of sports. / (→そのうえ) He is doing well in classes, and "*what is more* [*moreover*], he is good at any kind of sports.

かつ³　活　彼女にふられて気落ちしているから, 彼に活を入れてやろう *I'll cheer* [*pep*] him *up* because he is discouraged by having been dropped by her.

-がつ　-月　新居へ引っ越すのは何月ですか In what *month* of the year will you move into your new house?

かつあい　割愛　──割愛する omit 他 ⇒しょうりゃく, はぶく

かつお　鰹　bonito [bəní:tou] 回 (複 ~, ~s)

‖かつお節 dried bonito; (削り節) dried bonito shavings

かっか¹　❶【激する】──かっかする (口語的) get* steamed-up; (興奮する) get excited; (怒る) get angry [(口語的) mad] / そんなにかっかしなさんな Don't *get so steamed-up* [*excited, angry*].

❷【熱・光などが】熱が高く顔がかっかする I *feel very hot* [*flushed*] in the face because of the high fever.

かっか²　閣下　(大臣・大使・総督・司教など) Your Excellency; (裁判官・市長など) Your Honor [《英》Honour]; (市長・高官など) 《英》Your Worship ❖いずれも直接の呼びかけには Your, それ以外には性, 人数に応じて His, Her, Their とともに用いる) / イギリス大使閣下 *His Excellency* the British ambassador

◆大統領閣下 Mr. [Madam] President

がっか　学科　(大学の科) department 回 (しばしば Department); (科目) a subject (of study) ⇒かもく(科目) / 英文学科 *the Department* of English Literature / the English Literature *Department* / どの学科がいちばん好きですか Which *subject* do you like best?

‖学科試験 a written test

かっかい　各界　⇒かくかい

がっかい¹　学会　learned [scientific] society 回, academic community 回; (会合) meeting 回, conference 回 / 学会で研究発表する read a paper at *an academic meeting*

◆英文学会 the English Literature *Society*

がっかい²　学界　the academic world, academic circles

かっかざん　活火山　active volcano 回

かつかつ　かつかつの生活をする eke out a living ⇒ぎりぎり

がつがつ　がつがつ食べる eat *hungrily* [*greedily*] / 彼は昼食をがつがつ食べた He *devoured* his lunch.

がっかり　──がっかりする (失望する) be disappointed; (やる気をなくす) be discouraged [disheartened]

決勝戦で負けて, みんながっかりした All of us *were disappointed at* losing (in) the finals.

彼らのニューアルバムにはがっかりしたよ I *was disappointed with* their new album. / Their new album *was disappointing.*

がっかりするな Don't *be discouraged!* / Don't *lose heart!*

◆がっかりしたことに, 遊園地は休園日だった *To my disappointment,* the amusement park was closed. / 遅刻しないと約束したでしょう. 私をがっかりさせないで You promised not to be late. Don't *let me down.*

🅔「田中君は私たちといっしょに遊園地に行かないってさ」「ええ, がっかり」"Tanaka said he wouldn't come to the amusement park with us." "Oh no. *What a disappointment!*"

かっき　活気　(生気) life 回; (精力) energy 回; (元気) vigor, 《英》vigour 回; (活力) activity 回 / このクラスは活気に満ちている This classroom is full of *life* [*vigor, energy, activity*]./ (→このクラスの生徒たちは) The students of this class are full of *life* [*vigor, energy, activity*]. ◆活気のある商店街 an *active* [a *lively*, a *busy*] shopping center / 活気のある討論 a *vigorous* [*spirited*] debate / 活気のない町 a *sleepy* town / 彼らの歌には活気がみなぎっていた They sang the song with great *spirit*. / 新しい政策は日本経済を活気づけるだろう The new policy will *liven up* [*enliven*] the Japanese economy.

がっき[1] 学期 (3学期制の) term [C]; (2学期制の) semester [C] ‖新学期 *a* new *term* / 1年の3学期 *the* third *term* of the first year / 僕は前学期は成績がよかった[悪かった] I had a good [bad] report card last *term*.
‖学期末試験 term [final] examinations, 《米》finals

がっき[2] 楽器 musical instrument [C] (❖単に an instrument ともいう)
💬「何か楽器はやりますか」「ええ,ギターを弾きます」 "Do you play any (*musical*) *instrument?*" "Yes. I play the guitar."
‖楽器店 a musical instrument store / 管楽器 a wind instrument; 《集合的》the wind / 金管楽器 a brass instrument; 《集合的》the brass / 弦楽器 a stringed instrument; 《集合的》the strings / 鍵盤(けんばん)楽器 a keyboard instrument / 打楽器 a percussion instrument; 《集合的》the percussion / 木管楽器 a wood instrument; 《集合的》the woodwind

かつぎあげる 担ぎ上げる 荷物を肩にかつぎ上げる *lift* a load *up* onto *one's* shoulder / 我々は彼をリーダーにかつぎ上げた We *put* him *forward* as our leader.

かつぎこむ 担ぎ込む 負傷したドライバーは病院へかつぎ込まれた The injured driver *was carried* [*rushed*] *to* (a) hospital.

かつぎだす 担ぎ出す ビルの中からけが人が次々とかつぎ出された Injured people *were carried out of* the building one after another. / 西川君が生徒会長にかつぎ出された (→生徒会長になるよう説得された) Nishikawa *was persuaded to be* president of the student council.

かっきてき 画期的 ━画期的な epoch-making, revolutionary ‖画期的な発明 an *epoch-making* [a *revolutionary*] invention

がっきゅう 学級 class [C] (❖特に《英》ではクラスの一人一人に重点をおくときは単数形でも複数扱いになることがある) ‖そのクラスはインフルエンザのため1週間学級閉鎖となった *The class was suspended* for a week due to the flu. / このクラスではたびたび学級崩壊を起こす This *class* often *gets out of control*.
‖学級委員 a class representative, a monitor / 学級委員長 a class president / 学級新聞 a class newspaper / 学級担任 a homeroom teacher / 学級日誌 a class diary

かっきょう 活況 市場は活況を呈している The market places are *active*. / 株価は経済の活況を測る物差しである Stock prices are a gauge of economic *activity*.

かっきり ➾きっかり

かつぐ 担ぐ ❶【荷物などを】shoulder [他], carry ... on *one's* shoulder ‖彼はバット数本を肩にかついでグラウンドへ向かった He headed for the field *carrying* several bats *on his shoulder*. / さあ,みこしをかつごう All right, let's *shoulder* [*lift*] the *mikoshi*.
❷【だます】play a trick on ..., 《口語的》take* in ...(❖しばしば受身で); (笑い物にする) make* a fool of ... ‖かつぐのはよせよ Stop *playing tricks on* me!/ Stop *making a fool of* me!/ 《口語的》Stop *putting* me *on*! / 僕は彼女の作り話にまんまとかつがれた I *was taken in* by her story. ➾えんぎ(縁起)

がっく 学区 school district [C] ‖学区制 the school district system

かっくう 滑空 glide [C] ━滑空する glide [自] ➾とぶ(飛ぶ)

がっくり 疲れてがっくりとひざまずく fall down on *one's* knees *suddenly* because of exhaustion / 彼が試合に負けたと聞いてがっくりきた I *was disappointed* [*dejected*] to hear that he had lost the game./ I *felt down* to hear that he had lost the game.

かっけ 脚気 beriberi [béribéri] [U] ‖脚気になる come down with *beriberi*

かっけつ 喀血 〖医学〗hemoptysis [U] ━かっ血する cough [spit*] up blood from the respiratory organs

かっこ[1] 括弧 (小かっこ) parenthesis [pərénθəsis] [C] (複 parentheses); (中かっこ) curly bracket [C], brace [C]; (大かっこ) (square) bracket [C] (❖順に( ), { }, [ ] のこと. かっこはいずれも対になるので,通例複数形で用いる) ➾[巻末付録] (句読法) ‖かっこ内に回答を入れる put the answer in *the parentheses* ◆その語をかっこで囲む *parenthesize* [*bracket*] the word

かっこ[2] 確固 確固たる信念の持ち主 a person with a *firm* [*strong*] belief / これが真実だと信じるに足る確固とした証拠がある There is *solid* evidence for believing that this is true.

かっこいい かっこいい(→流行の)服 *fashionable* [*stylish*] clothes / 君の新しい車かっこいいね Your new car *looks nice* [*great*]. / あのギタリストかっこいいよね Isn't that guitarist *cool* [*sexy*]? / 彼ってまあまあだけど,かっこいいっていうほどじゃないわね He's OK, but not really *good-looking*.

かっこう[1] 格好・恰好
❶【姿形】(外見) appearance [U] [C]; (形) shape [C] [U]; (体形) figure [C]; (姿勢) posture [U] [C]
格好のよい[悪い]木 a tree with *a* good [poor] *shape*; a well-[poorly-]*shaped* tree
彼は格好がよい He makes *a* good *appearance*./ (→体形がよい) He has [cuts] *a* fine *figure*.
彼女の格好は招待客全員の注意を引いた Her *appearance* caught the attention of all the guests.

彼は同じ格好で2時間，立ち続けた He kept standing for two hours in *the* same *posture*.
◆格好悪いセーター a *tacky* sweater / かぜをひかないように暖かい格好をしていなさい Keep warm [*Dress* warmly] so you don't catch a cold. / そんな格好(→服装)で学校へ行くつもりなの？ Are you going to school in those *clothes*? / そんな格好悪い服，着たくないよ I don't want to wear *unfashionable* clothes like that.

❷【体面】
彼はいつも文学について話すが，ただ格好つけてるだけだ He is always talking about literature, but he's just *trying to impress people*.
女の子がいるからって格好つけるなよ Don't 「*put on airs* [*show off*] just because girls are around.
たくさんの人の見ている前で転んでしまって格好悪かった I *felt embarrassed* when I tumbled down in front of a crowd.

❸【適当】——格好の(適した) suitable, likely; (よい) good
ここは勉強するのに格好の部屋だ This is a *suitable* [*likely*, *good*] room for studying.

かっこう² 郭公 cuckoo [kúːkuː] ⓒ
かっこう³ 滑降 descent ⓤ ⓒ ‖ 滑降競技 a downhill (race) / 斜滑降 a traverse / 直滑降 a schuss [ʃús]

がっこう 学校

school ⓒ (❖ふつう大学以外の学校，特に小・中・高校を指す．《米》では大学を含むことがある）; (芸術・軍事などの技術を習得・訓練するための) academy ⓒ

【語法】
(1)生徒や教師として学校について話す場合は通例無冠詞だが，修飾語句を伴う場合は冠詞を用いる ‖ 歩いて学校に通っているのですか Do you walk to *school*? / 彼女はオーストラリアの学校で日本語を教えている She teaches Japanese at *a school* in Australia. / 正平は地元の学校に通っている Shohei goes to *the* local *school*.
(2)建物・施設としての学校には冠詞を用いる ‖ 学校を経営する run *a school* / 息子の先生と話をしに学校へ行った I went to *the school* to talk to my son's teacher.

〖学校が・は〗
学校は9時［月曜日，4月］から始まる Our *school* begins 「at nine [on Monday, in April]. (❖×begin from ... とはいわない)
日本では学校は4月に始まり3月に終わる In Japan, *school* begins in April and ends in March.
学校は何時に終わりますか What time is *school* over?
学校が終わったらうちへ来ない？ Why don't you come to my house after *school* (is over)?
きょうは学校がありません We have [There is] no *school* today.
その学校は駅からの交通の便のよい所にあります The *school* is of easy access from the station. / The *school* is easily reached from the station.

〖学校の・に〗
学校に入る(→入学する) enter *school*
彼女は学校の成績がよい She is doing well at *school*.
急がないと学校に遅れますよ Hurry up, or you'll be late for *school*.
彼は学校に行く途中で交通事故にあった He had a traffic accident on his way to *school*.
彼はすぐ新しい学校に慣れた He soon got used to *the* new *school*.
弟は来年，中学校に上がる My brother will enter *junior high school* next year.
彼はなぜまだ学校に出てこないんだ Why is he still staying away from *school*?
その学校にはおよそ500人の生徒がいる The *school* has about five hundred pupils.
🔴「君はどこの学校に行ってるの」「緑高校です」 "Where do you go to *school*? / What *school* do you go to?" "I go to Midori High School."

〖学校を〗
学校を卒業する finish [graduate from] *school* (❖graduate from ... は《英》では大学卒業だけに用い，それ以外は finish を用いる．《米》ではすべての学校に graduate を用いることができる) / 学校をサボる cut [skip] *school*
彼は学校を卒業したばかりだ He's just graduated from *school*.
彼は家庭の事情で学校をやめなければならなかった He had to leave [quit, drop out of, give up] *school* for family reasons.
彼は病気のため学校を休んでいる He is absent from *school* because of illness.

〖その他〗
学校では法律を学んでいます I study law at *school*.
新しい学校でも元気でね I wish you well in *your* new *school*.
学校ではうまくいってるの？ Is everything going well at *school*?
学校中が彼のうわさでざわめいた *The* whole *school* buzzed with the rumor about him.
学校給食に不満がありますか Do you have any complaints about *school lunches*?
私のベストタイムは学校記録に及ばなかった My best time fell short of *the school record*.
学校生活は順調ですか How are you getting along at *school*?
私たちは学校新聞を発行することに決めた We decided to publish *a school paper*.

‖学校医 a school doctor / 学校5日制 the five-day school week / 学校教育 school education, schooling / 公立学校 《米》a public school, 《英》a state school / 私立学校 a private school / 専修学校 a special vocational school / 専門学校 a technical [vocational] school

かっこく 各国 (それぞれの国) each [every] country; (様々な国々) various countries ∥ 東京には世界各国から最新の情報が入ってくる Tokyo receives the latest information from *various countries*.

かっこわるい かっこ悪い ⇨ かっこう(格好・恰好)

かっさい 喝采 (拍手) applause ⓤ; (歓声) cheer ⓒ ——かっさいする (拍手する) applaud ⓗⓘ; (歓声をあげる) cheer ⓗⓘ ∥ 人をかっさいで迎える greet a person with *applause* [*cheers*] / その歌手は大きなかっさいを浴びた The singer received a storm of *applause* [*cheers*]. / 我々はその役者にかっさいを送った We *applauded* [*cheered*] the actor.

がっさく 合作 co-production ⓤ; (作品) collaboration ⓒ ∥ 日米合作映画 a movie *made together* by Japan and America

かっさらう ⇨ うばう, さらう(攫う)

かつじ 活字 type ⓒ ⓤ; (印刷された字体) print ⓤ ∥ イタリック体の活字 (an) italic type / 活字を組む set (up) *type* / 大きな活字の本 a book with large *print* ◆彼女の小説が近々活字になるらしい I heard that her novel would soon *be printed*. / 名前をここに活字で書いてください Please *print* your name here. / Please *write* your name *in print* here. / 若者の活字離れが問題になっている That young people *do not read many books* has become a problem.

かっしゃ 滑車 pulley ⓒ; (滑車装置) (block and) tackle ⓒ ⓤ

がっしゅうこく 合衆国 ∥ アメリカ

がっしゅく 合宿 training camp ⓒ ——合宿する have* [hold*] a training camp ∥ 夏合宿 a summer *training camp* / 私たちテニス部は軽井沢で1週間合宿した Our tennis club *had a training camp* in Karuizawa for a week.
◆強化合宿 intensive *training at camp*
∥合宿所 a training camp

がっしょう¹ 合唱 chorus ——合唱する chorus ⓗⓘ, sing* in chorus ∥ 男声[女声, 混声]合唱 a male [female, mixed] *chorus* / 三部合唱 a three part *chorus* / 課題曲を合唱する *chorus* the set piece; *sing* the set piece *in chorus*
∥合唱団 a chorus (❖単数形で複数扱いになることがある); (聖歌隊) a choir [kwáiər]

がっしょう² 合掌 ——合掌する put* one's palms together in prayer ⇨ おがむ
◆合掌造りの家 a wooden house with a steep rafter roof

かっしょく 褐色 brown ⓤ ——褐色の brown ⇨ ちゃいろ

がっしり がっしりした体格の男 a *sturdy* [*heavily built*] man; a man「*of heavy build [with a strong frame]* / がっしりした身体 a *muscular* [*massive*] body

かっすい 渇水 a shortage of water, water shortage ⓒ; (干ばつ) drought [dráut] ⓒ ⓤ ∥渇水期 the period of water shortage; (乾季) the dry season

かっせいか 活性化 町の経済活性化のため大型店を誘致する invite a large supermarket to open to *activate* [*rev up*, *spur*] the economy of the town

かっせいたん 活性炭 activated carbon [charcoal] ⓤ

かっせん 合戦 (戦闘) fight ⓒ; (大規模な戦闘) battle ⓒ ⓤ; (競演) contest ⓒ ∥ 歌合戦 a singing contest / PK合戦【サッカー】 a penalty shoot-out

かっそう 滑走 ——滑走する slide* ⓗⓘ, glide ⓗⓘ; (飛行機が) run* ⓗⓘ ∥滑走路 a runway; (特に緊急時の) an airstrip

がっそう 合奏 ensemble [ɑnsáːmbl] ⓒ ◆その曲を合奏する *play* the tune *together*
∥合奏曲 an ensemble

カッター ⚠ cutter ⓒ (❖「カッターナイフ」は和製英語)

かったるい いちいち説明するのはかったるい It's *a hassle* to explain in detail. / きょうは体がかったるい I *feel listless* today.

かつだんそう 活断層【地学】 active fault ⓒ

がっち 合致 ⇨ あう(合う), いっち

がっちり がっちり握手する shake hands *firmly* / 守りをがっちりと固める put up a *strong* defense / 彼はがっちりした体格の持ち主だ He's a *sturdy* [*heavily built*] man. / 彼は取り引きに関してはがっちりしている He's pretty *sharp* at bargaining.

ガッツ (口語的) guts ∥ あいつはガッツがある He has a lot of *guts*. / ガッツポーズをする raise [pump] one's fist in the air (❖「ガッツポーズ」は和製英語)

がっつく eat* greedily, gobble ⓗⓘ ⇨ がつがつ, よくばる

かつて once (❖肯定文の過去時制に用い, 完了時制では用いない. 位置は通例 be 動詞を除く動詞の前または文頭に置く), at one time, formerly (❖once よりかたい語), ever (❖疑問・否定文で, また, 比較級・最上級とともに用いる) ——かつての, former, one-time (❖共に名詞の前で用いる)
彼はかつてニューヨークに住んでいた He *once* [*formerly*] lived in New York. / *At one time* [*Formerly*], he lived in New York.
その歌手はかつてほどの人気はない The singer is not as popular as he「*once was* [*used to be*].
こんな豪邸はいまだかつて見たことがない This is the most luxurious house I have *ever* seen. / I have *never* seen such a luxurious house like this.
かつてのボーイフレンドに駅で偶然会った I happened to meet my「*former* boyfriend [ex-boyfriend] at the station.
これがジョンがかつて住んでいた家です This is the *former* house of John.

かって 勝手
❶ 【わがまま・自由】 selfishness ⓤ ——勝手な selfish, self-seeking ——勝手に (好きなように) as one likes [pleases]; (思いのままに) at will; (自由に) freely; (無断で) without permission [leave]

君は勝手すぎる You're too *selfish*.
ペンを勝手に使っていいよ You can use these pens「*as you like* [*at will, freely*].
僕の物，勝手にいじらないで Don't touch my things *without my permission*.
◆何をしようと私の勝手でしょ（→だれも私に何をしろとは言えない）*Nobody tells me* what to do./（→あなたには関係ない）*It's none of your business* what I do. / その本を買おうと買うまいとあなたの勝手ですよ *It's up to you* whether you buy the book or not. / 勝手を言って申しわけありませんが早退させていただきます *I'm sorry, but* I'd like to go home early.
💬「助けてくれなくて結構」「そう，それなら勝手にすれば！」"I can take care of myself." "Well, then「*please yourself* [*suit yourself, have it your own way*]!"
❷【事情】
めったに来たことがない町なので勝手が分からない I don't know *my way about* [*around*] the town because I've seldom been here.
どうもコンピュータは勝手が（→使い方が）分からない I don't know *how to use* a computer very well.
外国では何から何まで勝手が違う In a foreign country, everything (about getting around) *is unfamiliar*.
❸【台所】kitchen Ⓒ
‖勝手口 a kitchen door;（裏口）a back door

かってでる 買って出る volunteer (他) (自), come* forward ∥彼女はその会議の司会役を買って出た She *volunteered to* serve as the chairperson of the meeting.

カット（削減・削除）cut Ⓒ;（散髪）cut Ⓒ, haircut Ⓒ;（挿絵）illustration Ⓒ ━カットする cut* (他) ∥髪をカットしてもらう have *one's* hair *cut*; get [have] *a haircut* / 彼女の給料は5パーセントカットされた Her salary *was cut* by five percent. / 彼らは補足的なところをカットして話を短くした They shortened the story by *cutting* the subplot.
◆その映画のノーカット版がテレビ放映された *The uncut version* of the movie was broadcast on TV.

かっと 彼はすぐかっとなる He easily「*gets angry* [*goes into a rage*]./ He *has a hot temper*./ He's very *touchy*. / 彼はかっとして秘書をどなりつけた He yelled at his secretary *in a fit of anger* [*rage*]. / ケイの言葉に父親はかっとなった Her father *lost his temper* at what Kay said.

ガット[1] GATT（❖General Agreement on Tariffs and Trade（関税と貿易に関する一般協定）の略語. 1995年にWTO（世界貿易機関）に移行）

ガット[2]（ラケットなどの）gut Ⓤ ◆バドミントンのラケットにガットを張る *string* a badminton racket

かっとう 葛藤《公式的》conflict Ⓒ Ⓤ ∥心の葛藤に苦しむ suffer *a* psychological [*an* emotional] *conflict*

かつどう 活動 activity Ⓒ Ⓤ《しばしば複数形 activities》;（ある期間にわたる連続した行動）action Ⓤ Ⓒ;（作業）operation Ⓒ ━活動的な active;（精力的な）energetic ━活動する become* active;（作業する）work (自);（活躍する）play an active part
クラブ[ボランティア，政治]活動 club [volunteer, political] *activities* / 救助活動に参加する take part in *the* rescue *operation(s)*
人々は火山がまた活動を始めるのではないかと心配している They are worrying that the volcano may *become active* again.
警察はすぐに活動を開始した The police took *action* immediately.
彼は世界平和のために活動している He *is working* for world peace.
彼女は生徒会で活動している She *is playing an active part in* the student council.
彼は非常に活動的なタイプだ He is an *active* [*energetic*] type of a person.
‖活動家（行動の人）a man of action;（特に政治的な）an activist / 火山活動 volcanic activity / 消火活動 fire fighting / 宣伝活動 an advertising [a publicity] campaign / 平和維持活動 a peacekeeping operation

カットグラス cut glass Ⓤ

かっとばす かっ飛ばす ホームランをかっ飛ばす *hit* [*slug*] a home run

カツどん カツ丼 *katsudon*, a bowl of rice topped with breaded and deep fried cutlets of pork bound with egg and vegetables ➔どんぶり

かっぱ 河童
慣用表現 次郎はかっぱだ Jiro *swims like a fish*.（❖swim like a fishで「泳ぎがうまい」の意味）
ことわざ かっぱの川流れ Even Homer sometimes nods.（→ホメロスさえ時にはしくじる）; Nobody's perfect.（→完璧(かんぺき)な人間はいない）

かっぱはカメのような姿をした架空の動物で，常に水をたたえた頭の上の皿，とがった口，水かきのついた手足が特徴です．昔話や絵によく登場し，今でも水の神様の祭りには水の事故からお守りくださいとの願いをこめてかっぱを祭ります．
A *kappa* is an imaginary tortoise-like creature with a brimming dish of water on top of its head, a pointed muzzle, and webbed hands and feet. *Kappa* often appear in old stories and pictures and have been deified at water-god festivals for protection against water accidents.

かっぱつ 活発 ━活発な（活動的な）active;（元気のよい）lively;（激しい）vigorous;（市況などが）brisk;（議論などが）animated ━活発に actively; lively; vigorously; briskly; animatedly
活発な女の子 an *active* [a *lively*] girl / 活発な市況 an *active* [a *brisk*] market
委員会はその問題について活発な議論をした The committee had an *active* [a *lively*, an *animated*, a *vigorous*] discussion about the problem.

かっぱらい かっ払い （盗み） stealing ⓤ,《米口語的》steal ⓤ, snatching ⓤ;（万引き行為）shoplifting ⓤ;（万引きする人）shoplifter ⓒ

かっぱらう かっ払う steal* ⓣ,《口語的》rip off ‖このコーヒーカップ, レストランからかっぱらってきたんだ I *ripped off* this coffee cup from a restaurant.

かっぱん 活版 ‖活版印刷 typography

カップ （茶わん）cup ⓒ;（計量の）cup ⓒ,（主に）measuring cup ⓒ;（優勝記念の）cup ⓒ (しばしば the Cup), trophy ⓒ (※カップも含めた優勝記念品の意味) ‖コーヒー[ティー]カップ a coffee [tea] *cup*（※ティーカップは teacup とも書く）/（料理で）カップ1杯分の牛乳を加える add *a cup* [*cupful*] of milk
‖カップケーキ a cupcake / カップラーメン《商標名》Cup Noodles, instant ramen (in a cup)

かっぷく 恰幅 ‖かっぷくのよい紳士 a stout [*large*, *portly*] gentleman

カップル （夫婦・婚約者・恋人どうし） couple ⓒ（※一人一人に重点がおかれると複数扱いになることがある）‖お似合いのカップル *an* ideal [*a* well-matched] *couple*

がっぺい 合併 merger ⓤⓒ;（吸収）absorption ⓤ ——合併する merge ⓘ; absorb ⓣ（※しばしば受身で）‖2つの大銀行の合併 the *merger* of two big banks / 小さな会社が大組織に合併された The small companies *were absorbed into* a big organization. / 3つの町が合併して市になった Three towns *merged into* a city.
‖合併症《医学》a complication

かつぼう 渇望 thirst ⓤ（また a ～）, hunger ⓤ（また a ～） ——渇望する crave for ...,《文語》thirst for [after] ...,《文語》hunger for [after] ... ‖富と名声を渇望する *crave* [*thirst*, *hunger*] *for* riches and fame

かっぽう 割烹 ‖割烹着 an apron with long sleeves / 割烹料理 dishes (and alcohol) served at a Japanese-style restaurant

がっぽり 彼の会社は新商品を当ててがっぽりもうけた His company「*hit the jackpot* [*made a killing*] by selling lots of their new product.

かつやく 活躍 activity ⓤ ——活躍する play an active part, be active
‖彼は生徒会で活躍している He is「*playing an active part* [*active*] *in* the student council.
今後のますますのご活躍を期待しております I hope you'll *be* increasingly *active* in the future.
◆彼は甲子園で大活躍した He *was a standout player*「*at Koshien Stadium* [*in the summer high school baseball tournament at Koshien Stadium*].（※Koshien Stadium が通じなければ, 後の表現を用いる）

かつよう 活用
❶【利用】 ——活用する make* use of ..., take* advantage of ...,《公式的》utilize ⓣ ‖週末をうまく活用する make「*good use* [*the most*] *of* one's weekend; *take advantage of* one's weekend / 天然資源を活用する「*make use of* [*utilize*] natural resources
辞書をもっと[最大限に]活用しなさい Make better [*full*] *use of* your dictionary.
❷【語形変化】inflection ⓤ;（動詞の）conjugation ⓤⓒ;（名詞・代名詞・形容詞の）declension ⓤ ——活用する[させる] inflect ⓘⓣ; conjugate ⓘⓣ; decline ⓘⓣ
動詞の活用 verbal *inflection* [*conjugation*]
‖活用形 an inflected form, an inflection;（動詞の）a conjugated form, a conjugation

かつら 鬘 wig ⓒ;（部分的な）hairpiece ⓒ;（男性のはげ隠し用）toupee [tuːpéi] ⓒ ‖かつらをつけている wear *a wig*

かつらく 滑落 ‖斜面で滑落する *slip down* a slope

かつりょく 活力 vitality ⓤ, energy ⓤ;（元気）life ⓤ ‖活力あふれる若者 a young man full of *vitality* [*energy*, *life*]

カツレツ ⇨カツ

かつろ 活路 ‖活路を見いだす find *a way out of* the difficult situation; find *a means to get out of* the difficult situation

がつん 兄から頭にがつんとげんこつを食らった My brother *banged* me on the head with his fist. / 先生からがつんと一発食わされた（＝怒られた）I *was scolded* by my teacher.

かて 糧 （生計）《公式的》bread ⓤ;（心の）food ⓤ ‖日々の糧を得る earn [*gain*] one's daily *bread* / 音楽が私の心の糧になっている Music is *food* for my soul.

かてい¹ 家庭

home ⓒⓤ, family ⓒ ——家庭の domestic, home, household (※すべて名詞の前で用いる);（家庭的な）《米》homey ,《主に英》homely

私の夢は, すてきな人と結婚して幸せな家庭を作ることです It has been my dream to get married to some nice man [woman] and make *a happy home*.
彼女は裕福な家庭の出だ She is from *a rich family*.
彼は家庭の事情で学校をやめなければならなかった He had to leave school for *family* reasons.
仕事と家庭を両立させるのは大変だ It's hard to combine work and *home*.
中村さんは家庭的な人だ Mr. Nakamura is a *domestic* type.
そのホテルは家庭的な雰囲気が売りだ The hotel is known for its *homey* atmosphere.
コンピュータは家庭でもふつうに使われるようになってきている Computers are becoming more and more commonly used in *the home*.
家庭ごみは週に2度回収される *Household garbage* is collected twice a week.
その夫婦は幸福な家庭生活を送った The couple kept *a happy home life*.
彼は母子[父子]家庭に育った He's been

brought up in *a fatherless* [*motherless*] *family.*/ He's been brought up in *a one-parent* [*single-parent*] *family*. (❖one-parent, single-parent は「片親」の意味)

人格は家庭環境に大きく左右される One's personality is greatly influenced by *his home environment*.

その国では家庭崩壊が確実に進んでいる *Family break down* is definitely getting worse in that country.

◆彼は家庭教師に数学を教わっている He is studying math under *a 「private teacher* [*tutor*]*.

‖家庭科 home economics / 家庭菜園 a kitchen garden / 家庭裁判所 a family court / 家庭内暴力 domestic violence / 家庭訪問 a home visit by *one's* teacher / 家庭用品 household articles [goods, stores] / 家庭料理 home cooking

かてい² 仮定 (推測) supposition ©Ⓤ; (憶測) assumption ©Ⓤ; (仮説) hypothesis [haipάθəsis] © (複 hypotheses) ―仮定する suppose ⊕; assume ⊕

それが事実という仮定に基づいて on *the supposition* [*assumption*] *that it is true*

世界中のコンピュータが動かなくなったと仮定しよう Let's *suppose* computers go down all over the world.

彼に結婚を迫られたと仮定して, あなたならどうしますか *Assuming* [*Supposing, Suppose*] *that he proposed to you, what would you do then?* / *If he proposed to you, what would you do then?*

かてい³ 過程 process Ⓤ© / 子供の成長過程を写真で記録する record *the process* of *one's child's growth by taking photos*

◆実験の過程で我々の仮説の問題点がはっきりしてきた In *the course* of the experiment, we came to know what was wrong with our hypothesis.

‖製造過程 a manufacturing process

かてい⁴ 課程 course ©; (教科課程) curriculum © (複 curricula, ~s) ‖教職課程 courses for students going into teaching / 修士課程 a master's program / 博士課程 a doctoral program

かていほう 仮定法〔文法〕 subjunctive mood ©

法(mood)は, 表現内容に対する話し手の心理的な態度を表す動詞の語形変化のことをいう. 仮定法は法の一つで, その表現内容を事実としてではなく, 仮定・想像・願望などとして表現する場合に用いられる. 動詞の語形によって,「仮定法過去」「仮定法過去完了」などに分類できる.

〔仮定法過去〕
If you *were* right, I *would* jump into the Sumida River. あなたが正しいなら, 隅田川に飛び込むよ / ❖If you are right, I will jump into the Sumida River. ともいえるが, 仮定法過去の文では「あなたは正しくない」という話し手の判断が含まれているのに対して, この場合は含まれない.

〔仮定法過去完了〕
If I *had left* home before 7:30, I *could have caught* the 8-o'clock train. 7時半より前に家を出ていれば, 8時の電車に乗ることができたのに(→ Since I didn't leave home before 7:30, I didn't catch the 8-o'clock train.)

カテゴリ category © ⇨はんちゅう

-がてら (…しながら) while; (…のときに) when /散歩がてらコンビニに寄って雑誌を買ってきた I dropped by a convenience store and bought a magazine *while* (I was) taking a walk.

がてん 合点 彼の言い分には合点がいかない What he says *doesn't sound convincing* to me. / それですべて合点がいった That *explains* it all!

かでん 家電 ‖家電製品 a household (electrical) appliance / 家電メーカー a household (electrical) appliance manufacturer

がでんいんすい 我田引水 あなたの議論は我田引水(→自分のことを優先する)だよ You're just *looking out for number one*.

かど¹ 角

❶【物の】corner ©, edge ©
彼はテーブルの角にひざをぶつけた He hit his knee on *the corner* [*edge*] of the table.
川の流れで石の角が取れて丸くなった The *edges* of the stone have been worn smooth by the flow of the river.

❷【道の】(街角) corner ©; (分岐点) turn ©, turning ©
次の角を右に曲がりなさい Turn (to the) right at *the* next *corner* [*turn, turning*]. / Take *the* next *corner* [*turn, turning*] to the right.
郵便局は角にあります The post office is at *the corner*.
角を曲がった所に銀行があります There's a bank just around *the corner*.
私の家は角を曲がって4軒目です My house is the fourth one around *the corner*.
〔慣用表現〕角が立つ(→人の感情を害する)ような言い方は避けるべきだ You should avoid expressions which *offend* people. / 彼もだいぶ角が取れた(→温和になった) He's grown fairly *mild* [*moderate, peaceable*].

かど² 過度 ―過度の excessive, too much ―過度に excessively, too much /過度の運動は控えるように You shouldn't exercise *excessively*. / 過度の飲酒は健康に害を及ぼす *Excessive* [*Too much*] drinking is harmful to the health. / Drinking *excessively* [*too much*] is harmful to the health.

かど³ 廉 職務怠慢のかどで非難される be reproached *for neglecting one's duties* / その男は放火のかどで逮捕された The man was arrested *on a charge of* arson.

かとう 下等 ―下等な low, lower(❖通例名詞の前で用いる); (劣っている) inferior ‖下等動物 the lower animals

かどう[1] 華道 (the art of) flower arrangement ➡いけばな ‖華道部 a flower arrangement club

かどう[2] 稼働·稼動 ―稼働する[させる] run* [自][他] ‖稼働時間(機械の) a run

-かどうか ➡どうか[1]

かとうきょうそう 過当競争 excessive [immoderate] competition [U]

かとき 過渡期 transition [C] [U], transition period [C], a period of transition ∥思春期から成人期への過渡期 *the transition* from adolescence to adulthood / その国の経済は今市場経済への過渡期にある The economy of the country is now in *the transition* to a market economy.

かどで 門出 (出発) start [C] ∥彼の人生の門出を祝う celebrate *the start* of his new life; (→新たな人生での幸運を祈る) wish him good luck in his new life

かとてき 過渡的 ―過渡的な transitional

かどまつ 門松 🗻

門松はお正月に見られる伝統的な飾りつけの一つで，もともとは年神を迎え入れるために置かれました．松の枝が使われるのは，松が長寿の象徴だと信じられているためです．門松は一対で家やお店の玄関に飾ります．
Kadomatsu, traditional New Year's decorations, were originally used to welcome in the New Year's god. It is common to use pine branches for *kadomatsu* because they are regarded as a symbol of longevity. *Kadomatsu* are set up in pairs in front of the gateposts of houses and shops.

カドミウム 〖化学〗 cadmium [U] (❖元素記号 Cd)

かとりせんこう 蚊取り線香 mosquito coil [C]

カトリック (教義·信仰) Catholicism [U]; (教徒) Catholic [C] ―カトリックの Catholic ∥(ローマ)カトリック教会 the (Roman) *Catholic* Church / カトリックの司祭 a *Catholic* priest

かな 仮名 🗻 *kana*, the Japanese syllabary [síləbèri] ➡かたかな，ひらがな ∥正しい[間違った]仮名づかい the proper [improper] use of *kana*

かなあみ 金網 wire netting [U]; (囲い) wire fence [C] ∥泥棒は金網を破って侵入した The burglar broke in through *the wire netting* [*fence*].

かない 家内 (家族) family [C]; (自分の妻) my wife, my better half ∥家内安全を祈願する pray for *the well-being* [*safety*] *of one's family*
‖家内工業 a cottage [home] industry

かなう[1] 叶う come* true, be realized ∥彼女の夢がかなった Her dream *has* ｢*come true* [*been realized, become a reality*].
◆かなわぬ恋[夢] an *impossible* love [dream] / やっと望みがかなった I *have had* my desire *fulfilled* at last.

かなう[2] 適う suit [他]; (役立つ) serve [他]; (満たす) meet* [他], measure up to …; (こたえる) 《公式的》 answer [他][自] ∥目的にかなった道具 a tool that *suits* [*serves, answers, meets*] *one's* purpose / それは彼らの要求に十分かなっている It *meets* [*measures up to, answers*] their request adequately. / 私の理想にかなう人はなかなか見つからなかった I couldn't easily find a person who *met my ideal*.
◆礼儀にかなったふるまい *polite* behavior / 彼女の言い分は理にかなっている What she says ｢*makes good sense* [*is reasonable, is rational, is logical*].

かなう[3] 敵う 柔道で君にかなう者はいない No one can *beat* [*match, rival*] you in judo. / You are without (*an*) *equal* in Judo. / (→君がいちばん柔道が強い) You are the strongest Judo wrestler. ➡かなわない

かなえる 叶える fulfill, 《英》 fulfil [他]; (実現する) realize [他] (❖進行形にはできない); (聞き入れる) hear* [他], 《公式的》 grant [他] ∥彼らは私たちの願いをかなえてくれた They *fulfilled* [*realized, heard, granted*] our request.
◆君の願いをかなえてやろう I'll *make* your wish *come true*.

かながわ 神奈川

神奈川県は本州の中央部に位置し，北で東京都に接しています．かつて鎌倉幕府が置かれ，さらに後の江戸時代には江戸(東京)と京都を結ぶ交通の要所でもありました．県都である横浜市には，日本の主要な国際貿易港の一つである横浜港があります．この港は19世紀半ばに開港し，ここから西洋の新しい思想や文明が日本にもたらされました．
Kanagawa Prefecture is located in central Honshu, bounded by Tokyo to the north. It was once the seat of the Kamakura military government, and later, in the Edo period, it was an important point on the highway connecting Edo (Tokyo) and Kyoto. Yokohama, the capital city, has one of the major international ports in Japan. The port opened in the middle of the 19th century, and new ideas and inventions of the West were introduced to Japan from here.

かなきりごえ 金切り声 scream [C], shriek [C] ∥恐怖で金切り声をあげる *give a scream* [*shriek*] of terror; *scream* [*shriek*] with terror / 金切り声をあげて助けを求める *give a scream* [*shriek*] for help; *scream* [*shriek*] for help

かなぐ 金具 metal fittings

かなぐりすてる かなぐり捨てる 恥も外聞もかなぐり捨てる *throw one's* honor *away*; *shed* [*discard*] *one's* honor

かなしい 悲しい

sad; (ひどく) 《文語》 sorrowful, mournful
悲しげな歌 a *mournful* [*sorrowful*] tune
彼は悲しそうな表情をしていた He had a *sad*

[sorrowful, mournful] look on his face./ His face looked sad [sorrowful, mournful].

その悲しい知らせに彼らはみな泣いた They all cried at the sad news.

何がそんなに悲しいの What makes you so sad?

彼がほかの町へ引っ越すと聞いて悲しかった I was [felt] sad to hear that he would move to another town.

悲しいことに，彼女を助けようとする人はだれもいなかった Sad to say, but there was no one who tried to help her./ To our sorrow [Regretfully], there was no one who tried to help her.

◆彼は悲しそうに窓の外を見つめていた She was looking out the window sadly [sorrowfully, mournfully].

かなしばり 金縛り

🖋「けさ方ベッドに縛りつけられたような感じで，全然動けなかったよ．いったい何なんだろう」，**金縛りにあったんだね** "Early this morning, I felt as if I had been tied down to my bed, so I couldn't move at all. What was it?" "Aha, you experienced *kanashibari*."

かなしみ 悲しみ sadness Ⓤ；(死や不幸による深い) sorrow Ⓤ (❖個々の悲しいことは Ⓒ でしばしば複数形で用いる)；(特定の原因による短く激しい) grief Ⓤ ∥耐えがたい悲しみ unbearable sadness [sorrow, grief]／悲しみで包まれた His death filled his family with grief [sorrow]./ 彼はガールフレンドにふられて悲しみに沈んでいる He is ⌈deep in sorrow [in deep sorrow] after being dropped by his girlfriend./ その老人は喜びも悲しみも経験してきた That old man has known joy and sorrow./ その少年は悲しみに打ちひしがれた The boy was overcome [overwhelmed] with grief./ The boy was grief-stricken.

かなしむ 悲しむ feel* [be] sad, feel sorrow；(人の死などを嘆く) grieve 🖉, mourn 🖉🖥

我々は彼の死を悲しんだ We felt ⌈sad about [sorrow for] his death./ (→嘆き悲しんだ) We mourned [grieved] over [for] his death.; We mourned his death.

◆深く悲しんでいる be deep in sorrow; be in deep sorrow／みんな次郎の失敗を悲しんだ(→気の毒に思った) All of us felt sorry over [about] Jiro's failure./ 彼がそんな悪いことをしたなんて悲しむべきことだ It is sad that he has done such a bad thing./ 彼の言葉は両親を悲しませた His words made his parents sad.

かなた 彼方 はるかかなたに高層ビルが見える I can see the skyscraper ⌈in the far distance [far off, far away]./ その彗星(は)は宇宙のかなたへ去っていった The comet went away into deep space./ 渡り鳥は海のかなたからやってくる Migrant birds come from beyond the sea.

カナダ Canada ——**カナダ人** Canadian Ⓒ

——**カナダ(人)の** Canadian

かなづち 金槌 hammer Ⓒ ∥金づちで壁にくぎを打つ drive a nail into the wall with *a hammer*; hammer a nail into the wall

[慣用表現] 彼は金づちだ(→全然泳げない) He can't swim ⌈*a stroke* [*at all*].

カナッペ canapé Ⓒ (❖フランス語から)

かなでる 奏でる バイオリン[曲]を奏でる play ⌈the violin [a tune]

かなめ 要 (要点) the point; (扇の) pivot Ⓒ

かなもの 金物 hardware Ⓤ, ironware Ⓤ ∥金物屋(店) a hardware store, (英)an ironmonger's; (商人) a hardware dealer, (英)an ironmonger

かならず 必ず

❶【きっと】certainly, surely; (間違いなく) without fail; (何としても) at any cost [price], at all cost(s)

[語法] certainlyはsurelyとほぼ同義に用いられるが，surelyより客観的事実に基づき，確信の度合いが強い．

必ずあなたを幸せにします I will *certainly* [*surely*] make you happy./ I will make you happy *for sure*./ I'm *certain* [*sure*] I can make you happy.

彼は必ず試験に合格する He will *certainly* [*surely*] pass the exam./ He is *certain* [*sure*] *to* pass the exam./ He will pass the exam *for sure*. (❖He が主語であっても上記の例はすべて話者の確信を表している)

彼女は欲しい物は必ず手に入れるというタイプだ She is the kind of person who will get what she wants ⌈*at any cost* [*at any price, at all costs*].

◆レポートを必ず期限どおりに提出するように *Be sure* [*certain*] *to* hand in your reports on time./ *Make sure* [*certain*] *to* hand in your reports on time./ *Don't forget to* hand in your reports on time.

❷【例外なく・いつも】always

僕は新宿に来ると必ずその店に寄る I *always* visit this shop when I come to Shinjuku./ *Whenever* I come to Shinjuku, I visit this shop.

彼女は必ずと言っていいほど問題を起こす She is *nearly always* a problem. (❖この problemは「扱いにくい人，やっかいな人」の意味)

◆学校帰りに必ずその本屋に寄ることにしている I ⌈*make a point of* visiting [*make it a point to* visit] the bookstore on my way home from school./ 我々はみんないつかは必ず死ぬ We all *must* die some day.

❸【必ずしも…ない】not always [necessarily]

お金が必ずしも幸福をもたらすとは限らない Money does *not always* [*necessarily*] bring happiness.

◆サッカーを好きな人が必ずしも上手だというわけではない *Not all* people that like [*Not everyone* that likes] soccer can play it

かなり　《口語的》pretty, rather, fairly,《主に英》quite;（相当に）considerably　かなりの《口語的》fair, a good（❖共に名詞の前で用いるが, a goodは口語では形容詞の前で副詞的に用いることがある）; considerable

【語法】
(1) prettyは最も一般的で, 話し言葉で多く用いる.
(2) good, wellなど好ましさを表す語の前で用いた場合, pretty, rather, quiteは好ましさを強調するが, fairlyは「まずまず」「まあまあ」という程度を表す.
(3) ratherはほかの語と異なり否定的意味合いで用いる場合が多くある∥きょうはかなり暑い It's *rather* hot today. / It's *pretty* hot today.（❖前者は暑すぎるという否定的なニュアンス. 後者は中立的. この例でfairlyを用いるとニュアンスは肯定的なものに傾く）
(4) ratherは比較級やtooの前で用いることができる.
(5) quiteが〈a(n)＋形容詞＋名詞〉とともに用いられる場合, a *quite* interesting movie, *quite* an interesting movieの両方が可能である.

かなり高齢の男性 a *pretty* [*rather, fairly, quite*] old man; *rather* [*quite*] an old man / かなりの数の人 a *fair* [*considerable*] *number of* people; *quite a few* people; *a good many* people

彼はかなりギターがうまい He plays the guitar *pretty* [*rather, quite, considerably*] well.

その商品はかなり粗悪な物だった The product was of *rather* [*pretty, quite, considerably*] poor quality.

外は思っていたよりもかなり寒かった It was *rather* [*considerably*] colder than I had thought.

彼女はかなりの値段でその洋服を買った She bought the clothes at *considerable* expense.

僕の家から駅まではかなりある It's *a good* distance from my home to the station. /（→駅は僕の家からかなり遠い）The station is *quite* a distance away from my home.

私が高校を卒業してからもうかなりになる It's been a *pretty* [*rather, fairly*] long time since I graduated from high school. / It's been *rather* [*quite*] a long time since I graduated from high school.

◆外国語を習得するにはかなりの忍耐が必要だ You need *a lot of* patience to master a foreign language. / 増税が我々の生活にかなりの影響を及ぼした The tax increases affected our lives *greatly*.

💬「彼の絵はどう？」「すごいよ. 彼は画家としてかなりのものだ」"What do you think of his paintings?" "They're amazing. He's *quite* [《口語的》*something of*] an artist."

カナリア canary [kənéri]

かなわない 敵わない ❶【匹敵しない】be no match for ... ∥テニスでは彼にかなわない I *am no match for* him in tennis. / I *can't equal* [*rival*] him in tennis. /（→彼は僕よりすぐれたテニスプレーヤーだ）He is a better tennis player than I (am). ◆ギターの腕前にかけてはだれも彼にかなわない He *has no equal* [*rival*] in playing the guitar. / *Nobody can equal* [*rival*] him in playing the guitar.

❷【我慢できない】この部屋は暑くてかなわない I *can't stand* [*put up with, bear*] the heat in this room. / The heat in this room *is quite unbearable*.

💬「お金貸してよ」「えっ, またかい？ 全く君にはかなわないな（→こんなに寛大な僕で君は幸運だよ）」"Will you lend me some money?" "Again? You're lucky I'm so patient."

かに 蟹 crab Ⓒ（❖肉はⓊ）⇨かにざ∥カニのはさみ the pincers [claws] of *a crab* / カニ肉 canned *crab*(*meat*)

かにく 果肉 flesh Ⓤ ∥リンゴの果肉 *the flesh of an apple*

かにざ 蟹座【天文・占星】Cancer Ⓤ（❖「蟹座の人」の意味ではⒸ）

がにまた bandy legs, bowlegs ──がにまたの bandy-legged, bowlegged ∥がにまたで歩く walk *bandy-legged* [*bowlegged*]

かにゅう 加入（入ること）entry Ⓒ Ⓤ;（団体などに入ること）admission Ⓤ ──加入する join ⓐ, enter ⓐ;（会員になる）become* a member of ... ∥労働組合に加入する join [*enter*] a labor union; *become a member of* a labor union
◆携帯電話に加入する *sign up for* a cellular phone / 電話に加入する（→設置してもらう）*have* a telephone *installed* / 保険に加入する *take out* insurance

∥加入者（会員）a member;（サービスへの）a subscriber;（保険の）a policyholder, the insured

カヌー canoe [kənúː] Ⓒ ∥カヌーをこぐ paddle *a canoe*; canoe

かね¹ 金

money Ⓤ;（現金）cash Ⓤ;（通貨）currency Ⓒ Ⓤ;（硬貨）coin Ⓒ Ⓤ;（紙幣）《米》bill,《英》note Ⓒ

《～(の)金》
多額[小額]の金 a large [small] amount of *money* / 汚い金 dirty *money* / 外国の金 foreign *currencies* / 偽金 counterfeit *money*

彼は有り金すべてをギャンブルにつぎ込んだ He poured *all his money* into gambling. / *All of his money* went on [to] gambling.

《金が・は》
私にはお金がない I'm [*pressed for* [*out of*] *money* [*cash*]. /（→持ち合わせがない）I have no *money* [*cash*] with [on] me.

お金がなくなってきた My *money* is running out.

多少お金が入ったので旅行でもしようと思っている I'm thinking of going on a trip because I've got some *money*.

新しい車を買うお金はありません I don't have

enough *money* to buy a new car. / I can't *afford* a new car.

◆アパートを借りるのはお金がかかりすぎる Renting an apartment「*costs* too much [*is too costly*].

🅔「あした返すから、少し貸してくれないかな」「あいにく余分な金がないんだ」"Can you lend me some *money*? I'll pay you back tomorrow." "I'm afraid there's no *money* to spare."

【金を】
銀行に金を預ける *deposit money* in a bank /
銀行から金を下ろす *withdraw money* from a bank / 寄付でお金を集める *raise money* by subscription

彼は金(→紙幣と硬貨)をズボンのポケットに入れた He put *the bills and coins* into his trouser pocket.

他人からお金を借りるのは好きでない I don't like to *borrow money* from others.

彼女はなけなしの金を私にくれた She gave me what little *money* she had to me.

そのCDを買うお金をためておいた I *saved* some *money* for the CD.

お金をむだづかいしてはいけない Don't waste *your money*.

父は株で金をもうけた My father *made money* in the stock market.

スキーにかなりお金をかけた I *spent* a lot of *money* on skiing.

◆私が昼食のお金を払いますよ I'*ll pay for your lunch*. / 私はおじにお金を出してもらって大学に行った I went to university *at my uncle's expense*.

【金で】
お金で愛は買えない *Money* can't buy love.

真理子は自分の金でステレオを買った Mariko bought the stereo with her own *money*.

彼女は金で動くような人ではない She won't *be tempted by money*.

【金の】
彼は金のためだけにそれをした He did it just *for money*.

金の心配ならいらないよ Don't worry about *the money*. / Never mind *the cost*.

健一は稼いだお金のすべてをすぐに使い果たした Kenichi soon「*used up* [*spent*, *consumed*] all *the money* he had earned.

【金に】
彼は金に汚い He is tight [stingy] with [about] *money*.

この絵は相当な金になるぞ This picture may be *worth* a considerable amount of *money*. / This picture may *make* us a considerable amount of *money*.

◆この仕事はたいして金にならない This job「*doesn't pay* well [*is not* very *profitable*].

【その他】
お金いくら持ってる? How much *money* do you have on [with] you?

🅔「お金、持ってる?」「少しなら」"Do you have any *money* with [on] you?" "Yes, I have some."

慣用表現 最後は金がものを言って、ビル建設をめぐる騒動は収まった *Money talked* in the end, and the disagreements about the construction of the building settled down. / その車を手に入れるためには金に糸目はつけない If I could get that car, *I would pay however much it costs*. / 金のなる木 *a money tree*

ことわざ 金の切れ目が縁の切れ目 Nobody knows you when you're down and out. (→金がなくなるとだれからも見捨てられる) / 金は天下の回り物 Money comes and goes. (→金はやってきて去ってゆく); Money is a great traveler in the world. (→金は世界を回る偉大な旅行者だ) / 地獄のさたも金しだい ➡ じごく / 時は金なり Time is money.

かね² 鐘 bell ⓒ /教会の鐘 *a church bell* / 鐘を鳴らす ring [toll] *a bell* (✿toll は弔いなどで鳴らすこと) / お寺の鐘をつく strike *a bell* at a temple / 鐘が正午を告げた The bell rang out noon.

かねあい 兼ね合い 予算との兼ね合いで、旅行の日程を1日短くした *Because of* my budget, I shortened the trip schedule by one day.

かねかし 金貸し moneylender ⓒ

かねがね かねがね(→長い間)お会いしたいと思っておりました I've looked forward to seeing you *for a long time*. / その件に関してはかねがね(→何度も)伺っております I've heard [been told] about it *many times*. / (→たくさん)I've heard *a lot* about it.

かねそなえる 兼ね備える 当社の製品は実用性と独創性を兼ね備えています Our products *combine* practicality *and* [*with*] originality. / Our products *have both* practicality *and* originality.

かねつ¹ 加熱 heating ⓤ ──加熱する heat ⓗ あたためる、ねっする ‖加熱器具 a heater / 加熱処理 heat treatment / 非加熱血液製剤 an unheated blood product

かねつ² 過熱 overheating ⓤ ──過熱する overheat ⓗ ‖ヒーターが過熱した The heater *overheated*. ◆過熱ぎみのブーム an overheated fad

かねづかい 金遣い 妹は金づかいが荒い(→浪費する)My sister *is extravagant* [*wasteful of money*]. / (→湯水のごとくお金を使う)My sister *spends money like water*.

かねづまり 金詰まり (金融のひっ迫) tightness ⓤ, tight money ⓤ; (不足) shortage of money ⓒⓤ ‖金詰まりで計画の規模が縮小された The plan was reduced in scale because of *the shortage of money*.

◆金詰まりだ Money is tight.

かねて (ずっと) for a long time; (何度も) many times; (以前) before, previously; (すでに) already /かねてからの希望がついにかなった What I'd been wanting *for a long time* came true at last. / おうわさはかねてより伺っております I've been told about you *many times*. / (→あなたの名前は聞き慣れている) Your name is familiar to me.

-かねない would [could] do, be likely to do; (可能性がある) be capable of doing ∥あいつならやりかねない That guy would [could] do that. / That guy is capable of doing that.

かねまわり 金回り 金回りがいい be well-off [on easy street, flush] / 金回りが悪い be badly-off [hard up]

かねめ 金目 金めの物を学校に持ってこないように Do not bring「valuable articles [valuables] to school.

かねもうけ 金儲け moneymaking ◆金もうけをする make money / 彼は金もうけのためなら何でもする He'll do anything for money.

かねもち 金持ち rich [wealthy] person; (金持ちの人々) rich [wealthy] people, the rich [wealthy] ――金持ちの、rich, wealthy,《口語的/軽蔑的》made of money (❖rich がもっぱら金銭面での豊かさを表すのに対して、wealthy は社会的地位の高さなども含意する) ∥金持ちになる become [get] rich / 彼はものすごい金持ちだ He is really rich [wealthy]. / 彼は金持ちの家に生まれた He was born into a rich [wealthy] family. / 金持ちが必ずしも幸せだとは限らない The rich [wealthy] are not always happy.
◆金持ちと結婚する《口語的》marry into money / 大金持ち(→億万長者)になる become a billionaire

かねる 兼ねる (両方に役立つ) serve as both ... and ~; (2役を務める) double as ...; (両立させる) combine ... and [with] ~ ∥このソファーはベッドも兼ねる This sofa doubles as a bed. / This sofa serves as both a sofa and a bed. / This sofa serves as a bed as well.
◆彼は趣味と実益を兼ねて絵画を集めている He is collecting paintings for both business and pleasure.
ことわざ 大は小を兼ねる ⇨ だい(大)

-かねる cannot do, be unable to do ⇨ -かねない, できる ∥その件に関しては私には何とも申し上げかねます I'm afraid I can't [am unable to] say anything about the matter./ (→言える立場にない) I'm afraid I'm not in a position to say anything about the matter. / 困っている彼を見るに見かねて宿題を手伝ってやった (→彼が困っているのを知っていたので手伝わずにはいられなかった) Knowing he was at a loss, I couldn't help but help him do his homework. / 彼はちょっと紳士とは言いかねる He isn't quite a gentleman.

かねん 可燃 ――可燃性 (in)flammability, combustibility ――可燃性の inflammable, combustible ◆可燃ごみ burnable trash
‖可燃物 combustibles, inflammables

かのう¹ 可能 ――可能な possible;(容易に実行可能な) feasible
彼女はその計画は実行可能だと強調した She stressed that it was possible to carry out the plan. / 速読はだれにでも可能です Rapid reading is possible for everyone.
彼は可能なたかぎり資料を収集した He collected as much data as possible.
◆彼が無罪になる可能性はあるのですか Is there any possibility that he will be found innocent? / きょう雪になる可能性は二[高い] There's no [a strong] likelihood of snow today. / 彼女は名ピアニストになる可能性を秘めている She has potential as a great pianist. / この痛み止めを飲みすぎると心臓発作を引き起こす可能性がある An overdose of this painkiller can induce (a) heart attack. / 科学技術の発達は将来我々が宇宙で生活することを可能にするかもしれない The development of technology may enable us to live in outer space in the future.

かのう² 化膿 ――化膿する become* infected, fester;(吹き出物などが) come* to a head

かのじょ 彼女 ――代 (彼女は・彼女が) she; (彼女の) her; (彼女に・彼女を) her; (彼女の物) hers; (彼女自身) herself ――名 (恋人) girlfriend
きょうは彼女とデートかい Are you going on a date with your girlfriend (again) today?

かば 河馬 hippopotamus [hìpəpátəməs] (複 ~es, hippopotami),《口語》hippo

カバー cover, covering; (本の) (dust [book]) jacket ◆dust cover ともいう。英語の cover は表紙を指す ――カバーする (覆う) cover; (埋め合わせをする) cover, make* up for ...; (曲を) cover
いすのカバー a chair cover [covering] / 自動車にカバーをかける put a cover [covering] over a car / 体力の不足を気力でカバーする cover [make up for] a lack of physical power by willpower
‖ハードカバー a hardcover, a hardback / ベッドカバー(装飾用の) a bedspread / まくらカバー a pillowcase

かばう 庇う (守る) protect, shield; (弁護する) speak* (up) for ...; (支持する) stand* (up) for ...; (いたわる) take* care of ... ∥彼は暴漢の前に立ちはだかって彼女をかばった He protected [shielded] her by standing in front of the hoodlum. / 彼女は彼が何も悪いことをしていないと言ってかばった She spoke [stood] (up) for him saying that he did nothing wrong. / 彼は痛めた右足をかばうようにして歩いた He walked taking care of his injured right leg.

がはく 画伯 ⇨ がか

かばやき 蒲焼き ウナギのかば焼き spitchcocked eel (seasoned with sugar and soy sauce) (❖spitchcock は「ウナギなどを裂いて直火(じかび)で焼く」の意味だが、あまり一般的な語ではない)

かはん 河畔 the riverside ◆セーヌ河畔のホテル a hotel on the Seine

かばん 鞄 bag; (通学用) schoolbag, satchel (❖satchel は肩からさげたり、背負っ

たりする物）；（革製で書類用）briefcase ©；（書類・絵画用の折りかばん）portfolio ©（複 ～s）；（旅行かばん）suitcase ©；（大型の旅行かばん）trunk ©；（旅行時のかばん類）《集合的》baggage ⓤ, luggage ⓤ

かばんをあける［閉める］open [close] *a bag* / 中身の詰まったかばん *a fat bag* / かばんの中を捜す dig into *the bag*

彼は本をかばんに入れた He put the books in *his bag*.

彼女はかばんから教科書を出した She took a textbook out of *her schoolbag*.

がばん 画板 drawing board ©, panel ©

かはんしん 下半身 the lower part [half] of the body, the part of the body below the waist ➪ じょうはんしん

かはんすう 過半数 majority ©（通例単数形）/ 過半数を占めている be in *a* [*the*] *majority* / 過半数を獲得する gain [get, win] *a majority* / 過半数はその案に反対だった The majority were against the proposal.

かひ 可否 ➪ さんぴ, ぜひ

かび¹ 黴 mold ⓤ ©；（白かび）mildew ⓤ ◆パンにかびが生えた The bread *got* [*became*] *moldy*. / この部屋はかび臭い This room smells *musty* [*fusty*].

かび² 華美 ──華美な（はでな）showy;（華やかな）gorgeous;（けばけばしい）gaudy, loud / 華美な服装 *showy* clothes

かひつ 加筆 ➪ かきくわえる

がびょう 画鋲 《米》thumbtack [θʌ́mtæ̀k] ©, 《英》drawing pin © / 壁に画びょうでカレンダーをはる place a calendar on the wall with *thumbtacks*; pin [tack] up a calendar on the wall with *thumbtacks*; *thumbtack* a calendar on the wall

かびる 黴びる ➪ かび（黴）

かびん¹ 花瓶 (flower) vase ©

かびん² 過敏 ──過敏な（精神的に）(hyper)sensitive, nervous;（肉体的刺激に）(hyper)sensitive, nervous;（薬などに）hypersensitive / 特定の薬に対する過敏な反応 a *hypersensitive* reaction to a particular medicine / 彼は試験を前にして神経過敏になっていた He was *nervous* [*hypersensitive*] with the exam near at hand.

かぶ¹ 株

❶【株式】stock © ⓤ, share ©《通例複数形 ～s》

株に投資する put money into *stocks*; invest *one's* money in *stocks* / 株でもうける［損する］make [lose] money on the *stock market*

彼女はその会社の株の25パーセントを所有している She holds 25 percent of *the company's stock*. / She holds 25 percent of *the stocks* [*shares*] in that company.

ニューヨーク株式市場で株価が下がった［暴落した］*Stocks* fell [crashed] on the New York stock market.

鉄鋼株が値上がりをしている Steel *stocks* have been「going up [rising].

❷【植物】

セロリ1株 *a bunch of* celery

庭にアジサイを2株植えた I planted *two* hydrangeas in the garden.

‖株価 share [stock] prices / 株主《米》a stockholder,《主に英》a shareholder / 成長株（株の）a growth stock;（人）a hopeful [promising,《口語的》up and coming] person

<慣用表現> テストで満点を取って彼の株が上がった He got a perfect score on the exam, and it made his *stock rise*.

かぶ² 下部 the lower part ──下部の lower;（下位の）subordinate //下部組織 a *subordinate* organization; a subsystem

‖下部構造（建造物・組織などの）a substructure

かぶ³ 蕪 turnip © ⓤ

かふう 家風 family custom [tradition] ©

カフェ café, cafe [kæféɪ] ©, coffee house [《英》bar] © ➪ きっさてん

カフェイン caffeine [kæfíːn] ⓤ ◆カフェイン抜きのコーヒー decaffeinated [*caffeine-free*] coffee;《口語的》decaf（❖カフェインを含むコーヒーは regular coffee という）

カフェオレ café au lait ⓤ（❖フランス語から）

カフェテリア cafeteria © ➪ しょくどう（食堂）

がぶがぶ 走った後で水をがぶがぶ飲んだ I「*gulped* (*down*) [*guzzled*] water after running.

かぶき 歌舞伎 kabuki ⓤ

歌舞伎は17世紀に始まった日本の伝統演劇です。役者の化粧をくま取りといい、その色と形は役によって違います。赤は正義と勇気を意味し、藍（❖）色は悪を意味しているといったぐあいです。徳川幕府が女性が舞台に上がることを禁じて以来、女性の役も男性役者が演じることになりました。女性役の役者を女形（*）といいます。
Kabuki is a form of traditional Japanese theater that originated in the 17th century. The make-up of the actors is called *kumadori*, and the colors and designs differ according to the character of each part: red stands for virtue and bravery, dark blue for vice. Since the Tokugawa shogunate put a ban on women performing on the stage, even the female roles have been played by special male actors who are known as *oyama*.

かふくぶ 下腹部 the lower abdomen

かぶけん 株券 stock [share] certificate ©

かぶさる 被さる be over …, cover ⓗ；（部分的に重なる）overlap ⓗ ◆彼の失敗の責任が僕にかぶさってきた（→責任を負わされた）I *was made to assume* (the) responsibility for his failure.

かぶしき 株式 stock © ⓤ, share ©《通例複数形 ～s》‖株式会社《米》a corporation, an incorporated [a stock] company（❖社名中では《米》Corp. や Inc. または《英》Ltd などの略語を用いることもある）/ 株式市場 a stock market / 株式取引所 a stock exchange / 株式仲買人 a (stock)broker

カフスボタン ⚠ cuff link ©, cufflink ©（通

かぶせる

例複数形 ～s）（❖「カフスボタン」は和製英語）∥カフスボタンをかける[はずす] fasten [remove] *cuff links*

かぶせる 被せる ❶【物を】put* 󠄀on; (覆う) cover 󠄀∥母親は娘に帽子をかぶせた The mother *put* a cap *on* her daughter. / マジシャンは箱に毛布をかぶせた The magician *put* a blanket *over* the box. / The magician *covered* the box *with* a blanket.

❷【責任・罪などを】彼は事故の責任を私にかぶせた He *put* [*laid*] the blame for the accident *on* me.

カプセル capsule [kǽpsəl] ⓒ ∥カプセルホテル a hotel offering self-contained sleeping berths / タイムカプセル a time capsule

かふそく 過不足 クッキーを5人で過不足なく(→均等に)分け合う distribute cookies *equally* among the five

かぶと 兜 helmet ⓒ ∥彼の音楽にかける情熱にはかぶとを脱ぐよ(→脱帽する) My hat is off to his daring efforts in music.

かぶとむし 甲虫 beetle ⓒ (❖カブトムシを含む甲虫類をいう)

かぶぬし 株主 (米) stockholder, (主に英) shareholder ⓒ ∥株主総会 a stockholders' [shareholders'] general meeting

がぶり 犬をがぶりとかまれた The dog *sank his teeth into* my hand.

かぶりつく bite* 󠄀ⓗ, attack 󠄀ⓗ ∥彼はハンバーガーにかぶりついた He *bit* [*bit into*, *attacked*] the hamburger.

かぶる 被る

❶【帽子など】(かぶる動作) put* 󠄀on; (かぶっている状態) wear* 󠄀ⓗ, have* ... on
帽子をかぶる *put* 󠄀*on* a hat [a hat *on*]
彼は黄色い帽子をかぶっていた He 「*was wearing* [*wore*] a yellow hat. / He *had* a yellow hat *on*.
◆彼女は帽子をかぶったまま食事を始めた She began to eat *with* her hat *on*. / (→帽子を取らずに) She began to eat *without taking* her hat *off*. / 彼女は帽子を目深にかぶった She *pulled* her hat *over* her eyes. / 父はふとんを頭からかぶって寝ている My father is sleeping with the top quilt *pulled over* his head.

❷【覆われている】be covered with ...
僕の本はほこりをかぶっていた My books *were covered with* dust.
◆雪をかぶった木々 snow-*covered* trees

❸【浴びる】(自らかける) pour [dash] ... over oneself 󠄀ⓗ
バケツの水を頭からかぶった I *poured* a bucketful of water *over* my head. / (→かけられた) I *had* a bucketful of water *poured over* my head.
◆我々のボートは大量の水をかぶった Our boat *shipped* [*took on*] a lot of water.

❹【他人の罪などを】
男は友人の犯した罪をかぶった The man *took* the blame for his friend's crime.
彼女は友達の借金をかぶった She *paid* her friend's debt. / She *paid* the debt for her friend.

かぶれる ❶【皮膚が】(発疹(ほっしん)) come* 󠄀[break*] *out* in a rash; (炎症) get* 󠄀irritated ∥汗でかぶれる *break out in a rash* from sweat; *get irritated* by sweat

❷【考えなどが】be influenced ∥彼女は西洋哲学にかぶれている She *is influenced by* Western philosophy. / (→熱中している) She *is involved in* Western philosophy. / あいつはアメリカかぶれだ He *is* too much *influenced* by American ways of thinking. / He is too Americanized. ◆ロックにかぶれている(→夢中である) *be enthusiastic for* rock

かふん 花粉 pollen ⓤ ∥花粉症 hay fever, pollen allergy

かぶんすう 仮分数 improper fraction ⓒ

かべ 壁

❶【建物の】wall ⓒ; (間仕切り) partition ⓒ
壁の穴 a hole in *the wall* / 壁をこわす break down *a wall* / 壁に絵をかける hang a picture *on the wall* / 壁に寄りかかる lean against *a wall*
その車は壁に激しく衝突した The car bumped hard against [on, into] *the wall*.
家の壁にはツタがはっていた Ivy crept up *the wall* of the house.
1部屋を壁で仕切って2部屋にした I divided the room in two with *a partition*.

❷【障壁】barrier ⓒ
言葉の壁 a language *barrier*
マラソンで2時間の壁を破ることは可能だろうか Is it possible to break *the* two hour *barrier* in the marathon?
◆僕たちの計画は壁に突き当たった Our plan has run up against *a wall*.
∥壁かけ a wall ornament / 壁紙 (a) wallpaper / 壁新聞 a wall newspaper / ベルリンの壁 the Berlin Wall
ことわざ 壁に耳あり Walls have ears.

かへい 貨幣 money ⓤ; (通貨) currency ⓒ ⓤ; (硬貨) coin ⓒ; (紙幣) paper [soft] money ⓤ, (米) bill ⓒ, (英) note ⓒ ∥貨幣価値 monetary [currency] value / 貨幣制度 a monetary [currency] system / 貨幣単位 a monetary [currency] unit

かべん 花弁 petal ⓒ

かほう¹ 下方 最上階から下方を見下ろす look *downward* [*down*] from the top floor

かほう² 果報 (good) luck ⓤ ◆果報者 a *lucky* person
ことわざ 果報は寝て待て Good things come to those who wait. (→待つ者にはよいことがやってくる)

かほう³ 家宝 family treasure ⓒ; (先祖伝来の財産) heirloom [éərlùːm] ⓒ

かほご 過保護 overprotection ⓤ ——過保護な overprotective ∥過保護な親 *overprotective* parents / 過保護に育てられた子供 a child brought up *overprotected*

かぼそい か細い (やせた) thin; (ほっそりした) slender, slim; (弱々しい) feeble, weak, thin ∥か細い体の女性 a *thin* [*slender*, *slim*] woman / その子はか細い声で答えた

The child answered in a *feeble* [*weak, thin*] voice.

かぼちゃ 南瓜 (Japanese) pumpkin ⓒⓊ

かま¹ 釜 iron pot ⓒ
かまで炊いたごはん rice boiled in *an iron pot* ‖電気がま an electric rice cooker
慣用表現 同じ釜の飯を食う(→一つ屋根の下で暮らす) *live under one* [*the same*] *roof*

かま² 窯 kiln ⓒ; (炉) furnace ⓒ ‖かま元 a pottery

かま³ 鎌 (小型の) sickle ⓒ; (両手で使う大型の) scythe [sáiθ]
慣用表現 彼女にかまをかけて本当のところを聞き出した I *tricked* her into telling me the truth.

かまう 構う
❶【気にかける】mind ⓣ, care ⓘ
私のことはおかまいなく Don't *mind* me.
麻理は服装のことは全くかまわない Mari 「*doesn't care about* [*takes no thought for*] her appearance.
僕はどうなってもかまわない I *don't care* what happens to me.
◆美紀は私たちに「かまわないでよ」と言った Miki said to us, "*Leave me alone.*" / 君が来ようが来まいが僕にいっこうにかまわない(→何の違いもない) It *doesn't make any difference* to me whether you come or not. / 彼女は「待って」と頼んだが, 彼はかまわず歩き続けた She asked him to stop, but he walked on *regardless*. / 彼女は騒音にかまわず話し続けた She carried on talking *in spite of* the loud noise. / いたいならここにいてくれてかまわない You *can* stay here if you like. / どこに行ってもかまいません It *doesn't matter* where you go. / ここで写真を撮ってもかまいませんか *Are we allowed to* take pictures here? / どんな服でもかまいません Any clothes will *do*. / いくらかかってもかまいません Expense *is no object*. / それがどうした. かまうものか *What the heck!*

💬「ここでたばこを吸ってもかまいませんか」「ええ, かまいませんよ, どうぞ」"*Do you mind if* I smoke here?" "No, I don't. Go ahead." (❖「いいえ, 困ります」なら Yes, I do.)

💬「ごめんなさい. 間違ってあなたのペンを使ってしまいました」「いや, かまいませんよ」"I'm sorry. I used your pen by mistake." "*That's all right.*"

❷【相手をする】(…とかかわりをもつ) have* something to do with ...
あんなふざけたやつにかまってはいられない I have no time to *have anything to do with* such a silly guy.
◆ちょっと赤ん坊をかまって(→遊んで)やってくれないか Please *play with* the baby for a while.

かまえ 構え パンチの構えをする pull back *one's* arm for a swing / 19世紀風の構えの家 a house built in the 19th century *style*

かまえる 構える (姿勢をとる) take* a posture [stance, position]; (用意する) get* ready; (住居を) take* up (*one's*) residence ‖相手に殴りかかろうと *take an aggressive stance* / ボールが来てもいいように構えなさい(→用意しなさい) *Get ready* for the ball. / 彼は郊外に家を構えた He took up residence in the suburbs. ◆刀を構える *hold up* a sword / カメラを構える *point* a camera / のんきに構えている場合じゃないよ It's not the time for you to *take it easy*. / そう構えずに楽になさい *Don't be* so tense. Just relax.

がまがえる 蝦蟇蛙【動物】toad ⓒ

かまきり 蟷螂 (praying) mantis ⓒ

かまくら 🏠 *kamakura*, an igloo-like snow hut which is made for children to play in

-がましい 言い訳がましいかもしれませんが, 会議を休んだのは腹痛のためなんです *It may sound like I'm making excuses*, but I couldn't attend the meeting because of stomachache. ⇨ おしつけがましい, さしでがましい

かまぼこ 蒲鉾 🏠 *kamaboko*, a piece of boiled fish paste ◆かまぼこ型(→半円筒形)のビニールハウス a *semicylindrical* plastic greenhouse

かまわない 構わない (気にしない) do* not mind, do not care; (問題ではない) do not matter ⇨ かまう /彼が私のことをどう言おうとかまわない I *don't care* what he says about me.

がまん 我慢 (忍耐) patience Ⓤ; (継続的な忍耐・抵抗) endurance Ⓤ; (ねばり強さ) perseverance Ⓤ; (寛容) tolerance ⓒⓊ ──我慢する be patient; (痛み・不快な状況に) bear* ⓣ; (耐え続ける) endure ⓣ; (不快な状況に) stand* ⓣ; (許容する) tolerate ⓣ; (いつものことと受け入れる)《口語的》put* up with ...
あいつには我慢ができない I can't 「*put up with* [*bear, stand*] him. / I *have no patience* with him.
よくもまあ彼の言うことを我慢して聞けるね How can you *have the patience* to listen to him?
最後まで我慢して聞いて *Bear with* me till I finish talking.
歯医者の予約の日までこの歯痛を我慢しなければならない I must *endure* this toothache until my dental appointment.
あの音は我慢がならない I can't *stand* that sound.
私はもうこんなことには我慢できない This is more than I can *stand*.
それは君が我慢しなきゃいけないことだ That's something you have to *put up with*.
私は我慢の限界に達した I *reached the limits of my patience*.
我慢しなさい *Be patient*.
ここが我慢のしどころだ You *must be patient* now.
試合は0対0のまま終盤に入り我慢比べになりそうだった The game reached the last stage with a score of 0 to 0 and took on the appearance of *an endurance contest*.

◆遊びたいのをどうにか我慢して宿題を終わらせた I managed to *keep myself from* playing and finished my homework. / 彼女は我慢(→自制)できずにわんわん泣いた She lost *control* and wailed. / 差し当たりこのパソコンで我慢しよう(→間に合わせよう) We'll have to *make do with* this computer for the present. / いいよ、安いほうで我慢するよ(→手を打つ) All right, I'll *settle for* the cheaper one. / 今回だけは我慢してやる(→許してやる) I'll *forgive* you just this once. / お金がなかったのでその本を買うのを我慢した(→あきらめた) I *gave up* buying the book for lack of money. / 彼は彼女が戻るのを我慢強く待った He waited *patiently* for her to return.

かみ¹ 髪

hair Ⓤ (✤一本一本の毛を指す場合は Ⓒ)
⇒ 場面・状況別会話 p.1710

<u>コロケーション</u> –hair–
【形容詞＋～】薄い～ thin [spare] hair / 濃い～ thick hair / 黒い～ dark hair / 茶色い～ brown hair / 白髪まじりの～ gray hair / 長い～ long hair / 短い～ short hair / 縮れた～ frizzy hair / まっすぐな～ straight hair / カールした～ curly hair / ぼさぼさの～ disheveled hair / 結んでいない～ loose hair / つやのある～ lustrous hair / 細い～ fine hair

【髪が・は】
私の髪は硬くて量が多い My *hair* is stiff and thick. (✤「柔らかい」は soft,「量が少ない」は thin)
髪が1本抜けた A *hair* fell out.
彼の髪は肩まで垂れている His *hair* comes to his shoulders.

【髪を】
髪を洗う[シャンプーする] wash [shampoo] *one's hair* / 髪をブラシ[くし]でとかす brush [comb] *one's hair*
通子は髪を長く伸ばしている Michiko wears *her hair* long. (✤客観的に「彼女は髪が長い」という場合は She has long hair. という)
私は月に1度髪を切る I have *my hair* cut once a month.
きのう美容院で髪をセットしてもらった I had *my hair* set at the beauty parlor yesterday.
私はぬれた髪をドライヤーで乾かした I dried *my* wet *hair* with a hair drier.
彼は髪を赤く染めた He colored *his hair* red.
彼女は髪を編んでいる She wears *her hair* in braids.
妹は髪をお下げにした My sister let *her hair* down.
彼女は髪を真ん中で分けている She parts *her hair* in the middle.

【その他】
ひと房の髪 a strand of *hair* / 髪にパーマをかけてもらう have *one's hair* permed
彼女は髪にピンクのリボンをつけている She has [wears] a pink ribbon in *her hair*.
髪の毛を切っている間我慢していてね Be patient while I'm cutting *your hair*.
🗨「この新しい髪型、どう」「よく似合ってるよ」 "How do you like *my* new *hairstyle*?" "It looks nice."
‖髪飾り a hair ornament

かみ² 紙

paper Ⓤ

<u>語法</u>
paper を数えるときは、a piece [sheet] of paper, two pieces [sheets] of paper のようにいう。a sheet of paper は一定の大きさ・型をもつ紙を指し、それも含めた紙片一般を a piece of paper という。

1枚の紙を2つに折る fold a sheet of *paper* double
この紙には何か書いてあるぞ Something is written on this *paper*.
この人形は紙でできている This doll is made of *paper*.
クリスマスプレゼントをきれいな紙で包んだ I wrapped the Christmas present in pretty *paper*.
‖紙おむつ a disposable diaper / 紙コップ a paper cup / 紙製品 a paper product / 紙タオル a paper towel / 紙テープ a streamer, ticker tape / 紙飛行機 a paper plane / 紙袋 a paper bag / 紙やすり sandpaper / 厚紙 cardboard / カーボン紙 (a) carbon paper / 壁紙 (a) wallpaper / 画用紙 drawing paper / 銀紙 silver paper / 再生紙 recycled paper / 包み紙 wrapping paper, a wrapper / 白紙 blank paper / はり紙 a notice, a bill / ボール紙 chipboard / 和紙 Japanese paper

かみ³ 神

(多神教の男神) god Ⓒ; (多神教の女神) goddess Ⓒ; (キリスト教など一神教の) God (✤冠詞なしで単数形で用いる。代名詞は He, His, Him で受ける), (公式的に) the Deity
全能の神 Almighty *God*; *God* Almighty / 神の崇拝 the worship of *gods* [*God*] / やおよろずの(→無数の)神 myriads of *gods* / 福の神 the *god* of well-being / ギリシャ[ローマ]神話中の神々 *the gods* in the Greek [Roman] myths
この神社に祭られているのは何の神ですか Which *god* is this shrine dedicated to?
息子が無事戻るよう神に祈った I prayed to "*a god* [*the gods*, *God*]" for my son's safe return.
神を信じている人は多い Many people believe in *gods* [*God*].
<u>慣用表現</u> 神に誓ってうそは言いません *In God's name* [*In the name of God*], I won't tell a lie. / 成功するかどうかは神のみぞ知る *God* [*Heaven*] (*only*) *knows* whether we will make it or not. / そんな非道が許されるようでは神も仏もあったもんじゃない(→慈悲というものはない) If such barbarities were accepted, *there wouldn't be any mercy in the world*.

[ことわざ] 苦しいときの神頼み ⇒ くるしい / さわらぬ神にたたりなし Let sleeping dogs lie. (→眠っている犬は寝かしておけ)

かみ[4] 加味 ━━加味する (考慮する) take* ... into consideration / 彼の意見も加味して旅行先を決定した We decided the destination of our trip *taking his opinion into consideration*.

かみあう 嚙み合う (意見などが) mesh 自; (歯車などが) mesh 自, engage 自, bite* 自 ∥クラスメートと話がかみ合わない I *don't mesh with* my classmates. / 歯車がかみ合わない The cogs *don't mesh* [*engage, bite*].

かみがかり 神がかり 神がかり的な (→並みはずれた)テクニック exceptional [extraordinary] technique

がみがみ 母さんはいつももっと勉強しろとがみがみ言う My mother *is* always 「*nagging* (*at*) [*getting at*] me to study harder. / もう分かったからがみがみ言うのはやめてくれ All right, that's enough. So, don't *be such a nag*. (❖ a nag は「がみがみ言う人」の意味)

かみきりむし 髪切り虫 long-horned beetle 回, longicorn

かみきる 嚙み切る bite* off, gnaw [nɔ́ː] off ∥硬い肉をかみ切る *bite* [*gnaw*] *off* tough meat

かみきれ 紙切れ a scrap of paper; (細長いもの) a slip [strip] of paper, slip 回

かみくず 紙屑 wastepaper 回; (ごみ) litter 回 ∥…を紙くず同然に扱う treat ... *as if it were as worthless as wastepaper*

かみくだく 嚙み砕く (物を) crunch 他 自, chew 他 自; (やさしく言う) simplify 他
◆その件に関してかみ砕いて (→平易な言葉で) 説明する explain the matter *in simple terms*

かみころす 嚙み殺す (かんで殺す) bite* ... to death; (あくびなどをこらえる) stifle 他, suppress 他 ∥あくびをかみ殺す *stifle* [*suppress*] a yawn / 笑いをかみ殺す *stifle* [*suppress*] a smile [laugh]

かみざ 上座 (食卓・部屋の) the top; (食卓の) the head ∥テーブルの上座に座る sit at *the head* [*top*] of a table

かみさま 神様 ⇒ かみ(神)

かみしばい 紙芝居 *kamishibai*, storytelling illustrated by a series of pictures

かみしめる 嚙みしめる (かむ) bite* 他; (浸っている) be immersed in ...; (楽しむ) enjoy 他; (じっくり考える) chew 他 自; (公式的) ruminate on ... ∥唇をかみしめる *bite one's lip* / 成功の喜びをかみしめる *be immersed in the joy of one's success; enjoy one's success*

かみそり 剃刀 razor 回; (安全かみそり) safety razor 回; (電気かみそり) electric razor 回, (electric) shaver 回 ∥かみそりの刃 the edge of *a razor*; a *razor* blade (❖後者は替え刃) / かみそりでひげをそる shave with *a razor* / かみそり負けする get *razor burn*

かみだな 神棚 a *kamidana*, a household Shinto altar

かみつ 過密 ━━過密な (込み合った) overcrowded; (道路・場所などが混雑した) congested; (人口過剰の) overpopulated; (余裕のない) tight; (詰め込まれた) impacted ∥過密都市 an *overcrowded* [an *overpopulated*, a *congested*] city / 人口過密地域 an *overcrowded* [*overpopulated*] area; a *densely populated* area / 過密スケジュール a *tight* schedule / 過密ダイヤ a *tight* train schedule

かみつく 嚙みつく bite* 他 自; (くってかかる) (口語的) bite *a person's head off* ∥彼女の犬が私の手にかみついた Her dog *bit* me on the hand. / この犬はかみつきますか Does this dog *bite*? / 彼は上司にかみついた He *bit* his boss's *head off*.

かみて 上手 (観客に向かって舞台の左側) stage left, the left (side of the stage)

かみなり 雷 (雷鳴) thunder 回; (雷鳴を伴う稲妻・落雷) thunderbolt 回; (稲妻) lightning 回

雷の音 a clap [rumble, roll] of *thunder* (❖ clap は突然の音. rumble, roll はゴロゴロととどろく音)

その子は雷におびえた The child was frightened at [by] *the thunder*.

雷が校庭の木に落ちた *Lightning* hit [struck] a tree in the schoolyard. / A tree in the schoolyard was hit [struck] by *lightning*.

男性は雷に打たれて死亡した The man was struck dead by *lightning*.

◆ずっと遠くで雷が鳴っている It's *thundering* in the far distance. (❖動詞 thunder は it を主語とし「雷が鳴る」の意味)

[慣用表現] 彼は勉強を怠けてばかりいたのでついに父親の雷が落ちた His father *scolded* him at last for having neglected his studies for a long time.

∥雷雲 a thundercloud

かみのけ 髪の毛 ⇒ かみ(髪), け

かみはんき 上半期 the first half of the year

かみひとえ 紙一重 天才と狂人は紙一重だ There is *a thin line* between genius and insanity. / 紙一重でレースに勝った I won the race *by a nose*.

かみふぶき 紙吹雪 confetti 回

かみわざ 神業 (神の行い) an act of God; (人間業を超えた) superhuman feat 回; (並みはずれた) exceptional [surpassing] feat 回; (奇跡) miracle 回

かみん 仮眠 doze 回, nap 回, (口語的) snooze 回 ∥仮眠をとる take [have] *a doze* [*nap, snooze*]

かむ[1] 嚙む (かみつく) bite* 他 自; (かみこなす) chew 他 自.

つめをかむ癖 the habit of *biting one's* nails / ガムをかむ *chew* gum

犬に足をかまれた I *got* my leg *bitten* by a dog. / A dog *bit* me in [on] the leg.

よくかんで食べないとおなかをこわすよ *Chew* your food well before swallowing it, or you'll get a stomachache.

[慣用表現] 彼は負けた悔しさに唇をかんだ He bit

his lip, feeling frustrated that he had lost.

かむ² (鼻を) blow* [他] ∥ティッシュペーパーで鼻をかむ *blow one's nose* with tissue paper

ガム (チューインガム) (chewing) gum [U]; (風船ガム) bubble gum [U] ∥ガム1枚[1パック] a stick [pack] of (*chewing*) *gum* / ガムをかむ chew *gum*

がむしゃら がむしゃらに働く work *like a horse* / 試験に向けてがむしゃらに勉強した I studied *like mad* for the exams.

ガムテープ ⚠ packing tape [U], masking tape [U]

カムバック comeback [C]《通例単数形》 ──カムバックする come* back, make* [stage] a comeback

カムフラージュ camouflage [kǽməflɑ̀ːʒ] [U] [C] ──カムフラージュする camouflage [他]

かめ¹ 亀 turtle [C] (❖《主に英》では特にウミガメをいう); (陸ガメ) tortoise [tɔ́ːrtəs] [C]

[ことわざ] 亀の甲より年の功 Live and learn. (→長生きするほど物知りになる)

かめ² 瓶・甕 pot [C] (❖陶器の物は an earthenware pot); (広口の) jar [C]; (装飾用の) vase [C]

[短歌] 瓶にさす藤の花ぶさみじかければたたみの上にとどかざりけり (正岡子規)

For this vase of mine
the wisteria blossoms
were trimmed a bit too short,
so their petals could not reach
as far as the tatami.

かめい¹ 加盟 ──加盟する join [他]; (団体が他の団体に) 《公式的》 affiliate *oneself* (to [with] ...); (成員になる) become* a member of ... ∥国連に加盟する *join* [*affiliate oneself to, become a member of*] the United Nations

‖加盟国 a member state [country], a signatory / 加盟団体 a member organization / 加盟店 a member store [shop]

かめい² 仮名 (偽の) false [assumed] name [C], alias [C]; (作家などの用いる) pseudonym [sjúːdənìm] [C], anonym [C]

がめつい greedy, grasping, 《口語的》 moneygrubbing

カメラ camera [C]; (テレビカメラ) TV [television] camera [C]; (映画撮影用) 《米》 movie camera [C], 《英》 cine-camera [C]

➩ [場面・状況別会話] p.1718

一眼[二眼]レフのカメラ *a* single-lens [twin-lens] reflex *camera* / カメラにフィルムを入れる load *a camera* with film; load film in [into] *a camera* / 子犬にカメラを向ける point [aim, direct] *one's camera* at puppies / 彼女はカメラ嫌いだ She is *camera-shy*.

◆富士山をカメラに収める (→富士山の写真を撮る) *take a picture* [*photograph*] of Mt. Fuji

‖カメラマン (写真家) a photographer; (映画・テレビの) a cameraman (❖性差別を避けるため a cameraperson を用いるのが無難) / カメラ屋 a camera shop [store] / 胃カメラ〖医学〗 a gastroscope, a gastrocamera / インスタントカメラ an instant camera / 隠しカメラ a concealed camera / 水中カメラ an underwater camera / 使い捨てカメラ a single(-)use [disposable] camera / デジタルカメラ a digital camera / ビデオカメラ a video camera; (ポータブルの) a camcorder / ポラロイドカメラ a Polaroid, a Polaroid camera

カメレオン chameleon [kəmíːliən] [C]

かめん 仮面 mask [C] (❖比喩的な表現でも用いる) ∥仮面をかぶる[かぶっている] put on [wear] *a mask* (❖「正体を隠す[隠している]」の意味にもなる) / 仮面を脱ぐ take off *a mask*; throw off *one's mask* (❖後者は「正体を現す」の意味) / …の仮面をかぶって under *the* [*a*] *mask* of ... (❖「…を装って」の意味)

‖仮面舞踏会 a masked ball, a masquerade

がめん 画面 (スクリーン) screen [C]; (映像) picture [C]《通例単数形》 ∥25インチの画面のテレビ a television with *a* 25-inch *screen* / テレビ画面を調整する adjust *the picture* on the television

かも 鴨 ❶【鳥】 (wild) duck [C] (❖雌のみを指す場合もある); (雄の) drake [C]; (子ガモ) duckling [C]

❷【だまされやすい人】 victim [C], 《口語的》 sucker [C], 《米》 (easy) mark [C] ∥老人をかもにする *make a sucker* [*prey*] *of* an old person ◆彼は詐欺師のいいかもになってしまった He *fell* [*became*] (*a*) *prey to* a swindler.

-かも ➩ かもしれない

かもく¹ 科目・課目 (school) subject [C]

数学は私のいちばん好きな科目です Mathematics is my favorite *subject*.

‖一般教育科目 《主に米》 liberal arts, 《主に英》 liberal studies / 試験科目 an examination subject / 専攻[専門]科目 a major subject / 選択科目 《米》 an elective (subject), 《英》 an optional subject / 必修科目 an obligatory subject, 《米》 a required subject, 《英》 a compulsory subject

-科目のいろいろ-

英語 English / 音楽 music / 化学 chemistry / 家庭科 home economics / 漢文 Chinese classics / 現代社会 contemporary society / 国語 Japanese / 古文 Japanese classics / 数学 mathematics / 生物 biology / 世界史 world history / 体育 physical education / 地学 earth science / 地理 geography / 日本史 Japanese history / 美術 arts / 物理 physics / 倫理 ethics

かもく² 寡黙 寡黙な人 a person *of few words*

かもしか 羚羊 (ニホンカモシカ) Japanese serow [C]

かもしだす 醸し出す なごやかな雰囲気をかもし出す *produce* a friendly atmosphere

-かもしれない -かも知れない may, might (❖might は may に比べて実現の可能性の低い事柄について用いられるといわれるが, 実際にはほ

とんど差はない)
あれが富士山かもしれない That *may* [*might*] be Mt. Fuji./ *Perhaps* [*Maybe, Possibly*], that is Mt. Fuji.
あすは雨になるかもしれない It *may* [*might*] rain tomorrow.
彼はその飛行機に乗り遅れたのかもしれない He *may* [*might*] *have* missed the plane.
彼は頭がいいかもしれないが物事の道理が分かっていない He *may* be intelligent, but he doesn't know what's what.
彼の話は本当かもしれないし,そうでないかもしれない His story *may or may not be true.*/ *Maybe* his story is true, and *maybe* it isn't.
もう少し努力したらならば,彼女は成功していたかもしれない(が,実際にはうまくいかなかった) She *might have* succeeded if she had worked harder.
◆今晩帰りが遅くなるよ。11時ごろになるかもしれない I'll be back late tonight, *perhaps* [*maybe, possibly*] about 11 o'clock.
🅔「お母さんどこ」「台所にいるかもしれないよ」 "Where's Mom?" "She *may* [*might*] be in the kitchen./ (→台所にいると思うよ)*I think* she is in the kitchen."
🅔「あの人酔っ払っていたのかな?」「かもしれないね」 "Was that person drunk?" "*Perhaps./ Maybe./ Possibly./* (→そうだと思う) I *guess* so."
かもつ 貨物 freight ⓤ (✵(米)では列車・船・飛行機による輸送の積み荷,(英)では船・飛行機のものを指す);(トラック・船・飛行機の) cargo ⓒⓤ (複 ~es, ~s);(陸上運送の)(英) goods (複数扱い) ∥貨物を船に積み込む load *freight* onto a ship
∥貨物自動車(米)a truck,(英)a lorry/ 貨物船 a freighter, a cargo vessel/ 貨物輸送機 a freighter, a cargo plane/ 貨物列車(米)a freight (train),(英)a goods train
カモフラージュ ⇨ カムフラージュ
かもめ 鷗 (sea)gull
かや 蚊帳 mosquito net ⓒ ∥蚊帳をつる[はずす]「put up [take down] *a mosquito net*
◆私たちはその計画について全く蚊帳の外だった We *were* kept completely *in the dark* about the plan.
がやがや 教室内はがやがやしていた The classroom *was buzzing* (with the students' voices).
かやく 火薬 gunpowder ⓤ, explosive ⓒⓤ ∥火薬庫 a (powder) magazine
かやぶき 茅葺き ──かやぶきの thatched ∥かやぶき屋根 a *thatched* roof; a *thatch*
かゆ 粥 rice porridge [gruel] ⓤ
かゆい 痒い ──形 itchy 🅔
背中がとてもかゆい My back「*feels* terribly *itchy* [*itches* terribly.]/ I feel terribly *itchy* on my back.
慣用表現 かゆい所に手が届くようなサービス service which *satisfies each and every need*
かゆみ 痒み itch ⓤⓒ ∥かゆみ止め anti-itch medicine

かよい 通い 通いの学生 a *off-campus* student; a student *living off-campus*/ ここ1年医者通いが続いている I've been seeing a doctor for a year.
かよう 通う
❶【行く】 go* to ...;(出席する) attend 🅔;(通勤する) commute 🅔
どこの学校に通っていますか What school do you「*go to* [*attend*]?
私の姉は東京の大学に通っている My sister「*goes to* [*attends*] college in Tokyo.
父は職場まで電車で通っている My father *goes to* the office by train./ My father *commutes* by train.
学生時代には本屋へ通った I「*went to* [*visited*] book stores *frequently* when I was a student.
週に1度病院へ通っている I *am going to* the hospital to see my doctor once a week.
◆僕は学校まで毎日歩いて通った I *walked to* school every day.
❷【交通機関が】
2つの町の間をバスが通っている A bus *runs* between the two towns.
❸【心が】(意思が通じ合う) communicate 🅔;(理解する) understand* 🅔
心の通い合った夫婦 a husband and wife who「*communicate with* [*understand*] *each other well*
慣用表現 血の通った(→思いやりのある)福祉活動 *humane* welfare activities
かようきょく 歌謡曲 Japanese pop song ⓒ
かようし 画用紙 drawing paper ⓤ
かようび 火曜日 Tuesday ⓒⓤ ((略語)Tu., Tue., Tues.) ⇨ にちようび
かよわい か弱い feeble, frail, delicate
から¹ 空 ──空の ∥空の約束 an *empty* [*hollow, vain*] promise/ ポットが空だ The thermos is *empty*./ *There is no water* in the thermos. ◆その箱の中身を空にした I *emptied* the box./ みな帰宅し,競技場は空になった Everyone went home, and the stadium *emptied*.
から² 殻 (貝・卵・クルミなどの) shell ⓒⓤ;(卵の) eggshell ⓒⓤ;(木の実の) nutshell ⓒ;(穀物・種子・果物などの乾いた) husk ⓒ;(木の実・豆などの) shuck ⓒ ∥カタツムリの殻 *a snail shell*/ 穀物の殻を取る remove *husks* from grains; *husk* grains/ 自分の殻を破る come out of *one's shell*/ 彼女は自分の殻に閉じこもりがちだ She tends to crawl [withdraw] into her *shell*.

-から

❶ 場所の起点	from; out of ...
❷ 時間の起点	from, since
❸ 理由・原因・動機	because; from
❹ 原料・材料	from, of
❺ 根拠・基準	from
❻ 出所・動作主	from; by

❶【場所の起点】(運動の起点) from;(内部から

-から

外へ) out of ...

語法
(1) fromの目的語には名詞・代名詞だけでなく副詞や前置詞もくる // 上[下]から *from above* [*below*] / テーブルの下から *from under* the table
(2) from ... to 〜 の形では, 冠詞が省略され, 慣用的に用いられることがある // 頭のてっぺんからつま先まで *from* head *to* foot / 花から花へ *from* flower *to* flower

私たちは小諸から小海線に乗って清里まで行った We went *from* Komoro to Kiyosato on the Koumi line.

彼らは成田からシドニーに向けて出発した They started *from* Narita for Sydney./ They left Narita for Sydney.

冷たい風が北から吹いてきた A cold wind blew *from* the north.

音楽室からピアノの音が聞こえてきた I heard the sound of a piano *from* the music room.

私たちの学校は駅から歩いて10分の所にある Our school is a ten-minute walk *from* the station./ (→駅から学校まで歩いて10分かかる) It takes ten minutes to walk *from* the station to our school.

学校の屋上からは海が見える You can see the sea *from* the rooftop of the school.

ロッカーの後ろから鉄也が現れた Tetsuya appeared *from* behind the locker.

人込みの中から悲鳴が聞こえた I heard a scream *from* among the crowd.

ここから出ていけ Get *out of* here.

車のトランクからかばんを出して Please take my bag *out of* the trunk.

窓から頭を出してはいけない You must not put your head *out of* the window.

彼はタクシーから降りた He got *out of* the taxi. (❖get out of ... は小型の乗り物・タクシーなどから降りる場合. 列車・バスなど大型の乗り物から降りる場合は get off ... を用いる)

◆ 裏口からそのビルに入った I entered the building *at* [*by*] the back door. (❖×from the back door とはいわない) / 泥棒はこの窓から (→窓を通って) 侵入したらしい A thief seems to have got in *through* this window. / 太陽は東から昇る The sun rises *in* the east. (❖通例from the east でなく, in the east という) / 25ページから始めましょう Let's start *on* page 25.

❓「きょうはどちらからいらっしゃったのですか」「大阪からです」 "Where did you come *from* today?" "(I came) *from* Osaka."

❷【時間の起点】 from, since

英作文ノート 現在完了の文では since
いつから日本にいらっしゃるのですか
→ ×*From when* have you been in Japan?
→ ○*Since when* have you been in Japan?
→ ○*How long* have you been in Japan?

★「…から」が時間の起点を表す場合, 現在完了の文の中で用いられるときは from ではなく since を用いる. ただし, 最後の How long ...? がふつうの言い方.

きのうの夜は8時から11時まで勉強した I studied *from* eight till [until, to] eleven last night.

この美術館はきょうから1週間休館だ This art museum is closed for a week *from* today.

きのうからこのホテルに滞在している I've stayed [been staying] at this hotel *since* yesterday.

初めて中国へ行ったときから中国が好きだ I've liked China「*since* I first went there [*from* the first trip there]. (❖この since は接続詞)

◆ 学校が終わってから (→放課後) デパートに行った I went to the department store *after* school./ 学校は4月[4月5日, 8時半]から始まります School begins「*in* April [*on* April 5, *at* 8:30]. (❖×from April とはいわない)

❓「図書館は何時からあいていますか (→何時にあくか)」「9時からだったと思うけど」 "What time does the library open?" "*At* 9 o'clock, I think."

❓「早くおふろに入りなさい」「うん, 宿題終わってからね」 "Take a bath soon." "Yes, but *after* I finish my homework."

❸【理由・原因・動機】 ━ 前 from, out of ... ━ 接 because, since (❖because のほうが直接の原因を表す)

義務感から行動する act *from* a sense of duty

たいていの人は好奇心からたばこを吸い始める Most people begin to smoke *out of* curiosity.

彼女がいるから美術部に入った I joined the art club *because* she was a member of the club.

その野球チームの監督は成績不振から解雇された The baseball manager was fired *because* his team made a poor showing.

暗くなってきたから早く帰ろう Let's hurry home *since* it's getting dark.

❹【原料・材料】 from, of (❖通例材料が原形をとどめない場合には from を用い, 元の形をとどめる場合には of を用いる. どちらともはっきりしない場合はどちらを用いてもよい)

ワインはブドウから作られる Wine is made *from* grapes.

水は水素と酸素から成る Water is「made up [composed]*of* hydrogen and oxygen.

❓「みそは何から作られますか」「大豆からです」 "What is miso made *from*?" "It's made *from* soybeans."

❺【根拠・基準】 from

多くのデータからこの地方は昔海底だったと判断される *From* the large amount of data it can be concluded that this area was under the sea a long time ago.

私から見て, 彼は時間にルーズだ *From* my

point of view [*In my opinion*] he's not punctual.
❻【出所・動作主】from; (…によって) by
これ, 知子からのプレゼントです This is a present *from* Tomoko.
毎日アメリカにいる友達からEメールが届く I receive (an) e-mail *from* a friend of mine in America every day.
彼は遅刻しないよう先生からいつも注意されている He is always told *by* his teacher not to be late.
❼【数量】
その劇のチケットは5,000円からです The tickets for the play start *at* [*from*] 5,000 yen.
そのコンサートには1万人からの(→以上の)人が集まった *More than* 10,000 people attended the concert. / (→ 約1万の人) *About* 10,000 people attended the concert.
❽【文末に用いて】
ここで待ってて. 切符を買ってくるから Wait here. *I'll* get tickets.
いつか仕返ししてやるからな *I'll* pay you back some day.

がら 柄
❶【模様】pattern ⓒ, design ⓒ
花柄 *a* flower *pattern* [*design*] / はでな柄のシャツ a shirt with *a* loud *pattern* [*design*]
❷【品位・身分・性格】
柄の悪い連中とつきあうな Don't hang out with a *rough* [*rude, vulgar*] bunch.
僕は生徒会長なんて柄ではない I'm not *the right person* to be president of the student council.
彼は柄にもなくてれている It's quite *unlike* him to feel shy.
君はそんなことを言えた柄か(→そんなことを言う権利はない) You don't have any *right* to say such a thing.
彼は職業柄花のことには詳しい He knows a lot about flowers *because he's in* [*a related*] [*the*] *business*.

カラー¹ ❶【色】color, 《英》colour ⓤⓒ ‖スクールカラー school *colors* (❖服やバッジに使う学校独自の具体的な色で, 学校の特色・雰囲気のことではない) / その広告はカラー印刷されている The advertisements are printed in *color*.
❷【特色】color ⓤ, character ⓤⓒ, characteristic ⓒ ‖ローカルカラー local *color* / この学校には独特のカラーがある This school has its own *color* [*character, characteristics*].
‖カラーコピー a color copy / カラー写真 a color photo [picture] / カラーテレビ a color television [TV] / カラーフィルム a color film / パステルカラー pastels / ポスターカラー (a) poster paint

カラー²(衣服の) collar ⓒ ‖えり

がらあき がら空き 店内はがら空きだった There were *very few customers in* the store. / The store was *almost empty of customers*.

からあげ 空揚げ とりのから揚げ *deep-fried* chicken

からい 辛い
❶【味】(ひりひりと) hot; (香辛料のきいた) spicy; (ぴりっと) piquant [píːkənt]; (塩からい) salty; (酒が) dry, smart
からいカレー a *hot* [*spicy, piquant*] curry
みそ汁がからすぎたら, お湯をさして If your *miso* soup is too *salty*, pour some hot water into it.
❷【厳しい】severe; (厳格な) strict
数学の先生は点がからい Our math teacher is *severe* [*strict*] in grading our papers. / Our math teacher grades our papers *severely* [*strictly*].

からいばり 空威張り bravado ⓤⓒ (複 ～s, ～es), bluff ⓤ; (どなり散らすこと) bluster ⓤ ——からいばりする bluster ⓘ
➡ いばる, きょせい (虚勢)

カラオケ 場面・状況別会話 karaoke ⓤ
➡ 場面・状況別会話 p.1712

「カラオケ」という言葉は「空っぽ」を意味する「カラ」と,「オーケストラの最初の部分をとった「オケ」の合成語です. 歌なしの曲に合わせ, ビデオモニターに映し出された歌詞を見ながら歌を歌うことができるのです. 特に個室で仲間だけで楽しめるカラオケルームと呼ばれる店のはやっています.
Karaoke is a compound term consisting of *kara*, which means "empty," and *oke*, which is short for "orchestra." In karaoke, people sing along to music from which the vocals have been deleted. The song lyrics are displayed on a video monitor. A place called a *karaoke room*, where people can enjoy karaoke in small groups in private rooms, is very popular.

からかう (いじめる) tease ⓘⓣ; (冗談を言って)《口語的》kid ⓘⓣ, play a joke on *a person*; (笑い者にする) make* fun [a fool] of *a person*, poke fun at *a person*; (いたずらをして) play a trick on *a person* ‖彼女の服装をからかうのをやめるべきだ You should stop 「*teasing* her *about* [*making fun of* her *for*] her clothes. / 《口語的》You should stop *putting* her *down for* her clothes. / からかうのはよしてくれ Stop *kidding* [*fooling*] me. / Stop *putting* me *on*.

からから ❶【乾いた】——からからの (のどが) thirsty, (口語的) parched; (干上がった) dry, dried-up; (天気が) dry ‖からから天気 *dry* weather / 走ったらのどがからからになった I got *thirsty* [*parched*] after running. / 川はからからに干上がっていた The river was completely *dry* [*dried-up*]. / The river was *parched*.
❷【音】電車内の床をからから転がる空き缶 an empty can *rattling* across the floor of a train / 風車がからから回っていた The toy pinwheel *rattled* as it turned.

がらがら ❶【音】がらがらと雨戸を閉める put up the shutters *with a clatter* [*rattle*] / その建物はがらがらと音を立てて倒れた The building came *rumbling* down. / The building 「*crashed* down [fell with *a crash*]. / 父は帰宅するといつもがらがらと大きな音を立ててうがいをする My father usually *gargles loudly* when he gets home.

❷【おもちゃ】rattle [C]

❸【すいている】⇨ がらあき

‖がらがら声 a hoarse [husky] voice

がらがらへび がらがら蛇 rattlesnake [C]

からきし ⇨ すこしも，ぜんぜん，まったく，まるで

からくさもよう 唐草模様 arabesque [C]

からくじ 空くじ 空くじを引く draw *a blank*

がらくた (くず) junk [U]; (不要品) 《米》rummage [U], 《英》jumble [U]; (はんぱ物) 《口語的》odds and ends 《複数扱い》 ∥彼の部屋はがらくただらけだった His room was full of *junk*.

‖がらくた市 《米》a rummage sale, 《英》a jumble sale

からくち 辛口 ―辛口の (カレーなどが) hot, pungent; (ワイン・酒などが) dry ⇨ からい

からくり ❶【機械の】mechanism [C], the works《複数扱い》 ∥おもちゃを分解してからくりを調べた I took a toy apart to know 「*its mechanism* [*the works*]. / I took a toy apart to know *how it worked*.

❷【計略】trick [C] ∥手品のからくりを見破る find out *the trick* of the magic

‖からくり人形 a mechanical doll

からげんき 空元気 (見せかけの元気さ) false spirit [liveliness] [U]; (酒の上での) 《口語的》Dutch courage [U] ◆から元気を出す *pretend to be cheerful*

からさわぎ 空騒ぎ a fuss about nothing, a tempest [storm] in a teapot ―空騒ぎする make* a fuss about nothing

からし 辛子・芥子 mustard [U]

からす¹ 烏 crow [C] ∥カラスがかあかあ鳴いている *A crow* is cawing. / カラスがごみに群がっていた *Crows* were flocking to the garbage.

[慣用表現] 父はいつもからすの行水だ My father always *takes a hurried bath*.

からす² 枯らす wither [他], kill [他]; (虫害などで) blight [他] ∥庭の花をひどい霜で枯らしてしまった The flowers in the garden *were* 「*killed* by [*died* from] the heavy frost. / The heavy frost *withered* the flowers in the garden.

からす³ 嗄らす 声をからして叫ぶ shout *in a hoarse voice* / 大声を出して応援したので声をからしてしまった I cheered so loud that 「my voice *got* [I *became*] *hoarse*.

からす⁴ 涸らす 井戸をからす *run* [*draw*] a well *dry* / 資源をからす *exhaust* [*drain*] resources ⇨ こかつ

ガラス

glass [U]; (窓ガラス) pane [C], window [C], windowpane [C]

1枚のガラス a sheet of *glass* (❖窓ガラスは a pane of glass) / ガラスを吹く blow *glass*

窓にガラスをはめた I fit a pane of *glass* in the window.

彼はガラスの破片で指を切った He cut his finger on 「a piece of broken *glass* [a shard of *glass*]. (❖on の代わりに with を用いると「故意に切った」の意味になる)

あのビルは一面ガラス張りだ That building is covered with *glass*.

‖ガラス切り a glass cutter / ガラス工場 a glass works / ガラス細工 《集合的》glasswork / ガラス製品 《集合的》glass, glassware / ガラス繊維 《集合的》glass fiber / ガラスびん a glass bottle / ガラス屋(人) a glazier; (店) a glass store / 安全ガラス safety glass / 板ガラス plate glass / 色ガラス colored glass / カットガラス cut glass / 強化ガラス toughened [tempered] glass / 曇りガラス opaque glass / クリスタルガラス crystal glass / すりガラス frosted [ground, opaque, smoked] glass / 二重ガラス(窓) double-glazing / フロントガラス 《米》a windshield, 《英》a windscreen / 防弾ガラス bulletproof glass

[慣用表現] 彼は学校運営が実際にはガラス張りだと主張している He contends that in reality the school administration is *open for all to see*.

からだ 体

❶【身体】body [C]; (体格・体形) build [U] [C], physique [U] [C], figure [C] (❖physique は特に男性の体格. 女性の「体」には figure を使うほうが上品)

運動選手のような[力強い，ほっそりした]体の男 a man of athletic [powerful, slender] *build* / 筋骨隆々の体の男 a man of magnificent *physique* / 体を鍛える build up *one's body*; build *oneself* up / 体の線を保つ keep *one's figure*

誠は体は小さいが腕の力が強い Makoto has *a* small *build*, but he has strong arms.

彼は丈夫な体をしている He has *a* strong *body*.

彼女はすらりとした体つきをしている She has *a* slender [*an* angular, *a* trim] *figure*.

激しく運動をしたら，体中の筋肉が痛くなった After exercising hard, I had muscle aches *all over* (*my body*).

◆体の発達 *physical* development / きゃしゃな体つきの男の子 a slightly *built* boy / 体を洗う wash *oneself* (❖×wash *one's* body とはいわない) / バスタオルで体をふく dry *oneself* with a bath towel / 体の芯(しん)まで冷える be chilled to *the bone* / 私たちは火のそばで体を暖めた We warmed *ourselves* by the fire. / 彼女はベッドで体を起こすのを手伝ってもらった She was helped to *sit up* in bed.

❷【健康・体力】health [U], shape [U]

体のぐあいがよい 「be in [have] good *health* / 体のぐあいが悪い 「be in [have] bad [poor, ill] *health* / 体をこわす lose [damage, injure] *one's health*; get sick / 健康で丈夫な体を保つ stay [keep] in *shape*

朝食を抜くのは体によくありません It's not good for *your health* to skip breakfast.

◆体の弱い子供 a *sickly* [*delicate, frail*] child / 体によい食事 *wholesome* meals / お酒を控えたほうが体にいいよ It's *healthier* to be temperate in your drinking. / 働きすぎで体がぐったりした Hard work made me feel *physically* drained. / 私は心も体も健康だ I'm healthy「*physically* and mentally [in mind and *body*]. / 体に気をつけてください Take care of *yourself*. / 体の調子が悪い I am not feeling well. / こう暑くては体がもたない(→我慢できない) I *can't stand* such hot weather. / 卵が体に合わない Eggs *don't*「*agree with* [*suit*] me.

‖五体満足 physical integrity

[慣用表現]今体が空いている(→暇だ)から，君の仕事を手伝ってあげよう I'*m free* now, so I'll help you with your work. / 忙しくて体がいくつあっても足りない I'm busy *enough for two people*. / 彼は体を張って(→命がけで)おぼれている子供を助けた He *risked his life* to save a child from drowning.

からだき 空焚き なべを空だきする *heat* an *empty* pot

からっかぜ 空っ風 dry wind [C]

カラット (宝石の重量の単位) carat [C] (❖200 mg; 《略語》ct); (純金の含有度を示す単位) 《米》karat, 《英》carat [C] (❖純金は24カラット; 《略語》k., kt.) ‖2カラットのダイヤの指輪 a two-*carat* diamond

からっと からっとした空気 *dry* air / あらしが過ぎると空はからっと晴れた After the storm, the sky *cleared up*. / 彼女はからっとした性格だ She is *frank*.

がらっと ➩がらりと

からっぽ 空っぽ 部屋は空っぽだった(→だれもいなかった) I *found no one* in the room. / 彼は腕力は十分あるが頭は空っぽだ He has plenty of muscle but *no brains*. / He's all muscle and *no brains*. / すぐに彼の財布は空っぽになった(→お金を全部使ってしまった) He had spent all his money soon.

からつゆ 空梅雨 ➩つゆ(梅雨)

からて 空手 🗻 karate [kərɑ́ːti] [U]

> 元来中国や沖縄で発展した伝統的な護身武術です．空手には「打ち」「突き」「けり」の基本的な3つの技があります．第二次大戦後，1955年ごろまでは空手もほかの武道と同様に人気を失いましたが，今では国内外ともに広く普及しています．しかし，柔道と違ってオリンピック正式競技にはいまだ認められていません．
> Karate is a traditional martial art of self-defense that was in the past mainly practiced in China and Okinawa. There are three basic techniques in karate: *uchi* (arm strikes), *tsuki* (thrusts) and *keri* (kicks). Although from World War II until around 1955 karate and other martial arts lost popularity, karate is now practiced both inside and outside Japan. Unlike judo, however, the sport has not yet been authorized as an official event of the Olympics.

からとう 辛党 彼は辛党だ(→酒が好きだ) He *enjoys drinking* (*alcohol*).

-からには 始めたからには簡単に引き下がるわけにはいかない *Once* I've started, I can't back down so easily. / やるからには本気でやれ *If* you *do it*, do it in earnest.

からふかし 空吹かし エンジンを空ぶかしする *race* an engine

からぶき 乾拭き **─からぶきする** wipe ... with a dry cloth

からぶり 空振り **─空振りする** swing* wide (❖wide は副詞) ◆私は空振りの三振をした I struck out *swinging*. / 彼の計画は空振りに終わった His plan *has come to nothing*. / His plan *ended in failure*. / His plan *was a failure*.

カラフル **─カラフルな** colorful, 《英》colourful ‖カラフルなイラストが入った本 a book with *colorful* illustrations

からませる 絡ませる entwine [他], tangle [他] [自], twist [他] [自] ‖私は彼女と指をからませた I *entwined* my fingers with hers.

からまつ 唐松 (Japanese) larch [C]

からまる 絡まる tangle [自], get* tangled [entangled] ‖この受話器のコードはからまりやすい This receiver cord *tangles* easily. / 僕の釣り糸がジュリアンのとからまっちゃった My fishing line *got entangled* [*tangled up*] *with* Julian's. / 海草が足にからまり，彼はもう少しで溺死(できし)するところだった His feet *got tangled* (*up*) *in* the seaweed and he almost drowned.

◆テープを巻き戻そうとしたらテープがからまった When I tried to rewind the tape, it *got stuck*. / 家の壁にはツタがからまっていた Ivy *crept up* the wall of the house. / The house *was covered with* ivy.

からまわり 空回り エンジンを空回りさせる *idle* an engine / 議論が空回りして結論は出なかった The argument *went round in circles* and we didn't reach a conclusion.

からみ 辛味 (からい味) hot taste [C]; (塩味) salty taste [C]

からみあう 絡み合う 環境汚染は様々な要因が複雑にからみ合って起きる Environmental pollution is caused by various *interwoven* factors.

からみつく 絡み付く ロープが足にからみついた The rope *twisted around* my leg.

からむ 絡む ❶【巻きつく】twine [自], twist [自] ‖つるが松の木にからんだ Vines *twined* [*twisted*] *around* a pine tree. ◆コンピュータのケーブルがみんなからんでしまった All the cables of my computer *got tangled up*.

❷【困らせる】annoy [他], give* *a person* a hard time; (けんかを売る) pick a quarrel [fight]; (せがむ・ねだる) pester [他] ‖父は酔うと人にからむ My father *picks a quarrel with* someone whenever he gets drunk. / 彼は私に電話番号を教えろとしつこくからんだ He kept *pestering* me to give him my phone number.

❸【かかわりをもつ】彼女はこの活動にどの程度からんでいたのか To what degree was she *involved* in this activity? / その事件には彼がからんでいると思う I think (that) he *was behind* the scandal. / あいつは金がからむと鬼だ He's a demon for money.

からりと ⇒ からっと

がらりと 戸をがらりとあける *fling* the door open / その事故の後, 彼女は生活のしかたをがらりと変えた She changed her style of living *completely* after the accident.

かられる 駆られる 野心にかられて *by the spur of* ambition / 彼は怒りにかられた Anger *spurred* him *on*. / 私は突然恐怖にかられた Suddenly I *was seized* [*overtaken*] *by* terror. / 彼は逃げ出したい気持ちにかられた He *felt impelled* to escape. / 彼女は彼についていきたいという抑えがたい衝動にかられた She *felt* an irresistible impulse to follow him. / 嫉妬(とっ)にかられて彼はおかしな行動をとった Jealousy *drove* him to act irrationally. / *Driven by* jealousy he acted irrationally. / 彼は好奇心にかられてその箱をあけた He opened the box *out of curiosity*.

がらんと がらんとした部屋 an *empty* [a *bare*] room / がらんとした(→人けのない)通り a *deserted* street

がらんどう その木の幹は中ががらんどうだ The trunk of the tree is *hollow* (inside).

かり¹ 仮 ──仮の (一時的) temporary, tentative, provisional; (偽の) false / 仮の結論 a *tentative* conclusion / 仮の名 a *false* [an *assumed*] name / この時間割は仮のものだ This schedule is *temporary*. / 仮住まいする *live temporarily* / 彼女は仮採用になった She was *hired on probation* [*trial*].

‖仮契約 a temporary contract / 仮事務所 a temporary office / 仮釈放 parole
⇒ かりに

かり² 借り debt ⓒⓊ / 友人に1,000円の借りがある I'm *in debt* to my friend *for* 1,000 yen. / I'm 1,000 yen *in debt* to my friend. / I owe my friend 1,000 yen. / 金があればすぐ借りを返したいのだが, 実のところ文無しだ I'd like to pay (off [back]) *my debt* at once. As it is, though, I have no money. ◆彼女には借り(→恩義)がある I *owe her a favor* [*debt of gratitude*]. / I'm *indebted* to her. / あいつに借りを返してやる(→仕返ししてやる) I'll *get even* with him. / これで貸し借りなしだ(→おあいこだ) Now we're *even*. / That makes us *even*.

かり³ 狩り hunt ⓒⓊ (❖〖英〗では通例キツネ狩りfoxhuntを指す), hunting ⓊⓁ; (銃による) 〖英〗shooting ⓊⓁ (❖〖米〗では hunting) / 狩りに行く go on *a hunt*; go *hunting* / キツネ[シカ]狩り fox [deer] *hunting* ◆潮干狩り shellfish *gathering* / キノコ[イチゴ]狩り mushroom [strawberry] *picking*
‖狩人 a hunter

かり⁴ 雁【鳥】 wild goose ⓒ

かりあげる 刈り上げる (髪を)cut* ... short; (動物の毛を) clip ⓁⓁ; (きれいに整える) trim ⓁⓁ / ‖羊の毛を刈り上げる *clip* a sheep ◆弟は床屋で髪を刈り上げしてもらった My brother had his hair *cut close* [*very short*] *on the back and over his ears* at a barbershop.

かりあつめる 駆り集める 彼は近所の人たちを駆り集めて祭りの準備をした He *gathered* his neighbors to prepare for the festival. / 彼らは有能な人員を駆り集めている They *are recruiting* well-qualified staff.

かりいれ¹ 刈り入れ harvest ⓊⓁ / ‖刈り入れ間近の穀物 grain ripe for *harvest* ◆青森の農家は今, リンゴの刈り入れにおおわらわです Farmers in Aomori are very busy *harvesting* apples.

かりいれ² 借り入れ 彼女はその事業のために銀行から多額の借り入れをした She *borrowed* heavily *from* the bank for the business.

かりいれる 刈り入れる reap ⓁⓁ, harvest ⓁⓁ ⇒ しゅうかく(収穫)

カリウム【化学】potassium Ⓤ (❖元素記号K)

かりかり かりかりしたトースト[ベーコン] *crisp* toast [bacon] / トーストがかりかりにこげてしまった The toast (was) burned *to a crisp*. / そんなつまんないことでかりかりするなよ Don't *get angry about* [*at*] such trifles. / きょう彼はかりかりしているから, からかったりしないほうがいい He's very *touchy* today; better not make fun of him. / お父さん, 何をそんなにかりかりしているの What's *eating* [*gnawing at*] you, Dad?

がりがり がりがりにやせている 〖口語的〗be (all) skin and bone(s) / 彼は非常に太っているが, 奥さんはがりがりだ He is enormously fat, whereas his wife is *very skinny*. / 犬が骨をがりがりかじっている A dog *is gnawing* (*at*) a bone. / 車が壁をがりがりこすってしまった My car *scraped against* the wall. / I *scraped* my car *against* the wall.

カリキュラム curriculum ⓒ (複 curricula, ~s) / ‖カリキュラムを作る *design* [*draw up, frame*] *a curriculum* / 彼女の提案を来年のカリキュラムに取り入れよう We will incorporate her suggestions in next year's *curriculum*.

かりきる 借り切る charter ⓁⓁ, rent ⓁⓁ, 《主に英》hire ⓁⓁ / ‖バスを借り切る *charter* a bus

かりこむ 刈り込む cut*, trim ⓁⓁ, prune ⓁⓁ, clip ⓁⓁ; (羊の毛を) shear* ⓁⓁ; (芝生を) mow* ⓁⓁ / ‖生け垣を刈り込む *trim* [*prune*] a hedge / 羊の毛を刈り込む *clip* [*shear*] a sheep

カリスマ charisma [kərízmə] Ⓤ / ‖その政治家にはカリスマ性がある The politician has *charisma*. ◆カリスマ性のある指導者 a *charismatic* leader

かりずまい 仮住まい temporary home ⓒ

かりだす¹ 借り出す きょう学校の図書館から本を2冊借り出した I '*checked* two books *out of* [*borrowed* two books *from*] the school library today. / この本はすべて市立図書館から借り出したものです All these books are *on loan* from the city library.

かりだす² 駆り出す 戦争に駆り出される(→徴

兵される) *be drafted* [*conscripted*] (into the army) / 父は私をその仕事に駆り出した(→手伝わせた) My father *got* me *to help with* the work.

かりたてる 駆り立てる drive* [他] ∥人を狂気に駆りたてる *drive* a person crazy

◆馬を駆りたてる *spur* horses *on* / 彼を駆りたてているのは何よりも怒りだと思う I think what *motivates* him most is anger. / その事件が群衆を暴動へと駆りたてた The incident *stirred* the crowd *to* violence.

かりちん 借り賃 (借家・借地に対する) rent [U] [C]; (レンタカーなどの) rental [C] ∥この自転車の借り賃はいくらですか How much is *the rental* for this bicycle?

かりて 借り手 borrower [C]; (借家などの) tenant [C] ◆その家には借り手がつかなかった *There was nobody who would rent* the house.

かりとる 刈り取る (草・枝などを) cut* [他]; (作物を) reap [他]; (芝生・穀物などを) mow* [他]; (収穫する) harvest [他] ∥草を刈り取る *cut* [*mow*] the grass / 小麦を刈り取る *harvest* [*reap*] wheat

かりに 仮に

❶【仮 定】 if, suppose, supposing (that ...); (たとえ…でも) even if [though] ...

仮にご主人が失業したとしたらどうやって家族を養っていきますか *If* [*Suppose, Supposing* (*that*)] your husband lost his job, how would you support the family?

仮に彼らが「不可能だ」と言ったとしても私はあきらめない *Even if* they say "it is impossible", I'm not going to give up.

❷【一時的に】 for the moment, for the present, for the time being

仮に犯人をXとしよう Let's call the suspect X *for the moment*.

かりにも 仮にも 仮にも(→決して)そんなことを言ってはならない You should *never* say such a thing. / 仮にも大人なのだから(→もう子供ではないのだから)自分の行動に責任をもちなさい *Since* [*Now that*] you're no longer a child, you have to be responsible for your own conduct. / 仮にも一度やると言った以上, 最後までやり通すべきだ *Once* you say that you will do it, you should do it.

かりぬい 仮縫い (しつけ) tack [C]; (寸法合わせ) fitting [C] **—仮縫いする** baste [他] [自], tack [他]; fit* [他] ∥彼がスーツの仮縫いをしてもらっている間, 私は待っていた I waited while he *was fitted* for a suit.

かりぬし 借り主 borrower [C]; (債務者) debtor [C]; (借家・借地人) tenant [C]

カリフォルニア California (❖米国西部太平洋岸の州; 《略語》Cal., Calif., 〔郵便〕CA)

カリブかい カリブ海 the Caribbean Sea

カリフラワー cauliflower [kɔ́ːləflàuər] [C] [U]

がりべん がり勉 (がり勉する人) 《米口語的》 grind [C], drudge [C], 《英口語的》 swot [C] **—がり勉する** grind* away (at [for] ...), 《英口語的》 swot (up)

かりめん 仮免 《米》 learner's permit [C], temporary (driving-)license [C], 《英》 provisional (driving-)licence [C]

かりもの 借り物 borrowed thing [C] ◆その服は友達からの借り物だから, 汚さないように気をつけなければならない I must be careful not to get the dress dirty, because I *borrowed* it from a friend of mine.

かりゅう 下流 ナイル川下流 the *lower* Nile / アマゾン川の下流地域 the *lower* reaches of the Amazon / 久慈川下流にすむ魚 fish living in the *lower* Kuji / 下流へ行く go *downstream* [*down the river*] / この川の下流に温泉地がある There is a spa *down* this river. / この川は数キロ下流で荒川と合流する This river joins the Arakawa several kilometers *downstream*.

がりゅう 我流 僕のチェスは我流だ I play chess *in my own way*.

かりゅうど 狩人 hunter [C]

かりょく 火力 heating power [U] ◆このガスオーブンは火力が強い[弱い] This gas oven has *a* strong [weak] *flame*.

‖火力発電 thermal power generation / 火力発電所 a thermal power plant [station]

かりる 借りる

❶【物・金銭を】 borrow [他] [自] (↔lend); use [他]; owe [他] [自]; rent [他] [自], 《主に英》hire [他]; charter [他]; lease [他]

> borrow: 移動可能な物を無料で借りる.
> use: 移動不可能な物を無料で借りる. また比較的短時間その場で使うために借りる.
> owe: 金を借りている.
> rent, hire: 車・部屋・土地などを賃借りする.
> charter: 飛行機・船・車などを有料で借り切る.
> lease: 土地・建物・機械などを長期間, 賃借りする.

図書館から本を借りる *borrow* [*check out*] a book from a library / レンタカー[ビデオ]を借りる *rent* a car [video]

電話を借りてもいいですか Can I *use* [*borrow*] the telephone? (❖設置された電話の場合は use だが, 携帯電話は borrow も用いる)

ペンをお借りしてもよろしいですか May I *borrow* [*use*] your pen?

彼はその家を内藤氏から月 8 万円で[月ぎめで]借りている He *rents* the house from Mr. Naito 「for 80,000 yen a month [by the month].

車を担保にして金を借りた I *borrowed* money on the security of my car. / I used my car for collateral to *borrow* money.

私は彼に1,000円[その本の代金を]借りている I *owe* him 「1,000 yen [for the book].

◆アパート[家, ビルの 5 階]を借りる *occupy* an apartment [a house, the fifth floor of a building] / 来週の月曜日まで5,000円お借りできませんか(→貸してくれませんか) Could you *lend* me 5,000 yen until next Monday?

❷【助力などを】

辞書の助けを借りて *with* the assistance

[help] of a dictionary / 信仰の名を借りたテロ行為 acts of terrorism done *in the name of* religious conviction

子供たちは大人の手を借りずにその作品を完成させた The children accomplished the work *without the help of* adults.

彼は聖書の中の有名な言葉を借りて演説の結びとした He ended his speech *with* a famous quote from the Bible.

その件について知恵をお借りしたいのですが Could you *give* me some advice about [on] the matter?

この場を借りておわびしたいと思います I would like to *take* this opportunity to apologize to you.

かる¹ 刈る cut* 㐧; clip 㐧; (短く刈り込む) crop 㐧; (芝生・穀物などを) mow* 圓 㐧; (整える) trim 㐧; (羊の毛を) shear* 圓 㐧; (作物などを) reap

草を刈る *mow* [*cut*] the grass / 小麦を刈る *reap* wheat / 羊の毛を刈る *shear* [*clip*] a sheep / 生け垣を刈る *trim* a hedge

きのう床屋で髪を短く刈ってもらった I *had* my hair「*cut short* [*cropped*] at a barber's yesterday.

かる² 狩る hunt 㐧 圓 / 野ウサギを狩る *hunt* hares / オオカミはふつう群れで獲物を狩る Wolves usually *hunt* in packs.

-がる 「幽霊なんか怖いものか」と彼は強がってみせた(→平静を装った) "Ghosts don't scare me at all," he said, putting *on a brave face* [*front*]. / 彼女は来られないことを残念がっていた She *was sorry* that she couldn't come. / 人々は、なぜ彼はそんなことを言われても腹を立てないのだろうと不思議がった People *wondered* why he didn't get angry though he was told such a thing. ➪ -たがる

かるい 軽い

❶【重量】light (↔heavy)

この荷物は目方が軽い This load *is light* in weight.

彼女は軽いコートを探している She is looking for a *light* coat.

そのソファーは見た目よりもずっと軽かった The sofa *was* much *lighter* than it looked.

◆荷物[箱の中身]を軽くする *lighten* a load [box]

❷【程度】light, slight ━軽く lightly, slightly; (穏やかに) gently, softly

軽い運動 *light* exercise / 軽いかぜをひく catch a *slight* [*mild*] cold / 軽い被害 a *light* [*slight*] damage / 軽い味 *light* taste / 軽い読み物[税金, ビール] a *light* reading [tax, beer] / 肉に軽く火を通す cook meat *lightly* / 軽くウエーブした髪 *gently* waving hair

そんな軽い朝食ではお昼までもちませんよ Such a *light* breakfast won't sustain you until noon.

その事故で私は軽いけがをした I was *slightly* injured in the accident.

先生は彼に軽い罰を与えた The teacher gave him a *light* punishment.

道はここから緩い上り坂になっている The road rises *gently* from here.

私たちは初め相手チームを軽く見ていた At first we *made light* [*little*] *of* the opposing team. / At first we *took* the opposing team *lightly*.

彼の意見をそんなに軽く扱ってはいけない Don't *treat* his opinions so *lightly*. / Don't *trifle with* his opinions like that.

彼は軽く手綱(ミミ)を引いた He pulled *gently* at the reins.

私は赤ちゃんの頭を軽くなでてみた I tried stroking the baby's head *gently* [*softly*].

◆軽いたばこ *mild* tobacco / 軽い犯罪 a *minor* offense / 彼の協力のおかげで私の負担が軽くなった His cooperation *lightened* my burden.

❸【軽快な】light

軽い音楽 *light* music

彼女は足取りが軽い She *is light* on her feet.

◆その知らせを聞いて心が軽くなった(→安心した) I *felt relieved* at the news. / マッサージをしてもらって肩が軽くなった Massage *eased* the stiffness in my shoulders.

❹【簡単な】easy ━軽く easily

自転車を修理することなんて彼にとっては軽いもんさ It is very *easy* [*a breeze*] for him to fix a bicycle.

彼女は難しい数学の問題を軽く解いた She solved a difficult math problem *easily*.

僕は軽く100メートル泳げる I can *easily* swim 100 meters.

その質問は彼女に軽くいなされてしまった She *easily* dodged the question.

◆彼は70歳を軽く超えているように見えた He looked *well over* 70.

❺「おまえ、ボウリングで150出せるか」「そんなの軽いよ」 "Can you bowl a game of 150?" "It's a piece of cake. / No sweat."

|慣用表現| 口が軽い ➪ くち / しりが軽い ➪ しり

かるいし 軽石 pumice [pʌ́mis] (stone) Ⓤ Ⓒ

かるがる 軽々 ━軽々(と) easily / 彼はフェンスを軽々と飛び越えた He hopped the fence *easily*.

かるがるしい 軽々しい careless, thoughtless ━軽々しいふるまい *careless* [*thoughtless*] behavior / 彼の軽々しい発言がスキャンダルを引き起こした His *careless* [*thoughtless*] remarks caused the scandal.

◆彼には軽々しく話しかけられない(→話しかけづらい) He is hard to talk to.

かるく 軽く ➪ かるい

カルシウム 【化学】 calcium Ⓤ (◆元素記号 Ca) / 牛乳はカルシウムが豊富だ Milk is rich in *calcium*.

かるた karuta, a Japanese card game / かるたをする play *karuta*

カルチャー culture Ⓤ ‖カルチャーショック (a) culture shock / カウンターカルチャー counterculture / サブカルチャー a subculture

カルチャーセンター

日本にはカルチャーセンターと呼ばれる学校があり，生涯学習の普及に一役買っています．カルチャーセンターでは外国語会話，ジャズダンス，ヨガ，エアロビクス，テニス，生け花，お茶，文学といった様々なクラスが用意されています．子育てに手がかからなくなった主婦が多く利用しているようです．
In Japan, schools called "culture centers" help to promote lifelong education. A variety of classes are offered, including foreign language conversation, jazz dance, yoga, aerobics, tennis, flower arrangement, tea ceremony, literature and so on. They are popular among housewives who need to spend less time on child care as their children get older.

カルテ ⚠(診察記録) medical record [card, chart] [C] (❖日本語はドイツ語の Karte から)
カルテット (四重奏) quartet ,《英》quartette [C]
カルデラ caldera [C] ‖カルデラ湖 a crater lake
カルテル 〘経済〙 cartel [C]
カルト (新興宗教・カルト教団) cult [C] ‖カルトムービー a cult movie
かるはずみ 軽はずみ ━軽はずみな (不注意な) careless; (無思慮な) thoughtless; (性急な) hasty, rash ∥軽はずみな判断を下す make a *hasty* judgement / 自分の軽はずみな行動を恥じています I'm ashamed of my *careless* [*thoughtless*] behavior. / 次の仕事を見つけないで仕事を辞めるとは軽はずみだったね It was *rash* of you to quit your job without having found the next one.
◆軽はずみにものを言う speak *thoughtlessly*
カルビ (ばら肉) rib [C]
かるわざ 軽業 acrobatics《複数扱い》‖軽業師 an acrobat
かれ 彼 ━[代] (彼は・彼が) he; (彼の) his; (彼に・彼を) him; (彼の物) his; (彼自身) himself ━[名] (恋人) boyfriend [C], lover [C] (❖後者は性的関係を暗示する) ➩ かれら
彼はよく外国へ行く *He* often goes abroad.
私は彼とけんかをした I had a fight *with him*.
聡子に彼はいるのだろうか I wonder if Satoko has *a boyfriend*.
かれい[1] 華麗 ━華麗な (すばらしい) splendid; (豪華な) gorgeous, luxurious ∥華麗な衣装 a *gorgeous* costume / 観客はみな，彼女の華麗な演技に魅了された All the spectators were enchanted with her *splendid* performance. ◆チャーチルは華麗な演説で知られた Churchill was distinguished for his *rhetorical* speeches.
かれい[2] 鰈 flatfish [C] (複 ～s, ～es), flounder [C] (複 ～s, ～)
カレー curry [C][U]; (カレーライス) curry and rice, curry with rice ∥からいカレー *a* hot *curry* / ビーフカレー beef *curry and rice* / カレーのルー *curry* roux
‖カレー粉 curry powder
ガレージ garage [gərɑ́ːʒ] [C] ∥車をガレージに入れる put a car into *a garage*
‖ガレージセール《米》garage sale,《英》car-boot sale
かれえだ 枯れ枝 dead branch [C]
かれき 枯れ木 dead [withered] tree [C]
がれき 瓦礫 debris [dəbríː] [U], rubble [U], wreck [C] ∥今度の大地震でその建物はがれきの山と化した The building was reduced to a heap of *debris* [*rubble*] in this big earthquake.
かれくさ 枯れ草 dry [dead] grass [U]
かれこれ 高校を卒業してかれこれ10年になる It's been *about* [*almost, nearly*] 10 years since I graduated from high school. / 彼が私のことにかれこれ言ってくる(→干渉する)ので本当にいらいらした I got really annoyed with him for *interfering* in my affairs. / かれこれするうちに数年が過ぎた *In the meantime*, the years went by.
かれし 彼氏 boyfriend [C], lover [C] (❖後者は性的関係を暗示する)
カレッジ (大学) college [C][U] (❖建物の中で行われる内容を意味するときは，しばしば無冠詞)
かれは 枯れ葉 dead leaf [C] ‖枯れ葉剤 (a) defoliant
かれら 彼ら (彼らは・彼らが) they; (彼らの) their; (彼らに・彼らを) them; (彼らのもの) theirs; (彼ら自身) themselves
彼らは農場で働いている *They* work on a farm.
このコンピュータは彼らのものだ This computer is *theirs*.
かれる[1] 枯れる die [自]; (しおれる) wither [自]
森の木が年々枯れていく The trees in the woods *are dying* year by year.
旅行から戻ってみると，植物のいくつかが枯れてしまっていた On my return from my trip, I found some of my plants *had withered away*.
◆霜で草が枯れた The frost *killed* the grass. / 近ごろ彼の弾くギターは枯れてきた(→円熟してきた) Recently his guitar playing *has matured*.
かれる[2] 涸れる dry up, run* dry, go* dry ∥井戸がかれた The well「*dried up* [*ran dry, went dry*]. / 彼女は涙がかれるまで泣いた She cried *until her tears ran dry*.
かれる[3] 嗄れる 彼に危険を知らせようと，のどがかれるほど大声で叫んだ I *shouted myself hoarse* to warn him of the danger. / 彼は声がかれるまで大声でしゃべり続けた He kept speaking in a loud voice until he [his voice] was *hoarse*.
かれん 可憐 ━かれんな pretty, lovely
カレンダー calendar [C] ➩ こよみ
卓上[壁かけ，日めくり]カレンダー *a* desk [wall, page-a-day] *calendar* / 2004年用のカレンダー *a* 2004 *calendar*; *a calendar* for 2004 / カレンダーをめくる turn over (a page [leaf] of) *a calendar*
かろう 過労 overwork [U] ∥過労で病気になる fall ill from *overwork* / 彼の父は過労死した

His father *died from* [*of*] *overwork.*

がろう 画廊 (art [picture]) gallery ⓒ

かろうじて 辛うじて barely, narrowly; (苦労して) with difficulty ∥1か月暮らしていくだけの金がかろうじてあった I had *barely* enough money to last a month. / 彼は雪崩にあったがかろうじて助かった He *narrowly* [(*only*) *just*] escaped death in a snowslide. ◆レースにかろうじて勝つ win a race *by inches* [*a nose*]

カロチン carotene Ⓤ

かろやか 軽やか ━━軽やかな light ∥軽やかな動き a *light* movement / 彼女は軽やかな足取りで歩く She walks with *light* steps.

◆軽やかに踊る dance *lightly*

カロリー calorie ⓒ ∥低カロリー食品 (a) *low-calorie* food / 彼女は1日1,500(キロ)カロリーに制限した She restricted herself to 1,500 *calories* a day. / この料理は約500(キロ)カロリーある This dish has about 500 *calories*. / ポテトチップスはカロリーが高い Potato chips *are high in calories.*

∥カロリー計算 calorie counting

ガロン gallon ⓒ (❖(米)では3.785リットル, (英)では4.546リットル;(略語)gal., g.)

かろんじる 軽んじる make* light [little] of... ∥少数意見を軽んじてはいけない Don't *make light of* minority opinions. ◆この問題の研究は長い間軽んじられてきた The study of this subject *has long been neglected.*

かわ¹ 川・河
river ⓒ ((略語)R., r.); (小川) brook ⓒ, stream ⓒ (❖river より小さく brook より大きい)

> 基礎 川の固有名は《米》では the Tone River, 《英》では the River Tone のように表すが, Riverはしばしば省略される.

川のこちら[向こう]側 this [the other] side of *the river* / 川の左岸に on the left bank of *the river* / カヌーで川を渡る cross a *river* by canoe / 川へ泳ぎに行く go swimming in *a river* (❖ ×go swimming to a river とはいわない)

その川はいくつかの町を流れている The *river* flows through several towns.

それらの川はすべて日本海に注いでいる All those *rivers* flow [run] into the Sea of Japan.

この川は流れが速い The current is rapid in this *river.* / This *river* has a rapid current.

子供たちが川で遊んでいる Children are playing in *the river.*

大雨で川が増水した The *river* rose because of the heavy rain.

私たちはボートで川を下った[さかのぼった] We went down [up] *the river* by boat.

洪水で川の流れが変わった The flood diverted the course of *the river.*

かわ² 皮
❶【動物の】(人間の皮膚・動物の加工された皮) skin ⓤⓒ; (獣の皮) hide ⓒ; (小動物の皮) pelt ⓒ

牛皮のベルト a belt made of *calf skin*

脂を減らすためにとり肉の皮は取りなさい Take *the skin* off the chicken to reduce the fat.

◆日焼けで背中の皮がむけてひりひりする My sunburned back *is peeling* and painful.

❷【植物の】skin ⓤⓒ, peel ⓤⓒ; (メロンなどの厚い皮) rind ⓤⓒ; (樹皮) bark ⓤⓒ

レモンの皮 lemon *peel* [*skin*] / ジャガイモの皮 potato *skin* [*peel*] / 木の皮をはぐ strip *bark* off wood

◆ミカンの皮をむく *peel* an orange

❸【外側を覆うもの】
シュークリームの皮 a puff *shell*

このパイは皮がさくさくしている The *crust* of this pie is crunchy.

慣用表現 あの男は面の皮が厚い(→厚かましい) That man *is impudent.* / あいつもとうとう化けの皮がはがれた(→本性を現した) He finally *showed his true nature.* / ハムレットを演じて彼の演技もひと皮むけた(→大きく進歩した)感じだ His acting seems to *have greatly improved* after he played Hamlet.

∥皮むき器 a peeler

かわ³ 革 leather ⓤ ∥革の手袋 *leather* gloves / 本[模造]革 genuine [imitation] *leather* ∥革靴 *leather* shoes / 革細工 *leather* craft / 革ジャン a *leather* jacket / 革製品 a leather, leather goods

がわ 側 (競技・論争の) part ⓤ ∥コインの裏側 *the other side* of a coin / 湖のこちら[向こう]側 this [*the* opposite] *side* of the lake / 私たちはその店の日のあたる側の席に座った We sat down on the sunny *side* of the shop. / 郵便局は市役所の右側にあります The post office is on *the right*(*-hand*) *side* of the city hall. / 彼らは通りの両側に花を植えている They are planting flowers on *both sides* of the street. / 彼は彼女の側に立った (→彼女の味方をした) He took her *side* [*part*]. / 通路側[窓側]の席をお願いします I'd like an *aisle* [a *window*] seat.

かわいい 可愛い
❶【愛らしい】lovely; (きれいな) pretty; (小さい・幼い) cute

かわいい子供 a *lovely* [*cute*] child / かわいい人形 a *pretty* doll

いとこの赤ちゃんはピンクを着るととてもかわいい My cousin's baby looks very *cute* in pink.

駅でかわいい子を見かけた I saw a *pretty* girl at the station.

彼は一見怖そうだがけっこうかわいいところもある Though he looks stern, there is something *cute* about him.

◆その男の子はかわいらしくおじぎをした The boy bowed *cutely.* ◆この植物は毎年春になるとかわいらしい花を咲かせる This plant has *little* blossoms every spring. (❖small には

「かわいらしい」という感情的なニュアンスはない)
- 「見て, 子猫がいるわ」「まあ, かわいい」 "Look! there is a kitten." "Oh, it's so *cute*."
- 「あなたになんか助けてもらいたくないわ」「かわいくないなぁ」"I don't want you to help me at all." "*How cheeky of you!*"

❷ 【いとしい】dear

私のかわいい娘 my *dear* daughter
◆だれだって自分の子供はかわいい Everybody *loves* his or her own children.

❸ 【小さい】little; (とても小さい) tiny

かわいいメモ帳 a *tiny* memo pad
◆僕の苦労なんて彼の苦労に比べればまだまだかわいいものだ The trouble I have is much *less serious* than the trouble he had.

ことわざ かわいい子には旅をさせよ Spare the rod and spoil the child. (→むちを惜しめば子供がだめになる) / かわいさ余って憎さ百倍 Too strong a love may turn to hatred. (→強すぎる愛は憎しみに変わることがある)

かわいがる 可愛がる love ㊥

私は猫を3匹飼っていてとてもかわいがっている I have three cats. I *love* them very much.
◆おじには小さいころよくかわいがってもらった I *was taken* good *care of* by my uncle when I was a child. / 彼女は先生にかわいがられている (→先生のお気に入り) She is the teacher's *pet* [*favorite*].

かわいげ 可愛い気 かわいげのない (→素直でない)子 a *disobedient* [(→頑固な) an *obstinate*] child / あの子はかわいげがない (→子供らしいところがない) There's *nothing childlike* about that boy.

かわいそう 可哀相 ──かわいそうな poor; (哀れな) pitiful; (みじめな) miserable; (悲しい) sad; (残酷な) cruel

かわいそうな話 a *sad* story
私はかわいそうなその子供に同情した I felt pity for the *poor* child.
彼女が謝っているのに無視するなんて, あなたもかわいそうなことをするね It's *cruel* of you to ignore her apologies.
◆かわいそう! *What a pity!* / 彼女がかわいそうだ, みんなして彼女を責めてばかりいるんだもの I *feel sorry for* her. Everybody keeps blaming her.

かわいた 乾いた・渇いた dry; (のどが) thirsty /部屋の中の乾いた空気 *dry* air in a room

かわいらしい 可愛らしい pretty ⇨かわいい

かわうそ 川獺 otter ⓒ

かわかす 乾かす dry ㊥ /日なたで服を乾かしなさい *Dry* your clothes in the sun. ◆髪をドライヤーで乾かす *blow-dry one's* hair

かわかみ 川上 the upper reaches [area] (of a river) /この川の川上に温泉がある There is a spa *above* this river. / 川上へ進もう Let's go *upstream* [*up the river*].

かわき¹ 乾き /このペンキは乾きが早い[悪い] This paint *dries* quickly [badly].

かわき² 渇き (のどの) thirst ⓤ /(また a ~) / のどの渇きをいやす quench [relieve, satisfy] one's *thirst*

かわぎし 川岸 riverbank ⓒ, the riverside
◆その花は川岸に咲いていた The flower was on the bank of the river.

かわきり 皮切り 彼女のスピーチを皮切りに会が始まった The party *started with* her speech.

かわく¹ 乾く dry ㊥, get* dry /このTシャツはすぐ乾くでしょう This T-shirt will soon 「*dry out* [*get dry*].
◆髪がまだ乾いていない My hair *isn't dry* yet. / My hair *is* still *wet*.

かわく² 渇く get* thirsty; (渇いている) be [feel*] thirsty /炎天下で働いたのでのどが渇いた I worked under the burning sun, and I got *thirsty*. / 彼女はのどが渇いてそれ以上歩くことができなかった She was too *thirsty* to walk any longer.

かわざかな 川魚 (淡水魚) freshwater fish ⓒ; (川の魚) river fish ⓒ

かわしも 川下 the lower reaches [area] (of a river) ◆川下へ進もう Let's go *downstream* [*down the river*].

かわす¹ 交わす 握手を交わす *shake hands* / あいさつ[契約]を交わす greetings [contracts] / 彼らはその問題について激論を交わした They *had* a hot dispute about [over] the problem. / 彼とは言葉を交わすほどの仲ではない I'm not on *speaking* terms with him. / だれも彼と言葉を交わそうとはしなかった No one would *talk to* him.

かわす² 攻撃から身をかわす dodge an attack / しつこい質問をかわす evade an inquisitive question

かわせ 為替 (郵便為替) money order ⓒ (略語 MO), (主に英) postal order ⓒ (略語 PO), (外国為替) exchange ⓤ /郵便為替で5,000円送る send *a money order* for 5,000 yen; send 5,000 yen by *money order* / きょうの為替レートは1ドル100円です Today's *exchange rate* is 100 yen to the (U.S.) dollar.
‖為替ディーラー a currency trader / 為替手形 a bill of exchange / 為替取引 (an) exchange transaction / 外国為替相場[レート] a rate of exchange, an exchange rate

かわせみ 翡翠 〖鳥〗kingfisher ⓒ

かわぞこ 川底 riverbed ⓒ, the floor of a river

かわった 変わった

❶【変な】(奇妙な) strange, odd; (独特の) peculiar; (異常な) unusual; (珍しい) uncommon

変わった人 a *strange* [an *odd*] person / 変わった趣味 a *peculiar* taste
その部屋には何か変わったところがある There is something *strange* in the room.
何か変わったことが起こったら知らせてください Please let me know if anything *unusual* happens.

❷【目新しい】(新しい) new; (ふつうでない) unusual; (異なった) different

たまには何か変わった料理が食べたい Sometimes I feel like eating something *unusual*.

☎「変わったことはないかい」「ああ，特にないよ」"What's *new*?" "Oh, nothing particular."

か

かわべり 川縁 川べりのレストラン a restaurant *by a river* / 私たちは川べり(→土手)を歩いた We walked along *the bank of the river*. / 鉄道は川べりを(→川と平行に)走っている The railroad runs *parallel to the river*.

かわら[1] 瓦 tile [C] //かわら屋根の家 a house roofed with *tiles*; a *tile*-roofed house

◆かわら屋根 a *tiled* roof

かわら[2] 川原・河原 a shore of a river, river shore [C]; (川岸・土手) riverbank [C]

かわり[1] 代わり・替わり

❶【代理・代用】(代わりのもの) substitute [C], replacement [C]; (代理人) deputy [C]

どんなロボットも人間の代わりにはならないだろう No robot could be *a substitute for* a human being.

◆折り紙の代わりに新聞紙を使う use a piece of newspaper *for* origami / 私にあなたの代わりが務まるでしょうか I don't know if I can *substitute for* you. / 牛乳の代わりに水を使った I used water 「*instead of* [*in place of*] milk. / 美穂が休みなので，私が代わりに花に水をやった As Miho is absent, I watered the flowers *instead*. / 映画を見に行く代わりにビデオを借りたらどうかしら How about renting some videos *instead of* going to the movies?

❷【代償・交換】──代わりに (お返しに) in return (for ...); (交換に) in exchange (for ...)

夕食をごちそうしてもらったかわりに彼女にプレゼントをあげた I gave her a present *in return for* dinner.

◆彼は数学ができないかわりに英語ができる His good English skills *make up for* his poor math skills. / なくした時計の代わりに新しいものを買った I bought a new watch to *replace* the one I lost.

かわり[2] 変わり

❶【変化】change [U][C]

議題に変わりはありません There is no *change* in the subject of the discussion.

◆きょうもいつもと変わりなく(→いつもどおりに)学校に行った I went to school today *as usual*. / こちらも変わりなく(→元気に)暮らしています I'*m getting along well* here, too. / 久しぶりに会ったが彼女はそれほど変わりなかった(→ほとんど以前と同じだった) I met her after a long time, but she *was* almost *the same* as before.

☎「お変わりありませんか」「おかげさまで元気です」"*How have you been?*" "Quite well, thank you."

❷【相違】difference [U][C]

この2つの店で野菜の値段にたいして変わりはない There is little *difference* in the prices of vegetables between these two shops.

かわりばえ 代わり映え 人事異動後の顔ぶれはかわりばえがしない The new order *is no better than before* the staff reshuffle. / 一生懸命勉強したが私の成績はいっこうにかわりばえがしなかった My grades *have not improved* at all though I worked hard. / 最近，集会での彼の話はかわりばえがしない(→目新しいものがない) *There is nothing new* [*original*] in his speaking at the meetings these days.

かわりはてる 変わり果てる 過疎化によって彼の故郷は変わり果ててしまった Depopulation *has completely changed* his hometown.

かわりばんこ 代わり番こ by turns, in turn //僕とジョーはかわりばんこにかばんを持った Joe and I carried the bag *by turns*.

◆かわりばんこに運転しよう Let's *take turns* (at) driving.

かわりめ 変わり目 学年の変わり目に at *the end* of the school year / 母親を亡くしたことが彼女の人生の変わり目になった Losing her mother proved to be *a turning point* in her life. / 彼はよく季節の変わり目に病気になる He often falls ill at *the change* [*turn*] of the seasons.

かわりもの 変わり者 odd [strange, eccentric] person [C]

かわる[1] 代[替，換]わる

❶【代わりをする】take* *one's* place, replace [他]; (代用する) substitute [自]

彼に代わる人を探しています I'm looking for someone who can *take his place*.

◆彼女に代わって私が王女の役を演じた I played the role of the princess *instead of* her. / 帰りは兄が運転を代わった(→引き継いだ) My brother *took over* the wheel on our way home. / 社長に代わってごあいさつ申し上げます Allow me to say a few words *on behalf of* the president.

❷【入れ替わる】(とって代わる) replace [他]; (交換する) change [他]; (交代する) take* the place of ...

CDはレコードにとって代わった CDs *have replaced* records.

すみません，席を換わっていただけますか Excuse me, but could you *change* [*trade*] seats with me?

あのチームは監督が代わった That team *changed* its manager.

☎「もしもし，友子さんいますか」「はい．代わりますのでお待ちください」"Hello, may I speak to Tomoko, please?" "Yes. Hold (the line) please, I'*ll get* her (on the phone)."

かわる[2] 変わる

❶【変化する】change [自]; (形・性質が) turn [自]

【change [turn]＋into [名]】沸騰すると水は水蒸気に変わる Water *changes* [*turns*] *into* steam when it boils. / 雨が雪に変わった The rain *turned into* snow.

故郷の町はすっかり変わっていた My hometown *had* completely *changed*. / 彼は態度がころころ変わる His attitude often *changes*. / 君はちっとも変わってないね You *haven't changed* at all. / 信号が青に変わった The traffic light *turned [changed to]* green. / 彼女の興味はジャズに変わった Her interest has *turned to* jazz.

◆考えが変わりました(→考えを変えた) I've *changed* my mind. / 予定が変わりました(→変えられた) The schedule *has been changed*. / 秋の天気は変わりやすい Autumn weather *is changeable*. / 怒りはやがて悲しみに変わった Anger *passed into* sorrow. / 彼は高校に行ってから人が変わった He *has became a different person* since he went to high school. / 何か変わったことはありますか What's *the news*? / エアコンの売り上げは季節によって変わる Sales of air-conditioners *vary* with the season. / 住所が変わりました I *have moved to* a new address.

❷【異なる】 be different ➡かわった
事態は以前とはかなり変わった(→以前とはずいぶん異なっている) The situation *is now quite different from* before.

◆努力したことで彼女のテストの結果は大きく変わった Her efforts *made* a big *difference* in her test results.

ことわざ 所変われば品変わる ➡ところ

かわるがわる 代わる代わる by turns, alternately, one after the other / 父と兄が代わる代わる車を運転した My father and brother drove the car「*by turns [alternately]*. / My father and brother *took turns* (at) driving the car.

かん¹ 勘 (直感) intuition ⓊⒸ, hunch Ⓒ; (本能) instinct Ⓒ Ⓤ; (第六感) the sixth sense
勘に頼る trust *one's instinct*; play [follow, act on] *one's hunch*
私の勘は当たった[はずれた] My *hunch* was right [wrong]. / 僕は勘で答えた I answered *on a hunch*. / きょうは勘がさえてるね Your *instincts* are sharp today.

◆彼女は勘がいい[悪い] She *is quick [slow] to catch on*. / 新聞記者はスキャンダルをかぎつける鋭い勘をもっている Newspaper reporters *have a nose for* scandal.

e 「どうして分かったの」「勘さ」 "How did you find out about it?" "*I just knew it*. / My *intuition* told me."

かん² 間 ❶【時間】 for, during; (期間内で) in
1週間家を留守にする be away *for* a week
私は過去3年間、旅行をしていない I haven't taken a trip *for [during]* the past three years. / その間の事情については知りません I don't know what happened「*during that time [then]*. / 彼はたった4日間で論文を書き上げた He finished his thesis *in* only four days.

❷【場所・人の間】 (2者間の) between; (3者以上の) among
日米間の貿易 trade *between* Japan *and* the United States / 男女間の不平等 inequality *between* men *and* women / 東京-福岡間の飛行機便 a plane service *between* Tokyo *and* Fukuoka
国家間には相互理解が不可欠だ Mutual understanding is essential *between* nations.
慣用表現 そのとき彼は間髪を入れず私に質問してきた Then he *immediately* asked me a question.

かん³ 感 feeling Ⓒ, sense Ⓒ, sensation Ⓒ; (強い感情) emotion Ⓤ /【義務,責任,達成】感 *a sense* of duty [responsibility, achievement] / 解放[満足]感 *a feeling* of relief [satisfaction]

◆優越[劣等]感 superiority [inferiority] *complex* / その決定はやや性急の感があったように思う I have *the impression* that the decision was a little hasty. / 彼女の言葉に私は感極まって泣いた I *was moved to tears* by her words.

かん⁴ 缶 can Ⓒ, 《英》tin Ⓒ ➡かんきり //缶コーヒーを飲む drink *a can of coffee*

かん⁵ 管 pipe Ⓒ, tube Ⓒ, duct Ⓒ //水道[ガス]管 *a water [gas] pipe* / ブラウン管 *a cathode-ray tube* (略語) CRT

かん⁶ 棺 coffin Ⓒ, 《米/婉曲的》casket Ⓒ

かん⁷ 寒 (真冬) midwinter Ⓤ; (最も寒い季節) the coldest season /寒の入り[明け] the beginning [end] of *midwinter*

かん⁸ 癇 彼の話し方がかんにさわる(→いらいらさせる) His way of speaking *gets on my nerves*.

-かん¹ -巻 volume Ⓒ ((略語) vol., vols.); (内容を表す区分) ❖volume は外形上の区分); (映画のフィルムの) reel Ⓒ //第3巻 Vol. III (❖読み方は volume three) / 全7巻の著作 a work in seven *volumes* / 百科事典全巻 *a complete set of* encyclopedias

-かん² -観 view Ⓒ, outlook Ⓒ //世界観 *a world-view* / 彼女は肯定的な人生観をもっている She has *a positive「outlook on [view of]* life.

-かん³ -刊 その本は1999年刊だ The book *was published* in 1999.

がん¹ 癌 cancer Ⓤ Ⓒ /胃[乳,肺,皮膚]癌 *stomach [breast, lung, skin] cancer* (❖cancer of the stomach のようにもいう) / 末期癌 terminal *cancer* / 癌にかかる(かかっている) get [have] (*a*) *cancer* / 性差別は社会の癌だ Sexism is *a cancer* of [in] society.
‖癌細胞 a cancer cell / 発癌性物質 a carcinogenic substance, a carcinogen

がん² 雁 wild goose Ⓒ

がん³ 願 お地蔵様に願をかける *wish [make a wish] on a jizo*

がん⁴ 眼 人に眼をつける *scowl at* a person

かんい 簡易 ‖簡易書留 simplified registered mail / 簡易裁判所 a summary court / 簡易食堂 a buffet / 簡易保険 postal

[post-office] life insurance
がんい 含意 implication ©Ⓤ, connotation Ⓒ ──含意する imply ⊕, connote ⊕
かんいっぱつ 間一髪 私たちは間一髪で爆発事故を免れた We escaped the explosion *by a hair*. / かろうじて
かんえん 肝炎 〔医学〕hepatitis [hèpətáitəs] Ⓤ ∥A型［B型］肝炎 *hepatitis* A [B] / 急性［慢性］肝炎 acute [chronic] *hepatitis*
かんおけ 棺桶 coffin Ⓒ,（米／婉曲的）casket Ⓒ
|慣用表現| 棺おけに片足をつっこんでいる *have one foot in the grave*
かんか 感化 influence Ⓤ ──感化する influence ⊕ ∥当時の若者は彼の思想に感化された The young people of those days *were influenced* by his thinking.
がんか¹ 眼下 その山の頂上から眼下に町を一望できる From the hilltop we can command a view of the whole town *below*.
がんか² 眼科（眼科学）ophthalmology [àfθælmálədʒi] Ⓤ;（病院の）the department of ophthalmology ∥眼科医 an eye doctor, an oculist, an ophthalmologist;（検眼する人）an optometrist
かんがい 感慨 老人は長い人生を振り返って感慨にふけっていた The old man *was lost in deep emotion*, looking back on his long life. / 20年ぶりに故郷を訪れて感慨無量だった I *was deeply moved* when I visited my hometown for the first time in 20 years. / 彼からの手紙を感慨深く読んだ I read a letter from him *with deep emotion*.
かんがい² 灌漑 irrigation Ⓤ ──灌漑する irrigate ⊕ ∥灌漑用水 irrigation water / 灌漑用水路 an irrigation channel [ditch]
かんがい³ 干害 drought damage Ⓤ

かんがえ 考え

❶ 思考　thought; idea; notion
❷ 思いつき　idea
❸ 意見　opinion; view
❹ 意図　intention

❶【思考】thought Ⓤ Ⓒ（❖思考(力)の意味ではⓊ, 具体的な「考え」の場合はⒸ）;（心に浮かぶ）idea Ⓒ;（漠然とした）notion Ⓒ;（思考行為）thinking
考えをまとめる collect *one's thoughts* / 考えなしに行動する act without any *thought*
彼はずっと考えにふけっている He has been lost in *thought*.
自分の考えを人に押しつけるのはよくない It's not a good idea to force your *ideas* [*views*] on other people.
彼の考えは甘いと思う I think his *idea* is shallow.
◆彼女の考えは(→何を考えているか)理解できない I can't understand *what she is thinking*.
❷【思いつき】idea Ⓒ
それはいい考えだ That's *a good idea*.
彼の頭にふとある考えが浮かんだ Suddenly an *idea* "occurred to [struck] him. / Suddenly he hit on *an idea*.
僕にいい考えがあるよ I have *a good idea*.
❸【意見】opinion Ⓒ;（見解）view Ⓒ
この問題についてあなたの考えはどうですか What's your *opinion* of [What do you *think of*] this subject?
私の考えでは, もっとみんな政治に関心をもつべきだ In my *opinion* [*view*], everyone should have more interest in politics.
私は彼にはっきりと自分の考えを言うつもりだ I will frankly express my *opinion* [*view*] to him.
◆彼女は決して考えを変えなかった She never changed *her mind*.
❹【意図】intention Ⓤ Ⓒ
計画を変更する考えはありません We have no *intention* of changing the plan.
◆彼らは政府に対し法案の見直しを求める考えだ They *intend to* demand that the government reconsider the bill. / 彼はその事件をモデルに小説を書く考えだ He *is thinking* of writing a novel based on the event.
❺【思慮】prudence Ⓤ;（考慮）consideration Ⓤ
少し考えが足りませんでした I lacked a little *prudence*.
◆費用のことは考えに入れていなかった I didn't *consider* the cost.
❻【期待】expectation Ⓤ
私の考えとは違う結果になった The result was contrary to my *expectation*.
❼【想像】imagination Ⓤ
◆電気のない生活なんて考えもつかない I can't *imagine* life without electricity.

かんがえあわせる 考え合わせる すべてを考え合わせると, 私たちは引き返すべきだと思う *Taking* everything *into consideration*, I think we should draw back.
かんがえかた 考え方 *one's* way of thinking;（見解）view Ⓒ ∥女性の役割についての従来の考え方 traditional *views* about the roles of women / 彼の考え方は私とは全く異なる *His way of thinking* is completely different from mine. / 君の両親もうちと同じだよ. みんな考え方が古いんだ（→ 保守的だ）Your parents are the same as mine. They *are too conservative*. / 彼は考え方がしっかりしている His *thinking* is solid.
かんがえごと 考え事 考え事をしていて乗り過ごしてしまった I was *lost in thought* and missed my stop.
⚡「どうしたの」「う, うん, ちょっと考え事をしていたんだ」"What's the matter?" "Well, er ..., I was just *thinking*."
かんがえこむ 考え込む （過去の失敗などについて）brood over [on, about] ...;（深く考える）think* deeply ∥私はそれをどうやろうかと考え込んでしまった I *thought deeply* how to do it.
かんがえだす 考え出す think* up;（案・計画などを）come* up with ... ∥解決策を考え出す *come up with* a solution / 彼は英語の新し

い教え方を考え出した He *thought up [devised] a new way to teach English.*

かんがえちがい 考え違い，misunderstanding ⓒⓊ ⇨ おもいちがい，ごかい ◆失礼ながら，考え違いなさっているようです Excuse me, but I think you *have misunderstood.* / 考え違いをしていたと認めざるをえない I must admit I *was in error.*

かんがえつく 考え付く think* of ..., hit* on ... 〃おもいつく 〃いいことを考えついた I've *hit on [got] a good idea.* / その問題の解決法が考えつかない I *can't think of* a solution to the problem.

かんがえなおす 考え直す reconsider ⓒⓉⓕ, rethink* ⓒⓉⓕ; (考え直してやめる) think* better of ... 〃君の気持ちは分かるが，考え直してほしい I understand how you feel, but I would like you to *reconsider* [*think* it *over again*]. ◆バスで行くつもりだったが考え直してタクシーで行った I was going to go by bus, but *on second thought* I went by taxi.

かんがえぬく 考え抜く think* through [out] 〃考え抜いた末に彼はこの結論に達した He arrived at this conclusion after *thinking* it *through.*

かんがえぶかい 考え深い thoughtful; (慎重な) prudent

かんがえもの 考え物 その計画をそんなに早く実行に移すのは考えものだ It's *debatable [questionable]* whether we should carry out the plan so soon.

かんがえよう 考え様 考えようによっては (→ある意味では) 彼は正しい He's right *in a way.* / ものは考えようだ Everything *depends on your point of view.*

かんがえる　考える

❶ 考慮・検討する　think
❷ …という意見をもつ　think
❸ 想像・推測する　imagine
❹ 意図する　think of ...

❶【考慮・検討する】think* ⓒⓉⓕ; (じっくり考える) think over, consider ⓒⓉⓕ
慎重に考えてから行動しなさい *Think* carefully before you act.
【think＋about [of]＋名】 それを考えると憂鬱(ゆううつ)になった When I *thought about [of]* it, I sank into melancholy. / 彼は典子のことばかり考えている He *thinks about [of]* nothing but Noriko. / ホテルの部屋割りをどうしようか考えています I'm *thinking of* how to assign rooms at the hotel. (❖この例では of を省いてもよい．その場合 think は他動詞)
もう少しじっくり考える時間をくれないか Give me some more time to *think* it *over.*
君は環境問題についてもっと真剣に考えるべきだよ You ought to *consider* environmental issues more seriously.
まだ20歳だということを考えれば，彼はよくやったといえよう *Considering* that he is only 20, we can say he did very well.
考えてみればきのうの晩もカレーを食べた *Come to think of it*, I had curry and rice yesterday evening, too.
◆いろいろ考えた末に私はある結論に達した I finally came to a conclusion after much *thought [consideration]*. / ちょっと考えると，その問題は解けそうにもない At first *thought*, the problem seems to be insoluble. / 結果は考えずに全力を尽くしなさい *Don't worry about the result. Just try your best.* / 君が考えていることを私に話してくれないか Will you tell me what you *have in mind*? / 自分のしたことをよく考えて (→反省して) みなさい *Reflect on* what you have done. / もっと現実的に物事を考えろ *Be* more practically *minded.*

🔴「何を考えているの」「別に何も」"What *are* you *thinking of*?/ What do you *have on your mind*?" "Nothing at all."

🔴「僕とつきあってくれない？」「考えておくわ」"Will you go out with me?" "I'll *think about* it."

❷【…という意味をもつ・…とみなす】think* ⓒⓉⓕ; (みなす) regard ⓒⓉⓕ; (解釈する) take* ⓒⓉⓕ; (判断する) judge ⓒⓉⓕ

【think＋that 節】彼女のせいだと考えるのは間違っているよ You are wrong in *thinking that* she is to blame.

【think＋of [about]＋名】この事件についてあなたはどう考えますか What do you *think of [about]* this case?

【regard＋名＋as 名[形]】みんな美奈子はおしとやかだと考えています Everybody *regards* Minako *as* "a modest girl [modest]."

13は不吉な数だと考えられている Thirteen *is thought to be* an unlucky number.

電話をしなかったときは，参加するものと考えてくれていいよ You can *take it that* I'll join you, if I don't call you.

だれもその問題を深刻なものだと考えていなかった Nobody *judged* the problem (*to be*) serious.

◆彼女は国際線全便を禁煙にすべきだと考えている She *is of the opinion that* smoking should be prohibited on all international flights.

❸【想像・推測する】imagine ⓒⓉⓕ; (予期する) expect ⓒⓉⓕ
まあ考えてもごらんよ Just *imagine* that!
彼が試合に負けるなんて考えられないよ I can't *imagine* that he'll lose the game.
結果は我々が考えていたものとはかなり異なっていた The result was quite different from what we *had expected*.
◆これから僕たちがどうなるのか考えると怖くなる I dread to *think* what may happen to us. / テストのことを考えただけで憂鬱(ゆううつ)になる *The* very *thought of* the exam makes me feel depressed. / 彼の首に残っている跡から考えて，私は殺人ではないかと思う *Judging* by the marks on his neck, I suspect murder. / 彼が以前に彼女に会ったことがあるという

ことは考えられる(→可能性がある) It is *possible* that he has seen her before. / 彼が病気だとは考えられない It is *unlikely* that he is sick.

❹【意図する】think* of ...; (計画する) plan [他][自]

今度の日曜日に鎌倉へでも行こうかと考えています I'*m thinking of* going to Kamakura next Sunday.

家の増築を考えています We *are planning* to enlarge our house.

かんかく[1] 感覚

(寒暖・痛みなどの) feeling [C][U]; (五感・センス) sense [C]; (感受性) sensibility [U]《また a ～》

平衡感覚を失う lose *a sense of balance* / ビジネス感覚 business *sense* / 現代の感覚にマッチしたデザイン a design that matches *a* modern *sense*

私の右腕は全く感覚がなくなった I have lost all *feeling* [*sensation*] in my right arm.

あいつの美的感覚を疑うよ I doubt his *aesthetic sense*.

彼には金銭感覚がない He doesn't have *a sense of economy*.

◆母は最近の若い人の感覚は(→何を考えているのか)分からないと言っている My mother says she can't understand *what* young people these days *are thinking*.

‖感覚器官 a sense organ / 色彩感覚 a sense of color, a sensibility for color / 方向感覚 a sense of direction

かんかく[2] 間隔 (時間・空間の) interval [C]; (物と物の) space [U][C]; (距離) distance [C][U]

木を等[3メートル]間隔に植える plant trees at regular [three-meter] *intervals*

机と机の間隔をもう少しあけ[詰め]なさい Make「some more [a little less] *space* between the desks.

◆2台の車は5センチもないくらいの間隔ですれ違った The two cars passed each other not more than five centimeters *apart*.

[会]「どのくらいの間隔で電車は走っていますか」「5分間隔です」"*How often* do the trains run?" "They run「at five-minute *intervals* [*every* five minutes]."

かんかつ 管轄 《公式的》jurisdiction [U] ‖この種の事件は警察の管轄外だ Cases of this kind are *not within* [*under*] *the jurisdiction* of the police. / The police have *no jurisdiction over* cases of this kind.

かんがっき 管楽器 wind instrument [C]; (オーケストラなどの管楽器部) the wind

カンガルー kangaroo [C] (複 ～s)

かんかん 審判の判定にかんかんになって怒る *be furious* about the umpire's decision / きょうはかんかん照りだ It's *a sizzling hot day* today!/ It's *a scorcher* today!

がんがん 頭ががんがんする have *a splitting* headache / エアコンをがんがんきかせる have the air conditioner on *at full blast*

かんき[1] 換気 airing [U]《また an ～》, ventilation [U] ―換気する air [他], ventilate [他] ‖窓をあけて換気した I opened the window of the room and *gave* it *a good airing*. / この部屋は換気がいい[悪い] This room *is* well [badly] *ventilated*.

‖換気口 a vent / 換気扇 a ventilating [an extractor] fan / 換気装置 a ventilator

かんき[2] 喚起 ―喚起する arouse [他], call [他], evoke [他] ‖(…への)注意を喚起する *call a person's* attention (to ...) / その本は新しい科学の分野への我々の興味を喚起した The book *aroused* our interest in a new field of science.

かんき[3] 歓喜 delight [U], joy [U] ➔よろこび ‖選手たちは歓喜の声をあげた The players gave a cry of *delight*. ◆歓喜の表情 a *delighted* look

かんき[4] 乾季・乾期 the dry season

かんき[5] 寒気 the cold ‖寒気団 a body of cold air, a cold air mass

かんきつ(るい) 柑橘(類) citrus fruit [C][U]

かんきゃく 観客 (スポーツなどの) spectator [C]; (観衆・聴衆) audience [C] ‖そのボクシングの試合は観客を熱狂させた The boxing match drove *the spectators* wild. / 手品師は箱の中身を観客に見せた The magician disclosed the contents of the box to *the audience*. / 観客は多かった[少なかった] There was *a* large [small] *audience*.

◆この劇場は500人の観客を収容できる This theater can hold 500 *people*. / きょうのコンサートの観客動員数は5千人だった Today's concert *attendance* (*figure*) was 5,000.

‖観客席 a seat, a stand

かんきゅう 緩急 球に緩急をつける *mix the speeds* of the pitches

がんきゅう 眼球 eyeball [C]

かんきょう 環境

(人に影響を与える) environment [U][C]; (物理的な) surroundings; (状況) circumstances ➔ [場面・状況別会話] p.1738

自然環境 *the* natural *environment*

僕の家の周りはとても環境がいい I have *a* nice *environment* around my house.

このあたりは環境が悪い *The environment* around here is bad.

その建物は周りの環境にうまく溶け込んでいる The building fits well into *its surroundings*.

きっとすぐ新しい環境に慣れるよ You will become accustomed to「*a* new *environment* [new *circumstances*] soon.

子供の性格は家庭環境に大きく左右される A child's personality is greatly influenced by *his* [*her*] *home environment*.

◆電気自動車は環境にやさしいといわれている It is said that electric cars are *environmentally-friendly*.

‖環境アセスメント environmental assessment / 環境衛生 environmental hygienics / 環境汚染 environmental pollution / 環境音楽 environmental music / 環境学 ecology / 環境基準 an environmental standard / 環境庁 the Environment Agency (❖2001年環境省に改称) / 環境破壊 environmental destruction / 環境保護 environmental protection / 環境保全 environmental preservation / 環境保全運動 an environmental activism / 環境ホルモン an environmental hormone, a hormone-disrupting substance / 環境問題 an environmental problem

かんきょうしょう 環境省 the Ministry of the Environment

かんきり 缶切り can [《英》tin] opener [C]

かんきん¹ 監禁 confinement [U] ➾ なんきん // 監禁されて in *confinement* ◆彼は暗く狭い部屋に1週間監禁された He *was confined* [*imprisoned*] in a small, dark room for a week.

かんきん² 換金 トラベラーズチェックを換金する *cash* a traveler's check

がんきん 元金 principal [C]

がんぐ 玩具 toy [C] ➾ おもちゃ

かんぐる 勘ぐる 彼は仲間たちが自分を裏切ろうとしているのではないかと勘ぐった He *suspected* that his friends would betray him. / 何かあるなどと勘ぐるな Don't *read* anything into it.

かんけい 関係

❶【物事の間の】relation [C] [U], relationship [C] [U]; (結びつき) connection [C]

２国間の協力[緊張]関係 「cooperative *relations* [the strain in *relations*] between two countries / 日米関係 *the* US–Japan *relationship*

この物語は現実と何の関係もない This story 「has no *relation* [*is* not *related*] *to* reality. / There is no *relation between* this story and reality.

この２つの事件には密接な関係がある There is *a* close *connection between* these two incidents.

日本はその国との友好関係を確立した Japan established *friendly relations* with the country.

◆事実関係 *the facts* / 敵対関係にある２つのギャング間の抗争 a struggle between two *rival* gangs / 天候に関係なく試合は行われる The game will be played *regardless of* the weather. / その国では政治と宗教は切っても切れない関係にある In that country 「politics and religion *are inseparably connected* [politics *is inseparable from* religion].

❷【人と物事の】relation [C] [U], relationship [C] [U]; (結びつき) connection [C]

彼はその委員会と密接な関係がある He has close *relations* [*connections, links*] *with* the committee.

私たちはあの会社とよい関係を保っています We maintain good *relations with* that company.

その記事で彼と事件との関係が明らかになった The article revealed his *connection with* the case.

◆その問題は私たち全員に関係がある That problem *concerns* all of us. / 彼はその事件と何の関係もない He *has nothing to do with* the case. / 彼はその収賄事件に関係していた He *was involved in* the bribery scandal. / 彼女が私のことをどう思おうと私には関係ない It *doesn't matter* to me what she thinks of me. / おまえには関係ない(→余計なお世話だ) *That's none of your business.* / 授業と関係のない話をしてはいけません You may not talk about things *not related to* the class.

❸【人と人の】relation [C] [U], relationship [C] [U] ➾ なか(仲)

親子関係 *the relations* [*relationship*] *between parents and children* / 顧客との信頼関係を築く establish *a relationship of mutual trust* with customers

君と美幸ってどういう関係なの What is *the relationship between* you and Miyuki?

この出来事が私と彼の関係にピリオドを打った This event put an end to my *relationship with* him.

◆彼と従業員の関係はうまくいっている He *is on good terms with* his employees. / 彼は私の隣人だが，それ以上は何の関係もない He is my neighbor, but beyond that I *have nothing to do with* him. / あの人とは血縁関係はない I'*m* not *related to* that man. / その会社は上下関係が厳しい(→上司に従うよう強く求められる) In the company *the employees are required to strictly obey their bosses.* / 警察は被害者の交友関係を洗った The police checked out the victim's *circle of acquaintances.*

❹【分野・方面】

彼はコンピュータ[教育]関係の仕事をしている He is *in* computers [education].

❺【その他】

経済学関係の本 a book *about* [*on*] economics

それは関係者全員に知らされた It was told to all (*the people*) *concerned.*

父は仕事の関係でよく海外に行く My father often goes abroad *on business.*

紙面の関係で(→不足のため)彼の評論は大幅に削られた His essay was greatly reduced *for lack of space.*

‖関係書類 the relevant documents / 関係当局 the authorities concerned / 因果関係 a causal [cause–effect] relation / 外交関係 diplomatic relations / 男女関係 the relations between the sexes / 肉体関係 physical relations / 人間関係 human relations ➾ むかんけい

かんげい 歓迎 welcome [C], reception [C]
—歓迎する welcome [他]

心のこもった歓迎 *a* cordial [hearty] *welcome* / 歓迎のあいさつ a *welcoming* speech

私は新しい学校で温かい歓迎を受けた I received *a* warm *welcome* at the new school.

いつ訪ねようと彼女は君を温かく歓迎してくれるだろう Whenever you (may) visit her, she'll 「warmly *welcome* you [give you *a* warm *welcome*].

どなたでも入部歓迎 We would *welcome* anybody [Anybody is *welcome(d)*] to join our club.
◆ 初心者[経験者]歓迎 Beginners [Experienced people] *welcome* / 歓迎されない客 an *unwelcome* guest / どんな提案でも歓迎します Any suggestion is *welcome*.
‖歓迎会 a welcome party; (正式の) a reception

かんげいこ 寒稽古 midwinter practice ⓒ

かんけいしゃ 関係者 (手紙で)関係者各位 To whom it may concern / 関係者以外立入禁止 (掲示) *Staff Only* / その作品は映画関係者の間では有名だ That film is well-known among *people* in the film industry.

かんけいだいめいし 関係代名詞〔文法〕relative pronoun ⓒ

関係代名詞は接続詞と代名詞の働きをあわせもつ語で、関係代名詞以下の節は、先行する名詞・代名詞を修飾する。先行する名詞・代名詞は「先行詞」と呼ばれる。ただし、関係代名詞の what は先行詞を含んでいる。関係代名詞は、先行詞の種類と格によって次のように分けられる。

先行詞	主格	所有格	目的格
人	who	whose	who(m)
動物・物	which	whose/of which	which
人・動物・物	that	—	that
先行詞を含む	what	—	what

かんけいふくし 関係副詞〔文法〕relative adverb ⓒ

関係副詞は接続詞と副詞の働きをもつ語で、how, when, where, why が主なものである。関係副詞節が修飾する名詞・代名詞(先行詞)を伴う場合と伴わない場合がある / Spring is the season *when* flowers are most beautiful. 春は花がもっとも美しい季節である / This is *how* he became a rich man. (→これが彼が金持ちになった方法だ)彼はこうして金持ちになった

かんげき¹ 感激 (強い感情) emotion ⓤ; (感銘) impression ⓤⓒ ――感激する be moved, be touched, be impressed ⇨ かんどう(感動) / 感激して涙を流す be moved to tears / 私たちは彼のスピーチに非常に感激した We *were* greatly *moved* by his speech. / この感激は言葉では言い表せません I can't express in words how *impressed* I *was*. / 彼女は感激屋だ(→すぐ感激する) She is *moved easily*.

かんげき² 観劇 theater-going ⓤ ‖観劇に行く go to *the theater*; go to *see a play*

かんけつ¹ 完結 conclusion ⓤⓒ; (完成) completion ⓤ ――完結する be concluded, be completed / 次回完結 *To be concluded*. (⟜連載記事などで用いる) / この漫画は次号で完結する This comic *will be completed* in the next issue.
‖完結編 the final program of a series

かんけつ² 簡潔 ――簡潔な brief, concise

――簡潔に briefly, concisely ⇨ てみじか / 彼のスピーチは簡潔で要を射ていた His speech was *brief* [*concise*] and to the point. / 簡潔に説明してください Explain it *briefly* [*concisely, in brief*], please.

かんけつせん 間欠泉 geyser [gáizər] ⓒ

かんげん¹ 還元 reduction ⓤ ◆ 利益の一部を社会に還元する *return* a part of *one's* profit to society

かんげん² 換言 換言すれば *in other words*; *that is to say*; *namely* ⇨ すなわち

かんげんがく 管弦楽 orchestral music ⓤ

かんげんがくだん 管弦楽団 orchestra ⓒ (⟜構成員に重点をおく場合は複数扱いになることがある)

かんご 歓呼 観衆は最初にスタジアムに入ってきた走者を歓呼して迎えた The crowd *cheered* the first runner to enter the stadium.

かんご 看護 nursing ⓤ, care ⓤ ――看護する attend ⓔⓘ, nurse ⓔⓘ, look after *a person*, care for *a person*, take* care of *a person* / 手厚い看護 full *nursing care* / 彼女は看護の仕事に向いている She is made for *nursing*. / その患者は絶えず看護が必要だ The patient needs constant *care*. / 彼女は3か月間夫の看護をしている She *has been attending* (*to*) her husband for three months.
‖看護学校 a nurses' school / 看護士 a male nurse / 完全看護 complete nursing care

がんこ 頑固 ――頑固な stubborn, (かたくなな) obstinate; (しつこい) persistent
頑固な汚れ a *stubborn* stain
あの老人は頑固だ That old man *is stubborn* [*obstinate*].
あの頑固者を我々の意志に従わせるのは難しい It's no easy task to bend that *stubborn man* to our will.
◆ 彼は頑固に大統領を批判し続けた He *persisted in* criticizing the president. / 君はあまりにも考え方が頑固(→厳格)すぎる You are too *rigid* in your thinking.

かんこう¹ 観光 sightseeing ⓤ; (観光事業) tourism ⓤ
観光コースを見て回る do *a sightseeing course*
箱根に立ち寄りちょっと観光した We stopped off in Hakone and *did some sightseeing*.
私たちはパリへ観光に行った We went *sightseeing* in Paris.
その村は観光によって荒らされた The village was ruined by *tourism*.
◆ 私たちは寺院やその他の場所を観光してきた We *have seen the sights* at the temples and elsewhere.
‖観光案内所 a tourist office, a tourist information center / 観光ガイド a sightseeing [tour] guide / 観光客 a tourist, a sightseer / 観光シーズン the tourist season / 観光事業 tourism / 観光団 a tourist [sightseeing] party / 観光地 a tourist spot / 観光バス a sightseeing bus / 観光ビザ a tourist visa / 観光名所 a tourist attraction, a place of interest, the sights / 観光旅行 a sightseeing tour / 市内観光 (a) city sight-

かんこう² 刊行 publication Ⓤ ━━刊行する publish ⓗ, issue ⓗ ⇨ しゅっぱん(出版) ‖刊行物 a publication / 定期刊行物(日刊以外の) a periodical

かんこう³ 敢行 彼は悪天候にもかかわらず登山を敢行した He *dared to* climb the mountain in spite of the bad weather.

かんこう⁴ 感光 ‖感光紙 photosensitive paper / 感光度 sensitivity

かんこう⁵ 慣行 practice Ⓒ Ⓤ, custom Ⓤ Ⓒ ⇨ しゅうかん(習慣) ‖日本の商慣行 Japanese business *practices* / 慣行に従う follow *the practice*

がんこう 眼光 彼は眼光鋭くその男を見据えた He stared at the man *with a sharp look in his eyes*.

かんこうちょう 官公庁 government and municipal offices

かんこうへん 肝硬変 〖医学〗 cirrhosis [siróusis] Ⓤ

かんこく¹ 勧告 advice Ⓤ, recommendation Ⓤ Ⓒ ━━勧告する advise ⓗ, make* a recommendation ‖勧告に従う follow [take] *a person's recommendation* / 辞職の勧告を受ける be advised to resign / 父は医者の勧告で酒をやめた *On* his doctor's *advice*, my father gave up drinking.

かんこく² 韓国 South Korea (❖公式名 the Republic of Korea; 《略》ROK) ━━韓国人 Korean ━━韓国語 Korean Ⓤ ━━韓国(人[語])の Korean

かんごく 監獄 jail Ⓒ Ⓤ, prison Ⓒ Ⓤ ⇨ けいむしょ

かんこどり 閑古鳥 慣用表現 あのデパートは閑古鳥が鳴いている(→ほとんど客がいない) That department store *has* [*attracts*] *few customers*.

かんごふ 看護婦 nurse Ⓒ ‖付き添い看護婦 *an attendant nurse* / 献身的な看護婦 *a dedicated* [*committed*] *nurse*
‖看護婦長 a head nurse / 准看護婦 《米》a practical nurse / 正看護婦 《米》a registered nurse

かんこんそうさい 冠婚葬祭 ceremonial occasions

かんさ 監査 inspection Ⓤ Ⓒ; (会計監査) audit Ⓒ ━━監査する inspect ⓗ; audit ⓗ ‖内部[外部]監査 internal [external] *audit* / 会計を監査する *audit* accounts
‖監査報告 an audit report / 監査役(会計の) an auditor

かんさい 関西 (地方) the Kansai district ‖関西弁 (方言) the Kansai dialect; (なまり) the Kansai accent

かんざいにん 管財人 〖法律〗 administrator

かんざし 簪 ▨ a *kanzashi*, an ornamental hairpin

カンザス Kansas (❖米国中部の州;《略》) Kan., Kans., 〖郵便〗KS)

かんさつ¹ 観察 observation Ⓤ Ⓒ ━━観察する observe ⓗ, watch ⓗ
星を観察する *observe* [*watch*] the stars / 人をじっと観察する *watch* a person attentively / 観察力が鋭い have keen *powers of observation*; have a keen *eye*
朝顔の観察記録をつけた I kept *a record of observations* on the morning glories.
◆野鳥を観察しに行こう Let's go bird-*watching*. / 私は彼が話している間彼の顔をじっくり観察した I *studied* his face as he talked.
‖観察者 an observer

かんさつ² 鑑札 license, 《英》licence Ⓒ ‖犬の鑑札 a dog *license* / 鑑札を受ける get [gain, take] *a license*

かんさつ³ 監察 inspection Ⓤ Ⓒ ━━監察する inspect ⓗ ‖監察官 an inspector

かんさん¹ 換算 conversion Ⓤ Ⓒ ━━換算する convert ⓗ ‖ドルを円に換算する *convert* dollars into yen / 摂氏を華氏に換算する公式を覚えてますか Do you remember the formula for *converting* centigrade into Fahrenheit?
◆100ドルを日本円に換算するといくらになりますか How much is 100 dollars *in* yen?
‖換算値 a converted score / 換算表 a conversion table / 換算率 the exchange rate

かんさん² 閑散 閑散とした(→静かな) 神社の境内 the *quiet and calm* grounds of the shrine / その行楽地はシーズンオフは開散として いる(→人けがない) The tourist spot 「*is deserted* [*has few visitors*] in the off-season.

かんし¹ 監視 watch Ⓤ (また a ~), guard Ⓤ ━━監視する watch ⓗ, guard ⓗ, keep* an [one's] eye on ...
警官はその囚人を厳重に監視した The police kept (a) close *watch on* the prisoner. / The police *watched* the prisoner closely.
彼を厳重な監視下に置くべきだ You should put him *under* close *guard* [*watch*].
◆隣人たちの行動をひそかに監視する *spy on one's* neighbors
‖監視員 a guard, a lookout; (海・プールの) a lifeguard / 監視カメラ a surveillance camera

かんし² 冠詞 〖文法〗 article Ⓒ ‖定[不定]冠詞 *a definite* [*an indefinite*] *article*

かんし³ 漢詩 (個々の詩) Chinese poem Ⓒ; (形式) Chinese poetry Ⓤ

かんじ 感じ
❶【感覚】 feeling Ⓤ Ⓒ; (感触) the [a] feel; (手ざわり) touch Ⓤ
その葉っぱは表面がざらざらした感じだ The leaf has *a rough feel* on its surface.
◆きょうはいつもより暖かい感じがする Today I *feel* warmer than usual.
❷【印象】 impression Ⓒ; (心持ち) feeling Ⓒ
この絵はうまく描けた感じがする I have *the impression* [*a feeling*] that I painted this picture well.
◆あの転校生は感じがいい[悪い] The transfer student is a *pleasant* [*an unpleasant*] one.

/ 彼女はおとなしい感じの人です She *looks like* a quiet person. / 何だか夢を見ているような感じだ I *feel* as if I'm dreaming. / 聞いた感じでは(→話からすると)彼女は困ったことになっているらしい *By the sound of it*, she seems to be in trouble.

❢「福井さんってどんな感じの人」「とても明るい人だよ」"What's Ms. Fukui *like*?" "She's very cheerful."

❸[雰囲気] atmosphere ⓤⓒ, feeling ⓒ《また a ～》

アットホームな感じの店 a store with *a homey atmosphere* / 感じをこめて曲を演奏する play a tune with *feeling*

この映画は吹き替えでは感じが出ない。Watching the dubbed version, I cannot get the real *feeling* of this film.

❢「やあ、久しぶり」「剛かい? ずいぶん感じが変わったな」"Hi. Long time no see." "Tsuyoshi, is that really you? You've really *changed*. [You *look* quite *different*.]"

かんじ² 漢字 🖌 (a) *kanji*, a Chinese character / 8画の漢字 *a Chinese character* of eight strokes / 漢字で書く write in *kanji*

‖常用漢字 Chinese characters for daily use

かんじ³ 幹事 coordinator ⓒ, organizer ⓒ; (連絡係) liaison ⓒ ◆私は新年会の幹事を務めた I was in charge of arrangements for the New Year's party.

‖幹事長 the chief secretary; (政党の) the secretary-general

かんじいる 感じ入る be deeply impressed

がんじがらめ がんじがらめの(→厳格な)規則 *hard and fast* rules / 人をがんじがらめに縛り上げる tie a person up *heavily* / 規則にがんじがらめにされるのは嫌いだ I hate to be *bound* by rules.

かんしき 鑑識 (判断) judgment ⓤⓒ, (犯罪捜査のための) criminal identification ⓤ
◆彼女は骨董(ぶ)品に対する鑑識眼がある She has *an eye [a good eye] for* antiques.

がんじつ 元日 New Year's Day

かんして 関して ➡かんする、について

かんじとる 感じ取る (状況などを理解する) take* in; (気づく) perceive ⓣ ◆彼はひとめですべての状況を感じ取った He *took in* the whole situation at a glance. / 彼女はその子供の声が震えているのを感じ取った She *perceived* the child's voice trembling.

かんしゃ¹ 感謝 thanks; (感謝の念) gratitude ⓤ ──感謝する thank ⓣ; be grateful, appreciate ⓣ

➡ コミュニケーションスキル p.353

私の心は感謝の気持ちでいっぱいになった My heart filled with *gratitude*.

彼は感謝のしるしとして彼女にプレゼントを贈った He gave her a present as a token of *his gratitude*.

彼は彼らの援助に深く感謝の意を表した He showed deep *gratitude for* their help.

あなたのご助力に心から感謝します *Thank you very much for* your help. / I'm *grateful for* your help. / I really *appreciate* your help. (❢この順で丁寧な表現になる)

‖感謝祭 Thanksgiving Day / 感謝状 a letter of thanks, a thank-you note

かんしゃ² 官舎 government employee housing ⓤ

かんじゃ 患者 patient ⓒ; (特定の病気・けがの) case ⓒ; (病気で苦しんでいる人) sufferer ⓒ ‖はしかの患者 *a case* of measles / 末期患者 *a terminal patient* / 患者を治療する cure *a patient* / 患者を診察する see [examine] *a patient* ◆エイズ患者(→犠牲者) an AIDS victim; a PWA (❢ *person with AIDS* の略語)

‖外来患者 an outpatient / 入院患者 an in-patient

かんしゃく 癇癪 temper ⓤⓒ《また a ～》‖かんしゃくを起こして in a fit of *temper* / 彼はかんしゃくもちだ He has a quick [hot, short] *temper*. / 彼女がかんしゃくを起こすのを見たことがない I have never known her (to) 「*lose her temper* [*fly into a temper*].

かんじやすい 感じ易い、(敏感な) sensitive; (感化されやすい) impressionable ‖感じやすい年ごろの子供を扱うのは難しい It's hard to deal with a child at a *sensitive* age.

かんしゅ 看守 guard ⓒ, (英) warder ⓒ

かんじゅ 甘受 ──甘受する (従う) submit ⓘ; (耐える) endure ⓣ, put* up with … / 会議での決定を甘受する *submit to* the decision made at the meeting

かんしゅう¹ 慣習 custom ⓤⓒ, convention ⓤⓒ ‖慣習に従って by [according to] *custom* / 古い慣習を打ち破る [に従う] break [follow] *an old custom* / 人に会ったときおじぎをするのが日本人の慣習だ It is *a custom* of [for, with] the Japanese to bow when they meet someone.

‖慣習法 a customary law

かんしゅう² 監修 (editorial) supervision ⓤ ‖この百科事典は広田氏の監修で編纂(ん)された This encyclopedia was compiled under *the supervision* of Mr. Hirota.

‖監修者 an (editorial) supervisor

かんしゅう³ 観衆 《集合的》audience ⓒ; (スポーツなどの) spectator ⓒ ‖観衆を集める draw *an audience* / 彼の演技は多くの観衆を引きつけた His performance drew *a large audience*. / チームのメンバーたちは観衆に手を振った The team waved (their hands) to *the spectators*. ◆5万人の観衆がスタンドを埋めつくした A *crowed* of 50,000 filled the stands.

かんじゅく 完熟 完熟トマト a *fully ripe* tomato

かんじゅせい 感受性 sensibility ⓤ, a feeling / 音楽的感受性の豊かな人 a person of musical *sensibility* ◆明はとても感受性が強い Akira *is* very *sensitive*.

がんしょ 願書 application (form) ⓒ ‖入学願書を出す fill [send in] *an application for admission* / 願書の受け付けは1月10日から20日までです *Applications* will be accepted

かんしょう

コミュニケーションスキル —感謝—

①感謝を表したいときの表現

(A) **Thank you. / Thanks.**
ありがとう．

(B) **Thank you for** calling.
電話をありがとう．

(C) **I'm thankful to** you for supporting me.
支持していただき感謝しています．

(D) **I'm very grateful that** you came to see me.
会いに来てくださってありがとうございます．

(E) **It's nice [kind] of** you to bring me here.
ここに連れてきてくれてありがとう．

(F) I really **appreciate** your consideration.
ご配慮にたいへん感謝いたします．

(G) **I owe** Ms. Brown my deepest gratitude.
私はブラウン先生に感謝しています．

☞ 日常の話し言葉では (A) (B) がふつう．最もくだけた言い方で若者がよく使うThanks. は「どうも(ね)」の響きである．(A) を丁寧な言い方にすると **Thank you very much.** や **Thanks a lot.** などとなる．**Thank you (ever) so much.** は女性が好んで使う表現．相手が自分に何かをしてくれるとき，「どうもね」の軽い響きでは **I appreciate it.** といい，「感謝します」の丁寧な響きでは I really appreciate it. という．

☞「…してくれて」と感謝の理由を述べる場合は (B) のように Thank you for ... のようにする．「いろいろとありがとうございました」なら **Thank you very much for everything.** となる．

☞ (C) 以下はフォーマルな響きがあり，(C) は thank の形容詞を使った表現．また thank を名詞として使って **Thanks to him, I got this chance.** (彼のおかげでこのチャンスをものにできました) のような表現や，動詞の形で **I thanked my father for his heartfelt advice.** (父の心からのアドバイスに感謝した) などと表現することもできる．

☞ (E) (F) の形も会話でよく使われる．

☞ (G) の owe を使って **I owe you a lot.** とすると「(あなたに) とても感謝しています」という意味になる．

☞ 依頼したことや聞きたかったことがかなわなかったときでも，相手に対して **Thank you anyway. / Thank you just [all] the same.** (とにかくありがとう) などというのがエチケットである．

②感謝に対する受け答えの表現

(A) You helped me a lot. Thank you.
–**You are welcome. / That's O.K. / No problem.**
本当に助かったよ．ありがとう—たいしたことないよ．

(B) It's very kind of you to recommend me as a good translator.
–**Don't mention it. / It's my pleasure.**
優秀な翻訳家として推薦していただき光栄です—どういたしまして．

(C) I'm really grateful to you for coming to the party.
–**The pleasure is mine.**
パーティーにご出席いただきまことにありがとうございます—(こちらこそ) ありがとうございます．

(D) Thank you for showing me the way.
–**Not at all.**
道順を教えてくださってありがとうございました—いいえ，何でもありませんよ．

☞ (A) は最も一般的な返事のしかた．No problem. はくだけた言い方．ほかに **(It's) no big deal.** (たいしたことないよ) などもある．

☞ (B) は (A) よりフォーマルな印象を与える．

☞ (C) は「私のほうこそ楽しんでいますよ」と相手と喜びを共有していることを表す．

☞ (D) には「お礼を言ってもらうほどのことではないですよ」という意味が含まれている．

from January 10 through 20. / 願書の締め切り日は2月14日です The *application* deadline is February 14.

かんしょう¹ 干渉 interference ⓤ, intervention ⓒ ⓤ ——干渉する interfere ⓐ, meddle ⓐ, 《口語的》 poke [stick*] one's nose into ...
他国の内政に干渉する *interfere in* the internal affairs of other countries
彼女は他人のことに干渉しがちだ She is apt to *interfere* [*meddle*] *in* other people's affairs.

かんしょう² 鑑賞 appreciation ⓒ ⓤ ——鑑賞する appreciate ⓗ; (楽しむ) enjoy ⓗ
クラシック音楽の鑑賞 an *appreciation* of classical music / 音楽を鑑賞する *appreciate* music
鑑賞にたえる写真を撮りたい I want to take a photograph worthy of *appreciation*.

◆彼女は絵の鑑賞力がある She has *a good eye for* paintings. / 趣味は映画鑑賞です I like *watching* movies.

かんしょう³ 観賞 草花を観賞する *enjoy looking at* flowers
‖観賞植物 an ornamental plant

かんしょう⁴ 感傷 sentiment ⓤ ‖仕事には感傷の入る余地はない There is no place for *sentiment* in business.
◆感傷的な映画 *sentimental* films / これらの古い写真を見ると私はいつもちょっと感傷的になる Whenever I see these old photos, I *get a bit sentimental* about them. / 彼は浜辺でひとり感傷に浸った Alone on the shore, he *indulged in sentimentality*.

かんしょう⁵ 完勝 その試合で我々は相手チームに完勝した In that game we *won a complete victory over* our opponent.

かんしょう⁶ 環礁 atoll [ǽtɔːl] ⓒ

かんじょう

コミュニケーションスキル —感情—

①喜び・安堵(あんど)の表現

(A) **I'm glad [happy] you came to see me.**
あなたが会いに来てくれてうれしい.
(B) I've decided to accept your invitation to the party.
 –**I'm very glad [happy] to hear that.**
パーティーへのご招待、お受けすることにしました.
—そのことを伺ってとてもうれしいです.
(C) **I made it! [I did it!; All right!] I got a perfect score!**
やったあ！ 満点だ！
(D) **Guess what**, I won first place in the essay contest.
あのね、小論文のコンテストで優勝したんだよ.
(E) I'll buy you a bicycle as a Christmas present.
 –**Wow! [Gee!] That's great!**
クリスマスのプレゼントに自転車を買ってあげよう.—うわあ、すごいや！
(F) **What a relief!**
ああ、ほっとした[よかった].

☞ (A), (B) の glad と happy は「うれしい」という喜びの気持ちを表す最もふつうの語. (A)はやや改まった表現で, 親しい間柄では**(It's) good to see you.**でよい.
☞ (C)は何かを達成したときに口にする表現. ほかの人に対しては**You made it!**(やったね！)のようにいう.
☞ (D) の That's great! は単に**Great!**でもよい. この言葉は、相手の成功を賞賛したり、提案を受け入れたりするときにも使われる.
☞ (E) の Wow! は口を大きくあけて [wáːu] くらいの大げさな感じに発音する.

②怒りや不快の表現

(A) **That's ridiculous!**
そんなのばかげてるよ！
(B) **How stupid!**
なんとばかな！
(C) **This is not fair.**
フェアじゃないよ.
(D) **That really makes me mad.**
本当に頭にきたよ.
(E) **Shame on you!**
ばかだなあ！
(F) **He has such a nerve!**
あいつは全く厚かましいやつだ！
(G) **It's irritating.**
いらいらするなあ.
(H) **Quite disgusting!**
全くいまいましい！

☞ (A)は物事に対して, (B)は人と物事の両方に使うことができる.
☞ (E)は「恥を知りなさい」が原義で, 悪いことをした子供に親が「いけない子ね！」としかるような場合にも使う.

③悲しみ・失望の表現

(A) **I'm so sad.**
とても悲しい.
(B) **What a pity!**
残念だ！
(C) **How disappointing!**
がっかりだよ！
(D) **I miss you.**
あなたがいなくて寂しい.

☞ (B)は「かわいそうに」という同情の気持ちも表し, **What a pity** you couldn't join us! (あなたがいっしょに来られなくて残念でした)のように、後に文をつなげていうこともできる.
☞ (D)は別れる人に対しては **I'll miss you.** (あなたがいなくなると寂しくなります)という.

④驚きの表現

(A) **What a surprise!**
驚いた！
(B) **You scared me!**
びっくりした！
(C) **I was so scared.**
すっごく怖かった.
(D) **That's terrible [horrible].**
それはひどいね.
(E) **Oh, my God!**
おやまあ！[なんてこった！]

☞ (B)はだれかがぬっと現れたような場合に口にする表現.
☞ (E)は大変な驚き・恐怖に対して使われる.

かんじょう¹ 感情

(気持ち) feeling ©（❖ただし怒りなどの強い感情を意味するときはⓊ, 理性に対する感情を意味するときは feelings）, 《公式的》sentiment Ⓤ ©; (強い気持ち) emotion Ⓤ©; (理性的な判断がきかない) passion Ⓤ©
➡ コミュニケーションスキル

国民感情 national *sentiment* / 感情のこもった手紙 a letter with *feeling* / 感情をこめて歌う sing *with feeling*

彼は感情が顔に出やすい He shows *his feelings* [*emotions*] easily.
あまりにも腹が立って感情を抑えることができなかった I was so angry that I couldn't control *my feeling*.
彼の発言にほかの人たちは感情を害した His remark hurt the others' *feelings*.
彼はその国に特別な感情をいだいていた He had *a particular feeling* about the country.
我々はよく感情に流される We are often influenced by *sentiment*.
この絵は私の感情に訴えるものがある This picture appeals to my *emotions*.
このような政策はその国の対日感情をいたずらに悪化させるだけだ Such a policy will end up only worsening the country's *feeling toward Japan* needlessly.
◆感情が高ぶる get *excited* / 彼女は感情の起伏が激しい She *is very emotional*. / どうして

んなに感情的になるの Why do you get so *emotional?* / 主人公に感情移入しながら映画を見た I watched the movie *empathizing with* the heroine in it.

かんじょう[2] 勘定
❶【計算】calculation [U]; (数を数えること) count [C] ―勘定する calculate [他]; (1つずつ数えて) count [他]
どうも勘定が合わない Somehow *my calculation* is not correct.
彼を勘定に入れるのを忘れるところだった I nearly forgot to *count* him *in*.
キャプテンはチームメートの数をもう一度勘定した The captain *counted* the number of teammates again.
❷【支払い】(請求書) bill [C]; (レストランの) check [C]; (勘定書) account [C]
お勘定, お願いします *Check* [*Bill*], please.
お勘定はすませたの? Have you paid *the bill*?
勘定は私が払います I'll pay *the bill*./ (→私のおごりです) This is 「*on* me [my *treat*].
お勘定は別々でお願いします Separate *checks* [*bills*], please.
食事代は私の勘定につけておいてください Charge the cost of the meal (up) to my *account*.
❸【考慮】account [U], consideration [U]
それは勘定に入れてある I have taken it into *account*.
[慣用表現] 彼は勘定高い人だ He is *calculating*.

かんじょう[3] 環状 幹線道路はここで環状道路と交差している The main road intersects *the beltway* [《英》*ring road*] here.
‖環状線《米》a belt line

がんじょう 頑丈 ―頑丈な strong, stout, sturdy; (堅固な) solid ∥頑丈なかばん a *stout* bag / 頑丈な壁 a *solid* wall / 彼は頑丈な体をしている He has a *strong* body. ◆頑丈に作られた箱 a *strongly-built* box

かんしょく[1] 感触 the [a] feel, the [a] touch; (印象・予感) feeling [C] ∥この生地は柔らかくて感触がいい This cloth is soft to *the touch* [*feel*]./ This cloth *feels* soft. / 私はシルクの感触が好きだ I like *the feel* of silk. / 試験に合格する感触を得た I got *the feeling* [*impression*] that I would pass the exam.

かんしょく[2] 間食 snack [C] ―間食する snack [自], eat* between meals

かんしょく[3] 官職 (地位) government post [C]; (職務) government service [C] [U]

かんじる 感じる

feel* [他] [自]; (五感で) sense [他]; (印象を受ける) be impressed by [with] ...; (気づいている) be aware of ..., be conscious of ...
【feel＋名】春の息吹を感じた I *felt* the breath of spring.
【feel＋名＋*doing*】彼女は心臓が速く打つのを感じた She *felt* her heart beating fast.
【feel＋that節】彼女は最近野菜不足だと感じている She *feels that* she doesn't eat enough vegetables these days.
【feel＋形】私はたいへん幸せだと感じた I *felt* very happy. / それに対して多少責任を感じている I *feel* partly responsible for it.
その兵士はすぐに危険を感じた The soldier soon *sensed* danger.
群衆の中にいるとつくづく孤独だと感じる I *am* very *aware of* loneliness among the crowds.
◆彼のスピーチには自信が感じられた There was *a note* of confidence in his speech. / この制度には何か矛盾を感じる I *think* there is something contradictory in this system. / その地方の冬の厳しさを肌で感じてきた I have been to the district and *realized firsthand* the harshness of the winter there.

かんしん[1] 感心 admiration [U] ―感心な good; (感嘆すべき) admirable ―感心する (感嘆する) admire [他]; (感銘を受ける) be impressed
彼はとても感心な生徒です He is an *admirable* student.
私たちは彼が親切なのに感心した We *admired* him *for* his kindness.
私は彼の知識の深さに感心した I *was impressed by* the depth of his knowledge.
◆彼の記憶力にはほとほと感心する I *am amazed at* his memory. / 祖母は最近の若者の言葉づかいには感心しないと言っている My grandmother says she 「*doesn't like* [*isn't happy with*] the language young people use these days. / 見もしないで日本映画はおもしろくないなどと決めつけるのは感心しないな(→よくないと思う) I *don't think* it's *right* for you to conclude that Japanese films aren't interesting without giving them a try.

かんしん[2] 関心 (興味) interest [U] [C]; (気がかり) concern [C] ⇨むかんしん
英語に関心を持つ take *an interest* in English
私は茶道にとても関心があります I have *a* great *interest* in the tea ceremony./ I *am* very *interested in* the tea ceremony.
スポーツにはあまり関心がありません I have little *interest* in sports./ I *am* not very *interested in* sports.
彼女はその絵に並々ならぬ関心を示した She showed no ordinary *interest* in the picture.
◆健康に対する人々の関心が高まって[低くなって]きている People *have been* 「more and more [less and less] *interested in* their own health. / 彼は社会問題に無関心だ He *is indifferent* to social problems. / そのスポーツ選手は世界中の人々の関心(→注目)を集めている The sports player has attracted *the attention* of people all over the world.
‖関心事 a matter of concern

かんしん[3] 歓心 人の歓心を買おうとする try to win a person's *favor*

かんじん 肝心 ―肝心な (重要な) important; (必須(ひっす)の) essential; (決定的な) crucial ∥それはもっともですが一つ肝心なことを見落としていますね That's fair enough, but you

have missed one *important* thing. / 肝心なときに彼はいつも失敗をしてしまう He always makes a mistake at a *crucial* moment.
◆肝心なのはあなたにもう一度やってみる気があるかどうかだ *The thing is* whether you have the will to try again.

かんすい 冠水 畑は冠水していた The field was *submerged*.

かんすう 関数【数学】*function* ◎ / 一次[二次]関数 *a linear* [*quadratic*] *function* / 三角関数 *a trigonometric function*

かんする 関する *about*, *on* (❋*about* より専門的な内容であることを暗示)，《公式的》*concerning*,《公式的》*with respect* [*regard*] *to* ...

その地震に関するニュース the news *about* the earthquake / 大気汚染に関する科学的データ the scientific data *on* air pollution
その点に関しては全く異論はありません I have no objection *on* the point.
彼はその収賄事件に関する一切の質問に答えることを拒否した He refused to answer any questions *concerning* the bribery scandal.

かんせい¹ 完成
completion Ⓤ, *perfection* Ⓤ ——完成する[させる] *complete* ⑯, *finish* ⑯, *perfect* ⑯ ⇨みかんせい

新しい橋の完成は遅れている *Completion* of the new bridge has been delayed.
このジグソーパズルは完成間近だ This jigsaw puzzle is near *completion*.
来週までにこの仕事を完成させなければならない I must *finish* [*complete*] this work by next week.
市庁舎は来年の春完成(する)予定だ The city hall is due to *be finished* [*completed*] in the spring next year.
彼女の歌唱技術は今や完成の域に達した Her singing technique has now reached *perfection*.
◆彼女の作品は完成度が高い Her work *is very mature* [*sophisticated*].
‖完成品 a finished product

かんせい² 歓声 *cheer* Ⓒ, *a shout of joy* / 勝者のファンは歓声をあげた The fans of the winner「*gave a shout of joy* [*shouted for joy*]. / インタビューは途中で何度も観衆の大きな歓声にさえぎられた The interview was punctuated with loud *cheers* from the audience. ◆そのランナーに歓声を送る *cheer* the runner; *give* [*raise*] *a cheer for* the runner

かんせい³ 閑静 ——閑静な *quiet* ‖閑静な住宅地 *a quiet* residential area

かんせい⁴ 感性 *sensibility* Ⓤ; (敏感さ) *sensitivity* Ⓤ ‖芸術的感性の持ち主 a person of artistic *sensibility*

かんせい⁵ 慣性【物理】*inertia* [ɪnə́ːrʃə] Ⓤ ‖慣性の法則 the law of *inertia*

かんせい⁶ 管制 *control* Ⓤ; (検閲) *censorship* Ⓤ ‖地上管制 ground *control* / 航空管制 flight *control*; air traffic *control*

◆灯火管制[報道管制]を敷く impose 「*a blackout* [*news censorship*]
‖管制官 an air traffic controller / 管制塔 a control tower

かんぜい 関税 *customs*(単数または複数扱い), *customs duties*, *tariff* Ⓒ ‖ウイスキーの関税を払う *pay customs on* whiskey / 関税を撤廃する *eliminate tariffs* / 車の関税を上げる *raise the tariff* on cars
‖関税障壁 a tariff barrier / 関税率 a tariff rate

かんせいはがき 官製葉書 *post card* Ⓒ, *postal card* Ⓒ (❋英国には官製はがきはない)

がんせいひろう 眼精疲労 *eyestrain*

がんせき 岩石 *rock* Ⓒ Ⓤ ⇨いし(石), いわ
‖岩石標本 specimens of rock

かんせつ¹ 間接 ——間接的な *indirect* (❋通例名詞の前で用いる) ——間接的に *indirectly* / 人に間接的に言及する make an *indirect* reference to a person / 事件のことは間接的に聞いた I heard about the event *indirectly* [*secondhand*].
‖間接喫煙 passive smoking / 間接照明 indirect lighting / 間接税 an indirect tax / 間接選挙 an indirect election / 間接民主制 indirect democracy / 間接目的語【文法】an indirect object / 間接話法 ⇨わほう

かんせつ² 関節 *joint* Ⓒ ‖指の関節 finger *joints* / そのタックルで肩の関節がはずれてしまった That tackle *put* [*threw*] my shoulder *out of joint*. / 指の関節をぽきぽき鳴らす crack *one's* knuckles
‖関節炎 arthritis / 関節リューマチ articular rheumatism

かんせん¹ 感染 *infection* Ⓤ,《公式的》*contagion* Ⓤ ——感染する *catch** ⑯, be infected ‖正体不明のウイルスに感染する *be infected with* an unknown virus
◆その病気は感染しない The disease is not *infectious* [*contagious*, 《口語的》*catching*]. / インフルエンザは感染力が強い Influenza *is highly contagious*. / Influenza *has high infectivity*.
‖感染経路 an infection route / 感染症 an infectious disease / 空気感染 aerial infection, infection passed through the air / 二次感染 secondary infection

かんせん² 観戦 相撲を観戦する *watch* a sumo tournament

かんせん³ 幹線 *trunk* [*main*] *line* Ⓒ ‖幹線道路 a trunk [main] road, a highway

かんせん⁴ 汗腺【解剖】sweat gland Ⓒ

かんぜん¹ 完全
(必要なものがすべてそろった状態) *completeness* Ⓤ; (完璧(<small>ペキ</small>)) *perfection* Ⓤ ——完全な *complete*; *perfect*; (十分な) *full* ——完全に *completely*; *perfectly*; *fully*; (すっかり) *quite*, *entirely* ⇨ふかんぜん

恐竜の完全な骨格 the *complete* skeleton of a dinosaur / 完全な思い違い a *complete* [*perfect*, *total*] misunderstanding
ジムは自分の日本語を完全なものにするために日本

へやってきた Jim came to Japan to make his Japanese *perfect*.

そのデータは記録から完全に消去されていた The data had been *completely* erased from the record.

めんが完全に伸びてしまった The noodles have got *completely* soggy.

台所はまだ完全には設備が整っていない The kitchen is not *fully* equipped yet.

彼の言うことを完全に理解したわけではなかった I didn't *quite* [*entirely*] understand what he said.

完全無欠な人はいない Nobody is *perfect*.

‖完全看護 complete nursing care / 完全雇用 a full employment / 完全試合 a perfect game / 完全主義 perfectionism / 完全燃焼 complete combustion / 完全犯罪 a perfect crime

かんぜん² 敢然 ──敢然と (勇敢に) bravely, courageously; (恐れずに) fearlessly ‖彼女は組織の不正に敢然と立ち向かった She *courageously* faced the injustice in the organization.

かんそ 簡素 ──簡素な simple ‖簡素な食事 a *simple* meal / 簡素に暮らす live a *simple* life ◆式典を簡素化する *simplify* a ceremony

がんそ 元祖 (創始者) the originator; (生みの親) the father

かんそう¹ 乾燥 ──乾燥した (乾いた) dry ──乾燥する[させる] dry ⓗ ‖乾燥した気候 a *dry* climate / 乾燥肌 *dry* skin / きょうは空気が乾燥している The air *is dry* today. / 九州地方の乾燥続きも先週の台風で終わりを告げた The *dry* spell in Kyushu ended when a typhoon hit the area last week.

‖乾燥機 a (clothes) dryer [drier] / 乾燥剤 (a) desiccant / 乾燥室 a drying room / 乾燥注意報 a dry-weather warning

かんそう² 感想 (印象) impression ⓒ ⓤ; (意見) opinion ⓒ ⓤ, remark ⓒ ‖感想を述べる express [give, offer] *one's opinion* ‖僕たちの学校についての感想は？ What's *your impression* of our school?

◆本の感想文を書く write *an essay* on a book / 日本にお越しになったご感想は？ *How do you like* Japan? / 一通り読んだら感想を聞かせてね Let me hear *what you think of* it after you read it through.

かんそう 完走 ──完走する run* till the end ‖20 キロのコースを完走する *run* the whole course of 20 kilometers

かんぞう 肝臓 liver ⓒ ‖飲みすぎは肝臓障害を引き起こすことがある Too much drinking can cause *liver problems*.

かんそうかい 歓送会 farewell party ⓒ, 《口語的》send-off (party) ⓒ ‖歓送会を開く hold *a farewell party* (for *a person*)

かんそうきょく 間奏曲 〖音楽〗interlude ⓒ, intermezzo ⓒ (複 ～s, intermezzi)

かんそく 観測 observation ⓒ ⓤ ──観測する observe ⓗ ‖天体 [気象] 観測をする make *an astrological* [*a meteorological*] *observa-*

tion / 星の動きを観測する *observe* the movement of a star

◆希望的観測 wishful *thinking*

‖観測者 an observer / 観測所 an observatory / 定点観測 fixed-point observation

かんそん 寒村 (さびれた村) deserted village ⓒ

かんたい¹ 歓待 hospitality ⓤ, welcome ⓒ ──歓待する welcome ⓗ, entertain ⓗ ‖私たちは彼女を昼食に招いて歓待した We *entertained* her with lunch.

かんたい² 寒帯 the frigid zone ‖寒帯植物 polar vegetation

かんたい³ 艦隊 fleet ⓒ

かんだい 寛大 ──寛大な (心の広い) generous, broad-minded; (寛容な) tolerant; (情け深い) lenient ──寛大さ generosity ⓤ; tolerance ⓤ; leniency ⓤ ‖寛大な処置 *lenient treat* / 人の寛大さにつけ込む abuse a person's *generosity* / 彼女はだれに対しても寛大だ She is 「*generous to* [*tolerant toward*] anyone.

がんたい 眼帯 eye patch [bandage] ⓒ ‖眼帯をする wear *an eye patch*

かんだかい 甲高い (調子の高い) high-pitched; (金切り声の) shrill ‖かん高い声で in a *high-pitched* voice / かん高い叫び声をあげる give a *shrill* cry

かんたく 干拓 land reclamation by drainage ◆湿地を干拓する *reclaim* an area from a marsh *by drainage*

‖干拓工事 reclamation works / 干拓地 reclaimed land

かんたん¹ 簡単

──簡単な (やさしい) easy; (単純な) simple; (手短な) brief ──簡単に easily; simply; briefly

簡単な仕事 an *easy* [a *simple*] task / 簡単な英語で書かれた本 a book written in *simple* English

【be easy＋(for 名(人))＋to *do*】このパソコンは初心者でも簡単に操作できます This computer *is easy* even *for* a beginner *to* operate.

【it is easy＋(for 名(人))＋to *do*】この手の機械は手入れが簡単です *It's easy to* maintain this type of machine. / 彼にとって英語を覚えるのは簡単なことだ *It is easy for* him *to* learn English.

この問題は複雑そうだが実は簡単だ This question looks complicated, but really it's *simple*.

そんなに簡単に夢をあきらめるなんて君らしくない It is unlike you to give up your dream so *easily*.

事情を簡単に説明していただけますか Would you like to explain the situation *briefly*?

簡単に言えば彼は首になったということだ To put it simply, he was fired.

◆兄は簡単に (→軽い) 夜食をとって、また試験勉強を始めた After having a *light* midnight

かんたん

snack, my brother started to study for the examination again. / そんな簡単に(→順調に)事が運ぶのならだれも苦労はしないよ If things went so *smoothly*, nobody would have difficulty. / 彼女はいとも簡単に(→難なく)ハードルを跳び越した She cleared the hurdles *without any difficulty*. / だれにでも簡単に電話番号を教えないほうがよい You shouldn't *just* give your telephone number to anyone.

かんたん[2] 感嘆 (賞賛) admiration ⓤ; (驚嘆) wonder ⓤ ──感嘆する admire ⊕ /感嘆の声をあげる cry out in *admiration* / 彼女の描写の正確さに感嘆した I *admired* the accuracy of her description.
‖感嘆詞 an exclamation, an interjection / 感嘆符 an exclamation point [《英》mark]

かんだん[1] 歓談 pleasant talk /彼らは首相としばらくの間歓談した They *had a pleasant talk* with the Prime Minister for a while.

かんだん[2] 寒暖 寒暖の差が大きい There's a big difference between *the hot and cold*.
‖寒暖計 a thermometer

がんたん 元旦 New Year's Day

かんたんぶん 感嘆文 〔文法〕 exclamatory sentence ⓒ

> what, how で始まり、最後に感嘆符が付く文のことをいう。主語＋述語動詞が省略されることが多い。文の形式に関係なく驚き・喜びなど感嘆の気持ちを表す文を感嘆文ということもある // What a horrible story (this is)! (これはなんて恐ろしい話なんだろう) / How delicious this chocolate is! このチョコレートはなんておいしいんだろう

かんち[1] 感知 この装置は微弱な振動も感知する This device *senses* even very weak vibrations.

かんち[2] 関知 君が何をしようと私は関知しない *It's none of my business* what you do.

かんちがい 勘違い ──勘違いする misunderstand* ⊕ ⊕, mistake* ⊕, be mistaken /会合の時間を勘違いしていたようです I'm afraid I *was mistaken* about the time of the meeting.
◆きょうは日曜日だと勘違いしていた I *mistakenly believed that* it was Sunday today.

がんちく 含蓄 implication ⓒⓤ /彼の言葉には含蓄があった His remark was full of *implications*.

がんちゅう 眼中 彼は金のことしか眼中にない(→彼にとっては金がすべてだ) Money means *everything* to him. / 彼は彼女に夢中でほかの女の子たちのことは全く眼中にない He's crazy about her and *takes no notice* of other girls.

かんちゅうすいえい 寒中水泳 swimming in midwinter

かんちょう[1] 官庁 government office
‖官庁街 a government office quarter

かんちょう[2] 館長 director ⓒ; (図書館の) chief librarian ⓒ; (博物館・美術館などの) curator ⓒ, 《英》keeper ⓒ

かんちょう[3] 干潮 low tide ⓒⓤ; (引き潮) the ebb (tide) /干潮時に at *low tide*

かんちょう[4] 浣腸 〔医学〕 enema [énəmə] ⓒ /浣腸する[される] give [get, have] *an enema*

かんちょう[5] 艦長 captain ⓒ

かんつう 貫通 ──貫通する penetrate ⊕, pierce ⊕ ⊕ /弾が彼の肩を貫通した The bullet *pierced* his shoulder.
◆トンネルが貫通した(→完成した) The tunnel *was completed*.

かんづく 感付く sense ⊕, be aware; (怪しいと思う) suspect ⊕, 《口語的》smell* a rat /彼女は彼がうそをついていることに感づいていた[感づいた] She *was [became] aware* of his lying. / カンニングしようとしたがすぐに先生に感づかれた I tried to cheat on the exam, but the teacher *smelled a rat* at once.

かんづめ 缶詰 can ⓒ, 《英》tin ⓒ; (缶詰食品) canned food ⓤ, 《英》tinned food ⓒ /ツナの缶詰 *a can* of tuna
◆缶詰の桃 *canned* peaches / 停電のために乗客は列車の中に缶詰になった Because of a power failure the passengers *were confined* in the train.

かんてい[1] 鑑定 judgment, 《英》judgement ⓒⓤ, appraisal ⓒⓤ ──鑑定する judge ⊕, 《公式的》appraise ⊕ /専門家に…の鑑定を依頼する ask an expert to *judge* ... / 焼き物を鑑定してもらった I had my china *appraised*.
◆筆跡鑑定によって本人かどうかの確認がすぐに行われた Identification was quickly made by *examining the handwriting*.
‖鑑定書 a written statement of expert opinion / 鑑定人 《米》an appraiser, 《英》valuer;（美術品などの）a connoisseur

かんてい[2] 官邸 official residence ⓒⓤ ‖首相官邸 the Prime Minister's official residence

かんてつ 貫徹 初志を貫徹する carry out *one's* original intention / 計画を貫徹する *carry through* a plan

かんでふくめる 噛んで含める 事情をかんで含めるように説明する explain the things *in plain words*

かんてん[1] 観点 viewpoint ⓒ, a point of view

別の観点から問題を見る look at a problem from *a different viewpoint [point of view, angle]*
◆この問題を政治的な観点から議論しましょう Let's discuss this problem *in political terms*.

かんてん[2] 寒天 agar ⓤ, Japanese gelatin ⓤⓒ

かんでん 感電 (electric) shock ⓒ /感電する get *a [an electric] shock* / 感電死する *be killed by an electric shock*; be electrocuted

かんでんち 乾電池 dry cell (battery) ⓒ, battery ⓒ

かんど 感度 (フィルムなどの) sensitivity ⓤ; (ラジオなどの) reception ⓤ /ここはラジオの感度が悪い Radio *reception* is bad here. / こ

の携帯電話は感度がいい *Reception* of this cell phone is good. ◆このフィルムは感度が高い This film is highly *sensitive*.
‖高感度カメラ a high-sensitivity camera

かんとう¹ 完投 ——完投する go* the distance, pitch a complete game

かんとう² 巻頭 the opening of a book
‖巻頭言 a foreword, a preface

かんとう³ 敢闘 敢闘(→勇敢に戦ったこと)をたたえる praise *a person* for *fighting bravely*
‖敢闘賞 a fighting-spirit prize

かんとう⁴ 関東（地方）the Kanto district
‖関東大震災 the Great Kanto Earthquake / 関東平野 the Kanto plains

かんどう¹ 感動（感銘）impression ⓤⒸ ——感動する be moved, be touched, be impressed ——感動的な moving, touching

> 英作文ノート 「感動する」=「感動させられる」
> 私たちはみな彼の演説に感動した
> →×We all *moved* to his speech.
> →○We *were all moved* by his speech.
> ★日本語では「感動した」と自動詞的に表現するが, moveは「(人を)感動させる」という他動詞なので受身で用いる.

その試合は観客に深い感動を与えた The game made *a* deep *impression* on the spectators.
私たちは彼女の温かい心に感動した We *were moved* [*touched*] by the warmth of her heart.
私は彼のスピーチに心から感動した I *was* deeply *impressed* by his speeches.
◆そのお芝居はとても感動的だった The play was very *impressive* [*moving*].

かんどう² 勘当 ——勘当する disown ⓕ ◆彼が勘当されたのは当然だ It is natural that his family *disowned* him.

かんとうし 間投詞 [文法] interjection Ⓒ

> 驚き・喜び・怒りなどの感情を表す語を間投詞という. 通例英語ではほかの文から独立しており, 最後に感嘆符を付ける. 「感嘆詞」と呼ばれることもある. ‖ *Ouch*! 痛いっ! / *Oh*! おお! / *Wow*! うわあ!

かんとく 監督

❶【監督すること】supervision ⓤ; (指揮) direction Ⓒ; (統制) control ⓤ ——監督する supervise ⓕ; direct ⓕ
彼の監督のもとで働く work under his *supervision* / 従業員を監督する *supervise* the workers
◆試験の監督をする *proctor* an examination / すみません, 私の監督不行き届きです(→気をつけていなかった) I'm sorry, I *didn't take care of* them.

❷【監督する人】supervisor Ⓒ; (映画などの) director Ⓒ; (野球などの) manager Ⓒ; (バスケットボール・サッカーなど) coach Ⓒ
監督は選手たちを呼び集めた The manager called the players together.
‖監督官庁 the competent authorities / 映画監督 a (movie) director / 現場監督 a site supervisor / 試験監督 a proctor / 舞台監督 a stage manager

がんとして 頑として (頑固として) obstinately, stubbornly; (断固として) firmly; (強情に) insistently ‖市長はその計画に頑として反対している The mayor stands *obstinately* against the plan.
◆彼はいかなる種類の援助も頑として受けようとしなかった He *would* not accept help in any shape or form. (◆would notは「どうしても…しようとしなかった」の意味)

カントリークラブ country club Ⓒ

カンナ 〖植物〗canna Ⓒ

かんな 鉋 plane Ⓒ ◆板にかんなをかける *plane* a board
‖かんなくず (wood) shavings

かんにん 堪忍 [慣用表現] 心の広い彼女もついに堪忍袋の緒が切れた Though she is broad-minded, she *lost her patience* at last.

カンニング ⚠ cheat Ⓒ (◆英語の cunning は「ずる賢い」の意味) ——カンニングする cheat ⓕ; (カンニングペーパーを使って) crib ⓕ ‖カンニングが見つかる be caught *cheating* / 私は数学の試験でカンニングをした I *cheated* on [(英)in] a math exam.
‖カンニングペーパー a crib [cheat] sheet

かんぬき 閂（戸・門の横木）bar Ⓒ; (差し錠) bolt Ⓒ ◆戸にかんぬきをかける *bar* a door

かんぬし 神主 〖神〗 Shinto priest Ⓒ

かんねん 観念（考え）idea Ⓒ, notion Ⓒ; (意識) sense ⓤ (またa～) ——観念する give* up, resign *oneself* to ..., be resigned to ... ‖彼女は本を読んで日本について誤った観念をいだいた She had *a* false *idea of* Japan from reading books. / 彼には経済観念がない He has no *sense of economy.* / いまさら試験勉強をしても遅すぎる. 観念しろ It's too late to prepare for the exam. Just *give up*! / すべて運命だと観念した I've resigned *myself to* my fate.
◆彼の福祉に関する考えはかなり観念的(→抽象的)だ His opinion about welfare is fairly *abstract*.
‖観念論〖哲学〗idealism / 観念論者 an idealist / 固定観念 a fixed idea

がんねん 元年 the first year (of an era) ‖平成元年 *the first year* of Heisei

かんのう 官能 ——官能的な sensual, sexy ‖官能的な音楽 *sensual* music

カンパ ⚠ fund-raising campaign [drive] Ⓒ (◆日本語ではロシア語の kampaniya から)
◆卒業生が私たちのクラブにカンパしてくれた The graduates *donated* some money to our club.

かんぱ 寒波 cold wave Ⓒ ‖寒波に見舞われる be hit by *a cold wave*

かんばい 完売 全席完売 All the tickets *are sold out*.

かんぱい¹ 完敗 complete defeat Ⓒ ‖私たちのチームは準決勝で完敗した Our team 「*suffered a complete defeat* [*was completely defeated*] in the semi-final.

かんぱい² 乾杯 ——乾杯する

かんばしい

drink* 慣 自, toast 他 ‖人の健康を祈って乾杯する *drink* (*to*) *a person's health*; *drink his [her] health to a person* / 新婚夫婦への乾杯の音頭をとった I proposed *a toast* to the newly married couple. / 新社長に乾杯しよう Let's drink [give, have, make] *a toast* to our new president.

◆乾杯! *Cheers!* / *Here's to you!* 《英口語的》*Bottoms up!*

かんばしい 芳しい (香りが) fragrant, sweet; (よい) good; (満足のいく) satisfactory ‖新しい先生の評判はあまりかんばしくない The new teacher doesn't have a very *good* reputation. / 試験の結果はあまりかんばしくなかった The results of the exams were not *satisfactory*.

カンバス canvas U C

かんばつ 干魃 drought [dráut] U C

かんばつをいれず 間髪を入れず → かん(間)

がんばり 頑張り (努力) effort U C; (忍耐・根気) patience U ‖彼女のがんばりはとうとう報われた At last she was rewarded for her *efforts*. ◆彼女はがんばり屋(→勤勉)だ She is *a hard worker*.

がんばる 頑張る
❶【努力する】(一生懸命やる) work [try] hard; (全力を尽くす) do* *one's* best ‖優勝できるようがんばろう Let's *do our best* to win the championship.

◆そのオーケストラは演奏会が近いのでがんばって夜遅くまで練習している The orchestra is practicing *hard* until late at night because their concert is close at hand. / がんばって! *Stick to it!* / *Hang in there!* / (→元気を出せ)*Come on!* / あしたの試合がんばってね(→ 幸運を祈る) *Good luck* with your game tomorrow.

❷【もちこたえる】hold* on [out]
彼らは目的地に着くまでどうにか水なしでがんばった They managed to *hold on* [*out*] without water until they reached their destination.

❸【主張する】insist 自 他
彼女はそんなことはしていないとがんばった She *insisted* that she didn't do that.

かんばん 看板 sign C, signboard C
壁に看板を備えつける fix *a sign* [*signboard*] to the wall
私たちは店の前に看板を立てた We put up *a sign* in front of our store.

◆わが会社の社長は看板にすぎない(→名目だけの社長にすぎない) The president of the company *is so in name only.* / 店の看板に傷をつけるようなことをするな Don't do anything that may *hurt the reputation of the shop*.

慣用表現 その新しいテーマパークは看板倒れだ(→見かけほどよくない) The new theme park is *not as nice as it looks.* / そろそろ看板にします(→店を閉める) It's time to *close.* / 不況のためその店は看板を下ろした(→廃業した) The shop *gave up its business* because of the depression.

‖看板教授 a star professor / 看板娘 a draw / 看板屋 a sign maker [painter]

かんぱん 甲板 deck C

かんび¹ 完備 そのスポーツジムにはあらゆる設備が完備されている The health club *has every amenity.* / 各教室は冷暖房完備だ Each classroom *is fully air-conditioned*.

かんび² 甘美 甘美な記憶 *sweet* memories

かんびょう 看病 nursing U ——看病する nurse 他, take* care of ..., look after ... ‖病気の父を夜通し看病した I *took care of* my sick father all night. / 彼女は母の看病疲れで倒れた She got sick because of *fatigue from nursing* her mother.

かんぴょう 干瓢 *kampyo*, dried gourd shavings

かんぶ 幹部 (指導者) leader C; (経営陣) executive C; (集合的) management U C ‖幹部会議 an executive meeting / 最高幹部 top executives, top management

かんぶ² 患部 affected [diseased] part

かんぷ 還付 return U; (返金) refund C ——還付する return 他; (金を) refund 他 ‖税金の還付 *a tax refund* / 還付を受ける get [receive] *a refund*

‖還付金 a refund

かんぷ² 完膚 相手を完膚なきまでに論破する argue down the opponent *completely*

かんぷう 完封 shutout U ——完封する shut* out ‖彼はタイガースを3安打に完封した He *shut out* the Tigers on three hits.

かんぷう² 寒風 cold wind

かんぷく 感服 admiration U ——感服する feel* (great) admiration for ... → かんしん(感心)

かんぶつ 乾物 dried goods ‖乾物屋 a grocer's, a grocery (store)

カンフル camphor U ‖彼の参加はわがチームにとっていいカンフル剤になるだろう His joining will be *a shot in the arm* for our team.

かんぶん 漢文 (文章) (classical) Chinese writing U; (中国の古典) Chinese classics 《単数扱い》

かんぺき 完璧 perfection U, completeness U ——完璧な perfect, complete ‖彼のやることすべてに完璧を期待してはいけない Don't expect *perfection* in everything he does. / 彼女の英語はほぼ完璧だ Her English *is near perfect*. ◆あとコイン1枚で僕のコレクションは完璧だ One more coin *will complete* my collection.

‖完璧主義者 a perfectionist

がんぺき 岸壁 wharf C (複 wharves, ~s), 《主に英》quay C

かんべつしょ 鑑別所 the Juvenile Classification Office

かんべん¹ 勘弁 ——勘弁する (許す) forgive* 他 自; (我慢する) bear* 他, put* up with ... ‖勘弁してください Please *forgive* me. / 彼のうそにはもう勘弁ならない I can't *put up with* his lying. ◆勘弁してよ(→いいかげんにして) *Give me a break!*

かんべん² 簡便 ——簡便な (簡単な) simple, easy; (使いやすい) handy; (便利な) conven-

ient ∥簡便な手続き a *simple* procedure
かんぽう¹ 官報 official gazette ©
かんぽう² 漢方 ∥漢方薬は自然の原料から作られる *Chinese herbal medicines* are made out of natural materials.
∥漢方医 a herb doctor, a herbalist
がんぼう 願望 desire ©Ⓤ, will Ⓤ, wish ©
⇒ コミュニケーションスキル p.391 ∥彼女は人一倍結婚願望が強かった Her *desire* to marry was stronger than others.
かんぼうちょうかん 官房長官 ∥内閣官房長官 the Chief Cabinet Secretary
かんぼく 灌木 bush ©, shrub ©, (集合的) scrub Ⓤ
カンボジア Cambodia (❖公式名 the Kingdom of Cambodia) ──カンボジア人 Cambodian © ──カンボジア語 Cambodian © ──カンボジア(人[語])の Cambodian
かんぼつ 陥没 subsidence ©Ⓤ ◆大雨で道路が陥没した The road *subsided* because of the heavy rain.
がんぽん 元本 (基本財産) principal ©; (資本金) capital ©(また a 〜)
かんまつ 巻末 the end of a book
かんまん¹ 緩慢 ──緩慢な slow, sluggish, tardy ∥動作が緩慢だ be *slow* in action
◆緩慢な警備 *lax* security
かんまん² 干満 the ebb and flow; (潮) tide Ⓤ© ∥干満の差 the range of *the tides*
かんみりょう 甘味料 sweetener ©Ⓤ ∥人工甘味料 *an artificial sweetener*
かんむり 冠 crown ©; (王子や貴族などの宝冠) coronet © (❖*crown* より小さい) ∥冠をかぶる put on *a crown*
かんむりょう 感無量 ⇒ かんがい(感慨)
かんめい 感銘 impression ©Ⓤ ∥人に感銘を与える make *an impression* on a person
◆彼女の優しさに私は感銘を受けた I *was impressed* [*struck*] by her kindness.
がんめん 顔面 ∥その知らせを聞くと彼女は顔面蒼白(そうはく)になった *Her face* [She] turned pale at the news.
∥顔面神経痛 facial neuralgia
がんもく 眼目 ∥今回の調査の眼目は事故の原因を科学的に究明することにある The main *purpose* of this inquiry is to investigate the cause of the accident scientifically.
かんもん¹ 喚問 summons © ──喚問する summon Ⓔ ∥喚問に応じる obey *a summons* / 証人として喚問される be *summoned* to appear as a witness
かんもん² 関門 barrier ©, hurdle © ∥医者になるためには多くの関門を突破しなければならない You have to clear [overcome] many *hurdles* to be a doctor.
がんやく 丸薬 pill ©
かんゆう 勧誘 invitation ©, recruitment Ⓤ ──勧誘する invite Ⓔ, recruit Ⓔ ⇒ コミュニケーションスキル p.999 ∥チームに入るよう何人かの友人を勧誘した I *invited* [*recruited*] some of my friends to join the team.
◆保険の勧誘をする try to persuade a person to buy insurance

∥勧誘員(訪問販売員) a door-to-door salesperson; (保険などの) a canvasser
がんゆう 含有 ──含有する contain Ⓔ ∥この野菜はビタミンCの含有率が高い This vegetable *contains* a high percentage of vitamin C. / コイン1枚中の金の含有量 the gold *content* of a coin
かんよ 関与 (参加) participation Ⓤ, involvement Ⓤ ──関与する be involved / 彼は汚職事件への関与を否定した He denied *involvement in* the corruption case. / 彼女はこの活動にどの程度関与していたのだろうか To what degree *was* she 「*involved in* [*connected with*] this activity?
◆その件には全く関与していない I *have nothing to do with* that matter.
かんよう¹ 寛容 tolerance Ⓤ ──寛容な tolerant, generous ∥彼の母親は彼のわがままに寛容すぎる His mother is too *tolerant of* his selfishness.
◆彼女は寛容にも私のうそを許してくれた She *generously* forgave me for telling a lie.
かんよう² 肝要 ──肝要な important, essential ∥ここは我慢が肝要だ It *is important* [*essential*] that you (should) be patient now.
かんよう³ 慣用 usage Ⓤ© ∥その言葉は慣用的なものではない The word is not *in common usage*.
∥慣用句 an idiom, an idiomatic phrase / 慣用表現 an idiomatic expression
かんようしょくぶつ 観葉植物 leafy [leaf-bearing] plant ©; (室内用の鉢植え) houseplant ©, potted [(英)pot] plant ©
がんらい 元来 originally; (生まれつき) by nature ∥元来この家はある有名女優のものだった *Originally*, the house belonged to a famous actress.
◆彼を信用したこと自体が元来間違いなんだ You shouldn't have trusted him *in the first place*.
かんらく¹ 陥落 a [the] fall; (降伏) surrender ©Ⓤ ∥首都の陥落 *the fall* of the capital
◆そのチームは今期8位に陥落した The team *dropped* to eighth place this season.
かんらく² 歓楽 ∥歓楽街 an entertainment district, a red-light district
かんらん 観覧 ──観覧する (劇などを) see* Ⓔ; (試合などを) watch Ⓔ ◆この催しは観覧自由です This event is *open to the public*.
∥観覧車(主に米) a Ferris wheel, (英) a big wheel / 観覧者(観客) a spectator; (見物人) a visitor / 観覧席 a seat; (野球場などの) stands / 観覧料 an admission (fee)

かんり¹ 管理

(運営・経営) management Ⓤ; (政府・行政などの) administration Ⓤ; (統制) control Ⓤ; (監督) supervision Ⓤ ──管理する manage Ⓔ; administer Ⓔ; control Ⓔ; supervise Ⓔ

危機管理 crisis *management* / 人事管理 personnel *management* / 品質管理 quality *control* / 政府の管理下にある be under *the gov-*

ernment *control*
彼は財務管理に精通している He is experienced in financial *management*.
選挙管理委員会は候補者名簿を正式に発表した *The Election Administration Committee* officially revealed the list of candidates.
きょう1日だけ店の管理を任されている I *am* 「*trusted to manage* [*in charge of*]」 the shop only today.
政府は一定の食物の輸入を管理している The government *controls* the import of certain foods.
◆健康管理をしっかりする *take good care of one's health* / 貴重品を管理する *watch* [*keep track of*] *one's valuables* / あなたは体重管理が必要です You need to *watch* your weight. / この寺の庭園はよく管理が行き届いている The garden of this temple *is* well 「*looked after* [*taken care of*]」. / このアパートは毎月の管理費が高い The monthly *maintenance fee* of this apartment is high.
‖管理教育 control-oriented education; 管理社会 a controlled society; 管理職(地位) a managerial position; (人) a managing member / 管理人 a manager; (ビルやアパートなどの) a superintendent, 《米》a janitor, 《英》a caretaker; (公共施設の) a custodian

かんり² 官吏 government officer ⓒ, public [civil] servant ⓒ

がんりき 眼力 彼にはよい骨董(ﾄﾞｳ)品を見分ける鋭い眼力がある He has *a* quick [keen] *eye* for good antiques.

かんりゃく 簡略 ――簡略な (手短な) brief; (単純な) simple / 自分の葬式はできるだけ簡略にしたい I would like to make my funeral as *simple* as possible. ◆手続きを簡略化する *simplify the procedure*

かんりゅう¹ 貫流 この川は東京を貫流している This river *runs* [*flows*] *through* Tokyo.

かんりゅう² 寒流 cold current

かんりょう¹ 完了 completion Ⓤ ――完了する complete ⓗ, finish ⓗⓘ / 建設工事はほぼ完了している The construction work *is* almost *finished* [*completed*].
◆任務完了 Mission *accomplished*! / 出発の準備は完了しました I'm *all ready* [*set*] *to leave*.
‖現在[過去, 未来]完了《文法》the present [past, future] perfect

かんりょう² 官僚 (集合的) the bureaucracy; (個人) 《例軽蔑的》bureaucrat ⓒ ――官僚的な bureaucratic / 高級官僚 *a* high-ranking *bureaucrat* / 官僚的なところのある教師 a teacher who has something of *the bu-*

reaucrat about him [her]
‖官僚主義 bureaucratism; (官僚的形式主義) red tape / 官僚政治 bureaucracy, bureaucratic government

がんりょう 顔料 pigment Ⓤⓒ, color, 《英》colour Ⓤⓒ

かんれい¹ 慣例 (習慣) custom Ⓤⓒ; (因習) convention Ⓤⓒ; (商売・法律の) practice, 《英》practise Ⓤⓒ; (伝統) tradition Ⓤⓒ / 慣例に従う[を破る] follow [break] *a custom* / 毎週金曜日に会合を開くのが私たちの慣例になっている It has become *a common practice* for [with] us to hold a meeting every Friday.

かんれい² 寒冷 ‖寒冷前線 a cold front

かんれき 還暦 私たちは祖父の還暦を祝った We celebrated our grandfather's *60th birthday*. / 祖母は還暦を迎えた My grandmother has reached *the age of 60*.

かんれん 関連 relation ⓒ, connection ⓒ, link ――関連する be related [connected, linked]
この物語は現実と何の関連もない This story has no *relation* [*relevance*] to reality.
そのことに関連していくつか質問したい I would like to ask some questions *in connection with* that matter.
物理学は数学と深く関連している Physics *is* closely *related to* mathematics.
肺癌(ｶﾞﾝ)は喫煙と密接な関係があるという They say lung cancer *is* closely 「*related to* [*connected with, linked with*]」 smoking.
◆2つの関連した問題 two *related* matters / その問題に関連した研究 studies *related* [*relative*] *to* the matter / 1つの問題を別の問題と関連づける 「*relate* one problem *to* [*connect* one problem *with*]」 another
‖関連会社 an affiliated [associated] company / 関連記事 a related article

かんろく 貫禄 (威厳) dignity Ⓤ; (風采(ｻｲ)) presence Ⓤ / 貫禄がある人 a man of *dignity* [*presence*] / 彼は演説で貫禄を示した He has really *made his presence felt* through his speech.

かんわ 緩和 relaxation Ⓤ, relief Ⓤ ――緩和する ease ⓗ, relax ⓘⓗ, relieve ⓗ / 痛みを緩和する薬 a medicine to *ease* [*relieve*] pain / 通勤ラッシュ緩和のため列車が増発された More trains were put on to *ease* commuter rush hours. ◆重税を緩和する(→減らす) *reduce* heavy taxes
‖規制緩和 deregulation / 金融緩和 ease of money

かんわじてん 漢和辞典 a Japanese dictionary of Chinese characters

き

き¹ 気

日本語の「気」は性質・意欲・関心・感情・意識など，人の精神活動に関するあらゆる現象を表す．さらに，物や場所がもつ香気・精気や雰囲気など，目には見えないがそこにあるものを表す場合にも用いる．英語には1語でそれに当たる語はなく，「気が…」「気に…」「気を…」などを日本語の慣用表現としてとらえ，それぞれの意味に最も近い英語を使うのが望ましい．

❶【性格・性質】(天性) nature Ⓒ; (気性) temper Ⓒ

【気が合う】あいつとはどうも気が合わない Somehow I *don't get along well with* him. / 気の合う仲間2人といっしょに伊豆へ行った I went to Izu with two *good friends* of mine.

【気が荒い】彼は気が荒い He *has a violent temper.*

【気がいい】(性格のよい) good-natured ∥彼は見かけはごついが気のいい人だ He looks rough, but is really a *good-natured* person.

【気が大きい】そのとき彼は酒が入って気が大きく(→気前よく)なっていた He *was being generous* with alcohol at that time.

【気が小さい】(臆病な) timid ∥姉の子供は2人とも気が小さい My sister's two kids are both *timid*.

【気が強い】(簡単に意思を曲げない) strong-minded; (負けず嫌いの) unyielding ∥彼女は小さいころから気が強かった She's been *strong-minded* since she was small.

【気が短い】short-tempered, quick-tempered ∥父は気が短い My father is *short-tempered.* / My father *has a short temper.*

【気が弱い】weak; (臆病な) timid ∥彼は気が弱くて彼女に好きだと言えない He is so *timid* that he can't tell her that he loves her.

❷【気持ち・意欲・関心・心づかい】(知性・思考などの理性的な心) mind Ⓤ; (感情) feelings; (一時的な気分) mood Ⓤ; (気づいていること) awareness Ⓤ, consciousness Ⓤ

彼女はころころ気が変わる She easily *changes her mind.*

君の言葉で気が楽になった Your words *have set my mind at ease.*

彼は数学のテストで満点をとって気をよくしている He's *in a good mood* because he got a perfect score on the math test.

◆気を悪くしないでね *Don't get offended.* / *Don't take offense.*

【気がある】太郎はどうも彼女に気があるらしい Taro seems to *be interested in* her.

【気が多い】(気まぐれな) fickle, capricious ∥美人で気の多い女性がその小説の主人公だ A *fickle* beautiful woman is the main character of that novel.

【気がおけない】気がおけない友人たちを呼んでうちでパーティーをした I had a party at home with some *intimate* friends of mine.

【気が重い】休み明けの試験のことを考えると気が重い(→憂鬱だ) I *feel depressed* when I think about the exam after the vacation.

【気がきく】小池さんの娘さんは気がきく[気がきかない] Mr. Koike's daughter is *considerate [inconsiderate]*.

【気が気でない】私はその子猫たちが車にひかれはしないかと気が気でなかった I *was really worried* that those kittens might get run over by a car.

【気が知れない】そんなにいい申し出を受けないなんて君の気が知れない I just *don't understand* why you don't accept such a good offer.

【気が進まない】そこへ行くのは気が進まなかった I *was reluctant to go* there.

【気がすむ】彼は何でも自分でやってみないと気がすまない(→満足しない) He *is never satisfied* until he gives something a try himself. / 悲しいときは気がすむまで泣けばいい Go ahead and *cry your eyes out* when you are sad.

【気がせく】電車が遅れて気がせいていた I *was impatient* because the train was delayed.

【気が立つ】猫が背中の毛を逆立てたら，それは気が立っている証拠だ If a cat's hair stands on end, it means he's *angry*.

【気が散る】be distracted ∥ラジオがついていると気が散って本が読めない I *get distracted* and can't read books when the radio is on.

◆うちだと気が散って勉強できない(→勉強に集中できない) I *can't concentrate on* studying at home.

【気がとがめる】結果的に彼女を裏切ることになって気がとがめた(→罪悪感を感じた) I *felt guilty* because I unintentionally betrayed her.

【気がない】旅行に彼を誘ってみたが気のない返事だった(→関心がなさそうだった) I asked him if he wanted to come with us on a trip, but he *didn't seem interested*.

【気が抜ける】入試が終わってすっかり気が抜けてしまった All *my tension was gone* after the entrance exam was over. / 準決勝は最後まで気の抜けない(→集中力を要する)試合だった The semifinal was a close game *which required a lot of concentration*.

【気が乗る】映画に誘われたが何となく気が乗らなかった I was asked to go to the movies, but somehow I *didn't feel like it*.

【気が早い】もう冬休みの計画を立ててるの？ 気が早いね You're making plans for the winter vacation already？ You *are jumping the gun*! (❖jump the gun は「ピストルの合図より先にスタートする」の意味)

【気が晴れる】友達に悩みをすっかり話したら気が晴れた I *felt better* after telling my friend all that had been troubling me.

【気が引ける】自分だけ特別扱いしてもらうのは何だか気が引ける I *feel uncomfortable* [*uneasy*] getting special treatment. / あのかわいい子に声をかけるのは気が引ける I *hesitate to* speak to that pretty girl.

【気が回る】そこまで気が回らなかった I *could never think of* that.

【気が向く】気が向いたら遊びにいらっしゃい Come and see me *when you feel like it*.

【気がめいる】寒くてじめじめした日がこう続くと気がめいる The succession of cold, damp days like this *makes me depressed*.

【気が若い】祖父は気が若い My grandfather *is young* ｢*at heart* [*in spirit*].

【気に入る】そのイヤリング，気に入った？ Do you *like* those earrings? / 気に入らないことがあるなら私に言いなさい If you have any *complaints*, just tell me.

【気にかかる】けんか別れをした友達のことがずっと気にかかっている The thought of a friend I parted with in anger *has been weighing on* me.

【気に食わない】彼女は私のやることなすことすべて気に食わないらしい It seems that she *doesn't like* anything I do.

【気にさわる】お客様の気にさわることのないよう十分注意してください You should be particularly careful not to *offend* our customers.

💬「彼女，怒ってるみたいだよ」「何か気にさわるようなこと言ったかな」 "She looks angry." "Did I say *something wrong* to her?"

【気にする】(心配する) worry [自], care [自] //彼の言ったことなんか気にするな Don't *worry about* what he said. / 彼は服装はあまり気にしない He *doesn't care* much *about* clothes.

◆彼女は背が低いことを気にしている She *is sensitive about* her short height.

【気にとめる】だれも彼の言うことを気にとめなかった No one *took notice of* what he said.

【気になる】弟は隣に住んでいる女の子が気になっている(→興味をもっている)ようだ It looks like my brother *is interested in* the girl living next to us. / 何かに集中していれば多少の騒音は気にならない When you are concentrating on something, some noise *doesn't* really *bother* you.

【気に病む】彼女はその失敗をいまだに気に病んでいる She's still *worried about* that mistake.

【気のきいた】気のきいた描写 a *neat* description / もうちょっと気のきいたプレゼントは思いつかなかったの？ Couldn't you think of anything *nicer* as a present?

【気のせい】

💬「彼女，絶対私のこと嫌ってるわ」「気のせいだよ」 "I know she hates me." "*That's only your imagination*."

【気は心】気は心だ(→大切なのは気持ちだ) *It's the thought that counts.*

【気を入れる】今度の対戦相手は優勝候補の一角だ．気を入れていけ The next opponent is one of the top-favorites. *Get fired up*!

【気を落とす】そう気を落とすなよ．また挑戦すればいいじゃないか Don't *be discouraged* [*disappointed*]. You can try again.

【気を配る】彼はいつも周りの人たちみんなに気を配る He always ｢*thinks of* [*cares about*] other people around him.

【気をつかう】みんなは彼に気をつかってその話題を避けた Everyone avoided talking about it *for his sake*.

💬「これ，どうぞ．近所で大評判なのよ」「そんなに気をつかわなくていいのに」 "This is for you. It's very popular in my neighborhood." "Oh, *you shouldn't have* (*done this*)."

【気をつける】(用心する) take* care, be careful; (警戒する) watch [他] //健康に気をつける *take care of one's* health / 体に気をつけてね *Take care* (*of yourself*). / 赤ちゃんを起こさないように気をつけて *Be careful that* you don't wake the baby up. / 気をつけて！ そこはでこぼこになってるよ *Watch out*! It's bumpy there. ◆言葉づかいに気をつけなさい *Mind* your language.

【気をとられる】テレビのニュースに気をとられていて魚を真っ黒にこがしてしまった The fish got burned black while I *was distracted* by the TV news.

【気を取り直す】気を取り直してもう一度やってみよう Let's *pull ourselves together* and try it again.

【気を吐く】そのマラソンでは大勢がリタイアするなか，彼ひとり気を吐いた He was the only runner *full of energy* in the marathon, while a lot of runners dropped out.

【気を引く】(注意を引く) draw* *a person's* attention //彼女は彼の気を引くために彼の前でわざと財布を落とした She intentionally dropped her purse in front of him to *draw his attention*.

【気を回す】

💬「彼，誤解しなかったかなあ」「大丈夫だって．いつも気を回しすぎだよ」 "Don't you think he might have taken it wrongly?" "No, it should be OK. You'*re worrying too much*."

【気をもたせる】彼とつきあう気がないんだったらあまり気をもたせない(→期待させない)ほうがいいよ If you are not interested in him, *don't raise his hopes* too much.

【気をもむ】飛行機に乗り遅れたらどうしようと気をもんだ I *was worried* that I would miss the plane.

【気を許す】彼女は私にはすっかり気を許しているようだ She seems to be completely *unguarded* with me.

【気をよくする】母は懸賞に当たって気をよくしている My mother *is in a good mood* because she won a prize.

【気を悪くする】気を悪くしないでね Please *don't be offended*.| (→私のことを悪くとらないで) *Don't think badly of me.*

❸【意識・精神活動】

【気が狂う】go* crazy [mad], go out of *one's* mind ◆君のせいで僕はいつも気が狂いそうだ

You *are* always *driving me crazy*. (❖drive ... crazy で「…を狂わせる」の意味)

【気がつく】(意識を取り戻す) come* to (*oneself*), become* conscious; (気づく) notice [他]; (分かる) find* [他] ➩ きづく ∥気がつくと私は病院にいた When I *came to*, I found myself in the hospital. / はっと気がつくとみんなが私を見ていた(→みんなが私を見ていることに急に気づいた) I *suddenly noticed* that everyone was watching me.

◆いいところに気がついたね(→見解が的(まと)を射ている) *Your comment is to the point.*

【気が遠くなる】1万光年というのは気の遠くなるような距離だ Ten thousand light-years is *an unimaginable amount of* distance.

【気がふれる】彼女は恐怖で気がふれた She *went crazy* with fear.

【気は確か】気は確かなのか *Are* you *in your right mind*?

【気を失う】彼女はその知らせを聞いて気を失った She *fainted* at the news.

【気を確かにもつ】気を確かにもってね *Keep a clear head* [*Get a grip on yourself*], OK?

❹【…と感じる・…したい・…するつもりだ】(意思) intention [U][C]; (意志) will [U] ━気がする (…と感じる) feel* [自], have* a feeling that ...; (…したい) would like to *do*, want to *do*; (…したい気がする) feel like *doing*; (…するつもりだ) be going to *do*

きょうは何かよいことがありそうな気がした I *had* a kind of *feeling that* something good would happen today.

試験が終わって今は全然勉強する気がしない As the exams are over, I *don't feel like* studying at all now.

◆もっといいやり方がありそうな気がする There *seems to be* a better plan. / 彼とはどこかで会ったような気がする I *think* I have met him somewhere. / 君とはうまくやれるような気がしてたんだ I *had a hunch that* you and I would get along well. (❖have a hunch that ... は「直感で…と思う」の意味) / 彼を招待する気は毛頭ない I *wouldn't* invite him at any price. (❖would not で強い拒否を表す) / 何となく場違いな所にいる気がする Somehow I don't *think* I belong here. / 高校に入学したのはついこの間のような気がする It *seems like* only yesterday that I entered high school.

💬「できるだけ大きい本がいるんだ」「それでいったい何をする気なの」 "I need the biggest book possible." "*What are* you *going to do* with it?"

❺【その他】

一瞬の気のゆるみ a lapse of concentration / 何の気なしに *without intention* / 気のないほめ方 *faint* praise / (号令で)気をつけ! *Attention*! / このビールは気が抜けている This beer is *flat*. / この教会,完成まであと100年以上かかるの? 気の長い話だね It's going to take more than 100 years to complete this church? That's *a slow process*. / 彼女は町にあこがれの俳優が来ると聞いて気もそぞろだった She *was very excited* to hear her favorite actor was coming to the city. / いい気になるんじゃないぞ Don't *be* so *sure of yourself*. ➩ いいき / その気になれば君はプロのカメラマンになれるよ You can become a professional photographer *if you want to*.

き[2] 木・樹

❶【樹木】tree [C]

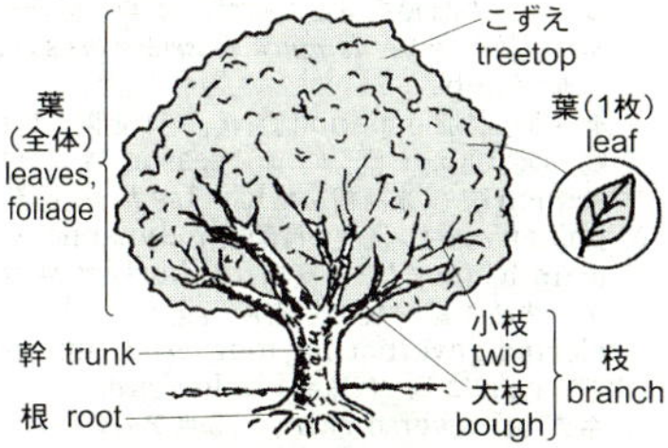

こずえ
treetop
葉(1枚)
leaf
葉
(全体)
leaves,
foliage
小枝
twig
枝
branch
幹 trunk
大枝
bough
根 root

リンゴ[桜]の木 *an* apple [*a* cherry] *tree*

その木は周囲[高さ]が5メートルある The *tree* is five meters around [high].

先月その木に雷が落ちた The *tree* was struck by lightning last month.

庭の木に小鳥が数羽とまっている Some birds are perched in *the tree* in the garden.

私たちは倒れた木に腰かけてひと休みした We sat on *a fallen tree* to have a rest.

彼が木の下で本を読んでいるのを見た I saw him reading a book under *a tree*.

◆木のない山 a *bare* [*bald*] mountain / 木の生い茂った山 a *wooded* [*tree-covered*] mountain

> [コロケーション] -tree-
> 〖動詞+～〗～を植える plant a tree / ～を切り倒す cut [chop] down a tree / ～に登る climb (up) a tree / ～の枝を切る cut a branch from a tree, chop a branch off a tree

❷【木材】wood [U] (❖製材は《主に米》lumber, 《英》timber, 丸太は log という) ━木の wood, wooden

木の机 a *wooden* desk; a desk *made of wood*

その庭は木の柵(さく)で囲われていた The garden was enclosed by a *wooden* fence.

その彫刻家は木で仏像を彫った The sculptor carved an image of Buddha from [out of] *wood*.

[慣用表現] 彼は木で鼻をくくったような(→そっけない)返事をした He gave a *blunt* reply. / その男は私に木に竹を接いだような話をした The man told me an *incoherent* story. / 君は木を見て森を見ていない You *can't see the forest* [《英》*wood*] *for the trees*. (❖英語でも日本語と同様,慣用表現になっている)

き[3] 生 ━生の (混じり気のない) pure ∥生じょうゆ *pure* [*raw*] soy sauce ◆生糸 *raw* silk / 彼はきまじめな人だ He is a *thoroughly se-*

rious [earnest] person.

き⁴ 奇 慣用表現 彼は奇をてらっている He「*makes a display of* [*shows off*] *his originality*. / 事実は小説よりも奇なり ➡ じじつ

き⁵ 黄 (黄色) yellow Ⓤ Ⓒ ➡ きいろ

き⁶ 機 chance Ⓒ; (時期) the time Ⓒ / 彼らがこの機を逃すはずがない They can't miss this *chance*. / まだ機は熟していない The time is not ripe yet.
慣用表現 姉は機を見るに敏だ(→素早く機会をつかむ) My sister *is quick to seize* [*grasp*] *an opportunity*.

-き 期 (期間) period Ⓒ; (一定の期間) term Ⓒ; (時代) age Ⓒ; (季節) season Ⓒ; (会期) session Ⓒ / 氷河期 an Ice *Age* / 全盛期 a golden *age* / 歴史の激動期 a dynamic *period* in history / 収穫期 the harvest *season* / 彼は4期連続で知事に当選した He was elected governor for four *terms* running.

ギア gear Ⓒ Ⓤ / 低速ギア *a low gear* / バックギア (*a*) reverse *gear* / 5ギアのオートマ車 an automatic with five *gears* / ギアをトップに入れる put the car in [into] high gear (❖「トップ(ギア)」は(米)high gear, (英)top gear という) / ギアをローからセカンドに入れる shift [(英)change] *gears* from low into second

きあい 気合 試験まであと少しだから気合を入れて(→集中して)勉強しなければ I've got to *concentrate on* studying because there are just a few days left until the exam. / 君には気合(→意気込み)が足りない You are lacking in *spirit*. / 相手が強いとこっちも気合が入る(→闘志がわく) I am full of *fighting spirit* against strong opponents. / 監督は選手に気合を入れた The manager *fired* the players *up*. / 挑戦者はチャンピオンに気合負けしている(→威圧されている) The challenger *is overawed* by the champion.

きあつ 気圧 (大気圧) (atmospheric) pressure Ⓤ; (空気圧) air pressure Ⓤ / 高[低]気圧 high [low] *atmospheric pressure* ◆ この地域に気圧の谷が近づいている A low pressure trough is approaching this region. / 中心気圧は965ヘクトパスカルです The central *barometric reading* is 965 hectopascals.
‖気圧計 a barometer [bərámitər] / 気圧配置 an atmospheric pressure pattern, the distribution of atmospheric pressure

ぎあん 議案 bill Ⓒ / 議案を立案する draft *a bill* / 国会に議案を提出する introduce *a bill* in the diet / 市議会はその減税議案を採択[可決, 否決]した The municipal assembly adopted [passed, rejected] the *bill* to lower taxes.

きい 奇異 —奇異な strange, odd; (人・行動などが) eccentric ‖ 私には彼女の格好は奇異に映った Her clothes seemed [looked] *strange* to me.

キー key Ⓒ ‖ マスターキー *a master key* / スペアキー *a spare key* / ピアノのキーをたたくpound [touch] *the keys* of the piano (❖ pound は「強く連打する」, touch は「軽くたたく」

の意味) / 車のキーをなくすなんて彼はなんてうかつだったんだ It was very careless of him to lose *his car key*.

きいきい オウムは鳥かごの中できいきい鳴いていた The parrots *were screeching* in their cage. / このドアはきいきいきしむ This door *creaks*. / そんなにきいきい声を出さないで Don't speak in *a squeaky voice*.

ぎいぎい いすを引くと床がぎいぎいいった The floor *creaked* as I pulled the chair. / 彼はぎいぎい音を立てながらバイオリンを弾いている He *is rasping* away on his violin.

きいてまわる 聞いて回る 私はいなくなった猫について近所の人に聞いて回った I went to my neighbors and *asked around* about my missing cat.

きいと 生糸 raw silk Ⓤ

キーパー (サッカー・アイスホッケーなどの) goalkeeper Ⓒ, (口語的) keeper Ⓒ, (口語的) goalie Ⓒ

キープ ドラゴンズが首位をキープしている The Dragons *keep* the lead.

キーポイント ⚠ この問題のキーポイント(→解く手がかり) *the key* to this problem / きょうの授業のキーポイント(→最も重要な部分) *the most important part* of today's class

キーボード keyboard Ⓒ

キーホルダー ⚠ key ring Ⓒ

きいろ 黄色 yellow Ⓤ Ⓒ ——黄色い yellow
黄色くなった葉が冷たい風にかさかさと音を立てた The *yellow* leaves rustled in the cold wind.
信号が黄色になった The traffic light turned *yellow*.
◆黄色がかった赤 *yellowish* red / 少女たちは黄色い声をあげて応援していた The young girls were cheering in *shrill* voices.

キーワード key word Ⓒ

きいん 起因 少年犯罪はほとんど家庭内の問題に起因している Almost all juvenile crimes *are*「*caused by* [*the result of*]」*family problems*.

ぎいん¹ 議員 (一般の議会の) a member of an assembly; (日本の国会議員) a member of the Diet, Diet member Ⓒ, (男性の) Dietman Ⓒ, (女性の) Dietwoman Ⓒ; (米国下院の) a member of Congress ((略語)MC), (男性の) Congressman Ⓒ, (女性の) Congresswoman Ⓒ, (米国上院の) senator Ⓒ; (英国の) a member of Parliament ((略語)MP) / 東京都選出の議員 *a Diet member* for Tokyo / 彼は国会議員に選出された He was elected *as a member of the Diet*.
◆党から汚職議員を追放する purge *corrupt members* from the party / 彼は衆議院[参議院]議員に立候補した He ran for「*the House of Representatives* [*the House of Councilors*]」.
‖議員会館 the Members' Hall / 議員立法 legislation by House members / 県[市, 町, 村]議会議員 a member of the prefectural [city, town, village] assembly / 都議会

議員 a member of the Tokyo Metropolitan Assembly
ぎいん² 議院 the House;（日本の）the Diet;（米国の）the Congress;（英国の）the Parliament／衆議院 *the House of Representatives*／参議院 *the House of Councilors*／議院内閣制 a parliamentary cabinet system／議院制度 the parliamentary system
キウイ（果物）kiwi [kíːwiː] (fruit)◎;（鳥）kiwi◎（❖ニュージーランド産の飛べない鳥）
きうん 気運 90年代終わりごろから環境保護の気運が高まってきている *There has been a growing tendency toward* protection of the environment since the late 90's.
きえい 気鋭 ――気鋭の spirited, energetic◆新進気鋭の画家 an *up-and-coming* artist
きえいる 消え入る その生徒は消え入るような声で返事をした The student replied in a *faint* voice.

きえる　消える

❶【見えなくなる・消えてなくなる】disappear ⓐ (↔appear)／（突然）vanish ⓐ／（だんだん薄れていく）fade away [out]
視界から消える *disappear* from sight／跡形もなく消える *vanish* without trace
私たちは水平線の下に消えるまでその船をじっと見ていた We watched the ship until it *disappeared* below the horizon.
3つ数えたら彼の手の中からそのコインが消えた The coin in his fist *vanished* on the count of three.
彼のセールボードが波間に消えた His sailboard *vanished* beneath the waves.
成功への希望は消えてしまった Any hope of success *has vanished*.
笑い声は徐々に消えていった The laughter *faded away* gradually.
◆水着の跡がまだ消えない I've still *got* marks from the bathing suit.／やがて飛行機は視界から消えた Soon the plane *went out of sight*.／民族間の憎しみはなかなか消えない Interracial hatred *dies hard*. (❖die hard は「（慣習などが）なかなか消えない」の意)／消印は消えかかっていて文字が読み取れなかった The postmark *was almost gone*, and I couldn't read the letters.／魚のにおいは洗ってもなかなか消えない The smell of fish *doesn't wash off* easily.／家賃だけで収入の半分が消えてしまう Just the rent *takes* half of my income.／とっとと消えろ！ *Get lost!*

❷【火・明かりなどが】go* out, die out
ろうそくが消えた The candle *went out*.
火が消えかかってるよ The fire *is dying out*.
◆部屋の明かりは消えていた The light in the room *was off [out]*.

ぎえんきん 義援金（寄付金）contribution ◎,《英》subscription ◎;（救援基金）relief fund ◎／地震の被災者のために義援金を募る collect *contributions* for the relief of the earthquake victims
きおう 気負う 彼らは気負いすぎているようだ They seem to *be too keen [eager]*.／彼には全く気負ったところがない（→本当の自分よりよく見せようとしない）He never tries to make himself look better than he really is.
きおうしょう 既往症 previous [past] illness◎;（病歴）medical [case] history◎

きおく　記憶

memory ◎ ⓤ;（思い出すこと）《公式的》remembrance ◎ ⓤ　――記憶する（覚えている）remember ⓗ;（意識的に覚える）memorize ⓗ

> **コロケーション**　-memory-
> 《形容詞＋～》あいまいな～ a vague memory／おぼろげな～ a dim [an indistinct] memory／かすかな～ a faint memory／鮮明な～ a vivid memory／はっきりした～ a clear memory

〖記憶～・～記憶〗
形状記憶合金 a shape memory alloy
私は人の顔に関しては記憶力がいい［悪い］I have a good [bad] *memory* for faces.
彼の記憶力にはほとほと感心する His *memory* amazes me.
◆形状記憶シャツ a *wash-and-wear* shirt
〖記憶が・は〗
あの事件の記憶がよみがえった The *memory* of that case recurred to me [my mind].
小さいころ祖母からそのような言い伝えを聞いた記憶がある I *remember* that I heard a legend like that from my grandmother in my childhood.
私の記憶が正しければ, 彼のお嬢さんはうちの息子と同い年だ *If I remember correctly*, his daughter is as old as my son.
〖記憶に〗
…を記憶にとどめる bear [have, keep] ... in memory
その光景は私の記憶に焼きついている The scene printed itself on my *memory*.
彼はわが校の名クオーターバックとして人々の記憶に残るだろう He'll always *be remembered* as a star quarterback in our school.
◆記憶に残る映画 an *unforgettable* [a *memorable*] film／彼のノーベル賞受賞はまだ我々の記憶に新しい His winning of the Nobel prize is still *fresh in our minds*.／彼女の名前はよくある名前だったので記憶に残らなかった Since her name was a common one, it *didn't register with* me.
〖記憶を〗
記憶を失う lose one's memory
その香水の香りは彼の古い記憶を呼び起こした The scent of the perfume awoke old *memories* in him.
私は記憶を頼りに昔住んでいた家を目ざした *By memory*, I headed for the house where I used to live.
〖記憶する〗
私はその事件を鮮明に記憶しています I *have a* vivid *memory* of the accident.
彼はそのころ神戸に住んでいたと記憶している I *remember* that he lived in Kobe at that

《その他》
ジョンは私の記憶ではとても背が高かった John, *as I remember*, was very tall.
子供のころは近所の子供たちと遊んだ記憶しかない I *don't remember anything* about my childhood *but* playing with neighbor children.
‖記憶喪失 loss of memory, 〖医学〗amnesia

きおくれ 気後れ 大勢の観客を見たとたん気後れしてしまった(→あがった) I *got stage fright* on seeing the large audience. / 面接官たちの前で私は気後れした(→勇気を失った) I *lost my nerve* in front of the interviewers.

キオスク (街頭・駅などの売店) kiosk [kíɑsk] Ⓒ; (新聞・雑誌売り場) newsstand

きおち 気落ち 母に先立たれて父はすっかり気落ちしてしまった My father *was* deeply *discouraged* after my mother's death. / 彼は試験の結果が悪くて気落ちしている He *is depressed* by his poor results on the examination.

きおん 気温 temperature Ⓤ Ⓒ
5月の平均気温 *the average temperature* for May
気温が高い[低い] *The temperature* is high [low].
きのうの最低気温はマイナス5度だった Yesterday's *minimum temperature* was five degrees below zero.
気温が氷点下になった *The temperature* dropped below zero.
ここのところ気温の変化が激しい There have been great *changes in temperature* these days.
その地方では気温が42度まで上がったことがある *The temperature* once rose to 42 degrees in that district.
◆きょうの予想最高気温は30度です Today's *high* will be 30 degrees.

きか¹ 気化 vaporization Ⓤ ──気化する vaporize ⑤ ‖気化熱 the heat of vaporization, evaporation heat

きか² 帰化 naturalization Ⓤ ◆彼女は日本で生まれ育ち21歳のときに米国に帰化した She was born and brought up in Japan, and she 「*was naturalized* in the U.S. [*became a U.S. citizen*] when she was 21.
‖帰化植物 a naturalized plant

きか³ 幾何 geometry Ⓤ ⇨ きかがく

きが 飢餓 starvation Ⓤ; (飢え) hunger Ⓤ / 飢餓に苦しむ子供たち children suffering from *starvation*

きかい¹ 機会

opportunity Ⓤ Ⓒ; chance Ⓒ; occasion Ⓒ
  opportunity:「機会」を意味する最も一般的な語.
  chance: 予期せずにめぐってきたという偶然性の高い機会を指す.
  occasion:「…のための特定の時・場合」を表す.

《~(の)機会》
絶好の機会 a golden *opportunity*
そんな有名な小説家と仕事できるなんてまたとない機会だ That's *the chance of a lifetime* to work with the famous novelist.

《機会が・は》
私には着物を着る機会が全く[ほとんど]ない I have no [little] *opportunity* to wear a kimono.
京都へ行く機会があればぜひその寺に行ってみるといい If you have *a chance* to go to Kyoto, you should visit that temple.
彼は機会(が)あるごとに外国人と英語で話すようにしている He tries to speak English with foreigners *every time he gets a chance*.
そのうち君の英語力が発揮できる機会があるかもしれない An *occasion* may arise when you can show your English ability.

《機会に》
アメリカに留学中,カナダに行く機会に恵まれた I had *an opportunity* to visit Canada while I was studying in the States.
◆また別の機会に彼にかけ直します I'll call him *another time*. / 出張でスペインに行ったのを機会に(→利用して)フランスに住むいとこを訪ねた I *took advantage of* my business trip to Spain by visiting my cousin in France.
🔴「この店入ってみたかったんだけど,もう時間ないかしら」「またの機会にしよう」"I've wanted to go in this shop, but I'm afraid there's not much time left." "*Let's make it some other time*."

《機会を得る[失う]》
機会を得る[失う] get [lose] *a chance*
僕は彼ら2人が話す機会をもてるように取り計らった I worked it so that the two of them had *a chance* to talk to each other.
そんなよい機会を逃すなんて本当に残念なことをしたね What a pity you *missed* such a *good chance*!
◆機会をうかがう *bide one's time*
‖機会均等 equal opportunity

きかい² 機械

machine Ⓒ, (集合的) machinery Ⓤ ──機械の・機械的な mechanical ──機械的に mechanically

《~機械》
欠陥のある機械 a defective *machine* / 最新式の[旧式の]機械 the latest model [an outmoded] *machine*

《機械が・は》
この機械は動きません This *machine* doesn't work.
機械は人間に代わって何でもできるというわけではない *Machines* cannot do everything for humans.

《機械に》
彼は機械に詳しい[うとい] He is 「familiar [unfamiliar] with *machinery*.
作動中は機械に触れないように Do not touch *the machine* while it is in motion.

《機械の》

彼はその機械の扱いに慣れている He is accustomed to operating the *machine*.
事故によってその機械の欠陥がいくつか明らかになった The accident revealed some defects in the *machine*.
〖機械を〗
彼は自分でその機械を修理した He repaired the *machine* himself.
機械を始動させる前に説明書を読みなさい Read the instructions before starting *the machine*.
〖その他〗
英単語を機械的に覚える memorize English words *mechanically*
方程式が立てば答えは機械的に求められる Once an equation is set up, the solution can be gotten *mechanically*.
そのブドウ園ではブドウの収穫が機械で行われている Grapes are *mechanically* picked in the vineyard.
‖機械工学 mechanical engineering / 機械翻訳 machine translation / 工作機械 a machine tool / 精密機械 a precision machine

きかい³ 器械 (道具・器具) instrument ◎
‖器械体操 apparatus gymnastics / 医療器械 medical instruments

きかい⁴ 奇怪 ──奇怪な (不可解な) mysterious; (奇妙な) strange //この間奇怪な事件が起きた There was a *mysterious* incident the other day. ◆彼はときどき奇怪な行動に出る He sometimes behaves *strangely*.

きがい¹ 危害 harm Ⓤ ◆うちの犬は人に危害を加えたりしません My dog won't *harm* anyone.

きがい² 気概 (気骨) spirit Ⓤ, backbone Ⓤ, (口語的) grit Ⓤ; (勇気) courage Ⓤ //彼らには最後までやり抜こうとする気概がない They have no *spirit* to carry it out.
◆気概のある男 a *spirited* man

ぎかい 議会 assembly ⒸⓊ; (国会) the Diet, 《米》Congress, 《英》Parliament //町[村, 市]議会 a town [village, municipal] *assembly* / 議会を解散[召集]する dissolve [convene] *the assembly* / 県議会は来週開かれる The prefectural *assembly* will meet next week. / 議会は開会中である The *assembly* is now in session.
‖議会政治 parliamentary government / 議会制度 the parliamentary system / 議会制民主主義 parliamentary democracy

きがえ 着替え (着替えること・着替え一式) a change of clothes; (余分の衣服) an extra [a spare] set of clothes //着替えを持っていく必要がある You need to take *a change of clothes*. ◆私たちは急いで着替えをすませた(→着替えた) We *changed* our clothes quickly.

きがえる 着替える change ⒾⓉ //タキシードに着替える change *into* a tuxedo / 彼はパジャマを脱いで制服に着替えた He *changed* out of the pajamas into the uniform. / もう着替えた? Have you *changed* your clothes?

きかがく 幾何学 geometry Ⓤ ──幾何学の, geometric ──幾何学的に, geometrically /

平面幾何学 plane *geometry* / 幾何学の定理 a *geometric* theorem
‖幾何学模様 a geometric pattern

きがかり 気掛かり (不安) anxiety ⓊⒸ; (心配) worry ⓊⒸ, concern Ⓤ //彼のいちばんの気がかりは病気の母のことだった His main *concern* was his sick mother.
◆彼女は面接の結果が気がかりだった She *worried* [*was anxious*] about the result of the interview.

きかく¹ 企画 planning Ⓤ; (計画) plan Ⓒ, project Ⓒ; (手はず) arrangements ──企画する plan Ⓣ; arrange Ⓣ //私はこの企画に全力を集中した I concentrated my energy on this *project*. / 彼は学園祭のイベントを企画している He *is planning* an event of the school festival.

きかく² 規格 standard Ⓒ 《しばしば複数形〜s》──規格化する standardize Ⓣ //日本工業規格 Japanese Industrial *Standard* (《略語》JIS) / ビデオテープのサイズを規格化する *standardize* the size of video tapes / これらの製品は規格に合っている These articles meet *the standards*.
◆規格外の製品 *nonstandardized* products
‖規格化 standardization / 規格品 a standardized article [product]

きがく 器楽 instrumental music Ⓤ

きかざる 着飾る dress (*oneself*) up; (着飾っている) be dressed up; (晴れ着を着る) be in *one's* best clothes //美穂はきょうやけに着飾っている Miho *is* awfully *dressed up* today. / 母は着飾って同窓会に出かけていった My mother *dressed up* and went to the class reunion.

きがする 気がする ⇨き(気)

きかせる¹ 利かせる もう少しコショウをきかせてください *Put* a little more pepper in it. / 彼女は気をきかせてその場を離れた(→その場を離れる思慮があった) She *had the good sense to* leave the place.

きかせる² 聞かせる あなたの夢を聞かせてください *Tell* me about your dreams. / チェロを弾いて聞かせてください Please *play* the cello *for* us.

きがつく 気がつく ⇨き(気), きづく

きがね 気兼ね 彼にはどうも気がねしてしまう(→彼といると落ち着かない) I somehow *feel* 「*ill at ease* [*uneasy*] in his presence. / 困ったことがあったら気がねしないで何でも聞いてください If you have any problems, *don't hesitate to* ask me.

きがまえ 気構え (心構え) preparation
◆最悪の事態に対する気構えをもたなくてはならない We must *be prepared* [*ready*] *for* the worst.

きがる 気軽 気軽に遊びに来てください Feel *free* to come and see us. / 散歩はだれでも気軽にできる運動だ Walking is an exercise that anyone can do *easily*. / 彼はいつでも気軽に(→快く)相談に乗ってくれる He *is* always *willing* [*ready*] *to* give me advice.

きかん¹ 期間 period Ⓒ; (契約などの) term

きかん ▯ ∥彼は短期間のうちに目に見えて進歩した He has made a visible advance *in a short period*. ◆どのくらいの期間イギリスに留学していたんですか *How long* have you studied in England? / この本の貸出期間は2週間です We *lend* you our books *for two weeks*. / このテレビはまだ保証期間中ですか Is this television still *under guarantee*?
∥契約期間 the term of contract / 有効期間 the period of validity

きかん² 機関 ❶【組織・機構】facility ▯; (公共施設) institution ▯ ❷【エンジン】engine ▯
∥機関士 an engineer / 機関誌 a journal, a bulletin / 機関車 a locomotive / 機関投資家 an institutional investor / 金融機関 banking facilities / 交通機関 means of transportation, transportation (facilities) / 蒸気機関 a steam engine / 報道機関 news media

きかん³ 気管 windpipe ▯, 〖解剖〗trachea [tréikiə] ▯ (複 tracheae, ~s) ∥気管支 the bronchial tubes / 気管支炎 bronchitis

きかん⁴ 器官 organ ▯ ∥感覚器官 sense organs / 呼吸器官 respiratory organs / 消化器官 digestive organs / 生殖器官 reproductive organs

きかん⁵ 季刊 ━━季刊の quarterly ∥季刊誌 a quarterly (magazine)

きかん⁶ 帰還 one's return (home) ◆スペースシャトルは10日間の任務を終え, 無事帰還した The space shuttle completed the 10-day mission and *returned* (*home*) safely.

きがん 祈願 (祈り) prayer ▯ ▯ ━━祈願する pray ▯ ∥必勝祈願 *a prayer* for victory

きかんさんぎょう 基幹産業 key [basic] industries

きかんじゅう 機関銃 machine gun ▯

きき¹ 危機 crisis [kráisis] ▯ (複 crises); (緊急事態) emergency ▯ ▯
財政[食糧]危機 *a financial* [*food*] *crisis*
患者はようやく危機を脱した(→乗り越えた) The patient *has* finally *gotten over the crisis*.
彼は人生の危機に直面している He is facing [confronting] *a crisis in his life*.
政府は将来のエネルギー危機に備えている The government has provided against *a future energy crisis*.
彼らはその問題に対してあまり危機感をいだいていないようだ They don't seem to have *a sense of crisis* about the problem.
◆父の会社は危機的な状況に陥った My father's company fell into *a critical situation*. / その鳥は絶滅の危機に瀕(ﾋﾝ)している That bird is [*threatened with* [*on the verge of*] *extinction*. / 私たちは危機一髪で死を免れた We *had a narrow escape* from death. / We *escaped* death *by a hair's breadth*.
∥危機管理(国家的な) crisis management; (経営上の) risk management

きき² 機器 (機械類) machinery ▯; (精密な) instrument ▯; (家庭用) appliance ▯; (ある目的のための) apparatus ▯ ▯ (複 ~, ~es); (設備・備品) equipment ▯ ∥医療機器 a medical instrument / AV機器 audiovisual apparatus [equipment] / 事務機器 office equipment / 精密機器 precision instruments / 電子機器 electrical equipment

きき³ 利き この自転車はブレーキの利きが甘い The brakes on this bike are *too loose*. / 私は右[左]利きだ I'm *right*-[*left*-]*handed*.

ききあきる 聞き飽きる その話は聞き飽きた I'*m sick and tired of hearing* that story.

ききいる 聞き入る 子供たちは彼の話に聞き入っていた The children *were listening attentively to* him. / 聴衆はその音楽に聞き入っていた The audience *was absorbed in* the music.

ききいれる 聞き入れる (願い・要求などを)《公式的》grant ▯; (忠告を) take* ▯, listen to ...; (申し出を) accept ▯ ∥彼は私の頼みを聞き入れてくれた He *granted* my request. / その生徒は先生の忠告を聞き入れようとしなかった The student *wouldn't take* [*listen to*] the teacher's advice. / 彼女は私たちの提案を聞き入れた She *accepted* our proposal.

ききうで 利き腕 one's dominant hand

ききおとす 聞き落とす miss ▯, fail to catch [hear] ∥何とおっしゃったのですか, 最後の2, 3語を聞き落としてしまいました What did you say? I *missed* the last few words.

ききおぼえ 聞き覚え その詩には聞き覚えがある The poem *sounds familiar to* me. / 聞き覚えのある声だった(→以前聞いたことを思い出した) I *remembered hearing* the voice *somewhere before*.

ききかえす 聞き返す そのおじいさんは店員に値段を聞き返していた The old man *was asking* a clerk the price *again*. / 英会話のテープを何度も聞き返した I *listened to* the English conversation tape *again and again*.
⇒ コミュニケーションスキル p.371

ききかじる 聞きかじった(→薄っぺらな)知識 *superficial* knowledge / 西洋史は聞きかじっただけです I *have* only *a smattering of* Western history.

ききぐるしい 聞き苦しい 彼の自慢話は聞き苦しい It is *disagreeable to hear* his bragging. / 回線の調子が悪くお聞き苦しい(→聞きづらい)点があるかもしれませんがご了承ください Please excuse *the poor sound quality* due to bad connection in the cables.

ききごたえ 聞き応え このCDは聞きごたえがある(→聞くだけの価値がある) This CD *is worth listening to*.

ききこみ 聞き込み (足で行う捜査) legwork ▯ ∥警察は聞き込み捜査を開始した The police started to do *legwork*.

ききすてる 聞き捨て 君が言ったことが本当なら聞き捨てならないな If what you said is true, I *can't* [*let it go by* [*pass it over*].

ききそこなう 聞き損なう 会場に遅れて着いたので彼の最初の曲を聞きそこなった I *missed* his first song because I got to the hall late.

ききだす 聞き出す 結局彼女の本心は聞き出せ

[コミュニケーションスキル] —聞き返す—

①相手の言葉が聞き取れなかったとき

(A) Will you make 10 copies of this for tomorrow's meeting?
–(I'm sorry, but) **Would you mind repeating that [Could you say that again, please]**?
これをあしたの会議のために10部コピーしてくれませんか. —(すみませんが)もう一度おっしゃっていただけませんか.

(B) **I beg your pardon**? [**Pardon**?; **Pardon me**?]
–I said, how long are you going to stay in Tokyo?
何ておっしゃったんですか. —東京にはどれくらいご滞在の予定ですか, とお尋ねしたのですが.

(C) I went to Shimo-Suwa yesterday.
–You went where?
きのう下諏訪に行ってきたんです. —どこへ行ったですって?

(D) Please help me carry this box upstairs.
–What? I didn't hear you.
この箱を2階へ運ぶのを手伝ってください. —えっ, 何? 聞こえませんでした.

(E) **Could you speak more slowly, please**?
–Oh, excuse me. I asked you where you took this photo.
もう少しゆっくり話していただけますか. —あ, 失礼. この写真をどこで撮られたのか, お聞きしたのですが.

(F) **Will you speak a little louder, please**?
–Let's meet at the front gate of the university at 3 o'clock. OK?
もう少し大きな声で言ってくれませんか. —大学の正門で3時に会いましょう. いいですか.

☞ 相手の言葉が聞き取れなかった場合は, (A) (B) (C) のような表現を使って聞き返す. (A) は最も丁寧な言い方. (C) のように, 聞き取れなかった部分だけを疑問詞の what, who, where などを使って聞き返すことが多い. このとき, 疑問詞でも上げ調子でいうことに注意.

☞ (D) はかなりくだけた言い方で, 身内とか同僚のように気心の知れた者どうしで使うほうが無難.

☞ 上記のほかに, **Excuse me, what did you say?** (すみませんが, 何とおっしゃいましたか)もよく使われる.

☞ (E) は相手の話すスピードが速すぎて聞き取れなかったとき, また (F) は相手の声が小さかったり, 電話などで声が遠くて聞き取れなかったときに使う表現. 親しい間柄では (E) には **Slow down, please.** (もっとゆっくり話してください), (F) には **Louder, please.** (もっと大きな声でお願いします)のような簡単な言い方も可能.

②相手の話の内容が分からないとき

(A) **I don't understand what you are saying.**
お話がよく分からないのですが.

(B) **I don't think I'm following you. /I'm afraid I'm not following you.**
おっしゃることがよく分からないんですが.

(C) **What do you mean by that?**
それはどういう意味ですか.

(D) "A provisional agreement," **did you say? What does that mean**?
「仮の契約」とおっしゃいましたか. それはどういう意味でしょう.

☞ 相手の話の内容が理解できない場合は, すぐにその意思表示をすることが必要である. 英米では話の内容を確認し合うのはふつうのことなので, 遠慮なく (A) ~ (D) のように聞きただせばよい.

☞ 相手の使った言葉が難解だったり, 意味不明であったりした場合には, (D) のように具体的にその語句を引用して尋ねる. また相手の意図がわからない場合には **I don't get it.** もよく使われる. 相手がためらっている場合には **Do you mean that ...?** のように問い直すことも必要である.

なかった I *couldn't find out* her real intention after all. / 彼から新しい情報を聞き出すのに成功した I succeeded in *getting* new information from him.

ききちがい 聞き違い すみません, **聞き違い**でした I'm sorry, 「I *heard it wrong* [I *didn't hear it right*].

ききちがえる 聞き違える mishear* [他] [自]; hear* wrongly [mistakenly] //「波」を「やみ」と**聞き違えた** I *misheard* "*nami*" as "*yami*."

ききつける 聞き付ける 悲鳴を**聞きつけて**人々はすぐその場に駆けつけた When they *heard* someone scream, people rushed to the scene immediately.

ききづらい 聞きづらい 彼からの電話は雑音が多くて**聞きづらかった** His voice was *hard to hear* on the phone, because there was a lot of noise. / そういうプライベートなことは彼女には**聞きづらい** I *hesitate to ask* her about such a private matter.

ききて[1] 聞き手 (対話などの) 《公式的》hearer [C]; (ラジオの) listener [C]; (聴衆) audience [C]; (インタビューの) interviewer [C]

ききて[2] 利き手 *one's* dominant hand

ききとり 聞き取り listening comprehension [U] ‖**聞き取り調査** fact-finding on the spot / **聞き取りテスト** a listening comprehension test

ききとる 聞き取る hear* [他], catch* [他]; (追う) follow [他] //彼女の声は騒音の中でほとんど**聞き取れなかった** Her voice *could hardly be heard* above [over] the noise. / 我々は彼の英語を**聞き取る**のに苦労した We had great difficulty (in) *following* his English.

ききなおす 聞き直す (もう一度尋ねる) ask again; (もう一度聞く) listen again //それについては彼に**聞き直してみる**必要がある We need to *ask* him *again* about that.

ききながす 聞き流す 彼女の言うことなんか**聞き流しなさい**(→無視しなさい) You should *ignore* what she says. / 彼はいつも先生の小言を**聞き流している**(→注意を払わない) He *pays*

ききなれる 聞き慣れる 彼女は聞き慣れない名前を口にした She mentioned an *unfamiliar* name.

ききにくい 聞き難い，(聞こえづらい) be difficult to hear; (尋ねにくい) hesitate to ask ∥入試に合格したかどうか彼本人には聞きにくい I *hesitate to ask* him whether he passed the entrance exam.

ききのがす 聞き逃す ほかのことを考えていて質問を聞き逃してしまった I was thinking about something else and I *didn't hear* the question.

ききほれる 聞き惚れる be enraptured with [by] ..., be charmed with [by] ..., be entranced by ... ∥このオーケストラの演奏にはいつも聞きほれる I *am* always *enraptured with* this orchestra's performance.

ききみみ 聞き耳 彼らの話に私の好きな俳優の名前が出たので聞き耳を立てた I *pricked up my ears* when my favorite actor's name was mentioned in their conversation.

ききめ 効き目 (効果) effect ∥このかぜ薬は効き目が速い This cold medicine 「*takes effect* [*works*] *quickly*.
◆頭痛に効き目のある薬 a medicine *effective* against headaches ∥ 彼にどんなに忠告しても効き目はないよ No matter how hard you warn him, it *is lost on* him.

ききもらす 聞き漏らす miss ⊕, fail to hear [catch] ∥記者たちはひと言も聞きもらすまいと彼の言葉に耳を傾けた The reporters listened closely to him not to *miss* a single word.

ききゃく 棄却 《法律》dismissal Ⓤ Ⓒ, rejection Ⓤ Ⓒ ―棄却する 《法律》dismiss ⊕, reject ⊕ ∥裁判所は控訴を棄却した The court *dismissed* [*rejected*] the appeal.

ききゅう 気球 balloon Ⓒ ∥気球に乗って空を飛ぶ fly in *a balloon* ∥ 気球を上げる fly *a balloon*
∥観測気球 an observation balloon ∥ 熱気球 a hot-air balloon

ききょう¹ 桔梗 Chinese bellflower Ⓒ

ききょう² 帰郷 homecoming Ⓤ ―帰郷する return to *one's* hometown, go* [come*] home ∥久しぶりに帰郷した I *went home* after a long absence.

ききょう³ 帰京 彼はあさって帰京する He *will return to Tokyo* the day after tomorrow.

きぎょう 企業 enterprise Ⓒ, business Ⓒ; (会社) company Ⓒ, corporation Ⓒ
∥企業イメージ a corporate image ∥ 企業家 a man of enterprise ∥ 企業合併 merger ∥ 企業広告 corporate advertising ∥ 企業コンサルタント a business consultant ∥ 企業秘密 a company secret ∥ 企業連合 a cartel ∥ 外資系企業 a foreign-affiliated corporation ∥ 公企業体 a public corporation ∥ 大企業 a big business [enterprise, company], a large enterprise ∥ 多国籍企業 a multinational (corporation) ∥ 中小企業 small and medium(-sized) enterprises ∥ 民間企業 a private enterprise ∥ 零細企業 a small business

ぎきょく 戯曲 drama Ⓒ, play Ⓒ (◆drama より口語的) ∥彼の新作の戯曲は大好評を博している His new *play* is a great hit. ◆その小説は戯曲化された The novel *was dramatized*.
∥戯曲化 dramatization ∥ 戯曲作家 a dramatist, a playwright

ききわけ 聞き分け 彼があんなに聞き分けのない人だとは思わなかった I didn't imagine he was so *unreasonable*.

ききわける 聞き分ける ❶【区別する】b と v を聞き分ける *distinguish* [*tell*] b *from* v ∥ 様々な楽器の音を聞き分ける (→聞き知っている) *recognize* different sounds of musical instruments
❷【納得する】understand* ⊕, listen to reason

ききわすれる 聞き忘れる パーティーの場所と日取りは聞いたのに時間を聞き忘れてしまった I asked the place and date of the party, but *forgot to ask* the time.

ききん¹ 飢饉 famine [fǽmin] Ⓤ Ⓒ ∥ききんに苦しむ suffer from *famine* ∥ その国をききんが襲った *A famine* struck the country.

ききん² 基金 fund Ⓒ; (基金運営の団体) foundation Ⓒ ∥その大学に基金を設立する establish *a fund* for the university ∥ 彼は孤児救済基金に1,000万円寄付した He donated 10 million yen to the relief *fund* for orphans.
∥国際通貨基金 the International Monetary Fund ((略認))IMF

ききんぞく 貴金属 precious [noble] metal Ⓒ ∥貴金属商 a jeweler ∥ 貴金属店 a jeweler's, a jewelry store

きく¹ 聞く・聴く

❶耳にする	hear
❷注意して聞く	listen
❸応じる	listen; obey
❹尋ねる	ask

❶【耳にする】hear* 自 ⊕
飛行機が離陸しようとしたとき異常な音を聞いた When the plane was about to take off, I *heard* a strange sound.
君の口からそんな言葉を聞くのはつらい It's painful for me to *hear* such words from you.
そんな話, 聞いたことある? *Have* you *ever heard of* such a thing?
彼女の海外留学の話, まだ聞いていないの? *Haven't* you *heard about* her studying abroad yet?
それは私がおととい彼女から聞いたのと同じうわさだ It's the same rumor as I *heard* from her the day before yesterday.
【hear+名+do】彼女は彼がフランス語を話すのを聞いた She *heard* him *speak* French.
【hear+名+doing】私は彼がイタリアのオペラを歌っているのを聞いた I *heard* him *singing*

an Italian opera.
【hear+名+done】彼は自分の名前が呼ばれるのを聞いた He *heard* his name *called*.
【hear+that[wh-]節】彼女が無事出産したと聞いてとてもうれしい I'm very happy to *hear that* she gave birth safely. / 私たちは彼が運転免許試験に合格したかどうか聞いていない We *haven't heard whether* he has passed the driving test.
◆ジョーンズ氏のことはうわさでは聞いているが面識はない I *know* Mr. Jones *by reputation* but I've never met him.
❷【注意して聞く】listen 自; (講演などを) hear* 他
よく(=注意して)聞きなさい *Listen* carefully.
そのとき私はCDを聴いていた I *was listening to* a CD at that time.
話を聞いてやる以外に彼に何をしてやれるというのですか What can I do for him besides *listen to* him?
私たちは彼女がピアノを弾くのを聴いていた We *were listening to* her *play* the piano.
私の話を最後まで聞きなさい *Listen to* me until I'm finished.
◆(私の話を)聞いているのですか *Are* you *with* me?/ Do you *follow* (what I'm saying)? / 彼の説明をよく注意して聞きなさい Please *pay close attention to* his explanation.
🔴「(人の話を)聞けよ」「ちゃんと聞いてるよ」 "*Listen*!" "I'm *listening*!"
❸【応じる】(耳を貸す) listen 自; (従う) obey 他, follow 他; (聞き入れる)《公式的》grant 他
私たちは彼を説得しようとしたが聞こうとしなかった We tried to reason with him, but he *wouldn't listen*.
彼の言うことを聞くくらいなら死んだほうがましだ I might (just) as well die as *obey* him.
私は姉のアドバイスを聞いて早めに出かけることにした I decided to *follow* my sister's advice and leave home early.
◆その子供たちには全然私の言うことを聞かない I *have no control over* the children. / 彼女はそこへ行くと言って聞かなかった She *insisted on* going there. / ちょっと頼みを聞いてくれないかな Do me a favor, will you?
❹【尋ねる】ask 他, inquire 他
僕に聞かないでくれよ *Don't ask* me!
健に聞いてごらん。彼なら知っているかもしれない *Ask* Ken. Maybe he knows.
もし分からないことがあれば何でも聞いてね If you have any questions, don't hesitate to *ask* me.
女性に年齢を聞くのは失礼だ It's not polite (of you) to *ask* a woman about her age.
◆まだチケットがとれるかどうかを聞いてみよう Let's *find out* if the tickets are still available.
🔴「どっちに行けばいいんだろう」「あのお巡(ま)りさんに聞いてみよう」 "Which way should we go?" "Why don't we *ask* that policeman?"
🔴「ちょっとお聞きしたいのですが」「はい、何でしょう」 "I'd like to *ask* you something."

"Yes. What is it?"
慣用表現 また爆弾テロだって？ 平和協定が聞いてあきれるよ A terrorist bombing again? So *what's the point of* the peace agreement? / 彼女は聞きしに勝る美人だ She is *even more beautiful than I've heard*. / 聞くところによると彼は5人兄弟だそうだ *From what I hear*, he has four brothers. / 私は彼らの話を聞くともなしに聞いてしまった I *overheard* their conversation. / 彼は私の言うことなど聞く耳を持たない He *won't listen to* me.
ことわざ 聞くは一時の恥、聞かぬは一生の恥 *Asking* is only a moment's shame, but not *asking* is a life-long shame.

きく² 効く・利く

❶【効果がある】(作用する) work 自; (効果がある) be effective, have* (an) effect; (効果が出る) take* effect; (…によい) be good for ...
この薬は鼻詰まりに効く This medicine *is effective against* a stuffy nose.
そのワクチンは新種のウイルスには効かなかった The vaccine *did not work on* the new virus.
2, 3か月たって漢方薬が効いてきた The herbal medicine *has taken effect* in two or three months.
◆チャンピオンのボディーブローが挑戦者に効き始めていた The champion's body blows *were beginning to tell on* the challenger.
❷【十分機能する】
このスープはコショウがききすぎている There is *too much* pepper in this soup.
自転車のブレーキがきかない The brakes on my bicycle 「*aren't working* [*don't work*]」.
彼は鼻がきく He *has a sharp sense of smell*.
けさ乗った電車は暖房がききすぎていた The heaters were turned up *too high* on the train I took this morning.
あの歌手の声にはパンチがきいている That singer's voice *has oomph*.
あの子は小さいのによく気がきくね Though he is a small child, he *is very attentive*.
❸【可能だ】
祖父は体の無理がきかない My grandfather *can't push himself too hard*.
このカメラは修理がきかない This camera *is not repairable*.
人生はいつでもやり直しがきく You *can make a fresh start* in life anytime.

きく³ 菊 chrysanthemum [krisǽnθimǝm]
‖菊人形 a chrysanthemum figure

きぐ⁎¹ 器具 (家庭用) appliance 回; (特定用途の) apparatus 回回 (複 〜, 〜es); (調理・掃除用) utensil 回 ‖ガス器具 a gas appliance / 暖房器具 a heating apparatus / 調理器具 cooking utensils / 電気器具 an electric appliance

きぐ⁎² 機具 implement 回 ‖農機具 *a* farming *implement*

きぐ³ 危惧 (不安) anxiety 回回; (将来への) misgivings, apprehensions ‖彼はその計画について危惧の念をいだいている He has *misgiv-*

ings [apprehensions] about the plan. ◆彼女は子供たちの将来を危惧している She *is apprehensive about* the future of her children.

きぐう 奇遇 博子じゃない！こんなところで会うなんて奇遇ね！ Oh, Hiroko! *What a coincidence* to meet you here! [*Fancy* meeting you here!]

ぎくしゃく 彼は緊張して歩き方がぎくしゃくしていた He was so nervous that he was walking *awkwardly* [*jerkily*, *unnaturally*]. / 彼らの関係はその出来事以来ぎくしゃくしている Their relationship *has been strained* since that incident.

きくばり 気配り (配慮) attention ⓤ; (注意) care ⓤ; (思いやり) consideration ⓤ ∥あなたはお年寄りに対する気配りが足りません You lack *consideration* for old people. / もう少し他人に対して気配りをしたほうがいい You should pay more *attention* to other people. ◆姉は目上の人に対して気配りが行き届いている My sister *is unfailingly attentive to* her seniors.

きぐらい 気位 彼女は気位が高くて僕たちには見向きもしない She is *so proud* that she isn't interested in us at all.

ぎくり 節子に弱点を指摘されてぎくりとした I *was startled* [(→うろたえた) *taken aback*] when Setsuko pointed out my weak point.

きぐろう 気苦労 worry ⓤⓒ, care ⓤⓒ ∥父は気苦労が多い My father has a lot of *worries*. ◆大人になるといろいろ気苦労が絶えない Adults always have *something to worry about*.

きけい 奇形 deformity ⓤ, malformation ⓤ ──奇形の deformed ∥奇形児 a deformed child

ぎけい 義兄 brother-in-law ⓒ (複 brothers-in-law, ~s)

きげき 喜劇 comedy ⓒ ──喜劇の comic, comical ∥どたばた喜劇 a slapstick *comedy* ∥喜劇映画 comedy film [picture], comic movie [film, picture] / 喜劇作家 a comic writer [dramatist] / 喜劇役者 a comic actor [actress], a comedian [comedienne]

きけつ¹ 既決 ──既決の decided, settled ∥既決事項 a matter *settled*

きけつ² 帰結 (成り行き) consequence ⓒ; (結論) conclusion ⓒ; (結果) result ⓤⓒ ∥当然の帰結 *a logical result*; *a natural consequence*

ぎけつ 議決 decision ⓒ; (決議) resolution ⓒ ──議決する decide 他自; resolve 他 ◆その新しい計画は議決された The new plan *was passed*.
∥議決権 voting rights, the right to vote

きけん¹ 危険

danger ⓤⓒ; (公式的) peril ⓤ; risk ⓒⓤ; hazard ⓒ ──危険な dangerous; (文語) perilous; (口語的) risky; hazardous
  danger: 「危険」を表す最も一般的な語.
  peril: 命にかかわるような差し迫った危険.
  risk: 自分から向かっていく危険.

| hazard: 危難の原因となる事物.

《危険が》
ダイビングには多くの危険が伴う There is considerable *danger* in diving.
彼はそのプロジェクトは危険が大きすぎると言った He said that the project was *too risky*.
津波の危険はありません There's no *danger* of a tsunami.

《危険に》
危険に気づく become aware of (*the*) *danger*
兵士はしばしば大きな危険にさらされる Soldiers *are* often *exposed to* great *dangers*.

《危険を》
それは大きな危険を伴う仕事だ It's an extremely *dangerous* task.
私は自分の金をすべて失うような危険を冒したくない I don't want to *run the risk of* losing all my money.

《危険な》
ロッククライミングは危険なスポーツだ Rock climbing is a *dangerous* sport.
家族を危険な目にあわせたくない I don't want to *put* my family *at risk*.
これが危険な投資であることはよく分かっている I'm well aware that this is a *risky* investment.
◆医者は患者が危険な状態を脱したと断言した The doctor pronounced that the patient had passed *the crisis*.

《その他》
危険，立入禁止《掲示》*Danger! Keep out!* / 危険物持ち込み禁止《掲示》*Dangerous Objects Prohibited* / 危険から自分の身を守る defend *oneself* from *danger*
シークレットサービスが大統領を危険から守っている The Secret Service *guards* the President (*against dangers*).
子供がその川で遊ぶのはとても危険だ *It is* very *dangerous for* children *to* play in the river.
∥危険信号 a danger signal / 危険人物 a dangerous person / 危険地帯 a danger zone

きけん² 棄権 (投票での) abstention ⓤⓒ; (競技での) default ⓤ ──棄権する (投票を) abstain 自; (競技を) withdraw* 自他; (競技の途中で) drop out of ... ∥彼女は気分が悪くなったレースを途中棄権した She *dropped out of* the race because she felt sick. / 今回の選挙で棄権者は全体の60パーセントにも及んだ Sixty percent of the voters *abstained from voting* at this election. / 相手が棄権したため彼は準決勝に進んだ He advanced to the semifinals because his opponent *withdrew*.

きげん¹ 機嫌

❶《気分》mood ⓒ, humor, 《英》humour ⓤ
治子はけさは機嫌がいい Haruko is *in a good mood* this morning.
彼はなぜか機嫌が悪い(→機嫌が悪い) He is *in a bad mood*.
お菓子をあげたら妹は機嫌を直した My sister

「*recovered her good humor [became cheerful again]* when I gave her some candy.
◆姉の機嫌を損ねてしまった(→怒らせた) *I've offended* my sister. / 子供の機嫌をとる(→喜ばせる)のも楽ではない It is not easy to *please* children. / 父は酒を飲んで上機嫌だった My father was drunk and *in high spirits*.

❷【あいさつ】⇨ ごきげん
彼は教授のところへご機嫌伺いに行った(→あいさつに行った) He went *to pay his respects* to his professor.
ご機嫌いかがですか *How are you*?

きげん² 期限 (指定期間) time limit ⓒ; (契約などの期間) term ⓒ; (締め切り) deadline ⓒ
申込書の提出期限はいつですか When is *the deadline for submission* of the application?
契約の期限は来月切れる *The term* of the contract will run out next month.
◆この回数券の有効期限は3か月だ This book of coupon tickets is *good for* three months. / もうすぐ請求書の支払期限だ The bill *is due* soon. / 報告書を必ず期限どおりに提出すること Be sure to turn in your reports *on time*. / 図書館で借りた本は返却期限を過ぎていた The books I borrowed at the library *were overdue*. / この割引券は期限切れだ This discount ticket *is no longer valid*.

きげん³ 紀元

> 紀元前を表す B.C. は before (the birth of) Christ の略で, 紀元を表す A.D. はラテン語の Anno Domini (= in the year of the Lord)「主イエスキリストの年に」の略。B.C. は年号の後に置く。A.D. は正式には年号の前に置くが, 後に置くこともある。

紀元前100年から紀元100年まで from 100 *B.C.* to *A.D.* 100 / 紀元2世紀に in the second century *A.D.* / この話ははるか昔, 紀元前4,000年にまでさかのぼる This story goes far back in the past, as far as 4,000 *B.C.*

きげん⁴ 起源・起原 origin ⓒ ⓤ /宇宙の起源 *the origin* of the universe / 中国語起源の言葉 a word of Chinese *origin*

きこう¹ 気候

climate ⓤ; (天候) weather ⓤ
⇨ 場面・状況別会話 p.1732
日本の気候は稲作に適している Japan's *climate* is favorable for the cultivation of rice.
房総半島は温暖な気候に恵まれています The Boso Peninsula is favored with *a mild climate*.
ここの気候は私に合う[合わない] *The climate* here agrees [disagrees] with me.

> コロケーション -climate-
> 【形容詞＋～】温暖な～ a mild [temperate] climate / 寒冷な～ a cold climate / 湿気の多い[乾燥した]～ a damp [dry] climate / 熱帯性～ a tropical climate / 大陸性～ a continental climate / 地中海性～ a Mediterranean climate

きこう² 機構 (しくみ) mechanism ⓒ ⓤ; (構造・構成) structure ⓤ ⓒ; (組織) organization ⓒ ⓤ /人体の機構 the body's *mechanisms*
‖経済機構 the economic structure / 経済協力開発機構 the Organization for Economic Cooperation and Development (《略語》OECD) / 社会機構 the structure [mechanism] of society / 流通機構 a distribution system

きこう³ 紀行 an account of travel [a journey] ‖紀行文 a travel note [sketch]

きこう⁴ 寄稿 ――寄稿する contribute ⓦ ⓘ, write* for ... /新聞に寄稿する a *write for* a newspaper / 彼女は毎週その雑誌に短い随筆を寄稿している She *contributes* a short essay to the magazine every week.
‖寄稿者 a contributor

きこう⁵ 寄港 ――寄港する put* in at [to] ...; call [stop] at ... /船は横浜に寄港した The ship *called at* Yokohama.

きごう 記号 sign ⓒ; (化学・数学の) symbol ⓒ; (文字・数字以外の印) mark ⓒ ――記号の symbolic /マイナス[プラス]の記号 *a* minus [plus] *sign* / H₂Oは水を表す記号です H₂O is *the symbol* for water. / この記号の意味が分かりません I can't see the meaning of this *mark*.
‖記号論 semiotics / 化学記号 a chemical symbol / ト音記号 a treble clef, a G clef / 発音記号 phonetic symbols [signs]

ぎこう 技巧 (技・こつ) art ⓤ ⓒ; (熟練による) skill ⓤ; (専門的な) technique ⓒ; (職人の) craftsmanship ⓤ ◆技巧を凝らした作品 an *elaborate* [a *polished*] *work* / この曲は技巧的で弾くのがとても難しい This piece is *technical* and very difficult to play.
‖技巧家 a technician

きこうし 貴公子 young nobleman ⓒ

きこうしき 起工式 ground-breaking ceremony ⓒ

きこえ 聞こえ 彼は名医の聞こえが高い(→評判がいい) He *has a good reputation* as a doctor. / マイペースと言えば聞こえはいいが, 実はやることがのろいだけだ "Doing something at his own pace" *sounds nice*, but actually it means "doing something slowly."

きこえよがし 聞こえよがし そんなこと, 聞こえよがしに(→わざと私のいる前で)言わなくたっていいじゃない You don't have to say such a thing *deliberately in* [*within*] *my hearing*.

きこえる 聞こえる

❶【耳に入る】(自然に) hear* ⓦ ⓘ (◆通例進行形にしない)
岩に打ち寄せる波の音が聞こえた I *heard* the wash of waves against the rocks.
私の位置から講義はほとんど聞こえなかった From my position, I *could hardly hear* the lecture.
その少女は聞こえないふりをした The girl pre-

tended *not to hear*.

【hear＋名＋*do*】外でだれかが叫ぶのが聞こえた I *heard* someone *shout* outside.

【hear＋名＋*doing*】うちに帰ると電話が鳴っているのが聞こえた When I got home, I *heard* the phone *ringing*.

◆彼は子供のころ耳が聞こえなくなった He *lost his hearing* in his childhood. / 彼女は私に聞こえる所で私を非難した She criticized me *in* [*within*] *my hearing*.

「もしもし，聞こえますか」「はい，聞こえます」 "Hello, *can you hear me*?" "Yes, *I can hear you*."

❷【響く】(…に思われる) sound [自]

彼女の歌は私にはどれもみな同じに聞こえる Her songs all *sound* the same to me.

まるで私を責めているように聞こえる It *sounds as if* you blame me.

◆彼の言うことはもっともらしく聞こえた What he said *rang true*.

❸【有名である】be famous, be well known (❖名詞の前では well-known とする)

彼女のおじさんは世に聞こえた歌手だ Her uncle is a *well-known* singer.

きこく 帰国 ―帰国する return [come* back, go* back] to *one's* country, return [come, go] home (❖come (back)は「帰ってくる」場合，go (back)は「帰っていく」場合，return はどちらの場合にも用いる) ‖俊明は先月帰国したばかりです Toshiaki just *came home* last month. / 無事に帰国されてうれしく思います I am delighted (that) you *have come home* safely. / リタは1年間の日本での生活を終えて帰国した Rita finished her year in Japan and *went back to her own country*.

◆使節団は帰国の途についた The mission *left for home*.

‖帰国子女 a student [child] who has lived abroad

きごこち 着心地 ゆかたは着心地がいい[悪い] A *yukata* is *comfortable* [*uncomfortable*] *to wear*.

きごころ 気心 由香と私は気心の知れた仲だ(→お互いによく知っている) Yuka and I *know each other well*. / 気心の知れた友人を呼んで誕生パーティーを開いた I invited *familiar* [*close*] friends to my birthday party.

ぎこちない awkward, clumsy; (堅苦しい) stiff ‖このロボットは動きがぎこちない This robot's movement is *awkward*./ This robot *moves awkwardly*. ◆ぎこちないほほえみ a *set* smile / 新しい先生の話し方はぎこちなかった The new teacher spoke *stiffly*.

きこつ 気骨 backbone [U], spirit [U]; (根性) grit [U] ‖兄にはそれをやるだけの気骨がなかった My brother didn't have *the backbone* to do it. / 彼はおとなしそうだが実は気骨のある人だ He seems quiet, but in fact he is *a man of backbone* [*grit*].

きこなす 着こなす wear* [dress] well ‖着物を着こなすのは難しい It is hard to *wear* kimono *well*.

◆スマートな着こなしの人 a neat *dresser* / 彼女はモデルのように上手に服を着こなしている She *is well-dressed* like a fashion model.

きこむ 着込む 外は寒いからしっかりと着込んでいったほうがいい It's cold outside, so you should「*bundle up well* [*dress warmly*].

きこり 樵 woodcutter [C], 《米》lumberjack [C], lumberman [C]

きこん 既婚 ―既婚の married ‖既婚男性[女性] a *married* man [woman]

‖既婚者 a married person; (総称) the married

きざ 気障 ―きざな (気取った) affected (❖言葉・態度などについて用いる); (うぬぼれた) conceited; (上流気取りの) snobbish ‖きざなせりふ *affected* words / あいつのきざな話し方が気に入らない I don't like his *snobbish* way of speaking. ◆あんなきざな男のどこがいいの What's so good about such *a snob*?

きさい 記載 (言及) mention [U]; (帳簿などへの記入) entry [C] ―記載する (言及する) mention [他]; (文章ではっきり述べる) state [他]; (帳簿などへ) enter [他]; (記録する) record [他] ‖彼の名前をリストに記載する *make an entry* of his name on the list / それについての記載はなかった No *mention* was made of it.

‖記載事項 an item mentioned / 記載もれ an omission

きざい[1] 器材 (器具や材料) instruments [tools] and materials

きざい[2] 機材 (機械と材料) machinery and materials; (機械の材料) machine parts

‖撮影機材 filming equipment

きさき 后・妃 (皇后) empress [C]; (女王) queen [C]

ぎざぎざ ―ぎざぎざの (のこぎりの歯のような) jagged, serrated; (硬貨が) milled ‖ぎざぎざのついたコイン a coin *with a milled edge* ◆ぎざぎざの海岸線 a *ragged* coastline (❖ragged は「(物の)へりなどが粗い」という意味)

きさく 気さく ―気さくな (人なつこい) friendly; (ざっくばらんな) frank; (寛大な) openhearted ―気さくに frankly ‖内気どころか彼女はとても気さくだった Far from being shy, she *was* quite *friendly*. / 隆はだれにでも気さくに話しかける Takashi speaks to everyone *frankly*.

◆尚夫は気さくに(→快く)私の相談に応じてくれた Hisao *was willing to* give me some advice.

きざし 兆し (しるし) sign [C]; (兆候) indication [C] [U]; (前兆) omen [C]; (よくないことの兆候) symptom [C] ‖春のきざし *a sign* of spring / 社会崩壊のきざし *symptoms* of social collapse / ようやく景気回復のきざしが見え始めた Finally the economy began to show *signs* of recovery.

きさま 貴様 貴様，何てことをしたんだ *You bastard*! What have you done?

-きざみ -刻み この時間だとバスは10分刻みで(→10分おきに)走っています During this hour, the buses come and go *every* 10 minutes. / きょうは分刻みのスケジュールをこなさなければならない Today I have to do the work on a schedule *arranged to the minute*.

きざみつける 刻み付ける *engrave* on [in] ... ∥その光景は記憶にしっかり刻みつけられている The scene *is* firmly *engraved on* [*in*] my memory.

きざみめ 刻み目 （V字形の）notch ⓒ; （小さな）nick ⓒ

きざむ 刻む （切る）cut*, chop 働; （細かく）mince 働; （細長く）shred 働; （彫る）carve 働; （心に）engrave 働 ∥母はタマネギを刻んでいる My mother *is chopping* an onion. / 彼は木に自分の名前を刻んだ He *carved* his name on a tree. / あのとき見た光景は私の心に深く刻まれている The scene I saw then *is* deeply *engraved in* my mind.

◆時計がカチカチと時を刻む音だけが聞こえる I hear only the clock *ticking away*.

きし¹ 岸 （川・湖などの）bank ⓒ; （海・湖・川の）shore ⓒ; （海の）coast ⓒ; （浜）beach ⓒ ∥カヌーは岸から流されていった The canoe drifted away from *the shore*. / 岸からはるか遠くにボートが見える I see a boat a long way off *the shore*.

◆小さなびんが岸に打ち寄せられていた A small bottle was washed *ashore*.

きし² 騎士 knight ⓒ ∥騎士道 chivalry
きし³ 棋士 professional *shogi* [go] player ⓒ

きじ¹ 記事 （新聞・雑誌の）article ⓒ, story ⓒ; （ニュース）news ⓒ; （1項目の記事）item ⓒ ∥きょうの新聞のトップ記事 *the lead article* in today's paper / 記事によると according to *the story* / 記事を読む [書く] read [write] *an article* / どの新聞もその事件の記事を載せていた All the newspapers carried *an article* about the incident. / 朝刊におもしろい記事があった There was *an interesting item* in the morning paper.

◆この事故はあしたの朝刊の記事になるな This accident *will appear* in the morning paper tomorrow.

∥三面記事 local [city] news / 特集記事 a feature story [article]

きじ² 生地 （布地）cloth ⓤ; （服地）material ⓤ; （パンやケーキの）dough [dóu] ⓤ ∥カーテン生地 curtain *materials* / パン生地をこねる knead *dough* / このスーツの生地は何ですか What *material* is this suit made of?

きじ³ 雉・雉子 pheasant [fézənt] ⓒ （複 ~s, ~）

ぎし¹ 技師 engineer ⓒ ∥電気 [機械] 技師 *an* electrical [*a* mechanical] *engineer*

ぎし² 義姉 sister-in-law ⓒ （複 sisters-in-law, ~s）

ぎし³ 義歯 false [artificial] tooth ⓒ; （架工歯）bridge ⓒ; （総入れ歯）dentures

ぎじ¹ 議事 proceedings, （会議事項）agenda ∥議事進行を妨害しないでください Don't obstruct *the proceedings*.

∥議事日程 an agenda, an order of the day / 議事妨害 obstruction of the proceedings, filibustering / 議事録 the minutes, (the records of) the proceedings

ぎじ² 疑似・擬似 ∥疑似餌(ぎ) a lure / 疑似体験 a virtual reality experience

きしかいせい 起死回生 彼は起死回生の一打を放った He got a hit which *turned the tables of the game*. (❖turn the tables は「形勢を逆転する」の意味)

ぎしき 儀式 ceremony ⓒ; （宗教などの）ritual ⓤⓒ ∥厳粛な儀式が執(と)り行われた A solemn *ceremony* was held.

◆儀式ばったあいさつ *ceremonious* greetings

ぎしぎし 階段を上るたびにぎしぎし音がする Every time I go up the stairs, they *creak* [*squeak*].

きしつ 気質 《公式的》disposition ⓒⓤ, temperament ⓤⓒ, nature ⓤ ∥おとなしい気質 quiet *disposition*

きじつ 期日 （定められた日）(fixed) date ⓒ; （約束の日）appointed day ⓒ; （締め切り）deadline ⓒ, time limit ⓒ ∥支払期日を決める fix *the date for payment* / このままでは期日に間に合わない We can't meet *the deadline* at this rate. / 感想文は期日までに提出してください Please submit an essay *by the deadline*.

∥期日指定預金 a certificate of deposit

ぎじどう 議事堂 assembly hall ⓒ
∥国会議事堂 (日本の) the Diet Building; (米国の) the Capitol; (英国の) the Houses of Parliament

きしべ 岸辺 （川・湖などの）bank ⓒ; （海・湖・川の）shore ⓒ ∥私たちは岸辺を散歩している We walked along *the shore*. / 波が岸辺に打ち寄せていた The waves were washing *the shore*.

きしむ 軋む （きいきいいう）creak 働, squeak 働; （こすれて耳ざわりな音を出す）grate 働 ∥最近台所の床がきしむ I've noticed the floor of the kitchen *is creaking* lately.

きしゃ¹ 汽車 train ⓒ ∥汽車に乗る get on *a train*

∥汽車賃 a railroad [railway] fare / 汽車ぽっぽ 《小児語》 a choo-choo (train)

きしゃ² 記者 （報道関係者一般）journalist ⓒ; （報道記者）reporter ⓒ; （特派員）correspondent ⓒ ∥彼はCNNの記者をしている He *is a reporter for* CNN. / He *reports for* CNN. ◆記者会見を開く hold *a press* [*news*] *conference*

∥記者クラブ a press club / 記者席 (議会の) the press gallery; (スポーツの) the press box / 記者団 the press corps[kɔ́ːr] / 雑誌記者 a magazine reporter / 女性記者 a woman reporter / 新聞記者 a newspaper reporter / スポーツ記者 a sports reporter

きしゅ¹ 旗手 日本選手団の旗手を務める serve as *a flag bearer* for the Japanese team

きしゅ² 機首 the nose (of an airplane) ∥パイロットは機首を上げた The pilot lifted *the nose*. ◆その飛行機は機首を下げた The airplane *nosed down*.

きしゅ³ 機種 model ⓒ ∥彼は携帯電話を新しい機種に変えた He changed his cell phone to *a new model*.

きしゅ[4] 騎手 (競馬の) jockey [C]; (馬に乗る人) rider [C]
きじゅ 喜寿 私たちは祖母の喜寿を祝った We celebrated our grandmother's *77th birthday.*
きしゅう 奇襲 敵は我々に奇襲をかけた The enemy *made a surprise attack on* us.
‖奇襲攻撃 a surprise attack / 奇襲戦法 shock tactics
きしゅく 寄宿 ―寄宿する (食事なしで) lodge at [with] ...; (食事付きで) board at [with] ... ‖寄宿学校 a boarding school / 寄宿舎 a dormitory, 《米口語的》a dorm / 寄宿生 a boarder
きじゅつ[1] 記述 (叙述・描写) description [U][C]; (説明) account [C] ―記述する describe [他]; give* an account of ... //この記述に間違いはありません There are no mistakes in this *description.* ◆記述式のテスト a *written* test / 19ページに詳しい記述があります The details *are written* on page 19.
きじゅつ[2] 奇術 magic [U] //奇術をする perform *magic*; do *a magic trick*
‖奇術師 a magician, a conjurer

ぎじゅつ 技術

(科学・芸術などの専門的な) technique [U][C]; (科学技術) technology [U]; (訓練で習得した技能) skill [C] ―技術的な・技術上の technical; (科学技術的な) technological ―技術的に technically; technologically
先端技術 *high technology* [*tech*] / 運転技術 driving *technique* / 技術を習得する acquire [master] *a skill*
情報通信の技術はこの10年の間に著しい進歩を遂げた Telecommunications *technology* has made remarkable progress in the last 10 years.
その仕事はきわめて高度な技術を要する That job requires highly *sophisticated techniques.*
それは技術的には可能だが, 相当時間がかかると思う That's *technically* possible, but I'm sure it'll take time.
◆父は30年間ずっと技術畑で働いてきた My father has been working *in the field of engineering* for 30 years.
‖技術援助 technical assistance / 技術革新 technical [technological] innovation / 技術・家庭(学科) technical arts and home economics / 技術官僚 a technocrat / 技術者 a technician; (技師) an engineer / 技術提携 technical cooperation [tie-up]

きじゅん 基準・規準 (標準) standard [C] 《しばしば複数形 ~s》; (尺度) measure [C] 《通例単数形》; (論拠) basis [C] (複 bases); (判断の) criterion [C] (複 criteria, ~s) //環境基準 *the environmental standards* / 基準を設ける set [establish] *standards* / 基準に達している be up to *the standard* / その建物は安全基準を満たしていない The building doesn't meet *safety standards.*
きしょう[1] 気性 (生来備わった特性) nature [U][C]; (性向) disposition [C]; (気質) temper [U][C] //気性の激しい人 a person *with a violent temper* / 彼女はさっぱりした気性の持ち主だ She has *an open disposition.*
きしょう[2] 気象 weather [U] //異常気象 *abnormal weather* / この地域は気象が変化しやすい *The weather* is changeable in this area.
‖気象衛星 a weather [meteorological] satellite / 気象学 meteorology / 気象観測 meteorological observation(s) / 気象情報 weather information / 気象台 a meteorological observatory, a weather station / 気象庁(長官) (the Director General of) the Meteorological Agency / 気象予報 a weather forecast [report] / 気象予報士 a certified weather forecaster
きしょう[3] 起床 ―起床する get* up, 《公式的》rise* [自] //あしたの朝は5時起床だ I have to *get up* at five tomorrow morning.
‖起床時間 the hour of rising
きしょう[4] 記章 (バッジ) badge [C]; (メダル) medal [C] //記章をつける wear *a badge*
きしょう[5] 希少 ‖希少価値 rarity value
きじょう[1] 机上 机上版の辞典 a *desk* dictionary / 机上の計画 a *desk* plan
[慣用表現] 机上の空論 *an armchair theory*; *a mere theory*
きじょう[2] 気丈 気丈な性格 a *strong-minded* personality / 両親の死の知らせにも彼女は気丈にふるまっていた She acted *bravely* at the news of her parents' death(s).
ぎしょう 偽証 〔法律〕 perjury [U][C], false testimony [U][C] ―偽証する commit perjury, perjure *oneself*, give* false testimony //彼は偽証罪に問われている He is accused of *perjury.* / 警察は彼が偽証しているのではないかと疑っている The police suspect him of *giving false testimony.*
ぎじょう 議場 assembly hall [C]; (議員席) the floor
きしょうてんけつ 起承転結 introduction, development, turn and conclusion
きしょく 気色 そんな気色の悪い物, よくさわれるね How can you touch such a *disgusting* thing?
きじん 奇人 eccentric (person) [C]; (変人・変わり者) 《口語的》oddball [C]
ぎしんあんき 疑心暗鬼 彼は疑心暗鬼になっている He *is filled with fear and anxiety.*
ぎじんか 擬人化 personification [C][U] ―擬人化する personify [他]
キス kiss [C] ―キスする kiss [他], give* *a person* a kiss //彼は彼女のほおにキスをした He *kissed* her on the cheek. / その歌手はファンに投げキスをした The singer *blew* [*threw*] his fans *a kiss.* / 母親は子供たちにおやすみのキスをした The mother *kissed* her children *good-night.* / その舞台ではキスシーンが何度もある There are many *kissing scenes* in that play. ◆上着の背中にだれかのキスマーク(→口紅)がついているのが分かってきまり悪かった I was embarrassed to find somebody's *lipstick* on the back of my jacket.

き

きす[1] 期す ❶【予期する・期待する】期せずして(→思いがけず)彼と私の考えが一致した *Unexpectedly* I agreed with him. / 私たちは旅先で期せずして(→偶然に)出会った We met each other「*by chance* [*accidentally*] while traveling.
❷【決意する】be determined [resolved] to *do* ∥彼らは試合での必勝を期している They *are determined* [*resolved*] *to* win the game.
❸【約束する】promise [他] ∥私は再会を期して彼らと別れた I parted from them, *promising to meet again.*
❹【日時を定める】6月20日を期して(→6月20日に)交渉を開始する enter into negotiations *on* June 20

きす[2] 帰す (結局…になる) come* to ...; (…に終わる) result in ... ∥彼の努力は水泡に帰した His effort *came to nothing.*

きず 傷

❶【けが】(事故などによる) injury [C][U]; (刃物・銃などによる) wound [wúːnd] [C]; (傷跡) scar [C]; (切り傷) cut [C]; (すり傷) scrape [C]; (引っかき傷) scratch [C]; (刺し傷) stab (wound) [C]

〖～傷〗
軽い[重い]傷 *a* slight [serious] *injury*
切り傷から血が出ていた *The cut* was bleeding.
ほんのかすり傷だ It's only [just] *a scratch.*

〖傷が・は〗
腕の傷がひどく痛んだ *The injury* [*wound*] on my arm hurt badly.
その男はほほに傷がある The man has *a scar* on his cheek.
傷はすぐ治った *The wounds* soon healed (over).
◆その手の傷はどうしたの How did you *injure* [*hurt*] your hand? (❖この injure, hurt は共に「傷をつける」の意味の動詞)

〖傷を・に〗
医者は傷を洗って消毒した The doctor washed *the cuts* and disinfected them.
ナイフで刺され足に深い傷を負った I was stabbed with a knife and *got a* deep *wound* on the leg.
看護婦さんが傷に包帯をしてくれた The nurse put a bandage on *the wound.* / The nurse bandaged *the wound.*

〖傷の〗
彼は傷の痛みに耐えた He bore *the pain of his injury* [*wound*].
病院で傷の手当を受けた I「*was treated* [*received treatment*] *for my injury* at a hospital.

〖その他〗
その猫は傷だらけだった The cat *was covered with wounds.*

❷【心の】scar [C],《公式的》wound [C],〖心理〗trauma [U][C]
幼児虐待は被害者の心に深い傷を残す Child abuse *leaves deep scars* in the victims.
音楽は心の傷をいやしてくれる Music heals *emotional wounds.*

❸【物の】(家具などの) scar [C]; (引っかき傷) scratch [C]; (ひび) crack [C], flaw [C] (❖crack は損傷を受けてできたもの. flaw は「欠陥」に相当するもの); (野菜・果物の傷み) bruise [C]
花びんの傷 *a crack* [*flaw*] in the vase
トマトは傷がつきやすい Tomatoes *easily get bruises.*/ Tomatoes *bruise easily.*
テーブルの表面にはたくさん傷がついていた There were a lot of *scratches* on the surface of the table. / The surface of the table *was scratched up.*

❹【汚点・不名誉】(汚点)《公式的》stain [C]; (不名誉) disgrace [U]
その失敗が彼の名声に傷をつけた The failure *left a stain on* his reputation./ The failure *damaged* his reputation.
彼女の逮捕は家名に傷をつけた Her arrest *brought disgrace on* her family.

きずあと 傷跡 scar [C] ∥その町にはいまだに内戦の傷跡が残っている The town still *bears the scars* of the civil war. / 手術後それほど傷跡が残ることはないでしょう There shouldn't be much of *a scar* after the operation. / 両親の離婚は彼女の心に傷跡を残した Her parents' divorce *left a scar* on her mind.

きすう[1] 奇数 odd [uneven] number [C] ── 奇数の odd

きすう[2] 基数 cardinal number [C]

ぎすぎす あれ以来, 彼との関係はぎすぎすしている(→お互いに冷たい) Since then, he and I *have treated each other coldly.* / 彼にはぎすぎすした(→つっけんどんな)ところがある There is something *surly* about him.

きずく 築く build* [他]; (建造する) construct [他]; (名声などを) establish [他] ∥とりでを築く *build* a fort / 信用を築く *establish* [*build*] a reputation / 彼は幸せな家庭を築いている He *is building* [*making*] *a happy family.*
◆ひと財産築く *make* a fortune / 彼はその国の経済の基礎を築いた He *laid the foundation for* the economy of the country.

きずぐすり 傷薬 ointment [U] ∥傷薬を塗る「put on [apply] *ointment*

きずぐち 傷口 wound [wúːnd] [C], cut [C] ∥傷口を消毒する disinfect *the wound* / まだ傷口がふさがらない *The wound* has not closed yet. / 腕の傷口を4針縫った It took four stitches to close up *the wound* [*cut*] on my arm.

きずつく 傷付く be injured [hurt, wounded]; (品物が) be damaged ∥彼の言葉で彼女のプライドは傷ついた Her *pride was hurt* [*wounded*] by what he said.
◆その犬は傷ついた足を引きずっていた The dog was trailing *its wounded leg.* / 妹は傷つきやすい年ごろだ My sister is at a *vulnerable* [*sensitive*] age.

きずつける 傷付ける (人・体・気持ちを) injure [他], hurt* [他], wound [他]; (物・事柄を) damage [他] ∥人の名声を傷つける *damage* a person's reputation / 君を傷つけるつもりはなかったんだ I didn't mean to *hurt* you.
◆机の表面を傷つける *scratch* the surface of

a desk

きずな 絆（結びつき）bond ⓒ《しばしば複数形 ～s》;（つながり）ties ∥会員間の強いきずな a close *bond* among the members / 家族のきずな *family ties* ◆彼らは強い友情のきずなで結ばれている They *are bonded* together by great *friendship*.

きずもの 傷物 defective [flawed, damaged] article ⓒ;（不良品）reject ⓒ ◆傷物の商品 *damaged* goods

きする¹ 期する ⇨きす(期す)

きする² 帰する ⇨きす(帰す)

きせい¹ 気勢 強豪相手に勝ったことでチームの気勢が上がった The win over a very strong team *put* our team *in high spirits*. / 彼のひと言で私たちは気勢をそがれた We *were discouraged* by what he said.

きせい² 既成 ―既成の（現存の）existing;（確立した）established;（完成した）completed ∥既成の政党 the *existing* [*established*] political parties ◆あなたは既成概念にとらわれすぎている You adhere to「*preconceived* ideas [*stereotypes*] too much.

∥既成事実 an established [accomplished, accepted] fact,《法律》a fait accompli [feit əkɑːmpliː]

きせい³ 既製 ―既製の（出来合いの）ready-made ∥既製のスーツ ready-made [off-the-rack] suits

∥既製品 a ready-made article / 既製服 ready-made [ready-to-wear] clothes

きせい⁴ 規制（取り締まり）regulation ⓤ ⓒ;（管理）control ⓤ ⓒ;（制限）restriction ⓒ ⓤ ―規制する regulate 他;control 他 ∥暴力シーンを含むテレビ番組に対する規制を厳しくする tighten *the regulations* on TV programs which contain violent scenes / 製品の販売を自主規制する *control* [*restrict*] the sale of the products *voluntarily*

∥規制改革 regulatory reform / 規制緩和 deregulation / 交通規制 the regulation of traffic / 銃規制法案 a gun control bill

きせい⁵ 帰省 homecoming ⓤ ―帰省する go* [come*, return] home ∥東京駅は夏休みの帰省客で混雑している Tokyo Station is very crowded with *people going home to stay* for their summer vacations.

◆彼女は今帰省中です She *is at home* now.

きせい⁶ 寄生 parasitism ⓤ ―寄生の parasitic, parasitical ―寄生する be parasitic on ... ∥寄生植物 a parasitic plant / 寄生虫 a parasite, a parasitic worm [insect] / 寄生動物 a parasitic animal

きせい⁷ 奇声（かん高い声）shrill cry ⓒ / 奇声を発する give out *a shrill cry*

ぎせい 犠牲 sacrifice ⓤ ⓒ;（被害者）victim

犠牲を払う make *a sacrifice*

彼は自分の命を犠牲にしてその少年を救った He saved the boy's life *at the sacrifice of* his own life. / He *sacrificed* his own life to save the boy's life.

多くの人がその火事の犠牲になった A lot of people「*fell victim to* [*became victims of*] the fire.

◆どんな犠牲を払ってもやりとげるつもりだ I will carry it out *at any cost*.

∥犠牲者 ⇨ ぎせいしゃ / 犠牲バント[フライ] a sacrifice bunt [fly]

ぎせいご 擬声語 onomatopoeia [ànəmætəpíːə] ⓤ, onomatopoeic word ⓒ

ぎせいしゃ 犠牲者（被害者）victim ⓒ;（事故・災害の死傷者）casualty ⓒ ∥戦争犠牲者 war *victims* / 犠牲者のほとんどは煙に巻かれた人々だった Most of *the victims* were overcome by smoke. / その地震でたくさんの犠牲者が出た There were a lot of *casualties* in the earthquake.

きせかえる 着せ替える 着せ替え人形 *a dress-up doll* / 人形の服を着せ替える *change*「the clothes on a doll [a doll's clothes]

きせき¹ 奇跡・奇蹟 miracle ⓒ ∥あの交通事故で彼女が死ななかったのは奇跡だった It was *a miracle* that she was not killed in that traffic accident. / そのとき奇跡が起こった Then *a miracle* happened. / パイロットは奇跡的に助かった The pilot escaped death「*by a miracle* [*miraculously*].

◆彼の逆転ホームランでジャイアンツは奇跡的な勝利を収めた The Giants achieved a *miraculous* victory with his come-from-behind home run.

きせき² 軌跡《数学》locus ⓒ（複 loci）;（跡）track ⓒ

ぎせき 議席 seat ⓒ ∥その党は今回の選挙で15議席を獲得した[失った] The party won [lost] 15 *seats* in the election.

きせつ 季節

season ⓒ ⇨ 場面・状況別会話 p.1732

春は木々が芽を出し、鳥が陽気にさえずる季節である Spring is *the season* when trees bud and birds sing merrily.

桜の咲く季節がやってきた *The* cherry blossom *season* has come.

エアコンの売り上げは季節によって変わる Sales of air-conditioners vary with *the season*.

夏は海の季節だ Summer is *the season* for the sea.

カキは今がちょうど季節だ Oysters *are in season* right now.(❖「季節でない」は be out of season)

季節の変わり目はかぜをひく人が多い Many people catch colds *at the change of the seasons* [*when the seasons change*].

◆季節の野菜 *seasonal* vegetables / 季節はずれの台風がその地域に大きな被害をもたらした The *unseasonable* typhoon caused extensive damage to the area. / 夏は1年でいちばん暑い季節だ Summer is *the hottest time of the year*.

💬「どの季節がいちばん好き？」「私は秋です」"Which *season* do you like best?" "I like fall best."

∥季節感 a sense of the season(s) / 季節風 a seasonal wind;（東南アジアで）a monsoon

/ 季節労働者 a seasonal worker

きぜつ 気絶 faint ◯ ━━気絶する faint ⾃, (口語的) pass out / 気絶して倒れる fall down in a faint / 彼は頭を強く殴られて気絶しそうになった He nearly *fainted* [*passed out*] when he was hit hard on the head.

キセル 煙管 pipe ◯ ◆キセルをする(→運賃をごまかす) *dodge the full train fare*

きせる 着せる ❶【服を】dress ⾃ / 姉は人形に服を着せていた My sister *was dressing* her doll. ◆彼女は子供にセーターを着せてやった She *helped* her child「*on with* [*put on*] a sweater.
❷【罪などを】彼は臆病(おくびょう)者の汚名を着せられた He *was branded* (as) a coward. / 彼女はぬれぎぬを着せられたと憤慨していた She was indignant about *being unjustly accused.* / みな、彼に罪を着せた Everyone *put* [*laid*] *the blame on* him.

きぜわしい 気忙しい 彼は気ぜわしい(→せっかちな)人だ He is a *restless* [an *impatient*] person. / 今月は何かと気ぜわしい(→落ち着かない) I *feel* somewhat *restless* this month.

きせん¹ 汽船 steamer ◯, steamship ◯ ((略語)) S.S.); (定期船) liner ◯ ((観光用の)) cruise ship

きせん² 機先 人の機先を制する *forestall* [*anticipate*] a person; 《口語的》*get a jump on* a person

きぜん 毅然 毅然とした態度をとる take a *firm* [*resolute*] attitude / 彼女は彼の要求を毅然として断った She *firmly* refused his demand.

ぎぜん 偽善 hypocrisy ◯ / いささか偽善めいた演説 a speech that smells of *hypocrisy* ◆偽善的な態度 *hypocritical* behavior
‖偽善者 a hypocrite

きそ¹ 基礎

base ◯, basis ◯ (複 bases), foundation ◯; (基本的な考え・原理) the basics ◯; (建物の) base ◯, foundation ◯ ━━基礎の basic, fundamental; (初歩的な) elementary
家の基礎を築く lay the *base* [*foundation*] for a house / 基礎英語コースを履修する take a *basic* English course
この夏に英文法の基礎を固めたい I want to master *the basics* of English grammar this summer.
彼は法律の基礎知識が足りない He lacks「*the basics* [*a basic knowledge*] of the law.
私は数学を基礎からやり直したい I want to study math again *from the basics*.
‖基礎工事 foundation work / 基礎体温 one's basal body temperature

きそ² 起訴 (検察の)《法律》prosecution ◯ ◯; (陪審の)《主に米》indictment [indáitmənt] ◯ ━━起訴する (検察が) prosecute ⾃; (陪審が) indict [indáit] ⾃ / 彼は強盗罪で起訴された He *was prosecuted* [*indicted*] *for* robbery.
‖起訴状 an indictment / 起訴猶予(よ) suspension of prosecution

きそう¹ 競う compete ⾃, contend ⾃; (勝利や賞を目ざして) contest ⾃ / 金賞を目ざして競う *compete for* the gold prize / 私はライバルとテストの点数を競い合っている I'm *competing with* my rival about the test score.

きそう² 起草 drafting ◯ ━━起草する draft ⾃ / 法案を起草する *draft* a bill

きそう³ 帰巣 ‖帰巣本能 the homing instinct

きぞう 寄贈 ━━寄贈する (与える) give* ⾃; (贈る) present ⾃; (慈善事業として) donate ⾃ / これらの本は市民団体からの寄贈です These books *were donated* by a group of citizens. / 卒業する学生は学校にピアノを寄贈した The graduating students *presented* a piano to the school.
‖寄贈者 a contributor, a donator / 寄贈品 a contribution, a donation

ぎそう¹ 偽装・擬装 (変装) disguise ⾃ ◯; (カムフラージュ) camouflage ⾃ ◯ ━━偽装する disguise ⾃; camouflage ⾃ / 彼は警備員に偽装した He *disguised himself as* a guard.
‖偽装結婚 fake [sham] marriage

ぎそう² 偽造 (文書・紙幣など) forgery ⾃ ◯, counterfeit ⾃ ━━偽造する forge ⾃, counterfeit ⾃ / 文書偽造 *forgery* of documents / 彼らはテレホンカードを偽造した They *forged* [*counterfeited*] telephone cards. ◆偽造ダイヤ a *fake* diamond
‖偽造硬貨 a counterfeit coin / 偽造紙幣 a counterfeit bill / 偽造パスポート a counterfeit [forged, fake] passport / 偽造品 a counterfeit, a fake / 偽造文書 a forged document, a forgery

きそうてんがい 奇想天外 ━━奇想天外な (驚くべき) amazing; (予期しない) unexpected / 奇想天外な冒険映画 an *amazing* adventure movie

きそく 規則

(公的なもの・法規) regulation ◯《しばしば複数形 〜s》━━規則的な regular ━━規則的に regularly ⇨ きそくただしい
厳しい規則 *a* strict *rule* [*regulation*] / 規則に従う obey *the rules* [*regulations*] / 規則を曲げる stretch [bend] *the rules* / 規則どおりに *by the rule* [*regulation*]
それは規則違反だ That's *against the rules*.
教師は規則を破った[守らない]生徒に罰を与えた The teacher punished the student for breaking [disobeying] *the rules*.
僕たちは新しい規則を作った We made [established] new *rules*.
当局は交通規則を厳しくした The authorities have tightened *the traffic regulations*.
この規則は全学生に適用される This *rule* is applied to all students.
例外のない規則はない There is no *rule* without exception. / Every *rule* has an exception.
規則に縛られるのは嫌いだ I hate to be bound by *rules*.
規則的に運動するとよいでしょう It's good to

きぞく　帰属　——帰属する《所属する》belong to ...;《権利・権限などが》《公式的》vest in ...
‖帰属意識 a sense of belonging

きぞく² 貴族　nobleman ⓒ《❖女性形は noblewoman》, aristocrat ⓒ;《英国の》peer ⓒ《❖baron, viscount, earl, marquis, duke などの爵位がある》;《総称》the nobility, the aristocracy,《英》the peerage ∥彼女はイタリアの貴族として生まれた She was born *an* Italian *aristocrat.* / 彼は貴族に叙せられた He was raised [elevated] *to the peerage.*
◆貴族の家柄 a *noble* [*blue-blooded*] family

ぎそく 義足　artificial leg ⓒ;《木製の》wooden [peg] leg ⓒ　∥義足を使う wear [use] *an artificial leg*

きそくただしい 規則正しい　regular ——規則正しく regularly ∥規則正しい脈拍 a *regular* pulse / もっと規則正しい生活をすべきです You should lead a more *regular* life.

きそつ 既卒　∥既卒者 a person who has finished school,《米》a graduate

きぞん 既存　——既存の existing　∥既存の権益 *existing* rights and interests

きぞん² 毀損　damage ⓤ　◆その会社はある雑誌を名誉毀損で訴えた The company sued a magazine for *libel* [*defamation*].

きた 北

the north　——北の north, northern [nɔ́ːrðərn]

北からの冷たい風 cold winds *from the north* / 北の空 the *northern* sky

どちらが北ですか Which direction [way] is *north*?《❖単に東西南北の一つとしての「北」は無冠詞》

目的地はここから 5 キロ北だ Our destination is five kilometers (*to the*) *north* from here.

神戸は淡路島の北にある Kobe is (*to the*) *north of* Awaji Island.

カナダはアメリカの北にある Canada is (*to the*) *north of* the U. S. / Canada is *on the northern border of* the U.S.《❖隣接している」ことをはっきりさせたい場合は後の表現を用いる》

彼の家はこの市の北の方に（→市の北部に）ある His house is「*on the north side of* [*in the northern part of*] this city.

私たちは 7 時に駅の北口で待ち合わせている We are to meet at *the north exit* of the station at seven.

◆北へ向かう列車 a *northbound* train / 僕の部屋は北向きだ My room *faces north.*《❖この north は副詞で「北へ, 北に」の意味》　飛行機は北へ飛んでいった The plane has flown *north* [*northward*].

ギター guitar ⓒ ∥ギターを弾く play *the guitar*
∥ギターアンプ a guitar amplifier / ギター奏者 a guitarist / アコースティックギター an acoustic guitar / エレキギター an electric guitar / スチールギター a steel guitar / ベースギター a bass (guitar)

きたアメリカ 北アメリカ　North America ——北アメリカの North American

きたい¹ 期待

expectation ⓒⓤ《しばしば複数形 ～s》, anticipation ⓤ, hope ⓒⓤ　——期待する expect ⓔ, anticipate ⓔ, hope ⓔⓤ

彼の成績は親の期待に添うものではなかった His grades didn't come [live] up to his parents' *expectations.* / His grades fell short of his parents' *expectations.*

あなたの期待におこたえできそうにありません I'm afraid I can't meet [live up to] your *expectations.*

我々の期待に反して彼は決勝で負けた Contrary to our *expectations*, he lost in the finals.

彼が成功するということはまず期待できない I see little *hope* of him succeeding.

子供に期待をかけすぎるな Don't *expect* too much of your child.

子供たちはサンタからのプレゼントを期待している Children *are expecting* presents from Santa.

その料理は期待したほどおいしくなかった The dish was not as good as I (*had*) *expected*.

エイズに対して政府が有効な対策をとることが期待されている It *is hoped* that the government will take effective measures against AIDS.

◆彼らのニューアルバムは期待はずれだった Their new album was *disappointing* [*a disappointment*] to me. / 彼らの期待を裏切るわけにはいかない I can't *disappoint* them. / I can't *let* them *down*.

🅔 「試合がんばってきてね」「もちろん. でも結果はあんまり期待しないでね」"Do your best in the game." "Of course, I will. But please don't *expect* too much (of me)."

きたい² 気体　gas ⓒ ⓤ (複 ～es, gasses);《蒸気》vapor,《英》vapour ⓤⓒ　∥気体燃料 gaseous fuel

きたい³ 機体　a body (of an airplane);《エンジンを除く機体》airframe ⓒ;《胴体》fuselage ⓒ

ぎたい 擬態【生物】mimicry ⓤ

ぎだい 議題《話題》topic ⓒ;《テーマ》subject ⓒ;《問題》issue ⓒ;《事項》item ⓒ;《協議事項リスト》agenda ⓒ　∥きょうの議題は「いかにしていじめを減らすことができるか」です Today's *topic* [*subject*] is "What can we do to reduce bullying?" / Today, we *discuss* what we can do to reduce bullying. / それは議題に含まれています It is on *the agenda.* / 次の議題に移りましょう Let's go on to *the* next *item on the agenda.*

◆その問題は議題にのぼらなかった The problem didn't come up for *discussion.*

き

ぎたいご 擬態語 imitative word [C]
きたえる 鍛える （訓練する） train [他]; （体を） build* up; （精神を） discipline [他]; （強くする） strengthen [他]; （鉄などを） forge [他]
精神を鍛える *discipline one's* mind
ジョギングで体を鍛えています I'*m strengthening* my body by jogging.
きょうからおまえたちをびしびし鍛えるぞ I'll *train* you really hard from today on. / I'll *give* you some really hard *training* from today on.
きたかいきせん 北回帰線 the Tropic of Cancer (↔the Tropic of Capricorn)
きたかぜ 北風 north wind [C]
きたく 帰宅 ―帰宅する go* [come*] home; （帰り着く） get* home; （家に戻る） return home ∥私はふつう6時に帰宅する I usually *get home* at six. / 姉はいつもより早く帰宅した My sister *came home* earlier than usual. / 彼はクラブ活動の後すぐ帰宅した He *returned home* immediately after his club activities. ◆私は帰宅途中いつもコンビニの前を通ります I always pass the convenience store *on my way home*.
きたぐに 北国 （地方） northern district [province] [C]; （国） northern country [C]
きたす 来す 彼のけがは日常生活に支障をきたすものではない His injury will not *be an obstacle to* his daily life. / 今それを発表すれば人々は混乱をきたすだろう Announcing the matter would 「*make* people *confused* [*lead* people *into a confused state*].
きたちょうせん 北朝鮮 （朝鮮民主主義人民共和国） North Korea（❖公式名 the Democratic People's Republic of Korea） ―北朝鮮人 North Korean [C] ―北朝鮮（人）の North Korean
きだて 気立て nature [U] [C], disposition [U] [C] ∥優子は気立てがよい Yuko 「*has a good disposition* [*is good-natured*].
◆奈央は気立ての優しい子だ Nao is a *sweet-tempered* girl.

きたない 汚い

❶【不潔な】dirty; （極度に） filthy; （空気・水などが） foul
汚い手で食べ物にさわるな Don't touch any food with your *dirty* [*filthy*] hands.
この地域の空気は汚い The air in this area is *dirty* [*filthy, foul*].
❷【整っていない】messy, untidy
研二の部屋はすごく汚い Kenji's room is really *messy* [*untidy*]. / Kenji's room is *in a* terrible *mess*.
彼の字は汚い His handwriting is *untidy*.
❸【卑劣な・けちな】mean, dirty, nasty; （不正な） unfair; （けちな）《口語的》tight, stingy
人のせいにするなんて汚いぞ It's *dirty* [*mean, nasty, unfair*] of you to blame it on me.
君にはそんな汚い商売に手を染めてほしくない I don't want you to be mixed up in that *dirty* [*nasty*] business.
彼は汚い手を使って試合に勝った He won the game *by* 「*unfair means* [*playing dirty*].
彼は金に汚い He is *tight* [*stingy*] with money.
❹【言葉が】（下品・卑わいな）《口語的》dirty, nasty, filthy, foul; （粗野な） coarse
汚い言葉づかいはやめなさい Stop using *dirty* [*nasty, filthy, foul, coarse*] language.

きたはんきゅう 北半球 the Northern Hemisphere
きたる 来たる coming, next; （今度の）《公式的》forthcoming; （間近に迫った） upcoming ∥来たるべき戦いに備える prepare for the *upcoming* battle / 来たる金曜日に生徒総会があります The student meeting will be held *this coming* Friday.
きたん 忌憚 忌憚のない意見 a *frank* [*a candid, an outspoken*] opinion / 忌憚なく言えばその案には反対です *To be frank*, I don't agree with the proposal.
きだん 気団 寒気団 *a* cold *air mass* / 大陸気団 *a* continental *air mass*
きち[1] 基地 base [C] ∥軍事基地 *a* military *base* / 空軍[海軍]基地 *an* air [*a* naval] *base*
きち[2] 機知 wit [U] ◆彼は機知に富んでいる He is very *witty*.
きち[3] 吉 good luck [fortune] [U]
きち[4] 既知 既知の事実 a *known* fact
きちきち きちきちの予算 a *very tight* budget / このスカートはきちきちだ This skirt is *too tight* for me. / スケジュールがきちきちに詰まっている I have a *tight* [*full, heavy*] schedule.
きちじつ 吉日 lucky day [C]
[ことわざ] 思い立ったが吉日 ⇨おもいたつ
きちゅう 忌中 祖母の忌中です I am *in mourning* for my grandmother.
きちょう[1] 貴重 ―貴重な （金で買えない） precious; （金銭的価値・有用性が高い） valuable ∥貴重な時間 *precious* time / 貴重な情報 *valuable* information / 貴重なガラス器と陶磁器のコレクション a *valuable* collection of glass and china / それは貴重な経験だ That's a *precious* experience.
‖貴重品 valuables
きちょう[2] 記帳 ―記帳する （帳簿に） make* an entry, enter [他]; （宿帳・名簿などに） register [自] [他] ∥フロントで記帳した I *registered* [*signed in*] at the front desk.
◆現金自動支払い機で通帳に記帳した I *updated* my bankbook at an ATM.（❖update は「…を最新のものにする」の意味）
きちょう[3] 基調 ヒューマニズムを基調とした作品 a work *based on* humanism
‖基調演説 a keynote speech [address]
きちょう[4] 機長 the captain of an airplane
ぎちょう 議長 chairperson [C], chairman [C]（❖女性形は chairwoman）（❖男女平等の考え方から chairperson が好まれる）; （衆議院・下院の） the Speaker; （参議院・上院の） the President ∥彼女はその会議の議長を務めた She acted as *the chairperson* of the meeting. / 加藤氏がその会議の議長に選ばれた Mr. Kato was elected *chairman* of the conference.

/ 議長，会議を2時間休会するよう提案いたします *Mr. Chairman*, I move that the meeting (should) adjourn for two hours. (❖女性議長には Madam Chairman) ◆だれがこの会議の議長を務めるのですか Who is going to 「*preside at* [*chair*] this meeting?

きちょうめん 几帳面 ―几帳面な (物事をきちんと行う) methodical, neat; (細心の注意を払う) meticulous; (厳密な) exact; (堅苦しい) precise //祖父はきちょうめんな人だった My grandfather was a *methodical* [*meticulous*] person. ◆木村君は時間にきちょうめんだ Kimura is always *punctual*.

きちんと

❶【整然と】(こぎれいに) neatly, tidily; (整然と) orderly
洋服はきちんとたたんであった The clothes were folded *neatly*.
美奈はいつもきちんとした服装をしている Mina is always *neatly* dressed.
お皿をテーブルの上にきちんと積み重ねなさい Pile up the dishes *neatly* on the table.
◆その部屋はきちんと片づいていた The room was *neat and tidy*. / 出かける前に髪をきちんとしたい I want to *fix* my hair before I go out.

❷【規則的に】regularly
1日3回きちんと食事をすれば健康が保てる Eating *regularly* three times a day keeps you fit.

❸【正確に・確かに】exactly, precisely
うちの犬は私の言うことがきちんと分かる My dog understands *exactly* what I say.
◆いつも隆志は約束の時間をきちんと守る Takashi *is* always 「*on time* [*punctual*] for appointments. / きちんと足に合った靴を履きなさい Wear shoes which fit your feet *well*. / 彼は約束をきちんと守る人だ He is a person who *surely* keeps promises.

きつい

❶【窮屈な】tight ―きつく tight(ly)
このセーターはちょっと首がきつい This sweater is a little *tight* in the neck.
包帯を腕にきつく巻いた I put the bandage around my arm *tight*(*ly*).
◆きついスケジュール a *tight* [*heavy*] schedule / ベルトをきつくした I *tightened* the belt.

❷【厳しい】severe, strict; (酷な) harsh, cruel ―きつく severely, strictly
きついお仕置き *severe* punishment
彼女はよく人に対してきついことを言う She often says *harsh* [*cruel*] things to others.
父にきつくしかられた I was *severely* scolded by my father.
[会話]「これとこれと，あとこれもきょう中に仕上げておいてね」「僕ひとりで？冗談きついよ」"I want you to finish this, this, and this by the end of the day." "All by myself? *You must be kidding*."

❸【気の強い】
あの子はきつい性格をしている That child is *strong-minded*.
この写真の少年はきつい目つきをしている The boy in this picture has a *sharp* look in his eyes.

❹【困難な】hard, tough, difficult
この宿題を月曜までにすませるのはかなりきつい It will be very *hard* to finish this homework by Monday.
彼は自分からそのきつい仕事を選んだ He chose the *tough* work himself.

❺【程度が激しい】
きつい日差し *intense* [*strong*] sunlight
きょうは風がきつい The wind is blowing *very hard* today.
このお酒はきつい This sake *is strong*.
頂上に近づくにつれて傾斜はきつくなった The slope *increased* as we got near to the top.

きつえん 喫煙 smoking [U] ―喫煙する smoke [自] [他] //室内での喫煙は禁じられています You are not allowed to *smoke* inside the room.
‖喫煙室 a smoking room / 喫煙者 a smoker / 喫煙車 a smoking car / 喫煙席 a smoking section / 間接喫煙 passive smoking

きづかい 気遣い どうぞお気づかいなさらないでください Please don't *worry* [*care*] *about* me. / お金が足りなくなる気づかい(→心配)はいらない You don't have to *worry about* running short of money.

きづかう 気遣う be anxious [concerned, worried] //彼女は地震のニュースを聞き，そこにいる親戚(しんせき)の安否を気づかった When she heard the news of the earthquake, she *became anxious about* the safety of her relatives there. / 私がけがをして以来，英子は私を気づかってくれる Ever since I got injured, Eiko *has been worried about* me.

きっかけ 切っ掛け (機会) chance [C], opportunity [C] //彼女に話しかけるきっかけがつかめない I can't get *a chance* [*an opportunity*] to speak to her. / 彼女はコンテスト入賞がきっかけで写真家になった Winning a prize in the photo contest gave her *a chance* to become a photographer.
◆水泳を始めたきっかけは何ですか *What made* you start to learn swimming? / 彼の発言は激しい論争のきっかけとなった His statement *triggered* a heated dispute.

きっかり (ちょうど) just; (正確に) exactly, precisely; (時刻が) sharp, 《口語的》on the dot //演奏会は6時きっかりに始まった The concert started at six *sharp* [*on the dot*]. / その飛行機は午後9時きっかりに着陸した The plane touched down at *exactly* 9:00 p.m. / その本は1,000円きっかりだった The book was *exactly* 1,000 yen.

きづかれ 気疲れ mental fatigue [U] ◆家にお客が来ると気疲れする I *get tired mentally* when people come to visit our house.

キック kick [C] ―キックする kick [他] //ボールをキックする *kick* a ball
‖キックオフ a kickoff / キックバック a kick-

back / キックボクシング kick boxing / コーナーキック a corner (kick) / ペナルティーキック a penalty kick

きづく 気付く

notice 他自;（感づいている）be aware;（分かる）find*他;（悟る）realize 他;（自覚している）be conscious

【notice＋名(人)】だれもその奇妙な音に気づかなかった Nobody *noticed* the strange sound. / 私はだれにも気づかれずにそこを通り過ぎた I passed by there without *being noticed* by anyone.

【notice＋名＋do[doing]】私は彼が部屋を出ていくのに気づいた I *noticed* him *leaving* the room. / 彼女はわたしが手を振っているのに気づかなかった She didn't *notice* me *waving* to her.

【notice＋that 節】彼が彼女を見ていたのに気づきましたか Did you *notice* that he was watching her?

彼女は自分の欠点に十分気づいていた She *was* fully *aware* [*conscious*] *of* her bad points.

彼は彼女が内心怒っているのに気づいていた He *was aware* [*conscious*] *that* she was inwardly angry.

だれも気づかない所に隠れた I hid where nobody could *find* me.

彼女はキーホルダーをなくしたのに気づいた She *found that* she had lost her key ring.

彼は自分の失敗に気づいていた He *realized* his mistake.

私は自分が全く間違っていたことに気づいた I *realized that* I was totally wrong.

チームの中で君がどれだけだいじな存在か気づいていないのか Don't you *realize* how important you are to the team?

◆気づいた(→意識が戻った)ときには保健室のベッドの上だった When I *came to*, I was lying on the bed in the school infirmary.

ぎっくりごし ぎっくり腰 strained back 回,【医学】（椎間板(ついかんばん)ヘルニア）slipped disk 回《通例単数形》◆父は立ち上がったときぎっくり腰になった My father *threw out his back* when he stood up.

きつけ 着付け dressing U ◆彼女は自分で着付けができる She can *put on* a kimono by herself.

きづけ 気付(in) care of ...《略記》c/o ◆松尾様気付, 佐藤健様 Mr. Satoh Ken, *c/o* Mr. Matsuo

きっさてん 喫茶店 coffee shop 回, café 回, tearoom 回《❖いずれも軽い食事をとることのできる軽食堂で, 日本のファミリーレストランに近い》

ぎっしり 道の両側には多くの屋台がぎっしり並んでいた A lot of stalls were lined up *closely* on both sides of the street. / スタジアムは何千人もの人でぎっしり埋まっていた The stadium *was crowded with* thousands of people. / 弁当箱にサンドイッチがぎっしり詰まっていた The lunch box *was stuffed with* sandwiches. / この予定表がぎっしり詰まっている

I *have a tight* [*full, heavy*] *schedule* ahead.

きっすい 生っ粋 生っ粋のパリっ子 a *native* [*trueborn, pure*] Parisian

きっする 喫する 私たちのチームは10対0で惨敗を喫した Our team *suffered* a crushing defeat by a score of 10 to 0.

ぎっちょ left-handed person 回,《主に米・口語的》lefty 回

きっちり ふたをきっちり閉めてね Screw the cap on *tight(ly).* / 面接は10時きっちりに始まった The interview started *exactly* at 10. / 遊びに行く前に宿題をきっちりやりなさい Do your homework *properly* before you go out.

キッチン kitchen 回

きつつき 啄木鳥 woodpecker 回

きって 切手 (postage) stamp 回

祖父の趣味は切手を集めることです My grandfather's hobby is collecting *stamps*.

1,000円分の切手を同封してください Please enclose 1,000 yen in *stamps*.

私ははがきに切手をはった I put *a stamp* on the postcard.

「80円切手5枚と50円切手10枚ください」「分かりました. 900円になります」"I'd like five 80-yen *stamps* and ten 50-yen *stamps*, please." "Okay. That'll be 900 yen."

◆切手をはった返信用封筒 a self-addressed *stamped* envelope / エアメールで出したいんですが, 切手代はいくらですか I'd like to send this letter by airmail. What's *the postage*? ‖切手アルバム a stamp album / 切手シート a sheet of stamps / 切手収集 stamp collecting / 切手収集家 a stamp collector / 記念切手 a commemorative stamp

-きっての 当代きっての名俳優 *the greatest* actor *of our time* / 彼はクラスきっての秀才だ He is *the brightest student in our class*.

キット kit 回 ◆模型飛行機組み立てキット *a* model aircraft *kit*

きっと¹（確かに）surely, certainly;（間違いなく）without fail;（おそらく）probably

きっと試験に合格してみせる I'll *surely* pass the test.

彼はきっと今ごろ京都に着いていることだろう *Probably* he has arrived in Kyoto by now.

◆これなら彼女もきっと気に入るわ I'm *sure* [*certain*] she'll like this. / 今, 富士山ではきっと雪が降っているでしょう It *must* be snowing on Mt. Fuji now.

「また会いに行くからね」「きっとよ」"I'll come to see you again." "*Be sure you do.*"

きっと² 彼女はその男をきっとにらみつけた She gave the man a *sharp* look. / (→怒って) She glared at the man *with anger*.

きつね 狐 fox 回（複〜es, 〜）;（雌）vixen 回;（子）cub 回

慣用表現 数か月前に訪れた店は跡形もなくなり, アパートが建っていた. まるできつねにつままれた気分だった The store I visited just a few months ago disappeared and there was an apartment house there. I *felt completely puzzled, as if I had been under a spell until then*.

きっぱり flatly; (完全に) completely ∥彼はそのうわさをきっぱり否定した He *flatly* denied the rumor. / 自分がしたくないことはきっぱり断る勇気が必要だ You need the courage to refuse *flatly* what you don't want to do. / 兄は子供が生まれてからたばこをきっぱりやめた My brother stopped smoking *completely* after his child was born.

きっぷ 切符 ticket ©; (切り取り式の) coupon ©

切符を切る punch *a ticket* / スピード違反の切符を切られる receive *a speeding ticket* / コンサートの切符がとれた I got *a concert ticket*.

鎌倉までの切符を2枚ください Two *tickets* to Kamakura, please.

前もって帰りの切符を買っておこう I'm going to buy *the return ticket* in advance.

切符を拝見いたします May I see *your ticket*? / *Ticket*, please.

切符のないかたは入場できません Admission by *Ticket* Only.

🗣「映画の切符が2枚あるんだけど、いっしょに行かない？」「いいわよ」"I have two movie *tickets*. Would you like to come with me?" "Sure."

∥切符売り場(売り場全体) a ticket office; (窓口) a ticket window; (カウンター式の) a ticket counter; (劇場・スタジアムなどの) a box office / 往復切符 a round-trip [(英)return] ticket / 片道切符 a one-way [(英) single] ticket

[関連語] 券売機 a ticket machine

きっぽう 吉報 good news

きづまり 気詰まり 席が彼の隣だったので気詰まりだった I *felt ill at ease* sitting next to him.

きつもん 詰問 ──詰問する question *a person* closely; (説明を求める) demand an explanation ∥警官は騒動の原因について彼らを詰問した The police officer *demanded an explanation* from them about the cause of the trouble.

きてい¹ 規定 (規則) rule ©; (公の規則) regulation ©; (法律による) provision © ──規定する (公式的) prescribe ⓜ; (法律で) provide ⓜ ∥規定の書式 a *prescribed* form / 規定に従う follow *a rule* [*regulation*] / 規定を設ける set up *a rule* [*regulation*] / 服装についてはここに規定があります Here is *a rule* about dress. / この法律はその種の犯罪に対し厳しい罰を規定している This law *prescribes* heavy penalties for that kind of crime.

∥規定種目 compulsory exercises / 規定料金 a regular fare

きてい² 既定 既定の事実 an *established* fact / これは既定の方針に反する That's against the *established* policy.

ぎてい 義弟 brother-in-law © (複 brothers-in-law, ~s)

ぎていしょ 議定書 protocol ©

きてき 汽笛 (steam) whistle ©; (警笛) horn ©; (船の) siren ∥船は汽笛を鳴らした The ship blew *a whistle*. / 汽笛が鳴るのが聞こえた I heard *a whistle* blow.

きてん¹ 機転 (機知) wit ©; (如才なさ) tact ⓤ ∥彼女は機転がきく[きかない] She has quick [slow] *wits*. ◆機転のきく[きかない]人 a *quick*-[*slow*-]*witted* person / 彼女はバッグをひったくられたとき機転をきかせ、持っていたカメラで犯人の姿をとらえた She *used her brains* [*head*] and took a picture of the purse snatcher with her camera when her bag was snatched away from her.

きてん² 起点 starting point © ◆この路線は東京駅を起点としている This line *starts from* Tokyo station.

きと 帰途 私たちは旅の帰途、祖父母の家に立ち寄った We dropped by our grandparents' house *on our way home* from a trip. / 彼らは1週間の合宿を終え帰途についた They *left* [*started*] *for home* after finishing their one-week training camp.

きど 木戸 (小門) gate ©

きどあいらく 喜怒哀楽 feelings, emotions ∥彼はおとなしくて喜怒哀楽をほとんど表に出さない He is so quiet that he hardly shows *his feelings* [*emotions*] at all. ◆彼女は喜怒哀楽が激しい She is *very emotional*.

きとう¹ 祈祷 prayer © (また複数形 ~s) ──祈祷する pray ⓐ ⓜ ∥祈祷師(悪魔払いの) an exorcist; (原始宗教の) a shaman; (信仰療法の) a faith healer / 祈祷書 a prayer book

きとう² 気筒 cylinder © ∥V型6気筒エンジン a six-*cylinder* V-type engine

きどう¹ 軌道 (惑星・人工衛星などの) orbit ⓤ; (線路) track © ∥円[楕円(だん)]軌道 *a circular* [*an elliptical*] *orbit* / 地球の軌道 the earth's *orbit* / スペースシャトルを軌道に乗せる put [launch] a space shuttle into *orbit* / 人工衛星は軌道に乗った[からはずれた] The satellite has gone into [out of] *orbit*.

◆おじの事業は軌道に乗ってきた My uncle's business *is getting well under way*.

∥軌道修正 a course correction

きどう² 機動 そのチームは持ち前の機動力を生かしたプレーで決勝に勝ち残った The team made full use of *its* remarkable *mobility* and advanced to the finals.

∥機動隊(警察機動隊) riot police; (分隊) a riot squad / 機動部隊 a task force

きどう³ 起動 コンピュータを起動させる *boot up* a computer

きとく¹ 危篤 危篤である be in *critical condition* / 彼は一時危篤状態に陥った He fell into *critical condition* for a while.

きとく² 奇特 ──奇特な (感心な) admirable, praiseworthy

きとくけん 既得権 vested rights

きどり 気取り このレストランは気取りがなく好感がもてる This restaurant doesn't have *an affected atmosphere* and so I like it here. / 彼女は芸術家気取りだ She「*pretends to be* [*poses as, acts as if she were*] an artist.

‖気取り屋 an affected person

きどる 気取る be affected, put* on airs, give* *oneself* airs; (…のふりをする) pose as … //映画スターを気取る *pose as* a movie star / 彼は有名になっても全く気取ったところがない Though he became famous, he「*is* not *affected* [does not *put on airs*] at all. ◆彼女はモデルのように気取って歩く She walks *in an affected way*, like a fashion model.

きない 機内 ‖機内映画 an in-flight movie / 機内サービス in-flight service / 機内食 an in-flight meal / 機内販売 in-flight sales / 機内持ち込み手荷物 carry-on baggage

きなが 気長 ―気長に patiently; (急がずに) without hurry //お返事は気長に待ちます I'll *patiently* wait for your reply.
◆気長にやりましょう Let's *take our time*.

きなくさい きな臭い 何かきな臭いにおいがしない？ Don't you smell something *burning*? / 両国間にきな臭い雰囲気が漂っている It seems like *trouble is brewing* between the two countries.

きなこ きな粉 🗻 soy flour [U]

きにいる 気に入る ➔き(気)

きにする 気にする ➔き(気)

きになる 気になる ➔き(気)

きにゅう 記入 ―記入する (書き記す) write* down; (書類などに書き込む) enter [他]; (必要事項を埋める) fill in [out] //彼は彼女の名前をリストに記入した He「*wrote down* [*entered*] her name on the list. / 入会希望のかたは申込用紙に記入してください *Fill in* [*out*] an application form if you want to join the club. ◆その申込書は記入もれが多かった There were a lot of *omissions* on the application.

きぬ 絹 silk [U] (❖種類を表す場合は [C]) //絹のスカーフ a *silk* scarf / この会社は主に絹製品を扱っている This company deals chiefly in *silk goods*.
‖絹糸 silk thread / 絹織物 silk fabrics

きね 杵 🗻 a *kine*, a mallet which is used to pound steamed rice in an *usu* (mortar) to make *mochi* (rice cakes)

ギネスブック the Guinness Book of Records

きねん 記念

commemoration [U], memory [U] [C], 《公式的》remembrance [C] [U] ―記念の commemorative, memorial ―記念する commemorate [他]

その偉大な俳優を記念する碑が建てられた A monument was set up *in memory* [*commemoration, remembrance*] *of* the great actor./ A monument was set up to *commemorate* the great actor.

ここへの旅行の記念にこの絵はがきをお持ちください Keep this picture postcard *as a remembrance of* your trip here./ (→みやげとして) Keep this picture postcard *as a souvenir of* your trip here.

これは牧場で馬に乗ったときの写真だ. いい記念になったよ This is a picture of me riding a horse at the ranch. It serves as *a* good *remembrance*.

◆このペンダント, 記念にあげる I'll give you this pendant *as a keepsake*. / 彼らのデビューアルバムは日本の音楽の歴史において記念すべきアルバムとなった Their debut album became a *memorable* one in the history of Japanese music. / 彼らは開店20周年を記念して(→祝って)パーティーを開いた They had a party to *celebrate* the 20th anniversary of their store's opening. / 新郎新婦を囲んで記念撮影をした(→彼らの結婚を祝って写真を撮った) We *took a picture* with the bride and groom *to celebrate* their wedding.

‖記念切手 a commemorative stamp / 記念硬貨 a commemorative coin / 記念祭 a commemoration, a memorial festival / 記念式典 a commemoration / 記念写真 a souvenir picture / 記念碑 a memorial, a monument / 記念日 a memorial day; (毎年の) an anniversary / 記念品 a memento, a remembrance; (みやげ) a souvenir

ぎねん 疑念 (不信) doubt [U] [C]; (疑い) suspicion [U] [C] //彼は彼女の言ったことに疑念をいだいているようだ He seems to have *doubts* about what she said.

きのう[1] 昨日

yesterday (❖副詞と名詞の用法があるが, 名詞の場合も常に無冠詞で用いる)

きのうは両親の結婚記念日だった *Yesterday* was my parents' wedding anniversary.

きのう駅で有史にばったり会った I came across Yuji at the station *yesterday*.

きのうの午後映画を見に行った I went to the movies *yesterday afternoon*.

きのうの最低気温はマイナス５度だった *Yesterday's* minimum temperature was five degrees below zero [freezing].

きのうから雨が降り続いている It has been raining since *yesterday*.

彼は「きのう学校を休んだ」と言った He said, "I was absent from school *yesterday*." (❖間接話法でいう場合, 言ったのがきょうならば He said that he was absent from school *yesterday*.でよい. ただしそうでない場合, yesterday の代わりに the day before や the previous day などを用いる)

高校に入学したのがついきのうのことのようだ It seems like *only yesterday* that I entered high school.

先週のきのうは何をしていたか思い出せない I can't remember what I did *a week ago yesterday*.

◆きのうの夜はいいテレビ番組がなかった There were no interesting TV programs *last night*.

き

慣用表現 彼の遅刻癖(へき)はきのうきょうに始まった話ではない He *has always been* prone to be late.

ことわざ きのうの敵はきょうの友 Yesterday's enemy is today's friend.

きのう² 機能 function ⓒ, faculty ⓒ ——機能的な・機能上の functional ——機能的に functionally ——機能する function ⓘ, work ⓘ ∥肺の機能 *a function* of the lungs / 視覚[聴覚]機能 *the faculty* of sight [hearing] / 腸の機能障害 *a functional disorder* of the bowels; *a dysfunction* of the bowels / 機能的な部屋 *a functional room* / このスイッチは正常に機能しない This switch doesn't *function* [*work*] properly. / This switch isn't *functional*. / この電話はファクシミリの機能を果たす This telephone also *functions* as a fax.

きのう³ 帰納 〔論理〕induction ⓤ ——帰納的な inductive ∥帰納法 induction

ぎのう 技能 skill ⓤⓒ ∥コミュニケーションの技能 communication *skills* / 技能を磨く brush up (on) one's *skill*
∥技能検定 a proficiency examination / 技能賞 a technical prize [award]

きのこ 茸 mushroom ⓒ; (毒キノコ) toadstool ⓒ ∥キノコをとる pick *mushrooms*
∥キノコ狩り mushroom gathering / きのこ雲 a mushroom cloud

きのどく 気の毒
私は彼女を気の毒に思い協力を申し出た I *felt sorry for* [*felt pity for, sympathized with*] her and offered to help.

彼の事故は本当に気の毒だ I'm dreadfully *sorry about* his accident.

そんなにお困りだったとはお気の毒に I'm *sorry* [*It's a pity*] *that* you were in such trouble.

彼らの不運を聞いてとても気の毒に思った I *was terribly sorry to* hear about their misfortune.

気の毒に思って彼に金を貸した I lent him money *out of pity*.

気の毒なことにその女性は二度と息子に会うことはなかった *Sadly*, the lady never saw her son again. / (→気の毒なその女性は) The *poor* lady never saw her son again.

デートをすっぽかしたりして彼にはひどく気の毒なことをしてしまった(→気の毒に思っている) I'm really *sorry that* I stood him up.

🔴「スキーで足を骨折したんです」「それはお気の毒に」"I broke my leg while skiing." "*That's too bad. / What a pity.*"

🔴「おなかが苦しいよ」「それはお気の毒様、ひとりでみんなの分食べちゃうからでしょ」"My stomach feels too heavy." "Well, well. *Tough luck.* You know you ate all of our food by yourself."

🔴「京子遅いね」「うん、京子には気の毒だけど先に行ってしまおうよ」"Kyoko is late, isn't she?" "She is. I'*m sorry for* Kyoko, but why don't we leave ahead of her?"

きのみ 木の実 nut

きのみきのまま 着の身着のまま 泊まっていたホテルが火事になり、私たちは着の身着のままで逃げた The hotel we were staying at caught fire, and we escaped *with nothing but the clothes we were wearing*.

きのめ 木の芽 bud ⓒ, sprout ⓒ, shoot ⓒ ∥木の芽が出始めた *Buds* are beginning to appear.

きのり 気乗り 気乗りのしない返事をする answer *halfheartedly*; give a *halfhearted* answer / きょうはテニスに行くのは気乗りがしない I *don't feel like* going [*am reluctant to go*] to play tennis today. / 彼女をコンサートに誘ってみたが、気乗り薄の様子だった I asked her to go to a concert with me, but she *didn't seem to be very interested*.

きば¹ 牙 (象などの) tusk ⓒ; (犬などの) fang ⓒ ∥オオカミはきばをむいた The wolf bared *its fangs*. ◆その犬は猫にきばをむいてうなった The dog *snarled at* a cat.

きば² 騎馬 ∥騎馬戦 a cavalry battle / 騎馬民族 a horse-riding people

きはく¹ 気迫 (気力) spirit ⓤ, soul ⓤⓒ; (やる気) drive ⓤ; (元気) vigor ⓤ ∥対戦相手は気迫に満ちていた The opponent was full of *spirit*. / きょうの日本チームからは気迫が感じられなった The Japanese team didn't seem to show any *spirit* today.
◆気迫のこもった表情 a *determined* look

きはく² 希薄 ——希薄な (液体・気体などが) thin / 山の希薄な空気 the *thin* air of the mountains ◆都会の希薄な(→うすべたい)人間関係 *superficial* human relations in the cities / 彼らは思いやりの気持ちが希薄だ(→欠けている) They *are lacking in* warmth.

きばく 起爆 その雑誌の記事が論争の起爆剤となった(→引き金となった) The article in the magazine *triggered* the dispute.
∥起爆装置 a trigger device

きはずかしい 気恥ずかしい 人前で歌うのは気恥ずかしい I *am embarrassed* to sing in front of other people.

きはつ 揮発 揮発性の液体 *volatile* liquid
∥揮発性 volatility / 揮発物 volatile matter / 揮発油 gasoline

きばつ 奇抜 ——奇抜な (新奇な) novel; (風変わりな) eccentric; (独創的な) original ∥奇抜な髪型 an *eccentric* hairstyle / 彼のアイディアはいつも奇抜だ His ideas are always *novel*.

きばむ 黄ばむ このワイシャツは黄ばんできた This shirt *has yellowed* [*turned yellow*].

きばらし 気晴らし (娯楽) pastime ⓒ, recreation ⓤⓒ; (気分転換) diversion ⓒ; (息抜き) relaxation ⓤⓒ ∥散歩はいい気晴らしになるよ To take a walk will be *a good diversion* for you. / 勉強ばかりしてないで気晴らしに出かけたら？ Why don't you go out *for relaxation* instead of studying all the time? ◆気晴らしに映画でも見に行こう Let's go to a movie *for a change*.

きばる 気張る (がんばる) exert *oneself*; (気前よく金を出す) pay* generously

きはん 規範・軌範 standard ©《しばしば複数形 ~s》,《公式的》norm ©/規範に従う keep to *the norms*
∥規範文法[文法] prescriptive grammar / 行動規範 the rules of conduct

きばん 基盤 base ©, basis © (複 bases), foundation ©/会社の基盤 *the foundation* of a company / 党の支持基盤を固める strengthen a party's *power base* / その国の経済基盤は安定している *The basis* of the country's economy is stable.

きひ 忌避 evasion Ⓤ©◆徴兵を忌避する *evade* conscription
∥徴兵忌避者《米》a draft dodger

きび¹ 黍[植物] millet Ⓤ

きび² 機微 この映画は人生の機微をうまく描いている This movie is successful in describing *the subtleties* of human life.

きびき 忌引き きょう川田さんは忌引きでお休みです Kawata *is absent* today *due to mourning* [*a death in the family*].

きびきび 母はきびきびと立ち働いている My mother is working *briskly.* / 彼女は私たちの質問にきびきびと答えた She answered our questions *crisply.* / 裕太は動きがきびきびしている Yuta is *nimble* in his movements.

きびしい 厳しい

❶【厳格な・容赦のない】strict, severe, rigorous;（規則などが）rigid;（冷酷な）harsh
——厳しく severely, strictly

厳しい父親 one's *strict* [*severe, rigorous*] father / 厳しい規則 *strict* [*severe, rigorous, rigid*] rules / 厳しい批判 *severe* [*harsh*] criticism

彼女は自分に厳しく他人に優しい She is *strict* [*severe*] with herself but gentle with others.

彼の両親はしつけが厳しい His parents keep *strict* [*rigid*] discipline in his house.

彼女はとても時間に厳しい She is very *strict* about punctuality.

先生は校則をさらに厳しくしようとした The teachers tried to make school regulations *stricter.*

淳を厳しくしからないで，まだ子供なんだから Don't scold Jun so *severely.* He is only a child.

規則を守らない者は厳しく罰せられます If you don't obey the rules, you will be *severely* punished.

💬「なかなかよく描けた水彩画だね．色さえ塗らなければなあ」「うわ，厳しいなあ」"That's a good watercolor. How I wish you hadn't painted it." "Come on, you're too *severe* [*harsh, cruel*]."

❷【過酷な】severe, harsh;（困難な）hard
——厳しさ severity Ⓤ, harshness Ⓤ

北国の冬の厳しさ *severity* [*harshness*] of winter in the northern part of the country / 厳しい生活環境に耐える endure *severe* [*harsh*] living conditions

今年の冬は寒さが厳しい We're having a *severe* [*hard*] winter this year. / It is *very* cold this winter.

現在の経済情勢はたいへん厳しい The economic situation now is very *severe.*

彼女は人生の厳しさ（→どれほど厳しいか）を思い知った She has realized how *severe* [*harsh, hard*] life is.

この作文をきょう中に仕上げるのは厳しい It will be *hard* to finish this composition today.

この給料では生活が厳しい It's *hard* for me to live on this salary.

きびす 踵 彼女はその家の前に犬がいるのを見てすぐにきびすを返した She *turned back* at once because [when] she saw a dog in front of the house.

きびょう 奇病 世の中には難病や奇病に悩まされている人も少なくない There are quite a few people in the world who suffer from serious or *strange diseases.*

きひん 気品 （優美）grace Ⓤ;（上品）elegance Ⓤ;（気高さ）dignity Ⓤ ◆気品のある装いをする wear *elegant* clothes / その老人の物腰には気品があった The old man had *graceful* manners.

きびん 機敏 ——機敏な（動作が）quick;（反応が）prompt ——機敏に quickly; promptly /緊急時には機敏な行動が要求される *Quick* [*Prompt*] actions are required in an emergency. / あの選手は動作が機敏だ That player is *quick* in his movements.

きひんしつ 貴賓室 a room for honored guests

きひんせき 貴賓席 seats for honored guests

きふ 寄付 contribution Ⓤ;（慈善事業などへの）donation Ⓤ《また a ~》❖いずれも「寄付された金品」の意味で ——寄付する contribute ⓗ⽬; donate ⓗ⽬

私たちは恵まれない子供たちのために寄付を集めています We are collecting *donations* [*contributions*] for disadvantaged children.

彼は持っていたレコードの大半を母校に寄付した He *donated* almost all of his records to his old school.

彼は大学に多額のお金を寄付した He *contributed* [*donated*] a large amount of money to the university.

∥寄付金 a contribution, a donation / 寄付者 a contributor, a donor

ぎふ¹ 義父 father-in-law © (複 fathers-in-law, ~s);（まま父）stepfather ©;（養父）foster father ©

ぎふ² 岐阜

岐阜県は日本のほぼ中央に位置する内陸県です．北東部には標高3,000メートル級の山々が連なる飛騨山脈があり，日本アルプスの一部を形成しています．数多くの観光名所がありますが，中でも有名なのは伝統的な合掌造りの家々が保存された白川郷で，世界文化遺産にも指定されています．
Gifu Prefecture is a landlocked prefec-

ture located near the center of Japan. To the northeast it is bordered by the Hida Mountains, which reach heights of 3,000 meters and form part of the Japan Alps. Among the many famous tourist sites in Gifu Prefecture is the village of Shirakawa, which has been designated a world cultural heritage site for its traditional houses in the "gassho-zukuri" style.

ギブアップ この問題は私には難しすぎる。ギブアップだ This problem is too difficult for me. I *give up*.

ギブアンドテーク もっとギブアンドテークを心がけて,役に立つ情報をもっているなら教えてよ *I'll scratch your back if you scratch mine.* If you have some useful information, tell it to me. (◈*I'll scratch ...* の文は「私の背中をかいてくれたらあなたの背中をかいてあげよう」という意味)

> 日本語の「ギブアンドテーク」は「相手に何かを与える代わりに自分も相手から何らかの利益を得ること」を意味するが,英語の give-and-take は「妥協,譲り合い」を意味する.

きふう 気風 (雰囲気) atmosphere ⓤⓒ; (精神) spirit ⓤ ‖私の母校は自由な気風で知られている My old school is known for *its* liberal *atmosphere*.

きふく 起伏 ups and downs ‖父の人生は起伏に富んでいる My father's life is full of *ups and downs*. ◆起伏のある山道 a *rolling* mountain path / このあたりの土地は起伏に富んでいる This region is *very hilly*. / 彼女は感情の起伏が激しい She is very *emotional*.

きぶくれ 着ぶくれ 寒がりなひとみは夏なのに着ぶくれしている Hitomi is cold-blooded, so she's *heavily dressed* even though it's summer.

きふじん 貴婦人 lady ⓒ, noblewoman ⓒ

ギプス ⚠ cast ⓒ, plaster cast ⓒ (◈日本語はドイツ語の Gips から) ‖彼女はまだ左腕にギプスをしている She still has a *(plaster) cast* on her left arm. / Her left arm is still in a *(plaster) cast*.

きぶつはそん 器物破損 property damage ⓤ, damage to property

ギフト gift ⓒ, present ⓒ ‖ギフトカード 《米》a gift certificate, 《英》a gift token [voucher] / ギフトショップ a gift shop

きふるす 着古す wear* out ◆着古したシャツ a *worn-out* shirt

きぶん 気分

〖気分〗
試験に受かったのできょうは気分がいい I *feel good* [I'm *in a good mood*] today because I passed the exams. (◈「気分が悪い」は good の代わりに bad を用いる)
食べすぎで気分が悪い I *don't feel well* [*feel sick*] because I ate too much. (◈「体調がよい」という場合は good ではなく well を用いる)

言いたいことをすべて言ったので気分がすっきりした I *feel refreshed* as I said everything I wanted to.
私はきょうは気分がふさいでいる I *feel blue* today.
大勢の人を目の前にして気分が落ち着かなかった I *felt ill at ease* in the presence of a large crowd. / The presence of a large crowd made me *nervous*.

〖~(の)気分〗
明るい[暗い]気分になる become cheerful [gloomy]
きょうは最高の気分だ I *feel great* today.
コンビニのお弁当ではいまいち旅の気分が味わえない A lunch bought at a convenience store is not enough to make me *feel like I'm on vacation*.
彼がお祭り気分を盛り上げてくれた He stirred up *a festive atmosphere* [*mood*].
君はまだ正月気分が抜けていない You haven't come out of *the New Year's holiday mood*.
きのうは外出する気分ではなかった I「*didn't feel like* [*was in no mood for*]」 going out yesterday.

〖気分を・に〗
彼女の不注意な言葉に彼は気分を害した様子だった He seemed to *be offended* by her careless words.
その話を聞いて幸せな気分になった That story made me *feel* happy.
彼の歌を聞いて私も歌いたい気分になった I *felt like* singing when I listened to him sing.

〖その他〗
4月になり私たちは気分も新たに新学年のスタートを切った April has come, and we have started our new school year *feeling refreshed* [*renewed*].
気分転換にテレビを見よう Let's watch TV *for a change*.
彼の意見はそのときの気分次第で変わる His opinions change「*depending on* [*according to*]」how he feels at the moment.
あしたは休みだと思うだけで気分的に楽だ It's *a relief* just to think tomorrow's a holiday.
🔊「映画を見に行かない?」「ごめんなさい.そんな気分じゃないの」"Would you like to go to the movies?" "Sorry, but I'*m not in the mood*."
🔊「気分はどうですか」「少しよくなりました」"*How do you feel*?" "I feel a little better now."
‖気分屋 a moody person

きべん 詭弁 sophistry ⓤⓒ, sophism ⓒ ‖詭弁を弄(ろう)する use *sophistry*
‖詭弁家 a sophist

きぼ 規模 scale ⓒ; (大きさ) size ⓤⓒ ‖世界的規模で on *a global scale* / 小規模な会社 a *small-scale* company / この地域では大規模な土地開発が進められている In this region the land is being developed on *a large scale*.

き

[コミュニケーションスキル] —希望・願望—

①「あなたに会いたい」と言いたいとき

(A) **I want to** see you.
(B) **I'd like to** see you.
(C) **I hope to** see you.
(D) **I need to** see you.

☞(A)は直接的だが最も一般的で，(B)はそれより控えめで丁寧な表現．また，例えば「電話で話すよりできれば直接会いたい」というニュアンスを含む場合は，**I'd rather** see you than talk on the phone. のようにI'd rather ... を使うこともある．
☞(C)は近い将来のことに関する希望を表し，(D)は「会う必要がある」という意味になる．

②「人に…してほしい」と言いたいとき

(A) **I want you to** help me.
手伝ってもらいたい．
(B) **I'd like you to** write to me.
手紙をいただきたいのですが．
(C) **I look forward to you** coming to the party.
パーティーに来ていただけたらと思います．

☞ここでも(A)は直接的な表現で親しい間柄でよく使われる．(B)は控えめで丁寧な言い方で，(C)は「期待している」という意味合いが含まれる．また婉曲的な依頼の表現として**I wonder if ...**がある．
I wonder if you have any extra money. 君にはお金の持ち合わせがあるだろうか．(❖「もしあれば貸してもらえないだろうか」を含意)

③wishを使った表現

(A) **I wish** you were here.
あなたがここにいてくれたらなあ．
(B) How **I wish** I could marry him.
彼と結婚できたらどんなにいいでしょう．
(C) **I wish** she had changed her mind.
彼女が気を変えてくれたらよかったのに．

☞かないそうもない，あるいはかなわなかったことに対しての願望を表すのにはI wish ... を用い，wishの後の節には仮定法の動詞がくる．wishにはほかに**I wish you every happiness.**(お幸せに)，**I wish you a merry Christmas!**(楽しいクリスマスを)のようなあいさつ的な表現もある．

④hopeを使った表現

(A) **I hope** you (will) pass the exam.
試験に受かるといいですね．
(B) **I'm hoping** you (will) pass the exam.
合格してくれるといいのだが．

☞hopeにはI hope to ... の表現のほかにこのような使い方があり，やはり近い未来への希望を表す．wishが実現性の少ない願望なのに対し，hopeは可能性のある希望を表す．また，助動詞willは付けても付けなくてもよい場合が多く，wantと異なり進行形にすることも可能である．進行形にするとよりていねいな希望の表現になる．

⑤希望・願望に対する受け答え

(A) **I want to** have lunch with you.
–O.K. / All right./ Sure.
お昼，いっしょに食べたいな．—いいよ．
(B) **I'd like to** try this hat on.
–Certainly.
この帽子かぶってみたいのですが．—はい，どうぞ．
(C) **I'd like you to** come to the party.
–Oh, I'd love to, but I have so much to do on Saturday.
土曜日のパーティーにいらしてくださいね．—行きたいのはやまやまなんですが，土曜日はやらなければならないことがいろいろありまして．
(D) **Will you** join us for some pizza?
–Thanks, but maybe some other time. [Sorry, but I can't make it. I'd like to take a rain check.] (❖take a rain checkは「次の機会にする」の意味)
ピザ食べに行くんだけどいっしょに行かない？—うれしいんだけど，またいつかね[ごめん，きょうはだめなんだ．また別の機会に誘ってよ]．

☞希望・願望を表す表現は，問いの形になっていても，yesかnoで答えればよいわけではない．したがって答えにもバリエーションがある．例えば(A)はMe, too. などで対応することもできる．I wishやI hopeなどに対する応答の仕方も会話の内容によることが多い．希望に添えないときは，I'm sorry, but ... で答えたり，Noだけではなくthank youなどを加えると感じが柔らかくなる．また，(D)のように「別の機会に」と付け加えることも多い．

◆本当に大規模なモーターショーですね It sure is a *big* motor show, isn't it?

ぎぼ 義母 mother-in-law [C] (複 mothers-in-law, ～s)；(まま母) stepmother [C]；(養母) foster mother [C]

きほう 気泡 bubble [C]《しばしば複数形 ～s》

きぼう 希望

hope [U][C]；(願望) wish [U][C]；(強い願望) desire [U][C]；(要求) request [U][C]；(夢) dream [C] ──希望する hope [他][自]；wish [他][自]；(欲する) want [他]
➜ [コミュニケーションスキル]
希望の光 a ray of *hope* / 希望をいだく have [cherish, entertain] *a hope* / 希望を捨てる give up *hope* / 親の希望に反して留学する study abroad against *the wishes* of *one's* parents
彼女の未来は希望に満ちている Her future is full of *hope*.
彼女は生きる希望を私に与えてくれた She gave me *hope* to live.
彼はいつでも希望を失わなかった He never lost *hope*.
場合によってはご希望に添えないこともございます Depending on the circumstances, we may not be able to fulfill *your wishes* [*requests*].
希望がかなうといいですね I hope *your wish* will be realized.

大学入学当時の兄は希望に燃えていた My brother was full of *hope* just after he entered the university.

弟の希望で動物園へ行った We went to the zoo at my brother's *request*.

彼は希望どおり明治大学へ入学が決まった He was admitted to Meiji University *as he had hoped [wished]*.

私は進学を希望します I *want* to continue my education after I graduate.

この映画の観覧希望者は、はがきに住所、氏名を明記してこちらまでお送りください *If you want to see* this movie, please send us a postcard with your name and address on it.

◆第一希望 the first *choice* / 希望がわいてきた I began to *feel hopeful*.

🍀「将来の希望を教えてください」「はい。私は画家になりたいと思っています」"Could you tell me "*your dream* for the future [*what you want to do* in the future]?" "Sure. I'd like to be a painter."

∥希望小売価格 a suggested retail price / 希望退職 voluntary retirement / 希望的観測 wishful thinking

ぎほう 技法 technique ⓤⓒ / 印象派の技法 Impressionist *techniques*

きぼり 木彫り wood carving ⓒⓤ / 木彫りの鳥 a bird *carved in wood*; a *wooden* bird

きほん 基本 basics, 《公式的》fundamental ⓒ (しばしば複数形～s); (基礎) basis ⓒ (複 bases) ——基本の・基本的な basic; (根本的な) fundamental ——基本的に basically; fundamentally / 基本に忠実なスイング a swing done truly to *the basics* / 彼女に料理の基本を教わった I was taught *the fundamentals* [*basics*] of cooking by her. / 基本的にはあなたの言っていることは正しい *Basically*, what you're saying is right.

∥基本給 base pay / 基本原則 first principles / 基本政策 a basic doctrine / 基本的人権 fundamental [basic] human rights / 基本料金 a basic charge

ぎまい 義妹 sister-in-law ⓒ (複 sisters-in-law, ~s)

きまえ 気前 generosity ⓤ ◆祖父は気前がよく頼まれれば何でもあげてしまう人だった My grandfather was so *generous* [*liberal*, *lavish*] *with his things* that he gave anything if asked for it. / 彼は気前よく夕食をごちそうしてくれた He treated me to dinner *generously*.

きまぐれ 気紛れ caprice [kəpríːs] ⓒⓤ; (思いつき) whim ⓒ ——気まぐれな capricious, whimsical / 一時の気まぐれでそうしたのではない I didn't do that on any momentary *caprice*. / 気まぐれでフランス語を習い始めた I started to learn French *on a whim*. / 彼女は気まぐれだ She is *capricious* [*whimsical*]. ◆山の天気は気まぐれだ (→変わりやすい) The weather in the mountains is *changeable* [(→予測できない) *unpredictable*].

きまじめ 生真面目 ——きまじめな very serious, very earnest / 彼女は見かけによらずきまじめだ She is *very serious* [*earnest*] despite her appearance.

きまずい 気まずい (ばつが悪い) awkward; (気持ちの落ち着かない) uncomfortable; (困惑した) embarrassed / 私たちの間に気まずい空気が流れた There was an *awkward* atmosphere between us. / 気まずい思いをさせてしまったのでしたらごめんなさい I am sorry if I made you feel *uncomfortable* [*embarrassed*]. ◆私は彼女と最近気まずい関係になっている (→うまくいっていない) I'm *not getting along well with* her these days.

きまつ 期末 the end of a term ∥期末試験 a term examination; (学年末の) a final exam, a final / 期末手当 a seasonal bonus

きまった 決まった regular, fixed ∥決まった仕事に就いている have a *regular* job / 学校は決まった時間に始まる School begins at a *regular* time. ◆彼はいつも決まった料理を注文する He always orders *the same* food.

きまって 決まって always ∥弟は決まって7時に学校へ出かけます My brother *always* leaves for school at seven.

◆彼は私に会うと決まって息子の自慢話をする *Whenever* he meets me, he brags about his son. / When he meets me, he *never fails* to brag about his son.

きまま 気儘 彼はいなかで気ままに暮らしている He leads a *carefree* life in the country. / 彼らは子供たちを勝手気ままにさせすぎだと思う I think they have gone too far in letting their children *have their own way*. / 彼は自由気ままなひとり暮らしにあこがれている He wishes to live *as he pleases* [*likes*] on his own.

きまり 決まり

❶【規則】rule

きまりを守る[破る] obey [break] *the rule*

ここで靴を脱ぐきまりになっています We have *a rule* that we take off our shoes here.

私たちは自分たちで服装についてのきまりを作った We made 「*rules about clothes* [*dress code*]」 ourselves.

ラブレターの書き方にこれといった決まりはない There are no fixed *rules* in writing love letters.

❷【決定】(解決・決着) settlement ⓤⓒ; (合意) agreement ⓒ

◆それで話は決まりだ *It's all settled* then. / きょう中にこの件に決まりをつけよう Let's *settle* this matter today.

❸【習慣】(個人の) habit ⓤⓒ; (一般の) custom ⓤⓒ

毎朝1杯の牛乳を飲むのがきまりになっている I *have a habit of* drinking a glass of milk every morning. / I *make it a rule to* drink a glass of milk every morning.

❹【その他】

この公園は犬の散歩をするときのお決まりのコースだ (→いつもこの公園に寄る) Every time I walk my dog, I visit this park on the way.

きまりの悪い思いをした I felt *embarrassed*.
きまりきった 決まりきった 決まりきった表現 a *fixed* [*stereotyped*] expression / 決まりきった仕事をやるのはもううんざりだ I'm fed up with my *routine* work. / そんなの決まりきったことだ(→明白だ) That's *obvious*.
きまりもんく 決まり文句 (慣用的な語句) set [fixed] phrase ⓒ; (陳腐な文句) stock phrase ⓒ, cliché [kli:féi] ⓒ /状況に応じた決まり文句を覚えておけば、英会話もぐんと楽しくなるでしょう When you've learned *set* [*fixed*] *phrases* to fit certain situations, English conversations will be more enjoyable. / 彼の詩は決まり文句ばかりで全然おもしろくない His poems are full of「*stock phrases* [*clichés*]」, so that they are not interesting at all.
きまりわるい 決まり悪い 彼はきまり悪そうにあいさつした He greeted me *with an embarrassed look*. / きまり悪くて「ごめん」なんて言えないよ I'll *feel awkward* [*embarrassed*] if I say "I'm sorry."

きまる 決まる
❶【定まる】be decided; (日取りなどが) be fixed; (取り決められる) be arranged
夏休みの予定が決まった The plan for summer vacation *was decided*.
私たちの学校の文化祭は9月26日に決まった Our school festival *was fixed* [*arranged, set*] for September 26.
◆みんなで公平にそれを分けることで話が決まった We *agreed* that we would divide it equally. / 彼が次期首相に決まった(→選ばれた) He *was elected* the next Prime Minister. / 姉の就職が決まった(→職を見つけた) My sister *found* a job.
❷【きっと…する】be sure [certain] to *do*
彼女は驚くに決まっている She *is sure to* be surprised. / *I'm sure* she will be surprised.
💬「学校やめるって本当？」「そんなのうそに決まってるだろ(→冗談を言っただけだ)」"Are you really going to quit school?" "You know that I was only joking."
💬「彼、私の提案をどう思うかしら」「あいつのことだから反対に決まってるさ」"I wonder what he thinks about my suggestion." "You know him. He's *surely* going to oppose it."
❸【うまくいく】
そのスーツ、とても決まってるね You *look perfect* in that suit.
彼のシュートが決まった He *made* a goal.
ぎまん 欺瞞 deceit ⓤⓒ, deception ⓤⓒ
◆欺瞞に満ちた言動 *deceitful* words and actions
‖自己欺瞞 self-deception
きみ¹ 君 you ⇒あなた
おい君、聞いてるか Hey *you*, do you hear me? (💬 Hey you! はやや乱暴な言い方. 呼びかけるときは Excuse me!, Sir!, Ma'am! などを用いるほうがよい)

きっと君は成功するよ I'm sure that *you* will succeed.
◆君の提案に賛成だ I'm for *your* proposal.
きみ² 気味 夜中に物音がして気味が悪かった I heard something late at night. It made me *feel uneasy*. / きょうは彼がやけに親切なので気味が悪い It's *weird* that he's so kind today. / 夜の学校は薄気味悪い Schools feel *creepy* [*eerie*] at night. / いい気味だ(→当然の報いだ) It *serves* [*Serves*] *you right*!
きみ³ 黄身 yolk [jóuk] ⓒⓤ, yellow ⓒⓤ /卵の黄身 the yolk of an egg
-ぎみ -気味 かぜぎみなので早く家に帰った I went home early because I *had a slight* [*touch of a*] *cold*. / 最近ちょっと疲れぎみだ I am *a little tired* these days. / 彼は太りぎみだ He is *on the plump side*. / 株価は下がりぎみだ The stock prices *are slipping*.
きみじか 気短 ──気短な (我慢できない) impatient; (怒りっぽい) quick-tempered, short-tempered
きみつ¹ 機密 secret ⓒ ──機密の secret, confidential, classified ‖最高機密 a top *secret* / 軍事機密を守る[もらす] keep [leak] a military *secret*
‖機密事項 secret information / 機密性 secrecy, confidentiality / 機密文書 a secret [classified, confidential] document
きみつ² 気密 ──気密の airtight ‖気密性の高い部屋 a *highly airtight* room
‖気密室 an airtight chamber [room]; (航空機の) a sealed [pressure] cabin; (潜水艦の) a pressure hull / 気密服 a pressure suit
きみどり 黄緑 yellowish green ⓤ
きみょう 奇妙 ──奇妙な (不思議な) strange; (変わった) odd; (好奇心をそそる) curious; (おかしな) funny /奇妙な夢を見た I had a *strange* [an *odd*, a *funny*] dream. / 東京の繁華街で奇妙な事件が起こった A *strange* [*curious*] thing happened in downtown Tokyo. / こんな遅くに教室の電気がついているなんて奇妙だな It's *strange* [*odd, funny*] that the lights should be on in the classroom at this late hour.
◆奇妙なことに、彼女は私の名前ばかりか誕生日まで知っていた *Strangely enough* [*Strange to say*], she knew not only my name but also my birthday.

ぎむ 義務
duty ⓤⓒ; obligation ⓤⓒ
| duty: 良心・正義感・道徳などによるもの.
| obligation: 慣習・約束・契約などの特定の条件により生ずるもの.
➡ コミュニケーションスキル p.394
人に義務を負わせる impose *a duty* [*an obligation*] on a person / 自らの義務を怠る neglect *one's* own *duty*
君は自分の義務を果たすべきだ You should 「do *your duty* [fulfill *your obligations*].
義務を逃れようとしてはいけない Don't try to get out of *your duties*.
自分の子供の世話をするのはあなたの義務だ It is

コミュニケーションスキル ―義務―

①must を用いる場合

(A) **You must** be quiet in the auditorium.
講堂の中では静かにすること.
(B) **You must** take this medicine after every meal.
この薬は毎食後に飲むこと.
(C) **We must** get out of here as soon as possible.
ここからできるだけ早く出たほうがよい.

☞ must は (A), (B) のように You must ... の形で用いると, 強制的できつい調子になるので, 会話では **You have to ...** や **You should ...** の形が好まれる.
☞ (C)のように We must ... とすると, 自分も含めて行動を促すような言い方になる.

②have to do を用いる場合

(A) **You have to** brush your teeth before you go to bed.
寝る前に歯を磨くんだよ.
(B) **I've got to** go there right away.
私は今すぐそこへ行かなければなりません.
(C) **We had to** explain to the police why we were at the murder scene.
私たちは警察に, なぜ殺人現場にいたのか説明しなければならなかった.

☞ (A) は must を使うより, やや穏やかな言い方になる.
☞ (B) のように, 口語では特に have to do が have got to do になることが多い.
☞ must には未来形, 過去形がないので, 未来の出来事には will [shall] have to do, 過去の出来事には had to do を用いる.

③should, ought to do を用いる場合

(A) **You should** think about it more seriously.
あなたはそのことについてもっと真剣に考えたほうがよい.
(B) **You should not** meet him anymore.
あなたはこれ以上彼に会うべきではない.
(C) **You ought to** consider environmental problems more seriously.
あなたは環境問題についてもっと真剣に考えるべきだ.
(D) **I should [ought to]** have studied harder last night.
昨夜はもっと一生懸命勉強しておくべきだった.

☞ (A) の should は相手に何か助言を与えるような場合に使う. 一方, (C) の ought to do は should よりもやや意味が強く, 「(当然)…すべきである」という意味合いが含まれるが, ①の must ほどは強くない.
☞ ought to do の否定形の語順は ought not to do となることに注意.
You ought not to talk back to your parents like that. 君はご両親に対してそのような口答えをすべきでない.
☞ should や ought to do は (D) のように, 〈should [ought to] have + 過去分詞〉の形で「(当然)…すべきであった(のに…しなかった)」の意味を表すことも多い.

④その他の義務の表現

(A) **We have a responsibility to** pay our taxes.
私たちには税金を払う義務がある.
(B) **You are supposed to** work on your assignment now.
今は宿題をする時間ですよ.
(C) When you're buying alcohol, **you are required to** show your ID to the clerk.
お酒を買うときは, 店員に身分証明書を見せなければならない.

☞ (B) の be supposed to do は「…することになっている」の意味で, 口語でよく使われる. あらかじめ決まっていることや, 規則や義務でそうするように期待されていることを表わす. **He was supposed to** attend the meeting this afternoon. (彼はきょうの午後は会議に出席するはずだった) のように過去形で使うと, 「実際にはそうしなかった」という意味になる.
☞ (C) の be required to do は「…するよう要求されている」が元の意味. 掲示や誓約書など, 形式的な場で用いられる表現で, 会話ではあまり用いない.

---

your *duty* [You have *a duty*] to take care of your children.
あなたは約束を果たす**義務がある** You *are under an obligation to* fulfill your promise.
◆法律は我々が税金を払うことを**義務づけている** The law *obliges* us to pay taxes.
‖義務感 a sense of duty / 義務教育 compulsory education

きむずかしい 気難しい (機嫌をとりにくい) hard to please; (扱いにくい) difficult ∥隣のおじいさんは気難しい The old man next door is *hard to please*. / 父は気難しい人だ My father is a *difficult* man. ◆あの先生はいつも気難しい(→不機嫌な)顔をしている That teacher always has a *sour* expression.

きめ 木目 (木目) grain ⓤ; (手ざわり) texture ⓒⓤ ◆きめの細かい[粗い]木材 *fine-grained* [*coarse-grained*] wood / きめ細かい肌 a *delicate* skin / きめ細かい注意を払う pay *close* attention

きめい 記名 signature ⓒ ――記名する sign *one's* name, register ⓔ ∥ここに記名してください Please *sign your name* here.
‖記名投票 an open [a signed] ballot

ぎめい 偽名 false [assumed] name ⓒ; (犯罪者が使う) alias [éiliəs] ⓒ ∥彼は偽名でホテルに泊まった He stayed at a hotel *under a false name*.

きめこむ 決め込む take* (it) for granted, assume ⓔ; (ふりをする) pretend ⓔ ∥その番

組は終わってしまったものと決め込んでいた I 「*took it for granted* [*assumed*] *that* the TV program had finished.
◆彼は英雄を決め込んでいるようだ It seems that he pompously *regards himself as* a hero. / 少年はそのことについてはだんまりを決め込んだ The boy *persisted in* keeping silent about that. / 私はずる休みを決め込んだ I *played hooky* shamelessly.

きめつける 決め付ける conclude ㊥, jump to a conclusion 《彼女は彼が悪いと決めつけた She *jumped to the conclusion* that he was to blame. / こんな理由では向かないと決めつけるのはまだ早いよ You shouldn't *conclude* so readily that you would not be the right person for such an important task.
◆我々は全員彼を有罪だと決めつけていた We all *firmly believed* he was guilty.

きめて 決め手 今のところ,あの男を犯人だとする決め手(→決定的な証拠)はない At the moment, there is no *conclusive evidence* that that man committed the crime.

きめる 決める

❶【決定する・決心する】decide ㊥ ㊒, determine ㊥ ㊒;(選択する)choose* ㊥;(決意する)make* up *one's* mind;(日取りなどを)fix ㊥, set* ㊥;(手はずを整える)arrange ㊥
態度を決める *determine one's* attitude / 予算を決める *set* a budget
彼女はその本を買うことに決めた She *decided to* buy the book.
今年は中国語をマスターしようと堅く心に決めている I *am firmly determined to* master Chinese this year. / I *have firmly decided that* I will master Chinese this year.
彼のシュートがその試合を決めた His goal *decided* the game.
このかばんに決めました I *chose* this bag.
彼らは値段を29,800円に決めた They *fixed* the price at 29,800 yen.
私たちはパーティーの日取りを次の日曜に決めた We *set* the party for next Sunday.
どこで会うかを決めよう Let's *arrange* where to meet.
それは前もって決められたとおりに行ってください Please do it as previously *arranged*.
🅒「本当にそこに行くの?」「うん,もう決めたんだ」"Are you really going there?" "Yes, I've already *decided*."
🅒「どの映画を見ようか」「君が決めてよ」"Which movie should we see?" "You *decide* [*choose*]."
◆私たちは議長を田中君に決めた(→田中君を選出した)We *elected* Tanaka as chairperson. / その力士は一瞬で勝負を決めた The sumo wrestler *finished* the bout in an instant.

❷【必ず…する】
私は毎朝犬の散歩をすることに決めている I *make it a rule to* take my dog out for a walk every morning.

❸【思い込む】take* (it) for granted, assume ㊥

彼の言ったことは本当だと決めてかかった I *assumed that* what he said was true.

❹【成功させる】
彼は最後の数分で2つのゴールを決めた He *got* two goals in the last few minutes.

❺【服装などを】
きょうの彼はスーツで決めている He *looks sharp* today in his suit.
彼はマットに着地すると両手を上げてポーズを決めた He *struck a pose* with both hands raised when he landed on the mat.

きも 肝 (肝臓) liver ㊒;(度胸) courage ㊚
[慣用表現] 君はなかなか肝がすわっているね You *are hard to surprise*. / 彼は肝が小さい He *is timid*. / 先生に言われたことを肝に銘じた I *took my teacher's words to heart*. / 彼女の悲鳴に肝をつぶした I *was astonished* by her scream. / 飛行機がガタガタ揺れるので肝を冷やした I *was terrified* by the plane's shaking.

きもいり 肝煎り おじの肝いりで就職が決まった I got a job *through the good offices of* my uncle.

きもだめし 肝試し 夜中に墓地で肝試しをした We *tested our courage* (by) going into a cemetery at night.

きもち 気持ち

(感じ) feeling ㊤ ㊒;(感情) feelings;(気分) mood ㊒
〘気持ちが・は〙
こんな気持ちは初めてだ It's the first time I've ever had this *feeling*.
彼女は人の気持ちがよく分かる人だ She is sensitive to other people's *feelings*. / She is sensitive to how other people *feel*.
◆このソファーはふかふかで気持ちがいい This sofa is soft and *comfortable*. / 大きな声で歌を歌うのは気持ちがいい It's *nice* to sing songs in a loud voice. / 船に乗ったら気持ちが悪くなった I *felt sick* when I was on the ship. / どんなに説得しても彼の気持ちは変わらなかった No matter how hard I tried to persuade him, he *wouldn't change his mind*. / 気持ちはよく分かるけど,彼女にあたるのはよくないな I *know exactly how you feel*, but you shouldn't be so hard on her.
〘気持ちを・に〙
君の言葉が彼女の気持ちを傷つけたんだよ What you said hurt her *feelings*.
その音楽は私の気持ちを明るくしてくれた The music 「*brightened up my mood* [*cheered me up*]」.
どうやって自分の本当の気持ちを伝えたらいいのか分からない I don't know how to get across my true *feelings*.
彼女の話を聞いて,悲しい気持ちになった I got 「*a sad feeling* [*sad*]」 listening to her story.
◆彼女の気持ちにもなってみなさい You should know how she *feels*. / その部屋からすぐさま逃げ出したい気持ちになった I *felt like* getting out of the room as soon as possible. / 気

持ちをこめて手紙を書いた I *put all my heart into* writing a letter. / 今は彼にそれを話す気持ちになれない I *can't bring myself to* say it to him now.

《〜(の)気持ち》
私たちは複雑な気持ちだった We had mixed *feelings*.
◆私の心は感謝の気持ちでいっぱいになった My heart filled with *gratitude*. / 大学生になるってどんな気持ちですか How do you *feel* about becoming a university student?

《気持ちの》
◆彼は気持ちの優しい人です He is a *kind* person. / 気持ちのいい風が吹いている A *pleasant* breeze is blowing.

《その他》
◆猫が気持ちよさそうに日なたぼっこをしている A cat is sitting *happily* in the sunshine. / 彼女は気持ちよくノートを貸してくれた She lent me her notebook *willingly*. / ああ, 気持ちいい. やっぱり温泉はいいね This *feels good* [*great*]. Hot springs are fantastic. / このぬるぬるしたものчто! 気持ち悪い What is this slimy thing? It's *unpleasant* [《口語的》*creepy*]. / ほんの気持ちですが, どうぞお受け取りください Would you please accept this *as a token of my gratitude*?

💬「手伝ってくれてありがとう. 何かお礼をしなくては」「どうぞおかまいなく. お気持ちだけで結構ですから(→役に立てただけでうれしい)」"Thank you for helping me. I feel I'm obliged to give you something to show my thanks." "Oh, no, please don't bother. I'm glad now that I have been of help to you."

💬「花びんはこのあたりでいいかな」「うぅん, 気持ち(→ほんの少し)右へ寄せて」"The vase should be here, right?" "Well, move it *just a little bit* to the right."

きもったま 肝っ玉 あいつは肝っ玉の太い男だ He is a *brave* man. / 彼は肝っ玉が小さい He is a *coward*.

きもの 着物 🏯 (衣服) clothes; (和服) kimono ⓤ (複 〜s) ◆英語化しているが,《米》では着物風の化粧着を指して用いることが多い)
着物を着て初もうでに行った I put on *a kimono* and visited a shrine on New Year's Day.
彼女は着物姿もとてもすてきです She looks very nice *in a kimono*, too.

日本の伝統的な衣服である着物は世界中でよく知られています. 日本では洋服が入ってくるまで, だれもがふだん着に着物を着ていましたが, 今では正月や成人式, 結婚式といった特別な機会にしか着ない人がほとんどです. そのためひとりで着物を着られる人は減っており, 着付けを教える学校に通う人もいます.
Kimonos, traditional Japanese clothing, are well known all over the world. Until the introduction of Western clothes, everybody wore kimonos as everyday clothing. Now, however, most people wear kimonos only on special occasions such as New Year's Day, Coming-of-Age Day or weddings. Therefore fewer people can put one on by themselves now, and some people go to special schools to learn how.

きもん 鬼門 an unlucky direction ◆私にとって理数系は鬼門だ(→苦手だ) I *am poor at* science and mathematics.

ぎもん 疑問 question ⓤ ⓒ; (疑い) doubt ⓤ ⓒ
疑問があったら今のうちに聞いてください If you have any *questions*, please ask me now.
彼の話にはいくつか疑問点がある I have some *doubts* about his story.
彼が犯人であることについては疑問の余地がない There is [I have] no *doubt* that he is the criminal.
彼の説明を聞いた後でもまだいくつか疑問が残った Some *doubts* remained after I heard his explanation.
◆多くの人々がその計画に疑問をいだいている Many people *are doubtful* about the project. / Many people find the project *questionable*. / 彼がその試合に勝てるかどうか疑問だ It is *doubtful* whether [if] he can win the game. / 我々は彼女にそんなことができるのかどうか疑問に思っている We *doubt* whether [if] she can do such a thing.
∥疑問詞 an interrogative / 疑問符 a question mark / 疑問文 an interrogative sentence / 付加疑問文 a tag question

ぎもんだいめいし 疑問代名詞〔文法〕interrogative pronoun ⓒ

「だれ」「何」など疑問を表す代名詞で, who, whom, whose, what, which がこれに当たる. 疑問代名詞を主語とする文では, 平叙文と語順が同じになる ∥ *What* is this table made of? このテーブルは何でできているのですか / *Who* jogs here every morning? 毎朝このあたりでジョギングをしている人はだれですか(❖ jogs の s は 3 人称単数・現在形の s)

ギヤ gear ⓤ ⓒ ⇨ ギア

きゃあきゃあ 隣の部屋から子供のきゃあきゃあ言う声が聞こえてきた I heard children *screaming* from the next room.

ぎゃあぎゃあ ぎゃあぎゃあ騒ぐほどのことではないだろう There's no need to make such *a big fuss*. / 赤ちゃんがぎゃあぎゃあ泣いている The baby *is bawling*.

きやく 規約 (規則) rule ⓒ; (協約) agreement ⓒ ∥規約を守る observe *rules*

きゃく 客
❶【来訪者】(招待客) guest ⓒ; (訪問客) visitor ⓒ, caller ⓒ
客を丁重にもてなす give *a guest* a fine reception
たくさんの客がパーティーに招かれた Many *guests* were invited to the party.
きょう思いがけない客があった I had *an* unexpected *visitor* today.

今晩お客さまがいらっしゃるのですか Are you expecting *visitors* tonight?
❷【顧客】(商店などの) customer ⓒ; (買い物客) shopper ⓒ; (依頼人) client ⓒ
固定客 *a* regular *customer*
新しくできたディスカウント店はいつも客でいっぱいだ The new discount store is always crowded with *customers*.
最近客があまり来なくなった We haven't been attracting many *customers* recently.
◆(呼びかけて)お客さん *Sir* [*Madam*]. / あのレストランは客の扱いが悪い That restaurant *gives poor service*.
❸【観客・乗客など】(聴衆・観衆) audience ⓒ; (見物客) spectator ⓒ; (乗客) passenger ⓒ; (宿泊客) guest ⓒ
その芝居は客の入りがよかった[悪かった] The play drew *a* large [small] *audience*.
そのホテルには200人の客が宿泊できる The hotel has accommodation(s) for 200 *guests*.

ぎゃく 逆
(位置・立場など) the opposite; (方向・順序など) the reverse; (内容・意見など)《公式的》the contrary;〘論理〙the converse ──逆の opposite; reverse(◆名詞の前で用いる); contrary
真実は全くその逆だった The truth was quite *the opposite*.
この電車, 逆方向に向かってるんじゃない? Isn't this train going in the *opposite* direction?
君と彼とは考え方が全く逆だよ Your view and his are completely *opposite* [*contrary*] *to each other*.
順番が逆だよ They're in *reverse* order.
彼を利用してやろうと思ったのだが, 逆にこちらがいいように使われてしまった I tried to take advantage of him, but *on the contrary*, he was successful in taking advantage of me.
逆もまた真なり *The converse* [*opposite*] *is also true*.
◆その絵は上下が逆だ This picture is *upside down*. / セーターを表裏逆に着ているのに気づいた I noticed that my sweater was *inside out*. / 靴が左右逆だよ You're wearing your shoes on the *wrong* feet. / 順序を逆にしてはいけない Never *reverse* the order. / 10から1まで逆に数えてごらん Count *backward* from ten to one.
🅔「こちらの方向に回すんですか」「いいえ, 逆です」"Do you turn it this way?" "No, *the other way*."
‖逆回転 backspin / 逆関数〘数学〙the inverse function

ギャグ《口語的》gag ⓒ; (冗談) joke ⓒ / 平田さんはよくギャグを飛ばす Mr. Hirata often tells *gags*.
きゃくあし 客足 店の近くにスーパーができてから客足が遠のいた Since a supermarket opened near our shop, we've had a sharp decline in the number of *customers*.
きゃくいん¹ 客員 ‖客員教授 a visiting professor / 客員研究員 a visiting research worker
きゃくいん² 脚韻 rhyme ⓤⓒ ◆この詩は脚韻を踏んでいる This poem *rhymes*.
ぎゃくこうか 逆効果 adverse effect ⓒ ◆弟をしかったが逆効果だった I scolded my brother, but it just *made matters worse*.
ぎゃくさつ 虐殺 slaughter [slɔ́ːtər] ⓤ; (大量虐殺) massacre [mǽsəkər] ⓒ ──虐殺する slaughter ⓗ; massacre ⓗ ‖虐殺者 a slaughterer / 大虐殺 a massacre, a mass killing
ぎゃくさん 逆算 ──逆算する count backward ‖彼女との待ち合わせの時間から自分が起きるべき時間を逆算した I *counted backward* from the time I had arranged to meet her and figured out the time I should get up.
ぎゃくしつ 客室 (旅館の) guest room ⓒ; (船・飛行機の) cabin ⓒ ‖客室係 a room clerk / 客室乗務員 a flight attendant,《集合的》a cabin crew
ぎゃくしゃ 客車《米》(passenger) car ⓒ,《英》(railway) carriage ⓒ, coach ⓒ(◆《英》では客車の公式名,《米》では食堂車・寝台車などと区別して普通客車の意味で用いる). day coach ともいう)
ぎゃくしゅう 逆襲 counterattack ⓒ ──逆襲する counterattack ⓘ ◆敵軍は逆襲に転じた The enemy troops started to *counterattack* [*make a counterattack*].
ぎゃくじょう 逆上 私は彼の言葉を聞いて逆上した I *flew into a rage* when I heard what he said. / 彼は逆上して彼女を殴った He *got really mad* and hit her.
きゃくしょうばい 客商売 the service industry
きゃくしょく 脚色 dramatization ⓤⓒ ──脚色する (劇化する) dramatize ⓗ; (改作する) adapt ⓗ ◆その漫画はテレビ用に脚色された The comic (book) *was dramatized* for television. ◆彼女は事実を脚色している She *is embellishing* [*coloring*] the truth.
きゃくせき 客席 seat ⓒ ‖ホールの客席は聴衆でいっぱいだった *The seats* in the hall were packed with people.
ぎゃくせつ 逆説 paradox ⓒ ⓤ ──逆説的な paradoxical ‖逆説的ではあるが, ペットはかわいいからこそ厳しくしつけなければならない It's *a paradox* that because pets are so cute we must train them strictly.
きゃくせん 客船 passenger boat [ship] ⓒ; (定期船) liner ⓒ ◆豪華客船 *a* luxury *ship*
きゃくせんび 脚線美 脚線美の女性 a woman *with beautiful legs*
きゃくそう 客層 このデパートの客層は20代, 30代の女性が中心だ(→顧客のほとんどは20代, 30代の女性だ) Most of *the clientele* of this department store are women in their 20s or 30s.
ぎゃくたい 虐待 mistreatment ⓤ; (残酷な行為) cruelty ⓒ; (保護されるべき人に対する)

abuse Ⓤ ──虐待する mistreat ⓔ; treat cruelly; abuse ⓔ ‖児童虐待 child *abuse* / 動物虐待 *cruelty* to animals / その虐待を受けた子供たちを思うと心が痛む My heart bleeds for those *abused* children.

ぎゃくたんち 逆探知 警察は容疑者からの電話を逆探知しようとした The police tried to *trace* the call from the suspect.

きゃくちゅう 脚注 footnote Ⓒ ‖そのことは本文ではなく脚注に書かれている That is referred to in *the footnotes*, not in the text.

ぎゃくて 逆手 ⇒さかて

ぎゃくてん 逆転 reversal ⓊⒸ ──逆転する reverse ⓔ ‖あれ以来私と彼女の立場は逆転した After that, my position and hers *were reversed.* / ドラゴンズはジャイアンツに4対3で逆転勝ちした The Dragons 「*came from behind* [*turned the tables*] *and defeated* the Giants by 4 to 3.
‖逆転判決 reversed ruling [decision] / 逆転ホームラン a come-from-behind home run

きゃくひき 客引き 彼はたちの悪い客引きにひっかかった He was caught by *a* wicked *barker*.

ぎゃくふう 逆風 unfavorable [adverse] wind Ⓒ ◆彼らは逆風をついて進んだ They went on *against the wind*.

きゃくほん 脚本 script Ⓒ; (映画の) scenario Ⓒ (複〜s), screenplay Ⓒ ‖脚本家 a scenario writer, a scriptwriter; (劇作家) a playwright

きゃくま 客間 (応接室) 《公式的》 drawing room Ⓒ; (客用寝室) guest room Ⓒ

ぎゃくもどり 逆戻り ──逆戻りする (元の方向に) turn [go*] back; (元の状態に) return ⓘ ‖手袋を落としたのでもと来た道を逆戻りした I dropped my glove somewhere, so I *went back toward* where I started. / その寺にいると奈良時代に逆戻りしたような気分になった In the temple, I felt as if I *had gone back to* the Nara period. / 夏休みが終わって忙しい生活に逆戻りした When summer vacation finished, I *returned to* my busy life.

きゃくよせ 客寄せ その店では客寄せのため週末にセールをする The shop holds a weekend sale to *draw* [*attract*] *more customers*.

ぎゃくりゅう 逆流 ──逆流する flow backward ◆水の逆流 the *backward flow* of water

ギャザー gathers ‖ギャザースカート a gathered skirt

きゃしゃ 華奢 ──きゃしゃな (ほっそりした) slender; (公式的) slight; (ひ弱な) weak, delicate; (こわれやすい) fragile ‖きゃしゃな作りの机 *a fragile* desk / その男の子はきゃしゃな体つきをしている The boy has *a slight* build.

きやすい 気安い 夏子とは気安い仲です I am *on friendly* [*familiar*] *terms with* Natsuko. / 彼は気安く質問に応じてくれた He answered my question *willingly* [*readily*]. / 気安く話しかけないでください Don't speak to me *in a familiar manner*.

キャスター ⚠ (解説者) newscaster Ⓒ, 《米》 anchor Ⓒ, 《英》 newsreader Ⓒ; (脚輪) caster Ⓒ, wheel Ⓒ ‖キャスター付きのテーブル a table *on wheels*

キャスティングボート ⚠ (議長の決定投票) casting vote Ⓒ 《通例単数形》
◆キャスティングボート(→決定権)を握る have *the deciding vote*

キャスト (全出演者) cast Ⓒ 《❖配役の1人は a member of the cast》 ‖オールスターキャスト *an all-star cast* / 豪華キャストの映画 a film with *a distinguished cast*

きやすめ 気休め (口先だけの慰め) empty consolation Ⓤ; (つかの間の安心) brief [temporary] relief Ⓤ ‖そんな言葉はただの気休めにしかならない Such words would be nothing but *empty consolation.* / Such words would give nothing but *brief relief.*
◆背中におできができたので気休めに消毒薬をつけておいた I put disinfectant on a rash on my back *just to ease my mind*.

きやせ 着痩せ 妹は着やせるタイプだ(→服を着たときにやせて見える) My sister *looks thinner when she is dressed*.

きたつ 脚立 stepladder Ⓒ

キャタピラー (無限軌道) caterpillar tread Ⓒ

きゃっ 彼女はクモを見てきゃっと叫んだ She saw a spider and *shrieked* [*screamed*]. 《❖叫び声そのものは eek [íːk]》

ぎゃっ 足を踏まれて彼はぎゃっと叫んだ He *yelled* when his foot was stepped on.

きゃっか 却下 ──却下する 〔法律〕 (訴えなどを) dismiss ⓔ; (請願・控訴などを) reject ⓔ, turn down ‖裁判所は控訴を却下した The court *rejected* the appeal. / 君の提案が却下されたのは残念だね It's too bad that your proposal *was turned down*.

きゃっかん 客観 客観的な意見 an *objective* opinion / 客観的に判断する judge *objectively*
‖客観性 objectivity / 客観テスト an objective test

きゃっきゃっ 猿たちはきゃっきゃっと言いながら駆け回っている The monkeys *are chattering* and running around. / 妹はその話を聞いてきゃっきゃっと笑った My sister *shrieked with laughter* when she heard the story.

ぎゃっきょう 逆境 adversity Ⓤ ‖勇気をもって逆境に立ち向かう face *adversity* with courage / 逆境に打ち勝つ overcome *adversity* / これまで何度も逆境と闘ってきた I've struggled with *adversity* many times. / 彼は今逆境にある He *is facing adversity* now. / He *is under adverse conditions* now. / 彼女は逆境に強い She bears *adversity* well.

きゃっこう 脚光 彼は新進気鋭の映画監督として脚光を浴びている He is in *the limelight* [*spotlight*] as a young and spirited movie director.

ぎゃっこう¹ 逆光 backlight Ⓤ ◆この前彼女と撮った写真は逆光だった The picture taken

キャンプ

with her the other day was shot *against the light*.
ぎゃっこう² 逆行 あの法案は時代に逆行している That bill *goes against* the times.
キャッシュ cash ◆キャッシュレス時代 the *cashless* age
🅔「お支払いは？」「キャッシュで」 "How are you paying?" "Cash."
‖キャッシュカード a bank [《英》cash] card / キャッシュディスペンサー 《米》an ATM, 《主に英》a cash dispenser
キャッシング cash advance ⓒ
キャッチ catch ——キャッチする catch* ㊛ ‖ナイスキャッチ！Nice *catch*! / ボールをキャッチする *catch* a ball
◆電波をキャッチする *receive* a radio wave
キャッチセールス ⚠ (街路での押し売り) high-pressure street sales ⓒ; (人) high-pressure street vendor ⓒ ‖キャッチセールスにつかまった A high-pressure street vendor caught me.
キャッチフレーズ catch phrase ⓒ, catchword ⓒ, slogan ⓒ
キャッチボール ⚠ catch Ⓤ ‖キャッチボールをする play *catch*
キャッチホン ⚠ call waiting service Ⓤ
◆(電話で)キャッチホンが入っちゃった。切らないでちょっと待っててね *I've got another call. Please wait for a minute and don't hang up*.
キャッチャー catcher ⓒ ‖キャッチャーフライ a pop-up to the catcher / キャッチャーミット ✤ a catcher's mitt
キャッツアイ (猫目石) cat's-eye ⓒ
キャップ (ふた) cap ⓒ, top ⓒ; (帽子) cap ⓒ; (キャプテン) captain ⓒ ‖このびんのキャップをはずしてもらえませんか Would you unscrew *the cap [top] of this bottle*?
ギャップ gap ⓒ ‖理想と現実のギャップは大きい There is *a big [wide] gap* between the ideal and the reality. / ジェネレーションギャップを埋めるのは容易ではない It is difficult to bridge *the generation gap*.
キャディー caddie, caddy ⓒ
キャパシティー (定員・容量・能力) capacity Ⓤⓒ
キャビア caviar(e) Ⓤ
キャビ ⚠ (写真のサイズ) cabinet size ⓒ
キャビネット cabinet ⓒ ‖ファイリングキャビネット *a filing cabinet*
キャビン (船室) cabin ⓒ
キャプション caption ⓒ
キャプテン (船長・主将) captain ⓒ
ぎゃふん 彼は僕が失敗すると言っていたけど、きっと成功してぎゃふんと言わせてやる(→全く間違っていたことを思い知らせてやる) He said I would fail. But I'm surely going to succeed and *make him realize he was completely wrong*.
キャベツ ⚠ cabbage Ⓤⓒ ‖キャベツを2玉買う buy 'two heads of *cabbage* [two *cabbages*] ‖芽キャベツ a Brussels sprout
キャミソール camisole ⓒ

ギャラ ⚠ performance fee ⓒ, pay Ⓤ (✤「ギャラ」は guarantee を省略した和製英語)
◆彼はギャラの安い番組には出ない He doesn't appear on TV programs that don't *pay* well.
キャラクター character ⓒ ‖キャラクター商品 goods featuring popular characters
キャラバン (隊商) caravan ⓒ
キャラメル caramel Ⓤⓒ ‖キャラメルソース caramel sauce
ギャラリー (美術館などを展示する) gallery ⓒ; (ゴルフの見物人)《集合的》the gallery
キャリア (経歴) career [kəríər] ⓒ; (保菌者) carrier [kǽriər] ⓒ ‖彼はこの道でのキャリアが長い He has *a long career* in this field.
◆彼女はジャーナリストとして20年のキャリアがある(→20年間ジャーナリストとして働いている) She *has been working* as a journalist for 20 years. / 彼女はキャリアアップを目ざして英会話学校に通い始めた She started attending an English language school to *get a more desirable job*.
‖キャリアウーマン a career woman / キャリア組 an elite bureaucrat / ノンキャリア組 a non-elite bureaucrat
ギャル girl ⓒ,《米口語的》gal ⓒ
キャロル (祝歌) carol ⓒ
きゃんきゃん (鳴き声) yap ⓒ, yelp ⓒ
◆子犬は物音にびっくりしてきゃんきゃん鳴きだした The puppy started *yelping [yapping]* with surprise when he heard the noise.
ギャング ⚠ (犯罪者の一味) gang ⓒ; (一員) gangster ⓒ (✤日本語の「ギャング」は犯罪者グループまたはそのメンバーを指すが、英語の gang はグループのみを表す) ‖ギャング映画 a gangster film [movie]
キャンセル ——キャンセルする cancel ㊛ ‖チケットの予約をキャンセルした I *canceled* the ticket reservation. ◆飛行機のキャンセル待ちをする be *on the waiting list* for a flight ‖キャンセル料 a cancellation fee
キャンデー 《米》candy Ⓤⓒ,《英》sweet ⓒ; (棒付きの) lollipop ⓒ
キャンドル candle ⓒ ‖キャンドルサービス a candlelight service

> a candlelight service はクリスマスなどにろうそくに火をともして行う礼拝をいう。結婚式の披露宴で行うものは During a wedding reception, the bride and groom visit their guests' tables and light candles. などと説明的に訳す。

キャンバス (油絵用の画布) canvas ⓒ; (帆布・テント) canvas Ⓤ ‖キャンバス地のバッグ a *canvas* bag
キャンパス campus ⓒⓊ ‖キャンパス内[外]で on [off] *campus*
キャンピングカー ⚠ (主に米) camper ⓒ, 《英》caravan ⓒ (✤「キャンピングカー」は和製英語)
キャンプ camp Ⓤⓒ; (トレーニングキャンプ) training camp ⓒ ——キャンプする camp ㊛ ‖サマーキャンプ *a summer camp* / ベース

キャンプ *a* base *camp* / 難民キャンプ *a* refugee *camp* / 我々はその夜，川のほとりでキャンプした We *camped* by the river for the night. / 弟はきのう秩父へキャンプに行った My brother went *camping* in Chichibu yesterday. / ジャイアンツは毎年宮崎でキャンプを張る The Giants have *their* training *camp* in Miyazaki every year. / きょう各球団がいっせいにキャンプインした All of the baseball teams *started their training camps* today.

◆キャンプファイアをする make *a campfire*
‖キャンプ施設 camping facilities / キャンプ場 a campsite, 《主に米》a campground / キャンプ村 a camping village / キャンプ用品 a camping outfit, camping equipment / オートキャンプ場 a car campground

ギャンブル ⚠(賭(か)け事) gambling◯ ‖彼は給料の大半をギャンブルに使ってしまった He spent most of his salary on *gambling*.

キャンペーン campaign◯ ‖スポーツ奨励のキャンペーンを実施する carry on *a campaign* to encourage sports / 彼女の新曲のキャンペーン *an advertising campaign* for her new song
‖キャンペーンガール a spokesmodel / キャンペーンセール a sales campaign

キャンベラ Canberra(✿オーストラリアの首都)

きゆう 杞憂 (根拠のない不安) groundless fears; (不必要な不安) needless fears
◆私の心配事は杞憂に終わった My worries proved *groundless*.

きゅう¹ 急
❶【急ぎ】──急な urgent; (即時の) immediate ──急に immediately
その話し合いは急を要する The discussion is *urgent*.
🖋「きのうは何で来なかったの」「急な用事で出かけていたんだ」"Why didn't you come yesterday?" "Because I went out *on urgent business*."
❷【突然】──急な sudden; (不意の) abrupt ──急に suddenly, all of a sudden; abruptly
急なお誘いなのですぐには返事ができません It's such a *sudden* invitation that I can't answer right away.
音楽が急にやんでラジオから臨時ニュースが流れてきた The music stopped *suddenly* and a news flash was broadcast on the radio.
運転手は急ブレーキをかけた The driver stepped on the brake *suddenly*.
◆その子供は急に笑い[泣き]だした The child *burst into* laughter [tears]. / きょうは急な(→思いがけない)来客があった We had *unexpected* visitors today.
🖋「あした帰ります」「ずいぶん急だね」"I'm going home tomorrow." "That's too *soon*."
❸【傾斜・角度が】──急な (坂などが) steep; (角度が) sharp
彼は急な坂道を滑り下りた He slid down the *steep* slope.
急な上りで息が切れた I was winded by the *steep* climb.
この先，急カーブがあるから気をつけて Be careful! There's a *sharp* curve ahead. [The road turns *sharply* ahead.]
❹【流れが速い】──急な fast, rapid, 《公式的》swift
この川は日本一流れが急だ This river has the *fastest* current in Japan.
❺【非常事態】emergency◯
急の場合に備えておくことが必要だ We need to prepare for *emergencies*.

きゅう² 級
❶【学校の】(学年) year◯, 《米》grade◯(✿小・中・高の学年); (クラス) class◯
兄は私の1級上です My brother is one 「*year* ahead of [*grade* above] me.
その少女は中学1年から3年へ飛び級した The girl *skipped* from seventh *grade* to ninth.
❷【等級】class◯; (段階) grade◯; (階級) rank◯; (水準) level◯
A級 *grade* A / 大使級の会談 talks at *the ambassadorial level*
彼女の作る料理はプロ級だ The food she cooks is at *the professional level*.
今度は3,000メートル級の山に登りたい I want to climb a 3,000-meter *class* mountain next time.
彼は世界でも第一級の建築家です He is *one of the world's top-class* architects. / He is *one of the best* architects in the world.
彼は国際級の選手だった He was a *world-class* athlete.
◆上級[中級，初級]学習者 an *advanced* [*intermediate*, *elementary*] learner
‖級長 a class president / 級友 a classmate

きゅう³ 旧 old; (以前の) former ‖旧体制 the *old* order / 旧ソ連 the *former* Soviet Union / 旧正月 New Year's Day *according to the old calendar*

きゅう⁴ 球 (球体) sphere◯, globe◯ ◆60ワット球 a 60-watt *bulb* / ピッチャーは第1球を投げた The pitcher threw the *first pitch*.

きゅう⁵ 九 nine; (9番目) the ninth

きゅう⁶ 灸 ⚠ 肩に灸をすえてもらった I had my shoulders *treated with moxibustion*.
慣用表現 先生は彼にお灸をすえた(→しかった) The teacher *scolded* [*reprimanded*] him.

伝統的な東洋医学療法である灸は，現代の日本でも評価されています。ヨモギの葉を乾燥して作った灸状のもぐさをつぼと呼ばれる位置(治療効果のある場所)に置き，燃やします。灸は西洋医学では治りにくいとされるアレルギーや肩こり，腰痛，また自律神経失調症などに効果があります。
Kyu (moxibustion), a traditional Asian medical treatment, is appreciated in modern Japan too. A small cone of moxa, made of dried *yomogi* (mugwort) leaves, is applied to and burned at points called *tsubo* (therapeutic points).

Kyu is effective for patients with allergies, stiff shoulders, lower back pains or problems of the autonomic nervous system, for which Western medicine is not regarded as having an effective remedy.

キュー (ビリヤードの) cue ⓒ
きゅうあい 求愛 ──求愛する court ⊕ ‖求愛行動 courtship behavior
キューアンドエー Q&A (質疑応答) Q and A (✧question and answer の略語)
きゅうい 球威 ピッチャーの球威は最後まで衰えなかった(→最後まで力の強い球を投げた) The pitcher kept throwing *powerful pitches* until the end.
きゅういん 吸引 ──吸引する (吸い込む) suck in [up] ◆この掃除機は吸引力が強い This vacuum cleaner has great *suction*.
きゅうえん¹ 救援 relief ⓤ; (救助) rescue ⓤⓒ ──救援する rescue ⊕ ‖彼らは洪水の被害者の救援に向かった They went out to *rescue* the flood victims.
‖救援活動 a relief [rescue] operation / 救援資金 relief funds / 救援隊 a rescue [relief] party / 救援投手 a relief pitcher / 救援物資 relief supplies [goods]
きゅうえん² 休演 本日は都合により休演いたします Today's *performance has been canceled* for certain reasons. / 主演女優は急病のため休演した The leading actress *canceled her appearance* because of a sudden illness.

きゅうか¹ 休暇 (主に米) vacation ⓒ, (主に英) holiday ⓒ (しばしば複数形 ~s) (✧大学の休暇は《米》《英》ともに vacation); (官庁・会社などの) leave ⓤ (✧通例病気や出産などのために願い出る休暇を指す)

夏期休暇 the summer *vacation* [*holidays*] / 病気[出産, 育児]休暇 sick [maternity, child-care] *leave* / 生理休暇 menstrual *leave* / 有給休暇 a paid *vacation* / 長期休暇 a long *vacation*

休暇はどうでしたか How was *your vacation*? / How were *your holidays*?

休暇は1か月です *My vacation* is [*My holidays* are] one month long.

来月2週間の休暇をとりたいのですが I'd like to take a two-week *vacation* next month.

彼は箱根で休暇を過ごしている He is spending *his vacation* [*holiday*(*s*)] in Hakone.

休暇中は猫を近所の人に預かってもらおう I'll leave my cat with a neighbor *during the vacation*.

彼女は今休暇でオーストラリアにいる She's in Australia *on vacation* [*holiday*]. (✧on vacation [holiday] では無冠詞)

◆法事のため1日休暇をとった I took a day *off* for a memorial service. / 彼女はまる1週間休暇をとった She took the whole week *off*.

きゅうか² 旧家 old family ⓒ ‖彼女は旧家の出だ She comes from *an old family*.
きゅうカーブ 急カーブ sharp turn [bend, curve] ⓒ ‖この急カーブではよく事故が起きている This *sharp curve* is the scene of many accidents.
◆道は急カーブしている The road *bends sharply*. / 赤い車は右へ急カーブを切った The red car *turned sharply* (to the) right.
きゅうかい 休会 recess ⓤⓒ; (一時的な) adjournment ⓒⓤ ──休会する recess ⊕; adjourn ⓒⓤ ‖議会は今度の金曜日まで休会になる The Diet *will adjourn* until [till, to] next Friday. / 国会は今度の金曜日まで休会になる The Congress is *in recess* now.
きゅうかく 嗅覚 a sense of smell ‖犬は嗅覚が鋭い Dogs have *a keen* [*a sharp, an acute*] *sense of smell*.
きゅうがく 休学 (公式的) a leave of absence from school ──休学する be absent from school, be away from school ‖彼は手術のために5か月間休学する He *will* ⌈*be absent* [*stay away*] *from school* for five months because of the operation. / 彼女は留学するために休学を願い出た She applied for *a leave of absence from school* to study abroad.
きゅうかくど 急角度 sharp angle ⓒ
◆道はトンネル内で急角度で右に曲がっている The road takes [makes] a *sharp* right turn in the tunnel.
きゅうかざん 休火山 dormant volcano ⓒ
きゅうがた 旧型 old type ⓒ ⇨ゅうしき
きゅうがわ 牛革 cowhide ⓒⓤ; (子牛の革) calfskin ⓤ ‖このジャケットは牛革でできている This jacket is made of *the cowhide*.
きゅうかん¹ 休刊 新聞休刊日 a newspaper holiday / この雑誌は来年まで休刊するらしい I heard (that) this magazine *will suspend publication* till next year.
きゅうかん² 休館 ──休館する close ⊕ⓒ ‖本日休館 (掲示) *Closed Today* / 図書館は月曜日休館です The library *is closed* on Mondays.
きゅうかん³ 急患 (急患患者) emergency patient [case] ⓒ ‖急患が出たらすぐに救急車を呼ぶこと If there's *an emergency case* [*patient*], you should call an ambulance right away.
きゅうかんちょう 九官鳥 (hill) myna(h) ⓒ
きゅうぎ 球技 ball game ⓒ (✧《米》では特に野球を指すことが多い)
きゅうきゅう¹ 救急 emergency ⓤⓒ ‖救急医療 emergency (medical) care / 救急医療体制 emergency (medical) care system / 救急救命士 a paramedic, an emergency medical technician / 救急箱 a first-aid [an emergency] kit / 救急病院 an emergency hospital / 救急病棟 an emergency ward / 救急用具 emergency equipment
きゅうきゅう² 汲々 彼は家族を養うためにきゅうきゅうとしている(→あくせく働いている) He is ⌈*working like a dog* [*slaving away*] to support his family. / 彼は昇進にきゅうきゅうとしている(→とらわれている) He *is a slave to* his promotion.

き

ぎゅうぎゅう ラッシュアワーの地下鉄はいつもぎゅうぎゅう詰めだ The subway *is* always *jam-packed* [*jammed*] during the rush hours. / 彼女はかばんに荷物をぎゅうぎゅうに詰め込んだ She *stuffed* [*crammed*] her things into the bag.

きゅうきゅうしゃ 救急車 ambulance [C] // 救急車を呼ぶ call *an ambulance* / 負傷した男性は救急車で最寄りの病院に運ばれた The injured man was taken *by ambulance* to the nearest hospital.

きゅうきょ 急遽 in a hurry, in haste //彼はクーデターの知らせに急遽帰国した He returned to his country *in haste* when he heard the news of the coup.

きゅうぎょう 休業 ―休業する close [他] [自] //本日休業《掲示》*Closed Today*; *Closed* / 年末は休業いたします We'll *be closed* at the end of the year.

◆臨時休業 *a special* [*an extra*] *holiday*

きゅうきょく 究極 ―究極の (最終的な) ultimate, final (❖共に名詞の前で用いる) ―究極的に ultimately, finally //究極のパソコン the *ultimate* personal computer / 彼は人生の究極の目的を求めてキリスト教に入信した He became a Christian in search of the *ultimate* [*final*] aim in life.

きゅうくつ 窮屈

❶【小さい・狭い】 ―窮屈な small; (衣服などがきつい) tight

この部屋にベッドを2つも置いたら窮屈だよ This room is too *small* for two beds.

このスカートは腰回りが少し窮屈だ This skirt is a little *tight* [*snug*] around the hips.

◆この靴はつま先が窮屈だ These shoes *are pinching* my toes.

❷【自由がきかない】(形式的な) formal; (融通がきかない) rigid; (経済的にひっ迫した) tight

君の考え方はあまりに窮屈だ You are too *rigid* in your thinking.

その国では食糧事情が窮屈になりつつある The supply of food is getting *tight* in that country.

❸【居心地が悪い】 uncomfortable

彼にとって日本の学校は規則ずくめで窮屈に感じられた He *felt uncomfortable* in a Japanese school because there were so many rules.

きゅうけい¹ 休憩 (仕事などの) break [C], rest [U] [C]; (授業間の) 《米》recess [U] [C], break [C] ―休憩する rest [自], take* [have*] a rest, take [have] a break

ここで15分の休憩をとりましょう Let's *take a* 15-minute *break* [*recess*] here.

ウサギはちょっと休憩するつもりがすっかり眠り込んでしまった The rabbit was going to *rest* just for a minute, but actually he fell into a deep sleep.

◆コーヒーを飲むために彼女は休憩した She *paused* for a cup of coffee.

‖休憩時間 (劇場などの) an interlude, 《米》an intermission, 《英》an interval; (授業間の) 《米》(a) recess; (仕事の合間の) a coffee [《主に英》tea] break / 休憩室 (ホテル・空港などの) a lounge (❖英語の a rest room は「トイレ」の意味)

きゅうけい² 求刑 検事は被告に終身刑[懲役5年]を求刑した The prosecutor *demanded* life [five years'] imprisonment for the accused.

きゅうげき 急激 ―急激な (突然の) sudden (❖通例名詞の前で用いる); (動きなどが) sharp; (増減などが) rapid (❖通例名詞の前で用いる) ―急激に suddenly; sharply; rapidly //気温の急激な変化 a *sudden* change in temperature / 急激な円高で輸出産業は苦境に立たされた A *sharp* rise in the yen caused difficulties for export industries. / インドの人口は急激に増加している India's population is growing *rapidly*.

◆急激なダイエット a *crash* diet / そんなに急激にやせるのはただ事ではない It is not normal to lose weight so *quickly*.

きゅうけつき 吸血鬼 vampire [C]

きゅうご 救護 《公式的》 aid [U], relief [U] ―救護する《公式的》aid [他] //ボランティアの人たちは地震の被災者の救護にあたった The volunteers 「*gave aid to* [*aided*] quake victims.

‖救護活動 relief activities / 救護所 a first-aid station [post, center] / 救護班 a relief squad [party, team]

きゅうこう¹ 急行 ❶【列車】 express (train) [C] //明石に急行で行く go to Akashi *by express* / 私たちは7時15分発の京都行きの急行に乗るつもりです We'll take *the* 7:15 *express train* for [to] Kyoto.

❷【急いで行くこと】 ―急行する rush [自], hurry [自] //レスキュー隊は墜落現場に急行した The rescuers *rushed* [*hurried*] to the scene of the crash.

‖急行券 an express ticket / 急行停車駅 an express station / 急行料金 express charges

きゅうこう² 休校 きのうは大雪のため休校だった We *had no school* yesterday because of a heavy snow.

きゅうこう³ 休講 本日休講《掲示》*No Lecture* [*Class*] *Today*; *Lecture* [*Class*] *Canceled Today* / 次の時間は山村先生が病気で休講だよ We'll have *no lecture* [*class*] for the next period because Mr. Yamamura is sick.

きゅうこう⁴ 旧交 [慣用表現] 私たちは久しぶりの同窓会で旧交を温めた We *renewed our friendship* at the class reunion after a long time.

きゅうこう⁵ 休耕 ‖休耕田 a fallow rice field

きゅうこうか 急降下 (飛行機の) nosedive [C] ―急降下する nosedive [自]; (飛行機・鳥などが) swoop [自] //私たちは飛行機が急降下するのをはらはらしながら見ていた We watched nervously as the plane *went into a nosedive*. / ワシがウサギを目がけて急降下した An eagle *swooped down* on a rabbit.

きゅうこうばい 急勾配 ━━急勾配の steep, perpendicular ∥急勾配の丘の斜面 a steep slope of the hill

きゅうこん¹ 求婚 proposal Ⓒ ━━求婚する propose 他自 ∥正夫は彼女に求婚した Masao *proposed* to her. / 彼女は彼の求婚を受け入れた［断った］ She accepted [declined] his *proposal*.

きゅうこん² 球根 bulb Ⓒ

きゅうさい 救済 help Ⓤ, relief Ⓤ; (援助)《公式的》aid Ⓤ;《キリスト教》salvation Ⓤ ━━救済する help 他;《公式的》aid 他 ∥今回の政府の計画に貧しい人たちの救済が目的のはずだった This government plan was supposed to *help* the poor. / 国連は難民のために救済活動を組織した The U.N. organized *a relief operation* for the refugees. / 彼は孤児のための救済資金として1,000万円を寄付した He donated 10 million yen to *the relief fund* for orphans.
∥救済策 relief measures / 救済事業 relief work

きゅうし¹ 九死 [慣用表現] 彼は交通事故で九死に一生を得た(→かろうじて死から逃れた) He「*had a narrow escape from* [*narrowly escaped*] *death* in the traffic accident.

きゅうし² 休止 (一時的に) suspension Ⓤ; (短い) pause Ⓒ ━━休止する suspend 他; pause 自 ∥小休止する take a pause
◆地震のため新幹線の運転は一時休止した The Shinkansen *was stopped temporarily* because of the earthquake.
∥休止符【音楽】a rest

きゅうし³ 臼歯 molar Ⓒ; (小臼歯) premolar Ⓒ ⇒は(歯)

きゅうし⁴ 急死 sudden death Ⓤ Ⓒ
◆その俳優は2日前に急死した The actor *died suddenly* two days ago.

きゅうじ¹ 球児 甲子園には毎年春と夏に全国から高校球児が集まってくる *High school baseball players* from all over the country gather at Koshien Stadium every spring and summer.

きゅうじ² 給仕 (男性の) waiter Ⓒ; (女性の) waitress Ⓒ (❖共に呼びかけにも用いる) ━━給仕する serve 他自, wait on [《英公式的》at] (table) (❖後者は「給仕として働く」という意味もある)

きゅうしき 旧式 ━━旧式な［の］ old-fashioned, outdated ∥そんな旧式な考え方, だれも理解できないよ Nobody could understand such an *old-fashioned* [*outdated*] view.
◆旧のカメラ an old type camera

きゅうしつ 吸湿 この繊維は吸湿性にすぐれている This fiber「*is highly absorbent* [*absorbs moisture*] well].

きゅうじつ 休日 (祝日・祭日) holiday Ⓒ (❖土曜・日曜は weekend); (非番) one's day off ⇒きゅうか(休暇)
彼女は休日はいつもデートに出かける She always goes out on a date on *her day(s) off*.
父は時々休日出勤をしなければならなくなる Sometimes my father has to *go to work on a holiday*.

● 「あすは休日ですか」「そうです. みどりの日という国民の祝日です」"Is tomorrow *a holiday*?" "Yes, it's a national holiday called Greenery Day."

きゅうしゃ 厩舎 stable Ⓒ

ぎゅうしゃ 牛舎 cowshed Ⓒ

きゅうしゅう¹ 吸収 absorption Ⓤ ━━吸収する absorb 他; (自分のものにする) assimilate 他; (吸い取る) suck 他
知識を吸収する assimilate [absorb] knowledge
このパジャマは汗をよく吸収する These pajamas *absorb* sweat well.
オゾン層は有害な紫外線を吸収し緩和している The ozone layer *absorbs* and reduces harmful ultraviolet rays.
植物は土から水分を吸収する Plants *suck* water from the soil.
その小さな会社は大会社に吸収された The small company *was*「*absorbed into* [*swallowed up*] *by* a big one.
∥吸収合併 (a) merger / 吸収剤 an absorbent

きゅうしゅう² 急襲 surprise attack Ⓒ ∥警察は反乱軍の拠点を急襲した The police「*made a surprise attack on* [*made a raid on, rushed*] the rebels' strongholds.

きゅうしゅう³ 九州 Kyushu; (地方) the Kyushu district; (島) Kyushu Island

きゅうじゅう 九十 ninety; (90番目) ninetieth

きゅうしゅつ 救出 rescue Ⓤ Ⓒ ━━救出する rescue 他 ∥救出活動 rescue operations / 消防士は倒壊したビルの中から少女を救出した The fire fighter *rescued* a little girl from a collapsed building.

きゅうしょ 急所 (生命に関する) vital organ Ⓒ; (弱点) weak point Ⓒ; (要点) the point ∥弾は彼の急所をはずれた The bullet missed his *vital organs*. / 彼の質問は簡潔で急所をついて(→的(㊀)を射って)いた His question was short and *to the point*.

きゅうじょ 救助 saving Ⓤ Ⓒ; (差し迫った危険からの) rescue Ⓤ Ⓒ; (助け) help Ⓤ ━━救助する save 他; rescue 他; help 他 (❖rescue は助けるという行為, save は助かるという結果に重点がある)
その男はおぼれている子供を救助した The man *saved* [*rescued*] a child from drowning.
乗組員は全員無事に救助された All the crew *was* [*were*] *rescued* safely.
巡視船が彼らの救助に向かった The patrol boats went to their *rescue*.
∥救助活動 a rescue operation / 救助犬 a rescue dog / 救助信号 an SOS call, a mayday [Mayday] / 救助隊 a relief team, a rescue party / 救助隊員 a rescue worker / 救助艇 a salvage boat

きゅうじょう 休場 その力士はけがのため春場所を休場した The sumo wrestler「*was absent from* [*skipped*] the spring tourna-

きゅうじょう² 球場 (baseball) stadium ⓒ, baseball field [ground] ⓒ, 《米》ball park ⓒ //甲子園球場 the Koshien Stadium

きゅうじょう³ 窮状 distress ⓤ //震災の被災者たちは政府に窮状を訴えた The victims of the earthquake complained to the government about distress [their miserable condition].
◆彼らは窮状を打開する手段を模索していた They were groping for a way to overcome the difficulties.

きゅうじょうしょう 急上昇 ──急上昇する rise* sharply, skyrocket ⓘ //そのグループは人気急上昇中だ The popularity of the group is skyrocketing.

きゅうしょく¹ 休職 (公式的)a leave of absence from work ──休職する be absent from work, be away from work //彼女は病気のため2か月間休職した She was absent [stayed away] from her work for two months because of her illness./ (→休職の許可を与えられた)She was given a sick leave for two months because of her illness.

きゅうしょく² 求職 (職探し) job hunting ⓤ
◆彼は先月から求職中だ He's been looking for a job since last month.
//求職者 a job-seeker, a job hunter; (志願者) an applicant

きゅうしょく³ 給食 (学校の) school lunch [《英》meal] ⓒ //学校給食に何か不満はありませんか Do you have any complaints about school lunches?
//給食費 school-lunch expenses

ぎゅうじる 牛耳る (支配する) control ⓘ, dominate ⓘ //その会社は清水一族によって牛耳られている The company is controlled [dominated] by the Shimizus./ (→一族の支配下にある) The company is under control of the Shimizus.

きゅうしん¹ 休診 本日休診 《掲示》Office Closed Today; Closed Today / その医院は木曜日が休診日です The clinic is closed on Thursdays.

きゅうしん² 急進 ──急進的な (過激な) radical; (極端な) (しばしば軽蔑的)extreme //急進的な見解[考え] a radical view [idea]
//急進主義 radicalism / 急進主義者 a radical / 急進派 a radical party

きゅうしん³ 球審 〔野球〕the chief umpire, the home plate umpire

きゅうじん 求人 job offer ⓒ //求人は年々少なくなっている Job offers are decreasing year by year.
◆きょうの新聞にはたくさんの求人広告が出ていた There were many want ads in today's newspaper.
//求人難 a labor shortage

きゅうしんりょく 求心力 〔物理〕centripetal force ⓤ (↔centrifugal force)

きゅうす 急須 teapot ⓒ

きゅうすい 給水 water supply, the supply of water //日照りが続き、東京では給水制限が始まった As the dry weather continued, the supply of water began to be rationed in Tokyo.
//給水施設 a water system / 給水車 a water wagon / 給水タンク a feed tank / 給水塔 a feed tower / 給水ポンプ a feed pump

きゅうする 窮する be at a loss //そう聞かれて、私は一瞬答えに窮した When I was asked so, for a moment I was at a loss [didn't know] how to answer.
ことわざ 窮すれば通ず It is when you come to a standstill that you will find a way out.; The darkest hour comes just before the dawn.(→最も暗いのは夜明け直前の時間だ)

きゅうせい¹ 旧制 the old system //旧制高校 a high school under the old system

きゅうせい² 旧姓 (以前の姓) one's former family name; (既婚女性の) one's maiden name ◆宇野夫人, 旧姓原 Mrs. Uno, née Hara(✿néeは[néi]と発音する)

きゅうせい³ 急性 ──急性の acute //急性アルコール中毒 acute alcoholism / 急性心不全 acute cardiac insufficiency

きゅうせいぐん 救世軍 the Salvation Army

きゅうせいしゅ 救世主 the Savior, the Messiah, the Redeemer

きゅうせき 旧跡 historic spot [site] ⓒ

きゅうせっきじだい 旧石器時代 the Old Stone Age, the Paleolithic period

きゅうせん 休戦 truce ⓒ, cease-fire, armistice ⓒ ⓤ ──休戦する make* a truce //休戦を宣言する declare a truce
//休戦協定 a cease-fire agreement

きゅうせんぼう 急先鋒 (指導者) leader ⓒ; (指導的立場) the vanguard //彼は反戦運動の急先鋒に立っている He is in the vanguard of the antiwar movement.

きゅうぞう 急増 sharp [rapid] increase ⓒ ⓤ ──急増する increase sharply [rapidly] //売上高の急増 a sharp increase in sales / 若者による犯罪が急増している The number of crimes committed by young people is increasing rapidly.

きゅうそく¹ 休息 rest ⓒ //かぜをひいたときは家に早く帰って十分な休息をとったほうがいいよ When you catch (a) cold, you should go home early and take a good rest.

きゅうそく² 急速 ──急速な fast, rapid; (素早い) quick //急速に fast, rapidly; quickly //急速冷凍 quick-freezing / 急速な進歩を遂げる make rapid progress / アジアの経済は急速に成長している The economies in Asia are growing very fast.

きゅうたい 旧態 その会社は社名こそ変わったが組織そのものは旧態依然だった(→実質的には変わらなかった) The company was renamed, but the organization itself remained unchanged.

きゅうだい 及第 ──及第する pass ⓘ ⓘ ⇒ごうかく //入学試験に及第する pass the entrance examination
//及第点 a pass mark

きゅうだん[1] 糾弾 ―糾弾する《公式的》censure [他], denounce [他] ∥彼らはその議員の汚職を糾弾した They *censured* [*denounced*] the politician *for* corruption.

きゅうだん[2] 球団 professional baseball team [C]

きゅうち[1] 窮地 awkward position [C],《口語的》corner [C], predicament [C] ∥窮地に陥る be driven [forced, put] into *a* (*tight*) *corner* / その会社はやっとのことで窮地を脱した The company got out of *the predicament* with great difficulty.

きゅうち[2] 旧知 石田氏とは旧知の間柄(→昔からの知り合い)だ I *have known* Mr. Ishida *for a long time*.

きゅうちゃく 吸着 タコの吸盤は吸着力が強い The suckers of an octopus *stick tight*.

きゅうてい 宮廷 court [C] [U]《しばしば Court》

きゅうていしゃ 急停車 sudden stop [C] ∥バスは急停車した The bus「*made a sudden stop* [*stopped suddenly*].

きゅうてん 急転 先月になって情勢は急転した The situation *changed suddenly* last month. / 証拠物件の発見によって事件は急転直下解決した As the evidence was found, the case was *suddenly* solved.

きゅうでん 宮殿 palace [C] ∥彼女は私たちをバッキンガム宮殿に案内してくれた She showed us Buckingham *Palace*.

きゅうとう[1] 急騰 sharp rise [C] ―急騰する rise* sharply ∥物価の急騰 *the sharp rise* in prices / 最近物価が急騰している Prices *are*「*rising sharply* [*skyrocketing*] these days.

きゅうとう[2] 給湯 (給湯設備) hot water supply [U] ‖給湯器 a water heater / 給湯室 a room where you can get hot water

きゅうどう 弓道 🗻

> 弓道は平安時代から室町時代にかけて大きく発展を遂げた日本の伝統武術の一つで，弓は木と竹，矢は竹でできています．まず，姿勢を正して足をしっかり固定し重心を安定させます．次に，弓に矢をつがえて弦をいっぱいに引き，ねらいを定めて矢を放ちます．弓道はかなりの集中力を必要とするため，精神鍛練によいとされています．
> *Kyudo* (Japanese archery) is a traditional martial art that developed largely from the Heian period (794–1192) through the Muromachi period (1338–1573). The bow is made of wood and bamboo and the arrow of bamboo. Archers first stand up straight and plant their feet properly for balance, and then they place an arrow on the bow string and draw it back as far as possible. Then they take aim and let the arrow go. It is said that *kyudo* is good to discipline the mind, for it requires high concentration.

ぎゅうどん 牛丼 🗻 *gyudon*, a bowl of rice topped with cooked beef (❖米国の一部では beef bowl として販売されている)

ぎゅうにく 牛肉 beef [U]

きゅうにゅう 吸入 inhalation [U] [C] ―吸入する inhale [他] ◆救急隊員はその男性に酸素吸入を行った The paramedics *gave* him *oxygen*.

ぎゅうにゅう 牛乳 milk [U] ∥牛乳1杯 a glass of *milk* / 牛乳2本 two bottles of *milk* (❖「パック入り」なら bottles の代わりに cartons を用いる) / この牛乳は脂肪分が少ない This *milk* is low in fat.
‖牛乳配達人 a milkman / 牛乳パック a milk carton / 牛乳びん a milk bottle / 低温殺菌牛乳 pasteurized milk / ホモ牛乳 homogenized milk

きゅうねん 旧年 last year, the past year ∥旧年中はたいへんお世話になりました Thank you for all of your help *during the past year*.

きゅうば 急場 (緊急事態) emergency [U] [C]; (危機的状況) crisis [C] (複crises) ∥彼は借金をして急場をしのいだ He borrowed some money and *got through the crisis*.
◆踏み台がこわれてしまったので急場しのぎにいすを使った Because the footstool broke, I substituted a chair *for the time being*.

きゅうばん 吸盤 (ゴム製の) suction cup [C]; (動物の) sucker [C]

キューピー 《商標名》kewpie (doll) [C]

キュービズム 〔美術〕cubism [U]《しばしば Cubism》

きゅうピッチ 急ピッチ 新しいスタジアムの建設工事が急ピッチで進められている Construction work on the new stadium is progressing *rapidly*.

キューピッド 〔ローマ神話〕Cupid

きゅうびょう 急病 sudden illness [sickness] [C] ∥父は急病で会社を休んだ My father was absent from the office because of *a sudden illness* [*sickness*].
◆急病人が出たため電車が少し遅れた The train was delayed a little because there was *an emergency medical case*.

きゅうふ 給付 grant [U] ―給付する grant [他] ◆給付を受ける receive *benefits*
‖給付金 benefits / 医療給付 medical benefits

きゅうブレーキ 急ブレーキ sudden braking ◆急ブレーキをかける *slam the brakes on*; *hit the brakes*

きゅうへん 急変 sudden change [C] ∥為替相場の急変 *a sudden change* in the exchange rate ◆天候が急変した The weather *changed suddenly*. / 彼の容体は3日前に急変した(→急に悪化した) His condition *took a sudden turn for the worse* three days ago.

きゅうぼう 窮乏 poverty [U] ∥窮乏生活を送る *live in poverty* ◆彼は失業し窮乏に陥った He lost his job and became *very poor*.

キューポラ (溶銑炉) cupola [C]

きゅうみん 休眠 dormancy [U]

きゅうむ 急務 urgent [pressing] issue [C] ∥日本の当面の急務は貿易障壁を減らすことだ Now *the urgent issue* for Japan is to reduce trade barriers. ◆被災地に物資の援助をすることが急務である It is *imperative* to give material assistance to the disaster area.

きゅうめい[1] 究明 (調査) investigation [U] [C] ―究明する investigate [他] [自] ∥彼は事件の真相を究明するために私立探偵を雇った He hired a private detective to *investigate* the fact of the matter.

きゅうめい[2] 救命 lifesaving [U] ‖救命いかだ a life raft / 救命具《米》a life preserver / 救命胴衣 a life jacket / 救命ブイ a life buoy / 救命ボート a lifeboat

きゅうやくせいしょ 旧約聖書 the Old Testament (《略語》OT)

きゅうゆ 給油 (燃料補給) refueling [U] ―給油する refuel [他] [自] ∥彼は給油のためにガソリンスタンドに立ち寄った He stopped his car at a gas station to *refuel.*
‖給油所 a gas station / 給油船 a tanker

きゅうゆう[1] 旧友 old friend [C] ∥久しぶりに旧友に会った I met *an old friend of mine* that I had not seen for a long time.

きゅうゆう[2] 級友 classmate [C]

きゅうよ 給与 pay [U]; (固定給) salary [C] ➔きゅうりょう(給料) ‖給与所得 (an) earned income / 給与所得者 a salaried employee / 給与水準 a pay level / 給与体系 the wage system / 給与明細書 a pay slip

きゅうよう[1] 休養 rest [C], 《公式的》repose [U] ―休養する rest [自], get* [have*, take*] a rest ∥休養をとる *rest*; *get* [*have, take*] *a rest* / きのうはゆっくり休養できましたか Did you *get a* good *rest* yesterday?

きゅうよう[2] 急用 urgent business [U] ∥父は急用で出かけました My father went out *on urgent business.*

きゅうらい 旧来 ―旧来の (因習的な) conventional; (伝統的な) traditional

きゅうらく 急落 sharp drop [C] ―急落する drop sharply ∥物価の急落 *a sharp drop* in prices / 先月株価はいっせいに急落した Stock prices *dropped sharply* across the board last month.

きゅうり 胡瓜 cucumber [C] [U] ∥キュウリの漬物 pickled *cucumbers*

きゅうりゅう 急流 (早い流れ) swift current [C]; (早瀬) rapids ∥急流を下る shoot *rapids*

きゅうりょう[1] 給料 pay [U]; (固定給) salary [C]; (賃金) wages

安い[高い]給料 *a* low [high] *salary*

兄の給料は月に20万円です My brother's *pay* is 200,000 yen a month. / My brother *is paid* 200,000 yen a month.

私は毎週金曜日に給料をもらう I get *my pay* [*wages*] every Friday.

あなたの給料は毎年上がりますか Does your *salary* increase every year?

社長は私たちの給料を上げてくれた[減額した] Our boss raised [cut] our *salaries.*

◆あの会社は給料がいいらしい They say that company *pays well.*

‖給料日 a payday / 給料袋《米》a pay envelope [《主に英》packet]

きゅうりょう[2] 丘陵 hill [C] ∥多摩丘陵 the Tama *Hills*
‖丘陵地帯 a hilly district

きゅうれき 旧暦 (太陰暦) the lunar calendar

きゅっと 唇をきゅっと結ぶ *compress one's* lips / ベルトをきゅっと締める *fasten one's* belt / 彼は冷酒をきゅっと(→一気に)飲み干した He *gulped* (*down*) a cup of chilled sake.

ぎゅっと 彼女は恐怖に震えているその子供をぎゅっと抱きしめた She *hugged* the frightened child *tightly.* / 彼はつかんでいた私の腕をぎゅっと握った He *tightened* his grip on my arm.

キュリー 〔物理〕curie [C] (❖放射能の強さの単位; 《略語》Ci)

キュロット(スカート) culottes (❖フランス語から)

きよ 寄与 contribution [U] [C] ―寄与する contribute [他] [自] ∥リンドバーグは航空の発展に大いに寄与した Lindbergh *made a* great *contribution to* aviation.

きょ 虚 emptiness [U] ◆虚と実 truth and *falsity* / 虚をつく *catch a person unprepared*

きよい 清い (清潔な) clean; (純粋な) pure; (澄んだ) clear ∥彼は山里で清く正しい生活を送っていた He was leading a *clean* [*pure*] life in the mountain village. / 五十鈴川の水は清く澄んでいた The Isuzu River was *clear* and transparent.
◆あなたの清き(→心からの)一票を私にお願いします Please cast your *heartfelt vote* for me.

きよう[1] 起用 ―起用する (任命する) appoint [他] ∥大統領はグレイ氏を副大統領に起用した The president *appointed* Mr. Gray (*as*) vice-president. ◆市原監督はついに森を先発投手に起用した Mr. Ichihara finally *made* Mori the starting pitcher.

きよう[2] 器用 dexterity [U] ―器用な (手先が) dexterous, handy ➔ぶきよう ∥彼女はたいへん器用にセーターを編む She weaves sweaters *with* great *dexterity.* / 君は器用に包丁を使うね You are *handy with* knives. ◆彼は手先が器用だ He *is good* [*skillful*] *with his hands.*
‖器用貧乏 a jack-of-all-trades (and master of none)

きよう[3] 紀要 bulletin [C]

きょう[1] 今日

―[名] today [U] ―[副] today, this day

来週のきょう《米》a week from *today*; 《英》*this day* week / 先週のきょう《米》a week ago *today*; 《英》*this day* last week

彼はきょう学校を休んだ He was absent from school *today.*

きょうはこれまで So much for *today.*

きょうの彼女は私に少しよそよそしかった She was rather cool toward me *today.*

さあ, きょうの授業を始めましょう Now, let's start *today's* lesson.

きょうの夕刊にその作家についての記事が載っているよ There's a story about the novelist in *today's* evening paper.

彼らはきょうかあすには出発するでしょう They will leave either *today* or tomorrow.

きょう中に宿題をやっておこう I'm going to finish my homework *today*.

きょうから3日間、陶器市が行われる There's a ceramics fair for three days *from today*.

きょうからダイエットを始めた I've started a diet *today*. (❖ start (始める) は、一時点で終わる行為なので×from today とはしない)

◆きょうの午後は暇ですか Are you free *this afternoon*? / きょうあす中にパーティーに出るかどうか決めなくてはならない I'll have to decide whether to go to the party or not *within a day or two*. / (手紙で)梅の花もほころんでだんだん春めいてきたきょうこのごろです The plum buds are starting to open, and spring is in the air. (❖「きょうこのごろです」は特に訳さなくてよい)

🔵「きょうは何曜日」「金曜だよ」"What day (of the week) is it *today*?" "It's Friday. / *Today* is Friday."

🔵「きょうは(何月)何日」「5月10日です」"What's the date *today*? / What's *today's* date?" "It's May 10."

きょう² 興 やっと興が乗ってきたところだったのに時間の関係で会はお開きになってしまった Though the party *had livened up* at last, it broke up on account of the time. / その光景を目にしてすっかり旅の興がそがれてしまった The scene *spoiled* completely (*the fun of*) my trip.

きょう³ 凶 evil ⓤⓒ, ill [bad] luck [fortune] ⓤ / おみくじを引いたら「凶」だった I drew an *omikuji* and it said "*Ill Luck.*"

きょう⁴ 経 sutra ⓒ / その僧侶(梵)は何時間もお経を唱えていた The Buddhist priest chanted *the sutra* for hours.

きょう⁵ 卿 Lord (❖英国の侯爵・伯爵・子爵・男爵の姓の前に置く); Sir (❖英国のナイトまたは準男爵の姓名または名前の前に置く)

-きょう¹ 狂 (口語的/軽蔑的) nut ⓒ, (口語的) freak ⓒ, buff ⓒ / 野球狂 a baseball *nut [freak, buff]*

-きょう² 強 ここから学校まで3キロ強ある It's *a little over* three kilometers from here to my school.

ぎょう 行 line ⓒ / そのページの最終行 *the last line* on the page / 1行おきに *on every other line* / 10ページの6行目から読みなさい Read from "*line six [the sixth line]*" on page ten. / 行を変えたらどう Why don't you begin *a new line* here?

🔵「riddle なんて単語どこにあるの」「上[下]から3行目だよ」"Where is the word 'riddle'?" "It's on *the third line from the top [bottom]*."

きょうあく 凶悪 ──凶悪な atrocious, 《公式的》heinous; (残忍な) brutal / 政府は凶悪犯罪に対して何らかの対策を講ずるべきである The government should take some measures against *atrocious crimes*.

‖凶悪犯 an atrocious criminal

きょうい¹ 胸囲 *one's* chest measurement; (女性の) bust ⓒ / 僕の胸囲は85センチです My *chest measurement* is 85 centimeters.

きょうい² 脅威 threat ⓤⓒ; (敵意の強い) menace ⓒⓤ / その民族紛争は世界平和に対する脅威となりかねない The racial dispute is likely to pose *a threat* to world peace. / オゾン層の破壊は人間の健康にとって大きな脅威だ The destruction of the ozone layer is *a serious menace* to human health.

きょうい³ 驚異 marvel ──驚異的な marvelous, amazing / 自然の驚異 *a marvel* of nature / 日本は戦後、驚異的な発展を遂げた Japan made *amazing [astonishing]* progress after the war. ◆驚異的な成功を収める make *a miraculous* success

きょういく 教育

education ⓤ (また an ~); (技術に関する) training ⓤ (また a ~) ──教育の・教育的な educational ──教育する educate ⓗ; train ⓗ

茂は高校までアメリカで教育を受けた Shigeru *was educated* in the United States through high school.

彼は子供によい教育を受けさせたがっている He wants to provide his children with *a good education*.

彼女は講演の中で教育の重要性を強調した She stressed the importance of *education* in her lecture.

彼らは子供たちの教育について全く意見が異なる They are in total disagreement with each other on *educating* their children.

彼らは正規の学校教育をほとんど受けていない They have received little formal *school education*.

日本では教育制度の改革が叫ばれている In Japan, reformation of *the educational [education] system* is being called for.

その映画は子供たちには教育上好ましくないとされている The movie is regarded as unsuitable for children *from the educational point of view*.

佐藤さんの奥さんはとても教育熱心だ Mrs. Sato is very *enthusiastic about education*.

真由美は新入社員の教育を担当している Mayumi is in charge of *training* new employees.

◆その少年は家庭教育(→しつけ)に問題があった There was a problem with *discipline* in the boy's home. / 彼は聡子が相当に教育のある女性だと思った He guessed (that) Satoko was a well-*educated* woman.

‖教育委員会 the Board of Education / 教育改革 an educational reform / 教育学 pedagogy / 教育学部 the faculty of education / 教育過程 a curriculum / 教育機関 an educational institution / 教育基本法 the Fundamental Law of Education / 教育産業 education industry [business] / 教育実

習 《米》student teaching, 《主に英》teaching practice / 教育実習生 a student teacher / 教育者 an educator, a teacher / 教育心理学 educational psychology / 教育水準 educational standards / 教育番組 an educational program / 教育費 educational expenses / 教育ママ a strict education-minded mother, an educationally conscious mother / 英才教育 education for gifted children / 家庭教育 upbringing / 義務教育 compulsory education / 高等教育 higher education / 再教育 reeducation / 生涯教育 lifelong education / 初等教育 primary education / スパルタ教育 severe education / 性教育 sex education / 通信教育 education by correspondence

きょういご 強意語《文法》intensifier ⓒ

きょういん 教員 teacher ⓒ; (学校全体の) the teaching staff, the faculty / 姉は教員の免状を持っている My sister is certified as *a teacher*.
∥教員室 a teachers' room / 教員免許 a teacher's certificate [license]

きょううん 強運 強運の持ち主 *a very lucky* person

きょうえい 競泳 swimming race ⓒ

きょうえん 共演 ──共演する (両者が主役で) costar ⓐ /シュワルツェネッガーとスタローンが初めて映画で共演するらしい I hear (that) Schwarzenegger and Stallone *will costar* in a movie for the first time.
∥共演者 a costar

きょうか¹ 強化 ──強化する strengthen ⓗ; (補強する) reinforce ⓗ; (管理などを) tighten ⓗ ⓘ; (兵力などを) build* up / 腹筋を強化する *strengthen* abdominal muscles / チームを強化する *reinforce* a team / 大統領の到着に備えて空港の警備が強化された In anticipation of the president's arrival, airport security *was tightened*.
∥強化合宿 a training camp / 強化ガラス hardened [toughened] glass / 強化プラスチック reinforced plastics / 強化米 enriched [fortified] rice

きょうか² 教科 subject ⓒ ⇨ かもく(科目)

きょうかい¹ 教会 church ⓒ /清水君は毎週日曜日に教会へ行く Shimizu goes to *church* every Sunday. (❖「礼拝のために教会へ行く」という場合は無冠詞)

きょうかい² 境界 (2国・2地域間の) border ⓒ; (ある地域の辺境) boundary ⓒ (❖両者とも区別なく用いられることも多い) /そこには隣国との境界を示す道標が立っていた There stood a guidepost which showed *the border of* the country. / うちの学校は調布市と世田谷区の境界線上にある Our school stands *on the border between* Chofu City *and* Setagaya Ward.
∥境界争い a border dispute / 境界線 a borderline

きょうかい³ 協会 association ⓒ, society ⓒ /作曲家協会 *a society* of composers

きょうかい 業界 industry ⓤ ⓒ; (芸能・娯楽などの) 《口語的》biz ⓤ ∥業界紙 a trade paper / 業界用語 a lingo, jargon / 音楽業界 the music biz / 建設業界 the construction industry / ファッション業界 the fashion industry

きょうがく 共学 coeducation ⓤ ──共学の coeducational, 《口語的》coed /私の志望校は共学の公立高校です I want to go to a *coeducational* [*coed*] public high school.

きょうかしょ 教科書 textbook ⓒ /教科書の85ページを開きなさい Open *your textbooks* to page 85.
∥教科書検定制度 the textbook authorization system / 検定(済み)教科書 an authorized textbook

きょうかつ 恐喝 blackmail ⓤ ──恐喝する blackmail ⓗ /その少年は金を巻き上げようと老女を恐喝した The boy *used blackmail* to extort money from an old woman.

きょうかん¹ 共感 sympathy ⓤ ──共感する sympathize ⓐ /彼女の考え方にはどうも共感できない I can't somehow *sympathize with* her view. / 彼の善行は世界中の人々の共感を呼んだ His good deed appealed to *the sympathy* of the people of the world.

きょうかん² 教官 teacher ⓒ, instructor ⓒ ∥指導教官 a supervising teacher

ぎょうかん 行間 行間を読む read *between the lines* / 行間をあける leave *space between the lines* / 本当の意味は行間に隠されている The actual meaning is hidden *between the lines*.

きょうき¹ 凶器 (lethal) weapon ⓒ /殺人に使われた凶器 *a murder weapon* / 銀行に凶器を持った男が現れた A man with *a* (*lethal*) *weapon* appeared in the bank.

きょうき² 狂気 madness ⓤ, insanity ⓤ ──狂気の mad, insane /破産が彼を狂気寸前まで追い込んだ The bankruptcy drove him to the brink of *madness*. / その仕事を君ひとりでやるなんて狂気のさただ It is *madness* to do the work all by yourself.

きょうき³ 狂喜 《公式的》rapture ⓤ ──狂喜する go* into raptures, be overjoyed ◆自分たちの市が次回のオリンピック開催地に決まって人々は狂喜乱舞した People *went wild with joy* when their city was chosen to be the host for the next Olympics.

きょうぎ¹ 競技 (競争) contest ⓒ, competition ⓒ; (試合) game ⓒ, match ⓒ; (競技会) 《米》meet ⓒ, 《英》meeting ⓒ; (競技種目) event ⓒ ⇨ しあい
ダンスの競技会 *a dance contest* [*meet*] / 競技に参加する participate in *a competition* / 次の競技は何ですか What is *the* next *event*?
∥競技者 a player, a contestant; (陸上の) an athlete / 競技場 (サッカーなどの) a playing field; (大きな) a stadium; (陸上の) an athletic field / 運動競技 athletics / 室内競技 indoor sports / 水上競技 aquatic sports / 馬術競技 equestrian events / 陸上競技 track and field events / 陸上競技会 an athletic meet

きょうぎ[2] 協議 discussion [C] [U]; (相談) consultation [U] **—協議する** discuss [他]; consult [自]; (話し合う) talk over … //協議の結果, 次のように決まりました *The consultation* resulted in the following agreement. / きょう国会では新しい税法について協議する Congress *will discuss* a new tax law today. / その問題について協議しよう Let's *talk over* the matter. ◆協議がまとまる(→合意に達する) *reach an agreement*
‖協議会 conference, a council / 協議事項 agenda (❖個々の事項は an item on the agenda) / 協議離婚 divorce by mutual agreement

きょうぎ[3] 狭義 narrow sense [C] //狭義においては in *a narrow sense*

きょうぎ[4] 教義 doctrine [C] [U], teachings, 《しばしば軽蔑的》dogma [C] [U] //カトリックの教義を信奉する accept Catholic *doctrine*

ぎょうぎ 行儀 (作法) manners; (ふるまい) behavior [U]

この高校の生徒は行儀がいい The students at this high school 「*have good manners* [*are well-mannered*]. (❖「行儀が悪い」は have bad [no] mannersまたは be ill-mannered)

(子供に対して)行儀よくしなさい *Where are your manners?* / *Behave yourself.* / *Be good.*

父は行儀作法にうるさい My father is strict about *proper behavior.*

◆行儀のよい[行儀の悪い]男の子 a *well-behaved* [*badly-behaved*] boy / 彼女は息子に人前では行儀よくしなさいと言った She told her son to *behave* in public.

> [英作文ノート] 「マナー」≠**manner**
> 食事中に音を立てるのは行儀が悪い
> →×It is *a bad manner* to make noise at the table.
> →○It is *bad manners* to make noise at the table.
> ★日本語では「行儀作法」の意味で「マナー」を用いるが, 英語の manner は「行儀, 作法」の意味では常に複数形 manners になる. 単数形の manner は「方法」「態度」の意味.

きょうきゅう 供給 supply [U] **—供給する** supply [他]

人々に食料を供給する *supply* people *with* food; *supply* food *to* [*for*] people

価格は需要と供給で決まる The price is determined by *supply and demand.* (❖日本語と語順が逆になるので注意)

◆ガスと電気の供給が止まった Gas and electricity *services* stopped. / この地図上の黒い部分ではまだガスが供給されていません The black area on this map *does not have* gas (*service*).
‖供給過多 oversupply, excess supply / 供給源 a source of supply / 供給不足 short supply

ぎょうぎょうしい 仰々しい 仰々しい肩書き the *high-sounding* titles / 彼の仰々しい話しぶりが耳についた His *pompous* manner of speech offended my ears.

きょうく 教区 parish [C]

きょうぐう 境遇 (暮らし向き) circumstances; (状況) condition [C], situation [C] //彼はみじめな[恵まれた]境遇に育った He grew up under miserable [good] *circumstances.* / 彼女は今の境遇に甘んじている She is content with *her* present *condition* [*situation*]. / どんな境遇にあっても希望を捨てないように Don't give up hope *no matter how the circumstances are.*

きょうくん 教訓 lesson [C]; (寓意(ぐう)) moral [C] **—教訓的な** instructive //物語から教訓を得る draw *a moral* from a story / 私はこれまで失敗から多くの教訓を得てきた I have learned a lot of *lessons* by failure.

ぎょうけつ 凝結 **—凝結する** condense [自] //水蒸気は冷えると凝結して水滴になる Steam *condenses* into water drops when it cools.

きょうけん[1] 狂犬 mad dog [C] ‖狂犬病 rabies, 〔医学〕hydrophobia

きょうけん[2] 強肩 強肩のキャッチャー a catcher with *a strong arm*

きょうけん[3] 強健 **—強健な** strong; (たくましい) robust, sturdy

きょうけん[4] 強権 (国家の権力) the power of the state //強権を発動する invoke *the power of the state*

きょうげん 狂言 🗻 *kyogen*, a Noh comedy [farce]
‖狂言自殺 sham [fake] suicide

> 狂言は対話と独白から成る一幕物の喜劇で, その舞台装置と衣装はたいへん簡素です. 狂言は能と深い関係があり, 基本的に能の幕間(まい)に演じられます.
> *Kyogen* is a one-act comedy made up of dialogues and monologues. Its stage setting and costumes are quite simple. It is closely related to *Noh* plays and is usually performed during intermissions at *Noh.*

きょうこ 強固 **—強固な** (強い) strong; (揺るぎない) firm; (断固とした) resolute **—強固に** strongly; firmly //強固な意志 a *strong* [a *firm*, a *resolute*, an *iron*] will / 強固な反対にあう meet with *strong* [*firm, resolute*] opposition

ぎょうこ 凝固 coagulation [U] **—凝固する** [させる] clot [自] [他], coagulate [自] [他]; (冷えて) congeal [自] [他] ‖凝固剤 a coagulant

きょうこう[1] 強硬 **—強硬な** (揺るぎない) firm; (強い) strong; (厳しい) hard **—強硬に** firmly; strongly //強硬手段をとる take *strong* [*extreme*] *measures* / 彼らはその政策に強硬に反対している They are *strongly* [*firmly*] opposed to the policy.
‖強硬派 a hard-liner; (タカ派) a hawk / 強硬路線 a hard [tough] line

きょうこう[2] 強行 **—強行する** force [他] //裁決を強行する *force* a vote / 道の反対側へ渡る

きょうこう ため人込みを強行突破した I *forced my way through* the crowd to the other side of the street.
◆雪の中, その試合は強行された The game *was played in spite of* the snow. / このツアーはたった2日間で数か国を訪れる強行軍だった This tour had *a very tight schedule.* We visited several countries in only two days.

きょうこう³ 恐慌 panic ⓊⒸ ‖金融恐慌 a financial panic / 世界大恐慌 the Great Depression

きょうこう⁴ 凶行 (暴力行為) violence Ⓤ; (残忍な犯罪) cruel [vicious] crime; (殺人) murder ⒸⓊ ‖凶行に及ぶ resort to (*an act of*) violence

きょうこう⁵ 教皇 the Pope

きょうごう¹ 強豪 excellent player Ⓒ; (強豪チーム) strong team Ⓒ, (口語的) powerhouse Ⓒ

きょうごう² 競合 駅の周辺ではいくつかのデパートが競合している Several department stores near the station *are competing with each other.*

きょうこく¹ 峡谷 ravine Ⓒ, gorge Ⓒ; (大きな谷) canyon Ⓒ

きょうこく² 強国 powerful nation Ⓒ, great power Ⓒ, power Ⓒ

ぎょうざ 餃子 ⇒ギョーザ

きょうさい 共催 joint sponsorship [auspices] Ⓤ ‖ー共催する cosponsor ⊕ ‖このサッカー大会は近隣3市の共催で行われている This soccer tournament *is cosponsored by* three neighboring cities. / このサッカートーナメントは *is held under the joint auspices of* three neighboring cities.

きょうざい 教材 teaching material ⓊⒸ ‖視聴覚教材 an audio-visual aid

きょうさいか 恐妻家 (口語的) henpecked husband Ⓒ

きょうさいくみあい 共済組合 (米) mutual aid society Ⓒ, (英) friendly society Ⓒ

きょうさく 凶作 bad [poor, lean] crop Ⓒ

きょうざめ 興醒め コンサート会場は音響が悪くてすっかり興ざめしてしまった The terrible acoustics in the concert hall completely *spoiled my enjoyment.* / (→がっかりした) I *was quite disappointed* because of the terrible acoustics in the concert hall.

きょうさん 協賛 (支援) support Ⓤ; (協力) cooperation Ⓤ ‖ー協賛する support ⊕; cooperate ⊕ ‖そのイベントに協賛する *support [cooperate in]* the event / その展覧会は市の協賛を得て行われた The exhibition was held *with the support of* [*in cooperation with*] the city.

きょうさんしゅぎ 共産主義 communism Ⓤ ‖共産主義国 a communist country / 共産主義者 a communist

きょうさんとう 共産党 the Communist Party ‖共産党員 a Communist, a member of the Communist Party

きょうし 教師 teacher Ⓒ; (指導者) instructor Ⓒ ‖高校の教師 a high school *teacher* / ピアノの教師 a piano *instructor*
彼女はこの学校の英語の教師です She is *an English teacher* at this school. / (→この学校で英語を教えている) She *teaches* English at this school.
◆彼は教師に向いていない He isn't cut out for *teaching.*

ぎょうし 凝視 gaze Ⓒ, stare Ⓒ ‖ー凝視する gaze ⊕, stare ⊕ ‖絵の一点を凝視する *gaze* [*stare*] *at* a point on a picture

ぎょうじ¹ 行事 event Ⓒ; (特別の) occasion Ⓒ; (公式の) function Ⓒ
その祭りは村の人々にとって特別の行事だ The festival is *a special event* [*occasion*] for people in the village.
‖学校行事 a school event [activity] / 公式行事 an official occasion [function] / 年中行事 an annual event [activity]

ぎょうじ² 行司 ⚟ a *gyoji*, a sumo referee ‖立て行司 the head sumo referee

きょうしつ 教室
❶[学校の] classroom Ⓒ, schoolroom Ⓒ; (階段教室) (lecture) hall [theater] Ⓒ
先生が教室に入ると生徒たちは話をやめた The students stopped talking when the teacher entered *the classroom.*
❷[けいこ事の] school ⒸⓊ, class ⒸⓊ
水泳教室に通う go to swimming *school* [*class*]
◆彼女は自宅でピアノの教室を開いている She *gives piano lessons* at her home.
‖LL教室 a language laboratory (❖LLは日本語でのみ用いる) / 料理教室 a cooking class

きょうしゃ 強者 the strong 《複数扱い》

ぎょうしゃ 業者 (ディーラー) dealer Ⓒ; (メーカー) manufacturer Ⓒ 《しばしば複数形 ~s》 ‖業者テスト a commercially prepared test

きょうじゃく 強弱 (強さと弱さ) strength and weakness; (音声の強勢) stress Ⓤ ‖強弱法 〔音楽〕 dynamics

きょうじゅ¹ 教授 ❶[教員] professor Ⓒ (《略語》 Prof.), (口語的) prof Ⓒ

> 米国の大学ではふつう assistant professor (助教授), associate professor (準教授), (full) professor (正教授) に分かれている. 英国の大学では学科 [講座] の長にのみ professor を用い, 以下 reader (助教授), senior lecturer, lecturer (専任講師) という. また, 米英とも客員教授は visiting professor という.

田中教授 *Professor* Tanaka / 彼女はブラウン大学の仏文学教授です She is *a professor* of French literature at Brown University.
❷[教えること] teaching Ⓤ; (レッスン) lesson Ⓒ ‖ーおしえる ‖英語の個人教授を受ける *take private lessons in* English
‖教授会 a faculty meeting / 教授陣 the faculty, the teaching staff / 教授法 a teaching method / 名誉教授 a professor emeritus

きょうじゅ² 享受 ―享受する enjoy [他] ‖豊かな生活を享受する *enjoy* a full life

ぎょうしゅ 業種 a type of industry [business]

きょうしゅう¹ 強襲 彼はピッチャー強襲のヒットで出塁した He got on base with a hit *blasted at* the pitcher.

きょうしゅう² 郷愁 (故郷への) homesickness [U]; (過去への) nostalgia [U] ◆郷愁にかられる *be* [*feel*] *homesick* [*nostalgic*]

きょうしゅうじょ 教習所 school [C][U] ‖自動車教習所 a driving school

きょうしゅく 恐縮 恐縮ですが, そこのバッグを取っていただけませんか *Excuse me, but* could you please get me that bag over there? / 遠くからお越しいただいて恐縮です *I'm grateful to* you *for* coming all this way. / *It's kind of you to* come all this way. / お待たせしてたいへん恐縮です *I'm* very *sorry* to have kept you waiting. / おほめの言葉をいただきたいへん恐縮しております I'*m* very *flattered* by your praise.

ぎょうしゅく 凝縮 condensation [U][C] ―凝縮する condense [他][自] ‖この短いフレーズに彼の様々な思いが凝縮されている His various feelings *are condensed into* this short phrase.

きょうじゅつ 供述 (申し立て) statement [C]; (宣誓供述) deposition [U][C]; (法廷での) testimony [U][C] ―供述する state [他]; depose [他]; testify [自][他] ‖うその供述をする make *a* false *statement* / 彼女は彼が現場にいなかったと供述した She *testified* [*deposed*] that he hadn't been present at the scene.

きょうしょ 教書 (米国大統領の) message [C]; (ローマ教皇の) bull [C] ‖(米国大統領の) 一般教書 the State of the Union *Message*

ぎょうしょう 行商 peddling [U], hawking [U] ―行商する peddle [他], hawk [他] ‖行商人《米》《英/古風》a peddler, 《英》a pedlar, a hawker

きょうしょく 教職 the teaching profession, teaching [U], schoolteaching [U] ‖教職に就く「go into [take up] *teaching*; become *a teacher*
‖教職員 (全教員) the teaching staff; (全職員) the staff of a school / 教職員組合 a teachers' union / 教職課程 a teacher-training course

きょうじる 興じる amuse *oneself*, have* fun ‖彼らはトランプに興じた They *amused themselves* (by) playing cards. / They *had fun* with cards.

きょうしん¹ 狂信 fanaticism [U] ―狂信的な fanatic(al) ‖狂信的集団 a *fanatic* group
‖狂信者 a fanatic

きょうしん² 強震 big [strong, severe] earthquake [C]

きょうじん 強靭 ―強靭な (強い) strong; (不屈の) tough, iron; (ねばり強い) tenacious ‖強靭な肉体 a *strong* body / 強靭な意志 a *strong* [a *tough*, an *iron*] will

きょうしんざい 強心剤 heart stimulant [C], 〔医学〕cardiotonic drug [C]

きょうしんしょう 狭心症 〔医学〕angina (pectoris) [U]

ぎょうずい 行水 ―行水する take* a quick bath

きょうする 供する (飲食物を) serve [他]; (提供する) offer [他] ◆図書館はその本を閲覧に供することにした The library decided to *make* the book *available for everyone to read.*

きょうせい¹ 強制 compulsion [U]; (おどしによる) 《公式的》coercion [U] ―強制する force [他], compel [他] (❖force のほうが強制力が強い); 《公式的》coerce [他] ―強制的な forcible (❖通例名詞の前で用いる), compulsory; 《公式的》coercive; (義務的な) obligatory
彼らはそこからの立ち退きを強制された They *were forced* [*compelled*] *to* leave there.
被告はその自白が警察に強制されたものだったと言った The accused said the confession *had been forced out* of him by the police.
私はなかば強制的にピアノを習わされた I *was* half *compelled to* take piano lessons.
その講座の履修は強制的なものではない The course is not *obligatory* [*compulsory*].
‖強制収容所 a concentration camp / 強制送還 forced [enforced] repatriation / 強制捜査 a compulsory investigation / 強制力 force / 強制労働 forced labor / 強制労働収容所 a labor camp / 強制わいせつ罪[行為] (an) indecent assault

きょうせい² 矯正 (病状・悪癖などの)《主に米》correction [U]; (罪人・悪癖などの) reform [U][C] ―矯正する correct [他]; reform [他] ‖視力を矯正する *correct one's* eyesight / 少年の悪い癖(くせ)を矯正する *correct* [*reform*] the boy's bad habits / 罪人を矯正する *reform* a criminal ◆歯列を矯正してもらった I *had* my teeth *straightened.*
‖矯正視力 corrected eyesight / 歯列矯正〔歯科〕orthodontics / 歯列矯正器 braces

きょうせい³ 共生 〔生物〕symbiosis [U]

きょうせい⁴ 強勢 〔音声〕stress [C]; (単語の) accent [C][U] ➔アクセント ‖第2音節に強勢をおきなさい Put *the stress* [*accent*] on the second syllable.

ぎょうせい 行政 administration [U]; (政治) government [U] ―行政の administrative, executive; governmental ‖行政改革 administrative reform / 行政官 an administrator / 行政機関 an administrative organization, the civil service / 行政区画 an administrative district / 行政権 administrative power / 行政指導 administrative guidance / 行政処分 administrative disposition / 行政府 the executive branch of government / 地方行政 local administration [government]

ぎょうせき 業績 achievement [C]; (事業の) (business) performance [C] ‖学問的な業績 academic *achievements* / 彼は医学の分野で数々のすばらしい業績をあげた He made many

き

remarkable *achievements* in the field of medicine. / わが社の業績は今期格段に伸びた Our *business performance* improved sharply this term.
‖業績不振 (a) poor performance

きょうそ 教祖 the founder of a religion [religious sect] ◆彼はロック界の教祖的存在だ He is *the high priest* of rock music.

きょうそう[1] 競争

competition [C] [U], rivalry [C] [U], contest [C]; (闘争) struggle [C] ―競争の competitive ―競争する compete [自]
他社との激しい競争に勝たねばならない We have to win *the* fierce *competition* with the other companies.
駅前の2つのデパートは熾烈(しれつ)な競争を繰り広げている There is intense *competition* [*rivalry*] between the two department stores near the station.
達也は優勝をかけて健次と競争しなければならなかった Tatsuya had to *compete* with Kenji for the championship.
競争の厳しいソフトウエア業界で生き残るのは大変だ It's difficult to survive in the *highly competitive* world of software business.
その高校の競争率は3倍だった *The rate of competition* to enter that high school was three to one.
◆そのデパートは売り上げで競争相手を上回った The department store outstripped *its rival* [*competitor*] in sales. / 料理の腕では, 姉とはまるで競争にならない My sister *is more than a match* for me in cooking.
‖競争社会 a competitive society / 競争心 a competitive spirit / 競争力 competitiveness / 生存競争 a struggle to survive

きょうそう[2] 競走 race [C]; (長距離) run [C]; (短距離) dash [C] ―競走する race [自] [他]
100[5,000]メートル競走に出場する take part in *the* 「100-meter *dash* [5,000-meter *run*] / 競走に勝つ[負ける] win [lose] *a race*
私は家まで妹と競走した I *had* [*ran*] *a race* with my sister to our home. / I *raced* my sister home.
‖競走者 a runner, a racer / 競走馬 a racehorse / 障害物競走(運動会の) an obstacle race; (陸上競技・競馬の) a steeplechase

きょうそう[3] 強壮 ➔じょうぶ(丈夫), つよい
‖強壮剤 (a) tonic

ぎょうそう 形相 道彦はものすごい形相で部屋に駆け込んできた Michihiko rushed into the room *with a furious* (*look on his*) *face*.

きょうそうきょく[1] 協奏曲 〔音楽〕 concerto [C] (複 ~s) ‖バイオリン協奏曲 *a* violin *concerto*; *a concerto* for violin and orchestra

きょうそうきょく[2] 狂想曲 capriccio [C] (複 ~s)

きょうそくほん 教則本 instruction book [C] ‖ギターの教則本 *a* guitar *instruction book*

きょうそん 共存 coexistence [U] ―共存する coexist [自], live together ‖自然と共存する *live together with* nature; *live in harmony with* nature / 近隣諸国との共存共栄をはかる try to *coexist* with neighboring countries *in mutual prosperity*
‖平和共存 peaceful coexistence

きょうだ 強打 (heavy [hard]) blow [C]; (野球などの) hard hit [C] ―強打する give* ... a heavy [hard] blow, hit* (...) hard ‖信夫は憲二の横っ面を強打した Nobuo *gave* Kenji *a heavy* [*hard*] *blow on* the side of his face. / 彼は倒れたときに床で頭を強打した He *hit* his head *hard* on the floor when he fell down. / 4番打者はライトへ強打を放った The fourth batter *hit hard* to right.
‖強打者 a slugger

きょうだい[1] 兄弟 (男の) brother [C]; (女の) sister [C]; (兄弟姉妹の一人) 《公式的》 sibling [C]

日本語では性別に関係なく「きょうだい」というが, 英語では brother「男のきょうだい」と sister「女のきょうだい」とを使い分ける. 男女の場合は, brother(s) and sister(s)という.

真子と誠は兄弟です Mako and Makoto are *sister and brother*.
ご兄弟はいらっしゃいますか Do you have any *brothers and sisters*?
私には兄弟がいない I have no *brothers or sisters*.
よく弟と兄弟げんかをしたものだ I used to *quarrel* [(→つかみ合いのけんか) *fight*] *with my brother*.
彼らは実の兄弟だ They are *real brothers*.
彼らは義理の兄弟だ They are *brothers-in-law*.
雄二には双子の兄弟がいる Yuji has *a twin brother* [*sister*].
[会話] 「兄弟は何人いますか」「兄が1人, 妹が2人います」 "How many *brothers and sisters* do you have?" "I have one (older) brother and two (younger) sisters." (❖年上・年下をはっきりさせる必要がある場合のみ older, younger などを用いる)
‖兄弟愛 brotherly [sisterly] love / 兄弟分 a sworn brother

[英作文ノート] 3人兄弟は **two** か **three** か うちは3人兄弟です →×I have *three* brothers. →○I have *two* brothers. ★日本語では「3人兄弟」といっても, これを言っているのがそのうちの一人の場合は, 自分を入れずに「2人の兄弟がいる」といわなければならない. 親が言う場合は, We have three sons.となる.

きょうだい[2] 強大 ―強大な (強力な) strong, 《文語》 mighty; (巨大な) great ‖強大な軍事力を持つ国 a country with *great* military strength / その会社は業界で強大な勢力を誇っている That company has *strong* [*great*] influence on the industry.

きょうだい[3] 鏡台 dressing table [C], 《米》 dresser [C], 《米》 vanity table [C]

きょうたく 教卓 teacher's desk [C]

きょうたん
きょうたん 驚嘆 wonder ⓤ; (感嘆) admiration ⓤ ──驚嘆する be amazed; admire ⓔ, marvel ⓔ ∥私は彼のピアニストとしてのすぐれた才能に驚嘆した I *was amazed at* his outstanding talent as a pianist.
◆ナイアガラの滝の光景は驚嘆に値する The sight of Niagara Falls *is wonderful*.

きょうだん¹ 教壇 platform ⓒ ◆教壇に立つ (→教師になる) *become a teacher*; (→学校で教える) *teach (at a) school*

きょうだん² 凶弾 その歌手は凶弾に倒れた The singer *was shot dead*.

きょうだん³ 教団 religious organization ⓒ

きょうち 境地 (状態) state ⓒ; (分野) ground ⓤ ∥無我の境地に達する reach *a state of selflessness* / 彼は科学の分野で新境地を開いた He *broke new ground* in the field of science.
◆何事もあきらめの境地になったら (→努力をやめては) だめよ You shouldn't *abandon your efforts in* anything.

きょうちゅう 胸中 胸中お察し申し上げます (→本当に気の毒に思っている) *I really sympathize with you.* / 私は彼女に胸中を語った I told her *everything that was in my heart*. / I told her *what I felt inside*.

きょうちょ 共著 この本は田中氏との共著だ This book is *a joint work* of Mr. Tanaka and me. / *I wrote* this book *in collaboration with* Mr. Tanaka.
∥共著者 a coauthor, a cowriter

きょうちょう¹ 協調 (調和) harmony ⓤⓒ; (協力) cooperation ⓤ ──協調する cooperate ⓘ ∥2国間の協調 *harmony* between the two nations / 我々は互いに協調して問題の解決にあたった We tried to solve the problem *in cooperation with* each other. / We *cooperated with* each other to solve the problem.
◆確かに彼女は有能だが, 協調性に欠ける There's no doubt that she's competent, but she *isn't cooperative*.
∥協調介入 concerted [joint] intervention / 労使協調 cooperation between management and labor

きょうちょう² 強調 emphasis ⓒⓤ (複 emphases), stress ⓤ ──強調する emphasize ⓔ, stress ⓔ ∥彼は教育の重要性を強調した He *emphasized* [*stressed*] the importance of education.

きょうちょうこうぶん 強調構文 cleft sentence ⓒ

> 強調構文は, It is [was] ... that ～ などの形で, 名詞・代名詞・副詞など (...の部分) を強調する構文である. 強調されるものが名詞・代名詞の場合は, that の部分を who (人の場合), which (物の場合) で表すこともある ∥ *It was* at the end of 1941 *that* the war broke out between Japan and the United States. 日本とアメリカとの間に戦争が勃発(ぼっ)したのは, 1941年末のことだった

きょうつう 共通 ──共通の common (❖比較変化なし), mutual
彼らは共通の趣味をもっている They share *common* interests.
公害は各国に共通の問題である Pollution is a problem *common to* all countries.
僕らには共通の話題がない We have nothing *in common* to talk about.
彼らには共通点が多い They *have a lot in common*.
彼女は私たちの共通の友人です She is our *mutual* friend.
◆この割引券は町内の全商店に共通です (→どの店でも使える) You can use this coupon at any store in this town.
∥共通語 a common language

きょうてい¹ 協定 agreement ⓒ; (国家間の) pact ⓒ, treaty ⓒ ∥2国間で協定が結ばれた (→調印された) *An agreement* [*A pact*, *A treaty*] has been signed by the two nations. / その協定は2年前に廃止された The *agreement* [*pact*, *treaty*] was abolished two years ago.
∥協定価格 a fixed price / 価格協定 price-fixing / 漁業協定 a fisheries agreement [pact] / 軍事協定 a military agreement [pact] / 紳士協定 a gentleman's agreement / 平和協定 a peace agreement [treaty]

きょうてい² 競艇 motorboat [powerboat] race ⓒ

きょうてき 強敵 strong [powerful, tough] opponent ⓒ

きょうてん¹ 経典 (仏教の) sutra ⓒ

きょうてん² 教典 scripture ⓒ 《しばしば複数形 ～s》

ぎょうてん 仰天 ──仰天する be flabbergasted [floored] ∥彼女の服装を見てびっくり仰天した I *was flabbergasted* by the clothes she wore.

きょうと¹ 教徒 (信者) believer ⓒ; (信奉者) follower ⓒ ∥イスラム教徒 a Muslim / キリスト教徒 a Christian / ヒンズー教徒 a Hindu / 仏教徒 a Buddhist

きょうと² 京都

> 京都府は人口の大部分が南部の京都市に集中しています. 京都市は, 1869年に東京が首都になるまでの約1,100年間, 日本の都として政治・文化・経済の中心地でした. そのため, かつての皇居であった京都御所や石庭で有名な竜安寺などの文化遺産が多く, また西陣織や清水焼などの伝統産業が盛んです.
> Most of the population of Kyoto Prefecture is concentrated in the south in Kyoto City. For some 1,100 years, Kyoto was the capital of Japan and the center of the country's politics, culture and economy until 1869, when the capital was moved to Tokyo. Many signs of Kyoto's cultural heritage remain, including the former Kyoto Imperial Palace and Ryoanji, a temple famous for its rock garden. Tra-

ditional crafts still flourish in Kyoto, including Nishijin silk fabrics and Kiyomizu ceramics.

きょうど¹ 強度 (物の) strength ⓊⒸ; (光・熱・音などの) intensity ⓊⒸ ◆彼は強度の衰弱で少しも動けなかった He was *extremely* [*very*] weak and he couldn't move at all.

きょうど² 郷土 hometown Ⓒ, home ⒸⓊ ∥彼はわが郷土の誇りだ He is the pride of our *hometown*.

∥郷土愛 love for *one's* home(town) / 郷土芸能 local performing arts / 郷土史 (a) local history / 郷土色 local color / 郷土料理 local dishes

きょうとう 教頭 vice-principal Ⓒ, assistant principal Ⓒ, 《英》deputy head-teacher Ⓒ

きょうどう¹ 共同 collaboration Ⓤ; (協力) cooperation Ⓤ ――共同の (合同の) joint; (共同使用の) communal ――共同する collaborate ⓘ; cooperate ⓘ

その２社が共同してこの商品を開発した The two companies developed this product *in collaboration* [*cooperation*] with each other. / The two companies *collaborated* [*cooperated*] *with* each other to develop this product.

この町には無料の共同浴場がある We have *a* free *communal bath* in this town.

彼らはこのビルの共同所有者だ They are *joint owners* of this building.

我々は共同声明を出した We issued *a joint statement*.

この映画は日米の共同製作だ This movie *was made in collaboration* by Japanese and American companies.

◆僕たちは柔道部と部室を共同で使っている We *share* the club room with the Judo Club.

∥共同記者会見 a joint press conference / 共同経営 (a) partnership / 共同研究 joint research / 共同作業 group work, teamwork / 共同事業 a joint venture / 共同住宅 《米》 an apartment house [building], 《英》 flats / 共同生活 community life / 共同責任 joint responsibility / 共同戦線 a (united) front / 共同体 a community / 共同募金 《主に米》 a community chest / 共同墓地 a (public) cemetery

きょうどう² 協同 産学協同の組織[プロジェクト] an *industry-university* organization [project]

∥協同組合 a cooperative / 消費者生活協同組合 a consumers' cooperative / 生協協同組合 a cooperative, 《口語的》 a co-op / 農業協同組合 a farmer's cooperative

きょうねん 享年 享年90歳 died at (*the age of*) 90

きょうばい 競売 auction ⓊⒸ ∥車を競売で買う buy a car at [by] *auction* / 楽器を競売にかける put musical instruments up for *auction*; sell musical instruments at *auction*

∥競売価格 a bid / 競売人 an auctioneer

きょうはく 脅迫 threat ⓊⒸ ――脅迫する threaten ⓣ ∥男は殺すぞと私を脅迫した The man *threatened* me with death. / 彼女はその男に脅迫されて犯罪を犯した She *was threatened* [*intimidated*] by the man *into* committing a crime. / She committed a crime *under threat* from the man.

∥脅迫罪 (the crime of) intimidation / 脅迫状 a threatening letter / 脅迫電話 a threatening phone call

きょうはくかんねん 強迫観念 obsession Ⓤ

きょうはん 共犯 《公式的》 complicity Ⓤ ∥彼女はその犯罪の共犯を疑われている She is suspected of *complicity* in the crime.

∥共犯者 an accomplice, a partner in crime

きょうふ 恐怖 fear ⓊⒸ; (激しい) terror Ⓒ; (ぞっとするような) horror Ⓒ; (突然の激しい) fright ⓊⒸ; (不安) dread 《しばしば a ～》 ∥死の恐怖 *the fear of death* / 失敗に対する恐怖心を克服する overcome *the fear of failing* / 少年たちは恐怖に震えていた The boys were trembling *with fear* [*terror, horror*]. / 彼女は恐怖のあまり悲鳴をあげた She screamed *with fear* [*terror, horror, fright*]. / 私は突然恐怖にかられた Suddenly I was seized by *fear*. / その事件は人々に恐怖を与えた The case struck *terror* [*horror, fear*] into the people.

∥恐怖政治 a reign of terror / 高所恐怖症 fear of high places, acrophobia / 対人恐怖症 fear of people, anthrophobia / 閉所恐怖症 fear of enclosed places, claustrophobia

きょうふう 強風 strong [high] wind Ⓒ, gale Ⓒ, 《口語的》 blow ∥強風にあおられる be fanned by *a strong wind*

∥強風警報 a gale warning

きょうへん 共編 coeditorship Ⓤ ∥共編者 a coeditor

きょうべん 教鞭 教鞭をとる (→教師になる) *become a teacher*; (→教壇に就く) *go into teaching*

きょうほ 競歩 【スポーツ】 (race) walking ◆競歩の選手 *a walker*

きょうぼう¹ 凶暴 ――凶暴な ferocious, fierce; (野蛮な) brutal ∥凶暴なクマ a *ferocious* [*fierce*] bear ∥犯人は非常に凶暴な性格の男だ The criminal is a very *ferocious* [*fierce, brutal*] man.

きょうぼう² 共謀 conspiracy ⓊⒸ, 《公式的》 complicity Ⓤ ――共謀する conspire ⓘ ∥彼女はその男と共謀して犯罪を犯そうとした She tried to commit a crime *in conspiracy with* the man. / She *conspired with* the man to commit a crime.

∥共謀者 a conspirator

きょうぼう³ 狂暴 ――狂暴な (暴力的な) violent; (逆上した) berserk ∥狂暴になる *go berserk*; get *violent*

きょうみ 興味
interest ――興味深い interesting

——興味がある be interested
陶芸に興味を示す show [express] *interest in* making pottery / 漢字に興味をもつ have *an interest in kanji* / 興味深い話 an *interesting* story

彼女は部活動に対する興味を失った She *has lost interest in* the club activities.

だんだん英語に興味がわいてきた I'm *beginning to take an interest in* English.

子供たちは興味をもってその動物の動きを見ていた Children were watching the movements of the animal *with interest*.

彼は音楽にたいへん興味がある He *has a deep interest in* music./ He *is deeply interested in* music.

そのような本には私は全然興味がない I'm *not interested in* that kind of book at all.

彼の宇宙に関する興味は尽きない(→ますます興味をもつようになっている) He's *becoming more and more interested in* the universe.

英国の大衆はそのスキャンダルに興味津々である The British public *is [are] very much interested in* that scandal.

◆ 彼の講義には興味がわかなかった His lecture *didn't interest* me. / 興味深いことにその島には数種の絶滅したとされていた動物がいた *Interestingly*, on the island there were some animals which were believed to have become extinct. / 興味本位で習い始めたダンスが結局彼女の本業になった She started taking dance lessons *for fun*, but dancing turned out to be her profession after all.

ぎょうむ 教務 school affairs ‖教務課 the registrar's office / 教務係 a registrar

ぎょうむ 業務 business Ⓤ; (職務) duty Ⓒ 《しばしば複数形 duties》 /業務用の車 a car *for business use* / その会社は一時業務を停止した The company suspended *business*. / 社員は昼食後それぞれの業務に戻った After lunch, the workers went back to their *duties [work]*.

🅔「秘書業務の経験は豊富ですか」「はい, 5年の経験があります」"Do you have much experience in *secretarial work*?" "Yes, I've had five years' experience."

‖業務上過失致死 professional negligence resulting in death / 業務提携 a business tie-up / 業務命令 an order (from *one's* superior)

きょうめい 共鳴 〖物理〗(音) resonance ⒸⓊ; (共感) sympathy Ⓤ ——共鳴する resonate ⓥ; sympathize ⓥ /その作家の主張に多くの読者が共鳴した Many readers *sympathized with* the writer's opinion.

‖共鳴者 a sympathizer

きょうやく 協約 agreement Ⓒ; (国家間の) entente Ⓒ ⇨ きょうてい(協定) ‖労働協約 a labor agreement

きょうゆ 教諭 teacher Ⓒ /高校教諭 *a high school teacher*

きょうゆう 共有 ——共有する (共通して持つ) share ⓥⓥ, have* ... in common; (共同所有する) own ... jointly /私は妹と部屋を共有している I *share* a room *with* my sister. / 我々はその土地を共有している We *own* the land *jointly*.

‖共有財産 common property; (公共の) public property / 共有者 a joint owner / 共有地 common land, a common

きょうよう¹ 教養 culture ⓤⒸ; (身につけた教育) education Ⓤ 《また an ~》

教養を身につける acquire *culture*; get *an education*

◆ 高度の教養のある人 a highly *cultured [educated]* person / あの男は教養がない That man *is uncultured [uneducated]*. / 彼女は教養を高めるためにその大学の公開講座をとっている She is taking an extension course at the college to *cultivate herself*.

‖教養学部 a college [school] of liberal arts / 教養課程 a liberal arts course, 《英》 a foundation course / 教養科目 the liberal arts / 教養番組 an educational program / 一般教養 general knowledge

きょうよう² 強要 ——強要する force ⓥ, compel ⓥ; (おどして) 《公式的》coerce ⓥ /自白を強要される be *forced [coerced] into* confessing / 王は国民に服従を強要した The king *compelled* his people to obey him.

きょうよう³ 共用 ——共用する share ⓥ, use ... jointly /私たちのアパートでは台所は共用です We *share* the kitchen in our apartment.

きょうらく 享楽 享楽にふける indulge (*oneself*) in *pleasure*

きょうらん 狂乱 frenzy ⓤⒸ, madness Ⓤ

◆ 半狂乱になる go *half-mad [half-crazy]* / その女性は夫が死んだと聞いて狂乱状態になった The woman became *frenzied [frantic, panicked]* when she was informed of her husband's death.

きょうり 郷里 *one's* hometown ◆ 郷里の友に手紙を書く write to a friend *back home*

きょうりゅう 恐竜 dinosaur Ⓒ

きょうりょく¹ 協力

cooperation Ⓤ; (芸術活動・研究などでの) collaboration Ⓤ; (助け) help Ⓤ ——協力する cooperate ⓥ; collaborate ⓥ; help ⓥ; (共に働く) work together ——協力的な cooperative

2国間の協力関係 *cooperative relations* between the two countries

その仕事をなしとげるには多くの人の協力が必要だ We need *cooperation* from many people to get the work done.

この番組は東京大学の協力により制作された This program was produced *in cooperation with* the University of Tokyo.

自治体は地元の人々にリサイクルへの協力を呼びかけた The local government appealed for *the cooperation* of local people in recycling.

その2社が協力してその橋を建設した The two companies *cooperated* in building the bridge./ The two companies *worked together* to build the bridge.

我々3人が協力してこの曲を書き上げた The three of us *collaborated (with each other)* in writing this song.

歓迎会を開くのに協力していただけますか Would you *help* us put on the reception?

ご協力をお願いいたします We'd like to ask for *your cooperation.*

彼らはみな協力的だった They were all *cooperative.*

ご協力ありがとうございます Thank you for *your help [cooperation].*

‖協力者 a cooperator

きょうりょく² 強力 ──**強力な** strong, powerful /強力な指導者 a *strong* leader / 強力な接着剤 a *powerful* adhesive / 政府は凶悪犯罪に対して強力な対策を講じた The government took *strong* measures against violent crimes. / そのトラックには強力なエンジンがついている The truck has a *powerful* engine. ◆ 彼はその案を強力に後押しした He *strongly* backed the proposal./ He *put his weight* behind the proposal.

きょうれつ 強烈 ──**強烈な** strong, powerful; (激しい) intense /強烈な一撃 a *powerful* blow / 彼女の印象は強烈だった (→私に強烈な印象を与えた) She made a *strong* impression on me. / 台所で強烈なガスのにおいがした There was a *strong [an intense]* smell of gas in the kitchen.

ぎょうれつ 行列 ❶【並んだ列】(順番待ちの) line ⓒ, (英) queue ⓒ, (行進) procession ⓒ, parade ⓒ /仮装行列 a costume *parade* / 店の前ではすごい数の人が行列を作って待っていた A lot of people were waiting *in (a) line* in front of the store./ (→長い行列ができていた) There was *a long line* of people waiting in front of the store.
❷【数学】matrix ⓒ (複 matrices, ~es)

きょうわこく 共和国 republic ⓒ ((略語) Rep.) /中華人民共和国 the People's *Republic* of China

きょうわとう 共和党 (米国の) the Republican Party, the Grand Old Party ((略語) GOP) ‖共和党員 a Republican

きょえいしん 虚栄心 vanity ⓤ /彼の言葉は彼女の虚栄心をくすぐった His words tickled her *vanity.* ◆ 虚栄心の強い人 a *vain* person

ギョーザ 餃子 a *gyoza*, a Chinese meat-and-vegetable (fried) dumpling

きょか 許可 permission ⓤ, (公式的) leave ⓤ; (公的な) license, (英) licence ⓤⓒ; (入場・入会・入学などの) admission ⓤ ──**許可する** permit ⓗⓔ, allow ⓗⓔ, (英) licence ⓗⓔ; admit ⓗⓔ コミュニケーションスキル p.417

先生は私に早退の許可をくれた My teacher gave me *permission* to leave early./ My teacher *let* me leave early.

私たちはその計画を続ける許可をもらった We got *permission [leave]* to continue with the plan.

体育館を使いたいのなら先生の許可をもらったほうがいい You should ask for your teacher's *permission* if you want to use the gym.

許可なくその部屋に入ってはいけない No one may enter the room *without permission.*

医者は私に1日2食しか許可しなかった The doctor *permitted [allowed]* me only two meals a day.

あなたはここで商売をする許可を得ていますか Are you *licensed* [Do you *have a license*] to do business here?

5名しか入部を許可されなかった Only five students 「*got admission* [*were admitted*] *to* the club.

‖許可証 a permit; (免許証) a license, (英) a licence; (入場〈通行〉許可証) a pass

ぎょかいるい 魚介類 fish and shellfish (複数扱い); (海産物) seafood ⓤ

きょがく 巨額 巨額の富 an *immense* fortune / 彼は巨額の金を株に投資した He invested *a large sum [amount] of* money in stocks.

ぎょかく 漁獲 今年のイワシの漁獲高は去年を上回った The sardine *catch* was larger [better] this year than last year.

ぎょがんレンズ 魚眼レンズ fish-eye lens ⓒ

きょぎ 虚偽 falsehood ⓤⓒ ◆ 虚偽の申し立てをする make *a false* statement

ぎょぎょう 漁業 fishing ⓤ, the fishing industry /漁業を営んでいる be engaged in *fishing* / 彼らは漁業で生活している They live by *fishing.*

‖漁業協定 a fisheries agreement / 漁業組合 a fishermen's association [union] / 漁業権 fishery [fishing] rights / 沿岸漁業 coastal [inshore] fishing / 遠洋漁業 deep-sea fishing

きょく¹ 曲 (旋律) tune ⓒ; (楽曲) music ⓤ (❖数えるときは a piece of ... とする); (歌) song ⓒ; (小品) piece ⓒ ⇒ 場面・状況別会話 p.1702 /静かな曲 a quiet *tune* / 楽しい曲 an enjoyable *tune* / ピアノで曲を弾く play a *tune* on the piano / 詩に曲をつける set *music* to a poem / 彼女はショパンの曲を弾いた She played *music* by Chopin. / この曲を聞くと子供のころを思い出します This *song* reminds me of my childhood. / この曲ではトランペットが主旋律をとる The trumpets play the melody in this *piece.* ◆ (ラジオで) この番組ではリクエスト曲[90年代のヒット曲]をお届けします We play *requests [the hits of the 90s]* on our radio program.

きょく² 局 ❶【部局】(官庁などの) office ⓒ, (米) bureau ⓒ (複 ~s, bureaux), (英) department ⓒ; (放送局) station ⓒ /テレビ[ラジオ]局 a television [radio] *station* / 郵便[電話]局 a post [telephone] *office* / 私は違う局にラジオを合わせた I tuned the radio to *a different station.*
❷【囲碁・将棋の】game ⓒ /将棋を一局指す

コミュニケーションスキル —許可—
①許可を求める表現

(A) **Can I** borrow your pen?
ペンをお借りしていいですか.

(B) **Could I** ask you a question about today's homework?
きょう出された宿題について質問してもよろしいでしょうか.

(C) **May I** come in?
入ってよろしいですか.

(D) **Do you mind if** I turn on the radio? / Do you mind my turning on the radio?
ラジオをつけてもかまいませんか.

(E) **Would you mind if** I opened the window? / Would you mind my opening the window?
窓をあけてもかまわないでしょうか.

(F) **Is it OK [all right] to** videotape the cartoon program tonight?
今晩のアニメ番組をビデオに録画してもいい?

(G) **Would it be OK [all right] for me to** visit your office at 2 p.m.?
午後2時にお宅の事務所に伺ってもよろしいでしょうか.

☞ (A)は親しい間柄で用いられることが多い.気軽な表現であるが,ふつうの状況なら失礼に当たることはない.語尾に please を付けて,**Can I ..., please?** のようにいうと少し丁寧になる. (B)の Could I ...? は Can I ...? よりも丁寧な言い方で,「できれば」という気持ちが含まれる.

☞ (C)は (A), (B) よりも丁寧な言い方. 面識がない人や目上の人に対しては,この形を用いたほうがよい. **Might I ...?** という言い方もあるが,あまり使われない.

☞ (D)は日本語の「…してもかまいませんか」に相当する表現. (E)は (D)より丁寧な言い方で,if 節は「もし…としたら」という仮定法過去を表すので,動詞には過去形を用いることに注意.

☞ (D), (E)の **Do [Would] you mind my doing?** は「(話し手自身が)…してもかまいませんか」という許可を求める表現だが,動名詞の前に代名詞を付けずに Do [Would] you mind **doing** ...? というと,「…してもらってもかまいませんか」という相手に何かを依頼する表現になる.

☞ (F)は,(A)に近く,親しい間柄では頻繁に用いられる. **Is it OK [all right] if ...?** もよく用いられる. (G)は (F)より丁寧な表現.

②許可に対する受け答え

Can [May] I use your bicycle?
 -(A) **Sure, go ahead. / Yes, of course.**
 -(B) **I'm sorry you can't. / I'm afraid you can't.**
自転車をお借りしていいですか
—いいですとも.どうぞお使いください.
—すみません.だめなんです.

Do you mind 「if I smoke [my smoking]?
 -(C) **No, not at all.**
 -(D) **Well, I'd rather you didn't. / Would you not, please?**
たばこを吸ってもよろしいですか
—ええ,かまいませんよ.
—できればご遠慮いただきたいのですが.

Would it be OK [all right] for me to go out for a while?
 -(E) **Certainly.**
しばらくの間外出してもよろしいでしょうか—いいですよ.

☞ Can I ...? または May I ...? と尋ねられたときの答え方は,肯定なら (A),否定なら (B)が一般的である.

☞ May I ...? と聞かれて Yes, you may. あるいは No, you may not. のように答えると,「よろしい」,「だめだ」といばった感じを相手に与えるので,目下の者や子供以外では失礼になる場合がある. I'm sorry や I'm afraid を最初に付けて,やんわりと断るのがよい.

☞ Do [Would] you mind ...? の場合,mind は「気にする」という意味なので,yes のように肯定で答えると「気になる」→「だめ」ということになる.「いいですよ」という場合は,(C)のように Not at all. などを使って否定で答えることに注意. (D)の didn't は,「ご遠慮ください」に当たる表現.過去形の did not を使って,「できれば」という控えめな気持ちを表す.

☞ (E)の Certainly. を使って許可を与えるのは,(A)の Sure. より改まった言い方.

---

play *a game* of *shogi* (with *a person*)

きょく³ 極 ❶【極限】疲労の極に達する(→疲れ果てる) be *completely* [*utterly*] exhausted **❷【地球・磁石・電極の】** pole ◯ //北[南]極 *the* North [South] *Pole* / 磁極 *a magnetic pole* / プラス[マイナス]極 *the* positive [negative] *pole* / N[S]極 *an* N [S] *pole*; *a* north [south] *pole*

きょくいん 局員 (事務員) clerk ◯; (職員)《集合的》staff ◯

きょく 極右 《集合的》the far [extreme] right, the ultraright《単数または複数扱い》

きょくげい 曲芸 acrobatics, (acrobatic) feat ◯; (離れ業) stunt ◯; (芸当) trick ◯ / 曲芸をする do [perform] *acrobatics* / 犬に曲芸を仕込む teach a dog *tricks* / 象の曲芸 *tricks* performed by an elephant
‖曲芸師 an acrobat / 曲芸飛行 stunt flying, aerobatics

きょくげん¹ 極言 極言すれば *to put it in an extreme way* / その絵に芸術的価値は全くないと極言する人たちもいる Some people *go so far as to say* that the painting has no artistic value.

きょくげん² 極限 limit ◯; (最大限) maximum ◯ (複 ~s, maxima)((略語)max.) //その瞬間,彼の恐怖は極限に達した At that moment, his fear reached *its limit* [*peak*].
‖極限状態 an extreme situation

きょくさ 極左 《集合的》the far [extreme] left, the ultraleft《単数または複数扱い》

きょくしょう 極小 〖数学〗minimum ◯ (複

〜s, minima)《略語》min.)　**—極小の** minimum

きょくせつ 曲折 (曲がりくねり) twists and turns; (浮き沈み) ups and downs ➡うよきょくせつ //様々な曲折の末に彼らは結婚した After many *twists and turns*, they finally got married.

きょくせん 曲線 curve [C], curved line [C] //グラフの曲線 *a curve* on a graph / 曲線を描く draw *a curve* / 川は町の東側をゆるやかな曲線を描いて流れている The river flows to the east of the city *in a* gentle *curve*.

きょくだい 極大 〔数学〕 maximum [C] (複 〜s, maxima)《略語》max.)　**—極大の** maximum

きょくたん 極端 extreme [C] [U]　**—極端な** extreme; (過度の) excessive　**—極端に** extremely; excessively

極端な例 an *extreme* example / **極端に走る** go to *extremes*

彼の意見は**極端すぎる** His opinions are too *extreme*./ His opinions *go* too *far*.

彼女は**極端に**臆病(おくびょう)だ She's *extremely* timid.

彼は彼女の気を引くために**極端な行動に出た** He went to *extremes* to attract her attention.

極端な話, ルールさえ守ってもらえれば後は適当でかまいませんから *To put it in an extreme way*, as long as you follow the rules, you can do the rest any way you like.

きょくち[1] 局地　**—局地的な** local,《公式的》localized　**—局地的に** locally　//けさ, 関東北部に局地的な大雨が降った There were *local downpours* in the northern Kanto area this morning.

‖局地戦 a local war

きょくち[2] 極地 pole [C]; (地方) polar region [C] ‖極地探検 a polar expedition

きょくち[3] 極致 美の極致 *the acme* of beauty; (→完璧(かんぺき)な美) *perfect* beauty / 芸の極致を極める (→奥義を極める) master *the secrets* of the art

きょくちょう 局長 (官庁などの) the chief [director] of a bureau; (郵便局長) postmaster [C]; (事務局長) secretary general [C]; (放送局の) the head of a television [radio] station

きょくてん 極点 pole [C]; (北[南]極点) the North [South] Pole

きょくど 極度　**—極度の** extreme; (過度の) excessive　**—極度に** extremely; excessively　//極度の疲労で倒れる break down from *extreme* [*excessive*] fatigue / 極度の緊張で言葉が出なかった I felt *extremely* tense and couldn't say anything. / 弟は極度の近視で眼鏡が手放せない My brother is *extremely* nearsighted and can't get by without glasses.

きょくとう 極東 the Far East　**—極東の** Far Eastern　//極東諸国[問題] *Far Eastern* countries [problems]

きょくどめ 局留め《米》general delivery [U],《英》poste restante [U]《また a 〜》//局留めで手紙を出す send a letter to *general delivery*

きょくのり 曲乗り trick [stunt] riding [U]; (飛行機) stunt flying [U], aerobatics

きょくばん 局番 telephone exchange number [C] ‖市外局番《米》an area code,《英》an STD code (❖STD は Subscriber Trunk Dialling の略語)

きょくぶ 局部 part [C]; (患部) the affected part; (陰部) private parts, genitals　**—局部の・局部的な** local　//局部的な痛み a *local* pain

‖局部麻酔 local anesthesia

きょくめん 局面 (段階) phase [C], stage [C]; (状況) situation [C]; (側面) aspect [C] //内戦の最終局面 *the* final *phase* of the civil war / 交渉は新しい局面に入った The negotiations entered *a* new *phase*. / 彼の論文はその問題のあらゆる局面を扱っている His article treats all *aspects* of the problem.

◆困難な局面(→行き詰まり)を打開する break *the deadlock* [*stalemate*]

きょくもく 曲目 (演目) program [C]; (個々の曲) number [C] //きょうのコンサートの曲目を知っていますか Do you know *the program* for today's concert?

きょくりょく 極力 (できるかぎり) as ... as possible [*one* can], to the best of *one's* ability; (何としてでも) by all means //極力むだを省くように Try to reduce waste *as much as possible*. ◆極力締め切りに間に合うようにします(→最善を尽くす) I'll *do my best* to meet the deadline.

きょくろん 極論 彼らの意見は極論だ Their opinion *goes too far*. / カレーも好きだしキムチも好きだ. まあ, 極論すれば, からいものなら何でも好きなんだな I like curry and also kimchi —— so, *to put it in* 「*an extreme* [*a very simple*] *way*, I like anything hot.

ぎょぐん 魚群 a school [shoal] (of fish) (❖shoal は大群を指す) ‖魚群探知機 a fishfinder

きょこう[1] 挙行　**—挙行する** hold* [他]; (祝典・儀式を) celebrate [他] [自]; (行われる) take* place //式を挙行する *hold* a ceremony

きょこう[2] 虚構 fiction [C] [U]　**—虚構の** fictional, fictitious //彼は現実と虚構の区別ができなかった He couldn't tell reality from *fiction*.

ぎょこう 漁港 fishing port [C]

きょしき 挙式 (結婚式) wedding (ceremony) [C] //二人は先月挙式した The two *held their wedding* last month.

きょしてき 巨視的 事態を巨視的につかむ(→細部にとらわれずに全体的に理解する) understand *the overall* [*whole*] *picture*; take *a broad view*

きょじゃく 虚弱　**—虚弱な** weak, delicate; (病気がちな) sickly //彼女は虚弱体質だ She has *a weak* [*delicate*] *constitution*.

きょしゅ 挙手 (採決の際の) a show of hands //挙手で決を採る decide by *a show of hands* ◆質問があれば挙手してください If you

きょじゅう 居住 ──居住する live ⓐ, reside ⓐ ∥この車は居住性にすぐれている This car is comfortable to *ride in*.
∥居住区域 a residential area / 居住空間 living space / 居住権 the right of residence / 居住者 an inhabitant, a resident / 居住地 *one's* place of residence

きょしゅつ 拠出 ──拠出する (寄付する) contribute ⓗⓐ, donate ⓗⓐ ∥拠出金 a donation

きょしょう 巨匠 grand master ⓒ; (特に音楽界の) maestro ⓒ (複 〜s, maestri) ∥映画界の巨匠 *a grand master* of the film world ◆彼は20世紀最後の巨匠画家といわれている He is said to *be* the last *great painter* of the 20th century.

ぎょじょう 漁場 fishing ground ⓒ, fisheries

きょしょくしょう 拒食症 【医学】anorexia ⓤ ◆拒食症患者 *an anorexic*

きょじん 巨人 (体の大きい人) giant ⓒ; (偉人) great figure ⓒ

きょすう 虚数 【数学】imaginary number ⓒ

キヨスク ⇒キオスク

きょせい¹ 去勢 (人・動物の睾丸除去) castration ⓤ ──去勢する castrate ⓗ; (動物を) neuter ⓗ (◆通例全身で) ∥彼は自分の犬を去勢した He *had* his dog *neutered* [(《口語的》) *fixed*].

きょせい² 虚勢 bluff ⓤⓒ
[慣用表現] 彼は虚勢をはっているだけだ He's only *bluffing* [*showing bravado*].

きょぜつ 拒絶 refusal ⓤⓒ, rejection ⓤⓒ, denial ⓤⓒ ──拒絶する refuse ⓗⓐ, reject ⓗ, deny ⓗ ∥市は住民の要求を拒絶した The city *refused* [*rejected*] the residents' request. / 彼らは我々の妥協案を受け入れるのを拒絶した They *refused* to accept our compromise. / 私たちの申し出はきっぱりと拒絶された Our offer *was* flatly *refused* [*rejected*]. ◆彼は日本食に拒絶反応を示した She *was averse to* Japanese food.
∥拒絶反応 【医学】rejection

ぎょせん 漁船 fishing boat ⓒ; (大型の) fishing vessel ⓒ

きょぞう 虚像 【光学】virtual image ⓒ ◆彼女は本当の自分とマスコミが作り上げた虚像とのギャップに苦しんだ She suffered because of the gap between her true self and *her false image* invented by the mass media.

ぎょそん 漁村 fishing village

きょたい 巨体 gigantic body ⓒ ∥彼は巨体をソファーに沈めた He lowered *his gigantic* [*huge*] *body* onto the sofa.

きょだい 巨大 ──巨大な huge, enormous, gigantic, giant ∥巨大なコンサートホール a *huge* concert hall / 巨大カボチャ a *giant* pumpkin
∥巨大都市 a megalopolis

きょだく 許諾 ──許諾する (承諾する) consent to ..., approve ⓗ, (許可する) permit ⓗ ◆許諾を得る get *consent*

ぎょたく 魚拓 a *gyotaku*, an ink impression of a fish kept as a trophy

きょだつ 虚脱 虚脱感に襲われる be seized with (*a sense of*) *listlessness*; feel *listless* / 彼女は恋人にふられてから虚脱状態だ She's *been in a state of collapse* ever since her boyfriend left her.

きょっかい 曲解 ──曲解する distort ⓗ, twist ⓗ ∥君は僕の言葉を曲解している You're *twisting* my words.

きょっけい 極刑 (死刑) the death penalty, capital punishment ⓤ ∥殺人犯を極刑に処する punish a murderer with [by] *the death penalty* ◆被告はおそらく極刑に処せられるだろう Probably the accused will *be executed*.

ぎょっと 彼女はその光景にぎょっとした She *was startled* at the sight. / 突然大きな物音がしてぎょっとした I *was taken by surprise* when I heard a loud noise suddenly.

きょてん 拠点 (足場・基盤) footing ⓤ (また a 〜); (とりで) stronghold ⓒ ∥彼らは大阪を拠点に事業を始めた They set *their base* in Osaka and started a business.

きょとう 巨頭 (指導者) leader ⓒ; (実業界などの) magnate ⓒ, tycoon ⓒ ∥巨頭会議 a top-level conference, a summit

きょどう 挙動 (ふるまい) behavior ⓤ; (英) behaviour ⓤ; (行動) action ⓒ
◆挙動不審な (→怪しげな) 男が銀行の近くをうろうろしている There's a *suspicious-looking* man hanging around near the bank.

きょときょと 彼女は友達はいないかとあたりをきょときょと見回した She looked around *restlessly* for her friend.

きょとん 何が起きているのか分からず彼はきょとんとしていた Not knowing what was going on, he *looked blank*.

きょねん 去年 last year
去年の今ごろはとても忙しかった I was very busy about this time *last year*.
今年は去年よりずっと雨が多かった We had much more rain this year than *last* (*year*).
◆1年前のきょう彼女は亡くなった She died *a year ago today*. / 彼らは去年の3月に結婚した They got married *last* March. (◆ last March は4月以降にいうと「この前の3月」の意味にもなるので「去年」であることを明確にするには in March last year のようにいう) / 去年の夏は雨がほとんど降らなかった We had little rain *last* summer.
🔴「いつから柔道を始めたの」「去年からです」"Since when have you been doing judo?" "Since *last year*."

きょひ 拒否 (申し出などに対する) refusal ⓒ; (提案・訴えなどに対する) rejection ⓤⓒ; (要求に対する) denial ⓤⓒ ──拒否する refuse ⓗ; reject ⓗ; deny ⓗ ∥きっぱりとした拒否 *a* flat [*resolute*] *refusal* / 要求を拒否する *refuse* [*reject, deny*] a request / 彼はその事件に関するいっさいの質問に答えることを拒否した He *refused* to answer any questions concerning the case. ◆彼女は英語に拒否反

応を示している She shows *an aversion to* English. / 大統領は拒否権を行使した The president exercised *his veto.*

ぎょふ 漁夫 fisherman [C]

[慣用表現] 両チームが星のつぶし合いをしている間にタイガースは漁夫の利を得て首位におどり出た While the two teams were trading losses, the Tigers *took advantage of their competition* and grabbed first place.

きょまん 巨万 巨万の富を築く make an *enormous* fortune

ぎょみん 漁民 fishermen

きょむ 虚無 虚無的な考え a *nihilistic* idea ‖虚無主義 nihilism / 虚無主義者 a nihilist

きよめる 清める purify ⑭ ‖心を清める *purify one's* soul

きょよう 許容 社会的に許容される範囲内で within socially *acceptable* limits / その程度の間違いは許容すべきだ We should *allow* a mistake like that. / 彼のその発言は許容しがたい That remark of his *is hardly tolerable.*

ぎょらい 魚雷 torpedo [C]

きよらかな 清らかな (けがれのない) pure; (澄んだ) clear; (清潔な) clean; (無邪気な) innocent ‖心の清らかな人 a person *pure* in mind / 清らかな生涯 a *pure* life / この川の水は清らかだ The water in this river is *clear.*

きょり 距離

❶【物理的】(2点間の) distance [C][U]; (間隔) interval [C]

地球から月までの距離 *the distance* from the earth to the moon

教会はここから2キロの距離にある The church is (at *a distance* of) two kilometers from here.

ここから駅までの距離はかなりある It's a good *distance* from here to the station.

彼女は私の家から歩いて行ける距離に住んでいる She lives *within walking distance* of my house.

車間距離を十分にとりなさい Keep a good *distance* from the car ahead.

片目をつぶると距離感がつかみにくい Closing one eye reduces *your sense of distance.*

◆長い距離を歩いて足が痛い My legs feel sore *from the long walk.* / その建物は駅から車で約20分の距離です The building is *about a twenty-minute ride* from the station.

💬「ここから最寄りの駅までの距離はどのくらいですか」「2, 3キロです」"*What is the distance* [*How far is it*] from here to the nearest station?" "It's two or three kilometers."

❷【比喩的】

その件に関して我々の意見には距離(→違い)がある There's *a difference* of opinion between us over that matter.

彼とは距離をおくようにしている I'm trying to *keep* him *at a distance.*

いっしょに旅行に行って彼女との距離が縮まった Traveling together *bridged the gap* between me and her.

ぎょるい 魚類 fish(es)

きょれい 虚礼 empty [mere] formality [C] ‖虚礼を廃する do away with *empty formalities*

きょろきょろ 彼はバスに乗っている間中あたりをきょろきょろ見回していた He *kept looking around* while he was riding on the bus.

ぎょろぎょろ 彼女はぎょろぎょろした目をしている She has *goggle eyes.*

ぎょろり からかうと彼はぎょろりとこっちをにらんだ When we teased him, he *glared at* us.

きよわ 気弱 ―気弱な (臆病(おくびょう)な) timid; (弱腰の)《口語的》weak-kneed ‖気弱で優柔不断な男 a *weak-kneed* and indecisive man

きらい[1] 嫌い

❶【好きでない】do* not like, dislike ⑭; (憎む) hate ⑭ (❖進行形にはできない)

僕はセロリが嫌いだ I *don't like* celery.

規則に縛られるのは嫌いだ I *hate* to be bound by rules.

歯医者に行くのが嫌いだ I *hate* going to the dentist.

彼は私の大嫌いなタイプだ He is the type of person I *hate.*

私のこと嫌いになったの? *Don't* you *like* me anymore? / (→飽きた) *Have* you *gotten tired of* me?

◆彼女は負けず嫌いだ(→2番目では満足しない) She *is never content to be* (*the*) *second best.* / エジソンの学校嫌いは有名だった Edison's *dislike of school* was well-known. / チョークが黒板できいっと音を立てるのが大嫌いだ(→耐えられない) I *can't stand* chalk squeaking against a blackboard. / 僕だって好き嫌いはあるさ I also have *my likes and dislikes.*

💬「彼のこと, 嫌いでしょう?」「そうでもないよ. 少しまじめすぎると思うだけだよ」"You *don't like* him, do you?" "Not exactly. I just think he's a little too serious."

❷【傾向】tendency [C] ➔けいこう(傾向)

彼女はしゃべりすぎるきらいがある She 「has *a tendency* [is *apt*] to talk too much.

きらい[2] 機雷 (underwater) mine [C]

きらう 嫌う

(好きでない)《口語的》do* not like, dislike ⑭; (ひどく嫌う) hate ⑭, detest ⑭ (❖いずれも進行形にはできない)

彼女は人と争うのを嫌う She *doesn't like* arguing with others.

光男がなぜ聡をそこまで嫌うのか分かりません I don't know why Mitsuo *dislikes* Satoru so much.

彼は自分がみんなに嫌われているのではないかと心配している He is worried that he *is disliked* by everybody.

病気の母は父がたばこを吸うのを嫌う My sick mother *hates* (for) my father to smoke.

◆どうやら彼女に嫌われてしまった It seems

like she *has taken a dislike* to me. / お茶の葉は湿気を嫌う(→湿気ですぐに悪くなる) Tea leaves *can go stale easily* in humidity.

きらきら 空に星がきらきらと輝いている Stars *are twinkling* in the sky. / 湖面は日の光を受けてきらきら輝いていた The surface of the lake *was sparkling* in the sunshine. / 子供たちは目をきらきら輝かせて彼の話を聞いていた The children were listening to him *with shining eyes*.

ぎらぎら 砂漠の太陽がぎらぎらと照りつけた The desert sun *glared down* on us. / 敵は私をぎらぎらとにらんだ The enemy stared at me with *glaring* eyes.

きらく 気楽 ──気楽な easy; (のんきな) easygoing; (心配のない) carefree; (安楽な) comfortable ──気楽に easily, at (*one's*) ease, at home /気楽な生活を送る lead an *easy* [*a carefree*] life / 気楽にしてください Please make yourself「*at home* [*easy*]. / 君は気楽でいいなあ(→僕も君みたいにのんきにやれたらなあ) I wish I were *easygoing* like you. / 彼には気楽に話しかけられる He's *easy* to talk to.

💬「ああ, うまくいかない」「気楽にやれよ」 "Oh, I can't make it!" "Take it *easy*."

きらす 切らす 切らす息を切らして階段を駆け上がった She ran up the stairs *out of breath*. / あいにく在庫を切らしています I'm sorry it *is out of stock*. / 塩を切らしてしまった I've *run out* of salt.

きらびやか ──きらびやかな (はでな) gorgeous; (華やかな) glamorous /きらびやかな衣装 a *gorgeous* dress / きらびやかな生活 a *glamorous* life

きらめく (きらきら輝く) glitter ⓐ; (星・光などが) twinkle ⓐ; (宝石などが) sparkle ⓐ /水面が朝日を反射してきらめいていた The surface of the water *was glittering* [*sparkling*] in the morning sun.

きらりと 彼女が振り向いたとき片方のイヤリングがきらりと光った When she turned around, one of her earrings *sparkled*.

きり¹ 霧 (視界を妨げるほど濃い) fog ⓒⓤ; (薄い) mist ⓒⓤ; (もや) haze ⓒⓤ

霧が晴れた[濃くなった]「*The mist* has 「*cleared up* [*thickened*].

山に深い霧がかかっていた The *dense* [*heavy, thick*] *fog* hung over the mountain.

町は霧に包まれていた The town was shrouded [wrapped] in *mist*.

◆霧の深い夜 a *foggy* night / スピードを落とせ! 霧が出てきたぞ Slow down! It's *getting foggy*. / 霧を吹いてからアイロンをかけたほうがいい You should *spray it with water* before pressing it.

きり² 切り (区切り) end ⓒ; (限度) bound ⓒ, limit ⓒ /欲を言えばきりがない There 「*are no limits* [*is no end*] to our desires. / Our desires *know no bounds*.

◆文句を言いだしたらきりがない There's *no end* to our complaints. / きりのいいところで終わろう Let's stop *when we get to a good* *place to leave off*. / 何とか仕事のきりをつけて伺います I'll try to find *a good knocking-off point* in this work and visit you.

きり³ 桐 paulownia ⓒ /桐のたんす a chest of drawers made of *paulownia wood*

きり⁴ 錐 (木工きり) gimlet ⓒ; (ドリル) drill ⓒ; (革などに穴をあける) awl ⓒ /箱にきりで穴をあける bore a hole in a box with *a gimlet*

-きり ❶【…だけ】寝たきりの老人 a *bedridden* old person / 今回は手伝ってあげよう, でもこれっきりだからね I'll help you this time, but *not* [*never*] *again.* / I'll help you, but *just* (*for*) *this once.* / 田中さん夫婦は何年も2人きりで暮らしている Mr. and Mrs. Tanaka have been living *alone* for years.

❷【…以来】それっきり彼女から連絡はありません I haven't heard from her *since then*.

きり 義理
❶【道義・道理】(義務) duty ⓒⓤ; (恩義) obligation ⓒⓤ

> 日本語の「義理」にぴったり当てはまる訳語はなく, duty は「良心・職責などによる義務」, obligation は「契約・道義上果たさなければならない義務」をそれぞれ意味する.

彼は義理がたい He *has a strong sense of duty*.

私は彼に義理がある[ない] I'm *under an* [*no*] *obligation* to him.

彼は私に同情すると言ってくれたが, お義理でそう言っているように見えた He said he felt sorry for me, but I think he said so *out of a sense of obligation*.

そのパーティーに出席しないと義理を欠くことになる It'll *be against social obligation* not to go to the party.

私は義理と人情の板ばさみに苦しんだ I was torn between *obligation and my personal feelings*.

バレンタインデーにはクラスの何人かの男の子に義理チョコを贈った I gave some male classmates *chocolates out of obligation* on St. Valentine's Day.

◆僕に義理立てする必要はないよ You don't have to *feel obliged* to me. / 君にとやかく言えた義理ではないが, もう少しまじめに英語を勉強したほうがいい. I know I'm *in no position to give you advice*, but you should study English a little harder. / 彼がいい歌手だとは義理にも(→どんなに思いやっても)言えない I can't say he's a good singer, *even to be nice*. / 寅さんは義理人情に厚い人だ Tora-san is a *loyal and warm-hearted* person.

❷【姻戚(☸)関係】
義理の兄弟 a brother-*in*-law (✿複数形は brothers-*in*-law) / 義理の母 a mother-*in*-laws

きりあげる 切り上げる (終わりにする) leave* off, wind* up; (仕事を) (口語的) knock off; (端数を) round up; (通貨を) 【経済】revalue ⓐ /58を60に切り上げる *round 58 up to 60* / 平価を切り上げる *revalue* the cur-

きりうり 切り売り 知識を切り売りする *peddle one's* knowledge

きりえ 切り絵 (a) *kirie*, a paper cut

きりおとす 切り落とす cut* off ∥母はカブの葉を切り落とした My mother *cut off* the turnip tops. ◆枝をのこぎりで切り落とす *saw* branches *of* a tree

きりかえ 切り替え (変更) change ⓒⓊ; (転換) switch ⓒ; (更新) renewal Ⓤⓒ
◆彼女は頭の切り替えが早い She is able to *shift mental gears* quickly.

きりかえす 切り返す ハンドルを切り返す *turn* the steering wheel *in the opposite direction* ∥ 彼はその質問に皮肉で切り返した He *countered* the question *with* sarcasm.

きりかえる 切り替える (変更する) change ⑭, switch ⑭ ∥君は頭(→考え方)を切り替えたほうがいい You should *change* your way of thinking. ∥ 政府は突然政策を切り替えた The government *changed* its policy abruptly.
◆彼女はしばらく落ち込んでいたがすぐに気持ちを切り替えた She had been disappointed for a while, but soon *bounced back*.

きりかかる 切り掛かる ナイフで切りかかる (→襲う) *attack a person* with a knife

きりかぶ 切り株 (木の) stump ⓒⓊ; (稲・麦などの刈り株) stubble Ⓤ

きりかわる 切り替わる change ⓘ; (とって代わられる) be replaced with ... ∥その制度はより柔軟なものに切り替わった The system *was replaced with* a more elastic one.

きりきざむ 切り刻む cut* ... into pieces, cut up, chop (up); (肉などを) mince ⑭

きりきず 切り傷 cut ⓒ; (深い) slash ⓒ; (大きく深い) gash ⓒ ∥軽い切り傷 *a* superficial *cut* ∥ 子供はちょっとした切り傷を作りやすい Children are prone to get small *cuts*.

きりきり 胃[頭]がきりきり痛む have a「*griping* stomachache [*splitting* headache]

ぎりぎり 彼はぎりぎりまで切り詰めた生活を送った He *scraped* a living. ∥ 私は列車にぎりぎり間に合った I was *just* in time for the train. ∥ その法案はぎりぎりの過半数で可決された The bill has been passed by a *bare* [*slim*] majority. ∥ 私は彼にそのことをぎりぎりまで話さなかった I didn't tell him about it *until the last minute*. ∥ 彼はぎりぎりひかれるのを免れた He *narrowly* escaped being run over.

ぎりぎりす grasshopper ⓒ

きりきりまい きりきり舞い 彼女はレポート提出の締め切りが迫っているのできりきり舞いしている She *is very busy* because the deadline for the paper is approaching.

きりくずす 切り崩す (ならす) level ⑭; (分裂させる) split* ⑭ ∥山を切り崩す *level* a mountain (*off*)

きりくち 切り口 (木の) cut end ⓒ; (断面) section ⓒ; (袋や包み物の目印) cut ⓒ
◆その問題を別の切り口から論じる *treat* the issue from another *viewpoint*

きりこむ 切り込む cut* into ...; (攻め込む) cut *one's* way into ... ∥まず彼が敵の中へ切り込んでいった He *cut his way into* the enemy first. ◆その件について鋭く切り込む (→問い詰める) *question a person* closely about the matter

きりさく 切り裂く rip*, tear* [téər] ⑭ ∥ 布を切り裂く *rip* a piece of cloth
◆夜のやみを切り裂くような悲鳴が聞こえた I heard a cry *piercing through* the night.

きりさげる 切り下げる (価格を) cut* ⑭, reduce ⑭; (通貨を) devalue ⑭ ∥平価を切り下げる *devalue* the currency

きりさめ 霧雨 drizzle Ⓤⓒ, fine [misty] rain Ⓤ ∥ きょうの午後霧雨が降った It *drizzled* this afternoon.

ギリシャ Greece (❖公式名 the Hellenic Republic) ──ギリシャ人 Greek ⓒ ──ギリシャ語 Greek Ⓤⓒ ──ギリシャ(人[語])の Greek ∥ギリシャ神話 the Greek myths [mythology] ∥ ギリシャ正教会 the Greek Orthodox Church ∥ ギリシャ悲劇 a Greek tragedy ∥ ギリシャ文字 the Greek alphabet

きりすてる 切り捨てる cut* off; (無視する) ignore ⑭, omit ⑭; (不用のものを) discard ⑭ ∥小数点以下を切り捨てる *discard* [*omit*] decimals ∥ 弱者[少数意見]を切り捨てる政策 a policy which *ignores* the weak [minority opinion]

キリスト (Jesus) Christ

キリストきょう キリスト教 Christianity Ⓤ ──キリスト教の Christian ∥キリスト教教会 a Christian church ∥ キリスト教徒 a Christian

きりそろえる 切りそろえる trim ⑭
◆野菜は全部同じくらいの大きさに切りそろえてください *Cut* all the vegetables *to* about the same size.

きりたおす 切り倒す cut* down, fell ⑭; (おのなどで) chop down ∥木を切り倒す *cut* [*chop*] *down* a tree

きりだす 切り出す (話を) broach ⑭ ∥彼女と別れたいがどうやって切り出していいか分からない I want to break up with her, but I don't know how to *broach* the subject.

きりたつ 切り立つ 切り立ったがけ a *sheer* cliff; a precipice

きりつ 規律・紀律 (統制・風紀) discipline Ⓤ; (規則) rule ⓒ; (公的な規則) regulation ⓒ(《しばしば複数形 ～s》; (秩序) order Ⓤ ∥規律を乱す violate *discipline* ∥ 厳しい規律を保つ maintain strict [harsh] *discipline* ∥ その高校は規律がやかましい[乱れている] *Discipline* is strict [loose] at the high school.
◆規律正しい生活をするべきだ You should lead an *orderly* life.

きりつ² 起立 ──起立する stand* ⓘ, (公式

的)rise* 圓 ∥起立！礼！着席！ *Stand up! Bow! Sit down!*
きりつける 切り付ける slash 他 ∥彼はその絵をナイフで切りつけた He *slashed* the painting with a knife.
きりっと その俳優はきりっとした(→輪郭のはっきりした)顔立ちだ The actor has *chiseled* features.
きりつめる 切り詰める (節約する) cut* down [back] on ..., reduce 他 (短くする) shorten 他 ∥支出を切り詰める *cut down on expenses*
◆切り詰めた生活をする lead a *frugal* life
きりとりせん 切り取り線 dotted line C (ミシン目の入った) perforated line C
きりとる 切り取る cut* off [out]; (不要なものを) trim off ∥雑誌から写真を切り取る *cut out* a picture from a magazine
きりぬき 切り抜き《主に米》clipping C, 《英》cutting C(❖×scrapとはいわない)∥新聞の切り抜き a newspaper *clipping*
きりぬく 切り抜く clip 他, cut* out ∥雑誌から記事を切り抜く *clip* an article from [out of] a magazine
きりぬける 切り抜ける (困難を乗り切る) get* [pass] through ...; (困難な状態から脱する) get out of ...; (生き残る) survive 自他; (克服する) get over, overcome* 他自 ∥難しい段階を切り抜ける *get through* a difficult phase / 彼らは人生で幾多の困難を切り抜けてきた They *have passed through* much hardship in their lives.
きりばな 切り花 cut flowers
きりはなす 切り離す cut* off; (分離する) separate 他; (取りはずす) detach 他 ∥シートから切手を1枚切り離す *separate* [*detach*] a stamp from a sheet / 宗教は政治と切り離すべきだ Religion should be *separated* from politics. ◆この2つの問題は切り離して検討すべきだ These two problems should be examined *separately*.
きりひらく 切り開く 森を切り開いて道路を造る *cut* a road *through* the forest / 自らの運命を切り開く *work out* one's own destiny / 自然科学の新しい分野を切り開く *open* a new field in natural science / 多くの人が移住してその土地を切り開いた A lot of people moved there to *develop* the land.
きりふき 霧吹き sprayer C; (香水などの) atomizer C
きりふだ 切り札 (トランプの) trump (card) C ∥切り札を出す play *one's trump card*(❖「とっておきの手を使う」という比喩的な意味でも用いられる) ◆その選手はチームの切り札だ The player is the team's *ace in the hole*.
きりまわす 切り回す (運営・管理する) manage 他; (経営する) run* 他 ∥おばは店をたった一人で切り回している My aunt *is managing* [*running*] the shop all alone.
きりみ 切り身 cut C; (薄い) slice C; (骨のない) fillet C; (厚い) steak C
きりもり 切り盛り management U; (家事・家計の) housekeeping U ◆彼女は若いのに

く家を切り盛りしている She's *managing* her house very well though she is young.
きりゅう 気流 air current C ∥上昇[下降]気流 an ascending [a descending] air current / 乱気流 turbulence
きりゅうさん 希硫酸 dilute sulfuric acid
きりょう 器量 ∥彼の娘は器量がいい[悪い] His daughter *is good-looking* [*plain-looking*]. ∥彼には我々のリーダーになる器量がある He has *the capability* [*ability*] to be our leader.
ぎりょう 技量 (技術) skill U C; (能力) ability U C ∥彼の歯医者としての技量はだれもが認めている Everyone recognizes *his skill* as a dentist.
きりょく 気力 (精力) energy U; (元気) vigor U; (活力) vitality U; (やる気) drive U; (意志力) willpower U ∥気力が衰える lose *one's energy* [*vigor*, *vitality*] / 彼は気力が充実している He's full of *energy*. / 最近何をやっても気力が続かない Lately I haven't had enough *energy* [*drive*] to finish anything. / 私にはこれ以上その件について話し合う気力がない I don't have *the energy* to discuss it any longer. / 彼女は気力だけで仕事を終わらせた She managed to finish the work *by willpower alone*.
きりりと きりりとした顔立ち *chiseled* features
きりわける 切り分ける cut* 他; (肉料理などを) carve 他自 ∥ケーキを6つに切り分ける *cut* a cake *into* six pieces / 客に肉を切り分ける *carve* the meat for the guests
きりん giraffe C (複 ~s, ~)

きる¹ 切る

❶[切断する] cut* 他; (薄く) slice 他; (たたくように) chop 他; (のこぎりで) saw* 他; (はさみで) clip 他; (切りそろえる) trim 他
木の枝を切る *cut* a branch from a tree / チーズを薄く切る *slice* cheese / タマネギをざくざく切る *chop* an onion *roughly* / つめを切る *trim one's* nails / 木をのこぎりで切って丸太にする *saw* a tree *into* logs
彼女はリンゴを6つに切った She *cut* the apple *into* six pieces.
私は髪を短く切ってもらった I *had* [*got*] my hair *cut* short.
【cut+名+形】父は急いでその手紙の封を切った(→手紙を切ってあけた) My father hurriedly *cut* the letter *open*.
【cut+名(人)+名】≒【cut+名+for 名(人)】彼女はすべての子供に1枚ずつパンを切ってやった She *cut* every child a slice of bread. / She *cut* a slice of bread *for* every child.
◆切符を *punch* a ticket / 川の水がせきを切った The river *has burst* the dam. / 船は波を切って進んだ The ship *plowed through* the waves.
❷[傷つける] cut* 他; (切り裂く) slash 他
ガラスの破片で指を切る *cut one's* finger on a piece of glass
彼は誤ってナイフで指を切った He *cut* his finger with a knife by mistake.

彼女は転んで唇を切った She fell down and *cut* [*split*] her lip.
ひげをそっていて顔を切ってしまった I *cut* myself [my face] shaving.
彼は手首を切って自殺した He committed suicide by *slashing* his wrist(s).

❸【流れを止める】
電灯のスイッチを切る *turn off* the light switch / ラジオを切る *turn* [*switch*] *off* the radio / エンジンを切る *cut* [*turn off*] an engine / 言葉を切る *stop talking*
彼はさよならと言って電話を切った He said good-bye and *hung up*.
(電話で)切らずにそのままお待ちください *Hold* [*Hang*] *on*, please.

❹【関係・つながりを】
彼女とは縁を切った I *broke off my relationship with* her.
彼は悪い友達と手を切った He「*broke up* [*is done*]*with* his bad friends.
彼は突然首を切られた(→解雇された) He *was fired* suddenly.
彼女と私は切っても切れない間柄だ She and I lead *intertwined* lives.

❺【限界・基準を】
その選手は100メートル走で10秒を切る The athlete runs 100 meters in *under* [*less than*] 10 seconds.
日本を発(た)つまで1週間を切った We *have less than one week* before we leave Japan.
円が1ドル100円を切った The value of the yen against dollar *has broken* the 100 yen mark.

❻【…しきる】⇒-きる

❼【その他】
トランプを切る *shuffle the cards* / 左にハンドルを切る *turn the wheel* (to the) left / 100万円の小切手を切る *write* (*out*) *a check* for one million yen
その子犬がとてもかわいくて思わずシャッターを切った The puppy was so cute that I *pressed the shutter* without realizing it.
彼女はそのレースでいいスタートを切った She *made a good start* in the race.

きる² 着る

❶【衣類を】put* on; (身につけている) wear*, have* ... on, be (dressed) in ...

put on　　wear

制服[黄色い服]を着た少女 a girl (*dressed*) *in* uniform [yellow]
きちんとした服を着なさい *Put on* a neat dress.
着物を着る機会が全くない I have no opportunity to *wear* a kimono.
彼女はグリーンの服を着ていた She *was dressed in* green.
彼女はこの服を着るといちばん美しく見える She looks most beautiful *in* this dress.
◆彼はパーティーに着ていく服を間違えた(→不適切な服装だった) He *was* inappropriately *dressed* for the party. / 早く服を着なさい *Get dressed* quickly. / コートを着ないで外に出ちゃいけません You must not go out *without* a coat *on*. / このシャツ着てみていいですか May I *try* this shirt *on*? / 母はしょっちゅう私の着るものに関してとやかく言っている My mother is always complaining about my *clothes*.

❷【身に引き受ける】
罪を着る *take the blame* / ありがとう、恩に着るよ Thank you. I'*m so grateful*.

-きる -切る 疲れ切る *be completely exhausted* / 本を読み切る *read a book to the end* / 手持ちの金をあっという間に使い切った I *used up* the money I had in an instant. / どうすればいいのか分からず困り切っている I'*m utterly at a loss* not knowing what to do. / 私の計画に父が反対するのは分かり切っていた It *was quite clear that* my father would object to my plan. / 彼女はマラソンで逃げ切って優勝した She *kept the lead* (*all the way*) *to the finish* and won the marathon race.

キルティング quilting ⓊⒸ
キルト (スコットランドの男性の民族衣装) kilt Ⓒ; (キルティングした掛けぶとん) quilt Ⓒ
きれ 切れ (布切れ) cloth Ⓒ; (ぼろ切れ) rag ⒸⓊ / きれのいいカーブ a *sharp* curve / 彼女は頭の切れがいい She's *very smart*. / この包丁は切れがいい This kitchen knife *cuts well*.
-きれ -切れ (小片) piece Ⓒ; (薄い) slice Ⓒ; (細長い一片) strip Ⓒ; (細長い紙) slip Ⓒ // 紙切れ *a piece* [*scrap*] *of paper* / ベーコン1切れ *a piece* [*slice, strip*] *of bacon* / 肉をもう1切れいかがですか Would you like *another slice of* meat?
◆燃料切れだ The fuel *ran out*. / 彼は昼食にツナサンドを2切れ食べた He ate *two* tuna sandwiches for lunch. / 時間切れで最後の問題ができなかった I *ran out of time* before I could finish the last question.

きれあじ 切れ味 切れ味のよい[悪い]ナイフ a *sharp* [*dull, blunt*] knife / 刃の切れ味が鈍る lose *edge* / このナイフは切れ味がよい[悪い] This knife *cuts* [*doesn't cut*] *well*.

きれい 奇麗

❶【美しい】―きれいな beautiful; (魅力的な) lovely; (かわいい) pretty ―きれいに beautifully
きれいなバラにもとげがある Even *beautiful* roses have thorns.
きょうの彼女はいつもよりずっときれいだ She *is*

much 「*more beautiful* [*prettier*]」 than usual today.
石川さんはきれいな声をしている Ms. Ishikawa has a *beautiful* voice.
彼はきれいな字を書く He has *beautiful* handwriting./ His handwriting is *neat*.
女性たちはみなきれいに着飾っていた The ladies were all dressed up *beautifully*.
◆彼女の家の玄関にはいつも花がきれいに生けられている Some flowers are always *elegantly* arranged at the entrance of her house.
❷【清潔な・整頓(贛)された】 ――きれいな clean; (澄んだ) clear, pure; (整頓された) neat, tidy ――きれいに cleanly; neatly, tidily
きれいな下着 *clean* underwear / きれいな川の水 (the) *clear* water of the river / 心のきれいな人 a person with a *pure* mind; a *good-hearted* person / きれいな白 *pure* white / 部屋をきれいにしておく[する] keep [make] a room *neat and tidy* / 服をきれいにたたむ fold one's clothes *neatly*
食べる前に手をきれいに洗いなさい Before you eat, wash your hands *clean*.
友子は本当にきれい好きだ Tomoko really *likes to keep everything clean and tidy*.
猫はとてもきれい好きな動物です Cats are very *neat* [*tidy*] animals.
◆窓をあけてきれいな(→新鮮な)空気を入れた I opened the window and let in some *fresh* air.
❸【完全に】
そんなにはきれいさっぱり忘れてしまった I *completely* [*clean*] forgot it. / I've forgotten *all* about it.
彼は3年で借金をきれいに返した He *paid* his debt *off* in three years.
びんのラベルはきれいにはがれた The sticker on the bottle peeled off *cleanly*.
その計画をめぐって私たちの意見はきれいに2つに分かれた We were divided *perfectly* in two about the plan.
❹【その他】
きれいな(→公正な)選挙 a *clean* election
このテレビはきれいに(→鮮明に)映らない This television doesn't have a *clear* picture.
その政治家の演説はいつもきれいごとばかりだ The politician always gives *glib* [*high-sounding*] speeches. (❖glib は「口先だけの」, high-sounding は「仰々しい」という意味)

きれい 儀礼 (礼儀正しいこと) courtesy Ⓤ Ⓒ; (形式的な行為) formality Ⓒ / 儀礼訪問をする pay a *courtesy* call / その会議は儀礼的なものにすぎなかった The conference was just *a formality*.

きれぎれ 切れ切れ 彼は息も切れ切れに部屋に駆け込んできた He rushed into the room *out of breath*.

きれつ 亀裂 crack Ⓒ; (人間関係の) rift Ⓒ; (岩・地表などの) fissure Ⓒ / 家の壁に亀裂を見つけた I found some *cracks* in the wall of my house. / この出来事がきっかけで彼らの間に亀裂が生じた This event caused *a rift* between them.

-きれない 今度の日曜日が待ちきれない I just *can't wait for* this coming Sunday. / 彼の無礼にはもう耐えきれない I *can't bear* his rudeness *any longer*. / 彼は生涯で使いきれないほどのお金を手に入れた He got *more money than* he *could spend* in his lifetime. / こんなにたくさん食べきれないよ I *can't eat* this much.

きれなが 切れ長 切れ長の目の人 an *almond-eyed* person (❖almond-eyed は「アーモンド形の」の意味で, 特に東洋人の目を形容して用いる)

きれはし 切れ端 (小片) scrap Ⓒ, piece Ⓒ / 紙の切れ端に落書きをする scribble on a *scrap* of paper / 鳥にパンの切れ端をやる feed the birds some *scraps* of bread

きれま 切れ間 break Ⓒ, rift Ⓒ / 雲の切れ間から日がさしている The sun shines through *a break* [*rift*] in the clouds.

きれめ 切れ目 (途切れ) break Ⓒ; (小休止) pause Ⓒ; (すき間) gap Ⓒ; (裂け目) rift Ⓒ; (終わり) end Ⓒ / 雲の切れ目から山頂がのぞいた The mountaintop was revealed through *a break* in the clouds. ◆切れ目なく続く車の列 *a continuous* line of cars

きれもの 切れ者 sharp-witted person Ⓒ

きれる 切れる

❶ 切断される	break; snap
❷ なくなる	be running short; expire
❸ とぎれる	
❹ 鋭い	cut
❺ キレる	

❶【切断される】 break* Ⓘ; (ぴしっと) snap Ⓘ
あまり強く引っぱらないで. この糸はすぐ切れてしまうから Don't pull too hard. This thread *breaks* easily.
輪ゴムがぷちんと切れた The rubber band *snapped*.
◆電球が切れた The bulb *has burned out*. / 大雨で堤防が切れた The embankment *gave way* because of the heavy rain.
❷【なくなる・終わる】 (じきに使い果たす) be running short; (満期になる) expire Ⓘ
燃料が切れそうだ Fuel *is running short*. / We're *running short of* fuel.
君の定期, 期限が切れてるよ Your commuter pass *has expired* [*run out*].
◆電池が切れた[切れている] The battery 「*has gone dead* [*is dead*]」. / ガソリンが切れた We're *out of gas*.
❸【とぎれる・途絶える】
あれ？電話が切れちゃった Huh? My call *was cut off*.
彼はやっと彼女と手が切れた He *has* finally *broken up with* her.
急な上りで息が切れた I *was winded* by the steep climb.
雲が切れて太陽が出た The clouds *broke* and the sun came out.

エアコンは1時間後にスイッチが切れるように設定されている The air conditioner has been set to *turn itself off* in an hour.

❹【鋭い】cut* ⾃

このはさみはよく切れる These scissors *cut well*.

◆よく切れる[切れない]ナイフ a *sharp* [*dull, blunt*] knife / 彼女は私のクラスでいちばん頭の切れる生徒だ She is the *sharpest* student in my class.

❺【キレる】

あいつはちょっと注意しただけですぐキレる(→かんかんに怒る) He easily *loses it* [*snaps*] at the slightest rebuke.

彼女の話を聞いてもうちょっとでキレそうになった I *almost* '*lost it* [*snapped*] when I heard her story.

❻【その他】

ボールが左に切れた(→曲がった) The ball *curved to the left*.

キロ (キログラム) kilo ⌀, kilogram ⌀; (キロメートル) kilometer ⌀ ∥時速300キロの速度で at a speed of *300 kilometers per hour* (*kph* と略す) / この豚肉は1キロいくらですか How much is this pork *a kilo*? / 私の体重は60キロです I weigh 60 *kilos*.

∥キロカロリー a kilocalorie ((略語)kcal) / キロバイト a kilobyte ((略語)KB) / キロヘルツ a kilohertz ((略語)kHz) / キロリットル a kiloliter ((略語)kl) / キロワット a kilowatt ((略語)kW, kw) / キロワット時 a kilowatt-hour ((略語)kWh)

きろ¹ 岐路 crossroads (単数または複数扱い); (重大な局面) crisis ⌀ (複 crises) ∥人生の岐路に立っている stand [be] at *the crossroads* of *one's life*

きろ² 帰路 帰路につく leave [start] for *home* / 学校からの帰路, 彼女は誘拐された She was kidnapped *on her way home* from school.

きろく 記録

❶【書き記すこと】record ⌀ ⓤ; (書類) document ⌀, file ⌀; (議事録) minutes ――記録する record ⊕, (登録する) register ⊕; (書き留める) write* [put*, note] down

実験の結果を記録する *record* the results of the experiment / 記録上最も暑い日 the hottest day *on record*

この卒業アルバムは私たちの学生時代の記録です This yearbook is *a record* of our school days.

古い記録によれば彼はこの村で生まれた According to *an old document*, he was born in this village.

私は夏休みの間毎日天気を記録した I *kept records* of the weather every day during the summer vacation.

この地震は被害の規模において記録にあるすべての地震を上回った This earthquake caused more damage than any other *on record*.

◆得点を記録する *keep* (*the*) *score*

❷【結果・成績】record ⌀ (◈「記録的な」の意で形容詞的にも用いる) ――記録する (計器などが) record ⊕, register ⊕

記録を樹立する[破る] set [break] *a record* / 世界[国内]記録を持つ hold *the world* [*national*] *record* / 記録に及ばない fall short of *the record* / よい記録を出す make *a good record* / 記録破りの猛暑 *record-breaking* heat

温度計はきょう摂氏30度を記録した The thermometer *registered* 30℃ today.

彼は幅跳びで自己記録を更新した(→破った) He broke *his personal record* in the long jump.

彼女はマラソンの記録保持者だ She '*holds the record* [*is the record-holder*] for [in] the marathon.

∥記録映画 a documentary film / 記録係 a recordkeeper; (計時係) a timekeeper / 記録文学 documentary literature / 公式記録 an official record

ギロチン guillotine ⌀

ぎろん 議論

(話し合い) discussion ⌀ ⓤ; (論争) argument ⌀ ⓤ, dispute ⌀ ⓤ; (討議) debate ⌀ ⓤ ――議論する discuss ⊕; argue ⊕ ⾃, dispute ⊕ ⾃; debate ⊕ ⾃
⇒ 場面・状況別会話 p.1766

【議論の】

彼に罪がないことは議論の余地がない His innocence *is beyond dispute*.

それはまだ議論の余地がある There's *room for further discussion*.

◆臓器移植は議論の分かれる問題だ Transplantation of organs is *a controversial* issue. / この本はこのごろ議論の的(まと)になっている This book *has been much talked about* these days.

【議論を・に】

彼らは議論を重ねてやっと結論に達した After much *discussion* they finally came to a conclusion.

我々はその問題について活発な議論を戦わした We *had a lively discussion* [*argument*] about the issue.

その決定をめぐって白熱した議論になった We *got into a* heated *argument* over the decision.

【議論が・は】

死刑の是非については様々な議論がある There is a lot of *discussion* [*debate*] about whether the death penalty is right or wrong.

その議論は次の会議まで持ち越された The *discussion* was carried over to the next meeting.

【議論する】

そのことを議論してもむだだ It is no good *discussing* the matter.

きわ 際 (端) edge ⌀; (わき) side ⌀ ∥がけの際に立つ stand on *the edge* of a cliff

◆別れ際に彼と握手をした I shook hands with him *when we parted*.

ぎわく 疑惑 (嫌疑) suspicion ⌀ ⓤ; (不信)

doubt [dáut] ⓒ ⓤ ‖疑惑を晴らす clear *the suspicion* / 彼には収賄の疑惑がある He's under *suspicion* of bribery. / 彼の行動は世間の疑惑を招いた His behavior aroused public *suspicions*. / 新しい証拠が出現して彼への疑惑が深まった *Suspicion* of him increased as new evidence appeared. / 人々は彼女を疑惑の目で見た People *viewed* her *with suspicion*.

きわだつ 際立つ (目立つ) stand* out ―際立った outstanding ‖この花に際立った特徴はない This flower has no *outstanding* characteristics. / 彼はスキーが際立ってうまい He is「*outstanding* at skiing [an *outstanding* skier].

きわどい 際どい ‖きわどい勝負をものにする win a *close* game / きわどいところで事故を免れた I *just* [*narrowly*] escaped the accident. / 私たちはきわどいところで(→ぎりぎり)間に合った We made it (*just*) *in the nick of time*.

きわまる 極まる ‖私は感極まって泣いてしまった I *was moved to tears*. / 彼の無礼極まりないふるまいに腹を立てた We were angry at his *extremely* rude behavior.

きわみ 極み ‖これはぜいたくの極みだ This is *extreme* luxury. / 彼の無礼な言動は遺憾の極みだ His rude remark was *most* regrettable.

きわめつき 極め付き ―極めつきの (評判のよい) reputable, esteemed; (悪名高い) notorious; (最高の) the best

きわめて 極めて very, extremely, exceedingly, highly ▶たいへん, とても ‖きわめて重要な問題 an *extremely* important issue / きわめて高度な技術 *highly* sophisticated techniques

きわめる 極める・窮める ‖山頂を極める *reach the top of a mountain* / その調査は困難を極めている They *are facing the greatest difficulty* in their investigation. / その芸を極めるには一生かかるだろう It would take your whole life to *master the art*.

きをつけ 気を付け (号令で) Attention!
きをつける 気を付ける ▶き(気)

きん¹ 金 〔化学〕 gold ⓤ (❖元素記号 Au) ―金の (金製の) gold; (金色の) golden ‖金の指輪 a *gold* ring / 金の延べ棒 a *gold* ingot [*bar*] / 金を掘り当てる strike *gold* ◆スプーンに金メッキをする *gild* a spoon ‖金運 luck with money / 金本位制〔経済〕 the gold standard / 金メダル a gold medal

きん² 菌 (ばい菌・病原菌) germ ⓒ; (桿菌(カンキン)) bacillus (複 bacilli); (バクテリア) bacteria《複数扱い》

きん³ 斤 loaf ⓒ (複 loaves) ‖パン1斤 *a loaf of* bread

ぎん 銀 〔化学〕 silver ⓤ (❖元素記号 Ag) ―銀の silver ‖銀の食器 *silver plate* ‖銀細工 silverwork / 銀製品 silverware / 銀メダル a silver medal

きんいつ 均一 ―均一な uniform; (温度・速度などの) even; (価格の) flat ‖大きさの均一なれんが bricks *uniform* in size / 均一料金 *a flat fee* [*rate*] ◆均一セール *a one-price sale* / あの店はすべて100円均一だ At that shop they *sell everything for* [*at*] *100 yen*.

きんいっぷう 金一封 a gift of money

きんえん 禁煙 禁煙〔掲示〕*No Smoking* / 禁煙運動を行う carry out *an anti-smoking campaign* / 父は禁煙中です My father *has been refraining from smoking*. / ここは禁煙です *Smoking*「*isn't allowed* [*is forbidden*] here. / 禁煙にご協力お願いします Thank you *for not smoking*.
‖禁煙車 a nonsmoking [smoke-free] car

きんか 金貨 gold coin
ぎんか 銀貨 silver coin ⓒ
ぎんが 銀河 galaxy ⓒ, the Milky Way ‖銀河系 the Galaxy, the Milky Way

きんかい 近海 ‖日本の近海ではたくさんの魚が捕れる We can catch a lot of fish in *the seas near* [*off*] *Japan*.
‖近海漁業 inshore fisheries

きんがく 金額 a sum (of money), an amount (of money); (値段・額) price ⓒ ‖この計画には莫大(ベメダィ)な金額が費やされた Huge *sums* were spent on this project.

きんがしんねん 謹賀新年 (I wish you a) Happy New Year

ぎんがみ 銀紙 (アルミ箔(ハク)) tin [aluminum] foil ⓤ; (銀色の薄紙) silver foil ⓤ, (英) silver paper ⓤ

きんかん¹ 近刊 ―近刊の (最近刊行された) recently published; (間もなく刊行される) near publication, forthcoming ‖近刊書 *forthcoming books*

きんかん² 金柑 〔植物〕(米) kumquat ⓒ

きんがん 近眼 《主に米》nearsightedness ⓤ, 《主に英》shortsightedness ⓤ ◆弟は近眼だ My brother *is nearsighted*.

きんかんがっき 金管楽器 brass instrument ⓒ;《集合的》the brass《単数または複数扱い》

きんかんしょく 金環食 an annular eclipse of the sun

きんき 近畿 (地方) the Kinki district

きんきゅう 緊急 emergency ⓤ ⓒ, urgency ⓤ ―緊急の urgent ―緊急に urgently
緊急着陸する make *an emergency landing*
緊急の場合はこの番号に電話してください *In an emergency* [*In case of emergency*], please call this number.
緊急事態に備えて食料を蓄えておかなければならない We must keep reserves of food *in case of emergency*.
父は緊急の用事で出かけました My father went out on *urgent* business.
地震の後すぐに緊急物資が供給された *Emergency supplies* were issued immediately after the earthquake.
‖緊急会議 an emergency meeting / 緊急措置 emergency measures

きんぎょ 金魚 goldfish (複 ~, ~es) ‖金魚をすくう scoop *a goldfish*

‖金魚すくい goldfish scooping / 金魚鉢 a goldfish bowl
慣用表現 女の子はお母さんの後をどこへでも金魚のふんのようについていった The girl *tagged along* her mother wherever she went.

きんきょう 近況 近況をお知らせください Please let me know *how you are getting along [on]*. / 私は時々両親にメールで近況報告をしている I sometimes e-mail my parents and *tell how I'm getting along*.

きんきょり 近距離 short distance ◎ ‖その店は駅から近距離にある The shop is (at) *a short distance* from the station.
‖近距離列車 a local train

きんきんごえ きんきん声 (かん高い声) shrill [high-pitched] voice ◎

きんく 禁句 taboo ◎ ⓤ (複 ～s), taboo word ◎ ‖その話は彼の前では禁句だ The subject is *a taboo* around him.

キング (チェス・トランプ) king ◎ ‖ハートのキング *the king* of hearts ◆キングサイズのベッド *a king-size* bed (✤英語の king-size は主にたばこの長さやベッドの大きさについていう語)

きんけい 謹啓 (個人あて) Dear Sir [Madam]; (会社・団体あて) (主に米)Dear Gentlemen, (主に英)Dear Sirs

きんけつ 金欠 私は今金欠だ Now I'm *broke*.

きんきん¹ 近県 (隣接する) neighboring prefecture ◎; (近くの) nearby prefecture ◎

きんきん² 金券 ‖金券ショップ a discount ticket broker's shop

きんげん 謹厳 ——謹厳な serious, sober ‖おじは謹厳実直な人だ My uncle is *serious and honest*.

きんけんせいじ 金権政治 money politics ⓤ ‖金権政治家 a money-driven politician

きんこ¹ 金庫 safe ◎ (複 ～s), strongbox ◎; (銀行などの金庫室) strong room ◎, vault ◎ 《しばしば複数形 ～s》 ‖金庫を破る crack [break open] *a safe* / 貸し金庫 a safe-deposit box

きんこ² 禁固 prison ⓤ, imprisonment ⓤ ‖裁判官は彼に5年の禁固刑を言い渡した The judge sentenced him to「five years *in prison* [*five years' imprisonment*].

きんこう¹ 均衡 (つり合い) balance ⓤ 《また a ～》, (公式的) equilibrium ⓤ ⓒ (複 equilibria) 《ふきん''》 ‖勢力の均衡を保つ keep *the balance* of power
◆8回裏の古田のホームランが試合の均衡を破った Furuta's home run in the bottom of the eighth inning broke *the deadlock*.

きんこう² 近郊 (郊外) the suburbs, the outskirts, (公式的) environs ——近郊の suburban ‖彼は東京近郊に住んでいる He lives in *the suburbs* of Tokyo. / この野菜はすべて近郊でとれたものだ All these vegetables were grown in *the suburbs*.

きんこう³ 金鉱 (鉱山) gold mine ◎, gold field ◎; (鉱石) gold ore ⓤ

きんこう 銀行 bank ◎ ‖銀行にお金を預ける deposit money in *a bank* / 銀行から金を下ろす withdraw [draw] money from *a bank* / 銀行から融資を受ける get *a bank* loan
銀行に50万円預金がある I have 500,000 yen in *the bank*.
新しいカメラを買うために銀行口座から5万円引き出した I withdrew 50,000 yen from *my bank account* to buy a new camera.
彼女はその事業のために銀行から多額の借金をした She borrowed heavily from *the bank* for the business.
‖銀行員 a bank employee [clerk], a teller / 銀行家 a banker / 銀行強盗 (行為) a bank robbery; (犯人) a bank robber / 銀行預金[口座] a bank account / 血液銀行 a blood bank / 信託銀行 a trust bank / 世界銀行 the World Bank / 地方銀行 a regional bank / 都市銀行 a city bank / 日本銀行 the Bank of Japan

きんこつ 筋骨 ‖筋骨たくましい若者 a *muscular* [*brawny*] young man

きんこんしき 金婚式 golden wedding anniversary ◎

きんこんしき 銀婚式 silver wedding anniversary ◎

きんさ 僅差 (わずかな差) narrow margin [difference] ◎ ◆7対6の僅差で勝つ win *by a close score of* 7 to 6 / 私たちのチームは僅差で彼らに勝った Our team *narrowly* defeated them. / 彼は僅差で知事に当選した He was elected governor *by a narrow* [*slim*] *majority*.

きんさく 金策 彼は金策に奔走している (→金を集めるのに忙しい) He's busy *raising* [*rounding up*] *money*.

きんし 禁止 prohibition ⓤ ◎; ban ◎ ——禁止する forbid* ⓜ; prohibit ⓜ; ban ⓜ
　forbid: 規則で禁止する場合と人が個人的に命令する場合の両方に用いる.
　prohibit: 法的・公的権威によって禁止する.
　ban: 特に社会的・道徳的な問題に関して, 法的に禁止する.
うちの学校ではバイク通学は禁止されている Our school *forbids* [*does not allow*] students *to* come to school by motorcycle.
夜11時以降の自動販売機による酒類の販売は法律で禁止されている The law *forbids* [*prohibits*] selling alcohol from vending machines after 11:00 p.m.
シンガポールでは, 路上につばを吐くことを法律で禁止している Spitting on the street *is prohibited* by law in Singapore.
離陸時の喫煙は禁止されています You *are prohibited from* smoking during take-off.
政府は銃の使用を禁止している The government *bans* the use of guns.
その雑誌は発売禁止になった The magazine *was banned*.
◆追い越し禁止 (掲示)*No Passing* / 横断禁止 (掲示)*No Crossing* / 立入禁止 (掲示)*Keep Out*; *Off Limits* / 駐車禁止 (掲示)*No Parking* / 入場禁止 (掲示)*No Entry* / はり紙禁止 (掲示)*Post No Bills*

きんし (がん) 近視 (眼) (主に米) nearsight-

edness Ⓤ,《主に英》shortsightedness Ⓤ;〖医学〗myopia Ⓤ　―近視の・近視眼的な《主に米》nearsighted,《主に英》shortsighted;〖医学〗myopic ∥近視眼的な見方 a *nearsighted* view ∥ 僕は近視だ I am *nearsighted*.
∥仮性近視 false nearsightedness [myopia]

きんジストロフィー 筋ジストロフィー 〖医学〗muscular dystrophy Ⓤ

きんじち 近似値 approximate value Ⓒ;〖数学〗approximation Ⓤ

きんしつ 均質（均質性）homogeneity Ⓤ　―均質な homogeneous

きんじつ 近日 近日開店《掲示》*Opening Soon* ∥『ミッション・インポッシブル３』近日公開 *Mission Impossible 3 coming soon!* ∥ 近日中にそちらに伺いたいと思います I'd like to visit you *one of these days*.

きんじとう 金字塔（不朽の功績）monument Ⓒ ◆彼は近代科学の分野に金字塔を打ち立てた（→多大な貢献をした）He made a *monumental contribution* to modern science.

きんしゅ 禁酒 abstinence Ⓤ　―禁酒する give* up drinking;（酒を断つ）abstain from drinking ∥父は医者から禁酒を言い渡された The doctor told my father to *give up drinking*. ◆彼は今禁酒している《口語的》He is *on the wagon* now.

きんしゅく 緊縮 curtailment Ⓤ, austerity Ⓤ,《公式的》retrenchment Ⓤ ∥緊縮政策 a *retrenchment* policy ∥緊縮予算 a *curtailed* [an *austerity*] budget

きんじょ 近所 neighborhood,《英》neighbourhood Ⓤ;（近所の人々）neighbors,《英》neighbours;（周辺一帯）vicinity Ⓤ Ⓒ　―近所の neighboring;（すぐ近くの）nearby (✦名詞の前で用いる)

この近所にある映画俳優が住んでいるという話だ They say (that) some movie star lives *in this neighborhood*.

彼女は近所づきあいが悪い[よい] She「*doesn't get along* [*gets along*] well with neighbors.

都会の人は以前ほど近所づきあいをしない傾向にある People in big cities tend to *mix with their neighbors* less than before.

ステレオの音量を下げなさい．近所迷惑よ Turn down the volume of the stereo. It must *be bothering the neighbors!*

母は今近所のスーパーへ行っています My mother has gone to a *nearby* supermarket.

◆近所のおばさん a *neighbor* lady ∥ 休暇中は猫を近所の人に預かってもらおう I'll leave my cat with *a neighbor* during the vacation.

この近所に花屋さんはありますか Are there any flower shops「*around here* [*in this area*]?

ぎんじょう 吟醸（吟醸酒）premium sake Ⓤ

きんじる 禁じる
❶【禁止する】forbid* ⓖ,《公式的》prohibit ⓖ;（人に…しないように言う）tell* *a person* not to *do* ⇨ きんし

何年間もその倶楽部への女性の入会は禁じられていた For many years entry to the club *was forbidden* [*closed*] *to* women.

モルモン教ではアルコールは禁じられている Alcohol *is prohibited* among Mormons.

私は父に夜の外出を禁じられている My father *told* me *not to go out* at night.

◆ロビーでの喫煙は禁じられています You *are not allowed to* smoke in the lobby.

❷【抑える】keep* [hold*] back

彼女の話を聞いて涙を禁じえなかった I *couldn't keep* [*hold*] *back* my tears at her story.

きんしん¹ 近親（近い親戚(⁀)）close relative Ⓒ ∥近親結婚 intermarriage ∥ 近親相姦(⁀) incest

きんしん² 謹慎 彼は担任の先生から１週間の自宅謹慎を言い渡された His homeroom teacher ordered him「*not to leave home* [*to be confined to his house*] for a week.

きんせい¹ 均整（つり合い）balance Ⓤ, proportion Ⓤ Ⓒ ◆彼女は均整のとれた体をしている She has a *well-proportioned* body.

きんせい² 近世 (early) modern ages [times] (✦日本史では江戸時代を指すのでふつう early を付けるが西洋史では「近代」と同義なので early は不要)

きんせい³ 金星 〖天文〗Venus

きんせい⁴ 禁制　―禁制の forbidden, prohibited ∥その寮は男子禁制だ The dorm is「*closed to* [*off limits to*] men.

ぎんせかい 銀世界 目がさめると外は一面の銀世界だった（→雪に覆われていた）When I woke up, I found the whole place *covered with snow*.

きんせつ 近接（近いこと）nearness Ⓤ,《公式的》proximity Ⓤ　―近接した near, close ∥社宅は会社に近接している The company housing is *close to* the office.

きんせん 金銭 money Ⓤ;（現金）cash Ⓤ ∥彼は金銭欲が強い He has a keen *desire for money*. ∥ 彼は金銭感覚がない He has no *sense of the value of money*. ∥ 彼女は金銭感覚がまひしている She is *insensitive to the actual value of money*.

◆金銭的に余裕があればギリシャに行ってみたい I'd like to visit Greece「*if my financial condition permits* [*when I can afford it*]. ∥金銭上の問題さえ解決すればその計画に着手できる Once *the financial problems* are solved, we can set about the plan.

きんせんか 金盞花 〖植物〗pot [common] marigold Ⓒ

きんぞく¹ 金属 metal Ⓒ Ⓤ　―金属の metal, metallic

金属製の棒 a *metal* bar ∥　金属音 a *metallic* sound

これらの化学薬品は金属を腐食する These chemicals corrode [eat into] *metals*.

∥金属探知器 a metal detector ∥　金属バット a metal bat ∥　金属板 sheet metal, a metal plate ∥　金属疲労 metal fatigue ∥　貴金属 precious [noble] metals ∥　軽金属 light metals ∥　重金属 heavy metals ∥　卑金属 base metals

きんぞく² 勤続 高橋さんは今年でこの会社に勤

続25年になる Mr. Takahashi *has worked* in this company *for 25 years* this year. / 同 の会社では勤続10年で特別休暇がもらえる A special vacation is given to those who *have served for 10 years* in the company.
‖勤続年数 the length of *one's service*

きんだい 近代 the modern age, modern times ──近代の・近代的な modern ‖近代的な都市が砂漠の中に突然現れた A *modern* city sprang up in the middle of the desert.
◆産業の近代化 *modernization* of industry / 近代化された工場 a *modernized* factory
‖近代国家 a modern nation [state] / 近代文学 modern literature

きんたいしゅつ 禁帯出 (For) Reference Only ◆百科事典は禁帯出だ It is forbidden to *take out* encyclopedias.

きんたま 金玉 (卑語) balls, nuts

きんだん 禁断 禁断の木の実 (the) *forbidden fruit* ‖禁断症状 withdrawal symptoms

きんちゃく 巾着 pouch ©

きんちょう 緊張 tension ⓤ; strain © ⓤ ──緊張する become* tense; (あがる) be [get*] nervous

> tension: 精神的な緊張のほか，対人または国家間の緊迫した情勢なども表す.
> strain: 過労・精神的な重圧などによる緊張.

テストの当日はとても緊張していた I *was* very *nervous* on the day of the test.
彼女は面接で緊張のあまり簡単な質問にすら答えることができなかった She *was* so *nervous* at the interview that she couldn't answer even simple questions.
彼女の声は緊張で震えた Her voice vibrated with *tension* [*nervousness*].
2国間の緊張が高まって戦争へと発展した The war was a result of *the increasing tensions* between the two countries. (◆「緊迫した情勢」の意味では ⓤ また複数形 tensions となる)
僕はその場の緊張をほぐすために冗談を言ってみた I told some jokes in order to 「*ease the tension in the place* [*break the ice*].
◆彼の顔の緊張が解けた(→リラックスした) All his facial muscles *relaxed*. / 彼は緊張した面もちで部屋に入っていった He went into the room with a *tense* expression on his face.
🗣"選手宣誓なんて想像しただけで緊張するよ"｢気楽にやれよ｣ "I *get nervous* just from thinking of making an oath representing all the athletes." "Take it easy."
‖緊張緩和 (a) détente

きんてい 謹呈 With compliments (◆著者が贈呈本に書く言葉)

きんとう 均等 equality ⓤ ──均等な equal, even ──均等に equally, evenly ‖男女間の機会均等 *equal opportunity* between the sexes / リーダーはメンバーにそれぞれ均等に利益を分配した The leader divided the profits *equally* among all the members.

きんとう² 近東 the Near East ──近東の Near Eastern ‖近東諸国 the *Near Eastern countries*

ぎんなん 銀杏 ginkgo [gíŋkou] nut ©

きんにく 筋肉 muscle [mʌ́sl] © ⓤ ──筋肉の muscular [mʌ́skjələr] (◆名詞の前で用いる) ‖筋肉をほぐす loosen up (*one's muscles*) / 盛り上がった筋肉 bulging *muscles* / 彼は筋肉質だ He's got a *muscular* body. / 水泳は筋肉を鍛えるのに効果がある Swimming is effective in developing *your muscles*.
‖筋肉注射 an intramuscular injection / 筋肉痛 muscle [muscular] pain / 筋肉疲労 muscle fatigue / 筋肉労働 physical [manual] labor

きんねん 近年 in recent years, in late years ‖近年地価が急激に下落している Land prices have been dropping sharply *in recent years*.
◆今年の冬は近年になく暖かかった This year we had a warm winter *compared to the last few years*.

きんぱく¹ 緊迫 ──緊迫する become* [get*] tense, become [grow*] strained ──緊迫した tense, strained ‖緊迫した中東情勢 *strained* situation in the Middle East / 事態は緊迫してきた The situation *has become tense*. / 会議室は緊迫した雰囲気に包まれていた The conference room was in a *tense* mood.

きんぱく² 金箔 gold foil [leaf] ⓤ; (金メッキ) gilt ⓤ

きんぱつ 金髪 blond hair ⓤ, fair hair ⓤ ──金髪の blond ◆金髪の人 a *blond(e)*

ぎんぱつ 銀髪 silver hair ⓤ ──銀髪の silver-haired

ぎんばん 銀盤 銀盤の女王 a queen of *the ice*

きんぴか 金ぴか ──金ぴかの (ぴかぴか光る) glittering; (金メッキした) gilded; (けばけばしい) gaudy

きんぴらごぼう 🍲 *kimpira-gobo*, sliced burdock root (and carrot) sautéed in oil, soy sauce and sugar

きんぴん 金品 金品を奪われる have *one's money and valuables* stolen / 政治家は有権者に金品を贈ってはいけない Politicians are not allowed to give *money or gifts* to the electorate.

きんぶち 金縁 gold rim © ──金縁の gold-rimmed ‖金縁の眼鏡 *gold-rimmed* glasses

ぎんぶち 銀縁 silver rim © ──銀縁の silver-rimmed

きんぷん 金粉 gold dust ⓤ

きんべん 勤勉 (特定のことに熱心なこと) diligence ⓤ; (性格的にまじめなこと) 《公式的》industry ⓤ ──勤勉な (熱心な) diligent; (よく働く) hard-working, industrious ──勤勉に diligently; industriously ‖勤勉な学生 a *diligent* student / よく日本人は勤勉だといわれる It is often said the Japanese are *industrious*.
◆彼女は勤勉だ She *is a hard worker*. / She *works hard*.

きんぺん 近辺 (近所) neighborhood, (英) neighbourhood ⓤ

◆彼女はロサンゼルス近辺に住んでいる She lives *somewhere around* Los Angeles.
きんぽうげ 金鳳花〔植物〕buttercup [C]
きんぼし 金星 金星をあげる score [have] *an upset win* (*over a person who is stronger*)
きんボタン 金ボタン（真ちゅうのボタン）brass button [C]
ぎんみ 吟味 examination [U] ──吟味する（念入りに調べる）examine [他];（精選する）select [他] ∥大学をよく吟味して選ぶ *select* a college with care / 計画の内容を吟味する *examine* the substance of the plan; *put* the substance of the plan *under examination*
きんみつ 緊密 ──緊密な（密接な）close [klóus] ──緊密に closely ∥人と緊密に連絡をとる keep in *close* contact with a person / 2国間の緊密な関係を築く establish a *close* relationship between two countries / 日本経済はアジア近隣諸国の経済と緊密に結びつくようになるだろう Japan's economy will be *closely* [*tightly*] tied into those of its Asian neighbors.
きんみゃく 金脈 gold vein [C];（資金を出してくれる人）financial supporter [C], patron [C]
きんむ 勤務（仕事）work [U];（会社などに勤めること）service [U] ──勤務する（働く）work [自]
姉はその病院に勤務している My sister *works for* the hospital.
彼は今勤務中です He's *at work* now. / He's *on duty* now.（❖on duty は警官・消防士などの勤務について用いる）
わが社の通常勤務時間は午前9時30分から午後5時までです *The normal working hours* in my office is from 9:30 a.m. to 5:00 p.m.
新聞の求人広告で勤務条件のいい会社を見つけた I've found a job with good *working conditions* in the newspaper's want ads.
私用の電話は勤務時間外にかけるようにしてください Private phone calls should be made *outside* (*of*) *working hours*.
彼女は勤務態度が悪い[いい] She *has a bad* [*good*] *attitude while at work*.
∥勤務先 *one's* office / 勤務成績 a job performance / 勤務評定 an efficiency rating / 在宅勤務 telecommuting, teleworking / 時間外勤務 overtime work / 超過勤務手当 overtime pay / 夜間勤務 a night shift
きんもくせい 金木犀〔植物〕fragrant olive [C]
きんもつ 禁物（一般に禁じられていること）forbidden thing [C];（禁句）taboo [C]（複 ～s）∥髪の毛の話は彼の前では禁物だ Talking about hair is *a taboo* ⌜in front of [around] him.
◆いくら運転に慣れているからとはいえ油断は禁物だ You *must not be too relaxed* even if you're accustomed to driving.

きんゆ 禁輸（通商禁止令）embargo [C] ∥禁輸品 embargoed goods
きんゆう 金融 finance [U];（金）money [U] ∥金融引き締め[緩和]政策をとる adopt *a tight* [*an easy*] *money policy*
∥金融会社 a finance company / 金融機関 a financial institution / 金融業 the financial [moneylending] business / 金融恐慌 a financial crisis / 金融業者 a moneylender, a money broker / 金融公庫 a (government-sponsored) finance corporation / 金融市場 a money market / 金融情勢 the financial situation / 金融政策 a monetary policy
きんようび 金曜日 Friday [U] [C]（《略語》Fri.）
➡にちようび ∥きょうは花の金曜日だ *Thank God it's Friday*!（《略語》TGIF）
きんよく 禁欲 ──禁欲的な ascetic;（独身主義の）celibate ∥禁欲生活を送る lead *an ascetic life*
∥禁欲主義 asceticism, stoicism / 禁欲主義者 an ascetic, a stoic
きんらい 近来 今年は近来まれに見る大豊作だった This year we had the richest harvest *in recent years*.
きんり 金利（利率）interest rate [C];（利子）interest [U] ∥金利の自由化 deregulation of *interest rates* / 金利が引き上げられた[引き下げられた] *The interest rate* was raised [lowered]. / ローンの金利は年3パーセントです The loan's annual *interest rate* is three percent.
∥高[低]金利 high [low] interest
きんりょう[1] 禁猟 prohibition of hunting
∥禁猟期《米》a closed season,《英》a close season / 禁猟区 a sanctuary, a preserve
きんりょう[2] 禁漁 prohibition of fishing
∥禁漁期《米》a closed season,《英》a close season / 禁漁区 a marine preserve
きんりょく 筋力 muscle [muscular] power [U];（体力）physical strength [U]
◆筋力トレーニングをする exercise to develop *one's muscles*
きんりん 近隣 ──近隣の neighboring,《英》neighbouring ∥近隣諸国 *neighboring* countries
きんるい 菌類（カビ・キノコなどの）fungus [C] [U]（複 fungi）
きんろう 勤労（働くこと）work [U];（肉体労働）labor,《英》labour [U]
◆勤労意欲がわく[なくなる] feel [lose] *one's will to work*
∥勤労学生 a student worker / 勤労感謝の日 Labor Thanksgiving Day / 勤労者 a worker, a laborer / 勤労所得 an earned income

く

く¹ 苦 (苦痛) pain ⓊⒸ; (心配) worry Ⓤ; (困難) difficulty Ⓤ ◆いじめを苦にする *worry about [over] being bullied* / 祖母は階段を上るのをちっとも苦にしていない My grandmother *thinks nothing of* going up the stairs. / 彼女は苦もなく難問を解いてみせた She solved the difficult question *easily* [*without any difficulty*]. / 寒さは全然苦になりません The cold *doesn't bother* me at all.
ことわざ 苦あれば楽あり No pain, no gain. (→苦労なくして利益はない)

く² 区 (都市の) ward Ⓒ; (区画) zone Ⓒ; (選挙区) constituency Ⓒ ∥神奈川2区 *the second constituency* of Kanagawa / 私の学校は千代田区にあります My school is in Chiyoda *Ward*. (❖手紙の住所としてはChiyoda-kuのように書く)
➔くぎかい, くちょう, くやくしょ

く³ 句 (語句) phrase Ⓒ; (俳句) haiku Ⓤ ∥前置詞句 *a prepositional phrase* / 一句ひねる compose *a haiku*
慣用表現 二の句が継げない ➔ にのく

く⁴ 九 nine; (9番目) ninth

ぐ¹ 具 ingredients ∥このスープは具が多い There are a lot of *ingredients* in this soup.

ぐ² 愚 stupidity Ⓤ, folly Ⓤ ∥そんなものに金を使うなんて愚の骨頂だ It is *the height of folly* to spend your money on such things. ◆愚にもつかないことを言うな Don't talk *nonsense!*

ぐあい 具合
❶【物事の状態・調子】
新しいコンピュータのぐあいはどうですか How *does* the new computer *work*?
このカメラはちょっとぐあいが悪いようだ It seems that *something is wrong* with this camera.
ステーキの焼きぐあいはどういたしましょうか *How* would you like your steak *done*?
実験はどんなぐあいでしたか *How* did you *do* on the experiment?
試験勉強の進みぐあいは順調ですか Are you doing all right in preparing for exams?
❷【健康状態】
ぐあいがよくないので学校を休むことにした I'm *in bad shape* and decided not to go to school.
ここ数日ぐあいがいい I've been feeling well for the past few days.
●「ぐあいはどう」「きょうはきのうよりずっといいよ」 "*How are you?*" "I'm feeling much better today than yesterday."
❸【都合】
きょうは仕事が立て込んでいてぐあいが悪い Today *is inconvenient* for me because I have a lot of work to do.
ぐあいの悪いことに(→運の悪いことに)彼が入ってきた *Unfortunately*, he came in here.
そこへうまいぐあいにタクシーが通りかかった *Luckily* a taxi came along then.
❹【方法】
そういうぐあいにやればよかったんですね I should have done it「*that way* [*like that*].

グアム Guam [gwáːm]

クアラルンプール Kuala Lumpur (❖マレーシアの首都)

くい¹ stake Ⓒ; (建築物の) pile Ⓒ; (テントの) peg Ⓒ ∥くいを抜く pull up *a stake* / 彼はくいを地面にしっかりと打ち込んだ He drove *a stake* into the ground firmly.
∥くい打ち機 a pile driver
ことわざ 出るくいは打たれる A nail that sticks up [out] gets hammered down.; A tall tree catches much wind. (→背の高い木は風当たりが強い)

くい² 悔い regret ⓒⓊ, repentance Ⓤ ∥悔いのない人生を送る lead a life with no *regret* ◆選手たちは悔いが残らないよう全力を尽くした The players did their best *not to regret* the game *later*.

くいあらす 食い荒らす 猿が畑の野菜を食い荒らした The monkeys *attacked* the vegetables in the garden.

くいあらためる 悔い改める 《公式的》repent ⓘⓒ ∥過ちを悔い改める *repent one's* sins

くいあわせ 食い合わせ ウナギと梅干しは食い合わせが悪いといわれている It's been said that *eating* eel and pickled plum *together will make you feel ill.*

くいいじ 食い意地 彼女は食い意地がはっている She *is a glutton.*

くいいる 食い入る その子供はテレビを食い入るように見ていた The child *was staring hard at* the television.

クイーン queen Ⓒ

くいき 区域 (行政上の) district Ⓒ; (ある特色をもつ) zone Ⓒ; (漠然と区分した) area Ⓒ; (特定の人々が住む) quarter Ⓒ; (警官の担当する) beat Ⓒ ∥居住区域 a residential *area* / 危険区域 a danger *zone* / 飛行禁止区域 a no-fly *zone*

ぐいぐい この小説にはぐいぐい引き込まれてしまった I *got absorbed* in this novel. / 子供たちは綱をぐいぐい引っぱった The children pulled the rope *hard* [*with all their strength*]. / のどが渇いていたので水をぐいぐい飲んだ I was so thirsty that I *gulped down* the water. / 彼はみんなをぐいぐい引っぱっていく He leads and manages everyone *enthusiastically*.

くいけ 食い気 appetite ⓊⒸ ◆彼女はまだまだ色気より食い気だ She still prefers *food* to love.

くいこむ 食い込む 肩にロープがくいこんだ

The rope *cut into* my shoulder.
◆体育の授業は3時間目にくいこんだ The P.E. class *ran over into* the third period. / テストで何とかクラスの上位半分にくいこんだ I just managed to *place* in the top half of the class on the test.

くいさがる 食い下がる 彼女はその花びんを売ってくれと彼に食い下がった（→しつこく頼んだ）She *asked* him *persistently* to sell the vase to her.

くいしばる 食い縛る 彼は歯を食いしばって痛みに耐えた He *endured* the pain *with his teeth clenched*.

くいしんぼう 食いしん坊 （大食家）big eater ⓒ, 《軽蔑的》glutton ⓒ
◆あなたって本当に食いしん坊ね You really *eat a lot*. / You really *like to eat*.

クイズ quiz ⓒ（複 quizzes）∥クイズ番組 a *quiz* program [show] / クイズを解く answer *a quiz* / 今からクイズを出すからよく聞いてね Now I'll give you *a quiz*, so listen carefully.

くいたりない 食い足りない 夕食にそば1杯だけでは食い足りない Only a bowl of *soba* for dinner *is not enough for my appetite*. / 彼が相手じゃ食い足りない（→僕の相手としては物足りない）He's *no match for me*. / 彼女のレポートはもうひとつ食い足りない（→不十分だ）Her report *is a little inadequate*.

くいちがい 食い違い 両国間に意見の食い違いは見られなかった There was no *difference of* opinion between the two countries. / 彼女の発言と行動には食い違い（→矛盾）があった There were some *contradictions* between her words and actions.

くいちがう 食い違う （異なる）differ from ..., be different from ...; （矛盾する）contradict ⓗ ∥結果は予想と食い違っていた The results *were different from* expectations. / 彼の言うことは著書で述べられていることと食い違っているようだ What he says seems to *contradict* his books.

くいちぎる 食い千切る bite* off ∥肉を食いちぎる *bite off* a piece of meat

くいちらす 食い散らす 彼はいつも食い散らす（→食べ物をこぼす）He always *spills a lot of food* as he eats.

くいつく 食い付く bite* ⓗⓘ ∥魚がえさに食いついた A fish *bit (at)* the bait.
◆彼はうまい話に食いついた He *jumped at* a good offer. / その子供は私の足に食いついて離れなかった The child *clung to* my leg and wouldn't go away.

くいつなぐ 食い繋ぐ 彼は貯金で食いつないだ He *is eking out a living on* his savings.

くいつぶす 食い潰す 彼は親からの遺産を食いつぶした He *ran through* the inheritance from his parents.

くいつめる 食い詰める （一文なしになる）become* penniless, 《口語的》go* broke

ぐいと 子供は父親のそでをぐいと引っぱった The child *pulled* his father's sleeve *with a jerk*. / The child *jerked at* his father's sleeve. / 彼はコップの水をぐいと（→一気に）飲み干した He *drank* a glass of water *in one gulp*. / He *gulped down* a glass of water.

くいどうらく 食い道楽 epicurism ⓤ, epicureanism ⓤ; （人）epicure ⓒ, gourmet ⓒ

くいとめる 食い止める （抑える）check ⓗ; （防止する）prevent ⓗ ∥彼らは敵の攻撃をうまく食い止めた They successfully *checked* the enemy's attack.
◆火事の被害を最小限に食い止めた We *minimized* the damage done by the fire.

くいにげ 食い逃げ 食い逃げをする「*skip out [run away] without paying the bill*, 《口語的》*dine and dash*

くいはぐれる 食いはぐれる きのうの夜は忙しくて夕食を食いはぐれた I was busy last evening, so I *missed* my dinner. / 手に職をもっていれば食いはぐれることはない（→生活が保証される）だろう If you acquire some kind of skill, you will *be assured of a living*.

くいもの 食い物 （食べ物）food ⓤ, （犠牲）prey ⓤ, victim ⓒ ∥暴力団の食い物にされる *fall prey [victim] to* gangsters ◆詐欺師は彼らを食い物にした The swindler *preyed on* them. / 彼らは国民を食い物にして（→搾取して）いる They *exploit* their people.

くいる 悔いる （悪いことをしたと）repent ⓗⓘ; （失敗や間違いを）regret ⓗ ∥彼は自らの罪を悔いた He *repented of* his sins. / 彼を殴ったことを悔いている I *regret* hitting him.

くう　食う

❶【食べる】eat* ⓗ, have* ⓗ; （虫などが刺す）bite* ⓗ ➡たべる

時間があるなら、いっしょに昼飯でも食わないか Why don't we *have* lunch together if you have time?

昨晩ひどく蚊に食われた I *was* badly *bitten* by mosquitoes last night.

◆このセーター、虫が食ってる This sweater *is moth-eaten*. / リンゴのいくつかには虫が食った穴があいていた Several of the apples had *worm holes*.

❷【消費する】use ⓗ, 《公式的》consume ⓗ; （時間・スペースを）take* ⓗ; （燃料を大量に）guzzle ⓗ; （浪費する）waste ⓗ

この冷蔵庫はとても電気を食う This refrigerator *uses [consumes]* a lot of electricity.

この車はガソリンをあまり食わない This car *does not use [consume] much* gas. / （→燃費がいい）This car *gets good gas mileage*.

このベッドは場所を食う This bed *takes up* a lot of room.

彼とむだ話をしていて時間を食ってしまった I *wasted a lot of time* talking idly with him.

❸【暮らす】live on ...; （生計を立てる）make* [earn] a living

そんなわずかな収入で食っていけるのか Can you *live on* such a small income?

役者で食っていくのは難しい It's difficult to *make [earn] a living* as an actor.

❹【被る】
私は置いてきぼりを食った I *was left behind*.

彼女は先生からお目玉を食った(→しかられた) She *was scolded* by her teacher.
❺【領分を侵す】
今度の選挙で彼は対立候補にだいぶ地盤を食われた A lot of his constituency *was taken* by his rival in this election.

慣用表現 一杯食わされた *I've been taken in.* / 食うか食われるかの世の中 a *dog-eat-dog world* / その家族は食うや食わずの生活をしている In that family *there's not enough food to go around.* / あいつは食えない(→狡猾(こうかつ)な)男だ He is *as cunning as a fox.* / その手は食わないよ *I won't fall for that trick.* / あいつの人を食った(→横柄な)態度が気に入らない I don't like his *insolent* attitude.

くう² 空 彼のバットは空を切った His bat *swung through the space.*

ぐう (じゃんけんの石) rock ©

くうかん 空間 space ⓤ; (…するための) room ⓤ ――空間の spatial /時間と空間 time and *space* / 狭い空間をうまく使う make good use of narrow *space* / 快適な居住空間 comfortable *residential space*

‖宇宙空間 outer space / 生活空間 living space

くうき 空気

❶【気体】air ⓤ
《~空気》
きれいな[汚染された]空気 clean [polluted] *air* / 乾いた[湿った]空気 dry [humid] *air* / さわやかな空気 refreshing *air*

《空気が~空気は》
山の空気はすがすがしい *The air* in the mountains is refreshing.
もし空気がなかったら、私たちは生きていけないだろう If it weren't for *air*, we could not live.

その小さな部屋は空気が悪かった *The air* was bad [stale] in the small room.
◆空気が抜けたタイヤ a *flat* tire

《空気を》
新鮮な空気を入れる let in some fresh *air* / 新鮮な空気を吸う breathe *the fresh air*
◆タイヤに空気を入れる *pump up* a tire; *inflate* a tire / 部屋の空気を入れ替えよう Let's *air out* the room.

❷【雰囲気】atmosphere ⓤ《また an ~》
その夜わが家には重苦しい空気が漂っていた There was *an* unpleasant *atmosphere* in our house in the evening.

‖空気入れ an air pump / 空気感染 airborne infection, infection passed through the air / 空気銃 an airgun, an air rifle / 空気清浄器 an air cleaner / 空気抵抗 air resistance

くうきょ 空虚 emptiness ⓤ ――空虚な (むなしい) empty; (うつろな) vacant ‖空虚な人生 *empty* life / 彼の慰めの言葉も空虚に響いた Even his words of comfort sounded *empty*.

ぐうぐう まだ11時なのにおなかがぐうぐう鳴っている My stomach *is growling* [*rumbling*] though it is only 11 o'clock. / 彼はぐうぐういびきをかいている He is snoring *loudly*.

くうぐん 空軍 air force © 《しばしば Air Force》/アメリカ空軍 the U.S. *Air Force*
‖空軍基地 an air base

くうこう 空港 airport © → 図版

成田空港 Narita *Airport* / 空港から出発する [に着陸する]「take off from [land at] *an airport*

私が彼を空港まで迎えに行きましょう I'll go to *the airport* to pick him up.
大統領の到着に備えて空港の警備が強化された In anticipation of the president's arrival,

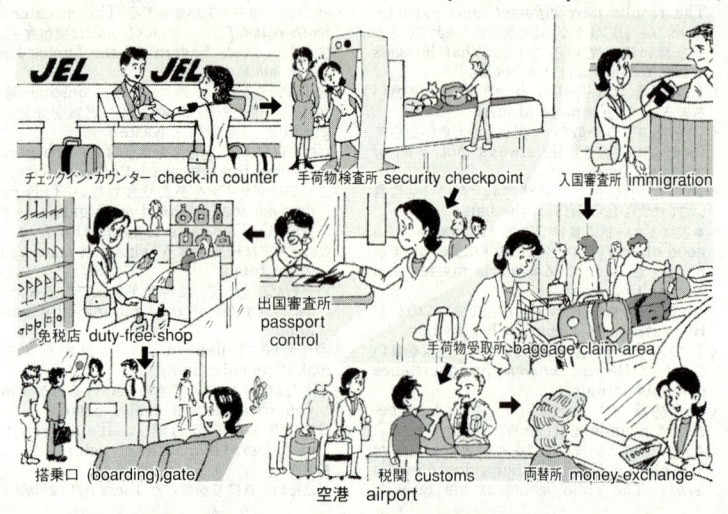

チェックイン・カウンター check-in counter / 手荷物検査所 security checkpoint / 入国審査所 immigration / 免税店 duty-free shop / 出国審査所 passport control / 手荷物受取所 baggage claim area / 搭乗口 (boarding) gate / 税関 customs / 両替所 money exchange

空港 airport

くうしゃ 空車 empty car [taxi] ◎
◆空車《掲示》*Vacant*; *For Hire*
くうしゅう 空襲 air raid ◎ ――空襲する make* an air raid on ...
◆その日東京はB29の空襲を受けた Tokyo *was bombed* by B29s that day.
‖空襲警報 an air-raid alarm [warning]
くうしょ 空所 blank ◎ ‖空所に答えを記入する fill in *the blanks* with answers
ぐうすう 偶数 even number ◎ (↔odd number) ――偶数の even, even-numbered
くうせき 空席 vacant seat ◎; (職・地位などの) vacancy ◎ ‖場内には空席が目立った There were a conspicuous number of *vacant seats* in the hall.
◆空席待ちの乗客 a passenger *on a waiting list* / 議長のいすが空席になっている The position of chairperson is *vacant*.
くうぜん 空前 ――空前の (前例のない) all-time, unprecedented; (記録的な) record; (記録破りの) record-breaking ‖空前の大惨事 an *unprecedented* disaster / その歌は空前の大ヒットとなった The song was a *record-breaking* hit.
◆きのうその遊園地は空前の人出を記録した An *unprecedentedly* large number of people visited the amusement park yesterday. / そのデモは空前絶後の規模で行われた The demonstration was held *on an unprecedentedly large scale that would perhaps be the largest ever*.

ぐうぜん 偶然

(運・不運に左右される) chance ⓤ◎; (偶発的な出来事) accident ◎ⓤ; (偶然の一致・出来事) coincidence ⓤ ◎ ――偶然の accidental, chance; (たまたまの) casual ――偶然に by chance [accident], accidentally
偶然の出会い a *chance* meeting / 奇妙な偶然の一致 a funny *coincidence*
我々がその店で会ったのは全くの偶然だった It was quite *a coincidence* that we met at the store.
同じ場所でこれだけ事故が起こるというのは単なる偶然とは思えない It doesn't seem *accidental* that so many accidents happen at the same point.
◆私は買い物をしているとき偶然彼に会った I 「*came across* [*ran into*] him while shopping. / I met him *by chance* while shopping.

くうそう 空想 (気まぐれな) fancy ⓤ◎; (とりとめもない) daydream ◎; (想像) imagination ⓤ ――空想する fancy ⓗ; daydream ⓘ; imagine ‖空想力を働かせる use *one's imagination* / 彼はさっきから空想にふけっている He *has been daydreaming* for some time. / 自分が空を飛んでいるところを空想してみた I *imagined* myself flying in the sky.
◆空想上の動物 an *imaginary* animal / 彼は空想の世界に閉じこもっている He has retreated into a world of *fantasy*.
‖空想家 a daydreamer / 空想科学小説 science fiction (《略記》SF)
ぐうぞう 偶像 idol ◎ ‖偶像崇拝を禁止する forbid 「*idol worship* [*idolatry*]
ぐうたら slob ◎; (怠け者) lazybones ◎ (複 ~) ――ぐうたらな lazy, idle ‖ぐうたらな学生 a *lazy* student
くうちゅう 空中 the air; (空) the sky; (宙) midair ◎ ――空中の aerial, in the air, midair ‖枯れ葉が空中に舞い上がっていた Dead leaves were flying up into *the air*. / たこが空中でくるくる舞っていた A kite was whirling about in *the sky*.
◆私は空中を歩いている夢を見た I dreamt that I was walking *on air*.
‖空中衝突 a midair collision / 空中戦 an air battle / 空中ブランコ a trapeze / 空中分解 midair explosion
くうちょう 空調 air conditioning ⓤ ‖空調設備(機械) an air conditioner
クーデター coup d'état [kùː deitáː] ◎ (複 coups d'état), coup (❖いずれもフランス語から) ‖クーデターを実行する carry out *a coup (d'état)*
くうてん 空転 審議は空転している The discussion *is going round in circles*.
くうどう 空洞 hollow ◎, 《公式的》cavity ◎
◆産業の空洞化 a *hollowing-out* of industry / その木の幹は空洞だ The trunk of the tree *is hollow*.
ぐうのね ぐうの音 彼女の理路整然とした説明に私たちはぐうの音も出なかった Her logical explanation 「*silenced* us [*left us in silence*].
くうはく 空白 blank ◎, vacuum ⓤ ‖政治的空白 a political *vacuum* ◆そこは空白にしてください Please leave that *blank*.
くうばく 空爆 air strike ◎ ‖敵機の空爆を受ける receive *an air strike* by enemy planes
ぐうはつ 偶発 それは偶発的に起こった It happened *accidentally*. / 偶発的な事件が続けて起こった *Accidents* happened in succession.
くうひ 空費 時間を空費する *waste one's time*
くうふく 空腹 hunger ⓤ ――空腹な hungry ‖空腹を感じる feel *hungry* / 彼らは水で空腹を満たした They satisfied *their hunger* by drinking some water. / 空腹でおなかが鳴っている My stomach is growling with *hunger*.
クーペ coupe [kúːp] ◎ (❖フランス語から)
くうぼ 空母 (aircraft) carrier ◎
くうほう 空砲 blank (shot) ◎
クーポン coupon ◎; (商品引換券) voucher ◎ ‖クーポン券 a coupon ticket
くうゆ 空輸 air transportation ⓤ, airlift ◎ ――空輸する send* [transport] ... by air, airlift ⓗ ‖彼らは被災者に生活必需品を空

輸した They *airlifted* daily necessities to the victims.
クーラー ⚠(ルームクーラー) air conditioner ©; (冷却器) cooler ©
◆この電車はクーラーがよくきいている This train is well *air-conditioned*.
くうらん 空欄 blank ©/空欄に意見を書いてください Write your comment in *the blanks*./適切な単語で空欄を埋めなさい Fill in *the blanks* with the appropriate words.
クーリングオフ (期間) cooling-off period ©
クール 彼はクールな人だ He *is cool-headed*.
くうろ 空路 air route ©◆彼らは空路ロンドンに向かった They left for London *by air* [*plane*]./They *flew* to London.
くうろん 空論 impracticable theory ©
◆机上の空論 *an armchair theory*
ぐうわ 寓話 (動物や物事を擬人化した教訓的な話) fable ©; (抽象観念を比喩的に表現した話) allegory ©
クエスチョンマーク question mark © ➡巻末付録 (句読法)
クオーター quarter ©
クオーターバック quarterback ©
クオーツ quartz Ⓤ∥クオーツ時計 a *quartz* watch [clock]
クオーテーション quotation ©, quote ©∥クオーテーションマーク quotation marks, quotes ➡巻末付録 (句読法)
クオリティー quality Ⓤ∥ハイクオリティーな画像 a picture of *high quality*
くかく 区画 (区分) division ©; (1片の土地) lot ©; (街区) block ©∥行政区画 *an administrative division*/その土地は小さな区画に分けられた The land was divided into small *lots*.◆2区画の土地が売り出されていた Two pieces of *land* were for sale.
∥区画整理 land readjustment
くがく 苦学 彼は苦学して大学を出た He *worked his way through* college.(❖英語には「苦学」のもつ暗いイメージはない)
くがつ 九月 September Ⓤ© ((略語)Sept., Sep.) ➡いちがつ
くかん 区間 section ©/その区間の電車は現在不通になっている Train services on that *section* are suspended now.
くき 茎 (草花の) stem ©, stalk © (❖通例 stalk はトウモロコシなどの太い茎をいう)/花の茎を切る cut off *the stem* of a flower
くぎ 釘 nail ©; (留めくぎ) peg ©
くぎを抜く draw [pull out] *a nail*
タイヤにくぎが刺さっていた I found *a nail* stuck in the tire.
そでがくぎに引っかかった I caught my sleeve on *a nail*.
父は壁にくぎを打ち込んだ My father hammered [drove] *a nail* into the wall.
◆そのふたはくぎで打ちつけてあった The lid *was nailed* down.
∥くぎ抜き(やっとこ) pincers; (てこ式の) a nail puller
慣用表現 子供たちはテレビの前にくぎづけだった The kids *were glued to* the TV./私たちは恐怖でその場にくぎづけになった We *were riveted* [*transfixed*] *to* the spot with fear./彼に忘れ物をしないようにとくぎを刺した I *warned* him not to forget his things.
くぎかい 区議会 ward assembly
くきょう 苦境 difficult situation ©, difficulties, predicament ©∥苦境に陥っても彼は最後まであきらめなかった Although got into *a difficult situation*, he didn't give up to the last./彼女は苦境に立たされている She is in *a difficult situation* [*predicament*].
くぎり 区切り・句切り 区切りのいいところで休憩しよう Let's have a break *when we come to a good place to stop*./彼は仕事に区切りをつけた He *ended* [*stopped*] his work.
くぎる 区切る・句切る (分ける) divide ⓗ; (分離する) separate ⓗ; (仕切る) partition ⓗ; (句読点で) punctuate ⓗ∥部屋はカーテンで3つに区切られていた The room *was divided* [*partitioned*] *into* three sections with curtains.◆単語を読点で区切る *put a comma between words*
くく 九九 multiplication table © (❖ただし、日本とは異なり通例12×12の表を指す. 単に table ともいう)/九九を暗記する learn *the multiplication tables* by heart
くくりつける 荷物を荷台にくくりつける *tie* baggage *to* a carrier
くぐりど 潜り戸 small side gate ©
くぐりぬける 潜り抜ける トンネルをくぐり抜ける go [*pass*] *through* the tunnel/法の網をくぐり抜ける *evade* the law/これまで何度も困難をくぐり抜けてきた(→経験してきた) I *have gone through* a lot of difficulties.
くくる 括る tie (up); (縛る) bind* (up)∥雑誌をひもでくくる *tie* [*bind*] *up* the magazines with string
◆文をかっこでくくる *put the sentence in* parentheses/腹をくくる(→覚悟する) *make oneself ready*/男は首をくくって死んだ The man *hanged himself*.
くぐる 潜る (間を通り抜ける) go* [*pass*] through ...; (下を通る) go [*pass*] under ...∥私たちは大きなお屋敷の門をくぐった We *went through* the gate of the mansion./あのガードをくぐってまっすぐ行ってください *Pass under* that overpass and go straight.◆彼らは法の目をくぐって悪事を働いた They *got around* [*evaded*] the law and committed crimes.
くげん 苦言 苦言を呈する(→率直な忠告をする) give *frank* [*candid*] *advice*; criticize candidly
ぐげん 具現 embodiment Ⓤ ——具現する embody ⓗ
ぐこう 愚行 foolish act ©, an act of folly
くさ 草 grass Ⓤ (❖種類を指すときは ©); (雑草) weed ©
草を刈る mow [cut] *the grass*
花壇に草が生えてきた *Grass* has grown in the flower bed.
私は草の上に横になって本を読んだ I lay down

on *the grass* and read a book.
庭には草が生い茂っていた The garden was covered with *weeds*.
私たちは畑の草を抜いた We pulled *the weeds* out of the field.
その空き地は草ぼうぼうだった The vacant lot *was overrun [overgrown] with weeds*.
◆草の生えた急な斜面 a steep *grassy* slope / 羊が丘の上で草を食(は)んでいた Sheep *were grazing* on the hills.
‖草色 green / 草競馬 a local horse race / 草野球 ⇨ くさやきゅう

くさい 臭い
❶【悪臭がする】—動 smell* 他; (ひどく臭い) stink* 自 —形 bad-smelling, nasty-smelling, 《口語的》smelly, foul
ごみが臭い The garbage 「*smells bad [stinks]*.
父は酒[たばこ]臭い My father *smells of* alcohol [cigarettes].
更衣室は汗臭かった The locker room *smelled sweaty*.
わあ, 臭い God, *that stinks*!
◆ここはガス臭い I *smell* gas here. / 彼の息は臭かった He had *bad* breath.
❷【怪しい】suspicious; (まゆつばの) fishy
その件に関しては彼が臭い I'*m suspicious of* him about it.
そのうわさはどうもいんちき臭いな The rumor *sounds fishy*.
◆何か臭いぞ I *smell a rat*. (❖smell a rat は「怪しいと思う」という意味の口語的表現)
❸【感じがする】
彼女の考え方は古くさい Her ideas *are old-fashioned*.
彼の映画には説教くさいところがある His films have *a moralistic tinge*.
彼はいなかくさい He *looks like a hick*.
❹【大げさな】
臭い演技 an *exaggerated* performance
あまりにくさいせりふを聞いているほうが恥ずかしくなる It's embarrassing to hear such *over-the-top* expressions.
慣用表現 その男は2年間臭い飯を食った That man *had* two years of *prison slop*. / 臭い物にふたをするようなやり方では問題の根本的な解決にならない *Covering up [Putting a lid on] a problem* can't be a fundamental solution.

くさかり 草刈り mowing ◘ ◆そろそろ庭の草刈りをしなければならない I have to *mow the grass* in my yard soon.
‖草刈りがま (小さいかま) a sickle; (大がま) a scythe / 草刈り機 (雑草などの) a weed cutter, a weed cutting machine; (芝刈り機) a lawn mower, a mowing machine

くさき 草木 plant ◘, 《集合的》vegetation ◘

ぐさっと 彼の言葉がぐさっときた His words *went straight to my heart*.

くさとり 草取り weeding ◘ ◆庭の草取りをする *pull out weeds in* a garden

くさのね 草の根 警察は草の根を分けてもその男を捜し出すと言った The police said they would 「*leave no stone unturned* [*make every possible effort*] to find the man.
‖草の根運動 a grass-roots movement

くさばな 草花 flower ◘; (花の咲く植物) flowering plant ◘ / 花壇に草花を植える plant *flowers* in a flower bed

くさはら 草原 grassy plain ◘; (牧草地) meadow ◘

くさび 楔 wedge ◘; (輪止め) chock ◘
‖くさび形文字 a cuneiform character

くさみ 臭み (bad) smell ◘; (強いにおい) odor ◘ / ショウガは肉の臭みを消す Ginger removes *the smell* from meat.

くさむら 草むら grass ◘; (茂み) thicket ◘ / ウサギは草むらに姿を消した The hare disappeared into *the grass*.

くさやきゅう 草野球 amateur baseball ◘; (特に子供の) sandlot baseball ◘

くさり 鎖 chain ◘ / 犬を鎖につなぐ keep a dog on *a chain*; chain up a dog / ドアに鎖をかけるのを忘れないでね Don't forget to put *the chain* on the door.
◆彼は鎖で自転車を柱につないだ He *chained* his bicycle to a post. / 私は犬の鎖をはずしてやった I *unchained* the dog.

ぐさりと 被害者は腹をぐさりと刺された The victim was stabbed *deep* in the stomach. / 彼の言葉は私の胸にぐさりと突き刺さった What he said struck *home* with me.

くさる 腐る
❶【腐敗する】《口語的》go* bad; (かびなどがついて) rot 自; (徐々に) decay 自; (だめになる) spoil* 他
野菜が腐ってしまった The vegetables *have gone bad*.
この魚は腐りかけている This fish *is going bad*.
夏場は食べ物が腐りやすい In summer, food *spoils [goes bad] easily*.
床板が完全に腐ってしまった The floorboard *has* completely *rotted away*.
◆腐った卵 *rotten [bad]* eggs / このリンゴはすっかり腐っている This apple *is rotten right through*.
❷【堕落する】
あいつは根性が腐りきっている He *is completely corrupt* at heart.
❸【その他】
彼は計画が失敗したので腐っている He *is very depressed* because his plan has failed.
あの男は金を腐るほど持っている That man *is rolling in money*.
ことわざ 腐っても鯛(たい) An old eagle is better than a young crow. (→老いたワシでも若いカラスよりはよい)

くされえん 腐れ縁 彼とは子供のころからの腐れ縁だ He and I *have been hopelessly tied since childhood*.

くさわけ 草分け (先駆者) pioneer ◘ / 彼は日本演劇界の草分け的存在だ He is *a pioneer* in the Japanese theatrical world.

くし¹ 串 (小さな) skewer ◘; (大きな) spit ◘ / 彼女は魚をくしに刺した She 「*put fish on*

skewers [skewered] some fish].
‖くし焼き(料理法) broiling on a stick

くし² 櫛 comb ⓒ ‖彼女は髪をくしでとかしていた She *was combing* her hair.

くし³ 駆使 私は参考書を駆使して数学の宿題をやった I did my math homework by *making full use of* study aids. / 彼女は5か国語を駆使する She *has a good command of* five languages.

くじ 籤 lot ⓒⓤ; (宝くじ・賞品分配のための) lottery ⓤ; (くじの券) lottery ticket ⓒ
⇒ くじびき ‖私たちはくじを引いてだれが最初に行くかを決めた We drew *lots* to see who goes first. / 彼はくじで議長に選ばれた He was chosen as a chairman *by lot*. / 彼はくじ運がいい[悪い] He *has good [bad] luck in lotteries*.
◆当たりくじ[空くじ]を引く draw a 「*winning number [non-winning number]*」

くしカツ 串カツ a broiled cutlet on a skewer

くじく 挫く (手足を) sprain ⓣ, twist ⓣ, wrench ⓣ; (挫折 (ざ) させる) frustrate ⓣ; (落胆させる) discourage ⓣ ‖転んで足をくじいた I took a tumble and *sprained [twisted, wrenched]* my ankle. / 彼の野望はくじかれた His ambition *was frustrated*.
[慣用表現] 弱きを助け強きをくじく *help the weak and crush the strong* / 彼らは出鼻をくじかれた They *were frustrated at the start*.

くしくも 奇しくも くしくもその日は彼の誕生日でもあった *By coincidence [Coincidentally]* the day was also his birthday.

くじける 挫ける (落胆する) be discouraged [frustrated]; (がっかりする) lose* heart ‖そんなことでくじけないで *Don't*「*be discouraged [give up]*」*over such a thing.*

くしざし 串刺し 肉をくし刺しにして焼く broil some bits of meat *on a skewer*

くじびき 籤引き くじ引きをする draw *lots* / 順番をくじ引きで決める decide on the order *by lot* / くじ引きでノートが当たった I won a notebook in *a lottery*.

くじゃく 孔雀 (雄の) peacock ⓒ; (雌の) peahen ⓒ; (雌雄とも) peafowl ⓒ

くしゃくしゃ くしゃくしゃのシャツ a *rumpled* shirt / 髪の毛がくしゃくしゃだよ Your hair *is rumpled*. / 彼女は紙をくしゃくしゃに丸めてごみ箱に投げ込んだ She *crumpled (up)* a piece of paper and threw it into a wastebasket. / 彼の顔は涙でくしゃくしゃになった His face *wrinkled up* in tears.

ぐしゃぐしゃ 雨が降って道がぐしゃぐしゃだ The road *is muddy [soggy]* after the rain. / ケーキはぐしゃぐしゃにつぶれていた The cake *was completely squashed*. / 車は事故でぐしゃぐしゃになった The car *was crushed into a heap* in the accident.

くしゃみ sneeze ⓒ ‖私はアレルギーでよくくしゃみが出る I *sneeze* a lot because of an allergy.

くじょ 駆除 extermination ⓤ ―駆除する《公式的》exterminate ⓣ; (取り除く) 《口語的》get* rid of ... ‖家から害虫を駆除する *get rid of* injurious insects in the house

くじょう 苦笑 wry [rái] smile ⓒ ‖彼は自分がなんとばかだったのかと思い苦笑した He *smiled wryly* to think what a fool he had been.

くじょう 苦情 complaint ⓒ; (不平・不満) grievance ⓒ ‖商品についての苦情が殺到している *Complaints* about our goods pour in.
◆隣の人から犬のことで苦情を言われた Our neighbor *complained* to us about our dog.

ぐしょう 具象 ‖具象画 a representational painting

ぐしょぐしょ 走ったらシャツが汗でぐしょぐしょになった My shirt *was soaking [dripping] wet* with sweat after running.

ぐしょぬれ ぐしょ濡れ 傘を持っていなかったのでぐしょぬれになった I got「*dripping wet [soaked to the skin]*」because I didn't have an umbrella.

くじら 鯨 whale ⓒ (複 ~s, ~) ‖鯨の一群 a school [pod] of *whales* / 鯨が潮を吹いている *A whale* is blowing [spouting].
‖シロナガスクジラ a blue whale / マッコウクジラ a sperm whale

くしん 苦心 pains; (努力) effort ⓤⓒ ―苦心する take* pains, work hard
このレポートには彼女の苦心の跡が見られる This report bears traces of her *pains and efforts*.
その作家は苦心の末、やっと小説を書き上げた The author finally finished writing a novel *after making great efforts*.
彼は苦心して大作を完成させた He *took pains to* complete a great work.
彼らは資金集めに苦心惨憺(たん)した They *took great pains* in collecting funds.
◆この機械は私たちの苦心の作です This machine is *the fruit of* our *labors*.

くず 屑 《米》trash ⓤ, 《英》rubbish ⓤ; (散らかった) litter ⓤ; (廃物) waste ⓤ
◆この世のくずども *the scum* of the earth / そのへんの紙くず拾ってくれる? Can you pick up *the wastepaper* around here?
‖くずかご(室内の)《米》a wastebasket, 《英》a wastepaper basket; (駅・公園の)《米》a trash basket, 《英》a litter basket / くず鉄 scrap iron / 糸くず (a) loose thread / おがくず sawdust / パンくず bread crumbs

ぐず dawdler ⓒ, 《米》slowpoke ⓒ ‖おい、ぐず！早くしろ Come on *slowpoke*. Hurry up!

くすくす 妹はテレビを見ながらくすくす笑っている My sister *is chuckling [giggling]* at the television.

ぐすぐす 彼は一日中鼻をぐすぐすいわせていた He kept *sniffing* all day.

ぐずぐず ❶【のろのろしている】ぐずぐずしていたら集合時間に間に合わないよ Hurry up [*Don't dawdle*], or you'll be late for the meeting time. / 何をそんなにぐずぐずしているの What's *taking you so long*? / ぐずぐずしないで早く学校に行きなさい *Be quick about* going to school. / ぐずぐずしてはい

られない There's no time to lose.
❷【文句を言う】終わったことをぐずぐず言ってもしようがない There is no use *grumbling* [*complaining*] *about* what is done.

くすぐったい 足の裏がくすぐったい The sole of my foot *tickles*.

くすぐる *tickle* 他; 〖好奇心をくすぐる *tickle a person's* curiosity / 彼女は弟のわき腹をくすぐった She *tickled* her brother's ribs./ She *tickled* her brother *on* the ribs.

くずす 崩す
❶【こわす・乱す】
山を崩す *level* a mountain / アリバイを崩す *break one's* alibi
列を崩さないように *Don't fall out of* line.
足を崩してくださってかまいません(→楽にしてください) *Make yourself comfortable.*
この手紙は崩した字で書いてあるので読みにくい This letter is hard to read because it is written in *cursive*.
私はきのうから体調を崩しています I *have been out of condition* since yesterday.
❷【お金を細かくする】*break* 他; (両替する) *change* 他
❢「500円玉を100円玉にくずしてもらえませんか」「いいですよ」"Will you *change* [*break*] this 500-yen coin *into* 100-yen coins?" "Sure."

くすだま くす玉 a *kusudama*, a colorful hanging decorative ball that is split open during celebrations

ぐずつく 今週はぐずついた天気が続いている The weather has been *unsettled* this week.

くすっと 彼女は私を見てくすっと笑った She looked at me *with a chuckle*./ She *gave a short chuckle* when she looked at me.

くすねる *pilfer* 他, 《口語的に》*filch* 他

くすのき 楠 *camphor tree* ⓒ

くすぶる 燻る (ぶすぶすと) *smolder* ⓘ; (煙を出す) *smoke* ⓘ 〖火事のあった家はまだくすぶっている The burnt house *is* still *smoldering*./ 彼らの不満はずっとくすぶり続けている Their discontent *has been smoldering*. ◆きのうは一日中家でくすぶっていた I *stayed* [*was stuck*] at home all day yesterday. (❖*be stuck* は「出かけたいが出かけられない」の意味)

くすむ くすんだ色 a *dull* [*dark*] color

くすり 薬

❶【薬剤】*medicine* ⓤⓒ; *drug* ⓒ
medicine: 主に調合された内服薬を指す。
drug: 薬品一般を指すが、現在は麻薬の意味で用いられることが多い。
3回分の薬 three doses of *medicine* / 薬を処方する *prescribe a medicine*
薬が効いてきた The *medicine* has begun to work.
頭痛によく効く薬はありますか Do you have any good *medicine* for a headache?
この薬を飲むと痛みがやわらぎますよ This *medicine* will relieve your pain.
私はかゆい所に薬を塗った I applied *medicine* [*ointment*] on the itchy place.
この薬を食後に飲んでください Take this *medicine* after meals.
家でゆっくりすることがいちばんの薬だ Relaxing at home is *the* best *medicine*.
祖父は薬漬けにされている My grandfather *is loaded up with medicine*.
❷【教訓】
この失敗は彼にとっていい薬になるだろう This failure would be 「good *medicine* [*a good lesson*] for him.
‖薬アレルギー a drug allergy / 薬箱 a medicine chest; (救急薬品の) a first-aid kit / 薬びん a medicine bottle / 薬屋 a pharmacy; (化粧品なども売る)《米》a drugstore, 《英》a chemist's / 薬湯 a medicated bath / かぜ薬 cold medicine, medicine for a cold / 丸薬 a pill / 粉薬 a powder / 座薬 a suppository / 湿布薬 poultice
慣用表現 ばかにつける薬はない ⇒ばか
関連語 カプセル a capsule / 錠剤 a tablet / 軟膏(なんこう) ointment

くすりゆび 薬指 the third finger; (主に左手の) the ring finger

ぐずる (だだをこねる) *get* peevish; (不機嫌になる) *get cranky* 〖その男の子は眠くなるとぐずりだす The boy *gets cranky* when he's sleepy.

-くずれ -崩れ 小説家くずれ a *failed* novelist / 化粧くずれを防ぐ prevent makeup from *being washed away* / 彼は刑事くずれだ He is a *has-been* detective.

くずれおちる 崩れ落ちる (天井・屋根などが) cave in; (崩れる) *fall* down; (崩壊する) *collapse* ⓘ 〖その建物は今にも崩れ落ちそうだ The building *could collapse* at any moment.

くずれる 崩れる
❶【こわれる】*collapse* ⓘ, *break* down, *give* way; (崩れ落ちる) *fall* down; (ぼろぼろに) *crumble* ⓘ; (音を立てて) *crash* ⓘ
地震で家の壁が崩れた The wall of my house *collapsed* due to the earthquake.
❷【形が】*lose* one's shape, *become* out of shape
そのジャケットはすぐに形が崩れた The jacket soon *lost its shape*.
◆その女優は50を過ぎているのに全く体型が崩れていない The actress *keeps up her figure* perfectly though she's over 50.
❸【天気が】
天気は夕方から崩れるでしょう The weather will 「*change for the worse* [*deteriorate*] in the evening.
❹【その他】
汗をかいて化粧が崩れた Sweat *ruined* my makeup.
1,000円くずれる？ Can you *break* [*change*] a 1,000-yen bill?

くせ 癖
❶【習慣】*habit* ⓒ; (奇癖) *peculiarity* ⓒ
癖を直す break *a habit* / 毎朝6時に起きる癖をつける form [get into] *the habit* of get-

ting up at six every morning
彼は頭をかく癖がある He has *a habit of* scratching his head.
髪をいじる癖がついた I *fell into [developed] a habit* of playing with my hair.
なかなか悪い癖が抜けない I can't easily get out of bad *habits*.
いつもの癖で上野行きのバスに乗ってしまった I got on a bus for Ueno *out of habit*.
それは癖になりそうだ It may get to be [become] *a habit*.
❷【特徴】
その先生はくせのある話し方をする The teacher has a *peculiar* way of speaking.
私の髪はくせがある I have *curly* hair.
‖くせ毛 naturally curly [wavy] hair
慣用表現 なくて七癖 Everyone has their *faults*. (→人にはそれぞれ欠点がある)

-くせに 何も知らないくせに口出ししないでよ Don't interfere *when* you don't know anything. / 彼はできないくせに何でもやりたがるんだ He wants to do everything *though [although]* he can't do it.
🗨 「ひえぇっ、おれゴキブリだめなんだ」「男のくせに、情けない！」 "Eek! I'm afraid of cockroaches!" "What a shame! *Are you a man or not?*"

くせもの 曲者（怪しい者）suspicious person ◎；(泥棒) thief ◎ (複 thieves)
◆この問題は簡単そうに見えるところが曲者だ(→実はそうでないから油断してはならない) This problem looks easy, but in fact it's not, so you must be careful.

くせん 苦戦（厳しい戦い）hard [severe] fight ◎；(接戦) close [tough] game ◎, close contest ◎ ‖私たちはそのチームとの試合で苦戦を強(し)いられた We had *a tough game* against the other team.

くそ 糞 ❶【大便】(卑語) shit ◎；(排泄(はいせつ)物) feces；(牛馬などの) dung ◎；(鳥や動物の) droppings
❷【怒り・失望・困惑などを表す】(卑語)Shit!, (俗語)Damn! ‖くそ、財布落っことしちゃったよ *Oh, shit! [Damn (it)!, God damn it!]* I dropped my wallet.
◆くそくらえ！(→地獄へ落ちろ) *Go to hell! / (God) damn you! /* 勉強なんかくそくらえだ(→勉強が何だっていうんだ) *To hell with* studying! / くそばばあ！ *You (old) hag [bag]! /* くそじじい！ *You (old) goat [fart]!*

くそまじめ 彼らはくそまじめだ(→まじめすぎる) They *are too serious*.

くそみそ 彼は僕のことをくそみそにけなした(→さんざん悪口を言った) He *called* me *all sorts of names*.

くだ 管（細めの）tube ◎；(太めの) pipe ◎ ‖穴に管を差し込む insert *the tube* into the opening
慣用表現 父は酔って管を巻いている My father is drunk and *babbling*.

ぐたい 具体 先生は具体例を示した The teacher gave us *a concrete [specific] example.* / 彼の説明は具体性に欠ける His explanation lacks *concreteness [specificity]*.

ぐたいか 具体化 ——具体化する（形をとる）take* form, take (complete) shape；(実現する) materialize ⓤ ‖彼らの計画は具体化された Their plan *materialized [was realized]*.
◆彼女の考えは絵の中に具体化されている Her idea *is embodied* in the pictures she draws.

ぐたいてき 具体的 ——具体的な concrete；(明確な) specific ‖具体的に concretely ‖具体的な証拠 *concrete* proof / 具体的なデータが必要だ We need *concrete* data. / もう少し具体的に説明してもらえませんか Could you explain more *concretely*?

くだく 砕く break* ⓤ；(粉々にする) shatter ⓤ；(粉々に砕く) smash ⓤ；(押しつぶす) crush ⓤ
彼は花びんを粉々に砕いた He *broke* the vase into pieces.
彼の夢は打ち砕かれた His dreams *were shattered*.
◆両親は弟の入試のことで心を砕いている My parents *are very worried about* my brother's entrance examination. / 私は彼女に事情を砕いて説明した I explained the circumstances to her *plainly*.

くたくた 長い距離を走ってくたくただった I *was exhausted [really tired]* from running long distance. / 姉はくたくたになって仕事から帰ってきた My sister came home from work *entirely exhausted*. / このぬいぐるみはくたくただ(→古くてだめになった) This stuffed animal *is worn out*.

ぐだぐだ 同じことをぐだぐだ言うな Don't *repeat* the same thing *over and over*.

くだけた 砕けた（親しい）friendly；(簡単な) easy, simple, plain；(形式ばっていない) informal ‖くだけた会話 *informal* conversations / くだけた言葉で説明する explain in *simple [plain]* language / 彼女はくだけた人だ She is a *friendly* person. / 校長先生はくだけた態度で私たちに接してくれた The principal received us in a *friendly* manner.

くだける 砕ける（こわれる）break* ⓤ, be broken；(破片が飛び散る) shatter ⓤ；(粉々になる) smash ⓤ ‖石でフロントガラスが粉々に砕けた The windshield *broke [was broken]* into pieces because of a stone. / コップが床に落ちて砕け散った The glass fell and *shattered* on the floor.
🗨 「彼、絶対彼女いるよね」「とにかく告白してみれば？ 当たって砕けろ、だよ」 "He must have a girlfriend." "But why don't you tell him you like him anyway? *You have nothing to lose.*"

ください 下さい
❶【もらう】
何か荷物を入れる物をください *I'd like* something to carry my things in.
すみません、ハンバーガーとオレンジジュースをください Excuse me, a hamburger and an orange juice, *please*.
もう一度チャンスをください *Give me* one

more chance.
🇪 「この靴と同じサイズで黒いのはありますか」「はい、こちらになります」「では、それをください」 "Do you have black ones in the same size as these shoes?" "Yes, here they are." "I'll take them, *please*."
❷【依頼】
【please を用いて】

> 語法
> please はふつう話し手の利益になる場合に用いる。聞き手の利益となる内容や単なる指示の場合に please を用いると、なかば強制的な意味となり不自然なこともある。

ドアを閉めてください Shut the door, *please*.
できるだけ早く戻ってきてください *Please* come back as soon as possible [you can].

【will, would, can, could などを用いて】
美術館へ行く道を教えてください *Would* [*Will*] you tell me the way to the museum? ◆would のほうが will より丁寧
荷物を移動してくださいませんか *Would you mind* shifting your baggage?
島田さんの電話番号を教えてください *Could* [*Can*] you tell me Mr. Shimada's number? ◆could のほうが can より丁寧
辞書を使わせてください *May* I use your dictionary?

くださる 下さる 加藤先生は親切にもこの本をくださった Mr. Kato was kind enough to *give* me this book.

くだす 下す ❶【命令】当局はその地域にだれも立ち入らないよう命令を下した The authority *gave* [*issued*] orders that no one (should) enter the area.
❷【判断などを】私たちが下した決定は適切だったと思いますか Do you think the decision we *made* was all right? / 裁判所は彼に無罪の判決を下した The court *found* [*adjudged*] him (to be) not guilty. / 委員会はその計画を採用すべきだとの結論を下した The committee *concluded* that the plan should be adopted.
❸【負かす】日本はフランスを2対1で下した Japan *beat* France by a score of 2 to 1.
❹【腹をこわす】腹を下している have「*loose bowels* [*diarrhea*]

くたばる くたばってしまえ *Go to hell!* / Kick the bucket! / 僕らは3時間の猛練習でくたばった We *were utterly exhausted* from three hours of hard training.

くたびれる be tired; (着古されている) be worn out ⇒つかれる(疲れる) ⇒待ちくたびれる / *be tired of* waiting / 長い間歩いたのでくたびれた I *was tired* after the long walk. / 彼のコートはくたびれている His coat *is*「*worn out* [*the worse for wear*]. ◆みんなくたびれ果てた Everyone *got totally exhausted*.

くだもの 果物 fruit ⓤⓒ ◆集合的に果物の総称としては ⓤ、種類をいうときは ⓒ /果物の缶詰 a can of *fruit* / マンゴーやパパイヤなどの果物 *fruits* such as mangoes and papayas / 姉はいろいろな果物を買った My sister bought various kinds of *fruit*.
‖果物ナイフ a fruit knife / 果物屋 a fruit store [《米》shop]

くだらない (取るに足りない) trivial, trifling; (価値のない) worthless; (ばかげた) nonsense, (《英口語的》) rubbishy ⇒つまらない /そんなくだらないことで電話をしてくるなよ Don't call me about [over] such a *trivial* matter.
◆彼女の本は全くくだらない Her book is a load of *rubbish* [《口語的》*poppycock*]. / 私たちは彼のくだらないジョークに飽き飽きしている We are weary of his *silly* jokes. / くだらないことを言ってないで勉強しなさい Stop talking *nonsense* and study.

🇪 「この湖にはネッシーという怪獣がいるんだよ」「くだらない、そんなの信じないね」 "There's a monster called Nessie in this lake." "*Nonsense*. I don't believe it."

くだり¹ 下り ━下りの down /下りのエスカレーターはどこですか Where's the *down* escalator? ◆下り線のプラットホーム a platform *for outbound trains*
‖下り列車《米》an outbound [《英》a down] train

くだり² 件 passage ⓒ /僕はその小説のこのくだりが大好きなんだ I like this *passage* of the novel very much.

くだりざか 下り坂 downward slope ⓒ
◆あの峠を越えれば道はそこから下り坂になる When we cross over the mountain pass, the path *goes down* from there. / あの会社も景気が下り坂だという話だ They say (the) business at the company *is declining*. / 天気は下り坂らしい I hear that the weather *will change for the worse*.

くだる 下る ❶【下降】go* down, descend ⓦ ⇒おりる /私たちはボートで川を下った We *went down* the river in a boat. / We *boated down* the river.
◆山道を下ると目の前に湖が見えてきた When we *climbed down* the mountain path, a lake came into sight before us.
❷【判決】その男に殺人罪の有罪判決が下った The man *was found* guilty of murder.
❸【下回る】その事故の犠牲者はおそらく300人は下らない(→300人以上)だろう The number of victims in the accident will be *more than* 300.
❹【腹が】腹が下っている have「*loose bowels* [*diarrhea*]

くち 口

❶体の部位	mouth; lip
❷言葉	
❸味覚	taste
❹開口部	mouth

❶【体の部位】mouth ⓒ (複 ～s [máuðz]); (唇) lip ⓒ
口をあける[閉じる] open [close] *one's mouth* / 口をすすぐ rinse out *one's mouth* / 口をす

ほめる pucker (up) *one's lips* / 口をとがらす pout *one's lips* / 口をきっと結ぶ pull in (*one's lips*)

ナプキンで口をふきなさい Wipe *your mouth with your napkin.*

食べ物で口をいっぱいにしたままでしゃべってはいけません Don't speak with *your mouth full.*

その犬は骨を口にくわえている The dog has a bone *in his mouth.*

トムはクッキーを口に詰め込んだ Tom stuffed *his mouth* with cookies.

子供は口をぽかんとあけてグライダーに見とれていた The child admired the glider 「*with open mouth* [*with his mouth open*].

◆驚いたことに彼はそのケーキをひと口で食べてしまった To our surprise, he ate the cake *in one bite.* / 彼女はコーヒーをひと口(→少し)飲んだ She 「*drank a bit of* [*took a sip of*] *coffee.* / このカレーはからく口の中(→舌)がひりひりする This curry is very hot and burns *my tongue.*

❷【言葉】

彼女はそのことについていまだに口を閉ざしたままだ She *hasn't told* anything about it yet.

口では言えないほどうれしかった I just *can't tell* you how glad I was.

彼は口ばかりで行動が伴わない He's *all talk* and no action.

君の口からそんな言葉を聞くのはつらい It's painful for me to hear such words *from you* [*your own lips*].

彼女は名前を聞かれ口から出まかせを言った When she was asked her name, she answered *what popped into her head.*

❸【味覚】taste ⓊU

これは僕の口には合わない This food *doesn't* 「*suit my taste* [*agree with me*].

◆お口に合うとよいのですが I hope you *like it.*

❹【開口部】mouth ⒸC

びんの口 *the mouth* of a bottle

◆新宿駅の西口 *the west exit* [(→改札口)*gate*] *of Shinjuku station* / 地面に大きな穴がぽっかり口を開いた A yawning gulf *opened up in the ground.*

❺【その他】

彼はいつも僕に仕事の口を紹介してくれる He always gets *a job* for me.

酒はいける口ですか Are you *a drinker*? / Do you *like alcoholic drinks*?

❻【慣用表現】

【あいた口がふさがらない】彼の無作法な態度にはあいた口がふさがらなかった I 「*was dumbfounded* [*gaped*] at his rude attitude.

【口がうまい】あいつは口がうまいからだまされないようにしろ You should take care not to be cheated by him because he *has a smooth tongue.*

【口が重い】正は口が重い(→言葉数の少ない人だ) Tadashi *is a man of few words.*

【口がかたい】心配しなくてもいい. あいつは口がかたい(→秘密を守れる)から Don't worry. He *can keep a secret.*

【口が軽い】彼女は口が軽い She *has* [*is*] *a big mouth.* / 彼は酒を飲むと急に口が軽くなる Alcohol suddenly *loosens his tongue.*

【口が裂けても】このことは口が裂けても(→どんなことがあっても)口外しないと約束するよ I promise not to tell anybody about this *whatever happens.*

【口が過ぎる】文句ばかり言って, ちょっと口が過ぎたよ I *went too far in complaining* to you.

【口が滑る】ごめん, つい口が滑っちゃったんだ I'm sorry. It *was just a slip of the tongue.*

【口が達者だ】彼は口が達者だ He 「*has a glib tongue* [*is glib*].

【口が減らない】おまえも口が減らないやつだな You *never shut up*, do you?

【口から先に生まれる】彼は口から先に生まれたような男だ He must *have been born with a big mouth.*

【口が悪い】彼女は口が悪いが気は優しい She *has a sharp tongue*, but she is kind.

【口にしない】彼女は肉をいっさい口にしない She *never eats* meat. / 彼は決して病気のことを口にしなかった He *never* 「*referred to* [*mentioned*] his illness.

【口に出す】自分の感情を口に出す *give utterance to one's emotions* / 我々はみんな彼が怪しいと思っているが決して口には出さない We are all suspicious of him, but *never express it.*

【口まで出かかる】その言葉, 口まで出かかっているんだがなあ The word is *on the tip of my tongue.*

【口八丁手八丁】彼は口八丁手八丁だ He *is as good at his job as he is at talking.*

【口をきく】speak* ⾃他; (気持ちや意見を伝える) tell* ⾃他; (言う) say* ⾃他; (話をする) talk ⾃他 / 真理とはまだ口をきいたことがない I *have never talked to* Mari. / 自分の母親にそんな口をきいてはいけない Don't *talk like that to your mother.* / 大きな口をきくな Don't *talk big.* / その子供はおびえて口がきけなかった The child *was too terrified to speak.* / The child was so terrified that he lost his speech.

◆口のきき方に気をつけろ Watch *your mouth* [*language*].

【口を極めて】みんな彼女のことを口を極めてほめそやした Everyone *praised her to the skies.*

【口をすっぱくする】あいつに金を貸してはだめだと口をすっぱくして(→何度も)言ったのに I told you *again and again* that you shouldn't lend him money.

【口をそろえる】隆介のことになるとみんな口をそろえて「あいつは頭がいい」と言う When it comes to Ryusuke, everyone says "He is clever" 「*with one voice* [*in chorus*].

【口を出す】彼女はいつも僕のやることなすことに口を出す She *is* always 「*meddling in* [*sticking her nose into*] my affairs.

【口をつく】不満の言葉が彼らの口をついて出た Words of complaint *poured from* their

lips.
【口をつぐむ】その件に関し，関係者は一様に口をつぐんだ Every person concerned *clammed up* about the matter.
【口を慎む】口を慎みなさい *Hold your tongue!*
【口を濁す】彼は結婚の話になると口を濁した He *spoke evasively* when the subject of marriage came up.
【口をはさむ】「私はどうなるのよ」と彼女は私たちの話に口をはさんだ "What about me?" she *interrupted* [*cut in, put in*].
【口を割る】ついに犯人は口を割り始めた(→白状し始めた) At last the murderer began to *confess* [*come clean, open his mouth*].
[ことわざ] 口は災いのもと Out of the mouth comes evil. / 死人に口なし ➾しにん / 人の口に戸は立てられぬ ➾と(戸) / 良薬は口に苦し ➾りょうやく

ぐち 愚痴 complaint [C], grumble [C] ∥彼のぐちにはみなうんざりしている Everyone is weary of his *complaints.*
◆彼がぐちをこぼすのも無理はない It is natural (that) he should *complain.* / 彼女はいつも仕事のぐちばかりこぼしている She *is* always *grumbling about* her job.

くちあたり 口当たり 口当たりのよいウイスキー a *smooth* whiskey

くちうつし 口移し ―口移しの mouth-to-mouth ➾くちづたえ ◆この技は代々口移しに伝えられてきた This technique has been inherited *orally* for generations. / 親鳥はひな鳥に口移しでえさをやった The mother hen *passed food from her beak to* the chick's beak.

くちうら 口裏 彼らはその事故を見なかったことにしようと口裏を合わせた(→前もって申し合わせた) They *agreed in advance to* pretend not to have seen the accident.

くちうるさい 口煩い nagging, 《口語的》picky ◆母は私の着るものに関しては口うるさい My mother *nags* about what I wear.

くちえ 口絵 frontispiece [C]

くちかず 口数 口数が多い(→おしゃべりだ) *be talkative* / 父は口数の少ない人だ My father is a man *of few words.*/ My father *doesn't talk much.*

くちがね 口金 (留め金) clasp [C]; (びんのふた) cap [C]

くちきき 口利き おじの口ききでその会社に就職することができた I got a position in the company *by* [*through*] *the good offices of* my uncle. ➾あっせん

くちぎたない 口汚い foul-mouthed, abusive ◆人を口汚くののしる *call* a person *names*

くちくかん 駆逐艦 destroyer [C]

くちくする 駆逐する drive* off [out], repel [他] ∥敵を駆逐する *drive off* an enemy

くちぐせ 口癖 a habit of saying ...; (好きな言葉) favorite [pet] phrase [C] ∥「英語は毎日勉強しないとだめだ」というのが父の口癖だった My father *had a habit of saying,* "You should study English every day."

くちぐちに 口々に (いっせいに) in unison ➾いっせい(一斉) ∥子供たちは「ディズニーランドに連れてって」と口々に叫んだ "Take us to Disneyland!" the children shouted *in unison.*
◆彼らは口々に先生に対する文句を言った(→だれもが文句を言った) *Every one* of them complained about their teacher.

くちぐるま 口車 (甘い言葉) sweet [honeyed] words ◆彼女は店員の口車に乗せられて高価な指輪を買ってしまった She *was sweet-talked* [*cajoled*] by a clerk *into* buying an expensive ring.

くちげんか 口喧嘩 quarrel [C], argument [C] ―口げんかする quarrel [自], have* words [an argument] (with *a person*) ∥彼らの間では口げんかが絶えない They *are* always *quarreling with* each other.

くちごたえ 口答え ―口答えする talk [answer] back ∥よくも私に向かって口答えができるね How dare you *talk back to* me!

くちコミ 口コミ ―口コミで by word of mouth ∥そのレストランの評判は口コミで広がった The rumor about the restaurant spread [got around] *by word of mouth.*

くちごもる 口籠る (ぼそぼそ言う) mumble [自][他]; (どもる) stammer [自][他]; (ためらって) 《米》hem [《英》hum] and haw ∥口ごもっておわびを言う *stammer out* an apology

くちさき 口先 彼らの方針に口先だけで賛同する give [pay] *lip service* to their policy / 口先だけの約束 an *empty* promise / 彼は口先ばっかりだ He's *all talk* [*mouth*]./ He never does what he says he'll do.

くちずさむ 口遊む croon [他][自], sing* to *oneself* ∥童謡を口ずさむ *croon* a children's song

くちぞえ 口添え recommendation [U][C] ―口添えする recommend [他] ∥友人の口添えでそのクラブに入会した I joined the club on my friend's *recommendation.*

くちだし 口出し ―口出しする interfere [自], 《口語的》stick* *one's* nose into ..., 《口語的》horn in (to ...) ∥私たちのことに口出ししないで Don't 「*interfere in* [*stick your nose into*] our affairs.
◆他人のことに口出しするな *Mind your own business.*/ *That's none of your business.*

くちづけ 口付け kiss [C] ―口づけする kiss [他][自] ∥彼は彼女の唇に口づけをした He *kissed* her lips./ He *kissed* her *on* the lips.

くちづたえ 口伝え 物語を口伝えに伝える hand down tales *orally* [*by word of mouth, from mouth to mouth*]

くちづて 口伝て 彼女がアメリカに留学したと口づてに聞いた I heard *by word of mouth* that she had gone to America to study.

くちどめ 口止め それについて話すことはかたく口止めされている I *am told never to talk* about it.
‖口止め料 hush money

くちなおし 口直し お口直しに果物でもいかがですか How about some fruit *to* 「*kill the aftertaste* [(→口をすっきりさせるために) *re-*

fresh your mouth]?
- **くちなし** 梔子 《植物》 gardenia Ⓒ
- **くちパク** 口パク lip synch Ⓤ
- **くちばし** 嘴 (ハト・スズメなどの) bill Ⓒ; (ワシなど猛禽(ﾓｳｷﾝ)類の) beak Ⓒ
  【慣用表現】**くちばしが黄色い**(→若くて経験が浅い) be callow; be wet behind the ears
- **くちばしる** 口走る (わけの分からないことを言う) babble ⾃⾃; (秘密をうっかりもらす) let* out ∥彼は酔っ払ってわけの分からないことを口走っていた He was drunken and *babbled*.
- **くちはてる** 朽ち果てる rot away, fall* into ruin [decay]; (世に知られずに死ぬ) die in obscurity ⇨くちる
- **くちばばったい** 口幅ったい (生意気な) presumptuous ∥口はばったい言い方 a *presumptuous* expression
- **くちび** 口火 pilot burner [light] Ⓒ
  ◆議論の口火を切る start an argument ∥紙面上での彼の発言が論争の口火となった His utterance on the paper *caused* [*triggered*] the argument.
- **くちひげ** 口髭 mustache, 《英》moustache Ⓒ ⇨ひげ 図版 ∥おじさんは口ひげを生やしている My uncle wears *a mustache*.
- **くちびる** 唇 lip Ⓒ (◆日本語の「唇」よりも広範囲を指し,鼻の下や唇の周辺部も含む.上下にあるので複数形で用いることが多い) ∥上[下]唇 the upper [lower] *lip* ∥薄い[厚い]唇 thin [thick] *lips* ∥荒れた唇 chapped *lips* ∥彼は唇をすぼめて口笛を吹いた He rounded *his lips* and whistled. ∥彼は悲しみをこらえて唇をかんだ He *bit his lip* to try to overcome his sorrow.
- **くちぶえ** 口笛 whistle Ⓒ ◆口笛を吹く *whistle*; give a whistle ∥歌を口笛で吹く *whistle* a song
- **くちぶり** 口振り 孝之はまるでそれを見たかのような口ぶりだった Takayuki *talked as if he had seen it*. ∥あの口ぶりでは彼は会に参加しそうにもない *Judging from his way of talking*, he won't attend the meeting. ∥彼女は仕事に満足していないような口ぶりだった She *hinted* that she was not satisfied with her work.
- **くちべた** 口下手 bad [poor] talker Ⓒ ∥彼は口下手だが正直者だ He is *a poor talker*, but an honest man.
- **くちべに** 口紅 lipstick Ⓒ Ⓤ ∥口紅をつける put on *lipstick* ∥口紅を落とす remove *lipstick*
- **くちまね** 口真似 mimicry Ⓤ ◆彼女は先生の口まねがうまい She is good at *mimicking* our teacher's voice.
- **くちもと** 口元 (口) mouth Ⓒ; (唇) lip Ⓒ ∥その少女は口元がかわいらしかった The girl had *a lovely mouth*.
  ◆それを聞いて彼女の口元はほころんだ(→ほほえんだ) Hearing it, she *smiled*.
- **くちやかましい** 口喧しい nagging, 《口語的》picky ∥口やかましく言う naggingly ∥母は行儀よくしなさいと口やかましく言う My mother tells me *naggingly* to behave

well. ◆戸田先生は私たちの服装にとても口やかましい(→厳格だ) Mrs. Toda *is* very *strict* about our clothes.
- **くちやくそく** 口約束 verbal promise Ⓒ
- **くちゃくちゃ** 彼はいつでもガムをくちゃくちゃかんでいる He *is* always *chewing* gum *noisily*.
- **ぐちゃぐちゃ** きのうの豪雨で運動場はぐちゃぐちゃになった The playground got *sloppy* [(→泥んこに) *muddy*] because of the heavy rain yesterday. ∥探し物をしていて部屋の中がぐちゃぐちゃになった My room was in *such a mess* after I had looked for something. ∥本の順番がぐちゃぐちゃだ The order of the books is *messy*. ∥もう頭の中がぐちゃぐちゃだ(→すっかり混乱した) I am *completely confused*.
- **くちょう¹** 口調 tone Ⓒ ∥穏やかな[命令, 自信のある]口調で話す speak *in a gentle* [*commanding, confident*] *tone* ∥林先生は怒ったような口調で「静かにしなさい」と言った "Be quiet!," said Mr. Hayashi *in an angry tone*.
- **くちょう²** 区長 the chief of a ward
- **くちる** 朽ちる (腐る) decay ⾃, molder, 《英》moulder ⾃, rot ⾃ ──朽ちた rotten ∥その古い橋は朽ちて流されてしまった The old bridge *became rotten* and washed away.
  ◆朽ちた古木 a *decayed* old tree
- **ぐちる** 愚痴る 彼はよく先生についてぐちる He often *gripes* about the teacher. ⇨ぐち

くつ 靴
(短靴) shoes (◆数えるときは a pair of ... とする); (長靴) boots (◆《米》では短靴 (low shoes) とくるぶしまでの靴 (high shoes) を shoes と呼び, 長靴 (boots) と区別する. 《英》では短靴のみを shoes と呼び, これ以外は boots となる); (運動靴) sneakers
靴を履く[脱ぐ]「put on [take off] *one's shoes*

舌革 tongue
靴ひも shoelace
かかと heel
底 sole
パンプス pumps
スニーカー sneakers
サンダル sandals
スリッポン slip-ons
ローファー loafers
ブーツ boots

/ 靴のひもを結ぶ lace (up) one's shoes; tie one's shoelace

美樹はきょう新しい靴を履いている Miki has new *shoes* on today. / Miki is wearing new *shoes* today.

この靴はつま先がきつい These *shoes* pinch my toes.

この靴は小さすぎて足が入らない These *shoes* are too small for me to put on.

この靴は履き心地がとてもよい These *shoes* are very comfortable.

この靴の片方が見つからない I can't find the mate to this *shoe*.(❖「片方の靴」を指すときは単数形を用いる)

そろそろ靴がすり減ってきた My *shoes* are showing (signs of) wear.

靴のサイズはどれくらいですか What size *shoes* do you take?

🔴「この靴いいなあ」「履いてみたらどう」"These *shoes* look nice." "Why don't you try them on?"

‖ 靴ずみ shoe polish / 靴底 a sole / 靴ひも a shoestring, a shoelace / 靴ブラシ a shoe brush / 靴べら a shoehorn / 靴磨き a (shoe) shine / 靴屋(店) a shoe store; (人) a shoemaker / 運動靴 sneakers

くつう 苦痛 (痛み) pain ⓤⓒ; (苦しみ) suffering ⓤⓒ; (苦悶(もん)) agony ⓤⓒ (❖通例 pain, suffering よりも強い) ‖ 苦痛を受ける suffer *pain [suffering]* / 苦痛に耐える bear *pain [suffering]* / 苦痛を訴える complain of *a pain* / 苦痛をやわらげる ease *pain [suffering]* / 精神的[肉体的]苦痛 mental *[physical] pain* / 彼は苦痛に顔をゆがめた His face was contorted with *pain [suffering]*.

◆彼の長ったらしい講釈を聞いているのは本当に苦痛だ It's quite *painful* to listen to his lengthy lectures.

くつがえす 覆す (体制などを) overthrow*ⓣ; (決定などを) overrule, overturnⓣ ‖ 政construireをくつがえす *overthrow* the government / 決定をくつがえす *overrule [overturn]* the decision

◆その発見によって彼の学説は根本からくつがえされてしまった His theory *was turned over* completely by the discovery.

くつがえる 覆る (既成のものが崩壊する) be overthrown, be overturned; (判決が逆転する) be overruled, be reversed

クッキー 《主に米》cookie, cookyⓒ, 《英》biscuitⓒ ‖ クッキーを焼く bake *cookies*

くっきり ―くっきりと clearly, sharply; (他のものとの対比で) distinctly ➡はっきり ‖ ここからは富士山がくっきりと見える We can see Mt. Fuji *clearly* from here. / 水平線が空と海をくっきりと分けている The horizon separates the sky and the sea *distinctly*.

クッキング cooking ⓤ ➡りょうり
‖ クッキングスクール a cookery [cooking] school / クッキングブック 《米》a cookbook, 《英》a cookery book

ぐつぐつ(と) シチューがぐつぐつ煮立っていた The stew *simmered [bubbled]*.

くっし 屈指 この小説は日本文学の中でも屈指の名作だ This novel is *one of the best [greatest]* works in Japanese literature.

くつした 靴下 (短い) socks; (長い) stockings(❖共に数えるときは a pair of ... とする) ‖ 靴下を履く[脱ぐ] "put on [take off] one's *socks* / 片方の靴下に穴があいている There is a hole in one of *my socks*. / 健, 靴下が裏返しよ Ken, *your socks* are (on) inside out.

くつじょく 屈辱 humiliation ⓤ, disgrace ⓤ ―屈辱的な humiliating, disgraceful ‖ 屈辱的敗北を喫する suffer *a humiliating* defeat / 私は心中ひどい屈辱感を味わった I felt so *humiliated* in my mind.

ぐっしょり 通り雨にあってぐっしょりぬれてしまった I was caught in a shower and *got wet to the skin [dripping wet, soaked]*.

クッション cushion ⓒ ‖ クッションに心地よく座る nestle down on *a cushion*

◆このソファーはクッションがきいている This sofa *is well-padded*.

くっしん 屈伸 ―屈伸する (柔軟運動として) flexⓣ ◆ひざの屈伸運動 knee *bend exercise*

グッズ (商品·品物) goods

ぐっすり fast, sound, well ‖ 赤ん坊はぐっすり眠っている The baby is *fast [sound]* asleep. / きのうはぐっすり眠れた I slept *well* last night. / ひと晩ぐっすり眠れば気分がよくなるよ Have a *good* night's sleep, and you'll be all right.

くっする 屈する give* in, yield ⓘ, submit ⓘ ‖ 誘惑に屈する 「*give in [yield] to* temptation / 彼はついに彼女のしつこい要求に屈した He *yielded to* her persistent demand at last.

くつずれ 靴ずれ (まめ) blister ⓒ, shoe sore ⓒ ‖ 新しい靴を履いたら靴ずれができてしまった When I wore new shoes, I got *shoe sores*.

くっせつ 屈折 〘光学〙refraction ⓤ, 〘文法〙inflection ⓤ ―屈折した (性格などが) warped ‖ 若者たちの屈折した心 *warped* minds of young people / にじは光の屈折によって起こる現象です The rainbow is a phenomenon caused by *refraction* of the light.

‖ 屈折望遠鏡 a refracting telescope / 屈折率 an index of refraction

くったく 屈託 屈託のない笑顔 a *carefree [an open]* smile

ぐったり 疲れてぐったりとしている be *dead* tired / 彼女はぐったりとしてソファーに座り込んだ She sank *limply* onto a sofa. / 暑さでシクラメンの花もぐったりしている The cyclamens *are drooping [wilting]* in the heat.

くっつく stick* ⓘ, cling* ⓘ (❖stick は主に接着剤などで, cling は自然の作用でつく場合などに用いることが多い) ‖ この切手はどうしても封筒にくっつかない This stamp *won't stick [adhere] to* the envelope. / その少女は怖くて母親にぴったりくっついていた The little girl *clung to* her mother in fear.

◆くっついて座る sit *side by side* / 子犬が家ま

で私にくっついてきた The puppy *tagged along behind* me all the way home.

くっつける (はりつける) stick* [他]; (接着剤で) paste [他], glue [他] //割れた茶わんを接着剤でくっつけた I *glued together* the broken cup. ◆子供たちは窓ガラスに顔をくっつけて外を眺めている The children are looking out with their faces *against* the windows. / 机をもう少し壁にくっつけてください *Put* the desk a bit *closer* to the wall.

くってかかる 食ってかかる 彼女は彼に猛然とくってかかった She *turned on* him fiercely.

ぐっと 恵美は涙をぐっとこらえてさよならを言った *Holding back* her tears, Megumi said goodbye. / あの映画のラストシーンにはぐっときた I *was deeply moved* by the last scene of the movie. / 彼女はワインをぐっと(→ひと口で)飲み干した She emptied her wine glass *at* [*in*] *one gulp*. / 地下鉄が開通したおかげで通学がぐっと楽になった The opening of the subway made it *much* easier to go to school. / その役を演じてから, 彼の演技にぐっと味が出てきた After he played the role, his performance improved *markedly* [*mightily*].

グッド good //グッドアイディア a *good* idea

くっぷく 屈服・屈伏 submission [U] ——屈服する yield [自], submit [自]; (降伏する) surrender [自] //権力への屈服 *submission to* the power

くつろぐ 寛ぐ relax [自], be [feel*] at home, make* *oneself* at home //自分の家がいちばんくつろげる I *can relax* best at home. / (客に)どうぞおくつろぎください Please *make yourself at home*. ◆くつろげる小さなレストラン a small *intimate* restaurant / この音楽を聴くといつも私はくつろいだ気分になる This music always *relaxes* me.

くつわ 轡 (馬具の一種) bit [C]

ぐでんぐでん ぐでんぐでんに酔っ払っている be *dead* [*blind*] drunk; 《口語的》be plastered

くどい (冗長な) wordy, lengthy, 《公式的》verbose; (繰り返しが多い) repetitious //彼の話はいつもくどい What he says *is* always *wordy* [*lengthy*]. ◆このレストランの料理は少しくどい The food *is seasoned* a little *too much* in this restaurant.

くとう 苦闘 ——苦闘する struggle [自] ➔ あくせんくとう

くどう 駆動 4輪駆動車 a *four-wheel-drive* car

くどうし 句動詞 〔文法〕phrasal verb [C]

> 動詞に副詞や前置詞が結びつき, それらがまとまって1つの動詞のような働きをするものを句動詞という(例: look after ... …の面倒を見る, look up to ... …を尊敬する).
>
> [目的語の位置]《動詞＋前置詞》の場合は前置詞の後ろにくる // Alice *looked after* the children. アリスは子供たちの面倒を見た.
> 《動詞＋副詞》の場合は副詞の前にくる場合と後ろにくる場合があるが, 目的語が代名詞の場合は副詞の前にくる // Tom *switched off* the light./ Tom *switched* the light *off*. トムは明かりを消した / Tom *switched* it *off*. トムはそれを消した.
>
> [アクセントの位置]ふつう前置詞にアクセントはないが, 副詞の働きをするものにはアクセントがある // He was called ón to stop the conflicts. 彼はその争いをやめさせるよう求められた.

くとうてん 句読点 punctuation mark [C] ➔ [巻末付録] (句読法)

くどく[1] 口説く (説得する) persuade *a person* to *do*, talk *a person* into *doing*; (異性を) make* advances [approaches] to *a person*, 《口語的》make a pass at *a person* // 友達をくどいて山登りに行った I *talked* my friends *into* climbing a mountain together. / あいつは女の子をくどく天才だ He is a genius for *making a pass at* girls. / 親をくどき落としてパソコンを買わせた I *talked* my parents *into* buying a PC.

くどく[2] 功徳 (善行) good deed [C] //功徳を積む do *a good deed*

くどくど tediously; (長々と) at great length //彼はくどくどと言い訳をした He excused himself *at great length*. ◆彼は同じ話をくどくどと繰り返した He *kept harping on the same thing*. (❖keep harping on は「くどくどと繰り返す」という意味の口語的表現)

くないちょう 宮内庁 the Imperial Household Agency

くなん 苦難 hardship [U] [C], suffering [U] [C]; (試練) trial [C] ➔ こんなん, しれん //苦難を乗り越える overcome *hardships* / 人生は苦難に満ちている Life is full of *trials*.

くに 国

❶【国家】country [C]; (国民の集まり) nation [C]; (行政上のまとまり) state [C][U]
➔ こっか(国家)

その国は4つの地域に分かれる The *country* has four regions.

その国では何語が話されていますか What language do people speak in that *country*?

日本はアジアのほかの国々から多くのことを学んできた Japan has learned a lot from other Asian *countries*.

自転車で国中を旅行したいな I want to travel *all over the country* by bicycle.

その国は独立を宣言した The *nation* declared independence.

新しい指導者は国の統一に成功した The new leader succeeded in unifying *the nation*.

その工場は国の管理下にある The factory is under the control of *the state*.

◆日出(ᵢ)ずる国(日本) *the Land* of the Rising Sun / ロシアはわが国の北方の隣国である Russia is *our* neighbor on the north.

❷【政府】government [C]《しばしばGovernment》

国を相手取って訴訟を起こす file a suit

against *the government*
国民は国に対して強い不信感をいだいている The people have a strong distrust of *the government*.
❸【地方・地域】
上総の国 *the Province* of Kazusa
❹【故郷】home ⓒⓊ, hometown ⓒ
◆ 私はもう何年も国に帰っていない I haven't been *home* for [(米)in] years.
🗣 「お国はどちらですか」「富山です」"*Where are you from? / Where do you come from?*" "*I'm from Toyama. / I come from Toyama.*"

くにがら 国柄 (国民性) national character ⓒ; (地方色) local color Ⓤ // 休日の過ごし方にもお国柄が表われる A way of spending holidays also shows *the national character.*

くにく 苦肉 苦肉の策 *desperate measures*

くにざかい 国境 border ⓒ, (公式的) frontier ⓒ ➡ こっきょう (国境)

くにゃくにゃ この針金は太いのにくにゃくにゃ曲がる This wire is thick, but it bends *easily*. / この鳥肉はくにゃくにゃしてかみ切れない This poultry is *rubbery* and difficult to chew.

ぐにゃぐにゃ そのジャングルジムは原爆の熱でぐにゃぐにゃに曲がってしまったらしい I hear that the jungle gym *was twisted* [*bent*] *out of shape* in the heat of the atomic bomb.

くぬぎ 櫟 〔植物〕Japanese oak*

くねくね くねくねと曲がった小道 a *winding* [*snaky*] path / その川は山岳地帯をくねくね流れている The river *meanders* through the mountain district. / そのロック歌手は腰をくねくねさせながら歌った The rock singer sang while *shaking* his hips.

くねる (川・道などが) wind* ⓘ
◆ 彼らは体をくねらせて踊った They danced with their bodies *twisted*. / 私は体をくねらせて縄を抜けた I *wriggled* (*myself*) free of the ropes.

くのう 苦悩 (公式的) affliction ⓒⓊ, anguish Ⓤ, distress Ⓤ, agony ⓒⓊ // 苦悩している *be in distress* / 彼女の顔には苦悩の色がにじみ出ていた She showed *her anguish* [*agony*].

くはい 苦杯 慣用表現 苦杯をなめる (→つらい経験をする) *undergo hardship*; (→負ける) *be defeated*

くばる 配る hand out, pass out; (配達する) deliver ⓘ; (トランプのカードなどを) deal* ⓘ
き(気)、め(目)
先生は試験問題を配り始めた The teacher began *handing* [*passing*] *out* the test papers.
駅の近くで女の子たちがちらしを配っていた Girls *were passing* [*handing*] *out* fliers near the station.
彼はこの地域で新聞を配っている He *delivers* newspapers in this area.
彼女は私たちにトランプを7枚配った She *dealt* us seven cards. / She *dealt* seven cards to us.

くび 首
❶【体などの部位】neck ⓒ; (頭部) head ⓒ
びんの首 *the neck* of a bottle / 短い[細い、太い]首 *a short* [*slender, thick*] *neck* / 首をしめる squeeze *a person's neck* / 首にスカーフを巻く wear a scarf around *one's neck*
キリンは首が長い The giraffe has *a long neck.*
このセーターはちょっと首がきつい This sweater is a little tight in *the neck.*
私は首を伸ばして人垣の向こうを見た I craned *my neck* to see over the crowd.
窓から首を出してはいけません Don't stick *your head* out of the window.
◆ 彼は首をつろうとした He tried to *hang himself.* / 彼女はベッドで首をしめて殺されていた She *was strangled* in her bed.
❷【解雇】(口語的) the sack, (口語的) the boot ➡ かいこ (解雇)
◆ 従業員を首にする *fire* an employee; *give* an employee *the boot* / おまえは首だ You *are fired.* / 仕事を首になった I *got fired* [*the boot*] from the job.
慣用表現 首に縄をつけてでも (→何が何でも) あいつをここへ連れてくるよ I'll bring him here, *no matter what.* / その猿はどうやっておりから抜け出したのだろうと彼女は首をかしげた She *wondered* how the monkey escaped from the cage. (❖首をかしげる動作は cock *one's head* というが、この表現には「疑問に思う」という意味はない) / 私がいくら頼んでも父は首を縦に振らなかった My father *wouldn't*「*nod his head* [*say yes*] no matter how hard I asked. / 行夫は何にでも首をつっ込みたがる Yukio tends to *stick his nose in* everything. / 僕たちは夏休みが来るのを首を長くして待った We *waited eagerly*「(→しびれを切らして) *impatiently*]*for* the summer vacation. / デートに誘ってみたが彼女は首を横に振った I asked her to go out with me, but she *shook her head.* / 彼は借金で首が回らない He *is in debt up to his ears.*
‖首飾り a necklace / 首筋 a nape (of *one's neck*) / 首輪 a collar

くびったけ 首ったけ 彼はその女の子に首ったけだ He is「*head over heels* [*madly*] *in love with* that girl.

くびっぴき 首っ引き 私は辞書と首っぴきで、ある難解な小説を翻訳している最中だ I am translating a difficult novel with a dictionary *at my side*.

くびつり 首吊り 彼は首つり自殺をしようとした He attempted to *hang himself*.

くびねっこ 首根っこ the scruff of *one's neck*

くびれる ウエストがくびれている *have a narrow* [*slim*] *waist* / ウエストがくびれていない *have no waist*

くふう 工夫 (アイディア) idea ⓒ; (方策) device ⓒ; (発明) invention Ⓤ (❖発明品の意味では ⓒ) ——工夫する (方法・装置などを) devise ⓘ, (発明する) invent ⓘ

この机にはいろいろと独自の工夫が凝らされている This desk is full of original *ideas*.
この装置は私が工夫して作ったものだ This device is my *invention*. / This device is what I *invented*.
◆このパソコンは初心者にも使いやすいように工夫されている This personal computer *is designed* to be easy to use for even a beginner. / このホームページは読みやすくするためにもうひと工夫が必要だ You should *rethink* this web site *a little* to make it easier to read. / ちょっとした工夫で辞書をもっと有効に使うことができる A little *ingenuity* makes a dictionary more useful.

くぶくりん 九分九厘 《口語的》ten to one / 九分九厘彼が勝つだろう *Ten to one* he will win.

くぶどおり 九分通り 新築の家は九分どおり完成した The new house has *almost* been completed. / 彼女の小川大学合格は九分どおり間違いないだろう It is *almost* certain that she will pass the entrance examination for Ogawa University.

くぶん 区分 division Ⓤ (❖区分されたものはⒸ); (分類) classification Ⓤ ──区分する divide ⑯; classify ⑯; (境界を定める) demarcate ⇒ わける ∥土地を区分する *demarcate* the land

くべつ 区別

distinction Ⓤ Ⓒ; (差別) discrimination Ⓤ ──区別する distinguish ⑯ (❖進行形にはできない), tell* ⑯, draw* [make*] a distinction; discriminate ⑯
AとBを区別する *draw* [*make*] *a distinction between* A *and* B
これらの植物は葉の形によって区別することができる You can *distinguish* these plants by the form of their leaves.
【distinguish [tell]＋名＋from 名】私にはサラブレッドとアラブ馬との区別がつかない I *can't distinguish* [*tell*] a thoroughbred *from* an Arab.
◆私には本物の宝石と偽物との区別がつかない I *can't tell the difference between* real jewels *and* fake ones. / 若若男女の区別なくだれでもこのメーリングリストに参加することができる Anybody, *regardless* [*irrespective*] *of* age or sex, can subscribe to this mailing list.
🗨「彼女と彼女のお姉さんとの区別がつきますか」「いいえ、どっちがどっちか区別できません」"*Can you tell* her *from* her sister?" "No. I can't tell who is who." (❖物の場合は、I can't tell which is which.となる)

くべる 火にまきをくべる put wood *on* a fire / まきを炉にくべる *feed* the furnace *with* wood; *feed* wood *into* the furnace
くぼち 窪地・凹地 hollow Ⓒ, depression Ⓒ
くぼみ 窪み・凹み hollow , depression Ⓒ; (へこみ) dent Ⓒ
くぼむ 窪む・凹む sink* (in), become* hollow [sunken] ∥彼の目は心労でくぼんでしまった His eyes *were sunken* from worry.

くま¹ 熊 bear Ⓒ ∥子グマ a (bear) *cub* ∥シロクマ a white [polar] bear / ヒグマ a brown bear
くま² 隈 彼は目の下にくまができている He has *dark rings* under his eyes.
くまで 熊手 (bamboo) rake Ⓒ ◆落ち葉を熊手でかき集める *rake up* dead leaves
くまなく 隈なく 私は家中くまなく探したが、結局かぎは出てこなかった I looked *everywhere* in the house for the key, but couldn't find it.

くまもと 熊本

熊本県は九州のほぼ中央に位置しています。温暖な気候と豊かな水に恵まれたこの県では、古くから文化が栄え、旧石器・縄文時代の遺跡や古墳が数多く発掘されています。また県内には世界で最も雄大なカルデラをもつ阿蘇山があり、毎年多くの観光客が訪れています。
Kumamoto Prefecture is located almost in the center of Kyushu. Blessed with a mild climate and abundant water, its culture has flourished since ancient times. Many burial mounds have been excavated as well as ruins from the early Stone Age and the Jomon period. Kumamoto is also known for Mt. Aso, which has the grandest caldera in the world and receives many visitors every year.

くまんばち 熊ん蜂 〖昆虫〗hornet Ⓒ

くみ 組

❶【学級】class Ⓒ (❖特に《英》ではクラスの一人一人に重点をおくときには単数形でも複数扱いになることがある), homeroom Ⓒ
私たちは同じ組だ We're in *the same class*.
佐藤先生は C 組の担任だ Ms. Sato is in charge of *Class* C.
🗨「あなたは何年何組ですか」「1 年 2 組です」"What grade and *class* are you in?" "I'm in *the second class* of *the first grade*."
❷【集団】group Ⓒ (❖《英》では複数扱いになることがある); (競技などの) team Ⓒ (❖チームの構成員を個々に指す場合は複数扱い)
5 人ずつ組になりなさい Make up [Form] *groups* of five.
白組が赤組を 2 点リードしている *The* white *team* has a two-point lead over *the* red *team*.
◆予選, 第 5 組 the preliminary, *Heat* 5
❸【ひとそろい】set Ⓒ; (2 個から成る) pair Ⓒ; (男女の) couple Ⓒ (❖一人一人に重点がおかれると複数扱いになることがある)
5 個組の食器 a five-piece *set* of tableware / スキー板一組 *a pair of skis* / 2 人一組になって踊る dance in *pairs*
◆トランプ一組 *a deck* [*pack*] *of cards*

くみあい 組合 (労働組合) union Ⓒ (❖正式には《米》labor union, 《英》trade union); (生活共同組合) (consumers') cooperative , 《口語的》co-op [kóuɑ̀p] Ⓒ ∥労働組合に加入する

join *a labor union*
‖組合員 a (labor) union member, a unionist / 組合運動 union activities

くみあげる 汲み上げる draw*; (ポンプで) pump (up) ‖井戸から水をくみ上げる *draw* water *from* a well ◆ほかの人の意見をくみ上げる *accept* other people's opinions

くみあわせ 組み合わせ combination; (2つの) pairing; 〔数学〕combination ‖試合の組み合わせをくじで決める decide「game *pairings* [*who plays who(m)*] by lot / そのセーターはオレンジ色と緑色の組み合わせがすばらしい The sweater's orange and green「make *a fine combination* [*are a good match*].

くみあわせる 組み合わせる 強いチームどうしを組み合わせた They *matched* the strong teams *with* each other. / このシャツに合うネクタイを組み合わせるつもりだ I'll try to *match* this shirt *with* the right tie.

くみいれる 組み入れる include, 《公式的》incorporate ‖歓迎会のプログラムに彼女のスピーチを組み入れた I *incorporated* her speech *into* the program of the welcoming party.

くみかえる 組み替える・組み換える 予算を組み替える *revise* a budget / 遺伝子を組み換える *splice* genes

くみかわす 酌み交わす 酒をくみ交わしながら (→いっしょに飲みながら) 語り合った We *had a drink together* and talked with each other.

くみきょく 組曲 suite [swíːt]

くみこむ 組み込む IC が組み込まれたカード a card with a *built-in* IC / このスケジュールには国会見学も組み込まれている A study visit to the Diet *is included in* this schedule.

くみだす 汲み出す (ひしゃくなどで) dip; (ポンプで) pump (out) ‖ポンプで船から水をくみ出す *pump* water *out of* a ship; *pump out* a ship

くみたて 組み立て (作業) assembly; (構造) structure, construction ‖コンピュータの組み立て作業 *the assembly* of computers / 文章の組み立て *the structure* [*construction*] of a composition ◆組み立て式のいす a *sectional* [*knockdown*] chair

くみたてる 組み立てる put* together; (機械などを) set* up, assemble; (文章を) compose ‖プラモデルを組み立てる *put together* a plastic model / 文章を組み立てる *compose* sentences / この机は簡単に組み立てられる This desk is easy to *assemble*.

くみとる 汲み取る 水槽の水をくみ取る *scoop up* water from the water tank / 言外の意味をくみ取る (→行間を読む) *read* between the lines / 人の事情をくみ取る (→考慮する) *take* a person's circumstances *into consideration*

くみふせる 組み伏せる 地面に男を組み伏せた I *held* [*pinned*] the man *down* to the ground.

くみん 区民 私は世田谷区の区民だ I'm *a resident of* Setagaya *Ward*.
‖区民税 a ward tax

くむ¹ 組む ❶【交差させる】(腕などを) fold; (足などを) cross ‖彼は腕を組んで何を考えているんだろう What's he thinking about *with his arms folded*? ‖彼は足を組んで公園のベンチに座っていた He was sitting on the bench *with his legs crossed* in the park. ◆健太は女の子と腕を組んで歩いていた Kenta was walking *arm in arm with* a girl. / 彼らは肩を組んで写真に写っていた They were in the picture *with their arms over each other's shoulders*.

❷【協力する】彼女と組んで (→彼女といっしょに) 新しいロックバンドを作るつもりだ I'm going to form a rock band *together with* her. ‖野党の1つが与党と手を組んだ (→いっしょになった) One of the opposition parties *joined* (*up*) *with* the ruling party. ‖私は彼とペアを組んでダンスを踊った I *was paired with* him in a dance. / (→彼は私のダンスパートナーだった) He was my dance partner.

❸【作成する】スケジュールを組む *make up* a schedule / コンピュータのプログラムを組む *make* [*write*] a computer program / いかだを組む *make* a raft / 足場を組む *put up* scaffolding ‖私たちは家を買うために2,000万円のローンを組んだ We *took out a mortgage* of 20 million yen to buy a house.

くむ² 汲む ❶【液体を】(くみ出す) draw*; (ポンプで) pump (up) ‖井戸から水をくむ *draw* water *from* a well
❷【気持ちを】consider, take* ... into consideration [account] ‖彼の気持ちをくんでやりなよ You should *consider* his feelings.

くめん 工面 金を工面する (→調達する) *raise* money / 何とか工面してお金を返した I *managed to* repay the money.

くも¹ 雲
cloud

薄い [厚い] 雲 thin [thick] *clouds* / 雲の上を飛ぶ fly above [over] *the clouds*
雲が切れた *The clouds* have broken.
だんだん雲が出てきた *Clouds* began gathering in the sky.
雲の切れ間から山頂がのぞいた The mountaintop was revealed through *a break* [*rift*] *in the clouds*.
海にはどんよりと厚い雲が垂れこめていた Thick gray *clouds* hung over the sea.
残念ながら富士山は雲に隠れて見えなかった To our regret, we couldn't see Mt. Fuji because it *was hidden in clouds*.
空には雲ひとつなかった There was not a (*single*) *cloud* in the sky. / The sky *was* (*completely*) *cloudless*.

くも

◆雲の多い天気 cloudy weather / 雲のない空 a *cloudless* sky

‖雲海 a sea of cloud(s) / 雨雲 rain clouds / いわし雲 fleecy clouds / きのこ雲 a mushroom (cloud) / 巻雲(¼ん) (a) cirrus / 積雲 (a) cumulus / (積)乱雲 (a) nimbus / 入道雲 a thunderhead / 飛行機雲 a vapor trail / 雷雲 a thundercloud

慣用表現 彼の話は雲をつかむような(→とてもあいまいな)話だった His story was *very vague*. / 雲をつくような大男 *a towering giant*

短歌 ゆく秋の大和の国の薬師寺の塔の上なる一ひらの雲(佐佐木信綱)
The end of autumn
in the land of Yamato.
Above the tower
of the Yakushi Temple
floats a single wisp of cloud.

くも² 蜘蛛 spider ⓒ / クモの糸 *a spider's thread* / クモが巣を張っていた I left for home spinning a web. / その部屋はクモの巣だらけだった The room *was full of spider webs*. / The room *was cobwebbed*.

慣用表現 人々はクモの子を散らすように(→四方八方へ)逃げた People ran away *in all directions*.

くもがくれ 雲隠れ ──雲隠れする (いなくなる) disappear 圓; (突然) vanish 圓; (隠れる) hide* (*oneself*)

くもまく 蜘蛛膜 〔解剖〕 the arachnoid membrane ‖くも膜下出血 subarachnoidal hemorrhage

くもゆき 雲行き 雲行きが怪しかった(→雨が降りそうだった)ので早めに家に帰った I left for home a little early because *it looked like rain*. / ひざの故障で彼が次の試合に勝てるかどうか雲行きが怪しくなってきた(→勝てそうもない) He *seems unlikely* to win the next game because of trouble with his knees. / それ以来、彼らの関係は雲行きが怪しくなってきている Their relationship *has been getting worse* since then.

くもらす 曇らす cloud ⓣ 圓; (霧・もやが) fog, mist ⓣ; (まゆをひそめる) frown ⓘ / 息でガラスを曇らせた I *fogged up* the glass with my breath. / 私が彼の名前を口にすると彼女は顔を曇らせた She *clouded over* when I mentioned his name. / 怒りが彼の判断を曇らせた Anger *clouded* his judgement.

くもり 曇り ❶【天候】 ──曇りの cloudy / 曇り空 a cloudy sky / 午前中は曇りだった It was *cloudy* in the morning. / 曇りのち時々雨 *Cloudy*, later occasional rain.

❷【汚れ】(ガラス・鏡などの) mist Ⓤ (また a ~), fog Ⓤ Ⓒ; (大理石などの) cloud Ⓤ Ⓒ / 眼鏡の曇りをふき取る wipe *the mist* from *one's* glasses

‖曇りガラス frosted glass

くもる 曇る

❶【空が】 become* [get*] cloudy, cloud over
きのうは一日中曇っていた It was *cloudy* all day yesterday.

空が曇ってきた.雨が降るかもしれない It [The sky] *is getting cloudy*. It might rain.

❷ (ぼんやりする) cloud 圓, fog up [over], mist up [over]
湯気で彼の眼鏡が曇った His glasses (*were*) *fogged up* with steam.
彼女の目は涙で曇った Her eyes *misted over* with tears.

❸【表情が】
そのニュースを聞いて父の顔は一瞬曇った My father's face *was clouded* for a moment at the news.

くもん 苦悶 agony Ⓤ Ⓒ, anguish Ⓤ / 彼女は自責の念に苦悶している She's *in the agony [anguish]* of a guilty conscience.

◆苦悶の表情 an *anguished* expression

ぐもん 愚問 silly [stupid] question Ⓒ

くやくしょ 区役所 ward office Ⓒ

くやしい 悔しい ──動 be [feel*] frustrated; (後悔する) regret ⓣ; (恥ずかしい) be [feel] ashamed; (屈辱を感じる) be [feel] humiliated ──形 frustrating; regrettable; (がっかりさせる) disappointing

ああ悔しい! How *frustrating [disappointing]*!
私が5,000円で買った服がその店では4,000円で売られていて, 何だか悔しい思いをした I *felt* somehow *frustrated* because the dress I had bought at 5,000 yen was sold at 4,000 yen at the store.

◆彼がうそをついていたことを知って私はすごく悔しかった I *felt very bitter* to know that he had told me a lie. / 試合で負けた日の晩は悔しくてよく眠れなかった I *was so upset* that I couldn't sleep very well the night after we lost the game. / 悔しいけど(→認めたくないが)君の勝ちだ I *hate to admit it*, but you win.

くやしがる 悔しがる be [feel*], get* frustrated; (後悔する) regret ⓣ / 彼女は自分の運の悪さを悔しがった She *was frustrated at [with]* her misfortune.

くやしさ 悔しさ (不満) frustration Ⓤ Ⓒ; (後悔) regret Ⓒ Ⓤ / 悔しさをばねに彼は猛練習した *The frustration* motivated him to practice harder.

くやしなき 悔し泣き ──悔し泣きする cry in frustration

くやしなみだ 悔し涙 tears of vexation / 私は悔し涙をこらえた I kept [held] back *my tears of vexation*.

くやしまぎれ 悔し紛れ 彼は悔しまぎれに私をののしった He cursed at me *out of frustration [bitterness]*.

くやみ 悔やみ ⇒ おくやみ

くやむ 悔やむ regret ⓣ, be sorry ⇒ こうかい (後悔) / 自分のしたことを悔やんでいる I *regret* what I did. / I'm sorry for what I did. (◆後の表現のほうが口語的) / 過ぎたことを悔やんでも始まらない There's no point in *regretting* the past. ◆友人の死を悔やむ *mourn* the death of *one's* friend

くよう 供養 (追悼式) memorial service Ⓒ

──供養する hold* a memorial service
くよくよ ──くよくよする worry 圓; (考え込む) brood 圓 // つまらないことでくよくよするな Don't *worry over* trifles. / 失敗をくよくよ考えるな Don't *brood over* [*on*] your failure.
くら¹ 蔵・倉 storehouse ⇒そうこ
くら² 鞍 saddle; /馬に鞍を置く *put a saddle on* a horse; *saddle* a horse

くらい¹ 暗い

❶【光が少ない】 dark; dim; gloomy
> dark: 光がなくて暗い. 最も一般的な語.
> dim: 物の輪郭がはっきりつかめないような暗さ.
> gloomy: 薄暗いこと. 陰気さ・もの悲しさを含意することが多い.

暗くならないうちに[なってから] before [after] *dark*
外は暗くなり始めた It began to *get* [*grow*, *become*] *dark* outside.
こんなに暗い明かりで勉強したら目を悪くするよ You'll damage your eyes if you study in this *dim* light.
◆父は暗いうち(→夜明け前)に出かけていった He went out *before daybreak*. / この部屋の明かりはいつも暗くしてある The light in this room *is always turned down*.

❷【心の晴れない・陰気な】 dark; (ふさぎ込んだ・希望のない) gloomy; (意気消沈させる) depressing; (気落ちした) depressed
物事[彼の性格]の暗い面 the *dark* side of things [his character] / 暗いニュース a *gloomy* [*depressing*] news
彼は性格が暗い He *is a gloomy sort*.
我々の将来の見通しは暗い Our prospects for the future *are looking gloomy*.
母の死は家族みんなに暗い影を落とした The death of my mother cast a *dark* shadow on the whole family.
テストのことを考えただけで暗い気持ちになる The very thought of the exam makes me *feel depressed*.
彼には暗い過去があるようだ He seems to have a *dark* past.

❸【知らない】
私は法律に暗い I *don't know much about* the law.
私はこのあたりの地理に暗い I'm *a stranger* here.

❹【色が】 dark
暗い色 a *dark* color / 暗い赤 *dark* red

くらい² 位 (地位・階級) rank ⓒ Ⓤ; (等級) grade ⓒ; (王位) the throne; 〖数学〗 place ⓒ // 位の高い[低い]人 a person of high [low] *rank* / 王の位につく come to *the throne* / 千の位 *the thousand's place* / 彼はあなたよりも位が上[下]だ He is *above* [*below*] you *in rank*.

-くらい -位

❶【およそ】 about, (《口語的》) around, approximately (❖*about* より文語的); (数詞の前で) some; (…かそのくらい) ... or so

本棚には50冊くらいの本があった There were *about* [*around*, *some*] fifty books on the bookshelf.
彼は30歳くらいでしょう I guess him to be *about* [*around*] thirty.
私たちはそこに1か月くらいいた We stayed there a month *or so*.
◆その女性は30から35歳くらいに見えた The lady seemed *somewhere between* 30 and 35. / 2台の車は10センチもないくらいの間隔で止まっていた The two cars were parked *not* 10 centimeters apart (from each other).(❖距離・時間を表す語に not が付く場合はそれより少ないことを表す)
🗨「このビルは建てられてからどれくらいですか」「20年ぐらいです」 "*How old* is this building?" "*About* twenty years old."
🗨「ここからお宅までどのくらいありますか」「2キロくらいです」 "*How far* is it from here to your house?" "*About* two kilometers."
🗨「プールにはどれくらい行きますか」「週に2回くらいです」 "*How often* do you go to the swimming pool?" "*About* twice a week."
🗨「どのくらいでこちらに来られますか」「1時間ぐらいで行けると思います」 "*How soon* will you get here?" "I guess I'll arrive in *about* an hour."

❷【比較の基準】 as ... as ~, so ... that ~
彼女は私くらいの背丈だ She is *as* tall *as* I [me].(❖asの後に人称代名詞がくる場合, 口語では目的格を用いることが多い) / She is *about* my height.
彼くらい運のいい人はいない No one is *as* [*so*] fortunate *as* him. / No one is *more* fortunate *than* him.
そのゴキブリは私の親指くらいの大きさだった The cockroach was 「*as big as* [*about the size of*] my thumb.
しばらく口がきけなくなるくらいその知らせに驚いた I was *so* surprised at the news *that* I couldn't speak for a while.
◆先生は私にも分かるくらいはっきりと英語を話す The teacher speaks English clearly *enough* for me to understand. / 前置きはこれくらいにして,さて本論に入りましょう *So much for* the introduction; now let's proceed to the main theme.

❸【軽い程度】
ごめんなさいくらい彼女は言ってもいいと思わない？ Don't you think she might *at least* say sorry?
1つくらいちょうだいよ Give me *just* one.
そのくらい僕でも分かる Even I can understand *that much*.
子供の知恵はせいぜいそのくらいだ A child does *not* know *any better*.
🗨「彼の話,分かる？」「少しぐらいならね」 "Do you understand what he is saying?" "*Some*, I guess."

❹【忌避・嫌悪】
生き恥をさらすくらいなら死んだほうがましだ I'd

グライダー

rather die *than* live in shame./ I *might as well* die *as* live in shame.
⇒ほど

グライダー glider ⓒ

くらいつく 食らいつく うまい話に食らいつく *jump at* a good offer / ライオンは獲物に食らいついた The lion *bit* his prey.

クライマックス climax ⓒ /徐々にクライマックスへと向かう work up to *a climax* / 試合はついにクライマックスを迎えた The game has 「come to [reached] *its climax* at last.

くらう 食らう（食べる）eat*,《口語的》put* away;（むさぼり食う）devour [dívə́uər] ⓔ /鼻にパンチを食らう *get a punch in the nose*

グラウンド ground ⓒ, field ⓒ（❖「運動場」の意味では通例 a baseball field（野球場）のように複合語で用いる）;（学校などの）playground ‖グラウンドコンディション the condition of the field [grounds] / ホームグラウンド a home field

くらがえ 鞍替え ──くら替えする change ⓔ, switch ⓔ /彼女はもっと楽な仕事にくら替えした She *changed* her job *to* an easier one. / いつから彼にくら替えしたの When did you *switch to* him?

くらがり 暗がり the dark;（薄暗がり）gloom Ⓤ /うっそうとした森の暗がりの中で in *the gloom* of a dense forest / 猫は暗がりでも物が見える Cats can see in *the dark*.

くらく 苦楽 私たちはそれ以来苦楽を共にしてきた We've shared *our joys and sorrows* since then.

クラクション ⚠ horn ⓒ（❖「クラクション」は商標名 Klaxon から）‖クラクションを鳴らす sound [blow, toot (on)] *a horn*

くらくら ──くらくらする（めまいがする）feel* dizzy [giddy];（混乱・興奮して）whirl ⓔ ‖熱で頭がくらくらする I *feel dizzy* because of (a) fever.
◆ くらくらするような高さ a *dizzy* [*giddy*] height / 彼のあまりのかっこよさにくらくらっとしてしまった(→恋をしそうになった) He was so cool that I *almost fell in love with* him.

ぐらぐら ぐらぐらする歯 a *loose* tooth / このいすは少しぐらぐらする This chair *is* a little *unsteady* [*wobbly*]. / 地震で家の中の物がぐらぐら揺れた Things in the house *shook* in the earthquake. / スープがなべの中でぐらぐら煮えている The soup *is boiling* in the pot.

くらげ 水母・海月 jellyfish ⓒ

くらし 暮らし（生活）life ⓒⓊ（複 lives）;（生計）living（通例単数形）/質素な[穏やかな, ぜいたくな, 切り詰めた]暮らし *a simple* [*quiet, luxurious, frugal*] *life* /彼らは何とか暮らしを立てている They *make* [*earn*] *their living* somehow. / They manage to *make ends meet*.
◆ 暮らし向きがよい[悪い] *be well* [*badly*] *off* / その日暮らしをする *live from hand to mouth* / 私は都会[いなか]暮らしのほうが好きだ

I prefer *living in the city* [*country*]. / 遺跡から昔の人々の暮らしぶりを知ることができる Ruins tell us *how* ancient peoples *lived*. / 兄はひとり暮らしを始めた My brother began to *live alone*.

グラジオラス gladiolus ⓒ（複 gladioli ~es,《米》）

クラシック（古典・一流の作品）classic ⓒ
◆ クラシックな家具 *classic* furniture
‖クラシック音楽 classical music（❖×classic music とは言わない）/ クラシックカー a classic car / クラシックバレエ (a) classical ballet

クラス
❶【学級】class ⓒ（❖特に《英》ではクラスの一人一人に重点をおくときには単数形でも複数扱いになることがある）
初級[中級, 上級]クラス a beginners' [*an* intermediate, *an* advanced] *class*（❖この class は course と言い換えることもできる）
麻里が私たちのクラスの代表委員に選ばれた Mari was chosen our *class president* [*representative*].
私の英語の点数はクラス平均より少し下だった My marks in English were a little below *the class average*.
◆彼女は自分の趣味についてクラスメートに話した She spoke about her hobbies to *her classmates*.
❷【等級】class ⓒ, rate ⓒ
ファースト[エコノミー]クラスで旅行する travel in (*the*) *first* [*economy*] *class*
彼はトップクラスの野球チームに所属している He belongs to a *top-class* [*top-rate*] baseball team.
‖クラス会 a class reunion / クラス替え rearrangement of classes

くらす 暮らす
（生活する）live ⓔ;（生計を立てる）make* a living;（日々を過ごす）get* along
快適に[質素に, 仲よく]暮らす *live comfortably* [*simply, in harmony*]
私は両親と弟といっしょに暮らしている I *live with* my parents and a brother.
祖父は厚生年金で暮らしている My grandfather *lives on* a company pension.
彼はフランス語を教えて暮らしている He's *making a living* (by) teaching French.
◆ 1か月そこで暮らす(→滞在する)だけの金がかろうじてあった I had barely enough money to *stay there for a month*. / 宝くじで10億円当たったら一生遊んで暮らせるよ If you win one billion yen in a lottery, you'll be able to *idle away your life*.

グラス（コップ）glass ⓒ ‖ウイスキーグラス a whiskey glass / カクテルグラス a cocktail glass / ワイングラス a wine glass

グラスゴー Glasgow（❖英国の都市）

グラスファイバー fiberglass,《英》fibreglass Ⓤ, glass fiber Ⓤ

グラタン gratin ⓒ（❖フランス語から）‖マカロニグラタン macaroni au *gratin*（❖au gratin

は [òu grǽtn] と読む)
クラッカー （食品）cracker ©, （爆竹）cracker ©, firecracker ©　∥クラッカーを鳴らす set off *a cracker*

ぐらつく ━ 働 shake*, wobble 圓; （決心・勇気が）waver 圓 ━ 形 shaky, wobbly　∥このいすはぐらつく This chair *is wobbly*. / 私の家はあのくらいの弱い地震ではぐらつかない My house doesn't *shake* in such a light earthquake. / けがのせいで彼は足元が少しぐらついている He's a little *shaky* on his feet because of the injury. / 画家になるという彼女の決意はぐらつくことがなかった She never *wavered* in her determination to be a painter.

クラッチ clutch ©　∥クラッチを入れる[切る] let in [out] *the clutch* / クラッチが入っている *The clutch* is in.

グラニューとう グラニュー糖 granulated sugar Ⓤ

グラビア gravure [grəvjúər] Ⓤ©, photogravure Ⓤ©

クラブ
❶【同好会】club ©
⇨ ぶ（部），場面・状況別会話 p.1748
クラブに入る[をやめる] join [quit] *a club*
🔵「学校では何のクラブに入ってるの」「美術部に入っています」"What *club* are you in at school?" "I'm in the art club."
🔵「クラブの部員はどのくらいですか」「20人くらいです」"How big is *your club*?" "We have about twenty members."
❷【ゴルフ】(golf) club ©; （ヘッドが木製の）wood ©; （ヘッドが金属製の）iron ©
❸【トランプ】club ©
クラブの7 the seven *of clubs*
∥クラブ活動 club activities; （課外活動）extracurricular activities

グラフ graph ©; （図表）chart ©　∥グラフを書く make [draw] *a graph* / このグラフは1年間の気温の変化を示している This *graph* shows a year's temperature changes.
∥グラフ用紙 graph paper / 円グラフ a pie graph [chart] / 帯グラフ a rectangle graph / 折れ線グラフ a line graph / 棒グラフ a bar graph [chart]

グラブ glove © ⇨ グローブ

グラフィック　∥グラフィックアート the graphic arts / グラフィックデザイナー a graphic designer / グラフィックデザイン graphic design

-くらべ -比べ　力比べ *a contest* of strength / 修と背比べをした Osamu and I *compared heights*.

くらべもの 比べ物　ビニールは本物の革とは比べものにならない Vinyl *can't compare with* real leather. / テニスの腕では私は彼とは比べものにならない（→彼にはかなわない）I'm *no match for* him in tennis.

くらべる 比べる

compare 働 圓（❖ 圓 の場合，しばしば favorably, unfavorably を伴う）

2冊の辞書を比べてみれば，この辞書のほうがすぐれていることが分かる *Compare* these two dictionaries, and you will find that this one is better.
日本の文化とアメリカの文化を比べて，レポートを書いた I *compared* Japanese culture *with* American culture and wrote a report.
1学期に比べて2学期は英語の成績が上がった *Compared with* the first term, my English grades went up in the second.
彼の家と比べたら私の家はとても小さい My house is very small *when compared with* his.
このパソコンはあのパソコンと比べてすぐれている［劣っている］This PC *compares favorably* [*unfavorably*] *with* that one.
◆中国と比べれば日本は小さな国だ Japan is a small country *in comparison with* China. / Japan is a smaller country than China. / パソコンの売り上げが去年に比べアップした Sales of PCs are higher *than* last year.

グラマー¹ ━ グラマーな 《米俗語》stacked, built　⇦英語の glamorous は「魅力的な」の意味で，必ずしも「豊満な肉体」を意味しない）；（胸・しりが大きい）voluptuous　∥彼女はグラマーだ She is *stacked* [*built*].

グラマー² （文法）grammar Ⓤ

くらます　なぜ彼が突然姿をくらましたか知っていますか Do you know why he suddenly *disappeared*? / 彼は警察の目をくらまして（→欺いて）逃げた He *deceived* the police and ran away.

くらむ 眩む　目がくらむような高さ a *dizzy* height / 目もくらむほど高いビル a *dizzyingly* tall building / ヘッドライトの光で目がくらんだ（→私の目を眩ませた）The glare of headlights *blinded* [*dazzled*] me. / だれでもこんな大金を見せられると目がくらむよ Anybody *would be blinded* by so much money.

グラム gram © （《略語》g, gm., gr.）　∥300グラムの牛肉 three hundred *grams* of beef

くらやみ 暗闇 darkness Ⓤ, the dark　∥妹は暗やみを怖がる My sister is afraid of *the dark*. / 暗やみで何かが動いた Something moved in *the dark*. / 町は暗やみに包まれていた The town *was shrouded in darkness*. / 彼らは暗やみに紛れて逃げた They ran away *under the cover* [*cloak*] *of darkness*.

クラリネット clarinet ©　∥クラリネットを吹く（→演奏する）play *the clarinet*
∥クラリネット奏者 a clarinet(t)ist

くらわす 食らわす　彼女は彼のほほに平手打ち［パンチ］を食らわせた She *gave* him a slap [punch] on the cheek.

グランド ⇨ グラウンド

グランドピアノ grand piano ©

グランプリ Grand Prix [grɑ́ːn príː] © （複 Grands Prix, ～）（❖フランス語から）; （大賞）(the) first prize　∥日本グランプリ *the* Japan *Grand Prix*

くり 栗　（実）chestnut [tʃésnʌt] ©; （木）chestnut tree ©　∥クリを拾う pick up *chest-*

nuts ◆栗色の髪 *chestnut* hair

クリアー 2メートルのバーをクリアーする *clear* a two-meter bar / 問題点をクリアーする(→解決する) *solve* a problem / (テレビゲームで) 1面をクリアーした I *cleared* [*got past*] the first stage.

くりあがる 繰り上がる 3時間目の英語が2時間目に繰り上がった The third-period English class *was moved up to* second period.

くりあげ 繰り上げ その候補者が彼の代わりに繰り上げ当選した The other candidate *was declared elected* as a result of his disqualification.

くりあげる 繰り上げる (期日などを) advance [他], move up [forward]; (数を) carry [他] ∥予定を繰り上げる *advance* [*move up*] a schedule / 出発の日が1週間繰り上げられた The date of departure *has been advanced* [*moved up*] by a week.

クリアランスセール (在庫一掃セール) clearance sale [C]

グリース (潤滑油) grease [U]

クリーナー (掃除機·洗剤) cleaner [C] [U]

クリーニング ⚠(ドライクリーニング) dry-cleaning [U]

◆スカートをクリーニング(→クリーニング店)に出す *send* a skirt *to the laundry* [*cleaners*, 《英》*cleaner's*] / コートがクリーニングから戻ってきた The coat came back from *the laundry*. / そのセーターはクリーニングに出してある The sweater is at *the laundry*.

クリーブランド Cleveland(❖米国の都市)

クリーム cream [U]; (化粧用) cream [C] [U]; (アイスクリーム) ice cream [U] [C] ―クリームの (形状) creamy; (色) cream-colored, cream(y) ∥クリーム入りコーヒー coffee with *cream* / クリームをかけたイチゴ strawberries and *cream* / 手にクリームを塗る apply *cream* to *one's* hands

💬「クリームと砂糖は入れますか」「ええ, ちょっとだけ」 "Do you take *cream* and sugar?" "Just a touch."

∥クリームソーダ ice-cream soda (❖《米》では単に soda ともいう) / クリームチーズ cream cheese / コールドクリーム cold cream / サワークリーム sour [soured] cream / シェービングクリーム shaving cream / 生クリーム whipping cream / 日焼け止めクリーム sunscreen, sunblock / ホイップクリーム whipped cream / リップクリーム lip salve

くりいれる 繰り入れる その経費は次年度予算に繰り入れられた The expense *was carried forward* [*over*] *to* the next year's budget.

クリーン クリーンな選挙 a *clean* election

∥クリーンナップ(トリオ) the middle of the (batting) order (❖×cleanup trio とはいわない. 日本語では「クリーンナップ(トリオ)」で3番, 4番, 5番打者を指すが, 英語の cleanup (hitter)は4番打者のみを指す)

グリーン (緑色) green [C] [U]; 〖ゴルフ〗 (putting) green [C] ∥グリーン車 (日本の) a "green" first-class car / グリーンベルト a green belt

グリーンピース (エンドウマメの実) (green) peas [píːz]; (環境保護団体) Greenpeace

クリーンヒット レフト前にクリーンヒットを放つ(→ライナーのシングルヒットを放つ) *hit a sharp* [*clean*] *single* to left field (❖clean hit という表現もあるが, あまり一般的ではない)

くりかえし 繰り返し repetition [C] [U]; (詩·歌の) refrain [C]

くりかえす 繰り返す repeat [自] [他] ―繰り返して repeatedly

山田先生は質問を繰り返した Mr. Yamada *repeated* the question.

「おなかがすいたよ」と彼は繰り返し言った "I'm hungry," he *repeated*.

◆同じ間違いを繰り返すな(→二度とするな) Don't make the same mistake *again*. / その物語は何度も繰り返し読んだ I read the story 「*again and again* [*over and over* (*again*)].

くりくり その赤ちゃんはくりくりした(→丸々としてかわいらしい)目をしている The baby has *cute round* eyes. / 彼は中学に入学するときくりくり坊主にした He *had his head* 「*shaved clean* [*cropped*] when he entered junior high school. (❖shave clean は「つるつるにそる」, crop は「短く刈り込む」という意味)

クリケット cricket [U] ∥クリケットをする play *cricket*

くりこし 繰り越し ∥繰越残高(来期への) the balance carried forward; (前期からの) the balance brought forward

くりこす 繰り越す transfer [他]; 〖簿記〗(来期へ) carry forward, (前期から) bring* forward ∥残金を次年度に繰り越す *carry* the balance *forward* to the next fiscal year

くりさげる 繰り下げる (延期する) put* off, postpone [他] ∥試験は大雪のため1時間繰り下げて行われた The examination *was put off* for an hour because of the heavy snow.

◆その式典は1週間繰り下げられた The ceremony *was moved back* a week.

クリスタル (水晶) crystal [U] ∥クリスタルガラス crystal (glass)

クリスチャン (キリスト教徒) Christian [C] ∥クリスチャンネーム a Christian name

クリスマス Christmas [U] [C]; (ポスターなどで) Xmas (❖X'mas と書くのは一般的ではない)

> Christmas は, 12月25日の「キリスト降誕祭」(Christmas Day)当日だけでなく, それ以前に始まるシーズンとしての「クリスマスの期間」(Christmastime)も指す.

クリスマスの日に on *Christmas* Day; at *Christmas* / クリスマスを祝う celebrate *Christmas*

💬「メリークリスマス, レイチェル」「メリークリスマス, 一郎」 "*Merry Christmas* to you, Rachel." "And to you, too. Ichiro."

∥クリスマスイブ Christmas Eve / クリスマスカード a Christmas card / クリスマスケーキ a Christmas cake (❖ふつう英米でクリスマスに食べるケーキはフルーツケーキ. ただし, 通例, 米国ではとりたてて Christmas cake という呼び

方はしない) /　クリスマスツリー a Christmas tree / 　クリスマスプレゼント a Christmas present [gift]

グリセリン 〖化学〗 glycerin Ⓤ ‖ニトログリセリン nitroglycerin

くりだす　繰り出す　(集まりなどに) turn out; (出かける) go* out ‖今夜は花見に繰り出そう Let's *go out* to see cherry blossoms tonight.

クリック　click Ⓒ ──クリックする click ⓥ ‖アイコンをクリック[ダブルクリック]する *click* [*double-click*] *on* an icon

クリップ　(paper) clip Ⓒ ‖書類をクリップで留めなさい *Clip* the papers together.

グリップ　grip Ⓒ ‖ラケットのグリップ *the grip* of a racket

クリニック　(外来患者用の診療所) clinic Ⓒ

グリニッジ　Greenwich [grénɪtʃ] ‖グリニッジ標準時 Greenwich (Mean) Time (《略語》GMT)

くりぬく　刳り貫く　丸木をくりぬいてカヌーを作る *hollow out* a tree trunk to make a canoe / 　ナシの芯(し)をくりぬく *core* a pear

くりのべる　繰り延べる　(延期する) put* off, postpone ⓥ

くりひろげる　繰り広げる　ワールドカップサッカーでは連日熱戦が繰り広げられている Exciting games *are being played* every day at the Soccer World Cup.

くりょ　苦慮　問題の解決に苦慮する *rack one's brains* to solve a problem

グリル　(レストラン) grillroom Ⓒ, grill Ⓒ; (焼き網) grill Ⓒ; (料理) grill Ⓒ

クリンチ　〖ボクシング〗 clinch Ⓒ ──クリンチする clinch ⓥ

くる¹ 来る

❶【話し手の方へ近づく】come* ⓥ
⇨ いく (行く)
早く来い *Come* quick [quickly].
彼はいつも遅れて来る He always *comes* late.
順子はきのうパーティーに来なかった Junko *didn't come* to the party yesterday.
きょうアメリカ人の友達が家に来る My American friend *is coming* to my house today.
彼は間もなくここに来るだろう He will *come* [*be*] here soon. (❖will の後では be が come と同じ意味で使われることがある)
彼女は走ってきた She *came* running.
向こうから人が来る Someone *is coming* from over there.
あ, 彼女が来た Look, here she *comes*. (❖主語が代名詞のときは《here＋主語＋動詞》の語順)
バスが来た Here *comes* the bus. (❖主語が代名詞でなければ《here＋動詞＋主語》の語順。また, 日本語は「来た」であるが×Here came the bus.とはしない)
いつでも遊びに来てください *Come* (*and*) *see me* any time.
どこから来たのですか Where did you *come from*? (❖Where do you come from?だと通例出身を聞くことになる)
彼女からきのう手紙が来た A letter *came* from her yesterday.
◆ここへは以前来たことがある I've *been* here before. / 　後から来るバスに乗ろう Let's take a *later* bus.
🅔「待った?」「いや, 今来たところ」"Have you been waiting?" "No. *I've just come*."
🅔「日本に来てからどのくらいになりますか」「もう 5 年になります」"How long *have* you *been* in Japan?" "Five years already."
🅔「新しい英語の先生が来るんだよ」「そうみたいだね」 "We are going to *have* a new English teacher." "So it seems."

❷【季節・時間・順序】come* ⓥ
北海道に夏が来た Summer *has come* to Hokkaido.
私の番が来た My turn *has come*.
◆その年の夏は来る日も来る日も(→毎日)雨だった It rained *every day* in the summer of the year. / 　高度情報化時代がついにやってきた The age of the information highway *has finally arrived*.

❸【由来・原因】come* from ...
この言葉はオランダ語からきている This word *comes* [*is derived*] *from* Dutch.
父の病気は過労からきているらしい My father's illness seems to 「*come from* [*be caused by*]」 overwork.

❹【事態の推移】
暑くなってきた It's *getting* hot.
彼女のことが好きになってきた I *have come* to like her.
雪が降ってきた(→降り始めた) It *began* to snow.

❺【ある段階に至る】
その力士の体力は限界にきている The sumo wrestler *has reached the limit* of his physical strength.
このテレビはがたがきている This TV *is worn out*.

❻【継続】
この伝統は300年続いてきた(→300年の歴史がある) This tradition *has a history of 300 years*. / 　This tradition *has been around for 300 years*.

❼【その他】
友達の家に遊びに行ってきます I'm going to my friend's house *to see him*.
どこへ行ってきたの? Where *have* you *been*?
電車の中に傘を忘れてきた I *left* my umbrella in the train.
そうこなくっちゃ *That's the spirit*.
もう頭にきた I've *had it up to here*.
彼女がだれのことを言っているのか私にはすぐぴんときた Who she was talking about *clicked with* me immediately.
今年のかぜはおなかにくるらしい I hear this year's flu *affects* the stomach.

くる² 繰る　(糸などを) reel ⓥ; (ページを) turn ⓥ ‖糸を繰る *reel in* the thread / 　ページを繰る *turn* (*over*) the pages

ぐる　僕は友人たちとぐるになって先生にうそをつ

いた I lied to my teacher *in cahoots with* my friends. / 健一はやつらとぐるにちがいない Kenichi must *be in cahoots with* them.

くるい 狂い (混乱) disorder Ⓤ ⇨くるう 〘事故のためにダイヤに狂いが生じた There was *disorder* in the train schedule because of the accident.

◆私の目に狂いはなかった I *was right* in my judgment. / My judgment *has proved right*. / 僕の時計は1秒の狂いもない My watch *keeps perfect time*.

くるう 狂う
❶【人の気が】──狂った《口語的》crazy, mad, insane(❖いずれも実際に精神異常の場合にもそうでない場合にも用いる)
妻の死によるショックで彼は(気が)狂ってしまった He *went insane* from the shock of his wife's death. / (→妻の死が彼を狂わせた) His wife's death *drove* him *insane*.
酒を飲んで運転したなんてあいつは狂ってるよ It *was crazy of* him [He must *be crazy*] to have driven under the influence of alcohol.
◆彼女は狂ったように試験勉強をした She studied *crazily* [《口語的》*like mad*] for the examination.
❷【夢中になる】
彼はギターに狂っている He *is crazy* [*mad, enthusiastic*] about the guitar.
◆踊り狂う dance *like crazy*
❸【調子が】
私の時計はよく狂う My watch often *has the wrong time*.
彼の歌は音程が狂っている He sings *out of tune*.
寒さで体の調子が狂ってしまった I've got [*become*] *out of shape* because it has been too cold.
手元が狂って違うボタンを押してしまった I *accidentally* pushed the wrong button.
❹【順序・予定などが】
本の並べ方が狂ってるよ The books *are out of order*.
雨で予定がすっかり狂った Our schedule *was completely upset* by the rain.
順番が狂った The order *got mixed up*.

クルー (乗組員)(集合的) crew Ⓒ
クルーザー (cabin) cruiser Ⓒ
グループ group Ⓒ(❖《英》では単数形で複数扱いになることがある) / ロックグループ a rock *group* / グループを作る form a *group* / 生徒たちはグループ別にその問題に取り組んでいる The students are working on the problem *in groups*. / 彼女は30人の生徒を3グループに分けた She separated 30 students into three *groups*.
◆彼は不良グループとつきあいがある He hangs around with *a gang*.

くるくる スケート選手はくるくる回った The ice skater *spun* [*turned*] *around (and around)*. / たこが空中でくるくる舞っていた A kite *was whirling about* in the sky. / 彼女はバトンをくるくる回した She *twirled* the baton. / 彼女はくるくると気が変わる She *easily* changes her mind.

ぐるぐる 地球は太陽の周りをぐるぐる回っている The earth *goes* [*spins*] *around (and around)* the sun. / 両腕をぐるぐる回して *Move* your arms *in circles*. / *Swing around* your arms. / 医者は彼の腕を包帯でぐるぐる巻きにした The doctor *wound* his arm *heavily* with a bandage. / 彼はバットをぐるぐる回していた He *was twirling* a bat.

くるしい 苦しい
❶【つらい・困難な】(困難な) hard, difficult, tough; (苦痛を与える) painful; (生活が) badly off, poorly off ⇨つらい
この苦しい仕事は早く終えたい I want to finish this *hard* job as soon as possible.
私は苦しい立場におかれている I am in a *difficult* position.
失恋は苦しいものだ Losing love is always *painful*.
当時はさんざん苦しい思いをした I suffered a lot of *painful* experiences at that time.
今がいちばん苦しい時だ. お互いがんばろう This is the *hardest* time. Let's keep trying.
彼らは生活が苦しい They *are badly* [*poorly*] *off*.
◆そんな苦しい言い訳はやめておけ Don't make such *a poor* [*bad, feeble*] *excuse*. / うちの会社は経営が苦しい Our company *is in financial difficulties*.
❷【息・胸などが】
胸が苦しい I *feel a pain* in my chest.
食べすぎておなかが苦しい I've eaten too much, and *my stomach feels heavy*.
走ったので息が苦しい I'm *short of breath* from running.
ことわざ 苦しいときの神頼み We pray to God only when we are in difficulties.; Danger past, God forgotten.(→危険が去れば神のことは忘れてしまう)

くるしさ 苦しさ pain Ⓤ, suffering Ⓒ Ⓤ ⇨くるしみ

くるしまぎれ 苦し紛れ 私は苦しまぎれに(→窮地に追い込まれて)うそをついてしまった *Put into a corner*, I couldn't help telling a lie. / (→やけになって) I told a lie *in desperation*.

くるしみ 苦しみ pain Ⓤ, suffering Ⓒ Ⓤ; (困難) difficulty Ⓤ Ⓒ; (苦難) hardship Ⓤ / 苦しみを味わう go through *hardships* / 苦しみに耐える bear [endure] *suffering* / 苦しみを克服する overcome *difficulties* [*hardships*] / だれも僕の苦しみを分かってくれない Nobody can understand my *pain*.
慣用表現 その会社は新事業の産みの苦しみを味わっている The company is suffering *growing pains* in its new enterprise.

くるしむ 苦しむ
❶【苦痛を感じる】suffer 自 他; (苦労する) have* difficulty (in) *doing*
彼は長いこと病気で苦しんでいる He's been *suffering from* (a) disease for a long time.

飢えに苦しむ人々を助けなければならない We must help people *suffering from* hunger.
その国の国民は重税に苦しんでいた People of the country *were suffering from* [*under*] a heavy tax burden.
私は英語の単語を覚えるのに苦しんでいる I *have difficulty* learning English words by heart.
❷【困る】be troubled;（当惑する）be at a loss
隣の部屋の騒音に毎晩苦しんでいる I *am troubled* [*annoyed*] *by* the loud noises from the next room every night.
思わぬ質問をされて返答に苦しんだ Receiving an unexpected question, I *was at a loss* [*for*] an answer [what to answer].
◆君のしていることは理解に苦しむよ *It's hard to understand* what you're doing.

くるしめる 苦しめる 今回のテストにはとても苦しめられた I *had a lot of trouble* answering the questions on this exam. / 彼は子供のころからぜんそくに苦しめられてきた He *has suffered from* asthma since he was a kid. / 重い税金が貧しい人たちを苦しめた（→圧迫した）The heavy taxes *oppressed* the poor.

くるぶし 踝 ankle ⓒ

くるま 車

❶【自動車】car ⓒ,（米）automobile ⓒ,（英）motorcar ⓒ（❖いずれも自動車を表す一般的な語で，通例バスやトラックなどは含まない）;（陸上の乗り物全般）vehicle ⓒ;（車の往来）traffic ⓤ ⇨じどうしゃ 図版
【車で】
彼女は北海道へ車で行った She went to Hokkaido *in her car* [*by car*].（❖byの後では無冠詞）
◆病院はここから車で30分のところにある The hospital is 30 minutes' *drive* from here. / It's a 30-minute *drive* from here to the hospital. / よかったら，今夜8時に車で迎えに行くよ If you don't mind, I'll *pick* you *up* at eight tonight. / 学校に車で行けるなんて便利だね It is convenient that you *can drive* to school.
🅔「家に帰る途中です」「じゃ，車で送らせてください」"I'm on my way home." "Then, let me *drive you*."
【車を】
車を運転する drive [steer] *a car* / 車を止める stop *a car*; pull *a car* up;（→駐車する）park *a car*
彼は車をバックで車庫に入れた He backed *his car* into the garage.
ピクニックに車を出せる人はいますか Is there anyone who can use *his or her car* for a picnic?
◆大通りで車（→タクシー）を拾おう Let's catch *a taxi* on the main street.
🅔「ここに車を止めちゃだめだよ」「すみません，知りませんでした」"You are not supposed to *park* (*your car*) here." "Sorry, I didn't know about that."
【車に・から】
車に乗る[から降りる] get in(to) [out of] *a car*
子猫が車にひかれた A kitten was run over by *a car*. /（→はねられた）A kitten was hit by *a car*.
◆車に乗せていただいてありがとうございます It's kind of you to *give me a lift* [*ride*].
【車が・は】
この通りは車が多い *Traffic* is heavy in this street.
◆日本では車は左側通行だ In Japan, *drivers* keep to the left.
【その他】
排気量3,000ccの車 *a car* with a 3,000-cc engine
雪のため車の流れはのろかった The *traffic* was slow because of snow.
◆車の部品 *auto* parts / トヨタ(社製)の車 a Toyota
❷【車輪】wheel ⓒ;（いすなどのキャスター）caster ⓒ
車付きのテーブル a table on *wheels* [*casters*]
‖車社会 a car-oriented society / 車酔い carsickness / オートマチック車 an automatic / 乗用車 a passenger car / 中古車 a used [secondhand] car / 手押し車 a barrow, a cart,《主に英》a trolley / 電気自動車 an electric [a battery] car / マニュアル車 a car with a manual transmission / レッカー車《米》a wrecker, a tow truck,《英》a breakdown truck [lorry]

くるまいす 車椅子 wheelchair ⓒ ‖彼は私の車いすを戸口まで押していってくれた He pushed 「my *wheelchair* [me in *a wheelchair*] up to the door. / 以前より車いすで利用できる施設が増えてきた There are more *wheelchair-accessible* facilities than before.

くるまえび 車海老 prawn ⓒ

くるまる wrap* *oneself* up;（くるまっている）be wrapped up ‖彼は毛布にくるまって横になった He *wrapped himself up in* a blanket and lay down.

くるみ 胡桃 walnut ⓒ ‖クルミ割り器 nutcrackers

-ぐるみ 家族ぐるみでスキーに出かけた I went skiing with my *whole* family. / 町ぐるみでごみ問題に取り組んでいる The *whole* town addresses the problem of waste. / 加藤さんとは家族ぐるみのつきあいです We enjoy a friendly relationship with Mr. Kato and his family.

くるむ wrap* ⑭ ‖彼は子犬を毛布でくるんだ He *wrapped* a blanket *around* the puppy. / He *wrapped up* the puppy *in* a blanket.

グルメ gourmet [gúərmei] ⓒ（❖フランス語から）

くるり 彼はくるりと向きを変え一塁に投げた He *turned swiftly around* and threw to first base. / 彼女は新しい服を着てくるりと回ってみせた She *spun around* to show me her

ぐるり

new clothes.

ぐるり 城は塀にぐるりと囲まれていた The castle *was surrounded* by walls. / 警察はその家をぐるりと取り囲んだ The police *surrounded* the house. / 山手線は東京都心をぐるりと回っている The Yamanote line *circles* the center of Tokyo. / 学校の周りを走ってぐるりと1周した I ran one lap *around* the school. / 彼女はぐるりと現場を見回した She looked *around* the scene. / 彼女の目はぐるりと一帯を見回した Her eyes traveled over the scene.

くるわせる 狂わせる (人を) drive* *a person* mad; (計画などを) upset* ⇒くるう / 娘の死が彼を狂わせた His daughter's death *drove* him *mad*.
◆その偏見が彼の判断を狂わせた The prejudice *confused* his judgement. / 金が彼の人生を狂わせた Money *perverted* the course of her whole life.

くれ 暮れ (年末) the year-end, the end of the year ∥もう暮れが迫ってきた It's getting near *the end of the year*.
◆暮れの大掃除 a *year-end* general house cleaning / 去年の暮れに鎌倉に行った I visited Kamakura at *the end of last year*.

グレー gray, 《英》grey ⓒⓊ ──グレーの gray, 《英》grey

クレーター crater ⓒ

クレープ (薄いパンケーキ) crepe, crêpe [kréip] ⓒ

グレープ 〔植物〕 grape ⓒ ∥グレープジュース grape juice

グレープフルーツ 〔植物〕 grapefruit ⓒⓊ (複 ~s)

クレーム ⚠ (苦情) complaint ⓤⓒ (❖英語の claim は「(損害賠償などの)請求」の意味) ∥彼らはその商品に関して会社にクレームをつけた They *made complaints* to the company about the product. / They *complained* to the company about the product.

クレーン crane ⓒ ∥クレーン車 a crane truck

くれぐれも くれぐれもお体をおだいじに *Be sure to* take good care of yourself. / ご家族の方々にくれぐれもよろしくお伝えください Please *give my best regards [wishes]* to your family. / 集合時間にはくれぐれも遅れることのないように *Please be very careful* not to be late for the meeting time.

クレジット credit ⓤ; (映画などの字幕に示される制作関係者の名前) the credits ∥パソコンをクレジットで買った I bought a personal computer *on credit*.
💬「お支払いはどのようになさいますか」「クレジットカードで」"How will you be paying?" "*By credit card*."

クレソン ⚠ 〔植物〕watercress ⓤ (❖日本語はフランス語の cresson から)

ぐれつ 愚劣 foolishness ⓤ, stupidity ⓤ, 《公式的》folly ⓤ ──愚劣な foolish, stupid

くれない 紅 vivid red, cerise [sərí:z] ⓤ ──紅(色)の vivid red, cerise

クレバス (氷河などの深い割れ目) crevasse [krəvǽs] ⓒ

クレパス ⚠ pastel crayon ⓒ (❖「クレパス」は商標名)

クレムリン the Kremlin(❖ロシア連邦政府のある建物)

クレヨン crayon ⓒ ∥クレヨンで絵を描く draw a picture with *crayons*

くれる¹ 呉れる
❶【与える·よこす】 give* ⓜ
彼が僕にこの本をくれる He *gave* me this book. / He *gave* this book *to* me.
彼女は毎日電話をくれる She *gives* me *a call* every day.
◆彼は私に金をくれと言ってきた He *asked* me *for money*. / こんなものおまえにくれてやるよ Here, *take* it.
❷【…してくれる】(親切にも…する) be kind enough to *do*, be nice to *do*; (わざわざ…する) take* the trouble to *do* ⇒やる

> **語法**
> 上記の表現のほか、英語では単に「(人に)…する、…した」に当たる表現を用いればよい場合が多い ∥お母さんがドレスを作ってくれた My mother *made* me a dress. / My mother *made* a dress *for* me.

彼は忙しいのに私を手伝ってくれた He 「*was kind enough* [*took the trouble*] *to* help me when he was busy.
その女性は私に市役所への行き方を教えてくれた The woman *told* me how to get to the city hall.
父は誕生日のお祝いにCDを買ってくれた My father *bought* me a CD for my birthday.
お金を貸してくれてありがとう Thank you for *lending* me money.
彼は私に優しくしてくれる He *is kind to* me.
だれか、助けてくれ! Somebody, *help* me!
◆こんなとき彼がいてくれたらなあ *I wish* he were [《口語的》was] around at times like this. / 彼がアメリカでも元気でいてくれたらいいな *I hope* he is doing fine in America. / このバッグを運ぶのを手伝ってくれませんか *Would* [*Could*] *you* help me carry this bag? / この部屋をよくもめちゃめちゃにしてくれたよね Now, you've messed up this room.
❸【…してくれるよう頼む】ask ⓜ ⇒たのむ
友人にいっしょに職員室へ行ってくれるよう頼んだ I *asked* my friend *to* go to the teachers' office with me.
彼女は入院中の友達に会わせてくれるように頼んだ She *asked to be allowed to* visit her friend in the hospital.

くれる² 暮れる
❶【日が】 get* [grow*] dark
日が暮れてきた It's *getting* [*growing*] *dark*.
暮れないうちに帰ってきなさいよ Come back home *before* (*it gets*) *dark*.
彼は日が暮れても帰ってこなかった He didn't come back even *after* (*it got*) *dark*.
❷【年が】come* to an end
今年もあと2時間ほどで暮れる This year will

come to an end in two hours or so.
❸【悲しみ・思案などに】
彼は職を失い途方にくれている He has lost his job and 「*doesn't know what to do* [*is at a complete loss*].
恋人を亡くし彼女は悲しみにくれた She *was deep in sorrow* over her boyfriend's death.
ぐれる go* wrong ∥彼は高校時代にぐれていた He *went wrong* while in high school.
◆ぐれた少年 a *delinquent* boy
クレンザー cleanser ©Ⓤ

くろ 黒

❶【色】black Ⓤ ——黒い black;（髪・目・肌などが）dark
黒いスーツの男 a man in a *black* suit
彼女は色が黒い She *has dark skin*. / She *is dark-skinned*.
トーストが黒くこげてしまった The toast burned *black*.
あの黒い雲だと大雨になるかもしれない Those *dark* [*black*] clouds may mean heavy rain.
◆信也は海で真っ黒く焼いた（→日焼けした）Shinya *got a nice suntan* at the seaside. / 君のシャツはえりが黒いよ（→汚れている）The collar of your shirt *is dirty* [*stained*].

> 英作文ノート「黒い目」は **dark eyes**
> 彼女は黒い目で黒い髪をしている
> →○She has *dark* eyes and *dark* hair.
> →○She is *dark*-eyed and *dark*-haired.
> ★目・髪・肌などが黒いというときは dark を用いるのがふつう。免許証などでは日本人の目の色は brown と表示されることが多い。なお She has「a black eye [two black eyes].の black eye は「目の周りの青あざ」の意味。

❷【その他】
我々はあの男を黒（→罪を犯した）とにらんだ We were quite sure that the man *was guilty*.
その政治家は黒いうわさが絶えない There are always lots of *dark rumors* about the politician.
∥黒帯（柔道・空手などの）a black belt / 黒こしょう black pepper / 黒ビール porter, stout / 黒魔術 black magic

くろう 苦労

（面倒）trouble Ⓤ《また複数形～s》;（困難）difficulty ⓊⒸ;（苦難）hardship ⓊⒸ;（努力）effort ⓊⒸ;（苦心）pains;（心配）worry Ⓤ ——苦労する（困難を味わう）have* trouble, have difficulty;（骨を折る）take* trouble, take pains;（苦しい思いをする）have a hard time, suffer hardships
今度の英語のテストでは苦労した I *had trouble* on this English exam.
我々は彼の英語を聞き取るのにとても苦労した We *had great difficulty* (*in*) understanding his English.

そのころの彼は苦労が多かった He *suffered many hardships* then. / He *had a hard time* then.
うちは苦労が絶えない *Troubles* [*Worries*] *fall on* our family *one after another*.
ここであきらめたら今までの苦労が水の泡だ If we gave up here, all our *efforts* would come to nothing.
その老人は苦労して階段を上った The old man mounted the stairs *with difficulty*.
私は苦労して彼を説得した I *took pains* to persuade him.
金ですむ話ならだれも苦労はしない If the problem could be solved with money, nobody would *have* any *difficulty* with it.
彼は何年もの苦労の末に成功した He finally succeeded *after years of effort*.
苦労のかいあって彼女は希望の職に就くことができた Her *efforts*「*were rewarded* [*paid off*] and she was able to get the job she wanted.
彼女は何の苦労もなく暮らしている She is living *without any trouble* [*worry*].
ご苦労さまでした *Thank you very much for your trouble.*
この本の著者はなかなかの苦労人のようだ The author of this book seems to *have suffered many hardships*.
◆若いころは親にずいぶん苦労をかけた（→親を悩ませた）I *worried* my parents a lot when I was young. /（→私が親の悩みの種だった）I *was a big worry* for my parents when I was young. / 私の部屋を掃除するのはひと苦労だった It *was a bit of work* cleaning my room. / 彼女は苦労性だ She is *a worry-wart*. / 父は若いころの苦労話をした My father told me *a hard luck story* from his youth.

ぐろう 愚弄 ——愚弄する ridicule ⑯, make* a fool of *a person*, make a mockery of *a person*

くろうと 玄人（本職の人）professional Ⓒ;（専門家）specialist Ⓒ;（熟練した人）expert Ⓒ ⇨プロ
慣用表現 彼のギターの腕前はくろうとはだしだ（→プロに勝るとも劣らない）He *is no less skilled* in guitar *than* a professional guitarist. /（→プロでさえその腕前に感嘆するだろう）*Even a professional guitarist would admire* his skill.

クローク ⚠cloakroom Ⓒ,《米》checkroom Ⓒ, coatroom Ⓒ ∥英語の cloak は「マント」の意味 ∥クロークにコートを預ける check *one's* coat at *the cloakroom*

クローズアップ（大写し）close-up [klóusÀp] ⓊⒸ
慣用表現 その番組では環境問題がクローズアップされていた（→主要なテーマだった）Environmental problems were the「*main subjects* [*focus*] of the program.

クローゼット《主に米》closet Ⓒ,《英》cupboard [kÁbərd] Ⓒ

クローバー clover ⓊⒸ ∥四つ葉のクローバー a four-leaf [four-leaved] *clover*

グローバル ──グローバルな global 〘グローバルな視点で物事を見る see things from a *global* point of view

グローブ glove [glʌ́v] C (❖野球のグローブ, ボクシングのグローブはそれぞれ baseball glove, boxing glove ともいう)

クロール the crawl 〘クロールで泳ぐ swim *the crawl*

クローン 〘生物〙clone C 〘クローン羊 *a clone* of a sheep; a *cloned* sheep

くろかみ 黒髪 dark [black] hair C
◆緑の黒髪の女性 a *raven-haired* woman; a woman *with raven hair*

くろこげ 黒焦げ 黒こげ死体 a *charred* body / ちょっと目を離している間に魚は黒こげになってしまった The fish *was「burnt black [charred]* when I looked away for a moment.

くろざとう 黒砂糖 brown sugar U; (精製されていない) unrefined sugar U

くろじ 黒字 (貿易の) surplus U C 〘日本の貿易黒字 Japan's *trade surplus* ◆今月は5万円の黒字だ We are 50,000 yen *in the black* this month. / その会社は今黒字だ The company is now *in the black*.

くろしお 黒潮 the Black Stream, the Japan Current

クロス ボールをクロスに打ち返す hit the ball back *diagonally* / この道は100メートルほど先で国道20号線とクロスします This street *crosses [intersects (with)]* Route 20 about a hundred meters ahead.

クロスカントリー cross-country C U
〘クロスカントリースキー cross-country skiing

クロスプレー ⚠ close play (❖この close は「きわどい, 接戦の」の意味. cross ではないことに注意) 〘ランナーは本塁クロスプレーでタッチアウトになった The runner was tagged out on *a close play* at the (home) plate.

くろずむ 黒ずむ (黒くなる) blacken 自; (黒みがかる) become* blackish; (汚れる) become stained [dirty] 〘すすで黒ずんだ柱 a pillar *blackish [blackened]* with soot / Tシャツの首がだいぶ黒ずんだ The neck of the T-shirt *has become very stained [dirty]*.

クロスワード(パズル) crossword (puzzle) C 〘クロスワードパズルを解く work out *a crossword puzzle*

クロッカス 〘植物〙crocus [króukəs] C

グロッキー ──グロッキーの (疲れ・病気などで足元がふらふらの) 〘口語的〙groggy [grági]; (疲労困憊した) tired out, exhausted

グロテスク ──グロテスクな grotesque; (醜い) hideous

くろパン 黒パン (ライ麦の) black [rye] bread U; (糖みつ入りの蒸しパン) brown bread U

くろぼし 黒星 (負け) loss C, defeat U C 〘その力士は黒星が3つ続いた The sumo wrestler has had three *losses [defeats]* in a row.

くろまく 黒幕 a puller of (the) strings ◆事件の黒幕はあの男(→あの男が陰で事件の糸を引いていた)にちがいない The man must *have been pulling the strings* in the case. / (→背後にいる) The man must *have been behind the scenes* in the case.

クロム 〘化学〙chrome U, chromium U (元素記号 Cr)

くろめ 黒目 (眼球の虹彩(こうさい)) iris C

くろやま 黒山 その歌手の周りには黒山の人だかりができた There was *a large crowd of people* gathering around the singer.

クロレラ 〘植物〙chlorella C

クロロホルム 〘化学〙chloroform U

クロワッサン croissant [krwɑːsɑ́ːŋ] C (❖フランス語から)

くわ¹ 桑 mulberry C

くわ² 鍬 hoe C

くわえて 加えて イワシはうまいし, 加えて安い Sardines are delicious; *besides* they are inexpensive. (❖上の例はうまいことを強調. besides の代わりに moreover を用いると安いことを強調する) / その店は洋服に加えて化粧品も売っている They sell cosmetics *along with* clothes at that store.

くわえる¹ 加える

❶【足す・増す】(付け足す) add 他; (増す) increase 自 他; (含める) include 他; (数える) count 他 自

7に3を加える *add* three to seven / 塩ひとつまみ加える *add* a pinch of salt

我々は彼を候補者リストに加えた We *included* him in the list of candidates.

消費税を加えて2,000円払った I paid 2,000 yen, *including* consumption tax.

◆明も仲間に加えようよ Why don't we *let* Akira *join* us? / 3に5を加えると8になる Three *and* five make(s) eight.

❷【与える】
ここにいる動物は人に危害を加えたりしない Animals here won't *do any harm to* people.

大部分の固体は熱を加えられると膨張する Most solids expand when they (*are*) *heated*.

彼は強盗に一撃を加えた He struck [dealt, delivered] *a blow* to the robber.

くわえる² 咥える 犬は口にくわえた獲物を私に見せた The dog showed me the wild game it *held in its mouth*. / 父はたばこをくわえて火をつけた My father *held* a cigarette *in his mouth* and lit it.

くわがたむし 鍬形虫 stag beetle C

くわけ 区分け (分類) classification U C; (分離) separation U ──区分けする classify 他; separate 他

くわしい 詳しい

❶【詳細な】detailed; (十全な) full ──詳しく in detail

詳しい説明をする give a *full [detailed]* explanation

もっと詳しい地図が欲しい I want a more *detailed* map.

それについて詳しく話してくれませんか Would

you tell me about it *in detail*?
◆(さらに)詳しいことを知りたい方は1234番にお電話ください For (further) *details*, please call 1234. / 詳しいことは後でお知らせします I'll let you know *the details* later on. / その昆虫の生態は詳しくは知られていません *Not much is known* about the habits of the insect. / この本は日本の歴史に詳しい This book will give you *in-depth* information about the history of Japan.
❷【精通している】
私はこのあたりには詳しい I *am familiar with* this neighborhood.
相撲について詳しいですね You *know a lot* about sumo, don't you?

くわずぎらい 食わず嫌い 父は漫画が嫌いだと言うがそれはただの食わず嫌いだ(→偏見にすぎない)と思う My father says he doesn't like comic books, but I think he *is just prejudiced*.

くわせもの 食わせ者 あいつはとんだ食わせ者(→詐欺師)だ.危うくだまされるところだった He was such *an impostor* that I was almost deceived by him.

くわせる 食わせる (えさをやる) feed* ⓗ; (養う) 養う ⓗ
慣用表現 あいついに一杯食わせてやるいいチャンスだ This is a good chance to *play a trick on* him.

くわだて 企て (試み) attempt ⓒ; (努力) effort ⓤⓒ; (計画) plan; (たくらみ) plot ⓒ /彼らの企てはすぐに明るみに出た Their *plot* was soon brought to light.

くわだてる 企てる (試みる) try ⓗ ⓘ, attempt ⓗ (❖try より形式ばった語. 失敗に終わることが多い); (計画する) plan ⓗ; (たくらむ) plot ⓗ ⓘ /政府は首都の移転を企てている The government *is planning* the relocation of the capital. / 彼らは政府の転覆を企てた They *plotted* to overthrow the government. / 彼らはカンニングを企てたが失敗に終わった They *attempted* to cheat on the exam but ended in failure.

くわわる 加わる
❶【加入する】join ⓗ ⓘ; (参加する) take* part, participate ⓘ
彼らは私たちの仲間[討論]に加わった They *joined* us [(*in*) our discussion].
彼はその計画に加わっていないと思う I don't think he *took part in* the plan.
❷【足される・増す】
12月になっていちだんと寒さが加わった It grew even *colder* in December.
収蔵品にモネの絵が加わった(→加えられた) A Monet *was added to* the collection.
◆この本は2,000円でそれに消費税が加わります This book costs 2,000 yen *plus* consumption [sales] tax.

-くん -君 (❖「君」に当たる英語はない. 親しい間柄ではファーストネームやニックネームで呼び合う) /やあ, 均君, 仕事は順調かい Hi, Hitoshi. How are you getting along with your work?

ぐん¹ 軍 army ⓒ; (陸海空軍) the (armed) forces; (軍隊) troops // 軍の放出品 *army surplus*

ぐん² 郡 《米》county ⓒ (❖state(州)の下位の行政区画; 《略語》Co., また,日本の「郡」もこれに当たるが,手紙などのあて名書きは Kaifu-gun「海部郡」のようにローマ字で書くのがふつう),《英》district ⓒ

ぐん³ 群 彼女はクラスで群を抜いて数学ができる She is *far ahead of the others* in her class in mathematics.

ぐんい 軍医 army surgeon ⓒ; (海軍の) naval [navy] surgeon ⓒ; (軍隊内で) medical officer ⓒ

ぐんか 軍歌 war song ⓒ, martial song ⓒ

くんかい 訓戒 admonition ⓒ /訓戒を受ける receive *an admonition*

ぐんかん 軍艦 warship ⓒ, battleship ⓒ

くんかいだ 犬は新しいドッグフードのにおいをくんくんかいだ The dog *sniffed at* the new dog food.

ぐんぐん ぐんぐん背が伸びる grow *taller and taller* / その歌手はぐんぐん(→急速に)人気が出てきた The singer has *rapidly* become popular. / 彼はスキーがぐんぐん上達した He made *rapid* progress in skiing. / 株価がぐんぐん上昇した Stock prices have gone up *sharply*.

ぐんこくしゅぎ 軍国主義 militarism ―軍国主義の militaristic ‖軍国主義者 a militarist

くんし 君子 (賢者) wise person ⓒ; (有徳者) a person of virtue ◆聖人君子ぶる play *the saint*
ことわざ 君子危うきに近寄らず Discretion is the better part of valor. / 勇敢さの大半は慎重さである) / 君子は豹変(ʊxɔ)す A wise man changes his mind, a fool never.

くんじ¹ 訓示 instruction ⓒ /新しい上司が訓示した Our new boss「gave *instructions* to [*instructed*] us.

くんじ² 訓辞 admonitory address ⓒ

ぐんじ 軍事 military affairs ‖ 軍事演習 (military) maneuvers / 軍事援助 military assistance / 軍事基地 a military base / 軍事拠点 a military post / 軍事行動 military action (activities, operation) / 軍事裁判 a court-martial / 軍事裁判所 a provost court / 軍事施設 a military installation / 軍事政権 a military regime / 軍事戦略 military strategy / 軍事同盟 a military alliance / 軍事費 military expenditures [spending] / 軍事予算 an arms budget / 軍事力 military power [strength, force]

ぐんしきん 軍資金 war chest ⓒ, war funds; (運動資金) campaign funds

くんしゅ 君主 monarch [mánɚk] ⓒ; (公式的) sovereign [sávərən] ⓒ ‖ 君主国 a monarchy / 君主制 monarchy / 専制君主 an absolute monarch / 立憲君主 a constitutional monarch

ぐんじゅ 軍需 ‖軍需産業 munitions industry / 軍需品 munitions, military supplies

ぐんしゅう 群衆・群集 crowd C, 《文語》throng U 《単数または複数扱い》; (暴徒) mob C ∥彼女は大群衆を押しのけて進んだ She thrust her way through the large crowd. / 日本が決勝ゴールを決めると群衆は熱狂した When Japan scored the winning goal, the crowd went mad. / 怒った群衆が本社の周りに集まってきている An angry mob is gathering outside the head office.
∥群集心理 mass [mob] psychology

ぐんしゅく 軍縮 disarmament U, arms reduction U ∥軍縮会議 a disarmament conference / 核軍縮 nuclear disarmament

くんしょう 勲章 decoration C; (メダル) medal C; (勲位を示す) order C ∥勲章をもらう be awarded a decoration

ぐんじょう 群青 ultramarine U, sea blue U ──群青色の ultramarine

ぐんじん 軍人 serviceman C, servicewoman C, soldier C (◆特に陸軍の軍人を指すこともある); (海軍の) sailor C; (空軍の) airman C; (将校) officer C ∥職業軍人 a professional soldier / 退役軍人 《米》a veteran,《英》an ex-serviceman

くんせい 薫製 ──薫製の smoked ∥サケの薫製 smoked salmon

ぐんせい 群生 ──群生する grow* in crowds ∥群生植物 a gregarious plant

ぐんたい 軍隊 (陸・海・空軍の総称) the (armed) forces, army C; (軍勢) troops / 軍隊を派遣する send [dispatch] an army / 軍隊を補強する harden troops / 軍隊に入隊する join the army
∥軍隊生活 an army life

ぐんて 軍手 (cotton) work gloves

ぐんと 彼の英語力はぐんとのびた His English has remarkably improved.

ぐんとう 群島 (a group of) islands, archipelago [à:rkəpéləgòu] C (複 ~s, ~es) ∥フィリピン群島 the Philippine archipelago; the Philippines

ぐんばい 軍配 (相撲の行司が持つ) fan C
◆この前の試合はタイガースに軍配が上がった(→タイガースが勝った) The Tigers won the previous game.

ぐんぱつじしん 群発地震 a series of concentrated random earthquakes

ぐんび 軍備 armaments ∥軍備を縮小[拡張,増強]する reduce [expand, reinforce] armaments
∥軍備拡張 the expansion of armaments, an arms buildup / 軍備縮小 disarmament, arms reduction / 軍備撤廃 disarmament / 再軍備 rearmament

ぐんぶ 軍部 the military 《複数扱い》;(軍当局) the military authorities

ぐんぷく 軍服 military uniform C

ぐんぽうかいぎ 軍法会議 court-martial C ∥人を軍法会議にかける try a person by court-martial; court-martial a person

ぐんま 群馬

群馬県は本州の中部、東京都の北西に位置する内陸県です。県南東部を除いてほぼ全県的に山がちで、北部には2,000メートル級の山々がそびえています。多くの湖沼や渓谷などの美しい自然に恵まれていますが、中でも珍しい植生の見られる尾瀬の湿原はとても有名です。
Gumma Prefecture is a landlocked prefecture, located in central Honshu to the northwest of Tokyo. The whole area is mountainous except for the southeastern part, and in the north there's a high range of mountains in the 2,000-meter class. This prefecture is blessed with natural beauty such as many lakes and ravines. The high moorland of Oze is especially famous for its unique flora.

ぐんゆうかっきょ 群雄割拠 携帯電話業界は群雄割拠の(→競争の激しい)時代を迎えた The cell phone industry has become highly competitive.

ぐんよう 軍用 ──軍用の military, for military use ∥軍用機 a warplane / 軍用犬 a sniffer dog / 軍用トラック an army lorry / 軍用品 military supplies

くんよみ 訓読み 漢字を訓読みする read kanji in the Japanese way [pronunciation]

ぐんらく 群落 colony C, community C

くんりん 君臨 ──君臨する reign [réin] ⊕, dominate ⊕⊕ ∥政界に君臨する dominate the political world ◆彼はヘビー級の王座に君臨している(→王座を保持している) He retains the heavyweight championship.

くんれん 訓練 training U (また a ~); (反復練習) drill C U; (しつけ) discipline U ──訓練する train ⊕⊕; drill ⊕
その猿たちはたくさんの芸をするように訓練されていた Those monkeys were trained to do many tricks.
彼女は看護の訓練を受けた She was trained in nursing [as a nurse, to be a nurse].
その選手はトーナメントに備えて厳しい訓練を始めた The athlete started hard training for the tournament.
∥職業訓練 professional [job, vocational] training / 避難訓練 (火事の) a fire drill; (地震の) an earthquake drill

け

け 毛 hair ❶❷; (羊毛) wool ❶; (動物の柔らかい毛) fur ❶; (動物・ブラシの硬い毛) bristle
- 私は髪の毛が硬い[柔らかい] I have stiff [soft] *hair*.
- 父は最近毛が薄くなってきた My father's *hair* has gotten thinner these days.
- サラダに毛が1本入っていた I found *a hair* in the salad.
- このセーターは毛100パーセントだ This sweater is 100 percent *wool*.
- うちの犬は初夏に毛が抜け変わる Our dog sheds *its* winter *fur* in early summer.

◆羊の毛を刈る *shear* [*clip*] a sheep / 鶏の毛をむしる *pluck* a chicken / 足の毛をそる *shave* one's legs

‖毛抜き (a pair of) tweezers / くせ毛 naturally curly hair / 縮れ毛 kinky [frizzy] hair / 付け毛 hair extension / 抜け毛 a fallen hair

[慣用表現] 私の英語力は中学生に毛の生えた程度だ My English ability is *just a hair better than* that of a junior high school student. / 彼は心臓に毛が生えている(→鋼鉄の神経をもっている) He *has nerves of steel*. / 身の毛もよだつ話 a *hair-raising* [*horrible*] story

-け¹ -気 しゃれっ気がある(→ユーモアのセンスがある) have *a sense of humor*; (→外見に気を配る) be *careful about one's appearance* / 塩気の強いみそ汁 *salty miso* soup / 祖母は少しリューマチの気がある My grandmother has *a touch of* rheumatism. / ふだんは全く火の気のない所から出火した The fire started from a spot where there didn't seem to be *a fire hazard*.(❖a fire hazard は「火事を起こす危険のあるもの」の意味) / うちのクラブは女っ気がない Our club is *all males*.

🅔「ちょっと寒けがする」「かぜをひきかけてるんじゃない? たっぷり休養をとったほうがいいよ」"I *feel a bit chilly*." "You might be catching a cold. I think you'd better take a good rest."

-け² -家 山本家 *the* Yamamotos / 天皇家 *the* Imperial *family* / ウィンザー家 *the House* of Windsor (❖現英国王室)

げ 下 下の下 *the worst of all* / その小説の(上・下巻のうち)下のほうはまだ読んでいない I haven't read *the second volume* of that novel.

-げ -気 少女は悲しげな目で私を見た The girl looked at me with *sad* eyes. / 子供たちは楽しげに走り回っていた The children were running around *cheerfully*. / 彼は何か言いたげな顔をしている He looks *as if he wants to* say something.

けあな 毛穴 pore ❶

けい¹ 刑 (判決) sentence ❶❷; (刑罰) punishment ❶ / 重い[軽い]刑 *a severe [light] sentence* / 死[終身]刑 *a death [life] sentence* / 刑を執行する administer *punishment* / 彼は10年の刑を終えた He has served *his* 10-year prison *sentence*.

◆裁判官は被告を懲役1年の刑に処した The judge *sentenced* the accused *to* a year in jail. (❖この sentence は「…を刑に処する」の意味の動詞)

けい² 計 (合計) total ❶, the sum; (計画) plan ❶ / このコンテストには計35名がエントリーした *A total of* 35 people were entered in the competition. / 一年の計は元旦にあり Your *plans* for the year should be made on New Year's Day.

けい³ 罫 (罫線) (ruled) line ❶ ◆罫線入りの紙 *ruled* paper / 罫線のない紙 *plain* [*unruled*] paper

けい⁴ 軽 軽自動車[トラック] a「compact car [light pickup truck] with an engine smaller than 660cc

-けい -系 ❶【系統・体系】system ❶ ‖太陽系 *the* solar *system* / 生態系 *an* ecological *system*

◆文系と理系 *the* humanities and *the* natural sciences / 日系ブラジル人 *a Japanese* Brazilian / ラテン系の人々 people of Latin *origin* / 佐藤氏は保守系無所属の新人候補だ Mr. Sato is a new candidate of conservative independent *bent*.

❷【系列】関西系のお笑い芸人 a comic performer of *the* Kansai *style* [*school*] / このホテルはJR系だ This hotel is a part of *the* JR *chain*.

ゲイ gay (❖gay は一般に「同性愛者」を指す. 女性に対しても用いる. 軽蔑的な含みはない) — ゲイの gay ‖ゲイバー a gay bar / ゲイボーイ a host in a gay bar

げい 芸 (技芸) art ❶❷, (artistic) skill ❶; (演技) performance ❶; (芸当) trick ❶
- その歌舞伎役者は先代の芸を引き継ぐと同時に自分の芸も磨いている The kabuki actor not only preserves *the art* of his predecessor but is polishing his own *skills*.
- 弟はわが家の犬に芸を仕込んでいる My brother is teaching our dog to do some *tricks*.

◆私は芸のない人間です I'm a person *of no accomplishments*. (❖accomplishments は「たしなみ」の意味)

🅔「バレンタインのプレゼントがいつもチョコじゃ芸がないと思わない?」「そんなことないよ. だって毎回手作りなんでしょ?」"I always give chocolate as a Valentine's present. Don't you think it's *a bit boring*?" "Not at all. Because you always make them yourself, don't you?"

‖芸達者 a versatile entertainer

[ことわざ] 芸は身を助ける It always pays to

learn a skill.(→技術を学ぶことは利益になる) / 多芸は無芸 ▶ ただ芸

けいあい 敬愛 (尊敬) respect ⓤ; (崇拝) worship ⓤ, adoration ⓤ ——敬愛する respect ⓣ; adore ⓣ, worship ⓣ

けいい¹ 敬意 (尊敬の念) respect ⓤ, (公式的) deference ⓤ; (オマージュ) homage ⓤ ∥彼らは女王に多大な敬意を表した They showed great *respect* for the queen. / その店員はいつも客に対して敬意をもって接している The salesclerk always treats customers *with respect*. / 彼の偉大な業績に対して敬意を払います We *pay homage to* his great achievements.

けいい² 経緯 (詳細) details, particulars; (経過) course ⓤ ∥私は事件の経緯についてはよく知らない I don't know about *the details* of the case.

◆事の経緯(→何が起きたか)をお話ししましょう I'm going to tell (you) *what happened*.

けいえい 経営 management ⓤ, administration ⓤ ——経営する manage ⓣ; run* ⓣ; operate ⓣ; keep* ⓣ; own ⓣ

> manage: 通例, 比較的大きな会社に用いる.
> run: manage より経営に関する責任・権限が大きいという含みがある.
> operate: 「組織を運営する」というニュアンスで用いる.
> keep: 小さな個人商店などの経営を指す.
> own: 資産として所有していることを指す.

上手な[下手な]経営 good [bad] *management* / 会社を経営する *manage* [*run*, *operate*, *own*] a company

彼女の両親は長野で旅館を経営している Her parents *keep* a Japanese-style inn in Nagano.

あなたに経営を一任します I'll leave you to *run* the business.

彼は父親が経営するみやげ物店で働いている He works at [in] a gift shop *managed* [*kept*] by his father.

この劇場は今は経営者が交代している This theater is now under new *management*.

経営側は労働者の賃上げ要求を受け入れなかった *The management* didn't give way to the workers' demands for higher wages.

◆経営能力 administrative ability / 彼は経営上の問題を処理する才にたけている He has great skill in dealing with *managerial* problems. / その会社は経営状態がよい[悪い] The company *is in good* [*bad*] *shape*. / その会社は深刻な経営難に陥っている The company is facing serious *financial difficulties*. / 多くの企業が多角経営に乗り出している A lot of enterprises have started to *diversify*.

∥経営学 business administration [management] / 経営学修士 a master of business administration, an MBA / 経営学部 the college of business administration / 経営コンサルタント a management consultant / 経営者 an administrator, a manager; (所有者) an owner / 経営陣 (集合的) the administration, the management / 経営方針 a management [business] policy

けいえん 敬遠 ——敬遠する (避ける) avoid ⓣ; (近寄らないようにする) stay [keep*] away from ... ∥その先生はみんなに敬遠されていた(→みんなはその先生を避けていた) Everybody *avoided* the teacher. / 以前は納豆を敬遠していたが,今では毎日食べている I used to *stay away from* natto, but I eat it every day now.

◆ピッチャーは森を敬遠した(→歩かせた) The pitcher *walked* Mori *intentionally*. / The pitcher *gave* Mori *an intentional walk*.

けいおんがく 軽音楽 light [popular] music ⓤ

けいか 経過 (推移) progress ⓤ; (過程) process ⓒⓤ; (成り行き) course ⓤ; (時がたつこと) passage ⓤ; (時間の隔たり) lapse ⓒ ——経過する (時間が) pass ⓣ, lapse ⓣ, go* by

時の経過 *the passage* of time / 試合の経過 *the progress* of a game

患者の術後の経過は良好だ The patient is making good *progress* after the operation.

彼が失踪(ﾉっｰ)してからすでに10年が経過している Ten years *have* already *passed* since he disappeared.

彼は教授に研究の途中経過を報告した He reported to the professor about *the progress* of his study. / He reported to the professor *how* his study *was going*.

◆二人のその後の経過が知りたい I want to know *what happened* to the two of them after that.

💬「先生,私はいつ退院できますか」「経過を見て順調なら来週には退院できますよ」"When can I go home, Doctor?" "Well, I'd like to *see how it goes* and if it's good, you can go home next week."

けいかい¹ 警戒 (用心) caution ⓤ; (予防) precaution ⓒⓤ; (見張り) watch ⓤ (また a ~), lookout ⓤ (また a ~); (警備) guard ⓤ ——警戒する (見張る) look [watch] out; (警備する) guard ⓣ; (警戒している) be on the lookout [watch] for ...; (見張っている) keep* a close watch

今夜は大雪に対する警戒が必要です We must *watch out for* heavy snow tonight.

常に地震に対する警戒を怠ってはいけません You should always take *precautions against* earthquakes.

警察はその男たちを厳重に警戒した The police *kept* (*a*) *close watch on* the men.

◆あいつは警戒したほうがいい You'd better *keep guard against* him. / You'd better *be on your guard against* him. / 500人の警官が厳重な警戒態勢で配置された Five hundred policemen were put on strict *alert*. / その川は警戒水位に達している The river has risen to *the danger level*. / 馬は警戒心の強い動物だ Horses are *cautious* animals.

∥警戒警報 a precautionary warning [alert]

けいかい² 軽快 ——軽快な (軽やかな) light;

(素早い) nimble ―軽快に lightly, light; nimbly ∥軽快な足取りで with *light* steps
◆軽快な服装 *sporty* [*casual*] clothes / どこからか軽快な音楽が聞こえてきた I heard a *rhythmical* music coming from somewhere.

けいかく 計画

plan [C]; project [C]; program,《主に英》programme [C]; scheme [C]; plot [C] ―計画する plan [他] [自]; project [他] [自]; scheme [他] [自]; plot [他] [自]

plan:「計画」の一般的な語.
project: ダムの建設など長期にわたって綿密に組み立てられた大規模な計画.
program: 特に政府による長期的な技術開発計画・社会問題を解決する計画.
scheme: 通例, よからぬたくらみ, 陰謀.《主に英》では政府による福祉・教育などに関する計画.
plot: 人に危害を加えたり失脚させようとする秘密の計画.

〖計画が・は〗
その計画はうまくいった The *plan* worked out.
世論の反対にもかかわらずその計画は実行された In spite of the public opposition, the *project* was carried out.
彼の計画が実現するかどうかは疑わしい I doubt whether [if] his *plan* will be realized.
ダムを造る計画は中止された *The project* of building a dam was cancelled.
その計画は結局失敗に終わった The *plan* ended in failure.
突然のあらしで私たちの計画は狂ってしまった The sudden storm upset our *plans*.
〖計画を〗
計画を立てる make *a plan* / 計画を練る consider *a plan* / 計画を実行する「carry out [execute] *a plan* / 計画をあきらめる give up *a plan* / 計画を変更する change *a plan*
議会は政府の新しい計画を承認した The parliament approved *the* government's new *plan*.
この計画を成しとげるには大変な努力がいるだろう This *project* would require [take] a great deal of effort.
〖計画に〗
彼らは我々の計画に賛成[反対]した They were favorable [opposed] to our *plan*.
彼らはその計画に本腰を入れて取り組んだ They bent their minds to the *project*.
〖計画する〗
彼女はこの夏アメリカに行くことを計画している She *is planning to* go to America this summer.
私たちは祖母の80歳の誕生パーティーを計画した We *planned for* our grandma's 80th birthday party.
〖その他〗
今のところすべて計画どおりに運んでいます Everything is going *as we planned* so far.
◆その殺人は計画的な犯行だった The murder was *deliberate* [*premeditated*]. / 彼女のダイエットはいつも計画倒れで終わる(→成功したことがない) She *has never succeeded in* carrying out her diet. / 彼の金の使い方には計画性がない He spends money *extravagantly*.
‖計画経済 planned economy / 5か年計画 a five-year plan / 長期計画 a long-term [-range] plan / 都市計画 city planning

けいかん[1] 警官 police officer [C] (❖男女を区別しない言い方. 呼びかけでは通例 officer という); (男性の) policeman [C]; (女性の) policewoman [C] ∥私服警官 *a* plainclothes *policeman* [*policewoman*]
◆暴動鎮圧のため警官隊が出動した *The police force* was sent to suppress the riot.

けいかん[2] 景観 (景色) scene [C]; (全体の風景) scenery [U]; (眺め) view [C] ∥景観を損ねる spoil *the view*

けいき[1] 景気

❶【経済活動の活発さ】(商売の様子) business [U]; (経済状態) economy [U], economic conditions; (時勢) times ⇨ ふけいき
景気がよい[悪い] *Times* are good [bad]. / *Business* is brisk [slow].
景気回復が政策の中心課題だ *Reviving business* is central to the government's policy.
専門家は今年の後半には景気が上向きになるだろうと語った The expert said *the economy* would improve later this year.
景気にかげりが見えてきた *Business* began to slow down. / *The economic trends* began to show a downturn.
[会話]「景気はどうだい」「あまりよくないよ[まあまあだね]」"*How's everything?*" "Not very good. [Not bad.]" (❖商売について尋ねる場合は "How's your business?" と聞くことが多い)
❷【威勢のよさ】
今夜は景気よくぱあっと騒ごうよ *Let's live it up* tonight! / *Let's have a spree* tonight!
景気の悪い顔してどうしたの You look *gloomy*. What's wrong?
彼は昔は景気よく金を使ったものだ He used to spend money *lavishly* [*extravagantly*].
[会話]「最近あいつ何だか浮かない顔してるなあ」「じゃあ, ちょっと景気つけてやろう」"He looks kind of gloomy lately." "Why don't we *cheer him up*, then?"
‖景気後退 (economic) recession / 景気対策 stimulative [stimulus] measures / 景気停滞 economic stagnation, a slump / 景気動向 economic trends / 景気予測 a business forecast

けいき[2] 刑期 a term of imprisonment, prison term [C] ∥彼は20年の刑期を務めた He served *a* 20-year *prison term*. / He served 20 years in prison.

けいき[3] 契機 (機会) chance [C], opportunity [C]; (転機) turning point [C] ∥これを契機にアメリカ史の知識を深めたい I'd like to use this as *an opportunity* to learn more about American history.

けいき⁴ 計器 (使用量を示す) meter ⓒ; (雨量・圧力などの) gauge [géidʒ] ⓒ; (飛行機などの) instrument ⓒ ‖計器盤 an instrument panel / 計器飛行 instrument flying

けいきんぞく 軽金属 light metal ⓒ

けいぐ 敬具 Sincerely (yours), (英) Yours sincerely, (親しい間柄で) Yours (❖いずれも最後にコンマを置き, 改行して署名する)

けいけん¹ 経験

experience ⓤⓒ ――経験する experience ⓗ ――経験を積んだ experienced

〖経験が・は〗
経験が豊富である have a lot of *experience*
彼はまだ教師としての経験が浅い He doesn't have much *experience* as a teacher.
彼女は外国人に日本語を教えた経験が少しある She has some *experience* in teaching Japanese to foreign people.
彼らには貧乏の経験がない They *have* never *experienced* the taste of poverty.
🔴「秘書業務の経験はありますか」「はい, 5 年間経験しました」 "Do you have any *experience* in secretarial work?" "Yes, I've had five years' *experience*."

〖経験を〗
経験を積む gain [accumulate, gather] *experience*
君は自分の経験を最大限生かすべきだ You should make the most of your *experience*.
彼は経験を積んだ医師だ He is an *experienced* doctor.

〖経験する〗
以前にも似たような症状を経験しましたか Have you *experienced* similar symptoms before?
こんな寒さは今まで経験したことがない I've never *experienced* such cold before.
◆苦難を経験する meet disaster / つらい時期を経験する go through a difficult [hard] time / 彼らは戦争中多くの苦難を経験した They *have undergone* many hardships during the war.

〖その他〗
経験不足 lack of *experience* / 経験から学ぶ learn by [from] *experience* / 実務経験が 3 年以上ある人 a person with more than three years' *working experience*
(求人広告で) 経験不要 No *experience* required [necessary].
(求人広告で) 経験者優遇 *Experienced workers* especially welcome.
あなたたちの中にアルバイトの経験者は何人くらいますか How many of you *have experience* in part-time jobs?
中国でのおもしろい経験談を少ししましょう I'll tell you about a few interesting *experiences* I had in China.
ボランティア活動はとてもいい経験になった Volunteer work was *a very good experience* for me.
彼の長年の経験と訓練があればこの仕事は完璧 (かんぺき) にできる His years of *experience* and training fit him for this job perfectly.
◆ケーキ作りなんて初めての経験なのでうまくいくかどうか Because this is *my first time to* bake a cake, I wonder if it will turn out well.

┌─ コロケーション ─ -experience- ──┐
│ 〖形容詞＋～〗 いやな～ an unpleasant experience / 得るものの多い～ a fruitful experience / 思い出深い～ a memorable experience / 過去の～ past experiences / 貴重な～ a valuable experience / 奇妙な～ a strange experience / 楽しい～ a pleasant experience / つらい～ a painful experience / 苦い～ a bitter experience / 忘れられない～ an unforgettable experience │
└──────────────────────┘

‖経験主義 empiricism / 経験主義者 an empiricist

[慣用表現] 経験がものを言う *Experience will tell.*

けいけん² 敬虔 ――敬虔な pious, devout (❖devout には「教義を厳格に守る」というニュアンスがある) ‖敬虔なキリスト教徒 a *pious* Christian

けいげん 軽減 (減らすこと) reduction ⓤ; (痛み・苦しみなどの緩和) relief ⓤ ――軽減する reduce ⓗ; relieve ⓗ ――税を軽減する *reduce* taxes / 患部を冷やせば痛みは軽減される Cool the affected part, and the pain *will be relieved.*

けいこ 稽古 (練習) practice ⓤⓒ; (訓練) training ⓤⓒ; (習い事) lesson ⓒ; (リハーサル) rehearsal ⓤⓒ ――けいこする practice ⓗ; (レッスンを受ける) take* lessons ‖けいこ中の芝居 a play *in rehearsal* / 彼女は毎日ピアノのけいこをしている She *practices* the piano every day. / 私は週に 3 回バレエのけいこに通っている I'm *taking* ballet *lessons* three times a week.
◆先生が私にけいこをつけてくれた The teacher *coached* [*trained*] me.

けいご¹ 敬語 (尊敬語) honorific ⓒ; (丁寧な言い方) polite expression ⓒ (❖英語には日本語の敬語のような複雑なきまりはない. 場面や状況に応じて改まった表現や丁寧な表現を用いる) ‖敬語を使えない若者が多い A lot of young people don't know how to use *honorifics* [*polite expressions*].

けいご² 警護 guard ⓤ ――警護する guard ⓗ

けいこう¹ 傾向 (個人的な) tendency ⓒ; (ある分野における) trend ⓒ
一般的な傾向 *a general tendency* / インフレ傾向 *a tendency toward* inflation / 物価の上昇傾向 *an upward trend in prices* / 最近の入試の傾向 *the recent trends* in entrance examinations
最近若者の間に保守主義の傾向がある There is *a tendency toward* conservatism among young people these days.
◆スポーツ紙は事実を誇張して伝える傾向がある

Sports newspapers *tend [are inclined] to* exaggerate the facts. / 日本人は集団に従う傾向がある Japanese *are apt to* conform to the group. (❖be apt to do は通例悪い意味で用いる)

けいこう² 蛍光 fluorescence [flɔːrésəns] Ⓤ ─蛍光の fluorescent ‖蛍光塗料 luminous paint / 蛍光ペン a highlighter (pen)

けいごう 迎合 彼はすぐ人に迎合する He's overly *accommodating* to other people.

けいこうぎょう 軽工業 light industry ⒸⓊ

けいこうとう 蛍光灯 fluorescent light [lamp]Ⓒ

けいこうひにんやく 経口避妊薬 oral contraceptive Ⓒ, 《口語的》the pill [Pill]

けいこく¹ 警告 warning Ⓒ Ⓤ; (注意) caution Ⓤ ─警告する warn Ⓣ, give* a warning; caution Ⓣ ‖彼らは彼の警告を軽く考えた They made light of his *warning*. / 警官は駐車違反のことで運転手に警告をした The policeman *cautioned* the driver about illegal parking. / 彼は私に暗くなってからひとりで出かけるなと警告した He *warned* me [*gave* me *a warning*] not *to* go out alone after dark. ◆そのサッカー選手は2度の警告(→2枚のイエローカード)を受け退場となった The soccer player got two *yellow cards* and was ordered to leave the field.

けいこく² 渓谷 ravine [rəvíːn] Ⓒ, gorge Ⓒ; (深くて大きな) canyon Ⓒ

けいさい 掲載 ─掲載する carry Ⓣ, run* Ⓣ ‖その週刊誌は毎号最新のファッションに関する記事を掲載している The weekly magazine *runs* an article on the latest fashion in every issue. ◆新聞に広告を掲載する *put* an advertisement in the paper / 彼の漫画は金曜の夕刊に掲載されている His comic strip *appears in* Friday's evening paper.

けいざい 経済

❶【経済活動一般】economy ⓊⒸ ─経済の economic ─経済的な financial ─経済的に financially

経済の立て直しをはかる try to revive *the economy* / 発展途上国に対する経済援助 *economic support* for developing countries

新空港はその地域の経済発展を促すだろう The new airport will help *the economic development* of the area.

彼は現在の経済の動向について鋭い意見を述べた He made a keen observation about the current *economic* trend.

その国の経済はかなり落ちこんでいる The country's *economy* is in deep recession.

現在の経済情勢はたいへん厳しい The *economic situation* now is very severe.

観光産業はその国の経済にきわめて重要な役割を果たしている Tourism plays a vital role in the country's *economy*.

私の大学時代, 父は経済的に援助してくれた My father assisted me *financially* in my college days.

彼女には経済観念というものがない She has no *sense of economy*.

◆わが家の経済状態では学費は自分で稼がなくてはならない On my family's *budget*, I must work for school fees.

❷【節約】─経済的な economy (❖名詞の前で用いる), economical ─経済的に economically

このへんではタクシーを使うのは経済的でない It is not *economical* to use taxis in this area.

ふつうはまとめ買いのほうが経済的だ Bulk buying is usually more *economical*.

‖経済界 the economic world / 経済改革 economic reform / 経済学 economics / 経済学者 an economist / 経済学部 the college [school] of economics / 経済企画庁 the Economic Planning Agency (❖2001年内閣府に統合) / 経済協力開発機構 the Organization for Economic Cooperation and Development(《略語》OECD) / 経済水域 economic waters / 経済制裁 economic sanctions / 経済政策 economic policy / 経済成長率 the economic growth rate / 経済大国 economic powers / 経済白書 an economic white paper / 経済発展 economic development / 経済評論家 an economic analyst / 経済封鎖 a blockade / 経済復興 economic recovery / 経済摩擦 economic friction / 計画経済 a planned [command] economy / 国内経済 the domestic economy / 市場経済 a market economy / 自由経済 a free economy

けいざいさんぎょうしょう 経済産業省 the Ministry of Economy, Trade and Industry

けいさつ 警察 the police 《複数扱い》; 《口語的》the law 《単数または複数扱い》 ─警察の police

> 【語法】 police は組織としての警察, または集合的に警察官全体を表し, 常に複数扱いになる. 通例 the を付けるが, 新聞などでは省略されることもある. 警察官1人をいう場合は a police officer, または a policeman [a policewoman]を用いる. the law は「法律の見張り番」というニュアンスで用いる口語的な表現で単数または複数扱い.

〖警察が・は〗
警察が彼女を追っている *The police* are after her.
警察はその容疑者を逮捕した *The police* captured [arrested] the suspect.
警察はその事件の調査に乗り出した *The police* have begun to investigate the incident.

〖警察を・に〗
警察に突き出す hand over to *the police*
彼女は警察に出頭しなければならない She has to report to *the police*.
彼女は庭に不審な男がいると警察に通報した She notified *the police* that a strange man was in her yard.
彼は誘拐の容疑で警察に指名手配されている He's

wanted by *the police* for kidnapping.
帰らないのなら警察を呼びますよ I'm going to call *the police* if you don't leave!
〖その他〗
警察ざたにはしたくない I don't want to *get the police involved*.
その男は今警察の監視下にある The man is now under the eye of *the police*.
∥警察学校 a police school [academy] / 警察官 a police officer, a policeman, a policewoman / 警察犬 a police dog / 警察署 a police station / 警察署長 the chief of police / 警察庁 the National Police Agency / 警察手帳 a police handbook / 国際警察 Interpol / 秘密警察 the secret police

けいさん 計算 calculation Ⓤ Ⓒ, （口語的） figures; （算数の） sum Ⓒ ──計算する calculate ⊕ 📖, make* [do*] a calculation, 《口語的》figure out; （１つずつ）count ⊕
計算間違い an error [a mistake] in *calculation* / その仕事に要する期間を計算する *calculate* how long the job will take
彼女は計算が速い［遅い］ She is quick [slow] at *figures*.
彼はいつも計算に間違いがない He is always accurate in *his calculations*.
彼の計算にはいつもたくさんの間違いがある There are always a lot of mistakes in his *calculations*.
私の計算はあなたのと合わない My *figures* don't agree with yours.
◆店の売り上げを計算する（→合計する）*total one's* shop sales / 私は計算問題（→算術）が苦手だ I'm weak at *arithmetic*.
∥計算機 a calculator / 計算尺 a slide rule
慣用表現 物事は計算ずくではいかないものだ Things just don't go as *you've figured*. / 彼は計算高い男だ He's a *calculating* man. / 予定を立てたとき遅れる可能性を計算に入れた（→考慮した） When I planned the schedule, I *took* the possibility of delay *into consideration*.

けいし¹ 軽視 （軽蔑） contempt Ⓤ; （無視・怠ること）neglect Ⓤ ──軽視する make* little of …, take* … lightly ∥彼の忠告を軽視してはならない You shouldn't *take* his advice *lightly*.

けいし² 警視 《米》deputy inspector Ⓒ, 《英》superintendent Ⓒ（◆日本の「警視」は通例後者で表す）∥警視総監 the Superintendent-General of the Metropolitan Police / 警視庁 the Metropolitan Police Department

けいじ¹ 掲示 （はり紙・告示）notice Ⓒ; （広報・通知）bulletin Ⓒ; （標示・標識）sign Ⓒ
▶ 場面・状況別会話 p.1764 / 掲示を出す put up *a notice* / 壁に「ホール内飲食禁止」の掲示があった There was *a notice* on the wall saying "No eating or drinking in the hall."
∥掲示板 a bulletin board, 《英》a notice board

けいじ² 刑事 （刑事巡査）(police) detective Ⓒ ──刑事の （犯罪に関する）criminal（◆名詞の前で用いる）∥私服刑事 *a* plainclothes *de-*tective / 刑事は容疑者を尾行した *The detective* shadowed the suspect.
∥刑事事件 a criminal case / 刑事責任 criminal liability / 刑事訴訟 a criminal suit / 刑事犯 a criminal offense

けいじ³ 啓示 revelation Ⓤ Ⓒ

けいしき 形式 （一定のやり方）form Ⓤ Ⓒ; （形式的な行為）formality Ⓤ Ⓒ ──形式的な formal ∥彼は形式を重んじる人だ He *has a formal* manner. / 形式にはこだわらなくていい You don't have to stick to *formalities*. / その小説はほとんどの部分が対話形式で書かれている A great part of the novel is written in *the form of* dialog. / 形式ばったあいさつは抜きにしましょう Let's skip *formal* greetings. / 大臣の謝罪は形式的なものにすぎなかった The Minister's apology was *a mere formality*. ◆歓迎会は立食形式で行われた The reception was held in *a buffet style*.
∥形式主義 formalism / 形式主義者 a formalist

けいしきしゅご 形式主語〖文法〗formal subject Ⓒ

後ろにくる単語・句・節の代わりに, 文の形式上の主語になる it のこと. 不定詞句や動名詞句, that 節が主語になるときに, 文頭にくる主語が長くなることを防ぐために, 形式主語が使われる ▷ *It* is clear *that* you are wrong. あなたが間違っているのは明白だ

けいしゃ 傾斜 slant Ⓒ, slope Ⓤ《また a ～》, incline Ⓒ, 《公式的》inclination Ⓒ Ⓤ ──傾斜する slope ⊕, slant ⊕ ∥急な傾斜 *a* steep *slant* [*slope*] / 頂上に近づくにつれて傾斜はきつくなった *The slope* increased as we got near to the top. / この道は川に向かって傾斜している This road *slopes down* toward a river.

げいしゃ 芸者 geisha Ⓒ, a professional female entertainer in kimono who performs at a meal with traditional Japanese music and dancing

げいじゅつ 芸術 art Ⓤ Ⓒ ──芸術の art ──芸術的な artistic
芸術的感性の持ち主 a person of *artistic* sensibility
父は全く芸術を理解しない My father has no eye for *art*.
君は芸術的才能に恵まれている You are endowed with *artistic* talent. / You have a talent for *art*.
そのシェフの作る料理はまさに芸術品だ The dishes the chef cooks are true *works of art*.
∥芸術家 an artist / 芸術祭 an art festival / 芸術作品 a work of art, an artwork / 芸術大学 a university of fine arts (and music), an art college

けいしょう¹ 継承 succession Ⓤ; （相続）inheritance Ⓤ ──継承する succeed to …; （相続）inherit ⊕ ∥王位を継承する *succeed to* the throne / 皇太子は王位継承権第１位である The prince is the first in *succes-*

sion to the throne.
∥継承者 a successor

けいしょう² 軽症 (軽い症状) mild case ⒞; (軽い病気) slight illness ⒞
◆彼はマラリアにかかったが，さいわい軽症ですんだ He got malaria, but fortunately it *didn't get too serious*.

けいしょう³ 軽傷 slight injury [wound] ⒞
◆彼はその事故で軽傷を負った He *got slightly injured* in that accident.

けいしょう⁴ 警鐘 warning [alarm] bell ⒞
◆警鐘を鳴らす(→警告する) warn; give a warning

けいしょう⁵ 敬称 title ⒞ (❖Mr., Dr., Princessなど。英語では名前の前に付けるのでprefix ともいう); honorific (title) ⒞ ∥敬称略 *Honorific titles* are omitted from names.

けいしょう⁶ 景勝 松島は景勝地として(→景色の美しさで)有名だ Matsushima is well known for *its scenic beauty*.

けいじょう¹ 形状 shape ⒞⒰, form ⒞⒰
∥形状記憶合金 a shape memory alloy

けいじょう² 計上 —計上する (予算に繰り込む) appropriate ⊕ ∥政府はそのプロジェクトに多額の金を計上している The government *has appropriated* a large sum of money for the project.

けいじょうひ 経常費 operating [running] expenses

けいしょく 軽食 (軽い食事) light meal ⒞; (間食) snack ⒞; (軽い飲み物) refreshments ∥3時ごろに軽食が出ます *Refreshments* will be served at around three.
∥軽食堂(カウンター式の) a snack bar; (セルフサービス式の) a cafeteria

けいしん 軽震 (軽い地震) slight [small] earthquake

けいず 系図 (系譜) genealogy ⒞; (家系図) family tree ⒞

けいすう 係数 〖数学・物理〗coefficient ⒞ ∥摩擦係数 the coefficient of friction

けいせい¹ 形勢 (情勢) the situation; (物事の流れ) the tide, the current; (成り行き) things ∥形勢を見守る watch how *the situation* develops ∥ 形勢が悪化してきている *Things* are getting worse. ∥ 形勢は我々に有利になった *The tide* turned in our favor. ∥ 中田のゴールで形勢が一変した Nakata's goal *turned the tide*.
◆形勢は互角だ *The chances* are even.

けいせい² 形成 formation ⒰ —形成する form ⊕⊕, build* up ∥人格を形成する *form one's* character; mold *one's* character
◆言語の形成期 the period in life when language is first acquired
∥形成外科 plastic surgery; (美容の) cosmetic surgery ∥ 形成外科医 a plastic surgeon

けいせき 形跡 (証拠) evidence ⒰, (しるし) sign ⒞; (痕跡) trace ⒞⒰ ∥だれかが私の引き出しをあけて何か捜した形跡がある There is *evidence* that someone has searched my drawer. ∥ 火星に生命が存在する形跡は今のところ見つかっていない No *signs* of life have been known on Mars so far.

けいせん 経線 a line of longitude; (子午線) meridian

けいそう¹ 軽装 light clothes ∥彼女は軽装で出かけた She went out in *light clothes*.
◆軽装で旅行する travel *light* (❖この light は「軽装で，身軽に」の意味の副詞)

けいそう² 係争 係争中である(→問題となっている) be *in dispute*; be *at issue* ∥ その件は法廷で係争中だ The case *is* still *pending* in court.

けいそく 計測 measurement ⒰ —計測する gauge [géidʒ] ⊕, measure ⊕ ∥計測は正確だった *The measurement* was exact.

けいぞく 継続 continuation ⒰, 《公式的》 continuance ⒰ (また a 〜); (継続性) continuity ⒰ —継続する continue ⊕, go* on —継続的な continuous, continual —継続的に continuously, continually
その問題は継続して話し合うことになった We decided to *continue* discussion on that issue.
外交政策には継続性が重要だ *Continuity* is important in diplomacy.
◆法案を(次期国会での)継続審議にする carry a bill *over* to the next (Diet) session ∥ 継続定期券は使用期間の2週間前から購入できます(→2週間前から更新できる) Commuter passes can *be renewed* two weeks before the expiration date. ∥ 継続は力なり *Persistence* brings strength.

けいそつ 軽率 —軽率な (不注意な) careless; (思慮を欠いた) thoughtless, rash; (早まった) hasty —軽率に carelessly; thoughtlessly; hastily ∥彼の軽率な行動がスキャンダルを引き起こした His *careless* behavior caused the scandal. ∥ 次の仕事を見つけないで仕事を辞めたのは軽率だったね It was *rash* of you to quit the job before you found another one.

けいたい¹ 携帯 —携帯する carry ⊕ ➡ 場面・状況別会話 p.1690 ∥電子辞書は携帯に便利だ Electric dictionaries are handy to *carry*. ∥携帯用ラジオ a *portable* radio ∥ 遅れる場合には携帯(電話)にかけるよ I'll call you on *your cell phone* if I'm late.
∥携帯電話《米》a cell(ular) phone, 《英》a mobile (phone) ∥ 携帯品 *one's* personal belongings ∥ 携帯品預り所 a checkroom, a cloakroom

けいたい² 形態 (形) form ⒞, shape ⒞; (構造) formation ⒰ ∥政治形態 *a form* of government ∥ 核兵器の発明は戦争の形態を一変させた The invention of nuclear weapons changed the whole *shape* of warfare.
∥形態素〖言語〗a morpheme ∥ 形態論〖言語〗morphology

けいだい 境内 the precincts of a temple [shrine]

けいだんれん 経団連 (経済団体連合会) the Federation of Economic Organizations

けいちょう 傾聴 —傾聴する 《公式的》attend, listen (attentively) to ... ∥彼の意

けいてき 警笛 horn ⓒ；警笛鳴らせ《掲示》Sound *Your* Horn / トラックが警笛を鳴らしながら轟音(ごう)を立てて通り過ぎていった A truck roared past with *its horn* blaring.

けいと 毛糸 (knitting) wool ⓤ ――毛糸の woolen, 《英》woollen ∥毛糸玉 a ball of *wool* / 毛糸の帽子 a *woolen* cap
◆母が毛糸でマフラーを編んでくれた My mother *knitted* me a scarf.

けいど¹ 経度 longitude ⓒⓤ (略語》long.)

けいど² 軽度 ――軽度の slight, mild /軽度のやけど a *slight* burn

けいとう¹ 系統 system ⓒ ――系統的な systematic ――系統的に systematically /神経[消化器]系統 *the* nervous [digestive] *system* / 私はスペイン語を系統的に勉強したことはない I haven't studied Spanish *systematically*. ◆命令系統 *the* chain *of* command / 計画を系統だてて説明してくれませんか Would you explain the plans *in sequence?* / 彼女は青系統の服をたくさん持っている She has a lot of *blue* clothes.

けいとう² 傾倒 ――傾倒する (賞賛する) admire ⓗ /彼はジミ·ヘンドリックスに傾倒している He *admires* Jimi Hendrix.

けいとう³ 継投 継投策が裏目に出て彼らはその試合を落とした *The change of pitchers* didn't work out and they lost the game.

げいとう 芸当 (曲芸) trick ⓒ；(妙技·離れ業) feat ⓒ；(演技) performance ⓒ /曲芸師は綱の上で側転するという芸当をやってのけた The acrobat performed *the feat* of doing cartwheel on a tightrope.
◆僕にはそんな芸当(→こと)はできない I could never do such *a thing*.

けいどうみゃく 頸動脈 《医学》carotid (artery) ⓒ

げいにん 芸人 (芸能人) entertainer ⓒ；(寄席の) vaudevillian [vɔ̀ːdvíljən] ⓒ /旅芸人 an itinerant *entertainer* ◆物まね芸人 *an* impressionist; *an* impersonator / 大道芸人 *a* street performer

げいのう 芸能 entertainment ⓤ ∥芸能界 show business / 芸能人 an entertainer / 芸能ニュース entertainment news / 芸能番組 an entertainment TV program / 芸能プロダクション a theatrical agency / 伝統芸能 traditional performing arts

けいば 競馬 horse racing ⓤ, the races(❖1つのレースは a race) ∥競馬をやる play [bet on] *the races* / 彼は競馬で大もうけ[大損]した He made [lost] a lot of money at *the races*.
∥競馬馬 a racehorse / 競馬場 the turf, 《米》a racetrack, 《英》a racecourse / 草競馬 a local horse race

けいはく 軽薄 ――軽薄な (浮ついた) frivolous; (不まじめな) flippant

けいはつ 啓発 (公式的) enlightenment ⓤ ――啓発する enlighten ⓗ /その教授の講義で私は大いに啓発された I *was* greatly *enlightened* by the professor's lecture.

けいばつ 刑罰 punishment ⓒⓤ, penalty ⓒⓤ /刑罰を科する impose *punishment* / 彼は自分の罪に対する刑罰を受けた He paid *the penalty* for his crime.

けいはんざい 軽犯罪 minor [petty] offense ⓒ, 《法律》misdemeanor ⓒⓤ ∥軽犯罪法 the Minor Offense Law

けいひ 経費 (一般的な費用) expenses, cost ⓒ; (会社などの経常経費) 《米》overhead ⓤ, 《英》overheads; (維持費) upkeep ⓤ /経費を切り詰める cut down on *expenses* / タクシー代を経費で落とす write off taxi fares as *business expenses* / 搭乗員には月10万円の必要経費が支給される Crew members are allowed 100,000 yen a month for *expenses*. / 直接仕入れを行えば経費を削減できるかもしれない We may cut *our costs* by buying direct. / 東京では経費がかさむため, その会社は移転を計画している The company is planning to move out of Tokyo because *the overhead* is too high there. ◆そのプロジェクトは経費がかかりすぎる The project *costs* too much. (❖このcostは「経費がかかる」という意味の動詞)

けいび 警備 guard ⓤ; (保安) security ⓤ ――警備する guard ⓗ /大統領の到着に備え空港周辺の警備が強化されている In anticipation of the President's arrival, *security* was tightened around the airport. / 大使館は厳重に警備されている The embassy *is* heavily *guarded*.
∥警備員 a (security) guard / 警備会社 a security company / 警備隊 a garrison / 警備艇 a guard ship

けいひん 景品 free gift ⓒ, giveaway ⓒ, 《主に米·口語的》freebie ⓒ
◆1等の景品は特製ジャンパーです *The first prize* is a specially made jacket.

げいひんかん 迎賓館 the State Guest House

けいふ¹ 系譜 (系図) genealogy ⓤⓒ; (家系) ancestry ⓒⓤ; (ルーツ) roots

けいふ² 継父 《米》stepfather ⓒ

けいぶ 警部 《米》captain ⓒ, 《英》chief inspector ⓒ ∥警部補《米》a lieutenant, 《英》an inspector

けいふく 敬服 ――敬服する (尊敬する) respect ⓗ /彼のがんばりには敬服している I *respect* him for his efforts.

けいべつ 軽蔑 contempt ⓤ; (激しい嫌悪感を伴う) scorn ⓤ ――軽蔑する scorn ⓗ, (嫌悪する) despise ⓗ, (見下す) 《口語的》look down on ... ――軽蔑的な contemptuous; scornful ――軽蔑的に contemptuously; scornfully
軽蔑的な態度 a *contemptuous* attitude
あいつは軽蔑にさえ値しない He's beneath *contempt*.
彼女は喫煙者を軽蔑しきっていた She had [felt] *nothing but scorn for* smokers.
貧しい人々を軽蔑してはならない Don't *despise* the poor.
彼女は彼のことを俗物だとひそかに[あからさまに]

けいぼ 継母 stepmother

軽蔑した She secretly [overtly] *scorned* him as a snob.
彼女は軽蔑のまなざしで私を見た She gave me a *scornful* look.
◆軽蔑すべき人間 a *contemptible* person

けいほう¹ 警報 alarm, warning ‖暴風[津波]警報 a storm [tsunami] *warning* / 警報を発する give [raise, sound] *the alarm* / 大雪警報は先ほど解除された The heavy snow *warning* was cancelled a short time ago.
‖警報器 an alarm

けいほう² 刑法 the criminal law, the penal code

けいぼう 警棒 《米》nightstick, 《英》truncheon

けいみょう 軽妙 ——軽妙な (軽快な) light; (気のきいた) smart, witty ‖軽妙なしゃれ a *witty* joke / 軽妙な筆致のエッセー an essay in a *light* style

けいむしょ 刑務所 prison, jail (❖《英》では gaol とも書く) ‖刑務所に入る go to *prison* (❖無冠詞で用いる) / 刑務所から出る be released from *prison* / その強盗は刑務所に入れられた The burglar was put in *prison*. / 彼は刑務所から脱走した He fled from *the prison*.

げいめい 芸名 (職業上の) professional name; (映画での) screen name; (舞台での) stage name

けいもう 啓蒙 enlightenment ——啓蒙する enlighten ——啓蒙的な enlightening ‖啓蒙運動 the Enlightenment / 啓蒙思想家 an Enlightenment thinker

けいやく 契約

contract; agreement; lease ——契約する contract, make* a contract; (契約書にサインする) sign (a contract)
- contract: 文書による正式な契約一般を指す.
- agreement: 双方の同意による契約を指し、法的拘束力はない.
- lease: 家屋・土地などの賃貸借契約.

〖契約が・は〗
X社とY社の間で代理店契約が成立した An agency *contract* has been reached between companies X and Y.
この家の賃貸契約は来年切れる The *lease* on this house expires next year.

〖契約を・に〗
契約を交わす sign *a written contract* / 契約を実行する execute [carry out] *a contract* / 契約を破棄する cancel *a contract* / 契約を履行する fulfill *a contract* / 契約を解除する terminate *a person's contract* / 契約を更新する have one's *contract* renewed / 契約に違反する breach [break, violate] *a contract*
その会社は大きな契約をものにした The firm landed *a big contract*.
その農家はあるレストランのために無農薬野菜を栽培する契約をした The farmer *contracted* with a restaurant *to* grow organic vegetables for them.
彼らは契約をとるためにある政治家のコネを使った They used a politician's influence to get *the contract*.
その選手は新設チームと契約を結んだ The player *signed with* a new team.
古田はスワローズと5年契約を結んでいる Furuta *is under a five year contract with* the Swallows.

〖その他〗
彼らは契約違反でその会社を提訴した They filed a suit against the company for *breach of contract*.
そのグループは新しいレコード会社と契約した The group *signed with* a new record label.
‖契約期間 a term of contract / 契約金 contract money / 契約者 a contractor, a contracting party / 契約社員 a contract worker / 契約書 a contract / 契約条件 the terms of a contract / 仮契約 a temporary contract / 売買契約 a sales contract / 本契約 a formal contract

けいゆ¹ 経由 その飛行機はフランクフルト経由でパリへ飛んだ The plane flew to Paris 「*by way of* [*via*] Frankfurt.

けいゆ² 軽油 light oil

けいよう 形容 ——形容する (描写する) describe; (言い表す) express
◆形容できないほどの美しさ beauty *beyond description* / それは何とも形容しがたい (→今まで見た中でいちばん) 奇妙な形をしていた It had *the strangest* shape I'd ever seen.

けいよう² 掲揚 ——掲揚する raise, hoist ‖国旗を掲揚する *raise* [*hoist*] the national flag

けいようし 形容詞〚文法〛adjective ‖形容詞句 an adjective phrase / 限定形容詞 an attributive adjective / 叙述形容詞 a predicative adjective

(1)形容詞は名詞を修飾する語で, 大部分の形容詞は比較級・最上級を作ることができる. 名詞の前または後からその意味を限定する「限定用法」と, 補語として主語や目的語の状態を説明する「叙述用法」がある. ‖ This is an *interesting* novel. これはおもしろい小説だ / I want to drink something *hot*. 何か温かい物が飲みたい / Don't speak with your mouth *full*. 口に食べ物をいっぱいにしたままでしゃべるな (❖以上限定用法) / Personal consumption remains *sluggish*. 個人消費はいまだ伸び悩んでいる (❖叙述用法)
(2)名詞の前に形容詞を複数並べるときは, ふつう次のような語順となる: (冠詞など) + 序数・数量+性質+大小+新旧・老若+形状・色+材料+名詞. ただし実際には, 4つ以上の形容詞を付けるのはまれである.

けいようどうし 形容動詞 (日本文法の) adjectival verb

けいり 経理 accounting ‖彼女は経理を担当している She is in charge of *accounting*.
‖経理課 the accounting section / 経理係 an accountant / 経理部 the accounting di-

vision [department]

けいりし 計理士 accountant [C]

けいりゃく 計略 (策略) trick [C]; (わな) trap [C]; (陰謀) plot [C] ∥計略を見抜く see through *a trick* / 彼らはみごとに彼女の計略にはまった They completely fell into her *trap.* / あいつは何か計略をめぐらせているにちがいない He's got to be devising some *plots.*

けいりゅう[1] 係留 ―係留する (船などをつなぐ) moor [他]

けいりゅう[2] 渓流 mountain stream [C] ∥父は渓流釣りが趣味だ My father likes *fishing in mountain streams.*

けいりょう[1] 計量 ―計量する measure [他]; (重量を) weigh [他][自] ∥ボクサーは試合前に計量を受ける Boxers *weigh in* before a match.
‖計量カップ a measuring cup / 計量器 a measure / 計量スプーン a measuring spoon

けいりょう[2] 軽量 ―軽量の lightweight

けいりん 競輪 keirin [U], bicycle [cycle] race [C] ‖競輪場 a bicycle racetrack / 競輪選手 a cycle racer

けいるい 係累 (扶養家族) dependent [C]

けいれい 敬礼 (挙手) salute [C] ―敬礼する salute [他][自] ∥国旗に敬礼する *salute* the national flag

けいれき 経歴 (素性・学歴) background [C]; (職歴) career [C]; (記録) record [C]; (履歴) *one's* personal history ∥経歴を調べる look into *one's background* / 彼は自分の経歴については何も言わなかった He said nothing with respect to *his personal history.* / 後藤氏は市長としてすぐれた経歴の持ち主だ Mr. Goto has *an* excellent *record* as a mayor.

けいれつ 系列 その会社は西武の系列だ That company is *a member of* the Seibu group.
‖系列会社 an affiliated company; (子会社) a subsidiary (company)

けいれん 痙攣 spasm [C][U], cramp [C][U] ∥けいれんを起こす go into *a spasm*; get *a cramp* / 胃けいれん stomach *cramps*

けいろ[1] 経路 (ルート) route [C]; (情報・伝達などの) channel [C]; (方法・手段) means [C] ∥感染経路 *an* infection *route* / これらの野菜はどのような経路をたどって消費者の手元に届くのだろうか By what *route* are these vegetables sent to the consumers?
◆彼はその商品の入手経路は明かさなかった He didn't tell us *how he got* that item.

けいろ[2] 毛色 この曲はアルバムの中のほかの曲とちょっと毛色が違うね This tune *is* a bit *different* (*in type*) from other tunes on the album.

けいろう 敬老 ‖敬老の日 Respect-for-the-Aged Day

けう 稀有 ―稀有な rare ➾めずらしい

ケー K 2Kのアパート a two-bedroom apartment with *a kitchen* ➾ディーケー

ケーオー (ノックアウト) KO [C] (複 KO's), knockout [C] ―KOする KO [他], knock out ∥KOで勝つ win by (*a*) *KO*; *knock a person out*
‖TKO(テクニカルノックアウト) a TKO, a technical knockout

ケーキ cake [U][C] (❖大きなケーキまるごと1つをいう場合には [C] だが, 切り分けたケーキの1切れを指す場合や, 漠然とした意味で用いるときは [U] として扱う)
ケーキ1切れ a piece [slice] of *cake* / ケーキを食べる eat *cake* / ケーキを焼く bake *a cake* / ケーキを6つに切り分ける cut *a cake* into six portions
‖ケーキカット cake-cutting (in ceremony) / ケーキセット (コーヒー[紅茶]付きケーキ) cake with coffee [tea] / ケーキ屋 a pastry shop / ウエディングケーキ a wedding cake / カップケーキ a cupcake / クリスマスケーキ a Christmas cake / ショートケーキ (切り分けたケーキ一般) a slice of cake; (種類としての) shortcake / チーズケーキ (a) cheesecake / デコレーションケーキ a fancy cake / バースデーケーキ a birthday cake / パウンドケーキ a pound cake / フルーツケーキ (a) fruitcake / ホットケーキ a pancake

ゲージ gauge [géidʒ] [C]

ケース ❶【容器】case [C] ∥彼はギターをケースにしまった He put the guitar in *the case.*
❷【事例】case [C] ∥これは非常にまれなケースだ This is *a* very rare *case.* / それらの問題はケースバイケースで検討しましょう Let's examine the issues *on a case-by-case basis.* (❖on a case-by-case basisは「一件一件別々に」の意味)
💬「だれがそれを担当するの」「それはケースバイケースだな」"Who's going to be in charge of that?" "*That* [*It*] *depends.*" (❖「場合による」の意味で case-by-case は用いない)
‖ケーススタディー a case study / ケースワーカー a caseworker

ゲート gate [C] ∥(競馬で)ゲートインする *enter the starting gate* / 7番ゲートへお進みください Please proceed to *Gate* 7.

ゲートボール 🗻

ゲートボールは, クロッケーをヒントに日本で考案されたゲームです. スティックでボールを打ち, 3つのゲートを順に通過させ, 最後にゴールポールに当てれば上がりです. ふつうは1チーム5人から成る2チームで争います. 日本では特に高齢者向けのスポーツとして普及しています.
Gateball is a game invented in Japan, inspired by croquet. The players hit balls with a stick through three wire gates in sequence. Players finish playing when they succeed in hitting the central pole. Usually the game is played by two teams of five players each. In Japan, gateball is especially popular among elderly people.

ケープタウン Cape Town (❖南アフリカ共和国南端の港市で立法上の首都)

ケーブル cable [C][U] ∥海底ケーブル *a* submarine *cable*
‖ケーブルカー a cable car / ケーブルテレビ cable television (《略語》CATV)

ゲーム game ⦿ ‖テレビゲーム a video game(❖ ×TV game とはいわない) / ゲームをする play a game / ホークスはライオンズに3ゲーム差をつけている The Hawks are three games ahead of the Lions.(❖「3ゲーム差をつけられている」は three games behind) / ゲームセット! Game!／The game is over!／(テニスなどで) Game, set and match.(❖ ×game set とはいわない)

‖ゲームセンター a video arcade,《英》an amusement arcade(❖ ×game center とはいわない)

けおとす 蹴落とす 彼は同僚をけ落として(→同僚を犠牲にして)今の地位を得た He got that position *at the expense of* his colleagues.

けおりもの 毛織物 woolen fabrics [textiles]

けが 怪我

(事故などによる) injury ⦿ ⦿, hurt ⦿(しばしば複数形 ~s);(刃物・銃などによる) wound ⦿
——けがをする get* [be] injured, get [be] hurt; get [be] wounded;(自分の過失によって) hurt* *oneself* ——けがをさせる injure ⦿, hurt; wound ⦿

⇒ 場面・状況別会話 p.1694

私は左足にけがをした I *was injured in* the left foot.

その事故で彼は軽いけが[大けが]をした He *was slightly* [*badly, severely*] *injured* in the accident.

その事故でバスの乗客にけがはなかった No passengers on the bus *were hurt* in the accident.

気をつけないとけがをしますよ Be careful or you'll *hurt yourself*.

私たちはけが人を急いで病院に運んだ We hurried *the injured* to the hospital.(❖ the injured は集合的に「けが人」を指す.1人のときは an injured person)

◆彼は誤ってナイフでけがをした He *cut himself* by mistake with a knife.

🔵「おけがはありませんでしたか」「ええ、大丈夫です」"Didn't you *hurt* yourself?" "No, I'm all right."

🔵「きのう道に迷ってしまったんだけど、そのおかげですてきなお花屋さんを見つけたの」「それはけがの功名だったね」"I got lost yesterday, but as a result I found a nice flower shop." "That was *a blessing in disguise!*"

ことわざ 生兵法は大けがの元 ➡ なまびょうほう

げか 外科 surgery ⦿ ——外科の surgical(❖名詞の前で用いる) ‖脳[心臓]外科 brain [heart] *surgery* / 形成外科 plastic *surgery*
‖外科医 a surgeon / 外科手術 a surgical operation

げかい 下界 (人間の住む世界) this world;(地上) the earth

けがす 汚す《公式的》soil ⦿;(名誉などを) dishonor ⦿,《英》dishonour ⦿, disgrace ⦿ / 彼は家名をけがした He *disgraced* the family name./ He brought disgrace on his family. ◆そのスキャンダルが彼の名声をけがした That scandal *injured* his reputation.

けがらわしい 汚らわしい (汚い) dirty;(不潔な) filthy;(むかむかするような) disgusting;(わいせつな) obscene / そんな言葉は口にするのもけがらわしい It's *disgusting* just to say those words.

けがれ 汚れ けがれを知らない(→無邪気な)子供 an *innocent* child

けがれる 汚れる そんなけがれた金は受け取れない I can't accept such *dirty* money.

けがわ 毛皮 fur ⦿ ⦿ ‖毛皮のコート a *fur* coat

げき¹ 劇 (芝居) play ⦿;(戯曲) drama ⦿ ⦿(❖ play よりもかたい語で、内容のまじめなものを指す)‖シェークスピア劇の研究 a study on Shakespeare's *plays* / 劇に出演する appear in *the play* / 劇を上演する「put on [perform, stage] *a play*
‖劇作家 a playwright, a dramatist

げき² 檄 監督は試合前に選手たちにげきを飛ばした The manager *harangued* the players before the game.

げきか¹ 劇化 dramatization ⦿ ——劇化する dramatize ⦿

げきか² 激化 ——激化する intensify ⦿ / 2つの部族間の争いが激化している The conflict between those two tribes *is intensifying*.

げきが 劇画 (realistically drawn) comic book ⦿ ‖まんが

げきげん 激減 ——激減する (著しく減る) decrease sharply [markedly];(急激に減る) decrease rapidly / 野生動物はここ数十年間で激減している Wild animals *have been decreasing sharply* in number in the last few decades.

げきじょう¹ 劇場,《主に英》theatre ⦿;(映画館) 《米》movie theater [house] ⦿,《英》cinema ⦿ ‖国立劇場 the National Theater / その劇場では今何をやっていますか What's playing at the *theater* now?

げきじょう² 激情 (激しい感情) violent [strong] emotion ⦿;(熱情) passion ⦿ ⦿ / 激情にかられて in a fit of *passion*

げきしん 激震 severe earthquake ⦿

げきせん 激戦 (激しい戦闘) fierce battle ⦿;(激しい競争) bitter [close] contest ⦿;(選挙の) hot contest ⦿ / 硫黄島は第二次世界大戦の激戦地だった Iwo Jima was *the scene of a fierce battle* in World War II.

‖激戦区(選挙の) a hotly contested election district

げきぞう 激増 ——激増する (著しく増える) increase markedly;(急激に増える) increase rapidly / 近年外国人居住者の数が激増している These days the number of foreign residents *is increasing rapidly*.

げきたい 撃退 ——撃退する (追い払う) drive* away [off],《公式的》repel ⦿;(克服する) fight* off / 痴漢を撃退する *drive* a molester *away* [*off*]

げきだん 劇団 theatrical [dramatic] company ⦿ ‖劇団員 a member of the theatrical company; (ベテランの) a trouper

げきつい 撃墜 ──撃墜する (撃ち落とす) shoot* [bring*] down

げきつう 激痛・劇痛 sharp [acute] pain ◎; (突然の) pang ◎ ∥突然腰に激痛が走った Suddenly I felt *a sharp pain* in my [the] lower back.

げきてき 劇的 ──劇的な dramatic; (徹底的な) drastic ──劇的に dramatically; drastically ∥劇的な出来事 a *dramatic* event / 劇的な変化 a *drastic* change / 彼女は劇的な一生を送った She led a *dramatic* life.

げきど 激怒 great anger ◎, fury ◎, rage ◎◎ ──激怒する get* [become*] furious, fly* into a fury [rage], rage ◎ ∥審判の判定に激怒する *get furious* about the umpire's decision / 彼は激怒してその男に殴りかかった He struck at the man *in a fit of rage*.

げきどう 激動 激動の時代 a *dynamic* era in history

げきとつ 激突 crash ◎; (2つの移動物の) collision ◎ ──激突する crash ◎; (2つの移動物が) collide ◎ ∥車は壁に激突した The car *crashed against* the wall.

げきひょう 劇評 drama criticism ◎

げきへん 激変・劇変 (急激な変化) sudden change ◎; (徹底的変化) drastic change ◎ ──激変する change suddenly; change drastically ∥90年代初頭にその国の政治形態は激変した The country's political system *underwent a drastic change* in the early 90s.

げきむ 激務・劇務 hard work ◎ ∥激務に耐える endure [stand] *hard work*
◆彼は毎日激務に追われている He is *extremely busy* at the office every day.

げきめつ 撃滅 ──撃滅する (完全に打ち負かす) defeat completely

げきやく 劇薬 (強力な薬) powerful drug ◎; (毒薬) poison ◎

げきらい 毛嫌い ──毛嫌いする hate ◎ ∥彼女は彼のことを毛嫌いしている She just *hates* him. ◆父はピアスをしている男を毛嫌いしている My father *is prejudiced against* men with pierced ears.

げきりゅう 激流 rapid [swift] current ◎; (ほとばしる水) torrent ◎

げきれい 激励 encouragement ◎ ──激励する encourage ◎, cheer ◎ ∥彼女のもとに全国から激励の手紙が寄せられた Letters of *encouragement* to her poured in from all over the country. / 大勢のクラスメートが彼の激励に駆けつけた A lot of his classmates came to *cheer* him *up*.
∥激励会 a pep rally

げきれつ 激烈 彼らは顧客獲得をめぐって激烈な競争を繰り広げている They are carrying on a *keen* competition for customers.

げきろん 激論 heated argument [discussion] ◎ ∥その問題について評論家の間で激論が交わされた There were *heated arguments* among the critics over the issue.

げけん 怪訝 ──けげんな (半信半疑の) dubious; (当惑した) puzzled ∥彼はけげんそうな顔をしていた He had a *puzzled* expression on his face.

げこ 下戸 私は下戸です (→ 酒が飲めない) I can't drink (alcohol) at all. / I am a teetotaler.

げこう 下校 ──下校する go* [come*] home (from school); leave* school (❖「学校を卒業[退学]する」の意味もある)
◆少年は下校途中に何者かに連れ去られた A boy was kidnapped by someone *on his way home from school*.

けさ 今朝 this morning

げざい 下剤 laxative ◎, purgative ◎

げざん 下山 ──下山する climb [come*] down a mountain

けし 芥子 〔植物〕poppy ◎ ∥ケシの実 a *poppy* seed

げし 夏至 the summer solstice

けしいん 消し印 postmark ◎ ◆ 2月28日の消印まで有効 Entries must *be postmarked* not later than Feb. 28. / その手紙にはモスクワの消印があった The letter was *postmarked* Moscow.

けしかける (犬などを) set* [sic] (a dog) on ...; (人をそそのかす) egg *a person* on ∥侵入者に犬をけしかける *set* [sic] *a dog on* a trespasser / 私は妹をけしかけて父に新しいテレビをねだらせた I *egged* my sister *on to* ask my father to buy a new TV set.

けしからん (恥ずべき) shameful; (とんでもない) scandalous; (無礼な) rude ∥大人をからかうとはけしからん It's *rude* of you to play a trick on adults. / 授業をサボるとはけしからん It's *a crime* to cut a class.

けしき 景色 scenery ◎; landscape ◎; view ◎

> scenery: 特に地方などの美しい景色全体.
> landscape: 個々の景色で, 主に内陸の景色.
> view: ある一定の場所から目に入る眺め.

美しい景色 beautiful *scenery*
展望台からはすばらしい景色を一望できる You can have *a splendid view* from the observation tower.
その景色は言葉にできないほど美しかった The *landscape* was beautiful beyond expression.
◆そこへ行く途中には景色のよい所がたくさんある There are a lot of *scenic spots* on the way there.

げじげじ 〔虫〕house centipede ◎
◆げじげじまゆ *bushy* eyebrows

けしゴム 消しゴム 《主に米》eraser ◎, 《英》rubber ◎ ∥消しゴム付きの鉛筆 a pencil with *an eraser* on the end / 間違いを消しゴムで消す erase a mistake with *an eraser*

けしさる 消し去る erase ◎, blank out, blot out ∥いやな思い出をすっかり消し去ってしまいたい I want to *blot* every unpleasant memory *out* of my mind.

けしとめる 消し止める put* out, extinguish ◎ ∥ついに消防隊は火を消し止めた Finally the fire fighters *put out* the fire.

けじめ (区別) distinction ⓒ ‖公私のけじめをはっきりすべきだ You should make *a* clear *distinction* between public and private issues.

◆遊びと仕事のけじめをつけなさい(→一線を画しなさい) You've got to *draw a line* between play and work. / 社長が辞任したからといって一連の不祥事にけじめがついた(→決着した)わけではない The resignation of the president didn't *put an end to* the series of scandals.

げしゃ 下車 ──下車する (降りる) get* off
◆福島で途中下車する「*stop over [make a stopover]* in Fukushima

げしゅく 下宿 (食事付きの) boardinghouse ⓒ; (部屋のみの) 《米》 rooming house ⓒ, 《英》 lodging house ⓒ ──下車する (食事付きで) board ⓘ; (部屋のみ) 《米》 room ⓘ, 《英》 lodge ⓘ ‖彼は大学時代, 本郷に下宿していた He used to *live in a rooming house* in Hongo while he was in college. / 彼はいとこの家に下宿している He *is boarding [rooming]* at his cousin's house.

◆彼女は5万円の下宿代を払うためにアルバイトをしている She works part-time to pay 50,000 yen for *her room [room and board]*. (✿room and board は「部屋と食事」の意味)

‖下宿人(食事付き下宿の) a boarder; (部屋のみの) 《米》a roomer, 《英》a lodger

げじゅん 下旬 (月の最後の10日間) the last 10 days of a month
◆法廷は5月下旬に開かれる The court will convene *in late* May.

けしょう 化粧 makeup ⓤ ──化粧する make* (*oneself*) up, put* on (*one's*) makeup ──化粧の cosmetic

厚[薄]化粧 heavy [light] *makeup*
彼女はドレッサーの前で化粧をしていた She *was putting on her makeup* at the dresser.
母はふだん化粧をしない My mother usually *doesn't wear makeup.*
寝る前には必ずきれいに化粧を落としなさい Be sure to 「*take off [remove] your makeup* before going to bed.
ちょっとお化粧を直してきます I'm going to fix *my makeup* quickly.
けさは化粧の乗りが悪い My skin just won't take *makeup* this morning.

🔊「毎朝化粧にかける時間はどれくらい」「せいぜい10分くらいかな」 "How much time do you take to *do your face* every morning?" "About ten minutes at the longest."

‖化粧板 veneer / 化粧室 a powder room, 《米》a rest room / 化粧水 (a) lotion / 化粧せっけん a toilet soap, a hand soap / 化粧台 《米》a dresser, a vanity 《英》dressing table / 化粧箱 a gift box / 化粧品 cosmetics / 化粧品店 a cosmetic(s) shop / 化粧ポーチ a vanity case, a vanity bag

―化粧品のいろいろ―
アイシャドー eye shadow / アイライナー eyeliner / アフターシェーブローション aftershave lotion / おしろい powder / 口紅 lipstick / クリーム cream / 化粧水 skin [moisturizing] lotion / 香水 perfume / 乳液 milk, milky liquid / 日焼け止め sunscreen / ファンデーション foundation / ヘアスプレー hair spray / ヘアトニック hair tonic / ほお紅 blusher, rouge / マスカラ mascara / マニキュア 《米》nail polish, 《英》nail varnish / まゆ墨 eyebrow pencil / ムース mousse / ローション lotion

けしん 化身 (権化) incarnation ⓒ; (具体化されたもの) the embodiment ◆悪魔の化身 a devil *incarnate* (✿*incarnate* は「化身の」の意味の形容詞. 通例名詞の後で用いる)

けす 消す

❶ 火を	put out, extinguish
❷ スイッチを切る	turn off, switch off
❸ 文字・録音などを	erase
❹ 姿を	disappear
❺ 取り除く	remove
❻ 殺す	kill

❶【火を】put* out, 《公式的》extinguish ⓕ
ろうそく[たばこ]を消す *put out* a candle [cigarette] / 火事を消す 「*put out [extinguish]* a fire
地震が起こったらまず第一に火を消さなければならない The first thing to do when an earthquake occurs is (to) *put out* any fire.

◆ろうそくの火を吹き消す *blow* a candle *out* / 彼はたばこを踏み消した He *stamped* his cigarette *out.*

❷【スイッチを切る】turn off, switch off
(栓をしめて)ガスを消す *turn off* the gas
彼女は部屋の明かりを消した She *turned [switched] off* the light in her room.
うちでは食事のときはいつもテレビを消す We usually *turn* the TV *off* during meals.

🔊「おふろ場の電気がつけっぱなしよ」「今, 消してくる」 "Somebody left the light on in the bathroom." "I'll go *turn* it *off.*"

❸【文字・録音などを】erase ⓕ; (消しゴムで) 《英》rub out; (録音・録画したものを) wipe out; (線を引いて) cross out; (こすって) rub off

黒板を消してくれますか Could you *erase* the blackboard?
僕は誤ってそのフロッピーの中のデータをすべて消してしまった I *wiped out* all the data on the floppy disk by mistake.
間違った箇所はすべて2本線で消して印鑑を押してください Any mistake must *be crossed out* with a double line and stamped with a seal.

❹【姿を】disappear ⓘ; (突然) vanish ⓘ
飛行機は視界から全く姿を消し暗やみの中に入った The plane completely *disappeared* from view into the dark.
恐竜は太古の昔に地球上から忽然(こつぜん)と姿を消した Dinosaurs *vanished* from the face of

the earth a long time ago.
❺【取り除く】remove [他]; (ふき取る) wipe [他]; (こすり取る) rub off; (きれいにする) clean off
コーヒーのだしがらは冷蔵庫のにおいを消すのに役立つ Coffee grounds help *remove* smells from refrigerators.
❻【殺す】kill [他], murder [他], 《俗語》eliminate [他], 《米俗語》rub out
じゃま者はだれであろうと消す I'*ll rub out* anyone who gets in my way.

げす 下衆 (品性のいやしい人) vulgar person [C], a person of low character; (身分のいやしい人) a person of low position
[慣用表現] げすの勘ぐりはよせ Don't have *a petty-minded suspicion.*
[ことわざ] げすの後知恵 It is easy to be wise after the event. (→事がすんでから賢明な判断を下すのは簡単だ)

げすい 下水 sewage [sú:idʒ] [U], drainage [U]; (設備) sewerage [sú:əridʒ] [U]; (排水管) drain [C] //下水が詰まった *The drain* is blocked [stopped up]. / その地区ではまだ下水道が完備していない *The sewerage system* isn't yet complete in that area.
‖下水管 a drainpipe / 下水工事 sewage work / 下水処理 sewage disposal / 下水処理場 a sewage disposal plant

ゲスト guest [C] //今夜のスペシャルゲスト tonight's special *guest* / ゲスト出演する make a *guest* appearance

けずりとる 削り取る (薄くそぎ取る) shave* (off); (こすり落とす) scrape (off)

けずる 削る
❶【刃物で薄くそぎ取る】(かんななどで) shave* [他], plane [他]; (鉛筆を) sharpen [他]
かつお節を削る *shave* dried bonito
ナイフで鉛筆を削った I *sharpened* the pencil with a knife.
◆壁のペンキを削って落とした I *scraped* the paint *off* the wall.
❷【取り除く・削減する】cut* [他]; (削減する) reduce [他]
予算を10パーセント削る *cut* [*reduce*] a budget by 10 percent
◆名簿から彼の名前を削る *take* his name *off* a list / 最後の文は削ったほうがいい You should *cross* the last sentence *out*. (❖cross out は「線を引いて消す」の意味)

げせない 解せない (理解できない) incomprehensible //解せない話 an *incomprehensible* story ◆彼がなぜそんなことをしたのかどうも解せない I just *can't understand* why he did such a thing.

げせん 下船 《公式的》disembarkation [U] [C]
━下船する get* off (a ship), 《公式的》disembark [自]

けた 桁 ❶【数学】(0から9までの数字) figure [C], digit [C]; (位) place [C] //3けたの数 three-*digits* number / 小数点以下3けたまで計算して四捨五入しなさい Calculate to three decimal *places*, and then round up. / 年収が8けたに達した My annual income has reached eight *figures*.
💬「これがたった1万円だって. 安いわね」「よく見て. 1けた間違えてるわよ(→もう1つのゼロを見落としている)」 "This is just 10,000 yen. It's a real bargain!" "Look carefully. You'*re missing another zero*."
❷【建物などの】(建物の) beam [C]; (橋の) girder [C]
[慣用表現] 彼はうちとはけた違いに大きな家に住んでいる His house is *incomparably* larger than ours. / そのホームランボールはけたはずれの高値で落札された The home-run ball was knocked down to an *extraordinarily* [*incredibly*] high price.

げた 下駄  *geta*, a pair of wooden clogs //げたを履く[脱ぐ] 「put on [take off] *geta*
‖げた箱 a shoe cupboard
[慣用表現] 君にげたを預けよう(→一任しよう) I'*ll leave everything to* you. / 得点にげたをはかせる(→点数を水増しする) *increase* [*jack up*] a score / 勝負はげたをはくまで(→終わってみなければ)分からない Nobody knows who will win the game *until* the game *is over*.

げたは木で作られた日本固有の履き物です. 裏に2本の歯がついた厚板でできているのがふつうです. 中にはつま先の部分に布やビニールのカバーのあるものや, 歯の形が違うものなどもあります. 一般的には夏, ゆかたを着るときに素足で履きます.
Geta are a kind of wooden clogs unique to Japan. They are usually made of a flat wooden platform with two supports projecting downward from the sole. Some of them have a cloth or vinyl cover for toes and some have supports of a different shape. Generally, *geta* are worn with bare feet to go with *yukata* in summer.

けだかい 気高い (高貴な) noble ━気高く nobly //気高い心 a *noble* mind

けたたましい (かん高い) shrill, piercing //けたたましい叫び声 a *shrill* cry
◆そのときベルがけたたましく鳴り始めた The bell started to *shrill* [*ring loudly*] at that moment. / 猿がおりの中でけたたましく鳴いている The monkeys *are chattering* in the cage.

けだま 毛玉 pill [C] ◆このセーターは毛玉ができにくい This sweater won't *pill* easily.

けだもの 獣 beast [C], brute [C] (❖いずれの語も日本語の「けだもの」同様,「人でなし」の意味を含む. 前者はいやしい欲望, 後者は理性の欠如・凶暴性を暗示する) //あの男は人間の皮をかぶったけだものだ That man is *a beast* in human form.

けだるい 気だるい lazy, 《文語》languid; (元気のない) listless //けだるい午後 a *lazy* afternoon

けち (難癖(なんくせ)) quibble [C]; (出し惜しみする人) miser [C] ━けちな (出し惜しみする) 《口語的》stingy, tightfisted; (心の狭い) mean

けちな根性 a *stingy* personality
あいつはけちな男で自分の金は使わない He's a *stingy* man and doesn't part with his money.
彼にチップをあげなかったなんてけちだね It was *mean* of you not to give him a tip.
◆けちな身なりの男 a *shabbily* dressed man / 君は僕のやることにいちいちけちをつけるんだね You *are* always *finding fault* with whatever I do. / 僕なんかたいした者じゃない、けちな絵描きですよ I'm not a great man at all — just a *worthless* painter. / けちくさいこと言うなDon't be so *small-minded*.
🅔「それはあげられないよ」「けち！」"I can't let you have it." "*You are stingy*."

けちけち ——けちけちする be stingy *∥*何をそんなにけちけちしているんだ Why *are* you so *stingy*? ◆金にけちけちしない be liberal with [*of*] *one's* money

ケチャップ ketchup ⓤ,《主に米》catsup ⓤ

けちる skimp ⓜⓙ, be stingy *∥*彼は食事代をけちってお昼をハンバーガー１つですませた He ate only one hamburger for lunch, *skimping on* food expenses.

けちんぼう けちん坊 penny pincher ⓒ, miser ⓒ,《米口語的》cheapskate ⓒ

けつ¹ 決 vote ⓒ *∥*決を採る take *a* vote

けつ² 穴 (しり)《主に米・俗語的》butt ⓒ,《米俗語》ass ⓒ,《英俗語》arse ⓒ ⇨しり
慣用表現 マラソン大会で僕はけつから３番目だった I was the third *from bottom* in the marathon race. / あいつはけつの穴が小さい (→度量が狭い) He *is narrow-minded*. / 彼は間違いをとがめられ、「それがどうした」とけつをまくった He *turned defiant* [*aggressive*] saying "What's wrong with it?" when he was accused of a mistake.

けつあつ 血圧 blood pressure ⓤⓒ *∥*血圧の測定 the measurement of *blood pressure* / 父は血圧が高い [低い] My father has high [low] *blood pressure*. / 私の血圧は上が125で下が90だった My *blood pressure* was 125 over 90. / 摂取する塩分を控えることで血圧を下げることができる You can lower *your blood pressure* by taking less salt. ◆高 [低] 血圧 (症)《医学》hypertension [hypotension]
∥血圧計 a blood pressure gauge

けつい 決意 determination ⓒ《また a ～》, resolution ⓒ ——決意する《公式的》determine ⓜ, resolve ⓜ *∥*決意を新たにする renew *one's determination*; make *a* fresh *determination*. / 彼の辞職の決意は堅い His *determination* to resign is firm. / 彼はオーストラリアに留学しようと決意した He *determined* to study in Australia. / He *determined* that he would study in Australia.

けついん 欠員 vacancy ⓒ, vacant post [position] ⓒ *∥*この欠員を埋める人が見つからなかった No one was found to fill this *vacant post*. ◆欠員が出る fall *vacant*

けつえき 血液 blood ⓤ *∥*運動すると血液の循環がよくなる Exercise stimulates the circulation of *blood*.

🅔「あなたの血液型は何ですか」「B 型です」"What's your *blood type* [《英》*group*]?" "It's B." / I have B-*type blood*."
∥血液銀行 a blood bank / 血液検査 a blood test / 血液製剤 a blood product

けつえん 血縁 blood relationship ⓤ;（血縁者）blood relation [relative] ⓒ ◆彼とは血縁関係にある I'm *related to* him *by blood*.

けっか 結果

（結末・成果）result ⓒⓤ;（最終的な結果）outcome ⓒ《通例単数形》;（効果）effect ⓒⓤ;（成り行き）consequence ⓒ
最悪の結果 the worst *result* / 原因と結果 cause and *effect*
試験の結果はあす発表される The *results* of the exam will be announced tomorrow.
私はそのレースの結果を知りたい I want to know *the outcome* of the race.
努力の結果、彼は試験に合格した As *a result* of his efforts, he passed the examination.
結果的には私は間違っていなかった *Judging only from the result*, I was not wrong.
結果論にすぎないかもしれないが、あのとき親の忠告をちゃんと聞いておくべきだった I may be able to say this *just because I already know the result*, but I should have obeyed my parents' advice that time.
◆調査の結果(→調査によって), 事の真相が明らかになった The truth of the matter emerged *from the investigation*. / ロケットの発射は失敗という結果に終わった The launch of the rocket *resulted in* a failure.
🅔「試合の結果はどうだった」「私たちの勝ちよ」"How did the game *turn* [*come*] *out*?" "We won."

けっかい 決壊 rupture ⓒⓤ ——決壊する burst* ⓙ *∥*豪雨で土手が決壊寸前になった Because of the heavy rain, the bank almost *burst* [*gave way*].

けっかく 結核 tuberculosis ⓤ(《略語》TB) *∥*結核患者の数はここ数年着実に増えている The number of *tuberculosis patients* has been steadily increasing for the last few years.

げつがく 月額 会費は月額2,000円です The fee is 2,000 yen *per month*.

けっかん¹ 欠陥（機械などの）fault ⓒ, defect ⓒ;（理論などの）flaw ⓒ;（弱点）weakness ⓒ;（コンピュータの）bug ⓒ *∥*性格的な欠陥 a *defect* in *one's* character / 事故によってその機械の欠陥がいくつか明らかになった The accident revealed some *defects* [*faults*] in the machine. / この建物には構造上の欠陥がある This building has *a structural fault* [*weakness*]. / 彼の議論には致命的な欠陥がある There is *a fatal flaw* in his argument.
∥欠陥車 a defective car / 欠陥住宅 a defective house / 欠陥商品 a defective product,《口語的》a lemon

けっかん² 血管 blood vessel ⓒ;（静脈）vein ⓒ(❖一般に「血管」の意味でも用いる);（動脈）artery ⓒ *∥*血管の詰まりを防ぐ prevent *blood*

げっかん

vessels from clogging
∥血管注射 an intravenous injection / 毛細血管 a capillary

げっかん¹ 月刊 ——月刊の monthly ∥この雑誌は発行部数が月刊50万部である This magazine has a *monthly* circulation of 500,000.
∥月刊誌 a monthly (magazine)

げっかん² 月間 交通安全月間 Traffic Safety *Month*

けっき¹ 血気 血気にはやる若者たち *hot-blooded* young people / 彼は相変わらず血気盛んだ (→若々しい活力を維持している) He still *keeps his youthful vitality*.

けっき² 決起 ——決起する rise* ⊕ ∥市民は圧政に対して決起した The citizens *rose against* the tyranny.
∥決起集会 a rally

けつぎ 決議 resolution ⓒⓤ; (決定) decision ⓤⓒ ——決議する resolve ⊕ ∥決議案を採択[否決]する adopt [reject] *a resolution* / 政府は輸入拡大を決議した The government *resolved* 「*that* imports should be expanded [*to expand* imports].
∥決議文 a resolution

げっきゅう 月給 monthly pay ⓤ, (monthly) salary ⓒⓤ ∥安月給をとる get [draw] *a small salary* / 彼の月給はだいたい30万円だ His *monthly salary* is about three hundred thousand yen. / 彼は月に三十万円ほど支払われている He *is paid* about three thousand yen *a month*.
∥月給取り a salaried employee [worker]

けっきょく 結局 (予想・期待に反して) after all (❖通例文末で用いる); (最終的に) finally, at last, in the end; (要するに) in short [brief]; (長い目で見れば) in the long run
本を買いに町へ出たが, 結局1冊も買わなかった I went to town to buy some books, but didn't buy any *after all*.
僕たちは善戦したが, 結局試合に負けてしまった We played well, but lost (the game) *in the end*.
結局, 彼は信頼に足る人間ではないということだ *In short*, he is not trustworthy.
品質のよいもののほうが結局は得だ Quality goods are profitable *in the long run*.
◆彼の計画は結局失敗に終わった His plan *ended in* failure. / 結局その政治家はわいろとは何の関係もなかった As it turned out, the politician had nothing to do with the bribe. / それは結局金を取るか安全を取るかの問題に帰着した It *came down to* a choice between money and safety. / 彼らは何度も試みたが結局失敗に終わった They tried many times *only to* fail miserably. (❖only to には否定的な結末が続く)

けっきん 欠勤 absence ⓤⓒ ——欠勤する be absent from …,《公式的》absent *oneself* from …(❖故意に欠勤することを意味することが多い)∥長期欠勤 a long(-term) *absence* / 彼は3日間欠勤している He *has been absent from work* for three days. / アルバイトだからといって無断欠勤が許されるわけではない Just because you work part-time doesn't mean you can 「*absent yourself from* [*miss*] *work without notice*.
∥欠勤者 an absentee / 欠勤届 a report of absence

けづくろい 毛繕い ——毛づくろいをする groom ⊕

げっけい 月経《公式的》menstruation ⓤ,《公式的》menstrual period ⓒ (❖口語では単に period ともいう), 〔医学〕menses
∥月経不順 irregular periods

げっけいじゅ 月桂樹 laurel ⓒ, bay tree ⓒ

けっこう¹ 結構

❶ よい　　good, nice
❷ 不要だ
❸ 満足だ・用が足りる
❹ …してもよい　can, may
❺ かなり　　fairly

❶【よい】 ——結構な good, nice;(申し分ない) excellent;(すばらしい) wonderful
結構なお品をありがとうございました Thank you very much for the *nice* present.
◆彼らがあれこれ口出ししてくれるのはまことに結構だが実際はそんな必要はない It's all very *well* for them to make suggestions, but they don't actually have to do it.
🍃「どうだい, 僕の料理の腕は」「結構なお腕前で」 "What do you think of my cooking?" "*Excellent*."

❷【不要だ】
あなたの援助などは結構です I *can do without* your help.
お見送りいただかなくても結構です There's no *necessity* for you to see me off.
🍃「もう少しいかがですか」「いいえ, 結構です」 "Would you like some more?" "*No, thank you*."
🍃「紅茶かコーヒーはいかがですか」「どちらも結構です. のどは渇いていません」 "Would you like a cup of tea or coffee?" "*Neither, thanks*. I'm not thirsty."

❸【満足だ・用が足りる】
私はこの席で結構です This seat *is all right* with me.
こちらにお名前だけ書いていただければ結構です *All we'd like you to do is* just to write your name here.
🍃「書く物は鉛筆しかありませんが」「それで結構です」 "I only have a pencil to write with." "*That will do*. / *That's good enough*."
🍃「500円貸してほしいって? ほら, 1,000円貸してあげるよ」「いや, 本当に500円で結構です」 "You want me to lend you 500 yen? Here, you can take 1,000 yen." "Thank you, but 500 yen *is* really *enough*."

❹【…してもよい】 can, may (❖may は can より堅苦しく, 「自分が許可してやる」と権威的に聞こえることがあるので注意が必要)
横のドアから出ても結構です You *can* [*may*] exit from the side door.
もし助けが必要なら, いつでも電話してくれて結構

です You *can* call me any time if you need some help.

◆どんな提案でも結構です Any 「suggestion *is* [suggestions *are*] *welcome.* / いつでも私たちの別荘を使って結構ですからね You *are welcome to* use our villa at your pleasure.

❺【かなり】fairly, pretty

彼はけっこう英語がうまい He speaks English *fairly* [*pretty*] well.

兄は昔はけっこうスキーが上手でした My brother used to be a *fairly* [*pretty*] good skier.

◆私はその映画がけっこう気に入った I *rather* liked the movie.

[会]「その靴高そうだね」「うん，結構な値段だったよ. 1万5千円したんだ」"Your shoes seem to have cost a lot." "Right, they cost *quite a lot*. They were 15,000 yen."

けっこう[2] 決行 ストを決行する *go out on* strike / あしたのハイキングは雨の場合でも決行します We'*ll go* hiking *on schedule* tomorrow even if it rains.

けっこう[3] 欠航 欠航する cancel [他] ∥台風のためにすべての(航空)便は欠航となった Owing to the typhoon, all flights *were canceled.*

◆神戸行きの船は今晩欠航します The ship for Kobe *will not sail* tonight.

けっこう[4] 血行 (blood) circulation [U][C] ∥血行がよい[悪い] have good [bad] *circulation* / 血行をよくする improve *blood circulation*

けつごう 結合 (化合) combination [U][C]; (団結) union [U] ━結合する combine [他][自]; unite [他][自]; (つなぐ) join [他] (❖しばしば together, up を伴う) ∥保守・革新派の結合 *the union* of a conservative with a reformist / 酸素と水素を結合させる *unite* hydrogen and oxygen

げっこう 月光 moonlight [U]

けっこん[1] 結婚

marriage [C][U] ━結婚する marry [他][自] (❖「…と結婚する」を×marry with ... としないことに注意), get* married; (結婚している) be married

〖～(の)結婚〗

彼女は娘の結婚を許した She gave her consent to her daughter's *marriage.*

◆姉夫婦は社内結婚だった My sister *met her husband working in the same company.* / My sister's *marriage was the result of an office romance.*

〖結婚を・に〗

両親は姉の結婚に反対している My parents are against my sister's *marriage.*

彼女に結婚を申し込むつもりです I'm going to *propose* (*marriage*) *to* her.

彼とは結婚を前提につきあっています I'm seeing him *with marriage in mind.*

〖結婚の〗

結婚の予定はありますか Are you going to *get married* (soon)?

◆私は彼と結婚の約束をしている I *am engaged to* him.

〖結婚する〗

僕は彼女と結婚したい I want to *marry* her. / I want to *get married to* her.

浩と裕子は結婚した Hiroshi and Hiroko *got married.*

私と結婚してくれませんか Will you *marry* me?

彼らは結婚したばかりです They *have just married.* / They *are newlyweds.*

彼は結婚していますか，それとも独身ですか *Is* he *married* or single?

両親は結婚して20年になります(→20年間結婚している) My parents *have been married* for 20 years.

彼女の両親は彼女を医者と結婚させようとした Her parents tried to *marry* her (*off*) *to* a doctor.

◆結婚している女性 a *married* woman

〖その他〗

結婚おめでとう Congratulations on *your marriage.* (❖以前は新郎に対して用いる表現だったが，現在は新婦に対しても用いる)

結婚後も仕事を続ける女性が増えている More and more women continue their careers *after marriage.*

姉は結婚相手を探している My sister is looking for *someone to marry.*

彼女は結婚願望はないと言っている She says she doesn't have *a desire* 「*to get married* [*for marriage*].

彼らは毎月いくらかのお金を結婚資金としてためている They put aside some money every month *for their marriage.*

◆結婚後の姓 *one's married* name / 結婚のお祝い a *wedding* gift / 私たちの結婚披露宴にご出席していただきたいと思っております We are hoping that you'll attend our *wedding reception.*

‖結婚記念日 a wedding anniversary / 結婚生活 married life / 結婚制度 the institution of marriage / 結婚相談所 a matrimonial bureau [agency] / 結婚適齢期 a marriageable age / 結婚指輪 a wedding ring / 国際結婚 (an) international marriage / 見合い結婚 an arranged marriage / 恋愛結婚 a love match

けっこん[2] 血痕 bloodstain [C] ∥警察は容疑者の衣服に血痕を発見した The police found *bloodstains* on the suspect's clothes.

◆血痕のついたタオル a *bloodstained* towel

けっこんしき 結婚式 wedding (ceremony) [C] ∥結婚式の日取り the date of *a wedding* (*ceremony*) / 彼らはその教会で結婚式を挙げた They held *their wedding* (*ceremony*) at the church.

‖結婚式場 a wedding hall

> 日本では，神前式，仏前式，キリスト教式などいろいろな形の結婚式があります. どの形をとるかは必ずしも宗教的理由によらず，新郎新婦の好みで決められることもよくあります. 例えば信者でなくとも教会で式を挙げることができます. また最近では，海外で結婚式を挙げるカップルもたく

さんいます.
In Japan, many different styles of weddings — Shinto, Buddhist or Christian — can be seen. The decision as to which one to choose is not necessarily made for religious reasons, but in many cases according to the couple's taste. For example, it is not necessary to be Christian to hold a ceremony at a church. Recently, there are also many couples who hold wedding ceremonies abroad.

けっさい¹ 決済 settlement ◎Ⓤ ——決済する settle ⊕; (手形・小切手などを) honor, 《英》honour ⊕

けっさい² 決裁 部長にその案の決裁を仰ぐ submit the proposal to the department head for *approval*

けっさく 傑作 masterpiece ◎ 『椿姫』はベルディの傑作の一つ *La Traviata* is one of Verdi's 「*great masterpieces* [*best works*]」
◆このアルバムが彼らの最高傑作とされている This album is said to be *the greatest of all their works*. / その質問に対する彼の答えが傑作だった(→おかしかった) His answer to the question *was quite funny*.

けっさん 決算 closing ◎Ⓤ, settlement of accounts ——決算する settle [balance] accounts / 3月に決算する settle [balance] accounts in March
‖決算期 the end of an accounting period; (年度末) a fiscal year-end / 決算日 the closing [settlement] date; (年度末) a fiscal year-end / 決算報告書《商業》a financial statement

げっさん 月産 monthly output [production]Ⓤ /その工場におけるCDプレーヤーの月産台数 the monthly output [*production*] of CD players at the factory

けっし 決死 ——決死の do-or-die; (自暴自棄の) desperate /彼らは決死の覚悟で村を守った They guarded the village with a *do-or-die* attitude.
◆彼はかけから決死の(→命をかけて)ダイビングをした He dived from the cliff *at the risk of his life*.
‖決死隊 a suicide squad

けつじつ 結実 ——結実する bear* fruit, 《公式的》come* to fruition; (よい結果を得る) get* results

けっして 決して

(絶対に…ない) never; (全く…どころでない) no (❖be 動詞の補語となる名詞・形容詞の前に用いる.強く否定し「むしろその逆だ」の意味をもつ); (全然…ない) not … at all, by no means; (いかなる理由があろうと…ない) on no account, not … on any account
彼は熱があっても決して学校を休まない He is *never* absent from school even when he has a fever.
君のことを決して忘れはしない I'll *never* forget you.
このことは決して口外してはならない *Never* tell this to anybody.
彼は決して初心者などではない He is *no* beginner.(❖「経験を積んでいる」という含みがある.He is not a beginner.とすると単に「初心者でない」ことを表し,その含みは消える)
私はひとりぼっちだったが,決して寂しくはなかった Although I was all alone, I was 「*not sad at all* [*by no means* sad].
君のしたことは決して許されることではない What you did will 「*not* be forgiven *on any account* [*on no account* be forgiven].
◆何が起ころうとも彼女は決してその場を動こうとしなかった No matter what happened, she *wouldn't* move there. / 彼女は決して人の悪口を言うような人ではない(→最も人の悪口を言いそうにない人だ) She is *the last person to* say bad things about others.

けっしゃ 結社 association ◎Ⓤ /政治結社 a political *association* / 秘密結社 a secret *association*

げっしゃ 月謝 monthly fee ◎, monthly tuition Ⓤ

けっしゅう 結集 ——結集する (集中する) concentrate ⊕; gather ⊕ /我々の総力を結集してその企画にあたった We 「*concentrated* all of our efforts on [*gathered* all of our efforts for] the project.

げっしゅう 月収 monthly income ◎; (月給) monthly salary

けっしゅつ 傑出 ——傑出した (すぐれた) outstanding, excellent; (卓越した) prominent /傑出した演奏家 an *outstanding* [an *excellent*, a *prominent*] musician

けつじょ 欠如 lack Ⓤ《しばしば a ~》, 《公式的》want ⊕《また a ~》 ——欠如する lack ⊕, be lacking in … /常識の欠如 a lack of common sense / 彼は誠実さが欠如している He *lacks* [*is lacking in*] sincerity.

けっしょう¹ 決勝 the final(s), the final game, the final match /ワールドカップの決勝戦 the World Cup *final* / わがチームは決勝戦へ進んだ Our team 「*went on* [*advanced*, *got through*] *to the finals*. / 私たちのチームは決勝で4対1で敗れた Our team was defeated by 4 to 1 in *the finals*. / 我々は決勝でロシアに敗れた We lost *the final* to Russia.
‖決勝進出者 a finalist / 決勝点(ゴール地点) the finish [goal] (line); (勝敗を決める得点) a winning score [goal] / 準決勝 a semifinal / 準々決勝 a quarterfinal / 同点決勝戦 a tie-breaker

けっしょう² 結晶 crystal ◎; (結晶作用) crystallization Ⓤ; (成果) fruit ◎《通例複数形 ~s》 /雪の結晶 snow *crystals* / 努力の結晶 *the fruits of one's effort* / この子は私たちの愛の結晶だ This child is *the fruit* of our love.

けつじょう 欠場 ——欠場する (棄権する) default ⊕; (欠席する) be absent from …

けっしょく 血色 color, 《英》colour ◎Ⓤ; (顔色) complexion ◎ /血色がいい[悪い]

have good [little] *color*

げっしょく 月食 lunar eclipse [C], an eclipse of the moon ‖皆既月食 a total eclipse of the moon / 部分月食 a partial eclipse of the moon

けっしん 決心

decision [U] [C]; (決意) determination [U] 《また a ～》, resolution [C] [U] ──決心する decide [他] [自], make* up *one's* mind; (堅く) 《公式的》determine [他], resolve [他] [自]

漫画家になろうという彼女の決心は堅い Her *decision* [*determination*, *resolution*] to be a cartoonist is firm.

彼は毎朝ジョギングしようと堅く決心した He *made a* firm *resolution* [*determination*] to jog every morning.

友人たちの話を聞いて彼女の決心は揺らいだ Her *decision* [*determination*, *resolution*] got shaky at her friends' story.

彼は決心を変えそうになかった He didn't seem to change *his decision* [*mind*].

彼はその大学へ行く決心をした He *decided* to go to the university. / He *decided* that he would go to the university.

由紀はまだそのことで決心がつかずにいる Yuki *hasn't decided* [*made up her mind*] about it yet.

彼女は医者になろうと決心している She *is determined* to become a doctor.

けっする 決する decide [他] ‖両チームの雌雄を決する試合 the game to *decide* which is the stronger of the two teams ◆運命を決する日 the *fatal* day / 意を決して火の中に飛び込んだ I jumped into the fire 「*with firm resolution* [(→勇気をもって)*with bravery*].

けっせい[1] 血清 〔医学〕 serum [síərəm] [U] [C] (複 ～s, sera)

けっせい[2] 結成 ──結成する form [他]; (組織する) organize [他] ‖ロックバンドを結成する *form* a rock band / 政党を結成する *organize* a political party

けつぜい 血税 彼らに血税(→苦労して稼いだ金)のむだづかいはやめてもらいたい I want them to stop wasting *taxpayers' hard-earned money*.

けっせき 欠席 absence [U] [C] ──欠席する do* not go, stay away, 《公式的》absent *oneself* (❖absent *oneself* は故意に欠席することを意味する場合が多い); (欠席している) be absent

和美は先生に前日欠席した理由を告げた Kazumi told her teacher the reason for *her absence* the day before.

きょうはかぜのため学校を欠席した I 「*didn't go to* [*stayed away from*, *was absent from*] school today because of a cold.

彼は(学校の)欠席が多い He *is* frequently *absent from* school.

彼女は学校を無断欠席した She *absented herself from* school *without notice*.

‖欠席者 an absentee / 欠席届 a notice [report] of absence, (an) excuse

けっせん 決戦 (戦闘) decisive battle [C]; (試合) decisive game [match] [C]; (決着をつける最後の対決) showdown [C]《通例単数形》

けつぜん 決然 ──決然とした determined, resolute, strong-minded ──決然と determinedly, resolutely, strong-mindedly

けっせんとうひょう 決選投票 the final ballot, runoff (election) [C] ‖決選投票を行う take *the final ballot*

けっそう 血相 彼女はその知らせに血相を変えて怒った(→怒りに顔を赤らめた) Her face *turned red with anger* at the news. / 彼は血相を変えて(→青ざめた顔で)僕の部屋へ飛び込んできた He burst into my room *with a pale face*.

けっそく 結束 (統一性) unity [U]; (団結) union [U] ──結束する unite [他] [自] ‖メンバー間の結束を固める *strengthen the unity* of the members / 私たちのクラス全員が結束してその作業にあたった Our class *united* to do the work. / 党員たちの結束は固い The members of the party *are closely united*.

けつぞく 血族 blood relation [C] ‖血族関係 blood relationship

げっそり げっそりやせこけたほお *hollow* [*sunken*] cheeks / 彼女は病気のためげっそりやせていた She was *very thin* because of illness.

けっそん 欠損 (不足額) deficit [C]; (損失) loss [U] [C] ‖5,000万円の欠損を出す make *a deficit* [*loss*] of 50 million yen ◆沈没船は欠損している部分が目立った Many parts of the sunken ship *were broken off and lost*.

けったく 結託 conspiracy [U], 《公式的》collusion [U] ──結託する conspire [自], 《公式的》collude [自] ‖その警察官は暴力団と結託した The police officer *conspired* [*colluded*] *with* the gang. / The police officer *was in conspiracy* [*collusion*] *with* the gang.

けつだん 決断 (決定・決断力) decision [C] [U] ──決断する make* a decision, decide [他] [自] ‖今政府は最終的な決断を迫られている The government is now being pressed for *the* final *decision*. / 決断を下さねばならない時が近づいている The time is approaching when we must 「*make a decision* [*decide*]. / 紀子は決断が早い Noriko is quick to *decide*. / Noriko *makes decisions* quickly.

◆彼は決断力のある[ない]人だ He is a *decisive* [an *indecisive*] man.

けっちゃく 決着 settlement [C] [U]; (終わり) end [C] ‖試合はまだ決着がついていない The game *hasn't* yet *come to an end*. / (→続いている)The game *is* still *going on*.

◆その論争に決着をつける *settle* [*end*, *conclude*] the dispute

けってい 決定

decision [U] [C]; (結論) conclusion [C] ──決定する decide [他] [自]; (日時などを) fix [他], set* [他] ──決定的な decisive; (最終的な) conclusive; (確定的な) definite

速やかな[最終, 重大な]決定 *a* prompt [final,

けってん

crucial] *decision*
私はあなたの決定に従います I'll follow [respect] your *decision*.
その件についてはまだ決定ではないが、ほぼ確実だろう This matter *hasn't been decided* yet, but it seems sure.
私の上司は後にその決定をくつがえした My boss overturned the *decision* afterward.
我々は彼らと協力することに決定した We *decided* [*determined*, *made a decision*] to cooperate with them.
スキーとの出会いが彼女のその後の人生を決定した Her encounter with skiing *decided* the rest of her life.
パーティーの日取りを次の日曜日に決定した We *set* [*fixed*] the party for next Sunday.
警察はその男が現場にいたという決定的証拠をつかんだ The police got the *decisive* [*conclusive*, *definite*] evidence that the man was at the scene.
そのチームの勝利は決定的だ It *is definite* that the team will win the game.
◆決定的瞬間をとらえた写真 a photograph of 「*a crucial moment* [*the moment of truth*] /
彼の理論には決定的な間違いがある There is a *fatal* [*crucial*] mistake in his theory.
‖決定権 the say, the last word / 決定打(野球の) a winning hit / 決定版(本の) a definitive edition

けってん 欠点 fault ◯; (短所) shortcomings, bad point ◯; (弱点) weak point ◯; (欠陥) defect ◯; (わずかな欠点) flaw ◯
欠点を直す correct *one's faults* [*shortcomings*]
彼女の唯一の欠点はとてもわがままなことだ Her only *defect* [*bad point*] is that she is so selfish.
他人の欠点を探すのはやめるべきだ You should stop *finding fault with* others.
この計画にはいくつかの欠点がある There are some *faults* in this plan.
彼の理論には欠点がない His theory *is free of flaws.* / (→完璧(かんぺき)だ) His theory *is perfect*.

けっとう¹ 血統 (血筋) blood ◯, bloodline ◯; (動物の) pedigree ◯; (生まれ) birth ◯ /
うちの犬は血統がいい Our dog has a good *pedigree*. / その家は彼の代で血統が途絶えた The *bloodline* of the house came to an end in his time.
◆血統書付きの犬 a *pedigreed* dog
‖血統書 a pedigree

けっとう² 決闘 duel ◯ ──決闘する duel ⊕, fight* a duel / 彼に決闘をいどむ challenge him to *a duel*

けっとう³ 血糖 blood sugar ◯ ‖血糖値 the blood sugar level

けっぱく 潔白 innocence ◯, guiltlessness ◯ ──潔白な innocent, guiltless /身の潔白を証明する show [prove] *one's innocence* /
私は潔白だ I am *innocent*.
◆彼は清廉潔白な人物だ He is a man of *integrity*.

けつばん 欠番 missing number ◯
‖永久欠番 a retired number

げっぷ¹ 月賦 《米》 monthly installment plan ◯, 《英》 monthly hire purchase ◯ ◯; (分割払いの1回分) monthly installment ◯ /月賦でソファーを買った I bought a sofa *on a monthly installment plan.* / 毎月1万円の月賦でギターを買った I paid for a guitar *by monthly installments* of 10,000 yen each.
◆車の月賦は今回が最後だ This is *the last installment on* the car.

げっぷ² belch ◯, 《口語的》 burp ◯ ◆彼は食事中にげっぷをした He *belched* [*burped*] while eating. (❖英米では人前でげっぷをするのは無作法とされ、げっぷが出てしまったときには必ず Excuse me. などと言う)

けっぺき 潔癖 ──潔癖な (清潔好きな) 《公式的》 cleanly [klénli]; (誠実な) scrupulous
◆彼女は潔癖症だ (→清潔を保つことにとても神経質だ) She is *too nervous about cleanliness*. / (→清潔を保つにうるさい) She is *a stickler for cleanliness*.

けつべつ 決別 (別れること) parting ◯ ◯; (やめること) quitting ◯ ──決別する (かかわりを絶つ) break* with ...; (放棄する) 《公式的》 renounce ⊕; (やめる) 《口語的》 quit* ⊕ /今までの生活と決別する *renounce* [*break with*] *one's past life* / 彼は仲間と決別して町を去った He *broke with* his friends and left the town.

けつぼう 欠乏 lack ◯ 《しばしば a～》, deficiency ◯ ◯, shortage ◯ ◯ ──欠乏する lack ⊕ /その地域では食糧が欠乏している *There is a shortage of* food in the district. / 口内炎はビタミンB₂欠乏症の一つだ Stomatitis is *a vitamin B_2 deficiency disease*.

けつまくえん 結膜炎 【医学】 conjunctivitis [kəndʒʌŋktiváitəs]

けつまずく stumble ⊕, trip ⊕ ⇨ つまずく

けつまつ 結末 (終わり) end ◯; (映画・物語などの) ending ◯; (結果) result ◯ ◯ /論争に結末をつける *put an end to* the dispute / その話の結末はどうなったの What was *the ending of* the story? / How did the story *end?* / その映画は意外な結末だった The movie had *a surprising end* [*ending*]. / 事件は不幸な結末を迎えた The case *came to an unhappy end.* / The case *met with an* unhappy *result*.

げつまつ 月末 the end of the month /月末に[までに]アパートの家賃を払います I will pay rent for the apartment *at* [*by*] *the end of the month.* / 給料は月末払いです We get our salaries *at the end of the month*.

げつめん 月面 the surface of the moon, the moon's surface ‖月面着陸 a landing on the moon

けつゆうびょう 血友病 【医学】 hemophilia [hi:məfíliə] ◯ ‖血友病患者 a hemophiliac [hi:məfíliæk]

げつようび 月曜日 Monday ◯ ◯ (《略語》 Mon.) ⇨ にちようび

けつらく 欠落 (失うこと) loss ◯ ◯; (欠如)

lack ◎《しばしば a ～》——欠落する（失われている）be lost;（失う）lose*◎;（足りない）lack ◎ ‖彼は記憶が一部欠落していた A part of his memory *was lost*. / He *lost* a part of his memory.

げつれい 月例 ——月例の monthly ‖月例会議 a monthly meeting

けつれつ 決裂 breakdown ◎,《公式的》rupture ◎◎ ——決裂する break* down,《公式的》rupture ⊜ ‖２国間の交渉は決裂した The negotiations between the two countries「broke down [ruptured, were broken off].

けつろ 結露 condensation ◎ ‖窓と壁にたくさんの結露ができていた There was a lot of *condensation* on the windows and walls.

けつろん 結論 conclusion ◎◎
必然的な[正しい, 誤った]結論 *a necessary [right, wrong] conclusion* / 結論に達する「come to [reach] *a conclusion*
私たちはその議論から最終的結論を引き出した We drew *a final conclusion* from the discussion.
この問題はなかなか結論が出そうもない I don't think we can easily come to *a conclusion* about this matter.
結論として, 我々は以下の点を明らかにしておきたい *In conclusion*, we'd like to make the following things clear.
結論を急ぐべきでない You shouldn't *jump [rush] to a conclusion*.
◆委員会はその計画を採用すべきだとの結論を下した The committee *concluded that* the plan should be adopted. / 結論から言えば, 君は合格できなかったのだ *Let me tell you the results first*. You couldn't pass.

げてもの 下手物（奇妙な物）bizarre [odd] things;（異様な食べ物）bizarre [odd] foods

けど 僕はパーティーに行ったけど, 僕の彼女は行かなかった I went to the party, *but* my girlfriend didn't. / その時計はとても高かったけど, クリスマスに彼女に買ってあげた I bought her a watch for Christmas *though* it was very expensive. / 私だったら彼の誘いに乗らないけどな If I were you, I *wouldn't* accept his invitation. ➡けれど(も)

げどく 解毒（解毒作用）detoxification ◎
◆これらの漢方薬にはいろいろな解毒作用がある These Chinese medicines *counteract* various *poisons*.
‖解毒剤 an antidote

けとばす 蹴飛ばす kick ⊜ ‖少年は缶をけとばした The boy *kicked* the can (*away*).

けなげ 健気 ——けなげな（賞賛に値する）admirable, praiseworthy;（勇敢な）brave ‖よく働くけなげな少年 an *admirable* [a *praiseworthy*] boy who works very hard / けなげにも彼はひとりで病床の親の世話をした It was *admirable* [*praiseworthy*] of the little girl to take care of her parents sick in bed all by herself.

けなす《口語的》run* down;（悪く言う）say* bad things about, criticize,《英》criticise ⊜ ‖すべての評論家が彼の映画をけなした All the critics *ran* his movie *down*. / 彼はこのアルバムをけなしていたけど, 僕は好きだな He *criticized* this album, but I like it. / 彼女はいつも人をけなしてばかりいる She always *says bad things about* others.

けなみ 毛並み うちの犬は毛並みがいい[よくない] Our dog has *a fine [bad] coat (of hair)*. / 彼女は毛並みがいい（→家柄がいい）She *comes from [of] a good family*.

げねつざい 解熱剤（熱の薬）(a) medicine for fever,《薬》antifebrile ◎

けねん 懸念（将来への不安）《公式的》misgiving ◎《しばしば複数形～s》;（恐れによる）fear ◎◎;（心配）anxiety ◎;（気がかり）concern ◎◎ ——懸念する fear ⊜; be anxious ‖行方不明の飛行機は墜落したのではないかとの懸念が高まっている There is growing *fear [anxiety, concern]* that the missing airplane may have crashed. / 陽子は自分の将来に対して懸念をいだいている Yoko *has misgivings about* her future. / 今はこのような状況で人質たちの安否が懸念されている Now *there is concern for* the safety of the hostages in this situation.

けはい 気配（形跡）sign ◎;（傾向）tendency ◎;（感じ）feeling ◎
火災の後, 生存者がいる気配はなかった There was no *sign* of life after the fire.
景気はいっこうによくなる気配がない There is no *tendency* toward improvement in the economy. / The economy shows no *signs* of improvement.
空の色に秋の気配が感じられる There is *a feeling of fall* in the color of the sky.
◆後ろに人の気配を（→人がいるのを）感じて振り向いた I *felt someone* at my back and turned around. / 敵は我々の銃撃に応戦する気配を見せなかった（→応戦してくる様子はなかった）The enemy *didn't seem to* return our fire.

けばけばしい（はでで安っぽい）gaudy;（色がはですぎる）loud;（人目を引く）showy ‖けばけばしい服装の女性 a woman dressed in *gaudy [loud, showy]* clothes ‖ホテルのけばけばしい内装 the *gaudy* interior of a hotel

けばだつ 毛羽立つ fluff ⊜, become* fuzzy ——毛羽立った fuzzy ‖毛羽立った生地 *fuzzy* cloth

げばひょう 下馬評（うわさ）rumor,《英》rumour ◎◎ ‖下馬評では新大統領はヒル氏が有力だということだ *There is a rumor [Rumor has it] that* Mr. Hill will most likely be the new President. /（→世間では）*People say that* Mr. Hill will most likely be the new President. ◆そのチームは下馬評どおり最下位に終わった That team finished last *as everyone had expected*.

けびょう 仮病 pretended illness [sickness] ◎ ‖彼は時々仮病を使って（→ 病気のふりをして）学校を休む He sometimes stays away from school *pretending to be ill*. / He sometimes

げひん *plays sick* to skip school.

げひん 下品 ──下品な vulgar;（みだらな）rude, indecent, foul,《口語的》dirty;（低俗な）low ──下品さ vulgarity ⓤ; indecency ⓤ ‖下品な冗談 rude [indecent] jokes;（→いやらしい冗談）dirty [off-color] jokes ／ 彼は食べ方が下品だ He has *vulgar* table manners. ／ そんな下品な言葉づかいはやめなさい Don't use such a *foul* [*dirty*] language. ／ その格好は下品すぎるんじゃない? Aren't your clothes rather *indecent*?

けぶかい 毛深い、hairy ‖毛深い腕 a *hairy* arm ／ 私は毛深い体質だ I have a naturally *hairy* body.

けむ 煙 smoke ⓤ ◆彼女の話に取材者たちはすっかり煙に巻かれた(→惑わされた) Interviewers *were* completely *mystified* [*confused, puzzled*] by her story.

けむい 煙い smoky ‖たばこの煙で煙い部屋 a room *smoky* with cigarette smoke ／ たき火が煙くて目が痛い My eyes are sore because of the *smoky* fire.

けむくじゃら 毛むくじゃら ──毛むくじゃらの shaggy;（毛深い）hairy ‖毛むくじゃらの犬 a *shaggy* dog ／ 毛むくじゃらの胸 a *hairy* chest

けむし 毛虫 (hairy) caterpillar ⓒ

けむたい 煙たい ❶【煙で】smoky ‖この部屋煙たいな This room *is smoky*. ❷【近づきにくい】父は私にとって煙たい存在だ(→父の前では落ち着かない) I feel *ill at ease* in the presence of my father. ／（→父にそばにいてほしくない）I *don't want* my father *to be around* me.

けむたがる 煙たがる 彼は父親のことを煙たがっていた He felt *uncomfortable with* his father. ／（→遠ざけていた）He *kept* his father *at a distance*. ／ あの先生は生徒から煙たがられている That teacher is「*kept at a distance* [*avoided*] by students. ／（→生徒にあまり好かれていない）That teacher *isn't liked* by students very much.

けむり 煙 smoke ⓤ
一筋の煙 a thread of *smoke* ／ 煙にむせる be choked by *smoke*
工場の煙突から煙がまっすぐ立ち昇っている *Smoke* is rising straight up from the factory chimney. ／ There is a column of *smoke* from the factory chimney.
ちょっと、電子レンジから煙が出ているよ！ Hey, *smoke* is coming out of the microwave!／ Hey, the microwave *is smoking*!
その部屋はたばこの煙がもうもうとたちこめていた The room was thick [heavy] with cigarette *smoke*.
煙がしみて目をあけられない I can't open my eyes because *the smoke* is stinging them.
犠牲者のほとんどが煙に巻かれた人々だった Most of the victims were overcome by *smoke*.
ことわざ 火のない所に煙は立たぬ ⇨ひ (火)

けむる 煙る （煙を出す）smoke ⓐ;（くすぶる）smolder ⓐ;（かすむ）look dim [blurred] ‖たき火が煙っていた The bonfire *is smoking* [*smoldering*]. ／ 東京タワーは雨に煙っていた Tokyo Tower *looked dim* in the rain. ／ The rain *blurred* the view of Tokyo Tower. ／ 彼の部屋はたばこで煙っていた His room *was full of* cigarette *smoke*.

けもの 獣 animal ⓒ;（特に大きな）《文語》beast ⓒ ‖獣道 an animal trail

けやき 欅 zelkova [zélkəvə] (tree) ⓒ

けやぶる 蹴破る 彼はドアをけ破って部屋に入った He *kicked* the door *in* [*down*] and went into the room.

ゲラ 〔印刷〕galley ⓒ ‖ゲラ刷り a galley (proof)

けらい 家来 《古風》retainer ⓒ, follower ⓒ;（召使）servant ⓒ ◆おまえはおれの家来だ。言うことを聞け You are *my man*. Obey me.

げらく 下落 fall ⓒ ──下落する fall* ⓐ, drop ⓐ ‖原油価格の下落 a *fall* [*drop*] in oil prices ／ 近年地価が急激に下落している Land prices *have fallen* [*dropped*] sharply in recent years.

けらけら その幼い少女はピエロを見てけらけら笑った The little girl *giggled* at the clown.

げらげら 私たちは彼の格好を見てげらげら(→大声で)笑った We *laughed aloud* [*out loud*] at the way he dressed. ／（→ばか笑いした）We *guffawed* at the way he dressed. ／（→爆笑した）We *gave* (*out*) *a roar of laughter* at the way he dressed.

けり きょう中にこの仕事にけりをつけなければならない I have to *finish* this work today. ／ その問題にやっとけりがついた(→解決した) We could finally *settle* the matter. ／ The matter *was* finally *settled*.

げり 下痢 diarrhea [dàiərí(ː)ə] ⓤ,《口語的》the runs ‖下痢をしている have diarrhea [*the runs*]; have loose bowels ／ きょうはちょっと下痢ぎみだ I have *a touch of diarrhea* today.
‖下痢止め a medicine for diarrhea

ゲリラ (ゲリラ兵) guer(r)illa [gəríla] ⓒ ◆彼らはあちこちの街頭でゲリラ的に(→散発的に)演奏活動を展開した They played music on various streets *sporadically*.
‖ゲリラ活動 guerrilla activities ／ ゲリラ戦 guerrilla warfare ／ ゲリラ戦術 guerrilla tactics ／ ゲリラ部隊 a band of guerrillas

ける 蹴る
❶【足で】kick ⓐ
その男はドアをけってあけた The man *kicked* the door open.
だれかに足をけられた Somebody *kicked* me *in* [*on*] the leg.
❷【拒絶する】refuse ⓐ ⓒ, reject ⓐ, turn down
申し出をける *refuse* [*reject, turn down*] a proposal
彼はA大学をけってB大学に入った He *turned down* A university and entered B university.

げれつ 下劣 ──下劣な vulgar;（低俗な）low;（卑劣な）mean ‖下劣なテレビ番組 a *vul-*

gar [low] TV program / あいつは下劣な趣味をしている He has *vulgar* [*low*] tastes.

-けれど(も) (しかし) but; (…だけれども) though, although (❖though よりやかたい語); (それにもかかわらず) yet

今は天気がいいけれど、おそらく雨になるだろう It's fine now, *but* it'll rain later. / *Though* it's fine now, it'll rain later.

よくないことだと分かっているけれどやめられない I know it's wrong to do so, *yet* I can't stop it.

あのピッチャーはすごいとは聞いていたけれども本当にすごいなあ *Though* I'd heard the pitcher was great, now I know it to be true.

彼は帰るらしいけれども、君はどうする He says he's going home. *But* what will you do?

すいません、お尋ねしたいことがあるんですけれども Excuse me, *but* may I ask you something?

◆もう少し速く走れたらいいのだけれど I *wish* I could run a little bit faster. / 彼女の病気が早くよくなってくれるといいのだけれど I *hope* she will get better soon. / 手伝っていただけるとありがたいのですけれども I'd be grateful if you could help me. / (電話で)馬場ですけれども、祐子さんいらっしゃいますか Hello, this is Baba speaking. Can I speak to Yuko?

ゲレンデ ⚠ ski slope ⓒ (❖日本語はドイツ語のGelände から)

げろ vomit Ⓤ, (俗語) puke Ⓤ, (米俗語) barf Ⓤ ⇨おうと

ケロイド keloid [kíːlɔɪd] Ⓤ Ⓒ /腕のやけどの跡がケロイドになっている The burn on my arm has become *a keloid* [*scar*].

けろりと 薬のおかげで歯痛はけろりと(→完全に)治まった My toothache *completely* disappeared [went away] after taking medicine. / 僕は彼女と会う約束をけろりと(→すっかり)忘れてしまった I *entirely* [*completely*] forgot the appointment to meet her. / 彼はいやみを言われてもけろりとしていた(→全然気にしていないようだった) He *didn't seem to care at all* about people's sarcastic words. / (→何も感じていないようだった)He *seemed to feel nothing* about people's sarcastic words. / 彼女は彼の事故を聞いてもけろりとしていた(→まるで何もなかったかのように冷静だった) When she heard about his accident, she *was as calm as if nothing had happened*.

けわしい 険しい (山などが) steep; (いかめしい) grim /険しいがけ *a steep cliff* / 父は険しい表情をしていた My father had *a grim look*. / My father was *grim-faced*.

◆この状態では我々の前途は険しい(→数々の困難が待ち受けているだろう) *Many difficulties will lie ahead* of us under this condition.

けん¹ 件 matter Ⓒ; (問題点) issue Ⓒ; (出来事) affair Ⓒ, 《公式的》incident Ⓒ; (事件) case Ⓒ /その件に関しては私は何も知らない I don't know anything about the *matter* [*affair*]. / 例の件についてお尋ねしたいのですが I'd like to ask you about *the matter*. / この件について質問はありますか Are there any questions about this *issue*? / 彼はその一件で逮捕された He got arrested for that *matter* [*affair*].

◆その店には1日に何百件もの電話がかかってくる The shop received *hundreds of calls* a day. / あしたの旅行の件で(→旅行について)二、三の確認をしたいのですが I need to check a few things *about* tomorrow's trip.

けん² 券 ticket Ⓒ ⇨きっぷ(切符) /電車[バス]の乗車券 *a train* [*bus*] *ticket* / エコノミークラスの航空券 *an economy class plane ticket* / コンサートの招待券 *a complimentary ticket for a concert* / 映画の券が2枚あるんだけど、いっしょに行かない？ I've got two movie *tickets*. Won't you come with me?
∥券売機 ⇨けんばいき

けん³ 県 prefecture Ⓒ (❖日本・フランス・イタリアなどの県をいう) ──県の prefectural

[語法] 手紙のあて名などに書くときはふつう prefecture や -ken などを付けない / 愛媛県松山市 Matsuyama-shi, Ehime

僕は埼玉県出身だ I am from Saitama *Prefecture*. / 兵庫県と鳥取県は隣接している(→隣接している県どうしだ) Hyogo and Tottori are neighboring *prefectures*. / 彼は剣道の県大会に出場した He took part in *the prefectural kendo competition*. / 私の学校の野球部は県下で最も強い The baseball team of our school is the strongest *in the prefecture*. / 彼女は神奈川県民だ She is *a citizen of* Kanagawa *Prefecture*. / (→彼女は神奈川県に住んでいる) She *lives in* Kanagawa *Prefecture*.

∥県営スタジアム a prefectural stadium / 県議会 a prefectural assembly / 県議会議員 a member of a prefectural assembly / 県知事 a prefectural governor / 県庁 ⇨けんちょう / 県道 a prefectural road

けん⁴ 剣 sword Ⓒ; (短剣) dagger Ⓒ /剣を抜く[納める] draw [sheathe] *a sword*
∥剣豪 a master swordsman / 剣士 a swordsman / 剣術 swordsmanship / 剣舞 a sword dance
慣用表現 ペンは剣よりも強し ⇨ペン

けん⁵ 険 =険のある (厳しい) harsh; (とげとげしい) waspish; (悪意ある) malicious /険のある言い方は避けるべきだ You should avoid *harsh* [*waspish, malicious*] words. / 彼女は険のある目でこちらを見た She gave me a *harsh* [*malicious*] look.

けん⁶ 腱 【解剖】 tendon Ⓒ, sinew Ⓒ Ⓤ
∥アキレス腱 an Achilles(') tendon, an Achilles(') heel

けん⁷ 鍵 (ピアノなどの) key Ⓒ /88鍵のオルガン an organ with 88 *keys*

-けん¹ -軒 この地区には10軒の家がある There are 10 *houses* in this district. / 私の家は角から4軒目です My house is *the fourth one* from the corner. / 彼女はこの家から5軒目

(→5軒先)に住んでいる She lives *five doors up* [*down, away*] from this house. / 彼は一軒一軒車のセールスに回った He went *from door to door* trying to sell cars. / 彼は丘の上の一軒家に住んでいる He lives in *a solitary house* on the hill.

け

-けん² -兼 書斎兼居間(→書斎付きの居間) a study-*cum*-living room / 彼はその曲の作曲家兼編曲者だ He is the arranger *as well as* the composer of the song./ He *both* composed *and* arranged the song.

-けん³ -圏 (範囲) sphere [C]; (地域) area [C]; (政治・経済上の) bloc [C]
◆英語圏(→英語を話す国)の人々 people in *English-speaking countries*
‖共産圏 the Communist bloc / 首都圏 the Tokyo (metropolitan) area / 勢力圏 a sphere of influence

-けん⁴ -権 right [U][C] //20歳以上は選挙権(→投票する権利)がある We have *the right to vote* from the age of 20.

げん¹ 弦 string [C]; 〖幾何〗 chord [C]
◆ギターに弦を張る *string* a guitar
‖弦楽器 a string(ed) instrument, 《集合的》 the strings

げん² 験 omen [C][U] ➔えんぎ(縁起) //験をかつぐ *believe in omens*; (→迷信深い) *be superstitious*

げん³ 元 (中華人民共和国の貨幣単位) yuan [juɑ́ːn] [C] (複〜)

げん- 現- (現在の) present; (現職の) incumbent; (前回勝利した) reigning //現住所 *one's present* address / 現首相 the *present* [*incumbent*] prime minister / 現チャンピオン a *reigning* [*present*] champion
◆現段階ではその件についてはっきりしたことは言えない We can't say anything clear about the matter *at this stage*.

-げん -減 今年度の売り上げは昨年度の10パーセント減だった Our sales for this fiscal year *decreased* [*dropped, were reduced*] by 10 percent compared to last year.

けんあく 険悪 **━険悪な** (緊迫した) strained, tense; (危険をはらんだ) touchy; (天気・事態などが) ugly, nasty; (今にも降りそうな) threatening; (とげとげしい) harsh; (悪意のこもった) malicious //彼とガールフレンドの仲は険悪になってしまった The relationship between him and his girlfriend has become *tense* [*ugly*]. / 彼の発言で話し合いは険悪な雰囲気になった His comment turned the atmosphere of the meeting *strained* [*touchy*]. / 険悪な雲行きだ It is *threatening* (to rain). / 彼は険悪な目つきで僕を見た He gave me a *harsh* [*malicious*] glance.

けんあん 懸案 pending issue [problem] [C] //懸案を片づける settle *a pending issue* [*problem*]
◆その企画案はここしばらく懸案になったままだ(→解決しないまま残されている) The project *has been left undecided* for a long time.

げんあん 原案 (議案) the original bill; (計画) the original plan //原案は彼によるものだ *The original bill* [*plan*] was made by him.
◆彼らは議案を原案どおり採択した They adopted the bill 「*in its original form* [(→何の修正もせずに) *without any changes*].

けんい 権威 authority [U]; (人) authority [C]; (専門家) expert [C] //彼はそのスキャンダルでほかの者に対する権威を失った He lost *his authority over* others because of the scandal. / 彼は地球物理学[その分野]の権威である He is *an authority* 「*on* geophysics [*in* the field].
◆権威のある病院 an *authoritative* hospital; (→一流の) a *prestigious* hospital
‖権威主義 authoritarianism / 権威主義者 an authoritarian

けんいん 牽引 (牽引力) traction [U] **━牽引する** tow [他] //車を牽引する *tow* a car
◆彼女がこの協会の牽引車だ She is *a force* of this society.
‖牽引車(自動車) a tractor; (機関車) an engine / 牽引療法〖医学〗 traction

げんいん 原因

cause [C]; (起源) origin [C][U], source [C]; (問題の根本原因) the root
原因と結果 *cause* and effect(❖この場合通例無冠詞) / 事故の直接の[間接的な]原因 *the* direct [indirect] *cause* of the accident / 原因不明の火事 a fire of *unknown origin*
スピードの出しすぎがその交通事故の原因だった Speeding was *the cause* of the traffic accident./ (→原因となった) Speeding *caused* the traffic accident.
けんかの原因は何なの What is *the cause* of the quarrel?/ (→何があなたにけんかを始めさせたのか) *What made* you start quarreling?
彼の病気の原因はまだ分かっていない *The cause* of his illness is not known yet.
彼らは協力して事故の原因の究明にあたった They made a concerted effort to determine *the cause of the accident*.
彼らは墜落事故の原因を調査した They examined *the cause of* a plane crash.
その問題の原因は彼らの怠慢にある The problem has its *origin* [*source*] in their negligence.
◆そのスキャンダルが原因で彼は職を失った The scandal *caused* him *to* lose his job. / 彼は足の骨折が原因で学校を1か月休んだ He stayed away from school for a month *because of* a broken leg.

げんえい 幻影 (目の錯覚) (optical) illusion [C]; (実体を伴わないもの) shadow [C]; (宗教的体験に伴う) vision [C]; (かなわぬ夢) mirage [C] //幻影を見る see *an illusion* / 彼は敵の幻影におびえている He's haunted by *the shadow* of his enemy.

けんえき¹ 検疫 quarantine [kwɔ́ːrəntìːn] [U] **━検疫する** quarantine [他] //海外から持ち込まれた動物や植物は検疫を受ける必要がある All animals and plants which have been brought from overseas need to *be quaran-*

tined [*put in quarantine*].
‖検疫所 a quarantine
けんえき[2] 権益 rights and interests
げんえき 現役 ―現役の active ∥現役時代 *one's active period* / 現役最年長の力士 the oldest *active* sumo wrestler / そのジャズピアニストはまだ現役だ The jazz pianist is still *active*.
◆そのピッチャーは去年現役から退いた The pitcher *retired from* baseball last year. / 彼はこの大学に現役で(→高校卒業後すぐに)入った He entered this university *right* [*directly*] *after graduating from high school*.
けんえつ 検閲 inspection [U] [C]; (出版物などの) censorship [U] ―検閲する inspect [他]; censor [他] ∥検閲を通る go through *inspection* / 検閲を受けていない本 a book that *has not been censored*; an *uncensored* book / 彼の荷物が税関の検閲に引っかかった His baggage couldn't pass *the* customs *inspection*. / その映画は一部検閲でカットされている A part of the movie *has been censored out*.
‖検閲官 an inspector; (出版物・映画・手紙などの) a censor
けんえん 犬猿 謙一と信夫は犬猿の仲だ Kenichi and Nobuo *are on cat-and-dog terms*. (❖英語では猫と犬になる)
げんえん 減塩 ―減塩の low salt ‖減塩食 a low salt diet / 減塩食品 low salt food
けんえんけん 嫌煙権 nonsmokers' [nonsmokers'] rights, the right to be free from secondhand smoke
けんお 嫌悪 (好まないこと) dislike [C] [U]; (憎悪) hatred [U] 《またa ～》; (むかむかするほどの) disgust [U]; (反感) antipathy [U] [C] ―嫌悪する dislike [他]; hate [他]; feel* disgust ∥彼は金持ちを嫌悪していた He「*had a hatred for* [*hated*] the rich. / 彼女は彼の下品さに嫌悪感をいだいていた She *was*「*feeling disgust* [*disgusted*] *at* his indecency. / 彼は自己嫌悪に陥っていた He *was immersed in self-disgust*.
けんか[1] 喧嘩 (口論) quarrel [C], argument [C]; (殴り合いの) fight [C]; (大勢でのはでな) brawl [C] ―けんかする quarrel [自], argue [自]; fight* [自] [他]
けんかを始める start *a quarrel* [*fight*] / 人にけんかを売る pick *a quarrel* [*fight*] with a person / けんかを買う「take up [accept] a challenge to *fight*
彼はクラスメートとけんかした He「*had a quarrel* [*quarreled*] *with* a classmate.
私はどのテレビ番組を見るかでいつも弟とけんかする I always *have quarrels* [*arguments*] *with* my brother about what TV program to watch.
先生は2人の生徒のけんかを仲裁した The teacher「put an end to [reconciled] *the fight* between the two students.
君たちのけんかに彼女を巻き込むな Don't involve her in your *quarrel*.
彼はけんかが強い He is good at *fighting*.
彼はけんか慣れしている He *is accustomed to fighting*.
彼らはけんか別れした They *quarreled with each other and ended their relationship*.
◆ちょっとしたけんかが元で彼女と別れてしまった *A little spat* caused me to break up with her. / 彼女はいつもけんか腰で話す She always speaks *with a defiant manner*. / あいつはすごくけんかっ早いから気をつけろ Be careful with him because he *is* very *quarrelsome* [*pugnacious*].
[ことわざ] けんか両成敗 In a quarrel [fight], both parties share the blame [fault].; It takes two to make a quarrel.
けんか[2] 献花 floral tribute [C] ◆献花(→亡くなった人へ花を供えるため)に並んだ人の列 a line of people waiting to *offer flowers* to a deceased person
げんか 原価 〖商業〗 cost price [U], cost [U] [C] ∥原価で[を割って]売る sell at [below] *cost*
‖原価計算 cost accounting
げんが 原画 original (painting) [C] ∥マチスの原画 *an original painting* by Matisse
けんかい 見解 (意見) opinion [C] [U]; (見方) view [C]; (評価) judgment, 《英》judgement [C] ∥個人的な見解 *one's* personal *opinion* / 肯定的[否定的]な見解 *a* positive [negative] *opinion* / 彼女は演説でその件に関する見解を述べた She expressed *her opinions* [*views*] on that matter in a public speech. / その問題に関して私は彼女と見解を異にする[同じくする] My *view* of the problem is「different from [the same as] hers. / それは見解の相違だ That's *a matter of opinion*.
けんがい 圏外 この町はその台風の勢力の圏外だった This town was *out of the range* of the typhoon's influence. / 彼の携帯電話は圏外だったので通じなかった He couldn't be contacted because his cellular phone was *out of range*. / その力士はすでに優勝圏外にいる(→優勝の可能性はない) That sumo wrestler *has no chance to win the championship*. / その候補者は当選圏外だ That candidate *is out of the running*.
げんかい[1] 限界 limit [C] 《しばしば複数形 ～s》, bounds; (能力・行動などの) limitations
それはもうすでに私の能力の限界を超えている It's already *beyond the limits* [*bounds*] of my abilities.
彼はついに我慢の限界に達した He reached *the limits* of his patience.
彼は体力の限界を感じて現役を退いた He recognized *his* physical *limits* and retired.
そのカーレーサーはスピードの限界に挑戦した The racing car driver tried to exceed *the limits* [*bounds*] of speed.
彼の欲望には限界がない His desire has no *limits*./ His desire knows no *bounds*.
げんかい[2] 厳戒 市内には厳戒体制が敷かれた The whole city was「put on [under] *strict alert*.
げんがい 言外 言外の意味をくみ取る(→行間の意味を読み取る) read *between the lines* / その選手は引退を言外にほのめかした The ath-

け

けんがく 見学 visit ◯, tour ◯; (授業などでの) field trip ◯ ——見学する visit 他 自, tour 他 自, go* on a tour, make* a tour
私たちは先週, 国会議事堂を見学した We took a field trip to the Diet Building last week. / We made a tour of the Diet Building last week.
◆体育の授業を見学させて(→休ませて)ください I want to be absent from the P.E. class. / (→見るだけにさせてください) I just want to watch the P.E. class. ‖見学者は動物にえさを与えてはいけません Visitors may not feed the animals.

げんかく¹ 厳格 ——厳格な strict; (妥協を知らない) stern; (冷酷なまでの) severe; (融通のきかない) rigid ——厳格に strictly; sternly; severely; rigidly ‖厳格な区別 a rigid distinction / 新しい先生はとても厳格だ The new teacher is very strict with us.

げんかく² 幻覚 hallucination ◯ ◯ ‖麻薬を常用し続けると様々な幻覚に襲われる If you use drugs habitually, you will have all kind of hallucinations. / 最近私は奇妙な幻覚に悩まされている I've been suffering from weird hallucinations. ◆彼女は高熱で幻覚を見ているにちがいない She must be hallucinating because of a high fever.
‖幻覚剤 a hallucinogen, a hallucinogenic drug

げんがく¹ 弦楽 string music ◯ ‖弦楽合奏団 a string ensemble [orchestra] / 弦楽器 a string(ed) instrument, (集合的) the strings; (弦楽部門) the string section

げんがく² 減額 cut ◯, reduction ◯ ◯ ——減額する cut* 他, reduce 他 ‖授業料の減額 reduction of school fees / 上司は私たちの給料を減額した Our boss cut our salaries.

げんかしょうきゃく 減価償却〔会計〕depreciation ◯ ◯

けんがん 検眼 (視力検査) vision test ◯
◆きのう新しい眼鏡を作るために検眼してもらった I had my eyes tested [examined] yesterday to get new glasses.

げんかん 玄関 (戸) the (front) door; (屋根付きの空間) the porch; (入り口) the entrance; (玄関の広間) the (entrance) hall
玄関から入る enter at [through] the front door
母が玄関に(応対に)出た My mother answered the door.
だれかが玄関に来ている There is someone at the front door.
荷物は玄関に置いてください Leave your luggage in the hall.
直宏は美奈子に会いに家へ行ったが玄関払いを食わされた(→玄関で追い払われた) Naohiro went to Minako's house to see her, but he was turned away at the door.
◆彼は玄関のベルを鳴らした He rang the doorbell. / 成田空港は日本の玄関です I'll see you out. / 成田空港は日本の玄関だ Narita Airport is the gateway to Japan.

けんぎ 嫌疑 suspicion ◯ ◯ ‖嫌疑を晴らす clear oneself of a suspicion / 私の友人に殺人の嫌疑がかかった A suspicion of murder fell on a friend of mine. / A friend of mine is under suspicion of murder.

げんき 元気

(活力) energy ◯; (精力) vigor, 《英》vigour ◯; (活気) vitality ◯; (気分) spirits; (健康) health ◯; (体力) strength ◯ ——元気な fine, well; (精力的に) energetic, vigorous; (陽気な) cheerful, high-spirited; (活発な) lively, alive; (健康な) healthy ——元気に (精力的に) with energy, with vigor; (陽気に) cheerfully, in high spirits
〖元気が〗
母はいつも元気がいい My mother is always cheerful [full of energy].
先生はきょう元気がない Our teacher is 「in low spirits [depressed] today.
若くて元気があるうちにいろいろな国へ旅行に行きたい I want to go on a trip to various countries while I'm young and have enough energy.
その映画を見て元気が出た The movie 「lifted my spirits [cheered me up].
どうかしたの. きょうは元気がないね Is anything wrong? You don't look well today.
だんだん元気が出てきた I'm feeling better and better.
◆彼は元気が出る(→勇気づけられる)話をしてくれた He told me an encouraging story.
〖元気を〗
元気を取り戻す recover one's vigor
彼女にふられて彼は元気をなくしてしまった He's lost his vigor since his girlfriend left him.
◆元気を出しなよ Cheer up!
〖元気な〗
元気な赤ん坊 a lively [bouncing] baby
祖父も元気なころはたばこを吸っていた My grandfather used to smoke when he was healthy [in good health].
〖元気に〗
子供たちが公園で元気に遊んでいた Children were playing cheerfully in the park.
すっかり元気になりました I've recovered my health completely.
早く元気になって(→よくなって)ください I hope you'll get better [well] soon.
◆彼は米国で元気にやっている He is doing all right in America.
〖元気だ〗
彼女はきょうはとても元気だ She is pretty well today.
彼女は年のわりにはびっくりするほど元気だ She is amazingly alive [(→ 活動的だ) active, spry] for her age.
新しい学校でも元気でね I wish you well in your new school.
◆元気でね Good luck.
🅔「久しぶり. 元気?」「元気だよ」"Long time

no see! *How are you*?" "(*I'm*) *fine, thank you*."

🗣「お母さんは元気？」「相変わらず元気だよ」 "*How's* your mother?" "She's *as strong as ever*."

【その他】
彼らは若者らしい元気さに欠ける They are lacking in youthful *vigor*.

◆彼女の手紙に元気づけられた I *felt* [*was*] *encouraged* by her letter. / 彼女を元気づけるにはどうしたらいいだろう What should we do to *cheer* him *up*? / 子供たちにあいさつをしたら元気のない返事が返ってきた When I said hello to the children, they answered me *cheerlessly* [*in a cheerless tone*]. / 疲れきって口をきく元気もなかった I *was too exhausted to* say a word.

けんきゃく 健脚 彼は健脚(→足の力が強くてよく歩ける人)だ He is *a strong walker*.

けんきゅう 研究

study ⓊⒸ《しばしば複数形 studies》; (特定分野の) research ⓊⒸ《しばしば複数形 〜es》(❖複数形でも単数扱い。数えるときは a piece of … とする) ——研究する study 他自; research 自他, do* [carry out] research

詳細な[徹底した, 独創的の] 研究 detailed [thorough, original] *research* / ハチの科学的研究 the scientific *study* of bees

彼女は自分の研究に熱心だ She is very earnest about her *studies*.

この問題の研究は長い間おろそかにされてきた The *study* of this subject has long been neglected.

この問題は現在研究中だ This problem is now *under study*.

研究によると過度の運動は健康に害を及ぼすということだ *Research shows that* excessive exercise is harmful to the health.

私は日本文学を研究している I'm *studying* Japanese literature.

彼の研究分野は経済学だ His *field of study* is economics.

◆核物理学の新しい研究方法 a new *approach* to nuclear physics / 彼は歴史の研究家だ He is *a student* of history. / 兄は大学で落語研究会に入っている My brother belongs to *the rakugo club* at college.

‖研究員 a research worker / 研究開発 research and development / 研究活動 research (activities) / 研究施設 research facilities / 研究室 a study (room); (実験室) a laboratory; (大学教官の) an office / 研究所 a laboratory, a research institute / 研究助手 a research assistant / 研究生 a research student / 研究発表会 a meeting for the presentation of research / 研究費 research funds [expenses] / 研究論文 a (research) paper, a treatise

けんきゅう¹ 言及 reference ⓊⒸ; (簡単に触れる) mention ⓊⒸ ——言及する refer 自他; mention 他 / 彼はその事実に言及した He "*referred to* [*mentioned*, *made reference to*] the fact. / この本は米国の生活について多く言及している This book *has* many *references to* life in the U.S. / その記者会見で刑事は容疑者についての具体的な言及を避けた The detective *avoided* specific *reference to* the suspect in that press conference.

けんきゅう² 原級 〖文法〗 the positive

けんきゅう³ 減給 a cut in wages [salary] ‖ 減給になる take *a cut in salary* / 彼は15パーセントの減給処分を受けた(→罰として15パーセントの減給を科せられた) He *was punished with a 15 percent cut in salary*.

けんきょ¹ 謙虚 ——謙虚な (控えめな) modest; (うぬぼれのない) humble ——謙虚さ modesty Ⓤ; humility Ⓤ ‖ 彼は自分の演技の才能にいつも謙虚だ He is always *modest* about his abilities in acting. / 彼は有名人だったが, 謙虚な人だった Although he was famous, he had a *humble* manner.

◆私はいつも他人の忠告には謙虚に耳を傾けようと思っている I always try to listen *humbly* to other people's advice.

けんきょ² 検挙 arrest ⓊⒸ; (一斉検挙) roundup ——検挙する arrest 他; round up ‖ 彼は飲酒運転で検挙された He *was arrested for* drunk driving. / 警察は不法入国者たちを一斉検挙した The police *rounded up* the illegal aliens.

けんぎょう 兼業 彼は本屋と文房具屋を兼業している He *runs both* a bookstore *and* a stationery store. / うちは兼業農家です We *run a farm on the side*. (❖*on the side* は「副業として」の意味)

けんいん 元凶 寝たばこは多くの火事の元凶だ Smoking in bed is *the prime cause* of many fires.

げんきょう² 現況 the present state, actualities

けんきん 献金 contribution ⓊⒸ, donation ⓊⒸ; (教会などでの) collection Ⓒ ‖ たくさんの会社がその政党に合計で5,000万円の献金をした Many companies *made contributions* [*donations*] to that political party totaling 50 million yen.

‖政治献金 a political contribution [donation]

げんきん¹ 現金 cash Ⓤ

私は現金を持ち合わせていない I have no *cash* with [on] me.

彼女は車の代金を現金で払った She paid *cash* for the car. / (→車を現金で買った) She bought the car *in* [*with*] *cash*.

現金でお買い上げいただいた物すべて25パーセント割引します We will give you a 25 percent discount on all *cash* purchases.

◆彼らは現金輸送車から現金を強奪しようともくろんでいた They were scheming to steal *the money* from *a security van*. / あいつは本当に現金な(→計算高い)やつだ He's really *mercenary* [*calculating*].

🗣「お支払いは現金ですか、それともカードになさいますか」「現金でお願いします」 "*Cash* or credit?" "*Cash*."

げんきん

‖現金書留 registered mail(❖英米ではふつうの書留で現金が送れるので特別な言い方はない) / 現金自動預け払い機 an automated [automatic] teller machine(《略称》ATM) / 現金取引 a cash transaction

げんきん² 厳禁 火気厳禁《掲示》*Flammable(s)* / 私語厳禁《掲示》*No Whispering* / 土足厳禁《掲示》*No Shoes Please* / はり紙厳禁《掲示》*Post No Bills* / 開放厳禁 *Close the door after you.* / 館内での写真撮影は厳禁です Photography *is strictly forbidden* in the museum.

げんけい¹ 原形 地震の後,私の家は原形をとどめていなかった(→すっかり変わってしまった) My house *had changed beyond recognition* after the earthquake.
◆原形不定詞〘文法〙a bare infinitive
⇨ふていし

げんけい² 原型 (見本となるもの) archetype ⓒ, model ⓒ; (機械などの) prototype ⓒ

げんけい³ 減刑 a reduction in a sentence, commutation ⓒ ⓤ ──**減刑する** reduce [commute] a sentence ∥まじめな態度が認められ彼の終身刑は懲役30年に減刑された His life prison *sentence was reduced* to a 30-year sentence for good behavior.

けんけつ 献血 blood donation ⓒ ──**献血する** donate [give*] blood ∥献血者 a blood donor / 献血車 a bloodmobile

けんげん 権限 power ⓒ ⓤ (しばしば複数形～s), authority ⓤ ∥権限を乱用する abuse *one's authority* / 私にはその計画を公式に認可する権限はありません I have no *authority* to approve the plan. / 首相の権限は日本国憲法によって規定されている *The powers* of the Prime Minister are defined by Japan's Constitution.
◆彼は最終決定を下す権限を与えられた He *was authorized to* make a final decision.

けんご 堅固 ──**堅固な** (堅い) firm; (頑丈な) solid; (強い) strong /**堅固な決意** firm resolution / 彼は何事も最後までやり通す堅固な意志をもっている He has a *strong* will to carry on to the end in everything he does.

げんこ 拳固 ⇨げんこつ

げんご¹ 言語 language ⓤ ⓒ,《文語》tongue [tʌ́ŋ] ⓒ; (話し言葉) speech ⓤ ◆言語に絶する戦争の光景 an *indescribable* war scene
∥言語学 linguistics / 言語学者 a linguist / 言語障害 a speech impediment / 言語表現 (a) verbal expression

げんご² 原語 the original language
◆シェークスピアを原語で読む read Shakespeare *in the original*(❖*the original* は「原文・原典」の意味)

けんこう 健康

health ⓤ ──**健康な** healthy; well,《口語的》fine; sound; fit
⇨ 場面・状況別会話 p.1696

healthy: 長期間にわたって健康であること.
well: ある時点において病気ではないこと.
sound: 心身ともに健康であること.

fit: 運動などの結果,健康であること.

《健康が・は》
おじは何か月も健康がすぐれない My uncle has been in poor [bad] *health* for months.
1日3回きちんと食事をすれば健康が保てる Eating regularly three times a day keeps you *fit*.
喫煙により健康が害されることがある Smoking can damage your *health*.
彼の健康は最近衰え始めた His *health* has recently begun to decline.

《健康に》
健康に気をつける take care of 「*one's health* [*oneself*]」 / 健康によい[悪い] be good [bad] for *the health*
彼女はずっと健康に恵まれてきた She has always enjoyed good *health*.
彼は健康になるまで母親の面倒を見た He nursed his mother back to *health*.

《健康を》
健康を回復する recover [regain, restore, return to] *one's health* / 健康を損なう damage [injure, ruin] *one's health*
健康を維持するために水泳を始めた I began to do swimming to 「*keep fit* [*stay healthy*]」.

《健康だ》
健康でない be in bad [poor, ill] *health*
彼はすこぶる健康だ He is in excellent [perfect] *health* [*condition*].
私は肉体的にも精神的にも健康だ I'm *sound* of mind and body.

《その他》
心の健康 mental *health* / 健康のために運動する take exercise for *one's health*
私の母は健康そのものだ My mother is the picture of *health*.
彼は健康そうだ He is looking *well* [*fit*].
私は常に健康的な食事を心がけている I always keep a *healthy* diet in mind.
彼女はまだ健康状態が思わしくない She is still in a poor *state of health*.
あなたの健康法は何ですか(→どのようにして健康を維持していますか) How do you *keep fit*?
‖健康管理 health care / 健康食品 health food / 健康診断書 a certificate of health / 健康保険 health insurance / 健康保険証 a health insurance card

---
英作文ノート 「健康診断を受ける」は何ていう?
私はあす健康診断を受けます
→ ✕ I'm taking *a medical checkup* tomorrow.
→ ○ I'm having *a medical checkup* tomorrow.
★take は学科の試験(test, examination)などを受けるときに用い,健康診断のときは have または undergo (専門的)を用いる.have [get] a medical [physical] examination ともいう.

げんこう¹ 原稿 (手書き・タイプの) manuscript ⓒ; (草稿・下書き) draft ⓒ; (印刷の) copy ⓤ ∥ペン書きの[タイプした]原稿 a pen-written [type-written] *manuscript* /

原稿を印刷する put *a manuscript* into print / 彼は原稿が遅れがちだ He's often behind in submitting *his manuscript.* / その原稿を仕上げるのにあらゆる努力をした I made every effort to finish the *manuscript.* / 原稿の棒読みは避けるべきだ You should avoid reading *your manuscript* in a monotonous tone.

◆日本の文化に関する原稿を頼まれた I was asked to *write about* Japanese culture. / その政治家は原稿なしで演説をした The politician made a speech *without notes.*

‖原稿用紙 manuscript paper / 原稿料 a manuscript fee, payment for writing a manuscript

げんこう² 言行 言行一致の(→約束を守る)人 a person *of his word* / 彼は言行不一致だった He was *false in word and deed.*

げんこう³ 現行 現行の制度 the *present* [*current*, *existing*] system / 現行の教科書 the textbooks *now in use* / 今月いっぱい料金は現行のままです The fare *remains the same* all this month.

‖現行法 the existing law, the law in force

げんごう 元号

> 日本には西暦のほかに年を表す特別な言い方があります。天皇即位の際に新しい時代を表す名称が中国の古い文献から選ばれることになっており、これを元号と呼んでいます。元号は中国で始まり、日本には 7 世紀に伝えられましたが、現在元号を用いているのは日本だけです。
> In Japan there is a special way of counting years in addition to the Western calendar style. At the accession of an emperor a new era's name is chosen from Chinese classic sources. This is called *gengo*. It originated in China and was introduced to Japan in the seventh century. Japan is the only country that employs *gengo* now.

げんこうこつ 肩甲骨 scapula [skǽpjələ] ◯ (複 scapulae, ~s)

げんこうはん 現行犯 盗みの現行犯で捕らえる catch *a person in the act of* stealing / そのすりは現行犯でつかまった The pickpocket *was caught red-handed* [*in the act*].

げんこく 建国 the founding [foundation] of a country ‖建国記念の日 National Foundation [Founding] Day

げんこく 原告 plaintiff ◯ (↔defendant), complainant ◯; (告発者) accuser ◯

げんこつ 拳骨 fist ◯; (こぶし) knuckles, punch ◯ ‖正平が僕をげんこつで殴った Shohei struck me with *his fist.* / Shohei gave me *a punch.*

けんさ 検査

(詳しく調べること) examination ◯◯; (主に公的機関による調査) inspection ◯◯; (基準を満たすか) test ◯; (点検) check ◯ ──検査する examine ◯; inspect ◯; test ◯◯
精密な[徹底的な, いいかげんな]検査 *a close* [*thorough, cursory*] *inspection* / 飛行機を故障がないかどうか検査する *inspect* an airplane for defects

新しいエンジンは必要な検査をすべて受けた[通過した] The new engine underwent [passed] all *the necessary tests.*

空港でかばんを検査された My bags *were examined* at the airport.

きのう学校で身体検査を受けた We *had a physical examination* at school yesterday.

父は糖尿病の検査を受けた My father *was tested for* diabetes.

彼女は目の検査を受けた She *had her eyes* [*vision*] *tested.*

◆警官はその男の身体検査をした The officer *searched* the man. / 先生は突然私たちの持ち物検査を始めた The teacher suddenly started *checking our stuff.*

‖検査官 an inspector / 学力検査 an achievement test / 血液検査 a blood test / 適正検査 an aptitude test / 抜き取り検査 a spot check

けんざい¹ 健在 私の祖父母はまだ健在です My grandparents are still *alive and well.*

けんざい² 建材 construction [building] materials

げんざい¹ 現在

the present; (今) now ◯, (今日 (*こんにち*)) today ◯ (❖now, today は副詞としても用いられる) ──at present; (現行の) current; (現在する) existing

過去を振り返るのはやめて現在のことを考えなさい Stop looking back on the past, and think about *the present.*

パソコンは現在広く使われている Personal computers are *now* in widespread use.

現在の私があるのはあなたのおかげだ I owe what I am *now* to you.

私は現在の住所に 3 年間住んでいる I have been living at my *present* address for three years.

現在の状況ではこの計画は成功しないだろう This plan will not succeed under the *present* [*existing*] condition.

現在まではすべて順調に進んでいる Everything has gone all right「*up to now* [*so far*].

現在のところ予定の変更はありません There are no changes in the schedule「*for the present* [*at present*].

◆ 4 月 1 日現在の人口 the population *as of* April 1 / それは現在の社会ではとても考えられない出来事だ That would be an unthinkable incident *in present-day society.*

‖現在形〖文法〗the present form / 現在時制〖文法〗the present tense / 現在進行形〖文法〗the present progressive form / 現在地(案内板などでの掲示) You are here.

げんざい² 原罪〖キリスト教〗original sin ◯

げんざいかんりょう(けい) 現在完了(形)〖文法〗the present perfect

> 完了形の一つで、《have [has] ＋ 過去分詞》の

げんざいぶんし

形で表される. 現在を基準にして過去に起こった出来事との時間的な関係を表現するのに用いられる.「完了(結果)用法」「経験用法」「継続用法」がある.

[完了(結果)用法] 動作が完了したことや完了した動作の影響が現在まで続いていることを表す // I *have* just *come back* from the trip. ちょうど旅行から帰ってきたところだ / Spring *has come*. 春が来た

[経験用法]「今までに…したことがある」という経験を表す // I *have seen* the movie several times. その映画は何度か見たことがある / *Have* you ever *been to* China? 中国へ行ったことがありますか

[継続用法] 現在まである動作・状態が続いていることを表す // He *has been* sick since Sunday. 彼は日曜日からずっと病気だ / She *has been taking* flamenco lessons for five years. 彼女は5年間フラメンコを習っている (❖(have+been+-ing)の形を現在完了進行形という. 動作が現在も続いていることを表すために現在完了進行形を用いることがある)

げんざいぶんし 現在分詞 〔文法〕 the present participle

(1)現在分詞は, 原則として動詞の原形に -ing を付けて作る.

(2)現在分詞は形容詞的な働きをする.「状態」や「動作の進行」を表すことが多い // a *sleeping* baby (=a baby who *is sleeping*) 眠っている赤ちゃん / the dog *barking* at the door (=the dog that *is barking* at the door) ドアのところでほえている犬

(3)現在分詞は「動詞+現在分詞」の形で用いたり, see, hear などの感覚動詞といっしょに用いたりすることができる // Let's go *skiing* next Sunday. 今度の日曜日にスキーに行こう / Keep *waiting* here. ここで待っていなさい / Through the window, I saw many people *passing by*. たくさんの人が通り過ぎるのを窓越しに見た

(4)現在分詞は, 上記以外に, 進行形の文・分詞構文でも用いられる // The telephone *was ringing* when I came home. 帰宅したとき電話が鳴っていた ⇨ぶんしこうぶん

げんざいりょう 原材料 raw material(s)
◆この薬の原材料は自然の物だ(→自然の物から作られている) This medicine *is made out of* natural materials.

けんさく 検索 〔コンピュータ〕 retrieval Ⓤ ──検索する search 他自, retrieve 他;(参照する) refer 自 /データ[単語]を検索する *search* data [*for* a word] / 索引を検索する *refer to* the index

げんさく 原作 the original (work)
◆原作の小説より映画のほうがずっといい The film is far better than the *original* novel.
∥原作者 the (original) author

けんさつ¹ 検札 ticket inspection Ⓒ ◆その乗客は検札のため切符を取り出した The passenger took out his ticket for *inspection*. / 電車が動きだすとすぐに車掌が検札に来た As soon as the train started to move, a conductor came to *check* [*inspect*] *our tickets*.
∥検札係(列車・バスなどの) a ticket inspector

けんさつ² 検察 《集合的》the prosecution 《単数または複数扱い》/ 検察側の尋問 questioning of *the prosecution*
∥検察官 a prosecutor / 検察庁 the Public Prosecutors Office

けんさん 研鑽 彼は外国の大学で10年間研鑽を積んだ He *studied* at a foreign university for 10 years.

けんざん¹ 検算 ──検算する check [go* over] the accounts

けんざん² 剣山 frog Ⓒ, spiked flower base Ⓒ (❖frogは花をさす小穴をあけたものなども含む)

げんさん¹ 原産 この植物は日本原産だ This plant is「*native to Japan* [*a native of Japan*]. / ジャガイモの原産地はどこですか Where is *the origin of the potato*?

げんさん² 減産 (a) decrease in production; (計画的な) (a) reduction of production ──減産する cut* [reduce] production
◆今四半期は生産量が5パーセント減産となった Production *decreased* [*was down*] five percent this quarter.

けんし¹ 検死 〔法律〕 inquest Ⓒ; (検死解剖)《主に米》autopsy Ⓒ / 殺人の疑いがある場合は検死をわなければならない An *inquest* must be *held* [*conducted*] if murder is suspected. / 検死の結果, その男は麻薬を常用していたことが分かった The *autopsy* on the man *showed* that he had been using drugs.
∥検死官 a coroner

けんし² 犬歯 canine [kéinain] (tooth) Ⓒ; (上あごの) eyetooth Ⓒ

けんじ¹ 検事 (public) prosecutor Ⓒ ∥検事総長 the Public Prosecutor General

けんじ² 堅持 我々は立場を堅持せねばならない We have to *stand* our ground.

げんし¹ 原子 atom Ⓒ / 酸素分子は酸素原子2つをもつ A molecule of oxygen has two *atoms of* oxygen.
∥原子価 valence / 原子記号 the symbol of an element / 原子爆弾 an atomic bomb / 原子番号 an atomic number / 原子物理学 nuclear physics / 原子量 atomic weight / 原子力 ⇨げんしりょく / 原子炉 a nuclear reactor

げんし² 原始 ──原始的な primitive ∥原始時代 the primitive [primeval] ages / 原始人 a primitive man / 原始林 a virgin wood [forest], a primeval forest

けんしき 見識 (判断力) judgment,《英》judgement Ⓤ Ⓒ; (洞察力) insight Ⓤ Ⓒ; (識別力)《公式的》discernment Ⓤ; (見解) view Ⓒ / すぐれた見識を示す show [exercise] good *judgment* / 高い見識の持ち主 a person of good *judgment* [*insight*] ◆美術に関して私たちの中では彼女がいちばん見識がある She *is the best judge* of art among us.

けんじつ 堅実 ──堅実な (安定した)

げんじつ　現実

reality ⓊⒸ《しばしば the ～》; (事実) fact Ⓒ ―現実の real, actual ―現実的な realistic, practical ―現実に really, actually
人生の厳しい現実に直面する face *the* harsh *reality* of life / 現実から逃避する run away from *reality* / 現実的な人生観 a *realistic* view of life

彼女は君のことをもう愛していないんだ. それが現実だ She doesn't love you any more, and that's *a fact*!

君は世の中の現実が何も分かっていない You know nothing about the *real* world.

時には現実を受け入れるのは難しいことだ It's sometimes hard to accept *reality*.

現実から目を背(そむ)けてはいけない Don't shut your eyes to the *reality*.

今の時代, 核戦争は現実に起こりうることだ A nuclear war can *actually* happen in this day and age.

現実問題としてその計画は実行不可能だろう As *a practical matter*, that plan is probably unfeasible.

彼の夢はだんだんと現実味を帯びてきた His dream is gradually becoming *a reality*.

君の考えはおもしろそうだが現実的ではない Your ideas sound interesting, but they're not *practical* [(→実現が難しい)*feasible*].

◆敦子は現実的な人だ Atsuko is *a realist* [*down-to-earth person*]. / 私の夢は現実になった My dream *came true*. / 恐れていたことがとうとう現実になった My fears *were realized* at last. / その計画は現実性に欠ける The plan is *unrealistic*.

∥現実主義 realism / 現実主義者 a realist

げんじてん　現時点 このレースの現時点でのトップはだれですか Who is the *current* leader in this race? / 現時点では応募者数は予想を上回っている As *of now*, the number of applicants is larger than expected.

げんしゅ¹　厳守 交通規則を厳守する *observe* traffic rules *strictly* / 彼はいつも時間を厳守する He *is* always *punctual*. / 彼は秘密を厳守すると約束した He gave me his promise *never to reveal* the secret.

げんしゅ²　元首 (国家元首) a head of state, 《公式的》sovereign [sάvərən] Ⓒ (◆皇帝・国王・女王など)

けんしゅう　研修 (訓練) training Ⓤ (また a ～); (研究) study ⓊⒸ ∥私たちはコンピュータの研修を受けた We got *training* in the use of computers.

◆彼は夏休みにパリへフランス語の研修に行く He's going to Paris to *study* French during the summer vacation.

∥研修生 a trainee / 研修旅行 a study trip

けんじゅう　拳銃 pistol Ⓒ; (銃) gun Ⓒ ∥拳銃を標的に合わせる aim [level] *a pistol* at the target / 警官が誤って子供に拳銃を発射した A policeman fired *his pistol* at a child by mistake.

げんしゅう　減収 a decrease in income
◆今月は3パーセントの減収だった Our income *decreased* three percent this month.

げんじゅう　厳重 ―厳重な strict; (容赦のない) severe; (注意深い) close; (程度の強い) strong ―厳重に strictly; severely; closely; strongly ∥厳重に抗議する protest *strongly* / 厳重に処罰される be punished *severely* / 500人の警官が厳重な警戒態勢に置かれた Five hundred policemen were put on *strict* alert. / 警官はその囚人を厳重に監視した The police guarded the prisoner *closely*. / 今後, 暴風雨に対する厳重な注意が必要だ We have to take *strict* precautions against the storm from now on.

げんじゅうしょ　現住所 こちらにあなたの現住所をお書きください Please write down your *present* [*current*] *address* right here.

げんじゅうみん　原住民 (軽蔑的) native Ⓒ; aborigine Ⓒ; (民族) aboriginal [indigenous] people Ⓒ ∥タヒチの原住民 the aboriginal [indigenous] *people* of Tahiti

げんしゅく　厳粛 ―厳粛な solemn ∥厳粛な儀式 a *solemn* ceremony
◆儀式を厳粛に行う conduct a ceremony *solemnly* / 私たちはその事実を厳粛に(→深刻に)受け止めるべきだ We should face the fact *seriously*.

けんしゅつ　検出 detection ―検出する detect ⦿ ∥高濃度の放射能が大気中から検出された A high level of radiation *has been detected* [*found*] in the air.

げんしょ　原書 the original ∥『赤毛のアン』を原書で読む read *Anne of Green Gables in the original*

けんしょう¹　懸賞 prize ⓊⒸ; (報酬金) reward Ⓒ; (懸賞金) price Ⓒ ∥懸賞に当選する win *a prize* / 懸賞のかかった試合 a *prize* match / 犯人に関する情報には100万円の懸賞がかけられている A *reward* of one million yen is offered for information on the criminal.

∥懸賞論文 a prize essay

けんしょう²　検証 inspection ⓊⒸ ―検証する inspect ⦿ ∥その事件により詳しい検証が必要だ The case needs closer *inspection*.

∥現場検証 an on-the-spot inspection

けんしょう³　憲章 charter Ⓒ ∥国際連合憲章 the Charter of the United Nations, the United Nations Charter / 児童憲章 the Children's Charter

けんしょう⁴　健勝 ご健勝をお祈りします We wish you *good health*.

けんじょう¹　献上 ―献上する offer ⦿, present ⦿

けんじょう²　謙譲 modesty Ⓤ, humility Ⓤ ∥謙譲の美徳 the virtue of *modesty*
∥謙譲語 humble language

げんしょう¹　減少 decrease ⒸⓊ, drop Ⓒ,

fall [C], decline [U] ―減少する decrease [自], decline [自]
人口の10パーセントの減少 a 10 percent *decrease in* population / 出産率の減少 *decline* in the birthrate
日本の学生の数は減少している The number of students in Japan *is decreasing* [*declining*].
この地区では犯罪発生率が急激[着実, 徐々]に減少してきている There *has been a* sharp [steady, gradual] *decrease in* the crime rate in this area.

げんしょう² 現象 phenomenon [C] (複 phenomena) ∥不思議[一時的, 世界的]な現象 *a* strange [passing, worldwide] *phenomenon* / 社会現象 *a* social *phenomenon* / 地震や台風のような自然現象 *natural phenomena* such as earthquakes and typhoons

げんじょう 現状 the present condition(s) [situation], the present state of things ∥現状を維持する[打破する] maintain [break] *the present condition(s)* / 現状では私たちが成功する見込みはまるでない There's no hope of success for us *under the present condition(s).* / 彼の意見は現状をふまえていない His opinion is not based on *the present situation.*

けんじょうしゃ 健常者 healthy person [C], a person with no physical or mental defects

げんしょく¹ 原色 primary color [C] (❖赤・黄・青); (鮮やかな色) vivid color [C]

げんしょく² 現職 現職の市長 the *incumbent* mayor / 現職の(→現役の)教師 a teacher *in active service* / 現職(→現在の職)にとどまる remain in *one's present post*

げんしょく³ 減食 医者は私に減食(→ダイエットすること)を勧めた The doctor advised me to「*go on a diet* [(→食事の量を減らすこと)*cut down on meals*].

げんしりょく 原子力 atomic [nuclear] energy [U], atomic [nuclear] power [U]
◆この事故は政府の原子力政策に深刻な影響を及ぼすかもしれない This accident could have serious implications for the government's *nuclear policy.*
∥原子力潜水艦 a nuclear submarine, a nuclear-powered submarine / 原子力発電 nuclear power generation / 原子力発電所 a nuclear power plant

けんしん¹ 献身 devotion [U]; (自己犠牲) self-sacrifice [U] ―献身的な devoted, self-sacrificing ∥彼女の献身的な世話のおかげで彼はすぐに元気になった Thanks to her *self-sacrificing* [*devoted*] care, he recovered his health quickly.
◆彼は貧しい人々の救済に献身してきた He *has devoted himself to* helping poor people.

けんしん² 検診 medical [physical] examination [C], (medical [physical]) checkup [C] ∥癌(がん)の検診を受ける have *a checkup* for cancer
∥集団検診 a group checkup / 定期検診 a regular checkup

けんしん³ 検針 ガスの検針をする(→計器の目盛りを読む) *read* the gas meter

けんすい 懸垂 chin-up [C], pull-up [C]
[会]「懸垂何回できる」「10回ぐらいかな」"How many *chin-ups* can you do?" "About ten."

げんすい 元帥 (陸軍)《米》a general of the army,《英》field marshal [C]; (海軍)《米》fleet admiral [C],《英》an admiral of the fleet; (空軍)《米》a general of the air force,《英》a marshal of the Royal Air Force

げんすいばく 原水爆 atomic and hydrogen bombs, A- and H-bombs, nuclear bombs; (核兵器) nuclear weapon [C]
∥原水爆禁止運動 a movement against nuclear weapons / 原水爆禁止世界大会 World Conference Against Atomic and Hydrogen Bombs

けんすう 件数 the number of cases
◆最近若者による交通事故の件数が増えている *The number of* traffic accidents caused by young people has increased recently.

げんすん 原寸 原寸大の模型 a *full-size* model
∥原寸図 a full-scale drawing

げんせ 現世 this world ―現世の worldly ∥現世と来世 *this world* and the next

けんせい¹ 牽制 彼はけん制球を投げた He made *a pick-off throw.* / ピッチャーは一塁ランナーをけん制でアウトにした The pitcher *picked* the runner *off* first base. / 両ランナーは互いにけん制し合って(→同じ速さを保って), 前へ出ようとはしなかった The two runners *kept pace with* each other, and neither tried to move ahead.

けんせい² 権勢 (権力) power [U]; (勢力) influence [U]

げんせい 厳正 厳正な裁判[審査] a *strict and fair* [*impartial*] trial [judgment]

げんぜい 減税 tax reduction [cut] [C] ―減税する reduce [cut*] taxes ∥人々は大幅な減税を要求している People are calling for big *tax cuts.*
◆所得税が減税されるらしい I hear (that) the income tax *will be reduced.*

げんせいりん 原生林 virgin [primeval] forest [C]

けんせき 譴責 reprimand [C] ―けん責する reprimand [他] ∥彼は厳しいけん責処分を受けた He received *a* stiff *reprimand.*

げんせき 原石 (原鉱) raw ore [C] [U]; (鉱石) ore [C] [U]; (宝石用の) gemstone [C]

けんせつ 建設 construction [U]; (設立) establishment [U] ―建設する build* [他], construct [他]
ここに団地が建設される予定だ A new housing complex is going to *be constructed* [*built*] here.
新しい駅は今建設中だ The new station is「*under construction* [*being built*] now.
建設工事はほぼ終了している *The construction*

work is almost finished.
◆平和な社会を建設する *establish* a peaceful society / 彼は私の論文に建設的な批評をしてくれた He made some *constructive* criticisms of my thesis.
‖建設会社 a construction company / 建設業 the construction industry / 建設業者 a builder / 建設現場 a construction site / 建設省 the Ministry of Construction (◆2001年国土交通省に統合) ⇒ こくどこうつうしょう / 建設費 construction costs / 建設用地 a building lot [site]

けんぜん 健全 ——健全な sound; (健康的な) healthy; (道徳的に) wholesome ‖健全な財政 *sound* finance / 健全な読み物 *wholesome* reading / 健全な生活を送る lead [live] a *healthy* life

げんせん¹ 源泉 source ⓒ ‖温泉の源泉 a *source* of hot springs
‖源泉課税 《米》withholding taxation, 《英》pay-as-you-earn (《略語》PAYE) / 源泉徴収 withholding [deducting] taxes at the source of income

げんせん² 厳選 これらの紅茶は厳選されたものです These teas *have been carefully selected*.

げんぜん 厳然 それは厳然たる事実だ It's a *hard* [*solid*] fact.

げんそ 元素 element ⓒ ‖元素記号 the symbol of an element, an atomic symbol

けんそう 喧騒 彼らは都会の喧騒を逃れていなかにやってきた They came to the country to get away from *the noise* [*din*] *and bustle* of the city.

けんぞう 建造 building Ⓤ, construction Ⓤ ——建造する build*, construct ‖建造中の船 a ship *under construction* / 橋を建造する *build* [*construct*] a bridge
‖建造物 a building, a structure

げんそう 幻想 (夢のような) fantasy Ⓤ ⓒ; (錯覚) illusion ⓒ ‖幻想の世界 a *fantasy* world / 彼女は有名になれるという幻想をいだいていた She 「*had fantasies* [*fantasized*] about becoming famous. / その場所には幻想的な雰囲気が漂っていた There was a *fantasy* mood in that place.
◆幻想的な音楽 *dreamy* music
‖幻想曲 a fantasy, a fantasia

げんぞう 現像 development Ⓤ ——現像する develop ⓐ ⓑ ‖フィルムを現像してもらう have film *developed*

げんそく 原則 (根本の規則) principle ⓒ; (一般的な規則) rule ⓒ ‖原則的にはその考えに賛成です *In principle*, I agree with that idea. / 原則としてだれもここに入ってはいけないことになっている *As a* (*general*) *rule*, no one is allowed to enter here. / それは基本原則に反する That is contrary to *the fundamental principles*.

げんそく² 減速 slowdown ⓒ, deceleration Ⓤ ——減速する slow down, 《公式的》decelerate ⓐ

けんそん 謙遜 modesty Ⓤ ‖彼は謙遜してそう言ったのだろう Maybe he said so *out of modesty*.

げんそん 現存 ——現存の (存在する) existing; (生きている) living ‖現存の画家 a *living* painter / これは日本に現存する最も古い寺です This is the oldest *existing* temple in Japan.

けんたい¹ 倦怠 fatigue Ⓤ, weariness Ⓤ
◆このごろ倦怠感を覚える I'm *feeling weary* [*tired*] these days. / 彼ら（夫婦）は倦怠期にきている(→結婚生活に飽きてきている) They *have become bored with their marriage*.

けんたい² 献体 ——献体する donate *one's body after death to* ... *for medical research*

げんたい 減退 (衰え) decline ⓒ; (喪失) loss Ⓤ ——減退する decline ‖食欲の減退 *loss* of appetite / 年をとると体力が減退する Your strength *declines* when you get older.

げんだい 現代 the present day [age]; (今日〈にち〉) today Ⓤ ——現代の present-day; (当世の) modern, contemporary
現代的な建築 a *modern* building
環境問題は現代における最も重要な問題の一つだ Environmental problems are one of the most important issues of *the present day*.
◆現代は情報化社会である *Today* we live in an information-oriented society.
‖現代音楽 contemporary music / 現代化 modernization / 現代史 contemporary history / 現代人 people of today / 現代生活 present-day life / 現代っ子 a modern kid [child], a child of today / 現代文学 contemporary literature

ケンタッキー Kentucky (◆米国中東部の州; 《略語》Ky., Ken., 《郵便》KY)

けんだま 剣玉 a cup and ball ‖子供のころよくけん玉をして遊んだ I used to *play with a cup and ball* when I was a child.

げんたん 減反 米の減反 (→作付け面積の削減) *reductions in* rice *acreage*

けんち¹ 見地 standpoint ⓒ, (観点) viewpoint ⓒ, a point of view ‖教育的見地からすればそれはすべきではない *From an educational point of view*, it should not be done.

けんち² 検知 この装置はガスもれを検知する This device *detects* gas leaks.
‖検知器 a detector

げんち¹ 現地 現地の(→地元の)人々 local people / 私たちは現地からの(→現場の)報告を待った We waited for an *on-the-spot* report. / 事件は現地時間午後8時に起こった The incident happened at 8:00 p.m. *local time*. / 11時に現地集合することに決まった We decided to *meet at the place* at 11.
‖現地調査 an on-site [on-the-spot] survey [investigation] / 現地法人 a local subsidiary

げんち² 言質 (約束) promise ⓒ; (誓い) pledge ⓒ ‖言質を与える make *a pledge* [*commitment*] / 言質をとる get *a person's promise*

けんちく 建築 (建築術) architecture Ⓤ; (建

築すること) construction; (建築物) building ──建築する build*, put* up, construct

私は西洋建築について多少知識があります I know something about *Western architecture*.

兄は大学で建築を専攻している My brother is majoring in *architecture* in college.

彼らは新しい家を建築している They *are building* a new house.

◆彼は日本で十指に数えられる建築家だ He is one of *the top 10 architects* in Japan.

∥建築学 architecture / 建築基準法 the Building Standard Law / 建築業 the building industry / 建築業者 a builder / 建築現場 a construction site / 建築工事 construction work / 建築資材 building materials / 建築費 building expenses / 建築物 a building / 建築面積 building area / 建築様式 a style of architecture

けんちょ 顕著 ──顕著な (注目に値する) remarkable; (際立った) marked, noticeable ∥人口の増加が顕著に見られる There has been a *marked* increase in population.

けんちょう 県庁 (行政庁) prefectural government; (県当局) the prefectural authorities ∥県庁舎 a prefectural office / 県庁所在地 the prefectural capital, the seat of the prefectural government [office]

げんちょう 幻聴 auditory hallucination

げんつき 原付き scooter, moped; (小型オートバイ)《米》motorbike

けんてい¹ 検定 official approval ──検定する approve, authorize ∥検定教科書 an authorized textbook / 検定試験 a licensing examination / 検定料 a certification fee

けんてい² 献呈 ──献呈する present, dedicate

げんてい 限定 limitation; (制限) restriction ──限定する limit, restrict ∥コンテストの参加者は高校生に限定されている Entry in the contest *is limited* [*restricted*] *to* high school students. / その商品は期間限定[夏季限定]で販売される That item will be sold「*for a limited time* [*only in summer*]」.

◆この部屋に入れる人数はちょうど5人に限定されている The capacity of this room is just five people.

∥限定版 a limited edition / 限定販売 a limited sale

げんてん¹ 減点 スペルミスで5点減点されていた I *had* five points *subtracted* [*taken off*] because of spelling mistakes.

∥減点法 the demerit system; (レスリングなどで) the bad-mark system

げんてん² 原点 (出発点) starting point; (初め) the beginning; (数学の) the origin ∥私たちはもう一度原点に立ち返ってみる必要がある We need to go [get] back to *the beginning* again.

げんてん³ 原典 the original (text)

げんど 限度 limit ∥何事にも限度というものがある Everything has *its limit*. / There is *a limit* to everything.

◆がんばってみましたがこれが限度です(→私のできる最善だ) I tried hard, but this is *the best I could do*.

けんとう¹ 見当

その国がどこにあるのか見当もつかない I *can't guess* [(→ 想像できない) *imagine*] where that country is.

彼がなぜそう言ったのか見当もつかない(→分からない) I *have no idea* why he said that.

君の考えることぐらい見当がつくよ I *can imagine* what you're thinking.

私の見当では(→私が見積もったところでは)2時間くらいでそこに着くでしょう I *estimate* it will take about two hours to get there.

君の推測は見当違いだったね Your guess *was way off*. / You *made a wrong guess*. / You *guessed wrong*.

あなたの意見は見当はずれの(→的(穷)がはずれている) Your comment is *beside the point*.

パーティーの会費は1人5000円見当です The fee for the party is *about* five thousand yen each.

けんとう² 検討 (調査) examination; (考慮) consideration ──検討する examine; consider

家に持ち帰って検討してみます I'll take it home and *consider* it.

この問題はもう一度検討する必要がある We have to *examine* this problem again.

その計画はまだ検討中である That plan is still *under consideration*.

けんとう³ 健闘 負けはしたものの選手たちは健闘した Though the players lost the game, they「*put up a good fight* [*fought hard*]」/ ご健闘を祈ります *Good luck (to you)*! / 受賞者たちはお互いの健闘をたたえ合った The winners *praised* one another *for their ceaseless efforts*.

けんどう 剣道

剣道は英語で日本式フェンシングと呼ばれることがありますが、竹製の刀(竹刀(しない))を用いたり、特別な防具を身に着けたりする点でフェンシングとは異なります。相手の面・胴・小手を打つか、のどを突くとポイントになります。試合では2ポイント先取、または制限時間内に1ポイントのリードをしていたほうが勝ちになります。

Kendo is sometimes referred to as Japanese fencing in English, but it is different from fencing in that, for example, a bamboo sword (*shinai*) and elaborate protective gear are used. A point is scored by hitting the opponent's head, trunk or forearms, or by thrusting at the throat. The winner is the first one to score two points, or the one with a one-point lead at the end of the allotted time.

げんどう 言動 もう少し言動に気をつけたほうがいいよ You should be more careful about 「*your words and actions* [*what you say and do*]／上司の言動がおかしい My boss *is acting* [*behaving*] *strangely*.

げんどうりょく 原動力 motive power ⓤ; (駆りたてる力) driving force ⓤ ∥彼の活躍がチーム大躍進の原動力となった His active play was *the driving force* behind the team's remarkable progress.

けんない 圏内 圏内の核実験 an *atmospheric* nuclear test／その国はかつてフランスの勢力圏内にあった The country *was* once *within* the French *sphere of influence*.／関東地方は暴風雨圏内にある The Kanto area *is in a storm zone*.／彼女は関西大学の合格圏内にいる (→合格の可能性が十分ある) She *has a good chance of passing the exam* for Kansai University.

げんなり 練習の後,選手たちはげんなりしていた (→疲れ果てていた) The players *were exhausted* after practice.／彼女の自慢話にはげんなりした (→飽き飽きする) I *am fed up with* her bragging.

げんに 現に (実際に) actually; (本当に) really; (自分の目[耳]で) with *one's* own eyes [ears]; (今) now, at this moment ∥それは本当です。現に見ましたから It's true, because I「*saw it with my own eyes* [*actually saw it*].◆現に(→事実として)世界のどこかで餓死している人が大勢いる The truth is that a lot of people are dying of hunger in the world.

けんにょう 検尿 urinalysis ⓤ, urine test ⓒ ─検尿する have* *one's* urine tested [checked], get* a urine test

けんにん 兼任 首相は3か月間,外相を兼任した The Prime Minister「*held the additional* [*concurrently held the*] *post* of the Foreign Minister for three months.

げんば 現場 (事故・事件などの) scene ⓒ; (地点) spot ⓒ; (建築などの) site ⓒ ∥人々が事故現場に群がった People crowded around *the scene of the accident.*／その男は犯行現場でつかまった The man was seized at *the scene of the crime.*／その火事の現場では人々が助けを求めて叫んでいた People were shouting for help at *the scene* [*site*] *of the fire*.

◆店員たちは男の盗みの現場を押さえた The salesclerks caught the man *in the act of stealing.*／上司たちは現場の声を反映させることなく結論を下した The top management made decisions without taking into account the opinions of those *in the field*.

∥現場監督 a field overseer, a site foreman／現場検証 an on-the-spot investigation [inspection]／工事現場 a construction site

けんばいき 券売機 ticket (vending) machine ⓒ

げんばく 原爆 atom(ic) bomb ⓒ, A-bomb ⓒ ∥原爆実験 an atomic test／原爆症 illness caused by atomic-bomb radiation／原爆ドーム Genbaku Dome, the Atomic Bomb Dome

げんばつ 厳罰 severe [heavy] punishment ⓤⓒ ◆彼は厳罰に処せられた He *was punished severely*.

げんぱつ 原発 (原子力発電所) nuclear power plant ⓒ

けんばん 鍵盤 (全体) keyboard ⓒ; (1本1本) key ⓒ ∥鍵盤楽器 a keyboard instrument

げんばん 原盤 (レコードなどの) master ⓒ

けんびきょう 顕微鏡 microscope ⓒ ∥我々は血液標本を採取し顕微鏡で調べた We took a blood sample and examined it under *the microscope*.

∥顕微鏡検査 a microscopic examination／顕微鏡写真 a (photo)micrograph／電子顕微鏡 an electron microscope

げんぴん 現品 こちらは現品限り (→展示してある品物のみ) 3 割引です We give a 30 percent discount *only on the displayed items*.

げんぶがん 玄武岩 〔鉱物〕 basalt [bəsɔ́ːlt] ⓤ

けんぶつ 見物 sightseeing ⓤ ─見物する (名所を訪れる) see* the sights (見る) see ⑯ (動きのあるものを) watch ⑯ (訪れる) visit ⑯

彼らは大阪見物に行った They went to *see the sights of* Osaka.／They went to Osaka for *sightseeing*.／They went *sightseeing* in Osaka.

私たちは何百という花火があがるのを見物した We *watched* hundreds of fireworks set off.

大勢の人がパレード見物に集まった A big crowd of people gathered to *watch* the parade.

ロンドンではいろいろな所を見物した I *visited* many places in London.

∥見物席 a seat; (球場などの) the stands／見物人 (観光客) a sightseer, a visitor; (観客) a spectator; (傍観者) an onlooker

げんぶつ 現物 (実物) the (actual) article [thing] ∥現物はこれよりもう少し大きいです The actual article [*thing, one*] is a little bigger than this.

◆支払いは現物でなされた I was paid *in kind*.

∥現物支給 payment in kind

ケンブリッジ Cambridge (❖英国 England 東部の都市; 米国 Massachusetts 州の都市)

けんぶん 見聞 (知識) knowledge ⓤ; (情報) information ⓤ; (経験) experience ⓒ ∥彼は海外を旅行して見聞を広めた He「*widened his knowledge* [(→より多くの世の中を見てきた) *saw more of the world*] by traveling abroad.／彼女は見聞が広い (→よく知っている) She *is well-informed*.

げんぶん 原文 the original (text), the text ∥この次はこの本を原文で読んでみよう Next time I'll try to read this novel *in the original.*／そんなに原文に忠実に訳さなくてもいいよ You don't have to make your translation so faithful to *the original*.

けんぺいりつ 建蔽率 building coverage ratio ⓒ

けんべん 検便 stool test [examination] ⓒ

けんぽう 憲法 constitution ⓒ (❖自国の憲法は the Constitution とする)

憲法の精神 the spirit of *the Constitution* / 憲法第25条 Article 25 of *the Constitution* / 憲法を制定[発布]する establish [proclaim] *a constitution*

憲法を改正することは容易ではない It is not easy to revise [amend] *the Constitution*.

日本国憲法にはすべての国民に対する平等の権利が含まれている *The Constitution of Japan* includes equal rights for all people.

その権利は憲法で保障されている That right is guaranteed under *the Constitution*.

それは憲法違反だ It is 「*against the Constitution* [*unconstitutional*].

‖憲法改正 a constitutional amendment / 憲法記念日 Constitution Day

げんぽう 減俸 salary [pay] cut Ⓒ, a cut in salary ──減俸する cut* [reduce] *a person's pay* / 彼は3パーセント減俸された He had his pay cut [*reduced*] by three percent. / He had a pay cut of three percent.

けんぼうしょう 健忘症 (忘れっぽいこと) forgetfulness Ⓤ; (記憶喪失) [医学] amnesia Ⓤ
◆このところ健忘症ぎみだ(→忘れっぽい) I've been *a bit forgetful* lately.

げんぽん 原本 the original (work); (文書) the original document; (原文) the text

けんま 研磨 ──研磨する (つやを出す) polish 他; (硬い物で磨く) grind* 他 ‖研磨機 a grinder / 研磨剤 abrasives

げんまい 玄米 brown [unpolished] rice Ⓤ
‖玄米茶 tea mixed with roasted rice

けんまく 剣幕・見幕 彼はものすごいけんまくで(→激しく)その店にどなり込んだ He stormed *ferociously* into the shop. / 彼女は恐ろしいけんまくで(→ものすごい顔つきで)私たちをにらみつけた She stared at us *with such a fierce* [*an angry*] *look*.

げんみつ 厳密 ──厳密な strict; (柔軟性のない) rigid; (綿密な) close ‖語の厳密な意味では in the *strict* sense of the word / 厳密な調査をする make a *close* [(→徹底的な) *thorough*] investigation

◆厳密に計算する make a *precise* calculation; calculate *precisely* / 厳密に言うと、この2つの箱は同じ大きさではありません *Strictly speaking*, these two boxes are not the same size.

けんみん 県民 an inhabitant of a prefecture ◆埼玉県民 the people of Saitama *Prefecture*

けんむ 兼務 父は2つの部長職を兼務している My father *holds* two managerial posts *concurrently*.

けんめい¹ 賢明 ──賢明な (賢い) wise; (思慮分別のある) sensible ‖あなたは賢明な選択をした You made a *wise* choice. / そのことは彼には言わないほうが賢明だ It would be *wise* [*sensible*] of you not to tell him about that.

◆ 賢明にも達郎は沈黙を守った *Wisely*, Tatsuro kept silent.

けんめい² 懸命 ──懸命な (熱心な) hard, eager; (精力的な) strenuous ⇒いっしょうけん

めい、‖懸命な努力 strenuous efforts / 彼女はコンピュータを覚えようと懸命です She is *eager* to learn how to use the computer.

◆彼は勝ちたい思いで懸命に練習した He trained *hard* because of his desire to win.

けんめい³ 件名 (電子メールの) subject Ⓒ

げんめい 言明 (宣言) declaration Ⓒ; (明確な声明) definite statement Ⓒ ──言明する declare 自他; state definitely [clearly] ‖知事はその問題については言明を避けた The governor avoided *making any definite statement* on the matter. / 彼はその話は事実であると言明した He *declared* that the story was true.

げんめつ 幻滅 disillusionment Ⓤ
◆姉は仕事に幻滅したと言っている My sister says she *was disillusioned with* her job.

けんもほろろ 彼にお金を貸してほしいと頼んだが、けんもほろろに(→きっぱりと)断られた I asked him to lend me some money, but he *flatly* refused.

けんもん 検問 check Ⓒ, inspection Ⓒ
◆その男は空港の検問で引っかかった(→検問所でつかまった) The man was caught at *the checkpoint* at the airport.
‖検問所 a checkpoint

げんや 原野 field Ⓒ; (荒れ地) wilderness [wíldərnəs] Ⓤ; (未開地) the wilds

けんやく 倹約 (質素であること) frugality Ⓤ (❖倹約の度合いがいちばん強い); (慎重にお金を使うこと) thrift Ⓤ; (時間・金などを浪費しないこと) saving Ⓤ ──倹約する save 他 自; (経済的に使う) economize 自; (切り詰める) cut* back [down] (on ...)

彼女は電気を倹約して使うように心がけている She is careful to *save* [*cut down on*] electricity.

母は毎月の家計を倹約している My mother *economizes on* our monthly living expenses.

彼はむだづかいをやめて今は倹約に努めている He has stopped wasting money and now is trying to 「*save some* [*be frugal*].
‖倹約家 a thrifty person, a saver

げんゆ 原油 crude oil Ⓤ

けんよう 兼用 この部屋は居間と兼用です(→居間としても使われる) This room 「*also serves* [*is also used*] as a living room.

けんらん 絢爛 絢爛たる文体 a *flowery* style of writing / 役者たちはみな絢爛豪華な衣装を着ていた All the actors and actresses were *gorgeously* dressed.

けんり 権利 right Ⓒ; (請求する権利) claim Ⓤ Ⓒ

権利を獲得する gain *a right* / 権利を行使する exercise *a right* / 権利を主張する insist on [assert] *a right* / 権利を侵害する infringe on *a person's right* / 権利を放棄する give up *a right* / 権利を保護する protect *a person's right* / 権利を乱用する abuse *a right* / 権利を勝ち得る win *a right*

彼らはその土地を使用する権利をめぐって激論を交

わしている They have a hot dispute over *the right to* use the land.
すべての人が平和に暮らす権利をもっている Every person has *a right to* live in peace.
君に私のプライバシーを侵す権利はない You have no *right to* violate my privacy.
彼女はその財産に対して法的権利がある She has *legal claim to* the property.
独裁者は市民から政治的権利を奪った The dictator deprived the citizens of *their political rights*.

‖権利金 premium; (貸家などの) key money

げんり 原理 (根本原則) principle ⓒ; (理論) theory ⓒ ‖民主主義の原理 *the principle of democracy* / てこの原理 *the principle of the lever*

‖原理主義 fundamentalism

けんりつ 県立 ──県立の prefectural
‖県立高校 a prefectural high school

げんりゅう 源流 (起源) origin ⓒ; (水源) source ⓒ, headwaters ‖その習慣の源流 *the origin of the custom*

げんりょう¹ 原料 raw material(s) ‖原料を輸入する import *raw materials*
◆豆腐は大豆を原料として作られる Tofu *is made from* soybeans.

げんりょう² 減量 a loss in weight ──減量する lose* weight ‖減量のためバターの代わりにオリーブ油を使っている To *lose weight*, I use olive oil instead of butter.
◆5キロ減量するように医者に言われた I was told to *lose* five kilograms by a doctor. / 私は環境のためごみの減量に努めている I'm trying to *reduce waste* for the sake of the environment.

けんりょく 権力 (支配力) power Ⓤ; (法的権力) authority Ⓤ; (影響力) influence Ⓤ ‖権力を得る[失う] gain [lose] *power* / 権力の座に就く[就いている] 「come into [be in] *power* / 権力に訴える assert *one's authority* / 権力を振るう exercise *one's power* [*authority*] / 彼の父親はこの町の権力者だ His father *has great influence* in this town.

‖権力闘争 a struggle for power, a power struggle

げんろん 言論 (話すこと) speech Ⓤ; (書くこと) writing Ⓤ ‖言論の自由 freedom of *speech* / 言論の統制 control of *speech and writing*

‖言論界 the press / 言論機関 an organ of public opinion

げんわく 眩惑・幻惑 彼はその景色の美しさに眩惑された He *was dazzled by* the beautiful scenery.

こ

こ¹ 子 child ⓒ (複 children); 《口語的》kid ⓒ; (男の子) boy; (女の子) girl; (息子) son ⓒ; (娘) daughter ⓒ; (赤ん坊) baby ⓒ; (動物の) young ⓒ《集合的》《複数扱い》
⇒こども

ひとりっ子 *an only child* / 末っ子 *the youngest (child)*

お子さんは何人いらっしゃるのですか How many *children* do you have?

お子さんはいつ生まれる予定ですか When is *your baby* due?

一夫, いい子にしていなさい Be *a good boy*, Kazuo.

受付の子はかわいいね The「*girl at the reception desk* [*receptionist*] is cute.

その子は自分のおもちゃを人に使わせたがらない That *kid* is possessive with [about] his toys.

うちの子は数学が得意です My *kid* [*son, daughter*] is good at math.

ことわざ かわいい子には旅をさせよ ⇒ かわいい

こ² 弧 arc ⓒ / ブーメランは弧を描いて空高く飛んだ The boomerang *arced* high in the sky.

こ³ 個 individual ⓒ

こ- 故- 故安藤氏 *the late* Mr. Ando

-こ¹ -個

語法 ふつうは、名詞の前に one (または a, an), two, three などを置いて表す。ただし不可算名詞で表されるものを数える場合、例えば「せっけん」には cake または bar,「角砂糖」には lump などの語を用いる。

パン1個 *a loaf* of bread / せっけん3個 *three cakes* of soap / 角砂糖4個 *four lumps* of sugar / キャンディー5個 *five pieces* of candy

🅔「いらっしゃいませ。ご注文をどうぞ」「はい。チーズバーガーを2個ください」 "May I help you?" "Yes. *Two* cheeseburgers, please."

-こ² -戸 house ⓒ / その地域の各戸には防音装置が施された Each *house* in the area was soundproofed. ◆ 世帯数20戸の村 a village of 20 *households* [*families*]

-こ³ -湖 lake ⓒ / 浜名湖 *Lake* Hamana; *the Lake* of Hamana (❖ of を用いない場合は the を付けない)

ご¹ 語 (単語) word ⓒ; (専門用語) term ⓒ; (言語) language ⓒ; (古典語) *a classical language* / この語はどういう意味ですか What does this *word* mean?

🅔「ブラジルでは何語が話されていますか」「ポルトガル語です」 "What *language* 「do they speak [is spoken] in Brazil?" "Portuguese."

ご² 五 five; (5番目) fifth ‖ 五大湖 the Great Lakes

ご³ 碁 go ⓤ / 碁を打つ play *go* ‖ 碁石 a go stone / 碁盤 ⇒ ごばん

> 碁は囲碁とも呼ばれ、2人のプレーヤーが碁盤の上に交互に黒と白の石を置き、できるだけ広い領域を囲んでゆくゲームです。
> Go (or *igo*) is a game in which two players take turns placing black and white stones on a grid in an attempt to capture as much territory as possible.

-ご -後 ━ 前 after; (今から…後に) in; (…以来ずっと) since (❖ 通例現在[過去]完了形とともに用いる) ━ 副 (…後になって) later, afterward, after ⇒ あと (後)

今から50年後の世界 the world *in* 50 years; the world 50 years *from now*

私たちは朝食後ドライブに出かけた We went for a drive *after* breakfast.

それから2, 3日後, 健から返事が来た A few days *later* [*afterward*], I got an answer from Ken.

その後, 彼はどうしてるの How has he been *since* then?

1時間後に駅で会おう Let's meet at the station *in* an hour.

その後, 彼らはずっと幸せに暮らしましたとさ They lived happily ever *after*. (❖ 童話などの結語)

◆選挙は2日後だ The election is two days *away* [*from now*].

コアラ 〔動物〕koala (bear) ⓒ

こい¹ 濃い

❶〔色〕deep; (黒ずんだ) dark

濃い灰色 *dark* [*deep*] gray

空は濃い青色だった The sky was *deep* blue.

❷〔濃度・密度〕thick, dense

濃いスープ *thick* soup / 濃いまゆ毛 *thick* eyebrows

とても内容の濃い映画だった It was a very *dense* film.

◆内容の濃い討論 a *substantial* debate / 霧が濃くなった The fog *thickened*. / 彼女は化粧が濃い She wears *heavy* makeup.

❸〔味〕strong

コーヒーは少し濃いめにして Make my coffee a little *strong*.

◆塩味の濃いみそ汁 *overly salted miso* soup / このラーメンは味が濃すぎる This ramen *is seasoned too heavily* [*strongly*].

❹〔可能性〕strong

彼がうその証言をした疑いが濃い There is a *strong* suspicion that he testified falsely.

こい² 恋 love ⓤ ━恋(を)する love 他 ⓖ ⇒ 場面・状況別会話 p.1692

私は勉に恋をしている I *am in love with*

Tsutomu. / 尚夫は博子に恋をした Hisao *fell in love with* Hiroko. / 彼らはひとめで熱烈な恋に落ちた They *fell passionately in love with* each other at first sight.
● 「実ったらこのごろ変ね」「絶対恋わずらいよ」 "Minoru is not himself these days." "He's *lovesick*, I'm sure."
‖恋がたき a rival in love / 恋文 a love letter / 恋物語 a love story
慣用表現 恋は盲目 *Love is blind*.

こい[3] 故意 ──故意の deliberate, intentional ──故意に on purpose, deliberately, intentionally /故意の侮辱 a *deliberate* insult / 彼女は故意に私に難しい質問をしたにちがいない. She must have asked me a difficult question 「*on purpose* [*deliberately*].

こい[4] 鯉 (一般の) carp ©(複 ~, ~s); (ニシキゴイ) koi ©(複 ~)

ごい 語彙 vocabulary ©Ⓤ /語彙を増やす increase [build up] *one's vocabulary* / 登は英語の語彙が豊富だ [乏しい] Noboru has *a large* [*small*] English *vocabulary*.

こいし 小石 small stone ©, 《米》rock ©; (海辺や河原の丸い小石) pebble ©

こいしい 恋しい (…を) long for …; (ないことを残念に思う) miss ⓗ /私は時々落ち着いたいなかの生活が恋しくなる I sometimes *miss* [*long for*] a quiet country life. / こたつが恋しい季節になった The season has come when we *long for* a kotatsu.

こいする 恋する ⇨ こい(恋)

こいつ こいつがおれの金を盗んだんだ *This guy* stole my money. / こいつはなかなかうまいから食べてみなよ *This* tastes very good. Try it. / (親しみや皮肉をこめて) こいつめ Oh, you!

こいぬ 子犬 puppy ©, pup ©

こいのぼり 鯉幟

5月5日の子供の日のころになると, コイの形をしたのぼりが高いさおに揚げられます. コイは滝さえも上るほどたくましいとされることから, このぼりには子供がすくすく健康に育つようにとの親の願いがこめられています.
Koinobori, carp-shaped streamers, are hoisted on tall poles around Children's Day (May 5). Carp are believed to possess enough strength and vitality even to swim up waterfalls. They represent the parents' wishes for their children to grow up in sound health.

こいびと 恋人 (男性から見た女性の) girlfriend ©, 《古風》sweetheart ©; (女性から見た男性の) boyfriend ©, lover ©(❖loverは「愛人」のニュアンスが強い); (特定の)《口語的》steady ©; (カップル) couple ©, lovers ©/彼に新しい恋人ができたそうだ I've heard that he's got *a new girlfriend*. / 二人は恋人どうしだ They are *lovers*.

コイル 〖電気〗coil ©

コイン coin ©/コイン入れ a *coin* purse

コインランドリー 《米》laundromat [lɔ́:ndrəmæt] ©(❖商標名から), 《英》laund(e)rette [lɔ̀:ndrét] ©, coin laundry ©

コインロッカー ⚠ (coin-operated) locker ©

こう[1] this; (このように) like this, (in) this way /こううるさくては眠れない I can't sleep in *this* noise. / 君のためを思ってこう言っているんだ I'm saying *this* for your sake. / こうなったからには, 私はここを出ます After *this* I will leave here.
● 「できないよ」「ほら, こうすればいいのよ」 "I can't do it." "Look. Do it 「*like this* [(*in*) *this way*]."

こう[2] 請う・乞う beg ⓗⒶ, 《公式的》request ⓗ /慈悲を請う *beg for* mercy / 私は彼女に許しを請うた I *begged* her *for* forgiveness. / I *asked* her pardon.
慣用表現 乞うご期待 *Don't miss it!*

こう[3] 功 (成功) success Ⓤ; (功績) achievement Ⓤ
◆内助の功 (→妻の支え) one's wife's support / 年の功 the wisdom of age / 作戦が功を奏した The operation *succeeded*. / 彼はその薬を発明するのに功があった (→貢献した) He *contributed to* the invention of the medicine.

こう[4] 項 (条項) clause ©, section ©; (項目) item ©; (方程式) member ©/条約の第5項 *section* five of the treaty

こう[5] 幸 happiness Ⓤ
慣用表現 幸か不幸かそのとき私にはお金の持ち合わせがなかった *Fortunately or unfortunately*, I had no money with me at that time.

こう[6] 甲 (手の) back; (足・靴の) instep ©; (カメの) tortoise shell ©Ⓤ /汗を手の甲でぬぐう wipe away sweat with *the back of one's hand*
ことわざ 亀(⁎)の甲より年の功 ⇨ かめ(亀)

こう[7] 香 incense Ⓤ /香をたく burn *incense* / 香を聞く guess [identify] *incense*

こう- 好~ 好成績をあげる make *good* grades / 新しい秘書は, 私に好印象を与えた The newly-employed secretary 「impressed me *favorably* [gave me *favorable* impression]. / 彼女のおとなしさは姉の快活さと好対照をなしていた Her pleasant calm *presented a striking contrast to* her sister's exuberant cheerfulness. ⇨ こうせいえん, こうりょくみ

-こう -港 port ©Ⓤ /横浜港 Yokohama *Port*; *the Port* of Yokohama

ごう[1] 合 富士山の5合目 *the fifth station* on the trail up Mt. Fuji / 米を2合炊く boil two *cups* of rice

ごう[2] 郷 ことわざ 郷に入っては郷に従え *When in Rome, do as the Romans do.*

ごう[3] 業 karma Ⓤ; (運命) destiny Ⓤ; (運命づけられた罪) one's predestined sin
慣用表現 彼はどうしても箱があかないのに業を煮やし, それをたたきつぶした He *became irritated* that the box wouldn't open, so he smashed it.

-ごう -号 (番号・順番) number ©; (雑誌などの) issue ©; (臨時増刊号) *a special issue; an extra number* / ニューヨーカー誌の最新号 *the*

latest *number* of *The New Yorker* / 7月11日号のニューズウイーク *the July 11 issue of Newsweek* ◆博士号 *a doctor's degree* / 66号線 *Route 66* / クイーン・エリザベス号 *the Queen Elizabeth* / 彼は306号室にいる He is in Room 306.

こうあつ 高圧 〔電気〕 high voltage [tension]ⒸⓊ ――高圧的な high-handed //高圧的な態度で in a *high-handed* manner //高圧ガス high-pressure gas / 高圧線 a high voltage [tension] wire / 高圧電流 high voltage [tension] current

こうあん¹ 考案 ――考案する (工夫する) deviseⒽ; (考え出す) figure out, 《公式的》originateⒽⓊ //乳製品の新しい製法を考案する *devise* a new process for producing dairy products / このアイディアはある有名な化学者が考案したものです This idea *originated* with a famous chemist.
//考案者 an originator, an inventor

こうあん² 公安 public peace [safety]Ⓤ
//公安委員 a public peace commissioner / 公安委員会 a public peace commission / 公安条例 public peace regulations

こうい¹ 行為

actⒸ; actionⓊⒸ (✻act が1回1回の行動を指すのに対し, action はある期間にわたる連続した行動を指す);《公式的》deedⒸ; (ふるまい) behavior, 《英》behaviourⓊ

コロケーション -act-
【形容詞＋～】思いやりのある～ a kindly act / 愚かな～ a foolish act / 軽はずみな～ a thoughtless act / 残忍な～ a cruel act / 尊敬に値する～ a respectable act / 恥ずべき～ a shameful act / 犯罪～ a criminal act / 卑劣な[汚い]～ a foul act / 不正～ a wrong act / 凶暴な～ a violent act / 無分別な～ a senseless act / 勇敢な～ a brave act / りっぱな～ an honorable act

侵略行為 *an act* of aggression / …に対する裏切り行為 *an act* of treachery against …
彼は違法[不法]行為をした He committed *an illegal act*.
君の行為は法律に反している Your *behavior* is against the law.
//行為者 a doer, a performer

こうい² 好意 (支持) favor,《英》favourⓊ; (親切) kindnessⓊ; (善意) goodwillⓊ; (厚遇) hospitalityⓊ ――好意的な favorable, friendly

ご好意に甘えさせていただきます I will trespass on *your hospitality*.
あれは彼なりに好意を示してるんだ That's his way of showing *his goodwill*.
みんなアンには好意的だった Everyone was *friendly* to Ann.
その劇は雑誌で好意的な論評を得た The play got *favorable* [*good*] reviews in the magazine.
◆著者の好意で *by courtesy* of the author (✻転載などの断り書き) / 加藤君はあの子に好意をもっているようだった It seemed that Kato *liked* that girl. / 彼女はキャプテンに好意を寄せている She *feels affection for* the captain.

こうい³ 厚意 kindnessⓊ /ご厚意に感謝します Thank you for *your kindness*.

こうい⁴ 校医 school doctorⒸ

ごうい 合意 agreementⓊ; (同意) 《公式的》consentⓊ ――合意する agreeⒽⒾ 《大筋で合意する *reach* broad *agreement* / 合意を破る *break an agreement* / 私たちはようやく合意に達した We finally reached [came to] *an agreement*. / この新しいルールは双方合意のうえで作られた This new rule was made *by mutual consent*.

こういう こういう服は趣味じゃないわ I don't like clothes *like this*. / こういう音楽はあまり好きでない I don't like *this kind of* music very much. / 事の起こりはこういうことなのです *This is how it happened*. / こういう理由でパーティーには出席できません For this reason [*This is why*] I can't attend the party. / こういう場合, どうすればいいのだろう What should I do in *this kind of* situation?
⇒ こんな

こういき 広域 wide areaⒸ ――広域に widely //その植物は広域に分布している The plant is distributed *widely* [*over wide areas*].
◆広域にわたる被害 *widespread* damage

こういしつ 更衣室 (体育施設の) locker [changing] roomⒸ; (劇場などの) dressing roomⒸ

こういしょう 後遺症 aftereffects / 彼は病気の後遺症に苦しんでいる He suffers from *the aftereffects* of his illness. / けがから6か月たって重い後遺症が出た Serious *aftereffects* appeared six months after the injury.

こういっつい 好一対 好一対の夫婦 a *well-matched* couple

こういってん 紅一点 the only girl [woman] (in a group)

こういん¹ 工員 (工場労働者) factory workerⒸ

こういん² 光陰 ことわざ 光陰矢のごとし Time flies (like an arrow).

こういん³ 行員 (銀行員) bank clerkⒸ

ごういん 強引 ――強引な forcible; (高圧的な) high-handed; (押しの強い) pushy //強引なセールスマン a *pushy* salesman / 私は彼の強引なやり方が嫌いだ I don't like his *forcible* ways.
◆彼女は強引にドアをあけた She opened the door *by force*. / 彼は強引にそのクラブに入会させられた He *was forced to* join the club.

こうう 降雨 rainfallⓊⒸ /年間降雨量 *an* annual *rainfall* / 英国はこの冬例年になく降雨量が多かった England had unusually heavy *rainfall* this winter.

ごうう 豪雨 heavy rainⓊⒸ, downpourⒸ; (滝のような雨) torrential rainⓊⒸ; (突然の) cloudburstⒸ //局地的な集中豪雨 localized *torrential rain* / 豪雨でその列車は2時間遅れた The train was delayed two hours by *the heavy rain*.

こううん 幸運 (good) luck ⓤ, (good) fortune ⓤ ——幸運な lucky, fortunate 幸運にも luckily, fortunately
幸運に恵まれる be favored by *fortune* / 幸運をもたらす bring *good fortune [luck]*
私は思いがけない幸運をつかんだ I had a stroke of *good luck*.
幸運を祈るよ *Good luck (to you)*! / *I wish you good luck.*
彼は幸運なやつだ He's a *lucky* guy.
1,000人の中から選ばれるなんて、君は幸運だよ You *are lucky* to have been selected from among 1,000 people.
彼は幸運の星のもとに生まれた He was born under a *lucky [fortunate]* star.
幸運にも私たちは村に通じる道路に出た *Luckily* we hit a road which led to a village.
幸運の女神が私にほほえんだ「*Lady Lucky [Fortune]* smiled on me.

こううんき 耕耘機 cultivator ⓒ

こうえい¹ 光栄 honor, (英) honour ⓤ (また an ～), (公式的) privilege ⓒ ⓤ /ご招待いただいて光栄に存じます It's a great *honor* to be invited. / 大統領にインタビューできたのは光栄だった It was a *privilege* to be able to interview the President.
◆お会いできてたいへん光栄です I *am*「*greatly honored* [*very glad*] to meet you.

こうえい² 公営 ——公営の public ‖公営住宅 (総称)《米》public housing,《英》council flat [house] / (個々の) a unit of public housing

こうえい³ 後衛 〖スポーツ〗back (player) ⓒ; 〖軍事〗the rear (guard)

こうえき 公益 ‖公益事業 a public utility [service] / 公益法人 a public corporation

こうえん¹ 公園 park ⓒ /国立公園 *a national park* / 上野公園 Ueno *Park* (✜特定の公園名にはふつう the を付けない)
🇪「犬を公園の中へ入れてもいいですか」「いいえ、許可されていません」"Can I take my dog into *the park*?" "No, dogs are not allowed."

こうえん² 講演 lecture ⓒ; (演説) speech ⓒ ——講演する give* a *lecture*, *lecture* ⓘ /日米貿易交渉に関する連続講演 a series of *lectures on* U.S.-Japan trade negotiations / 岡博士があす講演する予定です Dr. Oka is due to *give a lecture* tomorrow.
◆彼は米国の大学で日本の政治について講演した He *spoke* on Japanese politics at a university in the United States.
‖講演会 a lecture meeting / 講演者 a lecturer, a speaker

こうえん³ 後援 support ⓤ, backing ⓒ; (金銭的な) sponsorship ⓤ ——後援する support ⓘ, back (up); sponsor ⓘ /この展覧会は地元の新聞社が後援している This exhibition is sponsored by a local newspaper. / その美術展はフランス大使館の後援で開催された The art exhibition was held *under the sponsorship of* the French Embassy.
‖後援会 a supporters' association; (芸能人の) a fan club / 後援者 a backer, a supporter; (金銭的な) a sponsor

こうえん⁴ 公演 performance ⓒ ——公演する perform ⓘ ‖定期公演 a regularly scheduled *performance* / 私たちは時々海外で公演します We sometimes *perform* [*put on a performance*] abroad.
◆その演劇は長期公演が続いている That play has had *a long run*.

こうえん⁵ 好演 excellent performance ⓒ
◆彼は貧しい芸術家の役を好演した He *performed* the role of a poor artist *excellently*.

こうおつ 甲乙 その絵はどちらもとてもよく描けていて甲乙つけがたい Both pictures are painted very well and I *can't tell which is better*.

こうおん¹ 高音 high(-pitched) note ⓒ; (音符上の) high tone ⓒ; (合唱団の) treble ⓤ /この高音は私には出せない This *high note* is beyond my range.

こうおん² 高温 high temperature ⓒ /この物質は高温に耐えられる This material can withstand *high temperatures*.
◆日本の夏は高温多湿だ It is *hot and humid* in summer in Japan.

こうおん³ 恒温 ‖恒温動物 a warm-blooded animal

ごうおん 轟音 roar ⓒ /轟音とともに爆発する explode with *a roar*
◆トラックが轟音を立てて通り過ぎた The truck *roared* past. / The truck went past, *making a roaring sound*.

こうか¹ 効果 effect ⓒ ⓤ ——効果的な effective ——効果的に effectively, with effect
政府の政策はインフレに効果がなかった The government's policy *had no effect on* the inflation.
薬の効果が現れ始めた The medicine began to *take effect*.
英語を覚えるのに何か効果的な方法を教えてください Please tell me some *effective* ways to learn English.
適量の酒は体によいが飲みすぎは逆効果だ A moderate amount of alcohol is good for your health, but drinking too much has *the opposite effect*.
‖効果音 sound effects / 温室効果 the greenhouse effect / 特殊効果 special effects / 舞台効果 stage effects

こうか² 校歌 school song ⓒ ⓤ,《米》alma mater [ǽlmə mɑ́ːtər] ⓒ

こうか³ 降下 descent ⓒ ⓤ, fall ⓒ ——降下する descend ⓘ ◆パラシュートで降下する *make a parachute jump*

こうか⁴ 高価 ——高価な expensive; costly (✜通例悪い意味で用いられる); (価値のある) valuable /高価な時計 an *expensive* watch

こうか⁵ 高架 ‖高架線 overhead wires / 高架鉄道 an overhead railway,《米》an elevated railroad, an el / 高架道路《米》an overpass,《英》a flyover

こうか⁶ 硬化 〖医学〗 sclerosis [skləróusis] ⓒⓊ (複 scleroses) ――硬化する harden ⓐ, stiffen ⓐ /態度を硬化させる stiffen one's attitude
‖動脈硬化 hardening of the arteries, arteriosclerosis

こうか⁷ 硬貨 coin ⓒ /記念硬貨 a commemorative coin / 硬貨で払う pay with coins / この自動販売機は500円硬貨が使える This vending machine accepts 500-yen coins.

こうが 黄河 the Huang He [hwàːŋ hə́ː], the Yellow River

ごうか 豪華 ――豪華な（高級な）deluxe; (ぜいたくな) luxurious; (華やかな) gorgeous; (壮麗な) splendid /豪華なホテル a deluxe [luxurious] hotel / 豪華なドレス a gorgeous dress / きょうの夕食はずいぶん豪華だね What a luxurious dinner tonight!
‖豪華客船 a luxury ship / 豪華版 a deluxe edition

こうカード 好カード drawing card ⓒ

こうかい¹ 後悔 regret ⓒⓊ; (良心の呵責(ㄎ㉈)) remorse Ⓤ ――後悔する regret ⓐ, be [feel*] sorry (for ...) (◆後者のほうが口語的); (悔いる) repent ⓐⓘ
私は自分のしたことを後悔しています I regret what I did. / I'm sorry for what I did.
彼はひとりでパーティーに来たことを後悔した He regretted coming to the party alone.
彼女は両親を裏切ったことを深く後悔していた She was filled with remorse for [over] betraying her parents.
彼は後になって暴言を吐いたことを後悔した He repented of his rude remarks later.
ことわざ 後悔先に立たず It's (much) too late for regrets.; It's no use crying over spilt milk. (→こぼれた牛乳を嘆いてもしかたがない)

こうかい² 航海 (長期の) voyage [vɔ́iidʒ] ⓒ; (遊覧) cruise ⓒ; (帆船などでの) sailings; (船旅) passage ⓒ ――航海する make* a voyage; sail /世界一周の航海に出る make [take, go on] a voyage around the world / 私たちは北へ向かって航海している We are sailing to the north.
◆彼は航海に出ている He is at sea.
‖航海士 a mate / 航海日誌 a logbook / 処女航海 a maiden voyage

こうかい³ 公開 ――公開する (施設などを) open ⓐ, (展示する) exhibit ⓐ; (映画などを) release ⓐ, come* out /その施設の一部がマスコミに公開された Part of the facilities was opened to the media. / その会議の議事録は一般に公開されている The minutes of the meeting are open to the public. (◆「公開されている」という状態を表す場合は ×be opened とはいわない) / その美術館では日本各地の陶器が公開されている The museum exhibits pottery from every part of Japan. / Pottery from every part of Japan is on display at the museum. / その映画は来月公開予定な The film is due to 「come out [be released] next month.
◆その事故に関する情報の公開が強く求められている The disclosure of information about the accident is badly needed.
‖公開講座 an extension (course) / 公開状 an open letter / 公開捜査 an open criminal investigation / 公開討論会 an open forum / 公開放送 public broadcasting / 公開録音 a public recording

こうかい⁴ 公海 the high seas, international waters

こうがい¹ 公害 (environmental) pollution Ⓤ
公害をなくす get rid of pollution / 公害を引き起こす cause pollution; pollute
そのテレビ番組では騒音公害の問題を取り上げていた The TV program dealt with noise pollution.
‖公害対策 antipollution measures / 公害病 a pollution-related disease / 公害病認定患者 an officially certified patient of a pollution disease / 公害防止条例 pollution control ordinance / 公害問題 a pollution problem / 産業公害 industrial pollution / 低公害車 a low-polluting car, an eco-friendly car / 無公害工場 a pollution-free factory

こうがい² 郊外 (近郊) the suburbs; (1 地区) suburb ⓒ; (町はずれ) the outskirts /東京郊外にある大学 a university in the suburbs of Tokyo / 大阪郊外の住宅地に住む live in a residential suburb of Osaka / その事件は静かな郊外で起こった The incident occurred in a quiet suburb.

こうがい³ 口外 ――口外する (言う) tell* ⓐ; (秘密などをもらす) let* out /口外しないと約束するよ I promise not to tell.

ごうかい 豪快 豪快に笑う laugh heartily / その力士は相手力士を豪快に投げ飛ばした The sumo wrestler threw his opponent powerfully.

ごうがい 号外 an extra (issue of a newspaper) /号外を出す issue [publish] an extra

こうかいどう 公会堂 public hall ⓒ; (市・町の)・town hall ⓒ

こうかがくスモッグ 光化学スモッグ photochemical smog Ⓤ

こうかく 降格 relegation Ⓤ, demotion ⓒ ――降格する downgrade ⓐ, relegate ⓐ, demote ⓐ /そのチームは去年2部リーグに降格された The team was relegated to the second division.

こうがく¹ 工学 engineering Ⓤ ‖工学部 the department of engineering / 遺伝子工学 genetic engineering / 化学工学 chemical engineering / 機械工学 mechanical engineering / 社会工学 social engineering / 電気工学 electrical engineering / 土木工学 civil engineering

こうがく² 光学 optics Ⓤ ――光学の optical ‖光学機器 optical instruments

こうがく³ 後学 後学のために話を聞かせてほしいな I want you to tell me the story for my future reference.

こうがく⁴ 高額 ‖高額紙幣 a bill of a high

denomination / 高額所得 high income / 高額所得者 a person with high income

こうかく 合格 pass Ⓤ, success Ⓤ ━━合格する pass 圓他, succeed 圓
英語の試験に合格する *pass in* English / オーディションに合格する *pass* an audition / 三重大学に合格する *pass* [*succeed in*] the entrance examination for [to, of] Mie University (❖ ×pass Mie University とはいわない)

◆合格発表はいつですか When will *the results of the exam be announced*? / 私は明治大学の合格圏内にいる I *am within the acceptable range* for Meiji University.

🗨「入試に合格したよ」「それはよかったね、おめでとう！」"I *passed* the entrance examination." "That's wonderful news. Congratulations!"

‖合格者 a successful candidate / 合格点 a passing mark / 合格率 the ratio of successful applicants

こうがくしん 向学心 a love of learning
◆みんな向学心に燃えていた Everyone *was very eager to learn*.

こうがくねん 高学年 the upper grades
こうかくるい 甲殻類〖動物〗crustacean
こうかくレンズ 広角レンズ〖写真〗wide-angle lens
こうかつ 狡猾 ━━狡猾な cunning, sly ‖狡猾な策略 a *cunning* trick

こうかん¹ 交換
exchange Ⓤ Ⓒ, change Ⓒ, 《口語的》swap Ⓒ; (新しい物と取り換えること) replacement Ⓤ; (物々交換) barter Ⓤ ━━交換する exchange 他, change 他, swap 他, trade 他; replace 他, renew 他
タイヤを交換する *change* a tire
私のブローチとあなたのブレスレット，交換しない？ Won't you *exchange* [*trade*] your bracelet *for* my brooch?
私と席を交換してくれませんか Would you *exchange* seats *with* me? (❖seat のように同種の物を交換する場合は複数形を用いる)
私は彼と贈り物を交換した I *swapped* [*exchanged*] gifts *with* him.
我々は情報と意見を交換し合った We *exchanged* information and ideas.
うちは古い電話機を新しいコードレスに交換した We *have replaced* our old phone *with* a new cordless one.
私たちの学校は3人のアメリカ人を交換留学生として受け入れた Our school accepted three Americans as *exchange* students.
◆この腕時計は電池を交換しないといけない(→新しい電池が必要だ) This watch *requires* a new battery.
‖交換条件 a bargaining point / 交換レンズ（カメラの）an interchangeable lens / 電話交換手 a telephone operator / 電話交換台 a switchboard

こうかん² 好感 good [favorable, agreeable] impression Ⓒ, favor, 《英》favour Ⓤ ‖その少年の態度は人々に好感を与えた The boy's behavior made *a favorable impression* on people.
◆好感のもてる青年 a *likable* [*pleasant*] young man / 彼女は明に好感をいだいている She has *friendly feelings* for Akira.
こうかん³ 高官 high official
ごうかん¹ 厚顔 厚顔無恥な男 a shameless [brazen] man
こうかん² 睾丸 the testicles
ごうかん 強姦 rape Ⓤ Ⓒ;〖法律〗assault Ⓒ ━━強姦する rape 他
こうがんざい 抗癌剤 anticancer agent Ⓒ
こうかんしんけい 交感神経〖解剖・生理〗sympathetic nerve Ⓒ ‖副交感神経 a parasympathetic nerve

こうき¹ 好機 (good) opportunity Ⓤ Ⓒ, (good) chance Ⓒ ‖一生にまたとない好機 *the chance* of a lifetime / 好機を逸する miss *the chance* / 好機を待つ wait for *a chance*; bide *one's time* / 好機がめぐってきた *A good chance* presented itself.

慣用表現 好機逸すべからず *Make hay while the sun shines.*(→干し草は日が照っているうちに作れ)

こうき² 後期 the latter [second] half (of the period); (2学期制の) the second semester ━━後期の late ‖室町時代後期 the *late* Muromachi period
◆後期印象派 *Post-*Impressionism
‖後期試験 the second semester examination
こうき³ 高貴 nobility Ⓤ ━━高貴な noble ‖高貴な生まれの人 a person of *noble* birth
こうき⁴ 後記 postscript ‖編集後記 editor's note [postscript]
こうき⁵ 校旗 school flag Ⓒ
こうき⁶ 綱紀（公人の規律）(official) discipline Ⓤ ‖綱紀を粛正する enforce (*official*) *discipline*

こうぎ¹ 抗議 protest Ⓤ; (反対) objection Ⓒ ━━抗議する protest 圓他; object 圓他
彼らは核実験に抗議した They「*made a protest* [*protested*] *against* the nuclear test.
地元の人々は新空港の建設に強く抗議している The local people strongly *object to* the construction of a new airport.
彼らは抗議デモを行った They staged a「*protest march* [*demonstration*].
◆賃金カットに抗議してストをする strike *against* a wage cut / 彼は審判に抗議した He *appealed to* the umpire.
‖抗議集会 a protest rally / 抗議声明 a statement of protest / 抗議文 a note of protest

こうぎ² 講義 lecture Ⓒ ━━講義する give* a lecture ‖講義をサボる cut [skip] *a lecture* / フェミニズムについて講義する give *a lecture* on feminism / 彼の講義には興味がわかなかった His *lecture* didn't interest me. / 学生たちは講義のノートをとった The students took [made] notes at *the lecture.* Ⓒ
こうぎ³ 広義 broad [wide] sense Ⓒ ‖…を広

こうきあつ 高気圧〔気象〕high pressure

こうきしん 好奇心 curiosity／好奇心をそそる arouse [excite] one's curiosity
◆恵美は好奇心がとても強い Emi is 「very *curious* [full *of curiosity*].
🔑「なぜそんなこと聞くの」「単なる好奇心からさ」"Why do you ask that?" "Just out of *curiosity*."

こうきゅう¹ 高級 ——高級な high-class, high-grade; (高品質の) (high-)quality; (高価な) expensive; (店などが) exclusive (✦「一部の(裕福な)人だけが利用する」というニュアンスがある)
高級ホテル an *exclusive* hotel ／ 高級ブティック an *exclusive* boutique
彼はいかにも高級感のある時計をしている He wears a watch that *looks very expensive*.
◆高級リゾート地 a *fashionable* resort ／ 彼の話は私には高級すぎる(→知的すぎて理解できない) His story was too *intellectual* [*deep*] for me.／ 彼女は高級住宅地に住んでいる She lives in *a wealthy neighborhood*.
‖高級官僚 a high-ranking official ／ 高級車 a high-class car, a prestige car ／ 高級品 quality goods, an article of high quality

こうきゅう² 恒久 permanence Ⓤ ——恒久的な permanent, lasting ‖恒久の平和 a *permanent* [*lasting*] peace

こうきゅう³ 高給 high salary Ⓒ, high pay Ⓤ ／高給をもらって働く work for *high pay*
‖高給取り a highly paid worker

こうきゅう⁴ 硬球 hardball

ごうきゅう 号泣 ——号泣する wail ⓘ

こうきゅうび 公休日 public holiday Ⓒ, 《米》national holiday Ⓒ, 《英》bank holiday Ⓒ

こうきょ 皇居 the Imperial Palace ‖皇居前広場 the Imperial Palace Square

こうきょう¹ 公共 the public; (共通の) common ‖公共の土地 *common* land ／ 公共の福祉 *public* welfare ／ 公共交通機関 《主に米》*public* transportation, 《英》*public* transport ／ そのような発言は公共の場でなされるべきではなかった Such a statement shouldn't have been made in a *public* place.
‖公共機関 a public institution ／ 公共事業 public works, a public-works project ／ 公共施設 public facilities ／ 公共団体 a public corporation ／ 公共投資 public investment ／ 公共料金 public utility charges, utilities

こうきょう² 好況 (繁栄) prosperity Ⓤ; (にわか景気) boom Ⓒ ／当時は鉄鋼業界が好況を呈していた The steel industry showed signs of *prosperity* in those days.

こうぎょう¹ 工業 industry Ⓤ Ⓒ ——工業の industrial
阪神工業地帯 the Hanshin *Industrial* District ／ 日本の主要な工業都市 chief *industrial cities* in Japan
工業は19世紀に著しく発展した *Industry* greatly developed in the 19th century.
◆先進工業国 an *industrialized nation* [*country*] ／ 電子工業はわが国の代表的産業の一つである *Electronics* is one of our country's main industries.
‖工業化 industrialization ／ 工業技術 technology ／ 工業高校 a technical high school ／ 工業国 an industrial nation ／ 工業生産 industrial production ／ 工業製品 industrial products ／ 工業団地 an industrial park ／ 工業地区 an industrial area ／ 工業デザイナー an industrial designer ／ 工業用水 water for industrial use ／ 家内工業 a cottage industry ／ 軽工業 light industry ／ 重工業 heavy industry ／ 日本工業規格 Japanese Industrial Standard (《略語》JIS)

こうぎょう² 興行 (上演) performance Ⓤ; (見せ物) show Ⓒ ——興行する perform ⓜ, play ⓜ ‖地方興行 a road show ／ 5大都市で興行する *play* [*give performances in*] five large cities ◆サーカスを興行する *present* [*put on*] a circus

こうぎょう³ 鉱業 mining Ⓤ, the mining industry ‖鉱業所 a mining station

こうきょうがく 交響楽 symphony Ⓒ ‖交響楽団 a symphony orchestra

こうきょうきょく 交響曲〔音楽〕symphony Ⓒ ‖モーツァルトの交響曲第40番 Mozart's *Symphony No. 40*

こうきん¹ 公金 public money Ⓤ, public funds ‖公金を横領する embezzle *public money*

こうきん² 抗菌 ——抗菌性の antibacterial ‖抗菌グッズ *antibacterial* products

ごうきん 合金 alloy Ⓒ Ⓤ ‖真ちゅうは銅と亜鉛との合金である Brass is *an alloy* of copper and zinc.

こうぐ 工具 tool Ⓒ ‖工具一式 a *tool* kit ‖工具箱 a toolbox

こうくう 航空 (航空術) aviation [èiviéiʃən] Ⓤ ‖民間航空 civil *aviation* ／ 航空網が発達したおかげで世界中どこへでも行けるようになった The development of *aviation* networks has made it possible to go anywhere in the world.◆航空便でベスに手紙を出した I sent a letter to Beth *by airmail*.
‖航空宇宙産業 the aerospace industry ／ 航空運賃 an airfare ／ 航空会社 an airline (company) (✦会社名に使うときはしばしば Airlines, Airways で単数扱い) ／ 航空貨物 (an) air cargo ／ 航空管制官 an air traffic controller ／ 航空管制塔 a (control) tower ／ 航空機 (一般に空を飛ぶ乗り物) an aircraft ／ (特に飛行機) an airplane, a plane ／ 航空券 an airline ticket ／ 航空工学 aeronautical engineering ／ 航空産業 the aviation industry ／ 航空自衛隊 Air Self-Defense Force ／ 航空写真 an aerial [air] photograph ／ 航空測量 an aerial survey ／ 航空母艦 an aircraft carrier ／ 航空輸送 air transportation ／ 航空路 an air lane, an airway

こうぐう 厚遇 (warm) reception Ⓒ, hospitality [U] ―厚遇する receive hospitably ∥私はそこで特別な客として厚遇された I *was received hospitably* as a special guest there.

こうけい[1] 光景 sight [C]; (見晴らし) view [C]; (出来事の場面) scene [C]; (印象的な) spectacle [C] ∥恐ろしい光景 *an* awful *scene* [*sight*] / ぞっとする光景 *an* appalling *scene* [*sight*] / 痛ましい光景 *a* cruel *scene* [*sight*] / ありふれた光景 *a* common *sight* / ロッキー山脈の雄大な光景 *the* grand *spectacle* of the Rockies / 私はこれまでこんなに美しい光景を見たことがない I have never seen such *a* beautiful *sight* in all my life. / 濃い霧が湖の光景を覆い隠した A thick fog obscured *the view* of the lake.

こうけい[2] 口径 (レンズ) aperture [C]; (銃口) caliber [C] ∥12口径の銃 a 12-*caliber* gun

こうげい 工芸 (industrial) arts; (手芸) craft [C] ‖工芸家 an industrial artist, a craftsman, an artisan / 工芸品 a craft work / 伝統工芸 traditional arts [crafts]

ごうけい 合計 the sum, total [C] [U] (❖ the sum は単純に足していった数, total は(その時点での)最終的な総計というニュアンスがある) ―合計する add [sum, total] up

これを合計してください. 合計はいくらになりますか Please *add up* these (figures). What's *the total*?

死者と行方不明者の合計は現在のところ5,000人を超えている *The total* of the dead and the missing is, at present, over 5,000.

私は服に合計1万円使った I spent *a total* of 10,000 yen on clothes.

◆生活費は合計でいくらになりますか How much do the living expenses *come to*?

「おいくらですか」「合計で800円になります」 "How much?" "Eight hundred yen *in all* [*altogether*]."

こうけいき 好景気 (繁栄) prosperity [U]; (にわか景気) boom [C]

◆この不況の中にあってもコンピュータ業界は好景気に沸いている The computer industry *is booming* in spite of the recession.

こうけいしゃ 後継者 successor [C]; (相続人) heir [éər] [C] ∥我々は現在, 彼の後継者を探しています We're presently searching for his *successor*.

こうゲーム 好ゲーム (接戦) close game [C], good game [C]

こうげき 攻撃 attack [C] [U], offense [U] ―攻撃する attack [他] [自] ―攻撃的な aggressive

先制攻撃 *a* preemptive *attack* / 武力攻撃 *an* armed *attack* / 奇襲攻撃 *a* surprise *attack* / 個人攻撃 *a* personal *attack* / 攻撃的な態度 an *aggressive* manner / 攻撃の的(まと) the target of *the attack* / …に攻撃を加える[開始する] make [open] *an attack* on [against] ... / 敵の背後を攻撃する *attack* the enemy in the rear

◆敵に総攻撃をかける make *an all-out assault* against the enemy / 政府の政策は野党から激しく攻撃された(→非難された) The government policy *was* sharply *criticized* by opposition parties. / (野球で)私たちのチームが攻撃中だ Our team *is* now *at bat*.

‖攻撃側 offense

[慣用表現] 攻撃は最大の防御である *The best defense is a strong offense.*

こうけつ 高潔 ―高潔な high(-minded), noble ∥高潔な人 a man of *high* character

ごうけつ 豪傑 (大胆不敵な) bold man [C]; (勇敢な) brave man [C]

◆豪傑笑いをする roar with laughter

こうけつあつ 高血圧 high blood pressure [U], 〔医学〕hypertension [U] ∥父は高血圧だ My father has *high blood pressure*.

こうけっか 好結果 good results ∥彼の様子から見て好結果が期待できそうだ By the look of him, we can expect *good results*.

こうけん 貢献 contribution [U] ―貢献する contribute [自], make* a contribution ∥日本の国際社会への貢献 Japan's *contribution to* the international community / 多田君は学園祭の成功に大いに貢献した Tada *has contributed* greatly *to* the success of our school festival.

こうげん[1] 高原 plateau [plætóu] [C] (複 ~s, plateaux), tableland [C]; (山岳地方) highlands; (高地・高台) heights ∥那須高原 *the* Nasu *Heights*

こうげん[2] 公言 profession [U] [C]; (断言) declaration [U] [C] ―公言する profess [他]; declare [他] ∥彼は自分には天分があると公言してはばからなかった He *professed himself* to be gifted.

こうげん[3] 光源 light source [C]

ごうけん 合憲 ―合憲の constitutional

こうけんにん 後見人 〔法律〕guardian [C]

こうこ 公庫 住宅金融公庫 the Government Housing Loan *Corporation* / 国民生活金融公庫 National Life Finance *Corporation*

こうご[1] 交互 ―交互に by turns, alternately ∥沿道には紅白の旗が交互に並んでいた Red and white flags were placed along the street *alternately*. ◆父と兄が交互に車を運転した My father and brother *took turns* (*at*) *driving* the car. / 男女交互に並びなさい Line up *boy-girl boy-girl*.

こうご[2] 口語 the spoken [colloquial] language ―口語の spoken, colloquial ∥口語的表現 a *colloquial* expression

‖口語体 (a) colloquial style

ごうご 豪語 (大言壮語する) talk big; (自慢する) boast [他] ∥彼は自分が学校でいちばん速く走れると豪語している He *boasts* that he is the fastest runner in his school.

こうこう[1] 高校 (senior) high school [C]

工業[商業]高校 *a* technical [commercial] *high school* / 高校へ入学する enter (*a*) *high school* / 高校を卒業する graduate from (*a*) *high school*

姉は高校へ通っています My sister goes to *high school*.

弟は高校1年生です My brother is a first-

year student at [of] *high school*. 僕らは高校時代よくいっしょに遊んでいた We used to run around together *when we were in high school*.
彼は高校を出ると家業を継いだ He succeeded to the family business after finishing *high school*.
∥高校生 a high school student / 高校中退者 a high school dropout / 高校入試 a high school entrance examination

こうこう² 孝行 孝行息子[娘] a *dutiful* son [daughter](✤ dutiful は「忠実な, 義務を果たす」の意味)/ おじさんは僕の顔を見るといつも「親孝行するんだよ」と言う When my uncle sees me, he always says, "*Be good to your parents. [Take care of your parents.]*"
ことわざ 孝行のしたい時分に親はなし You never miss your parents until they're gone [dead].

こうこう³ 航行 navigation, sailing ──航行する navigate, sail ∥星を頼りに航行する *navigate* by the stars / 船は沿岸沿いに航行した The ship *sailed* along the coast.

こうこう⁴ 皓々・煌々 ──こうこうと(明るく) bright(ly); (まぶしいほど) brilliantly ∥夜空に月がこうこうと輝いている In the night sky the moon is shining *bright(ly)*. / 遠くにこうこうと光るネオンが見える I can see the neon lights shining *brilliantly* far away.

こうこう⁵ 後攻 後攻になる(→先に守備につく) take to the field first / うちのチームが後攻です Our team *fields first*.

こうごう¹ 皇后 empress ∥皇后陛下 Her Majesty *the Empress*

ごうごう¹ 轟々 滝がごうごうと水しぶきを上げている The waterfall is *roaring [thundering]* and whipping up spray.

ごうごう² 囂々 ごうごうたる(→厳しい)非難を浴びる be showered with *bitter [devastating]* criticism

こうごうしい 神々しい divine; (神聖な) holy; (畏敬(い)の念をいだかせる) awe-inspiring ──神々しく divinely ∥その晩は月が神々しく輝いていた The moon shone *divinely* that night.

こうごうせい 光合成 〔生物〕 photosynthesis

こうこうやきゅう 高校野球

日本ではプロ野球のほかに高校野球も人気があります。年に2回, 春と夏に全国高校野球大会が兵庫県にある甲子園球場で開かれ, 都道府県の代表校が出場します。試合の模様は全国にテレビ中継され, 連日何万もの人々が球場を訪れます。High school baseball is very popular in Japan in addition to professional baseball. Twice a year, in summer and spring, the National Senior High School Baseball Tournament is held at Koshien Stadium in Hyogo Prefecture. The chosen teams represent their prefectures. The games are telecast nationwide and many thousands of people visit the stadium every day.

こうこがく 考古学 archaeology ∥考古学者 an archaeologist

こうこく¹ 広告 advertisement,《口語的》ad ──広告する advertise
人目を引く広告 *a* prominent [*an* outstanding] *advertisement* / 車[店]の広告 an *advertisement* for a car [store]
雑誌の求人広告に応募した I answered *a help-wanted ad* in the magazine.
彼は販売員募集の広告を出した He 「*put out an ad* [*advertised*] *for* a salesclerk.
新聞に広告を出すのに200万円かかった It cost us two million yen to *advertise* [*run an ad*] *in* the newspaper.
◆広告のちらし an *advertising* flyer
∥広告キャンペーン an advertising campaign / 広告業 advertising (business) / 広告業者 an advertising agent / 広告収入 advertising revenue / 広告代理店 an advertising agency / 広告主 an advertiser; (スポンサー) a sponsor / 広告面 an advertising page / 広告欄 an advertisement column / 広告料 an advertisement rate / 意見広告 an opinion advertisement / 折り込み広告 an (advertising) insert, an insertion / 企業広告 a corporate advertisement / 個人広告 a personal advertisement / 誇大広告 an exaggerated advertisement / 新聞広告 a newspaper advertisement / 全面広告 a full-page advertisement / 比較広告 comparative advertising

こうこく² 公告 public notice [announcement]

こうこつ 恍惚 聴衆は彼女の名演奏に恍惚として聞き入った The audience listened to her playing *in ecstasy*. / 彼女は山に沈む夕日に恍惚として見とれていた She *was* 「*in rapture at* [*enchanted by*] the sight of the sunset in the mountains.

ごうコン 合コン 今晩男子テニス部と女子テニス部の合コンがある The male and female tennis clubs *will have a party together* tonight.

こうさ¹ 交差 crossing, intersection (✤「交差点」の意味では) ──交差する cross, intersect ∥立体交差 *an* overhead *crossing* / ナイフとフォークを交差させて皿に置く *cross one's* knife and fork on *one's* plate / この通りは, すぐそこで国道6号線と交差します This street *crosses* Route 6 right up there. / パン屋は交差点の少し先です The bakery is a little past *the crossing* [*intersection*].
◆この2本の線は互いに交差している These two lines *cut across* each other.

こうさ² 考査 test, 《公式的》examination

こうざ¹ 口座 account ∥普通預金口座 *a* savings *account* / 銀行に口座を開く[解約する] open [close] *an account* with the bank /

料金を銀行口座に振り込む transfer [pay] the charge into *the* bank *account* / 私は銀行口座から1万円引き出した I withdrew [drew] 10,000 yen from *my* bank *account*.
‖口座番号 one's bank account number

こうざ² 講座 (放送・出版物の) course ⓒ; (大学の) chair ⓒ / 英文法の集中講座 *an intensive course* in English grammar / ラジオの英語講座を聴き始めて3年になる I have listened to *a* radio English *course* for three years. / 彼はその大学で心理学の講座を担当している He holds *the chair* of psychology at the university.
‖公開講座 an extension course / 通信講座 a correspondence course

こうさい¹ 交際 association ⓤ; (親交) company ⓤ; (友好関係) friendship ⓤⓒ ——交際する associate ⓘ, hang* around [about]; (恋人として) go* out with ..., see*
10年来の交際 *a friendship* of 10 years
英語のネイティブスピーカーと交際していたおかげで彼の英語力はぐんと高まった His *association with* native speakers of English helped to improve his English remarkably.
両親が信夫との交際を許してくれない My parents won't allow me to *go out with* Nobuo.
息子が不良グループと交際していることに気づきませんでした I didn't notice that my son "hung around [was mixed up] with the gang.
もう彼女とは交際していません I'm not seeing her anymore.
彼とは交際を断つべきだ You'd better *break off your friendship* with him.
◆健二は交際範囲が広い Kenji has *a large circle of friends*.
‖交際費 social expenses; (娯楽費) entertainment expenses

こうさい² 公債 public bond [loan] ⓒ

こうざい¹ 功罪 advantages and disadvantages / 功罪相半ばする The *advantages and disadvantages* offset each other.
◆その本では教育制度の功罪が論じられている *The good and bad points* of the educational system are dealt with in the book.

こうざい² 鋼材 steel ⓤ

こうさく¹ 工作 (作ること) handicrafts; (働きかけ) maneuver ⓒ, move ⓒ ——工作する make* ⓘ, maneuver ⓘ, move ⓘ / 政治工作 a political *maneuver*; political *manipulation* / 秘密工作 a secret *maneuver* / 和平工作 a peace *move* / 工作の時間 a *handicrafts [crafts]* class / 彼は選挙戦が有利に運ぶように裏で工作した He *maneuvered behind the scenes* to improve his chances of winning in the election.
‖工作機械 a machine tool / 工作室 a shop, a workshop / 工作机 a workbench / 図画工作 arts and crafts

こうさく² 交錯 彼女の心の中では不安と期待が交錯していた She had a feeling of expectation *mingled with* worry.

こうさく³ 耕作 cultivation ⓤ ——耕作する cultivate ⓘ, work ⓘ; (すきを使って) plow [pláu] ⓘⓘ / 多くの人が移住してその土地の開発と耕作を行った A lot of people moved there to develop and *work* the land.
‖耕作機械 a cultivator / 耕作地 cultivated land

こうさつ¹ 考察 (考慮) consideration ⓤ; (検討) examination ⓒⓤ; (研究) study ⓒ ——考察する consider ⓘ; examine ⓘ; study ⓘ / 流行の変遷に関する一考察 *a study* of the changes in fashions / 問題に十分な考察を加える give careful *consideration* to a matter / 彼の提案は真剣に考察するに値する His suggestion deserves serious *consideration*.

こうさつ² 絞殺 strangulation ⓒ ——絞殺する strangle ⓘ

こうさん¹ 公算 probability ⓤⓒ, chance ⓤ / 彼が成功する公算は全く[ほとんど]ない There is no [little] *chance* of his succeeding. (❖「公算が大きい[小さい]」は a high [low] probability という)

こうさん² 降参 surrender ⓒⓤ ——降参する surrender ⓘ, give* in, (口語的) throw* in the towel; (あきらめる) give* up 降参だ *I give up*. / (→君の勝ちだ) *You win*.
🔊「降参か？」「まだまだ」"Do you *give up*?" "No!"

こうざん¹ 高山 high mountain ⓒ ‖高山植物 an alpine plant / 高山病 altitude sickness

こうざん² 鉱山 mine ‖産出量の多い鉱山 *a rich mine*
‖鉱山労働者 a miner

こうし¹ 講師 lecturer ⓒ, 《米》instructor ⓒ / 非常勤講師 *a part-time lecturer [teacher]* / 彼はその大学に専任講師として招かれた He was asked to join the university as *a full-time instructor*.

こうし² 行使 (武力などの) use ⓤ (また a ~), (公式的) employment ⓤ; (権力などの) (公式的) the exercise ——行使する use ⓘ, 《公式的》employ ⓘ; exercise ⓘ / 国連の名による武力の行使 *the employment [use] of force* under the name of the UN / 大統領は拒否権を行使した The president *exercised* his veto.

こうし³ 格子 (窓や戸の) lattice ⓒ; (鉄格子) grating ⓒ, grille ⓒ, grid ⓒ ‖格子縞(縞) (a) check / 格子戸 a lattice door / 格子窓 a lattice window

こうし⁴ 公私 public and private matters ‖公私混同する mix *public and private matters*

こうし⁵ 公使 minister ⓒ ‖駐日ロシア公使 *the* Russian *Minister* to Japan
‖公使館 a legation / 公使館員(個人) a member of the staff of a legation; (集合的に) the staff of a legation

こうし⁶ 子牛 calf [kǽf] ⓒ (複 calves)

こうじ¹ 工事 construction (work) ⓤ, works
土木工事 civil engineering *works* / 道路工

事 road construction /
工事中《掲示》Under Construction /
あの橋は今工事中です That bridge is *under construction* now. /
建設工事はほぼ終了している The construction work is practically finished. /
‖工事現場 a construction site

こうじ² 公示 official [public] announcement ―公示する announce officially [publicly] /あした総選挙が公示される The general election *will* ⌈*begin with the official announcement* [*officially begin*]⌉ tomorrow. /
‖公示価格 the declared value; (原油の) the posted price

こうじ³ 麹 koji, a form of yeast derived from sake or barley used in making soy sauce, sake, and *miso*

こうしき¹ 公式 (数学などの) formula (複 ~s, formulae) ―公式の (正式な) formal; (公務の) official ―公式に formally; officially /公式発表 a *formal* [an *official*] announcement / 公式記録 an *official* record / 公式の認可を得る get *official* permission / 公式訪問をする pay a *formal* [*state*] visit / 彼の引退が公式に発表された His retirement has been announced *officially* [*publicly*]. / 数学の小テストに備えて公式の復習をしなければならない I have to review some *formulas* for a math quiz. /
‖公式戦 a regular-season game, an official game

こうしき² 硬式 (❖欧米には「軟式」の野球・テニスがないので baseball, tennis は「硬式」を指す) /硬式テニス tennis / 硬式野球 baseball

こうせい 高姿勢 (高圧的な態度) high-handed attitude /彼は交渉の場で高姿勢に出た He took *a high-handed attitude* in the negotiations.

こうしつ 皇室 the Imperial [Royal] Family

こうじつ 口実 (言い訳) excuse; (真実を隠すための) pretext /もっともらしい口実 *a plausible excuse* / 口実をもうける invent *excuses* / 外出する口実を見つけなくては I have to find *an excuse* for going out. / 彼は頭が痛いという口実で学校を休んだ He was absent from school *on the pretext that* he had a headache.

こうして ナイフとフォークはこうして使うんです You should use your knife and fork ⌈*in this way* [*like this*].⌉ / 彼はこうして金持ちになった *That is how* he became a rich man.

こうしゃ¹ 校舎 school building; (村の小さな学校の) schoolhouse

こうしゃ² 後者 the latter (↔the former) /この二つの解決策のうちでは後者のほうがいいと思う Of these two solutions, I prefer *the latter* (one).

こうしゃ³ 公社 public corporation

-ごうしゃ -号車 食堂車は8号車です The dining car is *car number eight*.

こうしゃく¹ 公爵 duke; (英国以外の)

prince /公爵夫人 a duchess; (英国以外の) a princess

こうしゃく² 侯爵 marquess [máːrkwis]; (英国以外の) marquis [máːrkwəs] /
‖侯爵夫人 a marchioness [máːrʃənəs]; (英国以外の) a marquise [maːrkíːz]

こうしゃほう 高射砲 antiaircraft gun

こうしゅ 攻守 offense and defense; (野球の) batting and fielding

こうしゅう¹ 講習 (training) course, class ◆この夏休みは夏期講習を受けなければならない I have to take *summer school* this summer vacation. /
‖講習会 a class, a course, a workshop

こうしゅう² 公衆 the public ―公衆の public /彼らは公衆の面前で口論を始めた They began to quarrel with each other *in public*. /
‖公衆衛生 public health [hygiene] / 公衆電話 a public telephone, a pay phone / 公衆道徳 public morality / 公衆便所 a public restroom; (男性用) a men's room; (女性用) a women's room / 公衆浴場 a public bath

こうしゅう³ 口臭 bad [foul] breath; 〔医学〕halitosis /口臭がある have bad [foul] breath

こうしゅうは 高周波〔電気〕high frequency

こうしゅけい 絞首刑 hanging ◆彼は殺人罪で絞首刑になった He *was hanged* for murder.

こうじゅつ¹ 口述 ―口述する dictate ―口述の oral /彼は生徒に聖書の一節を口述して書き取らせた He *dictated* a passage from the Bible to the class. /
‖口述試験 an oral examination / 口述筆記 dictation

こうじゅつ² 後述 ―後述する say* [mention, write*] later /この問題に関しては後述する We'll mention this problem *later*.

こうしょ 高所 height 《しばしば複数形 ~s》, high place /彼女は高所恐怖症だ She *is afraid of heights*. / She *has acrophobia*. ◆状況を大所高所から見る *take a broad view of* the situation

こうじょ 控除 deduction, subtraction; (税金の) exemption ―控除する deduct, subtract; exempt /給料からの税の控除 the deduction [exemption] of taxes from *a person's* salary /
‖控除額 a deduction / 医療費控除 deduction for medical expenses / 基礎控除 a basic deduction / 所得控除 tax deductions and allowances / 配偶者控除 deduction for the spouse / 扶養控除 deduction for dependents

こうしょう¹ 交渉
❶【話し合い】negotiation 《しばしば複数形 ~s》, talks ―交渉する negotiate, talk; (かけ合う) bargain /労使間の交渉 *the negotiations* between labor and management / …と交渉を始め

open [enter into] *negotiations* with ... / …と交渉を続ける[打ち切る]「carry on [break off] *negotiations* with ... / 和平交渉を再開する renew *peace negotiations*
交渉は首尾よくまとまった *The negotiations* concluded successfully.
交渉はうまくいかなかった *The negotiations* didn't get anywhere.
交渉は新しい局面に入った *The negotiation* entered a new phase.
古田は新たな契約についてスワローズと交渉中だ Furuta *is negotiating* [*in negotiation*] *with* the Swallows on a new contract.
その件についてはまだ交渉中だ That matter is still *under negotiation*.
ついに両国が交渉の席についた At last both countries *sat down at the negotiating table*.
家主と家賃についての交渉をした I *negotiated* [*bargained*, *haggled*] *with* the landlord about the rent.
❷【人間関係】(接触) contact [U][C]; (関係) relations
最近彼とは全く交渉がない I have not been in *contact* [*touch*] with him recently.
‖外交交渉 diplomatic negotiations / 団体交渉 collective bargaining / 団体交渉権 right to bargain collectively / 予備交渉 preparatory negotiations

こうしょう[2] 高尚 ──高尚な (レベルが高い) high; (洗練された) elegant, refined //高尚な趣味 an *elegant* [a *refined*] taste
◆彼の演説は高尚すぎて私には理解できなかった His speech was too *advanced* for me to understand. / His speech was over my head. (❖over *a person's* head は「難しくて理解できない」の意味)

こうしょう[3] 校章 school badge [emblem, pin] [C]

こうしょう[4] 公証 ‖公証人 a notary (public) / 公証役場 a notary public's office

こうじょう[1] 工場 factory [C]; (大規模な) plant [C]; (製材・製紙などの) mill [C]; (ガラス・製鉄) works
自動車工場 *an* automobile *plant* / 工場で働く work at [in] *a factory* / 工場を経営する operate [run] *a factory*
この工場では自動車部品を生産している This *factory* produces automobile parts.
‖工場廃水 industrial waste water / ガラス工場 a glass works / 缶詰工場 a cannery / 自動車修理工場 an auto repair shop / 製紙工場 a paper mill / セメント工場 a cement plant

こうじょう[2] 向上 (品質などの) improvement [U][C]; (地位) rise [C][U] ──向上する improve [自], get* better //彼女の英語力は少しずつ向上している Her English *is* gradually *improving* [*getting better*]. / 彼女は向上心を持ち続けている She keeps having *a desire for self-improvement*.
◆各自動車メーカーは安全性の向上に努めている Every carmaker makes efforts to *improve* the safety of its cars. / 近年，女性の社会的な地位は向上したといわれている It is said that the social status of women *has risen* recently.

ごうじょう 強情 (言うことを聞かないこと) obstinacy [U]; (意志を変えないこと) stubbornness [U] ──強情な obstinate; stubborn // 強情な少年 a *stubborn* boy / どうしてそんなに強情をはるのか Why must you *be* so *obstinate*?

こうじょうせん 甲状腺 〘解剖〙 the thyroid [θáirɔid] (gland)

こうしょく[1] 公職 《公式的》(public) office [C][U] //公職に就く take [enter] *public office* / 公職に就いている hold *public office* / 公職を退く retire from *public office*
‖公職選挙法 the Public Office Election Law

こうしょく[2] 好色 ──好色な lecherous, lustful, 《公式的》libidinous ‖好色漢 a lecher / 好色文学 pornography, erotic literature

こうじる[1] 講じる 経済学を講じる *lecture* [*give a lecture*] *on* economics / 学校でのいじめを防止する対策を早急に講じなければならない We must *take* measures at once to prevent bullying in schools.

こうじる[2] 高じる 彼は趣味が高じて陶芸家になってしまった He got *so* interested in pottery that he became a potter.

こうしん[1] 交信 communication [U][C]; (連絡) contact [U][C] ──交信する communicate [他][自] //人と無線で交信する *communicate with* a person by radio / その飛行機との交信が途絶えた We lost *contact with* the plane.

こうしん[2] 行進 march [C]; (パレード) parade [C] ──行進する march [自]; parade [他][自] //彼らは市内の通りを行進した They *paraded* the streets of the city.
‖行進曲 a march

こうしん[3] 更新 renewal [U][C] ──更新する renew [他]; (記録を) break* [他] //運転免許証を更新する *renew one's* driving license / 彼女は200メートル走の世界記録を更新した She *broke* the world record for the 200-meter dash [sprint]. ◆最高[最低]記録を更新する *hit* a new high [low]

こうしん[4] 後進 (後輩) younger person [C], junior [C]; (若い世代) the younger generation //彼は辞任して後進に道を譲った He resigned his post to make way for *his younger people*.

こうじん 公人 public person [C]

こうしんこく 後進国 backward country [C] (❖軽蔑的なニュアンスがあるので，ふつう developing country (発展途上国)を用いる)

こうしんじょ 興信所 detective agency [C]; (商業用の) credit bureau [C]

こうしんりょう 香辛料 spice [C][U] ◆香辛料のきいた食べ物 *spicy* food

こうず 構図 composition [U]
◆この写真はうまく構図が取れている This photo *is* well *composed*. / 政官癒着(ゆちゃく)の構図が

こ

浮かび上がってきた *The* cozy *relationship* between some politicians and bureaucrats came to light.

こうすい[1] 香水 perfume [U] [C], 《主に英》scent [C] ‖香水1びん a bottle of *perfume* / 香水をつける[つけている] 「put on [wear] *perfume* / ハンカチは香水のいい香りがした The handkerchief was scented with *perfume*.

こうすい[2] 硬水 hard water [U]

こうずい 洪水 flood [C] ‖この町は去年洪水に襲われた This city suffered from 「*a flood* [*flooding*] last year. / 洪水で橋が流された The bridge was washed away by *the flood*. / 洪水で多くの村が水につかった *Flood waters* have swamped many villages. / 北京では毎朝, 自転車の洪水が見られる In Beijing you can see *a flood of bicycles* every morning.

こうすいかくりつ 降水確率 〔気象〕the probability of precipitation

こうすいりょう 降水量 〔気象〕precipitation [U]

こうせい[1] 構成 composition [U]; (文・論理などの) structure [U] [C]; (組織) organization [U] ―構成する 《公式的》compose [他], make* up

この交響曲は4楽章から構成されている This symphony *is composed* [*made up*] *of* four movements.

その委員会は5人の教員で構成されている The committee 「*is made up* [*is composed, consists*] *of* five teachers.

◆その映画は2部構成だった The film *consisted of* two parts. / あなたの家の家族構成を教えてください What is *the make-up* of your family?

‖構成員 a member / 構成要素 a component

こうせい[2] 公正 ―公正な (平等な) fair; (正しい) just ‖公正な判断 a *fair* judgment / 公正な取り引き *fair* [*honest*] dealing / 公正な裁判を受ける権利 the right to a *fair* trial / 陪審の評決は公正ではなかったと思う I don't think the jury's verdict was *just*.

‖公正取引委員会 the Fair Trade Commission

こうせい[3] 攻勢 offensive [C] 《しばしば the ～》‖平和攻勢 *a* peace *offensive* / 攻勢に出る take [go on, go over to] *the offensive*

こうせい[4] 更生 rehabilitation [U]; (改心) reformation [U] [C] ―更生する rehabilitate *oneself*; reform *oneself*, reform [自] ‖彼は私たちに更生を誓った He promised us to *reform himself*.

◆彼はその少年たちを更生させようとした He tried to *reform* the boys. (❖この reform は「更生させる」の意味の他動詞)

‖更正会社 a reorganized corporation / 更正施設 rehabilitation facilities

こうせい[5] 厚生 welfare [U]; (公共の) public welfare [U] ◆彼は厚生年金で暮らしている He lives on *a company pension*.

‖厚生施設 welfare facilities / 厚生省 the Ministry of Health and Welfare (❖2001年厚生労働省に統合) ➾こうせいろうどうしょう

こうせい[6] 後世 the future; (後世の人々) future generations, 《集合的》posterity [U] ‖後世のために美術品を保護する preserve art works for *posterity* / 彼の業績は後世まで語り継がれるだろう His achievement will be passed on to 「*the future* [*future generations*].

こうせい[7] 恒星 (fixed) star [C]

こうせい[8] 校正 〔印刷〕proofreading [U] ―校正する proofread* [他] [自] ◆ゲラ刷りを校正する *read* [*correct*] galley proofs

‖校正係 a proofreader / 校正刷り a galley proof

ごうせい[1] 合成 composition [U]; 〔化学〕synthesis [U] ―合成する compound [他]; 〔化学〕synthesize [他] ‖合成語 a compound (word) / 合成ゴム synthetic rubber / 合成写真 a composite (photograph) / 合成樹脂 a synthetic resin / 合成繊維 (a) synthetic fiber / 合成洗剤 a (synthetic) detergent / 合成肥料 a compound fertilizer / 合成物質 a compound substance

ごうせい[2] 豪勢 ―豪勢な luxurious ‖豪勢な夕食 *luxurious* dinner / 豪勢な暮らしをする lead a *luxurious* life; live in a *grand* style

こうせいねん 好青年 pleasant young man [C]

こうせいのう 高性能 ―高性能の high-performance; (能率のよい) highly efficient; (馬力のある) high-powered ‖高性能車 a *high-performance* car

こうせいぶっしつ 抗生物質 antibiotic [C]

こうせいろうどうしょう 厚生労働省 the Ministry of Health, Labour and Welfare

こうせき[1] 功績 (貢献) contribution [U] [C], 《公式的》service [C]; (業績) achievements ‖輝かしい功績 *a* brilliant *achievement* / みんなは心から彼の功績をたたえた Everyone heartily praised his *achievements*.

こうせき[2] 鉱石 ore [C] [U] ‖鉄鉱石 iron *ore*

こうせつ 降雪 snowfall [C]; (1回の) snow [C] ‖降雪量 (the amount of) snowfall

ごうせつ 豪雪 heavy snowfall [C] ‖豪雪地帯 a heavy snow area

こうせん[1] 光線 ray [C], beam [C]; (光) light [U] ‖太陽の光線 *the rays* of the sun; sunshine; sunlight / レーザー光線 *a* laser *beam*

こうせん[2] 交戦 (戦争) war [C] [U]; (戦闘) battle [C] [U] ‖日本は当時その国と交戦状態にあった Japan *was* 「*at war* [*fighting*] *with* the country in those days.

‖交戦国 a warring nation, a belligerent / 交戦状態 a state of war

こうせん[3] 公選 (an) election by popular vote

こうせん[4] 抗戦 resistance [U] ◆彼らは徹底抗戦に出た They *resisted* to the end.

こうせん[5] 鉱泉 mineral spring [C]

こうせん[6] 高専 (高等専門学校) technical college [C]

こうぜん 公然 ―公然の open; (周知の)

こうせん —公然と openly; publicly, in public ∥公然の秘密 an open secret / 彼女は公然と政府の政策を非難した She openly attacked the government's policy.

こうせんてき 好戦的 —好戦的な belligerent, warlike

こうそ¹ 控訴 appeal ⓒⓊ —控訴する appeal ⓐⓦ ∥控訴を退ける reject [dismiss] an appeal / 控訴を差し戻す refer the appealed case back to the lower court / 控訴を取り下げる withdraw an appeal / 被告はその判決を不服として高等裁判所に控訴した The defendant appealed the decision to the high court.

こうそ² 酵素 【生化学】 enzyme ⓒ ∥酵素洗剤 (an) enzyme detergent

こうそう¹ 構想 (計画) plan ⓒ; (着想) conception ⓒ; (小説などの) plot ⓒⓊ ∥大まかな構想を立てる make a rough plan / 彼はちょうど新しい小説の構想を練っているところだった He was just working out a plan [plot] for a new novel.

こうそう² 高層 —高層の high-rise ∥高層雲 an altostratus / 高層ビル a high-rise building; (超高層の) a skyscraper

こうそう³ 抗争 struggle ⓒⓊ, (公式的) strife Ⓤ ∥派閥抗争 party strife / 権力抗争 a power struggle / 対立する暴力団間の抗争 a struggle between two rival gangs

こうそう⁴ 高僧 high priest ⓒ

こうぞう 構造 structure ⓒⓊ —構造(上)の structural ∥中国の社会構造 the social structure of China / 人体の構造 the structure of the human body / この車には構造上の欠陥がある This car has a structural defect. ◆耐震構造の家 an earthquake-proof house / そもそも彼女は僕とは頭の構造が違うんだ She is constitutionally more than a match for me in intelligence.
∥構造改革 a structural reform / 構造主義 structuralism / 構造不況 a structural recession

ごうそう 豪壮 —豪壮な grand, magnificent ∥豪壮な邸宅 a magnificent residence

こうそく¹ 拘束 restraint ⓒⓊ —拘束する restrain ⓦ, bind* ⓦ ∥容疑者の身柄を拘束する restrain the suspect; take the suspect into custody ◆法的に拘束力のある取り決め a legally binding agreement
∥拘束時間 compulsory (working) hours / 拘束力 binding force

こうそく² 高速 high speed ⓒⓊ ∥オートバイが高速で通り過ぎた A motorcycle passed by at a high speed. ◆この機械は絵や文字を高速で印刷することができる This machine prints pictures and text very fast.
∥高速増殖炉 【物理】 a fast breeder reactor / 高速道路 (米) an expressway, a speedway, (英) a motorway / 高速度撮影 high-speed photography

こうそく³ 校則 school regulations [rules] ∥校則を破る [守る] break [obey] school regulations / 私たちの学校は校則が非常に厳しい[ゆるい] Our school regulations are very strict [lax]. / 髪を染めるのは校則違反です It's against school regulations to color your hair.

こうそく⁴ 光速 the speed [velocity] of light

こうぞく¹ 後続 —後続の following; (次の) next ∥彼はヒットを許したが, 落ち着いて後続のバッターを打ち取った He gave up a hit, but calmly got the following batters out.

こうぞく² 皇族 (全体) the Imperial [Royal] Family; (個人) a member of the Imperial [Royal] Family

ごうぞく 豪族 powerful family [clan] ⓒ

こうそつ 高卒 (高校卒業者) high school graduate ⓒ ◆彼は高卒だ (→学校教育は高校で終わった) His education ended at high school. / この仕事への応募者は高卒の資格 (→高校の卒業証書) が必要だ The applicants for this job are required to have a high school diploma.

こうたい 交替・交代 relief Ⓤ (❖「交代者」を表すときは ⓒ); (2者間の) alternation ⓒⓊ; (輪番) rotation ⓒⓊ; (交替勤務) shift ⓒ —交替する relieve ⓦ; alternate ⓦ; rotate ⓐⓦ; (順番に行う) take* turns; (役割などを) take a person's place —交替で alternately; by turns

きのうは交替なしで5時間働き詰めだった I worked for five hours with no relief yesterday.

謙と交代して明が主将になった Akira took Ken's place as captain.

委員長の役職は会員が交替で務める The chairmanship of the committee rotates among its members.

私と妹は交替で食事の後片づけをします My sister and I wash the dishes by turns. / My sister and I take turns (at) washing the dishes.

ガードマンは8時間交替で働く The guards work (in) eight-hour shifts.

政治の世界では世代交代が進んでいる There has been a generational shift in the political world.
∥交替制 a shift system

こうたい² 後退 (退却) retreat ⓒⓊ; (景気の) recession ⓒⓊ —後退する (後ろに下がる) go* back; (しだいに遠のく) recede ⓐ ∥相次ぐ埋め立てで海岸線は遠くに後退してしまった After repeated reclamation, the original coastline has receded into the distance.
◆3歩後退する back up three steps

こうたい³ 抗体 【生化学】 antibody ⓒ

こうだい 広大 —広大な vast, extensive ∥広大な雪原 a vast area of snow / 宮殿の広大な庭園 the extensive [huge] garden of the palace ◆広大無辺の宇宙 the infinite universe

こうたいごう 皇太后 Empress Dowager [dáuədʒər] ⓒ; (現国王[現女王]の母) the Queen Mother

こうたいし 皇太子 the Crown Prince; (英

こうたく 光沢 luster ◎《またa～》, sheen ◎《またa～》;（磨いて出した）polish ◎;（塗料などで出した）gloss ◎《またa～》 ‖真珠の光沢 the luster of pearls
◆彼女は柔らかく光沢のある髪をしている She has soft and *glossy* hair.

ごうだつ 強奪 robbery ◎ ◎;（輸送中の貨物などの）hijacking ◎ ——**強奪する** rob ⊕（※人・場所が目的語になるので，受身にするときに「奪われたもの」を主語にすることはできない）
⇒うぼう ‖現金輸送車から現金を強奪する *rob* a security van *of* the money

こうたん 降誕（誕生）birth ◎ ◎;（特にキリストの）the Nativity
‖降誕祭《キリストの》Christmas

こうだん[1] 公団 public corporation ◎ ‖日本道路公団 the Japan Highway *Public Corporation* ◆都市基盤整備公団 the Urban Development *Corporation*
‖公団住宅 a Housing Corporation apartment house

こうだん[2] 講談 🈁 *kodan*, (oral) storytelling of chronicles of wars and revenge

こうち[1] 耕地（耕された土地）cultivated land ◎, cultivated field ◎;（耕作可能な土地）arable land ◎ ‖耕地面積 cultivated acreage

こうち[2] 高地 highlands, height ◎《しばしば複数形 ～s》

こうち[3] 拘置 detention ◎ ——**拘置する** detain ⊕ ‖拘置所 (a) jail, (a) prison

こうち[4] 高知

高知県は四国の南部に位置し，太平洋に面しています．北部の深い山と南の陽光あふれる海，温暖な気候，これらの自然環境が"いごっそう"（「頑固一徹，反骨」の意味）と呼ばれる県民気質を形成したといわれ，坂本龍馬など近代日本の礎（いしずえ）となった人々が輩出しています．
Kochi Prefecture is situated on the south side of Shikoku Island facing the Pacific Ocean. With high mountains to the north, the sun-drenched ocean to the south, and a temperate climate, the prefecture's natural environment is said to be the source of the stubborn, rebellious spirit called "igosso" for which the people of Kochi are known. Many people who built the foundations for modern Japan came from Kochi, including Ryoma Sakamoto.

こうちく 構築 理論を構築する *develop* [*construct*] a theory

こうちゃ 紅茶 (black) tea ◎（※種類をいうときは ◎．英米では緑茶 (green tea) と区別するときに black tea を用いる．ふつうは単に tea という）‖紅茶をいれる make *tea* ‖イギリス人は紅茶を飲むのが好きだ English people like to drink *tea*.
💬「何になさいますか」「紅茶を2つお願いします」 "What would you like?" "Two *teas*, please."

こうちゃく 膠着 膠着状態にある be at *a deadlock* [*standstill*] ‖交渉は膠着状態に陥った The negotiation has reached *a deadlock* [*standstill*].
‖膠着語《言語》an agglutinative language

こうちょう[1] 好調 すべては好調だ Everything is 「*going well* [*all right*]. ‖ 出足好調だ We made a good start. ‖ 今, わがチームは絶好調です Our team is now *at its best*.

こうちょう[2] 校長 principal ◎,《英》headmaster ◎（《米》では私立学校の校長を指す．また女性は headmistress）
‖校長室 the principal's office

こうちょう[3] 紅潮 flush ◎《通例単数形》
◆彼女は恥ずかしさでほほを紅潮させていた Her cheeks *were flushed with* shame.

こうちょうかい 公聴会 public hearing ◎ ‖公聴会を開く hold *a public hearing*

こうちょく 硬直 硬直した考え rigid [*inflexible*] ideas ‖ 彼女は恐怖で体が硬直するのを感じた She felt herself *stiffen* with terror.
‖死後硬直《医学》rigor mortis

こうつう 交通

traffic ◎;（輸送機関）《主に米》transportation ◎,《主に英》transport ◎
‖交通の流れ the flow of *traffic* ‖海上交通 sea *traffic* ‖交通規則を「破る［break］ *traffic rules* ‖交通渋滞に巻き込まれる get into *a traffic jam* ‖交通事故にあう have [meet with] *a traffic accident*

大雪で交通はまひ状態になった The traffic was paralyzed by the heavy snow.

ここは交通の便がいい This place is convenient to public transportation.

警察官が交差点で交通整理をしていた A police officer *was directing* (*the*) *traffic* at the intersection.

今日ほとんどの大都市では交通量の多さが大きな問題となっている Today heavy *traffic* is a major problem in most big cities.

彼は昨年交通事故で亡くなった He was killed in *a traffic accident* last year.

飛行機は最も重要な交通機関の一つだ The airplane is one of the most important *means of transportation*.

‖交通安全 traffic [road] safety ‖交通安全運動 a campaign for traffic [road] safety ‖交通安全週間 Traffic [Road] Safety Week ‖交通違反 traffic (rules) violation [infraction] ‖交通規制 the regulation of traffic ‖交通巡査 a traffic police officer ‖交通情報 a traffic report ‖交通信号 a traffic light [signal] ‖交通費 transportation expenses ‖交通標識 a traffic sign ‖交通網 a public transportation system

> 英作文ノート 「交通が激しい」は何ていう？
> 国道1号線は交通が激しい
> →×Traffic is *busy* on Route 1.
> →○Traffic is *heavy* on Route 1.

→ ○There is *a lot of* traffic on Route 1.
★traffic は不可算名詞。交通量が多い[少ない]というときの形容詞は heavy [light] を用いる。a busy street は「にぎやかな通り、繁華街」の意味。

こうつごう 好都合 ━━好都合な (便利な) convenient; (有利な) favorable; (英) favourable; (適切な) right ‖それは好都合だ That's 「*convenient* for [*all right* with] me. ◆円高はわが社にとって好都合だった The strong yen was *advantageous* [*favorable*] to our company.

こうてい¹ 肯定 affirmation ━━肯定する affirm ━━肯定的な affirmative; (積極的な) positive ‖彼女は肯定的な人生観をもっている She has a *positive* outlook on life. ◆彼女と知り合いかと尋ねると彼は否定も肯定もしなかった When I asked him if he knew her, he *answered neither yes or no*. ‖肯定文〖文法〗an affirmative sentence

こうてい² 校庭 schoolyard; (運動場) playground; (学校の構内) school grounds

こうてい³ 高低 (起伏) ups and downs

こうてい⁴ 工程 (手順) process ◆「過程」の意味では ‖作業工程の一部を機械化する mechanize some parts of *the process* of work

こうてい⁵ 公定 公定歩合を引き下げる reduce [cut] *the official bank rate* ‖公定価格 an official price

こうてい⁶ 行程 (旅) journey; (1区間) leg; (旅行の日程) itinerary ‖2か月の行程 a two-month [(*a*) two months'] *journey*; *a journey* of two months ‖北海道旅行の行程 the itinerary for a trip to Hokkaido ‖きのうは予定の半分の行程しか進めなかった Yesterday we made only half the progress we had planned for *the journey*.

こうてい⁷ 皇帝 emperor (◆女性形は empress) ‖ローマ皇帝 a Roman *emperor*; *an emperor* of Rome
‖皇帝ペンギン〖鳥〗an emperor penguin

ごうてい 豪邸 (luxurious) mansion

こうてき¹ 公的 ━━公的な public; (公務上の・公式の) official ‖彼女はその経験がもとで公的な仕事をするようになった The experience stimulated her to enter *public* service.
‖公的資金 public funds ‖公的生活 public life ‖公的年金制度 a public pension plan

こうてき² 好適 ━━好適な (適した) suitable; (理想的な) ideal ‖彼らは保養に好適な土地に引っ越した They moved to a place *suitable* for recuperation.

こうてきしゅ 好敵手 (good) match 《また a～》, one's match to find [meet] *one's match* ‖彼らはテニスでは好敵手どうしです They are *a good match for* each other in tennis.

こうてつ¹ 更迭 ━━更迭する replace; (人事異動する) reshuffle; (免職する) dismiss ‖法務大臣を更迭する *replace* the Minister of Justice ‖この不祥事で役員全員が更迭された The entire management *was replaced* because of this scandal.

こうてつ² 鋼鉄 steel ‖このナイフは鋼鉄製です This knife is made of *steel*.

こうてん¹ 公転〖天文〗revolution ━━公転する revolve (around)

こうてん² 交点〖幾何〗vertex (複 ～es, vertices)

こうてん³ 好天 fine [fair] weather ‖この好天が2, 3日続くといいのですが I hope *the fine weather* will last a few days.
◆好天続き a run of *sunny days*

こうてん⁴ 好転 ━━好転する improve, become* [get*] better ‖状況が好転しているという確かなきざしがある There is every indication that the situation *is* 「*improving* [*taking a turn for the better*].

こうてん⁵ 荒天 stormy [rough] weather

こうでん 香典 (a) koden, a monetary offering to a departed spirit

こうてんてき 後天的 ━━後天的な acquired ‖後天的な病気 an *acquired* disease

こうど¹ 高度 ❶ 〖高さ〗height ‖高度を上げる[下げる] gain [lose] *height* ‖本機は高度1万メートルを飛行中です We are flying at *a height* [*an altitude*] of 10,000 meters.
❷ 〖程度〗高度経済成長 *high* economic growth ‖高度先端技術 *highly* developed technology ‖高度な技術を用いる apply a *high-level* technique ‖イルカは非常に高度な知能をもつといわれている Dolphins are said to have a very *high* degree of intelligence.
‖高度計 an altimeter

こうど² 光度〖天文〗luminosity; (等級) magnitude

こうど³ 硬度 hardness

こうとう¹ 高等 ━━高等な high, higher; (上級の) advanced ‖高等科 an advanced course ‖高等教育 higher education ‖高等裁判所 a high court ‖高等動物 a higher animal

こうとう² 口頭 ━━口頭の oral, verbal ━━口頭で orally, verbally ‖口頭試問 an *oral* test [examination] ‖その教師は彼に口頭による指示をした The teacher gave him *verbal* [*oral*] instructions.

こうとう³ 好投 good [nice] pitching ━━好投する pitch well

こうとう⁴ 高騰 sudden [sharp] rise ━━高騰する rise* suddenly [sharply] ‖円の高騰 *a sharp rise* in the yen ‖首相の発言を受けて株価は高騰した After the Prime Minister's statement, stock prices *rose sharply*.

こうどう¹ 行動

act; action (◆act が1回1回の行動を指すのに対し、action はある期間にわたる連続した行動を指す); (ふるまい) behavior; (行為)〖公式的〗conduct ━━行動する act; take* action; behave

勇気ある行動 courageous *conduct* / 考えを行動に移す translate ideas into *action*

行動を起こす前に慎重に考えなさい．Think carefully before you *act*.

彼女の行動は素早かった Her *action* was immediate.

彼がどうしてあんな行動をとったのか理解できない I can't understand why he 「*acted* the way he did [took such *action*].

行動に気をつけなさい．Mind how you *behave*. / Be careful what you *do*.

もう子供ではないのだから自分の行動に責任をもちなさい．Since you're no longer a child, you have to be responsible for your own *conduct*.

彼女はなかなかの行動派だ She's really *a woman of action*.

◆軍事行動を行う conduct *a military operation* / 彼の行動について逐一私に報告してください．Keep me posted on all his *activities*. / 常に団体行動をとること Whatever you do, do it as [in] *a group*. / 3時までは自由行動にします You will be *free* until three.

‖行動範囲 the range of activities / 行動様式 behavior patterns

こうどう² 講堂 (lecture) hall ⓒ, 《米》auditorium ⓒ (複 ~s, auditoria), 《英》assembly hall

こうどう³ 公道 (私道に対して) public street [road] ⓒ; (幹線道路) highway ⓒ

ごうとう 強盗【人】robber ⓒ; (夜盗) burglar ⓒ; (押込み強盗) housebreaker ⓒ; 【行為】robbery Ⓤ (◆個々の事件としては ⓒ); burglary Ⓤⓒ; housebreaking Ⓤ / 強盗を働く commit *robbery* / 近所の銀行で強盗殺人事件が発生した There was *a case of robbery and murder* at the neighborhood bank. / 最近強盗事件が多発している These days *robberies* occur frequently. / その強盗は刑務所に入れられた The *burglar* was put in prison. / 昨夜銀行に強盗が入った The bank *was robbed* last night.

ごうどう 合同 (連合) combination Ⓤⓒ; (団結) union Ⓤ; (政党などの) coalition Ⓤ; 〔数学〕congruence Ⓤ ——合同の joint (◆名詞の前で用いる); 〔数学〕congruent

——合同する combine ⓘ; unite ⓘ /合同演奏会 a joint concert / 次の2つの三角形が合同であることを証明せよ Prove that the following two triangles are *congruent*.

◆来月この2社は合同して新会社を作る予定だ These two companies are due to form a new company *together* next month. / 私たちのチームは彼のチームと合同で練習した Our team practiced *together with* his team.

‖合同会議 (両院の) a joint session

こうとうがっこう 高等学校 (senior) high school ⓒ (◆通例《高校》)

こうとうせんもんがっこう 高等専門学校 technical college ⓒ

こうとうぶ 後頭部 the back of the head

こうとうむけい 荒唐無稽 ——荒唐無稽な absurd, preposterous

こうどく¹ 購読 subscription ⓒ ——購読する subscribe ⓘ, take* ⓘ / 雑誌を定期購読する subscribe to a magazine / 私はその雑誌を1年間予約購読している I have a year's *subscription to* the magazine.

‖購読者 a subscriber / 購読料 a subscription rate [fee]

こうどく² 講読 reading Ⓤ ——講読する read* ⓘ / 授業で『老人と海』を講読する read *The Old Man and the Sea* in class

こうとくしん 公徳心 sense of public morality; (公共心) public spirit Ⓤ

こうとりくみ 好取組 good bout [báut] ⓒ

こうない¹ 構内 (土地・建物を含む) premises; (建物の構内) grounds; (大学の) campus ⓒ Ⓤ / 駅の構内で on the station *premises* / 構内立入禁止 (掲示) Keep off the *premises*. / 多くの学生が大学の構内を自転車で行き来している Many students use bicycles to move about *on the campus* of the university.

こうない² 校内 —— 校内で in (the) school —— 校内の (主に米) intramural / 校内で1番の生徒 the best student *in (the) school* / 校対抗試合 an *intramural* match

◆放課後，校内に残ってはいけない You must not remain *on school grounds* after school hours.

‖校内放送 a school PA announcement / 校内暴力 school violence

こうないえん 口内炎 〔医学〕stomatitis ⓒ, oral ulcer ⓒ / 口内炎ができる contract *stomatitis*

こうにゅう 購入 purchase Ⓤⓒ ——購入する (公式的) purchase ⓘ, buy* ⓘ / 学校は新しいコンピュータを購入した The school *purchased* a new computer.

‖購入価格 the purchase price / 購入者 a purchaser, a buyer

こうにん¹ 公認 official recognition [approval] Ⓤ ——公認する (公に認可する) recognize ... officially, authorize ⓘ; (よいと認める) approve ⓘ ——公認の (役割・地位などが) approved; (公式の) official / 彼は平泳ぎの公認日本記録をインターハイで出した He set an *official* Japanese record in the breast stroke at the inter-high school athletic meet. / 彼らは親も公認の仲だ Their relationship *is approved* by both of their parents. ◆民主党公認の候補者 a candidate *officially endorsed* by the Democratic Party of Japan

‖公認会計士 《米》a certified public accountant (《略語》CPA), 《英》a chartered accountant / 公認候補 a nominated candidate

こうにん² 後任 successor ⓒ ——後任の incoming / 彼女が党首の後任です She is *the successor* to the party leader. (◆×the successor of ... とはしない) / 後任の大使には後藤氏が内定している Mr. Goto will be appointed *incoming* ambassador.

こうねつ 高熱 (一般に) a high temperature; (病気による) a high fever / このガラスは高熱に耐える This glass withstands a

high temperature. / インフルエンザで高熱が出た I had *a high fever* with flu.

こうねつひ 光熱費 lighting and heating expenses; (公共料金) utility bills

こうねん¹ 光年 light-year ⓒ

こうねん² 後年 later, in later years

こうねんき 更年期 menopause ⓤ, the change of life ‖更年期障害 menopausal disorders

こうのう 効能 (薬などの効き目) effect ⓒⓤ, 《公式的》efficacy ⓤ ——**効能がある** effective / その薬の効能 the efficacy of the drug / そこの温泉は神経痛に効能がある That hot spring *is effective [good]* for neuralgia.
‖効能書き a statement of indications

こうのとり 鸛 stork ⓒ

こうは 硬派 ❶【強硬派】hard-liner ⓒ; (タカ派) hawk ⓒ
❷【男らしさを誇示する若者】(力にものをいわせる) young tough ⓒ; (きまじめな) strait-laced young person ⓒ
❸【かたい内容の記事】——硬派の hard ‖硬派記事 hard news

こうば 工場 factory ⓒ ⇨ こうじょう (工場)

こうはい¹ 後輩 one's junior; (高校・大学などの下級生) lowerclassman ⓒ (❖英米には日本の「先輩・後輩」に当たる概念がないため説明的に表すことも多い)
生意気な後輩 a cheeky *lowerclassman*
◆彼は中学で2年後輩だった He was two years *under [below]* me in junior high school. / 彼は私より年上だが会社では私の後輩だ(→後に入った) He is older than me. But he *joined* the company *after* me.

こうはい² 荒廃 (土地・建物などの) devastation ⓤ, ruin ⓤ; (心などの) desolation ⓤ
——**荒廃させる** devastate ⓗ ——**荒廃した** ruined ‖荒廃した山林 a *ruined* forest / 空襲による荒廃 *devastation* by air raids
◆心の荒廃 mental *despair* / 教育現場の荒廃が долго続いて久しい *The loss of order* in schools has long been a topic.

こうはい³ 交配 cross ⓒ ——**交配する** crossbreed* ⓗ; (植物の) cross-fertilize ⓗ ——**交配種の** crossbred / 2種類のバラを交配する *cross-fertilize* two kinds of roses
‖交配種 a crossbreed

こうばい¹ 購買 purchase ⓤ ——**購買する** purchase ⓗ ◆この車の広告は消費者の購買意欲をそそる This ad is trying to get [stimulate] consumers to *buy* that new car.
‖購買者 a purchaser, a buyer / 購買部 (学校の) a school shop; (生協の) a co-op / 購買力 purchasing power

こうばい² 勾配 (傾斜) slope ⓤ (また a ~); (鉄道・道路などの) 《主に米》grade ⓒ, 《英》gradient ⓒ; (屋根の) pitch ⓤ (また a ~); 【電気・物理】gradient ⓒ / 60度の勾配 *a slope* of 60 degrees / あの家の屋根の勾配は急[ゆるやか]だ That house's roof has *a steep [gentle] pitch*.

こうばい³ 紅梅 a plum tree with red blossoms

こうばいすう 公倍数 common multiple ⓒ ‖最小公倍数 the least [lowest] *common multiple*(略語 L.C.M., l.c.m.)

こうはく 紅白 (赤と白) red and white ‖日本では紅白はめでたいことの象徴です Red and white is a symbol of auspicious occasions in Japan. / NHKの紅白歌合戦を家族そろって見た Our whole family watched *the Red & White Song Contest* on NHK.
◆紅白試合 an *inter-team* match [game]

こうばしい 香ばしい aromatic, sweet-smelling, pleasant smelling ‖焼きたての香ばしいパン *pleasant smelling* bread fresh from the oven ◆喫茶店はコーヒーの香ばしいにおいでいっぱいだった The cafe was filled with *the aroma* of coffee.

こうはつ 後発 後発隊がきょうやっと到着した The group that *departed [started] later* finally arrived today.

こうはん¹ 後半 the latter [second] half ‖20世紀後半にハイテク産業が急速に発展した High-tech industry developed rapidly in *the second half* of the 20th century.
◆あの女優は40代後半です That actress is *in her late* forties.
‖後半生 the latter half of *one's life* / 後半戦 the second half of the game

こうはん² 公判 trial ⓒⓤ ⇨ さいばん ‖殺人事件の公判 a murder *trial* / 彼は詐欺罪で公判中だ He is going *on trial* for fraud.

こうはん³ 広範 ——**広範な** wide, extensive

こうばん¹ 交番 police box ⓒ (❖英米にはふつう日本の交番に当たるものはない) ‖私は交番で道を尋ねた I asked for directions at *the police box*. / 財布を拾って交番に届けた I picked up the wallet and took it to *the police box*.

こうばん² 降板 ——**降板する**〔野球〕leave* the mound

ごうばん 合板 plywood ⓤ

こうはんい 広範囲 (面積) large [wide] area ⓤ ——**広範囲な** extensive, widespread ‖広範囲にわたる調査 *extensive* research / 台風の被害は広範囲に及んだ The typhoon caused *widespread* damage.

こうひ¹ 公費 public expenses ‖市役所は公費で新年会を開いた The city hall held a New Year's party *at public expense*. (❖at public expense では expenses にならないことに注意)
◆公費をむだづかいする waste *public money*

こうひ² 工費 the cost of construction, construction costs

こうび 交尾 copulation ⓤ, mating ⓤ ——**交尾する** copulate ⓘ, mate ⓘⓗ ‖交尾期 the mating season

ごうひ 合否 (試験の結果) the results of the exam ◆試験の合否は1週間以内にお知らせします We'll notify you whether you *have passed (or not)* within a week. / たった5点が合否を分けた There was only a five-point difference *between passing and failing*.

こうひょう¹ 公表 (public [official]) announcement ⓒⓤ; (発表・公布) publication ⓤ ——**公表する** announce (officially [publicly]), make* ... public, disclose 働; (新聞・雑誌などで) print 働 ∥その被害者の名前は公表しないことに決定した They decided not to *announce* the name of the victim. / 彼は真実を公表した He *made* the truth *public*. / これはオフレコだから公表しないでください Don't *print* this — it's off the record.

こうひょう² 好評 (評判) (good) reputation Ⓤ《また a ~》; (人気) popularity Ⓤ; (本・映画など) favorable [good] review Ⓒ ∥彼女の待ち望まれていた新しい小説は大好評です Her long-waited new novel has received [got] *a very good review*. / Her long-waited new novel is *a big hit*.

◆当店ではこの料理が好評です This dish is *popular* in our restaurant. / 私の手作りのチーズケーキはみんなに好評だった(→みんなが気に入った) Everyone *loved* the cheesecake I baked.

こうひょう³ 講評 comment ⒸⓊ ——講評する comment 自 他, make* a comment on ... ∥音楽の先生が合唱コンクールについて講評した Our music teacher *made a comment on* the choral contest.

こうふ¹ 交付 delivery Ⓤ ——交付する (金品など) grant 他; (発行する) issue 他 ∥年金を交付する *grant* a pension / パスポートを交付する *issue* a passport
∥交付金 a grant; (助成金) a subsidy

こうふ² 公布 (法律・規則などの)《公式的》promulgation Ⓤ; (重要な事柄の)《公式的》proclamation Ⓤ ——公布する promulgate 他; proclaim 他 ∥新しい法が公布された A new law *was promulgated*. / 日本国憲法は 1946年に公布された The Constitution of Japan *was proclaimed* in 1946.

こうふ³ 鉱夫・坑夫 miner Ⓒ, mine worker

こうぶ 後部 the back, the rear; (船の) the stern ——後部の back, rear ∥後部座席 a back [rear] seat / バスの後部に荷物を置いてください Could you put your baggage at *the back* of the bus?

こうふう 校風 (気風) school tradition Ⓤ, the atmosphere of a school; (精神) school spirit Ⓤ ∥我々の学校の校風は自由です Our *school tradition* is liberal.

こうふく¹ 幸福 happiness Ⓤ; (福祉) welfare Ⓤ ——幸福な happy ——幸福に happily ⇨しあわせ
幸福に満ちあふれた生活 a life filled with *happiness* / 幸福に暮らす live *happily*; live a *happy* life / 幸福を追い求める pursue *happiness*
「世界中の子供たちの幸福」が会議のテーマです "*The welfare* of children all over the world" is the theme for the conference.
靖子さんと幸福な家庭を築いてください I heartily wish you to have a *happy* family life with Yasuko.
私は温泉につかっているときにいちばん幸福を感じる I feel *happiest* when I'm soaking in a hot spring.

こうふく² 降伏 surrender ⒸⓊ; (条件つきの) capitulation Ⓤ ——降伏する surrender 自; (条件つきで) capitulate 自 ∥敵に降伏する *surrender to* the enemy / 無条件降伏を飲む accept unconditional *surrender*

こうぶつ¹ 好物 one's favorite (food) ∥カキフライは私の好物です Fried oysters are *my favorite food*. ◆たいていの女の子は甘いものが大好物だ Most girls are very fond of sweets. / Most girls *love* sweets.

こうぶつ² 鉱物 mineral Ⓒ ◆日本は鉱物資源に乏しい Japan has few *mineral resources*.

こうふん 興奮

excitement Ⓤ; (ぞくぞくするような) thrill Ⓒ; (神経・器官の) stimulation Ⓤ ——興奮する be [get*] excited, be [get] thrilled ——興奮させる excite 他; thrill 他; stimulate 他 ——興奮した excited

実験の結果に僕らは興奮した The results of the experiment *excited* us. / We *were excited* by the results of the experiment.

世紀の大発見に彼らは興奮の色を隠せない様子だった Their great discovery seemed to fill them with *excitement*.

オリンピックの興奮さめやらぬうちにワールドカップが始まった While we *were* still *excited* by the Olympics, the World Cup started.

試合の前の晩は興奮してよく眠れなかった The night before the game, I couldn't sleep well *with excitement*.

子供たちは彼の冒険話にすっかり興奮していた The children *were* quite *thrilled* by his story of adventure.

濃いコーヒーは神経を興奮させる Strong coffee *stimulates* the nervous system.

◆スピルバーグの映画はいつ見ても興奮させられる I always find it *exciting* to watch Spielberg's movies. / 興奮した民衆は大統領官邸へ向かった The *agitated* crowd marched to the presidential residence.

🅔「あのゲーム買ったんだって? 早く見せて!」「そう興奮するなよ、今見せてやるから」"I hear you've bought that game. Let me see it!" "*Calm down*! I'll show you."

こうぶん 構文 the construction of a sentence, sentence structure Ⓒ ∥分詞構文 a participle construction

こうぶんし 高分子【化学】high polymer Ⓒ; (巨大分子) macromolecule Ⓒ ∥高分子化学 high polymer chemistry / 高分子化合物 a high polymer

こうぶんしょ 公文書 official document Ⓒ ∥公文書偽造で逮捕される be arrested for *forgery of official documents*

こうへい 公平 ——公平な fair; impartial; just; unbiased ——公平に fairly; impartially; justly ——公平さ fairness Ⓤ; impartiality Ⓤ; justice Ⓤ

> fair:「公平な・公正な」の意味で用いる最も一般的な語。
> impartial:「中立を守る・偏らない」というニュ

アンスがある.
just: 判断・判決などが道徳的に正しいという意味.
unbiased: 偏見・先入観がないことを表す.

公平な裁判 a *fair* trial / 第三者による公平な意見 an *impartial* opinion from a third party / 生徒を公平に扱う treat students *fairly*

私は2人の間で公平な立場を守った I remained *impartial* between the two.

救援物資は避難民に公平に分配された Relief supplies were distributed *fairly* to the refugees.

公平にやろうじゃないか *Fair's fair*.

選挙には公平さが重要だ *Fairness* is important in an election.

公平を期して言えば，この仕事に関して彼女はまったくの初心者だ *To be fair*, she's totally new to this job.

こうへん 後編 (本・映画などの) sequel ⓒ, the second part; (後の巻) the latter volume (❖ 3巻の場合は the third [last] volume) ⓒ

ごうべん 合弁 [日中合弁会社] a Japanese–Chinese *joint venture* / 某企業と合弁事業を設立する set up *a joint venture* with a certain corporation

こうほ 候補 candidate ⓒ; (指名された人) nominee ⓒ; (スポーツなどの優勝候補) favorite, 《英》favourite ⓒ

大統領候補 *a candidate* for President

新政党の候補が約3万票を獲得した The *candidate* from the new political party received about thirty thousand votes.

あの作家は芥川賞候補のひとりです That writer is one of *the nominees* for the Akutagawa Prize.

ブラジルはいつもワールドカップの優勝候補だ Brazil is always *the favorite* to win the World Cup.

その党は同じ地区に2人の候補者を立てた The party put up two *candidates* in the same district.

私の友達が次期生徒会長の最有力候補です A friend of mine is *the most likely candidate* for the next president of the student council.

◆チャップリンは一度もアカデミー賞候補にならなかった Chaplin *was never nominated* for an Academy Award. / その都市は2008年のオリンピックの候補地だ The city is one of *the sites* [*places*] *proposed* for the 2008 Olympic Games.

‖公認候補 a nominated candidate / 花婿[花嫁]候補 a prospective bridegroom [bride] / 無所属候補 an independent candidate

こうぼ 公募 ──公募する (論文・小説などを) invite public contribution; (参加を) invite public participation; (求人) advertise for ... /『アイドル雑誌に載せる写真を公募している They *are inviting public contribution of* photos for a teenage magazine. / その大学は日本語の講師を2人公募した The university *advertised for* two lecturers in Japanese.

こうぼ² 酵母 yeast Ⓤ ‖酵母菌 yeast fungus

こうほう¹ 後方 the rear, the back /『後方部隊 a *rear* (guard) / バスの後方に座る sit in *the back* of a bus ◆後方へ退く step *backward*

こうほう² 広報 (広報活動) public relations (❖ 単数扱い;《略語》PR); (宣伝) publicity Ⓤ /『広報活動にはお金がとてもかかる *Public relations* costs a lot of money.

‖広報課 a public relations section / 広報官 a spokesman (❖女性形は spokeswoman. 性差別を避けるため spokesperson を用いることも多い) / 広報誌 a PR magazine

こうほう³ 公報 official bulletin [report] ⓒ

こうぼう¹ 興亡 the rise and fall

こうぼう² 攻防 offense and defense

こうぼう³ 工房 studio ⓒ; (画家の), atelier ⓒ

こうぼう⁴ 弘法 ことわざ 弘法筆を選ばず A bad workman blames his tools. (→下手な職人は道具のせいにする) / 弘法も筆の誤り Even Homer (sometimes) nods. (→ホメロスでさえしくじることがある)

ごうほう 合法 ──合法的な (法で認められた) legal; (法に適した) lawful; (法的に正当な) legitimate ──合法的に legally; lawfully; legitimately /『合法的手段で by a *lawful* [*legal*] act / 合法的な事業 a *legitimate* business ◆中絶を合法化する *legalize* abortion

こうぼうせん 攻防戦 a battle in which the momentum shifts

◆両軍は激しい攻防戦 (→戦い) を繰り広げた Both armies fought *a fierce battle*.

こうま 子馬 (1歳未満の) foal ⓒ; (4歳未満の雄) colt ⓒ; (4歳未満の雌) filly ⓒ

こうまい 高邁 ──高邁な noble, lofty /『高邁な精神 *noble* [*lofty*] spirit

こうまん 高慢 ──高慢な haughty; (うぬぼれた) conceited /『冷酷で高慢な性格 *one's* cold and *haughty* nature / 我々は彼の高慢な態度に我慢ならない We cannot stand his *conceited* [→傲慢(㌔)な] *arrogant* attitude.

◆彼女は高慢ちきだ She's so *stuck-up* [*snobbish*].

ごうまん 傲慢 ──傲慢な arrogant; (横柄な) haughty /『彼の傲慢な態度はみんなの反感を買った His *arrogant* manner provoked everyone's antipathy. / あいつはだれに対しても傲慢だ He is *haughty* to everyone.

こうみょう¹ 巧妙 ──巧妙な (考え・言葉などが) clever; (抜け目ない) smart; (巧みな) skillful ──巧妙に cleverly; smartly; skillfully /『巧妙な手口 a *clever* trick / 巧妙な技 a *skillful* task / 彼は巧妙にその場を切り抜けた He handled the situation *cleverly* [*skillfully*].

こうみょう² 功名 功名心にかられる be eager for *fame*; be ambitious

こうみん 公民 (国民・市民) citizen ⓒ; (学科としての) civics (❖単数扱い) ‖公民館 a community center / 公民権 civil rights

こうむ 公務 official duty ⓤ(❖具体的業務を表す場合は ⓒ), official business ⓤ ‖首相は公務で多忙だ The Prime Minister is busy with *his official duties*.
◆公務執行妨害で逮捕します You are under arrest for *obstructing police duties*.
‖公務員 a public [civil] servant; (国家公務員) a national public [civil] servant; (地方公務員) a local public [civil] servant / 公務員住宅 an apartment house for government employees

こうむてん 工務店 construction company ⓒ

こうむる 被る (被害・損失などを) suffer ⓗ; (恩恵を) receive ⓗ, be indebted to ... ‖大災害を被る *suffer* a catastrophe / その会社は今年深刻な損失を被った The company *has suffered* heavy losses this year. / 我々はみな自然の恩恵を被っている We all *receive* benefit from nature. / トムには多大な恩恵を被っている I *am* greatly *indebted to* Tom.
◆君のへまのしりぬぐいなんてごめん被るよ I'd like to *be excused* from making up for your silly mistakes.

こうめい 高名 ──高名な (有名な) famous, well-known, celebrated, 《公式的》renowned; (専門的な分野で) eminent ‖山田教授はバイオテクノロジーの分野で高名な科学者です Professor Yamada is a *renowned* scientist in the field of biotechnology.
◆ご高名はかねがね伺っております I've heard much about *you*.

こうめい(せいだい) 公明(正大) ──公明(正大)な fair, fair and square ──公明(正大)に fairly, fairly and squarely ‖公明正大な態度 a *fair* attitude / 公明正大にふるまう play *fair* (*and square*)

こうもく 項目 (表・目録などの) item ⓒ; (新聞・本などの題目) heading ⓒ ‖内容を項目ごとに並べる arrange the contents *item by item*
◆…を項目別に分ける sort ... *by category* / (ニュースで) きょうの主な項目です Here are *the headlines* for today's news.

こうもり 蝙蝠 bat ⓒ ‖こうもり傘 an umbrella

こうもん¹ 肛門 anus [éinəs] ⓒ ──肛門の anal [éinəl]

こうもん² 校門 school gate ⓒ

ごうもん 拷問 torture ⓤ ──拷問する torture ⓗ, put* *a person under torture* ‖多くの無実の人が拷問にあい死んだ Many innocent people *were tortured* to death. / あの男は拷問にかけられて白状した That man confessed *under torture*. / 1時間も正座しているなんて私には拷問に等しい Just sitting upright (on the floor) for an hour is sheer *torture* for me.

こうや¹ 荒野 wasteland ⓒ ⓤ, the wilds, wilderness [wíldərnəs] ⓒ (通例単数形) ‖オーストラリアの荒野をさまよう wander in *the wilds* of Australia

こうや² 広野 vast [wide] plain ⓒ

こうやく 公約 pledge ⓒ; (選挙の) platform ⓒ, campaign [election] promise ⓒ ‖選挙公約を実行する[破る] fulfill [break] *a campaign promise*
◆政府は7パーセントの所得税減税を公約した The government *pledged* to make a seven percent cut in income tax.
‖公約違反 a breach of *one's* pledge

こうやくすう 公約数 common divisor ⓒ ‖最大公約数 the greatest common divisor ((略記)) G.C.D., g.c.d.

こうやさい 後夜祭 学園祭の後夜祭で私たちはたき火を囲んで歌ったり踊ったりした We sang and danced around the bonfire at *a closing party* of the school festival.

こうゆう¹ 交友 (友人) friend ⓒ; (知人) acquaintance ⓒ ‖彼女は交友関係が広い She has a large circle of *friends*.

こうゆう² 校友 school friend ⓒ; (男子の同窓生)《主に米》alumnus ⓒ (複 alumni [əlʌ́mnai]); (女子の同窓生)《主に米》alumna ⓒ (複 alumnae [əlʌ́mni:])
‖校友会 an alumni [alumnae] association

こうゆう³ 公有 ──公有の public, publicly owned ‖公有地 public land

ごうゆう 豪遊 ──豪遊する live it up ‖彼は毎晩会社の金で豪遊していた He *had been living it up* every night on the company's money.

こうよう¹ 公用 (公務) official business ⓤ; (公務員の使用) public use ⓤ ‖きょうの午後は公用で外に出ています I'll be out *on official business* this afternoon.
‖公用語 an official language / 公用車(会社の車) a company car; (公的機関の車) an official car

こうよう² 効用 (有用) use ⓒ; (効能) effect ⓒ ‖漢方薬の効用 *the effect* of drinking / その漢方薬には様々な効用がある That Chinese medicine *has* various *effects*. / That Chinese medicine *is effective* in various ways.

こうよう³ 高揚 (精神・意欲の) uplift ⓤ; (集団意識の) consciousness raising ⓤ ◆気分が高揚する feel *uplifted* / 士気を高揚させる raise [boost] morale

こうよう⁴ 紅葉 red leaves; (紅葉した風景) autumn colors ──紅葉する turn red ‖箱根は今燃えるような紅葉だ Hakone is now ablaze with *autumn colors*. / カエデは秋に紅葉する Maple leaves *turn red* in fall.

こうようじゅ 広葉樹 broadleaf tree ⓒ

ごうよく 強欲 ──強欲な greedy; (金銭欲の強い)《公式的》avaricious,《口語的》money-grubbing

こうら 甲羅 (カメ・カニなどの) shell ⓒ ◆プールサイドで甲羅干しする (→日光浴をする) *sunbathe* [*bathe in the sun*] at the poolside

こうらく 行楽 (ピクニック) excursion ⓒ; (団体での小旅行) excursion ⓒ; (遠出) outing ⓒ ‖春は行楽のシーズンだ Spring is a good season for *outings*.
‖行楽客《米》a vacationer,《英》a holiday-maker / 行楽地 a holiday resort / 行楽

和(びより) ideal weather for an outing

こうり[1] 小売り retail [U] ―小売りする retail [他][自] //あの問屋は小売りもする That wholesale store sells *at retail* as well. / このコートは小売りで2万円です This coat *retails* for [at] 20,000 yen.
‖小売価格 a retail price / 小売業 a retailer / 小売店 a retail store [shop]

こうり[2] 高利 (高い利息) high interest [U]; (巨利) large profits //高利で金を貸す lend money *at high interest*
‖高利貸し(人) a leech,《軽蔑的》a loan shark; (行為)《公式的》usury

こうり[3] 公理〔数学・論理〕axiom [C]

ごうり 合理 ―合理的な (理性的な) rational; (理屈に合った) reasonable; (実際的な) practical ―合理的に rationally; reasonably; practically //合理的な考え a *rational* [*reasonable*] idea / 食器はこのようにして洗えば手間がかからず合理的です Washing dishes in this way *is reasonable* [*practical*] because it will save you trouble.
◆その会社の組織は合理化された(→能率的になった) The company's organization *has been streamlined*.
‖合理化 rationalization; (特に企業などの) streamlining / 合理主義 rationalism / 合理性 rationality

こうりしゅぎ 功利主義〔哲学〕utilitarianism [U] ‖功利主義者 a utilitarian

こうりつ[1] 公立 ―公立の (公営の) public; (区・市・町・村立の) municipal; (道・府・県立の) prefectural; (都立の) metropolitan //公立図書館 a *public* library / 公立学校《米》a *public* [《英》*state*] school (❖英国で public school というと一部の名門私立校を指す)

こうりつ[2] 効率 efficiency [U] ―効率的な efficient ―効率的に efficiently //エネルギー効率を高める increase energy *efficiency* / 彼女は非常に効率的に仕事をする She works「very *efficiently* [*with great efficiency*].
◆効率の悪い仕事 *inefficient* work

こうりてき 功利的 彼は常に功利的だ(→利益を優先する) He always *gives priority to profit*.

こうりゃく 攻略 (攻め取ること) capture [U]; (打ち負かすこと) defeat [U] ―攻略する capture [他] //敵地を攻略する *capture* enemy land ◆そのコンピュータゲームの攻略本(→虎(とら)の巻)が発売されている *A playing guide* for that computer game has been published.

こうりゅう[1] 交流 ❶【交換】exchange [C][U], interchange [C][U] //市民交流 *exchange* of citizens / 日仏間の文化交流を促進する promote cultural *exchange* between Japan and France
❷【電気】alternating current [U]《略語》AC)

こうりゅう[2] 拘留 custody [U]; detention [U] (❖custody は主に裁判を待つ間拘置所に置かれる場合, detention は取り調べなどのために拘束される場合に用いる) ―拘留する take* ... in [into] custody; detain [他] //拘留中である be *in custody* / 男を殺人の罪で拘留する take a man *in* [*into*] *custody* for murder
‖拘留者 a detainee

こうりゅう[3] 興隆 (隆盛) rise [C]; (繁栄) prosperity [U] //オスマン帝国の興隆 *the rise* of the Ottoman Empire / 文化の興隆 cultural *prosperity*

ごうりゅう 合流 ―合流する join [自][他] //1時間もすればあなたたちに合流できます I can *join* you in an hour or so. / この川は数キロ下流で荒川と合流する This river *joins* [*merges into*] the Arakawa several kilometers downstream.
‖合流点 a meeting, a junction

こうりょ 考慮 consideration [U] ―考慮する consider [他], take* account of ..., take ... into account,《口語的》think* over
費用を考慮する *consider* the cost
その提案は考慮に値しない The proposal is not worth *considering*.
その点を十分考慮してください Please「*think* it *over* [*consider* it *thoroughly*].
その計画にはまだ考慮すべき点が多い A lot of points *to be considered* still remain in the plan.
報道関係者は被害者の気持ちも考慮しなければならない Journalists must *take into account* the feelings of the victims.
彼らは作業員の安全を考慮に入れていなかった They didn't *take* the security of the workers *into account* [*consideration*].
◆彼女が初心者であることを考慮すると, 彼女は本当にうまく役を演じた *Considering* (that) she is a beginner, she played her role very well.

こうりょう[1] 荒涼 ―荒涼とした (寒々と暗い) bleak; (不毛な) barren; (住む人のない) desolate //荒涼とした景色 a *bleak* landscape

こうりょう[2] 香料 (人工香料) artificial flavor [U][C]; (香辛料) spice [U][C]; (化粧品の) perfume [C] //バラの香料 rose-scented *perfumes*

こうりょう[3] 綱領 (要点) outline [C]; (政党などの基本方針) platform [C]

こうりょく 効力 (法律・薬などの) effect [U][C]; (法的拘束力) force [U]; (有効性) validity [U] ―効力のある effective; valid //その薬はすぐに効力が現われる The medicine has *an* immediate *effect*. /《口語的》The medicine *works* immediately. / その法律は2003年1月1日より効力を発する The law comes into *effect* [*force*] on January 1 of 2003. / 本契約は3年間効力を有する This contract「*is valid* [*holds good*] for three years.

こうりん 後輪 rear [back] wheel [C]

こうれい[1] 恒例 (毎年1回の行事) annual event [C]; (確立した習慣) established custom [C] ―恒例の (毎年行われる) annual; (習慣的な) customary //恒例の冬のバーゲン an *annual* winter sale / 毎年恒例の夏祭り the *annual* summer festival
◆優勝すると選手たちが監督を胴上げするのが恒例

テーマ別表現集

●高齢化と介護

❶高齢化に関する表現

1. 高齢化社会についてどう思いますか。
   What do you think about the aging [graying] society?
2. 近い将来3人に1人は60歳以上になるでしょう。
   One in three people will be over 60 years old in the near future.
3. 日本では高齢者の数が急速に増えつつあります。
   The number of elderly people in Japan is increasing rapidly.
4. 父は会社を退職して、今は年金で生活しています。
   My father has retired from his company and now he lives on a pension.
5. 私たちは祖父を特別養護老人ホームに入れました。
   We sent our grandfather to a special nursing home.
6. 母にとって祖父の世話がすごく負担になってきています。
   It's getting to be a big burden for my mother to take care of my grandfather.
7. 父は最近白髪が増えて、耳も遠くなってきています。
   My father's hair is turning gray now and he is hard of hearing.
8. 母は最近小さい字が読めなくなってきています。
   My mother has a hard time reading small print these days.
9. 母は最近物忘れをするようになってきています。
   My mother has become forgetful lately.
10. 祖父の老人性痴呆(ちほう)症［アルツハイマー病］がひどくなってきています。
    My grandfather's senility [Alzheimer's disease] is getting worse.

❷定年と老後に関する表現

1. 定年が60歳に上がり［下がり］ました。
   The retirement age has been raised [lowered] to 60.
2. 定年後も働きたいという人が多くいます。
   There are many people who want to work after retirement.
3. 高齢者のために働く機会を保証する必要があります。
   It is necessary to secure working opportunities for the elderly.
4. 祖父は老後の生きがいは庭いじりだと言っています。
   My grandfather says that gardening is what he lives for in his old age.
5. 年金は65歳から受けられます。
   We can receive a pension from the age of 65.

❸老人介護・老人ホームなどに関する表現

1. 老人介護保険［公的介護保険］が2000年から施行されました。
   Elderly care insurance [Public long-term care insurance] was implemented in 2000.
2. その保険は高齢者のための様々なケアをカバーしています。
   The insurance covers various types of care for the elderly.
3. お年寄りの家族の介護をするために仕事を辞めなければならない人もいます。
   There are people who have to quit their jobs in order to take care of elderly family members.
4. 老人介護ができる人をもっとたくさん養成する必要があります。
   We need to train more people who can provide care for the elderly.
5. 在宅介護を助けるためのサービスが導入されつつあります。
   Services that help with home care are being introduced.
6. ホームヘルプサービスやデイサービス等を利用したいというお年寄りはたくさんいます。
   There are many senior citizens who wish to use the home-help services or day services.
7. 老人用の養護施設は十分にありません。
   There aren't enough nursing homes for the aged.
8. 高齢者のための温泉施設があちこちにできています。
   Spas for the elderly have been built in many areas.
9. 家族と暮らすより老人ホームに入るのを好む人もいます。
   There are people who prefer to live in a nursing home rather than with their families.
10. 特別養護老人ホームは、常に介護が必要な老人のための施設です。
    Special nursing homes are institutions for seniors who need constant care.
11. 政府は老人福祉にもっとお金をつぎ込むべきです。
    The government should put more money into the welfare system for older people.

になっている The manager of the winning team is *usually* tossed into the air by his players.

こうれい[2] 高齢 advanced age [C], advanced years ⇒ [高齢化と介護] p.522 ‖私の祖母は100歳の高齢で亡くなりました My grandmother died at *the advanced age* of 100 years old.

◆日本では急速に高齢化が進んでいる Japanese society *is* rapidly *aging*.

‖高齢化社会 an aging society / 高齢者 an elderly [old] person, an elderly [old] man [woman], 《集合的》the elderly, the aged, elderly [old] people / 高齢出産 childbearing in later years

こうれい[3] 好例 good example [C]

ごうれい 号令 (命令) command [C]; (指示) order [C] ‖私のクラスでは学級長が起立の号令をかける The class leader gives *a command* [*an order*] to stand up in our class.

こうれつ 後列 back [rear] row [C] ‖後列に座る sit in *a back row*

こうろ 航路 route [C], course [C]; (船・飛行機などの定期の) lane [C] ‖遠洋航路 *a* sea *lane*

‖定期航路 the regular line

こうろう 功労 (貢献) contribution [U], services; (賞賛に値する) merits ‖功労者 a person who has done distinguished *services* / 彼は地域に対する功労により表彰された He was rewarded for *his contribution* [*services*] to the local community.

こうろん 口論 (口げんか) quarrel [C]; (激しい言い争い) argument [C]; (論争) dispute [C]

━口論する quarrel [自], have* a quarrel, 《婉曲的》have words with ...; argue [自]; dispute [自] ‖ゆうべ父とアルバイトのことで口論した I *had a quarrel with* my father about [over] my part-time job last night. / ささいなことで姉と口論になった I *got into a quarrel with* my sister about [over] trifles.

こうわ 講和 peace [C] ‖講和条約を結ぶ[破棄する] conclude [terminate] *a peace treaty*

‖講和会議 a peace conference

こうわん 港湾 harbor, 《英》harbour [C]

ごうわん 剛腕 剛腕投手 a *strong-armed* pitcher

こえ 声

❶【人の】voice [C] [U]

〚声が・は〛

彼は声が大きい He speaks in *a* loud *voice*.

表で声がした I heard *voices* outside.

彼女の声はよく通る Her *voice* carries well.

かぜをひいて声が出ない I have caught a cold, and lost *my voice*.

彼らの声が静かな場内に響いた Their *voices* sounded through the silent hall.

あの歌手は声がいい That singer has *a* good *voice*.

彼は怒りで声が震えた His *voice* shook with anger.

◆(電話で)声が遠いのですが I *can't hear you*.

〚声を・に〛

もっと声を出して *Raise your voice*.

彼らは声を潜(ひそ)めた They lowered *their voices*.

乗客は声を限りに助けを求めた The passengers shouted for help *at the top of their voices*.

彼は珍しく声を荒げた He *raised his voice*, which was unusual for him.

声に聞き覚えがあった It was *a* familiar *voice*.

◆彼女はその悲しい話を聞くと声をあげて泣いた She *cried out loud* when she heard the sad story. / 原宿でスカウトに声をかけられた A talent scout *approached* [*stopped*] me in Harajuku. / 今度野球の試合を見に行くときは私にも声をかけてください(→誘ってください) Please *ask* [*invite*] me next time you go to see a baseball game. / 声を合わせて歌いましょう Let's sing「*along together* [*in chorus*]. / その子供たちは声に出して本を読んだ Those children read a book *aloud*. / 彼は怒りで声を詰まらせていた He *was choking* with anger.

💬「こんなに遅くまでどこに行ってたんだ」「そんなに大きな声を出さないでよ」"Where have you been so late!" "Don't *shout* at me!"

〚声で〛

私たちは満員のエレベーターの中で小さな声で話した We talked in low [quiet] *voices* in a crowded elevator.

◆大きな声では言えないが(→我々の間の秘密だが)… *This is just between us, but* .... / もっと大きな[小さな]声で言ってください Could you *speak louder* [*more quietly*]? / Could you「*speak up* [*keep your voice down*]?

[コロケーション] -voice-

〚形容詞+～〛落ち着いた～ a steady voice / かすれ～ a husky [hoarse] voice / 金切り～ a shrill voice / かん高い～ a high-pitched voice / 澄んだ～ a clear voice / 力強い～ a firm voice / どら～ a gruff voice / 太い～ a deep voice / 震え～ a quivering voice / 細い～ a weak voice / 耳ざわりな～ a harsh [an abrasive] voice / 優しい～ a gentle voice

❷【動物の】(獣・鳥の) cry [C]; (小鳥・虫の) chirp [C]

オオカミの声 *the cries* of the wolves

けさは小鳥の声で目がさめた I woke to *the chirps* of the birds this morning.

◆鳥や虫の声を楽しむ enjoy birds and insects *singing*

⇒なきごえ(鳴き声)

❸【意見】

声なき声 *the silent majority*

先生たちに生徒の声をもっと真剣に聞いてもらいたい We want the teachers to listen to *the opinion* [*voice*] of the student body more seriously.

彼らは平和の尊さを声を大にして訴えている They *are emphasizing* the preciousness of peace.

ごえい

根本的な財政改革を求める声が高い There is a cry for radical financial reform.

今度の人事異動に関して一部の社員から不満の声が上がっている Some employees *are complaining* about this personnel change.

❹【時期】

英国では春の声を聞くころ(→春になると)水仙の花が咲き乱れる *When spring arrives*, daffodils are in full bloom all over Britain.

慣用表現 彼女は社長からお声がかかって、新規プロジェクトのメンバーとなった She became a member of the new project *on the recommendation* of the president.

ごえい 護衛（見張り）guard ⓤ; (同行) escort ⓤ (❖いずれも人を表す場合は ⓒ) ──護衛する guard ⓗ; escort ⓗ //護衛されて *under guard* [*escort*] / 彼らはヨーロッパ諸国を訪問した首相を護衛した They *escorted* the Prime Minister on his European tour.

◆マフィアのボスは多くの護衛をつけている The Mafia don has many *bodyguards*.

こえがわり 声変わり the change [breaking] of *one's* voice //僕は14歳のとき声変わりした I had *the change of my voice* when I was 14. / 彼は声変わりし始めた His *voice* began to *change*.

こえだ 小枝 twig ⓒ; sprig (❖twig より小さく、花や葉がついている); (地面に落ちている) stick ⓒ //たき火をする小枝を集めよう Let's pick up *sticks* to make a fire.

ごえつどうしゅう 呉越同舟 While the thunder lasted, two bad men were friends. (❖「雷が鳴っている間は2人の悪人も友達になった」の意味)

こえる¹ 越える・超える

❶【向こう側へ行く】go* [get*] over ..., cross ⓗ

国境を越える *cross* the border

車は丘を越えて見えなくなった The car *went over* the hill and disappeared.

◆この鳥たちは毎年冬になると大陸からはるばる海を越えてやってくる These birds come *over* the sea all the way from the continent every winter.

❷【上回る】(より多い) be over ..., be more than ...; (数量・限度などを) exceed ⓗ, go* beyond ...; (よりすぐれている) excel ⓗ

制限スピード[定員]を超える *exceed*「the speed limit [the capacity]

あの先生は30を超えているに違いない That teacher must *be over* 30.

その動物園の入場者数はついに100万人を超えた At last the number of the people who visited the zoo *exceeded* one million.

◆音速を超える *break* the sound barrier / 彼女の踊りは師匠を超えたね She came to dance *better than* her teacher. / ダム建設反対の運動に5万を超える署名が集まった *More than* fifty thousand people signed the petition against building the dam. / 大雪は予想を超える被害をもたらした Heavy snow caused *greater* damage *than expected*.

❸【超越する】go* [get*] over ..., 《公式的》transcend ⓗ

言葉の壁を越える *get over* a language barrier

◆あなたの行動は我々の理解を超えている Your behavior *is beyond our understanding*. / 名画は時代を超えて(→すべての時代の人々から)愛される Great movies are loved *by people of all generations*. / 15という年の差を越えて二人は結婚した They got married *despite an age difference* of 15 years. / そのコンサートにはジャンルの壁を越えて多くのミュージシャンが集まった Many musicians came together for the concert, *overcoming their different genres*.

⇨こす(越す・超す)

こえる² 肥える ❶【人・動物が】grow* [get*] fat ──肥えた fat, 《婉曲的》stout

❷【土地が】grow* fertile [rich] ──肥えた fertile //肥えた土地 *fertile* land

❸【感覚が】…に関して目[耳]が肥えている have an eye [ear] *for* ... / 彼は舌が肥えている He *has a delicate palate*.

こおう 呼応〖文法〗agreement ⓤ, concord ⓤ ──呼応する agree (with ...)

ゴーカート go-kart, 《米》go-cart ⓒ

コークス coke ⓤ

ゴーグル ⚠ goggles (❖数えるときは a pair of ... とする)

ゴーサイン ⚠ the go-ahead, the green light //知事はウォーターフロント開発にゴーサインを出した The governor gave「*the go-ahead* for [*the green light* to] the waterfront development.

ゴージャス ゴージャスな装い a *gorgeous* dress

コース (道筋・順序) course ⓒ, route ⓒ; (水泳・陸上などの) lane ⓒ; (料理の) course ⓒ (❖コース料理の1品を指す)

進学コースに進む go on to *the* college preparatory *course* / (ゴルフで)コースに出る play on a golf *course* / コース上にいる[コースをはずれる] be *on* [*off*] *course*

京都を見て回るならこのコースがお勧めです We would recommend this *route* to you for sightseeing in Kyoto.

姉は英会話集中コースで勉強しています My sister studies in *an* intensive English conversation *course*.

彼は第2コースを泳ぐ He is going to swim in *Lane* 2.

私たちはゆうべ評判のフランス料理店でフルコースの食事をした We had a *full course* dinner last night at a popular French restaurant.

◆景色のよいハイキングコース a scenic hiking *trail* / インコースの[アウトコースの]球 an *inside* [*outside*] pitch / 出世への最短コース *the* fast *track* for promotion

コースター coaster ⓒ; (ビールの) beer mat ⓒ

ゴースト (幽霊) ghost ⓒ //ゴーストタウン a ghost town / ゴーストライター a ghost

(writer)
コーチ (指導する人) coach ◎; (指導すること) coaching ◎ ──コーチする coach ◆兄はテニスのコーチだ My brother is *a* tennis *coach*. / 私はナショナルチームをコーチするように任命された I've been appointed to *coach* the national team.

コーディネーター coordinator ◎ ‖インテリアコーディネーター an interior coordinator

コーディネート ⚠(衣服の組み合わせ) coordinates ──コーディネートする coordinate

コーティング coating ◎◎ ◆この本の表紙はビニールでコーティングしてある The cover of this book *is coated* with vinyl.

コーデュロイ corduroy ◎

コート¹ (上着) coat ◎, overcoat ◎ ‖毛皮のコート *a* fur *coat* ‖ダッフルコート a duffel coat / トレンチコート a trench coat / レーンコート a raincoat

コート² (スポーツの) court ◎ ‖テニスコート *a* tennis *court* / 芝の[クレー]コート a grass [clay] *court*

コード¹ (電気) (electric) cord ◎

コード² (規則・暗号) code ◎ ‖コードネーム a code name

こおどり 小躍り ◆彼女はその知らせを聞くと小躍りして喜んだ She *danced for joy* when she heard the news.

コードレス ──コードレスの cordless ‖コードレス電話 a *cordless* phone

コーナー corner ◎; (競技場の) turn ◎, bend ◎; (特定の区画・売り場) section ◎, department ◎ ‖イン[アウト]コーナー the inside [outside] *corner* / 喫煙コーナー *a* smoking *section* / コーナーぎりぎりに right in *the corner* / 第3コーナーを回る round *the* third *turn* / あの投手はコーナーワークがうまい The pitcher has good *control in pitching to the corners*. ◆コーナーに追い詰める *corner a person* (◆この corner は動詞)
‖コーナーキック『サッカー』a corner kick

コーナリング cornering ◎ ◆私の車はコーナリングがよい My car *corners* well.

コーヒー coffee ◎ (◆ coffee はふつう a cup of coffee, two cups of coffee などと数えるが, 喫茶店などで注文する場合は a coffee, two coffees などということが多い. 豆の種類をいう場合は ◎)
◆濃い[薄い]コーヒー strong [weak] *coffee* / ブラック[ミルク入り]コーヒー black [white] *coffee* (◆単に black, white ともいう)
彼女は喫茶店でコーヒーを飲んでいた She was drinking a cup of *coffee* in a coffee shop.
コーヒーでもいかがですか Would you like some *coffee*?
コーヒーを入れてあげましょう I'll make *coffee* for you.
我々はコーヒーを飲みながら話をした We talked over a cup of *coffee*.
コーヒーはブラックでお願いします I like *my coffee* black.
姉は紅茶党だが私はコーヒー党だ My sister is a tea drinker, but I'm a coffee drinker.
彼は大のコーヒー好きで自分で豆をひいてブレンドするほどだ He *loves coffee*, and even grinds and blends his own beans.

> 英作文ノート 「アメリカン」は好きですか？
> 私はアメリカンコーヒーが好きです
> →×I like *American coffee*.
> →○I like *weak coffee*.
> ★アメリカのレストランなどで出されるコーヒーは一般に「薄い」が,「薄いコーヒー」の意味で American coffee とはいわない.「濃いコーヒー」(strong coffee) を好まない場合は, Make it weak, please. などといえばよい.

‖コーヒーカップ a coffee cup / コーヒー牛乳 coffee-flavored milk / コーヒーゼリー coffee-flavored jelly (◆「コーヒーゼリー」は和製英語) / コーヒーブレイク a coffee break (◆〖英〗では a tea break も同じ意味で使われる) / コーヒーポット a coffee pot / コーヒー豆 a coffee bean / コーヒーミル a coffee mill [grinder] / コーヒーメーカー a coffee maker / アイスコーヒー iced coffee / インスタントコーヒー instant coffee / 缶コーヒー canned coffee
関連語 エスプレッソ (an) espresso / カプチーノ (a) cappuccino / キリマンジャロ Kilimanjaro / サイフォン a coffee siphon / デミタス (a) demitasse / ブルーマウンテン Blue Mountain / モカ Mocha

コーラ cola ◎◎;〖商標名〗Coca-Cola ◎◎, Coke ◎◎, Pepsi-Cola ◎◎

コーラス (合唱・合唱団) chorus ◎ ‖コーラスで歌う sing in chorus

コーラン the Koran, the Quran [kərάːn]

こおり 氷

ice ◎ ──氷の(ような) icy
氷の1片[ひと塊] a piece [block] of *ice* / (製氷皿で作った)角氷 an *ice* cube
氷の上で滑って転んだ I slipped on *the ice*.
ゆうべ池に氷が張った The pond was covered with *ice* last night. / *Ice* formed on the pond last night.
はれた足首を氷で冷やした I treated my swollen ankle with *ice*.
オレンジジュースに氷を入れてください I'd like some *ice* in my orange juice.
けさは水が氷のように冷たかった The water *was icy* cold this morning.
魚はすぐに氷詰めにされた The fish *was* soon *packed in ice*.
◆氷に閉ざされた港 an *icebound* harbor
‖氷砂糖 sugar [rock] candy / 氷まくら an ice pillow, an ice bag / 氷水 ice water

こおりつく 凍り付く ◆凍りついた道 an *icy* road / 凍りついたような表情 a *stony* expression / きのうは凍りつくような寒さだった It *was freezing cold* yesterday.

こおる 凍る freeze* ◎; (凍っている) be fro-

zen ——凍らせる freeze 他 ∥水は摂氏0度で凍る Water *freezes* at zero degrees Celsius [centigrade]. / 水道管が凍ってしまった The water pipe *has frozen*. / 肉が冷凍庫の中でかちかちに凍っている The meat *is frozen* hard in the freezer. / その湖は湖面が凍っていた The surface of the lake *was frozen*. / 残ったスープは凍らせておけばよい You can *freeze* the leftover soup.
◆血も凍るような光景を見てしまった I saw a *bloodcurdling* scene.

ゴール (サッカーなどの得点) goal ⓒ; (目標) goal ⓒ; (トラック競技などの) finish (line) ⓒ ∥彼が決勝ゴールを決めた He scored [got] *the winning goal*. / ランナーが次々とゴールインしている The runners *are* now *crossing the finish line*. (❖×goal in とはいわない)
◆ついに二人はゴールインした (→ 結婚した) They finally *got married*.
∥ゴールキーパー a goalkeeper / ゴールキック a goal kick / ゴールポスト a goalpost / ゴールライン a goal line

コールタール coal tar ⓒ

ゴールデンアワー ⚠ prime [peak] time ⓒ ∥ゴールデンアワーの視聴率競争 a battle for *prime time* ratings

ゴールデンウイーク 🏔
> 4月の終わりから5月の初めにかけて、祭日と土曜・日曜がつながって連休となる週のことを「ゴールデンウイーク」といいます。多くの人々がいっせいに休みをとるため、行楽地はどこも混雑し、高速道路は大渋滞になります。
> "Golden Week" covers the period from the end of April to the beginning of May, during which there are several national holidays linked by a weekend. As a lot of people go on vacation at the same time, every holiday resort becomes crowded with people and the expressways are jammed with traffic.

ゴールド gold ⓤ ∥ゴールドラッシュ a *gold* rush / ゴールドメダリスト a *gold* medallist

コールドクリーム cold cream ⓤ

コールドゲーム called game ⓒ ◆試合は7回裏、雨のためコールドゲームとなった The game *was called* at the end of the seventh inning because of rain.

こおろぎ 蟋蟀 cricket ⓒ (❖英米ではコオロギに限らず、秋に鳴く虫を一般的に cricket と呼ぶことが多い) ∥コオロギの鳴き声が聞こえる I can hear *crickets* chirping.

コーン (トウモロコシ) (米) corn ⓤ, (英) maize ⓤ; (ソフトクリームなどの) cone ⓒ ∥コーンベルト the *Corn* Belt
∥コーンスープ corn soup / コーンスターチ corn starch / コーンフレーク cornflakes

ごおん 除夜の鐘がごおんと鳴った The New Year's bell resounded *with a deep gong*. / 頭を壁にごおんとぶつけた I banged my head against the wall.

こがい 戸外 the outdoors 《単数扱い》, the open air ——戸外で outdoor, open-air 《名詞の前に用いる》 ——戸外で outdoors, out of doors, in the open air

ごかい 誤解 misunderstanding ⓒⓤ ——誤解する misunderstand* 他, (口語的) get *a person* wrong ∥このような報道は視聴者に誤解を与えかねない Such a report can give rise to *misunderstandings* among viewers. / 僕に対する彼女の誤解は解けなかった I couldn't clear up *the misunderstanding* she had toward me. / 私のことを誤解しないでください Please don't *get me wrong*.
◆誤解を招くような態度 *misleading* behavior / 電話の相手は私を母と誤解して話し始めた A caller *mistook* me *for* my mother and began to speak.
🔊「ごめん、君のこと誤解してたよ」「分かってくれたならもういいよ」"I'm sorry, I *had misunderstood* you." "That's all right if you understand now."

こがいしゃ 子会社 subsidiary (company) ⓒ

コカイン cocaine [koukéin] ⓤ

ごかく 互角 ——互角の even, equal; (接戦の) close [klóus] ——互角に evenly, equally ∥互角の競争 a *close* race / 学校の成績では彼女は彼と互角だった In terms of school grades she was *even* with him.
◆あの2人のランナーはゴール直前まで互角の勝負だった Those two runners were *neck and neck* right up to the finish line.

ごがく 語学 (言語) language ⓒ (❖個々の言語ではなく言語一般をいう場合は ⓤ); (言語の学習) language study ⓤ ——語学の linguistic ∥あの子には語学の才能がある That child has「a talent for *languages* [a *linguistic* talent]. / 私は語学に強い[弱い] I'm good [bad] at *languages*. / きのうの語学の授業をさぼった I skipped *a language class* yesterday.
◆その仕事に就きたいのなら語学力は必須だ If you want to get that job, *a command of foreign languages* is a must.
∥語学学校 a language school / 語学教育 language education / 語学教材 language teaching materials / 語学教師 a language teacher

ごかくけい 五角形 pentagon ⓒ ——五角形の pentagonal ∥正五角形 *a regular pentagon*

こかげ 木陰 the shade of a tree ∥木陰でひと休みする have a rest in *the shade of a tree*
◆その通りは木陰になっている The street *is shaded by trees*.

コカコーラ 《商標名》Coca-Cola ⓤ ⓒ, Coke ⓤ ⓒ

こがす 焦がす burn* 他; (アイロンなどで) scorch 他; (衣類などの表面を) singe 他 ∥肉を焦がさないように気をつけて Be careful not to *burn* the meat. / 父はたばこで畳を焦がしてしまった My father *burned* a tatami mat with a cigarette. / 私はお気に入りのシャツをアイロンで焦がしてしまった I *scorched*

[singed] my favorite shirt when ironing.

こがた 小型・小形 (じじんまりした) compact; (持ち運びに便利な) portable; (ポケットサイズの)《口語的》pocket-sized ∥小型車 a small [compact] car / 小型テレビ a portable TV / 小型辞典 a pocket-sized [compact] dictionary
◆小型バス a minibus / 小型飛行機 a light plane / 超小型カメラ a micro-camera / モバイル機器はますます小型化している Hand-held devices [gadgets] are getting smaller and smaller.
∥小型化 miniaturization

こがたな 小刀 (small) knife ⓒ (複 knives); (折りたたみ式) pocketknife ⓒ, penknife ⓒ

こかつ 枯渇 ─枯渇する (干上がる) dry up; (欠乏する) run* out; (使い果たす) be exhausted ∥井戸が枯渇した The well dried up. ◆財源が枯渇した a drain on financial resources / 乱開発で国の資源が枯渇した(→乱開発が枯渇させた) Destructive development exhausted the country's resources.

ごがつ 五月 May Ⓤ ⇨小見出し
∥五月人形 a warrior doll for the Boy's Festival on May 5 / 五月病 hypochondria that afflicts many college freshmen or new employees in May

こがね 黄金 gold Ⓤ ──黄金色の golden

こがねむし 黄金虫 gold beetle ⓒ (❖日本のものとは別種)

こがら 小柄 ──小柄な (背が) short, small; (体つきが) of small build; (女性が) petite ∥うちの息子はどちらかというと小柄だ My son is rather small.

こがらし 木枯らし cold winter wind ⓒ ∥木枯らし一号は例年11月ごろに吹く The first cold winter wind usually blows in around November.

-こがれる ─焦がれる (切望する) long for ..., be impatient for ...; (恋する) be ardently in love with ... ∥彼は彼女からの電話を待ちこがれている He is longing [impatient] for her call. / He is impatiently waiting for her call.
◆彼女はその二枚目俳優に恋いこがれている She has a crush on the good-looking actor.

ごかん¹ 互換 この2つのワープロソフトは互換性がある[互換性がない] These two word processors are compatible [incompatible].

ごかん² 語感 (言葉に対する感覚) a sense of language; (語のもつ感じ) connotations, nuance ⓒ (❖connotationsはその言葉が含意するもの, nuanceは意味の微妙な違いを指す) / 詩人は鋭い語感をもっている Poets have a keen sense of language.

ごかん³ 五感 the five senses ∥五感をフルに働かせる use the five senses fully

ごがん 護岸 ∥護岸工事 shoreline protection works

こき 古希 the age of 70 ∥古希を迎える reach the age of 70

ごき 語気 a tone of voice ◆語気を荒げる raise one's tone / 語気を強めて言う speak emphatically

ごぎ 語義 the meaning of a word; (定義) definition Ⓤ

こきおろす 扱き下ろす 《口語的》 run* down, criticize severely ◆音楽雑誌は彼女の新しいCDをこきおろした The music magazines savaged [ran down] her new CD.

ごきげん 御機嫌 あの男はご機嫌とりだ He is ingratiating./《米口語的》He is an apple polisher./ ご機嫌いかがですか How are you?/ きょうは山本先生のご機嫌がいい Mr. Yamamoto is in a good mood today./ ご機嫌ななめだね You are not happy, are you?/ その赤ちゃんは高い高いをしてもらってご機嫌だった The baby looked very happy being raised high in the air.

こきざみ 小刻み 失業率は小刻みに上昇している The unemployment rate is slowly [little by little] increasing./ 恐怖のため彼女は小刻みに震えていた She was trembling slightly with fear.

こぎたない 小汚い そんな小汚い格好で出かけちゃだめだよ You shouldn't go out dressed so sloppily.

こきつかう こき使う work [drive*] a person hard,《口語的》push a person around ∥彼は従業員をこき使った He worked his employees hard.

こぎつける 漕ぎ着ける (何とか…する) manage to do; (合意などに達する) reach ⓖ ∥彼らはやっと開店にこぎつけた They finally managed to open their shop./ 両国は長い話し合いの末合意にこぎつけた Those two countries reached agreement after long talks.

こぎって 小切手 check,《英》cheque ⓒ ∥旅行者用小切手 a traveler's check / 不渡り小切手 a dishonored check / 20ドルの小切手を書く write a check for 20 dollars / この小切手を現金に換えてください I'd like to cash this check./ I'd like to get this check cashed./ 小切手にサインをお願いします Could you sign for the check?/ 小切手で払えますか Can I pay by check?
∥小切手帳 a checkbook,《英》a chequebook

ごきぶり cockroach ⓒ,《口語的》roach ⓒ ∥ゴキブリ捕り a cockroach trap

こきみ 小気味 ネギを刻む小気味のいい音 the pleasant sound of chopping leeks / 和郎がドリブルで相手選手をかわしてゆく姿は見ていて小気味がいい I get a kick out of watching Kazuro dodge his opponents while dribbling.

こきゃく 顧客 customer ⓒ; (弁護士などの) client ⓒ ⇨きゃく ∥顧客リスト a list of customers

こきゅう 呼吸
❶【息】breath ⓒ; (呼吸すること) breathing Ⓤ;《公式的》respiration Ⓤ ──呼吸する breathe [bríːð] ⓐⓖ
人に人工呼吸を施す give artificial respiration to a person; practice artificial respiration on a person / 深呼吸する take a deep

breath / 呼吸を整える catch *one's breath* / 呼吸を数える count *one's breathing rate*

魚はえらで呼吸する Fish *breathe* through their gills.

運動をすると呼吸が速くなる Your *breathing* gets faster when you do exercise.

その患者は呼吸が荒い The patient is *breathing heavily [hard]*.

救急車が到着したときにはすでに病人の呼吸は止まっていた The patient had already stopped *breathing* when the ambulance arrived.

彼は心臓発作を起こし，呼吸困難になった He had a heart attack, and *had difficulty (in) breathing*.

❷ 【調子】
彼と私は呼吸が合う（→気が合う） He and I *get along well*.

そのロシアのペアはぴったり呼吸の合ったスケーティングを見せた The Russian pair skated *in perfect harmony*.

❸ 【こつ】 knack [nǽk] ◯
走り幅跳びでは助走の呼吸をつかまなければだめだ You need to get *the knack* of an approach run in the long jump.

‖呼吸器 a respiratory organ / 呼吸器疾患 a respiratory disease / 複式呼吸 abdominal breathing

こきょう 故郷

（出身地・国）home ◯; （生まれた市・町・村）hometown ◯; （故国）homeland ◯; （出生地）*one's* birthplace ――故郷の home ――故郷に[へ] home

学生のほとんどが故郷に帰っている Most students have gone [returned] *home*.

故郷がなつかしい I miss *my hometown [home]*.

彼は18℃故郷を後にした He left *his hometown* at the age of 18.

彼女は故郷の北海道に戻った She returned *home* to (*her native*) Hokkaido.

私はこの町を第二の故郷と思っている I regard this town as *my second home*.

🔴「マイク，君の故郷はどこなの」「シドニーで生まれたんだけど，4歳から大学に行くまではケアンズにいたよ」 *"Where are you from, Mike?" "I was born in Sydney, but I lived in Cairns from when I was four years old until I went to university."*

慣用表現 その小説家は故郷に錦を飾った The novelist *returned home with a great success.*

こぎれい 小奇麗 ――小ぎれいな neat ――小ぎれいに neatly /妹はいつも部屋を小ぎれいにしている My sister always keeps her room *neat and tidy [clean]*. / 彼女は小ぎれいな身なりをしている She dresses *neatly*.

こく¹ （酒類の）body ⓤ ――こくのある full-bodied; (こってりした) rich /こくのある風味 a rich taste; *rich* flavor /こくのある赤ワイン *full-bodied* red wine

こく² 酷 ――酷な （残酷な）cruel; (非常に厳しい) severe, harsh /その仕事をすべて彼女にやらせるなんて酷だ It's *cruel* of you to make her do all that work. / 酷な言い方かもしれないけど，君にはそれは無理だよ It may sound a little too *harsh*, but I don't think you can do it.

こぐ 漕ぐ （ボートを）row 自他; （カヌーを）paddle 自他; （ブランコを）get* [go*] on a swing; (自転車・ペダルなどを) pedal 自他 /私たちは公園の池でボートをこいだ We *rowed* a boat on the pond in the park. / 自転車をこいで坂道を上るのは重労働だ It's very tiring to *pedal* (a bike) up a hill.

慣用表現 彼は授業中よく舟をこいでいる（→居眠りしている）He often *nods off* during a class.

ごく¹ 極 very, extremely /ごく少数の人々 *very few people* / この魚は日本近海ではごくまれにしか見られない We see this fish in the sea near Japan only *very* occasionally.

◆この事故はごく最近起こった This accident happened *quite* recently.

ごく² 語句 words and phrases

ごくあく 極悪 ――極悪の very bad; (残忍な) atrocious, 《公式的》heinous /極悪犯罪 a *heinous* crime / 極悪非道の所業 *atrocious [outrageous]* conduct

‖極悪人 an arch villain, a devil

ごくい 極意 (真髄) the essence; (秘伝) the secret /空手の極意をつかむ master *the essence [secret]* of karate

こくいっこく 刻一刻 every moment [second], moment by moment /刻一刻と自分の番が近づいてきた My turn approached *moment by moment*.

こくえい 国営 national [state] management ⓤ ――国営の national, state-run, government-run /国営企業 a *state-run* enterprise / 国営放送 *national* broadcasting

◆たばこ産業を国営化する *nationalize* the tobacco industry

こくえき 国益 the national interest /国益に反する be against *the national interest*

こくえん 黒煙 black smoke ⓤ /黒煙を吐く emit *black smoke*

こくおう 国王 king ◯; (君主) monarch ◯ /ヨルダン国王 *the King* of Jordan / 国王陛下 His Majesty *the King*

こくがい 国外 ――国外の foreign, overseas ――国外へ[に] overseas, abroad, outside the country /国外のニュース *foreign* news / その俳優は日本だけではなく国外でも人気がある That actor is popular both in Japan and *abroad*. / うちの両親はまだ国外へ出たことがない My parents have never been *abroad [overseas, outside the country]*. / その犯人は（飛行機で）国外へ逃亡した The criminal *took flight abroad*.

◆国外に住んでいる日本人 (an) *expatriate* Japanese / 元大統領は国外に（→自分の国から）追放された The former president was expelled [exiled] *from his country*.

‖国外追放 exile

こくがく 国学 the study of native Japanese thought through classical Japanese literature

こくぎ 国技 the national sport [game] ∥相撲は日本の国技だ Sumo wrestling is *the national sport* of Japan.

こくご 国語 (日本語) Japanese Ⓤ, the Japanese language; (公用語) national [official] language Ⓒ; (母国語) native language Ⓒ, mother tongue Ⓒ ∥国語の先生 a *Japanese (language)* teacher / 現代国語の授業は１週間に４時間ある There are four *modern Japanese* classes a week. / カナダの国語は英語とフランス語だ The *national languages* of Canada are English and French.

◆彼女は３か国語を話す She speaks three *languages*./ She is trilingual.

∥国語科(日本語科) a Japanese language course / 国語教育(日本語教育) Japanese language teaching / 国語辞典(日本語)の a Japanese dictionary

ごくごく 水をごくごく飲む gulp (down) water

こくさい¹ 国際 ━国際的な international; (全世界にわたる) cosmopolitan ━国際的に internationally

国際試合 an *international* match / 国際会議に出席する attend an *international* conference / 国際性を身につける acquire *an international way of thinking*

ロンドンやニューヨークは本当に国際色豊かだ London and New York are very *cosmopolitan*.

国際結婚は離婚率が高いという統計がある Some statistics say that a higher divorce rate is found in *international marriages*.

大臣の失言は国際問題にまで発展した The Minister's gaffe developed into *an international problem*.

その歌手は国際的に人気がある That singer is *internationally* popular.

◆兄は国際結婚をした(→日本人以外と結婚した) My brother *married a non-Japanese*.

∥国際運転免許証 an international driving licence / 国際化 internationalization / 国際関係 international relations / 国際協定 an international agreement / 国際協力 international cooperation / 国際空港 an international airport / 国際語 an international language / 国際社会 international society / 国際収支 the international balance of payments / 国際情勢 an international situation / 国際人 a cosmopolitan / 国際親善 international goodwill / 国際赤十字 the International Red Cross / 国際線 an international airline [flight] / 国際電話 an international call / 国際都市 a cosmopolitan city / 国際紛争 an international dispute / 国際法 international law / 国際見本市 an international trade fair / 国際理解教育 education for international understanding / 国際連合 the United Nations ((略語)) UN, U.N.)

こくさい² 国債 government [national] bond Ⓒ ∥国債を発行する issue *government bonds*

ごくさいしき 極彩色 極彩色の(→けばけばしい)Tシャツ a *garishly colored* T-shirt / 極彩色の施された神社の社殿 a *richly-colored* main hall of a shrine

こくさく 国策 national policy Ⓒ

こくさん 国産 ━国産の domestic, domestically produced; (農産物が) domestic-grown; (日本製の) Japanese, Japanese-made ∥国産品 *domestic* products [goods] / 国産車 a *domestic* car / 国産のマツタケ a *domestic-grown matsutake* mushroom / この国産ワインは非常にすばらしい This *domestically produced* wine is fantastic.

◆国産第１号のロケットがきのう打ち上げられた The first rocket *made in Japan* was launched yesterday.

こくし 酷使 ━酷使する (人などを) overwork ⓗ, work [drive*] ... hard; (機械などを) overuse ⓗ 体を酷使して働く *work one's body hard* / その雇用主は外国人労働者を酷使した The employer *overworked* the foreign laborers./ 長時間のＴＶゲームは目を酷使する Playing video games for hours *overworks* your eyes.

こくじ¹ 告示 (掲示) notice Ⓒ; (正式な) notification ⓊⒸ; (発表) announcement Ⓒ ━告示する notify ⓗ ∥政府告示 a government *notification*

こくじ² 酷似 close [striking] resemblance Ⓒ ━酷似する resemble closely ∥この新製品のブランド名とあの商標名は酷似している There is *a close resemblance* between the brand name of this new product and that trademark.

こくじ³ 国事 national [state] affairs

◆天皇の国事行為 the Emperor's *constitutional* functions

こくしょ 酷暑 intense [fierce, scorching] heat Ⓤ ◆去年の夏は酷暑だった Last summer it was *terribly* [*fiercely*] *hot*.

こくじょう 国情・国状 (事の事情) conditions of a country [nation]; (国内情勢) the state of affairs in a country [nation] ∥彼は中東各国の国情に明るい He is well informed about *the state of affairs in* Middle Eastern countries.

ごくじょう 極上 ━極上の (最高の) best; (高品質の) of the highest quality; (精選された) prime, choice ∥極上牛肉 *prime* beef / この品物は極上だ This merchandise is *of the highest quality*.

こくじん 黒人 black Ⓒ; (集合的) black people (◆Negroやcoloredには軽蔑的な含みがあるとされ, 現在はblackが好まれる. また最近ではアフリカ系アメリカ人という意味のAfro-Americanを好む人もいる) ━黒人の black ∥黒人の少年 a *black* boy / 黒人を差別する discriminate against *black people*

∥黒人英語 Black English / 黒人居住区 a

black neighborhood / 黒人霊歌 a spiritual

こくすいしゅぎ 国粋主義 ultranationalism ⓤ ‖国粋主義者 an ultranationalist

こくせい 国政 (national) administration ⓤ ‖国政選挙 a national election

こくぜい 国税 national tax ⓒ ‖国税庁(長官) (the Director General of) the National Tax Administration

こくせいちょうさ 国勢調査 (national) census ⓒ ‖国勢調査を行う take *a national census*

こくせき 国籍 nationality ⓤ; (市民権) citizenship ⓤ

日本国籍を失う lose *one's* Japanese *nationality*

彼は二重国籍です He has dual *nationality* [*citizenship*].

彼女はドイツ国籍です She has German *nationality*. / She is *a* German *citizen*.

彼がアメリカ国籍を取得した He *acquired* U.S. *nationality* [*citizenship*]. / He *was naturalized* in the U.S.

◆国籍不明機 an *unidentified* plane / 無国籍者 a *stateless* person

🖊「あなたの国籍は？」「日本です」 "What is your *nationality*?" "I'm Japanese." (❖外国に入国する際に出入国カードにも国籍欄は Japan ではなく Japanese と記入する)

⇒たこくせき

こくせんべんごにん 国選弁護人 court-appointed attorney ⓒ, public defender ⓒ

こくそ 告訴 (個人が刑事・民事事件を訴えること) accusation ⓒⓤ; (当局が主に刑事事件を訴えること) charge ⓒ; (個人の民事上の訴え) complaint ⓒ ──告訴する accuse ⓔ, charge ⓔ; complain to ...; (当局・個人が民事事件を訴える) sue ⓔ ‖告訴を取り下げる drop *an accusation* [*a charge*] / 彼女は上司をセクハラで告訴した She *accused* her boss of sexual harassment. / 警察はその男を窃盗罪で告訴した The police *charged* the man with theft. / 我々は損害賠償を求めて政府を告訴した We *sued* the government for damages.

‖告訴状 a letter of complaint / 告訴人 an accuser; (民事の原告) a complainant

こくそう 国葬 state [national] funeral ⓒ

こくそうちたい 穀倉地帯 granary ⓒ, grain belt ⓒ

こくたい 国体 (国民体育大会) the National Sports Festival; (国のあり方) national essence ⓤ

こくち 告知 notice ⓒ,《公式的》notification ⓤⓒ ──告知する notify ⓔ

◆現在は多くの人が癌(㋐)の告知を受ける Today many patients *are informed* that they have cancer.

こぐち 小口 小口の融資を受ける get *a small* loan

こくてい 国定 ‖国定教科書 a government-approved textbook / 国定公園 a seminational park

こくてん 黒点 (黒い点) black spot ⓒ; (太陽の) sunspot ⓒ

こくど 国土 country ⓒ; (土地) land ⓤ; (領土) territory ⓒ ‖日本の国土のおよそ70パーセントは山地だ About seventy percent of Japan's *land* is mountainous.

‖国土開発 national land development [planning] / 国土庁 the National Land Agency (❖2001年国土交通省に統合) / 国土地理院 the Geographical Survey Institute

こくどう 国道 national highway ⓒ ‖国道16号線 *National Highway* 16; *Route* 16

こくどこうつうしょう 国土交通省 the Ministry of Land, Infrastructure and Transport

こくない 国内 ─国内の domestic, home ‖国内ニュース home [*domestic*] news

◆この車種は国内だけでなく海外でも大人気だ This type of car is very popular both *at home* and abroad. / 彼はマラソンランナーとして国内では第一人者だ He is the best marathon runner *in the country*.

‖国内産業 domestic industry / 国内線 a domestic airline / 国内総生産 gross domestic product (《略語》GDP) / 国内便 a domestic flight / 国内放送 domestic broadcasting / 国内問題 a domestic issue / 国内旅行 a domestic trip

こくはく 告白 (罪・過ちなどの) confession ⓒⓤ ──告白する confess ⓔⓘ; (打ち明ける) tell* frankly ‖私は母に花びんを割ったことを告白した I *confessed* to my mother that I had broken the vase. / ポールはカレンに愛を告白した Paul *told* Karen (*frankly*) that he loved her. / Paul *declared* his love to Karen.

こくはつ 告発 accusation ⓤⓒ, indictment [indáitmənt] ⓤ, charge ⓒ ──告発する accuse ⓔ ‖彼女は詐欺の罪で告発された She *was accused* of fraud.

◆内部告発者によってその専務の汚職が発覚した The executive's corruption was brought to light by *a whistle-blower*.

‖告発者 an accuser / 告発状 a bill of indictment, a charge paper

こくばん 黒板 blackboard ⓒ,《米》chalkboard ⓒ (❖単に a board ともいう) ‖黒板に書く write on *a blackboard* / 黒板を消す clean *the blackboard*

‖黒板消し an eraser

こくひ 国費 (出費) national expenditures, national spending ⓤ; (予算) (national) budget ⓒ; (資金) government funds ‖国費をむだづかいする waste *government funds*

◆その外交官は国費で留学した The diplomat studied abroad *at government expense*.

‖国費留学生 a student studying abroad on a government scholarship

ごくひ 極秘 (極秘事項) top secret ⓒ; (極秘の状態) strict secrecy ⓤ ──極秘の top-secret, strictly secret, classified ‖極秘情報 *classified* information / 話し合いは極秘のうちに行われた The talks were held *in strict secrecy*.

‖極秘文書 top-secret documents
こくひょう 酷評 severe [sharp] criticism ⓤ ⓒ ――酷評する criticize ... severely [sharply] ◆その雑誌に彼の新著の酷評が載っていた There was *severe criticism* of his new book in the magazine.
こくひん 国賓 national [state] guest ⓒ ◆大統領は国賓として来日した The President visited Japan as *a state guest*.
こくふく 克服 conquest ⓤ ――克服する（打ち勝つ）conquer ⓗ;（乗り越える）overcome* ⓗ;（病気を）recover from ...,《口語的》get* over ... ◆彼女は引っ込み思案な性格を徐々に克服していった She managed to *overcome* her shyness little by little.
こくぶんがく 国文学（日本文学）Japanese literature ⓤ ◆国文学を専攻する major in *Japanese literature*
‖国文学科 the department of Japanese literature
こくぶんぽう 国文法（日本語の文法）Japanese grammarⓤ
こくべつしき 告別式 funeral (service) ⓒ ◆祖母の告別式を行った We *held* my grandmother's *funeral service*.
こくほう 国宝 national treasure ⓒ ◆人間国宝 *a living national treasure* ◆この仏像は国宝に指定されている This Buddhist image is designed as *a national treasure*.
こくぼう 国防 national defense [《英》defence] ⓤ ◆国防費 *defense spending* ／ 国防予算 the *defense budget*
‖国防省（英国の）the Ministry of Defence ／ 国防省（米国の）the Department of Defense, the Pentagon ／ 国防大臣（英国の）the Defence Minister ／ 国防長官（米国の）the Secretary of Defense
ごくぼそ 極細 ――極細の extrafine ◆極細のペン an *extrafine* pointed pen
こくみん 国民 nation ⓒ《単数扱い》;（文化的・地理的に見た場合の）people ⓒ;（国籍をもつ者）citizen ⓒ ――国民の national
国民的英雄 a *national* hero ／ 国民の声 the voice of *the nation* ／ 国民の祝日 a *national* holiday
全国民が核実験に反対した The whole *nation* [*country*] was opposed to the nuclear tests.
イギリス国民はよく紅茶を飲む The British (*people*) drink a lot of tea.
投票は国民の権利だ Voting is *a citizen's* right.
◆海外在住の日本国民は毎年増えている The number of Japanese *nationals* living abroad is increasing every year.
‖国民栄誉賞 a people's honor award ／ 国民感情 national mood [climate of opinion] ／ 国民休暇村 a national recreation village ／ 国民健康保険 national health insurance,《英》National Health Service ／ 国民宿舎 a public hostel run by the local council ／ 国民性 national characteristics [traits] ／ 国民総生産 gross national product（《略語》GNP）／ 国民体育大会 the National Sports Festival ／ 国民投票 a national referendum ／ 国民年金 national pension
こくむ 国務 state affairs ‖国務省（米国の）the State Department ／ 国務大臣 a Minister of State ／ 国務長官（米国の）the Secretary of State
こくめい 克明 ――克明な（詳しい）detailed;（念入りな）elaborate ――克明に in detail; elaborately ◆克明な記録 a *detailed* report ／ 事故の様子を克明に伝える tell *a person* about the accident *in detail*
こくもつ 穀物 cereal ⓒ ⓤ,《集合的》grain ⓤ,《主に英》corn ◆穀物市場 the *grain* market ／ 穀物畑 a field of *grain*
こくゆう 国有 ――国有の national, government-owned ――国有化する nationalize ⓗ ◆政府は石油産業を国有化した The government *nationalized* the oil industry.
‖国有財産 national property ／ 国有地 government-owned land ／ 国有林 a national forest
こくようせき 黒曜石〔鉱物〕obsidian ⓤ
ごくらく 極楽 (Buddhist) paradise ⓒ ◆その離島はこの世の極楽だった The isolated island was *a paradise* on earth. ◆（温泉につかって）ああ、極楽だ How *pleasant*! ◆祖父は85歳で極楽往生を遂げた（→安らかに死んだ）My grandfather *died peacefully* at the age of 85.
‖ゴクラクチョウ〔鳥〕a bird of paradise ／ 極楽とんぼ an easygoing fellow
ことわざ 聞いて極楽見て地獄 Though I heard the place was like a paradise, I see it is like Hell.; There's a big difference between what you see and what you hear.（→見ると聞くとでは大違いだ）
こくりつ 国立 ――国立の national ‖国立競技場 the National Stadium ／ 国立劇場 the National Theater ／ 国立公園 a national park ／ 国立大学 a national university ／ 国立博物館 a national museum
ごくりと 水をごくりと飲む gulp (down) water ／ ごくりとつばを飲み込む swallow hard
こくりょく 国力（勢力）national power [strength] ⓤ;（経済力）national wealth ⓤ
こくれん 国連 the United Nations（《略語》UN, U.N.）◆日本は1956年に加盟してJa-pan joined *the UN* in 1956. ／ Japan became a member of *the UN* in 1956.
‖国連安全保障理事会 the United Nations Security Council（《略語》UNSC）／ 国連加盟国 a member [nation] of the United Nations ／ 国連軍 the United Nations Forces ／ 国連憲章 the Charter of the United Nations ／ 国連事務総長 the Secretary-General of the United Nations ／ 国連総会 the United Nations General Assembly ／ 国連大学 the United Nations University ／ 国連大使 the Ambassador to the United Nations ／ 国連平和維持活動 a United Nations peacekeeping operation ／ 国連平和維持軍 a United Nations peacekeeping force ／ 国連本部 the United Nations Headquar-

ごくろう 御苦労 ご苦労さま *Thank you very much for your trouble.* / ゲームソフトを買うためにこの寒い中開店を待っているなんてご苦労なことだ(→どうかしている) *They're crazy to wait so long for the opening of the store to buy the game software in this cold weather.* ⇨くろう

こけ 苔 moss◎ ∥庭にコケが生えた *Moss has grown in the garden.*
◆こけむした石 *a mossy stone*
慣用表現 転石こけむさず *A rolling stone gathers no moss.* (✿元米「転々と職を変える人は成功しない」という意味だったが，《主に米》で「常に活動的であればさびつかない」という意味にも解されるようになった)

こけい 固形 ──固形の solid ∥固形食 solids, solid food / 固形スープ a stock cube / 固形燃料 a solid fuel

ごけい 語形 word form◎ ∥語形変化 inflection (✿個々の活用形は an inflection); (動詞の) conjugation

こけおどし 虚仮威し bluff◎ ∥そんなこけおどしは私には通じない *Such a bluff doesn't work with me.*

こげくさい 焦げ臭い 何かこげ臭いよ I (*can*) *smell something burning.*

こけこっこう cock-a-doodle-doo◎

こけし
こけしはもともと東北地方で作られていた木製の郷土人形です．円筒形の胴体に丸い頭がついているだけの素朴な形ですが，その素朴であたたかみのある表情は多くの人々を魅了してきました．
A kokeshi is a wooden doll originally made as a folk craft in the Tohoku district. It is characterized by its simple shape: it has nothing but a cylindrical body and a round head. Kokeshi, however, are appealing to many people because of their warm and charmingly innocent looks.

こげちゃ(いろ) 焦げ茶(色) dark brown◎
──こげ茶(色)の dark brown

こけつ 虎穴 ことわざ 虎穴に入らずんば虎児を得ず *Nothing ventured, nothing gained.* (→危険を冒さなければ何も得られない)

こげつく 焦げ付く ❶【焼けつく】burn* ⦿ ∥肉がなべにこげついてしまった *The meat has burned and stuck to the pan.*
❷【貸付金が回収不能になる】become* uncollectible [unrecoverable] ∥貸した金がこげついた *The loan became uncollectible.*

コケティッシュ ──コケティッシュな coquettish (✿英語の coquettish はあまりよい意味では用いない)

こげめ 焦げ目 肉にさっとこげ目をつけてからオーブンに入れます *Brown the meat quickly before putting it in the oven.* (✿この brown は「表面が軽く茶色になる程度に焼く」の意味，日本語と必ずしも一致しない)

こけらおとし 柿落とし the (formal) opening (of a new theater)

こける¹ 痩ける 長い療養生活の後, 彼女はほおがこけてしまった *Her cheeks have become hollow after spending a long time under medical treatment.*

こける² 転ける (転ぶ) fall* down, tumble down ⇨ころぶ

こげる 焦げる burn* ⦿; (表面が) scorch ⦿ ∥魚がこげてるよ! *The fish is burning*! / 何かこげるにおいがしませんか *Can you smell something burning*?

こけん 沽券 彼に金を借りるなんて私のこけんにかかわる *It is beneath my dignity to borrow money from him.*

ごけん 護憲 the support for the Constitution (in its current form) ∥護憲派 the supporters of the Constitution

ごげん 語源 the origin of a word, etymology◎ ∥辞書でその言葉の語源を調べてごらん *Look up the origin of the word* in the dictionary.

ここ¹

❶【場所】here; (この場所) this place; (これ・この) this
【ここが・は】
ここが私の母校だ *This is the school I used to go to.*
ここは札幌より寒い *It's colder here than Sapporo.*
🅔「ここはどこなんだろう(→私たちはどこにいるのだろう)」「ピカデリーサーカスの近くのはずなんだけど」 *"Where are we?" "Somewhere near Piccadilly Circus, I guess."*
【ここから】
ここから先は立入禁止です *You are not allowed to proceed from here.*
ここから出よう *Let's get out of here.*
ここから駅まで歩いてどのくらいですか *How long does it take from here to the station on foot?*
【ここに・へ】
ここへ来なさい Come (*over*) *here.* (✿over は相手が遠くにいる場合に用いる)
ここに越してくる前は横浜に住んでいました *We used to live in Yokohama before we moved here.*
荷物をここに置いていいですか *Can I leave my baggage here?*
助けがいるときはここ(→この番号)に電話して *Call this number if you need any help.*
🅔「僕の本知らない?」「ここにあるよ」 *"Have you seen my book?" "Here it is."*
🅔「なんだ, ここにいたのか. 探してたんだよ」「きょうはずっとここにいたよ」 *"You are here! I've been looking for you." "I've been here all day today."*
【ここ(の)～】
ここパリより実況生中継しております *I'm reporting live from here in Paris.*
ここ(→このパン屋)のパンは有名でよく雑誌に紹介されている *The bread of this bakery is very popular and often appears in magazines.*

【ここで】
ここではたばこはご遠慮ください Please refrain from smoking *here*.
ここかしこでそのうわさを聞く I hear the rumor *here and there*.
🔊 (タクシーで)「ここで降ろしてください」「はい、どうぞ」"*This* is fine./ Please stop *here*." "Here you are."

❷【時点・事態】
ここまでは大丈夫です *So far*, so good.
ここまで来たらもう後には引けない I cannot give up *at this point*.
ここがいちばんだいじだ *This* is the crucial point.
彼女はここ一番というときにいつも体調を崩してしまう She always gets sick *when the chips are down*.
ここぞというときにかぎって彼はどこかへ行ってしまう He's always gone *at the critical moment*.
ここらでひとつ実力をお見せしよう You'll see *now* what I can really do.
彼らはここぞとばかりに相手ゴールに攻めこんだ They attacked the opponent's goal *as if it were now or never*.

❸【期間】
ここ2、3日暖かい日が続いている It's been warm for the *past* few days.
ここしばらくは忙しくなるだろう I'll be busy *for a while*.
姉はここのところ毎日プールに泳ぎに行っている *Recently* my sister has been going to the swimming pool every day.

❹【その他】
ここだけの話だが… *This is (just) between you and me*, ….
彼のぐあいがここまで悪かったとは知らなかった I didn't know his condition was *this* bad.

ここ² 個々 ——個々の (独立した) individual; (各々の) each; (別々の) separate ——個々に individually; separately ∥個々のケースによって異なるので何とも言えない I can't comment on that because it depends on *each case*./ これらの問題は個々に検討する必要がある We'll have to consider these problems *individually* [*separately*].

ここ 古語 (廃語) obsolete word ⓒ; (古風な語) archaic word ⓒ

ごご 午後
(正午から夕方まで) afternoon ⓤⓒ; (正午から真夜中の0時までの時刻) p.m., P.M. ❖ラテン語で「正午の後」を意味する post meridiem の略. 時刻を表す数字の後に付けて用いる.
午後早く[遅く]に *in the* early [late] *afternoon* ∥ 日曜の午後に *on* Sunday *afternoon* ∥ きょう[あす、きのう]の午後 this [tomorrow, yesterday] *afternoon*
午後には雨もあがるだろう The rain will stop in *the afternoon*.
私は午後ずっと本を読んでいた I was reading a book all *afternoon*.
その店は午前11時から午後8時まであいている The shop is open from 11 a.m. to 8 *p.m.*
私は午後6時55分発の福岡行きの便を予約した I made a reservation on the flight for Fukuoka leaving at 6:55 *p.m.*

ココア hot chocolate ⓤ, cocoa [kóukou] ⓤ (❖いずれも店で注文するときは)

ここう 孤高 孤高の人 *a loner* (who has high ideals)

ごこう 後光 halo [héilou] ⓒ (複 ~(e)s), nimbus ⓒ (複 ~es, nimbi) ∥その優しい老婦人はまるで後光でもさしているかのように思われた It seemed as if the gentle old woman had *a halo* around her head.

こごえ 小声 (低い声) low voice ⓒ; (ささやき) whisper ⓒ ∥小声で話す speak in *a low voice*

こごえじに 凍え死に (凍死) death from cold [hypothermia]
◆寒さで凍え死にしそうになった I *was* almost *freezing to death* with cold.

こごえる 凍える freeze* 圓 ◆その朝は凍えるような寒さだった It was *freezing* cold that morning.

ここく 故国 one's home (country), one's homeland

ここち 心地 心地よい音楽 *pleasant* music ∥ この新しい化粧水は使い心地がよい This new skin lotion *is comfortable to apply*. ∥ 鳥の鳴き声で目がさめるのは心地よいものだ It is *pleasant* to wake up to the song of birds. ∥ 若者たちが心地よさそうに浜辺に寝そべっている Young people are *comfortably stretching out on the shore*. ∥ 生きた心地がしなかった I felt *more dead than alive*.

こごと 小言 (しかること) scolding ⓒ, telling-off ⓒ (複 tellings-off); (説教) lecture ⓒ ——小言を言う scold 他, tell* *a person off*; (説教する) lecture 他 ∥きのう両親にテストのことで小言を食らった I *was told off* about the exam by my parents yesterday.

ココナッツ coconut ∥ココナッツミルク *coconut* milk

ここのか 九日 9日間 for *nine days* ∥ 8月9日 August (*the*) *ninth*

ここのつ 九つ nine ⓤⓒ ⇨ きゅう(九)

こころ 心
❶【感情・精神】(感情) heart ⓒⓤ; (知性) mind ⓤⓒ; (魂) soul ⓒⓤ; (精神) spirit ⓤⓒ
私には彼の心が分からない I can't understand what's on his *mind*.
この曲を聞いていると心がなごむ *My heart softens* when I hear this tune./ This tune *soothes* me.
よく現代人は心が病んでいるといわれる It is often said that modern people *have diseased minds*.
なんて美しい景色だろう. 心が洗われるようだ How beautiful this scenery is! It *cleanses my heart*.
離れていても心はひとつだ I'll always *be with you in spirit*.

彼はいつか自分の手で家を建てようと心に決めた He *made up his mind* to build his own house by hand some day.

彼には心を打ち明けられる友達がいない He has no friends to *open his heart* to.

彼女は人の心を読むことができる She can *read others' minds*.

心から君のことを思っている I think of you *with my heart and soul*.

あなたには心から感謝しています I thank you *from the bottom of my heart*.

心の底から愛しています I love you *from the bottom of my heart*.

目は心の窓だ The eyes are the windows of *the soul*.

彼女はその仕事に身も心もささげた She devoted herself *body and soul* to the work.

◆心の病 *mental* troubles／心の広い［心の狭い］人 a *broad-minded* [*narrow-minded*] person／心優しい人 a *kind-hearted* person／心温まる話 a *heartwarming* story／その勇壮な祭りに日本の心を見た気がした I felt *Japanese* sensitivities in the heroic and violent festival.／「そんなの無理だ」と彼は心の中で叫んだ "It's impossible," he shouted *on the inside*.／彼は心の奥で何を考えているか分からない I have no idea what he's thinking *deep inside*.／彼女は遠い日本のふるさとを心に描いた She *pictured to herself* her hometown in faraway Japan.／あの夫婦は互いに心が通じ合っている That couple *understands each other*.

❷【慣用表現】

【心が痛む】君が悲しんでいるのを見ると心が痛む It *breaks my heart* to see you sad.

【心が動く】その提案に心が動いた I *was attracted* by the proposal.

【心が弾む】喜びに心が弾んだ My heart *leaped* with joy.

【心ここにあらず】彼女は心ここにあらずといった状態です She *pays no attention*.

【心に浮かぶ】ふとある疑念が彼女の心に浮かんだ Suddenly a doubt *occurred to her*.

【心に刻む】彼の勇姿は子供たちの心に深く刻み込まれた His valiant figure *was deeply engraved on* the children's minds [*memory*].

【心に留める】このことは心に留めておきなさい *Keep* this *in your mind*.

【心に残る】そのシーンはいまだに私の心に残っている The scene *is* still *imprinted on* my mind.

【心にもない】私は心にもないことを言ってしまった I said what I *really didn't mean*.

【心を入れ替える】心を入れ替えてまじめに働きます I'll *make a fresh start* and work hard.

【心を打つ】その少女の言葉に私は心を打たれた I *was moved* by what the girl said.

【心を奪う】彼は彼女の笑顔にすっかり心を奪われてしまった He *was* totally *fascinated* by her smile.

【心を鬼にする】彼は心を鬼にして息子を警察に連れていった He *hardened his heart against pity*, and took his son to the police.

【心をこめる】心のこもった贈り物 a *thoughtful* present／彼女は心をこめてマフラーを編んでいた She was knitting a scarf *with tender loving care*.

【心をつかむ】この新しいファッションは若い女性たちの心をつかんだ This new fashion *appealed to* young women.

【心を閉ざす】その少年はだれに対しても心を閉ざしていた（→開かなかった）The boy *didn't open his heart* to anyone.

【心を引く】のみの市を見ていて、私はなぜかその古い柱時計に心を引かれた When I went to the flea market, I *was* somehow *attracted to* the old wall clock.

【心を許す】あいつとは心を許し合った仲だ（→互いに信頼している）He and I *trust each other*.

【心を寄せる】彼女は大介に心を寄せている She *feels affection for* Daisuke.／She *is in love with* Daisuke.

こころあたり　心当たり（見当）idea ⓒ；（手がかり）clue ⓒ／この手紙の主がだれなのか全く心当たりがない I have absolutely no *idea* who wrote me this letter.
◆心当たりの場所は全部探してみたがその本は見つからなかった I checked *every likely place*, but I couldn't find the book.／その名前に心当たりはありますか Does the name *mean anything to you*?／Does the name *ring a bell*?

こころある　心ある（分別がある）sensible；（良心的な）conscientious；（情け深い）thoughtful／心ある人々が援助を申し出た *Thoughtful* people offered help.

こころいき　心意気（気迫）spirit ⓤ；（決意）determination ⓤ／その心意気だよ That's *the spirit*!／社長は君の心意気に引かれたんだ The president was impressed by your *spirit* [*determination*].

こころえ　心得（知識）knowledge ⓤ；（規則）rules／私にはいくらか茶道の心得がある I have some *knowledge* of the tea ceremony.
◆旅行中の心得（→すべきこととしてはいけないこと）*the dos and don'ts* during the trip

こころえる　心得る（会得している）know* ... very well；（理解する）understand* ⓘ／武術の奥義を心得ている *know* the heart of martial arts *very well*／彼女はその事情については心得ています He *understands* the situation.
◆君は仕事を何と心得ているんだ What do you *think of* your job?

こころおきなく　心置きなく（思う存分）to *one's heart's content*；（心配することなく）without worrying；（遠慮なく）without reserve／宿題も終わったして心おきなく（→目一杯）遊べるぞ Now that I have finished my homework, I can enjoy myself *to my heart's content* [*without worrying about anything*].

こころがけ　心掛け　みんなの信頼を得られるかどうかはふだんの君の心がけ（→態度）しだいだ Whether you can get everyone's trust depends on your everyday *attitude*.／早寝早起きするのはよい心がけだ（→賢明だ）It's *wise*

こころがける 心掛ける (留意する) keep* ... in mind; (努力する) try to do ∥そのことは心がけておきます I'll keep that in mind. / 少なくとも週2回は運動するように心がけている I try to get exercise at least twice a week.

こころがまえ 心構え one's mental attitude ◆そのことに関して心構えができていなかった I wasn't prepared for that.

こころがわり 心変わり a change of mind; (裏切り) betrayal Ⓤ ——心変わりする change one's mind; (裏切る) betray ⊕ ∥彼女は貴明の心変わりを責めた She blamed Takaaki for his change of mind.

こころくばり 心配り (配慮) consideration Ⓤ; (思いやり) thoughtfulness Ⓤ; (親切) kindness Ⓤ ∥みなさんのお心配りに感謝します I thank all of you for your consideration. ◆彼女は心配りのできる人だ She is a considerate person.

こころぐるしい 心苦しい 両親に仕送りを頼むのは心苦しい I hate to ask my parents to send me money.

こころざし 志 ❶【意志】(意向) will Ⓤ, wishes; (目標) aim Ⓒ, goal Ⓒ; (決心) resolution Ⓒ ∥彼は父の志を継いで教師になった Following his father's will [wishes], he became a teacher. / 彼女は志半ばで亡くなった She died before she achieved her aim. ◆僕は弁護士になる志を立てた I resolved [made up my mind] to become a lawyer. / 彼女は志が高い[低い] She has「lofty ambitions [no lofty ambitions].
❷【親切】kindness Ⓤ ∥お志に感謝します Thank you very much for your kindness. ◆これはほんの志(→感謝のしるし)です This is just a token of my gratitude.

こころざす 志す (意図する) intend to do; (ねらう) aim to do; (決意する) decide ⊕, make* up one's mind to do ∥父は若いころ野球選手を志していた My father had intended to become a baseball player when he was young. / 彼は小学生のころからF1レーサーを志していた He made up his mind to become a F1 driver when he was in elementary school.

こころづかい 心遣い (配慮) consideration Ⓤ; (思いやり) thoughtfulness Ⓤ ∥いろいろお心づかいいただきありがとうございます I thank you for your thoughtfulness.

こころづくし 心尽くし ——心尽くしの (心のこもった) hearty ∥心尽くしのもてなし hearty hospitality

こころづけ 心付け tip Ⓒ,《公式的》gratuity Ⓒ

こころづもり 心積もり 彼はひとりで宿題ができなければ姉に手伝ってもらう心積もりでいた He expected his sister to help him with his homework if he couldn't do it by himself.

こころづよい 心強い (安心させる) reassuring; (勇気づける) encouraging ∥心強い応援 an encouraging cheer ◆君といっしょだと心強いよ I feel reassured being with you.

こころない 心ない (思慮のない) thoughtless, inconsiderate; (無情な) heartless ∥心ない人々 thoughtless people / 私は彼の心ない言葉に傷ついた I was hurt by his heartless words.

こころなしか 心なしか 彼女はきょう心なしか元気がないように見えた She looked in low spirits today, unless I imagined it.

こころならずも 心ならずも (不本意にも) against one's will, unwillingly; (いやいや) reluctantly; (思わず) in spite of oneself ∥彼は心ならずも上司の提案を承諾した He accepted his boss' proposal reluctantly [against his will]. / 私は心ならずも彼女にうそをついてしまった I told a lie to her in spite of myself.

こころにくい 心憎い (みごとな) excellent, super; (感心するような) admirable ∥その酒のまろやかな味わいは心憎いばかりだ The mellow taste of the sake is excellent. ◆彼らの心憎いほどに凝ったもてなしに私はすっかり感激した I was deeply touched by their marvelously elaborate reception.

こころのこり 心残り (後悔) regret Ⓒ Ⓤ; (気が進まないこと) reluctance Ⓤ ∥僕には何の心残りもない I have no regrets. / I have nothing to regret. ◆彼と別れのあいさつを交わせなかったのが心残りだ I regret that I couldn't exchange good-byes with him.

こころばかり 心許り 心ばかりの物ですがどうぞお納めください Please accept this as a small token of my gratitude.

こころぼそい 心細い (寂しい) lonely; (不安な) uneasy ∥ひとり暮らしを始めたばかりで心細い I've just started living by myself and feel lonely.

こころまち 心待ち ——心待ちにする look forward to ...(❖to の後には名詞または動名詞が来る) ∥お帰りを心待ちにしています I'm looking forward to your return.

こころみ 試み attempt Ⓒ, try Ⓒ; (実験) experiment Ⓒ ∥勇気ある試み a brave attempt / 廃油をリサイクルするこの新しい試みに大きな期待が寄せられている They are expecting much of the new waste oil recycling experiment. ◆凶悪犯罪を減らそうとする政府の試みは失敗した The government's efforts to reduce violent crime failed.

こころみる 試みる try ⊕ ⊕; (特に困難なことを)《公式的》attempt ⊕ ∥逃亡を試みる attempt an escape / 私は何度も彼に学校へ来るよう説得を試みた I kept trying to persuade him to come to school.

こころもち 心持ち (幾分) a little, rather,《口語的》a bit ∥この靴は私には心持ち大きい These shoes are a bit too big for me.

こころもとない 心許ない (不安な) uneasy; (信頼がおけない) unreliable; (不安定な) unstable ∥彼にその仕事を任せるのは心もとない He is too unreliable to leave the work to. ◆手持ちの金だけでは心もとない I am uncom-

こころやすい 心安い （親しい）close, friendly ‖心安い友人 a *close* friend

こころゆくまで 心行くまで ▸彼らはホテルの窓からのすばらしい眺めを心ゆくまで堪能した They enjoyed the wonderful view from the hotel window *to their hearts' content*.

こころよい 快い nice; （気持ちのよい）pleasant; （さわやかな）refreshing ‖快いそよ風 a *refreshing* breeze ‖ 快い緊張感を楽しむ enjoy the *pleasant* feeling of tension

こころよく 快く （喜んで）gladly, with pleasure; （進んで）willingly; （即答で）readily ‖彼は私の願いを快く引き受けてくれた He accepted my request *willingly*. ‖ 先生は私の質問に快く答えてくれた My teacher *readily* answered my questions.

◆あの新しく来た生徒は同級生の間であまり快く思われていない The new student is not very *popular* among his [her] classmates.

ここん 古今 ancient and modern times

◆古今東西の恋愛小説 love stories of *all ages and countries*

ごさ 誤差 error ‖3パーセントの誤差 an *error* of three percent

◆風による誤差を計算に入れる take *the effect* of the wind into account

ござ rush mat

こざいく 小細工 cheap trick ‖…に小細工を弄する play a *cheap trick* on …

コサイン 〔数学〕cosine （（略語）cos）

こざかしい 小賢しい （ずるい）shrewd, cunning; （生意気な）presumptuous

こさく 小作 tenant farming ‖小作地 tenant land ‖小作人 a tenant (farmer)

こさじ 小匙 teaspoon ‖ （分量）teaspoonful ‖砂糖小さじ2杯 two *spoonfuls* of sugar

こざっぱり ──こざっぱりした （服装などが）neat (and tidy); （部屋などが）clean and tidy ◆彼はいつもこざっぱりした格好をしている He's always dressed *neatly*.

こさめ 小雨 a light rain; （ばらばらと降る雨）sprinkle ‖ drizzle; （通り雨）shower ‖けさ小雨がぱらついた There were *sprinkles* this morning.

◆小雨が降っている It's raining *lightly*.

こさん 古参 （古顔）old-timer

ごさん 誤算 （計算間違い）miscalculation ‖ （判断を誤ること）misjudgment ‖ miscalculation ──誤算する miscalculate; misjudge ‖私たちの最大の誤算は風が順風だと思っていたことだった It was our greatest *miscalculation* that the wind would be in our favor.

◆新人選手たちのめざましい活躍は監督にはうれしい誤算だった（→予想していなかった） The manager *didn't expect* that the rookies would achieve such remarkable results.

ごさんけ 御三家 the big [top] three

こし 腰

❶【体の部位】（胴のくびれた部分）waist; （左右に張り出した部分）hip （❖左右どちらか一方を指す。両方は hips）; （背中の下部）the lower back

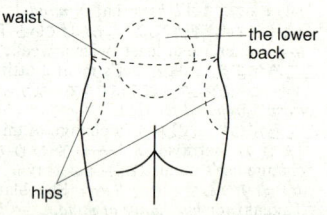

waist ─── the lower back
hips

彼女は腰が細い She has *a slender waist*.

きのうから腰が痛い I *have had a pain in my lower back* [*I've had a backache*] since yesterday.

山本先生は腰に手を当てて立っていた Mr. Yamamoto was standing with his hands on *his hips*.

パソコンを長時間使用すると肩や腰に負担がかかる When you use PC for a long time, a burden will be imposed on your shoulders and *your lower back*.

彼女は階段から落ちて腰を打ってしまった She fell down the stairs and bashed *her hip*.

このスカートは腰回りが少し窮屈だ This skirt is a little snug *around the hips*.

父はぎっくり腰になった（→腰の筋を違えた） My father strained *his lower back*.

◆腰を伸ばす stretch oneself ‖ 私の祖父は年で腰が曲がっている My grandfather is *bent* with age. ‖ 彼らはベンチに腰を下ろした They *sat down* on the bench. ‖ 彼女は腰をかがめて落としたものを拾った She *crouched* [*stooped*] down to pick up the thing she dropped. ‖ 彼は突風に飛ばされないように腰を落としてふんばった He stood firm, *bending low* not to be blown over by a gust of wind. ‖ このジーンズは腰ではくように作られている These jeans are *hip-huggers*.

❷【ねばりのある力】

腰の強い（→丈夫）紙 *strong* [*tough*] paper

このうどんは腰があっておいしい These noodles are *firm* and tasty.

❸【慣用表現】

【腰が重い・軽い】彼女は何をするにも腰が重い[軽い] She *is slow* [*willing*] to do anything.

【腰が低い】新井さんは礼儀正しくて腰の低い（→謙虚な）人だ Arai is polite and *modest*.

【腰を上げる】政府はやっと重い腰を上げてその問題に取り組み始めた The government *finally decided* to tackle the problem.

【腰を入れる】もっと腰を入れて（→真剣に）練習しなきゃだめだ You need to practice more *seriously*.

【腰を落ち着ける】私たちはしばらくその村に腰を落ち着ける（→滞在する）ことにした We decided to *stay* in the village for a while.

【腰を折る】母はいつも話の腰を折る（→話を中断する） My mother always *interrupts* [*cuts* in on] other's conversation.

【腰をすえる】弟も腰をすえて働くことにしたようだ My brother seems to *have settled down* to work.
【腰を抜かす】私は幽霊を見て腰を抜かした(→席を立てなくなった) I *froze to my seat* when I saw the ghost.

こじ¹ 孤児 orphan◯ ‖彼は2歳のとき孤児になった He *was left an orphan* at the age of two./ He *was orphaned* at the age of two. ‖孤児院 an orphanage / 中国残留日本人孤児 ➪ ざんりゅう

こじ² 故事 (歴史的事実) historical fact◯; (伝説) legend ‖故事来歴 the legend and history

こじ³ 誇示 ──誇示する (見せびらかす) show* off; (はっきり示す) display⊕ ‖富と権力を誇示する *show off one's* wealth and power

こじ⁴ 固持 田中教授は自説を固持した Professor Tanaka *persisted in* his own theory.

こじ⁵ 固辞 佐藤氏は選挙出馬依頼を固辞した Mr. Sato *firmly refused* the request to run for election.

-ごし -越し 窓越しに *through* a window / 肩越しに *over one's* shoulder / 新聞越しに *from behind* a newspaper / 小林さんとおじは20年越しの(→20年にわたる)つきあいだ Mr. Kobayashi and my uncle have been friends *over* 20 years.

ごじ 誤字 wrong letter [character]◯; (つづりの間違い) misspelling ‖彼の答案は誤字だらけだった His answer sheet was full of *wrong characters*.

こじあける こじ開ける pry [prize] ... open; (無理に) force ... open; (壊して) break* ... open ‖泥棒はドアをこじあけた The burglar *pried* [*broke*] the door open.

こしかけ 腰掛け (いす) chair◯; (一時的な仕事) temporary work◯,《口語的》temp work◯, ‖木製の腰かけ a wooden chair
◆姉は結婚までの腰かけのつもりで働いている My sister plans to keep working *only until* she gets married.

こしかける 腰掛ける sit* down, have* [take*] a seat ➪ すわる(座る)

こしき 古式 (古い儀式) ancient rite◯; (古くからの慣習) ancient custom◯
◆彼らの結婚式は古式ゆかしく(→伝統にのっとって)執り行われた Their wedding ceremony was held *according to the traditional custom*.

こじき 乞食 (人) beggar◯,《米口語的》panhandler◯; (行為) begging◯ ──乞食をする beg⊕,《米口語的》panhandle⊕

こしぎんちゃく 腰巾着 (おべっかを使って有力者にまとわりつく者) hanger-on ◯ (複 hangers-on)
◆あいつは支配人の腰ぎんちゃくだ(→影のように付き従っている) He *follows around* the general manager *like a shadow*.

こしくだけ 腰砕け 横綱は土俵際で腰砕けになった(→崩れた) The *yokozuna fell over backwards* at the edge of the ring. / その折衝は途中で腰砕けになった(→だめになった) The negotiations *broke down* in the middle.

ごしごし 手をごしごし洗う *scrub one's* hands / ごしごし磨いたらなべはぴかぴかになった I gave the pan *a good* scrubbing, and it became clean and shiny.

こしたんたん 虎視眈々 彼は虎視眈々と復讐(ふくしゅう)の機会をねらっていた He *was biding his time* until he could get his revenge.

こしつ¹ 固執 (頑固) persistence◯; (固守) adherence◯; (主張) insistence◯ ──固執する persist with [in] ...; adhere to ...; insist on ...; (執着する) cling* to ... ‖彼らは自分たちの計画に固執した They *persisted with* their own plan. / 祖母は昔ながらのやり方に固執する My grandmother *clings to* the old ways.

こしつ² 個室 one's (own) room◯; (病院などの) private room◯; (列車の) private compartment◯ ‖この寮では学生は各自個室を与えられている Each student has *their own room* in this dorm.

ごじつ 後日 (後で) later (on); (そのうち) some (other) day; (将来) in the future ‖この件については後日相談しましょう Let's talk about it *some other day*.
‖後日談 a sequel to the story

ゴシック ゴシック ❶【建築・美術】──ゴシックの Gothic ‖ゴシック様式の聖堂 a *Gothic* church
❷【印刷】(太字体) bold (type)◯; (ゴシック体) Gothic (type)◯ ──ゴシックの bold; Gothic
‖ゴシック建築 Gothic architecture

こじつけ ──こじつけの (不自然な) unnatural; (無理やりの) strained, forced; (ありそうもない) far-fetched ‖こじつけ話 a *strained story* / 君のその文章の解釈はかなりこじつけだ Your interpretation of the passage is rather *far-fetched*.

こじつける (ゆがめる) distort⊕, (曲解する) strain⊕ ‖彼女は話をいいようにこじつけようとしている She *is distorting* [*twisting*] the story to her advantage.

ゴシップ gossip◯◯ ‖彼女たちはその俳優のゴシップですっかり盛り上がっていた They were quite excited at *the gossip* about the actor./ 彼はゴシップ好きだ He is *a gossip* [*gossipy person*].
‖ゴシップ記事 a gossip item / ゴシップ欄 a gossip column

ごじっぽひゃっぽ 五十歩百歩 彼の案も君の案も五十歩百歩だ Your plan *is not much better than* his.

こしぬけ 腰抜け coward◯,《口語的》chicken◯

こしゃく 小癪 ──こしゃくな saucy ‖こしゃくなまねをする do a *saucy* thing

こしゅ 固守 古い習慣を固守する *stick to* the old customs

こしゅう 固執 ➪ こしつ(固執)
ごじゅう 五十 fifty;(50番目) fiftieth
ごじゅうおん 五十音 the Japanese (*kana*)

ごじゅうかた 五十肩 stiff and painful shoulders due to age (especially around fifty)

ごじゅうそう 五重奏 quintet(te) ◎

こじゅうと 小舅・小姑 brother-in-law ◎ (複 brothers-in-law, ~s)

こじゅうと(め) 小姑 sister-in-law ◎ (複 sisters-in-law, ~s)

ごじゅうのとう 五重の塔 five-storied pagoda [pəɡóudə] ◎

ごじゅん 語順 word order ⓤ

こしょ 古書 (古い時代の本) old book ◎; (古本) secondhand book ◎ ◆古書市 an *antiquarian* fair

ごしょ 御所 the ancient Imperial Palace

こしょう¹ 故障 (機械・体の) breakdown ◎; (機械の突然の) failure ⓤ ◎ ——故障する break* down; (機械が) be [get*] out of order
エンジンの故障 engine *trouble*
その国では信号機故障で毎日のように電車が止まる Trains stop almost every day due to signal *failures* in that country.
何もない所で車が故障した My car *broke down* in the middle of nowhere.
故障中 (掲示) *Out of Order; Out of Use*
◆この計算機は故障している This calculator *is broken.* / ATMが故障していてお金が下ろせない I can't withdraw cash as the ATM *doesn't work.* / バレーボールの選手にひざの故障は付き物だ Volleyball players tend to *get injured* in the knee.

こしょう² 胡椒 pepper ⓤ ◆コショウの実 *a peppercorn*
‖コショウ入れ 《米》a pepper shaker, 《英》a pepper pot / コショウひき a pepper mill

ごしょう 後生 後生だから(→お願いだから)そんなこと言わないでくれ For God's [Pete's, goodness, heaven's] *sake*, please don't say that!
◆祖母は祖父からもらった最初のラブレターを後生大事にしている My grandmother *treasures* the very first love letter from her husband.

ごじょかい 互助会 mutual-aid society ◎

ごしょく 誤植 misprint ◎, 《公式的》typographic error ◎, typo ◎ (複 ~s)

こしょくそうぜん 古色蒼然 古色蒼然とした山荘 a *very old-looking* cottage

こしらえる 拵える (作る) make* ⓔ; (準備する) prepare ⓔ / ごちそうをこしらえる *prepare* a feast / 先週スーツを1着こしらえた I had a suit *made* last month.
◆言い訳をこしらえる *make up* an excuse / けんかをして目の周りにあざをこしらえた I was in a fight, and *got* a black eye.

こじらせる (物事を) make* ... complicated; (病気を) make ... worse /彼はいつも事をこじらせる He always *makes* matters *complicated.* / かぜをこじらせてしまった I *made* my cold *worse.*/ My cold *got worse.*

こじれる (物事が) become* complicated; (人間関係が) go* sour; (病気が) get* [grow*] worse ∥2人の仲はこじれた Their relationship *went sour.* / 話がますますこじれてきた Things *are becoming* more and more *complicated.*

こじわ 小皺 fine wrinkles; (目じりの) crow's feet, laugh lines

こじん¹ 個人 individual ——個人の (個々の) individual; (私的な) private; (個人に関する) personal
個人の権利を守る protect the rights of *the individual* / 個人の好み an *individual* preference / 個人攻撃をする make *personal* remarks [attacks]
個人の自由とは何をしてもよいということではない *Individual* freedom does not mean that you can do anything you like.
赤ん坊が話し始める時期には個人差がある There is *individual variation* in when babies begin to talk.
◆私個人としてはその温泉のひなびた雰囲気が気に入っている *Personally*, I like the rustic atmosphere of the hot spring. / 僕は個人経営の塾に通っている I go to a *privately-run* cram school.
‖個人競技 an individual event / 個人主義 individualism / 個人主義者 an individualist / 個人崇拝 a personality cult / 個人タクシー a privately owned taxi / 個人面談 private consulting, private guidance / 個人レッスン a private lesson, 《英》a private tuition
⇒ こじんてき

こじん² 故人 the deceased, 《婉曲的》the departed (単数または複数扱い) ◆故人となる(→死ぬ) die;《婉曲的》pass away

ごしん¹ 誤診 misdiagnosis ◎, wrong diagnosis ◎ ——誤診する misdiagnose ⓔ, make* a wrong diagnosis of ... /医者は彼の胃癌(がん)を潰瘍(かいよう)と誤診した The doctor *misdiagnosed* his stomach cancer as an ulcer.

ごしん² 護身 self-defense ⓤ ∥護身術 the art of self-defense

こじんてき 個人的 ——個人的な (一人一人の) individual; (個人に関する) personal; (私的な) private ——個人的に personally /個人的な意見 a *personal* opinion / あなたの個人的な問題には干渉するつもりはありません I don't want to stick my nose into your *private* affairs. / 個人的にはあなたに賛成だ I *personally* agree with you.

こじんまり ⇒ こぢんまり

こす¹ 越す・超す
❶【越える】 go* [get*] over ..., cross ⓔ; (通過する) pass ⓔ
暗くならないうちにあの山を越してしまおう We'll go [get] *over* the mountain before it gets dark.
❷【引っ越す・来る】 move ⓔ
佐藤さんの家族は横浜に越した The Satos *moved to* Yokohama.
◆近くに(→近所に)お越しの節は私たちの家にもお立ち寄りください Please drop in on us

when you *come* into the neighborhood.
❸【上回る】(be) over ..., (be) more than ...
その地方では2メートルを超す積雪を記録した The snow accumulated to a depth of「*more than* [*over*] two meters in the area.
空港には500人を超すファンが詰めかけた *More than* [*Over*] 500 fans crowded the airport.
◆その国では夏の気温が40度を超す(→より高くなる)ことも珍しくない It's not surprising in that country that the temperature *goes higher than* 40℃ in summer.
❹【時間を過ごす】(時を過ごす) spend*⊕, pass⊕
沖縄で冬を越す *spend* the winter in Okinawa
◆去年はハワイで年を越した(→新年を迎えた) We *greeted the New Year* in Hawaii last year. / リスは秋の間にひと冬を越す(→乗り切る)ための食糧を蓄える Squirrels stock food in fall to *get through* the winter.
❺【勝る】
お金はたくさんあるに越したことはない(→あるほうがよい) The more money you've got, *the better*.
用心するに越したことはない(→いくら注意してもしすぎることはない) You *can never* be *too careful*.
慣用表現 運転免許を取るのでは彼に先を越された He *beat* me in obtaining a driving license. / 彼女の病気は峠を越した(→危機を乗り切った)ようだ She seems to *have passed* [*gotten over*] *a crisis* in her illness. / やっと寒さも峠を越した(→過ぎ去った) Finally the coldest days「*have passed* [*are over*].
⇨こえる(越える見・超える見)

こす² 漉す・濾す (ろ過する) filter⊕; (料理などで) strain⊕ ∥1回使った油はこしてから缶に入れたほうがよい You'd better *strain* the used oil before putting it in the can.

こすい¹ (ずるい) cunning, shifty ∥こすい手を使う take a *cunning* [*shifty*] measure

こすい² 湖水 lake◎ ∥(英国イングランドの)湖水地方 *the Lake District*

こすう¹ 個数 リンゴの個数を数える count *the number of* apples

こすう² 戸数 the number of houses [families]

こずえ 梢 (木の先) treetop◎; (枝の先) the end of a branch

コスチューム costume◎Ⓤ

コスト cost Ⓤ◎ ∥生産コスト production *costs* ◆その企画はコストがかかりすぎる That plan will *cost* too much. (❖この cost は「コストがかかる」の意味の動詞)
∥コストアップ an increase in cost / コストダウン a reduction in cost(❖「コストアップ」,「コストダウン」は共に和製英語) / コストパフォーマンス cost performance

コスモス cosmos [kázməs]◎

コスモポリタン (国際人) cosmopolitan◎

こする 擦る (手や布などで) rub⊕; (磨く) scrub⊕; (こすり落とす) scrape⊕ ∥手をこする *rub one's* hands / 彼はあくびをして目をこすった He yawned and *rubbed* his eyes. / こげたなべをたわしでこすった I *scrubbed* the burned pan with a scrub brush. / 彼はブーツについた泥をこすり落としていた He *was scraping* the mud off his boots.

こすれる 擦れる rub㉭; (激しく) scrape㉭

こせい 個性 (性格) personality Ⓤ◎; (異なる特徴) individuality Ⓤ; (独創性) originality Ⓤ ∥個性が強い have *a strong personality* / 個性を伸ばす develop *one's personality* / 個性を発揮する show *one's individuality* / 個性豊かな人 a person *of marked individuality* / 彼女はきれいだが個性に欠ける She's pretty, but lacks *individuality*. / その人の個性を生かすのが化粧の極意だ The most important thing in makeup is to make use of the person's *individuality*. / 彼は個性的な作品を次々発表している He has been producing works *of great originality*.

こせいぶつ 古生物 the life of past geological periods ∥古生物学 paleontology

こせき 戸籍 family register◎ ∥彼女の名を戸籍に入れる[から抜く] have *her* name「listed in [deleted from] *the family register* ◆彼女は戸籍上は(→法律上は)私たちの娘ではない She is not *legally* our daughter.
∥戸籍係 a registrar / 戸籍抄本 a copy of part of *one's* family register / 戸籍謄本 a full copy of *one's* family register

こせこせ こせこせする(→つまらないことで思いわずらう) *fuss about small things* / 彼のこせこせしたところが嫌いだ What I don't like about him is that he's *fussy*.

こぜに 小銭 small change Ⓤ; (硬貨) coin◎ ∥小銭入れ a change purse,《英》a purse

こぜりあい 小競り合い skirmish◎ ──小競り合いをする skirmish㉭

ごせん 互選 委員会は互選で議長を決めた The committee *elected* a chairperson *from among its own members*.

ごぜん 午前

(夜明けから正午まで) morning Ⓤ◎; (真夜中の0時から正午までの時刻) a.m., A.M.(❖ラテン語で「正午の前」を意味する ante meridiem の略。時刻を表す数字の後に付けて用いる)

語法 「午前(中)に」という場合、一般的には in the morning を用いるが、特定の日の午前の場合は on になり、this (きょう の)、yesterday (きのう の)などを伴う場合は前置詞は付かない ∥ 午前9時に at nine *in the morning* / 土曜日の午前に on Saturday *morning* / きょう[あす]の午前(中)に this [tomorrow] *morning*

姉は5月1日の午前に出産した My sister gave birth *on the morning* of May 1.
日曜の午前中はずっと寝ていた I slept *all morning* on Sunday.

あしたの午前中までには書き終えます I'll finish writing by tomorrow *morning*.
私たちは午前10時12分の電車に乗るつもりだ We're planning to take the 10:12 *a.m.* train.
【慣用表現】父はゆうべ新年会で午前様だった My father went to a New Year's party last night and *got home after midnight*.

ごせんし 五線紙 music paper [sheet] ⓤ
ごせんふ 五線譜 score ⓒ

-こそ
【語法】
英語では，状況に応じて強調構文や意味を強める形容詞などを用いて表す．また，単に強調したい語を強く発音するだけでそのニュアンスが伝えられることもある．．

これこそ私が探し求めていた本です This is the *very* book I've been looking for.
今度こそうまくいきますように Better luck *next time*!
ご両親は君のためを思えばこそ厳しくしているんだ Your parents are strict with you *for your own sake*.
私はフランス語は読みこそすれ，話すのはさっぱりだめです *It's true that* I read French, *but* I can't speak it at all.
彼のほうこそ謝るべきだ *It is* he [《口語的》him] *who* must apologize.
データは有効に活用されてこそ(→初めて)意味がある *It is not until* the data are made good use of *that* they are significant.
今でこそ彼の名を知らない人はいないが当時は無名の俳優だった Though everyone knows his name *now*, he was an unknown actor in those days.
● 「お会いできて光栄です」「こちらこそ」 "It's a pleasure to meet you." "*The pleasure is mine*."

こぞう 小僧 (少年) boy ⓒ; (子供)《口語的》kid ⓒ; (寺の) novice priest ⓒ ‖いたずら小僧 a naughty [mischievous] *boy*

ごそう 護送 犯人を護送する *send* a criminal to jail *under guard* ‖ルーブル美術館からの絵画を護送する *escort* the painting from the Louvre
‖護送車 a patrol [police] wagon

こそく 姑息 —姑息な (間に合わせの) makeshift, stopgap ‖姑息な手段をとる take a *makeshift* measure

ごぞく 語族 language family ⓒ ‖インド・ヨーロッパ[ウラル・アルタイ]語族 the Indo-European [Ural-Altaic] *language family*

ごそくろう 御足労 御足労いただきありがとうございます Thank you very much for *taking the trouble to come*.

こそげる scrape ... off [away]

こそこそ (こっそり) secretly; (人の陰で) behind *a person's* back; (気づかれないように) sneakingly ‖弟はこそこそ何かやっている My brother is doing something *secretly* [*behind our back*].
◆ その男はパトカーを見るとこそこそと逃げた The man *sneaked away* when he saw a police car.

ごそごそ 何かが暗やみの中でごそごそ動いた Something *rustled* in the dark.

こそだて 子育て child raising [rearing] ⓤ, child care ⓤ, parenting ⓤ ‖どの親も子育ての問題を抱えている All parents have *child raising* problems.

こぞって 女子高生はこぞってその歌手の髪型をまねた *All* high school girls tried to have the same hairstyle as that singer.

こそどろ こそ泥 petty [sneak] thief ⓒ

こそばゆい そんなにほめられるとこそばゆい That's too much. I *feel embarrassed* [*awkward*].

ごぞんじ 御存じ 彼をご存じですか Do you *know* him? / ご存じのようにこれが有名なシドニーのオペラハウスです This is the famous Sydney Opera House, *as you know*. / ご存じかもしれませんが彼女のお父さんは有名な作家です *As you may know*, her father is a famous writer. / 後はご存じのとおりです The rest is *history*.

こたい 固体 solid (body) ⓒ ——固体の solid / 固体燃料 *solid* fuel

こだい 古代 ancient times / 古代の ancient / 古代遺跡 an ancient monument / 古代史 ancient history / 古代人 ancient people / 古代文明 ancient civilization

こだい² 誇大 —誇大な exaggerated ‖誇大広告 an exaggerated advertisement / 誇大妄想 megalomania

ごたい 五体 五体満足の赤ん坊 a *normal and healthy* baby

こたえ 答え

(解答) answer ⓒ; (問題集などの解答書) key ⓒ; (解決法・結論) solution ⓒ; (返答) answer ⓒ, reply ⓒ,《公式的》response ⓒ; (計算結果) result ⓒ
正しい[間違った]答え a correct [*an incorrect*] *answer*
私はその質問の答えに詰まった I couldn't think of any (good) *answers to* the question.
パズルの答えは次のページにあります *The solution to* the puzzle is on the next page.
彼らは協議を重ねたが結局答えは出なかった They had a lot of discussions, but they couldn't find any *solutions* [*answers*].
ノックに答えはなかった There was no *answer* [*response*] *to* the knocks.
君の答えは答えになっていないよ Your *answer* is no *answer*.
彼は問題をすべて解いて答え合わせをした He solved all the problems and *checked his answers*.

こたえる¹ 答える

(解答する) answer ⓥ; (返答する) answer ⓥⓘ, give* an answer,《公式的》reply ⓥⓘ,《公式的》respond ⓥⓘ
アンケート[問題]に答える *answer* a question-

naire [question]
「はい」か「いいえ」で答えてください Please *answer* with yes or no.
その質問は答えるのが難しい The question is difficult to *answer*.
兄は今のところ結婚する予定はないと答えた My brother *answered* that he had no plan to get married at the moment.
彼女は大学へは行く気はないと先生に答えた She *replied* to the teacher that she did not intend to go to a university.
彼は私たちの質問に対して率直に答えてくれた He *gave* us *a* direct [straight] *answer* to our question.

こたえる[2] **応える** (期待・要望などに) meet* [他], satisfy [他]; (応答する) respond [自]
ご期待にこたえられるよう努力します I'll try to *meet* [*satisfy*] your expectations.
選手たちは手を振って観衆の声援にこたえた The players *responded to* cheers from the spectators by waving their hands.
◆この寒さは身にこたえる This cold *is* really *hard on* me. / あいつ, あんなにしかられたのにまるでこたえて(→落ち込んで)いないみたいだ Though he was scolded so much, he seems not to *be depressed* at all. / もし彼がメジャーリーグに行ったらそのチームはこたえるだろうね I'm sure the team would *really feel it* if he went to the Major Leagues.

こたえる[3] **堪える** ひとふろ浴びた後のビールはこたえられない *There's nothing like* beer after a bath.

こだかい **小高い** slightly elevated ◆小高い丘 *a small hill* / その駅は小高い所にある The station is on *a slight rise*.

こだから **子宝** 姉は子宝に恵まれている My sister *has been blessed with many children*.

ごたごた ❶【問題】trouble [U] [C]; (論争) dispute [C] [U] ∥ごたごたを起こす cause *trouble* / 彼らと近隣の住民との間にはごたごたが絶えなかった There were always *troubles* between them and their neighbors.
❷【無秩序】(混乱) disorder [U]; (散らかっていること)《口語的》mess [U] ∥引っ越しの準備で家中がごたごたしている The whole house *is in disorder*, in preparing for moving.
◆月末はいつもごたごたしている(→忙しい) *I'm* always *busy* at the end of the month.

こだし **小出し** 貯金を小出しに使う use *one's* savings *little by little*

こだち **木立ち** grove [C], a cluster [clump] of trees

こたつ **炬燵・火燵** 🗻

こたつは特に寒い冬の夜などに足を暖める日本の伝統的な暖房器具です. 昔は炭火の掘りごたつを使いましたが, 現在ではテーブルの裏側にヒーターのついた電気式のものが主流です. どちらの場合も上にこたつぶとんと呼ばれる上かけをかけます.
A *kotatsu* is a traditional Japanese heater that people can use to warm their feet especially on cold winter nights. It used to be a charcoal burner recessed into the floor, but these days it is usually an electric heater built into the underside of a table. In either case, the table is covered by a special quilt called a *kotatsu* futon.

ごたつく その党は党内がごたついている *There is a dispute* in the party.

ごたぶん **御多分** 彼女は箱入り娘でご多分にもれず世間知らずだ She was brought up in a sheltered environment, and *as a matter of course* doesn't know much of the world.

こだま **木霊** echo [C] ―こだまする echo [自] ∥母校の校歌が球場内にこだました Our school song *echoed* in the stadium.
[俳句] 谺(こだ)して山ほととぎすほしいまま
(杉田久女)
Echoing its hoot,
a cuckoo on the mountain
makes all sound its own.

こだわる 彼女は着るものにこだわる She's *particular about* what to wear. / 結果にはあまりこだわらないほうがいい You shouldn't *take* the results too *seriously*. / つまらないことにこだわるな Don't *make a fuss over* trifles. / 私は日本酒に関してはちょっとこだわりがあるんです I'm a bit *fussy* about sake.

こちこち ❶【硬い】―こちこちの hard; (石のように) rock hard ∥この冷凍肉はこちこちだ This frozen meat *is rock hard*.
❷【緊張】―こちこちの tense ∥音楽の歌のテストではいつもこちこちになる I always *get tense* during a singing test in the music class. ◆初めての舞台でこちこちになった I *had stage fright* at the first performance.
❸【頑固】―こちこちの stubborn; (融通がきかない) inflexible ∥うちの父は頭がこちこちだ My father *is so stubborn*.

ごちそう **御馳走** (豪華な食事) feast [C]; (もてなし) treat [C] ―ごちそうする (夕食に招く) invite *a person* for dinner; (おごる) treat [他] ∥すごいごちそうですね What *a feast*! / きょうのお昼はごちそうするよ Today's lunch *is* 「*my treat* [*on me*]. / 私は先週の土曜日友人のうちで夕食をごちそうになった I *was invited for dinner* at my friend's last Saturday.
◆ごちそうを作る prepare 「*something special* [*special dinner*] / テーブルには手のこんだごちそうがたくさん並んでいた There were a lot of *elaborate dishes* on the table.

ごちそうさま

英語には日本語の「ごちそうさま」に当たる決まり文句はないが, 食事に招かれた場合などは食後や帰り際に「おいしかった」という気持ちを伝えるのがふつう. その場合はI really enjoyed the meal. や That was a wonderful meal. などという. あるいは料理をした人に対してMy compliments to the cook [chef]. ということもある. また, 日本語ではのろけ話に対しても「ごちそうさま」ということがあるが, その場合はYou're lucky to have her [him]. といえば

ごちゃごちゃ こんなごちゃごちゃ散らかした部屋ではとても勉強なんてできない I can't possibly study in such a *messy* room. / みんないっせいにしゃべりだしたので頭の中がごちゃごちゃになった I *got mixed up* because everyone started speaking at once. / ごちゃごちゃ言うな Stop *complaining*!

ごちゃ混ぜ 彼はよく彼女の名前と昔のガールフレンドの名前をごちゃ混ぜにする He often *mixes up* her name with that of his former girlfriend. / 兄の机の上には本とノートがごちゃ混ぜにして積んであった Books and notebooks *were jumbled up* on my brother's desk.

こちょう 誇張 exaggeration Ⓤ, overstatement Ⓤ (❖どちらも具体的な発言を指すときはⒸ) ─誇張する exaggerate 他 自, overstate 他 /彼はその事件を誇張して報告した He gave an *exaggerated* account of the incident.

◆それはちょっと誇張しすぎじゃない？ Isn't that *stretching the truth* a little too far?

ごちょう 語調 a tone (of voice) ◆語調をやわらげる[強める] soften [raise] *one's voice*

こちら

❶ 場所・方向	here; this way
❷ 事物・人	this
❸ 自分	I; we

❶【場所・方向】(場所) here; (方角) this way
─こちらの this
川のこちら側 *this side* of the river
こちらは大雪だった We had a lot of snow *here*.
どのくらいでこちらに来られますか How soon can you get *here*?
こちらの物価は東京よりずっと安い The prices *here* are much lower than in Tokyo.
あちらこちらにチューリップが咲いている Tulips are in bloom *here and there*.
こちらに来てください Come *this way*, please.
もしこちらにおいでになることがあれば、ぜひともお立ち寄りください If you ever come「*this way* [*here*], be sure to come and see us.
🅒「こちらの方向に回すんですか」「いいえ、その逆です」 "Do you turn it *this* way?" "No, it's the other way."

❷【事物・人】this
(紹介して)洋子、こちらがブライアンです。ブライアン、こちらが洋子です Yoko, *this* is Brian. Brian, *this* is Yoko.
こちらは山田さんのお宅ですね *This* is Mr. Yamada's residence, isn't it?

❸【自分】(私) I; (私たち) we
(かかってきた電話に対して)10分後にこちらからかけ直します *I'll* call you back in 10 minutes.
こちらでは化粧品は扱っておりません *We* don't carry cosmetics.

◆こちらの身にもなってください Please consider *my position*, too.
🅒「お話しできてうれしかったです」「こちらこそ」 "It's been nice talking to you." "*The pleasure is mine.*"

こぢんまり こぢんまりとした部屋 a *cozy* [*snug*] *little room* / こぢんまりしたアパート a *small and cozy* apartment

こつ ❶ [a] knack, 《口語的》the hang /こつをつかむ get *the hang* / こういう問題を解くにはこつがあるんだ There is *a knack* to answering this kind of question. ◆彼は聴衆を笑わせるこつを知っている He knows *the trick* for making the audience laugh.

ごつい rough; (体格などが) burly; (顔つきなどが) rugged [rʌ́gid]

こっか¹ 国家 (政治的な) state Ⓒ; (民族集団としての) nation Ⓒ; (主に地理的な) country Ⓒ ─国家の national
国家間の不和 discord between *nations*
その裁判は国家的関心を集めた The trial drew *national* interest.

‖国家管理 state [government] control / 国家権力 state power, the power of the state / 国家公安委員会 the National Public Safety Commission / 国家公務員 a government official [worker, employee], a public servant / 国家試験 a state [national] examination / 近代国家 a modern state [nation] / 資本主義国家 a capitalist country / 多民族国家 a multiracial nation

こっか² 国歌 national anthem Ⓒ
こっか³ 国花 national flower Ⓒ
こっかい 国会 (日本の) the (National) Diet Ⓤ (❖米国議会は Congress, 英国は Parliament という) /国会を召集[解散]する summon [dissolve] *the Diet* / 国会は今開会中です *The Diet* is now「*in session* [*sitting*]. / 新しい法案が国会で承認された The new law was passed by *the Diet*.

‖国会喚問 a summons to the Diet / 国会議員 (日本の) a member of the Diet, a Dietman [Dietwoman]; (米国の) a Congressman [Congresswoman], a Member of Congress; (英国の) a Member of Parliament / 国会議事堂 (一般に) the Diet Building; (米国の)the Capitol; (英国の)the Houses of Parliament / 国会図書館 the National Diet Library / 通常国会 an ordinary Diet session / 特別国会 a special Diet session / 臨時国会 an extraordinary Diet session

こづかい 小遣い (定期的に子供などに与える) allowance Ⓒ; (自分が使う) pocket [spending] money Ⓤ /私のいとこは私よりもたくさんこづかいをもらっている My cousin gets *a bigger allowance* than I do. / 兄はこづかい稼ぎにアルバイトをしている My brother works part-time to *earn pocket* [*spending*] *money*.

◆彼女は毎日こづかい帳をつけている She keeps *a record of her expenses* every day.

こっかく 骨格 (体格) build Ⓒ, frame Ⓒ; (建物などの) framework Ⓒ

◆骨格のがっしりした男 a *sturdily-built* man

こっき 国旗 national flag [C] ∥国旗を掲揚する raise [hoist] *the national flag*

-国旗の呼称のいろいろ-
アメリカ国旗 the Stars and Stripes, the Star-Spangled Banner / 英国国旗 the Union Jack / 中国国旗 the Five-Star Red Flag / 日本国旗 the Rising Sun / フランス国旗 the Tricolor

こっきしん 克己心 self-restraint [U]

こっきょう[1] 国境 border [C], frontier [C]; (国境線) (national) boundary [C] ∥国境を越える cross *the border* [*national boundary*] / 国境を警備する guard *the border* / 愛に国境はない Love has no *boundaries*.

◆フランスはライン川に沿ってドイツと国境を接している France *borders* Germany along the Rhine. / France *is bordered* along the Rhine by Germany.

‖国境地帯 a border region / 国境紛争 a border dispute

こっきょう[2] 国教 state religion [C]

‖英国国教会 the Church of England, the Anglican [Established] Church

コック[1] cook [C] ‖コック長 a chief cook, a chef

コック[2] (水道・ガス・たるなどの) cook [C], 《米》 faucet [C], 《英》 tap [C]

こづく 小突く (指・棒などで) poke [他]; (ひじで) nudge [他] ∥人を軽くこづいて起こす *nudge* a person awake

コックス (ボートのかじとり) cox [C], coxswain [C]

コックピット cockpit [C]

こっくり 彼はよほど疲れていたのだろう, 授業が始まるとすぐにこっくりし始めた He must have been very tired; he began to *nod off* as soon as the class started. / 彼女は同意してこっくりとうなずいた She *nodded her head* in agreement.

こっけい 滑稽 ―こっけいな (笑いを誘う) funny, comic; (おどけた) comical; (ユーモアのある) humorous; (嘲笑(ちょうしょう)を誘う) ridiculous ∥こっけいなことを言う say *funny* things / まさかそのこっけいな帽子をパーティーにかぶっていこうというのではないでしょうね I certainly hope you're not planning on wearing that *ridiculous* hat to the party. / 君が彼の代わりに謝らなければならないなんてこっけいな話だ *It's ridiculous that* you're supposed to apologize for him.

こっこ 国庫 the national [state] treasury ‖国庫債券 a treasury bond / 国庫収入 national revenues / 国庫補助(金) a government [state] subsidy

ごっこ ごっこ遊び *make-believe* / 鬼[お店屋さん]ごっこをする *play* tag [shops]

こっこう 国交 diplomatic relations ∥国交を断絶する[結ぶ, 正常化する] 「break off [establish, normalize] *diplomatic relations* / 両国は5年前に国交を回復した The two countries restored *diplomatic relations* five years ago.

こっこく 刻々 夕暮れの空の色は刻々と変わった The sunset changed colors *minute by minute.* / 締め切りが刻々と迫っているのによいアイディアがなかなか思いつかない I can't come up with any good ideas even though the deadline is getting *closer and closer*.

こつこつ こつこつ働く work *diligently* [*hard*]; *plod* [*plug*] *away* at the work / 妹は毎月こつこつおこづかいをためている My sister puts away money *steadily* every month. / 彼女はいつもこつこつ努力している She always *keeps trying.* / ドアをこつこつたたく音が聞こえた I heard someone *knock* [*rap, tap*] *on* [*at*] the door.

ごつごつ ごつごつした岩 a *rough* rock / ごつごつした山 a *rocky* [*craggy*] mountain / ごつごつした手 *bony* hands

こっし 骨子 (要旨) the gist; (主要な点) the main point

こつずい 骨髄 (bone) marrow [U] ‖骨髄移植 a bone marrow transplant / 骨髄炎 osteomyelitis / 骨髄バンク a bone marrow bank

こっせつ 骨折 fracture [C] ―骨折する break* (a bone), fracture [他] [自] ∥彼はサッカーの練習中に右足を骨折した He *broke* his right leg during soccer practice.

◆そのチームのエースは指を骨折している The ace pitcher of that team *has a broken finger*.

‖複雑骨折 a compound fracture

こつぜん 忽然 彼は忽然と姿を消した He disappeared *abruptly* [*suddenly, all of a sudden*].

こつそしょうしょう 骨粗鬆症 osteoporosis [àstioupəróusəs] [U]

こっそり (ひそかに) secretly, in secret; (人目を忍んで) stealthily, on the sly ∥彼女が答えをこっそり教えてくれた She *secretly* told me the answer.

◆彼はこっそり家に入ろうとしているところを見つかった He was caught trying to *sneak* [*steal*] *into* the house. / 彼女が部屋をこっそり抜け出すところを見た人はいなかった No one saw her *sneak* [*slip, steal*] *out of* the room.

ごっそり (全部) all; (すっかり) completely, entirely ∥貴重品をごっそり盗まれてしまった *All* our valuables were stolen. / We had *all* our valuables stolen.

ごったがえす ごった返す (込んでいる) be crowded ∥駅は休暇で帰省する客でごった返していた The station *was crowded with* people on their way home for the holidays.

◆祭りで町全体がごった返していた *There was a lot of hustle and bustle* in the whole city because of the festival.

ごったに ごった煮 《米》 hodgepodge [C] [U], 《英》 hotchpotch [C] [U]

こっち here, this way ➔こちら ∥こっちへおいでよ Come *here*.

こづち 小槌 (small) mallet [C]; (議長などが持つ) gavel [C] ∥打ち出の小づち *a* magic *mallet*

ごっちゃ ➔ごちゃごちゃ, ごちゃまぜ

こつつぼ 骨壺 an urn (for cremated ashes), cinerary [cremation] urn

こづつみ 小包 (postal) parcel ⓒ, (postal) package ⓒ ∥祖母に小包を送った I mailed a package [parcel] to my grandmother. / これらの本を小包郵便で送っていただけますか Could you send these books by parcel post?

こってり こってりした料理 rich food / 彼は遅刻をして先生にこってり油をしぼられた The teacher gave him a really hard time for being late.

こっとう(ひん) 骨董(品) antique ⓒ, curio ⓒ ∥骨董品の腕時計 an antique watch ∥骨董商 an antique [a curio] dealer / 骨董屋 an antique [a curio] shop

コットン cotton ⓤ

こっぱみじん 木っ端微塵 置物は彼女の手から滑り落ち, こっぱみじんに砕けた The ornament slipped from her hands and broke [was smashed] into smithereens.

こつばん 骨盤 pelvis ⓒ (複 ～es, pelves)

こっぴどく 植木鉢を割って父にこっぴどくしかられた I was bawled out by my father for breaking a flowerpot.

こつぶ 小粒 (小さい粒) small grain ⓒ, (小さい種類) small type [kind] ⓒ ──小粒の small ∥小粒のサクランボ a small (type [kind] of) cherry

コップ glass ⓒ, (取っ手付きの) mug ⓒ (❖日本語はオランダ語の kop から) ∥コップ1杯のミルク a glass of milk
∥紙コップ a paper cup

コッペ(パン) (bread) roll ⓒ (❖×roll bread とはいわない)

こつん 母に頭をこつんとたたかれた My mother rapped me on the head.

ごつん 彼は頭を柱にごつんとぶつけた He bumped his head on a post.

こて 鏝 (裁縫用) iron ⓒ; (壁を塗るための) trowel ⓒ; (理髪用) curling tongs [irons]; (はんだ用) soldering iron ⓒ

ごて 後手 後手で打つ[指す] take [have] the second move; move [play, go] second / 彼らは相手チームの後手に回ってしまった They fell behind the opposing team.

こてい 固定 ──固定する fix ⓤ, fasten ⓒ ⓤ ∥このホールの座席はすべて床に固定されている All the seats in this hall are fixed to the floor.
∥固定観念 a fixed idea / 固定客 a regular customer / 固定給 a fixed salary / 固定金利 a fixed interest rate / 固定資産 fixed assets [property], capital assets / 固定資産税 a fixed property tax / 固定資本 fixed capital / 固定収入 a fixed income

こてきたい 鼓笛隊 drum and fife corps [band] ⓒ

こてこて こてこての大阪弁 a thick [heavy] Osaka accent

ごてごて heavily, thickly, gaudily ∥彼女のごてごて着飾った様子はその場にふさわしくなかった She was too gaudily dressed for the occasion.

こてさき 小手先 小手先のごまかし cheap tricks

こてしらべ 小手調べ (試し) trial ⓤ (❖抽象的な意味では ⓒ); (練習) practice ⓤ; (準備運動) warm-up ⓒ ∥小手調べにその問題を解いてみた I answered the question 「as a trial [as a warm-up, for practice].

こてん¹ 古典 (評価の高い一流の作品) classic ⓒ; (古典文学) the classics, classical literature ⓤ ──古典の (古典的な) classic; (古典派の) classical ∥日本の古典 the Japanese classics / 彼女にはどこか古典的な美しさがある There is a classic beauty about her.
◆古典的な(→ 古くさい)ジョーク a stale joke
∥古典音楽 classical music / 古典主義 classicism

こてん² 個展 one-person exhibition [show] ⓒ ∥個展を開く hold a one-person exhibition [show]

ごてん 御殿 palace ⓒ ∥御殿のような家に住む live in a house like a palace; live in a palatial house

こてんこてん こてんこてんにやっつけられる be beaten to a pulp

こてんぱん ➡ こてんこてん

こと¹ 事

[事柄] thing ⓒ; matter ⓒ; affair ⓒ

| thing: 日本語の「こと」に相当する最も一般的で意味の広い語.
| matter: thing とほぼ同意だがやや改まった語.
| affair: 個人のすべきこと, 計画的な行動.

大切なこと an important thing / 悪い[よい]ことをする do a bad [good] thing
おもしろいことを教えてあげよう I'll tell you an interesting thing.
君はそんなこともひとりでできないのか I can't believe you can't do such a thing by yourself!
世の中には私の知らないことがたくさんある There are a lot of things in the world I don't know.
それは笑い事ではない That's no laughing matter.
事の真相はまだ分からない The truth of the matter is still in doubt.
◆何かおもしろいことない? Is there anything interesting? / 高校を卒業したらやりたいことがある There's something I want to do after graduating from high school. / きょうは何もすることがない There is nothing to do today. / 本当のことを言おう I'll tell you the truth.

❤「僕は何をやってもだめだ」「そんなこと言うなよ」"I can't do anything well." "Don't say that [such a thing]."

❷ [出来事]
へえ, 学校で本当にそんなことがあったんだ Wow! So that really happened at school.

あした学校で健康診断があることを知ってる? Do you know *that* a medical check will be held at school tomorrow?

弟はきょう学校であったことを私に話した My brother told me *what* happened at school today.

そんなことがあってから彼は無口になった He hasn't talked much since *that event*.

❸【事情・内容】

詳しいことは後で説明します I will explain *the details* later.

事によっては私があなたの代わりに行ってもいいよ *Depending on the circumstances*, I'll go instead of you.

私事で恐縮ですが、この度山形に引っ越すことになりました Excuse me for mentioning *a personal subject*, but I will be moving to Yamagata.

自分のことは自分でしろ Handle your own *affairs* [*things*] yourself.

子供たちのこと面倒を見てくれてありがとう Thanks for taking care of my children.

おまえ、本当に純のこと好きなんだね You really like Jun, don't you?

パーティーのこと彼に伝えた? Did you tell him *about* the party?

パソコンのことなら僕にまかせてくれ If *it's related to* computers, just let me handle it.

❹【伝聞】

山田が中央大学に合格したとのことだ I heard *that* Yamada passed the entrance examination of [for] Chuo University.

❺【経験】

その映画は見たことがある I*'ve seen* the movie.

田中さんにはまだお会いしたことがない I*'ve never met* Mr. Tanaka.

❻【必要】

わざわざ会員名簿を作り直すことはない You *don't have* [*need*] *to* make the list of members again.

❼【習慣・きまり】

英語力をつけるため毎日英語で日記をつけることにしている I *keep* a diary in English every day to improve my English. (❖現在形で現在の習慣を表す)

私たちの学校では自転車で通学してはいけないことになっている Our school *forbids* us to go to school by bicycle.

❽【予定】

鉄也と5時に校門の所で会うことになっている Tetsuya and I *are* (*going*) *to* meet at the school gate at 5 o'clock. (❖be to *do* で予定を表す)

❾【すなわち】

この小説は小泉八雲ことラフカディオ・ハーンの作だ This novel was written by Lafcadio Hearn, *also known as* Koizumi Yakumo.

❿【命令】

マニュアルをよく読むこと *Read* the manual carefully.

廊下を走らないこと *Do not* run in the halls.

⓫【その他】

驚いたことにそのうわさは本当だった *To my surprise*, the rumor was true.

この話は聞かなかったことにしてください Please *act as if you never heard* that story.

慣用表現 彼らは事あるごとに口論になる *Whenever anything happens*, they start arguing with each other. / それは事だぞ(→問題だぞ) That's *the problem*. / 作業中に脚立(きゃたつ)がこわれたが、事なきを得た(→けがをせずにすんだ) Though the stepladder collapsed while I was working, *I didn't get injured*.

こと² 琴 🎵 koto ⓒ, a traditional Japanese「harp-like instrument [zither]」with thirteen strings

こと³ 古都 ancient city [capital] ⓒ; (歴史のある都市) historic city ⓒ

-ごと¹ (そっくり) ... and all; (…とともに) (together, along) with ... ∥土地を家ごと売る sell the land *together with* the house / トマトを皮ごと食べる eat a tomato「*together with the skin* [*skin and all*]」/ 教科書をかばんごと学校に忘れてきた I left my textbooks *in my bag* at school.

-ごと² 毎 ⇨ -ごとに

ことう 孤島 solitary [isolated] island ⓒ

こどう 鼓動 (心臓の) (heart)beat ⓒⓊ; (脈拍) pulsation Ⓤ ―― 鼓動する beat* ⓔ; pulsate ⓔ ◆幕が上がるにつれ胸の鼓動が高まった *My pulse* quickened as the curtain rose. / 戸をおそるおそるあけたとき、まるで心臓の鼓動が聞こえるかと思った I thought I could almost hear *the pounding* of my heart as I cautiously opened the door.

こどうぐ 小道具 (舞台の)(口語的) prop ⓒ, (公式的) property ⓒ; (小さな道具) small tool ⓒ; (部品) gadget ⓒ

ことかく 事欠く 話題に事欠かない *have a lot to talk about* / 食べる物には事欠かない *We have enough* [*a sufficient supply of*] *food*.

ことがら 事柄 (問題) matter ⓒ; (個人的な) affair ⓒ ⇨ (事) ∥きわめて重要な事柄 a very important *matter* / 私的な事柄 one's private *affairs*

こどく 孤独 (ひとりぼっちで寂しいこと) loneliness Ⓤ; (ひとりでいること) solitude Ⓤ ―― 孤独な lonely; solitary ∥孤独な生活を送る lead a *solitary* [*lonely*] life

ごとく 如く like, as; (まるで…のよう) as if [though] ... ⇨ まるで ∥当然のごとく *as a matter of course* / 電光石火のごとく (*as*) *quick as* lightning [a flash]; *like* lightning

ことこと 肉をことこと煮込む *stew* meat

ごとごと 荷車がいなか道をごとごと通っていった The cart *rattled* along the country road. / 2階で何かごとごといっているのが聞こえた I heard some *rattling* noises upstairs.

ことごとく (全く・すっかり) entirely; (全部) all, every ∥私の提案はことごとく拒否された *All* my proposals were rejected.

ことこまか 事細か　警察はその火事について彼らに事細かに質問した The police questioned them *in detail [closely]* about the fire.

ことさら 殊更　(特に) especially, specially, particularly; (わざと) on purpose, intentionally ∥この問題についてことさら取り上げる必要はない This problem is not *particularly* worth mentioning.

ことし 今年　this year
今年の学生採用数 *this year*'s intake of students
今年は雪が多い There has been a lot of snow *this year*.
今年の後半には景気が回復するだろう The economy will improve later *this year*.
今年中にもう一度ここに来たい I want to come here once again *by the end of this year*.
◆今年の冬 *this* winter; (→過ぎ去った) *last* winter／今年の夏はとても暑い It is very hot *this* summer.／今年は2003年だ *This* is the year 2003.

ことづけ 言付け　message ⓒ ∥彼女に何かおことづけがおありですか Would you like to leave *a message* for her?／Shall I take *a message* for her?

ことづける 言付ける　(伝言を残す) leave* *a message*; (人に…するよう頼む) ask *a person to do* ∥彼女に電話をくれるようお母さんにことづけた I *left a message* with her mother for her to call me.

ことづて 言づて ⇨ことづけ

ことなかれしゅぎ 事なかれ主義　the principle of peace-at-any-price; (消極的な[受身の]態度) negative [passive] attitude ⓒ
◆彼はいつも事なかれ主義だ He always *plays it safe*.

ことなる 異なる　(違っている) be different, differ ⓘ; (多様である) vary ⓘ
彼の意見は私とは全く異なる His opinion *is* completely *different from* mine.／We *differ* completely in opinion.
駐車料金は車の大きさによって異なります The parking fee *varies* depending on the size of the car.
◆我々は彼らとは異なったやり方をしている We do things *differently* from them.／その地名の由来については2つの異なる説がある There are two *different* views about the origin of the place name.／彼らは子供の教育について全く意見が異なる They *are in* total *disagreement* with each other on the education of their children.

ことに 殊に　(とりわけ, 特に) especially; (格別に) particularly, in particular; (例外的に) exceptionally; (何よりも) above all ∥彼女は映画, ことに恋愛映画が好きだ She likes films, *especially* romantic films.／今シーズン, チームの成績はことによかった The team did *exceptionally [unusually]* well this season.／今年の夏はことに雨が少なかった There was *especially* little rain this summer.

-ごとに -毎に　every, each; (…するごとに) whenever, every [each] time ∥4年ごとに知事を選出する elect a (new) governor *every four years*／彼は会う人ごとに自分の成功の話をする He talks about his success to *everyone [every person] he meets*.／日ごと[ひと雨ごと]に涼しくなる It gets cooler「*day by day [with every rainfall]*.

ことにする 異にする　differ ⓘ ∥この点については私は彼女と意見を異にする My opinion *differs [is different] from* hers on this point.

ことによると 事によると　(もしかすると) perhaps, 《口語的》maybe; (ひょっとすると) possibly ∥ことによるとこの問題には答えがないのかもしれない *Perhaps* this problem has no answer.　◆ことによると彼女の状態は思ったより悪いかもしれない *It may be that* her condition is worse than we thought.

ことのほか 殊の外　(いつになく) unusually; (例外的に) exceptionally; (とりわけ) particularly ∥今年の冬はことのほか寒い It is *unusually* cold this winter.／コレクションの中でも彼はことのほかこの絵を愛していた Of all the paintings in the collection, he *particularly* liked this one.　◆試験はことのほか(→思っていたより)やさしかった The examination was easier *than I (had) expected*.

ことば　言葉

❶ 語句 word; term; phrase
❷ 表現 word; talk
❸ 言語 language; dialect; speech

❶【語句】(単語) word ⓒ; (専門用語) term ⓒ; (句) phrase ⓒ
オランダ語起源の言葉 *a word* of Dutch origin／慎重に言葉を選ぶ choose *one's words* carefully
この言葉はどういう意味ですか What is the meaning of this *word*?／What does this *word* mean?
彼に何か言ってあげたかったがうまい言葉が見つからなかった I wanted to say something to him, but I couldn't find *the* right *words*.
「什器(じゅうき)」という言葉の意味を知っていますか Do you know the meaning of *the word* "juki"?
日本語は英語から多くの言葉を取り入れている Japanese has borrowed many *words* from English.
私の気持ちは言葉では言い表せない I have no *words* to express my feelings.
その景色は美しくて言葉にできない The landscape was beautiful *beyond words*.
◆私は怒りのあまり言葉を失った I *was speechless* with rage.

❷【表現】words; (話し方) talk ⓤ
赤ちゃん言葉 baby *talk*／別の言葉で言えば in *other words*
彼女は彼と二, 三言葉を交わしてから部屋を出た She *exchanged* a few *words* with him and then left the room.
私たちは先生にお礼の言葉を述べた We said a

few *words* of thanks to our teacher.
◆母の言葉どおり，翌日には体調が少しよくなった As *my mother had said*, I did feel a bit better the next day. / あなたの言葉を信用します I believe *you* [*what you say*]. / 緊張して言葉に詰まってしまった(→何と言っていいか分からなくなった) I was nervous and *didn't know what to say*. / 彼の言葉には鹿児島なまりがある He *speaks* with a Kagoshima accent.

❸【言語】language Ⓤ (◆個々の言語をいうときは Ⓒ)；(方言) dialect Ⓒ Ⓤ；(話し言葉) speech Ⓤ

書き［話し］言葉 *written* [*spoken*] *language* / 男［女］言葉 *men's* [*women's*] *language*

2 人の間には言葉の壁があった There was *a language barrier* between the two.

アメリカに行って言葉が通じたときはうれしかった I was happy to be able to speak *the language* when I went to the United States.

その土地の言葉が理解できなかった I didn't understand *the local dialect*.

🅴「オーストラリアではどんな言葉が話されていますか」「ドイツ語が公用語になっています」 "What *language* is spoken in Austria?" "German is the official language there."

慣用表現 お言葉に甘えてこのお金をお借りします *I'll accept your offer* and borrow this money. / お言葉を返すようですが，もう一度考え直してみてはどうですか *I don't mean* [*I'm sorry*] *to contradict you, but* I think you should think about it again. / それは言葉が過ぎるよ You've *said more than enough*. / それは言葉のあやというものだ It's just *the figure of speech*. / いくら言葉を飾ったって君の魂胆は見えついている You *spoke in a flowery way, but* I know that you have some secret plan. / 彼女はその質問に対して言葉を濁した(→あいまいな答えをした) She *gave a vague answer* to the question.

ことばづかい 言葉遣い，language Ⓤ /言葉づかいに気をつけなさい Watch [Mind] *your language* [*tongue*]. / 彼女はだれに対しても丁寧な言葉づかいをする She uses polite *language* with everyone.

こども 子供

❶【大人に対して】child Ⓒ (複 children)；(◆通例14歳以下)，(《口語的》) kid Ⓒ

子供向けのテレビ番組 a *child-oriented* TV program; a TV program *for children*

大人 1 枚，子供 2 枚ください One adult and two *children*, please.

僕はもう子供ではない I'm no longer *a child*.

子供のようなまねをするな Don't act like *a child*!

10歳未満の子供は入場できない *Children* under 10 (years old) are not admitted.

彼はほんの子供だ He is just [merely] *a child* [*kid*].

子供のころよくこの公園で遊んだ I used to play in this park *when I was a child*.

彼はいつも私を子供扱いする He always *treats* me *as* [*like*] *a child*.

子供心にも家計が苦しいことは分かっていた *Even as a child*, I knew that our family had a tight budget.

◆子供のころの思い出 memories of *one's childhood* / 彼女は子供のように澄んだ目で私を見た She looked at me with pure, *childlike* eyes. / 彼女は言うことが子供っぽい She makes *childish* remarks. (◆childlike はよい意味で，childish は悪い意味で用いられる)

❷【親に対して】child Ⓒ (複 children)；(赤ん坊) baby Ⓒ；(息子) son Ⓒ；(娘) daughter Ⓒ

子供を育てる bring up *a child* / 子供の日 *Children's Day*

もうすぐいとこに子供が生まれる My cousin is going to have *a baby* soon.

彼らには 2 人の成人した子供がいる They *have* two grown-up *children*.

子供連れのかたは子供から目を離さないでください Parents *with children* should keep their eye on them.

うちの子供がお宅におじゃましていませんか Is *our son* [*daughter*] at your place?

🅴「子供さんは何人ですか」「息子が 3 人です」 "How many *children* do you have?" "I have three sons."

/子供だまし a childish trick [prank] / 子供服 children's wear [clothing] / 子供部屋 a child's room / 子供料金 children's fare, fare for children

俳句 雪とけて村いっぱいの子どもかな (小林一茶)
The snow has melted
and the village is now full.
Kids everywhere.

ことも あろうに 事もあろうに (数ある…の中で) of all (the) things [people, places] / こともあろうに彼にその話をするなんて *Of all people*, you had to tell him.

こともなげ 事もなげ 「失敗したらまた一からやり直せばいい」と彼はこともなげに言った "We could always start over again if it doesn't work out," he said *quite indifferently*. / 彼はこともなげに難しい数学の問題を解いた He whipped through the difficult math problems *as if they were nothing*.

ことり 小鳥 (small [little]) bird Ⓒ /小鳥を飼う keep *a* (*small*) *bird*

ことわざ 諺 (格言) proverb Ⓒ；(言い習わし) (common) saying Ⓒ；(処世訓) maxim Ⓒ / ことわざにあるとおり *as the proverb* [*saying*] *goes* [*runs, says*]

ことわり 断り (拒絶) refusal Ⓒ；(許可) permission Ⓤ；(予告) notice Ⓤ /断り状を出す send *a letter of refusal* / 断りもなく図書室の本を持ち出してはいけません Don't take books out of the library *without permission*. ◆入場お断り 《掲示》 *No Admittance* / 未成年者お断り 《掲示》 *No Minors* (*Allowed*) / 切符をお持ちでないかたの入場お断り 《掲示》 Admission [Entrance] by Ticket Only

ことわる 断る

❶【拒絶する】refuse 🅗; reject 🅗; decline

⓸; turn down
- refuse: 申し出・要求・招待などをはっきり拒否する.
- reject: 激しく拒絶すること.
- decline: 丁重に断ること.
- turn down: decline より口語的な表現.

彼は私の申し出を断った He *refused* my offer.
彼女は彼のプレゼントを受け取ることを断った She *refused* to accept his present.
彼女は彼のプロポーズを受けようか断ろうか迷った She wavered between accepting and *refusing* his proposal.
私は彼の要求をきっぱりと断った I *rejected* his request. / I *flatly refused* his request.
彼女は申し出をせっかくですがと断った She *declined* the offer with thanks.

❷【許可を得る】
ビルの管理人さんに断ったの? Did you *get* the janitor's [caretaker's] *permission*?
次の授業を休むなら先生に断ったほうがいいよ You should *ask for* your teacher's *permission* if you want to be absent from the next class.
断っておくけど二度と私の日記を読まないでね I'm warning you! Never read my diary again.

こな 粉 powder ⓤ;(穀物の) flour ⓤ;(チョークなどの) dust ⓤ ∥コーヒー豆をひいて粉にする grind coffee beans into *powder*

こなぐすり 粉薬 (medical) powder ⓤ, powdered medicine ⓤ

こなごな 粉々 to [into] pieces ∥お皿がテーブルから落ちて粉々に割れた A plate fell from the table and *broke* [*smashed*] *into pieces*.

こなし 身のこなしが軽い have *an* easy *carriage*; *carry oneself* easily

こなす (行う) do* ⓸;(終わらせる) finish ⓸;(扱う) manage ⓸, (演じる) perform ⓸ ∥仕事をこなす *do* [*finish*] the work / 難しい役をこなす *perform* [*play*] a difficult part / 新しいコンピュータシステムをちゃんと使いこなせるのはジョンだけだ John is the only one who can really *manage* the new computer system. ◆荒馬を乗りこなす *break* a wild horse / 彼女は英語を自由に使いこなす She *has a good command of* English.

こなせっけん 粉石鹸 soap powder ⓤ

こなミルク 粉ミルク powdered [dried] milk ⓤ, milk powder ⓤ

こなゆき 粉雪 powdery [powder] snow ⓤ

こなれる (消化する) digest ⓸, be digested;(人柄が円熟する) mellow ⓸, mature ⓸ ∥彼女はこのごろ人柄がこなれてきた She *has mellowed* recently. ◆こなれた文章を書く write in a *natural* style

こにもつ 小荷物 (主に米) package ⓒ, (主に英) parcel ⓒ

コニャック cognac ⓤⓒ

ごにん 誤認 ─誤認する mistake* ◆事実関係の誤認 *a misunderstanding* of the facts ∥誤認逮捕 false arrest

こにんずう 小人数 a small number of people ⇒しょうにんずう

こぬかあめ こぬか雨 fine [light] rain ⓤⓒ;(霧雨) drizzle ⓤ (またa ~), drizzling rain ⓤⓒ

コネ (縁故) connections;(交際) contacts;(影響力) influence ⓤ;(有力な引き) pull ⓤⓒ ∥彼はその会社にコネがある He has *pull* with the company. / 彼女はコネで就職した She got a job *through connections*. / その会社は契約をとるためにある政治家のコネを使った The company used a politician's *influence* to get the contract.

こねこ 子猫 kitten ⓒ, 《口語的・小児語》kitty ⓒ

コネチカット Connecticut (❖米国北東部の州;《略語》Conn., 《郵便》CT)

ごねどく ごね得 彼らはごね得をねらって立ち退きを拒否した They refused to move out thinking that they would 「*do better* [*profit*] *by holding out*.

こねる 捏ねる (練り粉などを) knead ⓸ ∥粉をこねてパンを作る *knead* flour [dough] to make bread ◆理屈をこねる *quibble* / だだをこねる *whine*

ごねる (不平を言う) complain (about ...), 《口語的》bitch (about ...)

この
❶【手近の】this (複these)
このカメラはとても使いやすい *This* camera is very easy to use.
この人たちはみんな英語が話せます *These* people can all speak English.
このようにやればいいんです You should do it *like this*.
この人が山田健太さんです *This* is Mr. Yamada Kenta.
◆このうそつきめ *You liar*!

❷【最近の】this (複these);(この前の) last;(過去の) past
この春は杉花粉の量が多かった There was a lot of cedar pollen *this* spring.
この1か月間雨が降っていない It hasn't rained for the *last* [*past*] month.

このあいだ この間 (先日) the other day;(何日か前) a few [several, some] days ago;(最近) recently (❖通例過去形・現在完了形とともに用いる), lately (❖通例現在完了形とともに用いる)
この間の体育の授業なぜ休んだの Why were you absent from gym class *the other day*?
この間の話はみんなにはないしょにしておいてください Please don't tell the others what I said *the other day*.
ついこの間まで京都に住んでいました I lived in Kyoto until quite *recently*.
◆この間の月曜日 *last* Monday / この間の晩[週末] *the other* evening [weekend] / この間からずっと体の調子が悪い I've been feeling bad *for some time*. / 高校に入学したのはついこの間のような気がする It seems like

only yesterday that I entered high school.
- 「お願いだから手伝ってよ」「いやだね,この間こっちが頼んだときは助けてくれなかったんだから」"Will you help me, please?" "No way. You didn't help me *the last time* I asked you to."

このあたり この辺り around here
➡ このへん

このうえ この上 (これ以上) more, further; (これに加えて) besides (this) ∥このうえ望むものは何もありません There is nothing *more* that I (could) want. / 私のことでこのうえあなたにご迷惑をおかけするわけにはいきません I can't put you to *further* trouble on my account. ◆私はこのうえなく幸せだった I was *as happy as* (I) could be.

このかた この方 (以来) since ∥委員会の発足このかた *since* the establishment of the committee; *since* the committee was established ◆生まれてこのかた外国に行ったことがない I have never been to a foreign country *all my life*.

このかん この間 meanwhile, in the meantime ∥会議は3時間続いたが,この間彼はひと言もしゃべらなかった The meeting lasted for three hours; *meanwhile*, he did not say a word.

このくらい この位 about this; (数[量]が) this many [much] ∥このくらいの背丈の男性を見かけませんでしたか Did you happen to see a man *about this* tall? / このくらい私にだって分かります I know *this much* myself. ◆きょうはこのくらいにしておきましょう *So much* for today. / *Let's call it* a day. / 私が教えてあげられるのはこのくらいです This is *about all* I can tell you. / 彼はこのくらいのことでへこたれる人ではない He's not a person who gives up over *something like this*.

このごろ この頃 these days; (現今) now, nowadays; (近ごろ) lately, recently ∥このごろはレコードプレーヤーの需要がほとんどない There is little demand for record players *these days*. / このごろ彼女はよく遅刻してくる She's been coming in late quite often *recently* [*lately*].
◆このごろの若者 young people (*of*) *today*

このさい この際 (今) now; (現状では) under [in] these circumstances; (この場合) on this occasion ∥この際だからしかたがない There is no help for it *under* [*in*] *these circumstances*. / この際一つだけはっきりさせておきたい Let me make one thing clear *on this occasion*.

このさき この先 (今より先) from now [this time] on, in the future; (ここより先) ahead ∥この先道路工事中《掲示》Road Construction *Ahead* / この先どうするつもりですか What are you going to do *from now on*? / この先予定がぎっしり詰まっている I have a tight [full, heavy] schedule *ahead*. / お探しの建物は,この先をもう少し行った所にあります The building you are looking for is a little further *ahead*.

このたび この度 この度京都へ引っ越すことになりました I will be moving to Kyoto *very soon*. / この度事務所は下記の住所に移転しました Our office has moved to the following address. / この度はご結婚おめでとうございます Congratulations on your marriage. / この度はご愁傷さまでした Please accept my sincerest condolences. (❖以上の3文では「この度」は訳出不要)

このつぎ この次 (今度) next, next time ──この次の next ∥この次はもっとうまくやるようにすべきだ You have to try to do better *next time*. / この次はどこに止まりますか What is the *next* stop? / この次の土曜はあいてる? Are you free *next* [*this coming*] Saturday?

このとおり この通り (このように) like this, in this way; (ご覧のように) as you (can) see ∥このとおりにやってください Please do it *like this*. / 私たちはこのとおり元気にしています We are all quite well, *as you can see*.

このとき この時 (at) this time [moment, point](❖過去の文脈であればこの代わりにthatを用いる) ∥このとき私はまだほんの子供にすぎなかった I was only a child *at that time*. / 彼女はこのときとばかりに文句を言ってきた She had to pick *this time* to come and complain.

このところ (このごろ) these days, nowadays; (最近) recently, lately ∥彼女はこのところあまり寝ていない She hasn't been getting much sleep *lately*.

このは 木の葉 leaf ◯ (複 leaves); (総称) foliage ◯ ∥風が木の葉を揺らした The wind stirred *the leaves*.

このぶん この分 この分では週末も仕事をしないと締め切りに間に合わないだろう *At this rate*, I will have to work on the weekend in order to meet the deadline. / この分だと(→空の様子から判断すると)あしたも雨になりそうだ *From the look of the sky* [*Judging from the weather now*], I think it will rain tomorrow as well.

このへん この辺 around [near] here; (この地域に) in this area; (この近所に) in this neighborhood ∥このへんに銀行はありますか Is there a bank 「*around here* [*in this neighborhood*]?
◆すみません,このへんのことはよく分からないので Sorry, but I'm a stranger *here*. / きょうはこのへんで終わりにしましょう *So much* [*That's all*] *for today*. / 私はこのへんで失礼します I must be leaving *now*.

このほか この他 (このうえ) besides this; (これに加えて) in addition to this; (これ以外に) else, except this ∥このほかに何か言っておきたいことはありますか Is there anything you want to tell us 「*besides this* [*in addition to this*]?

このまえ この前 (先日) the other day; (前回) (the) last (time); (最近) recently, lately ──この前の last, previous, former ∥この前の木曜日に *last* Thursday / この前会っ

このましい

たときから君はちっとも変わってないね You haven't changed at all since we *last* met. / この前泊まった部屋にしてほしいのですが I'd like the room I had *the last time*. / この前君の彼女を偶然街で見かけたよ I saw your girlfriend by chance in town *the other day*.

このましい 好ましい (感じがいい) nice, fine, agreeable, pleasant; (望ましい) desirable; (好都合な) favorable, 《英》favourable; (適している) suitable ‖好ましい人物 a *desirable* person / 好ましい[好ましくない]印象を与える make a *favorable* [an *unfavorable*] impression; make a *good* [*bad*] impression / その学生寮は勉強に好ましい環境にあった The dormitory was located in an environment that *was suitable* [*favorable*] for studying. / この映画は子供には好ましくない This film *is not suitable* for children.

このまま as it is, as they are ‖部屋はこのままにしておいてください Please leave the room *as it is*.
◆彼はこのままだときっと失敗するでしょう He will fail for sure *if he stays the way he is*. / (→この調子だと) *At this rate*, he is bound to fail. / いじめの問題をこのままにしておけない We *must do something* about the bullying problem.

このみ¹ 好み (一般的に) liking ⓤ《また a ～》; (趣味) taste ⓒⓤ; (気まぐれな) fancy ⓒ; (選択) choice ⓒ, preference ⓤ ——好みの favorite ‖食べ物[服]の好み one's taste in food [clothes] / 好みにかなう suit [be to] one's taste / それはただ好みの問題だ It's just a matter of preference [*taste*]. / 調味料はお好みで加えてください Add seasoning *to taste*. / 特に好みはありません I have no particular *preference*.
◆私好みの音楽 *my kind of* music / 好みがうるさい be particular [*choosy, picky*] / 彼は好みのタイプじゃない He is not my *type*.

このみ² 木の実 (クルミなどの硬い木の実) nut ⓒ; (果実) fruit ⓒ ‖(イチゴなどの柔らかい木の実) berry ⓒ

このむ 好む like ⓜ, be fond of ..., care for ...(❖通例否定文・疑問文で用いる); (大好きである) love ⓜ; (…のほうを好む) prefer ⓜ ‖彼はひとりで外食するのを好まない He *doesn't like to* eat out alone. / 彼女は好んでへんぴな地域を旅行している She *is fond of* traveling in remote areas. / 好むと好まざるにかかわらず我々はそれをしなければならない We just have to do it, *whether we like it or not*.

このよ この世 (世界) the world; (現世) this world; (人生) this life ——この世の (世俗的な) worldly(↔spiritual); (天国に対して地上の) earthly ◆彼は若くしてこの世を去った He ⌜*departed this life* [*passed away, died*]⌝ young.

このように このようにしてください Please do it *like this*.

こはく 琥珀 amber

ごはさん 御破算 その計画はご破算になった The plan *fell through*. / (そろばんで)ご破算で願いましては *Set everything to zero*.

こばしり 小走り 彼は小走りに通りを横切った He *trotted* across the street.

ごはっと 御法度 僕たちの学校では髪を染めるのはご法度だ(→禁止されている) Dyed hair *is forbidden* at our school.

こばな 小鼻 小鼻の周りは脂が浮きやすい The area around *the base of the nose* is often oily.

こばなし 小話 (短いこっけいな話) short funny story ⓒ; (冗談) joke ⓒ

こばなれ 子離れ 息子はもう30歳だというのに, 彼女はいつまでたっても子離れできないようだ Even though her son is 30 years old, she doesn't seem able to *let him go*.

こばむ 拒む (拒否する) refuse ⓜ, turn down; (激しく拒否する) reject ⓜ; (否定する) deny ⓜ ‖申し出を拒む refuse [*turn down*] the offer / 彼は私たちの要求を受け入れるのを拒んだ He *refused* to accept our request.

コバルト 〖化学〗cobalt ⓤ(❖元素記号 Co)
‖コバルトブルー cobalt blue

こはるびより 小春日和 (暖かい秋の陽気) mild autumn weather ⓤ; (11月ごろの一時的に暖かい陽気) 《米》Indian summer ⓒ《英》St. Martin's summer ⓒ

こはん 湖畔 lakeside, lakeshore ‖湖畔のホテル a *lakeside* hotel; a hotel *on* [*by*] *the lake* ◆湖畔を散歩する take a walk *along the lake*

こばん 小判 a *koban*, an oval coin formerly used in Japan in the Edo period
ことわざ 猫に小判 ⇒ねこ

ごはん 御飯 (飯) rice ⓤ, cooked [boiled] rice ⓤ; (食事) meal ⓒ
ごはんを炊く cook *rice*
わが家では朝はごはんと決まっている We always have *rice* for breakfast at our home.
もうごはん, 食べた? Have you finished *your meal*?
食器にこびりついたごはん粒がなかなか落ちない *The pieces of rice* stuck to the dishes are hard to wash off.
◆ごはんですよ *Dinner* [*Lunch, Breakfast, Supper*] *is ready*. (❖時間に応じて dinner, lunch などを使い分ける)

ごばん 碁盤 board ⓒ, a board used in the game of go
◆碁盤の目 a *grid*; (*checkerboard*) *squares*

こび 媚 (へつらい) flattery ⓤ, coquetry ⓤ ‖こびを売る *flatter*

ごび 語尾 the end(ing) of a word ‖語尾変化 〖文法〗inflection

コピー (写し) copy ⓒ, duplicate ⓒ; (複写) photocopy ⓒ; (複製品) reproduction ⓒ; (広告文案) (advertising) copy ⓤ ——コピーする copy ⓜ, make* a copy, duplicate ⓜ ‖この報告書のコピーを2部とってくれませんか Would you make two *copies* of this report? / このソフトをコピーすることは違法です It is illegal to *duplicate* this software.
‖コピー機 a copy machine, a photocopier

/ 両面コピー a double-sided copy

コピーライター copywriter [C]

こびじゅつ 古美術 classical art [U]; (骨董(こっとう)品) antique [C] ‖古美術店 an antique shop

こひつじ 子羊 lamb [C]

こびと 小人 dwarf [C] (複 ~s, dwarves)

こびりつく 靴に泥がこびりついている Mud *is stuck* [*clinging*] *to* my shoes. / 彼女の言葉が頭にこびりついて離れない I *can't get* her words *out of* my mind./ Her words *are stuck in* my mind.

こびる 媚びる (お世辞を言う) flatter [他]; (へつらう) fawn on [upon] ..., brown-nose [他]

こぶ[1] 瘤 (打撲による) bump [C]; (はれもの) lump [C]; (ラクダの) hump [C]; (木の) knot [C], gnarl [C] ‖頭にこぶができる get *a bump* on *one's* head

[慣用表現] 彼は目の上のこぶ (→自分の前に立ちはだかる人) だ He is *the one who's standing in my way.*/ (→悩みの種) He is *a pain in the neck.*

こぶ[2] 昆布 ➔こんぶ

ごぶ 五分 (100分の5) five percent ━五分の (互角の) even ➔ごぶごぶ

こふう 古風 ━古風な (旧式な) old-fashioned; (古くて味わいのある) antique, quaint; (文体などが古い) archaic ‖古風な考え an *old-fashioned* idea / 古風な文体 an *archaic* style (of writing)

ごぶがり 五分刈り 五分刈りの頭 *close-cropped* hair; a *short-cropped* head / 五分刈りにする *have one's hair cut* [*cropped*] *short*

ごふく 呉服 (絹織物) silk fabrics [U] [C]; (着物の生地) kimono fabrics [U] [C]; (一般的に) 《米》dry goods, 《英》drapery [U] ‖呉服商 a kimono merchant, a dealer in kimono fabrics / 呉服店 a kimono shop, a store dealing in fabrics for kimonos

ごぶごぶ 五分五分 ━五分五分の fifty-fifty; (互角の) even ‖五分五分のチャンス a *fifty-fifty* [an *even*] chance / 勝ち目は五分五分だ The odds [chances] are *even*.

◆五分五分の試合 an *evenly-matched* game

ごぶさた 御無沙汰 長い間ごぶさたして申しわけありません Please excuse *my long silence.* / ごぶさたしています *It's been a long time since I saw you last.*/ *I haven't seen you for a long time.*/《口語的》*Long time, no see.*

こぶし 拳 fist [C] ‖こぶしを握りしめる clench *one's fist* / 父は弟に向かってこぶしを振り上げた My father raised [shook] *his fist* at my brother.

◆こぶし大の石 a *fist-sized* rock [stone]

こぶた 子豚 young [baby] pig [C], piglet [C]

こぶつ 古物 (骨董(こっとう)) antique [C]; (中古品) secondhand [《米》used] article [C] ‖古物商 a secondhand dealer [store]

こぶとり 小太り ━小太りの (ぽっちゃりした) plump; (女性が肉づきのよい) buxom ‖小太りの男性 a *plump* man

こぶね 小舟 small [light] boat [C]; (ボート) 《米》rowboat [C], 《英》rowing boat [C]

コブラ 〔動物〕cobra [C] ‖キングコブラ a king cobra

こぶり 小降り (小雨) light rain [U] 《または a ~》; (霧雨) drizzle [C] ◆雨が小降りになってきた The rain *is letting up*.

こふん 古墳 ancient tomb [C], tumulus [C] (複 ~es, tumuli); mound [C] (❖丘状になっているものをいう)

‖古墳時代 the Tumulus period

こぶん[1] 子分 follower [C]; (総称) following [C]; (部下) man [C] (複 men); (暴力団などの) henchman [C] ‖子分が多い have *a* large *following* / 彼は食事の間子分に見張りをさせた He had *his men* keep watch as he ate his meal.

こぶん[2] 古文 (昔に書かれた作品) ancient [archaic] writings; (日本の古典) the Japanese classics

ごぶん 誤文 ungrammatical [incorrect] sentence [C] ‖誤文訂正 correction of (grammatical) mistakes in a sentence

ごぶんけい 5文型〔文法〕five major sentence patterns

> (1)英語の基本的な語順で作られる5つの文のことを5文型という. 文の主題となる部分を「主語」(または「主部」), 主題について述べる部分を述語(または「述部」)という. 通例主語となるのは名詞·代名詞で, 述語の中心となるのは動詞である.
>
> 1. S+V (主語+動詞) ‖The sun is shining. 太陽が輝いている
> 2. S+V+C (主語+動詞+補語) ‖That sounds interesting. それはおもしろそうだ
> 3. S+V+O (主語+動詞+目的語) ‖He wrote five novels. 彼は5冊の小説を書いた
> 4. S+V+IO+DO (主語+動詞+間接目的語+直接目的語) ‖He gave her some flowers. 彼は彼女に花を贈った
> 5. S+V+O+C (主語+動詞+目的語+補語) ‖We named the puppy Pooh. 私たちはその子犬をプーと名づけた
>
> (2)5文型は, 文の理解を助けるために, 文の骨格について述べたもので, 実際の文ではたいてい副詞(句)や形容詞(句)のような修飾語句が必要になる. 特に副詞句は, 文を成り立たせるうえで重要な役割を果たすことがある ‖ She walked *fast*. 彼女は足早に歩いた (❖5文型でいうと第1文型) ‖ My brother is lying *on the bed*. 弟はベッドで横になっている (❖5文型でいうと第1文型だが, この場合, on the bed のような修飾語句がある場合が多い)

ごへい 語弊 こう言うと語弊があるかもしれないが… *It may not be entirely correct* to say this, *but* ....

こべつ[1] 戸別 ━戸別の (家から家への) door-to-door, house-to-house (❖共に名詞の前で用いる) ━戸別に from door to door, from house to house ‖戸別訪問 (販売) door-to-door sales; (選挙の) a door-to-door canvass

こ

こべつ² 個別 ―個別の (個人個人の) individual; (おのおのの) each ―個別に individually, separately; (一つ一つ) one by one ‖個別指導 individual guidance

コペルニクス Copernicus ◆コペルニクス的転回 a *Copernican* revolution

ごほう¹ 語法 (言葉の使われ方) usage [U] (❖具体的には[C]) ‖アメリカ語法 *American usage*; *an Americanism*

ごほう² 誤報 (新聞などの) false [incorrect] report [C]; (間違った情報) wrong information [U], misinformation [U]

ごぼう 牛蒡 burdock (root) [C] (❖英米では食用にしない)
[慣用表現] 彼女は5人をごぼう抜きにした(→一気に追い越した) She *overtook* five others *in a single spurt*.

ごぼごぼ 栓を抜いたとたん，水はごぼごぼ流れていった The water *gurgled down* the drain as soon as I pulled (out) the plug.

こぼす 零す

❶【物を落とす】(液体・粉を) spill* [他]; (個体を) drop [他]; (涙を) shed* [他]
彼は床にコーヒーをこぼした He *spilled* coffee on the floor.
パンくずをこぼさないようにね Be careful not to *drop* any crumbs.
❷【不平を言う】complain [自][他], grumble [自][他]
彼女はいつも夫に思いやりがないとこぼしている She *is* always *complaining* [*grumbling*] *about* how inconsiderate her husband is.

こぼね 小骨 (小さい骨) small [fine] bone [C]

こぼれる 零れる (落ちる) fall* [自], drop [自]; (液体が) spill* [自]; (あふれる) overflow [自]; (刃などが欠ける) be chipped, be nicked ‖こぼれたワインがテーブルクロスを真っ赤に染めた The *spilt* wine stained the tablecloth a bright red. / 知らせを聞いて彼女の目から涙がこぼれた Tears *fell* from her eyes at the news. ◆少年の顔から笑みがこぼれた The boy *had a charming smile* on his face.

ごほん ごほんとせきをする *cough harshly* / 先生は説明に入る前にごほんとせきをした The teacher *coughed* before he began the explanation.

こぼんのう 子煩悩 彼は子煩悩な父親だ He is a *loving* [*fond, tender*] father.

こま¹ 駒 (将棋・チェスなどの) piece [C], man [C] ‖こまを動かす move *a piece*; *make a move*
[慣用表現] 私たちのチームは決勝戦にこまを進めた Our team *advanced to* the finals.

こま² 独楽 top [C] ‖こまを回す spin *a top*

こま³ 齣 (フィルムなどの) frame [C], exposure [C]; (場面) scene [C]; (大学の授業の) class [C] ‖歴史のひとこま *a scene* from history / 4こま漫画 a *four-frame* comic strip / 週に4こま英語の授業がある We have *four* English *classes* a week.

ごま 胡麻 sesame (seed) [C] ‖ゴマをいる[する] roast [grind] *sesame seeds* / ゴマであえる dress with ground *sesame seed* / 開け，ごま! Open *sesame*! ‖ゴマ油 sesame oil
[慣用表現] 先生にごまをする *butter up* the teacher

コマーシャル (ラジオ・テレビの) (radio [TV]) commercial [C] (❖CMは和製略語); (広告) announcement [C], advertisement [C]
‖コマーシャルソング a commercial jingle

こまかい 細かい

❶【非常に小さい】small; (微細な) fine
きめの細かい砂 *fine* sand / 目の細かい網 a *fine* net / 細かな霧 a *fine* mist
そのメモは細かい字で書かれていたので読みにくかった The note was difficult to read because it was written in *small* letters.
◆目の細かい織物 a *tight* weave / タマネギを細かく刻む *cut* an onion *into pieces*
❷【詳しい】(詳細な) detailed; (綿密な) close
その交通事故について細かい説明を警察に求められた I was asked for a *detailed* explanation of the traffic accident by the police.
◆どんな細かいことも省略するな Don't omit any *details*. / この点については細かく検討してみる必要がある We need to consider this point *in detail*.
❸【ささいな】(小さな) small; (取るに足りない) trivial, trifling
そんな細かいこと気にするなよ Don't worry about such *small* [*trivial*] things.
❹【こまやかな】sensitive
彼は神経が細かい He *is sensitive*.
❺【小額の】small
細かいお金(→小銭)を持っていませんか Do you have some *small* change?
◆この1,000円札を細かくしてください Please *change* this 1,000-yen bill.
❻【勘定高い】stingy
彼はやたらお金に細かい(→けちだ) He *is* extremely *stingy* with his money.

ごまかし (欺瞞(ぎまん)) deception [U]; (詐欺) trickery [U] ◆彼にはごまかしがきかない You *can't fool* [*trick*] him.

ごまかす 帳簿をごまかす *cook* (*up*) the books (❖cook upは「でっちあげる」の意味) / スーパーでおつりをごまかされた I *was shortchanged* at the supermarket. (❖shortchangeは「おつりを少なく渡す」の意味) / 彼は失敗を笑ってごまかそうとした He tried to *laugh off* his mistake. / その歌手は年をごまかしていた The singer *lied about her age*.

こまぎれ 細切れ (細かい切れ端) scrap [C], fragment [C]; (肉の) chopped [hashed] meat [U]
◆肉を細切れにする *mince* [*chop up*] meat / 古代史については細切れの知識しかありません I have only a *fragmentary* knowledge of ancient history.

こまく 鼓膜 eardrum [C], tympanum [C] (複 ~s, tympana) ‖鼓膜が破れそうなほど大きな音 a noise loud enough to break *one's eardrums*; an ear-splitting noise

こまごま 細々 こまごまと説明している時間はな

いんだ There is not enough time to go into *particulars*. / 彼は仕事の進め方について、いちいちこまごまとした指示を出す He always gives very *detailed* instructions as to how the job should be done. / こまごまとした用事を片づけるだけで午前中いっぱいかかってしまった It took all morning just to do *a lot of little chores*.

ごますり (おべっかを言う人) flatterer ⓒ, apple polisher ⓒ

こまどり 駒鳥 robin ⓒ

こまねく 慣用表現 手をこまねく (→何もしないでいる) look on and do nothing

こまめ ――こまめに (勤勉に) diligently; (きびきびと) briskly; (たびたび) (very) often ∥ こまめに働く work *diligently* [*like a beaver*] / できるだけこまめに辞書を引くようにしなさい Try to consult your dictionary *as often as possible*.

こまやか 細やか ――こまやかな (温かい) warm; (優しい) tender; (友情が) close; (情が厚い) affectionate ∥ こまやかな愛情 *warm* [*tender*] affection ◆こまやかな気配り *meticulous* attention; attentiveness / 彼女はたいへん感情がこまやかな女性だ She is a woman with very *delicate* feelings.

こまらせる 困らせる (いらいらさせる) annoy ⓦ, bother ⓦ, trouble ⓦ (当惑させる) embarrass ⓦ, (困惑させる) perplex ⓦ, puzzle ⓦ ∥ そんな自分勝手なことを言って私を困らせないでよ Don't *bother* me by saying such selfish things. / 彼女は先生を質問攻めにして困らせた She *annoyed* the teacher with questions. ◆人を困らせる質問をする ask *embarrassing* questions

こまる 困る

❶【苦労する・悩む】be in trouble [difficulty], have* trouble [difficulty]; (困惑する) be puzzled; (途方にくれる) be at a loss; (当惑する) be embarrassed; (ひどい目にあう) have* a hard time; (金・時間がなくて) be hard pressed

困ったことがあったらいつでも電話してください Please call me anytime *if you are in trouble*.

私たちは新しい家のことでとても困っている We *are having* a lot of *trouble with* our new house.

パソコンが突然動かなくなって困っている I'm *puzzled* because my computer suddenly won't run.

あの質問には答えるのに困ってしまった I *was at a loss* (about [as to]) how to answer that question.

ロンドンではかばんを盗まれてとても困った In London, I *had a* very *hard time* when my bag was stolen.

彼はお金[時間]がなくて困っている He *is hard pressed for* money [time].

◆人を困らせる What's *the trouble*? / 彼女は困った顔をした She had a *troubled* expression. / 彼女みたいにあんまりまじめすぎるの

も困る I *don't like* girls like her who are too serious.

🗨「何か困ったことがおありですか」「はい，財布が見つからないんです」"*Are you in* some *trouble*?" "Yes, I can't find my wallet."

❷【迷惑する】be troubled; (いらいらする) be annoyed; (悩まされる) be bothered

隣の家の犬には本当に困っている We *are* really *troubled by* our neighbor's dog.

彼女の忘れっぽいのに困っている I'm *annoyed at* her forgetfulness.

彼には困ったものだ I'm *annoyed with* him.

◆彼はいつも仕事をサボって困る It *annoys* us *that* he is always loafing on the job. / 彼は親を困らせてばかりいる He always *bothers* his parents. / 困ったことに彼女はいつも遅刻する The *trouble is that* [*The trouble is,*] she always comes late.

❸【都合が悪い】

いなかでは車がないと困る Not having a car *is inconvenient* in the country.

雨が降ると困るから (→雨が降るといけないから) 傘を持っていくのを忘れないようにね Don't forget to take an umbrella with you, *just in case* it rains.

こまわり 小回り 日本で運転するなら小回りのきく車にしたほうがいい It is better to get a car *that can turn around easily in a small space* [*with a small turning circle*] if you're going to drive in Japan. / 彼は小回りのきく男だ He is a *flexible* man. / He is *flexible*.

コマンド 〘コンピュータ〙command ⓒ

ごまんと ブロードウェーで有名になることを夢見る若いダンサーはごまんといる There are *millions* [*zillions*] *of* aspiring young dancers looking for a chance to become famous on Broadway.

こみ 込み すべて込みの値段 an *all-inclusive* [《英》*all-in*] price / 配達料込みの値段です The price *includes* delivery. / 全部込みでいくらですか How much is it *altogether*?

🗨「このシャツはいくらですか」「税込みで5,250円になります」"How much is this shirt?" "It's 5,250 yen, *tax included*."

ごみ 《米》trash ⓤ, 《英》rubbish ⓤ; (生ごみなどの) 《米》garbage ⓤ; (粗大の) refuse ⓤ; (廃棄物) waste ⓤ; (道路などの) litter ⓤ; (ちり) dust ⓤ ⇒場面・状況別会話 p.1736

ごみを捨てるな《掲示》No [*Don't*] *Litter*

海岸はごみで散らかっていた The beach was littered with *trash*.

きょうは燃える[燃えない]ごみの日だ *Burnable* [*Nonburnable*] *trash* is collected today.

あすの朝忘れずにごみを出しておいてね Don't forget to take [put] out *the garbage* [*rubbish, trash*] tomorrow morning.

◆目にごみが入った I got *something* in my eye.

∥ ごみ収集車《米》a garbage truck, 《英》a dust cart / ごみ焼却炉 an incinerator / ごみ処理場 a land disposal site, a landfill / ごみ捨て場《米》a (garbage) dump, a dumping ground, 《英》a tip / ごみ箱《米》a

こみあう 込み合う (混雑している) be crowded; (いっぱいである) be packed [jammed] / 会場はたいへん込み合っていた The hall *was very crowded* [*packed*] *with people*.

こみあげる 込み上げる (感情が) well up within one / 彼の話を聞いているうちに涙がこみ上げてきた *Tears welled up within me* [*Tears came into my eyes*] *as I listened to his story*.
◆ 彼女がついに日本に帰ってくると知って喜びがこみ上げてきた *I was filled with joy when I learned that she will be coming back to Japan at last*.

こみいる 込み入る (複雑である) be complicated [intricate, involved] / このあたりは道がこみ入っている The streets *are complicated* around here.
◆ こみ入った事情 *complicated* circumstances

ごみごみ ごみごみした町 a *squalid* town

こみち 小道 (細道) path ◯; (路地) alley, lane ◯; (野山の) trail ◯, track ◯, footpath ◯

コミック (漫画) comic (book [strip]) ◯, cartoon ◯ ⇒ まんが

コミッショナー (最高責任者) commissioner ◯

コミッション charge ◯; (手数料) commission ◯

こみみ 小耳 ちょっと小耳にはさんだのですが… I just *happened to hear* that ….; I *heard a little rumor* that ….; *A little bird told me* that ….

コミュニケ communiqué [kəmjúːnɪkèɪ] ◯ (◆フランス語から) / 共同コミュニケを読み上げる [発表する] *read* [*issue*, *release*] *a joint communiqué*

コミュニケーション communication ◯ / コミュニケーションの手段 a means of *communication* / 親子のコミュニケーション *communication* between parents and children; parents-and-children *communication* / そのチームは監督と選手のコミュニケーションが不足しているようだ There seems to be a lack of *communication* between the manager and the players on the team.

コミュニティー community ◯ / コミュニティーセンター a community center

こむ 込む・混む
❶ (混雑する) be crowded; (道路などが) be congested [jammed]
バスは込んでいて身動きがとれなかった The bus *was so crowded that I couldn't move at all*.
その新しいデパートは買い物客で込んでいた The new department store *was crowded with shoppers*.
この時間は電車が最も込む The trains *are most crowded* at this hour.
高速道路は込んでいましたか Is the express-way *congested* [*jammed*]? / (→交通量が多かったか) Is traffic *heavy* on the express-way?
❷ 【精巧な】
手の込んだ言い訳 an *elaborate* excuse / 手の込んだ細工 *elaborate* work

ゴム ⚠ rubber ◯ (◆英語の gum は「材料としてのゴム、ゴムの木」などの意味) / ゴム底のスニーカー *rubber-soled* sneakers
‖ ゴム印 a rubber stamp / ゴム園 a rubber plantation / ゴム手袋 rubber gloves / ゴム長靴 rubber boots, 《主に英》wellington boots / ゴムの木 (観賞用) a rubber tree [plant]; (ゴムの採取用) a gum tree / ゴムのり gum, mucilage / ゴムひも an elastic (string) / ゴムボート a rubber raft (boat, dinghy) / ゴムまり a rubber ball / 天然[合成]ゴム natural [synthetic] rubber / 生ゴム crude [raw] rubber / 輪ゴム an elastic [a rubber] band

こむぎ 小麦 wheat ◯, 《英》corn ◯ ◆ 島の子供たちの肌は小麦色に焼けていた The children of the island had *golden brown* tans.
‖ 小麦粉 (wheat) flour / 小麦畑 a wheat field, a field of wheat

こむらがえり 腓返り (a) cramp in the calf [leg]

こめ 米 rice ◯
1粒の米 a [one] grain of *rice* / 米を研ぐ [炊く] wash [cook, boil] *rice*
米は日本人の主食である *Rice* is the staple food of Japanese people.
アジアでは広く米が栽培されている *Rice* is widely grown in Asia.
‖ 米蔵 a rice granary / 米俵 a straw rice bag [sack] / 米作り rice farming / 米粒 a grain of rice / 米どころ a rice-producing region / 米問屋 a rice wholesaler / 米ぬか rice bran / 米屋(店) a rice store; (人) a rice dealer

こめかみ temple ◯ / こめかみのあたりが痛む My head hurts around *my temples*.

コメディアン (喜劇俳優) comedian ◯, comic ◯; (喜劇女優) comedienne ◯ (◆現在は男女とも comedian を用いるのがふつう)

コメディー comedy ◯ ⇒ きげき / コメディータッチのメロドラマ a melodrama with a touch of *comedy*

こめる 込める
❶ 【詰める】 load, charge
ライフル銃に弾をこめる *load* a rifle
❷ 【集中する】
力をこめてくいを打ち込んだ I drove the stake in *with all my strength*.
彼は心をこめて彼女のためにピアノを弾いた He played the piano for her *with all his heart*.
彼女は感情をこめてフラメンコを踊った She danced the flamenco *with feeling*.
「本当にご親切さま」と彼女は皮肉をこめて言った "It's very kind of you," she said 「*with irony* [*ironically*].

こめん 湖面 the surface of the lake ◆ 彼ら

は湖面に映った月を見つめていた They gazed at the reflection of the moon *in the lake*.

ごめん　御免

❶【謝罪】(軽く謝るとき) Excuse me., Pardon me.; (自分の落ち度・過失を認めてわびるとき) I'm sorry, Sorry.; (小さな過失・非礼をわびるとき) I beg your pardon.

(人にぶつかって) ごめんなさい. 大丈夫ですか *Oh, excuse me*. Are you all right?

せっかく誘ってくれたのに行けなくてごめんね Thanks for the invitation. *I'm sorry* I can't go.

電話するのを忘れてごめんなさい *I'm sorry「for* forgetting [*to* have forgotten] to call you.

きのうはごめんなさい *I'm sorry about* yesterday.

ごめん, 遅くなっちゃって *Sorry* I'm late.

ごめんなさい. ミーティングは3時からだと思っていました *I beg your pardon*. I thought the meeting began at three.

❷【断り】

(部屋に入るとき) ごめんください *Hello* [*Excuse me*]. May I come in?

(座をはずすとき) ちょっとごめんなさい *Excuse me* (for) a minute.

❸【拒否・拒絶】

そんなことはごめん被る (→かかわりたくない) *I would rather be excused from* that./ (→何の関係ももちたくない) *I won't have anything to do with* it.

彼はお役ごめんになった (→その立場からはずされた) He *was「relieved of* [*dismissed from*] *his position*.

コメント (解説) comment Ⓤ Ⓒ ──コメントする comment ⓥ/ノーコメントです *No comment*!/ 私たちは校長先生に制服の着用についてコメントを求めた We *asked* the principal *to comment* on the wearing of school uniforms.

ごもくずし　五目鮨 〓　*gomokuzushi*, vinegared [sushi] rice mixed with various delicacies

ごもくならべ　五目並べ gobang Ⓤ, five-in-a-row Ⓤ/五目並べをする play *gobang* [*five-in-a-row*]

ごもくめし　五目飯 〓　*gomokumeshi*, rice steamed in stock with various seasoned ingredients

こもごも　人生の悲喜こもごも *the joys and sorrows* of life

こもじ　小文字 small [lower-case] letter Ⓒ

こもち　子持ち 彼女は3人の子持ちだ She *has three children*.

こもの　小物 (こまごました品々や道具) small article Ⓒ, accessory Ⓒ; (小人物) unimportant [insignificant] fellow Ⓒ
‖小物入れ an accessories case

こもり　子守 nursing Ⓤ; (親の留守中の) baby-sitting Ⓤ, (主に英) childminding Ⓤ; (人) baby-sitter Ⓒ ◆おばさんに赤ちゃんの子守をするよう頼まれた My aunt asked me to *look after* [*take care of*] her baby.
‖子守歌 a lullaby, a cradle song

こもる　籠る (気体が) be full of ..., be filled with ...; (人が) shut* *oneself* up, be confined ‖たばこの煙が部屋にこもっている The room *is filled with* tobacco smoke./ 彼は5時間も自分の部屋にこもりっきりだ He *has shut himself up* in his room for five hours.
◆愛情のこもった言葉 *affectionate* words/ 心のこもった贈り物 a *kind* [*heartfelt, thoughtful*] present/ 感情のこもっていないせりふ words said *without feeling*

こもれび　木漏れ日 sunlight filtering [streaming] down through the leaves of trees

こもん　顧問 (助言者) adviser Ⓒ; (専門的な相談相手) counselor, (英) counsellor Ⓒ, consultant Ⓒ ‖バレー部の顧問 *a staff adviser* to the volleyball club
‖顧問弁護士 a legal adviser; (会社の) a corporation lawyer, (米) a general counsel; (家の) a family lawyer/ 技術顧問 a technical [an expert] adviser

こや　小屋 (掘っ建て小屋) hut Ⓒ; (物置) shed Ⓒ; (丸太などの) cabin Ⓒ/犬小屋 a doghouse, a kennel/ 牛小屋 a cowshed/ 馬小屋 a stable/ サーカス小屋 a circus tent/ 芝居小屋 a playhouse/ 丸太小屋 a log cabin/ 山小屋 a (mountain) hut

こやく　子役 (役者) child actor [actress] Ⓒ; (役) child's part [role] Ⓒ

ごやく　誤訳 (間違った訳) mistranslation Ⓒ, incorrect translation Ⓒ ──誤訳する mistranslate ⓥ, make* a mistake [an error] in translation

こやし　肥やし (牛馬のふんなど) manure Ⓤ; (化学肥料) fertilizer Ⓤ

こやす　肥やす enrich ⓥ; (土を豊かにする) fertilize ⓥ; (家畜を太らせる) fatten (up); (判断力などを養う) cultivate ⓥ

こやみ　小止み 雨が小やみになってきた The rain *is letting up*./ There is *a lull* in the rain.

こゆう　固有 ──固有の (特有の) peculiar, proper; (自分自身の) one's own; (特徴的な) characteristic; (本来備わっている) inherent, instinctive; (土着の) native ‖日本固有の習慣 customs *peculiar* [*proper*] *to* Japan

こゆうめいし　固有名詞〔文法〕proper noun Ⓒ

固有名詞は大文字で書き始め, 通例冠詞が付かず, 複数形にならない. ただし, 以下のような場合は普通名詞と同じように考えて, 冠詞を付けたり, 複数形にしたりする ‖ My uncle has *a Picasso*. おじはピカソ(の絵)を持っている(❖作品など)/ There are three *Yamadas* in this class. このクラスには山田さんが3人いる(❖複数の同じ名前をもった人)/ *A Mr. Baker* came to see me a few minutes ago. ベーカーさんとかいう人が数分前にあなたに会いに来た(❖「…とかいう人」の意味)/ I want to be *a Ms. Mukai.* 向井さんのような人になりたい(❖「…のような人」の意味)

こゆき 小雪 light snow(fall) [C] ∥昨夜は小雪がぱらついた We had *a light snow* last night.

こゆび 小指 (手の) little finger [C],《米》pinkie [C]; (足の) little toe [C]

こよう 雇用 employment [U], hire [U] ―雇用する employ [他], hire [他] ◆雇用を生み出す create [generate] (*new*) *jobs*
∥雇用期間 a period of employment / 雇用契約 an employment contract / 雇用条件 the terms of employment / 雇用主 an employer / 雇用保険 unemployment insurance / 完全雇用 full employment / 終身雇用制 lifetime employment system / 男女雇用機会均等法 the Equal Employment Opportunity Law / 被雇用者 an employee

ごよう 御用 何かご用ですか *What can I do for you?*/ *May I help you?* / お安いご用です *Certainly.*/ *Of course.*/ *With pleasure.*/ *No problem.* / いつでもご用をお申しつけください I'm always at *your service.*/ I'm at *your service* any time.
∥御用納め the last business day of the year at government offices / 御用聞き an order taker / 御用始め the reopening of business after the New Year's holidays at government offices

こよなく 本をこよなく愛する love books *dearly*

こよみ 暦 calendar [C]; (年鑑) almanac [C] ∥暦の上ではもう夏だ It is already summer *according to the calendar.*/ *The calendar says* it is already summer.

こより paper string [C] ◆こよりをよる twist *paper into a string*

こら (相手の注意を喚起して) Hey (you)!, Look here! ∥こら, こんな所で何してるんだ *Hey*! What are you doing here?

コラージュ 〔美術〕 collage [U][C]

こらい 古来 (古代から) from old [ancient] times ―古来の old, ancient; (由緒ある) time-honored ∥古来の風習 *old* customs

ごらいこう 御来光 the sunrise seen from the top of a high mountain

こらえしょう 堪え性 最近の子供はこらえ性がない Children these days have no *perseverance.*

こらえる 堪える (耐える) bear* [他], stand* [他], put* up with ..., endure [他]; (抑制する) control [他], keep* [hold*] back, suppress [他] ∥笑いをこらえる *suppress* [*stifle*] *one's* laughter / 痛みをこらえる *stand* [*endure*] the pain / 涙をこらえる *hold back one's* tears
◆眠気をこらえる *withstand* sleepiness

ごらく 娯楽 (楽しみ) amusement [C]; (余興など) entertainment [U][C]; (休養·気晴らし) recreation [U][C]; (暇つぶし) pastime [C] ∥娯楽映画 an entertaining movie / 娯楽施設 amusement [recreational] facilities / 娯楽室 a recreation [games] room / 娯楽番組 an entertainment program

こらしめ 懲らしめ (懲罰) punishment [U][C]; (懲戒) discipline [U]; (教訓) lesson [C]

こらしめる 懲らしめる (罰する) punish [他], discipline [他]; (思い知らせる) teach* *a person* a lesson ∥ひとつ彼をこらしめてやらなくては I'll *teach* him *a lesson.*

こらす 凝らす 息を凝らして *with bated breath* / 趣向[工夫]を凝らす *elaborate* [*work out*] a plan; *make* elaborate [ingenious] plans / 私は目を凝らしてマジシャンの手を見た I *fixed my eyes* on the magician's hands.

コラム column [C] ∥スポーツ[音楽]のコラム *a column* on sports [music]

コラムニスト columnist [C]

ごらん 御覧 ご覧のとおり *as you* (*can*) *see* / ご覧に入れたいものがあります There is something I would like to *show* you. / ちょっとあれを見てごらん Just *look at* that./ Just *take a look at* that. / もう一度やってごらん *Try* it again./ *Give* it another *try.* / 見てごらん (→きっとこうなるよ) *You watch.*/ *Just watch.* / ほらごらんなさい(→言ったとおりでしょう) *I told you so*!/ *There you are.*

コリー 〔動物〕 collie (dog) [C]

ごりおし ごり押し ―ごり押しする (無理やり押し通す) force [他], bulldoze [他]; (計画·要求などを) push [他]

こりかたまる 凝り固まる (熱中する) be fanatical [crazy]; (偏執的である) be bigoted ∥一つの考えに凝り固まったりしない柔軟な人材を求めています We are looking for flexible people who *are* not *fanatical about* any one fixed idea.

こりこり この漬物はこりこりしていておいしい These pickles are nice and *crunchy.*

こりごり こんな仕事はもうこりごりだ *I've had enough of* this job.

ごりごり ごりごり削り取る *scrape ... off*

こりしょう 凝り性 彼女は凝り性(→熱中する人)だ She is *an enthusiast.*

こりつ 孤立 isolation [U] ―孤立する be isolated ∥台風のために海浜都市は完全に孤立してしまった The seaside city *was isolated* [*cut off*] by the typhoon.
◆社会から孤立する「*cut oneself off* [*be cut off*] from society / 彼は孤立無縁で(→ひとりで)戦った He fought *alone.*
∥孤立主義 isolationism

ごりむちゅう 五里霧中 五里霧中である(→どうしていいかさっぱり分からない) *be in a fog*; *be* (*all*) *at sea*; *not have a clue*

ごりやく 御利益 お寺にお参りしたらご利益があった *My prayers were answered* [*heard*] after I visited the temple.

こりょうりや 小料理屋 small restaurant [C]

ゴリラ gorilla [C]

こりる 懲りる (十分経験する) have* enough of ...; (教訓を得る) learn* a lesson (from ...) ◆これで彼もこりるだろう This will *teach* him *a lesson.* / この前ふられたのにまた告白するなんてこりないやつだ So you told her you love her again even though she dumped you recently. *You never learn.*

ごりん 五輪 the Olympic games, the Olympics ➡ オリンピック

こる 凝る (筋肉が) be [get*] stiff; (熱中する) be into ..., (口語的) be crazy about ...; (細かいことにこだわる) be particular about ... ∥私はいつも肩が凝っている My shoulders *are* always *stiff.* / 有里は最近編み物に凝っている Yuri *is into [crazy about]* knitting these days. ◆凝った料理を作る cook some *complicated* dishes / 肩の凝らない本 a book *for light reading*

コルク cork ⒰Ⓒ ∥コルクの栓を抜く pull out a *cork* ◆びんにコルクの栓をする *cork* a bottle
∥コルク抜き a corkscrew

コルセット corset Ⓒ

ゴルフ golf Ⓤ ∥彼は月に2，3回ゴルフをする He *plays golf* two or three times a month. ◆ゴルフに行く go *golfing*
∥ゴルフクラブ a golf club / ゴルフコース a golf course, golf links / ゴルフバッグ a golf bag / ゴルフボール a golf ball / ゴルフ練習場 a (golf) driving range

ゴルファー golfer Ⓒ

これ this (複 these)
これのふたどこにあるか知らない？ Do you know where the lid for *this* is?
これとこれをください I'll take *this* and *this.*
これ, 借りていい？ Can I borrow *this one*?
◆きょうはこれで終わります *That's all for today.* / *So much for* today. / これ以上歩けない I can't walk *any more.*
🄮「これは何」「知らないの？ DVD ドライブだよ」 "What's *this*?" "Don't you know? It's a DVD drive."
🄮「日曜日はおもしろいことあった？」「いや，これといってなかった」"Was there anything interesting last Sunday?" "No, nothing *in particular.*"

これから (これ以後) after this; (今後はずっと) from now on; (将来は) in the future ∥これからは遅れないようにしてください Please don't be late *from now on.*
◆これからの世代 the *coming* generation / これからどうしようか What shall we do *now*? / これから電話しようと思っていたところだったんだ I *was just about to* call you. / これから会えない？ Can we get together *now*? / これから勉強しなければならないことがたくさんある I have a lot of work *ahead of* me. / そのスポーツ選手はまだこれからというときに引退した The athlete retired *when he [she] still had a lot of promise.*

これきり (一度だけ) once and for all; (二度と…しない) never again; (これで全部) this is all ... ∥お金はこれきりしか持っていません *This is all* the money I have.
◆この話はもうこれきりにしましょう Let this be *the last time* we discuss this subject. / Let's *not* discuss this subject *again.*

コレクション (収集) collection Ⓒ ∥彼女は自分のコレクションを美術館に寄贈した She donated her *collection* to the museum.

コレクトコール (受信者払いの通話) collect call Ⓒ, (英)reverse-charge call Ⓒ
◆コレクトコールで電話していいですか Can I *call you collect*?

これくらい (これだけ) this; (このように) like [as] this; (そのように) so ➡ ーくらい, このくらい ∥箱の大きさはこれくらいです The box is about *this* big. / これくらいのことで疲れてはだめよ You shouldn't be tired after *something like this.*

これこれ 休むときは，これこれこの理由で休むとちゃんと言ってくださいWhen you're going to be absent, explain why *in detail*. / これこれ, やめなさい *Hey,* cut it out!

これしき これしきのことで泣くな Don't cry about *such a little thing.* / なんのこれしき Oh, *it's nothing.*

コレステロール cholesterol Ⓤ ∥そういう物を食べると血中のコレステロール値が増える That sort of food will raise *the cholesterol level* in your blood.

これだけ これだけは本当だ *This much* is true. / チームにこれだけの大物選手がそろっているんだから，とにかく負けるわけにはいかない With *so many* great players on the team, we simply cannot lose. / 言うべきことはこれだけです *This is all* 「there is [I have] to say.

これっぽっち これっぽっちのお金しか残っていない I only have *this much* money left. / 彼は相手を思いやる気持ちをこれっぽっちも持ち合わせていない He hasn't got *an ounce of* consideration for other people in him.

これで これで彼も僕の言ったことが分かっただろう *After that*, he should have understood what I said. / これで話を終わります *That's all I have to say.*

これでは これでは問題が解決したことにはならない *That* doesn't mean that the problem has been solved.

これでも これでも(→信じてくれないかもしれないが)中学のときの成績はクラスで1番だったんだ *You may not believe it, but* my grades in junior high school were the highest in the class.

これという particular ∥これという理由もなく without any *particular* reason / 日曜日にはこれといった予定はありません I have no *particular* plans for Sunday. / これといった趣味はありません I have no *particular* interests *to speak of.*

これほど so, such ∥彼女がこれほどすばらしい料理の腕前をもっていたとは知らなかった I had no idea she was *such* a wonderful cook. / これほどきれいな景色は見たことがない I have never seen *such* a beautiful scene as this. ◆これほど言ってもまだ分からないのか *Even after all I've said,* you still don't understand?

これまで so far, until now, up to now ∥彼の人生はこれまでのところ何もかもうまくいってい

これみよがしに

る Everything has gone well *so far* in his life. / これまでクラシック音楽には興味がなかった I wasn't interested in classical music *until now*.
- ◆きょうはこれまで *That's all for* today. / *So much for* today. / これは私がこれまで見た中でいちばんおもしろい映画です This is the most interesting movie that I've *ever* seen. / もはやこれまでだ *It's all over with* me.

これみよがしに これ見よがしに（人目を引くように）ostentatiously;（見せびらかすために）for show, to show off ‖彼は上着のそでから新しい腕時計をこれ見よがしにのぞかせた He held his wrist out of his jacket sleeve *ostentatiously* to show off his new watch.

コレラ〖医学〗cholera ‖コレラ患者 a cholera patient;（症例）a case of cholera / コレラ菌 a cholera bacterium [bacillus]

これら these (❖thisの複数形) ➡ これ ‖これらの商品は合計で7,000円になります *These* items add up to 7,000 yen.

ころ 頃
子供のころ，よくこの公園で遊んだ I used to play at this park *when* I was a child.
あのころはとても忙しかった I was very busy 「*at that time* [*in those days, then*].
もうそろそろ娘が電話してくるころだ *It's about time* for my daughter to call.
うそをつくのをやめて真実を話してもいいころじゃないか Isn't it *high time* you stopped lying and told me the truth?

ゴロ ⚠ grounder, ground ball ‖ゴロを打つ *hit a grounder*; ground ◆彼はセカンドゴロに倒れた He *grounded out* to second.

ごろ 語呂 この店の名前はごろがいい The name of this shop 「*has a nice ring* [*sounds nice*].
‖ごろ合わせ a play on words, a pun

-ごろ -頃（だいたいの時）about,《口語的》around;（…に近づいた時間に）toward
彼女は7時ごろに戻ります She'll be back (at) *about* seven thirty.
昼ごろ激しく雨が降りだした *Toward* noon, it began to rain heavily.
- ◆このメロンは食べごろだ This melon is *ready to eat*.

ころあい 頃合い 彼にはころ合いを見て話したい I want to 「*wait for* [*find*] *a good time* to tell him about it.

ころがす 転がす roll ‖ボウリングの球は投げるんじゃなくて転がすんだよ You don't throw a bowling ball; you *roll* it.
- ◆土地を転がして大もうけする make a fortune *by land speculation*

ころがりこむ 転がり込む（転がって入る）roll [tumble] into …;（不意に現れる）turn up (unexpectedly) ‖彼は疲れきってベッドに転がり込んだ He was exhausted and *tumbled into* bed. / 突然昔の友達が転がり込んできた An old friend of mine *turned up* suddenly at my home.
- ◆莫大(ばくだい)な財産が突然彼女に転がり込んだ She unexpectedly *came into* a large fortune. / A large fortune *fell into* her hands unexpectedly.

ころがる 転がる（回転する）roll;（倒れる）tumble [fall*] down;（横たわる）lie* (down) ‖ボールは転がって池に落ちた The ball *rolled* into the pond. / 彼はあおむけに芝生に寝転がった He *lay* on the grass with his face upward. / チャンスはいくらでも転がっている Opportunities *are lying around* everywhere. / You *can find* opportunities everywhere.

コロケーション〖文法〗collocation

ころげまわる 転げ回る roll [tumble, toss] about

ころころ ころころ転がる roll *over and over* / ころころと太った犬 a chubby dog / 彼女は意見をころころ変える She changes her opinion *frequently*.

ごろごろ 雷がごろごろ鳴っている *It's thundering.* / 猫はのどをごろごろ鳴らした The cat purred. / 岩が斜面をごろごろ転がっていった Boulders *rumbled down* the slope. / きのうからおなかがごろごろする My stomach *has been upset* since yesterday. / 家でごろごろしているのはもったいないくらいいい天気だ It's much too nice a day to *spend lying about* at home. / その部屋には空のびんがごろごろ転がっていた Empty bottles *were scattered* around the room. / 身長2メートルの選手なんてNBAにはごろごろいる The NBA *is full* of players who are two meters tall.

ころし 殺し murder ➡ さつじん

ころしもんく 殺し文句 telling phrase [expression];（決め手）clincher

ころしや 殺し屋 hired [professional] killer,《米俗語》hit man [woman]

ころす 殺す

❶【生命を奪う】kill; murder; assassinate; massacre, slaughter

> kill: 「殺す」の意味の一般的な語。人にも動物にも用いる。
> murder: 殺意をもって人を殺すこと。
> assassinate: 重要人物を暗殺すること。
> massacre, slaughter: 人を残虐な方法で大量に殺すこと。slaughter は食肉用に動物を殺すことにも用いる。

男は女を銃で殺した The man *killed* him with a gun. / The man shot and *killed* him.
彼はナイフで刺し殺された He *was killed* [*murdered*] with a knife.
- ◆彼女はひもでしめ殺された She *was strangled* with a cord.

❷【抑える】hold*;（押し殺す）suppress, stifle
あくびをかみ殺す suppress [stifle] a yawn
今の仕事のままでは彼の才能を殺すことになるだろう His current job will *stifle* his abilities.
私は戸の陰に隠れて息を殺した I hid behind the door and *held my breath*.

ごろつき（悪党）ruffian;（不良）hooligan

[C], hoodlum [C]; (やくざ) gangster [C]
コロッケ croquette [C] (❖フランス語から)
‖カニコロッケ a crab croquette
コロッセウム the Colosseum
ころっと 母に買い物を頼まれていたのをころっと忘れていた I had *completely* [*clean*] forgotten my mother had asked me to do some shopping.
コロナ 〘天文〙 corona [C] (複 ~s, coronae)
ごろね ごろ寝 ―ごろ寝する lie* down; (着替えないで寝る) sleep* [fall* asleep, drop off] with *one's* clothes on ‖家に帰ると父がソファーの上でごろ寝していた My father *was sleeping* on the sofa *with his clothes on* when I came home.
ころぶ 転ぶ (倒れる) fall* (down [over]), tumble (over) ‖その男の子は石につまずいて転んだ The boy stumbled on [over] a stone and *fell down.* / 床がとても滑りやすくてもう少しで転ぶところだった The floor was so slippery that I almost *fell over.*
[慣用表現] 彼女は転んでもただでは起きない(→すべてをうまく利用する) She *makes the best of everything.*/ She *takes advantage of every situation.* / どっちに転んでも損はない I have nothing to lose *either way.*
[ことわざ] 転ばぬ先の杖 Look before you leap. (→跳ぶ前によく見よ)
ころも 衣 (法衣) robe [C]; (てんぷらなどの) coating [U], batter [U] (❖前者は揚げたもの, 後者は揚げる前のものをいう); (ケーキなどの) frosting [U], icing [U]
‖衣替え a seasonal change of clothing
ころり ころりと死ぬ die *suddenly* / (女性に) ころりと参る fall *madly* in love (with a woman) / 彼女は態度をころりと変えた She changed her attitude *completely.* / そのチームは優勝候補だったが初戦でころりと負けてしまった The team was *easily* beaten in the first match though they had been expected to win the tournament.
ごろり 重いたるをごろりと転がす *roll* a heavy barrel / 彼はベッドにごろりと横になった He *lay down* on his bed.
コロン 〘文法〙 colon [C] ➾ [巻末付録] (句読法)
ごろん 彼は大きなカボチャを床にごろんと置いた He put the big pumpkin on the floor *with a thud.*
コロンブス (イタリアの航海家) Christopher Columbus
[慣用表現] コロンブスの卵 *Columbus's egg; a thing that looks easy once it has been done* (❖Columbus's egg はあまり一般的な表現ではない)
こわい 怖い ―[形] (恐ろしい) terrible, fearful, dreadful, horrible, scary; (厳しい) strict, stern ―[動] be afraid [frightened] of ..., have* a fear [dread] of ...
怖い目にあう have a *terrible* [*dreadful*] experience
そのころの私は怖いもの知らずだった I *wasn't afraid of anything* in those days.
彼女は蛇が怖いと打ち明けた She confessed to *being afraid of* snakes.
◆怖い顔をする look *fierce* [*threatening*] / 体育の先生はとても怖い先生だ Our gym teacher is really *frightening.* / 彼女は怖くなって顔を背(そむ)けた She turned away *in horror.* / あのときは死ぬほど怖かったよ I *was scared to death* then. / 怖いもの見たさでその部屋の中をのぞいた *Curiosity overcame my fear,* and I peeked into the room. / 彼には怖いものは何もない Nothing can make him *afraid.*/ He *is afraid of* nothing.
こわいろ 声色 a tone of voice
こわがる 怖がる fear [他][自], be afraid; (おびえる) be frightened, be scared ‖何も怖がることはない Don't *be afraid.*/ You have nothing to *fear.* / 彼女は暗やみをひどく怖がる She *is* very *afraid* [*frightened, scared*] *of* the dark. / 彼女はその手術を受けるのを怖がった She *was afraid* 「*of* having [*to* have] the operation.
こわき 小脇 本を小わきに抱える carry a book *under one's arm*
こわごわ (おずおずと) timidly; (おそるおそる) fearfully, with fear ‖彼らはこわごわ穴をのぞき込んだ *Fearfully,* they looked into the hole. / 彼女はこわごわとその動物にさわった She touched the animal *timidly.*
ごわごわ ごわごわした髪 *stiff* [*rough*] hair / このシーツはのりがききすぎてごわごわしている This sheets is *stiff* with too much starch.

こわす 壊す

❶【破壊する】break* [他]; (完全に) destroy [他]; (解体する) pull [tear*] down; (部分的に) damage [他]
夢をこわす *destroy* a dream
このいすをこわしたのはだれだ Who *broke* this chair?
データがウイルスによってこわされた The data *were* [*was*] *damaged* by a (computer) virus.
彼らは古い家屋をこわして新しいオフィスビルを建てた They *tore* [*pulled*] *down* the old houses and built a new office building.
❷【健康を害する】ruin [他]
毎晩夜ふかししていると体をこわすよ If you keep staying up late every night, you *will ruin* your health.
◆食べすぎておなかをこわした I ate too much and *got an upset stomach.*
❸【よい状態を悪くする】
美しい景観をこわす *ruin* [*destroy, spoil*] the beautiful scenery
彼のひと言がいい雰囲気をこわした What he said *destroyed* [*ruined*] the good atmosphere.
こわだか 声高 ―声高に (大声で) loudly, in a loud voice; (厳しく) severely ‖声高に批判する criticize *severely*
こわばる 強ばる stiffen [自], get* [become*] stiff ‖彼は緊張のあまり顔がこわばった His face *stiffened* [*tightened*] with tension. / 恐怖で体がこわばった I *stiffened* [*frozen*]

こ

こわれもの 壊れ物 (こわれやすい品物) fragile article ⓤ, (割れ物)《集合的》breakables
◆こわれ物-取扱い注意 Fragile: Handle with Care (❖箱などの表示)

こわれる 壊れる ❶【破壊される】break* ⓔ, be broken; (割れ物)《完全に》be destroyed; (部分的に) be damaged
それはこわれやすい It *breaks easily.* / It's *fragile.*
皿が床に落ちて粉々にこわれた The plate fell on the floor and *broke into pieces.*
この腕時計はこわれている This watch *is broken.*
またパソコンがこわれた The computer *has broken down* again.
その事故で彼の車はこわれた His car *was damaged* in the accident.
❷【よい状態が悪くなる】
姉の縁談がこわれてしまった My sister's engagement *was broken off.*

こん¹ 根 〔数学〕root ⓒ; (根気) endurance ⓤ /平方[立方]根 the square [cube] *root* / 根比べをする have an *endurance* contest
◆根を詰める devote all one's energy [energies] (to ...) / 根負けする give in to a person's *tenacity [persistence]* ⇨ こんき(根気)

こん² 紺 dark [navy] blue ⓤ

こん- 今- 今シーズンの終わりに at the end of *this* season / 今世紀 *this* [*the present*] century / 今学期中 during *this* session

こんい 懇意 ─懇意な friendly, (親密な) close, intimate (❖intimate は男女間の性的な関係をいうときに使われることもあるので注意); (親しい) familiar
◆…と懇意になる make friends with ...; become close to ... / 彼はその会社の社長と懇意にしている He 「*is good friends* [*has a close acquaintance*] *with* the president of the company.

こんいん 婚姻 marriage ⓤ ⇨ けっこん(結婚) / 彼らは婚姻届を出した They *registered their marriage.* / They *had their marriage registered.*
‖婚姻届 marriage registration, registration of *one's* marriage

こんかい 今回 this time ─今回の *this* /
彼女は今回は少し違った態度をとった She took a slightly different attitude *this time.* /
神戸を訪れるのは今回が初めてです This is my first visit to Kobe. / 税制改革が今回の選挙戦の争点だ Tax reform is the main issue of *this* election campaign.

こんがらかる (糸などが) get* [become*] tangled (up); (話などが) get confused; (事件などが) get [become] complicated / 頭がこんがらかってきた I'm getting confused.

こんがり こんがりと焼けたトースト *golden brown* toast / パンをこんがりきつね色になるまで焼いてください Toast the bread until it's *nice and brown.*

こんかん 根幹 (根本) basis ⓒ (複 bases); (基本) the fundamentals /外交の根幹 the *basis* of diplomacy

こんがん 懇願 entreaty ⓤ ⓒ ─懇願する entreat ⓔ, beg ⓔ, implore ⓔ; (哀願する) plead* with ...; (訴える) appeal to ... /援助を懇願する *entreat a person for* help; *beg a person to* help / 懇願を聞き入れる listen to *a person's entreaty* / 再三懇願したが彼の許しは得られなかった I 「*pleaded with* [*entreated*, *begged*, *appealed to*] him again and again, but I could not get his permission.

こんき¹ 根気 (忍耐力) patience ⓤ (↔impatience); (長期にわたる) endurance ⓤ; (ねばり強さ) perseverance ⓤ; (精力) energy ⓤ ⓒ /この仕事はたいへん根気がいる This job requires a lot of *patience* [*perseverance*].
◆根気のある人 a *patient* [*persevering*] person / 根気よく続ける continue *stubbornly* / 根気がなくなる *give up*

こんき² 婚期 marriageable age ⓤ /婚期に達した娘 a girl of *marriageable age* / 婚期を逸する be past *marriageable age*; lose *one's chance to get married*

こんきゅう 困窮 (貧困) poverty ⓤ; (困難) hardship ⓤ ⓒ; (苦境) plight ⓒ ─困窮する (貧乏に苦しむ) be poor [in poverty], 《口語的》be hard up
◆生活困窮者 *the poor and needy*

こんきょ 根拠 ground ⓤ ⓒ 《しばしば複数形~s》; (基礎となるもの) basis ⓒ (複 bases), foundation ⓤ; (理由) reason ⓒ ⓤ; (典拠) authority ⓒ
確かな根拠に立脚して on secure *ground*
何を根拠にそう言うのですか What is *the basis of* [*for*] your saying that?
この報道には根拠がない This report is without *foundation.* / This report has no *foundation* in fact.
◆根拠となるべき事実がなかった We had no facts to *go on.*
‖根拠地 a base (of operations)

ゴング ⚠(ボクシングなどの) bell ⓒ (❖英語の gong は「どら」の意味)

コンクール ⚠ contest ⓒ, competition ⓒ (❖日本語はフランス語の concours から) /合唱コンクールの参加者 competitors in *a* chorus *contest* / コンクールに参加する enter [participate in] *a contest* / コンクールで1位に入賞する win first prize in *a contest*

コンクリート concrete ⓤ ‖コンクリートミキサー a concrete mixer / 鉄筋コンクリート reinforced concrete

ごんげ 権化 incarnation ⓒ /悪の権化 the *incarnation* of evil

こんけつ 混血 彼は日本人とイギリス人の混血だ He is *half-Japanese, half-English.*
‖混血児 a child of mixed parentage

こんげつ 今月 this month
今月15日に on the 15th of *this month* / 今月の行事 *this month*'s events
私は今月末までにレポートを3つ提出しなければならない I've got three papers to hand in by the end of *this month.*

◆今月号の雑誌 the current issue of the magazine

こんげん 根源・根元 (根本) the root; (源泉) the source ∥諸悪の根源 the root [source] of all evil

こんご 今後 (これ以後) after this, from now on; (将来は) in the future ——今後の future, coming
今後は学校に遅刻しないように From now on, don't be late for school. /
彼らの新手法は今後の研究によい手本を示してくれた Their new methods set a pattern for future research. /
今後ともよろしくお願いいたします I look forward to your continued cooperation in the future.
◆事態は今後数年間変わらないでしょう The situation will continue for 「a few [the next few] years.

こんごう 混合 mixture ⓒ ——混合する mix 他自; (コーヒーなどを) blend 他自 ∥空気はいろいろな気体の混合物だ Air is a mixture of many different gases. / 水と油は混合できない You can't mix oil and [with] water. / Oil and water don't mix.
∥混合ダブルス mixed doubles / 混合物 a mixture; (酒・コーヒーなどの) a blend

コンコース (駅などの中央広場) concourse ⓒ

ごんごどうだん 言語道断 言語道断な (→けしからぬ) 要求 an outrageous demand / 高校生が酒を飲むなど言語道断だ It's outrageous for high school students to be drinking.

こんこんと¹ 懇々と (繰り返し) repeatedly; (熱心に) earnestly ∥先生は生徒たちを懇々と諭した The teacher admonished the students repeatedly [earnestly].

こんこんと² 滾々と 泉から水がこんこんとわき出ていた Water was gushing [bubbling] out from the spring.

コンサート concert ⓒ ⇨ 場面・状況別会話 p.1702 ∥今度の日曜日, グレイのコンサートに行くの I'm going to the GLAY concert next Sunday.
∥コンサートマスター《米》a concertmaster, 《英》a leader / 野外コンサート an open-air concert

こんさいるい 根菜類 root vegetables [crops]

こんざつ 混雑 (密集) congestion Ⓤ; (ぎゅうぎゅう詰め) jam ⓒ ——混雑する be jammed, be crowded; be congested ∥店は買い物客で混雑していた The store was crowded [jammed, packed] with shoppers.
◆通勤の混雑を緩和するため電車が増発される予定だ They are running more trains to ease the commuting crush.

コンサルタント consultant ⓒ ∥経営コンサルタント a management consultant

こんしゅう¹ 今週 this week
今週の月曜日 Monday of this week; this Monday
今週はずっと試験勉強で忙しかった I've been busy studying for the exam all (this) week.
今週中にお会いしましょう Let's get together sometime this week.
◆今週末 this weekend

こんしゅう² 今秋 《米》this fall,《主に英》this autumn

こんしゅん 今春 this spring

こんじょう 根性 (気力) spirit Ⓤ; (度胸) (口語的) guts, grit Ⓤ; (性質) nature Ⓤⓒ ∥根性のあるところを見せる show spirit [fight] / 彼女は根性がある She has (a lot of) guts. / 彼にはその仕事をこなすだけの根性はない He doesn't have the guts to do the job.
◆根性の悪い ill-natured

こんしん¹ 渾身 渾身の力をこめて by using all one's strength; with all one's might

こんしん² 混信 (ラジオなどの) interference Ⓤ

こんしんかい 懇親会 social (gathering) ⓒ; (形式ばらない集まり)《米口語的》get-together ⓒ; (パーティー) party ⓒ

こんすい 昏睡 (意識不明の状態) coma ⓒ ∥昏睡状態に陥る fall [go] into a coma

コンスタント 彼女はどうやってあのようにコンスタントに正解できるのか分からない I don't see how she can constantly come up with the right answer like that every time. / 彼はコンスタントに新曲を発表している He releases a steady stream of new songs.

こんせい 混成 mix ⓒ, melange ⓒ ——混成の mixed; (合成の) composite ∥混成物 (混合物) a mixture; (合成物) a compound; (異種の要素の) a hybrid

こんせいがっしょう 混声合唱 mixed chorus ⓒ

こんせいき 今世紀 this century ⓒ

こんせき 痕跡 (跡) mark ⓒ Ⓤ; (存在・通過の跡) trace ⓒ Ⓤ; (証拠) evidence Ⓤ Ⓒ; (印) sign ⓒ ∥痕跡をとどめない leave no trace(s) [mark(s)] / 事件現場に犯人の痕跡は残っていなかった No evidence of the criminal remained at the scene of the crime.

こんせつ 懇切 懇切丁寧な説明 a detailed explanation / 彼女は懇切丁寧に申込用紙の記入のしかたを教えてくれた She explained to me politely and in detail how to fill out the application form.

こんぜつ 根絶 ——根絶する (撲滅する) eradicate 他; (一掃する) wipe [stamp] out; (根こそぎにする) root out; (取り除く) get* rid of ... ∥犯罪を根絶する wipe out crime

コンセプト concept Ⓤ ⓒ

こんせん¹ 混戦 (乱戦) confused fight ⓒ; (接戦) close contest ⓒ ◆今月に入ってセ・リーグのペナントレースは混戦模様になってきた The Central League pennant race has been very close since the beginning of this month.

こんせん² 混線 (電話で) 混線しています The lines are crossed.

こんぜんいったい 渾然一体 渾然一体となる be indistinguishably [completely] fused; form a harmonious whole

コンセンサス consensus ◎◎ ∥コンセンサスを得る get [gain] *a consensus*
コンセント ⚠(wall) socket ◎, 《米》outlet ◎, 《英》power point ◎ (❖英語のconsent は「同意するの意味」) ∥プラグをコンセントに差し込む *plug in*; *put* [*insert*] *a plug into an outlet* / コンセントを抜く *unplug*
コンソメ consommé ◎ (フランス語から)
コンダクター (指揮者・導体) conductor ◎
コンタクト(レンズ) contact lens ∥コンタクトをしている wear *contact lenses* / コンタクトを入れる[はずす]「*put in* [*take out*] (*one's*) *contact lenses*
こんだて 献立 (献立表・料理) menu ◎; (献立表) a bill of fare ◆献立(→食事)を考える *plan a meal* / 今夜の献立は何ですか What's for *dinner* tonight?
こんたん 魂胆 secret intention [plan, design] ◎, ulterior motive ◎ ∥彼には何か魂胆があるようだ He seems to have some *secret design*.
こんだん 懇談 ──懇談する have* a friendly [an informal] talk; (雑談する) chat ⊜ ∥懇談会 a get-together
コンチェルト (協奏曲) concerto ◎
こんちくしょう 今畜生 (口語的) Damn it [you]!
こんちゅう 昆虫 insect ◎, 《米口語的》bug ◎ ∥昆虫学 entomology / 昆虫学者 an entomologist / 昆虫採集 insect-collecting
コンツェルン ⚠(企業合同) a group of companies; (複合企業体) conglomerate [kənɡlámərət] ◎ (❖日本語はドイツ語の Konzern から)
こんてい 根底 (根本) root ◎; (底) bottom ◎; (基礎) basis ◎ (複 bases); (土台) foundation ◎ ∥…の根底を成す form *the basis of* … / …を根底からくつがえす *knock the bottom out of* …; *overturn* … *completely*
◆根底にある理由 the *underlying* reason
コンディション (調子・状態) condition ◎◎, 《口語的》shape ◎; (運動選手などの体調) form ◎ ∥グラウンドのコンディションがいい[悪い] The field is good [bad] *condition.* / きょうは体のコンディションがいい[悪い] Today I'm in good [bad] *condition.* / 彼はコンディションを崩している He is out of *condition* [*shape*]. / 選手たちはベストコンディションで試合に臨んだ The players played the game in *their best condition.* / 彼は試合を前にコンディションを整えた He got himself into good *shape* before the match.
コンテキスト context ◎◎
コンテスト contest ◎ ∥写真コンテスト *a photo contest*
コンテナ container ◎ ∥コンテナ車 (自動車) a container truck; (列車) a container train / コンテナ船 a container ship
コンデンサー ⚠[電気] capacitor ◎
コンデンスミルク condensed milk ◎
コント ⚠(舞台などでの) comic skit [sketch] ◎ (❖日本語はフランス語の conte から)
こんど 今度 (この度) this time; (今) now; (次回) next time, another time; (近々) soon ──今度の (現在の) this, present; (新しい) new; (次の) next, coming; (最近の) last, recent

*今度の週末 this weekend / 今度の日曜 *next* [*this*] Sunday / 今度だけは *just this once*; (*just*) *for once*
今度は君の番だ Now it's your turn. / It's your turn (*next*).
今度彼女に会ったらよろしくお伝えください The *next time* you see her, please give her my best regards.
今度の英語の先生はよく宿題を出す Our *new* English teacher often gives us homework.
オーケストラは今度のコンサートに向けて猛練習している The orchestra is [are] practicing hard for the *coming* concert.
今度の選挙で彼女は市議会議員に当選した She was elected to the city assembly in the *recent* [*last*] election.
◆今度という今度はもう我慢できない I'm not going to put up with that *anymore*.
こんどう 混同 confusion ◎ ──混同する confuse ⊕, mix (up) ∥私はよく彼を弟さんと混同してしまう I often *confuse* him *with* his brother. / 彼は公私混同している He *mixes up* public and private matters.
コンドーム condom ◎, 《米俗語的》rubber ◎, skin ◎
ゴンドラ gondola ◎; (ロープウエーの) (cable) car ◎
コントラスト contrast ◎◎
コントラバス double bass ◎, contrabass ◎
コンドル condor ◎
コントロール control ◎ ──コントロールする control ⊕ ∥コントロール(→制球力)がいい[悪い] have good [poor] *control* / 感情をコントロールする *control one's* feelings
∥コントロールキー (コンピュータの) the control key
こんとん 混沌・渾沌 chaos ◎, confusion ◎ ∥現在その国の政情は混沌としている The political situation in that country *is* now 「*in a state of chaos* [*in complete confusion*].
こんな (このような) such, like this; (この) this
私はちょうどこんな本を探していたんです I have been looking for just 「*such a book* [*a book like this*].
こんな話し合いをしてもむだだ *This* discussion will get us nowhere.
こんな寒さの中、泳ぐなんてばかげている It's ridiculous to swim 「*in this* cold weather [*in such* cold weather, on a cold day *like this*].
こんなとき彼がいてくれたらなあ I wish he were around [here] *at times like this*.
◆こんなことは言いたくないが… I hate to say *this*, but …. / I'm sorry to say that ….
どうして彼女は私にこんな仕打ちができるのだろう How could she do *this* [*such a thing*] to

me? / 君とこんなところで会うとはね Fancy seeing you *here*! / もうこんな時間だ *Look what time it is*!

こんなに so ‖どうしてこんなに遅くなったのですか Why are you *so* late? / こんなに驚いたことはない I've never been *so* [*this*] surprised before.

◆私はこれまでこんなに美しい光景を見たことがない I have never seen *such* a beautiful sight in all my life. / こんなに暗い部屋で勉強したら目が悪くなるよ You'll hurt your eyes if you study in *such* a dark room. / 車の修理にこんなにお金がかかるとは思わなかった I didn't expect that it would cost *this* much to repair my car.

こんなん 困難 difficulty ⓊⒸ; (苦労) trouble ⓊⒸ; (苦難) hardship ⓊⒸ ──困難な difficult; hard, tough

困難な問題 a *difficult* problem / 様々な困難に打ち勝つ 「get over [overcome] various *difficulties* / 困難に陥る get into *difficulties*

彼女は困難に直面しても、勇気をもって立ち向かった Even when she encountered *a difficulty*, she faced it with bravery.

その会社は困難な状況にある The company is in a *difficult* [*tough*] situation.

この本の初版は今や入手困難である The first edition of this book is now *difficult* to obtain.

戦時中人々は多くの困難に耐えなければならなかった People had to bear [put up with] many *hardships* during the war.

こんにち 今日 (きょう) today; (このごろ) today, these days, nowadays ‖今日の若者 young people (*of*) *today*; *today's* young people / 今日の日本 the Japan *of today*; Japan *today* / 今日コンピュータがこなす仕事には目をみはるものがある It's wonderful what computers can do *today*.

こんにちは 今日は Hello., Hi., Good afternoon.

> Good afternoon.は正午過ぎから日没までのあいさつだが、改まった言い方で、最近はあまり用いられない。親しい間柄ではHello., Hi.が一日を通してよく用いられる。

🔖「こんにちは、文男」「やあ、ポリー. 元気？」 "*Hi*, Fumio!" "Oh, Polly! How are you?"

🔖「山本先生、こんにちは」「こんにちは、修二君」 "*Hello* [*Good afternoon*], Mr. Yamamoto." "*Hello* [*Hi*], Shuji."

こんにゃく 🔺

> こんにゃくはコンニャクイモの粉から作る弾力のあるゼリー状の食品です。ノーカロリーで食物繊維を豊富に含み、健康食品とされています。それ自体では味にくいが、果物の味をつけたこんにゃくゼリーなどにも加工されて人気が高まっています。
>
> *Konnyaku* is a firm gelatin-like food made from the starch of *konnyaku-imo*, a kind of taro. Because it has no calories and is rich in dietary fiber, it is considered a health food. *Konnyaku* is almost tasteless and can be processed into foods like fruit-flavored *konnyaku* jelly, which is popular among Japanese and foreigners alike.

こんにゅう 混入 ──混入する mix ... in, add ⓜ ‖その缶ジュースには毒物が混入されていた Poison *was mixed in with* the canned juice.

コンパ 🔺 party Ⓒ,《米口語》get-together Ⓒ

> コンパは英語のcompanyからとった学生言葉で、主に学生が計画してするパーティーのことをいいます。特に大学のクラブのメンバーで行うことが多く、新入生歓迎のための新歓コンパや卒業する4年生のための追い出しコンパが有名です。また、ほかの大学とのコンパで合コン（合同コンパ）というのもあります。コンパがきっかけで交際を始めるカップルも少なくありません。
>
> *Kompa* is student slang that comes from the English word "company." It refers to a party organized by students, especially by club members. Among the most popular club *kompa* are *shinkan-kompa* (welcome parties) and *oidashi-kompa* (farewell parties). And there are also *go-kon* (short for *godo-kompa*) arranged among different universities. Students often take advantage of *kompa* to find girlfriends or boyfriends.

コンパクト (化粧道具) compact Ⓒ ──コンパクトな (小さい) small, compact

◆この帽子はコンパクトに折りたためる You can fold this hat *compactly*.

‖コンパクトディスク a compact disk, a CD

コンパス (製図用の) compasses《単数扱い》; (羅針盤) (mariner's) compass Ⓒ ◆彼はコンパス(→足)が長い He has long *legs*.

コンパニオン ⚠(催し物での接待役の女性) (female) guide Ⓒ (❖英語の companion は「仲間, 友達」などの意味)

こんばん 今晩 this evening, tonight

⇒ こんや ‖今晩何か予定がありますか Do you have anything planned for *this evening*? / 今晩泊まるホテルの部屋の手配をしてもらえますか Will you see about a hotel room for *tonight*?

こんばんは 今晩は Hello., Hi., Good evening. (❖Good evening.は日没後に用いられる改まったあいさつ. 最近ではHello., Hi.を用いることが多い)

コンビ ⚠(2人組) pair Ⓒ; (芸人の) duo Ⓒ; (相手) partner Ⓒ (❖「コンビ」は combination を省略したもの) ‖彼女とコンビを組む form a *pair* [*team*] with her; *pair* [*team*] *up* with her / 名コンビ a good [perfect] *combination*; good *partners*

コンビーフ ⚠ corned beef Ⓤ

コンビナート ⚠ industrial [chemical] com-

コンビニ(エンスストア) convenience store

plex ◎ (❖日本語はロシア語の kombinat から)
∥石油(化学)コンビナート a petrochemical complex

コンビニ(エンスストア) convenience store

コンピュータ computer ◎
→ 場面・状況別会話 p.1698

コンピュータにデータを入力する put [feed, input] data into *a computer* / 情報をコンピュータで処理する process information with [by means of] *a computer* / コンピュータで制御された機械 a *computer-controlled* machine; a machine *under computer control* コンピュータの操作を覚えたい I want to learn how to [use] *a computer*.
◆コンピュータ化する *computerize*
∥コンピュータウイルス a computer virus / コンピュータグラフィックス computer graphics ((略記)) CG / コンピュータゲーム a computer game / コンピュータ言語 a computer language / コンピュータ時代 the computer age

こんぶ 昆布 *kombu*, kelp, a (sea) tangle

コンプレックス ⚠ (劣等感) inferiority complex ◎ (❖complex 単独では「劣等感」の意味はなく、抑圧された無意識の感情をいう) ∥彼女は姉に対して常にコンプレックスをいだいてきた She has always had *an inferiority complex* toward her older sister. / She has always felt *inferior* to her older sister.

コンペ ⚠ (ゴルフの) (golf) tournament [competition] ◎; (建築・設計の) competition ◎

こんぺき 紺碧 deep [dark] blue ⓤ ∥紺碧の空 a [the] *deep-blue* sky

コンベヤー conveyor ◎ ∥ベルトコンベヤー a conveyor belt

コンポ ⚠ (セットになったステレオ) stereo components

こんぼう 棍棒 club ◎, heavy stick ◎; (短い) cudgel ◎ ∥人をこん棒で殴る *hit* [*beat, strike*] a person *with a heavy stick*; *club* a person

こんぽう 梱包 (包むこと) packing ⓤ; (包み) package ◎, (主に英) parcel ── 梱包する pack ⓗ

こんぽん 根本 (基礎) the foundation, the basis (複 bases); (根元) the root ── 根本的な basic, fundamental ── 根本的に basically, fundamentally ∥問題の根本まで掘り下げてみよう Let's get to *the root* of the problem.
◆政治体制の根本的な改革 a *radical* reform of the political system
∥根本原理 fundamental [basic, radical] principles / 根本問題 a fundamental [root, basic] problem

コンマ (句読点) comma ◎; (小数点) decimal point ◎ → 巻末付録 (句読法) ∥コンマを入れる put [insert, use] *a comma* / コンマ以下 after *the decimal point*

こんめい 混迷 confusion ⓤ ∥混迷に陥る be thrown into *confusion* ◆情勢は混迷の度を深めている The situation has become more and more *chaotic* [*confused*].

こんもり その部分は土がこんもりと盛り上がっている The earth rises *into a little mound* at that spot.

こんや 今夜 tonight (❖間接話法では tonight が that night などに変わることがある. this night とはいわない); (今晩) this evening 今夜ぜひ夕食を食べに来てください You must come and have dinner with us *tonight*.
◆今夜はここに泊まりましょう Let's stay here *for the night*.

こんやく 婚約 engagement ◎ ── 婚約する be [get*, become*] engaged (to ...) ∥人との婚約を発表する announce one's *engagement* to a person / 婚約を解消する break (off) one's *engagement* / 彼は姉と婚約している He *is engaged to* my sister.
∥婚約者(男性) one's fiancé [fiːɑːnséi]; (女性) one's fiancée [fiːɑːnséi] / 婚約指輪 an engagement ring

こんよく 混浴 mixed bathing ⓤ
◆ここの露天ぶろは混浴です In this open-air bath, *"men and women [people of both sexes] bathe together.*

こんらん 混乱 (入り乱れて個々の区別がつかない状態) confusion ⓤ, muddle ◎; (順序や位置が整っていない状態) disorder ⓤ, (口語的) mess ◎ (しばしば a ～); (手がつけられないほどの無秩序状態) chaos ⓤ ── 混乱する be confused [disordered, muddled (up)], (口語的) be mixed up

混乱状態に陥る be thrown into *confusion* [*disorder, chaos*]

その大統領選挙では多少の混乱があった There was some *confusion* over the presidential election.

事件のショックで頭が混乱していた My mind *was confused* by the shock of the incident.
◆そのホテルの火事はすさまじい混乱を引き起こした The fire in the hotel caused (*a*) terrible *panic*.

こんりゅう 建立 (建設) erection ⓤ ── 建立する erect ⓗ

こんりんざい 金輪際 彼女とは金輪際口をきかない I *shall certainly never* [*I won't ever*] *talk* with her again. / *I'll be damned if I ever talk* with her again.

こんれい 婚礼 wedding ◎ → けっこん(結婚)
∥婚礼衣装 a wedding dress [outfit]

こんろ 焜炉 (cooking) stove ◎, (portable) cookstove ◎

こんわく 困惑 embarrassment ⓤ, perplexity ⓤ ── 困惑する be embarrassed [perplexed, puzzled]; (途方にくれる) be at a loss ∥彼は彼女の態度に困惑していると告白した He confessed that he *was puzzled* by her attitude.
◆彼にきのう休んだ理由を聞いたら困惑した表情になった He *looked embarrassed* when I asked him why he had been absent yesterday.

さ

さ 差

difference ⓊＣ《また a ～》；（見解などの） gap Ｃ；（数の） margin Ｃ
需要と供給の差を縮める[広げる] narrow [widen] *the gap* between supply and demand
私たちの考えにはそれほど差はないと思う I don't think there's much *difference* [*of a gap*] between our opinions.
15という年の差を超えて二人は結婚した They got married despite *an age difference* of 15 years.
我々の年齢差は4歳だ *The difference between* our *ages* is four years.
その国は貧富の差が大きい There is *a great gap between rich and poor* in that country.
その男性は若者と接して世代間の差を感じた The man felt [recognized] *a generation gap* when he talked with young people.
◆その会社は男女間に給与の差をつけている The company *differentiates* between male and female salaries. / 内陸部は寒暖の差が激しい The inland area has *a wide range of temperatures*. / 我々は3点差で負けた We were defeated *by* three points. / ジャイアンツはタイガースに2ゲーム差をつけられて[つけて]いる The Giants are two games *behind* [*ahead of*] the Tigers. / 彼女は最新のファッションを取り入れて周りに差をつけようとする She's always trying to *get ahead of* others by wearing the latest fashion. / 稔にはずいぶん数学で差をつけられたよ Minoru *has gotten* far *ahead of* me in math.

-さ¹

語法
文末あるいは文節末に用いる「…さ」は意味を強めたり，軽く言い放ったりするときに用いられるが，この「…さ」に当たる英語の決まった表現はない．場面に応じて強調の表現を用いたり，言葉のイントネーションで「…さ」のニュアンスを表すようにする．

あんなに勉強したんだもの，彼が合格するのは当たり前さ It's quite natural for him to pass the exam after studying that much. / 分かってくれなくても，まあいいさ Even if you don't understand me, 「it's all right [I don't mind]. / 君はいったい僕にどうしてほしいのさ What on earth do you want me to do?

-さ² -ness, -th, -(i)ty, -hood

語法
-ness, -th, -(i)ty, -hood などは，英語の形容詞・分詞・動詞などに付いて名詞を作る接尾辞．形容詞・形容動詞の語幹に付いて名詞を作る日本語の「さ」には必ずしも対応しない / 明るさ bright*ness* / このビルの高さ the *height* of this building

ざ 座
❶【席】 seat Ｃ / 座をはずす leave *one's seat*
❷【地位】 position Ｃ / 彼は社長の座に就いた He got *a position* as a company president. / 彼はライバルからトップの座を奪った He seized *the top position* from his rival.
◆権力の座に就く assume *power* / 彼は10年間チャンピオンの座を守り続けた He kept *the championship* for 10 years.
❸【集まり】 gathering Ｃ；（一座の人々）《集合的》the table / 彼女の軽率な発言で座がしらけてしまった Her thoughtless words cast a chill over *the table*. / 彼が座を取りもった He entertained the people at *the gathering*.
❹【星座】⇒ せいざ(星座)

さあ
❶【催促など】 さあ, 注意して見てくださいよ *Now* watch carefully. / さあ, 出かけよう *Come on*! Let's go. / さあ, みんないっしょに (やろう[歌おう])! *All together now*! / さあ, どうぞ *Here* you are. / *Here* it is.(◆前者は相手に, 後者は物に重点をおいた表現) / さあ空港に着きましたよ *Here* we are at the airport. / さあさあ, もう泣くのはおやめ *Here* [*Come on*], don't you cry anymore. / さあ, 終わったぞ *There*! It's all done!
❷【ためらいの気持ち】
●「彼女はきょうパーティーに来るんだろうか」「さあ, どうだかね」"Will she come to the party today?" "*Well*, 「I don't know [you never know]."

サーカス circus Ｃ
巡回サーカス a traveling *circus* / サーカスを興行する present [put on] *a circus* / サーカスを見に行く go to *the circus*
∥サーカス団 a circus (troupe)

サーキット
（カーレースなどの）(racing) circuit Ｃ；（電気回路）circuit Ｃ / サーキットトレーニング circuit training

サークル ⚠(同好会) club Ｃ (◆英語の circle は「(共通の趣味などで結ばれた)仲間」という意味で，「同好会」にはふつう club を用いる) ⇒ 場面・状況別会話 p.1748
テニスサークルに入る join *a tennis club* / サークル活動 *club* activities

ざあざあ
雨がざあざあ降っている The rain's *pouring down*. / *It's pouring*. / 湯ぶねにつかるとお湯がざあざあ流れ出た The water *cascaded* from the bathtub when I got into it. / 放送終了後のテレビがざあざあいっていた After all broadcasts were over, the TV produced nothing but *hissing static*.

サーチライト searchlight Ｃ

サード〚野球〛 third (base) Ｃ (◆通例無冠詞)；(三塁手) third baseman Ｃ；(車のギアの) third (gear) Ｕ / ギアをサードに入れる shift into *third* (*gear*)

サーバー (球技の) server ©; [コンピュータ] server ©; (給仕用具) server © ‖サーバーにアクセスする access *a server* ‖ サラダサーバー salad *servers*

サービス service ⓤ ©

> 英語のserviceは日本語のサービスのように「値引き」や「おまけ」を意味することはない ‖ちょっとサービス(値引き)してよ Can you give me a little discount, please? ‖ 取りつけはサービス(無料)です The installation is free of charge.

顧客サービス customer *service* ‖ ピザの宅配サービス a door-to-door pizza *service*

あのレストランはサービスがいい That restaurant gives good *service*. / *The service* is good at that restaurant.

◆それはサービス(→無料)になっています You can have it *for free* [*nothing*]. / It's *complimentary*. ‖ 5,000円のところを4,000円にサービス(→値下げ)しよう I'll reduce its *price* from 5,000 yen to 4,000 yen for you. ‖ 彼は土日を家族サービスにあてている(→家族と過ごすことにしている) He makes it a rule to *spend* weekends with his family. ‖ 彼はサービス精神旺盛(おうせい)だ(→他人に尽くすのが大好きだ)He really likes to *serve* [→他人を楽しませるのが]*entertain*] others.

‖サービスエース an ace, a service ace ‖ サービスエリア a service area ‖ サービス産業 (a) service industry ‖ サービス料 a service charge ‖ テレホンサービス a helpline

サーブ serve ⓤ ©, service ⓤ ──サーブする serve 他 自 ‖サーブを受ける[返す] receive [return] *a serve* ‖ 日本にサーブ権が移った It's Japan's *serve* now.

サーファー surfer ©

サーフィン surfing ⓤ ‖あしたは近くの海にサーフィンをしに行く I'll go *surfing* at a nearby beach tomorrow.

‖ネットサーフィン net surfing

サーフボード surfboard ©

サーモスタット thermostat ©

サーモン salmon [sǽmən] © ⓤ

サーロイン (牛の腰上部の肉) sirloin © ⓤ ‖サーロインステーキ (a) sirloin steak

さい¹ 才 (能力) ability © ⓤ, faculty ©; (天分) talent ⓤ © ‖彼は野球に天賦(てんぷ)の才がある He has native *ability* [*talent*] for baseball. ‖ 彼は数学の才がある He has *a faculty* for mathematics. / 彼は数学の才がある He has a *faculty* for mathematics.

さい² 犀 rhinoceros [rainɑ́sərəs] © (複 ~es), (口語的) rhino [ráinou] © (複 ~s)

さい³ 際 (…のときに) when; (もし…ならば) if ‖ご用の際はこちらにお電話ください Please call us *when* [*if*] you need some help.

◆緊急の際にはこの階段を使ってください Use these stairs *in case of* emergency. ‖ この際いらない物は全部捨ててしまおう I'll take *this opportunity* to throw away all of these unnecessary things.

さい⁴ 差異・差違 difference © ⓤ ⇒さ

さい-¹ 最─ -est(❖形容詞・副詞の最上級を作る接尾辞) ── most (❖通例3音節以上の形容詞・副詞とともに最上級を作る) ‖最新情報 the *latest* news ‖ 最高級品 the *most luxurious* product ‖ 最北[最南]端の町 the *northern-most* [*southernmost*] town

さい-² 再─ re-(❖「再び, 改めて, …し直す」の意味の接頭辞) ‖再選挙 *reelection* ‖ その件については再検討を要する It is necessary to *reconsider* the matter. ‖ 学生証を再発行してもらった I had my student ID card *reissued*. ‖ 再検査の結果, 異状が見つかった The medical *reexamination* proved that there was something wrong.

◆再就職する(→新たな仕事を得る) get a new job ‖ 容疑者を再逮捕する *arrest* the suspect *again* ‖ 彼はチャンピオンに再挑戦するつもりだ He is willing to *challenge* the champion to fight *again*.

-さい ─歳 year(s) old(❖… year(s) old は数詞の後に置く. また数詞だけで年齢が表せるので実際には省略されることも多い)

10歳未満の子供たち children *under* 10 (*years old*)

◆5歳児向けの本 a book for five-*year-olds* ‖ 彼女は3歳のときにピアノを始めた She started to play the piano *at* (*the age of*) three. ‖ 彼女は彼より3歳年上だ She is three *years older than* him. ‖ 彼には4歳と1歳の弟がいる He has two brothers, *aged* four and one.

🅔「あなたのお兄さんは何歳ですか」「20歳です」 "*How* old is your brother?" "He's 20 (*years old*)."

> [英作文ノート] 「…歳の」の英語は?
> 10歳の女の子
> →×a girl *of* ten *years old*
> →○a girl of ten (*years*)
> →○a girl *who is* ten *years old*
> →○a ten-*year-old* girl
> ★「彼女は10歳です」は She is ten years old. というが, この old は形容詞なので, ×a girl of ten years old とはいわない.

さいあい 最愛 ──最愛の darling, dearest, beloved(❖いずれも名詞の前で用いる) ‖最愛の夫 one's *darling* [*dearest, beloved*] husband

◆最愛の人 one's *darling* [*dearest*]

さいあく 最悪 ──最悪の the worst ‖試験の結果は今までで最悪だった The result of the exam was *the worst* ever. ◆最悪の事態を覚悟する prepare for *the worst* ‖ その蛇にかまれると最悪の場合, 死に至ることがある If you are bitten by the snake, *if worst comes to worst*, you might die from it. ‖ 最悪でも2週間の入院ですみそうだ I'll be in hospital only for two weeks *at* (*the*) *worst*.

ざいあく 罪悪 (道徳・宗教上の) sin © ⓤ; (法律上の) crime © ◆罪悪感にさいなまれる be 「consumed with [racked by] *a guilty conscience*

ざいい 在位 reign [réin] © ‖ジョージ3世の在位中に *in* [*during*] *the reign* of George III

◆王の在位30周年を記念して記念切手が発行された The commemorative stamps were issued to celebrate the 30th anniversary of *the* king's *accession to the throne.*

さいえん[1] 菜園 (vegetable) garden [C] ‖家庭菜園 a kitchen *garden*

さいえん[2] 才媛 intelligent [talented] woman [C]

さいかい[1] 再会 reunion [U] ─再会する meet* again ‖彼は家族との再会を切望している He yearns for *a reunion* with his family. / 彼らは固く再会を約束した They made a strong promise to *meet* [*see each other*] *again.*

さいかい[2] 再開 《公式的》resumption [U]《通例 a ～》, restart [C]; (店・裁判などの) reopening [U] ─再開する 《公式的》resume [他][自], restart [他][自]; reopen [他][自] ‖核実験の再開に抗議する protest against *the resumption* of nuclear testing / 休憩の後，私たちは討論を再開した After a break, we *resumed* [*reopened*] our discussions. / 行方不明の子供の捜索はけさ再開された The search for the missing child *was resumed* this morning. / その店はきのう営業を再開した The store *reopened* yesterday.

さいかい[3] 最下位 (順位) (the) last place, the bottom; (地位) the lowest rank [position] ‖最下位を脱する escape *last place* / 彼は数学ではクラスの最下位だった He was (*at*) *the bottom* of his class in math. / lord は英国貴族の最下位の階級だ "Lord" is *the lowest rank* in the British peerage.

さいがい 災害 disaster [C][U], calamity [C][U]; (大災害) catastrophe [C] ‖災害を被る suffer *a disaster* / 災害を防ぐ prevent *disasters* / その災害による死者はひとりもいなかった Nobody was killed in the *disaster* [*catastrophe*]. / この地域はこれまで数多くの自然災害に見舞われている This district has been stricken by a lot of *natural disasters.*

‖災害対策 disaster relief measures / 災害対策本部 disaster relief headquarters / 災害保険 casualty insurance / 災害補償 disaster compensation, financial aid after a disaster / 二次災害 a secondary disaster

[関連語] 被災者 a victim (of a disaster) / 被災地 a disaster area

ざいかい 財界 the economic world; (金融業界) the financial world; (実業界) the business world ‖財界首脳の一人が逮捕された One of *the major figures in the economic world* was arrested.

‖財界人 (金融家) a financier; (実業家) a business executive

ざいがい 在外 ‖在外公館 governmental establishments abroad / 在外邦人 Japanese living abroad

さいかいはつ 再開発 redevelopment [U][C], renewal [U] ─再開発する redevelop [他] ‖都市再開発 urban *redevelopment* [*renewal*] / 駅周辺は再開発が進められている The area surrounding the station *is being redeveloped.*

さいかく 才覚 gumption [U], resourcefulness [U]; (機知) wit [U] ‖才覚を現す show *one's gumption* [*resourcefulness*]

ざいがく 在学 彼女はアメリカの大学に在学している She *is* 「*in college* [*studying at college*] in the U.S. / 彼は高校在学中に母親を亡くした He lost his mother *while* (*he was*) *in high school.*

‖在学証明書 a certificate of enrollment

さいかくにん 再確認 double-check [C]; (予約などの) reconfirmation [U] ─再確認する double-check [自][他]; reconfirm [他] ‖計算違いのないことを再確認する *double-check* that there's no miscalculation / 飛行機の予約を再確認する *reconfirm one's* flight reservation

さいき[1] 才気 (知性) intelligence [U]; (機知) wit [U]; (頭の切れること) (sharp-)wittedness [U]; (すぐれた才能) brilliance [U] ‖才気あふれる青年 a young man *full of intelligence*; a *sharp-witted* [*brilliant*] young man

さいき[2] 再起 (復帰) comeback [C]《通例単数形》; (回復) recovery [U]《また a ～》 ─再起する come* back; recover [自] ‖そのボクサーは再起不能だろう The boxer will *be unable to*「*make a comeback* [*come back*].

さいぎしん 猜疑心 suspicion [U][C] ‖彼は猜疑心の塊(かたまり)だ He is full of *suspicion.*/ He is *suspicion* itself.

◆彼女は猜疑心が強い She is *very suspicious.*

さいきだいめいし 再帰代名詞 〘文法〙 reflexive (pronoun) [C]

> 再帰代名詞には，myself, yourself, himself, herself, itself, ourselves, yourselves, themselves, oneself がある．再帰代名詞の用法には，主語，目的語を強調する用法と，目的語として用いて主語と同じもの[人]であることを表す用法がある ‖ I *myself* don't know what to do. 私自身どうしてよいか分からない (❖I を強調) / He killed *himself* five years ago. 彼は5年前に自殺した (❖He killed him. とすると主語と目的語は別の人物であることを表す)

さいきょういく 再教育 reeducation [U]; (技術に関する) retraining [U] ─再教育する reeducate [他]; retrain [他]

さいきん[1] 最近 recently; lately; these days, nowadays; not long ago; (この前) last ─最近の recent, the [*one's*] latest, last; (今日(こんにち)の) today's

> recently: 過去形・現在完了形とともに用いる．
> lately: 通例現在完了形とともに用いる．過去形で用いることもあるが，その結果が現在まで継続している場合に限られる．また，最近では特に《米》で現在形とともに用いられるようになってきた．
> these days, nowadays: 現在形，また現在完了形で用いる．
> not long ago: 通例過去形の肯定文に用いる．

最近の出来事 recent events / 最近の若者 today's young people; the young people of today

父は最近太った My father has become stout recently [lately].

最近彼女に会っていない I haven't seen her recently [lately].

ごく最近まで彼はそのニュースを知らなかった He didn't know the news until quite recently.

彼と知り合ったのはつい最近だ It's only recently [lately] that I have gotten to know him.

彼はここ最近ふさぎ込んでいる He is in low spirits these days.

最近では子供は野球よりもサッカーが好きだ These days [Nowadays] children like soccer better than baseball.

このカメラは最近買った I bought this camera 「not so long ago [recently, lately].

いちばん最近彼に会ったのはいつ When did you see him last?

最近出た彼の小説は期待していたほどよくはなかった His latest novel was not as [so] good as I (had) expected.

その件に関する最近5年間のデータを集めた I collected the data from the last five years on that matter.

さいきん² 細菌 bacteria (❖bacterium の複数形), germ Ⓤ ∥この薬品は細菌の繁殖を抑える This chemical product prevents the propagation of bacteria [germs].

∥細菌学 bacteriology / 細菌学者 a bacteriologist / 細菌戦争 biological warfare / 細菌兵器 a bacteriological weapon

さいく 細工 ❶ 〔作ること〕〔工芸〕 craft Ⓒ; 〔職人技〕 workmanship Ⓤ, craftsmanship Ⓤ; 〔作られた物〕 work Ⓤ ∥紙[竹]細工 a paper [bamboo] craft item / このいすには美しい細工が施されている This chair has ornaments made with beautiful craftsmanship. ◆妹が粘土細工で人形を作った My sister worked the clay into a doll.

❷ 〔ごまかし〕 trick Ⓒ, 《公式的》artifice Ⓒ, deception Ⓤ Ⓒ ──細工する (だます) deceive ⓗ; 〔帳簿・資料などに〕 manipulate ⓗ ∥下手な細工は失敗を招く A poor trick should lead you to failure. / 彼に小細工は通用しないだろう He won't fall for cheap tricks./ He won't be deceived easily.

さいくつ 採掘 mining Ⓤ, digging Ⓤ ──採掘する (石炭などを) mine ⓗ; (鉱山などを) work ⓗ ∥石炭を採掘する mine [dig] coal / 金鉱を採掘する work a gold mine

∥採掘権 mining rights / 採掘地 diggings

サイクリング cycling Ⓤ ∥サイクリングに行く go cycling

∥サイクリングコース a cycleway

サイクル (周期) cycle Ⓒ ∥ライフサイクル a life cycle / サイクルヒットを打つ hit for the cycle ◆ 2サイクルエンジン a two-stroke engine / レンタサイクル a rent-a-bike

さいけいこくたいぐう 最恵国待遇 most favored nation status Ⓤ 《略語》MFN

さいけいれい 最敬礼 deep bow Ⓒ ──最敬礼する make* a deep bow, bow deeply

さいけつ¹ 採決 vote Ⓒ (❖挙手や起立によるものも含まれる) ──採決する take* [have*] a vote on ..., vote on ... / 法案を採決する 「take a vote [vote] on a bill / 採決の結果、その案は圧倒的多数で可決された The result of the vote was that the proposal was overwhelmingly passed. ◆議会で議案を強行採決する railroad a bill through an assembly

さいけつ² 裁決 (決定) decision Ⓤ Ⓒ, (判決) judgment, 《英》judgement Ⓤ Ⓒ ──裁決する decide ⓗ; judge ⓗ ∥裁決に不服を申し立てる complain about the decision [judgment] / その件に関し裁決を下す judge the matter; pass judgment on the matter

さいけつ³ 採血 ──採血する take* [collect] blood; (検査で) take a blood sample

∥採血車 a bloodmobile

さいげつ 歳月 (時) time Ⓤ; (年) year Ⓒ ∥彼女に最後に会ってから5年の歳月が流れた Five years have passed since I met her last.

ことわざ 歳月人を待たず Time and tide wait for no man.

さいけん¹ 再建 reconstruction Ⓤ, rebuilding Ⓤ ──再建する reconstruct ⓗ, rebuild* ⓗ ∥地震で倒壊した建物を再建する reconstruct a building ruined by an earthquake / 組織を再建する reconstruct [rebuild] the organization

さいけん² 債券 (国公社債) bond Ⓒ ∥債券を発行する issue bonds

∥債券所有者 a bondholder / 債券取引 bond trading

さいけん³ 債権 credit Ⓤ, claim Ⓤ Ⓒ ∥債権国 a creditor nation / 債権者 a creditor / 不良債権 nonperforming loans, bad debts

さいげん¹ 再現 reproduction Ⓤ Ⓒ; (犯罪の様子などの) reconstruction Ⓤ ──再現する reproduce ⓗ ∥犯行現場の再現 the reconstruction of a crime scene / これは江戸時代の一般的な民家を再現したものだ This is a reproduction of an ordinary house in the Edo period. / それは複雑すぎて再現不可能だといわれている It is said to be too complicated to reproduce.

さいげん² 際限 (終わり) end ∥際限なく食べ続ける keep eating without end (❖without end は成句で無冠詞) / 彼の欲望には際限がない There is no end to his desire./ His desire knows no bounds.

ざいげん 財源 (financial) resources; (資金) funds ∥我々は財源に乏しい We are poor in financial resources. / 新たな事業のために財源を確保する必要がある We need to secure financial resources for a new business.

さいけんとう 再検討 review Ⓒ Ⓤ; (再考) reconsideration Ⓤ ──再検討する review ⓗ, reexamine ⓗ; reconsider ⓗ ∥再検討中である be under review / これらの点は再検討が必要である These points need a review. / It is necessary to *review* these points.

さいこ 最古 ━━最古の the oldest ∥それらは北米最古の壁画です They are *the oldest* mural paintings in North America.

さいご¹ 最後

❶【終わり】the last, the end ━━最後の the last; (最終的な) final ━━最後に last (◆動詞の修飾に用いる), finally (◆文修飾にも動詞の修飾にも用いる); (最終的に) in the end

《最後の》

最後の手段 a *last* resort

これが最後のチャンスだ This is *the last* [*final*] chance.

とうとう最後の10ドルになってしまった I was down to my *last* 10 dollars.

彼は最後の数分で2つのゴールを決めた He scored two goals in *the last* few minutes.

その映画は最後の最後にどんでん返しがある The movie has an unexpected twist *at the very end*.

最後の最後まであきらめてはいけない Don't give up *till the very end*.

《最後を・に》

私が最後に教室を出ました I left the classroom *last*. / (→私が教室を出た最後の人だった) I was *the last* person to leave the classroom.

最後にあなたの夢を聞かせてください Finally [*Lastly*], let me ask you about your dreams.

最後に君に会ってから7年たった Seven years have passed since I saw you *last*.

最後になりましたが、私をいつも励まし支えてくれた家族に感謝しています *And last but not least*, I'd like to thank my family who have always encouraged and supported me. (❖last but not least は「最後に挙げるが非常に重要だ」という意味で、スピーチなどでよく用いられる)

◆その学者は最後には大統領になった The scholar *ended up as* President. / 「これを最後にたばこをやめる」と父は言った My father said, "I'm going to quit smoking *one and for all*." / 舞台の最後を飾ったのは出演者全員による合唱だった The play *was finished off* by a song sung by all of the actors.

《最後まで》

患者は最後までがんばった The patient endured *to the last* [*end*].

それはとても難しい仕事だったが麻衣子は最後までやり抜いた It was very difficult work, but Maiko stuck it out *to the end*.

◆最後まで聞いてよ！ *Hear* me *out*, please!

《その他》

夏休みもきょうが最後だ This is *the last day* of (the) summer vacation.

彼女と話したのはそれが最後となった It was *the last time* I talked with her.

最後から3番目を走っているのはだれですか Who is running the third *from last*?

❷【いったん…すれば】once

彼女はカラオケで歌い出したら最後, なかなかマイクを放さない *Once* she begins to sing at karaoke, she will never leave the microphone voluntarily.

さいご² 最期 *one's* [*the*] death; (終わり)《婉曲的》end ◎; (末路) fate ◎◎ ∥不運な最期を遂(と)げる meet *an* unhappy *end* [*fate*]; die *an* unhappy *death* ∥父の最期の日 *one's* dying day / 我々は父の最期を看取(みと)った We were present at our father's *deathbed*.

さいこ 在庫 stock ◎◎ ∥在庫を調べる check *the stock* / その新製品は今在庫があります The new product *is in stock* now. / 申しわけありませんが, ただ今在庫を切らしております I'm sorry, but we are *out of stock* now.

∥在庫一掃セール a clearance sale ∥ 在庫品 goods in stock,《米》(an) inventory

さいこう¹ 最高 ━━最高の (いちばんよい) the best (❖「いちばん…な」という場合は形容詞の最上級を用いる); (高さ・程度が) the highest; (権力・地位などが) supreme; (最大限の) maximum

最高の品質の品 a product of *the best* [*highest*] quality

うちのチームでは彼が断然最高の選手だ He is easily *the best* player on our team.

彼の作品の中でこれが最高だ This is *the best* of his works.

修二はテストで最高点を取った Shuji got *the highest marks* in the test.

◆あしたはこの夏最高の暑さになるでしょう It will be *the hottest* day of this summer tomorrow. / 私は最高に幸せです I'm *as happy as can be*. / 最高に気分がいい I *feel just great*. / ビデオは一度に最高3本まで借りられます You can borrow *a maximum* of three videos at a time. / 彼女はマラソンで自己最高記録を出した She set *her best record* in the marathon. / あのテレビ番組は最高におもしろかった That TV program was *really* [*so*] fun! / 彼って最高ね He's so *cool*.

🅔「コンサートどうだった」「もう最高！」"How was the concert?" "It was *terrific*!"

∥最高裁判所 ⇒ さいこうさいばんしょ ∥ 最高殊勲選手 the most valuable player (《略語》MVP)

さいこう² 再考 reconsideration ◎ ━━再考する reconsider ⦿ ⓔ ∥再考の余地なし There's no room for *reconsideration*. / その件に関しては再考を要する We *need to reconsider* the matter. / The matter *needs to be reconsidered*.

さいこう³ 採光 採光のための窓 a window to *let in light* / この部屋は採光がよい This room *gets plenty of sun*.

さいこう 在校 校長先生は何時までご在校ですか Until what time *is* the principal *at school*?

∥在校生 a student; (卒業生に対して) a current student

さいこうきゅう 最高級 ∥最高級品 articles of the highest quality

さいこうけんさつちょう 最高検察庁 the Supreme Public Prosecutor's Office

さいこうさいばんしょ 最高裁判所 the Supreme Court ‖最高裁判所長官 the Chief Justice of the Supreme Court

さいこうちょう 最高潮 (劇・演説などの) climax [C]; (絶頂) peak [C] ‖芝居は終わりに近づき, 最高潮に達した The play 「came to [reached] *its climax* as it drew to a close. / 中村が決勝のゴールを決めると観衆の興奮は最高潮に達した The crowd reached *the peak* of excitement when Nakamura made the winning goal.

さいこうふ 再交付 reissue [C] ━再交付する reissue [他] ‖パスポートを再交付してもらった I *had* my passport *reissued.*

さいこうほう 最高峰 (山の) the highest mountain, the highest peak ◆この作品は英文学の最高峰(→最高の作品)だ This is *the highest pinnacle* of English literature.

さいごつうちょう 最後通牒 ultimatum [C] (複 ~s, ultimata) ‖最後通牒を出す issue [deliver] *an ultimatum*

さいころ dice [C] (複~) (❖dice は本来 die の複数形だが, さいころはふつう2個一組で使うため単数形 die よりも複数形 dice で用いることが多い) ‖さいころを振る throw [roll] *the dice*

さいこん 再婚 remarriage [C] [U]; (2度目の結婚) second marriage [C] ━再婚する marry again, remarry [自] [他]

さいさき 幸先 チームはさい先のいいスタートを切った The team made a *good* start. / そいつはさい先がいい(→縁起がいい) That's *a good sign.*

さいさん[1] 再三 母親の再三にわたる説得にもかかわらず彼女は仕事を辞めた She quit the job in spite of her mother's *repeated* advice not to. / 先生は彼に再三再四注意した The teacher warned him *over and over.*

さいさん[2] 採算 (利益) profit [U]; (利得) gain [U] ‖彼らは採算を無視して商品を売っている They sell goods with no thought of *profit.* ◆この事業は採算が取れない This business 「*doesn't pay* [*is not profitable*].

ざいさん 財産 property [U] (❖「所有物」の意味では [C]); (莫大(ばくだい)な金額) fortune [C]; (貴重なもの・人) asset [C]

〖財産を〗

彼は一夜にして財産を失った He lost *his fortune* overnight.

彼女は親戚(しんせき)から莫大な財産を相続した She inherited *an* immense *fortune* from a relative.

彼は一人息子に財産を譲渡した He delivered *the property* over to his only son.

おじは宝くじに全財産をつぎ込んだ My uncle spent *all his fortune* on lottery tickets.

〖財産は・が〗

彼女の財産は2人の娘の間で平等に分けられた Her *property* was equally divided between her two daughters.

莫大な財産が彼の手に入った *A* large *fortune* came into his possession.

〖その他〗

彼は財産の管理を弁護士に委ねた He left *his property* in the hands of his lawyer.

おじは株でひと財産築いた My uncle *made a fortune* on the stock market.

家族が元気なことは大きな財産だ The health of the family is *a* great *asset.*

‖財産家 a man of property [wealth] / 共有財産 common property / 国有財産 national property / 私有財産 private property / 知的財産 intellectual property

さいし 妻子 *one's* wife and children; (家族) *one's* family ‖妻子のある人 a man with *a family* / 彼は妻子を養わなければならない He has to support *his family.*

さいじき 歳時記 🗻 (俳句の季語集) a *saijiki*, a book on the seasonal terms used in haiku; (季節の随筆集) a book of essays on seasonal themes

さいしけん 再試験 reexamination [U], 《米口語的》makeup (exam) [C] ‖あした英語の再試験を受けなくてはならない Tomorrow I have to 「*take the makeup* English *exam* [*retake the* English *exam*].

さいじつ 祭日 holiday [C]; (国民の祝日) national [《英》bank] holiday [C]; (祭りの日) festival (day) [C]

ざいしつ 材質 この机は材質がいい This desk is made with good *materials.* / この食器棚の材質は何ですか(→何でできているか) What *is* this cupboard *made of*?

さいして 際して 緊急事態に際しては冷静に行動しなさい *In case of* emergency, act calmly. / 彼らは困難に際して(→直面して)どうしてよいか分からなかった They didn't know what to do *in the face of* difficulty.

さいしゅ 採取 ━採取する (拾う) pick [他]; (集める) collect [他], gather [他]; (血液・指紋などを) take* [他] ‖彼らは容疑者の指紋を採取した They *took* some fingerprints of the suspect.

さいしゅう[1] 採集 collection [U] ━採集する collect [他]; (拾い集める) gather [他] ‖夏休みは昆虫採集に出かけたものだ I used to go *collecting insects* during summer vacations.

さいしゅう[2] 最終 ━最終の (最後の) the last; (決定的な) the final ━最終的に finally ‖最終列車に間に合った I could catch *the last train.* / 首相は最終的な決定を記者団に発表した The Prime Minister announced his *final* decision to the press. / 私たちの提案は最終的に受け入れられた Our proposal has *finally* been accepted.

‖最終回(競技・試合の) the final round; (野球の) the last inning; (ドラマなどの) the last installment / 最終日 the last day

ざいじゅう 在住 マレーシア在住の日本人 a Japanese *living in* Malaysia

さいしゅつ 歳出 annual expenditure [U]

さいしゅっぱつ 再出発 彼女はレポーターとして再出発した She *made a fresh start* as a reporter.

さいしょ 最初 the first; (始まり) the beginning ━最初の (the) first ━最初(に) first

【最初に】
まず最初にどこへ行こうか Where shall we go *first*?
最初に私の目を引いたのは美しい日本庭園だった *The first thing* that caught my eye was a beautiful Japanese garden.
私たちがいちばん最初にここに着いた We were *the first* to get here.

【最初の】
今のところ最初の２章を何とか終わらせただけです I've only managed to finish *the first* two chapters so far.
最初のころは新しいクラスになじめなかった *At first* I couldn't get used to my new class.

【最初から】
もう一度最初からやり直せたらなあ If only I could do it again *from the beginning*!
彼はその詩を最初から最後まで暗唱した He recited the poem *from beginning to end*.

【その他】
その映画は最初はつまらなかったが, だんだんおもしろくなってきた *At first* the movie was boring, but it became more and more interesting.
海外旅行をしたのはそれが最初だった It was *the first time* that I traveled abroad.
これは我々にとって最初で最後のチャンスかもしれない This might be *the first and last* chance for us.

さいじょ 才女 talented woman ⓒ
さいしょう¹ 最小 ──最小の (数・量が) the smallest; (量が) the least; (最小限の) minimum ∥世界最小の動物 *the smallest* animal in the world
∥最小公倍数 the least [lowest] common multiple (《略語》LCM, l.c.m.) / 最小値 the minimum value

さいしょう² 最少 ──最少の the least; (最低の) the lowest; (最少限の) minimum ∥最少の量[金額] *the least* amount [sum]

さいじょう 最上 ──最上の the best; (品質などが) the finest; (最も高い) the highest ∥最上位 *the highest rank*
◆彼はあのアパートの最上階に住んでいる He lives on *the top floor* of that apartment.

さいじょう 罪状 crime ⓒ ∥法廷は罰を罪状に見合うものにするべきだ The court should make the punishment proportionate to *the crime*.
∥罪状認否【法律】(an) arraignment

さいじょうきゅう 最上級【文法】superlative degree ⓒ

最上級は, 形容詞・副詞の比較変化の一つであり, ３つ以上のものの性質・数量・程度などを比較し,「最も…」の意味を表す. ➡ ひかくきゅう
[規則変化] １音節の語と２音節の語の一部は, 原級に-est を付ける. ２音節の語の多くと３音節以上の語は, 原級に most を付ける ∥ Nohara is *the tallest* in the class. 野原がクラスで最も背が高い / My father gets up (*the*) *earliest* in my family. うちでは父が最も早起きだ (❖-est を付ける際, y を i に変える, 子音字を重ねるなど, つづりに変化が生じるものもある) / What is *the most popular* sport in your country? あなたの国ではどのスポーツが最も人気がありますか
[不規則変化] 次のように全く違う語に変化するものもある ∥ This is *the best* movie that I have ever seen. これがこれまで見た中で最もいい映画だ (❖この best は good の最上級) / Who of the three eats (*the*) *most*? ３人の中ではだれが最も大食いだ (❖この most は much の最上級)

さいしょうげん 最小限 minimum ⓒ ──最小限の minimum ∥出費は最小限に抑えなければならない We have to keep the cost to *a minimum*.

さいしょく 菜食 (野菜の食事) vegetable diet ⓒ; (菜食主義者の食事) vegetarian diet ⓒ ∥私は医者の勧めで菜食している I'm on *a vegetarian diet* on my doctor's advice.
∥菜食主義 vegetarianism / 菜食主義者 a vegetarian

ざいしょく 在職 山田さんには在職中お世話になった Mr. Yamada was a great help to me *during my time in office*.

さいしょくけんび 才色兼備 彼女は才色兼備だ She is *both beautiful and intelligent*.

さいしん¹ 最新 ──最新の the newest; (最近の) the latest; (時代遅れでない) up-to-date
最新の情報[ニュース] *the latest* information [news] / 雑誌の最新号 *the latest number* [*issue*] of a magazine
彼女の小説の最新作が来月出版される Her *latest* novel will be published next month.
この工場には多くの最新式機械が設置されている A lot of *up-to-date* machinery is installed in this factory.

さいしん² 細心 ──細心の (注意深い) careful; (慎重な) prudent; (用意周到な) scrupulous ∥その機械の取り扱いには細心の注意が必要だ You should be *very careful* when you handle the machine.

さいしん³ 再審 retrial ⓒ ∥彼は再審で無罪となった He was found not guilty in *the retrial*.
∥再審請求をする appeal *for a new trial*

サイズ size ⓒⓤ ∥キングサイズのベッド a *king-size* bed / フリーサイズのトレーナー a *one-size-fit-all* sweatshirt / 同じサイズで違う色はありますか Do you have the *same size* in another color? / サイズを測っていただけますか Would you mind measuring me for *size*? / このスカートはサイズが合いません This skirt is *not my size*. / サイズが合うかどうかこれを試着してみたいのですが I'd like to try this on for *size*. ◆このシャツのS[M, L]サイズはありますか Do you have this shirt in *a small* [*medium, large*]?
🅔「ワイシャツのサイズは何ですか」「Mサイズです」"What *size* shirt do you wear? / What is your shirt *size*?" "I wear *a medium*. / I'm *a medium*."

●「いかがですか」「ちょっときついです. もっと大きいサイズはありますか」 "How does it fit?" "It's a bit tight. Do you have *a larger size*?"

ざいす 座椅子 legless chair ⓒ

さいせい 再生 (録音・録画したものの) playback ⓒ; (音・映像の) reproduction ⓤ; (廃物の) recycling ⓤ; (再び生まれること) regeneration ⓤ ──再生する play back; reproduce ⓣ; recycle ⓣ; regenerate ⓣ *ビデオテープを再生する play back* a video tape / この工場は再生部品から車を製造している This factory produces cars from *recycled* parts. / 破壊された森林が再生するには長い年月がかかるだろう It will be many years before destroyed forests *regenerate (themselves)*.

◆産業を再生させる *revive* an industry
‖再生紙 recycled paper / 再生装置 playback equipment / 再生品 a recycled article, recycled goods

さいせい 財政 finance ⓤ (また複数形 ~s) ──財政の financial ‖国家[地方]財政 national [local] *finance* / 財政を引き締める tighten *finances* / 県の財政を建て直す set the prefecture's *finances* in order / その国の財政は健全[赤字]だ The country's *finances* are sound [in the red]. / 彼si>はその財団に財政援助を求めた He made an appeal to the foundation for *financial aid*. / その会社は財政難に陥っていた The company was embarrassed by *financial difficulties*.
‖財政学 public finance / 財政危機 a financial crisis / 財政政策 a fiscal policy / 赤字財政 deficit financing

さいせいき 最盛期 (人生などの) the prime; (黄金時代) the golden age; (出盛り) the season *そのサッカー選手は今が最盛期だ He is now *in his prime* as a soccer player.

◆スイカは今が最盛期だ Watermelons are *in season* now.

さいせき 採石 ──採石する quarry ⓣ ‖採石場 a quarry

ざいせき 在籍 ──在籍する be enrolled *その高校には約1,200人の生徒が在籍している About twelve hundred students *are enrolled* in the high school.
‖在籍証明書 a certificate of enrollment

さいせん¹ 再選 reelection ⓒ ⓤ ──再選する reelect ⓣ *再選を目ざす seek *reelection* / 彼は知事に再選された He *was reelected* as governor.

さいせん² 賽銭 さい銭をあげる make *an offering of money*
‖さい銭箱 an offertory box [chest]

さいぜん 最善 the [*one's*] best ──最善の the best *人は何事にも最善を尽くすべきだ One should do [try] *one's best* in everything. / 確かにこれは最善の方法ではないかもしれません I admit this may not be *the best* way of doing it.

さいぜんせん 最前線 the front; (活動などの) the forefront ‖戦闘の最前線 the *forefront* [*front line*] of a battle

さいせんたん 最先端 最先端の技術 *the most advanced* technology / 彼女は流行の最先端を行っている (→流行を生み出している) She is *setting the fashion*. / (→最新の流行を追いかけている) She *follows the latest fashion*.

さいぜんれつ 最前列 the front [first] row

さいそく 催促 ──催促する (要求する) ask ⓣ, demand ⓣ; (せきたてる) urge ⓣ; (せがむ) press ⓣ *彼は私に金を返すようにと催促した He *urged* me to pay him back. / 彼女に返事を催促された I *was pressed for* an answer by her.
‖催促状 a reminder

さいそく² 細則 detailed regulations

さいた 最多 ──最多の the most *彼はそのトーナメントの最多出場記録をもっている He holds the record for *the most* entries into the tournament.

サイダー ⚠ (soda) pop ⓤ ◆英語の cider は, 《米》では「リンゴ果汁」, 《英》では「リンゴ酒」の意味)

さいだい¹ 最大 ──最大の the biggest, the largest; (最も偉大な) the greatest; (最高の) maximum *世界最大の自動車メーカー *the largest* car maker in the world / 私の最大の関心事 my *greatest* concern / 最大の効果 a *maximum* effect / 最大級の賛辞 *the greatest [highest] possible* praise
‖最大公約数 the greatest common divisor (《略語》GCD, g.c.d.) / 最大(瞬間)風速 the maximum (instantaneous) wind velocity / 最大値 the maximum value

さいだい² 細大 その件に関する事実を細大もらさず報告する report the facts of the matter 「*down to the smallest detail* [*in full detail*]

さいだいげん 最大限 maximum ⓒ ──最大限の maximum *彼は入試に合格するため最大限の努力をした He made *maximum* efforts to pass the entrance exams.

◆この機会を最大限に利用するべきだ We should *make the most of* this opportunity.

さいたく 採択 adoption ⓤ ──採択する adopt ⓣ ‖法案を採択する *adopt* the bill

ざいたく 在宅 ──在宅する be at home
●「すみません, 田中先生はご在宅ですか」「いいえ, 今, 外出しています」 "Hello. *Is* Mr. Tanaka *at home*?" "No, he is out now."
‖在宅介護 home care / 在宅勤務 telecommuting

さいたま 埼玉

埼玉県は東京都の北に位置しています. 首都圏を主な市場にした農業が盛んな一方で, 県南部を中心に都市化が進み, 人口増加率は全国でもトップクラスです. 2001年には浦和市, 大宮市, 与野市が合併し, さいたま市という人口100万人を越える大都市が誕生しました. かつて城下町として栄えた川越市やブドウなどの観光農園が多い秩父市などには県外から観光に訪れる人も多くいます. Saitama Prefecture is located to the north of Tokyo. Although it has a prosperous agricultural economy that serves the Tokyo area, the prefecture has also become increasingly urban, especially in the south. Saitama's population has increased at one of the fastest rates in Japan. In 2001, the cities of Urawa, Omiya and Yono merged to form Saitama City, a metropolis with a population over one million. Many tourists come to Saitama from other areas to visit attractions such as the former castle town of Kawagoe and the city of Chichibu, which has many vineyards and other agricultural facilities that are open to visitors.

さいたん 最短 ——最短の the shortest ‖私たちは地図で目的地までの最短ルートを調べた We found *the shortest route* to the destination on the map.

さいだん 祭壇 altar [ɔ́ːltər] ⓒ

さいだん² 裁断 (切ること) cutting Ⓤ; (判断) judgment Ⓤ; (決定) decision Ⓤ ——裁断する cut* ⊕ ‖裁断機 a cutter

ざいだん 財団 foundation ⓒ ‖財団法人 an incorporated foundation

さいちゅう 最中 夕食の最中に電話が鳴った The telephone rang *while* I was eating dinner [*in the middle of* dinner]. / そのビルは工事の最中だ The building is *under* construction.

ざいちゅう 在中 写真在中 Photo(s); Photo(s) Enclosed; Photo(s) Only (❖いずれも封筒に書く言葉. 最後の例はほかに何も同封しない場合)

さいちょう 最長 日本で最長の橋 *the longest* bridge in Japan

さいてい 最低 ——形 minimum ⓒ 《通例単数形》 ——副 (少なくとも) at least ——最低の the lowest, (公式の) minimum; (最悪の) the worst ‖最低条件を満たす meet the *minimum* requirements / 費用を最低限に抑える keep the cost to *the minimum* / 私は英語のテストで最低点を取った I got *the lowest mark* in the English exam. / このピアノを動かすには最低3人必要だ It takes 「*at least* [*not less than*]*three people to move this piano. / この製品は品質が最低です These products are of *the worst* quality. / きのうの最低気温はマイナス5度だった Yesterday's *minimum temperature* was five degrees below zero. / あいつは今まで会った中で最低のやつだ He's *the lowest* [*meanest*] person I've ever met.

🅔「あの映画, どう思う」「最低だね」 "What do you think about that movie?" "It's *absolutely terrible*!"

‖最低賃金 a minimum wage

さいてい² 裁定 decision ⓒⓊ ‖裁定を受け入れる accept [hand out] *a decision*

さいてき 最適 ——最適な the best; (理想的な) ideal ‖その仕事には彼が最適だ He's *the best* [*most suitable*] person for the job.

◆この種の植物の生育には湿った環境が最適だ (→湿った環境でいちばんよく育つ) This kind of plant grows *best* in moist surroundings.

さいてん 採点 (答案の)《主に米》grading Ⓤ, 《主に英》marking Ⓤ; (試験・競技などの) scoring Ⓤ ——採点する 《主に米》grade ⊕, 《主に英》mark ⊕; score ⊕ ‖答案を採点する *grade* [*mark*] exam papers / あの先生は採点が甘い[からい] That teacher is generous [strict] in *grading*.

‖採点者 a grader, a marker

さいてん² 祭典 festival ⓒ ➡まつり

サイト 〔コンピュータ〕 site ⓒ, web site ⓒ ➡[場面・状況別会話] p.1700

サイド side ⓒ ‖生産者サイドにつく take *the producer's side*

◆ワンサイドゲーム a *one-sided* game

‖サイドカー a sidecar / サイドスロー a sidearm throw / サイドテーブル an end table, a side table / サイドビジネス a second job / サイドブレーキ《米》an emergency brake, a hand brake, 《英》a handbrake / サイドミラー a sideview mirror, 《英》a wing mirror / サイドライン〔スポーツ〕a sideline / サイドリーダー a supplementary reader

さいど 再度 人に再度チャンスを与える give a person *another* [*a second*] chance / 私は再度挑戦した I tried *again*. / I gave it *another try*.

さいどく 再読 本を再読する read a book *again*

さいなむ 苛む torture ⊕, rack ‖罪の意識にさいなまれる be tortured [racked] by guilt

さいなん 災難 (災害) disaster ⓒⓊ; (不運) misfortune ⓒ; (面倒) trouble Ⓤ; (事故) accident ⓒ ‖災難にあう「meet with [suffer] *a disaster*; have [meet with] *an accident* / 私はさいわい災難を免れた Fortunately I escaped *the disaster*. / 私たちは思いもよらぬ災難に襲われた *An unexpected disaster* befell us. / 彼らはこのところ災難続きだ They have had *a series of misfortunes* these days.

🅔「電車ですりにあっちゃったよ」「それは災難だったね」"I had my pocket picked on the train." "*That's too bad*."

ざいにち 在日 在日外国人 foreign residents *in Japan* / 在日米軍 the U.S. Forces *in Japan*

さいにゅう 歳入 (annual) revenue Ⓤ

さいにん 再任 彼女は議長に再任された She was appointed chairperson *again*.

ざいにん 罪人 (法律上の) criminal ⓒ; (違反者) offender ⓒ; (道徳・宗教上の) sinner ⓒ

さいにんしき 再認識 私たちは問題の重要性を再認識した (→十分に認識した) We *fully realized* the importance of the problem.

さいねん 再燃 問題の再燃を避ける avoid *a repeat* of the problem / 汚職事件が再燃した (→再び持ち出された) The scandal *has been brought up again*.

さいねんしょう 最年少 ——最年少の the youngest

さいねんちょう 最年長 ——最年長の the oldest

さいのう 才能

(能力) ability ⓊⒸ; (生まれつきの) talent Ⓤ Ⓒ, gift Ⓒ; (素質) aptitude ⓒⓊ

才能を伸ばす develop *one's talent* / 語学の才能がある[ない] have *a [no] talent for* languages / 音楽の才能を発揮する show「*talent for [ability in]* music / 才能豊かな女性 a woman *of many abilities*

彼女はピアニストとしてすぐれた才能がある She has a great *talent* as a pianist. / She is a highly *talented* pianist.

才能を生かせばきっと成功しますよ Use *your ability* and you will surely succeed.

あれだけの才能がありながら、彼はまだマイナーリーグにいる With all that *talent*, he is still in the minor league.

> コロケーション －talent－
> 《形容詞＋～》音楽的～ (a) musical talent / 芸術的～ (an) artistic talent / ずば抜けた～ (an) outstanding talent / すばらしい～ (a) remarkable talent / 特殊な～ (a) special talent / 文学的～ (a) literary talent / 平凡な～ (an) average [(a) mediocre] talent / もって生まれた～ (a) natural talent

さいのめ 賽の目 ||ニンジンをさいの目に切る dice [cube] a carrot; cut a carrot *into cubes*

さいはい 采配 彼がそのグループの活動の采配を振るっている He *directs* the activities of the group. / そのチームが負けたのは監督の采配ミスのせいだ The defeat of the team is due to the manager's *poor directions*.

さいばい 栽培 cultivation Ⓤ ——栽培する grow*⊕, raise ⊕, cultivate ⊕ /綿花の栽培 *the cultivation* of cotton / この地区ではたくさんの農家が米を栽培している In this area, a lot of farmers *grow* rice.

さいはつ 再発 (病気の) return ⒸⓊ, relapse Ⓒ ——再発する return ⊕, relapse ⊕ / 病気が再発する have [suffer] *a return of* the disease / 不幸にも肺癌(がん)が再発した Unfortunately the lung cancer *returned*.

◆そのような事故の再発は防がなければならない We must prevent an accident like that from *happening again*.

ざいばつ 財閥 ▨ a *zaibatsu*, a financial combine

さいはっこう 再発行 reissue Ⓒ ——再発行する reissue ⊕ /パスポートを再発行してもらった I *had* my passport *reissued*.

さいはて 最果て 最果ての地 the *farthest land*

さいはん¹ 初版 (増刷) reprint Ⓒ; (第2版) the second edition ⊕ ——再版する reprint ⊕

さいはん² 再販 ||再販価格 a resale price / 再販(価格維持)制度 the resale price maintenance system

さいばん 裁判 trial Ⓒ Ⓤ, (訴訟) suit Ⓒ Ⓤ, lawsuit Ⓒ

殺人事件の裁判 a murder *trial* / 裁判を開く hold *a trial* / 公正[不公正]な裁判を受ける get a fair [an unfair] *trial* / …を相手に裁判を起こす bring [file] (*a*) *suit* against … / 容疑者[事件]を裁判にかける bring a suspect [case] to *trial*; put a suspect [case] on *trial* / 裁判で勝つ[負ける] win [lose] *a suit* / 裁判で証言する testify at *a trial*

彼女は窃盗容疑で裁判を受けている She *is on [standing] trial* for theft.

彼は汚職容疑で裁判にかけられた He *was*「*put on trial* [*tried*] for bribery.

◆裁判(→法廷)で争う fight *in the courts* / そのもめごとは裁判沙汰にならずにすんだ(→法廷外で解決した) The trouble was settled *out of court*.

||軍事裁判 a military tribunal / 刑事裁判 a criminal suit / 民事裁判 a civil suit

サイパン Saipan (✽マリアナ諸島の島)

さいばんかん 裁判官 judge Ⓒ (✽法廷で呼びかけるときは Your Honor という); 《集合的》bench(単数または複数扱い) ◆殺人事件の裁判官を務める *preside over* a murder case

さいばんしょ 裁判所 (法廷) court Ⓒ Ⓤ; (建物)《主に米》courthouse Ⓒ ||下級裁判所 a lower court / 家庭裁判所 a family court / 簡易裁判所 a summary court / 交通裁判所 a traffic court / 高等裁判所 a high court / 国際司法裁判所 the World Court / 最高裁判所 the Supreme Court / 少年裁判所 a juvenile court / 地方裁判所 a district court

さいばんちょう 裁判長 the presiding judge, the chief justice

さいひょうか 再評価 revaluation Ⓒ Ⓤ ——再評価する revalue ⊕ ◆資産を再評価する *reassess (the value of) one's* assets / その作家の作品は最近再評価されている The works of the writer *are now reappraised*.

さいひょうせん 砕氷船 icebreaker Ⓒ

さいふ 財布 (小銭入れ)《米》change purse Ⓒ, (主に英) purse Ⓒ; (札入れ) wallet Ⓒ, (米) billfold

change purse　　wallet

私は財布を盗まれた I had my「*change purse* [*wallet*] stolen.

私は財布をあけて1万円札を取り出した I opened *my wallet* and took out a 10,000-yen bill.

慣用表現 財布のひもを締める[ゆるめる] tighten [loosen] *the purse strings* / うちは母が財布のひもを握っている My mother *holds* [*controls*] *the purse strings* in our family.

さいぶ 細部 details ||細部がいかに精密に描かれているか注目してください Note how precisely *the details* are drawn.

さいぶん 細分 subdivision [U] ―細分する subdivide [他] ◆学問分野の細分化(→専門化)がますます進んでいる Each field of science is becoming more and more *specialized*.

さいへん(せい) 再編(成) reorganization [U], realignment [U][C] ―再編(成)する reorganize [他][自], realign [他][自] //チームを再編成する *reorganize* a team / 政界再編 political *realignment* / 中央省庁再編 *reorganization* of the Central ministries and agencies

さいほう 裁縫 sewing [U], needlework [U] ―裁縫する sew* [他][自], do* needlework //裁縫がうまい be good at *sewing* [*needlework*] / 母が私に裁縫を教えてくれた My mother taught me *how to sew*.
‖裁縫道具 a sewing kit / 裁縫箱 a sewing box

さいぼう 細胞 cell [C] //癌(がん)細胞 cancer *cells*
‖細胞学 cytology / 細胞分裂 cell division / 細胞膜 (a) cell membrane

ざいほう 財宝 treasure [U]; (富) wealth [U]

さいほうそう 再放送 rerun [C], rebroadcast [U] ―再放送する rerun* [他], rebroadcast* [他], repeat [他][自] //番組の再放送 *a rerun* of a program / このテレビ番組は多くの人の要望で再放送されている This TV program *is being rerun* by popular demand.

サイボーグ cyborg [C]

サイホン siphon [sáifən] [C]

さいまつ 歳末 the end of the year, the year-end //歳末大売り出し a *year-end* sale / 歳末助け合い運動 a *year-end* charity drive

さいみん 催眠 hypnosis [U] //催眠状態で under *hypnosis*
‖催眠療法 hypnotherapy

さいみんじゅつ 催眠術 hypnotism [U] ◆人に催眠術をかける *hypnotize* a person; *put* a person *under hypnosis*
‖催眠術師 a hypnotist

さいむ 債務 (借金) debt [C][U]; (義務) obligation [C] //債務がある be in *debt* / 債務を弁済する pay off *one's debt*
‖債務国 a debtor nation / 債務者 a debtor

ざいむ 財務 financial affairs ◆財務記録をつける keep *financial records*
‖財務管理 financial management / 財務局 a local finance bureau / 財務長官(米国の) the Secretary of the Treasury

ざいむしょう 財務省 (日本の) the Ministry of Finance; (米国の) the Department of the Treasury

さいもく 細目 (細部) details; (契約・規定書などの) the small [fine] print

ざいもく 材木 wood [U][C]; (製材した)《米》lumber [U], 《英》timber [U] ‖材木置き場《米》a lumber yard, 《英》a timber yard

さいゆうしゅう 最優秀 ―最優秀の the best ◆彼は野球チームの最優秀選手に選ばれた He was voted *MVP* of the baseball team. (❖MVPはthe *m*ost *v*aluable *p*layerの略語)
‖最優秀新人賞(スポーツなどの) the Rookie-of-the-Year Award

さいよう 採用 (雇用) employment [U]; (取り入れること) adoption [U] ―採用する employ [他]; adopt [他] //会社の採用試験を受ける take *an employment test* for a company / その会社は来春50人採用する The company is going to *employ* 50 people next spring. / 彼のプランは毎回採用された His plans *were adopted* every time. ◆今年の学生採用数 this year's *intake* of students
‖採用通知 (a) notification of employment

さいらい 再来 その作家はプルーストの再来(→第2のプルースト)だと騒がれている The writer has the reputation of being a *second* Proust. / ボウリングブームが再来した Bowling *is booming again*. / Bowling *has become popular again*.

ざいらい 在来 ―在来の (ありきたりの) usual; (旧来の) conventional ‖在来線 the old railroad line

ざいりゅう 在留 ―在留する (滞在する) stay [自]; (住む) live [自]

さいりよう 再利用 ―再利用する reuse [他], recycle [他] ➲リサイクル //空きびんを再利用する *reuse* an empty bottle / ペットボトルを再利用して作られたTシャツ a T-shirt made from *recycled* plastic bottles

さいりょう[1] 最良 ―最良の the best //人生最良の日 *the best* day of *one's* life / この方法がいつも最良だとは限らない This method is not always *the best*.

さいりょう[2] 裁量 discretion [U] //自由裁量で at *the discretion* of *a person*; at *a person's discretion* / その提案を受け入れるかどうかは彼の裁量に任せた We left it to his *discretion* whether we should accept the proposal. ◆自由裁量を与える give *a person a free hand*

ざいりょう 材料 material [U][C], 《口語的》stuff [U]; (食材) ingredient [C]; (要因) factor [C]
建築材料 building [construction] *materials* / 論文を書くための材料を集める collect *material* for a thesis / 景気好転の材料 *a factor* in the improvement of the economy
この料理の材料は何ですか What *ingredients* are in this dish?
ヒノキは家具を作るのによい材料です Japanese cypress is *a* good *material* for making furniture.
‖原材料 raw materials

ざいりょく 財力 financial power [U]; (富) wealth [U]

ザイル ⚠climbing rope [C] (❖日本語はドイツ語のSeilから)

さいるいガス 催涙ガス tear gas [U]

さいるいだん 催涙弾 tear-gas grenade [C]

サイレン siren [C] //サイレンを鳴らす sound *a siren* / 救急車のサイレンがけたたましく鳴るのが聞こえた I heard *an* ambulance *siren* wail. / サイレンが試合の開始を告げる *A siren* signals the beginning of the game.

サイロ silo [C] (複 ~s)

さいわい

さいわい 幸い，(幸福) happiness ⓤ; (幸運) good luck ⓤ ──**幸いな** happy, lucky, fortunate ──**さいわいに** fortunately, luckily 〔お役に立てれば幸いです I'd be *happy* to help you if I can. / 幸いなことにその事故でけが人は出なかった *Luckily* nobody was injured in the accident.
◆彼はその列車に乗り遅れたのが幸いし，事故にあわずにすんだ He missed the train, but *as it turned out*, he escaped the accident.

サイン¹ ⚠ (署名) signature ⓒ; (有名人の) autograph ⓒ; (合図) sign ⓒ; (野球の) signal ⓒ ──**サインする** sign ⓗ; autograph ⓗ; signal ⓗ ⓒ ⇒ 場面・状況別会話 p.1762
領収証にサインしてください Please *sign* this receipt.
(有名人などに対して)サインをもらえますか May I have *your autograph*?
監督はランナーにホームスチールのサインを送った The coach 「*sent the signal to* [*signaled* (*to*)] the runner to steal home.
∥サイン会 an autograph session / サイン帳 an autograph album / サインペン a felt(-tip) pen

サイン² 〖数学〗 sine ⓒ; (略語) sin)

サウジアラビア Saudi Arabia(❖公式名 the Kingdom of Saudi Arabia) ──**サウジアラビア人** Saudi (Arabian) ⓒ ──**サウジアラビア(人)の** Saudi (Arabian)

サウスカロライナ South Carolina(❖米国南東部の州; (略語) S.C., 〖郵便〗 SC)

サウスダコタ South Dakota(❖米国中北部の州; (略語) S.D., S.Dak., 〖郵便〗 SD)

サウスポー (左利き) southpaw ⓒ

サウナ sauna [sɔ́ːnə] (bath) ⓒ

サウンドトラック soundtrack ⓒ

さえ 冴え 羽生の指し手にはいつものさえが見られなかった Habu's playing was less *skillful* than usual.

-さえ
❶【…ですら】even
そんなことは子供でさえ分かる *Even* a child can understand such things.
裕子は母親にさえ本当のことを言わなかった Yuko didn't tell the truth *even* to her mother.
とても疲れていたので歩くことさえできなかった I was so tired that I couldn't *even* walk.
◆彼の言葉には真実のかけらさえもない *There is not a grain of* truth in his words.
❷【…だけで】only, if only(❖if only は通例仮定法の動詞とともに独立した形で用いる); (…かぎり) as long as
江利さえここにいてくれたらなあ *If only* Eri were here.
君はここにいさえすればいいんだ You *have only to* stay here.
彼の母親は彼がいい成績さえ取っていればそれで満足だった His mother was content *as long as* he got good grades.
◆おまえは彼女に謝りさえすればいいんだよ *All you have to do* is (to) apologize to her.
❸【…に加えて】in addition to …
両親ばかりか兄でさえ私の留学に反対した *In addition to* my parents, my brother objected to my studying abroad.

さえき 差益 marginal profit ⓒ
∥為替差益 an exchange profit

さえぎる 遮る (光・音などを) shut* out; (ふさぐ) block ⓗ; (口をはさむ) interrupt ⓗ ⓒ 〔高い木々が暑い日差しをさえぎっていた The tall trees *blocked* [*shut out*] the blazing sun. / その道は土砂崩れでさえぎられていた The road *was blocked* by a landslide. / インタビューは歓声にさえぎられた The interview *was interrupted* by cheers.
◆ガードマンが私の行く手をさえぎった A guard *barred* [*stood in*] my way.

さえずり (鳥の) song ⓤⓒ, the twitter; (チュンチュンという声) chirp ⓒ, chirrup ⓒ; (さえずること) singing ⓤ, twittering ⓤ 〔鳥のさえずり the *songs of* birds

さえずる sing* ⓗ, twitter ⓗ; (チュンチュンと) chirp ⓗ, chirrup ⓗ 〔鳥たちは楽しそうにさえずっていた The birds *were singing* [*chirping*] cheerfully.

さえる 冴える ❶【色・音が】夜空にさえる星 (the) stars *shining bright*(*ly*) in the night sky / 静寂の中にさえた太鼓の音が響き渡った The *clear* sound of drum rang through the silence.
❷【頭・気分が】今夜は頭がさえない My head is *not clear* tonight. / 顔色がさえないね You *don't look well*. / きのうは一日中気分がさえなかった I *felt blue* [*depressed*] all day yesterday. / ゆうべは目がさえて一睡もできなかった I was *wide awake* and didn't get a wink of sleep last night.
❸【技が】きょうも彼の包丁さばきはさえている As always he *is* very *deft at* handling a kitchen knife today.

さお 竿・棹 pole ⓒ, rod ⓒ ∥さお竹 a bamboo pole / 釣りざお a fishing rod [pole] / 旗ざお a flagpole

さか 坂 slope ⓒ, hill ⓒ
急な[なだらかな]坂 *a steep* [*gentle*] *slope* / 坂を上る[下る] go up [down] *a slope*
私の家はこの坂の上[下]にあります My house stands at the top [foot] of this *slope*.
◆道はここからゆるやかな上り[下り]坂になっている The road *rises* [*goes down*] gently from here.

さが¹ 性 nature ⓤⓒ 〔それが人間の悲しい性だ That's (*the*) miserable human *nature*.

さが² 佐賀

佐賀県は九州の北西部に位置し，北で日本海に，南で有明海に面しています。朝鮮半島や中国大陸に近いことから，古くから大陸文化の影響を強く受けてきました。この県の伝統工芸として知られる有田(伊万里)・唐津などの陶磁器は朝鮮半島からの陶工によって発展したものです。
Saga Prefecture is located in northwest Kyushu. It faces the Sea of Japan to the north and the Ariake Sea to the

south. Because of its proximity to the Korean Peninsula and China, it has long been influenced by the culture of the Asian continent. The traditional Arita (or Imari) and Karatsu ceramics for which Saga is famous were developed by potters from the Korean Peninsula.

さかあがり 逆上がり backward flip (on the horizontal bar)Ⓒ

さかい 境（境界線）boundary Ⓒ；(国境・その周辺) border Ⓒ ‖両家の境に塀がある There is a fence along *the boundary* between the two houses.

◆その日を境に彼は学校に来なくなってしまった He hasn't come to school *since* that day.

慣用表現 彼女は生死の境をさまよっていた She *was hovering between life and death*.

さかいめ 境目 boundary line Ⓒ, borderline Ⓒ ‖彼は合格できるかどうかの境目にいる He is on *the borderline* between pass and fail.

さかうらみ 逆恨み 親切のつもりで彼に忠告したのに逆うらみされてしまった Though I advised him out of kindness, he *unjustly held a grudge against* me.

さかえる 栄える（繁盛する）《公式的》prosper Ⓘ；(活発になる) flourish Ⓘ；(事業などが) thrive* Ⓘ ‖その町はかつて観光名所として栄えた That town once *prospered* as a place of interest.

◆大阪はそれ以来商人の町として栄えてきた Since then Osaka has been *prosperous* as a city of business.

さがく 差額 difference Ⓤ《また a ～》；(貸し借り・収支の) balance Ⓒ ‖差額を支払う pay *the difference*

‖差額ベッド代 an extra charge of hospital room

さかさ(ま) 逆さ(ま) ――逆さ(ま)に（上下が）upside down；(頭から) headfirst, headlong；(前後が) backward(s) ⇨ぎゃく ‖真っ逆さまに落ちる fall *headfirst* [*headlong*] ‖弁当箱を逆さにしないでね Don't turn the lunch box *upside down*.

‖逆さまつ毛 ingrown eyelashes

さがしあてる 捜し当てる・探し当てる find* (out) ‖やっとのことで友達の家を探し当てた At long last I *found* my friend's house.

さがしもの 捜し物・探し物 彼は何か捜し物をしているようだった He seemed to *be looking for* something.

さがす 捜す・探す

look for ..., 《公式的》seek* Ⓘ； search Ⓘ（❖search の後ろにさがす対象の人や物がくる場合は search for ... となり，対象を求めて場所をさがすという場合は search の直後に場所を表す語がくる）；(辞書などで) look up

これが彼の探している本にちがいない This must be the book which he's *looking for*.

私はポケットを捜してかぎを捜した I *searched my pockets for* the key.（❖×I searched the key in my pockets. とはいわない）

私たちは迷子になった子供を捜した We *searched for* the lost child.

地図で僕のいなかを探してごらん *Look up* my hometown on a map.

私はもっと給料のいい仕事を探している I'*m looking for* a better-paying job.

◆彼は手探りで眼鏡を捜した He *groped* [*felt about*] *for* his glasses.

🅔「何を捜しているの」「片方の靴を捜しているんだ」"What *are* you *looking for*?" "I'*m looking for* my other shoe."

🅔「スカートを買いたいのですが」「どんな色をお探しですか」"I want to buy a skirt." "What color *are* you *looking for*?"

さかずき 杯 (sake) cup Ⓒ ‖杯を干す drain *a cup*；drink *a cup* dry ‖ 杯を交わす exchange *cups*

慣用表現 父はよくひとり静かに杯を傾けている（→酒を飲んでいる）My father often quietly *drinks* (*sake*) alone.

さかせる 咲かせる このバラはとてもきれいな花を咲かせる This rose *has a* very beautiful *bloom*.

さかだち 逆立ち handstand Ⓒ ――逆立ちする stand* on *one's* hands

慣用表現 彼よりも速く走るなんて逆立ちしてもできないよ I *can never* run faster than him [he].

さかだてる 逆立てる bristle Ⓘ ‖彼女はその話を聞くと怒りで毛を逆立てた She *bristled* with anger at the story.

さかだる 酒樽 cask Ⓒ

さかて 逆手 彼はうまくそのトラブルを逆手にとった He skillfully *turned* the trouble *to his advantage*.

さかな¹ 魚

fish Ⓒ (複 ～, ～es) （❖複数形 fishes は種類の異なる魚についていう場合に用いる．また魚肉としての fish は Ⓤ）

私は大きな魚を3匹釣った I caught three big *fish*.

日本の近海ではたくさんの魚が捕れる We can catch a lot of *fish* in Japanese waters.

海にはたくさんの(種類の)魚がいる Many *fishes* live in the sea.

私たちは夕食に魚のフライ[焼き魚，煮魚]を食べた We had *fried* [*grilled, simmered*] *fish* for dinner.

‖魚釣り fishing ‖魚屋(人) a fish shop owner,《主に英》a fishmonger；(店) a fish shop,《主に英》a fishmonger's

さかな² 肴（添え料理）side dish Ⓒ ◆この料理は酒のさかなにぴったりだ（→酒とよく合う）This dish *goes well with sake*. ‖彼とはよくクラスメートの話をさかなに（→うわさ話をして）酒を飲んだ I used to drink with him and *gossip about* our classmates.

さかなで 逆撫で 彼の一言一言が私の神経を逆なでした His every word *rubbed* me *the wrong way*.

さかのぼる 遡る

(川を) go* up; (時代を) go back; (ある時代まで) date back to ... // 川をさかのぼる go up a river / 話はさらに1920年代にまでさかのぼる The story goes further back to the 1920s. / その銅貨が作られたのは7世紀にさかのぼる The copper coin dates back to the seventh century.
◆サケは産卵のために川をさかのぼる Salmon swim up rivers to lay eggs.

さかば 酒場
bar ⓒ, 《英口語的》pub ⓒ

さかみち 坂道
slope ⓒ, hill ⓒ // ケーブルカーはゆっくり坂道を登った The cable car slowly climbed the slope.

さかもり 酒盛り
drinking party [bout] ⓒ; (どんちゃん騒ぎ)《口語的》binge ⓒ

さかや 酒屋
(人) liquor shop owner ⓒ; (店) liquor store ⓒ

さからう 逆らう
go* against ...; (反対する) contradict ⓕ, oppose ⓕ; (従わない) disobey ⓕ ⓒ; (抵抗する) resist ⓕ ⓒ // 彼はいつも大勢(ﾀｲｾｲ)に逆らおうとする He always tries to go against the stream. / 親に逆らうものじゃない Don't disobey [go against] your parents. / いいか! 私に逆らうな I warn you! Don't contradict me.
◆彼は潮の流れに逆らって泳ごうとした He tried to swim against the tide.

さかり 盛り
❶【絶頂】the height, peak《通例単数形》; (全盛期) prime Ⓤ / 春の盛りに in the height [full] of spring / その選手はすでに盛りを過ぎている The player has already passed his prime.
◆ブドウは今が盛りです Grapes are now 「at their best [in season]. / 弟は遊びざいり盛りだ My brother is at his most playful age.
❷【発情】盛りのついた(→性的に興奮した)犬 an aroused dog; (→特に雌が) a dog in heat

さかりば 盛り場
(人出の多い場所) a place of popular resort; (繁華街) busy street ⓒ

さがる 下がる

❶【下降する】go* down, come* down, fall* ⓕ, drop ⓕ ⇒ おちる
石油の値段が下がった Oil prices have fallen [dropped, gone down].
ドルが先月から下がり続けている The dollar has been going down since last month.
明け方になると気温が下がり始めた The temperature began to fall at dawn.
湖の水位が下がってきた The level of the lake has come down.
熱がなかなか下がらない My temperature won't come down.
◆成績が下がってしまった My grades got worse. / 最新の世論調査では首相の支持率が下がった In the latest poll, support for the prime minister has decreased.
❷【垂れ下がる】hang* ⓕ
窓にはブラインドが下がっていた There were blinds hanging over the window.
軒先につららが下がっている Icicles hang under the eaves.
❸【退く】step [move] back

1歩下がりなさい Move back a step. / Take 「a step backward [one step back].
◆後ろに下がって絵がまっすぐかどうか見てくれない? Please stand back and see if the picture is straight. / 下がってよろしい You may leave now.
慣用表現 彼の勇敢さには頭が下がる I take my hat off to his courage.

さかん 盛ん
――盛んな (繁栄している) flourishing; (活発な) active; (人気がある) popular; (熱心な) enthusiastic ――盛んに enthusiastically
この地方ではリンゴの生産が盛んだ The production of apples is flourishing in this district.
僕たちの学校ではスポーツが盛んだ Sports are popular at our school.
沿道の観衆はランナーたちに盛んに声援を送った Spectators along the street cheered enthusiastically for the runners.
この問題については方々で盛んに議論がなされている This problem is discussed enthusiastically everywhere.
環境保護運動はますます盛んになってきている People are becoming more and more enthusiastic about the environmental protection movement.
◆あの老人は老いてなお盛んである That old man is still going strong. / かまの火は盛んに燃えていた The fire was blazing in the kiln. / 彼は私に盛んに酒を勧めた He tried hard to get me to drink.

さがん 砂岩
sandstone Ⓤ

さき¹ 先

❶ 先端	the end; point
❷ 順番が前	first; before
❸ 未来	(the) future
❹ 前方に	ahead

❶【先端】the end; (とがった) point ⓒ, tip ⓒ
棒の先 the end of a pole / 鉛筆の先 the point of a pencil / 指[舌]の先 the tip of one's finger [tongue]
◆キツツキは先のとがったくちばしをしている The woodpecker has a pointed beak.
❷【順番が前】(初めに) first; (…の前に) before
先に宿題をすませなさい Finish your homework first.
ジムは僕より先にそこに着いた Jim arrived there before [ahead of, earlier than] me.
◆私が遅れたら先に行ってください In case I'm late, please go ahead of me. / 母は毎朝いちばん先に起きる My mother gets up the earliest every morning.
🇪 「お先にどうぞ」「ありがとう」 "You go first, please. / After you, please." "Thank you."
❸【未来】(the) future
先のことは分かりません I can't tell the future.

◆夏休みはまだ1か月も先だ Our summer vacation is still one month *away*. / これから先本腰を入れてその計画に取り組まなければならない We have to focus our minds on the project *after this* [*from now on*]. / 二人は半年先に結婚する予定だ They are going to get married *in half a year* [*half a year from now*]. / 君の夢がかなうのもそう先のことではないだろう It won't be long before your dream comes true. / この先1週間は$1,000でやっていかなければならない I only have 1,000 yen *for the week ahead*. / この力士は先が楽しみだ(→有望だ) This sumo wrestler *is promising*.

❹【前方に】ahead
郵便局は1キロ先です The post office is one kilometer *ahead* [*off*].
この通りは300メートル先で行き止まりです This street ends 300 meters *ahead* [*off*].
彼女の家はすぐ[だいぶ]先です Her home is just [well] *ahead*.
◆この道はこの先150メートルの間直線だ This road is straight for the *next* 150 meters. / 彼は我が家の5軒先に住んでいる He lives five doors *away* [*down, up*] from my house. / あの銀行の先を左折してください Turn left *past* [*beyond*] that bank. / この電車は名古屋より先へは行きません This train doesn't go *beyond* Nagoya. / その先どうなったのか教えてよ Tell me what happened *after that*.

❺【慣用表現】
【先が長い】この仕事は完成までまだ先が長い(→長い時間がかかる) It *will take me a long time* to finish this work. / その老犬はもう先が長くないだろう I'm afraid the old dog *won't live much longer*.
【先が見える】そんな卑劣な手を使うようではあの会社も先が見えたな That company *has no future* because of its use of dirty tricks.
【先に立つ】彼はみんなの先に立って署名を集めた He *took the initiative* in gathering signatures.
【先を争う】人々はそのゲームソフトを買おうと先を争って店内になだれ込んだ People *scrambled* into the store to buy the game software.
【先を急ぐ】私たちは先を急ぐ救急車に道をあけた We made way for the *speeding* ambulance.
【先を越す】車の免許を取ろうと思っていたら弟に先を越されてしまった I was going to get a driver's license, but my brother *has beaten* me to it.

さき² 左記 ──左記の following (◆名詞の前で用いる) ◆詳しくは左記までお問い合わせください For further information, address inquiries to *the following*. / 出席者は左記のとおりです The attendees are *as follows*.

さぎ¹ 詐欺 swindle ⓒ, fraud ⓤ (◆個々の行為の意味では ⓒ) ‖詐欺を働く commit *a fraud* ◆彼は詐欺にあって大金をだましとられた He *was swindled* out of a large sum of money.

‖詐欺師 a swindler, a fraud
さぎ² 鷺 heron ⓒ
-ざき -咲き 遅咲き[早咲き]の桜 a *late-blooming* [an *early-blooming*] cherry blossom / 公園の桜は五分咲きぐらいだ The cherry trees in the park are about *fifty percent in bloom*. / 彼女は役者としては遅咲きだ She is *a late bloomer* as an actress.
さきおくり 先送り ⇨えんき
さきおととい 一昨々日 three days ago
さきおととし 一昨々年 three years ago
さきがけ 先駆け (先導) the lead; (主導) the initiative; (先駆者) pioneer ⓒ ◆彼のこの主張は環境保護運動の先駆けとなるものだった This claim of his *led* the environmental protection movement. / その雪は厳しい冬の先駆けだった The snow was *the harbinger* [*herald*] of the severe winter.
さきがけて 先駆けて 日本は他の国々に先駆けてこの制度を導入した Japan introduced this system *earlier than* other countries.
さきごろ 先頃 (先日) the other day; (しばらく前に) some time ago
さきざき 先々 (将来) the future; (訪問先) every place, everywhere ‖先々のことを案じる worry about *the future* / 私たちは行く先々で温かく迎えられた We received a warm reception *everywhere* [*wherever*] we went.
サキソホン〔音楽〕 saxophone ⓒ
‖サキソホン奏者 a saxophonist
さきそろう 咲き揃う 6月になって庭のアジサイが咲きそろった In June *every* hydrangea *came into flower* in my garden.
さきだつ 先立つ (先行する) (公式的に) precede ⓗ ‖交渉に先立って歓迎会が行われた A reception *preceded* [was held *before*] the negotiations. ◆彼女は不幸にも息子に先立たれた Unfortunately her son *died before* her. / 海外に行きたいが先立つもの(→十分なお金)がない I want to go abroad, but I don't have *enough money*.
さきどり 先取り ──先取りする (先端を行く) be ahead of …; (先を見越す) anticipate ⓗ ‖時代を先取りする *be ahead of the times* / メーカーはユーザーのニーズを先取りしなければならない Manufacturers must *anticipate* what users will need.
さきばしる 先走る 《口語的に》jump the gun; (性急になる) be hasty ‖先走ったまねをするな Don't *be hasty*.
さきばらい 先払い advanced payment ⓤ ──先払いする pay* … in advance
さきぼそり 先細り 景気の先細りが懸念されている It is feared that the economy may *taper off*. / ファックスの需要は先細りになるだろうといわれていた It was said that the demand for the facsimile would *decrease*.
さきほど 先程 a short time ago; (つい先ほど) just now ‖吉田さんは先ほどお帰りになられました Mr. Yoshida left *a short time ago*. ◆先ほど言ったようにあなたの意見には反対です *As I said*, I disagree with you.

さきまわり 先回り 彼らは近道して私たちの先回りをした(→私たちより先に着いた) They took a shortcut and *arrived ahead of* us. / その会社はわが社の先回りをしてその土地を買い占めた The company bought up the land *ahead of* our company.

さきみだれる 咲き乱れる 野原一面にスミレの花が咲き乱れていた Violets were *in bloom* all over the field.

さきゅう 砂丘 (sand) dune Ⓒ, sand hill Ⓒ

さきゆき 先行き (将来) the future; (見込み) prospects /計画の先行きには若干の不安がある There is some uncertainty about *the future* of the plan. / 景気の先行きは依然として不透明だ *Economic prospects* are still gray.

さぎょう 作業 (仕事) work Ⓤ, (工程) operation Ⓒ ──作業する work Ⓐ
作業中《掲示》Men at Work; Men Working
みないっせいに作業を開始した Everyone started *working* together.
私たちは慎重に作業を進めた We carried on with *the work* carefully.
彼女は精密な作業が得意だ She is good at delicate *operations*.
‖作業員 a worker / 作業時間 working hours / 作業場 a workshop / 作業服 work(ing) clothes

さきわたし 先渡し (商品の) payment after delivery; (賃金の) advance payment Ⓒ

さきん 砂金 gold dust Ⓤ

さきんじる 先んじる be ahead, anticipate Ⓐ /ヨーロッパは環境問題において日本よりも先んじている Europe *anticipates* [*is ahead of*] Japan on environmental issues.
慣用表現 先んずれば人を制す(→早い者勝ち) *First come, first served.*

さく¹ 咲く (草木・特に観賞用の花が) bloom Ⓐ, come* out; (特に木の花が) blossom Ⓐ
チューリップの花がきのう咲いた The tulips *bloomed* yesterday. /
桜はもう間もなく咲くだろう The cherry trees will *blossom* pretty soon.
わが家の庭には今色とりどりの花が咲いている Flowers of various colors *are in bloom* in our garden now.

さく² 割く (時間を) spare Ⓐ; (紙面などを) give* Ⓐ / 2、3時間ほどお時間を割いていただけますか Would it be possible for you to *spare* a few hours for me? / その新聞は誘拐犯逮捕の記事に第一面を割いた The newspaper *gave* the article about the arrest of the kidnapper front-page coverage.

さく³ 裂く (破る) tear* Ⓐ, (縦に) split* Ⓐ; (乱暴に) rip Ⓐ, (はさみなどで) cut* up; (関係などを) separate Ⓐ /彼はその布を裂いて捨てた He *tore* [*ripped*] *up* the cloth and threw it away. / 彼女は私たちの仲を裂こうとしている She's trying to [*separate* us [*break us up*, *break up* our relationship].

さく⁴ 柵 fence Ⓒ; (横木の) railing Ⓒ; (防御用の) stockade Ⓒ /彼は自分の土地の周りに柵をめぐらした He *put a fence* around his land. / He *fenced off* his land.

さく⁵ 策 (計画) plan Ⓒ; (たくらみ) scheme Ⓒ; (対策) measures; (方針) policy Ⓒ /策を練る *draw up a plan* / 政府は急激な円安を防ぐ策を講じた The government *took measures* to prevent a sharp fall in the yen.
◆策の施しようがない Nothing can be done.

さく⁶ 作 (作品) work Ⓤ /会心の作 *the best work; a masterpiece* / 駄作 *a poor work*
◆漱石作の小説 a novel *by* Soseki

さく── 昨── 昨夏 *last summer* / 昨シーズン *last season* / 一昨年 two years *ago*

さくい 作為 ──作為的な (不自然な) artificial; (故意の) deliberate /作為的行動 a *deliberate* action
◆その書類には作為の跡が見られる There is evidence of *fabrication* in the document.

さくいん 索引 index Ⓒ /索引を引く use [consult] *the index*

さくがら 作柄 crop Ⓒ, harvest Ⓒ /今年は米の作柄がよい We had *a good rice crop* this year.

さくげん 削減 cut Ⓒ, 《公式的》reduction Ⓤ Ⓒ ──削減する cut* (down), 《公式的》reduce Ⓐ, curtail Ⓐ /人員削減 *a personnel reduction* / 経費を10パーセント削減する「*cut down on* [*reduce, curtail*] expenses by 10 percent

さくご 錯誤 error Ⓒ, mistake Ⓒ /試行錯誤 trial and error / 時代錯誤 anachronism

さくさく 子供たちは霜の上をさくさくと歩いた The children walked *crunching* the frost under their feet. / このリンゴはとてもさくさくしている This apple is very *crispy*.

ざくざく キャベツをざくざく切る *chop* a cabbage / 参詣者たちは参道の砂利道をざくざく歩いた(→砂利音を立てた) The gravel approach to the shrine *crunched* under the visitors' feet. / 箱の中には古い硬貨がざくざく(→たくさん)あった There were *a lot of* old coins in the box.

さくさん 酢酸 acetic [əsíːtik] acid Ⓤ

さくし 作詞 山田太郎作詞 *words* [*lyrics*] *by* Yamada Taro / ジョン・レノンがこの歌の作詞と作曲をした John Lennon *wrote* both *the words* and the music for this song.
‖作詞家 a lyricist; a songwriter (❖作曲家の意味もある)

さくじつ 昨日 yesterday ➪ きのう(昨日)

さくしゃ 作者 (著者) author Ⓒ; (筆者) writer Ⓒ /この小説の作者はだれですか Who is *the writer* of this novel? / Who *wrote* this novel?
◆作者不詳の絵 an *anonymous* painting

さくしゅ 搾取 exploitation Ⓤ ──搾取する exploit Ⓐ /産業革命当時には女性や年少者が搾取された Women and children *were exploited* in the industrial revolution.

さくじょ 削除 deletion Ⓤ, elimination Ⓤ ──削除する delete Ⓐ, eliminate Ⓐ; (線などで) cross out /不要なファイルは削除したほうがいいよ You should *delete* files you don't need. / 私の名前が名簿から削除された My name *was deleted* [*crossed out*] from the list.

さくず 作図〘数学〙construction [U] ―作図する draw* [他];〘数学〙construct [他]

さくせい[1] 作成 ―作成する make* [他], draw* up;（用意する）prepare [他];（リストなどを）make up;（書類・小切手などを）make out ∥試験問題を作成する *make* examination questions / 読書リストを作成する *make up* a reading list / 請求書を作成する *make out* a bill / この契約書を2通作成してください Please *make* this document in duplicate. / 父はあすの会議の書類を作成しなければならない My father must *prepare* the documents for tomorrow's meeting.

さくせい[2] 作製 ➡せいさく(製作)

さくせん 作戦（大規模な軍事行動）(military) operation [C];（戦略）strategy [U];（個々の戦術）tactics《単数または複数扱い》∥作戦を練る［立てる］discuss [plan] *tactics* / 救出作戦 *a* rescue *operation* / 連合軍は砂漠の嵐(あらし)作戦を実行した *Operation* Desert Storm was conducted by an allied military force.
‖作戦会議 a strategy meeting / 共同作戦 a joint operation

さくそう 錯綜 ―錯綜した complicated;（非常に複雑な）intricate ―錯綜する get* complicated ◆その事故に関する情報は錯綜している（→混乱している）Information about the accident *is confused*.

さくづけ 作付け planting [U] ‖作付け面積 the planted area [acreage]

さくねん 昨年 last year ➡きょねん

さくばん 昨晩 last night ➡さくや

さくひん 作品 work [C];（小品）piece [C];〘音楽〙opus [óupəs] [C]《しばしば Opus》(複 opera, ～es;《略語》op., Op.)
芸術作品 *a work* of art / 文学作品 *a* literary *work* / 夏目漱石作品集 *the collected works* of Natsume Soseki / 三島由紀夫の作品を研究する approach Mishima Yukio's *works* / チャイコフスキーのピアノコンチェルト第1番作品23 Tchaikovsky's piano concerto No.1, *Op*. 23
◆シェークスピアの作品を英語で読む read *Shakespeare* in English

さくふう 作風 style [C][U]

さくぶん 作文 composition [C];（随筆）essay [C];（作文を書くこと）composition [U]; essay writing [U] ∥次の金曜日までに作文を書かなければならない I must write *an essay* by the next Friday. / 日本の学校で行う英作文は実際は和文英訳だ *English composition* done at Japanese schools is actually Japanese-English translation.

さくもつ 作物 crop [C];（農作物）farm products ∥作物を栽培する grow [raise] *crops* / 作物を収穫する harvest *the crops*

さくや 昨夜 last night, yesterday evening（❖通例 last night を用いる）∥昨夜は夕食をごちそうになりありがとうございました Thank you very much for the great dinner *last night*. / 昨夜から熱がある I've had a fever since *last night*.

さくら[1] 桜（木）cherry tree [C];（花）cherry blossoms ∥庭の桜は今満開だ *The cherry trees* in my garden are in full bloom now. / 嵐山の桜は今が見ごろだ *Cherry blossoms* in Arashiyama are now at their best.
‖桜色 pink / 桜前線 a cherry-blossom front, a line on the weather map showing when and where cherry trees have begun to bloom / 桜並木 a row of cherry trees
[短歌] 世の中にたえて桜のなかりせば春の心はのどけからまし（在原業平(ありわらのなりひら)）
If this world of ours
did not have cherry blossoms
that bloom and soon fall,
then the human soul in spring
would be quiet, restful, calm.

さくら[2]（露天商などの）shill [C];（劇場などで拍手する人）plant [C] ∥さくらにまんまと引っかかった I was really had by *the shill*.

さくらえび 桜海老 a *sakuraebi*, a small shrimp from the Pacific Ocean

さくらそう 桜草〘植物〙primrose [C]

さくらん 錯乱（取り乱すこと）distraction [U];（精神の）derangement [U], mental disorder [C] ―錯乱する become* distracted;（気が狂う）go* crazy [mad] ∥彼女は恋人の死を知り錯乱状態に陥った She *went crazy* after learning of her boyfriend's death.

さくらんぼ 桜ん坊・桜桃 cherry [C]

さぐり 探り その件について彼に探りを入れてくれますか Could you *sound* [*feel*] him *out* on the matter? / 彼らは腹の探り合いの状態だ They *are sounding each other out*.

さぐりあてる 探り当てる 暗やみの部屋で目覚まし時計を探り当てた I *groped about and found* the alarm clock in the dark room.

さぐりだす 探り出す find* [dig*] out;（特に秘密を）spy out ∥報道陣はどこで王女が休暇を過ごしているかを探り出した Journalists *found out* where the Princess was spending her vacation. / 彼らは彼女の秘密を探り出した They *spied out* her secret.

さくりゃく 策略（たくらみ）trick [C],《公式的》stratagem [C] ∥あらゆる策略を用いる use every *trick* / 策略をめぐらす devise *a stratagem*

さぐる 探る（手などで）feel* for ...;（捜索する）search [他];（ひそかに見張る）spy on ... ∥ポケットの中でかぎを探った I *felt* in my pocket *for* the key. / 警察は彼の行動を探っていた The police *were spying on* him.
◆その女性は私を探るような目で見た The woman looked at me *searchingly*. / 私たちは解決の糸口を探った（→見つけようとした）We *tried to find* the clue to the solution.

さくれつ 炸裂 explosion [U] ―炸裂する explode [自] ∥爆弾が炸裂した音を聞いた I heard a bomb *explode*.

ざくろ 石榴・柘榴（実・木）pomegranate [C]

さけ[1] 酒（アルコール飲料）alcohol [U], alcoholic drink ①, 《公式的》alcoholic beverage ①; (ウイスキー・ジンなどの強い酒)《米》liquor ①, (主に英) spirits

彼は酒の勢いで上司を非難した *Emboldened by alcohol, he criticized his boss.*

酒くさいよ *You smell of alcohol.*

◆酒の上のけんか a *drunken* brawl / 酒を断つ「*give up* [*quit*] *drinking*」/ この酒(→日本酒)は強い *This sake is strong.* / 私は酒が好きだ *I like drinking.* / 彼は全く酒を飲まない *He doesn't drink* at all. / 彼女は酒が強い *She can「drink quite a lot [hold her liquor]*」. / おじは酒が弱い *My uncle can't drink much.* / 父はすぐ酒に酔う *My father easily gets drunk.* / 彼は酒癖が悪い *He behaves badly when he gets drunk.* / 酒が回ってきた(→だんだん酔ってきた) *I'm getting drunk.* / 彼はきょうは酒が入っていない *He is sober today.* / 酒はつきあい程度です *I'm a social drinker.* / ストレスを酒で紛らわすのはよくない *You shouldn't drown stress in drink.* / 今夜は楽しい酒だ *It's fun to drink tonight.*

ことわざ 酒は百薬の長 *Sake is the best of all medicines.*; *Good wine makes good blood.*(→よいワインはよい血を作る)

―酒のいろいろ―

ウイスキー whiskey / ウオツカ vodka / カクテル cocktail / シェリー sherry / シャンパン champagne / 焼酎(しょうちゅう) shochu / ジン gin / 日本酒 sake / ビール beer / ブランデー brandy / ラム rum / ワイン wine

さけ² 鮭 salmon ①(複 ~); (❖「サケの肉」の意味では ①) / 塩ザケ a salted *salmon* / 缶詰のサケ canned [《英》tinned] *salmon*

‖サケマス漁業 salmon fishing

さけかす 酒粕 sake lees

さげすむ 蔑む despise ⑩, 《口語的》look down on ... ◆彼女はさげすむような目で僕を見た *She looked at me contemptuously.*

さけのみ 酒飲み drinker ①, (大酒飲み) heavy drinker ①, (飲んだくれ) drunkard ①

さけび 叫び (声) cry ①; (大声) shout ①; (悲鳴) scream ①; (きんきんした悲鳴) shriek ① / 救いを求める叫び a *cry* for help / 抗議の叫び *a cry* of protest / 叫び声をあげる give *a cry* [*shout, scream*]

さけぶ 叫ぶ

❶【声をあげる】shout ⓐ⑩; cry ⓐ⑩; scream ⓐ⑩; shriek ⓐ⑩; 《公式的》exclaim ⓐ⑩

| shout: 叫ぶ内容に関係なく最も一般的な語. |
| cry: 驚き・苦痛などで思わず叫ぶ. 必ずしも大声とは限らない. |
| scream: 驚き・恐怖・苦痛などで悲鳴をあげる. |
| shriek: scream よりかん高い声で叫ぶ. |
| exclaim: 喜び・驚き・賞賛・非難などの感情で急に叫ぶ. |

我々は助けを求めて叫んだ *We「cried out [shouted, yelled]」for help.*

多くのけが人が苦痛で叫んでいた *Many injured people were crying with pain.*

女性が叫んでいるのを耳にした *I heard a woman screaming.*

そんなに叫ばなくても聞こえますよ *Don't shout, I can hear you.*

❷【要求する】clamor ⓐ

彼らは彼女の無実を叫んでいる *They are clamoring for her innocence.*

◆英語によるコミュニケーションの重要性が叫ばれている *The importance of English communication skills is asserted.*

さけめ 裂け目 (壁・岩・地面などの) crack ①; (細長い) slit ①; (布などの) tear ①, rip ①

さける¹ 避ける avoid ⑩; (未然に防ぐ) prevent ⑩; (近寄らない) keep* [stay] away from ...; (義務などを)《公式的》evade ⑩

近ごろ彼女は僕のことを避けているみたいだ *Lately she seems to be avoiding me.*

高齢化は避けて通れない問題だ *Aging is a problem we can't avoid.*

彼らは人目を避けて体育館の裏で会った *They met behind the gym to avoid the public eye.*

あの連中は避けたほうがいい *You should keep away from those guys.*

注意して運転することで多くの交通事故は避けられる *Many traffic accidents can be prevented by careful driving.*

証人は質問の答えを避けた *The witness evaded answering the question.*

さける² 裂ける (布などが) tear* ⓐ⑩; (勢いよく) rip ⓐ; (板などが縦に) split* ⓐ⑩ / くぎに引っかかってシャツが裂けた *I tore my shirt on a nail.*

慣用表現 それだけは口が裂けても(→何が起こっても) 言えない *No matter what happens, I can't talk about that.*

さげる 下げる

❶【低くする】(程度・価値・位置などを) lower ⑩; (引っぱり下ろす) pull down; (価格などを) reduce ⑩; (価格・温度などを) bring* down; (音量などを) turn down; (賃金を) cut* down

あの店は全品価格を下げた *That shop lowered [reduced, brought down] all its prices.*

ブラインドを下げてくれない? *Could you please「pull down [lower]」the blinds?*

ボリュームを少し下げてください *Please turn the volume down a little.*

熱を下げる注射を打ってもらった *I got an injection to bring my fever down.*

◆私は祖母の墓に頭を下げた *I bowed my head at my grandmother's tomb.*

❷【つるす】hang* ⑩; (身につける) wear* ⑩

首にペンダントを下げる *wear a pendant around one's neck*

彼は店先に看板を下げることにした *He decided to hang a sign in front of the shop.*

◆その男は右手に紙袋を下げていた *The man was carrying a paper bag in his right hand.*

❸【後ろに動かす】move back; (後ろに引く) pull back; (後ろに押す) push back

いすを下げる *move [pull, push] back a chair*

❹【片づける】
食器を下げてください Please *take* [*clear*] *away* the dishes.
(レストランなどで)お下げしてもよろしいでしょうか *Have* you *finished*?

ざこ 雑魚 (various kinds of) small fish; (下っ端の者) small fry ◯

ざこう 座高 one's height sitting down ◆ 彼は座高が低い[高い] He *has a short* [*long*] *torso*. (✿torso は「胴体」の意味)

さこく 鎖国 national isolation [seclusion] ◯ //鎖国政策をとる adopt *a policy of national isolation* ◆ かつて日本はオランダと中国以外の国に対して鎖国した Formerly Japan *closed its doors to foreign countries* except Holland and China.

さこつ 鎖骨 collarbone ◯, 〔解剖〕 clavicle

ざこね 雑魚寝 3等船室に入ると20人ほどの乗客が雑魚寝していた When I went into the third-class cabin, I found about twenty passengers *were sleeping packed like sardines* on the floor. (✿packed like sardines は「缶詰のイワシのようにびっしり詰まって」という意味)

ささ 笹 bamboo grass ◯; (葉) bamboo leaf ◯

ささいな 些細な (取るに足りない) trivial, trifling; (小さな) small; (重要でない) unimportant //ささいなことでもいいから質問してください Please ask me even if it's a *trivial* [*trifling, small*] thing. //ささいなことで口論する quarrel over *trifles*

ささえ 支え (援助) support ◯; (支柱) support ◯; (つっかえ棒) prop ◯ //心の支え emotional *support* ◆ この木は支えをしなければならない This tree must *be propped up*.

さざえ turbo (shell) ◯ //サザエのつぼ焼き *a turbo cooked in the shell*

ささえる 支える support ◯; (つっかえ棒などで) prop (up); (重さなどに耐える) hold* ◯ //一家を支える *support one's family*
松葉づえで支えていないと立っていられない I need to *support* myself with a crutch to stand.
その棚はこんなにたくさんの本を支えるには弱すぎる That shelf is too weak to *hold* so many books.
母はひとりでこの店を支えてきた My mother *has kept up* this store by herself.

ささくれ (指先の) hangnail

ささげる 捧げる ❶【時間・努力・金銭・心などを】dedicate ◯; (心・人生などを) devote ◯; (犠牲にする) sacrifice ◯ //彼女は生涯を物理学の研究にささげた She *devoted* her life to the study of physics. //その詩は彼の亡き妻にささげられている The poem *is dedicated to* his dead wife.
❷【神・支配者などに】offer ◯ //神々に祈りをささげる *offer* prayers to gods
❸【両手で】hold* [lift] up //その男はひざまずき王に宝をささげた The man kneeled down and *held up* the treasure to the King.

ささつ 査察 inspection ◯ ◯ ——査察する inspect ◯ //査察官 an inspector

さざなみ さざ波 ripple ◯ //そよ風が吹いて池にさざ波が立った The breeze *rippled* the pond. / The pond *rippled* in the breeze.

ささみ 笹身 chicken breast ◯

ささやか ——ささやかな (わずかな) modest; (小さい) small //このささやかな贈り物をお受け取りください Please accept this *small* gift. / ささやかな給料だがないよりはましだ I get a *modest* [*small*] salary, but it is better than nothing.

ささやき 囁き (声・風の) whisper ◯; (小川などの) murmur ◯ //ささやき声で話す speak *in a whisper* / 風[小川]のささやきだけが聞こえた I heard only「*a whisper* of wind [*a murmur* of a stream].

ささやく 囁く whisper ◯ ◯, speak* in a whisper; (ぼそぼそと) murmur ◯ ◯ //恋人たちは愛の言葉をささやいた The lovers *whispered* words of love to each other. ◆ 彼は何か彼女の耳元でささやいた He *murmured* something in her ear. ◆ 彼らはもうじき結婚するといううわさがささやかれている It's *rumored* that they will get married soon.

ささる 刺さる stick* ◯; (突き通す) pierce ◯ //タイヤにくぎが刺さっているのを見つけた I found a nail *sticking* in the tire. / 魚の骨がのどに刺さった A fish bone *stuck* in my throat.

さざんか 山茶花 〔植物〕 sasanqua [səsǽŋkwə]

さし 差し それについては差しで(→ 2 人だけで)話そう Let's talk about it *just*「*by ourselves* [*between us*].

さじ 匙 spoon ◯; (小さじ) teaspoon ◯; (大さじ) tablespoon ◯ //塩小さじ 2 杯 *two teaspoons* [*teaspoonfuls*] of salt / 砂糖大さじに山盛り[すりきり] 3 杯 *three heaping* [*level*] *tablespoons* of sugar
慣用表現 このことに関してはもうとっくにさじを投げている I *have* already *given up* on this matter.

さしあげる 差し上げる ❶【与える】give* ◯ //もし気に入ったのでしたら差し上げます I'll *give* it to you if you like it. / (→取っておいてください) You *can keep* it if you like it.
❷【持ち上げる】lift ◯, hold* up //優勝チームは高々と優勝杯を差し上げた The winning team *lifted* the championship cup high (*up*) above their heads.

さしあたり 差し当たり (現在) at the moment, now, at present; (当分の間) for the moment [present], for the time being //差し当たり問題はない We have no problem *at the moment*. / 差し当たり食料は十分だ We have enough food *for the moment*.

さしいれ 差し入れ present ◯; (服役者への) articles sent to a person in prison

さしいれる 差し入れる 文化祭の準備をしていた私たちに先生がアイスクリームを差し入れてくれた Our teacher *got* ice cream for us when we were preparing for the school festi-

さしえ 挿絵 picture ⓒ, illustration ⓒ; (カット) cut ⓒ ∥この本にはたくさんの挿絵がある There are many *illustrations* in this book.
◆挿絵入りの辞書 an *illustrated* dictionary
∥挿絵画家 an illustrator

さしおく 差し置く (意図的に無視する) ignore ⊕ ∥彼はほかの意見をさしおいてそれを勝手に決めてしまった He decided it *ignoring* what others thought. ◆きょうは何をさしおいてもすることがある I have things to do *before anything else* today.

さしおさえ 差し押さえ seizure ⓤ; 【法律】 attachment ⓤ; (動産の) distraint ⓤ ∥財産の差し押さえを命じる order *the seizure [attachment]* of the property
◆彼は財産の差し押さえにあった He *had* his property *seized [attached]*.

さしおさえる 差し押さえる seize ⊕,【法律】attach ⊕, (動産を) distrain ⊕

さしかえる 差し替える この記事を別の記事と差し替える *replace* this article *with* the other one; *change* this article *for* the other one

さしかかる 差し掛かる 交差点にさしかかったらそこを右折してください When you *come to* the crossing, turn right there. / レースはもう終盤にさしかかっている The race *is reaching* the final stage.

さじかげん 匙加減 彼の昇進は上司のさじかげんひとつで決まる His promotion entirely depends on *how his boss decides to handle* it.

さしがね 差し金 (背後で操ること) instigation ⓤ; (入れ知恵) suggestion ⓤ ∥これはだれの差し金だ Whose *suggestion* is this?

さじき 桟敷 (劇場の 2 階桟敷) balcony ⓒ; (天井桟敷) gallery ⓒ

ざしき 座敷 [場面・状況別会話] p.1724

畳の敷かれた和室を座敷といい、特に客をもてなす部屋のことを指します。座敷にはふつう床の間と呼ばれる空間があり、そこには掛け軸や生けた花などが飾られています。
A *zashiki* refers to a tatami-matted Japanese-style room, and in particular a room for entertaining guests. A *zashiki* commonly has a Japanese-style alcove called a *tokonoma* that holds decorative materials such as *kakejiku* (a Japanese-style painting or piece of calligraphy) and a flower arrangement.

さしきず 刺し傷 (針などの) prick ⓒ; (ナイフなどの) stab wound ⓒ; (とげなどの) sting ⓒ

さしこみ 差し込み ❶【コンセント】outlet ⓒ, socket ⓒ; (プラグ) plug ⓒ
❷【急激な痛み】a sudden sharp pain; (わき腹などの) a stitch

さしこむ 差し込む ❶【挿入する】insert ⊕,《口語的》put* ⊕, (かぎなどを) fit* ⊕ ∥コンセントにプラグを差し込む *put [insert]* a plug *into* a socket / 錠にかぎを差し込む *fit* a key *into* a lock
❷【光などが】朝日が寝室に差し込んでいた The morning sun *was coming [shining]* into the bedroom.

さしころす 刺し殺す stab *a person to death*

さしさわり 差し障り さしさわりのないことを言う make *inoffensive* remarks / 私がそちらへ伺うと何かさしさわりがありますか Will it cause any *harm* if I visit you?

さししめす 指し示す point out, point at ..., 《公式的》indicate ⊕ ∥先生は地図でその場所を指し示した The teacher *pointed out* the place on the map.

さしず 指図 (やり方の) instructions; (方針) directions; (命令) orders, command ⓤ ──指図する instruct ⊕; direct ⊕; order ⊕, command ⊕ ∥私は君の指図は受けない I won't take your *orders*. / あいつの指図で働くのはいやだ I don't want to work *under his directions [instructions]*. / 私の指図どおりにやればうまくいく Follow my *directions [instructions]*, then everything goes well.
◆私に指図しないでくれ Don't *tell me what to do*.

さしずめ 差し詰め (今のところ) at present, at the moment, for the time being; (結局) after all

さしせまる 差し迫る 懸賞の締め切りが差し迫っている The deadline for the prize is 「*close at hand* [*coming near*]」. / それは差し迫った問題だ That is an *urgent* problem. / 差し迫った危険を回避しなければならない We must avoid *imminent* dangers.

さしだしにん 差出人 sender ⓒ

さしだす 差し出す ❶【前方へ】hold* out; (手をつかむため伸ばす) reach out ∥彼は立ち上がり私に手を差し出した He stood up and *held out* his hand.
❷【提出する】submit ⊕, present ⊕, 《口語的》hand in ∥書類を差し出す *submit* documents

さしつかえない 差し支えない さしつかえなければもう少し詳しく話していただけませんか I'd like you to give me some more information about it, if 「*it would be all right with you* [*you don't mind*]」. / あすお宅に伺ってもさしつかえないでしょうか May I come to your house tomorrow? / 彼がチームでいちばんの選手だと言ってもさしつかえないだろう It would be *fair* to say that he is the best player on our team.
💬「ここでたばこを吸ってもさしつかえないですか」「すみませんがご遠慮いただきたいのですが」 "*Would you mind if* I smoked here?" "I hope you won't mind not smoking here."

さしつかえる 差し支える (支障となる) interfere with ...; (悪影響を及ぼす) affect ⊕ ∥毎日バイトをやっていると学校の勉強にさしつかえませんか Doesn't working a part-time job every day *interfere with* your school work?

さして ⇨たいして(大して)

さしでがましい 差し出がましい (でしゃばりな) pushy; (ずけずけ言う) forward ∥差し出がましいようですがひと言言わせてください I may be a bit too forward [(→私には関係のないことですが) I know it's no my business], but let me say a word. / 彼は生意気で差し出がましい He is cheeky and *pushy*.
◆(私のことに)差し出がましいことをしないでくれ Don't *interfere* in my business.

さしでぐち 差し出口 人のことで差し出口をきく(→口出しする) *stick one's nose into* a person's business

さしとおす 刺し通す pierce ⊕, thrust* ... into〜 ∥魚をくしに刺し通す *thrust* a skewer *into* a fish

さしとめる 差し止める (やめさせる) stop ⊕; (一時的に) suspend ⊕; (禁止する) forbid* ⊕, ban ∥製品の輸入を差し止める *ban* [*forbid*] the import of a product / 彼らはその原発の運転差し止めを求めている They demand that the nuclear power plant *stop* [*suspend*] operations.

さしのべる 差し伸べる (手を) extend ⊕; (援助の手を) extend help, 《口語的》give* a helping hand ∥彼が手を差し伸べると彼女はその手を握った He *extended* his hand, and she shook it. / 困っている子供たちに援助の手を差し伸べなさい Give a helping hand [*Reach out*] *to* children in need.

さしはさむ 差し挟む 彼はいつも異論を差しはさむ He always *makes an objection*.

さしひかえる 差し控える (慎 む) refrain 自; (抑える) reserve ⊕ ∥コメントは差し控えさせていただきます I *refrain from* making comments. / I *reserve* my comments.

さしひき 差し引き (残り) the balance; (差し引くこと) deduction ⓤ ∥差し引き1万円の得[損]だ The balance is 10,000 yen for [against] me.
∥差引勘定 the balance of the account

さしひく 差し引く deduct ⊕, 《口語的》take* off ∥価格の15パーセントを差し引く *deduct* 15 percent *from* the price; *take* 15 percent *off* the price ◆必要経費を差し引くと赤字だ After we *take out* the necessary expenses, the balance is in the red. / その点は差し引いて(→大目に見て)この件を考慮してください I hope you could *overlook* that point and consider it.

さしみ 刺身 🗾

新鮮な魚介類などひと口サイズに切った「造り」ともいわれる料理で、ふつう千切りの大根や海草が添えられています。少量のすりおろしたワサビとともに、しょうゆにつけて生で食べます。刺身によく使われるものに、マグロ、カツオ、タイ、エビ、イカなどがあります。
Sashimi, also called *tsukuri*, is a dish of bite-sized fresh seafood usually served with shredded *daikon* (Japanese radish) and edible seaweed. People eat *sashimi* raw, dipping it into soy sauce with a little bit of *wasabi* (grated Japanese horseradish). Among the seafood common for *sashimi* are tuna, bonito, sea bream, shrimp and squid.

さしみず 差し水 なべが吹きこぼれる前に差し水をしてください *Add some water to* the pot before it boils over.

さしむかい 差し向かい そのカップルはテーブルに差し向かいで座った The couple sat *face to face* at the table.

さしむける 差し向ける send* ⊕ ∥編集長はレポーターを事件現場へ差し向けた The chief editor *sent* a reporter to the scene of the accident.

さしもどす 差し戻す send* back; (法案などを) refer back ∥その事件は地裁に差し戻された The case *was sent* [*referred*] *back to* the district court.

さしょう¹ 査証 visa ⓒ ∥入国査証 an entry visa

さしょう² 詐称 名前を詐称する(→偽名を使う) *use* a *false* name / 年齢を詐称する(→偽る) *lie about one's* age
∥学歴詐称 a false statement about *one's* educational [academic] background / 年齢詐称 misrepresentation of *one's* age

さじょう 砂上 砂上の楼閣(ろうかく) *a house built on the sand*; (→実現不可能な計画) *castle in the air*

ざしょう 座礁 ──座礁する go* [run*] aground; (岩礁に) go [run] on the rocks
◆我々の計画は座礁してしまった(→行き詰まってしまった) Our plan *has ended in deadlock*.

さしわたし 差し渡し (直径) diameter ⓒ

さじん 砂塵 a cloud of dust ∥突風が砂塵を巻き上げた The gust threw up *clouds of dust*.

さす¹ 指す

❶ [示す] point at [to] ... (❖at は指す「対象」を, to は指す「方向」を表す), 《公式的》indicate ⊕
友子は好きな男の子をそっと指さした Tomoko discreetly *pointed at* the boy she liked.
時計の針は7時を指していた The hands of the clock were「*pointing to* [*indicating*] 7 o'clock.

❷ [指名する] (教室などで) call on ...
数学の先生はいつも出席番号順に指す The math teacher always *calls on* us in roll-call order.
先生に指されたが質問に答えられなかった I *got* [*was*] *called on* by the teacher, but I couldn't answer his question.

❸ [意味する] mean* ⊕; (言及する) refer to ...
けちなやつとはだれのことを指しているのですか Who do you *mean* [*refer to*] by a stingy person?

❹ [将棋を]
週末はいつも父と将棋を指す I *play shogi* with my father every weekend.

さす² 差す

❶【光が】
雨がやんで薄日がさしてきた The rain has stopped, and the sun *is beginning to shine*.
私の部屋は一日中日があまりささない My room *doesn't get much sunshine* throughout the day.
❷【入れる・加える】put*⓪; (液体などを) pour ⓪; (目薬を) drop ⓪, apply ⓪
彼女はバラの花を花びんにさした She *put* roses in the vase.
吹きこぼれそうになったらなべに水をさしなさい *Pour* some water *into* the pot when it is about to boil over.
◆機械に油をさす *oil* a machine
❸【傘を】put* up; (使う) use ⓪
雨が降ってきたから傘をさしたほうがいいよ You'd better *put your umbrella up* because it's starting to rain.
❹【色・気持ちなどが】
西の空に赤みがさしてきた The western sky was「*turning* red [*gaining* a red tint].
大学受験の勉強にいやけがさしてきている I'm *getting tired* [*sick*] *of* studying for college entrance exams.

さす³ 刺す
❶【突く】(ナイフなどで) stab ⓪; (針などで) prick ⓪; (突き通す) pierce ⓪; (深く) thrust*⓪
通り魔は通行人の背中をナイフで刺した The phantom killer *stabbed* a passerby in the back.
針で指を刺した I *pricked* my finger with a needle.
◆肉をくしに刺す *skewer* meat / 肌を刺すような風 a *piercing* [*biting*] wind / その部屋にはアンモニアの鼻を刺すにおいがこもっていた The room was filled with *a pungent* [*sharp*] *smell* of ammonia.
❷【虫が】(蚊などが) bite*⓪; (ハチなどが) sting*⓪
蚊に刺された I *was bitten* by a mosquito.
首をハチに刺された I *got stung* on my neck by a bee.
❸【野球で】throw* out; (けん制球で) pick off
二塁走者はけん制球で刺された The runner *was picked off* second base.

さす⁴ 砂州 (河口などの) sandbank ⓒ, sandbar ⓒ (❖sandbank よりも小さいものをいう)

さすが
❶【何といっても】(当然予想されるとおり) as may [might] be expected (of ...); (…らしい) just like ...
さすがは元オリンピック選手の両親をもつだけあって,彼はスポーツ万能だ *As may be expected from* having parents who are both ex-Olympic athletes, he is good at all kinds of sports.
おぼれかけていた男の子を救出するなんてさすがは君だ It's *just like* you to save a drowning boy.
❸「通知表はオール5だったよ」「さすが！」"I got straight A's on my report card." "*That's just like you*!" (→君は本当に頭がいい) "You're *truly* a smart person!"
❷【そうはいうものの】even, although, even though
ふだんはおとなしい彼もさすがに今回は怒った *Although* [*Even though*] he is usually quiet, he got angry this time.
さすがの彼もその問題は解けなかった *Even* he couldn't solve the question.

さずかる 授かる 祖父は去年文化勲章を授かった (→授与された) My grandfather *was awarded* the Cultural Medal last year. / 兄夫婦は結婚10年目にしてようやく子供を授かった (→恵まれた) My elder brother and his wife *were blessed with* a child after having been married for 10 years.

さずける 授ける (学位・称号などを) confer ⓦ; (伝授する) teach*ⓦ, initiate ⓦ ∥ハーバード大学は彼に名誉教授職を授けた Harvard University *conferred* an honorary professorship on him. / 彼は父からバスフィッシングの秘伝を授けられた He *was initiated into* the art of bass fishing by his father.

サスペンス suspense ⓤ (❖予測のつかない不安感を表し「なぞ」の意味はない) ∥その映画はスリルとサスペンスに満ちている That movie is full of thrills and *suspense*.
∥サスペンス小説 a thriller, a mystery story

サスペンダー suspenders, (英)braces (❖数えるときはa pair of ... とする) ∥サスペンダーをする wear *suspenders*

さすらい さすらいの旅人 a *wandering* traveler

さすらう (放浪する) wander ⓘ, drift ⓘ

さする rub gently; (なでる) stroke ⓦ; (マッサージする) massage ⓦ ∥彼女は私の背中をやさしくさすってくれた She gently *rubbed* me on the back.

ざせき 座席 seat ⓒ / 前方[後方]の座席 a front [back] *seat* / 窓側[通路側]の座席 a window [an aisle] *seat* / 座席にはまだ十分の空きがあります There are plenty of *seats* available. / 私は列車の座席を2つ予約した I reserved [(英)booked] two *seats* on the train.
∥座席指定券 a reserved-seat ticket / 座席番号 the seat number / 座席表 a seating plan [chart]

させつ 左折 left turn ⓒ ──**左折する** turn (to the) left ∥左折禁止《掲示》*No Left Turn*

ざせつ 挫折 (失敗) failure ⓤ; (途中で破綻(はたん)すること) collapse ⓤ ──**挫折する** fail ⓘ; collapse ⓘ / 深い挫折感を味わう feel *a deep sense of failure* / 資金不足でその事業は挫折した The business *collapsed* due to lack of money. / みんなそれぞれの挫折を乗り越えて大きく成長する Everybody matures a lot as they overcome their own *failures*.

させる
make*... *do*; have*... *do*; let*... *do*, allow ... to *do*; get*... to *do*; force ... to *do*

(❖make, have, let の 3 語は後ろに原形不定詞が, get, allow, force の 3 語は to 不定詞がくることに注意)

make: 強制的に「…させる」の意味.
have: 頼んで「…してもらう」の意味で消極的な使役を表す.
let, allow: 「(人が)…する」のを許すという意味.
get: 説得して, あるいは依頼・命令して「…させる」の意味.
force: 無理やり「…させる」の意味で, make よりさらに強制の意味が強い.

僕は弟に部屋を掃除させた I *made* my brother clean the room.
私は野球部をやめさせられた I *was made to* leave the baseball team. (❖make は受身になると to 不定詞をとる)
出版社は私に原稿を書き直させた The publisher *had* me rewrite the manuscript.
その父親は子供たちの好きなようにさせた The father *let* the children do whatever they liked.
私にやらせてください *Allow* me *to* do that.
あいつに今すぐこの散らかった物を片づけさせろ *Get* him *to* tidy up this mess right now!
◆彼女を満足させるのは難しい It's hard to *please* her. / 君に大変な思いをさせて悪いと思っている I'm sorry I'*m giving* you a hard time.

させん 左遷 demotion [U] [C] ━左遷する demote [他] ∥父は地方の支店へ左遷された My father *was demoted* to a post in a local branch.

ざぜん 座禅 🗻 *zazen*, Zen meditation ∥座禅を組む practice *Zen meditation* in the lotus position ➡ぜん

さぞ さぞお疲れでしょう You *must* be very tired. / さぞかしご家族の皆様もお喜びでしょう *Surely* [*I'm sure*] all of your family are pleased.

さそい 誘い (招き) invitation [U]; (誘惑) temptation [U] (❖いずれも具体的な行為は [C]) ∥近ごろ彼女からよく誘いを受ける I often get *invitations* from her recently.
◆彼は新しい会社を興すという私たちの誘いには乗らなかった He *wasn't tempted* by our plan to start a new business.

さそいこむ 誘い込む (誘惑して) lure *a person* into …; (だまして) 《口語的》rope *a person* in ∥少年は不良グループに誘い込まれた The boy *was roped in* to the gang of hoodlums.

さそいだす 誘い出す 僕らは彼女を公園に誘い出した We *asked* her *out* to the park.

さそう 誘う
❶【勧める】(招待する) invite [他]; (…しようと) ask *a person* to *do*
私は誕生パーティーに友達を 5 人誘っている I'*ve invited* five friends of mine to my birthday party.
僕は友達から彼の家族といっしょにスキーに行かないかと誘われた I *was invited* by a friend of mine *to* go skiing with his family.
◆私は他社から来ないかと誘われている I'*ve been offered* a job by [at, with] another company. / I'*ve been approached* by another company. / 浜田君にデートに誘われちゃった Hamada *asked* me *out*. / 皆様お誘い合わせのうえ, パーティーにお越しください (→パーティーにあなたの友達を連れてきてください) *Bring your friends to* the party.
[e]「この映画のチケットが 2 枚あるんだけど, だれか興味のありそうな人知らない」「恵美を誘ってみたら?」"Do you happen to know somebody who might be interested in this movie? I've got two tickets here." "Why don't you *ask* Emi?"
[e]「これからカラオケに行くんだけど, いっしょにどう」「ごめん, きょうはほかに予定があるんだ. またの機会に誘って」"We're going to karaoke now. Will you join us?" "Sorry, I've got another appointment today. *Try* me some other time."
❷【促す】
陽気に誘われて私たちはピクニックに出かけた The fine weather *tempted* us to go on a picnic.
昼食の後の授業は眠気を誘う Lessons after lunch *make* us sleepy.
そのドラマの最終回は多くの人の涙を誘った The last episode of the TV drama *moved* many people to tears.

さそり 蠍 scorpion [C]

さそりざ 蠍座 〘天文・占星〙Scorpio [U] (❖「さそり座の人」の意味では [C])

さた 沙汰 少年たちのけんかはとうとう警察ざたになってしまった The fight between the boys *was* finally *reported to the police*. / この事件が裁判ざたになるのは必至だ It is inevitable that this case *will be brought to court*. / 君のしようとしていることはとても正気のさたとは思えない What you are going to do *is* completely *insane*. / 台風が接近しているのにヨットに乗るなんて狂気のさただ It is *madness* to go yachting while the typhoon is approaching.
[ことわざ] 地獄のさたも金しだい ➡じごく

さだか 定か ━定かな (確かな) certain ∥彼がまだそこに住んでいるかどうかは定かでない It's not *certain* whether he still lives there or not. ◆それは定かな情報ではない That is not *reliable* information.

さだまる 定まる (決定する) be decided; (固定する) be fixed; (落ち着く) be settled ∥やっと住所が定まった I *have* finally *settled down* in one place.
◆天候が定まらない (→変わりやすい) The weather *is changeable* [*unsettled*].

さだめ 定め (法律) law [C]; (規則) rule [C], regulation [C]; (運命) destiny [U], fate [U] ∥この世の定め *the fate* of this world

さだめる 定める ❶【制定する】(法律などを)《公式的》provide [他]; (条件として)《公式的》stipulate [他]; (規則などを) lay* down ∥法の定めるところにより as *provided* by law / ルールを定める *lay down* rules

❷【決定する】decide [他] [自]; (日程・計画などを) fix [他]; (目標などを) set* [他] //方針を定める *decide (on)* a policy / 目標を定める *set up one's* own goal
❸【ねらいをつける】猟師は銃で鳥にねらいを定めて撃った The hunter *aimed at* a bird and shot it.

サタン Satan [séitən]

ざだんかい 座談会 round-table talk [discussion] [C], discussion meeting [C]

さち 幸 (幸福) happiness [U]; (幸運) luck [U]
◆私たちは海の幸山の幸を堪能(たんのう)した We ate all sorts of *delicacies from land and sea* to our heart's content.

さちゅうかん 左中間〔野球〕left center (field) [U] //左中間へ二塁打を打つ hit a double to *left center*

さつ 札 《米》bill [C], 《英》note [C] //1,000円札 *a* 1,000-yen *bill* [*note*]
💬「1人2,500円だね」「私, 1万円札しかないんだけど, だれかくずせる」"It will be 2,500 yen per person." "I've only got *a* 10,000-yen *bill*. Can anybody give me change for it?"

-さつ -冊 (部) copy [C] //この本を5冊ください I'd like five *copies* of this book. ◆近藤君から本を数冊借りている I've borrowed several *books* from Kondo. / その大学の図書館には200万冊を超える蔵書がある The university library has over two million *volumes*.

ざつ 雑 ―雑な (大ざっぱな) rough; (いいかげんな) 《口語的》sloppy; (不注意な) careless ―雑に roughly; carelessly //雑な仕事 *careless* [*sloppy*] work / 荷物を雑に扱う handle baggage *roughly* [*carelessly*]

さつい 殺意 murderous intent [U]
◆彼は彼女に殺意をいだいていた He *intended to kill* her.

さついれ 札入れ wallet [C], 《米》billfold [C]

さつえい 撮影 (写真の) photography [U]; (映画などの) filming [U], shooting [U] ―撮影する (写真を) take* a picture [photo, photograph] (of ...); (映画などを) film [他], shoot* [他] //撮影禁止《掲示》*No Photography* [*Pictures*] / 私は姉の披露宴の写真を撮影した I *took photos of* my sister's wedding reception. / 彼は3月に新作の撮影を開始するそうだ I hear (that) he will start *shooting* his new movie in March. / この映画は全編中国で撮影された This movie *was filmed* entirely in China.
‖撮影会 a photo session / 撮影所(映画の) a movie [film] studio

ざつえき 雑役 (家庭での) chores; (会社などでの) odd jobs //雑役をする do *chores* [*odd jobs*]
‖雑役夫[婦] 《米》a janitor, 《英》a caretaker

ざつおん 雑音 noise [U] [C]; (電波障害) static [U] //このラジオはよく雑音が入る There's too much *static* on this radio. / あれが音楽だって? あんなものは雑音だ Do you call that music? That's sheer *noise*!

さっか 作家 writer [C]; (著者) author [C]; (小説家) novelist [C] ‖劇作家 a playwright [dramatist] / 陶芸作家 a ceramic artist

ざっか 雑貨 miscellaneous goods, 《公式的》sundries
◆東南アジアから雑貨を輸入する import *general merchandise* from Southeast Asia
‖雑貨店 a general store; (食料雑貨店) a grocery

サッカー soccer [U], 《英》football [U] ⇨ [サッカー] p.589 //サッカーをする play *soccer* [*football*] / サッカーくじ a *soccer* lottery

さつがい 殺害 killing [U]; (故意の) murder [U]; (殺意のない) manslaughter [U] ―殺害する kill [他]; murder [他]
‖殺害現場 a murder scene

さっかく 錯覚 illusion [C] //目の錯覚 *an optical illusion* / 昼寝からさめたとき朝だと錯覚した When I woke up from a nap, I *had an illusion* that it was morning. / 私は一瞬, 大富豪になったような錯覚を起こした I *was under the illusion* for a split second that I had become a millionaire. / For a split second, I *felt as if* I had become a millionaire. ◆あれ, ここに郵便ポストがあったと思ったけど. 私の錯覚かな? Oh, I thought there was a mailbox here. Or was it my *imagination*? / 彼女は彼の優しさを彼女への愛と錯覚していた(→混同していた) She *had been confusing* his kindness with love for her.

ざつがく 雑学 knowledge of various [miscellaneous] subjects, trivia [U]
◆彼は雑学の大家だ(→何でもよく知っている) He knows *something about everything*.

さつき 五月・皐月 (5月) May [U];〔植物〕azalea [C] //五月晴れ *fine May weather*

さっき[1] (少し前) a little [short] while ago; (しばらく前) some time ago ◆さっきの電話だれから? Who was *that* call from?
💬「さっきからそわそわしてるけど, どうしたの」「そろそろ合否通知が来るころなんだ」"You've been nervous *for some time*. What is it?" "I'll be receiving the results of the entrance exam soon."
💬「近藤君は?」「あれ, おかしいな. ほんのさっきまでここにいたんだけど」"Where's Kondo?" "Oh, that's strange. He was here *until just a minute ago*."

さっき[2] 殺気 観客は殺気立っていた The spectators *were wildly excited*.

ざっきちょう 雑記帳 notebook [C]

さっきゅう 早急 ―早急に (ただちに) immediately; (遅れずに) without delay; (緊急に) urgently //早急に対処します We'll deal with it *immediately*. / A型の血液が早急に必要だ We *urgently* need type A blood.

ざっきょ 雑居 ‖雑居ビル a building tenanted by various shops, offices and restaurants

さっきょく 作曲 composition [U] ―作曲する compose [他], write* music ‖作曲家 a composer; (歌謡曲などの) a songwriter (❖songwriterには「作詞家」の意味もある)

さっきん 殺菌 sterilization [U]; (低温殺菌)

テーマ別表現集

●サッカー

❶得点・試合結果などに関する表現

1. 私たちのチームは前半に田中のシュートで点を取りました.
   Our team scored a goal on Tanaka's shot in the first half.
2. エスパルスは後半残り10分前に何とか点を入れることができました.
   S-Pulse managed to score a goal 10 minutes before the end of the second half.
3. そのチームは現在2勝1敗2引き分けです.
   The team now has two wins, one loss and two draws.
4. 日本は1対0で韓国に敗れ［勝ち］ました.
   Japan「lost 1-0 to [won 1-0 over] Korea.
5. 前半の2つのゴールでイタリアは2対0でブラジルに勝ちました.
   Two goals in the first half earned Italy a 2-0 win over Brazil.

❷技に関する表現

1. センターバックがすばらしいゴールを決めました.
   The center back made a nice shot into the goal.
2. キャプテンが続けて2つゴールを決めて得点しました.
   The captain scored two goals in a row.
3. そのチームは佐藤のヘディングシュートで1点を入れました.
   The team got one point on Sato's header shot.
4. 彼のうまいコーナーキックのおかげで林はヘディングでゴールを決めることができました.
   His nice corner kick allowed Hayashi to make a header into the goal.
5. ゴールキーパーはストライカーのシュートを止めました.
   The goalkeeper blocked a shot from the striker.
6. マークされていないストライカーにミッドフィールダーがうまいパスをしました.
   The midfielder made a nice pass to the unmarked striker.
7. 野村が最初のゴールをアシストしました.
   Nomura assisted on the first goal.
8. ディフェンダーがゴール前を横切るヘディングパスでチャンスを作りました.
   The defender created a chance with a header across the face of the goal.
9. そのゴールキーパーのゴールキックは直接タッチラインを割りました.
   The goalkeeper missed a goal kick directly over the touchline.
10. 彼のペナルティーエリア外からのきわどいシュートは相手チームにプレッシャーをかけました.
    His close shots from outside the「penalty area [box]」put pressure on the opposing team.
11. 彼のドリブルシュートは相手の選手を惑わしました.
    His dribble shot confused the opposing players.
12. レフェリーは彼の反則に対してイエローカードを出しました.
    The referee showed him a yellow card for his foul.

❸その他

1. どちらのチームを応援していますか.
   Which team are you cheering [rooting] for?
2. 磐田から来た多くのファンはジュビロを応援しました.
   Many supporters from Iwata cheered on Jubilo.
3. 日本がワールドカップに進出したことがサッカーブームを引き起こしました.
   Japan's qualifying for the World Cup has produced a soccer boom.
4. 何万人ものサポーターたちがワールドカップに集まりました.
   Ten of thousands of supporters gathered at the World Cup.
5. 多くのサポーターたちがその試合のチケットを買うために長い列を作りました.
   Many supporters made long lines to get tickets for the game.

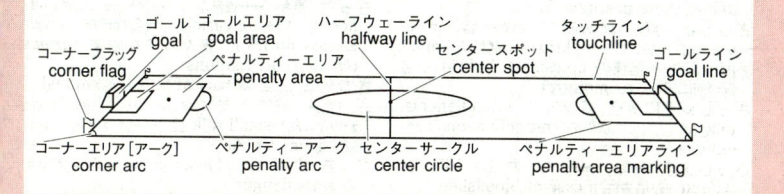

ゴール goal
ゴールエリア goal area
ハーフウェーライン halfway line
タッチライン touchline
コーナーフラッグ corner flag
ペナルティーエリア penalty area
センタースポット center spot
ゴールライン goal line
コーナーエリア［アーク］ corner arc
ペナルティーアーク penalty arc
センターサークル center circle
ペナルティーエリアライン penalty area marking

pasteurization ⓊⒸ ──殺菌する sterilize Ⓔ; pasteurize Ⓔ
‖殺菌剤 disinfectant / 殺菌力 sterilizing power / 低温殺菌牛乳 pasteurized milk

ざっきん 雑菌 various kinds of harmful germs [bacteria]

ザック (リュックサック) rucksack [rǽksæk] Ⓒ; (ナップサック) knapsack

サックス 《口語的》sax, saxophone Ⓒ

ざっくばらん ──ざっくばらんな (率直な) frank; (遠慮のない) candid; (形式ばらない) informal ──ざっくばらんに frankly; candidly; informally ◆ざっくばらんに言えば、その計画は現実的じゃない *Frankly* speaking, that plan is not realistic.

ざっくり 彼女はざっくりした(→ゆったりしていて目が粗い)セーターを着ていた She was wearing a *fairly large and coarsely woven* sweater.

さっこん 昨今 (最近) recently, lately; (このごろ) these days, nowadays

さっさと (急いで) quickly, at once; (敏速に) promptly; (遅れずに) without delay ◆さっさと歩け Walk *quickly*! / さっさと自分の部屋を片づけろ Clean up your room *at once*! / さっさとしなさい *Hurry up*! / 彼はいつも学校が終わるとさっさとうちに帰る He always goes home *right* after school.

サッシ sash Ⓒ, window frame Ⓒ ‖アルミサッシ an aluminum sash

さっし¹ 察し 彼女はとても察しがいい She *is* very quick 「*at guessing* [*to understand*]. / お察しのとおりです(→あなたは正しく推察した) *You've guessed it right*. / そのとき彼がどうしたか容易に察しがつく I *can* easily *imagine* what he did at that time.

さっし² 冊子 (本) book Ⓒ; (小冊子) booklet

ざっし 雑誌 magazine Ⓒ; (専門誌) journal Ⓒ; (定期刊行物) periodical Ⓒ
◆わが家は毎月3冊雑誌をとっている We take [subscribe to] three *magazines* every month.
◆その雑誌の8月号におもしろい記事が出ていた I found an interesting article in the August issue of that *magazine*.
‖雑誌記事 a magazine article / 雑誌記者 a magazine reporter / 科学雑誌 a science journal / ファッション雑誌 a fashion magazine / 漫画雑誌 a comic magazine [book]

ざつじ 雑事 miscellaneous affairs
◆ここ2、3日身辺の雑事(→個人的な用事)に追われて忙しい I've been busy with *personal affairs* these past few days.

ざっしゅ 雑種 (動植物の) cross, crossbreed Ⓒ, 《公式的》hybrid Ⓒ; (雑種犬) mongrel Ⓒ ──雑種の crossbred, hybrid (❖名詞の前に用いる。); mongrel

ざっしゅうにゅう 雑収入 miscellaneous income Ⓒ; (公共機関の) miscellaneous revenue Ⓤ

さっしょう 殺傷 ──殺傷する kill or wound ‖殺傷事件 a case of bloodshed

ざっしょく 雑食 ──雑食の 《公式的》omnivorous

さっしん 刷新 (改革) reform ⓊⒸ; (新しいものを取り入れること) innovation Ⓤ; (人事の) reshuffle Ⓒ ──刷新する reform Ⓔ; innovate Ⓔ; reshuffle Ⓔ ‖政界の刷新 political *reform* / 新しい社長は人事を刷新した The new CEO *carried out a* personnel *reshuffle*.

さつじん 殺人 (故意の) murder ⓊⒸ; (殺意のない) manslaughter Ⓤ; (総称)《法律》 homicide ⓊⒸ ‖殺人を犯す commit (*a*) *murder* / 殺人罪に問われる be charged with *murder* / 彼女に殺人の容疑がかかっている She is suspected of *murder*. ◆殺人的な(→極度な)忙しさだ I'm *extremely* busy. / ラッシュ時の山手線は殺人的に(→非常に)込む The Yamanote Line gets *horribly* [*terribly*] crowded during rush hours.
‖殺人罪 murder / 殺人事件 a murder (case) / 殺人犯 a murderer / 殺人未遂 attempted murder

さっする 察する (推察する) guess Ⓔ, suppose Ⓔ; (同情する) sympathize with …; (理解する) understand* Ⓔ ‖察するところ彼は彼女のことを気に入っているらしい I *suppose* [*guess*] he likes her. / そのあたりのことは(→私が意味することは)察してください I hope you *understand* what I mean. / 胸中お察しします I *do sympathize with* you. ◆彼女の心労は察するに余りある(→本当によく分かる) I *can just imagine* how worried she is.

ざつぜん 雑然 雑然とした部屋 a *messy* room / 本や新聞が雑然とテーブルの上に積まれていた Books and papers were in a *disorderly* pile on the table.

さっそう 颯爽 彼女はいつもさっそうとした格好をしている She always dresses *smartly*. / 剛はさっそうと(→軽やかな足取りで)町を歩いた Tsuyoshi walked *with a jaunty step* through the town.

ざっそう 雑草 weed Ⓒ ◆きょうは一日中庭の雑草取りをした I *weeded* the garden all day today.

さっそく 早速 (すぐに) immediately, at once, 《口語的》right now, 《口語的》right away ◆本当にそんなことができるのなら早速この場でやって見せてくれ If you really can do such a thing, show us right here, *right now*. ◆早速本題に入りましょう *Now* let's get to the main point. / 早速のお返事、ありがとうございます Thank you for your *quick* [*prompt*] reply.

ざった 雑多 ──雑多な (寄せ集めの) miscellaneous; (種々の) various ‖雑多な仕事 *miscellaneous* duties / 種々雑多な職業 *various* (*kinds of*) occupations

さつたば 札束 a wad of bills [《英》notes]

ざつだん 雑談 (気楽なおしゃべり) chat Ⓒ; (たわいない話) small talk Ⓤ ──雑談する chat Ⓔ, have a chat

さっち 察知 (気づく) sense Ⓔ ‖危険を察知する *sense* danger

さっちゅうざい 殺虫剤 insecticide ‖殺虫剤をまく spray (an) insecticide

さっと (素早く) quickly; (敏捷に) nimbly; (すぐに) immediately; (急に) suddenly, all of a sudden ‖弟はさっと電話を取った My brother *quickly* picked up the phone. / 自転車がつっ込んできたが，彼女はさっと身をかわした The bicycle came at her, but she dodged *nimbly* out of the way. / 彼はさっと立ち上がって部屋を出ていった *Suddenly* he stood up, and then left the room. / それを聞くと彼女の顔がさっと赤くなった She *suddenly* blushed when she heard that.

◆ホウレンソウをさっと(→軽く)ゆでる *blanch* spinach; *boil* spinach *lightly*

ざっと ❶(大ざっぱに)(手短に) briefly;(あわてて) hurriedly; (素早く) quickly ‖ざっと片づける tidy up *hurriedly* [*quickly*] / 重要な点をざっと説明する explain the points *briefly*
◆新聞にざっと目を通す *skim* (*through*) the newspaper

❷(ほぼ) roughly, approximately, about ‖今月の収益はざっと200万円ほどになる This month's profit is *roughly* two million yen. / メニューにはざっと20種類ほどのカレーが出ていた There were *about* twenty kinds of curry on the menu.

さっとう 殺到 ——殺到する (駆けつける) rush into [to] ...; (押し寄せる) pour in, flood ‖大勢の買い物客がそのデパート(のドア)に殺到した A crowd of customers *rushed* 「*into* the department store [*to* the door]. / 彼女の新曲へのリクエストがラジオ局に殺到した Requests for her new single *flooded* into the radio station.
◆その新型コンピュータに注文が殺到している *There's a rush* [*flood*] of orders for the new model of the computer.

ざっとう 雑踏 (混雑) congestion; (人込み) crowd ‖雑踏に巻き込まれる be caught in *the crowd* / 都会の雑踏 the hustle and bustle of the city

ざつねん 雑念 雑念を取り払う push [throw] *distracting thoughts* out of *one's* mind

さつばつ 殺伐 殺伐とした風景 dreary [bleak] scenery / 世紀末の殺伐とした世相 *the turbulence* of the end of the century

さっぱり
❶【全く】(全然…でない) (not) at all; (完全に) completely
フランス語はさっぱり話せません I *can't* speak French *at all*.
そんなことはきれいさっぱり忘れていた I had *completely* forgotten about that.
◆私には何が何だかさっぱり分からない I have *absolutely* no idea. / 開店当初そのレストランの客の入りはさっぱりだった(→客はほとんど入らなかった) There were *very few* customers when the restaurant was first opened.

❷【爽やかな】(味が) light, plain; (身なりが) neat and clean; (性格が) frank, open-minded
この肉はさっぱりした味のソースをかけるとおいしい This meat tastes good with a *light* sauce.
彼はさっぱりした性格だ He is a *frank* person.
◆あの姉妹はいつもさっぱりした格好をしている Those sisters are always dressed *neatly*. / ジョギングの後は気分がさっぱりする I feel *refreshed* after jogging.

💬 「何かさっぱりした物が食べたいな」「じゃあ，そばにしようか」 "I want to eat *something light*." "How about some *soba* [buckwheat noodles], then?"

ざっぴ 雑費 miscellaneous expenses

さつびら 札びら [慣用表現] 彼は世界中で札びらを切って(→惜しげなく金を使って)絵画を買いあさっている He *spends money freely and lavishly* in his hunt for paintings all over the world.

さっぷうけい 殺風景 (荒涼とした) bleak, desolate; (がらんとした) bare ‖殺風景な部屋 a *bare* room / 殺風景な眺め a *bleak* view

ざつぶん 雑文 miscellaneous writings; (随筆) essay

さつまいも 薩摩芋 sweet potato

ざつむ 雑務 (はんぱな仕事) odd jobs; (ちょっとしたこと) small things, trivialities ‖雑務に追われてなかなか自分の仕事に集中できない I'm kept busy with *trivialities* and can't concentrate on my own job.

ざつよう 雑用 (家庭の) chores ‖雑用をする do *the chores*

さつりく 殺戮 massacre

さて well, now ‖さて，そろそろ始めようか *Well*, shall we start now? / さて，もう帰らなくては *Well*, I must be leaving now.

さてい 査定 assessment ——査定する assess ‖査定価格 assessed value

さておき 冗談はさてさておそろそろ本題に入りましょうか *Joking aside* [*apart*], shall we get down to business now? / さておき(→差し当たって)私たちにできることをやろう Let's do what we can *for now*. / 彼の問題はさておき(→別にして)それにどのくらい費用がかかるのだろうか *Apart* [(主に米) *Aside*] *from* his problem, how much will it cost?

さては さてはあいつ逃げたな(→逃げたにちがいない) He *must* have run away. / さてはやつのしわざだったんだ *So*, it was him who did that.

サテライト satellite ‖サテライトスタジオ a satellite studio

さと 里 ❶【村】village ‖クマが里に下りてきた A bear came down to *the village*.
❷【生まれた所】(出身地) hometown; (実家) one's parents' home ‖妻は今出産のため里に帰っています My wife *is now staying at her parents' home* to have a baby.

さといも 里芋 taro (複 ~s)

さとう 砂糖 sugar ❖スプーンで何杯などというときには
角砂糖2個 two lumps [cubes] of sugar
私は紅茶には砂糖を入れません I don't take *sugar* in my tea.

ドーナツは油で揚げて砂糖をまぶしてあるから太るよ Donuts are fattening because they are deep-fried and *dusted with sugar*.
砂糖を取りすぎないようにしなさい Don't take too much *sugar*.
◆砂糖の入っていない清涼飲料 *sugar-free soft drinks*
🖋「コーヒーにお砂糖は入れますか」「はい、2つお願いします」 "Would you like *sugar* in your coffee?" "Yes, two please."
∥砂糖入れ a *sugar bowl* / 砂糖きび a *sugar cane* / 砂糖大根 a *sugar beet* / 氷砂糖《米》*rock candy*,《英》*rock sugar* / 白[黒]砂糖 *refined [brown] sugar*

さどう¹ 作動 ──作動する work ⊕, operate ⊕, run* ⊕; (始動する) start ⊕ ∥機械は順調に作動している The machine *is working [operating, running]* well. / 僕のパソコンが作動しないんだ My PC *doesn't work*. / やっとエンジンが作動した The engine *started* at last. ◆作業員は機械を作動させた The factory worker *turned* the machine *on*. / The factory worker *started* the machine.

さどう² 茶道

茶道、あるいは茶の湯は茶をたて、客にすすめ、味わう洗練された茶の芸術です。簡素な美と閑寂な趣を貴ぶ「わび」の精神を追求した千利休によって16世紀に完成しました。茶道の本質は、作法そのものよりも、繊細な美を味わい、静寂の中での人との交流を通じて精神性を向上させることです。
Sado, or the tea ceremony (also called *chado* or *chanoyu*), is the sophisticated art of tea preparation, serving and drinking. It was perfected in the 16th century by Sen no Rikyu, who pursued the idea of *wabi*, which lays stress on beauty in simplicity and tranquil elegance. The essence of *sado* lies in the elevation of the spirit through aesthetic sensitivity and social interchange in a calm atmosphere rather than in the technique itself.

さとおや 里親 foster parent ⊂; (父親) foster father ⊂; (母親) foster mother ⊂

さとがえり 里帰り 彼の奥さんは子供たちを連れて里帰りした His wife *went home* with their children *to see her parents*.

さとご 里子 foster child ⊂; (息子) foster son ⊂; (娘) foster daughter ⊂ ◆里子に出す *send one's child to foster parents*

さとす 諭す (注意する)《公式的》admonish ⊕; (納得させる) persuade ⊕; (理を説く) reason with ... ∥祖母は孫娘の不作法を諭した The grandmother *admonished* her granddaughter *for* her misbehavior. / 先生は学校を続けるようにその生徒を諭した The teacher *persuaded* [*reasoned with*] the student to stay on at school.

さとり 悟り (禅の) satori ⊔, spiritual enlightenment [awakening] ⊔ ∥男は悟りを開くためにインドの山奥へ行った The man left for the heart of the mountains in India to *attain spiritual enlightenment*.

さとる 悟る (認識する) realize ⊕, become* aware (of ...); (理解する) understand* ⊕; (感づく) sense ⊕ ∥自分がどんなに未熟かを悟ったよ I've *realized* how immature I am. / やっと祖父の言葉の意味を悟った I could finally *understand* the words my grandfather said to me. / 彼女は危険を悟った She *sensed* danger. ◆彼はいかにも悟った(→すべてを知っている)ようなことを言う He talks like he *knows everything*.

サドル (座席) seat ⊂, saddle ⊂ ∥自転車のサドルを高くする[低くする] raise [lower] *the bicycle seat*

さなか 最中 夏のさなかに *in the middle of summer* ∥この忙しいさなか(→忙しいときに)次々と来客があった I had guests one after another *when* I was very busy.

さながら 夜空の星はさながら宝石のようだ The stars in the night sky *look like* jewels.

さなぎ 蛹 (昆虫の) pupa [pjúːpə] ⊂ (複 pupae, ~s); (チョウ類の) chrysalis ⊕ (複 chrysalides, ~es)

サナトリウム (療養所) sanatorium ⊂ (複 ~s, sanatoria)

さは 左派 (革新的な党派) the left (wing); (人) leftist ⊂

さば 鯖 mackerel ⊂ (複 ~, ~s) 慣用表現 彼女は3、4歳はさばを読んでいる(→年をごまかしている)はずだ I believe she *fudges (the count) on* her age by three or four years. / (→若く言っている) I believe she *gives her age as* three or four years *younger than she really is*.

さばき 裁き judgment ⊔,《英》judgement ⊔; (決定) decision ⊔ ∥彼はその犯罪者に公平な裁きを下した He *passed* fair *judgment* on the criminal. ◆彼は厳しい裁きを受けるべきだ He should *be judged* [*tried*] strictly.

さばく¹ 砂漠 desert ⊂⊔ ∥サハラ砂漠 the Sahara (*Desert*)
∥砂漠化 desertification / 砂漠化緑化 desert reclamation

さばく² 捌く (処理する) deal* with ...; (巧みに扱う) handle ⊕; (解決する) settle ⊕; (売る) sell* ⊕ ∥たくさんの商品をさばく *sell* a lot of products / 彼はその難問をうまくさばいた He *handled* [*dealt with*, *settled*] the difficult problem successfully.
◆(野球で)フライをさばく *field* a fly ball / 魚をさばく *clean* a fish

さばく³ 裁く judge ⊕; (裁判にかける) try ⊕; (判決を下す) pass judgment (on ...) ∥人が人を裁くことは本当に正しいのだろうか Can a person really *pass judgment* on other people? / わが社の社長は脱税で裁かれた Our president *was tried* for tax evasion.

さばけた 捌けた (世慣れた) worldly-wise; (率直な) frank ∥彼はとてもさばけた人だ He is a really *worldly-wise* person.

さばける 捌ける (売れる) be sold; (売り切れる) be sold out

さばさば 言いたいことを言ってさばさばした(→胸につかえていたことを打ち明けてさっぱりした) I felt *relieved* as I got it off my chest. / 彼女はさばさばした(→くよくよしない)人だ She is a person who *never niggles*.

サバンナ savanna(h)◯

さび¹ 錆 rust ◯ ‖さびがつく gather *rust* / 自転車のさびをこすって落とす rub *the rust* off a bicycle
慣用表現 それは身から出たさびだ(→自業自得だ) You *asked for it*.(⬥ask for it で「自ら災難を招く」の意味) / It's *your own fault*.

さび² 寂 (俳句の) *sabi*, the tranquil, restrained aesthetic sensibility that is fundamental to the haiku of Matsuo Basho and others

さびしい 寂しい・淋しい

(人・場所が) lonely, 《主に米》lonesome; (人けのない) deserted
寂しい思いをする feel *lonely* / 寂しい暮らしを送る lead a *lonely* life
寂しい通りは歩かないようにしなさい You shouldn't walk on *deserted* streets.
私は恥ずかしがり屋で友達がいなくて寂しい I'm *lonely* because I'm shy and have no friends.
◆ (私たちは)あなたがいなくなると寂しくなります We *will miss* you.
🗨「この格好、どう」「うーん、首元がちょっと寂しいね。スカーフでも巻いてみたら？」"How do I look?" "Well, it looks a little *too bare* around the neck. Why don't you put on a scarf or something?"

さびしがり(や) 寂しがり(屋)・淋しがり(屋) 彼女は寂しがり屋だ(→いつもだれかにいっしょにいてもらいたがる) She *always wants company*. / (→ひとりでいるのをいやがる)She *doesn't like to be alone*.

さびしがる 寂しがる・淋しがる (寂しく思う) feel* lonely; (いない人を) miss⊕ ‖子供たちは母親がいなくて寂しがっている The children *miss* their mother.

さびつく 錆び付く (さびる) rust ⊕, get* rusty; (さびで動かなくなる) be stuck with rust; (能力などが) be rusty ‖はさみがさびついた The scissors *have gotten rusty*. / 雨戸がさびついて動かない The shutter *is stuck with rust*. / 大学でロシア語をやったけれどもさびついしまった I studied Russian in college, but it's *rusty* now.

さびどめ 錆止め rustproofing ◯; (さび止め剤) rust preventive ◯◯

ざひょう 座標 〖数学〗coordinate ◯
‖座標軸 a coordinate axis / 縦座標 the ordinate / 横座標 the abscissa [æbsísə]

さびる 錆びる rust ⊕, get* [become*] rusty ‖この包丁はすぐさびる This cooking knife *rusts* [*gets rusty*] easily. / ちょうつがいはさびてぼろぼろだ The hinge *has rusted away*.

さびれる さびれた(→人口が減少した)村 a *depopulated* village

サファイア sapphire ◯

サファリ safari ◯◯ ‖サファリジャケット a safari jacket / サファリパーク an animal park, a safari park

ざぶざぶ このスニーカーは水でざぶざぶ(→水の中でぱしゃぱしゃ動かして) 洗える You can wash these sneakers by *sloshing* them in water. / 彼はジーパンのすそをまくり上げてざぶざぶと川に入っていった He rolled up his jeans and *splashed* into the river.

サブタイトル (副題) subtitle ◯ (⬥複数形 subtitles には「字幕」の意味があるので注意)

ざぶとん 座布団 a *zabuton*, a small square cushion used for sitting on a *tatami* mat

サフラン 〖植物〗saffron ◯◯

ざぶり 頭から水をざぶりとかぶった I *poured* water over my head.

サブリミナル ‖サブリミナル効果 subliminal effects

ざぶん 彼は水の中にざぶんと(→水をはね上げて)飛び込んだ He jumped into the water *with a splash*.

さべつ 差別 discrimination ◯ ――差別する discriminate ⊕ ――差別的な discriminatory ➡ むさべつ
その国にはまだ少数民族に対する差別がある There still exists *discrimination* against minorities in the country.
雇用差別をなくすために彼らは立ち上がった They took action to stop *discrimination in employment*.
肌の色で人を差別してはいけない You must not *discriminate against* people by (their) skin color.
◆ 教師は生徒を差別なく(→平等に) 扱うべきだ Teachers should treat their students *equally*.
‖差別語 a discriminatory word, discriminatory language / 逆差別 reverse discrimination / 宗教差別 religious discrimination / 人種差別 racial discrimination / 性差別 sexual discrimination, sexism / 年齢差別 age discrimination (特に高齢者差別) ageism, agism

さほう 作法 (行儀) manners; (礼儀) etiquette ◯ ➡ ぶさほう ‖彼の無作法にいらいらした I was irritated by his *bad manners*. / 彼女の作法は上品だった Her *manners* were refined. / 母は食事の作法にやかましい My mother is strict about *table manners*.

サポーター (支持者) fan, supporter ◯; (スポーツ用の) supporter ◯; (男子選手用の) athletic supporter ◯, 《口語的》jockstrap ◯ ‖ひじにサポーターをする wear *a supporter* on the elbow

サボタージュ ⚠(怠業) 《米》slowdown ◯, 《英》go-slow ◯ ――サボタージュする 《米》go* on a slowdown (strike), 《英》go slow (⬥日本語はフランス語のsabotageから. ただし sabotage は本来「破壊活動, 妨害工作」の意味)

サボテン cactus 《複 ～es, cacti》

さほど さほど気にする必要はない You don't

サボる (学校・授業を) cut*, skip, play truant, 《主に米・口語的》play hooky; (仕事を) shirk, 《怠ける》be lazy, 《口語的》goof off; (逃れる) 《口語的》dodge ❖「サボる」は「サボタージュ」が転じたもの // 学校[会議, 英語の授業]をサボる cut [skip] school [a meeting, an English class] / 彼はいつもうまいこと自分の仕事をサボる He always manages to *dodge* his tasks. / サボっていないでさっさとやりなさい Stop *goofing off* and get to work right now.

ザボン 〖植物〗shaddock, pomelo (複 ~s)

さま 様 その新しいスーツ、さまになってるよ (→似合っている) You *look nice* in that new suit. / 彼女の満足しているさまが (→いかに満足しているかが) 目に浮かぶ I can imagine *how* satisfied she is.

🔴「スケートをするのは初めてなんだ」「初めてにしてはさまになってるよ(→上手だ)」"This is my first time to skate." "You're very good for a beginner."

-さま -様 (男性) Mr.; (女性) Ms.; (既婚女性) Mrs.; (未婚女性) Miss ➪ -さん

◆お母様によろしくお伝えください Please give my best regards to *your mother*. / 自分を何様だと思ってるんだ Who do you think you are? / おれを無視するとは何様のつもりだ Who are you to ignore me?

ざま ざまあ見ろ (→当然の報いだ) Serves you right! / なんてざまだ What *a sight* you are! / (→恥を知れ) Shame on you!

サマータイム 《米》daylight saving(s) time, 《略語》DST), 《主に英》summer time

さまがわり 様変わり 私の故郷はすっかり様変わりしてしまった My hometown *has completely changed*.

さまざま 様々 ――様々な various; (異なった) different // 様々な角度から問題を検討する examine a problem from *different* angles / 彼は様々な困難を克服した He overcame *various* difficulties.

◆様々な(→たくさんの)うわさが飛び交っていた There were *a lot of* rumors going around. / この図書館には様々な(→幅広い)分野の本がそろっている This library has *a wide variety of* books.

さます 覚ます・醒ます (目を) wake* up, awake*, awaken; (酔いを) sober up

けさは電話の音で目をさました This morning, I *woke up* to the sound of the telephone.

酔いをさますにはこの薬を飲むといいですよ This medicine will help *sober* you *up*.

慣用表現 彼女はつらい目にあってやっと目をさました She finally *woke up* after a painful experience.

さます² 冷ます (温度を下げる) cool; (興味・熱意をそぐ) spoil*, dampen // お茶が熱すぎたのでしばらく冷ました The tea was too hot, so I *cooled it off* for a while.

さまたげ 妨げ (障害) obstacle, hindrance // それは助けというよりむしろ妨げになるだろう It will *be more of a hindrance than a help*. / 資金不足が私たちの計画の大きな妨げとなった Lack of money was *a major obstacle* to our plan.

さまたげる 妨げる (じゃまする) disturb; (遅らせる) hinder; (進行・視界などを) obstruct; (不可能にする) prevent // 眠りを妨げる *disturb one's* sleep / 粗食は子供の自然な発育を妨げることがある A poor diet can *hinder* the natural growth of a child. / スキャンダルが彼の出世を妨げた The scandal *prevented* him *from* getting a promotion [his promotion]. / 濃い霧が視界を妨げた A thick fog *obstructed* our view.

さまつな 瑣末な trivial, trifling

さまよう さ迷う wander; (ぶらつく) roam; (放浪する) drift // 世界中をさまよう *roam around* the world / 私は森の中をさまよった I *wandered through* the woods.

◆生死の境をさまよう *hover between life and death*

さみしい 寂しい・淋しい (孤独な) lonely; (人けのない) deserted ➪ さびしい

さみしがり(や) 寂しがり(屋)・淋しがり(屋) ➪ さびしがり(や)

さみだれ 五月雨 early summer rain

俳句 五月雨をあつめて早し最上川(松尾芭蕉)
Early summer rain
in a hurry to rush on:
Mogami River

サミット (先進国首脳会議) summit (meeting) // ジェノバ・サミット the Genoa Summit (Meeting) ❖この場合は通例大文字で始める)

さむい 寒い

cold; (凍りつくように寒い) freezing; (うすら寒い) chilly

ひどく寒い天候 bitter *cold* weather

だんだん寒くなってきている It's *getting colder and colder*.

10月にしては寒いと思いませんか Don't you think it is *cold* for October?

この寒い中、外にいてはいけません Don't stay out *in this cold weather*.

山頂は凍りつくように寒かった It was *freezing cold* at the top of the mountain.

🔴「寒くない？」「そんなに」"Aren't you cold? / Don't you feel cold?" "Not really."

短歌 「寒いね」と話しかければ「寒いね」と答える人のいるあたたかさ(俵万智)
"Brrr! It's cold!" I say
to start a conversation.
"Yes, it is," he says,
"It's really cold." And I feel
the warmth of someone nearby.

さむがり 寒がり 彼はとても寒がりだ He's very *sensitive to* cold.

さむけ 寒気 chill ❖主に病気からくるもの)

◆けさは寒けがする I *feel chilly* this morning. / そのことを考えただけで寒けがする Just the thought of it *gives me the shivers*.

さむさ 寒さ cold ◻; (寒い天候) cold weather ◻; (寒け) chill ◻ ‖寒さに震える shiver [shudder] with *cold* / 寒さが身にしみた *The cold* pierced me to the bone. / このジャケットは厳しい寒さから身を守るように作られている This jacket is designed to protect against severe *cold*. / こんな寒さの中泳ぐなんてばかげている It is absurd of you to swim in this *cold weather*.

さむざむ 寒々 寒々とした冬の空 a dreary [bleak] winter sky / その小屋は寒々とした丘に立っていた The hut stood on a *bleak* hill.

さむらい 侍 🔍 samurai ◻, (Japanese) warrior ◻

さめ 鮫 shark ◻ ‖さめ肌 rough skin

さめる¹ 覚める・醒める
❶【眠りから】wake* up; awake*; waken ㊥, awaken ㊥
| wake up: 最もふつうの言い方.
| awake: 特に「目がさめる」の意味で書き言葉でよく用いられる.
| waken, awaken: 特に「目をさまさせる」の意味で使われるかたい語.

夢からさめる *awake* from a dream
私は笑い声で目がさめた I *woke up* to the sound of laughter.
濃いコーヒーを飲めば目もさめるだろう A cup of strong coffee *would wake* you *up*.
◆そのころにはすっかり目がさめていた By then I *was* wide *awake*.
❷【迷いから】(正気に戻る) come* to *one's* senses
彼は突然迷いからさめて，熱心に勉強し始めた Suddenly he *came to his senses* and began to study hard.
❸【酔いから】sober up; get* sober
水を1杯飲めば酔いがさめるよ A glass of water *will sober* you *up*.
❹【その他】
麻酔からさめる *wake up* from the anesthesia
今の若者はさめている(→現実的だ)といわれる Young people today are said to *be very realistic*.
みんな興奮したが彼女だけさめていた(→冷静だった) Everyone got excited, but only she 「*remained calm* [*kept cool*]」.
慣用表現 寝てもさめても彼女のことを考えている I think of her *awake or asleep*. / 海は目のさめるようなエメラルドグリーンだった The sea was *vivid* emerald green.

さめる² 冷める (温度が) cool (down [off]), get* cold; (興奮などが) cool (down [off]) ‖コーヒーが冷めますよ Your coffee *is getting cold*. / スープが冷めてしまった The soup *has cooled down*. / 彼らの愛はすぐに冷めるだろう Their love will soon *cool down*.
◆彼のスポーツに対する熱意は冷めることがなかった(→熱意を失わなかった) He *never lost* his *enthusiasm* for sports.

さめる³ 褪める fade ㊥ ‖壁紙の色がすっかりさめてしまった The wallpaper *has* completely *faded*.

さも 彼はさも満足そうにその話をした He told me the story with *great* satisfaction. / 彼女はさも何か聞きたそうに私を見た She looked at me *as if* to ask something.

さもしい base, mean, low ‖全部自分の手柄にしようなんてさもしいことを考えるな Don't be so *low* as to take all the credit for yourself.

さもないと or (else)(❖or else とすると強調される), otherwise ‖動くな，さもないと撃つぞ Don't move, *or* I'll shoot. / 二度と遅刻するなよ，さもないと(ひどい目にあわせるぞ) Don't be late again, *or else*.(❖or else の後の節を省略するのと脅迫的な意味になる) / だれにも言うな，さもないと後悔するぞ Don't tell anybody, *otherwise* you'll regret it.

さや¹ 莢 pod ◻; (硬い) shell ◻ ◆豆のさやをむく *shell* peas

さや² 鞘 (剣・ナイフなどの) sheath ◻; (刀・剣の) scabbard ◻; (ナイフの) case ◻ ‖ナイフをさやに戻す put a knife back in *its sheath*
慣用表現 私たちは元のさやに収まった We got *back together again*.

さやいんげん 莢隠元 《米》 string [green] bean ◻, 《英》 runner [French] bean ◻

ざやく 座薬 suppository ◻ ‖座薬を入れる insert *a suppository*

さゆう 左右 ❶【左と右】―左右に[へ] right and left, left and right, from side to side; (両側に) on both sides, on either side ‖彼は左右を見て通りを渡った He looked 「*right and left* [*both ways*]」, then crossed the street. / 車はでこぼこ道で左右に揺れた The car rocked *from side to side* over the rough road.
◆左右対称の図形 a *symmetrical* figure / その街路の左右には桜の木が並んでいる Cherry trees line 「*both sides* [*either side*] of the street. / 彼は音楽に合わせて体を左右に揺らした He *swayed* his body to the music.
❷【影響・決定】―左右する (影響する) influence ㊥; (支配する) rule ㊥, control ㊥; (決定する) decide ㊥ ‖幼年期の経験が人の人生観を左右する The experiences of childhood *influence* one's whole outlook on life. / 感情に左右されてはいけない *Don't let your heart rule your head*.
◆農業は天候に大きく左右される職業である Farming is a business 「*at the mercy of* [*dependent on*] the weather.

ざゆうのめい 座右の銘 私の座右の銘は人生は一度きりということです My *motto* is this: You only live once.

さよう 作用 action ◻《また an ~》; (効果) effect ◻◻; (自然の) process ◻◻; (影響) influence ◻ ㊥ ――作用する act (on …), work (on …); (直接的に) affect ㊥; (間接的に) influence ㊥
この薬は人体にすぐに作用する This medicine *acts* quickly *on* the human body.
月の引力は地球に作用する The moon's grav-

ity *exerts an influence on* the earth.
◆このせっけんには殺菌作用がある This soap *kills germs*.
‖作用反作用の法則〔物理〕the action-reaction law / 化学作用 chemical action / 消化作用 the process of digestion / 相互作用 interaction / 反作用〔物理〕reaction / 副作用 a side effect

さようなら

goodby(e), good-by(e), bye, bye-bye
🗣「山田先生，さようなら」「さようなら」*"Good-bye*, Mrs. Yamada." *"Goodbye."*

[語法]
(1) 別れのあいさつの最も一般的なものはGood-by(e)., Good-by(e).で，くだけた言い方にBye., Bye-bye.がある.
(2) また，親しい間柄ではSo long., See you soon [again, later]., Take care., Good night.（夜別れるとき）なども用いられる.

さよく 左翼（思 想）《集合的》the left (wing), the Left《単数または複数扱い》;（左翼思想の持ち主）leftist [C], left-winger [C];（野球の）left field [C];（左翼手）left fielder [C];（飛行機の）left wing [C] ―左翼の・左翼的な left, left-wing
‖左翼思想 leftism / 左翼団体 a leftist organization [party]

さよなら goodby(e), good-by(e) ∥彼女はさよならも言わないで帰っていった She went home without even saying *goodbye*. / 彼女は私たちに手を振ってさよならをした She waved us *goodbye*./ She waved *goodbye* to us.
‖さよならパーティー a farewell party / さよならホームラン[ヒット] a game-ending 「home run [hit]

さら 皿 dish [C]; platter [C]; plate [C]; saucer [C]

dish: 料理を盛るための深い皿のこと. また1皿分の料理のこともいう. さらに the dishes でナイフ・フォークを含めた食器一般を指す.
platter: 大型の盛り皿のこと.
plate: 料理を取り分けるめいめい皿のこと. また1皿分の料理のこともいう.
saucer: カップ・茶わんなどの受け皿のこと.

皿を洗う do [wash] *the dishes* / 皿の水気を切る drain *the dishes* / 皿を片づける[ふく，乾かす]「clear away [wipe, dry] *the dishes* / 皿に料理を盛りつける put food into *dishes*
私たちは野菜サラダを2皿注文した We ordered *two dishes* of vegetable salad.
‖皿洗い機 a dishwasher / 皿回し spinning plates (on a stick) / 紙皿 a paper plate / ケーキ皿 a cake plate / スープ皿 a soup plate;（深いもの）a soup bowl / 製氷皿 an ice tray / プラスチック皿 a plastic plate
[慣用表現] 彼らは手品師のマジックを目を皿のようにして見つめた They were *all eyes* as the magician did some tricks.

ざら この手の事件はその地域ではざらにある（→とてもよくある）ことだ Incidents of this kind are *very common* in that area. / 彼が遅刻するなんてざらだ（→珍しくない）It *is not unusual* for him to be late.

さらいげつ 再来月 the month after next

さらいしゅう 再来週 the week after next
◆再来週の（→次の次の）日曜日，暇？ Will you be free on the Sunday *after next*?

さらいねん 再来年 the year after next

さらう[1] 攫う（誘拐する）kidnap [他];（押し流す）carry off, wash away;（賞などを）carry off, run* [walk] away with … ∥すべての賞をさらう「*run away with* [*carry off*] all the prizes / 波にさらわれる *be washed away* by a wave
◆（思いがけない人が）人気をさらう *steal* the show / この歌はあっという間に若者の人気をさらった（→人気を呼んだ）This song *caught on with* young people in no time.

さらう[2] 浚う（網などで）drag [他];（港・川などを）dredge [他] [自];（きれいにする）clean [他] [自] ∥どぶをさらう *clean* a ditch / 警察は凶器を探して川をさらっていた The police *dragged* the river for the weapon.

サラきん サラ金（消費者金融会社[業]）consumer credit company [business] [C];（高利貸し）《軽蔑的》loan shark [C]

さらけだす 曝け出す 自分をさらけ出す *reveal one's true self*; *show one's true colors* / 試合に負けて彼の弱点がさらけ出された His weak point *was brought to light* when he lost the match.

さらさら[1] さらさらした粉 *dry* powder / さらさらと書く write *smoothly* / 林の中を小川がさらさらと流れていた A brook *was murmuring* in the woods. / 木の葉が風でさらさら音を立てた The leaves *rustled* in the wind. / 彼女の髪はさらさらしている Her hair *is smooth and silky*.

さらさら[2] あなたの言うことを聞く気などさらさらない I'm *not* going to follow you *at all*./ I *have no intention* of following you.

ざらざら ざらざらした砂 *coarse* sand / どうしてこんなに床がざらざらしているのかしら I wonder why the floor *is* so *gritty*. / 手ざわりがざらざらしている It's *rough* to the feel.

さらしもの 晒し者 私はさらし者になった（→みんなの前で恥をかかされた）I *was publicly disgraced*.

さらす 晒す expose [他] ∥危険に身をさらす

expose oneself to danger / 肌をあまり長い間日光にさらしてはだめない Don't *expose* your skin *to the sun's rays* too long. ◆非難[疑惑]に身をさらす *lay oneself (wide) open to* criticism [suspicion] / 彼はパーティーで酔っ払って恥をさらした He *got* drunk *and disgraced himself* at the party. / ジャガイモをスライスしてしばらく水にさらしなさい Slice a potato and *soak it in water* for a while.

サラダ salad ⓒⓤ ‖サラダをドレッシングで軽く和(あ)える toss *a salad* in dressing ‖サラダオイル salad oil ‖サラダサーバー a salad server / サラダドレッシング (a) salad dressing / サラダ菜 lettuce / サラダボウル a salad bowl / チキンサラダ chicken salad / ポテトサラダ potato salad
短歌「この味がいいね」と君が言ったから七月六日はサラダ記念日 (俵万智)
"This tastes really good,"
you said. And since you said it,
the sixth of July
shall now and forever be
Salad Memorial Day.

さらち 更地 (空き地) vacant lot ⓒ; (建物用) building lot ⓒ

ざらつく 机の表面がざらついている The surface of the desk *is sandy*.

さらっと (軽く) lightly; (簡単に) easily
➡さらりと

さらに 更に
❶【そのうえ・おまけに】besides, (and) what is more, in addition, 《公式的》moreover
車がパンクし、さらに雨が降りだした My car got a flat tire, *and what is more*, it started raining.
◆締め切りをさらに半年(→もう半年間)延ばす extend the deadline for *another* six months / さらにもう1つの理由がある There's *still* another reason. / 私はこの本を読んで、さらにそのレポートを書かなければならない I have to read this book, *and then* I have to write a paper on it. / 私たちはさらに1キロ川をさかのぼった We went up the river one kilometer *further*.
❷【いっそう】(比較級の強調) even, still, yet; (程度) further
(私も背が高いが)妹は私よりさらに背が高い My sister is *even* [*still*] taller than me [I].
雨はさらに強くなった The rain became *even* harder.
彼の病気はさらに悪化した(→ますます悪くなった) His illness *got even worse*.
私はその発想をさらに進めて新しい計画を立てた I carried the idea *further* and made a new plan.
警察はその事件をさらに詳しく調べた The police inquired *further* into the case.
◆これで我々はさらに困ることになるだろう(→これで困難が増すであろう) This will *add to* our difficulties.

サラブレッド thoroughbred ⓒ ‖サラブレッドの種馬 *a thoroughbred* stallion / 彼は相撲界のサラブレッドだ He's *a thoroughbred* in the sumo world.

サラミ salami [səlάːmi] ⓒⓤ

サラリー salary ⓒⓤ, pay ⓤ

サラリーマン ⚠salaried worker ⓒ (❖「サラリーマン」は和製英語。salaried workerは「月給をもらって働く人」の意味だが、あまり一般的ではない); (会社員) company employee ⓒ, office worker ⓒ; (頭脳労働者) white-collar worker ⓒ

さらりと さらりとした布 *smooth* texture / 彼女はその質問をさらりと(→巧みに)かわした She evaded the question *skillfully*. / 彼はその仕事をさらりと(→いとも簡単に)こなした He carried out the task *easily* [*without difficulty*]. / 先生はそのことについてさらりと(→なにげなく)触れただけだった Our teacher just made *passing* reference to that matter.

ざりがに crayfish ⓒ, 《米》crawfish ⓒ

さりげない さり気ない、さりげなく (→間接的に) そのことに言及する refer to the matter *indirectly* / さりげなく彼の本心を聞き出そうとした I *casually* tried to draw out his real intention. / 彼女はいつもさりげない(→控えめな) おしゃれを心がけている She always tries to dress *in an understated way*.

サリン sarin (gas) ⓤ ‖地下鉄サリン事件 the *nerve gas* attack on the Tokyo subway system

さる¹ 去る
(場所・人のもとを) leave* ⓗⓘ; (会社・職などを) resign ⓗⓘ; (引退する) retire ⓗ; (通り過ぎる) pass ⓗⓘ, be over
ほとんどの人が村を去り、今では30人しか残っていない Most people *left* the village and now only 30 remain.
どういうわけか彼は突然私たちのもとから去った For some reason he suddenly *left* us.
彼女は家庭の事情で会社を去った She *left* [*resigned (from)*] the company for family reasons.
そのテニスプレーヤーは30歳でコートを去った (→引退した) The tennis player *retired* when he was 30.
あらしは去った The storm 「*is over* [*has passed*].
◆彼女のお母さんは去年この世を去った Her mother *passed away* last year. (❖pass away は die の婉曲的表現) / その式典は去る (→この前の) 8月に行われた The ceremony was held *last* August.
ことわざ 去るものは日々にうとし Out of sight, out of mind. (→視界からなくなると記憶からもなくなる)

さる² 猿 monkey ⓒ; (類人猿) ape ⓒ (❖チンパンジー・ゴリラなど) ‖猿たちが木の上でうるさく鳴いていた *The monkeys* were chattering noisily in the tree.
◆そんな猿芝居(→浅はかなたくらみ)にはだれもだまされないよ No one will be deceived by *shallow tricks* like that.
ことわざ 猿も木から落ちる Even a monkey sometimes falls from a tree.; Nobody's

perfect.(→完璧(%)な人間はいない)
俳句 初しぐれ猿も小蓑(%)をほしげなり(松尾芭蕉)
The first winter rain.
Even the poor monkeys want
raincoats of their own.
さる[3] 申 (十二支の第9番目) the Monkey
⇒申

ざる 笊 (水切り) bamboo [plastic] colander ◎ ‖研(%)いだ米をざるにあげる drain rice in a *bamboo [plastic] colander* after washing ‖ざる法 a law full of loopholes(❖loophole は「抜け穴」の意味)

さるぐつわ 猿ぐつわ gag ◎ ◆彼はその女性にさるぐつわをはめて自分の部屋に監禁していた He *had gagged* the woman and confined her in his room.

さるすべり 百日紅 〔植物〕 crape [crepe] myrtle ◎

ざるそば 笊蕎麦 *zarusoba*, cold buckwheat noodles served on a wicker plate made of bamboo ⇒そば(蕎麦)

ザルツブルグ Salzburg(❖オーストリアの都市)

サルビア (観賞用) salvia ◎◎; (薬用) sage ◎◎

サルベージ salvage ◎ ‖サルベージ船 a salvage boat

さるまね 猿真似 slavish imitation ◎◎ ‖彼の作品は漱石の猿まねだと非難された His work was criticized as *a slavish imitation* of Soseki.

-ざるをえない -ざるを得ない have* to *do*, be forced [compelled] to *do*; (…せずにはいられない) cannot help *doing*, cannot help but *do* ‖雨のためにピクニックを中止せざるをえなかった Because of the rain, we 「*were forced to* [*had to*] call off the picnic. / 彼女がうそをついていると考えざるをえない We *can't help thinking* that she's lying.

-される
❶ (受身)
歓迎会に招待された I *was* [*got*] *invited* to the reception.
その事実は彼女の死後に公にされた The fact *was made public* after her death.
数名の志願者が不合格にされた Several applicants *were rejected*.
風で帽子が飛ばされた I *had* my hat *blown off* by the wind. (❖×I was blown off my hat by the wind. とはいわない)
❷ (尊敬)
浜田さんは毎日夜遅くまで仕事をされています Mr. Hamada *works* very late every day.(❖英語には「される」に当たる特に決まった敬語表現はない)
⇒れる

サロン salon ◎; (客間・応接室) reception room [hall] ◎

さわ 沢 (湿地) marsh ◎◎ (複 ~, ~es), swamp ◎◎; (谷川) mountain stream ◎

さわがしい 騒がしい noisy ‖なんて騒がしい所なんだ What a *noisy* place! / 部屋はとても騒がしかったので彼に向かってどならなければならなかった I had to shout at him because it was very *noisy* in the room.

さわがせる 騒がせる ‖そのニュースは世間を大いに騒がせた(→センセーションを巻き起こした) The news *caused* [*produced*] *a great sensation*. / お騒がせしました(→迷惑をかけてすみません) I'm sorry to have troubled you.

さわぎ 騒ぎ
❶【騒々しいこと】(騒音) noise ◎◎; (大騒ぎ) fuss ◎《しばしば a ~》
あの騒ぎは何だ What's that *fuss* about?
そう大騒ぎするな Don't make such a *fuss*.
隣の部屋の騒ぎはしばらくすると収まった The *noise* in the next room stopped after a while.
❷【騒動・混乱】(面倒) trouble ◎《また複数形 ~s》; (混乱) confusion ◎; (大騒ぎ) uproar ◎《また an ~》
騒ぎに巻き込まれる get involved in *trouble*
また君は学校で騒ぎを起こしたらしいね I hear you *got into trouble* at school again.
君の不注意がこんな騒ぎを引き起こしたんだぞ Your carelessness caused this *confusion*.
その知らせに私たちのクラスは大騒ぎだった Our class *was in an uproar* over the news.
❸【その他】
試験勉強が忙しくてスキーに行くどころの騒ぎではない(→スキーに行く暇などない) I'm *too busy* preparing for the exam *to go* skiing.
外は寒いどころの騒ぎじゃない(→凍るほど寒い) It is *freezing* cold outside.

さわぐ 騒ぐ make* (a) noise; (小さなことで騒ぎたてる) make a fuss, fuss ◎
騒ぐのはやめなさい Stop *making noise*.
騒ぐほどのことじゃないよ It's not worth *making a fuss (over)*.
何を騒いでるんだ What *are* you *fussing* about?
◆試験も終わったことだし、きょうは思いきり騒ごうよ Since the exams are over, let's *enjoy ourselves* to our hearts' content. / 人々は市長の辞職を求めて騒いだ People *clamored for* the resignation of the mayor.(❖clamor for [against] …は、「声高に…を要求する[…に反対する]の意味」) / 父も若いころは女の子たちに騒がれた(→人気があった) My father *was popular with* girls when he was young.
慣用表現 ボクシングの試合を見て血が騒いだ(→興奮した) I *got excited* at the boxing match. / 彼のいつもと違う真剣な表情を見て胸が騒いだ(→不安になった) I *felt uneasy* looking at his unusually serious expression.

ざわざわ ざわざわした街は嫌いだ I don't like a *noisy* city. / 木の葉が風にざわざわと音を立てた The leaves *rustled* in the wind.

ざわつく 彼が入ってくると教室はざわついた The classroom *buzzed* as he came in.

ざわめく 会場は興奮でざわめいていた The hall *was buzzing with* excitement. / 隣の部屋から人のざわめく声が聞こえた I heard *the hum* of conversation in the next room.

さわやか 爽やか ——さわやかな refreshing, fresh /朝のさわやかな空気を胸いっぱいに(→深く)吸い込んだ I breathed in the morning *fresh* air deeply. / けさはさわやかな気分だ I feel *fresh* this morning.
◆彼女は弁舌さわやかな(→話しぶりが流暢な)人だ She is *a fluent* [(→雄弁な) *an eloquent*] *speaker*. / 彼女はとてもさわやかだ(→感じがいい) She's very *pleasant*. / 彼はさわやかな笑顔で私の方へやってきた He came to me with a *pleasant* [*sunny*] *smile*. / きょうはとてもさわやかな顔をしてるよ You look very *refreshed* today. / 熱いシャワーを浴びてさわやかな気分になった A nice hot shower *refreshed* me.

さわり 触り (最も印象的なところ) the most impressive part; (最も重要なところ) the high point

さわる 触る・障る
❶【接触する】 touch 他, feel* 他; (勝手にいじる) meddle 自
アイロンにさわっちゃだめよ, 熱いから *Don't touch* the iron; it's hot.
彼は熱があるかどうか額にさわってみた He *felt* his brow to see if he had a fever.
大理石はさわるとつるつるしている Marble *feels* smooth. / Marble is smooth *to the touch.*
私のコンピュータにさわるな Don't *meddle* with my computer.
さわらないでください 《掲示》*Don't Touch*; *Hands Off*
◆コンピュータに初めてさわった(→使った) I *used* a computer for the first time.
❷【害する】 (傷つける) hurt* 他; (怒らせる) offend 他
彼女のなにげない言葉が彼の気にさわった Her casual words 「*hurt* his feelings [*offended* him].
◆その音が気にさわった The noise *got on my nerves.* / たばこを吸いすぎると体にさわりますよ Too much smoking *is harmful to your health.*
ことわざ さわらぬ神にたたりなし ⇨かみ(神)

さわん 左腕 《米》southpaw /(❖《英》では左利きのボクサーを指す), left-hander C, left-handed pitcher C, (主に米・口語的) lefty C

さん¹ 三 three; (3番目) third /三人称《文法》the third person / 第三者 a third party

さん² 酸 【化学】 acid U C

さん² 桟 (戸・障子の骨) frame; (戸締まり用) bolt

-さん¹
(男性) Mr.; (女性) Ms. [míz]; (既婚女性) Mrs.; (未婚女性) Miss

語法
(1) 姓名または姓の前に付けるが, 名前だけの場合には用いない ∥ ○*Ms.* Yamada Yuri / ○*Ms.* Yamada / ×*Ms.* Yuri
(2) 親しい間柄にはふつう敬称を付けずに名前で呼ぶ ∥ May I speak to Masao? (電話で)正夫さん, いらっしゃいますか
(3) Mr., Ms., Mrs.の語末のピリオドは《英》では置かれることが多い.
(4) Ms.は女性が既婚か未婚か分からない場合, あるいは既婚・未婚を問題にしたくない場合に用いる.

金田さん夫妻 *Mr. and Mrs.* Kaneda / 木田さんと水田さん *Mr.* Kida and *Mr.* Mizuta; *Messrs.* Kida and Mizuta

-さん² 産 /山梨産のブドウ grapes *from Yamanashi* / チリ産のワイン *Chilean* wine / 外国産[国内産]の小麦 *foreign-grown* [*home-grown*] wheat

-さん³ -山 Mount (❖山の名の前に付ける; 《略語》Mt.) /富士山 *Mt.* [*Mount*] Fuji

さんいん 産院 maternity hospital [home, clinic] C

さんか¹ 参加 participation U, entry C U ——参加する take* part (in ...), 《公式的》 participate (in ...); (組織・活動などに) join (in ...) (❖join in は組織などではなく, 活動・行為に加わる場合のみに用いる); (競技・コンテストなどに) enter 他 自; (競争する) compete (in ...)
平和維持活動への参加 participation *in* a peacekeeping operation / 競技への参加 *entry to* a competition
ほとんどの学生がその会議に参加した Almost all the students 「*took part* [*participated*] *in* the meeting.
彼女はツアーに参加しないと言った She told me that she *wouldn't join* (*in*) the tour.
彼は快くボランティアのグループに参加した He *joined* the volunteer group with pleasure.
彼は生徒会活動に積極的に参加した He *took* an active *part in* the student council activities.
彼女はそのレースに参加した She *entered* the race. / She *competed in* the race.
勝つことではなく参加することに意義がある It's not the winning that is important, it's *taking part*.
◆自由参加競技 an *open* competition / 育児に参加する *share in* child care
∥参加校 a participating school / 参加国 a participating country / 参加者 a participant; (競争・競技などへの) an entrant, an entry / 参加賞 a prize for participation

さんか² 産科 obstetrics U ——産科の obstetric /産科の看護婦 an *obstetric* nurse
∥産科医 an obstetrician / 産科病棟[病院] a maternity ward [hospital]

さんか³ 傘下 ——傘下の (従属する) subsidiary; (提携した) 《公式的》affiliated /彼の会社はその巨大企業の傘下に入った His company became 「*subsidiary to* [*affiliated with*] the gigantic company.

さんか⁴ 酸化 【化学】 oxidation U ——酸化する[させる] oxidize 自 他 ∥酸化鉄 iron oxide / 酸化物 (an) oxide / 一酸化炭素 carbon monoxide / 二酸化炭素 carbon dioxide

さんか⁵ 賛歌 a song of praise, anthem C,

hymn

さんが 参賀 a *sanga*, a visit to the Imperial Palace to celebrate a particular event or day

さんかい¹ 山海 山海の珍味 delicacies *taken from mountains and seas*

さんかい² 散会 議会は6時に散会となった The assembly 「*broke up* [*closed, ended*] at 6 o'clock.

さんがい 三階 《米》the third floor [story], 《英》the second floor [storey] ⇒ かい (階) // 彼はアパートの3階に住んでいる He lives on *the third floor* of the apartment. ♦ 3 階建ての家 a *three-story* [*three-storied*] house

ざんがい 残骸 wreck ⓒ, wreckage Ⓤ; (残った部分) the remains //墜落機の残骸 *the wreckage* [*wreck*] of a crashed plane

さんかいき 三回忌 the second anniversary of *a person's* death; (法要) a memorial service held on the second anniversary of *a person's* death

さんかく¹ 三角 (三角形) triangle ⓒ ――三角の triangular ⇒ ずけい 図説
ハンカチを三角に折る fold a handkerchief into *a triangle* [*triangular shape*]
♦ 彼は逆三角形の体つきをしている He has a *V-shaped* torso.
‖三角関係 a love triangle, 《英》an eternal triangle / 三角関数〔数学〕trigonometric functions / 三角定規《米》a triangle, 《英》a set square / 三角州 a delta / 三角すい a triangular pyramid / 三角柱 a triangular prism / 正三角形 an equilateral triangle / 直角三角形《米》a right [《英》right-angled] triangle / 二等辺三角形 an isosceles triangle

さんかく² 参画 ――参画する take* part in ..., (公式的) participate ⓘ, join in ... // その企画に参画する「*take part* [*participate, join*] in the project

さんがく 山岳 mountain ⓒ; (高い山々) high mountains //その部族はタイ北部の山岳地帯に住んでいる The tribe lives in *the mountain* [*mountainous*] *district* of Northern Thailand.
‖山岳信仰 the worship of mountains / 山岳部 a mountaineering [an alpine] club

ざんがく 残額 (分割払いなどの未払い分) the remainder《単数または複数扱い》; (残高) the balance //借金の残額を支払う pay *the remainder* of one's debt

さんがつ 三月 March Ⓤ ⓒ ((略語)Mar.) ⇒ いちがつ

さんがにち 三箇日 the first three days of a new year ⇒ しょうがつ

さんかん¹ 山間 山間の小さな村 a small village *surrounded by mountains* // 山間部では大雪となった There was a heavy snowfall in *mountainous areas*.

さんかん² 参観 visit ⓒ ――参観する visit ⓘ; (観察する) observe ⓘ //きょうは教育委員による授業参観がある Today the members of the Board of Education are scheduled to observe our classes.
‖参観者 a visitor / 授業参観日 Parents' Day, class observation day (❖class observation day は説明的な訳. 米国は学校によって呼び方が異なる)

さんかんおう 三冠王 the Triple Crown //三冠王になる win [get] *the Triple Crown*

さんぎいん 参議院 the House of Councilors (❖公式の英語名は Councillors) ‖参議院議員 a member of the House of Councilors / 参議院議長 the President of the House of Councilors

さんきゃく 三脚 tripod [tráipəd] ⓒ

ざんぎゃく 残虐 ――残虐な atrocious, cruel ♦ 彼らは幾多の残虐行為を受けた They were submitted to many *atrocities* [*cruelties*].

さんきゅう 産休 maternity leave Ⓤⓒ

サンキュー Thank you., Thanks. (❖Thanks. のほうが親しい間柄で気軽に使う「サンキュー」のニュアンスに近い) ⇒ ありがとう

さんぎょう 産業 industry Ⓤⓒ ――産業の industrial
この市がこの地方の産業の中心地だ This city is the center of *industry* of this local area.
エレクトロニクスはわが国の代表的な産業の一つである Electronics is one of our country's representative *industries*.
町のこの区域は産業開発区域として設定された This part of town was zoned for *industrial development*.
‖産業界 industry, the industrial world / 産業革命 the industrial revolution, the Industrial Revolution / 産業スパイ an industrial spy / 産業廃棄物 industrial waste [discharges] / 映画産業 the movie [film] industry / コンピュータ産業 the computer industry / 自動車産業 the auto(mobile) industry / 地場産業 a local industry / 第一 [二, 三] 次産業 a primary [secondary, tertiary] industry / ハイテク産業 the high-tech industries / レジャー産業 the leisure industry

ざんぎょう 残業 overtime work Ⓤ ――残業する work overtime //彼はきょう3時間残業した He *worked overtime* for three hours today. / He *did* three-hours *overtime* today.
‖残業時間 overtime / 残業手当 overtime pay [allowance]

ざんきん 残金 (残高) the balance; (未払いの金) the remainder《単数または複数扱い》 // 口座の残金は1万円を切った *The balance* in my account became less than 10,000 yen. / 今月末までに残金を支払います I'll pay *the remainder* by the end of this month.
♦ 財布の中の残金はもうわずかしかない I've got little *money left* in my wallet.

サングラス sunglasses, dark glasses (❖いずれも数えるときは a pair of ... とする) ‖サングラスをかける put on *sunglasses*

ざんげ 懺悔 (告白) confession ⓒⓤ; (改悛

(ざん)《公式的》penitence Ⓤ ——懺悔する confess ⊕⊖ ∥彼女は自分の罪を神に懺悔した She *confessed* her sin to God.

さんけい¹ 山系 mountain range Ⓒ ∥ヒマラヤ山系 the Himalayan *mountain range*

さんけい² 参詣 ——参詣する visit a temple [shrine] ∥ 参詣客 a visitor to a temple [shrine]

さんげき 惨劇 (悲劇的なこと) tragedy ⓊⒸ; (むごたらしい事件) gory incident ∥この部屋でその惨劇が起こった *The tragedy* happened in this room.

さんけつ 酸欠 a shortage of oxygen, oxygen shortage ⓊⒸ ∥その動物は酸欠で死んだ The animal died from *a shortage of oxygen*.

さんけづく 産気づく 彼女は産気づいている She *is in travail*.

さんげんしょく 三原色 the three primary colors ∥光の三原色 *the three primary colors* of light

さんけんぶんりつ 三権分立 the separation of powers

さんご¹ 珊瑚 coral Ⓤ ∥サンゴ礁 a coral reef; (環礁) an atoll

さんご² 産後 彼女は産後の肥立ちがよい[悪い] She is doing well [badly] *after delivery*.

さんこう 参考 reference ⓊⒸ, (情報) information Ⓤ

参考のためにこの本を読んでごらんなさい Read this book for *reference*.

作文するときにはこの本がいい参考になるよ This will *make a* good *reference* when you write a composition.

今後の参考のために伺いますが, それはどこで入手されましたか For (future) *reference*, where did you get it?

ご参考までに申しますが, こちらの商品のほうがあちらより幾分お高くなっております *For your information*, this product costs a little more than that one.

◆この問題は教科書を参考にして解いた I solved this problem by *referring to* the textbook. / あのときの君の話はとても参考になった(→役に立った) What you told me then *was* really *helpful*.

∥参考書(学習用) a study aid [guide] / 参考資料 reference materials / 参考図書 a reference book / 参考人 a witness / 参考文献 a reference / 参考文献一覧 (a list of) references, a bibliography

ざんごう 塹壕 〖軍事〗 trench Ⓒ, entrenchment Ⓒ

ざんこく 残酷 cruelty Ⓤ; (残忍さ) brutality Ⓤ ❖「残酷な行為」の意味ではいずれも Ⓒ; (非情) mercilessness Ⓤ, ruthlessness Ⓤ ——残酷な cruel; brutal; merciless, ruthless ——残酷に cruelly; mercilessly

彼女の誘いをにべもなく断るなんて君は残酷なやつだな You are *cruel* [It is *cruel* of you] to reject her invitation so flatly.

犯人は残酷にもその一家全員を殺害した The murderer *had the cruelty* [*mercilessness*] to kill the whole family.

動物たちに対する残酷な仕打ちは許されるべきでない. *Cruelty* [*Brutality*] to animals should never be forgiven.

さんさい 山菜 edible mountain [wild] plants

さんざい¹ 散在 ——散在する be scattered; (点在する) be dotted ∥この地区には小さな池が散在している Small ponds *are scattered around* this district./ This district *is scattered with* small ponds.

さんざい² 散財 ——散財する spend* a lot of money, waste money ∥とんだ散財をかけてすみませんでした I'm sorry to *have you spend a lot of money* on me. / そんなつまらない物に散財してはいけない Don't *waste your money on* such worthless things.

さんさく 散策 (散歩) walk Ⓒ; (ぶらぶら歩き) stroll Ⓒ, ramble Ⓒ ——散策する walk ⊖; stroll ⊖, ramble ⊖ ∥公園を散策してきた I *took a walk* [*stroll, ramble*] in the park.

さんざし 山査子〖植物〗hawthorn ⒸⓊ

さんさろ 三叉路・三差路 (3つの道の交差点) an intersection of three roads
◆この道は坂の下で三叉路になっている(→二またに分かれている) This road *forks* at the end of the slope.

さんさん 燦々 沖縄に到着すると太陽がさんさんと輝いていた The sun was shining *bright* [*brightly, brilliantly*] when I arrived in Okinawa.

さんざん 散々 (何度も) repeatedly, again and again; (ひどく) terribly, badly; (厳しく) severely ∥そんなことするなとさんざん言って聞かせたじゃないか Don't you remember that I told you *repeatedly* [*again and again*] not to do it? / 窓ガラスを割ったことで先生にさんさんしかられた I was told off *severely* [*terribly*] by my teacher for breaking a window.

◆彼は人にさんざん迷惑をかけておきながら知らん顔している Though he has caused us *so much* trouble, he doesn't seem to care a bit. / 船酔いでさんざんな目にあった I was seasick and *had a really hard time*. / ひどい天気でピクニックはさんざんだった The picnic was *terrible* because of the bad weather. / 人をさんざん待たせていったい何してたの You've kept me waiting *such a long time*. What on earth were you doing?

さんさんくど 三三九度 〖📛〗

三三九度とは, 夫婦になろうという二人が結婚の契りの酒杯を交わす重要な伝統儀式です. 新郎新婦が大きさの違う三つ組の杯で3回ずつ杯をやりとりします.
Sansankudo is an important traditional wedding rite performed by the couple through which they make a wedding vow. It is a ritual exchange of sake: three formal sips by the bride and groom from a set of three cups of different sizes.

さんさんごご 三々五々 in twos and threes ‖人々は三々五々パーティー会場を後にした People left the party hall *in twos and threes*.

さんじ¹ 惨事 disaster ⓒⓤ, calamity ⓒⓤ; (悲劇的なこと) tragedy ⓤⓒ ‖彼の不注意運転が惨事を引き起こした His careless driving caused *a disaster* [*tragedy*]. / その船舶事故は大惨事となった The ship accident turned out to be *a terrible disaster* [*tragedy*].

さんじ² 賛辞 compliment ⓒⓤ, praise ⓤ, tribute ⓒⓤ ‖…に賛辞を呈する pay *a compliment* [*tribute*] to … / 彼は彼女の演技に対し惜しみない賛辞を送った He lavished *praise* on her performance.

さんじ³ 参事 ‖参事官 a counselor, 《英》a counsellor

さんじげん 三次元 three dimensions ――三次元の three-dimensional, three-D, 3-D

さんしすいめい 山紫水明 山紫水明の地 a place of *beautiful mountains and rivers*

さんじせいげん 産児制限 birth control ⓤ

さんじゅう¹ 三十 thirty; (30番目) thirtieth

さんじゅう² 三重 ――三重の triple, three-fold ◆三重の塔 a *three-storied* pagoda ‖三重苦 a triple handicap / 三重唱[奏]《音楽》a trio

さんしゅうき 三周忌 ⇒さんかいき

さんしゅつ 産出 production ⓤ; (作物の) yield ⓤ (しばしば複数形～s) ――産出する produce ⓔ; yield ⓔ ‖石油産出国 an oil *producing country* / その山はダイヤモンドを産出することで知られる The mountain is known for *producing* diamonds.
‖産出高[量] (an) output, production, yield

さんじょ 賛助 support ⓤ ――賛助する support ⓔ ‖賛助会員 a supporting member

ざんしょ 残暑 late summer heat ⓤ, lingering summer heat ⓤ ◆まだまだ残暑が厳しい Severe *summer heat is lingering* yet.
‖残暑見舞い a late summer greeting card

さんしょう¹ 参照 reference ⓤⓒ ――参照する refer to …, make* reference to …; (確かめる) see* ⓔ (◆通例進行形にはできない); (比較する) compare ⓔ
星印は脚注参照のマークだ The asterisks *refer to* footnotes.
別紙の解説を参照のこと *Compare* the explanation in the attached sheet.
下記[下図]参照 *See below* [*chart below*].
60ページ注5参照 *See* note 5, p. 60. / *cf.* note 5, p. 60 (◆cf. はラテン語 confer の略で「…を参照せよ」の意味．ふつう [kəmpéər] または [sí:ef] と読む)
‖参照符号 a reference (mark) / 相互参照 a cross reference

さんしょう² 山椒 (木) Japanese pepper tree ⓒ; (香辛料) Japanese pepper

さんじょう¹ 惨状 震災後の町は惨状を呈していた (→ひどい状態にあった) The town *was in a terrible* [*horrible*] *state* after the earthquake. / 事故現場は目を背(そむ)けたくなるような惨状だった The scene of the accident *was so terrible* [*horrible*] that I felt like turning my eyes away from it.

さんじょう² 三乗 《数学》cube ⓒ, the third power ――3乗する 《数学》cube ⓔ (◆通例受身で) ‖2の3乗は8 *The cube* of two is eight. / Two *cubed* is eight. / Two (raised) to *the third power* is eight.
‖3乗根 the cube [cubic] root

さんしょううお 山椒魚 salamander ⓒ

さんしょく 三色 ――3色の three-color, tricolor(ed) ‖三色旗 a tricolor; (フランス国旗) the Tricolor

さんしょくすみれ 三色菫 pansy ⓒ

さんしん 三振 strikeout ⓒ ――三振する[させる] strike* out ‖そのバッターを三振にする *strike out* the batter / 佐藤は空振りの三振をした Sato (*was*) *struck out* swinging.

ざんしん 斬新 ――斬新な (目新しい) novel; (独創的な) original; (型にはまらない) unconventional ‖斬新なアイディア a *novel* [an *original*] idea / 彼の映画は斬新な映像にあふれている His movie is full of *novel* [*unconventional*] scenes.

さんすい 散水・撒水 芝生に散水する sprinkle the lawn *with water*; sprinkle *water* on the lawn
‖散水車 a sprinkler

さんすいが 山水画 a landscape painted in the Eastern Asian way

さんすう 算数 arithmetic [ərίθmətik], 《口語的》figures; (計算) sum ――算数の arithmetic(al) ‖算数のテスト an *arithmetic test* / 彼は算数がよくできる[できない] He is good [bad] at *arithmetic* [*figures*].

さんすくみ 三竦み 三すくみの状態になる reach *a three-party deadlock*

サンスクリット Sanskrit ⓤ

さんずのかわ 三途の川 the *sanzuno-kawa*, the river which the dead are believed to cross on the way to the other world

さんする 産する produce ⓔ; (作物を) yield ⓔ ‖その地域は良質のワインを産する That region *produces* wine of fine quality.

さんせい¹ 賛成

(意見の一致) agreement ⓤ; (是認) approval ⓤ ――賛成する agree ⓔ; (是認する) approve ⓔ ⇒ コミュニケーションスキル p.603

市長の計画は市民の賛成を得られなかった The mayor's plan didn't get *the approval* of the people.

賛成の方は挙手を願います If you *agree* [*approve*], please raise your hand.

彼らは彼の案に賛成の意を示した They showed *their approval* of his plan.

修正案は賛成多数で可決された The amendment was passed by *the majority's approval*.

【agree＋with 名 (+about [on] 名)】彼の意見に全面的に賛成しているわけではない I don't completely *agree with* his opinion. (◆

コミュニケーションスキル —賛成・反対—

①相手の言うことに賛成する

(A) I think he should be more careful with his words. Don't you think so?
　—Yes, **I think so, too**.
彼は自分の言葉にもっと気をつけるべきだと思うわ. そう思わない？—ええ, 私もそう思うわ.

(B) I cannot stand his bragging any more.
　—**You can say that again! / You said it!**
彼の自慢話にはもううんざりだ. 一同感！

(C) It was an exciting game.
　—**Absolutely!**
すごいゲームだったね. 一本当に！〔全く！〕

(D) So she accepted his offer?
　—**Exactly. / Right.**
それじゃ, 彼女は彼の申し出を受け入れたんですね？—そのとおりです.

(E) John is the type of person who always creates some problems.
　—**That's true.**
ジョンはいつも何かしら問題を起こす人だね. 一確かにそうだね.

(F) I think I'll keep a diary in English.
　—**That's a good idea! / That sounds great!**
英語で日記をつけようと思うんだ. —それはいい考えだね.

☞ (A) の I think so, too. は同意・賛成を表す最も平易で一般的な表現. 実際には, このひと言では足りないので, 状況に応じて (B) ～ (F) のように使い分けることになる. I think so, too. と同様に **I agree.**（同感です）, **I agree with you.**（あなたに同意します）もよく使われる.

☞ (B) の You can say that again. は, 文字どおりには「それをもう一度言ってもよい」ということで,「何度言ってもよいくらい本当のことだ」の意味になる. You said it! は「言ってくれたね」という感じで,「言えてる」に近い.

☞ (C) の Absolutely は, [ǽbsəlùːtli] と後ろを強く発音し, 全面的な賛成を表す.

☞ (F) の That's a good idea. は **Good idea!**, That sounds great! は **Sounds great!** ともいう. どちらも相手の提案に賛成する

意思表示である.

②相手の言うことに反対する・異論を唱える

(A) He couldn't help but keep the plan a secret. He did the right thing.
　—Well, **I don't think so**.
彼はその計画を秘密にしておかざるをえなかったんだ. 彼は正しいことをしたんだよ. —いや, 私はそうは思わないね.

(B) Will he come to the party?
　—**I'm afraid not [he won't].**
彼はパーティーに来るだろうか—いや, 来ないと思うけど.

(C) Aren't you tired of listening to me?
　—**Absolutely not!**
僕の話を聞くのに飽きてない？—いや, とんでもない！

(D) You don't like baroque music, do you?
　—**Not exactly**. It all sounds about the same to me.
バロック音楽がお好きではないんですね？—いや, そういうわけでもないんです. どれもみな同じように聞こえますけど.

☞ (A) の I don't think so. は率直に反対の意思表示をする場合に適した表現. また, 文字どおり **I don't [can't] agree.** や **I disagree.**（いずれも「賛成できません」の意味）と率直にいう表現もある. これらの表現では少し直接的すぎると感じる場合は, (B) の I'm afraid not. (残念だけどそうではないと思う) のように, 前に I'm afraid を付けると間接的で柔らかな響きになる.

☞ 強い反対の意思表示には, **That's what you think!**（それはあなたの考えでしょ！）という言い方もあるが, 議論が白熱しているときなどに使われる.

☞ (C) は相手の言ったことを強く否定する表現. ① (C) の Absolutely! と違い, [ǽbsəlùːtli] のように最初を強く発音する. **Definitely not!** も同じ意味.

☞ (D) の Not exactly. は相手の言うことが「必ずしも正しくない」ことを表す表現. この後に, 相手の言葉どおりではないという根拠を述べる内容が続くのがふつう.

---

agree with ... の後には「人・意見・考え」などを表す名詞がくる) / そのことについてはあなたに賛成です I *agree with* you *about* that.

【agree＋to 名(事柄)】私たちはしぶしぶ彼女の提案に賛成した We reluctantly *agreed to* her proposal. (❖agree to ... の後には「提案・計画」などを表す名詞がくる)

【agree＋to *do*】クラス全員が先生にプレゼントをすることに賛成した All the class *agreed to* give a present to our teacher.

◆ 法案に賛成票を入れる cast *a vote for* the bill / 君のアイディアには大賛成だね I'm *all for* your idea. / I *couldn't agree more with* your idea. / 核実験に賛成しているのは住民の少数にすぎない Only a minor part of the population *favors* [*is in favor of*] nuclear testing. / 彼女の案は賛成30, 反対10で可決された Her proposal was accepted by 30 votes *for* and 10 *against*.

🅔「あなたは賛成なの, 反対なの？」「私は反対です」"Are you *for* or *against* it?" "I'm *against* it."

🅔「わあ, すごい雨だよ. 駅までタクシーで行かない？」「賛成！」"Oh, it's pouring! Why don't we take a taxi to the station?" "*I'm for it!*"

賛成者 a supporter, a person who agrees

さんせい² 酸性 acidity Ⓤ ──酸性の acid, acidic ‖酸性雨 acid rain / 酸性食品 acid food / 酸性土壌 acid soil / 酸性反応 an acid reaction / 弱酸性 subacidity

さんせい³ 三世 the Third ‖ナポレオン 3 世

Napoleon *the Third*; Napoleon *III* ◆日系3世のアメリカ人 a *third generation* Japanese-American; a *Sansei*

さんせいけん 参政権 suffrage ⓤ, political rights ‖ 婦人参政権 female [women's] suffrage

さんせき 山積 ━━山積する pile up, be piled up ∥問題が山積している Problems *are piling up*./ Problems *are piled up*.
◆やっかいな仕事が山積している I've got a pile [*lot*] of troublesome work to do.

さんせん 参戦 ━━参戦する (参加する)「take* part」(公式的) participate (in …) ∥第二次世界大戦に参戦した国 a country that 「*took part* [*participated*] in World War II / 彼はそのカーレースに参戦した He 「*took part* [*participated*] in the car race.

さんぜん 燦然 ━━さん然と brilliantly, bright(ly) ∥さん然と輝く金メダル a *brilliantly* shining gold medal

さんそ 酸素 〔化学〕oxygen ⓤ (❖元素記号 O) ∥酸素化合物 an oxygen compound, 〔化学〕(an) oxide / 酸素吸入 oxygen inhalation / 酸素吸入器 an oxygen inhaler / 酸素マスク an oxygen mask / 活性酸素 activated oxygen

さんそう 山荘 (登山・避暑などのための) lodge ⓒ; (山中の小屋) mountain cottage ⓒ

ざんぞう 残像 afterimage ⓒ

さんぞく 山賊 bandit ⓒ

さんそん 山村 mountain village ⓒ

ざんそん 残存 ━━残存する remain ⓘ; (生き残る) survive ⓘⓣ ∥この地方に残存する風習 customs *remaining* in this region

ざんだか 残高 the balance ∥銀行の残高を照会する check *one's* bank *balance* ∥銀行預金残高 the bank balance

サンタクロース Santa Claus, 《口語的》Santa, 《英》Father Christmas

サンダル sandals (❖数えるときは a pair of … とする)

さんたん 惨憺 実験の結果は惨憺たるもの(→完全な失敗)だった Our experiment ended in *disaster*./ チームは惨憺たる(→ひどい)敗北を喫した The team suffered a *terrible* defeat. / 焼け跡は惨憺たる(→恐ろしい)光景だった The site of the fire presented a *horrible* sight. / 作文を書くのに苦心惨憺した(→大変な苦労をした) I took great pains to write the essay.

さんだん¹ 散弾 (集合的に) shot ⓤ; (小弾丸) pellet ⓒ ∥散弾銃 a shotgun

さんだん² 三段 3段のウエディングケーキ a *three-tiered* wedding cake / 彼女は剣道3段です She has *the third degree* [*grade*] in kendo.
‖3段ロケット a three-stage rocket

さんたんげん 単現 (三人称単数現在)〔文法〕third person singular present form

さんだんとび 三段跳び the triple jump

さんだんろんぽう 三段論法〔論理〕syllogism

さんち¹ 山地 mountainous district ⓒ; (高地) highlands

さんち² 産地 producing district ⓒ ∥青森はリンゴの産地として有名だ Aomori is famous as apple-*producing district*. ◆産地直送のサクランボ cherries *direct from the orchard*

さんちょう 山頂 the top [summit] of a mountain, mountaintop ⓒ; (先のとがった) peak ⓒ ∥雲が山頂を覆った The clouds covered *the mountaintops*.

さんてい 算定 (計算) calculation ⓤ ⓒ; (見積もり) estimate ⓤ ━━算定する calculate ⓣ; estimate ⓣ ∥修理費を算定する *calculate* [*estimate*] the costs of repair

ざんてい 暫定 ━━暫定的の provisional, temporary ∥彼らは暫定的な措置をとった They took *temporary* measures.
‖暫定政権 a provisional government / 暫定予算 a provisional budget

さんディーケー 3DK a three-room apartment with a kitchen and dining room

サンデー (日曜日) Sunday ⓤⓒ; (アイスクリーム) sundae ⓒ

サンド ⚠(サンドイッチ) sandwich ⓒ

さんど 三度 three times ∥祖母は1日に3度薬を飲む My grandmother takes medicine *three times* a day.
◆彼女は3度目の挑戦に成功した She made it on the *third* try.
慣用表現 彼は三度の飯よりサッカーが好きだ He would rather play soccer than *eat*.
ことわざ 三度目の正直 Third time lucky.; The third time's a charm. (→ 3度目にはうまくいく) / 二度あることは三度ある ➪にど

サンドイッチ sandwich ⓒ (❖3枚のパンを使った二重サンドイッチは double-decker,《主に米》club sandwich という) ∥ハムとキュウリのサンドイッチ a ham and cucumber *sandwich*

さんとう 三等 (等級) the third class; (第3位) (the) third place; (3等賞) the third prize ∥彼女はコンテストで3等を獲得した She won *third place* in the contest.

さんどう¹ 賛同 approval ⓤ ━━賛同する approve ⓘⓣ ∥彼の案はみんなの賛同を得た His plan won [obtained] everyone's *approval*. / 彼らは彼女の意見に賛同した They *approved of* her opinion.

さんどう² 参道 the approach to a shrine [temple]

サンドバッグ sandbag ⓒ

さんにん 三人 three (people)
ことわざ 三人寄れば文殊の知恵 Two heads are better than one. (→ 2人の頭があれば1人の頭よりもよい)

ざんにん 残忍 ━━残忍な brutal; (人が) cruel; (冷酷な) cold-blooded ∥残忍な犯罪 a *brutal* crime / 残忍な殺人者 a *brutal* [*cruel*] murderer

さんにんしょう 三人称〔文法〕the third person

ざんねん 残念
彼女が参加できないのは残念だ I am *sorry* [I *regret*, It's *a pity*] that she cannot join us.
残念ですがあなたの申し出をお受けできません I

regret to say that I cannot accept your offer.
彼女は自分の意見が通らず残念そうだった She appeared to be *sorry* that her idea was turned down.
残念なことに遠足は中止になった *To our disappointment*, the excursion was canceled.
残念ながら在庫はありません *I'm afraid* we are out of stock.
彼女は彼が来ないと聞いて残念がっていた She *was disappointed to* hear he wasn't coming.
● 「かぜをひいてパーティーに行けなかったの」「それは残念だったね」"I caught cold, so I couldn't go to the party." "*That's too bad.*"
‖残念賞 a consolation prize

さんねんせい 三年生 third-year student ⓒ; (大学の)《米》junior ⓒ; (高校の)《米》senior ⓒ; (小学校の)《米》third grader ⓒ ➡ ☆がくねん / 姉は高校3年生です My sister is *a third-year student* in senior high school.

サンバ samba ⓒ ‖サンバを踊る dance *the samba*

さんばい 三倍 three times ‖ 7の3倍は21です *Three times* seven is twenty-one. / 彼の部屋は僕の部屋の3倍の広さがある His room is *three times* as large as mine.

さんぱい 参拝 ──参拝する visit a shrine [temple], worship at a shrine [temple]
◆明治神宮の参拝者は数万人に達した *Visitors* [*Worshipers*] to Meiji Shrine numbered in the tens of thousands.

ざんぱい 惨敗 crushing defeat ⓒ ──惨敗する suffer a crushing defeat, be beaten completely

サンバイザー sun visor ⓒ

サンパウロ São Paulo (❖ブラジルの都市)

さんばがらす 三羽烏 (3人組) trio ⓒ (複 〜s)

さんばし 桟橋 pier ⓒ; (浮き桟橋) landing stage ⓒ ‖彼らは桟橋の近くにいかりを下ろした They anchored the boat near *the pier*.

さんぱつ¹ 散髪 haircut ⓒ ‖私はきのう散髪した(→してもらった)ばかりだ I just *got* [*had*] *a haircut* yesterday. / I just *had my hair cut* yesterday.

さんぱつ² 散発 東北地方で地震が散発的に起こっている In the Tohoku district earthquakes happen *sporadically*. / タイガースはその投手に散発5安打に抑えられた The Tigers were limited to five *random* hits by that pitcher.

ざんぱん 残飯 remains of a meal; (残り物) leftovers

さんび 賛美 praise ⓤ ──賛美する praise ⊕ ‖自然の美しさを賛美する *praise* the beauty of nature
‖賛美歌 a hymn

さんぴ 賛否 彼の意見には賛否両論あるだろう There must be *pros and cons* of his opinion. / 議長は新しい計画について投票で賛否を問うた The chairman *put* the new plan *to the vote*.

さんびょうし 三拍子 triple time
慣用表現 彼は走・攻・守の三拍子そろった(→万能の)野球選手だ He is an *all-around* [《英》*round*, (→理想的な) *ideal*] baseball player with textbook batting, fielding and base running. / (→3分野にすぐれた人)He is *a triple threat*: batting, fielding and base running.

さんぶ 三部 (3つの部分) three parts; (3冊) three copies ‖ 三部合唱 a chorus in three parts, a trio / 三部作 a trilogy

さんぷ 散布 ──散布する (まき散らす) scatter ⊕; (水・砂などを振りかける) sprinkle ⊕; (吹きかける) spray ⊕ ‖作物に農薬を散布する *spray* agricultural chemicals *on* the crops
‖散布器(噴霧器) a sprayer

さんぷく 山腹 mountainside ⓒ《通例単数形》; (丘の) hillside ‖その小屋は山腹にある The hut is on *the mountainside*.

さんふじんか 産婦人科 obstetrics and gynecology ‖産婦人科医 an obstetrician and gynecologist

さんぶつ 産物 product ⓒ; (農産物)《集合的》produce ⓤ; (成果) result ⓒ ‖米がこの地方の主要産物だ Rice is *the main product* [*produce*] in this district.
◆これは私たちの努力の産物だ This is *the fruit* of our efforts.
‖海産物 marine products / 農産物 agricultural products

サンフランシスコ San Francisco (❖米国の都市)

サンプル (見本) sample ⓒ; (血液・尿検査などのための) specimen ⓒ

さんぶん 散文 prose ⓤ ‖詩を散文で書く write a poem in *prose*
‖散文詩 a prose poem

さんぽ 散歩 walk ⓒ, stroll ⓒ ──散歩する take* a walk, (散歩に行く) go* for a walk, (ぶらぶら歩く) stroll ⊕
散歩に行きませんか Shall we *go for a walk*?
父は日曜は散歩のためにいつもより早く起きる On Sundays my father gets up earlier than usual to *take a walk*.
彼は海岸を散歩していた He *was strolling* [*taking a stroll*] along the beach.
朝の散歩に行こう Let's go for *a morning walk* [*stroll*].
◆私は朝と晩に犬を散歩させる I「*take my dog for a walk* [*walk my dog*] mornings and evenings.
‖散歩道 a walk; (遊歩道) a promenade

さんぼう 参謀 (軍隊の) staff officer ⓒ; (総称)《集合的》the staff; (会社などの相談役) adviser ⓒ ‖参謀会議 a council of war / 参謀長 the chief of staff / 参謀本部 the General Staff Office

さんぽう 三方 その空き地は三方を塀に囲まれていた The vacant lot was surrounded by walls *on three sides*.

さんま 秋刀魚 (Pacific) saury [sɔ́ːri] ⓒ

-ざんまい 三昧 王女はぜいたくざんまいの日々

を送っていた(→ぜいたくに暮らしていた) The princess lived in *luxury*. / この夏休みはテニスざんまいでした(→テニスばかりしていた) I *did nothing but* play tennis during this summer vacation.

さんまいめ 三枚目 (喜劇役者) comedian ⓒ, comic actor [actress] ⓒ; (こっけいな人) clown ⓒ

さんまん 散漫 彼の演説は散漫だった His speech was *rambling*. / 考え事をしていて注意力が散漫になっていた My attention *wandered* (from what I was doing). (❖「考え事をしていて」の意味はwanderに含まれる)

さんみ 酸味 acidity ⓤ, sourness ⓤ ◆このブドウは少し酸味がある This grape *tastes a little sour*.

さんみゃく 山脈 mountain range [chain] ⓒ ◆ロッキー山脈 *the Rocky Mountains* / ヒマラヤ山脈 the Himalayas(❖複数扱い)

ざんむ 残務 remaining work [business] ⓤ / あしたは残務整理をすることになるだろう Tomorrow, I will have to *clear up the remaining business*.

さんめんきじ 三面記事 city [local] news ⓤ

さんめんきょう 三面鏡 three-paneled [triple] mirror ⓒ

さんもん¹ 山門 temple gate ⓒ, a gate of a temple

さんもん² 三文 その本は三文の値打ちもない That book is not worth *a cent* [*penny*].
‖三文小説 a cheap novel / 三文判 a *sammomban*, a ready-made and inexpensive seal ⇒はんこ
ことわざ 早起きは三文の得 ⇒はやおき

さんやく 三役 (政党などの) the three key officials; (相撲の大関・関脇・小結) the three high ranks in sumo below *yokozuna*

さんゆこく 産油国 oil-producing country ⓒ

ざんよ 残余 (残り) the rest, the remainder; (残金) the balance

さんようすうじ 算用数字 Arabic numerals [figures]

さんらん¹ 産卵 ——産卵する (鳥などが) lay* eggs; (魚介類が) spawn 🔵 🔴 ‖産卵期 the breeding [spawning] season

さんらん² 散乱 ——散乱する be scattered ∥空き缶が公園中に散乱していた Empty cans *were scattered* all over the park.

さんりゅう 三流 ——三流の third-rate, third-class /三流の作家 a *third-rate* writer

ざんりゅう 残留 ——残留する remain behind, stay behind ‖中国残留日本人孤児 a Japanese child left behind in China after World War II

さんりん 山林 mountains and forests; (森林) forest ⓒ; (森林地帯) woodland ⓤ (《また複数形~s)

さんりんしゃ 三輪車 tricycle ⓒ, 《英口語的》trike ⓒ

さんるい 三塁 third (base) ⓤ ‖彼は三塁を守っている He plays *third base*.
‖三塁手 the third baseman / 三塁打 a three base hit, a triple

ざんるい 残塁 ランナーは3者残塁に終わった Three runners *were left on base*.

サンルーフ (自動車の) sunroof ⓒ

サンルーム sunroom ⓒ, 《米》sun porch ⓒ, 《英》sun lounge ⓒ

さんれつ 参列 attendance ⓤ (❖参列者の意味では) ,presence ⓒ ——参列する attend 🔴, be present ‖式には多数の人が参列した A lot of people *attended* [*were present at*] the ceremony. / There was *a large attendance* at the ceremony.
‖参列者 an attendant; (集合的に) (an) attendance

さんろく 山麓 the foot [base] of a mountain ‖私たちは山麓の村を訪れた We visited a village at *the foot of a mountain*.

シ 〖音楽〗 ti [tíː] ⓤ ⓒ

し¹ 死

❶【死ぬこと】death ⓤ ⓒ
生と死について考える consider life and *death* / 死に直面する face *death* / 不慮の[安らかな]死を遂げる die *an* accidental [easy] *death* / 死を選ぶ choose *death*

彼女は息子の死を悲しんだ She mourned 「*the death* of her son [her son's *death*].

彼女はかろうじて死を免れた She narrowly [just] escaped *death*.

酒の飲みすぎが彼の死を招いた Too much drinking caused his *death*.

多額の借金が彼を死に追いやった A large amount of debt drove him to *his death*.

その患者は死に瀕(ひん)している The patient is *at death's door*.

◆死の灰 (*radioactive*) *fallout* / その若者は事故死した The young man *was killed in an accident.* / それが彼女が死の間際(→死ぬ直前)にもらした言葉だ That was what she said just before she *died.* / そこは草木1本生えていない死の世界だった It was a *dead* world without a single plant.

❷【野球のアウト】【野球】out ⓒ
二死満塁です The bases are loaded with two *outs*.

‖安楽死 euthanasia, (a) mercy killing / 過労死 death from overwork / 事故死 an accidental death / 自然死 a natural death / 水死 (death by) drowning / 戦死 death in 「(the) war [battle] / 即死 instant death / 尊厳死 death with dignity / 突然死 a sudden death / 脳死 brain death / 病死 death from a disease / 変死 an unnatural death

短歌 死に近き母に添寝のしんしんと遠田(とおだ)のかはづ天に聞こゆる〈斎藤茂吉〉
As she nears the end,
I lie beside my mother,
and through the quiet
from a field far away
a frog's cries rise to heaven.

し² 詩 (1編の) poem ⓒ; (文学形式としての) poetry ⓤ (❖集合的に特定の詩人・時代の詩全体も意味する); (韻文) verse / 詩の・詩的な poetic(al) / 散文体で書かれた詩 *a poem written in prose; a prose poem* / ワーズワースの詩 the poetry of Wordsworth / 詩を朗読する recite *a poem* / 詩的な表現 *a poetic* expression / 佐藤春夫詩集 the 「*Collected Poems* [*Poetic Works*] of Sato Haruo

‖自由詩 free verse / 叙事詩 an epic / 叙情詩 a lyric

し³ 市 city ⓒ (通例 City) ――市の municipal, civic (❖名詞の前で用いる) / 川越市 Kawagoe *City*; the City of Kawagoe (❖手紙のあて先などでは Kawagoe-shi または Kawagoe だけでよい)

‖市議会 ⇨しぎかい / 市当局 a municipality, the city authorities

し⁴ 氏 (男性) Mr.; (女性) Ms. [míz] (❖既婚女性には Mrs., 未婚女性には Miss をも用いる) / 杉田氏 *Mr.* [*Ms.*] Sugita / 東, 西両氏 *Mr.* Azuma and *Mr.* Nishi

◆藤原氏(→藤原一族) the Fujiwara *clan* / 氏は(→彼は)かつてアメリカで生活していた *He* once lived in the U.S.

し⁵ 四 four ⓤ ⓒ ⇨ よん / 四半世紀 a quarter of a century

慣用表現 四の五の言わないで(→おまえの不平など聞きたくない)さっさとやれ I *don't want to hear your complaints*. Do it immediately.

し⁶ 師 (先生) teacher ⓒ; (経験を積んだ指導者)《公式的》mentor ⓒ / 師の教えを守る follow the precepts of *one's teacher* [*mentor*] / 人を師と仰ぐ respect a person as *one's teacher* [*mentor*]

-**し¹** 彼女の作業は速いし正確だ She gets the work done fast *and* accurately (*as well*). / 飼い猫のニャンは家の中にもいなかったし庭にもいなかった Our cat Nyan was *neither* in the house *nor* in the yard. / 彼はフランス語もできるし, そのうえドイツ語もできる He can speak French, *and* what's more, he can speak German, too. / 試験も終わったし, きょうは一日友達と思いっきり遊ぼそ *Now that* the exams are over, I'm going to hang out with my friends all day today.

-**し²** -視 その事実を重要視みなす(→重要とみなす) *regard* [*consider*] the fact *as important*; *attach importance to* the fact / 彼は富と幸福を同一視している He *identifies* [*equates*] wealth *with* happiness. / 彼がその仕事に適格かどうか疑問視する人もいる Some people *question* his fitness for the job.

-**し³** -史 history ⓤ / 日本史 *the history of* Japan; Japanese *history* / 西洋音楽史 *the history of* Western music / 古代[中世, 近世]史 ancient [medieval, modern] *history*

じ¹ 字 (漢字・仮名など) character ⓒ, symbol ⓒ; (アルファベットなど) letter ⓒ; (筆跡) hand ⓒ, handwriting ⓤ; (印刷されたもの) print ⓤ,《集合的》type ⓤ

大きな字の本 a book in large *print* [*type*]

この字は何と読むのですか How do you read this *character* [*letter*]?

彼女は字がきれいだ[うまい] Her *handwriting* is neat [good]. / She has neat [good] *handwriting*.

◆彼は左手で字を書き右手ではしを使う He *writes* with his left hand and uses chopsticks with his right hand. / その子供はもう字が読める The child is already able to *read.* / この先にS字カーブがあります There is *an S-curve* [《英》*S-bend*] ahead. / 彼は帰

るなりベッドに大の字になった As soon as he got home, he 「*sprawled out* [*stretched out*]」 on the bed. / 彼は恋愛のれの字も知らない (→恋愛に関して何も知らない) He knows *nothing about love*. / (→恋愛したことがない) He's *never* been in love.

じ² 地 (本性) *one's* true character [nature]; (模様などの) background ◯ /酔うとその人の地が出るという People say that *your true character* is revealed when you are drunk. / 私のハンカチは白地に青のストライプだ My handkerchief has blue stripes on *a white background*. ◆ウール地の (→ウールの) コート a wool coat / 地の文 (→引用句以外の文) *prose other than quotes*; (→物語の説明的な部分) *a narrative* / 彼は地黒だ He has *naturally dark* [*brownish*] *skin*. / その歌手は自分の歌の内容を地で行くような人生を送った (→その歌手の人生は歌の再現だった) The singer's life *reflected* his [her] songs.

じ³ 痔 (いぼ痔)《口語的》piles,《医学》hemorrhoids [hémərɔ̀idz]; (切れ痔) anal fissure (痔瘻《ろう》) anal fistula

じ⁴ 辞 address ◯, speech ◯ (❖ address is speech よりやや公式的)/開会[閉会]の辞を述べる give *an* opening [*a* closing] *address*

じ- next ⇒つぎ(次) /次ページ the next page

-**じ** -時 o'clock

【語法】
(1) o'clock は「…時ちょうど」という場合に用い,「…時〜分」のように端数の付く場合には用いない. // 今は朝の10時です It's 10 (*o'clock*) in the morning now. (❖ o'clock は省略可能) / 今は9時20分です It's nine-twenty now. (❖ × It's nine *o'clock* twenty now.)
(2) o'clock は a.m., p.m. とともに用いることはできない.

8時のバスに乗る take the 8 *o'clock* bus

3時ごろにそちらへ伺います I will be there about three (*o'clock*).

試合は午後1時ちょうどに始まる The game starts at one (*o'clock*) sharp in the afternoon.

◆4時半に at half past four; at four-thirty (❖書く場合は at 4:30 とする) / 彼は9時6分発の電車に乗り遅れた He missed the 9:06 train. (❖ 9:06 は nine-o [óu]-six と読む) / 私は毎朝6時45分(→7時15分前)に起きる I get up at quarter to [《米》before] seven every morning. / 16時の便は欠航となった The 16:00 *hours* flight was canceled. (❖ 16:00 は sixteen hundred と読む) / 花粉症の姉はこの時期外出時には必ずマスクをして出かける *Whenever* she goes out, my sister wears a mask at this time of the year, because she suffers from hay fever.

🅔「今何時ですか」「6時10分過ぎです」"*What time is it?*" "(It's) ten past [《米》after] six."

🅔「アルバイトは何時から何時までやってるんですか」「午後5時から7時半までです」"*What* are your part-time *hours?*" "From 5 p.m. to 7:30 p.m."

しあい 試合 game ◯; match ◯; competition ◯; tournament ◯ ——試合(を)する play ⑭⑭, play [have*] a game [match]

| game: 団体競技に用いられる傾向がある.《米》では -ball のつく競技には通例 game.
| match: 個人競技に用いられる傾向がある.《米》ではゴルフ・ボクシングなどに用いる.《英》では -ball のつく競技にもゴルフ・ボクシングなどにも用いる.
| competition: 競技会, 大会.
| tournament: トーナメント.

【〜の試合】
ボクシングの試合 a boxing *match* / 互角の試合 *a close game* [*match*] / 退屈な試合 *a boring game* [*match*] / 白熱した試合 *a heated game* [*match*]

あす再試合が行われる The game will be 「*played again* [*replayed*]」 tomorrow.

テレビゲームで野球を2試合やった I played *two games* of baseball on the video game.

第1試合の開始時刻は午前10時だ *The first game* [*match*] starts at 10 a.m.

【試合に・を】
私たちは試合に勝った[負けた] We won [lost] *the game* [*match*].

彼女はかぜで試合に出られなかった She couldn't take part in *the game* due to a cold.

彼のシュートがその試合を決めた His goal decided *the game*.

我々は2対0でその試合に勝った We won *the game* [*match*] 2 to 0.

選手たちは試合を前にして緊張していた The players were nervous before *the game*. ◆我々は太田高校の柔道部に試合を申し込んだ We challenged the judo club of Ota High School to *a meet*.

【試合が・は】
あしたバレーボールの学内対抗試合がある We have *an intramural* volleyball *game* tomorrow.

大雨のため野球の試合は中止となった[中断された] *The* baseball *game* was canceled [stopped] because of the heavy rain.

試合は7対7の引き分けに終わった The game ended in a tie [draw], 7 to 7.

【試合の】
父はその試合の結果を予想した Father predicted *the game's* [*match's*] results.

5回の彼のホームランが試合の流れを変えた His fifth-inning home run changed the course of *the game*.

【その他】
審判が試合終了のホイッスルを吹いた The referee blew the *game-ending* whistle.

ライオンズはそつのない試合運びでその一戦を制した The Lions tactically *controlled the game* and won it.

‖練習試合 a practice game [match]

じあい¹ 慈愛 affection ⓒ Ⓤ, love Ⓤ《また a～》◆慈愛に満ちた笑み an *affectionate* smile

じあい² 自愛 ご自愛ください Please take good care of yourself.

しあがり 仕上がり (できばえ) workmanship Ⓤ; (完了すること) finishing Ⓤ; (完成) completion Ⓤ ∥すばらしい仕上がりのソファー a sofa made with good *workmanship* / 彼の新曲の仕上がりが遅れている The *finishing* [*completion*] of his new song has been delayed.

しあがる 仕上がる be finished, be completed; (作られている) be made ∥やっと壁画が仕上がった The wall painting *is finished* [*completed*] at last. / この模型は本物そっくりに仕上がっている This model *is made* to look just like the real one.

しあげ 仕上げ finish Ⓤ(また a～); (できばえ) workmanship Ⓤ; (加筆) (finishing) touch ⓒ ∥ラッカー仕上げのギター a guitar with *a lacquer finish* / そのたんすは凝った仕上げがなされている The chest of drawers has *an elaborate finish*. / 幹江は絵に仕上げの筆を入れた Mikie put *the finishing touches* to her painting.

じあげや 地上げ屋 🔺 a *jiageya*, a person who uses force or threats to buy land in order to sell it to developers at high prices

しあげる 仕上げる finish ⊕ (❖ しばしば off を伴う), complete ⊕; (困難な仕事などを) get* through ... ∥その宿題を仕上げるのに5時間かかった It took five hours to finish (*off*) the homework. / 彼はテーブルを透明のニスで仕上げた He *finished off* the table with a clear varnish.

しあさって three days from now [today]

シアター (劇場) theater, 《英》theatre ⓒ; (映画館) 《米》(movie) theater ⓒ, 《英》cinema ⓒ

しあつ 指圧 🔺 *shiatsu*, acupressure ∥指圧師 a *shiatsu* [an acupressure] therapist

シアトル Seattle (❖米国の都市)

しあわせ 幸せ happiness Ⓤ; (幸運) fortune Ⓤ ——幸せな happy; (幸運な) fortunate, lucky ——幸せに happily
幸せな生活を送る lead a *happy* life; (→幸せに暮らす) live *happily* [*in happiness*]
末永くお幸せに I wish you everlasting *happiness*.
私は今最高に幸せです I'm *as happy as* can be now.
私たちは幸せな家庭を築きたい We want to make a *happy* family [home].
必ずあなたを幸せにします I'm sure I can make you *happy*.
いい友人がたくさんいてとても幸せです I'm very *happy* [*fortunate*] to have a lot of good friends.
きょうは私の人生でいちばん幸せな日だ Today is *the happiest* day of my life.

彼女と結婚するんだってね, この幸せ者！ I heard you're marrying her. What *a fortunate man* you are!
彼らはその後ずっと幸せに暮らしましたとさ They lived *happily* ever after. (❖ 童話などの結語)

シアン 《化学》cyanogen [saiǽnədʒən] Ⓤ
∥シアン化物 cyanide

しあん¹ 思案 (考えること) thought Ⓤ; (考慮) consideration Ⓤ; (熟考) (公式的)deliberation Ⓤ ⓒ ——思案する think* ⊕ ⊜; consider ⊕ ⊜; deliberate ⊜ ∥思案の末 after much *thought* [*consideration*, *deliberation*] / 今, どうすべきか思案中です Now I'm *thinking about* what I should do. / どちらの案を採るべきか思案のしどころだ We need to 「*consider carefully* [*deliberate carefully on*] which plan we should take.

◆彼女に何と言うべきかと思案にくれた I 「*was at a loss* to [*didn't know*] what to say to her. / 彼は思案顔をして座っていた He was sitting with *a thoughtful look* on his face.

しあん² 試案 tentative plan ⓒ, pilot scheme ⓒ

しい¹ 恣意 ——恣意的な arbitrary ——恣意的に arbitrarily
∥恣意性 arbitrariness

しい² 椎 《植物》chinquapin ⓒ

じい¹ 辞意 one's intention [decision] to resign ∥首相は辞意を表明した The Prime Minister declared 「*his intention to resign* [*that he would resign*]. / 彼は辞意を撤回した He withdrew *his decision to resign*.

◆彼女の辞意は堅い(→辞めようと堅く決心している) She *is firmly determined to resign*.

じい² 自慰 masturbation Ⓤ

シーアイエー CIA (❖ **C**entral **I**ntelligence **A**gency ((米国)中央情報局)の略語)

シーアイエス the CIS (❖ **C**ommonwealth of **I**ndependent **S**tates (独立国家共同体)の略語)

ジーエヌピー GNP (❖ **G**ross **N**ational **P**roduct (国民総生産)の略語) ∥日本のGNPは世界第2位である Japan's *GNP* is ranked second in the world.

シーエム CM ⚠ commercial ⓒ (❖ CM は commercial を日本式に略したもので, 英米では用いられない) ∥テレビCM a TV *commercial*
∥CMソング a jingle

しいか 詩歌 poetry Ⓤ, poems

しいく 飼育 (繁殖などのための) breeding Ⓤ; (食用にするための) raising Ⓤ, rearing Ⓤ ——飼育する breed* ⊕; raise ⊕, rear ⊕ ∥豚を飼育する *raise* [*rear*] hogs
∥飼育係 a keeper; (動物園の) a zookeeper / 飼育小屋 (小動物の) a hutch; (畜舎) a pen / 飼育場 a breeding ground, a farm

シーシー cc (❖ **c**ubic **c**entimeter(s) (立方センチメートル)の略語) ∥排気量3,000ccの車 a 3,000 *cc* car

じいしき 自意識 self-consciousness Ⓤ
◆彼は自意識過剰だ He is *too self-conscious*.

シーズン season ⓒ ∥クリスマスシーズン the

シーズンオフ

Christmas *season* / スキーのシーズンが近づいてきた *The ski season* is coming. / この浜辺はシーズン中多くの海水浴客でにぎわう This beach is crowded with swimmers during *the season*. / スワローズが今シーズンの優勝候補として浮かび上がってきた The Swallows emerged as the team to beat *this season*. / カキは今、シーズン(→旬(ピミ゚))だ[ではない] Oysters are now *in* [*out of*] *season*.

シーズンオフ ⚠ the off-season ——シーズンオフの[に] off-season //そのピッチャーはシーズンオフ中にだいぶ太った The pitcher got rather fat during *the off-season*. / そのホテルはふだんは高いが，割安のシーズンオフ料金もある That hotel is usually expensive, but it has affordable *off-season* rates too.

ジーセブン G7 (❖the Group of Seven (先進7か国(蔵相会議))の略語)

シーソー seesaw ⓒ, 《米》teeter-totter ⓒ // シーソーで遊ぶ play on a seesaw
‖シーソーゲーム a seesaw [close] game

しいたけ 椎茸 shiitake (mushroom) ⓒ

しいたげる 虐げる oppress 働; (暴威を振るう) tyrannize 働; (虐待する) ill-treat 働; (迫害する) persecute 働 //虐げられた人々 *oppressed* people; *the oppressed* / ある地域の住民を虐げる *oppress* [*tyrannize, ill-treat*] the people living in a particular area

シーツ sheet ⓒ //ベッドにシーツを敷く put *sheets* on a bed / シーツを替える change *the sheets*

しいっ hush [ʃː, hʌʃ], sh, shh, ssh [ʃ] //しいっ，隣の部屋で物音がしないか *Hush* [*Sh, Shh, Ssh*]! Do you hear something from the next room?

しいて 強いて 強いて言えば、野球よりサッカーのほうが得意だ *If I had to choose one*, I'd say I'm better at soccer than baseball. / 強いて答える必要はありません You don't need to answer 「*against your will* [*if you don't want to*].

シーディー CD ⓒ, compact disc ⓒ //CDをかける play [put on] *a CD* / CDを聴く listen to *a CD* / 私は彼よりずっとたくさんCDを持っている I have a lot more *CDs* than he does.
‖CDプレーヤー a CD [compact disc] player / CD屋[ショップ] a CD store [shop] / CDラジカセ a CD radio cassette player

シーディーロム 〔コンピュータ〕 CD-ROM ⓒ (❖compact *d*isc *r*ead-*o*nly *m*emory (読み取り専用メモリーCD)の略語)

シート¹ (1枚の紙など) sheet ⓒ; (覆い) cover(ing) ⓒ; (タールなどを塗った防水の) tarpaulin ⓒ //切手1枚 *a sheet* of stamps / 彼らは地面にビニールシートを敷いた They spread *a plastic sheet* on the ground. / 彼は荷物にシートをかぶせた He put *a cover* [*tarpaulin*] over the load.

シート² (座席) seat ⓒ //シルバーシート *a seat* for elderly or handicapped people (❖「シルバーシート」は和製英語)

シード 第1シードの選手 a top-*seeded* player; *a number-one seed* (❖名詞のseedは「シード選手、シードチーム」の意味) / 彼らのチームは第5シードになった Their team *was seeded* number five.
‖シード校 a seeded school team

シートノック ⚠ fielding practice Ⓤⓒ

シートベルト (自動車・飛行機の) seat belt ⓒ; (自動車の) safety belt ⓒ //(機内アナウンスで)シートベルトをお締めください Please fasten *your seat belt*.
◆運転する人はシートベルトをしなければならない Drivers must strap themselves *into their seats*.

ジーパン Gパン ⚠ jeans (❖日本語の「ジーパン」は jeans と pants を組み合わせた和製英語。数えるときは a pair of ... とする) //ジーパンを買う buy *a pair of jeans* / 彼女はジーパンをはいている She's wearing *jeans*.

ジープ jeep

シーフード seafood ⓤ

シーラカンス 〔魚〕 coelacanth [síːləkænθ] ⓒ

しいる 強いる force 働, compel 働, press 働; (意見などを押しつける) impose 働 //その地震で人々は長期にわたり不便な生活を強いられた People *were forced* [*compelled, pressed*] to lead inconvenient lives for a long time because of the earthquake. / 自分のやり方を他人に強いるべきでない You shouldn't *impose* [*force*] *your ways on* others.

シール seal ⓒ, sticker ⓒ //たんすにシールをはる put *seals* [*stickers*] on a chest of drawers

しいれ 仕入れ stocking ⓤ, buying ⓤ
◆直接仕入れを行えば経費を削減できるかもしれない We may be able to cut our costs by *buying* direct.
‖仕入れ価格 (a) prime [purchase] cost / 仕入れ係 a buyer, a purchase clerk / 仕入れ先 a supplier

しいれる 仕入れる stock 働; (買う) buy* 働; (手に入れる) get* 働 //店はその歌手のCDを大量に仕入れた They *stocked* the store *with* a lot of the singer's CDs. / (→仕入れて在庫がある) The store *stocks* a lot of the singer's CDs. / 私はテレビからその情報を仕入れた I *got* the information from TV.

しいん¹ 子音 consonant ⓒ //有声[無声]子音 *a* voiced [voiceless] *consonant*
‖子音字 a consonant (letter)

しいん² 死因 the cause of *a person's* death //彼の死因は肺癌(ポポ)だった Lung cancer was *the cause of* his *death*. / (→彼は肺癌で死んだ) He *died of* lung cancer.

しいん³ 試飲 sampling ⓤ, tasting ⓤ ——試飲する sample 働, taste 働 //ワインを試飲する *sample* [*taste*] wine
‖試飲会 a tasting

シーン scene ⓒ //暴力[ラブ]シーン *a* violent [love] *scene* / その映画のラストシーンは非常に感動的だ The movie's last *scene* is very moving.

じいん 寺院 (仏教・ヒンドゥー教などの) temple ⓒ; (イスラム教の) mosque ⓒ

ジーンズ jeans, 《米》blue jeans (❖数えるとき

は a pair of ... とする ‖はき古したジーンズ ragged jeans

しいんと 先生が怒って教室はしいんとなった The teacher got furious and the students became *perfectly silent.* ‖洞窟(ぢ)の中はしいんとしていた There was *a deep silence* in the cave.

じいんと 彼女の話は胸にじいんときた（→とても感動的だった）Her story *was very moving [touching].* ‖何かにひじをぶつけてじいんとしびれた My elbow hit something and *felt numb.* ‖I hit my funny bone.（❖funny bone は「ひじの、ぶつけるとじいんとなる場所」を指す口語的な表現。実在する骨ではない）

しうち 仕打ち bad treatment ⓤ
◆彼は仲間からひどい仕打ちを受けた He *was treated very badly* by his fellows.／He *got a raw deal* from his fellows.

しうんてん 試運転 trial [test] run ⓒ;（機械・飛行機などの）shakedown ⓒ;（車の）test drive ⓒ ──試運転する（機械・飛行機などを）shake* down;（車を）test-drive* ⓗ ‖新しい機械の試運転をする *shake down* a new machine;*give a new machine a trial run* ‖父が新車の試運転をした Father *test-drove* a new car.

シェア（市場占有率）(market) share ⓒ（通例単数形）‖市場の60パーセントのシェアを占める have *a 60 percent share of the market* ‖その会社はここ数年オーディオ業界でのシェアを伸ばしてきている The company has increased *its share* in the audio industry during the last several years.
‖シェアウエア [コンピュータ] shareware

しえい 市営 ──市営の municipal, city-operated;（市が所有する）city-owned ‖市営バス a *municipal* [*city*] bus ‖彼は市営住宅に住んでいる He lives in *municipal* [*city-owned*] *housing.*

じえい¹ 自営 おじは自営業を営んでいる My uncle *does business on his own.*／My uncle *is self-employed.*
‖自営業者 a self-employed person;（総称）the self-employed

じえい² 自衛 self-defense ⓤ ──自衛する defend [protect] *oneself* ‖自衛手段を講じる take *measures to defend oneself;* take *defensive measures*
‖自衛権 the right of self-defense ／自衛隊 the Self-Defense Forces（《略語》SDF）／自衛隊員 a Self-Defense Forces officer ／自衛本能 self-preservation ／陸上 [海上, 航空] 自衛隊 the Ground [Maritime, Air] Self-Defense Force

シェイプアップ ⚠姉はシェイプアップのためにスポーツジムに通い始めた My sister has started working out at a gym regularly to「*slim down* [*improve her figure*].（❖slim down は「やせる」、improve one's figure は「スタイルをよくする」の意味。「シェイプアップをする」の意味で×shape up とはいわない）

ジェーアール JR（❖*J*apan *R*ailways の略語）‖JR東日本 *JR East*（❖正式には East Japan Railway Company）／次の駅でJR線に乗り換えてください Transfer [Change] to *the JR line* at the next station.

シェーバー shaver
シェービングクリーム shaving cream ⓤ
ジェーリーグ J リーグ J League, Japan Professional Football League
しえき 使役 ‖使役動詞 a causative verb
ジェスチャー gesture ⓒ ⇨ 場面・状況別会話 p.1762 ‖その人にジェスチャーを交えて駅までの道を教えた I showed the person the way to the station *with gestures.*
‖ジェスチャーゲーム (a game of) charades [ʃəréidz]

ジェット ジャンボジェット機 a jumbo *jet* ‖ジェット機でウィーンへ行く fly to Vienna *by jet*（❖by の後では無冠詞）
‖ジェットエンジン [航空] a jet engine ／ジェット気流 [気象] a jet stream ／ジェットコースター a roller coaster,《英》a switchback（❖「ジェットコースター」は和製英語）／ジェット旅客機 a jetliner

ジェネレーション generation ⓒ ‖ジェネレーションギャップを感じる feel *the generation gap*

シェパード ⚠ [動物]《主に米》German shepherd ⓒ,《主に英》Alsatian ⓒ（❖単に shepherd というと「羊飼い」の意味になる）

シェフ chef ⓒ ‖一流のシェフ a master chef
シェリー（シェリー酒）sherry ⓤ
しえん 支援 support ⓤ;（特に金銭的な）backing ⓤ ──支援する support ⓗ, back ⓗ, give* ... support;（味方する）stand* by ... ‖支援を求める ask for *support* [*backing*] ‖その企業は彼らの活動を支援した The company *supported* [*backed* (*up*)] their activities.／ご支援いただきまことにありがとうございます I'm very grateful to you for「*your support* [*supporting* me].
‖支援活動 supporting activities ／支援者 a supporter ／支援団体 a support group

しお¹ 塩 salt ⓤ
塩をひとつまみ加える add a pinch of *salt* ／ゆで卵に塩を振る sprinkle *salt* on a boiled egg ／お清めに塩をまく ritually purify with *salt*
母は肉に塩コショウで味つけした Mother seasoned the meat with *salt and pepper.*
◆白菜の塩漬け *pickled* Chinese cabbage ／彼女は彼に塩かげんを見てと頼んだ She asked him to taste the dish for saltiness.
💬「塩を取ってくれませんか」「はい、どうぞ」"Would you pass me *the salt*, please." "Yes, here you are."
‖粗塩 raw salt ／岩塩 rock salt ／食卓塩 table salt

しお² 潮 tide ⓤ ⓒ ‖大 [小] 潮 a spring [neap] *tide* ‖潮の満ち引き the「*rise and fall* [*ebb and flow*] *of the tide* ‖潮が満ちて [引いて] いる *The tide* is in [out].
◆ここは潮の流れが非常に速い *The tidal current* is very strong here.／窓をあけると潮の香りがしてきた When I opened the win-

dow, I smelled *the sea*. / 鯨が潮を吹くのが見えた I could see a whale *spout*.
‖潮風 a sea breeze / 渦潮 a whirlpool / 引き潮 an ebb tide / 満ち潮 a flood tide
[和歌] 熟田津(にぎたつ)に船乗りせむと月待てば潮もかなひぬ今は漕ぎ出でな(額田王(ぬかたのおおきみ))
The Nikita shore.
We have come to leave by boat.
We wait for the moon,
and the tide begins to rise.
Come, then. Let's begin to row.

しおから 塩辛 イカの塩辛 *salted* squid
しおからい 塩辛い salty
しおくり 仕送り 私は親からの月13万円の仕送りで生活している I live on *a monthly allowance* of 130,000 yen *sent* by my parents. / I live on 130,000 yen *sent* by my parents each month.
しおけ 塩気 salty taste ◻ (また a~); (塩) salt ◻ ‖この料理は塩気が足りない(→もう少し塩が必要だ) This dish needs a little more *salt*. ◆私は医者の忠告どおり塩気のある食べ物を減らした I cut down on *salty* food as the doctor had advised.
しおどき 潮時 (high) time ◻; (機会) opportunity ◻◻ ‖彼らもそろそろ別れる潮時だ It's about *time* (that) they parted. / It's about *time* for them to part. (※前の表現ではthatは通例省略し, 節内の動詞は仮定法過去)
◆彼は潮時を見はからって部活をやめた He had been waiting for *the right moment* to leave the club.
しおひがり 潮干狩り clam [shellfish] gathering ◻ ‖潮干狩りに行く go to a beach to *gather clams*
しおみず 塩水 salt water ◻; (食塩水) saline (solution) ◻
しおやき 塩焼き (塩焼きの魚) fish broiled [(英)grilled] with salt ◆魚を塩焼きにする *broil* [*grill*] fish *with salt*
しおらしい (遠慮がちな) modest; (従順な) obedient; (おとなしい) gentle ‖きょうの彼女は妙にしおらしい She is being curiously *modest* [*obedient, gentle*] today.
しおり 栞 (本にはさむ) bookmark ◻; (旅行・遠足などの案内書) guide ◻, guidebook ◻ ‖(本の)ページにしおりをはさむ insert *a bookmark* between the pages
しおれる 萎れる wilt ◉, droop ◉; (枯れる) wither ◉ ‖花びんの花がしおれてしまった The flowers in the vase *have wilted* [*drooped*].
しか¹ 鹿 deer ◻ (複 ~); (雄ジカ) buck ◻, stag ◻ (複 ~, ~s); (雌ジカ) doe [dóu] ◻; (子ジカ) fawn ◻
◆(枝状の)シカの角(つの) an antler
‖シカ皮 buckskin / (食用の)シカ肉 venison
しか² 歯科 dentistry ◻ ‖歯科医 a dentist, (公式的) a dental surgeon / 歯科医院 a dental clinic / 歯科衛生士 a dental hygienist / 歯科大学 a dental college
しか³ 市価 market (price) ◻ ‖その商品は市価の30パーセント引きで売られている That product is being sold at 30 percent off *the*

market price.

-しか only ➡ -だけ

> [語法] only は日本語の「…しか～ない」に当たるので not などの否定語は不要. 強調する語の直前に置き, その語を強く発音する. ただし口語では位置は比較的自由で, 強勢のある場所で only が強調する語が分かる ‖ 彼女は好きなものしか食べない(→好きなものだけを食べる) She eats *only* what she likes. / (口語的)She *only* eats what she likes. (※likesに強勢がある)

私は今300円しか持っていない I have *only* [*as little as*] 300 yen now.
彼女しか彼の言ったことを信じていない *Only* she believes what he said. / She is the *only* person who believes what he said.
僕は1度しか東京へ行ったことがない I've been to Tokyo *only* once.
君にしか本当のことは話せない I can tell the truth *only* to you. / (→君以外のだれにも)I can tell the truth to *nobody but* you.
私があなたにしてあげられるのはこれくらいしかない This is the *only* thing I can do for you. / (→これがすべてだ)This is *all* I can do for you.
由紀子に告白するなら今しかないぞ Now is the *only* time to tell Yukiko that you love her.
◆その話を聞いてあきれるしかなかった I felt *nothing but* disgust when I heard the story. / 彼がそれを盗んだとしか思えない I *can't but* conclude that he is the one who stole it. / この道路では時速40キロまでしか出せない (→時速40キロ以上の速さで運転することが禁じられている) You are prohibited from driving faster *than* 40 kilometers per hour on this road.

しが 滋賀

> 滋賀県は本州中央部の西にあり, 四方を山に囲まれています. この県の中央部には日本最大の湖, 琵琶湖があります. 湖の周辺には多くの都市や町があり, 昔から水運の中心として栄えてきました. この地域にはまた比叡山延暦寺や大津の石山寺, 三井寺などの有名な寺があります.
> Shiga Prefecture is located in the western part of central Honshu and is surrounded by mountains on all sides. In the center of this prefecture lies Lake Biwa, the largest lake in Japan. Around this lake there are many cities and towns, which have flourished as centers for shipping on the lake. Some famous temples are also in this area, including Enryakuji on Mt. Hiei, Ishiyamadera, and Miidera in Otsu.

じか 時価 current price ◻; (市価) market (price) ◻ ‖その絵は時価数億円といわれている The painting is said to be worth a few hundred million yen *at the current* [*market*] *price*.

じが 自我 self ◎, 〖哲学・心理〗ego ◎ ◎ //自我に目ざめる become conscious of *one's self [ego]* / 自我を確立する establish *one's self [ego]* / 自我の崩壊を招く(→こうむる) suffer collapse of *one's self [ego]*
◆自我を主張する assert *oneself* / 彼は自我が強い He is *self-assertive*.

しかい¹ 司会 (催し物・番組などの司会者) a master of ceremonies(❖《米》では emcee ともいう;《略記》MC),《英》compère ◎, host ◎ (❖女性は hostess ともいう);(会議などの司会者) chairperson ◎, the chair ──司会する《米》emcee 他 自,《英》compère 他 自, host 他 自; take* the chair, chair //番組の司会者がゲストを紹介した *The emcee [host]* of the program introduced the guest. / 今夜,司会進行を務めさせていただきます山田です My name is Yamada and I will be *your MC* this evening. / 勝也がミーティングの司会をした Katsuya「*took the chair [presided]* at the meeting.

しかい² 視界 view ◎, sight ◎;(見通し) visibility ◎ //視界から消える go out of *sight*; disappear from *sight* / 霧で視界が悪かったので山登りは中止となった The hike was canceled because *the visibility* was bad [poor] due to fog. / そのビルが視界に入ってきたら目的地もすぐだ You are near the destination when the building comes into *view [sight]*.

しがい¹ 市外 彼女は市外からこの学校に通っている She attends this school from *outside the city*.
‖市外局番《米》an area code,《英》a dialling [an STD] code / 市外通話 an out-of-town call, a long-distance call

しがい² 市街 (都市の中心部・繁華街) town ◎
◆旧市街 (→かつての中心街) *the former center of a city*; (→古くからある区域) *the old part of a city* / この道を10分ほど行けば川越市街です It takes about ten minutes along this road to get to *downtown* Kawagoe.
‖市街地 town / 市街地図 a city map

しがい³ 死骸 (dead) body ◎; (人の) corpse ◎; (動物の) carcass ◎

じかい 次回 next time ──次回の next //次回はもっとがんばります I'll try harder *next time*. / 次回のミーティングの日取りを決めよう Let's determine the date for our *next* meeting. ◆(連続ドラマなどで)次回に続く *To be continued.*

しがいせん 紫外線 ultraviolet rays

しかえし 仕返し revenge ◎ ──仕返しする get* [take*] *one's* revenge on *a person*, revenge *oneself* on *a person* //仕返しに兄の靴を隠した She hid her brother's shoes *in revenge for* his bullying her. / 今いつにはきっとこの仕返しをしてやるぞ I'll「*take revenge on* [*revenge myself on, get back at*]*him for* this. / いじめっ子の仕返しを恐れて大人に助けを求められない子もいる Some children don't ask for help from adults because they're afraid the bullies will take revenge on them.

しかく¹ 資格 qualification ◎ 《しばしば複数形 ~s》; (免許証) license,《英》licence ◎; (必要条件) requirement ◎
応募資格を満たす meet [satisfy] *the* application *requirements*
この仕事にはどういう資格が必要ですか What are *the* necessary *qualifications* for this job?
彼女はロシア語教師の資格を持っている She has *a license* to teach Russian./ She *is qualified* as a teacher of Russian.
彼は保育士の資格を取った He obtained *a license [qualification]* to be a nursery school teacher.
彼は教師の資格を奪われた He was deprived of *his license* to teach school. / He *was disqualified from* teaching school.
◆彼に対してあなたがそんなことを言う資格はない You *are not qualified* to say that to him. / (→権利はない) You *don't have any right* to say that to him. / 彼女には市議会議員になる資格がある She is *eligible* to be a member of the city assembly.
‖資格試験 a qualifying examination / 資格所有者 a qualified person, a license holder / 資格審査 screening

しかく² 四角 (正方形) square ◎; (一般に四辺形) quadrilateral ◎ ──四角の square
四角い布 *a square* of cloth; a *square* piece of cloth / 板を真四角になるように切る cut a board into *a (perfect) square*
‖四角すい a square pyramid / 四角柱 a quadratic prism
[慣用表現] 四角四面なあいさつ a *cut-and-dried* greeting / そう四角張らずに Don't be so *formal*.

しかく³ 視覚 sight ◎, eyesight ◎,《公式的》vision ◎ ──視覚の visual //彼は幼いころに視覚と聴覚を失った He lost *his sight* and hearing when he was a child. ◆人々の視覚に訴える be appealing to *the eye*
‖視覚教材 visual aids / 視覚効果 visual effects / 視覚障害 an impaired vision

しかく⁴ 死角 (道路などの) blind spot ◎ //自転車が運転手の死角に入った A bicycle entered the driver's *blind spot*.

しがく¹ 私学 private school ◎; (私立大学) private college [university] ◎ ‖私学助成金 government subsidies to private schools

しがく² 史学 history ◎

しがく³ 歯学 dentistry ◎

じかく 自覚 awareness ◎《また an~》, consciousness ◎《また a~》──自覚する become* aware [conscious] (◆「自覚している」状態を表すには become の代わりに be を用いる); (気づく) realize 他 (❖進行形にはできない) //彼は自分が間違っていたことを自覚しているのだろうか Is he *aware that* he was wrong? / 彼は高校生としての自覚が足りない (→もっと自覚をもつべきだ) He should *be more aware [conscious]* that he is now a high school student. / 彼女は生徒会長として

の責任を自覚している She *is aware* [*conscious*] *of* her responsibility as the president of the student council.

◆我々は常に本校生徒としての自覚をもって行動するべきだ We should always *keep in mind* that we are students of this school.

‖自覚症状 a subjective symptom

しかけ 仕掛け (装置) device [C]; (気のきいた道具) gadget [C]; (機構) mechanism [C] [U]; (わな) trap [C]; (トリック) trick [C]; (釣りの) fishing tackle [U] ∥このおもちゃはどういう仕掛けで動くの What kind of *device* [*mechanism*] makes this toy move? / ネズミを捕るための仕掛けを台所に置いた I put *a* mouse *trap* on the kitchen floor. / ご覧のとおり, 種も仕掛けもございません As you can see, there's no *trick* here. ◆ぜんまい仕掛けのおもちゃ a *spring-driven* toy

‖仕掛け花火 set-piece fireworks

しかける 仕掛ける ❶【設置する】(わななどを) set* [他], lay* [他]; (爆弾などを)《口語的》plant [他] ∥ネズミ捕りを仕掛ける *set* [*lay*] a trap for mice / テロリストたちは銀行に爆弾を仕掛けた Terrorists *planted* a bomb in the bank.

❷【働きかける】敵の基地に攻撃を仕掛ける「*make a strike on* [*attack*] an enemy base / 彼がけんかを仕掛けてきたんだ He *picked* a fight [quarrel] with me. (❖fight はつかみ合いのけんか, quarrel は口論)

❸【…し始める】begin* [start] to *do* ➾ -かける ∥外出の準備をしかけたところで友人が訪ねてきた A friend of mine visited me when I *had* just *begun to* get ready to go out.

◆弟はテレビゲームをしかけたまま寝てしまった My brother fell asleep *while playing* a video game.

シカゴ Chicago (❖米国の都市)

しかざん 死火山 extinct volcano [C]

しかし

❶【けれども・だが】── [接] but; (それにもかかわらず) yet ── [副] however (❖but とほぼ同意だがやや公式的. 文頭・文中・文末のいずれの位置にも用いられ, コンマで区切るのがふつう), 《公式的》nevertheless ➾ -けれど(も), だが

彼女はそこへ行ったと言っていた. しかしそれはうそだった She said she went there, *but* that was a lie.

彼女は必死で勉強をした. しかし試験には通らなかった She studied very hard. *But* [*However, Yet, Nevertheless*] she couldn't pass the exam.

❷【それにしても】

しかしきょうの試合はすごかったね *Well*, [*Anyway, Really*] today's match was exciting, wasn't it?

じがじさん 自画自賛 self-congratulation [U], self-praise [U] ── 自画自賛する praise *oneself*, 《口語的》blow* *one's* own horn [trumpet]

じかせい 自家製 ── 自家製の homemade ∥自家製のソーセージ *homemade* sausages

じがぞう 自画像 self-portrait [C] ∥彼は自画像を描いている He is painting *a self-portrait.*

しかた 仕方 way [C], 《公式的》manner [C] 《通例単数形》; (…する方法) how to *do*; (体系的な方法) method [C] ➾ ほうほう ∥返事のしかたが悪いと怒られた I got scolded for *my* improper *way* [*manner*] *of* replying. / データの保存のしかたを教えて Show [Teach] me *how to* save data.

しかた(が)ない 仕方(が)ない

❶【やむをえない】(人が…を避けられない) can't help [avoid] ...; (事態が避けられない) can't be helped, be unavoidable [inevitable]; (当然だ) it is natural (that ... / to *do*)

失敗してしまったのはしかたないことだよ It *couldn't be helped* [It *was unavoidable*] that you failed.

僕といっしょに行きたくないというのならしかたがない I *can't help* it if you don't want to come with me.

君は悪いことをしたのだから怒られてもしかたがない You *can't avoid* being scolded [*It is natural that* you should be scolded] because you did something wrong.

◆こんな状況ではクラブをやめるよりしかたがない *There is nothing for it* [I *have no choice*] *but to* leave the club under these circumstances. / すんだことはしかたがない What is done「*is done* [*cannot be undone*].

🗨「ちょっとお金貸してよ」「またか. しかたがないなあ(→君も学ばないなあ)」"Can you lend me some money?" "Again? *You'll never learn*, will you?"

❷【むだだ】it is no use *doing* [to *do*], there is no use (in) *doing* ➾ むだ

いまさらそのことでぶつぶつ言ったってしかたがないよ *It's no use* [*There is no use*] complaining about that now.

❸【こらえられない】(…せずにはいられない) cannot help *doing* [but *do*], 《公式的》cannot but *do*; (我慢できない) can't stand [bear, 《口語的》put up with ...]; (…したくてしかたがない) be eager [《口語的》dying, 《口語的》itching] to *do*

映画の悲しいシーンに涙が出てしかたなかった I *couldn't*「*help* shedding tears [*help but* shed tears, *but* shed tears] at a sad scene in the movie.

私に対する彼の態度には腹が立ってしかたがない I *can't stand* [*bear, put up with*] his attitude toward me. / His attitude toward me is *unbearable.*

私はそのことを彼に話したくてしかたがない I'*m eager* [*dying, itching*] *to* tell him about it.

しかたなく 仕方なく (意志に反して) against *one's* will; (しぶしぶ) reluctantly, unwillingly ∥彼はしかたなく周りの意見に従った He complied with others' decisions *against his will.* / He *reluctantly* complied with others' decisions.

しかたなし(に) 仕方なし(に) ➾ しかたなく

じかため 地固め ── 地固め(を)する (地面を) level and harden the ground; (基礎を固め

じかだんぱん 直談判 direct negotiations 　—直談判する negotiate [talk] with *a person* directly [personally]

-しがち 芸能界というと華やかな世界を想像しがちだ We *tend* [*are inclined, are apt*] *to* think of show business as flamboyant. ⇒-がち

しかつ 死活 それは我々にとって死活問題だ It is *a* 「*matter of life and death* [*life-and-death matter, vital issue*] for us.

しがつ 四月 April ⓒⓊ ((略語)Apr.). ⇒いちがつ ‖四月ばか(人) an April fool; (日) April Fools' Day

じかつ 自活 self-support Ⓤ 　—自活する lead* an independent life, support [maintain] *oneself*, make* [earn] *one's* own living

しかつめらしい (堅苦しい) formal, stuffy; (いかめしい) severe, grim; (まじめくさった) solemn ‖しかつめらしい態度 a *formal* [*stuffy, severe, solemn*] attitude

しがない (つまらない) humble; (一介(炒)の) simple; (みすぼらしい) miserable; (貧しい) poor ‖しがない暮らしをする lead a *humble* [*poor, miserable*] life / 私はしがないサラリーマンさ I am just a *humble* [*simple*] company employee.

じかに 直に directly; (個人的に) in person, personally ⇒ちょくせつ ‖分からないところがあったら, じかに彼に聞いてみるといいよ If there's anything you don't understand, go ask him *directly* [*in person*].
◆最近道端にじかに座る若者が多い There are many young people who sit *right on* the ground these days. / 兄は素肌の上に(→肌着を着ないで)じかにワイシャツを着ている My brother wears a shirt *next to* his skin without an undershirt.

じがね 地金 (加工前の金属) raw metal Ⓤ; (メッキの素地) base metal Ⓤ

-しかねない (…しそうだ) might very well *do*, be likely to *do*; (可能性がある) be capable of *doing* ‖彼ならずる休みもしかねない He 「*might very well* [*is likely to*] play hooky.

じかび 直火 ソーセージを直火で焼く broil [(英)*grill*] sausages *over the fire*

しがみつく cling* to …, hang* onto [on to] …, hold* onto [on to] … ‖その子供は母親にしがみついた The child 「*clung to* [*hung onto, held onto*] his [her] mother.

しかめ(っ)つら しかめ(っ)面 (まゆをひそめた表情) frown Ⓒ; (苦痛などでゆがんだ表情) grimace Ⓒ ‖彼はしかめっ面で私を見た He looked at me *with a frown* [*grimace*].

しかめる (まゆをゆがめる) frown ⓘ; (嫌悪・苦痛などで顔をゆがめる) grimace ⓘ ‖彼の身勝手さに僕らは顔をしかめた We *frowned at* his selfishness. / 彼女は痛みに顔をしかめた She grimaced with pain.

しかも ❶【さらに】(そのうえ) (and) besides, 《公式的》(and) moreover, and ⇒ そのうえ ‖このテーブルは質がよく, しかも値段がてごろだ This table is of good quality, *and besides* [*moreover*, (→さらによいことには) *what is more*] it is reasonably priced. / This table is of good quality *and* reasonably priced, *too.* / 彼女はフルマラソンを走ることができる. しかもかなり速く She can run a full marathon, *and* at a good speed.
◆彼は作業が遅い. しかも(→さらに悪いことには)いいかげんだ He does his work very slowly *and*, what is worse, sloppily.
❷【それでもなお】(and) yet, still ‖彼は他人に迷惑をかけて, しかもひと言も謝らずにいる He bothered others, *and yet* he won't apologize.

じかよう 自家用 (自分用) for *one's* own use; (家庭用) for *one's* home use ‖自家用車 a family car; (個人の) a private car

しかる 叱る 《口語的》tell* off, 《公式的》dress down, 《公式的》rebuke ⓘ; (特に子供を) scold ⓘ; (とがめる) reprimand ⓘ
母親はその子をしかった The mother 「*told off* [*scolded*] the child.
彼はうそをついたため先生にひどくしかられた He was 「*severely scolded* [*told off* severely] by the teacher *for* telling a lie.
◆あの子は厳しくしかってやらねばならない That boy [girl] needs *a good scolding* [*telling-off, dressing-down*]. / このことが親に知れたら, 君は絶対しかられるぞ If your parents find out about this, you'll surely *catch it*.
(❖catch it は子供について使われる口語的表現)

しかるに 然るに yet, still, 《公式的》nevertheless ⇒ かかわらず

しかるべき 然るべき (適切の) proper, appropriate, suitable; (最適な) right; (正当な) 《公式的》due (❖名詞, 特に不加算名詞の前で用いる) ‖ふさわしい ‖そのことにしかるべき方法で対処する take *proper* [*appropriate, suitable*] measures against it / 当日はしかるべき服装で来てください Please come dressed in *proper* [*appropriate, suitable*] attire on the day. / それをするにはしかるべき人の許可が必要だ You need permission from the *right* person. / 彼は我々の質問に答えてしかるべきだ He 「*ought to* [*should*] answer our questions. / あの選手は退場させられてしかるべきだ That player *deserves* to be thrown out of the game.

しかん 士官 (commissioned) officer Ⓒ

しがん 志願 (申し込み) application ⓒⓊ 　—志願する (進み出る) volunteer ⓘ, come* forward; (申し込む) apply ⓘ ‖軍隊に志願する *volunteer for* the army / 彼は被災者救援活動を志願した He *volunteered* [*came forward*] to help the victims. / 友人と私は同じ大学を志願した My friend and I *applied to* the same university.
◆その大学の今年の入学志願者数は過去最高だった The number of *applicants* to the uni-

versity this year was the largest ever.
‖志願者(応募者) an applicant; (ボランティア) a volunteer; (立候補者) a candidate / 志願兵 a volunteer

じかん¹　時間

❶ (長さをもつ)時	time
❷ 単位(60分)	hour
❸ 時刻	time
❹ 区切られた一定の時・時限・授業	hour; class

❶【(長さをもつ)時】time Ⓤ (また a ~)
《時間が》
この料理は作るのに相当時間がかかるだろう This dish will take a lot of *time* to cook.

そう急がなくてもいいよ．時間はたっぷりあるんだから Don't hurry. We have a lot of *time*.

時間が足りなくて問題が全部はできなかったよ I was short of *time* and couldn't solve all the problems.

彼が買い物に出てからだいぶ時間がたった *A long time* has passed since he left to go shopping.

寝る時間がない I have no *time* to sleep.

このごろ忙しくて本を読む時間がほとんどない I'm so busy these days that I have little *time* for reading.

そんなことをしている時間があったら，勉強しなさい You should study if you have *time* to do such a thing.

◆その技を習得するまでにどれくらい時間がかかりましたか How long did it *take* you to acquire the technique?

🄬「今お時間はありますか」「今はありませんが3時ごろなら時間をとれます」"Do you have *time* now?" "No, I don't. But I can spare *time* for you at about three."

《時間を・に》
今すぐには答えられません．少し考える時間をください I can't answer right now. Please give me some *time* to think about it.

私たちはそのイベントの構想に多くの時間を費やした We spent much *time* in planning the event.

時間をむだに使うな Don't waste *your time*.

彼はわざわざ時間を割いて引っ越しの手伝いに来てくれた He kindly found *the time* to come and help me move.

彼はたくさんの仕事を抱え毎日時間に追われている He's got so many tasks that he is pressed for *time* every day.

◆ちょっとお時間をよろしいでしょうか Could you spare me *a minute*?

《時間の》
彼の話なんか聞くだけ時間のむだだよ It's *a waste of time* to listen to him.

その会には時間の都合がついたら参加します I will attend the meeting if I can manage *the time*.

犯人がつかまるのも時間の問題だ It's only *a matter of time* before the criminal gets arrested.

きのうは時間のたつのも忘れて1日中本を読みふけっていた I was so engaged in a book that I forgot *the (passage of) time* and spent the whole day yesterday reading it.

《その他》
空き時間は本を読んで過ごします I spend my *free time* reading books.

残り時間があまりない There is not much *time left*.

時間つぶしにそのへんを散歩してきます I'm going to walk around here to *kill time*.

◆テレビを長時間(→何時間も)見続けるのは目によくない Watching TV *for hours* is not good for your eyes.

❷【単位(60分)】hour Ⓒ
1日は24時間です There are 24 *hours* in a day.

私は彼を2時間待った I waited for him *for two hours*.

そこから駅までは歩いて1時間を見込んでおいたほうがいい You should allow *an hour* to walk from there to the station.

豪雨でその列車は2時間遅れた The train was delayed two *hours* by the heavy rain.

その遊園地はここから車で1時間の所にあります The amusement park is *an hour's drive* from here.

1時間で戻ります I'll be back *in an hour*.

彼は勉強していても必ず1時間に1回，10分间休憩をとる He never forgets to take one 10-minute rest *an hour* when he studies.

その店は24時間営業だ The store *is open 24 hours* (a day).

🄬「あなたの家から新宿までは電車で何時間かかりますか」「1時間です」"*How many hours* does it take from your home to Shinjuku by train?" "It takes *a little more than an hour*."

❸【時刻】time Ⓤ, hour Ⓒ
《~(の時間)》
時間です．鉛筆を置いてください *Time is up*. Put down your pencils.

次のフライトの時間を確かめた I made sure of *the time of* the next flight.

彼は集合時間を間違えていた He was mistaken about *the meeting time*.

試合は現地時間で夜の8時に始まる The game starts at 8 p.m. *local time*.

開店時間前から店の前には行列ができていた There was a line of people waiting in front of the store before *its opening time*.(✿閉店時間は (a) closing time)

◆パーティーの時間と場所を教えてください Tell me *when* and where the party will be held.

《時間を・に》
ラッシュアワーを避けるため時間をずらして家を出た I changed *the time* I leave home to avoid the rush hour.

彼は時間にルーズだ He is careless about

time. / He is *unpunctual*.

こんな遅い時間に電話をかけてくるな Don't call me at *a* late *hour* like this.

◆彼女はきちっと時間を守る人だ She is a very *punctual* person.

〖その他〗

もう寝る時間だよ It's *time* for bed. / It's *time* you went to bed.

そろそろ出かける時間だよ It's about *time* to go.

あれ，もうこんな時間だ．帰らなくちゃ Look at *the time*! I should [must] be going.

彼は時間どおりに現れなかった He didn't turn up *on time*.

彼女は約束の時間より前に[時間に遅れて]ここに着いた She got here「*ahead of* [*past*] *the* appointed *time*.

夕食の時間帯にこんな番組を流さないでほしい I wish they wouldn't broadcast such programs at dinner *time*.

◆もう時間も遅いことだし，この話はまたあしたにしよう It's *late*. We should talk about this tomorrow. / 時間厳守でお願いします Please be *punctual*.

❹【区切られた一定の時・時限・授業】(何かをするための特定の) hour [C] (❖複数形で「勤務・営業などの時間」の意味); (学校の授業時間) class [C] [U], period [C]

面会時間は3時から6時までです *The visiting hours* are from three to six.

きょうは授業が6時間ある We have six *classes* today.

次回の数学の時間までにこの問題を解いておかなければならない I have to solve this problem by *the* next math *class*.

きょうの1時間目は体育だった Today's *first class* was PE.

‖時間給 an hourly wage / 時間差攻撃(バレーボールの) a delayed attack / 時間割《主に米》a (class) schedule, 《英》a timetable / 営業時間 (店などの) opening hours; (業務時間) business hours / 休み時間 (a) break; (小学校の)《米》(a) recess

➾とき(時)

じかん² 次官 (日本の事務次官) vice-minister [C] (❖省庁によって異なる場合がある); (英米の) undersecretary [C]

じかんがい 時間外 ━時間外の overtime (❖名詞の前で用いる) ━時間外に overtime ‖3時間の時間外勤務をする *work overtime* for three hours; do three hours of *overtime*

‖時間外手当 overtime (pay)

じかんぎれ 時間切れ 時間切れになる前にこの作業を終えねばならない I must finish this work before *the deadline* [*time limit*]. / 時間切れで最後の問題ができなかった(→最後の問題を解く前に時間を使い切ってしまった) I *ran out of time* before I could finish the last question. / はい，時間切れです Okay, *time's up*.

しき¹ 指揮 (楽団などの) conducting [U]; (軍隊などの) command [C] [U]; (監督) direction [U] ━指揮する (楽団などを) conduct [他] [自]; (軍隊などを) command [他] [自]; (活動・組織などを) direct [他], conduct [他] ‖オーケストラを指揮する *conduct* an orchestra / 先生の指揮で校歌を歌った We sang our school anthem *conducted* by the teacher. / 首相が自衛隊を指揮する The Prime Minister *commands* [*is in command of*] the Self-Defense Forces. / 消防団は彼の指揮下にある The fire brigade *is under* his *command*.

‖指揮官 a commander, a commanding officer / 指揮権 command / 指揮者 a conductor / 指揮台 a podium / 指揮棒 a baton

しき² 式 ❶【儀式】(式典) ceremony [C]; (結婚式) wedding ceremony [C] ‖開会[閉会]式 *an* opening [*a* closing] *ceremony* / 式の日取りを決める set the date for *a ceremony* / 式は今度の日曜日に行われます *The ceremony* [*rite*] is going to be held next Sunday. / 彼らは教会で式を挙げた Their *wedding ceremony* was held at a church.

❷【数式】expression [C]; (等式・方程式) equation [C]; (公式) formula [C] (複 ～s, formulae) ‖式を立てる set up *an expression* [*equation*] / 二酸化炭素の化学式を知っていますか Do you know *the chemical formula* for carbon dioxide?

‖式次第 the program of a ceremony

しき³ 四季 (the) four seasons ‖この公園では四季を通じて様々な花が楽しめる You can enjoy many types of flowers「*the four seasons* of the year [(→一年中) *all the year around*] in this park.

◆日本は四季の変化に富んでいる Japan has remarkable *seasonal* characteristics.

しき⁴ 士気 morale [mərǽl] [U] ‖彼の言葉が私たちの士気を高めた His words boosted [raised] our *morale*. / きのうの大敗で彼らの士気はくじかれた Their *morale* was broken by yesterday's complete defeat. / チームの士気が下がっている *The morale* of the team is low.

しき⁵ 死期 the time of *one's* death, *one's* end, *one's* time ‖彼は死期が迫っている *The time of his death* [*His end, His time*] is drawing near.

-しき -式 (様式) style [C] [U]; (やり方) way [C], style [C] [U]; (体系的方法) method [C], system [C] [U] ‖イギリス式のつづり *the* British *way* of spelling / 和式[洋式]トイレ a Japanese-*style* [Western-*style*] toilet

◆折りたたみ式自転車 a *folding* bicycle

じき¹ 時期 time [U] [C]; (期間) period [C]; (段階) stage [C]; (季節) season [C] ➾とき(時)

彼の励ましのおかげであのつらい時期を乗り越えられた Thanks to his encouragement, I got through「those hard *times* [that hard *period*].

この時期は1年のうちで最も天気が変わりやすい The weather is the most changeable at this *time* of year.

雅夫はお金を全部テレビゲームにつぎ込んでいるけど，今はそういうことをやってみたい時期なんだろう Masao spends all his money on

じき

video games. But I think he's just going through *a stage*.
秋は勉強にもスポーツにもいい時期だ Fall is *a good season* for study and for sports.
クリスマスの時期には街のあちこちからクリスマスソングが聞こえてくる Christmas carols are heard everywhere on the streets during [in] *the Christmas season*.
今がトマトのいちばんおいしい時期だ(→今トマトは旬(しゅん)だ) Tomatoes are *in season* now.
時期はずれの桜が咲いた The cherry blossoms bloomed *out of season*.
◆時期にそのことを言うのは時期尚早(しょうそう)だ It's *still too early* to tell him about it.

じき² 時機 (好機) opportunity ⓊⒸ; (偶然の好機) chance Ⓒ; (ふさわしい時) time Ⓤ ➡ きかい(機会) ‖彼らは攻撃の時機をうかがっていた They were waiting for *an opportunity* [*a chance*] to attack. / そうするつもりだったが時機を逃してしまった I intended to do that, but I missed *the opportunity* [*chance*]. / 彼には時機を見て話すつもりだ I will tell him *at the right time*.

じき³ 次期 (次の) next; (後任に決まっている) incoming ➡ つぎ(次) ‖多くの人は彼が次期首相になると見ている Many people see him as the *next* prime minister. / 次期生徒会長には大きな期待がかかっている Much is expected of the *incoming* president of the student council. ◆次期大統領 the president-*elect*; the president *designate*(❖共に就任前の大統領当選者を意味する)

じき⁴ 直 ──じき(に) (間もなく) soon, shortly, before long; (すぐに) in a moment [minute]; (ほとんど) almost ‖雪はじきに溶けてなくなるだろう The snow will *soon* melt away. / もうじき春だ Spring is coming *soon*. / 母ならじき帰ってくると思います My mother will be back *in a moment* [*minute*]. / 彼がアメリカへ行ってからもうじき2年になる It's *almost* two years [*Almost* two years have passed] since he left for the U.S.

じき⁵ 磁気 magnetism Ⓤ ‖磁気を帯びる become *magnetic*; become *magnetized* ‖磁気あらし a *magnetic* storm / 磁気ディスク a *magnetic* disk / 磁気テープ a *magnetic* tape / 磁気ヘッド a (*magnetic*) head

じき⁶ 磁器 porcelain ⓊⒸ, china Ⓤ, chinaware Ⓤ

しきい 敷居 threshold Ⓒ, doorsill Ⓒ
◆二度とこの家の敷居をまたぐな Never *come back* to this house again! / I'll never *let you in* this house again!
慣用表現 こちらから頼み事ばかりしているので、彼の家は敷居が高い(→訪問しづらい) I *hesitate to visit* him because I'm always asking him for favors.

しきいし 敷石 flagstone Ⓒ; (舗装用の) paving stone Ⓒ

しぎかい 市議会 municipal [city] council [assembly] Ⓒ ‖市議会議員 a member of the municipal council

しききん 敷金 (security) deposit Ⓒ ‖2か月分の敷金を払う pay *a deposit* of two months' rent

しきさい 色彩 color, (英) colour ⓊⒸ; (気味) a tinge ‖はでな色彩の衣装 clothes with loud *colors*; loudly-*colored* clothes / その行事は宗教的色彩を帯びていた The event had *a religious tinge*. / The event was religiously *tinged*. / 彼女は独特の色彩感覚をもっている She has *a unique sense of color*. / 彼の絵は色彩豊かだ His painting is *colorful*.

しきし 色紙 a *shikishi*, a square card for art or calligraphy, also used for autographs

しきじ 式辞 address Ⓒ ‖成人式で市長が式辞を述べた The mayor gave [delivered] *an address* at the coming-of-age ceremony.

しきじ² 識字 ‖識字運動 an anti-illiteracy movement / 識字率 the literacy rate

じきじき 直々 ──じきじきに personally, in person ‖彼には総理がじきじきに賞を贈ることになっている The prime minister is going to present the prize to him *personally*. / The prime minister *himself* is going to present the prize to him.

しきしゃ 識者 intellectual Ⓒ, intellect Ⓒ; (専門家) expert Ⓒ

しきじゃく 色弱 (slight) color blindness Ⓤ

しきじょう 式場 ceremonial hall Ⓒ
◆結婚式場 a wedding *hall*

しきそ 色素 pigment ⓊⒸ ‖メラニン色素〖生物〗melanin

じきそ 直訴 ──直訴する make* a direct appeal to *a person* (without going through proper channels)

しきたり 仕来たり habitual practice ⓊⒸ, convention ⓊⒸ, custom ⓊⒸ ➡ かんしゅう(慣習), かんれい(慣例)

しきち 敷地 (用地) site Ⓒ; (1区画の土地) plot Ⓒ, (主に米) lot Ⓒ; (土地・建物を含む) premises ‖ビル建設用の敷地 *a site* for a building / その家の敷地は100坪ある The house's *plot* [*lot*] is「100 *tsubo* [330 square meters]. / その敷地内での飲酒はかたく禁じられている Drinking on the *premises* is strictly forbidden.

しきちょう 色調 tone Ⓒ; (濃淡) shade Ⓒ ‖柔らかい[暖かい]色調の絵 a picture in *a soft* [*warm*] *tone*

しきつめる 敷き詰める lay* ... all over ~
◆菜の花畑は一面に黄色のじゅうたんを敷き詰めたようだった The rape blossoms made the field look as if it *had been laid* with a yellow carpet.

じきに 直に ➡ じき(直)

じきひつ 直筆 one's own hand [handwriting] ‖その歌手直筆のサイン an autograph in the singer's *own hand* [*handwriting*]
◆直筆の原稿 an *autograph* manuscript

しきふ 敷布 sheet Ⓒ

しきぶとん 敷き布団 a *shiki-buton*, a futon used for sleeping on

しきべつ 識別 differentiation ⓊⒸ, discrimination Ⓤ ――識別する tell* 働 (❖通例 can, could, be able to を伴う)、distinguish 働 ⾃ (❖進行形にはできない)；(細かな違いを見分ける) discriminate 働 ⾃；(同類の2者の差を厳密に指摘する) differentiate 働 ⾃ ⇒くべつ ∥彼は食用キノコと毒キノコとを識別できる He can *tell* [*distinguish*, *discriminate*, *differentiate*] an edible mushroom *from* a poisonous one. / その2者を識別するのは難しい It is difficult to *distinguish* [*discriminate*, *differentiate*] *between* the two. / 遠くからだったので車の種類は識別できなかった I could not *distinguish* the type of car from so far away.

しきもう 色盲 color [《英》colour] blindness Ⓤ ――色盲の color-[《英》colour-]blind

しきもの 敷物 rug Ⓒ (❖通例床の一部を覆うもの)；(じゅうたん) carpet Ⓒ (❖通例部屋全体に敷き詰めたもの)；(マット・ござなど) mat Ⓒ

しきゅう¹ 至急 (すぐに) immediately, right away, at once; (急いで) quickly; (できるだけ早く) as soon [quickly] as possible; (緊急に) urgently ――至急の urgent, pressing ⇒すぐ ∥柔道部員は至急体育館に集まるように Members of the judo club, come gather *immediately* [*right away*, *quickly*] in the gymnasium. / 田中さんが至急お電話くださいとのことです Mr. Tanaka would like you to call him *as soon as possible*.(❖メモ書きなどでは as soon as possible を ASAP と書くことも多い) / この手紙を大至急ポストに入れてきてくれ Please go mail this letter *immediately* [*right away*].

しきゅう² 支給 provision Ⓤ Ⓒ；(特に定期的な) supply Ⓤ Ⓒ；(支払い) payment* Ⓤ ――支給する provide 働；supply 働；pay* 働；(必要経費などを) allow 働 ∥会社は作業員に作業服とヘルメットを支給した The company *provided* work clothes and helmets *for* the workers. / The workers *were provided with* work clothes and helmets. / 1日 2,000円までの交通費を支給します We will *allow* [*pay*] you up to 2,000 yen a day for transportation expenses. / 社員には夏と冬にボーナスが支給される The employees *are paid* a bonus in summer and winter.

∥現物支給 payment in kind

しきゅう³ 子宮【解剖】womb [wúːm] Ⓒ；【解剖】uterus Ⓒ (複 uteri, ～es) ――子宮の uterine ∥子宮外妊娠 ectopic pregnancy / 子宮癌 uterine cancer / 子宮筋腫(きんしゅ) hysteromyoma

しきゅう⁴ 四球 【野球】a base on balls, walk ⇒フォアボール

しきゅう⁵ 死球 死球を受ける be *hit by a pitch* ⇒デッドボール

じきゅう¹ 時給 hourly wage Ⓒ, time Ⓤ ∥私の仕事は時給1,500円です *The hourly wage* for my job is 1,500 yen. / My job *pays* me 1,500 yen *an hour*. / 残業には時給の5割増しで支払われる Overtime is paid at *time and a half*. ◆あなたの給料は時給で支払われます You *are paid by the hour*.

∥時給制 hourly wage system

じきゅう² 自給 彼らは食物を自給している They *produce* food *for themselves*. / They *are self-sufficient in* their food. / 彼の家族はいなかで自給自足の生活をしている His family lives a *self-sufficient* life in the country.

しきゅうしき 始球式 the ceremonial first pitch ∥人気歌手がきのうの始球式を務めた A popular singer threw out *the ceremonial first pitch* yesterday.

じきゅうせん 持久戦 endurance test Ⓒ, a test of endurance;（消耗戦）a war of attrition ∥持久戦に持ち込めば僕らの勝ちだ We can win if we make the game「*an endurance test* [*a test of endurance*]. / 軍は武器を備蓄し持久戦に備えた The army stocked arms to prepare for *a war of attrition*.

じきゅうそう 持久走 long-distance run Ⓒ

じきゅうりょく 持久力 staying power Ⓤ, stamina Ⓤ；(忍耐力) endurance Ⓤ ∥私にはフルマラソンを完走できるほどの持久力はない I don't have enough「*staying power* [*stamina*] to run a full marathon. / この仕事は相当な持久力を要する This job requires a lot of *endurance*.

しきょ 死去 *a person's death* ――死去する die ⾃,《婉曲的》pass away ⇒しぬ

しきょう 司教【カトリック】bishop Ⓒ ∥司教区 a bishopric, a diocese

しぎょう 始業 父の会社は午前9時始業だ My father's company *starts* [*opens*] at 9 a.m. / 始業のベルが鳴ると生徒は全員席に着いた All the students took their seats when *the period's bell* rang.

∥始業時間 opening time / 始業式 the ceremony at the opening of a new term

じきょう 自供 confession Ⓒ Ⓤ ――自供する confess 働 ⾃ ∥その女は犯行を自供した The woman *confessed* (*to*) the crime. / The woman *made a confession of* guilt.

じぎょう 事業 (商売・業務・会社) business Ⓤ Ⓒ；(特に困難で大胆な) enterprise Ⓒ；(十分に練られた) project Ⓒ；(新しくて冒険的な) venture Ⓒ

《事業を～に》

事業を営む manage [run] *a business* / 新しい事業を興す start *a new business*

彼は事業に成功した He succeeded in *business*.

彼女は父親の事業を継いだ She has taken over her father's *business*.

その出版社は事業を拡大した The publisher expanded [extended] *its business*.

《事業が～は》

その事業は失敗に終わった The *business* [*enterprise, project*] ended in failure.

その会社は事業がうまくいかず先月倒産した The company went bankrupt last month because of its poor *business* practices.

《その他》

わが社は事業の縮小を迫られている Our compa-

しきょく

ny needs to cut [reduce] the size of our *business*.
その会社は海外事業に積極的だ The company is active in *overseas business*.
合弁事業の条件が取り決められた The conditions for *the joint venture* were laid down.

||事業家 a person of business; (企業家) an entrepreneur / 事業所 an office; (会社) a company / 事業所得 earnings [profit] from a business / 事業税 an enterprise tax / 事業主 a business manager / 営利事業 a commercial enterprise [project] / 開発事業 a development project / 公共事業 public works / 慈善事業 a charity / ベンチャー事業 venture business

しきょく 支局 branch (office) ⓒ, bureau ⓒ ‖新聞社のロンドン支局 the London branch [bureau] of a newspaper

じきょく 磁極 (magnetic) pole ⓒ

しきり 仕切り partition ⓒ, screen ⓒ ‖その部屋の一部は仕切りで見えないようになっていた A part of the room was hidden by *a partition*.
◆この机の引き出しには仕切りが 2 つある(→仕切られた部分が 3 つある) The drawer of this desk has three *compartments*. / 土俵上で力のこもった仕切りが続いている In the ring the tension is growing as the sumo wrestlers *square off*.
慣用表現 その議論は後日仕切り直しということになった The dispute *ended without resolution only to be taken up again* later on.

しきりに 頻りに ❶【頻繁に・絶えず】(頻繁に) very often, 《公式的》frequently; (何度も) many times; (繰り返し) repeatedly; (絶えず) continuously ‖彼は授業中しきりに彼女の方を見ていた He looked at her *frequently [many times, repeatedly]* during the class. / うちの犬がさっきからしきりにほえている Our dog has been barking *continuously* for a while.
❷【熱心に】彼女はしきりにコンサートに行きたがっている She *is eager [anxious] to* go to the concert. / おじは私にその大学を受けるようしきりに説得していた My uncle tried *hard [eagerly]* to persuade me to take the entrance examination to the university.

しきる 仕切る ❶【場所・空間を】partition ⓗ; (分ける) divide ⓗ; (隠すために) screen ⓗ ‖部屋を3つに仕切る *partition [divide]* the room *into* three parts / 展示場にはついたてで仕切られたたくさんのブースがあった There were many 「*partitioned* booths [booths *divided* by partitions] in the exhibition hall. / 警察は事件現場の周囲をビニールシートで仕切った The police *screened off* the site of the crime with plastic sheets.
❷【取りしきる】(管理・経営する) manage ⓗ, run* ⓗ; (監督する) supervise ⓗ ‖彼がこの会社を仕切っている He *manages [runs, supervises]* this company. / 兄の友人が兄の結婚披露パーティーを仕切っていた One of my brother's friends *managed* [(→あれこれ世話をした) *looked after everything at*] my brother's wedding reception.
◆野球部は彼が仕切っている(→いばっている) He *is the bossy one* in the baseball club.

-しきれない ここでは紹介しきれないほどたくさんのお手紙をいただきました We received *many more* letters *than* we can read here now.

しきん 資金 (所持金・財源) funds; (金) money ⓤ; (基金) fund ⓒ; (資本金) capital ⓤ (また a〜) ⇒かね(金) ‖結婚資金 *funds for one's* marriage / 選挙[政治, 公的]資金 electoral [political, public] *funds* / 運転資金 the operating *capital* of a company / 我々には海外旅行をするのに十分な資金がある We have enough *funds* to travel abroad. / その計画に資金を割り当てることにした We decided to commit *funds* to the project. / 資金不足のため計画を断念した We abandoned our plan due to *lack [a shortage] of funds*. / 新しい図書館建設のための資金を集めた We raised 「*a fund [money]* for the construction of a new library. / その会社は資金繰りが苦しい The company is having a hard time *raising funds*. / その政治家は資金集めのパーティーを開いた The politician held a *fund-raising* party. ◆資金援助を受ける receive *financial assistance*
||資金源 a source of money

しぎん 詩吟 *shigin*, reciting Chinese poems, *tanka*, haiku, etc. in a sing-song voice

しきんきょり 至近距離 彼女は至近距離から腹部を撃たれた She was shot in the stomach *point-blank* [*at point-blank range*].

しきんせき 試金石 touchstone ⓒ, test ⓒ ‖この 1 戦が彼の実力を試す試金石となる This match will be *the touchstone [test]* of his abilities.

しく 敷く lay* ⓗ; (広げる) spread* ⓗ; (置く) put* ⓗ; (覆う) cover ⓗ
芝生の上にビニールシートを敷いた I *laid [spread, put]* a plastic sheet on the grass.
ウサギ小屋にわらを敷いてやった I *laid [spread, put]* straw in the rabbit coop.
フライパンに油を敷いた I *spread* oil over the surface of the frying pan.
都心から郊外までの新たな鉄道が敷かれた A new railroad *was laid* from the city center to the suburbs.
コップの下にコースターを敷いた I *put* a coaster under the glass.
小さなころには母がふとんを敷いてくれたものだった My mother used to *lay out* the futon for me when I was a little child.
その小道には砂利が敷かれた The path *was covered with* gravel.
◆市内には戒厳令が敷かれていた The city *was under* martial law.

じく¹ 軸 ❶【回転するものの中心】(2つの車輪を結ぶ棒) axle ⓒ; (仮想される中心線) axis

(複 axes); (中心点)〖機械〗pivot ⓒ; (巻き物などの芯(レ)) roller ⓒ ∥地球の軸 the earth's *axis* / 自動車の車輪は軸を中心に回転する The wheels of a car turn *on axles.* / 巻き物の軸が抜けてしまった The *roller* came off of a scroll. ◆彼は左足を軸にしてくるっと回った He turned around *on* his left foot. / He *pivoted on* his left foot.

❷【活動などの中心となるもの】pivot ⓒ; (中心) center ⓒ ∥わがチームには攻めの軸となる選手がいない We have no player on our team who can be *the pivot* on offense.

❸【掛け軸】scroll ⓒ

❹【数学】(座標軸) axis ⓒ ∥ x [y] 軸 *the x-axis [y-axis]*

∥軸足 a pivot leg / 軸受け〖機械〗bearings

じく² 字句 words (and phrases) ∥文書中の字句を訂正する correct *words (and phrases)* in a document

しぐさ 仕草・仕種 (身ぶり) gesture ⓒ, motion ⓒ; (ふるまい) behavior ⓤ; (動作) movement ⓒ ∥おどけたしぐさ playful *gestures* [*motions, behavior, movements*] / その子のかわいらしいしぐさにみんなほほえんだ Everybody smiled at the child's cute *gestures* [*behavior, movements*]. ◆そのチンパンジーがえさを食べるときのしぐさが(→食べ方が)おかしかった *The way* [*The manner* in which] the chimp ate was quite funny.

ジグザグ zigzag ⓒ ∥ジグザグの線を引く draw *a zigzag* / ジグザグの道 *a zigzag* road / 彼らは茂みの中をジグザグに進んでいった They went *in a zigzag* through the bushes. / They *zigzagged* (their way) through the bushes. ◆警官はジグザグ運転をしているそのバイクを止めた The police officer stopped the *zigzagging* motorcycle.

しくしく おなかがしくしく痛む have a *nagging* pain in the stomach / 女の子はしかられるとしくしく泣き始めた The girl began to *cry* [*weep*] *quietly* when she was scolded.

じくじく じくじくした傷 an *oozing* sore

しくじる (失敗する) fail ⓔ ⓘ, 《口語的》screw [mess] up; (不注意で大失敗する) blunder ⓔ; (間違う) make* a mistake ∥数学の試験をしくじる *fail* the math exam / 今回はしくじるなよ Don't *screw up* this time. ◆彼がしくじったせいで計画は失敗に終わった The plan ended up in failure because of his *blunder*.

🗣「最後の問題, 答えは 2 だよね」「2? あ, そうか. しくじった. 3 にしちゃったよ」"The answer to the last question was 'two', wasn't it?" "'Two'? Oh, yes, you're right. I *made a mistake.* I answered 'three'."

ジグソーパズル jigsaw puzzle ⓒ

シグナル signal ⓒ ➡あいず, しんごう

しくはっく 四苦八苦 四苦八苦して宿題を終わらせた I finished my homework *with a lot of difficulty.* / 彼女は夫の給料で家計をやりくりするのに四苦八苦している She *struggles* to manage a household on her husband's salary.

しくみ 仕組み (構造) structure ⓤⓒ; (機構) mechanism ⓤ ∥社会のしくみ *the structure* of society ◆このおもちゃはどういうしくみで動くの What makes this toy move?

しくむ 仕組む (たくらむ) plot ⓔ ◆巧妙に仕組まれたわな a cleverly *devised* trap / それは偶然だろうか, それとも仕組まれたものだろうか I wonder if it was done by accident or *by design.*

シクラメン cyclamen ⓒ

しぐれ 時雨 autumn shower ⓒ

しけ 時化 (暴風雨) storm ⓒ ∥しけで船は大きく横揺れした The ship rolled heavily in *the storm.* ◆台風のため海は大しけだった The sea was *very rough* [*wild, stormy*] because of a typhoon.

しけい 死刑 the death penalty, capital punishment ⓤ ∥死刑制度を廃止する abolish *the death penalty* / 死刑を執行する carry out *an execution* / 犯罪者に死刑を宣告する pass *the death sentence* on a criminal; *sentence* a criminal *to death* / その死刑囚はきょう死刑を執行された The *condemned criminal was executed* today.

∥死刑執行人 an executioner

しげき 刺激 stimulation ⓤ; (刺激物) stimulus ⓤⓒ (複 stimuli); (興奮) excitement ⓤ ⓒ ── 刺激する stimulate ⓔ; (興奮させる) excite ⓔ; (奮起させる) inspire ⓔ; (怒らせる) provoke ⓔ ── 刺激的な stimulating; (興味深い) interesting; (わくわくさせる) exciting; (挑発的な) provocative; (扇情的な) sensational

刺激に反応を示す respond to *a stimulus* / 知的[物理的, 精神的, 性的]な刺激を与える *give* intellectual [physical, mental, sexual] *stimulation; stimulate* intellectually [physically, mentally, sexually] / 刺激に満ちた都市生活 city life full of *excitement*

いいにおいが食欲を刺激した The aroma *stimulated* my appetite.

その経験に刺激されて彼女はいっそう力を入れて英語を勉強するようになった The experience *stimulated* [*inspired*] her to study English harder.

その作家の作品は私にとって常に刺激的だ The works of that writer are always *stimulating* to me.

この映画は子供には刺激が強すぎる This movie is too *sensational* for children.

◆刺激のない(→退屈な)生活を送る lead a *boring* [*dull*] life / 硫黄の刺激臭 the sharp [*pungent*] smell of sulfur / 煙が目を刺激する(→ひりひりする) Smoke *irritates* my eyes. / 彼は今機嫌が悪いから, 刺激しちゃいけない(→そっとしておけ) He's in a bad mood now, so *leave him alone.* / 医師は父にコーヒーのような刺激物をとらないようにと言った The doctor advised my father not to take *stimulants* such as coffee.

しげしげ(と) 私は以前その店にしげしげと通った I used to go to that shop *very often.* /

彼はその絵をしげしげと見た He *gazed* [*stared*] *at* the painting.

しけつ 止血 ―止血する stop bleeding
‖止血剤 a styptic

しげみ 茂み thicket [C]; (灌木(かんぼく)の) bush [C] ‖茂みの奥深くに身を隠す hide *oneself* deep in *a thicket* / 茂みの中から人影が現れた A figure emerged from *the bushes*.

しける[1] 時化る 海はしけている The sea *is stormy* [*rough*]. / ずいぶんしけた顔してるな You look really *glum*.

しける[2] 湿気る get* damp, become* soggy ◆クッキーがしけてしまった The cookies *have become soft*.

しげる 茂る (密集して生える) grow* thick; (…でいっぱいである) be thick with …; (場所一面に…が生えている) be overgrown with … ‖湖畔にはアシが茂っている Reeds *grow thick* around the lake. / 庭の木々が青々と茂っている The trees in the garden *are thick with* green leaves. / 留守にしている間に庭に雑草が茂ってしまった The garden *became overgrown with* weeds while I was gone.

しけん[1] 試験

❶【学校などの】examination [C], 《口語的》exam [C]; test [C]; quiz [C] (複 quizzes)

➔ [場面・状況別会話] p.1742

examination, exam: 長期間に学んだ成果を試したり資格などを与えたりするために行われるもの.
test:「試しに行う検査」の意味合いが強い.
quiz: 学校などで行われる小テスト.

〚試験が・は〛
きょう漢字の書き取りの試験があった We had *a test* on writing *kanji* today.
試験が終わってほっとした I was relieved to finish *the exams*.
試験が始まったとたん, 頭の中が真っ白になった My mind went blank as soon as *the exam* began.
あしたから期末試験がある *The*「*final exams* [《米》*finals*] start tomorrow.
数学の試験は簡単だった[難しかった] *The* math *exam* was easy [difficult].
💬「試験はどうだった」「まあまあだったよ」"How did you do in *your exams*?" "Not so bad."

〚試験の〛
中間試験の準備はしましたか Have you prepared for *the*「*midterm exams* [《米》*midterms*]?
僕の試験のできは最悪だった My performance on *the exams* was terrible.
試験の結果は2週間後に発表される The results of *the exam* will be announced two weeks later.
◆先生は試験の採点で忙しそうだ The teacher seems busy scoring *papers*.

〚試験に〛
試験に落ちる[受かる] fail [pass, succeed in] *an examination*
この問題はきっと試験に出るよ I'm sure that this question will be asked on *the examination*.
彼女は競争の激しい試験に備えて一生懸命勉強した She studied very hard for *the* highly competitive *examination*.

〚試験を〛
試験を行う give *an examination* / 試験を受ける take [《英》sit (for)] *an examination* / 試験を免除される be exempt from *examinations*

〚試験で〛
試験でカンニングをする cheat on [《英》in] *an exam* / 試験でよい[悪い]点を取る get a good [poor] grade on *an exam* / 試験で1番になる come out first [top] on *an exam*

〚その他〛
ABC大学の入学試験 *the entrance examination for* [*to*] ABC University / 試験勉強をする *study* [*prepare*] *for an examination*
💬「今度の試験範囲を教えてください」「1課から10課です」"Please tell us *what the* next *exam covers*." "It covers lessons one to ten."

❷【試すこと・検査すること】test [C]; trial [C][U]; experiment [C][U] ―試験する test [他]

test: 基準に合格するかどうか確かめること.
trial: 実際に役に立つかどうか前もって調べる.
experiment: 発見・実証を目ざす実験.

新車の性能を試験する *test* the performance of a new car / 人を試験的に雇う employ a person *on a trial basis*
新製品は必要な試験をすべて受けた The new product underwent all *the* necessary *tests*.
◆この新しいカードシステムはまだ試験段階にある This new card system is still in *the experimental stage*.
‖試験科目 an examination subject / 試験官 an examiner / 試験監督 《米》a proctor, 《英》an invigilator / 試験場 an examination room / 試験対策 a strategy for an examination / 試験問題 an examination question / 一次[二次]試験 a preliminary [secondary] examination / 口頭試験 an oral examination / 国家試験 the state [national] examination / 再[追]試験 a make-up examination, 《米》a makeup / 実地試験 a practical examination / 司法試験 the Bar Examination / 入学[入社]試験 an entrance examination / 筆記試験 a written examination / 面接試験 an interview / 模擬試験 a trial examination

しけん[2] 私見 私見では in *my opinion*

しげん 資源 resources ‖鉱物[水産, 地下]資源 mineral [marine, underground] *resources* / 人的資源 human *resources*; manpower / 資源を開発[利用]する develop [exploit] *resources* / 天然資源に乏しい[富んでいる] be poor [rich] in natural *resources* / 地球の持つ資源は限られている The earth's *resources* are limited.

じけん 事件 event [C]; incident [C]; case [C];

affair ◯; **happening** ◯
　event: 重要な事件・出来事.
　incident: 小事件.
　case: 犯罪事件など，調査を必要とする事件.
　affair: 特定の個人・場所などと結びついた事件.
　happening: 日常的に起こる偶然の事件・出来事.

2002年の10大事件 *the* 10 major *events* of 2002 / 歴史的[国際的]事件 historical [international] *events* / 民事[刑事]事件 *a* civil [criminal] *case* / ウォーターゲート事件 *the* Watergate *affair* / 不正事件を捜査する[解明する, もみ消す] investigate [clear up, cover up] *a case* of injustice

2つの放火事件は同じ日に起きた Both arson *cases* took place on the same day.
きょう学校で奇妙な事件があった There was *a* strange *incident* at my school today.
判事はその殺人事件を審理中です The judge is hearing *the murder case*.
彼はその事件と何の関係もない[大いに関係がある] He has nothing [a lot] to do with *the incident*.

じげん¹ 次元〚数学・物理〛 dimension ◯ / 第4次元 the fourth *dimension* ◆ 3次元の three-*dimensional* / 次元の低い[高い]話 *a vulgar* [*an elevated*] conversation / 彼の技術は私のとは次元が違う His skills are on *a* different *level* [*plane*] from mine.

じげん² 時限（授業時間）period ◯, hour ◯ / 1時限は50分です One *period* lasts 50 minutes. / 3時限目は数学です We have math class during third *period*.
‖時限ストライキ a time-limited strike / 時限装置 a timing device / 時限爆弾 a time bomb

しけんかん 試験管 test tube ◯ ‖試験管ベビー a test-tube baby

しご¹ 死後 life *after death* / その事実は彼女の死後に公にされた The fact was made public *after her death*. / その男性の遺体は死後数週間たっていると発表された It was announced that the man *had been dead* for several weeks.
‖死後硬直〚医学〛rigor mortis

しご² 死語（使われなくなった言語）dead language ◯;（廃れた言葉）obsolete word ◯

しご³ 私語 授業中に私語はいけません You must not *talk to each other* during class.

じこ¹ 事故

accident ◯

ひどい事故 *a* bad [serious] *accident* / 恐ろしい事故 *an* awful [*a* dreadful, *a* horrible] *accident* / 事故にあう have [meet with] *an accident* / 事故を起こす[防ぐ, 免れる] cause [prevent, escape] *an accident*
事故はいつ何時起こるか分からない *An accident* can happen at any moment.
その列車事故は人為的なミスによって起きた *The train accident* was caused by human error.

スピードの出しすぎは多くの交通事故の原因となる Speeding causes many *traffic accidents*.
その事故で私たちは来ることができなかったのです *The accident* prevented our [us from] coming.
人々が事故現場に群がった People crowded around *the scene of the accident*.
定められた手順を守って作業をすることが事故防止につながる Following the set procedures while working「leads to *the prevention of accidents* [*prevents accidents*].
◆彼らは飛行機の墜落事故に巻き込まれた They were involved in *a plane crash*. / バスどうしの衝突事故で多数の死者が出た A lot of people were killed in *a collision* between two buses. / レッカー車が事故車を引っぱっていった The tow truck took away *the wrecked car*. / その俳優は映画の撮影中に事故死したと報じられた It was reported that the actor *died an accidental death* while shooting a movie.

じこ² 自己 ── 名 self ◯ ◯ (複 selves) ── 代 oneself
自己嫌悪に陥る despise [hate] *oneself*
◆自己流で in *one's own way* / 費用は自己負担でお願いします Please *pay your own expenses*. / 彼はとても自己中心的だ He's very *selfish*. / 弟は自己顕示欲が強い (→注目されるのが好きだ) My brother *likes to attract attention*. / 彼女はきのう自己ベスト (→自分のベストタイム) を出した She recorded *her best time* yesterday.
‖自己暗示〚心理〛autosuggestion / 自己犠牲 self-sacrifice / 自己啓発 self-development / 自己主張 self-assertion / 自己紹介 ⇒じこしょうかい / 自己責任 responsibility for oneself / 自己破産 self-declared bankruptcy / 自己批判 self-criticism / 自己表現 self-expression / 自己分析 self-examination / 自己弁護 self-justification / 自己満足 self-satisfaction

じご 事後 ── 事後の[に] after the fact
◆彼らは総力を挙げてその事故の事後処理にあたっている They devote all of their energies to *dealing with the aftermath* of the accident.
‖ 事後承諾 an ex post facto [èks poust fǽktou] approval / 事後報告 an ex post facto report

しこう¹ 思考 thought ◯ ◯, thinking ◯
⇒かんがえ / プラス[マイナス]思考 positive [negative] *thinking*; optimistic [pessimistic] *thinking* / 明晰(めいせき)な[論理的な]思考 clear [logical] *thinking*
‖思考力 thinking ability

しこう² 施行 ── 施行する put* ... into effect [force] / 新法は来月から施行されます The new law *will go* [*be put*] *into effect* next month.

しこう³ 歯垢〚歯科〛(歯石(せき)) plaque ◯;（歯石）tartar ◯

しこう⁴ 嗜好 taste ◯ ◯ ◆このみ(好み) / この食べ物はあまり私の嗜好に合わない This food is

not much to my *taste*.
∥嗜好品(ぜいたく品) a luxury, luxury goods; (好物) one's favorite food

しこう⁵ 志向 映像志向の映画監督 an image-oriented film director / 彼女はブランド志向だ(→ブランド品に目がない) She *has a weakness for* name brands.

じこう¹ 事項 (事柄) matter ⓒ; (項目) item ⓒ; (題目) subject ⓒ ∥調査事項 *matters* for investigation / 関連事項 related *matters*
◆機密事項 *a top secret* / 申込用紙に必要事項を書き込む *fill in [out]* an application form / 安全の維持が私たちの最優先事項だ The maintenance of safety is our *top [first] priority*. / 使用する前にここに記されている注意事項をよく読んでください Please carefully read *the warning* printed here before you use it.

じこう² 時効 【法律】 (出訴期限法) the statute of limitations; (時効取得) prescription ⓤ ∥その事件は来週時効になる The *statute of limitations* on the case runs out next week. ◆そんな古い約束はもう時効だ An old promise like that *is no longer valid*.

じこう³ 時候 時候のあいさつ the compliments of *the season*

じごう 次号 the next number [issue]
◆次号に続く *To be continued*.

しこうさくご 試行錯誤 trial and error ∥試行錯誤して学ぶ learn *by trial and error*

じごうじとく 自業自得 ask for it [trouble], have* it coming (to one) ∥いまさら泣き言を言っても遅いよ. 自業自得だ It's too late to complain. You *asked for it*.

しこく 四国 Shikoku; (地方) the Shikoku district; (島) Shikoku Island

しごく¹ 至極 至極残念だ be *awfully [terribly] sorry* / あなたが怒るのは至極もっともだ It's *quite* natural for you to get angry.

しごく² 扱く ひげをしごく *stroke one's beard* / 私たちはコーチにずいぶんしごかれた We *were trained* very *hard* by the coach.

じこく¹ 時刻 time ⓤ; (1日のうちのある時刻) hour ⓒ ⇒ じかん(時間), とき(時)
列車の出発[到着]時刻 the departure [arrival] *time* of a train / 早い[遅い]時刻に出発する start *at an early [a late] hour* / 帰りの列車の時刻をメモする note *the time* of a return train
現在の時刻は7時30分です *The time* is 7:30.
彼は約束の時刻に来た He came at *the appointed time*.
列車は時刻どおりに到着した The train arrived *on time [schedule]*.
◆列車[飛行機, バス]の時刻表 *a train [flight, bus] schedule*

じこく² 自国 *one's* (own) country ∥自国語 *one's* native language, *one's* mother tongue

じごく 地獄 hell ⓤⓒ (しばしば Hell) ∥この世の地獄 (a) *hell* on earth / 受験地獄 examination *hell* (❖日本での場合にしか使わない) / 地獄に落ちろ! Go to *hell*! / 彼はその困難を乗り越えるのに地獄の苦しみ(→地獄)を味わった He went through *hell* to overcome the difficulties.
◆生き地獄 (a) *living death* / 地獄のような戦場 a *hellish* battlefield / 通勤地獄 *hellish* commuting on crowded trains [buses] / 彼女は地獄耳だ She *has big ears*.
ことわざ 地獄のさたも金しだい Money makes the world go round. (→金が地球を回す); Money talks. (→金がものを言う)

しこしこ (着実に) steadily; (ひたむきに) single-mindedly ◆しこしこした歯ざわりのめん *chewy* noodles

じこしょうかい 自己紹介 self-introduction ⓤⓒ ⇒ 場面・状況別会話 p.1760
◆自己紹介したいと思います I'd like to *introduce myself*.

しごせん 子午線 meridian ⓒ

しこたま 新しい事業で彼はしこたまもうけた He *made a lot of money* in his new business. / His new business *has brought* him *a lot of money*.

しごと 仕事

(働くこと) work ⓤ; (具体的な仕事・職) job ⓒ; (職業) 《公式的な》 occupation ⓒ, career ⓒ; (商売・業務) business ⓒ; (課せられた仕事) task ⓒ; (骨の折れる仕事) labor ⓤⓒ; (任務) duty ⓒ (しばしば複数形 duties)
⇒ 場面・状況別会話 p.1730

《~(の)仕事》
これは技術を要する仕事だ This is 「a skilled *job* [skilled *work*].
彼女は短期の仕事を探していた She was looking for *a temporary job*.
彼らはみんなやりがいのある仕事に就きたがっている All of them want to get 「a challenging *job* [challenging *work*].
◆毎日の決まった仕事 a daily *routine*

コロケーション ~work~
《形容詞+~》 安定した~ stable work / 住み込みの~ live-in work / 単調な~ monotonous work / つらい~ hard work / パートの~ part-time work / フルタイムの~ full-time work / 難しい~ difficult work / やさしい[楽な]~ easy work / やりかけの~ unfinished work

《仕事が・は》
たくさん仕事がある have a lot of *work* (*to do*)
仕事がたまっている There is a lot of *work* left undone.
まだ仕事が終わっていない I have not finished *my work* yet.
父は仕事が忙しい My father is busy with *his work*.
きょうは仕事がはかどっている I'm making progress with [in] *my work* today.
この仕事はかなり時間がかかりそうだ This *work* will take a lot of time.
あすまでにこの仕事は仕上がると思います I will have finished this *work* by tomorrow.

◆仕事が早い[遅い] be *a rapid [slow] worker* / 彼は仕事ができる(→有能な働き手だ) He's *an able worker*. / 兄はきょう[月曜日は]仕事がない(→休みだ) My brother「*is off* today [has Monday *off*]. / ナイチンゲールの仕事(→したこと)は高く評価されている *What* Nightingale *did* is highly regarded.

💬「お仕事は何ですか」「消防士です」 "What do you do?" "I'm a fire fighter."

💬「新しい仕事はどう」「快適だよ」 "How's *your new job*?" "It's fine."

〘仕事を〙
仕事を辞める quit [leave] *one's job* / 仕事を変える change *one's job* / 仕事を引き受ける undertake *a job*

君はこの仕事をやる必要はない You don't have to do this *work*.

結婚後も仕事を続ける女性が増えている More and more women continue *their careers* after marriage.

8時までにその仕事を片づけます I'll finish the *work* by 8 o'clock.

彼はやっと新しい仕事を見つけることができた He finally managed to find *a new job*.

彼にその仕事を任せてはどう? How about letting him do the *job*?

彼女は家の仕事をよく手伝う She is willing to do *household tasks*.

◆1日仕事を休む take *a day off* / 彼女は秘書の仕事をしている She *is* a secretary. / She *works* as a secretary. / 彼は毎日8時まで仕事をする He *works* until 8 o'clock every day.

〘仕事に〙
仕事に取りかかる start [set to] *work* / 仕事に精を出す attend to *one's business*

君はこの仕事に向かない You're not suitable for this *job*.

父は最近仕事に追われている My father has been very busy with *his work* recently.

騒音で仕事にならなかった(→騒音が仕事から私の注意をそらした) The noises distracted me from *work*.

〘仕事の〙
私はこの種の仕事の経験がない I have no experience in this kind of *job*.

少し仕事の手を休めて私の話を聞いてください *Put your work aside* for a minute and listen to me.

仕事の件できょうの午後彼女と会う約束をしている I have *a business* appointment with her this afternoon.

〘仕事で・だ〙
父は仕事でパリにいる My father is in Paris *on business*.

言っておくが大変な仕事だよ That's *a tough job*, I promise you.

ホテルを経営するのは大変な仕事です Managing a hotel is hard *work*.

〘その他〙
この大きな石を動かすのはひと仕事だ It's *a real job* to move this big stone.

◆今仕事中だからまた後で電話するよ I'm *working* now, so I'll call you later.

‖仕事着 work clothes / 仕事場 a workplace / 仕事始め the first work day of the year / 仕事部屋 a workroom

しこみ 仕込み (訓練) training ⓤ(またa ～); (準備) preparation ⓤ

◆彼の英語は英国仕込みだ His English *was learned* in England.

しこむ 仕込む (訓練する) train ⓗ; (教える) teach* ⓗ; (準備する) prepare ⓗⓘ ‖犬に芸を仕込む *teach* a dog tricks

しこり (はれもの) lump ⓒ; (腫瘍(ㄌㄨˊ)) tumor, (英)tumour ⓒ; (感情の) bad [ill] feeling ⓤⓒ ‖祖母は胸にしこりができたので病院に行った My grandmother developed *a lump* in her breast and went to the hospital. / 私たちの間にはしこりが残った Some *bad feelings* remained between us.

しさ 示唆 suggestion ⓤⓒ, hint ⓒ ‖示唆に富んだ提案 a proposal *full of good suggestions* ◆記事はその会社が不正な取り引きをしていたことを示唆している The article *hints* that the company had unfair dealings.

じさ 時差 time difference ⓤ(またa ～) ‖東京とリオデジャネイロの時差は12時間です *The time difference* between Tokyo and Rio de Janeiro is 12 hours.

◆時差通勤する(→通勤時間をずらす) *stagger commuting times* / 彼女はまだ時差ぼけが治らない She is still suffering from *jet lag*.

しさい 司祭 priest ⓒ

しざい¹ 私財 彼は町の復興のために私財をなげうった He offered *his own money* to rebuild the town.

しざい² 資材 materials ‖建築資材 building *materials*

じざい 自在 ━自在に (容易に) easily; (難なく) effortlessly; (自由に) freely; (巧みに) skillfully

◆英語を自由自在に操る speak English *fluently*; have *a good command* of English

しさく¹ 思索 (思考) thinking ⓤ, thought ⓤⓒ; (熟考) contemplation ⓤ ━思索する think* ⓗⓘ; contemplate ⓗⓘ ‖思索にふける be lost in *thought* [*contemplation*]
‖思索家 a thinker

しさく² 試作 trial manufacture [production] ⓤ ◆このソーラーカーはまだ試作段階にある This solar car is still in *the experimental stage*.
‖試作品 a trial product

じさく 自作 彼は自作の歌を披露してくれた He sang us a song *that he wrote* [*composed*]. / 彼女はその映画を自作自演した She *both* directed and acted in the movie.
‖自作農 a landed farmer

じさけ 地酒 local sake ⓤ

しさつ¹ 視察 inspection ⓤ ⓒ ━視察する inspect ⓗ, make* an inspection; (訪問する) visit ⓗⓘ ‖工場を視察する *inspect* a factory / 首相は被害の視察のために被災地を訪れた The Prime Minister visited the disaster area to *inspect* the damage.

‖視察団 an observation team, a group of inspectors / 視察旅行 a tour of inspection

しさつ² 刺殺 ──**刺殺する** stab *a person* to death

じさつ 自殺 suicide ⒰⒞ ──**自殺する** kill *oneself*, commit suicide(❖前者のほうが口語的) / 自殺をはかる attempt *suicide*; try to kill *oneself* / がけから飛び降り自殺をする kill *oneself by jumping* from a cliff; *jump* from a cliff *to (one's) death*
◆首つり自殺をする hang *oneself* / 焼身自殺する burn *oneself (to death)* / 列車に飛び込み自殺をする throw *oneself* in front of a train / ピストル自殺をする shoot *oneself (to death)* / こんな悪天候の中、山に登るなんて自殺行為だ Climbing mountains in this bad weather is *suicidal*.
‖自殺者 a suicide / 自殺未遂 an attempted suicide

しさん¹ 資産 (財産) 《集合的》 property ⒰; (個人・会社の) assets; (富) fortune ⒰⒞ / 莫大(煦)な資産を築く [持っている] make [possess] *a large fortune*
‖資産家 a rich [wealthy] person / 固定資産 fixed assets / 流動資産 current assets

しさん² 試算 ある試算によればその建物の建設費は10億円だ According to *a trial calculation*, the construction of the building would cost one billion yen.

しざん 死産 stillbirth ⒞⒰ ──**死産の** stillborn / 彼女の子は死産だった Her child *was stillborn*.

じさん 持参 ──**持参する** (持ってくる) bring* ⓣ; (持っていく) take* ⓣ / 筆記用具を持参してください Please *bring* your writing materials.
‖持参金 (a) dowry

しし 獅子 (雄) lion ⒞; (雌) lioness ⒞ ⇨ **しし座** ‖獅子舞い *shishimai*, a dance performed in a lion's mask as an exorcism

しじ¹ 支持 support ⒰; (支援) backing ──**支持する** support ⓣ, give* [offer] support; (支援する) back (up)
彼女の音楽は若者から圧倒的に支持されている Her music *has* overwhelming *support* from [among] young people.
彼らの意見は広範な支持を得た Their opinion got [won] broad *support*.
彼の政策は大衆の支持を失った His policy has lost *the support* of the public [public *support*].
何が起きようとも私はあなたを支持します Whatever may happen, I'll *back you up*.
あなたの支持政党はどこですか What party do you *support*?
最新の世論調査では内閣の支持率が下がった According to the latest poll, *support* for [the approval rating of] the cabinet has decreased.
◆私は彼女の意見を支持します I'm *in favor of* her opinion.
‖支持者 a supporter

しじ² 指示 directions, instructions ──**指示する** direct ⓣ, instruct ⓣ
指示を仰ぐ ask *a person* for *instructions*; ask for *a person's instructions* / 指示を与える give *a person* directions [*instructions*]
私の指示どおりにやればうまくいきます You can't go wrong if you follow my *directions* [*instructions*].
私たちは彼の指示に従ってその計画を実行した We carried out the plan under his *directions*.
私たちはその事故を調査するよう指示された We *were instructed* to inquire into the accident.

しじ³ 私事 one's private [personal] affairs / 私事にわたって恐縮ですが… Excuse me for bringing up *my personal affairs*, but .... / 私事に及ぶ質問をする ask *personal questions*

じじ 時事 current events ◆時事問題について議論する discuss *current affairs* [*topics*]
‖時事英語 (ニュース報道などで使われる英語) media English, news English / 時事解説 comments on current affairs [topics]

ししざ 獅子座 【天文・占星】 Leo [líːou] ⒰, the Lion(❖「獅子座の人」の意味では ⒞)

しじだいめいし 指示代名詞 【文法】 demonstrative pronoun

⑴指示代名詞は、this (複 these), that (複 those)のことで、「これ」「あれ」などとはっきり人・事物を指し示す場合に用いられる. 名詞的用法と形容詞的用法がある. 名詞的用法のものを指示代名詞、形容詞的用法のものを指示形容詞と呼ぶこともある / *This* comic book is more amusing than *that* one. この漫画の本はあの漫画の本よりおもしろい (❖形容詞的用法) / *This* is my house, and *that* is Mike's. これは私の家で、あれはマイクの家です (❖名詞的用法)
⑵指示代名詞の that は名詞の繰り返しを避けるためにも用いられることがある / The climate here is milder than *that* of Sapporo. ここの気候は札幌の気候よりも穏やかです

ししつ 資質 (性質) nature ⒰⒞; (特質) quality ⒰⒞; (才能) talent ⒰⒞ / 彼はこの仕事をするのに必要な資質を備えている He possesses *the* necessary *qualities* to do this job.

しじつ 史実 (事実) historical fact ⒞⒰; (証拠) historical evidence ⒰ / 史実に基づいた小説 a novel based on 「*historical facts* [*history*]

じじつ 事実
(現実の事柄) fact ⒞⒰; (真実) (the) truth; (真相) the case; (現実) reality ⒰⒞ 《しばしば the ～》
【～事実】
明らかな事実 a clear [an obvious] *fact* / 驚くべき事実 a surprising *fact* / 既成の事実 an established *fact* / 厳然たる事実 a cold [hard] *fact* / 周知の事実 a well-known *fact* / 偽りのない事実 the stark *truth*

〖事実が・は〗
彼女はその事実がもれるのを防ごうとした He tried to prevent the *fact* from leaking out.

今日(にち),地球が太陽の周りを回っているという事実はだれもが知っている Today the *fact* that the earth travels around the sun is known to everyone.

その事実は彼女の死後,明らかになった The *fact* came to light after her death.

〖事実を〗
事実を確かめる[隠す]「make sure of [hide] *the truth*

ありのままの事実を話してください Tell me *the plain [bare] facts.*

その事実を否定することはできない There is no denying that *fact.*

〖事実に〗
彼女の話は事実に反する Her story *doesn't agree with the facts.*

その物語は事実に基づいている The story is based on *facts.*

〖その他〗
彼女は英語が好きだし,事実よく勉強している She likes English and *in fact* she studies it very hard.

◆二人が結婚するというのは事実だ It is *true* that they will get married soon./彼がそのチームの事実上のリーダーだ He's *virtually [practically]* the leader of the team.

そのうわさは事実無根であることが判明した The rumor turned out to「*be groundless [have no basis in fact].*

慣用表現 事実は小説よりも奇なり *Truth [Fact] is stranger than fiction.*

ししゃ¹ 死者 dead person ⓒ; (総称) the dead; (事故・戦争による) (公式的) fatality ⓒ; (犠牲者) victim ⓒ ‖死者と行方不明者の合計は5,000人を超える The total of *the dead* and the missing is over 5,000.

◆その火災による死者は25人だった Twenty-five people *were killed* by the fire./交通事故による死者の数が確実に増加している The number of *deaths* in [The *death* toll from] traffic accidents is steadily increasing./地震で多くの死者が出た(→地震が多くの命を奪った) The earthquake *took* many *lives.*/(→多くの命が奪われた) Many *lives* were lost in the earthquake.

ししゃ² 支社 branch (office) ⓒ ‖その会社はフランスに支社がある The company has *a branch* in France. ◆大阪支社に勤めている work at *the Osaka office* (of a company)

ししゃ³ 使者 messenger ⓒ ‖…に使者を送る send *a messenger* to …

ししゃ⁴ 試写 preview ⓒ ‖映画の試写会を行う give *a preview* of a film; *preview* a film

ししゃく 子爵 viscount [váikàunt]

じしゃく 磁石 magnet ⓒ; (方位磁石) compass ⓒ ——磁石の magnetic

ししゃごにゅう 四捨五入 ——四捨五入する round (❖厳密には「端数を切り上げて,または切り捨てて整数にする」という意味) ‖1.73205を小数点以下第2位まで四捨五入する *round off*

1.73205 to two decimal places / 2.236を四捨五入すると2.24となる We can *round (off)* 2.236 to 2.24.

ししゅ 死守 チャンピオンは王座を死守した The champion *fought desperately and managed to defend* his title.

じしゅ¹ 自主 (自立) independence Ⓤ ‖自主性に欠ける lack *independence*

◆自主規制する adopt *voluntary controls* / 私たちはその議論に自主的に参加した We took part in the discussion *voluntarily.*

‖自主トレーニング independent training

じしゅ² 自首 警察に自首する「*give oneself up [surrender (oneself)]* to the police

ししゅう¹ 刺繍 embroidery ⓒⓊ ——ししゅうする embroider 他 ‖花のししゅうの入ったブラウス a blouse with flowery *embroidery* / 帽子の裏に名前をししゅうする *embroider* one's name on the reverse of one's hat

‖ししゅう糸 embroidery thread

ししゅう² 詩集 a collection of poems

◆ボードレール詩集「*Collected Poems [Poetical Works]* of Baudelaire

しじゅう¹ 始終 (いつも) always, all the time; (頻繁に) very [quite] often ‖父は始終私のやることに文句を言っている My father is *always* complaining about what I do./彼は始終,映画館に通っている He goes to the movies *quite often.*

しじゅう² 四十 forty Ⓤⓒ ⇒よんじゅう

じしゅう¹ 自習 ——自習する study by *oneself* ‖自習時間 a self-study [free-study] hour;(米) a study hall (❖米国の高校などでは時間割に自習時間を組み込むことがあり,その時間またはその部屋のことを study hall という)/自習室 a study room

じしゅう² 次週 (来週) next week

じじゅう 侍従 (宮廷の) chamberlain [tʃéimbərlin]; (英国王室の) equerry [ékwəri] ⓒ

ししゅうから 四十雀 titmouse (複 titmice), tit

しじゅうそう 四重奏 〔音楽〕quartet ⓒ ‖弦楽四重奏曲[団] *a string quartet*

ししゅうびょう 歯周病 periodontal disease ⓒ

じしゅく 自粛 その会社はテレビCMを流すのを自粛した The company *refrained from* putting commercials on TV./私たちはその商品の取り扱いを自粛した We *voluntarily stopped* dealing in the product.

ししゅつ 支出 (公式的) expenditure Ⓤⓒ, expense Ⓤⓒ, outgo Ⓤⓒ, (主に英) outgoings ——支出する (払う) pay* 他 自, (費やす) spend* 他 自 ‖支出を抑える limit *expenditures* / その計画を成功させるためには支出を惜しまない We'll spare no *expense* to make the project a success./その町は社会福祉に多額の支出をしている The town *spends* a lot of money on social welfare.

ししゅんき 思春期 adolescence Ⓤ; (年ごろ) puberty Ⓤ ‖思春期に達する reach (*the age of*) *puberty [adolescence]*

◆思春期の少年 an *adolescent* boy
ししょ[1] 司書 librarian [C]
ししょ[2] 支所 branch (office) [C]
しじょ 子女 child [C] (複 children), sons and daughters ➔きこく
じしょ[1] 辞書 dictionary [C]; (特に古典語の) lexicon [C] ∥単語の意味を辞書で調べる look up a word in *a dictionary* / 辞書を引いてみましたか Did you 「look in [consult] *your dictionary*? / この言葉は僕の辞書には出ていない This word doesn't appear in my *dictionary*. / 私は辞書と首っぴきでその本を読み通した I managed to read the book through to the end with *a dictionary* at my side.
じしょ[2] 地所 (土地) land [U] 《また複数形 ～s》; (広大な土地) estate [C]
じじょ 次女 *one's* second daughter
ししょう[1] 支障 (障害) obstacle [C]; (妨害) interference [U], hindrance [U][C]; (問題) problem [C] ∥その計画には何の支障もないように思えた There seemed to be no *obstacle* to the plan. / 台風のため試験のスケジュールに支障が出た The typhoon caused some *interference* with the exam schedule. / もし何か支障があれば知らせてください Let me know if you have any *problems*.
◆会議は何の支障もなく行われた The meeting went off without *a hitch*.
ししょう[2] 師匠 teacher [C]; (芸術の巨匠) master [C]
しじょう[1] 市場 market [C]
石油は市場に出す前に精製しなければならない Oil must be refined before it is put on *the market*.
東南アジア製のコンピュータが大量に市場に出回っている A lot of computers made in Southeast Asia *are on the market*.
日本はもっと市場を開放すべきだ Japan should open *its markets* to a greater extent.
2つの会社は市場を拡張するために合併した The two companies merged to expand *the market*.
日本は輸入革製バッグのよい市場です Japan is *a* good *market* for imported leather bags.
∥市場価格 a market price / 市場価値 a market value / 市場経済 a market economy / 市場占有率 a market share / 市場調査 market research / 売り手市場 a seller's market / 海外市場 an overseas [a foreign] market / 買い手市場 a buyer's market / 株式市場 a stock market / 金融市場 a money market / 国内市場 the home [domestic] market / 世界市場 the world market / 通貨市場 the currency markets
しじょう[2] 史上 in history; (記録上) on record ∥史上最も暑い日 the hottest day *on record* / それは史上初の試みだった It was the first attempt *in history*.
しじょう[3] 紙上 紙上討論 a discussion *in the newspaper* / その話題は紙上をにぎわしている The topic has been splashed *across the newspapers*.
しじょう[4] 誌上 彼の小説は最新号の誌上に掲載された His story appeared *in* the latest issue of *the magazine*.
しじょう[5] 試乗 test drive [C] ◆彼はその車を買う前に何度か試乗した He *test-drove* the car several times before he bought it.
しじょう[6] 私情 *one's* personal feelings ∥仕事に私情を差しはさむ interject *one's personal feelings* into business ◆私情を交えない意見を述べる give an *impartial* opinion
しじょう[7] 詩情 そのダンサーは詩情あふれる舞台を見せた The dancer gave a *richly poetic* performance.
じしょう 自称 自称芸術家 a *self-styled* artist / そのペテン師は大学教授を自称した The swindler *called himself* a professor.
じじょう[1] 事情 (周囲の状況) circumstances; (情勢) situation [C]; (状態) condition [C]; (理由) reason [C][U]
〖～事情〗
特別な事情 special *circumstances* / 交通事情を改善する improve *traffic conditions*
その国の食糧事情は悪化している *The food situation* in that country is getting worse.
東京は住宅事情の悪さで有名だ Tokyo is notorious for *its* terrible *housing situation*.
◆国内[海外]事情 domestic [foreign] *affairs* / 彼らがけんかになった詳しい事情を知りませんか Don't you know *the details* of how they got into a fight?
〖事情が〗
どんな事情があっても彼にその話をしてはいけない *Under no circumstances* should you tell him that story.
事情が許せば会議に参加します *If circumstances permit*, I'll attend the meeting.
◆英語は読めるが書くとなると事情が異なる I can read English, but writing *is a different matter*.
〖事情で〗
彼は家庭の事情で学校をやめた He quit school *for family reasons*.
その計画はやむをえない事情で中止になった The plan was cancelled due to *circumstances* beyond our control.
〖事情に〗
◆彼は中国の事情に通じている He「*knows a lot* [*is well-informed*] *about* China.
〖その他〗
そういう事情なのでパーティーは中止します Under those *circumstances*, the party will be called off.
◆警察は事情聴取をするために彼を呼んだ The police called him in for *questioning*.
じじょう[2] 自乗・二乗 〖数学〗 square [C] (《略語》sq) ―自乗する square [他] ∥3の自乗は9である *The square* of three is nine. / Three *squared* is nine.
ししょうしゃ 死傷者 casualty [C] ∥死傷者数 a *casualty* toll / その列車事故は多数の死傷者を出した The train accident caused heavy *casualties*.
ししょく 試食 ―試食する try [他], sample [他] ∥試食会 a tasting [sampling] party

しずおか

じしょく 辞職 resignation ◯ ⓤ ——辞職する resign ⓐ ⓔ /辞職願を提出する hand in one's resignation / 彼女は辞職した She resigned (from) her job. / 彼はチームの監督を辞職した He resigned (his post) as manager of the team. / 内閣は総辞職した The entire cabinet resigned.

じじょでん 自叙伝 autobiography ◯

ししょばこ 私書箱 post-office box ◯ (《略語》)POB, P.O. Box) (❖手紙などでは P.O. Box 1234 のように書く)

ししん¹ 指針 guide ◯; (政策などの) guidelines; (計器の針) indicator ◯, needle ◯ / 困ったときにはこの本がよい指針となるだろう This book will be a good guide for you when you get into trouble.

ししん² 私信 personal [private] letter ◯

ししん³ 私心 私心のない人 an unselfish [a selfless] person / 彼は私心を捨てて問題解決に取り組んだ He selflessly [unselfishly] tried to solve the problem.

じしん¹ 詩人 poet ◯
じじん² 私人 私人として式に参列する attend the ceremony in a private capacity

じしん¹ 地震 earthquake ◯, 《口語的》quake ◯ ➡ 場面・状況別会話 p.1734

《〜地震》
軽い地震 a light [slight] earthquake / 激しい地震 a big [strong, severe] earthquake / 海底[火山性, 断層]地震 a submarine [volcanic, dislocation] earthquake / 群発地震 a series of earthquakes

《地震が》
きのう地震があった There was [We had] an earthquake yesterday.
地震がいつ起こるかは予測できない You can't predict when an earthquake will take place.
夜明けに大きな地震が私たちの町を襲った A big earthquake struck our city at daybreak.

《地震で》
地震で家が揺れた An earthquake shook the house.
その古い建物は地震で崩壊した The old building gave way in the earthquake.
その地震で多くの被害が出た The earthquake caused great damage.

《その他》
地震の被災者を援助する aid earthquake victims
水戸の地震は震度3を記録した The earthquake in Mito registered three on the Japanese scale.
‖地震学 seismology / 地震学者 a seismologist / 地震計 a seismograph

じしん² 自信 confidence ⓤ, self-confidence ⓤ

《自信が》
…に自信がない lack confidence in …
その経験で自信が増した[揺らいだ] The experience boosted [shook] my confidence.
彼のスピーチには自信が感じられた There was a note of confidence in his speech.

◆彼には成功する自信がある He is confident of success. / He is confident that he will succeed. / 泳ぎには自信がない(→得意でない) I'm not good at swimming.

《自信を・に》
自信をつける[失う] gain [lose] confidence / 質問に自信をもって答える answer the questions with confidence [confidently] / 人に自信を与える give a person confidence / 自信にあふれている brim with confidence
試合に勝って彼は自信を取り戻した Winning the game restored his confidence.
試験の結果に彼女は英語に対する自信を深めた The exam result confirmed her confidence in her English.
君はもっと自分に自信をもつべきだ You should have more confidence (in yourself).

《その他》
自信満々である have an abundance of confidence; be full of confidence
◆自信に満ちた態度で in a confident manner / 自信過剰は禁物だ Don't be too confident. / 彼は自信家だ He is a confident person.

> **英作文ノート** **He is sure** … の後は？
> 彼はその入試に合格する自信がある
> →×He is sure to pass the entrance exam.
> →○He is sure that he will pass the entrance exam.
> →○He is sure of passing the entrance exam.
> ★He is sure to …. は, I'm sure that he will …. という"話し手"の確信を表す.

じしん³ 自身 oneself /自分自身を責める punish oneself / あなた自身本当にそう思うのですか Do you really think so yourself?
◆彼の成功は彼自身の努力によるものだ His success is due to his own efforts.

ジス JIS (❖Japanese Industrial Standard (日本工業規格)の略語) /ジスマーク the JIS mark

じすい 自炊 ——自炊する cook for oneself, do* one's own cooking

しすう 指数 index ◯, 〔数学〕exponent ◯ /《物価[株価]》指数 a price [stock] index
◆知能指数 an intelligence quotient (《略語》IQ)

しずおか 静岡

静岡県は本州の中央部, 太平洋岸に位置しています. 気候は温暖でミカンや茶の栽培に適しており, それらはこの県の主要な特産品となっています. 浜名湖ではウナギの養殖が盛んで, また工業品では楽器やオートバイ, 自動車が多く生産されています. 湯が島, 熱川などの温泉は富士箱根伊豆国立公園の一部を成し, 景色のよい所も多く, 多くの観光客が訪れています.
Shizuoka Prefecture is located in central Honshu on the Pacific coast. Its mild climate favors the cultivation of mandarin oranges and green tea, which are the most famous specialties

of this prefecture. On Lake Hamana people are engaged in eel cultivation. In the industries of this prefecture, musical instruments, motorcycles and automobiles are important items. Hot springs such as Yugashima and Atagawa are part of the Fuji-Hakone-Izu National Park. And with its many spots of beauty, the park attracts many tourists.

しずか 静か
——静かな quiet; (静まり返った) silent; (音・動きのない) still; (落ち着いた) calm; (穏やかな) soft (❖通例名詞の前で用いる) ——静かに quietly; silently; calmly; softly

静かな夜 a quiet [still, silent] night / 静かにしている keep quiet / 静かに暮らす lead a quiet life; live quietly / 静かな声で in a soft [quiet] voice

静かにしなさい Be quiet!

日が沈むとあたりは急に静かになった After sunset it suddenly 「became quiet [fell silent] all around.

静かな川が夕日を映し出していた The calm [still] river reflected the sunset.

医者は私に静かに寝ているようにと言った The doctor told me to lie quietly in bed.

車は静かに走りだした The car started quietly.

私はいつも部屋に静かな音楽をかけておく I always have soft music on in my room.

-しすぎる -し過ぎる 運動しすぎる overdo exercise; exercise too much / 車を運転するときにはいくら注意してもしすぎることはない You cannot be too careful when driving. ⇒-すぎる

しずく 滴 drop / 雨のしずく drops of rain; raindrops

◆彼のほおにひとしずくの涙が光った A tear [teardrop] glistened on his cheek.

しずけさ 静けさ quietness ⓤ, quiet ⓤ, stillness ⓤ; (落ち着き) calm ⓤ (また a ~) / 朝の静けさは1発の銃声によって破られた The quiet [stillness] of the morning was broken by a gun shot. / それはあらしの前の静けさにすぎなかった That was only the calm before the [a] storm.

システム system ⓒ / 新しい交通輸送システムが最近使われるようになった A new transportation system came into use recently.

‖システムエンジニア a systems engineer / システムキッチン a kitchen with built-in appliances / システム工学 systems engineering / システム手帳 a personal organizer

ジステンパー (犬などの急性伝染病) distemper ⓤ

じすべり 地滑り landslide ⓒ / その候補者は選挙で地滑り的勝利を収めた The candidate won a landslide victory in the election.

しずまる 静まる・鎮まる (止まる) stop; (静になる) become* quiet; (落ち着く) calm down; (暴動などが鎮圧される) be suppressed, be put down / 私たちは風が静まるのを待った We waited for the wind to stop [calm down]. / その知らせを聞くと騒々しい群衆は静まり返った The noisy crowd 「became quiet [fell silent] when they heard the announcement. / 彼の気が静まるまでひとりにしておこう Leave him alone until he 「calms down [feels better]. ◆静まり返った森 a silent forest / その痛みはなかなか鎮まらなかった The pain wouldn't go away.

しずむ 沈む
❶【位置が下がる】sink* ⓐ, go* down; (太陽・月が) set* ⓐ

船は房総沖で沈んだ The boat sank [went down] off Boso.

太陽は西に沈む The sun sets in the west.

太陽が山の向こう[地平線の下]に沈もうとしている The sun is sinking 「behind the mountains [below the horizon].

彼女はぐったりとソファーに沈み込んだ She sank deeply into the sofa.

❷【心・気分が】sink* ⓐ, feel* [get*] depressed, feel low [down]; (悲しむ) feel sad

その知らせを聞いて彼の心は沈んだ His heart sank when he heard the news.

彼女は試験に落ちて気分が沈んでいる She's feeling low because she failed the exam.

◆沈んだ顔をしている look blue [depressed]

❸【その他】

物思いに沈む sink into thought

しずめる¹ 静める・鎮める (静かにさせる) quiet ⓗ; (落ち着かせる) calm ⓗ ⓐ; (騒ぎなどを) put* down, suppress ⓗ; (なだめる) soothe ⓗ; (痛みなどを) relieve ⓗ / 騒がしい子供を静める quiet the noisy children / 痛みを鎮める relieve the pain / 彼女は気持ちを静めるために深呼吸をした She took a deep breath to calm down [herself]. / 警察はどうにか暴動を鎮めた The police managed to put down the riot.

しずめる² 沈める sink* ⓗ ⓐ / 敵の船を沈める sink an enemy ship / いすに身を沈める sink [lower oneself] into a chair

◆彼は強烈なパンチで対戦相手をマットに沈めた He knocked his opponent down on the mat with a strong punch.

じする 辞する 議長の職を辞する resign one's post as chairperson / 彼らは法的手段をとることも辞さない構えだ They are ready to take legal action.

しせい¹ 姿勢
❶【体の構え】posture ⓤ ⓒ; (体の置き方) position ⓒ; (ポーズ) pose ⓒ

姿勢がよい[悪い] have good [bad] posture / 直立の[座った]姿勢で in an upright [a sitting] position

楽な姿勢で座れるようにいすを調節した I adjusted the chair so that I could sit in a comfortable position.

その姿勢のままでいてください Please hold that

pose.
◆姿勢を正す(→背筋を伸ばす) *straighten (up) one's back* / 気をつけの姿勢をとる *stand at attention*
❷【態度】attitude
…に積極的[消極的]な姿勢を見せる *show a positive [negative] attitude toward ...*
私たちは環境問題に前向きの姿勢で取り組むべきだ *We should take a constructive attitude toward environmental issues.*

しせい² 施政 government ⓤ; (政治) administration ⓤ ◆施政方針演説をする *deliver a speech on administrative policies*

しせい³ 私製 ――私製の private ‖私製はがき *a postcard, a postal card* (❖英語では「私製はがき」「官製はがき」を区別しない)

しせい⁴ 市制 municipal system ⓒ /市制を敷く *implement a municipal system*

しせい⁵ 市政 municipal [city] government ⓤ; (市の業務) municipal [city] administration ⓤ /市政に参加する *participate in municipal [city] government*

じせい¹ 時勢 (the) times /時勢に逆らう[順応する] *go against [with] the times* / 父は時勢に遅れまいとコンピュータを買った *My father bought a computer to keep up with the times.*

じせい² 時制【文法】tense ⓤ ⓒ /未来時制 *the future tense*

じせい³ 自制 self-control ⓤ /自制する control *oneself* /自制心が欠けている[を失う] *lack [lose] self-control*
◆自制心のある人 *a self-controlled person*

じせい⁴ 自生 ――自生する grow* wild /ここには貴重な植物が自生している *Rare plants grow wild here.*

じせい⁵ 時世 days, times ⇨ じだい(時代)

しせいかつ 私生活 私生活に立ち入らないでください。*Don't stick your nose into my private life.*

しせいじ 私生児 illegitimate child ⓒ;《婉曲的》love child ⓒ (❖主にマスコミ用語)

じせいのいっち 時制の一致【文法】a sequence of tenses

(1)主節が現在時制の場合,従属節の時制は主節の時制の影響を受けない.
I *think* she *reads* the newspaper every day. 彼女は毎日,新聞を読んでいると思う
I *think* she *read* the newspaper yesterday. 彼女はきのう新聞を読んだと思う
I *think* she *has* already *read* the newspaper. 彼女はもう新聞を読んでしまったと思う
I *think* she *will read* the newspaper. 彼女は新聞を読むと思う
(2)過去の時点を基準にして従属節を表現するとき,従属節の時制は主節の時制の影響を受ける.上記文の主節の時制が過去形になると従属節の時制は以下のようになる.
I *thought* she *read* the newspaper every day. 彼女は毎日,新聞を読んでいると思った
I *thought* she *had read* the newspaper the day before. 彼女は前日,新聞を読んだと思った
I *thought* she *had* already *read* the newspaper. 彼女はもう新聞を読んでしまったと思った
I *thought* she *would read* the newspaper. 彼女は新聞を読むと思った
(3)従属節の内容が現在でも事実であるとの前提で発話するときは,従属節の時制は主節の時制の影響を受けない.歴史上の事実や不変の真理であると考えられている事柄などがこの場合に当たる.
He *knew* the earth *is [was]* round. 彼は地球が丸いことを知っていた
Yesterday we *were taught* at school that the Civil War *broke out* in 1861. きのう学校で,南北戦争が1861年に起こったと習った

しせき¹ 歯石 tartar ⓤ

しせき² 史跡 historic site [spot, place] ⓒ / 私たちは京都の史跡巡りをした *We toured the historic sites in Kyoto.*

じせき¹ 次席 ――次席の second ◆次席検事 *an assistant public prosecutor*

じせき² 自責 自責の念にかられる *have [suffer from] a guilty conscience*
‖自責点【野球】an earned run

しせつ¹ 施設 (設備) facilities; (収容施設) home ⓒ; (公共機関) institution
公共施設の拡充 *expansion of public facilities* / 孤児[老人]のための施設 *a home for orphans [senior citizens]*
私の町は文化施設が充実している *My town has excellent cultural facilities.*
‖医療施設 medical facilities / 教育施設 educational facilities / 軍事施設 military facilities [installations] / 研究施設 research facilities / 厚生施設 welfare facilities / 更生施設 a halfway house / 娯楽施設 amusement [recreation] facilities / 宿泊施設 lodging facilities

しせつ² 使節 (外交上の) envoy ⓒ; (公式の場への) delegate ⓒ (❖代表者個人を指す.代表団は delegation); (特別な任務を帯びた) mission ⓒ /経済使節団 *an economic mission* / 彼は親善使節として来日した *He came to Japan ⌈as a goodwill envoy [on a goodwill mission].*

しせつ³ 私設 ――私設の private ‖私設秘書 *a private secretary*

じせつ¹ 自説 one's (own) opinion [view]

じせつ² 時節 (季節) season ⓒ; (時期) time ⓤ ⓒ; (機会) chance ⓒ /時節の到来を待つ *wait for a chance* ◆時節柄(→暑い[寒い]天候の中)お体を大切に *Please take care of yourself in this hot [cold] weather.*

しせん¹ 視線 視線を向ける[落とす] *turn [drop] one's eyes* / 彼と視線が合った *My eyes met (with) his.* / 彼女は私から視線をそらした *She looked away from me.*

しせん² 支線 branch line ⓒ

しぜん 自然

❶【山川草木・生物・天候など】nature ⓤ ――自

然の natural
自然の美しさ[脅威] the beauty [forces] of nature; natural beauty [forces] / 自然の中に暮らす live in the midst of nature / 自然に帰る go [get] back to nature / 自然死する die a natural death; die of natural causes / 自然環境を守る preserve [protect] the natural environment

当時はこのあたりにもまだ自然が少し残っていた In those days there was still a bit of nature around here.

これは自然に親しむいい機会だ This is a good opportunity to be in close contact with nature.

この国の自然破壊は非常に深刻だ The destruction of nature in this country is very serious.

漢方薬は自然の原料から作られる Chinese medicines are made of natural materials.

❷【ひとりでに】——自然な natural; (自発的な) spontaneous; ——自然に naturally; spontaneously; (無意識に) unconsciously

この花は家の庭に自然に生えてきた This flower has grown naturally in my garden.

観客から自然に笑いがわき起こった The audience roared with spontaneous laughter.

◆自然の成り行きにまかせるしかない There's no help but to let nature take its course. / その傷は自然に治った The cut healed by itself. / 心配しなくてもその問題は自然に解決しますよ Don't worry. That problem will work itself out.

❸【無理がない】——自然な natural ——自然に naturally

自然にふるまう behave naturally

栄養の不足は子供の自然な発育を妨げる Lack of nutrition prevents the natural growth of children.

あなたの英語はとても自然ですね Your English is quite natural.

試験の前に緊張するのはごく自然なことだ It's quite natural to get nervous before an exam.

‖自然界 the natural world / 自然科学 natural science / 自然科学者 a natural scientist / 自然現象 a natural phenomenon / 自然災害 a natural disaster / 自然主義 naturalism / 自然主義者 a naturalist / 自然食品 natural food(s); (有機栽培による) organic food(s) / 自然淘汰 natural selection / 自然発火 spontaneous combustion / 自然発生 spontaneous generation / 自然保護 the preservation [conservation] of nature

じぜん¹ 事前 (選挙の)事前運動 a preelection campaign / 事前の通告 previous [advance] notice / 今度来るときは事前に電話してね When you come next time, give me a call beforehand [in advance].

じぜん² 慈善 charity / ‖慈善事業[慈善団体]に寄付する make a contribution to charity [a charitable organization]

じぜん³ 次善 次善の策 the next [second] best measure

しそう¹ 思想 thought; (観念) idea; (考えること) thinking

近代[自由主義]思想 modern [liberal] thought / 急進的[進歩的, 保守的]な思想 radical [progressive, conservative] thought / 思想の自由 freedom of thought / 思想を弾圧する suppress a thought / 思想統制をする maintain thought control

マルクスの思想が共産主義を生んだ Marx's ideas gave birth to communism.

‖思想家 a thinker

しそう² 死相 the shadow of death

しそうのうろう 歯槽膿漏 [医学] pyorrhea [páiəríːə] (❖口語では gum disease)

じぞう(ぼさつ) 地蔵(菩薩)

地蔵は左手に宝珠(ほうじゅ), 右手に錫杖(しゃくじょう)というつえを持っている石仏で, 昔から子供や旅人, また苦しむすべての人々の守護者として祭られてきました. 道端にはよだれかけをかけたり足元に花が供えられた地蔵が見られます.
A *jizo* is a stone Buddhist image, usually with a gem in the left hand and a staff called *shakujo* in the right. It has been respected as the guardian deity of children, travelers and all suffering beings since ancient times. It is often seen along roadsides with a bib around its neck and flowers offered by worshipers at its feet.

シソーラス (分類語彙(い)集) thesaurus

じそく 時速 時速50キロを保って運転する drive at a steady speed of 50 kilometers *per hour* (❖kilometers per hour は kph または k.p.h.と略す)

じぞく 持続 ——持続する (続く) last; (維持する) maintain, keep* up / ‖集中力を持続する keep up one's concentration

しそこなう fail to *do*, miss ——しそこなう ‖忙しくて彼女にその話をしそこなった I was so busy that I *failed* to tell her the story.

しそん 子孫 descendant; (子供たち) offspring (❖単数でも不定冠詞は付けない); (後世の人々) 《集合的》posterity / …の直系の子孫 a direct *descendant* of … / 子孫に財産を残す leave one's estate to one's *offspring*

しそんじる 仕損じる fail to *do*, miss ことわざ せいては事を仕損じる Haste makes waste. (→あわてるとむだができる)

じそんしん 自尊心 self-respect; (誇り) pride (また a 〜) ‖自尊心を保つ[失う] keep [lose] one's self-respect / その言葉に彼の自尊心はひどく傷ついた His *pride* was badly hurt by the remark.

◆自尊心の強い人 a *self-respecting* person

した¹ 下

❶ 低い所 bottom, foot; below, under; down

❷ 年齢 younger

❸【地位・能力・程度】 below, under; lower, worse, inferior

❶【低い所】── 图 (底) bottom ⓒ; (足部) foot ⓒ (複 feet) ── 前 (相対的に低い位置に[の]) below (↔above); (真下に[の]) under (↔over) ── 副 (より低いところへ[に]) down (↔up); (低い所で[に]) below; (下の方向に) downward (↔upward) ── 形 (下の部分の) lower (↔upper)(❖名詞の前で用いる)

[語法]
(1) below は「…より低い位置に」の意味で,「真下」を意味する場合は under と置き換えられる.
(2) under は真上にあるものと接触している場合とそうでない場合の両方を意味する. また, 真上を覆われた感じも表す.

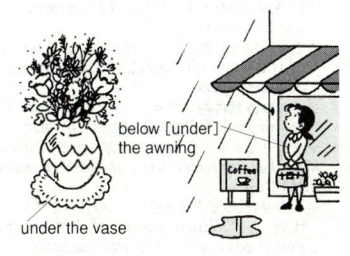

below [under] the awning

under the vase

【下に・へ】
海峡の下にトンネルを掘る dig a tunnel *under* the channel / 単語の下に線を引く「draw a line *under* [underline] a word / ページの下に書き込みをする write notes *at the foot of* the page
私たちはベッドの下に隠れていた We were hiding *under* the bed.
船は水平線の下に消えた The ship disappeared *below* the horizon.
飛行機から下に山が見えた From the plane we could see the mountain *below*.
夕飯ですよ. 下へ降りてきなさい Dinner is ready. Come *down* [*downstairs*].

【下で】
一つ屋根の下で暮らす live *under* one [the same] roof
私の猫はいすの下で眠っている My cat is sleeping *under* the chair.
◆下(→階下)で待ってくれるように彼に頼んだ I asked him to wait *downstairs*.

【下の】
下の歯[階] the *lower* teeth [floor]
志津子は私のすぐ下の部屋に住んでいる Shizuko lives in the room immediately *below* mine.
辞書は下の棚にある Dictionaries are on the *lower* shelf.

【下を】
下を見ちゃだめだ Don't look *down*!
ボートは橋の下を通った The boat passed *under* the bridge.
ほら, 孝が下を歩いてる Look, Takashi is walking *below* (us).

【下から】
下から5行目の文 the sentence on the fifth line *from the bottom*
ドアの下から明かりがもれていた Light was escaping *from under* the door.

❷【年齢】 younger (↔older)
彼には下に弟が2人いる He has two *younger* brothers.
年は彼女より2つ下です I am two years *younger than* she [her]. (❖口語では通例 than her を用いる)
◆この春いちばん下の妹が学校に上がる My *youngest* sister will start school this spring.

❸【地位・能力・程度】── 前 below, under ── 形 (下位の) lower (↔upper, higher); (…より劣った) worse (than …) (↔better), inferior (to …) (↔superior)
下のクラス a *lower* class
私の英語の点数はクラス平均よりはるかに下だった My marks in English were well *below* the class average.
妹は私よりも学年が2つ下です My sister is two grades *below* me at school.
私のパソコンは彼のよりも性能の点では下だが気に入っている I like my computer, though it is *inferior to* his in performance.
だれも彼の下では働きたがらない No one wants to work *under* him. (❖under は直接の監督・指揮下にある場合. below は階級の上下を表す)

❹【その他】
下に記すように as written *below* / 下に「男」のつく言葉(→「男」で終わる言葉) a word that *ends with* "otoko"
彼は上着の下にシャツを2枚着ていた He was wearing two shirts *under* his coat.

した[2] 舌 tongue [tʌŋ] ⓒ
舌の先 the tip of *one's tongue* / 舌を出す stick [put] *one's tongue* out (❖軽蔑(けいべつ)のしぐさ)
トウガラシのせいで舌がひりひりする *My tongue* is stinging from the red pepper.
アルコールのせいで舌がもつれた *My tongue* got tangled because of the alcohol.
[慣用表現] 彼は舌が肥えている He's *a gourmet*. (❖gourmet は「グルメ, 美食家」の意)
彼は彼女がいると緊張して舌が回らなくなる I get nervous and *tongue-tied* in her presence. (❖tongue-tied は緊張や恥ずかしさのために口がきけない状態をいう) / きょうはよく舌が回るね You're very *talkative* today. / 彼女は彼と別れると言ったのに, その舌の根も乾かぬうちに彼に会いたくてたまらないと言いだした She said she was sure to break up with him, *but in the next breath* she said she was dying to see him. / 舌をかみそうな名前 a *tongue-twisting* [*jawbreaking*] name / 私たちは彼の並はずれた才能に舌を巻いた(→驚嘆した) We *were astonished at* his outstanding talent.
⇒したたらず

しだ 羊歯 fern ⓒ

じた 自他 彼女は自他ともに認める無類の犬好きだ She considers herself a great lover of dogs and everyone acknowledges it.

したあご 下顎 the lower jaw; (あごの先端) chin ◎

したい¹ 死体 (dead) body ◎; corpse ◎ ∥死体の身元を確認する identify *a body* / 彼は死体遺棄の容疑で起訴された He was prosecuted for *abandoning a dead body*.
◆その行方不明者は死体で見つかった The missing person *was found dead*.

したい² 肢体 (体) body ◎; (手足) limb ◎
◆肢体の不自由な *physically* handicapped

-したい want [wish, would like] to *do*, feel* like *doing* ⇒ -たい¹
したいようにしていいよ You can do as you *want* (*to do*).
◆これ以上おまえのしたい放題にはさせないぞ I won't let you *have your own way* any longer.

しだい¹ 次第 ❶【…によって】勝つか負けるかは運しだいだ Whether we'll win or not *depends on* luck. / 天候しだいでは, 計画の変更もありうる *Depending on* the weather, we may change our plan.
🅔「ちょっと高くても質のいい物を買ったほうがいいのかな」「それは君しだいだよ」 "Should I buy the one of high quality even though it's a little expensive?" "It's *up to you*."
❷【…したらすぐ】as soon as /決心がつきしだい知らせてください Please let me know *as soon as* you decide.
◆ご都合しだいお電話をください Please call me *at your earliest convenience*.
❸【事情】事の次第を教えてください Tell me *how it happened*. / 事と次第によってはめんどうなことになるかもしれない *Depending on the circumstances*, we might run into trouble. / こういう次第できょうは行けません *That's why* I can't go today.
🅔「手伝ってくれない？」「事と次第によるね」 "Can you help us?" "*That* [*It*] (*all*) *depends*."
❹【順序】式次第 *the order* of a ceremony; *the running order* for a ceremony
⇒ しだいに

しだい² 私大 private university [college] ◎

じたい¹ 事態 (状況) situation ◎, the state of affairs; (漠然とした) things, matters ∥事態を受け入れる [収拾する] accept [settle] *a situation* / 事態は緊迫している *The situation* is very tense. / 事態は確実によくなってきている *Things* are getting steadily better.
◆非常事態を宣言する declare *a state of emergency* / 最悪の事態に備える[を覚悟する]「prepare for [expect] *the worst*

じたい² 辞退 ──辞退する (丁寧に) decline ⊜ ⊜; (断固として) refuse ⊜ ⊜ ∥申し出を辞退する *decline* an offer / 彼がパーティーに誘ってくれたが辞退した He invited me to the party, but I *declined* (his invitation).

じたい³ 自体 問題自体はそれほど複雑ではない The problem *itself* is not so complicated.

じだい¹ 時代

❶【歴史上の一期間】period ◎; era ◎; age ◎; epoch ◎
| period: 特に学問的な区分による時代.
| era: 重要な出来事・人物の出現によってほかと違いが際立つ時代.
| age: 文明・機械などの発展段階で区分された時代.
| epoch: 大きな出来事・変化のあった時代.

江戸時代 *the* Edo *period* / 明治[大正, 昭和]時代 *the* Meiji [Taisho, Showa] *era* / 原始時代 *the* primitive *ages* / 先史時代 *a* prehistoric *period* / 石器[鉄器]時代 *the* Stone [Iron] *Age*
高度情報化時代がやってきた *The* information *age* has arrived.
冷戦の終結は新時代の幕あけとなった The end of the Cold War marked the beginning of *a new epoch*.
ジャズの時代に続いてロックの時代が来た *The age* of rock followed *the age* of jazz.
◆ピカソはダリと同時代の画家である Picasso was 「*a contemporary of* [*contemporary with*] Dali.
🅔「どの時代の歴史を勉強してるの」「ルネサンス時代だよ」 "Which *period* of history are you studying?" "*The Renaissance*."

❷【時流・時勢】time ◎ (しばしば複数形 ~s), day ◎ (しばしば複数形 ~s)
古きよき時代 *the* good old *days* [*times*] / 時代の先端を行く get ahead of *one's time*
いつか私たちの時代も来るだろう Our *day* will come someday.
彼は時代に取り残されない (→時代についていく) ようにパソコンを始めた He began learning how to use a PC to keep up with *the times*.
そんな考え方は時代遅れだ That way of thinking is 「*behind the times* [*out-of-date*].

❸【生涯の一期間】days
学生時代を振り返る look back on *one's school days* / 現役時代に in *one's days as a player*
高校時代に多くの友人を作った I made a lot of friends 「in *my high school days* [*when I was in high school*].
◆彼女は幸せな子供時代を送った She had *a* happy *childhood*. / この曲を聞くと青春時代を思い出します This song reminds me of *my youth*.

❹【長い年月】
時代物の(→骨董(こっとう)品の)家具 *antique* furniture
∥時代劇 a samurai [historical] drama / 時代錯誤 an anachronism / 時代小説 a historical novel

じだい² 次代 (次の時代) the next age [era]; (次の世代) the coming [next] generation ∥次代をになうのは私たちだ *The next age* depends on us.

じだい³ 地代 land [ground] rent [C] [U]
しだいに 次第に gradually; (少しずつ) little by little //天気はしだいによくなるだろう The weather will *gradually* change for the better.
したう 慕う (愛する) love [他]; (愛着をもっている) be attached to ...; (尊敬する) respect [他]; (後を追う) follow [他] //真奈は洋を慕っている Mana *is attached to* Hiroshi. / あの先生はみんなに慕われている That teacher *is respected* by everyone.
◆故郷を慕う *long for one's* hometown
したうけ 下請け subcontracting [C] ◆その会社は仕事の一部を下請けに出している The company *subcontracts* part of the work.
‖下請け業者 a subcontractor / 下請け工場 a subcontracting factory
したうち 舌打ち 彼は電車の中に傘を忘れてきたことに気づいて舌打ちした He *clicked his tongue* when he noticed he had left his umbrella on the train.

したがう 従う

❶【後についていく】follow [他] [自]
私たちはガイドの人に従って工場を見学した We toured the factory, *following* the guide. / We *followed* the guide around the factory.
❷【服従する・応じる】(命令・規則・目上の人などに) obey [他] [自]; (忠告などに) follow [他] [自]
規則[命令]に従う *obey* rules [orders] / 先生の助言に従う *follow* [*take*] *one's* teacher's advice / 大勢(たいせい)に従う *follow* [*go with*] the crowd
委員会の決定には従います I *will follow* the decision made by the committee.
以下の説明に従ってください *Follow* the instructions below.
緊急の際は乗務員の指示に従ってください In case of emergency, please *follow the instructions* of the crew.
❸【…につれて】
頂上に近づくに従って空気は薄くなった The air got thinner *as* we got near to the top.
年をとるに従って彼はより頑固になった *The older he grew*, the more stubborn he became.

したがえる 従える そのボクサーはセコンドを2人従えていた The boxer *had* two seconds *with* him.
したがき 下書き (草稿) draft [C]; (下絵) sketch [C] //手紙の下書きをする「make *a draft* of [*draft*] a letter
したがって 従って ❶【それゆえ】therefore, so //失敗は予想されていた. したがってだれもがっかりすることはなかった The failure was expected, and *therefore* nobody was disappointed.
❷【…につれて】as ➾したがう //薬が効き始めるに従って痛みがやわらいだ The pain eased *as* the medicine began to work.
-したがる want to *do*; (切望する) be eager to *do*, be impatient to *do* ➾-たい¹

したぎ 下着 《集合的》underwear [U]

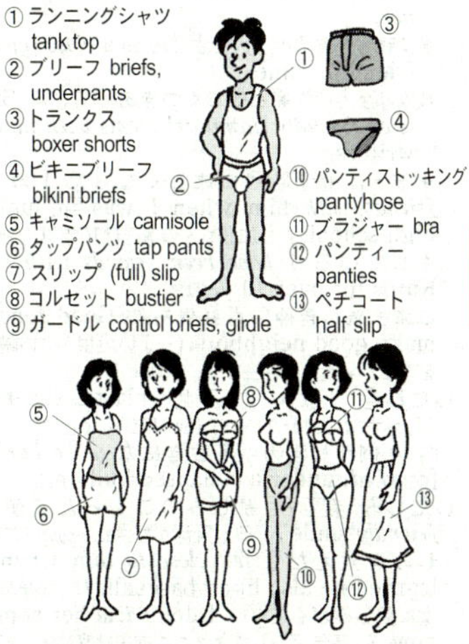

①ランニングシャツ tank top
②ブリーフ briefs, underpants
③トランクス boxer shorts
④ビキニブリーフ bikini briefs
⑤キャミソール camisole
⑥タップパンツ tap pants
⑦スリップ (full) slip
⑧コルセット bustier
⑨ガードル control briefs, girdle
⑩パンティストッキング pantyhose
⑪ブラジャー bra
⑫パンティー panties
⑬ペチコート half slip

したく 支度 preparation [U] [C]; (身じたく) dressing [U] ―したくする prepare [他] [自], get* ready; (身じたくする) get dressed //母は食事のしたくをしている My mother *is preparing* a meal. / 出かけるしたくをしなさい You'd better *get ready to* go.
じたく 自宅 *one's* home //自宅にいる be [stay] *at home* / 自宅で待機する wait *at home* / 自宅の住所 *one's home* address
したくちびる 下唇 the lower lip
したごころ 下心 (隠された意図) secret intention [C], ulterior motive [C] //弟が進んで家事を手伝うなんて何か下心があるにちがいない My brother must have some *ulterior motive* for doing housework voluntarily.
◆あいつの下心は見え見えだ His *intention* is obvious to me.
したごしらえ 下拵え 肉を下ごしらえする *prepare* [*dress*] meat for cooking / 下ごしらえした魚 *dressed* fish
したじ 下地 (基礎) the groundwork, foundation [C]; (基礎知識) a grounding //彼はその授業でしっかりした英語の下地を作った He got *a* thorough *grounding* in English in the class.
しだし 仕出し catering [U] ◆パーティーの仕出しをする *cater* a party
‖仕出し屋 a caterer
したしい 親しい friendly; familiar; close, intimate

> friendly: 友人としての親しさをいう最も一般的な語.
> familiar: うちとけた間柄であることを表す.
> close, intimate: 親密な交遊関係についていう. intimate は異性間に用いると性的な関係を暗示するので避けたほうがよい.

私の親しい級友たち classmates *close to* me

したじき

その女の人は私に親しげに話しかけてきた The woman spoke to me *in a friendly manner*.
彼は親しい友人の一人です He is a *close* [*good*] *friend of mine*.
彼女は多くの作家と親しくつきあっている She *is on friendly* [*familiar*] *terms with* many writers.
◆彼とは中学時代に親しくなった I *made friends with* him when I was in junior high school. / 加藤さんの家とは10年以上親しくしている I *have been friends with* the Katos for over 10 years.
ことわざ 親しき仲にも礼儀あり Good fences make good neighbors.(→よい垣根がよい隣人を作る)

したじき 下敷き (文房具) plastic sheet ◎ (❖英米では使わない); (皿・花びんなどの) mat ◎ ◆倒れた建物の下敷きになる *be buried* [*crushed*] *under a collapsed building*

したしみ 親しみ 親しみのこもった笑顔 a *friendly* smile / 彼も野球が好きだと分かって親しみを覚えた I *felt close to* him when I learned he also liked baseball. / なぜか彼女に親しみがもてない I don't *like* her somehow. / 長年暮らしてきたここ神田は私にとって親しみのある町だ Kanda is *very familiar* to me because I've lived here for many years.

したしむ 親しむ 読書に親しむ(→時間を費やす) *spend a lot of time* reading / 彼女はとても親しみやすい人柄だ She has a very *friendly* personality. / この本は世界中で親しまれている(→人気がある) This book *is popular* all around the world. / これは自然に親しむよい機会だ This is a good opportunity to *get closer to* nature.

したじゅんび 下準備 preliminary arrangements, preparation ◎◎ /会議の下準備をする *make preliminary arrangements for* a meeting

したしらべ 下調べ (準備・予習) preparation ◎◎; (予備調査) preliminary research ◎ ―下調べする prepare ⓐ; do* preliminary research /授業の下調べはしましたか Did you *prepare for* your class?

したたか (強く・ひどく) hard, severely ― **したたかな** (手強い) tough / 彼はしたたかな男だ He's a *tough guy*. / 暗い部屋で足をいすにしたたかぶつけた I struck my leg *hard* against a chair in a dark room. ◆したたかに(→抜け目なく)生きる live *shrewdly*

したたらず 舌足らず 舌足らずな(→不十分な)説明 an *unsatisfactory* explanation / 彼女は舌足らずのしゃべり方をする She speaks *with a childish lisp*.

したたる 滴る (しずくとなって落ちる) drip ⓐ; (伝い落ちる・しずくとなって落ちる) trickle ⓐ /傷口から血がしたたり落ちていた Blood *was dripping* from the wound. / 蛇口から水がしたたる音が聞こえた I heard the faucet *dripping*.

したつづみ 舌鼓 彼らは新鮮な海の幸に舌鼓を打った They *enjoyed* the fresh seafood *with gusto*.

したっぱ 下っ端 underling ◎ /人を下っ端扱いする treat a person like *an underling*

したづみ 下積み (無名) obscurity ◎; (最下位) the bottom /長年の下積みを経てついに彼はすぐれた役者として認められた After long years of *obscurity*, he was at last recognized as a good actor.

したて¹ 仕立て 仕立てのよい[悪い]スーツ a *well-*[*badly-*]*tailored* suit / 仕立て下ろしのスーツ a *brand-new* suit / 服を仕立て直す *re-make* a dress
‖ 仕立屋 (紳士服の) a tailor; (婦人服・子供服の) a dressmaker

したて² 下手 人に対して下手に出る take a *modest* [*humble*] *attitude* toward a person
‖ 下手投げ (野球) an underhand throw; (相撲) a *shitatenage*, an underarm throw

したてる 仕立てる ❶【服を】make* ⓐ /オーバーを仕立ててもらう *have* an overcoat *made*
❷【育てる】train ⓐ /人をエンジニアに仕立て上げる *train* a person to be an engineer
❸【それらしく見せる】私は彼らによって悪者に仕立て上げられた I *was made out* to be bad by them.

したどり 下取り trade-in ◎ /この古いテレビを下取りしていただけますか Will you *give me a trade-in* on this old TV?
◆彼は古い車を下取りに出して新車を買った He *traded in* an old car for a new one.
‖ 下取り価格 a trade-in price

したなめずり 舌なめずり オオカミは獲物を前に舌なめずりした The wolf *licked his chops* at the game before him.(❖chopsは動物に用いる。人間の場合は lick *one's* lips)

したばき 履き (outdoor) shoes

じたばた ―じたばたする (もがく) struggle ⓐ; (騒ぎたてる) make* a fuss; (抵抗する) resist ⓐ /いまさらじたばたしてもしようがないよ It's no use *making a fuss* now.

したばたらき 下働き assistant ◎ /彼女は姉のもとで下働きをしている She is working under her sister *as an assistant*.

したび 下火 火事はようやく下火になってきた The fire *is finally dying down*. / その番組の人気も下火になってきた The TV program *is losing* its popularity.

したびらめ 舌平目 〘魚〙sole ◎◎

-したほうがいい ⇨ほう(方)

したまち 下町 the old traditional districts (of a city) ❖英語のdowntownは街の中心地区・繁華街・商業地区を指すので、日本語の「下町」とは一致しない。

したまわる 下回る (…以下である) be below …; (…より少ない) be less than …; (…より低い) be lower than …; (…に足りない) fall* [come*] short of … /今年の8月の平均気温は平年を下回った The average temperature this August *was below* that of past years. / 今月は収入が支出を下回った Income *was less* [*lower*] *than* expenditures this month. / 売り上げは予想をはるかに下回った The sales *fell* far *short of* our expectations.

したみ 下見 preliminary inspection ⓒ / 彼らはイベント会場の下見に行った They made *a preliminary inspection* of the event hall.

したむき 下向き 彼はコップを下向きに(→逆さに)置いた He turned the glass *upside down*.

-したら (もし…なら) if …; (…するときに) when …. ⇨ -たら / 願い事が1つだけかなうとしたら何をお願いしますか *If you could have one wish come true, what would it be?* / 帰宅したらすぐ寝ます I'll go straight to bed *when* I get back.
◆もし彼が本当にやっていないとしたらいったいだれがやったんだ *Suppose* he really didn't do it, who on earth did?

したりがお したり顔 彼は教授をやり込めたとしたり顔に(→勝ち誇って)話した He told me *triumphantly* that he had argued his professor down.

しだれざくら しだれ桜 drooping cherry (tree) ⓒ

しだれやなぎ しだれ柳 weeping willow ⓒ

しだん 師団〔軍事〕 division ⓒ ‖師団長 the divisional commander; (自衛隊の)the Commanding General of the Division

じたん 時短 (労働時間短縮) reduction of working hours

じだん 示談 out-of-court settlement ⓒ / 彼は10万円で示談にすることを受け入れた He accepted *an out-of-court settlement* of 100,000 yen. ◆私たちはその件を示談ですませた We *settled* the case *out of court*.

じだんだ 地団駄 地団駄を踏んで悔しがる *stamp one's feet* in frustration

しち¹ 七 seven; (7番目) seventh

しち² 質 私の腕時計は質に入れてある My watch *is in pawn* [hock]. / 彼女はネックレスを質に入れた She *pawned* [*hocked*] her necklace.
‖質草 an article for pawning / 質流れ foreclosure / 質流れ品 a forfeited pledge / 質屋 a pawnshop

じち 自治 self-government Ⓤ, autonomy Ⓤ / その国は植民地に自治を認めた The country granted *self-government* to its colonies.
‖自治会 (地域の) a neighborhood self-governing body; (学生の) a student council [union] / 自治権 autonomy, the right of self-government / 自治省 the Ministry of Home Affairs (✦2001年総務省に統合) ⇨ そうむしょう / 自治体 a self-governing body; (地方自治体) a local government, a municipality

しちがつ 七月 July ⓤⓒ ((略語)) Jul.
⇨ いちがつ

しちかっけい 七角形 heptagon ⓒ

しちごさん 七五三

七五三は11月15日に子供たちのすこやかな成長を願う伝統行事です。3歳・5歳・7歳の子供たち(ふつうは3歳と7歳の女の子と5歳の男の子)が晴れ着を着て,両親といっしょに神社にお参りします。お参りのあと,両親は子供たちに千歳あめと呼ばれる特別なあめを買ってやります。
Shichigosan (November 15) is a traditional event to pray for the healthy growth of children. Three-, five- and seven-year-olds (usually three- and seven-year-old girls and five-year-old boys) are dressed up in their best clothes and brought to shrines by their parents to pray for their happy and healthy future. After the visit many parents buy their children special candy called *chitose-ame* (thousand-year-candy).

しちごちょう 七五調 the seven-and-five-syllable meter

しちじゅう 七十 seventy; (70番目) seventieth

しちてんばっとう 七転八倒 腹痛に七転八倒する *writhe in agony* from stomach pains

しちふくじん 七福神

七福神信仰は中国の7人の聖人に関する故事にならって,室町時代のころから人々の間に広がりました。7人の神々はインド,中国,日本の福の神の集まりで,宝船に乗った七福神の絵がしばしば描かれています。
The belief in *Shichifukujin* (the seven gods of good luck) was spread in Japan around the Muromachi period (1338-1573) following Chinese anecdotes of seven sages. Among the seven are gods from India, China and Japan, all of which are said to bring good luck. In a picture, they are often on board a ship called *Takarabune*.

しちめんちょう 七面鳥 turkey ⓒ

しちゃく 試着 ―試着する try on / これを試着してもいいですか Can I *try* this *on*?
‖試着室 a fitting room

しちゅう 支柱 prop ⓒ, support ⓒ, stay ⓒ / 祖母は私の精神的支柱になっている My grandmother is my emotional *support*.
◆その家族は一家の支柱(→稼ぎ手)を失った The family lost *their breadwinner*.

シチュー stew [stjúː] Ⓤⓒ / ビーフシチュー beef *stew*

しちょう¹ 市長 mayor ⓒ / 名古屋市長 *the mayor* of Nagoya
‖市長選挙 a mayoral election

しちょう² 試聴 CDを試聴する *listen to a CD before buying it*

じちょう¹ 自重 君はもう少し自重したほうがいい You should *be more prudent* [*cautious*].

じちょう² 自嘲 彼は自嘲ぎみにそう言った He said so *as if he were mocking himself*.

じちょう³ 次長 assistant manager ⓒ

しちょうかく 視聴覚 ―視聴覚の audio-visual / 視聴覚教育 audio-visual education / 視聴覚教材 audio-visual education materials / 視聴覚室 an audio-visual room

しちょうしゃ[1] 視聴者 viewer ⓒ, 《集合的》audience ⓒ / 視聴者参加番組 an audience participation program(❖電話で参加するものは《米》a call-in, 《英》a phone-in)

しちょうしゃ[2] 市庁舎 city hall ⓒ

しちょうそん 市町村 cities, towns and villages; (地方自治体) municipalities

しちょうりつ 視聴率 (audience) rating ⓒ / 視聴率がいい have good *ratings* / そのドラマの先週の視聴率は15パーセントだった The TV drama had *ratings* [*an audience share*] of 15 percent last week.

しつ[1] 質 quality Ⓤ / 質の高い商品 goods *of high quality* / 質を向上させる improve *the quality* / このカメラは質がいい This camera is of good *quality*. / This is a (good) *quality* camera. / 量より質を重視すべきだ *Quality* should be regarded as more important than quantity.

しつ[2] 室 (部屋) room ⓒ / 504号室 Room 504 (❖room five o[óu] four と読む) / 音楽室 a music *room*

しっ (静かにさせる声) sh(h), hush [ʃːː]; (追い払う声) shoo [ʃúː]

じつ 実 実を言うと来月引っ越すんです As *a matter of fact* [*To tell the truth*], I'll move next month.
慣用表現 名を捨てて実を取る ➡な
➡ じつに, じつの, じつは

しつい 失意 (失望) disappointment Ⓤ; (絶望) despair Ⓤ / そのとき私は失意のどん底にいた I was in the depths of *despair* at that time.

じついん 実印 registered seal

じつえき 実益 profit Ⓤ ◆姉は趣味と実益を兼ねて庭で野菜を育てている My sister grows some vegetables in her garden *for fun and (for) practical reasons*.

じつえん 実演 demonstration ⓒ ――実演する demonstrate ⓒ, give* a demonstration of ... / 店員はビデオカメラの使い方を実演してみせた The salesperson *demonstrated* how to use the video camera.
‖実演販売 demonstration sales

じっか 実家 (両親の家) one's parents' home [house]; (自分の生まれた家) one's home / 夏休みは実家に帰る予定です I'm going to go back to *my parents' home* during the summer vacation.

じっかい 十戒 〔聖書〕 the Ten Commandments

じつがい 実害 substantial harm [damage] Ⓤ

しっかく 失格 disqualification Ⓤ ――失格する be disqualified / 彼はそのレースに失格した He *was disqualified* from the race.
◆彼女は先生としては失格かもしれない She may be *a failure* as a teacher.

しっかり
❶【丈夫に・きつく】firmly, tightly
くぎをしっかり打つ drive a nail *firmly*
おばあさんは私の手をしっかり握りしめた The old woman grasped my hand *tightly*.
私は箱をしっかりと縛った I roped the box *tightly*.
◆母親は小さな息子をしっかりと抱きしめた The mother held her little son *tight*. / しっかりつかまっていなさい Hold tight [*tightly*].
❷【きちんと・十分に】
朝食をしっかりとる eat breakfast *properly*
彼女は社交上のたしなみをしっかり身につけている She is *well* versed in the social graces.
このことをしっかり覚えておくように Keep this in mind *firmly*.
しっかり勉強しなさい Study *hard*.
❸【励ましの言葉】
しっかりして(→元気を出して)! *Cheer up!*
しっかりするんだ,すぐに医者が来るから *Hold on*. The doctor is coming soon.
❹【堅実な】
彼女はまだ若いのにしっかりしている She is *reliable* though she is young.

しっかん 疾患 disease ⓒⓊ

じっかん 実感 (認識) realization Ⓤ《また a ~》――実感する realize ⓒ / 健康のありがたさをつくづく実感した I fully *realized* the value of good health. ◆まだ高校生になったという実感がわかない I still *can't believe* that I became a high school student. / 彼女の話には実感がこもっていた Her story *was full of feeling and expression*.

しっき 漆器 lacquer(ed) ware Ⓤ

しつぎ 質疑 (質問) question ⓒ; (問い合わせ) inquiry ⓒ
‖質疑応答 questions and answers

じつぎ 実技 体育実技 gymnastic *exercises* / 彼は自動車の実技試験に受かった He passed *his driving test*.

しっきゃく 失脚 (地位からの) loss of position; (没落) downfall ⓒ ――失脚する (地位を喪失する) lose* one's position / その政治家は収賄で失脚した The politician *lost his position* because of bribery. ◆彼は革命で失脚した(→権力の座から追放された) He *was ousted from power* by the revolution.

しつぎょう 失業 unemployment Ⓤ ――失業する lose* one's job / 失業者数が300万人に近づいている *Unemployment* is approaching the three million mark. / 政府は失業問題に真剣に取り組まなければならない The government must tackle *the unemployment problem* seriously. ◆私は現在失業中だ I am「*out of work*[*jobless, unemployed*] now.
‖失業者 an unemployed person,《集合的》the unemployed / 失業対策 an unemployment policy / 失業手当 unemployment compensation [allowance] / 失業保険 unemployment insurance / 失業率 the unemployment rate

じつきょう 実況 この試合は実況でお送りしています We are broadcasting this game *live*.
‖実況中継 a relay from the scene / 実況放送 an on-the-spot broadcast; (野球などスポーツの解説) a play-by-play commentary

じつぎょう 実業 business Ⓤ ‖実業家 a busi-

シック ━シックな chic [ʃíːk]; (いきな) stylish 〃彼女はシックなジャケットを着ていた She had on a *chic* jacket.

しっくい 漆喰 (壁などに塗る) plaster ⓤ; (モルタル) mortar ⓤ; (仕上げに使う) stucco ⓤ

しっくり 彼女はこのごろ母親としっくりいっていないようだ She doesn't seem to *be getting along with* her mother these days. / この花びんはこの部屋にはしっくりこない This vase *doesn't suit* [*fit*] this room.

じっくり (注意して) carefully; (十分に) thoroughly; (綿密に) closely 〃はんこを押す前に契約条件をじっくり読みなさい You should read the terms of contract *carefully* before putting your seal on it.
◆じっくり考える時間が必要だ We need some time to *think* it *over*. / そのことについて両親とじっくり話し合った I had a *heart-to-heart* talk with my parents about it. / 彼は夏休みの課題にじっくり取り組んでいる He *is taking his time* doing his summer vacation homework.

しつけ 躾 (精神的な) discipline ⓤ; (行儀) manners 〃しつけがいい have good *manners*; *be* well *disciplined* / この店は店員のしつけがなっていない The salespeople aren't trained in good *manners* at this shop. / 両親のしつけは厳しかった My parents were strict about *manners*.

しっけ 湿気 (湿度) humidity ⓤ; (不快な) damp(ness) ⓤ; (湿り気) moisture ⓤ 〃湿気を取る draw *the moisture*
◆湿気を含んだ風 a *damp* [*moist*] wind / 梅雨の時期は湿気が多い It's *humid* in the rainy season. / 湿気のない所に保存してください Please keep this in a *dry* place.

しっけい 失敬 あいつは本当に失敬なやつだ He is really a *rude* man. / 父の万年筆を失敬してきた I *took* my father's fountain pen *without permission*.

じっけい 実刑 (刑務所に入れること) imprisonment ⓤ; (実刑判決) prison sentence ⓒ
◆裁判官は彼に懲役5年の実刑判決を言い渡した The judge sentenced him to five years *in prison*.

しつける 躾る (訓練する) train ⓗ, discipline ⓗ; (行儀作法を教える) teach* good manners 〃ペットをきちんとしつける *train one's pet properly*

しつげん 失言 (口を滑らせること) a slip of the tongue; (不適切な発言) improper remark ⓒ; (特に政治家の) gaffe ⓒ 〃失言を取り消す take back *one's improper remarks* / すみません、失言でした I'm sorry, I made「*a slip of the tongue* [*an improper remark*].

しつげん² 湿原 marsh ⓒ ⓤ, marshland ⓒ ⓤ

じっけん¹ 実験 experiment ⓒ ⓤ; (テスト) test ⓒ ━実験する experiment ⓗ, do* [perform, carry out] an experiment; (試す) test ⓗ 〃動物実験 *an experiment* on animals / 地下核実験 *an* underground nuclear *test* / 化学の実験をする do *a* chemical *experiment*
彼らの実験はうまくいった Their *experiment* worked well.
その仮説が正しいかどうか実験してみよう Let's *do* [*conduct*] *an experiment* to see if the hypothesis is true.
◆実験的にこの方法を用いています We are using this method *experimentally*. / この新しい薬はまだ実験段階にある This new medicine is still in *the experimental* [*testing*] *stage*.
‖実験材料 experimental materials / 実験室 a laboratory, 《口語的》a lab / 実験台 (被験者) an experimental subject; (モルモット) a guinea pig / 実験道具 a chemistry apparatus

じっけん² 実権 (実際の権力) real [actual] power ⓤ; (完全な支配力) full control ⓤ 〃実権を握る hold *real power*

じつげん 実現 realization ⓤ, fulfillment ⓤ ━実現する realize ⓗ, fulfill ⓗ; (夢などが) come* true
選挙公約を実現する *fulfill* campaign promises
彼女の夢はいつか実現するだろう Her dream will *come true* someday.
その計画は実現不可能だ It is *impossible to realize* that plan.

しつこい
❶【執拗な】persistent ━しつこく persistently
ここ2、3週間しつこいかぜに悩まされている I've been suffering from a *persistent* cold for the last few weeks.
彼にしつこく質問された I was *persistently* questioned by him.
◆しつこい汚れ a *stubborn* stain / あまりしつこくつきまとうと彼女に嫌われるよ She'll get sick of you if you *keep on following her all the time*.
🄔 「ねえ、カラオケ行こうよ」「しつこいなあ、きょうは行けないって言ったでしょ」 "Say, let's go and sing karaoke." "*Give it a rest!* I told you I couldn't go today, didn't I?"
❷【料理が】(もたれる) heavy; (油っこい) greasy; (こってりした) rich
彼女の作った料理は少ししつこかった The dish she had cooked was a little *heavy*.

しっこう 執行 execution ⓤ ━執行する execute ⓗ; (実行する) carry out 〃強制執行 compulsory [forcible] *execution* / 刑を執行する *carry out* a sentence ◆その男は懲役1年、執行猶予(ᵍᵘ)3年の判決を受けた The man was sentenced to one year in prison with three years' *probation*.
‖執行委員会 an executive committee / 執行部 the executives

じっこう¹ 実行 (実践) practice ⓤ; (行動) action ⓤ ━実行する carry out; (実行に移す) put* ... into practice; (約束・義務などを)

fulfill [他]; (公務などを) execute [他]
契約を実行する *execute* [*carry out*] a contract
彼女は口だけで実行が伴わない She is all talk and no *action*.
この企画を実行に移す前によく検討しなければならない We have to consider this project carefully before we *carry* it *out*.
◆彼の言ったことは実行不可能だと思います I *don't think* what he said *is feasible*. / 彼は実行力がある He *is capable of getting things done*.
‖実行委員会 an executive committee

じっこう² 実効 actual [practical] effect [C]

しっこく 漆黒 漆黒の髪 *jet-black* hair

しつごしょう 失語症 〔医学〕aphasia [əféiʒə] [U]

じっさい 実際 (事実) fact [C]; (現実) reality [U] [C]; (真実) truth [U]; (実地) practice [U] ━実際の (現実の) actual; (実在の) real; (本当の) true; (実地の) practical ━実際に actually; really; truly; practically

〖実際(は)〗
彼女は, 彼は米国人だと言っていたが実際は英国人だった She said he was American, but *actually* [*in fact, in reality*] he was British.
彼女は実際は何と言ったのですか What did she *actually* say?
彼は実際頭がいい He is *really* intelligent.

〖実際に〗
それは実際にあった話ですか Is it a *true* story?
実際に見るのと聞くのとでは大違いだ There's a big difference between hearing about something and *actually* seeing it.
彼が予想したことが実際に起こった What he expected has *really* come to pass.
◆ああだこうだ言ってないで, 実際にやってみよう Let's stop fussing around and *try it*.

〖実際の〗
実際の値段 the *real* [*actual*] price
予測と実際の結果との違いは大きかった There was a great difference between the prediction and the *actual* results.

〖その他〗
実際問題として *as a matter of fact*; *in practice*
この写真だと彼は実際よりずっと若く見える This photo makes him look much younger than he *really* is.

じつざい 実在 existence [U] ━実在の (現実の) real; (生存している) living; (人・物などが存在する) existent ━実在する exist [自] ‖実在の人物 a *real* [an *actual*] person / その動物は実在するのですか Does the animal *exist*?

しっさく 失策 mistake [C], error [C] ‖彼は大失策を犯した He made *a great mistake*.

じっし¹ 実施 ━実施する (実行する) carry out; (実行に移す) put* ... into practice; (施行する) put ... into effect ‖新幹線の新しいダイヤは3月15日から実施される The new schedule of the Shinkansen *will be put into effect* on March 15. ◆きょう都立高校でいっせいに入学試験が実施された The entrance exam *was held* at the same time in all metropolitan high schools today.

じっし² 実子 *one's* own child

じっし³ 十指 彼は日本で十指に数えられる建築家だ He is counted among the *top ten* architects in Japan.

じっしつ 実質 (中身) 《公式的》substance [U]; (本質) essence [U] ━実質的な substantial; (本質的な) essential; (実際上の) practical; (事実上の) virtual ━実質的に substantially, in substance; essentially; practically; virtually ‖実質的な損害 *practical* damage / それは実質的な値上げだ It is *practically* a price increase. / それら2つの案は実質的には同じだ Those two plans are *virtually* the same.
‖実質賃金 real wages

じっしゃかい 実社会 the (real) world ‖実社会に出る go out into *the world*

じっしゅう 実習 (訓練) training [U]; (練習) practice [U] ━実習する practice [他] ‖調理実習 cooking *practice* / 彼女は自分の出身中学で教育実習をした She「*did her teaching practice* [*practiced teaching*] at the junior high school from which she had graduated.
‖実習生 a trainee / 教育実習生 a student teacher

じっしゅきょうぎ 十種競技 decathlon [C]

じっしょう 実証 ━実証する prove* [他] ‖その説が正しいことは実証済みだ It *has been proved* that the theory is right.
‖実証主義 positivism

じつじょう 実情 the actual [real] state of affairs ◆その国の実情を把握する understand *the real situation* in the country / 商品の需要に生産が追いつかないのが実情だ *Actually* the production of the goods can't keep up with the demand.

しっしん¹ 湿疹 eczema [igzíːmə] [U] ‖その子は顔に湿疹ができていた The child had *eczema* on his face.

しっしん² 失神 faint [C] ━失神する faint [自], 《口語的》pass out ‖彼女はショックのあまり失神しそうになった She was so shocked that she almost *fainted*.

じっしんほう 十進法 the decimal scale [system]

じっすう 実数 real number [C]

しっする 失する 遅きに失する(→遅すぎる) be *too* late / 礼を失する *be rude*

じっせいかつ 実生活 real [actual] life [U]

じっせき 実績 (結果) result [U] [C]; (業績) achievement [C] ‖彼には医者としての実績がある He has *achievements* as a doctor.

じっせん¹ 実践 practice [U] ━実践する practice [他] ‖学んだことを実践に移す put what *one* learned into *practice* / 彼は自分の主義を実践している He *is practicing* his principle.

じっせん² 実戦 (実際の戦い) actual fighting ⓤ, real combat ⓤ ◆彼は実戦に強い(→本試合で強い)タイプの選手だ He is the type of the player who is strong in *actual games*.

じっせん³ 実線 solid line ⓒ

しっそ 質素 ——質素な (簡素な) simple; (飾りけのない) plain ——質素に simply; plainly ∥質素な食事 a *simple* meal / 質素な暮らしをする live *simply* [a *simple* life] / 彼女は質素な身なりをしている She *is plainly* dressed [wears a *plain* dress].

しっそう¹ 失踪 disappearance ⓤ ——失踪する disappear ⓐ; (逃げる) run* away ∥彼が失踪して半年になる It has been six months since he *disappeared*.

しっそう² 疾走 ——疾走する run* at full speed, dash ⓐ

じつぞう 実像 (実態) the actual conditions

しっそく 失速 stall ⓒ ——失速する stall ⓐ ∥飛行機は突然失速した The plane suddenly *stalled*.

じつぞんしゅぎ 実存主義 〔哲学〕 existentialism ⓤ ∥実存主義者 an existentialist

しった 叱咤 ——叱咤する (しかる) reprimand ⓐ, 《公式的》rebuke ⓐ; (激励する) encourage ⓐ ∥選手たちを叱咤激励する *encourage* the players *in a loud voice*

しったい 失態 彼はとんだ失態を演じた He made *an* awful *blunder*.

じったい¹ 実態 the actual conditions [circumstances] ∥現代の学生の実態を調べる investigate *the actual conditions* of present-day students

じったい² 実体 substance ⓒ ◆実体のない会社 a *paper* company

しったかぶり 知ったかぶり 知ったかぶりをする (何でも知っているふりをする) pretend to know everything

じつだん 実弾 (弾丸) live ammunition ⓤ; (小銃弾) bullet ⓒ; (大砲の) live shell ⓒ ∥実弾射撃 a firing practice with live ammunition

しっち¹ 湿地 damp ground ⓤ; (沼地) marsh ⓒ, bog ⓒ

しっち² 失地 lost territory ⓤ ∥失地を回復する recover *the lost territory*

じっち 実地 (実際に行われること) practice ⓤ ——実地の practical ∥その理論を実地に応用してみよう Let's put the theory into *practice*. ◆警察は犯行現場の実地検証をした The police did *the on-the-spot investigation* at the scene of the crime. ∥実地訓練 practical training, on-the-job training / 実地試験 (運転免許の) a driving test / 実地体験 a practical experience / 実地調査 an on-the-spot survey

じっちゅうはっく 十中八九 ◆十中八九彼は勝つだろう Ten to one he will win. / He is *most likely* to win.

じっちょく 実直 ——実直な (誠実な) sincere; (正直な) honest; (良心的な) conscientious

しっつい 失墜 ——失墜する lose* ⓐ ∥知事は収賄事件で権威を失墜した The governor *lost his prestige* in the bribery scandal.

じつづき 地続き その列島はかつて大陸と地続き (→大陸の一部) だった The archipelago was once *a part of the continent*.

しっと 嫉妬 jealousy ⓤ; envy ⓤ (✽ jealousy は自分にないものをもっている人を憎悪する気持ち. envy は人の幸運・能力などをうらやむ気持ち) ∥彼女は嫉妬心からそんなことを言ったのだろう She would have said that *out of jealousy*. ◆彼女は姉の成功に嫉妬している She *is jealous* [*envious*] *of* her sister's success. / 彼はとても嫉妬深い He *is* very *jealous*.

しつど 湿度 humidity ⓤ ∥現在の湿度は70パーセントです *The humidity* is 70 percent now. ◆日本では夏は湿度が高い In Japan, it *is humid* in summer. ∥湿度計 a hygrometer

じっと
❶ 【動かずに】
外は寒かったので家でじっとしていた I *stayed* at home because it was cold outside.
ベッドでじっと横になっているうちに眠ってしまった I fell asleep while lying *quietly* on the bed.
子供たちはコンサートが終わるまでどうにか座っていた The children somehow sat *still* through the concert.
しばらくじっとしていなさい Stay [Keep] *still* for a while.
その子供は母親が帰ってくるまでじっとしていられなかった (→落ち着かなかった) The child *was restless* until his mother came back.

❷ 【集中して】
彼女は私をじっと見ていた She *was staring* [*gazing*] *at* me.
弟は部屋でじっと考え込んでいた My brother *was lost* [*absorbed*] *in thought* in his room.
じっと耳をすますと波の音が聞こえた I listened *attentively* [*intently*] and heard the sound of the waves.

❸ 【忍耐強く】 patiently
彼女は傷の痛みにじっと耐えた She bore the pain of her wound *patiently*.
彼が来るのを校門の前でじっと待った I *patiently* waited in front of the school gate for him to come.

しっとう 執刀 来週の父の手術は武藤先生が執刀する Dr. Muto *will perform the operation* on my father next week.

しっとり このケーキは風味が豊かでしっとりしている This cake *is* rich *and moist*. / この街にはしっとりした (→落ち着いた) 雰囲気がある This town has a *quiet* atmosphere.

じっとり 彼の手は汗でじっとりしていた His hands *were wet* with sweat.

しつない 室内 ——室内の indoor ◆雨だったので子供たちは室内で遊んだ The children played *indoors* because it was raining. ∥室内楽 chamber music / 室内競技 indoor

じつに

athletics / 室内装飾 interior design [decoration] / 室内プール an indoor pool

じつに 実に (本当に) really; (全く) quite; (非常に) very, so; (ものすごく) terribly, awfully; (極度に) extremely; (まことに) indeed

彼は実によく勉強する He *really* studies hard.
聴衆は実に静かだった The audience was *quite* silent.
彼女は実に個性的だ She has got a *very* individual personality.
きょうは実に寒い It is *terribly* cold today.
この本は実におもしろかった This book was *extremely* interesting.

じつの 実の (真の) true; (本当の) real; (事実上の) actual ‖実の父 one's real [(→生物学的な)*biological*] father
◆きのうは出かけたって言ったけど, 実のところ一日中家にいたんだ I told you I went out yesterday, but *to tell the truth*, I stayed at home all day.

じつは 実は (本当を言えば) to tell (you) the truth; (事実は) the fact is (that)..., actually, in fact

時計がこわれてたんじゃないんだ. 実は寝坊したんだよ My clock wasn't broken. *To tell the truth*, I got up late.
彼は若く見えるけど実は40歳を超えているんだ He looks young, but *actually [in fact]*, he's over 40.
実はお願いがあるのです *Actually*, I have a favor to ask of you.
⮕「この間貸した本, そろそろ返してくれない?」「実はまだ1ページも読んでないんだ」 "Isn't it time you returned the book I lent you the other day?" "Well, 「*the fact is [as a matter of fact,]* I haven't read a single page of it."

ジッパー 《米》zipper ◎, 《英》zip ◎

しっぱい 失敗

(不成功) failure ◎; (誤り) mistake ◎; (大失敗) blunder ◎ ——失敗する fail ⾃他

失敗に終わる end in *failure*
彼の最初の試みは完全な失敗だった His first attempt was *a total failure*.
同じ失敗を繰り返してはいけない Don't repeat *the same failure*.
私はひどい失敗をしてしまった I made *a「big mistake [blunder]*.
彼は事業に失敗した He *failed in* his business.
弟は試験に失敗した My brother *failed (to pass)* the examination.
その映画は失敗作だ The movie was *a failure [flop]*.
ことわざ 失敗は成功の元 Failure is a stepping stone to success. (→失敗の外の足がかりとなる)

じっぱひとからげ 十把一絡げ 僕をあんなやつらと十把ひとからげにしないでくれ Don't *lump me together* with those fellows.

じっぴ 実費 (実際にかかる費用) actual expenses; (原価) cost ◎ ‖実費を払う pay *the actual expenses*

しっぴつ 執筆 writing ◎ ——執筆する write* ⾃他 /小説を執筆する *write* a novel / 雑誌に執筆する *write* for a magazine ‖執筆者(著者) a writer, an author; (寄稿者) a contributor

しっぷ 湿布 compress ◎ / 温[冷]湿布 *a warm [cold] compress* / 私は足首に湿布をした I put *a compress* on my ankle.
‖湿布薬 poultice

じっぷ 実父 one's real father

しっぷう 疾風 (強風) gale ◎, strong wind ◎

じつぶつ 実物 (実際の物) real thing ◎, actual object ◎; (本物) genuine object ◎; (美術品の対象) life ◎ / 実物の (本当の) real; (本物の) genuine ◆その歌手の似顔絵は実物そっくりだった The portrait of the singer was *quite lifelike*. / この写真は実物大だ This photograph is *life-size*.

しっぺい 疾病 disease ◎

しっぺがえし しっぺ返し (仕返し) tit for tat, retaliation ◎ / しっぺ返しをする *give a person tit for tat* / いずれしっぺ返しを食らうだろう You'll *get tit for tat* someday.

しっぽ 尻尾 (動物の) tail ◎; (端) the end ◎ / 犬はうれしそうにしっぽを振った The dog wagged *its tail* happily.
慣用表現 彼もそのうちしっぽを出す(→本性を現す) He will *show his "true colors" [real character]* soon. / いつかあいつのしっぽをつかんでやる(→相手の弱みを見抜く) I'll *find out his weak point* someday. / 男はしっぽを巻いて逃げ出した The man ran away *with his tail between his legs*.

じつぼ 実母 one's real mother

しつぼう 失望 (期待はずれ) disappointment ◎; (落胆) discouragement ◎; (絶望) despair ◎ ——失望する (がっかりする) be disappointed; (やる気をなくす) be discouraged ‖彼女の顔に失望の色が浮かんだ A look of *disappointment* came to her face.
[be disappointed+with 名 [in 名(人)]] その映画[彼女]には失望した I *was disappointed 「with the movie [in her]*.
[be disappointed+to do] 彼は試験に通らなかったと知ってすっかり失望してしまった He *was completely disappointed to* know he hadn't passed the exam.
◆試験の点数が悪くて両親を失望させてしまった I *disappointed* my parents by getting a bad grade on the exam.

しつむ 執務 執務中である be *at work*

じつむ 実務 business ◎ / 私には5年の実務経験があります I have five years' *business experience*.

しつめい 失明 彼は6歳で失明した He 「*lost his sight [went blind]* at the age of six.

じつめい 実名 one's actual [real] name / その雑誌は容疑者の実名を挙げてその事件を報道した The magazine published the case giving the suspect's *actual name*.

しつもん 質問 question [C]; (問い合わせ) inquiry [U] [C] **―質問する** ask a question, question [他]
ほかに質問はありますか Do you have any more *questions*?
その件について質問があります I have *a question* about the matter.
記者たちはその女優に質問を浴びせた Reporters showered *questions* on the actress.
どうぞ自由に質問してください Please feel free to *ask* any *question*.
ひとつ質問してもいいですか May I *ask* you *a question*?
彼はその質問に答えられなかった He couldn't answer the *question*.
その歌手は質問攻めにあった The singer faced *a barrage of questions*.
‖質問書 a written inquiry

しつよう 執拗 **―執拗な** (しつこい) persistent; (頑固な) obstinate **―執拗に** persistently ‖労働者は賃上げを執拗に要求した The workers *persistently* demanded higher wages.

じつよう 実用 practical use [U] **―実用的な** practical ‖この商品は実用的だ These goods are *practical*. ◆彼の発明が実用化された His invention *was put into practice*.
‖実用英語 practical English / 実用新案 a utility model / 実用性 practical use / 実用品 a useful article; (日用品) daily necessities

しつりょう 質量 〔物理〕 mass [U] ‖…の質量を測定する measure *the mass* of …

じつりょく 実力
❶【実際の能力】ability [U] [C]
学歴よりも実力を重視する value *ability* above educational background
彼女は実力でその地位を得た She won the position *through her ability*.
彼らはきょうの試合で十分に実力を発揮した They showed *their ability* in full in today's game.
◆実力に応じて according to *one's merits* / 彼は実力のあるサッカー選手だ He is a *competent* soccer player.
❷【腕力】
実力を行使する resort to *force*
話し合いは決裂し彼らは実力行使に出た(→行動を起こした) Negotiations ended in failure and they *moved into action*.
‖実力者(政界などの) an influential person / 実力主義 the merit system, a meritocracy / 実力テスト an achievement test

しつれい 失礼
❶【無礼】 **―失礼な** (粗野な) rude; (丁寧さに欠ける) impolite
知っている人に会ってあいさつをしないのは失礼だ It *is rude* [*impolite*] not to say hello when you run into someone you know.
彼は先生にとても失礼な態度をとった He was very *rude* to the teacher.
彼はなんて失礼なやつなんだ What a *rude* man he is!
❷【謝罪・断り】
失礼ですが，美術館へ行く道を教えてくださいませんか *Excuse me, but* would you tell me the way to the museum?
(中座するとき)すみません，ちょっと失礼します *Excuse me* for a moment.
お待たせして失礼しました *I'm sorry* to have kept you waiting.
お話し中失礼しますが，お電話です *I'm sorry* to interrupt you, but there is a phone call for you.
(電話で)失礼ですが，どちら様でしょうか May I have your name, *please*?
では失礼します(→帰ります) Well, *I must be going now*.

[語法]
(1) Excuse me.は，(a)知らない人に話しかけたり，聞き返す場合，(b)失礼な行為などに対するおわびを言う場合，(c)人前を通ったり，中座する場合，(d)相手の意見に反論したり，相手と話したくない場合などに用いられる．Excuse me.よりも丁寧なかたい言い方としては，I beg your pardon., Pardon me.がある．
(2) I'm sorry.は，自分が悪いということをはっきり認め，謝罪の意味が強い．

じつれい 実例 example [C] ‖彼はその理論を実例を挙げて説明した He illustrated the theory by giving some *examples*.

しつれん 失恋 disappointed [lost] love [U]; (失意) broken heart [C]
◆彼は失恋した(→彼女にふられた)らしい I hear *his girlfriend left* him.

じつわ 実話 true story [C]

してい[1] 指定 designation [U]; (日時・場所の) appointment [U] **―指定する** designate [他]; appoint [他] ‖会合の日時を指定する *designate* [*appoint*] the time for the meeting / その仏像は重要文化財に指定されている The statue of Buddha *is designated* as an important cultural property. / 私たちは指定の時間に着いた We arrived at the *appointed* time. ◆この列車は全席指定です All seats *are reserved* on this train.
‖指定券 a reserved seat ticket / 指定席 a reserved seat

してい[2] 師弟 master and pupil, teacher and student(❖冠詞は付けない) ‖彼らは親子だが，師弟の関係でもある They are parent and child, and also *master and pupil*.

-していた
❶【過去の行為・出来事の継続】was [were] *doing*(❖過去進行形)
子供たちは一日中公園で遊んでいた The children *were playing* in the park all day.
妹が部屋に入ってきたとき，私は勉強していた I *was studying* when my sister came into my room.
❷【過去の状態】

[語法]
過去の状態は，(1)状態動詞(動詞自体に「…している」という状態の意味が含まれるもの．例:

-している

be, have, remain, know, believe, see, hear などの過去形，(2)be＋形容詞[過去分詞]などで表すことができる．

彼はしばらくそこに立ち尽くしていた He *stood* there for a while.
彼女はプレゼントをもらってとても喜んでいた She *was* very *glad* to receive the present.
弟の部屋にはおもちゃが散らかっていた My brother's room *was littered* with toys.

❸【過去の行為の繰り返し・習慣】(❖過去の行為の繰り返し・習慣は通例過去形を用いて表す)
母は高校で英語を教えていた My mother *taught* English at a high school.
私は毎日バスで学校に通っていた I *went* to school by bus every day.
当時この通りには路面電車が走っていた Streetcars *used to run* along this street in those days.

❹【現在までの行為・出来事・状態】have *done*, have been *doing*(❖現在完了形または現在完了進行形)
彼の言うことは正しいと思っていた I *have thought* he was correct.
午後はずっとテニスをしていた I *have been playing* tennis this afternoon.

❺【過去のある時点よりも前に起こった事柄】

[語法] 過去に起こった2つの出来事について，時間的にどちらが先に起こったかを示すため，先に起こったほうを過去完了(進行)形で表す．

彼の家に行くと，彼はもう出かけていた When I went to his house, he *had* already *gone out*.
一晩中勉強していたので，とても眠かった I was sleepy because I *had been studying* all night.

❻【未来のある時点での完了】will have *done*, will have been *doing*(❖未来完了形あるいは未来完了進行形)
来月でこの家に15年住んでいたことになる I *will have lived* in this house for 15 years by next month.

❼【仮定】(仮定法過去で) *did*; (仮定法過去完了で) had *done*
お金を持っていたら，貸してあげるんだけど If I *had* the money, I could lend it to you.
バスに乗っていたら，今ごろは駅に着いていただろう If I *had taken* a bus, I would have arrived at the station by now.

❽【名詞を修飾】(❖現在分詞・関係詞節などを用いて表す)
木にとまっていた鳥が突然飛び立った The bird *sitting* in the tree suddenly flew away.
私は彼女に借りていたCDを返した I returned the CD *that I had borrowed* from her.

—している
❶【行為・出来事の継続】
《現在》is [am, are] *doing*(❖現在進行形)
彼女は雑誌を読んでいる She *is reading* a magazine.
母はまだ電話をしている My mother *is* still *talking on the phone*.
《過去から現在まで》have *done*, have been *doing*(❖現在完了形，あるいは現在完了進行形)
子供のころからここに住んでいます I've *lived* here since I was a child.
きのうからずっと雨が降っている It *has been raining* since yesterday.
《過去》was [were] *doing*(❖過去進行形)

[語法] 日本語では，「…しているときに～した」のように過去の行為・出来事でも「…している」の形で表すことがあるが，英語の場合は，主文の時制に合わせて，「…している」の部分は過去進行形を用いて表す．

テレビを見ているときに父が帰ってきた My father came home when I *was watching* TV.
《未来》will be *doing*(❖未来進行形)
あすの今ごろ私は列車で旅行をしているだろう I *will be traveling* by train this time tomorrow.

❷【結果の状態】

[語法] 「…している」の形は，過去の行為や作用が完了して，その結果の状態が今でも残っている様子を表す場合がある．例えば，「帽子をかぶっている」は，過去に「かぶる」という行為が行われ，その結果である「帽子が頭にある」という状態が今でも続いていることを表す．この場合の「…している」を英語に訳すときは，英語の動詞によっては，進行形や現在完了形にせずに，状態を表す動詞の単純な現在形や be＋形容詞[過去分詞]を用いて表すことができる．この場合，通例，進行形にすると一時的な状態を意味することになる / 彼はいつも黒い帽子をかぶっている He always *wears* a black hat. / 彼は(一時的に)黒い帽子をかぶっている He *is wearing* a black hat.

《単純な現在形》
その川にはたくさんの橋がかかっている There *are* a lot of bridges across the river.
バケツに穴があいている There *is* a hole in the bucket.
彼の住所を知っている I *know* his address.
《be＋形容詞[過去分詞]》
彼女の祖母は死んでいる Her grandmother *is dead*.
彼女は疲れているようだ She seems to *be tired*.
空は暗い雲に覆われている The sky *is covered* with dark clouds.
❸【恒常的な状態】
彼女はお姉さんに本当によく似ている She really *resembles* her sister.
南には高い山がそびえている A high mountain *rises* to the south.
❹【繰り返し・習慣】(❖行為の繰り返し・習慣は通例現在形を用いて表す)
彼女は毎週月曜日にピアノを習っている She *studies* the piano every Monday.
私は自転車で通学している I *go* to school by bicycle.

❺【完了・経験】（完了）have *done*, will have *done*, had *done*; （経験）have *done*

昼食はもうすませている I *have* already *had* lunch.

あしたにはこの本を読み終えているだろう I *will have finished* reading this book tomorrow.

この曲はこれまでに何度も聴いている（→聴いたことがある）I *have listened to* this music many times.

❻【仮定】（仮定法過去）*did*; （仮定法過去完了）had *done*

答えを知っていれば教えてあげるのですが If I *knew* the answer, I *would tell* it to you.

彼の気持ちを分かっていればあんなひどいことは言わなかったのに If I *had known* how he felt, I *wouldn't have said* such a terrible thing to him.

❼【名詞を修飾する】

《現在分詞》
眠っている子供 a *sleeping* child（※単独で用いられる場合は、通例名詞の前に置かれる）

隣に座っている女の子が話しかけてきた The girl *sitting next to me* spoke to me.（※他の語句を伴う場合は、通例名詞の後に置かれる）

《関係詞節》
彼が歌っている歌の題名が思い出せない I can't remember the title of the song *that he is singing*.

《形容詞・前置調》
その映画館に空いている席はひとつもなかった There was not one *vacant* seat in the movie theater.

あの赤いコートを着ている女の人が私の姉です That woman *in* the red coat is my sister.

しでかす 彼らは何をしでかすか分からない There is no telling what they *will do*.

してき¹ 指摘 ──指摘する point out ‖先生は私のつづりの間違いを指摘した The teacher *pointed out* some misspellings to me.
◆それはいい指摘だね It's *a good remark*.

してき² 私的 ──私的な （公に対して）private; （個人の）personal ‖私的な意見 one's *personal* opinion

してき³ 詩的 ──詩的な poetic, poetical ‖詩的な表現 a *poetic* expression

してき⁴ 史的 ──史的な historical ‖史的唯物論 historical materialism

-してしまう

【語法】
「…してしまう」は、日本語では完了の意味を表すほかに、(1)好ましくない結果を表すとき（例：電話番号を間違えてしまった）、(2)強調を表すとき（例：その光景を見て驚いてしまった）などに用いることがあり、英語で表すときは、必ずしも完了形にするとは限らない。

宿題はもうやってしまった I *have finished* my homework. / 君が次に訪ねてくるまでにはこの絵を完成してしまっているだろう I *will have finished* this painting by the time you visit me next time. / 私はよく彼と弟さんを混同してしまう I often「*confuse* him [*mix* him *up*] with his brother. / ノートを家に置いてきてしまった I *left* my notebook in my house.

してつ 私鉄 private railroad [《英》railway] ◯

-しては きょうは3月にしては暖かい It is warm today *for March*. / 初めてにしては上出来だ You have done well *for a beginner*. / 私としてはその考えには賛成できない *As for me*, I can't agree with the idea.

-してみる 彼女はそのドレスを試着してみた She *tried on* the dress. / 私はそのボタンをもう一度押してみた I *pushed* the button once more. / 彼に聞いてみたらどうですか *Why don't you ask* him? / 彼は学校のバンドを指揮してみたいと思っている He *wants to lead* the school band.

してみると （そうすると）then

-しても 今すぐ家を出たとしてもそこに10時には着かないだろう *Even if I leave* home right away, I won't arrive there at 10. / 雨が降っても試合は予定どおり行われる *Even if it rains*, we'll have the game on schedule. / いつ遊びに行っても彼女は歓迎してくれる *Whenever I visit* her, she welcomes me. / どんなに勉強しても数学では彼にかなわない *No matter how hard I study*, I can't match him in math.

-してもらう （…を～してもらう）have* [get*] ... *done*; （人に…してもらう）have *a person do*, get *a person to do* ‖私は時計を修理してもらった I *had* my watch *repaired*. / 彼に宿題を手伝ってもらった I *had* him *help* me with my homework.
◆あなたにいっしょに来てもらいたいのです I *want* you *to come* with me. / 円をドルに両替してもらえませんか Can you *change* Japanese yen into American dollars?

してやられる またしても彼にしてやられた I *have been deceived* [*taken in*] by him again.

してん¹ 視点 a point of view, viewpoint ◯ ‖視点を変えてその問題を考えてみよう Let's think about the matter from *a different point of view*.

してん² 支店 branch (office) ◯ ‖札幌支店 *the* Sapporo *branch* / その会社は福岡に支店を開いた The company opened [established] *a branch* in Fukuoka.
‖支店長 a branch manager

してん³ 支点 （てこなどの）fulcrum ◯ （複 ～s, fulcra)

しでん 市電 《米》streetcar ◯, trolley ◯, 《英》tramcar

じてん¹ 辞典 dictionary ◯ ⇒ じしょ（辞書）‖和英辞典を引く consult *a Japanese-English dictionary*
‖英和辞典 an English-Japanese dictionary / 人名辞典 a biographical dictionary

じてん² 事典 （百科事典）encyclopedia ◯; （通俗的に）dictionary ◯ ‖生物学事典 *an encyclopedia* of biology

じてん³ 自転 rotation ⓊⒸ ——自転する rotate ⓐ ∥地球の自転 *the rotation* of the earth *on its axis*

じてん⁴ 時点 現時点ではその事故については何も分からない We know nothing about the accident *at this point* [*time, moment*]. ∥ 雨が降り始めた時点で私たちは行かないことに決めた We decided not to go *when* it started raining.

じてん⁵ 次点 彼は写真コンテストで次点だった He 「was *a runner-up* [finished *second*] in the photo contest.

じでん 自伝 autobiography Ⓒ

じてんしゃ 自転車 bicycle Ⓒ, cycle Ⓒ, 《口語的》 bike Ⓒ → 図版 ∥自転車をこぐ pedal *a bicycle* ∥ 自転車を押して歩く walk *one's bicycle* ∥ 私は毎日自転車で学校に通っています I go to school *by bicycle* every day. ∥ 妹は自転車に乗れるようになった My sister has learned to ride *a bicycle*.
∥自転車置き場 a bicycle parking lot ∥ 自転車競争 a bicycle [cycle] race ∥ 自転車屋 a bicycle shop ∥ 自転車旅行 a bicycle trip

しと¹ 使徒《キリスト教》apostle [əpάsl], disciple [disáipl] Ⓒ ∥十二使徒 the Apostles

しと² 使途 彼は金の使途を明らかにした He made clear *how* the money *was spent*.
∥使途不明金 unaccounted-for expenses

しとう 死闘 fierce battle [struggle] Ⓒ, desperate struggle Ⓒ ∥彼らは死闘を繰り広げた They fought *a fierce battle*.

しどう¹ 指導

instruction Ⓤ; (助言) guidance Ⓤ; (競技などの) coaching Ⓤ; (監督・指示) direction Ⓤ
——指導する instruct ⓐ; guide ⓐ; coach ⓐ; direct ⓐ

よろしくご指導をお願いいたします(→指導を期待する) I look to you for *guidance*.

消防団員が救急用具の使い方について指導した The fire fighters *instructed* people *in* how to use emergency equipment.

彼は野球チームの指導をしている He *coaches* a baseball team.

彼女は現役引退後、後進の指導にあたっている She *has been coaching* [*working as a coach for*] the younger generation since she retired from active play.

私たちは中野先生の指導のもとに劇の練習をした We practiced the play *under* (*the guidance of*) Mr. Nakano.

◆剛は私たちのクラブで指導的役割を果たしている Tsuyoshi is playing *a leading part* in our club. ∥ 彼は指導力をいかんなく発揮した He showed *his* full *leadership*.

∥指導案 a guidance [teaching] plan ∥ 指導教官 a guidance teacher, a counselor; (大学の) an (academic) adviser ∥ 指導者(リーダー) a leader, (勉強の) an instructor, (スポーツの) a coach ∥ 指導書 a guide; (教科書の) a teacher's manual ∥ 指導法 a teaching method ∥ 学習指導要領 the course of study ∥ 行政指導 administrative guidance ∥ 進路指導 guidance counseling

しどう² 私道 private road [path] Ⓒ

しどう³ 始動 ——始動する[させる] start ⓐ ⓗ ∥機械を始動させる *start* a machine ∥ エンジンは静かに始動した The engine *started* (*up*) quietly.

じどう¹ 自動 ——自動の・自動的な automatic ——自動的に automatically ∥このホテルの客室のドアは全部自動でかぎがかかる All the guest-room doors lock *automatically* in this hotel.
∥自動改札機 an automatic ticket gate ∥ 自動小銃 an automatic rifle ∥ 自動制御 auto-

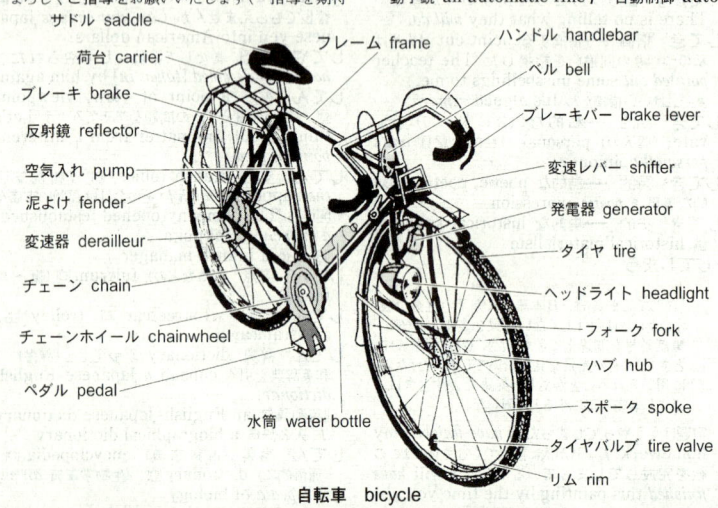

自転車 bicycle

- サドル saddle
- 荷台 carrier
- フレーム frame
- ハンドル handlebar
- ベル bell
- ブレーキ brake
- ブレーキバー brake lever
- 反射鏡 reflector
- 空気入れ pump
- 変速レバー shifter
- 泥よけ fender
- 発電器 generator
- 変速器 derailleur
- タイヤ tire
- チェーン chain
- ヘッドライト headlight
- チェーンホイール chainwheel
- フォーク fork
- ハブ hub
- ペダル pedal
- スポーク spoke
- 水筒 water bottle
- タイヤバルブ tire valve
- リム rim

matic control / 自動操縦装置 an automatic pilot / 自動ドア an automatic door / 自動販売機 a vending machine

じどう² 児童 (子供) child (複 children) // 彼女は児童向けの本をたくさん書いている She has written many「books for *children* [*juvenile* books].
‖児童館 a children's recreation center / 児童教育 child education / 児童憲章 the Children's Charter / 児童公園 a park for children / 児童心理(学) child psychology / 児童福祉法 the Child Welfare Law / 児童文学 juvenile [children's] literature / 未就学児童 a preschool child

じどうし 自動詞《文法》intransitive verb

(1)目的語をとらない動詞をいう。通例，相手や対象がなくてもできる動作や状態を示す。ただし，副詞(句)などがその動詞の意味を明確にする場合が多い。// Birds *fly*. 鳥は飛ぶ / He often *goes* to church. 彼はよく礼拝に行く / There *is* a fine library in the park. その公園にはりっぱな図書館がある
(2)自動詞には，be ...「…である」，become ...「…になる」，look ...「…のように見える」などのように，「…」の部分(補語)がないと意味が明確にならないものがある。// Ann *is* a cheerleader. アンはチアリーダーだ / I *became* sick. 私は病気になった
(3)動詞には，自動詞と他動詞の両方の働きをもつものが多い。// Suddenly the door *opened*. 突然ドアがあいた(❖この open は自動詞) / Nobody *opened* the door. だれもドアをあけなかった(❖この open は他動詞)

じどうしゃ 自動車 car, 《米》auto (複 〜s), automobile ⇒図版 / 自動車を運転する drive *a car* / 父は毎日自動車で会社に行く My father goes to work *by car* every day. ◆彼女が家まで自動車に乗せてくれた She gave me *a ride* to my house.
‖自動車学校 a driving school / 自動車産業 the auto(mobile) [car] industry / 自動車事故 a car accident / 自動車修理工場 an auto-repair shop, a garage / 自動車税 an automobile [a vehicle] tax / 自動車専用道路 an expressway,《英》a motorway / 自動車販売店 a car dealership / 自動車保険 automobile insurance / 自動車メーカー an automaker, a carmaker, a car [an automobile] manufacturer

しとげる (成しとげる) accomplish; (計画などを実行する) carry out; (仕上げる) finish, complete

しどころ し所 今が我慢のしどころだ These are hard times but *we must endure them*.

しとしと 一晩中雨がしとしと降っていた It *drizzled* all night long.

じとじと 今週はじとじとした(→湿気のある)日が続いている *Damp* weather has continued this week. / 汗でシャツがじとじとする(→ぬれている) My shirt *is wet* with sweat.

シドニー Sydney (❖オーストラリアの都市)

しとめる 仕留める (殺す) kill; (撃ち落とす) shoot* down; (撃ち殺す) shoot ... dead / 獲物をしとめる *shoot down* the game

しとやか ーしとやかな (優美な) graceful; (上品な) gentle; (物静かな) demure ーしとやかに gracefully; gently; demurely / 彼女はしとやかな人だ She is a *demure* lady. / 彼女はしとやかにおじぎをした She made a *graceful* bow.

じどり 地鶏 local chicken

しどろもどろ 彼女はしどろもどろの(→筋の通らない)返答をした She gave an *incoherent* [a *confused*] answer. / 彼女の思いがけない質問に

自動車 car

- グラブコンパートメント glove compartment
- スピードメーター speedometer
- ハンドル steering wheel
- アンテナ antenna
- フロントガラス windshield
- 送風口 air vent
- タコメーター tachometer
- バックミラー rearview mirror
- 空気調整 air control
- クラクション horn
- 屋根 roof
- アクセル accelerator
- ワイパー windshield wiper
- オーディオ装置 audio system
- ブレーキ brake
- ドアミラー sideview mirror
- チェンジレバー gear lever
- クラッチ clutch
- 運転席 drivers seat
- シートベルト seat belt
- 助手席 passenger seat
- ハンドブレーキ parking brake
- ドア doors
- トランク trunk
- ボンネット hood
- ヘッドライト headlight
- ラジエーターグリル grille
- バンパー bumper
- 方向指示器 turn signal
- フェンダー fender
- ドアハンドル door handle
- 泥よけ mud flap
- ナンバープレート license plate
- タイヤ tire
- ホイールキャップ hubcap

彼はしどろもどろになった Her unexpected question *confused* him.

しな 品 ❶【品物】(個々の) article ◯, item ◯; (商品) goods (❖通例複数や many は付けない); (在庫品) stock ◯◯ ‖このスーパーは品ぞろえが豊富だ This supermarket has a wide selection of *goods*. ‖ けっこうなお品をありがとうございました Thank you very much for your nice *present*.
❷【品質】quality ◯ ‖ この時計は品がいい[悪い] This watch is (*of*) *good [poor] quality*.
ことわざ 所変われば品変わる ⇒ところ

しない¹ 市内 市内無料配達《掲示》*Free Delivery within the City* ‖ 彼らは市内見物に出かけた They went sightseeing *in the city*. ‖ 彼女は横浜市内に住んでいる She lives *in the city of* Yokohama.
‖市内電話 a local call

しない² 竹刀 a *shinai*, a bamboo sword

-しない ❶【打ち消し】このコンピュータは正常に作動しない This computer *doesn't* function properly. ‖ 彼は私たちの考えに絶対に同調しないだろう He will *never* come around to our view. ‖ 彼はめったに遅刻しない He is *rarely* late for school.
❷【勧誘】休憩しない? *Why don't* we take a break? / *How about* taking a break? ‖ 学校まで競走しない? *Let's* race to school.
❸【軽い禁止・命令】遠慮しないで電話してください *Don't* hesitate to call me. ‖ 私のことは心配しないでください Please *don't* worry about me.

しなう 撓う bend* ⓔ ‖ 風で竹がしなっている The bamboo *is bending* in the wind.
◆この枝はよくしなう(→曲がりやすい) This branch is very *flexible*.

しなうす 品薄 この CD は現在品薄です This CD is *in short supply* at present.

しなおす し直す ⇒やりなおす

しなかず 品数 当店は品数が豊富です We have *a large variety of goods*.

しなぎれ 品切れ そのノートは品切れです The notebook *is* "*sold out* [*out of stock*]".

しなさだめ 品定め 彼女はその店でバッグの品定めをしていた She *was looking over* the bags at the shop.

しなびる 萎びる (しおれる) wither ⓔ ⓣ; (しわが寄る) shrivel ⓔ ‖ 野菜がしなびてしまった The vegetables *have withered*.

しなぶそく 品不足 ⇒しなうす

しなもの 品物 (個々の) article ◯; (商品) goods (❖通例複数や many は付けない); (在庫品) stock ◯◯ ‖ 品物を仕入れる stock *goods* (❖この stock は動詞) ‖ あの店では高価な品物を売っている That shop sells expensive *articles*. ‖ その品物は在庫がない The *goods* are out of stock.

シナモン cinnamon ◯

しなやか 撓やか ― しなやかな (曲がりやすい) flexible; (柔軟な) supple, limber, soft; (優雅な) graceful ‖ しなやかな動き *graceful movements* ‖ 猫はしなやかな体をしている A cat has a *flexible* [*supple*] body.

じならし 地均し ground leveling ◯
◆ローラーで地ならしをする *level the ground* with a roller

じなり 地鳴り a rumbling [rumble] of the earth ◆地鳴りがする I hear *the ground rumbling*.

シナリオ scenario ◯ (複 ～s); (映画の) screenplay ◯ ‖ シナリオライター a script writer

しなん 至難 これを私ひとりで運ぶのは至難の業だ It *is extremely difficult* for me to carry this by myself. ‖ 彼を説得するのは至難の業だ(→ほとんど不可能だ) It *is almost* [*next to*] *impossible* to persuade him.

じなん 次男 the [*one's*] second son

しにがみ 死神 Death

しにぎわ 死に際 彼は死に際に何と言いましたか What did he say *on* [*at*] *his deathbed*?

しにせ 老舗 (昔創業した店) long-established store [shop] ◯; (古い店) old store [shop] ◯ ‖『虎屋』は老舗の菓子店だ "Toraya" is a *long-established* confectionery *store*.

しにそこなう 死に損なう 男は自殺しようとしたが死にそこなった The man tried to kill himself but *failed*.

しにたえる 死に絶える その鳥は死に絶えてしまった The bird *is extinct*. ‖ The bird *has died out*.

しにめ 死に目 私は祖父の死に目に会えなかった I *wasn't able to be at* my grandfather's *bedside when he died*. ‖ I could not see my grandfather *on his deathbed*.

しにものぐるい 死に物狂い 彼女は宿題を終わらせようと死にものぐるいだった She was *desperate* to finish her homework. ‖ 彼らは死にものぐるいで走った They ran *desperately* [*for dear life, like hell*].

しにわかれる 死に別れる 彼は小学生のとき母親に死に別れた He *lost* his mother when he was in elementary school.

しにん 死人 dead person ◯; (総称) the dead
ことわざ 死人に口なし Dead men tell no tales.

じにん¹ 辞任 resignation ◯◯ ―辞任する resign ⓔ ‖ 議長を辞任する resign (*one's*) post) as chairman ‖ 首相の辞任を求める声 a clamor for *the resignation* of the Prime Minister ‖ 彼の辞任の意志は堅い His determination to *resign* is firm.

じにん² 自任 ―自任する (うぬぼれる) fancy oneself ‖ 彼女は自分が一流の歌手だと自任している She *fancies herself* an excellent singer.

じにん³ 自認 過失を自認する admit *one's* mistake; *admit* that *one* made a mistake

しぬ 死ぬ

die ⓔ (❖ふつう病気・飢え・老齢などで死ぬときには die of ..., けがや不注意で死ぬときには die from ... を用いるとされているが, die of ... の代わりに die from ... を用いることもある), 《婉曲的》pass away; (事故・戦争などで) be killed

──死んだ dead ⇨し(死)
若くして死ぬ die young / 老衰で死ぬ die of old age / 死んだふりをする play dead; feign death

彼は癌(がん)で死んだ He died of cancer.
彼女は傷が元で死んだ She died from a wound.
若い女性が交通事故で死んだ A young woman was killed in a traffic accident.
戦争中大勢の人が飢えで死んだ A lot of people died of hunger during the war.
戦場で数千人が死んだ Thousands were killed on the battlefield.
我々はみんないつかは必ず死ぬ We all must die someday.
彼は妻と2人の子供を残して死んだ He died, leaving a wife and two children.
おじが死んでから10年になる It is [has been] ten years since my uncle died. / My uncle has been dead for ten years. / Ten years have passed since my uncle died.
林の中で男性が死んでいるのが発見された A man was found dead in the woods.
死んだ男の血液から少量の毒物が検出された Traces of poison were found in the dead man's blood.
彼女は夫は死んだものとあきらめていた She gave up her husband for [as] dead.
この歌を聞くと死んだ兄を思い出す This song reminds me of my dead [late] brother.
死んでしまいたいと思ったこともあった At one time I wished myself dead.
暑くて死にそうだ I'm dying of the heat.
生き恥をさらすくらいなら死んだほうがましだ I'd rather die than live in shame.
彼は死んだように寝ていた He was sleeping like the dead.
彼女は幼い子供たちを残して死ぬに死ねなかった She couldn't die and leave her young children.

◆死ぬ間際に on one's deathbed / 出血多量で死ぬ bleed to death / 彼は湖に身投げして死んだ He drowned himself in the lake. / 彼は父親にショックを受けた He was shocked by the loss of his father. / このご恩は死ぬまで(→生きているかぎり)忘れません I'll remember your kindness as long as I live. / 彼の授業は死ぬほど退屈だった I was bored to death in his class. / His class was so boring that I could have died. / 彼女はフグにあたって危うく死にかけた(→何とか死を免れた) She got food poisoning from a globefish and barely escaped death. / この額では絵が死んでしまう This frame kills the picture.

じぬし 地主 landowner ⓒ; (男性の) landlord ⓒ; (女性の) landlady ⓒ ‖地主階級 the landed gentry

しのぎ 鎬 慣用表現 自動車メーカー各社は環境にやさしい車の開発にしのぎを削っている Each car manufacturer is in fierce competition with the others to develop environmentally friendly cars.

-しのぎ 痛み止めを飲んでも一時のしのぎにしかならないよ Taking a painkiller will be only a temporary remedy. / 彼は退屈のしのぎに漫画を読んでいる He is reading comics to kill time. / 彼らは寒さしのぎにたき火をした They built a fire to warm themselves (against the cold). / 大臣の答弁は単にその場のしのぎのものだった The Minister's replies were just meant to buy time.

しのぐ 凌ぐ
❶ 【耐える・乗り切る】(耐える) bear*, stand*, endure; (乗りきる) get* by
今年の夏はしのぎやすかった It was easy to bear this summer.
彼らは敵の猛攻をしのぎ切れなかった They couldn't defend against the fierce attack of the enemy.
この金で当座をしのがなければならない I must get by on [with] this money for the present. / This money must tide me over for the present. (※tide a person over で「(人に)困難などを乗り切らせる」の意味)

◆飢えをしのぐ stave off one's hunger / 彼らは近くのほら穴で雨をしのいだ They took shelter from the rain in a cave nearby. / その古い建物はすっかり朽ち果てていて雨風をしのぐのがやっとだった The old building had fallen into ruin and it barely gave me shelter from the rain and wind.

❷ 【勝る】surpass, outdo*
英語の力で同級生をしのぐ surpass one's classmates in English ability
彼女の新作映画は前作をしのぐできばえだった(→新作で今までの自分を超えた) She has surpassed [outdone] herself with her new film.

◆彼のピアノの腕は先生をしのぐまでになった He came to play the piano more skillfully than his teacher.

しのばせる 忍ばせる 足音を忍ばせて廊下を歩く walk in the corridor stealthily / 声を忍ばせて話す speak in a whisper / 泥棒は物陰に身を忍ばせて夜がふけるのを待った The thief hid himself and waited till late at night. / 隆明はかばんに漫画を忍ばせて学校に行った Takaaki went to school with comic books hidden in his bag.

しのびあし 忍び足 忍び足で歩く walk stealthily [(→つま先で)on tiptoe]
しのびこむ 忍び込む steal* [sneak*] into... ‖彼は2階の窓からその家に忍び込んだ He stole [sneaked] into the house through an upstairs window.
しのびよる 忍び寄る steal* [sneak*, creep*] up, (獲物などに) stalk ‖彼らは敵に忍び寄った They sneaked [stole] up on the enemy. / 秋の気配がもうそこまで忍び寄ってきている Autumn has already crept up on us. / トラはシカにそっと忍び寄っていった The tiger stalked [crept up on] the deer.
しのぶ 忍ぶ (耐える) bear*, stand*; (隠れる) hide* oneself ‖その木が切り倒される

しのぶ のは見るに忍びなかった I *couldn't bear to see* the tree being cut down.
◆彼らは人目を忍んで(→ひそかに)デートを重ねた They dated over and over *in secret*. / 彼は恥を忍んで彼女に金を貸してくれるよう頼んだ He *swallowed his pride* and asked her to lend him some money.

しのぶ² 偲ぶ (思い出す) recall 働 /故郷をしのぶ *recall* [*reminisce about*] one's home
◆亡き友をしのんでささやかな会を開いた We held a small gathering *in memory of* a friend of ours. / この遺跡にローマ帝国の当時の繁栄がしのばれる These remains *show* the prosperity of the Roman Empire in those days.

しば¹ 芝 (芝草) grass ⓤ; (芝生) lawn ⓒ /芝刈りをする cut *the grass*; mow *the lawn* / 芝を植える plant *grass*
‖芝刈り機 a lawn mower

しば² 柴 brush(wood) ⓤ /しば刈り brush-wood gathering

じば 磁場〔物理〕magnetic field ⓒ

じば 地場 /地場産業 local industry

しはい 支配 (権力による) rule ⓤ; (行動の統制) control ⓤ; (影響力による) dominance ⓤ; (統治) government ⓤ ——支配する rule 働; control 働; dominate 働; govern 働 ——支配的な dominant; (優勢な)《公式的》predominant
法の支配 the *rule* of law / 支配的な意見 *dominant* opinion / 英国の植民地支配下にある be *under the colonial rule* of Great Britain
徳川幕府は日本を約260年間支配した The Tokugawa shogunate *ruled* Japan for about 260 years.
彼はそのグループを支配しようとした He tried to *dominate* the group.
そのとき彼女は先入観にすっかり支配されてしまっていた She *was* completely *ruled* by prejudice at that time.
◆彼はこの地域の支配権を握っていた He *had a hold over* this area. / 世界全体が自然の法則に支配されている The whole world *is subject* to the laws of nature.
‖支配階級 the ruling classes / 支配者 a ruler / 支配人 a manager

しはい² 賜杯 the Emperor's Trophy [Cup]

しばい 芝居 (演劇) play ⓒ, drama ⓤ; (見せかけ)《口語的》act《通例単数形》/芝居をする "put on [perform] *a play*" / 芝居がはねた *The play* is over. / その芝居は客の入りがよかった[悪かった] The *play* was well [poorly] attended. / 彼女の同情は全くのお芝居だった Her sympathy was *all an act*. / She *pretended to* sympathize. ◆芝居を見に行く go to *the theater* / 芝居がかったしぐさをする make a *theatrical* gesture
‖芝居見物 theatergoing / 芝居小屋 a play-house
慣用表現 彼らは苦境を脱するためにひと芝居打った They *put on an act* to get out of trouble.

650

じはく 自白 confession ⓒ ⓤ ——自白する confess 働 ⓒ /犯行を自白する *confess one's crime* / 彼は時計を盗んだことを自白した He *confessed* (to) stealing a watch. / 警察は犯人から自白を引き出した The police extracted *a confession* from the criminal.

じばく 自爆 ——自爆する make* a suicide bombing

しばしば often, frequently /彼女はしばしば学校を休む She is *often* absent from school. / 彼はしばしばその寺を訪れた He *frequently* visited the temple.

じはだ 地肌 (皮膚) skin ⓤ ⓒ; (地面の表面) the surface of the ground

しはつ 始発 (始発列車) the first train /仙台行きの始発は何時ですか What time does *the first train* for Sendai leave [depart]?
◆青森始発の列車 a train *starting from* Aomori / 私が毎朝利用している駅は始発駅だ The station I use every morning is *the one where the train starts*.
‖始発駅 the first station

じはつてき 自発的 ——自発的な voluntary ——自発的に voluntarily, of one's own will [accord] /それは僕たちが自発的にやったことです We did it *voluntarily* [*of our own will*]. / 彼らは週末も自発的に働いてくれた They worked *voluntarily* even on the weekend.

しばふ 芝生 lawn ⓒ; (芝草) grass ⓤ; (球場などの) turf /芝生の上に寝転ぶ lie on *the grass* / 芝生に入るな《掲示》*Keep off the grass.*

じばら 自腹 慣用表現 彼女は自腹を切ってその百科事典を買った She *paid* for the encyclopedia *out of her own pocket*.

しはらい 支払い payment ⓤ /出来高に応じた支払い *payment* proportional to work done ◆授業料の支払いはすんでいる(→すでに支払った) I *have* already *paid* the school fees. / 電話代の支払いが2か月滞っている I *haven't paid* my telephone bills for two months. / 家賃の支払いはいつですか When is the rent *due*?《◆due は「支払われるべき」という意味の形容詞》
「現金でお支払いになりますか」「いいえ、カードでお願いします」"Will you *be paying* cash?" "No, I'll charge it."
‖支払い期限 the date of payment, the due date / 支払い先 a payee / 支払い条件 the terms of payment / 支払い高 the amount of payment / 支払い停止 suspension of payment

しはらう 支払う pay* 働 ⓒ /勘定を支払う *pay* an account / クレジットカードで支払う *pay* with a (credit) card / 私は彼に5,000円支払った I *paid* him 5,000 yen. / 彼女は車の代金を現金で支払った She *paid* cash for the car.《◆「現金で支払う」はpay in [by] cash ともいう》

しばらく

❶【少しの間】for a while, for a [some] time, some time; (ほんの少しの間) (for) a

minute, (for) a moment ∥僕たちはしばらくの間サッカーを楽しんだ We enjoyed playing soccer *for a while*. ∥容疑者はしばらく黙っていた The suspect remained silent *for some time*. ∥しばらくお待ちください Just a minute [*moment*], *please*.
◆しばらくしてバスが来た The bus came *after a while*. / しばらく山道を歩くと突然視界が開けた After a *short* walk along the mountain path, suddenly a view opened up. / しばらくは(→当座は)状況を静観しなければならない We have to watch the situation calmly *for the time being*.

❷【長い間】(for) a long time
∥しばらくぶりです We haven't seen each other *for a long time*. / It's been *a long time*. ∥彼はしばらくぶりで日本に帰ってきた He came back to Japan *after a long time*.
◆その出来事を忘れるのにしばらく時間がかかった It took me *a while* to forget the incident.

しばる 縛る bind*⦿, tie ⦿ ∥人の手足を縛る *bind a person* hand and foot / 彼はロープで荷物を縛った He *tied* [*bound*] the package with a rope. / 男は木に縛りつけられていた The man *was tied* to a tree. / 規則に縛られるのはいやだ I hate to *be bound* by rules. ◆彼は仕事に縛られていて、めったに休暇がとれない He *is chained* to his job and can seldom take a vacation.

しはん 市販 ―市販する put* [sell*] ... on the market ◆市販の薬 an *over-the-counter* medication ∥この紅茶は市販されていません This tea *is* not *sold commercially*.
∥市販品 goods on the market

じばん 地盤 ground ⦿ (しばしば複数形 ~s); (基盤) foundation ⦿ (しばしば複数形 ~s); (選挙の)(集合的)constituency ⦿ ∥地盤を固める make *the ground* firm; build a firm *foundation* / このあたりは地盤が弱い *The ground* is soft around here. / その政治家は農村に地盤を築いてきた The politician has established *a constituency* in farming areas.
∥地盤沈下 (a) subsidence, sinking of the ground

しはんき 四半期 quarter ⦿ ∥向こう四半期の販売予測 a sales forecast for *the quarter* ahead

しひ 私費 ∥彼は実験用の器材を私費で購入した He bought the apparatus and materials for the experiment *at his own expense*.
∥私費留学生(外国から来た) a student from abroad studying at his [her] own expense; (外国へ行った) a student studying abroad at his [her] own expense

じひ¹ 自費 ∥本を自費出版する publish a book *at one's own expense*/ foot the bill to publish *one's* book

じひ² 慈悲 mercy ⓤ ∥慈悲を請う beg for *mercy*/ …に慈悲をかける have *mercy* on …
◆慈悲深い神 *merciful* god

シビア ―シビアな (厳しい) severe, hard; (深刻な) serious ∥これはとてもシビアな問題だ This is a very *serious* problem.

じびいんこうか 耳鼻咽喉科 otolaryngology [òutoulærɪŋɑ́(ː)lədʒi] ⓤ; ear, nose and throat (《略記》ENT) ∥耳鼻咽喉科医 an otolaryngologist

じびき 字引 dictionary ⦿ ⇒じしょ(辞書)
∥生き字引 a walking dictionary

じびきあみ 地引き網 seine [séɪn] (net) ⦿, dragnet

じひつ 自筆 自筆の原稿 a *hand-written* manuscript; a manuscript *written in the handwriting of the author* / この書は徳川慶喜の自筆だ This calligraphy *was written by* Tokugawa Yoshinobu *himself*.

じひびき 地響き (ぢしんという音) thud ⦿; (とどろき) rumbling ⦿ ∥その古い塔は地響きを立てて崩れ落ちた The old tower fell to the ground *with a heavy thud*.
◆馬の大群は地響きとともに走り去っていった A large herd of horses *roared* away.

しひょう 指標 《公式的》index ⦿, indicator ⦿, barometer ⦿ ∥消費は経済成長の指標である Consumer spending is *an index* of economic growth.

じひょう 辞表 resignation (letter) ⦿ ∥彼は辞表を提出したが受理されなかった He handed in *his resignation*, but it wasn't accepted.

じびょう 持病 chronic disease ⦿
◆彼女は持病の喘息(ぜんそく)に苦しんでいる She is suffering from *chronic* asthma.

しびれ 痺れ numbness [nʌ́mnəs] ⓤ
慣用表現 いくら待っても彼が来ないので、彼女はしびれを切らして帰ってしまった She waited for a long time, but since he didn't appear she *lost patience* and went home.

しびれる 痺れる be numbed [nʌ́md]; (手足が) go* to sleep ∥足がしびれて立てないよ I can't stand up because my legs *have gone to sleep*. / 麻酔がきいて口のあたりがしびれている My mouth *is numbed* under the effect of the anesthesia.
◆彼女はその俳優にすっかりしびれてしまった The actor *made* her *weak in the knees*. / She *fell under the actor's spell*.

しぶ 支部 branch (office); (協会などの) chapter ⦿ ∥支部長 the chairperson of a branch

じふ 自負 (自信) self-confidence ⓤ, self-esteem ⓤ; (誇り) pride ⓤ
◆彼には設立当初から会社を支えてきたという自負がある He *is proud* 「to have supported [that he has supported] the company since it was established. / 彼は自負心が強い He *has high self-esteem*./ He *has a high opinion of himself*.(❖後の表現には「うぬぼれている」というニュアンスがある)

しぶい 渋い

日本語の「渋い」には味覚に関する意味とそこから派生した意味とがあるが、そのいずれについても英語にはぴったり相当する言葉がないので、場合に応じて適宜意訳しなければならない。衣服や装

しぶおんぷ

飾品，内装などに関してそのまま *shibui* を用いるケースも見られるが，まだ英語としての市民権を得るには至っていない．

❶[味が]（苦(にが)い）bitter
渋いお茶 *bitter* [(→濃い) *strong*] tea
このカキは渋い This persimmon tastes *bitter*.

❷[不満そうな] cross, sour [sáuər]
彼女は渋い顔をしていた She had a *sour* face.
◆その話を聞いて彼は一瞬渋い顔をした Hearing the story, he「*made a wry* face [*wore a frown*] for a moment.

❸[落ち着いた趣のある]（地味な）quiet, subdued, sober；（洗練された）refined, elegant
彼は若いのに渋い好みをしている Young as he is, he has *austerely elegant* [*refined*] tastes. (❖*austerely* は「簡素に」の意味)
彼女はいつも渋い色の服を着ている She always wears clothes of *quiet* [*subdued*, *sober*] colors.

◆渋い声 a *seasoned* voice / 渋い当たりの（→いい所に飛んだ）ヒット a *well-placed* hit / 渋い（→落ち着いた）演技を披露する show a *low-keyed* performance / 彼は渋いネクタイをしている He wears an *elegantly simple* tie. /『純粋理性批判』とはまたずいぶん渋い（→堅い）本を読んでいるね Are you reading *Critique of Pure Reason*? You are reading a very *serious* [(→難しい) *difficult*] book, aren't you?

❹[けちな]（口語的）stingy [stíndʒi]，（口語的）tight-fisted

しぶおんぷ 四分音符《音楽》《米》quarter note ⓒ，《英》crotchet ⓒ

しぶがっしょう 四部合唱 (vocal) quartet，《英》quartette ⓒ

しぶき（水煙）spray ⓊⒸ；（水はね）splash ⓒ ◆彼はしぶきを上げて川に飛び込んだ He jumped into the river *with a splash*. / 滝のしぶきがかかってきた The *spray* from the waterfall fell on us.

しふく¹ 私服 plain clothes ◆学園祭の日は私服で登校できる We can wear *our own clothes* to school on the day of the school festival.
‖私服警官 a policeman in plain clothes

しふく² 私腹 [慣用表現] 彼は社長の地位を悪用して私腹を肥やした He「*lined his (own) pockets* [*feathered his nest*] by abusing his position as president.

しふく³ 至福 bliss Ⓤ, supreme happiness Ⓤ / 至福の時 a moment of *bliss*

ジプシー gypsy ⓒ, Romany ⓒ

しぶしぶ 渋々 reluctantly, under protest；（不本意ながら）unwillingly ‖彼はしぶしぶその忠告に従った He *reluctantly* accepted the advice.

しぶつ 私物 *one's* own property, personal belongings ‖この辞典は私の私物です This dictionary is *my own property*.

◆彼は会社のパソコンを私物化している He *uses* the company's personal computer *as if it were his own*.

じぶつ 事物 things, affairs ‖日本の事物 *things* Japanese (❖*things* は後ろに形容詞が付くと「風物」「文物」を意味する) ◆私は抽象的な観念よりも具体的な事物を考察したかったのです I wanted to consider concrete *matters* [*things*] rather than abstract ideas.

ジフテリア〔医学〕diphtheria [difθíəriə] Ⓤ

シフト（野球で）バント［松井］シフトを敷く deploy a defensive *shift* against「a bunt [Matsui] / 会社は土日はシフト制だ In our company we work *in shifts* on Saturdays and Sundays.

しぶとい（強情な）stubborn, obstinate；（ねばり強い）persistent；（屈しない）unyielding ‖あいつはしぶといやつだ He's a *stubborn* guy. / 敵はしぶとく抵抗した The enemy resisted *unyieldingly*. / ゴキブリはしぶとい Cockroaches *are too tough to* die.

しぶみ 渋味（味）astringency Ⓤ；（洗練）refinement Ⓤ, elegance Ⓤ

しぶる 渋る be reluctant, be unwilling；（ためらう）hesitate ⓘ ‖返answerをしぶる *hesitate* to answer / 彼はこの件で彼女と交渉するのをしぶっている He *is reluctant* to approach her about this matter. / 彼女はまだ支払いをしぶっているの？ Is she still *unwilling* to pay?

じぶん¹ 自分 oneself ——自分の *one's* (own) ——自分で (by [for]) oneself

【自分の】
自分の机で勉強しなさい Study at *your* (own) desk.
弟は自分の部屋を欲しがっている My brother wants to have「*his own* room [a room *of his own*].
そんなこと自分の目で確かめないかぎり信じられないね I won't believe such a thing unless I see it with *my own* eyes.
あいつは自分のことばかり考えている He always thinks only of *himself*.
◆自分の好きなようにしなさい You can do as *you* choose. / 自分のしたことは自分で責任をとるべきだよ *You* are responsible for what *you've* done.

【自分に・で】
彼は自分に厳しい He is strict with *himself*.
ついに自分に合う仕事が見つかった I finally found a job suitable for *me*.
この人形，全部自分で（→独力で）作ったの？ Did you make this doll all *by yourself*?
自分で（→自ら）行って確かめなきゃだめよ You have to go and see *for yourself*.
自分で決めたことなのだから最後までやり通しなさい Carry it through, since you decided *yourself* to do it.
⚡「なぜあんなことをしたのかわけを話して」「自分でもどうしてなのか分からないんだ」"Tell me why you did a thing like that." "I'm wondering why *myself*."

【自分を】
あまり自分を責めてはいけない Don't blame *yourself* too much.
◆自分を何様だと思ってるんだ Who do you think *you* are?

〖自分は〗
◆彼は自分はどうなってもかまわないと言った He said that he didn't care what would happen to *him.*
〖その他〗
彼女は自分自身に腹を立てていた She was furious with *herself.*

じぶん[2] 時分 若い時分はよく彼といっしょに飲みに行ったものだ I used to go drinking with him *when* I was young. ⇒ころ

じぶんかって 自分勝手 ―自分勝手な selfish; (利己的な) egoistic //その歌手は自分勝手だと非難された The singer was criticized for *being selfish.* / 彼は息子の自分勝手なふるまいに激怒した He got upset about his son's *selfish* behavior.
◆自分勝手にふるまう *get* [*have*] *one's own way; do one's own thing* / ここでは自分勝手に行動してはいけない You cannot do *whatever you want* here.

しぶんしょ 私文書 private document [C]
‖私文書偽造 the forgery of a private document

しへい 紙幣 (硬貨に対し) paper money [U]; (1枚の札) 《米》 bill [C], 《英》 (bank) note [C] //20ドル紙幣をくずす break *a* 20-dollar *bill* / 林の中で大量の紙幣が発見された A lot of *paper money* was found in a wood.

じへいしょう 自閉症 〔心理〕 autism [U] ―自閉症の autistic

じべた 地べた 若者たちは地べたに座り込んだ The young people sat (down) *on the ground.*

しべつ 死別 ―死別する (亡くす) lose* [他] // 彼女は3歳のときに父親と死別した She *lost* her father at the age of three.

シベリア Siberia [saibíəriə] ―シベリアの Siberian

しへん 詩篇 (旧約聖書中の一書) the Book of Psalms [sɑ́ːmz], the Psalms

じへん 事変 incident [C] // 満州事変 *the* Manchurian *Incident*

しへんけい 四辺形 quadrilateral [C] ‖平行四辺形 a parallelogram

しほう[1] 四方 all directions, all sides //四方を見渡す look 「in *all directions* [(*all*) *around*] / 日本は四方を海に囲まれている Japan is surrounded by the sea on *all sides.* / ガラスの破片が四方八方に飛び散った Bits of glass scattered *in* 「*all directions* [*every direction*].
◆5メートル四方の部屋 a room five meters *square* / その町から高速道路が四方に延びている Freeways *radiate* from the city.

しほう[2] 司法 the administration of justice; (司法機関) 《集合的》 the judiciary ―司法の judicial
‖司法権 judicial power / 司法試験 the Bar Examination / 司法書士 a judicial scrivener, a person who prepares legal documents (❖米国にはこれに当たる職業はない)

しぼう[1] 死亡 death [U] (❖「死亡者」や「死にざま」を表す場合は [C]) ―死亡する die [自]; (事故や戦争で) be killed //新聞に死亡通知を載せる insert 「*a notice of death* [*an obituary*] in a paper / 新聞でその女優が死亡したのを知った I saw in the paper that the actress *had died.* / その事故で2人が死亡, 6人が負傷した Two people *were killed* and six were wounded in the accident.
‖死亡記事 an obituary / 死亡者数 a death toll / 死亡証明書 a death certificate / 死亡届 a report of *a person's* death / 死亡率 a death rate, a mortality rate

しぼう[2] 志望 wish [C]; (強い願望) desire [C] [U] ―志望する wish [他] [自]; want [他] (❖wish よりも実現する可能性が高いと見込まれている); 《公式的》 desire [他] //高司はテレビタレント志望だ Takashi *wishes* to be a TV personality. / 彼女の第一志望は京都大学なのだそうだ I hear that the school she *most wants to enter* is Kyoto University.
‖志望校 the school of *one's* choice

しぼう[3] 脂肪 fat [C] [U]; (豚の) lard [U] //脂肪分をとりすぎだよ You eat too much *fat.* / このおなかの脂肪がいやだ I hate these rolls of *fat* on my belly. ◆脂肪の多い肉 *fatty* meat
‖低脂肪乳 low-fat milk / 動物[植物]性脂肪 animal [vegetable] fats / 皮下脂肪 subcutaneous fat

しぼう[4] 子房 〔植物〕 ovary [C]

じほう 時報 the time signal //時計を時報に合わせる set a clock by *the time signal*

じぼうじき 自暴自棄 彼は失恋して自暴自棄になっていた He 「was *desperate* [*gave up on himself*] after losing at love.

しぼむ (植物などが) wither [自], fade [自]; (風船などが) deflate [自] //この花も夕方にはしぼんでしまうだろう This flower will *wither* in the evening. / 風船はしゅうと音を立ててしぼんでしまった The balloon made a hissing sound as it *deflated* [*shrank*].

しぼり 絞り・搾り ❶【カメラの】 diaphragm [dáiəfræ̀m] [C]; (開きの程度) aperture [C]
❷【染め物】 tie-dye [C] ◆しぼり染めのゆかた a *tie-dyed yukata*

しぼりだす 絞り出す (液体などを) squeeze [他] //チューブから歯みがきをしぼり出す *squeeze* toothpaste out of a tube ◆老人はしぼり出すような声で私に助けを求めた *Speaking with an effort* the old man asked me for help.

しぼりとる 搾り取る squeeze [他], exploit [他] //彼は私が稼いだお金を残らず搾り取った He *squeezed* all the money I had earned out of me.

しぼる 絞る・搾る

❶【水分を出す】 squeeze [他], wring* [他]; (乳を) milk [他]
ぬれたぞうきんをしぼる 「*wring out* [*twist*] a wet rag
私は毎朝搾りたてのオレンジジュースを飲んでいる I drink a glass of *freshly squeezed* orange juice every morning.
砂漠に住む人々はラクダの乳を搾る Desert people *milk* the camels.
❷【無理に出す】

彼は何とか作業の効率を上げられないものかと知恵をしぼっている He *is racking his brains for* a way to increase the efficiency of the work.

❸【狭】める・小さくする】
レンズをしぼる *stop down* / ラジオのボリュームをしぼる *turn down* the volume on a radio

彼は要求を2つにしぼった He *narrowed his requests down* to two.

僕は戦後の日本の歴史に的(まと)をしぼって勉強した I studied *with a focus on* the history of postwar Japan.

この段階で候補者は5人にしぼられた The candidates *have been narrowed down* to five at this stage.

❹【しかる・鍛える】
いたずらがばれて父にこってりしぼられた I *was chewed out [put on the grill]* by my father when he learned of my pranks.

合宿では新しいコーチにみっちりしぼられた The new coach *worked us hard* at the training camp.

しほん 資本 capital ◯ (また a ～)
資本の自由化 capital liberalization / 資本を投じる invest *capital* / 資本金800万円の会社 a company *with a capital of [capitalized at]* eight million yen

多くの企業が資本不足に苦しんでいる Many companies suffer from *a lack of capital*.

彼には十分な資本がある He has great reserves of *capital*.

◆この仕事は体が資本だ(→体力がなければできない) We *cannot* do this work *without physical strength*.

‖資本家 a capitalist, capital / 資本金 capital / 資本主義 capitalism / 資本主義経済 capitalistic economy / 資本主義国 a capitalist country / 金融資本 financial capital

しま¹ 島 island [áilənd] ◯ ─島の insular
地中海の島々 Mediterranean *islands* / 島巡りをする make *a tour of the islands*

あの島には人が住んでいない No one lives on that *island*.

彼らは神津島の出身です They are from 「*Kozu Island* [*the Island of Kozu*].

しま² 縞 stripe ◯ ─縞の striped
青い縞の入ったシャツ a shirt with blue *stripes* ◆そのリスの背中には美しい縞模様があった The squirrel had a beautiful *striped pattern* on its back.

‖縦縞 a vertical stripe / 横縞 a lateral [horizontal] stripe

しまい¹ 姉妹 sister ◯ ⇒きょうだい(兄弟) ‖ その2人の姉妹はとてもよく似ている The two *sisters* are very alike. / 神戸市とシアトル市は姉妹都市だ Kobe and Seattle are 「*sister cities* [《英》*twin cities*].

‖姉妹校 a sister school / 姉妹編(ある本の) a companion volume

しまい² 仕舞い、(終わり) end ◯ ⇒おしまい
先生はしまいには怒り出した *In the end* my teacher got angry. ◆しまいまで話を聞きなさい *Hear me out.* / 結局何も買わずじまい

で(→買わないで)帰ってきた I ended up *buying nothing* and came back.

しまいこむ 仕舞い込む (片づける) *put* away; (金などを) tuck (away); (かぎをかけて) lock (away) ‖ 母は高価な食器類を戸棚にしまい込んだ My mother *put* the expensive dishes *away* in the cupboard.

しまう 仕舞う
❶【片づける】(入れる) *put* (in); (しまっておく) *keep* (in); (片づける) put away

筆入れをかばんにしまいなさい *Put* your pencil case *in* your bag.

キャビネットにこのファイルをしまうスペースはありますか Is there enough space to *keep* these files *in* the cabinet?

彼女は悲しみを胸にしまっておいた She *kept* the grief *in* her bosom.

貴重品は金庫にしまっておいてください Please *keep* valuables in the safe.

◆母は冬物の服をクローゼットにしまった Mother *has stored* winter clothes *away* in the closet.

❷【終える】finish ⓗ, get* through (with ...); (...してしまう) have *done*

7時までに宿題をやってしまいたい I *want to finish [get through (with)]* my homework by seven.

ジムは預金を全部使ってしまった Jim *has used up* all the money in his bank account.

どうして彼女はひとりで行ってしまったのだろうか I don't know why she *has gone* alone.

しまうま 縞馬 zebra [ziːbrə] ◯ (複 ～, ～s)

じまえ 自前 彼は自前のトロンボーンを学校に持ってきた He brought *his own* trombone to school. / 父は仕事で使うパソコンを自前で購入した My father bought a PC for his work *at his own expense.*

じまく 字幕 (せりふの) subtitles ◆そのフランス映画には英語の字幕がついていた The French film was shown with English *subtitles.*

しまぐに 島国 island country ◯ ‖ 日本は島国です Japan is *an island country.*

‖島国根性 insularity

-しませんか
散歩に行きませんか How about going for a walk? / Why don't we go for a walk?

ワインをもう少し召し上がりませんか Won't you have some more wine?

💬「昼食を一緒にしませんか」「ええ、ぜひ」 "Would you like to join me for lunch?" "Yes, I'd love to."

しまつ 始末 ─始末する (処分する) dispose of ...; (処理する) deal* with ..., do* with ... ‖ ごみは自分で始末してください *Dispose of* waste by yourself. / こんなにたくさんのチョコレート、始末に困っちゃうよ I don't know *what to do with* this much chocolate. ◆出かけるときはきちんと火の始末をして(→火を消して)ください Make sure that you *put out the fire* when you go out.

‖始末書 a written apology

慣用表現 カラスはいくら追い払ってもすぐ舞い戻ってくるから始末が悪い However hard we

drive away the crows, they soon return. They *are out of our hands*. / あの子供は始末に負えない That noisy child *is unmanageable* [*unruly*].

しまった Oh, my God!(❖God という語を直接使用することを避けて gosh, goodness, Heavens, Lord などが用いられることもある); Shit! (❖かなり下品な言い方なので用いないほうがよい) /しまった! 電車が行っちゃった *Oh, my God!* [*Oh, dear!*] I missed the train.

しまながし 島流し 彼は島流しになった They *banished* him *to an island*.

しまね 島根

> 島根県は本州の西部に位置し, 県北部は日本海に面しています. 島根県の経済に最も重要な役割を果たしているのが, 米作を中心とする農業および漁業です. 観光名所の一つに大社町の出雲大社があります. ここは神道にとって最も重要な神社の一つで, 古代の神話によると, 日本中の神々が毎年10月に出雲に集まる習わしがあったとされています.
> Shimane Prefecture is located in western Honshu and faces the Sea of Japan to the north. Agriculture centered on rice production and fishing plays an important role in the prefecture's economy. Major tourist attractions include Izumo Taisha Shrine in Taisha-cho. This is one of the most important shrines in Shintoism. According to an ancient myth, all of Japan's gods made it a practice to gather there each October.

しまり 締まり 締まりのない口元 a *loose* mouth / 締まりのない額 a *stupid* face / 締まりのない服装 *sloppy* clothes / 父の体は昔に比べ, だいぶ締まりがなくなってきた My father's body is much less *firm* than it used to be. / 彼は若いころから締まり屋だった He has been *frugal* since he was young.

しまる¹ 閉まる (店・戸などが) close 自; (戸などが) shut* 自; (ばたんと) slam 自
窓がどうしても閉まらない The window *won't close* [*shut*].
日曜日だったので, その店は閉まっていた As it was Sunday, the shop *was closed*.
ドアがばたんと閉まった The door *slammed shut*. (❖この shut は形容詞)
🅔「図書館は何時に閉まるんですか」「7 時です」 "What time does the library *close*? / What time *is* the library *closed*?" "At seven."

しまる² 締まる ねじがきつくしまっている The screws *are* firmly *tightened*. / その水泳選手は締まった体をしている The swimmer has a *firm* body. / (野球などで) 締まっていこう! Let's *pull together*! / 彼の好投で試合が締まってきた Because of his fine pitching, the game became *tense*.

じまん 自慢 (自慢の種) pride Ⓤ, boast Ⓒ; (自画自賛) self-praise Ⓤ ——自慢する be proud of ..., brag 自他; (口に出して) boast 自他
健太は妹のことを自慢にしている Kenta *is proud of* his sister.
トムはルアーのコレクションを自慢している Tom *boasts of* his collection of lures.
4 か国語を話せることが彼の自慢だ It is his *boast* that he can speak four languages.
彼は両親の自慢の息子だ He is *the pride* of his parents.
自慢じゃないが, 数学でいい点を取ったためしがない *Though it's nothing to boast about*, I have never got good grades in math.
◆社長ご自慢の社内伝達システム the president's *much vaunted* internal communication system / 彼の自慢たらたらの話はうんざりだ I've had enough of his *boastful* talk.
🅔「君は運転がうまいね」「ありがとう. 事故を起こしたことがないのが自慢なんだ」 "You're a good driver." "Thanks. I'm *proud* that I've had no accidents."

しみ 染み stain Ⓒ Ⓤ, spot Ⓒ; (インクなどの) blot Ⓒ /シャツのしみを取る remove *a stain* from a shirt / しょうゆのしみはなかなか落ちない Soy sauce *stains* don't come [*wash*] out so easily. / カードにしみをつけてしまった I've made *a blot* on the card.
◆この生地はしみがつきやすい This cloth *stains* easily. / 日焼けのしすぎはしみの原因になる Tanning too heavily can cause *blotches* on the skin.

じみ¹ 地味 ——地味な (飾りけがなく簡素な) plain, simple; (色などが) quiet, subdued; (落ち着いた) sober; (控えめな) conservative /地味な黒いスーツ a *conservative* black suit / その色はあなたには地味すぎる That color is too *subdued* [*quiet*] for you. / このネクタイはそのスーツには地味すぎる This tie is too *plain* [*sober*] for that suit. / 近ごろ地味な結婚式がはやっている Recently, *simple* weddings are popular.

しみこむ 染み込む soak into ..., soak through /靴の中に雨がしみ込んだ The rain *has soaked through* my shoes.

しみじみ(と) しみじみと思い出に浸る be lost *deep in one's* memories / しみじみ語る talk *with feeling* / 親のありがたみをしみじみ感じる I feel *keenly* how much I owe my parents.

しみず 清水 springwater Ⓤ

じみち 地道 ——地道な steady; (不断の) constant ——地道に steadily; constantly /地道に努力する make *constant* [*steady*] efforts ◆これからは地道に (→まじめに正直に) 働くつもりです From now on, I'll work *soberly and honestly*.

しみつく 染み付く たばこのにおいが服にしみついてしまった The smell of cigarette smoke *got into* my clothes. / 学生時代に朝寝坊の癖(△)がしみついてしまった A habit of oversleeping *got* me when I was a student.

しみったれ そんなしみったれたこと言うなよ

しみでる 染み出る　seep (out), ooze (out) ‖油が包み紙を通してしみ出てきた Oil *seeped out* through the wrapping paper.

しみとおる 染み透る　soak through ‖汗が上着までしみ通ってしまった Sweat *has soaked through* to my coat.

しみぬき 染み抜き　stain remover ◻

シミュレーション simulation ◻ ◻

しみる 染みる　(水などが) soak ⊕ ◻; (痛む) smart ⊕, sting* ⊕ ‖インクが紙にしみた The ink *soaked* the paper. / The paper *soaked up* the ink. ‖このおでんはよく味がしみている The flavor *has soaked into* this oden. ‖煙が目にしみた The smoke made my eyes *smart* [*sting*]. ‖このごろ冷たい物が歯にしみる These days, cold things *make my teeth sting*.

◆彼女の言葉は私の胸にしみた Her words *hit home* with me.

-じみる -染みる　年寄りじみた話し方をする talk *like an old man* / 彼は時々子供じみたことを言う He sometimes says *childish* things. / 彼女もすっかり所帯じみてしまった She *has been* completely *domesticated*.

しみん 市民　citizen ◻ ‖市民の civil ‖大阪市民 the *citizen* of Osaka / これらの本は市民団体から寄贈されたものです These books were given by *a group of citizens*.

◆彼は米国の市民権を獲得した He acquired American *citizenship*.

‖市民運動 a citizens' movement / 市民会館 a civic center / 市民交流 an exchange of citizens / 市民大学 a community college / 名誉市民 an honorary citizen

じみんとう 自民党　the Liberal Democratic Party ((略語)) LDP)

ジム gym ◻ (✿gymnasium の短縮形)

じむ 事務　office [desk, clerical] work ‖—事務的な businesslike 事務的に処理する deal *in a businesslike* way 彼は事務の仕事に向いている He is suited to *office [desk] work*.

◆事務レベルの折衝　*working-level* contacts / 日曜日だったので事務所はみな閉まっていた Since it was Sunday, all *the offices* were closed.

🖉「どういうお仕事ですか」「貿易会社で事務をしています」"What kind of work do you do?" "I do *clerical work* at a trading company."

‖事務員 a clerk, an office worker / 事務局 a bureau, a secretariat / 事務次官 a vice-minister / 事務職員 the office staff / 事務総長 a secretary-general / 事務用品 office supplies

しむける 仕向ける　(強く勧める) urge ⊕; (導く) lead* ⊕ ‖その男は彼らが仲たがいするように仕向けた The man *led* them *to* be estranged from each other.

しめ 締め　しめにデザートを注文しよう Let's *finish up* by ordering dessert.

しめあげる 締め上げる　tighten up ‖ボルトを締め上げる *tighten up* the bolts

◆彼らは容疑者を締め上げて泥を吐かせた They *questioned* the suspect *severely* and made him confess his crime.

しめい¹ 指名　——指名する (役職などに) name ⊕, designate ⊕, appoint ⊕; (候補者として) nominate ⊕; (先生があてる) call on ‖私たちは全員,平野さんをキャプテンに指名した We all *named* Hirano (as) captain. ‖だれが大統領候補に指名されるだろうか Who will be *nominated* for President? ◆彼は誘拐の疑いで警察に指名手配されている He's *wanted* by the police for kidnapping.

‖指名打者 a designated hitter

しめい² 氏名　(full) name ◻ ‖住所氏名を書いてください Please write down *your full name* and address.

しめい³ 使命　mission ◻; (聖職・公職への) vocation ◻ ‖使命を果たす accomplish *one's mission* / 彼は重要な使命を帯びてアフリカに渡った He went to Africa *on an* important *mission*. / 彼女は使命感に燃えていた She had a strong *sense of mission*.

じめい 自明　——自明な self-evident ‖自明の理 a *self-evident* truth

しめきり 締め切り　(締め切り日) the closing date, deadline ◻ ‖締め切りに間に合う [間に合わない] meet [miss] *a deadline* / 締め切りが近づいてきた *The deadline* is drawing near.

◆締め切り(掲示) *Closed* ‖申し込みの締め切りはいつですか When does the application *have to be in*?

しめきる¹ 締め切る　close ⊕ ⊕ ‖遠足の参加申し込みはあすで締め切られます Applications for the outing *will be closed* tomorrow.

◆定員になりしだい応募は締め切らせていただきます We'll *stop* accepting applications when they reach the limit.

しめきる² 閉め切る　close up, shut* up; (閉ざしたままでおく) keep* ... closed [shut] ‖彼は一日中部屋の窓を閉めきっていた He *kept* the windows of his room *closed [shut]* all day.

しめくくり 締め括り　(終わり) end ◻; (結論) conclusion ◻ ◻

しめくくる 締め括る　conclude ⊕, end ⊕, finish ⊕ ⊕ ‖彼は有名なことわざで演説を締めくくった He *concluded* his speech with a famous proverb.

◆手紙を締めくくる *bring* a letter *to a close*

しめころす 締め殺す　strangle ⊕, choke *a person to death* ‖その男はネクタイでしめ殺されたと見られている It is suspected that the man *was strangled* with a tie.

しめし 示し　上級生が練習を怠けていたのでは下級生に示しがつかない (→悪い見本になる) It will *set a bad example to* underclassmen if upperclassmen neglect their practice.

しめしあわせる 示し合わせる　arrange previously [beforehand]; (共謀する) conspire ⊕ ‖少女たちは示し合わせたかのように同じ色の服を着てきた The girls came in the same color as if they *had arranged it previously*.

◆彼らは示し合わせておいたとおり同じ時刻に暴動を起こした They started riots at the same time as they *had planned*.

しめしめ しめしめ. どうやらひともうけできそうだぞ *Aha*! It seems that I'll make money.

じめじめ ─じめじめした damp; (空気が) humid ∥じめじめした天気 *damp* weather / ここ数日じめじめした日が続いている The weather has been *humid* for a few days.

しめす¹ 示す

show*, indicate; (指し示す) point (out); (図などで) illustrate; (数値などを) read*, stand* at ...

指で方向を示す *point* the direction with *one's* finger

このグラフは1年間の気温の変化を示している This graph *shows* the temperature changes for the year.

×印は事故現場を示している The cross *shows* where the accident took place.

彼女は私の話に興味を示した She *showed* interest in my story.

彼は何事にも積極的な態度を示す He *shows* a positive attitude toward everything.

彼は量子論の考え方を図で示そうとした He *tried to illustrate* the idea of the quantum theory with a chart.

温度計は30度を示している The thermometer *reads [stands at, indicates]* 30 degrees.

◆弟によいお手本を示さなければいけないよ You should *set* your brother a good example. / You should *set* a good example *for* your brother.

しめす² 湿す moisten [mɔ́isən] ∥ハンカチを水で湿す *moisten* a handkerchief with water

しめた Good!; (やったぞ) I've got [done] it!; (ありがたい) Thank Heaven!

しめだす 締め出す・閉め出す shut* [lock] out, exclude∥法廷から報道陣を締め出す *exclude* reporters from the court / かぎを忘れて家から締め出されてしまった I *was locked out* of my house because I left the key.

しめつ 死滅 extinction Ⓤ ─死滅する become* extinct, die out

じめつ 自滅 self-destruction Ⓤ; (自殺行為) suicide Ⓤ ─自滅する self-destruct Ⓤ, cut* *one's* (own) throat ∥彼女はダブルフォールトを重ねて自滅した She *cut her own throat* by serving a lot of double faults.

しめつける 締め付ける (きつく締める) tighten ∥ねじを締めつける *tighten* a screw

◆その先生は締めつけが厳しいので生徒から嫌われている The teacher is disliked by the students because he *controls* them *strictly [tightly]*. / 彼女の話を聞いて胸が締めつけられる思いだった I felt *distressed* to hear her story.

しめっぽい 湿っぽい damp; (空気が) humid; (ぬれた) wet∥部屋の中が湿っぽい It is *damp* in the room. ◆話が湿っぽくなってきた The story became *gloomy*.

しめて 締めて 売上高はしめて200万円になる見込みだ The sales will be two million yen *altogether*.

しめなわ 注連縄

しめ縄はわらをより合わせて作る神聖な縄で、邪悪なものや病気を寄せつけない特別な力があると信じられてきました。神社の神棚や鳥居、神々が宿るとされる古い木や岩などにかけられます。さらに正月には、一般家庭の玄関や車にも取りつけられます。
Shimenawa are sacred cords made of twisted strands of rice straw. They are believed to have the special power to ward off evil spirits or sickness. They are hung from *torii* (the entrance gates of shrines) and before the altars of Shinto shrines, and also around trees or rocks considered to be places of the divine. It is also common to find *shimenawa* over doorways of houses or on the front of cars at New Years.

しめやか 葬式がしめやかに(→ 厳(ﾞ)かに)執(ﾞ)り行われた The funeral was held *solemnly*.

しめる¹ 閉める (店・戸などを) close; (戸などを) shut*; (ばたんと) slam

ドアは静かに閉めなさい *Close [Shut]* the door quietly.

彼女は怒ってドアをばたんと閉めた She *slammed* the door angrily.

彼女は店をひと月閉めなくてはならなかった She had to *close* her store for a month.

◆窓は閉めたままにしておいてください Please keep the window *closed*.

しめる² 締める・絞める (しっかり留める) fasten; (結ぶ) tie; (きつくする) tighten ∥帯を締める *tie* an *obi* / ねじをしめる *tighten* a screw

シートベルトをお締めください *Please fasten* your seat belt.

◆蛇口をしめる *turn off* a faucet / ネクタイを締める *put on* a tie / 犯人は電話のコードで被害者の首をしめて殺した The murderer *strangled* the victim with a telephone cord.

慣用表現 今新しい事業に手を出すのは自分の首をしめるようなものだ(→ 自殺行為だ) If you set about new business now, that will *be suicidal*.

しめる³ 占める occupy; (場所・位置を) take*; (割合を) account for ... ∥重要な地位を占める *occupy [hold, have]* an important position / 半導体が当社の輸出の6割を占める Semiconductors *account for* 60 percent of our company's exports.

◆過半数を占めている *be in the majority* / 首位を占める *be at the top* / 物価は上昇するとの見方が大勢(ﾞ)を占めている The *prevalent* view is that prices will go up.

しめる⁴ 湿る become* damp; (少し) moisten [mɔ́isən]; (ぬれる) get* wet ─湿った moist; (不快で) damp; (空気が) humid ∥湿った紙 *moist* paper / 湿った靴

しめん

damp shoes / 地面はまだ湿っている The ground is still *wet*. / 湿った空気が部屋に流れ込んできた *Humid* air flew into the room.

しめん¹ 紙面 space ⓤ /…に紙面を割く give *space* to … / 彼の評論は紙面の都合で(→紙面不足のために)割愛された His essay had to be cut *for lack [want] of space*. / 連日その話題が紙面をにぎわせて(→大きな紙面を与えられて)いる The topic *has been given extensive space* in the newspapers day after day.

しめん² 四面 ‖(正)四面体(数学) a (regular) tetrahedron [tetrəhíːdrən]
[慣用表現] 大統領は腹心の部下からも見放され四面楚歌の状況に陥った The president, abandoned by his confidential staff, found himself to *be surrounded by enemies*.

じめん 地面 the ground, the earth ‖地面を掘る dig *the ground* / その少年は宝物を地面に埋めた The boy buried his treasure in *the ground*.

しも¹ 霜 frost ⓒⓤ ‖けさ,霜が降りた There was [We had] (a) *frost* this morning. / 庭の花が霜で枯れてしまった The flowers in the garden died from (a) *frost*. ◆この肉は霜降りだ This meat *is marbled with fat*.
‖霜取り装置 a defroster / 霜柱 needles of frost
[短歌] かささぎの渡せる橋に置く霜の白きを見れば夜ぞふけにける(中納言家持)
On the palace bridge
like the star bridge in the sky
(both called Magpies' Bridge)
I see the white of the frost
and I know the night is late.

しも² 下 下の句 *the latter half* of a tanka poem / 老人の下の世話をする help an old person with *bodily functions*

しもざ 下座 食卓の下座に座る sit at *the foot* of a table

しもて 下手 (観客に向かって舞台の右側) the right (side of the stage), stage right ⓤ

じもと 地元 ―地元の local ‖地元住民 *local* residents / 地元の人々は新空港の建設に強く反対している The *local* people strongly object to the construction of a new airport.
◆地元のチーム the *home* team

しもはんき 下半期 the latter [second] half of the year

しもやけ 霜焼け chilblain ⓒ, frostbite ⓤ (❖chilblain のほうが程度が軽い) ‖手が霜焼けになった I *got chilblain(s) [frostbite]* on my hands. / My hands *are chilblained [frostbitten]*.

しもん¹ 指紋 fingerprint ⓒ ‖指紋をとる take [get] *one's fingerprints* / 指紋によってその男性の身元が確認された The man was identified by *his fingerprints*.
‖指紋押捺(おう) fingerprinting

しもん² 諮問 consultation ⓤ ―諮問する consult ⓣ ―諮問の advisory ‖環境問題について専門家に諮問する *consult* specialists about the environmental problems
‖諮問委員会 an advisory committee / 諮問機関 an advisory organization

じもんじとう 自問自答 私の決断は正しかったろうか、私は幾度となく自問自答した I *wondered* a hundred times if I had made a good decision.

しや 視野 (見える範囲) *one's* field [range] of vision, view ⓤ; (見通し) outlook ⓒ; (知識・興味などの範囲) horizons ‖広い視野でものを見る take *a broad view of things* / カメラが彗星(ほい)を視野にとらえた The camera captured the comet in *its field of view*. / 彼は視野が狭い His *horizons* are narrow. / He is a *narrow* man. / 留学すると視野が広がるよ Studying abroad will broaden your *horizons*. / 私たちは長期的な視野に立ってこの問題に対処しなければなりません We have to take *a long-term view* in dealing with this problem.

しゃ 斜 [慣用表現] 彼にはどこか斜に構えたところがある There is something *cynical* about him.

じゃあ well, then ⇒ では ‖じゃあ、また今度 *Well*, see you soon. / じゃあね *Well, then.* Good-bye!
◆じゃあ始めよう *Now* let's begin.
🄔「家に帰る途中です」「じゃあ、お宅まで車で送らせてください」 "I'm on my way home." "*Then*, let me give you a lift home."
🄔「映画を見る気分じゃないな」「じゃあ、何する」 "I don't feel like watching a movie." "What shall we do, *then*?"

ジャー ⚠ (広口の魔法びん) wide-mouthed thermos ⓒ, (英)thermos flask ⓒ; (炊飯ジャー) insulated rice cooker ⓒ (❖英語の jar は「広口のびん」の意味)

ジャーキー jerky ⓤ

じゃあく 邪悪 ―邪悪な (反道徳的な) evil; (行為などが) wicked; (性格などが) vicious

ジャージー (生地) jersey ⓤ; (セーター・シャツ) jersey ⓒ; (運動用) sweat suit ⓒ

しゃあしゃあ 失敗してもしゃあしゃあと(→平然と)している *remain indifferent* after failing / 私に向かってよくしゃあしゃあとそんなことが言えるね You *have a lot of nerve to* say that to me.

じゃあじゃあ バケツからじゃあじゃあ水がもっている Water *is gushing* from the bucket.

ジャーナリスト journalist ⓒ

ジャーナリズム journalism ⓤ

シャープ 〔音楽〕sharp ⓒ ―シャープな (鋭い・鮮明な) sharp

シャープペンシル ⚠《米》mechanical pencil ⓒ,《英》propelling pencil ⓒ (❖「シャープペンシル」は和製英語。英語の sharp pencil は「とがった鉛筆」の意味)

シャーベット 《米》sherbet ⓒⓤ,《英》sorbet ⓒⓤ

シャーマニズム shamanism ⓤ

シャーマン shaman ⓒ

シャイ ―シャイな (内気な) shy

しゃい 謝意 gratitude ⓤ ‖…に謝意を表する express *one's gratitude* to …

しゃいん 社員 (従業員) employee ⓒ; (職員)

clerk, 《集合的》staff ‖私の会社には200名の社員がいる My company has *a staff of 200*. ◆彼はうちの会社の社員ではない He is not on our *payroll*. (◆payroll は「給与者名簿」の意味) / 社員旅行は毎年行われる *A company outing* is held annually.
‖社員食堂 a company cafeteria / 新入社員 a new employee / 正社員 a regular employee

しゃおく 社屋 a building of the company

しゃおん 謝恩 ‖謝恩会 a party held to thank teachers / 謝恩セール a customer appreciation sale

しゃか 釈迦 (the) Buddha [búdə]
ことわざ あなたにパソコンの使い方を説明するなんて, 釈迦に説法(→よく知っていることを説明しただけ)でしたね When I explained to you how to use the computer, *I was just telling you what you already know very well*.

ジャガー 〔動物〕jaguar

しゃかい 社会

society; (共同体) community; (世間) the world ——社会の social [sóufəl]
中国の社会構造 *the social structure* of China / 社会の一員 a member of *society* / 社会の変化についてゆく keep up with the changes in *society*

現代社会はますます複雑になってきた *Modern society* has become more and more complicated.

家族は社会の基本的な単位である The family is the basic unit of *society*.

彼にとっては社会的地位など何の価値もない *Social status* [*position*] has no meaning at all for him.

アリは高度な社会性をもつ昆虫だ Ants are highly organized *social* insects.

◆反社会的行為 an *antisocial* activity / 社会に出る(→学校を卒業する) get out of school / 彼女は身体障害者の社会復帰(→仕事に戻ること)を助ける仕事をしている Her work is helping disabled people to *return to work*. / 社会の窓があいているよ *Your fly* is open [down]. (◆子供どうしでは"XYZ!"ということもある. Examine *your zipper*.の略記)
‖社会科 social studies / 社会科学 (a) social science / 社会学 sociology / 社会環境 social environment [surroundings] / 社会現象 a social phenomenon / 社会主義 socialism / 社会主義者 a socialist / 社会情勢 social conditions / 社会人 a member of society, a working adult / 社会生活 a social life / 社会制度 a social system / 社会秩序 (a) social order / 社会不安 social unrest / 社会福祉 social welfare / 社会奉仕 social [public] services / 社会保障 social security / 社会問題 a social problem / 車社会 a car-oriented society / 競争社会 a competitive society / 高齢化社会 an aging society

じゃがいも じゃが芋 potato (◆サツマイモ (sweet potato)と区別して Irish [white] potato ともいう)

しゃがむ crouch; (完全に腰を落として) squat (down) ‖しゃがんで鉛筆を拾った I *crouched down* to pick up the pencil.

ジャカルタ Jakarta (◆インドネシアの首都)

しゃがれごえ 嗄れ声 しゃがれ声で in a hoarse [husky] voice

しゃがれる 嗄れる get* hoarse [husky] ——しゃがれた hoarse, husky ‖かぜで声がしゃがれてしまった The cold made my voice *hoarse* [*husky*].

しゃかんきょり 車間距離 the distance between two cars ◆前の車との車間距離をもっととりなさい Leave *a larger space between you and the car ahead*.

しゃきしゃき ——しゃきしゃきした (歯ごたえ) crisp; (動作) brisk, crisp ——しゃきしゃきと crisply; briskly ‖しゃきしゃきしたレタス *crisp* lettuce / しゃきしゃきと働く work *briskly*

しゃきっと 冷たい水で顔を洗ったら気分がしゃきっとした Washing my face with cool water, I felt myself *refreshed*.

しゃく¹ 癪 彼のものの言い方がしゃくにさわる His way of speaking *gets on my nerves*. / ここまで来て引き返すのもしゃくだ It's *annoying* [*irritating*] to have to turn back after coming all the way here.

◆しゃくなことに子供たちは私の言うことを聞こうとしなかった *To my vexation*, the children wouldn't listen to me.

しゃく² 酌 ——酌をする serve *a person* sake

-じゃく -弱 ここから病院まで車で20分弱だ It takes *a little less than* 20 minutes to drive from here to the hospital.

しゃくし 杓子 (丸底) ladle; (平底) dipper
慣用表現 しゃくし定規に考える think *inflexibly* [*by the rules*]

じゃくし 弱視 〔医学〕amblyopia

じゃくしゃ 弱者 weak people, the weak

しやくしょ 市役所 municipal office, 《主に米》city hall

じゃくしょう 弱小 ——弱小の small and weak ‖弱小国 a *small and weak* nation

しゃくぜん 釈然 彼女の説明ではどうも釈然としない I'm *not* quite *satisfied with* her explanation.

じゃくたい 弱体 その国では農業の弱体化が深刻だ Agriculture *is weakening* seriously in the country.

しゃくち 借地 leased land ‖借地権 leasehold / 借地人 a leaseholder, a tenant

じゃぐち 蛇口 《米》faucet, tap ‖蛇口をしめる[あける] turn off [on] *a faucet*

じゃくてん 弱点 weak point, weakness; defect ‖敵の弱点を突く hit the enemy's *weak point* / 弱点を克服するよう努力しなさい Try to overcome *your weak points*.

しゃくど 尺度 measure; (通例単数形); (基準) standard (しばしば複数形 ~s) /

名声や金は必ずしも人生の成功を測る最良の尺度ではない Fame and money are not always *the* best *measure* of success in life.

しゃくどういろ 赤銅色 brown [U] ―赤銅色の brown, tanned

しゃくとりむし 尺取り虫 measuring worm [C], cankerworm [C], looper [C]

しゃくなげ 石南花 〖植物〗rhododendron [C]

じゃくにくきょうしょく 弱肉強食 弱肉強食の世界 the world where *the stronger prey upon the weak*; a *dog-eat-dog* world

しゃくねつ 灼熱 ―灼熱の (燃えるような) burning; (焼けつくような) scorching, blazing; (情熱的な) passionate //灼熱の恋 a *passionate* love / 灼熱の太陽の下で under a *burning* sun

じゃくねん 若年・弱年 若年層 the young generation / 若年労働者 a *young* worker

じゃくはい 若輩・弱輩 ―若輩の young and inexperienced ➾みじゅく

しゃくはち 尺八 🗻

尺八は竹に小さな穴を5個あけただけの笛です. 巧みな指づかいと息の調節によって様々な音を出すことができます. 微妙な音を出すためにはあごの位置を変えることも重要です. 尺八はその単純な作りからは想像できないほど幅広い音色を生みます.

A shakuhachi is a simple bamboo flute with five small holes in it. It can produce various tones by subtle fingerwork and proper breath control. It's also important to move one's chin to make slight changes in the tone. *Shakuhachi* have an amazingly wide range of tone color for such a simple instrument.

しゃくほう 釈放 release [U][C], discharge [U][C] ―釈放する release [他], discharge [他] set* *a person* free //囚人を釈放する *set* a prisoner *free* / 警察はハイジャック犯と人質釈放の交渉をした The police negotiated *the release* of the hostages with the hijackers. / 彼は仮釈放された He *was released on parole*.

しゃくめい 釈明 explanation [C][U] ―釈明する explain [他], account (for …) //釈明を求める call *a person* to *account* / あなたはこの事態をどう釈明するのですか How do you *account for* this situation?

しゃくや 借家 rented house [C] //借家に住む live in *a rented house*
‖借家人 a tenant

しゃくやく 芍薬 peony [píːəni] [C]

しゃくよう 借用 ―借用する borrow [他][自] ➾かりる ‖借用語 a loanword / 借用証書 a bond of debt, 《口語的》an IOU (❖"I owe you."(私はあなたに借金がある)の音をアルファベットで表したもの)

しゃくりあげる しゃくり上げる sob convulsively, give* a sob

しゃくりょう 酌量 consideration [U], allowance [U] ➾じょうじょうしゃくりょう //…を酌量して in *consideration* for …; making *allowance(s)* for …

しゃげき 射撃 shooting [U]; (1回の) shot [C] ‖射撃演習 rifle practice / 威嚇(いかく)射撃 a warning shot / 一斉射撃 a volley

ジャケット (上着) jacket [C]; (レコードの) 《米》jacket [C], 《英》sleeve [C]

しゃけん 車検 automobile safety inspection [C], 《米》car safety check [C], 《英》MOT test [C] ◆車検に出す(→車を点検してもらう) *have one's car inspected*
‖車検証 a car inspection certificate

じゃけん 邪険 ―邪険な (不親切な) unkind; (粗暴な) harsh; (冷淡な) cold ―邪険に unkindly; harshly; coldly //人を邪険に扱う treat *a person unkindly* [*harshly, coldly*]

しゃこ[1] 車庫 (自動車の) garage [gərɑ́ːʒ] [C]; (電車[バス]の) train [bus] depot [díːpou] [C] //車庫付きの家に住む live in a house with *a garage*

しゃこ[2] 蝦蛄 〖動物〗mantis shrimp [C], squilla [C]

しゃこう[1] 社交 ―社交的な sociable ―社交上の social //姉は社交的な人だ My sister is *a sociable person*. / My sister is *a good mixer*. (❖good [bad] mixer は「社交術にたけている[いない]人」の意味) ◆社交界の花 a *society* beauty / 彼は社交辞令で彼女のドレスをほめた He admired her dress *just to be polite*.
‖社交家 a sociable person / 社交クラブ a social club / 社交性 sociability / 社交ダンス social dancing / 社交パーティー a social party

しゃこう[2] 遮光 ‖遮光カーテン a curtain which shuts out the light

じゃこう 麝香 (香料) musk [U]

しゃこうしん 射幸心 gambling spirit [U]
◆射幸心をあおる広告 a commercial which stirs up *one's urge to gamble*

しゃさい 社債 corporate bond [C]; (無担保の) debenture [C] //社債を発行する issue *a corporate bond*

しゃざい 謝罪 apology [C] ―謝罪する apologize [自] //儀礼的な謝罪 *a* superficial *apology* / …に謝罪を要求する demand *an apology* from [of] … / そのテレビ局社長は誤報に関して視聴者に謝罪した The president of the TV station *made* [*gave*] an *apology to* the viewers for the false report.

しゃさつ 射殺 ―射殺する shoot* … to death, shoot and kill //老人を襲ったクマは射殺された The bear which attacked the old man *was shot* 「*to death* [*and killed*].

しゃし[1] 社史 company history [C]

しゃし[2] 斜視 squint [C] ―斜視の squint-eyed, cross-eyed

しゃじ 謝辞 (感謝の言葉) words of thanks [gratitude] //謝辞を述べる say [give] *words of thanks*

しゃじく 車軸 axle [C]

しゃじつ 写実 ―写実的な realistic ―写実的に realistically ‖写実主義 realism / 写

実主義者 a realist

じゃじゃうま じゃじゃ馬（気性の荒い女）shrew ⓒ;（おてんば娘）《口語的》tomboy ⓒ

しゃしゃりでる しゃしゃり出る あのおばさんはよその家庭の問題にいつもしゃしゃり出る That woman always *sticks her nose into* other families' problems.

しゃしゅ 車種（型・年式）model ⓒ;（種類）type ⓒ

しゃしょう 車掌《米》conductor ⓒ,《英》guard ⓒ

しゃしょく 写植《印刷》photocomposition ⓤ, filmsetting ⓤ

しゃしん 写真

photograph ⓒ, picture ⓒ,《口語的》photo ⓒ（複 ～s）（◆正式には photograph だが, 日常的には picture, photo を用いることが多い）
→ 場面・状況別会話 p.1718

《写真を》
写真を現像する［焼き増しする］develop [reprint] *photographs* / 写真を撮ってもらう have *a [one's] photo* taken
ここで写真を撮ろうよ Let's take *a picture* here.
彼女はオーストラリアで動物の写真をたくさん撮った She took a lot of *pictures* of animals in Australia.
あなたの写真を1枚送ってください Will you send me *a picture [photo]* of you?
この写真を引き伸ばしてもらいたいんですが I'd like to have this *picture* enlarged.
その写真を見ると私は苦(⑤)い経験を思い出す The *picture* reminds me of a bitter experience.
💬 「すみません, 写真を撮っていただけますか」「いいですよ, ここを押せばいいんですね？」"Excuse me, but would you take *a picture* (for us)?" "Sure. I just press here, right?"

《写真が・は》
この写真はピンぼけだ This *picture* is out of focus.
この本には写真がたくさん載っている This book includes many *pictures*.
写真がうまく撮れているといいなあ I hope the *pictures* will come out nicely.
◆ 彼女は写真が嫌いだ She's *camera-shy*.

《写真の》
彼はこの写真の最前列の右にいます In this *picture*, he is in the front row on the right.
彼女は写真のほうが美人だ She looks more beautiful in the *picture* than in real life.

《その他》
写真撮影禁止《掲示》*No Photos*
この写真だと彼は実際よりずっと若く見える This *photo* makes him look much younger than he really is.
この写真ではよく分からないが彼女はすごく背が高い You can't see it clearly in this *picture*, but she's really tall.
（写真屋で）この写真, いつでき上がりますか When will these *photos* be ready?

レースは写真判定に持ち込まれた The race was left up to *the examination of the* finish line *photograph*.（◆「写真判定で勝つ」なら win in a photo finish）
◆ 彼女は写真写りがよい［悪い］She *photographs* well [badly].（◆この photograph は「写真に写る」という意味の動詞）
∥写真家 a photographer / 写真館 a photo studio / 写真コンテスト a photo(graph) contest / 写真集 a photograph collection / 写真立て a photo stand

---
-写真のいろいろ-
顔写真（証明用の）a portrait shot;（犯人の）《口語的》a mug shot / カラー写真 a color photograph / 記念写真 a souvenir photograph / 航空写真 an aerial photograph / 上半身の写真 an upper-body photograph / 証明写真 an ID photo / 白黒写真 a black and white photograph / スナップ写真 a snapshot / スピード写真 an instant photograph / 全身の写真 a full-length photograph / ヌード写真 a nude (photograph) / 報道写真 a news photograph / ポラロイド写真 a Polaroid picture(◆商標名) / モンタージュ写真 a montage,《米》a composite (photograph) / レントゲン［X線］写真 an X-ray (photograph)

ジャズ jazz ⓤ ∥ジャズを演奏する play *jazz*
∥ジャズシンガー a jazz singer / ジャズダンス jazz dancing / ジャズバンド a jazz band

-しやすい ❶【容易に…できる】be easy to *do*（◆このはさみは使いやすい These scissors *are easy to use*. / この辞書は字が大きくて見やすい This dictionary is printed in large type and *is easy to read*.

❷【…しがちだ】彼は感情を顔に出やすい He *shows* his feelings *easily*. / 彼は人の言うことを信じやすい He *easily believes [is apt to believe]* what other people say. / 彼は酔うとかっとしやすい He *is given to losing his temper* when he's drunk. / 私は車に酔いやすい I *am prone to get carsick*. / 冬の間はかぜをひきやすい People *are more subject [susceptible] to colds* in winter. / 山の天気は変わりやすい The weather in the mountains *is changeable*.

じゃすい 邪推
💬 「彼女, その仕事を僕に押しつけるためにわざと遅刻したんじゃないのかな」「それは邪推だよ」"I think she came late on purpose in order to force the work on me." "That's only *your imagination*."

ジャスト ⚠

日本語では「ちょうど…」「…きっかり」の意味で用いるが, 英語の just にはほかに「たった…」「…したばかり」の意味があり, 日本語とずれる場合があるので注意する. 日本語の「ジャスト」は exactly で表せる場合が多い.

このテーブルはジャスト1万円だ This table

costs *exactly* 10,000 yen. / きょうは8時ジャストに学校に着いた I got to school at 「8 o'clock *sharp* [*exactly* 8 o'clock]. / 高橋は直球をジャストミートした Takahashi *hit* the fast ball *squarely*.

ジャスミン jasmine [C] [U] ‖ジャスミン茶 jasmine tea

しゃせい¹ 写生 sketching [U] ━写生する sketch [他] [自] ‖写生画 a sketch

しゃせい² 射精 ejaculation [U] [C] ━射精する ejaculate [他] [自]

しゃせつ 社説 editorial [C], 《英》leader [C], 《英》leading article [C]

しゃぜつ 謝絶 ━謝絶する refuse [他] ‖面会謝絶《掲示》No Visitors

しゃせん¹ 車線 (traffic) lane [C] ∥1[2]車線の道路 a 「single *lane* [two-*lane*] road / 車線変更をする change *lanes*
‖追い越し車線 the fast lane / 対向車線 the opposite lane

しゃせん² 斜線 oblique (line) [C]; (区切りの記号) slash [C] ◆斜線部分 a *shaded* part

しゃそう 車窓 train [car] window [C] ∥車窓の風景 a view *from the train* [*car*] *window*

しゃたい 車体 the body (of a car)

しゃたく 社宅 company house [C], 《集合的》company housing

しゃだん 遮断 ━遮断する (さえぎる) block [他]; (止める) stop [他]; (電気などを) cut* ... off ∥この道は土砂崩れのために交通が遮断されている Traffic *has been blocked* [*stopped*] on this road by a landslide.
◆その防音装置は完全に外の騒音を遮断するものではない The soundproofing can't completely *shut out* the noises from outside.
‖遮断機 a crossing gate

しゃだんほうじん 社団法人 corporate juridical person [C] (❖法律上の正式名称. ふつうは corporation でよい)

シャチ 鯱〔動物〕killer whale [C]

しゃちほこばる 鯱張る (緊張して硬くなる) become* stiff ◆そんなにしゃちほこばらなくていいよ Don't *be* so *formal*.

しゃちゅう 車中 ━車中の[で] (電車) in [on] the train; (車) in the car ∥車中1泊 an overnight stay *in the car*

しゃちょう 社長 《主に米》president [C], 《英》chairman [C]; (最高経営責任者) chief executive (officer) [C] (《略語》CEO) ‖社長室 the president's office / 副社長 a vice-president

シャツ shirt [C]; (下着) 《米》undershirt [C], 《英》vest [C] ∥長[半]そでのシャツ *a* long-[short-]sleeved *shirt* / シャツを着る[脱ぐ] 「put on [take off] *a shirt*
‖Tシャツ a T-shirt / ポロシャツ a polo shirt

しゃっかん 借款 loan [lóun] [C] ‖円借款 yen credit [loan]

じゃっかん 若干 (少し) a little; (いくらか) somewhat ━若干の some; (量) a little; (数) a few ∥席はまだ若干残っています There are still *a few* seats left. / こっちのほうが若干値は張るが断然品質がよい This is *a little* more expensive, but it has much better quality. / その店ではアルバイトを若干名募集している They are looking for *some* part-time workers at the store.

ジャッキ jack [C] ◆ジャッキで車を持ち上げる *jack* a car *up*

しゃっきん 借金 debt [dét] [C] [U] (❖借金を表すときは [C], 借金状態を表すときは [U]); (貸付金) loan [lóun] [C] ━借金(を)する borrow money; (借金状態に入る) get* [run*, fall*, go*] into debt; (借金をしている) owe [他]
借金を返す pay (back [off]) *one's debt* / 借金を踏み倒す dodge paying *one's debts* / 借金の担保 security for *a loan* / 借金の返済 settlement of *a debt*
うちは銀行に300万円の借金がある We *are* three million yen *in debt* to the bank.
僕は友人に5,000円の借金がある I *owe* my friend 5,000 yen. / I *owe* 5,000 yen *to* my friend.
彼は借金をしていない He is free [out] of *debt*.
車を買うのに借金をしなければならなかった I had to *borrow money* to buy a car.
彼らは彼の借金をすべて帳消しにした They wrote off all his *debts*.
彼女は多額の借金を抱えている She's deep *in debt*.
友人が私の借金の保証人になってくれた A friend of mine became a guarantor for my *debt*. / My friend guaranteed my *debt*.
彼は借金で首が回らない He *is up to his ears in debt*.
‖借金取り a debt collector

ジャックナイフ jackknife [C]

しゃっくり hiccup [híkʌp] [C]《しばしば複数形～s》 ━しゃっくりをする hiccup [自] ∥しゃっくりが止まらない I can't stop *my hiccups*.

ジャッジ (審判員) judge [C]; (判定) judgment, 《英》judgement [C]

シャッター (カメラの) shutter [C]; (よろい戸) shutters ∥シャッターを切る press *the shutter* ◆昼飯を食べにその店に行ったらシャッターが下りていた The restaurant *was shuttered* when I went there for lunch.
‖シャッタースピード a shutter speed / シャッターチャンス a chance for a good shot

シャットアウト (野球などの完封) shutout [C] ━シャットアウトする shut* out ∥報道陣は完全にシャットアウトされた The press *was* completely *shut out*.

しゃてい(きょり) 射程(距離) range [U]《また a～》 ∥そのミサイルの射程距離は5,000マイルだ The missile has *a range* of 5,000 miles.
◆この一勝でジャイアンツは優勝を射程圏内にとらえた With this victory, the Giants *came within reach of* the championship.

しゃてき 射的 (射撃) shooting [U] ‖射的場 a shooting gallery

しゃど 斜度 平均斜度 *the* average *grade* (of a ski slope) / このコースは斜度がかなりきつい

This course *is* very *steep*.

しゃとう 斜塔　ピサの斜塔 the Leaning Tower of Pisa

しゃどう 車道　the roadway, road ◯

じゃどう 邪道　(正当でないやり方) unorthodox way [method] ◯ ◆邪道かもしれないが，このほうがふつうのやり方よりうまくいくんだ *This might be unorthodox*, but it works better than the usual way.

しゃない 車内　(電車で)車内でのおたばこはご遠慮ください Please refrain from smoking *in [on] the train.* / (バスの)車内はかなり込み合っていた *The bus* was pretty crowded.
‖車内販売 sales in [on] the train / 車内放送 announcement in [on] the train

しゃない² 社内　彼女の能力は社内で正当に評価されている Her abilities are justly estimated *in the company.* / 兄は社内結婚をした My brother *married a woman working in the same company.*
‖社内報 an in-house bulletin [newsletter]

しゃにくさい 謝肉祭　carnival ◯◯

しゃにむに 遮二無二　(一生懸命) very hard; (一心に) earnestly; (狂ったように) madly

じゃねん 邪念　(悪い考え) evil thought ◯; (雑念) distracting thought ◯　‖邪念を払う shake off *one's evil thought*

ジャブ 〖ボクシング〗 jab ◯

しゃふう 社風　(会社の気風) the company's style

しゃぶしゃぶ 🗻　*shabu-shabu*, a dish of thinly sliced beef cooked briefly in boiling water and then dipped into citrus flavored soy sauce

じゃぶじゃぶ 子供たちは浅瀬でじゃぶじゃぶ遊んでいた The kids *were splashing around* in the shallows.

しゃふつ 煮沸　——煮沸する boil ⨁ ‖煮沸消毒する sterilize by *boiling*

しゃぶる suck ⨁ ◯ ‖骨までしゃぶる *suck* *(on)* a bone / 指をしゃぶってはいけません Don't *suck* your thumb.

シャベル shovel ◯ / 雪かき用シャベル *a* snow *shovel* / シャベルが何か硬いものに当たった *My shovel* struck against something hard. ◆彼らは競技場の雪をシャベルで取り除いていた They *were shoveling* the snow *off* the field.

しゃべる 喋る　(話す) talk ⨀ ⨁; (おしゃべりする) chat ⨀; (ぺちゃくちゃと) chatter ⨀ ‖彼とはまだ一度もしゃべったことがない I've never *talked to [with]* him yet. / ゆうべ彼女と電話で2時間しゃべった I *chatted with* her on [over] the telephone for two hours last night.
◆あの男は本当によくしゃべる That guy is really *talkative.* / 私は彼女が彼と結婚することをうっかりしゃべってしまった I *let slip* that she was going to marry him.

しゃへん 斜辺　oblique side ◯ ; (直角三角形の) the hypotenuse [haipátənùːs]

しゃほん 写本　manuscript ◯

シャボンだま シャボン玉　soap bubbles
◆シャボン玉を吹く blow *bubbles*

じゃま 邪魔

❶ 〖妨害・障害〗 (障害物) obstacle ◯ ; (気になること・物) disturbance ◯ ◯ , interference ◯ ◯ , hindrance ◯　——じゃまする disturb ⨁, interfere ⨁, hinder ⨁; (うるさがらせる) bother ⨁

勉強してるんだからじゃまをしないで *Don't disturb* [*bother*] *me. I'm studying.*

きょうは一日電話にじゃまされずに仕事に集中できた I could concentrate on my work *without the interruption* of phone calls today.

すみません，ちょっとおじゃまします I'm sorry to *interrupt* you. (❖人の話の途中で割り込むときの言い方)

前髪が伸びてじゃまになってきた My bangs have grown long and come to *bother* me.

◆その箱，じゃまだからわきにどけてちょうだい That box *is blocking the way.* Will you move it aside? / 前に座っている人の頭がじゃまで舞台がよく見えなかった My view of the stage *was obstructed* by the head of the person sitting in front of me. / この部屋に大きいソファーはじゃまだ (→場所をとりすぎる) A big sofa *will take up too much space* in this room. / そこをどけ．じゃまだ *Move!* *You're in my way.* / 人をじゃま扱いしないでくれ *Don't* *treat me as a nuisance.*

💬「おじゃまじゃないですか」「大丈夫．ちょうど仕事も片がついたから」 "I hope I'm not *disturbing* you." "It's all right. I've just finished my work."

❷ 〖訪問〗 ➡ おじゃま

> 【語法】日本語の「おじゃまします」「おじゃましました」は訪問・入室の際のあいさつに用いるが，英語にはこれに当たる決まった言い方はない．状況に応じて様々な表現を使い分ける必要がある．入室のときに許可を求める意味では "May I come in?" を，相手に時間をとらせてわびる意味では "I'm sorry I've taken so much of your time." などを用いる．

あすおじゃましてもよろしいですか May I *visit* you tomorrow?

💬「どうもおじゃましました」「いいえ，またいつでも遊びにいらしてください」 "*I must be going now.*" "Please come again anytime." (❖ I must be going now. は，いとまごいをするときの決まり文句)

しゃみせん 三味線　🗻

三味線はバンジョーのような形をした楽器で，3本の弦をばちで弾いて演奏します．三味線は中国から琉球（沖縄）経由で日本に入ってきました．現在，沖縄の三味線は本土のものとやや異なり，「三線 (㊗)」と呼ばれています．英語ではshamisen または samisen とつづりますが，英語圏ではそれほど広く知られているわけではありません．
The *shamisen* is a banjo-like instru-

ment with a long neck and three strings. The strings are played with a plectrum. The *shamisen* was brought to Japan from China via the Ryukyu (Okinawa) Islands. In Okinawa the instrument is called the *sanshin* now and is somewhat different from in the rest of Japan. The word is spelled either "shamisen" or "samisen" in English, but the instrument is not widely known in the English-speaking world.

ジャム jam ◎; 《主に米》jelly ◎(❖特に果肉の入っていないものを指す) ‖ジャムのびん a *jam jar* ◎ ‖ アンズ[イチゴ]のジャム apricot [strawberry] *jam* ‖ パンにジャムを塗る spread *jam* on bread

ジャムセッション jam session ◎

シャムねこ シャム猫 Siamese [sàiəmíːz] (cat) ◎

しゃめん 斜面 slope ◎ ‖急[緩]斜面 a steep [gentle] *slope* ◆丘の斜面を滑り降りる slide down *a hillside*

しゃもじ 杓文字 rice paddle [scoop] ◎

しゃよう 斜陽 the setting sun ‖斜陽産業 a declining industry

じゃらじゃら 歩くとポケットの中で小銭がじゃらじゃら音を立てた The coins in my pocket *jingled* as I walked.

じゃり 砂利 gravel ◎ ‖その日本庭園には砂利が敷き詰められていた The Japanese garden was covered with *gravel*.
◆道に砂利を敷く *gravel* the road
‖砂利道 a gravel [graveled] path

じゃりじゃり 浜辺で食べたホットドッグは砂でじゃりじゃりしていた The hot dogs we ate at the beach were *gritty* with sand.

しゃりょう 車両 vehicle ◎; (車) car ◎; (列車の) 《米》carriage / 《英》carriage ‖橋を渡るのにすべての車両は通行料を払わなければならない All *cars* are required to pay a toll to cross the bridge. / 偶然小田君と同じ車両に乗り合わせた I happened to be on the *same car* as Oda.
◆車両通行止《掲示》*Closed to Vehicular Traffic* / 車両故障のため, この駅でしばらく停車します We are now experiencing *mechanical difficulties*, so we will stop at this station for a few minutes. (❖ mechanical difficultiesは婉曲的な表現)
‖車両故障 a vehicle breakdown / 連結式車両 an articulated vehicle

しゃりん 車輪 wheel ◎

しゃれ 洒落 (冗談) joke ◎; (ごろ合わせ) pun ◎, a play on words, wordplay ◎ ‖うまい[下手な]しゃれ a clever [poor] *joke* / しゃれを飛ばす make a *joke* / 僕はそのしゃれが分からなかった I didn't get *the joke*.
◆きのうはしゃれにならないほど暑かった It was *extraordinarily* hot yesterday.
🔴「この旅館, 真夜中になると白い服を着た幽霊が出るんだって」「しゃれにならないよ. ゆうべ白い服の女の人見たぜ」"I hear a ghost in white haunts this hotel at midnight." "*It's like a bad joke!* I saw a woman like that last night."

しゃれい 謝礼 reward ◎; (弁護士などに支払う) fee ◎ ‖犬を見つけてくださったかたには謝礼として1万円差し上げます We'll give 10,000 yen *as a reward* for finding our dog.

しゃれこうべ (頭蓋骨《ずがい》) skull ◎

しゃれた 洒落た nice; (素敵などが) smart, stylish; (趣味のよい) tasteful; (洗練された) chic [ʃíːk], sophisticated; (機知に富んだ) witty ‖しゃれたスーツ a *stylish* suit / このあたりにはしゃれたレストランが多い There are a lot of *nice* restaurants around here. / その店は内装がとてもしゃれていた The decor of the shop was very *tasteful*. / 彼はしゃれたことを言った He made some *witty* remarks.

しゃれっけ 洒落っ気 しゃれっけを出す *pay attention to one's appearance* ‖ 彼女には全くしゃれっけというものがない She is quite *indifferent to her appearance*.

じゃれる (恋人たちが) じゃれ合う *touch each other playfully* ‖ うちの猫はビニールのふくろにじゃれるのが大好きだ Our cat loves *playing with* plastic bags. / その子犬は私にじゃれてきた The puppy was *nuzzling* me. (❖nuzzleは「鼻をすりつける」の意味) / (→気を引こうと戯れた) The puppy *was frolicking to get* my attention.

ジャワ Java ‖ジャワ原人 Java man, Pithecanthropus erectus

シャワー shower ◎ ‖彼女は毎朝シャワーを浴びる She *takes a shower* every morning.
‖シャワーカーテン a shower curtain / シャワーキャップ a shower cap / シャワー室 a shower room

ジャングル jungle ◎ ◎ ‖ジャングルジム 《米》a jungle gym, 《英》a climbing frame

じゃんけん じゃん拳 🗾

いわゆる石・紙・はさみのゲームをじゃんけんといい, 石をグー, 紙をパー, はさみをチョキと呼びます. ふつう勝ち負けや順番を決めるのにじゃんけんをしますが,「じゃんけんぽん」の掛け声とともにいっせいに3つのうち1つの形の手を出して勝負します. グーはチョキに, チョキはパーに, パーはグーに勝ちます.
The game of rock-paper-scissors is called *janken* in Japan. The stone is called *gu*, the paper *pa* and the scissors *choki*. It is a common way to decide who is the winner or who will take precedence. Everybody shows his or her hand in one of the three shapes at the signal of "*janken pon*." Rock beats scissors, scissors beats paper and paper beats rock.

じゃんじゃん けさから事務所に電話がじゃんじゃんかかっている Phone calls *have been pouring* into the office since this morning. / おばさんは料理をじゃんじゃん(→次から次へと)出してくれた My aunt served us dishes *one after another*. / そんなにじゃんじゃん使

わないでよ. そのローションが高かったんだから Don't *drench yourself* with my lotion. It was expensive!(❖*drench oneself*は「びしょぬれになる」の意味)

シャンソン chanson [ʃɑ̃ŋsɔ́ːŋ] C (❖フランス語から)

シャンデリア chandelier C

しゃんと 背筋をしゃんと(→まっすぐ)伸ばす *straighten one's* back / その大学教授は80歳になるがまだしゃんとしている That professor is 80, but still *hale and hearty*. (❖*hale and hearty*は「(老人が)元気だ」の意味の決まり文句)

ジャンパー ⚠ (上着) jacket C; (スポーツ用の) windbreaker C (❖英語の jumper は (英) ではセーターを, (米) ではジャンパースカートを指す)

ジャンパースカート (米) jumper C, (英) pinafore C

シャンハイ 上海 Shanghai [ʃǽŋhái] (❖中国の都市)

シャンパン champagne [ʃæmpéin] U (❖フランス語から)

ジャンプ jump C ——ジャンプする jump 自 他 ‖猫が塀の上にジャンプした A cat *jumped up* onto the wall. / ここをクリックするとテキストの冒頭にジャンプする Click here, and you'll *jump* to the head of the text.
‖ジャンプスーツ a jumpsuit / ジャンプ台(スキーの) a ski jump

シャンプー shampoo [ʃæmpúː] C U ——シャンプーする shampoo 他 ‖彼女は髪のシャンプーとセットをしてもらった She had her hair *shampooed* and set.

ジャンボ (ジェット機) jumbo jet C ——ジャンボな jumbo

ジャンル (公式的) genre [ʒɑ́ːnrə] C (❖フランス語から. 文学・芸術などに用いる); (種類) kind C, type C ‖どんなジャンルの音楽を聞くのですか What kind of music do you listen to? / 彼の作品は散文詩のジャンルに属する His work belongs to *the genre* of prose poetry.

しゅ¹ 主 ❶【神】《キリスト教》the Lord ‖主よ, わたしをあわれんでください Have mercy upon me, O *Lord*. (❖詩篇/第六章より)
❷【主な】この会議の主たる目的 the *main* purpose of this meeting / その植物は主として亜熱帯地方に分布する That plant is *mainly* distributed in subtropical regions.

しゅ² 朱 vermilion U ——朱色の vermilion ‖朱塗りのわん a *vermilion-lacquered* bowl
ことわざ 朱に交われば赤くなる He who touches pitch shall be defiled therewith. (→ピッチにさわる者は汚れる)

しゅ³ 種 (種類) kind C, sort C; (生物分類上の) species U (複〜) ‖新種のウイルス *a new kind* of virus / 絶滅の危機に瀕(ﾋﾝ)している種 an endangered *species* / 最近はこの種のテレビ番組が多い Recently there are many TV programs of this *sort*.

しゅい 首位 the top, (the) first place; (先頭) the lead ‖首位を奪回する[譲る] 「take over [give up] *first place* / 首位を争う compete for *first place* / 彼らは首位を分け合った They tied for *first place*. / パ・リーグでは現在, 西武が首位に立っている The Lions are *at the top of* the Pacific League now.
‖首位打者 the leading hitter

しゆう 私有 ——私有の private ‖私有財産 private property / 私有地 private land

しゅう¹ 週 C ⇨ こんしゅう(今週), せんしゅう(先週), らいしゅう(来週)
週5日制 *a five-day week* (system) / 週に2回アルバイトをする do a part-time job twice *a week*
週に4時間英語の授業があります We have four periods of English *a week*.
不燃ごみは週に1度回収される Non-burnable garbage is collected once *a week*.
そのレストランは毎週メニューを変える The restaurant varies its menu *every week*.
彼は週ぎめで給料をもらっている He is paid *by the week*.
◆週の中ごろには結論が出るだろう A conclusion will be made *by midweek*. / その雑誌は隔週発行されている That magazine is issued 「*every other week* [*biweekly*].

しゅう² 州 (米国の) state C; (英国の) county C; (カナダの) province C ‖ワシントン州 Washington *State*; *the state* of Washington / アメリカ合衆国には州が50ある There are 50 *states* in the United States of America.
◆インディアナポリスはインディアナ州の州都である Indianapolis is *the capital* of Indiana.
‖州議会 a state assembly / 州知事 a state governor / 州立大学 a state university

しゅう³ 宗 (宗派) sect C ‖真言宗 the Shingon *Sect*

-しゅう¹ -周 (スポーツ競技の1周) lap C ⇨ いっしゅう(一周) ‖校庭を10周走る run 10 *laps* of the school ground

-しゅう² -集 collection C; (選集) anthology C, selection C ‖アメリカ短編選集 *a selection* of American short stories / 写真集 *a collection* of photographs

じゆう 自由

freedom U; (公式的) liberty U (❖freedom は「束縛されない」という意味で広く一般的に用いられる. liberty は freedom よりかたい語で, 特に国家・政府による制限からの自由を指す) ——自由な free ——自由に freely ⇨ ふじゆう
〖〜(の自由)〗
選択 [言論] の自由 *freedom of* choice [speech] / 出版[報道]の自由 *freedom of* the press
自分の考えを述べる自由が欲しい I want *freedom* to express my thoughts.
信教の自由は憲法で保障されている *Freedom of* religion is guaranteed by the Constitution.
◆彼はその事故で左腕の自由がきかなくなった(→使えなくなった) He lost *the use of* his left arm in the accident.
〖自由を〗
自由を得るための闘い the fight for *freedom* /

じゅう

自由を手に入れる[尊重する] gain [value] *liberty*

その物語の主人公は自由を求めて奮闘していた The hero of that story was struggling for *freedom*.

【自由な・の】

自由な選択 a *free* choice / 自由の喜びを味わう taste the joy of *freedom*

ここでは君は自由の身だ You *are free* here.

この学校は自由な雰囲気がある This school has a *free* atmosphere.

【自由に】

自由に通れる道 a *free* [an *open*] road

どうぞ自由に意見を述べてください Please *feel free to* express your opinion. / Please express your opinion *freely*.

このデータは自由に利用できる You *are free to* use this data. / You *can* use this data *freely*.

10歳未満の子供はこの遊園地に自由に出入りできる Children under 10 are given *free* admission to this amusement park.

◆サラダを自由にお取りください *Help yourself to* the salad. (❖*help oneself* は「(飲食物を)自分で取って食べる」という意味) / 生徒たちは学習する外国語を自由に選択できる The students *have a choice* of foreign languages to study. / 私のお金は自由になるお金はほとんどない I have little money *at my disposal*.

【自由だ】

仕事さえ終えれば君は自由だ You *will be free* once you have finished your work.

◆そう考えるのは自由だ *That's a matter of opinion.* / 値段は1万円、買う買わないは自由です The price is 10,000 yen. You *can take it or leave it.* / 私たちといっしょに行くか行かないかは君の自由だ *It's up to you* whether you go with us or not.

【その他】

僕は自由気ままな暮らしが気に入っている I am happy with my *free and easy* life.

◆彼女は自由奔放な(→社会的慣行にとらわれない)人だ She is an *uninhibited* person. / (→好きなようにふるまう) She behaves *as she pleases*. / その少年はヨーヨーを自由自在に操ることができる The boy can handle yo-yos *just as he pleases*. / これは私の自由裁量では決断できない問題だ This issue cannot be dealt with *at my discretion*. / ローマでは自由行動の日がまる1日あった We had one whole day 「*to go around on our own* [*free, of free time*]」 in Rome.

‖自由意志 free will / 自由化 ⇨じゆうか / 自由形 freestyle / 自由業 a freelance profession / 自由競争 free enterprise, free [open] competition / 自由経済 free economy / 自由契約選手 a free agent / 自由研究 independent research / 自由作文 a free composition / 自由時間 free time / 自由主義 liberalism / 自由主義者 a liberalist / 自由席 a nonreserved seat / 自由の女神 the Statue of Liberty / 自由貿易 free trade

じゅう¹ 銃 gun ◎ ‖銃を携帯する carry *a gun* / 銃を抜く draw *a gun* / 銃を撃つ fire *a gun* / 銃に弾を詰める load *a gun* / 彼は標的に銃を向けた He *pointed* [*aimed*] *a gun* at the target. / 政府は銃の使用を禁止している The government has banned the use of *guns*. / 彼は銃でオオカミを撃った He shot a wolf with *a gun*. / (→銃で) He shot at a wolf with *a gun*.; He shot [fired] *a gun* at a wolf. ◆人質は2時間もの間、銃を突きつけられていた The hostages *were held at gunpoint* for two hours.

‖銃規制法案 a gun control bill / カービン銃 a carbine / 機関銃 a machine gun / 空気銃 an airgun / 拳銃 a pistol / 散弾銃 a shotgun / ライフル銃 a rifle

じゅう² 十 ten; (10番目) tenth ◆何十人もの人 *dozens of* people / そのレストランへは何十回となく行ったことがある I've been to that restaurant *dozens of times*.

⇨じっちゅうはっく、じゅうにんといろ

じゅう³ 焼けたフライパンを水にいつけるとじゅうと音がした The hot pan *sizzled* when I put it in water.

-じゅう -中

❶【場所】all over …

彼女のもとには国中から激励の手紙が届いた She received letters of encouragement *from all over the country*.

彼は若いころ世界中を旅して回ったそうだ I hear he traveled *all over the world* when he was young.

妹はその俳優のポスターを壁中べたべたはっている My sister has put up the actor's posters *all over the walls*.

目がさめたら体中に発疹(ほっしん)が出ていた I woke up to find I had a rash *all over my body*.

その浜辺はそこら中ヤドカリだらけだった There were hermit crabs *all over* the beach.

◆そのうわさはあっという間に学校中に広まった That rumor spread *across the school* like wildfire. / そのアルバムを家中捜したが見つからなかった I searched for the album *everywhere in the house* but I couldn't find it.

❷【期間】throughout, all through …

彼は講演の間中、居眠りをしていた He was sleeping *all through* the lecture.

父はよくゴルフをするので一年中日焼けしている My father often plays golf, and is tanned *throughout the year*.

その患者は一晩中痛みでうめいていた The patient kept groaning with pain *all through the night*.

◆きのうは一日中うちでごろごろしていた I stayed home *all day* yesterday doing nothing. / きょう中に電話します I'll call you *today*. / 私は夏休みの間中、毎日近所のパン屋さんでバイトをした I worked part-time at a nearby bakery every day *during the summer vacation*.

❸【全部の】all, whole

この冬はうち中でインフルエンザにかかってしまった *The whole family* got flu this winter.

祖母の米寿のお祝いに親戚(しんせき)中が集まった All

the relatives got together to celebrate our grandmother's 88th birthday.

しゅうあく 醜悪 **―醜悪な**（醜い）ugly；（ぞっとするような）disgusting

じゅうあつ 重圧 great [heavy] pressure [U] [C] //彼は責任の**重圧**に耐えかねて仕事を辞めてしまった He couldn't bear *the great pressure* of responsibility and quit the job. / 彼は世論の**重圧**をはね返して（→屈しないで）権力の座に居座り続けた He withstood *the great pressure* of public opinion and continued to maintain power.

しゅうい 周囲 （周りの状況）surroundings；（環境）environment [U] [C]；（円周）circumference [C] [U]

カメレオンは周囲の状況に合わせて素早く体の色を変える Chameleons quickly change the color of their bodies according to *their surroundings.*

この島の周囲がどれくらいか知っているかい Do you know *the circumference* of this island?

◆この木の**周囲**は3メートルくらいある This tree is about three meters *around* [*in circumference*]. / 私は**周囲**の変化に全く気づいていなかった I had no realization of *the changes occurring around me.* / 彼は**周囲**の心配をよそにひとりで出かけた He went out by himself ignoring *other people's* concerns. / **周囲**の目なんか気にするな Don't worry about *what other people think.* / その町はかつて高い壁に**周囲**を囲まれていた The city *was* once *surrounded by* high walls.

じゅうい 獣医 《口語的》vet [C]，《米公式的》veterinarian [C]，《英公式的》veterinary surgeon [C] ‖**獣医学** veterinary medicine

じゅういち 十一 eleven；（11番目）eleventh

じゅういちがつ 十一月 November [U] [C]（《略語》Nov.）➾いちがつ

しゅうえき 収益 （利益）profit [C] [U]；（収入・売上高）the proceeds //去年，その会社は新しいゲーム機を発売して大きな**収益**をあげた Last year, that company *made a* big *profit* from selling a new game system. / この催し物の**収益**は慈善団体に渡される *The proceeds* of this festival will go to charity.

しゅうえん 終演 **終演**（→幕が下りるの）は午後10時です *The curtain falls* at 10 p.m.

じゅうおう 縦横 東京には地下鉄が**縦横**に（→東京全体に）張りめぐらされている The subway system covers the *whole* city of Tokyo. / 小野はその試合で**縦横**無尽の（→すばらしい）活躍を見せた Ono did a *very good* job in that game.

じゅうおく 十億 a [one] billion //負債は数**十億**ドルに達する The debts amount to *billions of* dollars.

じゆうか 自由化 liberalization [U] **―自由化する** liberalize [他] //資本の**自由化** capital *liberalization* / 米の輸入を**自由化する** *liberalize* the import of rice

しゅうかい 集会 meeting [C]；（非公式でうちとけた）gathering [C]；（特定の目的をもった）assembly [C] [U]；（政治的・宗教的な大集会）rally [C] //**集会**の権利 the right of *assembly* / 全校**集会**が体育館で開かれた *School assembly* was held in the gym.

‖**集会所** a meeting place, an assembly room / **抗議集会** a protest rally / **臨時集会** an extraordinary meeting, a special meeting

しゅうかく[1] 収穫 crop [C], harvest [U] [C]（❖crop は作物の収穫量に，harvest は収穫の作業に重点をおく）**―収穫する** harvest [他] [自]

作物を収穫する *harvest* [*gather*] a crop / 今年の穀物の**収穫** this year's grain *harvest*

去年はジャガイモの収穫が多かった[少なかった] We had *a* good [poor] potato *crop* last year.

秋は収穫の季節だ Fall is the *harvest* season.

この地方ではもうすぐ米の収穫が始まる *The* rice *harvest* is about to start in this region.

◆それについてインターネットで調べてみたが**収穫**はなかった I did a web search on that, but I *didn't get anything.* / 今回のバーゲンはあまり**収穫**がなかった I *didn't buy* much at the sale this time. / 2年間のイギリス留学は**収穫**が多かった The two years of studying in Britain *were fruitful.*

‖**収穫高** a crop, a yield

しゅうかく[2] 臭覚 the sense of smell

➾きゅうかく

しゅうがく 就学 **―就学する** enter school

◆**就学**前の子供 *preschool* children / **就学**年齢に達する arrive at *school age*

‖**就学率** the percentage of children attending school

しゅうがくりょこう 修学旅行 🗻 school trip [C] //僕たちは**修学旅行**で北海道に行った We went on *a school trip* to Hokkaido.

> 日本の学生は，ふつう中学・高校のときに学校主催の団体旅行に出かけますが，これを修学旅行といいます．一般的に奈良や京都などの歴史的に重要な都市を訪れ，文化遺産を見学します．最近私立の学校の中には中国や韓国，オーストラリアまで出かける学校もあります．
>
> In Japan, most junior and senior high school students go on a school trip called *shugaku ryoko.* Generally students visit historical cities such as Nara and Kyoto and see cultural treasures. Recently trips to China, Korea and even all the way to Australia have also been made by some private schools.

じゅうがつ 十月 October [U] [C]（《略語》Oct.）

➾いちがつ

しゅうかん[1] 習慣

custom [U] [C]; habit [C]; practice [C] [U], rule [C]; ritual [C]

custom：基本的には社会的慣習を指すが，個人の定着した習慣も指す．
habit：個人的な習慣や癖(くせ)を表す．
practice, rule：慣習・習わしを表す．

ritual: 社会的なしきたりや日常の決まりきった行為などを指す.

【習慣が・は】
長年の習慣は振り払うのが大変だ It's hard to shake (off) *an old habit*.
夜遅くにお菓子を食べるという悪い習慣がついてしまった I *fell* [*got*] *into a* bad *habit* of eating snacks late at night.
その国にはチップの習慣はない They *don't have the custom* of tipping in that country.
◆日本ではバレンタインデーに女性から男性へチョコレートを贈る習慣がある *It is customary* in Japan for women to give chocolate to men on Valentine's Day.

【習慣に】
私は毎朝新聞を読むのを習慣にしている I *make a habit* of reading the newspaper every morning.
父は1日に2回犬の散歩に行くのを習慣にしている My father *makes a rule to* walk our dog twice a day. / My father *usually* [*always*] walks our dog twice a day.
私はその仕事を始めてから早起きが習慣になった Getting up early *has become a habit* with me since I got that job.

【習慣を】
よい[悪い]習慣をつける *form* good [bad] *habits*
彼は夜ふかしの習慣を改めようとしている He is trying to「*get rid of* [*break*] *his habit* of staying up late.

【習慣だ】
朝食の前に散歩をするのが彼の習慣だ It is his *rule* to take a walk before breakfast.
その国では3日間にわたって結婚披露宴を行うのが習慣だ It's *the custom* in that country to hold a wedding reception for three days in a row.

【その他】
つい習慣でいつも同じシャンプーを買ってしまう I always buy the same shampoo just *out of habit*.
コーヒーには習慣性がある Coffee is *habit-forming*.

しゅうかん² 週刊 ―週刊の weekly
◆その雑誌は週刊だ That magazine *is published weekly* [*every week*].
‖週刊誌 a weekly (magazine)

しゅうかん³ 週間 week ◎ ‖好天はあと1週間続くでしょう Clear weather will continue for another *week*. / 我々は2週間でヨーロッパ6か国を回った We covered six European countries *in two weeks*. / 2, 3週間前に渋谷で有子を見たよ I saw Yuko in Shibuya a couple (of) *weeks ago*. / 私は何週間もまともな食事をとっていない I haven't had a proper meal *for weeks*.
‖交通安全週間 Traffic Safety Week / 読書週間 Book Week

しゅうき¹ 周期 cycle ◎; (期間) period ◎ ―周期的な cyclic; periodic(al) ―周期的に in cycles; periodically ‖肌の細胞は約28日周期で生まれ変わるといわれている The cells of the skin are said to replace themselves *in* about a 28-*day cycle*. / 彼は周期的なうつ状態に悩まされている He suffers from *periodic* nervous breakdowns. / 私の母は周期的にてんかんの発作を起こす My mother has fits of epilepsy *periodically*.
◆来週1週間, お天気は周期的に変わるでしょう The weather next week will *cycle through* rainy and sunny periods.

しゅうき² 臭気 (悪臭) bad smell ◎; (強烈な悪臭) stink ◎, stench ◎ ‖腐った肉から臭気を放っていた The rotten meat was giving off *a bad smell*. / あたりにはひどい臭気が漂っていた There was *an* awful *stench* in the air.
◆その部屋に入ると臭気が鼻をついた When I entered the room, it *stunk*. (✤ stunk は stink「悪臭がする」の過去形)

しゅうき³ 秋季 autumn ◎, fall ◎

-しゅうき ―周忌 the anniversary of *a person's* death ‖きのうは彼の三周忌だった Yesterday was *the second anniversary of* his *death*. (✤「三周忌」は亡くなって2年目なので second という)

しゅうぎ 祝儀 (心づけ) tip ◎, (公式的) gratuity ◎ ‖ご祝儀をはずむ(→ 多額の心づけをあげる) give *a generous tip*

しゅうぎいん 衆議院 the House of Representatives ‖衆議院議員 a representative, a member of the House (of Representatives) / 衆議院議長 the Speaker

しゅうきゅう¹ 週休 weekly holiday ◎ ◆私たちの会社は週休2日制(→週5日制)だ We are on *a five-day* (*work*) *week*. / We work *five days a week*.

しゅうきゅう² 週給 weekly pay ◎, weekly salary ◎
◆僕は週給2万円のバイトをしている I work part-time and *get* 20,000 yen *a week*.

じゅうきょ 住居 (家) house ◎ (複 houses [háuziz]), (公式的) residence ◎ ‖横浜に住居を構えた He「*took up residence* [*settled down*] *in* Yokohama. ◆その村で古代の住居跡が発見された The remains of ancient *dwellings* were found in that village.

しゅうきょう 宗教 religion ◎; (信仰) faith ◎ ―宗教の religious (✤ 名詞の前で用いる)
宗教の自由 freedom of *religion* / 宗教を信じる believe in *religion*
彼女は宗教上の理由から豚肉を食べません She doesn't eat pork *for religious reasons*.
その戦争は宗教的対立から起こった The war started out of *a religious conflict*.
彼の息子は家を飛び出してある新興宗教に入った His son ran away from home and went into *a religious cult*.
🅔「あなたの宗教は何ですか」「仏教です[無宗教です]」 "What's your *religion*?" "I'm a Buddhist. [I *don't have any particular religion*.]"
‖宗教家 (布教活動に従事する人) a person of religion; (熱心な信者) a religious person / 宗教画 a religious painting / 宗教改革 reli-

gious reformation; (16世紀の) **the Reformation** / 宗教裁判(中世の異端審問) **the Inquisition** / 宗教戦争 **a religious war** / 宗教団体 **a religious organization** / 宗教法人 **a religious corporation**

しゅうぎょう¹ 修業 日本の中学校の修業年限は3年です Junior high school in Japan requires three *years of study*.
‖修業証書 **a diploma**

しゅうぎょう² 終業 終業のベルが鳴るまでは席についていなければいけない We have to stay in our seats until *the bell* rings. / 彼女はいつも終業時刻ばかり気にしている She is *a real clock-watcher*.
‖終業時間 (a) **closing time** / 終業式 **an end-of-term ceremony**

しゅうぎょう³ 就業 彼女は正規の就業時間以外は働かない She never works outside regular *working hours*.
‖就業規則 **office regulations**

じゅうぎょういん 従業員 **employee** ◯; (労働者) **worker** ◯; (従業員全体) **the staff, the workforce** / JRの従業員 *a JR employee* / この規則は全従業員に適用される This rule refers to *all the employees*. / その会社は従業員の数を徐々に減らしている The company is gradually running down its *workforce*. / 従業員専用《掲示》 **Staff Only**
‖従業員組合 **an employees' union**

しゅうきょく 終局 (終末) **an end, a close** / その事件もようやく終局を迎えた The case finally *came to an end*.

しゅうきん 集金 **collection of money** ──集金する **collect money**
🔴「どちら様ですか」「新聞の集金です」"Who is it?" "I've come to *collect money* for the paper."
‖集金人 **a (money) collector**

じゅうきんぞく 重金属 **heavy metal** Ｕ ◯

じゅうく 十九 **nineteen**; (19番目) **nineteenth**

ジュークボックス **jukebox** ◯

シュークリーム ⚠**cream puff** ◯ (❖日本語はフランス語の *chou à la crème* から)

じゅうぐん 従軍 ──従軍する **serve in a war** ‖従軍慰安婦 (集合的)**comfort women, women forced into prostitution by the Japanese military during World War II** / 従軍記者 **a war correspondent**

しゅうけい 集計 **totaling** Ｕ ──集計する **add up, total** ◯ /売上金を集計する *add up [total] sales* / 3日間の入場者数を集計すると約10万人にのぼった The number of the visitors *added up [came] to* about a hundred thousand in three days. / ◆公式の集計結果が出た *The official count was announced*.

じゅうけい 重刑 **severe penalty** Ｕ

じゅうけいしょう 重軽傷 その事故で3人が死亡, 20人が重軽傷を負った Three people were killed, and twenty *were injured either severely or slightly* in the accident.

しゅうげき 襲撃 **attack** ◯ Ｕ; (猛攻撃) **assault** ◯ Ｕ; (急襲) **raid** ◯ ──襲撃する **attack** ◯; **assault** ◯; **raid** ◯ /その町は夜明けに襲撃された The city 「*came under attack [was attacked]* at dawn.

じゅうげき 銃撃 **shooting** ◯ ──銃撃する **shoot** ◯ ◯ ◆ 銃撃を始める[やめる] **open [cease] fire**
‖銃撃戦 **a gunfight, a firefight, an exchange of gunfire [shots]**

しゅうけつ¹ 集結 **concentration** Ｕ ◯ ──集結する **concentrate** ◯ ◯, **gather** ◯, 《口語的》**get together** /全国からボランティアが被災地に集結した The volunteers from all over the country *concentrated* at the disaster area.

しゅうけつ² 結 (終わり) **end** ◯ ──終結する **come to an end, end** ◯ /冷戦の終結は新時代の幕あけとなった *The end of the Cold War* marked the beginning of a new epoch. / 人々は戦争の終結を心から願っていた The people longed for the war to *end*.

じゅうけつ 充血 **congestion** Ｕ ──充血した **congested**; (目が) **bloodshot** /目が充血してるよ Your eyes *are bloodshot*.

じゅうご 十五 **fifteen**; (15番目) **fifteenth**

しゅうこう¹ 周航 **cruise** ◯ ──周航する **cruise** ◯ /今度の夏休みは瀬戸内海周航を計画している I'm planning to spend next summer vacation *cruising* the Inland Sea.

しゅうこう² 就航 ラスベガスへは直行便が就航している They have a nonstop flight to Las Vegas. / その船は今度の月曜日に就航する This ship will *set off on its maiden voyage* next Monday.

しゅうごう 集合 **gathering** Ｕ; 《数学》**set** ◯ ──集合する (1か所に) **gather** ◯; (約束して会う) **meet** ◯
あしたは新宿に朝8時集合よ. 遅れないでね We're supposed to *meet* at Shinjuku at 8 a.m. tomorrow. Don't be late!
1時間後ここに集合するということにしよう Let's *meet* here an hour from now.
全員, 集合! *Gather around*, everybody!
集合場所はどこですか *Where are we supposed to meet?*
集合時間と集合場所を確認したいのですが I'd like to confirm *when and where to meet*.
◆もし私が集合時間に来なかったら待たずに先に行ってください If I'm late for *the appointed time*, go ahead and don't wait for me. / 全員集合ですか *Is everybody here?*
‖集合写真 **a group picture** / 集合住宅 **an apartment house** / 集合名詞 ⇒しゅうごうめいし / 集合論 **set theory** / 空集合 **a null set** / 全体集合 **a universal set, a universe** / 部分集合 **a subset**

じゅうこう¹ 重厚 ──重厚な (態度・様子が重々しい) **grave**; (威厳のある) **dignified**; (知識・理解が深い) **profound** /重厚な作品 *a profound work; a work of great depth* / 彼は重厚な人柄だ He has a *dignified* personality.

じゅうこう² 銃口 **muzzle** ◯

じゅうこうぎょう 重工業 heavy industry ⓊⒸ

しゅうごうめいし 集合名詞 〖文法〗collective noun Ⓒ

> (1) 集合名詞は、その集合をまとまった1つのものとみなした場合は単数名詞扱いになり、構成するメンバー一人一人［一つ一つ］を重視した場合は複数扱いになる ▶ How large *is* your family? ご家族が何人ですか(❖家族を1つのまとまりとみなした場合) / My family *are* all early risers. 家族はみんな早起きです(❖家族の一人一人を意識した場合)
> (2) people という名詞は特殊な可算語で、複数扱いにすると「人々」という意味になるが、1つのまとまりとみなして a people のように単数扱いにすると「国民, 民族」という意味になる.
> (3) 集合名詞の中には、police「警察」や cattle「牛」のように形は単数形でも常に複数扱いのものもある.

じゅうごや 十五夜 a night when the moon is full ◆きょうは十五夜だ We have *a full moon* tonight.

ジューサー juicer Ⓒ

しゅうさい 秀才 (頭のいい人) bright [intelligent] person Ⓒ, 《口語的》brain Ⓒ

じゅうざい 重罪 serious crime Ⓒ,〖法律〗felony ⓊⒸ

しゅうさく¹ 習作 study Ⓒ; (特に芸術作品の) etude [eitúːd] Ⓒ

しゅうさく² 秀作 (すぐれた作品) excellent work Ⓒ

じゅうさつ 銃殺 ——銃殺する shoot* to death ◆その元大統領は銃殺刑になった The ex-president *was executed by firing squad*. (❖firing squad は「銃殺隊」の意味)

じゅうさん 十三 thirteen; (13番目) thirteenth

しゅうさんち 集散地 distribution center Ⓒ

しゅうし¹ 収支 (収入と支出) income and expenditure; (収支の差額) balance ▶ 収支を合わせる make (both) ends meet / ‖国際収支 the (international) balance of payments / 貿易収支 balance of trade

しゅうし² 修士 (修士号) master's degree Ⓒ; (文学修士) a Master of Arts (《略語》M.A.); (理学修士) a Master of Science (《略語》M.S.) ▶ 彼はアメリカで経営学の修士号を取った He got「*a master's degree* in business administration [*an M.B.A.*] in the U.S. ❖M.B.A. は Master of Business Administration の略語)
‖修士課程 a master's degree program / 修士論文 a master's thesis [dissertation]

しゅうし³ 終始 (ずっと) throughout; (始めから終わりまで) from beginning to end ▶ ミーティングはお互いの主張に終始した We asserted our points *throughout* the meeting. ◆知事は終始一貫して県内に米軍基地を置くことに反対した The governor *consistently* opposed having the U.S. base in the prefecture.

しゅうじ¹ 習字 (書道) calligraphy ⓊⒸ; (ペン習字) penmanship Ⓤ ▶ 私の妹は週に1回習字を習っている My sister *takes calligraphy lessons* once a week.

しゅうじ² 修辞 rhetoric Ⓤ

じゅうし¹ 重視 ——重視する (重きをおく) attach importance to ...; (重要とみなす) make* much of ...; (真剣に受け止める) take* ... seriously; (強調する) put* emphasis [stress] on ... (❖put の代わりに lay も可) ▶ もっと人間性を重視するべきだ You should *attach* more *importance to* human nature. / 彼は学生の授業の出席を重視します He *makes much of* students' class attendance. / 私たちはその問題を重視している We *take* that matter *seriously*. / その学校は英語教育を重視している The school *puts emphasis [stress] on* English education.

じゅうし² 十四 fourteen; (14番目) fourteenth

じゅうじ¹ 従事 ▶ 彼は酪農に従事している He「*is engaged* [*engages* (*himself*)]*in* dairy farming.

じゅうじ² 十字 cross Ⓒ ▶ 十字を切る *make the sign of the cross*; *cross oneself*
‖十字路 ⇨ じゅうじろ / かぎ十字 (ナチスの) swastika

じゅうじか 十字架 cross Ⓒ ▶ 十字架はキリスト教の象徴だ *The cross* is the symbol of Christianity.
◆イエス・キリストは十字架にかけられた Jesus Christ *was crucified*.

しゅうじぎもん 修辞疑問〖文法〗rhetorical question Ⓒ

じゅうじぐん 十字軍〖歴史〗Crusade Ⓒ; (戦士) crusader Ⓒ

じゅうしち 十七 seventeen; (17番目) seventeenth

しゅうじつ¹ 終日 (一日中) all day (long) ▶ 終日立ちっぱなしだったので足がむくんだ My legs got swollen from standing *all day (long)*.
◆終日禁煙《掲示》*No Smoking Any Time*

しゅうじつ² 週日 (平日) weekday Ⓒ

じゅうじつ 充実 ——充実した full; (満足のいく) satisfactory; (内容のある) substantial ▶ 充実した生活を送る lead a *full* life / 彼は気力が充実している He *is full of* energy. / このCD-ROMはコンテンツが充実している This CD-ROM has a *substantial* data content.
◆わが国は何よりも国民の福祉の充実をはかる(→促進する)べきだ Above all things, we should *promote* the welfare of the citizens. / あの店は品ぞろえが充実していない There's not much choice in that shop.
‖充実感 a sense [feeling] of fulfillment

しゅうしふ 終止符〖文法〗《米》period Ⓒ, 《英》full stop Ⓒ
[慣用表現] 彼らは和平条約を結ぶことで長い紛争の歴史に終止符を打つことができた They were able to *put*「*a period* after [*an end* to] the long history of the dispute by concluding a peace treaty.

しゅうしゅう¹ 収拾 (コントロール) control

Ⓤ; (解決・決着) settlement Ⓤ, solution Ⓤ ─ー収拾する (解決する) settle 他, solve 他 / 会議は収拾がつかなくなった The session *got out of control.* / 彼は事態の収拾をはかろうとした He tried to *settle* things *down.*

しゅうしゅう² 収集 collection Ⓤ Ⓒ (❖「収集物」の意味では Ⓒ) ─ー収集する collect 他 / 外国のコインを収集する *collect* [*make a collection of*] *foreign coins*
‖収集家 a collector / 収集癖 a collecting mania

じゅうじゅう¹ 鉄板の上で肉がじゅうじゅういっている The meat *is sizzling* on the iron plate.

じゅうじゅう² 重々 リスクが大きいことは重々承知しています I know *very well* that there's a high risk.

しゅうしゅく 収縮 (筋肉・金属などの) contraction Ⓤ; (布などの) shrinkage Ⓤ Ⓒ ─ー収縮する contract 自; shrink* 自 / 筋肉の収縮 *the contraction of muscles*

しゅうじゅく 習熟 ─ー習熟した proficient
◆その仕事はフランス語に習熟していることが要求される That job requires *proficiency* in French. / うちの学校では習熟度別の(→生徒の能力に従った)クラス編成になっている In our school, the classes are grouped *according to the students' abilities.*

じゅうじゅん 従順・柔順 obedience Ⓤ ─ー従順な obedient (↔disobedient) ─ー従順に obediently / 父に対して私は従順だった I was *obedient to* my father.

じゅうしょ 住所 address Ⓒ
自宅の住所 *one's* home *address* / 住所不定である have *no fixed address*

ここにあなたの名前と住所を書いてください Please write your name and *address* here.

住所はどちらですか What is *your address*?

私の郵便物をこの住所に転送していただけますか Would you forward my mail to this *address*? (❖「転送先住所」は a forwarding address という)

私は現在の住所に3年間住んでいる I have lived at *my* present *address* for three years.

‖住所変更届 a notification of change of address, a change-of-address notification / 住所録 an address book

しゅうしょう 愁傷 このたびはまことにご愁傷さまでした Please accept my sincere condolences. (❖I'm very sorry (to hear about your grandmother). などというほうがふつう)

じゅうしょう¹ 重症 serious illness Ⓤ
◆彼は重症だ He's *seriously ill.*
‖重症患者 a serious case

じゅうしょう² 重傷 serious [severe] injury Ⓤ / 10人の通行人がその爆発で重傷を負った Ten passers-by *were seriously injured* by the explosion.

しゅうしょく¹ 就職 employment Ⓤ ─ー就職する get* [find*] employment; (職を得る) get [find] a job ⇒ 場面・状況別会話 p.1730 / 会社に就職する *get employment* in a company / 彼は大学卒業後, 銀行に就職した After graduation from college, he *got a job* in a bank. / ここ数年就職難が続いている *It's been hard to get a job* in the last few years.

◆姉は今就職口を探しています My sister is now looking for *a job.* / 父の友人が就職の世話をしてくれた A friend of my father's found me *a job.* / 10名が就職の面接を受けた Ten people were interviewed for *the job.*

🅔「就職先は決まったの?」「いや, 大学院に進もうかと思っているんです」 "Have you *got a job* yet?" "No, I'm thinking of doing graduate study."

‖就職課 (大学の) a placement bureau (of a university) / 就職活動 job hunting / 就職試験 an examination for employment / 就職率 the rate of employment; (大学生の) the percentage of graduates who have found a job

しゅうしょく² 修飾 〖文法〗modification Ⓤ ─ー修飾する 〖文法〗modify 他
‖修飾語(句) a modifier ⇒ ごぶんけい

じゅうしょく 住職 the chief priest (at a Buddhist temple)

じゅうじろ 十字路 (交差点) intersection Ⓒ, crossroads / 次の十字路を右に曲がると郵便局があります If you turn at *the* next *intersection*, you'll see the post office.

しゅうしん¹ 執心 彼女は彼にご執心だ(→夢中になっている) She's *crazy about* him.

しゅうしん² 終身 ‖終身会員 a life member / 終身刑 life imprisonment / 終身雇用 lifetime employment / 終身年金 a lifetime pension

しゅうしん³ 就寝 ─ー就寝する go* to bed
‖就寝時間 (a) bedtime

しゅうじん 囚人 prisoner Ⓒ, inmate Ⓒ; (有罪判決を受けた) convict Ⓒ
‖囚人服 a prison uniform

じゅうしん¹ 重心 〖物理〗the center of gravity / スキーでは重心移動をするのが大切だ In skiing it's important to *shift your center of gravity.* ◆重心を保つ[失う] keep [lose] *one's balance*

じゅうしん² 銃身 barrel Ⓒ

しゅうじんかんし 衆人環視 衆人環視の中(→大勢の目撃者の前で), その事件の容疑者が逮捕された The suspect in that incident was arrested *in front of a lot of witnesses.*

ジュース¹ ⚠(果汁) juice Ⓤ Ⓒ; (清涼飲料水) soft drink Ⓒ (❖果汁100パーセントのものだけを juice と呼ぶ) ‖オレンジ[トマト]ジュース orange [tomato] juice

ジュース² 〖スポーツ〗deuce [djúːs] Ⓤ / ジュースになる go to *deuce*

しゅうせい¹ 修正 (法律などの) amendment Ⓤ Ⓒ; (改訂・改定) revision Ⓤ Ⓒ; (誤りの訂正) correction Ⓤ Ⓒ; (部分的な手直し) modification Ⓤ Ⓒ ─ー修正する amend 他; revise 他; correct 他; modify 他 / 誤りを修正する *correct* an error / その法律は修正の必要がある

That law needs *amendment*. / 私たちは彼の企画に一部修正を加えた We made some *revisions* [*modifications*] to his plan. / 予算案は何度も修正された後, やっと国会を通過した The budget finally passed the Diet after it *had been revised* many times.
‖修正案 an amendment / 修正液 correction fluid, 《米》whiteout / 修正予算 a revised budget

しゅうせい[2] 修整 (写真の) retouch [C] ━修整する retouch [他] ∥その写真はかなり修整されている That picture *is* heavily *retouched*.

しゅうせい[3] 終生 (一生) all *one's* life ━終生の lifelong (❖名詞の前で用いる) ∥彼は終生独身を貫いた He remained single *all his life*.

しゅうせい[4] 習性 habit [U] [C] ∥これらの昆虫は光の周りに集まる習性をもっている These insects have *the habit* of gathering around light.

しゅうせい[5] 集成 (収集) collection [U]; (編纂(へんさん)) compilation [U] [C] ➔ しゅうたいせい

じゅうせい 銃声 shot [C], gunshot [C], 《公式的》the report (of a gun) ∥隣の部屋で銃声が聞こえた I heard *a shot* in the next room.

じゅうぜい 重税 heavy tax [C]; (輸出入の際の) heavy duties ∥国民に重税を課す impose *heavy taxes* on the nation / 人々は重税に苦しんでいた People were suffering from *heavy taxes*.

しゅうせき 集積 accumulation [U] ━集積する accumulate [他], heap [pile] (up) ∥貨物を集積する *accumulate* cargo
‖集積回路 an integrated circuit (《略語》IC)

じゅうせき 重責 heavy responsibility [C] ∥重責をになう shoulder *a heavy responsibility*

しゅうせん[1] 終戦 the end of the war
◆両国間の戦争はようやく終戦を迎えた(→戦争が終わった) *The war* between the two countries *came to an end* at last.
‖終戦記念日 the anniversary of the end of World War II

しゅうせん[2] 周旋 ‖周旋業 brokerage / 周旋屋 a broker

しゅうぜん 修繕 repair [C] [U]; (つくろうこと) mending [U]; (機械などの) 《米口語的》fixing [U] ━修繕する repair [他]; mend [他]; 《米口語的》fix [他] ➔ しゅうり ∥こわれたいすを修繕する *repair* a broken chair

しゅうそ 臭素 〔化学〕 bromine [bróumiːn] [U] (❖元素記号 Br)

じゅうそう[1] 縦走 日本アルプスを縦走する(→アルプスの尾根に沿って歩く) *walk along the ridge* of the Japan Alps

じゅうそう[2] 重曹 〔化学〕 sodium bicarbonate [U], bicarbonate of soda, baking soda [U]

しゅうそく[1] 終息 ━終息する (終わる) end [自], come* to an end ∥ついに内乱は終息した At last the civil war *ended* [*came to an end*].

しゅうそく[2] 収束 ━収束する (収まる) calm down; 〔数学〕 converge [自] ∥事態は収束に向かっている Things *are calming down*.

じゅうぞく 従属 subordination [U] ━従属する be subordinate [subject] (to ...) ∥その国は長い間隣の大国に従属させられた That country *was subordinate to* its large neighbor for a long time.
‖従属国 a dependency / 従属節〔文法〕 a subordinate [dependent] clause / 従属接続詞〔文法〕 a subordinating conjunction
➔ せつぞくし

しゅうたい 醜態 disgraceful [shameful] behavior [U] ◆人前で醜態を演じる *behave disgracefully* [*shamefully*] in public

じゅうたい[1] 渋滞 (交通の) traffic jam [C], holdup [C] ➔ まひ ∥渋滞に巻き込まれる get caught in *a traffic jam* / 渋滞で動きがとれない be stuck in *a traffic jam* / 6号線はひどく渋滞している There is *a* terrible *traffic jam* on Route 6. / こっちへ行けば渋滞が避けられるよ If you go this way, you can avoid *the traffic jam*.

じゅうたい[2] 重体・重態 serious [critical] condition [U] (《また a ～》) ∥彼女は癌(がん)で重体です She *is* 「*in* (*a*) *serious condition* [*seriously ill*] with cancer.

じゅうたい[3] 縦隊 file [C], column [C] ∥2列縦隊で行進する march *in double file* [*columns*] (❖「4列縦隊で」なら march in fours)

じゅうだい[1] 重大 (重要性) importance [U]; (深刻) seriousness [U], 《公式的》gravity [U]; (危機) crisis [C] ━重大な important; serious, grave; critical ➔ じゅうよう
重大な誤り a *serious* [*grave*] fault / 重大な局面を迎える 「come to [reach] *a crisis*
これは重大な問題だ This is an *important* [a *serious*] problem.
我々の計画にとって重大な決定がなされた An *important* decision for our project was made.
君の責任は重大だ You have a *serious* responsibility.
その時点ではだれも事の重大さに気づいていなかった Nobody realized *the gravity* of the situation at that time.
‖重大事件 a serious affair

じゅうだい[2] 十代 *one's* teens ∥彼女は10代で子供を産んだ She had a baby *in her teens*.
◆聴衆の多くは10代だった Many of the audience were *teenagers*.

> [英作文ノート] 10代後半は「ハイティーン」?
> 彼女は今10代後半だ
> →×She is now in her *high teen*.
> →○She is now in her *late teens*.
> ★英語の teens は, 厳密には数に -teen の付く13歳から19歳までを表す. 英語では「ハイティーン」,「ローティーン」とはいわず, late teens, early teens と表現する. teens と複数でいうことにも注意.

しゅうたいせい 集大成 compilation [C] [U] ━集大成する compile [他] ∥この本は彼の長年にわたるバルザック研究の集大成である This book is *a compilation* of his many years of research on Balzac.

じゅうたく 住宅 (集合的) housing ⓤ; (一戸建て) house ⓒ (複 houses [háuziz])

住宅事情を改善する improve *the housing conditions*

近所に新しい住宅が建った *A new house* was built near us.

その火事で住宅2棟が全焼した Two *houses* were totally destroyed by the fire.

東京では住宅問題が緩和しつつある *The housing problem* is getting less serious in Tokyo.

大都市では住宅難が深刻な問題になっている *Housing shortages* have been a serious problem in the big cities.

‖住宅金融公庫 the Housing Loan Corporation / 住宅地 a residential area / 住宅手当 a housing allowance / 住宅都市整備公団 the Housing and Urban Development Corporation / 住宅ローン a home loan, a mortgage / 公営住宅 public housing / 2世帯住宅 two-generation housing

じゅうだつ 収奪 ──奪する take*-away ‖人々から土地を収奪する *take* land *away from* people

しゅうだん 集団 group ⓒ (✱(英)では単数形で複数扱いになることがある); (群集) mass ⓒ; (目的などを共にする比較的小さな集まり) band ⓒ; (暴力的な群れ) 《軽蔑的》mob ⓒ
➡だんたい

反逆者の小さな集団 *a* small *band* of rebels

私は集団で行動するのは好きじゃない I don't like to do things *in a group*.

20キロ地点で健男は先頭集団から飛び出した Takeo broke away from *the leading group* [*pack*] at the 20 kilometer mark.

子供たちは集団登校している Children *go to school in groups*.

弟は林間学校で初めて集団生活を経験した My brother experienced *living in a group* for the first time at the open-air school.

‖集団安全保障 collective security / 集団虐殺 mass murder / 集団検診 a group medical examination / 集団自殺 mass suicide / 集団食中毒 mass food poisoning / 集団療法 group therapy

じゅうたん 絨毯・絨緞 (床全面に敷く) carpet ⓒ; (一部に敷く) rug ⓒ ‖床に赤いじゅうたんを敷いた We spread [laid] *a* red *carpet* over the floor. ‖彼のマンションの床には高そうなじゅうたんが敷き詰めてあった The floor of his apartment was covered with *a carpet* that looked expensive.

‖じゅうたん爆撃 carpet bombing

じゅうだん¹ 銃弾 bullet ⓒ ‖市長の家に数発の銃弾が撃ち込まれた A few *bullets* were shot into the mayor's house. ‖彼は頭に銃弾を受けた He took *a bullet* in his head.

じゅうだん² 縦断 ──する go* [run*] through ‖その地下鉄は都心部を縦断している The subway *runs through* the center of the city. ‖いつか自転車で日本列島を縦断してみたい Someday I want to *go* [*travel*] *through* the Japanese islands by bicycle.

◆オレンジの縦断面 *a vertical cross-section* of an orange

しゅうち¹ 周知 周知の事実 a *well-known* fact / 周知のとおり, 鷗外は漱石と同時代の文豪である *As everybody knows*, Ogai was a great writer who was a contemporary of Soseki.

しゅうち² 衆知 衆知を集める(→多くの人に助言を求める)「*ask counsel of* [*take counsel from*] many people

しゅうちしん 羞恥心 (a sense of) shame ‖彼には羞恥心というものがない He is without *shame*./ He has no *shame*.

しゅうちゃく 執着 persistence ⓤ, tenacity ⓤ; (愛着) attachment ⓒⓤ ──執着する cling* ⓘ, persist ⓘ; be attached ‖地位に執着する *cling to one's* post ‖多くの宗教が執着を捨てるよう説いている Many religions advocate that people should give up *their attachments*. ‖彼女は金もうけへの執着心が強い(→金もうけに固執している) She is「*persistent in* [(→ 取りつかれている) *obsessed with*] making money.

しゅうちゃくえき 終着駅 terminal (station) ⓒ, 《口語的》last stop ⓒ, terminus ⓒ (複 termini, ～es)

しゅうちゅう 集中 concentration ⓤⓒ ──集中する concentrate ⓜⓘ, center ⓜⓘ

…に注意[精力]を集中する *concentrate one's* attention [*energy*] *on* … ‖大都市への人口集中 *the concentration of population* in big cities

そのとき私は食べることだけに神経を集中していた I *focused my concentration on* nothing but eating at that time.

もっと勉強に集中しなさい *Concentrate* more *on your* work.

彼の外交政策に人々の非難が集中した People's criticism *centered on* his foreign policy.

彼は試合に備えて気持ちを集中させている He *is building up his concentration* in preparation for the game.

僕は何に対しても飽きっぽい. 集中力が足りないのだろうか I get tired of everything quickly. I wonder if I lack *concentration* [*the ability to concentrate*].

どんなスポーツも集中力を養ってくれる All kinds of sports develop *your concentration* [*ability to concentrate*].

◆英文法の集中講座 *an intensive course* in English grammar / 彼は1つのことに集中できない He *can't keep his mind on* one thing./ 彼はマスコミから集中攻撃[砲火]を浴びた He *came under heavy fire* from the media./ The media *concentrated its criticism* on him.

‖集中豪雨 a local downpour / 集中治療室 an intensive care unit (《略語》ICU) / 集中爆撃 intensive bombing

しゅうちょう 酋長 chieftain ⓒ, chief ⓒ

じゅうちん 重鎮 dominant [influential] figure ⓤ, heavyweight ⓒ

しゅうてん 終点 terminal ⓒ, terminus (複 termini, ~es), the last station [stop], the end of the line ∥終点の1つ手前で降りなさい Get off at the next to *the last stop*. ◆このバスの終点は渋谷です(→渋谷へ行く) This bus *goes to* Shibuya.

じゅうてん 重点 (強調) stress ⓤ, accent ⓤ, emphasis ⓒⓤ (複 emphases) ∥この番組の重点は環境問題にある *The emphasis* of this program is on environmental issues. / 井田先生は授業で英文法に重点をおいている Mr. Ida *puts emphasis* [*stress*] *on* English grammar in his class. (❖ put の代わりに place, lay も可)
◆英語を重点的に(→集中的に)勉強しよう Let's study English *intensively*.

じゅうでん 充電 charge ⓒ ——充電する charge ⓥ ∥バッテリーは今充電中です The battery *is being charged* now.
◆この電気かみそりは充電式です This electric shaver is *rechargeable* [*cordless*]. / 彼らは2年の充電期間の後で活動を再開した They restarted their activities after *recharging their batteries* for two years.
∥充電器 a (battery) charger

しゅうでん(しゃ) 終電(車) the last train ∥急がないと終電に乗り遅れるよ Hurry up or you'll miss *the last train*.

しゅうと 舅 father-in-law ⓒ (複 fathers-in-law, ~s)

シュート (サッカーなどの) shot [ʃát] ⓒ; (野球のシュートボール) screwball ⓒ ——シュートする shoot* ⓥ, make* [take*] a shot ∥シュートを失敗する miss *a shot* / (サッカーで)孝が試合終了寸前にすばらしいシュートを決めた Takashi *shot* [*kicked*] *a beautiful goal* just before the end of the game. (❖ バスケットボールの場合なら made a beautiful shot という)
∥ダンクシュート a dunk shot / ロングシュート a long shot

しゅうとう 周到 ——周到な (注意深い) careful; (慎重に・冷静な) prudent, scrupulous ——周到に carefully; prudently, scrupulously / 周到な計画 a *careful* [*well thought-out*] plan / あいつは用意周到な男だ He's a *prudent* guy.

じゅうとう 充当 appropriation ⓤ ——充当する appropriate ⓥ, allot ⓥ ⇒あてる(充てる) ∥彼らは利益を施設費に充当した They *appropriated* [*allotted*] the profits *for* the facility cost.

じゅうどう 柔道 [図] judo ⓤ ∥柔道をする practice *judo* / 僕は柔道初段です I have a first *dan* rank in *judo*.

🅒「いつから柔道を始めたの」「去年からです」 "Since when *have* you *been practicing judo*?" "Since last year."

∥柔道着 a *judogi*, a judo uniform

日本の伝統武道である柔道は、単に肉体を鍛えるというより、精神鍛練と護身に重点をおいています。主な柔道の技に投げ技・固め技・当て技がありますが、公式の試合では最初の2つだけを用います。柔道は1964年よりオリンピック公式種目となっており、現在は世界中に愛好家がいます。
Judo is one of the traditional Japanese martial arts. Stress is laid on moral training and self-defense rather than simply on physical strength. Among the main *waza* (techniques) of judo are *nagewaza* (throwing), *katamewaza* (grappling) and *atemiwaza* (attacking vital points), but only the first two are used in official competition. Judo has been included in the Olympics since 1964 and is now popular worldwide.

しゅうどういん 修道院 religious house ⓒ; (男性の) monastery ⓒ; (女性の) convent ⓒ
関連語 修道士 a monk, a brother / 修道女 a nun, a sister

しゅうとく¹ 習得 acquisition ⓤ ——習得する acquire ⓥ; (熟達する) master ⓥ; (学ぶ) learn* ⓥ ∥言語習得の過程 the process of language *acquisition* / 外国語を習得するには忍耐が必要だ You need the patience to *master* a foreign language.

しゅうとく² 拾得 ——拾得する (見つける) find* ⓥ; (拾う) pick up ⇒ひろう(拾う) ∥拾得物は交番に届けるべきだ You should take *something found* to a police box.
∥拾得者 a finder

しゅうとく³ 修得 ——修得する (単位などを取る) earn ⓥ, get* ⓥ

しゅうとめ 姑 mother-in-law ⓒ (複 mothers-in-law, ~s)

じゅうなん 柔軟 (柔軟性) flexibility ⓤ ——柔軟な (融通のきく) flexible, elastic; (体が) supple; (態度が) soft ——柔軟に flexibly ⇒やわらかい ∥柔軟な考え方 a *flexible* [an *elastic*] way of thinking / 柔軟路線をとる take *a soft line* / 柔軟な体を保つためには運動を怠らないこと You should exercise whenever possible in order to keep「your body *supple* [yourself *supple*]. / どんな問題にも柔軟に対処することが必要だ You need to deal with all kinds of problems *flexibly*.
∥柔軟剤(洗濯用) a conditioner / 柔軟体操 stretching

じゅうに 十二 twelve; (12番目) twelfth
∥十二使徒 the (Twelve) Apostles / 12進法 the duodecimal system

じゅうにがつ 十二月 December ⓤ ⓒ (《略語》Dec.) ⇒いちがつ

じゅうにきゅう 十二宮 ∥黄道十二宮 the twelve signs of the zodiac

じゅうにし 十二支 the twelve signs of the Japanese zodiac ⇒えと

じゅうにしちょう 十二指腸 [解剖] duodenum [djùːədíːnəm] ⓒ (複 duodena) ∥十二指腸潰瘍(かいよう) [医学] a duodenal ulcer

じゅうにぶん 十二分 その実験は十二分の成果

をあげた The experiment gave *more than enough* results. / もう十二分にいただきました I've had *quite enough*. ⇨ じゅうぶん(十分)

しゅうにゅう 収入 income ◯ ◯; (稼ぎ高) earnings; (歳入) (公式的) revenue ◯ ◯
収入に見合った[以上の]生活をしていく live within [beyond] one's *income*
彼女は2か所から収入がある She has two *incomes*.
山田家は収入が多い The Yamadas have *a large income*.
兄は月30万円の収入がある My brother has *an income* of 300,000 yen a month. / (稼ぐ) My brother *earns* 300,000 yen a month.
私は自分の収入では暮らしていけない I can't live on my *income*.
彼は収入のすべてを競馬につぎ込んでしまった He put all *his income* into horse racing.
彼の収入は4年前の2倍になった His *income* is double what it was four years ago.
◆収入は手取り[税込み]でいくらですか What do you *earn* after [before] taxes?
‖収入印紙 a revenue stamp / 収入源 a source of income / 総収入 gross income / 定収入 a fixed [steady, regular] income / 年間収入 annual income / 副収入 a subsidiary income / 臨時収入 extra income

しゅうにん 就任 (公式的) assumption ◯ ◯; (大統領などの) inauguration ◯ ◯ 就任する take* [enter upon, come* into] office, assume ⊕; be inaugurated /彼は大統領に就任した He *was inaugurated as president*. / 鈴木氏が次期全日本チームの監督に就任することが決まった It was decided that Mr. Suzuki would *take office as* the next manager of the all-Japan team.
‖就任演説 an inaugural address / 就任式 an inauguration

じゅうにん 住人 (長期にわたる) inhabitant ◯; (在住者) resident ◯; (借家人) tenant ◯ ⇨ じゅうみん / きょうからは君もこの町の住人だ You are *an inhabitant* of this town starting today.

じゅうにんといろ 十人十色 ことわざ Different strokes for different folks. (→違う人には違うやり方で); To each his own. (→人それぞれの好みがある)

じゅうにんなみ 十人並み 僕の妹の器量は十人並み (→ふつう)だ My sister 「is *average-looking* [has *average* looks]. / 彼の絵の才能は十人並み (→平均) 以上[以下]だ His talent for art is above [below] *the average*. / He is above [below] *the average* in art.

しゅうねん 執念 (しつこさ) persistence
━━執念深い persistent, tenacious; (復讐 (ふくしゅう) 心に燃えた) revengeful; (うらみを忘れない) vindictive ━━執念深く persistently, tenaciously /彼女は執念深い人だ She is a *tenacious* person. / 彼は自分をふった女性を執念深く捜し回った He searched *tenaciously* for the woman who had turned him down.
◆彼らは再び優勝することに執念を燃やしている They 「are *enthusiastic about* [*devote all of their energies to*] winning the championship again.

-しゅうねん -周年 anniversary ◯ /きょうはわが校の開校10周年記念です Today is *the 10th anniversary* of the foundation of our school. / 両親は結婚20周年を祝った My parents celebrated *their 20th wedding anniversary*.

じゅうねん 十年 ten years; (10年間) decade ◯
慣用表現 その学者は十年一日 (いちじつ) のごとく (→何年も何の変化もなく) ナマズの研究を続けている The scholar has been studying catfish *for years without any change*. / 十年ひと昔だ (→この10年の間に多くのものが変わった) *Many things have changed during the past ten years.*

しゅうのう 収納 (貯蔵・保管) storage ◯ ━━収納する store ⊕, put* away /この部屋には本を収納するスペースが足りない There isn't enough space in this room to *store* the books.
‖収納庫 a repository

しゅうは 宗派 (分派) sect ◯; (教派) denomination ◯ (❖sect よりも大きい) /葬儀の執(と)り行われ方は宗派によって異なる The way funerals are conducted varies among *sects*.

しゅうはい 集配 collection and delivery ━━集配する collect and deliver /あなたの地区では郵便の集配は日に何度ありますか How many times a day is the mail *collected and delivered* in your area?
‖集配人 (米) a (mail) carrier, a mailman (❖性差別を避けるため a (mail) carrier を使うほうがよい); (英) a postman, a postwoman

じゅうばこ 重箱 a jubako, a tier of lacquerware boxes
慣用表現 こんな重箱の隅をつつく (→ささいなことにこだわる) ような議論はやめよう Let's stop discussing this. It's just 「*splitting hairs* [(→あら探しをする) *nitpicking*].

しゅうバス 終バス the last bus /終バスは何時に出ますか What time does *the last bus* leave?

しゅうはすう 周波数 [物理] frequency ◯ / このラジオ局は周波数96.5メガヘルツで放送している This radio station is broadcasting on *a frequency* of 96.5 megahertz.

じゅうはち 十八 eighteen; (18番目) eighteenth ‖18金 eighteen-karat gold
慣用表現 ホットケーキ作りが彼の十八番だ His *specialty* is cooking pancakes.

しゅうばん¹ 終盤 final [last] stage ◯ /試合は終盤戦に突入した The game entered *its final stage*. / 選挙戦は終盤にさしかかっている The election campaign is reaching *the last stage*.

しゅうばん² 週番 weekly duty ◯ ◆今週の週番はだれですか Who is *on duty this week*?

じゅうはん 重版 reprint ◯

じゅうびょう 重病 serious illness ◯, seri-

しゅうふく 修復 (老朽化した物の改修) renovation; (復元) restoration ——修復する renovate; restore ‖その絵は今修復中だ The picture *is* now *being restored*. / 大聖堂は修復工事のため閉まっている The cathedral is closed for *restoration work*.

じゅうふく 重複 (繰り返し) repetition; (部分的な重なり) overlap ——重複する repeat; overlap ⇒ちょうふく

しゅうぶん¹ 秋分 the autumnal equinox [í:kwinəks] ◆秋分の日 *Autumnal Equinox Day*

しゅうぶん² 醜聞 scandal ⇒スキャンダル ‖醜聞をもみ消す cover [hush] up *a scandal* / その醜聞が元で,彼は辞任した The *scandal* caused him to resign.

じゅうぶん¹ 十分 ——十分な enough, sufficient; (ありあまるほどの) ample; (目的が果たせる) adequate; (よい) good ——十分に enough, sufficiently; adequately; well; (きちんと) fully ⇒ふじゅうぶん

【語法】形容詞の enough は,ふつう修飾する語の前に置くのに対し,副詞の enough は,必ず修飾する語の後に置く ‖僕はそのテープを買うのに十分なお金を持っている I have *enough* money to buy that tape. / この部屋の広さなら15人入るのに十分だ This room is large *enough* for 15 people.

2,000円もあれば十分です Two thousand yen will be *enough*.

健康には十分注意しなさい Take *good* care of your health.

彼女が病気だということは十分分かっています I know *very well* that she is sick.

彼らにはその試合に勝つチャンスが十分あった They had a *good* chance of winning the game.

その問題については十分議論が尽くされるべきだ The problem must be *fully* discussed.

翻訳では外国文学のよさが十分に味わえない We can't *fully* appreciate foreign literature in translation.

彼は十分に責務を果たした He discharged his duty *fully*.

6時にここを出ればその電車に十分間に合うよ We'll have *enough* [*ample, plenty of*] time to catch the train if we leave here at six.

◆私はこの結果に十分満足している I am *perfectly* content with this result.

🅒「卵が2個しかないよ」「それで十分だ」"I have only two eggs." "That'll be *enough*."

🅒「もう少しケーキをいかがですか」「ありがとう。十分にいただきました」"Would you like some more cake?" "No, thank you. I've had *enough*."

‖十分条件〖論理〗a sufficient condition

じゅうぶん² 重文〖文法〗compound sentence

しゅうへん 周辺 (周囲) surroundings; (付近) vicinity; (近隣) neighborhood ——周辺の surrounding ‖その海域[国々] the *surrounding* seas [countries] / その野鳥は私たちの学校の周辺で見かけることができます We can see that wild bird in *the vicinity* of our school. / 彼女の家の周辺には緑が多い There is much greenery "*in the neighborhood of* [*around*] her house.

◆土湯温泉周辺の観光地図はありませんか Do you have any tourist maps of *the area around* the Tsuchiyu Hot Springs?

‖周辺機器(コンピュータの) peripheral equipment [device]

じゅうほう 銃砲 gun, firearms
‖銃砲店 a gun shop

シューマイ Chinese steamed dumpling

しゅうまつ¹ 週末 weekend (◆土・日を指すが,金曜の夜から月曜の朝までをいうこともあり) ‖週末のデート a weekend date / 週末に釣りに行く go fishing on [〖英〗at] the weekend / 週末は何をしていたの How did you spend *your weekend*? / 週末に車で軽井沢へ行こう Let's drive to Karuizawa *for the weekend*. / 私は週末いっぱい鎌倉にいるつもりだ I will be in Kamakura *over the weekend*. / 私たちは先週末を祖父母の家で過ごした We spent the *last weekend* at my grandparents' house.

しゅうまつ² 終末 end ‖終末を迎える come to *an end*
‖終末論〖神学〗eschatology, apocalypticism

じゅうまん¹ 十万 a hundred thousand ‖30万 *three hundred thousand* (◆thousand は数詞または数を示す形容詞の後では複数の s を付けない) ‖数十万の人々 hundreds and [*of*] *thousands of* people

じゅうまん² 充満 ‖煙が台所に充満していた The kitchen was filled with smoke.

じゅうみん 住民 (ある場所に長期間住む人) inhabitant; (一時的な居住者) resident; (市民権を持つ) citizen
地元住民は彼らに対して団結した Local *residents* [*people, inhabitants, citizens*] teamed up against the gang.
ほとんどの住民が新空港建設に反対している Most of *the residents* oppose the construction of a new airport.
私はこの町の住民です I'm *a resident* of this town. / (→この町に住んでいる) I *live* in this town.
‖住民運動 a citizens' movement / 住民税 a resident tax / 住民投票 a vote by the residents, a referendum / 住民登録 resident registration / 住民票 a resident card

じゅうみんしゅとう 自由民主党 the Liberal Democratic Party (〖略語〗LDP)

しゅうめい 襲名 彼は24歳のときに辰之助を襲名した He *succeeded to the name of* Tatsunosuke when he was 24.

しゅうもく 衆目 その投手がたぐいまれなる逸材であることは衆目の一致するところだ Every-

body agrees that the pitcher is a man of unusual talent. / The pitcher is, *by common consent*, a man of unusual talent.

じゅうもんじ 十文字 cross [C] ―十文字の cross-shaped ―十文字に crosswise
➾ じゅうじ(十字)

しゅうや 終夜 (一晩中) all night (long); (夜通し) through [all through, throughout] the night ‖ニューヨークでは地下鉄が終夜運転している The subway *runs through the night* in New York.
◆家の近くに終夜営業の酒屋がある There is an *all-night* liquor shop near my house.

しゅうやく 集約 ―集約する (1つにする) bring* together, unite [他]; (要約する) summarize [他] [自] ‖様々な意見を集約する *bring* various opinions *together* / このひと言に彼の全思想が集約されている His entire philosophy *is summarized* in this single word.
‖集約農業 intensive agriculture

じゅうやく 重役 executive [igzékjətiv] [C], director [C] ‖重役会 a board of directors

じゅうゆ 重油 (重質油) heavy oil [U]; (燃料油) fuel oil [U]

しゅうゆう 周遊 (circular) tour [C], 《英》 round trip [C], excursion [C] ‖私たちは去年, 九州周遊の旅に出かけた We 「*went on a tour of* [*traveled around*] Kyushu last year.
◆彼女は今ヨーロッパを周遊中だ She *is touring* Europe now.
‖周遊券 an excursion ticket, 《英》 a circular ticket

しゅうよう[1] 収容 accommodation [U] [C] ―収容する (入る) hold* [他], accommodate [他], contain [他]; (座席がある) seat [他] ‖そのホールは500人収容できる The hall can *seat* [*hold*] 500 people.
◆遺体を収容する *recover* bodies / 負傷者は近くの病院に収容された(→運ばれた) The injured *were taken to* nearby hospitals.
‖収容所(難民の) a refugee camp; (強制収容所) a concentration camp / 収容力 (a seating) capacity

しゅうよう[2] 修養 彼は精神修養のために座禅を組んだ He practiced *zazen* in order to *mold* [*form*] *himself mentally*.

じゅうよう 重要

(重要性) importance [U], significance [U] ―重要な important, significant; (不可欠な) vital, essential; (かぎを握る) key

人命救助が何よりも重要です Saving human lives is the most *important* thing. / The most *important* thing is to save human lives.

彼は日本における農業の重要性を強調した He emphasized *the importance* of agriculture in Japan.

彼はその事実を重要視している He *attaches importance to* that fact.

教育は政治にとって重要な要素である Education is an *important* element of government.

結果よりも過程のほうが重要だ The process is more *important* than the result.

自動車産業はこの市の経済にきわめて重要な役割を果たしている The automobile industry plays a *vital* [*key*] role in the economy of this city.

◆重要な転機を迎える take a *serious* turn / 外見はそれほど重要ではない Appearance *is not* what really *counts* [*matters*]. / あした雨が降るかどうかは, 私たちにとってとても重要だ It *makes a* great *difference* to us whether it rains [will rain] tomorrow.
‖重要参考人 a material witness / 重要書類 important papers / 重要人物 a very important person (《略語》VIP) / 重要文化財 an important cultural property / 重要文書 an important document / 重要無形文化財 an important intangible cultural property

しゅうらい 襲来 ―襲来する (敵が) attack [他] [自]; (災害などが) hit* [他]; (侵入する) invade [他] [自] ➾ おそう ‖津波がその島に襲来した A tsunami *hit* the island.

じゅうらい 従来 ―従来の (慣習による) conventional; (伝統的な) traditional; (前の) previous, former ‖女性の役割についての従来の考え方 *traditional* [*conventional*] views about the roles of women / その新しい車は従来の車とどう違うのですか What differentiates the new car from the *previous* models? ◆大会は従来どおりこの体育館で行われます The meet will be held at this gym *as usual*. / この問題は従来から(→長い間)指摘されていた This problem has *long* been pointed out.

しゅうらく 集落 (村) village [C]; (小さな村) hamlet [C]

しゅうり 修理 repair [C] [U], 《米口語的》 fixing [U]; (比較的簡単な) mending [U] ―修理する repair [他], 《米口語的》 fix [他]; mend [他]

この靴は修理が必要だ These shoes need *repair* [*mending*].

このテレビを修理してくれませんか Can you *fix* this TV?

車を修理するのにこんなにお金がかかるとは思わなかった I didn't expect that it would cost this much to *repair* my car.

その橋は修理中です The bridge is *under repair*.

この車は修理不可能だ This car is *beyond repair*.

私はこわれたパソコンを修理に出した I *sent* my broken computer *out for repairs*.

私は時計を修理してもらった I *had* my watch *repaired*.

自転車を修理してほしいのですが I'd like to *have* my bicycle *repaired* [*fixed*].

‖修理工 a repairman / 修理工場 a repair shop; (車の) a garage

しゅうりょう[1] 修了 completion [U] ―修了する finish [他], complete [他] ➾ おえる ‖…の全課程を修了する *finish* [*complete*] the whole course of … / 彼は博士課程を修了し

た He *completed* [*passed through*] the doctoral course.
‖修了証書 a certificate, a diploma

しゅうりょう[2] 終了 end [C] ━終了する end [自] [他], finish [他] [自]; (話・会など) close [他] [自], 《公式的》conclude [他] [自] ⇒ おえる, おわる ∥会議は4時に終了した The meeting *concluded* [*was closed*] at four. / 2時までにこの作業を終了しなければならない We must *finish* this work before 2 o'clock. / 建設工事はほぼ終了している The construction work *is* practically *finished*. / 長く続いた試合が終了したのは真夜中だった It was at midnight when the long game *came to an end*. / その試合の終了時刻(→試合が終わるの)は4時ごろです The game will *end* [*be over*] around four.

じゅうりょう 重量 weight [U] ⇒ おもさ ∥このノートパソコンの重量は約2キログラムだ This notebook computer is about two kilograms in *weight*. / This notebook computer *weights* about two kilograms.
◆この時計は重量感のあるシンプルな材質でできている The watch is made of *sturdy* and simple materials. / 彼は500グラム重量オーバーで失格になった He was *overweight* by 500 grams and disqualified.
‖重量挙げ〘スポーツ〙weight lifting / 重量級 the heavyweight division / 重量制限 a weight limit

じゅうりょく 重力 gravity [U], gravitation [U] (❖gravity は地球の重力に, gravitation は物体間の力に用いる) ∥重力の法則に従う obey the law of *gravity*
◆宇宙飛行士は無重力状態の中で生活する Astronauts live in *a state of weightlessness*.

シュール ⚠ ━シュールな surrealistic [sərì(ː)əlístik] (❖日本語はフランス語の surréalisme を省略したもの)
‖シュールレアリスム〘芸術〙surrealism

じゅうれつ 縦列 column [C], file [C] ∥縦列で歩く walk *in a file*
‖縦列駐車 parallel parking

しゅうれっしゃ 終列車 the last train

しゅうれん 修練・修錬 修練を積む *go into training*; *discipline oneself*

しゅうろう 就労 ‖就労時間 working hours / 就労日数 the number of workdays [working days] / 就労ビザ a work(ing) visa / 不法就労者 an illegal worker

じゅうろうどう 重労働 hard work [U]

しゅうろく 収録 recording [U] ━収録する record [他]; (本などに) contain [他] ∥その音楽はステレオで収録されている The music *is recorded* in stereo. / このCD-ROMには辞書が4冊収録されている This CD-ROM *contains* four dictionaries.

じゅうろく 十六 sixteen; (16番目) sixteenth

しゅうわい 収賄 taking a bribe, 《主に米》graft [U] ━収賄する take* [accept] a bribe, 《主に米》graft [自] ∥収賄を否認する deny *taking a bribe* / 国会議員が収賄で免職になった A member of the Diet was removed from his seat for *taking bribes*. / 彼は裁判にかけられて収賄罪に問われた He was tried and convicted of *graft*.
‖収賄事件 a bribery scandal

しゅえい 守衛 guard [C], keeper [C]; (門番) doorkeeper [C]; (学校などの施設の) custodian [C]

じゅえきしゃ 受益者〘法律〙beneficiary [C]
‖受益者負担 the beneficiary's payment share

しゅえん[1] 主演 (男優) the leading actor; (女優) the leading actress ━主演する star [自], play the lead ∥その映画はブラッド・ピットが主演した The movie *starred* Brad Pitt. / Brad Pitt *starred* [*played the lead*] *in* the movie.
◆北野武主演の映画 a film *starring* [*featuring*] Kitano Takeshi (❖この star は他動詞で「…を主演させる」の意味) / 2001年度アカデミー主演女優賞 *the* 2001 *Academy Award for Best Actress*

しゅえん[2] 酒宴 drinking party [C]; (正式の宴会) banquet [C] ∥酒宴を張る *hold a drinking party*

しゅかく 主格〘文法〙nominative [U], subjective [U], the nominative [subjective] case ━主格の nominative, subjective
‖主格補語 a subject [subjective] complement

しゅかん[1] 主観 subjectivity [U] ━主観的な subjective ━主観的に subjectively ∥主観的に判断する judge *subjectively* / 君の考えは主観的すぎるよ I think your idea is too *subjective*. / 私は主観を交えずに判断したつもりだ I judged it 「*without being subjective* [(→客観的に) *objectively*].
◆実際, 主観を離れる(→客観的でいる)ことは容易なことではない In fact, it's difficult for us to *be objective*.

しゅかん[2] 主幹 chief [C] ‖編集主幹 the editor in chief

しゅがん 主眼 (主な目的) the main purpose, the chief aim, keynote [C] ∥この政策の主眼は景気の早期回復にある *The main purpose* of this policy is to make the economy recover quickly.

しゅき[1] 手記 (覚え書き) note [C]; (体験記) memoirs [mémwɑːrz] ∥手記を書く write *memoirs*

しゅき[2] 酒気 酒気を帯びている *smell of alcohol* / 彼は酒気帯び運転でつかまった He was caught for *drunk driving*.

しゅぎ 主義 (生活や行動の方針) principle [C] [U]; (個人や社会の大義) cause [C]; (習慣) rule [C]

主義に殉じる die for *one's cause*
それは僕の主義に反する It's against my *principles*.
彼は自分の主義にあくまで忠実だった He stood true to his *principles*. / (→決して主義を曲げなかった) He never compromised his *principles*.

し

彼女は肉類はいっさい食べない主義だ It's *her principle* [*rule*] never to eat meat./ She doesn't eat meat in any form *on principle*.

あの政党は主義主張がはっきりしない That political party does not have well-defined *ideas or principles*.

◆あの病院はもうけ主義だ(→金もうけだけのために運営されている) That hospital *is run only for making money*.

じゅきゅう[1] 需給 (需要と供給) supply and demand(❖日本語とは語順が逆になる)

じゅきゅう[2] 受給 ━受給する receive [他] // 年金を受給する *receive* [*draw*] *one's* pension ‖年金受給者 a recipient of a pension, a pensioner

しゅぎょう[1] 修行 (禁欲的な苦行) ascetic [əsétik] practices; (訓練) training [U]《また a ～》 //彼は師匠から修行が足りないと言われた His master told him that he needed more *training*.

◆山にこもって厳しい修行を積む seclude *oneself* in the mountains to *practice* severe *asceticism*

‖修行僧 a Buddhist ascetic

しゅぎょう[2] 修業 discipline [U], training [U]《また a～》 //彼女は現在花嫁修業中だ She is now undergoing *training in housekeeping*.

◆そのシェフはイタリアで料理の修業を積んできたそうだ They say that the chef *was trained in* cooking in Italy.

じゅきょう 儒教 Confucianism [U] ━儒教の Confucian

[関連語] 儒者 a Confucian, a Confucianist

じゅぎょう 授業

(時間割の単位) class [C]; (学校での授業全体) school [U]; (授業の内容) lesson [C]

英会話の授業 *an* English conversation *class* / 授業に出る attend *classes* / 授業でノートをとる take notes in *class*

きょうの午後は授業がない We *have no classes* [*school*] this afternoon.

きょうは授業が正午に終わる *School* ends at 12 noon today.

授業が始まる前に黒板を消してください Please erase the blackboard before *class*.

授業は週に何時間ありますか How many *classes* are there in the [a] school week?

僕は授業についてゆけない I can't keep up with *the lessons* [*class*].

授業に追いつくために一生懸命勉強した I studied hard in order to catch up with *the class*.

きょうの授業はよく分かった I understood today's *lesson* well.

私たちの学校の1こまの授業時間は90分です Each *class* [*period*] is 90 minutes at our school.

私たちの学校の授業時間は朝の8時から昼の3時までです Our *school hours* are from eight in the morning to three in the afternoon.

授業中におしゃべりしてはいけません Don't talk *in* [*during*] *class*.

私たちの学校では授業用にパソコンを20台購入した Our school purchased 20 PCs *for class use*.

◆宮田先生は今, 3組の授業中です(→3組を教えています) Ms. Miyata *is teaching* Class 3 now. / 鎌田先生は授業がうまい(→よい先生だ) Mr. Kamata *is a good teacher*./ (→教えるのがうまい)Mr. Kamata *is good at teaching*.

💬「数学の授業は何時間目だっけ」「5時間目よ」 "Which period is math *class*?" "Fifth."

💬「あいつまた英語の授業をサボったんだ」「そんなことだろうと思ったよ」 "He *cut* [*skipped*] English *class* again." "I thought so."

‖授業参観日 Parents' Day, class observation day (❖class observation day は説明的な訳. 米国では学校によって呼び名が異なる) / 授業料 school fees; (大学・個人授業の)《米》tuition (fee) / 課外授業 an extra curricular lesson [class] / 短縮授業 shortened school hours / 補習授業 a supplementary lesson [class]

しゅぎょく 珠玉 gem [C] ◆珠玉の名曲 an *excellent* piece of music

じゅく 塾 🗻 a *juku* (school), a private supplementary school; (受験などのための短期間の) cram school [C] (❖cram は「詰め込む」という意味) //彼は週に3日塾に通っている He goes to *cram school* three times a week. / きょうは学校が終わったら塾へ行かなくてはならない I have to go to (*a*) *juku* [*private supplementary school*] after school today.

‖塾長 the head of a *juku* / 進学塾(高校への) a cram school to prepare for entrance exams for high school; (大学への) a private preparatory school / そろばん塾 a private abacus school

> 塾は学校での授業の補習, または受験のための強化授業を行う民間の学校です. 主に小・中学生が通いますが, 学校が終わってから塾に行き帰宅は夜遅くということもしばしばです. また, 週末に行くこともあります. 高校生や卒業生は大学入試に備えて, 予備校と呼ばれる学校に通うようになります.
>
> A *juku* is a private school where students receive remedial or advanced lessons useful for entrance examinations. Mainly elementary and junior high school students go to *juku* after regular school, sometimes staying until late at night. Some even go on weekends. In addition, many high school students and graduates go to schools called *yobiko* to prepare themselves for university entrance examinations.

しゅくえん 祝宴 banquet [C], feast [C] //祝宴を催す hold [give] *a feast*

しゅくが 祝賀 celebration [U] (❖「祝賀会」の意味では [C]), congratulation [C] //式典後に盛大な祝賀会が催された After the ceremony, *a*

しゅくがん 宿願 one's long cherished wish; (夢) one's dream ∥やっと宿願を果たすことができました I realized my «long cherished wish [dream]» at last.

しゅくご 熟語 idiom ⓒ, (idiomatic) phrase ⓒ; (慣用表現) idiomatic expression ⓒ

しゅくさいじつ 祝祭日 national [public] holiday ⓒ ⇨ しゅくじつ

しゅくさつ 縮刷 ∥縮刷版 a reduced size edition

しゅくじ 祝辞 (言葉) congratulations; (スピーチ) a speech of congratulations, congratulatory address ⓒ ∥大会の冒頭, 市長が祝辞を述べた At the beginning of the competition, the mayor made a speech of congratulations.

しゅくじつ 祝日 (national) holiday ⓒ ∥祝日を祝う celebrate [observe] a holiday / きょうは祝日です Today is a holiday.

---- 祝日のいろいろ ----
元旦 New Year's Day / 成人の日 Coming of Age Day / 建国記念の日 National Foundation Day / 春分の日 Vernal Equinox Day / みどりの日 Greenery Day / 憲法記念日 Constitution Day / こどもの日 Children's Day / 海の日 Marine Day / 敬老の日 Respect-for-the-Aged Day / 秋分の日 Autumnal Equinox Day / 体育の日 Health-Sports Day / 文化の日 Culture Day / 勤労感謝の日 Labor Thanksgiving Day / 天皇誕生日 the Emperor's Birthday

しゅくしゃ 宿舎 (宿泊所) lodging ⓒ; (ホテル) hotel ⓒ ∥公務員宿舎 housing for government employees / 国民宿舎 a public hostel run by the local council

しゅくしゃく 縮尺 scale ⓒ ∥5,000分の1の縮尺の地図 a map to [with, on] a scale of 1 to 5,000

しゅくじょ 淑女 lady

しゅくしょう 縮小 reduction ⓤⓒ; (経費などの) cut, 《公式的》curtailment ⓤⓒ ── 縮小する reduce ⓗⓘ, cut* back [down], scale down, 《公式的》curtail ⓗ ∥事業を縮小する scale down the project / その工場は生産を縮小しなければならなくなった The factory had to «cut down on [reduce]» production. ◆大阪城の縮小模型 a miniature replica of Osaka Castle
∥縮小コピー a reduced-size copy / 軍備縮小 disarmament

しゅくしょうかい 祝勝会 victory celebration ⓒ

しゅくず 縮図 reduced scale drawing ⓒ; (比喩的な) microcosm [máikrəkàzm] ⓒ ∥ここで起こっていることは社会全体の縮図にほかならない What is happening here is nothing but a microcosm of our society.

じゅくす 熟す ripen ⓘ ──熟した ripe ∥熟した[熟していない]バナナ a ripe [an unripe, a green] banana / トマトはもう熟している The tomatoes are ripe now. / カキは秋に熟す Persimmons ripen in fall.
〖慣用表現〗機は熟した The time has come./ It is high time now./ The time is ripe.

じゅくすい 熟睡 ──熟睡する sleep* well [soundly], have a good sleep ∥ゆうべ熟睡した I «slept well [had a good sleep]» last night. ◆そのとき彼女は熟睡していた She was sound [fast] asleep then.

しゅくせい¹ 粛正 ──粛正する cleanse [klénz] ⓗ ⇨ こうき (綱紀)

しゅくせい² 粛清 purge ⓒ ──粛清する purge ⓗ; (政敵などを抹殺する) liquidate ⓗ

じゅくせい 熟成 aging ⓤ, maturation ──熟成する age ⓘ, mature ⓘ ──熟成した aged, mature, ripe ∥熟成したチーズ mature [ripe] cheese / 約6か月するとチーズは熟成する The cheese will mature in about six months. ◆ワインをたるの中で熟成させる age [mature] wine in casks

しゅくだい 宿題

❶【学校などで課される】homework ⓤ, 《主に米》assignment ⓒ
数学の宿題 a math assignment
きょうは宿題がたくさんある I have a lot of homework (to do) today.
きのうは宿題で忙しかった I was busy with my homework yesterday.
宿題を忘れてきた I forgot my homework.
松本先生は宿題をたくさん出す Mr. Matsumoto gives us a lot of homework.
夏休みの宿題がまだたまっている I still have a stack of unfinished homework for summer vacation.
宿題を全部片づけたら遊びに行ってもいいよ You may go out and play when you have done all of your homework.
クラスの全員が宿題を提出した All the people in the class handed in their homework.
🅔「もう宿題は終わったの?」「まだ, 後でやるよ」 "Have you finished your homework yet?" "No, not yet. I'll do it later."
❷【議題の持ち越し】
この問題は次回までの宿題にしよう(→未解決のままにしておく) Let's leave this problem open [unresolved] until next time.

じゅくたつ 熟達 mastery ⓤ, proficiency ⓤ ──熟達する master ⓗ ──熟達した proficient, accomplished ∥彼女はスペイン語に熟達している She is proficient in Spanish. / She has mastered Spanish.

じゅくち 熟知 彼女はこのあたりの地理を熟知していた(→よく知っていた) She knew her way around here very well./ She was familiar with this neighborhood. / これは社内事情を熟知した者の犯行にちがいない This crime must have been committed by someone who is well-informed about the company.

しゅくちょく 宿直 night duty ⓒ ◆ゆうべは彼が宿直だった Last night he was on duty.
∥宿直員 a person who is on night duty /

宿直室 a night duty room
しゅくてき 宿敵 (昔からのライバル) *one's* old [*long-standing*] enemy
しゅくてん 祝典 celebration ⓒ; (祝祭) festival ⓒ
しゅくでん 祝電 congratulatory telegram ⓒ ◆私たちは彼らに祝電を打った We *sent* them *our congratulations by wire*.
じゅくどく 熟読 ──熟読する read* carefully; (じっくり読んで研究する) pore over [through] ‖教科書を熟読してごらんなさい *Read* your textbook *carefully*.
じゅくねん 熟年 mature age Ⓤⓒ, mature years
しゅくはい 祝杯 toast ⓒ (❖祝杯にトーストを入れたことから) ‖出席者は新郎新婦に祝杯をあげた Those who were present *drank a toast to* the bride and groom.
しゅくはく 宿泊 stay ⓒ, lodging Ⓤ (また a ~) ──宿泊する stay ⓥ, lodge ⓥ, put* up ⇒とまる(泊まる) ‖ホテルに宿泊する *stay* [*lodge*] *at* a hotel
◆彼は二つのホテルの宿泊手続きをした He *checked in* at the hotel. / そのホテルには200人の客が宿泊できる The hotel *has accommodations* for 200 guests. (❖accommodationsは「宿泊設備, 収容能力」の意味)
‖宿泊客 a guest, a visitor / 宿泊施設 (米) accommodations, (英) accommodation / 宿泊所 a lodging / 宿泊料 (a) room charge, (a) hotel charge
しゅくふく 祝福 blessing ⓒ ──祝福する bless* ⓥ ‖神の祝福がありますように! (May) God *bless* you! / みんなが彼らの結婚を祝福した They all *gave their blessing to* their marriage. / 私たちはみんなの祝福を受けて結婚した We got married *with* everyone's *blessing*. ◆お二人の前途を祝福いたします I *wish* you two *good luck*.
しゅくほう 祝砲 祝砲を打つ fire *a salute*
しゅくめい 宿命 fate Ⓤⓒ (しばしば Fate), destiny Ⓤⓒ, *one's* (fated) lot ──宿命的な fatal, fateful (❖fatal は不幸な運命を暗示する) ⇒うんめい / 宿命的な出会い a *fateful* encounter / 宿命の対決 a *fatal* confrontation / 2人が出会ったことは宿命としか言いようがない It was *fate* [*destiny*] that brought them together. / すべて宿命とあきらめた I've *accepted my fate*. ◆宿命のライバル an old [a *long-standing*] rival
‖宿命論 fatalism
しゅくやく 縮約 ──縮約する abridge ⓥ; (語・句を)〖文法〗contract ⓥ ‖『失われた時を求めて』の縮約版 *an abridged version of In Search of Lost Time*
じゅくりょ 熟慮 careful consideration Ⓤ, 《公式的》long [much] deliberation Ⓤⓒ; (じっくり考えること) contemplation Ⓤ ──熟慮する consider carefully, deliberate ⓥ, contemplate ⓥ ‖熟慮の末の決断 a decision made after「*careful consideration* [*long deliberation*] / この問題は熟慮を要する This matter needs「to *be considered carefully* [*careful consideration*].

じゅくれん 熟練 ──熟練した (長年の経験によって) skilled, experienced; (器用な) skillful; (専門的知識をもった) expert ‖熟練した技師 a *skilled* [*skillful*] engineer / ゴルフに熟練している *be skilled at* golf / 熟練した運転手でも事故を起こすことがある Even an *experienced* driver may cause an accident. / この仕事は熟練を要する This is *skilled* work. (❖この skilledは「(仕事が)熟練を要する」の意味)
‖熟練工 a skilled worker / 熟練者 a man of skill
しゅくん¹ 殊勲 ‖殊勲賞 (相撲の) the outstanding performance award / 殊勲打 (野球の) a game-winning hit / 最高殊勲選手 the Most Valuable Player (《略語》MVP)
しゅくん² 主君 *one's* (liege) lord
しゅげい 手芸 handicrafts; (ししゅう・編み物) fancywork Ⓤ ‖手芸教室 a handicraft class / 手芸品 a handicraft
じゅけいしゃ 受刑者 convict ⓒ
しゅけん 主権 sovereignty [sávərənti] Ⓤ ‖これはわが国の主権を侵す行為だ This act violates *the sovereignty* of our country. / 主権在民 (→主権は国民にある) *Sovereignty rests with the people*.
‖主権者 the sovereign ruler
じゅけん 受験 ──受験する take* an examination ⇒うける, しけん (試験)
‖私は山川大学を受験する (→入学試験を受ける) つもりです I plan to *take the entrance examination for* Yamakawa University.
◆彼女は熱心に受験勉強をしている She *studied hard for the entrance examination*. / 彼は去年その大学の受験に失敗した He failed [didn't pass] *the entrance examination for* that university last year.
‖受験科目 the subject of an examination, an examination subject / 受験参考書 a study aid [guide] for an entrance examination / 受験資格 qualifications to take an examination / 受験地獄 examination hell / 受験者 an examinee, an applicant / 受験生 a student preparing for an entrance examination / 受験戦争 examination war, intense competition to pass entrance examinations / 受験番号 an examinee's (seat) number / 受験票 an applicant's identification card / 受験料 an examination fee
しゅご¹ 主語 〖文法〗subject ⓒ ⇒ごぶんけい
しゅご² 守護 protection Ⓤ ──守護する protect ⓥ ‖守護神 a guardian deity
しゅこう 趣向 (工夫) device ⓒ; (着想) idea ⓒ; (計画) plan ⓒ ‖斬新(ざん)な趣向 *an* original *idea* / 会を盛り上げるために様々な趣向を凝らす *come up with* various *devices* to enliven the meeting / 今年の合宿は今までと趣向を変えてみようと思う I think we'll *change the plan* for our training camp to something we've never done before.
しゅごう 酒豪 heavy drinker ⓒ

じゅこう 受講 ―受講する attend [take*] a course ∥私は去年, 彼のドイツ語の授業を受講した I *attended* [*took*] *his course* in German last year.
‖受講料 tuition

しゅこうぎょう 手工業 craft [C]
‖手工業者 a craftsperson

しゅこうげい 手工芸 arts and crafts, handicrafts
‖手工芸品 a handicraft, craftwork

ジュゴン〘動物〙dugong [dúːgɑŋ] [C]

しゅさい 主催 ―主催する (催し物などを計画する) organize [他]; (後援する) sponsor [他]; (主催者として) host [他] ∥大学主催の体育大会に参加した I took part in an athletic meet *organized* [*sponsored, hosted*] by the university. ◆フランス大使館の主催で *under the auspices* [*sponsorship*] *of* the French Embassy / その会合は日本政府が主催している The Japanese Government *is* (*acting as*) *host to* the meeting.
‖主催国 the host country [nation] / 主催者 (組織者) an organizer; (後援者) a sponsor, a promoter, (a) host

しゅざい 取材 coverage [U] ―取材する (事件などを) cover [他]; (資料などを集める) gather [他] ∥激しい取材競争 intense *competition in coverage* / その記者は政治から芸能に至るまで幅広く取材する That reporter *covers* a wide range of topics from politics to show business. / 彼は新しい小説のために韓国へ取材に出かけた He went to Korea to *gather information* [*data*] for his new novel.
‖取材記者 a reporter

しゅざん 珠算 abacus calculation [U][C]
◆珠算をする *calculate with an abacus*

しゅし[1] 趣旨 (目的) purpose [C]; (意味) meaning [U]; (要点) the point ∥会議の趣旨を理解する understand *the meaning* [*point*] of a meeting / そのような発言は本会合の趣旨に反する Such a statement 「is against [violates] *the purpose* of this meeting.
◆彼から計画に同意するという趣旨の手紙を受け取った I received a letter from him *to the effect that* he consented to the proposal.

しゅし[2] 主旨 the (main) point; (要旨) the gist ∥主旨をつかむ grasp *the* (*main*) *point* / 私は彼女の話の主旨が分からなかった I didn't see *the gist* [*main point*] of her speech. / I didn't see her *point*.

しゅし[3] 種子 seed [C][U] ⇒たね

じゅし 樹脂 resin [rézin] [C][U] ‖合成樹脂 synthetic resins [plastic]

しゅじい 主治医 (担当医) a physician in charge; (かかりつけの医者) family doctor [C]

しゅしゃせんたく 取捨選択 choice [C], selection [U][C] ―取捨選択する choose* [他], select [他] ⇒えらぶ ∥資料を取捨選択する *select* data (*carefully*)

しゅじゅ 種々 ―種々の various, miscellaneous, different ⇒さまざま ∥種々雑多な品々 *various* [*miscellaneous*] articles / 種々の理由で for *various* reasons
◆庭には種々の花が咲き乱れている *Many kinds of* flowers are in full bloom all around the garden.

しゅじゅつ 手術 operation [C], 《英口語的》op [C]; (外科手術) surgery [U] ―手術する operate [自]
癌(がん)の手術 *a* cancer *operation*; *an operation* for cancer / 手術を行う perform *an operation*
祖父は心臓を手術した My grandfather *had* a heart *operation*. / My grandfather *had* his heart *operated on*.
彼は大手術を受けた He *underwent* [*submitted to*] *a long operation*.
彼女はその手術を受けるのを怖がった She was afraid to *have* the *operation*.
彼は手術の間意識がなかった He was unconscious during *the operation*.
彼女の手術は成功した Her *operation* was successful.
‖手術室《米》an operating room, 《英》an operating theatre / 手術台 an operating table

じゅじゅつ 呪術 magic [U] ‖呪術師 a magician

しゅしょう[1] 首相 the prime minister (《略語》PM) ∥小泉首相 *Prime Minister* Koizumi / 新しい首相を支持しますか Do you support *the* new *prime minister*?
‖首相官邸 the prime minister's official residence / 副首相 the deputy prime minister

しゅしょう[2] 主将 captain [C] ∥彼女は私たちのバスケットボールチームの主将です She is (*the*) *captain* of our basketball team.

しゅしょう[3] 殊勝 ―殊勝な admirable, commendable ∥自分から親の手伝いをするとは殊勝な心がけだ It is *admirable* of you to help your parents voluntarily.

じゅしょう[1] 受賞 ―受賞する (賞を勝ち取る) win* a prize; (賞を与えられる) be awarded a prize ∥広昭は英語のスピーチコンテストで1等賞を受賞した Hiroaki *won* [*was awarded*] (*the*) first *prize* in the English speech contest.
◆彼はピューリッツァー賞の受賞者です He's *a* Pulitzer Prize *winner*.

じゅしょう[2] 授賞 ―授賞する award a prize ‖授賞式 an award ceremony

しゅしょく 主食 staple [principal] food [C], staple [principal] diet [C][U] ∥日本人の主食は米です Rice is *the staple food* [*diet*] of Japanese. / (→日本人は米を常食としている) Japanese *live on* rice.

しゅしん 主審 the chief umpire

しゅじん 主人 (夫) *one's* husband; (店の) 《主に米》storekeeper [C], 《主に英》shopkeeper [C]; (所有者) master [C], owner [C]; (旅館などの) landlord [C]; (客の接待役) host [C] (❖女性形は hostess)
主人役を務める *play the host*; *act as* (*the*) *host*
仮にご主人が失業したらどうやって家族を養ってい

きますか If *your husband lost his job, how would you support your family?*
店の主人が強盗を追いかけた *The storekeeper chased a robber.*
その犬は主人に対して非常に忠実だった *The dog was very faithful to his master.*
宿の主人があいさつに出てきた *The landlord came out to greet us.*
◆(電話で)ご主人(→森川氏)はいらっしゃいますか May I speak to Mr. Morikawa?(❖英語では上記のように名前をいうのがふつう)

じゅしん¹ 受信 ──受信する receive ⓔ/そのラジオ番組は日本のどこででも受信できる *The radio program can be received [heard] in every part of Japan.* / このあたりは受信状態が悪い *Reception is poor [bad] around here.*
‖受信機 a receiver / 受信局 a receiving station / 受信者 an addressee / 受信料 a subscription fee

じゅしん² 受診 ──受診する see* a doctor

しゅじんこう 主人公 main character Ⓒ; (男の) hero Ⓒ; (女の) heroine [hérouən] Ⓒ; (劇・物語などの)《公式的》 protagonist Ⓒ/悲劇の主人公を演じる *play a tragic hero*

しゅす 繻子 satin Ⓤ ‖繻子仕上げ(銀器の表面などの) a satin finish

じゅず 数珠 Buddhist beads, Buddhist rosary Ⓒ
慣用表現 高速道路では車が数珠つなぎになっていた *There was a string of cars on the freeway.*

しゅせい 守勢 the defensive ‖守勢に回る be [act] *on the defensive*

しゅぜい 酒税 liquor tax Ⓒ

じゅせい¹ 授精 insemination Ⓤ ──授精する(人工的に受精させる) inseminate ⓔ ‖人工授精 artificial insemination

じゅせい² 受精〔生物〕 fertilization Ⓤ ──受精される be fertilized ‖受精卵 a fertilized egg / 体外受精 in vitro fertilization

しゅせいぶん 主成分 principal ingredient Ⓒ, basis Ⓒ (複 bases)

しゅせき¹ 主席 chairman Ⓒ ‖国家主席 the head of state

しゅせき² 首席 the top, the head ──首席の top, chief /高校を首席で卒業する graduate *at the top of one's high school class*(❖「大学を」なら graduate *with highest honors from college*)
‖首席判事 the presiding judge

しゅせつ 主節〔文法〕 main clause Ⓒ
➾せつぞくし

しゅせんど 守銭奴 miser [máizər] Ⓒ, 《口語的》 skinflint Ⓒ

じゅぞう 受像 (受けること) reception Ⓤ; (映像) picture Ⓒ ──受像する receive a picture ‖受像機 a receiver, a television (set)

しゅぞく 種族 tribe Ⓒ《単数または複数扱い》; (生物の) race Ⓒ

しゅたい 主体 学生が主体となっている(→主に学生から成る)デモ a demonstration *mainly composed of* students / 彼は主体性がない(→自立心がない) *He has no independence of mind.* / (→他人に簡単に影響される) *He is easily influenced by others.* / どの会社でも主体的に行動できる有能な人材を求めている *Every company is seeking capable people who can act independently.*

しゅだい 主題 the subject, the theme [θi:m]; (文学などの) motif Ⓒ /兄はすべての本を主題別に分類した *My brother divided all the books by subject.* / 論文を書くにはまず主題を設定しなければならない *You have to set the theme first in order to write a thesis.*
‖主題歌 a theme song

じゅたい 受胎 conception Ⓤ ──受胎する conceive ⓔ
‖受胎告知〔カトリック〕 the Annunciation

じゅたく 受託 ‖受託者 a trustee / 受託収賄罪 the crime of accepting a bribe in return for a favor / 受託販売 selling on consignment

じゅだく 受諾 acceptance Ⓤ Ⓒ; (承諾)《公式的》consent Ⓤ ──受諾する accept ⓔ; 《公式的》consent Ⓤ ‖ポツダム宣言受諾 *acceptance of the Potsdam Declaration* / 申し入れを受諾する *accept a proposal*

しゅだん 手段

means Ⓒ (複 ~s); (対策) measures; (頼ること) resort Ⓒ; (やり方) way Ⓒ

最も効率のいい交通手段 *the most efficient means of transportation* / 自衛手段をとる *take defensive measures* / 効果的な手段を講じる *take effective measures*

私たちはあらゆる手段を尽くしてそれを手に入れようとした *We tried every possible means to get it.*

目的と手段を混同してはいけない *You shouldn't confuse the means with the end.*

コンピュータは新しい伝達手段です *Computers are a new means of communication.*

彼女は不正な手段で情報を入手した *She obtained information by dishonest means.*

彼らは問題の平和的手段による解決を目ざして努力した *They made an effort to solve the problem by peaceful means.*

医者は最後の手段として手術に踏み切った *The doctor decided to perform an operation as a last resort.*

◆彼女は父親が怒るといつも泣くという手段に出る *She always resorts to crying when her father gets angry with her.* / あの男は目的のためには手段を選ばない *That guy doesn't care how he does it as long as he gets what he wants.*

しゅちゅう 手中 慣用表現 敵の手中に落ちる *fall into enemy [the enemy's] hands* / もはや勝利は我々の手中にある *Victory is already* 「*in our hands [within our grasp].*

じゅちゅう 受注 order Ⓒ ──受注する receive an order ➾ちゅうもん ‖今年になって受注が落ち込んでいる *Orders have been dropping this year.*

しゅちょう 主張

claim [C], assertion [U][C], insistence [U], argument [C] ―主張する (権利などを) claim [他][自], assert [他], insist [自][他], argue [他], 《公式的》contend [他]; (断言する) affirm [他]; (根拠もなしに) 《公式的》allege [他]

筋の通った主張 a logical *argument* / 主張を取り下げる renounce [drop] *one's claim*

彼は試合の勝者は自分だと主張している He *insists that* he won the match.

彼女は自分の無実を主張した She *affirmed* [*claimed*] her innocence. / She *affirmed* [*claimed*] *that* she was innocent.

証人は彼の有罪を主張した The witness *alleged* his guilt.

彼は私たちの計画を変更すべきだと主張している He *argues that* we should change our plan.

証拠によって彼女の主張が立証された Her *claims* were supported by the evidence.

◆彼は自分の主張が通らないのでいらいらしていた He was irritated because he *couldn't carry his point.* / 彼女はとても自己主張が強い She *is* very *self-assertive.* / 私たちは最後まで自分たちの主張を曲げなかった (→意見を守り通した) We *stuck to* our *opinion* to the end.

じゅつ 術 (技術) art [U][C]; (技法) technique [tekníːk] [C][U]; (特殊な技術) skill [C]

‖護身術 the art of self-defense

しゅつえん 出演 appearance [U][C] ―出演する appear [自] ‖ゲスト出演する *make a guest appearance* / 彼はハムレットの役で劇に出演する He *will appear* as Hamlet in the play.

‖出演者 a performer / 出演料 a performance fee, pay

しゅっか[1] 出火 出火の原因を調べる investigate the cause of *a fire* / 昨夜近くのレストランから出火した Last night *a fire broke out in* a nearby restaurant. ➔かじ(火事)

しゅっか[2] 出荷 shipping [U] ―出荷する ship [他] ‖野菜を市場に出荷する *ship* vegetables to the market (❖船以外の輸送手段を用いる場合も ship を使うことができる)

じゅっかい 述懐 reminiscence [U] ―述懐する reminisce [自]

しゅっかん 出棺 出棺(→霊柩(れいきゅう)車が家を出る)は4時の予定です *The hearse is to leave the house* at four.

しゅつがん 出願 application [C][U] ―出願する apply [自], make* an application ➔しんせい(申請) ‖特許を出願する *apply* [*make an application*] *for* a patent / 彼は3つの大学に出願した (→願書を3大学に送った) He *sent applications to* three universities.

◆出願者は本人が直接申し込むこと *Applicants* should apply in person.

‖出願期日 the deadline for application / 出願手続き application procedure / 新案特許出願中 Patent Pending (《略語》pat. pend.)

しゅっきん 出勤 ―出勤する go* to work, go to *one's* office ‖父は毎朝電車で出勤します My father *goes to work* by train every morning. / 毎週土曜日は出勤日です (→出勤する) I *go to my office* every Saturday.

‖出勤時間 (家を出る時間) the time to leave for work [*one's* office]; (仕事を始める時間) the clock-in time / 出勤日数 the frequency of attendance, the number of days present / 出勤簿 an attendance book

しゅっけ 出家 (僧侶(そうりょ)) bonze [C], Buddhist monk [nun] [C] ―出家する leave* home to be a Buddhist monk [nun]

しゅつげき 出撃 ―出撃する leave* *one's* position to attack the enemy

しゅっけつ[1] 出欠 attendance or absence

◆出欠をとる take *attendance* [*a roll-call*] (❖roll-call は「名前を呼んで出欠をとる」の意味) / 今週末までに会への出欠をお知らせください Please let me know by the end of this week *whether or not you will attend* the meeting.

しゅっけつ[2] 出血 bleeding [U], loss of blood; (主に体内での多量の) 〔医学〕hemorrhage [hémərɪdʒ] [C][U] ―出血する bleed* [自]; 〔医学〕hemorrhage [自] ‖彼は傷口から出血していた His wound *was bleeding.* / そのけが人は出血がひどかった The wounded person *was bleeding* heavily. / やっと出血が止まった *The bleeding* finally stopped. / 腕にボールが当たって内出血を起こした I've got *internal bleeding* in my arm where a ball hit it. / その男は出血多量で死んだ The man died from *excessive bleeding.* / (→出血して死に至った) The man *bled* to death.

◆当店ではただ今出血大サービス中です Our store is now selling *at a great loss.*

しゅつげん 出現 (現れること) appearance [U][C]; (出来事・発明・人などの) the advent; (新しいもの) arrival [C]; (誕生) birth [C] 《通例単数形》 ―出現する appear [自]; (生まれる) be born ‖久々の大型新人投手の出現で野球界は大いに沸いている The baseball world is abuzz with *the appearance* [*debut*] of a long-waited promising rookie pitcher. / 携帯電話の出現で相手がどこにいても簡単に連絡がつくようになった *The advent* of cell phones has enabled us to get in contact with people easily wherever they are. / この現象は1,000回に1度の割合で出現する This phenomenon *appears* [(→生じる) *occurs*] once in 1,000 times.

じゅつご[1] 述語 〔文法〕predicate [C] (《略語》pred.) ➔ごぶんけい

じゅつご[2] 術語 technical term [C], 《集合的》terminology [C][U]

しゅっこう[1] 出航 ―出航する sail [自], set* sail ‖この船は今晩神戸へ向けて出航します This ship *will sail* [*set sail*] for Kobe tonight.

しゅっこう[2] 出港 (a) departure from (a) port, ship's departure [U][C] ―出港する leave* [depart from] port ‖台風のため出港が見合わされた *The ship's departure* [*The departure from port*] was canceled because of the typhoon.

しゅっこう³ 出向 彼女は子会社へ出向している She *has been sent to* a subsidiary *on loan*./ She *is on loan to* a subsidiary.

‖出向社員 a temporarily transferred worker, a loaned worker

じゅっこう 熟考 熟考の末, 申し出を受け入れることにした After *consideration* [*deliberation*], I decided to accept the offer. / その提案は熟考に値する The proposal is worth *considering* [*reflecting*, *pondering*].

しゅっこく 出国 an exit from a country, (a) departure from a country ——出国する exit [depart] from a country, leave* a country ◆ 出国手続きをすませた I went through *the departure formalities*.

‖出国ビザ an exit visa

しゅつごく 出獄 ——出獄する be released from prison

しゅっさつ 出札 the sale of tickets ‖出札係《米》a ticket agent,《英》a booking clerk / 出札口《米》a ticket window,《英》a booking window

しゅっさん 出産 delivery ⓤⓒ, childbirth ⓤ ——出産する give* birth to a baby ‖兄は出産に立ち会った My brother was present at *the delivery* [*childbirth*]. / 彼女は女の子を出産した She *gave birth to* a baby girl.
◆ 姉は今月出産の予定です My sister *is due to have a baby* this month.
‖出産祝い (祝いの品) a gift for a newborn baby;(祝い事) a celebration of a birth / 出産休暇 (a) maternity leave / 出産予定日 the expected date of delivery [birth], the due date

しゅっし 出資 investment ⓤⓒ, capitalization ⓤ ——出資する invest ⓗ, make* an investment;(資金を調達する)《公式的》finance ⓗ ‖その開発事業には父の会社が出資した My father's company 「*made an investment* [*invested*] *in* the development project. / その2社の共同出資で新たなスーパーマーケットができた A new supermarket was opened through *the joint investment* of the two companies.

‖出資額 the amount of an investment / 出資金 an investment / 出資者 an investor / 出資率 the investment rate

しゅっしゃ 出社 ——出社する come* [go*] to one's [the] office ‖彼は毎日10時半に出社する He *comes to the office* at 10:30 every morning. ◆ 彼女はまだ出社していない She *is* not *at the office* yet.

しゅっしゅっ やかんからしゅっしゅっと蒸気が出ている The steam is coming out with *a hiss* [*hissing sound*] from the kettle. / シャツのしみに霧吹きでしゅっしゅっと水をかけた I *sprayed water repeatedly* on the smear on my shirt. / 機関車はしゅっしゅっぽっぽと走っていった The locomotive *chugged* away.

しゅっしょ 出所 ❶(起源) source ⓒ,《公式的》provenance ⓤ ‖出所不明の情報 a piece of information from *an* unknown *source* [*provenance*]

❷【出獄】 ——出所する be released from prison ◆ 彼は仮出所の身だ He is on *parole*.

しゅっしょう 出生 ⇨しゅっせい

しゅつじょう 出場 (参加) participation ⓤ;(競技への) entry ⓒⓤ ——出場する (参加する) take* part in ...,《公式的》participate ⓗ;(競技などに) enter ⓗ
そのチームは今回が甲子園初出場だ This is *the first participation* for the team *in* the national high school baseball tournament held at Koshien.
コンテストには3人しか出場しなかった There were only three *entries* in the contest.
彼女は校内バレーボール大会に出場した She 「*took part in* [*participated in, entered*] the intramural volleyball tournament.
レースへの出場を希望のかたはこの用紙に記入してください Those who want to 「*take part in* [*participate in, enter, compete in*] the race should fill out [in] this form.
わがチームは全国大会への出場権を獲得した Our team won *the right to take part in* the national meet.
◆ 彼女はコンテストへの出場資格を失った She *was disqualified* from the contest. / その選手はオリンピック出場停止処分になった The athlete *was suspended from* the Olympic Games.
‖出場者 a participant;(コンテストなどの) a contestant / 出場停止 (a) suspension

しゅっしょく 出色 彼の新作映画は出色のできばえだった His new film was *excellent* [*an outstanding*] piece of work.

しゅっしん 出身
彼女は京都出身だ She *comes* [*is*] *from* Kyoto.
彼は名家の出身だ He *comes* [*is*] *from* a distinguished family.
上田君は海瀬高校出身だ (→卒業した) Ueda *graduated from* Kaise High School. / (→卒業生だ) Ueda *is a graduate of* Kaise High School.
🔴「どちらのご出身ですか」「埼玉です」 "Where 「*do you come* [*are you*] *from*?" "I *come* [*am*] *from* Saitama."
‖出身校 an alma mater / 出身国 the country *one* comes [is] from;(出生国) *one's* native country / 出身地 *one's* hometown

じゅっしんほう 十進法 the decimal scale [system]

しゅっせ 出世 (実社会での成功) success in the real world;(昇進) promotion ⓒⓤ ——出世する (社会的に高い身分になる) move [go*] up in the world;(成功する) succeed ⓗ, get* ahead;(昇進する) get promoted
新聞記者のインタビューを受けたりして, 彼もすっかり出世したものだ To be interviewed by newspaper reporters, he must *have moved* [*gone*] *up in the world*.
彼女は会社での出世が早かった She 「*got promoted* [*rose*] rapidly in her company.

彼は工場長に出世した He's *gotten promoted to* chief of the factory.
スキャンダルで彼は出世の道を断たれた (→スキャンダルが出世を妨げた) The scandal prevented him from *succeeding* [getting *a promotion*].
◆高校時代の仲間の中では彼女が出世頭だ She's been *the most successful* of my former high school friends. / 彼女は出世コースに乗っている She is on *the fast track* (to the top). / She is climbing *the ladder* (to the top). / その作品が彼の出世作となった The work *made* him *famous* [*popular*]. / 出世払いで(→成功したら返すという約束で)金を借りた I borrowed money *on the promise that I would pay it back when I succeeded.*

しゅっせい 出生 birth [U] [C] //出生届を出す *register the birth of one's baby*; hand in *the registration of a birth*
◆日本の出生率は低下している *The birthrate* in Japan is declining.
‖出生証明書 a birth certificate / 出生地 the place where *one* was born; (特に有名人の) *one's* birthplace

しゅっせうお 出世魚 🗻 a *shusseuo*, a type of fish with different names according to the stage of growth

しゅっせき 出席 attendance [U] [C] (❖「出席すること」の意味では[U],「出席回数」の意味では[C]), presence [U] ━出席する attend [他] [自]; (出席している) be present
私たちの結婚披露宴にぜひご出席ください *Your attendance* [*presence*] *at* our wedding reception is kindly requested.
その授業には5回出席した I *attended* the class five times.
彼らは純の歓迎会に出席した They *attended* [*were present at*] Jun's welcome party.
パーティーに出席できない場合にはお知らせください Please let us know if you are not able to *attend* [*come to*] the party.
岡村先生は出席をとり忘れた Mr. Okamura forgot to *take attendance*. (❖「出席をとる」は call [take] the roll などともいう)
彼は出席日数が足りないので留年になるかもしれない He might be unable to pass to the next grade because of poor *attendance*.
佐々木先生の講義はいつも出席する生徒が多い There are always a lot of students (*present*) *at* Mrs. Sasaki's lectures.
彼はこの授業への出席率が悪い He has *a* poor *attendance rate* in this class.
‖出席者 a person (who is) present; (集合的) (an) attendance, those (who are) present / 出席簿 the school attendance register, a roll (book)

しゅつだい 出題 今度のテストには先日配ったプリントから出題します (→プリントに基づく問題を出す) I'm going to *make questions* for the next examination based on handouts I gave you the other day. / (→プリントにあった問題からとる) *The questions* on the next examination *will be taken* from those on the handouts I gave you the other day. / 関西大学の入試の出題傾向を知る必要がある I need to know *the types of questions that tend to be asked* on Kansai University's entrance examination. / 松田先生の英語のテストは毎回出題数が多い Every English exam Mr. Matsuda prepares has *a* large *number of questions* in it. / あすの歴史のテストは出題範囲が広い Tomorrow's history test *will cover a lot of material.*
‖出題者 a person who prepares an examination question

じゅっちゅう 術中 敵の術中にはまる fall into the enemy's *trap*

しゅっちょう 出張 (商用の) business trip [C]; (公務員の) official trip [C] ━出張する 「go* on [make*] a business trip; (商用で) go to ... on business //名古屋へ長期[短期]出張する *go on a* long [short] *business trip to* Nagoya / 父は出張が多い My father often *goes on business trips.*
◆母は今,博多へ出張中です My mother *is* now *in* Hakata *on business.* / おじは年に数回海外出張する My uncle *goes abroad on business* several times a year.
‖出張所 a branch office / 出張手当 a travel(ing) allowance / 出張費 travel(ing) expenses

しゅってい 出廷 an appearance (in court) ━出廷する appear (in court), make* an appearance (in court)

しゅってん 出典 source [C]; (典拠) authority [C] //引用文の出典を示す show *the source* 「of the quoted sentence [from which the sentence is quoted] / この文の出典はシェークスピアだ *The source* of this sentence is Shakespeare. / (→シェークスピアから引用されている) This sentence *is quoted from* Shakespeare.

しゅつど 出土 ━出土する (発掘される) be excavated [unearthed] //その遺跡からは多くの土器が出土した Many pieces of ancient pottery *were excavated* [*unearthed*] from the ruins.
‖出土品 an excavated [unearthed] article

しゅっとう 出頭 appearance [C] ━出頭する appear [自], report [自], 《公式的》present *oneself* //彼は法廷へ出頭するよう命じられた He was summoned to *appear* [*make an appearance*] in court. / 彼女は警察に出頭した She 「*reported to* [*presented herself at*] the police station.
‖出頭命令 a summons

しゅつどう 出動 ━出動する (出発する) start [自]; (…を出る) leave* [他] [自]; (派遣される) be sent, 《公式的》be dispatched; (招集される) be called out //救急車数台が事故現場へ向けて出動した Several ambulances *started* [*left* the fire station] *for* the scene of the accident. / 暴動鎮圧のため警官隊が出動した The police force *was sent* [*dispatched, called out*] to suppress the riot.

しゅつにゅうこく 出入国 ‖出入国管理 immigration control / 出入国記録カード an embarkation and disembarkation card

しゅつば 出馬 run ◎《通例単数形》 ――出馬する 《主に米》 run* 自, 《英》 stand* 自 ‖彼は県知事選に初出馬で当選した He was elected in *his first run for* prefectural governor. / 阿部氏は市長選への出馬を表明した Mr. Abe declared that he *will run「in the mayoral election [for mayor]*.

しゅっぱつ 出発

❶ 【出かけること】 (場所を去ること) departure Ⓤ ◎, (旅などを始めること) start ◎ ――出発する (場所を去る) leave* 自 他, depart 自 (❖leave のほうが口語的); (旅などを始める) start 自, start off [out]

出発を早める [遅らせる] hasten [delay] *the departure*

出発の日が1週間繰り上げになった *The date of departure has been advanced by a week*.

出発の準備は万端整っています *I'm all set to leave [depart, start]*.

あす午後3時に札幌へ向けて東京を出発します *I'm leaving [departing from] Tokyo for Sapporo at three tomorrow afternoon*.

我々の乗った飛行機は1時間遅れて出発した *Our plane「left the airport [(→離陸した) took off]*one hour late*.

彼女は朝早く出発した *She left [started] early in the morning*.

あの電車は何時に出発するのですか *What time does that train leave [depart]?*

◆さあ出発しよう *Let's go! / Let's get going! / Off we go!*

❷ 【物事を始めること】

その女優は最初にレストランのウェートレスとして出発した *The actress started (out) as a waitress in a restaurant*.

彼女は歌手として再出発を果たした *She made a fresh start as a singer*.

‖出発時刻 the departure time, the time of departure / 出発点(旅行・行動などの) a starting point; (陸上競技の) a mark / 出発ロビー(空港の) the departure lounge

じゅっぱひとからげ 十把一からげ ⇨ じっぱひとからげ

しゅっぱん¹ 出版 publication Ⓤ ――出版する publish 他自, bring* out; (刊行する) issue 他; (活字にする) print 他自

彼女の最新作が来月出版される *Her latest novel will「be published [be brought out, be issued, come out]* next month*.

彼女は写真集を自費出版した *She published her photo collection at her own expense*.

Y社の新しい辞書の出版記念パーティーに招かれた *I was invited to a party to celebrate the publication of the Y Company's new dictionary*.

◆彼は出版の仕事をしている *He has a job in publishing*. / (→出版社で働いている)*He works for「a publishing company [publisher]*. / その本が出版されているかどうか確認しよう *I'll check to see if the book is in print*. / 彼女の本は今は出版されていない *Her books are now out of print*.

‖出版業 publishing / 出版(業)界 the publishing trade [world] / 出版物 a publication

しゅっぱん² 出帆 ――出帆する sail (for ...), set* sail (for ...)

しゅっぴ 出費 expense Ⓤ ◎, expenditure Ⓤ ◎ ――出費する money ‖先月は何かと出費がかさんだ *I spent a lot of money on this and that last month*. / 今月は出費を抑え [減らさ] なければならない *I need to try「not to spend much money [to reduce expenses]* this month*.

しゅっぴん 出品 ――出品する (送る) send* 他; (展示する) exhibit 他自, put* ... on exhibit [display] ‖彼は展覧会に油絵を出品した *He sent an oil painting to an exhibition*. / *He exhibited an oil painting at an exhibition*.

‖出品者 an exhibitor / 出品物 an exhibit; (コンテストなどの) an entry

しゅっぺい 出兵 dispatch of troops
◆海外の戦地への出兵を命ずる *order troops abroad to the front*

しゅつぼつ 出没 ――出没する (時々現れる) appear every now and then; (幽霊などが出る) haunt 他 (❖しばしば受身で用いられる) ‖最近うちの畑にタヌキが出没している *Recently, raccoon dogs have appeared every now and then in our field*. / そのトンネルでは交通事故で亡くなった人の霊が出没するという *It is said that the tunnel is haunted by the ghosts of the victims of traffic accidents*.

しゅつりょう 出漁 ――出漁する go* out fishing ‖悪天候にもかかわらず彼らは出漁した *They went out fishing in spite of rough weather*.

しゅつりょく 出力 output Ⓤ ◎; (発電力) generating power Ⓤ /出力50ワットのギターアンプ *a guitar amp with「a 50-watt output [50 watts of power]*

◆その発電所の出力は1万キロワットだ *The generating capacity of the power plant is 10,000 kilowatts*.

しゅつるい 出塁 ――出塁する〔野球〕 get* on base

しゅと 首都 capital (city) ◎ ――首都の metropolitan ‖首都の移転 the relocation of the *(nation's) capital*

❓「アメリカの首都はニューヨークです」「違いますよ、ワシントン D.C. です」 *"The capital of the U.S. is New York." "No, it's Washington, D.C."*

‖首都圏 the Tokyo metropolitan area / 首都高速道路 the Metropolitan Expressway

しゅとう 種痘 (a) vaccination (against smallpox) ◆種痘をする *vaccinate a person against smallpox*

しゅどう 手動 ――手動の manual (❖名詞の前で用いる) ‖手動式のズームレンズ *a manual zoom lens*

じゅどう

◆この自動ドアは非常時には手動であけられる This automatic door can be opened「*by hand* [*manually*] in emergency.
∥手動ブレーキ a hand brake

じゅどう 受動 ──受動的な passive ∥受動態【文法】the passive (voice) ⇨ うけみ

しゅどうけん 主導権 the initiative;（指導者の地位）leadership ⃝ ∥主導権争い a struggle for the *leadership* / その討論会では彼が主導権を握っていた He seized [held] *the initiative* in that discussion. / チャンピオンは挑戦者から試合の主導権を奪い返した The champion has gotten back the once-lost *initiative* in the match from the challenger.

しゅとく 取得 ──取得する（手に入れる）get*, 《公式的》obtain ⃝;（習得する・権利などを獲得する）acquire ⃝ ∥不動産を取得する *acquire* real estate / 彼女は東京大学で博士号を取得した She *got* [*obtained*] a doctor's degree at Tokyo University.
∥取得物 a thing one has gotten [obtained];（特に価値のあるもの）an acquisition

しゅとして 主として（理由などが）mainly, chiefly, largely,《公式的》primarily;（大部分は）mainly, largely, mostly ⇨ おもに（主に）◆彼の成功は主として彼自身の努力によるものだ His success is *mainly* [*chiefly, largely, primarily*] due to his own efforts. / コンサートの観客は主として10代の女の子だった The audience at the concert consisted *mainly* [*largely, mostly*] of teenage girls.

じゅなん 受難（苦しみ）suffering ⃝ ⃝ ∥キリストの受難 the *sufferings* of Christ; the Passion ◆昨年は天候不良で農家にとっては受難の年だった Last year was *a hard year* for farmers because the weather was bad.

ジュニア ⚠ ─图（若者）young person ⃝;（集合的）young people（❖英語の junior には「中高生くらいの若者」という意味はない）;（息子）son ⃝ ─圈（…2世）Junior（❖主に米）で、同名の父子の息子・2兄弟の弟の名の後に付けて用いる;（略記）Jr., Jnr., jr.）∥ジュニア向けファッション（→ 若者向けの衣類）clothing for *young people* / ケン・ノートン・ジュニア Ken Norton, *Jr.*
◆テニスのジュニア選手権で優勝した I won *a junior* tennis *championship*.

しゅにく 朱肉 vermilion inkpad [pad] ⃝

じゅにゅう 授乳 ──授乳する（母乳）nurse ⃝ ⃝, breast-feed* ⃝ ⃝;（母乳以外のミルク）bottle-feed* ⃝ ⃝ ∥何時間おきに授乳していますか How often do you *nurse* (your baby)?
∥授乳期間 the period of nursing

しゅにん 主任 head ⃝, chief ⃝,（学科などの）chairperson ⃝ ∥英文科の主任 *the chairperson* of the English literature department / 北島先生が2年の学年主任だ Mr. Kitajima is *the head* [*chief*] of the teachers for the second year students. / 吉田氏がその雑誌の編集主任だ Mr. Yoshida is *the editor in chief* of the magazine.
∥主任弁護人 a lead attorney

ジュネーブ Geneva [dʒəníːvə]（❖スイスの都市）

しゅのう 首脳 leader ⃝, head ⃝ ∥各国首脳 *the leaders* of various countries
◆両国の首脳会議が来週開かれる The summit [*top-level*] *meeting* between the two countries will be held next week.
∥首脳部（政府の）the leaders [heads] of the government;（会社の）the top management of a company

シュノーケル snorkel ⃝

しゅはん 主犯 the principal [main] offender ◆万引きグループの主犯格の少年がつかまった The boy who was *the leader* of the shoplifting band has been arrested.

しゅび¹ 守備【スポーツ】defense,《英》defence ⃝ ⃝; （野球の）fielding ⃝ ──守備の defensive ∥守備をする play *defense* / 守備につく take *the defensive position*;（→野球で）take *the fielding position* / ゴール前の守備を固めた We strengthened *our defense* in front of the goal. / あのチームは守備が堅い［弱い］That team has *a strong* [*weak*] *defense*. / 健二は守備がうまい Kenji is good at *defense* [*fielding*].
∥守備範囲 a fielding area

しゅび² 首尾 首尾一貫した方針 a *consistent* policy / 首尾（→結果）は上々だ The results have been perfect. / 君の態度は首尾一貫していないよ Your attitude is not *consistent.* / You are not *consistent* in your attitude. / 2か国間の交渉は首尾よくまとまった The negotiations between the two countries concluded *successfully*.

じゅひ 樹皮 bark ⃝

ジュピター【ローマ神話】Jupiter（❖最高神. ギリシャ神話の Zeus に当たる）

じゅひょう 樹氷 (a coat of snow and) ice on a tree

しゅひん 主賓 a guest of honor ∥彼がこのパーティーの主賓だ He is *the guest of honor* at this party. ◆関根氏を主賓に迎えて晩餐(ばん)会が開かれた The dinner was held *in honor of* Mr. Sekine.

しゅふ¹ 主婦 a wife who does housework;（専業主婦）《主に米/婉曲的》homemaker ⃝, housewife ⃝（❖女性の役割を規定する性差別的な言葉ともとられるので、最近ではふつう homemaker を用いることが多い）
◆主婦業（→家事）と仕事を両立させる strike a balance between *housework* and a job outside the house

しゅふ² 首府 capital (city) ⃝ ⇨ しゅと

シュプール ⚠ ski tracks (on the snow)（❖日本語はドイツ語の Spur から）∥美しいシュプールを描く leave beautiful *ski tracks*;（→美しく滑る）*ski down* beautifully

シュプレヒコール ⚠ chant ⃝, a chorus of shouts（❖日本語はドイツ語の Sprechchor から）◆デモ隊は「原発建設反対」のシュプレヒコールを繰り返した The demonstrators repeatedly *chanted* [*shouted in chorus*], "We don't need nuclear power plants!"

じゅふん 受粉・授粉 pollination ⃝ ──受粉

する be pollinated ‖自家受粉 self-pollination / 人工受粉 artificial pollination / 他家受粉 cross-pollination

しゅほう 手法 (様式) manner [C]《通例単数形》, style [C] [U]; (方法) method [C]; (技法) technique [U] [C] //古典的な手法で描かれた絵 pictures painted in *a* classical *manner* [*style*] / 商品を新たな手法で売り出す sell goods 「with *a* new *method* [in *a* new *way*]

しゅぼうしゃ 首謀者 ringleader [C] //テロ事件の首謀者が逮捕された *The ringleader* of the terrorist attack has been arrested.

しゅみ 趣味

❶【楽しみですること】(積極的に行う活動) hobby [C]; (気晴らし) pastime [C]; (関心事) interest [C] ⇨むしゅみ

あなたの趣味は何ですか What 「are your *hobbies* [*hobbies* do you have]?

何か趣味をおもちですか Do you have any *hobbies?*

彼女は絵を描くことが趣味だ Her *hobby* [*pastime*] is painting pictures.

彼は趣味が広い He has a wide range of *interests.*

僕ら2人は共通の趣味で結ばれている Two of us are bound by common *interests.*

◆おばは趣味と実益を兼ねて花屋を始めた My aunt opened a flower shop to *combine business with pleasure.*

❷【好み】taste [C] [U]

上品な[低俗な]趣味 refined [low] *taste* / 趣味のよい人 a man *of taste*

クラシック音楽は僕の趣味じゃない Classical music isn't to my *taste.*

好子は服の趣味がよい[悪い] Yoshiko has good [bad] *taste* in clothes.

彼の絵は悪趣味だ His painting is in *bad* [*poor*] *taste.*

僕と彼女とは音楽の趣味が異なる(→僕の音楽の趣味は彼女のそれと異なる) My *taste* in music is different from hers.

◆彼女は趣味のよい時計をしている She wears a *tasteful* watch.

じゅみょう 寿命

❶【生き物の】longevity [U]; (通例期待される) life span [C], life expectancy [C] [U]; (一生) life [U] [C] (複 lives)

その土地の人々は寿命が長い People there have long *life spans.* / (→長生きする) People there *live* a long time.

この動物の平均的な寿命は10年だ *The* average *life span* of this animal is 10 years.

彼はたばこは寿命を縮めると言っている He says smoking 「shortens *one's life* [reduces *one's life expectancy*].

日本人の平均寿命は延び続けている *The average life expectancy* of Japanese people has been increasing.

◆彼は90で寿命を迎えた He *died* at 90. / パスポートをどこかに落としてしまったことに気づいたときは寿命の縮まる思いがした I *was scared to death* when I found that I had lost my passport somewhere.

❷【電池などの】life span [C], life expectancy [C] [U]; (有効期間) life [U] [C]

このCDプレーヤーももう寿命だ This CD player seems to *have come to the end of its life.*

◆アルカリ電池は寿命が長い Alkaline batteries *last a long time.*

しゅもく 種目 event [C] //彼は3種目で優勝を果たした He won championships in three *events.*

‖個人種目 an individual event / 団体種目 a group event

じゅもく 樹木 trees //公園内には様々な種類の樹木が茂っている There are various kinds of *trees* growing in the park.

じゅもん 呪文 incantation [C] [U], spell [C] //呪文を唱える chant *an incantation* [*a spell*]

しゅやく 主役 (役) the leading role [part], lead [C]; (役者) leading man [lady] [C] (❖a leading actor [actress]ともいう) //その少年が映画の主役を演じた The boy played *the lead* [*leading role*] in the film.

◆結婚式では花嫁が主役だ(→主に花嫁のためにある) Wedding ceremonies *are mainly for* brides. / 運動会では彼が主役だった(→最も活躍した) He *played the most active part* at the athletic meet.

じゅよ 授与 (賞の) presentation [C]; (称号・学位などの) conferment [C] [U], conferral [C]

──授与する (賞を) award [他], present [他]; (称号・学位などを)《公式的》confer [他] //そのバンドにグラミー賞が授与された The band *was* 「*presented* a Grammy award [*awarded* a Grammy]. / 校長が卒業生に卒業証書を授与した The principal 「*presented* diplomas to [*conferred* diplomas on] the graduates.

‖授与式 a presentation, an awards ceremony

しゅよう[1] 主要 ──主要な (主な) chief, main; (大きくて重要な) major; (最も重要な) leading; (中心的な) central

話し合いの主要なテーマ the *main* [*central*] theme of the discussion / 劇の主要人物 *the main* [*central, leading*] *figure* in a drama

神戸は日本の主要な港湾都市の一つだ Kobe is one of the *major* port cities in Japan.

フランスはワインの主要な生産国である France is a *major* producer of wine.

この展覧会は全国の主要都市で開催される This exhibition will be held in *major* [*principal*] *cities* throughout the country.

主要科目のテストが終わった I've finished the exams in *the main subjects.*

委員会の主要メンバーが全員そろった All of *the leading members* of the council have gathered.

‖主要産業 a staple [key, major] industry

しゅよう[2] 腫瘍 〖医学〗 tumor [C], growth [C] [U] //脳に腫瘍がある have *a tumor* [*growth*] in *one's* brain

‖悪性腫瘍 a malignant tumor / 脳腫瘍 a brain tumor / 良性腫瘍 a benign tumor

し

じゅよう 需要 demand ⓊC(またa～); (販売) market ⓊC(通例単数形); (必要性) need Ⓤ(またa～)/需要と供給 supply and demand(❖日本語と語順が逆であることに注意)/ 消費者の需要を満たす meet consumers' demand/ その商品はまだ需要がある There is still *a demand* [*market, need*] *for* the product./ The product *is still in demand.*/ 健康食品の需要が多い There is 「*much demand* [*a big market, much need*] *for* health foods./ その国では日本車の需要が伸びている［減っている］ *The demand for* Japanese cars is growing [falling] in that country.

しゅよく 主翼 a wing (of an airplane)

ジュラき ジュラ紀 〖古生物・地学〗the Jurassic (period)

しゅらば 修羅場 紛争で市内は修羅場と化した The city has become *the scene of a gory battle* due to the conflict./ 彼は数々の修羅場を踏んできた He has been through many *terrible [difficult] situations.*

ジュラルミン 〖化学〗duralumin

じゅり 受理 acceptance Ⓤ ――受理する accept ⑭, receive ⑭ / その書類は受理されなかった The document *was not accepted* [*received*].

じゅりつ 樹立 （設立）establishment Ⓤ ――樹立する（記録を）set* ⑭;（設立する）establish ⑭ / 新政府の樹立 *the establishment* of a new government/ 彼はスピードスケートで2つの公認世界記録を樹立した He *has set* [*established*] two official world records in speed skating./ 2国間の国交が樹立された The two countries *have established* relations with each other.

しゅりゅう 主流 the mainstream ――主流の mainstream /その考えが党内の主流を占めていた That was *the mainstream* thought in the party. ◆今年はこの型のシャツが主流だ（→流行している）This type of shirt is *in vogue* this year.
‖主流派 the leading faction

しゅりょう¹ 狩猟 hunting Ⓤ(❖(英)では猟犬を使った狩猟を指し, 銃による狩猟を shooting として区別する) / 狩猟に出かける go *hunting* [*shooting*]
‖狩猟期 open [the hunting] season/ 狩猟禁止区域 an area where hunting [shooting] is prohibited/ 狩猟場 a hunting ground/ 狩猟民族 a hunting people

しゅりょう² 首領（長）head ⓒ;（悪事を働く集団の）ringleader ⓒ

じゅりょう 受領 《公式的》receipt [rɪsíːt] Ⓤ ――受領する receive ⑭ / 金2万円確かに受領しました I *received* the sum of 20,000 yen.
‖受領者《公式的》a recipient / 受領証 a receipt

しゅりょく 主力 科学者たちはその問題の解明に主力を注いでいる Scientists are *focusing their energies* on solving the problem.
‖主力艦 a principal warship, a military flagship / 主力商品 a company's principal product [item]/ 主力選手 a principal [leading] player (of a team)/ 主力メンバー principal [leading] members

しゅるい 種類

kind ⓒ, sort ⓒ;（型・タイプ）type ⓒ;（同種中の）variety ⓒ;（品種）breed ⓒ;（範疇(はんちゅう)）category ⓒ;（同じ性質をもつ）class ⓒ

【語法】
(1)「…の種類の～」はふつう ... kind [sort] of ～ を用いて英語に訳すことができる.
(2) kind [sort] of に続く名詞にはふつう冠詞を付けない / 新しい種類の植物 a new *kind* [*sort*] *of* plant
(3) 複数種である場合には kinds [sorts] と複数形にする / 庭には様々な種類の花が咲いている There are various *kinds* [*sorts*] *of* flower(s) in the garden./ 世界には様々な種類の音楽がある There are various *kinds* [*sorts*] *of* music in the world.

この種類の本 this *kind* [*sort*] *of* book; books *of this kind* [*sort*](❖前者の例で books は不可. 後者の例で用いる ～ of ... kind [sort] という表現は, ... kind [sort] of ～ よりもかたい表現) / あらゆる種類の動物[果物]all kinds *of* animals [fruit]

庭にはたくさんの種類の植物があります There are plants *of many kinds* [*sorts*] in the garden.

どんな種類の映画が好きですか What *kind* [*sort*] *of* movie do you like?

その店はいろいろな種類のワインを置いている The shop stocks 「*a large variety of* [*many kinds of*] wines.

この種類のスイセンは初春に花を咲かせる This *kind* [*sort, variety*] *of* daffodil blooms early in the spring.

何種類のバラを育てているのですか How many *kinds* [*sorts, varieties*] *of* roses do you grow?

これらの犬はみな同じ種類です These dogs are all *of a kind.*/ These dogs are all *the same kind* [*sort, breed*].

彼の猫はうちのとは種類が違う His cat is *a different kind* [*sort, breed*] from ours.

遠くから見たので車の種類は識別できなかった I could not distinguish *the type* [*model*] of car from so far away.

それらの皿は作られた年代によっていくつかの種類に分けられている The dishes are divided into several *categories* [*classes*] according to when they were made.

じゅれい 樹齢 the age of a tree ◆この杉は樹齢800年を超えている This cedar is more than 800 *years old.*

シュレッダー shredder ⓒ /書類をシュレッダーにかける put a document through *a shredder; shred* a document

しゅろ 棕櫚 hemp palm (tree)ⓒ

しゅわ 手話 sign language ⓤⓒ, sign Ⓤ /手話をする talk in *sign language*;（→手話を用いる）use *sign language* / 彼は彼女に手話で答えた He answered her 「*by means of*

しゅわ [in] *sign language*.
∥手話通訳者 a sign language interpreter / 手話放送(番組) a TV program broadcast with sign language interpretation

じゅわき 受話器 (telephone) receiver ⓒ / 受話器を置く put *the receiver* down; hang up (*the phone*) / 彼は電話が鳴るとすぐに受話器を取った He 「picked up [lifted] *the receiver* as soon as the phone rang. ◆受話器をはずしておく leave *the phone* off the hook

しゅわん 手腕 ability ⓒⓤ /政治的[外交的]手腕 one's political [diplomatic] *ability* / 彼は文化祭実行委員長としてその手腕を発揮した He showed [exerted] his *ability* as the head of the executive committee of our school festival.

しゅん¹ 旬 旬の果物 fruits *in season*; *seasonal* foods / 旬の味覚を堪能(弦)する enjoy tasting the food *of the season* / イチゴは今が旬だ Strawberries *are* now *in season*. / サクランボは旬を過ぎてしまった Cherries have gone out *of season*.

しゅん² ⇨ しゅんと

じゅん¹ 順 order ⓤ /50音[先着]順に *in order of*「*the Japanese syllabary* [*arrival*] / クラス全員が背の順に並んだ Everyone in the class lined up *in order of height*. / その店ではCDをアルファベット順に並べている The CDs at the store are arranged *in alphabetical order*. / ここで起こったことを順を追って話してください Please tell me what happened here *in order*. / 剛, 建治, 正雄の順でゴールインした Takeshi, Kenji and then Masao finished the race *in that order*.
◆順に自己紹介をしてください Please introduce yourselves *in turn*.

じゅん² 純 ――純な (純粋な) pure; (無邪気な) innocent /純和風の部屋 a room made in 「*pure Japanese* [*all-Japanese*] *style* / 彼女は純な少女だ She is a *pure* [an *innocent*] young girl.
∥純愛 pure love, love from the bottom of one's heart / 純文学 serious literature

じゅん- 準- 準会員 an *associate* member / 彼はテニス大会で準優勝した He「won *second place* [(→準優勝者となった) became the *runner-up*] in a tennis meet.

じゅんい 順位 ranking ⓒ, order ⓤ /3者の優先順位を決める decide *the order of precedence* of the three / その曲は今週, ヒットチャートでの順位が下がった The ranking of the song has gone down on the hit chart this week. ◆その走者の順位は現在8位だ The runner *is ranked* [*stands*] eighth right now. / 彼の歌に好きな順に順位をつけた I *ranked* his songs *in order* of how much I like them.
∥順位決定戦 a play-off / 順位表(競技などの) standings

じゅんえき 純益 net profit ⓒⓤ /その会社は1億円の純益をあげた The company made *a net profit* of 100 million yen. / The company netted 100 million yen.

じゅんえん 順延 遠足は雨天順延です If it rains, the outing *will be*「*put off* [*postponed*] *till the next clear day*.

じゅんおくり 順送り その問題はもう何年も未解決のまま責任者から責任者へと順送りにされてきた The problem *has been passed down* unresolved from one responsible person to another for years.

じゅんかい 巡回 round ⓒ (通例複数形 ~s), patrol ⓤⓒ ――巡回する (口語的) do* [go*, make*] the rounds, patrol ⓑⓘ /この地区は1日に数回警官が巡回している Policemen「*do the rounds of* [*patrol*] *this district several times a day*. / 巡回中の警官が何者かに襲われた A policeman *on his rounds* [*beat*] has been assaulted by someone.
∥巡回区域 rounds / 巡回図書館 (米) a bookmobile, (英) a mobile library

しゅんかしゅうとう 春夏秋冬 この町では春夏秋冬美しい景色が楽しめる You can enjoy beautiful sights *all year round* in this town.

じゅんかつゆ 潤滑油 lubricant ⓒⓤ (◆比喩的な意味でも用いる), lubricating oil ⓒⓤ / ユーモアは人間関係におけるよい潤滑油となる Humor can work as *a good lubricant* in human relations.

しゅんかん 瞬間 moment ⓒ, (口語的) minute ⓒ (通例単数形), instant ⓒ (◆*moment* よりさらに短い) ――瞬間の·瞬間的な momentary, instantaneous /決定的瞬間 *a crucial moment; the moment of truth* / これは彼が転んだ瞬間を撮った写真だ This picture is of *the moment* [*instant*] *that he fell*. / 彼女と目が合った瞬間, 顔が赤くなってしまった *The moment* [*instant, minute*] (that) my eyes met hers, my face flushed. / 彼女に電話しようとしたまさにその瞬間に彼女のほうから電話がかかってきた I received a call from her *at the very moment* I was about to call her.
∥瞬間芸 a momentary [an instantaneous] performance / 瞬間接着剤 quick drying glue / 瞬間湯沸かし器 a flash water heater, (英) a geyser / 最大瞬間風速 the maximum instantaneous wind velocity

じゅんかん 循環 (血液·空気などの) circulation ⓤⓒ; (ひと巡り) cycle ⓒ; (順序正しく交代すること) rotation ⓤ ――循環する·させる (血液·空気など) circulate ⓑⓘ /季節の循環 *the cycle* [*rotation*] *of the seasons* / 水槽の水を循環させる *circulate* water through an aquarium / 運動すると血液の循環がよくなる Exercise stimulates "*the circulation of blood* [*blood circulation*]. / 血液は体内を循環している Blood *is circulating* around [through] the body. ◆駅前から市内循環バスが出ています There is *a bus which runs around the city in a circular route*.
∥循環器 a circulatory organ / 循環器系 the circulatory system / 循環小数 (数学) a repeating decimal / 循環論法 circular reasoning

しゅんき 春季 spring ⓤⓒ, springtime ⓤ

‖春季大会 a spring [springtime] meet
しゅんぎく 春菊〘植物〙 crown daisy
じゅんきゅう 準急 semi-express (train) ⓒ
じゅんきょ 準拠 この資料集は教科書に準拠して作られている This data book *is based on [was made according to]* the textbook.
じゅんぎょう 巡業 tour ⓒ ― 巡業する tour ⓤⓘ /劇団は地方を巡業した The theater company *made a tour of [toured]* the provinces. / 彼らは北海道を巡業中だ They are *on tour* in Hokkaido now.
じゅんきん 純金 pure [solid, true] gold ⓤ /純金製のメダル a *solid gold* medal
じゅんぎん 純銀 pure [solid, true] silver ⓤ
じゅんぐりに 順繰りに in turn, by turns /家族中が順繰りにかぜをひいた Everyone in my family caught a cold「*in turn [by turns]*. / 先生は最前列の生徒から順繰りに当てていった The teacher called on the students to answer「*in turn [by turns]*, starting from the first row.
じゅんけつ 純潔 purity ⓤ; (処女・童貞であること) virginity ⓤ ― 純潔な pure; virgin /純潔を守る keep *one's purity [virginity]*
じゅんけつしゅ 純血種 purebred ⓒ ― 純血種の purebred (❖名詞の前で用いる); (血統のよい・血統書付きの) pedigree (❖名詞の前で用いる) /純血種のポインター a *purebred* pointer
じゅんけっしょう 準決勝 (個々の試合) semifinal (game [match]) ⓒ; (段階) the semifinals /わが校のサッカー部はついに準決勝まで進んだ Our school soccer team has finally advanced to *the semifinals*. / 彼らは準決勝で敗れた They lost in *the semifinal*.
‖準決勝出場者[チーム] a semifinalist
しゅんこう 竣工 completion ⓤ ― 竣工する be completed /2001年に新図書館が竣工した The new library *was completed* in 2001.
‖竣工式 a ceremony to celebrate the completion
じゅんこう 巡航 cruise ⓒ ― 巡航する cruise ⓘ /この船は東京湾を巡航している This ship *cruises* about [in] Tokyo Bay.
‖巡航速度 (a) cruising speed / 巡航ミサイル〘軍事〙a cruise missile
じゅんさ 巡査 police officer ⓒ,《英公式的》police constable ⓒ (《略語》PC); (男性) policeman ⓒ; (女性) policewoman ⓒ /巡査部長 a (police) sergeant / 交通巡査 a traffic policeman [policewoman]
しゅんじ 瞬時 私たちの感覚は膨大な量の情報を瞬時に処理している Our senses deal with an enormous amount of information *instantly*.
じゅんじ 順次 (次々に) one after another; (順を追って) in order /そのバンドのレコードが順次CD化される予定だ The band's records will be transferred onto CDs *one after another*.
じゅんしせん 巡視船 patrol boat ⓒ

じゅんしゅ 遵守・順守 obedience ⓤ, observance ⓤ /遵守する obey ⓣ, (公式的) observe ⓣ /交通法規の遵守 *observance* of the traffic laws / 法律を遵守する *obey [observe]* the law
じゅんじゅんけっしょう 準々決勝 (個々の試合) quarterfinal (game [match]) ⓒ; (段階) the quarterfinals
‖準々決勝出場者[チーム] a quarterfinalist
じゅんじゅんに 順々に (順繰りに) in turn; (1つずつ・1人ずつ) one by one; (順を追って) in order /私たち5人はカラオケで順々に歌った Five of us sang songs「*in turn [one by one]* at karaoke.
じゅんじょ 順序 order ⓤ; (連続した) sequence ⓤⓒ; (手順) procedure ⓤⓒ
順序が逆だよ *The order* is backward.
子供たちは順序よくバスから降りた The children got off the bus *in order [sequence]*.
本棚の本の順序が乱れている The books on the shelves are *out of order [sequence]*.
彼の手違いで作業の順序が狂ってしまった His mistake has upset *the order [sequence]* of our work.
ちゃんと順序どおりにやればうまくいくさ You can do it if you *follow the proper sequence [procedure]*.
◆彼は仕事のやり方を順序だてて説明してくれた He explained to me「*in a methodical way [methodically]* how to do the work.
じゅんじょう 純情 pure heart ⓒⓤ ― 純情な pure,《公式的》ingenuous /乙女の純情をもてあそぶ toy with *the pure heart* of a girl / 純情かれんな少女 a *pure [an ingenuous] and pretty* girl
じゅんしょく 殉職 警官1人が殉職した One police officer *died in the line of duty*.
‖殉職者 a person who died in the line of duty
じゅんじる¹ 準じる 彼は先例に準じて罰せられた He was punished *according to* precedent. / 彼女は正社員に準じる扱いを受けている She is treated *in the same way as* the regular workers.
じゅんじる² 殉じる (後を追って死ぬ) kill *oneself* following *a person's* death; (主義などのために死ぬ) die for ...
じゅんしん 純真 ― 純真な (無邪気な) innocent; (素朴な) simple; (無垢〔く〕な)《公式的》ingenuous; (子供のような) childlike /純真無垢な少女 an *ingenuous* girl / 彼は今もなお子供のように純真だ He is still as *innocent [simple]* as a child.
じゅんすい 純粋 ― 純粋な (混じり気のない) pure; (本物の) genuine ― 純粋さ purity ⓤ; genuineness ⓤ
彼は純粋な心の持ち主だ He is *pure* at heart.
僕は純粋に君のことを心配して言っているんだよ What I'm saying is「*from my pure concern about you [purely from my concern about you]*.
◆純粋のシェパード a *pure-blooded [purebred]* German shepherd

‖純粋培養 pure culture

じゅんぜん 純然 純然たる芸術作品 a work of art(,) *pure and simple* ∥ 彼女がその殺人を犯したのは純然たる事実だ It's a *sheer* [*simple*] fact that she committed the murder.

しゅんそく 俊足・駿足 彼はチーム一の俊足だ He is *the fastest runner* in our team. / 彼は俊足を飛ばして二塁盗塁を決めた *Putting his speed to work*, he stole second.

じゅんちょう 順調 ――順調な (支障のない) smooth; (好都合な) favorable, 《英》favourable; (満足のいく) satisfactory

その投手は今シーズン順調な滑りだしを見せた The pitcher made a *smooth* [*favorable, satisfactory*] start this season.

◆順調にいけば，1時間で着きます If things go well [*smoothly, favorably, satisfactorily*], we can arrive there in one hour. / 学校生活は順調ですか How *are* you *getting along* at school?

しゅんと 彼は先生に怒られてしゅんとなってしまった He *hung his head in silence* when scolded by a teacher.

じゅんど 純度 (純粋さ) purity ∥ 純度99パーセントまで精製した金 gold refined to 99 percent *purity*

しゅんとう 春闘 the spring labor offensive

じゅんとう 順当 ――順当な (当然の) natural; (理にかなった) reasonable ――順当に (うまく) well; (予想どおりに) as expected ∥ 様々なデータを考慮すると，彼が勝つのが順当といえよう Taking various data into consideration, we can conclude that it's *natural* for him to win the match. / 順当にいけば，作業は今週末には終了する If everything goes well, the work will be finished by the end of this week. / そのチームは予選を順当に勝ち進んだ The team kept on winning the preliminaries *as expected*.

じゅんのう 順応 ――順応する (新しい環境・生活などに) adapt, adjust; (規則・習慣などに) conform (to ...) ∥ 彼女はすぐにアメリカでの新しい生活に順応した She soon *adapted* [*adjusted*] (*herself*) to her new life in America. ◆その少年はとても順応性のある子だ The boy is very *adaptable* [*flexible*].

‖順応性 adaptability

じゅんぱく 純白 ――純白の pure white, snow-white ∥ 純白のウエディングドレス a「*pure white* [*snow-white*] wedding dress

じゅんばん 順番 (番) turn; (順序) order; (列などの順) place

順番を待つ wait for *one's turn*

あまり待たずに順番が回ってきた *My turn* has come without much waiting.

ページの順番が狂っている The pages are *out of order* [*in the wrong order*].

1人の男が順番を無視してタクシーを待つ列に割り込んできた A man broke into the taxi line *out of turn*.

生徒たちは列の端から順番に自己紹介をした The students introduced themselves *in turn*, starting with the one at the end of the row.

子供たちが順番にブランコに乗った The children「*took turns* (*at*) getting on the swing [got on the swing *in turn*].

ちょっとトイレに行ってくるから順番とっといて Can you *save my place in line* for a while? I'm going to the rest room.

◆店の前には順番待ちの列ができていた There was *a line of people* in front of the shop.

じゅんび 準備

preparation ❖「…のための具体的な準備」の意味では通例複数形で用いる); (手はず) arrangements ――準備する prepare, get* [make*] ready; (手はずを整える) arrange

私たちは旅行の準備をした We「*made preparations* [*prepared*] *for* a trip. / (→出かける準備をした) We *prepared to* go on a trip.

きょうは早く帰って夕食の準備をしなければならない Today, I have to go home early *to prepare* [*make*] dinner.

私たちが彼の誕生会を準備した We *arranged* [*made arrangements for*] a birthday party for him.

会の準備はすべてととのった Everything *was arranged* [*prepared*] for the meeting.

出かける準備はすべてととのいましたか Have you got everything *ready* to go?

最悪の事態に備えて心の準備をしておかねばならない We must *prepare ourselves for* the worst.

そのプロジェクトは現在準備中です The project is *in preparation* now.

準備不足で面接官の質問に答えられなかった I couldn't answer the interviewers' questions because of *lack of preparation*.

◆準備中《掲示》*Closed* / 彼はレースの前に準備運動をした He「*warmed up* [*did some warm-ups*] before the race.

🅔「もうパーティーの準備はできた？」「うん．準備万端だよ」"Have you *prepared for* the party yet?" "Yes.「*Everything is ready*. [*It's all set.*]"

‖準備委員会 a preparatory committee / 準備段階 a preparatory stage

じゅんぷう 順風 following wind ∥ 船は順風を受けて走った The ship sailed with *a following wind*.

◆その事故が起きるまでは彼の人生は順風満帆だった *Everything* in his life *had been going well* before the accident occurred.

じゅんふどう 順不同 それらは順不同です They *are listed in random order*.

しゅんぶん 春分 the vernal [spring] equinox [íːkwinάks] ◆春分の日 Vernal Equinox Day, the Spring Equinox

じゅんぽう 遵法・順法 ∥順法闘争 a work-to-rule strike

じゅんぼく 純朴 ――純朴な (素朴な) simple and honest; (世間ずれしていない) unsophisticated ∥純朴な少年 a *simple and honest* [an *unsophisticated*] boy

じゅんもう 純毛 pure wool [wúl] Ⓤ ──純毛の pure-wool, all-wool //純毛の毛布 a *pure-wool* [*an all-wool*] blanket

じゅんようかん 巡洋艦 cruiser Ⓒ

じゅんれい 巡礼・順礼 pilgrimage Ⓒ;（巡礼者）pilgrim Ⓒ //…へ巡礼の旅に出る「go on [make] *a pilgrimage* to …

じゅんろ 順路 (fixed) route Ⓒ //順路に従う take [follow] *the (fixed) route*

しょ 書（習字）calligraphy Ⓤ;（書物）book Ⓒ //書の達人 a master of *calligraphy*

しょ- 諸－（もろもろの）various（❖英語では特に訳出せずに名詞の複数形で表せばよい場合が多い） //諸外国からの旅行者 travelers from *various* countries ◆身体の諸機能 bodily *functions* / 近隣諸国 neighboring *countries*

じょ 序 preface Ⓤ

しょあく 諸悪 諸悪の根源 the root of *all evil*

じょい 女医 female [woman] doctor Ⓒ

しょいこむ 背負い込む shoulder ⟨他⟩, take* … upon [on] *oneself* //彼はいつも責任をひとりでしょいこむうとする He is inclined to「*shoulder* all the responsibility by himself [*take* all the responsibility *upon* himself]
◆彼女は多くの仕事をしょいこんでいる She *is burdened with* a whole lot of tasks.

しよう¹ 使用 use [júːs] Ⓤ（❖個々の用途の意味では Ⓒ） ──使用する use [júːz] ⟨他⟩
使用禁止《掲示》*Do Not Use*
銃の使用は法律で禁じられている The law forbids the *use* of guns.
この試験では辞書の使用が認められている The *use* of dictionaries is permitted for this examination.
この製品は激しい使用にも耐えるようにできている This product has been made to endure hard *use*.
その薬は現在一般に使用されていない The medicine *is not*「*in* general *use* [*used* generally] now.
その部屋を使用するには事前に許可をとる必要がある You need to be given permission in order to *use* the room.
体育館は現在使用中だ The gymnasium *is* now *in use*.
この機械の使用目的は非常に限られている The *uses* for this machine are very limited.
その機械は使用禁止になっている The *use* of the machine *is forbidden*. / この機械を使用してはならない You *are forbidden to use* the machine.
使用後はごみ箱へ捨ててください Please put them into trash cans *after using them*.
この装置の使用法を教えてください Please tell me *how to use* this device.

◆使用中（トイレや浴室などの）《掲示》*Occupied* / 使用上の注意を守る follow *directions* [*instructions*] / 使用説明書をよく読みましょう Read *directions* [*instructions*, *users' manuals*] carefully. / 貸し自転車の使用料はいくらですか How much does it cost to *rent* a bicycle? //彼は使用済み切手を集めている He collects *used* stamps.

‖使用者 a user;（雇い主）an employer / 使用人 an employee;（召使）a servant

しよう² 私用（個人的な用事）private [personal] business Ⓤ;（私的な目的）private [personal] purpose Ⓤ;（個人で使うこと）private [personal] use Ⓤ //彼女は私用で外出しています She is out *on private* [*personal*] *business*. / 彼は学校のコンピュータを私用に使っている He uses computers in our school *for private* [*personal*] *purposes*.

しよう³ 仕様 ❶【方法・手段】彼がどこにいるか分からないのだから連絡のしようがない Without knowing where he is, *there is no way* to get in touch with him. / 僕に何ができるっていうのさ．どうしようもないじゃないか What can I do? *It can't be helped*. / そんなしようもない(→ささいな)ことでかっかするなよ Don't get so angry at such a *trivial* matter. ⇒しようがない
❷【仕様書・デザイン】（仕様書）specifications;（デザイン）design Ⓤ //そのCDプレーヤーの仕様が変わった They changed *the specifications* [*design*] of the CD player.
◆この商品は特別仕様になっている This product has a *"special design* [*modification*].

しよう⁴ 試用 この製品は無料で2週間試用できます You *can try* this product *out* for free for two weeks.
‖試用期間 a trial period

しよう⁵ 枝葉 trivial [trifling] detail Ⓒ;（つまらぬこと・物）triviality Ⓤ Ⓒ //彼は枝葉末節にこだわりすぎる He cares too much about *trivial* [*trifling*] *details*.

しよう⁶ 子葉 cotyledon [kàtəlíːdən] Ⓒ

-しよう
❶【誘い】let's ⇒-しませんか
けんかはもうやめにしよう *Let's stop quarreling* now.
彼の悪口はもう言わないことにしよう *Let's* not [《英口語的》Don't *let's*,《米俗語》*Let's* don't] say bad things about him any more.
◆次は何をしようか What should we *do* next?
❸「いっしょにサッカーをしよう」「そうしよう」 "*Let's* play soccer together." "Yes, *let's*."
❷【…するつもりだ】be going to *do*;（意図している）intend to *do*;（計画している）plan to *do*
あしたは部屋の掃除をすることにしようと思う I'*m going* [I *intend*] *to* clean my room tomorrow.
彼に電話しようと思っていたが，忘れてしまった I *was going to* call him, but I forgot.
◆二度とあそこへは行かないことにしようと思う I won't [will never] go there again.

しょう¹ 省 ❶【中央官庁】（日本・英国・ヨーロッパ諸国などの）ministry Ⓒ;（主に米国の）department Ⓒ（通例 Department）;（英国の）Office（❖省の名称中で用いる） //《米国の》国防総

省 *the Department* of Defense / （英国の）国防省 *the Ministry* of Defence / （英国の）外務省 *the Foreign Office*
❷【中国の行政区画】*province* ⓒ

しょう² 賞 （競技などでの）*prize* ⓤⓒ; （業績・功労に対する）*award* ⓒ ∥絵画コンクールで賞を取った I won *a prize* at a painting contest. / 彼には県知事より賞が授与された He was awarded *a prize* by the prefectural governor. / その俳優が賞を総なめにした The actor carried off all *the awards*.
∥アカデミー賞 an Academy Award / 1等賞 the first prize / グラミー賞 a Grammy Award / 残念賞 a consolation prize / ノーベル賞 a Nobel Prize / ブービー賞 a prize for the second-to-last place（❖英語の booby prize は「最下位の人に贈る賞」の意）

しょう³ 章 *chapter* ⓒ ((略語)) chap., ch.) ∥その問題はその本の第3章で扱われている The problem is treated in「*chapter* three [*chapter 3*, *the third chapter*] of the book.

しょう⁴ 性 *nature* ⓤⓒ ∥ごまかしをして勝負に勝つなんて私の性に合わない It's not in my *nature* to win the game by using tricks. / It goes against my *grain* to win the game by using tricks.
◆その仕事は彼女の性に合っていると思う I think that「the job *suits* her *well* [she is *suited to* the job]. / 僕と彼女とはどうも性が合わない Somehow she and I *never agree* (with each other).

しょう⁵ 商 【数学】 *quotient* [kwóuʃənt] ⓒ

しょう- 小- 私の住む町は小京都といわれている My town is called *a little Kyoto*.
∥小アジア Asia Minor

-**しょう**¹ -勝 *win*, *victory* ⓒ ∥その力士は今場所9勝6敗だった The sumo wrestler has had「nine *wins* and six *losses* [nine *victories* and six *defeats*] in this tournament. ◆私たちはそのチームに対して現在6勝3敗 Our team is *6 and 3* against that team at present.

-**しょう**² -性 脂性の肌 *oily* skin / 彼はひどく心配性だ He *gets worried very easily*. / 《主に米・口語的》He *is a worrywart*. / 彼女は疑り性だ(→何にでも熱中する) She *becomes enthusiastic about everything*.

じよう 滋養 (滋養物) *nourishment* ⓤ ◆滋養に富んだ食物 *nourishing* [*nutritious*] food
∥滋養強壮剤 (a) tonic

じょう¹ 情 （感情）*feeling* ⓒ, *emotion* ⓒ; （愛情）*love* ⓤ, *affection* ⓤⓒ ∥親子の情 *love* [*affection*] between parent and child / 懐古の情 retrospective *affection* / 彼はその捨て犬に哀れみの情をいだいた He「*had a feeling of* [*felt*] *pity* for the abandoned dog.
◆彼はその犬に情が移ってしまい, 家で飼うことにした He *became attached to* the dog, and so decided to keep it at his house. / 彼女は情の深い[薄い]人だ She *has a warm* [*cold*] *heart*. / She is a *warm-hearted* [*cold-hearted*] person. / 母は情にもろい My mother is sentimental.

じょう² 錠 （錠前）*lock* ⓒ; （南京錠）*padlock* ⓒ ⇨かぎ(鍵) 図版

じょう³ 嬢 （未婚女性の姓・姓名に付けて）Miss ∥高橋香織嬢 *Miss Takahashi Kaori*
◆受付嬢 *a female receptionist* / うぐいす嬢 *a female baseball announcer* / お手伝いしましょうか Can I help you, *Miss*? / お嬢さんはどうしていますか How is *your daughter*? / お嬢ちゃん, どこから来たの Where have you come from, *little girl*?

じょう⁴ 上 （一級）the first class; （本の上巻）volume one ⓤ, the first volume — 上の（一級）*first-class*; （最高の）the best ∥寿司(♯)の上を頼んだ I ordered *first-class* sushi. ◆中の上の家庭 an *upper-middle-class* family

-**じょう**¹ -条 （条項）*article* ⓒ ∥日本国憲法第9条 *Article 9* of the Japanese Constitution / 一条の光 *a ray* [*beam*] *of light*

-**じょう**² -上 それは理論上は可能である It is possible *theoretically*. / 彼らは宗教上の問題でもめている They are arguing about *religious* matters. / この映画は教育上好ましくない This movie is unsuitable *for educational purposes*. / 地球上の全人口は60億を数えるという It is said that the number of human beings *on the earth* is six billion. / 彼は健康上の理由でクラブをやめた He quit the club *because of* his ill health.

-**じょう**³ -乗 【数学】*power* ⓒ ∥3の4乗 the fourth *power* of three; three to the fourth *power* / 5を3乗する *raise* five to the *power* of three

-**じょう**⁴ -畳 4畳半の部屋 a room with four and a half *tatami*(s) [*straw mats*] / 私の部屋は8畳間だ My room「has eight *tatami*(s) [is an eight-*tatami* room].

-**じょう**⁵ -錠 *pill*, *tablet* ⓒ ∥この錠剤を8時間ごとに3錠服用しなさい Take three of these *pills* [*tablets*] every eight hours.

じょうあい 情愛 *affection* ⓤⓒ ∥親の子に対する情愛 parental *affection* for *one's* child / 夫婦の情愛 *affection* between husband and wife

しょうあく 掌握 ——掌握する *get** [*assume*] *control* ∥政権を掌握する *get* [*assume*] *control* of the government / 部下を掌握する *get* [*assume*] *control over one's* subordinates

じょうい 上位 彼の成績はクラスでも上位だ His grade「*is at a high rank* [*ranks high*] in his class. / 彼女の成績は私より上位だ Her grades *are higher than* mine. / その選手は上位入賞を果たした The athlete won *a higher prize*. / その歌手は今週のヒットチャートで上位を独占した The singer occupied *the top spaces* on this week's hit chart. / このレースの上位3人までが次のレースに参加できる *The top three* runners in this race can enter the next race.

しょういん 勝因 the cause of victory ∥きょうの勝因は何だったと思われますか What do you think was *the cause of your victory* today?

じょういん[1] 上院 the Upper House; (米国の) the Senate; (英国の) the House of Lords (❖単に the Lords ともいう)

‖上院議員 a member of the Upper House; (米国の) a Senator; (英国の) a member of the House of Lords

じょういん[2] 乗員 crew member [C], 《集合的》 crew [C]

しょううちゅう 小宇宙 microcosm [máikrəkɑ̀zm] [C]

じょうえい 上映 ━上映する play [他], show* [他] (❖いずれも自動詞で「上映される」の意味がある) ∥この映画館はよく古い映画を上映する This theater often *plays* [*shows*] old movies. / J劇場では今フランス映画を上映中です A French movie *is* now *playing* [*showing*] at the J Theater. / A French movie *is* now *on* at the J Theater. ◆その映画は上映時間が短い That is a *short* movie. / 『ゴジラ』近日上映 *Godzilla coming soon*!

しょうエネ 省エネ ━省エネの energy-saving ∥省エネタイプのエアコン an *energy-saving* air conditioner / 省エネ対策を講じる take *energy-saving measures*; (→エネルギー節約のために策を講じる) take *measures to save energy*

じょうえん 上演 ━上演する (演じる) play [他] (❖自動詞で「(劇などが)上演される」の意味がある), perform [他][自], put* on; (舞台などにかける) stage [他] ∥そのミュージカルは来月上演される The musical is going to *be played* [*performed, put on, staged*] next month. / 帝国劇場では今何を上演していますか What's *playing* at the Imperial Theater now?
◆上演は何時に終わりますか What time does *the show* end? / そのミュージカルは3年以上上演され続けている The musical *has been running* for over three years.

じょうおう 女王 queen [C] ➾じょおう

しょうおん 消音 ‖消音器(銃の) a silencer; (車などの) 《米》a muffler, 《英》a silencer

じょうおん 常温 normal temperature [U]; (室温) room temperature [U] ∥この食品は常温で2週間もちます This food will keep at *room temperature* for two weeks.

しょうか[1] 消化

❶【食べ物の】digestion [U][C] ━消化する digest [他][自]
消化を助ける help *digestion*
焼き魚は大根おろしといっしょに食べると消化によい Grilled fish *can be digested easily* when eaten with grated radish.
この野菜は消化しやすい[しにくい] This vegetable *is easy* [*hard*] *to digest*.
◆消化のよい[悪い]食べ物 *digestible* [*indigestible*] food / 消化不良を起こす get *indigestion*

❷【理解】━消化する digest [他], understand* [他]
黒田先生の授業は進み方が速いので生徒は内容を十分消化できずにいる Mr. Kuroda's classes proceed so fast that his students *can't digest* the material well.

❸【処理】━消化する (満たす) meet* [他]; (終える) finish [他]
ノルマを消化する *meet one's* quota
‖消化液 digestive juices / 消化器官 a digestive organ / 消化器系 the digestive system / 消化作用 the digestion process / 消化試合 a mop-up game

しょうか[2] 消火 (消火活動) fire fighting [U] ━消火する 「put* out [《公式的》extinguish] the fire ◆そこに着くと彼らはすぐに消火活動にあたった As soon as they got there, they started to *fight the fire*.
‖消火器 a fire extinguisher, an extinguisher / 消火栓 a (fire) hydrant, a fireplug

しょうか[3] 商科 ‖商科大学 a commercial college [university], a college [university] of commerce ➾しょうがく(商学)

しょうが 生姜 ginger [U] ‖ショウガ湯 hot water with grated ginger and sugar / 紅ショウガ red-dyed ginger

じょうか 浄化 purification [U]; (悪癖・腐敗などの) cleanup [C]《通例単数形》 ━浄化する purify [他]; clean up ∥県政の浄化 *the cleanup* of the prefectural government / この装置は室内の空気を浄化する This device *purifies* [*cleans*] the air in the room.
‖浄化槽 a septic tank / 浄化装置 a purifier

しょうかい[1] 紹介

introduction [U][C] ━紹介する introduce [他]; (高い地位の人に対して) 《公式的》present [他]; (よい情報を与える) 《口語的》put* *a person* onto ... ➾[コミュニケーションスキル] p.697, [場面・状況別会話] p.1760

> [英作文ノート] 「…をご紹介します」の英語は?
> みなさんに山田さんをご紹介します
> →×I *introduce* Mr. Yamada to you.
> →○*Let me introduce* Mr. Yamada to you.
> →○*Allow me to introduce* Mr. Yamada to you.
> →○*I'd like to introduce* Mr. Yamada to you.
> ★会話表現は, 直訳すると意味が通じないだけでなく, 相手によくない印象を与える場合がある. I introduce ... は, 「紹介する」ことを習慣にしているようで不自然に聞こえる.

彼は私によい医者を紹介してくれた He *put* me *onto* a good doctor.
彼女はその画家を日本に初めて紹介した She first *introduced* the painter to Japan.
◆この近くでどこかいいレストランを紹介して(→推薦して)くれませんか Can you *recommend* any good restaurants near here?
[会話]「彼ってすてきだわ」「紹介してほしい?」"He's so attractive!" "Would you like to *meet* him?" (❖この meet は「…と知り合いになる, …に紹介される」という意味)
[会話]「みなさんに高橋さんをご紹介します」「ただ今ご紹介にあずかりました高橋です」"I would like to *introduce* Miss Takahashi to

コミュニケーションスキル ―紹介―

① 初対面で自己紹介し合うとき

(A) **May I introduce myself?** I'm Tanaka Kenji. I'm an exchange student from Japan.

自己紹介させてください。私は田中健二と申します。日本から来た交換留学生です。

(B) **How do you do?** My name is Higashida Ichiro.
　-**How do you do?** My name is Charles Marvin.

はじめまして。東田一郎と申します。―はじめまして。チャールズ・マービンです。

(C) **Hello [Hi]**, I'm Beth. **Nice to meet you.**
　-**Hello [Hi]**, Beth. I'm Hiroshi. **Nice to meet you, too.**

こんにちは、私、ベスです。よろしく。―こんにちは、ベス。僕は広志です。

(D) **Hello**, I'm Matsuoka Sadao. Please call me Sada.
　-**Hello**, Sada. **Nice to meet you.**

こんにちは。私は松岡貞夫といいます。サダと呼んでください。―やあ、サダ、よろしくね。

☞ 自己紹介のしかたとしては、(A)は丁寧、(B)はより丁寧な表現となる。同年輩の友人を紹介する場合は、(C)がふつう。Hi は Hello よりさらにくだけた表現.

☞ 公式の席では、(A)のように名前を言った後で自分の仕事や身分に簡単に触れることが多い.

☞ 互いに紹介し合う場合、しっかり相手の顔を見ながら自分の名前を名乗ることがポイント。英米で名乗るときに握手を求められることも多い.

☞ (C)のように相手が(It's) Nice to meet you. と言った場合は、こちらも Nice to meet you, too. と言うのがマナー。日本語の「(どうぞ)よろしく」に当たるもので、too を強く発音する。なお、ふつう meet は初対面のときに、see は2度目以降に使われる.

☞ 英米では on a first-name basis, on first-name terms (ファーストネームで呼び合う仲の)が親密さと信頼感を表すので、時には(D)のように自分から進んでそのような関係を作り出していくことも必要となる。また名は呼びやすいように nickname (愛称)が好まれるので、日本名の愛称を考えておくとよい.

② 知り合いを紹介するとき

(A) Yoko, **this is** my friend, Tracy Johnson. Tracy, **this is** Yoko.

陽子、私の友達のトレイシー・ジョンソンよ。トレイシー、こちら陽子よ。

(B) Yoko, Tracy. Tracy, Yoko.

陽子、こちらはトレイシー。トレイシー、こちら陽子よ。

(C) Kazuo, **have you met** Ted? Ted, this is my friend, Kazuo.
　-Hi, Ted. I've heard a lot about you.

和夫、テッドには前に会ったかな？ テッド、こちらは友達の和夫。―やあ、テッド、うわさは聞いてましたよ。

(D) Mr. Brown, **may I introduce** Mr. Mori? / Mr. Brown, **please let me introduce you to** Mr. Mori.
　-Hello, Mr. Mori. I've been looking forward to meeting you.

ブラウンさん、森さんをご紹介します。―はじめまして、森さん。以前からお会いしたいと思っておりました。

☞ (A)は友人を紹介する最も一般的な紹介のしかた。(B)のように簡単に相手のファーストネームだけですます場合も多い.

☞ 2人が初対面かどうかがはっきりしない場合は、(C)のように尋ねてから、紹介に及ぶ.

☞ (D)の May I introduce …? と Please let me introduce you to … はかしこまった表現. I've been looking forward to *doing* は「首を長くして待っていた」に近い表現.

③ 紹介された相手と別れるとき

(A) **I'm very glad to have met you [It was really nice meeting you]**, Mr. Thomas.

お会いできてうれしかったです、トーマスさん。

(B) **I look forward to** seeing you again soon.

近いうちにまたお目にかかりたいです。

☞ (A)、(B)とも、紹介された相手と別れる際にいう表現。(A)では、to have met you と現在完了形を用いるところがポイント.

---

you." "Thank you very much for your kind introduction." (❖英米では紹介してくれた人に礼を述べるだけで、改めて自分の名前を名乗ることはふつうない)
‖紹介状 a letter of introduction / 結婚紹介所 a marriage agency

しょうかい² 照会 reference Ⓤ Ⓒ; inquiry Ⓤ Ⓒ ―照会する refer ⓐ, inquire ⓐ ◆銀行の預金残高を照会する check the balance in *one's* bank account

しょうかい³ 商会 company Ⓒ ((略語) Co., co.), firm Ⓒ /田中商会 Tanaka and *Company*; Tanaka & *Co.*

しょうがい¹ 障害

(じゃま) obstacle Ⓒ, hindrance Ⓤ Ⓒ; (困難) difficulty Ⓒ; (心身の) disability Ⓤ Ⓒ; (身体機能の欠如) defect Ⓒ
➡ 場面・状況別会話 p.1750
言語障害 a speech *defect* [*impediment*] / 聴覚障害 a hearing *defect*
この問題は両国の関係改善の大きな障害となっている This problem is *a great obstacle* [*hindrance*] to the improvement of relations between the two countries.
彼はこれまでに数々の障害を乗り越えてきた He has overcome a lot of *difficulties*.
我々の学校は障害のある学生をもっと多く受け入れるべきだ We should accept more students *with disabilities* at our school. / We should accept more *disabled* students at our school.

◆飲酒は肝機能障害を引き起こすことがある Drinking can cause *functional disorders of the liver.*
‖障害競走(競馬の) a steeplechase / 障害児教育 education of disabled children; (特殊教育) special education / 障害者 a physically disabled [handicapped] person, (集合的) the physically disabled [handicapped] / 障害物競走(陸上競技の) a steeplechase; (運動会の) an obstacle race / 身体障害者 a physically disabled [handicapped] person, (集合的) the physically disabled [handicapped]

しょうがい² 生涯 life ⓤⓒ (複 lives), lifetime ⓒ ‖生涯の伴侶(はんりょ) one's life partner; one's partner for life / …に生涯をささげる devote *one's life* to … / 彼女は先日、15年という短い生涯を閉じた She ended *her* short *life* of 15 years a few days ago. / 彼女は生涯の大半を生まれた町で過ごした She spent most of *her life* in the town where she was born. / 彼女は生涯独身だった She remained single *all* [*throughout*] *her life.* / 生涯二度と彼女に会うことはないだろう I won't see her again in *my lifetime.* / 彼は生涯で使いきれないほどのお金を手に入れた He got more money than he could spend in *his lifetime.*
◆君のことは生涯(→生きているかぎり)忘れないだろう I will [shall] never forget you *as long as I live.* / 彼はアメリカで生涯の友を得た He made *a lifelong friend* in the U.S.
‖生涯学習 lifelong learning [study] / 生涯教育 lifelong education

しょうがい³ 傷害 injury ⓒⓤ ‖人に傷害を加える inflict *injury* on a person; injure a person / 彼は旅行中傷害事件に巻き込まれた He was involved in *an injury* during his trip. / 彼は傷害罪で逮捕された He was arrested on *a charge of inflicting injuries.*
‖傷害致死 (a) bodily injury resulting in death / 傷害保険 accident insurance

しょうがい⁴ 渉外 public relations (単数扱い)((略語)PR) ‖渉外課 the public relations department, the PR department / 渉外係 a public relations officer((略語)PRO)

じょうがい 場外 ‖そのレスラーは相手を場外に投げ飛ばした The wrestler threw the opponent *out of the ring.* / 彼はきのうの試合で場外ホームランを2本打った He hit two *out-of-the-park homers* in yesterday's game.
‖場外馬券売り場 an off-track betting place [office]

しょうかく 昇格 promotion ⓒⓤ, (公式的) elevation ⓤ ──昇格する be promoted [elevated] ‖そのチームは1部リーグに昇格した The team *was promoted* [*elevated*] to the first division.

しょうがく¹ 少額・小額 少額の金 *a small sum* [*amount*] *of money*
‖小額紙幣 a small bill [note]

しょうがく² 商学 commercial science ‖商学部 the school [faculty] of commerce

しょうがくきん 奨学金 (学校などからの) scholarship ⓒ; (国などからの) (student) grant ⓒ (✪scholarship, grant は共に給付金を指し、返済する必要はない); (学生向けの貸付金) student loan ⓒ ‖彼女は奨学金をもらっている She is on *a scholarship* [*grant*]. / 彼は奨学金を受ける資格がある He is qualified to get [receive] *a scholarship* [*grant*]. / 彼女は奨学金をもらって留学している She is studying abroad *on a scholarship* [*grant*].

しょうがくせい¹ 小学生 (elementary) schoolchild ⓒ; (男子の) schoolboy ⓒ; (女子の) schoolgirl ⓒ

しょうがくせい² 奨学生 scholarship student ⓒ

しょうがつ 正月

> 正月は日本でいちばん重要な年中行事です。元旦には多くの人が神社や寺へ初もうでに行き、家族や親戚(しんせき)とおせち料理や雑煮を食べ、おとそを飲みます。正月三が日の間、ほとんどの会社や商店は休みになります。
> The New Year is the most important annual event in Japan. On the first day of the year, called *gantan*, many people visit shrines or temples to make wishes for the New Year, and they enjoy *osechi* (special dishes for the New Year) and *zoni* (soup with *mochi*) with *otoso* (spiced sake) with family and relatives. Most companies and shops are closed for the first three days of the year.

しょうがっこう 小学校 《米》 elementary [《米》grade, 《英》primary] school ⓒⓤ ‖弟は今年小学校に上がった My brother started *elementary school* this year.
◆妹は小学校の4年生です My sister is 「*in the fourth grade* [*a fourth grader*].

しようがない あいつは本当にしようがないやつだ He is a really *helpless* guy. / いつまでもぶつぶつ言うなよ、すんだことはもうしようがないじゃないか Don't complain any more. 「*What is done is done.* [*It couldn't be helped.*] / 妹にせがまれてしようがなく遊園地へ連れていってやった I was pestered by my sister until I *had no choice but to* take her to an amusement park. / セーターなんか脱いじゃおう、もう暑くてしようがないよ I'm going to take my sweater off. *It's* simply *too hot.* / ほかに説明のしようがない There is no other way to explain it.

じょうかまち 城下町 castle town ⓒ

じょうかん 上官 superior [senior] officer ⓒ

しょうき 正気 (通常の精神状態) senses, (right) mind ⓤ; (狂気に対して) sanity ⓤ; (意識) consciousness ⓤ (また a ~) ──正気の sane ‖正気に返る (→分別を取り戻す) come to *one's senses*; (→意識を取り戻す) 「come to [regain] *consciousness* / 正気を失う (→分別を失う) lose *one's senses*; (→気が狂う) lose *one's mind*; (→意識を失う) lose con-

sciousness / 正気でない be out of one's senses [*mind*] / 彼女にあんなことを言うなんて, 彼は正気とは思えない I don't think he was in *his* senses [*right mind*] to say such a thing to her. / 大雨で増水した川に泳ぎに行くなんて正気のさたとは思えない They *must* 「*have lost their sanity* [*be insane*]」 to go swimming in the river swollen with the heavy rain.

しょうぎ 将棋 △ *shogi*, Japanese chess / 将棋を指す play *shogi*
慣用表現 列車が急停車して乗客は将棋倒しになった The train came to a sudden halt and the passengers *fell over like dominoes*.

> 将棋はチェスに似たゲームで, 2人の競技者が81ますに区切られた将棋盤の上で20個ずつのこまを動かし, 勝負を競います. 将棋はチェス同様インド発祥のゲームで, 王を詰めれば勝ちという点などは共通していますが, チェスと違い取った相手のこまを再度使うことができます.
> *Shogi*, or Japanese chess, is played by two people with 20 playing pieces for each on a *shogi* board divided into 81 small squares. The game originated in India like chess, and also like chess, you win by checkmating your opponent's king. *Shogi*, however, differs from chess in that you can use the pieces you have captured.

じょうき¹ 蒸気 steam ⓤ / この船は蒸気で走る This ship is driven *by steam*.
◆ やかんがこんろの上で蒸気を出している The kettle *is steaming* on the stove.
‖蒸気機関 a steam engine / 蒸気機関車 a steam locomotive / 蒸気船 a steam ship, a steamer / 蒸気暖房 steam heating

じょうき² 上記 上記の理由により計画は中止された For the *above* reason, the plan was canceled. / 上記のとおりスケジュールは変更されました *As mentioned above*, the schedule has been changed.

じょうき³ 上気 ──上気する (紅潮する) flush ⓘ, be flushed; (興奮する) be [get*] excited / 彼の顔は怒りで上気していた His face *was flushed* with anger.

じょうき⁴ 常軌 常軌を逸した行動 *eccentric* [(→異常な)*abnormal*] behavior

じょうぎ 定規 ruler ⓒ / 定規で線分の長さを測る measure a line *with a ruler*
‖雲形定規 a curved rule, a French curve / 三角定規 《米》a triangle, 《英》a set square / T(型)定規 a T square

じょうきげん 上機嫌 彼女は上機嫌に歌っていた She was singing *cheerfully* [*in high spirits*]. / 父はきょうボーナスをもらって上機嫌だった My father got a bonus and *was in a good mood* today.

しょうきぼ 小規模 小規模な会社 a *small-scale* company / 彼は小規模ながら新しい商売を始めた He started a new business, though *on a small scale*.

しょうきゃく 焼却 incineration ⓤ ──焼却する burn* up, incinerate ⓘ ‖焼却炉 an incinerator / ごみ焼却場 a refuse incineration plant

じょうきゃく 乗客 passenger ⓒ ‖飛行機の乗客・乗員 the *passengers* and crew of a plane / この飛行機には何人の乗客が乗れますか How many *passengers* can this plane accommodate?
‖乗客名簿 a passenger [boarding] list

しょうきゅう 昇給 (pay) raise ⓒ, 《英》(pay) rise ⓒ / 大幅な昇給を期待する[要求する] expect [demand] *a generous raise* / 今年は5パーセント昇給した I got *a five percent raise* this year.
‖定期昇給 a periodic [mandatory] pay raise

じょうきゅう 上級 ──上級の (程度が) advanced, higher; (等級・地位が) upper, senior ‖高校では私が彼女の1年上級だったが, 大学では彼女が私の1年上級だ I was one year *senior to* her in high school, but now at college she's one year *ahead of* me.
‖上級コース an advanced course / 上級生 an older student; (大学・高校の)《米》an upperclassman, an upperclasswoman (◆高校の3年生, 大学の3年生(junior)または4年生(senior)を指す) / 《英》a senior

しょうきょ 消去 ──消去する clear ⓘ, erase ⓘ ‖そのデータは記録から完全に消去されていた The data *had been* completely *erased* [*cleared*] from the record.
◆ 消去法で答えを出した I worked out the answer *by process of elimination*.

しょうぎょう 商業 commerce ⓤ; (事業) business ⓤ ──商業の・商業的な commercial ‖商業の中心地 a center *of commerce*; a *commercial* center / その映画は商業的に成功した(→商業的な成功を収めた) The film was a *commercial* success. ◆ 大学にも商業化の波が押し寄せている The wave of *commercialization* is sweeping the universities.
‖商業英語 business English / 商業高校 a commercial high school / 商業主義 commercialism / 商業地区 a commercial district / 商業道徳 commercial morality / 商業都市 a commercial city / 商業簿記 commercial bookkeeping

じょうきょう¹ 状況・情況 (情勢・事態) situation ⓒ; (周囲の) circumstances; (条件) conditions
困難な状況に立ち向かう face *a difficult situation*
状況は徐々に好転[悪化]している The situation is gradually improving [getting worse].
すべての状況を把握するのは不可能だ It's impossible to take in *the* whole *situation*.
君がうそをつけば状況はもっとこじれるだろう If you tell lies, you will complicate *the situation*.
もし状況が違っていたら, 彼は命を落としていたかもしれない If *the circumstances* had been otherwise, he could have lost his life.

いかなる状況にあっても彼らはあきらめなかった They never gave up *under any circumstances*.

現在の状況では我々には打つ手がない *Under the present circumstances*, there's nothing we can do.

◆まず被害の状況(→被害がどの程度であるか)を把握しなければならない We must first determine *how much damage* there is.

‖状況証拠〖法律〗circumstantial evidence

じょうきょう² 上京 ──上京する (東京へ行く[来る]) go* [come*] to Tokyo ◆父は今上京中です My father is *in Tokyo* now.

しょうきょくてき 消極的 ──消極的な (受動的な) passive; (否定的な) negative; (内気な) shy ‖消極的な性格 a *passive* nature / …に消極的な態度をとる show a *negative* attitude toward … / 消極策をとったことが功を奏した *Passive* measures worked well.

◆彼はその計画の実行に消極的だった(→乗り気でなかった) He was *reluctant* to carry out the plan.

しょうきん 賞金 prize (money)ⓊⒸ ‖100万円の賞金を獲得する win [get] *a prize* of one million yen

‖賞金獲得者 a prizewinner

じょうきん 常勤 常勤の仕事 a *full-time* job / 常勤で働く work *full-time* / うちの事務所の常勤スタッフは18名います Our office is staffed with 18 *full-timers*.

じょうくう 上空 the sky ◆羽田上空を飛ぶ fly *over* Haneda / 飛行機は現在3万フィート上空を飛行中です The plane is now flying *at* (an altitude of) *30,000 feet*.

しょうぐん 将軍 (幕府の) shogun Ⓒ; (軍隊の) general Ⓒ ‖徳川9代将軍家重 Ieshige, *the* ninth *shogun* of the Tokugawa shogunate

じょうげ 上下 ──上下の up-and-down ──上下に up and down ‖この部品の回転運動を上下運動に変える This part converts the rotary motion to an *up-and-down* motion. / メリーゴーラウンドの馬は上下に動く The horses on a merry-go-round go *up and down*.

◆背広の上下 *a suit* / 上下2巻の小説 a novel *in two volumes* / ポスターを上下逆さにしたピンアップする pin up a poster *upside down* / 私たちのボートは激しく上下に揺れた Our boat *pitched* heavily. / どんな箱にも上下と4つの面がある Every box has *a top*, *a bottom*, and four sides. / 大雪のため, 列車は上下線とも遅れている Because of the heavy snow, both 「*inbound and outbound* [《英》*up and down*] *trains* are delayed. / ここ数日, 最高気温は摂氏10度あたりを上下している The high temperatures *have been hovering* around 10℃ for the last few days. / 私の部は上下関係が厳しい My club has *a strict pecking order*.

しょうけい 小計 subtotal Ⓒ

じょうけい 情景 scene Ⓒ ‖絵のように美しい情景 *a picturesque scene*

しょうけいもじ 象形文字 pictograph Ⓒ; (古代エジプトの) hieroglyph [háiərəglìf] Ⓒ

しょうげき 衝撃 shock ⓊⒸ, impact Ⓒ ──衝撃的な shocking ‖爆発の衝撃で建物が揺れた *The shock* of the explosion rocked the building. / 彼の講演は聴衆に大きな衝撃を与えた His lecture had [made] *a strong impact* on his audience. / その出来事は私には大きな衝撃だった The event was *a great shock* to me. / I was greatly shocked by the event. / 彼女はその衝撃的なニュースを聞いて大声をあげた She exclaimed loudly at *the shocking* news.

‖衝撃波 a shock wave

じょうげすいどう 上下水道 water supply and sewerage [súːərɪdʒ]

しょうけん 証券 (有価証券) securities; (公債・社債) bond Ⓒ; (手形) bill Ⓒ ‖証券会社 a securities company / 証券市場 a securities market / 証券取引所 the stock exchange [market]

しょうげん 証言 testimony ⓊⒸ ──証言する testify 圓 他, give* testimony ‖うその証言をする give false *testimony* / 証人は被告に有利[不利]な証言をした The witness *testified for* [*against*] the accused. / 彼女は彼が現場にいなかったと証言した She *testified* that he hadn't been at the scene.

じょうけん 条件 condition Ⓒ; (支払いなどの) terms; (資格) requirement Ⓒ

〖~条件〗

気象条件 *meteorological conditions* / 雇用条件 *the conditions* [*terms*] *of employment* / 十分条件 *a sufficient condition* / 必要十分条件 *the necessary and sufficient conditions* / 必要条件 *a necessary condition* / 無条件で *without any condition(s)* / 労働条件 *working conditions*

期限を守ることがこの仕事の第一条件だ Being punctual is *the first requirement for* this job.

〖条件が・は〗

私たちが満たさなければならない条件がいくつかある There are some *conditions* we have to satisfy [meet].

支払いの条件が合わなかった We couldn't reach an agreement on *the terms* of payment.

契約の条件は彼らに有利なものだった *The terms* of the contract favored them.

〖条件に・を〗

条件をつける make [set] *a condition* / 条件を受け入れる accept 「*a condition* [*terms*] / 条件を提示する offer *terms*

私たちの条件に合う[条件を満たす]人がやっと見つかった We managed to find a person who *met our requirements*.

この地域は稲作に適した自然条件に恵まれている This region *enjoys favorable* natural *conditions* for the cultivation of rice.

〖条件で〗

どんな条件でその仕事を引き受けたの *On what conditions* did you take the job?

彼女はいい条件で雇われている She is employed *on* favorable *terms*.

利子をつけて返すという条件で彼から金を借りた I borrowed money from him *on* (*the*) *condition* (*that*) I pay it back with interest. (❖condition と同格の that 節中の動詞はしばしば仮定法現在)

〖その他〗

条件しだいでは協力してもいい *Depending on the conditions*, I may help you.

◆私たちは条件付きの合意に達した We came to a *conditional* agreement.

‖条件節〖文法〗a conditional clause / 条件反射〖心理〗a conditioned response [reflex]

じょうげん[1] 上限 the upper limit; (最大限) maximum [C]; (価格・賃金などの) cap [C] ‖予算に上限を設ける place [impose] *a cap* on a budget

じょうげん[2] 上弦 上弦の月(→半月) *a half-moon*; (→4分の1の) *the first quarter moon*

しょうこ[1] 証拠 evidence [U], proof [C] [U]; (徴候) indication [C] [U], sign [C]

〖～証拠〗

外的証拠 *external evidence* / 状況証拠 *circumstantial evidence* / 直接証拠 *direct evidence* / 物的証拠 *material evidence*

〖証拠は・が〗

彼が無罪だという確かな証拠がありますか Is there any certain *evidence* [*proof*] that he is innocent?/ Do you have any certain *evidence* [*proof*] of his innocence?

まだ具体的な証拠は見つかっていない We have not found any concrete *evidence* yet.

警察は証拠がないのに彼を逮捕した The police arrested him on no *evidence*.

〖証拠を〗

証拠を固める collect [gather] *evidence* / 動かぬ証拠を見つける find [dig up, turn up] unquestionable *evidence* / 警察に証拠を隠す withhold *evidence* from the police

その弁護士は彼女が無実だという強力な証拠を挙げた The lawyer produced strong *evidence* ｢of her innocence [that she was innocent].

〖その他〗

泥棒はわずかな証拠も残さなかった The thief has not left a scrap of *evidence*.

彼のあの態度は私に何か隠している証拠だ That attitude of his is *proof* that he is keeping something from me.

彼は証拠不十分で釈放された He was released for *lack of evidence*.

◆彼は何か悩みがあるにちがいない. 彼の表情が何よりの証拠だ He must be worried about something. His face *speaks for itself*.

‖証拠隠滅 destruction [concealment] of evidence / 証拠書類 documentary evidence / 証拠物件 (a piece of) evidence; (法廷で示された) an exhibit

[ことわざ] 論より証拠 ➡ろん

しょうこ[2] 礁湖 lagoon [C]

しょうご 正午 noon [U], midday [U] ‖正午に at *noon* / 正午前[過ぎ]に at before [after] *noon* ◆正午の時報 the *12-o'clock* signal

じょうご[1] 漏斗 funnel [C]

じょうご[2] 上戸 (strong) drinker [C] ‖泣き上戸 a maudlin drunk / 笑い上戸 a happy drinker

しょうこう[1] 小康 彼女の容態はここ数日小康(状態)を保っている(→安定している) Her condition *has been stable* for the last few days.

しょうこう[2] 将校 officer [C] ‖陸軍[海軍]将校 *a* military [naval] *officer*

しょうこう[3] 症候 symptom [C] ‖インフルエンザの最初の症候 *the* first *symptoms* of flu

しょうこう[4] 焼香 ―焼香する offer [burn*] incense

しょうごう[1] 照合 check [C] ―照合する check [他] ‖写しを原文と照合する *check* the copy with [against] the original / 残された指紋を容疑者のものと照合する *check* the fingerprints left behind with [against] those of the suspect

しょうごう[2] 称号 title [C]; (学位) degree [C]

じょうこう 条項 clause [C] ‖その協定に新たな条項が盛り込まれた *A* new *clause* was written into the agreement.

しょうこうかいぎしょ 商工会議所 the Chamber of Commerce and Industry

じょうこうきゃく 乗降客 passengers getting on and off

しょうこうぎょう 商工業 commerce and industry

しょうこうぐち 昇降口 entrance [C]; (船の) hatch [C]

しょうこうぐん 症候群 〖医学〗syndrome [C]

じょうこく 上告 〖法律〗appeal [C] [U] ―上告する appeal [自] ‖被告は最高裁判所に上告した The defendant *appealed* to the Supreme Court.

しょうこりもなく 性懲りもなく しょうこりもなく彼はもう一度彼女をデートに誘った *Undeterred*, he asked her for a date again.

しょうこん 商魂 彼はなかなか商魂たくましい(→抜け目がない) He *is a shrewd businessman*./ (→金もうけのチャンスを見逃さない) He *never misses a chance to make money*.

しょうさ 小差 小差で勝つ win by *a narrow margin* ➡さ

しょうさい[1] 詳細 details, particulars ―詳細な detailed ―詳細に in detail ‖…を詳細に説明する explain … *in detail*; give a *detailed* explanation of … / その事件の詳細が公表された *Details* of the case were released to the public. / 彼はその問題に関する詳細な報告書を書いた He wrote a *detailed* report on the problem. / 詳細は24ページ参照 See page 24 for *details*. / 詳細は追ってお知らせします I will let you know *the details* later.

しょうさい[2] 商才 business ability [talent] [U] ‖商才がある have ｢*business ability* [*a head for business*]

じょうざい 錠剤 tablet [C]; (丸薬) pill [C] ‖錠剤を飲む take *a tablet*

しょうさっし 小冊子 booklet [C], pamphlet [C]; (営業・宣伝用の) brochure [bróuʃuər] [C]

しょうさん[1] 賞賛・称賛 praise [U]; (感嘆) admiration [U] **—賞賛する** praise [他]; admire [他] ∥レスキュー隊の勇気を賞賛する *praise* the rescue team for their courage / 広く賞賛を浴びた映画 a widely *praised* film / 日本文化のすばらしさを賞賛した本 a book *in praise of* Japanese culture / 彼女の努力は賞賛に値する Her efforts are worthy of *praise.* / 彼の新しい小説は大いに賞賛された His new novel *won* high *praise.*/ He *won* high *praise* for his new novel. / 彼女は町中の賞賛の的(まと)だ(→町中の人に賞賛されている) She *is admired* by the whole town.

◆その消防士は賞賛に値する勇気の持ち主だ That fireman has *admirable* courage.

しょうさん[2] 勝算 次の試合の勝算は十分ある[ない] We have 「*a* good [no] *chance of winning* the next game.

しょうさん[3] 硝酸 〖化学〗nitric [náitrik] acid [U]

しょうし 焼死 **—焼死する** be burned to death ∥火事で焼死する *be burned to death* in a fire; (→火事で命を落とす)「lose *one's* life [be killed] in a fire

‖焼死体 a charred body

しょうじ 障子 🖼

障子は格子の木枠に和紙をはった日本の伝統的な引き戸で，ふつう２枚が引き違いになっています．障子は和室の間仕切りや扉として使われるほか，窓枠に取りつけることもできます．障子を通して柔らかい光が入り，部屋に温かみが感じられますが，プライバシーをだいじにする人にとってはかぎがかからず，周囲の雑音も容赦なく入ってくる障子の部屋は住みづらいものに感じられるかもしれません．

Shoji are traditional Japanese sliding doors. Japanese paper is pasted over a wooden latticework, and usually one door slides past the other. They are used in Japanese-style rooms as partitions or doors, and they can also be fitted into windows. The light shining through *shoji* can fill rooms with a nice and warm feeling, but people who care about privacy might find it difficult to live in such a room with no locks and no good way to shut out the outside noise.

じょうし[1] 上司 《口語的》boss [C], superior [C] ∥直属の上司 *one's* immediate *superior*

じょうし[2] 城址・城趾 the ruins of a castle

じょうじ[1] 常時 always, at all times ∥学生証は常時携帯のこと You should carry your student ID card *at all times.*

じょうじ[2] 情事 (love) affair [C]

しょうしか 少子化 日本では少子化が進んでいる(→出生率が低下している) *The birthrate* in Japan *has been declining.*

しょうじがいしゃ 商事会社 commercial [trading] company [C]

しょうじき 正直 honesty [U]; (率直さ) frankness [U] **— 正直な** honest; frank **—正直に** honestly; frankly

正直な人 an *honest* person / 正直な意見 an *honest* [a *frank*] opinion

どうしてそんなことをしたのか正直に言いなさい Tell me *honestly* why you did it.

正直なところ私には分かりません *Honestly* [*Frankly*] (*speaking*), I don't know./ *To be honest* [*frank*] (*with you*), I don't know.

彼はばか正直だ He is *honest to a fault.*

[ことわざ] 三度目の正直 ➔ さんど

じょうしき 常識 (判断力) common sense [U]; (知識) common knowledge [U]

➔ ひじょうしき

私にもそれくらいの常識はある I have that much *common sense.*

彼は頭はいいが，どうも常識に欠ける He may be smart, but he *hasn't got much common sense.*

常識的に考えるとそんなことが起きるはずはない *According to common sense*, that can't happen.

常識を働かせていればあんな間違いはしなかったはずだ If you had used [applied] *common sense*, you would have never made a mistake like that.

そんなの常識だよ *It's a matter of common knowledge.*/ (→だれでも知っている) *Everybody knows it.*

◆常識的な(→ふつうの)人 an *ordinary* person / 常識的な(→ありきたりの)意見 a *commonplace* opinion / 象をペットにするなんて常識はずれだ *It is crazy of* you *to* have an elephant as a pet.

しょうしつ 焼失 **—焼失する** burn* down, be burned down ∥その火事で10戸の家屋が焼失した Ten houses *were burned down* in the fire. ◆いくつかの建物は焼失を免れた Some buildings *survived the fire.*

じょうしつ 上質 **—上質な** fine, excellent

‖上質紙 fine quality paper

じょうじつ 情実 (個人的な感情) *one's* personal [private] feelings; (えこひいき) favoritism [U] ∥情実で出世する be promoted through *favoritism* / 私たちは情実に左右されてはいけない We must not be influenced by *our personal feelings.*

しょうしゃ[1] 商社 trading [commercial] company [C] ∥父は商社マンだ(→商社に勤めている) My father *works for a trading company.*

‖総合商社 a general trading company

しょうしゃ[2] 勝者 winner [C]

じょうしゃ 乗車 **—乗車する** (バス・電車に) get* on; (車・タクシーに) get in ◆無賃乗車する ride without a ticket; steal a ride / 乗車拒否をする refuse to take a passenger / みなさんご乗車ください *All aboard!* / 乗車中はおたばこをご遠慮ください Please refrain from smoking *while aboard.*

‖乗車口 the (entrance) door / 乗車券 a ticket / 乗車賃 a fare

じょうじゅ 成就（達成）accomplishment Ⓤ Ⓒ, achievement Ⓤ;（実現）realization Ⓤ《また a～》◆とうとう我々の悲願が成就した At last our long-cherished wish *has been realized*.

しょうしゅう¹ 召集・招集 会を招集する *call a meeting* / 総会に株主を招集する *invite stockholders to a general meeting* / 軍を召集する *raise an army* / あす臨時国会が召集される A special session of the Diet *is to be convened* tomorrow.
‖召集令状《米》a draft notice,《英》one's call-up papers

しょうしゅう² 消臭 消臭スプレー a *deodorant spray*

しょうじゅう 小銃 rifle Ⓒ ‖自動小銃 an automatic rifle

じょうしゅう 常習 ——常習的な habitual ‖麻薬の常習 habitual drug *use* / 強盗の常習犯 a *habitual* robber
◆麻薬の常習者 a drug *addict*
‖常習犯 a habitual [hardened] criminal 慣用表現 弟は遅刻の常習犯だ My brother is *habitually* late for school.

しょうじゅつ 詳述 ——詳述する explain in detail, elaborate Ⓘ ⇨ くわしい

じょうじゅつ 上述 上述したように *as mentioned above* / 上述の理論 the theory *above mentioned*; the *above-mentioned* theory

しょうじゅん 照準（銃などの）sight Ⓒ（しばしば複数形 ～s）;（ねらい）aim Ⓤ ‖私たちは次の試合に照準を合わせて練習している We are training hard *setting our sights on* the next game.

じょうじゅん 上旬 彼は来月上旬（→初め）に日本を離れる He's leaving Japan *early next month*.（◆英米では「上旬」「中旬」「下旬」のように月を区切る習慣はない）

しょうしょ 証書（文書）document Ⓒ;（契約書）bond Ⓒ;（証明書）certificate Ⓒ

しょうじょ 少女 girl Ⓒ ⇨ しょうねん
◆少女趣味の服 *girlish* clothes
‖少女時代 girlhood / 少女漫画 a *girls'* comic

しょうしょう 少々（少量）a bit;（少数）a few /「コショウを少々加える add "*a bit of* [*some*] pepper / 少々お待ちください Wait *a minute*, please.

しょうじょう¹ 症状 symptom Ⓒ;（病状）condition Ⓒ ‖コレラに特有の症状 *symptoms* specific to cholera / 彼にはしかの症状が出た He had [showed] *the symptoms of* measles. / 彼女の症状はよくなり［悪化し］始めた Her *condition* has begun to improve [get worse].
‖禁断症状 withdrawal symptoms / 自覚症状 a subjective symptom

しょうじょう² 賞状 a certificate of merit [award] ‖私たちはトーナメントに優勝して賞状をもらった We were awarded *a certificate of merit* for winning the tournament.

じょうしょう 上昇 rise Ⓒ ——上昇する rise* Ⓘ, go* up;（増える）increase Ⓘ ‖物価の急上昇 a (sharp) *rise* in prices / 気温が摂氏39度まで上昇した The temperature *has risen* [*gone up*] to 39℃. / 最近この歌手は人気が上昇中だ This singer *is rising in popularity* these days.
◆物価の上昇傾向 *an upward trend* in prices
‖上昇気流 an ascending air current, an updraft

じょうじょう¹ 上場 株式を上場する *list the company stock* / その会社は東証に上場された The company *has been listed* on the Tokyo Stock Exchange.
‖上場会社 a listed company / 上場株 listed stocks

じょうじょう² 上々 上々のでき a *fine* performance / 気分は上々だ I feel *fine*. / 上々の滑りだしだ We've made a *good* start.

じょうじょうしゃくりょう 情状酌量 告には情状酌量の余地はない There is no room for *taking the circumstances* of the accused *into consideration*.

しょうしょく 少食・小食 少食な人 a *light eater* / 妹は少食だ My sister *doesn't eat much*. / My sister *eats like a bird*.

じょうしょく 常食 staple [daily] food Ⓒ
◆米を常食とする *live on* rice

しょうじる 生じる（起こる）happen Ⓘ, come* about, take* place;（現れる）appear Ⓘ
その出来事があってから彼の生活には大きな変化が生じた A great change *took place* in his life after the event.
その大事故はわずかなミスから生じた The serious accident *happened* because of a slight mistake. /（→わずかなミスが大事故につながった）A slight mistake *led to* the serious accident.
壁に亀裂が生じた A crack *appeared* in the wall.
◆すぐに別の問題が生じた Soon another problem *came up*. / そのひと言から思わぬ誤解が生じた（→誤解を引き起こした）The comment *caused* unexpected misunderstandings.

じょうじる 乗じる（…につけ込む，…を利用する）take* advantage of ... ‖彼は彼女の人のよさに乗じて金をだまし取った He *took advantage of* her good nature and cheated her out of her money.
◆泥棒はやみに乗じてその家に忍び込んだ The thief sneaked into the house *under cover of darkness*.

しょうしん¹ 昇進 promotion Ⓒ Ⓤ ——昇進する be promoted ‖昇進の見込みのある仕事 a job with good *promotion* prospects / 父は支配人に昇進した My father *was promoted to* manager.（◆地位を表す名詞には冠詞を付けない，《英》では to を省略した，to の代わりに be を用いたりする）/ 彼女は勤勉さが認められて早い昇進をものにした She got *a quick promotion* because of her hard work. / 彼の昇進は見送られた He was passed over for *pro-*

しょうしん

しょうしん² 小心 ——小心な (自信のない) timid; (臆病(おくびょう)な) cowardly ∥小心者 a timid person; a coward

しょうしん³ 焼身 焼身自殺する burn *oneself* to death

しょうしん⁴ 傷心 grief Ⓤ, heartbreak Ⓒ ∥傷心をいやす heal *one's* grief / 傷心のあまり自殺する kill *oneself* in grief

しょうじん 精進 ——精進する (専念する) devote *oneself* to ...; (努力する) make* an effort ∥勉強に精進する devote oneself to *one's studies*
∥精進料理 Zen cooking [cuisine]

しょうしんしょうめい 正真正銘 (本当の) true; (現実の) real; (偽物でない) genuine, authentic ∥正真正銘のドガの絵 a *genuine* [an *authentic*] Degas / どこから見ても彼は正真正銘の紳士だ To all appearances, he is a *true* [*real*] gentleman.

じょうず² 上手 ——上手な good (↔bad, poor); (巧みな) skillful (↔awkward) —— 上手に good; skillfully
字が上手である have *good* handwriting / 聞き[話し]上手 a *good* listener [*talker*] / はしを上手に使う use chopsticks *skillfully*
彼は上手だ He is a *good* singer. / He is *good* at singing. / He sings *well*.
彼は小さな子供の扱いがとても上手だ He is very *skillful* with small children.
日本語が上手ですね You speak *good* Japanese. / You speak Japanese *very well*.
あいつの言うことを真に受けないほうがいい, うそが上手だから Don't take him at his word. He's a *good* liar.
◆言い争いを上手に(→円満に)収める settle an argument *peacefully* / ずいぶん英語が上手になったね Your English *has greatly improved*.

しょうすい 憔悴 彼女は憔悴しきった様子だった She looked *haggard*. ⇨やつれる

じょうすい 浄水 ∥浄水器 a water purifier, a water filtration system / 浄水場 a water filtering plant

じょうすいどう 上水道 waterworks《単数または複数扱い》

しょうすう¹ 少数 少数の人 *a small number of* people / ゴールまでたどり着けたのはほんの少数だった Only *a few* were able to reach the goal. / そのテレビ番組の視聴者は少数だ That TV program has a *small* audience. / 少数意見も尊重するべきだ We should respect *the minority* opinion. / この会社ではたばこを吸う人は少数派です Smokers are *in the minority* in this office.
∥少数民族 a minority ethnic group

しょうすう² 小数 decimal (fraction) Ⓒ ∥小数点以下を切り捨てる discard *decimals*
◆小数第2位まで計算する calculate to *the second decimal place*
∥小数点 a decimal point / 循環小数 a recurring decimal / 無限小数 an infinite decimal / 有限小数 a finite decimal

しょうする 称する 彼はジャーナリストだと称していた He *described himself as* a journalist. / 高田と称する男が父を訪ねてきた A man *called* [*named*] Takada came to see my father. / A Mr. Takada came to see my father. / 彼女は病気と称して授業をサボった She *pretended* to be sick and cut classes.

じょうせい 情勢・状勢 situation Ⓒ, affairs; (周囲の状況) circumstances ∥世界情勢 world *affairs* / 中東情勢 the *situation* in the Middle East / 情勢の進展を見守る watch how *the situation* develops / 現在の経済情勢はたいへん厳しい The economic *situation* now is very severe. / その国の政治情勢をどのように見ますか What's your reading of *the political situation* in that country?
◆2国間の戦争は避けられない情勢だ(→避けられないように思われる) War between the two countries *seems* inevitable.

じょうせい² 上製 ——上製の (質のよい) of superior quality
◆上製本 a *well-bound* book

じょうせき¹ 定石 (決まった方法) formula Ⓒ
◆定石どおりに by the book

じょうせき² 上席 テーブルの上席に座る sit at *the head of a table*

しょうせつ¹ 小説 (長編) novel Ⓒ (⇨短編小説は short story); (物語) story Ⓒ; (作り話) fiction Ⓤ (↔nonfiction) (⇨架空の物語の総称, 数えるときは a piece [work] of ... とする) ∥小説を書く write a *novel*
💬「だれの小説が好きですか」「大江健三郎の小説が好きです」 "Whose *novels* do you like?" "I like *novels* by Oe Kenzaburo."
∥小説家 a novelist; (著述家) a writer / 私小説 an "I" novel, a confessional novel / 推理小説 a mystery novel / 大河小説 a saga / 探偵小説 a detective story / 冒険小説 an adventure story / 歴史小説 a historical novel / 恋愛小説 a love story, a romance / 連載小説 a serial story [novel]
慣用表現 事実は小説よりも奇なり ⇨じじつ

しょうせつ² 小節 〔音楽〕 bar Ⓒ

じょうせつ 常設 ——常設の (永続的・永久的な) permanent; (効力の継続する) standing ∥委員会を常設する(→常設の委員会を設置する) establish a *permanent* [*standing*] committee ◆ (美術館などの) 常設作品(→収蔵品) museum *collection*
∥常設委員会 a standing committee

じょうぜつ 饒舌 饒舌な人 a *talkative* 《《公式的》*loquacious*》 person / ビールを2, 3杯飲むと彼は饒舌になった A few glasses of beer *loosened* his *tongue*.

しょうせん¹ 商船 merchant ship Ⓒ; (一国の全商船) the merchant marine [《英》navy]
∥商船隊 a merchant fleet / 商船大学 a merchant marine college

しょうせん² 商戦 sales battle Ⓒ ∥デパートはクリスマス商戦を迎えた Department stores entered *a sales battle* for Christmas.

じょうせん 乗船 boarding Ⓒ, embarkation Ⓤ Ⓒ ——乗船する go* [get*] aboard

(a ship), go [get] on board (a ship)
◆ご乗船ください All aboard! / ご乗船ありがとうございます Welcome aboard!
‖乗船客 a passenger (on a ship) / 乗船券 a boat ticket

しょうせんきょく 小選挙区 (1区1人の選挙区) small constituency ⓒ ‖小選挙区制 the single-seat constituency system

しょうそ 勝訴 原告が勝訴した The plaintiff *won the case* [*suit*]. ⇨ さいばん

じょうそ 上訴 ――上訴する appeal to a higher court

しょうそう¹ 尚早 その件に関して結論を下すのは時期尚早だ It's *too early* to make a conclusion on that matter.

しょうそう² 焦燥 impatience ⓤ ‖彼の顔に焦燥の色が浮かんだ A look of *impatience* came to his face. ◆焦燥にかられる feel *impatient*
‖焦燥感 a feeling of impatience

しょうぞう 肖像 portrait ⓒ ‖私は彼女に肖像画を描いてもらった I had *my portrait* painted by her.
‖肖像画家 a portrait painter / 肖像権 one's portrait rights

じょうそう¹ 上層 (地層の) the upper layer; (建物の) the upper floor; (空の) the upper air ◆会社の上層部 the *leading members* [*top management*] of a company
‖上層階級 the upper classes

じょうそう² 情操 《公式的》sentiment ⓤⓒ
‖情操教育 cultivation of aesthetic sentiments [sensibilities]

じょうぞう 醸造 ――醸造する (日本酒・ワイン・みそ・しょうゆなどを) make* ... by fermentation; (主にビールを) brew 他

‖醸造酒 non-distilled alcohol / 醸造所 (ワインの) a winery

しょうそく 消息 (知らせ・便り) news ⓤ; (情報) information ⓤ ‖それ以来彼からは何の消息もない I haven't had any *news* from him since then. / *I haven't heard from* him since then.

◆消息筋によると according to *informed sources* / 映画界の消息に通じている *know a lot* about the movie world / 昨年以来彼の消息を聞かない *I haven't heard of* him since last year. / 彼女は買い物に出たまま消息を絶った She *has disappeared* since she left home to go shopping. / その登山家は2日前から消息不明だ The climber *has been missing* for two days.

しょうたい 招待 invitation ⓤⓒ ――招待する invite 他

招待に応じる[を断る] accept [decline] *an invitation*

彼はガールフレンドを家に招待した He *invited* his girlfriend to his house.

ご招待いただきありがとうございます Thank you for "*inviting* me [*your invitation*].

そのパーティーには多くの人々が招待された Many people *were invited* to the party.

彼らの結婚式の招待状をもらった I received *an invitation* to his wedding.

友人の招待でアメリカを訪れた *At* my friend's *invitation*, I visited America.

◆コンサートの(無料)招待券 *a free* [*complimentary*] *ticket* for a concert / 彼のスピーチは招待客全員の注目を集めた His speech attracted the attention of all *the guests*.
‖招待試合 an invitational game [match] / 招待席 a reserved seat for a guest

しょうたい¹ 正体 (本来の姿) one's true character [nature]; (身元) identity ⓤⓒ ‖正体をあばく[隠す] reveal [conceal] *one's true character* / 彼はとうとう正体を現した He finally showed *his true character*. / 殺人犯の正体はまだ分からない *The identity* of the murderer is still unknown. / We still don't know *who* the murderer is.

◆正体不明のウイルスに感染する be infected with an *unidentified* virus / 彼は正体なく眠っていた He was *dead* asleep.

しょうたい³ 小隊 〔軍事〕platoon ⓒ

じょうたい¹ 状態
condition ⓤ (また a ~); state ⓒ; shape ⓤ; situation ⓒ; circumstance ⓒ《通例複数形 ~s》

> condition:「状態」を意味する一般的な語.
> state: しばしば悪い状態に用い,「物」の場合は長期的に,「人」の場合は一時的な状態を表すことが多い.
> shape: in ... shape の形で用い, 人の体や機械の調子を表すことが多い.
> situation: ある時点, ある場所での状況.
> circumstance: situation に影響を与える, 周囲の状況.

この車は多少修理が必要だが状態はよい This car needs some repairs, but it's in good *condition*.

その患者はまだ危険な状態だ The patient is still in critical *condition*.

あなたはまだ歩き回れる状態ではありません You are in no *condition* to walk around yet.

彼女は最近健康状態が思わしくない She is recently in *a poor state of health*.

この寺は保存状態がよい This temple is in a good *state of preservation*.

その化石は完全な状態で見つかった The fossil was found in perfect *condition*.

部屋の中がこんな状態では友達を呼ぶこともできない With the room in this *condition* [*state*], I can't invite my friends into it.

そんな状態では計画の実行は不可能だな In that *situation* [Under those *circumstances*], it's impossible to carry out the plan.

‖経済状態 an economic state / 精神状態 one's mental condition [state] / 天候状態 weather conditions / 無重力状態 a state of weightlessness

じょうたい² 上体 the upper part of the body ◆上体を前に倒す[後ろに反(ｿ)らす] lean down [back]

しょうだく 承諾 (同意) consent ⓤ; (許可) permission ⓤ; (是認) approval ⓤ ――承諾する consent 自; permit 他; approve 他

じょうたつ

‖承諾を得る[求める] obtain [ask] *a person's consent* / 父は私たちの結婚を承諾した My father *consented* [*gave his consent*] *to our marriage.* / 私たちは先生から体育館を使う承諾をもらっている We have our teacher's *permission* to use the gym. / 彼は両親の承諾なしに学校をやめた He quit school without his parents' *consent* [*permission*].
‖事後承諾 ex post facto consent

じょうたつ 上達 (進歩) progress Ⓤ; (改善) improvement Ⓤ ──上達する make* *progress*; improve ⊕ ⊖ ‖…の上達が早い[遅い] make rapid [slow] *progress* in … / 彼女の英語はずいぶん上達した She *has* made great *progress in* (her) English. / She *has improved* her English greatly. / Her English *has improved* greatly.

しょうだん 商談 (会談) business talk Ⓒ; (交渉) negotiation ⒸⓊ; (取り引き) business deal Ⓒ ──商談をする have *a business talk* / …との商談に入る enter into *negotiations with* … / 商談をまとめる put through *a business deal*

じょうだん 冗談 joke Ⓒ

冗談を言う crack [make] *a joke* / 冗談を真に受ける take *jokes* seriously

私の冗談は彼らにうけた My *joke* set them off laughing.

彼女は彼が言った冗談が分からなかった She couldn't *see* [*get*] the *joke* he made.

冗談にも程があるよ(→冗談がすぎるよ) You are carrying *a joke* too far.

まあまあ, ただの冗談だよ Come now, it's only *a joke*.

ほんの冗談でしたことが彼を怒らせてしまった What I only did *as a joke* has made him angry. *I can't believe it!*

◆冗談半分に言う say *half-jokingly* / 冗談はよせ Stop *joking!* / 彼女は冗談が通じない(→ユーモアのセンスがない) She *has no sense of humor.* / 冗談はさておき本題に入りましょう *Joking apart*, let's get to the point. / 冗談にもそんなことを言うもんじゃない You shouldn't say such a thing, *even as a joke.* / 彼はガラスを割ったのを僕のせいにしたんだ。全く冗談じゃないよ He blamed me for breaking the window. *I can't believe it!*

🗣「これから海に泳ぎに行くんだ」「冗談でしょ。こんな寒い日に」"I'm just going for a swim in the sea." "*Are you kidding*? [*You're joking*!] It's too cold."

コロケーション -joke-
《形容詞＋～》悪趣味な～ a sick joke / お決まりの～ a standing joke / おもしろい～ a funny joke / 気のきいた～ a witty joke / 下品な～ a low joke / 上品な～ a clean joke / 辛辣(しんらつ)な～ a bitter joke / 陳腐な～ a stale joke / 罪のない～ a harmless joke / とげのある～ an offensive joke / 下手な～ a poor joke

しょうち¹ 承知
❶【知る・知っている】know* ⊕ ⊖, be aware

ご承知のとおりその計画は延期されました As you *know*, the plan was postponed.

不利を承知で彼らの提案に応じた I *agreed to* their proposal, *though I knew* the disadvantage to me.

そんなことは百も承知だ I *am well aware of that.* / I *know* that *very well.*

お名前は承知しております I *know* you by name.

🗣「できるだけ早く返事をください」「承知しました」"Please give me your answer as soon as possible." "*Certainly.*"

❷【承諾】(賛成する) agree ⊕ ⊖; (受け入れる) accept ⊕ ⊖; (許可する) permit ⊕ ⊖; (許す) forgive* ⊕ ⊖

両親にやっと私たちの結婚を承知してもらった I managed to persuade my parents to *agree to* our marriage.

うそをついたら承知しないよ If you tell me a lie, *I'll never forgive* you.

しょうち² 招致 invitation Ⓤ ──招致する invite ⊕ ⊖ ⇨ゆうち

しょうちゅう¹ 掌中 私たちは勝利をほぼ掌中に収めた(→勝ったも同然だ) We've almost *had* the game *in our hands.*

しょうちゅう² 焼酎 🗾

焼酎は昔から日本にある蒸留酒ですが, もともとは東南アジアから沖縄を経由して伝わりました。様々な穀物や芋類などの原料にこうじを加え, 発酵・蒸留して作ります。地方色豊かな焼酎が多数あります中, 熊本の球磨焼酎(原料は米), 宮崎と長野のそば焼酎(原料はそば), 沖縄の泡盛(原料は米)などはよく知られています。
Shochu, a traditional distilled spirit, originally came from Southeast Asia by way of Okinawa. It is made from various grains or potatoes which are fermented and distilled together with rice malt. There are many regional varieties of *shochu*. The famous types include *Kumajochu* (made from rice) from Kumamoto, *Sobajochu* (made from buckwheat) from Miyazaki and Nagano, and *Awamori* (made from rice) from Okinawa.

じょうちゅう 常駐 このビルには3人の警備員が常駐している Three guards *are always stationed* at this building.

じょうちょ 情緒 (感情) emotion ⓊⒸ, 《公式的》sentiment ⓊⒸ; (雰囲気) atmosphere ⓊⒸ ‖彼は情緒たっぷりに歌った He sang with deep *emotion.* / このあたりには昔の東京の情緒がまだ残っている There still remains *the atmosphere* of the old Tokyo around here.

◆異国情緒のある町 an *exotic* town / それ以来, 彼は情緒不安定だ He's been *emotionally unstable* since then.

しょうちょう 象徴 symbol Ⓒ ‖ハトは平和の象徴だ The dove is *a symbol* [*symbolic*] *of* peace. ◆象徴的な出来事 a *symbolic* event / オリンピックの旗は5大陸を象徴している The Olympic flag *symbolizes* five continents.

‖象徴主義〖文学〗symbolism

しょうちょう² 省庁 ministries and agencies ⇨ しょう(省)

しょうちょう³ 小腸〖解剖〗small intestine Ⓒ

じょうちょう 冗長 ──冗長な (長ったらしい) lengthy;(言葉数の多い) wordy ‖冗長な演説 a lengthy speech

じょうでき 上出来 上出来,上出来! *Good job! Well done!* / あいつにしては上出来だ(→予想以上によくやった) *He's done better than I had expected.*
♣「試験はどうだった」「上出来だったよ」"*How was the exam?*" "*I did very well.*"

しょうてん¹ 商店 (主に米) store Ⓒ, (英) shop Ⓒ (❖(米)では特定の商品を扱う店に shop を用いる傾向がある) ‖商店街 a shopping street;(屋根のあるもの) a shopping arcade [mall] / 商店主 (主に米)a storekeeper, (英) a shopkeeper

しょうてん² 焦点 focus Ⓒ (複 ~es, foci),〖光学〗focal point Ⓒ ⇨ ピント ‖レンズの焦点 *the focus* of a lens / この写真は焦点が合っている[ずれている] This picture *is in* [*out of*] *focus.* ♣金星に望遠鏡の焦点を合わせる *focus* a telescope *on* Venus / 彼女は焦点の定まらない目をしていた She had a *blank* look in her eyes. / 彼の発言が問題の焦点をぼかしてしまった His remarks *have clouded* [*confused*] the issue.
‖焦点距離〖光学〗focal length [distance] / 自動焦点カメラ an auto focus camera

しょうてん³ 昇天〖宗教〗ascension Ⓤ (❖キリストの昇天を Ascension) ──昇天する (死ぬ) die ⑧,(婉曲的に) pass away

じょうてんき 上天気 ここ 2, 3 日上天気が続いている *The fine weather* has lasted for a few days.

しょうど 焦土 その国は戦争で焦土と化した *The country was reduced to the ashes* in the war.
‖焦土戦術 scorched-earth policy

じょうと 譲渡 transfer Ⓤ Ⓒ ──譲渡する hand over, transfer ⑧ ‖彼は一人息子に財産を譲渡した He *handed* the property *over to* his only son.

しょうとう 消灯 合宿の消灯時刻は 9 時半だった *Lights-out* was [*We turned off the lights*] at nine thirty in our training camp.

しょうどう 衝動 (一時の感情) impulse Ⓤ Ⓒ,(強い欲望) urge Ⓒ (通例単数形) ‖衝動的な人 a person *of impulse*; an *impulsive* person / ブラウスを衝動買いする(→衝動的に買う) buy a blouse *on impulse* / 先生に言い返したい衝動を抑えた I resisted *an impulse* to answer the teacher back. / 彼女は彼についていきたいという抑えがたい衝動にかられた She felt *an irresistible impulse* [*urge*] to follow him.

じょうとう¹ 上等 ──上等な good, fine, excellent
彼女はいちばん上等な服を着て出かけた She went out in her *best* dress.
♦上等の[ふだんより上等の]刺身を買った I bought *sashimi of "good quality* [*better quality* than usual]*."* / この仕事をするにはそれだけうまく英語を話せれば上等だ(→十分だ) You speak English fluently *enough* for this job.

じょうとう² 常套 ──常套的な (いつもの) usual;(古い) old;(習慣の) customary;(型にはまった) conventional ‖彼の話にだまされるな. それはあいつの常套手段だ Don't be taken in by his story. That's *an old trick* of his.
‖常套句 a cliché, a well-worn phrase

しょうどく 消毒 disinfection Ⓤ,(殺菌) sterilization Ⓤ ──消毒する disinfect ⑧; sterilize ⑧ ‖容器を煮沸消毒する *sterilize* the container *by boiling* / 傷もよく洗ってから消毒しなさい Wash the cuts thoroughly and then *disinfect* them. / このおしぼりは消毒済みです This hand towel *has been sterilized*.
‖消毒薬[剤] (an) antiseptic, (a) disinfectant / 消毒用アルコール《米》rubbing alcohol,《英》surgical spirit

しょうとつ　衝突

❶【物と物との】crash Ⓒ,(異なる方向へ動く物どうしの) collision Ⓒ ──衝突する crash ⑧;(動く物どうしが) collide ⑧
車は壁に激しく衝突した The car *crashed* hard *into* [*against*] the wall. (❖against には「衝突してはね返る」という含みがある)
バスとトラックが正面衝突した A bus and a truck *crashed* [*collided*] *head-on*. / A bus *crashed* [*collided*] *head-on* with a truck.
さいわいその衝突事故による死者はなかった Luckily nobody was killed in *the crash* [*collision*].
部屋に入ろうとしたとき彼と衝突しそうになった I almost *collided with* him when I was coming into the room.

❷【争い・対立】clash Ⓒ,(闘争) conflict Ⓒ Ⓤ,(口論) quarrel Ⓒ,(論争) argument Ⓒ ──衝突する clash ⑧; conflict ⑧; quarrel ⑧; argue ⑧
武力衝突を引き起こす cause *armed conflict*; cause *an exchange of fire*
その 2 つの会社の間には利害の衝突がある There is *a conflict of interest(s)* between the two companies.
デモ隊は警察と衝突した The demonstrators *clashed with* the police.
その問題に関して私と彼の意見が衝突した My opinion *clashed with* his on that problem.
兄は両親と衝突してばかりいる My brother always *argues* [*quarrels*] *with* our parents.

しょうとりひき 商取引 commercial transaction Ⓒ, business deal Ⓒ
‖電子商取引 electronic commerce, e-commerce

じょうない 場内 場内は禁煙です Smoking is not allowed *in the hall.* / 間もなく試合が始ま

るという場内アナウンスがあった *It said on the PA* that the game would start soon. (❖PAは*p*ublic-*a*ddress system(拡声装置)の略語)

しょうに 小児 infant [C], little child [C] ‖小児科 pediatrics / 小児科医 a pediatrician / 小児まひ polio, 〔医学〕poliomyelitis

しょうにゅうどう 鍾乳洞 limestone cave [C]

しょうにん[1] 承認 (是認) approval [U]; (認可) recognition [U], 《口語的》OK, O.K. [C] ━承認する approve [他]; recognize [他], 《口語的》OK, O.K. [他], give* *one's* OK [O.K.] ‖ 私たちは先生からやっとその計画を実行してよいという承認を得た We managed to win our teacher's *approval* to carry out the plan. / 国会は政府の新しい計画を承認した The Diet *approved* the new plan of the government. / 多くの国がまだその新政権を承認していない A lot of countries *have* not *recognized* the new regime yet.

しょうにん[2] 商人 merchant [C]; (小売商) trader [C]; (商店主) 《米》storekeeper [C], 《英》shopkeeper [C] ‖綿商人 *a* cotton *trader*; *a trader* in cotton

◆大阪は商人の町として栄えてきた Osaka has been prosperous as *a city of business*.

しょうにん[3] 証人 witness [C]; (目撃者) eyewitness [C] ‖重要証人 *a* key *witness* / その事件の生き証人 *a living witness* of the event / 証人台に立つ enter *the witness box*; 《米》take *the stand* / 証人に尋問する[反対尋問する] examine [cross-examine] *a witness* / 検察[被告]側の証人として喚問された I was called as *a* prosecution [defense] *witness* in court.

◆あなたがその事件に関係ないことは私が証人になります(→証言する) I'*ll testify* that you have nothing to do with the case.

‖証人喚問 summoning of a witness

じょうにん 常任 ━常任の permanent; (いつもの) regular ‖常任委員 a regular member of a committee / 常任委員会 a permanent [standing] committee / 常任指揮者 a regular conductor (of an orchestra) / 国連常任理事国 a permanent member of the U.N. Security Council

しょうにんずう 少人数 私の通う塾は少人数制をとっている The *juku* I attend has *a small class system*. / 私は少人数で旅行をするのが好きだ I like to travel with *a small number of people*.

しょうね 性根 性根のすわった人 a person *of spirit* / 彼は性根を入れ替えてまじめに働きだした He *has made a fresh start* as a good worker. / あいつは性根が腐っている(→芯(しん)まで堕落している) He *is rotten to the core*.

じょうねつ 情熱 passion [U] [C]; (熱中) enthusiasm [U][C] ━情熱的な passionate; enthusiastic ━情熱的に passionately; enthusiastically ‖情熱的な愛 *passionate* love / 彼らは野球に情熱を燃やしている They have *a passion for* baseball. / Baseball is *a passion* with them. / 彼女は情熱をこめてそのことについて語った She talked about that matter *with great passion*. / この本によって新しい研究への情熱をかきたてられた This book aroused *my passion* [*enthusiasm*] for a new study. / 彼は仕事への情熱を失いつつある His *passion* for his work is beginning to wither.

しょうねん 少年 boy [C] (❖通例誕生から17, 18歳まで); (少年・少女) 《公式的》juvenile [C] 16歳の少年 *a* 16-year-old *boy*

◆少年のような笑顔 a *boyish* smile / 彼は小学生のころはサッカー少年だった He *had a passion for soccer* when he was a schoolboy. / 父は少年時代をそこで過ごした My father spent *his boyhood* there.

‖少年院 《米》a reformatory, 《英》a community home / 少年鑑別所 《米》a detention home, 《英》a detention centre / 少年犯罪 (a) juvenile crime; (少年非行) juvenile delinquency / 少年法 the Juvenile Act / 少年漫画 comics for boys, boy's comics / 少年野球 Little League baseball

[ことわざ] 少年老い易(やす)く学成(な)り難(がた)し Art is long, life is short. (→学芸の習得には長い時間がかかるが, 人生は短い)

しょうねんば 正念場 弱音を吐くな. ここが正念場だぞ Never say die. We are now at *the crucial moment*.

しょうのう[1] 小脳 〔解剖〕cerebellum [C]

しょうのう[2] 笑納 つまらない物ですが, どうぞご笑納ください This isn't much, but *I hope you'll like it*.

しょうのう[3] 樟脳 camphor [U]

じょうば 乗馬 (horse) riding [U] ◆乗馬を教えてくれる人を探している I'm looking for someone to teach me *how to ride a horse*.

‖乗馬靴 riding boots / 乗馬クラブ a riding club / 乗馬服 a riding costume

しょうはい 勝敗 その得点が勝敗を決した(→試合を決めた) The goal *decided the game*. / 私たちは勝敗(→結果)にはあまりこだわらない We don't take *the result of the game* too seriously. / 勝敗はともかくベストを尽くすだけだ *Win or lose*, I'll just do my best.

しょうばい 商売

❶【商活動】business [U]

商売を始める[やめる] go into [out of] *business*

我々の商売はうまくいっている Our *business* is doing well.

父の会社はシンガポールと商売をしている My father's company is doing *business* with Singapore.

彼は商売がうまい He has a good head for *business*.

彼は神社で商売繁盛を祈願した He prayed at a shrine that *his business would thrive*.

◆うちは商売をやっています(→店を経営している) My family runs *a store*. / 会社を作った最初の年は商売にならなかった(→もうけがなかった) We *didn't make much profit* in the first year of setting up our company.

❶「商売はうまくいっていますか」「まあまあですね」 "How's *your business?*" "Not too bad."
❷【職業】job ⓒ,《口語的》line ⓒ, business Ⓤⓒ, trade Ⓤⓒ

もうかる商売 *a profitable business*

私は家の商売を継ぐつもりはありません I won't follow in *the family business.*

何の商売をなさっているんですか What's *your trade?*

商売柄彼女は英語が得意だ She's good at English *because of her job.*

この商売は夏がいちばん暇だ[忙しい] Summer is the slackest [briskest] season in this *business.*

◆彼は歌を商売にしている(→歌で生計を立てている) He makes his living「*by singing*「(→歌い手として)*as a singer*).

‖商売がたき a business rival / 商売道具 the tools of one's [the] trade / 商売人(商人) a merchant, a businessman;(専門家) a specialist, a professional

しょうばつ 賞罰 reward and punishment

じょうはつ 蒸発 evaporation Ⓤ ——蒸発する evaporate ⓗⓘ;(人が) disappear ⓘ ∥アルコールは水よりもずっと蒸発しやすい Alcohol *evaporates* much more easily than water.

父は私たちを残して蒸発してしまった My father *has disappeared*, leaving us behind.

じょうはんしん 上半身 the upper part [half] of one's body ◆上半身写真 a *half-length* photograph / 上半身裸になって診察を受けた I was stripped *to the waist* while seeing the doctor. / 彼女はベッドで上半身を起こした She *sat up* in bed.

しょうひ 消費 consumption Ⓤ ——消費する consume ⓗ;(時間・金を) spend* ⓗ;(使う) use (up);(カロリー・脂肪を) burn* off

電気の消費量 *the consumption* of electricity / その仕事に多大な時間を消費する *spend* a lot of time *on* the job

エネルギー消費が大幅に減少した *The consumption* of energy has largely decreased.

個人消費はいまだ伸び悩んだままだ *Personal consumption* [*Consumer spending*] remains sluggish.

この運動ではわずかなカロリーしか消費することができません You can *burn off* just a few calories by doing this exercise.

‖消費者 a consumer / 消費者運動 a consumer movement, consumerism / 消費者金融 a consumer credit / 消費者団体 a consumer organization / 消費者物価 consumer prices / 消費者物価指数 the consumer price index, the CPI / 消費税 the consumption tax

じょうび 常備 あの本屋はその辞書を常備している The dictionary *is always in stock* at that bookstore.

‖常備軍 the regular army / 常備薬 household medicine;(救急箱) a first-aid kit

しょうひょう 商標 trademark ⓒ(《略語》 TM) / 商標を登録する register *a trademark* / 商標権を侵害する infringe *trademark rights*

‖登録商標 a registered trademark(《略語》 R.)

しょうひん¹ 商品 goods(❖数詞や many などで修飾できない), an article [item] for sale, 《集合的》《公式的》merchandise Ⓤ;(製品) product Ⓤ

質の高い[悪い]商品 *goods* of high [low] quality

どんな商品を扱っていますか What sorts of *goods* do you deal in?

その店にはいろいろな商品が売られている They sell a large variety of *goods* in that shop.

棚にはわずかな商品しか並んでいなかった There were only a few *goods* on the shelf.

このシャツは穴があいてしまっているので商品価値がない This shirt has no *value as an item for sale* [(→売れない)We can't sell this shirt] because of a hole in it.

店はその商品を大量に仕入れた The store stocked the *product* in large numbers.

‖商品券《米》a gift certificate,《英》a gift token [voucher] ⓒ / 商品名 a trade name / 商品目録 a catalog,《英》a catalogue / 目玉商品 a loss leader

しょうひん² 賞品 prize ⓒ ⇨ しょう(賞) ∥賞品をかけて争う race for *a prize* / 豪華賞品が当たるクイズ a quiz with excellent *prizes*

じょうひん 上品 elegant, graceful(❖elegant は服装・動作などが洗練されて上品なことをいい, graceful は自然なふるまいの中の上品さ・優雅さをいう);(洗練された) refined;(繊細な) delicate ——上品に elegantly, gracefully ——上品さ elegance Ⓤ, grace Ⓤ‖上品な物腰 *elegant* manners / 彼女はいつも上品な服装をしている She always wears *elegant* clothes. / She always dresses *elegantly*. / あいつには少しも上品なところがない There's not a bit of *grace* about him.

◆上品ぶるんじゃないよ Stop *putting on airs.*

しょうふ 娼婦 prostitute ⓒ

しょうぶ¹ 勝負 (試合) match ⓒ, game ⓒ(❖個人対個人では match, チーム対チームではgameを用いる傾向がある) ——勝負する(競技をする) play ⓗⓘ;(戦う) fight* ⓘ

勝負に勝つ win *a match* [*game*] / 勝負に負ける lose *a match* [*game*] / 勝負を捨てる give up *a match* [*game*] / 真剣に勝負する *play for real*

あっという間に勝負がついた The match [game] *was over* in an instant.

彼にテニスで勝負をいどんだ I challenged him to *a match* [*game*] of tennis.(❖テニスではgame が集まって set, set が集まって match を成す)

この勝負はもらった This *match* [*game*] is all mine.

試合は予想以上にいい勝負(→接戦)になった *The game was closer* than we had expected.

◆全く練習していないから出たとこ勝負だ I've not practiced at all, and I'll have to play it by ear.(❖play it by ear は「ぶっつけ本番でやる」の意味) / 入試までそう日はないけど、あきらめないぞ. これからが勝負さ I know I don't have many days left before the entrance exam, but I won't give up. The result depends on how I study from now on.

💬「あいつが相手じゃ勝負にならないよ」「あきらめるのは早いよ」"I'm no match for him." "It's too early to give up."

‖勝負事 a match, a game; (賭(か)け事) gambling

しょうぶ² 菖蒲 〖植物〗 sweet flag ◎ / (アヤメ科の植物の総称) iris ◎

じょうぶ 丈夫

❶【健康な】 ──丈夫な (健全な) healthy; (たくましい) strong

胃が丈夫である have a「*strong* stomach [*good* digestion]

祖父はいたって丈夫で病気ひとつしたことがない My grandfather is quite *healthy* and has never been sick.

彼は丈夫な体をしている He has a *strong* body.

❷【頑丈な】 ──丈夫な strong, tough; (しっかりした) firm; (長もちする) durable

丈夫な家具 *strong* furniture / 丈夫な作りの靴 *tough* shoes / 丈夫な生地で作られた服 clothes made of *durable* material

この棚は丈夫だからその本を全部載せても平気だよ This shelf is *strong* enough to hold all those books.

じょうぶ² 上部 upper part ◎; (てっぺん) the top ──上部の upper ‖建物の上部 the *upper part* of the building

‖上部構造 a superstructure

しょうふだ 正札 price tag ◎ ◆正札どおりの値段で買う buy at *the fixed price*

じょうぶつ 成仏 君が結婚して落ち着くまでは亡くなったお父さんも成仏できないだろう Your dead father won't be able to *rest in peace* until you get married and settle down.

しょうぶん 性分 nature ‖父はきちょうめんな性分だ My father is of *a* meticulous *nature.* / こつこつやるのは私の性分に合わない It 「isn't in my *nature* [doesn't *agree with* me] to work steadily.

◆彼は何をやっても人からいやがられることがない. 本当に得な性分だ He does whatever he wants, and yet nobody hates him. He's really *a fortunate person*. (❖「損な性分」なら unfortunate を用いる)

じょうぶん 条文 (本文) text ◎; (条項) provision ◎ ‖それは憲法の条文に明記されている It is clearly stipulated in *the text* of the constitution.

しょうへき 障壁 barrier ◎, obstacle ◎ ➡かべ, しょうがい (障害) ‖障壁を崩す[乗り越える]「break down [overcome] *a barrier* / その国は貿易障壁を減らす努力をしている The country is trying to reduce trade *barriers*. / 言葉の障壁はあったが彼らはその国の生活にすぐ慣れた In spite of *the* language *barrier*, they soon got used to the life in that country.

‖関税障壁 a tariff barrier

じょうへき 城壁 castle wall ◎ ◆城壁をめぐらす surround a castle with *walls*

しょうべん 小便 urine ◎, 《卑語》piss ◎ (またはa ~), 《口語的》pee ◎ (またはa ~) ──小便する urinate 🅐, pee 🅐, have* [take*] a piss ‖小便が近い have the need to *urinate* frequently / 立ち小便する *urinate* on [in] the street ◆小便を我慢する hold *one's water* / 小便をもらす wet *one's* pants / 寝小便する wet *one's* bed

‖小便器 a urinal

じょうほ 譲歩 concession ◎ ◎ ──譲歩する concede 🅑 🅐, make* a concession (to ...); (歩み寄る) meet* *a person* halfway ‖私たちはお互いの譲歩によってようやく合意に達した We finally got to agreement through mutual *concessions*. / 彼らはその点では我々に譲歩した They *conceded* that point to us.

しょうほう 商法 〖法律〗 the commercial law ‖マルチ商法 pyramid selling

しょうぼう 消防 (消火活動) fire fighting ◆消防署に電話しろ Call *the fire department* [《英》*brigade*]! (❖消防署の建物は a fire station)

‖消防訓練 a fire drill / 消防士 a fireman, a fire fighter (❖性差別を避けるため最近では fire fighter を用いる傾向にある) / 消防自動車 a fire engine / 消防団 a fire brigade / 消防庁 the Fire and Disaster Management Agency / 消防艇 a fireboat

じょうほう 情報

information ◎ (❖教えるときは a piece [bit] of ... とする); (機密) intelligence ◎; (ニュース) news ◎ ◎

その地震に関する情報 *information* about [on] the earthquake / 情報不足だ Be short of *information* / コンピュータで情報を処理する process *information* with a computer / その事業の財務状況について情報開示を求める demand *the disclosure of information* on the project's financial situation

その情報は世界中に広まった The *information* [*news*] spread all over the world.

これは役に立つ情報だ This is *a useful piece of information*.

どうやってその情報を手に入れたのですか How did you get the *information*?

彼らは肝心な情報を隠していた They have kept the crucial *information* secret.

彼らのニューアルバムが完成したという情報が入ってきた We've got *information* that they've finished making their new album.

この本には最新の情報が載っている This book gives us *the latest* [*hot*] *information*.

◆ラジオで交通情報を聞いた I listened to *the traffic report* on the radio. / 情報によれば、彼はかなり重傷を負っているそうだ Reportedly, he is injured quite seriously.

[コロケーション] -information-
〖形容詞＋～〗 貴重な～ valuable information / 機密～ classified [confidential] information, intelligence / 詳しい～ detailed information / 正確な～ accurate information / 確かな～ reliable information / 内々の～ private information / 内部～ inside information / 秘密の～ secret information / 無用な～ useless information
〖動詞＋～〗 ～を集める collect [gather] information / ～を交換する exchange information / ～を提供する give [offer] information / ～を流す give [spread] information / ～を引き出す draw [extract] information / ～をもらす leak information

‖情報科学 information science / 情報革命 the information revolution / 情報化時代 the information age / 情報化社会 an information-oriented society / 情報機関 a secret service / 情報源 a source of information / 情報検索〖コンピュータ〗 information retrieval / 情報公開 information disclosure / 情報工学 information engineering / 情報サービス an information service / 情報産業 the information industry / 情報誌 an informational magazine / 情報処理 information processing / 情報提供者 an informant; (警察などへの) an informer / 情報番組 an informational program / 情報網 information network / 情報理論 information theory / 就職情報誌 a job-information magazine

しょうほん 抄本 (抜粋) extract [C] ‖戸籍抄本「an extract from [a copy of part of] *a person's* family register

じょうまえ 錠前 lock [C] ⇨かぎ(鍵) ‖錠前屋 a locksmith

じょうまん 冗漫 ―冗漫な (長ったらしい) lengthy; (言葉数の多い) wordy, 《公式的》 verbose //冗漫な記事 a *lengthy* [*wordy*] article

しょうみ[1] 正味 (表示で) 正味300グラム *Net Weight* 300 Grams / この砂糖は正味10グラムだ This sugar「has *a net weight* of 10 grams [weighs 10 grams *net*]. / 宿題を終わらせるのに正味 3 時間かかった It took me *fully* three hours to finish my homework.

しょうみ[2] 賞味 この牛乳は賞味期限を過ぎている This milk is past *its*「*use-by* [*best before*] *date*.

じょうみゃく 静脈 〖解剖〗 vein [C] ‖静脈注射 an intravenous injection / 大静脈 the main vein
[関連語] 動脈 an artery

じょうむ 常務 (executive) managing director [C]

じょうむいん 乗務員 (船・飛行機の) crew member [C], crewman [C], 《集合的》 crew [C]; (列車の車掌) 《米》conductor [C], 《英》 guard [C] //その飛行機には 8 名の乗務員が乗っている There are eight *crew members* on board the airplane.
‖乗務員室 a crew's cabin / 客室乗務員(飛行機の) a flight attendant

しょうむしょう 商務省 (米国の) the Department of Commerce

しょうめい[1] 証明

proof [U][C]; (論証) demonstration [U][C] ―証明する prove* [他]; demonstrate [自]; (公式に) certify [他]
ピタゴラスの定理を証明する *prove* [*demonstrate*] the Pythagorean theorem / …であることを証明します This is to [I hereby] *certify* that .... (❖証明書などの文句)
この事実が彼は無実であることを証明した This fact *proved*「that he is innocent [him (to be) innocent, his innocence].
私はあなたたちに彼のアリバイを証明することができる I can *prove* his alibi to you.
その絵は本物であることが証明されている The painting *has been proved* [*certified*] to be genuine.
身分を証明するものを持っていなかったので中へ入れてもらえなかった I had nothing to *prove* my identity and I was not allowed to get in.
‖証明書 a certificate / 結婚証明書 a marriage certificate / 出生証明書 a birth certificate / 成績証明書 《米》a transcript, 《英》 a certificate / 身分証明書 an identity card, an ID (card)

しょうめい[2] 照明 lighting [U], illumination [U]; (明かり) light [C] //柔らかい照明 soft *lighting*; *a* soft *light* / 照明が落ちて映画が始まった *The lights* were turned off, and then the movie started.
◆この劇場は照明がよい[悪い] This theater *is* well [poorly] *lighted.* / その建物には外から照明が当てられていた The building *was lighted* [*lit, illuminated*] from outside.
‖照明係 a lighting technician / 照明器具 a light, lighting equipment / 照明効果 lighting effects / 照明弾 a flare / 直接[間接]照明 direct [indirect] lighting / 舞台照明 stage lighting

しょうめつ 消滅 disappearance [U][C]; (慣習などの) extinction [U]; (権利などの) 〖法律〗 lapse [C] ―消滅する disappear [自]; lapse [自] //権利の消滅 *the lapse* of a right / 土地開発により、その地域の雑木林は完全に消滅してしまった The groves in the area *have* completely *disappeared* because of land development.
◆その計画は自然消滅した The plan *died out in the course of time.* / この契約の効力は消滅している This contract *has lost* effect.

しょうめん 正面
❶【前面】 the front; (建物の) facade [C]
建物の正面を飾る decorate *the front* of a building / 正面から建物の写真を撮る take a picture of a building from *the front*
❷【前方】

学校の正面にある建物 a building 「*opposite to* [*across from*] the school
その車は私の家の正面に止められていた The car was parked *in front of* my house. (❖in front は「直接の正面」, opposite, across は「道路などをはさんだ正面」.)
‖正面玄関 the front entrance [door] / 正面衝突 a head-on collision
慣用表現 問題に正面から取り組む tackle a problem *head-on* / 彼に正面切って本当のことを話すことができなかった I couldn't tell him the truth *straight to his face*.

しょうもう 消耗 (疲労) exhaustion ⓤ; (消費) consumption ⓤ ──消耗する (使い果たす) exhaust ⓗ; (消費する) consume ⓗ / 激しい運動で体力を消耗した I *was exhausted* by hard exercise. ◆この電池はすぐに消耗してしまう This battery *runs down* too soon.
‖消耗品 consumable goods

しょうやく 抄訳 (一部を訳したもの) a translation of selected passages; (全体を要約して訳したもの) abridged translation ⓒ

じょうやく 条約 treaty ⓒ / 条約に調印する sign *a treaty* / 条約を結ぶ [改正する, 批准(ひじゅん)する, 破棄する] conclude [revise, ratify, break] *a treaty* / その国はアメリカと友好 [通商] 条約を結んでいる The country has *a peace* [*commercial*] *treaty* with the U.S.
‖条約国 a treaty power

じょうやど 定宿・常宿 *one's* usual [regular] hotel

しょうゆ 醤油 🗻 soy sauce ⓤ

しょうゆは英語で soy sauce といいますが、この soy という言葉は日本語の「しょうゆ」に由来するとされています。しょうゆは中国から伝わり、その後日本人の好みに合わせて変化しました。蒸した大豆にいった小麦・こうじ・食塩水を加えて半年から1年の間発酵させ、それをしぼって液を取り除ければしょうゆのできあがりです。しょうゆは日本で最も多く使われる調味料で、あらゆる料理に利用されます。最近ではほかの多くの国でもしょうゆが売られています。
Shoyu is called "soy sauce" in English; the word "soy" comes from the Japanese word *shoyu*. It was introduced from China and went through some modifications to fit the taste of Japanese people. Steamed soybeans are mixed with roasted wheat, rice malt and brine, and the combination is fermented for six months to one year. Finally *shoyu* is squeezed out of the mixture, leaving the dregs behind. *Shoyu* is the most common seasoning in Japan, and it is used for a considerable number of Japanese dishes. Now it is sold in many other countries, too.

しょうよ 賞与 bonus ⓒ ● ボーナス
じょうよ 剰余 surplus ⓤ ⓒ; (収支の差額) balance ⓒ, (数学) remainder ⓒ ‖剰余価値 (経済) surplus value / 剰余金 (会計) a surplus (fund) / 剰余定理 (数学) the remainder theorem

しょうよう 商用 商用で旅行する travel *on business*
じょうよう 常用 彼はソフトコンタクトレンズを常用している He *always uses* [*wears*] soft contact lenses. / 私はこの薬を常用している I *take* this medicine *habitually*.
‖常用漢字 Chinese characters for daily use / 麻薬常用者 a drug addict
じょうようしゃ 乗用車 (passenger) car ⓒ

しょうらい 将来

── 图 future ⓤ (通例 the ～) (❖「前途, 将来性」の意味では ⓒ); (有望) promise ⓤ ── 圃 in the future; (いつの日か) someday, one day ──将来の future
日本の将来を予想する forecast Japan's *future* / 将来の夫 *one's future* husband / 将来性のある会社 a company with [which has] *a future* / 将来が楽しみな野球選手 a baseball player *of great promise*; a *promising* baseball player
あなたは将来何になりたいですか What do you want to be 「*in the future* [(→大人になったら) *when you grow up*]?
人類は近い [遠い] 将来滅亡するかもしれない The human race may perish *in the near* [*distant*] *future*.
私たちは自分たちの将来について語り合った We talked with each other about our *future(s)*.
将来の見通しは明るい *Our prospects for the future* are looking bright.
先生は私に将来の夢について尋ねた My teacher asked me about my 「*dreams for the future* [*future dream*].
彼女は歌手としての将来性を大いに感じさせる She shows real *promise* as a singer.

しょうり 勝利 victory ⓒ ⓤ (↔defeat); (競技などの) win ⓒ (↔loss, defeat); (大勝利) triumph ⓒ ⓤ ──勝利する win* ⓗ ⓘ
輝かしい [決定的な] 勝利 a glorious [decided] *victory* / 勝利の歓声 shouts of *triumph* / 勝利の栄冠を手にする win *the crown of victory* / 大勝利を収める win [have, gain] *a great victory* / 勝利を宣言する claim *victory*
彼のホームランがチームに勝利をもたらした His home run brought *a victory* to the team.
勝利は我々の手中にある *Victory* is within our grasp.
勝利の女神は我々にほほえんだ *Victory* smiled on us.
我々は東高校チームとの闘いに勝利した We *won* the game against the Higashi High School team.
私たちのチームは勝利を逃した Our team 「*missed winning the game* [(→負けた) *lost the game*].
チャンピオンは KO で勝利を飾った The champion *won* by (a) knockout.
‖勝利者 a winner / 勝利投手 a winning pitcher (↔a losing pitcher)

関連語 圧勝 a sweeping [an overwhelming] victory / 完勝 a clear victory / 辛勝 a hard-won victory / 楽勝 an easy victory

じょうりく 上陸 landing Ⓤ ―― 上陸する land ⓗ; (岸・浜に) go* [come*] ashore; (台風などに) make* landfall, hit*, strike* ⓗ (✲hit, strike は「襲う」の意味) ∥ペリーは 1853年, 久里浜に上陸した Perry *landed* [*went ashore*] at Kurihama in 1853. / 台風は関東地方に上陸する見込みだ The typhoon is expected to「*make landfall in* [*hit, strike*] the Kanto district. ◆その健康食品ブームは日本にも上陸した The craze for the health food *has reached* even Japan.

しょうりつ 勝率 the percentage of wins

しょうりゃく 省略 (省くこと) omission Ⓤ; (短縮) abbreviation Ⓤ ―― 省略する omit ⓗ, leave* out; abbreviate ⓗ (短くする) shorten ⓗ; (要約する) abridge ⓗ

"It's 10 o'clock now."の"o'clock"は省略可能だ You *can omit* "o'clock" in "It's 10 o'clock now."

以下省略 The rest is omitted.

細かい話は省略します I'll *leave out* the details.

Monday は Mon.と省略される "Monday" *is shortened* [*abbreviated*] to "Mon."

名前の「エリザベス」は「ベス」と省略される The name "Elizabeth" *is shortened* to "Beth." (✲人名の場合は通例 abbreviate は用いない)

AFはオートフォーカスを省略した形です AF is「*an abbreviation of* [*short for*] autofocus.

◆住所は省略せずに書いてください Write your address *in full*, please.

∥省略符号 an apostrophe(✲記号は')

じょうりゅう¹ 上流 ❶【川 の】the upper stream; (地域) the upper reaches of a river ――上流に upstream / この川の上流にある町 a town located *upstream* on this river / 私たちは上流で釣りを楽しんだ We enjoyed fishing on *the upper reaches of the river*. / ここから5キロ上流につり橋がある There's a suspension bridge five kilometers *upstream* [*up the river*] from here. / 彼らは流れに逆らって川の上流へとこいでいった They rowed *upstream* [*up the river*] against the current.

❷【社会の】その先生は上流家庭の出身だ That teacher comes from *an upper-class family*.

∥上流階級 the upper class(es) / 上流社会 high society

じょうりゅう² 蒸留 distillation Ⓤ ―― 蒸留する distill ⓗ ∥ブランデーはブドウ酒を蒸留して作られる Brandy *is distilled from* wine.

∥蒸留酒 distilled liquor / 蒸留水 distilled water / 蒸留装置 a distillation apparatus, a still

しょうりょう 少量 ―― 少量の a little, a small quantity [amount] of ..., a bit of ... ∥塩を少量加えてください Add *a small amount of* salt. / なべに少量の水が入っている There is *a little* water in the pot.

しょうりょく 省力 その会社では省力化に努めている The company tries to *reduce* [*save*] *labor*.

じょうりょくじゅ 常緑樹 evergreen (tree) Ⓒ

しょうれい 奨励 encouragement Ⓤ; (勧めること) recommendation Ⓤ ―― 奨励する encourage ⓗ, recommend ⓗ ∥先生は私たちに読書を奨励している The teacher *encourages* us *to* read books.

∥奨励金(国から団体へ) a grant, a subsidy; (生産向上のための) an incentive

じょうれい 条例 regulation Ⓒ ∥県の条例 prefectural *regulations*

じょうれん 常連 (客) regular customer Ⓒ, 《口語的》regular Ⓒ ∥彼らはこのレストランの常連だ They are「*regular customers* [*regulars*] at this restaurant.

じょうろ watering can Ⓒ

しょうわ 昭和 Showa ◆私は昭和60年生まれです I was born in 1985 [the 60th year of *the Showa era*]. (✲年号は日本独特のものなので西暦を用いるほうがよい)

∥昭和時代 the Showa era [period]

しょうわくせい 小惑星【天文】asteroid Ⓒ

しょえん 初演 (音楽・演劇などの) the first performance; (演劇・映画などの) the premiere ∥『蝶々夫人』は1904年に初演された *The first performance of Madame Butterfly* was in 1904. / *Madame Butterfly was first performed* in 1904.

じょえん 助演 ―― 助演する (わき役を演じる) play a supporting role

∥助演男優[女優]賞 an award for the best supporting actor [actress]

ショー show Ⓒ ∥私たちはファッションショーを見に行った We went to *a fashion show*.

∥ショービジネス show business, 《口語的》show biz / チャリティーショー a charity show / モーターショー an auto show

じょおう 女王 queen Ⓒ ∥ビクトリア女王 *Queen* Victoria / 銀幕の女王 *a movie queen* ∥女王バチ[アリ] a queen bee [ant] / 女王陛下 Her Majesty

ショーウインドー show window Ⓒ ∥ショーウインドーには夏物の服が飾ってある Summer clothes are displayed in *the show window*.

ジョーカー【トランプ】joker Ⓒ

ジョーク joke Ⓒ ⇨じょうだん

ショーケース (商品の陳列棚) showcase Ⓒ

ジョージア Georgia (✲米国南東部の州; 《略語》Ga., 〖郵便〗GA)

ショーツ ⚠《女性下着》panties

ショート (電気) short circuit Ⓒ, 《口語的》short Ⓒ; (野球) shortstop Ⓒ, 《口語的》short Ⓒ ∥ショートして停電になった The electricity was cut off because of *a short circuit*. / 兄はショートを守っている My brother plays *shortstop*. ◆髪をショートにした I had my hair cut *short*.

∥ショートカット a short haircut / ショート

ショート(超短編小説) a short short story / ショートスカート a short skirt / ショートパンツ shorts / ショートヘア short hair

ショートケーキ

> 1切れずつのケーキという意味で「ショートケーキ」という場合は a slice of cake という. 日本のいわゆる「イチゴのショートケーキ」は strawberry layer cake のようにいえばよい. 英語の shortcake はスポンジの代わりにさくさくした生地を用い, その上にイチゴとホイップクリームをかけたものをいうことが多い.

ショール (肩かけ) shawl C
ショールーム (商品展示室) showroom C / 新型車のショールーム *a showroom* for new model cars
しょか¹ 初夏 early summer U
しょか² 書架 (本棚) bookshelf C (複 bookshelves); (図書館の) stack C 《しばしば複数形~s》
しょか³ 書家 calligrapher C
じょがい 除外 (締め出し) exclusion U; (例外にすること) exception C ——除外する (締め出す) exclude 他; (除く) except 他 / 特殊なケースは除外する *exclude* [*except*] special cases ◆未成年者はこの規則の適用から除外される Minors *are exempt* from these regulations.
しょがくしゃ 初学者 beginner C
しょかつ 所轄 (公式的)jurisdiction U
◆所轄の警察署 *one's local* police station /所轄官庁 the responsible authorities
しょかん¹ 所感 (論評) comment C; (印象) impression C; (所見) remark C / この問題についてひと言所感を述べさせていただきます Let me make a few *comments* [*remarks*] on this problem.
しょかん² 書簡 (手紙) letter C; (総称) correspondence U C / その小説家の書簡集 the *correspondence* of the novelist
しょき¹ 初期 (初めのころ) the beginning; (早い時代) the early days; (病気などの) early stage C ——初期の[に] early / その小説は明治時代初期に書かれた The novel was written「*at the beginning* of the Meiji period [in the *early* Meiji period, *early* in the Meiji period]. / 祖父の癌(がん)は初期に発見された My grandfather's cancer was caught in *the early stages*. / これはピカソの初期の典型的な作品だ This is a typical example of Picasso's *early* works.
◆フロッピーディスクを初期化する *initialize* [*format*] a floppy disk
‖初期化 initialization, formatting
しょき² 所期 ——所期の (期待された) expected; (望まれた) desired / 私は所期の目的を達成した I achieved the *expected* results.
しょき³ 書記 (事務官) clerk C; (秘書) secretary C / ‖書記官 a secretary / ‖書記長 a chief secretary; (政党の) a secretary-general
しょきゅう 初級 ——初級の (初歩の) elementary; (初心者の) beginners'; (入門の) introductory / ‖初級ロシア語 *elementary* Russian / 妹は英語の初級者クラスに入っている My sister is in the *beginners'* class in English.
じょきょ 除去 removal U C ——除去する remove 他; (やっかいなものを) get* rid of ...; (排除かにて水を浄化する *purify water by *removing* [*getting rid of*] sludge / 彼らはその地域で地雷の除去作業にあたっている They are engaged in *mine removal* in the area.
じょきょうじゅ 助教授 《米》assistant [associate] professor C, 《英》senior lecturer C, 《英》reader C
じょきょく 序曲〔音楽〕overture C
ジョギング jogging U ——ジョギングする jog 自 / ジョギングに行く go *jogging* / 彼は毎朝家の周りをジョギングしている He jogs around his house every morning.
しよく 私欲 self-interest U / 彼は私欲に目がくらんだ He was blinded by *self-interest* [*selfish desires*].
しょく¹ 職
❶ [仕事] (働き口) job C, 《公式的》occupation C; (働くこと) work U; (重要な地位にある人の) position C, post C
職を失う lose *one's job*
彼は職を転々としている He drifts from one *job* to another.
彼女は職を変えた She changed *jobs*.
彼は職を解かれた He was relieved of *his post*.
父は会社内で重要な職にある My father holds *an* important *post* [*position*] in his company.
彼は部長の職に就いた He took *a post* as manager.
私は職探しをしているところです I'm looking for *a job* now.
◆おじは定年退職して今は職がない My uncle retired and *is unemployed* [*out of a job*, *out of work*] now.
❷ [技術]
将来は手に職をつけたい I'd like to「*acquire some kind of skill* [*learn a trade*] in the future.
しょく² 食 (食物) food U; (食事) meal C; (食欲) appetite U C / きょうは食が進まない I have *a poor appetite* today. / 休みの日は1日2食になることが多い On holidays I usually eat two *meals* a day.
◆食が細い be a light [small] *eater* / 日本の食文化 Japanese *gastronomic* culture
‖機内食 an in-flight meal / 主食 a staple food / 和食 Japanese food
しょくあたり 食あたり food poisoning U
しょくいん 職員 (1人の) staff member C; (全体) the staff; (特に官庁などの職員全体) the personnel / 姉は図書館の職員です My sister is「*a staff member* of [on *the staff* of] the library. / その団体には70人の職員がいる There are 70 *staff members* in the organization. ◆この学校は職員が多い This school

has *a* large *staff.*
∥職員会議 a staff meeting; (教員の) a teachers' meeting; 職員室 a staff room; (学校の) a teachers' room

しょぐう 処遇 treatment ⓤ ∥親切な[冷たい]処遇を受ける receive kind [cold] *treatment*; *be treated* kindly [coldly]

しょくえん 食塩 (一般に) salt ⓤ; (特に食卓用の) table salt ⓤ ∥食塩水 (a) saline [séiliːn] solution (❖salt water は「塩水」「海水」の意味)

しょくぎょう 職業

《公式的》occupation ⓤⓒ; (仕事・勤め口) job ⓒ; (知的な仕事) profession ⓒ; (技術を要する仕事) trade ⓤⓒ; (使命感をもってする仕事) vocation ⓒ (❖特に「社会に貢献する仕事」をいう); (一生の仕事) career ⓒ
職業を探す look for *work* [*a job*]
彼の職業はタクシー運転手です He is a taxi driver *by occupation.*
彼は自分にあった職業を見つけた He found「*a job* that suited him [*his vocation*].
翻訳を一生の職業にしたい I want to make translation *my career.*
🔴 「ご職業は何ですか」「弁護士です」 "*What do you do?*" "*I'm a lawyer.*" (❖職業を尋ねるとき "What is your occupation?" と聞くのは非常にかたい言い方)
∥職業安定所 a job placement office / 職業教育 vocational education / 職業訓練 vocational training / 職業指導 vocational guidance / 職業紹介所 an employment agency / 職業病 an occupational disease / 職業別電話帳 the Yellow Pages

しょくご 食後 この薬は食後に飲んでください Take this medicine *after meals.* / 食後のデザートにヨーグルトを食べた I had yogurt as *dessert.* (❖「食後の」という意味はdessertに含まれる)

しょくし 食指 そのドレスを見て食指が動いた (→欲しくなった) I *wanted to get* the dress when I saw it.

しょくじ 食事

meal ⓒ; (規定食) diet ⓒ
《食事を》
食事を作る cook *a meal*
彼は1日に4度食事をする He *has* [*eats*] four *meals* a day.
私は何週間もまともな食事をとっていない I haven't had *a proper meal* for weeks.
彼が食事をおごってくれた He treated me to *a meal.*
食事をすませてから行きます I'll go there after I finish *my meal.*
◆けさは寝坊したので食事を抜いてきた I skipped *breakfast* this morning because I got up late. / あのレストランで食事をしませんか Shall we *eat* at that restaurant?
《食事に》
彼らは私を食事に連れていってくれた They took me out for *a meal.*
◆この前の日曜日に彼女を食事に招いた I invited her to *dinner* last Sunday. / 山岡はただ今食事に出ています Yamaoka is out for *lunch* now. / まずは食事にしよう First let's *eat.*
《食事の》
母は食事のしたくをしている My mother is preparing [《口語的》fixing] *a meal.*
◆私が食事の後片づけをした I *cleared the table.*
《その他》
◆食事中に電話がかかってきた There was a phone call「*while we were eating* [*during the meal*]. / 医者に食事制限をするように言われた I was told by the doctor to *go on a diet.*

しょくしゅ 職種 a kind of occupation [job]

しょくじゅ 植樹 私たちは学校の創立100周年記念に植樹した We *planted a tree* in commemoration of the 100th anniversary of the founding of our school.
∥植樹祭 a tree-planting ceremony; (アメリカ・カナダなどの)《米》Arbor Day

しょくしょう 食傷 あの歌手の歌には食傷ぎみだ I「*am fed up with* [*have had enough of*] the songs of that singer.

しょくじりょうほう 食餌療法 diet ⓒ, dietary cure ⓒ ∥食餌療法をしている be on *a diet*

しょくせいかつ 食生活 現代人の食生活 *the diet of modern people* / 君は食生活を改善する必要がある You have to improve *your eating habits.*

しょくせき 職責 *one's* duty ∥彼は職責を果たすために全力を尽くした He did his best to fulfill *his duty.*

しょくぜん 食前 食前に2錠飲む take two tablets *before*「*each meal* [*meals*]
∥食前酒 an aperitif [əpèrətiːf]

しょくたく¹ 食卓 (dining) table ⓒ ∥夕食のために食卓の準備をする set *the table* for supper / 食卓にはおいしそうな料理がたくさん並べられていた *The table* was spread with delicious-looking food. / 子供たちはみな食卓に着いた The children all sat down at *the table.* / 兄は食卓を片づけている My brother is clearing *the table.* / 私たちは食卓を囲んで座った We sat around *the table.*
∥食卓塩 table salt

しょくたく² 嘱託 (非常勤の) part-time employee ⓒ; (臨時の) temporary employee ⓒ

しょくちゅうしょくぶつ 食虫植物 insectivorous plant ⓒ

しょくちゅうどく 食中毒 food poisoning ⓤ ∥彼女は食中毒にかかった She got [came down with] *food poisoning.* / そのレストランで集団食中毒が発生した There was *a mass outbreak of food poisoning* at the restaurant.

しょくつう 食通 gourmet [ɡúərmei] ⓒ

しょくどう³ 食堂 dining room ⓒ; (レストラン) restaurant ⓒ; (軽食堂) snack bar ⓒ;

(列車内・駅などの) buffet [bəféi] ⒞; (セルフサービスの) cafeteria ⒞ ‖食堂車 a dining car, (口語的) a diner / 学生[社員]食堂 a school [company] cafeteria

しょくどう² 食道 throat ⒞, 〖解剖〗esophagus [isáfəɡəs] ⒞ ‖食道癌(ガン) cancer of the esophagus

しょくにん 職人 craftsman ⒞ (❖女性は a craftswoman), artisan ⒞ ‖彼は腕のよい職人です He is a good *craftsman*. ‖職人かたぎ the craftsman [artisan] spirit / 職人芸 craftsmanship

しょくば 職場 one's place of work (❖英語では, 職場の種類を具体的に表して a company, an office, a factory などということが多い)
◆彼は職場を変わった He changed *jobs*. / 彼女は職場に復帰した She returned to *work*. / 職場は上野にあります My *office* is in Ueno. ‖職場結婚 an office marriage / 職場放棄 a walkout, a strike

しょくばい 触媒 〖化学〗catalyst ⒞

しょくはつ 触発 その事件に触発されて各地で暴動が起こった(→その事件が暴動を引き起こした) The event triggered [touched off] riots in many locations.

しょくパン 食パン bread ⓤ (❖ 1 切れは a slice of …, 1 斤は a loaf of … とする)

しょくひ 食費 (家計の中の) food expenses; (下宿の) (the) charge for board ‖食費を切り詰める cut down on *food expenses*
◆彼女は毎月食費に 3 万円使っている She spends 30,000 yen on *food* every month.

しょくひん 食品 (個々の) food ⒞ (❖総称として用いるときは ⓤ); (総称) foodstuffs ‖食品売り場は地下 1 階です The *food* department is on floor B-1. ‖食品衛生 food hygiene / 食品添加物 a food additive / インスタント食品 instant foods / 加工食品 processed foods / 健康食品 health foods / 自然食品 natural [organic] foods / 生鮮食品 perishable foods, perishables / 冷凍食品 frozen foods

しょくぶつ 植物 plant ⒞; (特定の場所の) vegetation ⓤ
父は庭の植物に水をやっている My father is watering the *plants* in the garden.
天候は植物の生育に影響を及ぼす Climate influences the growth of *plants*.
彼女はたくさんの植物を育てている She is growing many *plants*.
◆夏休みには植物採集に行くつもりだ I'm going to go *plant-collecting* during summer vacation. ‖植物園 a botanical garden / 植物界 the vegetable [plant] kingdom / 植物学 botany / 植物学者 a botanist / 植物人間 a (human) vegetable / 植物油 vegetable oil / 観葉植物 an ornamental [a decorative] plant / 高山植物 alpine plants / 熱帯植物 tropical plants / 被子植物 an angiosperm / 裸子植物 a gymnosperm

しょくべに 食紅 red food coloring ⓤ

しょくぼう 嘱望 彼は将来を嘱望されている (→前途有望な) 若者だ He is a *promising* young man.

しょくみんち 植民地 colony ⒞ ‖その国はイギリスの植民地だった The country was *a* 「British *colony* [*colony* of Britain].
◆その国を植民地化する *colonize* the country ‖植民地化 colonization / 植民地支配 colonial rule / 植民地主義 colonialism / 植民地政策 a colonial policy

しょくむ 職務 (任務) duty ⒞ ⓤ; (仕事) work ⓤ ‖彼らは職務を遂行した They performed *their duties*. / 彼女は職務に忠実な人だ She is faithful to *her duties*. / 彼は職務怠慢だ He neglects *his duties*. ‖職務規定 office regulations / 職務権限 official power / 職務質問 police questioning

しょくもつ 食物 food ⓤ (❖種類をいうときは ⒞) ‖消化のよい食物 digestible *food* / 鉄分を多く含む食物 *food* containing lots of iron ‖食物繊維 dietary fiber / 食物連鎖 the food chain

しょくよう 食用 ——食用の edible ‖このキノコは食用です This mushroom is *edible* [*good to eat*]. ‖食用油 cooking oil / 食用ガエル a bullfrog

しょくよく 食欲 appetite ⒞ ⓤ ‖かぜをひいてあまり食欲がない I have a cold, so I have *a* poor *appetite*. / 少し散歩すれば食欲が出ますよ A little walk will boost *your appetite*. / こう暑いと食欲がなくなる This heat makes me lose *my appetite*. / このにおいは食欲をそそる This aroma stimulates *my appetite*. / 弟は食欲旺盛(オウセイ)だ My brother *has a good* [*hearty*] *appetite*.
◆私にとって秋といえば食欲の秋だ To me, fall is the season to "*eat*."

しょくりょう¹ 食料 food ⓤ (❖種類をいうときは ⒞); (食料雑貨類) groceries
私たちは大量の食料を輸入している We import large amounts of *food*.
母は食料品を買いに出ていて留守だ My mother is out shopping for *groceries*. ‖食料品 food / 食料品店 a grocery [food] store

しょくりょう² 食糧 food ⓤ (❖種類をいうときは ⒞); (備蓄した) provisions ‖彼らは非常時に備えて食糧を大量に蓄えている They keep a large stock of *food* for emergencies. / 飢えに苦しむ人々を救うには食糧の供給が十分ではない The supply of *food* is not sufficient to save those who are starving. / その国では食糧が不足している The country is short of *food*. ‖食糧危機 food crisis / 食糧事情 the food situation / 食糧難 a scarcity of food / 食糧問題 the food problem

しょくりん 植林 afforestation ⓤ ——植林する plant trees, afforest ⓣ

しょくれき 職歴 (経歴) one's professional [occupational] career

しょくん 諸君 (男性に) Gentlemen; (男女に) Ladies and gentlemen; (全員に)

Everybody; (友人たちに) Friends
◆諸君の健闘を祈る I hope (*all of*) *you* will do your best./ Good luck to (*all of*) *you*.

じょくん 叙勲 (a) conferment of a decoration ——叙勲する confer a decoration (on *a person*) ‖勲一等を叙勲される receive [*be decorated with*] the First Class Order

しょけい 処刑 execution ⓊⒸ ——処刑する execute ⊕ ‖その反乱の指導者は処刑された The leader of the rebellion *was executed*.
‖処刑台 a scaffold; (絞首台)a gallows

しょげる (気落ちしている) be (down and) depressed; (がっかりしている) be discouraged ⇨がっかり ‖彼は先生に怒られてすっかりしょげていた He *was* very *depressed* after he was scolded by the teacher.

しょけん¹ 所見 one's view [opinion] ‖所見を述べる give one's opinion [view]/ その医者の所見では, 彼の熱はすぐ下がるということだった The doctor's *opinion* was that his temperature would come down soon.

しょけん² 初見 sight-reading Ⓤ ◆その曲を初見で演奏する *sight-read* the tune

じょげん 助言 (忠告) advice Ⓤ; (熟慮の上の専門的な) (公式的)counsel Ⓤ ——助言する advise ⊕; counsel ⊕ ‖私は彼女に助言を求めた I asked her for (*her*) *advice*./ 彼は弁護士の助言に従った He followed his lawyer's *advice*./ 先生は私の研究について助言してくれた The teacher [*advised me* [*gave me advice*] on my research.
‖助言者 an adviser

しょこ 書庫 library Ⓒ; (図書館の) stack Ⓒ (しばしば複数形 〜s)

じょこう 徐行 ——徐行する go* slow(ly); (速度を落とす) slow down ‖徐行《掲示》*Go Slow*; *Slow Down* ‖大雨のため電車は徐行運転をした The train *went slowly* because of the heavy rain.

しょこく 諸国 アラブ諸国 Arab *countries*/ 近隣諸国 neighboring *countries*

しょさい 書斎 study Ⓒ

しょざい 所在 (人の) one's whereabouts; (建物などの) location Ⓤ ‖彼女の所在は不明だ Her *whereabouts* are unknown./ (→どこにいるのか分からない)We don't know *where* she is./ 責任の所在(→だれに責任があるのか)をはっきりさせる必要がある We have to find out *who is responsible*./ それ以来男は所在をくらましている The man *has been in hiding* since then.
‖所在地 a location; (政府機関などの)a seat

じょさいない 如才ない (機転のきく) tactful; (抜け目ない) clever ‖如才ない人 a *tactful* person ◆彼女は如才なく立ち回った She acted *tactfully*.

じょさんぷ 助産婦 midwife Ⓒ

しょし 初志 彼は初志を貫徹することにした He decided to *carry out his original intention*.

しょじ 所持 possession Ⓤ ——所持する possess ⊕, have* ⊕ ‖彼は麻薬の不法所持で逮捕された He was arrested for *illegal possession* of drugs.

‖所持金 money on hand/ 所持品 *one's* belongings

じょし¹ 女子 (少女) girl Ⓒ; (成人女性) woman Ⓒ (複 women)
わが校の女子バレーボール部 the *girls'* volleyball club at our school
うちのクラスは男子の数と女子の数が同じだ The number of boys in our class is the same as that of *girls*.
‖女子学生 a girl [woman, female] student / 女子(高校) a girls' (high) school/ 女子高生 a female high school student/ 女子大 a women's university [college]/ 女子大生(女子の大学生) a female university [college] student; (女子大学の学生)a women's university [college] student/ 女子トイレ 《米》the ladies' room, 《英》the ladies/ 女子寮 a girls' [women's] dormitory

じょし² 女史 (既婚女性) Mrs.; (未婚女性) Miss; (既婚・未婚を問わず) Ms.

じょし³ 助詞 (postpositional) particle Ⓒ

しょしがく 書誌学 bibliography Ⓤ ‖書誌学者 a bibliographer

しょしかた 処し方 身の処し方(→ふるまい方) how to conduct oneself

しょしき 書式 form Ⓒ; (コンピュータの) format Ⓤ ◆書式に従って申込書に記入してください Please fill out the application *as indicated*.

じょじし 叙事詩 epic (poem) Ⓒ

じょしつ 除湿 dehumidification Ⓤ ——除湿する dehumidify ⊕
‖除湿器 a dehumidifier

じょしゅ 助手 assistant Ⓒ ‖彼はその教授の助手を務めている He works as 「the professor's *assistant* [*an assistant* to the professor].
‖助手席 the seat next to the driver, a passenger('s) seat

しょしゅう 初秋 early fall [《英》autumn]Ⓤ

じょじゅつ 叙述 description Ⓤ ——叙述する describe ⊕ ‖叙述形容詞《文法》a predicative adjective

しょしゅん 初春 early spring Ⓤ

しょじゅん 初旬 the beginning of the month; (月初めの10日間) the first 10 days of a month
◆そのCDは来月初旬に発売される The CD will be released *early* next month.

しょじょ 処女 virgin Ⓒ; (処女性) virginity Ⓤ ‖処女を失う lose *one's virginity*
‖処女航海 a maiden voyage/ 処女作 *one's* maiden [first] work/ 処女地 virgin soil/ 処女峰 an unclimbed peak/ 処女膜《解剖》the hymen

じょじょう 叙情 lyricism Ⓤ ——叙情的な lyric, lyrical ‖叙情詩 a lyric (poem); (総称) lyric poetry/ 叙情詩人 a lyric poet

じょじょに 徐々に gradually, by degrees; (少しずつ) little by little; (ゆっくり) slowly; (一歩一歩) step by step ‖状況は徐々に変化しつつある The situation is *gradually* changing./ 9月に入って徐々に涼しくな

り始めた September has come and it's beginning to get cool *little by little.* / 新しいクラスにも徐々に慣れてきた I have *slowly* begun to get used to the new class.

しょしん[1] 初心 初心に返る(→取り戻す) recapture *the beginner's fresh spirit*

[ことわざ] 初心忘るべからず Don't forget the earnestness you had when you began.; Humble hearts have humble desires. (→謙虚な心はつつましい望みをいだく)

しょしん[2] 初診 the first [initial] medical examination ◆初診の方(→患者)は保険証をお持ちください *New patients* are required to bring their health insurance cards.

‖初診料 an initial fee [charge]

しょしん[3] 所信 (信念) *one's* belief; (意見) *one's* opinion [view] //首相は所信を述べた The Prime Minister gave *his opinion*.

‖所信表明演説 a general policy speech

しょしんしゃ 初心者 beginner [C]; (新人) novice [C] //初心者用の教則本 an instruction book for *beginners* / 初心者コース[クラス] a *beginners'* course [class]

◆スキーの初心者 a *beginner* skier

‖初心者マーク(車の) a newly-licensed driver sticker

じょすう[1] 序数 ordinal number [C]

じょすう[2] 除数 〔数学〕divisor [C]

しょする 処する (処罰する) punish [他], sentence [他]; (対処する) deal* [cope] with ... //殺人犯は終身刑に処せられた The murderer *was sentenced* to life imprisonment.

じょせい[1] 女性 woman [C] (複 women), lady [C] (❖woman の丁寧な表現だが, 近年ではやや古風ともされる); (若い) girl [C]

働く女性 *a* working *woman* / 初の女性知事 the first *woman* governor(❖複数形は women governors だが, この例のように特に女性であることを示したい場合以外, 職業を表す語に性別を付けるのはなるべく避けるほうがよい)

この本は女性にとても人気がある This book is very popular among *women.*

あの女性と知り合いですか Are you acquainted with that *lady*?

◆彼の話し方は女性的だ(→めめしい) He has an *effeminate* way of talking. / 彼女は女性らしい服を好まない She doesn't like *feminine* clothes. / その山はなだらかで, 女性的な姿をしている The mountain slopes gently and has a *feminine* appearance.

‖女性解放運動 the women's [feminist] movement, women's liberation / 女性解放論者 a feminist / 女性(週刊)誌 a women's (weekly) magazine / 女性ホルモン a female hormone

じょせい[2] 助成 ━助成する (財政的に援助する) support [他]; (後援する) sponsor [他]; (政府が) subsidize [他] //政府はその学校を助成している The government *subsidizes* the school.

‖助成金(公共事業などへの) a grant, a grant-in-aid; (企業などへの) a subsidy

じょせい[3] 女声 ‖女声合唱 a female chorus

しょせいじゅつ 処世術 処世術(→世の中でうまくやっていく方法)を心得ている know *how to get along in the world*

じょせいと 女生徒 girl student [C], schoolgirl [C]

しょせき 書籍 book [C] //書籍売り場 *the book department*

じょせき 除籍 その少年は学校から除籍された *The name of the boy was removed* [*crossed out*] *from* the school register. / The boy *was expelled* from school.

しょせつ 諸説 その件については諸説入り乱れている There are too many *various opinions* on the matter.

じょせつ[1] 除雪 ━除雪する remove [clear] the snow from the road, clear the road of snow

‖除雪車 a snowplow,《英》a snowplough

じょせつ[2] 序説 introduction [C]

しょせん 所詮 (結局) in the end; (いずれにしても)《口語的》anyway //連中は口ではきれいごとを言っていても, しょせん金に動かされるようなやつらさ They may say things that are morally right, but「*in the end* [*even so*], they are people who are moved by money. / 何を言ったってしょせん負けは負けだよ Loss is loss *anyway*, whatever you may say.

◆しょせん無理だったんだ. あの大学に受かろうなんて I should have known it wasn't possible for me to pass the entrance exam for that university. / 説明したところでしょせん君には分かるまい You'll *never* be able to understand if I explain it to you.

しょぞう 所蔵 このつぼは本田氏の所蔵だ This vase「*is owned by* [*belongs to*] Mr. Honda. / This vase *is in* Mr. Honda's *possession*.

じょそう[1] 助走 approach run [C] ‖助走路(走り幅跳びなどの) a runway; (スキーの) an approach

じょそう[2] 除草 weeding [U] ━除草する weed [他][自]

‖除草剤 a herbicide, a weed killer

じょそう[3] 女装 彼はパーティー会場に女装して現れた He turned up at the party「*in drag* [*dressed as a woman*].

しょぞく 所属 ━所属する (属する) belong to ...; (配属されている) be attached to ... //彼女はバレー部に所属している She *belongs to* the volleyball club. / (→一員である)She *is a member of* the volleyball club. / 兄は海上自衛隊に所属している My brother *is attached to* the Marine Self Defense Force. / (→働いている)My brother *works for* the Marine Self Defense Force.

しょたい[1] 所帯 household [C]; (家庭) family [C] //彼女の家は大所帯だ She has *a large family.* ◆彼女は結婚して所帯じみてきた She *has become much more domestic* since she got married. / 彼は最近所帯を持った He *has set up house* recently. / (→結婚した)He *has gotten married* recently. / わが校の吹奏学部は100人を超える大所帯だ The wind orchestra (club) at our school is *a large one* with

more than 100 members.
∥世帯主 the head of the household ∕ 所帯持ち a married man [woman]

しょたい² 書体 (手書きの) handwriting ⓤ; (活字の)〔印刷〕typeface ⓒ

しょだい 初代 アメリカの初代大統領 *the first president of the United States*

じょたい 除隊 ——除隊する leave* the military ◆彼は除隊になった He *was discharged from the military.*

しょたいめん 初対面 新しい先生とはきょうが初対面だった I met the new teacher *for the first time* today. ∕ Today was *the first time* for me *to meet* the new teacher. ∕ 私たちは初対面のあいさつを交わした We *introduced ourselves to each other.*

しょだな 書棚 bookshelf ⓒ

しょち 処置 (手段・方策) measures; (治療) treatment ⓤⓒ; (1つの) step ⓒ ——処置する (治療する) treat ⓣ; (対策をとる) take* measures; (対処する) deal* with ...
傷をすぐに処置する *treat* the wound quickly
先生は規則を破った生徒に厳しい処置をとった The teacher *took* strong *measures against* the student who broke the rules.
医者はけが人に応急処置をした The doctor gave *first aid (treatment)* to the injured.
◆家の前に自転車を放置されて処置に困っている We are at a loss *what to do* with the bicycle left in front of our house. ∕ どれほど非難されても平気な顔をしているんだから, あの政治家は処置なしだね The politician doesn't care at all no matter how much we criticize him. He's「*beyond redemption* [*a hopeless case*].

しょちゅうみまい 暑中見舞い 🖂 先生方に暑中見舞いを出した I sent *summer greeting cards* to the teachers. ∕ 暑中お見舞い申し上げます How *are you spending this hot weather*?(◆英米には日本の暑中見舞いのような習慣はない)

しょちょう 所長 head ⓒ, chief ⓒ; (団体・研究所などの) director ⓒ

しょちょう² 署長 head ⓒ, chief ⓒ
∥警察署長 the chief of a police station

しょちょう³ 初潮 one's first period [menstruation]

じょちょう 助長 ——助長する encourage ⓣ; (促進する) promote ⓣ; (強める) strengthen ⓣ ◆その政策はインフレを助長しかねない That policy might *encourage* inflation.

しょっかく¹ 触角〔生物〕feeler ⓒ, antenna ⓒ (複 antennae)

しょっかく² 触覚 the sense of touch

しょっき 食器 (総称) tableware ⓤ(◆皿やナイフなど食器全般をいう); (皿類) the dishes (◆カップなども含む) ∥食器を片づける put away *the dishes* ∕ 食器を洗ってくれる? Could you wash [do] *the dishes*?
∥食器棚 a cupboard [kʌ́bərd]

ジョッキ ⚠ (beer) mug ⓒ

ジョッキー (騎手) jockey ⓒ

ショッキング ショッキングな事件が起きた A *shocking* event happened.

ショック shock ⓒⓤ(※「精神的な打撃」の意味でも「衝突などによる衝撃」の意味でも用いる. 個々のショック, ショッキングなことは ⓒ, ショックを受けることは ⓤ)
ショックをやわらげる[吸収する] soften [absorb] *a shock* ∕ 人に電気ショックを与える give a person *an electric shock*
落としたショックで MD ウォークマンがおかしくなってしまった My MD Walkman has been damaged by *the shock* of dropping it on the floor.
父の死は大きなショックだった My father's death was *a great shock* to me.
その事件は人々に大きなショックを与えた The case「*gave a* great *shock* to people [*shocked* people a lot].
彼がそのショックから立ち直るまで長い時間がかかった It took a long time for him to get over *the shock*.
その老人はその薬を飲んでショック死した The old man *died of shock* from taking the medicine.
◆彼女は彼の言葉にひどくショックを受けて食事ものどを通らないほどだった She *was so shocked* at what he said (that) she could hardly eat.
💬「彼らのきょうのコンサート, 中止だって」「うそ! すごいショック. 楽しみにしてたのに」"They say they decided to cancel today's concert." "No way! What *a shock*! I've really been looking forward to it."
∥ショック療法 shock therapy ∕ カルチャーショック culture shock

しょっけん 職権 (権限) authority ⓤ; (権力) (official) power ⓤ ∥職権を行使する exercise *one's authority*
∥職権乱用 an abuse of authority

しょっけん² 食券 meal ticket

しょっこう 職工 workman ⓒ

しょっちゅう (いつも) always; (四六時中) all the time; (頻繁に) very often ∥父はしょっちゅうテレビを見ている My father is *always* watching TV. ∕ 彼女はしょっちゅう髪型を変える She changes her hairstyle *very often*.

ショット (打った球)〔球技〕shot ⓒ ∥ナイスショット! Good *shot*!

しょっぱい salty

ショッピング (買い物) shopping ⓤ ➡ p.1682
場面・状況別会話 母とデパートへショッピングに行った I went *shopping* at a department store with my mother.
∥ショッピングカート a shopping cart [《英》trolley] ∕ ショッピングセンター a shopping center [《英》centre] ∕ ショッピングバッグ a shopping bag ∕ ショッピングモール a shopping mall ∕ ウインドーショッピング window-shopping ∕ テレビショッピング a TV home shopping

ショップ (店) shop / ‖コーヒーショップ a coffee shop / ディスカウントショップ a discount shop / ペットショップ a pet shop

しょてい 所定 ――所定の (指定された) appointed; (確定した) fixed; (規定された) prescribed / 所定の用紙 a *prescribed* form / 所定の場所に集まる come to the *appointed* place ◆みんな所定の(→自分の)位置についた Everyone took *their* place.

じょてい 女帝 empress; (女王) queen

しょてん 書店 《主に米》bookstore, 《主に英》bookshop

しょとう¹ 初冬 early winter

しょとう² 初等 ――初等の elementary ‖初等科 an elementary course / 初等教育 elementary [primary] education

しょとう³ 初頭 the beginning / 17世紀初頭に at *the beginning* of the 17th century

しょとう⁴ 諸島 islands ‖ハワイ諸島 the Hawaiian Islands

しょどう 書道 *shodo*, (Japanese) calligraphy ‖書道家 a calligrapher

> 書道は、墨をつけた毛筆で漢字や仮名文字を書くもので、多様な文字形態をもった一種の造形芸術です。伝統儀式である書き初めは今日(にち)でも行われており、また文化祭などでも書道作品の展示は恒例となっています。
> Japanese calligraphy is a figurative art with a diversity of character shapes. Japanese and Chinese characters are written in black ink using a brush. The traditional ceremony of *kakizome* remains popular. Calligraphy exhibitions are regular features at school festivals.

じょどうし 助動詞 〖文法〗auxiliary verb (《略語》aux.)

> 助動詞は、「…できる」(可能)、「…すべきだ」(義務)、「…する必要がある」(必要)、「…するつもりだ」(意志)などの意味を表したり、完了形・未来形・進行形・受動態・間接話法であることを示すために使われる。また、一般動詞で、疑問文・否定文を作るために使われる do, does, did も助動詞である。助動詞は、肯定文では通例動詞の前に置かれ、疑問文・否定文では以下の特徴がある。
> [疑問文]疑問文では、助動詞、主語、動詞の語順で表す ‖ *Can* she play piano? 彼女はピアノが弾けますか
> [否定文]否定文では、助動詞の直後に not を付ける ‖ She *can not* [*cannot, can't*] play the piano. 彼女はピアノが弾けません
> [否定の疑問文]否定の疑問文では、否定の助動詞、主語、動詞か助動詞、主語、否定語、動詞の語順になる ‖ *Can't* she [*Can* she *not*] play the piano? 彼女はピアノが弾けないのですか(❖Can she not …? は強調の意味や驚きの感情を表すために用いられるが、一般的にはあまり用いられない)

しょとく 所得 (収入) income; (稼ぎ) earnings
彼女は所得が多い She has *a* large [high] income.(❖「少ない」なら small, low を用いる)
兄は月に30万円の所得がある My brother has *a* monthly *income* of 300,000 yen. / My brother's monthly *income* is 300,000 yen.
‖所得隠し concealment of *one's* income / 所得控除 tax deductions and exemptions / 所得水準 *one's* income level / 所得税 an income tax / 給与所得 employment income / 勤労[不労]所得 earned [unearned] income / 高[低]所得世帯 a high-[low-]income family / 国民所得 the national income / 事業所得 business income / 年間所得 annual income / 年金所得 pension income

しょのか 初七日 祖父の初七日の法要に行った I attended the Buddhist memorial service for my grandfather held on *the sixth day after his death*.

しょにち 初日 the first [opening] day; (映画・オペラ・演劇などの) premiere

しょにんきゅう 初任給 大卒の初任給 *the starting salary* [*pay*] for a university [college] graduate

じょのくち 序の口 これは序の口にすぎない This is only [just] *the beginning*.

しょばつ 処罰 punishment; (罰金など具体的な) penalty ――処罰する punish ‖彼は公金を横領し厳しく処罰された He *was punished* [*received a punishment*] for embezzling public money.

しょはん 初版 the first edition
‖初版本 a first edition

じょばん 序盤 知事選はまだ序盤戦だ The gubernatorial election is still in *the early stages*.

しょひょう 書評 book review
◆彼は新聞で書評をしている He *reviews books* in the newspaper.
‖書評家 a book reviewer / 書評欄 a book-review column

しょぶん 処分 (始末) disposal; (処罰) punishment ――処分する (不要なものを) dispose of …; (取り除く) get* rid of …; punish ‖家を処分する「*dispose of* [(→売る)*sell*] a house / 彼女はいらない服を処分した She「*disposed of* [*got rid of*] her unnecessary clothes.
◆在庫処分セール a *clearance* sale / 彼はたばこを吸って(学校から)退学処分を受けた He *was expelled from school* for smoking.

じょぶん 序文 (著者による) preface; (主に著者以外の人による) foreword ‖本に序文を書く write *a preface* to a book

ショベルカー power shovel, excavator (❖「ショベルカー」は和製英語)

しょほ 初歩 (知識) the rudiments, the elements, the ABC('s); (基礎) the basics ――初歩の rudimentary, elementary ‖スキーの初歩 *the rudiments* [*ABC's*] of skiing / 初歩的な質問 an *elementary* question
◆英会話を初歩から(→始めから)習う learn English conversation *from the beginning*

/ 初歩的なミスを犯してしまった I made a *basic* [(→単純な) *simple*] mistake.

しょほう 処方 prescription [C] ―処方する prescribe [他] //医者は処方箋(せん)を書いてくれた My doctor wrote me *a prescription.* / 私は鎮痛剤を処方された I *was prescribed* painkillers.

しょぼくれる 男の子は母親にしかられてすっかりしょぼくれていた The boy *looked* completely *depressed* [*discouraged*] after being scolded by his mother.

しょぼしょぼ 目が疲れてしょぼしょぼする(→かすむ) My eyes are tired and *bleary.* / 朝から雨がしょぼしょぼ降っている *It has been drizzling gloomily* since morning.

じょまく 除幕 unveiling [U] ―除幕する unveil [他] //その像の除幕式がきょう行われた *The unveiling ceremony* of the statue was held today.

しょみん 庶民 the (common) people, ordinary people //庶民の声 the voice of *the people* / その画家は庶民の生活を描いた The artist depicted the lives of *ordinary people.*
◆ここはとても庶民的な(→気取らず気さくな)町だ This is a very *unaffected* [*unpretentious*] *and friendly* town.

しょむ 庶務 general affairs ‖庶務課 the general affairs section

しょめい[1] 書名 the title [name] (of a book)

しょめい[2] 署名 (手紙・契約書などの) signature [C]; (有名人などの) autograph [C] ―署名する sign [他] [自]; (自筆で) autograph [他] //契約書[書類]に署名する *sign* a contract [document] / ここにご署名願います Please *sign* here. / 我々は何千人もの署名を集めた We collected thousands of *signatures.* / 私はその作家の署名入りの本を持っている I have a book 「*with* the author's *autograph* [*signed* by the author].
‖署名運動 a petition [signature-collecting] campaign / 署名者 a signer

じょめい 除名 彼はそのクラブから除名された He *was expelled* from the club. / 彼女はリストから除名された *Her name was* 「*struck off* [*taken off* (*of*)] the list.

しょめん 書面 (文書) writing [U]; (手紙) letter [C] //結果は書面でお知らせします We'll let you know the results 「in *writing* [by *letter*].

しょもつ 書物 (本) book [C]

しょや 初夜 *one's* wedding night

じょや 除夜 🗻 *joya*, New Year's Eve //除夜の鐘 the ringing of temple bells on *New Year's Eve*

> 大みそかの夜に，過ぎゆく年を送り，新しい年を迎えるために寺でつく108回の鐘のことを除夜の鐘といいます．仏教では人間は生まれながらに108の煩悩(ぼんのう)をもつとされ，鐘を1度つくごとに煩悩が1つ取り払われるように，との願いがこめられているのです．
> *Joyanokane* is the ringing of temple bells 108 times on New Year's Eve to ring the old year out and see the new year in. Buddhist belief says that human beings have 108 earthly desires, and this ceremony is practiced in the hope that with each toll of the bell one will be driven away.

じょやく 助役 (市町村の) deputy mayor [C]; (駅の) assistant stationmaster [C]

しょゆう 所有 possession [U] ―所有する own [他], 《公式的》possess [他]
そのビルは市の所有になった The building *came into the possession of* the city.
これらの工場は父が所有している These factories *are owned* by my father.
◆私のおじがこの土地の所有権を持っている My uncle holds *the ownership* of this land.
‖所有格〔文法〕 the possessive case ➾ かく(格) / 所有者 an owner / 所有地 *one's* land / 所有物 *one's* possessions [belongings]; (財産) *one's* property

じょゆう 女優 actress [C] (❖特に女性であることを強調する場合以外 actor(男女を問わず「俳優」を意味する)を用いるほうがよい)

しょゆうだいめいし 所有代名詞 〔文法〕 possessive pronoun [C]

> (1)所有代名詞は，主として，前の名詞を受けて「所有格＋名詞」の代わりに用いられる // His son is five years old and *mine* is six. 彼の息子は5歳で，私の息子は6歳だ(❖この mine は my son のこと) / I bought the same dictionary as *yours.* 私はあなたと同じ辞書を買いました(❖この yours は your dictionary のこと)
> (2)所有代名詞は単数のものを指す場合も複数のものを指す場合も形は変わらない // This book is *mine.* この本は私のものだ / These books are *mine.* これらの本は私のものだ
> (3)所有格の代名詞の前に a, an, this, these, that, those, some, any を置くことができないため(×a my friend とはいわない)，名詞の後に「of＋所有代名詞」を置いて所有の意味を表す // She is an old friend *of mine.* 彼女は私の古い友達(の一人)です / I like that car of *his.* 私は彼のあの車が気に入っています

しょよう[1] 所用 (用事) business [U]

しょよう[2] 所要 駅までの所要時間は歩いて10分くらいだと思います *It* would *take* about ten minutes to go to the station on foot.

しょり 処理 (処分) disposal [U]; (取り扱い) management [U] ―処理する (物事を) handle [他], deal* with …; (何とか) manage [他]; (処分する) dispose of …; (薬品で) treat [他]; (データなどを) 〔コンピュータ〕 process [他] //下水処理 sewage *disposal* / ごみを処理する *dispose of* garbage / 金属を酸で処理する *treat* a metal with acid / 彼女は事務処理能力にすぐれている She is good at *handling* office work. / 私はその問題をどう処理したらよいか分からなかった I didn't know how to *deal with* the problem. / 彼らは困難な状況を

し

じょりゅう

うまく処理した They *managed* the difficult situation well. / コンピュータはたくさんの情報を処理できる Computers *can process* a lot of information.

じょりゅう 女流 ——女流の *woman* (❖特に女性であることを示したい場合以外，職業を表す語に性別を付けるのはさけるほうがよい) / 彼女は有名な女流作家だ She is a famous (*woman*) writer.

じょりょく 助力 help ⓤ; (援助) assistance ⓤ ——助力する help ⓗ; assist ⓗ / 助力を求める ask for *a person's help* / 彼の助力がなかったら問題を解決することはできなかっただろう Without his *help*, we could not have solved the problem.

しょるい 書類 (文書一般) papers; (証拠となるような) document ⓒ; (記入用紙) form ⓒ / 書類に書き込む fill out *a form* / 書類を提出する submit *papers* [*documents*] / その男を書類送検する send the documents on the man's *case to the public prosecutor's office*
‖書類かばん a briefcase / 書類審査[選考] a paper screening / 関係書類 the relevant documents / 機密書類 secret documents

ショルダーバッグ shoulder bag

じょれつ 序列 (地位) rank ⓤ; (格付け) ranking ⓤ
◆年功序列制度 the seniority system

しょろう 初老 ——初老の elderly / 初老の紳士 an *elderly* gentleman

じょろん 序論 introduction ⓒ

しょんぼり その子供は人形をなくしてしょんぼりしていた(→がっかりしていた) The child looked *dejected* [*depressed*] because she had lost her doll. / 彼女はしょんぼりした(→寂しそうな)様子で窓の外を眺めていた She was looking out of the window with a *lonely* [*forlorn*] expression.

じらい 地雷 (land) mine ⓒ / 地雷を仕掛ける[除去する] lay [remove] *a mine*

しらが 白髪 (白髪まじりの髪) gray hair ⓤ; (白い髪) white hair ⓤ; (銀髪) silver hair ⓤ (❖いずれも髪１本をいう場合はⓒ) / 白髪を抜く pull out *a white hair* / 兄は若白髪だ My brother *has gray hair* even though he is (still) young. ◆白髪まじりの髪 *grizzled* hair / 白髪頭の紳士 a *gray-headed* gentleman / 母は白髪が増えてきた My mother's *hair* is turning *gray*.
‖白髪染め a hair dye

しらかば 白樺 white birch ⓒ

しらける 白ける 彼のつまらない冗談でその場がしらけた His stupid joke 「*cast a chill over* [*spoiled*] the meeting. / 政治家たちの不祥事続きで, 有権者は今度の選挙をかなりしらけた目で見ている(→無関心である) Voters *are* quite 「*indifferent to* [*apathetic toward*] this election because of the succession of politicians' scandals.

しらさぎ 白鷺 〖鳥〗 white heron ⓒ

しらじらしい しらじらしい(→見えすいた)言い訳をする make a *transparent* excuse

-しらず —知らず 彼は礼儀知らずだ He has *no manners*. / そのテニス選手は，ここ２年間負け知らずだ The tennis player *has never lost a game* for the past two years.

じらす 焦らす じらさないで全部話してよ *Don't keep* me *hanging* [*in suspense*]. Tell me the whole story.

しらずしらず 知らず知らず 知らず知らずのうちに(→知らないうちに)英語が上達していた My English has improved 「*without* (*my*) *knowing it* [*before I knew it*].

しらせ 知らせ (ニュース) news ⓤ; (報告) report ⓒ; (情報) information ⓤ; (通知) notice ⓤ
東京都からのお知らせ *information* from the Tokyo Metropolitan Government
君によい[悪い]知らせがある I have some good [bad] *news* for you.
私たちはその知らせを聞いて驚いた We were surprised at [to hear] *the news*.
彼が試験に受かったという知らせがあった I heard *the news* that he had passed the examination.

しらせる 知らせる let* ... know, inform ⓗ; (告げる) tell* ⓗ
私は彼女に彼が退院したことを知らせた I 「*told* her [*let* her *know*, *informed* her] *that* he had left the hospital.
彼は私たちにそのニュースを知らせてくれた He 「*let us know* [*told* us, *informed* us *of*] the news.
出席できない場合にはお知らせください Please *let us know* if you can't attend.
彼女がアメリカに留学したことを手紙で知らされた I *was informed* by letter [Her letter *told* me] that she had gone to America to study.
◆すぐに警察に知らせたほうがいい *Notify* the police of it immediately. / *Report* it to the police immediately. / この話はだれにも知らせないでください Please keep this story *to yourself*.

しらは 白羽 劇の主役として彼女に白羽の矢が立った She *was singled out* for the leading part in the play.

しらばくれる しらばくれる しらばくれてもだめだよ It's no use *pretending not to know*. / おやおや, しらばくれちゃって. 本当は知ってるくせに Well, well, *as if you didn't* [*don't*] *know*. I'm sure you do know.

しらふ 素面 こんなことしらふじゃとても言えないよ I couldn't say these things 「*when sober* [(→酔わずに)*without being drunk*].

シラブル (音節) syllable ⓒ

しらべ 調べ ❶ 【調査】 examination ⓤⓒ, investigation ⓤⓒ, inquiry ⓤⓒ; (検査) inspection ⓤⓒ; (尋問) questioning ⓤ
◆私は警察の調べを受けた I *was questioned* [*examined*] by the police. / 調べはついているぞ. さっさと白状しろ We've *investigated* everything about you. Now you'd better confess.
❷ 【旋律】 melody ⓤⓒ; (曲) tune ⓒ / フルートの調べが聞こえてきた I heard *a melody*

played on a flute.

しらべる 調べる

❶【調査する】examine [他]; investigate [他]; inspect [他]; check [他]; (見つけようと) search [他] [自]

examine: 詳しく観察・調査すること.
investigate: 事実関係を突き止めるために, 組織的に調査すること.
inspect: 念入りに点検すること.
check: 正しいかどうか確かめること.

彼らは血液標本を採取し, 顕微鏡で調べた They took a blood sample and *examined* it under the microscope.
警察はその殺人について考えられる動機を調べた The police *investigated* [*looked into*] possible motives for the murder.
税関でかばんを調べられた I *had* my baggage *inspected* at customs.
僕の車のエンジンを調べてもらえませんか Could you *check* the engine of my car?
ポケットを調べたが, 小銭はなかった I *searched* my pockets, but there was no change.
◆彼らは水質汚染を世界的規模で調べている They *survey* water pollution worldwide. / その件を調べるために彼は私立探偵を雇った He hired a private detective to *inquire into* the matter.

❷【辞書などで探す】look up; (あたってみる) consult [他]
単語の意味が分からなければ辞書で調べなさい If you don't know the meaning of the word, *look* it *up* in the dictionary.
電話帳を調べてみたら? Why don't you *consult* the telephone book?

❸【尋問する】question [他]
彼は警察に調べられた He *was questioned* by the police.

しらみ 虱 louse [C] (複 lice) ∥シラミがわく be infested with *lice*
[慣用表現] 警察は証拠を得るためその家の中をしらみつぶしに調べた The police *combed* the house *for* evidence.

しらむ 白む 東の空が白み始めた The eastern sky *is turning light* [*bright*].

しらをきる 白を切る (知らないふりをする) pretend not to know ➾しらばくれる

しらんかお 知らん顔 (彼女に)手を振ったのに彼女は知らん顔をした(→無視した) She「*ignored* me [*gave* me *the cold shoulder*] when I waved to her. / 彼は私が困っていたのに知らん顔をした He「*didn't care at all* about [*was indifferent* to] my trouble.

しり 尻 (人・動物の) buttock [C]《通例複数形 ~s》,《口語的》bottom [C],《口語的》butt [C],《婉曲的》behind [C]; (腰骨の左右に張り出した部分) hip [C]《通例複数形 ~s》; (衣服のしりの部分) seat [C]《通例単数形》
赤ちゃんのおしめを取っておしりをふいてあげた I took off the baby's diaper and wiped *her bottom*.
野球選手はおしりが大きい Baseball players have large *buttocks* [*hips*].
左のしりに注射をしてもらった I got an injection in *the* left *buttock*.
彼はおしりのポケットに財布を入れた He put his wallet into his *hip* [*back*] pocket.
ズボンのおしりにペンキがついているよ There's paint on *the seat* of your trousers.
◆母親は子供のおしりをたたいた The mother *spanked* the boy. (❖spank は「罰としてしりをたたく」の意味)
[慣用表現] 彼は本当にしりが重いな He *is* so *slow to start anything.* / 彼は女房のしりに敷かれている He *is a henpecked husband.*/ He *is tied to* his wife's *apron strings.* / 武はいつもしりに火がつくまで何もしない(→最後の瞬間まで待つ) Takeshi always waits *until the last minute.* / しりの軽い女 an *easy* lay / あいつは女の子のしりばかり追いかけている He *is always chasing after girls.*

しりあい 知り合い acquaintance [C] (❖friend ほど親しい間柄ではない) ➾しりあう ∥彼女は私の知り合いです She is *an acquaintance* of mine. / 田中君はその高校に知り合いが多い Tanaka has a lot of *acquaintances* in that high school.
◆法的な手続きについては知り合いの弁護士に聞いてみましょう I'll ask a lawyer *I know* about the legal process. / あなたとは何年も前から知り合いの(→もう何年もあなたのことを知っている)ような気がする It seems like I'*ve known* you for years. / どうやって彼女と知り合いになったの How did you *get*「*to know* [*acquainted with*] her? / あなたと知り合いになれてうれしい I'm glad I *met* you./ I'm happy *to have met* you.
💬「あの女の子, お知り合い?」「ええ, でもただの知り合いです」"Do you *know* that girl?" "Yes, but she's just *an acquaintance*."

しりあう 知り合う get* [become*] acquainted with ... (❖やや改まった表現), get [come*] to know; (会う) meet* [他] [自] ∥トーマスさんとはワシントンD.C.滞在中に知り合った I *became acquainted with* Mr. Thomas during my stay in Washington D.C. / 彼女と知り合ってから5年になる It's five years since I *got to know* her.

しりあがり 尻上がり 勝ち進むにつれ彼の試合内容はしり上がりによくなっていった The way he played in a match *got better and better* as he went through the tournament. / 疑問文はしり上がりの調子で読まれるものが多い Many interrogative sentences are read with a *rising* intonation.

シリアル cereal [U] [C] ∥私はふだん朝食はシリアルです I usually have *cereal* for breakfast.

シリーズ series [C] (複 ~) ∥日本シリーズ *the* Japan *Series* / (米国の)ワールドシリーズ *the* World *Series* / テレビの刑事コロンボシリーズ *the* Columbo TV *series* / 日本の湖をテーマにした10回シリーズのテレビ番組 *a* TV *series* of 10 broadcasts on lakes in Japan

しりうま 尻馬 彼はいつも人の尻馬に乗っている (→無批判に他人に同調する) He *is* always *following* someone else *blindly*.

じりき[1] 自力 自力でたたき上げた人 a *self-*

じりき made man / 彼は沈没寸前の船から自力で脱出した He escaped from the sinking ship 「*without help* [*by himself*]」.

じりき² 地力 (本来もっている実力) *one's real ability* ⇨ じつりょく ∥地力を発揮する show *one's real ability*

しりきれとんぼ 尻切れとんぼ 小倉先生のスピーチはしり切れとんぼになった(→最後まで話し切れなかった) Mr. Ogura's speech *was left unfinished*. / Mr. Ogura *couldn't finish* his speech. / 君のレポートはしり切れとんぼのままだ(→不完全なままだ) Your report *is left incomplete*.

しりごみ 尻込み ── **しりごみする** (ちゅうちょする) hesitate ⓐ; (おじけづいてやめる)《俗語》chicken out; (後ずさりする) back away ∥その仕事はリスクが大きいと分かると彼らはしりごみした They found the job risky, and they 「*hesitated to do* [*chickened out of*] it. / ほら彼女が来たよ. しりごみせずに話しかけてごらんよ Hey, she's coming here. *Don't hesitate* and talk to her.

シリコン 〖化学〗(ケイ素) silicon [sílikən] Ⓤ (✦元素記号 Si); (有機ケイ素化合物・シリコーン) silicone [sílikòun] ∥シリコンゴム silicone rubber / シリコン樹脂 (a) silicone resin / シリコンチップ a silicone chip / シリコンバレー Silicon Valley (✦高度エレクトロニクス産業が集中している San Francisco 南東の盆地)

しりさがり 尻下がり 景気はしり下がりに悪くなっている Business *is「getting worse and worse* [*deteriorating, declining*]. / この文はしり下がりの調子で読みなさい Read this sentence with a *falling* intonation.

しりしよく 私利私欲 self-interest Ⓤ ∥私利私欲に走る pursue *one's self-interest* [*own interests*]

じりじり(と) ❶【ゆっくりと】slowly (but surely); (少しずつ) little by little; (徐々に) gradually ∥2番手の走者がじりじりと追い上げている The runner in second place is 「*catching up slowly but surely* [*gradually catching up*]. / 物価がじりじりと上がっている Prices are going up *little by little*.
❷【太陽が照りつける様子】太陽がじりじりと照りつけていた The sun *was scorching* [*burning fiercely*].
❸【待ち切れない様子】impatiently ∥私たちは救助隊をじりじりしながら待った We waited *impatiently* for the rescue team.

しりすぼみ 尻窄み 彼らの壮大な計画はしりすぼみに終わった Their grandiose plan *has fizzled out*.

しりぞく 退く ❶【後退する】彼は白線から1歩退いた He *made* [*took*] a step *back* from the white line. / 中隊は前線から退いた The squadron *withdrew* from the front line.
❷【引退する】retire ⓐⓑ, resign ⓐⓑ ∥父は60歳で現役を退いた My father *retired from* active work at the age of 60. / 高橋さんは理事の職を退いた Mr. Takahashi *resigned* his position on the board of directors. / 彼はマラソン選手としての第一線を退いてからはコーチとして活躍している Since he *retired from the front line* as a marathon runner, he has been active as a coach.

しりぞける 退ける ❶【断る・却下する】refuse ⓐⓑ, turn down; (拒否する) reject ⓐⓑ ∥彼は私の提案をにべもなく退けた(→きっぱりと断った) He flatly *refused* [*turned down*] my proposal. / 彼女の控訴は退けられた Her (intermediate) appeal *was rejected* [*dismissed*].
❷【撃退する】defeat ⓐ, beat* ⓐ ∥投票で, 民主党は共和党を完全に退けた The Democrats totally *defeated* [*beat*] the Republicans at the polls.

しりつ¹ 市立 ── **市立の** municipal, city ∥市立病院[図書館, 高校] a *municipal* [*city*] hospital [library, high school]

しりつ² 私立 ── **私立の** private ∥私立高校[大学] a *private* 「*high school* [*university*] / 私立探偵 a *private* detective

じりつ 自立 (独立) independence Ⓤ ── **自立する** become* independent; (経済的に) support *oneself*, stand* on *one's* own (two) feet ◆ 自立した人 a *self-sufficient* [*self-supporting*] person / 経済的に親から自立している学生は少ない Few students *are* financially *independent of* their parents. ∥自立心 a sense of independence

じりつしんけい 自律神経 autonomic nerve Ⓒ ∥自律神経系 autonomic nervous system / 自律神経失調症 autonomic imbalance

しりとり 尻取り

> しり取りは語の最後の音を次の語の最初の音として使って語をつなげていく言葉遊びの一つです. 例えば 1人が「とうふ」といえば次の人は「ふぐ」というように続けていきます. 適当な言葉を思いつかなかったり,「ん」で終わる言葉を言った人が負けになります.
> *Shiritori* is a word game in which players make a chain of words, using the last syllable of one word as the first syllable of the next. For example, one player says "*tofu*" and the next player says "*fugu*." If you can't come up with the right word, or if you end your word with the "n" sound, you lose.

しりぬぐい 尻拭い 君のしりぬぐいはごめんだよ I'm not going to 「*straighten up* [(→埋め合わせをする)*make up for*] your mess. / 父は父親の借金のしりぬぐいをさせられた(→代わりに借金を払わされた) He was made to *pay* his father's debt *for* him. / 彼が結局しりぬぐいをするはめになった He ended up being the 「*fall guy* [*patsy*]. (✦*fall guy, patsy*は《米》で「貧乏くじを引かされた人」の意味の口語的表現)

じりひん じり貧 妥当な策を講じなければ, わが社はじり貧だ Unless appropriate measures are taken, our company *will get worse and worse*.

しりめ 尻目 宝くじ売り場に並ぶ大勢の人々をしり目に見ながら私は家路を急いだ I hurried home *paying no mind to* the people in line for lottery tickets. / 美紀は親の苦労をしり目に(→無視して)優雅な学生生活を送った Miki enjoyed her easy school life *disregarding* her parents' hardships.

しめつれつ 支離滅裂 ――支離滅裂な(論理的でない・明確(%)でない) incoherent; (矛盾を含む) inconsistent /彼の話は全く支離滅裂だ What he says「is totally *incoherent* [(→一貫性を欠く)*lacks coherence*].

しりもち 尻餅 /滑ってしりもちをついてしまった I slipped and *fell on my bottom*.

しりゅう 支流 (本流に注ぎ込む) tributary ⓒ; (本流から分かれた) branch ⓒ /この川には支流が多い This river has many *tributaries* [*branches*]. / 秋川は多摩川の支流だ The Akikawa River is *a tributary* of the Tamagawa River.

じりゅう 時流 (the current of) the times, the current trends /時流に逆らう swim [go] against *the current of the times* / 時流に乗る follow [go with] *the current of the times* / 彼の考え方は全く時流に合わない His way of thinking doesn't fit *the times*.

しりょ 思慮 (考え) thought ⓤ; (慎重さ) prudence ⓤ; (熟慮) consideration ⓤ /そんなことを言うなんて彼も思慮が足りないな He *lacks prudence* [It's *imprudent* of him] to say such a thing. / (→配慮に欠ける)It's *thoughtless* of him to say such a thing.
◆思慮深い人 a *prudent* [*thoughtful*] person / 思慮に欠けた行い an *imprudent* [a *thoughtless*] act

しりょう¹ 資料 (素材) material ⓤ; (判断・立論の根拠となる) data (❖本来は datum の複数形だが、単数扱いされることも多い); (講義などでの配布資料) handout ⓒ /彼は論文執筆のために資料を集めている He is collecting [gathering] *material* to write his paper. / 彼は貴重な資料を提供した He contributed valuable *data*. ◆第1次[第2次]資料 primary [secondary] *sources* / その会社に新型カメラの資料(→パンフレット)を請求した I asked the company to send me *a brochure* about their new-model camera.
∥資料館 a museum / 資料室 a reference room / 統計資料 statistics

しりょう² 飼料 (家畜のえさ) fodder ⓤ, forage ⓤ; (動物一般のえさ) feed ⓤ

しりょく¹ 視力 eyesight ⓤ, sight ⓤ, 《公式的》vision ⓤ /私は視力がよい[悪い] I have good [poor] *eyesight*. / 近ごろ視力が衰えている My *eyesight* is failing [getting poorer] these days. / 彼は交通事故で視力を失った He lost *his eyesight* in the traffic accident. / 彼の右目の視力は手術ですっかり元どおりになった *His sight* in his right eye was completely restored by the operation. / この前,視力検査をしてもらった The other day I *had my eyesight tested*. / 視力は両眼とも1.0です I have 1.0 *vision* in both eyes. / Both of *my eyes* are 1.0.

(1)1.0などと表すのは日本式。
(2)おおよそ日本の1.0に相当する視力を米国では20/20と表し,これは20フィートの距離から指標番号20の確認ができることを意味する。
(3)英国では6メートルの距離から6番目の指標を確認するという意味で6/6と表記することがある。

∥視力矯正 vision [eyesight] correction / 視力検査 an eye examination [test] / 視力表 an eye chart

しりょく² 死力 /死力を尽くす make *a desperate* [*a frantic, an all-out*] *effort* / 彼は死力をふりしぼって走った He *gathered all his energy* and ran.

しりょく³ 資力 (財力) means 《複数扱い》; (富) wealth ⓤ; (資金・財源) funds, financial resources /並みはずれた[そこそこの]資力がある人 a person of excellent [moderate] *means* / 彼の資力は限られているので懸命に働かなければならない His *means* are so limited that he must work very hard.

じりょく 磁力 magnetic force ⓤ
∥磁力線 magnetic lines of force

シリンダー cylinder ⓒ

しる¹ 知る

❶【知識・情報をもっている】know* 他 ⓗ; (人から聞いたりして) learn* 他 ⓗ
彼がどこに行ったか知ってる? Do you *know* where he's gone?
美恵子はおいしいケーキ屋さんをよく知っている Mieko *knows* a lot about good cake shops.
真実を知っているのはおそらく彼だけだ Probably he is the only person who *knows* the truth.
それについては彼から聞いて知っているだけです I only *learned* it from him.
自分の町の歴史について知りたい I'd like to *learn* about the history of my town.
私が知るわけないでしょ How should I *know*!
彼はそのことについて何も知らないふりをした He pretended he *didn't know anything* about it.
ジョンははしの使い方を知らなかった John *didn't know* how to use chopsticks.
彼女にはこのことを知られたくなかった I *didn't want* her *to know* about this.
何か問題があれば、どんなことでも我々に知らせてください Please *let* us *know* if there is a problem of any kind.
私の知るかぎり,3時ごろその部屋にはだれもいなかった As far as I know, there was nobody in the room about three.
◆このあたりよく知りません I'm quite *a stranger* here. (❖*stranger* は「(ある場所に)不案内な人」の意味)

❷【理解する・認識する】know* 他 ⓗ; (悟る) realize 他; (気づいている) be aware
それがどれほど危険なことか彼はよく知っていた He *knew* very well how dangerous it was.
知らないうちに11時を回っていた I *didn't realize* that it was already past 11.

その作曲家の晩年についてはよく知られていない The last years of the composer's life *aren't known* well.
◆彼女はエッセイストとして広く知られている She *is well-known* as an essayist. / その町は温泉で知られている(→有名だ) The town *is famous* for its hot springs. (❖悪い意味で知られている場合は notorious を用いる)

❸【分かる・発見する】find*⓪, find out; (発見する) discover⓪
彼は自分が癌(がん)であることを知った He *found* that he had cancer.
この近くにこんな大きな公園があるとはつい2,3日前まで知らなかった I *didn't find out* that there was such a large park like this around here until just a few days ago.
彼女は夫が浮気しているのを知った She *discovered* that her husband was having an affair.

❹【面識がある】know*⓪
彼女の顔[名前]だけは知っている I *know* her only by sight [name]. (❖「顔」は face ではなく sight を用いる)
田中君のことは小学校のころから知っています I *have known* Tanaka since I was in elementary school.
彼のことは個人的には知らない I *don't know* him personally.
◆散歩をしていたら知らない人に声をかけられた *A stranger* called out to me while I was taking a walk.

❺【経験する】
今の子供たちは戦争を知らない Today's children *have never experienced* war.
彼らは何の苦労も知らない They *don't know* any of life's cares.

❻【関係する】
それは私の知ったことじゃない It's *none* of my business. / It's *no concern* of mine.
あいつがどうなろうと私の知ったことではない I *couldn't care less* what will become of him.

ことわざ 知らぬが仏 Ignorance is bliss. (→無知は幸せだ)

しる² 汁 (果物・野菜などの) juice ⓒⓊ; (肉汁) gravy Ⓤ; (汁物・つゆ) soup Ⓤ // オレンジの汁をしぼる squeeze *the juice* out of an orange / 弁当箱から汁がもれていた Some *juice* leaked from the lunchbox.
◆汁気の多い果物 *juicy* fruits
慣用表現 甘い[うまい]汁を吸う(→いちばんいい部分をさらう) *skim the cream off the top*

シルエット silhouette [silué̞t] ⓒ
シルク silk Ⓤ // シルクハット a silk hat, a top [tall] hat / シルクロード the Silk Road
しるこ 汁粉

しるこは小豆な砂糖と水、さらに少々の塩で煮て作る甘い汁状の食べ物で、多くの場合もちが入っています。しるこに使う小豆はふつうこしてありますが、粒状に残っているものは「ぜんざい」あるいは「いなかじるこ」と呼ぶ。
Shiruko is a thick, sweet soup. It is a simmered mixture of adzuki beans, sugar, water and a little salt. It is usually garnished with a few pieces of *mochi*. It is common for *shiruko* to be smoothly puréed, but if whole beans remain, then the soup is called *zenzai* or *inaka-jiruko*.

しるし 印 (記号) mark ⓒ; (感謝・記念のしるし) token ⓒ; (象徴・兆候) sign ⓒ
このチェックの印は「重要」の意味です This check *mark* means "important."
分からない単語に印をつけた I *put marks* on the words I didn't know.
私たちの感謝のしるしとしてこのささやかな贈り物をお受け取りください Please accept this small gift as *a token* of our gratitude.
ここでは黄色は注意や警告のしるしとして用いられている Here yellow is used as *a sign* of caution or warning.
彼がプレゼントをするなんて、あなたが好きなしるしよ He gave you a present? That's *a sign* that he likes you.
◆友情のしるし *a seal* of friendship / 地図でその場所に×印[○印]をつけた I *marked* the place on the map *with an X* [*a circle*]. / この星印(*)はどういう意味ですか What does this *asterisk* mean?

しるす 記す・印す (書き留める) write* [put*] down; (石碑や書物に) inscribe⓪; (印をつける) mark⓪ // 私は時間と日付をノートに記した I *wrote* [*put*] *down* the time and date in my notebook. / 彼らの名前は記念碑に金文字で記されていた Their names *were inscribed* in letters of gold on the memorial tablet.

ジルバ jitterbug [dʒítərbʌɡ] ⓒ
シルバー (銀・銀色) silver Ⓤ

「シルバー」は日本語では「高齢者」を表すことがあるが、英語の silver にその意味はない。「高齢者」の意味では、senior などを用いる。

‖シルバーエイジ(年齢) one's senior [golden] years; (人々) senior citizens / シルバーシート(優先席)《掲示》Priority [Courtesy] Seating; (個々の) a priority [courtesy] seat (❖「シルバーシート」は和製英語)

しれい¹ 司令 command ⓒ ‖司令官 a commander / 司令長官 a commander in chief / 司令部 headquarters

しれい² 指令 (命令) order ⓒ《しばしば複数形 ~s》, instructions ――指令する order⓪, instruct⓪ ‖指令を出す give *orders* [*instructions*] / 私は本部の指令を受けて行動した I acted on *the orders* from headquarters.

じれい¹ 辞令 (任命書) written order [appointment] ⓒ
◆私は辞令を受けて新しい役職に就いた I received *appointment* to a new post.

じれい² 事例 (例) example ⓒ; (実例) case ⓒ

しれつきょうせい 歯列矯正 orthodontics Ⓤ ‖歯列矯正器 braces

じれったい 彼の仕事のやり方は本当にじれったい(→人をいらいらさせる) His way of doing work *is* really *irritating*. / 彼women決断が遅いので、じれったくなる I always *feel irritated* because he is slow in making decisions. / 適切な例が見つからず本当にじれったかった I *was exasperated* because I couldn't find an appropriate example. / ねえ、教えてよ、じれったいわね Come on. What is it? I'*m getting impatient*.

しれる 知れる become* known, be made known; (明るみに出る) be revealed, come* to light / その政治家がわいろを受け取ったことはすぐに知れてしまった The fact that the politician took a bribe soon *became known to* everyone. / It *was revealed* in no time that the politician took a bribe.
◆それは学校に知れるとまずいな(→先生たちに知ってほしくない) I don't want my teachers to *know* it. / 真実はおのずと知れるものだ The truth will *speak* for itself. / Truth will *out*.
慣用表現 得体のしれない男 a *mysterious* man / 彼ったらあんな下品な話し方をして、お里が知れるね His vulgar way of speaking like that *gives him away*. / あんなつまらないものに夢中になれるなんて、彼の気が知れない(→理解できない) I *can't understand* why he is absorbed in such foolish things.

じれる 焦れる become* [be] impatient; (いらいらする) be irritated / そんなにじれるなよ Don't *be so impatient*.
◆彼女は勉強がはかどらないのでじれてきた She *became on edge* since her study wasn't coming along well.

しれわたる 知れ渡る become* known / 彼女の名は全世界に知れ渡った[知れ渡っている] Her name *became* [*is*] *known* all over the world.

しれん 試練 trial ⓒ; (つらい経験) ordeal ⓒ / 試練の時 a time of *trial*; a *trying* time / 人生の様々な試練に耐える endure [stand] *the trials* of life / それは自分の子供には決して経験させたくないようなつらい試練だった It was a terrible *ordeal* I would never want my children to go through.

ジレンマ dilemma [dilémə] ⓒ; (板ばさみ) double bind ⓒ / ジレンマに陥る be caught in a *dilemma*
◆多国籍企業の社員の多くが会社への忠誠か国への忠誠かというジレンマに陥っている Many people in multinational corporations *are torn between* loyalty to their companies and loyalty to their own country.

しろ¹ 白 white Ⓤ ──白い white; (肌が) fair
あなたは白がよく似合いますね You look great in *white*.
その花びらは雪のように白かった The petals were as *white* as snow.
彼女が笑うと口元から白い歯がこぼれた Her *white* teeth flashed when she smiled.
彼女は色白だ She *has a fair* [*light*] *complex-*

ion.
◆白っぽい服 *whitish* clothes / 父はだんだん髪が白くなってきている My father's hair *is graying* [*going gray*]. / その問いかけに頭の中が真っ白になった My mind *went blank* on that question. / こいつは白(→無罪)だと思う I think this guy is *innocent*.
慣用表現 近所の人たちは彼女のことを白い目で見た Her neighbors 「*gave her icy looks* [*looked at her coldly*].

しろ² 城 castle ⓒ / 城を築く build *a castle* / 王は敵に城を明け渡す決心をした The king decided to yield *his castle* up to the enemy.
∥城跡 the site [ruins] of a castle (❖site は「城があった場所」、ruins は「城の遺跡」の意味)

しろあり 白蟻 termite ⓒ / シロアリの駆除 extermination of *termites*

しろうと 素人 amateur [ǽmətʃuər] ⓒ; (専門家でない人) layperson ⓒ / 全くの素人 a rank *amateur*; (→初心者) a *greenhorn* / 彼女は素人にしては絵がうまい She paints pictures well for *an amateur*. / 素人考えですが、こうしたらどうでしょう It's only *a layperson's* [*an amateurish*] *idea*, but why don't we try this? / 素人にも分かるように説明してください Please explain it in *layperson's* terms.
◆私は政治は素人です(→専門家ではない) I'm *not an expert* in politics. / 彼のダンスは素人離れしている(→彼はプロのように踊る) He dances *just like a pro*. / この宝石は模造品だが、素人目には本物に見える This gem is a fake, but it looks like the real thing *to the untrained eye*.

しろくじちゅう 四六時中 (一日中) all day (long), around the clock; (昼夜を問わず) day and night; (いつも) always / 弟は四六時中テレビを見ている My brother is *always* watching TV.

しろくま 白熊 polar bear

しろくろ 白黒 ──白黒の black and white (❖日本語と語順が逆) / 白黒の映画 a 「*black and white* [*monochrome*] *movie*
◆2人のうちどちらが上か白黒をつけよう(→きっぱり決着をつけよう) *Let's get it settled once and for all* which of us is better. / 彼はそのニュースを聞いて目を白黒させた(→驚いた) He *was shocked* at the news.

じろじろ その男の子は私をじろじろ見た The boy *stared at* me. / 彼は私の顔をじろじろ見た He *stared* me in the face.

じろっと 老人は不機嫌そうに私をじろっと見た The old man *threw a* sullen *glance at* me.

シロップ syrup, (米) sirup Ⓤ
∥メープルシロップ maple syrup

しろバイ 白バイ (white) police motorcycle ⓒ ◆白バイの警官 a *motorcycle* police officer (❖英米では、警官のバイクは白とは限らないので a white motorcycle とはいわない。パトカー (a police car) は白黒に塗られていることが多いので a black and white ということがある)

しろぼし 白星 その力士は7連敗の後、やっと白星をあげた(→勝った) The sumo wrestler finally *won* [*got a win*] after seven consecu-

シロホン xylophone [záiləfòun]

しろみ 白身 (卵の) the white (of an egg); (魚などの) the white meat ∥卵の黄身と白身を分ける separate the yolk from *the white*

しろめ 白目 the white of the eye

しろもの 代物 (漠然とした物) stuff; (具体的な物) thing ◆これはなかなかの代物(→かなりよい物)じゃないか Isn't it *something*? ∥ 彼はその骨董屋でとんでもない代物(→かがくた)をつかまされた They palmed off *complete junk* on him at the antique shop.

じろりと 太田教授は振り返ると私をじろりと見た Professor Ota turned around and *glared at* me.

じろん 持論 (人生観・主義) theory, philosophy; (お気に入りの論) pet theory; (意見) view, opinion ∥プレッシャーが創造性を生むというのが彼の持論だ His *pet theory* is that pressure produces creativity. ∥ 父は決して持論を曲げない My father always tries to stick to his own *opinion*.

しわ 皺 (皮膚・布・紙の) wrinkle; (紙・布の) rumple; (たたみじわ) crease ∥ アイロンでしわを伸ばす iron out *wrinkles* ∥ そのおじいさんの顔はしわだらけだった The old man's face was *full of wrinkles*.
◆額にしわを寄せる wrinkle (up) one's brow ∥ しわの寄らないシャツ a *wrinkle-free* shirt ∥ このズボンはしわになりやすい These trousers *wrinkle* [*crumple*] *easily*. ∥ 彼女は立ってスカートのしわを伸ばした She stood up and *smoothed out* her skirt.

しわがれる 嗄れる (しわがれ声になる) become* hoarse [husky], have* a frog in one's throat
◆しわがれ声で話す speak *in a hoarse voice*

しわくちゃ しわくちゃの —しわくちゃの (紙・布・衣類が) wrinkled, rumpled, crumpled, creased; (皮膚が) wrinkled, lined ∥ しわくちゃのシーツ *rumpled* sheets ∥ 彼はポケットからしわくちゃのハンカチを取り出した He took a *crumpled* [*creased*] handkerchief out of his pocket. ∥ 彼のズボンはしわくちゃになっていた His pants got *wrinkled* all over.

しわけ 仕分け —仕分けする (分類・整理する) sort, classify ∥現在ではこの機械で手紙やはがきはすべてこの機械で仕分けされている New letters and cards *are all sorted out* by this machine. ∥ 商品の仕分けを手伝ってくれませんか Could you help me *sort out* these goods?

しわざ 仕業 人々はそれを悪魔のしわざだと信じていた People believed it was *the work of the Devil*. ∥ この犯罪はマフィアのしわざにちがいない This crime must be the Mafia's *handiwork*. ∥ これはだれのしわざだ(→だれがこんなことをしたか) Who *did* this?

じわじわ(と) (ゆっくりと) slowly; (徐々に) gradually; (少しずつ) little by little, bit by bit; (着実に) steadily ∥彼の打率はじわじわと上がっている His batting average is rising *little by little*. ∥ 売り上げがじわじわと伸びている Sales have been growing *steadily*.

しわす 師走 (12月) December; (年末) the year end

しわよせ 皺寄せ しわ寄せを受けるのはいつも下請け業者だ It is always subcontractors that *suffer most*. ∥ いいかげんな政策のしわ寄せで税金が上がった Taxes have increased *as a consequence of* sloppy policy.

じわれ 地割れ 地震で町の至る所に地割れができた The earthquake caused *fissures* [*cracks*] in many parts of the city.

しん¹ 心 伸治は冷たそうに見えるがしんはいいやつだ Shinji looks like a cold-hearted person, but he is good *at heart*. ∥ 校正はしんの疲れる(→精神的に疲れる)仕事だ Proofreading is a *mentally exhausting* job. ∥ 京子は物腰は柔らかいがしんは強い Kyoko has a gentle manner, but she *has a strong character deep down*. ∥ 我々が目ざしているのは心・技・体の充実 What we are aiming at is perfection of *mind, technique and physique*.

しん² 芯 (鉛筆の) lead [léd]; (果物の) core; (ろうそくの) candlewick ∥リンゴの芯を取る remove *the core* of an apple; *core* an apple ∥ 鉛筆の芯が折れた The lead of the pencil broke.
◆このごはんは芯がある(→調理不十分だ) This rice *is undercooked*. ∥ 雨の中を歩いて体の芯まで冷えきってしまった I walked in the rain, and got chilled [frozen] *to the bone*.

しん³ 真 (真実) truth; (現実) reality —真の true; real —真に truly; really ∥ 真の愛 *true* love ∥ 加藤教授は真の意味での学者だ Prof. Kato is a scholar *in the true sense of the word*. ∥ その戦闘シーンは真に迫っていた The combat scene was *very true to life*. ∥ 彼女は真にスターの素質がある若手女優だ She is a young actress with *real star quality*.
慣用表現 まさかのときの友こそ真の友 A friend in need is a *friend indeed*.

しん-¹ 新- 新古典主義 neoclassicism ∥ 新学期 a *new* school term ∥ 新製品 a *new* product ∥ 世界新記録を作る set [establish] a *new* world record ∥ このゲームソフトは発売されたばかりだ This game software *has just been released* [*put on the market*].

しん-² 親- pro- (↔anti-) ⇒しんにち ∥親米の *pro*-American

ジン gin ∥ジントニック gin and tonic ∥ ジンフィズ gin fizz

じん 陣 (陣営) camp; (陣地) position; (集団) group, staff ∥教授陣 the teaching *staff* ∥ 報道陣 a *group* of press people ∥ オリンピック選手団の第一陣がきょう成田を出発した *The* first *group* of Olympic athletes departed from Narita today.
慣用表現 初陣を飾る (初戦に勝つ) win one's *first game* ∥ 背水の陣 ⇒はいすいのじん

しんあい 親愛 deep [warm] affection ∥ 親愛の情をいだく[示す] have [show] *deep affection* ◆(手紙で)親愛なるトム *Dear* Tom

しんい 真意 (本心) one's true intention,

what *one* really means; (本当の意味) the true meaning ‖それは私の真意ではなかった That was not *what I really meant*. ‖ 私たちは彼の真意を見抜くことができなかった We couldn't discover his *true intention*.

じんいてき 人為的 人為的ミス *human* error

しんいり 新入り newcomer ◎, 《口語的》 new kid, rookie ◎ ‖あの新入りの面倒を見てやってくれないか Will you take care of that *new kid*?

じんいん 人員 (人数) the number of people; (職員全体) the staff, the personnel [pə̀ːrsənél] ‖人員を増やす[減らす] increase [reduce] *the number of staff* ‖ 深刻な不景気のために人員削減を余儀なくされた The serious recession necessitated a「*cut in personnel* [*personnel reduction*].
◆この事務所には人員過剰[不足]だ This office *is overstaffed* [*understaffed*].

しんえい 新鋭 ━━新鋭の new (and powerful); (最新の) up-to-date ‖新鋭兵器 *a new and powerful* weapon ‖ 最新鋭の設備 the *up-to-date* facilities ‖ 彼は野球界の新鋭だ He is *a new star player* in the baseball world.

じんえい 陣営 camp ◎; (党内の) faction ◎ ‖保守[野党]陣営 the conservative [*opposition*] *camp* ‖ その代議士は彼らを裏切って反対陣営に寝返った The Diet member double-crossed them and went over to *the opposing faction*.

しんえん 深遠 ━━深遠な deep; (思想・学問が) profound ‖深遠な思想 a *profound* thought

じんえん 腎炎 〔医学〕nephritis ◎

しんか[1] 進化 evolution ◎ ━━進化する evolve ◎ ‖進化がどのように生じるか知っていますか Do you know how *evolution* takes place? ‖ は虫類は両生類から進化したと言われている Reptiles are said to *have evolved* from amphibians.
‖進化論 the theory of evolution; (ダーウィン説) Darwinism

しんか[2] 真価 real worth ◎, true value ◎ ‖真価を認める appreciate [acknowledge] *true value* ‖ 「今こそ諸君の真価を発揮する時だ」とコーチは言った "It's time to show your *real worth*," said the coach.

じんか 人家 house ◎ ‖このあたりはけっこう人家が多い This area *is* pretty *crowded with houses*. ◆人家が密集した[まばらな]地域 densely [sparsely] *populated* area

シンガーソングライター singer-songwriter ◎

しんかい 深海 the deep sea ━━深海のdeep-sea ◆名詞の前で用いる)
‖深海魚 a deep-sea fish

しんがい[1] 侵害 (侵入) invasion ◎ ◎; (無理やりの) intrusion ◎ ◎; (権利の) infringement ◎, infringement ◎ ◎ ━━侵害する invade ◎; intrude ◎; violate ◎ ‖人権侵害 *a violation* of human rights; *a* civil rights violation ‖ 著作権侵害 (*an*) *infringement* of copyright ‖ プライバシーを侵害する invade [*intrude on, violate*] *a person's* privacy ‖ 政府は憲法で保証された私の権利を侵害した The government *committed a violation* of my constitutional rights.

しんがい[2] 心外 君がそんなことを言うとは心外だ (→残念だ) I'm very sorry to hear you say such a thing.

じんかいせんじゅつ 人海戦術 その会社は新製品の宣伝をするために人海戦術に出た(→非常に多くの人を派遣した) The company *sent out a great number of people* [*used sheer manpower*] to advertise their new product.

しんがお 新顔 new face ◎, newcomer ◎

しんがく[1] 進学 大学に進学する go on to university ‖ 私は卒業後は進学を希望しています After I graduate, I would like to *continue my education*.
‖進学校 a high school known for sending its graduates on to university ‖ 進学塾 a cram school ‖ 進学率(大学への) the ratio of students who go on to university

しんがく[2] 神学 theology ◎
‖神学校 a theological school; (キリスト教の) a seminary ‖ 神学者 a theologian

じんかく 人格 (品性・人徳) one's character; (人間性・個性) one's personality ‖人格を形成する build *one's character* ‖ 子供の人格を尊重する respect a child's *personality* ‖ 彼の人格が突然変わったのはどうしてだろう What's behind the sudden change of his *personality*? ‖ 逆境が人格を育てるのかもしれない Difficulties may develop *your character*. ‖ 新井さんは人格者だ Mr. Arai is a「*man of character* [*respectable man*]
‖人格形成 character-building ‖ 多重人格 a multiple personality ‖ 二重人格 a split [dual] personality

しんがた 新型 new model ◎ ◆新型のスポーツカー a *new-model* sports car ‖ 最新型 the latest model

しんがっき 新学期 new school term ◎ ‖日本では新学期は4月に始まる In Japan, *the new school term* starts in April.

シンガポール Singapore (❖公式名 the Republic of Singapore) ‖シンガポール人 Singaporean ◎ ━━シンガポール(人)の Singaporean

しんがり しんがりを務める(→行列などの最後尾を行く) bring up *the rear* [*tail*]

しんかん[1] 新刊 (新刊書) new book [publication] ◎ ‖新刊図書目録 a list of *new books* [*publications*] ‖ 新刊紹介 a *book* review

しんかん[2] 新館 new building ◎

しんかん[3] 神官 priest ◎

しんかんせん 新幹線 the *Shinkansen*, the bullet train
◆ 東海道新幹線 the New Tokaido Line; the Tokaido *Shinkansen* (Line)

最初の新幹線は、1964年の東京オリンピックに合わせて東京―大阪間に開通しました。それ以来、新幹線は日本の主要な交通機関として重要

な役割を果たしています．新幹線といえばその驚くべき速さですが，その速度もさらに増しています．例えば開通当初の1966年には６時間40分かかった東京―博多間が，今では「のぞみ」を利用してわずか５時間で行けるようになりました．
The first *Shinkansen* (bullet train) came on the scene between Tokyo and Shin-Osaka in time for the Tokyo Olympics of 1964. Since then, the *Shinkansen* has played an important role as a major means of transport in Japan. The *Shinkansen* is characterized by its amazing speed, which is still on the increase. For example, the *Shinkansen* between Tokyo and Hakata in Kyushu, which was put into operation in 1966, took six hours and forty minutes initially, but the new *Shinkansen* trains called Nozomi run the same distance in only five hours.

しんき 新規 ―新規の new ∥新規契約を結ぶ hold *a new contract* / 彼は新規に事業を始めた He started a *new* business.
◆新規まき直しをはかる *start all over again*

しんぎ¹ 審議 (検討) discussion [U][C]; (国会などの) 《公式的》 deliberation [U][C] 《しばしば複数形 ～s》 ―審議する discuss [他]; deliberate [他][自] ∥審議を打ち切る close *the discussion* / この問題は後回しにして，次回の会合で審議します We'll table this matter now, and *discuss* [*deliberate on*] it at the next meeting. / その法案は国会で審議中です The bill is *under deliberation* in the Diet. / 国会の審議は今中断されている Diet *deliberations* have been interrupted. / 陪審員は審議のうえ有罪の評決を下した The jury brought in a verdict of guilty after *its deliberations*.
‖審議会 a council

しんぎ² 真偽 その真偽(→本当かどうか)を確かめてみよう Let's find out *whether it is true or not*. / 真偽の程はともかく，そんなうわさが流れていることは残念だ *Whether it is true or not*, it is regrettable that such a rumor is spreading.

しんぎ³ 信義 faith [U]; (忠誠) a sense of honor [loyalty] ∥信義を守る[破る] keep [break] *faith* / これは信義に背(そむ)く行為である This is an act running against *good faith*.
◆信義にあつい人 a *trustworthy* person

しんきいってん 心機一転 兄は心機一転，たばこをやめる決意をした My brother *turned over a new leaf*, and decided to stop smoking.

しんきじく 新機軸 innovation [C][U], new line [C] ∥彼らは新機軸を打ち出すことに成功した They succeeded in introducing *innovations*.

しんきゅう¹ 進級 ―進級する be promoted, move up ∥彼は出席日数が足りなくて進級できなかった He couldn't *be promoted to a higher grade* due to lack of attendance.
◆息子は４月に３年に進級する(→３年生になる) My son will *be* a third grader in April.

しんきゅう² 新旧 old and new (❖語順に注意) ∥新旧の大臣が会見を行った The「*old and new* [*incoming and outgoing*] ministers held a press conference.
◆わが国の政治制度は時代遅れであり，もう新旧交代の時期だ Our political system is outdated, and it's time to *replace the old with the new*.

しんきゅう³ 鍼灸 acupuncture [U] ‖鍼灸師 a practitioner of acupuncture, an acupuncturist

しんきょ 新居 new house [home] [C] ∥彼らは郊外に新居を構えた They made *a new home* in the suburbs.

しんきょう¹ 心境 a state [frame] of mind, mood [C]; (気持ち) feelings ∥心境を打ち明ける express *one's feelings* / 今の心境では，どうしてもそんなことはできない I couldn't do it in *my* present *state of mind*. / 今はのんびりテレビを見ていられる心境ではない I'*m not in the mood* to sit still and watch TV now. / その話を聞いて私は複雑な心境だった I *had mixed feelings* when I heard the story.
◆今の心境はいかがですか(→どう感じていますか) How do you *feel* now?
[会]「どうして髪型を変えたの」「心境の変化よ」 "Why did you change your hair style?" "*Just for a change*." (❖for a change は「気分転換に」の意味)

しんきょう² 信教 (信仰・宗教) religion [U], religious belief [U] ∥信教の自由は憲法で保証されている Freedom of *religion* is guaranteed by the Constitution.

しんきょく 新曲 new tune [C]; (歌) new song [C]; (新発売曲) new release [C]

しんきろう 蜃気楼 mirage [mərɑ́ːʒ] [C]

しんきろく 新記録 new record [C] ∥彼女は100メートルで日本新記録を出した She set [established] *a new Japanese record* in the 100-meter dash.

しんきんかん 親近感 affinity [C] ∥須賀教授はこの国に対して特別な親近感をもっていた Professor Suga had *a* special *affinity* for this country.
◆私たちは新任の先生に親近感を覚えた We *felt very close to* our new teacher.

しんきんこうそく 心筋梗塞 myocardial [cardiac] infarction [U]

しんく¹ 深紅・真紅 crimson [U], deep red [U] ―深紅の crimson

しんく² 辛苦 (苦難) hardship [U][C] ∥辛苦をなめる(→つらい目にあう) have (*a*) *hardship*; have *a hard time*

しんぐ 寝具 (ベッド用の) bedding [U] (❖マットレスを含むことがある); (シーツ・毛布など) bedclothes ∥寝具を干す put *one's bedclothes* out to dry

しんくう 真空 vacuum [C] ―真空の vacuum ∥私たちは真空状態での実験を試みた We carried out an experiment in *a vacuum*.
‖真空管 《米》a (vacuum) tube, 《英》a valve / 真空パック a vacuum pack

じんぐう 神宮 Shinto shrine [C]

◆明治神宮 *the* Meiji *Shrine*
ジンクス （迷信） superstition [C], popular belief [C];（縁起の悪い） jinx [C]（❖英語の jinx は「縁起の悪い物」の意味でしか用いない） //ジンクスを破る break *a jinx* / 彼は下着を洗うと試合に負けるというばかげたジンクスを信じていた He believed in *a* silly *superstition* that if you wash your underwear you lose a game.
シンクタンク （頭脳集団） think tank [C]
シングル ━シングルの single //シングルの上着 a *single-breasted* jacket / シングルの部屋はまだ空いていますか Is there a *single* (room) left?
‖シングルヒット a single / シングルベッド a single bed / シングルマザー a single [an unmarried] mother
シングルス singles《単数扱い》 //テニスのシングルスの試合をする play *singles* [a *singles* match] in tennis / 男子シングルスで優勝する win in the men's *singles*; win a men's *singles* match
シンクロナイズドスイミング synchronized swimming [U]

しんけい 神経

nerve [C]
〚神経が・は〛
この仕事は神経が疲れる This job is *hard on the nerves.*
◆父は神経が細かい My father *is sensitive.* / 彼女は神経が図太い She *is bold.*/ She *has a lot of nerves.* / その晩は神経が高ぶって眠れなかった I *was so nervous* that I couldn't sleep that night. / 仕事上の悩みが尽きず，とうとう彼の神経は参ってしまった The constant worries of his job finally *broke* him *down.*
〚神経を・に〛
彼の話し方はどうも神経にさわる His way of speaking somehow *gets on my nerves.*
◆友人が失敗を笑ったことが彼の神経を逆なでした His friend's laughing at his failure *rubbed* him *the wrong way.* / 多くの人は通勤で神経をすり減らしている（→疲れ果てている） Many people *are exhausted* [*worn out*] by commuting. / そんなことに神経を使う必要はない（→心配する必要はない） Don't *worry* about such a thing.
〚その他〛
彼は神経過敏になっていた He was「*a bundle of nerves* [*hypersensitive*].
◆そんなことを言うなんて君はあまりにも無神経だったね It was too *insensitive* of you to say such a thing. / 彼女は運動神経が抜群だ（→すぐれた運動選手だ） She is *an excellent athlete.*
‖神経科 the department of neurology / 神経科医 a neurologist / 神経ガス nerve gas / 神経系統 the nervous system / 神経症 neurosis / 神経衰弱 a nervous breakdown / 神経痛 neuralgia / 自律神経 an autonomic nerve / 反射神経 a reflex
しんけいしつ 神経質 ━神経質な nervous //姉は入試を3日後に控えて神経質になっている My sister *is nervous* with the entrance examination three days away.
しんげき 進撃 （前進） advance [C] //敵の進撃を食い止める stop *the* enemy's *advance*
◆ライオンズは優勝に向かって快進撃を続けている（→驚異的なペースで勝っている） The Lions *have been winning at an amazing rate* in the pennant.
しんけつ 心血 彼はその企画に心血を注いだ He *devoted all his energies to* the project. / 彼女は女性解放運動に心血を注いだ She ardently *devoted herself to* the women's liberation movement.
しんげつ 新月 new moon [C]
しんけん[1] 真剣 ━真剣な（まじめな） serious;（熱心な） earnest ━真剣に seriously; earnestly //真剣な表情 a *serious* expression / 私は真剣なのよ I'm *serious.*/ I'm not joking. / もっと真剣に将来のことを考えなさい You should be more *serious* about your future. / 彼はその問題に真剣に取り組んでいる He is working *earnestly* on the problem. / もっと真剣に環境問題を考えなければならない We should consider environmental problems more *seriously.*
しんけん[2] 親権 parental rights
しんげん[1] 進言 ━進言する（提案する） suggest [他], propose [他] //私は上司に改善案を進言したが，聞き入れてもらえなかった I *suggested* a reform plan to my superior, but it was rejected.
しんげん[2] 震源 the focus of an earthquake //震源は宮城県沖50キロと推定されている It is estimated *the focus of the earthquake* was located 50 kilometers off the coast of Miyagi Prefecture.
◆そのうわさの震源地はどうも隣のクラスらしい It seems that *the source* of the rumor is the next class.
じんけん 人権 human rights //人権を尊重する respect *human rights* / 人権を最優先するべきだ You should put top priority on *human rights.* / それは人権問題につながるおそれがある That would possibly lead to *the question of human rights.*
‖人権侵害 a violation of human rights / 人権擁護 the protection of human rights / 基本的人権 fundamental [basic] human rights / 世界人権宣言 the Universal Declaration of Human Rights
じんけんひ 人件費 personnel expenses, staff costs //人件費を抑える keep *personnel expenses* down / これほど人件費が高くてはやっていけない We cannot go on with such large *personnel expenses.*
しんご 新語 new word [C];（新造語） newly-coined word [C]
しんこう[1] 信仰 faith [U][C], religious belief [U][C], religion [U][C] ━信仰する believe in ... //信仰の自由 freedom of *religion* / この奇跡を経験したことによって彼は神への信仰を深めた Experiencing this miracle deepened [strengthened] his *faith in* God. / 彼らは

迫害され，信仰を捨てることを余儀なくされた They were persecuted and compelled to 「give up [renounce] *their faith*. / 彼女はキリスト教を信仰している She *believes in* Christianity. / (→キリスト教徒だ)She is a Christian. ◆彼は信仰心があつい He is *a very devout person*.

しんこう[2] 侵攻 invasion Ⓤ ——侵攻する invade 他 ∥1939年ドイツはポーランドに侵攻した In 1939, Germany *invaded* Poland. / 堀は城を侵攻から守るために作られた Moats were built to secure the castle from *invasion*.

しんこう[3] 振興 promotion Ⓤ ——振興する promote 他 ∥学術振興 *the promotion* of science / 産業の振興 *the promotion* of industry / これは国内産業振興の一助となるだろう This will help *promote* the development of domestic industries.

しんこう[4] 進行（進歩）progress Ⓤ;（前進）advance ⒸⓊ ——進行する（物事が）progress 自, make* progress;（乗り物が）move 自 ∥仕事は私が思ったほど進行していない The work *is* not *making* as much *progress* as I expected. / 捜査は現在進行中である The investigation is 「*in progress* [*under way*] now. / プロジェクトは着々と進行している The project *is in* steady *progress*. / 流氷が船の進行を阻(はば)んだ Drift ice hindered the *advance* of the ship. / お仕事の進行状況はいかがですか How are you *progressing* with your work?
▶進行方向左側のドア the door on your left as you face ahead / この種の癌(がん)は進行が速い Cancer of this kind *spreads* quickly. / 私は電車でいつも進行方向いちばん前の車両に乗る I always ride in the first car of the train. (◈この場合「進行方向」は特に訳さない)
∥進行係（司会）a master of ceremonies, an MC / 進行形『文法』the progressive form

しんこう[5] 新興 ——新興の（新しい）new, young;（急成長の）rising, growing ∥新興国 a rising [young] nation / 新興宗教 a new religion / 新興住宅地 a newly-developed residential area / 新興勢力 a growing power / 新興都市 a boom town

しんこう[6] 親交 friendship Ⓒ, friendly relations ∥私の祖母は島崎藤村と親交があった My grandmother 「*enjoyed the friendship of* [*was on friendly terms with*] Shimazaki Toson. / 私たちは留学生たちといっしょに食事をして親交を深めた We promoted *friendly relations* with overseas students by having a meal together.

しんごう 信号

（交通信号）(traffic) light [signal] Ⓒ;（合図）signal Ⓒ
信号を守りなさい You must obey [observe] *the traffic lights*.
信号が青になるまで待ちなさい Wait until *the light* turns green. (◈信号の「青」は green という)
その車は赤信号で止まった The car stopped at *the red light*.
彼女は信号を無視して前の車にぶつかった She ignored *the traffic lights* and hit the car in front of her.
次の信号を右に曲がってください Please turn right at *the* next *light*.
∥信号機 a signal / 危険信号 a danger signal / 遭難信号 a distress signal, a mayday signal / 手旗信号 flag signaling / モールス信号 the Morse code

じんこう[1] 人口

population ⒸⓊ
人口の増加[減少] an increase [a fall] in *population*
東京の人口はニューヨークより多い The *population* of Tokyo is larger than that of New York. (◈人口の「多い・少ない」は large, small で表す)
その町の人口は3年間で倍増した The town's *population* has doubled in the last three years.
この町の人口は5万人に減った The *population* of our city decreased to 50,000.
急激な人口増加が多くの問題を引き起こしている Rapid *population* growth is creating many problems.
この地域の夜間人口は少ない This area has *a small nighttime population*.
◆大都市は人口が密集している Big cities *are heavily* [*densely*] *populated*. / インターネット人口はここ数年で急激に増加している The *number of Internet users* has been rapidly increasing for the last few years.
❢「日本の人口はどれくらいですか」「約1億2,000万です」"What [How large] is *the population* of Japan?" "About 120 million."
∥人口過剰 overpopulation / 人口過密 overcrowding / 人口調査 a census / 人口爆発 a population explosion / 人口密度 (a) population density

じんこう[2] 人工 ——人工の artificial, man-made ∥学校で人工呼吸のやり方を習った We were taught how to give *artificial respiration* at school. / その湖は人工的に造られたものです The lake is *artificial* [*man-made*]. / 新しい人工衛星が打ち上げられた *A* new (*artificial*) *satellite* was launched.
∥人工甘味料 (an) artificial sweetener / 人工芝 artificial turf / 人工授精 artificial insemination / 人工知能 artificial intelligence / 人工中絶 an abortion

しんこきゅう 深呼吸 deep breathing Ⓤ;（1回の）deep breath Ⓒ ∥深呼吸して肩の力を抜きなさい Take a deep breath and relax your shoulders.

しんこく[1] 申告（税関での）declaration Ⓒ;（税金の）tax return Ⓒ;（報告）report Ⓒ ——申告する declare 他;（税金の）file a tax return ∥税関で申告する物があれば，この用紙に記入してください If you have anything to *declare*, please fill in this form. / 所得税の確定申告書は3月15日までに提出することになって

いる You are supposed to file *an income tax return* by March 15.
◆その会社は2億円の申告もれが明らかになった It was revealed that the company *had undeclared income* of 200 million yen.
‖青色申告 a blue return

しんこく² 深刻 ――深刻な serious, grave ――深刻に seriously ∥彼は深刻な顔をして教室に入ってきた He came into the classroom with a *serious* face. / そんなに深刻に考えるよ Don't take it so *seriously*. / この事故は政府の原子力政策に深刻な影響を及ぼすかもしれない This accident could have *serious* implications for the government's nuclear policy. / その年、九州地方は深刻な水不足に苦しんだ That year, the Kyushu district suffered from a *serious* shortage of water. / 環境汚染はますます深刻化している Environmental pollution *is getting more and more serious*.

しんこっちょう 真骨頂 ∥この曲はエリック・サティの真骨頂(→本来の価値)を示すものだ This piece of music shows *the true worth* of Erik Satie.

しんこん 新婚 ――新婚の newly-married, newlywed ∥新婚生活 *newly-married [newlywed]* life ◆彼らは新婚ほやほやだ(→結婚したばかりだ) They've just got married. / 姉は新婚旅行でハワイに行った My sister went to Hawaii on *her honeymoon*.
‖新婚夫婦 a newly-married couple, newlyweds

しんさ 審査 (優劣の) judgment ⓒ; (検査・試験) examination ⓒ; (選定・選別) screening ⓤ ――審査する judge ⓗ; examine ⓗ; screen ⓗ ∥審査に通る pass *the examination*; be accepted / 応募者は審査のうえ最終面接に回されます Applicants are *screened* before the final interview. ◆写真コンテストの審査員を務める *act as judge* at a photo contest

しんさい 震災 earthquake (disaster) ⓒ (◆地震による災害を強調する場合は disaster を付ける) ∥阪神大震災 the *Great Hanshin Earthquake* / 震災にあう suffer from *an earthquake*

じんさい 人災 man-made disaster ⓒ
◆これは明らかに人災(→人間の過失によって引き起こされたこと)であって天災ではない This has obviously *been caused by human negligence* and not a natural disaster.

じんざい 人材 (有能な人) capable [talented] person ⓒ; (人的資源) human resources, manpower ⓤ ∥私たちは有能な人材を探している We are looking for *capable people*. / 人材の発掘にはかなりの時間と費用がかかる It takes a lot of time and money to 「dig up [find] *talented people*.
◆営業部には人材がそろっている The sales division *has an efficient staff*.(◆staff は集合的に「職員全体」を指す)
‖人材派遣会社 a temporary office staff agency

しんさく 新作 (新しい作品) new work ⓒ

◆ジャッキー・チェン主演の新作映画 *a new film* featuring Jackie Chan / 彼の新作の戯曲は大好評を博している His *new* play has made a great hit. / 彼の小説の最新作を読みましたか Have you read his *latest* novel?

しんさつ 診察 medical examination ⓒ ――診察する examine, see* ⓗ ∥患者を診察する see [*examine*] a patient / きのう大学病院で診察を受けた I had *a medical examination [checkup]* at the university hospital. / 山田先生はただ今診察中です Doctor Yamada *is seeing his patients* now. / すぐ医者に診察してもらいなさい You should *see a doctor* at once. ◆see a doctor で「医者の診察を受ける」の意味)
‖診察券 an appointment card / 診察時間 doctor's office hours / 診察室 a consulting room / 診察料 a doctor's medical fee, a doctor's bill

しんさん 辛酸 (困難・苦労) hardship ⓤⓒ ∥彼はありとあらゆる辛酸をなめてきた He has gone through all kinds of *hardship(s)*.

しんし¹ 紳士 gentleman ⓒ ∥紳士的にふるまう behave *like a gentleman*
‖紳士服 men's wear / 紳士服売り場 the men's clothing department / 紳士録 a Who's Who

しんし² 真摯 ――真摯な (誠実な) sincere; (真剣な) earnest ――真摯に sincerely; earnestly ∥彼の真摯な態度に私たちはみな感銘を受けた His *sincere* attitude impressed us all. / 真摯な努力はいつか必ず実を結ぶのだ *Earnest* efforts will bear fruit someday.

じんじ 人事 (人事に関する事務) personnel [pə́ːrsənél] affairs [matters]
◆私は人事課に配属された I was placed in *the personnel section*. / 彼は人事部長の職を得た He got a position as *personnel manager*.
‖人事異動 a staff reshuffle / 人事院 the National Personnel Authority / 人事部 the personnel division [department]
ことわざ 人事を尽くして天命を待つほかない We have to do what we can and hope for the best.

しんしつ 寝室 bedroom ⓒ

しんじつ 真実 (the) truth ∥真実を語る tell *the truth* / 真実を曲げる distort *the truth* / いずれ真実は明らかになる *The truth* will appear sooner or later. / *Truth* will out. / 彼らは真実を突き止めようと努力した They struggled to discover *the truth*.
◆彼の話には真実味がなかった His story *didn't ring true*.

シンシナティ Cincinnati (◆米国の都市)

じんじふせい 人事不省 ∥彼はよく人事不省に陥るまで酒を飲む He often drinks himself into *unconsciousness*.

しんじゃ 信者 believer ⓒ ∥ジョンはキリスト教の信者だ John is *a believer* in Christianity. / (→キリスト教を信じている)John *believes in* Christianity.
‖カトリック信者 a Catholic

じんじゃ 神社 a *jinja*, a (Shinto)

しんしゃく shrine /神社にお参りする visit *a shrine*

> 神社には神道の神が祭られています。入り口には鳥居と呼ばれる門があり、参拝者は鳥居をくぐって聖域に入ります。手水舎(ちょうずや)で手を洗い・口をすすいで心身を清めてから、拝殿にお参りします。御神体が祭られている場所は神殿あるいは本殿と呼ばれます。神社にお参りするのは主に七五三や正月の初もうでなどのときです。
> A *jinja* (shrine) is a sacred place for Shinto deities. At the entrance is a gate called a *torii*, and worshipers enter a place of deities through it. They go on to the *chozuya*, a trough with a roof over it, to purify themselves by rinsing their hands and mouths, and then they pray at the *haiden* (hall of worship). The place where the deity is enshrined is called the *shinden* or *honden*. People go to shrines on such occasions as *shichigosan* or *hatsumode* of the New Year.

しんしゃく 斟酌 ――斟酌する make* allowance(s) for … /彼の若さを斟酌しなければならない We must *make allowances for* his youth.

しんしゅ¹ 進取 彼は進取の気性に富む人だ He is an *enterprising* person.

しんしゅ² 新種 new variety [type, kind] © /アマゾン川流域で新種のワニが発見された *A new variety* of alligator was found in the Amazon Basin. / そのワクチンは新種のウイルスには効かなかった The vaccine did not work on the *new type* of virus.

しんじゅ 真珠 pearl /真珠のネックレス a *pearl* necklace / 真珠を養殖する culture *pearls*
‖真珠貝 a pearl oyster
ことわざ 豚に真珠 ⇒ぶた

じんしゅ 人種 race ©, ethnic group © (❖最近では後者のほうが好まれる) ――人種的 racial

人種的偏見 *racial* prejudice / 人種のるつぼ a *racial* melting pot
その学校には様々な人種の子供たちが通っている Children of various *ethnic groups* go to that school.
人種問題でどういう立場をとっていますか Where do you stand on *racial issues*?
‖人種差別 racial discrimination / 黄色人種 the Mongoloid race (❖yellow race は差別的な言い方とされる) / 白色人種 the Caucasian race, the white race

しんじゅう 心中 (恋人どうしの) love [lovers'] suicide ; (2人いっしょの自殺) double suicide © (❖2人が合意してそれぞれ自殺することを指す。欧米では相手の意志の有無にかかわらず、相手を殺して自殺する場合は「殺人」とみなされる) ――心中する commit a love [double] suicide

◆48歳の男性が妻と子供1人を道連れに心中した A man of 48 killed his wife and child, and then *committed suicide.* / きょうの新聞に茨城で起きた一家心中の記事が載っていた There was a story of *a family suicide* in Ibaraki in today's paper.
‖無理心中 (a) murder suicide

しんしゅく 伸縮 expansion and contraction; (伸縮性) elasticity ©
◆伸縮性のあるゴム *elastic* rubber / 伸縮性の釣りざお a *telescopic* fishing rod

しんしゅつ 進出 advance ©© ――進出する advance ⓐ /彼らのチームは決勝に進出した Their team *advanced to* the finals.

◆その会社は中国への進出を目ざしている The company aims to *branch out into* China. / 彼女は政界への進出を考えている She is thinking of *going into* politics. / わが社は海外進出を決めた We decided to *expand* our business *overseas*. / その俳優はついにハリウッドに進出した The actor finally *made his way into* Hollywood.

しんしゅつきぼつ 神出鬼没 彼は神出鬼没だ(→まるでどこにでもいるようだ) It looks like he *is everywhere at once.*

しんしゅん 新春 (新年) the New Year

しんしょ 親書 private [personal] letter ©; (自筆の手紙) signed [autographed] letter © /大統領の親書 *an autographed letter* from the President

しんしょう¹ 心証 (印象) impression © /被告の態度は裁判官の心証を害した The defendant's behavior gave *a negative impression* to the judge. / 私は彼の心証をよくしようと必死だった I was trying hard to make *a good impression* on him.

しんしょう² 辛勝 narrow [slender] victory © ――辛勝する win* a narrow victory, win by a narrow margin

しんじょう¹ 心情 one's feelings /彼女の心情を察してやってほしい I want you to understand her *feelings.* / 彼らのしたことがいいとは言えないが、心情的には理解できる I can't say what they did was good, but I understand *their feelings.*

◆心情お察しいたします(→深く同情する) I *sympathize deeply with you.*

しんじょう² 身上 (生い立ち) one's personal background; (とりえ) one's merit [good point] /彼らは探偵事務所に彼女の身上調査を依頼した They asked a detective agency to *look into* her *personal background.* / 正直が彼の身上です Honesty is his *merit.*

◆一身上の事柄(→私事) one's *private* affairs
‖身上書 a personal information form; (履歴書) a résumé [rézəmèi]

しんじょう³ 信条 principle © (通例複数形~s); (特に宗教上の) creed © /自分の信条を貫く stick to *one's principles* / 自分に正直に生きるというのが私の信条だ It's my *principle* to be honest to myself.

じんじょう 尋常 ――尋常の (ふつうの) ordinary, usual, normal

◆彼の食欲は尋常ではない He's got an *incredible* appetite.

しんしょうしゃ 身障者 physically disabled [handicapped] person, 《集合的》the physically disabled [handicapped]

しんしょうぼうだい 針小棒大 彼はいつも針小棒大に言う He always *makes a mountain out of a molehill*. (❖make a mountain out of a molehill は「つまらないことを大げさに言う」の意味)

しんしょく¹ 寝食 僕らは3年間寝食を共にした We *lived together under the same roof* for three years. / 彼女は寝食を忘れて病気の子供の看病をした(→病気の子供の看病で食事や睡眠の時間がとれないほど忙しかった) She was so busy nursing her sick child that she *had no time to eat or sleep*.

しんしょく² 浸食 erosion ──浸食する erode, eat* away ‖この谷は川の浸食によってできた This valley was formed by *erosion* of the river.

しんじる 信じる

❶【正しいと思う】believe
私は彼女の言葉を信じている I *believe*「her words [what she said].
当時人々は太陽が地球の周りを回っていると信じていた In those days people *believed that* the sun went around the earth.
彼らが優勝したなんて信じられない I *can't believe that* they won the championship.
信じられないかもしれないが(→信じようと信じまいと)この前UFOを見たんだ *Believe it or not*, I saw a UFO the other day.
◆そんな話にはわかに信じがたい(→話がうますぎる) That story is *too good to be true*. / 信じられないことが彼の身に起こった An *unbelievable* thing happened to him.

❷【信用する】trust; (人柄・存在などを) believe in ...
私たちはみなあなたを信じています We all *trust* you.
自分の直感を信じなさい *Trust* your instinct.
幽霊の存在を信じますか Do you *believe in* ghosts?
彼は薬よりも食餌(じ)療法のほうを信じている He *believes* more *in* diet than *in* drugs.

❸【確信する】be sure [certain]
私はきょうの試合に勝つと信じている I'm *sure* [*certain*] *that* I'll win today's game.
私たちは彼の成功を信じています We're *sure of* his success.

❹【信仰する】believe in ...
彼らはキリスト教を信じている They *believe in* Christianity.

しんしん¹ 新進 ──新進の rising; (有望な) (young and) promising, budding ‖新進のハープ奏者 a *budding* harpist

しんしん² 心身 mind and body ‖心身ともに健全な若者たち young people who are sound *both in mind and body* ◆ 私は心身ともに疲れきっていた I was completely exhausted, *physically and mentally*.
‖心身症 a psychosomatic disease

しんしん³ 深々 雪はしんしんと降り続いていた The Snow was falling silently [thick and fast].

しんじん¹ 新人 newcomer, rookie; (新顔) new face; (芸能界の) new star; (新入社員) recruit ‖新人王 the *Rookie of the Year* / 新人教育 *recruit* training
◆新人戦 a *rookie* match / その歌手は最優秀新人賞を取った That singer got *the award for Best New Artist*.

しんじん² 信心 (信仰) faith, devotion
◆私の両親はとても信心深い My parents are very *religious*.

じんしん 人身 …に人身攻撃をする make *a personal attack* against ... / 原宿駅で人身事故があった関係でダイヤが乱れています The train schedule has been disrupted due to *the accident with casualties* at Harajuku Station.

しんすい¹ 心酔 ──心酔する (崇拝する) worship; (深く敬愛する) adore ‖彼女はモーツァルトに心酔している She *worships* Mozart. / She *is an ardent admirer of* Mozart.
◆彼は学生時代, 三島由紀夫の心酔していた He *was intoxicated with* Mishima Yukio's ideas when he was in college.

しんすい² 浸水 ──浸水する be flooded [drowned] ‖ハリケーンによって1,000戸以上の家屋が床上[床下]まで浸水した Over 1,000 houses *were flooded* above [up to] the floor by the hurricane.

しんすい³ 進水 ──進水する (船が) be launched ‖私たちの船は3日後に進水の予定です Our ship will *be launched* in three days.
‖進水式 a launching ceremony

しんずい 真髄・神髄, 《公式的》the quintessence; (精神) the spirit, the soul ‖民主主義の真髄 *the quintessence* of democracy / 無私無欲こそ幸福の真髄である Self-forgetfulness is *the very essence* of happiness.

しんせい¹ 申請 application ──申請する apply for ... ‖パスポート[ビザ]を申請する *apply for* a passport [visa]
◆離婚申請する *file* [*sue*] *for divorce*
‖申請書(用紙) an application form

しんせい² 神聖 ──神聖な sacred, holy ‖インドでは牛は神聖とされている Cows are regarded as *sacred* in India. / メッカはイスラム教徒にとって神聖な場所です Mecca is the *holy* [*sacred*] place for the Moslems.

しんせい³ 真性 ──真性の genuine ‖真性コレラ *genuine* cholera

じんせい 人生 life (複 lives)

幸福な人生を送る lead *a happy life*
それは彼の人生で最も幸せな時期だった Those were the happiest hours of his *life*.
人生とはそんなものだ That's *life*! / That's *the way it is*.
彼は大病をして人生観(→人生に対する考え方)が変わった His *attitude to life* changed after his serious illness.
彼はその島で第二の人生を踏み出した He started *a new life* on that island.
◆人生設計を立てる make *one's plans for the*

future / 祖父は人生経験が豊富だ My grandfather *has seen much of the world.* / 母は新聞の人生相談を毎週欠かさず読んでいる My mother reads *an advice column* in the newspaper every week without fail.

🅔「イギリス行き，まだ迷ってるんだ」「やってみろよ。一度きりの人生じゃないか」"I still haven't decided yet whether to go to Britain or not." "Oh, come on! *You have only one life to live.* [*You only live once.*]"

しんせいじ 新生児 new(-)born baby ⓒ
しんせかい 新世界 new world ⓒ; (アメリカ大陸) the New World
しんせき 親戚 relative ⓒ ⇨ しんるい(親類) ‖母方[父方]の親戚 *relatives* on *one's* mother's [father's] side / 彼女は私の遠い親戚です She is *a remote* [*distant*] *relative* of mine.
◆最近はおばの家とは親戚づきあいをしていない We *don't associate with* my aunt's family these days.
慣用表現 遠くの親戚より近くの他人 *A good neighbor is better than a faraway relative.*
じんせきみとう 人跡未踏 ‖丘の向こうには人跡未踏の荒野が広がっていた Beyond the hill stretched *untrodden* wilderness. / 地球上に人跡未踏の土地はほとんどないに等しい There is almost no *unexplored* land left on our planet.
シンセサイザー synthesizer ⓒ
しんせつ¹ 親切 kindness ⓤ ⓒ ━━ 親切な kind, nice; (心の優しい) kindhearted ━━ 親切に kindly, with kindness
ご親切に感謝します Thank you for *your kindness.*
彼はだれにでも親切だ He *is kind* to everyone.
彼女は親切にもその男の子を病院まで連れていってあげた She *kindly* took the boy to the hospital. / She was *kind enough to take* the boy to the hospital.
彼らはみな私に親切にしてくれた They *were* all very *nice to* me.
私たちは親切心からそうしたのに，彼女は気に入らなかったようだ We did it *out of kindness*, but she didn't like it.
しんせつ² 新設 ━━する (組織・機関を) establish ⊕; (団体などを) organize ⊕; (創立する) found ⊕, (口語的) set* up ‖彼は昨年新設された高校に入学した He entered a high school that *was founded* last year. ◆バレー選手は新設チームと契約を結んだ The volleyball player signed with a *new team.*
‖新設校 a newly-founded school
しんせつ³ 新説 new theory ⓒ, new idea ⓒ ‖新説を唱える advance *a new theory*
しんせつ 新雪 fresh snow ⓤ
しんせん 新鮮 ━━新鮮な fresh ‖新鮮な果物[牛乳] *fresh* fruit [milk] / 窓をあけて新鮮な空気を入れましょうか Shall I open the window and let in some *fresh* air?
◆その商品もすぐに新鮮味が薄れるだろう *The novelty* of the product will soon wear off.

しんぜん¹ 親善 goodwill ⓤ; (友好) friendship ⓤ ━━の friendly ‖国際親善を深める promote *international goodwill* [*friendship*] / 留学生を交換したことは両国の親善に大いに役立った Exchanging students greatly helped to *promote friendly relations* between the two countries.
‖親善試合 a friendly match / 親善使節 a goodwill mission / 親善大使 an ambassador of goodwill
しんぜん² 神前 ‖神前結婚 a wedding (ceremony) according to Shinto rites
じんせん 人選 ‖人選をする choose [pick] *the wrong person* / 人選にもれる *be left out* / そのチームは彼に代わるコーチを人選中だ The team *is selecting* a person suitable as a coach to take his place.
しんそう¹ 真相 (真実) the truth, the real story ‖その事件の真相はやみの中である *The real story* behind the incident remains a mystery. / 調査の結果，真相が明らかになった *The truth* of the matter emerged from the investigation.
◆事件の真相究明にあたる start to *get to the bottom of* the case / 彼は真相を知る唯一の人だ He is the only person who knows *what's what.*
しんそう² 新装 refurbishment ⓤ ━━新装する refurbish ⊕ ‖新装された体育館 a *refurbished* gym / その店はあす新装開店の予定だ The shop will *reopen* tomorrow *after refurbishment.*

しんぞう 心臓
❶【体の】heart ⓒ
心臓がどきどきしていた My heart was beating [pounding] fast.
祖母は心臓が悪い My grandmother has「*a weak heart* [*heart trouble*].
急に大きな音がしたので心臓が止まるほど驚いた *My heart stood still* when I suddenly heard the loud sound.
彼女は心臓の手術を受けた She had an operation on *her heart.*
この痛み止めを飲みすぎると心臓発作を引き起こす可能性がある An overdose of this painkiller can induce *a heart attack.*
そのマラソンコースの終盤に心臓破りの坂がある There's a *really steep* slope in the final stage of the marathon course.
❷【中心部】the heart
組織の心臓部 *the heart* of the organization
❸【ずうずうしさ】
彼は心臓が強い He *is bold.*/ He's *got nerve.*
‖心臓移植 a heart transplant / 心臓外科 cardiac [heart] surgery / 心臓外科医 a heart surgeon / 心臓病 (a) heart disease / 心臓まひ heart failure
じんぞう¹ 人造 ━━人造の artificial, man-made ‖人造湖 an artificial [a man-made] lake
じんぞう² 腎臓 kidney ⓒ ‖彼は腎臓病だ(→腎臓が悪い) He *has kidney trouble.*
‖腎臓移植 a kidney transplant / 腎臓結石

a kidney stone

しんぞく 親族 relative ⓒ ➡ しんるい(親類)

じんそく 迅速 ――迅速な (素早い) quick, prompt; (即座の) swift; (てきぱきとした) speedy ――迅速に quickly, promptly; swiftly; speedily /迅速に行動する take action *quickly*; take *quick* action / 新しい市長は違法駐車に迅速に対処した The new mayor took *swift* action against illegal parking.

しんそこ 心底・真底 あいつには心底愛想が尽きた I'm *completely* fed up with him. / 彼女は彼のことを心底から愛していた She loved him *from the bottom of her heart*.

しんそつ 新卒 new graduate ⓒ

しんたい¹ 身体 body ⓒ ――身体の physical ――身体的に physically /身体の発達 *physical development* / あした学校で身体検査がある We'll have *a physical checkup* at school tomorrow. ➡ ボディーチェック
∥身体障害者 a physically disabled [handicapped] person, 《集合的》the physically disabled [handicapped]

しんたい² 進退 彼らには進退極まった状態だ (→追いつめられている) They *have their backs against the wall*. / They *are driven into a corner*. / 彼は進退を明らかにするよう迫られている He has been urged to decide on *his course of action*. / 彼は進退伺い (→辞めるべきかどうかを問う手紙) を出した He handed in *a letter asking whether to resign or not*.

しんだい 寝台 bed ⓒ; (船・列車の) berth ⓒ
∥寝台券 a berth ticket / 寝台車 a sleeping car, a sleeper / 寝台料金 a berth charge

じんたい¹ 人体 human body ⓒ ∥人体実験 an experiment on a human body

じんたい² 靭帯 ligament ⓒ

じんだい 甚大 ――甚大な (はなはだしい) great; (程度がひどい) heavy, serious /その地区は津波で甚大な被害をこうむった That area suffered *heavy* damage from a tsunami.

しんたいそう 新体操 rhythmic gymnastics

しんたく 信託 trust ⓒ
∥信託銀行 a trust bank / 信託統治 trusteeship / 投資信託 an investment trust

しんだん 診断 diagnosis ⓤ ⓒ (複 diagnoses) ――診断する diagnose ⓣ /正しい [誤った] 診断 a right [wrong] *diagnosis* / 彼の病気は糖尿病と診断された He *was diagnosed* as having diabetes.
◆健康診断を受ける have *a medical examination [checkup]* / 診断書を書く draw up *a medical certificate*

じんち¹ 陣地 (配置) position ⓒ; (野営地) encampment ⓒ /敵の陣地を攻撃する attack *the* enemy's *encampment*

じんち² 人知 これは人知の及ぶところではない This is far beyond the boundaries of human intelligence.

しんちく 新築 おじは去年家を新築した My uncle *built a new house* last year.
∥新築祝い (パーティー) a housewarming (party); (贈り物) a housewarming gift

じんちく 人畜 それは人畜無害です It is *harmless to both humans and animals*.

しんちゃ 新茶 the first tea of the season

しんちゃく 新着 (新製品) new arrival ⓒ
◆新着図書はこの棚にあります The *newly-arrived* books are on this shelf.

しんちゅう¹ 心中 心中を打ち明ける bare *one's soul* / 彼は心中穏やかでなかった (→満足していなかった) He wasn't happy *at heart*. / (→心を乱されていた) He was disturbed *at heart*. / 心中お察しいたします (→深く同情する) I *deeply sympathize with you*.

しんちゅう² 真鍮 brass ⓤ

じんちゅう 陣中 彼女は陣中見舞いにアイスクリームを持ってきてくれた She *visited* us with ice cream *to encourage* us.

しんちょう¹ 身長 height [háit] ⓤ
身長を測る measure *one's height*
選手の平均身長は190センチを超えている The *average height* of the players is over 190 centimeters.
生徒は身長順に並んでいた The pupils lined up *in order of height [by height]*.
◆身長が3センチ伸びる grow three centimeters *taller* / 私は母と身長が同じだ I'm as *tall* as my mother. / I'm *the same height as* my mother.
📞「身長はどれくらいですか」「165センチです」 "*How tall* are you?" "I'm 165 centimeters tall."

しんちょう² 慎重 ――慎重な (注意深い) careful; (言動に) discreet; (用心深い) cautious, prudent ――慎重に carefully; discreetly; cautiously, prudently
慎重に言葉を選ぶ choose *one's words carefully*
彼はその機械を慎重に扱った He was *careful* with the machine.
母の運転は慎重だ My mother is a *cautious* driver. / My mother drives *cautiously*.
服を買うときは慎重に選びなさい Be *prudent* in choosing which clothes to buy.
決める前に賛否両方の意見を慎重に比較検討するべきだ You need to weigh the pros and cons *carefully* before deciding.
◆彼の発言は慎重さに欠けていた His remark lacked *prudence*. / 人種間の問題はきわめて慎重に対処しなければならない Race relations are an extremely *sensitive* issue.

しんちょう³ 新調 兄は入社式のためにスーツを新調した My brother *had a new suit made* for the company's entrance ceremony.

じんちょうげ 沈丁花 〖植物〗daphne [dǽfni] ⓒ

しんちょく 進捗 仕事の進捗状況を報告する report on *the progress* of work / 交渉は大いに進捗した The negotiation *made* much *progress*.

しんちんたいしゃ 新陳代謝 metabolism ⓤ ⓒ ∥たくさん汗をかくのは新陳代謝が活発な証拠だ Sweating a lot is a sign of high *metabolism*.

しんつう 心痛 (心配) worry ⓤ; (不安・気苦

労) anxiety [U]

じんつう 陣痛 labor, 《英》labour [U] 《また a ～》, labor pains ∥陣痛が始まる go into *labor*

じんつうりき 神通力 (超自然的な力) supernatural powers

しんてい 進呈 presentation [U] ―進呈する present [他] ∥見本無料進呈 Samples *are presented* free (of charge). / 先着200名様に粗品を進呈します The first 200 people *will be presented with* a small gift.

じんてき 人的 ―人的な human ∥人的ミス a *human* fault / 人的資源 *human* resources ◆人的被害 *casualties*

しんてきがいしょう 心的外傷 〘心理〙 trauma [tráumə] [U] [C] ◆心的外傷後ストレス障害 post-*traumatic* stress disorder

シンデレラ Cinderella [sìndərélə]

しんてん[1] 進展 (発展) development [U] [C]; (進歩) progress [U] ―進展する develop [自]; progress [自] ∥事態の急速な進展 *the* rapid *development* of a situation / 交渉はなかなか進展しなかった The negotiations *didn't make* much *progress.* / その問題は意外な方向に進展した That problem *developed* [*went, moved*] in an unexpected direction.

しんてん[2] 親展 Confidential, Personal (❖手紙などの表書き)

しんでん 神殿 shrine [C]; (古代ローマ・エジプト・ギリシャの) temple [C]
◆パルテノン神殿 *the Parthenon*

しんでんず 心電図 electrocardiogram [C] (《略語》ECG, 《米》EKG) ∥心電図を撮る take *an ECG*

しんてんち 新天地 (新しい世界) new world [C]

しんと[1] 彼女の言葉にみんなしんとなった Everyone *fell silent* at her words. / 町はしんと静まり返っていた There was *complete silence* in the city.

しんと[2] 信徒 (信者) believer [C]

しんど[1] 震度 (地震の強さ) seismic [sáizmik] intensity [U]
◆けさの地震は水戸で震度4だった The earthquake this morning had *an intensity* of four *on the Japanese scale* in Mito.

しんど[2] 進度 progress [U] ◆うちのクラスは数学の進度が遅れている Our class *is behind* [*slow*] in math. / あの先生の授業は進度が速くてついていけない That teacher's class *goes fast* and I can't keep up.

しんど[3] 深度 the depth

じんと 彼女の言葉が胸にじんときた I was *deeply* touched by her words.

しんどい (疲れる) tired; (きつい) hard
◆この暑さの中, 駅まで歩くのはしんどい It's *tiring* to walk to the station in this heat.

しんとう[1] 神道 ⛩ Shintoism [U] Shinto [U]

> 明確な経典, 教義, 布教制度が整っていないという理由で, 神道を宗教と見るかどうかについては昔から論議されてきました. しかし, 一般的には日本固有の信仰とみなされ, 自然崇拝や先祖崇拝といった日本の原始信仰から始まったとされています. 神道には「八百万(ﾔｵﾖﾛｽﾞ)の神」といわれる多くの神々が祭られています.
> There has been an argument as to whether Shinto should be considered a religion, because it does not have a distinct scripture, dogmas or missionary work. In general, it is regarded as Japan's indigenous beliefs, which trace their origins back to the ancient worship of nature and ancestors. Shinto includes many gods collectively called *Yaoyorozu-no-kami*, which literally means "eight million deities."

しんとう[2] 浸透 penetration [U] [C] ―浸透する (液体などが) penetrate [他] [自], 《公式的》permeate [自] [他]; (考えなどが) pervade [他] ∥彼の生きた時代には虚無的な思想が若者に浸透していた Nihilistic thinking *pervaded* young people in his time. / そのテントは雨水が浸透しない素材でできている The tent is made of a material that rain *can't penetrate.*
‖浸透圧 osmotic pressure

しんとう[3] 親等 the degree of relationship
◆日本では, いとこは4親等の親族に当たる In Japan, a cousin is considered *a relative in the fourth degree.*

しんどう[1] 震動・振動 ❶【揺れること】(左右に) vibration [U] [C]; (激しい) shock [C] [U]; (上下左右に) shake [C] [U] ―震動する vibrate [自]; shake* [自] [他] ∥このあたりは火山の噴火による震動が激しかった *The shock* of the volcanic eruption was severe in this area. / 電車が通るたびに建物が震動する Every time the train passes, this building *vibrates.*
❷【左右に振れること】swing [C] ―振動する swing* [自] ∥振り子の振動 *the swing* of a pendulum

しんどう[2] 神童 child prodigy [C]

じんとう 陣頭 その事件の捜査では彼が陣頭指揮をとった He *took the lead* in the investigation of that case.

じんどう 人道 humanity [U] ―人道的な humane (↔inhumane), humanitarian ∥人道にもとる犯罪 a crime against *humanity* / 彼は人道的な理由から動物実験に反対している He's against animal experiments for *humane* reasons.
‖人道主義 humanitarianism / 人道主義者 a humanitarian

じんとく 人徳 *one's* natural virtue; (個人的な魅力) *one's* personal charm ∥人徳のある人 a person of *natural virtue*
💬「彼が困ってるのを見るとだれもが助けたくなるんだよね」「それは彼の人徳だよ」 "Everybody feels like helping him whenever they find him in trouble." "That's because he's got such *a charming character.*"

じんどる 陣取る (場所を占める) occupy [他] ∥追っかけの女の子たちが会場の最前列に陣取っていた Groupies *occupied* the very first row in the hall.

シンナー (paint) thinner ◎Ⓤ／シンナーでペンキを薄める dilute paint with *thinner*
◆シンナーを吸う sniff *glue*(◆glue は「接着剤」の意味)／シンナー遊び *glue*-sniffing

しんなり タマネギがしんなりするまでいためなさい Fry onions until (they become) *soft*.

しんにち 親日 ──親日の pro-Japanese／トルコはとても親日的な国だ Turkey is very *pro-Japanese*.
‖親日家 a pro-Japanese; (日本文化が好きな人)a Japanophile

しんにゅう¹ 侵入 (押し入ること) intrusion ⓊⒸ; (侵略) invasion Ⓤ ──侵入する intrude ⓘ; (建物に押し入る) break* into ...; (侵略する) invade ⓘⓣ; (私有地などへ) trespass ⓘ／泥棒は台所の窓から侵入した The burglar *broke into* the house through a kitchen window.／国籍不明の飛行機が日本の領空に侵入した A plane of unknown nationality *intruded into* Japanese airspace.
◆だれかが私のコンピュータに侵入した形跡がある There's evidence that somebody *hacked into* my computer.
‖侵入者 an intruder, an invader, a trespasser／家宅侵入 breaking and entering／不法侵入 (an) unwarranted intrusion, trespassing, (a) trespass

しんにゅう² 進入 ──進入する enter ⓘ／進入禁止 〖掲示〗Do Not *Enter*

しんにゅうせい 新入生 new pupil [student]; (高校・大学の) freshman Ⓒ(◆男女ともに用いる)

しんにん¹ 信任 confidence Ⓤ (↔nonconfidence)／議会の信任を得る gain [win] *confidence* of the Diet
‖信任状 credentials／信任投票 a vote of confidence

しんにん² 新任 ──新任の new(◆名詞の前で用いる); (新たに任命された) newly-appointed ‖新任の先生 a *new* teacher／(学校で) 新任のあいさつを述べる make *a speech as a new teacher at the school*

しんねん¹ 信念 belief Ⓤ(また a ~); (信条・主義) faith Ⓤ; (強い確信) conviction ⓊⒸ／強い[堅い]信念 strong [firm] *belief*／彼は決して信念を曲げない He's always steadfast in his *belief* [*faith*]．／彼は最後まで自分の信念を貫くだろう He will stick to his *convictions* till the end.／すべての人は平等だというのが私の信念だ It is my *conviction* that all people are equal.

しんねん² 新年 new year Ⓒ (◆特定の年はthe new year); (年始の数日間) the New Year ‖新年の抱負 one's New Year's resolution／新年を祝う[迎える] celebrate [welcome] *the New Year*／新年おめでとう (A) Happy *New Year*!(◆会話では通例 a を付けない。また言われたほうは Thank you. (The) same to you. などと答える)／新年早々に引っ越すことになった I'm going to move *at the beginning of the new year*.
‖新年会 a New Year's party

シンパ Ⓐ(同調者) sympathizer Ⓒ

しんぱい 心配

anxiety [æŋzáiəti] Ⓤ; care Ⓤ; concern Ⓤ; fear; uneasiness Ⓤ; worry Ⓤ(◆いずれも「心配事」の意味では Ⓒ となることが多い) ──心配する be anxious; be concerned; be afraid; be worried, worry ⓘ

> anxiety: 起こりつつある、または将来起こるかもしれないことに対する不安。
> care: 精神的な重圧や心に重くのしかかるような不安。
> concern: 関心のあることに対し、気にかけて不安に思うこと。
> fear: 恐れ・恐怖を表す。
> uneasiness: 不安で気持ちが落ち着かないことを表す。
> worry: 「あれこれ思い悩む、心配する」という意味の最も一般的な語。「取り越し苦労」の意味でも用いられる。

〖心配が・は〗
何も心配はいらないよ There's nothing to *worry about*.
あしたは雨の心配はないでしょう There will be *no need to worry about* rain tomorrow.
〖心配の・に〗
子供が成長するにつれて心配の種も増す Our *anxieties* grow as our child grows.
◆彼女に何かあったのではないかと心配になった I *was afraid* something had happened to her.
〖心配を〗
親に心配をかけまいとしてそのことを黙っていた Fearing to give my parents cause for *worry*, I didn't say anything about it.
◆いろいろご心配をおかけして(→迷惑をかけて)申しわけありません I'm sorry *to have caused you* so much *trouble*.
〖心配で〗
彼らはみな心配でやつれていた They were all struck *with anxiety*.
ゆうべは心配で全然眠れなかった I was so *worried* last night that I couldn't sleep at all.
〖心配する〗
みんな君のことを心配していたんだよ We *were all worrying about* you.
心配するな。時間はまだたっぷりあるんだから *Don't worry*. We've got plenty of time left.
心配したところでどうなるというんだ What's the use of *worrying*?
僕がどんなに心配したか君には分からないだろう You have no idea *how worried* I was.
◆費用のことは心配するな *Never mind* the cost.
〖心配だ〗
母親の体が心配だ I'm *concerned* about my mother's health.
妹の将来が心配だ I'm *worried* about my sister's future.
◆あさっての天気が心配だ The weather the day after tomorrow *is doubtful*.
〖その他〗

シンバル

何か心配事があるの Is there *something worrying you?* / 私のことでしたらご心配なく *Don't worry* on my account. / 彼は何の心配もないかのようにふるまった He behaved as if he *were free from care.*
◆彼女は心配症だ She is *a worrier* [*worrywart*]. / 「そうだと思う」と彼は心配そうに言った "I'm afraid so," he said *anxiously.*

シンバル cymbals ‖シンバルを鳴らす clash *cymbals*; play *the cymbals*

しんぱん¹ 侵犯 (権利の) violation ⓒⓊ; (領土の) intrusion Ⓤ ──侵犯する violate 他; intrude 自 ‖領空侵犯 (a) trespass of national airspace

しんぱん² 審判 (事件などの) judgment Ⓤ ──審判する judge 他⾃; (競技で) referee 他⾃, umpire 他⾃ ‖野球の審判をする *umpire* a baseball game; act as umpire in a baseball game
◆審判はそのスケート選手に5.4の評点をつけた *The judge* scored the skater 5.4. / 彼は審判に抗議した He appealed to *the umpire.*
‖審判員 (競技・コンテストなどの) a judge; (野球・テニスなどの) an umpire; (ボクシング・サッカー・ラグビーなどの) a referee

しんぴ 神秘 mystery ⓒⓊ ──神秘的な mysterious ‖生命の神秘 the *mysteries* of life / 神秘のベールに包まれている be wrapped in a shroud of *mystery* / 宇宙の神秘を探る explore the *mysteries* of the universe / この絵には神秘的な美しさがある This picture has a *mysterious* beauty.
‖神秘主義 mysticism / 神秘主義者 a mystic

しんびがん 審美眼 an eye for beauty, a sense of beauty

しんぴょうせい 信憑性 (信頼性) reliability Ⓤ ◆この記事には信憑性がある[ない] This article is *reliable* [*unreliable*]. / 私は彼の報告の信憑性を疑っている I suspect *the truth* of his report.

しんぴん 新品 new article ⓒ ◆新品の靴 *brand-new* [*new*] shoes / 新品同様のテレビが捨てられていた A TV set「*in mint condition* [*as good as new*]」had been discarded.

しんぶ 深部 depths ‖アマゾンの深部に分け入る go into *the depths* of the Amazon

しんぷ¹ 神父 priest ⓒ, father ⓒ (❖後者は呼びかけにも用い、その場合 Father と書く) ‖ドイル神父 *Father* Doyle

しんぷ² 新婦 bride ⓒ ‖新郎新婦が教会から出てきた *The bride and groom* came out of the church. (❖語順に注意)

しんぷう 新風 彼は文壇に新風を吹き込んだ He「*breathed new life* into [(→活力を与えた) *invigorated*]」the world of literature.

シンフォニー (交響曲) symphony ⓒ

しんぷく 振幅 〔電気〕 amplitude Ⓤ

しんふぜん 心不全 heart failure Ⓤ

しんぶつ 神仏 (神と仏) the gods and Buddhist deities; (神道と仏教) Shintoism and Buddhism ◆神仏の加護を祈る pray for *divine* protection

じんぶつ 人物 (人間) person ⓒ; (性格・人柄) character ⓒ, personality Ⓤ; (著名な人) figure ⓒ; (登場人物) character ⓒ ‖偉大な人物 *a great person* / 歴史上の人物 *a historical figure* / 反核運動の中心人物 a central [leading] *figure* in the anti-nuclear movement / 劇の主な登場人物 the principal *characters* in the play / 学歴よりも人物を重視する regard *personality* rather than educational background as important / 彼女は党内で最も影響力のある人物だ She is the most powerful *person* in the party.
◆その警察官は不審な人物を見かけなかったかと私に尋ねた The policeman inquired whether I had seen *anyone* suspicious. / 彼はひとかどの人物だ He's *really somebody.*
‖人物画 a portrait / 重要人物 an important person [figure] / 要注意人物 a marked man [woman]

シンプル シンプルなデザインの服 a *simply* designed dress

しんぶん 新聞

newspaper ⓒ, paper ⓒ; (媒体としての総称) the press

【～(の)新聞】

英字新聞 an English-language *newspaper* / スポーツ新聞 a sports *newspaper* / 学校新聞 a school *newspaper* / きょう[きのう]の新聞 today's [yesterday's] *paper* / 5月7日の新聞 a *paper* dated May 7; the May 7 *paper* / 古新聞 old *newspapers*
◆学級新聞 *a class newsletter*

【新聞が】

その新聞は彼の死の記事を大きく扱った *The paper* featured the story of his death.

【新聞を】

新聞を配達する deliver *newspapers*
わが家は3種類の新聞をとっている We「*subscribe to* [*take*]」three different *papers.*
🅔「何新聞をとっていますか」「朝日新聞です」 "*What newspaper* do you take?" "I take *the Asahi.*"

【新聞に・で】

新聞に広告を掲載する put an advertisement in *the paper*
その事件は新聞に出ていた That incident was in *the paper.*
新聞によるとその竜巻の犠牲者は50人以上にのぼるらしい *According to the paper,* the number of victims of the tornado comes to more than 50.
きょうの新聞でおもしろい記事を読んだ I read an interesting story in today's *paper.*
🅔「新聞に何て書いてある」「強い台風が来るらしいよ」 "What does *the paper* say?" "It says that a strong typhoon is coming."

【新聞の】

新聞の切り抜き a *newspaper* clipping / 新聞のテレビ[スポーツ]欄 the TV [sports] section of *the newspaper* / きょうの新聞のトップ記事 the leading article in today's *paper*
◆皇太子の結婚が新聞の一面を飾った The mar-

riage of the prince *made the front page*.
∥新聞売り場 a newsstand / 新聞記事 a newspaper article / 新聞記者 a (newspaper) reporter, a newspaperman / 新聞広告 a newspaper advertisement / 新聞紙 newspaper(❖数えるときは a piece of ... とする) / 新聞社 a newspaper publisher [company] / 新聞配達 newspaper delivery; (人) a paperboy, a papergirl(❖「新聞配達をする」は do a paper route [《英》round]) / 新聞発表 a press release
関連語 朝刊 a morning edition / 夕刊 an evening edition / 日刊紙 a daily paper / 全国紙 a national paper / 地方紙 a local paper / タブロイド紙 a tabloid / 号外 an extra / 日曜版 the Sunday edition (of a newspaper)

じんぶん 人文 ∥人文科学 the humanities / 人文主義 humanism / 人文地理学 human geography, anthropogeography

しんべい 親米 ──親米の pro-American / その政党は親米路線をとった The political party took *a pro-American policy*.

しんぺん 身辺 身辺を警護する guard *a person* / 身辺を整理する order *one's affairs* / 身辺の世話をする take care of *a person*

しんぽ 進歩

progress ⓤ; (前進) advance ⓒⓤ; (改善・上達) improvement ⓤⓒ ──進歩する progress ⓐ; advance ⓐ; improve ⓐ
進歩を妨げる obstruct *progress* ⓐ / 情報通信の進歩 *the progress* of telecommunications
最近の科学技術の進歩についていくのはとても難しい It's very hard to keep up with *the recent advances* in technology.
ここ数年でリサイクル技術は驚くほど進歩した Recycling technology *has made* surprising *progress* [*advances*] in the last few years.
英会話を習って半年になるのに私の英語はあまり進歩していない Though I have been learning how to speak English for six months, I *haven't made* much *progress* [*improvement*].
◆進歩的な意見の持ち主 a person of *progressive* [*advanced*] ideas / その国の農業技術は近隣諸国よりはるかに進歩している The country is far *ahead of* its neighbors in agricultural technology.

コロケーション -progress-
《形容詞＋～》著しい～ considerable progress / 大きな～ great progress / 驚くべき～ surprising progress / 科学の～ scientific progress / 科学技術の～ technological progress / 急速な～ rapid progress / 着実な～ steady progress / めざましい～ remarkable progress / ゆっくりとした～ slow progress

しんぼう¹ 辛抱 patience ⓤ; (がんばり) perseverance ⓤ ──辛抱する be patient; (不愉快さを)《口語的》put* up with ...; (苦しさ・不快な状況を) bear* ⓐ / 長年の辛抱が報われて彼らはとうとう成功した Their years of *perseverance* were rewarded and they finally succeeded. / もう少しの辛抱だ Have a little more *patience*. / Be a little more *patient*. / 彼女は辛抱しきれずに仕事を投げ出した She *ran out of patience* and gave up the job. / あんないいかげんなやつによく辛抱できるね How can you *put up with* such an irresponsible person?
◆辛抱強い人 a *patient* person / 彼は彼女を何時間も辛抱強く待った He waited *patiently* for her for hours.

しんぼう² 信望 (信用) confidence ⓤ; (人望) popularity ⓤ ∥信望を得る[失う] win [lose] *the confidence* / 彼はクラスメートの信望が厚い He *is popular and has the confidence* of his classmates.

しんぽう 信奉 民主主義を信奉する believe in democracy / 社会主義の信奉者 *a believer* in [*a follower* of] socialism

じんぼう 人望 (人気) popularity ⓤ ∥人望を得る[失う] win [lose] *popularity*
◆人望の厚い人 a *popular* person

しんぼく 親睦 friendship ⓤⓒ ∥私たちは親睦を深めるためのパーティーを開いた We held a party to promote (*mutual*) *friendship*.
∥親睦会 a social gathering

シンポジウム symposium [simpóuziəm] ⓒ (複 ～s, symposia) ∥…に関するシンポジウムを開催する hold *a symposium* on ...

シンボル symbol ⓒ ⇨ しょうちょう(象徴)
∥シンボルマーク a symbol; (学校・市などの) an emblem; (会社の) a logo

しんまい 新米 ❶【米】new rice ⓤ ❷【新人】novice ⓒ, newcomer ⓒ; (初心者) beginner ⓒ ∥新米教師 a *novice* teacher
◆新米記者 a *cub* reporter

じんましん nettle rash ⓤⓒ, hives《単数扱い》∥牛乳を飲んだらじんましんが出た I got (a) *nettle rash* from drinking milk.

しんみ 親身 親身に人の世話をする look after a person *kindly* [*warmly*] / 彼女は親身になって私の話を聞いてくれた She leant a *sympathetic ear* to me.

しんみつ 親密 ──親密な close [klóus]; (仲のよい) friendly; (よく知っている) familiar ∥親密な関係 a *close* relationship / 私は彼らとは親密な間柄だ I'm on *close* [*friendly, familiar*] terms with them. / We are very *close to* them. ◆あの2人は親密な仲だ Those two are *intimate* with each other.

じんみゃく 人脈 personal connections, human network ⓒ ∥彼は裏の世界にも人脈がある He has *personal connections* with the underworld. ◆それは人脈作りをするいいチャンスだ It's a good chance to do *networking*.

しんみょう 神妙 ──神妙な (おとなしい) quiet; (従順な) obedient; (真剣な) serious ∥みんな神妙な顔をして彼の話を聞いた Everyone listened to him with a *serious* look. / 彼らは先生の前で神妙にしていた They were *quiet and obedient* in front of the teacher.

しんみり(と) しんみりした(→悲しい)気持ちで彼を見送った I saw him off in a *sad* mood. / 彼らはしんみりと(→静かに)死んだ父親の話をした They talked *quietly* about their deceased father.

じんみん 人民 the people; (国民) the citizen ∥人民の, 人民による, 人民のための政治 government of *the people*, by *the people*, for *the people* (❖リンカーン(Lincoln)の言葉)
‖人民戦線 the popular [people's] front

しんめ 新芽 sprout [C]

じんめい¹ 人命 (human) life [U] [C] ∥その事故で多くの人命が失われた Many *lives* were lost in the accident.
‖人命救助 lifesaving

じんめい² 人名 person's name [C]
‖人名辞典 a biographical dictionary

しんもつ 進物 gift [C], present [C]
◆進物用に包んでいただけますか Could you *gift-wrap* this?

じんもん 尋問 questioning [U]; (警察による) interrogation [C] [U]; (証人・被疑者に対する) examination [C] ―尋問する question [他]; interrogate [他]; examine [他] ∥その窃盗に関して警察は彼を尋問した The police *questioned* [*interrogated*] him about the theft.
◆誘導尋問をする ask *a leading question*
‖反対尋問 (a) cross-examination

しんや 深夜 ―[名] the middle of the night; (真夜中) midnight [U] ―[副] late at night; at midnight ∥深夜の2時に at 2 o'clock *in the middle of the night* / 深夜まで起きている sit up (*till*) *late at night* / 深夜営業している(→深夜まであいている) *be open till late at night*
◆議論は深夜まで続いた The discussion went on *far into the night*.
‖深夜バス a late bus / 深夜番組(テレビの) a midnight TV program [show] / 深夜放送(ラジオの) a midnight radio program / 深夜料金 a late-night rate [charge]

しんやく 新薬 new medicine [drug] [C]

しんやくせいしょ 新約聖書 the New Testament (《略語》NT, N.T.)

しんゆう 親友 good [close] friend [C] ∥私たちは親友だ We are *good friends*. / 彼らはすぐに親友になった They soon became *close friends* with each other.

しんよう 信用

❶【疑わないこと】(直感的な) trust [U]; (根拠に基づく) confidence [U] ―信用する trust [他]; (信じる) believe [他] [自]
人の信用を得る[失う] win [lose] a person's *confidence*
私は彼を信用している I *have confidence* [*trust, faith*] *in* him.
彼は私たちを全く信用していない He *has no trust in* us. / He *doesn't trust* us at all.
どこまでその記事を信用していいのか分からない I don't know how far I can *trust* the article.
彼は信用できる人だと思う I feel that 「he *can be trusted* [he's *trustworthy*].
それ以来彼の言うことが信用できなくなった I've *lost confidence in* his words ever since.
信用してください. 必ず約束は守ります *Trust* me. I'll surely keep my promise.
だれも私の話を信用してくれなかった Nobody *believed* me.
◆私はこの情報を信用できる筋から得た I got this information *from a reliable source*. / 彼女の話は簡単に信用しないほうがいい(→用心しろ) You *have to beware of* what she says.
❷【評判・価値】credit [U]; (信用性) credibility [U]; (世評) reputation [U] 《また a ～》
信用で…を買う buy ... *on credit* / 信用を築く[回復する] establish [restore] *a reputation*
これは店の信用にかかわる問題だ This is a matter which will affect our shop's *credibility* [*reputation*].
その不正な取り引きは会社の信用に傷をつけた The unfair deal has damaged the company's *credit* [*reputation*].
彼の店の信用度は高い His store's *credit* is good.
◆信用できる店 a *reputable* store
‖信用金庫 a credit bank / 信用組合 a credit union / 信用販売 a credit sale

じんよう 陣容 (顔ぶれ) line(-)up [C], 《集合的》staff [C]; (隊形) battle formation [C] [U] ∥そのチームは次の試合に備えて陣容を一新した The team has revised *its line(-)up* for the next game.
◆その会社は不祥事の後, 経営陣の陣容を立て直した The company *reorganized* the executives after the scandal.

しんようじゅ 針葉樹 conifer [C]
‖針葉樹林 a coniferous forest

しんらい 信頼

(直感的な) trust [U]; (根拠に基づく) confidence [U]; (根拠のない一方的な) faith [U] ―信頼する trust [他]; (頼りにする) rely [自]
人の信頼を得る[失う] win [lose] a person's *confidence* / 2国間の信頼関係を築く establish *a relationship of mutual trust* between the two countries
失った信頼を取り戻すのは難しい *The* lost *trust* of others is hard to restore.
彼女に信頼を裏切られた She betrayed *my trust* in her.
みんなの信頼にこたえられるようがんばった I did my best to live up to everyone's *trust*.
私は彼を全面的に信頼している I *have* [*put*] absolute *trust* [*confidence, faith*] *in* him.
正光はみんなから信頼されている Masamitsu *is trusted* by everybody.
◆信頼できる筋からのニュース news from *a reliable source* / 彼が信頼できる人だということは分かっている I know him to be *reliable* [*trustworthy*]. / その製品の信頼性は世界中で認められている *The reliability* of that product is recognized all over the world.

しんらつ 辛辣 ―辛辣な (厳しい) severe; (敵意のある) bitter; (鋭い) sharp ∥辛辣な批

評 severe [bitter, sharp] criticism

しんらばんしょう 森羅万象 all things in nature, 《公式的》(all) creation ◎; (宇宙) the universe [Universe]

しんり¹ 心理 《口語的》psychology [saikάlədʒi] ◎◎; (心理状態) a state of mind; (物の見方・考え方) mentality ◎ ──心理的な psychological; mental ──心理的に psychologically; mentally

私には彼の心理が分からない I can't understand his *state of mind*.

彼女はその小説で青年期の心理を描いた She described *the psychology* of the adolescent in the novel.

私の腹痛は心理的なものだった My stomachaches were *psychological*.

彼は相手よりも心理的優位に立った He gained a *psychological* advantage over his opponent.

◆ 彼は女の子の心理が分かっていない He doesn't know a girl's *feelings*. / 彼女は人の心理を読むのがうまい She is「*good* at reading other people's *minds* [a *mind-reader*].

∥心理学者 a psychologist / 心理作戦 psychological tactics / 心理的効果 a psychological effect / 心理テスト a psychological test / 群衆心理 mass [mob] psychology

しんり² 真理 truth ◎◎ ∥絶対的[普遍的]真理 an absolute [a universal] *truth* / 真理を追求する search for *the truth* / 彼女の言うことにも一面の真理がある There is some *truth* in what she says.

しんり³ 審理 trial ◎◎ ──審理する try ⓣ / 彼は審理の結果, 収賄罪に問われた He *was tried* and convicted of graft. / 現在その事件は審理中だ The case *is now being tried*.

しんりゃく 侵略 invasion ◎◎, aggression ◎◎ ──侵略する invade ⓣⓘ ∥ノルマン人のイングランド侵略 the Norman *invasion* of England

∥侵略行為 an act of aggression / 侵略者 an invader, an aggressor / 侵略戦争 an aggressive war, a war of aggression

しんりょう 診療 (治療) medical treatment ◎; (診察) medical examination ◎◎ ∥診療時間 (doctor's) office hours / 診療室 a doctor's office / 診療所 a clinic

しんりょく 新緑 new [fresh] verdure ◎, fresh greenery ◎ ∥新緑の季節 the season of *fresh greenery* / 新緑を満喫する enjoy *fresh greenery* fully

じんりょく¹ 尽力 (努力) effort ◎◎; (はからい) 《公式的》good offices; (助力) help ◎ ──尽力する make* every (possible) effort; (最善を尽くす) do* one's best / 「…の尽力で by [through] *the good offices* of ... / ご尽力をいただけるとありがたいのですが I'd be glad of *your help*. / 彼はその学校設立のために尽力した He *made every effort* to help establish the school.

じんりょく² 人力 human power ◎ ∥人力の及ばない beyond *human power*

しんりん 森林 forest ◎◎, woods (◆《米》ではしばしば単数扱い) ➪ もり(森) ∥森林浴する enjoy *a walk in the woods*

∥森林公園 a wooded [forest] park / 森林資源 forest resources / 森林地帯 forest area, woodland(s) / 森林破壊 destruction of forests / 森林伐採 deforestation / 森林保護 forest conservation

しんるい¹ 親類 relative ◎
父方の親類 a *relative* on one's father's side
彼は私の遠い親類だ He is a distant *relative* of mine.
お正月にはおじの家に親類縁者が集まる *My relatives* get together at my uncle's house on New Year's day.
◆ 彼はその俳優と親類関係にある He *is related to* the actor.

しんるい² 進塁 ヒットとエラーで山田は一塁から三塁に進塁した Yamada *moved* from first to third on a single and an error.

じんるい 人類 the human race, humankind ◎, humanity ◎, mankind ◎, man 《無冠詞単数形》; (人間以外の物と区別して) human beings

[語法] 性差別を避けるために man や mankind を使わず, the human race, humankind, human beings を用いるのがふつう.

人類の歴史 the history of *humanity*; the *human* history / 人類に奉仕する仕事をする work to serve *humanity* / 地球上の全人類 all the human beings on the planet
◆ 彼らは人類の起源について研究している They are studying the origin of *Homo sapiens*.
∥人類愛 love for humanity / 人類学 anthropology / 人類学者 an anthropologist / 文化人類学 cultural anthropology

しんれい 心霊 ∥心霊現象 psychic [spiritual] phenomena / 心霊写真 a psychic photograph / 心霊術 spiritualism

しんろ¹ 進路 course ◎ ∥台風の進路に当たっている be in *the course* of a typhoon / 飛行機は進路を変えた The plane changed *its course*. ◆ 卒業後の進路(→何をするか)は決めた? Have you decided *what to do* after graduation?
∥進路指導 counseling on *one's* future course

しんろ² 針路 course ◎ ∥針路を誤る take *a wrong course* / 針路をそれる deviate from *a course* / 船は南へ針路をとった The ship took [steered] *a southward course*.

しんろう¹ 心労 worry ◎ ∥彼女の髪は心労が重なって白くなってしまった A lot of *worries* have turned her hair white. / 彼は息子のことで心労が絶えない He *is always worrying* about his son.

しんろう² 新郎 (bride)groom ◎

しんわ 神話 myth ◎◎, (集合的) mythology ◎◎ ∥ギリシャ神話 Greek *myths* [*mythology*] / 男性が女性よりすぐれているという神話 *the myth* of male superiority

す

す¹ 巣 (鳥・小動物・昆虫などの) nest ⓒ; (ハチの) honeycomb [hǎnikòum] ⓤ; (養蜂用の) beehive ⓒ; (クモの) (cob)web ⓒ; (獣の) den ⓒ ∥悪の巣 *a nest of vice* / 軒下に巣を作っているツバメがいる There are swallows「making their nest [nesting] under the eaves. / クモが巣を張ると翌日晴れると聞いたことがある I have heard when a spider spins [weaves] *a web*, the next day will be fine. ◆愛の巣 *one's love nest*

す² 酢 vinegar ⓤ ∥ラッキョウを酢に漬ける pickle [soak] shallots in *vinegar* / 酢の物 a vinegared dish / リンゴ酢 cider [apple] vinegar

ず 図 (図解) figure ⓒ; (挿絵) illustration ⓒ; (図表) chart ⓒ, graph ⓒ, diagram ⓒ; (線画) drawing ⓒ; (地図) map ⓒ ∥図2参照 See *Figure 2*. / 町の人口の変化を図にする(→図を作る) *make a graph* of the population changes in the town / 彼女は図を描いて実験のやり方を説明した She *drew a diagram* to explain how to do the experiment. ∥設計図 a plan / 地形図 a topographical map / 天気図 a weather chart [map] 慣用表現 彼はすぐに図に乗る He easily *gets carried away*.

すあし 素足 barefoot ⓒ ──素足の[で] barefoot(ed) ∥素足で歩く walk *barefoot* / 素足の子供 a *barefoot* [*barefooted*] child ◆素足に靴を履いている wear shoes *without socks*

ずあん 図案 design ⓒ ∥図案を描く draw *a design* / この校章の図案化したものだ The *design* of this school badge *is based on* a certain kind of bird.

すい 粋 (公式的の)essence ⓤ; (最良の部分) the best ∥日本文化の粋 the *essence* of Japanese culture ◆技術の粋を集めて作られた機械 a *state-of-the-art* machine

すい² 酸い 慣用表現 彼は世の中の酸いも甘いもかみ分けた人だ He *has tasted the sweets and the bitters of life.*

ずい 髄 〔植物〕 pith ⓤ; 〔解剖〕 (骨髄) marrow ⓤ

すいあげる 吸い上げる suck up; (ポンプで) pump (up) ∥ポンプで井戸から水を吸い上げる *pump* water *up* from a well ◆子会社の利益を吸い上げる *siphon away* the profits of a subsidiary

すいあつ 水圧 water [hydraulic] pressure ⓤ ∥水圧計 a water-pressure gauge

すいい¹ 水位 water level ⓤ ∥川の水位はいつもより高[低]かった The *water level* in the river was higher [lower] than usual.

すいい² 推移 (変化) change ⓒ ⓤ; (移行) transition ⓒ ⓤ ──推移する change ⓘ; (発展する) develop ⓘ ∥時代の推移とともに with *the change* of the times / 軍国主義から平和主義への推移 *the transition* from militarism to pacifism ◆事態の推移(→どうなるか)を見守るほかない There's nothing to do but to watch *how things will turn out*.

ずいい 随意 ──随意の(自由な) free; (自由に選択できる) optional ──随意に freely ⇒じゆう ∥ここにある物はご随意にお使いください You can use these things *freely*. ◆どうぞご随意に Please *do as you like*. ∥随意筋〔生理〕 a voluntary muscle / 不随意筋〔生理〕 an involuntary muscle

すいいき 水域 zone ⓒ, area ⓒ, (海域) waters ∥漁業専管水域 an exclusive fishery zone / 経済水域 an economic zone / 200海里水域 a 200-mile zone

ずいいち 随一 当代随一の学者 the greatest scholar of our time / その会社は自動車業界随一の売り上げを誇る The company's sales are *the largest* in the car industry.

スイートピー sweet pea

ずいいん 随員 (付き人) attendant ⓒ; (側近) 《集合的》 entourage ⓒ

すいえい 水泳 swim ⓒ, swimming ⓤ ∥水泳がうまい[下手だ] be good [poor] at *swimming*; be a good [poor] swimmer / プールへ水泳をしに行く go for a swim at [×to] the pool

彼女は週に2回水泳教室に通っている She takes *swimming lessons* twice a week. ◆私は父から水泳を習った I learned *how to swim* from my father. ∥水泳選手 a swimmer / 水泳大会 a swim(ming) meet / 水泳パンツ (米)bathing trunks, (英)swimming trunks / 水泳帽 a swimming cap
関連語 クロール (the) crawl / 個人メドレー an individual medley / 自由形 freestyle / 背泳 (the) backstroke / バタフライ (the) butterfly, (the) butterfly stroke / 平泳ぎ (the) breaststroke / メドレーリレー a medley relay

すいおん 水温 water temperature ⓤ

すいか 西瓜 watermelon ⓒ ⓤ ∥スイカ1切れ a slice of *watermelon* / 私たちはスイカ割りをした We *enjoyed trying to split a watermelon with a stick while blindfolded.*

すいがい 水害 (洪水) flood ⓒ; (洪水による被害) flood damage ⓤ, flood disaster ⓒ ∥水害の被害者 *flood* victims / 水害をもたらす cause *a flood* / この地域は毎年、深刻な水害に見舞われる This area suffers from severe *floods* every year.

すいがら 吸い殻 (cigarette) butt [end] ⓒ ∥吸いがら入れ an ashtray

すいきゅう 水球 〖スポーツ〗 water polo ⓤ

すいぎゅう 水牛 water buffalo ⓒ

すいきょ 推挙 (推薦) recommendation ⓤ; (指名) nomination ⓤ ──推挙する recommend [他]; nominate [他] ‖会長に推挙される *be* 「*nominated for* [*put forward as*] the president

すいきょう 酔狂 蛇をペットにするなんて君も酔狂な男だね You must be *crazy* to have a snake as a pet. / だてや酔狂でこの商売をやっているのではない I'm not doing this business *just for fun*.

すいぎん 水銀 〘化学〙 mercury [U] (❖元素記号Hg) ‖水銀柱(温度計・気圧計の) the mercury / 水銀中毒 mercury poisoning / 水銀電池 a mercury cell / 水銀灯 a mercury(-vapor) lamp [light]

すいけい 推計 (概算) estimate [C] ―推計する estimate [他][自]

すいげん 水源 (川の) the source [head] (of a river) ‖ナイル川は多くの水源を有する The Nile has a lot of *sources*. / この川の水源地はどこですか Where is *the source* of this river?/ Where does this river *rise from*?

すいこう[1] 推敲 ―推敲する (磨きをかける) polish [他]; (改良する) improve [他] ‖君のレポートはまだ推敲が足りない Your paper needs 「to *be polished* [more *polishing*].

すいこう[2] 遂行 execution [U], performance [U] ―遂行する execute [他], perform [他], carry out ‖任務を遂行する *execute* [*perform, carry out*] *one's* duty

ずいこう 随行 ―随行する accompany [他] ‖大勢の護衛が首相に随行した A large escort *accompanied* the prime minister.

‖随行員 an attendant / 随行団 a retinue

すいこみ 吸い込み この掃除機は吸い込みがいい[悪い] This vacuum cleaner *sucks up* dust well [badly].

‖吸い込み口 an intake

すいこむ 吸い込む (空気・息を) breathe [bríːð] (in), draw* (in); (吸収する) absorb [他], soak (up) ‖新鮮な空気を吸い込む *breathe* [*draw*] (*in*) fresh air / 乾いた地面は雨をみるみる吸い込んだ The dry ground *absorbed* [*soaked up*] the rain very quickly.

◆彼は深く息を吸い込んで水中に潜(もぐ)った He *took* [*drew*] *a* deep *breath* and dove into the water. / 滝つぼをのぞき込むと吸い込まれそうな感じだった When I looked down into the basin of the waterfall, I felt as if I *were* [*was*] *swallowed up* in it.

すいさい 水彩 水彩で絵を描く paint in *watercolors*

‖水彩絵の具 watercolors / 水彩画 a watercolor (painting) / 水彩画家 a watercolor painter

すいさつ 推察 guess [C] ―推察する guess [他][自]; (見聞したことから) gather [他] ‖ご推察のとおりです You *guessed* right./ *Your guess* is right. / 彼女の様子から困っているのだと推察した I *gathered* from her look that she was in trouble.

すいさん 水産 ‖水産業 fisheries [fishing] industry / 水産国 a fishing country / 水産資源 fishery resources / 水産試験場 a fisheries experiment [experimental] station / 水産大学 a fisheries college / 水産庁 the Fisheries Agency / 水産物 marine products / 農林水産省 the Ministry of Agriculture, Forestry and Fisheries

すいさんか 水酸化 ‖水酸化ナトリウム sodium hydroxide / 水酸化物 a hydroxide

すいし 水死 ―水死する drown [自], be drowned, drown *oneself* ⇒おぼれる ‖川で水死する *drown* [*be drowned*] in the river / 彼女は水死体で見つかった She was found *drowned*.

すいじ 炊事 (料理) cooking [U]; (台所仕事) kitchen work [U] ―炊事する cook [他][自] ‖炊事洗濯は自分でしている I do *the cooking and washing* by myself.

‖炊事道具 kitchen utensils / 炊事場 a kitchen

ずいじ 随時 (at) any time, always ‖その学校は随時生徒を募集している The school accepts applications *at any time*.

◆質問があったら随時私に聞いてください You can ask me *when* you have a question.

すいしつ 水質 water quality [U] ‖水質汚染 water pollution / 水質検査 (a) water analysis [examination]

すいしゃ 水車 waterwheel [C]

‖水車小屋 a water mill

すいじゃく 衰弱 ―衰弱した weak ―衰弱する become* weak ‖彼女は空腹で衰弱していた She was *weak* with [from] hunger. / その患者は日に日に衰弱してきている The patient *is becoming weaker* day by day.

すいじゅん 水準 (標準) standard [C][U]《しばしば複数形 〜s》; (程度) level [C][U]

学力水準を保つ maintain *a standard* of academic ability / 教育水準を高める improve *educational standards*

彼の書くものは水準以上[以下]だ His writing is *above* [*below*] *standard*.

彼女はすぐれたピアニストだが世界的水準には達していない She is a good pianist, but doesn't come up to *the international standards* [*level*].

その国の生活水準は飛躍的に上がった *The* 「*standard of living* [*living standard*] in that country has risen dramatically.

私の国の文化水準は高いと思う I think *the cultural level* of my country is high.

‖水準器 a level / 水準点〘測量〙 a bench mark

ずいしょ 随所 その渓谷では大小の滝が随所に(→渓谷の至る所に)見られる Various sizes of waterfalls can be seen *throughout* the gorge. / この映画は随所に(→たくさん)見せ場がある This film has *a lot of* good scenes.

すいしょう[1] 水晶 crystal [U] (❖「水晶製品」は[C]) ‖水晶体〘解剖〙 a (crystalline) lens / 水晶玉 a crystal ball / 水晶時計 a quartz clock [watch] / 紫水晶 an amethyst

すいしょう[2] 推奨 recommendation [U] ―推奨する recommend [他] ⇒すいせん(推薦), すすめる(勧める・薦める)

すいじょう 水上 水上で生活する live *on the*

water
‖水上競技 aquatic sports / 水上警察 the police that patrol waters; (川) the river police; (港湾) the port [harbor] police / 水上交通 water transportation / 水上自転車 a pedal boat / 水上スキー water-skiing / 水上飛行機 a seaplane, a hydroplane

すいじょうき 水蒸気 (気体の状態の水) vapor, 《英》vapour [U]; (湯気) steam [U]

すいしん[1] 水深 水深を測る measure [sound] *the depth of water* / この種類の魚は水深1,000メートルくらいのところに住んでいる This kind of fish lives at *depths* of about a thousand meters.
💬「この湖の水深はどれくらいですか」「5メートルくらいです」 "How *deep* is this lake? / What *depth* is this lake?" "It's about five meters deep [in depth]."

すいしん[2] 推進 ―推進する (促進する) promote [他]; (推し進める) push on [ahead]; (前進させる) propel [他] ‖世界平和を推進する *promote* world peace / 国民の強い反対にもかかわらず政府はその計画を推進した In spite of strong opposition from the people the government *pushed on* [*ahead*] *with* the plan. ◆彼女はそのチームの優勝の推進力となった She was *the driving force* behind the team's victory.

スイス Switzerland (❖公式名 the Swiss Confederation) ―スイス人 Swiss [C] ―スイス(人)の Swiss

すいすい (素早く) swiftly; (滞りなく) smoothly; (軽快に) lightly; (難なく) easily ‖アメンボは水面をすいすい移動できる Water striders can move *swiftly* on the surface of water. / 彼女は難しい仕事をすいすいと片づけてしまった She's finished the difficult work *easily* [*with ease*].

すいせい[1] 水性 ―水性の aqueous ‖水性塗料 water paint

すいせい[2] 水星 〔天文〕 Mercury

すいせい[3] 彗星 comet [C] (❖彗星の頭は coma, 核は nucleus, 尾は tail) ‖ハレー彗星 Halley's *Comet* / 百武彗星 *Comet* Hyakutake
[慣用表現] そのバンドは昨年，彗星のごとく音楽界に現れた The band「*came on* [*burst upon*] the music scene last year.

すいせい[4] 水生 ―水生の aquatic (❖通例名詞の前で用いる) ‖水生植物 an aquatic plant / 水生動物 an aquatic animal

すいせん[1] 推薦 recommendation [U] ―推薦する recommend [他]; (候補として指名する) nominate [他]
先生の推薦でこの辞書を買った I bought this dictionary *on* my teacher's *recommendation*.
彼女は私にその本を推薦した She *recommended*「the book to me [me the book].
私は彼を学級委員に推薦した I *recommended* him *for* [*as*] class representative.
推薦状を書いていただけるとありがたいのですが I would very much appreciate it if you could write me *a* (*letter of*) *recommendation*.
姉はその大学に推薦入学した My sister *was admitted to* the college *on* [*by*] *the recommendation* of her high school.
‖推薦候補 a recommended candidate / 推薦者 a recommender / 推薦図書 a recommended book

すいせん[2] 水仙 narcissus [C]; (ラッパズイセン) daffodil [C]; (キズイセン) jonquil [C]

すいせん[3] 垂線 perpendicular (line) [C] ‖垂線を引く draw *a perpendicular*

すいせんべんじょ 水洗便所 flush toilet [C]

すいそ 水素 〔化学〕 hydrogen [U] (❖元素記号 H) ‖水素爆弾 a hydrogen bomb, an H-bomb

すいそう[1] 吹奏 ―吹奏する play [自] [他] ➩えんそう ‖吹奏楽 wind (instrument) music / 吹奏楽団 a brass band / 吹奏楽器 a wind instrument

すいそう[2] 水槽 water tank [C]; (魚類を飼育する) aquarium [C] (複 ～s, aquaria)

すいそう[3] 水葬 ―水葬する give* *a person* a sea [river] burial

すいぞう 膵臓 〔解剖〕 pancreas [C]

ずいそう 随想 (おりおり思ったこと) occasional [random] thoughts; (随筆) essay [C]

すいそく 推測 guess [C]; (当てずっぽう) guesswork [U], 《公式的》 conjecture [C] [U]; (あれこれと) speculation [U] ―推測する guess [他] [自]; speculate [自] [他]; (見聞の内容から) gather [他] (❖進行形にはできない)
彼女の推測は当たった She *guessed right*. / Her *guess was right*.
我々は彼女が非常に教育のある女性だと推測した We *guessed*「(that) she was [her to be] well-educated.
彼の言葉から私に何か隠していると推測した I *gathered* from his words that he was hiding something from me.
それは私の推測したとおりだった That was just as I *had guessed*.
それは推測の域を出ない(→推測にすぎない) It's *only a guess*.

> [コロケーション] -guess-
> 〖形容詞＋～〗当てずっぽうな～ a wild guess / 大ざっぱな～ a rough guess / 鋭い～ a shrewd guess

すいぞくかん 水族館 aquarium [C] (複 ～s, aquaria)

すいたい 衰退 decline [U] 《また a ～》 ―衰退する decline [自] ‖ローマ帝国の衰退 *the decline* of the Roman Empire / その産業は衰退の一途をたどっている The industry *is*「*in terminal decline* [*steadily declining*].

すいだす 吸い出す (ポンプで) pump out (from ...); (口を使って) suck out (from ...) ➩すう(吸う)

すいちゅう 水中 ― 水中の underwater ―水中で[に] underwater, under water ‖水中には様々な生き物がすんでいる Various creatures live *underwater*. ◆彼は大きく息を

吸い込んで水中に潜(もぐ)った After taking a deep breath, he dove *into the water*. ‖水中カメラ an underwater camera / 水中眼鏡(水泳用) swimming goggles; (目・鼻を覆う) a diving [face] mask

すいちょく 垂直 ――垂直の(線・面と直角に交わる) perpendicular; (水平面に対して) vertical (↔horizontal) ――垂直に perpendicularly; vertically

垂直方向に in *a vertical direction* / 垂直に交わる2直線 two lines crossing *perpendicularly*

この線に垂直な線を引きなさい Draw a line *perpendicular* to this one.

彼は垂直に切り立った(→垂直な)がけを命綱なしで登っていった He climbed up the *vertical cliff* without a safety line.

‖垂直線 a vertical [perpendicular] line / 垂直跳び a vertical jump / 垂直二等分線 a vertical [perpendicular] line crossing at the center of another line / 垂直尾翼 a vertical fin

すいつく 吸い付く 子犬は母犬のお乳に吸いついてなかなか離れなかった The puppy kept *sucking at* its mother's teat and wouldn't leave it. / タコの吸盤が手に吸いついた The suckers of an octopus *stuck to* my hand. / 静電気で下敷きにほこりが吸いついた Dust *stuck to* a plastic sheet by the power of static electricity. ⇨つく(付く)

すいつける 吸い付ける 磁石がくぎを吸いつけた The magnet *attracted* a nail.

スイッチ switch ©/照明のスイッチ *a light switch* / スイッチを押す press *a switch* / スイッチが入っている[切れている] The switch *is on* [*off*].

◆CDプレーヤーのスイッチを入れる[切る] *switch on* [*off*] a CD player; *turn on* [*off*] a CD player / 彼のラジオにスイッチが入ったままだった[切れていた] His radio was *on* [*off*]. ‖スイッチバック〔鉄道〕 a switchback / スイッチヒッター〔野球〕 a switch hitter

すいてい 推定(推測) supposition ©Ⓤ; (見積もり) estimation ©; (推定する) suppose, judge ⊕ず; (見積もる) estimate ⊕ず ⇨すいそく/推定年齢 *a person's supposed age* / 洪水の被害者は1万人を超えると推定される The number of the victims of the flood *is supposed* [*estimated*] *to be* more than 10,000 people. / 彼らは土器の製作年代を推定した They *estimated* when the earthen pots were made.

すいてき 水滴 a drop of water, water drop ©

すいでん 水田 rice field ©, (rice) paddy ©
すいとう¹ 水筒 canteen ©, water bottle ©
すいとう² 出納 ‖出納係 a cashier; (銀行の) a teller; (会社などの) a treasurer / 出納簿 a cashbook

すいどう 水道

❶〔上水道〕(給水・設備) water supply Ⓤ/きょうの午後水道が止まる予定です The water *supply* will be cut off this afternoon.

このあたりにはまだ水道がない There is no *water supply* around here yet.

◆水道を出す[止める] *turn the faucet on* [*off*] / 水道を出しっぱなしにしたのはだれ Who left *the faucet* running? / この山小屋には水道が引かれていない *Water is not piped to* this mountain hut.

❷〔海峡〕strait ©(しばしば複数形 ~s), channel ©(❖strait よりも広い)

紀伊水道 the Kii *Channel*

‖水道管(引き込んだ) a water pipe; (本管) a water main / 水道局 the bureau of waterworks / 水道工事 construction [repairing] of a water main [pipe]; (建物内の) plumbing / 水道水 running [tap] water / 水道料金 water charges, 《英》a water rate / 下水道 a sewer

すいとる 吸い取る ❶〔液体などを〕(物が) absorb ⊕ず; (人・物が) soak (up); (掃除機などが) suck (up) ⇨すう(吸う) / このパジャマはよく汗を吸い取る These pajamas *absorb* [*soak up*] sweat well. / タオルでよく水気を吸い取ってください *Soak up* as much of the water as you can with a towel, please.

❷〔利益を〕(取る) take* ⊕; (搾取する) exploit ⊕; /彼より高い額を税金に吸い取られている A large amount of money *is taken* from his earnings as taxes.

すいなん 水難 ‖水難救助犬 a water rescue dog / 水難事故(川・湖・海などの事故) an accident on a river [a lake, the sea]; (溺死(でき)) a drowning

すいばく 水爆 hydrogen bomb ©, H-bomb ©/水爆実験 an H-bomb [a thermonuclear] test / 原水爆 atomic and hydrogen bombs

すいはんき 炊飯器 rice cooker ©/電気炊飯器 *an electric rice cooker*

ずいひつ 随筆 essay © ⇨ エッセー ‖随筆家 an essayist

すいふ 水夫 sailor ©

すいぶん 水分 (水) water Ⓤ; (湿気) moisture Ⓤ; (果汁) juice Ⓤ ⇨みず/肌に水分を与える supply *water* [*moisture*] to skin / 桃は水分が多い Peaches 「have a lot of *juice* [are *juicy*].

ずいぶん 随分

❶〔たいそう〕――ずいぶん(と) very, (very) much, a lot

> **語法**
> (1) very は形容詞, 副詞, 感情・心理状態を表す動詞の過去分詞(amused, interested など)とともに用いられる.
> (2) much は比較級, 最上級, 動詞の過去分詞を強めるために用いられる. very much は動詞の過去分詞や単に動詞を強めるために用いられる.
> (3) a lot は比較級, 動詞を強めるために用いられる.

きょうの彼女はずいぶん幸せそうだ She seems

to be *very* happy today.

けさはずいぶんと早起きした I got up *very* early this morning.

君の英語はずいぶん上達したね Your English has improved 「*very much* [*a lot*]」.

彼女はみんなからずいぶん愛されていたらしい She is said to have been 「*much* loved [*loved a lot*]」 by everybody.

母のぐあいもずいぶんよくなった My mother's gotten *much* [*a lot*] better.

◆ 彼女と初めて会ってからもうずいぶんになる It's been 「*quite a long time* [*a very long time*]」 since I first met her.

❷【ひどい】

約束の時間に3分遅れただけなのに僕を置いていっちゃうなんて，ずいぶんだなあ You were so *unkind* [*mean*] not to wait for me when I was only three minutes late for the appointed time.

🗨 「あんなやつ，どうなったって知るもんか」「ずいぶんなことを言うね」 "I don't care what's going to happen to him!" "You're so *hard on him*."

すいへい¹ 水平 ──水平な（平らな）level, even;（垂直に対して）horizontal（↔vertical）∥水平方向に in *a horizontal direction* / はかりは水平な場所に置いて使いましょう Scales should be used on a *level* [*an even*] surface. / 両腕を広げて床と水平に保ちなさい Spread your arms and keep them *horizontal* (*to the floor*). ◆ 太陽が水平線に沈んだ The sun has sunk below *the horizon*.

∥水平尾翼 a horizontal tail / 水平面 a horizontal plane

すいへい² 水兵 sailor Ⓒ,《海軍》seaman Ⓒ

すいほう¹ 水泡（ひと粒の泡）bubble Ⓒ（しばしば複数形 ～s），foam Ⓤ（❖bubble が集まってきたもの）➡ あわ(泡)

慣用表現 彼女の失敗ですべては水泡に帰した All 「*went up in smoke* [(→むだになった)*came to nothing*]」 due to her failure.

すいほう² 水疱（水ぶくれ）blister Ⓒ

すいぼくが 水墨画 🖼 a *suibokuga*, a black-and-white [monochrome] painting in India ink

すいぼつ 水没 submersion Ⓤ ──水没する [させる] submerge 自他 / その地区はダム湖に水没する予定 The district is going to be *submerged* in the dam lake.

すいま 睡魔（眠気）sleepiness Ⓤ, drowsiness Ⓤ ➡ ねむけ / 彼は電車を乗り過ごさないよう必死に睡魔と闘っていた He struggled against *sleepiness* [*drowsiness*] so as not to miss his train stop. ◆ 勉強中激しい睡魔に襲われた(→すごく眠くなった) I *got* very *sleepy* [*drowsy*] when I was studying.

ずいまくえん 髄膜炎〔医学〕meningitis Ⓤ

すいません Excuse me.;（ごめんなさい）I'm sorry. ➡ すみません

すいみゃく 水脈（地下水脈）an underground vein of water

すいみん 睡眠 sleep Ⓤ（また a ～）❖ ねむる / 十分な睡眠をとることはだいじなことだ It is important to *get enough sleep*.

きょうは睡眠不足です（→ゆうべ十分に睡眠をとっていない）I *didn't get enough sleep* last night.

ここ数日，試験勉強のために睡眠時間を削っている I have cut down *my hours of sleep* for the last few days to study for the examination.

◆ 彼女はたいてい8時間睡眠をとる She usually *sleeps* eight hours.

∥睡眠薬 a sleeping drug;（錠剤）a sleeping pill / レム[ノンレム]睡眠 REM [non-REM] sleep

すいめん 水面 the surface of the water

◆ 水面に浮かぶ float *on the water* / 湖の水面はきらきら光っていた The *surface* of the lake was sparkling. / 落ち葉が池の水面に浮かんでいた Fallen leaves were floating *on the surface* of the pond.

慣用表現 水面下で（→ひそかに）交渉が進められた They carried on negotiations *secretly*.

すいもの 吸い物 🖼

吸い物はみそ汁と並ぶ日本の代表的な汁物です。かつお節やこんぶのあっさりしただし汁に塩・しょうゆ・酒を加え，とり肉や魚，野菜を入れます。とり肉と魚は汁からにごらないようにあらかじめ火を通しておきます。
Suimono is one of the typical Japanese soups (the other one is *misoshiru*). It is a clear soup consisting of a light stock made from *katsuobushi* (dried bonito) or *kombu* (kelp) and seasoned with salt, soy sauce and sake. *Suimono* is served with chicken or fish and vegetables in it. The chicken or fish is cooked before being put into the soup in order to preserve the clarity of the broth.

すいもん 水門 water gate Ⓒ, floodgate Ⓒ;（ダムのせき）sluice Ⓒ

すいようせい 水溶性 ──水溶性の water-soluble

すいようび 水曜日 Wednesday Ⓤ Ⓒ (《略語》Wed.) ➡ にちようび

すいり¹ 推理 reasoning Ⓤ;（推論）inference Ⓤ Ⓒ ──推理する reason 自（❖他動詞の場合，後ろに that 節がくる）; infer 他 / 推理を働かせる show *one's* 「*reasoning ability* [*ability to reason*]」 / その少年の推理は正しいことが分かった The boy's *reasoning* was found to be right.

∥推理小説 a mystery (story),《口語的》a whodunit;（探偵小説）a detective story

すいり² 水利（灌漑かんがい）irrigation Ⓤ;（水上輸送の）convenience to water transportation ∥水利権 water rights

すいりく 水陸 land and water

◆ 水陸両用車 *amphibious* vehicles

すいりょう¹ 推量 guess Ⓒ;（推論）inference Ⓤ Ⓒ ──推量する guess 自他; infer 他 ➡ すいそく, コミュニケーションスキル p.749

∥当て推量 a wild guess, guesswork

すいりょう² 水量 the volume of water

コミュニケーションスキル —推量—

①think, believe, suppose, guess などの動詞を使って表す場合

(A) I'm looking forward to tomorrow's hike. What will the weather be like?
—**I think** it'll be fine.
あしたのハイキング，楽しみだなあ．天気はどうかなあ．—晴れると思うよ．

(B) I hear Tom will take the entrance exam for Springfield University.
—**I believe** he will pass it this time.
トムがスプリングフィールド大学の入試を受けるそうだよ．—今回は合格すると思うよ．

(C) My parents are on a trip to Europe.
—**I'm sure** they are having a good time.
両親がヨーロッパ旅行に出かけているんです．—きっと楽しんでいるでしょうね．

(D) Do you think Sue will come to today's class reunion?
—**I'm afraid** she won't.
スーはきょうの同窓会に来るかい？—たぶん来ないと思うよ．

(E) Where is Bill? Hasn't he come yet?
—**I suppose** he has missed the bus again.
ビルはどこにいるんだ．まだ来ていないの？—またバスに乗り遅れたんじゃないかな．

(F) **I guess** he's over forty.
彼は40を過ぎていると思うよ．

☞ 推量を表す代表的な動詞には，think, believe, suppose, guess がある．これらの動詞の中では，think が最も使用範囲が広い．

☞ (B)の believe は think よりもう少し確信がある場合に用い，(E)の suppose は「(何らかの根拠に基づいて)推定する」ことをいう．(F)の guess は Guess who? (だれだか当ててごらん)のような使い方から分かるように，「推量する」の意味で用いられる．

☞ (C)の be sure (that) ... は「きっと…だと思う」の意味で，確信をもって何かを推量する場合に用いる．

☞ (D)の be afraid (that) ... は「残念だが…」のように，好ましくないことを推測する表現．また，口語では I'm afraid not. のように，that 以下の内容を not で代表させていうのがふつう．

②助動詞を使って表す場合

(A) Alex **may** possibly come to see us.
アレックスはひょっとすると私たちに会いに来るかもしれない．

(B) Tina **will be** waiting for your call.
ティナは君からの電話を待っているでしょう．

(C) It **cannot be** true.
そんなことは本当であるはずがない．

(D) Bob **cannot have done** such a silly thing.
ボブがそんなばかげたことをしたはずがない．

(E) It **must be** true.
それは本当にちがいない．

☞ 推量を表す助動詞としては may, will, can, must がある．これらはしばしば probably (おそらく), perhaps (たぶん), possibly (ひょっとすると)などの可能性を表す副詞といっしょに用いられる．

☞ (B)の will be＋現在分詞は未来進行形と呼ばれ，ある時点で進行していると予想される出来事を表す．

☞ can は (C)の It cannot be .... のように否定文で用いると，「…であるはずがない」という推量を表すことがある．(D)の cannot have＋過去分詞は，過去の出来事について「…したはずがない」と推量を述べる表現．

☞ (E)の must は「…にちがいない」という断定の推量を表す．推量を表す助動詞の中では，この must が最も確実性が高い．

③その他の語句を使って表す場合

(A) **It's likely** my wife will agree with me.
妻はおそらく私に賛成してくれるだろう．

(B) **Chances are** he will win first place in the tennis tournament.
彼はおそらくそのテニス選手権大会で優勝するだろう．

(C) **There is a strong [high] possibility** of heavy snow tomorrow.
あしたはきっと大雪になるだろう．

(D) She will give you a call later **for sure**.
彼女は後できっと電話をしてきますよ．

(E) **Ten to one** she will accept his proposal.
十中八九，彼女は彼のプロポーズを受け入れるだろう．

(F) How about going to a movie?
—**Sounds like** a good idea.
映画を見に行かない？—いいね．

(G) I think he will be elected president this time.
—**Could be.**
彼が今度は大統領に選ばれると思うね．—かもね［かもしれないね］．

☞ (A)は My wife is likely to agree with me. と言い換えることができる．推定の可能性を高めるには **It's very likely ...** とか **It's quite likely ...** などとする．

☞ (B)の (The) Chances are (that) ... は，(A) It's likely ... のくだけた表現．

☞ (D)の for sure は **for certain** ともいうが，for sure のほうが多く用いられる．

☞ (E)の ten to one は **nine times out of ten** (十中八九)ともいえる．

☞ (F)は (That) sounds like ... (…のように聞こえる)の意味で，様態を表す表現．That's a good idea. という断定を避けた，一種の遠回しの推量．

☞ (G)は Could be. ＝ **Maybe.** (おそらく［たぶん］)の意味で，口語でしばしば使われるくだけた言い方．

すいりょく

◆川の水量が増した The river *rose*.
‖水量計 a water meter [gauge]

すいりょく¹ 水力 water power ⓤ ——水力の hydraulic ‖水力発電 water power (generation) / 水力発電所 a hydroelectric power plant, a water power plant

すいりょく² 推力〔力学〕thrust ⓤ

すいれい 水冷 水冷式エンジン a *water-cooled* engine

すいれん 睡蓮 water lily ⓒ

すいろ 水路 waterway ⓒ, watercourse ⓒ;(運河) canal ⓒ;(航路) channel ⓒ(しばしば複数形~s) ◆水路で *by water*

すいろん 推論 inference ⓒ, reasoning ⓤ, deduction ⓒⓤ ——推論する infer ⓐ, reason ⓐⓘ, deduce ⓐ (❖ reason の他動詞、deduce は後々に that 節をとる) / これらの事実から彼は以下のように推論した From these facts, he *inferred* the following.

スイング 〔スポーツ〕swing ⓒ;〔音楽〕swing (music) ⓤ ——スイングする〔スポーツ〕swing* ⓐ ‖鋭くスイングする take a sharp *swing*; *swing* sharply

すう¹ 吸う (空気を) breathe [bríːð] (in), inhale ⓐⓘ; (しゃぶる) suck ⓐⓘ; (吸収する) absorb ⓐⓘ;(たばこを) smoke ⓐⓘ
新鮮な空気を吸う *breathe* the fresh air
息を吸って、吐いて *Breathe in*, breathe out.
赤ん坊は母親のおっぱいを吸った The baby *sucked* (at) its mother's breast.
このシャツは汗をよく吸う This shirt *absorbs* sweat well.
⦿「たばこを吸ってもかまいませんか」「ええ、どうぞ」"Do you mind if I *smoke*?" "Not at all."

すう² 数 number ⓒ;〔文法〕number ⓒⓤ
➡かず ‖正の数 a positive *number* [quantity]

(1) 数(+)の概念を表す語形の変化を数(+)という。英語の名詞には、1つのものを表す単数形(singular number)と2つ以上のものを表す複数形(plural number)の区別がある。通例、複数形は、単数形の語形の変化で表される。最も一般的なのは、単数形に-s/ -es を付けて作る作り方である。動詞は、その文の主語の数によって支配され、代名詞は受ける名詞の数によって形が変わる / The *boy admires his* teacher. その少年は先生を尊敬している / The *boys admire their* teacher. その少年たちは先生を尊敬している
(2) しかし、名詞が複数形でも単数扱いされるものや、単数形でも複数扱いされるものもある(➡しゅうごうめいし) / Some *people are* very shy. とても恥ずかしがり屋の人たちがいる

すう- 数- several, some, a few ‖数年 a *few* years / 私は数人の男に取り囲まれた I was surrounded by *several* men.

◆この公園には数百本のカシの木がある There are *hundreds of* oak trees in this park.

スウェーデン Sweden (❖ 公式名 the Kingdom of Sweden) ——スウェーデン人 Swede ⓒ ——スウェーデン語 Swedish ⓤ ——スウェーデン(人[語])の Swedish

すうがく 数学 mathematics,《米口語的》math,《英口語的》maths(❖ いずれも単数扱い) ——数学の mathematical ‖私は数学が不得意だ I'm not very good at *mathematics*. ‖数学者 a mathematician

すうき 数奇 ——数奇な (波乱に富んだ) checkered, varied ‖数奇な運命をたどる have a *checkered* fortune

すうきけい 枢機卿〔カトリック〕cardinal ⓒ

すうこう 崇高 ——崇高な(公式的) sublime, noble; (思想などが高遠な) lofty ‖崇高な宗教心 *sublime* devotion to *one's* religion

すうし 数詞〔文法〕numeral ⓒ

数を表す語。1つ、2つ、3つともの数を数えるときに用いる基数詞(cardinal number)と第1、第2、第3と順序を表すときに用いる序数詞(ordinal number)がある.

[基数詞] *four* books 4冊の本 / *Four times seven is twenty-eight*. 4かける7は28(4 × 7 = 28)
[序数詞] the *first* president 初代大統領 / January (the) *first* 1月1日

すうじ 数字 (数) number ⓒ; (数値・アラビア数字) figure ⓒ; (文字としての) numeral ⓒ; (計算)《口語的》figures
数字の 1 the numeral 1 / 4けたの数字 a four-digit *number* / 正確な数字 an exact *figure* / 数字を合計する add *the figures* up / 具体的な数字を挙げる *give* actual *figures*
7は縁起のよい数字だと信じられている Seven is believed to be *a lucky number*.
この報告書の数字を信用できますか Can you trust *the figures* in this report?
母は数字に弱い My mother is poor at *figures*.
‖アラビア数字(総称) Arabic numerals [numbers] / 漢数字(総称) Chinese numerals [numbers] / ローマ数字(総称) Roman numerals [numbers]

すうしき 数式 numerical expression ⓒ; (等式) numerical equation ⓒ ➡巻末付録 (数と数式)

すうじつ 数日 some days, several days;(2、3日) a few days ‖そのチケットは数日で売り切れた The tickets sold out in *a few days*.

◆ここ数日いい天気が続いている The good weather has held *for the last few days*.

すうじゅう 数十《口語的》dozens (❖ dozen は本来「12」の意味、×tens とはいわない) / 彼はもう数十回もその地を訪れたことがある He has been there *dozens of* times.

ずうずうしい 図々しい (厚かましい)《公式的》impudent, bold; (恥知らずな) shameless; (生意気な) cheeky ——ずうずうしく impudently, boldly; shamelessly ‖お前、彼女にプロポーズするなんてずうずうしいにも程があるぞ It would be too *impudent* of you to propose to her. / 彼はずうずうしくもまた金を借りにやってきた *Shamelessly*, he came by again to borrow money.

◆あいつはなんてずうずうしいやつなんだ(→神

が図太い) He's *got a lot of nerve*.

すうせい 趨勢 (傾向) tendency ⓒ; (大勢) trend ⓒ, drift ⓒⓤ //世論のすう勢を見きわめる judge *the trends* in public opinion
◆時代のすう勢(→流れ)にあらがう go against *the flow of the times*

ずうたい 図体 body ⓤ (体格) frame ⓤⓒ //あいつは図体ばかり大きくて何の役にも立たない Though he has *a large frame* [Though he's big], he's of no use at all.

すうだん 数段 テニスの腕前ではあなたは彼より数段上だ You play tennis *much better* than he [him].

すうち 数値 value ⓒ ⇨あたい

スーツ suit ⓒ //スーツを着る「put on [wear] *a suit* / その新しいスーツ, よく似合っているよ You look nice in that new *suit*.

スーツケース suitcase

すうねん 数年 some years, several years; (2, 3年) a few years //数年後彼らは結婚した *A few years later* they married.
◆30数年 30-*odd years* / ここ数年で様々な変化があった There have been many changes *in recent years*.

スーパー ⚠(スーパーマーケット) supermarket ⓒ; (字幕) subtitles //スーパーに買い物に行く go shopping *at a supermarket*
‖スーパーコンピュータ a supercomputer / スーパースター a superstar / スーパーヒーロー a superhero / スーパーマーケット a supermarket / スーパーマン(超人) a superman; (米国漫画の主人公) Superman / スーパーモデル a supermodel

すうはい 崇拝 admiration ⓤ, worship ⓤ; (神に対する) adoration ⓤ ──崇拝する admire ⓗ, worship ⓗⓒ; adore ⓗ //彼はそのピアニストを崇拝している He *admires* [*worships*] that pianist.
‖偶像崇拝 the worship of idols

スープ soup ⓤⓒ; (だし汁) stock ⓤⓒ //1杯のスープ a bowl of *soup* / 濃い[薄い]スープ thick [thin] *soup* / けさスープを飲みました I ate [had] some *soup* this morning. (✤スプーンを使った場合の表現. スプーンを使わずに直接カップから飲むときは drink soup という)
‖スープ皿 a soup plate / コーンスープ corn soup / 固形スープ a stock cube / チキン[オニオン]スープ chicken [onion] soup

ズーム カメラは遠くにいる象の群れをズームインした The camera *zoomed in on* a distant herd of elephants.
‖ズームレンズ a zoom lens

すうりょう 数量 (分量) quantity ⓒⓤ; (総数) number ⓒⓤ ⇨ぶんりょう

すうれつ 数列 《数学》 progression ⓒⓤ
‖等差[比]数列 an arithmetic [a geometric] progression

すえ 末
❶ 〖終わり〗 the end
3月の末に *at the end of* March
今月の末までにこの宿題を終えなければならない I must finish this homework *by the end of* this month.
◆うちの末の息子 our *youngest* son / 警察官による犯罪がこう多発するんじゃ世も末だ(→世の中はどうなってしまうんだろう) There have been a lot of crimes by police officers recently. *What is the world coming to*?
❷ 〖…の後で〗 after
長い議論の末 *after* a long debate
これはよく考えた末に出した答えです I reached this answer *after some hard thinking*.
❸ 〖前途〗 future ⓒ
この青年は末が楽しみだ This young man 「*has a future* [*is promising*].
◆末永くお幸せに I hope you will be happy *for many years*.

スエード suede ⓤ //スエードの靴 *suede* shoes

すえおき 据え置き (凍結) freeze ⓒ; (支払いなどの延期)《公式的》deferment ⓤⓒ //会社側は賃金の据え置きを発表した The company announced *a wage freeze*.
‖据え置き期間 a period of deferment

すえおく 据え置く (凍結する) freeze* ⓗ; (支払いなどを延期する) defer ⓗ, put* off //賃金の支払いを据え置く *defer* the payment of wages / タクシー運賃は当面据え置かれることになった It was decided that the taxi fares would *be frozen* for the time being.

すえおそろしい 末恐ろしい (将来に不安のある) ominous ◆この男の子にはこんな小さいうちから大人を負かしてしまうのだから末恐ろしい(→この先どうなるのだろう) Even at his age, this boy can beat adults. *What will become of him in the future*?

スエズうんが スエズ運河 the Suez Canal

すえつけ 据え付け (取りつけ) installation ⓤ; (セットすること) the setting ──据えつけの fixed //据えつけの食器棚 a *fixed* cupboard

すえつける 据え付ける (取りつける) install ⓗ; (セットする) set* ⓗ; (固定する) fix ⓗ //オフィスに新しいコピー機が据えつけられた A new photocopy machine *was installed* in the office.

すえっこ 末っ子 the youngest (child),《口語的》the baby //末っ子は甘やかされる傾向がある *The youngest* tends to get spoiled.

スエットスーツ《米》sweat suit ⓒ

すえる 据える (置く) set* ⓗ, place ⓗ, (高い所に) mount ⓗ; (しっかり固定する) fix ⓗ //彫刻を台座の上に据える *mount* a statue on a pedestal
〖慣用表現〗社長は自分の息子を後がまに据えた(→地位を継がせた) The president *made* his son *his successor*.

ずが 図画 (鉛筆・ペンなどで描くこと) drawing ⓤ; (絵の具などで描くこと) painting ⓤ (✤描かれた絵を意味する場合はいずれも ⓒ)
◆図画の時間 *art* class

スカート skirt ⓒ
ひざ丈⑱のスカート *a knee-length skirt* / スカートをはく put on *a skirt*
そのブラウスはこの赤いスカートによく似合う That blouse matches this red *skirt*.

‖キュロットスカート culottes (❖×culotte skirt とはいわない) / ジャンパースカート《米》a jumper,《英》a pinafore / タイトスカート a tight skirt / フレアスカート flares / 巻きスカート a wraparound skirt / ミニスカート a miniskirt / ロングスカート a long skirt

スカーフ scarf [C] (複 ~s, scarves) ‖スカーフを首に巻く wear *a scarf* around *one's* neck

ずかい 図解 illustration [C] [U]; (図) diagram [C], figure [C] ―図解する illustrate [他]; diagram [他] ‖その先生は授業でよく図解説明をする The teacher often uses *illustrations* in his class.

ずがいこつ 頭蓋骨 skull [C]

スカイダイビング skydiving [U] ―スカイダイビングをする skydive [自]

スカイライン ⚠(景色のよいドライブウェー) scenic drive [C]

スカウト (スカウトマン) (talent) scout [C]
◆彼は新しい選手をスカウトしに(→探しに)アメリカに渡った He went to America to *scout for* new players. / 彼女はモデルとしてスカウトされた She *was scouted* (*and employed*) as a model.

すがお 素顔 (化粧をしていない顔) a face without makeup ◆彼女は素顔のほうがきれいだと思う I think she is more beautiful *without makeup.* / その俳優はだれにも本当の素顔を見せようとしなかった That actor would not show *his true face* to anybody. / この番組では京都の素顔に迫ります In this program, we will examine the *real* Kyoto.

すかさず at once, immediately; (…するとすぐに) as soon as, the moment ➩すぐ ‖彼はボールを受けるとすかさずシュートを決めた *The moment* he got the ball, he made a goal.

すかし 透かし watermark [C] ‖この外国紙幣には花の透かし模様が入っている This foreign bill has *a watermark* of flowers.

すかす[1] 透かす (物を通して見る) see* … through ~; (目を凝らす) peer into … ‖暗やみを透かして見る *peer into* the darkness
◆すりガラスの窓を透かして外を見た I looked out *through* the frosted glass window. / 封筒を明かりに透かして見た I *held* the envelope *up to* the light.

すかす[2] 空かす (腹を) be hungry
◆子供たちは腹をすかして彼女の帰りを待っていた The children waited *hungrily* for her return./ The *hungry* children waited for her return.

すかすか 給料日の前だから冷蔵庫はすかすかです It's before payday, so the refrigerator is *almost empty.* / 骨粗鬆(こつそしょう)症は患者の骨がすかすかになる病気だ Osteoporosis is a disease in which the patient's bones become *overly porous.*

ずかずか (無遠慮に) rudely ‖男はずかずか私の家に上がり込んできた The man came *rudely* into my house.

すがすがしい 清々しい refreshing, fresh ‖早朝のすがすがしい空気 *fresh* air in the early morning ◆久しぶりに運動をしてすがすがしい気分になった I felt *refreshed* when I exercised for the first time in a long time.

すがた 姿

❶【外観】(体つき) figure [C]; (外観) appearance [U] [C]; (形) shape [C] [U]; (心に描く像) image [C]

〘~(の)姿〙
人の姿をした化け物 a monster *in human shape* [*form*]
遠くに人の姿が見えた I saw *a human figure* in the distance.
彼女は公園でみすぼらしい姿をした老人に出会った She met an old man of *shabby appearance* in the park.
彼らは彼女のあで姿に見とれた They were fascinated by her *alluring figure* [*appearance*].
◆姉はゆかた姿で出かけた My sister went out *in her yukata.* / 彼がケーキを作っている姿なんて想像できない I can't imagine *him baking cakes.*

〘姿が・は〙
今でも彼の姿が脳裏に焼きついている His *image* [*appearance*] is still imprinted on my brain.
この山は姿が富士山に似ているといわれている It is said that this mountain resembles Mt. Fuji *in shape.*
◆すでに男の姿はそこになかった The man *had* already *disappeared.*

〘姿を〙
◆母親の姿を見て子供は泣きだした *At the sight of* her mother, the child began to cry. / 選手たちがフィールドに姿を現すと，ファンから声援が起きた The fans cheered when the players *appeared* on the field. / 恐竜は大昔に地球上から姿を消した Dinosaurs *disappeared* from the earth a long time ago. / それ以来彼の姿を見かけた者はいない Nobody *has seen* him since (then). / 人込みの中で母の姿を見失った I *lost* my mother in the crowd. / 彼はやみに乗じて姿をくらました He *went into hiding* under cover of darkness.

❷【ありさま】(状況) state [C]
彼は島の現在の姿を人々に伝えようとした He tried to tell people about *the* present *state* of the island.
破壊された自然が元の姿を取り戻すまでには気の遠くなるような時間がかかる It takes a huge amount of time to restore nature that has been destroyed to *its* original *state.*
◆その町は昔の姿を今にとどめている The town has been preserved *as it used to be.*

すがたみ 姿見 full-length mirror [C]

スカッシュ〘スポーツ〙squash [U], rackets《単数扱い》

すかっと すかっとする飲み物 a *refreshing* drink / 大声で歌ったら気分がすかっとした I *felt refreshed* after singing loudly.

スカル (ボート) scull [C]; (競技) sculls

すがる 縋る (しがみつく) cling* to …; (もた

れる・頼る) lean* on [upon] ...; (縋る) depend on [upon] ... ⇨ しがみつく, たよる 《つえにすがって歩く walk *by leaning on* a stick / 彼女は夫にすがって生きてゆこうなどとは全く考えていなかった She never thought that she would have to *depend on* her husband to live.

すかれる 好かれる 《人に好かれる性格 an *amiable* disposition ⇨ すく(好く)

ずかん 図鑑 illustrated [picture] book ⓒ 《植物図鑑 an illustrated [a picture] book of plants

スカンク 〔動物〕 skunk ⓒ

スカンジナビア Scandinavia(《略語》Scand.)
―― スカンジナビア人 Scandinavian ⓒ ――
スカンジナビア(人)の Scandinavian

すき¹ 好き

like ⓣⓘ; be fond of ...; care for ...; love ⓣⓘ; prefer ... (to 〜) ―― 好きな favorite (◆名詞の前で用いる. また「いちばん好きな」という意味が含まれているので比較変化はしない)

like:「好き」を表す最も一般的な語.
be fond of ...: like よりも強意. 長い間, 気に入っているものについて用いる.
care for ...: やや公式的. 否定文, 疑問文で用いる.
love:「大好き」の意味.
prefer:「…の方が好き」の意味.
(◆上記の語句はいずれも進行形にはしない)

語法 「…するのが好き」という場合, like の後にはふつう不定詞と動名詞が区別なく用いられるが, 特定の具体的な行為をいう場合には不定詞, その行為一般をいう場合には動名詞, と区別して用いることもある. 《君のチームとサッカーをするのが好きだ I *like to play* soccer with your team. / 私はサッカーをするのが好きだ I *like playing* soccer.

〖好きだ・好きです〗
私は明るい色が好きだ I *like* bright colors.
僕は海辺を散歩するのが好きだ I *like* walking [to walk] by the sea.
私はラップが大好きです I *like* rap *very much.* / I'm *very fond of* rap. / I *love* rap *so much.* (◆最後の例の I love ... so much. は女性がよく用いる表現)
私は都会で暮らすほうが好きだ I *prefer* living in the city.
浩二のどこがいちばん好きなの What do you *like* best about Koji?
❢ 「夏と冬ではどちらのほうが好きですか」「夏のほうが好きです」"Which do you *like* better, summer or winter?" "I *like* summer better."
❢ 「どんな種類の映画が好きですか」「アクション映画が好きです」"What kind of movies do you *like*?" "I *like* action movies."
❢ 「あいつこの冬20回もスキーに行ったらしいぞ」「あいつも好きだねえ」"I hear he went skiing 20 times this winter." "How *crazy* of him!"

英作文ノート like の後は単数, 複数？
私は猫は好きだが犬は嫌いだ
→ ×I like *a cat* but not a dog.
→ ○I like *cats* but not dogs.
★一般的な好みをいうとき, 目的語に数えられる名詞がくる場合は複数形になる.

英作文ノート prefer のとる前置詞は？
私は紅茶よりコーヒーのほうが好きだ
→ ×I *prefer* coffee *than* tea.
→ ○I *prefer* coffee *to* tea.
→ ○I *like* coffee *better than* tea.
★prefer は like better の意味だが, 前置詞は to をとることに注意.

〖好きな〗
好きな作家はだれですか Who's your *favorite* writer?
好きなだけ食べていいぞ You can eat *as much as you like.*
どこでも好きな所に行っていいよ You may go *anywhere you like.*
好きなようにしなさい Do *as you like.*
どちらの服でも好きなほうを買ってあげよう I'll buy you *whichever* dress *you like.*

〖好きに〗
彼の話し方がどうも好きになれない I *don't like* [*care for*] the way he talks.
近ごろ突然カキが好きになった Suddenly I *came to like* oysters recently. (◆come to do は「…するようになる」の意味)
私は素朴で正直な村人たちが好きになった I *became* [*grew*] *fond of* the simple and honest villagers.
どうか僕の好きにやらせてください Please let me do *whatever I like.* / Please let me *go my own way.*
◆彼女はひとめでその青年が好きになった (→恋した) She *fell in love with* the young man at first sight. / (→好意をいだいた) She *warmed to* the young man at first sight.

ことわざ 好きこそものの上手なれ What you like, you do well.

すき² 隙

❶〔時間・空間の空き〕opening ⓒ, room ⓤ 《割り込む隙を探す look for *room* to cut in
◆老人は仕事の隙をみては思い出話を聞かせてくれた The old man told me stories of his past *whenever he could find time* during work.

❷〔油断〕(油断しているとき) unguarded moment ⓒ; (機会) chance ⓒ ⇨ ゆだん
彼は看守の隙に乗じて脱走した *Taking advantage of* the guard's *unguarded moment*, he ran away.
猫はハトに飛びかかる隙をうかがっていた The cat *watched for a chance* to spring at a pigeon.
◆彼女の議論には寸分の隙もない Her argument *doesn't leave any opening(s).* / 油断したすきに相手チームに得点されてしまった The other team scored a goal *when we were off guard.*

すき³ 鋤 (牛・トラクターなどで引く) plow, 《英》 plough [pláu] ⓒ; (シャベル状の) spade ⓒ ∥すきで地面を掘る dig the ground with a spade ◆畑をすきで耕す plow (up) a field

すぎ 杉 Japanese cedar ⓒ ∥杉花粉 cedar pollen

-すぎ -過ぎ

❶【時刻・年齢】 (時刻) past, after; (年齢) over

7時10分過ぎ ten (minutes) *past* seven / 寝たのは12時過ぎだった It was *past* twelve when I went to bed. / 彼女の赤ちゃんは真夜中過ぎに生まれた Her baby arrived *just after* midnight. / 彼は若く見えるが、実際は50過ぎだ He looks young, but actually he is *over* [*past*] 50.

❷【程度】 too

食べすぎは健康によくない Eating *too much* is bad for the health. / きょうは寒すぎも暑すぎもしない It's *neither too cold nor too hot* today.
◆スピードの出しすぎは事故の元だ *Speeding* causes accidents.
🅔「日本人は働きすぎだね」「全く」 "I think Japanese *work too much* [*hard*]." "Absolutely."

-ずき -好き (愛好者) lover ⓒ, fan ⓒ ∥映画好き a movie *lover* / 彼は野球好きで有名だ He is well known as *a baseball fan*.
◆彼は酒好きだ He *is fond of drinking*. / 彼は大の犬好きだ He *loves* dogs very much.

スキー skiing ⓤ; (板) skis (❖数えるときは a pair of ... とする) ──**スキーをする** ski ⓘ (❖ ×do ski や ×play ski とはいわない) ⇨ スキーとスノーボード p.755 ∥蔵王へスキーをしに行く *go skiing* in Zao / ここでスキーが借りられます You can rent *skis* here. / スキーをしていて足を骨折した I broke my leg while *skiing*. / 彼はスキーが上手[下手]だ He is good [bad] at *skiing*. / 彼はスキーヤーだ He is a good [poor] *skier*.
∥スキーウエア skiwear, a ski suit / スキー靴 (a pair of) ski boots / スキー場 (リゾート地) a ski resort; (ゲレンデ) a ski slope / スキー帽 a ski cap / スキーヤー a skier / スキーリフト a ski lift

すきかって 好き勝手 彼はいつも好き勝手な行動をする He always *does whatever he wants*. / 彼女はその城の中を好き勝手に歩き回った She walked around in the castle *just as she pleased*.

すききらい 好き嫌い likes and dislikes ∥彼女は食べ物に好き嫌いがない She has no *likes and dislikes* about food.
◆彼は食べ物の好き嫌いが激しい He *is particular about* food. / He is *a picky eater*.

すきこのんで 好き好んで by choice ∥なにも好き好んでこんな狭い家に住んでいるんじゃないよ I don't live in such a small house *by choice*.

すぎさる 過ぎ去る pass by, go* by ∥過ぎ去りし夏の思い出 memories of the summer that *has passed* [*gone*] *by* / 3年の歳月はあっという間に過ぎ去った Three years *have passed* [*gone*] *by* so quickly.

すきずき 好き好き (好み) taste ⓒⓤ ∥食器も人によって好き好きがある Everyone has *their own tastes* in things like dishes.
ことわざ たで食う虫も好き好き ⇨ たで

ずきずき ──ずきずきする (脈打つように痛む) throb ⓘ ∥ずきずきする頭の痛み a *throbbing* pain in the head / 歯がずきずき痛む My tooth *is throbbing* with pain.

スキット skit ⓒ

すきっぱら 空きっ腹 空きっ腹にビールを飲む drink beer *on an empty stomach*

スキップ skip ⓒ ──**スキップする** skip ⓘ ∥男の子が道をスキップしながらやってきた A boy came *skipping* down the road.

すきとおる 透き通る (透明な) transparent; (澄んだ) clear ⇨ とうめい ∥透き通った水 *transparent water* / 透き通るように青い空 a *clear* blue sky

すぎない 過ぎない (単なる) only, mere, just; (…でしかない) nothing but ..., no more than ... ∥それは単なるうわさにすぎない It's *only* [*nothing but*] a rumor. / それはあらしの前の静けさにすぎなかった It was *only* the calm before the storm.
◆人生は夢にすぎない Life is *but* a dream. (❖この but は「ほんの…」という意味の副詞. 公式的な表現で用いる)

すきま 透き間・隙間 opening ⓒ, gap ⓒ; (裂け目) crack, chink ⓒ ∥生け垣のすき間からのぞく peep through *a gap* in a hedge / その子供は狭いすき間をはって通り抜けた The child crawled through *a narrow opening*.
◆冷たいすき間風 *a draft* of cold air / その部屋はふとんがすき間なく敷き詰められていた The floor of the room *was covered with* laid out futons.

すきやき すき焼き 🍲

> すき焼きは、寿司(1)などと並んで最も有名な日本料理の一つです。基本的な材料は、薄切りの牛肉、豆腐に、白菜、ネギ、春菊などの野菜です。食卓に置いた鉄製のなべで、それらの材料をしょうゆ、砂糖、酒、みりんなどの調味料で煮込みます。地域によって作り方は少し異なります。
> *Sukiyaki*, one of the most famous Japanese dishes like sushi, usually consists of thinly sliced beef, tofu and vegetables like Chinese cabbage, spring onions and chrysanthemum leaves. The ingredients are cooked at the table in an iron pot with soy sauce, sugar, sake and *mirin* (sweet sake). The way of cooking varies from region to region.

スキャナ [コンピュータ] scanner ⓒ

スキャンダル scandal ⓒⓤ ∥政治スキャンダル a political *scandal* / スキャンダルをあばく expose *a scandal* / スキャンダルをもみ消す cover [hush] up *a scandal* / 彼はこのスキャンダルで出世の道を断たれた This *scandal* prevented him from getting a promotion.

テーマ別表現集

●スキーとスノーボード

❶ゲレンデに関する表現

1. 蔵王の雪質はどうですか.
   How is the quality of the snow in Zao?
2. パウダースノーなので, スキーには最高です.
   It is dry and powdery and perfect for skiing.
3. 白馬では5月の初めまで春スキーが楽しめます.
   In Hakuba you can enjoy spring skiing until the beginning of May.
4. 多くのゲレンデがスノーボーダーでにぎわっています.
   A lot of ski slopes are crowded with snowboarders.
5. 初心者コースはつまらないです.
   The beginner slopes are boring.
6. 上級者用のコースに挑戦してみましょう.
   Let's try the advanced slopes.
7. 昨夜の雨でコースの表面がアイスバーンになって (→凍りついて) います.
   Because of the rain last night, the surfaces of the slopes are frozen.
8. 新雪の上を滑るのはとても難しいです.
   It's very hard to ski on fresh [new-fallen] snow.
9. 志賀高原は林間コースやこぶ斜面など, いろいろなコースがそろっています.
   Shiga Kogen has various kinds of trails, such as forest slopes and moguls.
10. このスキー場ではナイトスキーがおすすめです.
    I'd recommend night skiing at this ski resort.
11. 3日 (リフト) 券を買うとお得です.
    A three-day ticket is a「good buy [bargain].
12. リフト待ちが30分以上になっています.
    We have to wait for the lift for more than 30 minutes.
13. スキーリフトに乗るの怖いなあ.
    I'm scared to take the ski lift.
14. いっしょにリフトに乗ってもらえますか.
    Will you get on the lift with me?
15. スキーヤーとスノーボーダーの接触事故が頻発しています.
    Collisions between skiers and snowboarders happen frequently.
16. 屋内スキー場ができたので, 一年中スキーを楽しむことができます.
    There are indoor ski slopes available, so we can enjoy skiing all through the year.

❷スキーの技術などに関する表現

1. ブーツがビンディングに入りません.
   My boots don't fit in the binding.
2. ブーツの底に雪がついてますよ.
   You've got snow sticking to the sole of your boot.
3. ストックでたたくと雪を落とせますよ.
   You can knock off the snow with the pole.
4. まだボーゲンしかできないんです.
   So far I can only snowplow.
5. 今シュテムターン [パラレル, ウェーデルン] を練習中です.
   I'm now practicing「stem turns [parallel skiing, wedeln].
6. モーグルができるようになりたいです.
   I want to be able to ski moguls.
7. 転びそうになったら, 横に倒れるようにします.
   If you feel you're going to fall [If you're about to fall], fall sideways.
8. スキーがあまりよく滑らなくなってきたので, ワックスを塗らなくてはなりません.
   My skis are not running very smoothly, so I need to wax them.
9. 気をつけてください. スキーのエッジで簡単に手を切ってしまいます.
   Be careful. You can easily cut your hands on the edges of the skis.

❸スキーに関するその他の表現

1. スキーの後の疲れをいやすには温泉に入るのがいちばんです.
   The best way to relax after skiing is to go to a hot spring.
2. あまり荷物を持っていきたくないので, スキーをレンタルする予定です.
   I don't want to carry a lot of baggage, so I'm planning to rent skis.
3. この新しいスキーウエアが今年はやっています.
   This new ski suit is in style this year.
4. みんなでスキーに行く前に, 新しいスキーウエアを買わなければなりません.
   I must buy a new ski suit before we go skiing.
5. 初心者はスキースクールに参加したほうがよいと思います.
   I think beginners should go to a ski school.
6. スキーシーズン中は彼は毎週のようにスキーに出かけます.
   During the ski season, he goes skiing almost every week.
7. この前の3連休に友達とスキーの初滑りを楽しみました.
   During the last three-day holiday, I enjoyed skiing with my friends for the first time this winter.

8. クロスカントリーはとても疲れますが、すごく気持ちがいいです。
   Cross-country skiing is exhausting, but it makes me feel really good.
9. 先に行ってください。後からついていきます。
   Please go ahead. I'll follow you.
10. あと2回滑ったら終わりにしましょう。
    Let's come down two more times and call it a day.
11. だれか止めてぇ！
    Somebody stop me!

❹スノーボードに関する表現

1. 今年はスノーボードに挑戦しようと思っています。
   I think I'll try snowboarding this year.
2. スノーボードをしたことはありますか。
   Have you ever snowboarded?
3. まだ3回目です。やっと基本ターンができるようになりました。
   This is just my third time. I can finally do [handle] the basic turn.
4. 2年前にスノーボードを始めたばかりです。
   I started snowboarding just two years ago.
5. ジャンプ［ターン］ができるようになりたいです。
   I want to be able to jump [turn].
6. テクニックをマスターすれば、モーグルも楽しいですよ。
   Once you've mastered the technique, moguls can be fun.
7. 回転滑降を習得するには十分な練習が必要です。
   Learning to do [Mastering] the slalom takes a lot of practice.
8. これはハーフパイプ競技用のボードです。
   This is a snowboard for the half-pipe.
9. ハードブーツはレース用、ソフトブーツはフリースタイル用です。
   Hard boots are for racing, and soft boots are for freestyle.

ワンメイク

スプレッドイーグル / Spread Eagle
Spread your legs and arms wide.

ツイスター / Twister
Rotate the lower half of your body 90 degrees.

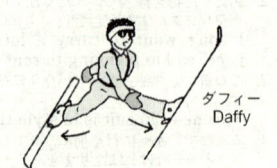

ダフィー / Daffy
Spread your legs, one in front and one in back.

ヘリコプター / Helicopter
Rotate your body 360 degrees.

インディー / Indy
Using your back hand, grab the toeside of the board between the bindings.

メランコリー / Melancholy
Grab the heel side of the board with your forward hand.

スキューバ scuba [C] ‖スキューバダイビング scuba diving

すぎゆく 過ぎ行く pass by ‖通りを過ぎ行く人々 people *passing by* on the street

すぎる 過ぎる

❶ 通過する	pass; go through
❷ 時がたつ	pass
❸ 程度を超える	

❶【通過する】pass [自] [他]; (通り抜ける) go* through ...; (そばを通り過ぎる) pass [go] by

私たちはあらしが過ぎるのをじっと待った We waited patiently for the storm to *pass*.

「もう甲府は過ぎたのかな」「いいえ, 今, 笹子トンネルを過ぎたところよ」"*Have* we *passed* Kofu yet?" "No, we'*ve* just *gone through* the Sasago Tunnel."

❷【時がたつ・ある時点を超える】pass [go*] (by)

あの出来事から3か月が過ぎた Three months *have passed* (*by*) since the incident.

夏休みはあっという間に過ぎた My summer vacation *went* (*by*) quickly.

◆10時を過ぎたというのに彼はまだ帰ってこない He hasn't come home yet, though it's *past* [*after*] 10. / ラッシュアワーはピークを過ぎた The rush hour is *past* its peak. / 小西先生は40代半ばを過ぎていると思う I think Ms. Konishi is *over 45*.

❸【程度を超える】

冗談がすぎるぞ You'*re carrying the joke too far*.

彼女の要求はちょっと度がすぎる Her request is a bit *too much*.

あいつにはすぎたかみさんだ She is *too good* to be his wife.

[ことわざ] 過ぎたるはなお及ばざるがごとし Too much is as bad as too little.

-すぎる -過ぎる too ➔ あまり[1], -すぎ

このカレーは辛すぎて僕には食べられない This curry is *too hot* for me *to* eat. / This curry is *so* hot *that* I *cannot* eat it.

このごろは自動車事故が多すぎる There are *too many* car accidents these days.

それではあまりに話がうますぎて信用できない That's *too good* a story *to* be true.

食べすぎるなよ Don't *eat too much*. / Don't *overeat*.

ちょっと, 言いすぎたかな I'm afraid I *went* a bit *too far in what I said*.

スキン (皮膚) skin [U] [C]; (コンドーム) condom [C] ‖スキンケア skin care / スキンヘッド a skinhead

ずきん 頭巾 hood [húd] [C]

スキンシップ ⚠(親子の) nurturing physical contact [U]

スキンダイバー skin diver [C]

スキンダイビング skin diving [U]

すく[1] 空く (腹が) be hungry; (込んでいない) be not crowded ‖帰りのバスはすいていた The bus *was not crowded* when I came home.

◆胸のすくような冒険談 a *delightful* [an *enjoyable*] adventure story / 今手がすいているから, 君の仕事を手伝ってあげよう I'*m free* now, so I'll help you with your work.

すく[2] 好く like [他], love [他], be fond of ... ➔ すき(好き) ‖その先生は生徒たちみんなから好かれている That teacher *is liked* by all the students.

すく[3] 透く 彼は歯の間が透いている He is *gap-toothed*. / There are *gaps* between his teeth.

すく[4] 梳く comb [kóum] [他] ➔ とかす(梳かす)

◆髪をすいてもらう *have one's* hair *thinned*

すく[5] 鋤く plow, 《英》plough [pláu] [自] [他]

すく[6] 漉く 紙をすく *make* (a sheet of) paper

すぐ 直ぐ

❶ まもなく	soon, before long
❷ ただちに	at once, immediately, right away
❸ 近くに	near, close
❹ 簡単に	easily

❶【まもなく】soon, before long

彼はすぐよくなるでしょう He should get well *soon*.

すぐ戻ります I'll be back *soon* [*in a little while*].

雨はすぐにやむよ The rain will stop *soon* [*before long*].

子供たちはすぐそのゲームに飽きてしまった The children *soon* got bored with the game.

もうすぐ夏休みだ Summer vacation is 「*coming soon* [*just around the corner*].

◆君の夢が実現するのももうすぐだ *It won't be long before* your dream comes true. / 祖父はもうすぐ90歳だ(→90歳に近づきつつある) My grandfather *is approaching* 90.

❷【ただちに】at once, immediately, right away

すぐ医者に診(み)てもらったほうがいい You'd better see a doctor *at once*.

何か困ったことがあればすぐ電話してください Should you have any trouble, call me *at once*.

彼は仕事を終えるとすぐに帰宅した He returned home *immediately* after work.

彼はひとめ見てすぐに私だと分かった He recognized me *immediately*.

◆今すぐここから出ていけ Get out of here *this minute*! / そのうわさはすぐに学校中に広まった The rumor *quickly* spread throughout the school. / 彼はその場ですぐに返事をした He replied 「*then and there* [*right on the spot*]. / 和歌子はロンドンに着くとすぐに私に電話をくれた Wakako called me 「*as soon as* [*the instant*] she arrived in London.

「出発する時間だよ」「今すぐ行くよ」"We must leave now." "I'm coming *right away*."

❸ 【近くに】 near, close
公園はすぐそこです The park is 「*near here* [*right over there*]*.*
小さな教会が農場のすぐ近くにあった A small church stood *close by* the farm.
◆すぐ近くの公園 a *nearby* park / 郵便局はここからすぐです The post office is *only a short way* from here. / It's *no distance* from here to the post office. / その事故は私のすぐ目の前で起こった The accident happened *right before my eyes*. / ドアのすぐ外で待っていてください Please wait *just outside* the door.

❹ 【簡単に】 easily
母はすぐ腹を立てる My mother gets angry *easily*.
彼はだれとでもすぐに仲良くなる He is a person who makes friends *easily*.
◆彼はつまらないことにすぐかっとなる He is *quick* to get angry about little things.

-ずく -尽く 相談ずくで決める *talk over before deciding* / 男は力ずくでその老婆から金を奪い取った The man robbed the old woman of her money *by force*. / 彼女は欲得ずくで(→金だけのために) 男とつきあう She goes around with men *only for their money*.

すくい 救い help ⓤ; (救助) rescue ⓤ; (救済) relief ⓤ;〖神学〗salvation ⓤ ∥ 救いを求める ask for *help* ◆彼らは難民に救いの手を差し伸べた They *gave a helping hand* to the refugees. / その仏像が焼失を免れたのがせめてもの救いだ(→感謝すべきだ) *We should be thankful* that the statue of Buddha escaped the fire.
∥救い主〖キリスト教〗the Savior

スクイズ 〔野球〕squeeze play ⓒ ——スクイズする squeeze (in)
∥スクイズバント a squeeze bunt

すくう¹ 救う (危険などから) save ⓤⓑ, rescue ⓤ ✤rescue は助けるという行為, save は助かったという結果に重点がある; (助ける) help ⓤ; (困難などから解放する) relieve ⓤ
須藤さんが僕を危険から救ってくれた Mr. Sudo *saved* [*rescued*] me from danger.
その医者が彼女の命を救った The doctor *saved* her life.
消防士たちは燃えている家から1人の老人を救い出した The fire fighters *rescued* an old man from the burning house.
ジョーンズ先生は患者を救うのに全精力を注いでいる Dr. Jones is investing all his energy into *helping* his patients.
◆あいつらは全く救いがたい連中だ They are really *hopeless*.

すくう² 掬う scoop (up [out]); (お玉で) ladle ⓤ; (手のひらで) cup ⓤ; (上澄みなどを) skim ⓤ ∥ 手のひらで水をすくう *skim* the fat from the surface of the soup / 弟は金魚を一度に2匹すくった My brother *scooped up* two goldfish at one time. ◆木の根に足をすくわれた I *tripped on* a tree root.

慣用表現 その計画は思わぬ問題に足元をすくわれた The plan *was tripped up* by an unexpected problem.

スクーター (motor) scooter ⓒ
スクープ scoop ⓤ; (独占記事) exclusive ⓒ ——スクープする scoop ⓤⓑ, get* a scoop ∥ 朝日は彼らの麻薬密輸をスクープした The Asahi 「*got the scoop* about [*scooped* the story of] their drug smuggling.
スクーリング (通信教育の) classroom lessons, schooling ⓤ
スクールバス school bus ⓒ
すぐさま at once, immediately ⇨ すぐ
すくすく その子供たちはすくすくと(→健康に)育った The children grew up *healthily*. / タケノコがすくすく(→急速に) 伸びている The bamboo shoots are growing *rapidly*.

すくない 少ない

(数が) few; (量が) little, small; (回数が) seldom, hardly ever
私の乗ったバスは客が少なかった There were *few* passengers on my bus. / There *weren't many* passengers on my bus.
僕の持っているCDは拓也のよりずっと少ない I have far *fewer* CDs than Takuya.
このことを知っている人は非常に少ない Very *few* people know this. / Only *a small number of* people know this.
今年の夏は雨が少なかった We had *little* rain this summer.
この店は靴の品数が少ない This shop has a *small* selection of shoes.
バスが時間どおりに来ることは少ない The buses *seldom* [*hardly ever*] come on schedule.
私のクラスは男子よりも女子のほうが10人少ない There are 10 *fewer* girls than boys in my class.
ごはんは少なめにしてください Give me *less than the usual amount of* rice, please. / *Go easy on* the rice, please.
少なからぬ若者がその葬儀に参列した *Quite* [〔公式的〕*Not*] *a few* young people attended the funeral.
彼らはみな,多かれ少なかれ似たような悩みを抱えていた All of them had *more or less* similar worries.
◆少ない時間だ. 有効に使おう We *don't have much* time. Let's make good use of it. / この通りは交通量が少ない Traffic is *light* on this street. / この牛乳は脂肪分が少ない This milk is *low* in fat. / お米が残り少なくなってきている Our stock of rice *is getting low*. / 池田先生は口数の少ない人だった Mr. Ikeda *didn't talk very much*. / Mr. Ikeda was a man *of few words*.

すくなからず 少なからず not a little [few]; (大いに) greatly, very much ∥ 風向きの変化がこの試合に少なからず影響している The shift in wind is having *"not a little* [*a great*] effect on this game.
すくなくとも 少なくとも at (the) least, not less than ∥ 1日に少なくとも1時間は勉強

going to *go skating* with my friends tomorrow. ◆スケート靴を履く put on *skates*
∥スケートリンク a skating rink / スピードスケート speed skating / フィギュアスケート figure skating

スケートボード (板) skateboard ©; (スポーツ) skateboarding Ⓤ ──スケートボードをする skateboard ⓥ

スケープゴート scapegoat © ∥今回の不祥事では彼がスケープゴートにされた He *was made a scapegoat* in this scandal.

スケール (規模) scale ©Ⓤ; (人間の度量) caliber Ⓤ; (はかり) scale © ⇒きぼ ∥スケールの大きな構想 a *large-scale* plan / スケールの大きな人間 a man *of high caliber*

スケジュール schedule © ∥スケジュールを立てる *make* (out) [*plan*] *a schedule* / すべてはスケジュールどおりに進んでいますか Is everything going *according to schedule*? / 今度の旅行はハードスケジュールだ We're going to have a *tight* [*heavy, full*] *schedule* during this trip.

ずけずけ 彼はだれに対してもずけずけとものを言う He is *outspoken* [*blunt*] with everyone.

すけだち 助太刀 (助け) help Ⓤ ∥人の助太刀をする give a person some *help* / 助太刀を頼む ask for *help*

スケッチ (作品) sketch ©; (写生) sketching Ⓤ ──スケッチする make* a sketch, sketch ⓥ ∥私は時々うちの犬をスケッチする I sometimes *sketch* my dog.
∥スケッチブック a sketchbook

すけっと 助っ人 helper ©

すげない (冷淡な) cold; (そっけない) flat ∥すげない返事 a *cold* reply / 彼女は彼の申し入れをすげなく断った She gave a *flat* denial to his proposal. / She turned his proposal down *flat*.

すけべえ 助平 (好色漢) lecher © ──助平な lecherous

すける 透ける 肌の透けて見えるブラウス a *see-through* blouse / その建物は壁がガラスでできていて骨組みが透けて見えるしくみになっている The frame of the building *can be seen through* its glass walls.

スケルトン ⚠ スケルトンモデル a *transparent* [*see-through*] model; (→半透明の) a *translucent* model (❖skeleton model は「骸骨(がいこつ)の模型」の意味)

スコア (競技の得点) score ©; (楽譜) score © ∥スコアをつける keep (*the*) *score* / 私たちは3対2のスコアで試合に勝った We won the game *by a score of* three to two.
∥スコアブック a scorebook / スコアボード a scoreboard
関連語 スコアラー a scorer, a scorekeeper / スコアリングポジション a scoring position

すごい 凄い
❶【程度が甚だしい】(ひどい) terrible; (激しい) heavy; (大変な) terrific, 《口語的》awful(❖名詞の前で用いる) ⇒ひどい
すごい大金 an *awful* lot of money / すごいスピードで at a *terrific* speed

すごいあらしになりそうだよ It looks like a *terrible* storm.
あなたの部屋, すごい散らかりようね Your room is in a *terrible* mess.
◆すごいごちそう 《口語的》a meal *and a half* / すごいどしゃ降りだね It's pouring *heavily*. / 彼はパーティーにすごい美人を連れてきた He brought a *real* beauty to the party.
❷【恐ろしい】 awful, terrible, dreadful, fearful ⇒おそろしい
彼女はすごい形相で私をにらんだ She glared at me with a *terrible* expression.
❸【すばらしい】 great, wonderful, 《口語的》terrific
私たちは彼のすごい記憶力に舌を巻いた We were amazed by his *wonderful* memory.
◆彼女はそのレースですごい(→ずば抜けた)記録を打ち立てた She set an *outstanding* record in the race.
🅒「試験にパスしたよ」「すごい, やったね」 "I passed the exam." "*Great* [*Terrific*]! You did it!"

ずこう 図工 arts and crafts

すごうで 凄腕 すご腕の記者 a *shrewd* journalist / ホテルの経営にすご腕をふるう *manage* a hotel *resourcefully*

スコール squall

すごく 凄く very, 《口語的》awfully, 《口語的》terribly, 《口語的》horribly ∥彼の話はすごくおもしろかった His stories were *very* interesting to me. / きのうはすごく寒かった It was *awfully* cold yesterday.

すこし 少し

❶ 数が	a few, some
❷ 量が	a little, some
❸ 時間・距離が	a little
❹ 程度が	a little

❶【数が】(少しある) a few, some; (少ししかない) few
外国の硬貨を少し持っています I have *a few* foreign coins.
クッキーをもう少しちょうだい Give me *some more* cookies, please.
そこには少ししか人がいなかった(→ほとんどいなかった) There were *few* people there.
❷【量が】(少しある) a little, some; (少ししかない) little

語法
a few, few は数えられる名詞の複数形とともに用い, a little, little は数えられない名詞とともに用いる. a few も a little も「少しはある」という肯定的な意味を表すが, a が付かないと「少ししかない」「ほとんどない」という否定的な意味合いになる.

シェフはスープを味見して少し塩を加えた The chef tasted the soup and added *a little* more salt.
紅茶をもう少しいかが Would you like *some more* tea?

します I study *at least* an hour a day. / 少なくとも君がうそをつかなかったことは認めよう *At least* you didn't tell a lie, I'll give you that.

すぐに ⇒すぐ

すくむ 竦む (こわばる) freeze* 圓; (たじろぐ) cringe 圓 ∥私はその事故を目の当たりにして身のすくむ思いだった I *froze* with terror at the sight of the accident. / 私は恐怖で足がすくんだ I *froze in my steps* in fear.

-ずくめ -尽くめ 彼女は黒ずくめの服装をしていた She *was (dressed) all in black*. / 先月はうれしいことずくめだった(→うれしいことがたくさん起こった) A lot of delightful things happened to me last month.

すくめる 竦める (肩を) shrug 囲 圓; (首を) duck 圓 圓 ∥彼女は私の質問に肩をすくめた She [*shrugged* (*her shoulders*) [*gave a shrug (of the shoulders*)] at my question.

スクラップ (不用品) scrap 回; (切り抜き) clipping 回 ⇒ きりぬき ◆ 古い車をスクラップにする *scrap* an old car / 彼は環境問題について書かれた新聞記事をスクラップしている He *clips* the articles on environmental problems out of the paper.

∥スクラップブック a scrapbook

スクラム 〖ラグビー〗scrum 回 ∥スクラムを組む form [make] *a scrum*

∥スクラムハーフ〖ラグビー〗a scrum-half

スクランブル この番組にはスクランブルがかかっている This program *is scrambled*.

∥スクランブルエッグ a scrambled egg / スクランブル交差点 an intersection with diagonal crosswalks

スクリーン screen 回 ∥スクリーン上の画像 the image on *a screen*

スクリプト script 回

スクリュー screw (propeller) 回, propeller

回 ∥スクリュードライバー a screwdriver / スクリューボール〖野球〗a screwball

すぐれない 優れない・勝れない きょうは気分があまりすぐれない I *don't feel very good* today. / 彼女は顔色がすぐれない She *looks pale*. / おじは何か月も健康がすぐれない My uncle *has been in poor health* for months.

すぐれもの 優れもの この自転車のライトは、周りが暗くなると自動的に点灯するすぐれものだ This bicycle light is *a special* [*neat*] *gadget* that automatically turns on when it gets dark.

すぐれる 優れる・勝れる be better (than ...), be superior (to ...), exceed 圓, surpass 圓 ━━**すぐれた** good, excellent; (傑出した) outstanding

健は数学にかけてはクラスのだれよりもすぐれている Ken *is better* in math *than* any of his classmates. / Ken *is superior to* his classmates in math.

良夫はユーモアのセンスにすぐれている Yoshio has a *good* sense of humor.

この賞は芸術性にすぐれた作品に贈られる This prize is to be awarded to an artistically *excellent* work.

◆ 犬の嗅覚は人間よりもずっとすぐれている Dogs can smell much *better than* people can. / この生地は吸水性にすぐれている This material absorbs water *well*. / これはすぐれて政治的な問題だ This is an *exceedingly* political problem.

スクロール ━━スクロールする〖コンピュータ〗scroll 圓 圓 ∥ウェブページをスクロールする *scroll* a web page

ずけい 図形 figure 回, shape 回 ⇒ 図版 ∥図形を描く draw *a figure* [*shape*]

スケート skating 回 ━━スケートをする skate 圓 ∥あしたは友達とスケートに行く I'm

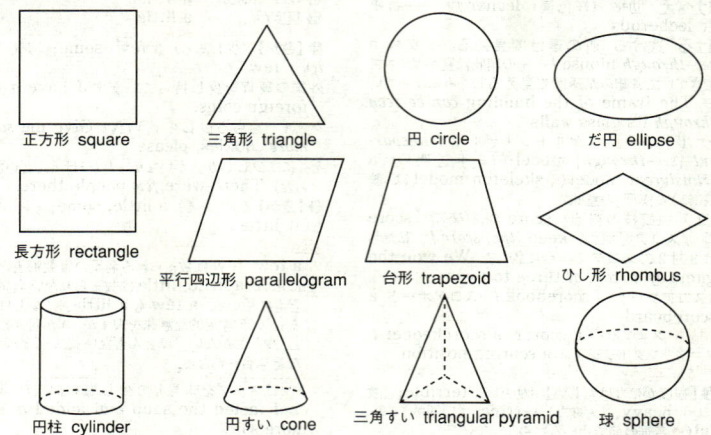

正方形 square	三角形 triangle	円 circle	だ円 ellipse
長方形 rectangle	平行四辺形 parallelogram	台形 trapezoid	ひし形 rhombus
円柱 cylinder	円すい cone	三角すい triangular pyramid	球 sphere

図形 shapes

お金は少ししか持っていません(→ほとんど持っていない) I have *little* money with me.
◆やかんの中には水が少し入っていた There was *a small amount of* water in the kettle.

💬「牛乳もうないの?」「まだ少し残ってるよ」 "Are we out of milk?" "No, we have *a little* left."

❸【時間・距離が】a little; (わずかの間) a minute, a while

少しお待ちください Just *a minute*, please.
少したって, 幸子がやって来た After *a while*, Sachiko came.
健があなたと少し話をしたいそうです Ken wants to speak with you *for a minute*.
少し席を詰めてもらえますか Will you sit closer together *a little*?
パン屋は交差点の少し先です The bakery is *a little* past the intersection.
◆彼はあと少しで退職だ He is *near* retirement. / 野球場は学校から少し離れた所にあります The baseball field is *at a distance* from our school.

💬「この番組は何時に終わるの」「10時少し前に終わるよ」 "What time does this program end?" "It ends *a little* before 10."

❹【程度が】a little; (幾分) some, somewhat; (わずかな) slight

彼女は君より少し若いと思う I think she's *a little* younger than you.
その上着はあなたには少し小さすぎる The jacket is *a little* too small for you.
もう少し背が高かったらなあ If only I were *a little* taller!
その知らせを聞いて少しほっとした The news gave me *some* relief.
彼は少し疲れているようだった He looked *somewhat* tired.
少し頭痛がする I have a *slight* headache.
彼女は少しでも気に入らないことがあると大騒ぎする She makes a big fuss if there's something she dislikes *even a little bit*.
少しでもお役に立てたのなら幸いです I'm glad if I've been of *some* help.
◆きょうの彼女は私に対して少しよそよそしかった She was *rather* cool toward me today. / 彼は彼女の話を少ししか理解できなかった He understood *little* of her story. / 少しは気分がよくなりましたか Do you feel *any* better now? / 少しはあいつの身にもなってみろ Try *to* put yourself in his position [(口語的) shoes]. / 彼女はもう少しでおぼれるところだった She *almost* drowned. / 彼のスペイン語の発音は少しずつよくなっている His Spanish pronunciation is improving *little by little*.

すこしも 少しも 私は少しも泳げません I *can't* swim *at all*. / 彼女は少しも怖がっていなかった She was *not* afraid *in the least*. / あなたを愛する気持ちは少しも変わっていません My love for you *hasn't* changed *a bit*. / コーヒーは少しも残っていない *None* of the coffee is left. / 彼女はそれを少しも知らなかった She knew *nothing* about that.

すごす 過ごす
❶【時を】spend*⊕, pass⊕
眠れぬ夜を過ごす *spend* a sleepless [restless] night
知子はビデオを見て1日を過ごした Tomoko *spent* [*passed*] the whole day watching videos.
彼はぶらぶらと時を過ごした He *passed* the time in idleness. / He *idled away* the time.
年をとるにつれて家で過ごす時間が長くなる As we grow older, we *spend* more time at home.
◆楽しい時を過ごす *have* a good [pleasant] time / 彼女は多忙な日々を過ごしている She is busy every day. / 私たちは海辺で休日を楽しく過ごした We *enjoyed* our vacation at the beach.

💬「夏休みはどう過ごすつもりですか」「海辺でのんびり過ごそうと思います」 "How *are* you going to *spend* summer vacation?" "I'm going to *spend* it relaxing at the beach."

💬「いかがお過ごしですか」「まあまあですよ. あなたは?」 "How *are* you *getting along*?" "We're getting along all right. And you?"

❷【限度を】
酒を過ごす(→飲みすぎる) drink sake *too much*

すごすご dejectedly, depressingly 〘彼は間違いを指摘されてすごすごと自分の席に戻った After his mistakes were pointed out, he returned to his seat *dejectedly*.

スコッチ Scotch (whisky)🆄
スコットランド Scotland ──スコットランド人 Scot🅲;(集合的) the Scottish ──スコットランド語 Scots🆄, Scottish🆄 ──スコットランド(人[語]) Scottish

スコップ (小型の) scoop [skúːp]🅲;(シャベル) shovel🅲

すこぶる 彼はすこぶる健康だ He is in *excellent* health. / 新緑が日の光に映えてすこぶる美しい The fresh green leaves, shining in the sun, are *very* beautiful. ⇨ とても

すごみ 凄味 すご味のある声 a *threatening* [*frightening*] voice / すご味のある(→迫真の) 演技 *realistic* acting / その男は「痛い目にあわせてやる」と, すご味をきかせて言った The man said *threateningly*, "You'll have a hard time."

すごむ 凄む threaten⊕ ⇨ おどす 〘強盗は私に命が惜しかったら金を出せとすごんだ The robber *threatened* that he would kill me if I didn't give him my money.

すこやか 健やか ──すこやかな healthy ──すこやかに healthily ⇨ けんこう 〘すこやかに育つ grow up *healthily* [*in good health*]

すごろく 双六 🆉
すごろくは日本に古くからある遊びの一つで, バックギャモンによく似たゲームです. たくさんの絵がついた紙の上でこまを動かします. 主に正月の

子供の遊びとして発達しましたが，最近ではかつてほどポピュラーな遊びではありません．
Sugoroku is a traditional game of Japan, much like backgammon. A piece of paper with a lot of little squares and pictures is used as the board. It was usually played by children at New Year's, but it's not as popular as it used to be.

すさまじい 凄まじい (恐ろしい) terrible, dreadful; (ものすごい) terrific, tremendous //爆発のすさまじい衝撃 the *tremendous* impact of an explosion / すさまじい交通事故だった It was a *terrible* [*dreadful*] traffic accident. / その小さな村はすさまじいあらしに襲われた The small village was hit by a *terrible* [an *awful*] storm.
◆彼はすさまじい(→激怒した)形相で私をにらんだ He glared at me with a *furious* look.

すさむ 荒む すさんだ生活を送る live a *wild* [*dissolute*] life / 彼の心はすさんでゆくばかりだ He is just becoming more and more of *a degenerate*.(❖degenerateは「堕落者」の意味)

ずさん 杜撰 ―ずさんな slipshod, sloppy //ずさんな仕事 *sloppy* work / 彼はずさんな経営の実態を指摘した He pointed out the *slipshod* management.

すし 寿司・鮨 🗻 sushi [U]
➔ [場面・状況別会話] p.1684

寿司にはいくつかの種類がありますが，最も典型的なものは握り寿司です．一般的な家庭料理ではなく，ふつうは寿司屋で食べます．板前はあらかじめ酢や砂糖で味をつけたごはんを握り，その上に生または調理した魚などをのせます．高級な寿司はかなり高価ですが，大衆的な回転寿司の店(コンベヤーに乗って回っている寿司の皿の中から好きなものを取ることができる)もあります．
Sushi comes in several kinds of forms, but the most typical one is *nigiri-zushi*. It is usually eaten at sushi restaurants rather than at home. To make *nigiri-zushi*, chefs take a small amount of rice (which is already seasoned with vinegar and sugar) and make it into a rice ball, topping it with raw or cooked fish or another delicacy. Sushi may be very expensive in some exclusive restaurants, but there are also reasonable ones called *kaiten-zushi*, where small plates of sushi go around on a conveyer belt so that customers can take whatever they want.

すじ 筋
❶【物語の】(具体的なストーリー) story [C], story line [C][U]; (構想) plot [C]
映画の筋 *the plot* of a movie
小説の筋を言わないで Don't tell me *the story line* of the novel.
❷【道理】(論理) logic [U]; (道理) reason [U]
―筋の通った (論理的な) logical; (道理にかなった) reasonable; (一貫した) coherent
筋の通った主張 a *logical* argument
彼女の意見は筋が通っている Her opinion *is reasonable* [*logical*].
◆筋の通らない返答 an *unreasonable* reply / 先方からあいさつに来るのが筋というものだ It is *proper* for them to come to greet us first.
❸【線】line [C]; (縞(しま)) stripe [C]; (細い線) thread [C]《通例単数形》
一筋の煙 *a thread of* smoke
❹【情報源】source [C]
この情報は信頼できる筋から得たものだ I got this information from *reliable sources*.
◆信頼できる筋からの情報によればその国の大統領は重体だということだ *I have* (*got*) *it on good authority that* the president of the country is in critical condition.
❺【筋肉・繊維】(筋肉) muscle [mʌ́sl] [C][U]; (腱(けん)) sinew [C][U]; (野菜などの繊維) fiber [C]
足の筋を違える strain *a* leg *muscle*
◆豆の筋を取るのを手伝ってくれない？ Could you help me *string* the beans?
❻【素質】aptitude [C][U]
君の将棋はなかなか筋がいい You *have a good aptitude* for *shogi*.

ずし 図示 illustration [U] ―図示する illustrate [他], diagram [他] ➔ ずかい

すじあい 筋合い おまえにとやかく言われる筋合いはない You have no *business* to say anything about it. / 文句を言われる筋合いはない《口語的》There's no *law* against it.

すじがき 筋書き (小説・劇などの) plot [C]; (計画・段取り) plan [C]
◆事は彼の筋書きどおりには運ばなかった Things didn't go *as* he *had planned*.

すじがね 筋金 ―筋金入りの staunch, stalwart //筋金入りの共産党員 a *staunch* [*committed*] Communist

ずしき 図式 diagram [C],《公式的》schema [C] (複 schemata, ～s); (図表) chart [C] //年間の気温の変化を図式で示す *show* the temperature changes for the year *in a diagram*

すじこ 筋子 salted salmon roe [U][C]

すじちがい 筋違い ―筋違いな (的はずれの) irrelevant; (不当な) unreasonable //私に文句を言うのは筋違いというものだ It is *unreasonable* of you to complain to me.

すしづめ 鮨詰め 公会堂は大勢の聴衆ですし詰めの状態だった The public hall was *jam-packed* with a large audience. / 帰りのバスはすし詰めだった We *were packed like sardines* in the bus on the way home.

すじみち 筋道 (論理) logic [U]; (道理) reason [U]; (話の脈絡) thread [C]《通例単数形》➔ すじ //彼女の意見は筋道が通っている Her opinion 「*has reason* [*is reasonable*].
◆筋道を立てて話す speak *in logical order* / 筋道の通らないことを言う say *illogical* things

すじむかい 筋向かい うちの筋向かいに本屋がある There is a bookstore *diagonally opposite* [*across from*] my house.

すじょう 素性・素姓 (生い立ち) background [C]; (身元) identity [U][C] //素性を明かす reveal *one's identity* / 素性の知れない男 a man with *an* obscure *background*

ずじょう 頭上 カモメが頭上を飛んでいた Seagulls were flying「*over my head* [*overhead*]. ◆頭上注意《掲示》*Watch Your Head*!

ずしり ―ずしりと heavily ⇒ ずっしり

ずしん(ずしん) 大木がずしんと音を立てて倒れた The big tree fell down with *a* heavy *thud*.

すす 煤 soot [U] //天井はすすだらけだった The ceiling was thick with *soot*.

すず[1] 鈴 bell [C] //鈴を鳴らす ring *a bell* / ほら, 鈴の音が聞こえるよ Listen, you can hear *a bell* ringing.

すず[2] 錫〘化学〙tin [U] (❖元素記号 Sn)

すすき 薄 Japanese pampas grass [U]

すすぐ rinse [他] //口をすすぐ *rinse out one's* mouth / 髪をすすいでシャンプーを落とす *rinse* the shampoo *out of one's* hair

◆皿をよくすすぐ *give* a dish *a* good *rinse*

すすける 煤ける ―すすけた sooty

すずしい 涼しい cool

涼しいそよ風 a *cool* breeze / 涼しげなシャツ a *cool* shirt

ここは涼しくて気持ちがいい It's *cool* and pleasant here.

9月以降徐々に涼しくなり始めた After September it gradually *began to get cooler*.

◆涼しい(→澄んだ)声 a *clear* voice / 彼は人から借りた本に書き込みをしておいて涼しい顔をしている He wrote in a book that he had borrowed from someone else, but he *doesn't care* about it.

すずなり 鈴生り 鈴なりの(→大勢の)見物人 *a lot of* onlookers / その木にはビワが鈴なりになっていた The tree *was loaded with* loquats.

すすむ 進む

❶ 前進する	go; move; advance
❷ 進歩する	advance, make progress
❸ 進行する・はかどる	go
❹ ある分野・段階に	advance
❺ 病気が	get worse
❻ 時計が	gain
❼ その他	

❶【前進する】go* [自]; make* *one's* way; move [自]; advance [自]; proceed [自]; travel [自]

> go:「進む」を表す最も一般的な語.
> make *one's* way: go とほぼ同義だが「苦労して進む」というニュアンスを伴うときがある.
> move: 移動する.
> advance: 目標に向かって進む.
> proceed: いったん停止した状態や中間地点からさらに進む.
> travel: 光や音が伝わる.

前へ進む *go* [*move*] forward

青信号は「進め」を意味する The green light means "*Go ahead*."

先に進むにつれて道は狭(せば)まった The road was becoming narrower as we *went on*.

後がつかえているのでどんどん進んでください There are so many people waiting. *Move on*, please.

渋滞に巻き込まれて全然進まなかった We got caught in a traffic jam and *didn't move* at all.

台風は内陸部に進んだ The typhoon *moved* inland.

パレードはゆっくり進んだ The parade *advanced* slowly.

一塁走者は二塁へ進んだ The runner on first base *advanced* to second.

(空港のアナウンスで) 7番ゲートへお進みください Please *proceed* to Gate 7.

光は音よりも速く進む Light *travels* faster than sound.

彼はやぶをかき分けて進んだ He *made his way* through the bush.

◆1歩前に進む *take* one *step forward* / (バスなどで乗客に)中ほどへお進みください *Please pass along*.

[語法]

> (1) make *one's* way は make の代わりに他の動詞を使うことで様々な進み方を表現することができる // 人の波を押し分けて進む *force one's way* through the crowd / 暗やみの中を手探りで進む *feel* [*grope*] *one's way* in the dark / 凍った道を慎重に進む *pick one's way* along an icy road
> (2) このほかに elbow *one's* way「ひじで押しのけて進む」, shoulder *one's* way「肩で押しのけて進む」, dodge *one's* way「身をかわしながら進む」, thread *one's* way「縫うようにして進む」, work *one's* way「(苦労して)徐々に進む」などがある.

❷【進歩する】advance [自], make* progress, progress [自]

その分野の研究はこの10年で驚くほど進んだ Studies in the field *have* surprisingly *advanced* over the past 10 years. / Surprising *progress has been made* in studies in the field over the past 10 years.

彼女は目標に向かって一歩一歩進んでいる She *is advancing* step by step toward her goal.

世の中が進むにつれ新しい問題も生まれている As the world *advances*, new problems have been arisen.

◆進んだ科学技術 *advanced* technology / 国民の福祉に関してはその国は日本よりずっと進んでいる That country *is* far *ahead of* Japan in terms of the welfare of its people.

❸【進行する・はかどる】go* [自]

すべてが我々が願ったとおりに進んだ Everything *went* as well as we wanted.

交渉はとんとん拍子に進んだ The negotiation *went* without a hitch.

勉強はうまく進んでいますか *Are* your studies *going* well?

この前の授業はどこまで進んだの How far did

you go [(→どこでやめたのか) Where did you leave off] in the last lesson?
私は円高がさらに進むと見ている I think the yen will *go* even higher.
◆彼の研究は順調に進んでいる He *is「coming on [getting along]* well *with* his research. / きょうは作業がだいぶ進んだ We *made good progress* in our work today. / 町の復興は着実に進んでいる The reconstruction of the city *is「steadily progressing [in* steady *progress]*.

❹【ある分野・段階に】advance ⊕
私たちは決勝戦に進んだ We *「advanced to [reached]* the finals.
◆彼は来年大学に進む He will *enter college* next year. / 私は工学部に進むつもりだ I will 「*enter the school of engineering [*(→専攻する)*major in engineering]*.

🔴「卒業後はどんな道に進むつもりですか(→何をするつもりか)」「広告業界に進みたい(→広告業界の仕事に就きたい)と思っています」 "*What will you do* after graduation?" "I'd like to *get into a career* in advertising."

❺【病気が】(悪化する) get* worse
翌年には彼女の病状はさらに進んだ She *got worse* the next year.
◆彼の癌(ガン)はすでに手がつけられないほど進んでいた His cancer was already too far *advanced* to be treated.

❻【時計が】gain ⊕ ⊖; (進んでいる) be fast
この時計は1日に2秒進む This watch *gains* two seconds a day.
その時計は5分進んでいる That watch *is* five minutes *fast*.

❼【その他】
食が進む[進まない] *have a good [poor] appetite*
ひとりでそこへ行くのは気が進まない I'm *reluctant* to go there alone.

すずむ 涼む cool *oneself*, cool off / ちょっとあの木陰で涼もう Let's *cool ourselves* for a minute under that tree.

すずむし 鈴虫 bell-ringing cricket ⓒ

すすめ 勧め・薦め (推薦) recommendation ⓤ; (助言) advice ⓤ; (提言) suggestion ⓒ / 彼の勧めでこの本を買った I bought this book *on his recommendation*. / 先生の勧めで音楽学校を受けることにした *On* my teacher's *advice*, I decided to take the entrance exam to a music school.
◆ (レストランなどで)本日のおすすめ《掲示》*Chef's Special [Choice]* / おすすめの品(→お買い得品) *a good value* / この辞書をお勧めするよ I *recommend* this dictionary to you.

すずめ 雀 sparrow
慣用表現 雀の涙ほどのボーナス *a tiny bonus*
ことわざ 雀百まで踊り忘れず A sparrow remembers how to hop until it's 100 years old.; What is learned in the cradle is carried to the grave.(→揺りかごの中で覚えたことは墓場まで運ばれる)
俳句 雀の子そこのけそこのけお馬が通る（小林一茶）

Hey, little sparrows!
Shoo! Shoo! Get out of the way! Shoo! The horses are coming through.

すずめばち 雀蜂 wasp ⓒ, hornet ⓒ

すすめる¹ 進める

❶【前進させる】(動かす) move ⊕
車をもう少し前に進めてください *Move* your car a little more *forward*.
◆彼は送りバントでランナーを二塁に進めた He *advanced* the runner to second with a sacrifice bunt.

❷【進行させる】(続ける) go* ahead [on] with ...; (促進する) promote ⊕
仕事を進める *go ahead [on] with* the work / 経営の合理化を進める *promote* the rationalization of management
この計画を進めよう Let's *go ahead [on] with* this plan.
お話を進めてください Please *go ahead [on] with* your story.
この運動は全国規模で進められている This campaign *is promoted* on a nationwide scale.
◆調査を進めるうちに意外な事実が明らかになった As we *pursued* the research, an unexpected fact was revealed. / 運動会の準備が進められている Preparations *are under way* for the athletic meet. / 彼らはひそかに交渉を進めていた They *had carried on* negotiations secretly. / 彼らはその発想をさらに進めて新製品を開発した They *carried* the idea *further* and developed a new product.

❸【時計を】advance ⊕, set* ... ahead [forward]
時計を1時間進める *advance* a clock one hour; *set* a clock an hour *ahead [forward]*
慣用表現 彼らは準々決勝にこまを進めた They *advanced to* the quarterfinal.

すすめる² 勧める・薦める

❶【助言・奨励する】(助言する) advise ⊕; (提案する) suggest ⊕; (奨励する) encourage ⊕; (推薦する) recommend ⊕
医者は私にもっと運動するように勧めた The doctor *advised* me *to* get more exercise.
彼は私に美術館に行ってみることを勧めた He *suggested [recommended]* that I (should) visit the museum.
先生は私にもう1つ語学の授業をとるよう勧めてくれた My teacher *encouraged* me *to* take another language course.

❷【差し出す】offer ⊕
彼女は僕に手作りのケーキを勧めた She *offered* me some cake she made herself.

すずらん 鈴蘭〚植物〛(a) lily of the valley

すずり 硯 inkstone ⓒ ∥ すずり箱 an inkstone box

すすりなき 啜り泣き sob ⓒ ◆電話の向こうから彼女のすすり泣きが聞こえてきた I could hear her *sobbing* over the phone.

すする 啜る sip ⊕ ⊖; (ずるずる音を立てて) slurp ⊕ ⊖, (鼻を) sniffle ⊕ / 彼女は熱いコーヒーをすすった She *sipped* the hot coffee.

すすんで 進んで (快く・喜んで) willingly; (自発的に) voluntarily ∥和男は進んで私の手助けをしてくれた Kazuo helped me *willingly*. / Kazuo *was willing* [*ready*] *to* help me.

すそ 裾 (衣服の) hem ⓒ ∥スカートのすそ *the hem* of a skirt / ワイシャツのすそ *the tail* of a shirt / ズボンのすそ *the bottom* of trouser legs / 山すそ *the foot* of a mountain / スカートのすそを上げる *take up* a skirt / 彼女はドレスのすそを引きずっていた She trailed her dress *on the ground*.

すその 裾野 the foot ∥阿蘇山のすそ野 *the foot* of Mt. Aso

スター star ⓒ ∥映画スター *a movie star* / この試合で彼はいちやくスター選手になった This game suddenly made him *a star player*.

スタート start ⓒ ──スタートする start ⊕ ⓘ ∥スタートラインにつく line up at *the starting line* / 健二はいいスタートを切った Kenji made a good *start*. / 彼はスタートの時点ですでに出遅れていた He was already late *at the start*.

スタイリスト (服飾の) fashion coordinator ⓒ, fashion stylist ⓒ

スタイル (型・様式) style ⓒ (❖英語の style は「(建築・芸術などの) 様式」,文体」を指し,「体つき」の意味では用いられない); (体つき) figure ⓒ (❖主に女性の体つきをいう語) ∥最新のスタイル *the latest style* / スタイルが崩れる lose *one's figure* / あなたはスタイルがいいです You have *a nice figure*. ◆彼はとてもスタイルがいい。He has *a nice physique*. (❖「男性の体つき」にはphysiqueを用いる)
∥スタイルブック a stylebook / ライフスタイル *one's style of living*, *one's lifestyle*

スタジアム stadium ⓒ (複 〜s, stadia)

スタジオ studio ⓒ (複 〜s) ∥レコーディングスタジオ *a recording studio*

すたすた すたすた(→きびきび)歩く walk *briskly* [(→せかせか) *hurriedly*]

ずたずた 彼はその手紙をずたずたに引きちぎった He *tore* the letter *to bits* [*shreds*]. / 彼女のひどい言葉に私の心はずたずたになった Her cruel remark *has broken* my heart.

すだつ 巣立つ (鳥が) leave* the nest ◆この大学からは毎年5,000人以上の学生が巣立ってゆく (→卒業する) More than 5,000 students *graduate from* this college every year.

スタッドレスタイヤ studless snow tire ⓒ

スタッフ (個々の) staff member ⓒ;《集合的》 staff ⓒ ∥編集スタッフ *the editorial staff* / 彼はこの店のスタッフです He's on *the staff* of this shop.

スタミナ stamina ⓤ ∥スタミナをつける build up *stamina* / スタミナ料理 food that helps to build up *stamina* / その挑戦者はスタミナが足りなかった The challenger lacked *stamina*. / この試合はスタミナ勝負だ This game will be a test of *stamina*. / You need *stamina* to win this game.

スタメン ⚠ the starting lineup (❖英語の starting member にはこの意味はない) ∥人をスタメンに入れる put a person into *the start-*

ing lineup

すだれ 簾 a *sudare*, a bamboo blind

すたれる 廃れる (使われなくなる) go* out of use; (はやらなくなる) go [drop] out of fashion ──廃れた obsolete ∥廃れた言葉 an *obsolete* word / この型の服はもう廃れてしまった This kind of clothing is *out of fashion*.
◆近くに新しい店がオープンしてからその店は急に廃れてしまった The business of the store suddenly *declined* after a new store opened nearby.

スタント stunt ⓒ ∥この映画のスタントシーンは圧巻だ *The stunt scenes* are the best part of this movie.
∥スタントマン a stunt man [woman, person] / カースタント a car stunt

スタンド (観客席) the stands; (屋根のない外野席)《米》bleachers; (売店) stand ⓒ; (電気スタンド) desk lamp ⓒ ∥レフトスタンドからの大声援 a loud cheer from *the* left-field *stands* / スタンドは大観衆に埋め尽くされた *The stands* were filled with spectators.
∥スタンドカラー a stand-up collar / スタンドプレー a grandstand play / ガソリンスタンド a gas station

スタンプ stamp ◆パスポートにスタンプを押してもらう have one's passport *stamped*
∥スタンプ台 an inkpad

スチーム steam ⓤ ∥私たちの家はスチーム暖房です Our house is「*heated by steam* [*steam-heated*].
∥スチームアイロン a steam iron / スチームバス a steam bath

スチール¹ (鋼鉄) steel ⓤ ∥スチールウール steel wool / スチールギター a steel guitar

スチール² 〔野球〕steal ⓒ ◆サードにスチールする *steal* third base / ホームスチールをする *steal home*

スチュワーデス stewardess ⓒ, flight attendant ⓒ (❖後者は男女の区別がなく, 現在はふつうこちらが用いられる)

スチロール 〔化学〕styrene ⓤ ∥発泡スチロール styrene foam,《商標名》Styrofoam

-ずつ 生徒は1人ずつ校長室に入った The students went into the principal's room *one by one*. / 生徒たちは1人1冊ずつ辞書を持っている Each of the students has *one* [*a*] dictionary. / 子供たちはリンゴを2個ずつもらった The children received *two* apples *each*. / 1日10ページずつ読むつもりだ I will read *10 pages a day*. / 3人ずつの組になりなさい Group together *in threes*. / 彼はとれたての野菜を1軒ずつ売って回った He sold fresh vegetables *from door to door*. / 彼の負傷した足は少しずつよくなっている His injured leg is healing *little by little*.

ずつう 頭痛 headache ⓒ ∥軽い [割れるような] 頭痛 a slight [splitting] *headache* / 朝からひどい頭痛なんだ I have had *a bad headache* since last night.
慣用表現 数学の成績が僕の頭痛の種だ My math grades are「*a big headache* [*a pain in the neck*].

すっかり (すべて) all; (全く) quite, fully; (完全に) completely
- 葉がすっかり散ってしまった The leaves have *all* fallen.
- 剛はすっかり大人になった Tsuyoshi is *fully* grown.
- 小百合に電話するのをすっかり忘れてた I *completely* forgot to call Sayuri.
- こちらの生活にもすっかり慣れました I'm *quite* used to the way of life here.
- 彼は教師になることをすっかりあきらめた He gave up *all* thoughts of becoming a teacher.
- 私の故郷の町はすっかり変わってしまっていた My hometown had changed *completely*.

ズッキーニ 〖植物〗zucchini ⓒ (複 ～, ～s)

すっきり(と) 目鼻立ちのすっきりした顔 a face with *clean-cut* features / どうも気分がすっきりしない I don't *feel refreshed* somehow. / やっと部屋がすっきり片づいた My room was cleaned up *neatly* at last. / この事件にはすっきりとしない点がある There is something *suspicious* about this case.

ズック ▲ (布地) canvas ⓤ; (靴) canvas shoes (⇨日本語はオランダ語の doek から)

すくと／すっくと すっくと立ち上がる stand up *straight*

ずっしり そのトロフィーはずっしりと重かった The trophy was *very heavy*. / 屋根の上に雪がずっしりと積もっている Snow accumulated *heavily* on the roof.

すったもんだ ado ⓤ, fuss ⓤ 《しばしば a ～》 /すったもんだする make [kick up] *a fuss* / すったもんだの末に我々は合意にこぎつけた After much *ado*, we arrived at an agreement.

すってんころり すってんころりと転ぶ *fall flat on one's back* [*face*] (⇨back は「あおむけに」, face は「うつぶせに」の意味)

すっと (不意に) abruptly; (静かに) silently; (すばやく) quickly / すっと席を立つ stand up *abruptly* / その犬はすっと姿を消した The dog vanished *silently*. / 痛みがすっとひいてゆくのが分かった I felt the pain go away *quickly*.
◆すっと伸びた枝 a *straight* branch / 思いきり叫んだら胸がすっとした After I shouted as loud as I could, I *felt relieved* [(→満足した) *satisfied*]. / 彼はポケットに両手をすっと入れて歩き去った He *slipped* his hands into his pockets and walked away.

ずっと
❶【程度・数量が】much, far, a lot
- 映画より原作のほうがずっといい The book is *much* [*far, a lot*] better than the film based on it.
- この写真だと彼は実際よりずっと若く見える In this photo he looks *much* [*far, a lot*] younger than he really is.

〘語法〙
much は数えられる名詞とともに用いることはできない。数えられる名詞には far, a lot, many を用いる / 今年は去年よりずっと雨が多かった We had *much* [*far, a lot*] more rain this year than last. / 彼女は私よりずっと多くの CD を持っている She has *many* [*far, a lot*] more CDs than me.

❷【時間的・空間的に離れて】
- その出来事はずっと前に起こった The incident happened 「*long ago* [*a long time ago*].
- 彼のことはずっと前から(→長い間)名前だけは知っている I have known him only by name *for a long time*.
- 私はずっと後になってからその事実を知った I learned of the fact 「*long afterward* [*much later*].
- 春はまだずっと先だ Spring is still *a long way off*.
- 先頭のランナーは私のずっと前を走っていた The leading runner was running *far* [*a long way*] *ahead of me*.
- ずっと遠くで雷が鳴っている It's thundering 「*far in the distance* [*far away*].
- 私は森のずっと奥まで行った I went *far* into the woods.

❸【続けて】(時間的に) all the time, (all) through; (距離的に) all the way; (まっすぐ先へ) straight

〘語法〙
「ずっと…している[いた]」という意味は完了形 (have [had] ＋ 過去分詞) の継続用法や,「続ける」という意味の動詞 continue, keep などを用いて表せる場合もある。

- 夏の間ずっと *all through* the summer
- 学校から家までずっと明と話して帰った I talked with Akira *all the way* home from school.
- この道をずっと行くと駅が見えます If you go *straight* along this street, you'll see the station.
- けさからずっと何も食べていない I *haven't eaten* anything since this morning.
- 彼女はアメリカに住むことを前からずっと夢見ていた She *has always dreamed* of living in America.
- 彼女は結婚後もずっと仕事を続けるつもりだ She will *continue* her career after marriage.
- 彼はずっとぶつぶつ文句を言っていた He *kept* grumbling about it.
◆きのうは1日ずっと家にいました I was home *all day* yesterday. / 公子はその間ずっと何も言わなかった Kimiko didn't say anything 「*the whole time* [*all the while*]. / 彼はずっとしゃべりっぱなしだった He talked *throughout*. / 以前はこの通りに沿ってずっと桜の並木があった There used to be cherry trees *all along* this street.

すっとぶ すっ飛ぶ その知らせを聞いて彼女は病院へすっ飛んでいった She *rushed* to the hospital at the news. / 彼と話をしたら頭の中のもやもやはすっ飛んでしまった Talking with him *cleared* the cobwebs from my brain.

すっぱい 酸っぱい sour / すっぱいリンゴ a *sour* apple / そのジュースはすっぱい味がした That juice 「*had a sour taste* [*tasted sour*].

ステレオタイプ

慣用表現 彼は子供たちにその川で泳いではいけないと口がすっぱくなるほど言った He told his children *again and again [over and over]* not to swim in the river.

すっぱだか 素っ裸 ──すっ裸の[で] stark-naked ∥子供たちが池ですっ裸で遊んでいる Children are playing in the pond *stark-naked*.

すっぱぬく 素っ破抜く (あばく) expose ⊕ ∥その新聞は彼らの裏取引をすっぱ抜いた The newspaper *exposed* their secret deal.

すっぱり 父は賭(か)け事をすっぱりとやめた My father quit gambling *completely*.

すっぴん 素っぴん 彼女は家ではほとんどすっぴんだ At home she *wears almost no make-up*.

すっぽかす (約束を) break*⊕; (デートを)《口語的》stand* *a person* up ∥きのうはまた彼女にデートをすっぽかされたよ She *stood me up* again yesterday.
◆彼は仕事をすっぽかして旅行に行った He *left* his work *unfinished* and went on a trip.

すっぽり 赤ん坊を毛布ですっぽりくるむ *wrap up* a baby in a blanket / 村はすっぽりと雪に覆われていた The village was *completely* covered with snow. / そのつぼは箱にすっぽりと収まった The pot fit *perfectly* into the box.

すっぽん soft-shelled turtle ◯
慣用表現 この絵とあの絵とでは月とすっぽんだ(→夜と昼ほどの差がある) This picture and that one are *as different as night and day*.

すで 素手 bare hands ∥素手でボールをつかむ catch a ball 「*with one's bare hands [bare-handed]* ◆素手で(→何も持たずに)戦う fight *unarmed [empty-handed]*

ステーキ steak ◯ ◯ ∥ステーキはレア[ミディアム, ウェルダン]でお願いします I'd like *my steak* rare [medium, well-done].
∥ビーフステーキ a (beef) steak (❖beef は付けないほうがふつう)

ステージ (舞台) stage ◯ ◯ ◯; (演技・演奏) performance ◯ ∥ステージに立つ appear [go] on *stage* / ステージを去る go off *stage* / 彼女の今夜のステージは最高だった She gave *a wonderful performance* this evening.

ステータス status ◯ ∥ステータスシンボル a status symbol

すてき 素敵 ──すてきな nice; lovely, cute (❖主に女性が用いる); (すばらしい) wonderful, great ∥わぁ, すてきな洋服. よく似合ってるわ What a *nice* [*cute*] dress! It looks great on you. / あなたの彼って, すてきな人ね Your boyfriend is a really *nice* guy.
⚡「すてきなプレゼントをありがとう」「どういたしまして」"Thank you for the *nice* present." "You're welcome."

すてご 捨て子 abandoned [deserted] child ◯

すてぜりふ 捨て台詞 parting shot ◯ ∥捨てぜりふを吐く make *a parting shot*

ステッカー sticker ◯ ∥…にステッカーをはる put *a sticker* on …

ステッキ (walking) stick ◯, cane ◯

ステップ (段) step ◯; (ダンスの) step ◯ ∥軽快なステップで with nimble *steps* / これは計画実現へ向けての最初のステップだ This is *the first step* toward realizing the plan.

すててこ suteteko, Japanese-style underpants

すでに 既に (肯定文で) already; (疑問文で) yet ∥警察が到着したときには強盗はすでに逃げ去っていた When the police arrived, the robber had *already* run away.
◆いずれにせよすでに(→今となっては)手遅れだ It's too late *now*, anyhow.

すてね 捨て値 (売る側から見て) giveaway price ◯ ◆私はそれを捨て値で売った I sold it 「*for a song* [*dirt-cheap*].

すてばち 捨て鉢 ──捨てばちな hopeless, desperate ∥捨てばちな態度 a *hopeless* [*desperate*] attitude / 彼は負けて捨てばちになった He 「*became desperate* [*gave up hope*]」 when he was defeated.

すてみ 捨て身 ──捨て身で (死にものぐるいで) in desperation; (死の危険を冒して) at the risk of one's life ∥彼は捨て身で敵に立ち向かった He fought against the enemy *at the risk of his life*.

すてる 捨てる

❶【手離す・廃棄する】throw* away [out], dump ⊕
このおもちゃ, 捨てるわよ I'll *throw away* this toy.
川にごみを捨ててはいけません Don't *dump* any trash in the river.
◆ごみ捨て禁止《掲示》*No Littering* / 銃を捨てろ! *Drop the gun(s)*!
⚡「ここに置いてあった雑誌知らない?」「ごめん, 捨てちゃった」"Have you seen the magazine I left here?" "Oh, sorry. I *threw* it *away*."

❷【断念する・見捨てる】(断念する) give* up; (見捨てる) abandon ⊕, desert ⊕
祖国を捨てる *abandon one's* country / 地位を捨てる *give up one's* position
望みを捨てても何にもならない There's nothing to be gained by *giving up* hope.
彼は自分の考えを捨てきれなかった He *simply couldn't abandon* his idea.
◆男は妻を捨てて別の女性のもとに走った The man *left [walked out on]* his wife for another woman. / 僕だってそう捨てたもんじゃないだろ僕はこの犬小屋, 僕が作ったんだ I made this doghouse by myself. *I'm not that useless, am I*?

ステレオ (装置) stereo (system) ◯; (効果・方式) stereo ◯, stereophonic ◯ ∥その曲はステレオで録音されていますか Is the music recorded *in stereo*?
∥ステレオコンポ stereo components / ステレオ放送 stereophonic broadcasting / カーステレオ a car stereo

ステレオタイプ stereotype ◯
◆ステレオタイプのイメージ a *stereotypical*

ステンドグラス

[*stereotyped*] image
ステンドグラス stained glass ⓤ
ステンレス stainless steel ⓤ ‖この自転車はステンレス製だ This bike is made of *stainless steel*.
スト strike ⓒ ‖スト中である be (out) *on strike* / 賃金カットに反対してストに突入する go (out) on *a strike* against a wage cut / バスのストのせいで学校まで歩かなければならなかった I had to walk to school because of the bus drivers' *strike*.
‖ゼネスト a general strike / ハンスト a hunger strike
ストア store ⓒ ‖コンビニエンスストア a convenience store / チェーンストア a chain store
ストイック ──ストイックな stoic, stoical
ストーカー stalker ⓒ
ストーブ heater ⚠ (※stove は一般に料理用こんろを指すことが多く, 暖房用の意味では通常 heater を用いる) ‖ストーブをつける[消す] turn on [off] *a heater*
‖ガスストーブ a gas heater / 石油ストーブ (米) a kerosene heater, (英) a paraffin heater / 電気ストーブ an electric heater
すどおり 素通り ──素通りする pass by (...) ‖その観光バスはバッキンガム宮殿を素通りしていった The sightseeing bus *passed by* Buckingham Palace.
◆我々はその問題を素通りする(→無視する)わけにはいかない We can't *ignore* the problem.
ストーリー (物語) story ⓒ; (筋) plot ⓒ
ストール (婦人用肩かけ) stole ⓒ
ストッキング stockings (※数えるときは a pair of ... とする) ‖ストッキングをはく[脱ぐ] 「put on [take off] *one's stockings* / ストッキングが伝線しちゃった I've got a run [(英) ladder] in *my stocking*. (※単数形はストッキングの片方だけを指す)
‖パンティーストッキング (米) pantyhose, (英) tights
ストック¹ (在庫) stock ⓤ
ストック² ⚠ (スキーの) ski poles [stocks] (※日本語はドイツ語の Stock から)
ストックホルム Stockholm (※スウェーデンの首都)
ストップ ジャイアンツはタイガースの5連勝にストップをかけた The Giants *stopped* the Tigers' five-game winning streak.
ストップウォッチ stopwatch ⓒ
すどまり 素泊まり 素泊まりで1泊いくらですか How much is *a room without meals*?
ストライキ strike ⓒ ⇒スト
ストライク 〔野球・ボウリング〕strike ⓒ ‖ストライクを取る get *a strike* / カウントはワンストライク, ツーボールです The count is *two (balls) and one (strike)*. (※日本語とカウントの順序が逆になることに注意)
ストライプ stripe ⓒ ‖青いストライプのシャツ a shirt with blue *stripes*
ストリップ strip ⓒ, striptease ⓒⓤ ‖ストリップショー a strip show
関連語 ストリッパー a stripper

ストレート ❶【滞らないこと】彼女は昨年の優勝者にストレートで勝った She won a *straight-set* victory over last year's champion. / She defeated last year's champion *in straight sets*. / 兄は医学部にストレートで合格した My brother entered a medical school *just after finishing high school*.
❷【酒類を薄めないこと】ウイスキーをストレートで飲む drink whisky *straight* [(英) *neat*]
❸【まっすぐ】ストレート(→直球)を投げる pitch *a fast ball* / ストレートのロングヘア long *straight* hair / ストレートな(→率直な)意見を言う a *frank* opinion
ストレス stress ⓤ ‖ストレスを感じる feel *stress* / 友達とのおしゃべりでストレスを解消する 「get rid of [relieve] *one's stress* by chatting with friends / これらの病気の多くはストレスが原因とされている Many of these diseases are considered to be caused by *stress*. / 彼はストレスがたまっている He is under *stress*.
◆ストレスの多い仕事 a *stressful* job
ストレッチ (直線コース) stretch ⓒ; (ストレッチ運動) stretching exercises ‖バックストレッチ a backstretch / ホームストレッチ a homestretch
ストロー straw ⓒ ‖ストローでレモネードを飲む suck lemonade (up) through *a straw*; drink lemonade *with a straw*
ストローク 〔スポーツ〕stroke ⓒ
ストロボ (electric) flash ⓒ, strobe (light) ⓒ ‖ストロボをたく use *a flash* / ストロボ内蔵のカメラ a camera *with a built-in flash*
すとん 子供がすとんと穴に落ちた A child fell *right* into the hole.
ずどん 森の中からずどんという銃の音が聞こえた I heard *the bang [boom]* of a gunshot in the woods.
すな 砂 sand ⓤ ‖1粒の砂 a grain of *sand* / 子供たちは砂遊びが大好きだ Children love playing with sand.
‖砂煙 a cloud of dust / 砂地 sandy soil / 砂時計 an hourglass, a sandglass / 砂場 (米) a sandbox, (英) a sandpit
慣用表現 彼のロンドン生活は友達もなく, 砂をかむようだった His life in London was *deadly dull* [*boring*] since he had no friends there.
すなお 素直 ──素直な (従順な) obedient, docile (※「人の言いなりになる」というニュアンスがある); (穏やかな) gentle, mild ──素直に obediently ──素直さ obedience ⓤ, docility ⓤ; gentleness ⓤ, mildness ⓤ
素直な子 an *obedient* [a *docile*] child / 素直な性格 a *gentle* [*mild*] nature
その犬は主人の言いつけに素直に従った The dog followed the master's order *obediently*.
◆くせのない素直な字 handwriting which is *natural and easy to read*
❓ 「そんなパーティーなんか行きたくないや」「本当は行きたいくせに素直じゃないんだから」"I don't want to go to such a party."

"Oh, don't kid yourself. I know you really want to go.".

スナック 【スナック菓子**】** snack food ⓤ, junk food ⓤ (✤snack はサンドイッチなどの「軽食」のことを指す)

❷【酒場】bar ⓒ, pub ⓒ (✤snack bar は通常酒類は出さない軽食堂を指す)

スナップ ❶【写真】snapshot ⓒ, snap ⓒ ∥ペットのスナップ写真を撮る take *a snap* of a pet

❷【手首の動き】スナップをきかす snap *one's wrist*

❸【留め具】《米》snap (fastener) ⓒ, 《英》(press) stud ⓒ

すなはま 砂浜 beach ⓒ ∥砂浜をジョギングする jog along *the beach*

すなわち 即ち that is (to say), namely, or (✤namely は具体的な例の提示, or は言い換えに用いる) ∥私は彼を信頼する理由があった. すなわち友情だ I had a good reason to trust him— *that is*, friendship. / 冷戦時代は2つの超大国が存在した. すなわちアメリカ合衆国とソビエト連邦だ There were two superpowers during the cold war, *namely* the U.S.A. and USSR. / 彼女は1マイル, すなわち約1,600メートルを走った She ran a mile, *or* about 1,600 meters.

スニーカー 《主に米》sneakers,《英》trainers, plimsolls (✤数えるときは a pair of ... とする)

すね 脛 (向こうずね) shin ⓒ; (脚部) leg ⓒ ∥すねを座卓にぶつける bang *one's shin* on a low table

∥すね当て a leg guard / すね毛 hair of the legs

慣用表現 あの男はすねに傷をもつ身だ(→やましいことがある) The man *has a guilty conscience*. / 親のすねをかじる live [*sponge*] *off one's parents*

すねる 拗ねる sulk ⓘ, get* sulky; (ふくれっ面をする) pout ⓘ ∥彼女は一日中すねていた She *had sulked* all day.

ずのう 頭脳 (知能) brains ⓤ; (頭の働き) head ⓒ ∥すぐれた頭脳 good *brains* / 彼は頭脳明晰(めいせき)だ He「*has a clever head* [*is clever-headed*].

∥頭脳流出 (a) brain drain / 頭脳労働 brainwork / 頭脳労働者 a brainworker

スノー snow ⓤ ∥スノータイヤ a snow tire / スノーボート a snow boat / スノーモービル a snowmobile

スノーボード (競技) snowboarding ⓤ; (板) snowboard ⓒ ――スノーボードをする snowboard ⓘ ⇒ スキーとスノーボード p.755 ∥今週末スノーボードに行く I'll go *snowboarding* this weekend.

すのこ 簀の子 a sunoko, a slatted wooden or plastic board laid on a bathroom floor

スパーク spark ⓒ ∥スパークプラグ a spark plug

スパート spurt ⓒ ――スパートする spurt ⓘ ⇒ ラスト

スパーリング 【ボクシング】sparring ⓤ

スパイ (人) spy ⓒ, secret [intelligence] agent ⓒ; (行為) espionage ⓤ ――スパイする spy ⓘ ∥あの外交官はスパイ活動をして逮捕された The diplomat was arrested for *spying*.

∥スパイ映画 a spy movie / スパイ衛星 a spy satellite / 産業スパイ (人) an industrial spy; (行為) industrial espionage / 二重スパイ a double agent

スパイク ❶【靴などの】(くぎ) spike ⓒ; (スパイクシューズ) spikes, spiked shoes, cleats (✤cleats はサッカーなどの靴. いずれも数えるときは a pair of ... とする)

❷【バレーボール】spike ⓒ ――スパイクする spike ⓗ

∥スパイクタイヤ a spiked tire, a studded tire

スパイス spice ⓒⓤ ◆スパイスのきいたソース *spicy* sauce

スパゲッティ spaghetti ⓤ (✤イタリア語から) ∥スパゲッティをゆでる cook *spaghetti* / スパゲッティミートソース *spaghetti* with meat sauce

すばこ 巣箱 (鳥の) birdhouse ⓒ; (ミツバチの) beehive ⓒ

すばしこい (素早い) quick; (敏捷(びんしょう)な) nimble, agile ――すばしこく quickly; nimbly ∥彼は体のわりにはすばしこい He's *quick* [*nimble, agile*] for someone that big.

すぱすぱ たばこをすぱすぱ吸う puff *on* a cigarette

ずばずば (あけすけに) outspokenly; (率直に) frankly ∥彼女はいつもずばずばものを言う She always speaks *outspokenly*. / She is always *outspoken*.

すはだ 素肌 (bare) skin ⓤ ∥きれいな素肌 clear [beautiful] *skin* / 素肌にゆかたを着る wear a *yukata* next to the skin

スパッツ ⚠ leggings (✤数えるときは a pair of ... とする. 英語の spats は「足首を覆う短いゲートル」の意味)

スパナ 《米》wrench ⓒ,《英》spanner ⓒ

ずばぬける ずば抜ける ずば抜けた学業成績 an *outstanding* academic record / 彼女はずば抜けて歌がうまい She sings [*exceptionally* well [*by far* (the) best]. (✤by far は比較級・最上級を強める) / 彼の英語力はうちのクラスの中でずば抜けている His English ability *stands out* in our class.

すばやい 素早い quick, swift ――素早く quickly, swiftly ∥素早い判断 a *quick* [*swift*] decision / 彼女は素早く異常を察知した She「*quickly* sensed [was *quick* to sense] something unusual. / 火事は素早く消し止められた The fire was *quickly* put out.

すばらしい 素晴らしい wonderful; splendid;《米》marvelous,《英》marvellous; excellent;《口語》great;《口語》fantastic

> wonderful: 最も一般的な語であらゆる場面で用いる.
> splendid: wonderful よりもやや誇張的.
> marvelous: wonderful よりも意味が強く, 予想以上にすばらしいとき.

excellent: 価値や質などがすぐれている.
great: 口語的であらゆる場面で用いる.
fantastic: 口語的で great よりもやや誇張的.

ここからはすばらしい眺めが見えますよ You have a *splendid* view from here.

彼女の料理はすばらしかった Her cooking was *marvelous*.

すばらしい映画だった That was an *excellent* movie.

これはすばらしい絵ですね This is a *great* painting.

彼は地区大会ですばらしい記録を残した He set a *fantastic* record in the local athletic meet.

◆その海はすばらしくきれいだった The sea was *fantastically* beautiful.

ずばり ❶【はっきり】(率直に) frankly ∥ずばり言うのもよいが、時と場合による It's fine to speak *frankly*, but it depends on the time and the situation. / ずばり言って彼の言うことは信用できない *Frankly*, I can't believe what he says.

❷【正確に】just, exactly ∥私の予想はずばり的中した I guessed *just* right. ◆ずばり核心をつく come *straight* to the point

すばる 昴【天文】the Pleiades

スパルタ ⚠ あの学校の教育はスパルタ式だ That school imposes *rigid* [*harsh*] *discipline* on its students.

「スパルタ(式)」は古代ギリシャの都市国家スパルタ Sparta で厳格な教育が行われていたことに由来し、日本語では「時にいきすぎと思われるほど厳しい」という意味で使われるが、英語のSpartanにはそのような含みがなく「(スパルタ人のように)簡素な、質実剛健な」の意味で用いられる.

ずはん 図版 (挿絵) illustration ⓒ; (全ページ大の) plate ⓒ, (図解) figure ⓒ

スピーカー (loud)speaker ⓒ; (拡声装置) public-address system ⓒ((略語)PA) ∥スピーカーから私の名前を呼ぶ声が聞こえた I heard my name called over *the loudspeaker*.

スピーチ (演説・あいさつ) speech ⓒ ⇒ [場面・状況別会話] p.1774 ∥友人の結婚披露宴でスピーチをするように頼まれた I was asked to 「*give a speech* [*say a few words*]」 at a friend's wedding reception.
∥スピーチコンテスト a speech contest

スピード speed ⓒⓊ
フルスピードで *at full speed* / スピード制限を守る observe *the speed limit* / 時速100キロのスピードで運転する drive *at a speed* of 100 kilometers (per hour)
◆彼女は高速に入るとスピードを上げた She *speeded up* after entering the expressway. / 我々は仕事のスピードを上げなければならない We must *speed up* our work. / 列車は徐々にスピードを落とした The train gradually *slowed down*. / (車の運転で)そんなにスピードを出すな Don't *drive too fast*. / そのときはどのくらいのスピードが出ていたんですか *How fast* was your car going then? / 古い世代は時代のスピードについていけない The older generation cannot keep up with *the pace* of the times.
∥スピード違反 speeding / スピード狂 a speed maniac / スピード写真 an instant photo / スピードメーター a speedometer

スピッツ 【動物】spitz

ずひょう 図表 (グラフ) chart ⓒ, graph ⓒ; (線図) diagram ⓒ ∥図表を作る draw *a chart*

スフィンクス sphinx ⓒ

スプーン spoon ⓒ ∥スープ用スプーン *a* soup *spoon* / スプーン3杯の塩 *three spoons* [*spoonfuls*] of salt / スプーンでスープを飲む eat soup with *a spoon*

ずぶとい 図太い (大胆な) bold; (厚かましい) impudent ∥彼女は図太い神経の持ち主だ She is *very impudent*. / She's got quite a nerve.

ずぶぬれ ずぶ濡れ 彼はどしゃ降りの中を歩いてずぶぬれだった He was 「*soaked to the skin* [*dripping wet*]」 after walking in the heavy rain. / 池に落ちてずぶぬれになった I fell into a pond and *got soaked to the skin*.

すぶり 素振り バット[竹刀(しない)]を素振りする *practice* 「*swinging* a bat [*swishing* a bamboo sword]」

スプリング spring ⓒ

スプリンクラー sprinkler ⓒ

スプリンター sprinter ⓒ

スフレ soufflé ⓒⓊ (❖フランス語から)

スプレー spray ⓒ ──スプレーする spray ⊕ ∥ヘアスプレー *a* hair *spray* / スプレー式の殺虫剤 *an* insect *spray* / 壁に塗料をスプレーする *spray* paint on the wall

すべ 術 もう私にはなすすべがない I *don't know what to do*.

スペア (予備) spare ⓒ ∥スペアインク a refill for a pen / スペアキー a spare key / スペアタイヤ a spare tire

スペアリブ spareribs

スペイン Spain ──スペイン人 Spanish ⓒ (複~) ──スペイン語 Spanish Ⓤ ──スペイン(人[語])の Spanish

スペース space Ⓤⓒ, room Ⓤ ∥駐車スペース (*a*) parking *space* / この部屋にはベッドを置くスペースはない There is no *space* to put a bed in this room. / 後ろの席にもう1人分のスペースありますか Is there any *room* for another person in the backseat?

スペースシャトル space shuttle ⓒ

スペード spade ⓒ ∥スペードのクイーン the queen of *spades*

スペクトル 【物理】spectrum ⓒ (複 spectra, ~s) (❖日本語はフランス語の spectre から)

すべすべ ──すべすべの (なめらかな) smooth; (絹のような) silky; (つやのある) sleek ∥赤ちゃんのすべすべした肌 a baby's *smooth* skin

すべて

(まとめて全部) all (❖可算名詞の集まりを指すときは複数扱い、不可算名詞の集まりを指すときは単数扱い); (一つ一つすべて) everything (《単数扱い》) ──すべての all; every (❖単数名詞に

用いる); (一つになって) whole(❖the または所有格の後で単数名詞とともに用いる)
すべて順調だ *All* [*Everything*] is fine.
すべてを白紙に戻す必要がある *Everything needs to go back to the drawing board.*
すべての点であなたに同意する I agree with you in *all* respects.
すべての新聞がその事故を一面のトップで報じた *All the papers* [*Every paper*] *carried the incident at the top of the front page.*(❖定冠詞, 数詞, 代名詞の所有格などは all の後に置く)
すべての計画がうまくいったわけではない *Not* 「*all the plans* [*every plan*] *worked out.*(❖部分否定には not all, not every とする)
勝敗がすべてではない *Winning is not everything.*
国民すべてが王の死を悲しんだ The *whole* nation grieved for the death of the King.
◆この件についてのすべての責任は私にあります I have *full* responsibility for this matter.

すべらす 滑らす 彼女は足を滑らせて階段から落ちた She *slipped* and fell down the stairs.
慣用表現 彼が鹿児島大学を受験することをうっかり口を滑らせて彼女に言ってしまった I *let slip* to her that he's going to take the entrance exam of Kagoshima University.

すべりおちる 滑り落ちる ワイングラスが彼の手から滑り落ちた The wine glass *slipped out of* his hand.

すべりこむ 滑り込む 一塁へ滑り込む *slide into first base* / 授業に何とか滑り込みセーフだった I *made it* to the class 「*just in time* [*in the nick of time*].

すべりだい 滑り台 slide ⓒ // 滑り台で遊ぶ play on *a slide*

すべりだし 滑り出し 滑り出しは順調だ We made *a good start*.

すべりだす 滑り出す (計画などが) get* under way

すべりどめ 滑り止め (坂道で使う車輪用の) skid ⓒ; (階段などの) strip ⓒ; (靴底の) cleats ◆私はすべり止めに蔵王大学を受けた I took the entrance exam of Zao University *to secure a place*.

スペリング spelling ⓤ ⇒ スペル

すべる 滑る
❶【なめらかに移動する】slide* ⓘ, glide ⓘ; (スキーで) ski ⓘ, (スケートで) skate ⓘ
彼は急な斜面を滑り降りた He *slid down* a steep slope.
私はあの山をスキーで滑り降りた I *skied down* that mountain.
引き出しの滑りがよくない The drawers *don't slide well.*
◆ボートは波の上を滑るように進んだ The boat *skimmed* over the waves.
❷【意図せずに】slip ⓘ; (車が) skid ⓘ
ぬれた石を踏んで滑る *slip* on a wet stone
凍った路面で車が滑った The car *skidded* on the icy road.

手が滑ってコップを割ってしまった The glass *slipped from my hand* and broke.
◆道は雨で滑りやすくなっていた The road was *slippery* with rain. / つい口が滑った It was just *a slip of the tongue*.
❸【試験などに】fail ⓘ
彼は国立大学の入学試験にすべった He *failed the entrance examination* for a national university.

スペル ⚠ spelling ⓒ (❖spell には名詞として「スペル, つづり」の意味はない) // これはイギリス英語のスペルだ This is *a British spelling*.
◆その単語のスペルを教えてください How do you *spell* that word, please? / この手紙はスペルミスだらけだ There are so many *misspellings* in this letter.

スポイト ⚠ dropper ⓒ (❖日本語はオランダ語の spuit から)

スポークスマン spokesperson ⓒ, spokesman ⓒ (❖最近では性差別を避けるため前者を用いることが多い)

スポーツ

sport ⓒ ⓤ (❖sport は運動だけではなくビリヤードなどのゲームや狩猟なども意味する)
私はスポーツが好きだ I like *sports* [《英》*sport*].
何かスポーツをやりますか Do you *enjoy* [*practice*, 《口語的》*do*] any *sports*?
父は週末はたいていテレビでスポーツを見ています My father usually *watches sports* on TV on weekends.
彼はなかなかのスポーツマンだ He's *good at sports.* / He's quite *an athlete.*(❖sportsman, sportswoman はフェアプレーをする人を指すため, 日本語の「スポーツマン」は用例のように表現する)
野球は日本では国民的スポーツだ Baseball is *a national sport* in Japan.
∥スポーツウエア sportswear / スポーツカー a sports car / スポーツ界 the sports world / スポーツ記者 a sports reporter / スポーツクラブ a health club / スポーツ新聞 a sports newspaper / スポーツニュース sports news / スポーツマンシップ sportsmanship / スポーツ用品 《米》sporting goods, 《英》sporting equipment / スポーツ欄 a sports section / アウトドアスポーツ outdoor sports / インドアスポーツ indoor sports / ウインタースポーツ winter sports

スポーティー ⚠ 彼はきょうはスポーティーな服装をしている He's wearing *casual* clothes today. (❖sporty は服装に用いると「はでな」の意味)

ずぼし 図星 友達が宏と朋子はつきあってると言っていたが図星だった My friend 「*hit the bull's eye* [*hit the nail on the head*] when he suspected Hiroshi was dating Tomoko.

スポット (場所) spot ⓒ // 山下公園は定番のデートスポットだ Yamashita Park is one of *the most popular date spots*.
◆その番組は問題のもう一つの側面にスポットを

当てた The program *highlighted* another side of the problem.
∥スポット広告 a spot / スポットニュース spot news
スポットライト spotlight © ∥スポットライトを浴びる come into *the spotlight*
すぼむ become* narrow
すぼめる 傘をすぼめる *fold* [*close*] *an umbrella* / 口[唇]をすぼめる *pucker* (*up*) *one's mouth* [*lips*] / 肩をすぼめるのはアメリカ人の典型的なジェスチャーだ *Shrugging one's shoulders is a typical gesture of Americans.*
ずぼら ーずぼらな（だらしがない）slovenly；（怠惰な）negligent ◆あいつはずぼらなやつだ《口語的》He is *a slob*.
ズボン trousers, 《米》pants（❖数えるときは a pair of ... とする。pants は《英》では下着のこと）/ ズボンをはく[脱ぐ]「*put on* [*take off*] *trousers*」/ ズボンのすそ上げをする *shorten trousers* / 新しい[白い]ズボンを買う buy「*a new pair of trousers* [*a pair of white trousers*]」(❖形容詞の位置の違いに注意)
このズボンは大きすぎる[きつすぎる] These *trousers* are too large [tight].
∥半ズボン shorts
スポンサー sponsor © ◆テレビ番組のスポンサーになる *sponsor* a TV program
スポンジ sponge ©Ⓤ ∥スポンジで浴槽を洗う wash the bathtub *with a sponge*
∥スポンジケーキ a sponge cake
スマート ースマートな （体型が）slim, slender（❖smart にこの意味はない）；（服装が）smart, stylish ∥彼女はスマートだから何を着ても似合う Because she is *slim*, she looks nice wearing anything.
◆彼女はいつも着こなしがスマートだ She always dresses *smartly*. / 彼はその交渉をとてもスマートにやってのけた He handled the negotiations *with such grace*.
すまい 住まい （家）house ©；（家庭生活の営まれる場所）home ©（❖《米》では home も「建物の意味でしばしば用いられる」）/ りっぱなお住まいですね You have *a wonderful house*. / 二人は郊外に住まいを持った The couple made *their home* in the suburbs. ◆ホテル住まいする「*stay at* [*live in*] *a hotel*」/ お住まいはどちらですか Where do you *live*?
すます¹ 済ます
❶【終える】finish ⓔ, get* through with ...
夏休みの宿題, もうすました? Have you *finished* your summer vacation homework yet?
それをすましたらもう帰ってもいいですよ After you「*get through* [*are done*] *with* that, you can go home.
◆もう支払いはすませた I've already *paid*. / 笑ってすますことではない It's no *laughing matter*. / 時間がないので堅苦しいあいさつは抜きですまして(→先に進んで)ください Please *move on* without formal greetings because we're running out of time.
❷【間に合わす】（不十分だが）make* do with ...
本当は6人必要だったが5人ですませた We actually needed six people, but *made do with* five.
◆昼は残り物ですませた I *just had* the leftovers for lunch. / 電話で用事はすませた I've done the work on the telephone.
すます² 澄ます ❶【耳を】耳をすましてごらん *Listen carefully*.
❷【態度を】姉はいつもすましている My sister *is always prim and proper*. / 容疑者はすました顔で自分は何も知らないと言った The suspect said that he knew nothing *with an innocent look*.
すませる 済ませる ➪ すます(済ます)
スマッシュ （テニスなどの）smash © ースマッシュする smash ⓔ ⓘ
すまない 済まない すまないが今回はあきらめてほしい *I'm afraid* I would like you to give it up this time. / あなたにはすまないことをしました *I am sorry* for what I did to you.
すみ¹ 隅 corner ©
部屋の隅には古雑誌がたくさん積み上げてある A lot of old magazines are heaped up in *the corner of* the room.
レポートは左上の隅をホチキスでとじなさい Staple your paper together in *the* top left *corner*.
このことは頭の隅においておいてください Keep this in *some corner of your mind*.
部屋を隅から隅まで捜したがかぎは見つからなかった I searched *every nook and corner* [*cranny*] of my room for the key, but I couldn't find it.
慣用表現 彼女をくどいてたなんてあいつも隅におけないね He made a play for her. He *isn't one to take lightly*.
すみ² 炭 charcoal Ⓤ ∥炭火でステーキを焼く broil steak *over charcoal* / 炭火焼きの料理 *charcoal-broiled* dishes
すみ³ 墨 （墨汁）India [Chinese] ink Ⓤ；（棒状の）ink stick ©；（タコ・イカの）ink Ⓤ ∥墨をする rub *an ink stick* (on a stone plate) to make ink
-ずみ -済み 売約済み《掲示》Sold / それは初めから計算済みだ It *has been taken into consideration* from the beginning. / もうそれは用済みだ We *don't need* it any more.
すみえ 墨絵

墨絵は墨だけで描く伝統的な絵画で, 日本には中国から伝えられました。墨絵は描き方によって白描画と水墨画の2つに分けられます。前者は輪郭を線だけで表したもの, 後者は墨の濃淡, ぼかしやにじみなどを生かしたものです。墨絵は使用する筆や紙の質によっても微妙に仕上がりの印象が変わります。
Sumie, traditional painting made only with *sumi* (India ink), was brought to Japan from China. Depending on the method of painting, *sumie* can be classified into two styles: *hakubyoga* and

すみか 住みか（家）house, 《公式的》dwelling;（犯罪者などの隠れ家）den

すみごこち 住み心地　新居は住み心地がいい Our new house is *comfortable to live in*. / この家の住み心地はいかがですか How do you *like living* in this house?

すみこみ 住み込み　あの店には住み込みの料理人が2人いる There are two *live-in* cooks in the restaurant. / その店の店員は住み込みで働いている That shop's clerk *lives in*.

すみずみ 隅々　車の中を隅々まで探す search *every inch* of the car / 隅々まで本を読む read a book *from cover to cover* / 彼の名前は世界の隅々まで知れ渡っている His name is known *all over* [*throughout*] the world.

すみなれる 住み慣れる　住み慣れたわが家 my (*dear*) *old* house / 彼は住み慣れた町を出ていった He left the town *where he had lived so long*.

すみません 済みません
❶【謝罪】I'm sorry.;（軽い謝罪）Excuse me., Sorry., Pardon me.（✥Excuse me., Sorry.よりも形式ばった言い方。I beg your pardon.はさらに丁寧な表現）

> 【語法】I'm sorry.は自分に非があることを認め謝罪する表現なので、人に軽くぶつかったときや人のすぐそばを通るとき、中座するときなど儀礼的に「すみません」という場合はExcuse me.がふつう。せきやくしゃみが出たときにもいう.

すみません、もう一度言ってもらえますか Excuse me [*Sorry*], could you say it again please?
すみません、きょうはもう閉店です I'm sorry, but we're closed today.
遅れてどうもすみません I'm sorry I'm [to be, for being] late.
ご迷惑をおかけして本当にすみませんでした I'm very [so] sorry to have troubled you.
◆すみません、お名前を思い出せなくて I'm afraid your name escapes me.（✥I'm afraid ... は好ましくないことを述べたり、遠慮がちに話す場合に用いる）

❷【呼びかけ】Excuse me.
（店先などで）すみません Excuse me./ Hello.
すみません、今何時ですか Excuse me. Do you have the time, please?
◆おじゃましてすみません、ちょっとお尋ねしたいのですが I'm sorry to bother you, but I'd like to ask you some questions. / すみませんが窓を閉めてもらえますか Could you do me a favor and close the window?

❸【感謝】Thank you.
いろいろとどうもすみません Thank you very much for everything.
🅔「頼まれた手紙、出しときましたよ」「すみません」"I posted the letter you asked me to." "*Thank you very much*."

すみやか 速やか　──速やかな prompt;（即刻の）immediate // 速やかな回答を要求する request a *prompt* answer
◆速やかに避難する evacuate *immediately*

すみれ 菫　violet // すみれ色 violet
(俳句) 山路来て何やらゆかしすみれ草（松尾芭蕉）
On a mountain path,
what is it that moves my soul?
Some wild violets.

すむ¹ 住む

live（✥一時的に住んでいることを強調する場合以外は通例進行形にしない）,《公式的》dwell*;（集団的に）inhabit（✥しばしば受身で用いる）

両親は北海道に住んでいます My parents *live in* Hokkaido.
私はかつてこの通りに住んでいた I used to *live on* [《英》*in*] this street.
妹は今（一時的に）おばの家に住んでいる My sister *is now living* 「*with* our aunt [*at* our aunt's].
オーストラリアに住んで5年たちます I've been *living in* Australia for five years.
この島には人も動物も住んでいない The island *is inhabited* by no humans nor animals.
◆この村には約100世帯が住んでいる This village *has* about a hundred families. / 庭に野良猫が住みついてしまった A stray cat *has settled* in my garden.

すむ² 済む
❶【完了する】finish, be finished;（終わった状態）be over
それがすんだらこっちを手伝ってください When you *finish* with that, please give me a hand.
会議は30分ですんだ The meeting (*was*) *finished* in half an hour.
試験がやっとすんだ The exam *is* finally *over*.
◆先生との話はすんだの? Have you *finished* talking with the teacher? / すんだことはしかたがない What is done 「*is done* [*cannot be undone*]. / すんだことは水に流そう Let bygones be bygones.
🅔「もうすんだ?」「まだ」"*Are you finished?*" "*Not yet.*"（✥Have you finished?より口語的）

❷【用が足りる】do*;（何とかこなす）get* by
それですみますよ That'll *do*.
借金をしないですみそうだ I seem to 「*get by* [*manage*] without borrowing money.
◆タクシーを拾えたので歩かずにすんだ Because I could get a taxi, I *didn't have to* walk. / 1,000円ですんだ It cost *only* 1,000 yen. / それは金ですむ（→解決する）問題ではない That's not a problem which can *be solved* by money.

❸【その他】
気がすむ（→満足する）まで何度でもやってみなさい

Try again and again until you *are satisfied*.

すむ³ 澄む ──澄んだ clear ‖澄んだ水 *clear water* / 青く澄んだ空 the *clear* blue sky / 澄んだ声 a *clear* voice ◆澄んだ(→けがれのない)瞳 *one's innocent* eyes

スムーズ 話し合いはスムーズに運んだ The talk went on *smoothly*. / 文化祭の準備はスムーズにいっている Preparations for the school festival are going *well*.

ずめん 図面 (設計図) plan ⓒ; (青写真) blueprint ⓒ ‖家の図面を引く draw (up) *the plans* for a house

すもう 相撲 🖼 sumo ⓤ ⇒ 相撲 p.775

相撲は長い歴史をもつ日本の格闘技ですが、現在見られる形式の基本ができあがったのは江戸時代です。まわしだけを身につけた2人の力士が土俵の上で闘います。取組の前には塩をまいて土俵を清め、しこを踏んで悪霊を追い払います。土俵の外に押し出されたり、足の裏以外の部分が少しでも土俵につけば負けになります。
Sumo is a combative sport of Japan with a long history. It was in the Edo period (1603-1867) that the basic style of what we see now was established. The two wrestlers, who wear nothing but *mawashi* (silken loincloths), compete in a round ring called a *dohyo*. Before each match, they scatter salt to purify the ring and stamp their feet to drive evil spirits away. If a wrestler is forced out of the ring or any part of his body except the soles of his feet touches the ground, he loses.

スモーク smoke ⓤ ‖スモークサーモン smoked salmon

スモッグ smog ⓤ ‖光化学スモッグ a photochemical smog

すもも 李 〖植物〗 plum ⓒ

すやき 素焼き (物) unglazed pottery ⓤ
◆素焼きの鉢 an *unglazed* pot

すやすや (ぐっすり) soundly; (穏やかに) peacefully ‖赤ちゃんは母親の腕の中ですやすや眠っていた The baby was sleeping *soundly* in its mother's arms.

-すら even ⇒ -さえ

スライス ❶ [薄いひと切れ] slice ⓒ
◆オニオンスライス *sliced* onion / タマネギをスライスする *slice* an onion
❷ [ボールの] slice ⓒ

スライダー 〖野球〗 slider ⓒ

スライディング 〖野球〗 sliding ⓤ
◆ホームにヘッドスライディングする *slide* into home *headfirst*

スライド slide ⓒ ‖スライドを映す project [show] *slides* ◆賃金は物価スライド制だ Wages *are indexed* to prices.
‖スライド映写機 a slide projector / スライドグラス a slide

ずらかる ずらかるぞ! *Let's get out of here!*

ずらす move ㉘, shift ㉘ ‖少しいすをずらしてください Could you please *move* [*shift*] the chair a bit? / きょうは昼休みをずらした I *shifted* my lunch break today.
◆計画をずらす(→延期する) *postpone* a plan; (→繰り上げる) *move up* a plan ‖この会社では部署によって始業時間をずらしている The starting times of this company's sections *are staggered*. (❖stagger は「(勤務時間、休日などを)重ならないようにずらす」の意味)

すらすら (容易に) easily, with ease; (流暢(りゅうちょう)に) fluently; (順調に) smoothly ‖彼は中国語をすらすら読める He can read Chinese *with ease*. / すらすら事が運んだ Things went on *smoothly*.
◆彼女は警官の質問にすらすら(→ためらいなく)答えた She answered the policeman's questions *without hesitation*.

すらっ ⇒ すらり

スラックス slacks (❖数えるときは a pair of ... とする)

スラッシュ slash ⓒ ⇒ 巻末付録 (句読法)

スラム slum ⓒ; (スラム街) the slums ‖スラム化する turn into *a slum*

すらり すらりとした女性 a *slender* woman / 彼女はすらりとした足をしている She *has long* (*slender*) *legs*. /《口語的》 She's *leggy*.

ずらり その通りには似たような家がずらりと並んでいる *There are rows of* similar houses on the street. / バス停にずらりと人が並んでいる *Many* people are lined up at the bus stop.

スラローム slalom ⓒ

スラング slang ⓤ ‖スラングを使う use *slang*

スランプ slump ⓒ ‖スランプを抜け出す come out of *a slump* / そのチームのエースピッチャーはこのところスランプに陥っている The ace pitcher on the team has hit [been in] *a slump* recently.

すり 掏摸 (人) pickpocket ⓒ; (行為) pickpocketing ⓤ ‖する (掏る) ‖すりに注意〖掲示〗 *Beware of Pickpockets*
◆すりにやられた I *had my pocket picked*.

すりあがる 刷り上がる 初版が刷り上がるのはいつごろですか When will the first edition *be off the press*?

ずりおちる ずり落ちる (するりと) slip off; (ずるずると) slide* down ‖かばんが肩からずり落ちた The bag *slipped off* [*down from*] my shoulder.

すりかえる すり替える 手品師はそのカードを他のカードにすり替えた The magician *secretly replaced* the card with another one. / 彼は話をうまくすり替えた He *cleverly changed* the subject.

すりガラス 磨りガラス frosted [ground] glass ⓤ

すりきず 擦り傷 scrape ⓒ, scratch ⓒ ‖ひざにすり傷を作る「*get a scrape* on [*scrape*] one's knee

すりきれる 擦り切れる wear* out ‖このシャツはそで口がすり切れてきた This shirt *has worn out* at the cuffs.
◆すり切れたコート a *worn-out* coat

すりこぎ 擂り粉木 wooden pestle [pésl] ⓒ

テーマ別表現集

●相撲

❶相撲のしきたりについての表現

1. すべての力士は相撲部屋に所属しています。
   Every sumo wrestler belongs to a stable.
2. 親方の妻はおかみさんと呼ばれ、母親のように力士たちの面倒を見ます。
   The wife of a stable master is called *okamisan*, and she takes care of the wrestlers like a mother.
3. 番付は各力士の位を示すもので、各場所の前に発表されます。
   The *banzuke* is a list that shows the rank of each wrestler. It is announced before each tournament.
4. 力士は上から横綱、大関、関脇のように番付がなされています。
   Wrestlers are ranked with yokozuna [grand champion] at the top, followed by ozeki [champion], sekiwake [junior champion], and so on.
5. 大相撲は日本各地で1年に6場所開催され、1つの場所は15日間続きます。
   There are six sumo tournaments a year held in different parts of Japan. Each tournament lasts 15 days.
6. 力士たちは日本中を巡業して回ります。
   Wrestlers go on tour and wrestle in tournaments all over Japan.

❷儀式についての表現

1. 幕内 [十両] 力士が化粧まわしを着けて土俵入りしました。
   The wrestlers in「the top [the second highest] division entered the ring wearing decorated aprons.
2. 行司は軍配と呼ばれる特別なうちわのようなものを使います。
   The *gyoji*, or referee, uses a special fan called a *gumbai*.
3. 取組の前に力士は呼び出しに名前を呼ばれ、土俵に上がります。
   Before matches, the wrestlers' names are called by a ring caller, and then they go up into the ring.
4. 力士は土俵を清めるために塩をまきます。
   Wrestlers toss salt to purify the ring.
5. 力士は実際の取組の前に塩まきと仕切りを繰り返します。
   Wrestlers repeat the salt-tossing and the getting-set routine before the real match.
6. 見せて回っているあの幕は、この取組にスポンサーの懸賞がかけられているということを表しています。
   The banners they are carrying around show the sponsors offering cash awards in this match.
7. 勝った力士は行司から懸賞を受け取ります。
   The winner accepts the prize money from the referee.

❸取組・勝負に関する表現

1. 相撲に使われる決まり手は82手あります。
   There are 82 winning techniques used in sumo.
2. 大ノ海は北ノ山を寄り切り [押し出し] で破りました。
   Onoumi beat Kitanoyama by「a force out [pushing him out of the ring].
3. 西ノ山は今までのところ7勝3敗です。
   So far Nishinoyama has won seven and lost three.
4. 東ノ海がついに全勝優勝を果たしました。
   Higashinoumi finally won a tournament without losing a single match.
5. 北ノ里は2場所連続の勝ち越しを決めました。
   Kitanosato achieved a winning record (8 or more wins out of a total 15 matches) in two tournaments in a row.
6. 彼はきょう負けると負け越しが決まります。
   If he loses today's match, he will have a losing record (8 or more losses out of a total 15 matches).
7. 西ノ里は、上手投げを打つ前に足が土俵から出ていたので、負けました。
   Nishinosato's foot was outside the rope before he did an overarm throw, so he lost.
8. ふつう力士は相手にまわしを取られたら勝ち目は少なくなります。
   Generally if the wrestler allows his opponent to get hold of his *mawashi* belt, he will have less chance of winning the match.
9. 立ち会いの呼吸が合わず、仕切り直しになりました。
   The wrestlers were unable to start the match simultaneously, so they had to get set on their starting lines again.
10. その取組は長引いて、行司が水入りを宣しました。
    The match went on for a long time, so the referee gave the wrestlers a water break.
11. 今の一番に物言いがついて、協議の結果取り直しとなりました。
    The referee's decision in this match was contested, and after a discussion it was decided that the wrestlers will have a rematch.

すりこむ 擦り込む 傷口に軟膏(な)をすり込む *rub* an ointment *into* the wound

スリット slit ⓒ ∥長いスリットの入ったチャイナドレス a Chinese dress with *a* long *slit*

スリッパ slippers (❖数えるときは a pair of ... とする. 英語の slippers はかかとの覆われた室内履きも指す)

スリップ ❶【滑ること】slip ⓒ; (自動車の) skid ⓒ ──**スリップする** slip ⓔ; skid ⓔ ∥ スリップした跡 a *skid* mark ∕ 我々の乗った車は凍った道路でスリップした Our car *skidded* [*went into a skid*] on the icy road.
❷【女性の下着】slip ⓒ
∥スリップ事故 an accident caused by a skid

すりつぶす 擂り潰す (柔らかい物を) mash ⓔ; (硬い物を) grind* ⓔ ∥ごまをすりつぶす *grind* sesame seeds

すりぬける 擦り抜ける (通り抜ける) pass through ... ∕ ∥人込みをすり抜ける *pass through* the crowd

すりばち 擂り鉢 mortar ⓒ ∥すり鉢で山芋をする grind yams *in a mortar*

すりへらす 磨り減らす wear* ⓔ ∥彼はその事件の取材に駆け回ったが靴をすり減らしただけだった He rushed around to cover the case, but just *wore* his shoes *out*. ∕ 私は不慣れな仕事に神経をすり減らした I *wore my nerves to a frazzle* doing that unfamiliar job.

すりへる 磨り減る wear* ⓔ; (すり減っている) be worn ∥靴のかかとがすっかりすり減ってしまった The heels of the shoes *have* completely *worn down*.

スリム ──**スリムな** slim ∥彼女は私よりスリムだ She is *slimmer* than me [I].
◆この運動はウエストをスリムにします This exercise *slims* your waist.

すりむく 擦り剝く scrape ⓔ, skin ⓔ ∥ひざをすりむいた I *scraped* [*skinned*] my knee.

すりよる 擦り寄る snuggle ⓔ ∥子犬が鼻をくんくんさせながらすり寄ってきた A puppy *was* whining *and snuggling* up to me.
◆あいつは昇進目的で上司にすり寄っている He *approaches* his boss for a promotion.

スリラー thriller ⓒ (小説・映画) thriller ⓒ

スリル thrill ⓒ ∥スリル満点のジェットコースターだった The roller coaster was「full of *thrills* [*thrilling*]. ∕ 私は最高のスリルを味わった I got *a* real *thrill*.

する¹ 為る

❶ 行う	do
❷ 状態にある	
❸ 仕事・役割が…である	be
❹ 人・物を…にする	make
❺ 決める	decide
❻ 感じられる	feel
❼ 値段が…である	cost

❶【行う】do* ⓔ ⓔ (❖「名詞＋(を)する」という表現(「洗濯(を)する」「話をする」など)は, 目的語に当たる名詞(「洗濯」「話」など)の項目を参照)
きょうはもう何もすることがない There's nothing left to *do* today.
言われたとおりにしなさい *Do* as you are told.
できるだけのことはするつもりです I'm going to *do* the best I can.
試験に落ちていたらどうしよう *What should I do* if I didn't pass the exam?
こんなに散らかして. 何とかしなさい What a mess! *Do something*!
あいつのすることはすべて気にくわない I hate *every little thing* he *does*.
◆どうしたら英語がうまくなるんだろう *How could I improve my English?*
💬「日曜日には何をするの」「たいてい友達とテレビゲームをするね」"What do you *do* on Sundays?" "I usually *play* video games with my friends."
💬「私の人形に何をしたの」「何もしてないよ」"What did you *do* to my doll?" "Nothing."

❷【状態にある】
静かにしなさい！ *Be* quiet!
彼女は細い腕をしている She *has* slender arms.
母親は心配そうな顔をして息子を見送った The mother saw off her son *with* an anxious look on her face.
機械が動かないんだ. いったいどうしたんだろう The machine won't work. *What* on earth *has happened*?
(医者が患者に)どうしましたか *What can I do for you*?

❸【仕事・役割が…である】be ⓔ
彼は服のデザイナーをしている He *is* a dress designer.
おじは高校の数学教師をしている My uncle *is* a high school math *teacher*. ∕ (→高校で数学を教えている) My uncle *teaches* math at a high school.
◆彼は北海道で医者をしている He *works as* a doctor in Hokkaido. ∕ 姉はこの町でパン屋をしている(→経営している) My sister *runs* a bakery in this town.

❹【人・物を…にする】make* ⓔ
我々は彼女をリーダーにした We *made* her a leader.
この料理はもっと甘くしたほうがいいようだ We'd better *make* this dish sweeter.
◆箱をいすにする(→いすとして使う) *use* a box *as* a chair ∕ 髪を短くする(→切ってもらう) *have* one's hair cut short

❺【決める】decide ⓔ, take* ⓔ; (選ぶ) choose* ⓔ
出発日を6月10日にした I *decided to* leave June 10. ∕ I *chose* June 10 for my departure
◆ええと, 僕はチャーハンにします Well, *I'd like (to have)* fried rice. ∕ さて, そろそろ行くとするか Well, I'd better get going now. ∕ 彼は朝, ふろに入ることにしている He *makes it a rule* to take a bath in the morning.
💬「どちらのシャツになさいますか」「こっちの白いほ

うにします」"Which shirt would you take?" "I'd take this white one."

❻【感じられる】(感じる) feel*; (聞こえる) hear*; (音がする) sound; (味がする) taste; (においがする) smell*

めまいがする I feel dizzy.

壁の向こうで人の話し声がする I can hear people talking through the wall.

この楽器は安っぽい音がする This instrument sounds cheap.

そのスープはトマトの味がした The soup tasted of tomato.

ジンチョウゲはいい香りがする Daphne smells good.

あんな言い方をされたらだれだっていい気はしないよ Nobody feels good when told something like that.

❼【値段が…である】cost*

この時計は5万円もした This watch cost as much as 50,000 yen.

そのギターはいくらしましたか How much did the guitar cost? / How much was the guitar?

❽【時間が経過する】

あと1時間もすればみんなに追いつけるだろう I will be able to catch up with them in an hour or so.

彼は1時間もしないうちに音を上げた He gave up within an hour.

❾【身につける】put* on; (身につけている) wear*

マスクをしてください Put on a mask.

彼は高価な時計をしている He wears an expensive watch.

❿【試みる・まさに…するところだ】(試みる) try to do; (今にも…しつつある) be about to do

びんのふたをあけようとしたが、固くてあけられなかった I tried to take the lid off the bottle, but it was so tight that I couldn't.

飛行機はまさに飛び立とうとしていた The plane was about to take off.

⓫【仮定する・立場をとる】

それが本当だとすれば大変なことになる If it is true, things will go terribly wrong.

彼女にすれば怒るのも当然だ It was natural for her to get mad.

する² 擦る (硬いものをすりつぶす) grind*; (マッチを) strike; (こする) rub; (金を) lose*, waste ∥ごまをする grind sesame seeds / マッチをする strike a match /

亮子は両手をすり合わせて暖めた Ryoko rubbed her hands together to warm them. / 男は競馬で持ち金を全部すった The man lost [wasted] all the money he had on the horse race.

する³ 刷る print ⇒いんさつ

する⁴ 掏る 電車の中で財布をすられてしまった I had my「wallet stolen [(→ポケットの中身を抜き取られた) pocket picked] in the train.

ずる ゲームでずるをするなよ! (→ずるをしようとするな) Don't try to cheat! / (→ずるをやめろ) Stop cheating! / 正はずるをして掃除をサボっている Tadashi unfairly shirks cleaning.

ずるい (ずる賢い) cunning, sly, wily; (不公平な) unfair; (不誠実な) dishonest

おべっか使うなんてあいつはずるいやつだ He's cunning [sly, wily] to flatter.

失敗を彼女のせいにするのはずるいよ It's unfair of you to blame her for the failure.

彼はずるい手を使って勝とうとした He tried to take unfair [dishonest] measures to win.

◆それはずるいよ That's not fair! / That's cheating!

ずるがしこい ずる賢い cunning, sly

するする 猿はするする木を登っていった The monkey climbed up the tree nimbly. / 彼は敵のディフェンスをするすると(→難なく)かわしていった He went easily through the opponents' defense. / 旗はポールをするする上がった The flag went up the pole smoothly.

ずるずる 私たちはその大きな袋を部屋までずるずると引きずっていった We dragged the large bag into the room. / 彼はラーメンをずるずるとすすった He slurped ramen. / 少年は鼻水をずるずるすすった The boy sniffed his runny nose noisily. / これといった案が出ず、ミーティングはずるずると長引いた The meeting dragged on without any good ideas. / 彼は借金の返済をずるずる延ばしている He keeps putting off the repayment of his loans. / 彼女は土手の上からずるずる滑り落ちた She slithered [slid] down the bank. / 彼は悪の道にずるずるとのめり込んでいった He got deeper and deeper into a life of vice.

-するために 彼は試験に合格するために一生懸命勉強した He studied hard (in order) to pass the exam. (❖in order to do は形式ばった表現で、目的を明確にした言い方) / 彼らは旅行をするためにお金をためなければならない They have to lay aside some money for traveling. ⇒ため

するっと コップが手からするっと滑り落ちた The glass slipped from my hand to the floor.

すると すると君は何も知らないんだね Then [So] you don't know anything about it, do you? / 階段を駆け上がった。するとそこで彼女が待っていた I ran up the stairs. And there she was waiting for me.

するどい 鋭い

❶【鋭利な・とがった】sharp,《文語》keen

鋭いナイフ a sharp [keen] knife

❷【感覚・頭の働き】sharp, keen; (小さな違いに気がつく) acute

犬は鋭い嗅覚(きゅうかく)をもっている Dogs have a sharp [an acute, a keen] sense of smell.

彼は彼女の鋭い質問にたじろいだ He winced at her sharp [keen] question.

彼は観察力が鋭い He makes sharp [keen, acute] observations.

◆彼はその案の問題点を鋭く(→的確に)指摘した He keenly pointed out the problems with the plan.

❸【痛み・音】sharp
鋭い痛み (a) *sharp* [*acute*] pain / 高く鋭い音 a high *sharp* sound
❹【その他】
目つきの鋭い男 a man with a *sharp* look in his eyes
彼の目が鋭く光った His eyes glinted *sharply*.

-するほうがいい -する方がいい ➔ほう(方)

するめ dried squid [C]

ずるやすみ ずる休み (学校の) truancy [U]
—ずる休みする (学校を) play truant [《主に米・口語的》hooky]; (サボる)《口語的》skip [他] //彼女は3日続けて学校をずる休みした She *played truant* [*hooky*] for three days in a row. / 兄はきょうかぜをひいたといって会社をずる休みした Today my brother pretended to have a cold and *skipped work*.

するりと 魚は私の手からするりと逃げた The fish *slipped* out of my hands *and went away*. / その選手は敵のディフェンスをするりと(→難なく)かわした The player evaded the opponent's defense *easily*.

ずれ (差異) difference [C] [U]; (隔たり) gap [C]; (時間の) (time-)lag [C] //彼らの間には意見のずれがある There is *a difference* of opinion between them. / 彼は息子と話していて世代間のずれを感じた He felt *a generation gap* as he talked with his son. / 到着予定の時間と実際に彼女が到着した時間とでは2時間もずれがあった There was *a lag* of as long as two hours between the estimated time of her arrival and the actual time she arrived.
◆机のずれを直しなさい(→正しい位置へ少しずらしなさい) *Move* the desk *a little to the right place*. / 大雨のためスケジュールにずれが生じた(→変更された) The timetable [schedule] *was changed* due to the heavy rain.

スレート slate [C] //スレートぶきの屋根 a *slate* roof

ずれこむ ずれ込む 最終的な決定は翌週までずれ込んだ The final decision *was put off* until the next week.

すれすれ ❶【触れそうなくらい近く】そのバイクは自動車のわきすれすれを(→もう少しでこすりそうになりながら)走っていった The motorcycle passed *almost* [*nearly*] *scraping* the side of a car. / ツバメが水面すれすれに飛んでいた A swallow *was skimming* the water.
❷【限度いっぱい】彼は時間すれすれで試験会場に現れた He turned up *just in time for* the examination. / 彼女はすれすれのところで入学試験に受かった She *narrowly* [*barely*] passed the entrance examination. / 彼のしたことは犯罪すれすれだ What he has done is *almost* [*close to*] a crime.

すれちがい 擦れ違い 私と彼とはちょうどすれ違いになったようだ He and I seem to *have* just *missed each other*. / 彼女はすれ違いざまに校長先生に会釈をした She nodded to the principal *as* she *passed* (*by* him [her]). / 彼ら夫婦は仕事の事情で，すれ違いの多い生活をしている He and his wife *don't see each other* very often at home due to their jobs.

すれちがう 擦れ違う ❶【通りなどで】pass [他] [自] //2台の車が道ですれ違った The two cars *passed each other* on the road. / 彼女は通りで私とすれ違ったが全然気づかなかった She *passed* (*by*) me on the street, but didn't recognize me at all.
❷【行き違いになる】時間に遅れて，わずかの差で彼女とすれ違ってしまった I *missed* her by a few minutes because I was late.
❸【意見などが】2人は話がすれ違っている(→互いの論点をつかみそこねている)ようだ Each one seems to *be missing the other's point*.

すれる 擦れる (摩滅する) wear* out, be worn out; (世間ずれする) become* too sophisticated; (ずる賢くなる) become cunning [sly] //ズボンがすれて穴があいてしまった My pants *are* so *worn out* that there's a hole in them.
◆この靴はかかとがすれる These shoes *rub* against my heels.

ずれる (滑って移動する) slide* [自], slip [自]; (移動する) move [自]; (規範などから逸脱する) deviate [自] //運動していて眼鏡がずれた My glasses *slid out of place* while I was exercising. / 机の位置がきのうと少しずれている The desk *has moved* a little from where it was yesterday. / 彼はふつうの人と金銭感覚がずれている His sense of money value *deviates from* that of ordinary people.
◆大雨のため電車の到着が15分ずれた(→遅れた) The train's arrival *was delayed* by 15 minutes due to the heavy rain. / その写真はピントがずれていた The photograph *was out of focus*. / ボーカルがバンドの演奏と少しずれている The vocals *are* slightly *out of sync* with the band. / 彼はバットを振るタイミングがずれている(→正しいタイミングで振っていない) He *doesn't swing* his bat *at the right time*.

スローガン slogan [C] //「ノー・モア・ヒロシマ」は有名な反核スローガンである "No more Hiroshimas" is *a* famous anti-nuclear *slogan*.

スロープ (斜面) slope [C]; (傾斜路) ramp [C]

スローモーション slow motion [U] //彼のプレーを今度はスローモーションで見てみましょう Let's watch his play in *slow motion* (on videotape) this time.

すわり 座り・据わり 座りのよい[悪い]植木鉢 a *stable* [an *unstable*] flowerpot

すわりごこち 座り心地 座り心地のよい[悪い]ソファー a *comfortable* [an *uncomfortable*] sofa; a sofa which is *comfortable* [*uncomfortable*] *to sit on*

すわりこみ 座り込み sit-in [C], sit-down [C] //座り込みスト *a sit-down strike* / 座り込みをする stage *a sit-in* [*sit-down*]

すわりこむ 座り込む (座る) sit* down; (しゃがむ) crouch [自]; (抗議などで) stage a sit-in [sit-down] //走り終えると彼は座り込んでしばらく動かなかった He *sat down* and wouldn't move for a while after running. / 彼らは市役所の前に座り込んで抗議した They *staged a sit-in* [*sit-down*] in front of the city hall (to protest).

すわる¹ 座る

sit* 圓, sit down (❖sit down は腰を下ろす動作を強調する); (席に着く) take* [have*] a seat, seat *oneself*

彼はいすに座った He *sat* (*down*) on the chair. (❖「(アームチェアなどに)深々と座った」なら on の代わりに in を用いる)

ここに座ってもいいですか Can I *sit* here?

どうぞお座りください Please [*sit down* [*take a seat, be seated*]]. (❖後の2つのほうがより丁寧な言い方)

彼女はピアノに向かって座った She *sat* at the piano.

彼は足を組んでいすに座っていた He *was sitting* on a chair with his legs crossed.

父は座って新聞を読んでいた My father *sat* reading a newspaper.

母親は子供にきちんと(→背筋を伸ばして)座るように言った The mother told her child to *sit up* (*straight*).

子供たちはコンサートの始めから終わりまで何とかじっと座っていた The children somehow managed to *sit still* through the concert.

クラス全員がキャンプファイアの周りに輪になって座った The whole class *sat in a circle* around the camp fire.

ポチ, お座り! *Sit*, Pochi!

◆電車は込んでいて座れなかった(→空席がなかった) The train was so crowded that「*there were no vacant seats* [(→立っていなければならなかった) I *had to stand*]. / 母親は子供をベビーカーに座らせた The mother *sat* [*seated*] her baby in the stroller. / 山田氏が市長の座に座る(→市長になる)ことになった It's been decided that Mr. Yamada is going to *be* the city mayor.

すわる² 据わる

その赤ちゃんはまだ首がすわっていない That baby *cannot* yet *hold his head up*. / 彼は酔って目がすわっていた He was drunk and *his eyes were glazed over*. / 彼は腹がすわっている(→容易に動じない) He *won't be upset easily*.

すんか 寸暇

彼女は寸暇を惜しんでピアノの練習をしている She *spends every spare moment* practicing the piano.

ずんぐり

おじはずんぐりした体型をしている My uncle is「*short and plump* [《口語的》*tub*-

by, 《口語的／軽蔑的》*dumpy*].

すんげき 寸劇 sketch 回, skit 回

ずんずん

(先へ先へと) on and on; (素早く) quickly; (早く) rapidly; (ためらいなく) without hesitation / 彼は森の奥へとずんずん進んでいった He went *on and on* into the woods.

◆きょうは宿題がずんずんはかどった I made *quick* [(→スムーズな) *smooth*] progress with my homework today.

すんぜん 寸前

電車に乗り込む寸前でドアが閉まってしまった The doors had shut *just* [*right*] *before* I got to the train. / その種は絶滅寸前といわれる / That species is said to be *on the brink* [*verge*] *of* extinction. / 彼は怒りで爆発寸前だ He *is about to* burst into fury.

すんだん 寸断

土砂崩れのためその道路は寸断されている The road *is blocked* [*closed*] *at many places* because of landslides.

すんでのところで

nearly, almost / すんでのところで川へ落ちるところだった I *nearly* [*almost*] fell into the river. / (→かろうじて落ちることを免れた) I *narrowly* [*barely*] *escaped* falling into the river.

ずんどう ずん胴

彼女はずん胴だ She has *no waist*.

すんなり(と)

(容易に) easily; (あっさり・快く) readily; (円滑に) smoothly / 彼はすんなり試験に合格した He passed the exam *easily*. / 彼女は僕の誘いにすんなり応じた She accepted my invitation *readily*. / 話はすんなりまとまった The negotiation has been settled *smoothly*.

すんぴょう 寸評 brief comment 回

すんぶん 寸分

その選手は相手に寸分の隙(ｷ)も与えない The player doesn't give his [her] opponent the *slimmest* chance to attack. / この原寸大の模型は本物と寸分違(ﾁｶﾞ)わぬできになっている This full-scale model is an *exact* [a *perfect*] copy of the real one.

すんぽう 寸法

❶ [長さ] (測った具体的な) measurements; (衣服などの) size 回 / スーツの寸法をとってください Could you *take my measurements* for a suit? / Could you *measure* me for a suit?

◆この布の寸法は25×25センチです This cloth is 25 centimeters by 25 centimeters. / コートの寸法直しをしてもらった I had my coat *altered*.

❷ [もくろみ] これで二人の仲もうまくいくという寸法だ So this is *how* [*the plan*] to make them get along.

せ

せ 背

❶〖背中〗the [one's] back;〖尾根〗ridge ⓒ
いすの背 *the back* of a chair / 山の背 *a mountain ridge*; *the ridge* of a mountain / 背を伸ばす[丸める] straighten [hunch] one's back

彼らは壁を背にして立っていた They stood *with their backs to* the wall.

彼女は私たちに背を向けた She *turned her back to* us.

彼は政治に背を向けている He *turns his back on* politics.

◆私たちは湖を背に写真を撮った We took a picture with the lake *in the background*.

❷〖身長・物の高さ〗height [háit] ⓤ
ここに背の順に並んでください Line up here *in order of height*.

◆背の高い木[グラス] a *tall* tree [glass] / 彼は僕より背が高い[低い] He *is taller* [*shorter*] than me [I]. / 妹はこの1年で5センチ背が伸びた My sister *has grown* five centimeters since last year. / このプールは子供では背が立たない Children *can't touch* (*the*) *bottom* in this pool.

💬「背はどのくらいあるの」「165センチです」"How *tall* are you?" "I'm 165 centimeters (*tall*)."

ことわざ 背に腹は替えられない Necessity knows no law.(→必要は法律を知らない)

せい¹ 性 ➡〖性〗p.781

❶〖性別〗sex ⓤ;〖主に文化・社会的な〗gender ⓤⓒ

性差別をなくす abolish *sex* [*sexual*] *discrimination*

❷〖性的な事柄〗sex ⓤ ──性の sexual
⇒ せいてき(性的)

性的魅力がある have *sex appeal*

週刊誌には性が氾濫している There is too much *sex* in weekly magazines.

その小説には性描写が多い The novel has much *sex* in it.

最近は性教育をする学校もある Recently some schools have been teaching *sex education*.

◆性に目ざめる become sexually aware

❸〖文法上の性〗gender ⓤⓒ

性・数・人称の一致 agreement of *gender*, number and person

∥性行為 sex, sexual intercourse / 性差 differences of sex [gender] / 性染色体 a sex chromosome / 性体験 sexual experience / 性的いやがらせ sexual harassment / 性転換 a change of sex / 性道徳 sexual morality / 性犯罪 a sexual [sex] crime

せい² 所為

❶〖過失・責任〗fault ⓒ
大丈夫. あなたのせいじゃないわ Don't worry. It's not your *fault*.

◆彼は自分の失敗を私のせいにした He *laid* [*put*] *the blame* for his failure *on* me. / He *blamed* me for his failure. / こんなことになった(→だれに責任がある)と思う Who do you think is *responsible* for this situation? / あいつのせいでせっかくのパーティーが台なしになった *Thanks to him*, the party was spoiled. / (→彼が台なしにした) He spoiled the party.

❷〖原因〗
きのう長時間歩いたせいで足が痛い My soles ache *because* I walked for a long time yesterday.

彼は生まれつきの童顔のせいで実際よりも若く見られがちだ *Because of* [*Owing to*] his inherently childish face, he is usually taken to be younger than he really is.

彼は映画好きの彼女のせいで(→影響されて)すっかり映画に詳しくなった *Influenced by* his girlfriend who is a movie fan, he came to know the movies very well.

💬「何か音がしなかった?」「ううん. 気のせいじゃない?」"Did you hear something?" "No. It's just *your imagination*."

せい³ 精

❶〖精霊〗spirit ⓒ;〖妖精〗sprite ⓒ / 花の精 the spirit of a flower

❷〖精力〗energy [énərdʒi] ⓤ;〖活力〗vigor ⓤ;〖体力〗strength ⓤ ∥ウナギを食べて精をつけよう Let's eat eels and gain *strength*.

[慣用表現] 彼は精も根も尽き果てた様子だった He looked *completely exhausted*. / 彼は学業に精を出している He studies *hard*.

せい⁴ 姓 one's family [last] name, one's surname ∥結婚して姓が変わりました I got married and *my family name* has changed.

◆姉は職場では旧姓を使っている My sister uses *her maiden name* in her office.

せい⁵ 正 ──正の〖プラスの〗plus, positive;〖正規の〗regular;〖副に対して〗original ∥正の数 a *positive* number ◆契約書は正と副の2通作成します The contract is prepared in *an official version* and a copy.

∥正会員 a regular member

せい⁶ 生 life ⓤ ∥彼は1899年にこの世に生を受けた He *came into the world* in 1899. / 生あるものは必ず死ぬ All *living* things must die.

せい⁷ 背〖身長・物の高さ〗height ⓤ ⇒ せ

せい- 聖 聖マルコ St. Mark (✦St.は Saint の略語)

-せい¹ -製 外国製のバッグ a *foreign-made* bag / お手製のネックレス a *handmade* necklace / このいすは木製だ This chair *is made of wood*. / イタリア製の靴は品質・デザインともにすぐれている The shoes *made in Italy* are superb in both quality and design.

-せい² -世 チャールズ2世 Charles *II* (✦IIは the Second と読む) / 彼は(日系)三世だ He is

テーマ別表現集

●性

❶性に関する一般的な表現

1. 男性と女性がお互いに興味をもつことは自然なことです.
   It is natural for men and women to be interested in each other.
2. 最近, 性体験のある若者の数は増えつつあります.
   These days, the number of young people experimenting with sex is increasing.
3. 10代の若者の中には避妊についてあまりよく知らない人もいるようです.
   It seems that there are some teenagers who don't know much about contraception.
4. 性教育は必要だと思いますか.
   Do you think sex education is necessary?
5. 安全な性行為についての教育は重要です.
   Education on safe sex is important.
6. 昔は日本では性について話すのはタブーとされていました.
   Talking about sex used to be a taboo in Japan.
7. 若者の間で性犯罪が増えつつあります.
   The number of sex crimes is increasing among young people.
8. テレビや映画に出てくる性的場面は子供たちに有害なときもあります.
   Sex scenes on TV and in movies are sometimes harmful to children.
9. 性転換手術に賛成ですか.
   Do you agree with sex change operations?
10. 女性を性の対象とだけ見るのは間違いです.
    It is wrong to see women only as sex objects.
11. 性の商品化が大きな社会問題になっています.
    The commercialization of sex has been a big social problem.
12. 自分が同性愛者であることを明言することは日本ではまだまれです.
    The coming out of homosexuals [gays or lesbians] is still rare in Japan.

❷セクハラ・性差別に関する表現

1. セクハラは職場でも学校でも問題になっています.
   Sexual harassment is a problem both in the workplace and in school.
2. セクハラを受けたことがありますか.
   Have you ever been sexually harassed?
3. セクハラは女性の健康に精神的および身体的影響を及ぼします.
   Sexual harassment affects women's mental and physical health.
4. セクハラが原因で仕事を辞めたり失ったりする人もいます.
   Some people quit or lose their jobs because of sexual harassment.
5. 彼の発言は彼が性差別主義者であることを物語っています.
   What he said proves that he is a sexist.
6. 女性は男性のお茶くみであると考えられていた時代はずっと前に終わりました.
   The days when women were supposed to serve tea to men are long gone.
7. 「スチュワーデス」という語は性差別的なので,「フライトアテンダント」に代わりつつあります.
   The word "stewardess" sounds sexually discriminatory. It has been replaced by "flight attendant."
8. 雇用機会均等法の施行によって性差別用語が禁じられていくでしょう.
   Language that discriminates between the sexes will be prohibited with the implementation of the Equal Employment Opportunity Law.
9. 育児は女性の仕事だという考えは間違っています.
   It is wrong to think that raising children is exclusively women's work.
10. 最近はバスやタクシーやトラックに女性の運転手をしばしば見かけるようになりました.
    These days we often see women bus, taxi and truck drivers.

―性差別と言葉―

1968年ごろにアメリカで始まった女性開放運動(women's liberation)を一つのきっかけとして, 性差別や女性蔑視(ﾍﾞｯｼ)とみなされるような英語表現が変わりつつあります. 例えば,「人間」は man から, person, one, human などに, chairman は chairperson に, policeman は police officer に, fireman は fire fighter に変わってきています. 女性形を表す-ess が語尾に付いた stewardess, hostess, actress といった語も flight attendant といった全く別の語にしたり, host, actor のように男性形に統一しています. さらに, その言葉自体に隷属的な響きがある secretary や housekeeper, maid といった語も, それぞれ administrative assistant, household worker, room attendant などになってきています. そのほか, boys and girls の語順を時には girls and boys と逆にしたり, someone, everybody, nobody などの代名詞を he ではなく they, he/she などにすることもあります.

せ

a *Sansei*.(❖一世 Issei, 二世 Nisei も英語となっている)

-せい³ -制 週休2日制 *a* five-day week *system* / 全日制[定時制]の高校 a *full-time* [*part-time*] high school / 4年制の大学 a *four-year* college

せい 税 tax [C][U]; (物品税) duty [C][U] ➔ぜいきん //民衆は重税に苦しんでいた People were suffering under *a heavy tax*. / 所得税が減税されるらしい I hear *income taxes* will be reduced. / この価格は消費税を含んでおりません This price doesn't include (*the*) *consumption tax*. / 税込みで3,000円になります It's 3,000 yen, *including tax*. / あなたの月収は税引き[税込み]でいくらですか How much is your monthly income *after* [*before*] *taxes*? ‖税額 the amount of (a) tax, the tax amount / 税収 tax revenues / 税制 tax system / 税率 tax rate, the rate of tax / 国税 a national tax / 住民税 a resident tax / 増[減]税 (a) tax increase [reduction] / 相続税 an inheritance tax / 地方税 a local tax / 直接[間接]税 a direct [an indirect] tax

せいあつ 制圧 control [U] ─制圧する control [他], bring* ... under control //この地域は敵の軍隊に制圧されている This district *is controlled* by enemy troops.

せいい 誠意 (正直) sincerity [U]; (誠実) good faith [U] //誠意を示す show *one's*「*good faith* [*sincerity*] / 彼の言葉には誠意が感じられなかった I felt his words lacked *sincerity*. ◆誠意のある人 a *sincere* [a *faithful*, an *honest*] person / 誠意をもって謝れば彼女も許してくれますよ She will forgive you if you make her a *sincere* apology.

せいいき 聖域 sanctuary [C]

せいいく 生育·成育 growth [U] ─生育する grow* [自] ➔せいちょう(成長·生長) //天候は植物の生育に影響を及ぼす Climate influences *the growth* of plants.

せいいっぱい 精一杯 (できるだけ) as hard as possible [*one* can]; (全力で) with all *one's* might //彼らは強豪を相手に精一杯戦った They played against the very strong team *as hard as they could*.
◆優勝を目ざし精一杯がんばります(→最善を尽くす) We'll *do* [*try*] *our best* to win the championship. / 返事をするのが精一杯だった It was *all I could do* to answer.

せいう 晴雨 試合は晴雨にかかわらず行います The game will be held「*whether it rains or not* [*rain or shine*]. / この傘は晴雨兼用です(→どんな天気でも使える) This umbrella *can be used in all weather*.
‖晴雨計 a barometer

せいうち 海象〔動物〕walrus [C]

せいうん 星雲 nebula [nébjələ] [C] (複 nebulae, ~s); (銀河系外の) galaxy [C]

せいえい 精鋭 the best, the pick //そのチームは精鋭がそろっている That team's members are *the pick of the litter*.
‖精鋭部隊 a crack unit

せいえき 精液 semen [U], sperm [U]

せいえん 声援 cheering [U], cheer [C] //大声援 *great cheers* ◆私たちはスタンドから選手に声援を送った We「*cheered* the players [*gave* the players *a cheer*] from the stands.

せいおう 西欧 (西洋) the West; (ヨーロッパ) Europe; (西ヨーロッパ) West [Western] Europe ‖西欧諸国 the Western countries / 西欧文明 Western civilization

せいか¹ 成果 (結果) result [C][U]; (努力などの) fruit [C] //よい成果を収める achieve good *results* / きょうの話し合いからは何も成果は得られなかった We could not get any *results* from today's meeting. / これは彼女の努力の成果だ This is *the fruit* of her effort.
◆彼らの実験は一応の成果をあげることはできた(→一部は成功した) Their experiment was only partly *successful*.

せいか² 聖火 the sacred fire; (オリンピックの) the Olympic Flame; (聖火リレーの) the Olympic Torch ‖聖火台(オリンピックの) the Olympic Flame holder / 聖火ランナー a torch bearer / 聖火リレー a sacred fire relay, an Olympic Torch Relay

せいか³ 生家 シェークスピアの生家 *the house where* Shakespeare *was born*

せいか⁴ 青果 fruits and vegetables
‖青果市場 a fruit and vegetable market

せいか⁵ 盛夏 (真夏) midsummer [U]; (暑い盛り) the height of summer

せいか⁶ 聖歌 sacred song [C]; (賛美歌) hymn [hím] [C]; (クリスマスの) carol [C]
‖聖歌隊 a choir [kwáiər]

せいかい¹ 正解 correct [right] answer [C] ─正解する answer correctly //その問題の正解者は彼と僕だけだった Only he and I *answered* the question *correctly*.
◆早めに家を出て正解だった(→よかった) *It was fortunate that* I left home early.

せいかい² 政界 the political world ─政界の political ◆彼は政界入りした He「went into [entered] *politics*. / 前首相は政界から引退した The former Prime Minister retired from *politics*.

せいかい³ 盛会 歓迎会は盛会だった The reception *was*「*a great success* [*very successful*]. / クラス会は盛会のうちに終わった The class reunion ended *successfully*.

せいかがく 生化学 biochemistry [U] ─生化学の biochemical
‖生化学者 a biochemist

せいかく¹ 正確

─正確な correct; accurate; precise, exact ─正確に correctly; accurately; precisely, exactly

> correct: 事実·基準·規則に照らして誤りがないこと.
> accurate: correct よりも意味が強い.
> precise, exact: 細部にわたって正確なこと.

〖正確な〗
正確な情報を知りたい I want to know *accurate* information.

せいかつ

今の正確な時刻が分かりますか Do you know what time *exactly* it is now?
これよりもっと正確な報告書を作成しなさい Make a more *precise* report than this.

〖正確に〗
状況を正確に把握する grasp the situation *accurately*
英語を正確に発音するのは難しい It is difficult to pronounce English *correctly*.
彼の年齢を正確には覚えていない I don't remember his *exact* age.
正確にいうと, 英会話を習い始めて2か月半です *To be exact*, it has been two and a half months since I began to learn English conversation.

〖正確だ〗
私の時計は正確だ My watch *keeps correct [accurate] time*.
計測は正確だった The measurement *was exact*.
◆彼女はいつも時間に正確だ She *is* always *punctual*.

せいかく² 性格 (固有の性格) character Ⓤ Ⓒ; (人柄) personality Ⓤ Ⓒ; (生来備わった特性) nature Ⓤ Ⓒ; (気質)《公式的》disposition Ⓒ Ⓤ ➡ 場面・状況別会話 p.1728

彼は性格がいい[悪い] He has *a* good [bad] *character*.
あの兄弟は性格が全く違う The brothers have quite different *characters*. / The brothers are quite different in *character*.
車の運転には性格が出ると聞く I hear how one drives a car shows *one's personality*.
問題の性格をよく理解しなければならない We have to understand *the nature* of the problem well.
◆性格の不一致を理由に離婚する divorce on the grounds of *incompatibility* / この作家は性格描写がうまい This writer is good at *characterization*. / 彼女とは性格的に合いません I'm *incompatible* with her. / 彼女は頼まれたら断れない性格だ When asked to do something, she's unable to refuse. / 2つの出来事は同じ性格のものだ The two incidents *are essentially the same*.
‖性格俳優 a character actor [actress]

せいがく 声楽 vocal music Ⓤ, singing Ⓤ ‖声楽家 a singer / 声楽科 a「vocal music [singing] course

せいかつ 生活

life Ⓤ Ⓒ (複 lives), living Ⓤ Ⓒ; (生計) livelihood Ⓤ《また a ～》——生活する live ⓘ

┌─ コロケーション ─ -life-
〖形容詞＋～〗忙しい～ a busy life / 気楽な～ an easy life / 孤独な～ a lonely life / 静かな～ a quiet life / 質素な～ a simple life / 充実した～ a full life / ぜいたくな～ a luxurious life / 怠惰な～ an idle life / 乱れた～ a disordered life (❖上記の句はすべて〈live [lead] a＋形容詞＋life〉の形で「～な生活を送る」という意

味を表すことができる)
─────
〖生活が・は〗
電気のない生活なんて想像もできない I can't even imagine *life* without electricity.
◆彼らは生活が苦しい(→貧乏だ) They *are badly off*. / 近ごろは以前より生活が楽になった Lately I *have been better off* than before. / 家族の生活がかかっている(→家族を養わなければならない)ので彼は一生懸命働いている He works hard because he *has to support his family*.

〖生活に〗
彼女は単調な生活に飽き飽きしていた She was sick and tired of *her* monotonous *life*.
コンピュータは私たちの生活に多大な変化をもたらした Computers *have brought about great changes in our lives*.
彼はなかなか東京の生活になじめなかった He couldn't get used to life in Tokyo.
彼が死んで家族は生活に困ってしまった Since his death, his family *had a hard time making a living*.

〖生活の・を〗
彼女は生活のために働かなければならなかった She had to work for *a living*.
彼はフランスで新しい生活を始めた He started *a new life* in France.
彼らは争い事のない平和な生活を営んでいた They「*led a* peaceful *life* [*lived* peacefully] without any quarrels.

〖生活する〗
彼の稼ぎは生活していくには不十分だ His earnings are insufficient to *live* (*on*).
彼らは漁業で生活している They *live* by fishing. / They *make their living* by fishing.
その老夫婦は年金で生活している The elderly couple *lives* on their pension.

〖生活〜〗
東京では生活費がとても高い *The cost of living* is [*The living expenses* are] very high in Tokyo.
彼女は急激な生活環境の変化についてゆけず体をこわしてしまった She ruined her health because of the sudden changes in *her living environment*.
◆彼の家族は生活保護を受けている His family is *on welfare*.

〖～生活〗
電話は日常生活には欠かせない Telephones are essential for *daily life*.
学校生活はどうですか How is *your school life*?
その俳優はあまり私生活について話さない The actor doesn't often talk about *his private life*.
‖生活指導 educational guidance / 生活習慣病 lifestyle-related diseases / 生活状態 living conditions / 生活水準 the standard of living, living standards / 生活反応 a vital reaction / 生活必需品 the necessities of life / 生活様式 a way of life, a lifestyle / 生活力(経済力) *one's* earning power; (生

命力) vitality / 家庭生活 *one's* home [family] life / 社会生活 social life / 大学生活 college life / 都会生活 city [urban] life / 独身[結婚]生活 single [married] life

せいかん[1] **生還** ──**生還する** (無事に戻る) return safely, return alive; (野球で) reach home, score [自] //遭難者は無事に生還した The survivor *returned* [*came back*] *safely*. / 彼の三塁打でランナーが生還した The runner「*reached home* [*scored*] on his triple.

せいかん[2] **精悍** 彼は精悍な顔つきをしている He has *strong, sharp* features.

せいかん[3] **静観** ──**静観する** (落ち着いて見守る) watch [observe] calmly; (しばらく様子を見る) wait and see*, stand* by watching

せいがん **請願** petition [C] ──**請願する** petition [他] //彼らはその法律を廃止するよう国会に請願した They *petitioned* the Diet to abolish the law.

‖請願書 a (written) petition

ぜいかん **税関** (機関) (the) customs (❖複数扱い. しばしば the Customs として単数扱い); (場所) customhouse [C] //税関を通る「get through [pass] *customs* / 私たちは税関で荷物を調べられた We got our baggage inspected at *the customs*. / 税関手続きをすませた I went through *the customs formalities*.

‖税関検査 customs inspection / 税関申告書 a customs declaration / 税関吏 a customs officer

せいき[1] **世紀** century [C]

今世紀最大の発明 the greatest invention of *this century* / 紀元5世紀に in *the* fifth *century* A.D. / 17世紀初め[終わり]に in *the* early [late] 17th *century*

その王の治世は半世紀に及んだ The king's reign spanned *half a century*.

世紀の大事件に国中が揺れた The great event *of the century* shook the entire nation.

‖世紀末 the end of a century / 四半世紀 a quarter of a century

せいき[2] **正規** ──**正規の** (本式の) regular; (正式の) formal //正規の手続きを踏む go through the *regular* procedures / 彼女は海外で正規の教育を受けた She received *formal* education abroad.

せいき[3] **生気** (生命) life [U]; (活力) vigor [U]; (生命力) vitality [U] //公園の木々は生気にあふれている The trees in the park are full of *life* [*vigor*]. ◆彼女は生気のない顔をしていた She had a *lifeless* face.

せいき[4] **性器** the sexual organs, the genitals

せいぎ **正義** justice [U] //正義の味方 a champion [friend] of *justice* / 彼らはみな正義のために戦った They all fought for *justice*. / 彼は正義感が強い He has *a* strong *sense of justice*.

せいきゅう[1] **請求** (強い要求) demand [C]; (権利としての要求) claim [C]; (要請) request [C] ──**請求する** ask [他]; (命令的に) demand [他]; (当然の権利として) claim [他]; (正式に) request [他]; (代金などを) charge [他]

彼は会社に損害賠償を請求した He *claimed* damages against the company.

カメラの修理代として7,000円請求された They *charged* me [I *was charged*] 7,000 yen for repairing the camera.

ご請求がありしだいサンプルをお送りします Samples will be sent *on request*. (❖この場合は無冠詞)

◆きのう電話代の請求書が送られてきた *The* telephone *bill* was sent to us yesterday.

‖請求額 the amount claimed [asked]

せいきゅう[2] **性急** ──**性急な** (早まった) hasty; (後先考えない) rash; (性格が) impetuous ──**性急に** hastily; rashly //性急な人 an *impetuous* person / 彼らは性急に結論を出した They made a *hasty* [*rash*] decision.

せいきょ **逝去** (死) death [U], 《婉曲的》passing [U] ──**逝去する** pass away //ご尊父様のご逝去を悼(いた)みお悔やみ申し上げます Let me express my deep regret over your father's *passing*.

せいぎょ **制御** control [U] ──**制御する** control [他] //制御がきかなくなる go out of *control* / 飛行機の航行はコンピュータで制御されている Navigation on planes *is controlled* by a computer.

‖自動制御装置 an automatic control device

せいきょう[1] **盛況** 彼らの公演は大盛況だった Their performance was *a great success*.

せいきょう[2] **生協** (生活共同組合) cooperative society [C]; (売店) 《口語的》co-op [C]

せいきょうと **清教徒** Puritan [C]

‖清教徒革命 the Puritan Revolution

せいきょうぶんり **政教分離** the separation of「religion and politics [church and state]

せいきょく **政局** the political situation //政局の行方を占う judge how *the political situation* will be / 政局は混迷している *The political situation* is confused.

ぜいきん **税金** tax [C][U] ➔ぜい

年末調整で税金がいくらか返ってきた Some *taxes* were refunded after a year-end tax adjustment.

私たちには税金を払う義務がある We have an obligation to *pay taxes*.

毎月10万円も税金に持っていかれる As much as a hundred thousand yen *goes to taxes* every month.

たばこには重い税金がかかっている *A* heavy *tax is imposed* on tobacco. / Tobacco *is* heavily *taxed*.

あの店の商品には税金がかからない The things sold at the shop *are tax-free* [*duty-free*].

今月から酒類の税金が下がった *The tax* on alcohol *has been reduced* [*cut*] starting this month. (❖「上がった」なら reduced, cut の代わりに increased, raised を用いる)

彼は税金を滞納している He *is in arrears with his taxes*.

せいく **成句** set phrase [C]; (慣用句・慣用表

現) idiomatic phrase [C]

せいくらべ 背比べ 彼と背比べをした I *compared heights* with him. / 背比べをしよう(→だれが高いか見る) Let's *see who is taller*.

せいけい[1] 生計 living [C], livelihood [C] (❖共に通例 a または *one's* を付けて用いる) ‖生計の道を断たれる be deprived of *one's living* / 彼女は子供たちに英語を教えて生計を立てている She *earns* [*makes*] *her living* by teaching English to children.

せいけい[2] 整形 彼女は胸を整形したにちがいない She must *have had cosmetic surgery on* her breasts.

‖整形外科 orthopedics; (形成外科) plastic surgery / 整形外科医 an orthopedist; (形成外科医) a plastic surgeon / 整形手術 orthopedic surgery; (形成手術) plastic surgery; (美容整形手術) cosmetic surgery

せいけい[3] 西経 アイスランドは西経20度に位置している Iceland is located at *longitude* 20 degrees *west*. (❖20°W long. と略す)

せいけい[4] 政経 politics and economics

‖政経学科 the department of politics [political science] and economics

せいけつ 清潔 cleanliness [klénlinəs] [U] ── 清潔な clean

清潔な政治 *clean* politics / 清潔な服装 *clean* clothes

部屋は清潔にしておきなさい Keep your room *clean*.

時々画面を清潔な布でふいてください Wipe the screen occasionally with a *clean* cloth.

彼女は清潔感がある(→清潔な印象を与える) She gives me *an impression of cleanliness*.

せいけん[1] 政権 (政治的権力) (political) power [U]; (政府) government [C]; (特に米国の) administration [C]; (非民主的な手段による) regime [C] ‖ブッシュ政権 *the* Bush *Administration* / ナチス政権下のドイツ Germany under *the* Nazi *regime* / 政権を握る[失う] come to [lose] *power* / 自民党が政権の座に就いている The Liberal Democratic Party has been *in power*. / その国では新政権が樹立された *A* new *government* was established in the country.

‖政権争い a struggle [scramble] for political power / 政権交代 a change of government [(political) power] / 軍事政権 a military regime / 単独政権 a single-party government / 連立政権 a coalition government

せいけん[2] 政見 党首は政見を述べた The party leader stated *his* [*her*] *political views*.

‖政見放送 a broadcast of a candidate's political views

せいげん 制限 restriction [C][U]; (限界) limit [C] ── 制限する restrict [他]; limit [他]

このトンネルでは通る車の高さに制限が設けられている They *set* [*put*] *a limit to* the height of cars that pass through this tunnel.

座席の数には制限があります *There is a limit to* the number of seats. / Seats *are limited in* number.

彼女は食事を1日1,000カロリーに制限した She *restricted* herself *to* 1,000 calories a day.

このあたりの制限速度は時速40キロです *The speed limit* around here is 40 kilometers per hour. / *Speed is restricted to* 40 kilometers per hour around here.

彼らは日本は輸入制限を撤廃するべきだと強く主張している They insist that Japan should lift *import restrictions*.

年齢制限はありません There is no *age limit*.

◆彼女は今食事制限をしている She is *on a diet* now. / 制限時間いっぱいです *The time is up*.

‖産児制限 birth control / 時間制限 a time limit / 重量制限 a weight limit

せいげんようほう 制限用法 〘文法〙 restrictive use [C][U] ➔ ひせいげんようほう

せいご[1] 正誤 ‖正誤表 (a list of) errata [erá:tə] / 正誤問題 true-and-false questions

せいご[2] 生後 生後7か月の赤ちゃん a *seven-month-old* baby / 彼は生後5か月で母親を失った His mother died five months *after his birth*.

せいこう[1] 成功

success [U][C] ── 成功する succeed [自], be successful

その新人歌手は成功の見込みがある The new singer has a chance of *success*.

ご成功をお祈りします I wish you *success*.

実験は大成功だった The experiment was *a great success*.

一生懸命努力すればいつかは成功するだろう If you try hard, you will *succeed* some day.

彼はその作家のインタビューに成功した He *succeeded* [*was successful*] *in* interviewing the writer.

彼女はジャーナリストとして成功した She *succeeded* as a journalist.

今度の新しい事業はぜひとも成功させなければならない We must *make* our new enterprise *a success* at all cost.

‖成功者 a success / 成功談 a success story / 成功率 (割合) a success rate; (可能性) a probability of success

[ことわざ] 失敗は成功の元 ➔ しっぱい

せいこう[2] 精巧 ── 精巧な elaborate; (手が込んでいて美しい) exquisite; (機械・技術などが) sophisticated ‖精巧な模型 an *exquisite* model / このオルゴールはとても精巧だ This music box *is* very *elaborate* [*exquisite*].

せいこう[3] 性交 (sexual) intercourse [U], sex [U] ➔ セックス

せいこうほう 正攻法 orthodox method [C] ◆彼らは正攻法で(→正々堂々と戦って)相手チームに勝った They *played fair* and beat the opposing team.

せいこつ 整骨 reset [C][U] ‖整骨医 an osteopath [ástiəpæθ]

せいこん[1] 精根 もう精根尽き果てた(→疲れきっ

せいこん

た) I'm completely exhausted.

せいこん² 精魂　精魂こめて作った料理 a dish one put his [her] heart and soul into / 彼はその交響曲の作曲に精魂を傾けた(→全精力を注いだ) He devoted all his energy [energies] to composing the symphony.

せいざ¹ 星座 constellation ◎; (占星術の) the signs of the zodiac
● 「星座は何座ですか」「双子座です」 "What is your sign?" "I am a Gemini."
‖星座表 a star chart

せいざ² 正座 ——正座する sit* on the floor Japanese style, sit erect with one's legs folded beneath one's body

せいさい¹ 制裁　(国際間の) sanction ◎; (罰) punishment ◎ /彼は何らかの社会的制裁を受けるだろう He will probably suffer some social punishment. / アメリカが日本に経済制裁を加えた The United States imposed [applied] economic sanctions against Japan.

せいさい² 精彩・生彩　(活気) life ◎
◆きょうの彼はプレーに精彩を欠いた(→活気がなかった) His playing was lifeless [dull] today. / 彼女の演技はひときわ精彩を放っていた (→目立ってすぐれていた) Her performance was remarkable [outstanding].

せいざい 製材 lumbering ◎ ‖製材業 the lumber [timber] industry / 製材所 a sawmill, 《米》 a lumbermill

せいさく¹ 政策 policy ◎◎
日本の対アジア政策 Japan's policy toward Asian countries / 財政政策を立てる shape a fiscal policy

政府は突然政策を変更した The government changed its policy abruptly.

新政府もこれまでの政策を引き継ぐだろう The new government will probably continue the former policy.

彼の経済政策は大衆の支持を得ている The public supports his economic policy.

‖政策協定 a policy agreement / 政策綱領 a platform / 政策論争 a policy dispute / 産業政策 an industrial policy / 社会政策 a social policy / 対外政策 a foreign policy / 福祉政策 a welfare policy

せいさく² 制作 (劇・映画などの) production ◎ ——制作する produce ⊕ /彼はテレビ番組を制作している He produces TV programs.
◆彼女は学園祭用のポスターを制作中だ She is painting a poster for the school festival.
‖制作者 a producer

せいさく³ 製作 (生産) production ◎; (製造) manufacture ◎ ——製作する (作る) make* ⊕; (製造する) manufacture ⊕ /この工場では機械部品を製作している We manufacture machine parts at this factory.
‖製作者 a maker, a manufacturer / 製作所 a factory / 製作費 production costs

せいさべつ 性差別 sexual discrimination ◎, sexism ◎ ——性差別的な sexist ‖性差別的な発言 a sexist remark

せいさん¹ 生産

production ◎ ——生産する produce ⊕; (機械で大量に) manufacture ⊕; (作る) make* ⊕

生産を増やす increase [step up] production

昨年は米の生産が落ち込んだ Rice production fell off last year.

彼らは生産を削減することに決めた They decided to cut back [down] production.

その工場では自動車部品を生産している The factory manufactures [produces] auto parts.

ここ3か月で生産が5パーセント増[減]となった Production has increased [decreased] five percent for the past three months.

◆この製品は工場で大量生産されている These goods are mass-produced at the factory. / 生産性を高める努力をしなければならない We must make an effort to increase productivity. / イタリアは世界有数のワイン生産国だ Italy is one of the greatest producers in the world. / そのような考え方は生産的ではない Such a way of thinking isn't productive.

‖生産過剰 overproduction / 生産管理 production control / 生産者 a producer / 生産者価格 a producer's price / 生産高 (単位・期間あたりの) (an) output / 生産地 a producing district / 生産物 (個々の) products; (集合的に) produce / 生産力 production capacity / 国内総生産 gross domestic product (《略語》GDP) / 国民総生産 gross national product (《略語》GNP)

せいさん² 清算 liquidation ◎, clearance ◎ ——清算する (負債を) clear ⊕, pay* off; (絶交する) break* up; (葬り去る) bury ⊕ /借金はすっかり清算した I completely cleared [paid off] my debts. / 彼女は彼との関係を清算した She broke up with him. / 彼は過去を清算した He「buried his past [put his past behind him].

せいさん³ 精算 adjustment ◎
◆その駅で運賃を精算しなければならなかった I had to pay the adjusted fare at the station. / 勘定は後で精算します I'll settle the bill with you later.
‖精算所 a fare adjustment office [window]

せいさん⁴ 凄惨 ——凄惨な (恐ろしい) horrible; (むごたらしい) gruesome /彼は凄惨な光景を目の当たりにした He saw the horrible [gruesome] sight with his own eyes.

せいさん⁵ 成算 (成功の見通し) hope of success; (見込み) prospect ◎◎
◆私には成算がある I am sure「of success [that I will succeed].

せいさん⁶ 青酸 hydrocyanic ◎
‖青酸化合物 cyanide [sáiənàid] / 青酸カリ potassium cyanide

せいさんかくけい 正三角形 equilateral triangle ◎

せいし¹ 生死 life and [or] death /祖父は数週間生死の境をさまよっていた My grandfather was hovering between life and death for a few weeks. / これは生死にかかわる問題

だ This is a matter of *life and* [*or*] *death.*
◆その3人はまだ生死不明(→行方不明)だ Those three people are still *missing.*

せいし[2] 制止 ―制止する (やめさせる) stop [他], restrain [他]; (押しとどめる) hold* back ‖ 彼は酔っ払いのけんかを制止した He *stopped* the drunks' quarrel. / He *restrained* the drunks *from* quarrelling. / 警官たちは暴徒を制止した The police *held back* the mob. / 何人かのファンが警備員の制止を振り切ってその歌手のそばに駆け寄った Some fans shook off the guards' *restraining arms* and rushed to the side of the singer.

せいし[3] 静止 ―静止する stand* still, come* to rest [a standstill]
◆その物体は静止している The object *is at rest.* / 突然パソコンの画面が静止した Suddenly the picture on the PC *froze.*
‖静止画像 a still picture / 静止軌道[衛星] stationary orbit [satellite]

せいし[4] 正視 その光景は正視に耐えなかった I *couldn't bear to look straight* [*directly*] *at* the scene.

せいし[5] 製糸 spinning [U] ‖製糸業 the silk reeling industry / 製糸工場 a silk mill

せいし[6] 製紙 paper manufacturing [U] ‖製紙会社 a paper manufacturing company / 製紙業 the paper industry / 製紙工場 a paper mill

せいし[7] 精子 sperm [C]

せいじ 政治

politics《単数または複数扱い》; (統治) government [U] ―政治の・政治的な political

彼らは政治にあまり関心がないようだ They don't seem to be very interested in *politics.*

彼らは国の政治を欲しいままにしていた They moved *the politics* of the country as they liked.

政治改革が今回の選挙戦の争点だ *Political reform* is the main issue of this election campaign.

彼女はいろいろな政治活動にかかわっている She engages in various *political activities.*

その国の政治情勢は変化しつつある *The political situation* of the country is changing.

彼はその問題の解決に政治生命を賭(か)けた He devoted *his political life* to solving the problem.

野党は首相の政治責任を厳しく追及している Opposition parties are intensely investigating *the political responsibility* of the Prime Minister.

みな彼の政治的手腕に期待している Everyone expects *political ability* [*skill*] of him.

この汚職事件は大衆の政治不信を招いた This scandal invited *distrust of politics* from the public.

‖政治運動 a political movement / 政治学 politics, political science / 政治学者 a political scientist / 政治献金 a political donation / 政治資金 a political fund / 政治資金規制法 the Political Fund Control Law / 政治団体 a political organization / 政治犯 a political prisoner / 政治力 political influence / 議会政治 parliamentary government / 金権政治 plutocracy / 地方[国際]政治 local [international] politics / 民主政治 a democratic government / 立憲政治 constitutional government

せいじか 政治家 politician [C], statesman [C] (❖前者が「私利私欲に走る政治家」という軽蔑的なニュアンスを含むのに対し，後者は「公正で聡明な指導者として尊敬されている政治家」を指す)

せいしき 正式 ―正式な (形式にかなった) formal; (正規の) regular; (公式の) official ―正式に formally; regularly; officially
正式な手続き *regular* procedure / 正式な名称 an *official* name / クラブに正式に入会を申し込む make a *formal* application for the club
それはいつ正式に発表されますか When will it be *officially* announced?

せいしつ 性質
❶【物の】(特性) property [C]; (本質) nature [U][C]
この金属には熱を通す性質がある This metal has *a property* of conducting heat.
父は仕事の性質上外国人と接する機会が多い *Due to the nature* of his job, my father often meets foreigners.
❷【人の】(生まれつきの) nature [U][C]; (傾向) disposition [C][U]; (情緒的な特性) temperament [U][C]; (気性) temper [C]; (性格) character [U][C]
彼女は穏和な[怒りっぽい]性質だ She has「*a* gentle *nature* [*a* hot *temper*].
うちの犬は性質が穏やかだ My dog is mild *by nature.*
⇒せいかく(性格)

せいじつ 誠実 (偽りのないこと) sincerity [U]; (正直) honesty [U] ―誠実な sincere; honest ―誠実に sincerely; honestly (❖sincere はふつう「その時々の自分の気持ちに忠実な」という意味で，人の性質のような永続的な状態を表さない)
誠実な人柄 *honest* personality
彼女の謝罪は誠実さが感じられなかった Her apology lacked [was lacking in] *sincerity.*
彼はだれに対しても誠実だ He is *honest* with everyone.

せいじゃ 聖者 saint [C]

せいしゃいん 正社員 full-time worker [C], regular employee [C]

せいじゃく 静寂 silence [U], stillness [U], quiet(ness) [U]; (喧騒(けんそう)の後の) hush [U]《また a ～》‖悲鳴が静寂を破った A cry broke *the silence* [*stillness*]. / 照明が暗くなると劇場は静寂に包まれた When the lights went down, *a hush* fell over the theater.

ぜいじゃく 脆弱 ―脆弱な (弱い) weak; (もろい) frail, fragile ‖脆弱な体質 a *weak* [*frail*] constitution / 脆弱な経済基盤 a *weak* basis of an economy

せいしゅく 静粛 ——静粛な quiet, silent ∥私の話が終わるまで静粛に願います Please keep *quiet* until I've finished my speech.
◆静粛に *Order! Order!*（※議長などの言葉）

せいじゅく 成熟 (人・動植物などの) maturity ⓤ; (果実の) ripeness ⓤ ——成熟する mature ⓘ; ripen ⓘ ——成熟した mature; ripe ∥成熟した女性 a *mature* woman / カキの実はまだ成熟していない The persimmons *have* not *ripened* [*become ripe*] yet. / この遺跡は当時の文化がすでにかなり成熟したものであったことを示している The remains show the culture *was* already quite *mature* in those days.

せいしゅん 青春 (*one's*) youth
彼らは青春を謳歌(ホゥ)している They are enjoying *their* youth.
娘は青春の真っただ中にいる My daughter is in the bloom of *youth*.
若いうちは青春のかけがえのなさを忘れがちだ We are apt to forget the preciousness of *our youth* when we are young.
青春時代にはいろいろ思い悩んだ I was worried a lot「*in my youth* [*when I was young*].

せいじゅん 清純 purity ⓤ ——清純な (純粋な) pure; (無邪気な) innocent ∥清純派の女優 an actress *with an image of innocence and purity*

せいしょ¹ 清書 clean [fair] copy ⓒ ∥作文を清書する *make a clean* [*fair*] *copy* of a composition

せいしょ² 聖書 (聖典としての) the (Holy) Bible; (1 冊の) Bible ⓒ ∥聖書の一節を引用する quote a verse from *the Bible*
∥旧[新]約聖書 the Old [New] Testament

せいしょう 斉唱 unison ⓤ ∥校歌を斉唱する *sing* the school song *in unison*

せいじょう¹ 正常 normality ⓤ ——正常な normal ——正常に normally ∥列車の運行は 10 時には正常に戻った The train service returned to *normal* by 10. / その男の行動は正常には見えなかった The man didn't appear to behave *normally*.
◆両国の国交を正常化する *normalize* diplomatic relations between the two nations / このコンピュータは正常に(→適切に)作動しない This computer doesn't work [function] *properly*.

せいじょう² 政情 political situation ⓒ ∥その国の政情は今のところ安定している At the moment *the political situation* is stable in the country.

せいじょう³ 清浄 cleanness ⓤ ——清浄な clean ∥清浄な空気 *clean* air
∥空気清浄器 an air cleaner [purifier]

せいじょうき 星条旗 (米国国旗) the Stars and Stripes (単数扱い), the Star-Spangled Banner(※米国国歌の名前でもある)

せいしょうねん 青少年 the youth (単数または複数扱い), young people; (若い世代) the younger generation
∥青少年犯罪 juvenile delinquency

せいしょく¹ 生殖 (繁殖) reproduction ⓤ; (発生) generation ⓤ; (出産) 《公式的》procreation ⓤ
∥生殖器 sex(ual) [reproductive, genital] organs / 生殖細胞 a reproductive cell

せいしょく² 聖職 sacred profession ⓒ
◆聖職に就く *take holy orders*;「*go into* [*enter*] *the church*
∥聖職者(牧師) a clergyperson, a churchman, a churchwoman

せいしん¹ 精神

(知力) mind ⓤ ⓒ; (肉体に対して) spirit ⓤ ⓒ; (魂) soul ⓤ ⓒ; (意志) will ⓤ ⓒ ——精神の・精神的(な) mental, spiritual → こころ

《精神が・は》
彼は人間の精神は無限の可能性をもつと考えた He thought human *mind* had infinite potential.
彼女の精神は過剰な自己中心主義にむしばまれている Her *soul* is eaten away by excessive self-centeredness.
◆彼はこのごろ精神が(→精神的に)不安定だ Recently he has been *mentally* unstable.

《精神に》
犯人は精神に異常をきたしていた The criminal was「*out of his mind* [*mentally* ill].
それは憲法の精神に反する It is against *the spirit* of the Constitution.

《精神を》
自立の精神を育てる cultivate *an independent spirit*
◆もう少し勉強に精神を集中しなさい Concentrate *your attention* a little more on your studies.

《精神的》
◆祖母は私の精神的支えだった My grandmother was *an emotional support* to me. / そのニュースを聞いたときの精神的ショックは大きかった I experienced *a great emotional shock* when I heard the news. / 選手たちは精神的にも肉体的にも疲れていた The players were tired both *mentally* and physically.

《その他》
彼女はとても精神力が強い She has great「*mental strength* [*willpower*].
このような映像を目にするのは精神衛生上よくない It is not good *for your mental health* to see such a picture.
◆あいつの精神年齢は小学生並みだ(→小学生と同じくらい精神的に未熟だ) That guy is as *mentally* immature as a schoolchild.

∥精神安定剤 a tranquilizer / 精神医学 psychiatry / 精神衛生 mental health / 精神科医 a psychiatrist / 精神鑑定 a psychiatric test / 精神障害 mental disorder / 精神状態 a mental condition, a state of mind / 精神薄弱 mental disability / 精神病 a mental disease [illness] / 精神病院 a mental hospital / 精神病患者 a mental patient / 精神分析 psychoanalysis / 精神分裂症[病] schizophrenia [skɪtsəfríːniə]

慣用表現 精神一到何事か成らざらん *Where*

there is a will, there is a way.(→意志あるところに道が開ける)

せいしん² 清新 ―清新な fresh, new

せいじん¹ 成人 (法律上成年に達した者) adult [C]; (子供に対して)《口語的》grown-up [C] ‖成人男性[女性] a *grown-up* man [woman]

◆息子たちはみな成人しました All my sons ⌈*came of age* [*grew up*].

‖成人映画 an adult [X-rated] movie / 成人教育 adult education / 成人式 a coming-of-age ceremony / 成人の日 Coming-of-Age Day

せいじん² 聖人 saint [C] ‖聖人君子ぶる play *the saint*

せいしんせいい 誠心誠意 (真心をこめて) wholeheartedly ◆両国の関係改善を目ざし誠心誠意努力する make *wholehearted* efforts to improve the relationship of the two countries / 彼らは誠心誠意(→最善を尽くして)その問題に対処した They *did their best* to deal with the problem.

せいず¹ 製図 (設計図などの下書き) drafting [U]; (図を引くこと) drawing [U]; (地図の) cartography [U] ―製図する (下書きを書く) draft [他]; (図を引く) draw* [他]

‖製図器具 a drafting [drawing] instrument / 製図版 a drafting [drawing] board

せいず² 星図 star chart [C]

せいすい 盛衰 the rise and fall, ups and downs《複数扱い》

[慣用表現]栄枯盛衰は世の習い ➔ えいこせいすい

せいすう 整数〔数学〕integer [C], whole number [C]

せいする 制する (抑える) control [他]; (鎮圧する) suppress [他] ‖はやる気持ちを制する *control one's* eagerness / 数時間後, 警察は暴動を制した The police *suppressed* the riot after a few hours.

[慣用表現]先んずれば人を制す ➔ さきんじる

せいせい 精製 refinement [U] ―精製する refine [他] ‖砂糖を精製する *refine* sugar

‖精製所 a refinery

せいせい 清々 言いたいことを言ったら気分がせいせいした I *felt relieved* as I said all I wanted to say. / 試験が終ってせいせいしたわ I'*m glad* that the exam is over.

せいぜい ❶【たかだか】(よくても) at (the) best; (多くて) at (the) most, not more than ...; (長くても) at (the) longest ‖頂上までせいぜい50メートルだ It's *not more than* 50 meters to the peak. / 出席者はせいぜい100人といったところだろう The number of attendants will be about a hundred *at* (*the*) *most*. / ミーティングはせいぜい10分くらいで終わるだろう The meeting will probably end in about ten minutes *at most* [*the longest*].

◆このメンバーでは準決勝に残るのがせいぜいだろう *It will be all* our team *can do* to advance to the semifinals.

❷【できるだけ】せいぜい楽しんできてください Enjoy yourself *as much as you can*. / 試験でいい点が取れるようせいぜい努力します I make *every* effort to get good grades on tests.

ぜいせい 税制 taxation [tax] system [U]

‖税制改革 a tax reform / 税制調査会 the Taxation [Tax] System Research Council

ぜいぜい 喘息(ぜんそく)でぜいぜいいう *wheeze* with asthma / 彼はぜいぜい息を切らしながら教室に入ってきた *Gasping for breath*, he came into the room.

せいせいどうどう 正々堂々 負けはしたものの, 彼らは正々堂々と戦った Though they lost the game, they played *fair*.

せいせき 成績

(試験・試合などの結果) result [C]《通例複数形 ～s》; (評価)《米》grade [C], 《英》mark [C]

➔ [場面・状況別会話] p.1742

〖成績が・は〗

生物の成績はAだった *My grade* in biology was an A./ I *got* an A in biology.

歴史の成績が上がった[下がった] *My grade* in history improved [dropped].

◆彼は学校の成績がよい[悪い] He *is doing well* [*poorly*] at school. / 彼女の成績はクラスで上の方だ She *ranks* high in our class.

〖成績を〗

数学でよい[悪い]成績を取った I *got a* good [bad] *grade* in math.

英語の成績を伸ばしたい I want to improve *my grade* in English.

◆日本チームは予想以上の成績をあげた The Japan team's *record* was better than we had expected.

〖その他〗

彼は優秀な成績で高校を卒業した He graduated from high school *with* high *grades* [*marks*].

彼はまあまあの成績だった He got fairly good *grades*.

タイガースは昨シーズン不本意な成績に終わった Tigers couldn't obtain satisfactory *results* last season.

‖成績証明書 a transcript / 成績表《米》a report card, 《英》a school report

せいせん 精選 ―精選する ⌈pick out [select] ... carefully ‖精選された材料 *carefully selected* materials

せいぜん¹ 整然 彼女の机の上は整然としている Her desk is kept *in perfect order*. / 体育館にはたくさんのいすが整然と並べられていた A lot of chairs were lined *in good order* in the gymnasium. / 式は整然と執(と)り行われた The ceremony was held *in an orderly manner*. / 彼の言うことは理路整然としている What he says is *logical*.

せいぜん² 生前 彼女の生前の遺志を尊重する respect her *last wishes* / 父は生前よくこの店に私を連れてきてくれた My father often took me to this restaurant *when he was alive*. / みんなでCDを聞いてそのギタリストの生前をしのんだ We remembered *the life* of the guitarist while listening to his CDs.

せいせんしょくひん 生鮮食品 (新鮮な) fresh foods; (腐りやすい) perishable foods,

せいそ perishables ∥スーパーの生鮮食品売り場 the 「perishable foods [perishables] department in a supermarket

せいそ 清楚 ──清楚な(こぎれいな) neat, tidy; (清らかな) clean ∥彼女は清楚な装いをしている She has *neat and tidy* clothes on. / She is dressed *neatly*.

せいそう¹ 清掃 cleanup ⓤ (通例単数形), cleaning ⓤ ──清掃する clean (up) ∥彼女はボランティアで公園の清掃をしている She *cleans up* the park as a volunteer.
∥清掃作業員 (米) a garbage collector, (米公式的) a sanitation worker, (英) a dustman / 清掃車 (米) a garbage truck, (英) a dustcart

せいそう² 正装 formal [full] dress ──正装する dress up ∥彼は正装で式に出た He attended the ceremony in *formal [full] dress*. / その演奏会に正装していく必要はないよ You don't need to 「*wear formal dress [dress up]* for the concert.

せいそう³ 盛装 gala [gorgeous] dress ⓤ, Sunday best ⓤ, one's best ∥会場には盛装した婦人たちがいた There are ladies in 「*gala dress [their best]* in the hall.

せいそう⁴ 政争 (政治的な反目) political conflict [strife] ⓤ; (政権争い) a struggle for political power

せいぞう 製造 production ⓤ; (機械での大量生産) manufacture ⓤ ──製造する make* ⓗ, produce ⓗ ⓤ; (機械で大量に) manufacture ⓗ ⇨つくる

新型ビデオの製造が開始された The new VCR model *went into production*.

その薬品は製造中止になった They *stopped the production [manufacture]* of the medicine.

この工場は再生部品から車を製造している This factory *makes [produces, manufactures]* cars from recycled parts.

∥製造過程 the process of production / 製造業 the manufacturing industry / 製造者[元] a maker, a producer, a manufacturer / 製造所[元] a factory, a plant / 製造年月日 the date of manufacture [production] / 製造物責任法 the Product Liability Law

せいそうけん 成層圏 〖気象〗 the stratosphere

せいそく 生息 ──生息する live ⓘ; (集団的に)(公式的) inhabit ⓗ ⇨すむ(住む) ∥ワニが生息する沼地 a swamp *inhabited* by alligators / シーラカンスはインド洋に生息している Coelacanths 「*live in* [*inhabit*] the Indian Ocean.

◆その地域ではパンダの生息数が急激に減っている *The number* of pandas is declining sharply in that area. / その山で、絶滅したと思われていた鳥の生息が確認された The bird, which had been thought extinct, was found to *be existing* in the mountains.

∥生息地 a habitat

せいぞろい 勢揃い、会場にはその映画の出演者全員が勢ぞろいした All the cast of the movie 「*got together* [*assembled*] at the hall.

せいぞん 生存 (生き残ること) survival ⓤ; (生きていること) life ⓤ (↔death); (存在すること) existence ⓤ ──生存する (生き残る) survive ⓗ ⓘ; (生きる) live ⓘ; (存在する) exist ⓘ ∥自然界における激しい生存競争 the fierce *struggle for existence* [*life*] in the natural world / 遭難者全員の生存が確認された They confirmed *the survival* of all the victims. / 水と大気は人間が生存するうえで欠かすことのできないものだ Water and air are indispensable for human beings to *live*.

◆その事故の生存者は100人中わずかに2名だけだった *The survivors* of the accident were as few as two out of one hundred. / (→わずか2名だけが生き残った) Only two out of one hundred *survived* the accident.

∥生存権 the right to live / 適者生存 survival of the fittest

せいたい¹ 生体 ∥生体解剖 vivisection / 生体肝移植 a liver transplant from a living body / 生体実験 an experiment on a living body / 生体反応 an organic reaction

せいたい² 生態 (自然界の生物の習性) behavior, (英) behaviour ⓤ, habit ⓤ; (人の暮らしぶり) *a person's* lifestyle; (生物と環境との関係) ecology ⓤ ⓒ ∥トラの生態を調べる study *the behavior* [*habits*] of tigers / 若者の生態を調べる study young people's *lifestyle*

◆その地域の生態系を破壊する damage *the ecosystem* of the area

∥生態学 ecology / 生態学者 an ecologist

せいたい³ 声帯 〖解剖〗 the vocal cords [chords] ◆人の声帯模写をする *mimic* a person's *voice* / 彼は声帯模写を得意としている He is good at *vocal mimicry* [*imitation*].

せいたい⁴ 政体 government ⓤ, a form [system] of government ∥専制政体 autocratic government / 立憲政体 constitutional government

せいだい 盛大 ──盛大な (豪華な) grand; (大きい) big, large ∥盛大なパーティーを開く hold a *grand* [*big, large*] party / (観客を促して) 盛大な拍手を! Give him [her, them] a *big* hand! / そのイベントは盛大に行われた The event was held *on a grand* [*big, large*] *scale*.

ぜいたく 贅沢 luxury [lʌkʃəri] ⓤ, extravagance ⓤ ──ぜいたくな luxurious [lʌgʒúəriəs], extravagant; (高価な) expensive ──ぜいたくに luxuriously, extravagantly

ぜいたくざんまいの暮らしをする live *in the lap of luxury*

彼女はぜいたくな生活にすっかり慣れてしまっている She's been too accustomed to 「*luxurious* living [living *in luxury*].

◆彼女は食事に関してはかなりのくちだ (→多くの金を使っている) She *spends a lot of money* on food. / (→高価な物を食べる) She eats very *expensive* food. / 昨夜はぜいたくをして

寿司(↓)を食べた I *splurged* and had sushi last night. / あれもこれもぜいたくばかり言うもんじゃないよ (→君は多く望みすぎだ) You say you want this and that — I think *you're asking for too much*. / コックは新鮮な食材をぜいたくに使った The cook *was lavish with* fresh ingredients.

‖ぜいたく品 a luxury

せいたん 生誕 birth Ⓤ Ⓒ ∥その作家の生誕200年を祝う式典が催された A ceremony was held to celebrate the 200th anniversary of the writer's *birth*.

◆ここが彼の生誕の地です This is his *birthplace*. / This is *where* he *was born*.

せいち¹ 精緻 ―精緻な (細心の) scrupulous; (詳細な) minute [mainúːt]; (綿密な) in-depth (❖名詞の前で用いる) ∥精緻な調査 a *scrupulous* [a *minute*, an *in-depth*] examination ◆精緻を極めた工芸品 a *very scrupulously* made craftwork

せいち² 聖地 sacred place ∥聖地を巡礼する make a pilgrimage to *sacred places*

◆ハリウッドはすべての映画ファンにとっての聖地である Hollywood is *a shrine* for all movie lovers.

せいち³ 生地 one's birthplace, the place where a person was born

せいち⁴ 整地 斜面を削って整地する remove soil to level a slope

せいちゅう 成虫 adult Ⓒ, imago Ⓒ (複 ~es, imagines)

関連語 変態 metamorphosis / さなぎ a pupa / 幼虫 a larva

せいちょう¹ 成長・生長 growth Ⓤ; (発達・発展) development Ⓤ ―成長する grow* ⓘ; (大人になる) grow up; (成熟する) mature ⓘ; (発達・発展する) develop ⓘ

〖成長する〗
彼は去年1年で15センチも成長した He *grew* as much as 15 centimeters last year.
彼女は美しい女性に成長した She *has grown up to be* a beautiful lady.
子供が成長するにつれて親の心配も増す Parents' anxieties grow as their children *grow*.
そのアジアの国は急速に成長している That Asian country *is developing* rapidly.

〖成長が・は〗
この植物は成長がかなり速い The *growth* of this plant is quite rapid. / (→かなり速く成長する) This plant *grows* quite rapidly.

〖~の成長〗
おじは娘の成長を記録し続けている My uncle has kept a record of *his daughter's growth*.

〖成長の〗
今度の舞台には役者としての彼の成長の跡 (→成長) が見られる This performance proves his *growth* [*development*] as an actor.

〖その他〗
ヒマワリの生長過程 *the process of the growth* of sunflowers
その国の経済は1960年代に高成長を遂げた The economy of the country *saw a period of rapid growth* in the 1960s.

◆海外での経験が彼を大きく成長させた His experiences abroad *matured* him considerably.

‖成長株 a growth stock; (有望な人物) a promising [an up-and-coming] person / 成長記録 the record of *a person's growth* / 成長産業 a growth [sunrise] industry / 成長ホルモン growth hormones / 成長率 a growth rate / (高度)経済成長 (high) economic growth

せいちょう² 清聴・静聴 ご清聴ありがとうございました Thank you (very much) for *your kind attention*.

せいちょう³ 整腸 ∥整腸剤 (a) medicine effective against intestinal disorders

せいつう 精通 ―精通する (よく知っている) know* a lot about …; (熟知・熟練している) be (well) versed in … ∥彼は物理学に精通している He「*knows a lot about* [*is well versed in*] physics. ◆彼女は財務管理に精通している (→経験を積んでいる) She *is experienced in* financial management.

せいてい 制定 establishment Ⓤ; (法律の) enactment Ⓤ Ⓒ ―制定する establish ⓘ; (法律を) enact ⓘ ∥その国で新たな法律が制定された A new law *has been established* [*enacted*] in that country.

せいてき¹ 性的 ―性的(な) sex (❖名詞の前で用いる), sexual ―性的に sexually ∥性的魅力がある have *sex appeal*; be *sexually attractive* / 人と性的な関係を持つ have *sexual relationships with a person* / 性的いやがらせを受ける suffer *sexual harassment*; *be sexually harassed*

せいてき² 政敵 political enemy [opponent] Ⓒ

せいてき³ 静的 ―静的(な) static (↔ dynamic) ―静的に statically

せいてつ 製鉄 iron manufacturing Ⓤ; (製鋼) steel manufacturing Ⓤ ∥製鉄業 the iron [steel] industry / 製鉄業者 an iron [a steel] manufacturer / 製鉄所 an ironworks, a steelworks

せいてん¹ 晴天 fine [fair, good] weather Ⓤ; (晴れた空) a fair [blue, clear] sky ∥ピクニック当日は晴天に恵まれた We *had fine weather* on the day of our picnic. / *The weather was fine* on the day of our picnic. / この晴天続きで水不足が心配される We anticipate a shortage of water due to this *long spell of fine weather*. / 子供たちは晴天のもと元気に遊んでいた Children were playing cheerfully *under a fair [blue, clear] sky*.

せいてん² 青天 a blue sky

慣用表現 彼らの離婚はまさに青天の霹靂(へきれき)だった Their divorce really was *a bolt from [out of] the blue*.

せいてん³ 聖典 scripture Ⓒ 《しばしば複数形 ~s》; (仏教経典) sutra Ⓒ; (キリスト教の) the Bible; (イスラム教の) the Koran

せいでんき 静電気 static electricity Ⓤ ∥空

せいと　生徒

student ◯ (◆(米)では通例中学生以上を,《英》では大学生以上を指す); pupil ◯ (◆(米)では小学生を指し,《英》では小中高生に用いる); (小中学生) schoolchild ◯ (◆男子生徒は a schoolboy, 女子生徒は a schoolgirl ともいう); (個人でやっている家庭などの) pupil ◯

彼は東西高校の生徒です He is *a student* at Tozai High School.

その学校の生徒数はおよそ1,000人です The school has approximately one thousand *students* [*pupils*].

全校生徒が体育館に集まった *The whole student body of the school* assembled in the gymnasium. / *The (whole) school* assembled in the gymnasium.

近所のバイオリン教室が生徒を募集している A violin school in my neighborhood is accepting *pupils*.

‖生徒会 a student council / 生徒会長 the president of a student council / 生徒指導 student guidance / 生徒手帳 a student handbook

せいど　制度

(社会的・政治的な) system ◯; (しきたり) institution ◯　——制度化する institutionalize ◯

日本の教育制度 Japan's *educational system* / 現在の学校制度を見直す reexamine *the present school system*

新たな制度を設ける必要がある We need to *establish a new system.*

その制度は20年前に廃止された The *system was abolished* 20 years ago.

今の制度では20歳未満の投票は認められていない *Under the present system*, people under 20 are not allowed to vote.

‖家族制度 a family system / 貨幣制度 a monetary system / 選挙制度 an election [electoral] system / 奴隷制度 slavery / 封建制度 the feudal system, feudalism

せいど² 精度
precision ◯, exactness ◯; (努力を要する) accuracy ◯ ‖精度の高い計測器 a measuring instrument with high *precision* / 実験の精度を高める increase the *exactness* [*accuracy*] of an experiment

せいとう¹ 正当
——正当な (適正な) fair (↔unfair); (妥当な) valid (↔invalid); (合法的な) legitimate (↔illegitimate)　——正当化する justify ⓗ

いかなる目的も正当な手段で達せられるべきだ We should achieve whatever end *by fair* [*legitimate*] *means*.

彼は正当な理由もなく[があって]クラブをやめさせられた He was removed from the club *without* [*for*] *a valid reason*.

彼は自分のすることを正当化したがる He tends to *justify* what he does.

◆彼女の能力は正当に評価されるべきだ We should judge her abilities *justly* [*fairly*].

その報告は彼の正当性を証明した The report proved his *justification* [(→合法性) *legitimacy*]. / 彼女がその男を刺したのは正当防衛だった It *was in self-defense* that she stabbed the man.

‖正当化 (a) justification

せいとう² 正統
——正統な (正しいと認められた) orthodox (↔unorthodox); (嫡出(ちゃくしゅつ)の) legitimate (↔illegitimate) ‖…の正統な継承者 the *legitimate* heir to … / その論の正統的な解釈 the *orthodox* interpretation of the theory

‖正統派 an orthodox school

せいとう³ 政党
(political) party ◯ ‖政党間の権力闘争 a battle for power *between the parties* / また新しい政党が結成された Another *new political party* was organized. / その政党内部に大きな変化が起こっている There has been a big change *within the party*.

‖政党政治 government by a political party / 政党内閣 a party cabinet / 革新政党 a progressive party / 保守政党 a conservative party

せいとう⁴ 製糖
sugar manufacturing ◯ ‖製糖会社 a sugar manufacturing company / 製糖業 the sugar industry / 製糖工場 a sugar manufacturing factory [mill]

せいどう¹ 青銅
bronze ◯ ‖青銅器時代〖考古〗 the Bronze Age

せいどう² 聖堂
(キリスト教の) church ◯ ‖大聖堂 (キリスト教の) a cathedral

せいとく 生得
——生得の innate ‖生得権 a birthright

せいどく 精読
intensive [careful] reading ◯　——精読する read* intensively [carefully]

せいとん 整頓
——整頓する put* [set*] … in order; (場所を) tidy (up); (整頓しておく) keep* … in order ‖机の上を整頓しなさい *Put* your things on the desk *in order*. / 君の部屋はいつもきちんと整頓してあるね Your room *is* always「*kept in order* [*neat and clean*].

◆整頓された部屋 an *orderly* [a *tidy*] room

せいなん 西南
the southwest　——西南の southwest

せいなんせい 西南西
the west-southwest　——西南西の west-southwest

ぜいにく 贅肉
excess fat ◯, 《口語的》flab ◯ ‖最近腰の周りにぜい肉がついてきた Lately, I've been putting on「*excess fat* [*flab*] around the waist. / Lately, I've been getting *flabby* around the waist. / ぜい肉を落として彼はすっかりスマートになった He's gotten rid of *the flab* and become quite slim.

せいねん 青年
(若い人[男性, 女性]) young person [man, woman] ◯; (若い人々) young people, 《集合的》youth ◯《単数または複数扱い》

町の青年がそのみこしをかついだ *Young people* [*The youth*] of the town carried the *mikoshi* on their shoulders.

彼はなかなかの好青年に育った He's grown up

into a quite *fine young man*.
◆父は若いころ文学青年だった My father was *a literature enthusiast* when he was young. / 彼は青年時代をここ札幌で過ごした He spent *his youth* [*younger days*] here in Sapporo. / He lived here in Sapporo in *his youth*.

‖青年海外協力隊 the Japan Overseas Cooperation Volunteers / 青年実業家 a young businessperson [businessman, businesswoman]

せいねん² 成年 【法律】one's majority (◆通例《米》では21歳, 一部の州では18歳を, 《英》では18歳を指す) ⇨みせいねん
◆彼はまだ成年に達したばかりだ He *has* just 「*come of age* [*become an adult*].

せいねんがっぴ 生年月日 the date of *one's* birth, *one's* date of birth, *one's* birthdate
C「生年月日はいつですか」「1985年9月12日です」 "What is *your* 「*date of birth* [*birthdate*]*?" "(It's) September 12, 1985."

せいのう 性能 (能力) performance ⓤ; (効率) efficiency ⓤ ⇨のうりょく
そのコンピュータよりこっちのほうが性能がいいよ This computer *has higher performance* than that one. / This computer *performs better* than that one.
彼は性能をよくするためにラジコンカーを改造した He remodeled his radio controlled car to *upgrade its performance*.
このヘッドホンステレオも長年の使用でだいぶ性能が悪くなった The *performance* of this personal stereo *has gotten* quite *worse* due to years of heavy use.
高性能のコンパクトカメラが次々に発売されている *High performance* compact cameras are being put on sale one after another.

せいは 制覇 (支配) domination ⓤ; (征服) conquest ⓤ ——制覇する (支配する) take* [gain] control over ..., dominate ⓗ; (征服する) conquer ⓗ; (試合に勝つ) win* ⓗ ‖ 彼らは軍事力で世界を制覇しようとたくらんでいた They conspired to 「*gain control over* [*dominate, conquer*] the world by resorting to military force. / わが校のサッカー部は全国制覇を果たした(→全国大会で優勝した) The soccer team of our school *won the championship* at the national soccer *tournament*. / 彼は4つの大会を制覇した He *won four tournaments*.

せいばい 成敗 punishment ⓒⓤ ——成敗する punish ⓗ

せいばつ 征伐 conquest ⓤ ——征伐する conquer ⓗ

せいはつりょう 整髪料 hairdressing ⓤ

せいはんたい 正反対 the (direct) opposite; (意見などに関して)《公式的》the contrary ——正反対の opposite; contrary ‖ はんたい 《これについての彼の意見は私とちょうど正反対だった His opinion on this matter was quite *opposite* [*contrary*] to mine. / 彼は目的地と正反対の方向へ向かって歩いていた He was walking *in the completely opposite direction from* [*of*] his destination. / 彼女はとても引っ込み思案だったが, 今は全く正反対だ She used to be very shy, but now she's gone to *the opposite* [*contrary*] *extreme*. / 悲観論と楽観論は正反対のものである Pessimism is *the very opposite of* optimism. / Pessimism and optimism are *opposites*.

せいひ 成否 (a) success (or failure); (結果) result ⓒⓤ ‖ この計画の成否はひとえに彼の働きにかかっている The success of this plan [Whether this plan turns out to be *a success or failure*] wholly depends on him.

せいび 整備 (保全) maintenance ⓤ; (車・機械などの修理点検) service ⓒ; (改善) improvement ⓤ ——整備する maintain ⓗ; (修理する) repair ⓗ; service ⓗ; improve ⓗ ‖ よく整備された町並み a *well maintained* row of houses
彼はバイクの整備を怠っている He is neglecting 「*the maintenance* of [*to maintain*] his motorcycle.
町は環境整備に力を入れている The town is putting a great effort into *environmental improvement*.
父は今車を整備に出している My father *is having* his car *serviced*.
大通りが整備されてだいぶきれいになった The main street *has been improved* and it's quite neat and clean now.
◆車のエンジンを整備する *tune* an engine of a car / その公園の芝はよく整備されている(→よい状態に保たれている) The grass in the park *is kept in good condition*.
‖整備員 a maintenance man; (公園・運動場などの)《米》a groundskeeper, 《英》a groundsman / 整備士 (車の) a car mechanic; (飛行機の) a ground crew / 整備新幹線 new *Shinkansen* plans / 自動車整備工場 a garage

せいひょう 製氷 ice making ⓤ ‖ 製氷機 an ice machine / 製氷皿 an ice tray

せいびょう 性病 venereal disease ⓒⓤ (《略語》VD), sexually transmitted disease ⓒⓤ (《略語》STD), 《婉曲的》social disease ⓒ

せいひれい 正比例 【数学】direct proportion ⓤ, direct ratio [réiʃou] ⓤ ‖ XはYに正比例する X *is in direct proportion to* Y.

せいひん¹ 製品 product ⓒ; (機械で大量生産されたもの) manufactures; (商品) goods (◆数詞や many などで修飾できない)
彼らは製品の販売にとても熱心です They are very diligent in selling *their products*.
その会社は新製品の発表を行った They gave a presentation of *their new product*.
手作りの製品はいつも形がいろいろだ *Handmade products* always vary in shape.
その店では様々な外国製品を扱っている They deal in various *foreign products* at the shop.
◆彼らは新型車の製品化を進めている They are preparing to *produce* a new type of car.
‖化学製品 chemical products / ガラス製品 glassware / 革製品 leather goods, leather

/ 絹製品 silk goods [manufactures] / 石油化学製品 a petrochemical / 電気製品 electrical appliances / 乳製品 milk [dairy] products / プラスチック製品 plastics / 羊毛製品 woolen goods

せいひん² 清貧 清貧に甘んじる be content [satisfied] to live honestly in poverty

せいふ 政府 government ⓒ (しばしば Government) (❖《英》では単数形で複数扱いになることがある)
政府の外交方針 the Government's foreign policy
彼らは新政府を樹立した They established a new government.
政府当局は企業経営者にもっと外国人を雇用するよう要請している The government authorities are appealing to business owners to hire more foreigners.
政府内には汚職が蔓延(まんえん)している The government is rife with corruption.
彼は反政府デモに参加した He joined a demonstration against the government.
‖政府開発援助 Official Development Assistance (《略語》ODA) / 政府機関 a government agency / 政府高官 a high-ranking government official / 政府首脳 the head of the government / 政府筋 government sources [circles] / 政府予算案 the government's budget / 暫定政府 an interim government / 州政府 a state government / 中央政府 the central government / 非政府組織 a non-governmental organization (《略語》NGO) / 無政府主義 anarchism

せいぶ 西部 the west, the western part; (米国の) the West ――西部の western ‖米国の西部開拓者たち pioneers of the American West / 彼は埼玉県西部のとある町に住んでいる He lives in a town in the west [western part] of Saitama.
‖西部劇 a western [Western] (movie)

せいふく¹ 制服 uniform ⓒ Ⓤ; (学校の) school uniform ⓒ ‖制服を着る put on a uniform; (→着ている) wear a uniform / 制服姿の看護師 a nurse in uniform; a uniformed nurse / 制服で登校する go to school in uniform; wear a uniform to school / あの高校には制服がない They 「don't have to wear [have no] uniforms in that high school.
|関連語| セーラー服 a middy (blouse) and a skirt (as a girl's school uniform) / 詰めえり(制服) a (school) uniform with a stand-up collar; (えり) a stand-up collar / ブレザー a blazer

せいふく² 征服 conquest Ⓤ ――征服する conquer ⓘ ‖16世紀, スペイン人はメキシコを征服した The Spanish conquered Mexico in the 16th century. / 彼らは悪条件の中ついにカンチェンジュンガ山を征服した They conquered Mt. Kanchenjunga at last in spite of the bad conditions.
‖征服者 a conqueror / 征服地 a conquest / 被征服者(総称) the conquered

せいふく³ 正副 正副委員長を選出する elect a chairperson and a vice chairperson / 申請書を正副2通提出した I handed in the application in duplicate.

せいぶつ¹ 生物 living thing ⓒ,《集合的》life Ⓤ; (植物以外の) (living) creature ⓒ; (科目) biology Ⓤ
彼は海の生物が好きだ He likes 「living things [creatures] in the sea.
地球上には様々な種類の生物が存在している Various forms of life exist on the earth.
地球外生物の存在を信じますか Do you believe in extraterrestrial life?
‖生物化学 biochemistry / 生物学 biology / 生物学者 a biologist / 生物工学 biotechnology / 生物兵器 a biological weapon

せいぶつ² 静物 still life Ⓤ ‖静物画 a still life

せいふん 製粉 flour milling Ⓤ ――製粉する grind* ... into flour, mill ⓘ ‖小麦を製粉する grind wheat into flour; mill wheat
‖製粉機 a mill / 製粉所 a (flour) mill

せいぶん 成分 (食品・薬などの) ingredient ⓒ; (構成要素) constituent ⓒ; (元素) element ⓒ ‖大気中の成分を調べる examine the constituent elements of the air / 使用説明書にこの薬の成分が表示されています The ingredients of this drug are listed in the instructions.
‖栄養成分表示 a nutrition information label [panel] / 主成分 the main ingredient

せいへき 性癖 (公式的) proclivity ⓒ,《公式的》propensity ⓒ ‖彼は物事を大げさに言う性癖がある He has a proclivity to exaggerate things.

せいべつ 性別 sex Ⓤ ⓒ,《公式的》gender Ⓤ ⓒ ‖この仕事に性別は関係ない You can do this job regardless of your sex.

せいへん 政変 political change ⓒ; (政府が変わること) a change of government

せいぼ¹ 歳暮 △ ⇨おせいぼ
せいぼ² 生母 (実の母) one's real mother
せいぼ³ 聖母 the Holy Mother, Our Lady, the Madonna ◆聖母マリア the Virgin Mary

せいほう¹ 西方 the west ――西方の west, western ‖ポルトガルはスペインの西方に位置している Portugal lies to the west of Spain.
◆西方への旅 a westward journey

せいほう² 製法 (manufacturing) process ⓒ ‖この薬は特殊な製法で作られている This drug has been made by a special process [(→方法) method].

せいぼう 制帽 (uniform) cap ⓒ; (学帽) school cap ⓒ ‖看護婦の制帽 a nurse's cap

ぜいほう 税法 tax law

せいほうけい 正方形 square ⓒ ――正方形の square ――《図版》‖1辺が10センチメートルの正方形 a 10-centimeter square

せいほく 西北 the northwest ――西北の northwest

せいほくせい 西北西 the west-northwest ――西北西の west-northwest

せいほん 製本 bookbinding ◯ ──製本する bind* ⦅他⦆ ∥製本業 bookbinding / 製本業者 a binder, a bookbinder / 製本所 a bindery, a bookbindery

せいまい 精米 rice polishing ◯; (精白米) polished rice ◯ ──精米する polish rice ∥精米所 a rice mill

せいみつ 精密 ──精密な (詳細にわたる) detailed, close [klóus]; (正確な) precise, accurate ──精密に in detail, closely; precisely, accurately ∥非常に精密な作りの腕時計 a watch which is made very *precisely* [*accurately*] / その昆虫の絵は細部まで精密に描かれていた The picture of an insect was *precisely* [*accurately*] drawn in every detail. / 精密な調査により、その壁画の制作年代が特定された On *close* [*minute*] inspection, they found out when the wall painting was made. / 彼らはそのコンピュータを精密に検査した They examined the computer *closely* [*minutely, in detail*].
◆彼は病院で精密検査を受けた He underwent *a thorough medical examination* at the hospital.
∥精密科学 the exact sciences / 精密機器 precision instruments

せいむ 政務 the affairs of state ∥政務官 a parliamentary secretary

ぜいむしょ 税務署 tax office ∥税務署員 a tax collector, a taxman; (事務員) a tax office clerk / 税務署長 a tax office superintendent

せいめい¹ 生命

life ◯ ◯ (❖個人の命,人命の意味では ◯) (複 lives) ⇒ いのち

〖生命が・は〗
その飛行機墜落事故で多くの生命が失われた A lot of *lives* were lost in the plane crash.
火星に生命は存在すると思いますか Do you think *life* exists on Mars?
〖生命の〗
生命の起源 the origin of *life* / 生命の神秘 the mysteries of *life*
彼はそんなつまらないことのために生命の危険を冒すほどばかではない He is not such a fool as to *risk his life* for such a trifling thing.
〖生命を・に〗
その医者が彼女の生命を救った The doctor saved her *life*.
人間の出した有害物質が生き物の生命を脅(おびや)かしている Toxic substances discharged by human beings are endangering *lives*.
患者の生命に別状はない The patient's *life* is not in danger.
〖～生命〗
彼は公約の実現に政治生命を賭(か)けた He staked *his political life* on the fulfillment of his pledge.
◆そのけがで彼の水泳選手生命は絶たれた The injury ended his *career as a swimmer*.

〖その他〗
アスファルトを突き破って生えてくる植物に生命力の強さを感じた Coming across a plant that had sprouted through the asphalt, I felt *its life* [*vital*] *energy*.
◆その地域は地震によって電気、ガスなどの生命線が断たれた *The lifelines* such as electricity and gas supplies were cut off in the district because of the earthquake. / ゴキブリは生命力が強い A cockroach has *a strong power to survive*.
∥生命維持装置 a life-support machine [system] / 生命科学 life sciences / 生命線(手相の) the lifeline / 生命保険 life insurance, (英) life assurance / 生命倫理 bioethics

せいめい² 声明 statement ◯, announcement ◯◯ ∥彼らはその法案に関する党声明を発表した They *issued* [*made*] *their party's statement* on the bill.
∥声明書 a statement / 共同声明 a joint statement / 公式声明 a communiqué, an official statement [announcement, declaration] / 犯行声明 a criminal statement

せいめい³ 姓名 one's (full) name
∥姓名判断 fortune-telling from the letters of *a person's* name

せいもん 正門 the front [main] gate; (入り口) the main entrance

せいや 聖夜 the holy night; (クリスマスイブ) Christmas Eve

せいやく¹ 制約 restriction ◯◯, (条件) condition ◯ ──制約する restrict ⦅他⦆, limit ⦅他⦆ ∥活動を法的に制約する put legal *restrictions* on the activities; *restrict* [*limit*] the activities legally / その国に入国するには様々な制約がある Various *conditions* are imposed on us to enter the country. / 私たちはその作業をするうえで時間的な制約を受けている Our time *is restricted* [*limited*] to do the work.

せいやく² 製薬 ∥製薬会社 a pharmaceutical company

せいやく³ 誓約 (固い誓い) pledge ◯; (神などに対しての) oath ◯, vow ◯ ──誓約する (公式的) pledge ⦅他⦆; vow ⦅他⦆
∥誓約書 a written pledge [vow, oath]

せいゆ 精油 (芳香油) essential oil ◯◯; (石油精製) oil refining ◯, (精製した石油) refined oil ◯

せいゆう 声優 (テレビ・映画の) dubbing artist ◯, voice actor [actress] ◯◯; (ラジオドラマなどの) radio actor [actress]

せいよう¹ 西洋 the West (↔the East) ──西洋の Western / 西洋風の建物 a *Western-style* building; a *westernized* building
◆ここ100年ほどで日本はすっかり西洋化した Japan *has been westernized* very much in the last one hundred years or so.
∥西洋医学 Western medicine / 西洋化 westernization / 西洋史 Western history / 西洋思想 Western thought / 西洋諸国 the Western countries / 西洋人 a westerner [Westerner] / 西洋ナシ〖植物〗 a pear

/ 西洋文化 Western culture / 西洋文明 Western Civilization / 西洋料理 Western food; (料理法) Western cooking [cuisine]

せいよう² 静養 rest ⓤⓒ; (病気などの回復) 《公式的》recuperation ⓤ ──静養する take* a (good) rest; (回復する) 《公式的》recuperate ⓐ ∥医者は彼にしばらく静養するように言った The doctor ordered him to「take a rest [rest] for a while. ◆彼女は自宅で静養中です She's resting [recuperating] at home.

せいよく 性欲 sexual desire ⓤⓒ; (非常に強い) lust ⓤ; ∥性欲が強い have strong「sexual desire [lust].

せいらい 生来 by nature, innately ──生来の natural (✿普通名詞の前で用いる), innate ∥浩は生来の怠け者だ Hiroshi is lazy by nature./ Hiroshi was born lazy.
◆洋子には生来数学の才能があった Yoko was mathematically inclined.

せいり¹ 整理

❶【整頓(%)】──整理する put* [set*] ... in order; (場所を) tidy (up); (整理しておく) keep* ... in order [(neat and) tidy]; (片づける) clear up; (まとめる) organize ⓐ; (書類などをとじる) file (away)

引き出しの中を整理しなさい Tidy the drawer up./ (→引き出しの中の物を) Put the things in the drawer in order.

彼の机の上はいつもきちんと整理されている His desk is always kept in good order.

考えを整理してから話しなさい You should organize your thoughts before you speak.

いずれ心の整理がついたら君にも話すよ When I put my feelings in order some day, I'll tell you about it.

整理整頓 (→この部屋を整頓された状態に保つように) Keep this room in order./ (→使用後は元へ戻すように) Put things back after using them.

◆身辺を整理する order one's affairs / 交通整理をする direct [regulate] the traffic / 写真をアルバムに整理する put photographs in an album

❷【捨てる・削減する】──整理する (捨てる) throw* away; (削減する) reduce ⓐ, cut* back (on ...)

本棚のいらない本を整理する throw away the unwanted books on the shelves

その会社は人員を整理する予定だ The company is going to reduce [cut back] the number of its employees.

∥整理券 a numbered ticket / 整理だんす a chest of drawers / 整理番号 a reference number / 書類整理箱 a file

せいり² 生理 ❶【月経】period ⓒ, 《公式的》menstrual period ⓒ, 《公式的》menstruation ⓤ ──生理の menstrual ∥今生理中です I'm having my period. (✿遠回しには It's that time of the month. という) / 生理が10日遅れている My period is 10 days late.

❷【生物の体に起こる現象】physiology ⓤ ──

生理的な physiological ∥生理的欲求を満たす meet one's physiological needs

◆ああいう人は生理的に好きになれない (→本能的に嫌いと) I don't like such a person instinctively./ (→理由は言えないが) I don't like such a person, though I can't tell you why.

∥生理学 physiology / 生理学者 a physiologist / 生理休暇 a (menstrual) period leave / 生理現象 a physiological phenomenon / 生理痛 menstrual pain [cramps] / 生理用ナプキン 《米》a (sanitary) napkin, 《英》a sanitary towel [pad] / 生理用品 sanitary goods

せいりし 税理士 certified tax accountant ⓒ

せいりつ 成立

❶【作られる・できあがる】──成立する (作られる) be made; (組織・団体などが) be formed, be organized, be established

先週, 新内閣が成立した A new cabinet was formed [organized] last week.

徳川幕府が成立したのは何年ですか When was the Tokugawa shogunate established?

❷【成り立つ】
彼のアリバイは成立する (→有効である) のだろうか Can his alibis be valid?

議長が来なければ会議は成立しない (→会議ができない) We can't have the meeting without the chairperson's attendance.

彼がいないとバンドが成立しない (→バンドに不可欠だ) He is indispensable to our band.

❸【まとまる】──成立する be reached; (協定・条約などが) be concluded

昨年, 2国間に条約が成立した A treaty was concluded last year between the two countries. / The two countries concluded a treaty last year.

商談が成立した Our business agreement has been reached. / We have reached the business agreement.

◆国の今年度予算が成立した (→国会で承認された) The budget for this fiscal year was approved by the Diet.

せいりゃく 政略 politics 《単数または複数扱い》, political tactics

∥政略結婚 a marriage of convenience, a political marriage

せいりゅう 清流 clear [crystal] stream ⓒ

せいりょう 声量 彼女は声量がある She has a big voice./ Her voice has plenty of volume.

せいりょういんりょうすい 清涼飲料水 soft drink ⓒ

せいりょうざい 清涼剤 refreshing substance ⓒ ∥道端の花々はあわただしい都会生活を送る私にとって一服の清涼剤となる Roadside flowers refresh me in the midst of life in the busy city.

せいりょく¹ 勢力 power ⓤ; (影響力) influence ⓤⓒ; (力をもつもの) force ⓒ, power ⓒ
勢力の均衡を保つ keep the balance of power / 世界経済の3大勢力 the three bigger forces [powers] in the world economy / 勢力争いに巻き込まれる get involved in a pow-

er struggle / 勢力を振るう wield *influence* [*power*]

その国は周辺地域に勢力を拡大しつつある The country is extending *its power* [*influence*] over its surrounding areas.

彼は実業界における勢力を完全に失った He lost *his power* [*influence*] in the business world completely.

彼はかつての勢力を取り戻そうと必死だ He's trying very hard to regain *his power* [*influence*].

その国はローマの勢力下に置かれた The country was placed *under the influence* of Rome.

台風の勢力はいまだ少しも衰えない The typhoon has not yet lost *its power* a bit.

∥勢力基盤 (政党・政治家などの) a power base / 勢力範囲 a sphere of influence / 反対勢力 an opposing force / 武装勢力 a military force

せいりょく² 精力 energy Ⓤ (❖個人の出せる力・能力の意味では複数形 energies); (元気) vigor, 《英》vigour Ⓤ ——精力的な energetic; vigorous ∥精力を使い果たす use up all *one's energy* / 精力の衰えを感じる feel a decline in *one's energy* / 精力絶倫である have *a lot of (sexual) energy* / 彼は精力旺盛(おうせい)な画家だ He is a *very energetic* painter. / その医者は患者を救うために全精力を注いだ The doctor invested *all his energy* [*energies*] in helping his patients. / その候補は精力的な選挙運動を行った The candidate conducted an *energetic* [*a vigorous*] campaign. / The candidate conducted a campaign *vigorously*.

∥精力家 a man of vigor, 《口語的》a live [láiv] wire / 精力剤 a tonic

せいれい 政令 (内閣による命令) cabinet order Ⓒ; (政府による命令) government ordinance Ⓒ ∥政令指定都市 an ordinance-designated city

せいれき 西暦 (キリスト紀元) the Christian era; (キリスト紀元後) A.D. (❖ふつう年号の若い場合に用い, 年号の前または後ろに付ける) ∥西暦90年に in *A.D.* 90; in 90 *A.D.*

◆これは西暦1999年に書かれた This was written in (the year of) 1999.

せいれつ 整列 ——整列する (1列に並ぶ) line up, stand* in a line [row], form a line [row] ∥生徒は先生の前に整列した Students *stood in a line* [*row*] in front of their teacher. (❖主に line は「縦に」, row は「横に」並ぶことを指す) / 私たちは2列に整列した We *stood in* [*formed*] *two lines*. / (→ 2列に) We *stood in two rows*. / (号令で) 整列！ *Line up!*

◆走者はスタートラインに整列した The runners *were lined up* on the starting line.

せいれん 精錬 refinement Ⓤ, smelting Ⓤ ——精錬する refine ⓣ, smelt ⓣ ∥製錬所 a refinery; (溶鉱所) a smelter

せいれんけっぱく 清廉潔白 清廉潔白な人 a man *of absolute integrity*

セイロン Ceylon (❖スリランカの旧称)

せいろん 正論 彼の言うことは全く正論だ I think what he says *is quite right* [*reasonable*].

セージ 〖植物〗sage Ⓤ Ⓒ

セーター sweater [swétər] Ⓒ; (頭からかぶって着る) pullover Ⓒ ∥手編みのセーター a hand-knitted *sweater*

セーフ 二塁はセーフだった The runner *was safe* at second. / 彼は三塁に滑り込みセーフとなった He slid into third and *was called safe*. / 猛ダッシュして試験時間に滑り込みセーフだった (→ ぎりぎりで間に合った) I ran as fast as I could and *made it just in time for the exam*.

セーブ 〖野球〗save Ⓒ ——セーブする 〖コンピュータ〗save ⓣ ⓘ; 〖スポーツ〗save ⓣ ∥データをセーブし忘れないように Don't forget to *save* your data. / 田原はその試合で20セーブ目をあげた Tahara recorded [was credited with] *the* 20th *save* in the game. / 彼はレース後半のために力をセーブして走っているようだ He seems to *be pacing himself and saving energy* for the latter half of the race.

∥セーブポイント a save point

セーフティーバント ⚠ 〖野球〗drag bunt Ⓒ

セーラーふく セーラー服 (女学生の制服) a middy (blouse) and a skirt (as a girl's school uniform); (上下そろいの子供服) sailor suit Ⓒ

セール (bargain) sale Ⓒ ∥今週いっぱい, あの店で夏物のセールをやっている They *are having a sale on* summer clothes throughout this week. / それはセールで買いました I bought it *on* [*at a*] *sale*.

∥ガレージセール 《米》a garage [yard] sale, 《英》a car-boot sale / 在庫一掃セール a clearance sale / バーゲンセール a bargain sale

セールス 父はかつて保険のセールスをしていた (→ 保険会社のセールスマンだった) My father used to *be a (traveling) salesman* for an insurance company.

セールスポイント ⚠ (商品の) selling point Ⓒ (❖ × sales point とはいわない); (長所) *one's* good point; (人の魅力的な特徴) winning characteristic ∥私のセールスポイントは明るいこと, そしてとても根気のあるところです My 「*good points* [*winning characteristics*] are that I'm cheerful and I'm very patient.

セールスマン (traveling) salesperson Ⓒ (❖男性は salesman, 女性は saleswoman ともいう); (営業マン) sales representative Ⓒ (❖口語では短縮して sales rep ともいう)

せおいなげ 背負い投げ shoulder throw Ⓒ

せおう 背負う ❶ 【背に乗せる】put* ... on *one's* back; (背に乗せて運ぶ) carry ... on *one's* back ∥彼は重い荷物を背負ってその山を登った He climbed the mountain, *carrying* a heavy pack *on his back*.

❷ 【責任などを】shoulder ⓣ ∥彼は多額の借金を背負っている He *is shouldering* heavy

せおよぎ

debt. ◆彼女は一家を背負っている She *supports her family on her own.*
せおよぎ 背泳ぎ backstroke ◯《通例the～》/背泳ぎをする do *(the) backstroke*; swim *(the) backstroke*; swim *on one's back*

せかい 世界

❶【地球上全体】the world, the earth ― 世界の・世界的の world, global, worldwide ― 世界的に globally, worldwide
世界の七不思議 the Seven Wonders of *the World* / 世界の国々 countries *on the earth*
彼女は愛が世界を救えると堅く信じている She has a firm belief that love can save *the world.*
富士山は日本が世界に誇れる名山だ Mt. Fuji is the mountain we can proudly introduce to *the world.*
全世界の人々が幸福を望んでいる *The whole world* [*earth*] desires happiness.
世界でいちばん高い山は何か知っていますか Do you know what the highest mountain *in the world* is?
彼は世界各地を旅行してきた He's traveled in *every part of the world.*
我々はみな世界平和を望んでいる We all are hoping for *world peace.*
彼女は200メートル平泳ぎの世界記録を破った She broke *the world record* for the 200 meter breaststroke.
彼の発見は世界中の注目を集めている His discovery has attracted attention 「*all over* [*throughout*] *the world.*
世界的に景気があまりよくない Business is rather slow *worldwide.*
彼らは世界的規模で水質汚染の調査をしている They are surveying water pollution *worldwide* [*on a global scale*].
その本は世界的なベストセラーです The book is a *worldwide* bestseller.
その国の国王は世界一の大金持ちだ The king of that country is the richest person *in the world.*
◆彼は世界的に有名な歌手である He is a *world-famous* singer.

❷【生活の場・世の中】world ◯
彼は自分の世界に閉じこもっている He's living in *a world* of his own.
君と僕とでは住んでいる世界が違う You and I are living in different *worlds.*
彼女に出会って全く新しい世界が開けた *A whole new world* was opened up in front of me when I first met her.

❸【特定の社会・特定の分野】the world
大人[子供]の世界 *the world* of adults [children]; the adults' [children's] *kingdom* /
学問の世界 *the academic world* / スポーツの世界 *the world* of sports / 動物の世界 *the animal world* / 政治の世界 *the political world*
彼は勝負の世界の厳しさを思い知らされた He learned how severe *the world of competition* is.

❹【宇宙全体・特定の宇宙】world
幻想の世界 *a fantasy world* / 想像の世界 *an imaginary world* / 未知の世界 *an unknown world*
世界全体が自然の法則に支配されている *The whole world* is subject to the laws of nature.
◆死後の世界は存在すると思いますか Do you believe in *life after death*?

‖世界観 one's outlook on the world / 世界記録保持者 the holder of the world record / 世界経済 the world economy / 世界史 world history / 世界情勢 world affairs / 世界人権宣言 the (Universal) Declaration of Human Rights / 世界選手権大会 a world championship (meet) / 世界大戦 a world war / 世界地図 a world map / 世界チャンピオン the world champion / 世界(復興開発)銀行 the World Bank / 世界貿易機関 the World Trade Organization 《略語》WTO / 世界保健機関 the World Health Organization 《略語》WHO / 新[旧]世界 the New [Old] World / 第三世界 the Third World

せかす 急かす hurry ⑭, rush ⑭ /母親は彼女に早く宿題をするようせかした Her mother *hurried* her 「*to do* [*into doing*] her homework very soon. / 彼は母親にせかされて学校へ行った He left for school, *being hurried* [*rushed*] by his mother. / せかさないでよ Don't *hurry* [*rush*] me.

せかせか せかせかと歩く walk *hurriedly* / 彼女は夕飯を食べ終わるなりせかせかと片づけ始めた She began to clear the table *busily* as soon as she finished dinner. / 彼はとてもせかせかした人だ He is a very *hurried* [(→落ち着きのない)*restless*] person.

せかっこう 背格好(背丈) height [háit] ◯ ◯; (男性の体つき) build ◯ ◯; (特に女性の体つき) figure ◯ /彼はお兄さんと背格好がよく似ている He and his brother are almost the same *in height and build.*

ぜがひでも 是が非でも at all cost(s), at any cost [price] /是が非でもそのコンサートには行きたい I want to go to that concert 「*at all cost* [*at any cost*].

せがむ pester ⑭; (強く迫る) press ⑭ ⑮; (請う) beg ⑭ ⑮ /少女は母親に人形を買ってとせがんだ The girl *pestered* her mother to buy her a doll.

せがれ 倅 one's son ⇨ むすこ

セカンド 【野球】(二塁) second (base) ◯; (二塁手) second baseman ◯; 【車のギア】second ◯

‖セカンドバッグ a carrying pouch

せき¹ 席

❶【座る場所】seat ◯, place ◯
席に着いてください *Please take* [*have*] *your seat(s).* / *Please sit down.* / *Please be seated.*
彼女は突然席を立つと,そのまま部屋から出ていっ

た She 「*stood up from* [*left*] *her seat* suddenly, and went out of the room.
私が戻るまで席を取っておいてくれませんか Will you *keep* [*save*] *my seat* [*place*] until I come back?
電車でお年寄りに席を譲った I *gave up my seat* [*place*] *to* an old person on the train.
試験中に席を離れてはいけません Don't *leave your seat* during the examination.
席を替わっていただけませんか Would you *change seats* [*places*] *with me*?
この席はお年寄りや体の不自由なかたのためのものです This *seat* [*place*] is for the old and disabled.
あいにく席は予約でいっぱいです I'm sorry but all *seats* are reserved.
通路側[窓際]の席をお願いします I'd like *an aisle* [*a window*] *seat*, please. (❖禁煙席[喫煙席]は non-smoking [smoking] seat)
僕の隣の席に座りなよ Come take *a seat next to* me.
◆少し席を詰めていただけませんか Could you *move over* a bit for me? / （電話で）花沢は今席をはずしております Hanazawa *is not here* [*at his desk*] right now.
🖋「この席空いてますか」「いえ, います」 "Is this *seat* free?" "No, it's occupied."

❷【場・機会】
懇親会の席を設ける *hold* a social gathering
彼は記者会見の席で重大発表を行った He announced a very serious matter *at the press conference*.
彼女が公の席に姿を現すのは久しぶりだ It has been quite a long time since she appeared *in public*.

❸[地位] position ⓒ, post ⓒ
副委員長の席に1つ空きがある One of *the positions* [*posts*] of vice-chairman is left unoccupied.
‖運転席 a driver's seat / 助手席 a passenger [front] seat / ボックス席 a box (seat) / 予約席 a reserved seat

せき² 咳 cough [kɔ́ːf] ⓒ《通例単数形》――せきをする cough 🔁, give* a cough 🔁 / 彼はここ数日せきがひどい He's *had a bad* [*heavy*] *cough* for the past few days. / He's been *coughing badly* for the past few days. / 彼のせきはまだ止まらない His *cough* is hanging on. / 彼はごほんごほんとせきをした He 「*coughed* harshly [*gave* harsh *coughs*]. / まだ少しせきが出ます I'm still *coughing* a bit.
‖せき止め cough medicine; (ドロップ) a cough drop [《英》sweet]; (シロップ) a cough mixture [《英》syrup]
関連語 かぜ (a) cold / くしゃみ a sneeze / 鼻水 nasal mucus, a runny nose / 鼻詰まり a stuffy nose

せき³ 堰 weir [wíər] ⓒ; (ダム) dam ⓒ
慣用表現 その部屋から出たとたん, 彼女はせきを切ったようにしゃべりだした She *burst into speech* as soon as she got out of the room. / ドアが開くと車内に人々がせきを切ったようになだれ込んだ People *rushed into* the train *like a dam breaking* as its doors opened.

せき⁴ 籍 (戸籍) family register ⓒ ‖籍を入れる[抜く] have *one's* name 「*listed in* [*deleted from*] *the family register*
◆彼はその高校に籍をおいている He *is enrolled in* that high school. / その選手はジャイアンツからドラゴンズへ籍を移した That player *was transferred* from the Giants to the Dragons.

せき⁵ 積【数学】product ⓒ ‖9と6の積は54である *The product* of 9 times 6 is 54.

せきえい 石英【鉱物】quartz ⓤ
せきがいせん 赤外線 infrared [ìnfrəréd] rays ‖赤外線カメラ an infrared camera / 赤外線写真 an infrared photograph, (写真術) infrared photography / 赤外線フィルム an infrared film
せきこむ 咳き込む have* [be taken with] a fit of coughing
せきじ 席次 (成績の順位) (class) ranking ⓤ; (席順) the order of seats ‖席次が上がった My *class ranking* went up.
せきじゅうじ 赤十字 the Red Cross (Society) ‖赤十字病院 Red Cross Hospital / 日本赤十字社 the Japanese Red Cross (Society)
せきじゅん 席順 seating arrangement [order] ⓤ ‖席順を決める[変える] fix [change] *the seating arrangement*
せきじょう 席上 彼は歓迎会の席上でスピーチを行った He made a speech *at the welcome party*.
せきずい 脊髄【解剖】the spinal cord ⓒ
‖脊髄炎【医学】myelitis [màiəláitəs] / 脊髄神経 the spinal nerve / 脊髄注射 a spinal injection
せきせつ 積雪 (雪が積もること) the accumulation of snow; (降った雪) snow ⓤ; (降雪) snowfall ⓒⓤ ‖5センチの積雪 five centimeters of *snow* / 東京の積雪は30センチに及んだ The snow 「*lay* 30 centimeters *deep* [*accumulated to a depth of* 30 centimeters] in Tokyo.
せきたてる 急き立てる hurry (up), rush 🔁; (駆りたてる) urge 🔁 ‖人をせきたてて仕事をさせる *hurry* a person *into* work / 先生は教室から出るようにと生徒たちをせきたてた The teacher *rushed* the students out of the classroom.
せきたん 石炭 coal ⓤ ‖石炭を掘る mine *coal* / 火に石炭をくべる put *coals* on the fire / 石炭を燃やして部屋を暖める burn *coal* to heat [warm] the room
‖石炭ガス coal gas / 石炭紀【地質】the Carboniferous (era [period])
せきちゅう 脊柱【解剖】spinal column ⓒ, spine ⓒ
せきつい 脊椎 spine ⓒ, backbone ⓒ
‖脊椎動物 a vertebrate (animal) / 脊椎湾曲 spinal curvature / 無脊椎動物 an invertebrate (animal)
せきてい 石庭 rock garden ⓒ, rockery ⓒ

せきどう 赤道 the equator, the Equator // 赤道地帯 the region of *the equator*; the *equatorial* region / 我々の船はきのう赤道を越えた Our ship crossed *the equator* yesterday.

> 英作文ノート 赤道の上か下か?
> その都市は赤道直下にある
> →×The city is (located) right *under the equator*.
> →○The city is (located) right *on the equator*.
> ★日本語で「赤道直下」というが, 英語では全く逆に「赤道上に」と表現する.「赤道付近」は near the equator という.

せきとめる 塞き止める dam (up), stem / 水の流れをせき止める *stem* the flow of water / 川をせき止めてダムを造る *dam* (*up*) a river

せきとり 関取 a *sekitori*, a professional sumo wrestler in the top two ranks, *juryo* and *makuuchi*

せきにん 責任

responsibility; (負債などに対する法律上の義務) liability; (釈明義務) accountability; (とがめ) blame; (落ち度) fault; (義務) trust ⇒むせきにん

《責任は・が》
僕たちの責任は重い Our *responsibility* is heavy. / We have *a big responsibility*.
彼らはみな, 自分には責任はないと言い張った Each of them insisted that they *were free of responsibility*.
航空会社は事故の原因について遺族に説明する責任がある The airline company *has a responsibility* to give an explanation of the cause of the accident to the bereaved. / The airline company *is accountable* to the bereaved for the cause of the accident.
◆失敗の責任は君にある You *are responsible for* the failure. / You *are to blame for* the failure. / 会社は労働者の安全に対して責任がある The company *is responsible to* the workers *for* their safety. / だれにその戦争を始めた責任があると思いますか Who do you think *is guilty of* starting the war?

《責任を》
人に責任をなすりつけるのはよせ Don't *attach the responsibility to* others.
どうやってその責任をとるつもりなんだ How do you intend to *take responsibility for* that?
彼はその試合で4番としての責任を果たせなかった He couldn't *fulfill his responsibility* as a cleanup in the game.
彼はその事故の全責任を負った He *accepted full blame* [*responsibility*] *for* the accident.
私に責任を転嫁しないでくれ Don't *shift the blame* onto me.
◆そのことに関しては責任を感じています I *feel responsible for* it. / 運転手は事故の責任を問われなかった The driver *was not to blame for* the accident. / 貴重品は各自が責任をもって管理してください Please remember (that) you *are responsible for* your own valuables. / (駐車に対し)当方は責任を負いません(→自分の責任で駐車してください) Park *at your own risk*.

《責任だ・です》
それは完全に彼の責任だ That's absolutely his *fault*.
チームをまとめるのが監督の責任だ It's the coach's *responsibility* to get the team together.

《その他》
彼は責任感が強い[ない] He has [*a strong* [*no*] *sense of responsibility*.
◆責任者に会わせてください Let me see *the person in charge*. / 何よりもまず責任の所在(→だれに責任があるか)をはっきりさせなければならない First of all we must make it clear *who is responsible*. / 彼は会社の中で責任ある立場にいる He is in a "*responsible* position [*position of trust*] in the company.
‖刑事責任 criminal liability / 連帯責任 joint liability

せきのやま 関の山 彼には負け惜しみを言うのが関の山だった(→彼ができることといえば負け惜しみを言うことだけだった) *All he could do was* (to) cry sour grapes. / あのチームと試合をしてもぼろ負けするのが関の山だ(→ぼろ負けするに決まっている) If we play a game against that team, we *are sure to* be completely defeated.

せきはい 惜敗 ——惜敗する (僅差で敗れる) lose* *by a narrow margin*; (接戦を落とす) lose a close game
◆我々はきのう1点差で惜敗した We *lost* the game *by a margin of* just one point.

せきばらい 咳払い cough ——せき払いをする (話を始める前に) clear *one's* throat; (注意を引くために) give* a cough

せきはん 赤飯

> 赤飯は結婚式, 誕生日, 祭りなどの特別な日に祝いの膳としてふるまわれる代表的な米料理です. もち米に小豆を入れて蒸しますが, 赤飯特有の赤っぽい色は小豆の煮汁の色です.
> *Sekihan* is a typical celebratory rice dish served on special occasions such as weddings, birthdays and festivals. Glutinous rice is steamed with red beans and takes on a pinkish color from the liquid that comes out of the beans.

せきひ 石碑 (記念碑) stone monument; (墓石) tombstone, gravestone // 丘の上に石碑を建てる raise [erect] *a stone monument* on the hill

せきぶん 積分 〔数学〕 integration ——積分する integrate

‖積分学 integral calculus / 定[不定]積分 a definite [an indefinite] integral

せきむ 責務（義務）duty ◯；（責任）responsibility ◯◯ ‖責務をまっとうする fulfill *one's duty* / 十分に責務を果たす do [perform] *one's duty* fully

せきめん 赤面 ──赤面する （一般に）turn red；（恥ずかしくて）blush ◉ ‖彼は怒りで赤面した His face *turned red* with anger. / その少女に見つめられ，彼は恥ずかしくて赤面した He *blushed* with embarrassment when the girl gazed at him.
‖ 赤面恐怖症《心理》erythrophobia [iriθrəfóubiə]

せきゆ 石油 oil ◯, petroleum ◯
100万バレルの石油 a million barrels of *oil* / 石油を精製する refine *oil* / 石油を掘り当てる strike *oil*
その国は石油が豊富だ That country is rich in *oil*.
石油不足が社会不安を引き起こした The *oil shortage* caused the social unrest.
私たちは石油に代わる新しいエネルギー源を見つけなければならない We need to find new energy sources in place of *oil*.
‖石油会社 an oil company / 石油化学 petrochemistry / 石油化学製品 a petrochemical / 石油缶 an oil drum / 石油危機 an oil crisis / 石油コンビナート a petrochemical complex / 石油産業 the oil industry / 石油産出国 oil-producing countries / 石油資源 oil resources / 石油ストーブ an oil heater / 石油製品 oil products / 石油タンク an oil tank / 石油輸出国機構 Organization of Petroleum Exporting Countries《略語》OPEC

せきらら 赤裸々 ──赤裸々な naked [néikid], bare ──赤裸々に nakedly, barely ‖赤裸々な事実 the *naked* truth

せきらんうん 積乱雲 cumulonimbus [kjùːmjəlounímbəs] ◯,（入道雲）thundercloud ◯, thunderhead ◯

せきり 赤痢《医学》dysentery ◯ ‖赤痢菌 a dysentery germ

せきりょう 席料 （レストランの）cover (charge) ◯；（会場の借り賃）a charge for a room；（寄席などの）admission fee ◯

せく 急く （急ぐ）hurry ◉, hasten ◉
[ことわざ] せいては事を仕損じる ⇒ しそんじる

セクシー ──セクシーな sexy,《米口語的》foxy ‖セクシーな声 a *sexy* voice

セクシャルハラスメント ⇒ セクハラ

セクション section ◯

セクト sect ◯ ‖セクト主義 sectarianism

セクハラ ⚠ sexual harassment ◯
◆上司からセクハラを受ける be sexually harassed by *one's* superior

せけん 世間 （世の中）world ◯《しばしば the ～》；（人々）people《複数扱い》；（公衆）the public
《世間が・は》
世間は狭い It's *a small world*.
世間が何と言おうと僕は気にしない I don't care what「*people* say [*the world* says].
とかく世間は根も葉もないうわさに踊らされがちだ *People* tend to be influenced by groundless rumors.
《世間に・で》
その作家は生前，世間に認められることはなかった The writer didn't *make his mark on the world* when he was alive.
世間では彼らが結婚するともっぱらのうわさだ *People* are saying that they are sure to get married.
彼の新しい作品は広く世間で認められた His new work *has received* wide *recognition from the public*.
《世間の》
世間の評判になる make a big noise *in the world*
彼は世間のことをよく知っている He has seen much of *the world*.
その泥棒はどじを踏んで世間の物笑いになった The stupid mistake made the thief *the laughing-stock of the world*.
彼女はいつも世間の目を気にしている She always cares about *how she appears to the world*.
◆世間の常識 *conventional* wisdom
《世間を》
この事件はもうひと月近くも世間を騒がせている This case *has been agitating the public* for almost a month.
彼女の快挙は世間をあっと言わせた Her accomplishment *astonished the world*.
《世間～》
彼女は世間ずれしている She *is too wise in the ways of the world*.
この言葉は世間一般で（→多くの人々によって）広く使われるようになった This word is now used *by many people*.
◆世間体がよい[悪い] look [do not look] respectable / 世間体を気にする pay attention to what other people think / 世間体を保つ keep up appearances / 世間並みの幸せな暮らしをする lead a life *as happy as the average* / 彼女は世間知らずだ She「*is naive* [*knows little of the real world*].
‖世間話 a chat, small talk, (a) gossip

せこい （性格がけちくさい）mean；（金銭的にけちな）stingy ‖それっぽっちの金をけちるなんてせこいよ It's *stingy* of you to grudge such a small sum of money.
◆せこいこと言わずに海外旅行に行こうよ Don't be such a tightwad [skinflint]. Let's take a trip abroad.

せこう 施工 construction ◯ ◆ダム工事が来月施工される（→始まる）ことになった It is decided that the building of the dam *will begin* next month.

セコンド 《ボクシング》second ◯

-せざるをえない -せざるを得ない
❶[⋯せずにはいられない] cannot help *doing*, cannot help but *do*
彼女の努力には感心せざるをえない I *cannot help admiring* her effort.

❷【余儀なく…する．…しなければならない】must *do*, have to *do*, be compelled [forced] to *do*
彼らは土地を手放さざるをえなかった They *had to part* with the land.
停電で仕事を中断せざるをえなかった We *were compelled* by the blackout *to stop* work.

セし 摂氏 Celsius Ⓤ (《略語》C.) —摂氏の centigrade /´セっし/

せじ 世事 (世の中のこと) the world, worldly affairs ‖彼女は世事にうとい She knows little of the (real) world.

せしめる (言いくるめて) wheedle ⊕; (策略などで)《口語的》wangle ⊕ ‖彼女は父親を言いくるめてこづかいをせしめた She *wheedled* pocket money *out of* her father.

せしゅう 世襲 —世襲の hereditary ‖その国では国王の地位は原則として世襲される As a rule, the position of the king *is hereditary* in the country.
‖世襲財産 hereditary property / 世襲制度 a hereditary system

せじょう 世情 (世の中のこと) the world, worldly affairs ‖彼は世情に通じている He knows much about *the world*.

せすじ 背筋 (背中) back Ⓒ; (背骨) spine Ⓒ ‖背筋が痛い have pains in *one's back* / 背筋を伸ばしなさい Straighten *your back.* / 背筋に寒けが走った Chills ran up *my spine.* / I got chills down *my back.* / その恐ろしい光景を見て私は背筋が寒くなった The terrible sight *sent shivers (up and) down my spine.*
◆ 背筋を伸ばして(→まっすぐに)立つ[座る] stand [sit] up *straight*

セスナ Cessna Ⓒ (✿米国セスナ社の軽飛行機); (軽飛行機一般) small airplane Ⓒ

-せずに ノックもせずに部屋に入ってくるな Don't come into my room *without knocking.* / 喜美子はさよならも言わずに行ってしまった Kimiko went away *without saying goodbye.* / タクシーに乗らずに(→乗る代わりに)歩こう Let's walk *instead of taking a taxi.*

ぜせい 是正 correction Ⓤ Ⓒ, rectification Ⓤ Ⓒ ‖是正する correct ⊕, rectify ⊕ ‖誤りを是正する *correct* errors [mistakes] / 日本は率先して貿易不均衡を是正するべきだ Japan should take the initiative in *rectifying* the trade imbalance. ◆国会議席数の是正 *reapportionment* of Diet seats

せせこましい (心の狭い) narrow-minded; (偏狭な) narrow ‖せせこましい考え方 a *narrow* idea / あの男はなんてせせこましいやつなんだ What a *narrow-minded* man he is!

せせらぎ murmur ‖《文語》babble ⊕ ‖また a ~ ‖小川のせせらぎの音 the *murmur* of a little brook

せせらわらい せせら笑い sneer Ⓒ, contemptuous [sneering] smile Ⓒ

せせらわらう せせら笑う laugh mockingly (at ...), sneer (at ...) ‖みんなは彼のことを陰でせせら笑っていた Everybody *laughed mockingly at* him behind his back.

せそう 世相 (社会情勢) social conditions ‖世相を反映する事件 a case which reflects 「*social conditions* [*an aspect of society*]
◆その政策は環境重視の世相を反映している The policy reflects *public opinion* that regards the environment as important.

せぞく 世俗 —世俗の (現世の) worldly; (非宗教的な) secular ‖世俗的な事柄 *worldly* matters / その僧は世俗の権力を利用した The priest took advantage of the *secular* power.

せたい 世帯 household Ⓒ《単数または複数扱い》; (家族) family Ⓒ ‖私たちの村には約100世帯が住んでいる Our village has about a hundred *families*.
‖世帯数 the number of households / 世帯主 the head of a household / 低所得世帯 families on low incomes / 2世帯住宅 a two-family home

せだい 世代 (集合的)generation Ⓒ ‖来るべき世代 future *generations* / 第5世代コンピュータ fifth-*generation* computers / 世代のずれを感じる feel *a generation gap* / 何世代にもわたって *for generations*
若い世代の間で自然食品を買う傾向が見られる There's a trend toward buying organic food among *the younger generation*.
彼は彼女と同世代だ He and she *are of the same generation.*
これらの物語は世代を越えて伝えられてきた These stories have been transmitted [handed down] *from generation to generation.*
◆そのチームは世代交代の時期を迎えている *A generational shift* has begun in the team.
‖次世代 the next generation

せたけ 背丈 height [háit] Ⓒ Ⓤ ‖彼女は私くらいの背丈だ She is about my *height*.

セダン 《米》sedan Ⓒ; 《英》saloon Ⓒ

せちがらい 世知辛い, せちがらい世の中 a hard [cold] world / あいつはせちがらい(→計算高い)やつだ He is a *calculating* guy.

せつ¹ 節 ❶【信念】one's principles ‖節を曲げない[守る] adhere to *one's principles* / 節を曲げる compromise *one's principles*
❷【…のとき】when ‖近くにお越しの節はぜひわが家にお立ち寄りください Please drop in [by] at my house *when* you come around here. ◆その節はたいへんお世話になりました Thank you for your kindness「*at that time* [*the other day*].
❸【文の】(詩・文章のひと区切り) passage Ⓒ; (章より小さい区分) section Ⓒ; (段落) paragraph Ⓒ; (聖書の) verse Ⓒ;《文法》clause Ⓒ (✿文の一部を構成するいくつかの集まりで、主語＋述語の構造をもっているもの) ‖従属節 a *subordinate clause* / 第2章の第5節で in *the fifth section* of Chapter II / 川端康成『雪国』からの一節 a *passage* from Kawabata Yasunari's *Snow Country*

せつ² 説 (意見) opinion Ⓒ, view Ⓒ; (学説) theory Ⓒ ‖新説を唱える advance *a new theory* / ご説ごもっともです Your *opinion* [*view*] is right. / 恐竜は温血動物だったという説がある

One *theory* says that dinosaurs were warm-blooded. / 宇宙の起源に関しては様々な説がある There are various *theories* on the origin of the universe.

せつえい 設営 ―設営する set* [put*] up ∥テントを設営する *set* [*put*] *up* a tent

ぜつえん 絶縁 〔電気〕insulation [U] ―絶縁する〔電気〕insulate [他]; (人との関係を絶つ) break* (off relations) with ... ◆彼とは絶縁状態にある I *am through with* him.
‖絶縁状 a letter terminating a relationship; (女性から男性にあてた)《米口語的》Dear John letter / 絶縁体 an insulator / 絶縁テープ insulating tape

せっかい[1] 切開 〔医学〕incision [U] ―切開する cut* open, incise [他] ∥傷口を切開してうみを出す *cut open* a wound and squeeze out pus; *lance* a wound
‖心臓切開手術 open-heart surgery

せっかい[2] 石灰 lime [U] ‖石灰岩 limestone / 石灰水 limewater / 生石灰 quicklime / 消石灰 slaked lime

せっかく 折角

❶【努力･尽力を惜しんで】

せっかく(→はるばる)来たんだから, 遊んでいこうよ We came *really a long way*, so let's enjoy ourselves.

塩を入れすぎてせっかくの(→苦労して作った)スープを台なしにしてしまった Too much salt spoiled the soup *I worked so hard on*.

ここで計画を断念しようものならせっかくの(→すべての)苦労が水の泡になってしまう *All* our efforts will have been for nothing if we abandon the plan now.

せっかくのお招きですがお伺いできません Thank you for your *kind* invitation, but I'm sorry I cannot come.

💬「あした僕とスケートに行かない?」「せっかくだけど(→誘ってくれてありがとう), ほかに約束があるの」"Will you go skating with me tomorrow?" "*Thank you for asking*, but I have a previous appointment."

❷【貴重な】

彼女はせっかくの(→貴重な)時間をむだにしたくなかった She didn't want to waste *precious* time.

彼はせっかくの(→数少ない)チャンスを生かしきれなかった He couldn't make use of the *rare* chance.

せっかくの(→楽しみにしていた)休日が雨で台なしになった The rain spoiled the holiday *I had looked forward to*.

せっかち ―せっかちな impatient; (性急な) hasty ∥そうせっかちになるな Don't be so *impatient* [*hasty*]. / あんなせっかちな人は見たことがない I've never seen such an *impatient* person.

せっかん 折檻 ―せっかんする punish ... by beating, 《公式的》chastise [他] ∥子供をせっかんする *punish* a child *by beating*; *chastise* a child

せつがん 接岸 船が岸壁に接岸した The ship *was brought alongside* the wharf.

せつがんレンズ 接眼レンズ eyepiece [C]

せっき 石器 stone implement [C] ‖石器時代 the Stone Age / 新[旧]石器時代 the Neolithic [Paleolithic] Age

せっきゃく 接客 上司は今接客中です My boss *is meeting a customer*. / あの店の店員は接客態度がいい(→客に対して親切だ) Clerks *are nice to customers* at that store.
‖接客係 an attendant

せっきょう 説教 (訓戒) lecture [C]; (主に宗教的な) sermon [C] ―説教する lecture [他]; (主に宗教上の) preach [他][自] ∥私たちは授業中におしゃべりをして先生にお説教された We *were lectured* by the teacher for having talked in class. / また貯金しろというあの長い説教だ That long *sermon* about saving money again! / 彼は私たちに慈悲について説教した He *preached* [*delivered a sermon*] to us about mercy. ◆彼の映画には説教くさいところがある His films have *a moralistic tinge*.

ぜっきょう 絶叫 (悲鳴) scream [C], shriek [C]; (大声) cry [C] ―絶叫する scream [自][他], shriek [自][他]; cry [自][他] ∥あらん限りの声で絶叫する *scream one's* head off / 彼女は恐怖のあまり絶叫した She *screamed* out of fear.

せっきょくせい 積極性 assertiveness [U], aggressiveness [U] ∥彼は積極性に欠ける He lacks *assertiveness* [*aggressiveness*].

せっきょくてき 積極的 ―積極的な (肯定的な) positive; (活動的な) active; (自分の意見をはっきり出す) assertive ―積極的に positively; actively; assertively ∥彼は何事にも積極的な態度を示す He shows a *positive* attitude toward everything. / 雅子はダイエットに成功して以来とても積極的になった Masako has become very *assertive* since she succeeded in her diet. / 僕たちは本田君の意見を積極的に支持した We *positively* supported Honda's opinion. / 彼女はボランティア活動に積極的に参加している She is taking an *active* part in volunteer work.

せっきん 接近 approach [U] ―接近する go* near, come* near, approach [他][自] ―接近した close ∥台風が九州に接近した A typhoon 「*came near* (*to*) [*approached*] Kyushu. ◆この近所では家と家とが接近して建っている Houses stand *near* (*to*) each other in this neighborhood. / 両チームの実力は接近している The two teams *are almost equal* in skills.
‖異常接近(航空機の) a near miss

せっく 節句 🗻

節句とは, 季節の変わり目などに年中行事を行う日のことをいいます. 現代ではふつう, 1月7日(七種(ななくさ)の節句), 3月3日(桃の節句), 5月5日(端午(たんご)の節句), 7月7日(七夕(たなばた)), 9月9日(菊の節句)の五節句を指します.
Sekku are days on the calendar for events that mark changes in the seasons. The *sekku* days now fall on January 7 (called the Seven Herb Festival), March 3 (Girls', or Dolls, Festival),

May 5 (Boy's Day), July 7 (Tanabata Festival), and September 9 (Chrysanthemum Festival).

ぜっく 絶句 ——絶句する become* speechless ◆ 突然の知らせに彼女はしばし絶句した The sudden news「*left her speechless* [*struck her dumb*] for a while. / She *couldn't speak* for a while due to the news.

セックス (性交) sex ⓤ, sexual intercourse ⓤ; (性別) sex ⓤ ⓒ,《公式的》gender ⓤ ⓒ (❖日本語の「セックス」は通例「性交」の意味で用いられるが, 英語の sex は本来的には「性別」の意味で用いられる) ——セックスする have* sex (with ...),《婉曲的》make* love (with [to] ...),《婉曲的》sleep* (with ...)
10代のセックス teenage sex
彼女は母親ともオープンにセックスの話をする She talks frankly about *sex* with her mother.
彼らはセックスに興味をもち始めている They are beginning to get interested in *sex*. / They are beginning to be *sexually* aware.
∥セックスアピール sex appeal / セックスシンボル a sex symbol / セックスチェック《スポーツ》gender verification

せっけい¹ 設計 design ⓤ (❖「設計図」の意味では ⓒ), plan ⓒ ——設計する design ⊕, plan ⊕ /家の設計図を描く draw *a design* [*plan*] of a house / このビルはだれが設計したのですか Who *designed* [*made the plans for*] this building? / この新しい家は特に老人向きに設計されている This new house *is* specifically *designed* for the elderly.
∥設計者 a designer / 生活設計 a plan for *one's* life

せっけい² 雪渓 snowy valley [ravine, gorge] ⓒ

ぜっけい 絶景 wonderful [superb, magnificent] view ⓒ ◆その展望台からの眺めは絶景だった The view from the observation tower *was wonderful* [(→言葉にならないほど美しい)*beautiful beyond description*].

せっけっきゅう 赤血球 red (blood) corpuscle ⓒ, red blood cell

せっけん¹ 石鹸 (固形の) soap ⓤ (❖数えるときは a bar of ... とする)
せっけんの香り the odor of *soap*
せっけんで手を洗った I washed my hands with *soap*.
このせっけんは汚れがよく落ちる This *soap* cleans [washes] well.
🗨「スカートに絵の具がついちゃった」「せっけんで洗えば落ちるわよ」"Some watercolors stained my skirt." "You can wash it out with *soap*."
∥せっけん入れ a soap dish / せっけん水 soapy water / 粉せっけん soap powder / 洗濯せっけん laundry soap / 薬用せっけん medicated soap

せっけん² 席巻・席捲 ——席巻する sweep* ⊕ /そのポップグループは日本全土を席巻した The pop group *swept* the whole of Japan.

せつげん 節減 reduction ⓤ ⓒ ——節減する reduce ⊕, cut* down /光熱費を節減する *reduce* [*cut down*] utility bills
◆当社の新車は燃料節減型です Our new model is *a real fuel-saver*!

ゼッケン ⚠ (racing) number (cloth) ⓒ /背中にゼッケンをつけて走る run with a participant's *number* (*cloth*) pinned on *one's* back / ゼッケン5番の選手 the *number 5 player* [*runner*]

せっこう 石膏 (鉱物) gypsum [dʒípsəm] ⓤ; (粉末) plaster ⓤ /石膏像 a *plaster* figure; (→胸像) a *plaster* bust

ぜっこう¹ 絶交 ——絶交する break* (off relations) with ... ——絶交している be through (with ...) /僕, 次郎と絶交しちゃったI've broken off relations with Jiro. / もうおまえとは絶交だ You and I *are through*.

ぜっこう² 絶好 絶好の (最高の) best; (完璧(ぺき)な) perfect; (理想的な) ideal /絶好のチャンスをつかむ have an *ideal* [a *golden*] opportunity / この季節は勉強するのに絶好の時期だ This season is *the best time for study*. / きょうは絶好のハイキング日和(びより)だ Today is a *perfect* [an *ideal*] day for hiking.

ぜっこうちょう 絶好調 カープの山田は今絶好調だ Yamada of the Carp is *in top shape* [*condition*] now.

せっこつ 接骨 bonesetting ⓤ ∥接骨医 a bonesetter

せっさたくま 切磋琢磨 彼らは切磋琢磨して(→互いに励まし合い, 競争しながら)碁の腕を磨いてきた They have gotten better at go *by encouraging and competing with each other*.

ぜっさん 絶賛 high praise ⓤ ⓒ,《口語的》rave ⓒ ——絶賛する praise ... very highly, acclaim ⊕, rave about [over] ... /絶賛の評 rave notices / だれもがその小説を絶賛した Everyone *praised* the novel *very highly*. / 彼の新しい映画は各紙で絶賛された He *won high praise* for his new film in every newspaper.
◆絶賛発売中 *Now Selling to Rave Reviews* (❖英語には掲示としての次のような表現がない)

せっし 摂氏 Celsius ⓤ ((略語)C.) ——摂氏の centigrade /気温は摂氏マイナス5度です The temperature is minus 5 degrees *centigrade*. / メタノールは摂氏64.65度で沸騰する Methyl alcohol boils at 64.65° *Celsius*.
∥摂氏温度計 a centigrade thermometer

せつじつ 切実 一切実な (深刻な) serious, acute; (差し迫った) urgent; (心からの) earnest ——切実に seriously; urgently; earnestly /切実な訴え an *earnest* [*urgent*] appeal / 教育制度の崩壊は社会全体にとって切実な問題だ The collapse of the educational system is a *serious* [an *acute*] problem for society at large.
◆現在多くの人々が公害対策の必要性を切実に感じている Now many people feel keenly

that we have to take some measures against environmental pollution. / 世界中で平和と友好が切実に求められている Peace and friendship are *eagerly* sought all over the world.

せっしゃ 接写 close-up [klóusʌ̀p] [U] [C] //野草を接写する *take a close-up photo* of wild grass

せっしゅ[1] 摂取 （食べ物などの）ingestion [U], intake [U]《また an ～》;（文化などの吸収）assimilation [U] ━摂取する ingest [他], take* (in); assimilate [他] //カルシウムの摂取（量）*intake* of calcium / 日本は諸外国の文化を摂取してきた Japan *has assimilated* [*taken in*] cultures of foreign countries.

せっしゅ[2] 接種 inoculation [U] [C];（ワクチン接種）〘医学〙vaccination [C] [U] ━接種する inoculate [他];〘医学〙vaccinate [他] //人にインフルエンザの予防接種をする *inoculate* a person *against* influenza

せっしゅ[3] 節酒 moderate drinking [U]
◆彼は最近節酒に努めている Recently he's been trying to *cut down on his drinking*.

せっしゅう 接収 requisition [U] [C],《公式的》expropriation [U] [C] ━接収する requisition [他],《公式的》expropriate [他] //家財道具を接収する *requisition* household goods

せつじょ 切除 《公式的》excision [U], removal [U] [C] ━切除する《公式的》excise [他], remove [他] //胸のしこりの切除 *the surgical removal* of a lump from *one's* breast / 父は大腸の一部を切除した My father *had* a part of his large intestine *excised*.

せっしょう[1] 折衝 negotiation [C] [U]《しばしば複数形 ～s》 ━折衝する negotiate [自] [他] //非公式な折衝 unofficial *negotiations* / 折衝にあたる engage *oneself* in *the negotiations* / 労使間で折衝が重ねられた Labor and management had several *negotiations*.

せっしょう[2] 殺生 （殺し）killing [U] ━殺生する kill [他] [自] //「殺生はやめなさい」と僧は言った The priest said, "Don't *kill*." ◆そんな殺生な（→薄情な）! Don't be so *heartless* [*cruel*]!

せつじょうしゃ 雪上車 snowmobile [C]

せっしょく 接触 touch [C]《通例単数形》;（連絡）contact [U] ━接触する touch [他];（連絡を取る）contact [他], come* [get*] in contact with ... //…と接触を保つ *keep in contact* [*touch*] *with* ... / 警察は犯人との接触を試みた The police *tried to get in contact with* the criminal. / 桜の枝が屋根に接触していたので切り落とした A branch of the cherry tree *was touching* the roof, and so I cut it off. / その病気は接触感染するといわれてきた It has been said that the disease *spread through casual contact*. / その政治家はマスコミ関係者との接触を避けている The politician avoids *contact* with people involved with the mass media. ◆バイクと接触する *have a minor collision with* a motorbike / 電気の接触が悪い *The* electrical *connection* is bad.
‖接触事故 a minor collision

せつじょく 雪辱 （スポーツなどの）revenge [U] //彼には2回続けて負けているので，今度こそ雪辱を果たしたい Because I've been beaten by him two times in succession, I want to *get my revenge with* him this time. / 敗戦後，彼は雪辱に燃えていた Since his defeat, he has panted for *revenge*.
‖雪辱戦 a return match [game]

ぜっしょく 絶食 fast [C] ━絶食する fast [自]（❖「宗教上の理由で絶食する」というニュアンスが強い）//2日間の絶食 *a* two-day *fast* ◆その検査の前は絶食しなければならない You *can't eat anything* before that examination.

せっすい 節水 water conservation [U] ━節水する conserve water //水不足で節水する *conserve water* because of a water shortage

せっする 接する
❶【触れる】touch [他] [自]
直線 *l* は円Oに接している Line *l touches* circle O.
町のはずれはその平野を囲む山々に接している The edge of the city *touches* the mountains surrounding the plain.
❷【隣り合う】be next to ...
うちの庭は畑に接している My garden *is next to* the field.
◆アメリカ合衆国はカナダ，メキシコと国境を接している The U.S.A. *shares borders with* [*borders*] Canada and Mexico.
❸【人と関わる】（扱う）treat [他];（会う）see* [他], meet* [他] [自]
以前に比べると外国人と接する機会が増えた We have more occasions to *meet* [*come in contact with*] foreigners than before.
彼はいつも彼女に対して敬意をもって接している He always *treat* [*deals with*] her respectfully.
❹【その他】
訃報(ふほう)に接する *hear* [*receive*] the news of *a person's* death
彼がドイツ文学に初めて接したのは18のときだった It was at the age of 18 that he *read* German literature for the first time.

ぜっする 絶する 言語に絶する苦しみ *indescribable* [*unspeakable*] suffering; suffering *beyond description* [*words*] / 古代の王たちは想像を絶するほどの強大な権力をもっていた Ancient kings held great power *beyond imagining*.

せっせい[1] 摂生 ━摂生する（健康に気をつける）take* (good) care of *one's* health

せっせい[2] 節制 moderation [U];（特に節酒）《公式的》temperance [U] ━節制する be moderate [temperate] //たばこを節制する *be moderate* [*temperate*] in smoking

ぜっせい 絶世 ━絶世の（比類ない）matchless //絶世の美女 a woman of *matchless* beauty

せつせつ 切々 切々たる願い *earnest* wish / 彼女は自分の思いを切々と手紙につづった She expressed herself in her letter *passionately* [*ardently*].

せっせと （一生懸命）hard;（勤勉に）diligent-

せっせん

ly; (忙しく) busily ∥せっせと働く work *hard* [*diligently*]; work *like an ant* [*a bee*] / 彼女はせっせと庭仕事をしていた She was working *busily* in the garden.

せっせん¹ 接戦 close [klóus] game ⓒ ∥僕たちは木曜、試合に勝った It was *a close game*, but we finally won it.

せっせん² 接線 〖数学〗tangent line ⓒ

せっそう 節操 (信条) principle ⓒⓊ《通例複数形~s》; (誠実さ) integrity Ⓤ; (品行) morals ∥彼は節操もなく考えを変える He changes his opinion *without principles*.
◆無節操なふるまい *unprincipled* conduct / 前の彼女と別れたと思ったらもう別の子とつきあい始めたなんてあいつも節操がないな He started to go out with a new girlfriend as soon as he broke up with the former one. He *is very fickle*.

せつぞく 接続 connection ⓒⓊ ──接続する connect ⾃⾃ ∥スピーカーをCDプレーヤーに接続してください *Connect* the speaker *to* the CD player. / この列車は博多行きに接続します This train *connects with* another for Hakata. / 電車の接続が悪くて約束の時間に遅れた I was late for the appointment because I had *a bad* train *connection*.
∥接続駅 a junction / 接続便 (飛行機) a connecting flight

せつぞくし 接続詞 〖文法〗conjunction ⓒ

> 語と語，句と句，節と節を結びつける働きをするものを接続詞という．接続詞には，「等位接続詞」と「従属接続詞」がある．等位接続詞と名詞節を導く従属接続詞は種類が少ないが，副詞節を導く従属接続詞にはいろいろな種類がある．
> [等位接続詞] 対等の関係にある語・句・節を接続する (and, but, for, nor, or) ∥ At the age of 17, my brother quit school *and* began to work. 私の兄は17歳のとき学校をやめて働き始めた / I have a bicycle, *but* its brakes are broken. 私は自転車を持っているが，ブレーキがこわれている
> [従属接続詞] 名詞節・副詞節を主節に従属させる (after, because, before, if, that, whether など) ∥ I insisted *that* I was right. 私は自分が正しいと主張した / She has been working for that company *since* she finished school. 彼女は学校を卒業してからずっとその会社で働いている / George was wet to the skin, *because* he played soccer in the rain. 雨の中でサッカーをしたので，ジョージはずぶぬれになっていた

せっそくどうぶつ 節足動物 arthropod ⓒ

せったい 接待 (応対) reception ⓒ《通例単数形》; (もてなすこと) entertainment Ⓤ ──接待する《公式的》receive ⾃; entertain ⾃ ∥きょうは客の接待で忙しかった I was busy *entertaining* guests today. / 私たちはパーティーで特別な客としての接待を受けた We were *received* as special guests at the party.
∥接待係 a receptionist / 接待費 entertainment expenses

ぜったい 絶対

──絶対の・絶対的な absolute ──絶対(に) absolutely

絶対的な信頼 *absolute* trust / 絶対的な真理 *absolute* truth

それは絶対に不可能だ It's *absolutely* impossible.

彼の計画には絶対反対だ I'm *absolutely* against his plan.

ここでは彼が絶対的な権力をもっている He has *absolute* authority here.

彼女は医者から3日間の絶対安静を言い渡された The doctor told her to *remain absolutely quiet* for three days.

◆わが家では父が言ったことは絶対である What my father says *is the law* in our house. / 彼は自分の罪を絶対に認めないだろう He would *never* admit his guilt. / 金なんか絶対に貸さないよ I wouldn't lend you money *for anything*. / 絶対に彼がそんなことを言うはずがない He is *the very last* man to say such a thing.（❖*the very last* は「最も不適」の意味） / この本は絶対に(→何があっても)なくさないでね Don't lose this book *no matter what may happen*. / その映画は絶対に見たほうがいい(→見なければならない) You've got to see this movie. / 絶対にうちに来て Be sure to come to my house tomorrow.

🔊「あれは絶対に聡史だよ」「絶対違うよ」 "That *must be* Satoshi." "*No way!*"

🔊「ニンジンを食べてしなさい」「絶対?」 "*Finish* your carrots." "*Must I?*"

🔊「私の代わりにこれをやってくれない?」「絶対いや」 "Will you please do this for me?" "*No way!*"

∥絶対音感 〖音楽〗perfect pitch / 絶対温度 absolute temperature / 絶対君主制 absolute monarchy / 絶対多数 an absolute majority / 絶対値 〖数学〗absolute value / 絶対服従 total obedience

ぜつだい 絶大 ──絶大な tremendous, enormous ∥彼女は宮廷内で絶大な権力を握っていた She had *tremendous* [*enormous*] power in the Court. / このシリーズは若者を中心に絶大な人気を誇っている This series boasts *tremendous* popularity mainly among young people. ◆彼らに絶大な(→全面的な)信頼をおいている I put *total* faith in them. / 絶大なる(→惜しみない)ご支援をたまわり，まことにありがとうございます I'm really grateful to you for your *wholehearted* [*most generous*] support.

ぜったいぜつめい 絶体絶命 私たちは絶体絶命だった We were *in a real bind*. / 主人公は絶体絶命のピンチに追いつめられた The hero *had his back to the wall*. / The hero *was driven into a corner*.

せつだん 切断 cutting Ⓤ; (手術で) amputation Ⓤⓒ ──切断する cut* off; amputate ⾃ ∥ワイヤーを切断する *cut off* a wire / 彼は事故で片足を切断した His leg *was cut off* in the accident. / 彼女は手術で腕をひじから切断

した She *had* her arm *amputated* at the elbow. ◆台風で通信網が切断された The lines of communication *were severed* because of the typhoon.
∥切断面 a section

せっち 設置（設立）establishment ⓊⒸ;（機関などの）formation Ⓤ;（設備などの）installation Ⓤ ——設置する establish ⓗ; form ⓗ; install ⓗ ∥新しい学部の設置 *the establishment* of a new faculty / 新しい委員会を設置する *form* [*set up*] a new committee / タイムレコーダを設置する *install* a time clock

せっちゃく 接着 割れた破片を接着剤でくっつけた I *put* the broken pieces *together with glue*. / I *glued* the broken pieces *together*.
∥瞬間接着剤 quick drying glue

せっちゅう 折衷（妥協）compromise ⓊⒸ ——折衷する compromise ⓘⓗ ∥これは彼の案と私の案を折衷したものです This is *a compromise* between his plan and mine.
◆現代の日本家屋のほとんどは和洋折衷だ Most houses in present-day Japan are *a blend of Western and Japanese styles*.
∥折衷案 a compromise / 折衷主義《公式的》eclecticism

ぜっちょう 絶頂（頂点）the top,《公式的》the summit;（最高潮）the height, peak Ⓒ《通例単数形》∥彼は現在人気の絶頂にある He is now *at the height* [*peak*] of his popularity. / 彼は幸福の絶頂にあった He *was at the summit* [*peak, height*] of happiness.

せっつく（せきたてる）press ⓗ;（催促する）urge ⓗ ∥子供にせっつかれてその人形を買った I *was pressed* [*urged*] by my child *to* buy the doll.

せってい 設定 setting Ⓒ ——設定する set* ⓗ ∥賃金の最高限度を設定する *set* [*place*] a ceiling on wages / オーブンの温度を摂氏180度に設定する *set* the temperature of the oven to 180°C / この洗濯機は全自動なので毎回設定を変える必要はない Since this washing machine is fully automatic, you don't need to change *the setting* every time.

せってん 接点〔数学〕a point of contact;（討論などの）a point of agreement;（異なるものの間の）interface Ⓒ ∥芸術と科学の接点 *the interface between* art and science / 私は彼との議論に接点を見いだそうとした I tried to find *a point of agreement* in the argument with him.

せつでん 節電 power saving Ⓤ ——節電する save electricity ∥このエアコンは節電型だ This air conditioner is *the power saving type*.

セット
❶【ひとそろい】set Ⓒ
家具の3点セット *a three-piece set* of furniture / ゴルフセット *a set* of golf clubs
このジャケットとこのスカートでセットになっている This jacket and this skirt *make a set*.
◆ステレオセット *a stereo system* / 日曜大工セット *a do-it-yourself kit*
❷【試合の区切り】set Ⓒ

3セットの試合 a three-*set* match
彼は第2セットの最初のゲームを取った He won the first game of *the* second *set*.
❸【舞台装置】set Ⓒ
映画［舞台］のセット *a film* [*stage*] *set*
❹【準備・設定】setting Ⓒ ——セットする set* ⓗ
夕食のためにテーブルをセットする *set* a table for supper
ビデオを10時にセットしなくちゃ I must *set* the video to go on at 10 o'clock.
◆セットポジションから投げる pitch from *a set position*
❺【調髪】set Ⓒ《通例単数形》——セットする set* ⓗ
髪をセットする *set one's* hair
私はきのう美容院で髪をセットしてもらった I *had* my hair *set* at the beauty parlor yesterday.
∥セットポイント a set point / セットローション setting lotion

せつど 節度 moderation Ⓤ;（節制）《公式的》temperance Ⓤ ◆節度ある生活 a *sober* life / 節度を守ってお酒を飲んだほうがいい You should *be moderate* in your drinking. / 彼のふるまいは節度を失したものだった His behavior was *immoderate*.

せっとう 窃盗 theft ⓊⒸ ∥彼は窃盗罪で逮捕された He was arrested for *theft*.
∥窃盗犯 a thief

せっとうご 接頭語〔文法〕prefix Ⓒ（❖単語の前に付けてその単語に意味を添えるもの）

せっとく 説得 persuasion Ⓤ;（説得して断念させること）dissuasion Ⓤ ——説得する（説き伏せる）persuade ⓗ, talk ⓗ; dissuade ⓗ
彼の気持ちを変えさせるにはかなりの説得が必要だろう It'll take a lot of *persuasion* to make him change his mind.

語法
日本語の「説得する」が用いられるのは，説得がうまくいった場合だけとは限らないが，persuade は説得に成功したことまで含意する。そのため「彼に新車を買うように説得したがだめだった」という文を英語にすると次のようになる ∥ I *tried to persuade* him to buy a new car, but he didn't [wouldn't]. (❖ × I persuaded him to buy a new car, but …. とはしない)

彼女は説得に応じなかった I tried to *persuade* her, but she wouldn't listen to me.
母は父を説得して酒をやめさせた My mother *persuaded* my father *to* give up drinking.
我々は彼を説得して学校をやめるのを思いとどまらせた We *persuaded* him *not to* quit school. /（→断念させた）We *talked* him *out of* quitting school. / We *dissuaded* him *from* quitting school.
彼に説得されてそのクラブに入ることにした He *talked* me *into* joining the club.
◆彼の意見はとても説得力がある His opinion is very *persuasive* [*convincing*]. / 彼の支持

が必要だが彼を説得できますか We need his support. *Can you win* him *over*? (◆*win a person over*は「人を説得して支持を得る」の意味)

せつな 刹那 moment ⓒ, instant ⓒ ◆刹那的な喜び *momentary pleasures*

せつない 切ない (つらい) painful, sad ∥切ない思いをする feel *painful* [*sad*] ◆彼がいなくてすごく切ない(→寂しい) I really *miss* him.

せつなる 切なる (熱心な) 望み an *ardent* [(→真剣な)*earnest*] hope

せつに 切に (熱心に) earnestly; (本心から) sincerely; (心の底から) from the bottom of *one's* heart ∥私たちはみな、幸福と平和を切に望む We all *earnestly* desire happiness and peace. ◆彼の成功を切に(→本当に)願っている I *do* hope for his success.

せっぱく 切迫 切迫した(→急を要する)状況 an *urgent* [*a pressing*] situation / 切迫した(→緊迫した)雰囲気 a *tense* atmosphere

せっぱつまる 切羽詰まる 有り金をすべて使い果たしてせっぱつまっている(→困っている) I have used up all my money, and now I *am in a fix* [*pinch*]. / せっぱつまって(→追いつめられて)やっと彼は行動を起こした He took action at last after he *was driven to the wall*.

せっぱん 折半 ―折半する split* [divide] ... equally, halve ⊕; (費用を) go* fifty-fifty ◆昼食代を折半する *go fifty-fifty on* lunch / もうけは折半した We *split* the profits *equally*./ We *halved* the profits.

ぜっぱん 絶版 その本は絶版になっている The book *is out of print*.

せつび 設備 《集合的》equipment ⓤ (◆数えるときはa piece of ... とする); (施設) facilities ―設備する equip ⊕
設備のよい [悪い] 部屋 a *well-*[*badly-*] *equipped* room / 化学実験用の設備 *equipment for* chemical experiments
このスポーツジムにはあらゆる設備がある This health club has every kind of *equipment*.
その会社は設備の改善を計画している The company is planning to improve *its facilities*.
あの工場はまだ完全には設備が整っていない That factory *is not* fully *equipped* yet.
私の学校は設備が整っている My school *is well-equipped*.
この研究室には非常に高価な機器が設備されている This laboratory *is equipped with* very expensive instruments.
∥設備投資 equipment investment / 設備費 the cost of equipment / 研究設備 research facilities

せつびご 接尾語 〖文法〗 suffix ⓒ (◆単語の後に付けてその単語に意味を添えるもの)

ぜっぴつ 絶筆 the last (piece of) work, swan song ⓒ

ぜっぴん 絶品 (すぐれた品) a superb piece of work; (傑作) masterpiece ⓒ ◆彼女が作ってくれたケーキは絶品だった The cake which she made for me was *a masterpiece*.
◆このソースはまさしく絶品の(→比類のない)味だ This sauce has an *incomparable* taste.

せっぷく 切腹 [絵] harakiri ⓤ ―切腹する commit harakiri

かつて切腹(日本ではあまり「ハラキリ」とはいわない)は、武士道の教えを守る名誉ある死に方だとされていました。武士道では、武士たる者、死ぬべきときは恥を忍んで生き延びるより潔く死ぬべしとされていたのです。腹を裂くのは、腹に魂が宿るとされていたからです。今日(註)ほとんどの日本人にとって、切腹は遠い過去のものです。
Seppuku (the term *harakiri* is not often used in Japan) used to be committed by samurai in the past as an honorable way of dying in accordance with *bushido* (the samurai code). The code taught that a samurai must kill himself when necessary rather than live with shame for the rest of his life. He slashed his stomach because his spirit was believed to reside there. *Seppuku* is ancient history for most of today's Japanese.

せつぶん 節分 [絵]

節分は元来、旧暦上で季節の分かれ目のすべてを指しましたが、今では立春(春の始まりの日、2月4日ごろ)の前日のことだけをいいます。節分の日(2月3日ごろ)には豆まきと呼ばれる伝統的な儀式があります。いった大豆を「鬼は外、福は内」と叫びながら家の中や外にまき、年の数だけ食べます。
Setsubun originally referred to the days which precede the beginning of the four seasons in the old calendar, but now it is applied only to the day before *risshun* (the first day of spring, around February 4). There is a traditional ceremony called *mamemaki* for *setsubun* (around February 3): people scatter roasted soy beans inside and outside the house shouting *"oni wa soto, fuku wa uchi,"* which means "devils out, fortune in," and they eat as many beans as their age.

せっぷん 接吻 kiss ⓒ ⇒キス

ぜっぺき 絶壁 precipice ⓒ; (特に海岸の) cliff ⓒ

せつぼう 切望 その国の国民は平和を切望している The people in that country *long* [*yearn*] *for* peace. / 彼はパリ留学を切望している He's *eager* [*anxious*] *to* study in Paris.

ぜつぼう 絶望 despair ⓤ ―絶望する despair ⊕, lose* hope ―絶望的な desperate, hopeless ∥絶望のどん底にいる be in the depths of *despair* / 彼女は絶望のあまり自殺した She killed herself *"out of* [*in*] *despair.* / たび重なる失敗が彼を絶望に追い込んだ The repeated failure has driven him to *despair*. / 彼は自分の将来に絶望している He

ぜつめつ

コミュニケーションスキル —説明—

①語句の意味を説明してもらいたいとき

"A"はどういう意味ですか.
- (A) **What is the meaning of "A"?**
- (B) **What do you mean by "A"?**
- (C) **What does "A" mean?**
- (D) **How do you define the term "A"?**

語句の意味を尋ねるには，(A)～(C)がよく使われる．(D)のようにdefine(定義する)を使うと形式ばった表現になり，授業や公式な会議などで使われる．term(用語)もフォーマルな言葉である．

②もっと具体的に説明してほしいとき

もう少し詳しく話してもらえますか．
- (A) **Would you give me a few more details on [about] that?**
- (B) **Would you explain that a little more fully?**
- (C) **Would you be more specific?**
- (D) **Can you give an example?**
- (E) **Perhaps you could give some examples of ....**

☞ 出だしをCould [Would]にするとCanより丁寧な響きになり，聞く側が複数いる場合はmeの代わりにusを使う．これらの表現の後に So what do you mean? などが入ることもある．もっとインフォーマルな言い方には **For example?** / **Like what?** などがあり，特に Like what? は親しい間柄で頻繁に使われている．その他， **Would you please elaborate on that?** (さらに詳しく…)という言い方もある．(D)や(E)は「例を挙げて詳しく…」の意味のときに使う．

③語句あるいは内容を明らかにしてあげる必要があるとき

私が言っているのは…ということです．
- (A) **What I mean is ....**
- (B) **By that I mean ....**
- (C) **I define it as ....**
- (D) **I'll define it this way.**

(A)と似た表現には **What I want to say is this.** というのがあり，(D)同様この後に説明を加える．また主語が人間ではなく，**It means ....** (それは…という意味です)という言い方もよくある．(C)や(D)のようにdefineを使うと「定義」について述べるややかたい響きの表現となる．

④例を挙げるとき

例えば…／例を挙げてみましょう．
- (A) **For example ....**
- (B) **Here is an example.**
- (C) **Let me give you some examples.**
- (D) **To take [give] an example ....**

☞ (A)が最もよく使われる表現．類似表現に **For instance ....** がある．

「*despairs of* [*feels hopeless about*] his future. / 難民たちは絶望的な状況の中で暮らしている The refugees live in *hopeless* conditions. / 残念ですがその患者は絶望的です I'm afraid「the patient *is a hopeless case* [*there's no hope* for the patient].
◆わがチームの優勝は絶望的だ Our team *has no hope* [*chance*] *of* winning. / *There's no hope* [*chance*] that our team will win. / ああ，もう絶望的だ *All hope is gone.* / 乗客は全員絶望視されていた(→死んだと思われていた) All the passengers *were believed* (*to be*) *dead*.

ぜつみょう 絶妙 絶妙のタイミングで with *perfect* timing / その役者は絶妙な演技を見せた The actor gave an *exquisite* [a *marvelous*] performance.

せつめい 説明

explanation ⓒ ⓤ; (口頭・文書による詳細な) account ⓒ; (図・絵・例などによる) illustration ⓤ ⓒ; (使い方の) instructions; (写真などの短い) caption ⓒ ――説明する explain 働 ⓔ; (理由・原因を) account for ...; illustrate 働
⇒ コミュニケーションスキル

納得のいく[詳しい，簡単な]説明 a convincing [detailed, brief] *explanation*

以下の説明に従ってください Follow *the instructions* below.

店員は私に時計の使い方を説明した The clerk *explained* the use of the clock to me.

彼女はこの現象を理論的に説明した She *gave* a theoretical *explanation* of the phenomenon.

あの先生の説明はいつも分かりやすい[分かりにくい] That teacher's *explanations* are always easy [hard] to understand.

彼女はいくつかの例を挙げて自分の考えを説明した She *illustrated* her idea with some examples.

これはほかに説明のしようがない *There is no other way to explain* this.

彼の理論ではこの現象の説明がつかない His theory *doesn't account for* this phenomenon.

事故の原因は明らかで説明するまでもない The cause of the accident is clear and *needs no explanation*.

彼の説明不足のせいで私たちは混乱してしまった We were confused because of his *insufficient explanation*.

◆警察にその男の特徴を説明する *describe* the man to the police / 説明のつかない事件がこの地区で相次いで起こっている *Inexplicable* events have happened in this area one after another. / あなたの計画を大まかに説明してくれますか Could you *outline* your plan to me?

‖説明会 an explanatory meeting / 説明書 (機械操作の) a manual; (使用説明書) instructions; (薬などの) directions

ぜつめつ 絶滅 extinction ⓤ ――絶滅する become* extinct, die out ／その鳥は絶滅の危機に瀕(ひん)している That bird is threatened

せつもん 設問 question ◯

せつやく 節約 (むだを省くこと) economy ◯ Ü, saving Ü◯; (倹約) thrift Ü ——節約する economize (on ...), save 他; (切り詰める) cut* down (on ...)

私たちは経費の節約を心がけている We try to ｢cut down [economize] on expenses.

バーゲンを利用してお金を節約しよう Let's take advantage of the sale and save money.

この機械を使えば時間と労力を節約することができる You can save time and energy by using this machine. / This machine can save (you) time and energy.

◆安い品物を買うことが節約になるとは限らない It is not necessarily economical to buy cheap articles.

せつり 摂理 自然の摂理 the laws of nature / 神の摂理 Divine Providence

せつりつ 設立 foundation Ü, establishment Ü ——設立する found 他, establish 他, set* up ∥その病院は1930年に設立された The hospital was founded [established, set up] in 1930. / 彼らはその会社の設立に参加した They took part in the foundation [establishment] of the company.

せとぎわ 瀬戸際 その銀行は倒産の瀬戸際にある The bank is on the edge [verge] of bankruptcy. / 彼らは瀬戸際になって計画の実行を断念した They gave up carrying out the plan at the last moment.

せとないかい 瀬戸内海 the (Seto) Inland Sea

せともの 瀬戸物 china Ü, chinaware Ü; (陶器) pottery Ü; (磁器) porcelain Ü (❖いずれも数えるときはa piece of ... とする)
∥瀬戸物屋 a china shop

せなか 背中 back◯
背中合わせに座る sit back to back / 背中を丸めて歩く walk with ｢one's back hunched [a stoop]｣
彼女は私の背中をぽんとたたいた She clapped me on the back.
背中が痛い I have an ache in my back. / I've got a backache. / My back hurts. (❖ ｢腰が痛い｣の意味にもなる)
このブラウスは背中で留める This blouse fastens (up) at the back.
彼は怒って私に背中を向けた He got angry and turned his back on me.

ぜに 銭 money◯ ∥あぶく銭 easy money / 小銭 small change
ことわざ 安物買いの銭失い ⇒ やすもの

ぜにん 是認 approval Ü ——是認する approve 自他 ∥その記事は彼の犯罪行為を是認しているかのようだ The article seems to have approved of his crime.

ゼネコン ⚠ general contractor ◯

ゼネスト ⚠ general strike ◯

せのび 背伸び ——背伸び(を)する (つま先で立つ) stand* on tiptoe ∥彼女は背伸びをして棚から本を取った She stood on tiptoe [her tiptoes] to take a book from the shelf.

◆彼はいつも背伸びをしすぎる (→自分の能力以上のことをしようとする) He is always trying to do more than he is able to do. / (→高望みしすぎる) He is always aiming too high.

セパタクロー sepak takraw Ü

せばまる 狭まる narrow 自, become* [get*] narrow ∥進むにつれて道は狭まった The road became narrower as we went on. / その2人の走者の差はあっという間に狭まった The gap between the two runners narrowed in an instant.

◆選択の幅が狭まった (→制限された) The choice has become limited.

せばめる 狭める narrow 他; (制限する) limit 他, restrict 他 ∥捜索の範囲を狭める narrow the range of an investigation

せばんごう 背番号 (jersey) number ◯ ∥｢背番号10の選手はだれですか Who's (that player wearing) number 10? / 彼は背番号5をつけている He is wearing (jersey) number five. / His (jersey) number is five.

ぜひ 是非

❶ [何としても] at all costs, at any cost; (ぜひどうぞ) by all means; (必ず…する) be sure to do

ぜひまたその国を訪れたいと思う I'd like to visit the country again at any cost.

もしこちらにおいでになることがあれば、ぜひお立ち寄りください If you ever come this way, ｢be sure [don't forget] to come and see us.

◆君にはぜひ我々のチームに加わってほしい We do [really] want you to join our team. / あなたの助けがぜひ必要なんです We badly [desperately] need your help. / 今夜ぜひ夕食を食べにいらっしゃい You must come and have dinner with us tonight. (❖mustは親しい間柄で用いるとき丁寧な勧誘を意味することがある) / それはいい機会だからぜひ行くべきだ (→逃すべきではない) That's a good chance and you should not miss it.

🗨 ｢お宅に伺ってもよろしいですか｣｢ええ，ぜひどうぞ｣ "May I visit your house?" "By all means."

🗨 ｢もう1杯ビールいかがですか｣｢ええ，ぜひ｣ "Would you like another glass of beer?" "Sure thing."

🗨 ｢あのレストランの料理はすごくおいしいらしいよ｣｢じゃあ，ぜひ行きましょう｣ "I hear that restaurant serves very good food." "Well, let's be sure to go there."

❷ [可否・善悪]
その計画の是非を論じるのはまだ早い It's too early to discuss whether the plan is

right or wrong. / 慣用表現 それは是非もないことだ(→しかたがないことだ) It *can't be helped.*

セピア sepia ◯ ──セピア色の sepia

せひょう 世評 (評判) fame ◯, reputation ◯(また a ～); (うわさ) rumor ◯◯ ◆彼女はすぐれた歌手として世評が高い She has *the reputation* of being an excellent singer. / 世評によればその試合は八百長だったということだ *Rumor has it that* the match was fixed. ◆世評(→人のいうこと)を気にする必要はないよ You don't have to care *what people will say.*

せびる 彼は両親に金をせびった He *pestered* his parents *for* money.

せびれ 背鰭 dorsal fin ◯

せびろ 背広 suit ◯; (ビジネススーツ)《米》business [《英》lounge] suit ◯ ／《シングル[ダブル]の背広 *a* single-[double-]breasted *suit*

せぼね 背骨 spine ◯, backbone ◯

せまい 狭い

(幅が) narrow; (面積が) small; (限られた) limited, restricted

狭い部屋 a *small* room(❖a narrow room は「細長い部屋」の意味) ／ 狭い意味では in a *narrow* sense / 視野が狭い have narrow [*limited*] views

その道は狭くて 2 人並んでは歩けなかった The road was too *narrow* to walk two abreast.

交通機関の発展に伴って世界が狭くなっている The world *is becoming smaller* with advances in transportation.

選択の幅は非常に狭い The choice is very *limited.*

◆心の狭い人 a *narrow-minded* person / 狭い額 a *low* forehead / この川はここから狭くなり始める This river begins to *narrow* here.

慣用表現 世間は狭い *It's a small world.* / ここ数年は不況のせいで就職は狭き門となっている(→就職するのが難しくなっている) Because of the depression *it's been hard to* get a job in recent years.

せまくるしい 狭苦しい cramped ／狭苦しい部屋 a *cramped* room / 彼の部屋はいつも散らかっていて狭苦しい His room is always messy and *cramped.*

せまる 迫る

❶ [近づく] approach ◯ ◯, draw* near, be near at hand

台風が九州に迫っている A typhoon *is approaching* Kyushu.

結論を出さねばならないときが迫っている The time *is approaching* [*near at hand, drawing near*] when we must come to a conclusion.

◆期末試験まであと 3 日に迫っている(→試験は 3 日後だ) The final exams *are only three days away* [*off*]. / 彼は間近に迫った演奏会のことで頭がいっぱいだ He is completely preoccupied with the *coming* concert. / 彼女は

迫りくる危険に気がつかなかった She didn't notice the *imminent* danger. / その家の裏には山が迫っている(→山がすぐ裏にある) There is a mountain *just* [*right*] *behind* the house. / その話は真に迫っている The story *is quite real* [*realistic*]. / 夕やみが迫っている(→しだいに濃くなっている) The dusk *is gathering.*

❷ [要求する] (せがむ) press ◯ ◯; (強制する) force ◯, compel

彼女は本当のことを教えてほしいと私に迫った She *pressed* me 「*to tell* [*for*] the truth.

大臣は辞任を迫られた The minister *was forced* [*compelled*] *to resign.*

◆彼は必要に迫られて土地を手放した He gave up his land *from* [*out of*] *necessity.* / 彼はその女性に復縁を迫った He *pestered* the woman *for* a reconciliation with him.

せみ 蝉 cicada [sikéidə]◯,《米》locust ◯ ／セミが鳴いている *The cicadas* are buzzing.

俳句 閑かさや岩にしみ入る蟬の声(松尾芭蕉)
Ah, it's so quiet,
they seep into the boulders:
cicada voices.

ゼミ ⚠seminar [séminɑ̀ːr] ◯ (❖日本語はドイツ語の Seminar(ゼミナール)から)

セミコロン semicolon ◯ ➡ 巻末付録 (句読法)

セミナー seminar ◯ ／昨日、環境保護についてのセミナーが開かれた *A seminar on* environmental protection was held yesterday.

セミファイナル (準決勝) semifinal ◯

セミプロ semiprofessional ◯,《口語的》semipro ◯ (複 ～s) ──セミプロの semiprofessional

せめ¹ 責め blame ◯, responsibility ◯◯ ／…の責めを負う take *the blame* [*responsibility*] *for* …

せめ² 攻め attack ◯ ◯, offense,《英》offence ◯ ◆攻めに出る[出ている] take [be on] *the offensive* / 敵を兵糧攻めにする(→飢えさせる) *starve* the enemy

せめて (少なくとも) at least; (…だけ) just ／せめて電話くらいしてくれてもよかったのに You should *at least* have called me. / あと 30 分あればなぁ I wish I had *at least* another 30 minutes. / せめてもう 1 週間だけでも締め切りを延ばしていただけませんか Couldn't you extend the deadline *just* for another week? ◆それが私のせめてもの(→唯一の)慰めです It's my *only* comfort.

せめよせる 攻め寄せる 敵は首都に攻め寄せた(→進軍した) The enemy 「*marched on* [(→包囲した) *besieged*] the capital.

せめる¹ 攻める attack ◯ ◯; (侵略する) invade ◯ ／敵を攻める *attack* [*make an attack on*] the enemy / 私たちは敵チームの陣地に一気に攻め込んだ We *attacked* our opponent *and got into* their position without stopping. ◆マスコミはその俳優を質問で攻めたてた The media *bombarded* the actor *with* questions.

せめる² 責める blame ◯, accuse ◯ ／そんなささいなことで彼女を責めることはない You

don't have to *blame* her *for* trifles like that./ 彼女は彼が本当のことを話していないと責めた She *accused* him *of* not telling the truth./ 彼らは私の失敗を責めたてた They *kept blaming* me *for* my mistake. ◆私は妻に安定した仕事に就けと責められている My wife *is pressing* me *to* take a stable job.

セメント cement ⓤ 〃塗りたてのセメント *wet cement*/ セメントを流す *pour cement*/ セメントはまだ固まっていない *The cement hasn't set yet.* ◆壁にセメントを塗る *cement* a wall; *cover* a wall *with cement*

せもたれ 背もたれ back ⓒ, backrest ⓒ
◆(座席の)背もたれを倒す *recline one's seat*

ゼラチン gelatin ⓤⓒ

ゼラニウム 〔植物〕geranium ⓒ

セラミックス ceramics《単数扱い》

せり¹ 芹 Japanese parsley ⓤ

せり² 競り auction ⓒ 〃…を競りにかける[出す] put ... up for *auction*/ …を競りで買う buy ... at [by] *auction*

せりあう 競り合う compete 圓 〃私たちは優勝をかけて競り合った We *competed with* each other *for* the first prize.

ゼリー (米)(商標名)Jell-O, jello ⓤ, (英)jelly ⓤⓒ 〃冷蔵庫のゼリーが固まった *The Jell-O* has set in the fridge.

せりうり 競り売り auction ⓒⓤ
⇒せり(競り)

せりおとす 競り落とす buy* ... at auction, knock down (◆しばしば受身で)/ その本は彼に100万円で競り落とされた The book *was knocked down* to him for one million yen.

せりだす 迫り出す (突き出る) stick* out 〃通りに木がせり出している The tree *sticks out* into the street./ 父はこのごろ腹がせり出してきた My father's stomach *has been sticking out* recently.

せりふ 台詞 (芝居の) lines; (言葉) words 〃せりふを覚える〔とちる〕 memorize [fluff, blow] *one's lines* ◆それはまさに彼女の言いそうなせりふだね That's just *what* she would say./ 彼は捨てぜりふを吐いて部屋を出ていった He made *a parting shot* and left the room./ それはこっちのせりふだ That's *what* I want to say to you!/ That's *what* I would say to you!/ Same to you!

セルフサービス self-service ⓤ 〃セルフサービスの食堂 *a self-service* restaurant
◆飲み物はセルフサービスでどうぞ Please *help yourself to* a drink.

セルフタイマー self-timer ⓒ

セルロイド celluloid ⓤ

セレナーデ 〔音楽〕serenade [sèrənéid] ⓒ

セレモニー ceremony ⓒ

ゼロ zero [zí(ː)rou] ⓒ (複 ～(e)s), nothing ⓤ, (英)nought ⓒ (◆電話番号・部屋番号などの0は[ou]と読むことが多い)⇒れい(零)
3対0で勝つ win 3 to *nothing* [*zero*]/ 人口のゼロ成長 *zero growth* in population; zero population *growth*
100万にはゼロが6個ある There are six *zeros* in one million.
今年の経済成長はゼロと見込まれている The economic growth of this year is estimated at *zero*.
その国に関する知識はほとんどゼロだ I know almost *nothing* about the country.
彼はゼロから事業を起こした He built his business *from nothing* [*scratch, zero*].

セロテープ ⚠ sticky [adhesive] tape ⓤ, (米)(商標名) Scotch tape ⓤ, (英)(商標名) Sellotape ⓤ (◆Cellophane は日本的商標名)

セロハン (商標名) Cellophane [séləfèin] ⓤ 〃セロハンに包まれた花束 flowers in the *cellophane* wrapping

セロリ 〔植物〕celery ⓤ 〃セロリ1株[1本] a bunch [stick] of *celery*

せろん 世論 public opinion ⓤ 〃世論に耳を傾ける listen [pay attention] to *public opinion*/ 政府は世論を無視するべきではない The government should not disregard *public opinion*./ 世論調査をする take [conduct] *an opinion poll*

せわ 世話
❶ [面倒を見ること] care ⓤ; (援助) help ⓤ ―世話(を)する care for ..., take* care of ..., look after ...; (助ける) help 圃 圓
ランは世話が大変だ Orchids need a lot of *care.*
私の留守中, 彼が犬の世話をしてくれた He took *care of* my dog while I was away.
本当にお世話になりました (→助けてくれてありがとう) *Thank you* very much *for your kind help.*/ (→いろいろありがとう) *Thank you* very much *for everything.*/ (→面倒をかけてすみません) *I'm really sorry to have troubled you.*
この花はよく世話されている This flower *is* well *taken care of.*
君の世話になるつもりはない *I don't need your help.*
◆私に猫の世話を任せて彼らは旅行に出かけた They went on a trip, *leaving* their cat *in my charge.*/ 英語を読むときはこの辞書の世話になっている I *always use* this dictionary when I read English./ いつまで親の世話になる(→親に頼る)つもりだ How long are you going to *depend on* your parents?/ おじのところに1週間世話になった(→泊まった) I *stayed*「*with my uncle* [*at my uncle's*] *for a week.*/ 弟は体が弱くてしょっちゅう医者の世話になっている My brother is weak and always *sees the doctor.*/ 同窓会の世話役は秋山君に決まった Akiyama was named *the organizer* of our class reunion.

❷ [やっかい・手数] trouble ⓤ
あいつは本当に世話のやけるやつだ He *gives* us a lot of *trouble.*/ He's really *a troublesome person.*
◆彼女は世話のいらない子供だった She was easy to look after when she was a child./ 父がいつもお世話になっています *Thank you for your kindness* to my father. (◆英米ではこのようなあいさつは一般的ではない)/ 怒られて

も笑っているなんて彼は世話がないよ(→どうしようもない) He's *hopeless*. He keeps laughing even when he is scolded.

❸【あっせん・仲介】

おじに仕事を世話してもらった My uncle *helped me find a job* [*found me a job*].

いい英語の先生を世話してもらえませんか Can you *introduce* a good teacher of English to me?

❹【おせっかい】

余計なお世話だ(→自分のやるべきことだけを気にしろ) *Mind your own business*! / (→君には関係ない) *That's none of your business*.

彼女は大の世話好きだ She *loves to do things for people*.

せわしい せわしい日々を送る lead a *busy* life / 彼はせわしなく部屋の中を行ったり来たりした He paced the room *restlessly*.

せん¹ 線

❶【細長い筋】line ⓒ

線を引く draw *a line* / 2つの点を線で結ぶ draw *a line* between two points; connect two points with *a line* / 細い線 *a* fine [thin] *line* / 太い線 a thick *line*

◆重要な単語の下に線を引く *underline* important words / 体の線が崩れる lose *one's figure*

❷【道路・鉄道・電話などの】(バス・列車などの) line ⓒ; (電線・電話線) wire ⓒ ⓤ, line ⓒ; (車線) lane ⓒ; (道筋) route ⓒ; (鉄道線路) track ⓒ

銀座線 the Ginza *Line* / 66号線 *Route* 66 / 6車線の高速道路 a six-*lane* freeway

その高速道路の上り[下り]線はひどく渋滞している There is a terrible traffic jam on *the inbound* [*outbound*] *lanes* of that expressway.

次の東京行きの列車は2番線から発車します The next train for Tokyo leaves from *Track (No.)* 2.

◆彼は国際線のパイロットをしている He is a pilot for *an international airline*.

❸【方向・方針】line ⓒ《しばしば複数形 ~s》

その線に沿って計画を立てた We've made a plan along [on] *those lines*.

◆ここまではなかなかいい線いってる(→君はうまくやっている)よ You're doing very *well* so far. / その線でいってみようじゃないか Let's try this *in that way*.

‖曲線 a curved line / 38度線 the 38th parallel / 実線 a solid line / 斜線 a diagonal line / 垂線 a perpendicular line / 対角線 a diagonal line / 直線 a straight line / 点線 a dotted line / 波線 a wavy line / 破線 a broken line / 平行線 a parallel line

せん² 千 thousand; (千番目) thousandth

[語法]
(1) 数詞または数を示す形容詞の後では複数の s を付けない / 5, 6千人 five or six *thousand* people
(2) 数字の読み方 / (ふつうの数字) 1,065 a [one] thousand (and) sixty-five (❖and は《米》では通例省略される) / (年号) 1999 nineteen ninety-nine / 2001 two thousand (and) one

何千回も *thousands of times* / 千分の1 *a* [*one*] *thousandth*

そのホールは3千人を収容できる The hall can accommodate three *thousand* people.

その地震で数千[何千]人もの人が死んだ Several *thousands of* [*Thousands of*] *people* were killed in the earthquake.

せん³ 栓 (びんの) cap ⓒ; (コルク栓) cork ⓒ; (水道・ガスなどの) stopcock ⓒ; (穴に詰めるもの) plug ⓒ, stopper ⓒ; (蛇口)《米》faucet ⓒ, 《英》tap ⓒ ‖ガスの栓をあける[閉める] turn on [off] *the gas* (*stopcock*) / ワインボトルに栓をする *put a cork in* a wine bottle; *cork* a wine bottle / ビールの栓を抜く *take the cap off* a beer bottle; *open* a beer bottle

◆栓をあけたびん *an open bottle* / 耳に栓をする *plug one's ears*

‖栓抜き a bottle opener;(コルク用の)a corkscrew

せん⁴ 腺《解剖》gland ⓒ

ぜん¹ 善 (よいこと) good ⓤ; (正しいこと) right ⓤ

「それじゃそれで決まりだ. いつから始める」「善は急げだ(→早ければ早いほどよい)」 "It's all settled then. When do we start it?" "*The sooner, the better*."

ことわざ 善は急げ Never hesitate to do good. (→よいことをするのにためらうな)

ぜん² 禅 Zen ⓤ

禅は座って足を組み、瞑想(めいそう)すること(座禅)によって悟りを得ようとする仏教の修行の一つです。禅は茶道・柔道など日本の文化にも大きな影響を与えました。
Zen is a form of Buddhist practice seeking enlightenment by meditating in the lotus position. Zen has had a great influence on aspects of Japanese culture such as sado (tea ceremony) and judo.

ぜん-¹ 全-(すべての) all;(全体の) whole;(完全な) complete;(まるまるの) full ‖全国(民) the *whole* country / その事故の全責任を負う accept *full* blame for the accident

◆うちの洗濯機は全自動です My washing machine is *fully* automatic.

ぜん-² 前-前社長 the *previous* president; the *ex*-president (❖「元社長」の意味でも用いる) / 前ページ参照 See the *previous* page. / 前夫 one's *ex*-husband

-ぜん -膳 ごはん1膳 *a bowl of* rice / はし1膳 *a pair of* chopsticks

ぜんあく 善悪 wrong and right, good and evil ◆おまえはもう善悪の区別がつく年ごろだ You are big enough to know [tell] *right* from *wrong*.

せんい¹ 繊維 fiber, 《英》fibre ⓤ ⓒ ‖もっと繊維質をとりなさい. Take more *fiber*.

‖繊維会社 a textile company / 繊維工場 a

せんい textile factory / 繊維産業 the textile industry / 繊維製品 textiles / 化学繊維 chemical fiber / 合成繊維 synthetic fiber / 食物繊維 dietary fiber

せんい² 戦意 fight ⓤ, fighting spirit ⓤⓒ ‖戦意を喪失する lose *one's fighting spirit*

ぜんい 善意(好意) goodwill ⓤ ‖彼らは善意でそうしたんだ They did it out of *goodwill.*/ They *meant well* when they did it. ◆善意の人 a *well-meaning[-intentioned] person* / 彼女は彼の行為を善意として受け止めた She took his behavior *as well intentioned.*

ぜんいき 全域 the whole [entire] area ‖関東全域はその地震で大きな被害を受けた *The whole [entire] Kanto area* suffered much damage from the earthquake.

せんいん 船員 sailor ⓒ, seaman ⓒ; 《集合的》crew ⓒ 《❖高級船員(officer)は含まない》

ぜんいん 全員 all (the members) ‖クラス全員 *all* the classmates; the *entire [whole] class* / 私たちは全員その案に賛成です We *all* agree to the plan.
◆うちは家族全員タイガースファンだ *Our whole family* are Tigers fans.

ぜんえい 前衛 (サッカー・ラグビーなどの) forward ⓒ / (の略語)fwd; (芸術の) the avant-garde [ɑ̀ːvɑŋɡɑ́ːrd]; (軍隊の) the vanguard ——前衛的な avant-garde ‖前衛芸術 avant-garde art

せんえつ 僭越 僭越ながら歓迎のあいさつをさせていただきます *Please allow me to* say a few words of welcome. / 彼は僭越にも(→ずうずうしくも)我々の議論に口出ししてきた *It was presumptuous of* him *to* cut in to our discussion.

ぜんおんぷ 全音符〖音楽〗《米》whole note ⓒ, 《英》semibreve ⓒ

せんか¹ 戦火 the flames [fires] of war; (戦争) war ⓤⓒ

せんか² 戦禍 その地域は戦禍を免れた The region didn't suffer any *damage in the war.*

せんが 線画 line drawing

ぜんか 前科 criminal [police] record ⓒ ‖前科がある have *a criminal [police] record*
◆前科2犯である(→ 以前に2度有罪判決を受けている) *have been convicted* twice *previously* ‖前科者 an ex-convict, 《口語的》an ex-con

せんかい 旋回 ——旋回する (輪を描いて) circle ⓘ; (向きを変える) turn ⓘ ‖東に旋回する *turn [take a turn] to* the east / ヘリコプターが私たちの頭上で旋回していた A helicopter *was circling* in the air above us.

せんがい 選外 私の作品は選外だった My work *was not selected [chosen].*
‖選外佳作 an honorable mention

ぜんかい¹ 全快 全快するには時間がかかるだろう It'll take a lot of time to *recover completely (from the illness).* / 彼の全快祝いにパーティーを開こう Let's have a party to *celebrate* his *recovery (from his illness).*

ぜんかい² 全開 エンジン全開で車を走らせる drive a car「*with the throttle wide open [at full throttle]*

ぜんかい³ 前回 前回の会合 the *previous [last]* meeting / 今回の作品は前回のより出来だ This work is an improvement on [over] *the last one.* / 前回と同じホテルに泊まります I'll stay at the (same) hotel I had *the last time.* / 彼女は前々回の水泳大会で優勝した She won first prize in the swim meet *before last.*

ぜんかい⁴ 全壊 私の家はその台風で全壊した My house *was completely destroyed* by the typhoon.

ぜんかいいっち 全会一致 その案は全会一致で採択された The plan was adopted *unanimously* [(→票決で)*by a unanimous vote*].

せんがく 浅学 浅学非才をかえりみず in spite of *my lack of knowledge and ability*

ぜんがく 全額 the total [full] amount; (総計) total ⓒ, the sum (total)
◆借金を全額返済する pay back *one's debt in full* / 銀行から全額下ろす withdraw *all one's savings* from the bank

せんかく(しゃ) 先覚(者) pioneer ⓒ

せんかん 戦艦 battleship ⓒ

せんき 戦記 a record of war

ぜんき¹ 前期 (前半) the first half; (2学期制の) the first semester; (初期) the early period; (前の期間) the former [preceding] term ‖前期試験 the first-semester exams

ぜんき² 前記 前記のとおり *as (is) mentioned above* / 詳しいことは前記の番号にお問い合わせください For further information, please call the number *above (mentioned).*

せんきゃく¹ 先客 彼が訪ねてきたときすでに先客がいた When he visited me, I *already had a visitor.*

せんきゃく² 船客 a passenger (on board)

せんきゃくばんらい 千客万来 その店はきのう千客万来だった The shop *was full of customers* yesterday.

せんきゅうがん 選球眼 彼は選球眼のよいバッターだ He is a batter who *has a good [sharp] batting eye.*

せんきょ¹ 選挙

election ⓒⓤ ——選挙する (選挙で選ぶ) elect ⓣ

選挙を行う hold *an election*

私たちは選挙で彼女を委員長に選んだ We *elected* her as chairperson.

今度の選挙でその党が勝つとはだれも予想していなかった No one had expected the success of the party in this *election*.

この選挙でわが国の将来の方向が決まるかもしれない This *election* might decide the future course of our country.

彼は次の選挙に出馬する He'll run [《英》stand] in the next *election*.

彼女は前回の選挙に当選[落選]した She won [lost] *the last election*.

その町ではあす選挙がある An election will「be held [take place]」 in the town tomorrow. / They are having *an election* in the town tomorrow.

選挙の結果は間もなく分かる The result of *the election* will be known soon.
◆私は選挙(→投票)に行かなかった I didn't go to *the polls*.

‖選挙違反 violation of the election law / 選挙運動 an election campaign / 選挙演説 a campaign speech / 選挙カー a campaign car / 選挙管理委員会 the Election Administration Committee,《米》 the board of elections / 選挙区 an election [electoral] district, a constituency / 選挙権 the right to vote, suffrage / 選挙公報 an election [a campaign] bulletin / 選挙公約 a campaign promise [pledge] / 選挙資金 a campaign fund / 選挙制度 the election system / 選挙戦 an election campaign / 選挙日 an election day / 選挙妨害 campaign obstruction / 選挙ポスター a campaign poster / 選挙民 a voter,《集合的》electorate / 間接選挙 an indirect election / 公職選挙法 the Public Offices Election Law / 参議院選挙 House of Councilors election / 衆議院選挙 House of Representatives election / 市長選挙 a mayoral election / 小選挙区制 the single-seat constituency system / 総選挙 a general election / 大統領選挙《米》a presidential election / 大統領予備選挙《米》a presidential primary (election) / 知事選挙 a gubernatorial election / 地方選挙 a local election / 中間選挙《米》an off-year election / 直接選挙 a direct election / 統一地方選挙 united local elections / 普通選挙 a popular election / 補欠選挙 a by-election

せんきょ² 占拠 occupation ⓤ ──占拠する occupy ⓗ ‖建物を不法占拠する *occupy* a building *illegally*

せんぎょ 鮮魚 fresh fish ⓒⓤ

せんぎょう 専業 私は専業主婦で2児の母親です I am *a (full-time) housewife [homemaker]* and mother of two children. (❖housewife は女性の役割を規定する言葉ともとれるので, 最近では代わりに homemaker が使われる. また主夫の場合もこれを使う)／父は野菜作りを専業にしている My father *specializes in* growing vegetables.

‖専業農家 a full-time farmer

せんきょうし 宣教師 missionary ⓒ

せんぎり 千切り キャベツの千切り *shredded* cabbage / ニンジンを千切りにする *shred* a carrot; *cut* a carrot *into shreds*

ぜんきんだいてき 前近代的 ──前近代的な premodern; (時代遅れの) old-fashioned

せんくしゃ 先駆者 (創 始 者) pioneer ⓒ, forerunner ⓒ ‖公民権運動の先駆者 *a pioneer* in the civil rights movement

ぜんけい 全景 complete [panoramic] view ⓒ, panorama ⓒ ‖その建物の屋上からは町の全景を見ることができた We had *a complete view* of the city from the roof of the building.

せんけつ 先決 宿題を終わらせることが先決だ *First of all*, I must finish my homework.

‖先決問題 the first question to be settled, the first thing to do

せんげつ 先月 ──先月の 10 日に on the 10th of *last month* / (雑誌の)先月号 *last month's* issue
彼は先月イギリスへ出発した He left for Britain *last month*.

せんけん 先見 先見の明のある女性 a woman of *foresight* [*vision*] / 彼は先見の明がある He *has foresight*./ He *is farsighted*.

せんげん 宣言 declaration ⓒ ⓤ; (重大事項の) proclamation ⓤ ⓒ ──宣言する declare ⓗ; (公式に) proclaim ⓗ / (政府などが) 非常事態を宣言する *declare* a state of emergency / 大統領はオリンピック大会の開会を宣言した The President *declared* the Olympic Games open. / その国は独立を宣言した The country *proclaimed* its independence. / 彼は次期選挙に出馬すると宣言した He *declared* [*announced*] that he will run in the next election.

‖世界人権宣言 the (Universal) Declaration of Human Rights / 独立宣言 the Declaration of Independence

ぜんけん 全権 full [complete] power ⓤ ‖人に全権を委任する give a person *full power* / その国では軍部が全権を掌握した The military *seized complete power* over the country.

‖全権大使 an ambassador plenipotentiary

ぜんげん 前言 *one's* previous [earlier] remarks ‖前言を撤回する withdraw [take back] *one's previous remarks* / 私は彼女に前言を撤回させた I *made* her *withdraw her previous remarks*.

せんご 戦後 ──戦後の postwar (↔prewar) ──戦後(に) after the war ‖戦後のベビーブーム the *postwar* baby boom / このドラマの舞台は戦後の日本である This drama is set in 「*postwar* Japan [Japan *after the war*].

‖戦後派 the postwar generation

ぜんご 前後

❶【位置・方向】(位置) front and back, in front of and behind … ──前後に back and forth

前後をよく見て！ Check *your front and back* carefully./ Be sure to look *in front and back of you*.(❖「前後左右を見る」なら look around を用いる)

車の前後を横切るのは危険だ It is dangerous to cross *in front of or behind* cars.

波のせいでマストが前後に揺れた The waves swayed the mast 「*back and forth* [*backwards and forwards*].

◆彼らは前後から襲われた They were attacked *front and rear*.

❷【時間・数が前か後】──前後に before or after …; (…くらい) about

体育祭の前後に武雄の歓迎会を開こう Let's have a welcome party for Takeo *before or after* the field day.

そちらに着くのは 6 時前後になります I will come over *about* [*around*] six.

彼は 30 歳前後に見えた He looked *about*

[around] 30. / He looked 30 *or so*.
◆卒業と前後して(→直後に)車の免許を取った I got a driver's license *just* [*right*] *after* graduation.
❸【順序】order ◫◉; (文脈) context ◫◉ 前後関係から判断すると judging from *the context*
◆話が前後しましたが… Well, the subjects seem to be *out of sequence*, but .... / 彼の話はよく前後する (→混乱する) His speech often *gets confused.* / 彼らは前後の見境もなく殴り合いのけんかを始めた They came to blows *recklessly.*
慣用表現 前後不覚に(→ぐっすり)眠る sleep *like a log*/ 彼は酔って前後不覚になった(→意識がなくなった) He was drunk and 「*dead to the world* [*had passed out*]. / 私は緊張のあまり前後を忘れた(→頭の中が真っ白になった) I was so tense that *my mind went blank*.

せんこう¹ 先行 時代に先行する be *ahead of the times* / 思惑が先行する(→期待しすぎ)expect too much / 我々のチームは2点先行している Our team *leads by two points.* / その会社に対しては実績よりも期待感が先行している(→上回っている) Expectations for that company *exceed* current earnings.
‖先行詞 ⇨ せんこうし   先行投資 a prior investment

せんこう² 専攻 one's specialty, 《米》one's major ——専攻する specialize in ..., 《主に米》major in ... / 私は米文学を専攻している I'm *majoring in* American literature. / 彼女の専攻は生物学です Her *major* is biology. / 専攻は何ですか What's *your major*?
‖専攻科目 a major subject

せんこう³ 閃光 a flash (of light); (反射光) a glint of light / 突然の閃光に目がくらんだ A sudden *flash of light* blinded my eyes.

せんこう⁴ 潜行 地下に潜行する go *underground* / 潜行性の病気 an *insidious* disease

せんこう⁵ 線香 *senko*, stick incense (◆線香1本は an incense stick という) / 仏壇に線香をあげる(→火をつける) light [(→供える) offer] *incense* (*sticks*) on a Buddhist altar
‖線香花火 a sparkler

> 線香は江戸時代に中国から入ってきましたが、それ以前の日本の香は粉状や丸く固めたものでした。線香の香りの元は白檀(びゃくだん)などの香木や、じゃこうなどの動物から抽出した香料です。葬式や法事などの仏教の儀式には必ず線香がたかれます。
> *Senko* (stick incense) came from China in the Edo period (1603–1867). The incense used until then was powder or tablets. *Senko* is scented with aromatic woods like sandalwood or animal products like musk. Buddhist rituals such as funerals and memorial services for the dead are always accompanied by *senko*.

せんこう⁶ 選考 (選抜) selection ◉◫; (審査) screening ◫◉ ——選考する select ◉; screen ◉ /その作品は選考からもれた The work *wasn't selected.* / 最終面接で2人の応募者が選考からはずされた Two applicants *were screened out* at the last interview. / 応募者の履歴書は慎重に選考されます Personal histories of applicants *will be screened* carefully.
‖選考委員 a member of a screening committee / 選考委員会 a screening committee / 選考基準 criteria for screening   書類選考 a screening of documents

せんこう⁷ 先攻 相手チームが先攻だ(→先に攻撃する) Our opponent *will attack* [(→野球で) *bat*] *first.* 先攻後攻(→どちらが先に攻撃するか)をくじを引いて決めた We drew lots to decide *which of us would attack* [*bat*] *first.*

ぜんこう¹ 全校 the whole school
‖全校生徒 all the students of a school / 全校朝会 schoolwide morning assembly

ぜんこう² 善行 good deed ◉ / 善行を積む keep on doing *good deeds*

ぜんごう 前号 (現在の前の号) the last issue [number]; (任意の号の前の号) the preceding issue [number] / 前号より続く Continued *from the last issue.*

せんこうし 先行詞【文法】antecedent ◉
⇨かんけいだいめいし

せんこく¹ 先刻 そんなことは先刻承知だ I knew it *all along.* / I already knew it. / 先刻から鈴木さんというかたがお待ちです A Ms. Suzuki has been waiting for you *for some time*.

せんこく² 宣告 pronouncement ◉; (刑の) sentence ◉◫; (スポーツでの) call ◉ ——宣告する pronounce ◉; sentence ◉; call ◉ / 被告に有罪を宣告する *pronounce* the defendant guilty / 死刑を宣告される be *sentenced* [*condemned*] *to death* / 審判はバッターアウトを宣告した The umpire *called* the batter out. ◆彼女はあと1か月の命だと宣告された(→言われた) She *was told that* she would die within a month.

ぜんこく 全国 the whole country ——全国的な national, nationwide ——全国(的)に all over the country

全国からボランティアが被災地に集まった The volunteers gathered at the disaster area *from all over the country*.
台風は全国的な災害を引き起こした The typhoon caused a *nationwide* [*national*] disaster.
この種のリサイクル運動が全国規模で進められている These kinds of recycling campaigns are promoted *on a nationwide scale*.
この番組は全国ネットで放映されている This program is broadcast *over a national network*.
◆あすは全国的に晴れるでしょう Tomorrow it will be fine *throughout* [*all across*] *the country.* / この花は日本全国で見られる This flower can be seen 「*all over Japan* [*in every part of Japan*].
‖全国区 the national constituency / 全国

紙 a national newspaper / 全国大会(スポーツなどの) a national meet / 全国地図(日本の) a map of all of Japan / 全国放送 nationwide broadcasting

せんごくじだい 戦国時代 the *Sengoku period*, the *Warring States period* (❖中国の「戦国時代」は the Warring States period)

ぜんごさく 善後策 corrective [remedial] measures ‖善後策を講じる take *corrective* [*remedial*] *measures*

センサー sensor ‖その音でセンサーが作動した The sound「set off [activated] *the sensor*. / このセンサーは温度の変化を感知する This *sensor* detects [picks up] changes in temperature.

せんさい¹ 繊細 fineness Ⓤ; (優美) delicacy Ⓤ; (感覚が) sensibility Ⓤ ――繊細な fine; delicate; sensitive ‖繊細な指 *delicate* fingers / 繊細なユーモア感覚 a *fine* sense of humor / 彼女は非常に繊細な感覚の持ち主だ She is a「*very sensitive* person [person of great *sensibility*].

せんさい² 戦災 war damage Ⓤ ‖戦災を被る[免れる] suffer [escape] *war damage*; suffer [escape] *damage during the war* ◆彼は戦災で家を焼かれた His house was burned *during the war*.
‖戦災孤児 a war orphan

せんさい³ 先妻 one's former wife, one's ex-wife, 《口語的》one's ex

せんざい¹ 洗剤 detergent Ⓒ Ⓤ; (粉末の) washing powder Ⓒ Ⓤ; (磨き粉) cleanser Ⓒ Ⓤ ‖合成洗剤 a synthetic detergent / 中性洗剤 a pH-neutral detergent

せんざい² 潜在 ――潜在的な (可能性のある) potential; (隠れた) latent ‖潜在能力を引き出す bring out one's *potential* [*latent*] *ability* / 両国の間には戦争の危険が常に潜在している *There is* always the *potential* danger of war between the two countries.
‖潜在意識 the [one's] subconscious / 潜在需要 potential demand

ぜんさい 前菜 hors d'oeuvre [ɔ́ːr dɔ́ːrv] (複~s, ~)

せんざいいちぐう 千載一遇 千載一遇のチャンスなんだからこれを逃す手はないよ You should seize the chance; it's *one in a million*.

せんさく 詮索 ――詮索する pry into ..., 《口語的》poke [stick*] one's nose into ... ‖あいつは他人のプライベートなことを詮索するのが好きだ He *likes to pry* [*stick his nose*] *into* other people's private affairs. / He *is inquisitive* [*nosy*] *about* other people's private affairs.
◆あまり詮索しないで *Don't be so inquisitive*.

せんさばんべつ 千差万別 人の性格は千差万別だ People *have an immense variety of* personalities.

せんし¹ 戦死 death in (the) war [battle, action] ――戦死する be killed in (the) war [battle, action] ‖私の祖父は戦死しました My grandfather *was killed in the war*.

‖戦死者 a person who was killed in the war, 《集合的》war dead

せんし² 戦士 fighter Ⓒ, warrior Ⓒ; (兵士) soldier Ⓒ ‖企業戦士 a corporate warrior

せんじ 戦時 wartime Ⓤ ‖戦時中には食べ物にも事欠いた We didn't even have enough food *during the war*.
‖戦時内閣 a war cabinet

せんしじだい 先史時代 prehistoric period Ⓒ, prehistoric times

せんしつ 船室 cabin Ⓒ ‖1[2]等船室 a first-[second-]class cabin

せんじつ 先日 the other day ‖先日街で真理を見かけた *The other day*, I saw Mari on the street. ◆先日来, のどが痛い I've had a sore throat *for several days*.

ぜんじつ 前日 the day before, the preceding [previous] day; (祝祭日などの) eve Ⓒ 《通例Eve》‖ハイキングの前日は早く寝ようと思っています I'll go to bed early *the day before* the hike.

せんじつめる 煎じ詰める boil down (❖「要約する」といった比喩的な意味にも用いられる) ‖この問題は煎じ詰めると組織が弱いということだ This problem *boils down to* poor organization. ◆煎じ詰めて言えば(→要するに), この計画は失敗だったのだ *In short* [*brief, a word*], this plan was a failure.

せんしゃ¹ 洗車 car washing Ⓤ ――洗車する wash a car 《洗車場》 a car wash

せんしゃ² 戦車 〖軍事〗tank Ⓒ

せんじゃ 選者 selector Ⓒ

ぜんしゃ 前者 the former (↔the latter) ‖2つの計画のうちでは私は前者がよいと思う *Of the two plans, I prefer the former*. / 前者の提案のほうが後者のそれよりも現実的だった *The former* suggestion was more realistic than the latter.

せんしゅ¹ 選手 (スポーツやゲームの) player Ⓒ; (運動の) athlete Ⓒ ‖「水泳の選手」a swimmer,「ボクシングの選手」a boxer など, 上記の訳語を使わないケースも少なくない) ‖テニスの選手 a tennis *player* / バスケットボールの選手 a basketball *player* / ❖シード選手 a seeded *player*

なれるかどうか分かりませんが, オリンピック選手になりたいと思います I don't know if I can, but I would like to be *an Olympic athlete*.

◆健は柔道のオリンピック代表選手(→チームの一員)に選ばれた Ken was picked for the Olympic judo team. / 彼はそのチームと選手契約(→チームでプレーする契約)を結んだ He signed a contract to play with the team.
‖選手権 a championship / 選手権試合 a title match / 選手権大会 a championship tournament / 選手権保持者 a champion / 選手生命 player's career / 最優秀選手 the most valuable player (《略記》MVP)

せんしゅ² 先取 3回の裏にスワローズが2点を先取した The Swallows *scored the first* two runs in the bottom of the third inning. / 我々のチームが先取点をあげた(→最初に得点し

せんしゅ

た) Our team *scored first*.
∥先取点 the point(s) [run(s), goal(s)] scored first (❖野球は run, サッカーは goal を用いるのがふつう)

せんしゅ³ 船主 shipowner ⓒ

せんしゅ⁴ 船首 bow ⓒ《しばしば複数形 ~s》
∥船首像〖海事〗a figurehead

せんしゅう¹ 先週 last week

> 「先週の木曜日」というときはふつう last Thursday というが, last は「すぐ前の」という意味なので, 土曜日に last Thursday といえば「先週の木曜日」ではなく「今週の木曜日」を指す場合もある. 先週ということをはっきりさせたいときは on Thursday last week のようにいう.

先週初雪が降りました We had the first snow of the season *last week*.
先週の火曜日に英語の小テストがあった We had an English quiz「*last Tuesday* [*on Tuesday last week*].
◆先週のきょう《米》*a week ago today*;《英》*this day last week* / 先週末は町を出ていました I was out of town *last weekend*.

せんしゅう² 選集 selection ⓒ;(名作集) anthology ⓒ ∥アメリカ短編選集 *an anthology of American short stories*

ぜんしゅう 全集 complete works ∥シェークスピア全集 Shakespeare's *complete works*; *a (complete) set of* Shakespeare's *works*

せんしゅうがっこう 専修学校 special vocational school ⓒ

せんじゅうみん 先住民 indigenous people,《軽蔑的》native ⓒ《しばしば複数形 ~s》

せんしゅうらく 千秋楽 夏場所もついに千秋楽を迎えた At last *the last day* of the Summer Sumo Tournament has come.

せんしゅつ 選出 election ⓒⓊ ——選出する elect ⓔ ∥4年ごとに知事を選出する We *elect* a (new) governor every four years.
◆彼は新潟県3区選出の参議院議員だ He *represents* the third district of Niigata Prefecture in the House of Councilors.

せんじゅつ 戦術 tactics; (戦略) strategy Ⓤいつもの戦術を使う use [employ] the usual *tactics* / 戦術にたけている be skilled in *tactics* / 新たな戦術を編み出す devise [think up] new *tactics*
∥戦術家 a tactician, a strategist / 戦術兵器 tactical weapons

ぜんじゅつ 前述 前述のとおり as (is) mentioned above / 前述の理論 the *above-mentioned* theory

ぜんしょ 善処 ご期待に添えるよう善処いたします(=適切な対処をとります) We'll take proper [*appropriate*] *measures* to meet your expectations.

せんじょう¹ 戦場 battlefield ⓒ, battleground ⓒ ∥戦場で数千人が死んだ Thousands were killed *on the battlefield* [*field of battle*]. / その国は戦場と化した That country turned into *a battlefield*.

せんじょう² 洗浄 ——洗浄する wash ⓔ, clean ⓔ;(医などを)〖医学〗irrigate ⓔ ∥傷口を洗浄する *irrigate* [*rinse out*] a wound
◆胃を洗浄してもらう have one's stomach *pumped*
∥洗浄液(コンタクトレンズなどの) lens cleaning solution

ぜんしょう¹ 全勝 ——全勝する win* all the games [matches] ∥彼は全勝で優勝を飾った He *won all the games* and gained the championship. / He won the championship *with a complete victory*. / 私たちは9戦全勝した We *won all* nine *games*.

ぜんしょう² 全焼 ——全焼する burn* down ∥わが家は昨夜の火事で全焼した Our house *burned down* in the fire last night.
◆その映画館は全焼した The movie theater *was completely destroyed by fire*.

せんしょうこく 戦勝国 victorious nation [country] ⓒ

ぜんしょうせん 前哨戦 preliminary skirmish ⓒ

せんじょうてき 扇情的 ——扇情的な sensational;(性的に) suggestive,《公式的》lascivious ∥新聞の扇情的な報道 a *sensational* report in a newspaper / 扇情的なポスター a *suggestive* poster

せんしょく 染色 dyeing Ⓤ ——染色する dye ⓔ ∥染色工場 a dye works

せんしょくたい 染色体 chromosome ⓒ
∥染色体異常 (a) chromosomal abnormality / 染色体地図 a chromosome map / X[Y]染色体 the X [Y] chromosome

せんじる 煎じる boil down, brew ⓔ ∥お茶を煎じる *brew* tea

せんしん¹ 専心 devotion ⓒ; (集中) concentration Ⓤ ——専心する devote *oneself* to ..., be devoted to ...; concentrate on ... ∥彼は作曲に専心している He「*is devoted* [*has devoted himself*] *to* composition.
◆彼女はその仕事に一意専心で取り組んでいる She is engaged in the task *with a singleness of purpose*.

せんしん² 先進 ∥先進工業国 advanced industrialized nations

せんじん 先陣 ...の先陣を切る be in *the vanguard* of ... / 先陣争いをする *compete to be first*

ぜんしん¹ 全身 the [one's] whole body ——副 all over *one's body*

彼女はその事故で全身を強く打った Her *whole body* was hit hard in the accident.
彼らは全身にやけどをしていた They had burns *all over their bodies*.
水泳は全身運動だ Swimming *works on the whole body*.
◆全身の力をふりしぼって with *all one's strength* / 全身泥まみれになる get muddy *from head to foot* [*toe*] / その画家はその作品に全身全霊を打ち込んだ The artist「*gave his body and soul to* [*put his heart and soul into*] the work.
∥全身麻酔 general anesthesia

ぜんしん² 前進 advance ◎ Ⓤ, progress Ⓤ ――前進する go* [move] forward, go [move] ahead, advance 働, progress 働 (号令で)前進! *Go ahead*! / *Forward*!

生徒たちは退場門の方に前進した The students *moved forward* to the exit gate.

軍隊は暗やみの中を前進した The troops 「*went ahead* [*advanced*] in the dark.

彼の論文には前進の跡が見られた His paper shows *signs of progress*.

計画はわずかながらも前進した The plan *moved ahead*, though only a little.

◆フランスへの留学を決断したことで彼女は自分の夢に向けて一歩前進することになる Deciding to go to France to study *takes her a step closer* to her dream.

ぜんしん³ 前身 国際連合の前身は国際連盟だった The United Nations *was preceded by* the League of Nations.

せんしんこく 先進国 advanced [developed] country ◎ ‖日本はG８を構成する先進国の一つである Japan is one of *the advanced [developed] countries* that compose the G8. ‖先進国首脳会議 a G8 Summit

ぜんじんみとう 前人未到・前人未踏 前人未到の(→前例のない)記録 an *unprecedented* record / 前人未踏の(→足が踏み入れられていない)島を探索する explore an *untrodden* island

センス sense ◎ Ⓤ; (服などの) taste Ⓤ; (才能) the [a] feel / 安奈にはユーモアのセンスがない Anna *has no sense of* humor. / 彼女は洋服のセンスが抜群だ[悪い] She has excellent [bad] *taste in* clothes. / 彼は芸術のセンスがある He *has* 「*a feel for* art [*an artistic sense*]. / 本当にそれがいいの？君の美的センスを疑うよ Do you really want that? It shows your lack of an esthetic *sense*.

せんす 扇子 a *sensu*, a (folding) fan ◆扇子で(顔などを)あおぐ *fan oneself*

扇子は竹の骨組みに和紙を張った折りたたみ式の扇で，開くと扇形，閉じると竹の棒のようになります．中国から持ち込まれたうちわを折りたたみ式の扇子にしたのは日本人でしたが，今度は扇子が日本から逆に中国へ伝わり，さらには遠くヨーロッパの国々にも持ち込まれました．
A *sensu*, a folding fan made of bamboo ribs covered with Japanese paper, is fan-shaped when opened and like a bamboo stick closed. It is said that the *uchiwa* (round fan) brought from China was remodeled into the *sensu* by Japanese and that the folding style was reintroduced to China and brought all the way to Europe.

せんすい 潜水 diving Ⓤ ――潜水する dive* 働 ➾ もぐる ‖潜水艦 a submarine / 潜水病 the bends, caisson disease / 潜水夫 a diver / 潜水服 a diving suit

せんする 宣する (宣言する) declare 働 働; (発表する) announce 働 働 ➾ せんげん ‖開会を宣する *announce* the opening of the meeting

ぜんせ 前世 *one's* previous life [existence] ‖彼の前世は何だったのだろう What was he in his *previous life*?
◆前世の因縁 *predestined* fate

せんせい¹ 先生

❶ [教師] teacher ◎; (大学の教授) professor ◎ ((略語) Prof.); (指導者) instructor ◎

[語法] teacher は先生を表す最も一般的な語だが，例えば「松井先生」という場合，Matsui teacher とはいわない．男の先生なら Mr. Matsui, 女の先生なら Miss Matsui (未婚) や Mrs. Matsui (既婚) または Ms. Matsui (未婚，既婚を問わない)などという．また名前を呼ばないときには男の先生には sir, 女の先生には ma'am を用いる．一方，professor は，Professor Matsui のような形でも用いられ，この表現は呼びかけにも用いられる．

担任の先生 a homeroom *teacher*

(木下)先生、おはようございます Good morning, *Miss* Kinoshita.

私は幼稚園の先生になりたい I want to be *a kindergarten teacher*.

(生徒が)先生、いくつか質問していいですか *Sir*, [*Ma'am*] may I ask a few questions?

父はその中学校の理科の先生です My father is *a science teacher* at the junior high school. / (→教えている) My father *teaches* science at the junior high school.

🔊「あの女性はどなたですか」「私たちの英語の先生のホワイト先生です」"Who is that woman?" "That's *Ms.* White, our English *teacher*."

❷ [医者] doctor ◎ ((略語) Dr.), 《口語的》 doc ◎ (✤docは主に医者に対する呼びかけに用いる)

山口先生は外科医です *Dr.* Yamaguchi is a surgeon.

先生はご不在ですか Is *the doctor* out? (✤医者に対してはこの例のような場合や呼びかけで doctor を用いることができるが，弁護士や代議士などに対しては，Mr. [Ms.] Tanaka のように相手の名前を挙げる)

せんせい² 宣誓 oath ◎ ――宣誓する take* [swear*] an oath, swear 働 働 ‖聖書に手を置いて宣誓する *swear* on the Bible / 選手宣誓！我々はスポーツマン精神にのっとり，正々堂々と闘うことを誓います *Athletes' oath*! We swear to play fairly and follow the rules of good sportsmanship. (✤欧米にはこのような選手宣誓の習慣はない)

せんせい³ 専制 (専制政治) despotism Ⓤ; (暴政) tyranny Ⓤ ◎ ‖専制君主 a despot, a tyrant, an absolute monarch / 専制国家 an autocracy

せんせい⁴ 先制 敵に先制攻撃を加える make *a preemptive strike* [*attack*] against the enemy / 相手チームが先制点をあげた(→最初に得点した) Our opponent *scored first*.

ぜんせい¹ 全盛 全盛期に達する[を過ぎる]

reach [pass] *one's prime* / 無声映画全盛の時代 *the golden age* of silent movies / そのころローマ帝国は全盛期にあった The Roman Empire was in *its prime* at that time. / その一族は当時全盛を極めていた The family was「*at the height of their prosperity* [*in their glory*] then.

ぜんせい[2] 善政 その国の王は善政を敷いた(→よく統治した) The king *governed* the country *well*.

ぜんせいき 前世紀 (現在の前の世紀) the last century; (任意の世紀の前の世紀) the preceding century

せんせいじゅつ 占星術 astrology / ‖占星術師 an astrologer

センセーショナル ――センセーショナルな sensational / その事件はセンセーショナルな見出しとともに新聞に載った The event was reported in the newspaper with a *sensational* headline.

センセーション sensation / ‖一大センセーションを巻き起こす create [cause] *a great sensation*

ぜんせかい 全世界 all the world, the whole world / その実験の結果に全世界の注目が集まった The results of the experiment were followed by「*all the* [*the whole*] *world*. / 彼は作曲家として全世界に知られている He is known「*all over* [*throughout*] *the world* as a songwriter.

せんせき 船籍 registry, the nationality of a ship / 日本船籍の貨物船 a cargo ship of Japanese *registry*

せんせん[1] 宣戦 …に対して宣戦布告する *declare war* on [upon, against] …; *proclaim war* against …
‖宣戦布告 a declaration [proclamation] of war

せんせん[2] 戦線 〔軍事〕front (しばしば Front), / これらの会社はその大企業に対して共同戦線を張った These companies formed *a united front* against the big company.
‖人民戦線 the people's front

ぜんせん 戦前 ――戦前の prewar (↔postwar) / 戦前(に) before the war / 彼は戦前、奈良に住んでいた He lived in Nara *before the war*.
‖戦前派 the prewar generation

ぜんせん[1] 前線 (気象の) front; (戦場の) front (しばしば Front), line; (最前線) the front line / 敵軍は前線から撤退した The enemy troops withdrew from *the front line*. / 梅雨前線が北上している *The seasonal rain front* is going [moving] north.
‖寒冷[温暖]前線 a cold [warm] front

ぜんせん[2] 善戦 ――善戦する put* up a good fight, fight* well; (最善を尽くす) do* *one's best* / 彼らは強豪を相手に善戦した They *put up a good fight* against a very strong competitor.

ぜんせん[3] 全線 来年その地下鉄は全線開通する予定だ The subway will open along *the entire line* next year. / その道路は事故のために全線(→完全に)通行止めになっている The road is *completely* closed because of the accident. / その(電車の)路線は大雪で全線不通になっている *All train services* on the line have stopped because of the heavy snow.

ぜんぜん 全然 (全く…ない) not (…) at all, not … any, no ◆まったく
彼は蛇を全然怖がらない He's *not at all* afraid of snakes.
厚着をしていたので全然寒くなかった I *didn't* feel cold *at all* because I was wearing heavy clothes.
私は全然楽譜が読めない I *cannot* read music *at all*.
全然金を持ち合わせていなかった I *didn't* have *any* money with me.
政治のことは全然知りません I *have no* knowledge of politics.
◆これは前に私が見たものと全然違う This is *quite* [*completely*] different from what I've seen before. / 彼女は全然淑女なんかじゃない She *is anything but* a lady. / 彼はコーチとして全然なっていない He *is no good* as a coach. / その映画、全然(→本当に)おもしろかったよ That movie was *really* exciting. / 綾子の彼氏って全然(→すごく)かっこいいじゃない Ayako's boyfriend is *so* cool.
⚫「緊張してる?」「全然」"Are you nervous?" "*Not at all.*"

せんせんきょうきょう 戦々恐々 彼女は先生に怒られるのではないかと戦々恐々としていた(→ひどく恐れていた) She *was terribly afraid* [*nervous*] that she would be scolded by the teacher.

せんせんげつ 先々月 the month before last

ぜんぜんじつ 前々日 two days ago; (おととい) the day before yesterday; (任意の日の2日前) two days before

せんせんしゅう 先々週 the week before last ◆その事件は先々週の火曜日に起きた The event happened *on* Tuesday *two weeks ago*.

せんぞ 先祖 ancestor, 《集合的》ancestry / ――先祖の ancestral
遠い先祖 remote *ancestors* / 先祖伝来の刀 a sword *handed down from one's ancestors*; *one's ancestral* sword / 先祖の霊を祭るworship the spirit of *an ancestor* / ご先祖様のお墓参りをする visit *one's ancestors'* grave
その武士は私の先祖に当たる That samurai is one of my *ancestors*.
◆その一族は先祖代々(→何代にもわたって)この土地に住み続けてきた The family has lived on this land *for generations*.

せんそう[1] 戦争

war; (❀戦争の状態は, 個別の戦いは), warfare; (戦闘) battle
〚戦争〜〛
戦争反対 No More *War*
戦争中に多くの人々が命を落とした Many peo-

ple lost their lives *during the war*.
両国は長い間戦争状態にあった The two countries *were at war* for a long time.
だれに戦争責任があると思いますか Who do you think *is responsible for* (*starting*) *the war*?
◆戦争ごっこをして遊ぶ play *soldiers*
〖～戦争〗
英国は百年戦争でフランスと戦った England fought against France in *the Hundred Years' War*.
湾岸戦争は1991年1月に始まった *The Gulf War* started in January 1991.
〖戦争が・は〗
その2国間に戦争が起こった *War* broke out between the two countries.
その戦争は1945年まで続いた The *war* lasted until 1945.
〖戦争に・で〗
戦争に勝つ[負ける] win [lose] *a war* / 戦争に突入する plunge into *war*
我々は戦争に反対だ We are against *war*.
彼女は一人息子を戦争で亡くした She lost her only son *in the war*.
〖戦争の〗
多くの人がその戦争の犠牲になった A lot of people fell victim to *the war*.
その戦争のために彼らは別れ別れになった They were separated from each other *by the war*.
その町のあちこちにまだ戦争のつめ跡が見られる *Traces of the war* can still be seen all over the town.
〖戦争を〗
戦争を放棄する renounce *war*
日本は1904年にロシアと戦争を始めた Japan *went to war* against Russia in 1904.
父は若いころ戦争を経験した My father *experienced war* when he was young.
‖戦争映画 a war film [《米》movie] / 戦争犠牲者 war victims / 戦争記念碑 a war memorial / 戦争孤児 a war orphan / 戦争犯罪人 a war criminal / 戦争捕虜 a prisoner of war / 核戦争 (a) nuclear war / 経済戦争 economic warfare / 宗教戦争 a religious war / 侵略戦争 an aggressive war / 全面戦争 an all-out war / 独立戦争 a war of independence / 貿易戦争 a trade war

せんそう[2] 船窓 porthole [C]
せんそう[3] 船倉 hold [C]
ぜんそう 前奏 introduction [C]
‖前奏曲 a prelude
せんぞく 専属 彼には専属のマネージャーがいる He has a manager who「has *an exclusive contract* with him [works for him *exclusively*]. / そのタレントはこの会社の専属だ The entertainer *is under exclusive contract with* this company.
‖専属契約 (an) exclusive contract
ぜんそく 喘息 asthma [ǽzmə] [U] ‖私は若いころから喘息を患っています I have had *asthma* since I was young. / けさ喘息の発作に襲われたがすぐに治まった I had *an asthma* [*asthmatic*] *attack* this morning, but it passed soon.
‖喘息患者 an asthmatic
ぜんそくりょく 全速力 ―全速力で at full [top] speed, with all speed ‖ランナーたちは全速力でゴールを駆け抜けた Runners ran through the goal「*at full speed* [*as fast as they could*].
センター (中心となる場所や施設) center [C]; (野球の) center field [U]; (選手) center fielder [C] ‖センターフライ a fly ball to center (field) / センターライン a center line / ショッピングセンター a shopping center / (大学入試)センター試験 the National Center for University Entrance Examinations examination
せんたい 船体 the body of a ship
せんだい 先代 (前任者) predecessor [C]
◆先代吉右衛門 the *former* Kichiemon

ぜんたい 全体

the whole ―全体の whole, all, entire ―全体で in all, altogether
全体の一部 a part of *the whole*
雪が村全体を覆っていた Snow covered「the *whole* village [*all* of the village].
彼の初回のホームランが試合全体の流れを決めた His first-inning home run set the tone for the *entire* game.
費用は全体で1万円かかります It will cost 10,000 yen *in all*.
全体的に見て，この計画は悪くない *On the whole*, this plan is not bad.
私たちはその問題を日本だけでなくアジア全体の問題としてとらえるべきだ We should regard that as a problem not only of Japan but of Asia *as a whole*.
◆事件の全体像 *an overview* of the affair / 体全体がかゆい I feel itchy *all over*. / 一体全体，彼は何をしているんだ What「*on earth* [*in the world*] is he doing?
‖全体会議 a general meeting; (総会) a plenary session / 全体主義 totalitarianism

ぜんだいみもん 前代未聞 ―前代未聞の (前例のない) unprecedented; (聞いたことのない) unheard-of ‖前代未聞の事件 an *unprecedented* [*unheard-of*] case / これは前代未聞の凶悪犯罪だ Such an atrocious crime is *unheard-of* [*unprecedented*]. / (→そんな凶悪犯罪は聞いたことがない) I *have never heard of* such an atrocious crime.
せんたく[1] 洗濯 wash [U]《また a ～》, washing [U] ―洗濯する wash [他], do* the washing [laundry]
洗濯物を干す hang [put] out *the washing* [*laundry*] to dry (❖「取り込む」なら bring in を用いる)
きょうは洗濯物がたくさんある I have *a* large *wash* today.
このズボンは洗濯しないといけない These trousers need *a wash*.
私はいつも日曜の朝に洗濯をする I always *do the washing* on Sunday morning.

せんたく

このしみは洗濯すれば落ちますか Can I *wash* this stain out? / Will this stain *wash* out?

このセーターは洗濯すると縮むかもしれない This sweater may shrink *in the wash.*

◆私のシャツ、洗濯に出してくれた？ Have you sent my shirt to *the laundry*? / これらは洗濯がきく These「*are washable*[*can be washed*]. / 洗濯した物を全部たたんだ I folded up all *the clean clothes.*

◆「私の白いブラウスはどこ」「洗濯中よ」 "Where's my white blouse?" "It's *in the wash.*"

∥洗濯かご a laundry basket, 《米》a hamper / 洗濯機 a washing machine, 《口語的》a washer / 洗濯せっけん 《米》laundry soap, 《英》washing powder / 洗濯ばさみ 《米》a clothespin, 《英》a clothes peg / 洗濯屋(店) a laundry, cleaners, (人) a launderer / 全自動洗濯機 a fully automatic washing machine

ことわざ 鬼のいぬ間の洗濯 ⇨ おに

せんたく² 選択 choice ⓤⓒ; selection ⓤⓒ (◆前者が好み・反映するのに対して、後者は客観的にいちばんよい物を念入りに選ぶ) ── 選択する choose* ⓜⓘ; select ⓜ ⇨ えらぶ

選択を誤る(→間違った選択をする) make a bad *choice* / 難しい選択を迫られる be pressed with *a difficult choice*

君は賢い選択をしたと思う I think you *made the* wise [intelligent] *choice.*

ほかにはどんな選択肢がありますか What are the other *choices* [*options*]?

学生はフランス語かドイツ語のいずれかを選択できる Students *have the choice* [*option*] to take French or German.

どちらも同じ条件なので選択に迷う The conditions are all the same, so I *don't know which one to choose.*

この件に関して君たちに選択の余地はない You guys *have no choice* in this matter.

∥選択科目 《米》an elective [《英》optional] subject / 選択問題 a multiple-choice question

センタリング 《サッカーなどで》centering ⓤ ── センタリングする center ⓜⓘ

せんたん 先端 ❶(とがった先) tip ⓒ, point ⓒ; (端) end ⓒ / 枝の先端 *the tip* of the branch / この道路は能登半島の先端まで延びている The road runs to *the tip* of the Noto Peninsula.

◆そのころは女子高生が流行の先端を行っていた High school girls *were leading* [*setting*] *the fashion* in those days. / その病院の医療器械は時代の先端を行っている The medical appliances in that hospital *are ahead of the times.* / 彼らはエイズウイルスの研究の先端を行っている They *are at the forefront of* research into the HIV virus.

∥高度先端技術 highly-developed technology

せんだん 船団 fleet ⓒ, convoy ⓒ

センチ ⇨ センチメートル

せんち 戦地 front ⓒ 《しばしば Front》; (戦場) battlefield ⓒ

ぜんち 全治 全治1週間のやけどを負う suffer a burn that takes a week to「*completely heal up* [*heal completely*]

ぜんちし 前置詞 【文法】 preposition ⓒ ((略語) prep.) ∥前置詞句【文法】a prepositional phrase

名詞または名詞句の前に置いて形容詞句または副詞句を作る語を前置詞という。前置詞は他の品詞といっしょになって句全体で前置詞と同じ働きをする場合もある // a friend *of mine* (◆*of mine* は形容詞句) 私の友達 / I live in Osaka. (◆*in Osaka* は副詞句) 私は大阪に住んでいる / She made herself understood *by means of* sign language. (◆*by means of sign language* は副詞句) 彼女は手話で意思を伝えた

ぜんちぜんのう 全知全能 全知全能の神 Almighty God; God *Almighty*

センチメートル centimeter, 《英》centimetre ⓒ 《略語》cm)

センチメンタル ── センチメンタルな (感傷的な) sentimental / センチメンタルな曲 a *sentimental* tune / その詩を読んで少しセンチメンタルな気分になった I got a bit *sentimental* reading the poem.

せんちゃ 煎茶 🗻 *sencha*, green tea (of medium quality)

せんちゃく 先着 先着30名様に1,000円分の商品券を差し上げます A 1,000-yen gift certificate will be given to the *first 30 people.* / チケットは先着順に販売いたします The tickets will be sold *on a first-come, first-served basis.* / 先着順にお座りください Please sit down *in the order of arrival.*

せんちゅう 戦中 戦中の大衆文化 popular culture *during the war*

∥戦中派 the generation that grew up during World War II

せんちょう 船長 captain ⓒ; (小型商船・漁船などの) 《口語的》skipper ⓒ (◆共に呼びかけにも用いる) ∥クック船長 *Captain* Cook

ぜんちょう¹ 全長 full [total] length ⓤ ∥ジャンボジェット機の全長は約70メートルだ *The full* [*total*] *length* of a jumbo jet is about seventy meters. / A jumbo jet is about seventy meters *long.*

ぜんちょう² 前兆 omen ⓒ, sign ⓒ; (凶事などの)《公式的》portent ⓒ ∥よい[悪い]前兆 a good [bad] *omen* / 動物たちが落ち着かなくなるのは地震の前兆といわれている Restless animals are said to be *a sign* of an earthquake.

せんて 先手 ❶【将棋・囲碁】the first move / 先手(→先手を打つの)は中山氏です Mr. Nakayama is *the one to make the first move.* / 彼に先手を譲った I let him make *the first move.*

❷【機先を制すること】その試合では彼が先手をとった(→最初に得点した) He *scored first* in the game. / 警察は先手を打って空港で犯人を

待ちかまえた The police *were ahead of* the criminal and waited for him at the airport. / あいつ彼女に告白したらしい．先手をとられちゃったよ He seems to have told her that he loved her. He really *got the jump on me.* / 先手必勝 *Whoever attacks first will win.*

せんてい[1] 選定 ―選定する select [他], choose* [他] ∥その都市はオリンピックの開催地に選定された The city *was selected* [*chosen*] to be the host city of the Olympic Games.
‖選定基準 selection criteria / 選定図書 books selected [recommended] for students [pupils]

せんてい[2] 剪定 ―剪定する prune [他]; (形を整える) trim [他] ∥父は一日中，庭木の剪定をしていた My father spent all day *pruning* [*trimming*] our yard trees.
‖剪定ばさみ pruning shears

ぜんてい 前提 (仮定) assumption [C], 《公式的》presupposition [U] [C]; (理論上の) premise [C] ∥君が参加することを前提に旅行を計画しよう I'm going to plan this trip *on the assumption that* you will go with us. / 君の論理は前提が間違っている Your logic is wrong in *its premises.*
◆綾には結婚を前提に(→結婚のことを考えて)つきあっている人がいる Aya is going out with a person *with* marriage *in mind.*
‖前提条件 a precondition, 《公式的》a prerequisite / 大[小]前提 a major [minor] premise

ぜんでら 禅寺 🗻 Zen temple [C]

せんでん 宣伝

(個々の広告など) advertisement [C], 《口語的》ad [C]; (広告すること) advertising [U], publicity [U]; (政治的な) 《しばしば軽蔑的》propaganda [U] ―宣伝する advertise [他] [自], publicize [他]; propagandize [他]

私たちはサークルの宣伝のためにたくさんのポスターをはった We put up a lot of posters to *advertise* our club.

その車が売れないのは宣伝が足りなかったからだ The car isn't selling well because it *hasn't been advertised enough.*

その会社はマスメディアで大々的に新しいゲームソフトの宣伝をしている The company *advertises* their new game software *in* the media on a large scale.

テレビで新しい化粧品の宣伝をしていた New cosmetics *were advertised* [*publicized*] *on* TV.

それテレビで宣伝してたやつだよね It *was advertised on* TV, wasn't it?

歌詞に店名が出てくるので，その歌はうちの店のいい宣伝になってくれている That song *serves as a good advertisement for* our shop because the name of our shop is mentioned in it.

◆彼女は一流大学に通っている兄のことを宣伝して回っている(→みんなに言い触らしている) She *is going around telling everybody that* her brother goes to the prestigious university.
‖宣伝カー a sound truck / 宣伝係 a publicity agent / 宣伝活動 an advertising campaign / 宣伝効果 the influence [effect] of advertising / 宣伝費 advertising expenses / 宣伝ビラ a handbill, a leaflet (❖leaflet は通例折りたたんだものをいう); (政治的な) a propaganda bill [leaflet] / 宣伝ポスター an advertising poster / 宣伝文句 an advertising pitch; (広告文) ad copy

ぜんてんこうがた 全天候型 全天候型トラック an *all-weather* track

せんてんせい 先天性 ‖先天性疾患 an inborn [an innate, a congenital] disease

せんてんてき 先天的 ―先天的な (性質などが) inborn, innate, inbred (↔acquired); (病気が) congenital ∥あの子には先天的な歌の才能がある The child has an *inborn* [*innate, inbred*] talent for singing. / この疾患は先天的なものだ This disease is *congenital.*

セント cent [C] (❖1ドルの100分の1；記号 ¢；《略語》c., ct.) ∥7ドル30セント seven dollars (and) thirty *cents* (❖$7.30 と記す．また《米》では seven thirty というほうがふつう)

せんと 遷都 the relocation [transfer] of the capital ―遷都する transfer the capital

せんど 鮮度 freshness [U] ∥鮮度の落ちた野菜はおいしくない Vegetables that have lost *their freshness* aren't good to eat.
◆野菜は冷蔵庫に入れておけば鮮度を保つことができる You can *keep* vegetables *fresh* in a refrigerator.

ぜんと 前途 future [C]; (見通し) the outlook ∥彼女の前途はとても明るい Her *future* is very bright. / 彼は前途多難だ There *will be many difficulties lying ahead of* him *in the future.* / コンピュータ産業は前途洋々だ *The outlook for* the computer industry *is good.* / 彼らの前途を祝して乾杯 Let's drink *to* their *bright future!*
◆前途有望な若いゴルファー a *promising* [《口語的》*coming*] young golfer

ぜんど 全土 そのニュースはたちまち日本全土に伝わった The news spread 「*all over* [*throughout*] *Japan* immediately. / その事件は日本全土を震撼(しんかん)させた The incident shook *the whole of Japan.*

せんとう[1] 先頭 the lead, the front ∥彼は39キロ地点で先頭に立った He *took the lead* at 39 kilometers from the start. / 彼女が先頭に立ってその作業を進めた She *took the lead* in doing the work. / 彼は列の先頭にいた He was at *the front of* the line.
◆生徒たちはバトントワラーを先頭にパレードを行った(→バトントワラーが先頭に立った) The baton twirler *headed* [*led*] the parade of students. / 先頭集団には6人のランナーがいる There are six runners in *the leading group.* / 先頭車両は冷房が弱められていた The air conditioning was turned down in *the front* [*first*] *car of the train.*

せんとう² 戦闘 combat ⓊⒸ, action ⓊⒸ; (大規模な) battle ⓊⒸ ∥戦闘を開始する go into *combat* [*action, battle*]
∥戦闘員 a combatant / 戦闘機 a fighter (plane) / 戦闘部隊 a combat command / 非戦闘員 a noncombatant, a civilian

せんとう³ 尖塔 steeple Ⓒ; (先端部分) spire

せんとう⁴ 銭湯

> 銭湯は入浴料を払って入る公共の浴場です. しかし最近では銭湯も日本中で少しずつ減少してきています. というのも現在ではほとんどの家にはふろがあるからです. しかし銭湯は, ふろのない部屋に住む人々にとって今でも欠かせないのはもちろんのこと, 地域社会の人々との交流の場として大切な役割を果たしています.
> A *sento* is a public bath which people have to pay for. But in recent years, *sento* are gradually decreasing in number all over Japan mainly because most people now live in houses with baths. Even now, however, *sento* are indispensable to some people who do not have baths at home, and they still play an important role as a community gathering place where people enjoy communication with others.

せんどう¹ 先導 lead 《通例単数形》 ——先導する lead* ⊕⊜, (公式的) precede ⊕ ∥2台の白バイがランナーたちを先導している Two police motorcycles *are leading* the runners. / (→白バイに先導されている) The runners *are led* by two police motorcycles.
∥先導車 a leading car

せんどう² 船頭 boatman Ⓒ; (渡し舟の) ferryman Ⓒ
ことわざ 船頭多くして船山に登る Too many boatmen cause the boat to climb a mountain.; Too many cooks spoil the broth. (→料理人が多すぎるとスープがだめになる)

せんどう³ 扇動 instigation Ⓤ; (暴力的・不法な) incitement Ⓤ; (世論喚起活動) agitation Ⓤ ——扇動する instigate ⊕; incite ⊕; agitate ⊕ ——扇動的な inflammatory ∥彼らは労働者を扇動してストを決行させた They *instigated* [*incited, agitated for*] the workers to strike. / 彼は扇動的なスピーチを行った He made an *inflammatory* speech.
∥扇動者 an instigator, an agitator

ぜんとうよう 前頭葉 the frontal lobe (of the brain)

セントバーナード 〔動物〕 Saint Bernard Ⓒ

セントラルヒーティング central heating Ⓤ ◆このビルはセントラルヒーティングで暖房されている This building *is centrally heated*.

セントラルリーグ the Central League

セントルイス Saint Louis (❖米国の都市)

せんない 船内 犯人はまだ船内に潜んでいる模様だ The criminal still seems to be hiding *inside the ship*. / 船内で豪華なパーティーが行われていた There was a luxurious party *on the ship*.

ぜんにちせい 全日制 full-time [regular] schooling ∥全日制高校 a full-time [regular] high school

ぜんにほん 全日本 ∥全日本選手権 the all-Japan championship [title] / 全日本選手権大会 the all-Japan championship meet / 全日本代表チーム the all-Japan team

せんにゅう 潜入 (情報を得るための) infiltration Ⓤ ——潜入する infiltrate ⊕⊜; (忍び込む) sneak* into ... ∥彼らは敵の基地に潜入した They *sneaked* [*infiltrated*] *into* the enemy's base.
∥潜入者 an infiltrator

せんにゅうかん 先入観 preconception Ⓒ; (偏見) prejudice ⓊⒸ, bias ⓊⒸ (❖後者は好意的である場合にも用いる) ∥彼はロックに対しある種の先入観をいだいている He has some kind of *preconception* about rock music. / 彼女はそれに対する誤った先入観にとらわれている She is possessed by *an* incorrect 「*preconception* about [*bias* against, *prejudice* against] it.

せんにん¹ 専任 英語の専任の教師 a *full-time* teacher of English
∥専任講師 (大学の) a full-time lecturer [《米》instructor]; (塾などの) a full-time teacher

せんにん² 選任 (選ぶこと) election ⓒⓊ; (任命) appointment Ⓤ ——選任する elect ⊕; appoint ⊕ ∥彼が学級委員に選任された He *was elected* class representative.

せんにん³ 仙人 彼は仙人 (→山の隠者) のような生活を送っている He leads the life of *a mountain hermit*.

ぜんにん¹ 善人 good [good-natured] person Ⓒ, 《集合的》the good

ぜんにん² 前任 ——前任の preceding, former ∥前任の会長 a *former* [*preceding*] chairperson
∥前任者 one's predecessor

せんぬき 栓抜き (びんの) bottle opener Ⓒ; (コルク栓の) corkscrew Ⓒ

せんねん 専念 ——専念する (集中する) concentrate on ...; (身をささげる) devote oneself to ... ∥彼は部活に専念している He *devotes himself to* club activities. / きょうは数学の勉強に専念する I *will concentrate on* studying math today.

ぜんねん 前年 (その年の前の年) the year before, the previous year; (去年) last year ∥前年度の会計報告 「*the previous* [*last*] *year's* financial report

せんのう 洗脳 brainwashing Ⓤ ——洗脳する (口語的) brainwash ∥彼女はすべてにおいて彼を信用するように洗脳された She *was brainwashed into* trusting him on everything.

ぜんのう¹ 全能 ——全能の almighty《しばしば Almighty》, 《公式的》omnipotent ∥全能の神 *Almighty* God; God *Almighty*

ぜんのう² 前納 payment in advance ——前納する pay* in advance ∥受講料の30万円を前納する 「*pay* 300,000 yen *in advance* [*prepay* 300,000 yen] as tuition

せんばい 専売 （販売の独占） monopolization [U]; （独占権·専売事業·専売品） monopoly [C] **──専売する** monopolize [他] ∥かつてたばこと塩は国の専売だった Tobacco and salt used to *be* 「government *monopolies* [*monopolized* by the government]. ◆16文キックは馬場選手の専売特許（→おはこ）だった The *jurokumon* kick was Baba's *unique specialty.*
‖専売特許 a patent

せんぱい 先輩 （年長者） *one's* senior（❖英米には日本の「先輩·後輩」のような上下関係の概念があまりないので説明的に表すこともある）
上杉さんは私の4年先輩です Mr. Uesugi *is* four years my *senior.* / Mr. Uesugi *is* my *senior* by four years.
◆徳川さんは高校の2年先輩です Tokugawa is two years *ahead of* me in high school. / 夏美さんは私の大学の先輩です（→私より先に卒業した） Natsumi graduated from our university *ahead of* me. / 鈴木さんはこの会社では2年先輩だが同い年だ Suzuki is the same age as me, but he began working at this company two years earlier. / 彼女は私より若いけれども経験の面では（大）先輩です（→私よりたくさんの経験を積んでいる） Even though she is younger than I am, she *has* (*much*) *more experience* than I do. / 田中先輩は私たちみんなのあこがれの人だ We all admire *Tanaka.*（❖「田中先輩」の「先輩」に当たる特別な英語はない） / 先輩，受験がんばってください I wish *you* good luck in the entrance examinations.（❖この場合の「先輩」に当たる特別な英語はない）

ぜんぱい[1] 全敗 **──全敗する** lose* all the games [matches]

ぜんぱい[2] 全廃 total abolition [U] **──全廃する** abolish totally; （廃止する） do* away with ... ∥核兵器の全廃を求める運動 a movement for *the total abolition* of nuclear weapons / 人々はその制度の全廃を望んでいる People want the system 「*totally abolished* [*done away with*].

せんぱく[1] 浅薄 **──浅薄な** （うわべだけの） superficial; （浅い） shallow ∥浅薄な考え a *superficial* [*shallow*] idea

せんぱく[2] 船舶 ship [C], 《公式的》 vessel [C], 《集合的》 shipping [U]
‖船舶会社 a shipping company

せんばつ 選抜 selection [U] [C] **──選抜する** select [他] ∥その大学は大勢の志願者の中から10人の学生だけを選抜する The college *selects* only 10 students from many applicants.
‖選抜試験 a screening test / 選抜チーム an all-star team / 全国選抜高校野球大会 the National Invitational High School Baseball Tournament

せんぱつ[1] 先発 きのうの試合では上原が先発した Uehara *was the starting pitcher* in yesterday's game.
‖先発隊 an advance party [team, group] / 先発投手 a starting pitcher / 先発メンバー the starting line-up, the starters

せんぱつ[2] 洗髪 hair-washing [U]; （シャンプーでの） shampooing [U] **──洗髪する** wash *one's* hair; shampoo *one's* hair

せんばづる 千羽鶴 🗻

> 千羽鶴とは1,000羽の折り鶴をつなげたもので，人が病気から回復することを願って家族や友達が作ります．千羽鶴はまた平和の祈願にも用いられます．
> A *sembazuru* is a string of a 1,000 origami cranes made by the friends or family of a sick person to express their wishes for the person's return to health. It can also be used as a prayer for peace.

せんばん 旋盤 lathe [C] ‖旋盤工 a lathe operator

せんぱん 戦犯 （戦争犯罪人） war criminal [C]

ぜんはん 前半 the first [former] half ∥7月前半に大雨が降った We had heavy rain *in the first half* of July. / あと5分で前半終了です There are five minutes left before the end of *the first half.*
◆おじは40代前半だ My uncle is in his *early* forties. / 気温は30度台前半になるものと思われます The temperature will be in the *low* thirties.

ぜんぱん 全般 （全体） the whole **──全般的な** whole; （全体にわたる） overall; （一般的な） general **──全般的に** generally, overall, in general ∥計画全般を見直す必要がある We need to remake the *whole* plan. / 彼は物理学全般に関心をいだいている He is interested in physics *generally* [*overall, in general*]. / この夏は全般的に平年より気温が低かった The temperature was *generally* lower this summer than the average.
◆それは社会全般にわたる問題だ That is a problem in society *at large.*

せんび 船尾 stern [C]

せんぴょう 選評 **──選評する** select and make* comments on ...

ぜんぶ[1] 全部

all 《単数または複数扱い》, everything 《単数扱い》; （全体） the whole **──全部の** all, every; whole, entire（❖共に名詞の前で用いる） **──全部で** in all, in total, altogether

〖全部〗

それは弟が全部食べてしまった My brother ate 「them *all* [*all* of them].

必要なものはこれで全部ですか Is this *all* you need?

彼は彼女の言うことを全部信じてしまう He believes *everything* she says.

宿題を全部片づけたら遊びに行ってもよい You may go out and play when you have done *all* (of) your homework.

それらの本を全部読んだわけではない I have not read *all* those books.

彼女はそのことについて全部話してくれた She gave me the *whole* story about it.

私は彼の作品を全部持っている I have an *entire* collection of his works.

ぜんぶ

【全部で】
全部でおいくらですか How much is it *altogether* [*in all*]／
わがチームのメンバーは全部で100人だ Our team has 100 members「*in all* [*altogether*].

【全部の】
全部の先生が厳しいわけじゃない Not *all* teachers are strict.

彼の本は全部がつまらないわけではない Not *all* of his books are boring.

● 「あの歌手のどこがいいの」「全部」 "What do you like about that singer?" "*Everything*."

ぜんぶ² 前部 the front (part), the fore part ‖バスの前部 *the front* (*part*) *of the bus*

せんぷう 旋風 (風) whirlwind ◯; (大評判) sensation ◯ ‖松坂の出現は野球界に大旋風を巻き起こした Matsuzaka's debut caused *a great sensation* in the baseball world.

せんぷうき 扇風機 (electric) fan ◯ ‖扇風機をかける[止める] turn on [off] *an electric fan* ／ 扇風機にあたる expose *oneself* to the breeze from *a fan*

せんぷく 潜伏 hiding ◯, concealment ◯; (病気の) incubation ◯ ──潜伏する hide* ◯; incubate ◯ ‖犯人はまだこの近辺に潜伏しているにちがいない The criminal must *be hiding* somewhere around here. ／ その病気は約2週間の潜伏期間を経て発病する The symptoms of the disease appear after *an incubation period* of about two weeks.

ぜんぷく 全幅 彼らは彼女に全幅の信頼をおいている (→完全に信頼している) They *trust* her *completely* [*totally*]. ／ They *have complete* [*total*] *trust* in her.

ぜんぶん¹ 全文 (書物・演説などの文章全体) the full text

ぜんぶん² 前文 (序文) preamble ◯; (前記の文) the above sentence, the sentence above

せんべい 煎餅 🍘 a *sembei*, a rice cracker ‖せんべいぶとん a thin, uncomfortable futon

ぜんべい 全米 水泳の全米代表チーム the *all-American* swimmers' team ／ その大学には全米から優秀な学生が集まってくる The university attracts many excellent students *from all over the U.S*. ／ その番組は全米で放送されている The program is broadcast *throughout the U.S.*

【全米オープン(テニスの)】 the U.S. Open ／ 全米バスケットボール協会 National Basketball Association ((略称)) NBA)

せんべつ¹ 選別 ──選別する (えり分ける) sort ◯; (選び出す) select ◯ ‖資源ゴミを選別して回収する *sort* and collect recyclable waste

せんべつ² 餞別 farewell gift ◯
◆おじが海外留学の餞別にと5万円くれた My uncle gave me 50,000 yen just before I went to study abroad. (❖英米には餞別に金銭を贈る習慣はない)

ぜんぺん¹ 前編 the first part; (最初の巻) the first volume

ぜんぺん² 全編 the whole story; (本・巻) the whole book [volume] ‖作者の自然を愛する心が物語の全編にあふれている The author's love of nature permeates *the whole story*. ／ (→最初から終わりまで) The story is filled with the author's love of nature *from beginning to end*.

せんぼう 羨望 envy ◯ (また an ～) ──羨望する envy ◯ ‖彼はテストでただ一人満点を取り、クラスの羨望の的(ま)となった He *became the envy of the class* [Everybody in the class *envied* him] for being the only one who got a perfect score on the exam. ／ みんなが彼女を羨望のまなざしで見ていた Everybody looked at her *with envy*.

せんぽう¹ 先方 (男性) he; (女性) she; (複数の人) they; (契約などの正式な場面で) the other party ‖先方の意見を聞いてから判断すべきだ We should decide after hearing *his* [*her, their, the other party's*] opinion. ／ 先方から何か言ってきたらすぐに教えてください If you hear *from him* [*her, them, the other party*], please let me know right away.

せんぽう² 戦法 tactics (単数または複数扱い); (戦略) strategy ◯ ‖奇襲戦法をとる use *shock tactics*

せんぽう³ 先鋒 the vanguard ‖反核運動の先鋒に立っている *be in the vanguard of* antinuclear movement

ぜんぼう 全貌 the whole story ‖いまだその事件の全貌は明らかになっていない *The whole story* about the incident has not been revealed yet.

ぜんぽう 前方 ──前方に[へ] ahead (❖動きを伴う場合にも伴わない場合にも用いる); forward (↔backward) (❖動きを伴う場合にのみ用いる) ‖隊はさらに前方へと進んだ The troops went farther *forward* [*ahead*]. ／ 我々の前方に川が見えた We saw a river 「*ahead of* [*in front of*] us. ／ 前方100メートルほどの所に交差点があります There is a junction about one hundred meters *ahead*.
◆姉は前方不注意で交通事故を起こした My sister had a traffic accident *because she wasn't watching where she was going*.

せんぼうきょう 潜望鏡 periscope ◯

せんぼつしゃ 戦没者 (集合的) the war dead (複数扱い)
‖戦没者慰霊碑 a war memorial

ぜんまい¹ spring ◯ ‖ぜんまいを巻く wind up *a spring* ／ オルゴールはぜんまいで動く A music box is driven by *a spring*. ／ この時計のぜんまいは切れている This clock's *spring* has broken. ◆ぜんまい仕掛けの人形 *a clockwork* [*windup*] doll

ぜんまい² royal fern ◯

せんまいどおし 千枚通し awl ◯

せんまん 千万 1 [2]千万円 10 [20] *million yen* ／ 数千万匹のバッタの大群 a swarm of *tens of millions of* locusts

せんむ 専務 ‖専務取締役 a senior managing director

せんめい 鮮明 (輪郭が) distinctness ⃝, sharpness ⃝; (見やすさ) clearness ⃝; (色彩・記憶などが) vividness ⃝; (色などが) brightness ⃝ ──鮮明な distinct, sharp; clear; vivid; bright ──鮮明に distinctly; clearly; vividly ∥鮮明な赤 vivid [bright] red / うちのテレビは映像があまり鮮明ではない Our TV doesn't have a very *sharp* [*clear*] picture. / 私はその事件を鮮明に記憶しています I can remember the incident *vividly*. / I have a *vivid* memory of the incident.

ぜんめつ 全滅 complete [total] destruction ⃝, annihilation [ənàiəléiʃən] ⃝ ──全滅する be destroyed completely, be annihilated, be wiped out ∥この地区の住人は敵の爆撃で全滅した People of the district *were annihilated* [*wiped out*] by the enemy bombing.
◆家中の害虫を全滅させる(→駆除する) *exterminate* insect pests throughout the house / 村は洪水で全滅した(→洪水が村を全滅させた) The flood *destroyed* the village *completely*. / 台風で畑の作物が全滅だった The typhoon「*completely destroyed* [*wiped out*] the crops in the field.

せんめん 洗面 ∥洗面器 a basin, 《米》a washbowl, 《英》a washing-up basin [bowl] / 洗面所 a bathroom ⇨ べんじょ / 洗面台 a washbasin, 《米》a sink / 洗面用具 toiletries, toilet articles

ぜんめん¹ 全面
❶【物の表面】the whole [entire] surface
板の全面 *the whole surface* of a board
◆ビルの壁は全面白く塗られた *All of* the walls of the building were painted white. / きょうの新聞の1面は全面その事件に関する記事で埋まっていた The first page of today's newspaper was filled *entirely* with articles about the incident.

❷【あらゆる方面】──全面的な (完全な) complete; (全体の) whole, entire(❖いずれも名詞の前で用いる) ──全面的に completely; wholly, entirely
この計画にはあなたの全面的な支持が必要だ We need your *entire* support for this project.
彼らは私の案に全面的に賛成してくれた They approved of my plan *completely*.
この企画にはY社が全面協力している(→全面的に協力を受けている) This project *is wholly* [*fully*] *supported* by company Y.
わが校の校則が去年全面的に改定された Our school rules were *entirely* revised last year.
◆彼らは核兵器全面禁止を訴えている They are appealing for *a total ban on nuclear weapons*.
∥全面広告 a full-page advertisement / 全面降伏 complete [total] surrender / 全面戦争 an all-out [a full-scale] war

ぜんめん² 前面 the front ◆その映画は戦争の恐ろしさを前面に押し出した(→戦争の恐ろしさが主なテーマの)作品だった The horrors of war were *the main theme* of the movie. / 彼が交渉の前面に出れば(→交渉を指揮すれば)何らかの問題が生じるだろう There will be some problems or other if he *directs* the negotiations.

ぜんもう 全盲 ──全盲の totally blind

せんもん 専門

specialty ⃝; (大学の専攻) 《米》major ⃝; (仕事・関心) 《口語的》line ⃝; (専門分野) field ⃝ ──専門の・専門的な (専門化した) specialized; (特別な) special; (職業的な) professional; (技術的な) technical

その教授の専門は法律です *The specialty* of that professor is law. / That professor *specializes in* law.

あなたの専門は何ですか What is your *major*?

私は大学でフランス文学を専門にしている My *major* at college is French literature. / I'm *majoring in* French literature at college.

彼は自分の専門(分野)以外のことは何ひとつ知らない He doesn't know anything *outside* his *field*.

彼女の講演は思っていた以上に専門的だった Her lecture was more *specialized* [*technical*] than I had expected.

その件に関して専門的な立場からのご意見を伺いたいのですが We'd like to hear your opinion from a *technical* point of view.
◆ここはてんぷら専門の店だ This restaurant *specializes in* tempura.

∥専門医 a specialist / 専門家 a specialist; (技術者) a technician; (本職の人) a professional; (熟練した人) an expert / 専門学校 a technical school, a vocational college / 専門科目 a major subject / 専門教育 technical [professional] education / 専門書 a technical book, a treatise / 専門職 a profession / 専門知識 specialized [technical] knowledge / 専門店 a specialty store / 専門病院 a special hospital / 専門用語 a technical term, (集合的) terminology

ぜんや 前夜 the night before, the previous night; (祝祭日などの) eve ⃝ ∥文化祭の前夜祭 *an eve* of the school festival / 試合の前夜に大けがをしてしまった I got hurt badly *the night before* the game. / 卒業式の前夜にパーティーをした We had a party *on the eve* of (the) graduation.

せんやく 先約 previous engagement [appointment] ⃝
🅔「今夜夕食でもどう」「ごめんね，先約があるの」"How about dinner tonight?" "I'm sorry but「*I'm booked* [*I have a previous appointment*]."

ぜんやく 全訳 complete translation ⃝
◆次の授業までにこの文章を英語に全訳しなければならない I have to *translate* this passage *completely into* English by the next class.

せんゆう¹ 専有 …の権利を専有している *possess* [*have*] *all* the rights to ...

‖専有権 an exclusive right / 専有物 a privately owned article, private property / 専有面積 a privately owned area, private property

せんゆう² 占有 occupation [U], 《公式的》 occupancy [U]; (所有) possession [U] ―占有する occupy [他]; possess [他] ∥その土地は代々わが家が占有している Our family *has occupied* [*possessed*] the land for generations.
‖占有権 the right of possession / 占有者 《公式的》 a possessor; (建物・部屋などの) an occupant / 市場占有率 a (market) share

せんゆう³ 戦友 a comrade [brother] in arms

せんよう 専用 *one's* exclusive [private] use ―専用の (特別の) special; (私有の) private; (個人の) personal ∥自分専用のテレビがあったらな I wish I had a TV *for my exclusive* [*private*] *use.*/ I wish I had *my own personal* TV. / あちらにお客様専用駐車場があります There is a parking lot for *the exclusive use of* our customers over there. / この専用の布でその金属を磨きなさい Rub the metal with this *special* cloth. / この車はわが社専用の車です This is our company's *private* car.
◆従業員専用の入口 an entrance for the staff *only* / 女性[男性]専用《掲示》 *Ladies* [*Men*] *Only* / この席は当クラブの会員専用になっています These seats are *exclusively for* the members of our club.
‖専用回線 a dedicated line; (予約などの) a hot line / 政府専用機 a government plane

ぜんよう 全容 the whole story ∥事件の全容がついに明らかになった *The whole story* of what had happened became clear at last.

ぜんら 全裸 ―全裸の (stark-)naked, nude ―全裸で (stark-)naked; (何も身にまとわず) with nothing on ∥その倉庫から男性の全裸死体が見つかった *The naked body* of a man was found in that warehouse.
‖全裸写真 a nude photograph

せんらん 戦乱 (戦争) war [U] [C]; (騒動・混乱) disturbance [U] [C] ∥戦乱の世 times of *war* [*disturbance*]

せんりがん 千里眼 second sight [U], clairvoyance [U]; (千里眼をもつ人) clairvoyant [C] ∥彼は千里眼をもつといわれている It is said that he「*has second sight* [*is a clairvoyant*].

せんりつ¹ 旋律 tune [C], melody [C] [U] ‖主旋律 the main melody

せんりつ² 戦慄 a shudder [frisson] (of fear) ∥戦慄が走る *have a frisson* [*shudder*] *of fear*; *shudder from fear*

ぜんりつせん 前立腺 〖解剖〗 prostate (gland) [C] ‖前立腺癌(がん) prostate cancer / 前立腺肥大症 enlargement of the prostate

せんりひん 戦利品 spoils (of war), loot [U]

せんりゃく 戦略 strategy [U], 《公式的》 stratagem [C] ―戦略[上]の strategic ―戦略的に strategically ∥戦略を練る discuss *strategy* / そこは戦略上非常に重要な地である The place is *strategically* very important.
‖戦略家 a strategist / 戦略核兵器 strategic nuclear weapons / 戦略物資 strategic materials / 戦略兵器削減条約 the Strategic Arms Reduction Treaty (《略語》 START) / 戦略兵器制限交渉 the Strategic Arms Limitation Talks (《略語》 SALT)

ぜんりゃく 前略

> 英文の手紙では日本の手紙のように時候のあいさつなどを書かないので，特に「前略」に当たる表現はない．Dear … で書き出し，その後用件に移ればよい．

せんりゅう 川柳 a *senryu*, a humorous haiku

せんりょう¹ 占領 occupation [U]; (攻略) capture [U] ―占領する occupy [他]; capture [他] ∥国土のほとんどが敵軍に占領された Most of the country *has been occupied* [*captured*] by the enemy. / ポーランドはかつてロシアの占領下にあった Poland was once *under* Russian *occupation*.
◆この部屋は彼の物で占領されている This room *has been taken up* by his stuff. / 兄はひとりで広い部屋を占領している My brother *has* a large room *all to himself*.
‖占領軍 occupation forces, an occupation army / 占領地 an occupied territory

せんりょう² 染料 dye [U] [C] ∥人工[天然]染料 artificial [natural] *dyes*

ぜんりょう 善良 ―善良な good; (まっとうな) right-minded ∥善良な市民 a *good* [*right-minded*] citizen

ぜんりょうせい 全寮制 彼は全寮制の学校へ入った He entered a *boarding* school.

せんりょく 戦力 military force [strength] [U]; (戦争につながる潜在的な力) war potential [U]; (軍隊) armed forces ∥戦力増強をはかる try to build up *military force* [*strength*]
◆彼ならわがチームの戦力になって(→選手として大いに貢献して)くれるだろう He will *make a great contribution to* our team as a player. / このチームで彼は戦力外の(→役に立たない)選手だ He is *not* a *useful* player in this team.
‖主戦力(チームの) the leading player (of a team) / 新戦力 new [fresh] blood

ぜんりょく 全力 (すべての力) all *one's* might [strength]; (全精力) all *one's* energy
彼は全力で岩を持ち上げようとした He tried to lift the rock *with all his might* [*strength*].
彼は部活動に全力を注いだ He *devoted all his energies to* club activities.
◆全力を尽くしてお助けします I will *do all* [*everything, anything*] *I can* to help you. / 結果は考えずに全力を出しなさい Don't worry about the result. Just *try* [*do*] *your best.* / 警察は犯人逮捕に全力を挙げている The police *are*「*making every effort* [*going all out*] *to* arrest the criminal. / 彼は100メートルを全力疾走した He *ran* 100 meters「*as fast as he could* [*for all he was worth*].

ぜんりょくとうきゅう 全力投球 僕はそのバ

ッターに対して全力投球した I threw my fastest pitch to the batter. / 全力投球で部活動に打ち込んだ I devoted all my energies to club activities.

ぜんりん 前輪 front wheel ◎ ‖前輪駆動 front-wheel drive((略語)FWD)

せんれい¹ 先例 《公式的》 precedent ◎ , previous instance [example] ◎ //先例にならう follow *precedent* / 先例を破る break with *precedent* / この判決は他の訴訟のよい先例となるだろう This court decision will set a good *precedent* for other lawsuits.

せんれい² 洗礼 baptism ⓤ ◎ , christening ⓤ ◎ //カトリックの洗礼を受ける *receive* Catholic *baptism*; *be baptized* a Catholic
◆その新人投手は初登板でプロの厳しい洗礼を受けた The rookie pitcher *had the usual tough time* in his first game as a professional.
‖洗礼式 (a) baptism, (a) christening / 洗礼名 a Christian [baptismal] name

ぜんれい 前例 《公式的》 precedent ◎ ⓤ , previous instance [example] ◎ //このような研究はまるで前例がない This kind of research *is* completely 「*without precedent* [*unprecedented*]」.
◆この計画は前例のない大きなスケールで進められている This project is being developed on a large and *unprecedented* scale.

ぜんれき 前歴 one's past record [history], one's past (※a past は「いかがわしい過去」の意味) //前歴を調べる check *a person's past record* [*history*] / その女は決して前歴を明かそうとしなかった The woman would never tell us *her past*.

◆その男には窃盗でつかまった前歴があった The man *had a record of* being arrested for theft. / 彼は前歴を偽ってその職に就いた He got that job using *a false résumé*. (※résumé は「履歴書」の意味)

せんれつ¹ 鮮烈 ━鮮烈な (鮮やかな) vivid; (強烈な) striking, powerful //その絵は人々に鮮烈な印象を与えた The picture made a *vivid* [*striking*] impression on people.

せんれつ² 戦列 a line (of battle) //戦列に加わる[を離れる] join [leave] *the line of battle*
◆その投手は帰国後すぐに戦列(→チーム)に加わる予定だ The pitcher is joining *the team* as soon as he gets back to Japan.

ぜんれつ 前列 the front row //この写真の前列左から2人目が私です I am the second from the left *in the front row* in this picture. ◆私たちは会場の最前列に座った We took our seats *in the first row* in the hall.

せんれん 洗練 refinement ⓤ , sophistication ⓤ ━洗練された refined, sophisticated //彼の書く文章はとても洗練されている His writing *is very refined* [*sophisticated, polished*]. / 彼女は洗練された着こなしをする She wears clothes in a *refined* [*sophisticated, polished, elegant*] way. / 彼女は音楽の趣味が洗練されている She has a *refined* [*sophisticated*] taste in music.

せんろ 線路 (railroad) track ◎ ; (レール) rail ◎ (通例複数形 ～s) //線路を渡る cross *a railroad track* ◆ 線路を敷く build [construct, lay] *a railroad*
‖線路工事(敷設工事) tracklaying; (保線工事) track maintenance

そ

ソ 〖音楽〗sol ⓊⒸ, so ⓊⒸ

そ 祖 (先祖) ancestor Ⓒ; (特に父方の先祖) forefathers; (創設者) founder Ⓒ; (ある分野の先駆者) originator Ⓒ, father Ⓒ

-ぞ (❖英語では強調の「ぞ」に相当する表現はないので意訳，イントネーションを変えるなどの必要がある) ∥なかなかいいぞ That's quite good. (❖goodを強く発音する)

そあく 粗悪 ――**粗悪な** (平均より劣った) poor, inferior; (悪い) bad ∥粗悪品 goods of poor [inferior] quality

-ぞい -沿い 道路沿いにはたくさんのみやげ物屋がある There are many souvenir shops along the street. / そのレストランは海岸沿いにある The restaurant is on the coast.

そいね 添い寝 赤ちゃんに添い寝する lie beside one's baby

そう¹

❶【そのように】so, it, that

> 語法
> soは「そのように」の意味で，指し示す内容がitやthatよりも漠然としている．it, thatは前に述べた内容をはっきりと表し，thatのほうがitより強意的．

本当にそう思いますか Do you really think so?
休憩したければ，そう言ってください If you want to have a rest, please say so.
そうらしいよ It seems so.
そうしよう Let's do it [that]!
そうしていただけるとありがたいのですが I would be grateful if you could do so [that].
我々はそういうことが二度と起こらないように注意すべきだ We must be careful that something like that will not happen again.

🍂「彼は私たちの提案に同意すると思いますか」「そう思います[そうは思いません]」"Do you think he will agree with our proposal?" "I guess so. [I guess not.]"

🍂「僕のせいだって言いたいんだろう?」「そうは言ってないよ」"Are you saying it was my fault?" "No, I'm not saying that."

🍂「和食が大好きなんです」「私もそうよ」"I love Japanese dishes." "So do I. / Me, too."

🍂「私は英語が話せません」「私もそうです」"I can't speak English." "Neither can I. / Me, neither."

🍂「先生に相談してみよう」「そうしたほうがいいよ」"I'll try to talk with my teacher." "It's a good idea."

🍂「きょうは暑いですね」「そうですね[そうですか]」"It's hot today." "Isn't it? [Is it?]"

❷【肯定】yes, no (❖yesは肯定疑問文に対して，noは否定疑問文に対して答えるときに用いる)

🍂「この教科書はあなたのですか」「そうです」"Is this your textbook?" "Yes, it is."

🍂「傘を持ってこなかったの?」「そうなの」"Didn't you bring your umbrella?" "No, I didn't."

🍂「英単語のテストは来週だよね」「そうだよ」"Is it next week that we are having an English vocabulary test?" "That's right."

❸【あいづちなど】

🍂「美代がイギリスに留学するんだって」「へえ，そうなんだ」"I hear Miyo will study in England." "Oh, 「will she [she will]?"

🍂「きのう横浜に行ったんだ」「そう．どうだった」"I went to Yokohama yesterday." "Really? How was it?" (❖関心のあるときは語尾を上げる)

🍂「あした映画を見に行くの」「あ，そう」"I'll go to a movie tomorrow." "Oh, 「will you [really]?" (❖関心のないときは語尾を下げる)

❹【程度】so, that

そう難しいことではない It's not so [that] difficult.
そう緊張しないで．リラックスしてください Don't be so nervous. Please just relax yourself.

🍂「おなかすいた?」「そうでもないです」"Are you hungry?" "Not really."

❺【その他】

そうだ，彼女に電話しなきゃ Oh, I forgot. I need to call my girlfriend.
そうそう，姉が来年結婚するんですよ By the way, my sister is going to get married next year.
そうか，分かったぞ Now I understand.
そうですねえ，こうしたらどうでしょう Let's see. How about doing it this way?

慣用表現 そうは問屋がおろさない ⇒ とんや

そう² 層 (地層・大気などの) layer Ⓒ, stratum Ⓒ (複 strata); (社会の) stratum Ⓒ, class Ⓒ; (所得・年齢などの) bracket Ⓒ ∥オゾン層 the ozone layer / 高額所得者層 a high income bracket / 多くの日本人は自分が社会の中間層に属していると思っている Many Japanese think they belong to the middle class. ◆この雑誌は若年層にターゲットをしぼっている This magazine is intended for young readers. / そのチームは選手の層が厚い The team has a good selection of players.

そう³ 沿う 川に沿って歩く walk along the river / 党の方針に沿って in accordance with the party line / 運河に沿って道が続いていた The street ran parallel to the canal.

そう⁴ 添う (期待・要求などを満たす) meet* ⓂⒺ; (期待・要求などに応じる) come* [live] up to ... ∥みんなの期待に添う meet everyone's expectations / ご希望に添えないこともあるかもしれません We may not be able to meet your wishes.
◆ご希望に添うことができませんでした We

couldn't *comply with your request*.

そう⁵ 僧 (僧侶) priest ⓒ; (修道院) monk

そう- 総- 総監督 a *general manager* / 総攻撃 an *all-out* assault / 総所得 a *gross income* / 総司令官 a commander-*in-chief* / 総人口 the *total* population

-そう¹ ⇨ーそうだ

-そう² -艘 1艘のボート a [one] boat (❖「艘」は数詞で表す)

ぞう¹ 象 elephant ⓒ /象の鼻 an elephant's trunk

ぞう² 像 (画像) image ⓒ; (影像) statue ⓒ; (人物像) figure ⓒ /自由の女神像 the Statue of Liberty / 光はスクリーン上に像を結んだ The light *created an image* on the screen. ◆その小説は現代の若者像を生き生きと描いている The novel vividly describes *present-day young people*.
‖虚像 a virtual image / 実像 a real image / 未来像 a vision

そうあたりせん 総当たり戦 round robin ⓒ

そうあん 草案 draft ⓒ /草案を書く make *a draft*

そうい¹ 相違 difference ⓒⓊ; (似たもの間の) distinction ⓒⓊ; (対照的な) contrast Ⓤ /わずかな[かなりの]相違 *a* slight [considerable] *difference* / 意見の相違 a *difference* of opinion / 人間と類人猿の相違は遺伝学的にはほとんどない The genetic *distinction* between humans and apes is very slight. ◆(書類などで)上記のとおり相違ありません I *affirm* the above *to be true in every particular*.

そうい² 創意 (独創性) originality Ⓤ; (アイディア) original idea ⓒ
◆創意に富んだ作品 *original* work / 創意工夫を凝らす come up with *an innovative idea*

そうい³ 総意 (大方の意見) the general opinion; (大方の意思) the general will; (一致した意見) the consensus /その決定は国民の総意に基づいていない The decision is not based on *the general will* [*opinion*] of the nation.

そういう (前述の) such, (《口語的》) like that; (その種の) that kind [sort] of ... /そういう食べ物は体によくない Such food is not healthy. / そういう映画はあまり好きではありません I don't like *that kind of* movie very much. ◆そういうわけで彼は大学をやめました *That's why* he quit the university. / そういう事情ならいくらかお金を貸しましょう If *that's the case*, I'll lend you some money. / 人生とはそういうものだ That's life.

🔴「カレーはどう」「そういうから辛い物を食べたい気分じゃないな」"How about curry?" "I don't feel like *such* spicy food."

そういえば そう言えば そういえば(→思い出したが)彼女はちょっと疲れていたみたいだ *That reminds me*, she looked a bit tired. / そういえば(→話題は変わるけれど)きのうの午後出かけた? *By the way*, were you out yesterday afternoon?

🔴「あいつ,彼女でもできたんじゃないか」「そういえば最近ファッションにこだわってるな」"He has a girlfriend, doesn't he?" "*Come to think of it*, he's concerned about fashion lately."

ぞういん 増員 その研究所では職員が40人増員された The staff *increased* by 40 members at the institute.

そううつびょう 躁鬱病 〔医学〕 manic-depression Ⓤ

ぞうえん 造園 landscape gardening Ⓤ
‖造園家 a landscape gardener [designer]

ぞうお 憎悪 hatred Ⓤ(また a ~), detestation Ⓤ, loathing Ⓤ (❖順に意味が強くなる) ——憎悪する hate ⓗ, detest ⓗ, loathe ⓗ /憎悪をむき出しにする display one's hatred [*loathing*] / …に憎悪の念をいだく have *a hatred of* …

そうおう 相応 ——相応の (適した) suitable; (ふさわしい) adequate; (妥当な) reasonable ——相応に suitably; adequately; reasonably /相応の給料 a *reasonable* salary / 英語が話せるようになるにはそれ相応の努力が必要だ It is necessary to make *adequate* efforts to speak English. ◆年相応にふるまう act *one's age* / 私は身分相応の暮らしをしている I live *within my income* [*means*].

そうおん 騒音 noise ⓒⓊ /隣のうちの騒音には我慢できない I can't stand *the noise* our next-door neighbor makes. / 線路のそばは騒音がひどい There is *a* terrible *noise* near the railroad.
‖騒音公害 noise pollution

ぞうか¹ 増加 increase ⓒⓊ; (伸び) growth Ⓤ(また a ~); (上昇) rise ⓒ; (加えること) gain ⓒⓊ ——増加する increase ⓗ
人口の増加 *an increase* [*a growth*] in population / 犯罪の急激な増加 *a sharp rise* in crime
町の人口はこの5年間で30パーセント増加した The population of the town *has increased* by 30 percent in the past five years.
失業者数は年々増加の一途をたどっている The number of (the) unemployed *is increasing* year by year.
外国人居住者の数はますます増加しつつある The number of foreign residents *is on the increase*.
‖増加率 a rate of increase

ぞうか² 造花 artificial flower ⓒ

そうかい¹ 爽快 ——爽快な refreshing; (元気が出る) bracing; (冷たくすがすがしい) brisk, crisp /山頂の空気は爽快だった The air on the top of the mountain *was refreshing* [*bracing*]. ◆気分爽快だ I *feel refreshed*.

そうかい² 総会 general meeting [assembly] ⓒ; (本会議) plenary session [meeting] ⓒ /生徒総会は来週開かれる The general student meeting will be held next week.
‖総会屋 a corporate racketeer / 株主総会 a general meeting of stockholders / 国連総会 the General Assembly

そうがかり 総掛かり 私たちは総がかりで仕事に取り組んだ We got on with the work *all together*.

そうがく　総額（全体の額）the total sum [amount]; (合計) the (sum) total ∥被害総額は1,000万円近い *The total amount of* the loss is almost 10 million yen. ◆費用の総額は100万円を超えた *The total cost* exceeded one million yen. / 今なら総額300万円相当の賞品が当たります We are giving away prizes *totaling* three million yen now.

ぞうがく　増額　increase ⓒ　──増額する increase ⓗ, raise ⓗ　∥賃金の増額を要求する demand *an increase* in wages / 予算を200万円に増額する *increase* the budget to two million yen

そうかつ　総括　summary ⓒ　──総括する summarize ⓗ　∥意見を総括する *summarize* [*make a summary of*] the opinions
∥総括質問 a general interpellation

そうかん¹　壮観（景色）magnificent [grand] view ⓒ; (見せ場) spectacle ⓒ ∥日没時のエアーズロックは壮観だった I had *a magnificent view* of Ayers Rock at sunset.

そうかん²　相関（相関的な）correlative　∥貧困と犯罪発生率には相関関係があるといわれている It's said that there is *a correlation* between poverty and the crime rate. / It's said that poverty and the crime rate *correlate* to each other.

そうかん³　送還（不法入国者などの）deportation ⓤ　──送還する deport ⓗ　∥彼は本国へ強制送還された He *was deported* to his native country.

そうかん⁴　創刊　1950年創刊 *First published* in 1950 / その雑誌は1985年に創刊された The magazine 「*was started* [*made its first appearance*] in 1985.
∥創刊号 the first issue [number]

ぞうかん　増刊　春の増刊号 a special [an extra] spring issue

そうがんきょう　双眼鏡　binoculars (◆数えるときは a pair of ... とする) ∥双眼鏡をのぞく look through *binoculars*

そうかんとく　総監督　general manager

そうき¹　早期　──早期の early　∥早期治療 *early* treatment / 癌（がん）を早期に発見する find cancer *in its early stages*
∥早期教育 early-childhood education

そうき²　想起　その名前を聞くと多くの人はあのいまわしい事件を想起する The name *reminds* many people of [*about*] the awful case.

そうぎ¹　葬儀（葬式）funeral (ceremony) ⓒ; (埋葬) burial ⓤⓒ　∥葬儀に参列する attend *a funeral ceremony* / 彼の葬儀はきのう執（と）り行われた His *burial* took place yesterday.
∥葬儀場 a funeral hall / 葬儀屋(人) an undertaker, a funeral director, 《米》 a mortician; (店) an undertaker's, 《米》 a funeral home [parlor]

そうぎ²　争議　dispute ⓒ; (ストライキ) strike ⓒ　∥労働争議 a labor *dispute* / 争議を始める start *a dispute*

ぞうき　臓器（internal）organs　∥臓器を提供する donate *one's organs*
∥臓器移植 an (internal) organ transplant

ぞうきばやし　雑木林　copse ⓒ; (低林) thicket ⓒ

そうきゅう¹　早急　──早急な（即座の）immediate, prompt; (緊急の) urgent　──早急に immediately, promptly; urgently ∥この問題には早急に対処する必要がある We must cope with this problem *immediately*.
◆できるだけ早急に連絡をください Please get in touch with me *as soon as possible*.

そうきゅう²　送球　throw ⓒ　∥彼の送球がそれたすきにランナーは二塁から三塁に進んだ The runner moved from second to third while he made *a bad throw*.

そうぎょう¹　創業（創立）the foundation; (設立) the establishment　──創業する found ⓗ; establish ⓗ　∥創業1900年 *Established* in 1900; *Since* 1900 / あの店は今年創業250年を迎える That shop celebrates the 250th anniversary of *its foundation* this year.
∥創業者 a founder

そうぎょう²　操業　operation ⓒⓤ　──操業する operate ⓐⓗ; (操業している) be in operation　∥操業を開始［停止］する start [stop] *operation* / その工場は操業の再開にこぎつけた The factory managed to get back in *operation*.
∥操業時間 operating hours / 操業短縮 the reduction of operations / 完全操業 full operation

ぞうきょう　増強（強化）strengthening ⓤ; (数・量の) increase ⓒ; (兵力などの) buildup ⓒ　──増強する strengthen ⓗ; increase ⓗ; build* up　∥軍備増強 a military *buildup* / 私は体力の増強をはかっている I'm trying to *strengthen* myself.

そうきょくせん　双曲線〖数学〗hyperbola ⓒ (複 ~s, hyperbolae)

そうきん　送金　remittance ⓤⓒ　──送金する send* money, 《公式的》 remit ⓐ ⓗ　∥小切手で1万円送金する *send (a remittance)* of 10,000 yen by check

ぞうきん　雑巾　cleaning rag ⓒ; (ほこり用の) duster ⓒ, dustcloth ⓒ; (床用の) floorcloth ⓒ　∥床の雑巾がけをする wipe the floor *with a cleaning rag*

そうぐう　遭遇　encounter ⓒ　──遭遇する meet* with ..., 《公式的》 encounter ⓗ　∥敵に遭遇する *encounter* the enemy / 私たちの乗った船はあらしに遭遇した The ship that we were on *encountered* a storm.

そうくずれ　総崩れ　rout ⓒ ◆ベイスターズの打線に火がつきカープ投手陣は総崩れになった Because the BayStars' batters were hot, the Carp's pitchers *were knocked out one after another*.

ぞうげ　象牙　ivory ⓤ　∥象牙色 ivory / 象牙細工 ivory work / 象牙の塔 an ivory tower

そうけい¹　総計（合計）the total, the sum (total); (総合計) the total sum [amount]　──総計する total ⓗ, add up　∥費用は総計12万円となった *The total* of expense came to

120,000 yen. / この欄の総計を出してください Please *add up* the figures in this column.

そうけい² 早計 ——早計な (せっかちな) rash; (急な) hasty 〃そう決めつけてしまうのは早計だ It *is rash* to decide like that.

そうげい 送迎 送迎いたします We get [drive] you *to* the station for free.
‖送迎バス (旅館などの) a courtesy bus; (空港などの) a limousine bus

ぞうけい¹ 造形 molding Ⓤ ‖造形美術 the plastic [formative] arts

ぞうけい² 造詣 knowledge Ⓤ《また a ～》ジョーンズ教授は日本の古典文学に造詣が深い Professor Jones has *a* profound *knowledge* of classical Japanese literature.

そうけっさん 総決算 (最終的な勘定) closing accounts ◆きょうの公演は半年間の練習の総決算だ Today's performance is *the fruit* of our rehearsals for over six months.

そうけん¹ 双肩 日本の将来はあなたたちの双肩にかかっています The future of Japan *rests on your shoulders.*

そうけん² 壮健 ——壮健な healthy, in good health 〃ご壮健で何よりです I'm glad to know you *are in good health.*

そうけん³ 送検 ——送検する send* *a person to the public prosecutor's office* ◆警察は男を業務上過失傷害の疑いで書類送検した The police *sent the papers on* the man's *case to the prosecutor's office* on charges of professional negligence resulting in injuries.

そうげん 草原 grassland Ⓤ《また ～s》; (平野) plain Ⓒ; (北米の) prairie Ⓒ; (南米の) the pampas

ぞうげん 増減 increase and [or] decrease; (変動) fluctuation Ⓤ ——増減する increase and [or] decrease; fluctuate ⓥ, vary ⓥ 〃人口の増減 the *fluctuation* of population / 年によって多少の増減があるが, 会員数はほぼ200人だ The number of members is about two hundred, though each year it *fluctuates* slightly.

そうこ 倉庫 warehouse Ⓒ 〃商品を倉庫に保管する store goods in *a warehouse*
‖倉庫会社 a warehouse company

そうご 相互 ——相互の mutual,《公式的》reciprocal ——相互に mutually,《公式的》reciprocally
相互の親睦を深める promote *mutual* friendship
国家間の相互理解が不可欠だ *Mutual understanding* is essential between nations.
◆相互に協力し合う cooperate *with each other* / 東西線と中央線は中野駅と三鷹駅の間で相互に乗り入れている The Tozai Line and the Chuo Line *use the same tracks* between Nakano and Mitaka stations.
‖相互依存 interdependence / 相互関係 mutual relations / 相互作用 interaction / 相互扶助 mutual [reciprocal] help

ぞうご 造語 (言葉を作ること) coinage Ⓤ; (作られた語) coinage Ⓒ, coined word Ⓒ

そうこう¹ 草稿 draft Ⓒ; (原稿) manuscript Ⓒ 〃エッセーの草稿を書く make *a draft* of an essay

そうこう² 彼女をデートに誘おうかどうか迷っていたが, そうこうするうちに彼女は友達と帰ってしまった I was hesitating whether to ask her out or not. *In the meantime* she went home with her friend.

そうこう³ 走行 (車内アナウンスで) 走行中, 窓から顔や手を出さないようお願いいたします Please don't put your head or arms out of the window *while the bus is moving.* / この車の走行距離はどれくらいですか What is *the mileage* on this car?

そうごう¹ 総合 ——総合する (1つにする) put* together; (意見などをまとめる) summarize ⓥ ——総合的の general ——総合的に as a whole, on the whole
専門家の話を総合するとこの計画の実行は不可能だろう *Putting together* what the experts said, it will be impossible to carry out this project.
総合的に見てみなさん賛成のようですね *On the whole,* everyone seems to agree.
◆わが校の陸上部は県大会で総合優勝した Our school's track club *won the all-around competition* at the prefectural track and field meet.
‖総合口座 a savings account / 総合雑誌 a general interest magazine / 総合商社 a general trading company [firm] / 総合職 a management position / 総合大学 a university / 総合病院 a general hospital

そうごう² 相好 彼は孫の写真を見て相好を崩した When he saw the picture of his grandchild, he *broke into a smile.*

そうこうかい 壮行会 send-off [farewell] party Ⓒ 〃壮行会を開く have *a send-off [farewell] party*

そうこうしゃ 装甲車 armored car Ⓒ

そうこん 早婚 early marriage Ⓒ ◆私の姉は早婚だった My sister *married young.*

そうごん 荘厳 solemnity ——荘厳な (厳粛な) solemn; (壮大な) magnificent 〃荘厳な音楽 *solemn* music

そうさ¹ 捜査 (捜すこと) search Ⓒ; (犯罪などの) investigation ⓤⒸ ——捜査する search ⓥⒸ; investigate ⓥ ⓥ, make* [conduct] an investigation 〃不正事件を捜査する *investigate [make an investigation into]* a case of injustice / 捜査は難航していた *The investigation* was running out of steam. / その会社に捜査の手が及んだ *The investigation* has been extended to the company. / 警察はついにその事件の公開捜査に踏み切った The police finally decided to make *an open criminal investigation* of the case. / 捜査線上に1人の男が浮かび上がった *The investigation* focused on a man as a suspect. / その事件は捜査中だ The case *is under investigation.*
‖捜査員 an investigator; (刑事) a (police) detective / 捜査本部 the investigation headquarters / 捜査網 a police dragnet / 捜査令状 a search warrant

そうさ² 操作 (機械などの) operation ⓤ, handling ⓤ; (市場・人・社会などの) manipulation ⓤ ──操作する operate ⓣ, handle ⓣ; manipulate ⓣ ‖この機械は操作が簡単です This machine is easy to *operate* [*handle*]. / その新聞社は世論を操作しようとした The newspaper company attempted to *manipulate* public opinion. ◆(車の)ハンドル操作を誤る lose *control* of a car
‖遠隔操作 remote control / 株価操作 stock (market) manipulation

ぞうさ 造作 彼にとってラジオの修理など造作ないことだ It's *easy* for him to repair a radio.

そうさい¹ 総裁 president ⓒ; (銀行・特定の公共団体などの) governor ⓒ (❖特定の総裁を表すときは President, Governor とする) ‖自民党総裁 *the President* of the LDP / 日銀総裁 *the Governor* of the Bank of Japan

そうさい² 相殺 ──相殺する offset* ⓣ; (帳消しにする) cancel ⓣ ‖原油価格の上昇分は円高で相殺されるだろう The increases in crude oil prices will *be offset* by the appreciation of the yen.

そうざい 惣菜 🗾

> 惣菜とはごはんといっしょに食べるおかずのことで、今では、スーパーマーケットや惣菜屋で買うこともできます。特に働く母親やひとり暮らしの若者たちには大助かりのようです。
> *Sozai* is a general term referring to prepared dishes served as a complement to rice. Now it is also common to buy *sozai* at supermarkets and *sozai* shops. That seems to be a big help especially for working mothers and young people living alone.

そうさく¹ 捜索 search ⓒ ──捜索する search ⓣⓘ ‖捜索を打ち切る call off *a search* / 行方不明の子供の捜索はけさ再開された The search for the missing child resumed this morning. / 彼女は警察に娘の捜索願を出した She *asked* the police *to search for* her daughter. (❖⟨search + 人⟩にすると「人の身体検査をする」の意味になる) / 彼らは警察の家宅捜索を受けた They *had their house searched* by the police.
‖捜索隊 a search party

そうさく² 創作 creation ⓤ; (作品) creative [original] work ⓒ; (小説) novel ⓒ ──創作する (作る) create ⓣ; (執筆する) write* ⓣ ‖これは彼の創作ではない This is not his *creation* [*original work*].
◆その話は彼女の創作(→でっちあげ)だった She "*made up* [*fabricated*]" the story.
‖創作意欲 zeal for creation [writing] / 創作活動 creative activities / 創作ダンス a creative dance

ぞうさく 造作 (建具・備品など) fittings; (顔の作り) features ‖彼女は顔の造作が整っている She has regular *features*.

ぞうさつ 増刷 reprinting ⓤ ──増刷する reprint ⓣ

そうざらい 総さらい 来週は今までやったところの総ざらいとしてテストをします Next week you'll have a test as *a general review* of what you've learned so far.

そうざん 早産 premature birth ⓒ
◆弟は早産で生まれた My brother was born *prematurely*.

ぞうさん 増産 an increase in production, production increase ⓤ ──増産する increase production ‖コンピュータを増産する *increase the production of* computers

そうし 創始 ──創始する (組織・団体などを) found ⓣ; (理論・考えなどを) originate ⓣ ‖日本の鉄道はイギリス人技術者によって創始された An English engineer *founded* the Japanese railway system.
‖創始者 (組織・団体などの) a founder; (理論・考えなどの) an originator

そうじ¹ 掃除 cleaning ⓤ (❖ただし1回のまとまった掃除を指す場合には a が付く) ──掃除する clean ⓣ; (掃(は)く) sweep* ⓣ; (ふく) wipe ⓣ; (こする) scrub ⓣ; (モップで) mop ⓣ; (ほこりを払う) dust ⓣ
部屋の掃除をする *clean* a room
私たちは年に1回校内の大掃除をする We *do a thorough* school *cleaning* once a year.
床を掃いた後, ふき掃除をした After sweeping the floor, I *wiped* it.
今週は私たちが掃除当番です It is *our turn to sweep the classroom* this week.
◆居間に掃除機をかける *vacuum* a living room / 彼女の部屋はいつも掃除が行き届いている Her room *is always clean*.
‖掃除機 a vacuum cleaner / 掃除道具 a dusting tool

そうじ² 相似 〖数学〗 similitude ⓤ; (似ていること) similarity ⓤ (❖具体的な相似点を表す場合は ⓒ) ──相似の similar ‖A は B の相似形である A is *a similar figure* to B.

そうじ³ 送辞 farewell speech ⓒ, 〖公式的〗 farewell address ⓒ ‖送辞を述べる make *a farewell speech*; deliver *a farewell address*

そうしき 葬式 funeral ⓒ ⇒ そうぎ(葬儀) ‖葬式を出す hold *a funeral*

そうじしょく 総辞職 general resignation ⓤ, resignation 「in a body [en masse]
◆内閣は総辞職した The cabinet *resigned* 「*in a body* [*en masse*].

そうしそうあい 相思相愛 太郎と花子は相思相愛の仲だ Taro and Hanako *love each other*. / Taro and Hanako *are in love with each other*.

そうした such ⇒ そのような, そんな

そうしたら and (then), then ‖バスで行きなさい. そうしたらもっと早く着くから Take a bus, *and* you'll get there earlier. / *If* you take a bus, (*then*) you'll get there earlier. / きのう大急ぎで駅に行ったんだよ. そうしたら電車が全部止まってたんだ I rushed to the station yesterday, *and found* all train services stopped.

そうしつ 喪失 loss ⓤⓒ ──喪失する lose* ⓣ ‖自信を喪失する *lose one's* confidence /

彼は事故の後一時的な記憶喪失に陥った He suffered from *a temporary memory loss* after he had had the accident.
‖喪失感 a sense of loss

そうして 姉が大学を卒業し,そうして今度は兄が大学を卒業した My sister graduated from college, *and* (*then*) my brother graduated as well. / 彼とは偶然クラブが同じだった.そうして時々個人的に話すようになった I happened to belong to the same club as he. *And this is how* I came to sometimes talk with him personally. / いつもそうして(→そのように)テレビゲームばかりやってるの? Do you always play video games「*like that* [*in that way*]」?

そうじて 総じて generally, in general, on the whole ∥その商品の輸入はここ5年間総じて増加傾向にある *On the whole*, the imports of those goods have tended to increase for the past five years.

そうしゃ¹ 走者 runner ⓒ ∥最終走者 *the last runner*; *an anchor*
◆佐藤は走者一掃の三塁打を放った Sato hit a triple and *cleared the bases*.

そうしゃ² 奏者 player ⓒ ∥サックス奏者 *a saxophone player*; *a saxophonist*

そうじゅう 操縦 (機械などの) operating ⓤ; (かじをとること) steering ⓤ ──操縦する operate 他; steer 他; (飛行機を) fly* 他, pilot 他; (ヨット・小型ボートなどを) sail 他 ∥ヨットを操縦する *sail* a yacht / 友人はヘリコプターの操縦ができる A friend of mine can *fly* [*pilot*] a helicopter.
◆彼女は夫をうまく操縦している She *is managing* [*manipulating*] her husband well.
‖操縦桿 a control lever [stick] / 操縦士 a pilot / 操縦席 a pilot's seat, a cockpit / 副操縦士 a copilot

ぞうしゅう 増収 (収入の) increased income ⓤⓒ; (利益の) increased profit ⓤⓒ; (歳入の) increased revenue ⓤ ∥来年はいくらか増収を見込んでいる I'm expecting some *increased income* next year.

ぞうしゅうわい 贈収賄 bribery ⓤ ∥贈収賄事件 a *bribery* scandal / 市長は贈収賄で逮捕された The mayor was arrested for *bribery*.

そうじゅく 早熟 ──早熟な precocious ∥早熟な子供 a *precocious* child

そうしゅん 早春 early spring ⓤ

そうしょ¹ 草書 (a) sosho, (a) Japanese cursive-style script

そうしょ 蔵書 library ⓒ, a collection of books ⓒ ∥3,000冊の蔵書 a *library* of 3,000 volumes; *a collection* of 3,000 books
◆私の学校の図書館は5万冊の蔵書がある The library of my school has 50,000 *books*.
‖蔵書家 a book collector / 蔵書目録 a library catalog [《英》catalogue]

そうしょう 総称 generic [general] term ⓒ ∥それらを総称しては虫類と呼んでいる "Reptiles" is *a generic* [*general*] *term* for them.

そうじょうこうか 相乗効果 (経済の) multiplier effect ⓒ; (薬の) synergistic effect ⓒ ∥隣接する2つのデパートは相乗効果をねらって同時にバーゲンセールを始めた The two neighboring department stores held sales at the same time relying on *the multiplier effect*. / これらのハーブはブレンドすることで相乗効果が期待できる The combination of these herbs is expected to have *a synergistic* [*cumulative*] *effect*.

そうしょく¹ 装飾 (きれいに見せること) decoration ⓤ; (華やかにすること) ornament ⓤ ──装飾する decorate 他; ornament 他 ∥商店街にはもうクリスマスの装飾が施されていた The shopping street *has been* already *decorated* for Christmas.
‖装飾品 a decoration, an ornament / 室内装飾 interior decoration [design]

そうしょく² 草食 ──草食の grass-eating,《公式的》herbivorous ∥草食動物 a herbivorous animal, a herbivore

ぞうしょく 増殖 (細胞などの) multiplication ⓤ; (増加) increase ⓤ ──増殖する multiply 自; increase 自
‖高速増殖炉 a fast breeder reactor

そうしん 送信 transmission ⓤ ──送信する transmit 他 ∥宇宙探査機が月の裏側の映像を送信してきた The space probe *transmitted* photos of the far side of the moon.
◆メールを送信する *send* an e-mail
‖送信機 a transmitter

ぞうしん 増進 (増加) increase ⓒ; (向上) improvement ⓒ; (促進) promotion ⓤ ──増進する increase 自; improve 他; promote 他 ∥祖母は健康増進のために毎朝散歩している My grandmother takes a walk every morning to *improve* her health. / 私は秋になると食欲が増進する My appetite *increases* in the autumn. / I have a *better* appetite in the autumn.

そうしんぐ 装身具 accessories; (宝石のついた) jewelry ⓤ

ぞうすい¹ 増水 ──増水する (水位が上がる) rise* 自; (水量が増える) swell* 自 他 ∥台風の後,川は4メートル近く増水した The river *rose* almost four meters after the typhoon.

ぞうすい² 雑炊 (a) zosui, a kind of rice porridge cooked with vegetables, fish meat, or eggs

そうすう 総数 the total number ∥応募総数は2万towards達した *The total number* of applicants reached 20,000.

そうすかん 総すかん 彼は勝手なことばかり言うのでクラスのみんなから総すかんを食った Everyone in the class *turned their backs on* him because he was always selfish.

そうすると そうすると (それでは) then (❖通例文頭か文尾で), so (❖文頭で); (もしそうならば) if so, in that case ∥そうすると今度は私の番だ It's my turn, *then*. / そうするとあしたは来ないんだね? *So*, you're not coming tomorrow? / 彼女が遅れるかもしれないって? そうすると代役を探さなければならないな You say she may

be late? *If so* [*In that case*] we need to find a substitute for her.
◆２つ目の信号を右に曲がってください．そうすると左手に黒い建物が見えます Turn to the right at the second light. *And* you will see a black building on your left.

そうすれば すぐに謝りなさい．そうすれば彼も分かってくれるでしょう You must apologize to him right now, *then* he will understand. / しっかり勉強しなさい．そうすればいい点数が取れるよ Work hard, *and* you can get a good mark. / 僕のラケットを貸してあげるよ，そうすれば買わなくてすむだろう I'll lend you my racket. *It*'ll save you buying one.

そうぜい 総勢 in all, strong（❖数詞の後で用いる）∥参加者は総勢80名だった There were 80 participants *in all.* / 総勢およそ２万の兵がここに駐留している The army of nearly twenty thousand *strong* is stationed here.

そうせい 造成 development [U] ―造成する develop [他] ∥宅地を造成する *develop* land for housing lots
‖造成地 a development

そうぜい 増税 tax increase [C] ―増税する increase [raise] taxes ∥増税に強く反対する be strongly opposed to *a tax increase*

そうせいき 創世記 （旧約聖書の） Genesis

そうせいじ 双生児 （２人） twins; （２人のうちの１人） twin [C]
‖一卵性[二卵性]双生児 identical [fraternal] twins

そうせつ 創設 foundation [U], establishment [U] ―創設する found [他], establish [他] ⇒そうりつ ∥大学を創設する *found* [*establish*] a university
‖創設者 a founder

そうぜつ 壮絶 壮絶な戦い a *fierce* [（→全力での）an *all-out*] battle / 彼女は壮絶な最期を遂げた She died a *heroic* [（→劇的な）*dramatic*] death.

そうせつ 増設 ―増設する （施設·設備などを） establish [他], set* up; （電話を） install [他] ∥新しい部署を増設する *establish* [*set up*] a new department / 電話を２本増設する *install* two *more* telephones

そうぜん 騒然 会場は騒然としていた The hall *was in a state of confusion.* / 彼らの突然の解散宣言に場内は騒然となった Their sudden announcement about breaking up the group *threw* the audience *into an uproar* [*a commotion*].

ぞうせん 造船 shipbuilding [U] ‖造船会社 a shipbuilding company / 造船業 the shipbuilding industry / 造船所 a shipyard, a dockyard

そうせんきょ 総選挙 general election [C] ∥来年早々総選挙があるとのうわさだ It's rumored that *the general election* will take place early next year.

そうそう[1] 早々 ❶【急いで】―早々に hurriedly, hastily ◆彼らは早々に引き上げた They beat a *hasty* retreat.
❷【…してすぐに】（時期の初め） early; （…するないなや） as soon as ... ∥来週早々にお電話します I'll give you a call *early* next week. / 母は帰宅早々夕飯のしたくに取りかかった My mother started preparing for dinner *as soon as* she came home.

そうそう[2] 草々

> 英語には「草々」に当たる表現はないが，手紙を終わらせるときの文句は Sincerely yours, Sincerely などを用いればよい．

そうそう[3] 葬送 葬送行進曲 a *funeral* march

そうそう[4] 錚々 パーティーには経済界のそうそうたる人たちが出席した *Leading* figures from the economic world attended the party.

そうぞう[1] 想像

imagination [U] [C]; （空想） fancy [U]; （推量） guess [C] ―想像する imagine [他]; fancy [他]; guess [自] [他]

想像を絶する *beyond all imagination*
君の考えていることくらい想像がつくよ I *can guess* what you think.
ご想像におまかせします I leave it to *your imagination.*
彼女は想像力が豊か[貧困]だ She *has a rich* [*poor*] *imagination.*
想像力を働かせなさい *Use your imagination.*
彼の話は私の想像力をかきたてる His story *stimulates* my *imagination.*
試験は想像していたよりずっとやさしかった The exam was much easier than I *had imagined* [*expected*].
テレビのない生活なんて想像できない I *can't imagine* life without a TV set.
私の想像したとおりだ I *guessed it right.*/ It's *just as* I *imagined.*
彼女は想像力をたくましくして物語を書いた She *gave free rein to her imagination* and wrote her story.
◆想像上の動物 an *imaginary* animal / 想像妊娠だった That was *a false pregnancy.* / 1,000年後の地球がどうなっているかなんて想像もつかない I *have no idea* what will become of the earth in 1,000 years. / 100万円が当たったらと想像するだけでわくわくする *Just thinking* about winning one million yen makes me excited.

そうぞう[2] 創造 creation [U] ―創造する create [他], make* [他] ∥新しい時代を創造する *create* a new age
◆彼女は創造性に富んでいる She *is creative.*
‖創造力 creative power

そうぞうしい 騒々しい noisy ∥教室は騒々しくて勉強どころではなかった The classroom was too *noisy* to study. / 騒々しい子供たちだな What *noisy* children they are!
◆その年は世の中がとても騒々しかった That year was a very *turbulent* time.

そうぞく 相続 inheritance [U]; （地位の） succession [U] ―相続する inherit [他]; （継ぐ） succeed [自] [他] ∥彼は莫大(ばくだい)な遺産を相続した He *inherited* [*succeeded to*] a large for-

tune. / 彼は昨年父親の跡目を相続してその会社の社長になった Last year he *succeeded* his father as president of the company.
‖相続争い a quarrel over an inheritance / 相続税 《米》an inheritance tax,《英》death duties / 相続人 an heir [éər]
そうそふ 曾祖父 great-grandfather ⓒ
そうそぼ 曾祖母 great-grandmother ⓒ
そうそん 曾孫 great-grandchild ⓒ

-そうだ
❶【…という話だ】 I hear [heard] (that) …; (うわさで) They [People] say (that) …, 《公式的》It is said (that) …

彼女は就職が決まったそうだ *I hear* she got a job.

今度のスター・ウォーズシリーズはおもしろいそうだ *They say* the latest in the *Star Wars* series is interesting.

山田先生が学校を辞めるそうだ *It is said that* Miss Yamada is leaving the school.

◆彼女はあした来られないそうだ *She said* she couldn't come tomorrow. / 康之は夏休みにオーストラリアに行くそうだ(→本人から言われた) *I'm told that* Yasuyuki will go to Australia during this summer vacation.

❷【…に見える・思われる】 look ⓛ; seem ⓛ; appear ⓛ; sound ⓛ

　look: 客観的に…のように見える.
　seem: 主観的に…のように思われる.
　appear: 外見上…のように見える.
　sound: 聞いて…のように思われる.

【look+(to be) 形[名]】 彼は元気そうだった He *looked* fine. / わあ、おいしそうなケーキ Oh, this cake *looks* good.

【look+like 名】 雨が降りそうだ It *looks like* rain.

【It seems [appears]+(to 名(人))+that 節】 それなら彼にもできそうだ It *seems to me that* even he can do that.

【seem [appear]+(to be) 形[名]】 彼らは幸せそうに見えた They *appeared to be* happy.

【sound+形[副]】 それはおもしろそうだね It *sounds* interesting.

英作文ノート「幸せそうに」の英語は?
彼女はいつも幸せそうに見える
→×She always looks *happily*.
→○She always looks *happy*.
★She is happy.(彼女は幸せだ)と比較すると形容詞 happy の働きが分かりやすい. 副詞 happily は, She danced with him happily.(彼女は幸せそうに彼とダンスをした)のように用いる.

---

❸【…しそうである】 (…する寸前だ) be going to *do*, be about to *do*; (おそらく…だ) be likely to *do*

花が枯れそうだ The flowers *are going to* die.

男の子は今にも泣き出しそうだった The boy *was about to* cry.

彼はあのパーティーに来そうにない He *is not likely to* come to the party tomorrow.

いかにもあいつの考えそうなことだ That's just what he *is likely to* think (of).

◆よそ見をしていて電柱にぶつかりそうになった I looked away and *almost* ran into a utility pole. / おなかが減って死にそうだ I *am dying* of hunger.

そうたい¹ 早退 彼女は気分が悪くなって学校を早退した She got sick and *left school early* [*earlier than usual*].

そうたい² 相対 ——相対的な relative ——相対的に relatively 〃偏差値というのは相対的なものだ Deviation value is *relative*. / 彼は相撲取りとしては相対的に見て小柄だ He is *relatively* small for a sumo wrestler.
‖相対性理論 the theory [principle] of relativity / 相対評価 grading on a curve

そうたい³ 総体 ——総体的に (全体的に) on the whole; (一般的に) in general, generally 〃総体的に今年の新入生はよく勉強する *On the whole* [*In general*], this year's new students study hard.

そうだい¹ 壮大 ——壮大な (雄大な) grand; (華麗な) magnificent 〃壮大な計画 a *grand* plan / 頂上からの眺めは壮大だった The view from the top of the mountain *was magnificent*.

そうだい² 総代 (代表) representative ⓒ; (卒業生の)《米》valedictorian ⓒ 〃小野は卒業生総代に選ばれた Ono was chosen as *valedictorian* for the graduation ceremony.

ぞうだい 増大 increase ⓒⓊ ——増大する (増加する) increase ⓛ, (大きくなる) grow* ⓛ ⇒ぞうか(増加) 〃需要の増大 *increase* in demand / 世界貿易におけるアジアの影響力は急激に増大している Asia's influence on world trade *is growing* rapidly.

そうだち 総立ち 観客はみな総立ちになった *All* the audience *rose from their seats* [*stood up*]. / 観衆は総立ちになって金メダリストに拍手を送った *All* the spectators *gave* the gold medalist *a standing ovation*.

そうだつ 争奪 (奪い合い) struggle ⓒ; (競争) competition ⓒ 〃彼をめぐって両球団の間で争奪戦が繰り広げられた There was *a struggle* for him between the two baseball teams.

そうだん 相談 (一般の) talk ⓒ; (専門家への) consultation Ⓤⓒ ——相談する talk ⓛ; consult ⓣⓛ

卒業後の進路を先生と相談した I「*talked to* [*had a talk with*] my teacher about what to do after graduation.

彼女はその件について弁護士に相談した She *consulted* a lawyer on the matter.

彼女は友達に結婚について相談を持ちかけた She *consulted* her friend about her marriage.

相談したいことがあるのですが I'd like to *talk to* you about something.

相談相手がだれもいない I have no *one to talk to*.

◆それについては家族と相談してからお答えします I'll give you an answer after I *have talked it over with* my family. / 彼のことを姉に相

そうち

談した(→アドバイスを求めた) I asked my sister *for advice* about my boyfriend. / 由美はいつも相談に乗ってくれる(→アドバイスをくれる) Yumi always *gives me advice*. / 価格は相談に応じます The price *is negotiable*.
∥相談員 an adviser [advisor], a counselor,《英》a counsellor;(専門の)a consultant / 相談役 a senior (corporate) adviser / 人生相談 advice on personal problems
慣用表現 それはつらい相談だ *You're asking the impossible*. / ものは相談だけどちょっとお金貸してもらえるかな *Could we discuss borrowing some money?*

そうち 装置 (仕掛け) device ⓒ;(設備) equipment Ⓤ;(器具一式) apparatus Ⓤⓒ /防火装置を取りつける install *fire prevention equipment* [*devices*]
◆すべての部屋に防音装置が設置されています All the rooms *are soundproofed*.
∥安全装置 a safety device / 制御装置 a control system / 舞台装置 a stage setting

ぞうちく 増築 extension Ⓤⓒ ──増築する (拡張する) extend 他;(建て増しする) build* an addition [extension] / 家を増築する *extend* a house / 校舎は一部増築された An *extension* was built onto the school building.

そうちゃく 装着 タイヤにチェーンを装着する *put a chain on a tire*

そうちょう¹ 早朝 early morning / きのうの早朝 *early* yesterday *morning*
/ 早朝に出発する leave *early in the morning*

そうちょう² 総長 (大学の)《米》president ⓒ,《英》chancellor ⓒ

そうちょう³ 荘重 solemnity Ⓤ ──荘重な solemn / 荘重な音楽 *solemn* music / 儀式は荘重に執(と)り行われた The ceremony was held *with solemnity*.

ぞうちょう 増長 ──増長する (思い上がる) be puffed up,《口語的》have* [get*] a swelled head / そんなことを言ったらますます彼を増長させてしまう If you say such a thing to him, he will *get* an even more *swelled head*.

そうっと ⇒そっと

そうで 総出 家族総出で弟の野球の試合を見に行った *All my* [*My whole*] *family* went to see a baseball game that my brother took part in.

そうてい¹ 想定 (推量) assumption ⓒ;(仮定) supposition ⓒ ◆阪神大震災クラスの地震を想定して避難訓練が行われた An evacuation drill took place *simulating* an earthquake of the Great Hanshin Earthquake level.

そうてい² 装丁 (製本) binding ⓒ;(デザイン) design Ⓤⓒ ──装丁する bind* 他; design 他 / 装丁のしっかりした本 a well-*bound* book / 彼は画家になる前、本の装丁の仕事をしていた He *had designed* books before he became a painter.

ぞうてい 贈呈 presentation Ⓤ ──贈呈する present 他 / 優勝者にトロフィーが贈呈された They *presented* a trophy to the champion.
∥贈呈式 a presentation ceremony

そうてん 争点 (要点) the point (at issue);(問題点) issue ⓒ / 政治改革が今回の選挙のいちばんの争点だ Political reform is *the main issue* in this election.

そうでん 送電 (電力を送ること) power [electric] transmission Ⓤ;(供給) power supply Ⓤ ──送電する transmit electricity [power] ∥送電線 a power line

そうとう 相当
❶〔かなり〕considerably, quite,《口語的》pretty;(ふつう以上に) rather ──相当な considerable
相当な額のお金が動いた They dealt with a *considerable* amount of money.
我々はもう相当な距離を走っている(→運転している) We've been driving a *considerable* distance.
あのつぼは相当古いらしい I hear the vase is *pretty* [*rather, quiet*] old.
彼の音楽に対する情熱は相当なものだ His enthusiasm for music is *considerable*.
◆彼は相当参っている様子だ He seems *very* upset. / それをするには相当な勇気がいる It takes *a lot of* courage to do it.
❷〔相応する〕──相当する (…に対応する) correspond to ...;(…に等しい) be equivalent to ..., be equal to ...
東京の区はニューヨーク市の borough に相当する Tokyo's wards *correspond to* New York City's boroughs.
1 フィートは30.48センチに相当する One foot *is equivalent* [*equal*] *to* 30.48 centimeters.
◆「わび」に相当する英語は何ですか What's the English word *for* "wabi"? / 100万円相当の指輪が盗まれた A ring *worth* one million yen was stolen. / 習い事をするにはそれ相当の(→ある程度の)お金がかかる We need *some* money to take lessons.

そうどう 騒動 (秩序・静寂などを乱すこと) disturbance ⓒ;(もめごと) trouble Ⓤ《また複数形～s》;(混乱) confusion Ⓤ;(暴動) riot ⓒ / 騒動を起こす make *a disturbance* / 騒動を鎮める quell *a disturbance* / 何やらひと騒動起きそうな予感がする I have a feeling that *some trouble* will come up. / 彼らがけんかしてクラス中が大騒動になった Their fight threw the whole class into *confusion*.
∥お家騒動 family troubles / 米騒動 a rice riot

ぞうとう 贈答 an exchange of gifts ◆贈答用に包んでください Please *gift-wrap* it.
∥贈答品 a gift

そうどういん 総動員 警官を総動員して警備にあたる *mobilize all* the police to guard

-そうな 彼女はうれしそうな顔をしていた She *looked* happy. / -そうだ

そうなめ 総なめ 無名のチームが強豪チームを総なめにした An unknown team *defeated* [*beat*] *all* the powerful teams. / マドンナはその年のグラミー賞を総なめにした Madonna *won most of* the Grammy awards of that

そうなん 遭難 accident ©; (船の) shipwreck © ∥山で遭難する have [meet] an accident in the mountains / この夏は山での遭難事故が多い There have been many accidents in the mountains this summer.
◆その船は日本海で遭難した The ship was wrecked in the Sea of Japan.
‖遭難救助隊 a rescue party / 遭難現場 the scene of an accident / 遭難者 a victim

そうに 雑煮

雑煮はおせちと同様に、正月の特別な料理です。地方によっていろいろな作り方があるますが、ふつう雑煮は、だし汁にしょうゆ、あるいはみそを加え、もち、とり肉、魚、様々な野菜などを入れたものをいいます。
Zoni is served as a special dish for the New Year like osechi. While zoni varies greatly from region to region, it usually consists of ingredients such as mochi, chicken, fish and vegetables in a broth of stock, soy sauce or sometimes miso.

そうにゅう 挿入 insertion Ⓤ© ——挿入する insert ⊕ ∥論文に図をいくつか挿入する insert some figures in the essay
◆挿入口に100円硬貨を入れる put a 100-yen coin in a slot
‖挿入句 a parenthesis

そうねん 壮年 彼はまだ壮年だ He is still in 「his prime [the prime of life].

そうは 走破 ——走破する run* the whole course ∥彼らは5,000キロを走破した They ran the whole course of 5,000 kilometers.

そうば 相場 (市価) market ©, market price ©; (為替の) rate ©; (投機) speculation Ⓤ© ∥相場に手を出す get engaged in speculation / 相場が上がっている[下がっている] The market is rising [falling]. / ここ1週間、相場は不安定な状態が続いている The market price has been unstable for a week. / スーパーのレジの時給は900円が相場だ The going rate of pay for a cashier at a supermarket is 900 yen per hour. (❖going rate は「現行の料金」の意味)
‖円相場 the exchange rates of the yen to other currencies / 株式相場 a stock market / 為替相場 the exchange rate
慣用表現 私が若いころは修学旅行といえば京都と奈良と相場が決まっていた When I was young, the standard destinations for school excursions were Kyoto and Nara.

そうはく 蒼白 彼は知らせを聞いて顔面着白になった He turned pale when he heard the news.

ぞうはつ 増発 ゴールデンウイークには列車が増発される They run extra trains during the "Golden Week" holidays.

そうばん 早晩 (遅かれ早かれ) sooner or later; (いずれは) in time ∥この問題は早晩決着するだろう This problem will sooner or later come to a conclusion.

ぞうはん 造反 rebellion Ⓤ© ——造反する rebel ⊕ ∥造反者 a rebel

そうび 装備 equipment Ⓤ ——装備する equip ⊕ ∥この船には無線が装備されている This boat is equipped with a radio. / 兵士たちは重装備をしていた The soldiers were equipped with heavy weapons. / 彼らは完全装備で登山に行った They went mountain climbing fully equipped.

そうひょう 総評 general comment ©

そうびょう 躁病 〖医学〗 mania ©Ⓤ

そうふ 送付 ——送付する send*⊕, deliver ⊕; (金銭・小切手などを)〖公式的〗remit ⊕ ∥客に請求書を送付する send bills to a customer
‖送付先 a destination

そうふう 送風 (換気) ventilation Ⓤ ——送風する ventilate ⊕ ∥送風機 a ventilator

ぞうふく 増幅 〖電気〗 amplification ——増幅する 〖電気〗 amplify ◆あたりの静けさが彼らの恐怖を増幅させた The silence around there increased their fear.

ぞうへいきょく 造幣局 mint ©

そうへき 双璧 彼女たちは女子テニス界の双璧だった They were the two greatest women tennis players.

そうべつ 送別 ——送別の farewell ∥送別会を開く have a farewell [send-off] party

そうほう 双方 both (sides) ——双方の both; (相互の) mutual ∥労資双方 both labor and management / 先生は双方の意見を聞いた The teacher heard both of their opinions. / 双方互角の戦いになった Both were well matched. / 彼らは双方合意のうえで離婚した They got divorced by mutual agreement.
◆その協議では双方とも譲ろうとしなかった Neither side would give up in the discussion. (❖neither は「双方とも…ない」の意味)

そうほんざん 総本山 the head temple ∥天台宗総本山延暦寺 Enryakuji, the head temple of the Tendai sect

そうむ 総務 (仕事) general affairs; (人) a person in charge of general affairs
‖総務庁 the Management and Coordination Agency (❖2001年総務省に統合) / 総務部 the general affairs department

そうむしょう 総務省 the Ministry of Public Management, Home Affairs, Posts and Telecommunications

そうめい 聡明 ——聡明な intelligent; (利発な) bright ∥彼女は聡明な人だと思う I think her (to be) an intelligent [a bright] woman.

そうめん 素麺

そうめんは日本で昔から食べられてきためんで、小麦で作る非常に細いめんです。そうめんを盛る器に冷水を入れて、いわゆる冷やしそうめんとして食べるのが最も一般的で、特製のつゆにつけて
Somen, a kind of traditional Japanese noodles, is made of wheat and is very

そうもくろく 総目録 general catalog ©; (完全なリスト) complete list ©

ぞうもつ 臓物 entrails ©; (鳥 の) giblets; (牛・豚などの) the pluck; (食用の) organ [variety] meat ©

ぞうよ 贈与 ―贈与する give*⊕, present ⊕; (寄付する) donate ⊕⊜
‖贈与税 a gift tax

そうらん 騒乱 disturbance ©; (暴動) riot ©. ‖騒乱を起こす[鎮める] cause [put down] *a riot* / その国ではいまだに騒乱が続いている *The disturbance* still continues in the country.

そうり 総理 ‖総理大臣 the Prime Minister, the Premier (《略語》PM) / 総理府 the Prime Minister's Office (❖2001年内閣府に統合)

ぞうり 草履

着物用の履き物をぞうりと呼んでいます。ぞうりもげたも鼻緒がついていますが、ぞうりを履くときには足袋(⊛)を履くのに対し、ふつうげたは素足です。また、げたは木でできていて2本の歯がついていますが、ぞうりは皮製からビニール製のものまで様々で、底は平らで歯はついていません。昔はわらやいぐさで作られたぞうりが一般的な庶民の履き物でした。

The sandals worn with *kimono* are called *zori*. Both *zori* and *geta* have a thong that comes between the big and second toes, but *zori* are usually worn with *tabi* (divided socks) while *geta* are worn barefoot. And while *geta* are made of wood and have two projections attached to the sole, *zori* can be made of various materials, including leather and plastic, and they have flat soles. In the past, *zori* made of woven straw or rushes were the usual footwear for ordinary people.

そうりつ 創立 foundation ⓤ, the founding, establishment ⓤ ―創立する found ⊕, establish ⊕, set* up ‖私たちの学校は1910年に創立された Our school *was founded* [*established*] in 1910. / その会社は創立60周年を迎えた The company celebrated the 60th anniversary of *its founding*.
‖創立記念日 the anniversary of the founding / 創立者 a founder

そうりょ 僧侶 (Buddhist) priest ©; (修道僧) (Buddhist) monk ©

そうりょう 送料 (郵便料金) postage ⓤ; (配達料) delivery charge ©©. ‖送料無料 *postage* free / 送料込みで *postage* included / 送料は800円[別]です *The delivery charges* are 「800 yen [extra]. / この小包の送料はいくらですか What is *the postage* for sending this parcel?

そうりょうじ 総領事 consul general ©
‖総領事館 a consulate general

そうりょく 総力 教育関係者はいじめの問題に総力を挙げて(→全力で)取り組まねばならない All those concerned with education must tackle the bullying problem *with all their might* [*power*]. / その事件を解決するために警察は総力を結集した The police *concentrated all their efforts on* solving the case.
‖総力戦 an all-out [a total] war

ソウル Seoul (❖韓国の首都)

そうるい 走塁 (base) running ⓤ ‖走塁妨害 obstruction

ソウルミュージック soul music ⓤ

そうれい 壮麗 ―壮麗な magnificent; (壮大な) grand; (華麗な) splendid ‖壮麗な寺院 a *magnificent* temple

そうれつ¹ 壮烈 ―壮烈な (英雄的な) heroic; (勇敢な) brave ‖壮烈な最期を遂げる die a *heroic* [*brave*] death

そうれつ² 葬列 funeral procession ©

そうろ 走路 (競技場の) track ©; (マラソンの) course ©

そうろん 総論 general remarks; (概論) introduction ©, outline © ◆総論から各論に移る go from *the general* to the particular

そうわ 挿話 episode ©

ぞうわい 贈賄 bribery ⓤ (❖「収賄」の意味もある) ‖彼らは贈賄事件に直接関与していた They were directly connected with *the bribery*.
‖贈賄罪 the crime of bribery

そえがき 添え書き (注記) note ©; (付記) (公式的) rider ©

そえもの 添え物 (付属物) (公式的) appendage ©; (料理の) garnish ©

そえる 添える attach ⊕; (料理の付け合わせを) garnish ⊕ ‖勝利に花を添える add glory to the victory / プレゼントには手紙が添えてあった A letter was *attached* to the present. / 彼女はハンバーグステーキにクレソンを添えた She *garnished* hamburger steaks *with* watercress.
◆カードを添えて仁美に花束を送った I sent Hitomi a bouquet (*together*) *with* a card.

そえん 疎遠 僕らは卒業以来疎遠になってしまった We *grew apart from* each other after our graduation.

ソース¹ ⚠ sauce ⓤ© (❖英語では、ドレッシングやしょうゆなど食べ物にかける液体調味料はすべて sauce という。日本で一般にいう「ソース」は Worcester(shire) sauce) ‖タルタルソース tartar [tartare] *sauce* / トマト味のソース tomato-based *sauce* / とんかつにソースをかける put *sauce* on a pork cutlet

ソース² (出所) source © ‖ニュースソース *a* (news) *source*

ソーセージ sausage ⓤ© ‖ウインナソーセージ (a) Vienna sausage, 《米》(a) wiener (❖「ウインナソーセージ」は和製英語) / フランクフルトソーセージ a frankfurter

ソーダ soda ⓤ; (ソーダ水) soda (water) ⓤ; (口語的) pop ⓤ / クリームソーダ *an* ice-cream *soda* (❖《米》では soda ともいう)

ソーラー ‖ソーラーカー a solar car / ソーラ

―システム a solar heating system
ゾーン zone ◯

そかい 疎開 evacuation ◯ ―疎開する evacuate 自 ∥彼女は戦時中, 両親のいなかに疎開していた She *evacuated* to her parents' (house) in the countryside during the war.

そがい¹ 阻害 obstruction ◯, hindrance ―阻害する obstruct 他, hinder 他 ∥子供の自然な発育を阻害する *obstruct* [*hinder*] the natural growth of a child

そがい² 疎外 alienation ◯ ―疎外する alienate 他, leave* out ∥彼女はクラスの仲間から疎外されていた She *was alienated* from her classmates. / 彼は社会からの疎外感を味わっていた He *felt alienated* from society.

そかく 組閣 ∥新内閣が組閣された A new cabinet *was formed*.

-そく -足 ∥靴1足 *a pair of* shoes / 靴下2足 *two pairs of* socks

そぐ 削ぐ (薄く削る) pare 他; (やる気などを) damp 他, deaden 他 ∥竹をそいでくしを作る *pare* [*whittle, shave*] a piece of bamboo to make a skewer ◆その話を聞いて勉強する意欲をそがれた(→失った) When I heard the story, I *lost* my drive to study.

ぞく¹ 俗 (卑俗な) vulgar; (世俗的) worldly; (低俗な) low ∥俗な趣味 *low* [*vulgar*] tastes
慣用表現 彼は母親がいないと何ひとつできない人間, 俗にいうマザコンだ He cannot do anything without his mother. *As is commonly said* [*As they say*], he's a mama's boy.

ぞく² 賊 (泥棒) thief ◯ (複 thieves); (強盗) robber ◯; (押し入り強盗) burglar ◯; (反逆者) rebel ◯, insurgent ◯《しばしば複数形～s》

ぞく³ 属 【生物】 genus ◯ (複 genera, ~es)

ぞく- 続- sequel [síːkwəl] ◯ ➡ ぞくへん

-ぞく -族 (家族・一族・語族) family ◯; (部族・生物学上の) tribe ◯ ∥インド・ヨーロッパ語族 the Indo-European *family* / ズールー族 the Zulu (*tribe*)

ぞくあく 俗悪 ―俗悪な coarse, vulgar ∥俗悪な番組 a *coarse* [*vulgar*] program

そくい 即位 enthronement ◯◯; (継承) (公式的) accession ◯ ―即位する mount [ascend] the throne

ぞくうけ 俗受け ∥その小説は俗うけしなかった The novel didn't *appeal to the general public*.

そくおう 即応 ―即応する (適する) fit* 自 他; (対処する) cope with ... ∥この福祉政策は時代の要求に即応したものだ This welfare policy *fits* (*to*) the demands of the times.

ぞくご 俗語 slang ◯ ―俗語的な slang, slangy ∥俗語的な言い回し a *slangy* expression / chickenは俗語で臆病(おくびょう)者のことだ "Chicken" is *slang* for a coward.

そくざ 即座 ―即座の immediate, ready ―即座に immediately, at once, right away; (その場で) on the spot ➡ すぐ, ただちに

に ∥即座の機転がきく人 a man of *ready* wit / 彼女は即座に彼の正体を見破った She found him out *at once*. / 彼女は彼の誘いを即座に断った She declined his invitation *on the spot*.

そくし 即死 instant death ◯ ―即死する be killed instantly ∥その墜落事故で乗客は全員即死だった All the passengers *were killed instantly* in the crash.

そくじ 即時 immediately, instantly, at once, right away ∥国連安全保障理事会は両国の即時停戦を求めた The UNSC demanded that the two countries (should) cease fire *immediately* [*at once*].
∥即時払い immediate [prompt] payment

ぞくじ 俗事 worldly [secular] affairs ∥俗事に追われる be busy with *worldly affairs* / 彼女は俗事にうとい She knows little of *worldly affairs*.

そくじつ 即日 the same day ∥試験の結果は即日発表される The results of the exam are to be announced *on the same day*.
∥即日開票 ballot counting on the day of the election / 即日仕上げ same day service / 即日配達 same day delivery

ぞくしゅつ 続出 ∥インフルエンザで学校を休む生徒が続出した Students were absent from school *one after another* due to flu.

ぞくしょう 俗称 (学名に対する) vernacular name ◯; (通称) common [popular] name ◯

そくしん 促進 promotion ◯◯; (奨励) encouragement ◯ ―促進する promote 他; encourage 他; (公式的) foster 他 ∥産業の発展を促進する *encourage* [*foster*] the growth of industries / 我々は販売促進のためのあらゆる可能性を検討してきた We have explored all the possibilities of *promoting sales*.

ぞくしん 俗信 popular belief ◯; (迷信) popular superstition ◯

そくする 即する ∥彼の提案は実情に即していない His suggestion does not 「*conform to* [*meet the needs of*] the present situation. / この物語は事実に即して作られている This story *is based on* the facts.

ぞくする 属する belong to ... (❖「属している」という場合も進行形にはならない); (部門に) come* [be] under ...
パンダは乳類に属する Pandas 「*come under* [*belong to*] the category of mammals.
ドイツ語はゲルマン語派に属している German *belongs to* the Germanic group of languages.
その島はかつて日本に属していた The island *was under* the rule of Japan once.
◆少数派に属している *be in* the minority

そくせい 速成 ∥プログラマーを速成する *train* programmers *in haste*

ぞくせい 属性 attribute ◯ ➡ せいしつ

そくせいさいばい 促成栽培 forcing culture ◯ ◆イチゴを促成栽培する *force* strawberries

そくせき¹ 即席 ―即席の (料理などが) in-

stant; (その場の・準備なしの) impromptu [imprámptu:] ∥即席チャーハン *instant* Chinese fried rice / 彼は即席ですばらしい講演をした He gave an excellent *impromptu* speech.
◆即席で橋を作る *improvise* a bridge

そくせき² 足跡 footprint [C]; (業績) achievement [C] ➔あしあと ◆女性解放運動の足跡をたどる *trace the history* of the feminist movement / 彼は20世紀の音楽史に偉大な足跡を残した He made *a* great *contribution* to the history of music in the 20th century.

ぞくせけん 俗世間 the secular world
◆俗世間を捨てる quit *secular life*

ぞくせつ 俗説 (根拠のない説) old wives' tale [C]

そくせんりょく 即戦力 彼はこの新事業の即戦力として期待されている He is expected to 「*be useful* [*work*] *immediately* for this new business.

ぞくぞく¹ ―ぞくぞくする (寒さ・恐怖で) feel* a chill, shiver [自]; (興奮して震える) be thrilled ∥彼は翌日の試合のことを考えるとぞくぞくした He *was thrilled* to think about tomorrow's game.
◆この小説はぞくぞくするほどおもしろい This novel *is thrilling* and enjoyable.
💬「体がぞくぞくする」「かぜよ, きっと」"I *feel a chill* [*shiver*]." "You've probably caught (a) cold."

ぞくぞく² 続々 コンサート会場に人が続々とやって来た People came to the concert hall *one after another.* / 救援物資が続々と被災地に到着した Relief supplies got to the disaster area *in succession.* / 人々が続々とスタジアムから出てきた *A stream of* people came out of the stadium.

そくたつ 速達 special delivery [C] [U], 《英》 express [U] ∥この手紙を速達で出すと, いつ着きますか If I send this letter by *special delivery*, when will it arrive (there)?
∥速達郵便 special delivery mail / 速達料金 a special [《英》an express] delivery charge

そくだん¹ 即断 prompt [immediate] decision [C] ―即断する decide promptly [immediately], make* a prompt [an immediate] decision

そくだん² 速断 (速やかな決断) quick decision [C]; (早まった決断) hasty decision [C] ∥速断は慎むべきだ We should not *make a hasty decision.*
◆速断を要するneed to *decide quickly*

ぞくっぽい 俗っぽい (世俗的な) worldly; (通俗的な) popular; (品のない) vulgar ∥俗っぽい言い方 a *popular* expression

そくてい 測定 measurement [U] ―測定する (長さ・量などを) measure [他]; (重さを) weigh [wéi] [他] ➔はかる(計る・測る・量る) ∥血圧の測定 *the measurement* of blood pressure / 耕地面積の測定を行う *measure* cultivated acreage
∥体力測定 a test of physical strength

そくど 速度 speed [C] [U]; 〔物理〕 velocity [C] ➔スピード
速度を上げる 「pick up [gather] *speed* / 速度を落とす lose [decrease, drop] *speed* / 一定の速度を保つ keep *a* steady *speed* / 時速60キロの速度で車を運転する drive a car at *a speed* of 60 kilometers an hour
光は音よりも速度が速い Light travels at *a* higher *speed* than sound.
この道路の制限速度は時速50キロです *The speed limit* on this road is 50 kilometers an hour.
その車はかなりの速度で走っていた The car was going *at quite a high speed.*
◆車はその建物の近くで速度を落として止まった The car *slowed down* to a stop near the building.
∥速度計 a speedometer / 速度制限 speed restrictions / 最高速度 the maximum speed / 瞬間速度 an instantaneous speed / 平均速度 an average speed

そくとう 即答 prompt [immediate, quick] answer [C] ∥即答を避ける avoid *giving a prompt* [*an immediate, a quick*] *answer* / 即答はできません I can't *give you an immediate* [*a ready*] *answer.*

ぞくとう 続投 そのチームの監督の来季の続投が決まった It was decided that the manager of the team would *continue to manage* next season.

そくどく 速読 speed reading [U] ―速読する read* speedily [rapidly], speed-read* [他] [自] ∥速読術 the art of speed reading

そくばい 即売 spot sale [C]
◆彼女はランの展示即売会に出かけた She went out to *the exhibition and sale* of orchids.

そくばく 束縛 (拘束) restraint [U] [C]; (制限) restriction [C] [U] ―束縛する restrain [他], tie [他]; restrict [他] ∥…の束縛から解放される be relieved from *the restraint* of … / 僕は何物にも束縛されたくない I don't like to *be restricted* at all. / だれも人の自由を束縛することはできない No one should *restrict* others' freedom.
◆時間に束縛されて, お寺をゆっくり見学することができなかった *Having limited time,* we couldn't visit the temples leisurely.

ぞくはつ 続発 先月この近所で事件が続発した *There was a rash* [*succession*] *of* cases in this neighborhood last month.

ぞくぶつ 俗物 snob [C]; (俗人) worldly person [C] ∥俗物根性 snobbery

ぞくへん 続編 (本などの) sequel [sí:kwəl] [C]; (番組などの) spin-off [C] ∥彼女は『明暗』の続編を書いた She wrote *a sequel to Meian.*

そくほう 速報 (news) flash [C], prompt report [C] ∥ニュース速報 *a news flash*
◆開票結果がインターネットで速報された The results of the election *were reported promptly* on the Internet.

ぞくほう 続報 later report [C], follow-up report [C]
◆続報が入りしだいお伝えします We'll give *fur-*

そくめん 側面 side ◯; (局面) aspect ◯, phase ◯ ∥彼の性格の優しい側面 the gentle *side* of his character / 問題をあらゆる側面から検討する discuss every *aspect* of a problem / 車の側面にオートバイがつっ込んだ A motorcycle crashed into *the side* of a car. / 当番組ではこの戦争の政治的内面に光を当ててみたいと思います We'll clarify the political *aspect* of the war in this program.
◆難民を側面から(→間接的に)援助する help refugees *indirectly*
∥側面図 a side view

そくりょう 測量 measurement ◯; (土地などの) survey ◯ ∥━━測量する survey 他自 / 土地の測量を行う *survey* [*make a survey of*] the land
∥測量機器 a surveying instrument / 測量技師 a surveyor

そくりょく 速力 speed ◯◯ ⇒ そくど, ぜんそくりょく

そぐわない その場にそぐわない音楽 an *unsuitable* [*inappropriate*] piece of music for the occasion / その法律はもはや現実にそぐわないものになっている The law *doesn't suit* this present situation any longer. / 彼女の服装はそのパーティーにそぐわなかった(→場違いだった) Her dress *was out of place* at the party.

そげき 狙撃 sniping ◯; (銃撃) shooting ◯ ━━狙撃する snipe at ...; shoot* 他自 / きのうそのビルで有名な政治家が狙撃された A famous statesman *was sniped* [*shot*] *at* in the building yesterday.

ソケット socket ◯ ∥この電球はソケットに入らない This bulb doesn't fit into *the socket*.

そこ¹ 底

bottom ◯《通例 the 〜》, floor ◯; (川・海などの) bed ◯; (靴の) sole ◯
海の底 *the sea bed*; *the bottom* of the sea
紙袋の底が抜けた *The bottom* fell out of the paper bag.
その箱は二重底(→上げ底)だ The box has *a raised bottom*.
ビーカーの底に白い粉が沈殿した White powder has settled down to *the bottom* of the beaker.
この人造湖の底には村が沈んでいる A village lies at *the bottom* of this artificial lake.
彼女は彼のことを心の底から愛していた She loved him *from the bottom of her heart*.
◆ゴム底のスニーカー *rubber-soled* sneakers
慣用表現 底の浅い(→表面的な)知識 *superficial* knowledge / 物価はついに底を打ったようだ Prices seem to *have hit bottom* at last. / 食料品の蓄えが底をついた(→尽きた) The food stock *ran out*. / 彼は腹の底から笑った He gave a *hearty* laugh.
⇒ そこなし

そこ²

❶【場所】there; (その場所) that place; (それ・その) that
《そこで・に》
うちの犬はいつもそこで寝る Our dog always sleeps *there*.
5時までにそこに着くのは難しい It is hard for me to get *there* by five.
そこにはたくさんの人がいた There were a lot of people *there*.
その地震のニュースを聞いて, そこにいる友人の安否を気づかった When I heard the news of the earthquake, I feared for (the safety of) my friends *there*.
◆私たちはニューヨークへ行き, そこに1週間滞在した We went to New York, *where* we stayed a week.
🅔 「そこにいるのはだれ」「私, 佳織よ」 "Who's *there*?" "Me, Kaori."
《そこまで》
そこまで歩いて10分ほどだった It took me about ten minutes to walk *there*.
◆そこまでしか行けませんでした I could go only *that far*.(❖that far は「その程度離れた所に」の意味) / クリスマスはもうそこまで来ている Christmas is *just around the corner*.
《その他》
そこがふろ場です *That* is the bathroom.
私の代わりにそこへ行ってくれますか Will you go *there* for me?
そこから何が見えますか What can you see *from there*?
私の家はすぐそこです My house is right *over there*.
◆そこをどいてください Get out of *my way*, please.
❷【程度・範囲】
そこまで自分を責めることはないよ You don't have to feel *so* sorry.
そこまでは思いつかなかった I couldn't think *that much*.
❸【そのとき】then
ちょうどそこへ父が帰ってきた My father came home just *then*.
❹【その点】that
そこのところを詳しく説明してください Please explain *that* (*point*) in detail.
私は彼のそこがいちばん好きなんです *That*'s the thing I like most about him.
問題はそこだ *That*'s the question. / It's *there* that the problem lies.

そこあげ 底上げ 国民の生活水準を底上げする *raise* [*improve*] the standard of living of the people

そこいじ 底意地 彼は底意地が悪い He *is mean* [*spiteful*] *at heart*.

そこう 素行 behavior, 《英》behaviour ◯; (道徳上の)《公式的》conduct ◯ ◆あの生徒は日ごろの素行が悪い That student always *behaves* badly. / 少年は素行を改めた The boy 「*reformed* (*himself*) [*mended his ways*].

そこく 祖国 *one's* homeland, *one's* (own) country ∥祖国を捨てる leave *one's country* / 彼らは祖国の名誉のために戦った They fought for the honor of *their country*.

そこしれない 底知れない その選手は底知れない可能性を秘めている The player has *fathomless* potential.

そこそこ そこそこの(→並みの)品質のダイヤモンド a diamond of *moderate* quality / 彼は宿題もそこそこに出かけた He *hurried through* his homework and then went out.

●「調子はどう」「そこそこだよ」 "How are you doing?" *"Just so-so."*

-そこそこ 秀夫は100メートルを11秒そこそこで走る Hideo runs 100 meters in *a little over* 11 seconds. / ホールには20人そこそこしかいなかった There were 20 people in the hall *at most*.

そこぢから 底力 (隠された力) hidden [potential] strength ◎;(本当の力) real strength ◎ /底力を発揮する show *one's hidden [real] strength*

そこつ 粗忽 —そこつな (不注意な) careless; (軽率な) rash /そこつ者 a careless [rash] person, a blunderer

そこで (だから) (and) so, therefore ⇒ そこ² / 今困っているんだ。そこで頼みがある I'm in trouble now, *(and)* so can I ask you a favor? ◆学校に着いて、そこで初めて忘れ物に気がついた I arrived at school, *and then* I realized I had forgotten something. / 前の方法ではコストがかかりすぎた。そこで考え出されたのがこの方法だ Our former method was too costly. *That's why* we thought out this one.

そこなう 損なう spoil*◎;(健康などを) injure ◎, damage ◎;(ひどく損なう) ruin ◎ / 人々はその橋が川の景観を損なうと考えた People thought that the bridge would *spoil [mar]* the beauty of the river.

◆彼の機嫌を損なうと大変なことになるぞ If you 「*hurt* his feelings [*offend* him], you'll be in big trouble.

-そこなう -損なう miss ◎, fail to *do* /キャッチャーはボールを取りそこなった The catcher *missed* the ball. / いつもの電車に乗りそこなった I *missed* my usual train. / 彼女はわずか1点差で賞を取りそこなった She *failed to win* the prize by only one point.

そこなし 底無し —底なしの bottomless / 底なし沼 a *bottomless* swamp

◆父は底なしの大酒飲みだ My father is an *extremely* heavy drinker. / My father drinks *like a fish*.

そこぬけ 底抜け 底抜けに明るい *extremely* cheerful / 彼は底抜けの楽天家だった He was *totally* optimistic. / He was optimistic *to the core*.

そこねる 損ねる バスに乗りそこねる *miss* a bus / 彼女は働きすぎで健康を損ねた Overwork *ruined [damaged]* her health. / 会話をところどころ聞きそこねた I *missed* fragments of the conversation.

⇒そこなう、-そこなう

そこのけ その少女の包丁さばきは料理人そこのけだった (→料理人を恥じ入らせた) The girl's knife handling *put* a (professional) cook *to shame*.

そこはかとない あたりにはバラの香りがそこはかとなく漂っていた The air was fragrant *with the faint scent of* roses.

そこびえ 底冷え 今夜は底冷えがする(→とても寒い) It's *very cold [chilly]* tonight. / I *am chilled to the bone* tonight.

そこまで ⇒そこ²

そこら(へん) (場所) around there; (およそ) ... or so /そこらへんを散歩に行こう Let's go for a stroll *around there*. / 飛行機はあと10分かそこらで到着するでしょう The plane will arrive in about ten minutes *or so*. ◆おもちゃや人形がそこら中にあった Toys and dolls were 「*all over the place* [*everywhere*]. / この新しい辞書はそこらの辞書とはわけが違う This new dictionary isn't one of *those usual* dictionaries.

そざい 素材 material ◎ ◎;(題材) subject matter ◎ /透明な素材 *a transparent material* / 素材の持ち味を生かす make good use of *the material* / この服の素材は何ですか What is *the material* used in this dress?

そざつ 粗雑 —粗雑な (ぞんざいな) careless, sloppy; (粗削りな) rough; (不完全な) crude —粗雑に carelessly, sloppily; roughly; crudely / 粗雑な工事 *careless work* / 物を粗雑に扱う handle a thing *crudely [roughly]*

そし 阻止 prevention ◎;(妨害) obstruction ◎ —阻止する prevent ◎; obstruct ◎ /コレラ菌の日本上陸を阻止する *prevent* the spread of cholera bacteria to Japan / 彼らはその法案の成立を阻止しようとした They tried to 「*obstruct* the passage of the bill [*prevent* the bill *from* being passed].

そじ 素地 (基礎・下地) a grounding /彼にはすでに画家としての素地があった He already had *a grounding* as a painter.

そしき 組織

organization ◎ (❖特定の集団を指す場合は ◎); (体系立った) system ◎;(構造) structure ◎ ◎ —組織する organize ◎ ◎ / 委員会を組織する *organize [form]* a committee

国連は難民のために救済活動を組織した The U.N. *organized* a relief operation for the refugees.

警察は組織ぐるみの犯行と断定した The police concluded that it was *organized crime*.

◆葉の組織 leaf *tissue* / 組織立った考え方 a *systematic* way of thinking / 彼らは自然保護のための組織的な活動を展開している They are developing a *systematic* environmental movement. / その団体は200名で組織されている The organization *is composed of* 200 people.

‖組織図 an organization chart / 組織票 organized votes / 神経組織 nervous tissue / 政治組織 a political organization / 犯罪組織 a criminal syndicate

そしつ 素質 (資質) the makings; (才能) ap-

titude ©Ⓤ, **talent** ©Ⓤ, **gift** © ⇨ さいのう ‖君には一流のバイオリニストになる素質がある You have 「*the makings* of [*what it takes to be*] a first-rate violinist. / 彼女には語学の素質がある She has *a gift* for languages.

そして （並列）**and**;（時の経過）**and then**
⇨ それから
彼女はとても聡明で, そして優しい人だった She was a very wise *and* kind woman.
彼らは翌朝まで大いに飲み, そして大いに語った They drank *and* talked a lot until the next morning.
彼は書斎に机, いす, そしてソファーを必要としている He needs a desk, a chair(,) *and* a sofa in his study.
顔を洗い, そして歯を磨いた I washed my face *and* brushed my teeth.
◆私はエプロンを作り, そして母にあげた I made an apron, *which* I gave to my mother.

そしな 粗品（ささやかな贈り物）**small gift** © (❖英語には日本語のように贈り物をするとき謙遜(けんそん)する表現がないので, 「ささやかな贈り物」と考える) ‖粗品ですがお受け取りください This is just *a small gift*. I hope you'll like it.

そしゃく 咀嚼《公式的》**mastication** Ⓤ, **chewing** Ⓤ ──咀嚼する《公式的》**masticate** ⊕, **chew** ⊕ ‖食べ物を咀嚼する *chew* [*masticate*] food
◆彼の言葉の意味を十分に咀嚼する（→理解する）には時間がかかるだろう It'll take you a long time to *understand* the meaning of his words well.

そしょう 訴訟〔法律〕**suit** Ⓤ ©, **lawsuit** ©, **action** © ‖訴訟に勝つ［負ける］**win** [**lose**] *a suit* / 訴訟を取り下げる **withdraw** [**drop**] *a suit* / 彼らはその会社を相手取って損害賠償の訴訟を起こした They filed *a suit* [*an action*] for damages against the company.
◆離婚訴訟を起こす *file for divorce*
‖訴訟手続き **legal proceedings** / 訴訟費用 **costs** / 刑事訴訟 **a criminal suit** / 民事訴訟 **a civil suit**

そしょく 粗食（簡素な食事）**simple diet** ©;（栄養的に乏しい食事）**unnourishing food** Ⓤ ‖戦時中はみんなが粗食を強(し)いられた Everyone had to live on *simple diets* during the war.

そしらぬ 素知らぬ 彼女は私たちの前をそ知らぬ顔で通り過ぎた She passed by *ignoring* us. / 「こんにちは」とあいさつしたのに彼はそ知らぬ顔をした Though I greeted him with "Hello," he *pretended not to recognize me*.

そしり 謗り 人々のそしりを受ける（→批判される）**be criticized** by people / そんなことをすれば早計のそしりは免れない（→責められる）だろう If you do such a thing, you will *be blamed* for hastiness.

そしる 謗る （悪く言う）**speak* ill of** ...;（非難する）**criticize** ⊕; （責める）**blame** ⊕

そすう 素数〔数学〕**prime number** ©

そせい 蘇生 **revival** Ⓤ © ──蘇生する［させる］**revive** ⊕ ⊕, **come*** [**bring*** *a person*] **back to life** ⇨ いきかえる

そぜい 租税（税金）**tax** ©Ⓤ;（課税）**taxation** Ⓤ ⊕; **ぜい, ぜいきん** ‖租税収入 **tax revenue**

そせいらんぞう 粗製乱造 安物の時計を粗製乱造する *mass-produce* watches *of inferior quality*

そせき 礎石〔建築〕**foundation stone** ©; （隅石）〔建築〕**cornerstone** ©; （基礎）**foundation** ©

そせん 祖先 **ancestor** ©, 《集合的》**ancestry** Ⓤ ⇨ せんぞ ‖人類の祖先 the *ancestors* of humans

そそう 粗相 **carelessness** Ⓤ; （大へま）**blunder** © ‖粗相をしてコップを割ってしまった I broke a glass *because of my carelessness*.
◆子供が粗相をした（→おもらしをした）My child *wet his* [*her*] *pants*. / くれぐれも粗相のないように（→失礼のないように）Take great care not to *be impolite*.

そそぐ 注ぐ
❶【つぐ】**pour** ⊕
カップにコーヒーを注ぐ *pour* coffee into a cup
❷【流れ込む】**flow into** ...
黒部川は日本海に注ぐ The Kurobe River *flows into* the Sea of Japan.
❸【集中する】（努力などを）**devote** ⊕;（愛情などを）**shower** ⊕;（視線などを）**fix** ⊕
彼は新しい事業に全力を注いだ He 「*devoted all his energies to* [*poured all his energies into*] the new project.
その母親は息子に深い愛情を注いだ The mother *showered* her son *with* deep affections.
全世界がその新技術に熱い視線を注いでいる The whole world *has* its eyes *fixed on* the new technology.
慣用表現 それは火に油を注ぐようなものだ That's just like *throwing fuel on the fire*.

そそくさ 彼はそそくさと出かけていった He 「*went out hurriedly* [*hurried away*].

そそっかしい **careless**; （軽率な）**rash**, **hasty** ‖雨の日に電車に傘を置き忘れるなんてそそっかしいね How *careless* of you to leave your umbrella on the train on a rainy day!

そそのかす 唆す （いたずらなどを）《口語的》**put*** *a person* **up to** ...; （よくないことをするように）**incite** *a person* (**to do**), **egg** *a person* **on** ... ‖マイクにそそのかされたんだ Mike *put me up to it*. ◆蛇はイブをそそのかしてそのリンゴを食べさせようとした The snake *tempted* Eve to try the apple.

そそりたつ そそり立つ **rise*** (**high**), **tower** ⊕ ‖そそり立つ岩山 the *towering* rocky mountain / 森の奥深くに巨木がそそり立っていた A huge tree *rose high* in the deep forest.

そそる 好奇心をそそる **arouse** [**excite**] *a person's* curiosity / パンを焼くにおいが彼の食欲をそそった The smell of baking bread *whetted* his appetite.

そぞろ 子供たちは旅行のことで一日中気もそぞろ

そだいごみ

だった Thinking about the trip, the children *remained restless* all day. / 私たちは夕方の町をそぞろ歩きした We rambled [strolled] about the town in the evening.

そだいごみ 粗大ごみ bulky garbage Ⓤ

そだち 育ち (教育・しつけ) breeding Ⓤ; (発育) growth Ⓤ /彼女の物腰から育ちのよさが分かる Her manner shows good *breeding*.

◆育ち盛りの子供 a *growing* child / 彼女は育ちがよい[悪い] She *is well-*[*ill-*]*bred*. / 礼子は生まれも育ちも大阪だ Reiko *was born and brought up* in Osaka. / 私は田舎[いなか]育ちだ I *was raised in the city* [*country*]. / 今年は稲の育ちが悪い Rice *is growing* poorly this year.

そだつ 育つ grow* ⾃; (しつけられて) be raised, be brought up, be reared

稲は日本中で育つ Rice *grows* all over Japan.

猛はりっぱな若者に育った Takeshi *has grown* (*up*) *into* a fine young man.

私は海岸の小さな村で生まれ育った I *was born and raised* [*brought up, reared*] *in* a small village by the sea.

◆この子は母乳[ミルク]で育った This baby *is breast-*[*bottle-*]*fed*. / その監督のもとで多くの一流選手が育った(→その監督は多くの選手を一流にした) The manager *made* many players first-class.

慣用表現 寝る子は育つ ➪ねる(寝る)

そだてあげる 育て上げる bring* up; (養成する) train ⾄ /彼女は女手一つで3人の子供を育て上げた She *brought up* three children by herself.

◆コーチは彼を超一流の選手に育て上げた His coach *made* him a really great player.

そだてのおや 育ての親 (養子縁組による) adoptive parent ⓒ; (里親) foster parent ⓒ

慣用表現 生みの親より育ての親 ➪うみのおや

そだてる 育てる raise ⾄; (人を) bring* up; (動物を) breed* ⾄; (植物を) grow* ⾄; (里親として) foster ⾄; (養成する) train

洋子はだいじに育てられた Yoko *was「brought up* [*raised*]*」with great care*.

私は朝顔を育てている I*'m raising* [*growing*] some morning glories.

その夫婦は子供の育て方についてよくけんかする The couple often disagrees *over how to raise* their children.

田中夫妻はその孤児を育てることにした Mr. and Mrs. Tanaka decided *to foster* the orphan.

◆才能を育てる *develop one's* talents / この大学は多くの学者を育ててきた(→生み出してきた) This university *has produced* a lot of scholars.

そち 措置 measure ⓒ; (一段階としての) step ⓒ ➪ たいさく(対策) /緊急措置を講じる take *emergency measures* / 麻薬が広まるのを防止するために断固たる措置がとられなければならない Strong *measures* must be carried out to block the spread of drugs.

そちら (場所) (over) there; (あなた) you;

(こちら(this)に対して) that /そちらの天気はどうですか How is the weather (*over*) *there*? / (店で)そちらのをください I'll take *that one*. / 彼女はそちらの方へ行ったのですね？ She went *that way*, didn't she? / そちらのかたは妹さんですか Is *that* your sister? / 私どもの販売員があすそちらに伺います Our representative will be calling on *you* tomorrow. / そちらはいかがお過ごしですか How are *you* getting along? / そちらのかたどうぞ *Over* (*to you*)!

そつ 彼は会の司会をそつなくこなした He presided at the meeting *tactfully*. / 彼女は何をやらせてもそつがない(→失敗せずにやる) She does everything *faultlessly* [*without making mistakes*].

そつう 疎通 understanding Ⓤ /両国の意思の疎通をはかる promote *the mutual understanding* between the two countries

◆彼らは意思の疎通を欠いていた There was a lack of *communication* between them.

ぞっか 俗化 vulgarization Ⓤ; (営利化) commercialization Ⓤ ——俗化する vulgarize ⾄; commercialize ⾄ /残念ながらこの町も年々俗化されつつある To my disappointment, this city *is becoming* more *vulgarized* [*commercialized*] year by year.

そっき 速記 shorthand Ⓤ, (米) stenography Ⓤ /彼は私が言ったことをすべて速記で書き留めた He took down everything I said *in shorthand*.

‖速記者 (米) a stenographer, (英) a shorthand typist

そっきゅう 速球 fastball ⓒ /ピッチャーは速球を投げた The pitcher threw *a fastball*.

‖速球投手 a fastballer

そっきょう 即興 improvisation Ⓤ ——即興の impromptu, improvised, ad-lib /即興演奏で有名なピアニスト a pianist well-known for *his* [*her*] *improvisation* / 即興でスピーチをする make an *impromptu* speech

‖即興曲 an improvisation, an impromptu

そつぎょう 卒業 graduation Ⓤ ——卒業する graduate ⾄ (英)では大学卒業だけに用い, 大学以外のときは finish を用いる. 《米》ではすべての学校に graduate を用いる)

卒業してから彼女に何度か会った I saw her several times *after graduation*.

高校を卒業したらどうするの What are you going to do after you「*graduate from* [*finish*]*」senior high school?*

卒業式は来週行われます *The graduation* (*ceremony*) [《米》*The commencement*] will be held next week.

彼らは卒業旅行に(→卒業を記念して)ヨーロッパへ行った They went to Europe *to commemorate their graduation*.

◆高校を卒業したての若者たち young people *fresh from* high school / 子供じみた習慣を卒業する *outgrow* [*grow out of*] *one's* childish habits / 彼女は名古屋大学の卒業生です She is *a graduate* of Nagoya University.

🔴「卒業おめでとう！」「ありがとう」"Congratu-

lations on *your graduation*!" "Thank you."
‖卒業アルバム《米》a yearbook / 卒業試験 a graduation examination / 卒業証書 a diploma, a graduation certificate / 卒業論文 a graduation thesis

そっきん¹ 即金 (現金) (spot) cash ⓤ ‖即金で払う pay *in cash*

そっきん² 側近 (補佐) aide ⓒ; (従者) attendant ⓒ; (取り巻き)《集合的》entourage ⓒ ‖首相の側近 *the aides* to the Prime Minister

ソックス socks (❖数えるときは a pair of ... とする) →くつした ‖ハイソックス knee *socks* / ルーズソックス baggy *socks*

そっくり
❶【似ている】
実物そっくりの絵 a *lifelike* drawing / マドンナのそっくりさん a Madonna *look-alike*
高子は母親そっくりだ Takako *looks just like* her mother. / Takako *is the spitting image of* her mother.
彼のしぐさはお父さんにそっくりだ His manners *are just like* his father's.
その姉妹の声はそっくりだ Those two sisters have *identical* voices.
❷【全部】all
僕はこづかいをそっくり貯金した I saved *all* my allowance.
泥棒の一味は部屋から金めの物をそっくり持ち去ってしまった The burglars stripped the room of *all* valuables.
◆彼はそれまで所有していたものをそっくり失ってしまった He lost *everything* he had owned before.
❸【そのまま】
机の上をそっくりそのままに(→今あるとおりに)しておきなさい Leave it *as it is* on the desk.
彼は見たことをそっくりそのまま(→見たとおりに)話した He described the thing *exactly as* he had seen it.
この遺跡をそっくりそのまま(→完全な形で)保存するのは難しい It's difficult to preserve these remains *in their entirety*.

そっくりかえる 反っくり返る lean* back
◆いすにそっくり返って(→尊大な態度で)座る sit back *arrogantly* [(→誇らしげに) *proudly*] in a chair

そっけつ 即決 prompt [immediate] decision ⓒ ──即決する decide promptly [immediately] ‖事態は即決を要していた The situation required that we should *decide promptly*.

そっけない 素っ気ない、(冷淡な) cold, dry; (ぶっきらぼうな) curt, blunt ‖そっけない態度[返事] a *curt* manner [reply] / 彼らにそっけなく扱われた I got *the cold shoulder* from them. / 彼女を映画に誘ったがそっけなく断られた I asked her to go to a movie with me, but she gave me a *blunt* [*flat*] refusal.

そっこう¹ 即効 immediate effect ⓒⓤ ‖この薬は腹痛に即効がある This medicine has *an immediate effect* on stomachache.
‖即効薬 a quick remedy

そっこう² 速攻 敵に速攻を仕掛ける make [launch] *a swift attack* on the enemy

ぞっこう 続行 continuation ⓤ ──続行する continue ⓜ, go* on (*doing*) ‖審議の続行 *the continuation* of the discussion / 悪天候の中, 試合は続行された Despite the bad weather, the game *was continued*.

そっこうじょ 測候所 meteorological [weather] station ⓒ

そっこく 即刻 immediately, at once, right away; (その場で) then and there, on the spot ‖計画を即刻中止する stop a project *immediately* / 彼は即刻解雇された He was dismissed *then and there [on the spot]*.

ぞっこく 属国 dependency (state)ⓒ, subject nation ⓒ

ぞっこん 彼は恵子にぞっこんだ He *is deeply* [*head over heels*] *in love with* Keiko.

そっせん 率先 彼は率先して事にあたるというところがない He shows the absence of *initiative*. / 日本は率先して貿易不均衡を是正するべきだ Japan should *take the lead* [*initiative*] in rectifying the trade imbalance.

そっち (場所) (over) there; (方向) that way; (こっち(this)に対して) that; (あなた) you ‖そこ², そちら ‖今そっちに行くよ I'm going [coming] *there* now. / 私はそっちのほうがいいと思うな I think *that one* is better.

そっちのけ 彼は勉強そっちのけで野球ばかりしている He always plays baseball, *putting his studies aside [neglecting his studies]*.

そっちゅう 卒中 stroke ⓒ,《古風》apoplexy ⓤ

そっちょく 率直 ──率直な (遠慮のない) frank; (包み隠さずずばりと言う) candid; (ずけずけ言う) outspoken; (単刀直入な) straightforward; (隠しだてしない) open ──率直に frankly; candidly; openly
率直な質問をする ask a *frank* question; ask a question *frankly*
率直なご意見を聞かせてください I'd like to hear your *frank* opinion.
彼女はいつも率直な言い方をする She always speaks *frankly* [*candidly*].
率直に話し合いましょう Let's discuss it *openly*.
率直に言って, その話は信じられない *To be frank with you* [*Frankly speaking*], I can't believe the story.

そっと
❶【静かに】quietly; (優しく) softly
彼女は姉を起こさないようにそっと部屋を出た She left the room *quietly* so as not to wake her sister up.
ドアはそっと閉めてください Close the door *quietly* [*softly*].
❷【優しく】gently, softly; (軽く) lightly
その子供は猫の頭にそっと触れた The child touched the cat's head *lightly* [*softly*].
彼女は花びんをテーブルの上にそっと置いた She

ぞっと

put the vase on the table *gently* [*softly*].
❸【ひそかに】secretly, stealthily
彼はその部屋をそっとのぞいた He *secretly* looked in the room.
◆私は彼女にテーブルの下からそっとメモを渡した I *slipped* her a note under the table.
❹【そのままに】
今は彼女をそっとしておこう(→ひとりにしておこう) Let's *leave* her *alone* now.

ぞっと 事故の現場を見てぞっとした I *shuddered* to see the scene of the accident. / ゴキブリは見ただけでぞっとする The mere sight of a cockroach *gives me the creeps*. / その話を聞いてぞっとした(→寒気がした) The story *gave me the shivers*. / それは本当にぞっとするような事件だった It was simply a *horrible* incident.

そっとう 卒倒 faint C ——卒倒する(気絶する) faint 自; (仰天する) be floored / 彼女はショックのあまり卒倒しそうになった She almost *fainted* with shock.

そっぽ 猫の写真を撮ろうとカメラを向けたらそっぽを向かれてしまった I pointed my camera at the cat to take its picture, but it 「*turned away* [*looked the other way*].

そつろん 卒論 graduation thesis C

そで 袖 sleeve C
男の子は母親のそでを引っぱった The little boy pulled his mother by *the sleeve*.
暑くなってきたのでそでをまくり上げた Because it became hot, I rolled *my sleeves* up.
◆長そで[半そで]のブラウス a *long-*[*short-*]*sleeved* blouse / そでなしのワンピース a *sleeveless* dress / 舞台そでで待機する wait *in the wings* / 新しい制服にそでを通した(→着た) I *put on* a new school uniform. / 彼は両親のそでにすがった(→頼み込んで助けを求めた) He *begged* his parents *for help*.
‖そで丈 the length of a sleeve
慣用表現 彼は市長にそでの下を使った(→わいろを贈った) He *bribed* the mayor.
ことわざ ないそでは振れぬ A man cannot give what he hasn't got. (→持っていないものは与えられない)

ソテー sauté [soutéi] U C (✤フランス語から)

そでぐち 袖口 cuff C

そてつ 蘇鉄〔植物〕cycad C

そと 外

❶【外部】(外側) the outside; (戸外) the outdoor ——外に[で] out, outside; (戸外で) outdoors
外の空気を吸う breathe the air *outside*
外はまだ雨が降っている It is still raining *outside*.
雨がやむと子供たちは外に出ていった The children went *out* [*outside*] after the rain had stopped.
外で遊ぼうよ Let's play *outside*.
ドアのすぐ外で待っていてください Please wait just *outside* the door.
彼女は窓から外を眺めていた She was looking *out* of the window.

❷【外出先】
外から帰ったら(→家に帰ったら)すぐうがいをしなさい Gargle right away *when you come home*.
今夜は外で食事をしましょう Let's eat *out* tonight.

そとがわ 外側 the outside, the exterior ——外側の outside, exterior /箱の外側にシールがはってある A sticker is put on *the outside* of the box. ◆そのドアは外側に開く The door opens *outward*.

そとづら 外面 彼女は外面がいい She *puts on a friendly face in public*.

そとば 卒塔婆 a *sotoba*, a thin wooden board stood up by a grave on which a sutra is written

そとまわり 外回り(外勤) outside work U; (環状線の) the outer track
◆兄は外回りの仕事が多い My brother often *works outdoors* [*outside the office*].

そなえ 備え(準備) preparations; (困難・災害などに対する) provision U C; (設備) equipment U; (防備) defense, 《英》defence C
◆地震に対する備えは十分だ We *are* fully *prepared for* an earthquake.
ことわざ 備えあればうれいなし Providing is preventing.

そなえつけ 備え付け 備えつけの(→作りつけの)戸棚 a *built-in* closet / 備えつけの(→用意された)ペンをご利用ください Please use the pens *provided*.

そなえつける 備え付ける(設備などを) equip 他; (必要な物を供給する) provide 他; (家具などを) furnish 他; (器具などを) install 他 /各教室にはクーラーが備えつけてある Every classroom *is equipped* with an air conditioner. / その部屋には本棚が備えつけられていた The room *was furnished* with a bookcase. / 部屋に電話を備えつけてもらった I had a telephone *installed* in the room.

そなえもの 供え物 offering C /供え物をする make *an offering*

そなえる¹ 備える

❶【準備する】prepare for ..., provide for ...
いつでも最悪の事態に備えておく必要がある We always need to *prepare for* the worst.
彼は将来に備えて貯金している He is saving money to *provide for* the future.
◆選手たちは試合に備えて一生懸命練習している The players are training hard *in preparation for* the game.

❷【設備する】equip 他; (家具などを) furnish 他
部屋に家具を備える *furnish* a room *with* furniture
その教室は最新のコンピュータを備えている The classroom *is equipped* [*furnished*] *with* the latest computers.
◆その病院は最新の設備を備えている The hospital *has* the latest conveniences.

❸【能力などを】

彼はリーダーとしての資質を備えている He *possesses* what it takes to be a leader.
彼女は生まれながらに芸術的才能を備えている She *is gifted* [*endowed*] *with* artistic talent.

そなえる[2] 供える offer [他], make* an offering //祖父の墓前に花を供えた I *offered* flowers before my grandfather's grave.

ソナタ 〔音楽〕sonata [C] ‖ソナタ形式 a sonata form

そなわる 備わる (生まれつきもっている) be gifted [endowed] with ...; (備えられている) be equipped with ..., be furnished with ... //最新設備の備わった工場 a factory *furnished with* the latest equipment / 彼には語学の才能が備わっている He *is gifted* [*endowed*] *with* a talent for languages.
◆その老婦人には気品が備わっている The old woman *has* a natural grace.

その that; the; its
that: 自分から離れている物や人，また，先に述べた事柄を指す．複数名詞に付くときは those.
the: すでに述べられた名詞や，前後関係から何を指すか分かる名詞の前に付ける．
its: 所有を表す．
その新聞を取ってくれる？ Will you get me *that* newspaper?
そのことはみんな知っている Everyone knows about *that*.
バス停に女の子が立っていた．その子はかわいい帽子をかぶっていた I saw a girl standing at the bus stop. *The* [*That*] girl wore a lovely hat.
その日は晴れていた It was fine on *that* day.
そのうわさは町中に広まった *The* [*That*] rumor spread throughout the town.
彼に貸した本が返ってきたが，そのカバーが少し汚れていた The book I had lent him was returned, but there were a few stains on *its* jacket.

そのうえ その上 besides; moreover; furthermore; in addition (to that); on top of that
besides: 前述の内容を軽く補足する．
moreover: 前述よりも重要な事柄を追加する．
furthermore: besides や moreover を使った後，さらに付け加える場合に用いる．
in addition: besides より少しかたくて回りくどい表現．
on top of that: くだけた言い方．不快なことに用いられることが多い．
彼女は勉強ができるし，そのうえスポーツも得意だ She does well at school. *Besides*, she is good at sports.
このスカートはとてもすてきで，そのうえ値段もてごろだ This skirt is very nice. *Moreover*, it is reasonably priced.
きょうは財布をなくし，そのうえ学校に遅刻した Today I lost my wallet, and *on top of that* I was late for school.
分厚い本を読み，そのうえそのレポートを書かなければならない I have to read a thick book. *In addition* (*to that*), I have to write a paper on it.

そのうち (すぐに) soon; (間もなく) before long; (近いうちに) one of these days; (いつか) someday, sometime
雨はそのうちやむでしょう The rain will stop *soon*.
彼もそのうち先生の言ったことが分かるだろう He will understand *someday* what the teacher said.
◆英語のテストで満点の人が3人いたが，彼もそのうちの一人だった Three people got a perfect score on the English test. He was one *of them*. / 彼女には兄が3人いる．そのうち2人は社会人だ She has three brothers, two *of whom* are working.

そのかわり その代わり (代わりに) instead; (引き換えに) in exchange; (しかし) but; (だから) so //彼女の誕生日に電話することができなかった．その代わりメールを送った I couldn't call her on her birthday. *Instead* I e-mailed her. / 私が食器を洗うから，その代わりテーブルをふいておいてね I'll wash the dishes. *In exchange* [*return*] wipe the table. / ゲームをやってもいいけど，その代わり終わったらすぐ寝なさい You can play a game. *But* go to bed at once when you finish it.

そのかん その間 in the meantime [meanwhile], meanwhile //彼はその間じっとしていた He kept still *in the meantime*.

そのき その気 彼女はおだてられてその気になった(→おだてが彼女をうぬぼれさせた) The flattery *went to her head*. / 彼は彼女をその気にさせておいてからふった He made her *fall for* him, and then ditched her.

そのくせ (しかし) but, and yet; (それにもかかわらず) nevertheless //彼は人には文句を言うが，そのくせ自分からは何もしない He is complaining to others, *but* [*and yet*] he doesn't do anything. / 彼女は好き嫌いはないと言っていたが，そのくせ野菜を残す She said she could eat anything, *nevertheless* she doesn't eat vegetables.

そのくらい (その程度の) that much; (同じくらいの数の) so [as] many; (同じくらいの量の) so [as] much ➔ それくらい //彼女のことについてはそのくらいしか知らない I know only *that much* about her.
◆そのくらいで結構です *That*'s enough.

そのご その後 after that; (以来) since (then) (❖完了形の動詞とともに用いる); (後で) afterward, 《主に英》afterwards, later
彼はその後ずっと忙しいそうだ I hear he has been busy ever *since*.
その後2年たって，彼らは再会した Two years *later*, they met again.
その後いかがお過ごしですか *How have you been* (*since then*)?
私たちはレストランで食事をし，その後映画を見に行った We ate at a restaurant and *afterward* [*after that*] we went to see a movie.

そ

そのころ その頃 (その当時) in those days; (その時) then, at that time
- そのころ彼はまだ有名ではなかった He had not yet become famous *in those days*.
- 私はそのころ本を読んでいた I was reading a book *at that time* [*then*].
- そのころには彼女も家に帰っているだろう She will have gotten home *by then* [*that time*].

そのせつ その節 その節は〔=先日は〕お世話になりました Thank you very much *for the other day*.

そのた その他 (残り全部) the others, the rest; (…など) and so on [forth], etc. ‖彼はバスで、その他の人たちは電車で家に帰った He went home by bus and *the others* went home by train. / 引き出しの中には鉛筆、消しゴム、定規その他が入っていた There were pencils, erasers, scales *etc.* [*and so on*] in the drawer.
◆彼は野球、サッカー、その他のスポーツが得意だ He is good at baseball, soccer and *other* sports.

そのため その為 (その理由で) for that reason, therefore, so; (その目的で) for that purpose; (その結果) consequently, as a result ‖そのため彼は学校を休んだ He was absent from school *for that reason*. / 彼女がアメリカに行くのはそのためだ She is going to America *for that purpose*. / *That is why* she is going to America. / あたりが暗くなってきた。そのため私たちは練習をやめた It was getting dark all around, and *consequently* [*so*] we stopped practicing.

そのつど その都度 each time ‖彼はいいアイディアが浮かんだらそのつど書き留めている He writes down good ideas *each time* he hits on them.

そのて その手 その手の商品はもう古い *That kind of* product is already out of date. / その手は食わないぞ You can't so easily cheat me with *that*.

そのとおり その通り そのとおりにします I'll do *just like that*.
🅔「つまり、机をもう少し右に動かしたほうがいいということだね」「そのとおり」 "So, you say I should move the desk to the right a little more." "*That's right.*/ *Exactly*."

そのとき その時 then, at that time; (その当時) in those days; (その瞬間) at that moment [instant]; (その機会に) on that occasion
- そのとき私はテレビを見ていた I was watching TV *at that time* [*then*].
- 私にはそのとき何が起こったのか分からなかった I couldn't understand what happened *at that moment*.
- 父はそのとき以来たばこを吸っていない My father hasn't smoked *since then*.
- 後で職員室に来てください。そのときにプリントを渡しましょう Come to the teachers' room later. I'll give you the handouts *then*.
◆私たちが夕食を食べ始めたちょうどそのとき父が帰ってきた My father came home *just when* we began to eat supper.
🅔「先生に知れたらどうするの」「そのときはそのときだよ」 "What will you do if the teacher knows that?" "*I'll think about that when the time comes*."

そのば その場 (場所) the place; (地点) the spot; (場合) the occasion; (場面) the situation; (そこ) there ‖彼はたまたまその場に居合わせた He happened to be 「*on the spot* [*there*]. / その場で決めることができなかった I couldn't decide it *on the spot*. / 彼女のひと言がその場を救ってくれた Her words saved *the situation*. / その場はどうにか切り抜けた I managed to get out *of the situation*.
慣用表現 その場しのぎの対策 *stopgap* measures / その場逃れの言い訳をする give an excuse *only to suit the occasion*

そのひ その日 that day, the day; (まさにその日) the very day; (その同じ日) the same day ‖その日は暑かった It was hot *that day*. / その日に限ってかぎをかけるのを忘れた *On that particular day* I forgot to lock the door.

そのひぐらし その日暮らし 兄はその日暮らしをしている My brother *lives from hand to mouth*.

そのへん その辺 (そのあたり) around there; (その近くに) near there ◆そのへんのことはよく覚えていない I don't remember *about it* clearly. / 遊ぶのはそのへんでやめにしなさい You should stop playing *now*. / そのへんまでご一緒しましょう I'll accompany you *to somewhere near hear*.
🅔「私のかばん見なかった?」「そのへんにあったよ」 "Didn't you see my bag?" "It was *around there*./ I saw it *near there*."

そのほか その外 (残りの物) the rest; (その他の物) the others ──そのほかの other ‖彼らは教室にいたが、そのほかの人たちは校庭で遊んでいた They were in the classroom, but *the others* were playing on the playground. / そのほかに何か質問はありますか Do you have any *other* questions?
◆そのほかに何を持っていけばいいですか What *else* should I take with me?

そのまま (電話は) 切らずにそのままお待ちください *Hold the line, please*. / テーブルの上はそのままにしておいてください Please leave the things on the table *as they are*. / 私は彼女から聞いたことをそのまま話した I told the story *exactly as* she had told it. / 彼は授業が終わると、家に帰らずそのまま友達の家に行った When school was over, he went *straight* to his friend's house without going home.

そのみち その道 彼はその道の専門家だ He is an expert 「*on the subject* [*in the field*].

そのもの その物 (当の物) the very thing; (それ自体) itself ‖それは私が捜していたまさにそのものだ It is *the very thing* that I was searching for. / 弟は健康そのものだ My brother is health *itself*. / My brother is

the picture of health.
◆今, 彼女はまさそのものだ She *is* now *as happy as can be.*

そのような such, 《口語的》like that ⇨ そんな ∥そのような言葉は一度も聞いたことがない I've never heard *such* a word. / そのような場所に行ってみたい I would like to go to a place *like that.*

そのように (in) that way, like that ⇨ そんな ∥そのように教わりました I was taught it *like that.* / 私はそのようには考えません I don't think *that way.*

そのわりに その割に 彼女, 英会話を習っているの? そのわりにはあまり上達していないみたい She takes lessons in conversational English? *Considering that,* her English doesn't seem to have improved.

そば¹ 側
❶【付近】——そばの (近所の) neighboring; (近くの) near, nearby; (すぐ近くの) close to ... ——そばに (かたわらに) by, beside; (わきに) by [at] the side of ..., by [at] one's side; (近くに) near, nearby, close to ...; (周囲に) around ⇨ ちかく (近く)
〖そばの〗
彼は駅のそばの本屋に寄った He stopped by a book store *near* [*close to*] the station.
それならすぐそばのスーパーで売っていたよ It was sold at 「a supermarket *nearby* [a *nearby* supermarket].
〖そばに〗
おじいさんが私のそばに座った An old man sat *beside* [*by*] me.
私が病気の間, 彼はそばについていてくれた He was *by my side* during my illness.
銀行は花屋のそばにある The bank is *close to* the flower shop.
◆彼女はいつも眼鏡をそばに (→手元に) 置いている She always keeps her glasses *at hand.* / そばに寄らないで! *Keep* [*Stay*] *away!*
〖そばを〗
車は湖のそばを通った The car passed *by* the lake.
その子供は母親のそばを離れなかった The child didn't leave his mother's *side.*
〖その他〗
子供たちは噴水のそばで遊んでいた The children were playing *near* the fountain.
❷【…するとすぐ】
兄はお金を稼いだそばから使ってしまう My brother spends his money *as soon as* he makes it.

そば² 蕎麦 (植物) buckwheat ©; (食品) *soba,* buckwheat noodles
⇨ 場面・状況別会話 p.1684
∥そば粉 buckwheat flour / そば屋 a *soba* [noodle] shop

そばは, うどんやそうめんと並ぶ日本の代表的なめんで, そば粉でできています。冷たいそばと温かいそばがあります。竹すに盛られた冷たいそばを「ざるそば」と呼び, つゆにつけて食べます。しょうゆ味の熱いつゆをかけて食べるそばにはいろいろあります。天ぷらをのせた「天ぷらそば」, 揚げ玉をのせた「たぬきそば」, 生卵を入れた「月見そば」などが人気があります。

Soba, like *udon* and *somen,* is a typical kind of Japanese noodles. It is made of buckwheat flour. You can eat it hot or cold. Cold *soba* served on a bamboo plate and dipped into sauce is called *zarusoba. Soba* eaten hot in soy-flavored broth has many types. Among the popular ones are *tempura soba* with tempura, *tanuki soba* with tempura crumbs, and *tsukimi soba* with a raw egg.

そばかす freckles ◆顔にそばかすがある have a *freckled* face

そばだてる 欹てる 彼女は彼らの話に耳をそばだてた She *pricked up her ears* when they were talking.

そびえる 聳える rise*⑮, tower ∥山が空に向かってそびえている Mountains *rise up* to the sky.

-そびれる そのことは彼女に言いそびれてしまった (→機会を逃した) I *missed the chance* to tell her about it. / 忙しくて手紙を出しそびれた (→出しそこなった) I was so busy that I *failed* to mail the letter.

そふ 祖父 grandfather ©
ソファー sofa ©, couch ©
ソフト ⚠
❶【柔らかい】——ソフトな soft ∥ソフトな手ざわりの生地 a cloth *soft* to the touch
◆彼は一見ソフトなイメージだが, 実はとても頑固だ He looks *gentle* [*mild*], but actually he is very stubborn.
❷【ソフトウエア】 software ◎ (❖×soft とはいわない) ∥その会社はパソコン用の新しいソフトを発表した The company released new *software* for PCs.

ソフトウエア software ◎
ソフトクリーム ⚠soft ice cream ◎© (❖「ソフトクリーム」は和製英語)
ソフトドリンク ⚠(アルコールを含まない飲料) nonalcoholic drink © (❖英語の soft drink は「アルコールを含まない炭酸飲料」の意味)
ソフトボール softball © (❖球の意味では ©)
そふぼ 祖父母 *one's* grandparents
ソプラノ 〖音楽〗 soprano ◎© (複 ~s, soprani) ∥ソプラノを歌う sing *soprano* / 彼女の声はきれいなソプラノだ She has a beautiful *soprano* voice.
∥ソプラノ歌手 a soprano

そぶり 素振り (態度) manner ©; (気配) sign ©; (ふるまい) behavior, 《英》behaviour ©; (身ぶり) gesture © ∥つれないそぶり *a cold manner* / 彼女は怒っているそぶりは見せなかった She showed no *sign* of anger.

そぼ 祖母 grandmother ©
そぼう 粗暴 ——粗暴な rough, violent; (手に負えない) wild ∥私たちは彼の粗暴なふるまいに耐えられなかった We couldn't bear his

rough behavior.
そぼく 素朴 ——素朴な (単純な・質素な) simple; (飾りけのない) unpretentious; (洗練されていない) unsophisticated ∥素朴な疑問 a *simple* question / 彼女はその素朴な人柄でみんなに好かれている She is liked by everybody because of her *unpretentious* personality. / 彼女はいなかでの素朴な生活にあこがれている She is attracted to the *simple* life in the country.

そまつ 粗末

❶【上等でない】 ——粗末な (質素な) plain, humble; (みすぼらしい) shabby, poor
粗末な食べ物 *plain* food / 粗末な暮らしをする live a *shabby* life
彼らは粗末な家に住んでいた They lived in *humble* [*shabby*] houses.
村人たちは粗末な服を着ていた The villagers wore *shabby* clothes.

❷【おろそかにする】
物を粗末に扱う *handle* a thing *carelessly*
彼は体を粗末にしている(→むとんちゃくである) He *is careless about* his health.
親を粗末にしては(→ひどく扱っては)いけない You must not *treat* your parents *disrespectfully* [*lightly*].

そまる 染まる dye ∥この生地はよく染まる This cloth *dyes* well. / 山々は夕日に赤く染まっている The mountains *are dyed* red by the setting sun.
◆彼らはいつの間にか悪に染まっていた They *had sunk* into vice without noticing it. / その子のシャツは血に染まっていた The child's shirt *was stained* with blood.

そむく 背く (命令などに) disobey; (法律などに違反する) violate; (約束などを破る) break*; (裏切る) betray
規則に背く *break* a rule
彼らは法に背いた They *violated* the law.
彼は親の意に背いて大学に進学しなかった He *disobeyed* his parents and didn't go on to college.
◆人の期待に背いて *contrary to* a person's expectation / 自分の意志に背いて父親の店を継いだ I *went against* my will and took over my father's shop.

そむける 背ける 彼は怖くなって顔を背けた He got frightened and *turned his face away*. / 現実から目を背けてはいけない You shouldn't *turn your eyes away* [*avert your eyes*] from reality.

ソムリエ sommelier (❖フランス語から)

そめ 染め dyeing; (着色) coloring
◆この着物は染めがいい This kimono *is well dyed*.

そめもの 染め物 (染めること) dyeing; (染めた物) dyed goods

そめる 染める (染料で) dye; (色づけする) color, 《英》colour; (薄く) tint
布を黄色に染める *dye* the cloth yellow / 彼は髪を茶色に染めた He *colored* [*dyed, tinted*] his hair brown. / 夕日が家々を赤く染めていた The setting sun *dyed* houses red.

◆彼女は恥ずかしがってほおを赤く染めた She *blushed* [*turned red*] with shame.

そもそも (まず始めに) to begin with; (第1番目に) in the first place; (いったい) on earth ∥そもそもどうしてそんなことを言ったんだ Why *on earth* did you say that? / 彼に話したのがそもそもの間違いだった It was a mistake to tell him about it「*in the first place* [*to begin with*].

そや 粗野 ——粗野な (下品な) vulgar; (乱暴な) rough; (無作法な) rude; (上品さのない) coarse ∥粗野な態度 a *rough* [*rude*] behavior / 彼は時々粗野な言葉づかいをする He sometimes uses *coarse* [*vulgar*] language.

そよう 素養 (知識) knowledge; (たしなみ) accomplishments; (基礎) a grounding ∥彼は美術の素養がある[あまりない] He has [doesn't have much] *knowledge* of the fine arts.

そよかぜ 微風 breeze, gentle [light] wind ∥そよ風が吹いている There is *a breeze*.

そよぐ 戦ぐ (さらさら音を立てる) rustle; (揺れる) sway; (軽く動く) stir ∥木の葉が風にそよいでいる The leaves of the trees *are rustling* [*swaying*] in the wind.

そよそよ (穏やかに) gently; (小さく快い音を立てて) softly ∥心地よい風がそよそよ吹いていた The breeze was blowing *gently*.

そら¹ 空

(天) the sky (❖形容詞が付くと通例aを伴う. また, 広がりを強調するときは複数形skiesも用いる. (空中) the air

> コロケーション -sky-
> 【形容詞＋～】青～ a blue sky / 曇り～ a cloudy sky / 晴れた～ a clear sky / 星～ a starlit sky / 夜～ a night sky

空が明るくなった *The sky* lightened.
空に星がきらめいていた Stars were shining in *the sky*.
鳥のように空を飛べたらどんなに楽しいだろう How wonderful it would be if I could fly in *the sky* like a bird.
彼らはいっせいに空を見上げた They looked up at *the sky* all at once.
鳥は空高く舞い上がった The bird flew *high up into the sky* [*air*].
◆空の旅は楽しかったですか Did you enjoy *your flight*?
∥空色 sky blue

そら² Look!, Here!, There! ∥そら, 向こうに山が見えるよ *Look*, you see mountains over there. / そら, 彼女が来た *Here* she comes. / そら, また始まった *There* you go again. ◆そら見なさい(→そう言ったでしょう) *I told you so.*

そらおそろしい 空恐ろしい 彼らの将来を考えるとそら恐ろしい I *feel a strong anxiety* about their future.

そらす¹ 逸らす (方向を) turn away; (注意などを) distract, divert; (いやなものから

目を) look away, avert [他]; (話を) change [他] //彼は私から目をそらした He *turned his eyes away* from me. / 話をそらさないでください *Don't change the subject*. / 彼女はその話題からみんなの注意をそらそうとした She tried to *distract* [*divert*] everyone's attention from the topic.

そらす² 反らす 体を後ろに反らす *bend oneself* backward

そらぞらしい 空々しい (空虚な) empty; (見えすいた) obvious, transparent //そらぞらしい言い訳 an *obvious* [a *flimsy*] excuse / 彼はそらぞらしいお世辞を言った He made *empty* compliments.

そらで 空で 彼はその詩をそらで言える He can recite the poem *from memory*.

そらとぶえんばん 空飛ぶ円盤 flying saucer [C], unidentified flying object [C] (《略語》UFO)

そらなみだ 空涙 false tears, crocodile tears //そら涙を流す shed *false* [*crocodile*] *tears*

そらに 空似 [慣用表現] 他人のそら似 ➔ たにん

そらまめ 空豆 broad bean [C]

そらみみ 空耳 何か聞こえたような気がしたがそら耳だった I thought I heard a noise, but in fact I *was merely hearing things*. (❖hear things は「幻聴が生じる」の意味. ふつう進行形で用いられる)

そらもよう 空模様 the look of the sky //空模様からするとあしたは雨になりそうだ Judging from *the look of the sky*, it may rain tomorrow. ◆空模様が怪しい *The sky* [*weather*] looks threatening.

そり¹ 反り (曲線) curve [C]; (板などの) warp [C] ◆小屋の床には少し反りがある The floor of the cabin *is* slightly *warped* [*curved*]. / 彼女とは反りが合わない I *can't get along well with* her.

そり² 橇 (小型の) 《米》sled [C], 《英》sledge [C]; (大型の) sleigh [C] //そりに乗る go [ride] on *a sled*

そりかえる 反り返る (反って後ろに曲がる) bend* backward; (板などが) warp [自], be warped //板が日に当たって反り返ってしまった The board *warped* in the sun. / (→日光が板を反り返らせた) The sun *warped* the board. ◆彼はいすに反り返って(→偉そうに)座っていた He sat back in the chair *arrogantly* [*pompously*].

ソリスト ⚠soloist [sóulouist] [C] (❖日本語はフランス語の soliste から)

そりゅうし 素粒子 〖物理〗 elementary particle [C]

そる¹ 反る curve [自]; (板などが) warp [自], be warped; (体・指などが) bend* over backward //本の表紙が反ってしまった The cover of the book *has* (*been*) *warped*. / 彼女は体を後ろに反らして頭を床につけることができる She can *bend over backward* and touch the floor with her head.

そる² 剃る shave* [自][他]; (そり落とす) shave off //頭をそる *shave one's* head / 父は毎朝ひげをそっている My father *shaves* (*himself*) every morning.
◆顔をそってもらう *get a shave*

それ¹

❶【相手に近いものを指して】that (複 those)
それは何に使うんですか What do you use *that* for?
それを取ってもらえますか Would you hand me *that*, please?

❷【前述の物・事を受けて】it; (指し示す気持ちがあるとき) that
それなら前に聞いたことがあります I have heard *it* before.
それはいい考えだ *That*'s a good idea.
◆それがどうしたっていうの *So what?*
💬「彼女が主役に選ばれたんだって」「それ本当？」 "I hear she was chosen to play the leading part." "Is *it* true?"
💬「そんなに早く起きなくても大丈夫だよ」「それもそうだね」 "You don't have to get up so early." "*That may be so*."
💬「君が言ってた本ってこれ？」「あ, それそれ」 "Is this the book you told me about?" "Oh, *that's it*."

❸【そのとき】then
それ以来彼の家には行っていません I haven't been to his house *since then*.

それ² それ, 行くぞ！ *Here* goes!

それから (その次に) (and) then; (その後) after that; (後で) afterward; (それ以来) since (then) (❖完了形とともに用いる)
夕食を食べて, それから宿題をした I had dinner, (*and*) *then* did my homework.
それからどこに行ったの Where did you go *after that*?
彼はそれからずっとアメリカに住んでいる He has lived in America ever *since*.
◆私はケーキとクッキー, それからアイスクリームも食べた I ate a piece of cake, cookies, *and* an ice cream. / それから1週間後, 彼女から電話があった She called me a week *later*.

それきり それきり彼からは連絡がない I haven't heard from him *since then* [*ever since*]. / ディズニーランドには5年前に行ったがそれきりだ I went to Disneyland five years ago, but *that was it*.

それくらい それ位 それくらいのことなら私にもできる *Something that easy* even I could do. / それくらいの(→そんな小さな)ことで騒ぐな Don't make a fuss about *such a small* thing. / それくらいの量なら食べられる I can eat *as much*. / もういい. それくらいにしておきなさい OK. *That*'s enough!

それこそ それこそまさに私が探していたCDです *That* is the very CD I was looking for. / この話が彼に知れたらそれこそ大変だ If he hears of this story, it will *really* be a big problem.

それじゃあ (じゃあね) bye; (それなら) then, so; (さて) now ➔ それでは //それじゃあ, またあした *Bye*. See you tomorrow.

それぞれ each; (順にそれぞれ) respectively
(✿ 文末で用いる)

彼らはそれぞれ能力がある *Each* of them has their own ability. / They *each* have their own ability.

人はそれぞれ自分の夢をもっている *Each* person has his or her own dream.

彼の弟は14歳と11歳です His brothers are 14 and 11 years old *respectively*.

このアイスクリームはそれぞれ100円です These ice creams are 100 yen *each*.

それだから (そういうわけで) That's why, 《公式的》therefore ➡ だから ‖ それだからきのうは学校を休んだのだ *That's why* I was absent from school yesterday.

それだけ
❶ [その物・事だけ]
知っていることはそれだけです That's all [*the only thing*] I know.

それだけは言えない(→それ以外なら何でも言う) I will say *anything but that*.

❷ [程度]
それだけあれば十分だ That (*much*) will be enough.

きょう中にそれだけやってしまいなさい Finish *that much* before the day is over.

それだけ一生懸命勉強したのだから、いい点数が取れるでしょう Since you studied *so hard*, you will get high grades.

試験に落ちた。ただそれだけのことだよ I failed the examination, *and that's that*.

早起きすればそれだけ時間を有効に使える If you get up earlier, you can make *that much more* use of your time.

その本を読むのには時間がかかったが、それだけの価値はあった It took a lot of time to read the book, but *it was worth it*.

それっきり その問題はそれっきりになっている (→未解決のままである) The problem is left *unsettled*. / それっきり彼からは電話がかかってこない I haven't had a phone call from him「*since then* [*ever since*].

それで (そういうわけで) so; (それでは) then; (そして) and
彼はきつい練習をしたので疲れていた。それで早く寝てしまった After a hard practice, he felt very tired, *so* he went to bed early.

それでどんな映画を見たの What movie did you see, *then*?

◆それで思い出した(→それが思い出させた) *That* reminds me.

💬「きのう駅で恵理子に会ったんだ」「それで?」 "I met Eriko at the station yesterday." "*And*? / *Well*?"

それでいて (それなのに) (and) yet ‖彼はふだん全く英語の勉強をしない。それでいて英語ができるようになりたいなどと言っている He usually doesn't study English at all, *and yet* he says he wants to be good at English.

それでこそ よく言った。それでこそ僕の弟だ Well said! *That's* my brother.

それでなくても 宿題を手伝ってくれって?それでなくても忙しいのに You want me to help you with your homework? I'm too busy *as it is*.

それでは then; (そうならば) if so; (ところで) well; (さて) now ‖それでは教科書を開いてください *Now*, open your textbook. / それではまた後で See you later, *then*. / それでは私が代わりに行きましょう *Then* I'll go instead. / それではしばらく忙しくなりますね *If so*, you will be busy for a while.

それでも (しかし) but; (それでもなお) still, and yet; (それにもかかわらず) nevertheless ‖いつものバスに乗りそこなったが、それでも学校には間に合った I missed my usual bus, *but* I arrived at school in time. / 彼の両親は反対したが、それでも彼はやることにした His parents objected, *still* [*even so*] he decided to do it. / 彼の説明を聞いたが、それでも全く分からなかった He explained it to me, *nevertheless* [*still*] I didn't understand it at all. / それでも私の父親ですか Now I don't believe you're really my father?

それどころ 映画を見に行きたいのはやまやまだけど、忙しくてそれどころじゃないんだ I really want to go to the movie, but I'm *too busy to do that*.

それどころか (反対に) on the contrary; (少しも…ない) far from …; (実は) in fact, actually ‖雨はやまなかった。それどころかますます激しくなった It didn't stop raining. *On the contrary*, it rained more and more heavily. / 全然怒ってなどいません。それどころかむしろうれしいくらいです I'm not angry at all. *In fact*, I'm glad.

それとなく (間接的に) indirectly; (遠回しに) in a roundabout way ‖私はそれとなく彼女の考えを聞いた I *indirectly* asked her about her opinion. / 彼女はそれとなく彼に注意した She warned him *in a roundabout way*.

それとも or ‖ミルクティーにしますか、それともレモンティーにしますか How would you like your tea, with milk *or* with lemon?

それなのに (しかし) but; (それでも) (and) yet ‖彼は熱があった。それなのに学校に来た He had a fever, *but* he came to school. / 彼女は忙しそうだった。それなのに私の話を聞いてくれた She seemed busy, *and yet* she listened to me.

それなら (もしそうなら) if so, in that case; (そういうことなら) then ‖図書館に行くの?それならバスで行ったほうがいいよ Are you going to the library? *If so*, you should take a bus. / それならあした電話します I'll call you tomorrow, *then*.

◆それならそうと早く言ってくれればよかったのに *If that was the case*, you might have told me so earlier.

それなり 彼らはそれなりに努力している They make an effort *in their own way*. / 試験はそれなりのできだった The results of the exams were good *up to a point*.

それに (そのうえ) besides (that), moreover; (それに加えて) on top of that ‖疲れて

いたし, それにおなかもすいていた I was tired; *besides that* I was hungry. / 彼女は正直だし, それに明るい She is honest, *moreover*, she is cheerful.

それにしても 彼はスキーは初めてだと言っていたが, それにしてはうまい *Even though* he said it was his first time to ski, he skis very well.

それにしても 彼が忙しいのは知っているが, それにしても電話ぐらいくれてもよさそうなものだ I know he is busy, *still* [*even so*] he might have called me. / それにしてもきょうは暑いね *At any rate*, it is hot today.

それにつけても それにつけても思い出されるのは優しかった祖母のことだ *What that* reminds me of is my grandmother who was kind to me.

それにひきかえ 君の弟さんは本当にしっかりしているね. それにひきかえうちの弟は… Your brother is really sensible. *On the other hand*, my brother …

それは 先週は用事がたくさんあってそれは忙しかった I was *really* busy last week because I had a lot of things to do.

そればかりか 彼女は夕食をごちそうしてくれた. そればかりか車で家まで送ってくれた She treated me to dinner, *moreover* she drove me home.

それはさておき それはさておき, お兄さんは最近どうしてるの *Putting that aside*, how is your brother doing these days?

それはそうと (ところで) by the way; (さて) well // それはそうと, 今何時? *By the way*, what time is it?

それはそれは
 🅒「荷物をお持ちしましょう」「それはそれは, おそれ入ります」 "Let me take your baggage." "Thank you very much *indeed*."

それほど それ程 (そんなに) so // 試験はそれほど難しくなかった The examination was not *so* difficult. / それほど欲しいのなら買えばいいのに If you want it *so much*, you should buy it.
 🅒「料理が上手ですね」「いえ, それほどでも」 "You cook very well." "No, *not really*."

それまで (それまでずっと) till [until] then // それまでずっと寝ていた I was sleeping *until then*. ◆ それまでに部屋を片づけておきなさい Clean up your room *by then* [*that time*]. / その店に行ってみてあいていなかったらそれまでだ If you go to the shop and it is closed, 「*that's that* [*that's the end of it*]. / それまで食べた中で最もおいしい食べ物だった It was the most delicious food I had *ever* had.

それみろ それ見ろ それ見ろ. ひとりで全部やろうったって無理だよ *I told you* it was impossible to do everything by yourself. / それ見ろ. やっぱり僕の言ったとおりだったじゃないか *See that*! It was just as I told you.

それも (しかも) (and) … at that // 傘をなくしたんだ. それも新しいのを I lost an umbrella, (and) a new one *at that*.

◆ 彼女はデジカメをこわしてしまった. それも買ってすぐにだ She broke her digital camera, *and* that was just after she bought it.

それもそのはず 彼は英語が上手だ. それもそのはず(→彼が英語が上手なのは当然だ. なぜなら), 彼は10年間アメリカに住んでいたんだ *It's natural* that he speaks good English, *because* he lived in America for 10 years.

それゆえ それ故 (公式的)therefore; (したがって) accordingly ➪ だから

それる 逸れる (弾などが) miss ⑩; (正道から) go* astray; (針路を急に変える) swerve ⑨; (話などが) wander ⑨, stray ⑨ // 矢がまとからそれた The arrow *missed* the target. / 車は大通りからわき道にそれた The car *swerved* from the main street into a side street. / どうやら話がわき道にそれてしまったようです Our conversation seems to *have 「wandered from the subject* [*got off the track*]*.*

ソロ 【音楽】solo ⓒ ♦ ソロで歌う sing *solo* ‖ ソロホーマー a solo homer

そろい 揃い (一式) set ⓒ // 家具ひとそろい *a set of* furniture

◆ 彼女と妹はそろいの服を着ていた She and her sister wore the *same* clothes.

慣用表現 彼らはそろいもそろってだらしない *Every one* of them is sloppy.

-ぞろい -揃い (全部が) all; (…のどれもが) every, every one of … // 彼の小説は傑作ぞろいだ His novels are *all* masterpieces.

◆ 三つぞろい *a three-piece suit*

そろう 揃う
❶【集まる】get* together; (1か所に) gather ⑨
テニス部員が全員そろった All the members of the tennis club 「*got together* [*gathered*].
◆ 必要な材料はすべてそろった All the necessary materials *were gathered*. (❖ この gatherは「集める」の意味の他動詞) / みんなそろっていますか *Is everybody here?* / その学校には頭のいい生徒がそろっている The school *has a lot of* bright students. / 彼らはそろって(→いっしょに)教室に入ってきた They came into the classroom *together*. / 家族そろってカラオケに行った *My family and I* went to sing karaoke.
❷【完全になる】
これで全集がそろう This book *makes the set complete*. / This book *completes* the set.
このコーヒーセットはカップの数がそろっていない (→ 足りない) This coffee set is 「*a few cups short* [*short of some cups*].
❸【同じになる】(数量などが) be equal; (形などが) be uniform
このリボンは全部長さがそろっている These ribbons *are all equal* in length.
このイチゴは粒がそろっていない These strawberries *aren't uniform in size*.

◆ 彼らのスポーツが得意だ *All of* them are good at sports.

そろえる 揃える
❶【並べる】(きちんと整える) arrange ⑩,

put* ... in order
棚の本をそろえた I *arranged* the books on the bookshelf.
◆靴をきちんとそろえてから入りなさい *Place* your shoes neatly *side by side* before you come in.
❷【同じにする】
私たちは声をそろえて校歌を歌った We sang a school song *in unison*.
彼女たちは口をそろえて(→全員一致して)彼の意見に反対した They *unanimously* objected to his opinion.
前髪の長さをそろえてください Could you *cut my bangs the same length*?
❸【集める】collect 🅼; (準備する) get* ... ready
旅行に必要な物をそろえておかなければならない, I have to *get* what I will need for the trip *ready*.
◆その店は家具を豊富にそろえている That shop *has a wide selection of* furniture. / キャンプ用品を買いそろえた I *bought a complete set of* camping outfit.

そろそろ (ほどなく) soon, before long; (ほぼ) almost //彼女もそろそろ来るだろう She will be here *soon* [*before long*]. / そろそろ出かける時間です It's *almost* time to go.
◆そろそろ失礼します I should be going *now*. / ここに越してきてそろそろ2年になる It has been *nearly* [*almost*] two years since we moved here. / 弟もそろそろ彼女ができてもいい年ごろだ My brother is old *enough to* have a girlfriend.
❷【ゆっくりと】slowly //彼は重い荷物を持って階段をそろそろと降りた He *slowly* went down the stairs carrying heavy baggage.

ぞろぞろ 私たちはぞろぞろと先生の後についていった We *filed along* behind the teacher. / 劇場から観客がぞろぞろと出てきた The audience *streamed* out of the theater. / パレードの周りに人々がぞろぞろ集まってきた People *crowded* along the parade route.

そろばん 算盤 abacus [ǽbəkəs] 🅒 (複 ～es, abaci) //そろばんで計算する calculate on *an abacus* / 妹はそろばんを習っている My sister learns how to use *an abacus*.
慣用表現 この商売はそろばんが合わない(→もうからない) This business *doesn't pay*.

ぞろめ ぞろ目 ぞろ目の日に発売される列車の乗車券を記念に買い求める人がいる Some people buy a train ticket as a memento on *the day when the year, the month and the day are the same number*.

そわそわ 彼は午後に面接を受けるのでそわそわしている He *is nervous* because he will have an interview in the afternoon. / 何をそわそわしているの Why *are* you *fidgeting* [*restless*]?

そん 損
❶【損失】loss 🅒🅤 ――**損する** lose* 🅼; (損失を被る) suffer a loss
彼は株で100万円損した He *lost* [*suffered a loss of*] one million yen on the stock.
その会社は取り引きで大損をした The company *suffered a heavy loss* in the deal.
今それを買うのは損だ It will be *a loss* [*waste of money*] to buy it now.
◆彼は自分の損になるようなことはしない He doesn't do anything that *is unprofitable* to him.
❷【不利】disadvantage 🅤🅒
そのことを知らなくて損をした I *was at a disadvantage* because I didn't know the thing.
彼女は口下手で損をしている Her inability to express herself well is *a disadvantage* to her.
◆一生懸命勉強しておいて損はない You *lose nothing* by studying hard. / 彼はいつも損な仕事を引き受けている He always takes *thankless* jobs. / 彼らは損な立場にいる They are in a *disadvantageous* position.

そんがい 損害 damage 🅤; (利益などの) loss 🅒🅤
台風は九州地方に大きな損害を与えた The typhoon did [caused] great *damage* to the Kyushu area.
その地震による損害額は10兆円と見積もられた The *damage* caused by the earthquake was estimated at 10 trillion yen.
◆彼らは会社に対して損害賠償を請求した They claimed *damages* against the company.
‖損害保険 accident insurance

そんけい 尊敬 respect 🅤 ――**尊敬する** respect, look up to ...
その先生は生徒たちの尊敬を集めている The teacher earns *the respect* of the students.
彼の努力は尊敬に値する His effort deserves [is worthy of] *respect*.
姉は祖母に深い尊敬の念をいだいている My sister *has great respect* for my grandmother.
私たちはみな彼女をリーダーとして尊敬している We all *respect* her as our leader.
彼女はだれからも尊敬されている She is 「*respected* [*looked up to*] by everyone.

そんげん 尊厳 dignity 🅤 //そういう発言は女性の人間としての尊厳を傷つけるものだ That kind of remark impairs human *dignity* for women.

そんげんし 尊厳死 death with dignity

そんざい 存在
existence 🅤, being 🅤 ――**存在する** exist 🅼
そのころまだ電話は存在していなかった In those days telephones hadn't *come into existence* yet.
宇宙人は存在すると思いますか Do you think aliens *exist*?
◆彼は子供たちにとってヒーロー的な存在だった He was *a hero figure* for children. / 彼女はクラブではいつも目立たない存在だった She always kept *a low profile* in our club. / 小さいころは幽霊の存在を信じていた I *believed in*

ghosts when I was a child. / 彼女はおとなしいが**存在感のある**人だ She is quiet but makes her *presence* felt.

ぞんざい ――**ぞんざいな** (がさつな) rough; (いいかげんな) sloppy; (不注意な) careless; (失礼な) impolite ――**ぞんざいに** roughly; carelessly //彼らは言葉づかいがぞんざいだ They use *rough* language. / (→ぶっきらぼうに話す) They speak *curtly*. / 彼女は物をぞんざいに扱う She handles things *roughly*.

そんしつ 損失 loss ⒰ⒸЕ //その会社の**損失**は50億円に達した That company suffered *a loss* of five billion yen. / 彼の死は政界にとって大きな**損失**だ His death is *a great loss* to the political world.

‖損失補填(てん) compensation for a loss

そんしょう 損傷 damage ⒰ //脳にひどい**損傷**を受ける suffer severe brain *damage*

そんしょく 遜色 この機械は新しい物と比べて少しも**遜色**がない (→劣っていない) This machine *is not inferior to* the new ones at all.

そんじょそこら あのおそば屋さんはそんじょそこらの店とはわけが違うんだ That *soba* shop is quite different from ones *around there*.

そんじる 損じる (人の機嫌を損ねる) offend ⊕; (失敗する) fail to *do* //彼女の機嫌を損じてしまった I have *offended* her.

◆あて名を書き損じた (→間違ったあて名を書いた) I wrote the *wrong* address.

ぞんじる 存じる (知っている) know* ⊕; (思う) think* ⊕; (信じる) believe ⊕

◆ご好意ありがたく存じます I *appreciate* your kindness.

🄮「では佐藤さんをご存じなんですね」「はい、よく存じております」 "Then you know Miss Sato, right?" "Yes, I *know* her very well."

そんぞく 存続 continuance ⒰ ――**存続する** (ずっと続く) continue ⊕; (もちこたえる) last ⊕ //会の**存続**が危ぶまれている It is doubted whether the association can *continue*.

そんだい 尊大 ――**尊大な** (横柄な) arrogant; (高慢な) haughty //**尊大な**態度をとる take an *arrogant* attitude; have a *haughty* air

そんちょう¹ 尊重 respect ⒰ ――**尊重する** respect ⊕; (敬意を払う) have* respect [regard] for ...; (高く評価する) value ⊕ //個性を**尊重する** *value* individuality / 彼本人の意思を**尊重**しましょう Let's *respect* his wishes. / 彼らの意見をもっと**尊重**するべきだ We should *have* more *respect for* their opinion.

そんちょう² 村長 the chief [head] of a village

そんとく 損得 profit and loss, loss and gain; (利害) interests //彼女はいつも自分の**損得**ばかり考えている She always thinks of「her own *interests* [personal *gain*].

◆**損得**は問題ではない I don't care *whether I gain or lose*. / 彼は**損得**抜きで(→お金のためでなく)その仕事を引き受けた He took the job *not for money*.

そんな (そのような) such; (そんなふうな) like that; (その) that

そんな話は聞いたことがない I've never heard「*such* a story [a story *like that*].

そんなことは子供にだってできる Even a child can do「*such a thing* [*that*].

彼女に**そんな**ひどいことを言ったの? Did you say *such* a terrible thing to her?

◆**そんなばかな**(→信じられない) I can't believe it! / ごめんなさい。**そんな**つもりじゃなかったんです I'm sorry. I didn't really mean it. / **そんな**のずるいよ *That*'s not fair. / **そんな**わけで一晩中眠れなかったんだ *That's why* I couldn't sleep all night. / 世の中なんて**そんな**ものだよ *That's the way* the world is.

🄮「きっと手帳は家に忘れてきたんだよ」「**そんな**はずないわ」 "You left your diary at home." "*That* can't be true."

🄮「彼、寝坊したからあと20分くらいで来るって」「**そんな**ことだろうと思ったよ」 "He said he overslept and would come here in about twenty minutes." "I thought「*as much* [*so*]."

そんなに (それほど) so, that; (数が) so [that] many; (量が) so [that] much

何を**そんなに**悩んでいるの What are you *so* worried about?

テストは**そんなに**難しくなかった The test wasn't *so* [*very*] difficult.

その番組が**そんなに**おもしろいなんて知らなかった I didn't know the program was *that* interesting.

そんなに CD を持ってるの? Do you have *that many* CDs?

そんなにテレビばかり見ていると目が悪くなるよ If you watch *so much* television, your sight will fail.

◆**そんなに**大きな音を立てないで Don't make *such* a big noise.

ソンブレロ sombrero Ⓒ (複 ~s) (❖スペイン語から)

ぞんぶん 存分 私たちはテニスを思う**存分**楽しんだ We enjoyed playing tennis *to our hearts' content*. / 思う**存分**食べました I ate *as much as I liked*.

そんぼう 存亡 その会社は**存亡**の危機に直面していた The company was facing *a crisis*.

そんみん 村民 villager Ⓒ; (全体) the village

ぞんめい 存命 亡き父**存命**中にはたいへんお世話になりました Thank you very much for everything you did for my father *while he was alive*.

そんらく 村落 village Ⓒ; (小さい) hamlet Ⓒ

た

た¹ 他 ──他の other, another ⇒ そのほか, ほか

だ² 田 paddy ⓒ, rice field [paddy] ⓒ ‖田に水を引く irrigate *a paddy* / 田を耕す plow *a rice field*

たあいない 他愛ない ⇒ たわいない

ダーウィン Darwin (❖オーストラリアの都市)

ダークホース dark horse

ターゲット この雑誌はティーンエージャーをターゲットにしている This magazine 「*is targeted at* [*targets*] teenagers.

ダース dozen ⓒ (《略語》doz., dz.)

> 【語法】
> (1) 数詞の後では単複同形 ‖ 1 [2] ダース a [two] *dozen*
> (2) 次に名詞がくるときは of を付けず形容詞的に用いることが多い ‖ 鉛筆 3 ダース three *dozen* pencils (❖×three dozens of pencilsとはいわない)
> (3) ある決まった物の一部を指すときは of を用いる ‖ この卵を半ダースください Give me 「a half [half a] *dozen* of these eggs, please.

ビールをダース単位で買う buy beers *by the dozen* / この箱には 1 ダースのリンゴが入る This box holds *a dozen* apples. / このボールは 1 ダースいくらですか How much are these balls *a dozen*?

ダーツ darts 《単数扱い》 (❖「ダーツの矢 1 本」は a dart) ‖ダーツをする play *darts*

タートルネック 《米》turtleneck ⓒ, 《英》polo neck ⓒ ‖ タートルネックのセーター a *turtleneck* sweater

ターバン turban ⓒ ‖ターバンを巻く wear *a turban*

ダービー the Derby ‖日本ダービー the Japan Derby

タービン 〘機械〙turbine [tə́:rbɪn] ⓒ

ターミナル terminal ⓒ ‖ターミナルケア terminal care [medicine] / ターミナルデパート a department store at a railroad terminal / ターミナルビル (駅の) a building built over a railroad terminal / ターミナルホテル a hotel near a railroad terminal (❖「ターミナルデパート」「ターミナルビル」「ターミナルホテル」はいずれも和製英語》 / エアターミナル an air terminal, a terminal building / バスターミナル a bus station

タール tar Ⓤ ‖低タールのたばこ a *low tar* cigarette

ターン turn ⓒ ‖氷上で完璧(ぺき)なターンをする make perfect *turns* on the ice
◆Uターンする make *a U-turn*
‖ターンテーブル a turntable

タイ¹ Thailand (❖公式名 the Kingdom of Thailand) ──タイ人 Thai ⓒ ──タイ語 Thai Ⓤ ──タイ (人[語]) の Thai

タイ² ❶【ネクタイ】tie ⓒ, 《主に米》necktie ⓒ (❖tie のほうがふつう)
❷【同点】tie ‖そのチームとうちとの対戦成績は 3 対 3 のタイだ The won-loss record between that team and ours is *a tie*, 3 to 3.
◆砲丸投げで世界タイ記録を出す *tie the world record* in the shot put
‖タイブレーク 〘テニス〙a tie-breaker, a tie-break

たい¹ 対 (競技などで) versus(《略語》vs., v.); (…の間の) between; (…を相手に) against; (…に向かって) toward ‖日本の対米政策 Japan's policy *toward* the United States / 日本対韓国の試合 a game *between* Japan *and* South Korea; a Japan *versus* South Korea game / きょうの名古屋ドームでの試合はドラゴンズ対タイガースだ Today's game at the Nagoya Dome is the Dragons *versus* the Tigers.
◆ 3 対 2 の割合で酢と油を混ぜる mix *three parts* of vinegar *and two parts* of oil / 我々は 2 対 0 で試合に勝った We won the game *2 to 0*.

たい² 他意 彼に他意があったとは思わない I don't believe he had any *other intentions*.

たい³ 隊 party ⓒ ‖救助隊 a rescue *party* / 捜索隊 a search *party* / 登山隊 a *party* of climbers

たい⁴ 鯛 sea bream
[ことわざ] 腐っても鯛 An old eagle is better than a young crow. (→年老いたワシでも若いカラスよりはよい)

> その名前が「めでたい」を連想させるタイは、日本では昔から祝い用の魚とされ、結婚式など祝い事の席でよくふるまわれます。
> Because *tai* (sea bream) is associated with the term *medetai*, which means auspicious, it has been regarded in Japan as a celebratory fish. *Tai* is a fish often served at happy occasions like weddings.

-たい¹ want (to *do*); would like (to *do*); hope (to *do*); wish (to *do*);

> want: 「…したい」を表す最も一般的な表現.
> would like: want より丁寧な表現. 会話などでよく用いられる.
> hope: 実現の可能性があることを望むときに用いられる.
> wish: want, would like より改まった表現. 仮定法とともに用いると実現の可能性が乏しい願望を表す.

いつかキューバに行ってみたい I *want to* go to Cuba someday.
みんなにお礼を言いたいと思います I'd *like to* say thank you to everyone.
この手紙を出しておいてもらいたいのですが I *want* [*would like*] you *to* post this letter.

(❖would like *a person* to *do* は want に比べて丁寧だが、命令的な響きをもつこともある)

またお目にかかりたいです I *hope* to see you again. / I *hope (that)* I'll see you again. (❖目上の人には want より hope がふつう)

私たちの結婚披露宴にぜひ出席していただきたいと思っております We *are [were] hoping* that you'll attend our wedding reception. (❖were hoping のほうがより丁寧)

夏までに3キロ落としたいと思っていたんだけど I *had hoped to* lose three kilos by summer. / I *had hoped (that)* I would lose three kilos by summer. (❖実現しなかったことを表すには had hoped を用いる)

象が飼いたいなあ I *wish* I could have an elephant as a pet.

◆言いたくないけど君にも責任があるよ I *hate to* 「*tell* you [*say this*], but you are partly responsible for it. / 外出するよりも家にいたい気分だ I *feel like* staying home rather than going out.

🗣「何が食べたい」「韓国料理がいいな」"What do you *want to* eat?" "I want to eat Korean food."

🗣「どうしてあんなことしたんだ」「したかったからだよ」"Why did you do that?" "I just *wanted to*." (❖口語ではしばしば to の後の動詞は省略される)

-たい² -帯 〖地理〗zone C // 寒 [温, 熱] 帯 *the* frigid [temperate, torrid] *zone*

◆この価格帯の車を探しています I'm looking for a car within this *price range*.

だい¹ 大 ── 形 (大きい) big, large; (偉大な) great ── 名 (大きさ) size C ⇒ おおきい[な]

大都市 a *big* city / 大選手 a *great* athlete / 10大ニュース *10 big* items of news / ピンポン玉大のしこり a lump about *the size of a* ping-pong ball; a lump *as big as a* ping-pong ball

私たちは大の仲よしです We're *great [good, close] friends*.

彼の新曲は大ヒットした His new song was *a big [smash] hit*.

この製品は大中小の3つのサイズがあります This product comes in three sizes: *large, medium and small*.

◆その提案には大賛成です I'm *all for* the proposal. / この試合はジャイアンツが負ける可能性が大だ *There's a strong probability* that the Giants will lose this game.

慣用表現 だれにだって大なり小なり(→その人なりの)悩みはある Everyone has troubles *of his or her own*. / ベッドに大の字になる *stretch oneself out* on the bed

ことわざ 大は小を兼ねる The greater includes the less(er).

だい² 代
❶ 〖時代・年代〗(世代) generation C; (時代) time C (しばしば複数形~s); (治世) reign [réin] C

次代の人々 *the coming generation* / 7代目の子孫 *a person's seventh generation* descendant

うちは祖父の代[何代も前]から農業をやっています My family has been farming 「*since my grandfather's time [for many generations]*.

◆5代目志ん生 Shinsho V (❖*Shinsho the fifth* と読む) / 先生は40代前半です Our teacher is *in his early 40s*. / その事件は1970年代に起きた The event took place in *1970s [1970's]*. (❖1970s [1970's] は nineteen seventies と読む) / 彼は何代目の首相ですか(→彼の前に何人首相がいましたか) How many prime ministers were there before him? / その店は最近代替わりした(→持ち主が変わった) The store *has changed hands* recently.

❷ 〖料金〗charge C; (乗り物の) fare C; (郵便・ガスなどの) rate C

クリーニング代 a cleaning *charge* / バス代 a bus *fare*

◆ガソリン代は割り勘にしよう Let's share *the cost* of gasoline. / お代は結構です(→無料です) *It's free*. / 電話代を払うのを忘れていた I had forgotten to pay *the telephone bill*.

だい³ 台
❶ 〖物を載せる〗(物を置くための) stand C; (踏み台) stool C; (彫像などの台座) pedestal C // 譜面台 a music *stand*

◆彼はいすを台にして(→いすの上に立って)電球を取り替えた He stood *on the chair* and changed the light bulb.

❷ 〖おおよその範囲〗テストで90点台を取る get *90 something* in the exam / 10時台の電車に乗れば家に帰れます I can get home if I catch a train *between 10 and 11*. / この手のパソコンなら9万円台で買える You can get a PC of this type for *90-something thousand yen*.

❸ 〖単位〗パトカーが2台家の前に止まっていた *Two* police cars were parked in front of my house.

だい⁴ 題 title C; (テーマ) theme C // その映画の題は何ていうの What is *the title* of the film? ◆『サーカスの少年』という題の本を彼らからもらった He gave me a book *entitled [titled] A Son of the Circus*. / 試験は5題出題された There were five *questions* in the exam.

だい- 第- (❖英語の「第」に当たる言葉は特にない) / 第3章 the third chapter; chapter three / モーツァルトの交響曲第40番 Mozart's Symphony No. 40 (❖*number forty* と読む)

たいあたり 体当たり 体 当 た り す る crash into ..., dash *oneself* at [against] ... // 泥棒を警官に体当たりした The robber *crashed into* a policeman.

◆彼の体当たりの演技が注目を浴びている He's *giving everything he has to his performance*, so all eyes are on him.

タイアップ 《口語的》tie-up C // 数社がタイアップして新しいブランドを立ち上げた Several companies *formed a tie-up* and started a new brand. // タイアップ商品 a tie-in

たいあん 大安

大安は旧暦の六曜の一つで、六曜には先勝, 友引, 先負, 仏滅, 大安, 赤口があります。最も縁

起がよいとされる大安に祝い事をすることが多く, 大安の日曜日には結婚式が集中します. 逆に縁起が悪いとされる仏滅には, 結婚式などの祝い事にはふつう避けられます.
Taian is one of the *rokuyo* (six days) in the traditional calendar. They roll around in the order of *Sensho, Tomobiki, Sembu, Butsumetsu, Taian* and *Shakko.* People tend to choose *Taian* to hold celebrations since it is considered to be the luckiest day. That is why many weddings fall on Sundays that are *Taian*. On the other hand, *Butsumetsu* is considered to be an unlucky day and tends to be avoided for weddings and the like.

だいあん 代案 alternative (plan) ⓒ
たいい¹ 大意 (概略) outline ⓒ; (要約) summary ⓒ; (要点) the point; (骨子) the gist ∥お話の大意は分かりました I grasped *the outline* of your story.
◆論文の大意をまとめる *summarize* a paper
たいい² 退位 abdication ⓤ ━━退位する (公式的) abdicate from the throne, give* up the throne
たいいく 体育 physical education ⓤ (《略語》PE, 《英》physical training ⓤ (《略語》PT); (学科) gymnastics《単数扱い》《❖ 短縮して gym ともいう》∥体育の先生 a *PE* teacher / きょうの午後体育の授業がある I've got *gym* [*PE*] this afternoon.
∥体育館 a gymnasium, a gym / 体育祭 a field day, 《英》a sports day; (競技会) an athletic meet [meeting] / 体育の日 Health-Sports Day

だいいち 第一 ━━ 形 first《通例the [one's] ～》《略語》1st); (主要な) primary, prime ━━ 副 first (of all), to begin with

勉強が君の第一の仕事だ Study is your *first* duty.

彼が第一の容疑者だ He is the *prime* suspect.

あなたが英語を勉強する第一の目的は何ですか What's your *primary* purpose in learning English?

私にはそれはとてもできそうにありません. まず第一にとても忙しいのです I'm afraid I can't do it. *To begin with* [*In the first place*], I'm very busy.

第一に自分のことを考えるべきだ You should think of yourself *first*.

地震が起きたらまず第一にガスの元栓をしめなさい When an earthquake occurs, *first* (*of all*) you should turn off the gas.

日本の第一印象はいかがですか What are *your first impressions* of Japan?

事故の第一報が入ってきた *The first report* of the accident came in.

安全第一 《掲示》*Safety First*
◆この仕事は信用が第一だ Credit is *the most important thing* in this business.
∥第一次産業 primary industry / 第一党 the dominant party / 第 1 面 the front page (of a newspaper)

だいいちにんしゃ 第一人者 彼女はその道の第一人者として雑誌で紹介された She was introduced in a magazine as *the leading authority* in the field.

だいいっせん 第一線 第一線を退く retire from *the front line* / 第一線で活躍する be active in *the front line* / 第一線の映画監督 a *front-line* movie director

だいいっぽ 第一歩 the first step ∥第一歩を踏み出す take *the first step* / 平和に向けての第一歩 *the first step* toward peace
◆彼女は新聞記者としての第一歩を踏み出そうとしていた She *was beginning* her career as a journalist.

たいいん¹ 退院 ━━退院する leave* [get* out of] (the) hospital; (退院している) be out of (the) hospital(❖《英》では the を省略する) ∥父はきのう退院した My father *left the hospital* yesterday. / 昨年来, 彼は入退院を繰り返している He *has been in and out of the hospital* since last year.

たいいん² 隊員 member ⓒ
たいいんれき 太陰暦 the lunar calendar
たいえき¹ 体液 (body) fluid ⓤ
たいえき² 退役 ━━退役する leave* [retire from] the service ∥退役軍人《米》a veteran,《英》an ex-serviceman

ダイエット diet ⓒ ➡ 場面・状況別会話 p.1696 ∥今ダイエット中です I'm *on a diet* now. / 急激なダイエットで彼は体をこわした A crash *diet* injured his health. / ダイエットしたほうがいいんじゃない You should go on *a diet*.
∥ダイエット食品 diet food

たいおう 対応 (一致) correspondence ⓤ ━━対応する (相当する) correspond to ...; (策を講じる) take* measures against ... ∥この日本語に対応する英語はありますか Is there any English phrase *corresponding* [*equivalent*] *to* this Japanese?
◆客の問い合わせに対応する (→答える) *answer* inquiries from customers / 時代の変化に対応する (→遅れないようにする) *keep up with* the changing times / 消費者のニーズに対応する *meet* the consumers' needs / 我々はその問題に対する対応策を協議した We discussed *countermeasures* against the problem.

だいおうじょう 大往生 大往生を遂げる (→穏やかに死ぬ) die peacefully; die a peaceful death

ダイオキシン《化学》dioxin [daiáksin] ⓤ ∥その地区の土壌から高濃度のダイオキシンが検出された A high density of *dioxin* was detected in the soil of that area.

たいおん 体温 temperature ⓤ ∥人の体温を測る take a person's *temperature* / 彼女の体温は上がり [下がり] 始めた Her *temperature* began to go up [down]. / 彼の体温はいつもより高い [低い] His *temperature* is higher [lower] than usual. / 大人の体温は36度前後です A human adult's *temperature* is

about 36℃. (❖ 36℃ は thirty-six degrees centigrade [Celsius] と読む)
‖体温計 a (clinical) thermometer

たいか¹ 大家 (巨匠) master ⓒ; (権威) authority ⓒ; (専門家) expert ⓒ ∥物理学の大家 an authority on physics ∥ その道の大家 an expert on the subject ∥ バイオリンの大家 a master of the violin

たいか² 大火 big [great, huge] fire ⓒ ⇨ かじ (火事)

たいか³ 対価 (報酬) reward Ⓤ ⓒ; (補償) compensation Ⓤ

たいか⁴ 耐火 ──耐火の fireproof
‖耐火建築 a fireproof building ∥ 耐火れんが (a) firebrick

たいか⁵ 退化 《生物》 degeneration Ⓤ; (退行) regression Ⓤ ──退化する degenerate ⓥⓘ; regress ⓥⓘ

たいが 大河 big [great] river ⓒ
‖大河小説 a saga

だいか 代価 cost Ⓤ ⓒ, price Ⓤ (また a ~) ∥我々は成功のためにあまりに高い代価を支払った We paid too high a price for success.

たいかい¹ 大会 mass meeting ⓒ; (総会) general meeting ⓒ; (競技大会) 《主に米》 meet ⓒ; (トーナメント) tournament ⓒ; (政治的・宗教的な) rally ⓒ ∥野球の全国大会に参加する take part in a national baseball tournament ∥ あす陸上競技大会が行われます The track meet will be held tomorrow.
‖水泳大会 a swim(ming) meet ∥ 花火大会 a firework(s) display ∥ 弁論大会 a speech contest

たいかい² 大海 the ocean ∥大海の一滴 a drop in the ocean

たいかい³ 退会 withdrawal Ⓤ ⓒ ──退会する withdraw* ⓥⓘ, leave* ⓥ ⓘ, 《口語的》 quit* ⓥ ⓘ ⇨ やめる (辞める)
‖退会届 a notice of withdrawal

たいがい¹ 大概 (いつもは) usually; (たいてい) mostly; (一般に) generally ──たいがいの (大部分の) most; (ほとんどの) almost all ∥日曜はたいがい遅くまで寝ています I usually [mostly, generally] sleep late on Sundays. ∥ たいがいの場合その病気はすぐ治る In most cases, the disease can be cured easily. ∥ たいがいの人はその政策に反対している Most people object to the policy.

たいがい² 対外 ──対外的な (外国に対する) foreign; (外部に対する) external
‖対外援助 aid to a foreign country ∥ 対外関係 foreign [external, international] relations ∥ 対外試合 games with other schools, interscholastic games ∥ 対外政策 an external policy

たいがいじゅせい 体外受精 in vitro [víːtrou] fertilization Ⓤ; ──体外受精児 Ⓤ ‖体外受精児 a test-tube baby

だいかいてん 大回転 giant slalom ⓒ

たいかく 体格 build Ⓤⓒ, physique ⓒ ∥体格がいい [に恵まれていない] have a good [poor] build ∥ がっしりした体格の男 a man of heavy build; a heavily built man

たいがく 退学 ──退学する leave* [《口語的》 quit*] school (❖ leave school は文脈によって「卒業する」の意味にもなる) ∥彼は家庭の事情で退学した He left school for family reasons.
◆その学生は退学になった The student was thrown [kicked] out of school. (❖ be thrown [kicked] out of school は「学校側からやめさせられる」の意味)
‖退学処分 expulsion from school ∥ 退学届 a notice of withdrawal from school ∥ 中途退学者 a dropout

だいがく 大学 university ⓒ, college ⓒ Ⓤ

【語法】
(1) university は大学院を設置した総合大学, college は単科大学だが, そのような制度上の区別を意識しない場合には, しばしば両者が区別なく用いられ, 特に口語では college を用いることが多い.
(2) university の前の冠詞は《米》では必ず用い, 《英》ではふつう省略されるが, 修飾語を伴う場合は不定冠詞が必要 ∥ 大学に通う go to college; go to (a [the]) university ∥ よい大学に通う go to a good college [university]

《大学に》
大学に進む go (on) to college
兄は今年, 大学に入った My brother entered college this year.
どこの大学に通っていますか What college [university] do you go to?
姉は大阪の大学に在学中です My sister is in a college [university] in Osaka.
あの大学に自分が合格するなんてとても想像できない I can't possibly see myself passing the entrance examination for that college [university].

《大学を》
大学を卒業する graduate from college ∥ 大学を中退する 「drop out of [quit] college
私は福井大学を受けるつもりだ I'll take the entrance examination for Fukui University.

《大学で》
彼は大学で日本文学を学んでいる He studies Japanese literature in [at] college.
この大学ではロシア語は教えていません Russian is not taught at this college [university].

《その他》
おじは私の大学時代, 経済的に援助してくれた My uncle assisted me financially in my college days.
彼女は別府大学の学生だ She is a student at Beppu University. (❖ × a student of Beppu University とはいわない)
◆彼は大学の構内をあちこち歩き回った He walked about the campus.
‖大学教育 university [college] education ∥ 大学教授 a (university [college]) professor ∥ 大学生 a university [college] student ∥ 大学生活 university [college, campus] life ∥ 大学入学資格検定 the University Entrance Qualification Examination ∥ 大学

だいがくいん　入試 a university [college] entrance examination / 大学入試センター the National Center for University Entrance Examinations / 大学入試センター試験 the「National Center for University Entrance Examinations [NCUEE] examination / 大学病院 a university hospital / 医科大学 a medical college / 教育大学 a college of education / 芸術大学 a college of fine arts / 工科大学 an institute of technology / 公立大学 a municipal university [college] / 国立大学 a national university [college] / 歯科大学 a dental college / 市民大学 a citizens' college / 商科大学 a commercial college / 女子大学 a women's university [college] / 私立大学 a private university [college] / 水産大学 a fisheries college / 短期大学 a junior college / 農業大学 an agricultural college / 四年制大学 a four-year college

だいがくいん　大学院 graduate school ⓒ ‖大学院で研究する study at *a graduate school*; do graduate work
‖大学院生 《米》a graduate (student), 《主に英》a postgraduate (student)

たいかくせん　対角線 diagonal [daiǽgənəl] (line) ⓒ

たいかん¹　耐寒　耐寒訓練 *training in endurance against the cold* (❖英語には決まった表現がない) / この花は耐寒性にすぐれている This flower *is very resistant to the cold*.

たいかん²　退官 retirement ⓤ ⓒ ──退官する retire ⓐ

たいがん　対岸 the other [opposite] side ‖川の対岸に人が立っているのが見えた I saw a man standing on *the other [opposite] side* of the river.
慣用表現 それは対岸の火事ではない(→我々にも起こりうる) It could happen to us. / (→人ごとではない) It's not just *other people's affair*.

だいかん　大寒 🈳 *daikan*, a day around January 20 marking the coldest time of the year

たいかんしき　戴冠式 coronation ⓒ

だいかんみんこく　大韓民国 ⇨ かんこく(韓国)

たいき¹　大気 (天体を取り巻く) the atmosphere; (空気) the air ‖高濃度の放射能が大気中から検出された A high level of radiation has been detected in *the air*. ◆大気の状態が不安定になり各地で強い雨が降った *Atmospheric conditions* became unstable, and heavy rain fell in many areas.
‖大気汚染 air pollution

たいき²　大器 その野球選手は大器晩成型だった The baseball player was *a late bloomer*.

たいき³　待機 ──待機する wait ⓐ, stand* by ‖自宅待機を命じられた I was ordered to *stand by at home*. ◆警官を待機させる *put police officers on standby*

だいぎし　代議士 (代表) representative ⓒ; (使節) delegate ⓒ

だいきぎょう　大企業 large company ⓒ, 《集合的》big business ⓤ

たいきけん　大気圏 the atmosphere ‖大気圏外に出る go out of *the atmosphere* ‖大気圏内の核実験 an *atmospheric* nuclear test

だいぎし　代議士 (日本の国会議員) a member of the Diet, Diet member ⓒ; (衆議院議員) a member of the House of Representatives

だいきぼ　大規模　──大規模な large-scale ──大規模に on a large scale ‖大規模な損害を被る suffer *large-scale* damage / 事業を大規模に展開する expand *one's* business *on a large scale*

たいぎめいぶん　大義名分 cause ⓒ ‖世界平和という大義名分のために戦う fight for [in] *the cause* of world peace

たいきゃく　退却 retreat ⓒ ⓤ, withdrawal ⓤ ⓒ ──退却する retreat ⓐ, withdraw* ⓐ ‖彼らは前線から退却するしかなかった They had no choice but to *retreat* from the front.

たいきゅう　耐久　耐久性のある生地 a *durable* material / 8時間耐久レース an eight-hour *endurance race*
‖耐久消費財 《米》durable goods, 《英》consumer durables / 耐久性 durability / 耐久力 stamina

だいきゅう　代休　代休をとる take a compensatory day off

たいきょ¹　大挙　報道陣が事故現場に大挙して押し寄せた The press「*rushed in force* [*thronged*] to the scene of the accident.

たいきょ²　退去　──退去する leave* ⓐ ⓐ; (危険な場所から) evacuate ⓐ ‖抗議者たちはその場から退去するように命じられた The protesters were ordered to *leave* there.
◆その犯罪者は国外に退去させられた The criminal *was deported* [*expelled*].

たいきょう　胎教 モーツァルトの曲は胎教によい(→胎児によい影響を与える)らしい I hear that Mozart's music has a good influence on one's unborn baby.

たいきょく¹　大局　物事を大局的に見る see things *in perspective* / それは大局的に見れば重要ではない That's not important *from a broad(er) point of view*.

たいきょく²　対局　将棋の対局をする play *a game of shogi*

たいきょくけん　太極拳 tai chi (chuan) [tái tʃíː (tʃwán)] ⓤ

だいきらい　大嫌い　あなたなんか大嫌いだ I hate you. / 蛇は大嫌いなものの一つだ Snakes are one of *my pet hates*.

たいきん　大金 a lot of money, a large sum of money ‖宝くじで大金を当てる win *a lot of money* in the lottery / 1,000円でも私には大金だ Even 1,000 yen is *a lot (of money)* to me.

だいきん　代金 (値段) the price; (費用) the cost ‖食事の代金は私の勘定につけておいてください Charge *the cost* of the meal to me.
◆注文した本の代金を払いましたか Did you *pay for* the books you ordered? / そのCDの代金はいくらですか *How much* is the CD?

だいく 大工（人）carpenter ©; (仕事・職) carpentry ⓤ ‖大工道具 carpenter's tools / 日曜大工 do-it-yourself (《略語》DIY)

たいくう 滞空 ‖滞空時間 the duration of a flight

たいぐう 待遇 (取り扱い) treatment ⓤ; (接客) service ⓤ; (給与) pay ⓤ ‖不当な待遇を受ける receive unfair *treatment* / 彼らは待遇改善を求めて立ち上がった They took action for *better treatment* [(→賃上げ)*pay*]. ◆国賓の待遇を受ける *be treated* as a national guest / あの会社は待遇がいい(→給与がいい) That company *pays* its employees *well*.

たいくつ 退屈 boredom ⓤ ——退屈な (うんざりさせる) boring; (おもしろくない) dull; (単調な) monotonous

退屈で死にそうだ I'm dying of *boredom*.

その試合はとにかく退屈だった The match was very *boring* anyway.

彼は少々退屈な男だ He's a bit of a *boring* person./ He's a bit of a bore.(❖a bore は「退屈な人[こと]」の意味)

退屈な仕事だが給料はいい It's a *boring* job but the pay is good.

◆退屈そうな顔をしている look *bored* / 彼の長ったらしいスピーチにはみんな退屈した We *were all bored with* his long speech./ 退屈しのぎに漫画を読んだ(→漫画を読んで時間をつぶした) I *killed time* reading comics./ 彼の話はテンポがよくて聞く者を退屈させない He speaks at a good tempo, so he *doesn't bore* his listeners.

たいぐん 大群 鳥の大群 a large flock of birds / イナゴの大群 a large swarm of locusts / 象の大群 a large herd of elephants / 魚の大群 a large school of fish / 夏になると観光客の大群がここへやってくる Crowds of tourists visit here during the summer.

たいけい¹ 体系 system ⓒ ‖給与体系 a *salary system* / 法体系 a *system* of law

◆体系的な *systematic* investigation / …を体系的に研究する make a *systematic* study of …; study … *systematically* / 日本語文法理論を体系化する *systematize* a theory of Japanese grammar

‖賃金体系 a wage system

たいけい² 体型・体形 figure ©, physique © (❖figure は主に女性に、physique は男女ともに用いる) ‖体型を保つ[が崩れる] keep [lose] *one's figure* / 彼女はスリムな[ぽっちゃりした]体型をしている She has a slim [plump] *figure*.

だいけい 台形 〖幾 何〗《米》trapezoid ©, 《英》trapezium © (複 ~s, trapezia)

→ ずけい 図版

たいけつ 対決 confrontation ©ⓤ; (決着をつけること) showdown © (通例単数形); (戦い) fight ——対決する confront ⓗ; fight* ⓗⓘ ‖世紀の対決 *the fight* of the century / 彼と直接対決することは避けたい I'd like to avoid a direct *confrontation with* him. ◆きょう1位と2位のチームの直接対決がある Today the first and second place teams *are going head to head*.

たいけん 体験 experience ⓗⓤ ——体験する experience ⓗ ‖実体験 a real *experience* / 貴重な[異常な, つらい]体験をする have *a* precious [*an* unusual, *a* trying] *experience* / その体験は私の信念を揺るがした The *experience* shook my beliefs./ 彼女は外国での体験談を聞かせてくれた She told us *the* [*her*] *experiences* she had in foreign countries.

◆その専門学校は体験入学することができる That vocational school *allows prospective students to observe lessons*.

→ はつたいけん

たいげんそうご 大言壮語 彼は日ごろから大言壮語している He's always *talking big*.

たいこ¹ 太鼓 drum © ‖太鼓をたたく beat *a drum*

‖太鼓腹 a potbelly / 太鼓持ち(おべっかを言う人) a flatterer / 大太鼓 a bass drum / 小太鼓 a snare drum

慣用表現 彼女の才能には太鼓判を押すよ(→保証する) I *guarantee* her ability.

たいこ² 太古 ——太古の ancient, primitive

たいこう¹ 対抗 (競争) competition ⓤ; (張り合い) rivalry ⓤ ——対抗する (匹敵する) match ⓗ, equal ⓗ; (競う) compete ⓘ; (反撃する) counter ⓗⓘ

数学では彼に対抗できない I *can't match* him in math./ I'm *no match for* him in math. (❖後の表現の match は名詞で「対等の人[物], 好敵手」の意味)

その会社は他社に対抗するために新製品を開発中だ The company is developing a new product to *compete with* [*against*] its rivals.

◆クラス対抗のバレーボール大会 an *interclass* volleyball game / 大学対抗駅伝 an *intercollegiate ekiden* race / …に対抗意識をいだいている have *competitive feelings* for … / …に対して対抗策を講じる take *countermeasures against* … / 地域住民は暴力団に対抗して団結した Local citizens teamed up *against* the gang./ 現職の市長の対抗馬はだれですか Who's *running against* the incumbent mayor? (❖run against *a person* で「…に対抗して選挙に立候補する」の意味)

たいこう² 退校 ——退校する leave* [quit*] school

たいこう³ 対向 ‖対向車 an oncoming car / 対向車線 the opposite lane

たいこう⁴ 大綱 (基本原則) fundamental principles; (大要) outline ©

だいこう 代行 校長の代行をする act for the principal / 社長代行 the *acting* president ‖代行機関 an agent

たいこく 大国 (強国) power © (しばしば Power), (大きい国) large country © ‖経済[軍事]大国 an economic [a military] power

だいこくばしら 大黒柱 (頼みの綱・支柱) mainstay ©(通例 the ~); (稼ぎ手) breadwinner © ‖チームの大黒柱 *the mainstay* of a team

だいごみ 醍醐味 釣りの醍醐味を味わう enjoy *the real pleasure* of fishing

だいこん 大根 a *daikon* (radish), a Japanese radish(❖*radish* はふつうの大根より小さくて丸いハツカダイコンを指す)
∥大根足(太い) fat legs;(太くて短い) stubby legs / 大根おろし(器具) a *daikon* grater;(食物) grated *daikon* / 大根役者 a bad actor [actress], a ham

たいさ 大差 大差をつけている have *a large lead* / 大差をつけて勝つ win *by a wide margin* / 両者の間には大差はない There's not much *difference* [of *a gap*] between the two. / いずれにしても大差はない It *doesn't make a big difference.*

だいざ 台座 (彫像・円柱などの) pedestal ⓒ;(宝石の) setting ⓒ

たいざい 滞在 stay ⓤ《通例単数形》;(客としての) visit ――滞在する stay ⓘ
短[長]期間滞在する *stay* (for) a short [long] time; make *a* short [long] *stay* / 滞在をもう1週間延ばす lengthen [extend] *one's stay* for another week
その島での滞在は短かったがとても楽しかった Our *stay on [visit to]* that island was short but a lot of fun.
どのくらい日本に滞在する予定ですか How long are you going to *stay* in Japan?
彼女は夏休みの間私の家に滞在した She stayed *with me [at my house]* during summer vacation.
それは彼女の米国滞在中に起こった It happened *during* her *stay* in the U.S.
∥滞在客 a guest / 滞在地 a place where *one* stays / 滞在費 expenses during *one's stay*

だいざい 題材 (資料) material ⓤⓒ《また複数形 ~s》;(主題) subject ⓒ, topic ⓒ /小説の題材 *the topic* of a novel / 私はレポートの題材を集めている I'm collecting *material* for a paper.

たいさく¹ 対策 measure ⓒ《しばしば複数形 ~s》;(対抗策) countermeasure ⓒ《しばしば複数形 ~s》/政府は凶悪犯罪に対して強力な対策を講じた The government took strong *measures* against violent crime(s). / 何らかの抜本的な対策がとられるべきだ I think that some drastic *measures* should be taken.
◆高3の夏休みには本格的な受験対策に取りかかるべきだ You should start *preparing* seriously *for college entrance examinations* during the summer vacation of senior year in high school.

たいさく² 大作 (大規模な作品) large-scale work ⓒ;(膨大な作品) voluminous work ⓒ;(偉大な作品) great work ⓒ;(傑作) masterpiece ⓒ

たいさん 退散 ――退散する (逃げる) run* away ◆ 群衆を退散させる disperse the crowd / 退散しよう(→帰ろう) We'd better be going now.

だいさん 第三 ――㊋ third 《通例 the ~》(《略語》3rd) ――㊌ third, thirdly, in the third place
◆第3巻 Vol. *III*(❖volume three と読む)
∥第三国 a third country / 第三次産業 the tertiary industry / 第三者 a third party / 第三世界 the Third World / 第三セクター a joint venture company of local government and private enterprise / 第三帝国(ナチス支配下のドイツ; 1933-45) the Third Reich [ráik]

たいし¹ 大志 ambition ⓤⓒ /彼女は宇宙飛行士になるという大志をいだいてアメリカへ渡った She went to America with *an ambition* to be an astronaut. ◆ 少年よ大志をいだけ Boys, *be ambitious*.(❖札幌農学校の教頭, クラーク(W.S. Clark)の言葉)

たいし² 大使 ambassador ⓒ《しばしば Ambassador》/駐仏日本大使 *the* Japanese *ambassador* to France / ワシントン駐在の韓国大使 *the* Korean *ambassador* in Washington
∥大使館 an embassy / 大使館員《集合的》 the embassy (staff);(個人) a member of an embassy

たいじ¹ 胎児 (妊娠3か月以後の) fetus [fíːtəs] ⓒ;(妊娠8週間以内の) embryo [émbriòu] ⓒ

たいじ² 退治 ――退治する (追い払う) get* rid of ...;(一掃する) wipe out;(根絶する) root out /ゴキブリを退治する *get rid of* cockroaches

だいし 台紙 (写真などをはる) mount ⓒ
◆写真を台紙にはる *mount* a picture

だいじ¹ 大事
❶【重要・大切】――だいじな (重要な) important;(貴重な) precious
だいじな手紙は安全な場所にしまっておきなさい Keep *important* letters in a safe place.
私たちにとって今がいちばんだいじなときだ This is the most *important* time for us.
十分な睡眠をとることはだいじなことだ It is *important* for us to get enough sleep.
彼女は私にとってとてもだいじな存在だ She is very *precious* to me.
◆(病気の人に)おだいじに Please take care of *yourself.*/ I hope you get better soon. / 彼は父親からもらった時計をとてもだいじにしている He greatly *cherishes* [*treasures*] the watch his father gave him. / 君はもっと友だちの気持ちをだいじにする(→尊重する)べきだ You should *respect* the feelings of your friends. / 彼はその花びんをとてもだいじに(→慎重に)扱った He handled the vase very *carefully.*/ He *was* very *careful with* the vase. / あなたがいちばんだいじにしている物は何ですか What's your most *treasured possession?* / このお金はだいじに使いなさい(→むだづかいしてはいけない) Don't waste this money.

❷【大きな出来事】
火事は大事に至らないうちに消し止められた The fire was put out *before it got serious.*

慣用表現 大事をとって医者に診(ﾐ)てもらった *To play* (*it*) *safe* I got checked by the doctor.

ダイジェスト digest ‖ダイジェスト版 an abridged edition

だいしぜん 大自然 nature; (母なる自然) Mother Nature

たいした 大した
❶【それほど】
彼はたいした芸術家ではない He *is not much of* an artist.
全然たいしたことじゃないから心配しなくてもいい *It's no big deal* [*It's nothing serious*], so you don't have to worry about it.
彼女のけがはたいしたことはなかった Her injury *was not serious*.
今度の試合では勝ち負けはたいした問題ではない It *matters little* whether or not we win the next game.
🖉「どうもありがとうございます」「たいしたことじゃありませんよ」"Thank you very much." "*It's nothing much.*"
❷【大変な】
これ,ひとりで作ったの? たいしたもんだね Did you make this by yourself? *That's great.*
あいつはたいしたやつだよ He's really *somebody* [*some guy*].
私に口答えするなんてたいしたものだね(→よくできるね) How dare you talk back to me!
それはたいした見ものだった It was *quite a sight*.

たいしつ 体質 《公式的》constitution ‖彼女は虚弱体質だ She has *a weak constitution*. / 彼は体質改善のために水泳を始めた He began swimming to *improve his constitution*.
◆この薬は私の体質に合わない This medicine *doesn't agree with* me. / 彼はアレルギー体質だ He *has allergies*. / 私は太りやすい体質だ(→すぐに太る) I put on weight easily.

たいして¹ 大して 風はたいしてなかった There was not *much* breeze. / 外はたいして寒くない It's not *very* cold outside. / 彼はたいして勉強しないのに学校の成績はよい He doesn't work *much*, yet he does well at school.

たいして² 対して 彼に対して反感をいだいているわけではありません I don't have anything *against* him. / 先生は質問に対してはっきりと答えてくれた Our teacher gave us a clear answer *to* the question. / 彼に対して私は複雑な気持ちだった I had mixed feelings *toward* him. / 先月の売り上げ50万に対して今月は300万を超えている This month's sales are over three million yen *compared with* five hundred thousand last month. ⇨たいする

たいしゃ¹ 代謝 ‖基礎代謝 basal metabolism / 新陳代謝 metabolism

たいしゃ² 退社 ——退社する (帰る) leave* the office; (辞職する) resign; (定年で) retire ‖6時に退社する *leave the office* at six / 阿部さんは先月退社した Mr. Abe *resigned (from the company)* last month.

だいじゃ 大蛇 big snake

たいしゃく 貸借 (簿記の) debit and credit; (貸すことと借りること) borrowing and lending(❖両者とも日本語と語順が逆であることに注意) ‖貸借対照表〔会計〕a balance sheet

だいしゃりん 大車輪 (鉄棒の) giant swing

たいしゅう¹ 大衆 the (general) public(❖ 1つのまとまりと見るときは単数扱い.個人に重点をおくときは複数扱い); (支配層に対する人民) the people; (庶民) the masses(❖軽蔑的な含みがある)
大衆に受ける appeal to *the public*
彼の政策は大衆の支持を得ている[失っている] His policy is in [out of] favor with *the public*.
◆この汚職事件は大衆の政治不信を招いた This scandal generated *public* distrust in politics. / 元来貴族の遊びだったテニスは19世紀に大衆化した Tennis, which used to be a pastime for nobles, *was popularized* in the 19th century.
‖大衆運動 a popular movement / 大衆教育 mass education / 大衆紙 a popular newspaper / 大衆車 a popular car; (経済的な車) an economical car / 大衆社会 a mass society / 大衆小説 a popular novel / 大衆食堂 a cheap restaurant / 大衆文化 mass culture

たいしゅう² 体臭 body odor ((略語) B.O.) ‖一般的にいうと日本人は体臭があまり強くない Generally speaking, Japanese people don't have strong *B.O.*

たいじゅう 体重 weight
体重が10キロ増えた I've gained [put on] 10 kilograms (of *weight*).
あまり食べないようにしているのに,全然体重が減らない I'm trying to eat less, but I've not lost *weight* at all.
医者は彼に体重を5キロ減らすように言った The doctor advised him to reduce his *weight* by five kilograms.
◆体重を量る *weigh oneself* / 姉は毎日おふろ上がりに体重計にのる My sister steps on *the scales* every day after taking a bath.
🖉「体重はどのくらいですか」「60キロぐらいです」"How much do you *weigh*?" "I weigh about sixty kilograms."

たいしょ 対処 難局に対処する cope [deal] *with* a difficult situation / 前向きに対処します We'll see what we can do.

たいしょう¹ 対照 contrast ——対照する contrast
彼はとても静かだが,対照的に妹のほうは活発だ He is so quiet, but *in* [*by*] *contrast*, his sister is active.
彼は私とは全く対照的な人である He is *a great contrast* to me.
その火山の噴煙は青空と奇妙な対照をなしていた The smoke of the volcano *made a strange contrast* with the blue sky. / The smoke of the volcano *contrasted* strangely with the blue sky.
私たちは自分たちの考えと彼らの考えとを比較対照してみた We *contrasted* our idea *with* theirs.

◆2つの対対照的な考え two *contrasting* thoughts

たいしょう² 対象 (感情・思考・行動などの) object ⓒ; (目標・的 (き)) target ⓒ; (主題) subject ⓒ ‖恋愛[研究, 課税]の対象 *an object of* love [study, tax] / 政治改革はこのごろよく議論の対象になっている Political reform is *a* controversial *subject* these days.
◆このコースは初心者が対象である This course *is* [(*intended*) *for* [*aimed at*]] beginners. / その調査は全校生徒を対象に行われた The survey was carried out *among* all the students.

たいしょう³ 対称 (左右対称) symmetry Ⓤ ⓒ (↔asymmetry) ──対称の symmetrical
◆その庭園は左右対称に設計されている The garden is designed *symmetrically*.

たいしょう⁴ 大将 (陸軍) general ⓒ (《略語》Gen.); (海軍) admiral ⓒ (しばしば Admiral) (《略語》Adm.); (空軍) (米) general ⓒ, (英) air chief marshal ⓒ; (上司・親方) boss ⓒ ◆がき大将 *a bully* / みんなにちやほやされているがあいつはしょせんお山の大将だ Everyone makes a fuss over him, but he's just *a big fish in a small pond*.

たいしょう⁵ 大勝 その試合で私たちのチームは大勝した Our team *won a great victory* in that game.

たいしょう⁶ 大正 [🗾] Taisho
◆祖母は大正5年生まれです My grandmother was born「in *1916* [in *the fifth year of the Taisho era*]. (❖年号は日本独自のものなので西暦を用いるほうがよい)
‖大正時代 the Taisho era [period]

たいじょう 退場 ──退場する leave* ⊕ⓘ; (劇の脚本で) exit ⊕, make* *one's* exit ‖その試合では3人の選手が退場を命じられた Three players were ordered to *leave the field* in that game. / (脚本のト書きで) ハムレット, 退場 *Exit* Hamlet. (❖主語の前に置き, 三人称・単数・現在でも s を付けない. 2人以上が退場する場合は exeunt)

だいしょう¹ 大小 大小によって [かかわらず] 「*according to* [*regardless of*] *size*」/ 水槽の中には大小様々な魚が泳いでいた There were 「*various sizes of* fish [fish *of various sizes*]」in the aquarium. / その国は大小50の島からなる The country consists of 50 islands, *large and small*.

だいしょう² 代償 (補償) compensation Ⓤ; (代価) price Ⓤ (また a 〜) ‖…の代償として *in compensation for* ... / どんな代償を払っても目標を達成するつもりだ I'll achieve my goal *at any price* [*cost*]. / 我々はその計画実現のためにあまりに高い代償を払った We paid too high *a price* for the realization of the plan.

だいじょうぶ 大丈夫 ──大丈夫な all right, OK, O.K., okay; (安全な) safe; (確かな) sure
医者はその子は大丈夫だと言った The doctor said the child was「*all right* [*OK*]」.
この水は飲んでも大丈夫です This water is *safe*「*for drinking* [*to drink*]」.
大丈夫, 君ならきっと試験に合格するよ I'm *sure* you'll pass the exam. / You'll *surely* pass the exam.
◆この牛乳まだ大丈夫かな? Is this milk still *good*? / その犬はかんだりしないから大丈夫だよ (→心配するな) *Don't worry*, the dog won't bite you. / 何が起こっても大丈夫だ (→準備はできている) I'm *ready for anything*. / この棚はその本を全部載せても大丈夫だよ (→載せられる) This shelf *can* hold all those books. / 彼女なら大丈夫だ (→信頼できる) You *can rely on* her. / She *can be relied on*.
💬「顔色が悪いけど, 大丈夫?」「大丈夫です」 "You look pale. Are you「*all right* [*OK*]」?" "I'm「*all right* [*OK*]」."
💬「こんな遅くに電話してごめん」「大丈夫だよ」 "I'm sorry for calling this late." "That's *all right*."
💬「手伝おうか」「いや大丈夫」 "Do you want me to help?" "*No, thank you*."
💬「何時くらいなら大丈夫 (→都合がいい)?」「5時過ぎたら何時でも大丈夫だよ」 "What time is *convenient* for you?" "Any time after five will *do*."

たいしょく¹ 退職 (定年) retirement Ⓤ ⓒ; (辞職) resignation ⓒ Ⓤ ──退職する retire ⊕; resign ⊕⊕, 《口語的》quit* ⊕⊕ ‖定年前に退職する take early *retirement* / 父は65歳で会社を退職した My father *retired from* the company at the age of 65.
‖退職金 retirement allowance; (会社の都合で退職させられた場合の) severance pay / 退職者 a retired employee / 退職願 notice of *one's* resignation

たいしょく² 大食 弟は大食だ My brother *eats a lot*. ‖大食漢 a glutton, a big eater

たいしん 耐震 この橋は耐震性がある This bridge is「*earthquake-proof* [*proof against damage from earthquakes*]」.

たいじん¹ 対人 彼は対人関係で悩んでいる He's worrying about *his* relations with other people. / そのことがあってから彼女は対人恐怖症になっている She *has had a phobia about meeting people* since that incident.

たいじん² 退陣 (辞職) resignation Ⓤ ⓒ ‖首相に退陣を迫る demand *the resignation of* the Prime Minister

だいじん 大臣 (ヨーロッパ諸国・日本などの) minister ⓒ; (米国各省の長官) secretary ⓒ; (英国の) secretary ⓒ, minister ⓒ (❖英国では省によって使い分ける. 「大蔵大臣」のみ the Chancellor of the Exchequer. いずれもしばしば大文字で始める) ‖大臣になる become [(→任命される) be appointed, (→就任する) take office as] *a minister*
‖外務大臣 the Minister of Foreign Affairs / 環境大臣 the Minister of the Environment / 経済産業大臣 the Minister of Economy, Trade and Industry / 厚生労働大臣 the Minister of Health, Labour and Welfare / 国土交通大臣 the Minister of Land, Infrastructure and Transport / 財

務大臣 the Minister of Finance / 総務大臣 the Minister of Public Management, Home Affairs, Posts and Telecommunications / 総理大臣 the Prime Minister / 農林水産大臣 the Minister of Agriculture, Forestry and Fisheries / 副大臣 a state secretary, a vice-minister / 法務大臣 the Minister of Justice / 文部科学大臣 the Minister of Education, Culture, Sports, Science and Technology

だいず 大豆 soybean ◎

たいすい 耐水 ――耐水(性)の water-resistant; (防水の) waterproof, watertight

たいすう 対数 〔数学〕logarithm ◎, (《口語的》log ◎ ∥対数表 a table of logarithms, a log table / 自然対数 a natural logarithm / 常用対数 a common logarithm

だいすう 代数(学) 〔数学〕algebra ◎ ∥代数の問題を解く solve a problem in *algebra*

だいすき 大好き 夏は私の大好きな季節です Summer is my *favorite* season. / 推理小説が大好きだ I *love* mystery novels.

たいする 対する

❶ 【向かい合う】face 他 自
2つの建物は川をはさんで対している The two buildings stand *facing* each other across a river.

❷ 【応対する】
愛想よくお客に対する「*wait on* [*attend to*] customers with courtesy

❸ 【比較対照】
西洋に対する東洋 the East *as opposed to* the West
ドルに対して円安である The yen is weak *against* the dollar.
その映画はアメリカでは不評なのに対して(→ところが一方)日本ではとても人気がある The film has a bad reputation in the U.S., *while* it is very popular in Japan.

❹ 【…に向けて】to, toward, (《英》towards; (感情・好み・趣味の対象) for; (反対・反抗) against (❖どの前置詞を用いるかは単語によって決まっていることが多い)
新しい規則に対する反発 reaction *to* [*against*] the new rules / 病人に対する励ましの言葉 words of cheer *for* the patients / 自分の将来に対する不安 a fear *for one's* future / 人に対する非難 blame *against* a person
彼女は最近私に対して冷たい She's cold *to* [*toward*] me these days.
あなたの発言は働く女性に対する侮辱だ Your remark is an insult *to* working women.
彼は何事に対しても積極的な姿勢を見せる He shows a positive attitude *toward* [*to*] everything.
彼のサッカーに対する熱意はけがをしても冷めることがなかった His enthusiasm *for* soccer wasn't tempered by the injury.
政府は覚醒(かくせい)剤の蔓延(まんえん)に対して強力な対策を講じるべきだ The government should take strong measures *against* the spread of drugs.

◆歴史に対する興味 (an) interest *in* history / 彼の名声に対する深い嫉妬(と) a deep jealousy *of* his good reputation / 健康に対する悪影響 a bad effect *on one's* health / 敵に対する勝利 a victory *over one's* enemy / 彼は私[私の言葉]に対して腹を立てていた He was angry「*with* me [*at* my words].

❺ 【…に関して】about, on
そのテーマに対していくつかおもしろい意見が得られた We got some interesting opinions *about* [*on*] the theme.
彼の意見は我々に対する誤解に基づいている His opinion is based on a misunderstanding *about* us.

たいせい¹ 体制 (制度) system ◎, (構造) structure ◎ ◎; (権力) the Establishment (❖しばしば軽蔑的・批判的に用いる) ➡ はんたいせい / 体制側の人間 a person *on the side of the Establishment*
∥旧体制 an old order / 経済体制 an economic system / 社会体制 a social system / 新体制 a new order / 政治体制 a political system

たいせい² 体勢 (姿勢) posture ◎, position ◎; (平衡) balance ◎ ∥体勢を崩して転んだ I lost *my balance* and tumbled.

たいせい³ 大勢 (全般的情勢) the general situation; (一般的傾向) the general trend [drift] ∥その地域の大勢は和平に傾いている *The general drift* of affairs in the area is toward peace.
◆大勢に従う[逆らう] go with [against] *the stream* / 若者の中で大勢を占める意見 an opinion *prevalent* among young people / 彼のホームランが試合の大勢を決めた His home run *almost decided* the game.

たいせい⁴ 態勢 留学生を受け入れる態勢を整える(→準備する) *make preparations* to accept foreign students / …できる態勢にある *be ready* [*prepared*] to *do* / 飛行機は着陸態勢に入った(→着陸のため降下を始めた) The plane *began its descent* to land.

たいせい⁵ 大成 作曲家として大成する *become a great* composer; *succeed* as a composer / あんなだらしない生活をしていたら彼は決して大成しないだろう He will never be *anybody* because he's leading a loose life like that. (❖anybodyは疑問文・否定文で「ひとかどの人物, 大人物」の意味)

たいせい⁶ 胎生 〔生物〕viviparity ◎ ∥胎生動物 a viviparous animal

たいせいよう 大西洋 the Atlantic (Ocean) ――大西洋の Atlantic ◆大西洋横断の船旅 a *transatlantic* voyage
∥北大西洋条約機構 the North Atlantic Treaty Organization(《略語》NATO [néitou])

たいせき¹ 体積 volume ◎ ∥この箱の体積はいくらか What is *the volume* of this box?

たいせき² 退席 ――退席する (席を離れる) leave* *one's* seat; (部屋を出る) leave the room

たいせき³ 堆積 accumulation ◎ ◎, heap ◎; (堆積作用) sedimentation ◎ ――堆積す

たいせつ 大切

一大切の (重要な) important; (決定的な) crucial; (貴重な) precious, valuable ——**大切に** (慎重に) carefully

大切な思い出 *treasured* memories

十分な休みをとることが彼女には大切だ It's *important* for her to take a good rest. / It's *important* that she (should) take a good rest.

それは我々にとって大切な問題だ That's 「an *important* matter [(公式的)a matter *of importance*] to us.

今夜は彼と大切な約束がある I have an *important* appointment with him tonight.

時間ほど大切なものはない Nothing is 「*more precious* than [so *precious* as] time.

大切なのは言葉ではなく行動である The *important* thing is not what you say but what you do.

もっと大切に扱わないとこわれてしまいますよ You have to handle it 「*more carefully* [*with more care*] or you'll break it.

◆彼女は彼がくれた指輪を大切にしている She *treasures* the ring which he gave her. / お体を大切に *Please take care of yourself.* / もっと両親を大切にしなさい *Take better care of* your parents. / 天然資源は大切にするべきだ(→むだづかいしてはいけない) We must *not waste* natural resources. / 牧師はお互いに助け合うことの大切さを説いた The minister preached *the importance of* helping each other. / 彼が私にとってどれほど大切な人かあなたに分かりっこない You never know *how much he means to* me.

たいせん¹ 大戦 (世界大戦) world war Ⓒ ‖第一次世界大戦 *World War* I (◆ I は one と読む); その老人は2度の世界大戦で戦った That old man fought in both *world wars*.

たいせん² 対戦 ——**対戦する** (試合をする) play 他, play a game with [against] …, meet* 他, (競う) compete 自, (戦う) fight* 自他 ‖私たちのチームは決勝で彼のチームと対戦した Our team *played (against)* his team in the finals. / そのチームとの対戦成績は3勝2敗だ Our team has *a 3-2 record against* that team. ‖対戦相手 an opponent

だいせんきょく 大選挙区 large constituency Ⓒ ‖大選挙区制 a large-constituency system

たいそう¹ 体操 gymnastics(◆教科名としては単数扱い.短縮して gym ともいう); (運動) exercise Ⓤ Ⓒ ‖私は寝る前に軽い体操をする I do [take] some light *exercise* before going to bed. / この本はいい頭の体操になる This book provides *a good exercise* for the brain.

◆ラジオ体操をする *exercise* to the radio

‖体操選手 a gymnast / 体操服 a gym suit / 体操用具 (a piece of) gymnastic apparatus / 器械体操 apparatus gymnastics / 柔軟体操 stretching / 準備体操 warm-up [warming-up] exercises / 新体操 rhythmic gymnastics / 美容体操 calisthenics

関連語 あん馬 pommel [side] horse / 段違い平行棒 uneven (parallel) bars / 跳馬 horse vault, long horse / つり輪 flying rings / 鉄棒 horizontal bar / 平均台 balance beam / 平行棒 parallel bars / 床運動 floor exercises

たいそう² 大層 very, much ‖彼は英語にはたいそう自信があるようだ He seems to be *very* confident of his English. ◆彼はいつもたいそうなことを言う He always *exaggerates*.

だいそう 代走 〔野球〕(代走者) pinch runner Ⓒ ◆…の代走をする *run for* …

だいそつ 大卒 (大学卒) college [university] graduate Ⓒ ‖大卒女子[男子]に対する求人 the job offers to *female* [*male*] *college graduates*

だいそれた 大それた (無謀な) wild; (常軌を逸した) outrageous; (向こう見ずな) reckless; (恐ろしい) terrible ‖大それた望みをいだく have a *wild* ambition / 彼らはひそかに大それた計画を立てていた They were making an *outrageous* plan in secret.

たいだ 怠惰 laziness Ⓤ, (何もしないこと) idleness Ⓤ ——**怠惰な** lazy; idle ‖怠惰な人 a *lazy* person / 怠惰な生活を送る lead a *lazy* [an *idle*] life

だいだ 代打 〔野球〕(代打者) pinch hitter Ⓒ ◆…の代打に出る *pinch-hit for* …

だいたい¹ 大体

❶【おおよそ】(約) about; (たいてい) almost; (たいてい) generally; (大ざっぱに) roughly; (全体的に見ると) on the whole ——**大体の** most; general; rough ➔およそ

君の答えはだいたい正しい Your answer is *almost* correct.

学校まではバスでだいたい10分くらいです My school is *about* ten minutes' bus ride.

夜はだいたいテレビを見て過ごします I *generally* spend the evening watching TV.

その計画はだいたい成功だった *On the whole*, the project was a success.

その仕事はどれくらい時間がかかるか大体の見当はついている I have a *rough* idea (of) how long it will take to finish the job.

◆大体の計画を教えてもらえますか Could you tell me *the outline of* your plan?

🗣「もう宿題はすんだの?」「だいたいね」 "Have you finished your homework yet?" "*Just about*."

❷【そもそも】
だいたいそんなうまい話があるわけがない *In the first place*, it's too good to be true.

だいたい² 大隊 〔軍事〕battalion Ⓒ

だいたい³ 大腿 (太もも) thigh [θái] Ⓒ ‖大腿骨〔解剖〕a femur

だいたい 代替 ——**代替の** alternative ‖代替エネルギー *alternative* energy (◆太陽エネルギー・風力エネルギーなど)

‖代替品 a substitute / 代替フロン a CFC substitute

だいだい¹ 代々 代々語り継がれている民話 a folk tale passed on *from generation to generation* / 私の家は代々この町で商売をしている Our family has been in business in this town *for generations*.

だいだい² 橙 〔植物〕bitter orange ◎
◆だいだい色 *orange*

だいだいてき 大々的 新製品を大々的に宣伝する advertise a new product 「*on a large scale*〔口語的〕*in a big way*〕/ 各紙が事件を大々的に報じた All the papers 「*gave a lot of coverage to* [*featured*] the incident.

だいたすう 大多数 the majority / その地震で大多数の家屋が倒壊した *The majority* of the houses were destroyed by [in] the earthquake.
◆大多数の学生がその提案に賛成だった *Most* of the students [*Almost all* (of) the students] were in favor of the proposal.

たいだん 対談 talk ◎; (会見) interview ◎; (対話) dialogue ⓤ ◎ ――対談する talk with ..., have* a talk with ...

だいたん 大胆 大胆な (危険をかえりみない) bold; (思いきった) daring; (恐れを知らない) fearless ‖私たちは彼女の大胆な発言に驚いた We were surprised at her *bold* remarks. / 彼の提案に反対するなんて君も大胆だね You are *bold* to be against his proposal. / It's *bold* of you to be against his proposal. / 彼女は大胆な服を着ていた She was wearing a *daring* dress. / 彼は授業ボイコットという大胆不敵な行動に出た He took the *bold* measure of boycotting classes.

だいち¹ 大地 the earth, the ground ‖母なる大地 Mother *Earth*

だいち² 台地 plateau [plætóu] ◎ (複 ~s, ~x), tableland ◎ ‖根釧台地 Konsen *Plateau*

たいちょう¹ 体長 length ⓤ
◆その虫は体長10センチくらいだった The insect was about ten centimeters *long*.

たいちょう² 体調 (physical) condition ⓤ, shape ⓤ ‖体調がいい be in good *condition* [*shape*] / 体調が悪い be 「in poor [out of] *condition* [*shape*] / 体調を整える get into *shape* / 彼は体調を崩している He is in bad *condition*. / 体調を保つために毎日運動している I get some exercise every day to keep myself in *shape*. / 彼女は徐々に体調が戻している She's gradually getting back into *shape*.

たいちょう³ 隊長 captain ◎; (指揮者) leader ◎; (司令官) commander ◎

だいちょう¹ 大腸 the large intestine ‖大腸炎〔医学〕colitis / 大腸菌 a colon bacillus

だいちょう² 台帳 〔会計〕(原簿) ledger ◎
タイツ tights (❖ 数えるときは a pair of ... とする

たいてい 大抵 generally; (ふつうは) usually; (ほとんど) mostly ――たいていの most 私はたいてい夕食前に宿題を終わらせる I *usually* [*generally*] finish my homework before dinner.
たいていの子供は甘い物が好きだ *Most* children like sweet things.
彼女はウインタースポーツならたいていこなす When it comes to winter sports, she's good at *most* kinds.
◆彼は野球のことならたいていのことは知っている He knows *almost everything* about baseball. / 彼女はたいていのことでは(→簡単には)驚かない She's not *easily* upset.

たいてき 大敵 great enemy ◎
慣用表現 油断大敵 ⇨ ゆだん

たいど 態度

(心構え) attitude ◎; (物腰) manner ◎; (ふるまい) behavior, 《英》behaviour ⓤ; (立場) stand ◎

態度をはっきりさせる make *one's attitude* clear / 態度を決める determine *one's attitude* / 態度が大きい have *a haughty attitude*

反省してるなら言葉じゃなくて態度で示してよ If you feel sorry, show it in *your behavior* instead of words.

彼は授業中の態度が悪い He has 「*a poor attitude* [poor *manners*] in class.

彼女は何にでも積極的な態度を見せる She shows *a positive attitude* toward everything.

彼は自分には関係がないという態度をとった He took the attitude that it was no concern of his.

彼女は好きな男の子の前ではころっと態度が変わる She *changes her attitude* completely in front of the boy she likes.

彼らは挑発的な発言に態度を硬化させた They stiffened *their attitude* at the provocative remark.

そのことに関しては我々は一貫した態度をとってきた We have been consistent in *our attitude* toward that matter.

彼女が私を好きでないことは態度で分かる *Her behavior* toward me shows that she does not like me.

◆何だ, その態度は(→お得意のつもりだ) *Who do you think you are*? / 人前でそんな態度をとってはいけない You shouldn't *behave* like that in public.

コロケーション –attitude–
〖形容詞＋~〗あいまいな~ an ambiguous [a noncommittal] attitude / 厚かましい~ a brazen [an impudent] attitude / 謙虚な~ a modest attitude / 傲慢(ごうまん)な~ an arrogant attitude / 消極的な~ a negative attitude / 慎重な~ a cautious attitude / 積極的な~ a positive attitude / 挑戦的な~ a defiant attitude / 卑屈な~ a subservient attitude / ぶっきらぼうな~ a surly attitude / 無礼な~ a rude attitude / 友好的な~ a friendly attitude / よそよそし

い～ a distant [an unfriendly] attitude / 冷淡な～ a cold attitude

たいとう¹ 対等 ──**対等な** equal, even / **対等に** equally, evenly / **…と対等の立場にある** be on an *equal* footing with … / どの生徒も対等に扱われるべきだ Every student should be treated *equally*. / 私は女性が男性と対等の条件で働ける職場に勤めたい I want to work in an office where women are on *equal* terms with men.
◆彼とテニスで対等に戦える人はいない He has no *equal* in tennis. (❖この equal は「対等の人[物]」の意味)

たいとう² 台頭 rise / ──**台頭する** rise; (力を増す) gain power ◆日本代表チームは若手選手の台頭がめざましい (→上達が著しい) The young players on the Japanese National Team *are improving dramatically*.

だいどうげい 大道芸 street performance / 大道芸人 a street performer

だいどうしょうい 大同小異 多くの提案がなされたがどれも大同小異だった Many proposals were made, but *there was not much difference* among them.

だいどうみゃく 大動脈 the main artery; (幹線道路) trunk [main] road

だいとうりょう 大統領 president (しばしば President); (略語)Pres. / ブッシュ大統領 *President* Bush(❖the は付けない) / 先月ロシアの大統領が代わった (→新しい大統領が就任した) *The* new *President* of Russia took office last month.
◆ジミー・カーターは大統領任期中に中東和平協定を取りまとめた *During his presidency*, Jimmy Carter arranged the Middle East peace accord.
‖大統領官邸 a presidential residence; (米国の)the White House / 大統領候補 a candidate for president, a presidential candidate / 大統領執務室 a presidential office; (米国の) the Oval Office / 大統領選挙 the presidential election / 大統領夫人 the President's wife, 《米》the First Lady / 大統領補佐官 a presidential aide / 副大統領 a vice-president(《略語》VP)

たいとく 体得 ──**体得する** (習得する) master; (体験によって身につける) learn* … by [through] experience

だいどく 代読 メッセージを代読する *read* a message *for* [*on behalf of*] *a person*

だいどころ 台所 kitchen / 台所仕事 kitchen work / 台所用品 kitchen utensils
慣用表現 台所が苦しい (→収支を合わせるのに苦労している) *have difficulties in making ends meet*

タイトスカート tight skirt

タイトル ❶【題名】title; (新聞記事などの見出し) caption, head / その本のタイトルを覚えてる? Do you remember *the title* of the book?
❷【選手権】title, championship / タイトルを獲得する take [win] *a title* / タイトルを失う[防衛する] lose [defend] *a title*
‖タイトルマッチ a title match

たいない 彼の体内にはまだ弾丸が残っている He's still got a bullet *in his body*.
‖体内時計 a biological clock

だいなし 台無し その事件が彼の人生を台無しにした The incident *has ruined* his life. / 突然の雨のせいでピクニックが台無しになってしまった The sudden rain *spoiled* [*upset*] our picnic.

ダイナマイト dynamite / 数本のダイナマイトを仕掛ける set some sticks of *dynamite*

ダイナミック ──**ダイナミックな** dynamic ──**ダイナミックに** dynamically

だいに 第二 ──第二の second (通例 the ～); (もう一つの) another / 第二に secondly, second, in the second place / 第2巻 *the second* volume; volume *two* / ここは私の第二の故郷です This is my *second* home. / 第二のチェルノブイリを作ってはならない We must not create *another* Chernobyl. ◆彼は画家として第二の人生を歩み始めた He started *a new life* as a painter.
‖第2アクセント〖音声〗(a) secondary stress / 第2言語 a second language / 第二次産業 a secondary industry / 第二次世界大戦 World War II, the Second World War

たいにち 対日 アメリカの対日貿易赤字 U.S. *trade deficit with Japan* / その国は対日関係の改善に努力している The country is trying to improve *the relations with Japan*. / その国の国民の対日感情はあまりよいものでない People in the country don't have good *feelings toward Japan*.

だいにゅう 代入 〖数学〗substitution / ──**代入する** substitute / *a* に 3 を代入する substitute "3" for "*a*"

たいにん 大任 important duty [task] / 彼は無事大任を果たすことができた He could carry out *his important duty* [*task*] safely.

たいにん² 退任 ──**退任する** (辞職する) resign; (定年で) retire

ダイニングキッチン ⚠a kitchen with a dining area (❖「ダイニングキッチン」は和製英語)

ダイニングルーム dining room

たいねつ 耐熱 ──**耐熱の** heatproof, heat-resistant ‖耐熱ガラス heat-resistant glass

だいの 大の 私たち 2 人は大の親友だ We two are *great* friends. / 桑田君は大の野球ファンだ Kuwata is a *big* [*great*] fan of baseball. / 私は蛇が大の苦手だ I dislike snakes *very much*. / 大の大人がそんな子供じみたことを言うもんじゃない A *full grown* adult like you shouldn't say such a childish thing.

たいのう 滞納 ──**滞納する** fall* into arrears; (滞納している) be behind with …, be in arrears ‖彼は家賃を 4 か月分滞納している He *is* four months *behind* [*in arrears*] *with* his rent. / His rent *is* four months *in arrears*.
‖滞納金 arrears / 滞納者 a defaulter

だいのう 大脳 〖解剖〗cerebrum (複 ～s,

cerebra) ‖大脳皮質 the cerebral cortex / 大脳辺縁系 the limbic system

だいのじ 大の字 彼は芝生の上に大の字になった He「*spread himself*[(→手足を投げ出した)*sprawled out*] on the grass.

たいは 大破 ―大破する be badly [completely] damaged, be wrecked ‖彼の車はダンプと衝突し大破した His car *was*「*completely damaged* [*wrecked*] by crashing into a dump truck.

ダイバー diver ⓒ ‖スカイダイバー a skydiver / スキンダイバー a skin diver

たいはい¹ 大敗 わがチームは15対0で大敗を喫した Our team *was completely defeated* by a score of 15 to 0.

たいはい² 退廃 decadence ⓤ, corruption ⓤ ―退廃的な decadent, corrupt ‖退廃的なムード a *decadent* atmosphere / 退廃的な音楽 *decadent* music / 退廃した生活 a *corrupt* life

たいばつ 体罰 corporal [physical] punishment ⓤ ‖生徒に体罰を加える inflict *corporal* [*physical*] *punishment* on a student

たいはん 大半 彼は休暇の大半をいなかで過ごした He spent *the major* [*greater*] *part* of his holidays in the country. / 本校の生徒の大半が市内に住んでいる *Most* [*The majority*] of the students of this school live inside the city. / 大半の観衆はそのグループの演奏がお目当てだった *A large part of* the audience came mainly to hear the group. / その競技では女性が参加者の大半を占めていた Women *were in the majority* at the competition.

たいひ¹ 対比 (対照) contrast ⓤⓒ; (比較) comparison ⓤⓒ ―対比する contrast ⓥ; compare ⓥ ‖彼の初期の作品と後期の作品を対比する *compare* [*contrast*] the works of his early days *with* those of his later days

たいひ² 待避 ―待避する take* shelter ‖待避所 a shelter

たいひ³ 堆肥 compost ⓤ

タイピスト typist ⓒ

だいひつ 代筆 僕は彼のラブレターを代筆してやった I *wrote* a love letter *for* him.

たいびょう 大病 serious illness ⓤ ‖彼は大病を患っている He is suffering from *serious illness*./ He is *seriously ill*.

だいひょう 代表 (代表者) representative ⓒ; (公式の場への使節) delegate ⓒ (❖代表者個人を指す) ―代表的な representative; (典型的な) typical ―代表する represent ⓥ; (特有である) be typical of ...
日本の国連代表 the Japanese *delegates to* the U.N.
我々は山田君と長谷川君をクラスの代表に選んだ We chose Yamada and Hasegawa to be our class *representatives*.
彼女はわが校を代表してその討論会に臨んだ She *represented* our school at the debate. / She took part in the debate *on behalf of* our school.
電子工業はこの国の代表的産業の一つである Electronics is one of this country's *representative* industries.
このいすはアールデコ様式の代表的なものだ This chair *is typical of* art deco design.
◆「花火」は北野武監督の代表作だ *Hanabi* is *the most famous film* directed by Kitano Takeshi. / 健は柔道のオリンピック代表選手に選ばれた Ken was selected to be a member of the Olympic judo team.
‖代表委員(クラスの) a class president / 代表作 one's masterpiece / 代表者 a representative / 代表団 a delegation / 代表取締役 a representative director

ダイビング diving ⓤ ‖(野球で)山田はその打球をダイビングキャッチした Yamada *made a diving catch of* the ball.
‖ダイビングスーツ a diving suit / ダイビングスクール a diving school / スカイダイビング skydiving / スキューバダイビング scuba diving / スキンダイビング skin diving

たいぶ 退部 彼は野球部を退部した He *quit* the baseball club.

タイプ
❶【型・種類】type ⓒ; (種類) kind ⓒ, sort ⓒ
彼はスポーツマンタイプだ He is *an athletic type*.
どんなタイプの靴が欲しいですか What *kind* [*sort*] of shoes do you want?
君みたいなタイプはこの仕事に向いている Your *sort* [*kind*] is suited for this job.
彼は私の好みのタイプじゃない He is not my *type*.
🅒「どんなタイプの女の子が好きなの」「物静かな子かな」 "*What type of* girls do you like?" "Well, I like the quiet type."
❷【タイプライター】typewriter ⓒ
◆タイプミス *typing* errors / 手紙をタイプで打つ *type* a letter

だいぶ 大分
(非常に) very (❖形容詞や副詞を修飾する), (very) much, a lot (❖動詞, 形容詞・副詞の比較級などを修飾する); (かなり) 《口語的》pretty, quite, rather
彼女はだいぶ眠そうだ She seems to be *very* [*pretty, quite, rather*] sleepy.
彼の英語はここ3か月でだいぶうまくなった His English has improved "*very much* [*a lot*] during these three months.
気分はだいぶよくなりました I feel *much* [*a lot*] better now.
◆きょうはだいぶ(→たくさんの)お金を使ってしまった I've spent *much* [*a lot of*] money today. / だいぶ(→かなり長い時間)待ったが, 結局彼女は来なかった I waited *for quite a long time*, but in the end, she didn't turn up. / その湖まではまだだいぶありますよ(→まだ遠い) The lake is still *far* from here.

たいふう 台風 typhoon ⓒ
➪ 場面・状況別会話 p.1734
小型で強い勢力の台風 *a small but powerful typhoon* / 台風の目 *the eye of a typhoon*
台風が東シナ海で発達している *A typhoon* is developing over the East China Sea.

だいふく

台風5号は房総半島に接近している *Typhoon No.5 is approaching the Boso Peninsula.*

台風は本州各地で猛威をふるった *The typhoon raged with fury all over Honshu.*

台風の中心気圧は970ヘクトパスカル，中心付近の最大風速は30メートルに達している *The atmospheric pressure of the center of the typhoon is 970 hectopascals, and the maximum wind around its center is measured at 30 meters per second.*

台風の進路を予測するのは難しい *It is hard to predict the path a typhoon is going to take.*

きのうは台風一過でいい天気だった *The typhoon had passed, so yesterday's weather was clear and sunny.*

‖雨台風 a rain typhoon / 大型台風 a big typhoon / 風台風 a wind typhoon / 小型台風 a small typhoon

慣用表現 このチームは今シーズン台風の目になりそうだ(→波乱を起こしそうだ) *This team is likely to upset people's expectations this season.*

関連語 サイクロン a cyclone / ハリケーン a hurricane

だいふく　大福

大福はやや甘みを加えたもちであんを包んだ代表的な和菓子です。一般的な白い大福のほか，もちにヨモギを加えた「よもぎ大福」，あんといっしょにイチゴがまるごと入った「いちご大福」などがあります。
Daifuku is a typical Japanese confectionery made from slightly sweetened mochi stuffed with bean paste. Besides the usual white daifuku, there are yomogi daifuku, whose mochi is kneaded with mugwort, and ichigo daifuku, in which a whole strawberry is stuffed into the mochi together with bean paste.

だいぶつ　大仏 a great statue of Buddha
◆奈良の大仏 *the Great Buddha* at Nara / 東大寺の大仏殿 *the hall for the Great Buddha* at Todaiji temple

だいぶぶん　大部分 ―图 majority ⓤ《また～》《◆全体を1つのまとまりとして考えるときは単数扱い，個々を強調するときは複数扱いになる》, the best [better] part ―副 mostly, largely, for the most part ―大部分の most ⇨ほとんど

彼女は蔵書の大部分を売ってしまった *She has sold the majority of her books.*

地球の表面の大部分は海に覆われている *The best [better] part of the earth is covered with water.*

大部分の人が彼の無実を信じている *Most people believe his innocence.*

そのコンサートの聴衆は大部分若者であった *The audience at the concert was mostly [largely] young.*

◆新しい校舎は大部分(→ほとんど)完成している *The new school building is almost [nearly] completed.*

タイプライター typewriter ⓒ

たいへい　太平・泰平 peace ⓤ ‖天下太平だ *All the world is at peace.* / *Peace is all around the world.*

たいべい　対米 対米政策 *a policy toward the United States* / 対米輸出 *export to the United States* / 日本の対米貿易黒字 *Japan's trade surplus with the United States* / その国の国民の対米感情はあまりよいものでない *People in that country don't have good feelings toward the United States.*

タイペイ　台北 Taipei (❖台湾の首都)

たいへいよう　太平洋 the Pacific (Ocean) ―太平洋の Pacific / 北[南]太平洋 *the North [South] Pacific* / 冬の間太平洋側では晴天の日が多い *The Pacific Coast is likely to have fine weather during winter.*
‖太平洋沿岸諸国 the Pacific countries / 太平洋高気圧 a Pacific high / 太平洋戦争 the Pacific War / 太平洋プレート the Pacific Plate / 環太平洋地域 the Pacific Rim

たいべつ　大別 ごみはリサイクルできるものとできないものとの2つに大別される *Trash can be classified [divided] roughly into two types — recyclable and nonrecyclable.*

たいへん　大変

❶**〖重大な〗** ――大変な（重大な）serious; （恐ろしい）terrible, awful

大変なへまをしてしまった *I've made a serious [terrible] mistake.*

大変なことが起こった *A terrible [An awful] thing has happened.*

◆大変だ, 財布をどこかに落としてしまった *Oh, no! I've dropped my wallet somewhere.* / 君のしたことが先生に知れたら大変だぞ *If the teacher finds out what you've done, you'll be in trouble.*

🗨「彼は仕事を失ったらしい」「それは大変だね」"*They say he's lost his job.*" "*That's tough. / That's too bad.*"

❷**〖容易でない〗**

辞書を作るのは大変な仕事だ *Making a dictionary is a tough [hard] job.*

その本を読むのは高校生には大変だ *The book is hard for high school students to read.*

不況でどの会社も大変らしい *Every company seems to be suffering difficulties because of the depression.*

❸**〖程度がはなはだしい〗**

彼女は大変な浪費家だ *She spends money a lot.*

彼は大変な野心家だった *He was a man of great ambition.* / *He was a very ambitious man.*

週末ともなるとこの通りは大変な人出でにぎわう *This street gets crowded with a great many people on weekends.*

この計画を成しとげるには大変な努力が要求されるだろう *This project would require much*

[a lot of] effort.
❹[とても] very(❖形容詞・副詞を修飾する), (very) much(❖動詞・形容詞・副詞などを修飾する)

たいへんお世話になりました Thank you *very much* for your kindness [help].
たいへん驚いたことに,彼はその試験に失敗した *Much* to my surprise, he failed to pass the exam.
その本はたいへん役に立つ The book is 「*very* helpful [*of great* help].
お待たせしてたいへん申しわけありません I'm *very* [*terribly, awfully*] sorry to have kept you waiting.

◆たいへんよくできました *Well done.*/ *Good job.*

たいへん 代返 ──代返する answer the roll (call) *for a person*

たいべん¹ 大便 (公式的)excrement ⓤ, feces,〖医学〗stool ⓒ(通例複数形 ~s)
◆大便をする move [empty] *one's* bowels

たいべん² 代弁 ──代弁する speak* for *a person* ◆彼の歌はその時代の若者の気持ちを代弁している His songs *express* the feeling of the young people of that era.
∥代弁者 a spokesperson

たいほ 逮捕 arrest ⓤⓒ,capture ⓤ,《公式的》apprehension ⓤ ──逮捕する arrest ⓣ, capture ⓣ,《公式的》apprehend ⓣ ◆彼女は窃盗容疑で逮捕された She *was arrested* for [on suspicion of] theft./ 警察は彼を窃盗の容疑で逮捕した The police *arrested* him on [for] a charge of robbery./ 彼は暴行の現行犯で逮捕された He *was arrested* [*captured*] in the act of assault./ 犯人はまだ捕まっていない The criminal *has not been arrested* yet./ The criminal *is* still *at large*./ おまえを逮捕する You *are under arrest*.(❖警察官の言葉)/ その男に逮捕令状が出された A *warrant* was issued *for his arrest*./ ここで誘拐犯が繰り広げられた Here is the scene of *the* dramatic *arrest of the* kidnapper.

◆すりは現行犯逮捕された The pickpocket *was caught red-handed*.

たいほう 大砲 (heavy) gun ⓒ,《集合的》artillery ⓤ;(旧式の)cannon ⓒ ∥大砲を撃つ fire *a gun* [*cannon*]

たいぼう¹ 待望 ──待望の long-awaited, long-expected(❖共に名詞の前で用いる) ∥待望の彼らのニューアルバムがもうすぐ出る Their *long-awaited* [*long-expected*] new album is coming soon.

たいぼう² 耐乏 耐乏生活をする endure a hard [poor] life

たいぼく 大木 big tree ⓒ;(高い木) tall tree ⓒ

だいほん 台本 script ⓒ;(芝居などの) scenario ⓒ(複 ~s);(映画の) screenplay ⓒ

たいま 大麻 〖植物〗hemp ⓤ;(マリファナ) marijuana ⓤ, cannabis ⓤ,《口語的》grass ⓤ

タイマー timer ⓒ ∥タイマーを5分にセットした I set *the timer* for five minutes./ 炊飯器のタイマーを朝6時にセットした I set the electric rice cooker's *timer* for 6 a.m.
∥セルフタイマー a self-timer

たいまつ 松明 torch ⓒ

たいまん 怠慢 (具体的な行為の)neglect ⓤ;(習慣的・傾向としての)negligence ⓤ ──怠慢な neglectful; negligent ∥彼は職務怠慢のため減給処分を受けた He had his salary reduced for *neglect* [*negligence*] *of his duty*.

だいみょう 大名 a *daimyo*(❖*daimio* ともつづる), a Japanese feudal lord
∥大名行列 a procession of a *daimyo* and his attendants

タイミング 彼はバットを振るタイミングがいい[悪い] He has good [bad] *timing* for swinging the bat./ 平田はいつもいい[悪い]タイミングでギャグを飛ばす Hirata tells gag *at the right* [*wrong*] *time*./ 彼女のうわさ話をしているところにタイミングよく[悪く]本人が現れた She made a *timely* [an *untimely*] appearance when we were talking about her./ 彼女に告白するタイミングを逃してしまった I missed *the chance* to tell her that I loved her.

タイム time ⓤⓒ;(試合の一時中断)〖スポーツ〗time-out ⓒⓤ ∥100メートル走で美樹は13秒1のタイムを出した Miki recorded *a time* of 13.1 seconds in the 100-meter dash./ タイムアップ *Time is up.*/ 監督はタイムを要求し選手を集合させた The coach called *a time-out* and gathered the players around him./ タイムカードを押し忘れた I forgot to punch *my time card*.(❖出社時には punch in,退社時には punch out ともいう)

◆タイム!信二がけがしてる *Time* (*out*)! Shinji is hurt./ 私のタイムを計ってください *Time* [*Clock*], please./ そのレースのタイムをとった I *timed* [*clocked*] the race.
∥タイムカプセル a time capsule / タイムキーパー a timekeeper / タイムサービス a discount offered during certain hours(❖× time service とはいわない)/ タイムトライアル〖スポーツ〗a time trial / タイムマシン a time machine / タイムリミット a time limit / タイムレコーダー a time clock

タイムリー ──タイムリーな timely,《公式的》opportune ∥彼女からの電話は非常にタイムリーだった She made a very *timely* [*opportune*] call to me.

◆彼はタイムリーヒットを放った He got an *RBI hit*.(❖RBI は *run batted in* の略. a timely hit は日本語の「タイムリーヒット」とは異なり,得点が入らない場合にも用いる)

だいめい 題名 title ⓒ ∥『ライ麦畑でつかまえて』という題名の本を読んだ I read a book with *the title The Catcher in the Rye*./ I read a book *entitled The Catcher in the Rye*.

だいめいし 代名詞 〖文法〗pronoun ⓒ

> (1)代名詞は,名詞,名詞句[節],文の代わりに用いられる語のことをいう.同じ名詞を繰り返すのを避けたり,はっきりと名詞をいわなくても分

かる場合などに用いる.
(2)代名詞には，関係代名詞，疑問代名詞，再帰代名詞，指示代名詞，所有代名詞，人称代名詞，不定代名詞がある.

◆「瀬戸物」は陶磁器の代名詞(→同義語)となっている We use the word "setomono" as *a synonym* for earthenware in general.
‖関係代名詞 a relative pronoun / 疑問代名詞 an interrogative pronoun / 再帰代名詞 a reflexive pronoun / 指示代名詞 a demonstrative pronoun / 所有代名詞 a possessive pronoun / 人称代名詞 a personal pronoun / 不定代名詞 an indefinite pronoun

たいめん¹ 体面 honor,《英》honour ⓤ; (尊厳) dignity ⓤ; (体裁(ﾃｲ)) appearance ⓤⓒ /それは私の体面にかかわることだ That affects my *honor* [*dignity*]. / 彼は体面上知ったふりをしているにちがいない He must be pretending to know about it [*for appearance's sake* [(→面目を失わぬよう) *not to lose face*]. ◆体面を保つ save (one's) face

たいめん² 対面 ─対面する meet* ⓦⓘ /彼らは30年ぶりに対面した They *met* (*each other*) for the first time in 30 years.

だいもく 題目 (書物の) title ⓒ; (研究・論文などの) subject ⓒ; (演題) topic ⓒ

タイヤ tire,《英》tyre ⓒ /タイヤに空気を入れる put [pump] air into *a tire* / タイヤを交換する change *a tire* / 自転車のタイヤがパンクした My bike got *a flat tire*.
‖タイヤチェーン a (tire) chain / スタッドレスタイヤ a studless snow tire / スノータイヤ a snow tire / スペアタイヤ a spare tire

ダイヤ ❶【列車の運行予定表】(train) schedule ⓒ, timetable ⓒ /ダイヤ改正 revision of *a schedule* / 事故のためダイヤが大幅に乱れている *The schedule* is very much disrupted due to an accident. / 電車はダイヤどおり運行されている様子だ Trains seem to be running *on schedule*.
❷【ダイヤモンド】diamond ⓒⓤ /ダイヤの指輪 *a diamond* ring
❸【トランプのマーク】diamond ⓒ /ダイヤのキング the king of *diamonds*

たいやく¹ 大役 important duty [task] ⓒ /大役を仰せつかる be charged with *an important duty* [*task*] / 彼女はみごとに大役を果たした She carried out *an important duty* [*task*] successfully.

たいやく² 対訳 この本は英和対訳の形式をとっている This book has the original English text and the Japanese translation printed next to each other.

だいやく 代役 substitute ⓒ, stand-in ⓒ; (代りの役的) understudy ⓒ
◆映画中のいくつかのシーンでは彼がその俳優の代役を務めた He *substituted* [*stood in*] for the actor in some scenes of the movie.

ダイヤモンド diamond ⓒⓤ; (野球の) the diamond ‖ダイヤモンドダスト diamond dust, ice crystals

ダイヤル dial ⓒ ─ダイヤルする (電話する) dial ⓦⓘ, call ⓦⓘ /うちの電話はダイヤル式だ Our telephone is *a dial phone*. / ダイヤルしてしまった I *dialed* [*called*] a wrong number by mistake.
‖ダイヤルイン direct-dialing / フリーダイヤル《米》a toll-free number,《英》a Freefone number

たいよ 貸与 制服は会社から貸与される Uniforms *are lent* by the company.

たいよう¹ 太陽 the sun(❖ある状態の太陽を表すときには《a [an]+修飾語句+sun》となることがある) ─太陽の sun, solar
太陽は東から昇り西に沈む *The sun* rises in the east and sets in the west.
太陽は明るく輝いていた *The sun* was shining bright(ly).
きょうは太陽が出ていない There is no *sun* today.
真っ赤な太陽が山の向こうに沈もうとしている *A glowing red sun* is descending behind the mountains.
地球や火星などの惑星は太陽の周りを回っている Planets such as the earth and Mars go around *the sun*.
彼らは太陽エネルギーを効率よく電力に変える研究をしている They are studying how to change *solar energy* into electricity efficiently.
◆君は僕の太陽だ You are my *sunshine*.
‖太陽系 the solar system / 太陽光線 a sunbeam, the sun's rays / 太陽電池 a solar cell; (solar cell を並べたもの) a solar battery / 太陽熱 solar heat / 太陽熱温水器 a solar water heater / 太陽暦 the solar calendar

たいよう² 大洋 the ocean

だいよう 代用 substitution ⓒⓤ ─代用する (…を～の代わりに用いる) substitute ... for～; (…を～として用いる) use ... as～ /サラダ油をオリーブ油の代用にした I *substituted* salad oil for olive oil. / 彼女は空きびんを花びんの代用にした She *used* an empty bottle *as* a vase. ◆段ボール箱は子犬の小屋の代用になる Cardboard boxes can *serve as* a kennel for a puppy.
‖代用食 substitute food / 代用品 a substitute

たいようねんすう 耐用年数 その機械の耐用年数は15年です The machine has *a 15-year life span*. / *The life* of the machine is 15 years.

たいら 平ら ─平らな flat (↔rough); (水平な) level; (でこぼこしていない) even (↔uneven); (なめらかな) smooth
材木にかんなをかけて平らにした I planed a piece of wood *flat* [*smooth*].
私たちは平らな場所にテントを張った We put up the tent on *level* [*even*] ground.
◆地面を平らにする *level* the ground / 彼はピザの生地を平らに伸ばした He *flattened* (*out*) the pizza dough.

たいらげる 平らげる eat* up, finish (off, up) /彼は出された料理をあっという間に平らげて

しまった He *ate* [*finished*] *up* all the dishes on the table in a flash.

だいり 代理
substitute ◎; representative ◎; agent ◎; deputy ◎ ——代理の acting(❖名詞の前で用いる)，representative

> substitute: 代わりを務める人．
> representative: 代わりに選ばれた・任命された人．
> agent: 業務を代行する人．
> deputy:「副…」に当たる地位にある人で，トップの不在時にその代わりを務める．

クラブの部長がいないときは僕が代理を務めます I *act as the substitute for* the club leader when he is absent. / I *substitute* [*act*] *for* the club leader when he is absent.
あの先生がうちの学校の校長代理です That teacher is *the acting* [*deputy*] *principal* of our school.
◆彼のぐあいが悪かったので僕が代理でレポートを提出した I handed in his report *for* him because he was ill. / 上野氏の代理として大塚氏が会議に出席します Mr. Otsuka will attend the conference *in place of* Mr. Ueno. / X社とY社の間で代理店契約が結ばれた *An agency agreement* has been reached between X and Y companies.
‖代理教員《米》a substitute teacher,《英》a supply teacher / 代理母 a surrogate mother / 広告代理店 an advertising agency [agent] / 総代理人 a general [the sole] agent / 法廷代理人 an attorney / 旅行代理店 a travel agency [agent]

だいリーガー 大リーガー major leaguer ◎

だいリーグ 大リーグ major league ◎《しばしば Major League》, (the) majors ◎ /近ごろは日本人が大リーグでプレーするのも珍しいことではなくなった It's not uncommon for Japanese to play in *the major leagues* nowadays.
[関連語] マイナーリーグ a「minor league [Minor League], the minors

たいりく 大陸 continent ◎ ——大陸の continental /ヨーロッパ大陸 the European Continent / 新[旧]大陸 the New [Old] Continent / オリンピックの旗は5大陸を象徴している The Olympic flag symbolizes five *continents*.
‖大陸移動説〖地学〗continental drift / 大陸横断鉄道 a transcontinental railroad / 大陸性気候 a continental climate / 大陸棚 a continental shelf

だいりせき 大理石 marble Ⓤ /大理石の床 a *marble* floor

たいりつ 対立 conflict ◎ Ⓤ; (敵対関係)《公式的》antagonism Ⓤ; (反対) opposition Ⓤ ——対立する conflict with …; (考えが) be opposed to …
両国間には激しい対立がある There is *a* sharp *conflict* [*antagonism*] between the two countries.
その戦争は宗教的対立から起こった The war grew out of *a religious conflict*.
彼らはその問題で意見が対立した They *conflicted with* each other on the issue. / (→対立する意見をもっていた) They had *opposing opinions* on the issue. / (→意見が分かれていた) They *were divided* (in opinion) on the issue.
◆対立する2つのグループ間に抗争があった There was a fight between the two *opposing* groups.
‖対立候補 a rival candidate

たいりゃく 大略 (あらまし) outline ◎; (要約) summary ◎ /…の大略を述べる give *an outline of* …

たいりゅう 対流 〖物理〗convection Ⓤ ‖対流圏〖気象〗the troposphere

たいりょう¹ 大量 ——大量の a lot of …, a (large) quantity of …, (large) quantities of … ——大量に in quantity /私たちは日々大量のごみを出している We discharge「*a lot* [*a large quantity, large quantities*] *of* waste every day. / We discharge waste *in quantity* every day.
◆その工場では車の部品を大量生産している They *are mass-producing* auto parts.
‖大量解雇 mass dismissal / 大量虐殺 a massacre / 大量消費社会 a mass consuming society / 大量生産 mass production

たいりょう² 大漁 good [large] catch ◎; (網で一度に捕れる魚が多いこと) good haul ◎ /昨年はサンマが大漁だった We had a *good* [*large*] *catch of* saury last year.

たいりょく 体力 (physical) strength Ⓤ, (physical) powers /患者はまだ体力が回復していない The patient has not regained *his strength* yet. / 彼は体力を消耗しきって, その場に倒れてしまった He used up all *his strength* [*energy*], and fell down there. / 次の試合のために体力を蓄えておきなさい You'd better save *your strength* for the next game. / 体力をつけるためにトレーニングは欠かせない We can't gain *strength* without training. / 彼女にはその仕事は体力的に(→彼女の体力を考慮すると) 無理だろう She seems unable to do the job, *considering her strength*. / (→その仕事をするほど体力がない) She doesn't seem to be *strong enough* to do the job.
◆健は体力がない Ken is *physically weak*.
‖体力測定 a physical test

たいりん 大輪 大輪の菊 a *large-flowered* chrysanthemum

タイル tile ◎ /その職人は床にタイルを張った The craftsman laid *tiles* on the floor. / The craftsman *tiled* the floor. ◆緑のタイル張りの台所 a green-*tiled* kitchen

ダイレクトメール direct mail Ⓤ,《軽蔑的》junk mail

たいれつ 隊列 (横列) rank ◎; (縦列) file ◎ /隊列を組む form *a rank* [*file*]

だいろっかん 第六感 sixth sense Ⓤ《また a 〜》, hunch ◎ /彼は第六感が働く His *sixth sense* is very keen. / 私は第六感で彼がうそを

ついていると思った My *sixth sense* told me [I *had a hunch*] that he was lying.

たいわ 対話 (2者間の) dialogue ⓊⒸ (❖《米》では dialog ともつづる); (うちとけた会話) conversation ⓊⒸ; (会話) talk ⒸⓊ ──対話する talk with ... ∥もっと親子の対話が必要だ Parents and children need to have more of *dialogue* [*conversation*] *between* them./ Parents and children need to *talk* more *with* each other.

たいわん 台湾 Taiwan ──台湾人 Taiwanese (台湾(人)の) Taiwanese

たうえ 田植え planting of rice seedlings in paddies ◆田植えをする *plant rice seedlings in paddies*

ダウへいきん ダウ平均〖経済〗Dow-Jones average [index] Ⓤ

タウン town Ⓒ ∥タウン誌 a magazine for town news / ニュータウン a new town / ベッドタウン a bedroom suburb

ダウン¹ 正二はかぜでダウンした Shoji *was down* [*in bed*] *with a cold*./ 挑戦者はそのラウンドにチャンピオンから2回のダウンを奪った (→2度ダウンさせた) The challenger *floored* [*downed*] the champion twice in the round./ 由美は理科の成績が今学期大幅にダウンした Yumi's science grade *fell* [*dropped*] significantly this term.
∥ダウンサイジング downsizing / ダウンロード〖コンピュータ〗download / ノックダウン〖ボクシング〗a knockdown

ダウン² (鳥の綿毛) down Ⓤ ∥ダウンジャケット a down jacket

ダウンしょうこうぐん ダウン症候群〖医学〗Down's syndrome Ⓤ

たえがたい 耐え難い unbearable, intolerable ∥耐えがたい悲しみ *unbearable* [*intolerable*] *sadness* / 部屋の中は耐えがたい暑さだった The heat in the room was *unbearable* [*intolerable*]./ I *couldn't stand* the heat in the room.

だえき 唾液 saliva [səláivə] Ⓤ
∥唾液腺(ᵏ) salivary glands

たえしのぶ 堪え忍ぶ endure ⑭, put* up with ...; ∥貧しさを耐え忍ぶ *endure* poverty

たえず 絶えず (常に) always (❖しばしば進行形とともに用いて, 話者の非難・嫌悪の気持ちを表す), all the time; (頻繁に) constantly; (とぎれることなく) continuously; (繰り返し) continually ∥彼は卒業後の進路のことで絶えず悩んでいる He is *always* [*continuously*] worried about what to do after graduation./ 山の天気は絶えず変化している The weather in the mountains is *constantly* changing./ 母は私の言葉づかいが悪いと絶えず文句を言っている My mother is *always* [*continually*] complaining about my language.
◆レギュラー選手の地位を保つため彼女は絶えず努力している She makes *constant* efforts to stay regular.

たえだえ 絶え絶え 患者は息も絶え絶えであった The patient could *breathe only feebly*./ 彼は息も絶え絶えに教室に駆け込んできた He came running into the classroom *out of breath*.

たえなる 妙なる 妙なる楽の音 *mellifluous* [(→人を魅了する)*entrancing*] musical sound

たえま 絶え間 絶え間ない努力 a constant effort / きのうは一日中絶え間なく雨が降っていた It rained *continuously* [*without a break*] all day yesterday./ We had a *continuous* rain all day yesterday./ 川の水は絶え間なく海へと注ぎ込む Rivers run *continuously* [*ceaselessly*] into the sea.

たえる¹ 耐える
❶【我慢する・辛抱する】bear*⑭, stand*⑭; (許容する) tolerate ⑭, 《口語的》put* up with ...; (長期間) endure ⑭
彼は傷の痛みにじっと耐えた He *bore* [*stood, tolerated, endured*] the pain of his wound.
この部屋の暑さにはもう耐えられない I *can't bear* [*stand, tolerate, endure*] the heat in this room any more.
その映画の暴力シーンは見るに耐えなかった I *couldn't bear* [*stand*] *to see* the violent scene in the movie.
彼は唇をかみしめて屈辱に耐えた He *bore* [*stood, tolerated, endured*] the humiliation and bit his lip.
❷【もちこたえる】withstand*⑭, resist ⑭; (重さに) hold*⑭, bear*⑭
この皿は高温に耐えられる This plate *can withstand* high temperatures.
精密機器は強い衝撃には耐えられないものが多い Many precision instruments *can't resist* strong impacts.
あのロープはそんなに重い荷物に耐えられますか *Will* that rope *hold* [*bear*] such a heavy load?
❸【価値がある】bear*⑭, be worth (doing), be worthy of ...
その本はくだらなすぎて読むに耐えない The book *doesn't bear* reading. It's trashy.

たえる² 絶える
その家は彼で血統が絶えた The bloodline of that family *came to an end* with him.
彼女は心配事が絶えない (→心配事から解放されることがない) She *is never free from* worries.
彼女は常に笑顔が絶えない She is *always* with a smile on her face.
彼との連絡が絶えてもうずいぶんになる It's been quite a long time since I *lost* contact with him.
彼女はついに息を絶えた She finally 「*passed away* [《文語》*breathed her last*].
この通りは夜7時を過ぎるとばったり人通りが絶えてしまう This street *empties* completely after seven in the evening.

だえん 楕円 ellipse Ⓒ; (卵形) oval Ⓒ ── 楕円の elliptic(al); oval ⇨ずけい 図版
∥楕円軌道 an elliptical orbit

たおす 倒す

❶【立っているものを横にする】(殴り倒す) knock [strike*] (down), down ⑭; (切り倒

す）cut* down, fell [他]; (投げ倒す) throw* down; (ひっくり返す) topple (over), tip (over)

浩は正雄を殴り倒した Hiroshi *knocked* [*struck*] Masao (*down*) *to the ground.*

彼はチェーンソーを使って大木を倒した He「*cut* the big tree *down* [*felled* the big tree] with a chainsaw.

猫が花びんを倒した A cat *toppled* [*tipped*] *over* the vase.

◆彼は座席の背もたれを倒した He *reclined* his seat.

❷【負かす】(競技・ゲームなどで) beat* [他]; (競技・ゲーム・戦争などで) defeat [他]

そのテニス選手は昨年のチャンピオンを倒した The tennis player *beat* [*defeated*] last year's champion.

❸【転覆させる】overthrow* [他], overturn [他], topple [他]

政府を倒す *overthrow* [*overturn, topple*] the government

タオル towel [C]; (浴用の) 《米》washcloth [C], 《英》facecloth [C], 《英》flannel [C]

私はタオルで手をふいた I dried my hands with [on] *a towel.*

ぬれたタオルをしぼった I wrung (out) *a* wet *washcloth.*

‖タオルかけ a towel rack [rail] / タオルケット a terry cloth blanket, a blanket made of toweling / タオル地 toweling / エアータオル a hand drier / バスタオル a bath towel / ハンドタオル a hand towel / ペーパータオル a paper towel

たおれこむ 倒れ込む 彼は部屋に入るなりソファーに倒れ込んだ As soon as he entered the room, he *dropped* [*flopped, collapsed*] *onto* a sofa.

たおれる 倒れる

❶【立っているものが横になる】fall* [自]; (転がるようにして勢いよく) tumble [自]; (ぐらついて) topple (over); (崩れるように) collapse [自]; (卒倒する) faint [自]

彼はバランスを失って床に倒れた He lost his balance and *fell down* on the floor.

彼は雪の上でうつぶせにばったり倒れた He *fell* flat on his face on the snow. (❖「あおむけに倒れる」は fall「on *one's* back [backward])

その建物はがらがらと大きな音を立てて倒れた The building *fell* [*collapsed*] with a great crash.

彼女は倒れてきた木の下敷きになって大けがをした She got severely injured under a *falling* tree.

彼は敷居につまずいて倒れた He *tumbled* over a doorsill.

うずたかく積んであった本がついに倒れた A tall pile of books finally *toppled over.*

彼は過労で倒れた He *collapsed from* exhaustion.

彼は今にも倒れそうなほど真っ青だった He was so pale that he looked as if he would nearly *faint.*

彼女は朝礼中に貧血で倒れた She *fainted from* anemia during a morning assembly.

❷【寝込む・死ぬ】

彼は熱で倒れてしまった He's *been laid up with* fever.

ジョン・レノンは自宅前でファンを名乗る男の凶弾に倒れた John Lennon *was shot to death* by a self-styled fan in front of his apartment.

❸【政府・会社などが】fall* [自]; (倒産する) go* bankrupt

政府はわずか1か月で倒れた The government *fell* after only a month in office.

たか[1] 高 あいつには簡単に勝てるとたかをくくっていたが，大間違いだった I'*ve been thinking it's easy to* beat him. But now I know I've been completely wrong. ➾たかが

たか[2] 鷹 hawk [C]; (鷹狩りに用いる) falcon [C] ‖鷹狩り falconry / 鷹匠 a falconer / タカ派 ➾タカは

[ことわざ] 能ある鷹はつめを隠す ➾のう[2]

たが (おけなどの) hoop [C]

だが (しかし) but, yet, however; (だけれども) though, although (❖though よりやや形式ばった語); (一方で) while ➾-けれど(も) ‖

彼の英語はゆっくりだが着実に上達している He is improving his English slowly *but* steadily. / 君の考えはおもしろそうではある．だが現実的ではない Your idea sounds interesting. *But* [*Yet, However*] it's not practical. / *Though* your idea sounds interesting, it's not practical. / なるほどお金はだいじだが，それがすべてというわけではない It is true that money is important, *but* it is not everything. / たいていの子供はハンバーガーが大好きだが，達也は嫌いだ Tatsuya doesn't like hamburgers, *while* most children love them.

◆お金があればすぐ借金を返したいのだが I'*d like to* pay my debt at once if I had some money.

たかい[1] 高い

❶高さ	high; tall
❷値段	high; expensive
❸音・声	high; loud
❹数値・程度	high
❺地位	high

❶【高さ】high (↔low); tall (↔short)
—高く high

high: 位置が高いことを示す語.
tall: 細長いものの長さに視点をおいた語.

私の町は高い山に囲まれている My town is surrounded by *high* [*lofty*] mountains.

キリマンジャロはアフリカ大陸でいちばん高い山です Mt. Kilimanjaro is the *highest* mountain in the continent of Africa.

このビルはすごく高い This building is very *tall.*

あの背の高い人が志穂です That *tall* person is

たかい

Shiho.
妹は私より背が高い My sister is *taller* than me.
この部屋は天井が高い This room has a *high* ceiling.
隆は高い所が苦手だ Takashi is afraid of *high* places.
鳥のように空高く飛べたらなあ I wish I could fly *high* (*up*) in the air like a bird.
日の高いうちにすべての作業を終えることができた We could finish the whole work while the sun was still *high up* in the sky.
彼はトロフィーを頭上高く上げてみせた He raised the trophy *high* over his head.
このズボンはウエストの位置が高い This pair of pants has a *high* waist.
◆ 彼女は鼻が高い She has a *big* [*prominent*] nose.(✿×a high nose とはいわない) / 高くした I *raised* the seat of a chair. / (子供を抱き上げてあやしながら)高い高い *Upsy-daisy*!/ *Up you come*!

❷【値段】(値段が) high (↔low); (お金のかかる) expensive (↔inexpensive)
日本は物価が高い Prices are *high* in Japan.
あのホテルは(宿泊料は)高い That hotel is *expensive*.
そのギターは高すぎて僕には買えない That guitar is *too expensive* [The price of that guitar is *too high*] for me to buy.
それはとても高かったが, いい品だったので満足している Though it was very *expensive*, I'm satisfied with it because of its good quality.
その本は古本屋に高く売れた I sold the book to a secondhand book store *at a high price*.
彼女は私より時給が高い She gets [draws] a *higher* hourly wage than I [me].
きのうより円が高くなった The yen is *higher* than it was yesterday.
◆ その雑誌は定価が300円も高くなった The price of the magazine *soared* by 300 yen. / 安い中古車は修理が必要になって結局新車を買うより高くつく場合がある Cheap used cars sometimes need to be repaired and may *cost* us more than new ones after all.

❸【音・声】high (↔low); (かん高い) shrill, piercing; (大きい) loud
彼女は声が高い She has a *high*-pitched voice. / She speaks in a *high* pitch.
この曲はすごくキーが高い The key of this tune is very *high*.
◆ しっ! 声が高いよ Shh! You're speaking too *loud*. / Shh! Don't speak so *loud*.

❹【数値・程度】(数値・品質などが) high (↔low) ── 高く high; (大いに・好意的に) highly (✿評価・賞賛を表す動詞を修飾する)
気温が高い The temperature is *high*.
アフリカの多くの国では乳児の死亡率が高い The death rate of infants is *high* in many countries in Africa.
深くもぐればもぐるほど水圧は高くなる The deeper you go in the water, the *higher*

the pressure gets.
この大学に入るには高い学力が必要だ Entering this university calls for *high* scholastic ability.
この試合はかなりレベルの高い一戦になりそうだ This game will be of quite a *high* level.
彼女は独創的な作品で高い評価を得た She 「*was highly estimated* [*received high estimation*] for her creative works.
私に恋人ができないのは男性に対する理想が高すぎるからだと思う I guess the reason I'm without a boyfriend is that I have *too high* an ideal of a man.
イルカは高い知能をもっているという It is said that dolphins have *high* intelligence.
◆ 彼が犯人である可能性が高い There's a *strong possibility* that he is the criminal.

❺【地位】high (↔low)
身分の高い人 a person with a *high* position [rank]
みんな高い地位に就きたがっている Everybody wants to rank *high*.
慣用表現 彼女はお高くとまっている She *is stuck-up*.

たかい² 他界 ──他界する 《婉曲的》pass away

たがい 互い each other, one another
二人は互いに顔を見合わせた The two looked at 「*each other* [*one another*].
彼らは互いに愛し合っていた They loved 「*each other* [*one another*].
この2本の線は互いに交差している These two lines cut across 「*each other* [*one another*].
僕と彼女は互いの性格をよく分かっている She and I understand 「*each other's* [*one another's*] characters very well.
二人は互いの電話番号を交換した(→互いに電話番号を教え合った) The two told 「*each other* [*one another*] their telephone numbers.
◆ 私たちは互いにもっと勉強をしなければならない *Both of* us need to study harder.

> 英作文ノート **each other** と前置詞
> あなたたちは互いにもっと話し合うべきだ
> → ×You should talk *each other* more often.
> → ○You should talk *with each other* more often.
> ★each other は副詞としてではなく代名詞として用いられるので, 自動詞の後では適切な前置詞が必要.

だかい 打開 ──打開する (解決する) solve 働; (乗り越える) get* over; (打ち勝つ) overcome* 働 / 難局を打開する solve [get over, overcome] the difficult situation
◆ 行き詰まりを打開する *break* the deadlock / まだ打開策を見いだせずにいる We haven't found *a way out* (*of* the problem) yet.

たがいちがい 互い違い ──互い違いに alternate [ɔ́ːltərnət] ──互い違いに alternately / その駅には普通列車と急行列車が互い違いにやってくる *Alternate* local and express trains come into the station. / スペードのカードとハートのカードを互い違いに並べた I laid out spades and hearts *alternately*.

たかいびき 高鼾 loud snore ◆高いびきをかく *snore loudly*

たかが たかがこれしきの痛みで騒ぐような僕じゃない I won't make a fuss over a *trifling pain like this*. / 彼がコンピュータを使ってできることなんてたかが知れている(→限られている) What he can do with computers *is limited*. / お金の残り少ない僕にとってはたかが100円, されど100円だ One hundred yen is *just* [*only*] one hundred yen, but still it means a lot to me now that I've got so little money left.

たがく 多額 large sum [amount], great deal //政府は環境保護に多額の予算をあてた The government budgeted 「*a large sum* [*a great deal*] *of* money for environmental protection. / 彼女はその事業のために銀行から多額の借金をした She borrowed *a large amount of money* from the bank for the business. / She borrowed *heavily* from the bank for the business.

たかくか 多角化 〖商業〗 diversification ──多角化する 〖商業〗 diversify //経営を多角化する *diversify* (the company's) business

たかくけい 多角形 〖数学〗 polygon

たかくけいえい 多角経営 〖商業〗 diversification, 〖商業〗 diversified management

たかくてき 多角的 ──多角的に(様々な観点から) from various points of view //この問題は多角的な検討を要する(→多角的に検討される必要がある) This issue needs to be examined *from various points of view*.

たかさ 高さ
❶【物の】 height [háit]; (高度) altitude

彼の背の高さを測った I measured his *height*. / I measured how *tall* he was.

このいすは高さを調節できる You can adjust *the height of* this chair.

そのとき飛行機は1万メートルの高さを飛行していた The plane was flying at *a height* [*an altitude*] of 10,000 meters then.

◆私は背の高さが母と同じだ I am as *tall* as my mother. / 彼は本を目の高さに持ち上げて読んでいた He was reading a book at eye *level*. / そのビルの最上階は目もくらむような高さだった The top floor of the building was so *high* that it made me feel dizzy.

🔑「あの木の高さはどのくらいですか」「約20メートルです」 "*How tall* is that tree?" "(It's) about twenty meters (tall)."

🔑「マッキンリー山の高さを知っていますか」「6,194メートルです」 "Do you know how *high* Mt. McKinley is?" "(It's) 6,194 meters (high)."

❷【値段の】
あまりの(値段の)高さにその時計を買うのはあきらめた I gave up on buying the watch because it was so *expensive*.

❸【音・声の】 pitch
❹【数値・程度の】
まだ5月だというのに, きょうの気温の高さは真夏並みだ Though it's still May now, the temperature today is as *high* as it is in midsummer.

その歌手の人気の高さに驚いた I was surprised at 「how *popular* the singer is [*the popularity* of the singer].

その新聞は記事の質の高さで知られる The newspaper is famous for the *high* quality of its articles.

だがし 駄菓子 confectionery made of cheap ingredients

たかしお 高潮 storm surge [tide]; (高波) high [tall] wave

たかだい 高台 height [háit] 《しばしば複数形~s》; (丘) hill

たかだか 高々 ❶【高さ】彼は高々とこぶしを上げてポーズをとった He posed by holding his fist *high* up.
❷【声】彼は声高々と作文を読み上げた He read out the composition *loudly*.
❸【せいぜい】 at (the) most, at (the) very most, not more than … //僕の演奏を聞きにくる人なんてたかだか10人がいいところだろう There will be 「*not more than* 10 people [10 people *at most*] who will come and hear me play. ◆たかだか500円で何をけちけちしてるんだ Don't be so stingy with *only* [*just*] 500 yen.

慣用表現 彼が優勝したからお母さんも鼻高々だろう His mother *must be very proud of* his winning the championship.

だがっき 打楽器 percussion instrument, (集合的)the percussion //打楽器奏者 a percussionist

たかとび¹ 高跳び (走り高跳び) the high jump ‖棒高跳び〖スポーツ〗the pole vault 関連語(走り)幅跳び《米》the broad jump, 《英》the long jump

たかとび² 高飛び 犯人はすでに海外へ高飛びしてしまった The criminal *has escaped* [*fled*] *abroad*.

たかとびこみ 高飛び込み 〖スポーツ〗 high diving

たかなみ 高波 high [tall, tidal] wave //数人が高波にさらわれた A few people were swept away by *high* [*tall*, *tidal*] *waves*.

たかなる 高鳴る beat* fast, throb //その知らせを聞いて胸が高鳴った My heart 「*beat fast* [*throbbed*] at the news.

たかね 高値 high price //その家はかなりの高値で売れた The house was sold *at a very high price*.

◆きょうの平均株価の終値は最高値を更新しました The closing price of the average stock today *was higher than ever*.

たかねのはな 高嶺の花 あんな大きな家が欲しいけど, 高嶺の花だな A big house like that *is beyond* [*out of*] *my reach*.

たかのぞみ 高望み 君は高望みしすぎだよ

You're aiming [《口語的》flying] too high.
タカは タカ派（個人）hawk 回（↔dove）;（全体）the hawks (↔the doves)
たかびしゃ 高飛車 ──高飛車な（常に人を支配しようとする）overbearing;（権威をかさに着た）high-handed ∥彼の高飛車な口調にみんな腹を立てた Everyone got angry at his *high-handed* way of speaking.
たかぶる 高ぶる（感情が激する）run* high;（緊張する）get* nervous,《口語的》get up-tight;（興奮する）get excited ∥彼は試合を前に神経が高ぶっている His *feelings are running high* [He *is nervous*] with the game near at hand.
たかまり 高まり 感情の高まり *a surge* of a feeling / 世論の高まり *a ground swell* of opinion
たかまる 高まる（増大する）grow* 自;（増える）increase 自;（地位などが）rise* 自 ∥ 人々の環境問題に対する関心が高まっている There is a *growing* interest among people in environmental problems. / People are getting *more and more* interested in environmental problems. / その事件により２国間の緊張はますます高まった The tensions between the two countries *increased* a lot because of the incident. / そのCDの大ヒットで彼女の人気は高まった Her popularity *rose* due to the big hit her CD made. / The CD's big hit made her *more* popular.
たかみのけんぶつ 高みの見物 彼は友人どうしのけんかに高みの見物を決め込んだ He *just stood around and watched* his friends' quarrel.
たかめる 高める（質・水準などを）raise 他;（よりよくする）improve 他;（増やす）increase 他;（地位などを）lift 他;（感情・効果などを）heighten 他 ∥効率を高める *raise* [*increase*] efficiency / 教育水準を高める *improve* [*raise*] educational standards / その展覧会で入賞したことが彼女の名声を高めた Winning a prize at the exhibition *lifted* [*raised*] her reputation. / その記事が事件に対する世間の関心を高めた The article *heightened* the people's interest in the case.
◆士気を高める *boost one's morale* / ネイティブスピーカーとの交際が彼の英語力を高めた His English *improved* through his association with native speakers.
たがやす 耕す cultivate 他;（くわで）hoe [hóu] 他;（すきで）plow,《英》plough [pláu] 他（※しばしば up を伴う）∥畑を耕す *cultivate* [*hoe*, *plow* (*up*)] a field
たから 宝 treasure 回（※大切な人といった意味では回）;（貴重な物・人）asset 回 ∥その宝はこのあたりに埋蔵されているといわれている The *treasure* is said to be buried around here. / 彼は日本の宝だ He is「*a treasure* to [*an asset* in] Japan. ◆骨董（ミネ）品の好きな彼にとってその古い蔵はまるで宝の山だった The old storehouse was like *a gold mine* for him, who likes antiques.
∥宝探し a treasure hunt

慣用表現 あんな高いピアノを買って全然弾かないなんて宝の持ち腐れだよ It's *a waste of* an expensive piano not to play it at all.

だから
（それで）(and) so,《公式的》(and) therefore,《公式的》(and) thus;（…なので）because, since (※意味は because より弱く as より強い．通例文頭で用いる．as は※付帯的な状況を表し、理由がそれほど重要でない場合や、すでに知られている場合に用いる．理由が重要である場合には because, since を用いる)
きょうは気分が悪いんだ．だから僕は家にいるよ I don't feel well today, (and) *so* I'll stay home. / I'll stay home *because* I don't feel well today.
きょうは休みだからどこかへ出かけよう I have no school today, (and) *so* I'm going out. / I'm going out *because* I have no school today.
夏なんだから暑いのは当然だ It is quite natural to be hot *because* [*since, as*] it is summer now.
もう子供じゃないんだから自分の行動に責任をもちなさい *Since* [*As*] you're no longer a child, you have to be responsible for your own conduct.
雪がふったからといって学校を休んでもいいことにはならない *Just because* it snows doesn't mean you are allowed to be absent from school.（※この意味のとき, because を since, as に換えることはできない）
◆お願いだからひとりにしないで *For God's sake*, don't leave me alone. / この仕事はとても簡単だからだれにだってできます This job is so easy *that* anyone can do it.

🔴「学校にまた遅刻しちゃった」「ほらね、だからいつも早く家を出なさいと言ってるでしょ」"I was late for school again." "You see! I'm always telling you to leave the house early."

🔴「アイスを食べすぎておなかこわしちゃった」「だから言ったじゃないの」"I've got a stomachache from eating too much ice cream." "*I told you so!*"

🔴「けさは寒すぎるよ」「だから何だっていうの．学校サボる気？」"It's too cold this morning." "*So what*? Are you going to skip classes?"

🔴「亮司君，今から彼女に告白するんだって」「あぁ，だからさっきからそわそわしてたんだ」"Ryoji is going to tell her that he loves her now." "Aha, *that's why* he's been restless for some time."

🔴「すごくおなかがすいてたんだ」「だからって私の分まで食べちゃうことないじゃない」"I was very hungry." "*That* can be no excuse for having eaten mine."

たからかに 高らかに みんなでその歌を声高らかに歌った We all sang the song「*in a loud voice* [*loudly*] together.
たからくじ 宝籤 lottery 回;（券）lottery ticket 回 ∥いつか宝くじで１億円当てるぞ I will

たからもの 宝物 treasure ◎(❖「大切な人」の意味では ◎) ∥あなたは私の宝物だ You are my *pride and joy*. / 私はその思い出を一生の宝物にしている I *treasure* the memory throughout my life.

たかる ❶【集まる・取りつく】(集まる) gather ⓐ; (群がる) crowd ⓐ, swarm ⓐ ∥ケーキにアリがたくさんたかった A lot of ants *swarmed* [*gathered*] on the cake. / その歌手の周りにサインを求めるファンがたかっていた Fans seeking for the singer's autographs *crowded* [*swarmed*] around him.
◆ほら、ごはんにハエがたかっちゃうよ Hey, a fly is going to *land on* your bowl of rice.
❷【せがむ・ねだる】(せがむ) pester ⓐ; (ただでもらう) sponge ⓐ; (要求する) ask ⓐ; (おどす) frighten ⓐ ∥正はいつも良夫に食事をたかっている Tadashi always 「*sponges* meals *off* Yoshio [*asks* Yoshio *for* meals, *pesters* Yoshio *for* meals]. / 不良グループにたかられた A group of gangsters *frightened* me *into giving* them *money*. / A group of gangsters *extorted* money *from* me.

-たがる want to *do*; (しきりに) be anxious [eager] to *do*; (できそうにないことを) long to *do*, 《公式的》yearn to *do*; (進んで) be ready to *do* ➪ ～たい¹ ∥彼が君と話したがっているよ He *wants* [*is anxious*, *is eager*] *to talk* with you. / 彼女は子供のころの友達に会いたがっている She *longs* [*yearns*] *to see* her childhood friends.
◆彼は他人の会話にすぐ口をはさみたがる He *readily cuts in* when others are talking. / 彼女は負けを認めたがらなかった She *was unwilling* [*reluctant*] *to admit* the defeat.

たかわらい 高笑い ――高笑いする give* a loud laugh, laugh loudly

たかん 多感 ――多感な (感じやすい・傷つきやすい) sensitive; (感傷的な) sentimental ∥彼女は今最も多感な年ごろだ She is at the age when people are most *sensitive* [*sentimental*].

たき¹ 滝 waterfall ◎, falls(❖しばしば地名の一部として用いられる); (大きな) cataract ◎; (急で小さな) cascade ◎ ∥ナイアガラの滝 (the) *Niagara Falls* ∥修行者が滝に打たれていた An ascetic was standing under a *waterfall*. ◆滝のような雨が降りだした The rain began to pour *in torrents*. / 彼は額から滝のような(→多量に)汗を流していた His forehead was sweating *heavily*.
∥滝つぼ the foot [base] of a waterfall

たき² 多岐 彼の趣味はガーデニングからパラグライダーまで多岐にわたる He has *various* [*diverse*] hobbies from gardening to paragliding.

たぎ 多義 ∥多義語 a polysemous word / 多義性 polysemy

だきあう 抱き合う hug [embrace] each other ∥10年ぶりに再会し彼らは固く抱き合った They met for the first time in 10 years and *hugged* [*embraced*] each other tightly. / 駅のホームでカップルが抱き合っていた A couple *were hugging each other* on a platform of the station.
◆二人は抱き合って泣いた They wept *in each other's arms*.

だきあげる 抱き上げる 私は赤ちゃんを抱き上げた I *lifted* the baby *in my arms*.

だきあわせ 抱き合わせ 抱き合わせ販売 a tie-in / このソフトは別のソフトと抱き合わせで売られている This application is sold *bundled with* another one.

だきおこす 抱き起こす 彼は転んだ老女を抱き起こした He *raised* a fallen old woman *in arms* to her feet.

だきかかえる 抱き抱える 彼女は花束を抱きかかえていた She *was holding* a bunch of flowers *in her arms*. / 彼女は子供を抱きかかえて病院に駆け込んだ She ran into the hospital *carrying* her child *in her arms*.

たきぎ 薪 firewood ◎, wood ◎ ∥たきぎを集める collect *firewood* [*wood*]

たきこみごはん 炊き込みご飯 rice boiled with fish [vegetables] and seasoning

だきこむ 抱き込む 彼は金で有力な議員を抱き込んだ(→味方につけた)He *won* an influential councilor *over to his side* by paying him money. / (→味方につくよう買収した)He *bribed* an influential councilor *to support* [*stand for*] him.

タキシード 《主に米》tuxedo ◎ (複 ～s), 《口語的》tux ◎, 《主に英》dinner jacket ◎

だきしめる 抱き締める hug ⓐ, embrace ⓐ (❖いずれも愛情をもって抱くこと) ∥彼は彼女をしっかりと抱きしめた He *hugged* [*embraced*] her tightly. / He *held* her tightly *in his arms*.

だきつく 抱き付く (勢いよく) throw* *one's* arms around ...; (しがみつく) cling* to ... ∥彼女は彼に抱きついた She *threw her arms around* him. / その子は雷の音を怖がって父親に抱きついた The child, scared of the sound of thunder, *clung to* his father.

たきつける 焚き付ける egg *a person* on to *do*; (人々を) incite ⓐ ∥弟をたきつけて父に新しいテレビゲームをねだらせた I *egged* my brother *on to* ask my father to buy a new video game.

たきび 焚き火 fire ◎ ∥たき火をする 小枝を集めよう Let's gather some sticks to *make a fire*. / たき火にあたった I warmed myself at a fire.

だきゅう 打球 打球は場外へ飛んでいった The ball flew out of the stadium.

だきょう 妥協 compromise ◎ⓒ ――妥協する compromise (with *a person*), make* a compromise with *a person* ∥両者が妥協して話がついた They settled the matter by *compromising* [*making a compromise*] *with* each other. / その点に関しては妥協の余地はない There's no room for *compromise* on that point. / 彼らはその妥協案を受け入れた They accepted *the compromise (proposal)*.

たぎる 血がたぎる *be boiling with excitement*

たく¹ 炊く boil; (加熱調理する) cook / ごはんを炊いた I *cooked* [*boiled*] rice.

たく² 焚く お父さんが帰るまでにおふろをたいておこう I will have「*heated the water in the bathtub* [(→準備する) *prepared the bath*] before my father comes home. / フラッシュをたいて(→使って)写真を撮った I took a picture by *using a flash*. / 暖炉に火をたいた I *made a fire* in a fireplace.

だく 抱く hold*; (愛情をもって) hug, embrace; (卵を) sit* on ...
少女はクマのぬいぐるみを抱いていた The girl *was holding* a teddy bear *in her arms*. 母親は息子をしっかり抱いた The mother *hugged* [*embraced*] her son tightly. その鳥は卵を抱いていた The bird *was sitting on its eggs*.
◆彼は彼女の肩を抱いた He *put his arm around* her shoulders.

たくあん 沢庵

たくあんは大根の漬物で, 干した大根をたるにつめ, 米ぬかと塩をその上にまぶし, ふたをのせて重しをします. たくあんはおにぎりやお茶漬けなどの付け合わせとしてよく出されます.
Takuan is a pickle made of *daikon* (Japanese radish). Dried radishes are put into a barrel, sprinkled with rice bran and salt, and pressed beneath a heavy lid, often with a stone on it. *Takuan* is often served together with *onigiri* (rice balls) or *ochazuke* (boiled rice in hot green tea).

たぐい 類 kind, sort / そういった類の質問にはお答えできません I can't answer such *kind* [*sort*] of a question. / I can't answer questions like that. ◆鉛筆やボールペンなど, 筆記用具の類はこの棚にあります Writing materials, such as pencils and ball-point pens, are on this shelf.

たぐいまれな 類い稀な (比類ない) incomparable, matchless; (まれに見る) rare; (並みはずれた) extraordinary / 彼女はたぐいまれな才能の持ち主だ She is a person with *incomparable* [*matchless, rare, extraordinary*] talent. ◆たぐいまれな美女 an *incomparably* [a *matchlessly*] beautiful woman

たくえつ 卓越 ——卓越した (非常にすぐれた) outstanding, excellent; (著名な・重要な) prominent, eminent; (比類のない)《文語》surpassing(❖名詞の前で用いる) / 卓越した技の持ち主 a person with an *outstanding* [an *excellent*, a *surpassing*] skill / 卓越したピアニスト an *outstanding* [an *excellent*, a *surpassing*] pianist

たくさん

❶【多数・多量】——たくさんの (多数の) many (↔few),「*a lot of* [《口語的》*lots of*] of ..., a large number of ...;(多量の) much (↔little),「*a lot* [《口語的》*lots*] of ..., a large amount of ...

語法
(1) 肯定文では a lot of ..., lots of ..., a large number [amount] of ... などを用いることが多い. many, much を肯定文で用いるのは公式的か, または前に too, so などを伴う場合.
(2) 否定文・疑問文では通例 many, much を用いる.

その役者はたくさんの映画に出演している He's appeared in「*a lot* [*lots*] of movies.
このあたりには猫がたくさんいる There are「*a lot of* [*a large number of*] cats around here.
彼はお金をたくさん持っている He has「*a lot of* [*a large amount of, plenty of*] money. (❖ plenty of ... は「十分(すぎるほど)の…」の意味で, 数にも量にも用いられる)
きょうの午後はやることがたくさんある I have *a lot*「*of* work [*to do*] this afternoon.
今年は雨がたくさん降った We had *a lot of* rain this year. / It rained *a lot* this year.
ゲームソフトをたくさん持っていますか Do you have *much* game software?
テレビ局には非常にたくさんの意見が寄せられた The TV station received「*an awful lot of* [*so many*] opinions.
会場にはそれほどたくさんの人はいなかった There were not *so many* people in the hall.
この花にはあまりたくさん水をやってはだめよ Don't give this flower *too much* water.
できるだけたくさんの本を読みなさい Read *as many* books *as you can*.
1泊旅行にそんなにたくさんの服を持っていってどうするの Why are you taking *so many* clothes for just an overnight trip?
私は彼女よりたくさんCD[お金]を持っている I have *more* CDs [money] than she (has).
3人のうちでいちばんたくさんハンバーガーを食べたのはだれですか Which of the three ate *the most* hamburgers?
◆彼は古いおもちゃをたくさん集めている He has a *large* collection of old toys.

❷【十分・これ以上いらない】
その作業には4人もいればたくさんだろう Four people will be *enough* [*sufficient*] to get the work done.
けんかはもうたくさんだ We've had *enough* of quarreling [fighting].
もうたくさんだ. それ以上何も言うな *That's enough*. Don't say any more!
●「もっと食べたら?」「ありがとう. でももうたくさんいただきました. おなかいっぱいです」"Why don't you have some more?" "Thanks, but *I've had enough*. I'm full."

たくしあげる たくし上げる tuck up, roll up / 彼はシャツのそでをたくし上げて作業にかかった He *tucked* [*rolled*] *up* his shirt sleeves and began to work.

タクシー taxi ©（複 〜s, 〜es），cab ©, taxicab ©
流しのタクシー a cruising *taxi* / タクシーを拾う catch [pick up] *a taxi*
駅までタクシーで行った I went to the station *by* [*in a*] *taxi*.（❖byの後では無冠詞）
タクシーを呼んでいただけませんか Could you call me *a taxi*?
タクシーにしよう。バスで行くよりそのほうが早いよ Let's take *a taxi*. It's faster than going by bus.
タクシーに乗ろうと思ったが，空車が全然なかった I wanted to take *a taxi*, but there weren't any that were unoccupied.
タクシーを止めた（→大声を出して）I hailed *a taxi*. /（→手を振って）I flagged down *a taxi*.
（呼びかけて）タクシー *Taxi*!
‖タクシー運転手 a taxi driver,《主に米・口語的》a cabdriver,《口語的》a cabby / タクシー会社 a taxi company / タクシー代 a taxi fare / タクシー乗り場 a taxi stand,《米》a cabstand,《英》a rank / 個人タクシー an owner-driven taxi

たくじしょ 託児所《米》day-care center ©,《英》crèche [kréʃ] ©,《英》day nursery © ‖彼女は仕事の間託児所に子供を預けた She put [left] her child in a *day-care center* while she worked.

たくじょう 卓上 卓上（電気）スタンド a *desk* [*table*] lamp / 卓上コンロ a *table* gas stove

たくす 託す ⓣ, leave* ⓣ ‖彼女は彼女にある調査を託した He *entrusted* [*left*] a certain investigation to her. / He *entrusted* her *with* a certain investigation. / 一郎は健二に美津子への手紙を託した Ichiro *left* a letter for Mitsuko with Kenji.
◆彼女はこの仕事に夢を託している She *lays* her dreams on this job. / 彼は彼女への愛を歌に託した（→歌の中に表現した）He *expressed* his love to her in a song.

たくち 宅地 housing site ©;（1区画）housing lot © ‖宅地を造成する develop *housing sites* [*lots*]
‖宅地開発[造成] the development of housing lots / 宅地開発[造成]業者 a developer / 宅地分譲 the sale of housing lots

タクト ⚠ baton ©（❖日本語はドイツ語のTaktstock から）◆そのオーケストラの演奏会では彼女がタクトを振った（→オーケストラを指揮した）At the concert, she *conducted* [*led*] the orchestra.

たくはい 宅配 その商品はうちへ宅配される（→宅配便で送られる）The purchase is going to *be sent* to my house *by delivery service*.
‖宅配会社 a delivery service company / 宅配ピザ屋 a pizza delivery shop / 宅配便 (a) delivery [parcel delivery] service;（直送の）door-to-door delivery service

たくばつ 卓抜 ――卓抜な outstanding,《文語》surpassing（❖名詞の前で用いる）

タグボート tugboat

たくましい 逞しい（筋肉の発達した）muscular, brawny;（肉体的・精神的に強い）strong;（体が健康的である）sturdy / たくましい体つきの青年 a young man with a *muscular* [*brawny, sturdy*] build / 少年は心もたくましく育った The boy grew up *strong* in (his) body and soul.
◆僕たちは想像力をたくましくして恐竜の模型を作った We made models of dinosaurs *using our wildest imagination*.

たくみ 巧み ――巧みな（うまい）good;（技にたけた）skillful;（器用な・巧妙な）clever ――巧みに skillfully; cleverly ‖彼は話術が巧みだ He is *good at* conversation. / そのカヌーは激流を巧みに通り抜けた The canoe *skillfully* shot the rapids. / 男は言葉巧みに老人に粗悪品を売りつけた The man *cleverly* persuaded the old man to buy the goods of poor quality.

たくらみ 企み（陰謀）plot《しばしば複数形〜s》;（策略）trick ©;（共謀）conspiracy © ‖麻薬密輸のたくらみ a *plot* [*conspiracy*] to smuggle drugs / 彼は連中のたくらみを素早く見抜いた He quickly saw through their *plots* [*tricks, conspiracies*].

たくらむ 企む plot ⓣ, scheme ⓣ;（共謀する）conspire ⓣ ‖彼らは大使館の襲撃をたくらんでいた They *were plotting* [*scheming, conspiring*] to attack the embassy.
◆僕の血液型なんか聞いたりして，彼女いったい何をたくらんでいるんだろう（→何をするつもりなんだろう）I wonder what she *plans* [*intends*] to do — asking my blood type.

だくりゅう 濁流 (swollen) muddy stream ©

たぐる 手繰る たこ糸をたぐる *pull* [*draw*] *in* a kite string / 記憶をたぐる *go back in one's* memory

たくわえ 蓄え・貯え reserve ©《しばしば複数形〜s》, stock ©, store ©;（貯金）savings ‖水の蓄えが尽きる run out of *the reserves* [*stocks, stores*] of water / 老後の蓄えは万全ですか Do you have enough *savings* for your old age?

たくわえる 蓄える・貯える
❶【とっておく】reserve ⓣ;（物・情報などを）store ⓣ;（お金などを）save ⓣ ©, set* [put*] aside
彼は地下室に食べ物を蓄えた He *reserved* [*stored*] food in the cellar. / He *stocked* the cellar *with* food.
重要なデータはこのコンピュータに蓄えている We *store* important data in this computer.
老後に備えて少し蓄えておくべきかな I wonder if I should *save* [*set aside*] some money for my old age.
今夜は早く寝てあすの試合のために体力を蓄えておかなければ I must go to bed early tonight to *save* my strength for tomorrow's game.
❷【ひげを】
彼はあごひげをたくわえている He *has* [*wears*] a beard.

たけ¹ 竹 bamboo © ⓤ（複〜s）‖竹製のいす a

bamboo stool
∥竹細工 bamboo work / 　竹ざお a bamboo pole / 　竹とんぼ a flying bamboo toy shaped like a propeller / 　竹ぼうき a bamboo broom / 　竹やぶ a bamboo grove [thicket]

慣用表現 彼は竹を割ったような性格をしている He is a *straightforward* person.

たけ²　丈　❶【長さ】length / ∥ひざ丈のスカート a *knee-length* skirt / 　このシャツは私には丈が長すぎる The *length* of this shirt is too long for me. / 　This shirt is too long for me. ◆スカートの丈を3センチ詰めてもらった I had my skirt shortened [taken up] three centimeters.

❷【すべて】思いのたけを語る tell *everything one has in mind*

-だけ
❶【限定】── 副 only, just; (ただ単に) simply, merely ── 形 only (❖名詞の前で用いる), alone (❖名詞・代名詞の後で用いる)

語法
[only] 公式的では強調する語の直前に置きその語を強く発音する. 口語的には位置は比較的自由で, 強勢により強調する語を示すことができる.
[just] 口語的に用いられることが多く, 強調する語の前に置く. 「ただ…, ほんの…」というニュアンスがあり, only のように限定の意味の強い語ではない.

彼だけが試験に合格した *Only* he [He *alone*, He was the *only* person who] passed the examination. (❖ ×Just he ... とはしない)
僕の持ち金は1,000円だけだ I have *only* [*just*] 1,000 yen with me.
これは僕たち2人だけの秘密だよ Let's make this a secret *just* [*only*] between you and me.
君にこれだけは言っておきたい I want to tell you *just* [*only*] one thing.
それを立証するにはその証拠だけで十分だ That evidence *alone* is sufficient to prove it.
私は見たままを言っただけです I *only* [*just, simply*] told you what I saw.
後はスイッチを入れるだけでよい Then, you *only* have to switch it on. / *All* you have to do then is switch it on.
答えを間違えたというだけでそんなに悲観することはないよ You don't have to be so disappointed *only* [*just, simply*] because you gave the wrong answer.
彼は彼女に会うためだけにロンドンへ行った He went to London *just* to see her.
そんなこと考えただけでぞっとするよ I shudder *just* thinking about it. / The *mere* thought of it makes me shudder.
そのペン, ちょっとだけ(→少しの間)貸してよ Let me use your pen *just a minute*.
彼女は勉強だけでなく運動でもすぐれている She excels *not only* in her studies *but also* in sports. / 　She excels in sports *as well as* in studying.
◆僕が知っているのはそれだけだ(→それが僕の知っているすべてだ) That's *all* I know. / 　トマトだけは食べられない(→トマト以外なら何でも食べられる) I can eat *anything but* tomatoes. / 　彼は口に出して言わないだけで(→言わないけれども), 本当は君の態度にあきれかえっているんだよ He is disgusted at your behavior, *though* he doesn't say so. / 　*It's true* he doesn't say so, *but really* he is disgusted at your behavior.

💬「何かお探しですか(→お手伝いしましょうか)」「いえ, 見ているだけです」"Can I help you?" "No thanks, *I'm just looking*."

💬「絵の具のついた隆の顔を浩が笑ったんだって」「えっ, それだけ(→そんなささいなこと)であんな大げんかになるかい」"They said Hiroshi laughed at the paint on Takashi's face." "No way! How could *such a trifling thing* be the reason for such a big fight?"

💬「お母さん, 500円だけでいいから貸して」「500円だけね. 今月はもう貸しますよ」"Lend me *just* [×*only*] 500 yen please, Mom." "You can have *only* [*just*] 500 yen and nothing more until next month."

❷【程度・比例】
好きなだけお取りください Take *as much as* you like.
駅で待っていてくれる? できるだけ早く行くから Will you wait for me at the station? I'll come *as soon as possible* [*I can*].
お金はこれだけあれば十分だ I don't need any more money when I have *this much*. / *This amount of* money is enough.
あれだけ練習したんだから彼は勝つだろう I'm sure he'll win because he practiced *so much*.
どれだけ心配したか分かってるの? Do you see *how much* I've worried about you?
できるだけのことはした I did *all I could* [*the best I could, my best*].
映画に誘うだけ誘っておいて自分は来ないなんて彼女もひどいなあ(→よく約束を破るものだ. 私を映画に誘ったのは自分なのに) How could she break her own promise? It was she who invited me to the movie.
相手が強ければ強いだけやる気がわいてくる The *stronger* the opponent is, *the more* motivated I get.

❸【見合う】
あの展覧会は行くだけの価値があるよ That exhibition *is worth* visiting.
長くアメリカに住んでいただけあって彼は英語がすごく上手だ *As may* [*might*] *be expected of* having lived in the U.S. for a long time, he speaks English very well.

たげい　多芸　彼は多芸多才な人だ He is *versatile*.
ことわざ 多芸は無芸 Jack of all trades and master of none. (→何でも屋はどれにおいても大家ではない)

たけうま 竹馬 stilts (made of bamboo and wood) ‖竹馬に乗って歩く walk on *stilts*

だげき 打撃 ❶【精神的打撃・損害・強打】《精神的打撃》shock ⓒⓊ, blow ⓒ;《損害》damage Ⓤ;《強打》blow ⓒ / 彼の引退はわがチームにとって大きな打撃だ His retirement is *a「great shock [big blow]* to our team. / その町の観光業は火山の噴火で大打撃を受けた The tourist business of the town suffered *「a huge blow [great damage]* from the eruption of the mountain. / The tourist business of the town *was hard hit* by the eruption of the mountain.
❷【野球】《野球》batting Ⓤ
‖打撃戦 a slugfest / 打撃練習 batting practice (※「打撃練習をする」なら practice batting)

たけだけしい 猛々しい 《勇猛な》brave, daring ◆あいつは我々全員をだましておいて平気な顔をしているよ, 全く盗人(ぬすっと)たけだけしい How *impudent [shameless]* he is to look as if nothing has happened after he'd deceived all of us!

だけつ 妥結 《解決》settlement ⓒⓊ;《意見の一致》agreement ⓒⓊ ──妥結する reach a settlement [an agreement] ‖難航していた交渉もついに妥結した The negotiations, which were not going smoothly, *have reached 「a settlement [an agreement]* at last.

だけど 海外旅行をしたいな. だけどお金がないから無理だな I want to travel abroad, *but* it's impossible because I don't have enough money. / 映画の券が2枚あるんだけど, いっしょに行かない？ I've got two movie tickets. Won't you come with me? / お願いがあるんだけど Could you do me a favor? / 彼がもっと頻繁に手紙をくれたらいいんだけどな I wish he wrote to me more often. → けれど(も)

たけなわ 宴たけなわというときに突然停電になった The party *was in full swing* when the blackout suddenly occurred. / 野山の紅葉も美しく, 秋まさにたけなわといったところだ With beautiful autumn colors in fields and mountains, fall [autumn] *is really at its peak* now.

たけのこ 竹の子・筍 bamboo shoot ⓒ
|慣用表現| ここ最近, 似たような新人バンドが雨後の竹の子のように (→ 次々と) デビューしている Recently, a lot of bands which resemble each other have debuted *one after another*. / ここ数年でこのあたりのコンビニは雨後の竹の子のように増えた Convenience stores around here *have mushroomed* in the last few years.

たこ¹ 《手足の》callus ⓒ;《足の》corn ⓒ ‖私は中指にペンだこがある I have *a callus* on my middle finger *which was made by writing too much*.
|慣用表現| 彼の自慢話はもう耳にたこができるくらい聞いたよ (→ 聞くのはうんざりだ) I'm *sick and tired of [fed up with]* hearing his boastful talk.

たこ² 蛸 octopus ⓒ《複 〜es, octopi》‖タコの足 *octopus's* arms [tentacles]
◆たこ足配線は火災の原因になることもある *Plugging many appliances into one outlet* may cause a fire.
‖タコつぼ a pot used as an octopus trap

たこ³ 凧 kite ⓒ ‖たこをあげる fly *a kite*
‖たこあげ kite-flying / たこ糸 a kite string

だこう 蛇行 ──蛇行する meander [miǽndər] ⓘ, wind* [wáind] ⓘ;《ジグザグに進む》zigzag ⓘ ‖その川は湿原を大きく蛇行して流れている The river *meanders [winds]* lazily through the marsh. / その車は蛇行運転していた The car *was zigzagging [weaving]* in the road.

たこく 他国 foreign country ⓒ

たこくせき 多国籍 ──多国籍の multinational ‖多国籍企業 a multinational corporation [enterprise] / 多国籍軍 the multinational forces

たこやき たこ焼き 🍢
たこ焼きは小麦粉にタコ, ショウガ, ネギを混ぜたものを半球状の小さい穴がついた特別な鉄板で焼いたもので, だんごのような形をしています. 祭りなどでは, たこ焼きの屋台がよく出ています.
Takoyaki is a kind of dumpling made by mixing flour with chopped octopus, ginger and minced green onions. It is then cooked on a special griddle with a lot of small hemispherical holes. Street stands selling *takoyaki* are often found at festivals.

たごん 他言 他言は無用 *Don't tell it to anybody.* / *Mum's the word*! / 今から話すことを他言しないと約束して Promise not to *repeat [tell anybody]* what I'm going to tell you.

たさい¹ 多才 ──多才な multitalented, versatile ‖多才な音楽家 a *multitalented [versatile]* musician; a musician of many talents [gifts]

たさい² 多彩 ──多彩な 《様々な》various ‖多彩な機能をもった新型MDプレーヤー a new MD player with *various* functions / 討論会には多彩な顔ぶれが (→ 様々な分野の人たちが) 集まった People from *various* fields gathered at the conference.

ださい 《服装などが》dowdy,《口語的》nerdy ‖あいついつもださい格好してるな He always wears *dowdy [nerdy]* clothes.
◆あんな帽子かぶっちゃって, あいつ本当にださいやつだな He's really *a nerd* wearing such a hat. / またふられたの, ださいなあ You've been turned down again? What *a loser* you are!

たさく 多作 ──多作な prolific, productive ‖多作な彫刻家 a *prolific [productive]* sculptor

ださく 駄作 《口語的》trashy work ⓒ

たさつ 他殺 murder ⓒⓊ ‖他殺死体 the body of a *murder* victim

ださん 打算 calculation Ⓤ ──打算的な《抜

け目のない) calculating; (欲得ずくの) mercenary ∥彼は打算的な考え方をする He has *calculating* ways of thinking.

たざんのいし 他山の石 (教訓となる具体例) object lesson ◎ ∥彼女の失敗を他山の石とする take her failure as *an object lesson*; (→彼女の失敗から学ぶ) learn from her failure

たし 足し (補足) supplement ◎; (助け) help ◎; (役に立つこと) use ◎ ∥私が英語を教えて得る収入は家計の足しにしている The money I get from teaching English is a *supplement* to the family budget. / I *supplement* the family budget by teaching English. / そんないいかげんな練習では何の足しにもならないぞ Sloppy training like that won't 「*be of* any *help* to you [*help* you at all]. / 少しですが何かの足しにしてください (→このお金があなたの役に立ってくれたらうれしい) I'd be glad if this money would *be of* some *help* [*use*] to you. (❖「少しですが」の部分を though a small amount のように訳出する必要はない)
◆ほかに何もなかったのでクッキーを食べて腹の足しにした (→短時間だけ空腹を満たした) Without anything else to eat, I *eased my hunger for a short time* by eating cookies.

だし¹ 出し ❶ [だし汁] stock ◎ ∥煮干しでだしをとる make (soup) *stock* with small dried sardines ◆このスープはだしがきいている This soup *is flavorful*. / This soup *has lots of flavor*.
❷ [口実] 姉はよく自分の子供をだしにしてデパートへ行く My sister often *uses* her child *as a pretext* for going to department stores.

だし² 山車 float ◎

だしあう 出し合う pool ⦿, chip in ∥私たちは文化祭で喫茶店を開くためにお金を出し合った We 「*pooled* our money [*chipped in* our money, *chipped in*] to run a tearoom at the school festival. ◆問題解決のためみんなで知恵を出し合った We *put our heads together* to solve the problem.

だしいれ 出し入れ このバッグは物の出し入れがしやすい構造になっている This bag's design makes it easy to *get things in and out*. / お金の出し入れはこの機械でできます You can *deposit and withdraw* money with this machine.

だしおしみ 出し惜しみ 彼は金を出し惜しみするやつだ He's *so stingy with* money. / 彼女はそれに関する情報を出し惜しみしている She *is unwilling to give* people information on the matter.

たしか 確か ❶ [確信している・確実である] ──確かな sure; certain; (明確な) definite; (疑いの余地のない) unquestionable ──確かに surely; certainly; definitely; (疑いなく) no doubt, undoubtedly

> sure:「きっと~だ」という話者の主観的な確信を表す.
> certain: 客観的な根拠に基づく確かさを表す.

彼が事件にかかわっていないことは確かだ We are *sure* [*certain*] that he has nothing to do with the case. / It is *certain* that he has nothing to do with the case. (❖He を主語にして He is *sure* [*certain*] to have nothing to do with the case. も可. ただし, ×It is *sure* that …は不可)

1つだけ確かなことがある One thing is (*for*) *sure*. / There is one thing I'm *sure of*.

彼がそれをやったという確かな証拠がある There is *unquestionable* [*solid*] evidence that he did it.

確かに彼女は偉大な芸術家だが, あまりに自己中心的だ *Surely* [*Certainly*] she is a great artist, but she is so selfish.

彼女は確かにそう言ったんだ She *definitely* said so.

◆確かに君の言うことにも一理ある (→一理あることは認めねばならない) I must admit there's a certain logic in what you say. / 確かなことは (→確実には) 言えないけど, 彼はそのうち引っ越すみたいだよ I can't *rightly* say, but he seems to be going to move one of these days.

❓「ドアのかぎをかけたのは確かですか」「確かですとも」"Are you *sure* [*certain*] you locked the door?" "Yes, I am. / *Positive*."

❓「彼はもっと積極的になるべきだと思うよ」「確かに」 "I think he must be more aggressive." "(*You're*) *right*. / (→私もそう思う) I think so, too."

❷ [正常な・正確な]
彼は計算が確かだ He is *accurate* [*correct*] in calculating.

私の記憶が確かなら, その日彼女がはいていたのは黄色のスカートだった *If my memory serves me* (*correctly* [*right*]), what she wore on the day was a yellow skirt.

❓「いったい何を言ってるんだ. 君, 気は確かかい?」「もちろんさ」 "What on earth are you saying? Are you *insane* [*out of your mind*]?" "Of course I'm not." (❖*insane*, *out of one's mind* はともに「正気でない」の意味)

❸ [たぶん]
彼女に初めて会ったのは, 確か去年の4月だったと思う I met her first in April of last year, 「*I believe* [(→間違えていなければ) *if I'm not mistaken*].

君は確か村田君だったよね You are Murata, aren't you?

❹ [信頼できる] ──確かな reliable, sure, safe

腕の確かな外科医 a *reliable* surgeon; (→熟練した) a *skilled* surgeon

その情報は確かな筋からのものだから, きっと本当だよ The information is from a *reliable* [*safe*] source, so it must be true.

その問題を解決する確かな方法を, 我々はまだ見いだせていない We haven't found the one *sure* way to solve the problem.

たしかめる 確かめる make* sure [certain], see* 他 自 (❖通例進行形にはできない), 《公式的》ascertain 他; (点検する・調べる) check (up) ⇨ かくにん

【make sure [certain]+that 節】間違いがないか確かめてください Please *make sure [certain]* (*that*) there are no mistakes.

【make sure [certain]+of 名】電車の発車時刻を確かめた I *made sure [certain] of* the departure time of the train.

【see+if 節】月曜日にお店がやっているかどうか確かめておいてよ Please *see if* the store is open on Monday. (❖see if の代わりに check whether も可)

私の言うことが信じられないのなら行って自分の目で確かめてきたらどうだい If you don't believe me, why don't you go and *see* for yourself?

そこまでの行き方を地図で確かめた I *checked (up)* the way to get there on a map.

それ，田中先生に確かめた(→確認のために聞く)ほうがいいよ You'd better *ask* Mr. Tanaka about it *to make sure*.

たしざん 足し算 addition ⓤ (↔subtraction) ◆その子はもう足し算ができる That child can already *add*.

たじたじ その俳優は記者団の質問攻めにたじたじになった The actor *got nonplused* by the barrage of questions from reporters.

たじつ 他日 someday; (別の機会に) some other time

だしっぱなし 出しっ放し 本を出しっぱなしにする *leave* a book *lying there* / 水を出しっぱなしにしないで Don't *leave* the water *running*.

たしなみ 嗜み accomplishment ⓒ (しばしば複数形 ~s); (慎み) modesty ⓤ; (礼儀作法) graces ∥彼女は女性としてのたしなみに欠ける She is lacking in *modesty* for a woman. ◆彼女は琴のたしなみがある She *is* skilled *at* (the) koto. / 彼はいくらか茶道のたしなみがある(→茶道の知識がある) He has some *working knowledge* of the tea ceremony.

たしなむ 嗜む (好む) have* a taste for ...; (技芸などを) practice 他 自; (酒は少々たしなみます(→少し飲む) I *drink* only moderately.

たしなめる (しかる) scold 他, 《公式的》reprove 他; (いさめる) 《公式的》remonstrate with *a person* ∥彼女はうるさくしてはいけませんと子供をたしなめた She *reproved* her children for making a noise.

だしぬく 出し抜く (裏をかく) outwit 他, 《口語的》outsmart 他; (機先を制す) forestall 他, steal* a march on *a person*, get* the jump on *a person* ∥その件では彼にみごとに出し抜かれた I *was* completely *outwitted* by him in the matter.

◆その雑誌はこの事件の特ダネで他誌を出し抜いた The magazine *scooped* other ones with this case.

だしぬけ 出し抜け ──だしぬけに (突然) suddenly, abruptly; (不意に) unexpectedly ⇨ とつぜん

◆彼はだしぬけに私のことが好きだと言った All of a sudden, he said he loved me.

だしもの 出し物 (プログラム) program ⓒ, bill ⓒ 《通例単数形》; (演技) act ⓒ ◆この劇場の来月の出し物は『ハムレット』だ *Hamlet* will *be on* at this theater next month.

だしゃ 打者 〖野球〗batter ⓒ, hitter ⓒ ∥強打者 *a power hitter*; 《口語的》*a slugger* / 指名打者 《米》*a designated hitter* 《略語》DH; 首位打者 *the leading hitter*

だじゃれ 駄洒落 (くだらない冗談) boring [poor] joke ⓒ; (ごろ合わせ) pun ⓒ ∥だじゃれを飛ばす make [cut, tell] *a boring joke*

たじゅう 多重 ──多重の multiplex ∥多重人格 multiple personality / 音声多重放送 multiplex sound broadcasting / 文字多重放送 teletext

たしゅたよう 多種多様 ──多種多様な various (kinds of ...), a wide [great] variety of ... ∥その植物園では多種多様な熱帯植物を見ることができる You can enjoy *a wide variety of* tropical plants at the botanical garden.

だじゅん 打順 〖野球〗batting order ⓒ, line-up ⓒ ∥彼のきょうの打順は5番だ He *is batting* fifth today.

たしょう 多少

❶〔幾分〕──多少の・多少(は) some (❖数にも量にも使える); (数が少し) a few; (量が少し) a little ⇨ すこし

場内にはまだ多少の空席があった There were still *some [a few]* vacant seats in the hall.

その選挙では多少の混乱が見られた There was *some [a little]* confusion over the election.

多少はポルトガル語が話せます I speak Portuguese *a little*.

多少なりともお役に立てたのであれば幸いです I'm glad if I've been of *some* help.

◆多少の失敗は(→ある程度は)大目に見てください Please overlook my fault *to some degree*. / 西洋建築については多少知識があります I know *something* about Western architecture. / 彼女は多少のことでは(→そう簡単には)驚かない She isn't surprised *so easily*.

💬「そのコーラ，もう飲んじゃった？」「いや，まだ多少あるよ」"Have you finished your Coke?" "No. There's still *some* left. [There still is *some* (left).]"

❷〔多さ〕(数) the number; (量) the quantity; (額) the amount

応募者の多少によって予定を変更する場合もあります We may change our plan according to *the number* of the applicants.

義援金は多少にかかわらず(→どんなに少なくても)受け付けております Contributions are welcome, *no matter how small* (*the amount is*).

たじろぐ (縮み上がる) flinch 自; (しりごみする) 《文語》shrink* back ∥彼女は犬にほえられて一瞬たじろいだ She *flinched [shrank back]* for a moment at the dog's bark.

だしん 打診 ──打診する sound out ∥彼にこ

たしんきょう

その計画についての考えを打診してみてくれないか Will you *sound out* his opinion about this plan?

たしんきょう 多神教 polytheism

たす 足す add / 3に7を足すといくつになりますか What do you get if you *add* seven *to* [*and*] three? / 私の紅茶にもう少しミルクを足していただけますか Could you *add* some more milk *to* my tea? / ここに1文字抜けていたので足しておきました I *added* one letter here because it was left out.

◆5足す1は6 Five *and* one make(s) six. / Five *plus* one is [equals] six.

だす 出す

❶ 中から外へ	put out; take out; let out
❷ 提出する・渡す	hand in, submit; present
❸ 送る	send (out); 《米》mail, 《英》post
❹ 発する	give off ..., send out
❺ 指示などを	issue

❶【中から外へ】put* out; (取り出す) take* out; (出してやる) let* out

ポケットから手を出しなさい *Take* your hands *out of* your pockets.

雅樹はかばんから漫画を出した Masaki *took* a comic book *out of* his bag.

鳥をかごから出しちゃだめよ Don't *let* the bird *out of* the cage.

あしたの朝忘れずにごみを出しておいてね Don't forget to *put out* the garbage tomorrow morning.

◆彼女は窓から顔を出した She *poked* [*stuck*] her head *out of* the window. / 彼女は何か失敗をすると舌を出す When she fails at something, she *sticks out* her tongue. / 竹の子が顔を出し始めた Bamboo shoots started to *come out*. / ヒマワリはじきに芽を出すだろう The sunflowers will soon begin to *grow* their shoots.

❷【提出する・渡す】hand [turn] in, submit; (提示する) present

解答用紙を出しなさい *Hand* [*Turn*] *in* your answer sheets.

彼は委員会に報告書を出すつもりだ He is going to *present* a report to the committee.

◆あすまでに子供の出生届を出さなければならない We must *register* the birth of our baby by tomorrow. / あり金を全部出せ! *Give me* [*Hand over*] all of your money! / 私は靴を修理に出さなければならない I have to *have* my shoes *repaired*. / あのジャケットは洗濯がきかないのでドライクリーニングに出さなければならない That jacket won't wash; it has to *be dry-cleaned*.

❸【送る】send* (out); (投函する)《米》mail, 《英》post

人を使いに出す *send a person* (*out*) on an errand

忘れずにこのはがきを出してね Please remember to *send* [*mail*] this postcard.

彼らは友人たちに結婚式の招待状を出した They *sent out* wedding invitations to their friends.

◆手紙に返事を出さないのは失礼だ It is impolite not to *answer* letters.

❹【発する】(光・音・香りなどを) give* off ..., send* out

その白い花は強い芳香を出していた The white flower 「*gave off* [*emitted*] strong perfume.

◆高熱を出す have [run] a high fever / その煙突は黒い煙を出している(→煙突から黒い煙が出ている) Black smoke *is coming out of* the chimney. / もっと大きな声を出しなさい *Say it louder.* (✿単にLouder.も可) / 教科書を声を出して読みなさい Read the textbook *aloud*. / この高音は私には出せない(→声域を越えている) This high note is *beyond my range*.

❺【指示などを】issue

彼に逮捕令状が出された A warrant *was issued* for his arrest.

◆彼は私になぞなぞを出した He *asked* me a riddle.

❻【公の場に】

浅草に店を出す *open* a store in Asakusa / 人の秘密を明るみに出す *bring* a person's secret *to light*

彼らは家を売りに出した They *put up* their house *for sale*.

石油は市場に出す前に精製しなければならない Oil must be refined before it *is marketed*.

名前は出さなかったけれど、彼は私のことを言っていたのです He *didn't mention* the name, but he meant me.

彼女はこれまで多くのヒット曲を出した She *has made* many hits.

彼らは来月新しい CD を出す They *release* their new CD next month.

その科学者はパトナム社から本を出している That scientist *publishes* with Putnum.

❼【覆われた物を】

医者は私にお腹を出すよう(→見せるように)言った The doctor told me to *show* him my belly.

❽【感情・思いなどを】show*, express

怒りを顔に出す *show one's* anger (on *one's* face)

◆我々はみな彼を怪しいと思っているが口には出していない We are all suspicious of him, but never *mention* it.

❾【力などを】

学業に精を出す *attend to one's* studies
元気を出せ! *Cheer up!*

彼女はその大会で十分に力を出しきれなかった She couldn't fully *show* her ability at the competition.

そのとき車は猛スピードを出して走っていた The car was running *at* a violent speed then.

❿【費用などを】pay*

旅行の費用はおばが出してくれた My aunt *paid* my traveling expenses.
◆私はおじにお金を出してもらって大学に行った I went to university *at* my uncle's expense.
⓫【食べ物・飲み物を】serve 他
デザートにアイスクリームを出す *serve* ice cream as a dessert
父は友人にウイスキーを出した My father *served* whiskey to his friend.
◆彼女はいつもごちそうを出してくれる She always *sets* a good table.
⓬【(結果として)生じさせる・記録する】
平均(値)を出す *calculate [find]* an average
その火事は多くの死者を出した The fire *left* many (people) dead.
その会社は海外プロジェクトで数百万ドルの損失を出した That company *lost [had a loss of]* several million dollars on its foreign project.
彼女はきのう自己ベストを出した She *recorded* her best time yesterday.
あわてて結論を出してはいけない Don't *come to* conclusions in a hurry. / Don't *rush [jump] to* conclusions.
彼の家系はこれまで多くの科学者を出してきた His family *has produced* a lot of scientists.
⓭【その他】
彼は電話して照美を出してほしいと言った He phoned and *asked for* Terumi.
その一覧表を出すにはこのアイコンをクリックすればいい You have only to click on this icon to *get* that list.
この前の旅行では彼が車を出した(→この前は彼の車で旅行した) Last time, we went on a trip *in his car*.
会議をするためグループごとに代表者を出した(→選出された) A representative *was elected* from each group to hold a meeting.
-だす —出す start 「to *do [doing]*, begin*「to *do [doing]*」/ トラックは前へ動きだした The truck *started to move* forward. / 突然雨が降りだした It suddenly *began raining [to rain]*. ◆彼女はわっと泣きだした She *burst into tears*.

たすう 多数 large number ◎; (大部分) majority ◎《また a ～》《単数または複数扱い》《全体を1つのまとまりとして考えるときは単数扱い。個々を強調するときは複数扱いになる》——多数の many, a lot of ..., a large number of ... ⇒たくさん
その地震で多数の村人が命を落とした *A lot of [A large number of]* the villagers lost their lives in the earthquake.
議員の大多数はその提案に賛成である *The majority* of the assembly members is [are] for the proposal.
その話し合いでは反対派が多数を占めた Those who were against it *were in a [the] majority* at the discussion.
私たちは多数決でそれを決めた We decided it *by majority vote*.

多数派の意見に従った I went along with the *majority* opinion.
その法案は圧倒的多数で可決された The bill passed *by an overwhelming majority*.
◆その店は中古家具を多数取りそろえている That shop has *a wide selection of* second-hand furniture.
だすう 打数 彼はきょう4打数3安打だった He hit three out of four *times at bat*.

たすかる 助かる
❶【救われる・生き残る】(救われる) be saved; (生き残る) survive 自他
その事故では1人しか助からなかった Only one person 「*was saved [survived]* in that accident.
◆医者は少年の両親に彼は助かるだろうと言った The doctor told the boy's parents that he would *live* [(→回復する) *recover*]. / 彼は雪崩(なだれ)にあったがかろうじて助かった He narrowly *escaped death* in the snowslide.
❷【労力などが省ける】
荷物を持ってくださってどうもありがとうございます. 本当に助かりました Thank you for carrying my baggage. You've been *a great help (to me)*.
このバイクは燃費がいいのでだいぶガソリン代が助かっている This motorcycle has good fuel efficiency and it *saves* me a lot of gas.
彼が機械に詳しいので本当に助かる His familiarity with machinery *helps* us (*out*) very much.

たすき 襷 (和服のそでをからげるためのひも) a *tasuki*, a cord used to tie up kimono's sleeves; (肩から斜めにかける布) sash ◎ //そのチームの最終走者に今たすきが渡りました The team's anchorperson has just been passed *the sash*. //かばんをたすきがけにする *sling* a bag *diagonally over the shoulder*

たすけ 助け (助力) help ◎; (救助) rescue ◎ ◎
彼のしてくれたことは私にとっては何の助けにもならなかった What he did for me was 「*of no help* [not any *help* at all] to me.
彼女はだれの助けもいらないと言った She said she needed nobody's *help*.
もし彼女の助けがなかったら私たちは道に迷っていただろう Without her *help*, we would have lost our way.
私は辞書の助けを借りて何とかその本を読破した I managed to read through the book *with the help [assistance] of* a dictionary.
その火事現場では, 人々が助けを求めて叫んでいた People were shouting for *help* in the fire.
私がおぼれかけたとき, 彼が助けに来てくれた He came 「*to my rescue* [to *rescue* me] when I almost drowned.

たすけあい 助け合い mutual help ◎; (協力) cooperation ◎ ◆歳末助け合い運動(→慈善活動) a year-end *charity* campaign
たすけあう 助け合う help 「*each other [one another]*; (協力する) cooperate 自 //私

たちはお互いに助け合わなくてはいけない We must *help* [*cooperate with*] *one another*.

たすけおこす 助け起こす 彼は老人を助け起こした He *helped* the old man (*get*) *up*.

たすけだす 助け出す rescue [他] //彼らはがれきの下からけが人を助け出した They *rescued* injured persons from under the debris.

たすけぶね 助け船 lifeboat [C]; (助け) help [U] ◆私が言葉に詰まると先生は助け船を出してくれた When I was at a loss for words, my teacher *gave* me 「*a helping hand* [(→アドバイスをしてくれた) some *advice*].

たすける 助ける

❶【手伝う】help [他]; (援助する) 《公式的》aid [他]; (補佐する) 《公式的》assist [他] ⇒ てつだう

盲導犬は目の不自由な人の生活を助ける (→生活の様々な場面で目の不自由な人を助ける) Guide dogs *help* blind people with various situations in their lives.

君以外に僕を助けてくれる友達はいない I have no other friend to *help* me but you.

その老人が道を渡るのを助けてあげた I *helped* the old man cross [across] the street.

[語法] 「人が…するのを助ける」「人を助けて…させる」は《help＋人＋(to) *do*》や《help＋人＋副》で表す. 上の用例で cross は前者, across は後者を用いた表現である.

彼女はアルバイトをして家計を助けている (→家族を経済的に助けている) She works part-time to *help* her family financially.

この酵素は消化を助ける This enzyme *helps* [(→促進する) *promotes*] digestion.

◆発展途上国の子供たちを助けるために募金が行われている Money is being raised *in aid of* children in developing countries. / 彼にはずいぶん助けてもらっている (→多くを負っている) I *owe* him a lot.

❷【救助する】save [他], rescue [他]; (救うために助力する) help [他][自] ⇒ きゅうじょ

僕たちは小さな女の子がおぼれかけているのを助けた We *saved* [*rescued*] a little girl from drowning.

助けて (→命を救って) いただいてありがとうございました I truly thank you for *saving my life*.

助けて! *Help* me!

◆(命ごいして) 私はどうなってもかまいませんが, 息子は助けてください I don't care about my life, but please *don't kill* my son.

たずさえる 携える 手に手を携えて *hand in hand* / 彼女は弁当を携えてピクニックに出かけた She went on a picnic *with* her lunch.

たずさわる 携わる (従事する) engage [be engaged] in ...; (関係する) be concerned with ... //父は教育に携わっている My father *engages* [*is engaged*] *in* education. / 彼女はこの本の編集に携わらなかった She *wasn't concerned with* editing this book.

たずねびと 尋ね人 missing person [C] ◆尋ね人広告 《主に米》*a personal* (*ad*)

たずねる[1] 訪ねる

visit [他][自], call 「on *a person* [at ...] (❖on の後には人, at の後には場所を表す言葉がくる)

夏休みに京都を訪ねた I *visited* Kyoto during the summer vacation.

パリには訪ねてみたい場所が数多くある There are a good number of places I want to *visit* in Paris.

私は久しぶりに恩師を訪ねた I 「*called on* [*visited*] my former teacher after a long absence.

父の会社を一度訪ねてみたい I want to *call at* my father's office once.

◆友達が訪ねてきた A friend of mine *came to see* me. / ある日曜日彼がひょっこり訪ねてきた He *dropped in on* me on a Sunday.

たずねる[2] 尋ねる

❶【質問する】ask [他][自], inquire [他][自]

「今何時」と広子は尋ねた "What time is it?" *asked* Hiroko.

ある婦人が私に近づいてきて道を尋ねた A lady came up to me and *asked* the way.

【ask＋名(人)＋about＋名】私は彼女に将来の夢について尋ねた I *asked* her *about* her dreams for the future.

【ask＋名(人)＋wh- 句】彼は彼女に次にすべきことを尋ねた He *asked* her *what* to do next.

【ask＋名(人)＋if 節】私はトムに留学したことがあるか尋ねた I *asked* Tom *if* he had studied abroad.

[会]「町田先生, お尋ねしたいことがあるんですが」「いいよ, 言ってごらん」"May I *ask* you a question, Mr. Machida?" "Sure, go ahead."

❷【探す・調べる】look [search] for ... ⇒ さがす

その子供たちは母親の行方を尋ねていた The children *were looking* [*searching*] *for* their mother.

だせい 惰性 〔物理〕 inertia [inə́ːrʃə] [U]; (習慣) habit [C] //彼女は惰性でそのドラマを見続けている She keeps on watching the drama *from* [*out of*] *force of habit*.

だせき 打席 打席に立つ be *at bat* / 松井, きょうの3打席目です This is the third time Matsui is *at bat* today.

だせん 打線 batting line-up [C] //強力打線 *a* powerful *batting line-up* ◆タイガースは最近打線が湿っている (→攻撃が不調だ) The Tigers are poor at *offense* lately.

たそがれ 黄昏 twilight [U], dusk [U] //たそがれ時に at *twilight*

[慣用表現] 彼女は人生のたそがれ時にある She is in *the twilight* of her life.

だそく 蛇足 (余計な補足) unnecessary addition [C] //蛇足ながら… This may be *an unnecessary addition*, but ....

ただ[1] 只

❶【ふつうの・ほんの…にすぎない】―ただの

──形 (ふつうの) ordinary; (ありふれた) common ──副 (ほんの…にすぎない) only, just
彼だってテレビに出るようになる前はただの高校生だったんだよ(→ふつうの高校生にすぎなかった) He was just an *ordinary* high school student before he started to appear on TV.
初め彼女はただのかぜだと思っていた At first she thought it was a *common* cold.
彼はただの腹話術師ではない He is *no ordinary* ventriloquist. (❖no ordinary で「特にすぐれた」の意味. He is not an ordinary ventriloquist. は単に「ふつうでない」という意味)
ただのかすり傷だよ It's *just* [*only*] a scratch.
❷【無料】──ただで free ──ただで (for) free, free of charge
このバッジ, ただでもらったんだ I got this badge (*for*) *free*.
◆彼はただ同然でそのチケットを手に入れた He got the ticket *for practically nothing*. / 彼らはただ働きさせられていた They were made to *work for nothing*.
慣用表現 そんなことをしたらただじゃおかないぞ(→ひどい目にあわせる) If you do such a thing, I'll *give you a hard time*. / こんなところを親に見つかったらただではすまない(→厳しく罰せられる)だろう I'll *be severely punished* if my parents find me doing things like this. / ただより高いものはない *There's no such thing as a free lunch.* (❖「ただで食べられる昼食はない」という意味の英語の決まり文句)

ただ² 唯

❶【単に】only, merely (❖only よりもかたい語), just ➡ 〜だけ
君はただここにいるだけでいい You have *only* to stay here.
彼女、ああしてただ格好つけているだけさ She is *just* showing off that way.
だれかが助けてくれるのをただ待っているだけではだめだよ You shouldn't be *just* waiting for someone to help you.
◆彼はただ単に自分がそうしたいからという理由でそうしたのだった He did it *simply* because he wanted to do it. / 彼女は私が何を言ってもただうなずくばかりだった She *did nothing but* nod at whatever I said to her.
❷【たった】
ピアノを弾くことが私のただ1つの趣味だ Playing the piano is my *only* hobby.
彼は私のただ一人の友達です He is my *one and only* friend.
私はただのひと言も話さなかった I didn't say *a single word*.
そのパーティーで私が知り合いになりたいと思う人はただのひとりもいなかった At that party there was not *even one person* that I'd like to meet.
❸【ただし】but
どこへ行ってもいい. ただ危ないことはするな You may go anywhere, *but* don't do anything dangerous.
だだ 駄々 そんなにだだをこねるもんじゃありません Don't *be so unreasonable*. (❖unreasonable は「聞き分けのない」の意味)
ただい 多大 ──多大な great; (深刻な) serious / 彼の思想は後の芸術家たちに多大な影響を及ぼした His idea had a *great* influence on later artists.

ただいま

❶【現在】now; (ちょうど今) just [《口語的》right] now; (たった今) just ➡ いま(今)
近藤さんはただ今外出中です Mr. Kondo is out *now*.
彼はただ今席をはずしています He isn't here *just now*.
江本先生はただ今お見えになりました Mrs. Emoto has *just* arrived.
❷【(今から)すぐに】right away [《口語的》now]
ただ今参ります I'm coming *right away*.
◆(レストランなどで)ただ今お持ちします Coming (*right*) up!
❸【あいさつ】

語法 英語には日本語の「ただいま」に相当する決まった言い方はない. Hi!, Hello!などのあいさつの言葉を用いたり, I'm home [back].などと言ったりする.

❷「ただいま」「お帰り, 浩. 学校はどうだった」 "*Hello. I'm home.*" "Hello, Hiroshi. How was school?"
たたえる¹ 称える praise ⑬; (賞賛する) admire ⑬ / 受賞者たちは互いにたたえ合った The winners *were praising one another*. / 彼は勝者ではあったが, 彼をたたえる者はだれもいなかった Though he was a winner, no one *admired* him.
◆谷山高校チームの勝利をたたえて球場内に校歌が流された *In praise of* the victory of Taniyama High School, the school song was played in the stadium.
たたえる² 湛える その湖は満々と水をたたえている The lake *is brimming with* water. / 少女は満面に笑みをたたえていた The girl *was all smiles*.

たたかい 戦い・闘い

❶【戦闘】fight ©; (大規模な) battle © ©; (戦争) war © ©(戦争) ➡ せんそう(戦争)
…との戦いに勝つ[負ける] win [lose] *a fight against* … / 関ヶ原の戦い *the battle* of Sekigahara
その戦いで7人の兵士が負傷した Seven soldiers were wounded in the *battle*.
❷【勝負・競い合い】
彼らはタイトルマッチで激しい闘いを繰り広げた They fought *a really hard fight* in the title match.
その選挙は4党による闘いだった The election was *a four-way fight* [*battle*].
❸【闘争・奮闘】fight ©, battle ©, war © ©, (…を求める闘争) struggle ©
自由を得るための闘い *the fight* [*battle, struggle*] *for freedom*
彼女の短い生涯は癌(がん)との闘いだった Her

short life was *a battle* [*fight, war*] *against* cancer.

たたかう 戦う・闘う

❶【戦闘する】 fight* 自他 ∥敵軍と戦う *fight against* [*with*] the enemy forces(◆*with* よりも *against* のほうが敵対の感じが強い)

米国は他の国々と連合してイラクと戦った The U.S. *fought with* other countries *against* Iraq.(◆この場合の *with* は「…と連合して」の意味)

彼らは祖国の名誉のために戦った They *fought* for the honor of their country.

❷【勝負する・競い合う】

その2人のボクサーは正々堂々と闘った The two boxers *fought* clean.

わが校の野球チームは優勝をかけて東高校チームと闘った Our school's baseball team *played a game against* Higashi High School for the championship.

彼は長谷川名人と闘った He *had a match with* the grand champion Hasegawa.

❸【闘争する・奮闘する】

不正と闘う *fight* (*against*) injustice / 人種差別撤廃を目ざして闘う *fight* [*battle, struggle*] *for* the elimination of racial discrimination

その患者は最後まで病気と闘った The patient 「*fought* (*against*) [*struggled with*] his disease to the end.

たたかわす 闘わす 彼らは長時間にわたり激しい議論を闘わせた(→激しく議論した) They *argued* heavily for a long time.

たたきあげる 叩き上げる 彼は一介(いっかい)の労働者からたたき上げて大企業の社長になった He *worked his way up* from an ordinary workman to the president of a big company.

たたきうり 叩き売り bargain [discount] sale © ◆バナナのたたき売りをする *knock down* the price of bananas

たたきおこす 叩き起こす (戸をたたいて起こす) knock at the door and wake* *a person* up;(手荒く起こす) wake *a person* up roughly ∥真夜中にたたき起こされた I *was woken up roughly* at midnight.

たたきおとす 叩き落とす (ハエなどを) swat 他

たたきこむ 叩き込む …にくさびをたたき込む *drive* a wedge *into* … / その男を牢獄(ろうごく)にたたき込む *put* the man *into* prison / 彼の助言を頭にたたき込んだ I *hammered* his advice *into* my head.

たたきころす 叩き殺す beat* … to death

たたきこわす 叩き壊す break* down, knock down,(粉々に) smash 他 ∥彼はハンマーで戸をたたきこわした He *broke down* the door with a hammer.

たたきだい 叩き台 (原案) original plan ©;(試案) tentative plan ©;(出発点) springboard © ∥これはよりよい計画を立てるためのたたき台にすぎない This is only *a springboard* to a better plan.

たたきだす 叩き出す turn [kick] *a person* out ∥彼は息子を家からたたき出した He turned his son *out of* the house.

たたきつける 叩き付ける throw* 他, fling* (down)(◆後者の方が荒々しい) ∥人に挑戦状をたたきつける *throw* [*fling*] *down* a challenge to a person / 彼はバットを地面にたたきつけた He *flung down* his bat on the ground. ◆彼は怒って本を机の上にたたきつけた He got angry and *banged* his book on the desk. ∥たたきつけるような雨の中、僕らは駅まで走っていった We ran to the station in *a beating rain*.

たたきなおす 叩き直す 曲がった性根をたたき直す *correct a person's* perverse disposition; *flog* a perverse disposition *out of a person*

たたきのめす 叩きのめす beat* up, knock down,《口語的》flatten 他

たたく 叩く

❶【打つ】 hit* 他 自,《公式的》strike* 他 自;(続けざまに) beat* 他 自;(こぶしなどで) knock 他 自;(トントン・コツコツと) tap 他 自

彼はこぶしでテーブルをたたいた He *hit* [*struck*] the table with his fist.

聡が僕の頭をたたいたんだ Satoru *hit* me *on* the head.

彼は毎晩ドラムをたたく He *beats* the drums every night.

だれかがドアをたたいている Somebody is *knocking* on [at] the door.

母はよいスイカをたたいて見分けることができる My mother can tell a good watermelon by *tapping* it.

◆ 雑誌でゴキブリをたたく *slap* [*smack*] a magazine at a cockroach / 母親は坊やのおしりをたたいた The mother *spanked* her boy.(◆*spank* は「罰としてしりをたたく」の意味) / 彼女は泣いている少年の背中をポンとたたいた She *patted* the crying boy *on* his back. / 私たちは音楽のリズムに合わせて手をたたいた We *clapped our hands* in rhythm to the music. / 私は母の肩をたたいてあげた I *massaged* my mother's shoulders. / I *gave my mother a shoulder massage*.(◆欧米ではこりをほぐすために肩をたたくという習慣がないので *massage* などで代用する)

❷【攻撃する】(攻撃する) attack 他 自;(批判する) criticize,《英》criticise 他

その政治家はマスコミにさんざんたたかれた The politician *was criticized* harshly by the mass media.

❸【その他】

大口[むだ口]をたたく *talk big* [*trash*] / ボギーをたたく *make a bogey*

[関連語] 日本たたき Japan bashing

ただごと 彼が青い顔をしているなんてただごとじゃないぞ He is pale. It's *out of the ordinary*.

ただし 但し but, however;(もし…なら) if;(…という条件で) on condition that … ∥今回はお前のためにやってやろう。ただしこれっきりだぞ I'll do it for you this time, *but* not again. / 外出してもよい。ただし6時には戻るこ

と You can go out *if* [*on condition that*] you come back by 6 o'clock.

ただしい 正しい
(道徳・事実に合った) right (↔wrong); (正確な) correct (↔incorrect); (適切な) proper (↔improper), right (↔wrong) ——正しく right(ly); correctly; properly

正しい答え the *right* [*correct*] answer / 正しい選択をする make the *right* choice / 単語を正しくつづる spell words *correctly*

だれの言うことが正しいのか分からない I don't know who is *right*.

彼は自分の理論が正しいことを証明した He demonstrated that his theory was *right*.

私の記憶が正しければ、森田先生は茨城出身だ Ms. Morita is from Ibaraki, if I remember *right*.

彼は私にレストランでの正しい食事のしかたを教えてくれた He showed me the *proper* way to dine at a restaurant.

◆礼儀正しいふるまい *polite* behavior

ただしがき ただし書き proviso ⓒ (複 ~s)
ただす¹ 正す (訂正する) correct 他, right 他 /不正を正す *right* a wrong / 誤りがあれば正せ *Correct* errors, if any.
◆姿勢を正す *straighten* oneself; (→背筋を伸ばして座る) *sit up*

ただす² 質す ask 他, (細かく質問する) question 他; (確かめる) make* sure /彼に真意をただしてみよう I'll *ask* him *about* his real intentions.

たたずまい 佇まい (雰囲気) atmosphere ⓤⓒ; (外観) appearance ⓤⓒ /その庭園は落ち着いたたたずまいを見せていた The garden had *a* calm *atmosphere*.

たたずむ 佇む 彼女は池のほとりにぼんやりとたたずんでいた She *stood still* absent-mindedly on the pond.

ただただ 彼女が勤勉なのにはただただ感心するばかりだ *All I can do* is to admire her for her diligence. ⇨ただ(唯)

ただちに 直ちに at once, right away, immediately; (…するとすぐ) as soon as …
⇨すぐ /ただちに帰ってきなさい Come back *at once*. / 彼が着いたらただちに出発しよう Let's start *as soon as* he arrives.

だだっこ 駄々っ子 (聞き分けのない子) unreasonable child ⓒ; (甘やかされた悪がき) spoiled brat ⓒ

だだっぴろい だだっ広い (家・部屋などが) overly spacious; (土地が) too vast /だだっ広い部屋にいすが1つだけ置いてあった A chair was all there was in an *overly spacious* room.

ただでさえ ただでさえ (→今のままでも) 金がないのに臨時出費だ I am running out of money *as it is*, but now I have unexpected expenses. / あの学生はただでさえ頭がよいのにそれに加えて勉強熱心だ That student is *not only* brilliant, *but (also)* diligent. / 彼らのチームはただでさえ強いのにさらに強力な選手たちを集めようとしている Their team is *already*

strong, *and moreover* [*besides*], they seem to recruit the best players.

ただならぬ (ふつうでない) unusual /彼はただならぬ気配を感じた He sensed something *unusual*.

ただのり 只乗り バスのただ乗りを防止する prevent *fare-beating* on a bus / その男は電車にただ乗りした The man *stole a ride* on the train.

たたみ 畳

畳は和室用のマットで、中心部分にわらを固め、表面を細かく編んだイグサで覆ってあります。縦180センチ、横90センチ (約 6 × 3 フィート) のサイズが一般的で、和室の広さは畳の数で表します。湿気の多い日本の気候には畳が適しているといわれています。
Tatami, floor mats for Japanese-style rooms, are filled with woven rice straw and covered with finely-woven rush. The normal size of one *tatami* is 180 centimeters long and 90 centimeters wide (approximately 6 feet by 3 feet); the size of Japanese-style rooms is measured by the number of *tatami*. It is said that *tatami* are a suitable material for the humid weather of Japan.

たたみかける 畳み掛ける たたみかけて質問する (→質問の砲火を浴びせる) *fire* questions / (スポーツで) たたみかけるような攻撃 *a quick succession of* attacks ◆野球「連打」の場合は attacks の代わりに hits を用いる

たたむ 畳む fold (up); (2つ折りにする) double 他 /毛布をたたむ *fold up* a blanket / 彼は傘をたたんだ He *folded* (*up*) [*shut*] his umbrella. ◆店をたたむ (→ 商売をやめる) *shut up* [*close down*] a shop / テントをたたむ *strike* [*pull down*, *lower*] a tent

ただもの やつはただ者ではない He *is no* [*not any*] *ordinary man*.

ただよう 漂う (水面・空中をゆっくり移動する) drift 自; (浮遊する) float 自 /1艘(含)の小船が波間に漂っていた A boat *was drifting* [*floating*] on the waves. / 空には白い雲が漂っていた There were white clouds *floating* [*drifting*] in the sky.
◆彼女にはどことなく気品が漂っている There is something elegant *about* her. / その部屋には緊迫した雰囲気が漂っていた The room *had* a tense atmosphere. / 梅の香りがあたり一面に漂っていた The fragrance of plum *was in the air* all around.

たたり 祟り (のろい) curse ⓒ /先祖のたたり one's ancestor's *curse* ◆蛇を殺さないほうがいいよ、たたりがあるっていうから You shouldn't kill snakes. It is said that you'll *be cursed* after that.
ことわざ さわらぬ神にたたりなし ⇨ かみ(神)

たたる 祟る curse 他 /悪霊にたたられる *be cursed* by evil spirit
◆無理(→過労)がたたって体をこわしてしまった The strain *made* me lose my health. / 去年は冷夏にたたられて (→冷夏のせいで) 米が不作

だった We had a poor crop of rice last year *because of* the cool summer.

ただれる 爛れる (化膿(かのう)する) fester ⓐ /傷がただれてきた The wound began to *fester*.

たち 質 (性質) nature ⓤ ⓒ; (気質)《公式的》disposition ⓒ ⓤ; (傾向) temperament ⓤ ⓒ /彼は飽きっぽいたちだ He「is capricious *by nature* [has *a capricious disposition*]. / He gets bored with anything *easily*. / 理佐はおとなしいたちだ Risa is quiet *by temperament*. / Risa is *a quiet type*. ◆たちの いいかぜをひく catch a *bad cold* / このいたずらはたちが悪い(→悪意がある) This mischief is *malicious*. / 彼は物事を深く考えるたち(→考える人)ではない He's not a deep thinker.

-たち -達 (❖名詞・代名詞の複数形で表す) /女の子たち girls / 子供たち children / あなたたち you

たちあい 立ち会い、(臨席) presence ⓤ /証人立ち会いのもとに現場検証が行われた They inspected the scene *in the presence of* the witness.
‖ 立会演説会 a joint campaign-speech meeting / 立会人 an observer; (証人) a witness

たちあう 立ち会う be present (at ...); (出席する)《公式的》attend ⓐ; (証人として) witness ⓐ /多くの友人が我々の結婚式に立ち会ってくれた Many friends *witnessed* our marriage.

たちあがる 立ち上がる
❶【起立する】stand* up, get* up,《公式的》rise* ⓐ
聴衆は立ち上がって拍手した The audience *stood* [*got*] *up* and applauded.
彼はいすから立ち上がって私を迎えてくれた He *rose* from his chair and greeted me.
◆ぱっと立ち上がる *jump* [*spring*] *to one's feet*
❷【行動を起こす】(反抗する)《公式的》rise* ⓐ;(要求を掲げて)《公式的》arise* ⓐ
人々は政府に反抗して立ち上がった People *rose* in revolt against the government.
黒人たちは公民権を要求して立ち上がった Black people *arose* to demand their civil rights.
❸【コンピュータが】start ⓐ; (システムが) boot up
僕のパソコン, 立ち上がるのが遅いんだよなあ My PC *boots up* so slowly.

たちあげる 立ち上げる start ⓐ; (システムを) boot up; (電源を入れる) turn on /夏子は彼にそのコンピュータの立ち上げ方を聞いた Natsuko asked him how to *start* that computer.

たちいふるまい 立ち居振舞い、(身のこなし) movement ⓒ /しとやかな立ち居ふるまい *one's* graceful *movements*

たちいり 立ち入り 立入禁止《掲示》*Keep Off*; *Keep Out*; *No Admittance*; *No Trespassing*; *Off Limits*; *No Entrance* / 芝生内立入禁止《掲示》*Keep off the grass*. / 関係者以外立入禁止《掲示》*Personnel Only*; *Private* / 法廷への立ち入りを禁じる refuse a person *admittance to* the courtroom / 工場の立ち入り検査をする make *an on-the-spot inspection of* the factory

たちいる 立ち入る ❶【入る】enter ⓐ ⓐ, go* into ...; (不法侵入する) trespass ⓐ /当局はその地域にだれも立ち入らないよう命じた The authority gave orders that no one (should) *enter* the area. / 彼らは私の土地に無断で立ち入った They *trespassed on* my land.
❷【介入する】interfere ⓐ, step in
◆そのような立ち入った(→個人的な)ことは聞くのではない You shouldn't ask about such *personal* affairs.

たちうち 太刀打ち 太刀打ちする compete with ... ◆英語ではとても彼女に太刀打ちできない I「*am no match for* [*have nothing on*] her in English.

たちおうじょう 立ち往生 ぬかるみにはまってバスが立ち往生してしまった The bus *was stuck* in the mud. / 交通ストのせいで私は大阪で立ち往生した The transportation strike *stranded* me in Osaka.

たちおくれる 立ち後れる・立ち遅れる スタートで立ち後れる start *too slow* / リサイクルに関するかぎり, 日本はドイツに大きく立ち後れている As far as recycling is concerned, Japan *falls* [*lags*] far *behind* Germany.

たちおよぎ 立ち泳ぎ ──立ち泳ぎする tread* water

たちがれる 立ち枯れる その工場の周辺の木々は立ち枯れていた The trees *were blighted* around the factory.

たちぎえ 立ち消え 結局その企画は立ち消えになった(→失敗に終わった) The project *fell through* after all. / (→完成する前に忘れられた) The project *ended in being forgotten before it was completed*.

たちぎき 立ち聞き ──立ち聞きする(盗み聞きする) eavesdrop ⓐ; (偶然耳にする) overhear* ⓐ /彼女は陰れて彼らの話を立ち聞きしていた She *was eavesdropping on* their conversation from her hiding place.

たちきる 断ち切る break* ⓐ; (関係などを) cut* off,《公式的》sever ⓐ /長年続いた慣習を断ち切る *break* conventions which have lasted for years
◆彼女は元の恋人への思いを断ち切れずにいる(→忘れられないでいる) She *can't get* her ex-boyfriend *out of her mind*.

たちぐい 立ち食い, (立食) stand-up meal ──立ち食いする eat* standing ‖立ち食いそば屋 a stand-up *soba* shop [restaurant]

たちくらみ 立ちくらみ 急に立ち上がったら立ちくらみがした I *felt dizzy* when I stood up suddenly.

たちこめる 立ち込める 部屋に煙がたちこめていた The room *was filled with* smoke. / 早朝の湖には霧がたちこめていた Mist *hung over* the lake early in the morning.

たちさる 立ち去る leave* ⓐ ⓐ, get* [go*] away /彼女はその場を立ち去ろうとしなかった She wouldn't *leave* there. / 今すぐここから

立ち去れ！ *Go away from here* right now!/ *Get out of here* right now!

たちしょうべん 立ち小便 ——立ち小便する urinate outdoors while standing

たちすくむ 立ちすくむ (恐怖などでぼう然とする) be petrified (with ...); (その場にくぎづけになる) be rooted to the spot; (凍りつく) freeze* 自 ‖彼女は恐怖でその場に立ちすくんだ She *was rooted to the spot* in terror.

たちつくす 立ち尽くす 彼は驚きのあまりしばらくその場に立ち尽くした He was so surprised that he *just stood still* there for some time.

たちっぱなし 立ちっぱなし 池袋から川越までずっと立ちっぱなしだった I had to *keep standing* all the way from Ikebukuro to Kawagoe.

たちどころに 立ち所に at once, right away, immediately; (…するとすぐ) as soon as … ⇒すぐ

たちどまる 立ち止まる stop 自 ‖彼は突然立ち止まって振り返った He *stopped* suddenly and turned around.

◆立ち止まらないで(→先へ進んで)ください *Move on*, please./ *Go along*, please.

たちなおる 立ち直る recover 自, get* over … ‖彼は試合に負けたショックから立ち直るまで長い時間がかかった It took a long time for him to「*recover from* [*get over*]」the shock of losing the game.

◆彼は非行少年だったが、今はすっかり立ち直って(→改心して)まじめに暮らしている He used to be a delinquent boy, but now *is* completely *reformed* and leading a serious life.

たちならぶ 立ち並ぶ stand* in a row; (…に沿って) line 他 ‖縁日には境内に屋台が立ち並ぶ Booths *stand in a row* in the precincts of the shrine on the festival day. / 海岸沿いにヤシの木が立ち並んでいる Palm trees *line* the coast.

たちのき 立ち退き eviction C U; (移転) removal U C ‖私たちはアパートからの立ち退きを求められた We were ordered to *leave* the apartment.

‖立ち退き命令 an eviction order / 立ち退き料 compensation for eviction

たちのく 立ち退く leave* 他, move out of …; (法的に) be evicted ‖長年住んできた土地を立ち退かなければならなくなった I had to *move out of* the place where I had long lived.

たちのぼる 立ち昇る go* up, rise* 自 ‖遠くで一筋の煙が立ち昇るのが見えた I saw a column of smoke「*go up*［*rise*］」in the distance.

たちば 立場

❶【境遇】 position C《通例単数形》; (状況) situation C

私の立場だったらあなたはどうしますか If you were in my *position*, what would you do?

私たちはとても難しい立場に立たされている We are in *a* very difficult *situation*.

私はあなたに忠告できる立場にない I'm「in *no position* [not in *a position*]」to give you advice.

彼らは互いの立場をもっと尊重すべきだ They should respect each other's *positions* more.

立場上、その質問にはお答えできません I'm not *in a position to* answer that question.

君にそんなことをされては私の立場がなくなる If you do that, it will *put* me *in an embarrassing position*.

❷【見地】 position C, stand C, standpoint C《通例単数形》

立場を明確にする clarify *one's position* / 教師の立場でその問題について議論する discuss the issue from *the standpoint* of a teacher

◆彼らは議論で共通の立場(→立脚点)が見いだせなかった They were unable to find any common *ground* in their discussion.

e「この計画に関してあなたはどういう立場をとっていますか」「私は反対です(→反対の立場をとっている)」 "What's your *stand* on this project?" "I've taken a stand against it."

たちはだかる 立ちはだかる stand* [block] in *a person's* way; (困難などが)《公式的》confront 他 ‖裏通りへ入ると数人の男が私たちの前に立ちはだかった Some men *stood in our way* when we went into an alley. / 我々の行く手に思いがけない困難が立ちはだかった Unexpected trouble「*stood in our way*［*confronted* us］」.

たちばなし 立ち話 彼女たちは駅で立ち話をしていた They *stood talking* [*chatting*] in the station.

たちふさがる 立ち塞がる 彼女の前にはいくつかの難問が立ちふさがっている Some difficult problems *were in her way*.

たちまち soon, at once, quickly, in no time ⇒すぐ ‖彼のうわさはたちまち学生の間で広まった The rumor *quickly* spread through the students.

たちまわる 立ち回る うまく立ち回る *act* tactfully [artfully]; *conduct oneself* with tact

たちみ 立ち見 《掲示》立ち見席のみ *Standing Room Only* / その映画は大入りで立ち見が出た The movie attracted so large a crowd that some people had to *see it standing*.

‖立ち見客 a standee

たちむかう 立ち向かう face 他,《公式的》confront 他, stand* (up to ...); (勇敢に) brave 他 ‖彼は強い決意をもって苦難に立ち向かった He *faced* his hardships with great resolution. / 彼らは勇敢に敵の攻撃に立ち向かった They「*bravely stood*［*braved*］」the enemy's attack.

だちょう 駝鳥 ostrich C

たちよみ 立ち読み 彼は友人を待つ間、コンビニで雑誌を立ち読みした He *browsed through* magazines in a convenience store (*without buying*) while waiting for his friend. (❖browse throughは「拾い読みする」の意味)

たちよる

たちよる 立ち寄る 《口語的》drop by, 《口語的》drop in (on [at] ...), call (on [at] ...) (*on* の後には人, *at* の後には場所を表す言葉がくる); (旅の途中で) 《口語的》stop off (at [in] ...), よる (寄る) ∥ 私が立ち寄ったとき彼女は家にいなかった She wasn't home when I *dropped by.* / 次に京都へいらっしゃる折にはぜひ私たちのところへお立ち寄りください Next time you visit Kyoto, please *call on* us. / 神戸へ行く途中京都に立ち寄ってお昼を食べた We *stopped off at* Kyoto for lunch on our way to Kobe.

だちん 駄賃 (チップ) tip ©; (報酬) reward ©© ◆買い物に行ったら母が駄賃をくれた My mother *paid* me for going shopping.

たつ¹ 立つ

❶ 足をついて　　　　stand up; stand
❷ 物が直立している
❸ 立場に身を置く

❶【足をついて】(起立する) stand* up; (起立している) stand ®
演壇に立つ *stand* on a platform
立ってください *Stand up*, please.
彼は立っているのもやっとだった He could barely *stand.*
背筋を伸ばして立ちなさい *Stand up* with your back straight.
私たちはフェンス際に立って野球の試合を見た We *stood* by the fence watching the baseball game.
私はそこにだれかが立っているのを見た I saw somebody *standing* there.
僕の犬は後ろ足で立てるよ My dog *can stand* (*up*) on her hind legs.
彼はじっと立ったまま次郎を待った He *stood still* and waited for Jiro.

❷【物が直立している】
境内には高い杉の木が立っていた Tall cedars *stood* [There *were* tall cedars] in the precincts of the shrine.
馬は耳が立っている A horse's ears *stick upright.*

❸【立場に身を置く】
人生の岐路に立っている *stand* [*be*] at the crossroads of *one's* life
正夫は微妙な立場に立っていた Masao *was* in a delicate situation.
日本チームは試合の間中守勢に立たされた Japan's team *had to be defensive* throughout the game.
彼はゴール手前でレースの先頭に立った He 「*took the lead in* [*headed*] the race just before the finishing line.
人の上に立つ者の責任は重大だ *Leaders* have a heavy responsibility.

❹【生じる】
どこからそんなうわさが立ったのだろう Where did such a rumor *start* from?
ラーメンからは湯気が立っていた Steam *was rising* from the ramen.
このせっけんは泡があまり立たない This soap *doesn't* 「*make* bubbles [*lather*] well.

❺【巧みである】
彼女は筆が立つ She is *a good* [*skillful*] *writer.*
その大学生はたいそう弁が立った The college student was *a very eloquent* [*good*] *speaker.*

❻【その他】
彼女はむっとして席を立った She was offended and *left her seat.*
この通りには毎週日曜日の朝に市が立つ *A market is held* in this street on every Sunday morning.
彼はチームをしょって立っている He *carries* the entire team.
今度の週末の予定はまだ立っていない The plan for the coming weekend hasn't *been made* yet.

ことわざ 立つ鳥跡を濁さず It is an ill bird that fouls its own nest. (→自分の巣を汚す鳥はよくない鳥だ)

たつ² 経つ
pass (by)
あれからすでに半年がたった Six months *have already passed* since then. / *It has already been* six months since then.
何年もたってから彼の説が正しかったことが証明された His theory was proven to be true *after years had passed* [*years later*].
◆数日たったら(→後には), 彼はこのことをけろっと忘れるに決まってるよ I'm sure he'll completely forget about this *in a few days.* /
彼と知り合ってからもうかなりたちます I have known him *for quite some time.* / 時がたつにつれてこの出来事は忘れられていった This incident went out of their mind 「*with* (*the passage of*) *time* [*as time went by*]. / 3分もたたないうちに救急車が到着した An ambulance arrived *in less than* three minutes. / その石段は何年もたつうちにすっかりすり減ってしまった The stone steps have worn away *over* the years. / どちらが正しいかは時がたてば分かる *Time will tell* which is right.

たつ³

❶【断絶・遮断する】(切り離す) cut* off, 《公式的》sever ®; (急に断絶する) break* off; (遮断する) interrupt ®
世間との関係を絶つ *cut oneself off* from the world
警察は犯人の逃走経路を断った The police *cut off* the criminal's escape route.
その事件を機に両国は関係を絶った The two countries 「*broke off* [*severed*] relations after the incident.
◆そのヘリコプターは2時間前から消息を絶っている The helicopter *has been missing* for two hours.

❷【やめる・断念する】give* up
酒を断つ 「*give up* [*quit, cut off*] drinking
◆悪習を絶つ *break oneself of* a bad habit

❸【その他】
悪の根を絶つ *root out* evils / 自らの命を絶つ *take one's* own *life*; *commit suicide*

たつ⁴ 建つ （建築される）be built; （建っている）stand* ⓐ; （碑などが）be set [put] up // 隣の町に新しい教会がたった A new church *was built* in the next town. / その２軒の家はかなりくっついて建っている The two houses *stand* [*are*] quite close.

たつ⁵ 発つ leave* ⓐ他, start ⓐ /彼は10時の列車で東京をたった He *left* Tokyo by the 10:00 train. / 彼女はきのう日本をたってブラジルへ向かった She *left* Japan *for* Brazil yesterday.

たつ⁶ 裁つ cut* ⓑ ➪ きる（切る）

たつ⁷ 辰 （十二支の第５番目）the Dragon
➪ えと

だつい 脱衣 ——脱衣する take* off *one's* clothes ➪ ぬぐ
∥脱衣所（更衣室）a changing room; （学校・体育館などのロッカールーム）a locker room

だっかい¹ 脱会 defection ⓤ ——脱会する defect ⓐ /彼女はそのクラブを脱会した He「*defected from* [*quit*] the club.

だっかい² 奪回 ——奪回する regain ⓑ, win* back /ペナントを奪回する *win* the pennant *back*

たっかん 達観 その若者はすでに人生を達観しているようだ The young man seems to *know the truth of* life already.

だっかん 奪還 ——奪還する recapture ⓑ, regain ⓑ

だっきゃく 脱却 ——脱却する escape ⓐ, free *oneself* from ...; （危機・困難から）emerge from ... /彼らはいまだに古い因習から脱却できずにいる They still can't *escape* [*free themselves*] *from* established convention.

たっきゅう 卓球 table tennis ⓤ, 《口語的》ping-pong ⓤ /卓球をする play「*table tennis* [*ping-pong*]
∥卓球台 a (ping-pong) table

だっきゅう 脱臼 〖医学〗dislocation ⓤⓒ
◆肩を脱きゅうした I *got* my shoulder *dislocated*.

タック （ひだ）tuck ⓒ, knife pleat ⓒ
◆ツータックのズボン *double-pleated* pants

ダッグアウト 〖野球〗dugout ⓒ

ダックスフント 〖動物〗dachshund ⓒ

タックル 〖スポーツ〗tackle ⓒ ——タックルする tackle ⓐ他 /彼はその選手に後ろからタックルした He *tackled* the player from behind.

だっこ 抱っこ 赤ん坊をだっこする hold [（→抱き上げる）lift] *a baby in one's arms* / もう疲れた。だっこして I'm so tired. *Carry me (in your arms).*

だっこく 脱穀 threshing ⓤ ——脱穀する thresh ⓐ他 /∥脱穀機 a threshing machine

だつごく 脱獄 prison break ⓒ, jailbreak ⓒ ——脱獄する break* (out of) prison, escape from prison /犯人は昨夜脱獄した The criminal *escaped from prison* last night.
∥脱獄囚 an escaped convict [prisoner]

だつサラ 脱サラ 彼は脱サラして（→会社勤めをやめて）農業を始めた He *quit white-collar work* and became a farmer.

だっしふんにゅう 脱脂粉乳 (powdered) skim milk ⓤ

だっしめん 脱脂綿 (absorbent) cotton ⓤ, 《英》cotton wool ⓤ

たっしゃ 達者 ❶【上手】——達者な good // 彼は英語が達者だ He *is good at* English. / （→流暢(りゅうちょう)に話す）He *speaks* English *fluently*. / 彼女は本当に口が達者だ She is really *a good*「《軽蔑的》*glib*]*talker*.
❷【丈夫】足が達者な（→健脚だ）be *a strong walker* / 祖母は達者にしています My grandmother is "*in good health* [*going strong, hale and hearty*]. / さようなら，お達者で（→体に気をつけて）Farewell. *Please take good care of yourself.*

ダッシュ ❶【記号】（（一）の記号）dash ⓒ; （（'）の記号）prime ⓒ（❖Á は [éi práim]と読む）➪ 巻末付録 （句読法）
❷【突進】——ダッシュする dash ⓐ, make* a dash

だっしゅ 奪取 ——奪取する seize ⓑ, take* ⓑ /彼はついにタイトル奪取に成功した Finally he succeeded in *taking* the title.

だっしゅう 脱臭 ——脱臭する deodorize ⓑ
∥脱臭剤 (a) deodorizer

だっしゅつ 脱出 escape ⓒ ——脱出する escape ⓐ他, get* away /国外脱出を企てる try to *escape* overseas / 彼は燃えている家から脱出した He *escaped* [*got away*] *from* the burning house.

ダッシュボード dashboard ⓒ

だっしょく 脱色 decolorization ⓤ ——脱色する decolorize ⓑ; （髪などを）bleach ⓐ他 /髪を脱色して茶色にする make *one's* hair brown *by bleaching*
∥脱色剤 bleach

たつじん 達人 expert ⓒ, adept ⓒ; （大家）master ⓒ /剣道の達人 *an expert of* kendo

だっすい 脱水 ——脱水する （回転式脱水機で）spin(-dry) ⓑ /衣類を脱水する *spin* clothes
∥脱水機（回転式の）a spin-dryer / 脱水症状 dehydration

たっする 達する
❶【ある場所に】reach ⓑ, get* to ...
➪ とうたつ

能力［我慢］の限界に達する *reach the limits of one's* abilities [patience]

登山隊は昼前に頂上に達した The climbing party *reached* [*got to*] the top before noon.

問題について我々は合意に達した We *reached* a consensus on the issue.

彼女のピアニストとしてのテクニックは今や完成の域に達している Her technique as a pianist *has reached* perfection.

◆私たちは長い協議の末結論に達した We *came to* a conclusion after a long discussion.

❷【ある数量に】reach ⓑ; （金額などが）amount to ... ➪ およぶ

その都市の人口は100万人に達した The popula-

tion of the city *has reached* a million.
募金額は200万円に達した The sum of the collection *reached* [*amounted to*] two million yen.
◆就学年齢に達する *arrive at* school age / 今年の輸入目標値に達する *meet* this year's import target / きょうは気温が35度に達した The temperature *hit* 35℃ today. / 雪の深さは2メートルに達した The snow *rose to* the level of two meters. / 負債は数十億ドルに達する The debts *run into* billions of dollars.
❸【目的などを】achieve [他]; (実現する) realize [他] ⇒たっせい
僕たちはついに目的を達した We finally *achieved* our purpose.

だっする 脱する escape [自] [他], get* out of ... ∥苦境を脱する *get out of* trouble / 医者は患者が危険な状態を脱したと言った The doctor said that the patient *had escaped from* the crisis.

たつせ 立つ瀬 それでは私の立つ瀬がありません (→私に面目を失わせる) That *makes* me *lose face*.

たっせい 達成 accomplishment [U]; (努力の末の) achievement [U], 《公式的》attainment [U] ―達成する accomplish [他]; achieve [他], 《公式的》attain [他] ∥達成感 *a sense of achievement* / 世界記録を達成する *accomplish* [*achieve*] a world record; (→樹立する) *set* a world record / 私たちはついに当初の目標を達成した We finally *achieved* [*accomplished*] our original goal.

だつぜい 脱税 tax evasion [U] ―脱税する evade [dodge] taxes
∥脱税者 a tax evader [dodger]

だっせん 脱線 derailment [C] [U]; (話の) 《公式的》digression [U] ―脱線する be derailed, run* off the rails; (話が) get* off ..., wander off ..., digress [自] ∥列車が脱線した The train *ran off the rails*. / いつの間にか話が脱線してしまった I *got off the subject* [*digressed*] without realizing.

だっそう 脱走 escape [C] ―脱走する escape [自], run* away, 《公式的》flee* [自]; (任務地などから) desert [自] ∥彼は刑務所から脱走して近くの森へ逃げ込んだ He *escaped* [*ran away, fled*] *from* the prison into some nearby woods.
∥脱走者 an escapee, a fugitive / 脱走兵 a deserter

たった
❶【わずか】only
私はたった103円しか持っていなかった I had *only* 103 yen.
彼はたった一度のチャンスをものにした He took advantage of his (*one and*) *only* chance.
彼はたったの一撃でその男を気絶させた He knocked the man unconscious with *only* one blow.
◆彼女はたったひとりでそこへ行った She went there *all by herself* [*all alone*]. / 彼女はたった500円でこのTシャツを買った She paid *no more than* 500 yen for this T-shirt.
❷【ちょうど】just
たった今, 宿題を終えたところです I (have) *just* finished my homework. / I finished my homework *just now*. (❖just now は現在完了の文には用いない)

だったい 脱退 (身を引くこと) withdrawal [U] [C]; (組織からの) 《公式的》secession [C] [U] ―脱退する withdraw* [自]; 《公式的》secede [自]; (クラブなどを) leave* [他] [自] ∥そのギタリストはバンドから脱退するだろうといううわさだ The rumor says that the guitar player is going to *leave* [*quit*] his band.

タッチ touch [C] ―タッチする touch [他] ∥タッチの硬いピアノ a piano with *a* stiff *touch* / 彼は粗いタッチで絵を描いた He drew a picture with *a* rough *touch*. / モニター画面上のこのボタンにタッチしてごらん *Touch* this button on the monitor. / (鬼ごっこで) 鬼は雅人にタッチした "It" *touched* [(→つかまえた) *caught*] Masato.
◆タッチアップする *tag up* (❖×touch up とはいわない) / 石井は二塁でタッチアウトになった Ishii *was tagged out* at the second base. (❖×be touched out とはいわない) / タッチの差で電車に乗り遅れた I missed the train *by a hair*. / 彼女はその件にはいっさいタッチしていなかった She *had nothing to do with* the matter.
∥タッチダウン〔アメリカンフットボール・ラグビー〕a touchdown / タッチパネル a touch panel / タッチライン〔ラグビーなど〕a touchline

たって その会議は首相のたっての希望で沖縄で開催されることになった The meeting was to be held in Okinawa *at the earnest request* of the Prime Minister.

-たって たとえ両親が反対したって, 僕は決意を変えないだろう I won't change my mind, *even if* my parents are against it. / どんなことが起こったってあきらめないぞ *Whatever happens* [*may happen*], I won't give up. / 彼を説得しようとしたってむだだよ It's useless *to* try to persuade him. / どんな犠牲を払ったってそれをするつもりだ I'll do it *at any price*. / あしたは早起きしなくたってかまわないよ You *don't have to* get up early tomorrow. ⇒-ても

だって (なぜなら) because; (しかし) but
謝る必要はないよ. だって君は何も悪いことはしてないんだから You don't have to apologize, *because* you did nothing wrong.
◆彼女がかわいそうだ, だってみんなして彼女を責めてばかりいるんだから I feel sorry for her *since* everybody keeps blaming her.
[会]「電話しなさいって言ったでしょ」「だって時間がなかったんだもん」"I told you to call me." "*But* I didn't have time."
[会]「なぜ笑ってるの」「だってセーターを裏返しに着ているんだもの」"Why are you laughing?" "*Because* you're wearing your sweater inside out."

-だって
❶【…でさえ】even; (…もまた) too, also

子供だってそのくらいできるぞ *Even* a little child can do that.
僕にだって言いたいことはあるんだ I want to say something, *too*.
◆速読はだれにだってできます Rapid reading is possible for *everyone*. / ごめん．それ以外の仕事なら何だってやるから Sorry. I'll do *anything* but that job. / 彼は子供たちが読みたいという本は何だって買ってやった He bought his children *whatever* books they wanted to read.

❷「私，そんなこと言ってないわ」「私だって」"I didn't say such a thing." "*Neither* did I."

❷【…(だ)そうだ】I *hear** (that) …, They *say** (that) …
最近引っ越したんだってね I *hear* you moved recently.
彼女，今入院してるんだって *They say that* [*It is said that*] she's now in the hospital.

❸【その他】
成績が何だっていうんだ *To hell with* grades! / (→気にしないぞ) I *don't care about* grades!
そんなことはどうだっていい That's *not the point*.
私が遅れたのがどうだっていうの *What does it matter that* I'm late?
あれが音楽だって？あんなものは雑音だ *Do you call* that music? That's noise!

❷「私，結婚するの」「何だって」"I'm getting married." "*You what?*"

だっと 脱兎 脱兎のごとく逃げる run away like *a scared hare*

たづな 手綱 rein ⓒ《しばしば複数形～s》‖馬の手綱をしめる tighten *the reins* on a horse / 彼はゆっくり手綱を引いた He pulled gently *on the reins*.
慣用表現 連中は部活動の間怠けてばかりだ．先生はもっと手綱をしめたほうがいい They are always lazy in the club activities. The teacher should *tighten the reins on them*.

たつのおとしご 竜の落とし子 sea horse ⓒ

タッパーウェア《商標名》Tupperware ⓤ

だっぴ 脱皮 脱皮する cast* ⓐ, shed* ⓐ ‖蛇は毎年脱皮する Snakes *shed* [*cast off*] their skins every year. / そんな古い考え方からは脱皮しなければならない We should *shed* such an old-fashioned way of thinking.

たっぴつ 達筆 彼は達筆だ He *writes in* [*with*] *a good hand*.

タップダンス tap-dancing ⓤ, tap dance ⓒ

たっぷり ユーモアたっぷりの話 a story *full of* humor / サラダはまだたっぷりあります There is still *plenty of* salad. / まだ買い物を楽しむ時間はたっぷりある We still have *enough* time to enjoy shopping. / たっぷり2時間かかります It takes me 「*two full* [*a good* two] hours to finish my homework. / 彼は浴槽にお湯をたっぷりと(→縁まで)はった He filled the bathtub with hot water *to the brim*. / 彼はたっぷり夕食をとった He had a *big* supper.

ダッフルコート duffel [duffle] coat ⓒ

だつぼう 脱帽 (号令で)脱帽 *Hats off!* / 彼の努力には脱帽するよ I *take*「*my hat off* [*off my hat*] to his efforts.

たつまき 竜巻 whirlwind ⓒ, tornado ⓒ (複～s, ~es); (海上の) waterspout ⓒ

だつもう 脱毛 loss of hair; (除毛) depilation ⓤ ──脱毛する depilate ⓐ ‖脱毛剤 (a) depilatory ‖脱毛症[医学] alopecia

だつらく 脱落 (落伍(ごう)) dropout ⓒ; (ページなどの) omission ⓤⓒ ──脱落する drop out; be omitted, be left off [out], be missing ‖彼女はついに先頭集団から脱落した At last she *dropped out of* the leading group. / その辞書には脱落があった There were *missing* pages in the dictionary.
‖脱落者 a dropout

だつりょくかん 脱力感 (消耗感) feeling of exhaustion; (虚脱感) feeling of emptiness

だつりん 脱輪 着陸時に飛行機の車輪の1つが脱輪した(→はずれた) One of the wheels *came off* as the plane landed. / 彼の車は脱輪して(→路肩を踏みはずして)5メートルほど下の畑に落ちた His car *ran off the shoulder* and fell about five meters down to a field.

たて¹ 縦

──縦の (垂直の) vertical ──縦に vertically; (長い辺の方向に) lengthwise ➾ よこ
縦線 *a vertical line* / 毛布を縦にたたむ fold a blanket *lengthwise*
彼は小さいころ縦縞(じま)のユニホームにあこがれていた He dreamed of wearing a uniform with *vertical stripes* when he was a child.
◆縦に1列に並ぶ line up *one behind another* / この板は縦が10センチ，横が5センチある This board is ten centimeters *long* and five (centimeters) wide. / This board is ten centimeters by five.
‖縦社会 a vertical society
慣用表現 彼はなかなか首を縦には振らなかった(→承知しなかった) He *wouldn't say yes*. / 父は縦の物を横にすることさえしない(→非常に怠惰で指一本動かさない) My father *is too lazy to lift a finger*.

たて² 盾 shield ⓒ (❖「優勝盾」の意味にもなる); (小型の丸い盾) buckler ⓒ
慣用表現 彼は法律を盾に(とって)彼らの要求を退けた *Using* the law *as a shield*, he rejected their request.

-たて -立て 入れたてのコーヒー *fresh* coffee / 焼きたてのクッキーを召し上がれ Have some cookies *hot from the oven*. / その青年は大学を出たてだ The young man is *fresh from* [*out of*] *college*. / 塗りたてのペンキにさわるな Don't touch the *wet paint*. / トウモロコシはとれたてがいちばんおいしい Corn is best when eaten *right after* picking.

たで 蓼[植物] smartweed ⓒ, knotweed ⓒ
ことわざ たで食う虫も好き好き There is no accounting for tastes. (→人の好みは説明できない)

だて 伊達 だて眼鏡をかける put on (a pair of) *glasses for show* / 彼女はだてに(→むだに)年をとっていない She didn't grow old *in vain.*
‖だて男 a fop, 《古風》a dandy

-だて¹ -立て 2本立て映画 a *double* feature / 2［4］頭立て馬車 a carriage and *pair* [*four*]

-だて² -建て 一戸建ての家 a *house*;《主に英》a *detached* house / 5階建てのアパート a five-*story* apartment house / 2階建てバス a *double-decker* (*bus*) / ドル建てのトラベラーズチェック traveler's checks in *dollars* / このビルは10階建てだ This building is ten *stories* high.

たてあな 縦穴・竪穴 ‖竪穴式住居 a pit dwelling

たていた 立て板 [慣用表現]立て板に水を流すように話す talk *very fluently*

たていと 縦糸 《集合的》the warp

たてうり 建て売り ‖建て売り住宅 a ready-built house;《分譲住宅》a tract house

たてかえる¹ 立て替える 悪いけど, タクシー代立て替えておいてくれる? Sorry, but will you *pay* the taxi fare *for me*? I'll pay you *back later*. (✿後半の文がないと「後で返す」という意味がなくなる)

たてかえる² 建て替える rebuild* ⓗ, reconstruct ⓗ ‖うちは去年家を建て替えた We had our house *rebuilt* last year.

たてがき 縦書き vertical writing Ⓤ ◆…を縦書きにする *write … vertically*

たてかける 立て掛ける lean* ⓗ ‖はしごは壁に立てかけてあった The ladder *was leaning against* the wall. / 私は傘を壁に立てかけた I *leaned* [*stood, put*] my umbrella *against* the wall.

たてがみ mane Ⓒ

たてかんばん 立て看板 standing signboard Ⓒ

たてぐ 建具 (移動可能な) fittings; (作りつけの) fixtures ‖建具屋 a joiner

たてごと 竪琴 harp Ⓒ

たてこむ 立て込む 仕事が立て込む be busy with *one's* work / 今立て込んでますのでまたにしてください I'm *busy* now. So please come again later. / 店内は客で非常に立て込んでいた The store was *very crowded* with customers. / このあたりは家が立て込んでいる This is a *built-up* area around here.

たてこもる 立て籠もる shut* oneself in … ‖テロリストたちは大使館に立てこもっている Terrorists *are shutting themselves in* the embassy.

たてじく 縦軸 vertical axis Ⓒ

たてつく 盾突く (公然と反抗する) defy ⓗ; (従わない) disobey ⓗⓘ ➡はんこう(反抗) ‖おれに盾突く気か Are you *disobeying* me?

たてつけ 立て付け このふすまは立てつけが悪い(→なめらかに開閉しない) This *fusuma* doesn't *open and close smoothly*.

たてつづけ 立て続け 立て続けにゴールを決める make goals *in quick succession* / おじは立て続けに大ジョッキ3杯のビールを飲み干した My uncle drank three big jugs of beer *in a row* [*on end*].

たてつぼ 建坪 ground area Ⓒ

たてなおす¹ 立て直す rebuild* ⓗ, reconstruct ⓗ ‖その党は国の経済を立て直すことを公約に掲げた The party made a public promise to *rebuild* [*reconstruct*] the country's economy. / 計画を立て直す(→もう一度最初から) go back to the drawing board; (→改める) *revise* the plan

たてなおす² 建て直す rebuild* ⓗ, reconstruct ⓗ

たてなが 縦長 ──縦長の(長方形の) oblong ⇨たて(縦)

たてひざ 立て膝 立てひざで座る sit *with one knee up*

たてふだ 立て札 signpost Ⓒ; (標識・掲示) sign Ⓒ ‖立て札を立てる put up *a signpost*

たてまえ 建て前 (原則) principle Ⓒ; (理屈) theory Ⓤ; (公的な立場) official stance Ⓒ《通例単数形》; (方針) (official) policy Ⓒ Ⓤ ◆「表向きの方針・原則」をぴったり表す英語はない) ‖遅刻は認めないというのが建て前だが, 実際には黙認されている *In theory* being late isn't allowed, but actually it's overlooked. / うちの店では値引きしないのを建て前としている It's our *official policy* not to reduce the price.
◆建て前と本音 *words and actual intention*

だてまき 伊達巻 <画> a *datemaki*, a rolled omelet mixed with fish paste

たてまし 建て増し extension Ⓒ《◆ただし具体的な「建て増し部分」を表すときは Ⓒ》──建て増しする extend ⓗ ‖ホテルの新たな建て増し部分 *a new extension* to the hotel

たてむすび 縦結び granny knot

たてもの 建物 building Ⓒ; (建築物) structure Ⓒ

たてやくしゃ 立て役者 (芝居の) lead(ing) actor [actress] Ⓒ ◆優勝の立て役者(→優勝に大きく貢献した選手) *a player who made a great contribution* to the victory

たてゆれ 縦揺れ (船や飛行機の) pitch Ⓒ《通例単数形》; (地震の) vertical shaking Ⓤ ──縦揺れする pitch ⓗ, shake* vertically

たてる¹ 立てる

❶【物を】set* [put*] up, stand* ⓗ
アンテナをどこに立てようか Where should we *set* [*put*] *up* the antenna?
私たちはバースデーケーキにろうそくを立てた We *stood* candles on the top of the birthday cake.
◆シャツのえりを立てる *turn up one's* shirt collar / 犬はその物音を聞いて耳を立てた The dog *lifted* [*cocked, raised*] its ears when it heard the noise.

❷【予定などを】
仮説を立てる *form* a hypothesis
私たちは夏休みの計画を立てた We *made* plans for the summer vacation.
私は年間10万円貯金する目標を立てた I *set* the goal of saving 100,000 yen a year.

❸【生じさせる】
声を立てて笑う laugh out *loud* / もうもうとほこりを立てる *raise* a cloud of dust
音を立てないで Don't *make* noise!
おまえが妙なうわさを立てたんだろう You *started* a strange rumor, didn't you?
❹【その他】
使者を立てる *send* a messenger / 大統領選挙に候補者を立てる *put up* a candidate for president
つまらないことで腹を立てるな Don't *get angry* over trivial matters.
彼女は生計を立てるために仕事を見つけなければならなかった She had to find a job to *make* [*earn*] *a living*.
彼は歯医者として身を立てた He *established himself* as a dentist.
彼はいつでも先輩を立てている He always *gives the credit to* his seniors.
彼女の顔を立ててやりなよ *Save* her *face*.

たてる[2] 建てる build* [他], 《口語的》 put* [set*] up; (記念碑などを) 《公式的》 raise [他] // 記念碑を建てる *raise* [*put up, set up*] a memorial / おじは最近3階建ての家を建てた My uncle *built* a three-storied house recently. / この学校は100年以上も前に建てられた This school *was built* more than 100 years ago.

たてわり 縦割り 縦割り行政 *vertical* administration

だてん 打点 〘野球〙 run batted in [C] (《略語》 RBI) //彼はきのう3打点あげた He had three *RBIs* yesterday. / He *batted in* three *runs* yesterday.
‖勝利打点 a game-winning RBI

だとう[1] 打倒 ―打倒する overthrow* [他], bring* down; (打ち負かす) defeat [他] //現政権を打倒する *overthrow* the present government
◆打倒メッツ! *Down with* the Mets!

だとう[2] 妥当 ―妥当な (適切な) appropriate, proper, sound; (正当な) valid; (値段などがてごろな) reasonable //妥当な処置 *proper* measures / 妥当な主張 a *sound* argument / 妥当な値段 a *reasonable* price / 彼がその賞を受けるのは妥当だ It is *appropriate* that he (should) be awarded the prize.
◆彼女の主張は妥当性を欠いていた Her claim lacked *validity*. / この法則はすべてのケースに妥当するものではない This law is not *true* in all cases.
[会話]「杉田は今シーズンどれくらいホームランを打つんだろうね」「ううん, 20本くらいが妥当な線だろう」 "How many home runs do you think Sugita will hit in this season?" "Well, I'd put it *right* at 20 or so."

たどうし 他動詞 〘文法〙 transitive verb [C]

> (1)目的語をとる動詞をいう. 通例相手や対象がなければできない動作や状態を示す. 次の文型になる //《主語+動詞+目的語》 She *cleans* her room every Saturday. 彼女は毎週土曜日に自分の部屋の掃除をする / 《主語+動詞+間接目的語+直接目的語》 I *showed* him my album. 彼に私のアルバムを見せた / 《主語+動詞+目的語+補語》 Everyone *calls* me Ken. みんな僕のことをケンと呼ぶ
> (2)動詞には, 自動詞と他動詞の両方の働きをもつものが多い ⇨ じどうし

たとえ[1] (…だとしても) even if …; (…ではあるが) even though … ⇨ -ても, -でも
たとえ彼らが「ノー」と言っても私はあきらめない *Even if* they say "no," I'm not going to give up.
たとえどんなに成功の可能性が低くても我々はそれをやらなければならない *Even though* we might have little chance of success, we must do it. / *No matter how* [*However*] little the chance of success is, we must do it.
◆たとえ何が起ころうと私はあなたを信じています *Whatever* [*No matter what*] happens, I believe you. / たとえ試験に落ちても, 彼はもう一度挑戦するだろう *If* he fails the exam, he will try again. / たとえ冗談でもそんなことを言ってはいけない You must not say such things *even* 「as a joke [in jest].
[慣用表現] 君のためならたとえ火の中水の中, 何だってやれるさ I would *go through fire and water* just for you.

たとえ[2] 譬え (直喩(ちょくゆ)) simile [síməli] [C] [U]; (隠喩(いんゆ)) metaphor [C] [U]; (例) example [C]; (ことわざ) proverb [C], saying [C] //たとえを挙げて説明する take *an example* to explain / 「壁に耳あり」とたとえにもいうように, 軽はずみなことは言わないほうがいい As *the proverb* says, "The walls have ears," so you shouldn't speak carelessly.
‖たとえ話 an allegory

たとえば 例えば for example (❖e.g. (ラテン語 exempli gratia の頭文字) と略すことがあり, [íːdʒi]または [fərigzǽmpl]と読む); (具体的には) for instance; (言ってみれば) say, let's say (❖文中で間投詞的に用いる); such as …, like … (❖補足的に例を列挙するときに用いる)
多くの言語が1つの語族に分類される. 例えば英語, ドイツ語, フランス語, イタリア語はインド・ヨーロッパ語族である Many languages can be classified into one language family. *For example*, English, German, French and Italian are Indo-European languages.
ヨーロッパを旅行中たくさんの物を買った. 例えばローマではアンティークな家具を買った During the trip to Europe, I bought a lot of things. *For instance*, I bought a piece of antique furniture in Rome.
だれでもいいから1人の作家, 例えば村上春樹だったら村上春樹の本を10冊読んでレポートを書きなさい Pick any writer, *let's say* Murakami Haruki, to read 10 of his books, and write a paper on him.
例えば宝くじで1,000万円当たったとしたら何をしますか What would you do if you won, *say*, 10 million yen in a lottery?

例えばロンドンやパリといった大都市よりも自然の豊かな土地を旅行したい I want to visit places with natural beauty rather than big cities *like* [*such as*] London and Paris.

💬「この街にはコンピュータ会社がたくさんあるんだよ」「例えば？」"There are many computer companies in this city." "*Such as?*"

たとえる 例える compare [他], liken [他] ∥人生はよく航海にたとえられる Life *is* often *compared* [*likened*] *to* a voyage.

◆彼の厳格さは何にもたとえようがない *There is nothing comparable to* his rigidness. / His rigidness *is beyond comparison.* / この山はたとえようもないほどに美しい This mountain is beautiful *beyond description*.

たどく 多読 extensive reading [U] ━多読する read* many books; (広範に) read extensively [widely]

たどたどしい (話し方・動作がなめらかでない) faltering, halting; (よろよろした) tottering ━たどたどしく falteringly, haltingly; totteringly ∥彼はたどたどしい日本語で話したが，我々は理解できた He spoke in *faltering* [*halting*] Japanese, but we could understand him. / その赤ちゃんはたどたどしい足取りだが何とか歩ける The baby manages to walk with *tottering* steps.

たどりつく 辿り着く reach [他], get* to …; (何とかして) find* *one's* way ∥7時間後やっとのことで富士山頂にたどり着いた Seven hours later, we finally *reached* [*got to*] the top of Mt. Fuji.

たどる 辿る (川・道に沿っていく) follow [他]; (跡を) trace [他] ∥うわさの出所をたどる *trace* the source of a rumor; *trace* a rumor to its origin / この道をたどっていくと海に出ます *Follow* [*Go along*] this path, and you will come to the sea. / この物語はとても複雑なので，筋をたどるのが難しい This story is so complicated that it is difficult to *follow* the plot. / 我々は雪の上に残された足跡をたどっていった We *traced* the footprints left on the snow.

◆彼女は記憶をたどりながら子供のころの話をした *Searching her memory*, she talked about her childhood. / 経済は衰退の一途をたどった The economy *kept declining.* / 2国間の紛争は激化の一途をたどった(→さらに激しくなった) The dispute between the two countries 「*got more and more intense* [*continued to intensify, got worse*]. / 彼女は結局母親と同じ運命をたどった She *ended up facing the same fate* as her mother.

たな 棚 shelf [C] (複 shelves); (網棚・陳列棚) rack [C]; (壁に取りつけた棚) ledge [C] ∥棚の上に花びんを載せる put [place] a vase on *the shelf* / 壁に棚を取りつける attach *a shelf* to the wall / 網棚の上にかばんを載せる put a bag on *the rack* / その大きな本棚は棚が10段ある That big bookcase has 10 *shelves*.
‖食器棚 a cupboard [kʌ́bərd] / 本棚 a bookshelf, a bookcase

[慣用表現] 彼は自分の欠点を棚に上げて人のことばかりあげつらっている He *shuts his eyes to* his own shortcomings, and is quick to blame others.

[ことわざ] 棚からぼたもち an unexpected piece of good luck ➾ たなぼた

たなあげ 棚上げ (計画・法案などの) shelving [U] ━棚上げする (計画を先送りにする) shelve [他] ∥その法案は2年間棚上げされたままだ The bill *has been shelved* for two years.

たなおろし 棚卸し・店卸し 《主に米》 inventory [U], 《主に英》 stocktaking [U] ━棚卸しをする make* an inventory, take* stock ∥棚卸しのため，あすの午前中は休業します We'll be closed tomorrow morning for *inventory*.

たなこ 店子 tenant [C]

たなざらし 店晒し 店の奥にはたくさんの缶詰がたなざらしになっていた A lot of canned products *were left unsold* at the back of the store.

たなばた(まつり) 七夕(祭り)

五節句の一つである七夕は，もともと中国の牽牛(けんぎゅう)星と織女星を祭る年中行事に由来しています．この2つの星が年に1度，7月7日(旧暦では8月7日)に天の川をはさんで会うとされています．七夕には，願い事を書いた短冊やいろいろな飾りを笹(ささ)の葉にさげるのが一般的で，仙台の七夕祭りは特に有名です．

Tanabata, one of Japan's five traditional festivals, originated in a Chinese legend about two stars: the Cowherd Star and the Weaver Star who can meet each other across the Milky Way only once a year on July 7 (August 7 on the old calendar). The common style of *tanabata* is the display of bamboo branches decorated with many ornaments and strips of colored paper on which people write their wishes. The *tanabata* festival in Sendai is especially famous.

たなびく 棚引く trail [自]; (かかる) hang* [自] ∥煙突からの煙が青空にたなびいていた Smoke *was trailing* out from a chimney into the blue sky. / 白いかすみが遠くの山にたなびいているのが見えた I could see a white mist *hanging over* a mountain far away.

たなぼた 棚ぼた (思いがけない幸運) an unexpected piece of good luck, a godsend; (特に遺産など) (unexpected) windfall [C] ∥ほとんど会ったこともないおじの遺産が入るなんてまさに棚ぼただった It was such *an unexpected windfall* that I inherited a fortune from my uncle whom [who] I had scarcely ever met.

たなん 多難 多難な年 a *hard* year / 我々の前途は多難である Our future is *full of difficulties.*/ *Many problems lie ahead* in our future.

たに 谷 valley [C]; (深く切り立った峡谷) ra-

vine [rəvíːn] ○, gorge ○; (気圧の谷) trough [trɔ́ːf] ○ ∥小さな川が谷間を流れている A stream runs in the valley. / 気圧の谷が関東地方に接近している An atmospheric [A low-pressure] trough is approaching the Kanto area.
◆景気の谷 the bottom of business

だに tick ○, mite ○; (社会の害虫) vermin ∪ ∥家ダニ a rat mite

たにがわ 谷川 mountain stream ○

たにそこ 谷底 the bottom of a ravine [gorge]

たにま 谷間 valley ○ ∥ビルの谷間 a valley between tall buildings
◆胸の谷間(女性の乳房の間) cleavage

たにん 他人 others, other people; (血縁関係にない人) unrelated person ○; (見知らぬ人) stranger ○; (部外者) outsider ○
他人の仕事のあら探しをするのは簡単だ It is easy to find fault with other people's work.
他人は当てにはできない You cannot rely on others [other people].
彼女は何でも他人まかせにする She leaves everything up to others.
他人のことに口をはさむな Don't interfere in other people's affairs. / (→自分のやるべきことだけを気にしろ) Mind your own business.
彼らは他人どうしだ They are strangers to each other. / They don't know each other.
彼女は僕とは赤の他人です She is an utter [a complete, a perfect] stranger to me.
これは他人事ではない This is not other people's business [affair].
慣用表現 他人行儀はよしましょう Don't be formal. / 他人のそら似 (an) accidental [(a) coincidental, (a) chance] resemblance

たにんずう 多人数 a great many people, a large number of people

たぬき 狸 raccoon dog ○ (❖(米)では「アライグマ狩り用の犬」を意味することもある) ∥たぬきおやじ a foxy old man / たぬきそば soba in (a) soy-flavored broth with a topping of tempura crumbs
慣用表現 彼は自分に都合の悪いことがあるといつも狸寝入りを決め込む Whenever there is something inconvenient for him, he always 「pretends to be asleep [《口語的》plays possum].
ことわざ 捕らぬ狸の皮算用 Don't count your chickens before they are hatched. (→ひながかえる前にその数を数えるな)

たね 種
❶ 【植物の種子】 seed ○ (❖集合的に用いられるときは ∪); (リンゴ・ミカンなどの小さい種) pip ○; (桃・梅などの真ん中に1つある大きい種) (米) pit ○,《主に英》stone ○; (仁) kernel ○
このスイカは種ばかりだ This watermelon is full of seeds [seedy].
子供たちは庭にヒマワリの種をまいた The kids planted sunflower seeds in the garden. / The kids seeded sunflower in the garden.
◆種なしブドウ seedless grapes / 小さいころ母はスイカの種を取ってくれた When I was a child, my mother would kindly seed the watermelon for me.
❷ 【原因】 cause ○; (源) source ○; (心配の種) worry ○; (自慢の種) pride ∪
彼らにけんかの種は尽きない There's no end to the sources [causes] of their quarrels.
娘の将来のことがいつも私たちの心配の種だった Our daughter's future has always been a worry to us.
広いキャンパスがわが校の自慢の種だ The spacious campus is the pride of our school.
◆あいつはいつも災いの種だ He is always planting the seeds of trouble. / 子供のころ彼はいつも物笑いの種にされていた As a child, he was always 「the target of jokes [a laughing stock]. / 30を過ぎていまだに定職についていない息子が頭痛の種です My son who is past 30 and still doesn't have a regular job is a headache for me.
❸ 【話題・材料】 (話題) topic ○, subject ○; (題材) material ∪ ○; (料理の材料) ingredient ○
私たちは話の種が尽きた We ran out of topics of conversation.
おでんの種では何が好きですか What are your favorite oden ingredients?
その作家は自分の小説の種探しに忙しい The novelist is busy looking for material for his novel.
❹ 【秘密】 secret ○; (手品の仕掛け) trick ○, gimmick ○
手品の種を明かす reveal [give away] magic tricks
種も仕掛けもありません There is no 「secret trick to [gimmick behind] this.
∥種牛 a seed bull / 種馬 a stallion, a stud (horse) / 一粒種 (ひとりっ子) one's only child
ことわざ まかぬ種は生えぬ No pain, no gain. (→苦労がなければもうけもない); Nothing comes from nothing. (→無からは何も生じない)

たねあかし 種明かし ——明かしする reveal ⦿, give* away / 手品の種明かしをする reveal [give away] magic tricks
◆では種明かしをしましょう I'll show you how it works.

たねぎれ 種切れ 私たちは話題が種切れになった We ran out of topics of conversation.

たねび 種火 pilot burner [light] ○; (おき火) embers

たねぼん 種本 source book ○

たねまき 種蒔き sowing ∪, seeding ∪ ——種まきする plant (sow*] seeds, sow a field with seed ∥今が種まきに絶好の時期だ This season is the best for sowing [seeding].
∥種まき機 a sowing [seeding] machine, a sower, a seeder

たねん 多年 many years ∥彼は多年にわたっ

てボランティア活動に従事している He has been engaged in volunteer activity *for many years*.
‖多年生植物 a perennial plant, a perennial

-だの 兄は物理だの化学だのを大学で勉強している My brother studies physics *and* chemistry at the university. / ああだのこうだの文句を言うんじゃない Don't complain of *this and that*.

たのしい 楽しい

(人を楽しませる) enjoyable; (人を満足させる) delightful, pleasant; (幸福な) happy; (陽気な) cheerful, merry; (愉快な)《米口語的》fun ──楽しく delightfully, pleasantly; happily; cheerfully

楽しい時を過ごす spend a *delightful* [*pleasant*] time; have a *good* time
テニスはとても楽しいスポーツだ Tennis is a very *fun* sport.
ピアノを弾くのはとても楽しい Playing the piano is「very *enjoyable* [a lot of *fun*]. (❖この fun は名詞で「楽しみ」の意味)
島田先生は話をしていて楽しい Mr. Shimada is *pleasant* to talk with. / It is *pleasant* to talk with Mr. Shimada.
彼は子供のころのことを話しているとき楽しそうだった He *looked happy* when he was talking about his childhood.
僕は楽しく生きられたらそれでいい I just hope to live *happily*.
子供たちが遊園地で楽しそうに遊んでいた Children were playing *cheerfully* [*happily*] in the amusement park.
◆パーティーは楽しかった We *had a good time* at the party. / We *enjoyed* the party. / We *enjoyed ourselves* at the party. / 彼の若いころは楽しい思い出に満ちていた His youth was full of *sweet* memories. / そのミュージカルはとても楽しかった The musical was very *entertaining*.

たのしさ 楽しさ フライフィッシングの楽しさがやっと分かった I finally found *the joy* of fly-fishing.

たのしませる 楽しませる entertain [他]; (愉快にさせる) amuse [他]; (喜ばせる) delight [他], please [他] ‖おじはいつも冗談を言っては私たちを楽しませた My uncle always *amused* us「with jokes [by making jokes]. / 秋にはこの一帯の紅葉が観光客の目を楽しませる Colored leaves in this whole area *delight* [*please*] *the eyes* of sightseers in the fall.

たのしみ 楽しみ

❶【喜び・娯楽】(喜び) pleasure [U][C]; (大きな喜び) delight [U][C]; (満足感を伴う喜び) enjoyment [U][C]; (喜びを与えるもの) fun [U]; (娯楽) amusement [U][C]; (気晴らし) pastime [C]; (趣味) hobby [C]
私の唯一の楽しみは旅行だ My only *pleasure* [*amusement*] is traveling. / I find *pleasure* [*amusement*] only in traveling.
スポーツ観戦が父のいちばんの楽しみです My father's favorite *pastime* is watching sports.
老後は何か楽しみをもつべきだ You should have some *hobbies* in your old age.

❷【期待】hope [U][C], expectation [U][C]
親は子供の将来を楽しみにするものだ Parents would *put* [*set*] *their hopes on* their children's future.
楽しみにしていたのに, 遠足が雨で延期になった *Contrary to our expectations* [*hopes*], the excursion was postponed due to rain.
◆将来が楽しみなスポーツ選手 a *hopeful* [*promising*] athlete / 近いうちにお目にかかれるのを楽しみにしています I'*m looking forward to* seeing you soon. / 弟は年に1度のお祭りを何よりの楽しみにしている Nothing gives my brother more *pleasure* than the annual festival.

たのしむ 楽しむ enjoy [他], enjoy *oneself*, have* a good [great] time, 《口語的》have fun
私たちはパーティーを大いに楽しんだ We *had a* very *good time* at the party. / We *enjoyed* the party very much. / We *enjoyed ourselves* at the party very much.
毎年わが家では冬休みにスキーをして楽しみます Every year, my family *enjoys* skiing during the winter vacation.
◆父は自分が楽しむためにピアノを買った My father bought a piano *for his own amusement*. / ディズニーランドは子供も大人も楽しめる Disneyland *is enjoyable* for both kids and adults.
💬「夏休みはハワイに行くんだ」「いいなあ. 楽しんできてね」"I'm going to Hawaii during the summer vacation." "That's great! *Have a good time*."

たのみ 頼み

❶【依頼】request [C]
頼みを聞き入れる grant *a request* / 頼みに応じる comply with *a request* / 頼みを断る refuse [decline, turn down] *a request*
私は息子の頼みでパソコンを買った I bought a computer *at* my son's *request*.
💬「一つ頼みがあるんですが」「はい. 何ですか」"*Would you do me a favor?* / *Can I ask you a favor?*" "Yes. What is it?"

❷【当て・希望】(信頼) reliance [U]; (信用) trust [U]; (依存) dependence [U]; (希望) hope [U]
彼女には一人息子だけが頼みの綱だった (→最後の頼みだった) Her only son was *her last hope*.
◆その党は数を頼みにその法案を通過させようとした The party tried to pass the bill *by force of numbers*.

たのみこむ 頼み込む (熱心に頼む) ask earnestly; (懇願する) plead* [自] ‖母はおばに私の面倒を見てくれるように頼み込んだ My mother *pleaded with* my aunt to take care of me.

たのむ 頼む

❶【依頼する】ask [他]; (懇願する) beg [他], request [他]; (嘆願する) implore [他]

彼女は私に自分の秘密を友達にはどうか黙っていてほしいと頼んだ She *begged* me not *to* tell her secret to her friends.

私はアメリカで勉強させてほしいと両親に熱心に頼んだ I *implored* my parents *to* let me study in the United States.

【ask＋名(人)＋for 名】私は父に金銭の援助を頼んだ I *asked* my father *for* financial support.

【ask＋名(人)＋to *do*】僕は彼に折り返し電話をくれるように頼んだ I *asked* him *to* call me back. / まゆみは人に頼まれるといやとは言えない Mayumi can't say no when someone *asks* her *to* do some favor.

【ask＋that 節】彼女は入院中の友達に会わせてくれるように頼んだ She *asked that* she (《英》might) be allowed to meet her friend in the hospital.

【ask＋名＋of 名(人)】≒【ask＋名(人)＋名】ちょっと頼みたいことがあるんだけど Can I *ask* a favor *of* you?/ Can I *ask* you a favor?

◆母に頼まれてやってきました I have come here *at* my mother's *request*. / 頼む！あと１日だけ待ってくれ Give me just one more day. *Please*! / 頼むから出ていってくれ *Would you please* get out of here?/ *For heaven's sake*, get out of here.

❷【任せる】

この仕事は彼に頼もう I will *ask* him to do this job./ I will *leave* this job *to* him.

この問題は弁護士に頼んだほうがいい You should *see* an attorney about this matter.

留守の間，母のことを頼みます(→面倒を見てください) Please「*take care of* [*look after*] my mother while I'm away.

❸【注文する・雇う】(注文する) order [他]; (予約する) reserve [他], book [他]

君は何を頼んだの What did you *order*?

その本は在庫がなかったから頼んでおいたよ Since the book was out of stock, I *have reserved* it for you.

◆タクシーを頼んで(→呼んで)いただけますか Would you *call* me a taxi? / 英語の家庭教師を頼んで(→雇って)やろう I will *hire* [*employ*] an English tutor for you.

💬「疲れた．もう料理したくないな」「じゃ，ピザでも頼もうか」"I'm exhausted. I don't feel like cooking now." "Then, shall we *order* some pizza?"

たのもしい 頼もしい (信頼できる) reliable, dependable; (前途有望な) promising, hopeful ‖彼には頼もしい父がついている He has a *reliable* [*dependable*] father. / 彼女は将来が頼もしい劇作家だ She is a *promising* playwright. ◆頼もしい娘さんだこと What a *good* [*nice*] daughter!

たば 束 bundle [C]; (花など同種の物の小さな) bunch [C]; (穀物・書類の) sheaf [C] (複 sheaves) ‖手紙の束 *a bundle of* letters / バラの花束 *a bunch of* roses / 分厚いラブレターの束 *a* thick *sheaf* [*bundle*] *of* love letters / 1束200円のホウレンソウを2束買った I bought two *bunches* of spinach for 200 yen each. / 彼は彼女に花束を持っていった He took her *a bunch of flowers*.

◆僕らが束になってかかってもあのレスラーには勝てない We couldn't beat that wrestler *even if we put all of our strength together*.

だは 打破 ━打破する break* down ◆因習を打破する *break through* old customs; *break away from* old customs (❖後の表現は「(自分たちの習慣を)自ら打ち破ること」の意味)

たばこ 煙草 tobacco [U] (❖種類をいうときは[C]); (紙巻きたばこ) cigarette [C]; (葉巻) cigar [C]; (植物) tobacco plant [C]; (喫煙) smoking [U]

〘たばこが・は〙

ここでのおたばこはご遠慮ください Please refrain from *smoking* here.

たばこは体に悪い *Smoking* is「not good [bad] for your health.

寝たばこがゆうべの火事の原因だった *Smoking in bed* caused the fire last night.

💬「一服，どうですか」「たばこは吸わないんです」"Would you like a smoke?" "No, thanks. I *don't smoke*. [I'm *a non-smoker*.]"

〘たばこの〙

たばこの灰 *cigarette* ash(es) / たばこの吸いがら a *cigarette* butt [end] / たばこの火を消す extinguish [put out] *a cigarette*

〘たばこを〙

たばこをもみ消す stub out *a cigarette* / 立て続けにたばこを吸う chain-smoke *cigarettes* / たばこをやめる give up [quit, stop, refrain from] *smoking*

◆おじは1日にたばこを2箱吸う My uncle *smokes* two packs [《英》packets] of cigarettes a day. / 彼はたくさんたばこを吸う He *smokes* a lot./ He is *a* heavy *smoker*.

💬「たばこを吸ってもいいですか」「いいですよ」"Would you mind if I *smoke*?/ Would you mind me [my] *smoking*?" "No, not at all." (❖「できればご遠慮いただきたい」ならば，Would you not, please?などという)

〘その他〙

くわえたばこで歩く walk *with a cigarette in one's mouth*

父がたばこに火をつけた Father lit (up) *a cigarette*.

‖たばこ入れ(巻きたばこ用) a cigarette case; (刻みたばこ用) a tobacco pouch / たばこ屋(人) a tobacconist; (店) a tobacco shop

タバスコ 《商標名》Tabasco (sauce) [U]

たはた 田畑 the fields; (農場) farm [C]

たはつ 多発 そのトンネルでは交通事故が多発している This tunnel is a spot where traffic accidents *occur frequently*.

たばねる 束ねる bundle [他]; (縛って束にする) tie up ... in a bundle [sheaf], bind* up ... in a bundle [sheaf] ‖古新聞を束ねる *bundle up* old newspapers / 麦わらを束ねる *bind up* straw *into sheaves*

◆髪を後ろで束ねる *tie one's* hair back / リーダーは私たちのチームを上手に束ねていた Our

た

leader *got* our team *together* well.

たび¹ 旅 trip ◯; (長旅) journey ◯; (周遊・観光旅行) tour ◯; (小旅行) excursion ◯; (船旅) voyage [vɔ́iidʒ] ◯, cruise ◯; (旅をすること) travel ⇨ 場面・状況別会話 p.1686

パリ7日間の旅が抽選で当たった I won *a 7-day trip* to Paris in a lottery. / 彼は3年に及ぶ放浪の旅から帰ってきた He came back from *a 3-year wandering journey.* / 列車での長旅には飽き飽きした I was fed up with *a long journey* by train. / 姉はヨーロッパ周遊の旅に出た My sister went on *a tour* of Europe. / その船旅で私は将来の妻に出会った I met my future wife on the *cruise.* / 宇宙への旅は間もなく現実のものになるだろう *Space travel* is going to be realized soon. / 旅は知識を広めてくれる *Travel* broadens your knowledge. / 友達が旅先で不慮の事故にあった A friend of mine encountered an unexpected accident *during his trip.*

◆一人旅をする travel *alone [by oneself]* / 私たちはこの前の夏休みに山陰地方を旅してきた We *traveled* in the Sanin district (during the) last summer vacation. / 空の旅は楽しかったですか Did you enjoy *your flight?* / 父は旅慣れている Father *is used to traveling.*

🅔「あすフランスに発(た)ちます」「よい旅を」 "I leave for France tomorrow." "*Bon voyage!* / *Have a nice trip!*" (✧Bon voyage [bàn vwaiáːʒ] は「よい旅を」の意味のフランス語)

‖旅芸人 an itinerant entertainer / 旅路 the course of *one's* journey / 旅人 a traveler

ことわざ かわいい子には旅をさせよ ⇨ かわいい / 旅の恥はかき捨て There is no need to worry about manners while traveling. (→旅行中は礼儀作法を気にすることはない) / 旅は道連れ世は情け In traveling what is wanted is a companion; in life, compassion. (→旅には道連れが必要で, 人生では親切が必要である)

短歌 幾山河越えさり行かば寂しさの終(は)てなむ国ぞ今日も旅ゆく (若山牧水)
Mountains and rivers:
crossing one, then another,
from one lonely place
to endless lonely places.
Today I journey again.

たび² 足袋

足袋は着物を着るときに履く綿製の靴下です。先端が2つに分かれているのは, ぞうりやげたを楽に履くための工夫です。靴を兼ねたゴム底の地下足袋は建築現場や農家の人々などが使います。
Tabi are a kind of socks made of cotton to wear with kimono. The toe is split so that you can wear *zori* or *geta* without difficulty. *Jikatabi* with rubber soles are used outdoors by construction workers and farmers.

-たび -度 会うたびに彼女は美しくなっていく *Every time [Each time, Whenever]* I see her, she becomes more beautiful.

だび 茶毘 (火葬) cremation ◯ ◯ ◆彼はその地で茶毘に付された He *was cremated* there.

たびかさなる 度重なる (繰り返しの) repeated; (頻繁な) frequent ‖その家族は度重なる不幸に見舞われた The family encountered *repeated [a series of]* misfortunes.

たびだつ 旅立つ set* off [out]; (ある場所を離れる) leave* ◯ ◯ ‖彼はアメリカに向けて旅立った He *set out on a journey* to the United States. / He *left* for the United States.

たびたび 度々 (しばしば) often, frequently; (何度も) many times; (繰り返し) repeatedly; (何度も何度も) again and again, over and over again ‖その少年はたびたびこの店に姿を見せる The boy *often [frequently]* appears at this store. / そのようなことは今までにもたびたび起こっている That kind of thing has occurred *many times.* / その歌手は覚醒(かくせい)剤所持でたびたび逮捕された The singer was arrested for possession of drugs *again and again.*

ダビング dubbing ◯ ──ダビングする make* a copy, dub ◯ ‖そのCD, 気に入ったらダビングしてあげるよ If you like that CD, I'll *make a copy* for you.

タフ ──タフな tough, strong ‖あいつはタフなやつだ He's a *tough* guy.

タブー taboo ◯ ◯ ──タブーの taboo ‖性の話はここではタブーだ Talking about sex is *a taboo* here. / Sex is a *taboo* subject here.

だぶだぶ ──だぶだぶの (大きすぎる) too big, too large; (ゆるい) loose [lúːs]; (袋のようにふくれた) baggy ‖だぶだぶのセーター a *loose [baggy]* sweater / そのワンピースは私にはぴったりだったが, 妹にはだぶだぶだった That dress fit me just fine, but it was *too big* for my little sister.

◆水を飲みすぎて腹がだぶだぶだ I drank too much water, and it is *sloshing* around in my stomach. / 彼はカツにソースをだぶだぶとかけた He *drowned* the cutlet in sauce.

だぶつく このところ父はおなかの肉がだぶついてきたようだ These days my father looks *flabby* around his waist. / 新型のゲーム機が発売され, 市場には旧型の製品がだぶついている As the latest model of computer game hardware has been put on sale, the market *is glutted with* old models.

だふや だふ屋 《米》(ticket) scalper ◯, 《英》(ticket) tout ◯

たぶらかす (欺く) deceive ◯, cheat ◯

ダブリューティーオー WTO (✧*World Trade Organization*(世界貿易機関)の略語)

ダブリン Dublin(✧アイルランド共和国の首都)

ダブル double ‖ダブルの部屋 a *double* room / ダブルの背広 a *double-breasted* jacket / ダブルパンチを食らう suffer *a* [*double punch [one-two punch]*] / そのアイコンをダブルクリッ

クすれば添付ファイルを開ける You can open the attached file by *double-clicking* the icon. ◆ズボンのすそをダブルにする *cuff* a pair of trousers
‖ダブルスチール〖野球〗a double steal **/** ダブルフォールト〖テニス〗a double fault **/** ダブルプレー〖野球〗a double play **/** ダブルヘッダー〖野球〗a doubleheader **/** ダブルベッド a double bed **/** ダブルボギー〖ゴルフ〗a double bogey

ダブる　(部分的に重なる) overlap ⊕; (留年する) repeat ⊕ ‖この写真は2つの画像がダブっている Two images *overlap* in this photo. **/** 彼は高校の1年生をダブった He *repeated* his first year at the senior high school. ◆目が悪いのであの高いビルがダブって見える I have poor eyesight, and I see the tall building *double*. **/** 彼女に亡くなった母の面影がダブった She *brought back images* of my late mother.

ダブルス　(競技) doubles [dʌ́blz]《単数扱い》; (試合) doubles match ◻ ‖混合[ミックス]ダブルス a mixed *doubles*

タブロイド(ばん)　タブロイド(版) tabloid ◻ ‖タブロイド版の新聞 a *tabloid* (newspaper)

たぶん　多分

❶【おそらく】(十中八九) probably, likely; (もしかすると) perhaps, 《口語的》maybe; (ひょっとすると) possibly

[語法]

[「たぶん」の示す確率] probably (80-90%ぐらい) → likely (70%ぐらい) → perhaps, maybe (30-50%ぐらい) → possibly (20%ぐらい)

[文中での位置] probably は通例 be 動詞・助動詞の後、一般動詞の前に置かれ、時に文頭・文尾で用いられる. perhaps, maybe は通例文頭に置かれ、時に文中・文尾で用いられる. possibly は文頭・文中・文尾のいずれでも用いられる. likely は文頭・文中で用いられる.

たぶん彼はきょう学校に来るでしょう He will *probably* come to school today. **/** It is *probable* that he will come to school today.

たぶんあすは雪が降るでしょう It *is likely* ⌈to snow tomorrow [*that* it will snow tomorrow]. (❖この用法は形容詞)

彼が言ったことはたぶん間違っている *Perhaps* [*Maybe*] what he said is wrong.

たぶん彼女は英語が話せるでしょう She can *possibly* speak English.

彼はたぶん彼女と結婚しないだろう He ⌈will *probably* not [*probably* won't] marry her. (❖probably は文全体を修飾するので否定語の直後には置かない)

▶「彼はもうニューヨークに着いただろうか」「たぶんね」"Has he already arrived in New York?" "*I hope so*." (❖hope は希望する)

▶「あしたパーティーに来ますか」「たぶん行けないと思います」"Will you come to the party tomorrow?" "No, I *am afraid not*." (❖afraid は心配するの意)

❷【たくさん】
彼の成功は多分に献身的な奥さんのおかげだ His success is due ⌈*very much* [*in large part*] to his devoted wife. **/** He owes his success *very much* to his devoted wife.

そのバスが乗っ取られた可能性が多分にある There is a *high* [*strong*] probability that the bus has been hijacked.

ご多分にもれず彼の会社もリストラせざるを得なかった *Like many others*, his company could not help resorting to restructuring.

たべあるき　食べ歩き　私は福岡で食べ歩きをした I *made an eating tour* of Fukuoka.

たべかけ　食べ掛け　食べかけのクッキー a *half-eaten* cookie **/** ごはんを食べかけでどこに行くんですか Where are you going *in the middle of the meal*?

たべかた　食べ方　私はこの魚の食べ方(→料理方法)を知りません I don't know *how to cook* this fish.

たべごろ　食べ頃　このメロンはちょうど食べごろだ This melon *is just ready to eat*. **/** 今はミカンが食べごろ(→旬(しゅん))だ Mandarin oranges *are in season* now.

たべざかり　食べ盛り　食べ盛りの子供 *a growing child with a good appetite*

たべすぎ　食べ過ぎ　━━食べ過ぎる eat* too much, overeat* ⊜ ‖食べすぎで胸やけがする I have heartburn from *eating too much*.

たべずぎらい　食べず嫌い　私はずっと納豆を食べず嫌いしてきた(→食べてみることもせずに嫌ってきた) I've hated natto for a long time *without even trying it*. **/** 弟は食べず嫌いが多い My brother *doesn't like* many kinds of food even though he doesn't try them.

タペストリー　tapestry ◻ ◻

たべのこし　食べ残し　leftovers, the leavings, the remains of a meal; (残飯) table scraps ‖けさの朝食はゆうべの食べ残しだった Today's breakfast was *the leftovers* from yesterday's dinner.

たべほうだい　食べ放題　あのレストランはランチが1,000円で食べ放題だ That restaurant has an *all-you-can-eat* lunch special for 1,000 yen. **/** 今晩のパーティーは食べ放題です You *can eat as much as you like* at tonight's party.

たべもの　食べ物　food ◻ ◻ (❖食べ物一般を指すときは ◻, 種類を指すときは ◻); (規定食) diet ◻

お寿司(すし)は私の好きな食べ物の一つだ Sushi is one of my favorite *foods*.

冷蔵庫の中に食べ物はほとんどなかった There was scarcely any *food* in the fridge.

彼はきのう手術を受けたので、食べ物がおかゆだけに制限された He had an operation yesterday, and *his diet* has been restricted to rice porridge.

◆猿に食べ物を与えないでください Please do not *feed* the monkeys. **/** 夏は食べ物に気をつ

けなさい Take good care of *what you eat during summer.*

たべる 食べる

❶【食する】eat* 他自；（食事をとる）have* 他；（摂取する）take* 他；（動物がえさを食べる）feed* 他

きょうはまだお昼ごはんを食べていない I *haven't eaten [had]* lunch yet today.

私たちは夕食にステーキを食べた We *ate* steak for dinner.

きょうはふらふく食べた I *ate「a lot [heartily]* today./《米》I *stuffed myself* today.

魚を生で食べられますか Can you *eat* fish raw?

羊が野原で草を食べていた Sheep *were feeding on* grass in the field.

彼はあれだけの量を1時間で食べてしまった He *ate up* that much within an hour.

何か食べるものはありませんか Is there something to *eat?*

きのうはうちでごはんを食べたから，今晩は外で食べることにしないか Since we *ate in* yesterday, let's *eat out* tonight, shall we?

魚は食べ飽きた I *had enough of* fish.

ケーキをもうひと口だけ食べた I *took [had]* another *bite* of the cake.

◆この果物をちょっと食べてみませんか Why not *taste [try]* this fruit? / お寿司(し)をご自由にお食べください Please *help yourself to* sushi. / このキノコは食べられるのだろうか Is this mushroom *edible*? / この食堂の食事は食べられないこともない The dishes in this restaurant are just *eatable*. (❖*edible* は「食用の」, *eatable* は「食べようと思えば食べられる」の意味) / うちの犬にはドッグフードを食べさせている We *feed* our dog dog food.

❷【生活する】

彼らは月々の年金だけでは食べていけない They cannot *live* on their monthly pensions.

彼は孝行な息子たちに食べさせてもらっていた He *was supported* by his dutiful sons.

だべる 駄弁る chat 自, have* a chat ‖私は喫茶店で友達とだべっていた I *was chatting with* my friends in a coffee shop.

たべん 多弁 ──多弁な talkative ‖父は飲めば飲むほど多弁になった The more my father drank, the more *talkative* he became.

だほ 拿捕 capture Ⓤ, seizure ⓊⒸ ──拿捕する capture 他, seize 他 ‖たくさんの船が北方領土周辺でだ捕されている Many ships *are captured [seized]* around the Northern Territories.

たほう 他方 一方はその案に賛成しているが他方は反対している One side is for the plan, but *the other (side)* is against it. / 彼は厳格だが，他方情にもろいところもある He's very strict, but *on the other hand*, he's easily moved.

たぼう 多忙 ──多忙な (very) busy ‖多忙な生活を送る lead a *busy* life / 父はここのところ研究で多忙を極めている My father has been *very busy* with his research these days.

◆彼女は仕事で多忙のため息子の卒業式に出席できなかった She could not attend her son's graduation (ceremony) because of *the pressure* of business.

たほうめん 多方面 多方面にわたる 知識 *wide-ranging* knowledge / 多方面にわたる才能の持ち主 a *multifaceted [versatile]* character; a man *of many [various] talents* / その歌手は多方面で活躍している The singer is active *in various fields*.

だぼく 打撲 blow Ⓒ ‖彼は全身打撲で病院に運ばれた He received *blows* all over his body and was sent to a hospital.

‖打撲傷 a bruise

たま¹ 玉 ball Ⓒ；（ガラスの小さい玉）bead Ⓒ；（水滴）drop Ⓒ；（眼鏡のレンズ）lens Ⓒ, glass Ⓒ；（めんの玉）small pile Ⓒ

毛糸玉 *a ball of yarn [wool]* / パチンコ玉 *a pachinko ball*

母はうどんを3玉ゆでた My mother boiled *three small piles of udon*.

僕の眼鏡の玉に傷が入っている There's a scratch on *the lens* of my glasses.

◆500円玉 *a 500-yen coin*

慣用表現 彼は人のあら探しをするのが玉に傷(→唯一の欠点)だ His *only defect [flaw]* is criticizing others. / 彼は額に玉のような汗をかいていた *Beads [Drops]* of *sweat* stood on his forehead. / The sweat stood *in beads* on his forehead.

たま² 球 ball Ⓒ；（投球）pitch Ⓒ；（送球）throw Ⓒ；（電球）(light) bulb ‖内角低めの球 *a low inside pitch* / 球を投げる[受ける, 打つ, ける] throw [catch, hit, kick] *a ball* / 彼は球が速い He *throws a fast ball*. / 電気の球が切れた The *light bulb* burned out.

たま³ 弾 （ピストル・ライフルの弾）bullet Ⓒ；（散弾）shot Ⓒ；（大砲の弾）cannonball Ⓒ ‖流れ弾 *a stray bullet*

◆銃に弾をこめる *load* a gun / 弾を発射する *fire a gun* / その兵士は弾に当たって死んだ The soldier *was shot* dead. / *The bullet* killed the soldier.

たまいれ 玉入れ 🏳 *tamaire*, field day event, especially in elementary school, where two teams compete by throwing red or white balls into a basket hung high on a pole

たまげる マグワイアの特大ホームランにはたまげた I *was flabbergasted at* the big home run by McGwire.

たまご 卵・玉子

❶【動物の卵】（鳥類・は虫類・昆虫の卵）egg Ⓒ；（魚類・両生類の卵）《集合的》spawn Ⓤ；（魚の食用の卵）roe ⓊⒸ

生卵 *a raw egg* / いり[ゆで, 落とし]卵 *a scrambled [boiled, poached] egg* / 半熟[固ゆで]卵 *a soft-boiled [hard-boiled] egg* / 卵を抱く sit on *eggs* / 卵をかき混ぜる beat *eggs* ペンギンが卵を産んだ The penguin laid *eggs*. ダチョウの卵がかえった The ostrich's *egg* hatched.

この料理では卵の白身ではなく黄身を使います In

this dish you use the yolk of *an egg*, not the white.
◆卵の殻 *an eggshell* / この髪型は卵形の顔にいちばん似合う This hairstyle goes best with an *oval* face.
❷【一人前になっていない人】
医者の卵 a doctor *in the making* / 弁護士の卵(→駆けだしの弁護士) a *fledgling* lawyer / 役者の卵(→新進の役者) a *budding* actor; an actor *in embryo* / 作家の卵(→将来の作家) a *future* writer
‖卵酒 eggnog / 卵立て an eggcup / 卵焼き an omelet

たましい 魂 (霊魂) soul Ū C̄; (肉体に対する魂) spirit Ū C̄
この仏像には作った人の魂が宿っているかのようだ It seems that *the soul* of the person who made this Buddhist image dwells in it.
ハロウィーンには死者の魂が帰ってくるといわれている It is said that *the spirits* of the dead come back during Halloween.
画家は自分の作品に魂を打ち込んだ The painter put *his heart and soul* into his works.
彼女は息子を失って、まるで魂が抜けたようだった She lost her son, and looked as if she *had no spirit at all.*
◆我々は彼女の美しさに魂を奪われた(→魅了された) We *were charmed [fascinated]* by her beauty.
ことわざ 一寸の虫にも五分の魂 ⇒ いっすん / 三つ子の魂百まで ⇒ みつご

だましとる だまし取る 彼は彼女から金をだまし取った He *cheated [swindled]* her *out of* her money.

だます 騙す (不正に) cheat ⊕; (うそをついて) deceive ⊕, take* in; (巧みな計画で) trick ⊕
我々は彼のうそに簡単にだまされてしまった We *were* easily *deceived [taken in]* by his lie.
彼女は妹をだまして相続財産を横取りした She *cheated* her sister *out of* her inheritance.
私は人にだまされやすい I'm *easily cheated* by other people.
彼は私たちをだましてこわれた車を買わせた He *tricked* us *into* buying the broken car.
◆だまされやすい人 *a dupe*, 《口語的》*a sucker* / だまされたと思ってあの本を買ってごらん *Just take my word for it* and buy that book. (❖take a person's word for it は「人の言葉を信用する」の意味) / その古いコンピュータをだましだまし使ってきたがもう限界だ I *have used every trick that I know to coax* the old computer into working, but it has had it. (❖coax は「(機械などを)注意深く取り扱う」の意味)

たまたま (偶然に) by chance, by accident, accidentally; (思いがけず) unexpectedly / きのう古本屋でたまたまその辞書を見かけた I saw the dictionary *by chance* in a used bookstore yesterday. / そのデパートでたまたまバーゲンをやっていたのでつい服を買ってしまった There was a bargain sale at the department store *unexpectedly,* and I bought some clothes in spite of myself.
◆幸運なことに、彼がけがをしたときたまたま医者が居合わせていた Luckily, a doctor *happened to* be there when he got injured.

たまつき 玉突き billiards (単数扱い) /玉突きをする play *billiards* ◆10台の車の玉突き事故で道路が通行止めになった Due to *the* 10-car *pileup,* the road was closed.
‖玉突き台 a billiard table / 玉突き場 a billiard room

たまに (時々) occasionally, once in a while /彼とはたまに会います I see him *occasionally* [*once in a while*]. / たまにはまじめな本も読みなさい Read serious books *occasionally.* / 遊園地にはたまにしか行きません(→めったに行かない) I *rarely* [*seldom*] go to an amusement park. / たまには(→気分でも変えて)映画でも見に行こう Why not go to the movies *for a change?*

たまねぎ 玉葱 onion C̄ (❖料理の材料としては Ū)

たまの (時々の) occasional; (めったにない) rare ◆たまの休みなんだから朝寝坊させてほしい Since I *rarely* have a day off, let me sleep late in the morning.

たまのこし 玉の輿 彼女は玉の輿に乗りたい(→金持ちの男と結婚したい)と思っている She wants to *marry a rich man.*

たまひろい 球拾い 1年生のうちはずっと球拾いをしなければならなかった I had to *pick up balls* all the time when I was a freshman.

たまむしいろ 玉虫色 iridescent color Ū
◆首相の玉虫色の(→あいまいな)発言に国民は憤りを感じた The nation was enraged at the Prime Minister's *ambiguous* [*equivocal*] speech.

たまもの 賜物 (成果) fruit C̄; (結果) result C̄ /彼の成功は日ごろの努力の賜物だ His success is *the result* [*fruit*] of his everyday efforts.

だまらせる 黙らせる hush ⊕, shut* up, silence ⊕ /彼の雷がみんなを黙らせた His thundering *shut* everyone *up.*

たまらない 堪らない
❶【耐えられない】
暑くてたまらない This heat is *unbearable* [*intolerable*]. / I *can't stand* this heat.
私はおかしくてたまらず、吹き出してしまった I *couldn't help* bursting into laughter.
こんな古ぼけた本がそんなに高いんじゃたまらない(→理不尽だ) It's *unreasonable* that such an old book is so expensive.
子供を亡くしたその母親の心中を思うとたまらない(→とても悲しい)気持ちになった When I thought of the feelings of the mother who had lost her child, I felt *so sad.*
❷【とても】(非常に) very (much), 《口語的》badly, 《口語的》awfully, 《口語的》terribly; (耐えられないくらいに) intolerably, unbearably
あの本が欲しくてたまらない I want that book

badly [so bad].

お母さんは君のことが心配でたまらないんだよ Your mother is *very* worried about you.

◆その俳優はたまらなくいい声をしている That actor's voice has *irresistible* charm. / パンダのしぐさはたまらなく愛らしかった The panda's behavior was *irresistibly* pretty. / 私はひとり暮らしがしたくてたまらない I'm *anxious* to live by myself. / がけから下をのぞいたときには怖くてたまらなかった When I looked down from the cliff, I was scared *to death*. / 彼女に会いたくてたまらない I'm *dying* to see her.

たまりかねる 堪り兼ねる (我慢できない) lose* patience; (気持ちを抑えられない) be unable to restrain *oneself* 僕はたまりかねて彼女をどなってしまった I *lost patience in the end*, and shouted at her. / 彼女はたまりかねて泣きだした *Unable to restrain herself any longer*, she began to cry.

だまりこくる 黙りこくる 私が何を言っても彼は黙りこくっていた He *remained quiet* no matter what I said.

だまりこむ 黙り込む fall* silent, fall [lapse, sink*] into silence, 《口語的》clam up / その事実を知らされると, 彼は急に黙り込んだ When he heard the fact, he suddenly *fell silent*.

たまりば 溜り場 (人が好んで行く場所) haunt ◎; (不良の集まる場所)《口語的》hangout ◎
◆そのコンビニは学生たちのたまり場になっている The students *hang out* at that convenience store.

たまる¹ 溜まる
❶【集まる】collect ⦿; (徐々に増す) gather ⦿; (積もる) accumulate ⦿, be accumulated; (山積みになる) pile up, be piled up; (金が) be saved

ほこりがテレビの上にたまっていた Dust *collected* [*gathered, accumulated*] on the TV set.

机の上には書類がいつもたまっている Documents *are* always *accumulated* [*piled up*] on the desk.

牛乳びんに雨水がたまっている Rainwater *has accumulated* in the milk bottle.

◆1年で100万円たまった(→貯金した) I *saved* a million yen in a year. / 年をとるにつれて疲れがたまるようになった As we grow older, *the fatigue gets worse and worse*. / 都会での生活はストレスがたまる Living in a city is *stressful*. / 彼の目には涙がたまっていた His eyes *were full of* tears. / Tears *stood* in his eyes.

❷【滞る】(仕事をやり残す) have* ... left unfinished [undone]; (借金が) run* up

あしたから新学期だというのに, 宿題がたくさんたまっている Though the new term begins tomorrow, I *have a lot of assignments left unfinished* [*undone*].

その店にはつけがたまっている I *have run up bills* at that shop.

◆家賃が半年もたまっている I *am* half a year *behind* [*in arrears*] *with* my rent. / たまった仕事を終えるには時間がかかる It takes a lot to finish *the backlog* of my work.

たまる² 堪る 負けてたまるか *I'll be damned if* I lose. / そんなことがあってたまるか *I'll be damned if* it's true. / It's *definitely* [*absolutely*] *impossible*. / おれの気持ちがおまえなんかに分かってたまるか *How would you know how I feel?* ➡ たまらない

だまる 黙る
❶【しゃべらない】(静かになる) become* quiet [silent] [❖become の代わりに be, fall も可]; (黙っている) keep* silent [quiet]; (話すのをやめる) stop talking [speaking]; (口を慎む) hold* *one's* tongue

先生が教室に入ってくるとすぐに生徒たちは黙った As soon as their teacher entered the classroom, the pupils *became* [*fell*] *quiet*.

黙りなさい *Stop talking*. / *Silence*. /《口語的》*Shut up*.

◆彼は会議中黙って座っていた He sat *silently* [*in silence*] during the meeting. / 黙って(→何も言わずに)部屋を出て行くとは無礼だ It is rude to leave the room *without saying anything*.

❷【口外しない】(沈黙を守る) keep* [remain] silent, keep silence; (口を慎む) hold* *one's* tongue; (何も言わない) say* nothing, do not say [any word [anything]; (秘密にしておく) keep ... *a secret* [*to oneself*]

彼女はその事件について黙っていた She 「*kept silent* [*said nothing, held her tongue*] about the accident.

そのことは黙っておいてください Please *keep* it 「*a secret* [*to yourself*].

◆どうしてそんなだいじなことを私に黙っていたんですか Why *didn't* you *tell* me such an important thing?

❸【文句を言わない】(我慢する)《口語的》put* up with ..., endure ⦿; (無関心でいる) remain indifferent

彼の無礼さにはもう黙っていられない I just *can't put up with* his rudeness any more.

何千という人々が餓死しているというときに黙っているわけにはいかない We cannot *remain* [*act*] *indifferent* when thousands of people are starving to death.

◆事情を話すと兄は黙って(→文句を言わず)金を貸してくれた When I told him the circumstances, my brother lent me some money *without complaining*.

❹【無断・無届けで】
彼は黙って(→無届けで)学校を欠席した He was absent from school *without* (*previous*) *notice*.

彼女は黙って(→無断で)彼のコンピュータを使った She used his computer *without* (*his*) *permission*.

ダミー dummy ◎ /ダミー会社 a *dummy* company

だみごえ 濁声 harsh [hoarse, guttural]

voice ◆だみ声の政治家 a *harsh-voiced* politician

たみんぞくこっか 多民族国家 multiracial [multiethnic] country

ダム dam ◆多目的ダム *a multipurpose dam* / 貯水ダム *a* water-storage *dam* / ダムを作る build *a dam*

たむける 手向ける （供える）offer; （餞別（せんべつ）を送る）send* ◆友人の墓前に花をたむける *offer* flowers on *one's* friend's grave

たむし 田虫 【医学】ringworm

たむろする 屯する (たまり場にする)《口語的》hang* out [around] ◆高校生がゲームセンターにたむろしている High school students *are* 「*hanging out* [*loitering*] at the video arcade.

ため 為

❶【利益】for; (…の利益のために) for the benefit [sake, good] of ... 留学生のための日本語クラス a Japanese class *for* international students
彼は息子のために死にものぐるいで働いた He worked like mad *for* his son.
彼女はあなたのためを思えばこそ、そう言ったのよ She told you so *just for your own good.*
戦争中多くの人々が自国のために死んでいった In wartime, a lot of people gave their lives *for the sake of* their own country.
◆ためになる講義 a *useful* lecture / この本は子供のためになる This book is 「*instructive to* [*good for*] children. / その授業は彼にとって何のためにもならなかった That class did him *no good*. / 吉田教授のために送別会を開いた We held a farewell party *in honor of* Professor Yoshida. (◆*in honor of* ... は「…に敬意を表して」の意味)

❷【目的】for; (…するために) to *do*
父は健康のために毎朝ジョギングをしている My father jogs every morning *for* his health.
あすの試験のために一生懸命勉強した I studied very hard *for* tomorrow's examination.
彼は何のためにそんなことをしたんだ What did he do such a thing *for?* / *Why* did he do such a thing?
新車を買うためにはアルバイトをしなければならなかった I had to work part-time *to* buy a new car.
◆英語が話せるようになるためにアメリカに行った I went to the United States *so that* I could speak English. / 彼女は児童心理学を学ぶため(→目的で)カナダへ渡った She went to Canada *for the purpose of* studying child psychology. / 彼女はスチュワーデスになるために一生懸命勉強した She studied hard *with the intention of* becoming a flight attendant.

❸【原因・理由・結果】because (of ...), due to ..., since; (…の結果) as a result of ..., in consequence of ...
大雨のため電車が遅れた *Because of* [*Due to*] heavy rain, the trains were delayed.
彼女は一生懸命勉強したため試験に合格した She passed the examination *because* [*since*] she studied very hard.
彼は寝不足のため講義に集中することができなかった He could not concentrate on the lecture 「*as a result of* [*in consequence of*] sleeplessness.
◆けがのために死ぬ die *from* a wound / 癌(がん)のために死ぬ die *of* cancer / 恐ろしさのために震える tremble *with* fear / 彼は怠けているためにいつも失敗する He always fails *through* his laziness. / 彼は助けてくれたために物理が分かるようになった I came to understand physics *thanks to* his help.

ことわざ 情けは人のためならず ⇒なさけ

だめ 駄目

❶【役に立たないこと】no good ——だめな (役に立たない) useless; (悪い) bad; (無能な) incompetent, incapable
このコンピュータはもうだめだ This computer 「*is no good* any more [(→ついにこわれた) *has finally broken*].
彼の勉強方法ではだめだ (→適切ではない) His way of studying 「*is no good* [*won't do*].
牛乳は冷蔵庫に入れておかないとすぐにだめになって (→腐って) しまう Keep the milk in the refrigerator, or it'll soon *go bad.*
この学校にはだめな教師はひとりもいない There are no *incompetent* teachers in this school.
◆靴が(履き古されて)だめになった My shoes *are worn out.* / あんなだめな(→ろくでもない)やつとつきあってはいけない You shouldn't go around with such a *good-for-nothing* guy. / あのバンドの今夜の演奏はだめだ(→ひどい) That band's performance tonight *is terrible.* / 日本では家を買うには1,000万円ではだめだ(→十分ではない) Ten million yen *is not enough* to buy a house in Japan. / 働きすぎて彼は体をだめにした His hard work *ruined* [*spoiled*] his health. / 干ばつで作物がだめになった(→干ばつが作物をだめにした) The drought *ruined* the crop.

❷【むだ】no use, no good
泣いたってだめだ(→むだだ) It's *no use* crying.
◆今ごろになってあわててもだめ(→遅すぎる)だよ It's *too late* to hurry now. / 彼は午前中に仕事を終わらせようとしたがだめだった(→むだだった) He tried *in vain* to finish the job by the noon. / だめでもともとだ(→失うものは何もない) We have nothing to lose.

❸【できない】cannot *do*; (下手だ) be 「*not good* [*poor*] *at* ...; (不可能だ) be impossible
私はパソコンはぜんぜんだめだ(→使えない) I *can't use* a computer at all.
土曜日は先約があるのでだめです Since I have a previous engagement, I *can't manage* [*make it* on] Saturday.
父は英語がだめだ My father *is* 「*not good* [*poor*] *at* English.

ためいき

💬「その本, 大きな書店に行けば買えるよね」「だめだと思う. もう絶版なんだよ」"Do you think I can get that book in some big bookstore?" "I'm afraid *not*. It's out of print now."

❹【望みがないこと】no hope ──だめな hopeless;（間違った）wrong
その患者はもうだめだ The patient *is hopeless*. / There *is no hope* for the patient.
君の答えはだめだ Your answer *is wrong*. / You *are wrong*.
◆私はもうだめだ *It's all over* with me. / *I'm finished*. / だめだとは思うが, 一応キャンセル待ちリストに載せてもらった *I don't think I can be fitted in*, but I had my name put on the waiting list. / 試験はだめだった I *failed* (*in*) the examination.

❺【禁止】(…してはいけない) must not *do*;（…するべきではない）should not *do*;（…しなければならない）must [have* to] *do*
彼にそんなことを言ってはだめだ You *must* [*should*] *not* tell such a thing to him.
そんな簡単なことぐらいひとりでできなくてはだめだ You *must* [*should, have to*] do such an easy thing by yourself.
◆ひとりでそこへ行っちゃだめよ (→行くな) *Don't go there alone*. / この喫茶店ではたばこはだめだ (→許されていない) Smoking is 「*not permitted* [*prohibited*]」 in this coffee shop.

💬「お母さん, 1万円ちょうだい」「だめよ亮司. きのうあげたばかりじゃない」"Mom, just give me 10,000 yen." "*No way*, Ryoji. I gave you some money only yesterday."

〖慣用表現〗母は日が暮れる前に帰るように弟にだめを押した My mother *made* (*it*) *doubly sure* that my brother would be back home before sunset. ⇨ だめおし

ためいき 溜め息 sigh [sái]Ⓒ /安堵(あんど)のため息をつく give [heave] *a sigh* of relief; *sigh* with relief / 母は私の成績表を見て深いため息をついた When my mother saw my report card, she *gave a deep sigh*. / 彼らのすばらしい演技に場内からはため息がもれた A great *sigh* of admiration for their splendid performance rose from the whole hall.

ためいけ 溜め池（貯水池・用水池）reservoir [rézərvwàːr]Ⓒ;（人工池）pond Ⓒ;（灌漑(かんがい)用）irrigation pond Ⓒ

ダメージ damage Ⓤ /一連のスキャンダルはその放送局に大きなダメージを与えた A series of scandals did [caused] great *damage* to the broadcasting station.
◆私の髪はパーマやヘアダイで相当ダメージを受けている My hair *has been* really *damaged* by permanents and hair dye.

だめおし 駄目押し 9回表にだめ押しの2点が入った They added two *insurance* runs in the top of the ninth inning.

ためこむ 溜め込む（蓄える）store 働;（ひそかに貯蔵する）hoard 働;（貯金する）save 働 /リスは冬に備えて食糧をたっぷり地中にため込む Squirrels *store* (*up*) a lot of food under the ground for winter. / 彼は金をたんまりため込んでいるようだ He seems to *have saved* a lot of money.

ためし¹ 試し（試み）try Ⓒ;（試用）trial Ⓒ;（試験）test Ⓒ;（実地・実験）experiment Ⓒ / 試しにやってごらん Give it *a try*. / *Try* it.
◆試しに自動翻訳機を使ってみた I used the automatic translator *on a trial basis*. / I *tried* (*out*) *using* the automatic translator.（❋try *doing*は「試しに…してみる」で, 実際に何かをしてみることだが, try to *do*は「…しようとする」で, 実際にやるかどうかは分からない）/ 試しにこれを食べてみなさい *Have a taste of* this. / *Try* this. / そのセーターを試しに着てみた I *tried on* that sweater. / ものは試しだ (→やってみるまで分からない) *You'll never know until you try*.

ためし² 例 このへんでは雪が降ったためしがない It *has never* snowed around here. / 彼の予想は当たったためしがない There is no *precedent* for his guesses being right.

ためす 試す（試みる）try 働, have* a try;（試用する）try out;（試験する）test 働, put* ... to the test
ありとあらゆる方法を試してみたがどれもうまくかなかった I *tried* every method under the sun, but nothing worked.
その機械がうまく動くかどうか試してみた I *tested* the machine to check whether it might work well.
新型のビデオカメラを試してみた I *tried out* the brand-new video camera.

ためつすがめつ つぼをためつすがめつ眺める take a *good* look at the vase; scrutinize the vase *carefully*

だめもと だめもとでやってみれば? Give it a try. *You have nothing to lose*.

ためらい hesitation Ⓒ Ⓤ /そのときは彼女に話すことに何のためらいもなかった At that time, I had no *hesitation in* telling her.

ためらう hesitate 働, be hesitant;（迷う）waver 働 /彼は彼女に本当のことを言うのをまだためらっている He *is still hesitating about* telling the truth to her. / 私は彼の申し出を受けるべきかどうかためらっている I'*m wavering* between accepting and refusing his offer. / 彼は自分の本当の父に会うのをためらった He *hesitated* [*was hesitant*] to meet his true father.
◆彼女は少しもためらわずにその提案を拒否した *Without any hesitation*, she said no to that proposal. / 彼女はためらいがちに彼を見つめた She *hesitantly* looked at him.

ためる 貯める・溜める

❶【蓄える】（貯蔵する）store 働;（節約する）save 働;（蓄積する）accumulate;（積み上げる）heap 働, pile 働;（集める）collect 働, gather 働
彼はオーストラリア旅行のためにお金をためている He *is saving* money for a trip to Australia.

彼らは日照りに備えて雨水をためている They *are storing* (*up*) rainwater for a drought.

後の競争に備えて体力をためておくべきだ You should *save* (*up*) your stamina for your later races.

押し入れには古新聞がためてあった Old newspapers *were piled up* in the closet.

◆彼女は目に涙をためて抗議した She protested *with tears in her eyes*. / 兄はいつも洗濯物をためている My brother always *lets* the laundry *pile up*. / ストレスをためないようにしなさい You shouldn't *let* the stress *accumulate*.

❷【滞らせる】（借金をためる）run* up, accumulate ⓔ

彼は公共料金の支払いを3か月ためている He *has run up* utilities bills for three months. / His utilities bills *have piled up* for three months.

ためん 多面 ━━多面的な multifaceted, many-sided ◆物事は多面的にとらえるべきだ You should look at things *from various angles* [*perspectives*].

‖多面体 a polyhedron

たもうさく 多毛作 multiple cropping ⓤ

たもくてき 多目的 ━━多目的の multipurpose, all-purpose ‖多目的ホール a *multipurpose* hall

たもつ 保つ（状態を保持する）keep* ⓔ ⓘ;（場所・位置を保持する）hold* ⓔ;（維持する）maintain ⓔ;（保存する）preserve ⓔ

秩序を保つ *keep* [*preserve, maintain*] good order / 均衡を保つ *keep one's* balance / 若さを保つ *keep* [*stay*] young / 威厳を保つ *maintain one's* dignity

省エネのため夏の間は部屋の温度を摂氏28度に保っておいた To save energy, I *kept* the temperature of the room at 28 degrees Celsius during the summer.

そのゴルファーは3年間賞金女王の座を保った The golfer *held the title* of prize-money queen for three years.

高い演奏水準を保つのは難しい It is difficult to *maintain* a high standard of performance.

健康を保つのはそれほど大変なことではないと思うよ I don't think it is so hard to *maintain your health*.

◆面目を保つ *save* (*one's*) *face*

たもと 袂（衣服の）sleeve ⓒ ◆かつて橋のもとには船着き場があった Formerly there was a wharf *by* [*near*] *the bridge*.

慣用表現 彼らは自民党だたもとを分かって新党を結成した They *broke with* the Liberal Democratic Party and formed a new party.

たやす 絶やす その少女はいつも笑顔を絶やさなかった The girl was *never without a smile* on her face. / 仏壇には花を絶やさないようにしている I see to it that there are *always* flowers at the family altar.

たやすい（容易な）easy ━━たやすく easi-

ly, with ease ‖彼にとってこの難解な問題を解くのはたやすい It is *easy* for him to solve this difficult problem. / 父はたやすくプラモデルの飛行機を組み立てた My father *easily* assembled the model plane.

たゆまぬ たゆまぬ努力 steady [*strenuous, ceaseless*] effort(s)

たよう 多様 ━━多様な various, diverse ‖その国には多様な民族がいた There were *various* [*a variety of*] peoples in the country. / 我々のもとには多様な意見が寄せられた We received *diverse* opinions.

‖多様化 diversification / 多様性 variety, diversity

たより¹ 頼り 頼りになる先生 a *reliable* [*dependable, trustworthy*] teacher / 頼りがいのある友達 a friend *one can trust*

彼女はお金の面で親を頼りにしている She *is dependent on* her parents *for* money. / She financially *relies on* her parents.

友人を頼りに上京した I came to Tokyo, *counting on* a friend of mine.

彼はいざというときに頼りにならない He'll *be no help* if something goes wrong.

彼は足をけがしたので，松葉づえを頼りに歩かなければならなかった Since he got his leg injured, he had to walk *using crutches for support*.

辞書を頼りにドイツ人の友達からの手紙を読んだ *Consulting* [*Referring to*] *a dictionary*, I read a letter from my German friend.

彼は地図を頼りに見知らぬ土地を歩くのが好きだった He loved to walk around unknown places *with the help of a map*.

記憶を頼りにふるさとを歩いた I walked around my hometown *from memory*.

たより² 便り（手紙）letter ⓒ;（消息）news ⓤ, word ⓤ ‖きのう母から便りがあった I received *a letter* from my mother yesterday.

◆最近息子から便りがない I *have not heard from* my son lately. / 風の便りでは，太郎がアメリカの女性と結婚したそうだ People say [《口語的》*A little bird told me*] that Taro got married to an American woman.

慣用表現 便りのないのはよい便り *No news is good news*.

-だより -便り ニューヨーク便り *news* from New York / 花便り *news* about the blooming of cherry trees

たよりない 頼りない，（信頼できない）unreliable, undependable;（不明確な）indefinite, vague ‖あの先生は何となく頼りない The teacher is somewhat *unreliable* [*undependable*]. / 彼からは頼りない返事があるだけだった We could just have an *indefinite* [a *vague*] answer from him.

たよる 頼る（依存する）depend on [upon] …;（信頼する）rely on …, trust ⓔ;（当てにする）count on …;（すがる）fall* back on …

私には頼るべき友達がいない I have no friends to *depend* [*rely*] *on*.

私は親戚(しんせき)を頼って上京してきた I came to Tokyo from the country, *counting on* my relative here.
ひとり暮らしなので，インスタント食品に頼ることが多い Since I am living alone, I often *fall back on* instant food.
◆彼は晩年酒に頼ることが多かった He often *turned to drink* in his later years.

たら 鱈 cod [C], codfish [C]

-たら (もし…ならば) if; (…するとき) when; (…の場合) in case of ..., in case (that) ... ∥彼に会ったらよろしくお伝えください *If* you see him, please say hello to him. / 家に着いたら電話をくださいね *When* you come home, please call me. / 雨が降ったら遠足は中止です *In case of* rain [*In case* it rains], the excursion will be canceled.
◆母が帰ってきたらすぐに出かけよう Let's go out *as soon as* my mother comes home. / 結果をよく調べてみたら間違っていることが分かった We examined those results thoroughly, *and* we found that they were wrong. / 絵でも描いてみたらどうですか *Why don't you* draw a picture? / もっと流暢(りゅうちょう)に英語が話せたらなあ *I wish* I could speak English more fluently. / 浩子ったら，またあいさつしてないわ *That* Hiroko! She hasn't said hello again!

たらい 盥 (洗濯用) washtub [C], washing tub [C]; (おけ) tub [C]

たらいまわし たらい回し その患者は病院をたらい回しにされた The patient *was sent from one* hospital *to another*.

だらく 堕落 (政治的・道徳的) corruption [U] ━堕落する be corrupted ━堕落した corrupt ∥政治の堕落 political *corruption* / 彼は堕落した生活を送った He led a *corrupt* life. / 最近の警察は堕落しきっている The police *are* completely *corrupted* these days.
◆世の中は堕落した人間ばかりだ The world is full of *degenerates*.

-だらけ (…でいっぱいの) full of ...; (…で覆われた) covered with ...; (…で汚れた) smeared with ... ∥彼の言うことは間違いだらけだ What he says is *full of* mistakes. / その眼鏡は表面が傷だらけだった The surface of those glasses was *full of* scratches. / そのシャツは血だらけだった The shirt was *smeared with* blood.
◆泥だらけの靴 *muddy* shoes / しばらく猫と遊んでいたら服が毛だらけになってしまった I got the cat's hair *all over* my clothes after playing with it for a while.

だらける (だらっとする) be listless; (怠ける) be lazy, be sluggish ∥このごろの酷暑のせいでだらけてしまった The extreme heat these days made me *listless*.
◆先生がいないのでみんな気分がだらけている Because their teacher is away, everybody *has loosened up*.

たらこ 鱈子 cod roe [U]

だらしない (身なりなどが) sloppy, slovenly; (整頓(せいとん)されていない) untidy; (道徳的に) loose [lúːs], immoral; (怠惰な) lazy; (不注意な) careless; (厳しさに欠ける) lax ∥あいつは本当にだらしないやつだ He's a really *slovenly* guy. / 彼女はだらしない生活をしている She leads a *lazy* [*loose*] life. / 彼は時間に関してはだらしなかった He *was lax* about keeping time.
◆彼は服装がだらしない He is *sloppily* dressed. / もう疲れたの？ だらしないわね You're already tired? *How pathetic*! [*Shame on you*!](❖Shame on you!は「恥ずかしいと思いなさい」の意味)

たらす 垂らす ❶【液体をしたたらせる】drip [他]; (よだれを) 《米》drool [自], 《英》dribble [自] ∥青インクを白いドレスにたらしてしまった I *dripped* blue ink on my white dress. / 赤ちゃんがよだれをたらしている The baby *is drooling*.
◆パンケーキの上にシロップをたらしてください Please *put* the syrup on that pancake. / 彼は小さいころいつも鼻をたらしていた He always *had a runny nose* when he was small.
❷【物体をぶら下げる】hang* [他] ∥人を救助するため屋上からロープを垂らした We *hung* a rope (*down*) from the rooftop to save people.
◆その少女は長い黒髪を後ろに垂らしていた The girl *had* her long black hair *flowing down* her back.

-たらず -足らず (…以下) less than ... ∥父は1週間足らずで帰ってくるでしょう My father will come home in *less than* a week.

ダラス Dallas(❖米国の都市)

たらたら 犯人は腕から血をたらたら流していた The criminal *was dripping* [*trickling*] blood from his arm. / 彼女は義理の父の前で冷や汗たらたらだった She *was in a cold sweat* in front of her father-in-law. / 彼はいつも学校に対して不満たらたらだった He *was* always *full of complaints* about his school. / He *was* always *complaining* about his school.

だらだら だらだらした(→長くてゆるやかな)上り坂 a *long, gentle* ascent / きのうはとても暑かったのでみなだらだらと(→のろのろと)仕事をした Since it was very hot yesterday, everybody worked *sluggishly*. / 彼のだらだらした(→退屈な)講演の間ずっと寝ていた I was sleeping during his *tedious* lecture. / 夏休み中，テレビを見て1日をだらだらと過ごすことが多かった During the summer vacation, I often *idled away* a day by watching TV. / 彼のひざからは血がだらだらと流れていた Blood *was running down* his knee. / 補講は8時までだらだらと長引いた The extra class *dragged on* until eight.

タラップ ⚠(飛行機の) ramp [C]; (船の) gangplank [C], gangway ladder [C] (❖日本語はオランダ語の trap から) ∥タラップを降りる descend *a ramp*

たらばがに 鱈場蟹 king crab [C]

たらふく 北海道で新鮮なカニをたらふく食べた

❸【疑問·思案】I wonder
ハワイまで飛行機でどれくらい時間がかかるのだろうか How long does it take to Hawaii by air, *I wonder*?
彼に以前会ったことがあっただろうか *I wonder* whether I have seen him before.
❹【感嘆】what, how
私はなんてばかだったんだろう *What* a fool I have been!
あなたの作ったパイはなんておいしいんだろう *How* delicious your pie is!
❺【念押し】
君はこの仕事を失いたくないんだろう? You don't want to lose your job, *do you*?
試験に落ちたんじゃないだろうね You didn't fail the exam, *did you*?
冗談だろう? You *must* be kidding.

タワー tower [C] ∥東京タワー (*the*) Tokyo *Tower*

たわいない (ささいな) trivial, trifling; (ばかげた) silly, foolish; (簡単な) easy **—たわいなく** (簡単に) easily ∥その兄弟はいつもたわいないことでけんかしていた The brothers were always quarreling over *trivial* matters. / あいつを負かすなんてたわいもないことさ It's *very easy* to defeat him.

たわごと 戯言 (ばかげた言葉) nonsense [U]; (ばかげたおしゃべり) silly [foolish] talk [C] ∥たわごとを言うな Don't talk *nonsense*.

たわし 《米》scrub [《英》scrubbing] brush [C]

たわむ 撓む (位置が下がる) sag [自]; (重さで下がる) be weighed down; (しなる) bend* [自], be bent ∥木の枝が雪の重みでたわんだ The branches of the tree *sagged* [*were bent*] under the weight of snow.

たわむれ 戯れ (楽しみ) fun [U]; (遊び) play [U]; (冗談) joke [C], jest [C][U]; (男女の恋) flirtation [C]

たわむれる 戯れる (遊ぶ) play [自]; (冗談を言う) joke [自]; (男女が) flirt [自] ∥子猫が毛糸玉に戯れていた The kitten *was playing* with the ball of yarn.

たわら 俵 straw bag [sack] [C] ∥米俵 a straw rice bag

たわわ つるにブドウがたわわになっている The vines are *heavy* [*loaded down, laden*] *with* grapes.

タン ⚠tongue [tʌ́ŋ] [C][U] ∥タンシチュー *tongue* stew

たん[1] 痰 phlegm [flém] [U] ∥たんを吐く spit out *phlegm* / たんがからみます I'm getting *phlegm* in my throat.

たん[2] 端 [慣用表現] 太平洋戦争は真珠湾攻撃に端を発した The Pacific War *originated in* the attack on Pearl Harbor. / The attack on Pearl Harbor *triggered off* the Pacific War.

だん[1] 段
❶【階段の】step [C]; (はしごの) rung [C]
この石段は100段ある These stone stairs have 100 *steps*.
階段を2段ずつ上がった I went up the stairs, *two steps* at a time.
❷【重なりの】(棚) shelf [C] (複 shelves); (層) tier [C], layer [C]; (ロケットの) stage [C]
花びんを棚のいちばん下の[いちばん上の]段に載せる put a vase on the *bottom* [*top*] *shelf* / 3段のウエディングケーキ a *three-tier* wedding cake / 3段式ロケット a *three-stage* rocket
打ち上げ後すぐにロケットの1段目が切り離されることになっている *The first stage* of the rocket is supposed to be detached soon after it is launched.
◆2段ベッド *a bunk bed*
❸【段落】paragraph [C]; (縦の) column [C]
3段抜きの見出し a *three-column* headline
最後の段にはこの論文の要旨が書かれている The summary of this article is written in *the* final *paragraph*.
❹【等級】rank [C], grade [C], a *dan*
もっと上の段を目ざすべきだ You should aim at *a higher rank* [*grade, dan*].
彼は柔道4段だ He is a judoka of *the fourth dan*. / He holds *the fourth dan* [*grade, rank*] in judo.
❺【場合·局面】
いざプロポーズという段になると彼はおじけづいてしまう *When it comes to* proposing, he loses his nerve.
❻【程度】
彼は技術的に私より数段上である He is *a cut above* me in skill. / I *am no match for* him in skill.
◆5段変速自転車 a *five-speed* bicycle
❼【九九の】
弟は九九を4の段まで言える My brother can run through the multiplication tables to *the fours*.

だん[2] 談 talk [C], story [C], account [C] ∥経験談 *a story* of *one's* experience; *one's* personal experiences / 成功談 *a* success *story* / 冒険談 *an* adventure *story* / 目撃者の談によると according to *the account* of an eyewitness
◆その話には後日談があるんだ There's *a sequel* to the story.

だん[3] 壇 platform [C]; (指揮者·講演者の立つ) podium [C] (複 ~s, podia); (説教壇) pulpit [C] ∥講演者は壇の上に立って経験談を話し始めた The lecturer「stood on [took] *the platform* and began to talk about his personal experiences.

-だん -団 (一般的な集団) group [C]; (共通の目的をもつ人々の集団) band [C]; (仕事や競技の組) team [C]; (一味) gang [C]; (塊(かたまり)·組織) body [C]; (外交団など) corps [kɔ́ːr] [C] (複 ~ [kɔ́ːrz]); (代表団·使節団) delegation [C]; (旅の一行) party [C]; (一座) company [C] ∥旅行団 *a group* [*party*] of tourists / 殺人事件の弁護団 *a* defense *team* in a murder case / 外交団 *a* diplomatic *corps* / 寒気団 *a body* of cold air / 麻薬の密輸団 *a gang* of drug smugglers / 記者団 *a* press *corps* / バレエ団 *a* ballet *company* / 選手団 *a delegation* of athletes

高校生ならだれでもそんな問題くらい解けるだろう *Any* high school student should be able to answer that question.

だれでも科学者になれるとは限らない *Not everyone* can become a scientist.

◆だれでもいいからここに来て Someone come here! I *don't care who it is*.

だれ(に)も 誰(に)も

❶〖だれでも〗(みんな) everyone, everybody; (どんな人も) anybody, anyone

だれもが試験に合格した *Everybody* [*Everyone*] passed the examination.

こんな簡単な仕事はだれにもできる *Anybody* [*Anyone*] can do this easy job.

だれもがこの図書館の利用を許されているわけではない *Not everybody* [*everyone*] is allowed to use this library. (❖not everybody [everyone]で部分否定になる)

❷〖だれ(に)も…ない〗nobody, no one, none, not anybody [anyone]

そこにはだれもいなかった There was *not anyone* there. / There was *nobody* [*no one*] there.

きのうだれにも電話をかけなかった I called *nobody* yesterday. / I *didn't* call *anybody* yesterday.

この豪雨の中だれも外出したいとは思わない *Nobody* [*No one*] wants to go out in this heavy rain.

私たちはまだだれも準備ができていない *None* of us is [are] ready yet. (❖noneの後には通常 of+複数名詞が続き、単数または複数扱い)

だれひとり 誰一人 (だれも…ない) nobody // だれ一人として彼の言うことを理解できなかった *Nobody* [*No one, Not a single person*] could understand what he said.

◆だれ一人席を立とうとしなかった *Everybody* stayed in their seats.

たれまく 垂れ幕 drop curtain Ⓒ, banner Ⓒ

たれめ 垂れ目 彼女は垂れ目だ Her *eyes turn down on the outside corners*. (❖欧米では目の形状についてあまり言及しない)

たれる 垂れる
❶〖物体が垂れ下がる〗hang*ⓘⒸ; (だらりと) dangle ⓘⒸ; (木の枝が) droop ⓘ

桜の木が道の上に枝を垂れていた Cherry trees *hung* [*drooped*] down over the road.

彼女は恥ずかしくなって頭(ホヘ)を垂れた She *hung* [*lowered*] *her head* in shame.

◆その少女の髪は後ろに垂れていた The girl's hair *flowed* [*hung*] *down* her back. / うちの犬は耳が垂れている Our dog *is floppy-eared* [*lop-eared*]. / 何も考えずに釣り糸を垂れているのが好きだ I like *dropping* a fishing line without thinking anything.

❷〖液体がしたたる〗drip ⓘ, drop ⓘ; (したた り落ちる) trickle ⓘ

屋根から雨水がたれていた Raindrops *were dripping* from the rooftop.

少女の額から汗がたれていた The girl's forehead *was dripping* with sweat.

❸〖説教・文句を〗

若造のくせに人に説教などたれるんじゃない Don't *give* me a lecture as you are a youngster.

彼はいつも学校のことで文句をたれている He *is* always *complaining* about his school.

だれる (つまらなくなる) get* dull; (だらける) get dull [lazy] //その劇は途中でだれてきた The play *got dull* in the middle.

◆午後になると気分がだれる I *feel dull* [*lazy*] in the afternoon.

タレント Ⓐpersonality Ⓒ, entertainer Ⓒ; (有名人) celebrity Ⓒ //テレビタレント *a TV personality* [*entertainer, celebrity*] / タレント議員 an *entertainer-turned* Diet member

タロいも タロ芋 taro Ⓒ (複 ~s)

-だろう

❶〖推量〗

〖語法〗

[動詞・助動詞を用いる場合]推量の意味を表す動詞としては、think「…と思う」が一般的だが、ほかにも suppose, guess(いずれも「…と推測する」の意味)や be afraid「よくないことを心配する」, be sure「…と確信する」, believe「…と信じる」などがある。また、助動詞には、will「…だろう」, must「…にちがいない」, cannot「…のはずはない」, may「…かもしれない」がある。

[副詞を用いる場合]推量の意味を表す副詞には、certainly, surely(いずれも「きっと」の意味), probably, likely, perhaps, maybe, possibly(いずれも「たぶん」の意味)などがある。 ⇒たぶん

息子は今晩帰ってくるだろう I *think* [*suppose, guess*] (that) my son will come home tonight. / *Probably* [*Perhaps*] my son will come home tonight.

あしたは雨が降るだろう I *am afraid* (that) it will rain tomorrow.

きっと彼がこの難問に答えるだろう I *believe* [*am sure*] (that) he would answer this difficult question. / *Certainly* [*Surely*], he would answer this difficult question.

お昼までにはこの仕事を終えているだろう I *will* have finished this job by noon.

彼女はゆうべ夜ふかしをしていたから眠たいだろう She *must* be sleepy because she sat up late last night.

❷〖仮定〗would, could, might

一生懸命勉強していたら今ごろは大学生だっただろうに If you had studied very hard, you *would* have been a college student by now.

君の助けがなかったらその問題は解けなかっただろう Without [But for] your help, I *could* not have solved the question.

たるみ 弛み (ひも・ロープなどの) slack ⓤ; (腹などの) flab ⓤ

たるむ 弛む slacken ⓐ, loosen ⓐ; (体の張りがなくなる) sag ⓐ ——たるんだ slack, loose; (体の張りがなくなった) flabby ∥ロープがたるんでいる The rope *is slack* [*loose*]. / 最近運動していないのでおなか周りがたるんできた Since I don't do exercise these days, my belly *has gotten flabby*.
◆息子は最近たるんでいて勉強に集中できていない My son *is lazy* [*slack*] these days, and he can't concentrate on his studies. / 気持ちがたるんでいるから何度も同じ間違いをするんだ You've been making the same mistakes again and again, because *you've let your mind wander*. / 彼は大学に入ってからというものたるんでいる (→意欲を失っている) ようだ It seems that he *has lost his willpower* since he entered the university.

たれ 垂れ (かけ汁) sauce ⓤ; (肉汁) gravy (sauce) ⓤ ∥ウナギのたれ *sauce* for broiled eels

だれ 誰

❶【だれ(が)】who
あの男の人はだれですか *Who* is that man?
そんなことだれが言ったんだ *Who* said such a thing?
だれがだれか分からない I don't know *who's who*.
だれが知るものか *Who* knows? (❖「だれも知らない」という意味を表す修辞疑問文)
◆だれだって人からほめられれば悪い気はしないよ *Nobody* [*No one*] feels unhappy if they are praised by others.
❡「だれがこの劇を書いたと思いますか」「シェークスピアです」"*Who* do you think wrote this play?" "Shakespeare did." (❖「だれがこの劇を書いたか知っていますか」の場合には Do you know who wrote …? の語順になる)
❡「こんな遅くにだれかしら」「僕が出るよ」"I wonder *who's* calling this late?" "I'll get it."
❡「だれ?」「僕だよ」"*Who is it*?" "It's me."
❷【の】whose
その本がだれの物か分からない I don't know 「*whose* book that is [*whose* that book is].
❡「それはだれのノートなの」「僕のだよ」"*Whose* notebook is that?/ *Whose* is that notebook?" "It's mine."
❸【だれを・だれに・だれと】《公式的》whom, 《口語的》who
いったいだれを探しているんだい *Who* [*Whom*] are you looking for?
その事実についてだれに聞いたんですか *Who* [*Whom*] did you ask about the fact?
いつもだれと学校に行きますか *Who* [*Whom*] do you always go to school *with*?
❡「剛が体育館の裏でけんかしてるぞ」「だれと」"Tsuyoshi is fighting behind the gym." "*Who with?*/ *With who?*"
❹【だれが…しようとも】《公式的》whoever, 《口語的》no matter who; (だれを[に, と]…しようとも)《公式的》whoever, 《公式的》whomever, 《口語的》no matter who [whom]
だれが止めようと私は続けるつもりだ *Whoever* [*No matter who*] may try to stop me, I will go on.
君がだれとデートしようと僕の知ったことじゃない I don't care about *whoever* [*whomever*] you have a date *with*.
⇨だれか, だれでも, だれ(に)も, だれひとり

だれか 誰か (肯定文で) somebody, someone (単数扱い); (疑問文・否定文・if [whether]節で) anybody, anyone (単数扱い)
だれかが本を買ってこなければならない *Somebody* [*Someone*] has to go and buy the book.
だれか答えが分かりますか Does *anybody* [*anyone*] know the answer?
もしだれかが私のことを聞いたら, 休暇をとっていると言ってください If *anybody* [*anyone*] asks about me, please tell them I am on vacation.
こんにちは. だれかいませんか Hello. Is *anybody* there?
だれか手伝ってくれませんか Would *somebody* [*someone*] help me? (❖肯定の答えを期待している場合は, 疑問文でも somebody [someone] を用いる)

たれこむ 垂れ込む squeal ⓐ, rat ⓐ ∥あいつが彼のことを警察にたれこんだのだろう The guy might *have squealed* [*ratted*] *on* him to the cops.

たれこめる 垂れ籠める hang* [lie*] low ∥空には雲が垂れこめていた Clouds *hung* low in the sky. / The sky was covered with *low-hanging* clouds.

たれさがる 垂れ下がる hang* ⓐ, droop ⓐ ∥柳の枝が川の上に垂れ下がっていた Willow branches *hung* [*drooped*] *down* over the river.

だれでも 誰でも (どんな人でも) anybody, anyone; (だれもみな) everybody, everyone; (…の人はだれでも) whoever; (どんな…でも) any
この仕事は簡単なのでだれでもできます This job is so easy that *anybody* [*anyone*] can do it.
だれでもその芸術家のことはよく知っている *Everybody* [*Everyone*] knows the artist well.
だれでも参加したい人はしていい *Whoever* wants to join may join.
俳優であればだれでもいいというわけではない It's not that *any* actor will do.

I *stuffed myself with* fresh crabs in Hokkaido.

だらりと (緊張感なく) loosely ‖彼は両腕をだらりとさせていた His arms were hanging *loosely*.

-たり 彼らは歌ったり踊ったりして楽しい時を過ごした They *sang and danced*, and had a good time. / 彼女はいいよと言ったりだめだと言ったりいつも優柔不断だ She cannot make up her mind at any time; *sometimes* she says yes, and *sometimes* no. / アルバイトをしたり勉強をしたりで大学のときはとても忙しかった What with working part time *and* (what with) studying, I was very busy when I was a college student. / 一日中雪が降ったりやんだりしていた It snowed「*on and off* [*off and on*] all day. / 男は通路を行ったり来たりした The man walked「*up and down* the aisle [*back and forth* in the aisle]. / 腹痛だったので食べたり飲んだりできなかった Because of stomachache, I could not *eat or drink*.(❖否定の並列の場合は or を用いる)

ダリア dahlia ◯

たりきほんがん 他力本願 他力本願では(→他人に頼っていては)何もできない You cannot do anything if you just *rely* [*depend*] *on others*.

だりつ 打率 batting average ◯ ‖打率が高い[低い] have *a high* [*low*] *batting average* / 彼の打率は2割3分9厘です He has a .239 *batting average*. / His *batting average* is .239. (❖.239 は two thirty-nine [three nine]と読む。また、.300 は three hundred と読む)

たりない 足りない (十分でない) be not enough; (不足している) be short, be lacking, lack ◯

300円では夕食を食べるには足りない Three hundred yen *is not enough* for dinner.

ケーキを作るには小麦粉が足りない We *don't have enough* flour to make a cake.

その会社は人手が足りなくて、新たに10人雇った The company *was short of* hands and it employed another 10 people.

あと500円足りない I'm 500 yen *short*.

2メートルに5センチ足りない It's five centimeters *short* of two meters.

この曲を演奏するのにバイオリン奏者が1人足りない We *are* one violinist *short* for playing this piece.

この調子ではすぐにお金が足りなくなってしまうだろう At this rate, we'll soon *run short of* money.

合格点に5点足りなかった I *was* five points *short* of passing.

彼には経験が足りない He *is lacking* in experience. / He *lacks* experience.

◆スプーンがあと2つ足りない We *need* two more spoons. / 彼は英語の力が足りない He *is「poor at* [*weak in*] English. / 自分はまだまだ勉強が足りない I still *have a lot to learn*. / 君には学生としての自覚が足りない(→学生だということを認識する必要がある) You *must realize* that you are a student. / 有能な人材が足りなくて困っている We are in trouble because *there's a shortage of* competent people.

●「毎月のおこづかいって足りてる？」「全然足りないよ」 "Do you get a sufficient allowance every month?" "No, they are *far from enough*."

慣用表現 あいつはちょっと(頭が)足りない He is a bit *short on brains*. / 彼の発言など取るに足りない(→考えるに値しない) What he said is *not worth considering*.

たりょう 多量 多量の水がタンクに残っている A *large amount* [*deal*] *of* water is left in the tank. / 果物にはビタミンが多量に含まれている Fruits「*have a lot of* [*are rich in*] vitamins. / 彼は出血多量で亡くなった He died of *an excessive loss of blood*.

だりょく¹ 打力 〖野球〗batting power ◯

だりょく² 惰力 (慣性の力) inertia [inə́ːrʃə] ◯

たりる 足りる
(十分である) be enough, be sufficient; (間に合う) do* ◯

1,000円あれば昼食を食べるには足りる A thousand yen will「*be enough* [*be sufficient, do*] *for* lunch.

僕はその本を買うのに何とか足りるお金を持っていた I had *barely enough* money to buy that book.

◆彼は信頼するに足りる男だ He's a *trustworthy* guy.

たる¹ 樽 (大だる) barrel ◯; (小だる) keg ◯; (酒だる) cask ◯ ‖ビールのたる a beer *barrel*

たる² 足る ⇒たりる

だるい 怠い (気力がない) sluggish, languid; (手足が) heavy ‖このところの暑さのせいで体がだるい I feel *sluggish* [*languid*] in the heat these days. / きのう長距離を走ったので足がだるい My legs feel *heavy* because I ran a long distance.

タルタルソース tartar(e) sauce

タルト tart(e) ◯

だるま 達磨 〖人形〗a daruma [Dharma] (doll)

‖だるまストーブ a potbellied stove

だるまは手足のない張り子の人形で、顔以外は赤く塗られ、底が重くなっています。これは6世紀の中国に実在した達磨という僧侶(宗派)の座禅姿を表したものです。だるまは倒してもすぐに起き上がることから縁起がよいとされています。目の入っていないだるまもありますが、これは願い事があるときに片方の目を入れ、願いがかなったときに残りの目を描き入れるようになっているのです。

A *daruma* (*Dharma*) doll is a papier-mâché doll which is painted red except for the face and weighted at the bottom. It represents the Buddhist priest Bodhidharma, who lived in sixth century China, sitting in a lotus position. The doll is considered to bring good

だんあつ 弾圧 oppression ⓤ, suppression ⓤ ——弾圧する oppress ㊗, suppress ㊗ / 隠れキリシタンたちは幕府からの厳しい弾圧に苦しんでいた The secret Christians suffered severe *oppression* from the shogunate. / 彼らは当局から弾圧を受けた They *were suppressed* by the authorities.

たんい 単位

❶【度量衡の単位】(計量の) unit ⓒ; (度量の) measure ⓒ
単位を間違えて計算してしまった I made my calculations in *the* wrong *unit*.
グラムは重さの単位です The gram is *a unit* of weight.
オランダの貨幣単位はギルダーである *The monetary unit* of the Netherlands is the guilder.

❷【構成要素】unit ⓒ
社会を構成する最小の単位としての夫婦 a married couple as *the* smallest social *unit*
◆クラス単位で行動する do things *as a class* / これらのビーズはグラム単位で売られている These beads are sold *by the gram*.

❸【授業の単位】《主に米》credit ⓒ, unit ⓒ; (科目) course ⓒ
このクラスは5単位のコースです This class is a *five-credit* course.
卒業するためには最低120単位必要である You will need at least 120 *credits* for graduation.
あの教授は簡単に単位をくれる That professor gives *credits* easily.
◆かろうじて数学の単位は取ったが英語の単位は落とした I barely *passed* in math but *failed* in English.

たんいち 単一 (電池) D battery ⓒ
たんいつ 単一 単一の (唯一の) single; (1つにまとまった) unitary /単一欧州市場 the *Single* European Market / 単一国家 a *unitary* state [nation] /単一民族国家 a *homogeneous* state [nation]
たんいん 団員 member ⓒ
たんおんかい 短音階 minor scale ⓒ
たんか¹ 担架 stretcher ⓒ /救急隊員らが患者を担架で運んだ The paramedics carried the patient on *a stretcher*.
たんか² 単価 unit price [cost] ⓒ ◆このボールペンの単価はいくらですか How much do these ball-points cost *each*?
たんか³ 啖呵 fighting [defiant] words
◆「もうおまえとは絶交だ」と彼はたんかを切った "I'll have nothing more to do with you," he *declared defiantly*.
たんか⁴ 短歌 [A] *a tanka*, a 31-syllable Japanese poem / 短歌をよむ compose *tankas* [*tanka*]

日本古来の歌、和歌に属する短歌は5-7-5-7-7の5句、31音節からできています。元来、和歌にはいくつかの異なる形式の歌がありました。短歌に対し長歌という形式もありましたが、ほかのいくつかの歌とともに姿を消し、事実上、和歌といえば短歌ということになったわけです.
Tanka (literally "short poem"), which belongs to the old Japanese poetry called *waka*, is a 31-syllable poem formed by five lines in the pattern of 5-7-5-7-7. Originally there existed other forms in *waka* such as *choka* (literally "long poem"), which was distinguished from *tanka*. With the disappearance of *choka* and other minor forms, *tanka* virtually became equivalent to *waka*.

だんか 檀家 [A] a *danka*, a family that belongs to a particular Buddhist temple
タンカー tanker ⓒ /石油タンカー an oil *tanker* / マンモスタンカー a mammoth *tanker*; a supertanker
だんかい¹ 段階 (局面) stage ⓒ, phase ⓒ, step ⓒ; (等級) level ⓒ, grade ⓒ, rank ⓒ ——段階的な gradual
この計画は初期[最終]段階にある This plan is in *its early* [*final*] *stages*.
クラスは試験の結果に基づいて4段階に分けられた The class was divided into four *levels* [*grades*], based on the results of the test.
◆その会社は従業員を段階的に削減した The company「reduced the number of employees *gradually* [*phased out* the employees]. / 国民の理解を得るには政府は新法について段階を追って説明する必要がある The government has to explain the new law *step by step* in order to obtain understanding from the nation.

だんかい² 団塊 団塊の世代 the *baby-boom* generation; (→団塊の世代の人たち) *baby boomers* (❖日本語の「団塊の世代」が1947～1949年ころに生まれた世代を指すのに対し、英語の baby-boom generation は第二次大戦後15年間ほどに生まれた世代を指す)
だんがい¹ 断崖 cliff ⓒ; (切り立ったがけ) precipice ⓒ; (川や海に面したがけ) bluff ⓒ
‖断崖絶壁 a precipitous cliff, a sheer cliff
だんがい² 弾劾 impeachment ⓤ ——弾劾する impeach ㊗ /弾劾裁判所 a Court of *Impeachment* / その大統領は不倫問題のために弾劾された the president *was impeached* as a result of extramarital affairs.

たんがん¹ 嘆願 《公式的》entreaty ⓒⓤ,《公式的》plea ⓒ; (文書による) petition ⓒ ——嘆願する《公式的》entreat ㊗, plead* ㊗; (文書で) petition ㊗ /国会は我々の嘆願を却下した The Parliament turned down our *entreaty*. / 5,000人を超える人がその嘆願書に署名した More than 5,000 people signed the *petition*. / 我々は学長に学部を新設するように嘆願した We *petitioned* the president to establish a new department.
たんがん² 単眼 (昆虫の) simple eye ⓒ
たんがん³ 単願 ——単願する (1つの学校のみに志願する) apply to only one school
だんがん 弾丸 bullet ⓒ /数発の弾丸がその男

に命中した Several *bullets* hit the man. /弾丸ライナー〖野球〗a line drive

たんき¹ 短気 ━━短気な (怒りっぽい) short-tempered, quick-tempered; (せっかち・性急に) hotheaded, impatient ◆短気を起こす *lose one's temper* / 短気なのを別にすれば彼女は申し分ない Apart from *her short* [*quick*] *temper*, she is perfect. / 私の父は非常に短気だ My father *has a very short temper*. / 彼は短気な人だ He is *a hothead*.
ことわざ 気は損気 Haste makes waste. (→急ぐとむだなことをしてしまう)

たんき² 短期 short period ◎, short time ━━短期の short-term /彼は短期の割のいいバイトを探している He is looking for a *short-term* part-time job that pays well.
◆あのチームは短期決戦に強い。That team is strong in *a short and decisive battle*.
‖短期貸付 a short-term loan / 短期集中講座 a crash course / 短期大学 a junior college / 短期留学 short-term study abroad

だんき 暖気〖気象〗warm air mass ◎

たんきゅう¹ 探求 quest ◎ ━━探求する seek* ⓗ /真の豊かさを探求する *seek* true wealth
‖探求者 a seeker

たんきゅう² 探究 (調査・研究) inquiry ⓤ◎, search ◎ /真理を探究する *search for* truth / 彼女は探究心にあふれた優秀な学生だ She is an excellent student with *an inquiring mind*.

たんきょり 短距離 short distance ◎ ◆この種の車両は短距離輸送専用に使われている These kinds of vehicles are used exclusively for a 「*short-distance transportation* [*transportation in a short distance*].
‖短距離走《米》a dash, a sprint / 短距離走者 a sprinter

タンク tank ◎ /燃料タンクはほとんど空だった The fuel *tank* was almost empty.

タンクトップ 《米》tank top ◎ /タンクトップを着る wear *a tank top*

タンクローリー ⚠ tanker ◎, 《米》tank truck ◎ (◆「タンクローリー」は和製英語)

だんけつ 団結 (結合) union ⓤ; (共通の利害・目的による) solidarity ⓤ◎; (一致) unity ⓤ ━━団結する unite ⓗ, band ⓗ
彼らには十分な団結力がある They have enough *power of unity*.
私たちの団結は固い We have strong *solidarity*.
従業員は企業のリストラに対して団結した The employees *united* against the restructuring of the corporation.
この難局を乗りきるためには私たちの団結が必要だ We have to *band together* to overcome this difficulties.
◆彼らの一致団結しての努力がとうとう実を結んだ Their *united* effort finally bore fruit. / いじめに対して団結して闘おう Let's fight 「*in body* [*as a body*] against bullying.
‖団結権 the right of organization
慣用表現 団結は力なり *Unity is strength*.

たんけん¹ 探検 (未知の地への) exploration ⓤ◎; (冒険旅行) expedition ⓤ◎ ━━探検する explore ⓗ /アムンゼンは1911年, 南極探検に成功した Amundsen succeeded in *his exploration of the Antarctic* in 1911. / 村の少年たちは洞窟(どう)の探検に出かけた The boys in the village went on *the expedition* into the cave.
‖探検家 an explorer / 探検隊 an expedition (party)

たんけん² 短剣 dagger ◎

たんげん 単元 unit ◎ /夏までに私たちは数学を5単元終えなければならない We have to cover five *units* of math before summer.

だんげん 断言 (根拠・信念に基づく) affirmation ⓤ◎; (自分の確信に基づく) assertion ⓤ◎ ━━断言する affirm ⓗ; assert ⓗ; (保証する) assure ⓗ; (表明する) declare ⓗ ◎ /彼女は自分が完全に無実だと断言している She *affirms* that she is completely innocent. / 彼は子供たちの言ったことは本当だと断言した He *asserted* that children's words were true. / 私はここにその話が事実であることを断言します I hereby *declare* the story to be true.
◆断言はできない I can't *say for sure*.

タンゴ tango ◎ (複〜s) /タンゴを踊る dance *the tango*

たんご 単語 word ◎; (ある個人・言語で用いる語の全体) vocabulary ⓤ
多くの英単語がラテン語に由来している Many *English words* are derived from Latin.
試験前にこの単語を全部覚えなければいけない I must learn all these *words* by heart before the exam.
単語のつづりが分からなければ辞書で調べなさい If you can't spell *the word*, look it up in the dictionary.
もっと勉強して中国語の単語力をつけたい I want to increase [build up] *my* Chinese *vocabulary* by studying harder.
‖単語帳 a word book

だんこ 断固 断固たる処置をとる take *decisive* [*firm*] measures / 彼には断固とした態度で臨もうと思う I will take a *firm* attitude toward him. / 彼女は断固として自分の正当性を主張した She *firmly* insisted her rightness. / 彼は断固としてわいろを受け取らなかった(→きっぱり拒絶した) He *flatly* rejected the bribe. / 彼女は断固として(→強い意志をもって)偏見と闘った She *resolutely* fought against prejudice. / 我々はその計画には断固反対だ We *are dead set against* the plan.

だんご 団子 dumpling ◎ ‖団子鼻 a bulbous nose
ことわざ 花より団子 ⇨ はな(花・華)

たんこう 炭坑・炭鉱 coal mine ◎,《英》colliery ◎ (◆建物・設備全般も含まれる) ‖炭坑労働者 a coal miner

だんこう¹ 断行 ━━断行する carry out resolutely /首相は行政改革を断行した The prime minister *carried out* administrative reform *resolutely*.

だんこう² 断交 ━━断交する break* off relations ◆首脳交渉の決裂は2国間の断交につながるおそれがある The collapse of the summit meeting could cause *the breaking off of diplomatic relations* between the two countries.

だんこう³ 団交（団体交渉）collective bargaining ⓤ ‖団交を行うことは労働者の重要な権利の一つだ *Collective bargaining* is one of the important rights of workers.

だんごう 談合 bid rigging ──談合する rig a bid ∥談合は消費者利益の保護のために禁止されている To *rig a bid* is prohibited for the protection of consumer's interests.

たんこうぼん 単行本 book © ∥彼女は彼のエッセーを単行本として出版した She published his essays「in *book* form [as *a book* itself].

たんこぶ（打撲によるもの）bump ©；（はれもの・しこり）lump © ∥彼は頭にたんこぶができている He has [gets] *a bump* on his head.
慣用表現 彼は私にとって目の上のたんこぶだ He is「really *troublesome* [such *a nuisance*] to me. / He's *a pain in the neck*.

だんこん 弾痕 bullet hole [mark] © ∥その壁には無数の弾痕が残っていた The wall was pitted with hundreds of *bullet holes*.

たんさ 探査 probe ©, exploration ⓤ© ──探査する probe 他⾃, explore 他⾃ ∥新しい埋蔵石油資源の探査 *an exploration* for new oil reserves / アメリカは月面の探査に成功した The United States succeeded in *its probe* of the surface of the moon.
∥月面探査機 a moon [lunar] probe / 無人宇宙探査船 a space probe

だんさ 段差 difference in level
◆この先段差あり《掲示》*Bump* Ahead

ダンサー（professional）dancer ©

たんさいぼう 単細胞 single sell ©; ──単細胞の single-celled, unicellular
◆彼は本当に単細胞（→単純）だ He is really *simple-minded* [*a simpleton*].
∥単細胞生物〖生物〗 a single-celled [unicellular] organism

たんさく 探索 search © ∥行方不明の少年を探索する *search for* a missing boy

たんざく 短冊 🔲 a *tanzaku*, an oblong card for writing poetry

たんさん¹ 炭酸 carbonic acid ⓤ
◆これは炭酸入りですか Is this *carbonated*?
∥炭酸飲料 carbonated drinks,《英》minerals / 炭酸ガス carbonic acid gas;（二酸化炭素）carbon dioxide / 炭酸カルシウム calcium carbonate / 炭酸水 Seltzer [seltzer] ©, soda, soda water / 炭酸ソーダ sodium carbonate

たんさん² 単三（電池）AA [dÁbl éi] battery ©

たんし 端子〖電気〗terminal ©

だんし 男子（少年）boy ©;（成人）man ©;（男性）male © ∥男子学生と女子学生 boy [male] students and girl [female] students
∥男子校 a boys' school / 男子トイレ a men's room

タンジェント〖数学〗tangent ©（《略語》tan）

たんじかん 短時間 a short time ──短時間の brief ∥短時間の休憩をとろう Let's have a *brief* break. / コンピュータのおかげで私は短時間で作業を終えることができた Thanks to the computer, I was able to finish the work *in a short time*.

だんじき 断食 fast ©;（断食する行為）fasting ⓤ ──断食する fast ⾃, go* on a fast ∥断食スト a hunger strike / 断食日 a day of fast [fasting]

だんじて 断じて（絶対に）absolutely;（決して…ない）never ∥あなたとの約束は断じて守る I'll *absolutely* keep my promise to you. / I'll *never* break my promise to you. / 彼のことは断じて許せない I'll *never* forgive him.

たんしゃ 単車 motorcycle ©,《英》motorbike ©（❖《米》では小型オートバイを指す）
➡ オートバイ

だんしゃく 男爵（英国の最下位の貴族）baron © ∥男爵夫人 a baroness

たんじゅう¹ 胆汁 bile ⓤ

たんじゅう² 短銃 handgun ©, pistol ©
➡ ピストル

たんしゅく 短縮 reduction ⓤ© ──短縮する shorten 他;（数量などを）reduce 他 ∥政府は勤労時間の短縮を推進している The government is promoting *a reduction* in the working hours. / きょうは短縮授業だ School hours are shortened today.
∥短縮形〖文法〗a contraction, a shortened form / 短縮ダイヤル a speed dial

たんじゅん 単純 simplicity ⓤ ──単純な simple;（人が）simple-minded ∥単純な仕事 a *simple* task / このゲームのルールはいたって単純だ The rules of this game are very *simple*. / 彼はなんて単純なやつなんだ What a *simple-minded* fellow he is! ◆単純な（→ばかげた）ミスを犯す make a *foolish* mistake

たんしょ¹ 短所（欠点）shortcomings,（公式的）demerit ©（↔merit）;（性質・制度上の）fault ©;（弱点）weak point ∥だれにだって短所の1つや2つはある Everybody has a few *shortcomings*. / その計画には長所と短所がある The program has merits and *demerits*. / 気が弱いのが彼女の短所だ Her *weak point* is that she is not assertive.

たんしょ² 端緒 この実験は遺伝子治療の実現の端緒を開いた This experiment *gave a start to* the realization of gene therapy.

だんじょ 男女 men and women;（両性）both sexes ∥当時，男女間の賃金格差は大きかった There was (a) great disparity in pay between *men and women* at that time.
◆男女を問わず regardless of *sex* / 男女兼用の服 *unisex* clothing / 私たちの美術部には男女合わせて15人の部員がいる There are 15 *boys and girls* in our art club. / 私たちの学校は男女共学だ Our school is *co-ed*.
∥男女関係 relations between men and women / 男女雇用機会均等法 the Equal Employment Opportunity Law / 男女差別

sex [sexual] discrimination / 男女平等 sexual equality

たんじょう 誕生 birth Ⓤ Ⓒ ――誕生する be born ⇒うまれる

新政党の誕生 *the birth* of a new party

◆宇宙はどのようにして誕生したのだろう How did the universe *come into existence [being]*? / 私たちは彼女の誕生パーティーを開いた We held *a birthday party* for her. / 誕生祝いに母からネックレスをもらった My mother gave me a necklace *for my birthday*.

‖誕生石 a birthstone

だんしょう 談笑 ――談笑する have* a pleasant chat [talk], chat ⓥ

たんじょうび 誕生日 birthday Ⓒ

誕生日おめでとう Happy *birthday* to you!

きょうは私の16歳の誕生日です Today is my 16th *birthday*. / It's my 16th *birthday* today.

私たちは祖母の80歳の誕生日をパーティーを開いて祝った We celebrated my grandmother's 80th *birthday* with a party.

妹に誕生日のプレゼントを買った I bought *a birthday present* for my sister.

🔊「誕生日はいつですか」「5月27日です」"When is *your birthday*?" "It's (on) May 27."

たんしょく 淡色 light color Ⓒ ‖淡色野菜 a light-colored vegetable

たんしん¹ 単身 (単独で) alone; (独力で) by oneself ‖彼女はダンスの勉強をしに単身ニューヨークへ渡った She went to New York *alone [by herself]* to study dance.

◆大阪に単身赴任する(→家族を残して転任する) 「*be transferred to [take up a post in]* Osaka *leaving one's family behind*

‖単身赴任 temporary dispatch without family / 単身赴任者 a business bachelor

たんしん² 短針 (時計の) hour [short] hand Ⓒ

たんす 箪笥 (引き出し式の整理だんす) a chest (of drawers); (洋服だんす) wardrobe Ⓒ, (靴つきの化粧だんす) (米)bureau Ⓒ (複 ~s, bureaux [bjúərouz]), (米)dresser Ⓒ

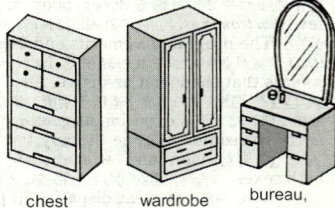

chest　　wardrobe　　bureau, dresser

ダンス dance Ⓒ; (踊ること) dancing Ⓤ ――ダンスをする dance ⓥ ‖人とダンスをする *dance with* a person ‖ダンス教室 a dance school / ダンスパーティー a dance; (大舞踏会) a ball / ダンスホール a dance hall, (英)a dancing hall / 社交ダンス social [ballroom] dancing

たんすい 淡水 fresh water Ⓤ ――淡水の freshwater(❖名詞の前で用いる) ‖淡水魚 a freshwater fish / 淡水湖 a freshwater lake

だんすい 断水 suspension of water supply ――断水する 「cut* off [suspend, stop] (the) water supply ‖あす午前10時から12時まで断水になります (*The*) *water supply will be cut off* from 10 a.m. to 12 noon tomorrow.

たんすいかぶつ 炭水化物 carbohydrate Ⓒ Ⓤ

たんすう 単数 〖文法〗singular (number) Ⓒ ――単数の singular ‖名詞の単数形 *the singular form* of a noun

たんせい 丹精 これは祖父が丹精こめて育てきた盆栽です This is a bonsai that my grandfather has raised *with great [loving] care*.

たんせい² 端正 ――端正な (顔立ちが整った) handsome; (きりっと引き締まった) chiseled ‖端正な顔立ち *chiseled* features

だんせい¹ 男性 Ⓒ man Ⓒ(複 men), gentleman Ⓒ (❖目の前にいる男性を指すときにman の代わりに使う丁寧語); (生物学的な性別を強調して) male Ⓒ; (生物学的に, 男性全体を指して) the male sex; (文法の) the masculine gender ――男性の male ――男性的な manly, masculine

男性的な声 a *manly* [*masculine*] voice

あそこに立っていらっしゃる男性はどなたですか Who is that *man* [*gentleman*] standing over there?

その話は男性の視点で語られている The story is told from *a man's* perspective.

‖男性美 masculine beauty / 男性ホルモン (a) male (sex) hormone

だんせい² 男声 male voice Ⓒ ‖男声合唱 a male chorus, (米) a glee club

たんせき 胆石 gallstone Ⓒ, 〖医学〗cholelith Ⓒ ‖胆石症 a cholelithiasis

だんぜつ 断絶 (隔たり) gap Ⓒ; (断絶すること) breaking off Ⓤ; (滅亡) extinction Ⓤ ――断絶する break* off ‖諸外国と国交を断絶する *break off* diplomatic relations with foreign countries / 世代間の断絶 *a* generation *gap*; *a* communications *gap* between generations

たんせん 単線 single track [line] Ⓒ ‖単線運転する run on *a single track* ◆単線の鉄道 *a single-track* [*single-tracked*] railroad

だんぜん 断然 (はるかに) by far, much, far and away(❖最上級や比較級とともに用いて意味を強める) ‖その映画は彼の他の作品と比べて断然おもしろかった The film was *much* more interesting than his other works. / 前売りを買ったほうが断然得だよ You'll benefit *much* by buying a ticket in advance.

たんそ 炭素 〖化学〗carbon Ⓤ (❖元素記号 C) ‖一酸化 [二酸化] 炭素 carbon monoxide [dioxide]

だんそう 断層 〖地学〗fault Ⓒ, dislocation Ⓒ ‖断層地震 a dislocation earthquake / 断層写真 〖医学〗a tomogram / 断層線 a fault

たんそく¹ 短足 short leg ━━短足の short-legged ‖彼は短足だ He has *short legs*.

たんそく² 嘆息 sigh ⓒ ━━嘆息する (ため息をつく) sigh ⓐ, heave a sigh (of grief)

だんぞく 断続 ━━断続的な intermittent ━━断続的に off and on, on and off, intermittently ‖あすは一日中断続的に雨が降るでしょう There will be *intermittent* showers all day tomorrow. / It will rain *intermittently* [*on and off*] all day tomorrow.

だんそんじょひ 男尊女卑 predominance of men over women; (男性優位主義) male chauvinism
◆男尊女卑の社会 a *male-dominated* society

たんだい 短大 junior college ⓒ

だんたい (集団) group ⓒ, party ⓒ; (組織) organization ⓒ;
団体行動をとる act as a group
10名以上だと団体割引になる A party of 10 or more receives *a group discount* [*rate*].
彼は団体旅行で中国へ行ってきた (→中国への団体旅行に加わった) He joined *a group tour* to China.
みやげ物屋に団体客がどやどやと入ってきた A *group* [*party*] *of travelers* noisily came into the souvenir shop.
‖団体競技 a team game [sport, event, competition] / 団体交渉 collective bargaining / 団体行動 group activity, collective [group] action, team-work / 団体生活 group life / 団体精神 an esprit de corps / 圧力団体 a pressure group / 宗教団体 a religious group [organization] / 地方公共団体 a local [regional] public body

たんたん 淡々 ━━淡々とした (冷静な) cool, calm; (感情を交えない) dispassionate, matter-of-fact ━━淡々と calmly; dispassionately, matter-of-factly ‖彼は淡々とした口調で話し始めた He started to speak in a *dispassionate* tone.
◆彼は試合に負けても淡々としていた He *was unconcerned* about losing the game.

だんだん 段々 ━━だんだん(と) (徐々に) gradually, little by little; (次々に) one after another; (ますます) more and more
しばらくいっしょに暮らしてみて, だんだん彼女のことが分かり始めた After living with her for some time,「I *gradually* began to understand her [I began to understand her *little by little*].
客がだんだん帰っていく The guests are leaving *one after another*.
そのテレビドラマはだんだんおもしろくなってきた The TV drama is getting *more and more* interesting.
◆雪が解け始めてだんだん暖かくなってきた The snow has begun to thaw and it is getting *warmer and warmer*.

だんだんばたけ 段々畑 terraced field [farm] ⓒ

たんち 探知 (見つけ出すこと) detection ⓤ ━━探知する detect ⓗ ‖未確認の航空機がレーダーで探知された An unidentified aircraft *was detected* on [by] radar.
‖探知機 a detector

だんち 団地 apartment [housing] complex ⓒ, housing development [《英》estate] ⓒ; (中低所得者向けの公営住宅団地) 《米》housing project ⓒ ‖私は団地に住んでいる I live in *an apartment complex*.
‖工業団地 an industrial park [《英》estate]

だんちがい 段違い 彼女は私たちより段違いに数学がうまい She is *far ahead of us* in mathematics. / 彼は私よりテニスが段違いにうまい I *am no match for* him at tennis. / I'm *not in the same league* as he is at tennis.
‖段違い平行棒 uneven (parallel) bars

たんちょう¹ 単調 ━━単調さ monotony ⓤ; (退屈) dullness ⓤ ━━単調な monotonous; dull ‖単調なリズム a *monotonous* rhythm / 単調な生活を送る lead a *monotonous* life / ここの景色は単調だ The scenery here「*is monotonous* [(→変化に乏しい) *lacks variety*].
◆単調な (→ほかの日と変わらない) 毎日だった One day was *very much like another*.

たんちょう² 短調 〔音楽〕minor (key) ⓒ ‖交響曲第9番=短調 Symphony No. 9 in D *minor*

だんちょう¹ 団長 a head [leader] (of a party)

だんちょう² 断腸 その計画を断念するのは断腸の思いだった We were *heartbroken* [*brokenhearted*] at abandoning the project.

たんてい 探偵 (私立探偵) (private) detective ⓒ (❖単に detective というと刑事の意味にもなる) ‖探偵小説 a detective story

だんてい 断定 conclusion ⓒ ━━断定する conclude ⓗⓐ ‖状況証拠のみでは彼が犯人だと断定できない One cannot *conclude* that he is guilty just from the circumstantial evidence. / にわかに断定はできない We must not *jump to conclusions*.
◆それについてはあまり断定的な言い方をしないほうがいい You shouldn't speak so *definitely* about that.

たんてき 端的 ━━端的な (率直な) straightforward, frank; (明らかな) plain ━━端的に straightforwardly, frankly; plainly ‖端的な表現 a *straightforward* expression ‖端的に言えば *frankly* speaking; to be *frank* with you
◆このグラフは世界的な気象異変を端的に示している This graph shows *clearly* the global climate change.

たんとう 担当 charge ⓤ ━━担当する take* charge, be in charge ‖迷ったときは担当の人に聞きなさい If [When] (you are) in doubt, ask *the person in charge*. / 母はその会社の経理を担当している My mother *is in charge of* accounting for the company.
◆英語の担当教師 an English *teacher*

たんとう² 短刀 (短剣) dagger ⓒ, short sword ⓒ

だんとう¹ 弾頭 (ミサイルなどの) warhead ⓒ ‖核弾頭 a nuclear warhead

だんとう² 暖冬 mild winter ⓒ ‖昨年は暖冬だった We had *a mild [warm] winter* last year.

だんどう 弾道 trajectory ⓒ ——弾道の ballistic ‖弾道弾 a ballistic missile ‖ 大陸間弾道弾 an intercontinental ballistic missile ((略語))ICBM／ 中距離弾道弾 an intermediate range ballistic missile ((略語))IRBM

たんとうちょくにゅう 単刀直入 単刀直入に言えば *frankly speaking; to be frank with you*／ 単刀直入な質問 a *point-blank [direct]* question／ 単刀直入に話してください。Please *get straight [right] to the point*.

たんどく 単独 ——単独の (ひとりの) solo; (独立の) independent ——単独で (ひとりで) alone; (独力で) by *oneself*, on *one's own*; (独立して) independently ‖単独飛行に成功する succeed in *a solo flight*／ この任務での単独行動は禁じられている You are forbidden to 「*take independent action [act independently, act alone]* on this mission.／ 旅行中に単独行動はしないでください。Please don't *go off on your own* during the trip.
◆その事件は彼女の単独犯行らしい It seems she *committed* the crime 「*without accomplice [on her own]*.
‖単独会見 an exclusive interview／ 単独内閣 a single-party [one-party] cabinet

だんとつ 断トツ 彼女はそのレースで断トツの1位だった She won the race *by a wide margin*.／ 彼はクラスで断トツに足が速い He runs fastest *by far* in his class.

だんどり 段取り (計画) plan ⓒ; (準備) arrangements ‖私たちは送別会の段取りを決めた We worked out the plan for the farewell party.

だんな 旦那 (主人) master ⓒ; (夫) husband ⓒ; (呼びかけで) sir, (口語的) mister

たんなる 単なる (ほんの) mere; (単純な) simple ‖単なる間違い *a simple mistake*／ それは単なる偶然にすぎない That's 「*a mere [only a, a pure]* coincidence.
◆彼は単なる友達です He is *just* a friend.

たんに¹ 単に (ただ) only, just, merely (❖ just はやや口語的. merely は only よりもかたい語); (単純に) simply ‖それは単に程度の問題だ That's *only* a matter of degree.／ 彼はただ単に自分がそうしたかったという理由でそうしたのだった He did it *simply* because he wanted to do it.／ それは単にあなただけの問題ではなく, クラス全体の問題だ It's *not only* your problem *but also* our entire class's.

たんに² 単二 (電池) C battery

タンニン 《化学》tannin ⓤ ‖タンニン酸 tannic acid

たんにん 担任 ——担任する take* [have*] charge of ...; (教える) teach* ⓣ
◆このクラスは田中先生が担任です This is Ms. Tanaka's class.／ Ms. Tanaka *is in charge of this class*.
‖担任教師 a homeroom teacher

だんねつざい 断熱材 insulating material ⓤ, insulator ⓒ

たんねん 丹念 ——丹念な (念入りな) elaborate; (細かすぎるほど念入りな) meticulous ——丹念に elaborately; (綿密に) closely ‖その町の方言について丹念に調査する make an *elaborate* survey of the dialect of the town／ 彼女は訳文を原文と丹念に突き合わせた She *closely* compared the work with its translation.◆丹念な風景描写 a *detailed* depiction of landscape

だんねん 断念 ——断念する abandon ⓣ, give* up ‖彼は大西洋横断の夢を決して断念しようとはしなかった He would never *abandon [give up]* the idea of crossing the Atlantic.／ 私たちは彼女が雪山に登るのを断念させた We *persuaded* her *to give up* climbing the snowy mountain.／ We *dissuaded* her *from* climbing the snowy mountain.

たんのう¹ 堪能 ❶《優秀》——堪能な proficient ‖彼女はフランス語に堪能である She *is proficient in* French.／ She *has a good command of* French.
❷《満足》——堪能する enjoy ⓣⓘ ‖本場のイタリア料理を堪能する *enjoy* genuine Italian food／ 私たちは昨夜, 彼のすばらしい演奏を十分に堪能した We 「*thoroughly enjoyed [enjoyed greatly, enjoyed every moment of]* his wonderful performance last night.

たんのう² 胆嚢 《解剖》gallbladder ⓒ ‖胆のう炎 《医学》cholecystitis; (一般的に) an inflammation of the gallbladder

たんぱ 短波 shortwave ⓤ (また a ～) (❖ short-wave, short wave ともつづる)
‖短波放送 short-wave broadcasting／ 短波ラジオ a short-wave radio／ 極超短波 ultrahigh frequency ((略語))UHF／ 超短波 very high frequency ((略語))VHF

たんぱく¹ 淡白 ——淡白な (味・色の) plain, simple, light; (率直な) frank, candid; (無関心な) indifferent ‖淡白な食物 *plain [light]* food／ 彼は金銭に淡白な男だった He was quite *indifferent* to money.

たんぱく² 蛋白 (タンパク質) protein [próutiːn] ⓒ ❖種類もいうときは ⓒ; (尿の) albumin ⓤ ‖タンパク源 *a source of protein*／ 卵はタンパク質が豊富だ Eggs are rich in *protein*.
‖動物[植物]性タンパク (an) animal [(a) vegetable] protein

だんぱつしき 断髪式 a *dampatsushiki*, a ceremony for cutting off the topknot of a retiring sumo wrestler

タンバリン tambourine ⓒ ‖タンバリンをたたく play [beat] *the tambourine*

たんパン 短パン short pants, shorts

だんぱん 談判 negotiation ⓒ《しばしば複数形 ~s》——談判する negotiate ⓘ, have* talks [a talk]

たんび 耽美 ——耽美的な aesthetic [esθétik] ‖耽美主義 aestheticism／ 耽美主義者 an aesthete

ダンピング dumping [U] ──ダンピングする dump [他] //半導体チップのダンピングを防止する prevent *dumping* of semiconductor chips

ダンプカー ⚠ dump truck [C], 《英》dumper (truck) [C], 《英》tipper lorry [truck] [C] (❖「ダンプカー」は和製英語)

タンブラー tumbler [C]

たんぶん 単文 〖文法〗simple sentence [C]

たんぺん 短編 (小説) short story [piece] [C], sketch [C] //ヘミングウェイ短編集 *the collected short stories* of Hemingway

‖短編映画 a short film / 短編作家 a short-story writer

だんぺん 断片 fragment [C], scrap [C] ──断片的な fragmentary ──断片的に in fragments //断片的な知識 *fragmentary* [*partial*] knowledge / 断片的な情報 *scraps* of information / 彼はその出来事について断片的にしか覚えていなかった He remembered the incident only *in fragments*.

たんぼ 田圃 rice field [paddy] [C], paddy field [C] ‖田んぼ道 a path [lane] through rice fields

たんぽ 担保 security [U], guarantee [C]; (不動産の抵当) mortgage [C]; (見返り担保) collateral [U] //土地を担保にしてお金を借りる borrow money with some land *as security*; *mortgage* some land

◆私の家は1,000万円の担保に入っている My house *is mortgaged* [*in mortgage*] for 10 million yen. / *There is a mortgage* of 10 million yen on my house.

‖担保付貸付金 a secured loan / 担保物件 security

だんぼう 暖房 heating [U] //暖房を入れる[切る] turn on [off] *the heating* ◆この部屋は暖房がきいている[いない] This room *is well* [*poorly*] *heated*. / 私たちの家はスチーム暖房です Our house *is heated by steam*.

‖暖房器具 a heater / 暖房装置 a heating system

だんボール 段ボール (corrugated) cardboard [U], corrugated paper [U] ‖段ボール箱 a (corrugated) cardboard box

たんぽぽ 蒲公英 dandelion [C]

たんまつ 端末 (コンピュータの) terminal [C]

だんまつま 断末魔 *one's* last moments, the [*one's*] hour of death ◆断末魔の苦しみ *death throes*; *the agonies* [*agony*] *of death* / 断末魔の叫び *one's final scream*

たんまり 金をたんまり持っている have *tons of* money

だんまり 黙り だんまりを決め込む *keep mum*; *clam up* ⇒だまる

たんめい 短命 short life [C] ──短命の short-lived ◆当時の人々は短命だった People in those days *died young*. / 今度の内閣はきっと短命に終わるよ I'm sure this Cabinet *won't last long*.

だんめん 断面 (cross) section [C] //日本社会の一断面を見る see *a cross section* of Japanese society

‖断面図 a cross section

たんもの 反物 🗻 (着物用の生地) cloth for kimono [U], piece [yard] goods; (織物) 《米》dry [soft] good, 《英》drapery [U]

だんやく 弾薬 ammunition [U]

‖弾薬庫 a (powder) magazine, an ammunition dump

たんよん 単四 (電池) AAA battery [C] (❖AAAはtriple Aと読む)

たんらく 短絡 (電気のショート) short circuit [C] ──短絡的な simplistic //短絡的な考えは避けるべきだ One should avoid *simplistic* thinking. / One should avoid *jumping to conclusions*.

だんらく 段落 (文章の) paragraph [C] //35ページの第1段落の2行目 the second line of *the* first *paragraph* of page 35

だんらん 団欒 これは食事の後の一家団らんの写真です This is a picture of *our family enjoying a pleasant conversation* after a meal.

たんり 単利 〖経済〗simple interest [U]

だんりゅう 暖流 warm current [C]

だんりょく 弾力 (伸縮性) elasticity [U]; (融通性) flexibility [U] ──弾力のある elastic; flexible //スポンジは弾力性がある Sponges are *elastic*. / Sponges have *elasticity*.

◆弾力的に考える think *flexibly*

たんれん 鍛練 (心身の) discipline [U], training [U]; (金属などの) temper [U] ──鍛練する discipline [他], train [他]; (金属などを) temper [他], forge [他] //精神[身体]の鍛練 mental [physical] *training* / 心身を鍛錬する *train one's* mind and body

だんろ 暖炉 stove [C]; (作りつけの) fireplace [C] //暖炉をたく light *a stove*; make a fire in *the stove* [*fireplace*] / 暖炉にあたる warm *oneself* at「*a stove* [*the fireplace*]

だんわ 談話 (informal) talk [C] [U], conversation [U] //事件に関する首相の談話が新聞に発表された The Prime Minister's (*informal*) *talk* on the incident was published in the newspaper.

‖談話室(ホテルなどの) a lounge

ち

ち¹ 血

❶【血液】 blood ⓤ

《血が》
切り傷から血が出ていた *Blood* was running [flowing] from the cut. / The cut *was bleeding*.
その戦闘ではたくさんの血が流された A lot of *blood* was shed in the battle.
◆ (→出血)がなかなか止まらなかった *The bleeding* wouldn't stop. / ひざから血が出てるよ Your knee *is bleeding*. / You *are bleeding* at [from] the knee.

《血を・に》
血を吐く vomit *blood* / 血に染まった包帯 a bandage covered with [in] *blood*
警察は一滴も血を流すことなく暴動を鎮圧した The police put down the riot without shedding a drop of *blood*.
◆血(→出血)を止める stop *bleeding*

《血の》
血の海 a sea [pool] of *blood*
◆血のついたシャツ a *bloodstained* shirt / その血の跡はなかなか洗い落とせなかった It was hard to wash *the bloodstains* out.

《その他》
血しぶき a fountain of *blood*
彼は頭を切って顔中血だらけだった He got a cut on his head and his face *was covered with blood*. ➡ ちのけ

❷【血統】 blood ⓤ

血を分けた兄弟 a *blood* brother
彼らは血がつながっている They *are*「*related by blood* [*blood relatives*]*.
彼女にはポーランド人の血が流れている She has Polish blood in her.
◆彼は皇族の血を引いている(→子孫だ) He *is descended from* the Imperial family.

慣用表現 頭に血が上って彼をどなりつけた *Blood rushed to my head* and I yelled at him. / その光景を見て全身の血が凍るようだった The sight made *my blood freeze* [*run cold*]. / 路上での演奏を目にして彼のギタリストの血が騒いだ The street performance *stirred his* guitarist's *blood*. / 子供のころに読んだものは君の血となり肉となっている What you read during childhood *has become a part of* you. / 血の通った政策 a *humane* policy / 彼は成功しようとあのにじむような努力を重ねた He made *desperate* efforts to succeed. / 血は争えない *Blood tells*. / *Blood will out*. / 血は水よりも濃い *Blood is thicker than water*. / あいつは血も涙もない男だ He's a *cold-blooded* man.

ち² 地

(大地) the earth; (地面) the ground; (場所) place ⓒ; (国) land ⓒ ‖地の果て the end of *the earth* ⓤ / 天と地 heaven and *earth* / 異国の地 *an* alien *land* / 安住の地を見つける find *a place* where *one* can live peacefully
◆ 私はついに韓国の地を踏んだ I finally *set foot in* South Korea.

慣用表現 彼は地に足が着いている(→現実的だ) He *has* [*keeps*] *his feet on the ground*. / このスキャンダルで彼の評判は地に落ちた(→完全に失った) He's *completely lost* his reputation because of this scandal.

チアガール ⚠ cheerleader ⓒ (❖「チアガール」は和製英語)

ちあん 治安 (秩序) order ⓤ; (平和) the peace ‖治安を維持する[乱す] keep [disturb] *order* / その町は治安がいい The town *is safe to live in*. / (→犯罪率が低い) *The crime rate is low* in the town.

ちい 地位 position ⓒⓤ; (社会的な) place ⓒ (通例単数形); (職務上の) post ⓒ; (階級) rank ⓒⓤ; (身分) status ⓤ
地位の高い人 a person *of rank* / 支配人の地位を得る get *the post* of manager
彼女は政府の重要な地位に就いている She occupies *an* important *position* in the government.
彼らの活動は女性の社会的地位の向上に大きく貢献した Their activities have contributed a great deal to the improvement of *the social status* [*standing*] of women.
◆ 歌手としての地位を確立する(→名声を得る) win *a reputation* as a singer / 私は会社では彼よりも地位が低い[高い] I *rank lower* [*higher*] than him in the company. / I *am under* [*above*] him in the company.

ちいき 地域 area ⓒ; (行政上の) district ⓒ; (特徴のある) region ⓒ ——地域の regional; (地元の) local
雨の多い地域 a rainy *region*
新空港はその地域の発展を促すだろう The new airport will help the development of *the area*.
政府は地域の人々の反対を無視している The government ignores the opposition of (the) *local* people.
広い地域で雨が降るでしょう It will rain over *a wide area*.
この言葉の意味は地域によって少しずつ異なる The meaning of this word differs a little *from region to region*.
‖地域活動 community activities / 地域経済 a regional economy / 地域研究 an area study / 地域差 regional differences / 地域社会 a (local) community / 地域住民 a local resident / 地域紛争 a regional conflict

ちいく 知育 (知能を伸ばす教育) intellectual education ⓤ

チーク teak ⓒ; (チーク材) teak ⓤ

チークダンス ⚠ cheek-to-cheek dancing ⓤ (❖「チークダンス」は和製英語) ——チークダンスをする dance cheek to cheek

ちいさい[な] 小さい[な]

❶【体積・広さ・長さなどが】small (↔large); little (↔big, great); tiny; (背が) short
　small:客観的・相対的に「小さい」を意味し,形・広さ・程度などに用いられる.
　little:「小さくてかわいい」という愛情・同情などの主観的感情が加わる.
　tiny:「驚くほど小さい」の意味.
小さな切り傷 a *small* cut / 小さくてかわいい鳥 a cute *little* bird / クッキーを小さく割る break a cookie up into *small* pieces
彼女はクラスでいちばん小さい She is the *smallest* [*shortest*] in the class.
その上着は私には少し小さすぎた The jacket was a little *too small* for me.

❷【年齢が】small, little; (若い) young
そのころ私はほんの小さな子供だった I was only a *small* [*little*] child at that time.
小さいころここへ来た覚えがある I remember coming here「*when I was small* [*in my childhood*].
姉の子供はまだとても小さい My sister's child is still very *young*.

❸【程度・規模が】small, little; (ささいな) trivial
小さな間違い a *small* [*trivial*] mistake / 小さな利益 a *small* profit / 小さい会社 a *small* company
小さなことでくよくよするな Don't worry about *trivial* [*trifling, small*] things.

❹【音・声が】low
小さい声で in a *low* voice
◆ステレオの音を小さくする *turn* the stereo *down* / 声を小さくする *drop* [*lower*] *one's voice*

❺【その他】
小さな数 a *small* number [figure] / 気の小さい人 a *timid* [*shy*] person

慣用表現 不良少年たちも柔道の小川先生の前では小さくなっていた The bad boys *looked small* in front of Mr. Ogawa, who is a Judo instructor. (❖発話者が「小さくなる」場合は feel small という)

ちいさめ 小さ目 ニンジンはそれより少し小さめに切りなさい Cut the carrots into *smaller* pieces than those.

チーズ cheese C U (❖チーズの種類や一定の形をした製品についていう場合は C) //チーズ1切れ a slice [piece] of *cheese* / (写真を撮るときに)はい, チーズ Say *cheese*!
‖チーズケーキ (a) cheesecake / チーズバーガー a cheeseburger

――― チーズのいろいろ ―――
エダムチーズ Edam cheese / エメンタールチーズ Emmenthaler cheese / カッテージチーズ cottage cheese / カマンベールチーズ Camembert cheese / クリームチーズ cream cheese / グリュイエールチーズ Gruyère cheese / ゴーダチーズ Gouda cheese / 粉チーズ grated cheese / ゴルゴンゾーラチーズ Gorgonzola cheese / スティルトンチーズ Stilton cheese / スモークチーズ smoked cheese / チェダーチーズ Cheddar cheese / ナチュラルチーズ natural cheese / パルメザンチーズ Parmesan cheese / ブルーチーズ blue cheese / プロセスチーズ processed cheese / モッツァレラチーズ Mozzarella cheese

チーター 〖動物〗cheetah C
チーフ chief C, head C
チーム team C //チームに加わる join *a team* / 新しいチームを組む organize [form] *a new team* / 彼はその野球チームのレギュラーだ He's a regular player on [《英》in] the baseball *team*. ◆我々のチームはチームワークがいい We have good *teamwork*.
‖チームプレー team play / チームメート a teammate

ちえ 知恵 (英知・分別) wisdom U; (考え) idea C; (頭脳) brain C U 《通例複数形 ~s》, head C
昔の人の知恵 *the wisdom* of the ancients / 知恵をしぼる rack *one's brains* / 知恵を出し合う put *ones' heads* together / 知恵を働かせる use *one's brains* [*head*]
いい知恵が浮かんだ I hit on *a good idea*.
弟はだんだん知恵がついてきた My little brother gradually began gaining *wisdom*.
彼にも善悪を見分けるくらいの知恵はある He 「*has the wisdom* [*is wise*] enough] to distinguish good from evil.
いったいだれの入れ知恵なんだ Who *put such an idea into* your *head*?
◆知恵の回る人 a *smart* [(→抜け目のない) *shrewd*] person / 知恵遅れの子 a「*mentally retarded* [*slow*] child / 知恵をお借りしたいのですが Could you give me some *advice*?
‖知恵熱 teething fever / 知恵の輪 a wire puzzle
ことわざ 三人寄れば文殊の知恵 ⇒ さんにん

チェアマン chairman C (❖性差別を避けるため最近では chairperson が好まれる)

チェーン chain C U; (タイヤに巻く) tire chains //自転車のチェーンがはずれた My bicycle *chain* came off.
‖チェーンソー a chain saw / チェーン店 ⇒ チェーンストア

チェーンストア chain store C, 《英》multiple store C

チェコ (チェコ共和国) the Czech Republic
――チェコ人 Czech C ――チェコ語 Czech U ――チェコ(人[語]) Czech

チェス chess U //チェスをする play chess
◆チェスのこま *a chessman*
‖チェス盤 a chess board

ちぇっ Tut!, Darn (it)!, Rats!

チェック ❶【照合・点検】check C ――チェックする check ⦿ //書類を入念にチェックする *check* a document carefully; *make* a careful *check of* a document

❷【格子模様】check C U ――チェックの checked //青と白のチェックのシャツ a blue-

and-white *checked* [*checkered*] shirt ‖チェックポイント a point (to be checked) (❖英語の checkpoint は「検問所」の意味) / チェックリスト a checklist / トラベラーズチェック a traveler's check [(英) cheque]

チェックアウト checkout ⓒⓊ ──チェックアウトする check out ‖ホテルをチェックアウトする *check out of* a hotel / チェックアウトの時間を教えてもらえますか Can you tell me when *the checkout time* is?

チェックイン check-in ⓒⓊ ──チェックインする check in ‖ホテルにチェックインする *check in at* a hotel / (ホテルで)チェックインをお願いします I'd like to *check in*, please.

チェリスト cellist ⓒ

チェロ cello ⓒ (複 ~s) ‖チェロを弾く play *the cello*
‖チェロ奏者 a cellist

チェンジ チェンジコートする change courts [sides] / イメージチェンジする change one's image / (野球で)チェンジになった The side *was retired*. / その車は去年モデルチェンジした The car *model was revised* last year.
‖チェンジアップ(野球) a change-up / チェンジレバー (米) a gearshift, (英) a gear lever

チェンバロ 〔音楽〕harpsichord ⓒ, cembalo ⓒ (複 ~s) (❖前者のほうがふつう)
‖チェンバロ奏者 a harpsichordist, a cembalist

ちか¹ **地下** (地階) basement ⓒ ──地下の underground ──地下に[で] underground
(活動家などが)地下に潜(ﾞ)る *go underground*
食料品は地下2階で売っています Foodstuffs are sold in the second *basement*.
このビルの地下に車を止めた I parked *underground* below this building.
その化石は地下20メートルの所で見つかった The fossil was discovered 20 meters *underground* [*below* (*the*) *ground*].
◆その建物は地上10階, 地下2階建てだ The building has 10 stories above and 2 *below* (*the*) *ground*.
‖地下街 an underground shopping arcade [mall] / 地下核実験 an underground nuclear test / 地下活動 underground activities / 地下資源 underground resources / 地下室 ➡ちかしつ / 地下水 underground water, groundwater / 地下組織 the underground / 地下鉄 ➡ちかてつ / 地下道 ➡ちかどう / 地下トンネル an underground tunnel

ちか² **地価** land prices, the price of land ‖東京の地価は近年急激に下落[上昇]している The land prices in Tokyo have dropped [risen] sharply in recent years.

ちかい¹ **近い**
❶【空間的に】near, close (❖near よりも接近の度合いが大きい)
私の学校は家から近い My school is *near*

[*close to*, ×*near from*] my house.
このあたりでいちばん近い病院はどこですか Where is *the nearest* hospital around here?
私は入り口にいちばん近い所にある絵が気に入った I like the picture *nearest (to)* the entrance. (❖比較変化した nearer, nearest は前置詞としても用いられるが, to を付けるほうがふつう)
彼女は明かりに近い方へいすを動かした She moved her chair *closer to* the light.
◆ゴールは近いぞ The goal is *right up ahead*. / これが家へ帰るいちばん近い道です This is *the shortest* way back home.

❷【時間的に】near, close
近い将来に in the *near* [*immediate*] future
試験が近い The exams are *near* [*close*] *at hand*. / The exams are *around the corner*.
◆近いうちに電話するよ I'll call you「*one of these days* [*soon*].
/ きのう寝たのは1時近かった It was *nearly* [*almost*] 1 o'clock when I went to bed yesterday.

❸【関係・程度・性質が】close
近い親戚(ﾞ) a *close* relative
英語はドイツ語に近い English is *close to* German.
彼女の答えは完璧(ﾞ)に近かった Her answer was「*close to* [*almost*] perfect.
(正解などに)近いですよ You're [That's] *close*.
彼の考え方が私のに最も近い His views are *closest* [*nearest*] *to* my own.
私たちは年が近い We are *close* in age.
◆私と彼女に将棋で勝つなんて不可能に近い It's *almost* [*nearly, next to*] impossible for me to beat her at *shogi*. (❖next to は否定語の前で用いられる) / 彼の野球選手生命も終わりに近い His career as a baseball player *is coming to an end*. / 冬になるとトイレが近くなるものだ In winter, people *go to the bathroom more often*.

❹【数が】almost, nearly;(およそ) about
100人近い人がバスを待っていた *Almost* [*Nearly*] one hundred people were waiting for the bus.
祖父は90近い My grandfather is *almost* [*nearly*] ninety.
➡ちかく(近く)

ちかい² **誓い**, vow ⓒ;(神にかけての) oath ⓒ;(固い約束) pledge ⓒ ‖誓いを守る[破る] keep [break] *one's vow* / うそをつかないという誓いを立てる make [take] *a vow* not to tell a lie / 結婚の誓いを交わす exchange marriage *vows*

ちがい **違い** difference ⓒⓊ ➡さ
性格の違い *differences* in character
新製品と従来のものとの違いは何ですか What is *the difference between* the new product and the previous one?
スポーツは実際にやるのと見るのとでは大違いだ There's *a big difference between* taking part in sports and seeing them.
ヒラメとカレイの違いが分かる? Can you tell

「*the difference between* a turbot and a halibut [a turbot *from* a halibut]?
だれが監督になろうとたいした違いはない It *doesn't make* much *difference* no matter who may be the coach.
◆妹とは5歳違いです My sister and I are five years *apart*. / I'm five years *older* than my sister.

> コロケーション　-difference-
> 《形容詞+~》大きな~　a big [wide] difference / 決定的な~　a crucial difference / はっきりした~　a clear [noticeable] difference / 微妙な~　a subtle difference / わずかな~　a minor [slight] difference

ちがいない　違いない

> 語法
> 「(…に)ちがいない」という推量を表す場合は must *do*, または口語で have to [hǽftu] *do* を用いる. ただし過去の推量(「…だったにちがいない」)の場合には must have+過去分詞, また未来の推量(「(これから)…にちがいない」)は will (certainly) *do*, be (certainly) going to *do* などの形になる. さらに「きっと…だ」という意味で I'm sure (that) … も用いられる. 「…ないにちがいない」と否定の推量を表す場合には I'm sure (that)+否定文の形にすればよいが,「…はずはない」という意味合いでは cannot *do* を用いることもできる.

あいつはうそをついているにちがいない He *must* [*has to*] be lying.
どこかに傘を忘れたにちがいない I *must* have left my umbrella somewhere.
君はいつか後悔するにちがいない You *are* [(*certainly*) *going* [*bound*] *to*] be sorry some day.
今年はタイガースが優勝するにちがいない I'*m sure* [*certain*] *that* the Tigers will win the pennant this season. / The Tigers *are sure* [*certain*] *to* win the pennant this season.
おそらくその時点ではだれもその事実に気づいていなかったにちがいない I'*m sure* nobody noticed the matter at that point.
そのとき彼はここにいなかったにちがいない He *can't* have been here at that time.

ちがいほうけん　治外法権【法律】extraterritorial rights, extraterritoriality

ちかう　誓う swear*, vow; (約束する) promise, 《公式的》pledge; (心に) decide, determine
神にかけて誓う *swear by* [*to*, *before*] *God* / 復讐(ふくしゅう)を誓う *vow* revenge
彼女は真実を話すと誓った She *swore* [*vowed*] *to tell the truth*. / She *swore* [*vowed*] *that* she would tell the truth.
誓って彼には一度も会ったことがありません *I swear that* [*On my* (*word of*) *honor*,] I have never seen him.
二人は将来を誓い合った仲だ They *pledged* [*promised each other*] *to marry in the future*.

ちがう　違う

❶【異なる】(be) different; (似ていない) (be) unlike ⇨ことなる
彼らは性格が全く違う They *are* quite 「*different from* each other [*unlike*] in character.
彼は毎日違う靴を履いている He wears *different* shoes every day.
人にはそれぞれ違った能力がある Each person has *different* abilities.
私と違って弟は英語が得意だ *Unlike* me, my brother is good at English.
実際に起こったことは私の予想とは違っていた What really happened 「*was different* [*differed*] *from* what I had expected.
その映画は今までに見たどの映画とも違っていた The movie *was unlike* anything I'd seen before.
その件に関しては私は彼と意見が違う My opinion on that matter *is different from* his. / I *disagree with* him on that matter.
きょうの彼女はどこかいつもと違う She *looks* somehow *different* today.
さっきと言ってることが違う It'*s different from* what you said a little while ago.
◆約束が違うじゃないか That's *not* what you promised. / 彼は他人と違ったものの見方をする He sees things *differently from* others. / 僕だったら違ったやり方でやった I would have done *otherwise*. / プロはさすがに違う (→世界が違う) The pros *are another world*. / この本は難しすぎます. 違うの(→ほかの)を見せてください This book is too difficult. Show me *another*. / 努力すればテストの結果はだいぶ違うだろう Your efforts will *make a big difference* in your test results. / この包丁はこれまで使っていたものとは切れ味がまるで違う(→ずっとよく切れる) This knife cuts *much better* than the one I have been using.

❷【間違っている】(be) wrong
その手紙はあて名が違っていた The address on the letter *was wrong*. / The letter was *wrongly* addressed.
彼女のせいだって考えるのは違うんじゃない？ I think you *are wrong* [(→思い違いしている) *mistaken*] in thinking that she is to blame.
(電話で)違う番号におかけのようです I'm sorry, you have the *wrong* number.
🔴「オーストラリアの首都はシドニーだよね, 違う？」「違うよ, キャンベラだよ」 "The capital of Australia is Sydney, *isn't it?*" "*No*, it's Canberra."

ちがえる　違える 足の筋を違える *strain* a leg muscle

ちかく¹　近く

❶【空間的に】——近くの nearby, near, close [klóus]　——近くに[で] nearby, near, close; (近所に[で]) in the neighborhood

《近くに》
近くにすてきな喫茶店がありますよ There's a nice coffee shop *nearby*.
私は学校の近くに住んでいる I live *near* [*close to*, *in the neighborhood of*] my school.
彼女は窓の近くにいすを動かした She moved her chair *closer to* the window.
近くにいるんだけど，ちょっと寄ってもいいかな？ I'm *in the neighborhood*. Can I stop in for a few minutes?

《近くの》
私はよく近くの公立図書館を利用します I often go to a public library *nearby*.
彼は夏休みを湖の近くの保養地で過ごした He spent the summer vacation at a resort *near* [*close to*] the lake.

> 語法
> 「近くの町」などの表現で near は原則では名詞の前には用いない ∥ 彼女は近くの町に住んでいる ×She lives in a *near* town.; ○ She lives in a *nearby* town. / She lives in a town *nearby*. (❖near the town は「その町の近くに」の意味) / いちばん近くの病院はどこですか Where's the *nearest* hospital (*from here*)?

《近くで》
この近くでどこかいいレストランを紹介してくれませんか Can you recommend any good restaurants *near* [*around*] *here*?
ゆうべ家のすぐ近くで火事があった There was a fire *very near* my house last night.

《近くを》
数日前，君の家の近くを通ったよ I passed *near* your house a few days ago.
祖母は近くを見るのに眼鏡が欠かせない My grandmother can't see things *close up* without glasses.

《その他》
ここから駅はすぐ近くだ The station is very *near* [×near from] here. / It's *no distance* from here to the station.
富士山をこんなに近くから見るのは生まれて初めてだ This is the first time I've ever seen Mt. Fuji *from so close*.

❷【近いうちに】soon, before long
首相は近く訪米する予定だ The prime minister is going to visit the United States *soon* [*before long*].

❸【ほとんど】nearly, almost; (およそ) about
それを終わらせるのに1時間近くかかった It took me *nearly* an hour to finish it.
父はきのう1時近くまで働いていた My father was working until *almost* 1 o'clock yesterday.
500人近くの人がその大会に参加した *About* five hundred people attended the grand meeting.

◆その事故は明け方近くに起きた The accident took place *toward* daybreak.

ちかく² 地殻 〖地学〗crust ⓊⒸ ∥地殻変動〖地学〗diastrophism

ちかく³ 知覚 perception ⓊⒸ; (感覚) sensation Ⓤ ——知覚する perceive ⓗⒺ ∥知覚過敏 hyperesthesia / 知覚神経 a sensory nerve

ちがく 地学 (地球科学) earth science Ⓤ (❖「地質学」geology,「地球物理学」geophysics,「海洋学」oceanography,「気象学」meteorology などを含む)

ちかごろ 近頃 recently, lately (❖過去時制・完了時制で用いる); these days, nowadays (❖現在時制で用いる) ➔ さいきん(最近) ∥近ごろめっきり涼しくなった It has gotten noticeably cooler *recently* [*lately*].
◆ 近ごろの若者 *today's* young people; young people *of today* / それは近ごろにない(→近年でいちばん)明るい話題だった It was the happiest news *in recent years*.

ちかしつ 地下室 (地階) basement Ⓒ; (地下貯蔵室) cellar Ⓒ

ちかちか ネオンがちかちかと点滅していた A neon sign *flashed on and off*. / 何時間もテレビゲームをやったので目がちかちかする(→痛い) After playing a video game for hours, my eyes are *sore*.

ちかぢか 近々 ➔ ちかく(近く), まもなく

ちかづき 近付き お近づきになれてうれしく思います I'm glad *to meet you*. / お近づきのしるしに一杯やりましょう Let's *seal our new friendship* with a drink.

ちかづく 近付く

❶【場所・状態などに】approach ⓗⒺ, get* near [close], come* up to ...
頂上に近づくにつれて傾斜はきつくなった The slope increased as we *approached* [*got near* (*to*)] the top.
ここ数日の大雨で川の水は警戒水位に近づいている The river water *is getting near* the danger level due to the heavy rain these past few days.
台風が本州に近づいている A typhoon *is approaching* [*getting closer to*] the mainland of Japan.
彼は私に近づいてきて自己紹介した He *came up to* me and introduced himself.
◆彼の作品は完成に近づいている(→間もなく完成する) His work will *be finished soon*./ (→ほとんど完成している) His work *is almost finished*. / おりに近づかないこと(→離れていろ) *Keep* [*Stay*] *away from* the cage.

❷【時期・時間が】approach ⓗⒺ, come* soon; (だんだん)〖文語〗draw* (near)
決断を下さねばならない時が近づいている The time *is approaching* when we must make a decision.
試合の日が近づいている The day of our match *is* 「*coming soon* [*drawing near*, *near at hand*].
夜が近づいてきた Night *drew on*.
◆夏休みも終わりに近づいてきた The summer vacation *is coming* [*drawing*] *to an end*.

❸【関わる】
あの人には近づかないほうがいいよ You should *keep* [*stay*] *away from* that man.
彼は近づきにくい人だ He's *difficult to ap-*

ちかづける 近付ける 売り上げを目標額に近づける try to get closer to a sales target / 彼はいすを引いてテーブルに近づけた He drew his chair closer [nearer] to the table. / 子供をこのあたりに近づけないでください Don't let the children come near here. / (→離しておく) Keep the children away from here. / この素材は火に近づけてもすぐには引火しません Even if you put this material close to the fire, it won't ignite easily.

ちがった 違った (異なる) different; (間違った) wrong ⇒ちがう

ちかてつ 地下鉄 《米》 subway ⓒ, 《英》 the underground; (ロンドンの) the tube; (特にパリなどの) metro ⓒ (しばしば Metro) 《通例単数形》 / 私は地下鉄で通学している I go to school by subway. (✦by の後では無冠詞)

ちかどう 地下道 underground passage ⓒ, 《英》 subway ⓒ; (坑道) tunnel ⓒ

ちかば 近場 こんな近場でバーベキューが楽しめるとは思わなかった I never knew we could enjoy a barbecue so close to our house.

ちかみち 近道 近道をする take a shortcut / これが家へ帰るいちばんの近道です This is the shortest way home.

ちかよりがたい 近寄り難い 彼女は美しすぎて近寄りがたいほどだ She's unapproachably beautiful.

ちかよる 近寄る come* [get*] close, come [get] near ⇒ちかづく / 私は彼に，それ以上近寄るなと叫んだ I shouted at him not to come any closer.

ことわざ 君子危うきに近寄らず ⇒くんし

ちから 力
❶ 【体力】 (physical) strength Ⓤ, power Ⓤ, force Ⓤⓒ

力をこめてボールをける kick a ball with all one's strength [might] / 力比べをする have a contest of strength / 力をつける build up one's strength / 力を合わせる join forces

この扉をあけるにはかなり力がいる It takes a lot of strength [energy] to open this door.

そのテーブルを1人で動かせるほどの力はない I 「don't have the strength [am not strong enough] to move the table by myself.

◆力の強い[弱い]人 a strong [weak] person / もっと力を入れて引っぱれよ Pull it harder. / 肩の力を抜くために深呼吸をした I took a deep breath to relax.

❷ 【能力・力量】 ability Ⓤⓒ, energy Ⓤ
英語の力がつく improve one's (ability in) English / 力を発揮する show one's ability / 自分の力を過信する be overconfident of one's own ability

彼にはその問題を解く力はない He 「doesn't have the ability [is not able] to solve the problem.

彼女は持てる力すべてを社会福祉にささげた She spent all her energy on social welfare.

力の及ぶ限り協力します I'll help you to the best of my ability [abilities].

◆力のある(→有能な)人 an able person / 彼女は自分の力だけでそれを成しとげた She's done it alone [by herself, on her own]. / 成功するために我々は力を合わせる(→共に努力する)べきだ We must work together in order that we may succeed. / 私はまだ英語を書く力が足りない I'm not able to write English well yet. / 数学では彼のほうが私より力が上だ He's more than a match for me in math. / 民子さんは英語の力がある(→得意だ) Tamiko is good at English.

❸ 【気力・元気】 strength Ⓤ; (活力) energy Ⓤ 《また複数形 energies》 ⇒ちからなく
仕事に力を注ぐ put one's energy [energies] into one's work / 力を使い果たす use up all one's energy [force] / 力が尽きる have all one's energy used up; (→息を引き取る) breathe one's last / 試合に備えて力を蓄える save one's energy for a match / 力を奮い起こす summon up one's strength

生きる力がわいてきた The strength to live came from within.

今晩宿題を終わらせなきゃいけないのに、もうそんな力は残ってない I have to finish my homework tonight, but I haven't got the energy [strength] left anymore.

◆力のない声 a weak voice

❹ 【助力・尽力】 (助け) help Ⓤⓒ, aid Ⓤⓒ; (支え) support Ⓤ
力になってほしいんだ I need your help.
他人の力は借りない I don't want any help. / I'm not going to ask for anybody's help.

◆いつでも力になるよ I'm always ready to help. / 彼の力で(→おかげで)そのごたごたは丸く収まった Thanks to him the quarrel was settled peacefully.

❺ 【暴力・勢力・権力】 power Ⓤ, force ⓒⓊ; (影響力) influence Ⓤⓒ
力で暴動を鎮圧する put down a riot by force / 力に訴える resort to force / 日米の力関係 the power balance between Japan and the United States

彼は人事に関して大きな力を握っている He has a lot of power over personnel matters.
その会社はある政治家の力を使って契約を取りつけた The company used a politician's influence to get the contract.

◆力のある国 a powerful [an influential] nation

❻ 【威力・効力】
自然の力を思い知る realize fully the forces of nature / 動力源として風の力を利用する harness wind as a source of energy
この車は電気の力で走る This car runs on electricity.
彼女は薬の力を借りないと眠れない She can't sleep without the help of a (sleeping) drug.
私は意志の力でその困難を乗り越えた I got over the difficulty by willpower.

彼はいつも金の力で人を動かそうとする He always *tries to buy people.*

❼【努力】

君はもう少し英語の勉強に力を入れたほうがいいね You should *put* a little more *effort into* studying English.

私たちの英語の先生は文法に力を入れている（→重視している）Our English teacher *puts* [*lays*] *emphasis on* grammar.

‖力うどん *udon* topped with *mochi* / 力仕事（重労働）heavy labor [work]；（肉体労働）physical [manual] labor

ちからいっぱい 力一杯 ボールを力一杯けとばす kick a ball「*as hard as one can* [*with all one's strength*]

ちからこぶ 力瘤（二頭筋）biceps [C]（複～）‖（腕を曲げて）力こぶを作る flex *one's biceps*

ちからずく 力尽く 力ずくで戸をあける *force* the door open / 私はその金を力ずくで取り返した I got back the money *by force.*

ちからぞえ 力添え お力添え願いたいのですが I'd like to ask for *your help* [*aid, support*].

ちからだめし 力試し（体力の）a test of *one's* strength；（能力の）a test of *one's* ability ‖彼は力試しにそのコンテストに応募した He entered the contest「*as a test of* [*to test*] *his ability.*

ちからづける 力付ける（勇気づける）encourage [他]；（元気づける）cheer up ⇨はげます

ちからづよい 力強い powerful, strong；（頼りになる）reliable ‖力強い演説 a *powerful* [*forceful*] speech ◆君が我々のチームに加わってくれると力強い We *will feel* more *reassured* if you join our team. / この参考書は私のように英語が不得意な者の力強い味方だ This study guide is *a great help* for someone as poor at English as I am.

ちからなく 力なく 彼は私の質問に力なく答えた He answered my question *feebly* [*weakly*].

ちからまかせ 力任せ 彼女は力まかせに私を殴りつけた She hit me「*with all her strength* [*as hard as possible*].

ちからもち 力持ち strong man [C] ◆縁の下の力持ち *an unsung hero* [*heroine*]

ちかん[1] 痴漢 groper [C], molester [C]；（変質者）pervert [C] ‖きょう電車で痴漢にあった *A groper* molested me on the train today.

ちかん[2] 置換（置き換えること）replacing [U]；〔化学〕substitution [U] ——置換する replace [他]；〔化学〕substitute [他]

ちき 知己（親友）good friend [C]；（知人）acquaintance [C]

ちきゅう 地球 (the) Earth, the earth, the globe（❖地球が「丸い」ことを強調する），the [our, this] planet

地球上の全人類 all the human beings *on the earth* / 地球にやさしい製品 *earth-friendly* products

◆地球規模の問題 *global* problems

‖地球温暖化 global warming / 地球儀 a globe / 地球人 an earthling（❖SF小説などで用いる）/ 地球物理学 geophysics

ちぎょ 稚魚 fry [C]（複～）

ちぎる 千切る（引きちぎる）tear* [téər] [他]；（小さく分ける）break* up ‖紙の端をちぎる *tear* the edge *off* a piece of paper / パンをちぎってハトにやった I *broke up* some bread and gave it to the doves.

ちぎれる 千切れる（裂ける）tear* [téər] [自]，be torn off；（取れる）come* off ‖紙袋の持ち手がちぎれてしまった The handle of the paper bag *tore* [*came*] *off.*

◆耳がちぎれそうなほどの寒さだった It was so cold that my ears nearly *fell off.*

チキン chicken [U] ‖チキンライス chicken pilaf（❖「チキンライス」は和製英語）

ちく 地区 area [C]；（行政上の）district [C]；（ある特定の人々の住む）quarter [C]；（特色のある）zone [C] ‖関東地区 *the* Kanto *district*

‖工業地区 an industrial area / 住宅地区 a residential area / 商業地区 a commercial area, a business district

ちくいち 逐一（一つ一つ）one by one；（詳細に）in detail ‖彼はそこで起こったことを逐一報告した He reported what had happened there *one by one.*

ちくごやく 逐語訳 literal translation [C] ——逐語訳する translate ... literally [word by word]

ちくざい 蓄財 saving [U] [C] ——蓄財する save (up)

ちくさん 畜産 stock raising [farming] [U], stockbreeding [U] ‖畜産業者 a stockbreeder / 畜産物 stock farm products

ちくじ 逐次（一つ一つ）one by one；（次々と）one after another

ちくしょう 畜生（けだもの）beast [C], brute [C]；（悪態）Damn (it)!, Son of a bitch!, Fuck it!, Shit!（❖これらはかなり強い言葉なので人前で使うべきではないとされる）

ちくせき 蓄積 accumulation [U] [C] ——蓄積する accumulate [他] [自]；（蓄える）store (up) ‖知識の蓄積 *the accumulation* of knowledge ◆疲労が蓄積して彼は倒れた He got sick because of *a buildup* of fatigue.

チクタク チクタクと時を刻む *tick the minutes* / 時計がチクタクいう音しか聞こえなかった I only heard「*the tick-tock* of a clock [*the ticking* of a clock].

ちくちく ちくちくする痛み *pricking* pain / この毛布は少しちくちくする This blanket *tickles* [*prickles*] a little.

ちくのうしょう 蓄膿症〔医学〕empyema [U]

ちぐはぐ 彼は言うこととすることがいつもちぐはぐだ（→一貫していない）What he says *is* always *inconsistent with* what he does. / その靴とスーツ，何だかちぐはぐだね（→靴がスーツと合わない）Your shoes *don't* seem to *match* [*go well with*] the suit.

ちくび 乳首（人の）nipple [C]；（動物の）teat [C]；（ほ乳びんの）《米》nipple [C]，《英》teat [C]

ちくり ちくりちくりといやみを言う make some *stinging* remarks / 彼女は誤って針で親指をちくりと刺してしまった She accidentally *pricked* her thumb with a needle. / ハ

チに指をちくりとやられた I *was stung* on the finger by a bee.

ちくる 彼が僕のことを先生にちくった He *snitched* [*told*] *on* me to the teacher.

ちくわ 竹輪 a *chikuwa*, a tube-shaped fish sausage

ちけい 地形 natural [geographical] features, topography Ⓤ ‖地形学 topography, geomorphology / 地形図 a topographical map

チケット ticket Ⓒ ⇒ きっぷ

ちけん 知見 (知識) knowledge Ⓤ; (情報) information Ⓤ ‖知見を広める expand *one's knowledge*

ちこう 地溝 〖地理〗rift valley Ⓒ

ちこく 遅刻 ──遅刻する be late

何分[どれくらい]遅刻したの How *late* were you?

きのうは学校に15分遅刻しちゃった I *was* 15 minutes *late for* school yesterday.

彼は約束の時間に遅刻してきた He *came late to* the appointment.

‖遅刻者 a latecomer / 遅刻届 a written excuse for being late

ちし¹ 地誌 (local) topography Ⓤ, a geographical description of an area ‖地誌学 topography

ちし² 致死 ‖致死量(薬の) a lethal dose / 過失致死罪 accidental homicide

ちじ 知事 (prefectural) governor Ⓒ 《しばしば Governor》《(略記)Gov.》‖岩手県知事 *the Governor* of Iwate

ちしき 知識 knowledge Ⓤ 《また a ~》; (情報) information Ⓤ

┌─ コロケーション ─────────────
│ **-knowledge-**
│ 〖形容詞＋~〗浅い~ superficial knowledge / 限られた~ limited knowledge / 完全な~ thorough knowledge / 基礎的な~ elementary [basic] knowledge / 初歩的な~ rudimentary knowledge / 正確な~ accurate knowledge / 専門的な~ specialized knowledge / 広い~ extensive knowledge / 深い~ profound knowledge / 不完全な~ imperfect knowledge / わずかな~ slight knowledge
└─────────────────────

知識を広げる expand [enlarge] *one's knowledge* / 知識を吸収する absorb [soak up] *knowledge* / 知識を得る gain [acquire] *knowledge*

彼はアメリカの文化に関する知識が豊富だ He has a good *knowledge* of American culture./ He's well *informed about* American culture.

私はその画家に関する知識が多少ある[ほとんどない、全くない] I have some [little, no] *knowledge* of the painter.

この本は環境問題に関する知識をたくさん与えてくれる This book gives a lot of *information on* [*about*] environmental problems.

彼は読書で知識を増やした He increased *his knowledge* by reading.

‖知識階級 the educated class(es), the intelligentsia / 知識人 an intellectual; (教養のある人) an educated person / 知識欲 a thirst for knowledge / 予備知識 background [preliminary] knowledge

ちじく 地軸 the earth's axis

ちしつ 地質 (土質) the nature of the soil; (地質学的特徴) geological features, geology Ⓤ

‖地質学 geology / 地質学者 a geologist / 地質調査 a geological survey

ちしま 千島 (千島列島) the Kuril(e)s, the Kuril(e) Islands

ちじょう 地上 (地面) the ground; (大地) earth Ⓤ; (地表) the surface of the earth ──地上の (この世の) earthly; (地表の) surface

地上最大の都市 the largest city *on earth* / 地上の楽園 an *earthly* paradise; a paradise *on earth*

◆このビルは地上40階、地下3階だ This building has 40 stories *above ground* and 3 below.

‖地上管制〖航空〗ground control / 地上軍 ground troops / 地上波放送 terrestrial broadcasting

ちじょく 恥辱 shame Ⓤ, humiliation Ⓤ Ⓒ, disgrace Ⓤ ⇒ くつじょく、はじ

ちじん 知人 acquaintance Ⓒ ⇒ しりあい

ちず 地図 map Ⓒ; (地図帳) atlas Ⓒ; (海図・航空図) chart Ⓒ

市街地図 a city *map* / 世界地図 a world *map* [*atlas*]; a *map* of the world / 道路地図 a road *map* [*atlas*] / 日本地図 a *map* of Japan / 白地図 a blank *map* / 5,000分の1の縮尺の地図 a *map* with [on] the scale of 1 to 5,000 / 地図で富士山を探す look up Mt. Fuji on *a map*

彼は駅までの地図をかいてくれた He drew me *a map* to the station.

自分の家がその地図では見つからなかった I couldn't locate my house on the *map*.

この地図の見方を教えて Please tell me how to read [use] this *map*.

私たちの学校はこの地図に出ていない Our school is not (shown) on this *map*.

地図のその場所に×印をつけた I marked the place on *the map* with an X.

地図を頼りにやっと彼の家にたどり着いた I managed to get to his home *with the help of a map*.

ちすい 治水 (洪水調節) flood control Ⓤ

‖治水工事[事業] a flood control project / 治水ダム a dam for flood control

ちすじ 血筋 blood Ⓤ; (家系) stock Ⓤ Ⓒ ⇒ けっとう(血統)、ち(血) ‖彼は血筋がいい He comes from good *stock*. / 血筋は争えない *Blood will tell*.

ちせい¹ 知性 (感情・意志に対する) intellect Ⓒ Ⓤ; (理解力) intelligence Ⓤ ──知性的な intellectual; intelligent ‖すぐれた知性の持ち主 a person of superior *intellect* [*intelligence*]

ちせい¹ 彼は知性に欠けている He lacks *intelligence*.

ちせい² 治世 reign [réin] ⓒ ∥その王の治世は半世紀に及んだ The king's *reign* lasted half a century.

ちせつ 稚拙 ──**稚拙な** (下手な・未熟な) poor ∥稚拙な文章 a *poor* piece of writing

ちそう 地層 〖地質〗stratum ⓒ (複 strata) ∥白亜紀の地層 a Cretaceous *stratum*
∥地層学 stratigraphy

ちたい 地帯 (地域) area ⓒ, region ⓒ; (用途・特徴によって区分された) zone ⓒ, belt ⓒ ∥工業地帯 an industrial *area* ∥ (道路中央の) 安全地帯 (米)a safety *zone* [*island*]; a traffic island

チタン 〖化学〗titanium Ⓤ (❖元素記号 Ti)

ちち¹ 父
father ⓒ; (創始者) the father
父の日 *Father's* Day ∥ 父親になる become *a father*
彼女は日本人の父とアメリカ人の母から生まれた She was born of a Japanese *father* and an American mother.
彼は2児の父親だ He「is *the father* of [has] two children.
ハイドンは「交響曲の父」と呼ばれている Haydn is called "*the Father* of the Symphony."
◆父親のいない子供 a *fatherless* child ∥ 父親らしい態度 a *fatherly* attitude
ことわざ この父にしてこの子あり Like father, like son.

ちち² 乳
milk Ⓤ; (乳房) breast ⓒ
赤ん坊に乳を飲ませる give a baby *the breast*; *nurse* a baby ∥ 乳を飲む take [(→吸う) *suck*] *the breast*
◆砂漠に住む人々はラクダの乳を搾(ﾋﾞ)る Desert people *milk* camels. ∥ この牛は乳の出がいい This cow *milks* well.
∥乳搾り milking

ちちおや 父親 father ⓒ ➡ちち(父)

ちちかた 父方 彼は父方のいとこです He's「my cousin *on my father's side* [my *paternal* cousin].

ちぢこまる 縮こまる (しりごみする) shrink* ⓐ; (丸まる) curl up ∥彼は縮こまって眠った He curled up and fell asleep.

ちちばなれ 乳離れ ──**乳離れする** be weaned; (自立する) become* independent
◆彼はまだ乳離れしていない He's still *dependent on his parents*. ∥ He still *hasn't cut the (umbilical) cord*. (❖umbilical card は「へその緒」の意味)

ちぢまる 縮まる トップとの差はなかなか縮まらなかった I couldn't easily *reduce* the gap behind the leader. ➡ちぢめる

ちぢみ 縮み shrinkage Ⓤ ∥ほとんど伸び縮みしない生地 material with little *stretch*

ちぢみあがる 縮み上がる shrink* ⓐ, cower ⓐ ∥我々は彼のけんまくに縮みあがってしまい，何も言えなかった We *shrank* [*cowered*] at his angry look and were speechless.

ちぢむ 縮む shrink* ⓐ; (短くなる・背が低くなる) get* short
このセーターは洗濯すると縮むかもしれない This sweater may *shrink* in the wash.
父は近ごろ少し背が縮んだようだ My father seems to *be getting* a little *shorter* these days.
◆赤ちゃんが階段の上で遊んでいるのを見て命の縮む思いがした I *was scared to death* [It *scared the life out of* me] when I saw a baby playing at the top of the stairs.

ちぢめる 縮める (短くする) shorten ⓑ, cut* short; (要約する) condense ⓑ; (削減する) reduce ⓑ
命を縮める *shorten one's* life ∥ スカートの丈(ﾀｹ)を縮める *shorten* (the length of) a skirt ∥ 滞在を5日 [5日に] 縮める *cut short one's* stay "by five days [to five days]
◆ 世界記録を5秒縮める *better* [*beat*] the world record by five seconds; *clip* five seconds off the world record ∥ 首を縮めてボールをよけた I *ducked* (my head) to avoid the ball.

ちちゅう 地中 電線を地中に埋める bury power lines in the *ground* [*earth*] ∥ 地中から(→地中に埋まっている) 財宝が見つかった Treasure was found buried in *the ground* [*earth*].

ちちゅうかい 地中海 the Mediterranean (Sea) ∥地中海の島々 *Mediterranean* islands ∥地中海性気候 a *Mediterranean* climate

ちぢれげ 縮れ毛 curly [frizzy] hair ⓒ

ちぢれる 縮れる (丸まる) curl ⓐ ∥彼女の髪は縮れている She has *curly* [*frizzy*] hair.

ちつ 膣 〖解剖〗vagina ⓒ

ちつじょ 秩序 order Ⓤ ∥法と秩序 law and *order* ∥ 秩序を乱す disturb [upset] *order* ∥ 秩序を確立する establish *order* ∥ 社会秩序を保つ maintain public [social] *order* ∥ その地域の秩序はようやく回復した At last *order* was restored in the area. ◆その都市は戦争ですっかり秩序を失ってしまった The city *has been thrown into* complete *disorder* by the war. ∥ その仕事はもっと秩序立ったやり方でするべきだ We should do that work "*in a more systematic way* [more *systematically*].

ちっそ 窒素 〖化学〗nitrogen Ⓤ (❖元素記号 N) ∥窒素酸化物 nitrogen oxide ∥ 窒素肥料 nitrogenous fertilizer

ちっそく 窒息 suffocation Ⓤ ──**窒息する [させる]** (酸素不足で) suffocate ⓐ ⓑ (❖自動詞は進行形で用いる); (首をしめられたり) choke ⓐ ⓑ ∥煙に巻かれて窒息(死)しそうだった I *was* almost *suffocated* by the smoke. ∥ えりがきつくて窒息しそうだ The tight collar *is choking* me. ∥ 彼女はもちをのどに詰まらせて窒息(死)しかけた She nearly *choked to death* on mochi.

ちっとも この前会ったときと君はちっとも変わってないね You've *not* changed *at all* since we last met. ∥ 君が彼と結婚するなんてちっとも知らなかった I *never* knew you were going to marry him. ∥ 彼の言うことなんかちっとも気にならない I *don't* care *a bit* about

what he says.
- 「寒くない?」「ちっとも」 "Aren't you cold?" "No, *not at all*."

チップ (心づけ) tip ⓒ; (集積回路) chip ⓒ; (野球の) tip ⓒ ∥チップを置いていく leave *a tip* / ドアボーイに1ドルチップをあげた I gave the doorman one dollar as *a tip*. / I tipped the doorman one dollar. / (ウェーターなどに)はい, チップです Here's *a tip* for you.
◆ボールをファウルチップする *tip* a ball *foul* / ウェートレスにチップをやってください Please *remember* the waitress.

ちてい 地底 the depth of the earth

ちてき 知的 ──知的な (知性を要する・教養のある) intellectual; (聡明の) intelligent ∥知的な人 an *intellectual* [*intelligent*] person; a person *of intellect* [*intelligence*] / 知的水準 *intellectual* standard / 彼は知的好奇心が旺盛(おうせい)だ He's full of *intellectual curiosity*. / 彼女は知的な顔をしている She looks *intelligent*.
∥知的所有権 *intellectual* property rights / 知的能力 mental faculties

ちてん 地点 (点) point ⓒ; (場所) spot ⓒ / 出発[ゴール]地点 *the* starting [finishing, winning] *point* / そのランナーはスタートから40キロ地点でトップに立った The runner shot ahead at *the* 40 kilometer *point* [*mark*]. / 川はこの地点で2つに分かれる The river divides into two at this *point*.

ちどうせつ 地動説 the heliocentric system; (コペルニクス説) the Copernican system

ちどりあし 千鳥足 酔っ払いが千鳥足で通りを歩いていた A drunken man *was staggering* [*reeling*] along the street.

ちなまぐさい 血生臭い 血なまぐさい事件 a *gruesome* [*gory*] incident

ちなみに 因みに (ところで) by the way, incidentally ∥ちなみに試合には勝ったんですか *By the way*, did you win the game?

ちなむ 因む …にちなんだ(→関係した) 話題 a topic *related to* … / …にちなんだ(→祝う) 行事 an event *in celebration of* … / 彼女はおばにちなんで洋子と名づけられた She was named Yoko *after* her aunt.

ちねつ 地熱 subterranean heat ⓤ, the heat from inside the earth
∥地熱発電 geothermal power generation

ちのう 知能 intelligence ⓤ ∥高い[低い]知能 high [low] *intelligence* / チンパンジーは高度な知能をもつといわれている Chimpanzees are said to「have a high degree of *intelligence* [be very *intelligent*]. / 知能の遅れた子供たち *mentally retarded* children
∥知能指数 an intelligence quotient (《略語》IQ) / 知能テスト an intelligence [a mental] test / 知能犯(犯罪) an intellectual crime, a white-collar crime; (人)an intellectual criminal

ちのけ 血の気 血の気の多い男 a *hot-blooded* man / 彼女の顔から血の気がうせた She turned pale. / The blood [color] drained from her face.

ちのみご 乳飲み子 (unweaned) baby ⓒ, infant ⓒ

ちのり 地の利 我々の会社はライバル会社に比べて地の利を得ている Our company has *a geographical advantage* over our rivals.

ちば 千葉

千葉県は本州中央部に位置し、太平洋に面しています。気候は一般的に穏やかで、県のあちこちには市場向け野菜の畑や牧場が、水田と同様に多く見られます。成田市には新東京国際空港があり、日本の国際的な窓口として重要な役割を果たしています。観光名所として、東京ディズニーランドが1983年に開業しました。
Chiba Prefecture is located in central Honshu on the Pacific Ocean. The climate is in general mild, and there are truck farms and dairy farms as well as rice fields here and there. The New Tokyo International Airport in Narita plays a key role in international air transport in Japan. A major attraction is Tokyo Disneyland, which opened in 1983.

ちばしる 血走る 血走った目 *bloodshot* eyes / 興奮で彼の目は血走っていた His eyes *were bloodshot* from excitement.

ちばなれ 乳離れ ⇒ ちちばなれ

ちび (背の低い人) small [short] person ⓒ, 《軽蔑的》 shorty ⓒ; (がき) brat ⓒ

ちびちび (少しずつ) little by little; (節約して) sparingly
◆ウイスキーをちびちび飲む *sip* whiskey / クッキーをちびちび食べる *nibble* a cookie

ちびっこ ちびっ子 little kid [child] ⓒ

ちひょう 地表 the surface of the earth

ちびる ちびた靴 *worn-out* shoes / ちびた鉛筆(→鉛筆の使い残り) a pencil stub / 出費をちびる *skimp on* expenses / 小便をちびる 《米口語的》*wet one's pants*

ちぶ 恥部 (陰部) private parts, genitals; (不名誉) disgrace ⓤ

ちぶさ 乳房 breast ⓒ

チフス 〖医学〗(腸チフス) typhoid ⓤ; (発疹(ほっしん)チフス) typhus ⓤ; (パラチフス) paratyphoid ⓤ

ちへいせん 地平線 the horizon ∥太陽が地平線の下に沈んだ[の上に昇った] The sun has *sunk below* [*risen above*] *the horizon*.

ちほう¹ 地方

❶【地域】area ⓒ; (行政上の・ある特色をもった) district ⓒ; (特徴による区分) region ⓒ; (部分) part ⓒ
関東地方 *the* Kanto *area* [*district*]
この地方では雪はめったに降らない It rarely snows in this *region* [*district*].
この虫は地方によって名前が違う This insect is called differently *from region to region*.
◆地方色豊かな小説 a novel with much *local color* [*character*] / 地方特有のなまり a *region-*

ちほう

al dialect [accent]

❷ 〔中央に対する〕 the provinces; (田園地方) the country ⇨ いなか

‖ 地方行政 local administration [government] / 地方銀行 a local bank / 地方検察庁 a district (public) prosecutor's office / 地方公務員 a local government employee / 地方債 a local [municipal] government bond / 地方裁判所 a district court / 地方紙 a local paper / 地方自治(体) (a) local government / 地方税 local taxes / 地方政治 local politics / 地方選挙 a municipal election / 地方都市 a provincial city

ちほう² 痴呆 〔医学〕 dementia Ⓤ ――痴呆の demented ‖ 老人性痴呆症 senile dementia

ちまき 粽 a *chimaki*, a rice confection wrapped in bamboo leaves

ちまた 巷 ちまたの声（=世論） *public* opinion ◆ ちまたのうわさではあの会社は経営難らしい *People say* [*Rumor has it*] *that* that company is in financial difficulties.

ちまなこ 血眼 彼女は落とした指輪を血眼になって捜していた She was looking *desperately* [*frantically*] for the ring she dropped.

ちまみれ 血塗れ 血まみれのシャツ a *bloody* [*bloodstained*] shirt / 彼は血まみれで倒れているところを発見された He was found lying *in a pool of blood*.

ちまめ 血豆 blood blister Ⓒ ‖ 足に血まめができる get *a blood blister* on *one's* foot

ちまよう 血迷う 〔正気を失う〕 go* mad, go out of *one's* mind ◆ 何を血迷ったのか彼は窓から飛び降りようとした *Something came over him*, and he tried to jump out of the window.

ちみつ 緻密 ――緻密な （綿密な） close [klóus]; (精密な) precise; (注意深い) careful; (詳細の) detailed; (手の込んだ) elaborate ‖ 緻密な計画 an *elaborate* [*a detailed*] plan / 緻密な調査を行う make a *careful* [*close*] examination ◆ この推理小説は非常に緻密に構成されている This detective story is very *elaborately* constructed.

ちみどろ 血みどろ 血みどろの戦い a *bloody* [*gory*] battle

ちめい 地名 place name Ⓒ, the name of a place ‖ 地名辞典 a geographical dictionary, a dictionary of place [geographical] names

ちめいしょう 致命傷 致命傷を受ける get *a fatal wound* [*injury*] / 彼はその銃撃戦で致命傷を負った He *was fatally* [*seriously*] *wounded* in the shoot-out. / そのスキャンダルがその政治家にとっての致命傷となった That scandal *was fatal* for the politician.

ちめいてき 致命的 ――致命的な fatal ‖ 致命的なミスを犯す make a *fatal* mistake / その遅れは私たちの計画には致命的だった The delay was *fatal* to our plan.

ちめいど 知名度 知名度の低い女優 a *lesser-known* actress / 彼は日本人としてはアメリカでいちばん知名度の高い映画監督だ He is the *most famous* [*best-known*] Japanese film director in America. / 彼は日本では知名度がない He *is not known* in Japan.

ちゃ 茶 tea Ⓤ (❖英米では紅茶を指す。種類をいう場合は Ⓒ); （緑茶） green tea Ⓤ

薄い, [濃い] 茶 weak [strong] *tea* / 茶を入れる [つぐ] make [pour] *tea*

‖ 茶会 a tea party; (日本の) a tea ceremony party / 茶菓子 a tea cake / 茶がら used tea leaves / 茶器 [茶道具] tea things, a tea service [set] / 茶こし a tea strainer / 茶さじ a teaspoon / 茶室 a tea ceremony room / 茶たく a saucer / 茶だんす a cupboard [kʌ́bərd] (for tea things) / 茶筒 a tea caddy / 茶摘み tea picking / 茶の間 ⇨ちゃのま / 茶柱 ⇨ちゃばしら / 茶畑 a tea field / 茶店 [茶屋] a teahouse / ウーロン茶 oolong tea / 紅茶 (black) tea / ジャスミン茶 jasmine tea / ほうじ茶 roasted tea / 抹茶 powdered green tea / 麦茶 barley tea / 緑茶 green tea ⇨ おちゃ, ちゃいろ

日本茶には様々な種類の茶があります。最も一般的な緑茶は、蒸した茶葉を乾燥させたもので、紅茶のように発酵はさせません。緑茶用の柔らかい葉を摘み取った後の硬い葉や茎を使ったものが番茶、そしてそれをあぶったものがほうじ茶と呼ばれます。ほかにも麦やそば、様々な薬草を使った茶を飲みますが、これらは最近健康によいということで注目されています。
Japanese tea comes in many varieties. *Ryokucha*, the most common green tea, is made by simply steaming and drying leaves without fermenting them like black tea. *Bancha* is made of the tough leaves and twigs left over after the more tender leaves are picked out for green tea, and *hojicha* is made by roasting *bancha*. Barley, buckwheat, other cereals and various herbs are also made into tea and have been more widely considered good for health recently.

チャージ （料金） charge Ⓒ Ⓤ; 〔スポーツ〕 charging Ⓤ ◆ 丸山は終盤で猛チャージをかけたがウッズに2打及ばなかった Maruyama *closed the gap* in the home stretch, but lost to Woods by two strokes.

‖ テーブルチャージ a cover charge / ルームチャージ a room charge

チャーシュー roast pork Ⓤ (❖中国語の発音を英語表記すると chashao となる)

チャーター 飛行機[バス]をチャーターする *charter* a plane [bus] / チャーター機[便] a *charter*(*ed*) plane [flight]

チャート （ヒットチャート） the charts ‖ ヒットチャートの1位になる top *the charts*

チャーハン (Chinese) fried rice Ⓤ

チャーミング charming; (かわいい) pretty

チャイム chime ‖ 玄関のチャイムが鳴った *The chimes* of doorbell rang.

ちゃいろ 茶色 brown Ⓤ ――茶色の brown ‖ こげ茶色 *dark brown* / 茶色っぽい

サングラス *brown-tinted* sunglasses

ちゃかす 茶化す (からかう) make* fun of ...; (冗談にする) turn ... into a joke ∥人を茶化さないで *Don't make fun of* me.

ちゃかっしょく 茶褐色 (dark) brown Ⓤ ―茶褐色の (dark) brown

ちゃきちゃき ちゃきちゃきの江戸っ子 a *true-born* Tokyoite

ちゃく 東京駅2時着の列車 the train *due to arrive* at Tokyo Station at 2 p.m. / 彼女は2着の服を試着した She tried on *two* dresses.
🔊「そのレースで彼は何着だったのですか」「2着です」 "Where did he *finish* in the race?" "He *finished* [*came in*] second."

ちゃくがん 着眼 君はいいところに着眼したね (→ 見るべきところを知っている) You *know where to look*./ (→ねらいは正しい) Your *aim is right*.
∥着眼点 a viewpoint, a point of view

ちゃくし 嫡子 (跡取り) heir [éər] Ⓒ; (嫡出子) legitimate child Ⓒ

ちゃくじつ 着実 ―着実な steady ―着実に steadily ∥着実な進歩 *steady* progress / 着実な進歩 steady progress / 物価の上昇はゆっくりだが着実に進んでいる The rise in prices is gradual but *steady*./ 彼女の英語力は着実に伸びていった Her English ability *steadily* improved.

ちゃくしゅ 着手 ―着手する (始める) start ⓐ, begin* ⓐ; (取りかかる) set* about ... ∥警察はようやくその事件の捜査に着手した At last the police 「*began* to investigate [*set about* investigating] the case.

ちゃくしょく 着色 coloring, 《英》colouring Ⓤ ―着色する color ⓐ, (塗る) paint ⓐ ∥(表示で)合成着色料使用 Contains Artificial *Coloring*

ちゃくせき 着席 ―着席する sit* down, take* a [*one's*] seat ∥ご着席ください Please *take* [*have*] *a seat*./ Please *be seated*.

ちゃくそう 着想 idea Ⓒ ∥この着想はおもしろいが実現にはもうひと工夫必要だ This *idea* is interesting, but you need a little more of something in order to realize it.
◆彼はその古い物語に着想を得てこの小説を書いた *Inspired by* the old story, he wrote this novel.

ちゃくだつ 着脱 このエアコンはフィルターの着脱が簡単だ It's easy to *attach and remove* this air conditioner's filter.

ちゃくち 着地 landing Ⓒ Ⓤ ―着地する land ⓐ ∥飛行機は無事着地した The plane *landed* safely./ その選手は着地をきれいに決めた The gymnast made *a beautiful landing*.

ちゃくちゃくと 着々と (着実に) steadily; (一歩一歩) step by step ∥文化祭の準備は着々と進んでいる The preparations for our school festival are 「*progressing steadily* [*making steady progress*].

ちゃくにん 着任 新しい先生が着任した The new teacher *arrived at his* [*her*] *post*.

ちゃくばらい 着払い cash (collect) on delivery (《略語》C.O.D.) ◆この品物の代金は着払いでいいですか Can I *pay* for this article 「*on delivery* [*when it is delivered*]?

ちゃくふく 着服 ―着服する pocket ⓐ; (横領する) embezzle ⓐ ∥公金を着服する *pocket* [*embezzle*] public money

ちゃくメロ 着メロ ring tone

ちゃくもく 着目 ―着目する pay* attention to ... ∥彼らは新事実に着目した They 「*paid attention to* [*focused their attention on*] the new facts.

ちゃくよう 着用 ―着用する (着ている) wear* ⓐ, (着る) put* on ∥式には制服を着用すること You should *wear* your school uniforms to the ceremony.
◆シートベルトを着用して(→締めて)ください *Fasten* your seat belt.

ちゃくりく 着陸 landing Ⓒ Ⓤ ―着陸する land ⓐ, make* a landing; (特に飛行機が) touch down ∥その飛行機は午後9時に無事着陸した The plane *landed* [*touched down*] safely at 9 p.m./ 宇宙飛行士たちの月面着陸は世界中に大きな興奮を呼び起こした The astronauts' *landing on the moon* caused great excitement all over the world./ 飛行機は着陸態勢に入った The airplane began *its approach for landing*./ 飛行機は成田空港に緊急着陸した The plane *made an emergency landing* at Narita Airport.
∥胴体着陸 (a) belly landing / 軟着陸 a soft landing / 無着陸飛行 a nonstop flight

ちゃち ―ちゃちな (安物の) cheap; (質の悪い) poor; (みすぼらしい) shabby; (見せかけだけの) shoddy ∥ちゃちな時計 a *cheap* watch ◆この家は造りがちゃちだ This house is *shoddily* built.

ちゃっかり 彼女は本当にちゃっかりしているよ (→抜け目ない) She is really *shrewd*./ 彼はちゃっかり(→ずうずうしくも)うちで食事をして帰った He *had the nerve* to eat at my house and then just go home.

チャック ⚠《主に米》zipper Ⓒ, fastener Ⓒ (❖「チャック」は日本の商標名) ◆ジャンパーのチャックを上げる[下ろす]「*zip up* [*unzip*] a jacket / 彼女はかばんのチャックをあけて財布を取り出した She *zipped open* her bag and took out her wallet.

ちゃづけ 茶漬け ⇒おちゃづけ

ちゃっこう 着工 新しい駅は9月に着工される *The construction* of the new station *will be started* in September.

ちゃのま 茶の間 (居間) living room Ⓒ, 《米》family room Ⓒ, 《主に英》sitting room Ⓒ (❖英米では家族がくつろぐ living room と食事をする dining room が分かれているので「茶の間」にぴったり当てはまる訳語はない)

ちゃばしら 茶柱 tea stem Ⓒ ∥茶柱が立っている *The tea stem* is floating on end in my cup.

ちゃばつ 茶髪 *chapatsu*, brown dyed hair

ちゃばん 茶番 farce Ⓒ ∥その合併はとんだ茶番だった The merger was *a real farce*.

チャペル chapel

ちゃぼ 矮鶏 〖鳥〗bantam

ちやほや 彼女はちやほやされて(→みんなにもてはやされて)いい気になっているようだ She seems to have become conceited because everyone *makes a big fuss over* her. / 彼は両親にちやほやされて(→甘やかされて)育った He *was spoiled* [*pampered*] by his parents when he was growing up.

ちゃめ 茶目 めいはとてもお茶目な(→ふざけているがかわいい)子だ My niece is a very *playful* [*いたずらっぽい*) *mischievous*] (*but cute*) girl. / 彼女は失敗したとき茶目っ気たっぷりに舌を出してみせた She stuck out her tongue *playfully* when she failed.

ちゃらちゃら ちゃらちゃらした格好をする(→はでな服を着ている) wear *showy* [*gaudy*] clothes / 男はポケットの中の小銭をちゃらちゃらいわせた The man *rattled* the coins in his pocket.

ちゃらんぽらん 彼女の言うことはいつもちゃらんぽらんだ(→無責任なことを言う) She always says *irresponsible things*. / 彼はちゃらんぽらんに(→いいかげんに)仕事をする He works *sloppily*.

チャリティー charity ‖ チャリティーコンサート a charity concert / チャリティーショー a charity show / チャリティーバザー a charity bazaar

ちゃりん かぎが床に落ちてちゃりんと音を立てた A key fell to the floor with *a clink*.

チャレンジ ⚠ (挑戦) try ――チャレンジする (物事に) try (取り組む) tackle ✦**challenge** は「人・組織に挑戦する」の意味。‖ 難しい問題にチャレンジする *tackle* a difficult problem / 今年の夏は山登りにチャレンジするつもりです I'll *try to* climb the mountain this summer.
◆彼女はチャレンジ精神旺盛(おう)だ She is full of *adventure*.

ちゃわん 茶碗 (食事用の) (rice) bowl; (湯のみ) teacup ‖ 茶わんにごはんをよそう serve rice *in a bowl* / 茶わん1杯のごはんを食べる eat *a bowl of* rice
‖ 茶わん蒸し a *chawammushi*, an egg dish steamed in a bowl

-ちゃん ❶【名前につける場合】

> 語法
> (1)「…ちゃん」は日本独特の表現なので、日本の名前を英語の中で用いるときは、呼び捨てがふつう。-chan の形をそのまま用いることもあるが、日本語に通じた人に対してしか通じない。‖ 真理ちゃん、何してるの Mari, what are you doing? / 賢ちゃん、元気だった? Ken-*chan*, how have you been?
> (2)英語の名前には、「…ちゃん」に相当するものとして、慣用的な愛称がある。例えば Michael には Mickey や Mike, Catherine には Cathy や Kate など。

❷【家族につける場合】お父ちゃん Dad; Daddy / お母ちゃん Mom; Mommy / おじちゃん Grandpa; Granddad / おばあちゃん Grandma; Grannie / おじちゃん Uncle / おばちゃん Aunt; Auntie (✦「お兄ちゃん」「お姉ちゃん」は本人の名前には愛称を用いる)

チャンス chance; opportunity

> chance: 予期せずにめぐってきたという偶然性の度合いが高いものを指す。
> opportunity: 意図的に作り出した機会というニュアンスがある。

千載一遇のチャンス *a chance* in a million
チャンスをつかむ seize *a chance*
まだ彼らが試合に勝つチャンスはある They still have *a chance* of winning the game.
チャンスがあればそこに行ってみたい If I have *a chance*, I would like to go there.
もう一度チャンスをください Please give me another *chance*.
彼は絶好のチャンスを逃した He missed a 「*wonderful chance* [*golden opportunity*].
思いがけず彼女にオリンピック出場のチャンスがめぐってきた She unexpectedly got *a chance* to participate in the Olympics.
今がチャンスだ Now is *your* [*my*] *chance*.

ちゃんと

❶【きちんと】(整然と) neatly; (適切に) properly; (正式に) formally
部屋をちゃんと片づけなさい Clean up your room *neatly*.
ちゃんと座りなさい Sit *properly*.
朝ごはんちゃんと食べた? Did you eat breakfast *properly* [*like you're supposed to*]?
演奏会にはちゃんとした服装で行きなさい You should dress *formally* [*properly*] for the concert.
◆(親が子に対して) ちゃんとしなさい Behave *yourself*!

❷【確かに】(完全に) perfectly; (正確に) exactly; (正しく) correctly
彼女のことはちゃんと覚えています I remember her *perfectly*.
言いたいことがあるならちゃんと言ってごらん If you have something you want to say, tell me *exactly* [*precisely*].
◆そのことは彼にちゃんと伝えました I'm sure I told him that.

❸【しっかりした】
そのタレントも昔はちゃんとしたバレーボールの選手だった The celebrity was once a *respected* volleyball player.
彼はまだ若いがちゃんとした考えをもっている Though he is still young, he has *grown-up* ideas.
彼はまだちゃんとした仕事に就いていない He doesn't have a *regular* job yet.

チャンネル channel ‖ チャンネルを変える change *channels* / 6チャンネルにしていい? Can I change it to *Channel* 6? / 1チャンネルでニュースをやっている The news is on *Channel* 1. / 野球は何チャンネルでやってるの What *channel* is the ball game on?
◆私と弟はしょっちゅうチャンネル争いをしている My brother and I *are* always *arguing about which program to watch*.

ちゃんばら sword [sɔ́ːrd] fight ◆ちゃんば

らごっこをする play at *sword fighting*
‖ちゃんばら映画 a samurai movie
チャンピオン champion ◎, (口語的)champ ◎ ‖彼はヘビー級の世界チャンピオンになった He became *the* world heavyweight *champion*.
‖チャンピオンベルト a champion belt
ちゃんぽん 兄はビールと日本酒をちゃんぽんに飲んでいた My brother was drinking beer and sake *at the same time*.
ちゆ 治癒 (傷などの) healing ⓤ; (病気などの) cure ◎ ——治癒する (傷が) heal (up); (病気が) be cured
ちゅう¹ 中 (平均) average ⓤ◎; (中くらい) medium ⓤ◎, middle ◎ⓤ ⇨ちゅうくらい ‖彼女の成績はいつも中の上だ Her grades are always a little above *average*.
ちゅう² 宙 (空中) the air; (虚空) space ⓤ ‖ (胴上げで) 野村監督の体が2度，3度と宙を舞った The manager, Nomura, *was tossed into the air* several times. / その構想は宙に浮いたままだ The plan is still 「*up in the air* [*pending*].
ちゅう³ 注 note ◎; (注釈をつけること・注釈) annotation ⓤ◎; (脚注) footnote ◎ ‖巻末に注がついている *The notes* are given at the end of the book. ◆注をつける *annotate*
ちゅう- 駐- 駐日アメリカ大使 the U.S. ambassador *to* Japan

-ちゅう -中

❶【期間】(…の中で) in; (…の間に) during; (…以内に) within; (…する間に) while
私は午前中に宿題を終わらせた I finished my homework *in* the morning.
夏休み中に10冊くらいは本を読むつもりだ I am going to read about ten books *during* the summer vacation.
授業中の私語は慎むんだ Don't talk *during* [*in*] class.
来週中には検査の結果が出るだろう The results of the examination will be released *within* the next week.
留守中に電話があったようだ It seems that someone called me *while* I wasn't (at) home [*during* my absence].
◆今月中はずっと忙しかった I was busy *all* this month. / 今週中にこの本を図書館に返さなければならない I have to return this book to the library *by the end of* this week.
❷【状態】
その美術館は修理中だ The museum is *under* repair.
社長は今電話中です The president is *on* the phone now.
彼は今会議中だ He's *in* a meeting now.
私の前で甘い物の話をするのはやめてよ．今ダイエット中なんだから Don't talk about sweet things in my presence. I am *on* a diet now.
その企画は検討中だ The plan is *under* consideration.
◆電話は話し中だった The line was *busy*. / 食事中にげっぷをするのはよいマナーではない It's not good manners to belch *at the table*.
❸【…のうちで】
エリート中のエリート the elite *of* the elite
5人中3人が彼の意見に賛成だった Three *out of* five agreed with his opinion.
大気中の二酸化炭素の割合は年々増加している The proportion of carbon dioxide *in* the air is increasing every year.
等伯の「松林図」は名画中の名画だ Tohaku's *Pine Trees* is a picture *to end all* pictures.

ちゅうい 注意

❶【気を配ること】attention ⓤ ——注意する pay* [give*] attention, (公式的) attend ⓘ
彼女は彼の注意を引くためにわざとハンカチを落とした She dropped her handkerchief intentionally to *get* [*catch*] his *attention*.
最初はその絵に特に注意を払わなかった I *didn't pay* much *attention to* that painting at first.
彼の説明をよく注意して聞きなさい Please *pay* close *attention to* his explanation.
もう少し注意していれば，彼女の変化に気がついたはずだ If you *had given* more *attention to* her, you would have noticed the changes in her.
その政策は人々の注意をその問題からそらすために立てられた That policy was developed to divert public *attention* from the problem.
その問題はよくテストに出るから要注意だよ We should *pay particular attention to* that question because it often appears on exams.
◆その保育園では園児に対する注意が行き届いている That kindergarten *takes very good care of* its pupils. / 彼は注意力散漫だ He *lacks concentration*. / He *has a short attention span*. / また同じミスをするなんて君は注意が足りないよ How *careless* of you to repeat the same mistake!
❷【気をつけること】caution ⓤ, care ⓤ ——注意する be careful, take* care of …; (注意して見る) watch ⓘ◎; (気をつける) mind ⓘ◎ (✤通例命令文で用いる)
取扱い注意《掲示》*Handle with Care*
足元注意《掲示》*Watch* [《英》*Mind*] *Your Step*
この化学薬品の取扱いには細心の注意が必要だ You must handle this chemical with great *care*.
車を運転するときにはいくら注意してもしすぎることとはない You cannot *be too careful* when driving (a car).
このカメラの扱いには注意してください Please *be careful with* this camera.
通りを横切るときは車に注意しなさい *Watch out for* cars when crossing the street.
◆猛犬注意《掲示》*Beware of the Dog*
❸【忠告】advice ⓤ, (警告) caution ⓤ, warning ◎ⓤ ——注意する advise ⓘ; caution ⓘ, warn ⓘ
出発前にひと言注意をしておきます Let me *give*

ちゅういぶかい

you *a word of caution* before we start.
遅刻は今回が初めてだったので彼は注意されただけですんだ This was his first time being late, so he *was only given a warning*.
父は医者にアルコールを控えるよう注意されている My father *has been advised* by his doctor *to* refrain from drinking.
注意事項をよく読みなさい Read *the warnings* carefully.
添乗員はツアー客に夜ひとりで出歩かないように注意した The tour guide *warned* [*told*] the tourists not *to* go out alone at night.
◆生徒たちは先生の注意(→指示)をよく守った The students followed their teacher's *directions* faithfully. / この装置をお使いになる前に使用上の注意をよくお読みください Read *the instructions* carefully before using this device.
‖注意書き(注・但し書き) a note; (使用法などの) instructions / 注意報 a warning / 注意力 attentiveness; (集中力) concentration / 要注意人物 a marked man [woman]

ちゅういぶかい 注意深い、(慎重な) careful, cautious; (気を配る) attentive; (油断のない) watchful ——注意深く carefully, cautiously; attentively; watchfully /事態の推移を注意深く見守る watch *attentively* how things develop / 彼女の運転は注意深い She drives *carefully*.

チューインガム (chewing) gum / チューインガムをかむ chew *gum*

ちゅうおう 中央 (中心) the center, the heart; (真ん中付近) the middle ——中央の central; middle
町の中央に大きな公園がある There is a big park in *the center* of the city.
生徒は体育館の中央に集まった The students got together in *the middle* of the gymnasium.
‖中央アジア Central Asia / 中央アメリカ Central America / 中央気象台 the Central Meteorological Observatory / 中央銀行 a central bank / 中央集権 centralization of power / 中央政府 the central government / 中央分離帯《米》a median (strip),《英》a central reservation / 中央郵便局 the Central Post Office

ちゅうか 中華 ‖中華街 Chinatown / 中華そば Chinese noodles / 中華なべ a wok / 中華料理(品) Chinese food; (料理法) Chinese cooking [cuisine] / 中華料理店 a Chinese restaurant

ちゅうかい 仲介 (調停) mediation / 仲介する mediate / 彼が両者の仲介に立った He *mediated* [*acted as a mediator*] between the two.
‖仲介者 a mediator, a go-between

ちゅうがえり 宙返り (とんぼ返り) somersault; (飛行機の) loop /その体操選手は最後に2回宙返りをして着地した At the end, the gymnast did two *somersaults* and landed. / 飛行機は宙返りをした The plane *looped the loop*.

ちゅうかく 中核 (中心部) the core; (核心) kernel; (集団の) nucleus (複 nuclei) / 彼らがその運動の中核を形成している They form *the nucleus* of the activity.

ちゅうがく 中学 junior high school, junior high ; (日本での正式英語名) lower secondary school
弟は中学2年生です My brother is *in his second year of junior high school.*/《米》My brother is *in the eighth grade*.
妹は地元の中学校に通っている My sister goes to *a local junior high school*.
彼は中学時代のクラスメートだ He was a classmate of mine *during junior high school*.
いとこは中学生です My cousin is *a junior high school student*. / My cousin *goes to junior high school*.

ちゅうかじんみんきょうわこく 中華人民共和国 ⇨ちゅうごく

ちゅうがた 中形・中型 medium [middle] size ——中型の medium-sized

ちゅうかん 中間 the middle ——中間の (真ん中の) middle; (場所などの) intermediate; (距離が) halfway, midway; (時期が)《公式の》interim; (学期の) midterm; (中庸の) moderate
中間的な立場をとる take a *moderate* [*neutral*] stance
彼らはレースの中間地点にさしかかった They approached *the halfway* [*midway*] *point* of the race.
◆病院は2つの町の中間にある The hospital is located *halfway* [*midway*] between the two towns.
‖中間管理職 a middle manager; (総称) the middle management / 中間試験 a midterm examination,《米》a midterm / 中間色 an intermediate color / 中間層 the middle class / 中間発表 a preliminary announcement / 中間報告 an interim report

ちゅうき 中期 the middle (period) ‖奈良時代中期に in *the middle* of the Nara period

ちゅうきゅう 中級 ——中級の intermediate /彼はドイツ語の中級コースを受講している He is taking an *intermediate* German course.

ちゅうきんとう 中近東 the Middle (and Near) East

ちゅうぐらい 中位 ——中ぐらいの medium; (平均的な) average; (程度が適度の) moderate /彼女は中ぐらいの背の高さだ She is of *medium* height. / この前の試験では中ぐらいの成績だった I got an *average* grade on the last exam. ◆中ぐらいの箱を持ってきて Bring me a *medium-sized* box.

ちゅうけい 中継 (放送) relay ; (放送局間の) hookup ; (放送する) broadcast* /『ワールドカップは世界中に中継された The World Cup *was broadcast* all over the world. / そのニュースはマイアミから衛星中継された The news *was broadcast* [*transmitted*] from Miami *by satellite*.
◆全国にテレビ中継される be televised [tele-

cast] over a nationwide network / この放送は生中継でお送りしています This program comes to you *live*.
‖中継局 a relay station / 中継車 a broadcast truck / 中継放送 a relay broadcast / 実況中継 an on-the-spot broadcast

ちゅうけん 中堅 (主力) backbone ⓒ /彼らは会社の中堅だ They form *the backbone* of the company.
◆その会社は中堅の出版社だ That company is a *midlevel* publisher.
‖中堅手 a center fielder

ちゅうげん 中元 ⇨ おちゅうげん

ちゅうこ 中古 ──中古の used, secondhand /中古の家具 *used* [*secondhand*] furniture ◆ピアノを中古で買った We bought a piano *secondhand*.
‖中古車 a used [secondhand] car / 中古品 a used article, secondhand goods

ちゅうこうせい 中高生 junior and senior high school students

ちゅうこうねん 中高年 (中高年齢層) the middle-aged and elderly

ちゅうこく 忠告 (助言) advice [ədváis] ⓤ; (専門的な)《公式的に》counsel ⓤ; (警告) warning ⓒ ⓤ ──忠告する advise [ədváiz] ⓗ, give* advice; warn ⓗ
私は彼女の忠告に従った I followed [took, accepted] her *advice*.
彼は両親の忠告を聞かなかった He wouldn't listen to his parents' *advice*.
兄は友人の忠告を聞いてたばこをやめた My brother stopped [gave up] smoking on his friend's *advice*.
【advise [warn] +名(人) +to *do*】医者は母に塩分を減らすよう忠告した The doctor *advised* my mother to cut down on salt.

ちゅうごく 中国 China (✤公式名は the People's Republic of China) ──中国人 Chinese ⓒ (複 ~) ──中国語 Chinese ⓤ, the Chinese language ──中国(人[語])の Chinese

ちゅうごく² 中国 (地方) the Chugoku district

ちゅうごし 中腰 half-rising[-sitting] posture ⓒ ◆2列目の人は中腰になってください People in the second row, please「*crouch halfway down* [*half-crouch*].

ちゅうざ 中座 会議の途中で中座する *leave in the middle of* a meeting

ちゅうさい 仲裁 (裁定) arbitration ⓤ; (調停) mediation ⓤ ──仲裁する arbitrate ⓘ ⓗ; mediate ⓘ ⓗ /労使紛争を仲裁する *arbitrate* [*mediate*] a labor dispute / 2人のけんかは彼の仲裁で解決した The quarrel between the two was settled through his *mediation*.
‖仲裁人 an arbitrator; (調停者) a mediator

ちゅうざい 駐在 residence ⓤ ⓒ ──駐在する be stationed; (配置されている) be stationed; (滞在する) stay ⓘ /彼は特派員としてパリに3年間駐在した He *stayed* [*was stationed*] in Paris for three years as a correspondent.

◆日本駐在のオーストラリア大使 the Australian ambassador *to* Japan /彼らはこの会社のメキシコ駐在員だ They are *representatives* of the company in Mexico.
‖駐在所 a police box / 海外駐在員 an overseas worker [representative]

ちゅうさんかいきゅう 中産階級 the middle class(es)

ちゅうし¹ 中止 (中断) discontinuation ⓤ; (一時的な) suspension ⓤ ──中止する discontinue ⓗ; suspend ⓗ; (やめる) stop ⓗ; (取り消す) cancel ⓗ, call off
工事は一時中止された The construction *was suspended* temporarily.
その工場ではコンピュータの生産を中止した The factory *stopped* producing computers.
大雨のため野球の試合は中止となった The baseball game *was canceled* [*called off*] because of heavy rain.
◆彼らは計画を中止するかもしれない They may [*give up* [*discontinue*] the plan.

ちゅうし² 注視 gaze ⓒ ──注視する (じっと見つめる) gaze at ..., fix *one's* eyes on ...; (注意して見守る) watch carefully

ちゅうじ 中耳 middle ear ⓒ;《解剖》tympanum ⓒ (複 ~s, tympana)
‖中耳炎 inflammation of the middle ear,《医学》tympanitis

ちゅうじつ 忠実 ──忠実な faithful; (裏切らない) true; (忠誠な) loyal ──忠実に faithfully /彼女は自分の主義に忠実だ She *is faithful* [*true*] *to* her principles. / この訳は原文に忠実だ This translation *is faithful* [*true*] *to* the original. / 彼は自分の任務を忠実に実行した He carried out his duties *faithfully*. / この犬は飼い主に忠実だ This dog *is loyal* [*faithful*] *to* his master.

ちゅうしゃ¹ 注射 injection ⓒ,《口語的》shot ⓒ ──注射する inject ⓗ /医者は彼女に栄養剤を注射した The doctor *injected* her *with* the nutrient. / The doctor *injected* the nutrient *into* her. / The doctor *gave* her *a* nutrient *injection*. / 学校でインフルエンザの予防注射をしてもらった I had *a* flu *shot* [*injection*] at school.
‖注射液 an injection / 注射器 a (hypodermic) syringe / 注射針 a (hypodermic) needle / 静脈注射 an intravenous injection

ちゅうしゃ² 駐車 parking ⓤ ──駐車する park ⓗ ⓘ /駐車禁止《掲示》*No Parking* / ここには駐車できません You *can't park* here. / 道路のわきに車が駐車してある A car *is parked* at the side of the road. / 彼は駐車違反で罰金を取られた He was fined for *a parking violation*. / 東京都心は駐車違反の車であふれている Downtown Tokyo is filled up with *illegally parked cars*.
🅒「駐車場(→駐車するスペース)どこか空いてる?」「いっぱいみたいだよ」"Are there any *parking spaces*?" "It looks like they are all full."
‖駐車場《米》a parking lot,《英》a car park / 駐車料金 a parking charge

ちゅうしゃく 注釈 note [C], annotation [U] [C] //…に注釈をつける add *notes* to ...
‖注釈者 an annotator / 注釈書 an annotated edition, a book with annotations

ちゅうしゅう 仲秋 仲秋の名月 *the harvest moon*

ちゅうしゅつ 抽出 extraction [C] [U]; (標本の) sampling [U] ―抽出する extract [他] // 木の幹から樹液を抽出する *extract* sap from the trunk of a tree
◆5歳以下の子供100人を無作為に抽出した We *selected* 100 children aged 5 and under *at random.* / We *randomly sampled* 100 children aged 5 and under.

ちゅうじゅん 中旬 the middle (10 days) of a month ◆彼女は7月中旬に日本へ帰国する She will come back to Japan *in* 「*the middle of* July [*mid*-July].

ちゅうしょう[1] 抽象 abstraction [U] ―抽象的な abstract //彼の説明は抽象的すぎて分からなかった His explanation was too *abstract* for me to understand.
‖抽象画 an abstract painting / 抽象画家 an abstract painter / 抽象名詞〖文法〗an abstract noun / 抽象論 an abstract argument

ちゅうしょう[2] 中傷 slander [C] [U], libel [U] ―中傷する slander [他] //その雑誌には彼を中傷する記事が載っていた There was an article *slandering* him in the magazine. / 彼らの発言は彼女に対する中傷だ What they said is *a slander* against her.

ちゅうしょうきぎょう 中小企業 small and medium-sized enterprises [companies, businesses]; (小さな企業) small companies [businesses]

ちゅうしょく 昼食 lunch [U] [C]
軽い昼食をとる have *a* light *lunch*
彼女はダイエットのために昼食を抜いている She skips *lunch(es)* because of her diet.
昼食にツナサンドを食べた I had a tuna sandwich *for lunch.*
‖昼食会 a luncheon / 昼食時間 lunchtime

ちゅうしん 中心

the center; (中心部) the middle; (町などの) the heart; (焦点) the focus
〖～の中心〗
話題の中心 *the focus* [*center*] of conversation / 円の中心 *the center* of a circle
彼の家は町の中心にある His house is located in *the center* [*heart*] of the town.
◆この若い選手たちがチームの中心(→主要メンバー)になるだろう These young players will be *the principal members* of the team.
〖中心に〗
◆世界は自分を中心に(→自分の周りを)回っていると彼女は思っている She thinks the world revolves *around* her. / 新党は彼を中心に(→リーダーとして)組織された The new political party was organized with him *as a leader.* / 会議は環境問題を中心に行われた The meeting *centered* [*focused*] *on* environmental problems.
〖その他〗
京都はかつて日本の政治の中心地だった Kyoto used to be *the* political *center* of Japan.
◆市の中心部 *the central part* of the city / 彼はその運動の中心人物だった He was *the leader* of the movement.
‖中心点 the central point

ちゅうすいえん 虫垂炎〖医学〗appendicitis [U]

ちゅうすう 中枢 (中心) the center; (活動・商業などの) the hub //政治の中枢 *the center* of politics
‖中枢機関 a central organization / 中枢神経 the central nerves

ちゅうせい[1] 中世 the Middle Ages ―中世の medieval ‖中世史 medieval history

ちゅうせい[2] 中性 (化学の) neutrality [U] ―中性の neutral ‖中性子 a neutron / 中性子爆弾 a neutron bomb / 中性脂肪 triglyceride / 中性洗剤 (a) neutral detergent

ちゅうせい[3] 忠誠 (忠節) loyalty [U] [C]; (国家・君主などへの)《公式的》allegiance [U] [C] //兵士たちは国への忠誠を誓った The soldiers swore *allegiance* to their country.

ちゅうぜつ 中絶 (妊婦の) abortion [U] [C] ―中絶する have* an abortion, abort [他] // 彼女は妊娠4か月で中絶した She *had an abortion* in the fourth month of pregnancy.

ちゅうせん 抽選 (くじ引き) lot [U] [C], drawing [C]; (宝くじ) lottery [C] //彼女は抽選でバリ島旅行を当てた She won a trip to Bali *in the lottery.* / 来週の日曜日に八雲商店街の抽選会を行います We will hold *the* Yakumo mall *lottery* next Sunday.
◆妹は抽選に当たった[はずれた](→当たり[はずれ]の番号を引いた) My sister *drew a winning* [*losing*] *number.*
‖抽選券 a lottery [raffle] ticket / 抽選番号 a lottery [raffle] number

ちゅうせんきょくせい 中選挙区制 the multiple seat district system

ちゅうぞう 鋳造 ―鋳造する cast* [他]; (貨幣を) coin [他], mint [他] ‖鋳造所 a foundry

ちゅうそつ 中卒 (中卒者) junior high school graduate [C] ◆私は中卒です(→受けた教育は中学校で終わった) My *education ended at junior high school.*

ちゅうたい 中退 ―中退する (意図的にやめる) leave* [quit*] school; (成績が悪くてやめる) drop out
◆彼は家庭の事情で大学を中退した He *left* [*quit*] the university for family reasons.
‖中退者 a dropout

ちゅうだん 中断 (停止) stop [C]; (妨害) interruption [U]; (一時的な) suspension [U] ―中断する stop [他] [自]; interrupt [他]; suspend [他] //勉強を中断して紅茶を1杯飲んだ I *stopped* studying and had a cup of tea. / 臨時ニュースのために番組が一時中断された The program *was* temporarily 「*interrupted* by [*suspended* because of] a news bulletin.

◆彼らとの交渉は意見の食い違いのため中断した(→打ち切られた) The negotiations with them *were broken off* because of a difference of opinion.

ちゅうちゅう ネズミがちゅうちゅう鳴いている A mouse *is squeaking.* / 妹はストローでジュースをちゅうちゅう吸っていた My sister *was sucking* juice through a straw.

ちゅうちょ 躊躇 hesitation [U] [C] ―ちゅうちょする hesitate [自] ∥私は一瞬部屋に入るのをちゅうちょした I *hesitated to* enter the room for a moment. / 彼女はちゅうちょせず彼に質問した She asked him *without hesitation.*

ちゅうづり 宙吊り その男性はがけから宙づりになった That man *was hung* [*suspended*] *in midair* [*the air*] from the cliff.

ちゅうと 中途 仕事を中途でやめる leave *one's* work *unfinished* [*half done*] / 彼らは中途で引き返した They turned back *halfway* [*midway*]. / 彼は中途採用だ(→通常の採用時期以外に採用された) He *was hired by the company out of the regular hiring period.*

ちゅうとう[1] 中東 the Middle East ―中東の Middle Eastern ‖中東諸国 the countries in the Middle East

ちゅうとう[2] 中等 ―中等の (中級の) middle; (程度が中くらいの) medium ‖中等教育 secondary education

ちゅうどう 中道 ―中道の middle-of-the-road ‖中道政治 middle-of-the-road politics / 中道政党 a centrist [middle-of-the-road] party

ちゅうどく 中毒 poisoning [U]; (麻薬などの) addiction [U] [C] ◆彼らはガス中毒を起こした They *were poisoned by gas.* / They *got* [*had*] *gas poisoning.* / 彼はアルコール中毒だ He is *an alcoholic.* / 兄は仕事中毒だ My brother is *a workaholic.* / 彼らはすっかりテレビゲーム中毒になった They *are* completely *addicted to* video games.
‖中毒患者(麻薬の) a drug addict / 中毒症状 toxic symptoms / 一酸化炭素中毒 carbon monoxide poisoning / 食中毒 food poisoning / 麻薬中毒 a drug addiction

ちゅうとはんぱ 中途半端 ―中途半端な (未完成の) unfinished; (半分やった状態で) half done; (不完全な) halfway ∥仕事を中途半端にする *leave one's* work *unfinished* [*half done*]
◆彼女に中途半端な(→優柔不断な)返事をしてしまった I gave her an *indecisive* answer. / 中途半端な気持ちなら(→気乗りがしないのなら)参加しないほうがいい If you are *halfhearted*, you should not take part in it.

ちゅうとん 駐屯 ―駐屯する be stationed ‖駐屯地 a post; (守備隊の) a garrison (town)

チューナー tuner [C]

ちゅうなんべい 中南米 Latin [South and Central] America

ちゅうにかい 中二階 mezzanine [C]

ちゅうにくちゅうぜい 中肉中背 中肉中背の男性 a man of「*medium height and build* [*medium size*]

ちゅうにち 駐日 駐日フランス大使 the French ambassador *to Japan*

ちゅうにゅう 注入 injection [U] [C] ―注入する inject [他] ∥金融機関に公的資金を注入する *inject* public funds *into* a financial institution

チューニング ―チューニングする tune (up) ∥彼はギターのチューニングをしていた He *was tuning up* his guitar.

ちゅうねん 中年 middle age [U] ―中年の middle-aged ∥中年の男性 a *middle-aged* man; a man *of middle age* / 私の両親は中年太りだ My parents *have developed middle-age spread.* / My parents *have gained weight as they reach middle age.*

ちゅうは 中波 〔電気〕medium wave [U] [C]

チューバ 〔音楽〕tuba [C]

ちゅうハイ 酎ハイ 🗻 a *chuhai*, a highball made from *shochu* mixed with soda and ice

ちゅうばん 中盤 試合は中盤戦に入った The game has reached [entered] *the middle stage.*

ちゅうび 中火 (中くらいの炎) medium flame [C]; (中くらいの熱) medium heat [U] ∥中火でよくいためてください Fry it well *over a medium flame.*

ちゅうぶ 中部 (中心部) the central part; (中央部分) the middle part; (地方) the Chubu district

チューブ tube [C]; (タイヤの) inner tube [C] ∥チューブ入り歯磨き *a tube of* toothpaste / 彼はチューブから絵の具をしぼり出した He squeezed paint from *a tube.*

ちゅうぶう 中風 paralysis [U]; (軽症のもの) palsy [U] ◆中風にかかる be [become] *paralyzed*

ちゅうふく 中腹 その学校は丘の中腹にある The school is *on*「*the side of a hill* [*a hillside*]. / 私たちは山の中腹で(→途中まで登って)休憩した We took a rest *halfway up the mountain.*

ちゅうぶらりん 宙ぶらりん その問題は宙ぶらりんになった(→未解決の)ままだ The problem is still「*up in the air* [*unsettled, pending*].

ちゅうべい[1] 中米 Central America ―中米の Central American

ちゅうべい[2] 駐米 駐米英国大使 the British ambassador *to the U.S.*

ちゅうもく 注目 attention [U], notice [U] ―注目する (注意を払う) pay* attention to ...; (見守る) watch [他]
注目すべき結果 a result *worthy of attention*
その事件は人々の注目を集めている The case has attracted [drawn] *the attention* of people.
その歌手は今最も注目を浴びている That singer *is* now *the center of attention.*
彼の発見は注目に値する His discovery *is worthy of attention.*

最初彼女の小説は批評家に注目されなかった（→批評家は彼女の小説に注目しなかった）At first the critics *didn't pay attention to* her novel.
選挙の結果にみんなが注目している Everyone is *paying attention to* [*watching*] the results of the election.
その新人作家は人々の注目の的(ま)だ The new writer is *the focus* [*center*] *of public attention*.

ちゅうもん 注文

❶【品物を注文すること】order Ⓒ ——注文する order ⓘⓣ, 《公式的》place an order
【注文が·は】
ご注文はおすみですか *Have* you *ordered* yet?
その人形は注文が殺到して生産が間に合わない状態だ There has been a rush of *orders* for that doll and the production has fallen behind.
💬「ご注文はお決まりですか」「はい，このバーベキューピーフサンドイッチをください」"Are you ready to *order*? / May I take *your order*?" "Yes. I'll have this barbecued beef sandwich."
💬「ほかにご注文は？」「いえ，それで結構です」"*Anything else*?" "No, thanks. That'll do."
【注文を·に】
注文に応じる fill [meet] *an order* / 注文を受ける receive [get, take, accept] *an order* / 注文を取り消す cancel *an order*
すみません，注文をお願いします Excuse me, I'd like to *order* now.
【注文する】
私はピザとサラダを注文した I *ordered* a pizza and a salad.
その会社は小麦を大量に注文した The company *placed a* large *order* for wheat.
その本はもう紀伊国屋書店に注文してある That book *is* already *on order* at Kinokuniya Bookstore.
これは私が注文したものとは違います This is not *what I ordered*.

英作文ノート 注文は書店にするものだけど…
私はその書店に本を3冊注文した
→ ×I *ordered* three books *to* the bookstore.
→ ○I *ordered* three books *at* [*from*] the bookstore.
→ ○I *placed an order* for three books *with* the bookstore.
★「その書店に」につられて to the bookstore としないよう注意．ふつう「店頭で注文する」場合は at を，「注文して…から取り寄せる」場合は from を用いる．order を名詞で用いるときは《place an order for＋物＋with＋店など》となる．

【その他】
ご注文の品は1週間以内にお届けいたします We will deliver *the ordered goods* within a week.

❷【条件をつけること】(条件) condition Ⓒ；(要求·要請) request Ⓒ, demand Ⓒ (❖ demand のほうがより強い要求を表す)
東京に行って歌手になると言いだした姉に父は1つ注文をつけた When my sister said she was going to Tokyo to become a singer, my father *made* one *condition*.
彼女はいつも無理な注文をつける She always *makes* unreasonable *demands* [*requests*].
◆この仕事をあしたまでに仕上げろだなんて，どだい無理な注文だ *It's too much to ask me* to get all this work done by tomorrow.
‖注文建築 a custom-built house / 注文書 an order form [sheet]

ちゅうや 昼夜 彼は昼夜兼行で(→24時間ぶっ通しで)働いた He worked 「*around the clock* [*day and night*]. / 一昼夜熱が下がらなかった My temperature didn't come down *for a whole day and night*.

ちゅうゆ 注油 lubrication Ⓤ ——注油する lubricate ⓣ / 自転車の車輪に注油する *lubricate* [*oil*] the hubs of bicycle wheels

ちゅうよう 中庸 (節度) moderation Ⓤ
◆中庸を得た行動 a *moderate* action; *moderate* behavior

ちゅうりつ 中立 neutrality Ⓤ ——中立の neutral
中立を守る observe [maintain] *neutrality*; remain *neutral*
日本はその問題に対して中立的態度をとっている Japan takes *a neutral stance* toward that problem.
‖中立国 a neutral nation / 中立主義 neutralism / 中立主義者 a neutralist / 中立地帯 a neutral [demilitarized] zone

チューリップ tulip Ⓒ

ちゅうりゅう¹ 中流 (川 の) the middle reaches (of a river); (社会の) the middle class ‖日本人の多くは中流意識をもっている(→中流階級に属すると思っている) Most Japanese *think they belong to the middle class*.
‖中流家庭 a middle-class family

ちゅうりゅう² 駐留 ——駐留する (滞在する) stay ⓘ；(特に軍隊などが) be stationed ‖駐留軍 occupation forces

ちゅうりん 駐輪 ——駐輪する park ⓘⓣ
‖駐輪場 a bicycle parking lot

ちゅうわ 中和 〖化学〗neutralization Ⓤ；(毒などの反作用) counteraction ⓊⒸ ——中和する neutralize ⓣ /『酸をアルカリで中和する *neutralize* acids with alkalis

ちゅんちゅん どこかで鳥がちゅんちゅん鳴いているのが聞こえる I hear birds *chirping* somewhere.

-ちょ -著 ジョン・アップダイク著『走れウサギ』*Rabbit, Run by* John Updike

ちょいちょい (たびたび) sometimes; (時々) sometimes, every now and then ‖おじはちょいちょいうちにやってくる My uncle *often* [*sometimes*] comes to my house.

ちょう¹ 蝶 butterfly Ⓒ ‖モンシロチョウ a cabbage butterfly
◆アゲハチョウ a swallowtail / ひもを蝶結び

にする *tie* a string *in a bow* / 蝶ネクタイ a *bow tie*
慣用表現 彼女は蝶よ花よと（→大切に）育てられた She was brought up *with the utmost care.*

ちょう² 腸 (全体) the bowels [báuəlz]；〔解剖〕(大腸・小腸) the intestines ──腸の intestinal ◆腸のぐあいが悪い have *bowel* [*intestinal*] *trouble*
‖腸カタル〔医学〕intestinal catarrh / 腸チフス〔医学〕typhoid (fever) / 腸捻転(ﾈﾝﾃﾝ)〔医学〕a twist in the intestines / 腸閉塞〔医学〕intestinal obstruction / 大［小］腸〔解剖〕the large [small] intestine

ちょう³ 長 (その集団で責任をもっている人) the head;（権威や権力をもって集団を統括する人）the chief; (指導者) the leader ‖一家の長 the *head* of the family
◆彼は泳ぎにかけては僕より一日(ｲﾁｼﾞﾂ)の長がある（→少しだけすぐれている）He *is just a bit better than* me in swimming.

ちょう⁴ 庁 agency ⓒ ‖防衛庁 the Defense Agency

ちょう⁵ 兆 trillion ⓒ ‖3兆円 three *trillion* yen

ちょう⁶ 町 (地方公共団体) town ⓒ; (区市町村の中の) -cho

ちょう⁷ (王朝) dynasty ⓒ; (時代) period ⓒ; (特定の人物で代表される時代) age ⓒ ‖平安朝 the Heian *period* / ビクトリア朝 the Victorian *Age, the reign* of Queen Victoria

ちょう- 超 super-, ultra- ◆彼女は超一流のバイオリニストだ She is a *really excellent* violinist. /（→群を抜いてすぐれている）She is *in a class of her own* as a violinist. / あいつ超むかつく He *really* makes me mad./ He is *really* disgusting.
🅒「で、映画はどうだった」「超おもしろかった」"So, how was the movie?" "It was *super* exciting."
‖超現実主義 surrealism / 超大国 a superpower / 超特急 ⇨ ちょうとっきゅう

-ちょう¹ 調 ハ長調［短調］C *major* [*minor*] / 会話調の文体 a conversational style / この詩は七五調だ This poem is written in *a seven-five syllable meter.*

-ちょう² 丁 ペンチ1丁 a *pair* of combination pliers and wire cutter / 豆腐1丁 a *block* [*cake*] of tofu

ちょうあい 寵愛 王の寵愛を受ける *be particularly loved* by the king

ちょうい 弔意 弔意を表す express *one's* condolences

ちょういん 調印 (署名) signing Ⓤ ──調印する sign ⓗ ‖両国は和平条約に調印した The two countries *signed* a peace treaty.
‖調印国 a signatory / 調印式 a signing ceremony

ちょうえい 町営 ──町営の municipal ‖町営体育館 a *municipal* gymnasium

ちょうえき 懲役〔法律〕penal servitude Ⓤ; (禁固刑) imprisonment Ⓤ ‖彼は懲役5年に処せられた He was sentenced to「five years' *imprisonment* [five years *in prison*].
‖無期懲役 life imprisonment

ちょうえつ 超越 ──超越する (理解・経験などの限界を)《公式的》transcend ⓗ;（感情・行動などを）rise* above … / 人力を超越している *transcend* [*go beyond*] human power / 彼は世俗を超越している He「*rises above* [*stands aloof from*] the world.

ちょうおんかい 長音階 major scale ⓒ

ちょうおんそく 超音速 supersonic speed Ⓤⓒ ‖超音速の supersonic ‖超音速旅客機 a supersonic transport(《略語》SST)

ちょうおんぱ 超音波 supersonic [ultrasonic] waves; (医療用の) ultrasound Ⓤ
‖超音波検査 ultrasonography

ちょうか 超過 excess Ⓤ《また an ～》; (余剰) surplus Ⓤⓒ ──超過する exceed ⓗ ‖新築費用は予算を大幅に超過した The cost of building a new house far *exceeded* our budget.
◆ビデオの返却が遅れたので超過料金を払わなければならなかった I was late returning some videos, so I had to pay *an extra charge. /* 私のかばんは重量制限を3キロ超過していた My bags *were overweight* by three kilos.
‖超過額 a surplus, an excess / 超過勤務 overtime work / 超過勤務手当 overtime pay, an overtime allowance / 輸入超過 (an) excess of imports (over exports)

ちょうかい¹ 町会 (町民会) town meeting ⓒ; (町議会) town council ⓒ

ちょうかい² 懲戒 彼は会社の極秘資料を持ち出し懲戒免職になった He took away some of the company's confidential documents and *received a disciplinary dismissal* [he *was dismissed for disciplinary reasons*].

ちょうかく 聴覚 (the sense of) hearing,〔医学〕auditory sense Ⓤ Ⓒ ‖聴覚が鋭い have *an* acute *sense of hearing /* 彼は聴覚を失った He lost his sense of hearing.
‖聴覚器官 an auditory organ

ちょうかん¹ 長官 (官庁などの) director general ⓒ; (内閣官房・アメリカの) secretary ⓒ ‖警察庁長官 the *Director General* of the National Police Agency / 内閣官房長官 the *Chief* Cabinet *Secretary /* （米国の）国務長官 the *Secretary* of State / 最高裁判所長官 the *Chief Justice* of the Supreme Court

ちょうかん² 朝刊 morning (news)paper ⓒ; (夕刊と区別して) morning edition

ちょうかんず 鳥瞰図 bird's-eye view ⓒ

ちょうき 長期 a long period (of time); (長い間) long time [term] ⓒ ‖交渉は長期にわたって続いた The negotiations lasted *for a long period of time.*
◆長期的には *in the long run /* その論争は長期戦の様相を呈してきた The dispute is showing signs of becoming *a prolonged war.*
‖長期計画 a long-range plan / 長期契約 a long-term contract / 長期欠席 (a) long absence / 長期予報 a long-range forecast

ちょうきょう 調教 training Ⓤ ──調教する train ⓗ ‖調教師 a trainer

ちょうきょり 長距離 long distance [C] ——長距離の long-distance ‖長距離電話をかける make a *long-distance* call
‖長距離競争[レース] a long-distance race / 長距離飛行 a long-distance flight / 長距離輸送 a long haul / 長距離列車 a long-distance train

ちょうけし 帳消し 借金を帳消しにする *write off* [*cancel* (*out*)] a debt / 彼はホームランを打ってさっきのエラーを帳消しにした He hit a home run and *wiped out* the error he had made earlier.

ちょうこう[1] 兆候・徴候 sign [C], indication [C]; (病気の) symptom [C] ‖景気回復の兆候が現れた *Signs* of improvement appeared in the economy. / 患者はインフルエンザの兆候を示していた The patient showed *the symptoms* of influenza.

ちょうこう[2] 聴講 ——聴講する sit* in on ..., 《米》audit [他] ‖後藤教授の講義を聴講した I 「*sat in on* [*audited, attended*] Professor Goto's lecture.
‖聴講生 an auditor / 聴講料 an admission fee

ちょうごう 調合 ——調合する prepare [他]; (薬を) make* up; (薬局で) dispense [他]; (混合して作る) compound [他] ‖いくつかの薬品を調合する *compound* several drugs / 薬剤師が処方の薬を調合してくれた The pharmacist *made up* a prescription for me.

ちょうこうそうビル 超高層ビル high-rise building [C], skyscraper [C]

ちょうこく 彫刻 (像) sculpture [C][U]; (木・象牙(ぞう)などの) carving [C][U]; (金属・石などの) engraving [C][U] (❖いずれも彫刻品の意味では[C]) ——彫刻する sculpt [他]; carve [他]; engrave [他] ‖大理石の彫刻品 *a* marble *sculpture* / 柱にツタの彫刻を施す *carve* vines on a pillar
‖彫刻家 a sculptor / 彫刻刀 a chisel

ちょうさ 調査

(組織的な) investigation [U][C]; (質問などによる) 《公式的》inquiry [U][C]; (学術上の) research [U]; (統計・測量などによる) survey [C] ——調査する investigate [他], make* an investigation; inquire into...; research into [on] ...; survey [他]

警察はその事件の調査に乗り出した The police started to *investigate* the incident.

その飛行機墜落事故の原因の徹底的な調査が行われた They *investigated* thoroughly the cause of the plane crash. / They *made a* thorough *investigation* of the cause of the plane crash.

彼らはその男の身元を調査した They *inquired into* the man's background.

調査の結果，半数近くの生徒が学校に満足していないことが分かった *The survey* showed that about half of the students are not satisfied with school.

事故の原因は現在調査中だ The cause of the accident *is under investigation* now.

‖調査委員会 a fact-finding committee / 調査員 an investigator, an examiner / 調査結果 findings / 調査書(成績の) a school report [record, transcript] / 調査団 an inquiry commission, a survey group / 調査報告 a report on an investigation / 調査用紙(アンケート用紙) a questionnaire / 国勢調査 a census / 市場調査 market research / 世論調査 a public opinion poll

ちょうざい 調剤 ——調剤する prepare [compound] a medicine; (処方に従って) fill [make* up] a prescription

ちょうし 調子

❶【ぐあい・状態】condition [U]《また a ～》; (体の状態) shape [U]; (機械などの) order [U]

最近体の調子がいい I'*m in good shape* [*condition*] these days.

彼はしばらく体調を崩していたが，だんだん調子が戻ってきたようだ He wasn't feeling well for a while, but he seems to *be returning to his normal condition* gradually.

選手たちは試合に備えて調子を整えているところだ The players *are getting themselves in good condition* [*form*] for the game.

◆きょうは体の調子が悪い I'*m not feeling well* today. / I *don't feel like myself* today. / 僕のコンピュータは調子が悪い *There's something wrong with* my computer. / 水泳を始めてからずいぶん体の調子がよくなった *My health has improved* a lot since I started swimming.

[会]「調子はどう」「元気でやってるよ」"*How are you doing?* / *How's it going?*" "I'm doing fine."

❷【声・言葉・音楽などの】(音の高低) tune [U], key [C]; (音色・口調) tone [C]

彼は調子はずれに歌った He sang 「*out of tune* [*off key*].

そのピアノは調子が狂っている The piano *is out of tune.*

彼女はいらいらした調子で話し続けた She kept on talking *in an* irritated *tone.*

彼は突然声の調子を変えて私を非難した He suddenly changed *his tone* and criticized me.

◆声の調子を上げる[下げる] raise [lower] *one's voice* / 彼女は足で調子をとりながらギターを弾いた She played the guitar *while beating time* with her foot. / 声の調子から彼女がとても怒っていることが分かった I could tell *by her voice* (that) she was very angry. / 彼の一本調子の演説を聞いているうちに私はうとうとしてしまった I nodded off while listening to his *monotonous* speech.

❸【勢い】

その調子！ *Way to go*! / *That's it*! / *That's the stuff* [*spirit*]! / *That's the way*!

その横綱は今場所はとても調子がいい That *yokozuna is doing very well* in this tournament.

彼もやっと本調子になってきた He's finally *getting into his stride.*

いつもの調子でやればいいんだよ You only have to do it *as you always do*.

松坂はペナントレースの終盤に入ってますます調子を上げてきた Matsuzaka *is getting better and better* in the final stages of the pennant race.

この調子ではすぐにお金が足りなくなってしまうだろう *At this rate*, we'll soon run short of money.

慣用表現 あいつらはいったん調子に乗ると(→夢中になると)手がつけられなくなる Once they are *wound up*, it's very difficult to stop them. / あまり調子に乗るなよ(→我を忘れて興奮するなよ) *Don't get* so *carried away*. / 彼はいつも調子のいいことを言う(→口がうまい男だ) He is a *smooth-tongued* man. / (→お世辞のうまい人だ) He's *a flatterer*. / 彼女は君に調子を合わせていただけだ She *was* only *playing along with* you.

ちょうじ[1] 弔辞 a message of condolence, condolences; (追悼説) funeral [memorial] address ⓒ ∥弔辞を述べる offer *one's condolences*; make *a memorial address*

ちょうじ[2] 寵児 shining star ⓤ ∥球界の寵児 *a shining star* in baseball circles

ちょうじかん 長時間 会議は長時間にわたった The conference continued *for a long time*.

ちょうししゃ 聴視者 (全体として) the audience; (テレビの) viewer ⓒ; (ラジオの) listener ⓒ

ちょうしぜん 超自然 ──超自然の supernatural ∥超自然現象 a supernatural phenomenon

ちょうじゃ 長者 (金持ち) rich [wealthy] person ⓒ; (大富豪) millionaire ⓒ ∥長者番付 a list of millionaires / 億万長者 a billionaire

ちょうしゅ 聴取 警察は事件の関係者から事情を聴取した The police *questioned* people involved in the case about the situation.
∥聴取者 (ラジオの) a radio listener; (全体) the radio audience

ちょうじゅ 長寿 long life ⓒ,《公式的》longevity ⓤ ◆彼の家は長寿の家系だ He comes from a *long-lived* family.
∥長寿番組 a long-running[-lived] program

ちょうしゅう 徴収 collection ⓤ; (税金の) levy ⓒ ∥─を徴収する collect 働; levy 働 / 税金を徴収する *levy* a tax / パーティーの会費を徴収した I *collected* the fees for the party.

ちょうしゅう[2] 聴衆 audience ⓒ (❖通例単数扱い。個々の聴衆を指す場合は複数扱い);(出席している人) attendance ⓤⓒ; (聞き手) listener ⓒ ∥彼はたくさんの[3,000人の]聴衆を前に演説した He gave a speech before「*a large audience [an audience* of 3,000]. / 聴衆はオーケストラの演奏に魅了されていた *The audience* was [were] enthralled by the orchestra's performance.

ちょうじゅう 鳥獣 birds and beasts
∥鳥獣保護区 a wildlife sanctuary

ちょうしょ[1] 長所 strong [good] point ⓒ; (すぐれた点) merits; (美点) virtue ⓒⓤ; (有利な点) advantage ⓒ ∥長所を伸ばす develop *one's strong* [*good*] *points* / 親切なところが彼女の長所です Her kindness is her *strong point*. / この機械の長所は軽くて持ち運びに便利なことだ This machine has *the advantage* of being light and easy to carry. / *The advantage* of this machine is that it is light and easy to carry. / どんな人にも長所と短所がある Everyone has *his* '*merits* and demerits [*good points* and bad *points*]. / この商品は素材の長所を生かしている This product makes good use of the material's *advantages*.

ちょうしょ[2] 調書 (法律で) record ⓒ; (報告書) report ⓒ ∥警察は容疑者を取り調べて調書を作成した The police interrogated [questioned] the suspect and made *a report*.

ちょうじょ 長女 *one's* [the] first daughter; (娘が2人の場合) *one's* [the] older daughter; (娘が3人以上の場合) *one's* [the] oldest daughter (❖(英)では older, oldest の代わりに elder, eldest を用いる)

ちょうしょう 嘲笑 (冷やかし) ridicule ⓤ; (悪意のある) derision ⓤ; (冷笑) sneer ⓒ ──嘲笑する ridicule 働; (あざ笑う) laugh at ..., sneer at ... ∥彼の発言はみんなの嘲笑を招いた His remark brought everyone's *ridicule*. / 彼は私たちを嘲笑した He *laughed* [*sneered*] *at* us.

ちょうじょう 頂上 (山の) the top, the summit; (とがった山の) the peak
山の頂上に到着する reach *the top* of the mountain
富士山の頂上は雲に覆われていた *The top* of Mt. Fuji was covered in clouds.
頂上からの眺めはとてもよかった The view from *the summit* was quite good.

ちょうじょうげんしょう 超常現象 paranormal [supernatural] phenomenon ⓒ, the paranormal, the supernatural
⇒ 場面・状況別会話 p.1722

ちょうしょく 朝食 breakfast ⓒⓤ
遅い朝食をとる have [eat] *a late breakfast* (❖形容詞が付くときは ⓒ)
私はいつも7時前に朝食をすませる I always finish *breakfast* before seven.
朝食にハムエッグを食べた I had ham and eggs *for breakfast*.

ちょうじり 帳尻 帳じりが合わない *The accounts don't balance*. / 先月は帳じりを合わすのに苦労した I had a hard time *making both ends meet* last month.

ちょうしん[1] 長身 その選手は2メートルの長身だ The player is *tall*, with a height of two meters.

ちょうしん[2] 長針 minute [long] hand ⓒ

ちょうじん 超人 (男の) superman ⓒ; (女の) superwoman ⓒ ◆彼は超人的な体力の持ち主だ He has *superhuman* strength. / 彼は新しい事業を成功させるために超人的な努力をした He made *superhuman* efforts to be successful in his new enterprise.

ちょうしんき 聴診器 stethoscope [C] ‖医者は私の背中に聴診器を当てた The doctor applied *a stethoscope* to my back.

ちょうしんせい 超新星〘天文〙supernova [C] (複 supernovae, ~s)

ちょうせい 調整 adjustment [U][C]; (機能などの) coordination [U] ─調整する adjust [他]; coordinate [他]; (意見などを) iron out ...

スケジュールを調整する *adjust* the schedule

このスイッチでテレビの画像を調整することができます You can *adjust* the picture on the TV with this switch.

時間調整のために少々停車します We will make a few minutes' stop 「*to adjust the time* [(→予定の発車時間を待つために) *to wait for the scheduled departure time*].

◆定期的にエンジンを調整してください Please *tune up* the engine regularly. / 佐々木は次の試合に向けての調整が遅れている Sasaki *is behind in training* for the next game.

‖在庫調整 inventory control / 年末調整(税金の) year-end tax adjustment

ちょうぜい 徴税 taxation [U], tax collection [U] ─徴税する collect a tax

ちょうせつ 調節 adjustment [U][C] ─調節する adjust [他]; (機器・温度などを) regulate [他]

いすの高さを調節する *adjust* the height of a chair / ラジオの音量を調節する *adjust* the volume on a radio

この机は背の高さに応じて調節することができる You can *adjust* this desk to your height.

この機械が水槽の温度を調節する This machine *regulates* the temperature of the water tank.

◆ランプの明るさはノブを回して調節できます You can *control* the brightness of the lamp by turning the knob.

ちょうせん[1] 挑戦 challenge [C]; (権威などに対する反抗) defiance [U] ─挑戦する (人に) challenge [他]; (試みる・試す) try [他]

挑戦状をたたきつける throw [fling] down *a challenge* / フランス料理に挑戦する *try one's hand at* French cooking

チャンピオンは私の挑戦に応じなかった The champion didn't accept my *challenge*.

私はチェスで鈴木さんに挑戦した I *challenged* Ms. Suzuki *to* a game of chess.

彼は100メートルバタフライの世界記録に挑戦した(→世界記録を破ろうとした) He *tried to* 「*break the world record* [(→新しい記録を打ち立てようとした) *set a new world record*] for the 100-meter butterfly.

学生たちはその数学の難問に挑戦した The students *tried* [*attempted*] *to solve* the difficult problem in mathematics.

◆デモ参加者たちは警官に挑戦的な態度をとった The demonstrators took [assumed] a *defiant* attitude toward the police officer. / 彼女は3度目の挑戦で試験に合格した She passed the examination *on* the third *try* [*trial*].

‖挑戦者 a challenger

ちょうせん[2] 朝鮮 Korea (❖朝鮮民主主義人民共和国 the Democratic People's Republic of Korea (通称, 北朝鮮 North Korea) と大韓民国 the Republic of Korea (通称, 韓国 South Korea) に分割されている) ─朝鮮人 Korean [C] ─朝鮮語 Korean [U] ─朝鮮(人[語])の Korean

‖朝鮮半島 the Korean Peninsula

➜かんこく(韓国), きたちょうせん

ちょうぜん 超然 黒川先生は世俗のことには超然としている Mr. Kurokawa *is detached from* the real world. / (→無関心だ) Mr. Kurokawa *is indifferent to* the real world.

ちょうぞう 彫像 statue [C], sculpture [C][U] ‖彫像を彫る carve *a statue*

ちょうそく 長足 夏休みの間に彼女の英語は長足の進歩を遂げた She *made rapid progress in* English during summer vacation.

ちょうそん 町村 (町と村) towns and villages; (地方自治体) municipalities ‖町村合併 the merger [amalgamation] of towns and villages

ちょうだ[1] 長打〘野球〙extra-base hit [C] ‖松井はその試合で3本の長打を放った Matsui made [got] three *extra-base hits* in the game. ◆高山には長打力がある Takayama has *the power to hit the long ball.*

‖長打者 a long-ball hitter

ちょうだ[2] 長蛇 クレープ屋の前には長蛇の列ができていた There was *a long line* [《英》*queue*] in front of the crepe stand.

ちょうだい 頂戴 ❶【もらう】─ちょうだいする receive [他] ‖お手紙をちょうだいしました I *received* your letter.

◆結構な物をちょうだいいたしましてどうもありがとうございました Thank you very much *for the nice present.*

❷【飲食】─ちょうだいする have* [他] ‖もう十分ちょうだいしました I'*ve had* enough, thank you.

❸【その他】ケーキをあとちょっとだけちょうだい *Give me* a bit more of the cake. / 京都に着いたら知らせてちょうだいね *Please* let me know when you arrive in Kyoto.

ちょうたいこく 超大国 superpower [C]

ちょうたつ 調達 ─調達する (物資を) provide [他], supply [他]; (資金を) raise [他] ‖村人が私たちのために食料を調達してくれた The villagers *provided* [*supplied*] us *with* food. / 父はお祭りに屋台を出すための資金をどうにか調達することができた My father managed to *raise* the money for a booth at the festival.

◆戦争中, 砂糖の調達(→手に入れること)は困難だった Sugar was hard to *get* during the war. / 日用品はロンドンで調達する(→買う)ことにした I decided to *buy* my daily necessities in London.

‖資金調達 finance

ちょうたん 長短 (長さ) length [U][C]; (長所と短所) good and bad points, advantages and disadvantages

ちょうたんぱ 超短波 very high frequency ①C ((略語))VHF), ultrashort waves

ちょうちょう¹ 蝶々 butterfly C
⇨ちょう(蝶)

ちょうちょう² 町長 (town) mayor C

ちょうちょう³ 長調 〖音楽〗 major (key) C
——長調の major ∥ト長調のソナタ a sonata in G *major*

ちょうちん 提灯 paper [Chinese, Japanese] lantern C
∥ちょうちん行列 a lantern procession
慣用表現 幸男はいつも山田先生のちょうちん持ちをしている Yukio *is* always *flattering* [*fawning on*] Mr. Yamada.

ちょうつがい 蝶番 hinge C ∥そのドアはちょうつがいがはずれているよ That door is off *its hinges*.

ちょうてい 調停 mediation Ⓤ; (法的強制力をもつ) arbitration Ⓤ ——調停する mediate 他⑯; arbitrate 他⑯ ∥紛争を調停する *arbitrate* a dispute / 争いは調停に持ち込まれるだろう The dispute will go [be referred] to *arbitration*. / その紛争では国連が調停に入った The UN *mediated in* the conflict. / 裁判所が労使間の調停をした The court *arbitrated between* labor and management. / 市が工場と近隣住民の調停に乗り出した The city government started *mediating between* the factory and the neighboring community.
∥調停案 a mediation [an arbitration] plan / 調停委員会 a mediation committee / 調停者 a mediator, an arbitrator

ちょうてん 頂点 the top, the summit, the peak; (三角形・円すい形などの)《公式的》the apex; (名声などの) the zenith ∥三角形の頂点 *the apex* [*vertex*] of a triangle / 彼女は苦労の末, 芸能界の頂点に上り詰めた She worked her way up to *the top* of show business. / 聴衆の興奮は頂点に達した The excitement of the audience reached *its peak*. / その物理学者は名声の頂点にある The physicist is at *the zenith* [*peak*] of his fame.

ちょうでん 弔電 a telegram of condolence ∥弔電を打つ send *a telegram of condolence*

ちょうでんどう 超伝導 〖物理〗 superconductivity Ⓤ ∥超伝導体 a superconductor

ちょうど¹ 丁度

just, right(❖ right は主に「場所」について用いる); (正確に) exactly, precisely
学校はちょうど4時に終わる School ends *just* [*exactly*] at four.
今7時ちょうどです It's *just* [*exactly*] seven. / It's seven *sharp*.(❖ *sharp* は時刻の後に置いて「…時きっかりで」の意味)
授業にちょうど間に合った I was *just* in time for the lesson.
裕子から電話があったとき, 僕はちょうど出かけるところだった I was *just* about to leave the house when Yuko called.

石井さんはちょうど到着したところです Ms. Ishii has *just* arrived. / Ms. Ishii has arrived *just now*.(❖ × Ms. Ishii has arrived just now. とはいわない)
家のちょうど向かいにコンビニができた They built a convenience store *right* across the street from my house.
湖の水面はちょうど(→まるで)鏡のようだった The surface of the lake was *just like* a mirror.
◆これはちょうど欲しいと思っていた CD です This is *the very* CD that I wanted. / ちょうどいいところへ来てくれた, 宿題を手伝ってくれない? You've come *at the right time*. Will you help me with my assignment? / このドレスは私にちょうどぴったりだ This dress fits me *perfectly*.

ちょうど² 調度 furniture Ⓤ ⇨かぐ(家具)

ちょうとうは 超党派 ——超党派の(2大政党制の場合) bipartisan;(政党が3つ以上ある場合) nonpartisan

ちょうとっきゅう 超特急 super express (train)C, bullet train C ◆この原稿を超特急で(→できるだけ急いで)仕上げてくれませんか Could you finish this manuscript *as quickly as possible* [*you can*]?

ちょうない 町内 (近所) neighborhood Ⓤ; (地域社会) community C;(4辺を道路で囲まれた区画) block C;(通り) street C (❖ 英語には「町内」にぴったり当てはまる言葉がないので, 状況に応じて次のように言い換える) ∥斉藤さんは同じ町内に住んでいます Mr. Saito and I live on *the* same *block*. / (→私の近所に住んでいる)Mr. Saito lives in my *neighborhood*.
∥町内会 a neighborhood association

ちょうなん 長男 one's [the] first son;(息子が2人の場合) one's [the] older son;(息子が3人以上の場合) one's [the] oldest son(❖《英》では older, oldest の代わりに elder, eldest を用いる)

ちょうにん 町人 townspeople 《複数扱い》; (商人) merchant C

ちょうのうりょく 超能力 supernatural power Ⓤ C;(超感覚的知覚) extrasensory perception Ⓤ ((略語))ESP ⇨ 場面・状況別会話 p.1722
∥超能力者 a person with supernatural power;(霊能力者) a psychic

ちょうは 長波 long wave Ⓤ C ((略語))LW

ちょうば¹ 帳場 (勘定台) cash desk C, counter C;(旅館の) front desk C

ちょうば² 跳馬 vaulting horse C

ちょうはつ¹ 長髪 long hair Ⓤ C ∥長髪の男性 a man *with long hair*

ちょうはつ² 挑発 provocation Ⓤ C ——挑発する provoke 他⑯ ——挑発的な provocative ∥挑発的な態度をとる take a *provocative* attitude / 挑発されて彼とけんかをしてしまった I had a fight with him *under provocation*. / I *was provoked into* fighting with him. / 彼女は挑発に乗ってこなかった She refused *to be provoked*.

ちょうばつ 懲罰 punishment Ⓤ C;(矯正の

意図を含む) discipline ⓤ
◆彼らは懲罰に付されるだろう They will *be punished* [*disciplined*].
‖懲罰委員会 a disciplinary committee

ちょうふく 重複 (部分的重なり) overlap ⓤⓒ; (繰り返し) repetition ⓤ; (余分) redundancy ⓤⓒ ——**重複する** overlap ⓐⓣ ‖英語で作文を書くときは，同じ語の重複を避けなさい When you write an essay in English, avoid 「*the repetition* of [*repeating*] the same word. / 君の質問は僕のと重複する Your question *overlaps* mine.

ちょうへい 徴兵 《主に米》the draft, conscription ⓤ ——**徴兵する** 《主に米》draft ⓣ, conscript ⓣ ‖彼は健康上の理由で徴兵を免除された He was excused from *the draft* for health reasons. / その国は30年前に徴兵制を敷いた The country introduced *conscription* 30 years ago. / 祖父は22歳のときに徴兵された My grandfather *was drafted* [*conscripted*] when he was 22.
‖徴兵制度 the draft [conscription] system

ちょうへん 長編 (長編小説) long novel ⓒ; (長編映画) long film ⓒ

ちょうぼ 帳簿 (account) book ⓒ (❖帳簿の内容を指す場合は books) ‖帳簿をつける keep *books* / 帳簿をごまかす doctor [《口語的》cook] *the books* / 帳簿にきょうの売り上げを記入する enter today's sales in *the book*
‖帳簿係 an accountant, a bookkeeper

ちょうほう¹ 重宝 電子レンジは本当に重宝なものだ Microwave ovens are really *convenient*. / 彼女はコンピュータに詳しいので，みんなに重宝がられている Everyone finds her *useful* because she knows a lot about computers. / この地図は旅行中に重宝する This map *comes in handy* on trips.

ちょうほう² 諜報 intelligence ⓤ
‖諜報活動 espionage / 諜報機関 a secret service, an intelligence organization / 諜報部員 a secret agent, a spy

ちょうぼう 眺望 view ⓒ, 《公式的》prospect ⓒ 《通例単数形》‖この塔からの相模湾の眺望はすばらしい *The view* of Sagami Bay from this tower is splendid.

ちょうほうけい 長方形 rectangle ⓒ, oblong ⓒ ——**長方形の** rectangular, oblong
⇨ずけい 図版

ちょうほんにん 張本人 (首謀者) the ringleader, the mastermind ‖いたずらの張本人 *the ringleader* [*mastermind*] of the practical joke / この騒ぎの張本人はだれだったの Who was *the ringleader* of this trouble? / (→だれがこの騒ぎを始めたのか) Who started this trouble?

ちょうまんいん 超満員 ——**超満員の** jam-packed, overcrowded ‖バスは学生で超満員だった The bus *was jam-packed* [*overcrowded*] with students.

ちょうみりょう 調味料 seasoning ⓤⓒ, 《公式的》condiment ⓒ ‖化学調味料 chemical seasoning

ちょうみん 町民 the townspeople 《複数扱い》

-**ちょうめ** -丁目 港町 3 丁目 Minatomachi 3-*chome*

ちょうめん 帳面 notebook ⓒ
⇨ちょうぼ，ノート

ちょうもん 弔問 condolence visit ⓒ ‖町長が被害者の遺族を弔問した The mayor *made a condolence visit to* the family of the victim.
‖弔問客 a condolence visitor

ちょうもんかい 聴聞会 聴聞会を開く hold *a hearing*

ちょうやく 跳躍 jump ⓒ, leap ⓒ ——**跳躍する** jump ⓐ, leap* ⓐ ‖跳躍選手 a jumper / 跳躍台 a springboard

ちょうらく 凋落 decline ⓤⓒ ——**凋落する** decline ⓐ ‖17世紀にはこの町は凋落の一途をたどった In the 17th century, the city fell into *decline*.

ちょうり 調理 cooking ⓤ ——**調理する** cook ⓐⓣ ‖調理師 a cook / 調理実習 cooking practice / 調理台《米》a counter,《主に英》a worktop / 調理場 a kitchen / 調理法 a recipe

ちょうりつ¹ 町立 ——**町立の** municipal (❖「地方自治体の」という意味なので，「市立」「村立」にも用いる) ‖町立図書館 a *municipal* [*town*] library

ちょうりつ² 調律 tuning ⓤ ——**調律する** tune ⓣ ‖ピアノを調律する *tune* a piano
‖調律師 a tuner; (ピアノの) a piano tuner

ちょうりゅう 潮流 current ⓒ, tide ⓒ ‖時代の潮流に乗る[逆らう] go with [against] *the current* of the times

ちょうりょく¹ 聴力 hearing ⓤ ‖左耳の聴力を失う lose *one's hearing* in the left ear / 祖母の聴力は衰えています My grandmother's *hearing* is 「getting worse [going]. / My grandmother is losing *her hearing*.
‖聴力検査 a hearing test

ちょうりょく² 張力 【物理】tension ⓤⓒ, tensile strength ⓤⓒ
‖表面張力 surface tension

ちょうるい 鳥類 birds ‖ 鳥類学 ornithology / 鳥類学者 an ornithologist

ちょうれい 朝礼 morning assembly ⓒ ‖毎週月曜日に運動場で朝礼がある We have *a morning assembly* on the playground every Monday.

ちょうろう 長老 elder ⓒ; (男性の)《公式的》the doyen; (女性の)《公式的》the doyenne ‖鉄鋼業界の長老 *the doyen* of the steel industry

ちょうわ 調和 harmony ⓤⓒ ——**調和する** harmonize ⓐⓣ, match ⓐⓣ, go* well ‖そのカーテンと壁は調和がとれている The curtain *harmonizes* [*goes well*] *with* the wall. / The curtain *matches* the wall. / The curtain and the wall *match*.
私たちは自然と調和して暮らすことを望んでいる We wish to live *in harmony with* nature.
この絵は色彩がよく調和している The colors in

this picture「*harmonize* nicely [*go well*] *with* each other.

新しいビルは周囲と調和していない The new building *doesn't harmonize [go well, fit in] with* its surroundings.

◆調和した色彩 a *harmonious* blend of colors / 絵画では光と影の調和を保つことが大切だ It is important to keep *a balance* of light and shade in drawing.

チョーク chalk Ⓤ (◆種類を表すときは Ⓒ) / チョーク 2 本 two pieces of *chalk* / チョークの粉 *chalk* dust / 黒板にチョークで答えを書く write the answer *with a piece of chalk* on a blackboard

ちよがみ 千代紙 🔲 *chiyogami*, Japanese paper with colored patterns

ちょき (じゃんけんの) scissors / ちょきを出す show *scissors*

ちょきちょき (はさみなどの音) snip-snap Ⓤ
◆はさみで紙をちょきちょき切る *snip* the paper with scissors (*rhythmically*)

ちょきん 貯金 savings; (預金) deposit Ⓒ ─貯金する save (up)

月に 2 万ずつ貯金する *save* 20,000 yen a month / 貯金を使う dip into *one's savings*

武は自転車を買うために貯金している Takeshi *is saving* (*up*) to buy a bicycle.

兄は貯金をはたいてコンピュータを買った My brother spent all *his savings* on a computer.

私は去年 50 万円貯金した I *saved* 500,000 yen last year.

哲也はオーストラリア旅行のためにこづかいを貯金している Tetsuya *is saving* his allowance for a trip to Australia.

◆貯金を(→銀行から)1 万円下ろす *withdraw* 10,000 yen *from the bank* / 私は貯金が(→銀行に)100 万円あります I *have* one million yen *in the bank*.

‖貯金通帳(銀行の) a bankbook; (銀行・郵便局などの) a passbook / 貯金箱 a money box; (子豚の形の) a piggy bank / 積立貯金 installment (savings) / 郵便貯金 postal savings

ちょきんちょきん ⇨ちょきちょき

ちょきんと 針金をちょきんと切る *snip* a wire

ちょくえい 直営 direct management / この店は JR の直営です This store *is under the direct management of* JR. / This store *is directly managed [run] by* JR.

ちょくげき 直撃 direct hit Ⓒ ─直撃する hit* hard / その海沿いの町は先週, 台風に直撃された The ocean-front town *was hit hard [directly, squarely] by* a typhoon last week.

◆弾丸が彼の右胸を直撃した A bullet *hit* him *squarely [right] in* the right chest.

ちょくご 直後 ─直後に[で] (時間的に) immediately [right] after ...; (空間的に) just [right] behind ... / 彼が新しい党首に選ばれた直後にその不祥事が明るみに出た The scandal broke *right after* he was elected the new party leader. / バスの直前直後で道路を横断するのは危険だ It is dangerous to cross a street *just before or behind* a bus.

ちょくし 直視 ─直視する look straight [squarely] at ... / 私たちは日本が今日(こんにち)抱えている問題を直視しなければなりません We must *look straight at* the problems of Japan today.

◆現実を直視する *face* reality [the facts]

ちょくしゃ 直射 direct rays / この植物は直射日光にあてないでください Don't expose this plant to「*the direct rays of the sun* [*direct sunlight*].

ちょくしん 直進 ─直進する go* straight (on, ahead) / この通りを直進して最初の信号を左に曲がってください *Go straight* along this street and turn left at the first traffic light.

ちょくせつ 直接

directly, immediately (◆後者のほうが原因と結果が仲介物なしに結びついているという意味が強い); (個人的に) personally ─直接の direct, immediate; personal

直接福岡に行く go *direct(ly)* [*straight*] to Fukuoka / 事故の直接の原因 the *direct* [*immediate*] cause of the accident

僕は彼女から直接聞いた I heard the story *directly* from her.

彼らはその事件に直接関与していた They were *directly* involved in the incident.

私は磯さんと直接話したいのです I'd like to talk with Ms. Iso *personally* [*in person*].

生徒会は校長と直接交渉をした The student council had *direct negotiations* with the principal.

◆警察は事件について被害者から直接情報を得た The police obtained *firsthand* information about the case from the victims.

‖直接税 a direct tax / 直接選挙 a direct election / 直接目的語《文法》 a direct object / 直接話法《文法》 direct speech

ちょくせん 直線 straight line Ⓒ / ペンで直線を引く draw *a straight line* with a pen / ここから学校まで直線距離で 5 キロです It is five kilometers from here to school「*in a straight line* [*as the crow flies*].

‖直線運動 linear motion / 直線距離 beeline distance / 直線コース(競技場の) a [the] stretch; (ゴール前の) the homestretch; (ゴールと反対側の) the backstretch

ちょくぜん 直前 ─直前に[で] (時間的・空間的に) just before ...; (空間的に) just in front of ... / 試験の直前にかぜをひいてしまった I caught a cold *just before* the exam. / バスの直前を横断しないでください Don't cross *just in front of* the bus.

ちょくそう 直送 これらのトマトは産地直送です These tomatoes *came direct* [*straight*] *from the farm*.

ちょくぞく 直属 加藤さんは私の父の直属の上司です Mr. Kato is my father's *direct* [*immediate*] superior. / (→父は加藤さんの直接の監督下にある) My father is under the *direct*

ちょくちょう 直腸〘解剖〙rectum ©
∥直腸(が)〘医学〙rectal cancer, cancer of the rectum

ちょくちょく often 〘孝志はちょくちょく僕の家に遊びに来る Takashi *often* comes to my house to see me.

ちょくつう 直通 〘この列車は松本まで直通ですか Does this train go *direct*(*ly*) to Matsumoto? / このホテルから空港までの直通バスが5分おきに出ている The *direct* [*through*] *bus* from this hotel to the airport runs every five minutes.
∥直通電話 direct dialing / 直通列車 a nonstop [direct] train

ちょくばい 直売 direct sales ——直売する sell* ... directly 〘生産者直売のナシ pears *sold directly by the producers* [*growers*]
∥直売店 a direct sales store, an outlet

ちょくめん 直面 ——直面する be faced [confronted] with ... 〘日本は今経済的な危機に直面している Japan *is* now *faced* [*confronted*] *with* an economic crisis.
◆私たちが今直面している問題についてもっと話し合うべきだ We have to discuss more the problem *before* us.

ちょくやく 直訳 literal [word-for-word] translation © 〘この表現は直訳では意味がわからない This expression cannot be understood if *translated literally*.

ちょくゆ 直喩〘修辞〙simile ©∪

ちょくゆにゅう 直輸入 direct import ∪ ——直輸入する import ... directly 〘その店はアメリカからスニーカーを直輸入している The store *imports* sneakers *directly* from the United States.

ちょくりつ 直立 ——直立する stand* straight [erect] ◆直立不動の姿勢をとる(→気をつけの姿勢をとる) *stand at attention*

ちょくりゅう 直流〘電気〙direct current ∪

ちょくれつ 直列 series ©(複〜) 〘電池を直列につなぐ connect batteries *in series*

ちょこちょこ 小さな女の子が私の方にちょこちょこ歩いてきた A little girl came *toddling* toward me. (※toddleは「幼児がちょこちょこ歩く」という意味です) / (→小さい歩幅で歩いてきた) A little girl *walked* toward me *with short steps*.

ちょこまか リスが芝生の上をちょこまか走り回っている Squirrels *are bustling* [*skittering*] *around* on the lawn. (※bustleは「せわしく動き回る」, skitterは「小動物がちょこまかと動き回る」という意味)

チョゴリ(韓国・北朝鮮の衣装) chogori

チョコ(レート) chocolate ∪© 〘1箱のチョコレート a package [box] of *chocolate*
∥板チョコ a chocolate bar

ちょこんと 黄色い小鳥が枝にちょこんと(→1羽だけで)とまっていた A little yellow bird was perched *alone* on the branch. / ベンチには男の子がちょこんと(→静かに)座っていた A little boy was sitting *quietly* on the bench. / 少女は観客にちょこんと(→小さな)おじぎをし

た The girl gave a *small* bow to the audience.

ちょさく 著作(著述) writing ∪; (著書) book ©; (作品) writings, work © 〘漱石の著作 *the writings* [*works*] of Soseki / 全7巻の著作 *a work* in seven volumes
∥著作権 (a) copyright / 著作権侵害 copyright infringement / 著作権料 royalties

ちょしゃ 著者 author ©, writer © 〘その本の著者 *the author* of the book

ちょじゅつ 著述 writing ∪
∥著述業 authorship

ちょしょ 著書 book ©, writings, work © 〘彼女には美術史に関する著書がいくつかある She has written a few *books* on the history of art.

ちょすい 貯水 〘貯水槽 a water tank, a reservoir / 貯水池 a reservoir / 貯水量 the amount of stored water

ちょぞう 貯蔵 storage ∪; (保存) preservation ∪ ——貯蔵する store ⊕; preserve ⊕ 〘肉を冷凍貯蔵する *keep* meat *in cold storage* / 私の家では地下室に食料を貯蔵しています We *store* (*up*) food in the basement.
∥貯蔵庫 a storehouse, a depository / 貯蔵室 a storeroom; (商品などの) a stockroom

ちょちく 貯蓄 savings ——貯蓄する save (up) (→ちょきん)
∥貯蓄型保険 savings-type insurance

ちょっか 直下 〘赤道直下の島 an island *right on the equator*
∥直下型地震 a major earthquake directly beneath a particular area, a direct-hit quake

ちょっかい 彼は人のことにちょっかいを出しすぎる(→干渉しすぎる) He 「*interferes with* [*meddles in*]」 others' affairs too much. / おれの女にちょっかいを出すな(→言い寄るな) *Don't make a pass at* my girl.

ちょっかく 直角 right angle © 〘2直線は直角に交わっている The two lines cross *at right angles*. / The two lines meet *at an angle of 90 degrees*.
∥直角三角形 (米) a right triangle, (英) a right-angled triangle / 直角定規 a square

ちょっかつ 直轄 direct control ∪ 〘環境省直轄の研究機関 a research institute *under the direct control* of the Ministry of the Environment

ちょっかっこう 直滑降 〘斜面を直滑降で降りる make *a straight descent* down the slope

ちょっかん 直感 intuition ∪©, hunch © ——直感的な intuitive ——直感的に intuitively, by intuition 〘彼女に初めて会ったとき, よい友達になれると直感した When I first met her, *my intuition told me that* we would be good friends. / 彼の直感は当たった His *intuition* proved right. / 彼女はいつも直感で行動する She always follows [acts on] *her hunches*. / 彼女がうそをついていると分かった I knew *intuitively* [*in my bones*] that she was telling a lie.

チョッキ ⚠ (米) vest ©, (英) waistcoat

‖防弾チョッキ a bulletproof vest, a flak jacket

ちょっきゅう 直球 fastball ◎ ‖直球を投げる throw *a fastball*

ちょっけい¹ 直系 夏目漱石の直系の子孫 a *direct* descendant of Natsume Soseki / ソニーの直系の会社 a company *under the direct control of* Sony

ちょっけい² 直径 diameter ◎ ‖その皿は直径が30センチある The plate has *a diameter* of 30 centimeters./ The plate is 30 centimeters *in diameter [across]*.

ちょっけつ 直結 direct connection ◎ ── 直結する be directly connected ‖日常生活に直結した問題 a problem that *is directly connected with* our daily lives

ちょっこう 直行 go* straight to ...,《口語的》make* a beeline for ... ‖新聞記者は事故現場に直行した The newspaper reporter *went straight to* the scene of the accident.
‖直行便(飛行機の) a direct [nonstop] flight

ちょっと

❶【時間】(ほんの少しの時間) a minute [second]; (しばらく) some time, a while
ちょっと待ってください *Just a minute [second, moment]*, please.
ちょっと待ってよ Wait *a minute [second]*./ Hold it.
このペン、ちょっと借りていい? Can I borrow this pen *for a minute [while, moment]*?
志郎はちょっと前に家を出た Shiro left home *a while [moment] ago*.
ちょっとお時間をいただけますか Could you spare me *a minute*?

❷【数量】(少数) a few; (少量) a little; (数・量がいくらか) some
昼食にはサンドイッチをちょっと食べただけだ I had only *a little bit* of a sandwich for lunch.
なべにはシチューがちょっとだけ残っていた There was *only a little* stew left in the pan.
もうちょっとしょうゆを加えてください Please add *a little more* soy sauce.
寝る前にお茶をちょっと飲んだ I had *some* tea before going to bed.
この車は100万円ちょっとだった(→100万円より少しかかった) This car cost *a little more than* one million yen.
🗨「お皿は5枚で足りるかな」「もうちょっと必要だと思うよ」"Are five plates enough?" "I guess we need *a few more*."

❸【程度】(少し) a little; (わずかに) slightly; (かなり) rather,《口語的》pretty,《主に英》quite
美奈子はフランス語がちょっと話せる Minako can speak「French *a little* [*a little* French].
このズボンはちょっとウエストがきつい These trousers are *a little* tight in the waist.
先学期、成績がちょっと上がった My grades improved「*a little* [*slightly*] last term.
きょうはちょっと暑い It's *rather* [*pretty*] hot today.(❖rather は暑すぎるという否定的なニュアンスがある. pretty は中立的)
このクロスワードパズルはちょっと難しい This crossword is *rather* difficult.
次の試合に彼が出られないのはちょっと痛い It's *pretty* [*quite*] hard on us that he can't play in the next game.
◆もうちょっとで(→ほとんど)電車に乗り遅れるところだった I *almost* missed the train.
🗨「彼がいなくて寂しい?」「ちょっとね」"Do you miss him?" "*Kind* [*Sort*] *of*."

❹【簡単に】easily (❖打ち消しの語を伴う)
このレースでだれが勝つかはちょっと予想がつかない You can't *easily* tell who will win this race.
彼女はちょっとやそっとでは君のことをあきらめないよ She won't give up on you *so easily*.
◆彼がいつ戻ってくるかはちょっと(→はっきりとは)分かりません I'm not *quite* sure when he will be back.

❺【呼びかけ】Hey.(❖Hey.はかなりくだけた表現),《米》Say.,《英》I say.
ちょっと、僕の自転車に何してんの *Hey*, what are you doing to my bike?
ちょっと! 何か落としましたよ *Hey*! [(→すみません) *Excuse me*!] You dropped something.
◆ちょっと聞いてよ *Guess what*!/ *You know what*?

❻【その他】
ちょっとあいさつでもと思って電話したんだ I *just* called to say hello.
学校からの帰りに彼女の家にちょっと寄ってみた I *dropped in at* her house on my way back home from school.
この写真をちょっと見てごらん *Just take a look at* this photo.
ちょっとお願いしたいことがあるのですが May I ask you a favor?(❖このように「ちょっと」が具体的な意味をもたない場合は特に訳出する必要はない)
宿題は1時間ではちょっと終わりそうにないんだよ I'm afraid I can't finish my assignment in an hour.
🗨「あしたカラオケに行かない?」「ごめん、あしたはちょっと(→いっしょに行けない)」"What about going to karaoke tomorrow?" "Sorry, *I can't go with you* tomorrow."
🗨「何かいいことでもあったの?」「うん、ちょっとね(→まあね)」"Did something good happen?" "Well, *yes*."

ちょっとした ❶【小さな】small, minor, little ‖ちょっとした違い a *minor* difference / ちょっとした誤解から論争が起こることもある A dispute can arise from a *small* [*simple*] misunderstanding. / 僕は香織にちょっとした贈り物をすることにした I decided to give Kaori a *little* [*small*] present.
❷【かなりの】quite ‖彼女はちょっとした考古学者だ She is *quite* an archeologist./ She is

ちょっぴり

something of an archeologist. / 彼の絵はちょっとしたものだ His paintings are *quite something*.
◆祖父はちょっとした財産を持っている My grandfather has a *small* fortune. ✤ a small fortune は口語で「ひと財産」の意味

ちょっぴり a little, 《口語的》a bit /ちょっぴり恥ずかしかった I was *a little* embarrassed.
◆ちょっぴりもうかった I made a *tiny* profit.

ちょとつもうしん 猪突猛進 headlong dash Ⓒ /妹は猪突猛進型だ My sister is *a type of person who makes a headlong dash*.

ちょびひげ ちょび髭 small mustache [《英》moustache] Ⓒ

ちょぼくじょう 貯木場 《米》lumberyard Ⓒ, 《英》timberyard Ⓒ

ちょめい 著名 ──著名な notable; (有名な) famous, well-known /著名な小説家 a *notable* novelist
‖著名人 a celebrity

ちょろい 彼をだますなんてちょろいもんだよ It's 「*very easy* [*a cinch, easy as pie*] to cheat him.

ちょろちょろ 蛇口から水がちょろちょろ流れている (→したたり落ちている) Water *is trickling* from the tap. / かごの中をハムスターがちょろちょろ動き回っていた Hamsters *were scurrying around* in the cage.

ちょろまかす (たいして価値のない物を) pilfer 働, 《口語的》filch 働 /彼は母親の財布から小銭をちょろまかした He *pilfered* [*filched*] a little money from his mother's purse. / 彼のレジの人はおつりをちょろまかした The cashier 「*pilfered* some of the change [→私につり銭を少なく渡した]*shortchanged*] me].

ちょんぎる ちょん切る cut* off; (ちょきんと) snip off /はさみでジーンズのすそをちょん切った *cut* [*snip*] *off* the bottom of some jeans with scissors

ちょんぼ 私たちはその仕事でちょんぼをしてしまった We 「*screwed up* [*goofed up, made a mess of*] the job.

ちょんまげ 丁髷 🔲 a *chommage*, a topknot /役者はみんな髪をちょんまげにしている All the actors *do* [*wear*] their hair *in chommage* [*a topknot*].

ちらかす 散らかす (物を) scatter 働; (ごみなどを) litter 働; (場所を) mess up
彼は机の上に書類を散らかしていた He *had scattered* papers *over* the desk. / He *had scattered* the desk *with* papers.
学生たちは公園にごみを散らかした The students *littered* the park *with* trash.
お客さんが来るから居間を散らかさないでね A guest is coming, so *don't* 「*mess up* [*make a mess in*] the living room.
ゴミを散らかすな (掲示) *No Littering*

ちらかる 散らかる (物が) be scattered; (ごみなどが) be littered; (場所が) be messy, be in a mess /部屋のあちこちにたくさんの本が散らかっている Many books *are scattered* [*lying*] *around* the room. / The room *is scattered* with many books. / 僕の部屋は今おそろしく散らかっている My room *is in a terrible mess* now. / ちょっと(家の中は)散らかっていますが、どうぞお入りください I'm afraid the house *is* kind of *messy*, but come on in please.

ちらし 散らし flier Ⓒ; (手で配る) handbill Ⓒ; (新聞などの) insert Ⓒ /駅の近くで学生たちがちらしを配っていた Students were passing out *fliers* [*handbills*] near the station.

ちらす 散らす scatter 働 /きのうのあらしが桜の花を散らした The storm *scattered* the cherry blossoms yesterday.
◆考え事をしてるから気を散らすようなことはしないでね Don't try to *distract* me *from* my thinking. / 彼らは議論で火花を散らした (→激しい議論をした) They *had a heated argument*. / 彼女は足が痛いとわめき散らした She *cried out* with pain in her leg. / 彼は何かにつけ他人に当たり散らす He always *takes it out on* others whenever he has the chance.

ちらちら 雪がちらちら (→軽く) 降り始めた It began to snow *lightly*. / A *light* snow began to fall. / 遠くで釣り船の明かりがちらちら光っていた The lights of the fishing boats *were shimmering* [*glimmering*] in the distance. / 車のヘッドライトで目がちらちらした (→ヘッドライトが私の目をくらませた) The headlights of the car *dazzled me*. / あそこのベンチの女性はさっきからこちらをちらちら見ている The woman on the bench over there *has been sneaking glances at* us. / 彼の悪いうわさがちらちらと (→時々) 耳に入る I *sometimes* happen to hear a bad rumor about him.

ちらつかせる (ちらっと見せる) flash 働; (ほのめかす) hint at …; (希望・誘惑などを) dangle 働 /やくざは刃物をちらつかせた The gangster *flashed* a knife. / 母はおこづかいアップをちらつかせて僕に勉強させた My mother made me study *by* [*hinting at* a raise in my allowance [*dangling* a raise in my allowance *in front of* me].

ちらつく ❶【ちらちら降る】fall* lightly /雪がちらついている Snow *is falling lightly*.
❷【光がまたたく】twinkle 働; (かすかに光る) shimmer 働; (点滅する) flicker 働 /遠くに港の明かりがちらついているのが見える I see harbor lights *shimmering* in the distance. / テレビの画面がちらついている The TV screen *is flickering*.
❸【心に浮かぶ】appear before *one's* eyes, cross *one's* mind /成績表をもらったとき怒った父の顔がちらついた When I got my report card, my father's angry face *appeared before my eyes*.

ちらっと 彼女は出ていくとき私をちらっと見た She *glanced* [*took a glance*] *at* me when she left.

ちらばる 散らばる scatter 働, be scattered /子供たちは遊園地のあちこちに散らばった The children *scattered* throughout the amusement park. / 私の親戚は日本全国

に散らばっています My relatives *are scattered* all over Japan.

ちらほら このあたりにもコンビニがちらほらと(→そこここに)でき始めた Convenience stores are beginning to open *here and there* in this area. / 二人が結婚するかもしれないといううわさをちらほら(→時々)耳にします I hear *now and then* a rumor that they are going to get married.

ちらりと 真弓をちらりと見たら笑いを抑えるのに必死だった When I *glanced* [*took a glance*] *at* Mayumi, she was having a hard time holding back laughter. / 電車がトンネルに入る直前, 空に大きな飛行船がちらりと見えた I *glimpsed* [*caught a glimpse of*] a big blimp just before our train went into the tunnel.

ちり¹ 地理 geography Ⓤ ∥彼は地理よりも歴史が得意だ He is better at history than at *geography*.

◆彼女はこのあたりの地理に詳しい She *knows her way around* here. / 私はこのあたりの地理には詳しくありません I'm *not familiar with* this neighborhood. / (→不案内です) I *am a stranger in* this neighborhood.

∥地理学者 a geographer

ちり² 塵 dust Ⓤ ∥本棚にちりが積もっている The bookshelf is covered with *dust*. / 彼女の部屋にはちりひとつ落ちていない There's not a speck of *dust* in her room.

◆電灯のかさのちりを払ってくれませんか Could you *dust* the lampshade, please?

∥ちり取り ⇒ちりとり

ことわざ ちりも積もれば山となる Steady efforts produce big results. (→努力を積み重ねると大きな成果が得られる) ; Many a little makes a mickle. (→少量でも多く集まれば多量となる)

ちりがみ 塵紙 (ティッシュペーパー) tissue Ⓒ (❖×tissue paper とはいわない) ; (トイレ用) toilet paper Ⓤ

∥ちり紙交換(行為) exchanging old newspapers for toilet paper ; (人)a newspaper recycler

ちりちり ちりちりに(→縮れた)パーマをかけている have a *frizzy* perm / 夏休み中に髪の毛をちりちりにした I *had* my hair *frizzed* during summer vacation.

ちりぢり 散り散り 駅は込んでいたので, 私たちのグループはちりぢりになってしまった The station was so crowded that our group *was scattered* [*became separated*]. / 戦争中, その一家はちりぢりになった The family *was broken up* [*dispersed*] during the war. / どなり声が聞こえると男の子たちはちりぢりに(→四方八方に)逃げた The boys ran away *in all directions* the moment they heard the angry shout.

ちりとり 塵取り dustpan Ⓒ

ちりばめる stud (❖通例受身で用いる) ∥アーモンドをちりばめたケーキ a cake *studded with* almonds / その箱には真珠がちりばめられている The box *is studded* [(→はめ込まれている)*inlaid*] *with* pearls.

ちりょう 治療 (手当て) (medical) treatment Ⓤ Ⓒ ; (治癒) cure Ⓒ ; (薬・手術によらないもの) therapy Ⓤ Ⓒ ──治療する treat ⨺ ; cure

最新のエイズ治療法 the latest *treatment* for AIDS / 放射線治療の効果が出る(→治療に反応する) respond to *radiation therapy*

彼は現在, 腕の骨折の治療を受けている He *is now being treated* for a broken arm.

【treat＋名(人)＋for 名】医者は抗生物質で私のインフルエンザを治療した The doctor 「*treated* me *for* the flu [*treated* my flu] with antibiotics.

【cure＋名(人)＋of 名】佐久間先生が彼の癌(ﾊﾞ)を治療した Dr. Sakuma 「*cured* him *of* his cancer [*cured* his cancer].

◆傷を治療する *heal* a wound / 虫歯の治療に3か月かかった It took three months to *fix* the cavities.

∥治療費 a doctor's bill [fee] / 集中治療室 an intensive care unit (《略語》ICU)

ちりょく 知力 intellect Ⓤ Ⓒ, intellectual power Ⓤ Ⓒ, mental ability Ⓤ Ⓒ ∥急速な知力の衰え a rapid loss of *mental ability* / 知力のすぐれた少女 a girl *of great intellectual power* ; an *intelligent* girl

ちりんちりん ベルがちりんちりんと鳴った The bell *went ting-a-ling*. / 風で風鈴がちりんちりんと鳴っている The wind chime *is tinkling* in the wind. / The wind *is tinkling* the wind chime.

ちる 散る

❶【分散する】scatter ⨺, be scattered

コンサートが終わると観客たちは散っていった The audience *scattered* [*broke up, dispersed*] after the concert.

この大学の卒業生は全国に散っている Graduates of this university *are scattered* all over Japan.

◆パンタグラフから火花が散った Sparks *flew* from the pantograph.

❷【花や葉が落ちる】fall*⨺

昨夜の強風で桜の花がみんな散ってしまった The cherry blossoms 「*all fell* [*are all gone*] because of the strong wind last night.

❸【気が】

隣の部屋から聞こえてくる音楽に気が散って本が読めない(→音楽が読書から私の注意をそらしている) The music from the next room *distracts* me *from* reading.

チルド ∥チルド食品 chilled food

ちんあげ 賃上げ a raise (in wages), pay raise Ⓒ, 《口語的》pay [wage] hike Ⓒ ∥3パーセントの賃上げを要求する demand *a three percent pay raise* [*hike*]

◆賃上げを要求してストをする strike for 「*higher wages* [*a wage increase*]

∥賃上げ闘争 a struggle for higher wages / 賃上げ要求 a demand for higher wages

ちんあつ 鎮圧 suppression Ⓤ ──鎮圧する suppress ⨺, put* down ∥暴動鎮圧のため機動隊が出動した The riot police were sent to

suppress [put down] the riot.
ちんか¹ 沈下 subsidence ⓤ ―沈下する sink* ⓘ, subside ⓘ ∥その建物は毎年1センチずつ沈下している The building sinks one centimeter every year.
∥地盤沈下 ground subsidence
ちんか² 鎮火 ―鎮火する extinguish ⓣ, put* out ∥火事は3時間後に鎮火された The fire was extinguished [put out] in three hours.
ちんがし 賃貸し ―賃貸しする rent [《英》let*] (out)(✤rentには「借りる」の意味もあるため、明確にするには out を用いる) ⇨ かす(貸す) ∥アメリカに行っている間、家を斉藤さん一家に賃貸しすることにした We decided to 「rent out [lease] our house to the Saitos while we are in the States.
ちんがり 賃借り ―賃借りする rent ⓣ ∥部屋を賃借りする rent [take a lease on] a room
ちんぎん 賃金 wages(✤特に肉体労働者への日給、週給についていう);(給料) pay ⓤ
安い賃金で働く work for [at] low wages / 賃金引き上げを要求する demand 「higher wages [a pay raise] / 男女間の賃金格差を是正する correct the disparity in wages between men and women / 賃金カットに反対してストをする strike against a wage cut
彼は週10万円の賃金をもらっている He gets weekly wages of 100,000 yen. / His wages are 100,000 yen a week.
会社側は賃金の引き下げを組合に通告した The management notified the union of a reduction in wages.
∥賃金水準 a wage level / 賃金スライド制 a sliding pay scale / 賃金生活者 a paid worker / 賃金凍結 a wage freeze / 最低賃金 a minimum wage
ちんしもっこう 沈思黙考 meditation ⓤ(また複数形～s)∥沈思黙考する be deep in meditation
ちんしゃ 陳謝 apology ⓒ ―陳謝する apologize ⓘ ∥その会社は事故に関して被害者に公には陳謝していない The company hasn't publicly apologized to the victims for the accident.
ちんじゅつ 陳述 statement ⓒ ∥虚偽の陳述を行う make a false statement / 陳述書を提出する submit [hand in] a statement
ちんじょう 陳情 petition ⓒ ―陳情する petition ⓣ ∥政府に陳情書を提出する submit a petition to the government / 彼らは市長に高校の新設を陳情した They petitioned [made an appeal to] the mayor to build a new high school.
∥陳情団 a group of petitioners,《米》a lobby
チンする (電子レンジで温める) warm [heat] ... in a microwave (oven); (電子レンジで調理する) cook ... in a microwave (oven),《米口語的に》zap ⓣ
ちんせい 沈静 首都の暴動は次の日に沈静化した The rioting in the capital calmed [qui-
eted, died] down the next day.
ちんせいざい 鎮静剤 鎮静剤を飲む take a tranquilizer [sedative]
ちんたい¹ 沈滞 stagnation ⓤ ◆景気は沈滞している Business is stagnant [slow]. / 沈滞ムードを吹き飛ばすために、我々のチームは強化合宿を行った Our team had a training camp to get rid of our depressed mood.
ちんたい² 賃貸 2年の賃貸契約で家を借りる rent a house on a two-year lease contract / このアパートの賃貸料は月7万円です The rent for this apartment is 70,000 yen a month. / 彼女は賃貸契約をさらに2年延長した She renewed her lease for another two years.
∥賃貸マンション a rental apartment
ちんちゃく 沈着 composure ⓤ ∥チャンピオンはピンチに追い込まれても沈着冷静だった The champion 「kept his composure [remained calm] even in a fix.
◆沈着な態度 a calm [collected, self-possessed] attitude / 沈着冷静に行動する behave calmly
ちんちょう 珍重 ―珍重する treasure ⓣ, prize [value] highly ∥このコインは世界中で珍重されている This coin is highly prized all over the world.
ちんちん ❶【音】自転車のベルをちんちん鳴らす tinkle the bell on the bicycle / やかんがちんちん鳴っている The kettle is whistling.
❷【犬の芸】ブラッキー、ちんちん Sit up, Blacky! / ポチがちんちんしている(→後ろ足で立っている) Pochi is standing on his hind legs.
ちんつう 沈痛 ―沈痛な (悲嘆にくれている) sorrowful; (悲しそうな) sad ∥彼女は沈痛な面もちで病室から出てきた She came out of the sickroom, looking sorrowful [sad].
ちんつうざい 鎮痛剤 painkiller ⓒ, analgesic ⓒ ∥鎮痛剤を処方される be prescribed painkillers
ちんでん 沈殿 sedimentation ⓤ ―沈殿する settle ⓘ ∥細かいお茶の葉がポットの底に沈殿した Fine tea leaves settled to the bottom of the pot.
◆フラスコの底に黄色い沈殿物ができた Some yellow sediment formed at the bottom of the flask.
ちんどんや ちんどん屋

> ちんどん屋とは新規開店の店や芝居などを伝統的なやり方で宣伝して回る人々のことです。彼らの格好は奇妙なもので、男性までもが大げさな化粧に日本髪のかつら、そしてはでな着物をつけ、太鼓や鐘を鳴らしながら商店街を練り歩きます。
> Chindonya are traditional advertisers for newly opened stores, plays and the like. They dress in a rather odd way: even the men wear exaggerated make-up, colorful kimono and wigs in traditional Japanese hairstyles. They walk around shopping areas playing drums and gongs.

チンパンジー chimpanzee ©
ちんぴら hoodlum ©, 《米俗語》punk ©
ちんぴん 珍品 curio ©(複 ～s), rarity ©
ちんぷ 陳腐 ——陳腐な (古くさい) trite; (使い古された) hackneyed; (平凡な) 《軽蔑的》banal; (ありふれた) commonplace //陳腐な考え a banal [trite] idea / 陳腐な表現 a hackneyed [(→月並みな) conventional] phrase; a cliché (✿発音は [kliːʃéi])
◆陳腐な言い訳 a ready-made excuse
ちんぷんかんぷん 彼の説明はちんぷんかんぷんだ His explanations are gibberish to me. / (→ギリシャ語のように理解不能だ) His explanations are all Greek to me. / (→全く理解できない) I can't understand his explanations at all.; I can't make head or tail of his explanations.
ちんぼつ 沈没 ——沈没する sink* ⑧ //船は100人の乗客を乗せたまま和歌山沖で沈没した The ship sank off Wakayama with 100 passengers aboard.
◆沈没船を引き揚げる raise a sunken ship
ちんみ 珍味 delicacy © //山海の(→あらゆる種類の)珍味 delicacies「of all kinds [taken from mountains and seas]
ちんもく 沈黙 silence ⓤ© //容疑者は最後まで沈黙を守った The suspect「maintained her silence [remained silent] to the end. / 彼は突然沈黙を破って,事件について話し始めた He suddenly broke his silence and began to talk about the case. / 彼女は10年の沈黙を破って新しい小説を発表した She published a new novel after 10 years of silence. / 部屋は気まずい沈黙に包まれた An awkward silence [hush] fell over the room.
ことわざ 沈黙は金なり Silence is golden.
ちんれつ 陳列 display ⓤ©; (展覧会などの) exhibition ⓤ© ——陳列する display ⑧; exhibit ⑧ //新しいおもちゃをショーウインドーに陳列する display new toys in a show window / エジプトの宝物はこの部屋に陳列してあります Egyptian treasures are exhibited [displayed] in this room. / 陳列してある商品には手を触れないでください Please do not touch the goods on display.
∥陳列室 a display room, a showroom / 陳列台 a display stand / 陳列棚 a showcase / 陳列品 an article on display

ツアー ⚠ (団体旅行) group [organized] tour ⓒ; (パックツアー) package tour ⓒ (✪日本語のツアーは団体で1か所または各地を訪れることだが, 英語のa tourは人数に関係なく, 1人または団体で各地を回ること. 1か所のみを訪れるときは人数に関係なく a trip を使う) ➡ 場面・状況会話 p.1686 ∥この夏は東南アジアツアーに行くつもりです I'm thinking of going to *a group* [*package*] *tour* of Southeast Asia this summer.
◆先週イチゴ狩りツアーに参加した I joined *a* strawberry picking *trip* last week. / その新人歌手は初の全国ツアー中だ The new singer is on *her* first *national tour.*
∥ツアーコンダクター a tour conductor

つい¹
❶【わずか】 (ほんの) only; (ちょうど) just; (たった今) just now (✪過去時制で用いる)
ついしか月ほど前 *only* a month ago
つい今しがた帰ってきた I've *just* got back. / I got back *just now.*
それはついきのうのことのように思い出される I remember that as if it were *only* yesterday.
その事故はここからつい数百メートル先で起きた The accident happened *only* a few hundred meters away from here.
◆つい最近まで知らなかった I didn't know *until quite recently.*
❷【うっかり】 (不注意に) carelessly; (間違って) by mistake; (思わず) in spite of *oneself*; (無意識に) unintentionally
ついうっかり同じ本を2冊買ってしまった I bought two of the same book *by mistake.*
つい大声をあげてしまった I shouted *in spite of myself.*
◆甘い物にはつい手が出てしまう I *can't resist* sweets. / 新製品を見るとつい買ってしまう I *can't help buying* new products whenever I see them. / 歯医者の予約をついうっかり忘れてしまった I *missed* the my dentist appointment. It slipped my mind.

つい² 対 pair ⓒ ∥1対の花びん *a pair* of vases / この2つの茶わんは対になっている These (two) teacups come as *a pair.*

ツイード tweed ⓤ; (ツイード製の服) tweed ⓒ ∥ツイードの上着 *a tweed* jacket

ついおく 追憶 (回顧) reminiscence [rèminísəns] ⓤ; (思い出) reminiscences, recollection ⓒ ∥追憶にふける be lost in *reminiscences*

ついか 追加 (付け足し) addition ⓤ; (物などの補足) supplement ⓒ ──追加の additional; supplementary ──追加する add ⓗ; supplement ⓗ
追加注文する make *an additional order*
ジャイアンツは8回に追加点を3点あげた The Giants *added three runs* in the eighth inning.
◆チーズバーガーをあと2つ追加してください Can I have two *more* cheeseburgers?
∥追加予算 a supplementary budget / 追加料金 a supplementary [an extra] charge

ついきゅう¹ 追及 (調査) investigation ⓒ (✪具体的な調査内容は ⓒ); (尋問) interrogation ⓤ ──追及する investigate ⓗ; interrogate ⓗ; (非難する) accuse ⓗ; search for ... ∥事故の原因追及 *an investigation* into the accident / 我々はなぜ彼がそのような行為に及んだのかを追及する必要がある We need to *investigate* what caused him to do such a thing. / 市長は公費による観光旅行の責任を追及された The mayor *was accused* of going on a sightseeing trip at public expense. / 警察はテロリストの追及に必死だ The police *are* desperately *searching for* the terrorists.

ついきゅう² 追求 (理想・目的・快楽などを追うこと) pursuit ⓤ; (捜し求めること) search ⓒ ──追求する pursue ⓗ; search for ... ∥幸福の追求 *the pursuit* of happiness / 若者は理想を追求する Young people *search for* an ideal. / 利潤を追求する *seek* profit

ついきゅう³ 追究 ──追究する pursue ⓗ, seek* ⓗ ∥哲学者は真理を追究する Philosophers *pursue* [*seek*] the truth.

ついげき 追撃 chase ⓒⓤ, 《公式的》pursuit ⓤ ∥NATO軍の戦闘機が領空に侵入した飛行機を追撃した The NATO fighter *gave chase to* the intruding plane.
∥追撃機 a pursuit [chase] plane, an interceptor

ついし (験) 追試(験) supplementary exam(ination) ⓒ, 《米》make-up (exam) ⓒ; (不合格による) retake ⓒ, 《英》resit ⓒ
◆英語の追試を受けた I *retook an* English *exam.*

ついしん 追伸 postscript ⓒ ((略語) P.S., PS)

ついずい 追随 ──追随する follow ⓗⓘ ∥戦後日本の防衛政策はアメリカに追随している Regarding its defense policy, Japan *has followed* in America's footsteps since the end of the last war.
◆バイオリンの演奏にかけては彼女は他の追随を許さない *No one comes close to* her in playing the violin.

ツイスト the twist ∥ツイストを踊る do [dance] *the twist*

ついせき 追跡 (つかまえるために) chase ⓒ, 《公式的》pursuit ⓤ ──追跡する chase ⓗ, pursue ⓗ; (足跡などを) track ⓗ ∥トラを巣穴まで追跡する *track* the tiger to its lair / 追跡の手を逃れる escape [evade] *pursuit* / FBIはその逃亡者を追跡中だ The FBI is in

pursuit of the fugitive.
‖追跡者 a chaser, a pursuer / 追跡調査 a follow-up survey

ついそう 追想 reminiscence [rèminísəns] [U]
➔ ついおく

ついたち 一日 the first day of a month
◆きょうは12月1日です It's「*the first* of December [December (*the*) *first*] today.

ついたて 衝立 screen [C]; (仕切り) partition [C]

ついちょう 追徴 additional collection [C]
──追徴する charge an additional amount
◆申告もれが明らかになり彼は所得税を50万円追徴された He *was charged* an additional 500,000 yen for income tax after some undeclared income was revealed.
‖追徴金 a forfeit / 追徴税 a penalty tax

ついつい 土曜日はついつい夜ふかしをしてしまう I *can't help staying up late* on Saturdays.

ついて

❶【…に関して】about, 《公式的》concerning, regarding; (軽く触れる場合) of; (専門的内容) on; (…をめぐって) over; (すでに述べられたことに関して) as for …
日本についての本 a book *about* Japan (❖内容が学術的な場合は on を用いる)
そのことについてどう思いますか What do you think *about* [*of*] it?
彼は家族のことについて話したがらない He's reluctant to talk *about* his family.
その話について耳にしたことはあるが, 詳しくは知らない I've heard *of* the story, but don't know much about it.
金銭についての質問はお断りします We won't accept any questions *concerning* [*regarding*] money.
彼女はその事件についてコメントするのを避けた She avoided commenting *on* the case.
その件について議論するのはしばらくやめよう Let's not argue *over* [*about*] the case for a while.
その3人については私が個人的に連絡しておきます *As for* those three, I'll personally contact them.
◆君たちはそれについてもっと率直に話し合うべきだ You should *discuss* it more openly. (❖discuss は他動詞なので about は付けない)
❷【そこで】➔ ついては
❸【…を単位として】➔ -つき

ついで[1] ついでのときに(→都合のよいときに)やっておいてくれればいいです If you could do it *at your convenience*, that would be fine. / (→時間のあるときに) That would be fine if you could do it *when you have time*. / 学校へ行くついでにこれをポストに出しておいて Will you mail this *on your way to* the school? / 横浜に来るついでがあれば(→機会があれば)遊びに来てください Please come and visit us *when you have a chance to come* to Yokohama. / 買い物ついでに10円切手を5枚買ってきてもらえるかな Could you get five 10-yen stamps *when* you go shopping?

ついで[2] 次いで (…の次に) next to …; (後に) after ‖私は彼に次いでよい成績だった I got the best grades *next to* him. / A社に次いでB社が大学生の間で就職先として人気のある企業だ *After* [*Next to*] A, B is the second most popular company to work for among college students.

ついていく 付いて行く (…の後に) follow [他]; (いっしょに) go* with …, come* (along) with … (❖話している相手についていく場合は相手の立場で考えて come を用いる); (同伴する) accompany [他]; (遅れずに) keep* up with … ‖子犬は主人についていった The puppy *followed* its master. / 知らない人についていっちゃだめだよ You must not *go with* strangers. / ついていってもいいですか Can I *come with* you? / 日本人学生が英語による授業についていくのは大変だ It's hard for Japanese students to *keep up with* lessons in English.
◆あなたの考え方にはついていけません I *can't go along with* your way of thinking.

ついている 付いている このランチにはサラダとコーヒーがついています Salad and coffee *come with* this lunch. / 歯に青のりがついてるよ You'*ve got* some green *nori* on your teeth.

ついて(い)る lucky ‖きょうはついてるぞ I'm *lucky* today. / Today is my *lucky* day. / 君はついてるね *Lucky* you!
◆ついてないね *Hard* [*Bad*] *luck*.

ついてくる 付いて来る (…の後に) follow [他]; (いっしょに) come* (along) with …; (同伴する) accompany [他]; (遅れずに) keep* up with … ‖私についてきてください Please *follow* [*come along with*] me. / 彼は親切にも駅までついてきてくれた He was kind enough to *accompany* me to the station.

ついでに ➔ ついで[1]

ついては 山田先生が来春退職されます. ついては先生を迎えて送別会を3月に開こうと思うのですが Mr. Yamada will retire next spring. *Therefore* I'd like to hold a farewell party for him next March.

ついてまわる 付いて回る 私はロシアからの視察団に通訳としてついて回った I *went around* with a Russian inspection team as an interpreter. / 犯罪歴は一生ついて回る A criminal record *is with* you for life.

ついとう 追悼 (服喪) mourning [U]; (お悔やみ) condolence [U] (❖condolences で「お悔やみの言葉」の意味) ──追悼の memorial ‖追悼の辞を述べる give *a memorial address*; deliver *a eulogy* (❖eulogy は死者への賞賛の言葉)
◆大統領は先日亡くなったその歌手に追悼の意を表した The President *paid tribute to* the singer who died the other day.
‖追悼式 a memorial service

ついとつ 追突 rear-end collision [C] ◆後ろの車に追突された My car *was rear-ended* by the car behind me.

ついに 遂に・終に at last; at length; in the

end; finally; after all(❖after all 以外は否定文に使わない)
- at last: 努力が報われて.
- at length: 長い休止期間の後に.
- in the end: 結末には.
- finally: 長い時間を経て.
- after all: 努力むなしく,または予想・意図に反して.

ついに彼は知子のハートを射止めた He won Tomoko's heart *at last*.

長い沈黙の後ついに彼女は口を開いた After a long silence she spoke *at length*.

彼はついには一文無しになってしまった He went broke *in the end*.

ついに真実が明かされた The truth *finally* came out.

ついに彼女は来なかった She didn't come *after all*.

ついばむ 啄む peck [pick] at ... ∥数羽の小鳥がえさをついばんでいた A few birds *were pecking at* seeds.

ついほう 追放 exile [éksail] Ⓤ; banishment Ⓤ; deportation Ⓤ; purge Ⓒ; elimination Ⓤ ──追放する exile 他; banish 他; deport 他; purge 他; eliminate 他; (学校・団体などで問題を起こした者を) expel 他; (取り除く)《口語的》get* rid of ...
- exile: 主に政治的理由により自国民を追放すること.
- banishment: 刑罰として自国民または他国民を追放すること.
- deportation: 好ましくない外国人を追放すること.
- purge: 組織などから人を追放すること.
- elimination: 好ましくない者を排除すること.

党から汚職議員を追放する *purge* corrupt members from the party

彼は国外に追放された He *was exiled* from the country.

その団体のワンマン会長は自分の気に入らない会員をすぐに追放する The dictatorial president of the organization easily *eliminates* members whom he doesn't like.

ポルノ雑誌は公共の場から追放すべきだ We should「*get rid of* [(→禁じる) ban]」pornographic magazines in public spaces.

その学校はいじめ追放(→いじめをなくすこと)に取り組んでいる The school is trying to *eliminate* bullying.

ついやす 費やす (お金・時間などを) spend* 他; (むだに) waste 他 ∥政府はその橋の建設に20億円を費やした The government *spent* two billion yen *on* building the bridge. / 彼は一人前の寿司(f)職人になるのに10年を費やした He *spent* 10 years to become a professional sushi chef. / 我々はささいな問題に多くの時間を費やすべきではない We shouldn't *waste* much time *on* trivial matters.

ついらく 墜落 (飛行機などの) crash Ⓒ; (落下すること) fall Ⓒ ──墜落する crash Ⓒ; fall* 自 ∥墜落現場 *the site of a crash* ∥ 行方不明の飛行機が墜落したのではないかとの懸念が高まっている There is growing concern that the missing plane may *have crashed*. / 彼女は がけからなぞの墜落死を遂げた She mysteriously *fell down the cliff and died*.

ツインベッド twin bed Ⓒ (❖通例複数形で用いる. 単数形はツインベッドの片方を指す)

ツインルーム twin room Ⓒ

つう 通 (食べ物・芸術などの) connoisseur Ⓒ [kànəsə́ːr]; (専門家) expert Ⓒ; (権威者) authority Ⓒ ∥私の父はワイン通です My father is *a connoisseur of wine*.
◆デイビッドはなかなかの日本通です David *really knows about Japan*.

-つう -通 (書類など) copy Ⓒ ∥英語の履歴書を3通送付してください Please send three *copies* of the résumé in English.
◆はがき2通と手紙1通が届いてますよ There are *two postcards* and *one letter* for you.

つういん 通院 彼は交通事故の後, 月に1回通院している Since the traffic accident, he「*goes to the hospital* [*sees a doctor*]」once a month. (❖go to (the) hospital は文脈によっては「入院する」の意味になるので注意が必要)

つうか¹ 通貨 currency Ⓤ Ⓒ; (金銭一般) money Ⓤ ➡ 巻末付録 (通貨一覧) ∥外国通貨 foreign *currency* / 米ドルに対して強い[弱い]通貨 *a* strong [weak] *currency* against the US dollars
∥通貨危機 a monetary crisis / 通貨切り上げ revaluation / 通貨切り下げ devaluation / 通貨制度 a monetary system / 国際通貨基金 the International Monetary Fund (《略語》the IMF)

つうか² 通過 《公式的》passage Ⓤ ──通過する pass 自他 ∥彼らはその法案の通過を懸命に阻止しようとした They worked hard against *passage* of the bill. / 列車は名古屋を通過したところだ Our train *has* just *passed* Nagoya.
◆日本チームは第1次予選を通過した The Japanese team *got through* the first round. / (飛行機のアナウンスで)当機は現在紀伊半島上空を通過しております We *are* now *flying over* the Kii Peninsula.
∥通過駅 a station the train doesn't stop at

つうかあ 田中と遠藤はつうかあの仲だ Tanaka and Endo are *of one mind*.

つうかい 痛快 痛快な漫画 a *very exciting* comic book 自他 ∥君のあの高慢ちきなやつをひっぱたいたのを見て痛快だったよ It *gave me great pleasure* to see you slap that boastful guy.

つうがく 通学 ──通学する go* to school; (バス・電車で) commute to school ∥兄は電車とバスで通学していた My brother *commuted* [*went*] *to school* by train and bus.
◆私は歩いて通学しています I *walk to school*.
∥通学路 one's route to school

つうかん¹ 痛感 ──痛感する strongly [fully] realize 他 ∥現在の仕事に英語の必要性を痛感している I *strongly realize* how English is necessary for my present job. / 大臣は「社会的責任を痛感している」と述べた The Minister said, "I *strongly realize* my social responsibility."

つうかん² 通関 ‖通関手続き customs procedure

つうき 通気 ventilation ◆天然素材の服は通気性がいい Clothes made of natural materials *breathe well*. ‖通気孔 a vent

つうきん 通勤 commuting ──通勤する go* to work;（バス・電車・車で）commute ◆‖通勤時間はどのくらいですか How long does it take you to *go to work*? / 私は横浜から東京まで電車で通勤している I *commute* from Yokohama to Tokyo by train.
‖通勤客 a commutation passenger / 通勤者 a commuter / 通勤手当 a transportation allowance / 通勤定期《米》a commuter pass,《英》a season ticket / 通勤電車 a commuter train / 通勤ラッシュ the rush-hour traffic

つうこう 通行《公式的》passage ◆;（車の往来）traffic ◆‖警官は通行車両に徐行するよう合図した The police officer signaled *the traffic* to go slowly. / この道路は通行止めです This road *is closed to traffic*.
◆通行止め《掲示》*No Through Road*/ *Road Closed* / 一方通行《掲示》*One Way* / 右側通行《掲示》*Keep to the Right* / この先通行禁止《掲示》*No Admittance Beyond This Point* / 日本では車は左側通行です In Japan cars *drive on the left*.
‖通行人 a passerby;（歩行者）a pedestrian / 通行料金 a toll

つうこく 通告 notice ◆,《公式的》notification ◆ ──通告する inform ◆, notify ◆‖球団は彼に戦力外通告を行った（→来季契約の延長はしないと通告した）The baseball team *notified* him *that his contract wouldn't be extended next season*.

つうこん 痛恨 彼がこの事件に巻き込まれたことは痛恨の極みだ It is *most regrettable* that he got involved in this incident.

つうさん 通算 total ◆ ──通算する total ◆‖私は通算12年カナダに住んでいました I spent *a total* of twelve years in Canada.
◆小田投手の昨年までの通算成績は27勝18敗9セーブだ Oda's *record* as a pitcher up to the last year is 27 wins, 18 losses and 9 saves.

つうさんしょう 通産省 the Ministry of International Trade and Industry（❖2001年経済産業省に改称）⇨けいざいさんぎょうしょう

つうじ 通じ bowel movement ◆‖もう2日ほどお通じがないんです I haven't had *a bowel movement* for two days. / ヨーグルトは通じをよくする Yoghurt helps your *bowel movements*.

つうじて 通じて 彼らはインターネットを通じて知り合った They got to know each other *through* the Internet. / 現代は様々なメディアを通じてあらゆる情報が入ってくる All sorts of information pour out *through* various media. / その国は一年を通じて高温多湿だ It's hot and humid *throughout* [*all through*] *the year* in that country.

つうしょう¹ 通称 この通りの通称は「肉屋通り」だ This street *is commonly called* "Butchers' Street."

つうしょう² 通商 trade ◆;（大規模な）commerce ◆ ‖アメリカ通商代表部 the Office of US *Trade* Representative（《略語》USTR）
‖通商交渉 trade talks / 通商条約 a commerce treaty

つうじょう 通常 usually, normally ──通常の usual, normal ‖川の水位は通常より低い The river is lower than *usual*. / 1月4日より通常どおり営業します We will be open *as usual* from January 4.
‖通常国会 an ordinary Diet session, a regular (session of the) Diet / 通常兵器 conventional weapons / 通常料金 a normal price

つうじる 通じる

❶【つながる】（道などが）lead* ◆, go* ◆;（鉄道などが）run* ◆;（部屋・戸などが）open ◆;（電話が）get* through
この道は東京湾に通じている This street *leads* [*goes*] to Tokyo Bay.
うちの近くの駅から銀座まで地下鉄が通じている The subway [《英》underground] *runs* from my local station to Ginza.
そのドアは中庭に通じている The door *opens* to the patio.
家に電話したが通じなかった I phoned home but I *couldn't get through*.

❷【了解される】（理解される）be understood;（自分の意思を理解させる）make* *oneself* understood;（互いに理解し合う）communicate with …

> **英作文ノート** lead では通じない！
> 私の英語は通じませんでした
> →×My English didn't *lead* to anyone.
> →○I couldn't *make myself understood* in English.
> ★「通じなかった」を「自分を分からせることができなかった」と解釈し, make myself understood で表現する.「通じる」=lead と考えて直訳しても意味をなさない.

◆彼女には彼の気持ちが通じた She *understood* his feelings. / 彼にいやみを言ったが通じなかった（→むだになった）I made a sarcastic remark about him, but *it was wasted*. / あの先生には冗談は通じない That teacher *doesn't get jokes*. / この文章は意味が通じない These sentences *don't make sense*.

❸【精通している】（よく知っている）be familiar with …;（知識が広い）be well informed about [on] …;（専門家である）be an expert in …
彼は最近の社会事情に通じている He *is familiar with* current affairs.
緒方氏はイギリス文学に通じている Mr. Ogata *is well-informed* about English literature.
◆弟はコンピュータに通じている My brother

is computer literate.
❹【その他】
私は彼の結婚を母を通じて知った I learned of his marriage *via* [*through*] my mother.
どうやらライバル会社に通じている者がここにいるようだ It seems that someone here *is secretly in contact with* our rival company.
そのチームにはそんな作戦は通じない Such a tactic won't *work* on that team.
その手は通じないよ That *doesn't work* on me!
彼は友達の奥さんと通じている(→浮気している) He *is having an affair with* the wife of his friend.
慣用表現 すべての道はローマに通ず ⇨ みち(道)

つうしん 通信 communication ⓤ (❖「通信機関「手段」」の意味では複数形も使われる. 「通信文」の意味では ⓒ); (文通) correspondence ⓤ ━━通信する communicate ⓥ; correspond ⓥ
すべての通信が途絶えている All *communications* are cut off.
姉は通信教育で簿記の勉強をしている My sister is taking *a correspondence course* in bookkeeping.
◆BBC からの通信 *a report* from the BBC / このテーブルは通信販売で買った I bought this table by *mail order*.
‖通信員 (特派員)a correspondent; (報道記者)a reporter / 通信衛星 a communications satellite / 通信機関 communications / 通信工学 communications engineering / 通信社 a news agency / 通信簿 《米》a school card, 《英》a school report / 通信妨害 jamming / 通信網 a communications network [system] / パソコン通信 communication using personal computers / 光通信 optical communications

つうせつ¹ 通説 (一般的に認められた説) generally accepted theory ⓒ; (一般的に信じられていること) popular belief ⓤ ‖通説とは異なり contrary to *popular belief* / 子供のころに外国語を習うほうが上達するというのが通説だ It's *a generally accepted theory* that younger children learn foreign languages more easily.

つうせつ² 痛切 高齢化社会は現代において痛切な問題だ The aging of society is a *serious problem* today. / 面接での礼儀作法の重要性を痛切に感じた I *fully realized* how important manners were at the interview.

つうぞく 通俗 popularity ⓤ (大衆向けの) popular; (一般的な) common; (低俗な) vulgar ‖テレビドラマの多くは通俗的だ Many TV dramas are for the *common* taste. / 何とも下品で通俗な雑誌だ It's a *vulgar* magazine.
‖通俗小説 a popular novel

つうたつ 通達 notification ⓤ (❖具体的な通達内容は ⓒ) ━━通達する notify ⓥ ‖通達を出す issue *a notification*

つうち 通知 notice ⓤ; (公の) notification ⓤ (❖notice, notification とも具体的な通知内容は ⓒ) ━━通知する inform ⓥ; (正式に) notify ⓥ
けさ ABC 社より採用通知を受け取った I received *a notice of employment* this morning from ABC.
面接の結果は2, 3日中に通知します We'll *notify* you of the result of your interview in a couple of days.
◆次の会合の日取りをご通知ください Please *advise* me of the date for the next meeting.
‖通知表 《米》a report card, 《英》a school report

つうちょう 通帳 (銀行の) bankbook ⓒ, passbook ⓒ ◆通帳を作る(→口座を開く) open *a savings account*

つうどく 通読 ━━通読する (最後まで読み通す) read* through / 評判の新刊を通読する *read through* a popular new book

つうねん 通念 generally accepted idea ⓒ ◆彼らの主張は社会通念上受け入れがたい Their arguments are not acceptable according to *current social standards*.

ツーバイフォー この住宅はツーバイフォー工法で建てられたものです This house is built by *the two-by-four method*.

つうはん 通販 mail order ⓤ ⇨ つうしん

ツーピース two-piece (suit) ⓒ ‖白いツーピースのスーツ a white *two-piece* suit / 山田さんはいつものツーピース姿だった Mrs. Yamada was in her usual *two-piece* suit.

つうふう¹ 通風 ventilation ⓤ ‖この部屋は通風がいい[悪い] This room *has good* [*bad*] *ventilation*. ‖通風孔 a vent

つうふう² 痛風 gout [gáut] ⓤ ‖痛風にかかる suffer from *gout*

つうぶん 通分 1/2と3/5を通分する reduce 1/2 and 3/5 *to a common denominator* (❖1/2, 3/5はそれぞれ one-half, three-fifths と読む. common denominator は「公分母」の意味)

ツーベース(ヒット) two-base hit ⓒ, double ⓒ ‖ツーベースヒットを打つ hit *a double*

つうほう 通報 report ⓤ ━━通報する report ⓥ ‖火事の通報 *a report* of a fire / 彼はこの事実を警察に通報すると言っておどした He threatened to *report* this fact to the police.

つうやく 通訳 interpretation ⓤ; (通訳者) interpreter [intə́ːrprətər] ⓒ ━━通訳する interpret [intə́ːrprət] ⓥ ‖通訳を通して[抜きで]アメリカ人と交渉する negotiate with an American through [without] *an interpreter* / 彼女はフリーの通訳者として働いている She works as *a freelance interpreter*. / 私は英語とイタリア語の通訳ができます I can *interpret* English and Italian.
‖同時通訳 simultaneous interpretation; (通訳者)a simultaneous interpreter

つうよう 通用 ━━通用する (受け入れられる) be accepted; (使用される) be used, be in use; (法的に有効な) be valid; (効力がある) hold* ⓥ
このクレジットカードは世界中で通用する This credit card *is accepted* all over the world.

君の意見は学校側には通用しないよ Your opinion *won't be accepted* by the school administration.
その硬貨は日本ではもう通用しない That coin *is no longer in use* in Japan.
その規制はまだ通用する That regulation *is still valid*.
この許可証は3月31日まで通用する This pass will *hold good* until March 31.
◆英語は主なホテルで通用する People *understand* English at major hotels. / そんなうそは私には通用しない Such a lie *won't work on me*.
‖通用期間 a valid length of a term / 通用門 a service entrance

ツーラン (ツーランホームラン) two-run homer [home run] ◎ ‖ツーランホームランを打つ hit *a two-run homer* [*home run*]

ツーリスト tourist ◎

ツーリング ⚠ (バイクでの) motorcycle tour ◎; (自転車での) bicycle tour ◎

つうれい 通例 (ふつうは) usually; (一般に) generally; (原則として) as a rule ‖通例このようなことは認められませんが、今回は例外です We *usually* can't accept this kind of thing, but this is an exceptional case.

つうれつ 痛烈 ——**痛烈な** (辛辣な) bitter; (厳しい) sharp; (打撃が) hard ——**痛烈に** bitterly; sharply ‖彼は痛烈な一撃でタイソンをマットにはわせた He knocked Tyson to the canvas with his *hard* blow. / 彼はその政策を痛烈に批判した He *bitterly* criticized the policy.

つうろ 通路 (廊下) passage ◎; (乗り物・劇場などの) aisle [áil] ◎ ‖通路に荷物を置かないでください Please don't put your things in *the aisle*. / 通路をあけてください (→障害物をどけて) Please clear *the passage* [*way*]. / (→わきに寄って) Please make *way*. / 通路側の席をお願いします I'd like an *aisle* seat please.
‖地下通路 an underpass, 《米》a subway

つうわ 通話 (tele)phone call ◎, call ◎ ‖携帯の通話料金は割高だ The charge for *a cellular* [《英》*mobile*] *call* is more expensive.
◆ただ今通話中です The telephone [line] *is busy* [《英》*engaged*].
‖通話料 telephone charges / 国際通話 an international [overseas] call / 市外通話 an out-of-town call, 《英》a regional call / 市内通話 a local call / 長距離(国内)通話 a long-distance call, 《英》a national call

つえ 杖 (walking) stick ◎; (藤(と)製の) cane ◎ ‖私の祖父はつえをついて歩く My grandfather walks with *a stick*.
ことわざ 転ばぬ先の杖 ⇒ ころぶ

つか¹ 塚 mound ◎ ‖アリ塚 an ant hill / 貝塚 a shell-mound
つか² 柄 (刀の) hilt ◎

つかい 使い
❶【用事】errand ◎
私は子供のころ喜んでお使いに行ったものです When I was a child, I used to enjoy going on *errands*.
ちょっとお使いに行ってきてくれる？ Will you go on *an errand* for me? / Can I ask you *a favor*?
❷【人】messenger ◎; (持参人) bearer ◎; (使い走り) messenger [errand] boy ◎
使いの者をそちらへよこします We'll send you *a messenger*.
使いの人が知らせを持ってきた The bearer brought news.
❸【その他】
人形使い a puppeteer / 蛇使い a snake charmer / 猛獣使い a trainer of wild animals
彼はなかなかの剣の使い手だ He is *a good swordsman*.

つがい 番 (動物の) pair ◎; (鳥の) brace ◎ ‖ひとつがいのカモ *a brace of* ducks

つかいかけ 使いかけ 使いかけの(→使い切っていない) ヘアムースがたくさんある There are many bottles of hair mousse *which I haven't used up*.

つかいかた 使い方 言葉の誤った使い方 improper *use* of a word / このビデオカメラの使い方をだれも知らない No one knows *how to use* this video camera. / 彼は人の使い方がうまい He knows *how to handle* people.

つかいがって 使い勝手 使い勝手のいいカメラ an *easy-to-use* camera / このキッチンは使い勝手がいい(→料理がしやすい) This kitchen is *easy to cook in*.

つかいこなす 使いこなす (機械などを) manage ⓜ; (上手に利用する) make* good [full] use of …; (言葉などを) have* a good command of … ‖新しく導入された機械を使いこなす *manage* the newly installed machine / 多くの人がコンピュータを使いこなしていない Many people don't *make full use of* computers. / 彼女は5か国語を使いこなす She *has a good command of* five languages.

つかいこむ 使い込む ❶【金を】misappropriate ⓜ; (会社などを) embezzle ⓜ ‖彼は奥さんにないしょで生活費を使い込んだ He *misappropriated* living expenses behind his wife's back. / 銀行員は支店の金を300万円使い込んだ The bank clerk *embezzled* three million yen from his branch.
❷【長く使う】使い込まれたテニスのラケット *a well-used* tennis racket / 長く使い込まれた万年筆 a fountain pen *used for a long time*

つかいすて 使い捨て ——**使い捨ての** disposable, throwaway / 使い捨てコンタクト *disposable* [*throwaway*] contact lenses
◆あの会社は派遣社員を使い捨てとしか思っていない That company thinks that temporary staff are *expendable*.

つかいで 使いで 1,000万円は使いでがあるだろう Ten million yen should *go a long way*.

つかいなれる 使い慣れる *get** used to …
◆このソフトは十分使い慣れている I'm well *used to* this software. / 使い慣れた(→長く使って信頼している)英和辞典をなくしてしまった I lost my (*old*) *trusty* English-Japanese dictionary.

つかいはしり　使い走り（用事）errand ◯;（人）errand [messenger] boy ◯,（口語的）gofer ◯ ∥彼は長年その俳優の使い走りをしていた He was *a gofer* for that actor for a long time.

つかいはたす　使い果たす　use up ..., spend* all ..., exhaust ⓗ ∥精力を使い果たす *exhaust one's* energy / 有り金を使い果たしてしまった I've *spent all* my money.

つかいふるす　使い古す　wear* out ⓗ ― 使い古しの much used;（ぼろの）worn-out ∥使い古した辞書 a *much used* dictionary ◆使い古された言葉 an *overused* expression;（→決まり文句）a cliché

つかいみち　使い道　use ◯ ∥この空きびんは使い道がない This empty bottle is *of no use*. / This empty bottle is *useless*.
◆これにはどんな使い道がありますか What do you *use* this *for*? / その機械は使い道がたくさんある That machine can *be used* in many ways.

つかいもの　使い物　このラジオはもう使い物にならない This radio is *useless* [*of no use*]. / 彼女はぜんぜん使い物にならないよ She's worse than *useless*.

つかいわける　使い分ける　敬語を使い分ける（→適切に使う）*use* honorific expressions *properly* / 私は2つのEメールアドレスを1つは個人用、もう1つは仕事用に使い分けている I have two *different* e-mail addresses; one for my personal use and the other for work. / 彼女は3か国語を使い分ける She *has command of* three languages.

つかう　使う

❶ 物・道具などを	use
❷ 金・時間を	spend
❸ 人を	employ; handle
❹ 言葉を	use; speak
❺ 気・神経を	
❻ 交通手段を	take, use
❼ その他	

❶【物・道具などを】use [júːz] ⓗ;（利用する）make* use [júːs] of ...;（特定の目的のために）employ ⓗ

父は私が車を使うのを許してくれた My father gave me permission to *use* his car.

この器具は何に使うんですか What *is* this tool (*used*) *for*?

働く女性が旧姓を使うのは珍しいことではない It's not uncommon for working women to *use* their maiden names.

英語を学ぶ際上手に辞書を使うことが大切である *Making* good *use of* your dictionary is important in learning English.

もし生物兵器が使われたら大変なことになる If biological weapons *are employed*, it will be a disaster.

◆浴室と台所を共同で使う *share* a bathroom and a kitchen

❷【金・時間を】（消費する）spend* ⓗ;（むだに使う）waste ⓗ;（有効に）use ⓗ, make* use of ...

趣味にお金を使う *spend* money on *one's* hobbies

むだづかいはやめなさい Don't just *waste your money*.

兄は上手にお金を使う My brother *uses* his money wisely.

私は暇な時間を詩を書くのに使っている I *spend* my spare time *in* writing poems.

君はもっと有効に時間を使うべきだ You should *use* your time more effectively.

❸【人を】（雇う）employ ⓗ;（きぎよく扱う）handle ⓗ;（利用する）use ⓗ

父の工場では外国人労働者を10人ぐらい使っている My father *employs* about ten foreign workers in his factory.

彼は人を使うのがうまい［下手だ］He is good [poor] at *handling* people.

彼はその女優を何度か自分の映画で使った He *used* the actress in some films of his.

❹【言葉を】use ⓗ; speak* ⓗ

目上の人には丁寧な言葉を使いなさい *Use* polite words to people who are older than you.

彼女は6か国語を自由に使う She fluently *speaks* six languages. / She *has a good command of* six languages.

❺【気・神経を】

お気をつかわないでください Please *don't bother*.

社長と食事すると気をつかう I *get nervous* when I eat at the same table as the president.

あれは神経を使う場面だった That was a *nerve-racking* situation.

❻【交通手段を】take* ⓗ, use ⓗ

タクシーを使って駅まで行った I *took* a taxi to the station.

◆今度の帰省には飛行機を使うつもりです I plan to fly home next time.

❼【その他】

頭を使いなさい *Use your head* [*brains*].

居留守を使った I *pretended I wasn't in*.

汚い手を使ってまで試合に勝ちたいとは思わない I don't want to win the game by *playing dirty*.

彼は仮病を使って練習をサボった He skipped practice *pretending to be sick*.

⇒ つかえる(使える)

つかえる¹　支える

❶【ふさがる・引っかかる】

道がつかえていて動けない I cannot move because the road *is jammed* [*congested*].

パイプに何かがつかえている The pipe *is blocked*. / Something *is blocking* the pipe.

まだ先がつかえている（→私たちの前にたくさんの人が待っている）There are so *many people waiting ahead of us*.

もちがのどにつかえた Some *mochi got stuck in my throat*.

買ったばかりのソファーがドアにつかえて（→大きす

ぎて)入らない The sofa I've just bought is [*too big to go through* [*so big that it's stuck in*] the door.

その部屋の天井はとても低くて立ち上がると頭がつかえそうになる The room has a very low ceiling, so my head almost *touches* it when I stand up.

彼女の言葉を聞いて胸につかえていたものがとれた Her words relieved me of *what had been bothering me*.

❷【言葉が滞る】

スピーチの途中2, 3回つかえてしまった I *stumbled* a few times in the middle of my speech.

つかえる² 使える (使用できる) usable; (役に立つ) useful; (有効な) valid //このペン、だれが捨てたの。まだ使えるよ Who threw away this pen? It's still *usable*. / この券はいつまで使えますか How long is this ticket *valid*? / あいつは使える男だ He is a *useful* man.

◆ビザカードは使えますか Do you *accept* [*take, honor*] VISA cards? / この自動販売機は1万円札が使える This vending machine *accepts* 10,000-yen bills. / そのアイディアは使える That's a *good* idea.

つかえる³ 仕える serve ㊥, work for *a person* //その男は王に40年間仕えた The man *served* the King for 40 years.

つかずはなれず 付かず離れず 彼とはつかず離れずの距離を保っている I get *neither too close to nor too far away from him*.

つかつかと 彼女はつかつかと(→ためらわずまっすぐに)その男に歩み寄り平手打ちを食らわせた She walked *right up* to the man *without hesitation*, and gave him a slap. / 彼はつかつかと職員室に入っていった He *strode* into the teachers' room. (❖stride は「(急いで、勢いよく)大またで歩く」)

つかぬこと 付かぬ事 つかぬ事を伺いますが、以前どこかでお会いしませんでしたか *Excuse me*, but haven't we met before somewhere?

つかのま 束の間 (一瞬) moment ⓒ ── つかの間の (一瞬の) momentary; (短時間の) brief; (短命の) short-lived //つかの間の幸せ *brief* happiness / 小さい子供がいるとつかの間も息が抜けない I can't have a rest even *for a moment* with a small child.

◆父の病気が治ってほっとしたのもつかの間、今度は自分が倒れてしまった My joy over my father's recovery from illness was *short-lived* as I soon after became ill.

つかまえる 捕まえる catch* ㊥; (力ずくで) seize [síːz] ㊥; (握る) catch [take*] hold of ...; (逮捕する) arrest ㊥

タクシーをつかまえる *catch* [*get*] a taxi

うちの猫がネズミをつかまえた My cat *caught* a mouse.

私は彼の腕をつかまえた I *caught hold of* his arm.

警察はすりを現行犯でつかまえた The police *arrested* [*caught*] a pickpocket in the act.

方々に電話して、やっと彼女が友達のところにいるのをつかまえた I telephoned around and finally *caught* her at her friend's.

◆彼女はよく先生をつかまえて質問をしていた She often *stopped* her teacher to ask questions.

つかませる 掴ませる 人に金をつかませる *bribe* a person *with* money / 彼女は偽物のダイヤをつかませられた She *had* an imitation diamond *palmed off on* her.

つかまる¹ 捕まる be caught; (逮捕される) be arrested //家を出ようとしたところを母につかまった I *was caught* by my mother when I was about to leave. / ついに犯人がつかまった Finally the criminal *was arrested*.

◆彼女は忙しい人なのでなかなかつかまらない She's such a busy person that it's difficult to *catch* her. / 彼はスピード違反でパトカーにつかまった He *was stopped* by a police car for speeding.

つかまる² 掴まる hold* on //手すりにしっかりつかまってください Please *hold on* tight *to* the bar. ◆子猿は母親の背中にしっかりつかまっていた The baby monkey *clung to* its mother's back.

つかみあい 掴み合い 彼らはつかみ合いのけんかを始めた They started *grappling*.

つかみどころのない 掴み所のない (要領を得ない) pointless; (あいまいな) vague; (はぐらかした) evasive //つかみどころのない答え a *vague* answer

◆彼女はつかみどころのない人だ(→どんな人か説明しづらい) It's *difficult to describe what kind of person* she *is*.

つかむ 掴む

❶【手でつかむ】catch* ㊥; take* ㊥; hold* ㊥; grasp ㊥; grip ㊥; grab ㊥; seize [síːz] ㊥; clutch ㊥

catch: 動くものをつかむ.
take: 動かないものを手に取る.
hold: 手に取ったものを放さずにつかんでいる.
grasp: がっしりとつかむ.
grip: きつく握りしめるように持つ. また、すべらないようにつかむこともいう.
grab: 素早く奪い取るようにつかむ.
seize: 力ずくでつかむ.
clutch: 恐怖心・不安などからぎゅっとつかむ.

彼はハエを手でつかんだ He *caught* a fly with his hand.

ママの手をつかんでいなさい *Hold* Mommy's hand.

彼は私の肩をぐいとつかんだ He *grasped* my shoulder.

海の中に落とされないようにロープをしっかりつかんでいた I *was gripping* [*firmly holding*] the rope not to be thrown away to the sea.

母は10円玉のつかみ取り大会で優勝した My mother won at *the contest of rough grabbing as many* ten-yen coins *as you could in one handful*.

❷【手に入れる】get* ㊥

つかる

大金をつかむ *get lots of money*
彼女はその映画に出演するチャンスをつかんだ She *got* a chance to be in the movie.
事件の重要な手がかりをつかんだ I *got* [*found*] an important clue to the case.
❸【理解する】understand*; (把握する) grasp
要点をつかむ *grasp* the point
彼の真意をつかむことはできなかった I couldn't *understand* what he really meant.
❹【人の心を】capture
彼女は人の心をつかむのがうまい She knows how to *capture* people's hearts.
ことわざ おぼれる者はわらをもつかむ ➡ おぼれる

つかる¹ 浸かる (洪水で) be flooded; (水面下に) be under water ∥大雨で床上まで水につかった The house *was flooded* above the floor level by heavy rain.
◆父は一日の終わりに熱いふろにつかるのを何よりも楽しみにしている My father loves *soaking himself to a hot bath* at the end of the day more than anything else.

つかる² 漬かる (漬物などが) be pickled ∥このキュウリはよく漬かっている These cucumbers *are well pickled*.

つかれ 疲れ tiredness; (非常な疲れ) fatigue; (極度の疲れ) exhaustion
疲れがたまって病気になった I got ill because of constant *fatigue*.
最近はなかなか疲れがとれない I can't shake off *fatigue* easily these days.
疲れをいやすには温泉につかるのがいちばんだ It's best to soak in a hot spring to relieve *fatigue*.
◆猛勉強の疲れが出た I *got tired* after studying hard. / まだ疲れが残っています I *still feel tired*. / 彼は疲れを知らない人だ He *never gets tired*.

つかれはてる 疲れ果てる 彼女は疲れ果てているようだ She seems to be *exhausted* [*completely worn-out*].

つかれめ 疲れ目 eyestrain

つかれる¹ 疲れる be [get*] tired; (極度に) be [get] exhausted, be [get] worn-out (be で「疲れている」状態、get で「疲れる」ことを表す)
長旅でさぞ疲れたでしょう You must *be tired* from the long journey.
私は精神的に疲れてしまった I *am* mentally *exhausted*.
きょうはくたくたに疲れた I'm absolutely *worn-out* today.
◆生活に疲れる *be tired* of the demands of everyday life / バス旅行は疲れる Traveling by bus is *tiring*.
🗨「疲れた顔をしてるね」「きのう2時間しか寝てないんだ」"You look *tired*." "I had only two hours of sleep last night."

つかれる² 憑かれる 弟はつかれたように勉強しだした My brother started studying *like mad* [*one possessed*].

つき¹ 月

❶【天体】the moon (❖ある特定の時期・形態の月をいうときは冠詞として a, an を用いる)
月の満ち欠け waxing and waning of *the moon* / 明るい月 *a* bright *moon* / 8月の月 *an* August *moon*
今夜は月が出ている[出ていない] There is *a* [*no*] *moon* tonight.
月は雲に隠れている The *moon* is behind the clouds.
月は東から昇り西へ沈む The *moon* rises in the east and sets in the west.
月が明るく輝いている The *moon* is shining bright.
◆月の軌道 the *lunar* orbit / 月のない夜 a *moonless* night
❷【暦】month ——月の(毎月の) monthly
毎月の予算 a *monthly* budget / 月の初め[半ば, 終わり] the beginning [middle, end] of *the month*
彼は少なくとも月に1度は映画を見に行く He goes to a movie at least *once a month*.
毎月試験がある We have an exam *every month*.
私は月々1万円のこづかいをもらう I get 10,000 yen as pocket money *a* [*per*] *month*.
∥新月 a new moon / 半月 a half moon / 満月 a full moon / 三日月 a crescent moon
ことわざ この絵とあの絵とでは月とすっぽんだ This picture and that one are as different as night and day. (❖as different as night and day は「夜と昼ほどの差がある」の意味)
俳句 月天心貧しき町を通りけり (与謝蕪村) The moon glows on high far above a poor village as I pass on through.

つき² 付き ❶【運】luck, fortune ∥つきが回ってきた *My luck* has turned in. / I've got *fortune* on my side.
❷【つきぐあい】このライターはつきが悪い This lighter doesn't *ignite* easily. / こののりはつきがいい This glue *sticks* [*adheres*] well.

-つき -付き ❶【付属して】社長付きの秘書 a secretary *to* a president / バス・トイレ付きの部屋 a room *with* a bathroom / このビデオデッキは1年間の保証付きだ This VCR *comes with* a one-year guarantee. / この民宿は1泊2食付きで1人7,000円です This Japanese guesthouse charges 7,000 yen for one night per person *including* breakfast and dinner.
❷【単位】(1つごと) a, per ∥1人につき *per* head [*person*] / 1時間につき3,000円支払います I'll pay you 3,000 yen *per* [*an*] hour.
❸【理由】because of ... ∥雨天につき試合は中止します The game is cancelled *because of* rain.

つぎ¹ 次

next (❖形容詞 next に続く名詞が省略された形) ——次の next; (第2の) second ——次

に next；(第2に) second, secondly
次のかたどうぞ *Next* please. / Who's *next* please?
次の日曜日に野球の試合がある We are having a baseball game *next* Sunday. (✿ × on next Sunday とはいわない)
出かけるのは今度の日曜じゃなくてその次の日曜にしないか Why don't we go out not this (coming) Sunday but *the next [following]* Sunday?
次のバスは何時ですか What time is the *next* bus coming?
あなたの降りる駅は次の次です Your station is *after the next one*.
では次に移りたいと思います Now, we'll move on to *the next*.
次にいらっしゃるときは何も持ってこなくていいですから When you come and visit us *next* (time), just bring yourself. / *Next* (time) you come and visit us, just bring yourself. (✿ 後の next time は接続詞的用法)
私たちは次にどうしたらいいか議論した We discussed what to do *next*.
まず砂糖を入れて,次に卵の黄身を加えます First you put in sugar, and *next* add an egg yolk.
カスピ海の次に大きい湖はスペリオル湖です The Lake Superior is the biggest lake 「*next to [after]* the Caspian Sea.
田中さん,次はあなたの番ですよ You'll be (*the*) *next*, Mr. Tanaka.
◆京都の次は新大阪に止まります This train will stop at Shin-Osaka *after* Kyoto. / 次から次へとよくそうりそがつけるもんだ How can you tell lies *one after another*?

英作文ノート 「次のとおり」は決まった表現
結論は次のとおり
→×The conclusion is *following*.
→○The conclusion is *as follows*.
★「次のとおり」は英語でも決まり文句で as follows という. as は関係代名詞.

つぎ² 継ぎ patch © / ひざに継ぎの当たったズボン a pair of trousers with *patches* on the knees ◆古い服に継ぎを当てる *patch* old clothes / 継ぎの当たった上着 a *patched* jacket

つきあい 付き合い
彼とは5年来のつきあいだ(→5年間友達でいる) I *have been friends with* him for five years.
彼女とはあいさつを交わす程度のつきあいでしかない I have only a nodding *acquaintance* with her.
私たちのつきあい(→関係)はもう終わった Our *relationship* has finished.
彼女はつきあいがいい[悪い] She is *sociable* [*unsociable*].
父はつきあいが広い[狭い] My father *has a large* [*small*] *circle of friends*.
ご近所づきあい(→うまくつきあうこと)は大切だ It's important *to* 「*get on well with* [*be friendly with*]* your neighbors.
つきあいもだいじだけれど勉強もしなさい I know *going out with your friends* is important, but you need to study as well.
父はお酒はつきあい程度に飲むだけです My father is a *social* drinker. (✿a social drinker は「つきあいで飲む人」の意味)
つきあいでカラオケに行った I went to karaoke *just to be sociable*.

つきあう 付き合う
❶【交際する】go* around with *a person*,《口語的》hang* around with *a person*,《公式的》associate with *a person*；(男女の比較的短い的浅いつきあい) see* *a person*；(男女の比較的長いつきあい) go out with *a person* (✿ see, go out with はしばしば進行形で用いる)
⇨ 場面・状況別会話 p.1692
あんな連中とはつきあうな Don't *go around with* those people. / (→近づくな) Stay away from those people.
息子が不良仲間とつきあっていて心配だ I'm worried that my son *hangs around with* a youth gang.
最近ちょっとつきあってる女の子がいるんだ I'm now *seeing* a girl.
◆ここの人たちとはみんなうまくつきあっている I *get along* well *with* everybody here.
🔴 「だれかつきあってる人いるの」「別に」 "*Are you going out with* anyone?" "Not really."
🔴 「僕とつきあってくれない」「ごめんなさい,私つきあっている人がいるの」 "Will you *go out with* me?" "Sorry, I have *a boyfriend*."
❷【いっしょに行動する】
友達につきあって原宿に買い物に行った I *went along* shopping in Harajuku *with* a friend.
これからボウリングに行くんだけどつきあわない? We are going bowling. Won't you 「*come with* [*join*]* us?

つきあかり 月明かり moonlight ©

つきあげ 突き上げ (圧力) pressure © / そのメーカーは消費者から突き上げを食っている The manufacturer is under *pressure* from consumers.

つきあげる 突き上げる こぶしを突き上げる *raise one's fist* / 国会議員を突き上げる(→に圧力をかける) *put pressure on* members of the Diet

つきあたり 突き当たり the end / この道のつきあたりを右に曲がってください Turn right at *the end* of this road.
🔴 「このへんにトイレはありますか」「この廊下のつきあたりにあります」 "Is there a toilet around here?" "There is one at *the end* of the corridor."

つきあたる 突き当たる その計画は壁に突き当たった The plan *ran up against* a wall. / 彼女は今難問に突き当たっている She's now *being faced with* a difficult problem.

つきあわせる 突き合わせる (…を〜と照合する) check ... against [with] 〜；(…を〜と比較する) compare ... with [to] 〜 / 帳簿と領収書を突き合わせる *check* the account book

つきおくれ

against [with] the receipts / 原文と翻訳を突き合わせる check [compare] the original with the translation
慣用表現 あんなやつと顔をつき合わせて仕事するのはまっぴらだ No way I want to work face-to-face with someone like that. / そのことについて彼らとひざをつき合わせて話をした I had「a face-to-face [an up-close-and-personal] talk with them about that.

つきおくれ 月遅れ・月後れ 月遅れの雑誌 a month-old magazine / 月遅れの(→旧暦の)正月 the lunar New Year

つきおとす 突き落とす 人を列車から突き落とす push a person off the train / 男はがけから女を突き落とした The man pushed a woman over the cliff.

つきかえす 突き返す (拒否する) reject 働, refuse 働; (押し戻す) push back / その申込用紙は不備なところがあったので突き返された The application form was rejected because it was not filled out properly. / 彼女はそのプレゼントを彼に突き返した She pushed the present back at him.

つきかげ 月影 (月の光) moonlight Ⓤ

つぎき 接ぎ木 grafting Ⓤ ──接ぎ木する graft 働 / リンゴの枝を台木に接ぎ木する graft an apple branch onto a rootstock

つきぎめ 月極め ──月ぎめの monthly / 月ぎめの購読者 a monthly subscriber
◆月ぎめで支払われる get paid by the month

つききり 付ききり 彼女は夫をつききりで看病した She nursed her husband night and day.

つぎこむ 注ぎ込む (精力・金などを) put* 働; (投資する) invest 働 / 彼は株に貯金をつぎ込んだ He put [invested] his savings in stocks.

つきささる 突き刺さる (とがった物が) stick* 働; (突き通す) pierce 働 / ピンが指に突き刺さった A pin stuck into my finger. / 彼女の冷たい言葉が胸に突き刺さった Her bitter words pierced my heart.

つきさす 突き刺す (とがった物で) stick* 働; (突き通す) pierce 働; (物を) thrust* 働; (刃物などで人を) stab 働 / 男の子は肉にフォークを突き刺した The boy stuck「the meat with a fork [a fork into the meat]. / 強盗は興奮し包丁で私の腕を突き刺した The robber got excited and stabbed me in the arm with a kitchen knife.
◆突き刺すような風 a piercing [biting] wind

つきすすむ 突き進む (押し分けて) push one's way; (…に向かって) head straight toward … / 彼は人込みの中を突き進んだ He pushed his way through the crowd. / 私は目標に向かって突き進むだけだ I only head straight toward my goal.

つきそい 付き添い (付き添うこと) attendance Ⓤ; (付き添う人) attendant Ⓒ; (護衛する人) guard Ⓒ / あの患者は24時間付き添いが必要だ That patient needs 24-hour attendance.
∥付き添い看護婦 an attendant nurse

つきそう 付き添う (世話をする) look after …; (同行する) accompany 働; (警護する) escort 働 / 父の入院中は母と私が交代で付き添っていた My mother and I were looking after my father in turn while he was in the hospital. / 息子の入園式に一家そろって付き添った The whole family accompanied our son at the kindergarten entrance ceremony. / 容疑者は友人に付き添われて警察に出頭した The suspect reported to the police station accompanied by his friend.

つきたおす 突き倒す push over / 彼は弟を突き倒した He pushed over his younger brother.

つきだす 突き出す (棒・身体などを) stick* out; (押し出す) push out; (警察などに) hand over / 少年は窓から顔を突き出した The boy stuck his head out of the window. / 店長は万引きした者を警察に突き出した The shop manager handed over a shoplifter to the police.

つぎたす 継ぎ足す・注ぎ足す (加える) add 働; (広げる) put* on an extension / コードを継ぎ足す add an extension cord / ワインをつぎ足す add some (more) wine; 《米》top off wine

つきたてる 突き立てる 氷の塊(ೇೌ)にアイスピックを突き立てる thrust an ice pick into a block of ice

つきたらず 月足らず 妹は月足らずで生まれた My sister was born prematurely.

つきづき 月々 every [each] month ──月々の monthly / 月々の支払い a monthly installment / 実家から月々10万円の仕送りを受けている I receive 100,000 yen from my parents every month.

つぎつぎ 次々 (次から次に) one after another; (連続して) in succession, successively / 記者たちは次々に質問を浴びせた The reporters shot questions one after another.
◆次々にすばらしい発見をして彼らは有名になった A series of brilliant discoveries made them famous.

つきっきり 付きっ切り ⇒つききり

つきつける 突き付ける (証拠などを) confront a person with …; (銃などを) point 働 / 彼女は私に証拠を突きつけた She confronted me with the evidence. / 男は我々にピストルを突きつけた The man pointed a gun at us.

つきつめる 突き詰める (まじめに考える) take* … seriously / そんなに突き詰めて考えないほうがいいですよ Don't take it seriously.

つきでる 突き出る stick* out; (張り出す) jut out, (公式的) project 働 / がけから突き出た岩 a rock jutting out from the cliff / くぎが板から突き出た A nail stuck out of the board.

つきとおす 突き通す ⇒つきさす

つきとばす 突き飛ばす push a person down / 強盗は通行人を突き飛ばして逃げ去った The robber pushed pedestrians down and ran away.

つきとめる 突き止める find* out; (跡をたど

つく

って）trace 働；（所在を）locate 働 ‖事故の原因を突き止める find out the cause of an accident ／ 私はうわさの出所を突き止めた I *traced* the rumor to its source. ／ 警察は犯人の居所を突き止めた The police *located* the criminal.

つきなみ 月並み ——月並みの（言葉・話などが）trite；（使い古された）hackneyed ‖月並みな言葉 *trite* [*hackneyed*] words

つきぬける 突き抜ける go* through ... ‖くぎが板を突き抜けた The nail *went through* the board.

つぎはぎ 継ぎ接ぎ patch ◻ ⇒つぎ（継ぎ）‖継ぎはぎ細工 a patchwork

つきはじめ 月初め the beginning of the month ‖月初めには会議がある We have a meeting at *the beginning of the month*.

つきはなす 突き放す ‖彼は友達に対して突き放した言い方をした He spoke coldly to his friends. ／ 前半終了直前にレッズはさらに１点を加えガンバを２-０と突き放した The Reds scored another goal just before half time and *broke away from* Gamba by a score of 2 to 0.

つきばらい 月払い（月々の支払い）monthly payment ◻；（毎月のローン）monthly installment ◻ ⇒げっぷ（月賦）

つきひ 月日（時）time ◻；（年月）years；（日々）days ‖月日がたつとともに as *time* goes by ／ あれからだいぶ月日がたったような気がする It seems many *years* have passed since then. ／ 月日がたつのは早いものだ *Time* goes by quickly. ／ *Time* flies.

つきびと 付き人（世話人）attendant ◻；（助手）assistant ◻

つきまとう 付きまとう（人の後を）follow *a person* around；（まつわりつく）《口語的》tag along（with ...）；（妄想などが）haunt 働（※通例受身で用いる）‖彼はまた発作が起きるのではという不安につきまとわれている He *is haunted* by the fear that he may have another fit.

🗨 「最近ジョンにつきまとわれてうっとうしいのよ」「それってストーカーみたいじゃない」"I've gotten annoyed lately because John *follows* me *around*." "Isn't that like stalking?"

つきみ 月見 🖼 *tsukimi*, moon-viewing ‖お月見をする enjoy viewing the moon

つきみそう 月見草〖植物〗evening primrose ◻

つぎめ 継ぎ目 joint ◻；（板・布などの）seam ◻ ‖継ぎ目のない板 a board *without joints*; *a seamless* board ／ かなり継ぎ目が目立ちますね *The joint* is pretty obvious, isn't it?

つきもの 付き物 日本の結婚披露宴に酒は付きものだ（→欠かせない）Alcohol is *essential* to wedding receptions in Japan. ／ There are *no* wedding receptions *without* alcohol in Japan. ／ スポーツにけがは付き物だ Injuries are *a part of* sports.

つきやぶる 突き破る break* through ... ‖バリケードを突き破る *break through* a barricade

つきゆび 突き指（手の指の）sprained finger ◻；（足の指の）sprained toe ◻ ——突き指する sprain 働 ‖小指を突き指した I *sprained* my little finger.

つきよ 月夜 moonlight [moonlit] night ◻（✦moonlit は詩的な感じ）◆今夜はいい月夜だ There's [It's] *a beautiful moon tonight*.

つきる 尽きる（なくなる）run* out；（使い切る）be used up；（資源・体力などが）be exhausted；（終わる）end 働 ‖食料が尽きそうだ Our food *has* almost *run out*. ／ We *have* almost *run out of* food.

◆そのマラソンランナーは力が尽きて途中棄権した The marathon runner gave up the race due to *exhaustion*. ／ 一晩中話が尽きなかった We *talked without end* all night. ／ 彼は仕事の悩みが尽きない He *has constant worries* about his work. ／ そんな話ばかばかしいの一言に尽きるよ That story *is sheer* [*complete*] *nonsense*.

つく¹ 付く

❶ くっつく — stick, adhere
❷ 付属する — have; include
❸ 跡が残る
❹ 同伴する — accompany; follow
❺ 味方する — take sides with *a person*

❶【くっつく】stick* 働, adhere 働；（ついている）be attached to，be on ...

切手がなかなか封筒につかない The stamp *won't stick* [*adhere*] *to* the envelope.

このボンドはよくつくよ This bond *sticks* well.

ほっぺにごはん粒がついてるよ A grain of rice *is stuck on* your cheek.

◆料理にハエがつかないように注意してね Be careful that flies *don't get on* the dishes. ／ セーターにたばこのにおいがついてしまった The sweater *has gotten* a tobacco odor. ／ 彼のシャツのえりにはしょうゆのしみがついている The lapels of his shirt *are stained* [*smeared*] *with* soy sauce.

❷【付属する】have* 働；（含む）include 働；（付属している）belong to ...

この辞典にはCDがついている This dictionary *has* a CD with it. ／ This dictionary *comes with* a CD.

カレーはサラダがついて600円です The curry is 600 yen *including* a bowl of salad.

そのベルトはこのコートについていたものだ The belt *belonged to* this coat.

◆ポケモンの絵がついたTシャツ a T-shirt *with* Pokémon *on it* ／ その部屋はバス・トイレつきだった The room was *with* a private bathroom. ／ 今そのビデオを全巻買うと専用ケースがついてくる（→無料で手に入る）If you buy the complete set of videotapes now, you *get* the special case *for free*.

❸【跡が残る】

床には点々と犬の足跡がついていた The floor

was dotted with dog pawprints [tracks].
この地図で印のついているのが現在地だ The place *marked* on this map is here.
❹【同伴する】(同伴する) accompany ⦿,《公式的》attend ⦿; (後をついていく) follow ⦿
首相にはいつも護衛がついている The prime minister *is* constantly *attended* by bodyguards.
少年は先生の後について教室に入ってきた The boy *followed* his teacher into the classroom.
⇨ついていく, ついてくる
❺【味方する】take* sides with *a person*
討論会で私は彼女の側についた I「*took sides with* her [*took* her *side*, *sided with* her] at the debate.
◆がんばれよ,僕がついている Come on! I'm *pulling for you*.
❻【備わる】
私の部屋にもやっとエアコンがついた I've got an air-conditioner in my own room at last. / I've had an air-conditioner *installed* in my own room at last.
❼【テレビ・電灯・火などが】(作動する) work ⦿; (電灯などが) go* on
このテレビ,つかないよ This TV doesn't *work*.
このボタンを押せば電気がつきます Press this button, and the light *goes on*.
◆彼の部屋に明かりがついている The light *is on* in his room. / テレビをつけたままにしておいて Leave the TV *on*. / テーブルクロスに火がついてしまった The tablecloth *caught fire*. / マッチがぬれていて火がつかなかった The match *didn't strike* because it was wet.
❽【実などが】(実をつける) bear* ⦿
昨年この木にはたくさんの実がついた The tree *bore* a lot of fruit last year.
❾【力などが】(得る) get* ⦿,《公式的》obtain ⦿; (達成する) achieve ⦿; (増える・増やす) gain ⦿⦿; (よくなる) improve ⦿
試合に勝って自分に自信がついた I've got [*obtained*] confidence in myself by winning the game.
もっと体力がついてから退院すべきだ You need to *gain* more physical strength before you leave the hospital.
彼女もだいぶ英語の力がついた Her English *has* quite *improved*.
❿【値段が】(金額がかかる) cost* ⦿; (…の価値がある) be worth ...
家電製品の修理は新品を買うより高くつく場合がある The repair of a household appliance sometimes *costs* more than buying a new one.
それは売ったらかなりの値がつくだろうね It would *be worth* a lot of money if you sold it.
◆競売で彼のギターには約500万円の値がついた His guitar *was priced* at approximately five million yen at an auction.
⓫【運が】

きょうは朝からついてる I'm in luck [I'm *lucky*, *Luck is with me*] from morning today.
新品の傘をなくしたとはついてないですね It *was hard luck* [You *were unlucky*] losing your new umbrella.

つく² 着く

❶【到着する】arrive ⦿; get* to ...; reach ⦿
> arrive: 特に遠方の目的地に到着すること.
> reach: 努力して到着するという含みがある. arrive よりもかたい語.
> get to: arrive, reach よりも口語的な表現.

【語法】
arrive は後ろに at, in, on を伴うことが多い. at は到着する場所を地点としてとらえた場合, in はそれよりも広い場所としてとらえた場合, on は the scene, the spot などの特定の場所および「島, プラットホーム」など平らな表面が意識される場合に用いる.

早く[遅れて]着く *arrive early* [*late*]
彼女は時間前に目的地に着いた She「*arrived at* [*got to*, *reached*] the destination ahead of time.
駅に着いたらお電話します I'll call you *when* I *arrive at* the station.
ジャックはきのう日本に着いた Jack *arrived in* Japan yesterday.
彼は今着いたところです He *has* just *arrived*. /《口語的》He *just arrived*.
我々はついに山頂に着いた We *reached* the summit at last.
暗くならないうちに家に着いた I *got* home before dark. (❖この home は「家に」という意味の副詞なので to は不要. 次の例の there (「そこに」) も同様)
彼女はもうそこに着いているころだろう She should *have gotten* there by now.
きょう夏子からの手紙が着いた Natsuko's letter *reached* me today. / I *received* a letter from Natsuko today.
◆さあ, 着いたぞ *Here we are*.
❷【届く・触れる】(届く) reach ⦿⦿; (触れる) touch ⦿ ⇨とどく, ふれる
この自転車はサドルが高すぎて足が地面に着かない The seat of this bicycle is so high that my feet can't *reach* [*touch*] *the ground*.
彼女の髪はちょうど肩に着くくらいの長さだ Her hair *reaches down* just *to* the shoulders.
❸【位置に】
どうぞ席に着いてください Please *sit down*. / Please *take a seat*.
家族全員が夕飯の食卓に着いた The whole family *sat at* the supper table.

つく³ 就く

❶【職・地位に】(職業に) enter ⦿; (地位に) take* ⦿; (得る) get* ⦿; (占める) occupy ⦿; (保持する) hold* ⦿
兄は教職に就いた My brother *entered* [*went into*] teaching. / My brother *became* a teacher.
彼は放送関係の仕事に就いた He took [got] a

job in broadcasting.
その女性は政府の重要な地位に就いている The woman *occupies* [*holds*] an important position in the government.
◆政権に就く *come into power* / 王位につく *mount* [*come to*] *the throne*; *be enthroned* / 姉はまだ職に就いていない My sister *is* still 「*out of* [*without*] *work*.
❷【師・先生の】
兄は久保田教授についてダニの生態を研究している My brother is studying the habits of ticks *under* Professor Kubota.
妹は先生についてバイオリンを習っている My sister is taking violin lessons *from* a teacher.
❸【その他】
彼は9時に床についた He *went to bed* at nine.
我々は夕方5時ごろ家路についた We *started* [*set out*] *on the road home* at about five in the evening.

つく⁴ 突く
❶【つっつく・押す】(棒などで) poke 他 自; (押す) push 他 自; (強く・急に) thrust* 他 自; (乱暴に) shove 他
小枝でカタツムリの頭を突いてみた I *poked* (*at*) *the head of a snail with a stick*.
彼に背中を突かれた He *pushed* [*shoved*] me *on the back*.
◆彼女はひじで僕の腕を突いた She *nudged* me on the arm with her elbow.
❷【鋭い物で刺す】(刃物で) stab 他; (もりで) spear 他; (針などで) prick 他 ⇒ さす(刺す)
男はナイフで彼の腹部を突いた The man *stabbed* him in the stomach with a knife.
彼はもりで大きな魚を突いた He *speared* a big fish.
❸【支えとして】
めまいがしたので私は壁に手をついて体を支えた Feeling dizzy, I *put* my hand on the wall to support myself.
食事のときにテーブルにひじをつくんじゃない Don't *rest* [*put*] *your elbows on the table* when you're eating.
老人はつえをついて歩いていた The old person was walking *with a cane*.
彼女はほおづえをついて雑誌をぱらぱら見ていた She was leafing through a magazine, *resting her cheek on one hand*.
彼は相手のパンチを受けリングに両ひざをついた He was punched by the opponent and 「*fell to his knees* [*knelt down*] on the ring.
❹【攻撃する】
問題の核心をつく *get* [*come*] *to the point* of a matter
我々は相手チームの左サイドをついた We *attacked* the left side of the opposing team.
彼の言葉が彼女の痛いところをついた His words *touched* her sore spot.
❺【吐く・言う】

彼女は窓の外を見てため息をついた She *sighed* looking out of the window.
うそをつくな Don't *tell a lie*! / *Tell me no lies*!
❻【その他】
大みそかにお寺の鐘をついた I *struck a bell* at a temple on New Year's Eve.
めいとまりをついて遊んだ I played with my niece *bouncing a ball*.

つく⁵ 搗く もちをつく *pound steamed rice to make mochi*
つく⁶ 憑く possess 他 ⇒ つかれる(憑かれる), とりつく

つぐ¹ 継ぐ・接ぐ
❶【受け継ぐ】(人の跡を) succeed 他; (仕事・財産などを) succeed to …; (仕事・商売などを) take* over; (地位・性格などを) inherit 他
彼は高校を卒業したら家業を継ぐと言っている He says he is going to 「*succeed to* [*take over*] *the family business* after finishing high school.
王子が王位を継いだ The prince *succeeded to the throne*. / The prince *succeeded the king*.
上村君の跡を継いで今田君が生徒会長になった Imada *succeeded* Uemura as president of the student council.
❷【言葉などを】(付け加える) add 他; (続ける) continue 他, go* on to say ⇒ つけくわえる
彼はパーティーは楽しかったと言ってから、君が来ればもっと楽しかったのにと言葉を継いだ He said "I enjoyed the party," and *added* [*continued*, *went on to say*] "I could have enjoyed it more if you had been there."
◆ここで息を継ぐと歌いやすいよ You *draw breath* here [at this point], and it's going to be easier to sing.
❸【つなぐ】
ユウガオにスイカを接ぐ *graft* a watermelon *onto* a calabash
医者が骨を接いでくれた The doctor *set my broken bone*.

つぐ² 次ぐ 日本で富士山に次いで高い山は何ですか Which is the highest mountain in Japan *after* [*next to*] Mt. Fuji? / 東高校に次いで西高校が入場してきた Nishi High School *followed* Higashi High School into the stadium. / Nishi High School came into the stadium *after* Higashi High School. / 敗北に次ぐ敗北で彼はすっかり落ち込んでいた He was completely disappointed by defeat *on* [*after*] defeat.

つぐ³ 注ぐ pour 他 //コップにジュースをついだ I *poured* juice into a glass. / (→コップをジュースで満たした) I *filled* a glass with juice. / 彼女は私にハーブティーをついでくれた She *poured* me a cup of herb tea.

つくえ 机 desk © //彼女はさっきから机に向かっている She's *been sitting* [(→勉強している) *studying*] *at her desk* for some time.

つくし 土筆 a field horsetail's shoot (with spore on its top)

つくす 尽くす

❶【あるだけのものを出す】
全力を尽くす do one's best
問題の早期解決に向けて最善を尽くします We'll do「our best [the best we can] to solve the problem as soon as possible.
私たちはあらゆる手を尽くして彼を捜した We tried every means available to find him.
彼らはそこで残虐の限りを尽くした They did all kinds of cruel things there.

❷【献身する】
人に尽くす devote oneself to a person / 地域のために尽くす serve one's community
彼は被災者援助に尽くしてきた He's devoted himself to helping the victims.

❸【…し尽くす】
したいことはし尽くした I did everything [all] I wanted to do.
火はその森全体を焼き尽くした The fire burned the whole forest up.
彼は料理をあっという間に食べ尽くしてしまった He ate up all the dishes in an instant.
その服はすべて売り尽くされた The clothes were all sold out.

つくだに 佃煮 tsukudani, preserved food made of small fish, shellfish, seaweed, etc. boiled down in sweetened soy sauce

つくづく こんな生活つくづくいやになった I'm really [quite, completely] sick and tired of this way of living. / 彼はそのはり紙をつくづくと眺めた He looked attentively [intently, closely] at the notice. / ごみ処理場を見学して、ごみ問題についてつくづく考えさせられた Visiting a waste treatment center made me think a lot about waste problems. / つくづく自分が情けなく思えた I couldn't help but feel that I was shameful. / 親のありがたさをつくづく感じた I couldn't help but feel grateful to my parents.

つぐない 償い (埋め合わせ) compensation Ⓤ; (宗教上の罪滅ぼし)《公式的》atonement Ⓤ ∥罪の償いをする make atonement for one's sin; atone for one's sin / せめてもの償いにお手伝いさせてください I would like to help you as compensation.

つぐなう 償う (埋め合わせをする) compensate 他自, make* up for …; (宗教上の罪・過ちなどを)《公式的》atone 自 ∥彼女は罪を償った She atoned for her sin. / 彼女は彼が受けた損失を償った She compensated him for the loss. / She made up for his loss.

つぐみ 鶫〘鳥〙thrush Ⓒ

つぐむ 噤む 何を聞いても彼女は口をつぐんだままだった She「kept her mouth shut [kept silent, wouldn't answer] no matter what I asked her.

つくり 作り・造り (構造) structure Ⓤ Ⓒ, build Ⓤ Ⓒ; (建築様式・組み立て方) construction Ⓤ; (設計) design Ⓤ; (できばえ) workmanship Ⓤ ∥簡単な作りのおもちゃ a toy with simple structure [construction] / この乗り物は一度に20人を運べる作りになっている The design of this vehicle permits 20 people to be carried at a time.

◆赤れんが造りの学校 a school built [made] of red brick(s) / このいすは作りがしっかりしている[悪い] This chair is strongly [poorly] built. / 僕と彼とでは作りがまるで違うんだから、僕が負けるのも当然だよ He and I have completely different frames. It's quite natural that I should lose.

つくりあげる 作り上げる それはマスコミが作り上げた虚像だ That's a false image the media created.

つくりかえる 作り替える 古くなった自分の服をクッションカバーに作り替えた I made my old dress over into a cushion cover. / 屋根裏を子供部屋に作り替えた We remodeled the attic into a children's room. / わがチームはユニフォームを新しく作り替えた We had our new uniforms made and exchanged our old ones for them.

つくりかた 作り方 フルーツケーキの作り方を知っていますか Do you know「how to make [the recipe for] fruit cake? / 彼がそのプラモデルの作り方を教えてくれた He showed me how to build the plastic model.

つくりごと 作り事 fabrication Ⓒ, invention Ⓒ ∥どうせそんなの彼の作り事だよ It must be his fabrication. / He must have fabricated it.

つくりだす 作り出す (製造する) produce 他; (考案する) invent 他 ∥彼は数多くのゲームソフトを作り出している He has produced a lot of game software.

つくりつけ 作り付け ─作りつけの built-in, fitted (❖共に名詞の前で用いる) ∥作りつけの本棚 a built-in bookshelf
◆その部屋には壁に作りつけのクローゼットがある The room has a closet built into the wall.

つくりばなし 作り話 (でっちあげ) invention Ⓒ, fabrication Ⓒ; (虚構) fiction Ⓒ Ⓤ ∥それは全く彼の作り話だ That's totally his invention [fabrication].
◆彼はいつも作り話ばかりしている He is always「making up [inventing] stories.

つくりもの 作り物 この植物は全部作り物だ These plants are all artificial.

つくりわらい 作り笑い artificial [forced, fixed] smile Ⓒ ∥彼女は彼に作り笑いをした She gave him an artificial [a forced, a fixed] smile.

つくる 作る・造る

❶製造・生産する	make; produce
❷建造する	build, construct
❸調理する	make; prepare; cook
❹作成する	make, draw up
❺組織する	set up, establish
❻創作する	make; write, compose

❶【製造・生産する】make* 他; produce 他; manufacture 他; create 他
make:「作る」を表す最も一般的な語. 非常に

幅広く用いられる．
  produce：make よりややかたい語．主に「製品・作物」を作ることを表す．
  manufacture：特に工場などで機械を使って大量に作る場合に用いる．
  create：神・自然などが「創造する」という意味で用いることが多い．

彼は巣箱を作った He *made* a bird house.

このジーンズは腰でフィットするように作られている These jeans *are made to* fit at the hips.

僕はスーツを初めてオーダーで作った I *had* a suit *made to order* for the first time.

ヒノキは家具を作るのによい材料です Japanese cypress is a good material for *making* furniture.

コンピュータ会社は毎年新しい機種を作っている Computer companies *produce* new models every year.

私たちは車の部品を作っている工場を見学に行った We visited a factory that *manufactures* car parts.

聖書によると神が造った最初の人間はアダムだ The Bible says Adam was the first man that God *created*.

【make＋名(人)＋名】≒【make＋名＋for 名(人)】
母は私にワンピースを作ってくれた My mother *made me* a dress. / My mother *made* a dress *for* me.

【make＋名＋(out) of＋名(材料)】(❖材料が変化せずそのまま物質に残る場合) 漢方薬は自然の原料から作られる Chinese medicines *are made out of* natural materials.

【make＋名＋from＋名(原料)】(❖材料が加工され変化してしまう場合) チーズは牛乳から作る Cheese *is made from* milk.

【make＋名＋into＋名(製品)】 ペットボトルから様々な衣類を作ることができる Plastic bottles *can be made into* various clothes.

◆その工場はテレビを作っている They *assemble* TV sets in that factory. (❖assemble は「組み立てて作る」の意味)

❷【建造する】build*, construct
交通渋滞を解消するため新しい道路が造られた A new road *was built* as a remedy for the traffic jams.

堀は城を侵攻から守るために造られた Moats *were built* to secure the castle from invasion.

その木の上にはカラスが巣を作っている Crows *have built* a nest on top of the tree.

❸【調理する】make*; (食事を準備する) prepare; (主に米・口語的) fix; (加熱調理する) cook
朝食を作る *make* [*prepare*] breakfast / サラダを作る *prepare* salad (❖火を使わないので cook は使えない)
彼女が帰宅したとき彼は夕食を作っていた He *was cooking* dinner when she came home.
キャンパーたちは火をおこして食事を作った The campers made a fire and *cooked* their meal.

シュークリームを作ったことがありますか Have you *tried making* cream puffs?

◆彼は私にカクテルを作ってくれた He *mixed* [*made*] a cocktail for me. / 彼はそのごはんで小さなおにぎりを作った(→小さなボールの形にした) He *shaped* the rice *into* little balls.

「何となくおなかがすいてきたな」「ちょっと待ってて．何か作るから」 "I'm getting a little hungry." "Just a second. I'll *fix* something."

「何を作っているの」「特製カレーだよ」 "What *are* you *cooking*?" "My special curry!"

❹【作成する】make*, draw* up
会員名簿を作る [*draw up* [*make*] a list of members / 報告書の草案を作る *make* [*prepare*] a draft of a report

私たちは契約書を作る必要がある We have to *draw up* [*write*] a contract.

私は旅行に持っていくもののリストを作った I *made* a list of what to bring for the trip.

◆この法律は1999年に作られた(→発効した) This law *was enacted* in 1999.

❺【組織する】organize; (設立する) set* up, establish, found
母は近所の人たちとバレーボールチームを作った My mother *organized* a volleyball team with the neighbors.

彼女はわが校に写真部を作った She *set up* a photography club in our school.

彼はネパールの小さな村に学校を作った He *founded* a school in a small village in Nepal.

兄は今の仕事を辞めて自分で新しく会社を作ろうとしている My brother is going to quit his present job and *set up* [*establish*, *start*] a new company of his own.

❻【創作する】make*; (文・詩・曲などを) write*, compose
詩を作る *write* [*compose*] a poem
私たちは村の人々を題材にした映画を作った We *made* a film on people in the village.

ジョン・レノンは数多くの名曲を作った John Lennon *wrote* a lot of good music.

◆新語を作る *coin* a new word

❼【形作る】form, mold, 《英》mould
サルは社会を作る Monkeys *form* a society.

様々な経験が今の彼を作っている A lot of experiences *have formed* what he is now.

すごい数の人が行列を作っているのを見てびっくりした I was surprised to see so many people *forming* a long line.

彼女は粘土で象を作った She *molded* an elephant out of clay. / She *molded* the clay into an elephant.

◆お二人で幸せな家庭を作ってください I hope you will *make a* happy *home* together. / 肩書きが人を作る(→成長させる)というのはあなたちうそではない You cannot deny that the responsibilities of a title *make one grow*.

❽【栽培する】grow*, raise
小麦を作る *grow* wheat
母は菜園で様々な種類の野菜を作っている My

mother *grows* [*raises*] many kinds of vegetables in her garden.

❾【でっちあげる】(話・言い訳などを) make* up, invent [他]

彼は口実を作ってその会議をサボった He *made up an excuse* and skipped the meeting.

💬「そんなのうそだよ. 話, 作ってない?」「作ってないよ. 本当だってば」 "No kidding! You've *invented* the story, haven't you?" "No! Believe me, it's true!"

❿【その他】

オーストラリアに行ったらたくさん友達を作りたい I hope I can *make* many *friends* when I go to Australia.

彼らは当分子供を作らないつもりでいる They have decided not to 「*have children* [*start a family*] for the time being. (❖start a family は「1人目の子供をもうける」の意味)

何とか時間を作って入院している祖母のお見舞いに行った I managed to *make time* and visited my grandmother in the hospital.

彼女は毎朝顔を作る(→化粧する)のにたっぷり30分かける She spends a good half hour every morning to *make herself up*.

裕子は女子マラソンの国内記録を作った Yuko *set* [*established*] *the national record* for the women's marathon.

彼はあちこちに借金を作っている(→金を借りている) He *borrows money* from everywhere.

彼の祖父は株でひと財産作った His grandfather *made a fortune* on stocks.

彼女が笑顔を無理に作っているのが分かった I knew she *was forcing herself* to smile.

つくろう 繕う ❶【修繕する】mend [他], 《米口語的》fix [他]; (かがる) darn (up); (継ぎを当てる) patch (up) //彼女はシャツのほころびをつくろった She *mended* [*fixed, darned*] a rip in a shirt.

❷【整える・取りつくろう】髪をつくろう *do* [*fix*] *one's hair* / 世間体をつくろう *keep up appearances* / 彼はうそをついてその場をつくろった He *smoothed things over for the moment* by telling a lie.

つけ 付け (掛け売り) 《米》charge [《英》credit] account [C] (❖単に an account ともいう), credit [U] //つけで物を買う buy things *on credit* [*account*] / これ, 私のつけにしておいてください I'd like this *charged to* my *account*. ◆つけをためる run up *a bill* / このまま勉強もせずに遊んでばかりいると, いずれそのつけが回ってくるよ If you keep on fooling around without studying at all, *you'll have to pay for* it someday.

-づけ -付け そのニュースは7月13日付けの朝刊で報道されていた The news was in a morning paper *dated* July 13. / 彼は4月1日付けで部長に昇進した He was promoted to department head *on* April 1.

つけあがる 付け上がる あの子は甘やかすとすぐつけ上がる That child is always ready to 「*take advantage of* [*abuse*] your generosity. (❖「take advantage of [abuse] *a person's* generosity は「人の寛大さにつけ込む」の意味)

つけあわせ 付け合わせ garnish [C], relish [C][U], 《米》the fixings //ニンジンの付け合わせ *a garnish* of carrots

◆ハンバーグにキャベツの千切りを付け合わせる *garnish* a hamburger steak *with* shredded cabbage

つけいる 付け入る 彼女は相手につけ入る隙(すき)を与えない She never lets a person *take advantage of* her.

つけかえる 付け替える 兄は車のCDプレーヤーを新しい物に付け替えた My brother 「*replaced* the CD player on his car *with* [*changed* the CD player on his car *for*] a new one.

つげぐち 告げ口 **—告げ口する** 《口語的》tell* [他][自], report [他] //正雄は良夫がカンニングをしたと先生に告げ口した Masao *told on* Yoshio to the teacher that he cheated on the exam./ Masao *reported* Yoshio to the teacher for cheating on the exam.

つけくわえる 付け加える add [他] //彼はさようならと言った後, 楽しいパーティーだったと付け加えた He said good-bye and *added* that he had enjoyed the party. / 彼はその本に参考文献一覧を付け加えた He *added* [*appended*] a list of references to the book. / 今彼女の言ったことに二, 三付け加えたいことがあるのですが I'd like to *add* a few things to what she's just said.

つけこむ 付け込む (利用する) take* advantage of ..., play on [upon] ... //あいつは他人の弱みにつけ込むようなやつだ He is a man who 「*takes advantage of* [*plays on*] your weakness.

つけたす 付け足す add [他] ➔つけくわえる

つけね 付け根 腕の付け根 *the* shoulder *joint* / 舌の付け根 *the root* of the tongue / 指の付け根 *the base* of a finger

つけねらう 付け狙う stalk [他]; (跡をつける) tail [他] //男はその女性を連れ去ろうとつけねらっていた The man *was stalking* [*tailing*] her in order to kidnap her.

つけひげ 付け髭 彼は付けひげをつけて変装した He put on *a false mustache* [*beard*] to disguise himself. (❖mustache は口ひげ, beard はひげ全体を指す)

つけまつげ 付け睫毛 彼女は鏡を見ながら付けまつげをつけた She put on *false eyelashes* looking into the mirror.

つけまわす 付け回す (ついて回る) follow *a person* around [about]; (ひそかに) stalk [他] //刑事はその男をつけ回した The detective *followed* the man *around*.

つけもの 漬物 *tsukemono*, vegetables preserved in salt, salted rice bran, or miso; (塩・酢で漬けたもの) pickle [U]《また複数形～s》 // 漬物を漬ける make *tsukemono* [*pickles*]

つけやきば 付け焼き刃 そんな付け焼き刃の知識では彼らの厳しい質問には答えられないだろう You won't be able to answer their intensive questions with such *hurriedly acquired* knowledge.

つける¹ 付ける

❶ くっつける	put
❷ 付け加える	put; install
❸ 跡を残す	
❹ 後についていく	follow
❺ 用意する	provide; hire
❻ 習得する・獲得する	acquire; gain
❼ 記入する	keep; write down
❽ 名づける・決める	name; settle
❾ 値段などを	price; bid
❿ 火・電気を	light; switch [turn] on ...
⓫ 実などを	bear

❶【くっつける】put*⊕;（塗る）spread*⊕;（薬などを）apply ⊕

すぐ傷口に薬をつけなさい *Put* some medicine *on* [*Apply* some medicine *to*] your cut at once.

トーストにイチゴジャムをつけて食べた I *spread* strawberry jam on the toast and ate it.

タオルにもっとせっけんをつけたほうがいいよ You should *apply* more soap to the washcloth.

◆スカートに油絵の具をつけてしまった（→汚してしまった） I *stained* my shirt *with* oil paint. / 母はきょう口紅をつけている My mother *is wearing* lipstick today. / 刺身はしょうゆをつけて食べます You *dip* sashimi *in* soy sauce before eating it.

❷【付け加える】put*⊕;（固定する）fix ⊕, fasten ⊕;（設置する）install ⊕;（添付する）attach ⊕;（縫いつける）sew*⊕

商品に値札をつける「*put* a price tag *on* [*attach* a price tag *to*] an article」/ タイヤにチェーンをつける *put* chains *on* tires

シャツのボタンもつけられないの？ Can't you even *put* [*sew*] a button *on* your shirt?

トランクに名札をつけた I *put* a name tag *on* my suitcase.

勉強部屋にエアコンをつけてもらった I *had* an air conditioner *installed* in my study.

◆本に索引をつける *append* an index *to* a book / これ買うから、何かおまけをつけてよ I'll buy this if you *throw in* something. / どうやって針にえさをつけたらいいの How do you *bait* the hook?

❸【跡を残す】

アイロンでズボンに折り目をつけた I *put* a crease in my trousers with an iron.

買ったばかりのたんすに傷をつけてしまった I've *damaged* the chest I just bought.

❹【後についていく】follow ⊕;（尾行する）shadow ⊕

だれかにつけられているような気がした I felt「*I was being followed* [*someone was following me*].

２人の刑事が容疑者の後をつけた Two detectives *shadowed* the suspect.

❺【用意する】provide ⊕;（雇う）hire ⊕, employ ⊕

被告に弁護士をつける *provide* a defendant *with* a lawyer

両親は中学受験の弟に家庭教師をつけた My parents *hired* [*employed*] a private teacher for my brother who's preparing for the entrance examination to junior high school.

❻【習得する・獲得する】（知識などを）acquire ⊕;（体力などを）gain ⊕

教養を身につける *acquire* culture

◆彼女は体力をつけるために空手を習っている She takes karate lessons to「*build up more strength* [*become stronger*]. / 君はもっと日本語の読解力を身につけるべきだよ You should *improve* your ability to read and understand Japanese.

❼【記入する】（日記・帳簿などを）keep*⊕;（書き留める）write* down

日記[帳簿]をつける *keep* a diary [an account book]

◆正しい答えの番号に丸印をつけなさい *Draw* [*Put*] a circle *around* the number of the correct answer. / これ、つけておいてください I'd like this *charged to* my account.

❽【名づける・決める】（名前を）name ⊕;（決着をつける）settle ⊕

姉は自分の赤ん坊に明子という名前をつけた My sister *named* her baby Akiko.

この論争にけりをつけるのはあなたしかいない You're the only one who *can settle* this argument.

◆私が行って彼と話をつけてくる I'll go and *have it out with* him.（❖have it out は「争いなどの片をつける」の意味）

❾【値段などを】price ⊕, put* [set*] a price on ...;（競売などで）bid*⊕ ⊜

競売で彼の絵には1,000万円の値がつけられた His picture *was priced* at 10 million yen at an auction [*was auctioned* for 10 million yen].

彼女はその盆栽に30万円の値をつけた She *priced* the bonsai at 300,000 yen.

彼は競売でその像に5,000万円の値をつけた He *bid* 50 million yen for the statue at an auction.

◆審査員の一人が彼の演技に10点満点をつけた One of the judges *gave* his performance a perfect score of 10.

❿【火・電気を】（点火する）light*⊕;（スイッチを入れる）switch [turn] on ...

たばこ[マッチ、ろうそく]に火をつける *light* a cigarette [match, candle]

テレビ[明かり]をつけてください Please *switch* [*turn*] on the television [light].

◆ゆうべはテレビをつけたまま眠ってしまった I slept *with* the television *on* last night.

⓫【実などを】bear*⊕

この桃の木は昨年たくさんの実をつけた This peach tree *bore* a lot of fruit last year.

◆校庭の桜はたくさんのつぼみをつけている The cherry trees on the school grounds *are covered in* buds.

つける² 着ける
❶【着用する】put* on; (身に着けている) wear*㊥, have*... on (❖ wear も have ... on も状態を表すが, 特に一時的な状態をいう場合には be wearing, have ... on を用い, wear はややまれ) ➡きる(着る)

ネクタイ[下着]を着ける *put on*「a tie [underwear]

彼は舞台衣装を身に着けた He *put on* his stage clothes.

彼はシャツにバッジを着けた He *put* a badge *on* his shirt.

彼女はきれいな髪飾りを着けていた She「*wore* a beautiful hair ornament [*had* a beautiful hair ornament *on*].

❷【乗り物を場所に】
彼はビルの玄関先に車を着けた He「*stopped his car* [*pulled up*] at the entrance of the building.

彼は渡し場に船を着けた He brought the boat *to* [*alongside*] the ferry.

つける³ 漬ける・浸ける
(浸す) soak㊥; (ちょっと浸す) dip㊥; (漬物にする) pickle㊥; (保存加工する) preserve㊥ // 洗濯物を水につけた I *soaked* the wash in the water. / 彼は湯かげんを見るためふろのお湯に手をつけた He *dipped* his hand in the bath water to see its temperature. / 野菜を2, 3日の間, 酢に漬けておきなさい *Pickle* [*Preserve*] the vegetables in vinegar for a few days.

つげる 告げる
tell*㊥; (公表する・アナウンスをする) announce

私には彼女に本当のことを告げる勇気がない I dare not *tell* her the truth. / I dare not *inform* her *of* the truth.

その祭りがこの地方に夏の訪れを告げる The festival *tells* people *that* summer has come in this area.

アナウンスで飛行機の到着時刻が告げられた The arrival time of the plane *was announced*.

◆時計が9時を告げた The clock *struck* nine. / ベルが電車の発車を告げた The bell *rang* [*sounded*] the departure of the train. / 彼は彼女に別れを告げ, 反対の方向に歩きだした He *said* good-bye to her and started to walk in the opposite direction. / その女性は名前も告げずに立ち去った That woman left *without giving* her name.

つごう 都合
❶【事情】circumstance ⓒ; (好都合) convenience Ⓤ (↔inconvenience) ――都合のよい(好都合な) convenient; (有利な) advantageous ――都合よく conveniently; advantageously ➡こうつごう, ふつごう

〖都合が・は〗
こちらに来ていただくのにあすはご都合はよろしいですか Would it be *convenient* for you to come here tomorrow?

ご都合がよろしければ夕食をご一緒しませんか *If it suits your convenience*, would you like to have dinner with me?

ご都合がつきしだい連絡をいただきたいのですが Please get in touch with me *at your earliest convenience*.

◆都合がつけば(→何も支障がなければ)参ります I'll come *if nothing interferes*. / 何時がいちばんご都合がよろしいですか What time would *suit* you best? / もし月曜にご都合がつかなければ火曜でもいいです If Monday is *inconvenient* for you, Tuesday is OK with me.

🅔「土曜か日曜のどちらかあいてる?」「ええっと…, そうだね, 土曜日なら都合がつくよ」"Are you free on either Saturday or Sunday?" "Let me see ... Yes, I'm *available* on Saturday."

🅔「今度の日曜にパーティーやるんだけど, 来ない?」「あいにくその日は都合が悪いんだ」"We're having a party next Sunday. Can you come?" "I'm afraid I *can't make it* that day." ❖make it は「(決められた時間に)行く, 来る」の意味

> **英作文ノート** convenient は主語に注意
> もしご都合がよろしければあすお会いしたいのですが
> →✕If *you're convenient*, I'd like to see you tomorrow.
> →〇If *it's convenient* for you, I'd like to see you tomorrow.
> ★convenient (都合のよい)の主語は「人」ではなく「物事」。この場合の it は「あす会うこと」という状況, 条件を表す。

〖都合の〗
ご都合のよいときに電話をください Please phone me *at your convenience*.

彼女はいつも自分の都合のいいことばかり言う She's always saying what's *advantageous* to her.

◆彼は自分に都合の悪いことはすぐ忘れてしまう He soon forgets things that are *disadvantageous* to him.

〖都合で・を〗
◆彼は一身上の都合で会社を辞めた He resigned from the company *for personal reasons*. / 前回イタリアに行ったときは時間の都合でベネチアに行けなかった(→行く時間がなかった) I *didn't have time* to visit Venice the last time I went to Italy. / 僕はみんなの都合(→予定)を聞いて集まる日にちを決めた I asked everyone about *their schedules* and set up the date for a get-together.

〖その他〗
円高はわが社にとって好都合であった The strong yen was *advantageous* to our company.

◆議論の都合上とりあえず彼の説が正しいとしよう Let us, *for the sake of argument*, assume that he is right. / いつも万事都合よくいくとは限らない You can't expect everything *will go well* all the time. / その通りに出ると都合よく空車のタクシーが来た *Luckily*, an empty taxi came just when we got to the street.

❷【やりくり】——都合する (時間・金などを作る)《口語的》manage ㊥; (手配する) arrange ㊥; (貸す) lend*

こちらに来て話し合う時間を都合していただけませんか Could you *manage* the time to come and talk with us?

今月末までに何とか都合をつけて会いに行きます I'll *manage* somehow *to* go and see you by the end of this month.

5万円ほど都合してもらえないでしょうか Could you *lend* me about fifty thousand yen?

◆金の都合がつかず(→資金集めがうまくいかず),その工事は中断されている The construction work is on hold because they haven't succeeded in *raising money*.

❸【全部で】in all

その旅行には都合3万円かかった It cost 30,000 yen *in all* for the trip.

つじ　辻 (十字路) intersection ㊒, crossroads; (街角) street corner ㊒

つじつま　辻褄　それは君がさっき言ったこととつじつまが合っていないよ That *is not consistent with* what you said a little while ago. / 彼はうそをついて話のつじつまを合わせた He lied to *make his story consistent [coherent]*. / 君の話はつじつまが合わない Your story *doesn't add up [hold water]*.

つた　蔦 ivy /áivi/ ㊒ /その壁にはツタがはっていた The wall was covered with *ivy*.

-づたい -伝い 彼らは沢伝いに(→沢に沿って)山を下った They descended the mountain *along* a stream. / 泥棒は屋根伝いに(→屋根から屋根へと)逃げていったようだ The thief seems to have fled *from* roof *to* roof.

つたう　伝う 鎖を伝って岩場を登った I climbed a rocky slope *on* a chain. / 涙が彼女のほおを伝って流れた Tears *ran* [*trickled*] *down* her cheeks. / 猿は木の枝を伝って(→枝から枝へと)逃げた The monkey escaped *from* branch *to* branch. / 暗い廊下を壁を伝って歩いた I went through the dark hallway *touching* the wall.

つたえきく　伝え聞く 伝え聞くところによると,彼はアメリカでプロの音楽家として活躍しているらしい I *heard from others* that he was active in the U.S. as a professional musician.

つたえる　伝える

❶【知らせる】tell* ㊥; (正式に) inform ㊥, notify ㊥; (分からせる) get* [put*] across; (考え・感情などを) communicate ㊥; (新聞などに書いてある) say* ㊥ (✱進行形にはできない); (報道する) report ㊥

彼女は上司に会社を辞めると伝えた She *told* [*informed, notified*] her boss *that* she was going to leave the company.

私に電話をくれるよう昭男に伝えてください Please *tell* Akio *to* call me.

太郎は次郎に手紙でパーティーの日時を伝えた Taro *informed* [*notified*] Jiro *of* the date and time of the party in a letter.

どうやって自分の本当の気持ちを伝えたらいいのか分からない I don't know how to *get* [*put*] *across* my true feelings.

新聞は行方不明の子供が無事発見されたと伝えている The newspaper *says* [*reports*] *that* the missing child was found safe and sound.

◆ご両親によろしくお伝えください Please「*remember me* [*give my best regards*] *to* your parents. / このメッセージを必ず彼に伝えるようにしてください Make sure that you *give* [*pass*] this message to him. / 伝えられるところによると,彼はかなりの重傷を負っているようだ *Reportedly*, his injury is quite serious.

❷【伝承する】(教える) teach* ㊥; (後世に) hand [pass] down ⇒ おしえる

ガラス職人は弟子にその技術を伝えた The glassworker「*taught* his pupil his techniques [*handed down* his techniques to his pupil].

これはこの家に代々伝えられてきた掛け軸である This is a hanging scroll *handed* [*passed*] *down* from generation to generation in this family.

❸【伝達する・伝播(ぱ)する】(思想などを) carry ㊥; (紹介する) introduce ㊥; (送信する) transmit ㊥

西洋文化はこれらの交易路に沿って東洋に伝えられた Western culture *was carried* to the East along these trade routes.

奈良時代には多くの中国文化が日本に伝えられた A lot of Chinese culture *was introduced* into Japan during the Nara period.

❹【電気・熱などを】conduct ㊥, transmit ㊥

鉄は熱をよく伝える Iron *conducts* [*transmits*] heat well.

つたない　拙い　私のつたない英語でも何とか彼と話が通じた I could manage to communicate with him in spite of my *poor* [*unskillful*] English.

つたわる　伝わる

❶【知られる】(知れ渡る) spread* ㊥; (知らされる) be told [informed]; (分かってもらえる) get* [come*] across

そのうわさは学校中に伝わった The rumor *has spread* all over the school.

パーティーの日時が彼にだけ伝わっていなかった Only he *was not told* [*informed of*] the date and time of the party.

僕の皮肉が彼女には伝わらなかった My sarcasm *didn't get* [*come*] *across to* her.

◆その選手の意気込みがファンに伝わった The fans *could feel* the athlete's enthusiasm.

❷【伝承される】come* down, be handed down

それはこの地域に古くから伝わる祭りだ It is a festival which *has*「*come down* [*been handed down*] from old times in this area.

わが家に代々伝わる大切なつぼを割ってしまった I have broken the precious vase *handed down* from generation to generation in my family.

❸【導入される】(紹介される) be introduced; (来る) come*⾃
キリスト教は16世紀に日本に伝わった Christianity 「*was introduced* [*came*] into Japan in the 16th century.
❹【光・熱などが】
光は音より速く伝わる Light *travels* faster than sound.
この建築材は熱が伝わりにくい Heat *can't be conducted easily* through this building material.
❺【物に沿って移動する】 ➡ つたう
彼女のほおを涙が伝わって落ちた Tears *ran* [*trickled*] *down* her cheeks.
壁を伝わって(→壁に触れながら)暗い廊下を進んだ I went through a dark corridor *touching* the wall.

つち 土(土壌) earth 🅤, soil 🅤; (地面) ground 🅤, (泥) mud 🅤, dirt 🅤; (土地・国土) soil 🅤🅒, 《公式的》 land 🅒
肥えた[やせた]土 fertile [poor] *earth* [*soil, ground*] / 土で汚れたジーンズ jeans *soiled with dirt*
ポチは土を掘って骨を埋めた Pochi dug *the ground* and buried some bones.
鉢に土を盛った I filled the pot with *earth* [*soil*].
彼女は花の周りの土を踏み固めていた She was stamping *the earth* [*soil, ground*] around the flower.
彼女はついに長年夢見たアメリカの土を踏んだ As she has long dreamed, *she set foot on* U.S. *soil* [*land*] at last.
◆きょう、ついに連勝していた大関に土がついた(→負けた) The *ozeki*, who had successively won the matches, finally *lost* today.
つちいろ 土色 earthlike color 🅤
つちかう 培う 長年の修業で培った技術 a skill *cultivated* in the training which has lasted for years
つちけむり 土煙 タンクローリーが土煙を上げて走り去った A tank truck ran past, raising *a cloud of dust*.
つちふまず 土踏まず the arch of a foot
つつ 筒(円筒) cylinder 🅒; (パイプ) pipe 🅒; (金属・ガラス・ゴムなどの管) tube 🅒
-つつ 状況が徐々に変化しつつある The situation *is gradually changing*. / 運動会の準備が進みつつある Preparations *are under way* for the athletic meet. / 日本の貿易黒字は増加しつつある Japan's trade surplus *is on the increase*. / 彼は母親の顔色をうかがいつつ意見を述べた He stated his opinion *while frequently* looking at his mother's face to see how she felt. / 勉強しなければと思いつつも遊んでしまう I can't help playing, *though* I know I have to study.
つづいて 続いて 続いてアメリカからのレポートです *Next*, a report from the U.S.
つつうらうら 津々浦々 全国津々浦々を旅してきた He's traveled *all over the country* [*throughout the country*].
つっかいぼう 突っ支い棒 prop 🅒 / 私たちは傾いた木につっかい棒をした We *put a prop* against the leaning tree. / We *propped up* the leaning tree with poles.
つっかえる パイプに何かがつっかえているようだ Something seems to *be blocking* the pipe. / 老人はのどにもちがつっかえた The old man *choked* on mochi. / 彼はつっかえつっかえ話をした He *stumbled a few times* while speaking. ➡ つかえる (支える)
つっかかる 突っ掛かる 木の根につっかかって転びそうになった I *stumbled over* the root of a tree and almost fell down. / 彼は人につっかかってばかりいる He *is* always *attacking* others.
つっかけ 突っ掛け (サンダル) sandals
つづき 続き(続く部分) continuation 🅒; (本・映画などの続編) sequel 🅒; (残り) the rest 🅒 / この続きを歌えますか Can you sing the *continuation* of this part of the song? / Can you *continue* this song? / 続きはまたあしたお話ししましょう I'll tell you *the rest* of this story tomorrow. / その本の続きが出た *The sequel* to the book was published.
◆きのうの続き(→きのうやめたところ)からお話ししましょう I'm going to tell you the story from *where we left off* yesterday. / 話には続きがある(→それが話のすべてではない) *That's not the whole story*. / *That's only part of the story*. / ここに加入者本人との続き柄(→血縁・親族関係)を記入してください Write your *relationship* to the subscriber in here.
‖続き番号 consecutive numbers / 続き物 a serial, a series
-つづき -続き 日照り続きで作物の被害が大きい Crops are badly damaged by *the* 「*spell of dry weather* [*dry spell*]. / 彼はここのところ失敗続きだ He's had *a run* [*succession, series*] *of failures* lately. / 今週はこれまで6日続きの雨だ We've had rain *for six days in succession* this week. / We've had rain *for six days in a row* this week. / おのおのが作った短いメロディーを合わせてひと続きの長い曲を作った We each made a short piece of melody, and then we combined them into *a long tune*.
つっきる 突っ切る 空き地をつっ切る *cut across* [*through*] a vacant lot / バイクが横断中の人々の間をつっ切っていった A motorcycle *went* [*sped*] *through* people crossing the street.
つつく(指・ひじ・棒などで) poke 🅗🅒; (鳥が) peck 🅗🅒 / はしでゆでたジャガイモをつついてみた I *poked* the boiled potato with a chopstick. / 鳥が米粒をつついていた The birds *were pecking at* grains of rice. / キツツキがその木をつついて穴をあけていた A woodpecker *was pecking* a hole in the tree. / 彼は眠りそうになっていた私をひじでつついた He *poked* [*nudged*] me with his elbow when I almost fell asleep. / 彼はその研究発表の不備な点をつついた He *poked* holes in the presentation of the study.
◆彼女は食欲がなさそうでちょっとつついただけで

夕食を終えた She seemed to have no appetite and ended her dinner just by *picking at* some dishes. / 友達となべをつついた(→同じなべから食べた) My friends and I *ate from the same pot*.

つづく 続く

❶ 継続する・持続する　continue; go on; last
❷ 同じようなことが次々に生じる
❸ 別のことが生じる　follow, come after
❹ 後に従う　follow
❺ 道などが　continue; lead; extend
❻ 並ぶ

❶【継続する・持続する】continue 他(❖動作や状態が「切れ目なく続く」場合と「中断後に続く・再開する」場合の両方に用いることができる); (切れ目なく) go* on; (もちこたえる) last 自
そのコンサートは3日間続いた The concert *continued* [*went on, lasted*] for three days.
工事は昼も夜も休みなく続いている The construction work *is continuing* [*going on*] day and night.
私たちの愛は永遠に続くだろう Our love will *last* forever.
練習は夜の10時まで続いた The practice *continued* [*went on, lasted*] until 10 at night.
会議は昼食後も続いた The meeting *continued* after lunch.
両国間の紛争はいつまで続くのだろうか I wonder how long the dispute between the two countries will *last*?
◆ 昨年の今ごろは日照りが続いた(→日照り続きがあった) We had *a dry spell* about this time last year. / 雨がもう5日間降り続いている It *has been* [*kept on*] *raining* for five days. / うちは祖父の代から続く酒屋だ My family runs a liquor shop which my grandfather founded. / 裏面へ続く *Over.*; *P.T.O.* (❖Please turn over.の略語) / 次回に続く *To be continued.* / 50ページに[から]続く *Continued on* [*from*] p. 50.

🗨「彼の勉強はどれくらい続くと思う？」「せいぜい数分しか続かないでしょう」"How long do you think his studying will *last*?" "It'll *last* only a few minutes at most."

❷【同じようなことが次々に生じる】
近ごろ飛行機事故が続いている(→一連の飛行機事故があった) Lately, there has been *a series of* airplane accidents.
悪いことは続いて(→次々に)起こるものだ Bad things tend to happen *one after another*.
僕らはこのところ負けが続いている(→連続して負けている) Recently, we've lost several games *consecutively*.

❸【別のことが生じる】follow 他自, come* after ...(❖進行形・受身にはできない), 《公式的》succeed 他自
ギターソロの後にドラムソロが続いた A drum solo *followed* [*came after, succeeded*] the guitar solo.
式典後にいくつかの祝賀会が続いて行われた After the ceremony, several celebrations *followed*. / *Following* the ceremony, several celebrations were held.

❹【後に従う】follow 他自
生徒たちはガイドさんに続いて寺の中へ入っていった Students *followed* the guide into the temple.
◆ 佐野に続いて佐々木がゴールした Sasaki reached the goal *after* [*next to*] Sano.

❺【道などが】continue 自; (至る) lead* 自; (延びる) extend 自
この道は海岸まで続いている This road *continues* [*leads, extends*] to the coast.
畑は線路に沿って3キロ続いていた The field *continued* [*extended*] for three kilometers along the railroad track.

❻【並ぶ】
通りには本屋が続いていた The street *was lined with* book stores.
駅前からその美術館まで延々と人の列が続いていた *There was* a long line of people from the station to the art museum.

つづけざま 続け様 ──続けざまに(連続して) in a row, in succession; (切れ目なく) consecutively; (次々に) one after another // 彼は4回も続けざまに転んだ He fell four times 「*in a row* [*in succession*]. / そのバンドは4枚のシングルを続けざまに発表した The band released four singles *one after another*.

つづけて 続けて 6日続けて雨だ It's been raining for six days 「*consecutively* [*in a row, in succession*]. / 5つのグループが続けて入場してきた Five groups came into the hall *one after another*.

つづける 続ける

❶【継続・持続させる】continue 他自(❖「切れ目なく続ける」場合と「中断後に続ける・再開する」場合のいずれにも用いる); (切れ目なく) go* [keep*] on; (再開する) 《公式的》resume 他
試験に合格するために努力を続ける *continue* [*go on with*] efforts to pass the exam
彼らは10年間研究を続けた They *went on with* their research for 10 years.
生存者の捜索が続けられた The search for survivors 「*was continued* [*continued*].
「だからね」と彼女は話を続けた "So," she *continued* [*went on*].
10分間の休憩の後、また会議が続けられた After a 10-minute break the meeting *was resumed*.
彼女は話し続けた She *continued* [*went on, kept* (*on*)] *talking*.
彼の負債は増え続けた His debts *continued to* mount up.
急がなくていいから自分のペースで続けなさい You don't have to hurry. Just *keep on going* at your own pace.

◆ずっと立ち続けていたのでくたびれた I'm tired because I *have been standing* for a long time. / 彼は缶ジュースを3本続けて飲んだ He drank three cans of juice「*in a row* [*successively, one after another*].

❷【すぐに別のことに移る】

バンドはその曲に続けて新曲を披露した The band played their new song *after* that one.

理科に続けて歴史のテストが行われた(→歴史のテストが理科のテストに続いた) The history exam *followed* the science exam.

つっけんどん ―つっけんどんな blunt, brusque; (そっけない) curt ―つっけんどんに bluntly, brusquely; curtly ∥彼のつっけんどんな話し方が気に入らない I don't like his *blunt* [*curt*] manner of speaking. / 駅への道を聞いたらその男性は「知らない」とつっけんどんに答えた When I asked the man whether he knew the way to the station, he just said *bluntly* [*curtly*], "No."

つっこみ 突っ込み (漫才で)ぼけとつっこみ the funny man and *the straight man* / つっこみを入れる(→気のきいた言葉や皮肉を言う) *make a wisecrack* [*gag*]

つっこむ 突っ込む

❶【突入する】(突進する) run* [dash] into ...; (ぶつかる) crash into ...; (飛び込む) plunge [dive] into ...

その選手はボールを抱えて敵陣へつっこんでいった The player *ran* [*dashed*] *into* the opponent's defense holding the ball in his arm.

車は花屋につっこんだ The car *ran* [*crashed*] *into* a flower shop.

彼はつまずいて頭から田んぼにつっこんでしまった He stumbled and *plunged* [*dived*] *into* the rice paddy headfirst.

❷【勢いよく入れる】thrust [他]; (すき間などに) poke [他]; (いいかげんに) shove [ʃʌv] [他], stick* [他]; (急いで詰め込む) stuff [他]

棒を穴につっこむ *thrust* [*poke*] a stick *in* a hole

彼はハンカチをポケットにつっこんだ He *stuck* the handkerchief *into* his pocket.

彼は衣類をたたまずに引き出しにつっこんだ He *shoved* [*stuck, stuffed*] his clothes *into* a drawer without folding them.

❸【核心に鋭く迫る】

彼はそれに関してつっこんだ(→問題の核心に触れる)質問をした He asked a question to *get to the point* of the matter.

もっとつっこんだ(→より詳細に及ぶ)議論が必要だ We need to discuss it *in more detail*.

[慣用表現] 私の個人的なことに首をつっこむのはやめてくれ Don't *pry* [*stick your nose*] *into* my private affairs [business].

つつじ azalea [C] (❖ツツジ科植物の総称)

つつしみ 慎み modesty [U]; (慎重) prudence [U]; (思慮分別) discretion [U]

◆彼女は非常に慎み深い女性だ She is a very *modest* [*humble, discreet*] woman.

つつしむ 慎む ❶【気をつける】be careful about [of] ..., be discreet ∥言葉を慎みなさい *Be*「*careful about* your words [*discreet in* what you say]. / Watch your language.

❷【控える】《公式的》abstain [《公式的》refrain] from ... ∥父は酒を慎むべきだと思う I think my father should *abstain* [*refrain*] *from* drinking *too much*. / I think my father should *try not to* drink *too much*.

つつしんで 謹んで 謹んで新年のお喜びを申し上げます Please accept my heartfelt wishes for a happy new year. / 謹んでお悔やみ申し上げます Please let me offer you my deepest condolences.

つったつ 突っ立つ そんなとこにつっ立ってないでこっちに来て手伝ってよ Stop *just standing* there. Come here and help us.

つつぬけ 筒抜け 我々の計画は彼らに筒抜けだった *Every detail of* our plan *leaked out to* them. / 隣部屋の会話がこちらに筒抜けだった We *could hear clearly the whole* conversation they had in the next room.

つっぱしる 突っ走る 彼は高速道路をつっ走っていた He *was driving swiftly along* the expressway. / (→彼の車は)His car *was speeding along* the expressway. / 彼女は後先を考えずにつっ走るタイプだ She's the type of person who *rushes* into things without thinking about the consequences.

つっぱねる 突っぱねる reject [他], turn down ∥彼女は彼の申し出をつっぱねた She *rejected* [*turned down*] his proposal.

つっぱり 突っ張り (相撲の) *tsuppari*, thrusting (as a sumo technique); (不良少年・少女) delinquent [C], hooligan [C]

つっぱる 突っ張る (反抗的にふるまう) behave defiantly; (筋肉などが) be stiff [tight]; (支える) prop up; (相撲で) thrust [他] ∥彼女は学校ではかなりつっぱっている She *behaves* rather *defiantly* at school. / ここの筋肉がつっぱってるんだ The muscle here *is tight* [*stiff*]. / 洗顔しすぎで顔がつっぱる感じがする My face *is tight* from overwashing.

つつましい 慎ましい (謙虚な) modest; (目立たない) unpretentious; (質素な) simple ∥つつましい女性 a *modest* [an *unpretentious*] woman / つつましい生活を送る lead a *simple* life; live *simply*

つつみ[1] 包み package [C], pack [C], 《主に英》parcel [C] ∥ひもで包みを縛る tie *a package* with string / 彼は大きな包みを抱えていた He was carrying *a* large *package*. / 私はその大きな包みをあけた I undid *the* big *package*.

‖包み紙 wrapping paper, a wrapper

つつみ[2] 堤 embankment [C]

つづみ 鼓 🖼 a *tsuzumi*, a Japanese small drum which is played on *one's* shoulder

つつみかくす 包み隠す 自分のしたことを先生に包み隠さず話した I told everything I had done *outright* [*straightforwardly, frankly*] to my teacher.

つつむ 包む wrap (up), fold [他]; (完全に) envelop [他]; (覆い隠す) shroud [他] (❖通例受身

で), veil 㕣
アルミホイルでサケを包む *wrap* [*fold*] *salmon in aluminum foil*
ふろしきはほとんど何でも包めて便利だ A *furoshiki* is convenient because it *can wrap* just about anything.
彼の生い立ちはなぞに包まれている His early history *is shrouded* [*veiled*] *in* mystery.
その湖は朝もやに包まれていた The lake *was shrouded* [*veiled, enveloped*] *in* a morning mist.
小屋はあっという間に炎に包まれた The whole shed *was enveloped in flames* in an instant.
◆熱気に包まれた会場 a hall *filled with excitement* / 彼女は最新のファッションに身を包んでいた She *was dressed in* the latest fashion. / 大学入学のお祝いにとおじが2万円も包んでくれた My uncle *gave* me as much as 20,000 yen to celebrate my entrance to the university. / これを贈り物用に包んでください Will you *gift-wrap* this?

つづり 綴り (語のつづり字) spelling Ⓒ (❖「つづり方」の意味では Ⓤ);(紙をとじ合わせたもの) file Ⓒ / 『アップル』のつづりを言ってごらん Give *the spelling* of the word "apple." / 彼女はつづりの間違いを指摘してくれた She pointed out some「*spelling mistakes* [*misspelled words*]」to me.
◆彼は自分の名前のつづりを間違えた(→間違えてつづった) He「*spelled* his own name *wrong* [*misspelled* his own name]. / 君の名前のつづりを教えてください(→どうつづりますか) How do you *spell* your name? / この伝票は3枚つづりになっています This form comes in *triplicate*.

つづる 綴る (語・文字を) spell 㕣;(日記などを) write* 㕣;(とじる) bind* 㕣 / 日記をつづる *write* a diary / 書類をつづる *bind* documents

🅔「ミック・ジャガーのジャガーってどうつづるか知ってる？」「うん、J-a-g-g-e-r だよ」"Do you know「how to *spell* [*the spelling* of] Jagger in Mick Jagger?" "Yes, that's J-a-g-g-e-r."

つて 伝 connections, 《口語的》contact Ⓒ / 私はこの会社につてがある I have *connections* [*contacts*] in this company. / 彼女はつてでその会社に入った She got the job at that company *by using connections* [*contacts*].
◆僕は親戚(しんせき)のつてを頼ってアメリカへ行った I went to America, counting *on the help of* my relative.

つど 都度 疑問に思うことがあったらそのつど質問してください Ask me *whenever* you have a question. / そのジェットコースターに乗るにはそのつど券を買わなければならない You have to buy a ticket *every time* you ride the roller coaster.

つどい 集い meeting Ⓒ;(非公式でうちとけた) gathering Ⓒ, get-together Ⓒ

つどう 集う gather 㕣 ⇨ あつまる

つとまる 務まる (力量を備えている) be equal to ...;(適任である) be fit for ... / 彼にその仕事が務まると思いますか Do you think he *is*「*equal to* [*fit for*]」*the task*?
◆彼には生徒会長は務まらない He *is*「*unfit for* [*unequal to*]」*the position of president of the student council*.

つとめ¹ 勤め work Ⓤ, job Ⓒ ⇨ しごと
母は近くの花屋へ勤めに出ている My mother *has a job at* a nearby flower shop. / My mother *works at* a nearby flower shop.
兄は先週勤めを辞めた My brother quit [left] *his job* last week.
父はきのう勤めを休んだ My father stayed home from *work* yesterday.
お勤めは？ (→どんな仕事をしていますか) *What kind of job do you have?* / (→どこに勤めていますか) *Where do you work?* ❖英米では勤め先よりも職種を尋ねるほうがふつう
◆おじの会社勤めももう長い My uncle's *been working* for the company for a long time.
‖勤め口 a job / 勤め先 one's workplace

つとめ² 務め (義務) duty Ⓒ Ⓤ;(職務) job Ⓒ, task Ⓒ / 両親を助けるのは私の務めだ It's my *duty* to help my parents. / あの飛行機は長年の務めを終え解体されることになった That plane ended *its duty* and was scheduled to be scrapped. / 彼女は生徒会長としての務めをりっぱに果たした She carried out *her duties* [*jobs, tasks*] as president of the student council satisfactorily.

つとめあげる 勤め上げる おじはその会社を定年まで無事勤め上げた My uncle *worked* for the company for many years *until* his retirement age without any trouble.

つとめて 努めて 彼女は努めて(→できるだけ)明るくふるまった She behaved *as cheerful as*「*possible* [*she could*]」/ (→明るく見えるよう努力した) She *tried her best* to look cheerful.

つとめる¹ 努める (努力する) try to *do*, make* an effort to *do*;(最善を尽くす) do* *one's* best to *do* / 彼らは問題の早期解決に懸命に努めた They「*tried hard* [*did their best*]」*to* solve the problem as soon as possible. / 私は早寝早起きをするよう努めている I'm *trying* [*making an effort*] *to* go to bed early and to get up early.

つとめる² 務める (…として任務を果たす) act as ...;(役割を演じる) play 㕣;(職務・任務を) serve 㕣 Ⓒ
彼女は会議の議長を務めた She *acted* [*served*] *as* the chairperson of the meeting.
彼はその映画でわき役を務めた He *played* a supporting role in the movie.
佐藤氏は知事を3期務めた Mr. Sato *served* three terms as governor.
◆だれが彼女の代理をするのですか Who will *take the place of* her?

つとめる³ 勤める work 㕣, serve 㕣 Ⓒ
彼はレストランに勤めている He *works for* [*in*] a restaurant. (❖work for は雇用主を、work at [in] は勤務先を意識した言い方)
彼女は出納係としてその銀行に勤めている She

ツナ　tuna ▢; ‖ツナ缶《米》canned [《英》tinned] tuna / ツナサンド a tuna sandwich

つな　綱　rope▢▢; (やや細い) cord▢▢
綱1本 *a* (piece of) *rope* [*cord*]
彼は2本の木の間に綱をぴんと張った He stretched *the rope* tight between the two trees.
◆その大関は今場所綱取りがかかっている(→よい成績をあげれば横綱になる) The *ozeki* will become a *yokozuna* if he gets a good score in this tournament.
‖命綱 a lifeline
慣用表現 あなたは私の最後の頼みの綱です You are my last *hope*.
⇒つなわたり

つながり　繋がり　connection ▢, relation ▢, link ▢ /2つの現象のつながりを調べる examine *the connection* [*relation, link*] *between* the two phenomenon / 男はその殺人事件と何らかのつながりがあると見られる The man seems to *have* some *connections with* the murder case. / The man seems to *have* something *to do with* the murder case.
◆私と彼とは血のつながりがある I *have a blood relationship with* him. / (→親戚(しんせき)である)I'm *related to* him.

つながる　繋がる
❶【ひと続きになる】connect ⊜, be connected; (じかに結合している) join ⊜, be joined; (物と物を連結する) link ⊜, be linked
その島は橋によって本土とつながった The island (was) *connected* [*joined, linked*] *to* the mainland by a bridge.
この線はどのコンセントにつながっているの Which outlet *is* this cord *connected* [*plugged in*] *to*?
◆兄の通っている高校は大学とつながっている My brother's high school *is related to* a university. / 彼女の電話は話し中でつながらなかった Her line was engaged [busy] and I *couldn't* [*get through to*] [*reach*] her.
❷【関連がある】be related to ..., be connected with ...
私はあのおばとは血がつながっていない I'm not *related to* [*connected with*] that aunt *by blood*. / That aunt and I *are not blood relatives.*
その問題はもう1つ別の問題ともつながっている The problem *is* *related to* [*connected with*] another one.
◆小さな事件が重なり戦争につながっていった A series of small incidents *led up to* the outbreak of war. / 飲酒運転は事故につながる (→結果として事故になる)ことが多い Drunk driving often *results in* accidents.

つなぎ　繋ぎ　(料理の) binder ▢▢; (衣類)《米》coveralls ◆卵と野菜をよく混ぜてつなぎに卵を入れなさい Mix the meat and vegetables well and add an egg *to bind the mixture.* ‖つなぎ資金 a stopgap fund

つなぎとめる　繋ぎ止める　ボートをロープで渡し場につなぎ止める *fasten* a boat to the ferry with a rope / 彼女の気持ちをつなぎ止めておくのは難しい It's difficult to *keep* her *attracted to* me.

つなぎめ　繋ぎ目　(接合部分) joint ▢, join ▢; (結び目) knot▢ ‖パイプのつなぎ目 *a pipe joint*

つなぐ　繋ぐ

❶【連結する】join (together); connect ⊜; link (up [together])

| join: 物と物を直接, またはワイヤーなどを介して接続する.
| connect: 物と物を, 間に何かを介して接続する.
| link: 間に何かを介して, あるいは介するようにして接続する.

手をつなぐ *join* hands
2本のロープをつないで長くした I *joined* two ropes to make a long one.
鉄道はY市とN村をつないでいる The railway *connects* [*links*] Y City *with* N Village.
このビデオをテレビにつないでくれる？ Will you *connect* [*hook up*] this VCR *to* the TV for me?
内線712番につないでください Will you *connect* me *to* extension 712? / Will you *give* me extension 712?
◆彼らは手をつないで歩いていた They were walking *hand in hand.*

❷【つなぎ止める】tie ⊜; (馬などを) hitch (up); (係留する) moor ⊜
彼女は犬をポールにつないだ She *tied* her dog *to* the pole. / She *leashed* her dog *to* the pole.
彼たちはボートを岸につないだ We *moored* our boat to the river bank.
◆犬を鎖につないでおきなさい *Keep* [*Hold*] the dog *on a leash.*

❸【命などを】
彼らはパンひと切れを分け合って命をつないだ They [*sustained their lives* [*survived*]] by sharing a slice of bread.
彼らは1敗を守り優勝への望みをつないだ They won their last game to stay at one loss, so they *still have a chance to* win the tournament.

つなひき　綱引き　(a) tug of war ‖綱引きをする have *a tug of war*; play *tug of war*

つなみ　津波　tsunami ▢ (◆英語化している), tidal wave ‖津波の危険はない There's no danger of *a tsunami.* / 村は津波に襲われた The village was hit by *a tsunami.*
‖津波警報 a tsunami warning

つなわたり　綱渡り　tightrope walking▢
◆きのう見たサーカスでは子供が綱渡りをしていた A child *walked the tightrope* in the circus we saw yesterday.
慣用表現 この商売は毎日が綱渡りだ We *are walking a tightrope* everyday in this trade.

つね　常　私は食事の後にお茶を飲むのが常です I *usually* have a cup of green tea after meals. / 彼は早朝にジョギングをするのが常だった He *used to* jog early in the morning. / それが世の常というものだ That's *the way it goes*.

つねづね 常々 君は実におもしろい人だと僕は常々(→いつも)思っていたよ I've *always* thought you are quite an interesting person.

つねに 常に always, all the time, at all times //彼は常に辞書を持ち歩いている He *always* carries a dictionary with him.

つねる 抓る pinch, nip 他 //僕はほおをつねって夢でないことを確かめた I *pinched* 「my cheek [myself *on* the cheek] to make sure I wasn't dreaming.
◆陽子は私の腕を思いきりつねった Yoko *gave* me *a hard pinch* [*nip*] *on* the arm.

つの 角 (牛・カタツムリの) horn ⓒ; (シカの枝角) antler ⓒ //羊に角が生えてきた The sheep has sprouted *horns*. / カタツムリが角を出した[引っ込めた] A snail 「*put out* [*drew in*] *its horns* [*antennae*]. / 角のある動物を挙げなさい Name 「animals *with horns* [*horned* animals].

‖角笛 a horn

慣用表現「もう遅いので急いで帰らないと家内が角を出して待ってる」と言って父の友人は帰っていった As he left our house, my father's friend said, "It's late and my wife's waiting. If I don't hurry home, she'll *be furious*."

つのる 募る ❶【強まる・高じる】(増大する) grow* 自, increase 自; (強まる) intensify 自 //彼女に対する僕の思いは募る一方だった My love for her *was growing* more and more (*intense*). / 洪水が起こるのではないかと地域住民の不安が募った The anxiety over the threat of flood *grew* [*increased, intensified*] among the people living in the area.
❷【募集する】(寄付を) collect 他; (参加者などを) look for ...; (受け入れる) accept 他 //寄付金を募る *collect* donations / 卓球大会への参加者を募ります We are 「*looking for* [*accepting*] applicants for the table tennis tournament.

つば¹ 唾 spit ⓤ; (唾液(だえき)) saliva ⓤ ◆彼は手につばをつけてから鉄棒に飛びついた He *spat on* his hands and then jumped up to the horizontal bar. / 道につばを吐く人をどう思う? What do you think about a person who *spits* on the street? / レモンを想像するだけでつばが出てきた My *mouth watered* at just the thought of a lemon.

慣用表現 あの女の子にはつばをつけてある I *have dibs on* that girl.

つば² 鍔 (帽子の) brim ⓒ; (刀の) (sword) guard ⓒ ◆つばの広い帽子 a *wide-brimmed* hat

つばき 椿 camellia ⓒ ‖ツバキ油 camellia oil

俳句 赤い椿白い椿と落ちにけり
(河東碧梧桐(かわひがしへきごとう))
Red camellias,
and white camellias, too,
landing on the ground

つばさ 翼 wing ⓒ //ワシは翼を広げた The eagle spread [expanded] *its wings*. / 飛行機の翼の一部が破損した A part of *the* plane's *wing* was broken off.
◆その鳥は翼を広げると約1メートルある *The* bird's *wingspan* is about one meter.

つばぜりあい 鍔迫り合い つばぜり合いの結果わが校が勝利した The result of *the close game* [*race*] was a victory for our school.

つばめ 燕 swallow ⓒ

つぶ 粒 (小麦・米などの穀物の) grain ⓒ; (麦・トウモロコシなどの) kernel ⓒ; (水の) drop ⓒ //米1粒 *a grain of* rice
大粒の雨が降っている It's raining in *large drops*.
◆机の上に1粒の涙が落ちた A tear [*teardrop*] fell onto the table. / このジュースはオレンジの粒(→果肉)入りだ This orange juice has *pulp* in it. / クリームの中にイチゴの粒々(→種)が入っている There are strawberry *seeds* in the cream. / このサクランボは粒(→サイズ)がそろっている All of these cherries have the *same size*.
慣用表現 このチームは選手の粒がそろっている(→みなすばらしい) The players of this team *are all excellent*.

つぶさに in detail, minutely //子供たちはその動物の生態をつぶさに観察し記録した The children observed and recorded *in detail* [*minutely*] how the animal lived.

つぶし 潰し 彼女はコンピュータに非常に詳しいからいくらでもつぶしがきくだろう(→どんな仕事にも就けるだろう) She can *take any job* because of her immense knowledge of computers.

つぶす 潰す
❶【平たくする】crush (up); (ゆでたジャガイモなどを) mash (up); (粉々に) smash (up); (ぺちゃんこに) squash 他
ペットボトルはつぶしてから箱に入れてください *Crush* plastic bottles before putting them into the box.
その箱をつぶさないで. 中にケーキが入っているの Don't *crush* the box. There's some cake inside.
ゆでたジャガイモをスプーンでつぶした I *mashed* boiled potatoes with a spoon.
◆水ぶくれをつぶしてはいけない Don't *burst* a blister.
❷【だめにする・役に立たなくする】
子供の個性をつぶす *suppress* a child's individuality
彼女は父親から受け継いだ店をつぶしてしまった She *bankrupted* the store she took over from her father.
彼は大声で歌いすぎて声をつぶした He sang too loud and *made his voice very hoarse*.
親の顔をつぶすようなことはするな Don't do anything that would 「*make* your parents *lose face* [*embarrass* your parents].
❸【時間を】kill 他; (むだに使う) waste 他

暇をつぶす *kill* time
漫画を読んで1時間つぶした I *killed* an hour reading comics.
せっかくの休日を弟の宿題の手伝いでつぶしてしまった I *wasted* my holiday helping my brother finish his homework.

つぶぞろい 粒揃い うちのテニス部は粒ぞろいだ The members of our tennis team are *all good*.

つぶつぶ 粒々 このゼリーにはオレンジの粒々(→果肉)が入っている This Jell-O has orange *pulp* in it.

つぶやき 呟き mumble ⓒ, murmur ⓒ; (不平などの) mutter ⓒ

つぶやく 呟く mumble ⓐ ⓗ, murmur ⓐ ⓗ; (不平などを) mutter ⓒ ‖彼は窓の外を眺めながら何やらつぶやいていた He *was mumbling* [*murmuring, muttering*] (something) to himself while looking out the window.

つぶより 粒より ─粒よりの picked (❖名詞の前で用いる); (食べ物などが) choice ‖粒よりのリンゴ *choice* apples ◆日本代表チームは粒よりの選手がそろっている The all-Japan team consists of *selected* [*chosen*] members.

つぶら 円ら つぶらなひとみ *cute round* eyes

つぶる 瞑る close ⓗ ‖さあ、目をつぶってごらん Now, *close your eyes*.
[慣用表現] 今回の遅刻には目をつぶってやろう I'm going to「*close my eyes to* [*overlook*]」your coming late this time.

つぶれる 潰れる
❶【崩れる・こわれる】be crushed, squash ⓗ, be squashed; (崩壊する) collapse ⓐ; (破壊される) be destroyed
彼に座られて帽子がぺちゃんこにつぶれてしまった My hat *was crushed* flat because he sat on it.
箱の底のオレンジはみんなつぶれていた The oranges at the bottom of the box *were* all *squashed*.
地震で多くの家がつぶれた Many houses「*collapsed* in [*fell down* in, *were destroyed* by] the earthquake.
◆足の裏のまめがつぶれた The blister on the sole of my foot *broke*.
❷【だめになる】spoil ⓗ, be spoiled; (中止になる) be canceled; (事業が) fail ⓐ, collapse ⓐ; (倒産する) go* bankrupt
父の会社がつぶれた My father's company *has failed* [*collapsed, gone bankrupt*].
その企画は資金繰りがうまくいかずつぶれた The project *collapsed* due to lack of funding.
◆レンズを通して太陽を見ると目がつぶれちゃうよ You will *lose your sight* if you look at the sun through the lens. / 彼女はカラオケで歌いすぎて声がつぶれた (→声がかれた) Her voice *got very hoarse* because she sang karaoke too much. / 角(ミ)の本屋は今にもつぶれそうだ The book store at the corner is on the brink of「*closing down* [*going out of business*]」. / あなたがパーティーに来てくれないと私の面目がつぶれてしまいます I'll *lose face* if you don't come to the party.
❸【時間をとられる】
庭の草むしりで半日つぶれてしまった I *lost* half of the day weeding the garden.

つべこべ つべこべ言わずにさっさとやれ I want *no ifs, ands or buts*. [*I don't want any of your complaints*.] Just do it!

ツベルクリン tuberculin [tjuːbáːrkjəlin] ⓤ
‖ツベルクリン検査 a *tuberculin* test / ツベルクリン反応 a *tuberculin* reaction

つぼ¹ 坪 [日] a *tsubo*, a Japanese unit of area of land equal to about 3.3 square meters ‖坪10万円の土地 the land priced 100,000 yen a *tsubo* / わが家の土地は100坪ある Our family owns 100 *tsubo* of land.

つぼ² 壺 ❶【容器】(金属・陶器・ガラス製の丸い容器) pot ⓒ; (陶器・ガラス製で広口の) jar ⓒ; (装飾用の) vase ⓒ ‖その芸術家は粘土でつぼを作った That artist formed *pots* from clay.
❷【身体】moxibustion [acupuncture, pressure] point ⓒ (❖moxibustion は「きゅう」, acupuncture は「はり」, pressure は「指圧」の意味)
❸【要点】the point, the key ‖彼はその作業をうまくやるつぼを心得ている He knows *the key* to doing the work successfully. / 石井先生のつぼを押さえた授業は生徒の評判がいい Mr. Ishii's lecture has a good reputation among students because he *always makes the point* when he teaches.
‖骨つぼ an urn / 滝つぼ the basin of a waterfall
→おもうつぼ

つぼみ 蕾 (flower) bud ⓒ ‖バラはまだつぼみだった The roses were still *in bud*. (❖in bud は無冠詞) / つぼみはまだ固い The *buds* are still closed. / チューリップのつぼみがふくらんだ The *buds* of tulips are swollen. / つぼみが開いた The *bud* opened into a flower.

つぼむ 窄む この花はあと2, 3時間でつぼんでしまう These flowers *close up* in a few hours.

つま 妻
❶【配偶者である女性】wife ⓒ (複 wives)
最愛の妻 one's beloved *wife* / 内縁の妻 a common-law *wife*
私には妻も子もいる I have *a wife* and children.
彼女はきっと彼のよき妻となろう She is surely going to「*make a good wife* for him [*make him a good wife*]」.
◆彼には美しい妻がいる He's *married to a beautiful woman*. (❖「私には妻がいます」は、通例 I'm married. という. I have a wife. は自分に妻がいることを「告白」するなどの限られた場面でしか用いない) / 彼はその女性を妻にした He *married* [*got married to*] the woman. / 彼は3年ぶりに別れた妻に会った He met *his ex-wife* for the first time in three years.
❷【食べ物】
刺身のつま a garnish for *sashimi*
‖新妻 a bride / 人妻 (他人の妻) another

man's wife; (既婚女性) a married woman

つまさき 爪先 tiptoe ⓒ; (足の指) toe ⓒ //この靴はつま先がきつい, These shoes are pinching *my toes*. / 彼女は頭のてっぺんからつま先まで泥だらけだった She was covered with mud *from head [top] to toe*. / 彼女はつま先立ちで歩いた She walked *on tiptoe*.

つまされる 彼女が試験に落ちたと聞いて身につまされる思いがした I *felt very sympathetic* [*My heart went out to* her] when I heard she didn't pass the exam.

つましい 倹しい; (質素な) simple; (倹約する) thrifty //つましい生活を送る live a *frugal* [*simple, thrifty*] life; live *frugally* [*in a small way*]

つまずく 躓く ❶ 【よろめく】stumble ⓘ, trip ⓘ //男の子が石につまずいて転んだ A little boy *stumbled* [*tripped*] *over* a stone and fell.
❷ 【失敗する・うまくいかない】その女性は事業につまずいた The woman *failed in* her business. / 計画は最初からつまずいた(→思いどおりに進められなかった) The plan *was not carried out* from the start *as had been expected*. / 彼は英語の受動態の学習でつまずいている He's *suffering difficulty* in learning the passive voice of English.

つまはじき 爪弾き クラスメートは彼女をつまはじきにした Her classmates *gave her the cold shoulder*. (❖give ... the cold shoulder は「…に冷たい態度をとる」の意味)

つまびく 爪弾く (米)pick ⓘ, pluck ⓘ ⓘ, strum ⓘ ⓘ //ギターをつまびく *pick* (the strings of) the guitar; *pluck* (at) the strings of the guitar

つまみ ❶ 【つまむ部分】(回すもの) knob ⓒ //CDプレーヤーの音量調節つまみ *the volume knob* [*control*] of a CD player / 時計の針を合わせるためにつまみを回す turn *a knob* to set the hands of a clock
❷ 【食べ物】(軽食) snacks //父はビールとつまみを注文した My father ordered beer and some *snacks*.

-つまみ a pinch of ... //塩ひとつまみ *a pinch of* salt

つまみぐい つまみ食い 彼は母親のいないすきにコロッケを1個つまみ食いした He *sneaked* a croquette when his mother was not there.

つまみだす つまみ出す 米に混じったごみをつまみ出した I *picked* unwanted things *out of* the rice. / 彼はその酔っ払いを店からつまみ出した He *threw* [*turned*] the drunk *out of* the shop.

つまむ pick ⓘ, pinch ⓘ //彼は泥だらけの靴下を(指先で)つまんで洗濯機に入れた He *picked* his dirty socks *up* (*with the tips of his fingers*) and put them into the washing machine. ◆ひどいにおいに鼻をつまんだ I *held* [*pinched*] *my nose* at the bad smell. / 私たちは菓子をつまみながら話をした We had a talk *over* some snacks.

つまようじ 爪楊枝 toothpick ⓒ

つまらない

❶ 【おもしろくない・退屈な】(興味を引かない) uninteresting; (退屈な) dull, boring; (退屈している) bored

つまらないパーティー an *uninteresting* [a *dull*, a *boring*] party

その映画はつまらなかった The movie *was boring* [*dull*].

いつも同じじゃつまらないからきょうは何か違うことをして遊ぼうよ It's *boring* to always do the same thing. Let's do something else today.

彼女はパーティー会場の隅でひとりつまらなそうにしていた She *seemed bored*, alone in a corner of the party hall.

◆つまらないだじゃれ a *cold* jest / 君が行かないんじゃつまらないよ If you don't go, it will be *no fun*. / ああ, つまらない. 何かおもしろいことないかしら Oh, *what a bore*! Isn't there anything exciting (to do)?

❷ 【取るに足りない】trivial, trifling, petty; (ばかばかしい) silly; (重要でない) unimportant; (価値のない) worthless

つまらないことでくよくよするな Don't worry over such a *trivial* [*trifling*] matter.

つまらない間違いをしてしまった I've made a *silly* mistake.

彼はつまらない人間だ He's「an *unimportant* [a *worthless*] person.

◆つまらないことから口論が始まった A quarrel started over *nothing*. / つまらない物ですが, どうぞ(→ここにあなたのために持ってきた物があります. 気に入ってくれるといいのですが) Here's *something* I've brought for you. I hope you'll like it. (❖英語ではふつう日本語でのように自分が贈る物を悪く言うことはない)

つまり (すなわち・換言すれば) that is (to say), in other words, I mean; (詳しく言えば) namely (❖文頭では用いない); (要するに) in short; (ひと言で言えば) in a word //例の2人の生徒, つまり良夫と正はきょうも遅刻した The two students,「*that is* [*namely*], Yoshio and Tadashi, were late again today. / つまり実験は失敗したのです *In short* [*In a word*], the test failed.

◆彼の言いたかったのはつまりそういうことだったのだろう *Anyway*, that would be what he wanted to say. / つまりこういうことなんです Let me put it this way. (❖後に説明が続く)

🔑「つまり犯行現場近くにはいなかったということですか」「そのとおりです」 "*You mean* you were not anywhere near the scene of the crime?" "Precisely."

つまる 詰まる

❶ 【管などが】be stopped (up), be stuffed (up), be blocked (up), clog (up)

このパイプには何か詰まっている This pipe is「*stopped* (*up*) *with* [*blocked* (*up*) *by*] something.

トイレが詰まっている The toilet *is clogged up*.

かぜで鼻が詰まっている My nose *is stuffed*

up from a cold. / I have a *stuffy* nose from a cold.

その男はもちがのどに詰まって窒息死した The man *got* his throat *blocked by mochi* and died. / The man *choked* to death *on* his *mochi*.

◆コピー機が詰まってしまった The copy machine *got jammed*. / その部屋はむんむんしていて息が詰まりそうだった The room was hot and humid and I *was* almost *stifled* [*suffocated, choked*].

❷【いっぱいである】be full, be filled, be stuffed

まくらの中にはもみがらが詰まっていた The pillow *was* 「*full of* [*filled with, stuffed with*] chaff.

◆この先予定が詰まっている I have a *tight* [*full, heavy*] schedule ahead. / バスの中は乗客でぎっしり詰まっていた The bus *was jam-packed* with passengers.

❸【縮まる】

洗濯したらシャツの丈(たけ)が詰まった Washing made my shirt *too short*.

前の車との距離が詰まった Our car *got nearer to* the one ahead. / The distance between our car and the one ahead *got shorter*.

◆詰まった当たりのゴロ a *slow* grounder

❹【行き詰まる】

彼女は言葉に詰まった She *was at a loss for words*.

私は涙で声が詰まった My voice *was choked* with tears.

つまるところ 詰まる所 (要するに) in short, 《公式的》in sum; (ひと言で言えば) in a word

つみ¹ 罪 (法律上の) crime [C] [U]; (道徳・宗教上の) sin [C] [U]; (罪を犯していること・罪悪感) guilt [U]; (違反) offense, 《英》offence [C]

〖罪を・に〗

罪を償う atone [pay] for *one's crime* [*sin, guilt*]

彼は罪を犯した He committed *a crime* [*sin*].

彼は絶対に自分の罪を認めないだろう I'm afraid he would never admit his *crime* [*sin, guilt*].

父の車を無断で借用したって罪にはならないだろう It won't be *a crime* to use my father's car without permission.

◆私は罪になるようなことは何もしていない I did nothing *criminal*. / 彼は彼女の犯した罪をかぶった He took *the blame* for what she had done. / その国会議員は収賄の罪に問われている The Diet member *has been accused of* taking bribes.

〖～(の)罪〗

重い[軽い]罪 *a* serious [minor] *crime*

彼は何の罪も犯していないことが分かった He was found innocent of any *crime*.

◆彼は強盗の罪で逮捕された He was arrested for *robbery*.

〖罪の〗

彼には全く罪の意識がないようだった He didn't seem to have any *sense of guilt* at all. / He didn't seem to *feel guilty* at all.

◆罪のないうそ a *white* lie / 罪のない冗談 a *harmless* joke

〖罪は〗

◆その件に関しては彼女に罪はない She is *not to blame* for that.

〖その他〗

彼は罪深い人間だ He is a *sinful* person.

◆彼女をふるなんて彼は罪なことをするやつだ(→残酷だ) It is *cruel* of him to turn her down.

つみ² 詰み checkmate [C]

つみあげる 積み上げる pile (up); (いいかげんに) heap (up); (きちんと) stack (up) ∥部屋の隅にはたくさんの古雑誌が積み上げてあった A lot of old magazines *have been piled* [*heaped, stacked*] *up* in the corner of the room. ◆きちんと積み上げられた本の山 *a* neat *stack* [*pile*] *of* books

つみおろし 積み降ろし 彼の引っ越しのとき荷物の積み降ろしを手伝った I helped him *load and unload* things when he moved.

つみかさなる 積み重なる get* piled [heaped, stacked] up, form a pile [heap, stack](❖get heaped up, form a heapは「いいかげんに」, stackは「きちんと」の意味. また, getの代わりにbe動詞を用いれば「積み重なっている状態」を意味する); (蓄積する) pile up

つみかさね 積み重ね (蓄積) accumulation [U]; (継続) continuation [U]

◆何事においても努力の積み重ねが大切だ The *continuous* [*constant*] efforts are what matter in everything.

つみかさねる 積み重ねる ❶【物を】pile (up); (いいかげんに) heap (up); (きちんと) stack (up) ∥お皿をテーブルの上にきちんと積み重ねなさい *Stack up* the dishes neatly on the table.

❷【事を】経験を積み重ねる *accumulate* [*pile up*] *one's* experience / 長年積み重ねてきた(→継続的な)努力がついに報われた The *constant* efforts I'd made for so long have finally been rewarded. / 彼はその後も同じような犯罪を積み重ねた(→繰り返した) He *repeated* crimes of the same kind after that.

つみき 積み木 《米》blocks, 《主に英》bricks

つみこむ 積み込む put* [他]; (大量の荷を) load (up) ∥トラックに家具を積み込む *put* [*load*] furniture *into* a truck; *load* a truck *with* furniture(❖一般に「荷物を積み込む」という場合はload a truckとする)

つみたて 積み立て accumulation [U] [C]

‖積立金 a reserve fund / 積立預金[貯金] installment [collection] savings

つみたてる 積み立てる (使わずにとっておく) put* aside; (預金する) save [他] [自] ∥彼は世界一周旅行の費用として毎月5万円ずつ積み立てている He 「*puts aside* [*saves*] 50,000 yen every month for a round-the-world trip.

つみとる 摘み取る pick [他], nip off; (引き抜く) pull (out) ∥花を摘み取る *pick* [*nip off*] flowers

◆悪の芽を摘み取る *nip* evil *in the bud*

つみに 積み荷 load ◎;(船・飛行機などの)cargo ◎◎(複 ～es, ～s);(陸・海・空による)《米》freight [fréit] ◎(❖《英》では船・空輸貨物を freight といい, 陸上運送貨物は goods を用いる)∥警察は船の積み荷を調べた The police inspected *the load* [*cargo, freight*] on the ship. ◆みんなでトラックの積み荷を下ろした We all *unloaded* the truck.

つみほろぼし 罪滅ぼし (公式的)atonement ◎∥親不孝をしたせめてもの罪滅ぼしにと, 彼は必死で店を守り続けている He's been trying hard to keep the store in business as *atonement* to his parents *for* having let them down.

つむ¹ 積む
❶【車などに】load (up)
トラックに家具を積む *load* a truck *with* furniture; *load* furniture *into* a truck
数台の車を積んだトレーラーが走り過ぎていった A trailer *loaded with* several cars went past me.
❷【重ねる】pile (up);(いいかげんに)heap (up);(きちんと)stack (up)
ダンボール箱はそこにきちんと積んでおきました I *piled up* cardboard boxes neatly there.
先生の机の上には書類が山のように積んであった Documents *were piled* [*heaped*] *up* high on the teacher's desk.
◆いくら金を積まれてもこの絵を手放すことはしません I'm not going to sell this painting no matter how much money you *offer*.
❸【経験などを】
その仕事は多くの経験を積んだ人にお願いしたほうがいい We'd better ask an *experienced* person to do the work.
彼はイタリアで10年間料理人になるための修業を積んできた He's got 10 years of *training* in Italy to be a cook.

つむ² 摘む pick ⊕;(集める)gather ⊕
私は彼女にタンポポを摘んでやった I *picked* some dandelions *for* her. / I *picked* her some dandelions.
ブルーベリーを摘んでジャムにした I *picked* [*gathered*] blueberries and made jam from them.
◆非行の芽を摘む *nip* juvenile delinquency *in the bud* / 否定するだけのしかり方では子供の好奇心の芽を摘んでしまう(→いろいろな物事に対する好奇心を台なしにしてしまう)ことになる Always saying "no" and "don't" to children will *ruin* [*spoil*] their curiosity about various things.

つむ³ 詰む 目の詰んだ織物 *tightly woven* fabrics / (将棋で)あと5手で詰むよ *Mate* in five.

つむぐ 紡ぐ spin* ⊕∥綿から糸を紡ぐ *spin* cotton *into* thread; *spin* thread *out of* cotton

つむじ 旋毛 a whorl of hair on *one's* head
慣用表現 あいつはつむじ曲がりだ He is a *contrary* [*an ill-natured*] guy. / 彼女をパーティーに呼ばないとつむじを曲げてしまうよ She'll *get angry* if you don't invite her to the party.

つむじかぜ 旋風 whirlwind ◎

つむる 瞑る close ⊕ ➪つぶる

つめ¹ 爪
❶【指の】nail ◎(❖「手の親指以外のつめ」は fingernail,「手の親指」は thumbnail,「足のつめ」は toenail ともいう);(鳥・獣の)claw ◎
つめの手入れをする do *one's nails* / …につめを立てる dig *one's nails* [*claws*] *into* …
だいぶつめが伸びてるね. 切りなさいよ *Your nails* have grown so long. You should trim [clip, cut] them.
彼女はつめを伸ばしている She's growing *her nails*. / She has long *nails*.
彼女はつめをかむ癖(½)がある She has the habit of biting *her nails*.
猫が柱でつめを研(½)いでいた A cat was sharpening *its claws* against a post.
その投手は投げすぎでつめが割れてしまった The pitcher got *his nails* torn from too much throwing.
❷【琴の】plectrum ◎ (複 plectra, ～s),《口語的》pick ◎
慣用表現 彼はつめに火をともすようにして(→極端に倹約した生活をして)ためた金で家を買った He bought a house with the money he had saved *by leading extremely thrifty life*. / 彼は本当によく練習するよ. 君も彼のつめのあかでも煎(½)じて飲みなさい(→彼を見習いなさい)He practices really hard. You should *follow his example*. / 彼の言葉にはつめのあかほどの思いやりも感じられない There is not *even the smallest* show of kindness in what he says.
ことわざ 能ある鷹(誓)はつめを隠す ➪のう²

つめ² 詰め (最終段階)the final stage ∥我々の計画は詰めが甘かったようだ It seems that we *weren't careful enough at the final stage* of planning.
∥詰め将棋 a *shogi* checkmate problem

-づめ -詰め びん詰めのピクルス pickles *in a jar* / そのジュースをびん詰めにする *bottle* the juice / 本を箱詰めにする *box* the books; *pack* the books *into a box* / 400字詰め原稿用紙 a sheet of *400-character* manuscript paper / 圭子は警視庁詰めの記者に Keiko is a reporter *accredited to* the Metropolitan Police Department. / 今週は働きづめだった I've been working throughout this week. / バスは満員で僕はずっと立ちづめだった The bus was packed, so I *had to stand all the way*.

つめあと 爪跡 木の幹にはクマのつめ跡が残っていた There were *scratches* made by a bear on the trunk of the tree. / その台風は日本各地に大きなつめ跡を残した The typhoon left terrible *scars* in various parts of Japan.

つめあわせ 詰め合わせ お菓子の詰め合わせをいただいた I received a box of *assorted* sweets.

つめえり 詰め襟 stand-up collar ◎;(制服)

a uniform with a stand-up collar

つめかえる 詰め替える（再び満たす）refill [他];（入れ替える）repack [他] ∥シャンプーを詰め替えた I *refilled* the bottle of shampoo. / 詰め換え用の洗剤を買った I bought a pack of detergent *to refill the bottle.* / 野菜を別の箱に詰め替えた I *repacked* vegetables *into* another box. ◆このボールペンは詰め替えができる This ball-point pen is *refillable.*

つめかける 詰め掛ける crowd [自] [他];（押し寄せる）throng [自] [他] ∥ライブ会場には多くのファンが詰めかけた A lot of fans *crowded* the concert hall./ The concert hall *was crowded with* a lot of fans. / 彼の周りに人々が詰めかけた People *crowded* [*thronged*] around him.

つめきり 爪切り nail clippers;（はさみ形の）nail scissors

つめこみ 詰め込み 詰め込み勉強で覚えたものは試験が終わるとじきに忘れてしまう *Crammed* [*Briefly acquired*] knowledge is forgotten soon after the examination. / あの先生は詰め込み教育をする That teacher *crams knowledge* into the students' heads.

つめこむ 詰め込む（詰める）pack [他], cram [他]（❖cramは知識などを詰め込む場合も用いる）;（柔らかい物を）stuff [他] ∥人に知識を詰め込む *cram* knowledge into a person / バッグに荷物を詰め込んだ I *packed* things *into* my bag./ I *packed* my bag *with* things. / 人質たちはその小さな部屋に詰め込まれていた The hostages *were packed into* the small room. / 勉はクッキーを口に詰め込んだ Tsutomu *stuffed* his mouth *with* cookies. / 真理子はクッションに綿を詰め込んだ Mariko *stuffed* the cushion *with* cotton./ Mariko *stuffed* cotton *into* the cushion.

つめたい 冷たい

❶【低温の】cold (↔hot);（心地よい程度に）cool (↔warm);（不快なほど）chilly;（氷のように）ice-cold, icy

冷たい色調 a *cold* [*cool*] tone

何か冷たい飲み物でもいかがですか Would you like something *cold* to drink?

風が冷たくなってきた The wind is getting *cold.*

由紀の手は氷のように冷たかった Yuki's hands *were* 「*as cold as ice* [*icy*].

私の手が何か冷たい物に触れた My hand touched something *cold.*

その子猫は冷たくなっていた The kitten *was dead and cold.*

❷【冷淡な】cold (↔warm);（よそよそしい）cool, chilly, unfriendly

彼女は冷たい心の持ち主だ She has *a cold heart.*/ She is a *cold-hearted* woman.

彼らはよそ者に冷たい They are *cold* to strangers.

彼は周囲の冷たい目に耐えた He endured *cold stares* from people around.

そんなに冷たくしないで Don't be so *cold!*

そんなに冷たいこと言わないで Don't say such *unfriendly* things.

◆彼女はちょっと冷たい感じの人だ She has a tinge of *coldness* [*coolness, chilliness, unfriendliness*] to others. / 彼女は彼を冷たくあしらった She *treated* him *coldly.*/ She *gave* him *the cold shoulder.*

つめもの 詰め物（歯の）filling [C] [U];（料理などの）stuffing [U];（物を保護するための）packing [U];（当て物）pad [C], padding [U] ∥歯の詰め物が取れた A piece of *filling* came out of my tooth. ◆歯に詰め物をする *fill* a tooth / まくらに詰め物をする *stuff* a pillow

つめよる 詰め寄る 彼らは彼女に詰め寄って釈明を求めた They *cornered* her, demanding the explanation for the matter.

つめる 詰める

❶【いっぱいにする】pack [他], cram [他];（柔らかい物を）stuff [他]

彼女は缶詰を箱に詰めた She *packed* a box *with* canned food. / She *packed* canned food *into* a box.

弁当を詰めているとき電話が鳴った The telephone rang while I *was packing* lunch.

出発の3時間前にようやくスーツケースを詰め終わった I finally *finished packing* my suitcase three hours before the departure time.

彼は人形に綿を詰めた He *stuffed* the doll *with* cotton.

❷【ふさぐ】fill [他], stuff [他]

穴にセメントを詰めてふさいだ I 「*filled* (*in*) [*stuffed* (*up*)] the hole *with* cement.

❸【席などを】move over [up], close up

少し詰めてもらえますか Will you 「*move over* [*move up, close up*] a little?

◆どうぞ奥へお詰めください *Move* to the rear, please.

❹【短くする】（丈(ﾀｹ)を）shorten [他], take* up;（幅を）take in

彼はジーパンの丈を4センチ詰めてもらった He *had* his jeans *shortened* [*taken up*] four centimeters.

彼女はドレスのウエストを詰めてもらった She *had* her dress *taken in* at the waist.

◆彼は徐々にトップの走者との差を詰めてきた He's gradually *gotten nearer to* the top runner.

❺【議論などを】

その件に関してはもっと議論を詰める必要がある We need to *discuss* the matter more *thoroughly.*

❻【職場に】

このビルには常時3人の警備員が詰めている There are always three security guards *on duty* in this building.

❼【将棋】

相手の玉(ｷﾞｮｸ)を7手で詰める *put* the opponent's king *in checkmate* in seven moves

つもり

❶【意図】――…するつもりである be going to *do*; intend to *do*; will *do*; plan to *do*;

mean* to *do*
be going to *do*: 近い未来の予定・計画・意図を表す。
intend to *do*: 近い未来の意志を表すややかたい語。
will *do*: 決意が堅いというニュアンスが強い。通例一人称の主語に用いる。主語が二人称・三人称の場合には通常 be going to *do* を用いる。
plan to *do*: きちんと計画されていることを強調する。
mean to *do*: 特に会話で用いられるくだけた表現。

これから食事するつもりだ I'm going to have a meal now.
来年はニュージーランドでホームステイをするつもりだ I'm going [*planning*] to do a homestay in New Zealand next year.
将来は弁護士になるつもりだ I'm going [*I intend*] to be a lawyer in the future.
彼は結婚するつもりがあるのかしら Is he ever *going to* marry?
彼が来なかったらどうするつもりなの What「*are you going to* do [*will* you do] if he doesn't come?
もう二度と彼に会うつもりはない I *will* never see him again.
うそをつくつもりはなかったんだ I didn't *mean to* tell you a lie.
夕食前に宿題をすませてしまうつもりだったができなかった I「*had intended* [*had meant, was going*] *to* finish my homework before dinner, but I couldn't.
◆今度の週末は横浜へ行くつもりです I'*m going to* Yokohama this weekend. (❖be going to の後に go や come がくる場合, be going to go [*come*] より be going [*coming*] とするほうがふつう) / あれは冗談のつもりだったんだよ That *was intended* [*meant*] *as* a joke. / I *meant* it *as* a joke.
❷【思う】
僕たちにあんなことを言うなんて, あいついったい何様のつもりなんだ Who on earth does he *think* [*believe*] he is to say such a thing to us?
妹はすっかりお姫様になったつもりでいる My sister *is making believe that* she is a princess. / (→お姫様になったかのようにふるまっている) My sister *is behaving as if* she has become a princess.
家中の戸締まりをしたつもりだったが, 寝室の窓があいていた I *thought* I had locked the house up, but the bedroom window was open.
❸【心構え】
きょうの夕方に電話するからそのつもりでいてよ I'll call you this evening. So *keep that in mind*.
今度こんなことをしたら退学だからな, そのつもりでいろよ (→退学になるということを覚えておけ) *Remember that* you'll be kicked out of school next time you do things like this.

つもる 積もる
❶【堆積する】pile up, accumulate 圓; (場所に残る) settle 圓; (積もっている) lie* 圓
雪が40センチ積もった The snow *accumulated* [*lay*] 40 centimeters deep on the ground.
この雪は積もらないだろう The snow *won't accumulate* [*stick*]. / (→じきに溶けるだろう) The snow will soon *be melted away*.
❷【たまる】accumulate 圓, pile up
彼女の借金は積もり積もって500万円を超えた Her debts *have accumulated* [*piled up*] to over five million yen.
◆数年ぶりに仲間が集まり, 積もる話に花が咲いた (→様々なことについてたくさん話すことを楽しんだ) We got together for the first time in a few years, and we enjoyed talking about many things.

つや¹ 艶 gloss Ⓤ(また a ~), luster Ⓤ(また a ~); (磨いて出た) polish Ⓤ(また a ~) ∥彼女はつやのある美しい髪をしている She has beautiful hair with *gloss* [*luster*] on it. / She has beautiful *glossy* hair. / おじはつぼを磨いてつやを出した My uncle rubbed his vase to bring out *the luster*.
◆つやのある肌 *bright and youthful* skin / あの歌手はつやのある声をしている That singer has *mellow voice*. / このギターはつや出し [消し] 塗装が施されている This guitar has *a glossy* [*matte*] *finish* on it.
つや² 通夜 wake ⓒ ∥今夜彼女の通夜が営まれる They are holding her *wake* tonight.
つやつや 彼女は肌がつやつやしている She's got healthily *glowing* skin.

つゆ¹ 梅雨 *tsuyu*, the rainy season
沖縄は梅雨に入った *The rainy season* has come in Okinawa.
やっと梅雨が明けた *The rainy season* is finally over.
∥梅雨入り the start of the rainy season / 梅雨空 the cloudy sky during the rainy season / 梅雨(ぜん)前線 a (seasonal) rain front

だいたい6月の中旬から約1か月間続く日本の雨季のことを梅雨といいます。北海道を除く日本列島はその間湿気の多さに悩まされます。高温多湿のため食べ物は傷みやすく, したがって食中毒も起こりやすくなります。しかし, 梅雨がもたらす雨は米作りにはとても重要です。
Tsuyu refers to the rainy season in Japan. It usually starts in the middle of June and lasts for about a month. *Tsuyu* brings a lot of humidity to Japan, except for Hokkaido. During the season, food easily goes bad because of the high temperatures and humidity, so there is a strong possibility of food poisoning. *Tsuyu*, however, is very important as it brings a large amount of the rain necessary for rice cultivation.

つゆ² 露 dew Ⓤ; (露のひとしずく) dewdrop

◎ ∥露が降りた The dew has fallen. / その花は露にぬれていた The flower was wet with dew. ◆彼女の物とはつゆ知らず,僕はそのケーキを食べてしまった I ate the cake up *without knowing at all* that it was hers.

短歌 秋の田のかりほの庵(いほ)の苫(とま)をあらみわが衣手は露にぬれつつ(天智天皇)
In the autumn field
my small hut for the harvest
is thatched, rough and crude,
and so the sleeves of my shirt
are growing damp with the dew.

つゆ³ 汁 (吸い物) soup ⓤ; (果汁) juice ⓤ ⓒ, nectar ⓤ ➡ しる(汁)
◆そばつゆ *sauce* into which buckwheat noodles are dipped when eaten

つよい 強い

❶【力・能力がある】 strong; (非常に) powerful ─ 強く strongly; powerfully

強いボクサー a *strong* [*powerful*] boxer / 体をもっと強くする *make one's body stronger* [*more powerful*]

彼は私たちのクラスで腕相撲がいちばん強い He is *the strongest* in our class in arm wrestling.

僕の学校の野球部はとても強い My school has a very *strong* [*powerful*] baseball team.

これは非常に強い接着剤だ This is a very *powerful* [*strong*] adhesive.

◆ほかの通貨に対して円が強くなった The yen *has strengthened* against other currencies.

❷【程度が著しい】 strong; (強烈な) intense; (厳しい) severe ─ 強く strongly; intensely; severely

強い信念 a *strong* [*firm*] belief / 強い好奇心 *intense* curiosity / 強い酒 *strong* alcohol; *hard* liquor

きのうは強い風が吹いていた There was a *strong* wind yesterday. / (→風が強く吹いていた) It was blowing *hard* yesterday.

きょうは快晴で日差しが強い Today the sky is clear and the sunlight is *strong* [*intense*].

子供に対する母親の愛情は非常に強い A mother's love for her child is very *strong*.

彼はいまだに政界に対する影響力が強い He still exerts a *strong* influence on the political world.

もっと度の強い眼鏡が必要だ I need *stronger* [*thicker*] glasses.

彼は強いなまりがある He has a *strong* [*thick*] accent.

彼らは新空港の建設に強く反対している They object *strongly* to the construction of a new airport.

それは旅行会社のミスなんだから強く言わないとだめだよ It's the travel company's fault, so you should complain *strongly* to them.

◆彼は転んで床で強く頭を打った He fell and hit his head *hard* on the floor. / 彼女は彼の手を強く(→固く)握った She held his hand *firmly* [*tight*]. / ストーブをもう少し強くしてくれる? Will you *turn up* the heater a bit?

❸【耐久力がある】

彼女は南国出身なので暑さに強い She *can tolerate* heat because she comes from the south.

この植物は乾燥に強い This plant *can withstand* dryness.

青木さんは酒が強い Ms. Aoki *can drink a lot*. / Ms. Aoki *can hold her liquor*.

ステンレスは酸に強い Stainless steel is *resistant to* acid.

彼は本番に強い(→ここ一番でうまくやる) He *does things well* when the chips are down.

❹【得意だ】 be good at [with] ... (❖「扱いがうまい」の意味では _with_)

彼は物理に強い He is「*good at* [*strong in*] physics. / Physics *is* his *strong point* [*area*].

彼女はコンピュータに強い She *is good with* computers.

つよがり 強がり (負け惜しみ) sour grapes; (からいばり) bravado ⓤ; (こけおどし) bluff ⓤ ⓒ / もう強がりを言うのはやめて,負けを認めなよ Don't *cry sour grapes* any more, and admit that you lost.

◆彼女は強がりを言ってるだけだ She's just *bluffing*. / She's just *whistling in the dark*. (❖*whistle in the dark* は「恐れていないふりをする」の意味の口語的表現)

つよがる 強がる その男の子は精一杯強がってみせた The boy *put on* as much of *a bold front* as he could.

つよき 強気 ─ 強気の (積極的な) aggressive; (大胆な) bold; (確固とした) strong / 強気の発言をする make an *aggressive* [a *bold*] statement ◆僕らは強気で攻めて試合に勝った We won the game by attacking the opponent *aggressively* [*boldly*].

つよく 強く ➡ つよい

つよさ 強さ strength ⓤ; (能力) power ⓤ; (堅固さ) firmness ⓤ; (物理的な威力) force ⓤ ⓒ; (光・熱・音などの) intensity ⓤ / 彼のパンチの強さを測る measure *the strength* [*power*] of his punch / 衝撃に対する強さ *strength* [*firmness*] against shocks / 意志の強さ *strength* [*firmness*] of will / その横綱はずば抜けた強さを誇っている The *yokozuna* has incomparable *strength*. / 台風は中型で並みの強さです The typhoon is of medium size and has medium *force* [*strength*, *power*].

つよび 強火 野菜を強火でいためる fry vegetables over *a high flame*; stir-fry vegetables / こんろを強火にする *turn up the flame* of a stove

つよまる 強まる become* strong(er); (痛み・感情などが) grow* (more) intense, intensify ⓘ / 夜には風雨がさらに強まる模様です The wind and rain will *become stronger* during the night. / その法案に対する反対の

声が強まってきている Opposition against the bill *is growing intense* [*strong*] among people. / 私の疑念はさらに強まった My suspicion *has intensified* more.

つよみ 強み advantage [C], strength [C] [U]; (長所) strong point [C] ∥バレーボールをするときには彼の背の高さは大きな強みだ His height is *a* great *advantage* [*strength*] when he plays volleyball.

つよめる 強める strengthen [他]; (威力などを徐々に) gather [他]; (音量・火力などを) turn up; (感情・活動などを) intensify [他] ∥こんろの火を強める *turn up* the stove / 台風は勢力を強めて北上中です The typhoon *is strengthening* [*gathering*] its force and is moving north. / 人々は大雨に対する警戒を強めた People *intensified* precautions against heavy rain. / People *took more* precautions against heavy rain. / 彼の言葉に私はますます疑念を強めた His remarks *intensified* my suspicion more and more.

つら 面 先輩面をする *posture* [*pose*] *as* 「an older student [a more experienced person]」/ いまさらどの面下げて彼女に会いに行けるというのか *How* can I dare to face her now?

➾ つらのかわ

つらあて 面当て 彼女のやっていることは私に対する面当てに違いない She must be doing things like that *just in order to trouble* me.

つらい 辛い (困難な) hard, tough; (耐えがたい) unbearable; (苦痛を与える) painful; (不幸な) bitter (❖名詞の前で用いる)

つらい練習に耐える bear *hard* training

炎天下での作業は非常につらい Working under the scorching sun is really *hard* [*tough, painful, unbearable*].

彼と別れるのはつらい It's *hard* for me to say good-bye to him.

彼女もいろいろつらい思いをしてきた She's had a lot of *hard* times.

君の口からそんな言葉を聞くのはつらい It's *painful* [*unbearable*] for me to hear such words from you.

◆彼は彼女につらくあたった He *was hard on* her. / He *treated* her *badly*. / このごろ足が痛んでつらい My leg pain *has been troubling* me these days. / 麻子はつらい立場に立たされている Asako is in a *difficult* position.

-づらい このペンは書きづらい This pen is *hard* to write with. / It's *hard* to write with this pen.

つらがまえ 面構え 男は不敵な面構えをしていた The man had *a* defiant [fearless] *look on his face*.

つらさ 辛さ (苦痛) bitterness [U], pain [U]; (悲しみ) sadness [U], grief [U] ∥好きな人にふられるつらさは君には分かるまい You wouldn't understand *the bitterness* [*pain*] of being turned down by the one you love.

つらなる 連なる range [自] ∥その山々は東西に連なっている The mountains *range* [*stretch*] from east to west. / 通りに沿ってずっと店が連なっている Shops *range* all along the street. ◆店の前には人々が連なっている (→人の列がある) *There is a line* of people in front of the store.

つらぬく 貫く ❶【通り抜ける】(貫通する) penetrate [他]; (通り抜ける) go* through ...; (とがったものが) pierce [他]; (道・川などが) run* through ... ∥矢は彼の心臓を貫いた The arrow *penetrated* [*went through*] his heart. / この道は県を南北に貫いている This road *runs through* the prefecture north to south.

❷【堅持する】stick* to ...; (やり抜く) carry out ∥彼は自分の信念を貫くだろう He will *stick to* his principles. / 彼は志を貫いた He *carried out* his intention.

つらねる 連ねる 通りには古本屋が軒(のき)を連ねている The street *is lined with* secondhand book stores. / Secondhand book stores *line* the street. / 彼はそのクラブの創設者に名を連ねている He *is on the list of* the founders of the club.

つらのかわ 面の皮 あいつは面の皮の厚いやつだ He is a *thick-skinned* guy. / あいつ失敗したんだって？ ふん，いい面の皮だ He failed? Humph, *it serves him right*. / 彼女に僕の失敗をばらされちゃって，全くいい面の皮だったよ I *was mortified* when she told everyone about my failure.

つらよごし 面汚し dishonor [C], disgrace [C] ∥あいつはわがクラブの面汚しだ He is *a dishonor* [*disgrace*] to our club.

つらら 氷柱 icicle [C] ∥軒先にはつららができていた *Icicles* had formed under the eaves.

つられる 釣られる おいしそうなにおいにつられて，買うつもりもなかったパン屋に入ってしまった *Lured* by a good smell, I went into a bakery although I didn't need any bread. / お菓子につられて多くの子供が公園に集まってきた (→お菓子が子供を引き寄せた) Sweets *attracted* many children to the park. / 1等賞金の額につられて宝くじをたくさん買ってしまった (→1等賞金の額が私に宝くじをたくさん買わせた) The amount of the first prize *made* me buy too many lottery tickets.

つり 釣り

❶【魚釣り】fishing [U] ──釣りをする fish [自]

おじはアユ釣りが趣味だ *Ayu fishing* is my uncle's hobby.

彼は息子を釣りに連れていった He took his son *fishing*.

> [英作文ノート] 釣りは川でするもの
> 私は家の近くの川へ釣りに行った
> →×I went *fishing to the river* near my house.
> →○I went *fishing in the river* near my house.
> ★《go to＋場所》はよいが《go *doing* to＋場所》とはいわない．「川での釣りに行った」と考える．類例に go *shopping at* the supermarket (スーパーに買い物に行く) がある．

つりあい

❷ [つり銭] change Ⓤ
おつりはいりません(→とっておいてください) Keep *the change*.
この自動販売機はつり銭切れだ This vending machine is *out of change*.
◆おつりの出ないようご用意ください(→きっかりの額を持ってきてください) Please bring the exact「amount of money [fare]」. (❖fareは「運賃」の意味)
🔴「じゃあ1人2,800円だね」「1万円でおつりある?」 "It's 2,800 yen per person, then." "Can you give me *change* for a 10,000-yen bill?"

‖釣り糸 a (fishing) line / 釣りざお a fishing rod (米pole), a rod / 釣り道具 fishing tackle / 釣り針 a (fish)hook / 釣り船 a fishing boat / 釣り堀 a fishing pond / 磯釣り surf-casting / 海釣り sea fishing / 川釣り river fishing / 浜釣り fishing from the shore / 船釣り fishing from a boat

つりあい 釣り合い (重さ・力などの) balance Ⓤ(また a 〜); (比率・均衡・調和) proportion Ⓤ Ⓒ (しばしば複数形〜s); (似合いの物) match Ⓒ ‖左右の重さのつり合いを保つ keep *the balance* of weight between both sides / 先生は力のつり合いを考えてクラスの生徒を2つのチームに分けた The teacher divided the class into two teams considering *the balance* of ability between them.
◆スウェットパンツにはでなシャツでは全然つり合いがよくない Sweat pants and a loud shirt *don't match* at all.

つりあう 釣り合う (重さ・力などが) balance 🅐; (組み合わせが) match 🅐 ‖左右の重さがつり合った The weight of both sides *balanced*. / この絵は部屋につり合っている This picture *matches* the room. / This picture *is in harmony with* the room.
◆この狭い部屋にそんな大きな本棚はつり合わない This small room and that big bookshelf *will be out of proportion*.

つりあげる¹ 吊り上げる (物を) lift 🅐, hoist 🅐; (値段などを) raise 🅐 ‖クレーンで鉄骨などつり上げる *lift [hoist (up))* steel beams with a crane / 商品価格を不当につり上げる *raise* the price of the products unreasonably / 彼は目をつり上げて怒った He glared angrily.

つりあげる² 釣り上げる catch* 🅐; (特に大物を) land 🅐 ‖彼は大きなブラックバスを釣り上げた He *caught [landed]* a big black bass.

つりがね 釣り鐘 a large bell suspended in a temple

つりかわ 吊り革 strap Ⓒ ‖つり革におつかまりください Please hold [hang] on to *the strap*.

つりせん 釣り銭 change Ⓤ Ⓒ ⇨つり

つりばし 釣り橋・吊り橋 (大きなもの) suspension bridge Ⓒ; (渓谷などにロープでつったもの) rope [hanging] bridge Ⓒ

つりわ 吊り輪【スポーツ】(flying) rings

つる¹ 釣る

❶【魚などを】(捕らえようとする) fish 🅐; (捕らえる) catch* 🅐; (大物を釣り上げる) land 🅐 ‖父はアユを釣りに出かけた My father went *fishing for ayu*.
川で大きなマスを釣った I *caught [landed]* a big trout in the river.
きのうはザリガニをたくさん釣った I *caught* a lot of crayfish yesterday.

❷【誘う】
彼女をケーキでつって宿題を手伝ってもらおう I'm going to *tempt* her with cake to help me finish my homework.

つる² 吊る,《公式的》suspend 🅐 ‖父が木の枝にブランコをつってくれた My father *hung [suspended]* a swing from a branch for us. ‖ 彼女が昨夜首をつったらしい I heard that she *hanged* herself last night. (❖「首をつる」の意味では過去・過去分詞はhangedとなる)‖ 彼は骨折した左腕を包帯でつっていた His broken left arm *was hung [suspended]* in a sling.

つる³ 攣る 足がつった I *got [had]* (a) *cramp* in my leg.

つる⁴ 蔓 ❶【植物】vine Ⓒ; (イチゴなどの地面をはうもの) runner Ⓒ; (キュウリなどの巻きひげ) tendril Ⓒ ‖つるが松の木に巻きついた *Vines* twined around a pine tree.

❷【眼鏡の】temple Ⓒ

つる⁵ 鶴 crane Ⓒ ➡おりづる, せんばづる
[慣用表現] 父の鶴の一声で家族旅行の目的地が決まった *Just one word* from our father decided the destination of our family trip.

つる⁶ 弦 (弓の) bowstring Ⓒ, string Ⓒ

つるしあげ 吊るし上げ 彼はみんなからつるし上げを食った He *was crucified* by everyone. / He *was condemned by a kangaroo court*.

つるしあげる 吊るし上げる《口語的》crucify 🅐, put* *a person* in a kangaroo court

つるす 吊るす hang* 🅐,《公式的》suspend 🅐 ‖軒(き)にカキをつるす *hang [suspend]* persimmons from the eaves ‖ シャツをハンガーにつるした I *hung* my shirt on a hanger.

つるつる 油をこぼしちゃって床がつるつるだから気をつけて Be careful. The floor is *slippery* because I spilled oil on it. / 大理石はさわるとつるつるしている Marble is *smooth* to the touch. / おじは頭がつるつるだ (→完全にはげている) My uncle is *completely bald*. / 彼はめんを1本だけつるつるとすすった He ate just one noodle by *slurping* it.

つるはし 鶴嘴 pickax Ⓒ,《口語的》pick Ⓒ

つるむ 彼はいつもあの悪友たちとつるんでいる He always「*hangs out [spends time]*」with those bad friends.

つるり 彼はスケートリンクでつるりとすべってしりもちをついた He *slipped* on the skating rink and fell on his bottom. / サトイモはゆでるとつるりと皮がむける Taros can be *easily peeled* when boiled.

つれ 連れ (友達) friend Ⓒ; (旅などでの) companion Ⓒ ‖連れがいるんだけどいっしょに君のうちに行ってもいいかな Can I visit you with *my friend*? / 僕たちは旅の途中で一人旅をする

高校生と連れになった During our trip, a high school student who was traveling alone became *our companion*.

◆お連れ様は何人でいらっしゃいますか How many people are there in *your company* [*party*]?

-づれ -連れ 遊園地は多くの**親子連れ**でにぎわっていた The amusement park was crowded with *parents and children*. / その俳優は**子供連れ**で動物園を訪れた The actor went to the zoo *with his children*. / 男女の2人**連れ**が手をつないで歩いていた *A couple* were walking hand in hand.

つれこ 連れ子 *one's* spouse's child from a previous marriage

つれこむ 連れ込む (連れてくる) bring* *a person* in [into] …; (連れていく) take* *a person* in [into] … ∥彼は彼女をホテルに**連れ込んだ** He *took* her *into* the hotel.

つれさる 連れ去る take* away; (誘拐する) kidnap [他] ∥彼女は帰宅途中に車で**連れ去られた** She *was kidnapped* in a car on her way home.

つれそう 連れ添う 40年**連れ添った**妻 *one's* wife *of* 40 years / 私たちは**連れ添って**30年になる We'*ve been married* for 30 years.

つれだす 連れ出す take* out ∥彼女を食事に**連れ出す** *take* her *out* for a meal / 彼を部屋から**連れ出す** *take* him *out of* the room

つれだつ 連れ立つ 友達2人と**連れ立って**映画に行った I went to see a movie *with* two of my friends./ Two of my friends and I went to see a movie *together*.

-つれて -連れて 時がたつに**つれて**失恋の痛手も消えるものだ *As* time goes [passes] by, you will recover from your broken heart. / 父も年をとるに**つれて**体力が衰えてきたようだ It seems that *the older* my father gets, *the weaker* he becomes.

つれていく 連れて行く take* [他]; (導く) lead* [他]; (聞き手の所へ) bring* [他]

彼は妹を遊園地へ**連れていった** He *took* his sister to the amusement park.

彼女は僕をドライブに**連れていってくれた** She *took* me for a drive.

彼女はアパートのある一室へ**連れていかれた** She *was taken* to a certain room in an apartment.

僕もいっしょに**連れていってよ** *Take* me with you.

彼らが人々を安全な場所に**連れていった** They *led* [*took*] people to a safe place.

君のうちに友達を**連れていっても**いいかい Can I *bring* a friend to your house?

つれてかえる 連れて帰る 彼は妹を**連れて帰った** He *took* his sister *home*.(❖話し手または聞き手の所へ「連れて帰った」なら took の代わりに brought を用いる) / 彼女は遊び場にいる息子を**連れて帰ってきた** She 「*went* (*and*) *got* [*fetched*] her son *back* from the playground.

つれてくる 連れて来る bring* [他] ∥今度来るときは妹さんも**連れてきてね** Next time you come, *bring* your sister with you. / 彼女はまだ家にいるようだから，君が行って**連れてきてくれ** She still seems to be at home. So you go and *bring* her.

つれない (冷たい) cold; (無情な) heartless, hard; (愛のない) loveless ∥人に対する**つれないそぶり** *one's cold* [*heartless, loveless*] behavior to a person / 人に**つれなくする** be *cold* [*heartless*] to a person / **つれない**なあ How *cold* [*heartless, loveless*] you are!

◆最近彼女が**つれない**んだ She's *giving* me *the cold shoulder* these days.

つれもどす 連れ戻す (この場所へ) bring* back; (元の場所へ連れていく) take* back ∥私が彼をここへ**連れ戻してみせる** I will *bring* him *back* here.

つれる[1] 連れる (付き添う) accompany [他] ∥女性は子供を**連れていた** The woman *accompanied* her child. / 大統領は護衛を**連れていた** The President *was accompanied* by bodyguards. / 少年は母親に**連れられて**登校した The boy went to school *accompanied* by his mother.

◆彼は彼女を**連れて**会場に現れた He came into the hall *with* her.

つれる[2] 釣れる ここはイワナがよく**釣れる**(→イワナ釣りによい場所だ) This is *a* good mountain trout *fishing spot*. / きょうはアユが10匹**釣れた** I *caught* 10 *ayu* today.

つわもの (勇者) brave man [C] ◆あの塾の講師陣は**つわものぞろい**だ(→経験豊富ですぐれた先生が大勢いる) *There are a lot of experienced and superior teachers* in that cram school.

つわり morning sickness [U] ∥姉は**つわり**がひどいそうだ My sister said she had terrible *morning sickness*.

つんざく 塀の向こうで耳を**つんざく**ような叫び声がした I heard an *earsplitting* [*a piercing*] shriek from behind the wall. (❖piercing は「かん高い」の意味)

つんつん 彼女はいつも**つんつん**している She *is* always *stuck-up* [*unfriendly, curt*].

つんと ❶【態度】彼女は**つんと**していて僕が話しかけても相手にしてくれない She *is* so *stuck-up* [*stand-offish, unfriendly*] that she doesn't pay attention to me when I talk to her. / その写真の少女は**つんと**おすましていた(→いっぱしの女性を気取っていた) The girl in the picture *put on airs* as if she had been a grown lady.

❷【におい】シンナーのにおいが**つんと**鼻をついた There was a *sharp* [a *pungent*, an *intense*] smell of paint thinners. / わさびが鼻に**つんと**きた Horseradish came *pungently* to my nose. (❖「(わさび・シンナーなどが)鼻につんときた！」は My nose is on fire.という)

ツンドラ tundra [tʌ́ndrə] [U] [C]

つんのめる 木の根っこにつまずいて**つんのめった** I stumbled over the root of a tree and *pitched forward*.

て 手

❶ 体の部分	hand
❷ 労働力・人手	hand, help
❸ 手段・方法・計略	means, way

❶【体の部分】(手首から先) hand ⓒ; (肩から手首まで) arm ⓒ; (犬・猫などの) paw ⓒ

《～手》
右[左]手 one's right [left] hand
反対の手も見せなさい Show me *your* other *hand*, too.
彼は両手に大きな花束を抱えていた He held a big bouquet of flowers *in his arms*.
その力士は子供を片手でひょいと持ち上げた The sumo wrestler lifted the child easily *with one arm*.

《手が》
水仕事で手が荒れた *My hands* have become rough from kitchen work.
先生が質問するといっせいに手が挙がった When the teacher asked a question, everybody raised *their hands* at once.
◆その棚は高すぎて彼女には手が届かない The shelf is too high for her to *reach*.

《手を》
手を合わせて祈る put [join] *one's hands* together and pray / 手を差し出す put out *one's hand* / 手をたたく clap *one's hands* / (人の)手を握る hold *a person's hand* / 手を引っ込める draw back *one's hand*
手を上げろ! *Hands up*!
答えが分かったら手を挙げなさい Raise *your hand* if you know the answer.
食卓に着く前に手を洗いなさい Wash *your hands* before sitting at the table.
彼はコートのポケットに手を入れて歩いていた He was walking with *his hands* in his coat pockets.
目をつぶって手を出してごらん Close your eyes and give me *your hand*.
彼らは手をつないで歩いていた They were walking *hand in hand*.
赤ちゃんはそのボールを取ろうと手を伸ばした The baby stretched out *its arm* to catch the ball.
ドアに手をはさまないよう気をつけて Be careful not to catch *your hand* in the door.
私はタオルで手をふいた I dried *my hands* with a towel.
子供たちは走り過ぎる電車に向かって手を振った The children *waved* (*their hands*) at the passing train.
彼はおばあさんの手を引いて道路を渡った He *took* the old woman *by the hand* and crossed the road.
◆(車の)ハンドルから手を離しちゃだめだよ *Don't let go of* the steering wheel. / 手を触れないでください Please *do not touch*. / 僕は床に手をついて彼女に謝った I *threw myself at her feet* and apologized.

《手に》
手に何を持っているの What's in *your hand*?
どうぞ手に取って素材の柔らかさをお確かめください Please *take* it *in your hands* and feel the softness of the material.
◆彼女はその雑誌を手に取った She *picked up* the magazine.

《手で》
手で口を隠す cover *one's mouth with one's hand*
下着はいつも手で洗っています I usually wash my underwear *by hand*. (❖手段を表す by の後にくる名詞には冠詞を付けない)
◆警官は私たちに出ていくよう手で合図した The policeman *waved* us out.

《その他》
汗を手の甲でぬぐう wipe sweat *with the back of one's hand*
(犬に)ポチ, お手! *Shake hands*, Pochi!
恵まれない子供たちに愛の手を! Please extend *a loving hand* to underprivileged children.
彼らは難民に救いの手を差し伸べた They gave *a helping hand* to the refugees.
◆捜査の手(→捜査)は元大臣にまで及んだ *The investigation* reached as far as the ex-minister. / 彼らは大量リードしながらも攻撃の手をゆるめなかった Even though they had a big lead, they *continued to fight hard*.

❷【労働力】(人手) hand ⓒ (❖「手助け」の意味では a hand とする), help ⓤ
◆その村では子供たちもりっぱな働き手だった In that village, even the children *worked hard to support their families*.

【手が空く】(暇である) be free ∥今手が空いているから君の仕事を手伝ってあげるよ I'm free now, so I'll help you with your work.

【手がかかる】私は非常に手のかかる赤ん坊だったらしい They say I was really a *troublesome* baby.

【手が込む】手の込んだ言い訳 an *elaborate* excuse

【手が足りない】多くの病院では手が足りない状態(→人手不足)が続いている Many hospitals *have been shorthanded*.

【手が離せない】彼は今手が離せません He *is engaged* right now.
🕿「啓子から電話よ」「今手が離せない(→忙しい)から後でかけ直すって伝えて」"Telephone for you from Keiko." "Tell her *I'm too busy* now and I'll call her back later."

【手がふさがっている】今は手がふさがっています I've got *my hands full* now.
🕿「こっちの机を動かすの手伝って」「ごめん, 今手

がふさがっているんだ」 "Help me move this desk." "Sorry, I've only got one pair of hands."
【手を貸す】手を貸していただけますか Could you lend me *a hand*? / もしあなたが手を貸して(→助けて)くれなかったら, 成功していなかっただろう I could not have succeeded if you had not *helped* me.
❸【手段・方法・計略】(手段) means ⓒ (複〜); (方法) way ⓒ; (計略) trick ⓒ; (将棋・チェスなどの) move ⓒ; (トランプの持ち札) hand ⓒ
ほかに手はないのか Isn't there any other *way*?
(将棋などで)それはいい手だ That's *a good move*.
◆それも手だなあ That's *an idea*! / もう打つ手がない There's *nothing I can do*. / 彼は奥の手(→切り札)を出した He played *his trump card*. / 彼は汚い手を使って(→不正に)今の地位を得た He got his present position *unfairly*.
【(〜の)手に乗る】だめだめ, その手には乗らないよ Oh no, I *won't fall for that trick*!
【手の施しようがない】彼のけがはもう手の施しようがなかった Nothing could have been done about his injury. / It was too late to do anything about his injury.
【手を尽くす】あらゆる手を尽くして捜したが, 彼女は見つからなかった We *tried* every possible *means to* find her, but in vain.
❹【所有・支配】
【手に入れる】get*ⓐ,《公式的》obtainⓐ, (買う) buy*ⓐ //その情報を公式のルートから手に入れた We *got* the information through official channels. / 僕はついに念願のギターを手に入れた Finally I *bought* the guitar I had long wanted to buy. / 彼は私のためにその試合の切符を2枚手に入れてくれた He *obtained* two tickets for me for the match.
【手に落ちる】ロンドン塔は一度も敵の手に落ちたことがない The Tower of London *has never fallen* to any enemy.
【手にする】(持つ) have*ⓐ, (得る) get*ⓐ //こんな大金, 今まで手にしたことがない I *have never had* such a large amount of money.
【手に入る】(入手可能である) be available //申込用紙は事務所で手に入ります Application forms *are available* at the office. ◆そのコンサートのチケットはどこで手に入りますか Where can I *get* a ticket for the concert?
【(人の)手に渡る】かつて暮らした家も今は人の手に渡ってしまった The house we had once lived in *has passed into* someone else's *hands*.
❺【種類】kind ⓒ, type ⓒ
この手の音楽は今大変なブームです *This kind of* music is really hot now.
◆あの手の男には気を許すな Don't let down your guard against *a man like him*.
❻【その他】
流れの急な川が我々の行く手を阻(ﾊﾊﾞ)んでいた A strong current *stood in our way*.
向こうの方で火の手が上がった A fire burst *into flames* over there.
【お手のもの】彼はケーキ作りはお手のものだ He's *no slouch at* baking cakes. (❖be no slouch at … は「…が得意だ」の意味の口語的表現)
【手が出る】アイスクリームにはつい手が出てしまう(→我慢できない) I *can't resist* ice cream.
【手がつけられない】あっという間に火事は手がつけられなくなった In seconds the fire *went out of control*.
【手が出ない】とてもじゃないがそんな高価なかばんには手が出ない I *couldn't afford to buy* such an expensive bag.
【手が届く】成功は今や彼の手の届く所にある Success is now *within his reach*. / 子供の手の届かない所に保管すること Keep *out of reach* of children.
【手が早い】あいつは女性には手が早いといううわさだ They say he's *fast with women*.
【手が離れる】彼女は子供の手が離れたら外で働きたいと思っている After her children *are off her hands*, she wants to work outside the home.
【手が回る】忙しくてとてもそこまでは手が回らない(→注意を払えない) I'm so busy that I *can't possibly pay attention to* that.
【手取り足取り】全くのパソコン初心者でもインストラクターが手取り足取り(→段階を踏んで)くれます Even if you have never touched a computer, the instructor will teach you *step by step*.
【手に汗を握る】彼は手に汗握るような物語を多数書いてきている He has written many *exciting* stories.
【手に余る】キャンプで30人の子供たちのリーダーになるというのは僕の手に余る It's *too much for me* to become a leader of 30 children at the camp.
【手に負えない】あの子供たちは手に負えない I *can't handle* those children. / この仕事は私の手に負えなくなってきた This work *has become too much for* me.
【手につかない】彼は息子の入試の結果が気になって仕事が手につかなかった(→集中できなかった) He was so anxious about the result of his son's entrance exam that he *couldn't concentrate on* work.
【手に取るよう】(はっきりと) clearly, distinctly; (正確に) exactly //僕には彼の考えていることが手に取るように分かった I knew *exactly* what he was thinking about.
【手の切れるような】手の切れるような札 a *crisp* bank note
【(〜する)手はない】千載一遇のチャンスなんだからこれを逃す手はないよ You *should seize* the chance; it's one in a million.
【手も足も出ない】その問題は難しくて手も足も出なかった(→何もできなかった) That question was so difficult that I *could do nothing about* it.
【手を上げる】父が私に手を上げたことは一度もない My father *has* never *raised his hand* to me.

【手を入れる】私はもう一度レポートに手を入れた I *revised* my paper once again.

【手を打つ】先に手を打つ(→行動を起こす) *make the* first *move* / あの子にいたずらさせないように何か手を打ってくださいよ *Do something* to keep that child out of mischief. / それで手を打とう(→それで決まりだ) *It's a deal.* / *That's the deal.* / *It's all settled.*

【手を変え品を変え】彼女は手を変え品を変え私に保険加入を勧めてきた She *tried every possible means* to convince me to take out an insurance policy.

【手を切る】彼は悪い友達と手を切った He *broke off with* his bad friends.

【手を組む】野党の1党が与党と手を組んだ One of the opposition parties *joined (up) with* the ruling party.

【手を加える】原稿に手を加える *revise* a manuscript / インスタントラーメンも手を加えればけっこうおいしくなる You can make even instant ramen taste pretty good if you *season it yourself*.

【手をこまねく】僕らが必死に車を押している間,彼はただ手をこまねいていた(→何もしないで)見ていた When we were trying hard to push the car, he just stood there *and did nothing*.

【手を染める】君にはそんな汚い商売に手を染めて(→かかわって)ほしくない I don't want you to *get mixed up in* that dirty business.

【手を出す】その会社は最近いろいろな事業に手を出し(→かかわり)始めた That company has begun to *be involved in* all sorts of businesses. / 僕の彼女に手を出すんじゃないぞ(→触れずにいろ) *Keep your hands off* my girlfriend. / あいつのほうが先に手を出した(→殴った)んだ He *hit* me first.

【手をつける】夕飯にほとんど手をつけてないじゃない You've hardly *touched* your dinner. / 宿題が多すぎてどこから手をつけていいのか分からないくらいだった I had so much homework that I didn't even know *where to start*. / 彼は会社の金に手をつけた(→金を横領した) He *pocketed* the company's money.

【手を抜く】彼は最近仕事で手を抜いている He's *been cutting corners* on his job recently.

【手を引く】事業から手を引く(→撤退する) *withdraw* from the business / その事件からは手を引いたほうがいい You should *wash your hands of* the incident.

【手を広げる】その会社は外食産業にまで手を広げている That company *has extended* its business to the food service industry.

【手を結ぶ】3つの大きな銀行が近々手を結ぶ(→提携する)ことになったらしい I hear three major banks are going to *link up* in the near future.

【手を焼く】そのわがままな男の子にはみんな手を焼いていた(→だれもどうしていいか分からなかった) *Nobody knew what to do* with that spoiled boy.

【手を休める】少し仕事の手を休めて(→手をわきへおいて)私の話を聞いてください *Put your work aside* for a minute and listen to me.

【手をわずらわせる】お手をわずらわせてしまって申しわけありません I'm sorry for *causing you trouble*.

-て

❶【そして】and
彼はドアをあけて客を中に入れた He opened the door *and* let the visitor in.
その部屋は夏涼しくて冬暖かい It's cool in summer *and* warm in winter in that room.
◆何時間も歩いて小さな村に着いた *After* walking for many hours, we arrived at a small village.
❢「だれか来て手伝ってよ」「分かった。ちょっと待って」"Can anyone come *and* help me?" "OK. Wait a moment."

❷【…しながら】
彼は腕組みをして物思いにふけっていた He was lost in thought *with* his arms folded.
私は特売品を探して店の中をあちこち歩き回った I wandered around the store looking for bargains.
父はいつも「よいしょ」と言って立ち上がる(→立ち上がるときに「よいしょ」と言う) My father always says "yoisho" *when* he stands up.

❸【…することによって】by *doing*
彼女はピアノを教えて生計を立てた She earned her living *by* teaching piano.
◆強盗は彼女をおどして金庫をあけさせた The burglar *frightened* her *into* opening the safe.

❹【…ので】because, for
歯が痛くて少しも眠れなかった I couldn't sleep at all 「*because* I had a toothache [*because of* my toothache].
◆このひもは短すぎて結べない This string is *too* short *to* tie. / 長いことお待たせしてすみません I'm sorry *to* have kept you waiting so long.

❺【…にもかかわらず】though
彼女はそのことを知っていて私に教えてくれなかった *Though* she knew that, she didn't tell me about it.
◆彼はそのけんかを見て見ぬふりをした He *closed his eyes to* the fight.

で 出 ❶【出身】大学出の人(→大学の卒業生) a college [university] *graduate* / 彼は裕福な家の出だ He *comes* [*is*] *from* a wealthy family.
❷【出現・出番】日[月]の出 *the rise* of the sun [moon] / 出を待つ俳優 an actor who is waiting for *his turn* / ゆうべ新宿は人の出(→人)が多かった There were many *people* in Shinjuku yesterday evening.
❸【出ぐあい】このきゅうすはお茶の出が悪い This teapot *doesn't pour well*. / 水の出が悪い The water *doesn't flow smoothly*.

-で

❶ 場所	at; in
❷ 時間・年齢	at; in; for
❸ 手段・方法	with, by, in, on
❹ 原因・理由	with, of, from, because of,

-で

❺ 材料	of, from
❻ 状態・条件	at, with, in
❼ 金額	for, at
❽ 話題・論題	about, on

❶【場所】at; in

語法
(1) 比較的狭い範囲の場所を表す場合は at, 広い範囲の場所を表す場合は in を用いる ∥ トムの家で *at* Tom's house / 駅で *at* the station / 世田谷区で *in* the City of Setagaya / 広島で *in* Hiroshima / 近畿地方で *in* the Kinki district / 日本で *in* Japan / ヨーロッパで *in* Europe
(2) 自分が生活している場所など, 小さくても「広がり」が感じられる場合は in を用い, 広くても通過点にすぎないような場合は at を用いる ∥ 私はこの小さな町に住んでいる I live *in* this small town. / 名古屋で列車を乗り換えた I changed trains *at* Nagoya.
(3) 前置詞の in, at ではなく, 副詞などを用いることによって表現する場合もある ∥ 沖で offshore / 上の階で upstairs

彼女と校門の所で5時に待ち合わせている I have arranged to meet her *at* the gate of our school at 5 o'clock.
新宿駅で山手線に乗り換えてください Change to the Yamanote Line *at* Shinjuku Station.
あす成田空港で彼らに会う I'm meeting them *at* Narita Airport tomorrow.
きょう部室で順子にチョコレートをもらった I was given a chocolate by Junko *in* the clubroom.
今年の冬は北海道でスキーをするつもりだ I'm going skiing *in* Hokkaido this winter.
◆姉は昭和商事で働いています My sister works *for* Showa Trading. / その交差点の手前で降ろしてください Please drop me off *just before* the intersection. / 電車で浩子に会った I met Hiroko *on* the train.
⚡「その靴, どこで買ったの」「東京デパート」"*Where* did you buy those shoes?" "At Tokyo Department Store."

❷【時間・年齢】(時の一点) at; (…たてば) in; (…の間に) for

きょうは中間試験の前日なので11時で学校が終わりだ School ends *at* 11 o'clock because today is the day before the midterm exams.
姉は19歳で結婚した My sister got married *at* (the age of) 19.
あと1時間で大阪駅に着く We'll arrive at Osaka Station *in* an hour.
あと1週間で夏休みだ Summer vacation begins *in* a week.
ここ数年で急速にパソコンが普及した Personal computers have quickly become widespread *in* the past few years.
たった3日間のアルバイトで5万円になった *For* only a three-day part-time job, I earned 50,000 yen.
◆こちらに引っ越してきてから来月で2年になる *Next month*, two years will have passed since I moved here. / 1時間で宿題を終わらせなさい Finish your homework *within* an hour.

❸【手段・方法】with, by, in, on

ほうきで庭を掃(は)きなさい Sweep the garden *with* a broom.
彼女は左利きだが文字は右手で書く She is left-handed, but she writes *with* her right hand.
バスで学校に通っている I go to school *by* bus.
私たちは電子メールで連絡をとり合っている We keep in contact with each other *by* e-mail.
飛行機のチケットを現金[クレジットカード]で買った I paid for the plane ticket「*in* cash [*by* credit card].
英語で手紙を書いた I wrote a letter *in* English.
ここにあなたの名前をペンで書きなさい Write your name here *in* pen.
ワープロで手紙を書いた I wrote a letter *on* a word processor.
弓子はその曲をピアノで弾いた Yumiko played the piece *on* the piano.
そのニュースはけさの新聞で知った I learned about the news *in* today's paper.
きのう彼女と電話で話をした I talked with her *on* [*over*] the phone yesterday.
彼はガラスの破片で指を切った He cut his finger *on* a piece of glass. (❖on の代わりに with を用いると「故意に切った」の意味になる)
◆徒歩で[車で]通勤する *walk* [*drive*] to work

❹【原因・理由】with, of, from, because of, in

母はかぜで寝ています My mother is in bed *with* a cold.
今夜のヤクルト対中日戦は雨で中止になった Tonight's Swallows-Dragons game was called off *because of* rain.
彼は胃癌(がん)で[けががもとで]死んだ He died「*of* stomach cancer [*from* an injury]. (❖通例病気・飢え・老齢などで死ぬときは of, けがや不注意などの場合は from を用いる)
その作家は交通事故で死んだ The writer was killed *in* a traffic accident.
◆青森はリンゴで有名だ Aomori is famous *for* its apples. / 彼は殺人容疑で逮捕された He was arrested *on* suspicion of murder.

❺【材料】of, from

クラリネットは木でできている Clarinets are made *of* wood.
豆腐で作ったアイスクリームを食べた I ate some ice cream made *from* tofu.
◆紙で風船を折ったことがありますか Have you ever folded paper *into* a balloon?

❻【状態・条件】at, with, in

全速力で走る run *at* top speed / 人に笑顔であいさつする greet a person *with* a smile
ひとりで旅行するのと団体で旅行するのとではどちらが好きですか Which do you like better,

traveling *alone* or *with a group*?

◆父はビール１杯で顔が真っ赤になる My father's face turns bright red *after* one glass of beer.

❼【金額】for, at

このＴシャツは300円で買った I bought this T-shirt *for* 300 yen.

その株は2,000円で売られている The stock is selling *at* 2,000 yen.

🅔「その時計, いくらで買ったか(→いくら支払ったか)」「3,000円で買ったよ(→支払った)」 "*How much* did you pay for that watch?" "I paid 3,000 yen for it."

❽【話題・論題】about, on

私たちは文化祭の件で話し合わなければならない We must talk *about* the school festival.

◆きょう英語の時間に, なぜ英語を勉強するのかというテーマで激論になった In today's English class, we had a hot argument *on* the topic of why we should study English.

❾【そして・それで】and

次の文を読んで問いに答えなさい Read the following passage *and* answer the questions.

◆あしたから期末試験なんだよ. で, この２, ３日はあまり寝ていないんだ Final exams begin tomorrow, *so* I haven't had a good sleep for several days.

🅔「高校をやめるつもりなんだ」「ああ, そう. で, やめた後どうするの」"I'm going to drop out of high school." "Oh, yeah? *Then* what are you going to do?"

❿【…しながら】

私たちは漫画を読んで２, ３時間過ごした We spent a few hours *reading* comic books.

彼女は化粧もしないで家を飛び出した She rushed out of the house *without putting* on her make-up.

彼女は私に何も言わないで帰ってしまった She went home *without saying* anything to me.

⓫【あまりに…ので】because, for

彼女はかぜをひいていたので泳ぎに行けなかった She was unable to go swimming *because* she had a cold.

◆あまりにも激しく泣いていたのでその子は答えることができなかった The child was crying so hard *that* he couldn't answer. / 急いでいたので私たちは駅まで走った *Since* we were in a hurry, we ran to the station.

であい 出会い meeting ⓒ 《通例単数形》; (思いがけない) encounter ⓒ 《偶然の出会い》 a chance *meeting* / 彼との出会いが私の一生を大きく変えた The *meeting* with him completely changed my life.

◆ローラとの初めての出会いは４年前です(→４年前に初めて会った) I met Laura for the first time four years ago.

であいがしら 出会い頭 ２人は廊下の角で出会い頭に(→すれ違いざまに)ぶつかった The two of them bumped into each other *in passing* at the corner of the corridor.

であう 出会う meet* ⓜ ⓔ ➪あう(会う) /私たちは偶然そのパーティーで出会った We *met* by chance at the party.

◆電車の中で小学校時代の友達にばったり出会った On a train I "*came across* [*ran into*, *happened to meet*] a friend from my elementary school days.

てあか 手垢 finger smudge ⓒ /テレビの画面は手あかで汚れていた The TV screen was dirty with *finger smudges*.

◆手あかのついた本 a *well-thumbed* book

てあし 手足 (腕と足) arms and legs; (手と足) hands and feet; (手足いっしょに) hand and foot(❖この表現は「人の手足となって」という比喩的な意味でも用いられる), limbs(❖複数形limbは手足の１本を指す) / (人の)手足を縛る bind *a person hand and foot* / 手足を伸ばす stretch *one's limbs* / 赤ん坊のぽちゃぽちゃ太った手足 the plump *arms and legs* of a *baby* / 彼女は手足が不自由だ She has trouble using *her arms and legs*. / 彼は兄の手足となって働いた He worked for his brother *hand and foot*.

てあし 出足 その企画は出足でつまずいた The project went wrong *from the beginning* [*start*]. / 雨で客の出足が鈍った The turnout was poor because of rain.

てあたりしだい 手当たり次第 ――手当たり次第に (順序なしに) in no particular order; (無作為に) at random /彼は友達に手当たり次第に電話をかけた He called his friends *at random*.

てあつい 手厚い 人を手厚く葬る bury a person *with the greatest respect* / 人を手厚く看護する nurse a person *tenderly* / 彼らは私を手厚くもてなしてくれた They *gave* [*showed*] me *hospitality*. / They *were hospitable* to me.

てあて 手当・手当て

❶【治療】(medical) treatment ⓤ ――手当てする ⓜ

私は病院で傷の手当てを受けた I "*was treated* [*received treatment*] for my injury at a hospital.

❷【報酬】(給与) pay ⓤ; (特定の目的のための) allowance ⓒ; (給付金) benefit ⓒⓤ; (特別手当) bonus ⓒ

残業手当はつきますか Can I get *overtime pay*?

‖応急手当 first aid / 家族手当 a family allowance / 失業手当 unemployment compensation [《英》benefits] / 通勤手当 a transportation allowance

てあみ 手編み 手編みの帽子 a *hand-knitted* cap / このセーターは手編みだ This sweater *was knitted by hand*.

てあらい 手洗い ❶【洗面所】(家庭の) (主に米) bathroom ⓒ; (レストランやデパートなどの) 《米》 rest room ⓒ ➪ おてあらい

❷【洗濯】このセーターは手洗いできます This sweater *is hand-washable* [*washable by hand*].

てあらい² 手荒い rough; (暴力的な) violent

コミュニケーションスキル —提案・勧誘—

①何かを提案するとき

(A) **Let's** talk [have a talk] over lunch. –OK. [All right.]
昼食をとりながら話をしましょう. —いいですよ.
(B) **How about** a drink after work? –That sounds good [great].
仕事の後で一杯どう. —いいね.
(C) **How [What] about** going for a drive to the beach next Sunday? –That sounds great. [I'm sorry, but I can't make it on that day.]
今度の日曜日に海岸までドライブに行くっていうのはどう. —すばらしいわね. [ごめん. その日は都合がつかないのよ.]
(D) I'll pick you up at the station tomorrow morning. **How about** 8 o'clock? –That will be fine (with me).
あしたの朝, 駅に車で迎えに行くよ. 8時でどうだい. —僕のほうはそれでいいよ.
(E) **Shall we** go for a walk? –Good idea.
散歩に行こうよ. —いいわね.

☞ 自分も含めて「何かをしよう」と提案する場合は, (A)〜(C)のようにいう. (A)の Let's ... はくだけた表現で, 親しい間柄で用いる. (B), (C)に比べると, (A)は「…しよう」という強い調子の提案になる. **Let's ..., shall we?** のようにいうことも多く, このほうが響きが柔らかくなる. (C)の How [What] about *doing*? の代わりに **Why don't we ...?**(…しませんか)という表現もよく使われる.
☞ 提案に対する答え方は, 賛成であれば OK. や All right. が最も簡単な意思表示になる. That sounds good [great]! は積極的に提案を歓迎する言い方で, 特に若者は Sounds good [great]! あるいは単に Great! ということが多い. 逆に断る場合は, (C)のように I'm sorry で始めて理由を述べればよい.
☞ How about ...? は提案のほか, (D)のように相手の都合を尋ねる場合にも使うことができる.
☞ Shall we ...? は, ちょっとした提案をする際に用いることが多い.

②何かを人に勧めるとき

(A) **Will [Won't] you** have another cup of coffee? –Yes, please. [No, thank you.]
コーヒーをもう1杯いかがですか. —ええ, いただきます. [いいえ, 結構です.]
(B) **Would you like** some ice cream for dessert? –Yes, please.
食後にアイスクリームはいかがですか. —はい, いただきます.
(C) You look tired. **Why don't you** take a break?
疲れてるみたいだね. ひと休みしたらどう.
(D) **It might be better for you to** consult a dentist.
歯医者に診(み)てもらったらどうですか.
(E) **You should** read that book.
あの本はぜひ読んでおくべきだよ.

☞ (A), (B)は食べ物や飲み物を人に勧めるときの最も一般的な表現. (A)では Will you ...? より Won't you ...? のほうがより丁寧な勧め方. (B)の Would you ...? は(A)よりさらに丁寧な勧め方となる. いずれの場合も, Yes, please. または No, thank you. で答えるのがふつう.
☞ (A), (B)以外にも, 食べ物や飲み物を勧める表現はいくつかあるが, 「コーヒーはいかがですか」と勧めるのならば, **Can I get you** some coffee?, **How about** some coffee?, **Do you want** some coffee? などがある.
☞ (C)の Why don't you ...? は「なぜ…しないのか」という元の意味から分かるように, 押しつけがましい響きをもつ勧誘となる.
☞ (D)は「…するほうがいいのではないでしょうか」と柔らかい調子で何かを促す場合に用いられる.
☞ (E)の You should ... は「ぜひ…するべきだ」の意味で, 提案というより積極的な勧めに近い内容となる. You had better ...(…しなさい)よりは控えめだが, 共に目上の人に用いるのは避けたほうがよい.

—手荒く roughly; violently ∥手荒な扱いを受ける be treated *roughly* ∥ 手荒なまねはよせ Don't get [be] *rough*!
-**である** ❶【断定】be ∥オゾンの化学式はO_3である The chemical formula for ozone *is* O_3.
❷【同格】商社マンである私の父は海外出張が多い My father, a trading company employee, often goes abroad on business.
であるく 出歩く（外出する）go* out;（うろつく）wander about [around] ∥最近忙しくて出歩く暇がないんだ I am too busy to *go out* these days.
-**であれ** たとえどんなことであれ, 分からないことは聞いてください Please ask me about *whatever* you don't understand. ∥ 国内であれ国外であれ, そんなことをしてはいけない You shouldn't do things like that, *whether* at home *or* abroad.

てい 体 体のいい(→もっともらしい) 言い訳 a *plausible* excuse ∥ 彼女はそ知らぬ体で(→ふりをして) 通り過ぎた She passed me by, *pretending* not to know. ⇨ ていよく
慣用表現 ほうほうの体で(→縮み上がって) 逃げ出す run away *with one's tail between one's legs*
てい- 低- 低価格 a *low* price ∥ 低所得 a *low* income ∥ 低賃金 *low* wages ∥ 低予算 a *low* budget ⇨ ていしき
-**てい -邸**《公式的》residence ©∥官邸 *an official residence* ∥ 水田邸 Mr. Mizuta's *residence*
ていあん 提案 proposal ©;（控えめな）suggestion © ——**提案する** propose ⊕; suggest ⊕ ⇨ コミュニケーションスキル
有益な提案 *a helpful suggestion* ∥ 提案を受け入れる accept *a proposal*
私は彼の提案に賛成した[反対した] I「agreed

with [objected to] his *proposal*.
あなたは私の提案に賛成ですか，それとも反対ですか Are you for or against my *proposal*?
彼女の提案で吉田先生の送別会をすることになった We decided to have a farewell party for Ms. Yoshida at her *suggestion*.
彼の提案は考慮に値する His *suggestion* deserves to be considered.
【propose [suggest]＋名 [*doing*]】計画を中止することを提案した I *proposed* [*suggested*] giving up the plan.
【propose [suggest]＋that 節】彼女に医者に診(み)てもらったらどうかと提案した I *suggested* [*proposed*] *that* she (*should*) see a doctor.(❖should を用いるのは主に《英》)
❢「私どもの提案にご賛成いただけますか」「もちろんです」 "Would you agree to our *proposal*?" "Of course."

ティー¹ (紅茶) tea ⓤ ∥ティーカップ a teacup / ティータイム a coffee break, a tea break,《主に英》teatime / ティーバッグ a tea bag / ティーポット a teapot / ティールーム a tearoom / アイスティー iced tea / ハーブティー herbal tea / ミルクティー tea with milk / ミントティー mint tea / レモンティー tea with (a slice of) lemon

ティー²〖ゴルフ〗tee ⓒ ∥ティーグラウンド a teeing ground / ティーショット a tee shot

ディーエヌエー DNA (❖*deoxyribonucleic acid*(デオキシリボ核酸)の略語)

ディーケー DK ⚠ 3 DK の賃貸マンション a three-room apartment [《英》flat] *with a kitchen and dining room*(❖DK は dining と kitchen の頭文字をとった和製語．英語では用いない)

ティーシャツ Tシャツ T-shirt ⓒ, tee shirt ⓒ ∥彼はいつも T シャツとジーパンだ He always wears jeans and *a T-shirt*.

ディーゼルエンジン diesel engine ⓒ

ディーピーイー DPE ⚠ photo finishing (service) ⓤ ∥DPE は developing「現像」, printing「焼きつけ」, enlarging「引き伸ばし」の頭文字をとった和製語．英語では用いない)

ティーピーオー TPO ⚠ the occasion(❖TPO は time「時」, place「場所」, occasion「場合」の頭文字をとった和製語．英語では用いない)∥TPO をわきまえた(→場面にふさわしい)服装 proper clothes for the occasion

ディーラー dealer ⓒ ∥車のディーラー a car dealer

ていいん 定員 (収容能力) capacity ⓤ(またa ～); (決まった数) fixed number ⓒ ∥このバスの定員は40人です This bus has *a capacity* of 40 seats. / *The* (*seating*) *capacity* of this bus is 40. / その大学の志願者数は定員に満たなかった The number of applicants to the university「didn't reach *the fixed number* [was under *strength*].
◆そのバスは明らかに定員オーバーだった The bus was clearly *overloaded*.

ティーンエージャー teenager ⓒ (❖13歳から19歳までを指す)∥このグループはティーンエージャーに大人気だ This group is very popular with *teenagers*.

ていえん 庭園 (皇帝) emperor ⓒ ∥屋上庭園 a roof garden / 日本庭園 a Japanese garden

ていおう 帝王 (皇帝) emperor ⓒ
◆暗黒街の帝王 *a boss* of the underworld

ていおうせっかい 帝王切開〖医 学〗Caesarean [sizέəriən] ⓒ, Caesarean section ⓤ,《米口語的》C-section ⓤ ∥帝王切開で生まれる be born by *Caesarean*

ていおん¹ 低音 low(-pitched) note ⓒ; (音符上の) low tone ⓒ; (合唱の) bass ⓤ ∥(最)低音部の声 a *bass* voice / 低音部を歌う[演奏する] sing [play] *low notes*

ていおん² 低温 low temperature ⓒ ∥低温殺菌 pasteurization / 低温殺菌牛乳 pasteurized milk

ていか¹ 低下 a drop, fall ⓒ; (体力・価値などの) decline ⓒ(またa ～); (減少) decrease ⓒ ──低下する drop ⓘ, fall* ⓘ; decline ⓘ
気温の低下 *a drop in* temperature
日本では出生率が低下している The birthrate in Japan *is declining*.
高校生の学力は低下していると思いますか Do you think that the academic level of high school students *is declining*?
最近の子供は運動不足で体力が低下している Recently the strength of children *has been falling* due to lack of exercise.
◆視力の低下 *failure of* eyesight / 近ごろ祖母は記憶力が低下してきている My grandmother's memory *is failing* these days.

ていか² 定価 fixed [list] price ⓒ; (値段) price ⓒ ➾ねだん ∥定価から5パーセント値引きする allow a five percent discount off *the fixed* [*list*] *price* / 彼女はそのドレスを定価の3割引で買った She bought the dress at 30 percent off *the fixed* [*list*] *price*.
∥定価表 a price list

ていがく¹ 停学 (a) suspension from school
◆彼はたばこを吸って1週間の停学処分になった He *was suspended from school* for a week for smoking. / He *was given a* week's *suspension* from school for smoking.

ていがく² 定額 fixed amount [sum] ⓒ
∥定額預金 fixed amount savings

ていがくねん 低学年 the lower grades [classes]

ていかんし 定冠詞〖文法〗definite article

ていき¹ 定期 ──定期的な regular; (周期的な) periodic ──定期的に regularly; periodically
そのオーケストラは定期的に演奏会を開いている The orchestra gives a concert *regularly* [*at regular intervals*].
目は眼科で定期的に検査するべきだ Eyes should be examined *periodically* by an oculist.
父はその雑誌を定期購読している My father *subscribes to* the magazine.
∥定期入れ a pass holder / 定期刊行物 a periodical / 定期券《米》a commuter pass, a

commutation ticket, 《英》a season ticket / 定期検診 a periodic [regular] medical checkup / 定期試験 a regular examination / 定期点検 a routine check / 定期便 (a) regular service; (大型船・大型飛行機の) a liner / 定期預金 a fixed [time] deposit

ていき² 提起 ──**提起する** raise ㊥, bring* up ∥彼は会議で重要な問題を提起した He *raised* [*brought up*] an important problem at the meeting.

ていぎ 定義 definition ⓒ (❖「定義すること」を表す場合は Ⓤ) ──**定義する** define ㊥ ∥厳密な定義を下す give *a rigorous definition* / 彼はこの言葉を次のように定義した He *defined* [*gave a definition of*] this word *as* follows.

ていきあつ 低気圧 low (atmospheric) pressure Ⓤⓒ, 《気象》depression ⓒ; (インド洋に起こる熱帯性低気圧) cyclone ⓒ
∥熱帯低気圧 a tropical cyclone

ていきゅう 低級 ──**低級な** low, low-grade; (低俗な) vulgar ∥低級な話題 *low-grade* [*vulgar*] topics

ていきゅうび 定休日 regular holiday ⓒ
◆ABデパートは木曜日が定休日です(→木曜日は休業する) AB Department Store *is closed* on Thursdays.

ていきょう 提供 offer ⓒ; (供給) supply Ⓤ ──**提供する** (与える) give* ㊥, provide ㊥; (差し出す) offer ㊥; (供給する) supply ㊥ ∥事件について警察に情報を提供する *supply* [*provide*] the police with information on a case / おじは自分の家をパーティーの会場に提供してくれた My uncle *offered* his house for the party.
◆腎臓の提供者 a kidney *donor* / この番組はアイレックス株式会社の提供でお送りいたしました This program *has been*「*brought to you* [*sponsored*] *by* IREX Corporation.
∥特価提供(商品の) a special offer

テイクアウト (持ち帰り用の料理) 《米》takeout ⓒ, 《英》takeaway ⓒ
◆ホットコーヒー2つ, テイクアウトでお願いします Two hot coffees *to go*, please.

ていくう 低空 low altitude ⓒ ∥飛行機が低空を(→低く)飛んでいた An airplane was flying *low*.
∥低空爆撃 low-level bombing / 低空飛行 (a) low altitude flight

ディクテーション dictation Ⓤⓒ

デイケア day care

ていけい¹ 定形 fixed form ⓒ ∥定形外郵便物 a nonstandard-sized letter / 定形郵便物 a standard-sized letter

ていけい² 提携 (口語的)tie-up ⓒ; (協力) co-operation Ⓤ ──**提携する** tie up; cooperate ㊥ ∥この会社は私のおじの会社と提携している This firm *is tied up with* my uncle's firm. / わが社はアメリカの会社と提携してこの商品を開発した We developed this product *in cooperation with* a company in the U.S.
∥技術提携 technical tie-ups

ていけつ 締結 conclusion Ⓤⓒ ──**締結する** conclude ㊥ ∥条約を締結する *conclude* a treaty

ていけつあつ 低血圧 low blood pressure Ⓤ, 《医学》hypotension Ⓤ

ていこう 抵抗 resistance Ⓤ 《また a ～》; (反対) opposition Ⓤ ──**抵抗する** resist ㊥ ∥その男は警察に抵抗しなかった The man *made no resistance* to the police.
その軍隊は激しい抵抗にあった The troops encountered *a strong resistance*.
抵抗してもむだだ. おとなしく出てこい There is no use *resisting* us. Come out peacefully.
彼女はかぜをひいて細菌に対する抵抗力が落ちていた She had a cold and *her resistance* to germs was lowered.
◆それが政府に対する彼らの最後の抵抗だった That was their last *stand* against the government. / 最初はテレビに出るのに多少抵抗があった(→あまり気が進まなかった) At first I *was* a little *reluctant to* appear on TV. / 彼女の傲慢(ごうまん)な態度には抵抗を感じる(→うんざりする) Her arrogant attitude *puts me off*.
∥抵抗器(電気の) a resistor / 空気抵抗 air resistance / 電気抵抗 electrical resistance

ていこく¹ 定刻 fixed time ⓒ, time Ⓤ; (予定時刻) schedule ⓒ ∥定刻より早く ahead of *time* / コンサートは定刻に始まった The concert began「*on schedule* [*as scheduled*]. / この列車は定刻より10分遅れている This train is 10 minutes *behind time* [*schedule*].
◆ 彼は定刻を過ぎても姿を見せなかった He didn't appear even though it was past *the appointed time*.

ていこく² 帝国 empire ⓒ (しばしば Empire) ∥神聖ローマ帝国 the Holy Roman Empire
∥帝国主義 imperialism / 帝国主義者 an imperialist

ていさい 体裁 (外見) appearance Ⓤⓒ; (見ばえ) presentation ⓒ ∥体裁をつくろう「*keep up* [*save*] *appearances*」/ 旅館としての体裁を整える adjust *appearance* as an inn / 彼はいつも体裁ばかり気にしている He always cares about *his appearance*.
◆この辞書は体裁がいい This dictionary「*looks nice* [*is presentable*]. / みんなの前で転んで体裁が悪かった(→恥ずかしかった) I *felt embarrassed* when I fell down in front of everyone. / 彼女はサラダを体裁よく盛りつけた She dished up the salad *beautifully*. / その小説は日記の体裁をとっている(→形式になっている) The novel *takes the form of* a diary.

ていさつ 偵察 scouting Ⓤ, 《軍事》reconnaissance ⓒⓊ; (人) scout ⓒ ──**偵察する** scout ㊥ ∥偵察に行く go out on *reconnaissance* / 偵察機 a reconnaissance plane

ていし 停止 stop ⓒ, stoppage Ⓤ; (一時的な) suspension Ⓤ ──**停止する** stop ㊥ ㊥; suspend ㊥
一時停止《掲示》*Stop* / 一時停止する make [come to] *a brief stop*
その車は赤信号で停止した The car *stopped* at

てuじ

the red traffic light.
彼女の口座に預金がないので銀行は小切手の支払いを停止した The bank *stopped* the check because there was no money in her account.
そのサッカー選手は反則で出場停止処分を受けた The soccer player *received a suspension* from play for a foul.
そのレストランは2週間の営業停止を命じられた The restaurant was ordered to *suspend business* for two weeks.

◆火山は活動を完全に停止している The volcano *is completely extinct.* / 停電で工場の作業は全部停止した The power failure brought the whole factory to *a standstill.*
‖停止信号 a stop signal, a stoplight / 停止線 a stop line / 一時停止ボタン a pause button / 心停止 cardiac arrest

ていじ¹ 定時 fixed time ◯ ‖定時に退社する leave *one's* office *at a fixed time*

◆渋滞のせいでそこへ定時に着けなかった(→間に合わなかった) Because of the traffic jam, we could not arrive there *on time.*

ていじ² 提示 presentation ◯Ｕ; (証拠などの) production Ｕ ──提示する (見せる) show* ◯; present ◯; produce ◯ ‖通過する際には身分証明書を提示してください Please *show [present, produce]* your ID card when you pass through.

ていせい 低姿勢 (目立たない) low profile ◯(通例 a ~); (控えめな態度) modest attitude ◯ ‖彼はいつも低姿勢だ He always keeps *a low profile.*

◆彼女は今度は低姿勢に出た(→謙虚だった) She *was modest* this time.

ていせい 定時制 ‖定時制高校 a part-time high school; (夜間の) high school evening classes

ていしゃ 停車 stop ◯ ──停車する stop ⓐ ‖この電車は次の駅で3分間停車します This train *will make a* three-minute *stop* at the next station. / バスは急停車した The bus *stopped suddenly.* / The bus *made a sudden stop.* / 私たちは次の停車駅で降ります We will get off at the next *stop.*

◆停車禁止〔掲示〕 *No Standing* / 停車中の電車は急行本川越行きです The *waiting* train is an express bound for Honkawagoe.

ていしゅ 亭主 (夫) *one's* husband; (店主) master ◯ ‖宿屋の亭主 the master of an inn / あの家は亭主関白らしい They say that *the husband is the boss* in that family.

ていじゅう 定住 settlement Ｕ ──定住する settle ◯ ‖彼は軽井沢に定住することにした He decided to *settle himself* in Karuizawa.

ていしゅう(にゅう) 定収(入) (一定の) fixed [regular] income ◯; (安定した) steady income ◯

ていしゅうは 低周波〔電気〕 low frequency ◯Ｕ

ていしゅつ 提出 (書類などの) submission Ｕ; (法案などの) introduction Ｕ ──提出する submit ◯, give* in; introduce ◯; (手渡す) turn in, hand in; (郵送で) send* in ‖申込書の提出期限 *the deadline for submission* of applications / 委員会に書類を提出する *submit* papers *to* a commission
私は罰としてレポートを提出するよう命じられた I was required to *submit* a paper as a penalty.
土曜日までに宿題を提出しなさい *Hand [Turn] in* your homework by Saturday.

ていしょう 提唱 proposal Ｕ◯; (唱道) advocacy Ｕ ──提唱する propose ◯; advocate ◯ ‖ダーウィンは進化論を提唱した Darwin *proposed* the theory of evolution.
‖提唱者 a proposer, an advocate

ていしょく¹ 定職 定職に就く get *a steady job* / 彼には定職がない He has no *regular work.*

ていしょく² 定食 set (meal) ◯ ‖トンカツ定食 a pork cutlet *set* / お昼の定食にはコーヒーとデザートがついています Coffee and dessert come with *the「lunch set [set lunch].*

ていしょく³ 停職 suspension ◯Ｕ ◆その弁護士は3か月間停職〔処分〕になった That attorney *was suspended* for three months.

ていしょく⁴ 抵触 この行為は法に抵触する This act *is against* the law.

ていじろ 丁字路 T-junction ◯

でいすい 泥酔 ──泥酔する 《口語的》get* [be] dead drunk; (酔いつぶれる) pass out ‖彼は泥酔していた He *was dead drunk.*

ていすう 定数 (決められた数) fixed number ◯, 〔数学・物理〕 constant ◯; (定足数) quorum ◯ (通例単数形) ‖議員の定数 the *fixed number* of Diet members / 定数に達しない be short of *a quorum* ◆国会の定数是正 *reapportionment* of Diet seats

ディスカウント (割引) discount ◯Ｕ ‖ディスカウントストア 《米》a discount store, 《英》a cut-price shop / ディスカウントセール a discount sale

ディスカッション discussion ◯ Ｕ ⇒ 場面・状況別会話 p.1766
‖パネルディスカッション a panel discussion

ディスク disk ◯, disc ◯ (❖コンピュータ関連では disk を用いる傾向がある) ‖ディスクジョッキー a disc jockey (《略語》DJ) / ディスクドライブ〔コンピュータ〕 a disk drive

ディスコ disco ◯ (複 ~ s), discotheque ◯ ‖渋谷のディスコに行く go to *a disco* in Shibuya

ディズニーランド Disneyland

ディスプレー (展示) display ◯; (コンピュータの) display ◯, monitor ◯ ‖カラーディスプレー a color *display*

ていする 呈する (状態を示す) show* ◯, assume ◯; (与える) give* ◯ ‖活況を呈する *show* activity; be active / 苦言を呈する *give* frank [candid] advice / 事態は複雑な様相を呈してきた The things began to *assume* a complicated aspect.

ていせい 訂正 correction Ｕ◯ ──訂正する correct ◯ ‖つづりの訂正 a spelling cor-

rection / （試験問題で）誤りがあれば訂正しなさい *Correct* errors, if any. / 試験問題に訂正箇所があった There were some *corrections* in the test questions.

ていせい² 帝政 imperial government ⓤ
◆帝政ロシア *Czarist Russia*

ていせつ¹ 定説 （学問的な）established theory ⓒ；（一般に認められている）accepted theory ⓒ ∥定説をくつがえす overturn *an established theory*

ていせつ² 貞節 fidelity ⓤ,《古風》chastity ⓤ ━━貞節な faithful,《古風》chaste

ていせん 停戦 cease-fire ⓒ, armistice ⓒ；（協定に基づく休戦）truce ⓒ ━━停戦する cease fire ∥2国間の停戦を模索する seek to bring about *a cease-fire* between two countries
∥停戦協定 a cease-fire agreement / 停戦交渉 cease-fire negotiations / 停戦命令 a cease-fire order

ていそ 提訴 ━━提訴する（事故などを法廷に持ち込む）bring* ... before the court；（告訴する）sue 働倉；（訴える）appeal 億 ∥国連に提訴する *appeal* to the UN

ていそう 貞操 《古風》chastity ⓤ ∥貞操を失う［守る］lose [defend] *one's chastity*

ていそく 低速 low speed ⓒⓤ ━━低速で at a low speed ∥低速ギア a low gear

ていぞく 低俗 ━━低俗な low, low-level, vulgar；（下品な）coarse ∥低俗なテレビ番組 *low* [*vulgar*] TV programs

ていそくすう 定足数 quorum ⓒ（通例単数形）∥定足数に達する have [achieve] *a quorum* / 定足数に達しない be short of *a quorum*

ていたい¹ 停滞 ━━停滞する stagnate 倉, be stagnant ∥景気が停滞している The economy *is stagnant*. ∥本州南岸付近に梅雨前線が停滞している The rain front *is lingering* near the south coast of Honshu.
∥停滞前線《気象》a stationary front

ていたい² 手痛い painful, severe ∥手痛い打撃を受ける suffer *painful* [*severe*] damage

ていたく 邸宅 residence ⓒ；（大邸宅）mansion ⓒ

ていち 低地 lowland ⓤ（また複数形 ～ s）

ていちゃく 定着 ━━定着する become* established, come* to stay；（定着している）be established；（根づく）take* root ∥この言葉は若者の間ですっかり定着した This word *has taken root* among young people.
◆その国に民主主義を定着させることは容易ではない It isn't easy to *establish* democracy *in* the country.

ていちょう¹ 丁重 ━━丁重な（礼儀正しい）polite；（礼儀正しく親切な）courteous；（慎重な）careful；（手厚い）hospitable ━━丁重に politely；courteously；carefully；hospitably ∥申し出を丁重に断る decline an offer *politely* ∥彼の家では丁重なもてなしを受けた He gave me a *hospitable* welcome at his house. / このバイオリンは丁重に扱わねばなりません This violin must be handled *carefully*.

ていちょう² 低調 ━━低調な（活気のない）dull, inactive, sluggish, slack；（活動の緩慢な）slow ∥低調な試合 a *dull* [an *inactive*] game / 滑り出しは低調だった We made a *slow* start. / わが社の先月の売り上げは低調だった Our sales were *sluggish* [*slack*] last month.

ティッシュペーパー ⚠tissue ⓒ（❖×tissue paper とはいわない）；（商標名）Kleenex ⓤ

ていっぱい 手一杯 彼は自分の仕事をこなすので手一杯だった He *had his hands full* doing his own job. / He *was occupied with* his own job.

ていでん 停電 blackout ⓒ；（事故などによる）power failure ⓒ；（電力の供給停止）《米》outage ⓒ ∥昨夜この地区は停電になった There was a『*power failure* [*blackout*] in this district last night. / 停電だ! *It's a blackout*! / *The lights have gone out*!
◆大型の台風のために停電になった *The electricity was cut off* by the big typhoon. / The big typhoon *cut off the electricity*.

ていど 程度

❶【度合い・範囲】（度合い）degree ⓒⓤ；（範囲）extent ⓤ《また an ～》

ある程度までは君にも責任がある You are also responsible *to some degree* [*extent*].

それは単に程度の問題だ That's only a matter of *degree*.

彼女はこの活動にどの程度かかわっていたのか *To what degree* [*extent*] was she involved in this activity? /《口語的》*How far* was she involved in this activity?

彼らはみな，程度の差こそあれ動物好きだった They all liked animals, *to* [*in*] *different degrees*.

◆海外旅行をするにはある程度の（→いくらか）お金が必要だ You need *some* money to travel abroad. / その程度のことしか彼にしてあげられなかった That was *the least* I could do for him.

❷【水準】level ⓒ；（基準）standard ⓒⓤ

この問題は程度が高すぎる The *level* [*standard*] of this question is too high.

その子供は高校程度の数学の問題は解いてしまう The child can solve mathematical problems of *a high school level*.

❸【およそ】about

その通りには当時20軒程度の本屋があった There were *about* twenty bookstores along the street in those days.

ていとう 抵当 mortgage [mɔ́ːrɡidʒ] ⓒ；（担保）security ⓤ ∥あの家は2,000万円の抵当に入っている There is *a mortgage* of 20 million yen on that house.
◆彼らは家を抵当に入れて500万円借りた They *mortgaged* their house *for* five million yen. / 私には抵当に入れるものが何もない I have nothing to offer as *collateral*.
∥抵当権 a mortgage

ていとく 提督 admiral ⓒ《しばしば Admiral》《《略語》Adm.》

ディナー dinner ⓤ ∥ディナーパーティー a dinner party

ていねい 丁寧

❶【礼儀正しい】politeness ⓤ;（思いやりがあって）courtesy ⓤ ――丁寧な polite; courteous ――丁寧に politely; courteously
丁寧におじぎする bow *politely*
彼女は丁寧な言葉づかいをする She uses *polite* language.
ご丁寧にお電話をいただき、ありがとうございました It is very *courteous* of you to call me.

❷【注意深い】――丁寧な careful, attentive ――丁寧に carefully, attentively
彼女はその書類を丁寧に書き写した She copied the documents *carefully* [*attentively*].
彼は容疑者の経歴を丁寧に調べた He *carefully* [*closely*] investigated the background of the suspect.
その花びんは丁寧に扱ってね、こわれやすいから Be *careful* with the vase [Handle the vase *with care*], because it breaks easily.
彼はその小説を最初から最後まで丁寧に読んだ He read the novel *attentively* from beginning to end.

◆彼女は丁寧に（→良心的に）仕事をするので有名だ Everyone knows that she works *conscientiously*.

ていねん 定年・停年 retirement age ⓤ;（年齢制限）age limit ⓒ ∥定年で退職する retire (because *one* reaches *retirement age*)（◆通例かっこ内は省略される）/ 父は来年定年を迎える My father will reach *retirement age* next year.
∥定年制 an age limit system / 定年退職者 a retired person,《米》a retiree

ていはく 停泊 ――停泊する anchor ⓘ;（停泊している）be [lie*, ride*] at anchor ∥多くの船が港に停泊していた Many ships *were* (*riding*) *at anchor* in the harbor.
∥停泊地 an anchorage

ていばん 定番 このセーターは定番商品だ This sweater is *a standard item*.

ていひょう 定評 an established reputation ◆英文法の定評ある参考書 a *standard* [an *established*] reference on English grammar / 彼は腕のよい歯医者として定評がある He 「*is established* [*has an established reputation*] as a good dentist.

ディフェンス （守備）defense ⓤⓒ ∥ディフェンスを固める strengthen *defense* / うちのチームはディフェンスが強い［弱い］ Our team's *defense* is strong [weak].

ディベート debate ⓒ ⇒ 場面・状況別会話 p.1770

ていへん 底辺〖幾何〗the base;（階層の）the bottom ∥三角形の底辺 *the base* of a triangle

ていぼう 堤防 bank ⓒ;（人工の）embankment ⓒ;（土手）dike ⓒ ∥大雨で堤防が決壊した Because of the heavy rain, *the bank burst*.

ていほん 定本 standard text ⓒ

ていめい 低迷 景気が低迷している（→不活発だ）The economy *is sluggish*. / そのチームは長い間下位に低迷してきた The team *has long floundered* near the bottom of the standings.

ていめん 底面〖幾何〗the base ∥円すいの底面 *the base* of a cone

ていよく 体よく （丁重に）politely;（巧みに）tactfully ∥私の申し出は体よく断られた My offer was refused *politely* [*tactfully*].

ていらく 低落 fall ⓒ, decline ⓤ（また a ～）――低落する fall* ⓘ, decline ⓘ

ティラミス tiramisu

ていり¹ 低利 low interest ⓤ ∥低利で資金を融資する finance *at low interest*
∥低利融資 a low-interest loan

ていり² 定理〖数学・論理〗theorem ⓒ ∥ピタゴラスの定理 *the Theorem* of Pythagoras

でいり 出入り ❶【出ることと入ること】――出入りする go* [come*] in and out ∥この店にはけさから多くの人々が出入りしていた Many people *have come in and out* of this store since this morning.
◆出入りの（→定期的に注文をとりに来る）業者 a dealer *who regularly comes for orders* / 車が出入りするのでここには駐車しないでください Cars *pass through* here, so please do not park here. / 私の家は人の出入り（→訪問者）が多い We have a lot of *visitors*. / 10歳未満の子供はこの遊園地に自由に出入りできる（→自由に出入りすることを許されている）Children under 10 *are given the run of* this amusement park. / 彼はその店の出入り（→入ること）を禁じられた He was forbidden to *enter* the store.

❷【収支】income and outgo [expenditure] ∥出入りの多い月 the month when *income and outgo* are high

でいりぐち 出入り口 doorway ⓒ, door ⓒ;（壁・垣などの）gateway ⓒ ∥出入り口に立たないでください Please don't stand in *the doorway*.

ていりゅう 底流 undercurrent ⓒ

ていりゅうじょ 停留所 stop ⓒ ∥バスの停留所 *a bus stop* / 渋谷行きのバスに乗って、3つ目の停留所で降りてください Take the bus for Shibuya and get off at *the third stop*.

ていりょう 定量 fixed quantity ⓒ ∥定量分析〖化学〗quantitative analysis

ていれ 手入れ ❶【世話】care ⓤ ――手入れする take* care of ...;（修理する）repair ⓘ;（切りそろえる）trim ⓘ ∥肌の手入れ skin *care* / つめ［芝］の手入れをする trim 「*one's* nails [the lawn] / 自転車の手入れをしなさい *Take care of* your bicycle. ◆手入れの行き届いた庭 a *well-kept* garden / この手の機械は手入れ（→管理）が簡単です It's easy to *maintain* this type of machine.

❷【警察の】raid ⓒ ――手入れする raid ⓘ ∥警察は彼の事務所の手入れを行った The police *carried out a raid on* his office.

ていれい 定例 ━定例の regular ‖定例の記者会見 a *regular* press conference
‖定例会議 a regular meeting

ディレクター director [C]

ディレクトリ 〘コンピュータ〙 directory [C]

ティンパニー 〘音楽〙 timpani [U] 《単数または複数扱い》; (1個の) kettledrum [C] (❖2つ以上組み合わせたものが timpani)
‖ティンパニー奏者 a timpanist

てうす 手薄 帽子の在庫が手薄だ(→不足している) The stock of hats *is running short.* / そのとき店の警備は手薄になっていた(→少なかった) The security of the store *was weak* [*slack*] then.

てうち 手打ち ‖手打ちうどん handmade *udon* noodles

デーゲーム day game [C]

テーゼ ⚠〘哲学・論理〙 thesis [θíːsis] [C] (複 theses) (❖日本語はドイツ語の these から)

データ data [U] 《単数または複数扱い》 (❖本来は datum の複数形) ‖データを検索する retrieve *data* / 手に入るあらゆるデータが集められた All available *data* were gathered.
‖データ処理 data processing / データ通信 data communication / データ入力 data entry / データバンク a data bank / データベース a database

デート date [C] (❖《米》では「デートの相手」の意味もある) ━デートする 《主に米》date [自] [他], have* a date ➩ [場面・状況別会話] p.1692
あしたは麻里とデートだ I'*ll have a date with* Mari tomorrow.
彼女は初デートの日にかぜをひいた She caught cold on *her* first *date*.
彼女はいつも休みの日にデートに出かける She always *goes out on* 「*a date* [*dates*] on her day off.
だれとデートだったの(→デートの相手はだれだったの) Who was *your date*?
◆拓也にデートに誘われちゃった Takuya *asked* me *out*. / お台場は若者に人気のデートコースだ Odaiba is *a* popular *spot for* young *couples*.

テープ tape [U] [C]; (紙テープ) paper streamer [C]; (セロテープ) 《米》《商標名》Scotch tape [C], 《英》《商標名》Sellotape [U]
(1着で)テープを切る breast *the tape* / テープを巻き戻す[早送りする] rewind [fast-forward] *a tape* / ビデオテープを再生する play back *a video tape* / 60分テープ *a* 60-minute *tape*
私は彼女のピアノのテープをかけた I played *a tape* of her piano performance.
このテープは空だ This *tape* is blank.
彼女の演説をカセットテープに録音した I recorded her speech on *a cassette* (*tape*)./ I taperecorded her speech.
‖テープカット ribbon cutting / オーディオテープ (an) audiotape / 磁気テープ a magnetic tape / 絶縁テープ insulating tape / デモテープ a demo (tape) / マスターテープ a master tape / 両面テープ a double-faced adhesive tape

テーブル table [C]
テーブルの上を片づける clear *the table*
どうぞテーブルに着いてください Please sit [take your seat(s)] at *the table.*
彼女はふきんでテーブルをふいた She wiped *the table* with a cloth.
彼らはレストランで4人用のテーブルを頼んだ At the restaurant, they asked for *a table* for four.
‖テーブルクロス a tablecloth / テーブルスピーチ an after-dinner speech / テーブルマナー table manners / ナイトテーブル a bedside table

テープレコーダー tape recorder [C] ‖テープレコーダーで録音する record on *a tape recorder*

テーマ theme [θíːm] [C]; (主題) subject [C]; (話題) topic [C] ‖ディスカッションのテーマ *the topic* of a discussion / 「環境」が今年の会議のテーマだった "The Environment" was *the theme* [*topic*] for this year's conference. / それらの絵はテーマ別に分けられた Those pictures were classified according to *subject*.
‖テーマソング a theme song / テーマパーク a theme park

テールライト taillight [C]

ておい 手負い 手負いのトラ a *wounded* tiger

ておくれ 手遅れ 手遅れにならないうちに歯医者に診(み)てもらいなさい You had better see the dentist before it's *too late*. / 彼が異変に気づいたときにはもう手遅れだった It was *too late* by the time he realized something unusual had happened.

でおくれる 出遅れる 選挙戦に出遅れる *get a late start* in an election campaign

ておけ 手桶 bucket [C], 《主に米》pail [C]

ておしぐるま 手押し車 handcart [C]; (買い物用の) pushcart [C]; (土木作業用の) wheelbarrow [C] (❖単に barrow ともいう)

ておち 手落ち fault [C]; (誤り) mistake [C]; (見落とし) oversight [C] [U] ‖主催者側の手落ち *the fault* [*mistake*] of the organizer / 作業に手落ちがあった There were some *oversights* in the work.

デオドラント このシャンプーにはデオドラント効果がある This shampoo is *deodorant*.
‖デオドラントスプレー a deodorant spray

ており 手織り ━手織りの hand-woven, homespun
‖手織物 hand-woven [homespun] fabrics

でかい big; (巨大な) huge ‖彼は態度がでかい He acts *big*.

てかがみ 手鏡 hand mirror [C]

てがかり 手掛かり (糸口) clue [C]; (問題解決のかぎ) key [C] ‖そのなぞ[問題]を解く手がかり *a key to* the mystery [problem] / 彼の発言が手がかりになった His remarks provided *a clue*. / 事件の手がかりは何かつかめましたか Have you found any *clues to* the case?
◆刑事は犯人の手がかりをたどっていった[途中で失った] The detective followed [lost] *the trail* of the criminal.

てがき 手書き handwriting [U] ━手書きの

て

handwritten 〃彼から手書きの年賀状が届いた I got a *handwritten* new year's card from him.

てがける 手掛ける deal* with ...; (うまく扱う) handle [他]; (育てる) bring* up 〃彼はこの手の仕事を数多く手がけてきた He *has dealt with* a lot of work of this kind.

でかける 出掛ける (外出する) go* (out); (出発する) start [自]; (場所を離れる) leave* [自]; (留守にする) be out

ちょうど出かけようとしたときに雨が降り始めた Just when I *was going out*, it began to rain.

あなたが出かけている間に木村さんから電話があったわよ Ms. Kimura called you while you *were out*.

そろそろ出かける時間だ It's about time to *go* [*leave*].

さあ出かけよう Let's *go*!

出かける準備はできてる? Are you ready to *go*?

父は朝の7時に仕事に出かけます My father *leaves for* work at seven in the morning.

◆この夏はまだどこにも出かけていません I *haven't been* anywhere this summer yet. / 日曜には僕たち兄弟はよく釣りに出かけたものだった On Sundays my brother and I would often *go fishing*.

[e]「お母さん, いらっしゃる?」「今買い物に出かけてるんですが」"Is your mother home?" "She'*s out shopping* now."

てかげん 手加減 彼はまだ子供なんだから手かげんしてやりなさい *Go easy with* [*on*] him because he is still only a child. / 彼は相手がだれでも手かげんしない He never *pulls his punches* whoever the opponent is.

でかせぎ 出稼ぎ 祖父は冬になると東京に出稼ぎに行っていたそうだ I hear my grandfather *went* to Tokyo *to work* in winters.

‖出稼ぎ労働者(季節労働者) a seasonal [migrant] worker

てがた 手形 ❶【有価証券】(為替手形)〘金融〙a bill of exchange, draft [C] 〃手形を引き受ける take up *a draft* [*bill*] / …あてに手形を振り出す draw *a draft* [*bill*] on ... / 手形に裏書きする back *a draft* [*bill*] / 小切手で支払いますか, 手形にしますか Will you pay by check or by *draft*?

❷【手の形】handprint [C] 〃赤ちゃんの手形をとる take *the handprint* of a baby

‖手形受取人[支払人, 振出人] the payee [payer, drawer] of a draft / 手形交換所 a clearing house / 銀行為替手形 a bank draft(《略語》B/D) / 不渡り手形 a dishonored draft / 約束手形 a promissory note

でかた 出方 move [C] 〃彼らは互いに相手の出方をうかがっていた Each of them watched to see what *moves* his opponent would make.

てがたい 手堅い 手堅い(→堅実な)商売 a *steady* business / ジャイアンツはバントで手堅く(→着実に)ランナーをセカンドに進めた The Giants *steadily* moved the runner to second on a bunt.

てかてか 彼はポマードでてかてかにした(→光る)髪をトレードマークにしていた He made his *shiny* hair with pomade a trademark.

でかでか 新聞の一面にでかでかと書きたてられる *be splashed across* the front page of the newspaper / どのポスターにも立候補者の名前がでかでかと書かれている On every poster the name of the candidate is written *in big letters*.

てがみ 手紙

letter [C]; (短信) note [C] ⇒ [巻末付録] (手紙・はがきの書き方)

〚〜手紙〛

お礼の手紙 *a* thank-you *letter* / 12月25日付けの手紙 *a letter* dated December 25 / 置き手紙をする leave *a note*

これはあなたあての手紙です This is *a letter* for you.

〚手紙が〛

きょうアンから手紙が来た I got *a letter* from Ann today.

もう今ごろは手紙が届いているだろう *The letter* will have arrived by now.

〚手紙に・の〛

手紙のあて先を書く address *a letter* / 手紙の封を切る open *a letter*

私はすぐに彼の手紙に返事を出した I answered his *letter* immediately.

彼の手紙には次のように書いてあった His *letter* read as follows.

〚手紙を〛

英語で手紙を書く write *a letter* in English

彼が私に手紙をくれた He wrote me *a letter*.

この手紙を書留にしたいのですが I'd like to have this *letter* registered.

◆きのう彼女に手紙を書いた I *wrote to* her yesterday.

[e]「この手紙を出してもらえますか」「いいですよ」"Could you mail [post] this *letter*?" "No problem."

てがら 手柄 (名誉) credit [U]; (偉業) exploit [C]《通例複数形〜s》〃手柄を立てる perform *exploits* / それは彼女の手柄だ *The credit* goes to her. / 彼は手柄をひとり占めしようとした He tried to take all *the credit*.

◆それは大手柄だ(→よくやった)! *Excellent*! / You *did* it!

でがらし 出涸らし このお茶は出がらしだ(→葉がすでに使用されたものなので薄い) This tea *is thin because the leaves have already been used*.

てがる 手軽 ──手軽な (容易な) easy; (てごろな) handy; (簡単な) light ──手軽に easily 〃手軽にできる運動 an *easy* form of exercise / このワープロは手軽に持ち運べる You can carry this word processor *easily*. / 昼食はそばで手軽にすませた I had a *light* lunch of *soba*.

てき 敵 enemy [C]; (競争相手) opponent [C] 敵と戦う fight with [against] *the enemy* /

敵を背後から攻撃する attack *the enemy* from the rear / 敵に包囲される be surrounded by *the enemy*

彼らは敵から国を守った They kept [defended] their country from *their enemies*.

彼らは敵の攻撃に耐え抜いた They withstood *the enemy's* attack.

その要塞(ようさい)は一度も敵の手に落ちたことがない The fort has never fallen to any *enemy*.

彼は敵前逃亡した He escaped from the face of *the enemy*.

私は彼を敵に回してしまった I've made *an enemy* of him.

彼は社内に敵が多い He has many *enemies* in his company.

今のところうちは敵を4対1でリードしている We are now leading *our opponent* 4 to 1.

エイズは人類の敵だ AIDS is *an enemy* of the human race.

◆我々は敵味方(→敵対するチーム)に分かれて試合に臨んだ We took part in the game, divided into *opposing teams*.

‖敵艦《公式的》an enemy vessel / 敵機 an enemy plane / 敵軍 an enemy [a hostile] army, enemy forces / 敵国 an enemy country / 敵陣 an enemy camp / 敵地 (an) enemy territory / 敵兵 an enemy soldier

慣用表現 わがチームは向かうところ敵なしだ Our team is *unbeatable*.

ことわざ きのうの敵はきょうの友 ⇒きのう(昨日)

-てき -滴 drop ⓒ / 1滴の血 a *drop* of blood ◆まじめな話,私は一滴も(→全く)飲めないんです Seriously, I can't drink *at all*.

でき 出来 (できばえ) performance ⓤ; (結果) result ⓒ《通例複数形 ~ s》⇒じょうでき / 上々のでき a fine *performance* / 試験のできはあまりよくなかった My *results* in the exams were not very good.

◆できのよい[悪い]生徒 a *bright* [*dull*] student / 去年は米のでき(→収穫高)がとてもよかった We had a very good *crop* of rice last year. / It was a bumper year for rice last year.(❖bumper year は「大豊作の年」の意味) / そのカメラマンは作品のでき(→自分の作品に)満足しているようだった The photographer seemed to be satisfied with *his works*. / その芝居の出来不出来(→成功するかどうか)は彼の演技ひとつにかかっている *Whether* the play is *successful or not* depends entirely on his performance.

💬「試験どうだった」「さんざんのできだったよ」"How was the exam?" "I *did* very *badly*."

できあい¹ 出来合い ──できあいの ready-made / できあいのコート a *ready-made* coat

できあい² 溺愛 祖母は姉を溺愛していた My grandmother *doted on* my sister. / (→盲目的に愛していた)My grandmother *loved* my sister *blindly*.

できあがり 出来上がり finish ⓤ《また a ~》 ◆できあがりはなかなかのものだった It was wonderfully *finished*.

できあがる 出来上がる (完成する) be completed, be finished; (準備が整う) be ready / このビルはもうすぐできあがる This building *will be completed* [*finished*] soon.
◆私が着いたときには彼らはすでにできあがっていた(→酔っていた) They *were* already *loaded* when I arrived.

てきい 敵意 hostility ⓤⓒ, 《公式的》enmity ⓤⓒ / 敵意をむき出しにする show *hostility* openly to *a person* / 彼女は私に敵意をいだいているようだった It seemed that she felt *hostility* to me.

◆敵意のある態度 a *hostile* attitude

テキーラ tequila (❖メキシコ産の蒸留酒)

てきおう 適応 adaptation ⓤⓒ, adjustment ⓤⓒ ──適応する adapt [adjust] *oneself* / 人は年をとるにつれて新しい環境に適応するのが難しくなる As we get older, it is difficult to *adapt* [*adjust*] *ourselves to* a new environment. ◆その小さなサボテンは東京の気候にすっかり適応してしまったようだった It seemed that the small cactus *was well-adapted* [*-adjusted*] *to* the climate of Tokyo.

‖適応性 adaptability / 適応能力 the ability to adapt

てきおん 適温 (ちょうどよい温度) suitable temperature ⓤⓒ; (ほどほどの温度) moderate temperature ⓤⓒ / 適温に保つ keep at *a suitable temperature*

てきがいしん 敵愾心 hostility ⓤ ⓒ, hostile feelingⓤ

てきかく¹ 的確 ──的確な (適切な) proper; (正確な) accurate; (緻密(ちみつ)な) precise / 的確な判断 *proper* judgment / 彼の解説はいつも的確 His commentary is always *accurate* [*precise*].

◆的確に処理する deal *properly* / 彼女の提案は端的かつ的確だった(→的(まと)を射ていた) Her suggestion was simple and *to the point*.

てきかく² 適格 ──適格な (資格のある) qualified; (ふさわしい) eligible; (能力のある) competent / 彼は教育者として適格だ He is *qualified* as a teacher.

‖適格者 a qualified person

てきぎ 適宜 塩を適宜(→好みに合わせて)加えてください Add salt *to taste*. / 集会終了後は適宜(→自分の裁量で)帰宅してよろしい You may home *at your own discretion* after the meeting is over.

てきごう 適合 adaptation ⓤ, fit ⓤ《また a ~》; (一致) conformance ⓤ ──適合する adapt ⓘ, fit* ⓘ; conform ⓘ ◆条件に適合する(→条件を満たす) *meet* a requirement

できごころ 出来心 (衝動) impulse ⓤⓒ; (気まぐれ) whim ⓒ / つい出来心で盗みを働いてしまった I committed a theft *on an impulse*.

できごと 出来事 occurrence ⓤ, (大きな) event ⓒ; (小さな) incident ⓒ; (偶然の) happening ⓒ

よくある出来事 a common *occurrence* / 今週の主な出来事 the chief *events* of this week / そのとき信じられない出来事が起こった Then, *an* unbelievable *occurrence* happened.

その2つの出来事の間には何の関係もありません There is no connection between those two *events*.

信じられないかもしれませんが, これは実際にあった出来事なのです You may not believe me but this was *a true-life incident*.

◆それは一瞬の出来事だった(→一瞬のうちに起こった) It *happened in a flash*. / 私たちは昨夜の出来事について話し合った We talked about *what had happened* last night.

てきざい 適材 彼は社長として適材だ He is the *right* [*good, suitable*] man to be president.

慣用表現 適材適所 *the right man in the right place*

テキサス Texas(◆米国南部の州; 《略語》Tex., 《郵便》TX) ‖テキサスヒット Texas leaguer

てきし 敵視 彼は僕を敵視している(→敵とみなしている) He *looks upon me as an enemy*. / (→敵意をもっている) He *is hostile to me*.

できし 溺死 drowning Ⓤ ──溺死する drown ⾃ ‖男が川で溺死した A man *drowned* in the river.

‖溺死体 a drowned body

てきしゃせいぞん 適者生存 survival of the fittest

てきしゅつ 摘出 extraction Ⓤ; (除去) removal Ⓤ ──摘出する extract ⾃; remove ⾃ ‖手術によって臓器を摘出する *surgically remove* organs

できすぎ 出来過ぎ その話はできすぎていると思う I think the story *is too perfect to be true*.

テキスト Ⓐ(教科書) textbook Ⓒ ‖このテキストは初心者向けだ This *textbook* is for beginners.

てきする 適する suit ⾃⾃; (適している) be suitable [fit, good]

この魚は生(⾷)で食べるのに適していない This fish *is not fit to eat* raw.

この靴は山道に適している These shoes *are suitable* [*fit*] *to wear* in the mountains.

日本の気候は稲作に適している Japan's climate *suits* [*is good for*] the cultivation of rice.

◆彼はリーダーに適さない He *is not cut out to be a leader*. (◆「生まれつき向いていない」の意味が含まれる) / He *is not fit to be a leader*.

てきせい¹ 適正 ──適正な (妥当な) fair; (適切な) proper; (理にかなった) reasonable ‖適正な賃金 a *fair* wage / 適正な処置をとる take *proper* measures

‖適正価格 a fair [reasonable] value

てきせい² 適性 aptitude ⓒⓊ ‖彼は医者としての適性を備えていた He had *an aptitude* to be a doctor.

‖適性検査 an aptitude test

てきせつ 適切 ──適切な (ふさわしい) proper, right, appropriate; (よい) good; (関係のある) relevant ‖ふてきせつ

適切な治療を施す give *proper* treatment / 気持ちを表現するのに適切な言葉を見つける find the *right* [*proper*] words to express what *one* feels

彼はいつでも適切な助言を与えてくれる He always gives me *good* [*sound*] advice.

地震のときは適切な行動をとらなければなりません You must take *proper* action at the time of an earthquake.

◆適切な (→的(⾃)を射た)例を挙げる take a case [an example] *in point* / 彼の発言は適切さを欠いていた (→不適切だった) His remark was *inappropriate*.

できそこない 出来損ない, (失敗作) failure ⓒ; (役立たず) a good for nothing ──できそこないの good-for-nothing(◆名詞の前で用いる) ‖彼の作ったこのマガジンラックはできそこないだ This magazine rack he made is *a failure* [(→大失敗) *a flop*].

◆できそこないのカレー *badly-cooked* curry / このできそこないめ! What *an idiot!*

てきたい 敵対 両国は長い間敵対関係にあった The two countries *have been hostile to* each other for a long time.

‖敵対行為 hostile acts

できだか 出来高 (収穫量) crop ⓒ, yield ⓒ (しばしば複数形〜s); (生産高) output ⓒ; (1回の仕事量) the piece; (株式の取引高) turnover Ⓤ ‖米の出来高 a rice *crop*; *yields* of rice / 従業員の給料は出来高で決められるべきだ Workers should be paid 「*by the piece* [*on a piecework basis*].

◆出来高払いの仕事をする do piecework

できたて 出来立て ──できたての just made, fresh, freshly made; (真新しい) brand-new; (あつあつの) hot ‖できたてのピザ a pizza *just made* / できたてのほやほやの (→オーブンから出したばかりであつあつの)パンを買ってきたよ I've got bread *fresh* [*hot*] *from the oven*.

てきちゅう 的中 ──的中する (的(⾃)に) hit* the mark [target]; (予想が) prove* [guess] right; (予言が) come* true ‖彼女の放った矢は的に的中した The arrow she shot *hit the mark* [*target*]. / 彼の予言は的中した His prophecy 「*came true* [*was fulfilled*].

てきど 適度 ──適度な (ほどよい) moderate; (適当な) suitable ‖君は適度な運動を心がけるべきだ You should take some *moderate* exercise.

てきとう 適当

❶【ふさわしい】 ──適当な suitable, appropriate, good

空欄に適当な語を入れなさい Fill in the blanks with the *appropriate* words.

この仕事を任せるのに適当な人を知りませんか Do you know 「*a suitable* [*the right*] *person for this job*?

彼らはテントを張るのに適当な場所を探していた They were looking for a *suitable* spot to pitch a tent.

適当なところで仕事を切り上げて家に帰った I stopped working at a *good* stopping point and went home.

◆ニンジンを適当な大きさに切る cut a carrot

to size / あとは適当に(→いいと思うように)やってくれ As to the rest, do *as you think* [*see*] *fit*.

💬「パーティーに何着ていくの」「適当な服がないのよねぇ」"What are you going to wear to the party?" "I don't have anything *suitable*."

❷【いいかげんな】
彼女の仕事は適当だ(→いいかげんに仕事をする) She does her work *anyhow*.
彼はいつも彼女に適当にあしらわれている He *is always trifled with* by her.
問題の意味が分からなかったので, 適当な答え(→当てずっぽう)を書いておいた I didn't understand the question, so I wrote down *a guess*.
だれかに私の居場所を聞かれたら適当にごまかしておいてね If anybody asks you where I am, just *make up something reasonable*.

てきにん 適任 適任の right; (最も適任の) perfect; (必要を満たした) suitable // 彼がその仕事に適任かどうかは疑問だ There is a question whether he is the *right* person for the job. / 彼女がその仕事の適任者です She is 「*a suitable* [*the perfect*] *person* for the job.

できばえ 出来栄え・出来映え performance ⓒ; (製品の) workmanship ⓒ
◆彼女の絵はみごとなできばえだった(→彼女の描いた絵はみごとだった) The picture she painted was *wonderful*.

てきぱき ——てきぱき(と) (素早く) quickly, promptly; (能率的に) efficiently // てきぱきと答える reply *quickly* [*promptly*] / 彼はやるべきことをてきぱきとこなした He did his duties *promptly* [*efficiently*].

てきはつ 摘発 exposure Ⓤⓒ ——摘発する expose ⓗ // 政治汚職の摘発に乗り出す start *the exposure* of political corruption

てきびしい 手厳しい severe // 手厳しい批判を受ける suffer *severe* criticism

てきほう 適法 legality Ⓤ ——適法の legal

てきめん 薬の効果がてきめんに現れて彼は眠りに落ちた The medicine 「had an *immediate effect* [*worked immediately*] and he fell asleep.

できもの 出来物 〔医学〕 boil ⓒ; (吹き出物) rash ⓒ

てきやく 適役 suitable [right] role ⓒ ——適役の suitable, right // ジュリエットは彼女にぴったりの適役だった Juliet was *the suitable* [*right*] *role* for her.

てきよう¹ 適用 application Ⓤ ——適用する apply ⓗ ⓒ // この規則は生徒には適用されない This rule 「*isn't applied* [*doesn't apply*] *to* students. / This rule *isn't applicable to* students. / 検察側は殺人罪の適用を検討している The prosecution considers whether murder *applies*. ◆この素材は適用範囲が広い This material *can be widely used*.

てきよう² 摘要 (要約) summary ⓒ; (概略) outline ⓒ

てきりょう 適量 suitable amount [quantity] ⓒ, proper amount [quantity] ⓒ // 適量 のアルコール *suitable amount* of alcohol

できる 出来る
❶【可能である】can, be able to *do*

【語法】
(1)現在形の be able to は助動詞 can とほぼ同じ意味であるが, 現在時制のときや物を主語にするときは can のほうが一般的.
(2) can には未来形や完了形がなく, またほかの助動詞の後で用いることができないので, 代わりに be able to を用いる // 将来, 人は自由に宇宙旅行をすることができるようになるだろうか Will people *be able to* travel through space freely in the future?
(3)過去の事実を述べる際, could が仮定法とまぎらわしいので was [were] able to を用いるほうがよい. また過去のある時点の1回かぎりの事実を表現する場合は was [were] able to を用いる // 私は終電に乗ることができた I *was able to* catch the last train.
(4)受身では can がふつう // その窓はあけることができなかった The window *could not* be opened.

彼女は100メートルを12秒で走ることができる She *can* [*is able to*] run 100 meters in 12 seconds.
私はクロールができない I *can't* [*I'm not able to*] swim the crawl.
私にできることであれば, 何でもやりますよ If there's anything I *can* do, I'll do it.
このパソコンを使うことができるのは山田だけだ Yamada is the only one who *can* really manage this personal computer.
やればできるじゃないか(→やったらできたじゃないか) You *could* do it if you tried.
一生懸命英語を勉強すれば英語の本を読むことができるようになるよ If you study English hard, you will *be able to* read books in English.
できることなら私が代わってあげたいのだが I wish I *could* do it for you.
3回目でやっとそのアプリケーションをインストールすることができた I *was* finally *able to* install the application on my third attempt.
◆せっかく空港まで見送りに行ったのに彼女に会うことができなかった I went all the way to the airport to see her off, but I *was unable to* see her. / このプログラムを使うと数秒でその計算をすることができる This program *is capable of* doing the calculation in a few seconds.

💬「今度の日曜日, パーティーに参加できる？」「残念だけど, 用があってだめなんだ」"*Can* you come to the party this Sunday?" "I'm sorry, but I can't. I have things to do."

💬「英語以外に何か外国語はできますか」「はい, 中国語ができます」"*Do* you *speak* any foreign languages besides English?" "Yes. I *can speak* Chinese."

❷【優秀である】
できる[できない]生徒 a *good* [*poor*] student

彼女は英語がよくできる(→得意だ) She *is good at* English./ (→成績がいい)She *is doing well in* English.

彼は数学ができない(→不得意だ) He *isn't good* [*is poor*] *at* math./ (→成績が悪い)He *is doing poorly in* math.

彼女は若いのによくできた女性だ She's *very mature* for someone so young. (❖mature は「分別のある」の意味)

山田さんはよくできる(→有能な)人だ Yamada is a *competent* person.

❸[作られる] be made of [from] ... (❖通例材料が変化せず残る場合は of, 加工され変化する場合は from を用いる); (建造される) be built; (組織される) be organized

豆腐は大豆からできる Tofu *is made from* soybeans.

このオルゴールはとてもよくできている This music box *is very well made*.

近くに新しい公園ができた A new park *was built* in the neighborhood.

私たちの学校に将棋クラブができた A *shogi* club *has been organized* at our school.

◆校門の前に新しいコンビニができた(→開店した) A new convenience store *has opened* across from the school gate.

❹[仕上がる] (完成する) be completed, finish ⾃; (準備が) be ready

そのサッカースタジアムは先月ようやくできた The soccer stadium *was* finally *completed* last month.

1か月前から作っていた自分のホームページがやっとできた I've finally *finished* my Web page that I've been working on since a month ago.

夕食の用意ができたよ Dinner's *ready*.

🔸「この写真いつできますか」「あさってになります」 "When *will* these pictures *be ready*?" "The day after tomorrow."

❺[起こる・生じる]

ほおにきびができた I *got* a pimple on my cheek.

雨上がりの道路にはあちこちに水たまりができていた *There were* some puddles here and there on the road after the rain.

彼女は美人なのになかなか彼氏ができない Even though she's beautiful, she *has hard time finding* a boyfriend.

彼女に赤ちゃんができた(→妊娠した) She *is pregnant*./ (→赤ちゃんが生まれた) She *had a baby*.

アメリカでもすぐに友達ができるよ You *will* soon *make friends* in America.

急用ができたので, いっしょにその映画を見に行けなくなりました Urgent business *has come up*, so I can't go to the movie with you.

❻[関係する]

彼らはきっとできてるよ(→つきあっている) I'm sure they're *going* [(→肉体関係がある) *sleeping*] *together*.

⇒ できるかぎり, できるだけ, できれば

できるかぎり 出来る限り できるかぎりのことはするつもりだ I'll do *whatever I can do* for you.

できるだけ 出来るだけ as ... as *one* can, as ... as possible //できるだけ早く帰ってきてね Come home *as soon as* 「*you can* [*possible*]./ できるだけたくさんの本を読みなさい Read *as many books as* 「*you can* [*possible*].

◆できるだけのことはした(→最善を尽くした) I did *my best*./ (→すべてした) I did *everything I could*./ あきらめる前にできるだけのことをしなさい Try *everything possible* before you give up.

てきれいき 適齢期 marriageable age ⓒ, a proper age for marriage //彼の娘は結婚適齢期だ His daughter is of *marriageable age*.

できれば 出来れば if (at all) possible, preferably //できればきょうの午後お目にかかりたいのですが I'd like to see you this afternoon, *if possible*./ 彼らは新築で, できれば職場の近くにある家を探していた They were looking for a new house, *preferably* near the office.

てぎわ 手際 絵美は手ぎわよく仕事を片づけた Emi did her job *efficiently* [(→素早く)*speedily*]./ 彼はまじめに働くがどうも手ぎわが悪い He works seriously but he's kind of *slow*.

てぐすね 彼女は彼が来たら文句を言おうと手ぐすねを引いて(→用意をして)待っていた She was waiting for him, all *set on* complaining to him.

てくせ 手癖 その子は手くせが悪い That child is *light-fingered*.

てぐち 手口 (やり方) method ⓒ, trick ⓒ; (犯罪などの) (公式的) modus operandi [móudəs ɑ̀pərǽndiː] Ⓤ (また a ~) ((略語) MO) //巧妙な手口 clever [skillful] *modus operandi*

でぐち 出口 exit ⓒ,《英》way out ⓒ (複 ways out) //出口の近くに立たないでください Don't stand near to the *exit*.
‖出口調査 an exit poll

てくてく 彼は美術館までバスに乗らずにてくてく(→全行程を)歩いた He walked *all the way* to the museum, not by bus.

テクニカル ‖テクニカルターム a technical term/ テクニカルノックアウト《ボクシング》a technical knockout《略語》TKO

テクニック technique [tekníːk] ⓒ; (こつ) (口語的) knack ⓤ (また a ~)
関連語 テクニシャン a technician

でくのぼう でくの坊 このでくのぼうめ! What *a loser*!

テクノロジー technology Ⓤ

てくび 手首 wrist ⓒ //手首を切る slash *one's wrists*/ 僕は彼の手首をつかんだ I took him by *the wrist*.

でくわす 出くわす come* across, happen to meet,《口語的》run* into ... //映画館で旧友に出くわした I *happened to meet* an old friend of mine at the movie theater.

てこ 梃子 lever ⓒ //てこの原理を応用する apply *the lever* principle

慣用表現 彼は一度決めたらてこでも動かない He won't budge an inch once he decides.

てこいれ 梃入れ ―てこ入れする（強化する・改善する）shore up, prop up ∥景気のてこ入れを行う *shore* [*prop*] *up* the economy

てごころ 手心（斟酌(しんしゃく)）allowance ⓤ ⓒ（しばしば複数形～s）；（考慮）consideration ⓤ ∥相手の年を考えて手心を加える *make allowance(s) for* the opponent's age

てこずる have* trouble (with ...), have a hard time ∥泣く子をあやすのにてこずる *have trouble* humoring a crying child ／ 彼は数学の勉強にてこずっている He *has a hard time* studying math.

てごたえ 手応え（反応）response ⓤ ⓒ；（効果）effect ⓒ ⓤ ∥あいつは何を言っても手ごたえのないやつだ He shows no *response* whatever I say to him. ／ 彼女は不買運動の呼びかけに対する確かな手ごたえを感じた She felt *a definite response* to her appeal for boycott. ／（釣りで）確かに手ごたえがあったんだが I'm sure I felt *a tug* on the line.（❖tug は「ぐいと引くこと」の意味）

でこぼこ 凸凹 ―でこぼこの rough, bumpy;（平らでない）uneven;（ごつごつした）rugged [rʌ́gɪd] ∥月の表面はでこぼこだ The face of the moon is *rough*. ／ 彼はでこぼこ道を自転車に乗っていった He rode a bicycle on the *rough* [*rugged*] road.

デコレーション（飾り）decoration ⓒ ⓤ ∥デコレーションケーキ a fancy [decorated] cake [❖「デコレーションケーキ」は和製英語]

てごろ 手頃 ―てごろな（使いやすい）handy;（値段が）reasonable,（ふさわしい）suitable ∥てごろな大きさの袋 a *handy-*sized bag ／ 彼女はてごろなエスニック料理の入門書を探していた She was looking for a *handy* guide to ethnic cooking. ／ 彼はギターをてごろな値段で手に入れた He got a guitar at a *reasonable* price. ／ パーティーを開くのにてごろなお店を知りませんか Do you know some restaurants *suitable* to have a party?

てごわい 手強い tough;（恐るべき）formidable;（頑強な）stubborn ∥今度の敵は手強いぞ Our next opponent is *tough* [*formidable*].

デザート dessert ⓒ ⓤ,《英口語的》afters ∥デザートにアイスクリームが出た Ice cream was served for [as] *dessert*.

デザイナー designer ⓒ ∥デザイナーズブランドの制服 a *designer* uniform
∥グラフィックデザイナー a graphic designer ／ 工業デザイナー an industrial designer ／ 服飾デザイナー a dress designer ／ ヘアデザイナー a hair stylist

デザイン design ⓒ ⓤ ―デザインする design ⓗ ⓘ ∥斬新(ざんしん)なデザインのドレス a dress of (*an*) original *design* ／ 彼はこの机を自分でデザインして作った He *designed* and made this desk by himself.

てさき 手先 ❶【手の先】彼女は手先が器用［不器用］だ She *is* good [*awkward*] *with her hands*. ／ She is「*dexterous* [*clumsy*] *with her hands*].

❷【手下】pawn ⓒ；（配下）agent ⓒ ∥彼は斉藤の手先だ He's Saito's *pawn*. ／ あいつはとうとう銀行強盗の手先に成り下がった At last he lowered himself to be *the agent* of the bank robbers.

でさき 出先 彼は出先から電話をかけてきた He gave me a phone call from *the place where he was*.
∥出先機関（官庁の）a local agency of the government;（会社の）a branch office

てさぎょう 手作業 handwork ⓤ ◆これらの民芸品はすべて手作業で作られています All these folk crafts are「made *by hand* [*hand-made*].

てさぐり 手探り 眼鏡を手探りで捜す「*feel about* [*grope*] *for one's* glasses ／ 彼らは洞穴の中を手探りで進んだ They *felt* [*groped*] *their way* in the cave. ／ 交渉はいまだに手探りの状態が続いている The negotiations *are still fumbling for a solution*.

てさげ 手提げ（袋）shopping [《米》tote] bag ⓒ;（かばん）briefcase ⓒ
∥手提げ金庫 a portable safe

てざわり 手触り the [a] feel, touch ⓤ ∥手ざわりがざらざらしている It's rough to *the feel*. ／ 絹は手ざわりがいい Silk「is soft to *the touch* [*feels* good]. ◆それは毛皮のような手ざわりがする It *feels* like fur.

でし 弟子（教え子）pupil ⓒ,（信奉者）disciple ⓒ, follower ⓒ;（見習い）apprentice ⓒ ∥有名なピアニストの弟子 *a pupil* of a famous pianist ／ 彼はだれひとりとして弟子をとらなかった He wouldn't take any *pupils*. ／ 彼は19のときにその料理人のところに弟子入りした He *became a pupil* [*an apprentice*] of the chef when he was 19.

てしお 手塩 彼らは一人娘を手塩にかけて育てた They brought up their only daughter *with special* [*tender loving*] *care*.

てしごと 手仕事 manual work ⓤ, handwork ⓤ;（手工芸）handiwork ⓤ

てした 手下 follower ⓒ, one's man,《軽蔑的》underling ⓒ;（集合的）following ⓒ ∥手下を引き連れて歩く walk with *his* [*her*] *following* behind

デジタル ―デジタルの digital ∥デジタルウオッチ a digital watch ／ デジタルオーディオテープ a digital audio tape (《略語》DAT) ／ デジタルカメラ a digital camera ／ デジタル通信 digital communication ／ デジタル放送 digital broadcasting ／ デジタル録音 (a) digital recording

てじな 手品（総称）magic ⓤ;（個々の）(magic) trick ⓒ ∥トランプの手品 *a card trick* ／ 彼はパーティーで手品をした He *performed magic* at the party. ／ 彼はその難しい問題を手品のように解いてしまった He solved the difficult problem like *a magic trick*.
∥手品師 a magician

でしゃばり 出しゃばり（おせっかいな人）meddler ⓒ, intruder ⓒ,《口語的》busybody ⓒ ―でしゃばりな meddlesome, in-

でしゃばる trusive, nosy ‖次郎はでしゃばりだ Jiro is *a meddler*. / (→何にでも首をつっ込みたがる)Jiro likes to *put his nose into everything*.

でしゃばる 出しゃばる butt in ..., put* *one's* nose into ... ‖知りもしないことにでしゃばるな *Don't butt in on* what you don't know!

てじゅん 手順 （手続き）procedure ⓊⒸ; （行程）process Ⓒ; （段取り）arrangements, plan Ⓒ ‖手順を踏む follow *a procedure* / この機械を組み立てる手順は比較的簡単だ *The process* for putting together this machine is relatively easy.

◆仕事を手際よく進める proceed with *one's* work *smoothly* / 彼が失敗したので仕事の手順が狂ってしまった His mistake upset *the order* of the tasks.

てじょう 手錠 handcuffs, 《口語的》cuffs
◆警官は容疑者に手錠をかけた The policeman *handcuffed* [*cuffed*] the suspect.

-でしょう will (❖「…と思う」の意味が強い場合は、I think, I'm afraid, I guess, I hope など発話の意図に応じた表現を用いる) ➡ -だろう
米国の学校を日本の学校と比較すれば多くの違いに気づくでしょう If you compare American schools with Japanese schools, you'll find many differences.

🅔「あしたは雨でしょうか」「おそらくそうでしょう」 "*Will* it rain tomorrow?" "*I'm afraid so*."

-です （断定）be (❖be 動詞を用いないで表現する場合も多い)
あすは休日です Tomorrow *is* [*will be*] a holiday.
今年の夏は暑いですね It's very hot this summer, isn't it?
◆きのうかぜをひいたので学校を休んだのです Yesterday I stayed home from school because of a cold. / きょうは学校はお休みです We have no school today. / クレーのこの絵が大好きです I *love* this painting by Klee.

🅔「ここにこの花びんを置いたのはだれ」「私です」 "Who put this vase here?" "*I did.*"

てすう 手数 trouble Ⓤ ➡てま
◆手数のかかる仕事 *troublesome* work / いつもお手数をおかけして申しわけありません I'm sorry to *trouble* you so often. / お手数ですが、駅へ行く道を教えてくれませんか *I'm sorry to trouble* [*bother*] *you*, but will you tell me the way to the station? / コンピュータのおかげでずいぶん手数が省けた My computer saved me a lot of *work*.

てすうりょう 手数料 （歩合）commission ⒸⓊ; （サービス料）(service) charge Ⓒ ‖料金には10パーセントの手数料が含まれています The price includes *a commission* of 10 percent.

ですが （逆接）but; （順接）and ➡ -が, だが ‖捜したのですが、かぎは見つかりませんでした I looked for the key, *but* I couldn't find it. / 故郷は日本ですが、ここは私の第二の故郷です My home is Japan, *and* this is my second home. ◆疲れたので少し休みたいのですが I'm tired, and *I'd like to* have a break.

🅔「もしもし、田中さんをお願いします」「私ですが」 "Hello. May I speak to Mr. Tanaka?" "*Speaking.*"

ですから so ➡ だから ‖あんなにピアノの練習をしたのですから、きっと発表会でもうまく弾けますよ You practiced the piano very hard, *so* you're sure to do well at the recital.

てすき 手すき お手すきなら手伝っていただきたいのですが I would like you to help me if you are *free*.

ですぎる 出過ぎる 出すぎたまねをするな Don't be *too meddlesome* [*nosy*].

デスク （机）desk Ⓒ; （新聞の編集部）《米》desk Ⓒ（通例 the ～）‖デスクトップコンピュータ a desktop computer / デスクワーク a desk job, desk work

テスト

test Ⓒ, exam Ⓒ, 《公式的》examination Ⓒ; （小テスト）《米》quiz Ⓒ ──テストする test ⊕ ⊜, give* a test
➡ しけん（試験）, 場面・状況別会話 p.1742

テストに受かる [落ちる] pass [fail] *a test* / 数学のテストを受ける take *a test* in math
きょう学校で英語のテストがあった We had *an English test* [*exam*] at school today. / We had *a test* [*an exam*] in English at school today.
彼はそのテストで90点を取った He got 90 (points) on the *exam*.
先生はテストの問題を配り始めた The teacher began distributing the *test* papers.
彼は新しいコンピュータの性能をテストした He *tested* the performance of the new computer.
毎週金曜日に英語の小テストがある We have *a quiz* in English every Friday.
母は私の期末テストの結果にがっかりした My mother was disappointed at the results of my *term exams*.
彼女は一生懸命英語のテスト勉強をした She *studied* very hard *for* the English *test*.

‖テストケース a test case / テストコース a test course / テストパイロット a test pilot / テストパターン a test pattern / 穴埋めテスト a fill-in-the-blanks test / 実力テスト an achievement test / 心理テスト a psychological test / 知能テスト a mental test, an intelligence test / ロールシャッハテスト a Rorschach test

てすり 手摺 handrail Ⓒ; （階段の）banisters; （ベランダ・橋などの）parapet ‖手すりにおつかまりください Hold on to *the handrail*, please. / 彼女は手すりから身を乗り出した She leaned out over *the parapet*.

てせい 手製 ──手製の handmade; （自家製の）homemade (❖「粗末な」という悪い意味合いもある); （手編みの）hand-knit ‖お手製のパイ a *homemade* pie

てぜま 手狭 この家は私たちには少し手狭になってきた This house has become a little *too small* for us.

てそう 手相 the lines on *one's* palm ∥よい手相をしている have lucky *lines on one's palm* ◆手相を見てあげよう Let me *read your palm.*
‖手相占い palmistry / 手相占い師 a palmist, a palm reader

でぞめしき 出初め式 the New Year Parade of the firefighters

でそろう 出揃う いつもの顔が出そろった All regulars「*got together* [*were present*].

てだし 手出し 先に手出しをした(→けんかを始めた)ほうが悪い The person who *started the fight* is wrong. / 手出しは無用 *Stay away from it.* / 彼女は決して余計な手出しをしない(→自分のすべきことを心得ている) She *knows her business very well.*

でだし 出だし (開始) the start; (初め) the beginning ∥好調な出だしを切る make [get off to] *a* good *start* [*beginning*] / その曲の出だしはとても印象的だ *The start* [*beginning*] of the music is very impressive.

てだすけ 手助け help [U], assistance [U], 《公式的》aid [U] ──手助けする help [他] [自], 《公式的》assist [他], 《公式的》aid [他] ∥彼は強盗が銀行に侵入するのを手助けしたとされる It is said that he *assisted* [*helped*] the robber to break into the bank.

てだて 手立て measures ∥早急に事故を減らす手立てを講じる必要がある We need to take *measures* to reduce accidents at once.

でたて 出立て 彼女は大学出たてだ She is *fresh from* college.

でたとこしょうぶ 出たとこ勝負 こうなったら出たとこ勝負だ(→すべてを運に任せよう) Now that I'm in this situation, I'm going to *leave all to chance.*

てだま 手玉 彼女はすっかり彼を手玉にとっている She *twists* him *around her* (*little*) *finger.*/ She's *got* him *under her thumb.*

でたらめ nonsense [U]; (うそ) lie [C] ──でたらめな (うその) false; (成り行きまかせの) random, haphazard ∥でたらめを言うな Don't talk *nonsense.* / 彼女は僕にでたらめな電話番号を教えた She gave me a *false* number. / あいつの言っていることはみんなでたらめだ What he says is all *lies* [《俗語》*bullshit*]. ◆この記事は全くのでたらめだ(→真実のかけらもない) There's *not a bit of truth* in this article.

てぢか 手近 ──手近な[に] (near) at hand, (close) at hand; (身近な) familiar ∥手近な例を挙げる give a *familiar* example / 私はいつも手近に辞書を置いている I always keep a dictionary (*close*) *at hand.*

てちがい 手違い mistake [C]; (ちょっとした) slip [C], 《口語的》slip-up [C] ∥ちょっとした手違いで計画がだめになってしまった Our plan was spoiled by *a slip.* / 私どもの手違いで皆様には多大なご迷惑をおかけいたしました We're very sorry to have troubled you so much because of our *mistakes.*

てちょう 手帳 (pocket) notebook [C]; (日付入りの) (pocket) diary [C] ∥彼女の電話番号を手帳に書き留めた I wrote down her telephone number in *my notebook.*
‖生徒手帳 a student's handbook, a student ID

てつ 鉄 〖化学〗iron [U] (❖元素記号 Fe); (鋼鉄) steel [U] ──鉄の iron ∥鉄の意志をもつ男 a man of *iron* will / 鉄はさびやすい *Iron* rusts easily. / このなべは鉄製ですか *Is* this pot *made of iron?*
‖鉄亜鈴 a pair of iron dumbbells / 鉄鉱石 ironstone / 鉄製品 ironwork / くず鉄 scrap iron / 製鉄 iron manufacturing
[ことわざ] 鉄は熱いうちに打て Strike while the iron is hot.

てっかい 撤回 withdrawal [U] [C] ──撤回する《公式的》withdraw* [他], take* back ∥前言の撤回 *the withdrawal of* previous remarks / 彼は要求を撤回することを拒否した He refused to「*take back* [*withdraw*] his claim.

てつがく 哲学 philosophy [U] ──哲学的な philosophical ∥ライプニッツの哲学 *the philosophy* of Leibniz; *the* Leibnizian *philosophy* / 「自分に正直であれ」というのが私の人生哲学です "Be honest to yourself": that's my *philosophy of life.*
‖哲学者 a philosopher / 哲学書 a philosophy book

てつかず 手付かず ──手つかずの untouched; (未使用の) unused ∥その島の自然は手つかずのまま残されている The natural environment of the island is left *untouched.* ◆まだ手つかずの宿題が残っている There is still some homework *which isn't started.*

てづかみ 手摑み …を手づかみで食べる eat … *with one's fingers* / 彼はその魚を手づかみにしようとした He tried to *catch* the fish *with his hands.*

てっかん 鉄管 (細い) iron tube [C]; (太い) iron pipe [C]

てっき 鉄器 《集合的》ironware [U]; (金物) 《集合的》hardware [U] ‖鉄器時代 the Iron Age

てつき 手付き hand [C] ∥慣れた手つきで *with* practiced *hands* / 忠はぎこちない手つきで鉛筆を削った Tadashi sharpened the pencil「*with* clumsy *hands* [*clumsily, awkwardly*].

デッキ (船の) deck [C]; (バス・列車の) platform [C]; (テープデッキ) (tape) deck [C] ∥デッキに出る go up *on deck*

デッキチェア deck chair [C], 《米》beach chair [C]

てっきょ 撤去 removal [U] [C]; (解体) dismantlement [U] ──撤去する remove [他]; (機械などを) dismantle [他]; (建物などを) demolish [他] ∥地雷を撤去する *remove* mines / 旧庁舎の撤去作業が始まった They started to *demolish* the old government building.

てっきょう 鉄橋 steel bridge [C]; (鉄道の) 《米》railroad [《英》railway] bridge [C]

てっきり 僕はてっきり彼女が新しい英語の先生なのだろうと思っていた I thought she was *surely* [*certainly*] our new English teacher. / 私はてっきりそれを彼のいつもの冗談だと思った I *put* it *down as* his usual type of joke.

てっきん 鉄筋 reinforcing bar ©
∥鉄筋コンクリート reinforced concrete

でつくす 出尽くす もうアイディアは出尽くしたよ I *ran out of* ideas.

てづくり 手作り ——手作りの (手製の) handmade; (自家製の) homemade (◆「粗末な」という悪い意味合いもある) ∥手作りのケーキ *homemade* cake / このおもちゃはどれも手作りだ All of these toys are *handmade*.

てつけ(きん) 手付け(金) deposit ©, 【法律】earnest money ⓤ ∥彼らは家の手付金を打った They *paid [made, put down] a deposit on* their house.

てっこう 鉄鋼 steel ⓤ
∥鉄鋼業 the steel industry

てっこうじょ 鉄工所 ironworks《単数または複数扱い》, iron factory ©

てっこつ 鉄骨 steel [iron] frame ©

デッサン ⚠(下絵) sketch ©; (概略的な絵) rough drawing © (◆日本語はフランス語の dessin から)
• リンゴのデッサンをする *sketch* an apple

てっしゅう 撤収(撤退) withdrawal ⓤ ——撤収する withdraw* ⓗ

てつじょうもう 鉄条網 barbed wire fence © ∥その研究所は鉄条網で張りめぐらされている The laboratory is surrounded by *a barbed wire fence*.

てつじん 鉄人 iron man © ∥鉄人レース an *iron man* race ◆料理の鉄人 a *master* chef (◆この master は「名人の, 一流の」の意味)

てっする 徹する 彼は夜を徹して勉強した I studied *all night*. / あの店は金もうけに徹している That shop *devotes itself to* moneymaking.

てっせん 鉄線 (針金) steel wire ⓤ; 【植物】clematis © ∥有刺鉄線 barbed wire

てっそく 鉄則 hard-and-fast rule © ∥英語で文の最初の文字は大文字というのが鉄則だ It's *a hard-and-fast rule* in English that the first letter of a sentence is a capital letter.

てったい 撤退 withdrawal ⓤ© ——撤退する withdraw* ⓗ; (特に軍隊の) pull out ∥香港の中国への返還に伴い多くの企業が市場から撤退することを決定した Many companies decided to *withdraw from* the Hong Kong market due to the reunification with China. / 全軍がその地域から撤退した All troops *pulled out of* the area.

てつだい 手伝い (行為) help ⓤ; (人) help(er) ©; (家政婦) housekeeper © ∥お手伝いさんを雇う employ *a housekeeper*
◆何かお手伝いしましょうか Is there anything I can「*help* you with [*do for* you]?

てつだう 手伝う

help ⓗ; (手を貸す) give* [lend*] *a person* a hand; (補佐する) assist ⓗ
君の仕事を手伝うよ I'll *help* you *with* your work. (◆help の目的語は常に人で手伝う内容は with の後に置く)
仕事を手伝ってくれて本当にありがとう Thank you for *helping* me *in* my work. (✿help が動名詞の場合は in を用いる)
彼らは私のかばんを捜すのを手伝ってくれた They *helped* me (*to*) find my bag.
彼女はベッドで体を起こすのを手伝ってもらった She *was helped to* sit up in bed. (✿受身の場合 to を省略することはできない)
このソファーを動かすのを手伝ってよ *Help* me move this sofa. / *Give* me *a hand to* move this sofa.

◆もともと病弱だったところに過労も手伝って彼女は今入院しています Overwork *aggravated* her poor health and she's hospitalized now. (✿aggravate は「悪化させる」の意味)

でっちあげ でっち上げ (作り事) fabrication ©; (作り話) fiction ⓤ, 【口語的】story ©; (人を罪に陥れる) 【口語的】frame-up © ∥とんでもない。それは彼のでっちあげだ No way! That's his *story*.

でっちあげる でっち上げる (話などを) 【口語的】make* [cook] up, fabricate ⓗ (犯人に) frame ⓗ ∥話をでっちあげる *make* [*cook*] *up* a story / 彼は犯人にでっちあげられてしまった He's *been framed*.

てつづき 手続き procedure ⓤ©; (法律・慣習上の) formalities; (訴訟の) proceedings
(飛行機などの) 搭乗手続き the boarding *procedure* / 手続きを踏まずに without *a procedure* / …に対する訴訟の手続きをする take [start] *proceedings* against …
2月20日までに入学手続きをすませなければならない We must complete *entrance procedures for* the school by February 20.
ビザを取得するには煩雑な手続きが必要だ You need to go through complicated *formalities* to get a visa.

てってい 徹底 ——徹底的な (完璧(ﾍﾟｷ)な) complete; (細部に至る所まで) thorough; (根本的な) radical ——徹底的に completely; thoroughly; (骨の髄まで) to the bone
彼は徹底した菜食主義者だ He's a *complete* vegetarian.
そのホテルはサービスが徹底している The hotel has *thorough* service.
彼女はすべてにおいて徹底しすぎている She is too *thorough* in everything.
今回の事故の原因についてはもう一度徹底的に調べ直す必要がある We have to *thoroughly* investigate the cause of this accident once again.
この継続的な不況を切り抜けるには徹底した改革が必要だ We need *radical* reform to get out of this prolonged recession.
彼女の教育方針は徹底してエリート主義だ She is elitist *to the bone* in her educational policy.

◆その男の子は徹底的にこらしめる (→その男の子に教訓を与える) べきだ We should *teach* the boy *a good lesson*. / 社長は省エネを徹底するようにとの通達を出した The president issued a notice that everyone should *be concerned about* energy-saving.

てっとう 鉄塔 steel tower ©; (高圧線用の)

pylon ◯

てつどう 鉄道 《米》railroad ◯, 《英》railway

鉄道を敷設する lay *a railroad* / 鉄道を開通させる open *a railroad*
オーストラリアでは鉄道網があまり発達していない *Railroads* are [*The railroad network* is] not well developed in Australia.
◆大雪のために東京の鉄道機能がまひした *Train services* in Tokyo were paralyzed by the heavy snow.
‖鉄道員 a railroad worker / 鉄道運賃 a railroad fare / 鉄道会社 a railroad company / 鉄道警察官 a railroad police officer / 鉄道工事 railroad work / 鉄道作業員 《米》a tracklayer, 《英》a platelayer / 鉄道事故 a railroad accident

てっとうてつび 徹頭徹尾 （徹底的に）completely, thoroughly; （始めから終わりまで）from beginning to end /私はいかなる核実験にも徹頭徹尾反対です I'm *completely* against all nuclear testing.

デッドヒート （接戦）dead heat ◯（◆同着の意味も含む）, close race [game, contest] ◯ / 2人のマラソン選手はゴール直前までデットヒートを繰り広げた The two marathon runners *were in a* 「*dead heat* [*close race*] up to the finish line.

デッドボール ⚠ そのピンチヒッターはデッドボールで一塁へ出た The pinch hitter *was hit by a pitch* and got to first. (◆英語の a dead ball は「ファウルなどでプレーの進行を停止させるボール」の意味)

てっとりばやい 手っ取り早い 英語が話せるようになる手っとり早い方法を知りませんか Do you know a *quick and easy* way to learn to speak English? / 手っとり早く言えば, あなたとはもう会いたくないのです *In short*, I don't want to see you again.

デッドロック deadlock ⓤ /両社の交渉はデッドロックに乗り上げた The negotiations between the two companies 「*came to a deadlock* [*were deadlocked*].

でっぱ 出っ歯 bucktooth ◯ (通例複数形 buckteeth) /姉は出っ歯だ My sister has *buckteeth*. / My sister is *buck-toothed*.

てっぱい 撤廃 （廃止）abolition ⓤ ——撤廃する abolish ⓗ; （規則などを解除する）lift ⓗ /輸入制限を撤廃する *abolish* import restrictions

でっぱなし 出っ放し 台所の水が出っぱなしだったよ You *left the water running* in the kitchen.

でっぱり 出っ張り （突起部分）projection ◯

でっぱる 出っ張る （突き出る）stick* out, 《公式的》project 画 / くぎが出っ張っている A nail *is sticking out*.

てっぱん 鉄板 iron [steel] plate ◯ⓤ; （薄い板）iron [steel] sheet ◯ⓤ, sheet metal ⓤ
‖鉄板焼き meat and vegetables grilled on a griddle

でっぷり fat; (かっぷくのよい) stout, portly (◆いずれも fat の婉曲的用法) /でっぷりとした ご婦人 a *portly* lady

てつぶん 鉄分 iron ⓤ /鉄分の多い食べ物 food which is rich in *iron*

てっぺい 撤兵 ——撤兵する 「pull out [withdraw*] *one's* troops

てっぺん 天辺 the top; (山頂) the summit /その少年は木のてっぺんまで登った The boy climbed up to *the top* of the tree.
慣用表現 彼女のファッションは頭のてっぺんから足の先まで完璧(%%)だ She dresses perfectly *from head to foot*.

てつぼう 鉄棒 (体操用の) horizontal bar ◯ (◆器械体操用の高い鉄棒を a high bar, 公園などにあるものを単に a bar ともいう); (鉄の棒) iron bar ◯ /体育の授業では最も鉄棒が苦手だ *Bar exercise* is my worst activity in PE class.

てっぽう 鉄砲 gun ◯ /シカをねらって鉄砲を撃つ fire *a gun* at a deer
‖鉄砲水 a flash flood

てづまり 手詰まり deadlock ⓤ /手詰まりの状況がもうだいぶ続いている The situation has been at *a deadlock* for quite a while.

てつや 徹夜 ——徹夜する stay [sit*] up all night /宿題を仕上げるためゆうべは徹夜した I *stayed up all night* last night to finish my homework.
◆徹夜作業 all-night work; 《米口語的》an all-nighter / 徹夜でテレビゲームをする play video games *all* [*throughout the*] *night*

でてくる 出て来る いろいろな意見が出てきた We've *heard* lots of different ideas. / 捜していた本が出てきた I *found* the book I've been looking for.

でどころ 出所 (情報などの) source ◯ /私はそのうわさの出所を知っている I know *the source* of the rumor. ◆彼は金の出所(→どのように金を手に入れたのか)を隠している He doesn't say 「*how he got* the money [*where* the money came from].

てどり 手取り (給料の) take-home pay ⓤ; (実質的な収入) net income ⓤ; (税引き後) after-tax income /手取りで30万円だ My salary is 300,000 yen *net* [*after taxes*].

てとりあしとり 手取り足取り 兄はガールフレンドに手取り足取りゴルフを教えた My brother *kindly* taught his girlfriend *step by step* how to play golf.

デトロイト Detroit (◆米国の都市)

テナー → テノール

てなおし 手直し (部分的修正) modification ⓤ◯; (改良) improvement ⓤ◯; (全体的修正) revision ⓤ◯ ——手直しする modify ⓗ; improve ⓗ; revise ⓗ /あなたの小説はちょっとした手直しでずっとよくなる Your novel will be much better with a little *modification*. / 君の論文は手直しが必要だ Your paper needs to *be revised* [*modified*].

でなおす 出直す (戻ってくる) come* back; (再び立ち寄る) call ... again; (新しく始める) make* a new [fresh] start, start (all) over again /彼女は一から出直す決心をした

She decided to 「*start* (*all*) *over again* [*make a new life*].

💬「店長は今食事で出ています」「ではまた後で出直します」"The manager is out for lunch at the moment." "*I'll come back* later then."

てなげだん 手投げ弾 ➔てりゅうだん

てなずける 手懐ける (味方に引き入れる) win* over; (動物を) tame [他] ∥野生の象を手なずける *tame* a wild elephant / 彼を手なずけておいて損はないよ You won't regret *winning* him *over*.

てなみ 手並み

💬「言っとくけどテレビゲームにかけてはちょっとしたもんだよ」「じゃあお手並み拝見といきますか」"Mind you, I'm an expert at video games." "Well, well, let's *see how good you are*."

てならい 手習い (習い事) learning [U]

[慣用表現] 六十の手習い *It's never too late to learn*. (→学ぶのに遅すぎることはない)

てなれた 手慣れた 小さい子供の世話をするのは手慣れている I'*m used to* looking after small children. / さすが手慣れたものですね You are *an expert*.

テナント tenant [C] (❖英米ではアパートなどの借家人のことも指す) ◆テナント募集《掲示》《米》*For Rent*; 《英》*To Let*

テニス tennis [U] ∥テニスをする play *tennis* / 私はテニスの試合でソフィーとペアを組んだ I was paired with Sophy for *the tennis match*.

‖テニスコート a tennis court / テニスシューズ tennis shoes / テニス選手 a tennis player / 軟式テニス tennis played with a soft ball (❖軟式テニスは日本で考案されたもので, 欧米では tennis といえば硬式テニスのこと)

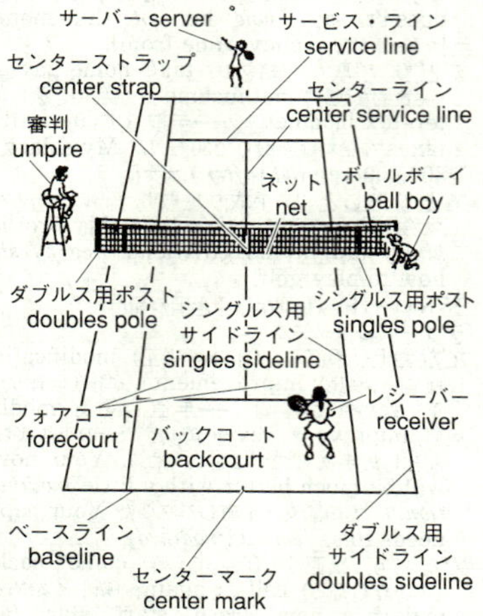
サーバー server
サービス・ライン
service line
センターストラップ
center strap
センターライン
center service line
審判
umpire
ネット
net
ボールボーイ
ball boy
ダブルス用ポスト
doubles pole
シングルス用ポスト
singles pole
シングルス用
サイドライン
singles sideline
レシーバー
receiver
フォアコート
forecourt
バックコート
backcourt
ベースライン
baseline
センターマーク
center mark
ダブルス用
サイドライン
doubles sideline

デニム denim [U] ∥デニムのシャツ a *denim* shirt ◆デニムのジーンズ《口語的》*denims*

てにもつ 手荷物 《主に米》baggage [U], 《主に英》(hand) luggage [U] (❖数えるときは a piece of ... とする) ∥手荷物を預ける check *one's baggage* / (機内)持ち込み手荷物はありますか Do you have any carry-on *baggage*?

‖手荷物預り所 (駅などの)《米》a baggage room, a checkroom, 《英》a left luggage (office); (劇場などの) a cloakroom / 手荷物預り証 a claim tag

てぬい 手縫い ―手縫いの hand-sewn ∥手縫いのゆかた a *hand-sewn yukata*

てぬかり 手抜かり (見落とし) oversight [C] [U]; (落ち度) fault [C] ∥どんな手抜かりも許されない We cannot afford any *oversights*. / それは私の手抜かりでした That was my *fault*.

てぬき 手抜き おいしい料理を作るには手抜きをしないことだ *Don't cut corners* if you want to make good food. / 彼の仕事はいつも手抜きだ (→中途半端にやる) He always *does his work halfway*.

‖手抜き工事 construction work with some corner-cutting

てぬぐい 手拭い 🗻 a *tenugui*, a thin Japanese-style (hand) towel

てぬるい 手緩い (甘い) soft; (寛大な) 《公式的》lenient ∥あの先生は生徒に手ぬるい The teacher *is soft with* students. / その刑罰は手ぬるすぎる The punishment is too *lenient*.

テネシー Tennessee (❖米国中南部の州; 《略語》Tenn., 〔郵便〕TN)

てのうち 手の内 *one's* hand [cards] ∥手の内を見せるほど私はばかじゃないよ I'm not so silly as to *show* you *my hand*.

テノール 〔音楽〕 tenor [U] [C] (❖ドイツ語から)

‖テノール歌手 a tenor

てのひら 手の平・掌 palm [C], the flat of *one's* hand ∥その猿は手のひらにのるほど小さい The monkey is so tiny that it can sit on *your palm*. ◆手のひらで水をすくう cup water with *one's hands*

[慣用表現] 手のひらを返すように (→急に) 態度を変える change *one's* attitude *abruptly* [(→完全に) *completely*]

デノミ(ネーション) ⚠ (通貨切り下げ) redenomination downward [U]; (通貨改革) currency reform [U] (❖英語の denomination は「貨幣単位」の意味)

◆ロシアの大統領はデノミを実施した (→ルーブルの価値を引き下げた) The President of Russia *has devalued the ruble*.

-ては 父は新しいライターを買ってはすぐになくしてしまう My father *keeps* buying a new lighter and losing it right away. / ばれてしまってはしかたがない. すべて話そう There's nothing to do but to tell you all about it *now that* you've already found out. / そんなことを言われてはだれだって頭にくる Everyone would get angry *if* such a thing were said.

では (話題を変えて) well; (次の話題へ) all right, OK; (ひと段落ついて) now; (話題を引

き継いで) then (❖日本語と英語は必ずしも上記のとおりに一致しないので，状況に応じて使い分けることが必要)

💬「きょうはいろいろとどうもありがとうございました」「ではまたお会いしましょう」 "Thank you very much for everything today." "(*Well*,) let's get together again."

💬「そのことに関して反対意見はありません」「では次の議題へ進みます」 "We have no objection to that." "*All right*, we'll move on to the next topic."

💬「全員食事から戻りました」「では午後の部を始めましょう」 "Everyone's back from lunch." "*Now* [*OK*], shall we start the afternoon session?"

💬「車がまだ修理から戻ってきていません」「ではドライブは来週末にしましょう」 "The car hasn't been fixed yet." "*Then* [*Well, then*] we'll take a drive next weekend."

-では

❶【関して】

彼はその点では安心です He's trustworthy *in* that respect.

ディベートでは吉田の右に出る者はいない *When it comes to* debating, no one can beat Yoshida.

❷【判断】

天気予報では午後に雨が降るらしい *According to* the weather forecast, it will rain in the afternoon. / The weather forecaster *says* it will rain in the afternoon.

私の意見では今回は取りやめたほうがいい *In* my opinion, we should cancel it this time.

彼の健康状態では運動をするのはまだ無理でしょう *Judging from* his health, I don't think he can exercise yet.

💬「しまった！ 3時から映画を録画しようと思ってたのに」「私の時計ではまだ5分前ですよ」 "Oh, no! I was going to record a movie at three." "It's still five to, *by* my watch."

❸【時間・場所】

あすでは遅すぎる．きょうやりなさい Tomorrow is too late. Do it today.

そのころ浩の家ではパーティーが開かれていた At that time, a party was being held *at* Hiroshi's house.

北海道では冬の終わりだが，沖縄ではもう初夏だ *In* Hokkaido the winter is drawing to a close while it's already the beginning of summer *in* Okinawa.

❹【対比・強調】

英語では通じなかったので，下手なフランス語で話した People didn't understand English, so I used my poor French.

💬「山田はまだ来ないのか」「コーチ，私ではだめですか」 "Hasn't Yamada arrived yet?" "Coach, how about me?"

💬「これで十分ですか」「それでは全然足りないよ」 "Is this enough?" "No, that's not enough at all."

デパート ⚠department store [C] (❖×depart とはいわない)

デパートへ買い物に行く go shopping at *a department store*

てはい 手配 (組織的・計画的な) arrangements; (警察の捜索) search [C] ━手配する arrange [他] [自]; search for ... ∥応援の者を何人かそちらに送るように手配します I'*ll arrange* to send some helpers to you. / タクシーの手配をしてあります I'*ve arranged for* a taxi. / 忘年会の手配はすべて幹事に任せてある We've asked an organizer to make all *arrangements for* a year-end party. / 警察は手配中の車を見つけた The police found the car that they *were searching for*.

◆その男は誘拐の容疑で警察に指名手配されている That man *is wanted* by the police for kidnapping.

ではいり 出入り 人の出入りが多いので防犯に気をつけている We're careful about security because people keep *coming in and out*. / 彼は私の家に自由に出入りしている He has *the run* of my house. / トムは不品行のためにクラブへの出入りを禁じられた Tom *was barred from* the club for bad behavior.

てはじめ 手始め ━手始めに first of all; (始めるにあたり) to begin with ∥手始めにこの問題から解いてみよう *First of all*, let's work on this question.

てはず 手筈 (手配・準備) arrangements; (計画) plan [C] ∥我々は結婚式の手はずを整えた We'*ve* 「*made the arrangements* [*arranged*] *for* our wedding.

◆彼女が彼とデートできるよう手はずを整えてあげた I'*ve arranged for* her *to* go out on a date with him. / これで手はずはすべて整った It's all *arranged* now.

でばな 出端 我々は先制点を取って，相手の出ばなをくじいた We scored first and *took the wind out of* their *sails*. (❖take the wind out of a person's sails は「人を出し抜く」の意味) / 雨のため，富士山に登る計画の出ばなをくじかれた The rain *put a damper* on my plan to climb Mt. Fuji.

てばなし 手放し 私は手放しで自転車に乗ることができない I can't ride a bicycle *with no hands*.

[慣用表現] 姉の大学合格の知らせにみんな手放しで喜んだ We *were overjoyed* at the news that my sister was admitted to a university. / 昇給したとはいえ税金も上がると思うと手放しでは喜べない I *can't be completely happy* about my raise because I'll just have to pay more taxes.

てばなす 手放す (物を) part with ...; (譲る) give* up; (売る) sell* [他] ∥その子犬を手放すのはつらい It's sad to *part with* the puppy. / 彼は必要に迫られて土地を手放した He *gave up* his land from necessity. / 彼女は5万円で指輪を手放した She 「*sold* a ring [*let* a ring *go*] for 50,000 yen.

◆現代社会で生きていくには携帯電話は手放せない (→必需品である) Cell phones *are necessities* for living in today's society.

でばぼうちょう 出刃庖丁 kitchen knife ◎

てばやい 手早い quick ——手早く quickly / 手早く荷造りをすませた I *quickly* packed up.

ではらう 出払う あいにく両親は今出払っています I'm afraid my parents *are both out* now.

でばん 出番 *one's turn* / 出番を待っている間はすごく緊張する I get very nervous while waiting for *my turn*.
◆マイク，ここで君の出番となるわけだ This is *where you come in*, Mike. / 僕の出番はなかった I had no *opportunity to play*.

てびき 手引き (案内書) handbook ◎, guidebook ◎; (指導書) manual ◎ / 夏山登山の手引き a *handbook* on summer mountain climbing / 実験の手引き a laboratory *manual*

てひどい 手ひどい 彼はその国で手ひどい扱いを受けた He was treated *terribly* in that country.

デビュー debut [deibjúː] ◎ / あの女優は10歳でデビューした That actress *made her debut* at 10 years old.
◆デビュー曲 *one's first song*

てびょうし 手拍子 お年寄りたちは手拍子をとりながら歌った Old people sang while「*beating time with their hands* [*clapping to the beat*].

てびろく 手広く (規模などが) on a large scale; (範囲が) extensively / おじは手広く商売をしている My uncle does business *on a large scale*.

でぶ (口語的) fatty ◎, 《口語的》fatso ◎

てぶくろ 手袋 (各指が分かれた) gloves; (親指だけが分かれた) mittens《❖共に数えるときは a pair of ... とする》/ ゴム手袋をはめる[はずす]「put on [take off] *rubber gloves*」/ 私たちは手袋をしたまま握手した We shook hands with *our gloves on*. / この手袋は左と右が違う These *gloves don't match*.

でぶしょう 出無精・出不精 (人) stay-at-home ◎ / 父は出無精だ My father is *a stay-at-home*.

てぶら 手ぶら 魚釣りに行って手ぶらで帰ってきた I went fishing, but came home *empty handed*. / どうぞ手ぶらで来てください Please *just bring yourself*.

てぶり 手振り (しぐさ) gesture ◎ ⇒ みぶり

デフレ(ーション) deflation ◎

でべそ 出臍 protruding navel ◎

てべんとう 手弁当 彼らは手弁当で(→自費で)地元候補を応援した They supported their local candidate *at their own expense*.

てほどき 手解き first lessons; (秘伝などの) initiation ◎ / 恋の手ほどきを友達の姉さんから受けた I received *my first lessons* in love from a friend's sister.
◆私は彼にスキーの手ほどきをしてもらった I *was initiated into* skiing by him. / He *taught me how to ski*.

てぼり 手彫り hand-carving ◎
◆手彫りの人形 a *hand-carved* doll

てほん 手本 (模範) model ◎; (典型) pattern ◎; (例) example ◎ / 子供たちに手本を示す set *a model* [*an example*] for children / 天文学は最も早く発展し，あらゆる科学の手本となった Astronomy was developed first and became *a model* for all other sciences. / 弟のよいお手本になりなさい Be *a good example* for your younger brother. / 私は母をお手本にした I *followed the example of* my mother. / 彼は私が政治家としてお手本とする人だ He is my *role model* as a politician.

てま 手間 (時間) time ◎; (手数) trouble ◎; (努力) effort ◎ ◎; (労力) labor,《英》labour ◎ ⇒ てまどる / 手間を省く save *time and labor* / お手間はとらせません It won't take much of *your time*. / この花は手間暇かけて育てただけのことはある It was worth *putting in a lot of time and effort* to grow these flowers. / この機械を組み立てるのはとても手間がかかる It's *a lot of trouble* to assemble this machine.
🍩「きのうはんこを忘れたのできょうまた区役所に行かなきゃならないんだ」「とんだ二度手間だね」"I forgot to bring my personal seal yesterday, so I have to go to the ward office again today." "Too bad you have to *make another trip*."
‖手間賃 wages

デマ ⚠ (根拠のない) groundless [false] rumor [《英》rumour] ◎《❖日本語はドイツ語の Demagogie から》/ あすは学校はないというデマが飛んだ There was a *groundless rumor* that we will have no school tomorrow. / それは結局デマだった It turned out to be *a false rumor*.

てまえ 手前
❶[こちら側] this side; (写真・絵などの前景) the foreground
私たちは橋の手前で花火見物をした We watched the fireworks *on this side* of the bridge.
その写真の手前で眼鏡をかけている人が岡田さんです The man wearing glasses in *the foreground* in the photo is Mr. Okada.
◆あの女の子は毎朝私の降りる駅の1つ手前で降りる That girl gets off the train one station *before* mine every morning. / この戸は手前に引けば開きます Pull the door and it will open. / 会社は破産の一歩手前だ The company is *on the brink of* bankruptcy.
🍩「すみません，郵便局はどこですか」「コンビニの手前を左に曲がった所です」"Excuse me. Could you tell me where the post office is?" "Turn left just *before* the convenience store."
❷[体裁]
彼女がいる手前，映画を見て泣けなかった I couldn't cry at the movie *in the presence of* my girlfriend.
大口をたたいた手前バンジージャンプをする羽目になった Since I talked big, I had to go bungee-jumping.

でまえ 出前 demae, delivery serv-

ice; (パーティーなどへの) catering service
◆寿司(すし)の出前をとろう Let's *have* sushi *delivered.*
‖出前持ち a delivery person

日本のそば屋，寿司屋，ラーメン屋などは出前のときに店で使うのと同じ食器を使います．そして食べ終わった食器を玄関の前に置いておけば取りにきてもらえます．
When restaurants in Japan especially for *soba*, sushi or ramen deliver food, they use regular plates and bowls that are supposed to be left outside the front door after the meal for the shop to come and pick up.

てまえがって 手前勝手 ──手前勝手な selfish, self-centered ◆手前勝手な行動をとる act [behave] *selfishly*

てまえみそ 手前味噌 手前味噌ですが，私は大学３年のとき司法試験に受かりました It may sound like I'm *blowing my own trumpet* [*horn*], but I passed the National Bar Examination when I was in my third [《米》junior] year at university. (❖ blow *one's* own trumpet [horn] は口語的表現で「自画自賛する」の意味)

でまかせ 出任せ あの男は口から出まかせばかり言う (→言うことが無責任だ) What he says is always *irresponsible.*/ (→何も考えずに話す) He always speaks *without thinking.*

でまど 出窓 bay window [C]

てまどる 手間取る take* time (❖事柄が主語になる)， spend* a lot of time (❖人が主語になる) ‖この問題に答えるのに手間どった It *took* me *time* to answer this question./ I *spent a lot of time* to answer this question.
◆どうしてそんなに手間どったの What *has kept* you so *long*?

てまね 手真似 gesture [C]

てまねき 手招き beckoning [U] ──手招きする beckon [他] ‖彼女はカウンターに来るよう私に手招きした She *beckoned* me (over) to the counter.

てまわし 手回し (準備) preparations; (手配) arrangements ──手回しする prepare [自]; arrange [他] [自] ◆太郎君は手回しがいいね Taro, you *are* always *well-prepared.*

てまわりひん 手回り品 *one's* belongings ‖お手回り品をお忘れなく Don't forget *your belongings.*

でまわる 出回る (市場に現れる) be [appear] on the market ‖６月にはサクランボが出回る Cherries *will be on the market* in June.
◆日本では偽のブランド品が大量に出回っている A lot of fake brand-name items *are available* in Japan.

てみじか 手短 ──手短な (文章などが短い) short; (簡潔な) brief ──手短に briefly ‖手短に言えば *in short* [*brief*] / そのことを手短に説明した I explained the matter *briefly.*/ I gave a *brief* [*short*] explanation of the matter.

でみせ 出店 (露店) stall [C], stand [C], booth [C]

てみやげ 手土産 present [C], gift [C]

でむかえ 出迎え 駅まで出迎えに行きますよ I'*ll come to meet* you at the station.

でむかえる 出迎える come* to meet *a person*; (公式に) receive [他]; (歓迎する) welcome [他], greet [他] ‖彼は満面に笑みを浮かべて私たちを出迎えた He *greeted* us with a big smile.

でむく 出向く go* [come*] to ... (❖話している相手の所へ出向くときは come を使う) ‖彼は月に１回アメリカの本社へ出向く He *goes to* the head office in the U.S. once a month. / こちらから出向きます I'*ll come to* your place.

デメリット (不利な点) disadvantage [C]; (短所) 《公式的》demerit [C] (❖日本語の「デメリット」は英語では disadvantage を用いることが多い)

-ても

❶【たとえ…しても】 even though, 《口語的》even if; (…にせよ〜にせよ) whether ... or 〜
たとえ失敗しても怒らないよ I won't get angry with you, *even if* you fail.
いまさら後悔しても始まらない *Even though* you regret it now, it's too late.
１個くらい多くても少なくてもたいした違いはない *Whether* there is one more *or* less, it doesn't make much difference.
◆電話が鳴っても取っちゃだめだ Don't answer the phone *if* it rings. / 君がいなくても何とかなるよ We can manage *without* you.
❷【何が…しても・どんなに…しても】
何があってもあきらめないぞ I'll never give up *whatever happens* [*no matter what* (*happens*)].
君がどんなに遅れても待っているよ *However* [*No matter how*] *late* you are, I'll wait for you.
どこへ行っても彼女は人気者だ *Wherever* [*No matter where*] she *goes*, she's always popular.
だれが何と言ってもそれは変えられない *No matter what anybody says*, we can't change it.
❸【…だけれども】 though, although
私の MD ウォークマン使ってもいいけど，こわさないでよ *Though* you can use my MD Walkman, don't break it./ You can use my MD Walkman, *but* don't break it.

デモ demonstration [C], 《口語的》 demo [C] (複 〜s) ◆多くの人々が増税反対のデモをするために広場に集まった A lot of people gathered in the square to *demonstrate* against higher taxes.
‖デモ行進 a demonstration march / デモ隊 demonstrators / デモテープ 《口語的》a demo

でも (しかし) but, however ‖今夜電話して．でも８時以降にね Call me tonight, *but* after eight. / みんな彼のことをよく言わない．でも私は信じている No one says anything good

て

about him, *but* I believe him.

-でも

❶【たとえ…でも】 even though, 《口語的》 even if

今回がだめでもまた次があるさ *Even if* you fail this time, you'll have another chance.
◆そんなこと子供でもできる *Even* a child can do that. / たとえそうでも私は認めない *Even so*, I cannot accept it.

❷【どんな(に)…でも】

いくら何でもそりゃひどいな *Whatever* [*No matter what*] *the reason is*, that's terrible.

何度でもお好きなだけ試してみてください Please try *as many times as* you like.

何が何でも勝ってみせるぞ I will win 「*at any cost* [*no matter what*].

🅔「いつ君に電話したらいい」「いつでもいいよ」 "When can I call you?" "*Anytime* 「*is OK* [*at all*]."

❸【…だけでも】

一生に一度でもいいから好きなだけ買い物をしたい I wish I could shop as much as I want *just* once in my life.

10円でもいいので寄付をお願いします Please donate something, *even* 10 yen.

彼女の名前だけでも聞いておけばよかった I should have asked her name *at least*.

❹【例えば】

お茶でも飲みましょうか Would you like to have a cup of coffee *or something*?

もし月曜が不都合なら火曜でもいいです If Monday is inconvenient for you, Tuesday is *also* OK with me.

サンドイッチでも買って外で食べない? Why don't we get *some* sandwiches and eat outside?

デモクラシー democracy Ⓤ

てもち 手持ち 今は手持ちの金がない I have no money *with* [*on*] me.

てもちぶさた 手持ち無沙汰 思ったよりずいぶん早く仕事が終わって何だか手持ちぶさただ(→時間がある) We've finished the work much earlier than we thought, so now we *have time on our hands*.

てもと 手元 ──手元の[に] (手近に) at hand; (そばに) by *one's* side; (手に合わせて) in hand /彼女はその薬をいつも手元に置いている She always keeps the pills *at hand*. / 父親が娘を手元に置いておきたいものだ Fathers want to keep their daughters 「*by their sides* [*at home*]. / お手元の資料をご覧ください Have a look at the data *in hand*.
◆今手元に1,000円しか持っていません I only have 1,000 yen *on* [*with*] me. / 手元が狂って(→ねらいをはずして)デッドボールを投げてしまった I *missed my aim*, and the ball I threw hit the batter.

デモンストレーション (実演) demonstration Ⓤ (❖具体的演出内容は Ⓒ) ⇒ デモ /ロボット犬のデモンストレーションをデパートでやっていた They were giving *a demonstration* of a robotic dog at the department store.

デュエット duet Ⓒ /彼とデュエットで歌った I sang *a duet* with him.

てら 寺 (Buddhist) temple Ⓒ

寺に参拝に行く go to worship at *a temple*

🅔「このお寺の名前は何というのですか」「東大寺です」 "What is this *temple* called?" "It's called Todaiji (*Temple*)."

てらい 衒い 彼は何のてらいもない男だ He is an *unpretentious* man.

てらう 衒う (見せびらかす) make* a show of ..., show* off, (ふりをする) pretend 🅐 🅑 /奇をてらった行動 an action *showing off one's eccentricity*

デラウェア Delaware (❖米国東部大西洋岸の州; 《略記》 Del., 〔郵便〕DE)

てらしあわせる 照らし合わせる (…と~を比較する) compare ... with ~; (…を~に照合する) check ... with [against] ~ /訳文を原文に照らし合わせる *compare* the translation *with* the original / 自分の答えを回答と照らし合わせた I *checked* my answers *with* the correct answers.

テラス terrace Ⓒ /テラスで昼食を食べよう Let's have lunch on *the terrace*.
‖テラスハウス 《米》a town house, 《英》a terrace(d) house

てらす 照らす

❶【光などが】 shine* on [over] ...; (光を当てる) light* (up); (照明する) illuminate 🅐; (明るくする) lighten 🅐

月が湖面を照らしている The moon *is shining on* the lake.

懐中電灯で暗い夜道を照らした I *lighted up* the dark road with a flashlight at night.

表通りは色とりどりの電灯で照らされていた The main street *was illuminated with* lots of colorful lights.
◆水たまりは日に照らされてすぐに蒸発してしまった The puddle soon evaporated *in the sunshine*.

❷【比較・照合する】

規則に照らすと *according to* the rule

現実に照らして考えるとやはりそれは無理だと思う I don't think it's possible *considering* reality.

デラックス ──デラックスな deluxe; (豪華な) gorgeous; (一流の) first-class /デラックスな客船 a *deluxe* [*first-class*] passenger ship / デラックスなペントハウス a *gorgeous* [*luxurious*] penthouse

テリア terrier Ⓒ

てりかえし 照り返し reflection Ⓤ; (照り返した光) reflected light Ⓤ; (照り返した熱) reflected heat Ⓤ /私の部屋は屋根の照り返しで暑い My room is hot because of the *reflected heat* off the roof.

てりかえす 照り返す reflect 🅐 🅑

デリカシー delicacy Ⓤ /彼にはデリカシーのかけらもない He hasn't got an ounce of *delicacy* in him./ There isn't an ounce of *delicacy* in his manner.

デリケート ──デリケートな (問題などが微妙な) delicate [délikət]; (微妙な・敏感な) sensitive 〃デリケートな問題 a *delicate* [*sensitive*] problem / デリケートな肌 *sensitive* skin(❖delicate skin は「きめ細かい肌」の意味) / 彼女はデリケートな人だ She is a *sensitive* [*vulnerable*] person. / She is *easily hurt*. (❖delicate person は「病弱な人」、「他人を傷つけないように自らの言動に気をつける人」の意味)

てりつける 照り付ける (ぎらぎら) glare ⊜ 〃砂漠の太陽が照りつけていた The desert sun *was glaring* [*blazing*] *down*.

てりやき 照り焼き *teriyaki*, a Japanese dish in which fish or meat marinated in soy sauce and sweet sake is grilled

てりゅうだん 手榴弾 (hand) grenade [grinéid] ⊡

てりょうり 手料理 homemade [home-cooked] dish ⊡ 〃花子さんの手料理を食べられるなんて幸せなやつだな You're a lucky man (that) you can enjoy Hanako's *homemade food*.

てる 照る shine* ⊜ 〃カリフォルニアといえばいつも太陽が照っているイメージがある My image of California is that the sun *is* always *shining*.

でる 出る

❶外へ出る	go (out); get out; leave
❷出発する・離れる	leave; depart; go
❸姿を現す	appear
❹出席・参加する	go [come] to ...; take part in ...
❺出演する	appear
❻卒業する	graduate

❶【外へ出る】(出ていく) go* (out); (立ち去る) get* out; (去る) leave* ⊕
ちょっと庭に出ませんか *Why don't we go out* into the yard?
彼は夕食後いつも散歩に出る He always *goes* (*out*) for a walk after dinner.
おまえなんかここから出ていけ You, *get out* of here!
解答し終わった者は教室を出てよい You may *leave* the classroom after you have finished answering the questions.
◆父は今ちょっと出ています My father *is out* [*not in*] at the moment.

❷【出発する・離れる】(去る) leave* ⊕ ⊜; (乗り物・人が) depart ⊜; (行く) go* ⊜
列車は午後4時に3番線から出ます The train *leaves* [*departs*] at 4 p.m. from Track 3.
私は毎朝7時半に家を出る I *leave* my house at seven-thirty every morning.
彼女は18で家を出た She *left* home when she was 18.
もうそろそろ出ようか Shall we *go* [*start*] now?

❸【姿を現す】(現れる) appear ⊜; (隠れていたものが) come* out; (下から) come up; (太陽・月などが) rise* ⊜
たまに家の庭にキツネが出る Foxes sometimes *appear* in my garden. / You can sometimes *see* foxes in my garden.
先週まいた種の芽がもう出てきた The seeds I planted last week *are* already *coming up*.
元日の朝、私たちは山頂で太陽が出るのを待った We waited on the top of the mountain for the sun to *rise* [*come up*] on the morning of the first day of the New Year.
雨がやんで月が出てきましたよ The rain has stopped, and the moon *is coming out*.
◆その夜は月が出ていた The moon *was out* that night. / シャツがセーターから出ているよ Your shirt *is sticking out* from under your sweater. / なくしたCDが車から出てきた (→見つけた) I *found* the missing CD in my car. / (→偶然見つかった) The missing CD *turned up* in my car. / そのホテルには幽霊が出るらしい The hotel is said to *be haunted*.

❹【出席・参加する】(出席する)《口語的》go* [come*] to ..., be present at ...,《公式的》attend ⊕; (参加する) take* part in ...,《公式的》participate ⊜; (競技・大会に) enter ⊕ ⊜; (選挙に)《米》run* [《英》stand*] for ...
私はきょうの数学の授業に出なかった I *didn't「go to* [*attend*] today's math class.
彼は式典に出た He「*was present at* [*attended*] the ceremony.
佐藤さんは傍聴者として会議に出た Mrs. Sato *attended* the meeting as an observer.
けがをして運動会に出られなかった I *couldn't take part in* the school sports day because of an injury.
野原はカラオケ大会に出たがっている Nohara *wishes to enter* the karaoke contest.
彼は都知事選に出ることを断念した He gave up *running for* Governor of Tokyo.

❺【出演する】appear ⊜; (主演する) star ⊜
私はテレビに出たことがある I *have appeared on* TV.
ハリソン・フォードは多くの映画に(主役で)出ている Harrison Ford *stars* in many movies.

❻【卒業する】graduate ⊜; (終える) finish ⊕; (学校を)《英》leave* ⊕ (❖《英》では「大学以外の学校を卒業する」の意味にgraduateは用いない)
彼女は山中大学の生物学部を出たばかりだ She just *graduated from* the biology department of Yamanaka University.
君が大学を出たのはいつですか When *did* you「*graduate from* [*finish*] university?
私は来年高校を出る I *will「graduate from* [《英》*leave*] high school next year.

❼【突き出る】stick* out,《公式的》protrude ⊜
塀からくぎが出ている A nail *is sticking out* of the fence.

◆このごろ腹が出てきた I have become pot-bellied recently.
❽【液体が流れる】(鼻水などが) run* ⾃; (血などが) bleed ⾃; (涙が) water ⾃
鼻水が出て止まらない My nose keeps running.
傷口から血が出ていた The cut was bleeding.
痛くて涙が出た My eyes watered because of the pain.
◆この水道は水が出ない This faucet doesn't work.
❾【与えられる】receive ⾃, get*, be given; (食べ物が) be served
この冬はボーナスが出なかった We didn't receive [get] any bonus this winter.
きょうは宿題がたくさん出た We've got lots of homework today.
彼女に入国の許可が出た She was given permission to enter the country.
披露宴では豪華なフランス料理が出た Wonderful French food was served at the wedding reception.
❿【生じる・発生する】(結果として) come* from ...; (火災・病気などが) break* out
それはてれくささから出た言葉だ They are the words「coming from [born out of] embarrassment.
どこからの話か分からない話は信じない I don't trust news that comes from an unknown source.
どこから火が出たのかまだ分からない It's not known yet where the fire「broke out [started].
その学校から結核患者が出た TB broke out in the school.
◆一晩中せきが出た I had a cough all night. / I was coughing all night. / これでいい味が出るはずだ This should bring out the good taste. / 一晩よく寝たら元気が出た I felt cheered up after a night's sleep. / その事故で多くのけが人が出た There were a lot of people injured in the accident. / 風が出てきた The wind has started blowing. / ごみがたくさん出た There was a lot of trash.
⓫【出版・掲載される】appear ⾃; (出版される) come* out, be published; (発行される) be issued
ダイアナ元王妃死亡のニュースは世界中の新聞の一面に出た The news of the former Princess of Wales' death appeared on front pages all over the world.
その雑誌は年2回出る The magazine「comes out [is published] twice a year.
◆私の名前がリストに出ていた My name was on the list. / I found my name on the list.
⓬【売れる】sell* ⾃
きょうはスイカがよく出るな Watermelons are selling very well today.
◆当店ではこのノートパソコンがよく出ています This laptop PC is a good seller in our store.
⓭【至る】(人がたどり着く) come* to ...; (道路が通じる) lead* to ...

私はパリで道に迷ったが, すぐにセーヌ川に出た I got lost in Paris, but I soon came to the Seine.
この道を行けば案内所に出る This road leads to the information center.
⓮【提出する】hand in; (持ち出される) be brought up
今度の金曜日の午後5時までにレポートを出すように You need to hand in the paper by 5 p.m. this Friday.
代案が会議に出された An alternative plan was「brought up [proposed] in the meeting.
◆あの二人には離婚話が出ている It is rumored that the couple may divorce.
⓯【結果を得る】(受け取る) receive ⾃, get* ⾃; (達する) reach ⾃, come* to ...
結果が出るまで1週間待った I waited (for) a week before I received [got] the results.
討論を繰り返したが結論は出なかった We didn't reach [come to] a conclusion even after repeated discussions.
◆やっとその数学の問題の答えが出た Finally I solved the math problem.
⓰【応答する】answer ⾃; (電話に) get* ⾃
だれか来ても出るんじゃないよ Don't answer the door no matter who comes.
◆山田はただ今電話に出ております I'm afraid Yamada is on the phone at the moment.
🔴「だれか電話に出てくれますか」「私が出ます」 "Could someone answer [pick up] the phone?" "I'll get it."
⓱【態度をとる】take* ⾃
強い態度に出る take a firm attitude
それは相手がどう出るかによる It depends on what「action they take [move they make].
⓲【その他】
彼は怒るとすぐ顔に出る When he gets angry, it shows on his face.
合計は1万円をちょっと出るくらいです The total sum is just over 10,000 yen.

デルタちたい デルタ地帯 delta (region) ⓒ
てるてるぼうず 照る照る坊主 🏞

てるてる坊主はちり紙や白い布で作る人形です。「早く雨がやみますように」とか「あした晴れますように」との願いをこめて軒(のき)にさげます。これは昔からの風習で, 特に翌日, 遠足などの行事を楽しみにしている子供たちが作ります
A *teruteru-bozu* is a kind of doll simply made of tissues or white cloth. Children hang it from the eaves hoping that it will stop raining soon or the weather will be clear tomorrow. It is an old custom done by children especially when they are looking forward to a special event like a field trip on the next day.

てれかくし 照れ隠し 私はてれ隠しに冗談を言った I made a joke to cover my embarrassment.
てれくさい 照れ臭い, (赤面する) bashful;

(ばつが悪い) embarrassed; (はにかんだ) shy ‖そんなこと言われると何だかてれくさいな I *feel embarrassed* to be told that.

テレックス telex ⓤⓒ

でれでれ あいつは女性といっしょだとすぐでれでれする He *gets spoony* when he's around women.

テレパシー telepathy ⓤ

テレビ
⚠ television ⓤ,《口語的》TV ⓤ,《英口語的》telly ⓤ (❖いずれも受信機を指す場合は ⓒ)
14インチのテレビ *a* 14-inch *TV* / テレビをつける[消す] turn on [off] *the TV*
テレビの映りが悪い *TV* reception is bad.
テレビに出たい I want to appear on *TV*.
今テレビ,何やってる What's on *TV* now?
父は毎晩テレビで野球のナイター中継を見る My father watches night baseball games *on TV* every night.
最近見たいテレビがない These days, there's nothing I want to watch on *TV*.
それはあまりに残虐な場面なのでテレビでは放送できない That is too cruel a scene to broadcast on *TV*.
その少年はテレビっ子だ That boy is *a TV addict*.
みんなテレビにくぎづけだった Everyone *was glued to the television*.
卒業したらテレビ関係の仕事をしたい I'd like to work in *television* after graduation.
もうちょっとテレビの音を小さく[大きく]してください Could you turn down [up] *the TV*?
◆今は本物の戦争も世界中にテレビ中継される These days even real war *is televised* [*broadcast*] worldwide. / 弟は毎日テレビゲームをしている My brother plays *video games* every day.
‖テレビアンテナ a TV antenna / テレビ映画 a TV movie / テレビカメラ a television [TV] camera / テレビ局 a TV station / テレビタレント a TV personality / テレビ電話 a TV phone, a videophone / テレビドラマ a TV drama / テレビ番組 a TV program / テレビ放送 a television broadcast / テレビ欄 a TV [channel] guide / カラー[白黒]テレビ a color [black-and-white] TV / ケーブルテレビ cable TV (《略語》) CATV)

テレホン (tele)phone ⓒ ‖テレホンショッピングで自転車を買う buy a bicycle *by phone*
‖テレホンカード a prepaid phone [telephone] card

てれや 照れ屋 shy [bashful] person ⓒ

てれる 照れる (赤面する) be bashful; (ばつが悪い) be embarrassed; (はにかむ) be shy ‖そんなに見つめられるとてれちゃうよ I *feel embarrassed* if you stare at me like that.

てれわらい 照れ笑い embarrassed [self-conscious] smile / ──てれ笑いする smile bashfully [in embarrassment]

てれんてくだ 手練手管 wiles ‖手練手管の限りを尽くす make use of all of *one's wiles*

テロ ⚠ terrorism ⓤ ‖やつのしていることはテロ行為だ What they are doing is *terrorism*. ◆モスクワで爆弾テロが発生した There was *a terrorist bombing* in Moscow.

テロリスト terrorist ⓒ

てわけ 手分け ──手分けする (分割する) divide ⓜ; (分け合う) share ⓜ ‖その仕事は手分けしてやろう Let's *divide* [*share*] the work.
◆我々は手分けして迷子の子供を捜した We *split up* and searched for the lost child.

てわたし 手渡し 手渡しで手紙を受け取った I *received a letter by hand*.

てわたす 手渡す hand ⓜ ‖私は母にお金を手渡した I *handed* money to my mother.

てん¹ 点
❶【印・記号】(小さな点) dot ⓒ; (小数点・場所) point ⓒ; (句読点のコンマ) comma ⓒ
0.123 (❖zero point one two three と読む)
i や j にいつも点をつけ忘れる I always forget to "put *a dot* over i and j [*dot* i and j]."
高層ビルの展望台から下を見ると人も車も点のようだ People and cars look like *dots* [*specks*] from the observation floor of a skyscraper.
点Aから直線lに垂線を引きなさい Draw a vertical line from *point* A to line *l*.
❷【成績】(段階評価) grade ⓒ; (得点) point ⓒ, mark ⓒ; (試験の得点) score ⓒ
よい点[満点]を取る get *a* good [perfect] *score*
国語の試験で90点取った I got *a* (*score of*) 90 on the Japanese test. (❖ 90 points [marks]などというより単に数字だけをいうほうがふつう)
合格するには200点満点中120点以上必要だ You need 120 *points* (*marks*) out of 200 to pass.
英語の試験の平均点は62点です *The average mark* on the English exam is 62.
◆岡田先生はテストの点が甘いから好きだ I like Mr. Okada because he *marks* [*grades*] exams generously. (❖この mark は「採点する」という意味の他動詞)
🅔「この前の数学何点だった」「けっこうよかったよ.72点だった」"*What mark* did you get on the last math test?" "Pretty good. It was 72."
❸【競技の】(得点) point ⓒ; (総得点) score ⓒ; (野球・クリケットなどの) run ⓒ; (サッカー・アメリカンフットボールなどの) goal ⓒ
日本は3点差で勝った Japan won by three *points*.
田中は一人で5点を入れた Tanaka alone *scored* five *points* [*runs*].
スワローズは7回に追加点を2点あげた The Swallows *added* two *runs* in the seventh.
(野球で)点が入るたびにファンが喜んだ The fans celebrated whenever *a run* was scored.
◆ジャイアンツは点差を広げた The Giants *widened their lead*.

てん

● 「今，何点」「3対1でうちが勝ってるよ」 "What's *the score*?" "We're leading 3 to 1."

❹ [事柄・問題] point ◎; (特定の箇所) respect ◎; (観点) viewpoint ◎

そこがかれのいい点だ That's his good *point*.

その点では同意します I agree with you *on that point*.

あらゆる点で私は彼女にかなわない In every *respect* [*way*] she is superior to me.

どういう点でこの絵は当時のほかの絵よりすぐれていますか In what *respect* [*How*] is this picture better than others from the same period?

人道主義の点から考えて空爆は中止したほうがよい From *the* humanitarian *viewpoint* [*point of view*], the bombing should be stopped.

◆この家は広さと価格の点では申し分ない This house is very good *in terms of* size and price. / 英語が話せるという点で，青木のほうが桜井よりも就職が有利だ Aoki has an employment advantage over Sakurai *in that* she can speak English. / ご不明な点がございましたらこちらまでお電話ください If there's *anything* unclear (to you), please call here.

❺ [品物の個数] piece ◎, item ◎, article ◎

家具3点 three *pieces* of furniture

100点を超す出展があった More than 100 *items* were exhibited.

‖決勝点(ゴール) the finish line; (勝負を決める得点) the winning run [point, goal]

[慣用表現] 金額を見て目が点になった My eyes widened when I saw the price.

てん² 天

❶ [空] the sky

天を仰ぐ look up to the sky

その山は天高くそびえていた The mountain rises *high up to the sky*.

❷ [神・天国] (神) God, Heaven; (天国) Heaven

赤ちゃんは天からの授かり物だ Babies are gifts from *Heaven*.

天に誓って私はそれをやっていない I swear *to God* that I didn't do that.

[慣用表現] 私は運を天に任せた I *left it to chance*. / 天高く馬肥ゆる秋(→空は高く，馬は豊富な草を食(は)んで肥える すばらしい秋の天候) *Good autumn weather under a high sky when horses fatten on rich grasses.* / 2つの映画の製作費は天と地ほどの差がある The production costs of the two movies are *as different as night and day*. / 彼女は彼にキスされたとき天にも昇る気持ちだった She *was* "*in seventh heaven* [*on cloud nine*]" when she was kissed by him.

[ことわざ] 天は二物を与えず God does not bless a person twice.

てん³ 貂 [動物] marten ◎

-てん 展 exhibition ◎, show ◎ ‖美術展 an art *exhibition* / 20世紀印象派展 an *exhibition* of 20th century impressionism

-でん 伝 チャーチル伝 a life [*biography*] of Churchill / 祖父は自分の武勇伝をよく私に語って聞かせた My grandfather used to tell me his *heroic episodes*.

でんあつ 電圧 voltage ⓤ ◎

‖電圧計 a voltmeter

てんい 転移 (変化) change ◎; (癌(がん)細胞などの) spread ⓤ, [医学] metastasis ◎ (複 metastases) ――転移する spread* ⓐ; (移る) transfer ⓐ ‖癌の転移を食い止める stop the cancer from *spreading* / 癌が肺に転移した The cancer *spread* to the lungs.

てんいん 店員 《米》salesclerk ◎, 《英》(shop) assistant ◎; (男性の) salesman ◎ (女性の) saleswoman ◎; (男女の区別なく) salesperson ◎ ‖あの店員の接客態度は悪い That *salesclerk* is impolite to customers.

でんえん 田園 (いなか) the country; (田園地帯) the countryside, the rural area [district] ――田園の country; (のどかな) rural ‖田園生活を楽しむ enjoy *country* [*rural*] *life*

◆目の前に田園風景が広がっていた *Pastoral scenery* spread out before us.

‖田園都市 a garden city

てんか¹ 天下 ❶ [世の中] (世界) the world; (全国) the whole country; (世間) the public ‖彼の作品は天下に知られている His work is well known *all over the world*. / His work is *world-famous*. / 秀吉はついに天下を取った Hideyoshi finally conquered *the whole country*. / 彼女が作るカレーは天下一品だ Her curry *is the best in the world*.

❷ [思うままにふるまうこと] 江戸時代は徳川家の天下だった The Tokugawa family *had dominance* during the Edo period. / 彼の家はかかあ天下だ He is *a henpecked husband*.

[慣用表現] 天下分け目の(→決定的な) 戦い, a *decisive* battle

てんか² 点火 lighting ⓤ; (エンジンなどの) 《公式的》ignition ⓤ ――点火する light* ⓐ; ignite ⓐ; (花火・ロケットなどに) set* off ‖ガスストーブに点火する *light* a gas heater

‖点火装置 an ignition

てんか³ 添加 addition ⓤ ――添加する add ⓐ ◆このお菓子には天然着色料が添加されている (→含有している) This candy *contains* natural coloring.

‖(食品)添加物 a food additive, an additive

てんか⁴ 転嫁 ――転嫁する (責任・罪などを) shift ⓐ, transfer ⓐ ‖他人に責任を転嫁しないでくれ Don't shift the responsibility onto others. / Don't pass the buck to others.

でんか¹ 電化 electrification ⓤ ――電化する electrify ⓐ ‖そのローカル線はまだ電化されていない The local line *isn't electrified* yet.

‖電化製品 electrical appliances

でんか² 殿下 (相手に直接呼びかけるとき) Your (Imperial) Highness; (間接的に指すとき) His [Her] (Imperial) Highness(❖いずれも三人称単数扱い。日本の皇室以外の王室の場合は Imperial の代わりに Royal を用いる) ‖(日本の)皇太子殿下 *His Imperial Highness* the Crown Prince (❖英国皇太子の場合は (*His*

Royal Highness) the Prince of Wales という / 皇太子妃殿下 (*Her Imperial Highness*) Crown Princess

てんかい 展開 （進展）development ⓊⒸ
━━展開する develop 自; （徐々に明らかになる）unfold 他; （広がる）spread* out ∥新たな展開を見せる show *a* new *development* / 理論を展開する *develop* a theory / この事件は思わぬ方向へ展開している This case *is developing* in an unexpected direction. / トンネルを抜けると美しい風景が目の前に展開した When we emerged from the tunnel, beautiful scenery *spread out* before our eyes.
∥展開図 an expanded [unfolded] diagram

てんかい² 転回 turn ⓊⒸ ━━転回する turn 自 ∥状況は180度転回した The situation *took a 180-degree turn*.

てんかん¹ 転換 change ⒸⓊ; （急な）switch Ⓒ ━━転換する change 他自; switch 他自 ∥市場経済への転換 *a switch* to a market economy / 車を方向転換する *change the direction of* a car / 気分転換に外で食事しよう Let's eat outside *for a change*. / この問題を解くには発想の転換が必要だ You need to 「*change your way of thinking* [(→別の角度から見る) *look at it from a different angle*] to solve this problem.
◆ 方針を180度転換する *do an about-face*[*-turn*] in *one's* policy / 戦後経済は当時転換期にあった The postwar economy was at *a turning point* then.

てんかん² 癲癇 〔医学〕epilepsy Ⓤ ━━てんかんの epileptic ∥てんかんの発作を起こす have *an epileptic fit* [*seizure*]
∥てんかん患者 an epileptic

てんき¹ 天気
❶【天候】weather Ⓤ（❖通例 the を付けるが、形容詞が付くときは不要）

山の天気は絶えず変わる The weather in the mountains 「changes constantly [(→変わりやすい) is changeable].

天気はよくなってきている *The weather* is improving.

天気がよければあしたのショーは行われます If *the weather* is nice [〖公式的〗*Weather* permitting], the show will take place tomorrow.

休暇の間天気には恵まれなかった We were unlucky with *the weather* during vacation.

この天気では外に出る気もしない I don't want to go outside in this *weather*.

天気予報によれば今夜は雪になるそうだ *The weather report* says it will snow tonight.

彼女は元お天気お姉さんだった She was *an* ex-*weather girl*.

◆ きょうは天気がいい It's fine [*sunny, clear*] today. / *The weather* is *fine* [*good*] today. (❖「悪い」なら fine などの代わりに bad を用いる。)
/ 天気に関係なく祭りは行われる The festival will go ahead *rain or shine*.

●「すばらしい天気ですね」「本当に」"Isn't it *a wonderful day*?" "Isn't it!"
●「あしたの天気はどう」「雨だよ」"What'll *the weather* be like tomorrow?" "It's going to rain."

❷【晴天】good weather Ⓤ ━━天気の fine
たぶんあしたも天気だろう Probably it's going to be *fine* [*sunny, clear*] tomorrow, too.

あすまでこの天気はもたないだろう This *good weather* won't last until tomorrow.

∥天気雨 a sun shower / 天気図 a weather map [chart] ⇨ 図版 / 天気予報 a weather forecast [report]

〖慣用表現〗彼女はお天気屋だ She is *moody*.
⇨ 場面・状況別会話 p.1732

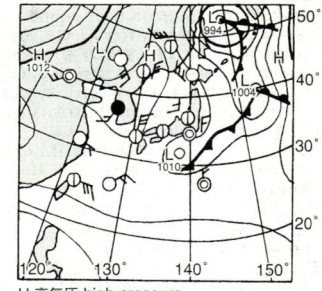

H 高気圧 high pressure
L 低気圧 low pressure
○ 快晴 clear ① 晴 fair ◐ 曇 cloudy
● 雨 rain ⊕ 雪 snow ◉ 霧 fog
⊚ 煙霧 haze ⚡ 雷雨 thunderstorm
⌇ 風向及び風速 wind direction and speed
▲▲▲ 温暖前線 warm front
▼▼▼ 寒冷前線 cold front
▲▼▲▼ 停滞前線 stationary front

てんき² 転機 turning point Ⓒ ∥40にして彼は人生の転機に立った At the age of 40, he was at *a turning point* in his life.

でんき¹ 電気
electricity Ⓤ; （電灯）(electric) light Ⓒ; （電流）(electric) current ⒸⓊ ━━電気の electric; （電気に関する）electrical

この地域には電気が通じていない There is no *electricity* in this area.

電気をむだづかいしないように Don't waste *electricity*.

太郎は料金滞納で電気を止められた *The electricity* was turned off because Taro hadn't paid the bill.

古いエアコンは電気をたくさん食う An old air conditioner uses [consumes] much *electricity*.

この機械は電気で動いている This machine runs on *electricity*.

電気をつけて[消して]くれますか Could you turn *the light* on [off]?

向かいの家の電気が消えた *The lights* in the

でんき

opposite house went off [out]. ゆうべふろの電気がつけっぱなしだったよ You left *the* bathroom *light* on last night. それは電気系統の故障だった That was an *electrical* fault.
◆作業員は電気の通った線に触れ感電した The worker got an electric shock by touching *live* wires.
‖電気いす an electric chair / 電気回路 an electric circuit / 電気がま an electric rice cooker / 電気かみそり an electric shaver / 電気機関車 an electric locomotive / 電気器具 electrical appliances / 電気技師 an electrical engineer, an electrician / 電気工学 electrical engineering / 電気自動車 an electric car / 電気スタンド (卓上の)a desk lamp; (床上の)a floor lamp / 電気ストーブ an electric heater / 電気抵抗 electrical resistance / 電気毛布 an electric blanket / 電気屋 an electrical appliances store / 電気料金 the electricity charge; (家庭に請求される料金)an electricity bill

でんき² 伝記 biography ⓒ; (書名などで) life ⓒ /エジソンの伝記 *a biography* of Edison
◆彼は伝記作家として名をはせている He is well known as *a biographer*.

でんきゅう 電球 (light) bulb ⓒ /電球が切れた The bulb has burned out.
‖裸電球 a bare light bulb

てんきょ¹ 転居 move ⓒ ──転居する move ⓐ /このたび下記の住所へ転居しました We *have moved* to the address given below.
‖転居先 one's new address / 転居通知 a change-of-address notice / 転居届 a removal notice

てんきょ² 典拠 source ⓒ; (権威のあるもの) authority ⓒ ◆引用文の典拠を示す cite *the reference* for a quotation

でんきょく 電極 electrode

てんきん 転勤 transfer ⓒ ──転勤する be transferred /彼女はシカゴ支店への転勤を願い出た She asked for *a transfer* to the Chicago branch. / イアンはロンドンから東京へ転勤になった Ian *was transferred* from London to Tokyo.

てんぐ 天狗 △ a tengu, one of the best known goblins in Japan
慣用表現 彼は英語が話せるというだけでてんぐになっている He "*is puffed up* [*has a big head*]" just because he can speak English.

> 天狗は日本で最もよく知られた妖怪(ようかい)で、長い鼻が特徴です。天狗は超自然的な力をもち、また善と悪の相反する要素を持ち合わせているとされています。
> *Tengu* are some of the best known goblins in Japan. They are noted for their long noses. It is said that *tengu* have supernatural powers and possess aspects of both good and evil.

でんぐりがえし でんぐり返し 弟はでんぐり返しができる My brother *can do somersaults*. (❖somersault は宙返りなどもいう)

てんけい 典型 (代表的なもの) type ⓒ; (模範) model ⓒ, (見本) specimen ⓒ ──典型的な typical; model /肩からカメラをさげている典型的な日本人観光客 a *typical* Japanese tourist with a camera hanging from his [her] shoulder / スーツにシルクハットに黒のこうもり傘、彼は英国紳士の典型だね With his suit, silk hat and black umbrella, he is *a good specimen* of an English gentleman.

てんけん 点検 check ⓒ, (公式的) examination ⓤ; (公式の検査) inspection ⓤⓒ ──検査する check ⓐ, examine ⓐ; inspect ⓐ /点検中(掲示) *Under Inspection* / エンジンを総点検する *check* an engine *thoroughly* / ガス屋さんがガス器具の点検に来た A gasman *came to inspect* the gas appliances.
‖定期点検 a routine check

でんげん 電源 power source ⓤ; (電力の供給) power supply ⓤ; (コンセント) (米)outlet ⓒ, (英) socket ⓒ /電源を遮断する cut off *the power supply* / 部屋の電源を探す look for *an outlet* in a room ◆ラジオの電源を入れる[切る] turn the radio *on* [*off*] / ビデオを電源につなぐ *plug in* the VCR

てんこ 点呼 (roll) call ⓒ ◆点呼をとる call the roll; take attendance

てんこう¹ 天候 weather ⓤ ⇨ てんき (天気) 図版, 場面・状況別会話 p.1732 /天候不順 unstable *weather* / 悪天候 bad *weather*

てんこう² 転校 ──転校する change schools /中学校のとき2回転校した I *changed schools* twice when I was in junior high school. ◆東京の学校へ転校する *change* [*transfer*] to a school in Tokyo
‖転校生 a transfer (student)

てんこう³ 転向 ──転向する (…になる) turn ⓐ, become* ⓐ; (宗教・思想などを) be converted to … /そのテニス選手は昨年プロに転向した The tennis player *turned* professional last year.

でんこう 電光 (電気の光) electric light ⓤ; (稲妻) lightning ⓤ ◆彼は電光石火の早業で相手ディフェンダーからボールを奪った He took the ball away from the defender on the opposing team *with lightning speed*.
‖電光掲示板 an electric billboard; (得点板) an electric scoreboard / 電光ニュース news on an electric billboard

てんごく 天国 heaven ⓤ (しばしば Heaven); (楽園) paradise ⓒ /天国にいる be in *Heaven* / スイスはスキー天国だ Switzerland is *a paradise* for skiers.
‖歩行者天国 a pedestrian-only street

でんごん 伝言 message ⓒ [mésidʒ] /鈴木さんへの伝言を頼んでもいいですか May I leave *a message* for Miss Suzuki (with you)? / ワンさんですか、近藤さんからの伝言があります Are you Mr. Wang? I have *a message* for you from Mr. Kondo. / 彼は午後3時までに戻るという伝言を残していった He left *a message* that he would be back by 3 p.m.
‖伝言板 a message board

てんさい¹ 天才 (…の才能) a genius for …;

テンション

(人) genius ⓒ 〃彼女は語学の天才だ She has a genius for languages. / She is a genius with languages.
◆彼女は天才的な作曲家だ She is a gifted composer. / 彼は生まれながらの天才バイオリニストだ He is a born violinist.
‖天才児 a child genius [prodigy]

てんさい² 天災 natural disaster ⓒ 〃天災に見舞われる be visited by a natural disaster 慣用表現 天災は忘れたころにやってくる A natural disaster strikes when we have forgotten about the previous one.

てんさい³ 転載 reproduction ⓤ ──転載する reproduce ⓗ 〃無断転載を禁ず Reproduction without permission is prohibited. / この記事は著者より許可を得て転載したものです This article was reproduced by permission of the author.

てんざい 点在 都会に点在する緑 patches of green in the city / その平原には高い木が点在している The plain is dotted with tall trees.

てんさく 添削 correction ⓤ ──添削する correct ⓗ 〃あしたまでに作文を10本添削しなければならない I need to correct 10 compositions by tomorrow.

てんし 天使 angel ⓒ 〃天使のような少女 an angel of a girl; an angelic girl
‖堕天使 a fallen angel

てんじ¹ 展示 exhibition ⓤ, show ⓤ;（陳列）display ⓤ 〃いずれも具体的内容を表すときは ⓒ ──展示する exhibit ⓗ, show*ⓗ; display ⓗ
その美術館にはフェルメールの絵がいくつか展示されている Some pictures by Vermeer are exhibited in the art museum.
その展示室には彼の彫刻が展示されていた His sculpture was displayed in the exhibition room.
このホールでは様々な展示会が行われる Various exhibitions [shows] are held in this hall.
来年のカレンダーの展示即売会に行かない？ How about going to an exhibition where next year's calendars are displayed and sold?
‖展示場 an exhibition hall / 展示品 an exhibit

てんじ² 点字 Braille [bréil] ⓤ（✦小文字でつづることもある）〃点字を読む［書く］read [write] Braille / 点字本 a book in Braille / 文章を点字に訳す put a text into Braille
‖点字ブロック tactile warnings

でんし 電子 《物理》electron ⓒ ──電子の electronic
◆電子音がピーと鳴った There was a beep.（✦There was an electronic beep. ともいえるが，あまり一般的ではない）
‖電子オルガン an electronic organ / 電子音楽 electronic [synthetic] music / 電子計算機 a computer / 電子顕微鏡 an electronic microscope / 電子工学 electronics / 電子辞書 an electronic dictionary / 電子ブック an electronic book / 電子マネー electronic money, e-money / 電子レンジ a microwave (oven)

でんじき 電磁気 electromagnetism ⓤ

でんじは 電磁波 electromagnetic wave ⓒ

でんしメール 電子メール e-mail, email, E-mail ⓤ ⓒ（✦mail は ⓤ だが, e-mail は ⓒ としても用いられる）➪ メール, 前・後見返し

でんしゃ 電車 train ⓒ
電車に乗る［を降りる］「get on [get off] a train
この電車は名古屋まで行きますか Does this train go to Nagoya?
これは大阪行きの電車です This train is (bound) for Osaka.
帰りの電車に傘を置き忘れた I left my umbrella on the train home.
電車の中ですりにあった I had my pocket picked on the train.
ちょうど急行電車に間に合った I caught an express train just in time.
北海道まで電車で行った I went to Hokkaido by train.
‖電車賃 a train fare / 最終電車 the last train / 通勤電車 a commuter train / 満員電車 a jam-packed train / 路面電車《米》a streetcar,《英》a tram

てんしゅ 店主《米》storekeeper ⓒ,《英》shopkeeper ⓒ（✦以上2語は所有者以外に店の管理者の意味もある）;（店の所有者）the owner of a store [shop]

てんじゅ 天寿 祖母は天寿をまっとうした（→老いて死んだ）My grandmother died of old age.

でんじゅ 伝授 女の子にもてる秘訣(ひけつ)を伝授してください Please teach me the secret of being popular with girls.

てんしゅかく 天守閣 castle tower ⓒ

てんしゅつ 転出 ──転出する move out 〃転出届を出す give notice of moving out

てんじょう 天井 （部屋の）ceiling ⓒ;（車・屋根裏の）roof ⓒ 〃ヨーロッパの家は概して天井が高い Houses in Europe have high ceilings in general. / その洞窟(どうくつ)の天井にはたくさんのコウモリがいる There are many bats on the roof of the cave.
◆東京の地価は天井知らずに高騰した The land prices in Tokyo went sky-high.
‖天井裏 an attic / 天井桟敷(さじき) the gallery

でんしょう 伝承 ──伝承する hand down ... from generation to generation
◆彼女は日本の民間伝承を研究している She studies Japanese folklore.

てんじょういん 添乗員 tour conductor ⓒ

てんしょく¹ 転職 a change of job, career change ⓒ;（転々と変えること）job-hopping ⓤ ──転職する change jobs, change one's job 〃彼はいろいろな理由があって転職した He changed his job for a variety of reasons.
‖転職者 a person who has changed jobs

てんしょく² 天職 vocation ⓒ 〃教師は私の天職だ Teaching is my vocation.

でんしょばと 伝書鳩 carrier [homing] pigeon ⓒ

テンション ⚠ 彼女はきょうテンションが高い

てんじる 転じる (変える) change 🔵; (向ける) turn 🔵 ‖話題を転じる *change* the subject / 攻撃に転じる *change* to the offensive / 私は窓辺に目を転じた I *turned* my eyes toward the window.

てんしん 転身 おじは弁護士から陶芸家へ転身した My uncle *transformed* himself from a lawyer into a ceramic artist.

でんしん 電信 telegraph ⓤ; (電信による通信) telegraphic communication ⓤ ‖電信為替 a *telegraphic* transfer / 電信柱 《米》a *telephone* pole, 《英》a *telegraph* pole

てんしんらんまん 天真爛漫 ——天真爛漫な (純真で無邪気な) innocent ‖天真爛漫な笑顔 an *innocent* smile

てんすう 点数 (成績) mark ⓒ; (競技の) point ⓒ ➡ てん(点)
‖点数制(交通違反などの) the *point* system
慣用表現 有権者の点数を稼ぐ *win brownie points* with voters

てんせい 天性 ——天性の (生まれつきの) born ‖天性の音楽家 a *born* [*natural*] musician
◆彼のジャンプ力は天性のものだ He *was born with* a special ability for jumping.

でんせつ 伝説 legend ⓒⓤ; (言い伝え) tradition ⓤ; (民間伝承) folklore ⓤ ——伝説上の legendary ‖アーサー王伝説 the Arthurian *legends* / 伝説上の怪物 a *legendary* monster / 伝説によるとこの山には宝物が隠されているそうだ According to *legend*, a treasure is hidden in these mountains. / その試合での彼のシュートは今や伝説と化している The shot he made in the game is now regarded as 「*a legend* [*legendary*].

てんせん 点線 dotted line ⓒ; (ミシン目の切り取り線) perforated line ⓒ ‖点線を引く draw *a dotted line* / 点線に沿って切り取ってください Tear (off) along *the perforated line*.

でんせん¹ 伝染 (空気・動物などによる) infection ⓤ; (接触による) contagion ⓤ ——伝染する spread* 🔵
◆この病気は伝染する This disease *is infectious* [*contagious*]. / あくびは伝染する Yawning *is infectious* [*contagious*]. / Yawning *spreads* from person to person.

でんせん² 伝線 (ストッキングなどの) run ⓒ, 《英》ladder ⓒ ‖ストッキングが伝線しちゃった I've got a *run* [*ladder*] in my stocking.

でんせん³ 電線 electric wire ⓤⓒ; (電信用の) telegraph wire [line] ⓒ ‖電線に数羽のスズメがとまっていた Several sparrows were sitting on the *electric wire*.

でんせんびょう 伝染病 (空気・動物などによる) infectious disease ⓤⓒ; (接触による) contagious disease ⓤⓒ; (短期間に大勢が感染する) epidemic ⓒ ‖難民キャンプでの伝染病が心配される We are concerned about *infectious* [*contagious*] *diseases* in the refugee camp. / その村ではなぞの伝染病が広まった An unknown *epidemic* spread through the village.
‖伝染病患者 a patient with an *infectious* [a *contagious*, an *epidemic*] *disease* / 法定伝染病 a legally designated *infectious disease*

てんそう 転送 ——転送する forward 🔵 ‖私の郵便物をこの住所に転送していただけますか Would you *forward* my mail to this address? / 松下さんからの電子メールを近藤さんと桜井さんに転送した I *forwarded* the e-mail from Mr. Matsushita to Mr. Kondo and Mrs. Sakurai.
‖転送先住所 a *forwarding* address

でんそう 電送 写真を電送する *transmit* a picture

てんたい 天体 heavenly [celestial] body ⓒ ——天体の astronomical,《公式的》celestial ‖アンドロメダ星雲はよく知られた銀河系外の天体だ The Andromeda nebula is *a* well-known *heavenly body* outside our galaxy.
‖天体観察 an *astronomical* observation / 天体図 a celestial map / 天体望遠鏡 an astronomical telescope / 天体物理学 astrophysics / 天体物理学者 an astrophysicist

でんたく 電卓 (pocket [desk]) calculator ⓒ

でんたつ 伝達 (意思の) communication ⓤ; (情報などの) transmission ⓤ ——伝達する communicate 🔵; transmit 🔵 ‖我々は様々な伝達手段をもっている We have various *means of communication*. / 今日(ёё)多くの情報が電話回線を使って世界中に伝達されている A lot of information *is transmitted* over telephone lines worldwide.
◆伝達事項はありません There's no *message* for you.

でんたつどうし 伝達動詞《文法》reporting verb ⓒ ➡ わほう

てんち¹ 天地 ❶〖天と地〗heaven and earth (※無冠詞で用いる); (宇宙) the universe ‖天地神明に誓う *swear*「*by heaven and earth* [*to God*]◆(キリスト教の)天地創造 the Creation

❷〖人間の住む場所〗(世界) world ⓒ; (国土) land ⓒ ‖新天地を求めて海を渡る sail across the sea in search of *a new world* / 夏の北海道は涼しくて別天地だ Hokkaido in summer is cool and *like*「*another world* [*a paradise*].

❸〖上下〗天地無用〖掲示〗*This Side Up*; *Do Not Turn Over*

てんち² 転地 医者は患者に転地療養を勧めた The doctor suggested that the patient should *go to the country for a change* (of air).

でんち 電池 battery ⓒ, cell ⓒ (※cellの集まったものがbattery) ‖電池が切れた The battery「*is dead* [*has run down*]. / 盗聴器は電池で動いている The bugging device is「*powered by a battery* [*battery*-powered]. / 時計の電池を換えてもらえますか Could you

change *the battery* in my watch?
∥アルカリ電池 an alkaline battery / 乾電池 a dry battery [cell] / 水銀電池 a mercury battery [cell] / 太陽電池 a solar battery [cell] / 単1 [2, 3, 4] 電池 a "D" ["C", "AA", "AAA"] battery (✣AA は double A, AAA は triple A と読む) / 蓄電池 a storage battery

でんちゅう　電柱　(総括的に) utility pole ◯; (電話線用の) telephone pole ◯; (電信用の) telegraph pole ◯

てんちょう¹　転調　〖音楽〗modulation Ⓤ◯
てんちょう²　店長　store [shop] manager ◯
てんてき¹　天敵　natural enemy ◯; (捕食動物) predator ◯
てんてき²　点滴　drip ◯, intravenous (drip) ◯ /点滴を受ける get *a drip*
∥点滴注射 an intravenous drip infusion

てんてこまい　てんてこ舞い　きょうは次から次に問い合わせの電話がありてんてこまいだった I *was frantically busy* today answering so many inquiring phone calls. / 父が会社の社長を今晩連れてくると突然言いだしたのでわが家はもうてんてこまいだ We *are in chaos* as my father suddenly said he would bring the president of his company home this evening.

でんてつ　電鉄　(鉄道会社) 《米》electric railroad [《英》railway] company ◯

てんてん¹　転々　彼は日本全国を転々としている He *is wandering around* all over Japan. / 彼女は職を転々としている She *drifts from one job to another.* / (→職を次々と変える人) She *is a job-hopper.*

てんてん²　点々　この部落ではまだわらぶき屋根の家が点々と(→あちらこちらに)見られる You can still find thatched houses *here and there* in this village. / 部屋には血の跡が点々とついていた The room *was spotted* with blood.

てんでんばらばら　みんなてんでんばらばらなことを言う Everyone says *different things.* / 彼らはやることがてんでんばらばらだ(→それぞれが勝手にやりたいことをやっている) Every one of them *does what he or she likes irrespective of the others.*

テント　tent ◯ /テントを張る pitch [put up] *a tent* / テントをたたむ strike [pull down] *a tent* ◆10日間のテント生活をする *camp out* for 10 days

でんと　conspicuously /彼はでんと構えて動こうともしなかった He stayed there *conspicuously* and showed no sign of moving. / 彼の部屋には大きな机がでんと置いてあった There was a huge desk sitting *conspicuously* in his room.

てんとう¹　店頭　クリが店頭に並んでいる Chestnuts are displayed *at the front of the store.* / すてきなバッグが店頭に飾られていた Lovely bags were displayed in *the show window.* / 最新のモデルはまだここでは店頭に出ていない(→売られていない) The latest model is not *on sale* here yet.
∥店頭株 an over-the-counter stock (《略語》OTC) / 店頭販売 over-the-counter sales

てんとう²　点灯　レインボーブリッジの明かりが点灯した The lights of the Rainbow Bridge came [turned] *on.*

てんとう³　転倒　❶〖転ぶ〗――転倒する fall* (down) /ふろ場で転倒する *fall down* in the bathroom
❷〖気持ちが〗彼女は気が転倒してただ泣くだけだった She *was very upset* and just kept weeping.

でんとう¹　伝統　(社会的習慣) tradition Ⓤ◯; (歴史) history ◯; (文化的・社会的遺産) heritage Ⓤ　――伝統的な　traditional　――伝統的に　traditionally

古い伝統を重んじる[復活させる] respect [restore] old *traditions*

わが校は創立100年の伝統がある Our school has *a history* of 100 years since its foundation.

京都の町は伝統的な日本のイメージを与えてくれる The city of Kyoto gives us an image of *traditional* Japan.

谷川大学は伝統的に法学部が有名だ The law department at Tanikawa University *traditionally* has a good reputation.

私の学校では運動会で先生がリレーを走ることが伝統になっている At our school, the teachers *traditionally* run a relay in the athletic meet.

◆伝統あるラグビー部 a *long-established* rugby club
∥伝統行事 a traditional event / 伝統芸術 traditional arts / 伝統工芸 traditional crafts

でんとう²　電灯　(electric) light ◯, electric lamp ◯ ⇨ でんき(電気)

でんどう¹　伝道　(伝道の仕事) mission [missionary] work ◯; (説教) preaching Ⓤ　――伝道する　preach ⊕ /伝道に携わる be engaged in *missionary work* / 彼女は日本でキリスト教の伝道をしている She *preaches* Christianity in Japan.
∥伝道者[師] a missionary

でんどう²　伝導　〖物理〗(熱・電気などの) conduction Ⓤ　――伝導する　conduct ⊕ ∥伝導体 a conductor

でんどう³　電動　――電動の　electric-powered /このエンジンは電動ですか Is this an *electric-powered* engine?
∥電動タイプライター an electric typewriter / 電動のこぎり a power saw

でんどう⁴　殿堂　palace ◯; (会館) hall ◯
◆(野球で)彼は殿堂入りした He *entered the Baseball Hall of Fame.*

てんどうせつ　天動説　the geocentric theory; (プトレマイオス説) the Ptolemaic system

てんとうむし　天道虫　《米》ladybug ◯, 《英》ladybird ◯

てんとりむし　点取り虫　《米》grind ◯, 《英》swot ◯

てんどん　天丼　(a) tendon, a bowl of rice topped with (prawn) tempura

てんにゅう

てんにゅう 転入 ━転入する（移り住む）move into ...;（転校する）enter another school ‖転入生 a transfer student ／ 転入届 a change-of-address notice

てんにょ 天女 celestial nymph ⓒ

てんにん 転任 ━転任する be transferred ／宮地先生は浜松の学校に転任した Mr. Miyaji *was transferred* to a school in Hamamatsu.
◆連絡は転任先にお願いします Please contact me at *my new post*.

てんねん 天然 natural ／このカキは養殖ではなく天然ものだ These oysters are *natural*, not cultured. ／ 彼は天然ボケだね He's a *natural* comedian.
◆彼女の髪は天然パーマです Her hair is *naturally* curly.
‖天然ガス natural gas ／ 天然資源 natural resources

てんねんきねんぶつ 天然記念物（自然物）natural monument ⓒ;（動植物）a rare species protected by law ／その鳥は国の特別天然記念物に指定されている The bird has been designated *a special rare species protected by law*.

てんねんとう 天然痘 smallpox Ⓤ

てんのう 天皇 emperor ⓒ;（現在即位しているの）the Emperor ／（日本の）天皇陛下（間接的に）*His Majesty the Emperor*;（直接呼びかけるとき）*Your Majesty* ／ 天皇に謁見（けん）する have an audience with *the Emperor* ／ 天皇は日本国の象徴である *The Emperor* is the symbol of the nation of Japan.
◆ここは天皇陛下ご一家がお泊まりになられたホテルです This is the hotel where the *Imperial* family stayed.
‖天皇制 the Emperor System of Japan ／ 天皇誕生日 the Emperor's birthday ／ 天皇杯 the Emperor's trophy

てんのうせい 天王星【天文】Uranus

でんぱ[1] 電波 radio wave ⓒ ／私は今電波の届かない場所にいる I'm now in a location out of the reach of *radio waves*.
◆（声が）電波に乗る go on *the air* ／ 携帯電話は地下では電波が入りにくい Cell phones have trouble getting *a signal* underground.
‖電波障害 interference, static ／ 電波望遠鏡 a radio telescope ／ 電波妨害 jamming

でんぱ[2] 伝播（普及）propagation Ⓤ;（広がること）the spread ━伝播する propagate ⓗ; spread* ⓗ ／知識の伝播 *the propagation* of knowledge

てんばい 転売 resale Ⓤ ━転売する resell* ⓗ ／転売するつもりでこのマンションを買った I bought this condo to *resell*.
‖転売価格 a resale price

てんばつ 天罰 divine retribution ／彼女のたび重なるうそに天罰が下ったんだ This must be *divine retribution* for her repeated lies.
◆天罰てきめん（→当然の報い）だ *It serves you right*!

てんび 天日 洗濯物を天日干しにする *dry* the washing *in the sun* ／ 天日干しのイカ sun-dried squid

てんびき 天引き deduction Ⓤ ━天引きする deduct ⓗ ／組合費は給料から天引きされる The union dues *are deducted* from the salary.

でんぴょう 伝票（商売上の）slip ⓒ;（レストランなどの勘定）（米）check ⓒ, 《英》bill ⓒ ／支払い伝票を切る issue *a payment slip* ／（レストランで）伝票をお願いします Can I have *the check* please?

てんびん 天秤（はかり）balance ⓒ;（はかりの皿）scale ⓒ;（はかりの器具）scales（◆数えるときは a pair of ... とする）／火薬を天秤で量る weigh gunpowder「in *the balance* [on *the scales*]
慣用表現 私たちは2つの案を天秤にかけた We *weighed* one plan against the other. ／ あいつは花子と恵子を（両）天秤にかけている He *is weighing* Hanako *against* Keiko.

てんびんざ 天秤座【天文・占星】Libra Ⓤ（◆「天秤座の人」の意味では ⓒ）

てんぶ 転部 私はバレー部からバスケ部へ転部した I *changed* from the volleyball club *to* the basketball. ／ 兄は法学部から文学部へ転部した My brother *changed* [*transferred*] *from* the law department *to* literature.

てんぷ[1] 添付 ━添付する（添える）attach ⓗ ／（Eメールなどの）添付ファイル *an attached file*; *an attachment* ／ 書類に手紙を添付する *attach* a letter to the papers

てんぷ[2] 貼付 ━貼付する（のりなどではる）affix ⓗ ／応募用紙に最近の写真を貼付してください *Affix* a recent photograph of yourself to your application form.

てんぷ[3] 天賦 だれでも何かしら天賦の才をもっているものだ Everyone has *a (natural) gift* for something.

てんぷく 転覆（政府の）overthrow Ⓤ ━転覆する（車両などが）roll over;（船が）capsize ⓗ ⓘ;（政府を）overthrow* ⓗ ／ボートが転覆した The boat *capsized*. ／ 彼らは政府の転覆を企てた They plotted to *overthrow* the government.

てんぷら 天麩羅 tempura ⓒ Ⓤ

てんぷらは様々な魚介類や野菜を油で揚げて作ります。材料に小麦粉、卵、冷水を溶いた衣をつけ、サラダ油かごま油でよく揚げます。衣をよく冷やしておくと、熱い油で揚げたときにからっと仕上がります。てんぷらは大根おろしを入れたつゆにつけて食べるのが一般的です。
Tempura is made by deep-frying many kinds of seafood and vegetables. They are dipped into a batter of flour, eggs and cold water and deep-fried in salad oil or sesame oil. The contrast between the cold batter and the hot oil makes the tempura coating especially light and crispy. People usually eat tempura by dipping it into a thin sauce mixed with grated radish.

てんぶん 天分 a gift (for ...), (a) talent (for ...) ━天分の gifted, talented ／父親

は息子に音楽の天分があると確信した The father was convinced that his son「had a gift for music [was musically gifted].

でんぷん 澱粉 starch ⓤ ─でんぷん質の starchy

テンペラが テンペラ画 tempera painting

てんぺんちい 天変地異 natural disaster ⓒ

テンポ〔音楽〕tempo ⓒ（複～s, tempi）❖比喩的に音楽以外の意味で用いるときはⓒで通例単数形；（ペース）pace ⓤ（またa～）；（速さ）speed ⓤ ∥テンポの速い[遅い]曲に合わせて踊る dance to a tune with a quick [slow] tempo / 生活のテンポ the tempo [pace] of life / 彼の会話のテンポにはついていけない I can't keep pace with him in conversation.

てんぼ 店舗《米》store ⓒ,《英》shop ⓒ

てんぼう 展望 ❶【眺め】view ⓤ ∥展望のきく場所 a place with a fine view
❷【見通し】（可能性）prospect ⓤ（また複数形～s）;（一般的予測）outlook ⓒ ∥長期的展望 a long-term outlook / その地域の民主化の展望は明るい The prospects for democratization in the area are good.
◆日本の政局を展望する predict Japan's political situation
∥展望車 an observation car / 展望台 an observation platform [tower], an observatory

でんぽう 電報 telegram ⓒ, telegraphic message ⓒ,《米口語的》wire ⓒ;（通信方式）telegraph ⓤ ∥友人に結婚祝いの電報を打った I sent a telegram on the occasion of my friend's wedding. / 大学の合格通知を電報で受け取った I received an offer from the university by telegram [telegraph].
◆彼は息子にすぐ帰るようにとの電報を打った He telegraphed [《米口語的》wired] his son to come home at once.
∥電報為替 a telegraphic remittance / 電報料 a telegraph fee [charge]

デンマーク Denmark（❖正式名 the Kingdom of Denmark）─デンマーク人 Dane ⓒ,（総称）the Danish ─デンマーク語 Danish ─デンマーク（人[語]）の Danish

てんまく 天幕（大テント）marquee ⓒ

てんまつ 顛末 everything, the whole story;（詳細）all details ∥事の顛末 everything about the event

てんまど 天窓 skylight ⓒ

てんめい 天命（運命）fate ⓤ;（寿命）the end of life
ことわざ 人事を尽くして天命を待つ ⇨ じんじ

てんめつ 点滅 blink ⓒ ─点滅する flash ⓘ ⓣ;（ちかちかと）flash on and off;（細かくちかちかと）blink ⓘ ∥彼は私に向かってヘッドライトを点滅させた He flashed the headlights at me. / ネオンがちかちかと点滅していた A neon sign was flashing on and off.

てんもん 天文 ∥見積もり額は天文学的数字になった The estimate reached astronomical figures.
∥天文学 astronomy / 天文学者 an astronomer / 天文台 an astronomical observatory

てんやく 点訳 ∥新聞を点訳する transcribe a newspaper into Braille
∥点訳者 a Braille transcriber

てんやもの 店屋物 food delivered from a restaurant

てんやわんや ∥その知らせに村中がてんやわんやの大騒ぎとなった The news threw the whole village into utter confusion.

てんよう 転用 ─転用する（土地・建物などを）convert ⓣ;（金などを）divert ⓣ ∥農地を駐車場に転用する convert farmland into a parking lot / 旅行資金を株に転用する divert the travel money into stocks

でんらい 伝来（導入・渡来）introduction ⓤ ─伝来する be introduced;（受け継がれる）be handed down ∥キリスト教は16世紀にポルトガルから日本に伝来した Christianity was introduced to Japan from Portugal in the 16th century. / これは先祖伝来の掛け軸だ This is a hanging scroll handed down from my ancestors.

てんらく 転落（落下）fall ⓒ;（破滅）downfall ⓒ ─転落する fall* ⓘ ∥バスががけから転落した The bus fell from the cliff. / ギャンブルで彼は転落の道をたどった Gambling caused his downfall. ◆彼女は世界ランク9位に転落した She dropped to ninth place in the world rankings.

てんらんかい 展覧会 exhibition ⓒ,《口語的》show ⓒ ∥展覧会を開く hold an exhibition / 私は展覧会に絵を出品する I'm going to show my painting at the exhibition.
∥展覧会場 an exhibition hall [gallery]

でんりそう 電離層 the ionosphere

でんりゅう 電流 electric current ⓒ ⓤ ∥電流を切る switch off the (electric) current / この物質は電流を通さない This material doesn't conduct「electric current [electricity]. ◆この線には電流が流れている This line is live.
∥電流計 an ammeter / 高[低]圧電流 a high-[low-]voltage current / 直流[交流]電流 direct [alternating] current

でんりょく 電力 (electric) power ⓤ ∥太陽電池は太陽のエネルギーを電力に変える A solar cell converts the energy of the sun into electric power.
∥電力会社 an electric power company / 電力供給 the supply of electric power / 電力事情 the (electric) power situation / 電力消費(量) power consumption

でんわ 電話

（通信手段）(tele)phone ⓤ;（電話機）(tele)phone ⓒ;（電話をかけること）call ⓒ, (tele)phone call ⓒ,《英》ring ⓒ;（回線）line ⓒ ─電話する call ⓣ, (tele)phone ⓣ ⓘ,《英》ring* (up) ⇨ 場面・状況別会話 p.1690, 巻末付録（電話の英会話）
〖～電話〗
今公衆電話からかけているので長く話せないんだ I

でんわ

can't talk long now because I'm calling from *a pay phone.*

メアリーは長電話だ Mary *talks for a long time on the telephone.*

ブラジルからあなたに国際電話ですよ There's *an overseas call* from Brazil for you.

【電話が】

電話が一日中鳴りっぱなしだった *The phone* was ringing all day.

電話が切れた(→出る前に) *The phone* stopped ringing. / (→話している最中に) *The line* was cut off.

最近彼女から電話がない I haven't received *a call* from her recently.

山崎から電話があったとお伝えください Please tell him [her] that Yamazaki *called.*

❖「すみません、電話が遠いのですがもう少し大きな声で話してもらえますか」「もしもし聞こえますか」 "Sorry, but *I can't hear you.* Could you speak up a little?" "Hello, can you hear now?"

【電話に・を】

電話に出る take [answer] *a call*

電話を切らずにそのままお待ちください Please hold *the line.*

実はまだ電話を引いていないんです Actually I haven't had *the line* installed yet.

こちらから後で電話をかけ直します I'll *call* you *back* later.

◆父は電話を切った My father *hung up.* (❖「…との電話を切る」は hang up on … とする)

【電話で】

彼女と電話で2時間しゃべった I talked with her *on [over] the (tele)phone* for two hours.

電話で寿司(ﾌﾞ)を注文した I placed an order for sushi *by phone.*

【電話する】

彼女に電話した I *called [made a call to]* her. / I gave her *a call.*

すぐに警察に電話してください *Call* the police immediately.

何回電話しても彼女のところは話し中だ No matter how often I *call* her, it's busy [《英》engaged].

彼にあしたの会議には出られないと電話しておいた I've *called*「*to tell [and told]* him *that* I can't attend tomorrow's meeting.

【その他】

あす電話をもらえますか Can you give me *a call [ring]* tomorrow? (❖give a ring to me は「指輪をください」の意味) / Can you *call* me (*on the phone*) tomorrow?

携帯のほうに電話をください Can you give me *a call* on my cell phone?

スミス部長、奥様からお電話です Mr. Smith, you've got *a phone call* from Mrs. Smith.

この電話番号は現在使われておりません This *telephone number* is not in service.

母は電話中です My mother *is on the phone.*

真理子は電話魔だ(→電話をかけすぎる) Mariko *makes too many phone calls.*

❖「今の電話だれからだったの」「間違い電話だったよ」 "Who was that *phone call* from?" "It was *a wrong number.*"

❖「電話つながった?」「うん、やっと今つながったよ」 "Did you *manage to get through*?" "Yes, it's ringing now."

‖電話加入者 a telephone subscriber / 電話局 a telephone company / 電話交換手 a (telephone) operator / 電話交換台 a switchboard / 電話線 a telephone line / 電話注文 a telephone order / 電話帳 a phone book / 電話ボックス 《米》a telephone booth,《英》a telephone [call] box / 電話料金 a (tele)phone bill / 電話連絡 contacting *a person* by phone / いたずら電話 (ふざけた) a prank call; (性的) an obscene call / 携帯電話 《米》a cell(ular) phone, a mobile phone / 公衆電話 a public telephone; (硬貨の) a pay phone; (カードの) a cardphone / コードレス電話 a cordless phone / 国際電話 an overseas [international] call / 市外電話 an out-of-town call / 市内電話 a local call / 留守番電話 an answering machine,《英》an answerphone

短歌 また電話しろよと言って受話器置く君に今すぐ電話をしたい (俵万智)
You say, "Call me back again sometime," and then you just hang up the phone.
And as soon as you hang up
I want to call you again.

と

ト 〖音楽〗 G ◎Ⓒ ∥ト長調[短調]で in (the key of) *G* major [minor]
∥ト音記号〖音楽〗a G clef, a treble clef

と¹ 戸 door Ⓒ
戸をあける[閉める] open [close, shut] *a door*
戸があかない *The door* won't open.
その戸は押せば[手前に引けば]あきます Push [Pull] the *door* and it will open.
戸にはかぎがかけてあった[なかった] *The door* was locked [unlocked].
指を戸にはさんだ I got my fingers caught in *the door*.
その戸は中庭に通じている The *door* opens onto the patio.
∥網戸(扉・戸) a screen door; (窓) a window screen / 格子戸 a lattice door / 引き戸 a sliding door
ことわざ 人の口に戸は立てられぬ People will talk.

と² 都 (東京都) Tokyo (Metropolis)(❖手紙のあて名などでは Tokyo だけでよい) ――都の metropolitan ∥都議会(議員) (a member of) the Metropolitan Assembly / 都知事 the Governor of Tokyo / 都庁 the Tokyo Metropolitan Government Office / 都民 a Tokyoite [tóukiouàit], a citizen of Tokyo

-と
❶【同伴・随伴】with
あした父と釣りに行きます I'm going fishing *with* my father tomorrow.
だれと映画に行ったの Who did you go to the movies *with*?
❷【動作の対象・相手】
私は弟とけんかをした I quarreled *with* my brother.
次はだれと試合をするの Who will you play *against* next?
何年も彼と会っていない I haven't seen him for years.
❸【結果・帰結】
彼はチームのレギュラーとなった He became a regular player on the team.
野球の試合は雨で中止となった The baseball game was canceled because of the rain.
❹【比較・対比】
中国と比べれば日本は小さな国だ Japan is a small country「in comparison *with* [compared *to*] China.
大介は美香子の姉と同じ高校に通っている Daisuke goes to the same high school *as* Mikako's older sister.
❺【思考・表現の内容】that(❖ 口語では省略されることが多い)
彼女は頭がいいとみんな言っている Everybody says (*that*) she's smart.
彼は君より少し若いと思うよ I think (*that*) he's a little younger than you.
彼が親切な人だと分かった We've found out (*that*) he is a nice person.
❻【限度】
特売品は1時間とたたないうちにすべて売り切れた All the bargains were sold out before an hour had passed.(❖ 強調のため before 節に過去完了を用いる)
❼【列挙】and
私は犬と猫と金魚を飼っている I have a dog, a cat(,) *and* goldfish.(❖ 3つ以上の語[句, 節]を並べる際には, 最後の語[句, 節]の前だけに and を置くことが多い. この and の前のコンマは省略可能)
◆紅茶とコーヒー, どちらがいいですか Which would you prefer [like better], tea *or* coffee?
❽【…するとき】when;(…するにつれて)as;(…するとすぐ)as soon as …
私は彼に会うといつも赤面してしまう I always turn red *when* I meet him. / I turn red *whenever* I meet him.
私が電話すると彼はすでに寝ていた He was already in bed *when* I called.
年をとると彼は父親に似てきた *As* he grew older, he resembled his father more and more.
彼は家に帰るとすぐに寝てしまった *As soon as* he got home, he went to bed.
❾【仮定・条件】if;(たとえ…でも)even if [though] …
3に7を足すといくつになりますか What do you get *if* you add seven to [and] three?
推薦状を書いていただけるとありがたいのですが I would appreciate it *if* you could write me a letter of recommendation.
たとえ腹が立とうと暴力はいけない You should not resort to force *even if* you get angry.
◆何が起きようと彼は決してうろたえない *Whatever* [*No matter what*] happens, he never gets upset.

ド 〖音楽〗do [dóu] Ⓤ Ⓒ

ど 度
❶【回数】time Ⓒ
私はその映画を何度も[1度, 2度, 3度]見た I saw the movie「*many times* [*once, twice, three times*].
彼と会ったのはそれが3度目だった That was *the third time* I had met him.
◆ 2度目の挑戦で試験に合格した I passed the examination on my *second* attempt [try].
❷【単位】degree Ⓒ
60度の勾配(話) a slope of 60 *degrees* / 東経90度, 北緯40度25分の地点 at 90° E longitude and 40° 25′ N latitude; at a longitude of 90° E and a latitude of 40° 25′ N(❖ 90° E

は ninety degrees east, 40°25′N は forty degrees (and) twenty-five minutes north と読む)
2 直線は30度の角度で交わっている The two lines meet at an angle of 30 *degrees*.
水は摂氏0度で凍る Water freezes at 0 *degrees* C [Celsius, centigrade]. (❖×0 degree とはしない)

◆度の強い眼鏡 *thick* [*strong*] glasses / この眼鏡は私には度が合わない These glasses *don't fit my eyes*. / このウオツカ(のアルコール度数)は60度だ This vodka contains 60 *percent* alcohol. (❖英米ではアルコール度数を proof という単位で表す. 60度の場合,《米》では 120 proof,《英》では 105 proof となる)

🅴「熱はどのくらいありますか」「38度です」 "What's your temperature?" "It's 38 *degrees* (*centigrade*)."

❸ [程度]
度を越した運動は健康に害を及ぼす Excessive [*Too much*] exercise is harmful to the health.
彼のいたずらはいつも度が過ぎる He always *carries* his tricks *too far*.

慣用表現 度を失う (→うろたえる) be [get] *upset*

ど- どでかい建物 a *huge* building / ど根性 *sheer* guts / 町のど真ん中に *right in the middle* of the city / あいつはどけちだ He's *really* stingy. (❖英語には「ど-」に当たる語は特にない)

ドア door ◎ ⇨ と(戸) ‖ ドアストッパー a doorstop(per) / ドアチェーン a door [night] chain / ドアノブ a doorknob / ドアボーイ a doorman(❖「ドアボーイ」は和製英語) / ドアマット a doormat / アコーディオンドア a folding door / 回転ドア a revolving door / 自動ドア an automatic door / スイングドア a swinging [《英》swing] door

どあい 度合い (程度) degree ◎ Ⓤ
とい¹ 問い question ◎ / 問いに答える answer *a question*
とい² 樋 (水平の) gutter ◎;(排水管) drainpipe ◎

といあわせ 問い合わせ inquiry Ⓤ ◎,(照会) reference Ⓤ ◎ / 電話でのお問い合わせには応じられません We don't answer telephone *inquiries*. / 新製品に関する問い合わせの手紙がその会社に殺到した Letters of *inquiry* about the new product flooded into the company. ◆お問い合わせはお電話で If you have any *questions*, please call us.

といあわせる 問い合わせる ask ⓜ ⓔ, inquire ⓜ ⓔ, make* inquiries about ... / その仕事にはどんな資格が必要なのか問い合わせてみた I *asked* [*inquired*] about the necessary qualifications for the job.

◆問い合わせてみるとその本はまだ在庫があることが分かった *On inquiry* I found the book was still in stock.

-という きのう岡田さんという人があなたに会いに来ましたよ *A* Mr. Okada [A man *named* Okada] came to see you yesterday. / 窓という窓が花で飾られている Every window is [*All* the windows are] decorated with flowers. / この近所にある映画俳優が住んでいるという話だ They say (*that*) a movie star lives in this neighborhood. / 私は彼がきょうの午後来るというメッセージを受け取った I received a message *that* he would come this afternoon. / テレビに出るという彼の夢が実現した His dream *of* being on TV has come true.

🅴「あすは休日ですか」「ええ, みどりの日という国民の祝日です」 "Is tomorrow a holiday?" "Yes, it's a national holiday *called* Greenery Day."

-というのに -と言うのに 雨だというのに試合は予定どおり行われた *Though* it was raining, the game was held on schedule.

-というのは -と言うのは 彼はアイスクリームが好きじゃないんです, というのは自分でそう言ってましたから I know he doesn't like ice cream, *because* he said so.

-というのも -と言うのも 彼は無実にちがいない, というのも完璧(㊗)なアリバイがあるからだ He must be innocent, *because* he has a perfect alibi.

-というより -と言うより 彼らはパートナーというよりライバルどうしだ They are not *so much* partners *as* rivals.

-といえども 日曜といえども仕事に行かなければならなかった *Even though* it was Sunday, I had to go to work.

-といえば -と言えば 映画といえば, 先日『タイタニック』を見ました *Speaking of* movies, I saw *Titanic* the other day.

といかえす 問い返す (聞き直す) ask again; (反問する) ask back
といかける 問い掛ける ask ⓜ ⓔ, ask a question ⇨ とう(問う)
といき 吐息 (ため息) sigh ◎
といし 砥石 whetstone ◎;(回転式の) grindstone ◎ / 砥石で包丁を研(と)ぐ sharpen a kitchen knife on *a whetstone*
といただす 問い質す question *a person* closely / 我々は彼の真意を問いただした We *questioned* him *closely about* his real intentions.

ドイツ Germany (❖公式名 the Federal Republic of Germany) ――ドイツ人 German ◎ ――ドイツ語 German Ⓤ ――ドイツ(人[語])の German

-といった 私にはこれといった特技もない I don't have any specialty *to speak of*.

といつめる 問い詰める 彼女になぜそんなことをしたのかと問い詰めたが答えようとしなかった I *pressed* her *for* the reason why she did such a thing, but she wouldn't answer.

トイレ (家庭の)《米》bathroom ◎,(公共の)《米》rest room ◎, toilet ◎,(公式的)lavatory ◎(❖《米》では toilet や lavatory は主に公衆トイレの標示に用いられ, 家庭用は bathroom, 公共用は rest room というが, 家庭ではトイレを toilet を用いるのがふつう);(女性用)《米》ladies' room ◎,《英》the ladies(単数扱い);(男性用)《米》men's room ◎,《英》the gents《単数扱い》/ トイレはどちらですか Where's *the bathroom* [*rest room*]? / すみませんがトイレをお借りできますか Excuse me, but may I use *the bathroom*? (❖× may I borrow ...? とはしない)

トイレットペーパー toilet paper [tissue] (❖数えるときは a roll of ... とする)

とう¹ 問う
❶【尋ねる】ask 🔄 😊, inquire 🔄 😊, question 🔄
人の安否を問う ask [inquire] after a person's safety
彼はその件に関する感想を問われた He *was asked* his views on that matter.
◆計画の賛否を問う住民投票を実施する hold a referendum *on* the plan
❷【問題にする】(気にする) care 🔄 😊; (重要である) matter 😊
値段は問いません. どうしてもそれが欲しいんです I *don't care about* the price. [It *doesn't matter* to me how much it costs.] I want it badly.
◆年齢・性別を問わず *regardless of* age or sex / (広告などで)経験は問いません *No* experience *necessary*.
❸【罪・責任を】
彼は殺人罪に問われている He *is*「*accused of* [*charged with*] murder.

とう² 当 当社 our company / 当の本人(→話題になっている人)が現れた *The person in question* appeared. / 当の本人もその結果には驚いていた He *himself* was surprised at the result. (❖女性なら She herself ... となる)

とう³ 党 party 🔄 //党を結成[解散]する form [break up] *a party* / 党に加わる[を脱退する] join [leave] *a party*
◆彼はコーヒー党だ He's *a coffee person*.
‖党員 a party member, a member of the party / 党首 the party leader, the president of the party / 党大会 a party convention / 第一党 the dominant party / 野党 an opposition party / 与党 the ruling party

とう⁴ 塔 tower 🔄; (仏教寺院などの) pagoda 🔄; (教会などの尖塔(せんとう)) steeple 🔄 //エッフェル塔 the Eiffel Tower / 五重の塔 *a* five-story pagoda / 広告塔 *an* advertising tower / テレビ塔 *a* television tower

とう⁵ 薹 とうの立った(→硬くなり食べごろを過ぎた)大根 a radish *that's too old and hard for eating*

とう⁶ 藤 〔植物〕cane 🔄, rattan 🔄 //藤のかご *a* cane [rattan] basket

とう⁷ 糖 sugar 🔄 //果糖 fruit sugar, fructose, levulose / ブドウ糖 grape sugar, glucose

-とう¹ -等 ❶【等級】1 等船室 a *first-class* cabin / 2 等星 a *second-magnitude* star / 宝くじで 1 等を当てる win (*the*) *first prize* in the lottery
💬「そのレースでは何等だったのですか」「2 等です」 "Where did you finish in the race?" "I finished [came in] *second*."

❷【など】and so on [forth] ⇨ など

-とう² -頭 head 🔄 (複~) //80頭の牛 80 (*head* of) cattle

どう¹

❶【方法を尋ねる】how
いちばん近い病院へはどう行けばいいですか *How do I get to* the nearest hospital?
この問題はどうやって解けばいいのですか *How should I solve* this problem?
ドイツ語で「さようなら」はどういいますか *How do you say* "goodbye" in German?
今それをどうやるべきかを思案中です I'm thinking *how* I should do it.

❷【内容・状態を尋ねる】how, what
きょうは気分はどうですか *How are you feeling* today?
足のぐあいはどうですか *How's* your leg?
景気はどうですか *How's* business?
天気はどうでしたか *What* was the weather *like*? / *How* was the weather?
1,000年後の地球はどうなるだろう *What* will become of the earth in 1,000 years?
彼は今どうしているだろうか I wonder *what* he's doing now.
今晩のご予定はどうなっていますか *What* are your plans for this evening?
どうしたの *What's wrong* [*the matter*] (*with you*)?
それからどうなりましたか *What* happened next?
このような音楽をどう思いますか *What do you think of* [*How do you like*] this kind of music?
💬「調子はどう」「元気でやってるよ」 "*How* are you doing?" "I'm doing fine."
💬「映画はどうだった」「なかなかよかったよ」 "*How* was the movie?" "Not bad."
💬「試験のできはどうだった」「いいできだったよ」 "*How* did you do on your exams?" "I got through with good grades."

┌─ 英作文ノート ─┐
「どう」≠how
この件をどう思いますか
→× *How* do you think of this matter?
→〇 *What* do you think of this matter?
★「どう」に当たる英語はいつも how とは限らない.「…をどう思いますか」の意味では What do you think of ... ? という.

❸【勧誘・提案】《口語的》How [What] about ...?, Why don't [not] ...?
💬「映画に行くのはどう」「いいね」 "*How* [*What*] *about* (going) a movie?" "That sounds like a good idea."
💬「この靴いいなあ」「履いてみたらどう」 "These shoes look nice." "*Why don't* you try them on?"
💬「2,500円でどう」「2,000円以上は払えないな」 "*How about* 2,500 yen?" "I can't pay more than 2,000 yen."

❹【その他】
どうしようもない状況 a *hopeless* situation

そんなことはどうでもいい It *doesn't matter to me*.
どう見ても彼はうそつきには見えなかった *To all appearances*, he didn't seem to be a liar.
どう, おもしろいでしょ *See*, that's interesting, isn't it?
理由はどうあれ人を見下してはいけない Don't look down on people *whatever* the reason.
教科書忘れちゃった. どうしよう Oh, no! I forgot to bring my textbook! *What should I do*?

🅔「彼女, 君があげたプレゼント気に入らなかったって」「それがどうした」"She said she didn't like the present you gave her." "*So (what)*?"

🅔「彼女はきょう来るかな」「さあ, どうだろう」"Will she come today?" "*Who knows*?"

どう² 胴 body ◯; (人間などの) trunk ◯ ∥ダックスフントは胴が長い A dachshund has *a long body* [*trunk*].
◆胴が太い [細い] have *a big* [*small*] *waist* / ずん胴である have *no waist*

どう³ 銅 copper ◯ (✤元素記号 Cu)
∥銅貨 a copper (coin) / 銅山 a copper mine / 銅線 copper wire / 銅メダリスト a bronze medalist / 銅メダル a bronze medal

どう⁴ 道 (行政区画) prefecture ◯ (✤英語では「県」と「道」を区別しない. 北海道はふつう Hokkaido でよい)

どう- 同- (同じ) the same; (前述の) the above(-mentioned) ∥同年齢の子供たち children of *the same age* / 同サイズの2着の服 two suits of clothes of *the same size*
◆同量のオリーブオイルと酢を混ぜる mix *equal amounts* of olive oil and vinegar

どうあげ 胴上げ 彼らは監督を胴上げした They *tossed* their manager *into the air*.

とうあつせん 等圧線 【気象】 isobar [áisəbàːr] ◯

とうあん 答案 (exam [examination]) paper ◯ ∥答案を提出する hand in *one's exam paper* / 答案を採点する [返す] mark [return] *an exam paper*
∥答案用紙 answer sheets

どうい 同意 (意見の一致) agreement ◯; (承諾) 《公式的》consent ◯; (是認・賛成) approval ◯ ──同意する agree (with [to] ...)(✤ agree with ... は「(人・考えに)意見が一致する」, agree to ... は「(提案などを)承諾する」); consent (to ...); approve (of ...) ∥そのことに関してはあなたの意見に同意します I *agree with* you [*your opinion*] about that. / 我々はその費用を負担することに同意しました We *agreed* 「*to* pay [*that* we (should) pay] the expenses. / 両親の同意は得られましたか Did you get [win] your parents' *consent*? / 彼の同意を得ずに計画を実行するわけにはいかない We can't carry out the plan without his *consent* [*approval*]. / 先生はうなずいて同意を示した The teacher nodded *in agreement* [*consent, approval*].

どういう what ∥どんな ∥いったいどういうつもりだ What do you mean by that? / この単語はどういう意味ですか What does this word mean? / 彼女が辞めたってどういうことなんだ What do you mean, she quit?
◆きのう僕と口をきかなかったのはどういうわけだい *How* is it that you didn't speak to me yesterday? / 彼はとても勤勉なのにどういうわけか成功しない He works very hard, *but somehow he never succeeds*.

どういご 同意語 synonym ◯ (↔antonym) ∥"joy"は "pleasure"の同意語です "Joy" is *a synonym for* "pleasure."

どういたしまして
❶【感謝に対して】You're (quite) welcome., Don't mention it., It's my [a] pleasure., My pleasure., No problem., That's 「all right [OK].

🅔「手伝っていただいて本当にありがとうございます」「どういたしまして」"Thank you very much for your help." "*You're welcome*."

❷【謝罪に対して】Never mind., No problem., Not at all., That's 「all right [OK].

🅔「お手数をかけてすみません」「どういたしまして」"I'm sorry to trouble you." "*That's all right*."

とういつ 統一 (単一・まとまり) unity ◯; (統合) unification ◯; (規格化・標準化) standardization ◯ ──統一する unite ◍; unify ◍; standardize ◍ ∥民族の統一 the unity [unification] of a people / 国家を統一する *unify* a nation / この家の内装は統一感がない The interior design of this house 「has no [lacks] *unity*.
◆精神の統一 mental *concentration*
∥統一見解 (a) consensus / 統一国家 a unified nation / 統一地方選挙 nationwide local elections

どういつ 同一 ──同一の the same, the identical ∥同一人物による犯行 crimes by *the same* person
◆富と幸福を同一視してはいけない We should not *equate* wealth *with* happiness.
∥同一性 identity

どういん 動員 mobilization ◯◯ ──動員する mobilize ◍ ∥洪水の被災者を救援するために軍隊が動員された The army *was mobilized* to help the flood victims.
◆その歌手のコンサートはいつもたくさんの観客を動員する That singer's concerts always *draw* large audiences.

とうえい 投影 この小説には作者の心境の変化が投影されている The change in the author's mental state *is reflected* in this novel.

とうおう 東欧 Eastern Europe ──東欧の East European
∥東欧諸国 Eastern European countries

どうおんいぎ 同音異義 homonymy ◯
∥同音異義語 a homonym (✤発音が同じで意味が違う語. ring (指輪)と ring (鳴る), knew (知った)と new (新しい)など)

とうか¹ 灯火 light ◯; (ランプの明かり) lamp-

light [U] ‖灯火管制 a blackout
[慣用表現] 灯火親しむ候となりました Now is *the best time of year for reading.*

とうか² 投下 爆弾を投下する *drop* a bomb / ヘリコプターによる援助物資の投下 *dropping* relief supplies from helicopters / 新プロジェクトに巨額の資本を投下する *invest* a great deal of capital in a new project

どうか¹
❶【依頼・懇願】please
どうか誤解しないでください *Please* don't get me wrong.
どうか入試に合格しますように *Please* let me pass the entrance examination!
◆どうかお幸せに *I wish* you all the best.
❷【正常でない】
どうかしましたか *What's the matter?* / *Is anything* 「*the matter* [*wrong*]?
そんなことをするなんて君はどうかしているよ It's *crazy* of you to do such a thing. / You are *crazy* to do such a thing.
彼女はきょうはどうかしている She *isn't* [*doesn't look*] *herself* today.
❸【疑問】(…かどうか) whether, if
まだチケットがとれるかどうか聞いてみよう Let's find out *whether* [*if*] the tickets are still available.
◆この仕事を彼に任せるのはどうかと思うんだけど I *don't think it's a good idea* to leave this job to him. / 彼は美術館を訪れてはどうかと言った He *suggested* that we (should) visit the museum. (❖ should を用いるのは主に《英》)

[語法]
[**whether** を **if** で代用できない場合]
(1) 直後に or not または to 不定詞が続く // なれるかどうか分かりませんが, オリンピック選手になりたいと思います I don't know *whether* or not I can, but I would like to be an Olympic athlete. (❖ただし I don't know *if* I can or not, ... は可) / その候補者に投票すべきかどうか分からない I don't know *whether* to vote for that candidate or not.
(2) 主語となるとき. ただし文頭にこない場合は if も可 // 彼女が本気で言ったのかどうかは判断しがたい *Whether* she really meant what she said is difficult to judge. / 彼がいっしょに来るかどうかは問題ではない It doesn't matter *whether* [*if*] he comes with us or not. (❖なお目的語であっても文頭にくる場合, if は不可)
(3) 主格補語となるとき // 問題は我々が彼を信頼できるかどうかだ The point is *whether* we can trust him or not.
(4) 名詞の同格節 // 彼がその仕事に適任かどうか疑問だ There is a question *whether* he is the right person for the job.

どうか² 同化 assimilation [U] ──同化する assimilate [自] [他] // 異文化に同化する *assimilate* (*oneself*) *into* a foreign culture

どうか³ 銅貨 copper (coin) [C]

どうが 動画 animation [C]

とうかい¹ 倒壊 collapse [U] ──倒壊する fall* down, collapse [自]; (破壊される) be destroyed // ビルの倒壊 *the collapse* of the building / 倒壊したビル a *collapsed* building / その地震で多くの家が倒壊した Many houses 「*fell down* [*collapsed, were destroyed*] in the earthquake.

とうかい² 東海 (地方) the Tokai district

とうがい 当該 ──当該の (関与している) concerned // 当該官庁 the authorities *concerned* / 当該人物 the person *concerned*; the *said* person

とうかく 頭角 彼はすぐれたゴールキーパーとして頭角を現してきた He began to *stand out* as a good goalkeeper.

どうかく 同格 同格である be *equal in rank* / みんなを同格に扱う treat everyone *equally*

どうかせん 導火線 fuse [C]; (原因) cause [C] // 導火線に火をつける light *the fuse* ◆それが紛争の導火線となった It *caused* the dispute.

とうかつ 統轄 supervision [U] ──統轄する supervise [他] [自], control [他] // 組織を統轄する *supervise* [*control*] an organization ‖統轄者 a supervisor

とうがらし 唐辛子 red pepper [C], cayenne (pepper) [C] (❖薬味としてはどちらも [U])

とうかん 投函 ──投函する mail [他], 《英》post [他] // 結局その手紙は投函されなかった The letter *wasn't mailed* after all.

どうかん 同感 その点に関しては私は全く彼に同感だ With regard to that point, I fully *agree with* him.
💬「こう暑いと食欲がわかないよ」「同感」 "I have no appetite in this heat." "*Same here.*"

どうがん 童顔 童顔である have *a baby* [*childish*] *face* / 童顔の人 a *baby-faced* person

とうき¹ 冬季・冬期 winter (season) [U] [C], wintertime [U] ‖冬季オリンピック the Winter Olympics

とうき² 投棄 ──投棄する throw* away, dump [他] // ごみを不法投棄する *dump* trash illegally

とうき³ 投機 speculation [U] [C] ──投機する speculate [自] // 株に投機する *speculate in* the stock market / 最近は何が投機の対象になるか分からない These days it's hard to tell what will become the object of *speculation.* ◆投機的な事業 a *speculative* venture ‖投機家 a speculator

とうき⁴ 陶器 pottery [U]; (陶磁器・瀬戸物) china(ware) [U]; (土器・陶器) earthenware [U] (❖いずれも数えるときは a piece of ... とする) // 陶器の置物 a *china* ornament
[関連語] 陶工 a potter / 製陶業 pottery / 製陶場 a pottery

とうき⁵ 登記 registration [U] ──登記する register [他] [自] ‖登記所 registry office / 登記簿 a register / 登記料 a registration fee

とうき⁶ 騰貴 rise [C] ──騰貴する rise* [自] // 物価の騰貴 *a rise* in prices

とうぎ 討議 discussion [C] [U], debate [C] [U] ──討議する discuss [他], debate [他] [自] // …を

討議にかける bring ... up for *discussion* / 討議に入る[を打ち切る] begin [close] *a discussion* / 討議に加わる join in *a discussion* / 我々はその問題について委員会と討議した We *discussed* the problem with the committee. / その問題は現在討議中です The matter is now *under discussion*.

どうき[1] 動機 motive ©; (理由) reason ©U /不純な動機から from *an impure motive* / スペイン語を始めた動機は何ですか What's *your motive* for learning Spanish? / What *made* you learn Spanish? / 彼が我々に近づいてきたのにはもう一つ別の動機があった He had another *motive for* approaching us.
◆政治的な動機のあるテロリスト a politically *motivated* terrorist

どうき[2] 同期 前年同期に比べて compared with *the same* [*corresponding*] *period* of the previous year / 私たちは学校で同期だった We *graduated in the same year*. / We *were in the same class* at school.
‖同期生 a classmate

どうき[3] 動悸 palpitations ◆動悸がする *palpitate*; *get palpitations*

どうぎ[1] 動議 motion © /動議を可決[否決]する pass [reject] *a motion* / 休会の動議を提出する propose *a motion* "to adjourn [that the meeting (should) be adjourned]
‖緊急動議 an urgent motion

どうぎ[2] 道義 morality U /彼の発言は道義にもとる His remark *goes against morality*.
◆道義的責任がある have *a moral responsibility*; be *morally responsible* / そんなことをして道義的に許されるのですか Is it *ethical* to do such a thing?

どうぎご 同義語 synonym ©(↔antonym)

とうきゅう[1] 投球 (投げること) pitching U; (投げた球) pitch © ──投球する pitch ⊕, throw* a ball

とうきゅう[2] 等級 grade ©, class ©
◆このオレンジは大きさによって等級分けされる These oranges *are graded* "according to [by] size.

とうぎゅう 闘牛 bullfighting U; (1回の試合) bullfight © ‖闘牛士 a bullfighter, a matador / 闘牛場 a bullring

どうきゅう 同級 誠と僕は高校時代同級だった Makoto and I were *classmates* [*in the same class*] in senior high school.
‖同級生 a classmate

どうきょ 同居 同居人 *a lodger* [*roomer*] / 祖母は私たちと同居している Our grandmother *lives with* us. / この家には2つの家族が同居している Two families *live together* in this house.

とうきょう 東京

東京都(または東京)は日本の首都であり,本州中部の太平洋岸に位置しています.市に相当する23の特別区と26の市,13の町村からなり,太平洋戦争の激戦地,硫黄島などの島々を含みます.23区のみを指して東京と呼ぶこともあります.東京は江戸時代の初めに政治上の中心となり,現在は人口約1,200万人と日本の約1割の人口が集中し,日本の政治・経済・文化の中心地となっています.東京の中心にある皇居はかつて江戸城と呼ばれ,江戸時代,徳川家の代々の将軍が住んでいました.現在は天皇とその家族が住んでいます.
The Tokyo Metropolis (also called just "Tokyo") is the capital of Japan. Located on the Pacific Ocean side of central Honshu, it consists of 23 *ku*, or wards, which correspond to cities; 26 cities; and 13 towns and villages. Tokyo also includes a number of islands such as Iwo Jima, which was a site of fierce battles during the Second World War. Sometimes the name "Tokyo" refers to only the 23 *ku*. Tokyo became Japan's political center at the start of the Edo Period. Now it is home to some twelve million people, about one-tenth of Japan's total population, and it is the country's political, economic and cultural center. At the heart of Tokyo is the Imperial Palace. Called "Edo Castle" during the Edo period, it was home to the shoguns from the Tokugawa family. Now the Emperor and some of his family live there.

どうきょう 同郷 私は彼女と同郷です I'm *from the same town* as she.

どうぎょう 同業 私たちはみんな同業です We *are all in the same business* [*trade*].
‖同業者 《集合的》the trade, the profession; (個人) a person in the same business [trade] / 同業者組合 a trade association

とうきょく 当局 the authorities /学校[市,政府]当局 *the* school [city, government] *authorities* / 関係当局 *the authorities* concerned

どうぐ 道具
❶{器具・用具} tool ©; instrument ©; implement ©; utensil ©; outfit ©, kit ©
 tool: 手に持って使う小さな道具.
 instrument: 医療用などの精巧な道具.
 implement: 簡単な道具.特に農耕具・園芸用品.
 utensil: 家庭用品.特に台所用品.
 outfit, kit: 道具一式.
❷{手段・方便} tool ©
彼は私をその地位を得るための道具にした He used me as *a tool* for getting the position.
‖道具箱 a tool box / 園芸道具 gardening implements / 大道具 a (stage) setting / 小道具 props, (stage) properties / 裁縫道具 a sewing kit / 商売道具 the tools of *one's* [the] *trade* / 大工道具 carpenter's tools / 調理道具 a cooking outfit

どうくつ 洞窟 cave

とうげ 峠 (山道) (mountain) pass ©; (絶頂) peak ©; (危機) crisis © (複 crises) /足柄峠 *the* Ashigara *Pass* / 峠を越える cross

a (mountain) pass / 彼の病気が峠を越したと聞いてひと安心した We were relieved to hear that his illness *had passed the crisis*. / 暑さもここ 2, 3 日が峠だろう The heat *will pass its peak* in a few days.
◆仕事はやっと峠を越した At last I've gotten *past the most difficult part* of the work.

どうけ 道化 (道化師) clown ◎ ∥道化を演じる play [act] *the clown*

とうけい¹ 統計 statistics《複数扱い》∥統計をとる collect [gather, take] *statistics* / 出産統計 *statistics on* births / 統計によるとその国では急速に少子化が進んでいる According to the statistics [The statistics show that] the birthrate has been declining rapidly in that country.
∥統計学 statistics《単数扱い》/ 統計学者 a statistician / 統計表 a statistical table

とうけい² 東経 the east longitude ◆東経 20 度 25 分 20° 25′ *east longitude* (❖20° 25′ は twenty degrees (and) twenty-five minutes と読む)

とうげい 陶芸 ceramics《単数扱い》, ceramic art ◎◎, pottery ◎ ∥陶芸家 a potter

どうけい 同系 ──同系の (起源が同じ) cognate; (会社などの系列が) affiliated
∥同系色 a similar color

とうけつ 凍結 freeze ◎, freezing ◎ ──凍結する freeze* ◎ ∥凍結した道路 a *frozen* [*icy*] road / 賃金の凍結 a wage *freeze* / 公共料金を凍結する *freeze* public utility rates / その会社は全資産を凍結された The company *had* all their assets *frozen*.

どうけん 同権 男女は同権であるべきだ Men and women should have *equal rights*.
∥男女同権 equal rights for men and women

とうげんきょう 桃源郷 (地上の楽園) earthly paradise ◎◎; (理想郷) utopia ◎◎

とうこう¹ 登校 go* [come*] to school ∥あすは 8 時までに登校してください Please *come to school* by eight tomorrow. / 8 月 1 日は登校日だ We *have to go to school* on August 1. (❖英米には休暇中に登校する習慣はない) / 妹が登校拒否している My sister *refuses to go to school*.
◆彼は登校途中に事故にあった He had an accident *on his way to school*.

とうこう² 投稿 contribution ◎ ──投稿する contribute ◎ ∥新聞に投稿する *contribute to* a newspaper / 彼は毎月雑誌にイラストを投稿している He *contributes* his drawings to a magazine every month.
∥投稿者 a contributor / 投稿欄 a readers' column, a letters-to-the-editor column

とうこう³ 投降 surrender ◎ ──投降する surrender ◎ ⇨ こうふく (降伏)

とうごう¹ 統合 integration ◎; (統一) unity ◎, unification ◎; (会社・組織の) consolidation ◎ ──統合する integrate ◎, unify ◎; consolidate ◎ ∥2 つの町を統合する *unite* [*unify*] the two towns / その会議の目的は世界経済のより緊密な統合にある The aim of the conference is *the closer integration* of the world's economy.

とうごう² 等号〔数学〕equal [equals] sign ◎

どうこう¹ 動向 (傾向) trend ◎; (動き) movement ◎◎ / 経済の動向 economic *trends* / 時代の動向 *the trends* of the times / 彼らは世論の動向を調査した They studied *trends* in [of] public opinion. / 警察は容疑者の動向をひそかに監視していた The police have been secretly monitoring *the movements* of the suspect.

どうこう² 同好 同好の士 a person *with* [*sharing*] *the same interest*
∥同好会 a club, a society

どうこう³ 同行 ──同行する go* [come*] with ..., accompany ◎ ∥通訳が 1 人我々に同行する An interpreter *is coming with* us.

どうこう⁴ 瞳孔〔解剖〕pupil ◎

どうこう⁵ 私はあなたにどうこう言える立場にない I'm in no position to tell you *this or that*.

とうこうせん 等高線〔地理〕contour line

とうごく 投獄 imprisonment ◎ ──投獄する put* *a person in* jail [prison], jail ◎, imprison ◎ ◆彼は 10 年間投獄されている He's *been in jail* for 10 years.

とうざ 当座 (しばらくの間) for the present, for the moment, for the time being ∥当座は 2 万円もあれば足りるだろう Twenty thousand yen should be enough「*for the present* [(→当座の必要には): *for our immediate needs*]. ◆当座しのぎの住まい makeshift [stopgap] housing
∥当座預金《米》a checking account, 《英》a current account

どうさ 動作 movement ◎◎; (身ぶり) gesture ◎; (ふるまい) manners ∥軽やかな[ぎこちない]動作 light [stiff] *movements* / 動作が機敏である[のろい] be quick [slow] in *one's movements*

とうさい 搭載 この車は 230 馬力のエンジンを搭載している This car *has* [*is equipped with*] a 230-horsepower engine.

とうざい 東西 east and west; (東洋と西洋) the East and the West ∥その道は東西に延びている The street runs「*east and west* [*from east to west*].
〔慣用表現〕洋の東西を問わず (→世界中で) *all over the world*

どうざい 同罪 君も同罪だ (→君にも責任がある) You *are also to blame*.

とうざいなんぼく 東西南北 north, south, east and west (❖英語では北南東西の順)

とうさく¹ 倒錯 (性的倒錯) perversion ◎◎
∥性的倒錯者 a (sexual) pervert

とうさく² 盗作 plagiarism ◎, 《口語的》crib ◎ ──盗作する plagiarize ◎, 《口語的》crib ◎ ∥盗作者 a plagiarist

どうさつ 洞察 insight ◎◎ / 深い洞察力の持ち主 a person of deep *insight* / 物事の本質を洞察する gain [get] *(an) insight into* the nature of things / 彼女は最近の著書で環境問題に対するすぐれた洞察を示した In her recent

とうさん

book, she showed remarkable *insights into* environmental problems.
とうさん 倒産 bankruptcy ⓊⒸ ――倒産する go* bankrupt, fail ⾃ ∥長引く不況でその会社は倒産に追い込まれた The long recession reduced the company to *bankruptcy*.
どうさん 動産 movable property Ⓤ,〖法律〗movables
どうざん 銅山 copper mine Ⓒ
とうし¹ 投資 investment ⓊⒸ ――投資する invest ⽥ ⾃ ∥彼は株に1,000万円投資した He *invested* [*made an investment of*] 10 million yen in stocks.
‖投資家 an investor / 投資信託 an investment trust, a mutual fund / 機関投資家 an institutional investor / 公共投資 public investment / 設備投資 capital investment
とうし² 凍死 death from cold ――凍死する freeze* to death, be frozen to death;《寒さで死ぬ》die of [from] cold
とうし³ 闘志 fighting spirit Ⓤ Ⓒ, fight Ⓤ ∥闘志にあふれている be full of 「*fighting spirit* [*fight*] / 闘志を見せる show *one's fighting spirit*
とうし⁴ 透視 ――透視する (見抜く) see* through … ‖透視能力 clairvoyant power
とうし⁵ 闘士 fighter Ⓒ;(政治運動などの) activist Ⓒ;(主義などの擁護者) champion Ⓒ
とうじ¹ 当時 at that time, in those days, then ∥私の住む町は当時それほど大きくはなかった My town was not that big 「*at that time* [*in those days, then*]. / 電球は当時としては画期的な発明だった The light bulb was a very novel invention *at that time*. / 当時から彼女の才能には注目していた I noticed her talent *even in those days*.
◆当時の日本の首相 the *then* Prime Minister of Japan (❖この then は形容詞) / 当時の記憶はあいまいだ My memories of *those days* are vague. / 私が学校を卒業した当時は大変な就職難だった It was very hard to get a job *when* I graduated from school.
とうじ² 冬至 the winter solstice
とうじ³ 湯治 温泉に湯治に行く go to a spa for *a hot-springs cure*
‖湯治客 a visitor at a hot spring / 湯治場 a spa
とうじ⁴ 答辞 彼女は卒業式で(校長の祝辞に対して)答辞を述べた She *made* [*gave*] *an address in reply to* the principal's address at graduation.
どうし¹ 動詞 〖文法〗verb Ⓒ ((略語))v, V)
‖動詞句 a phrasal verb / 規則動詞 a regular verb / 自動詞 an intransitive verb / 助動詞 an auxiliary verb((略語))aux.) / 他動詞 a transitive verb / 不規則動詞 an irregular verb
どうし² 同志 (組合・政党などの) comrade Ⓒ, fellow member Ⓒ;(仲間) companion Ⓒ
-どうし ―同士 バスどうしの衝突 a collision *between two* buses / 私たちはいとこどうしです We are *cousins*. / 彼らは仲間どうしで言い

争いを始めた They began to quarrel *among themselves*. / 彼女たちはお隣どうしだ They live next door *to each other*.
どうじ 同時 ――同時に at the same time, at once, simultaneously
∥2つのグループは同時に出発した The two groups started 「*at the same time* [*simultaneously, together*].
同時に2つのことをするのは私には無理だ I cannot do two things 「*at once* [*at one time*].
◆店は開店と同時に満員になった The shop filled 「*as soon as* [*just as, the moment*] it opened. / ピストルの音と同時に選手たちは飛び出した *At* the bang of the pistol the runners dashed off. / 彼らは卒業と同時に結婚した They got married *just after they graduated*. / 彼はコメディアンであると同時にすぐれた俳優でもあった He was *a good actor as well as* a comedian. / He was a comedian *and also* a good actor.
‖同時通訳 simultaneous interpretation;(人) a simultaneous interpreter
とうしき 等式 〖数学〗equality Ⓒ
とうじき 陶磁器 《集合的》ceramics,《集合的》china Ⓒ
とうじご 頭字語 acronym Ⓒ (❖複合語の各語の頭文字を組み合わせて作った語;UNICEF など)
とうじしゃ 当事者 (関係者) the person concerned;(契約・事件・訴訟の) the party (concerned) ∥その件は当事者どうしの話し合いで一応の解決に至った The issue was tentatively settled through the talks between *the persons* [*parties*] *concerned*.
どうじだい 同時代 the same age [period]
――同時代の contemporary ∥ピカソはダリと同時代の画家である Picasso was *contemporary with* [*a contemporary of*] Dali. (❖ a contemporary は「同時代の人」の意味)
とうしつ 等質 the same quality, homogeneity Ⓤ
とうじつ 当日 当日は快晴だった It was nice and clear *that day*. / テストの当日はとても緊張していた I was very nervous on *the day* of the test. / この入場券は発行当日限り有効です This admission ticket is valid [good] only for *the day of issue*.
‖当日券 a same-day ticket sold on the day of the performance
どうしつ¹ 同室 …と同室である (→部屋を共有している) share a room with … ∥彼らはホテルで同室だった They stayed in *the same room* at the hotel.
どうしつ² 同質 the same quality, homogeneity Ⓤ (↔heterogeneity) ∥同質の材料 material of *the same quality*
どうじつ 同日 the same day
どうして
❶【なぜ】why
どうして彼女は行ってしまったのだろうか I don't know 「*why* she's gone [*what made her go*].
どうしてきのうパーティーに来なかったの *Why*

didn't you [*How come* you didn't] come to the party yesterday? (❖*How come* の後は平叙文の語順)

💬「行ってドアを閉めてきなさい」「どうして私が」 "Go (and) shut the door." "*Why me?*"

💬「きょうは外出しちゃだめだよ」「どうして」 "You can't go out today." "*Why not?*" (❖否定・禁止などに対する返答には not を付ける)

❷【どうやって】how

テレビをつけっぱなしにしてどうして勉強できるんだ I don't know *how* you can study with the TV on.

◆その知らせを聞いたときどうしていいか分からなかった When I heard the news, I didn't know *what to do.*

❸【その他】

その映画はつまらないと聞いていたが, どうしてなかなかのものだった I had heard the movie was boring, but *actually* it was quite good.

どうして, どうして, あなたには到底かないませんよ *No, no*, I'm no match for you.

どうしても

どうしても今週中にその件に関して結論を下さなければならない We must make a decision on that matter by the end of this week *at all costs* [*by all means*].

有機食品はどうしても(→必然的に)やや高価になる Organic foods are *inevitably* [*necessarily*] more expensive.

この窓はどうしてもあかない This window *won't* open.

彼の名前がどうしても思い出せない I「*simply can't* [*can't for the life of me*] remember his name.

どうしても携帯電話が欲しいのなら自分で買いなさい If you *must* have a cell phone, buy one for yourself. (❖この must は主張・固執を表し, 強勢が置かれる)

金がどうしても必要なんだ I need money *badly*.

どうしても彼女に本当のことを話す気になれなかった I *couldn't bring myself* to tell her the truth.

彼女はどうしても家に帰ると言って聞かなかった She *insisted on* going home.

分かった, どうしてもというなら彼を助けましょう OK, I'll help him, *if you insist*.

とうしゅ¹ 投手 〖野球〗pitcher ◯ ‖投手陣 the pitching staff / 投手戦 a pitcher's duel / 救援投手 a relief pitcher / 左腕投手 a left-handed pitcher,《主に米》a lefty,《米》a southpaw / 勝利投手 the winning pitcher / 先発投手 the starting pitcher, the starter / 敗戦投手 the losing pitcher

とうしゅ² 党首 the leader of a (political) party, the party leader
‖党首会談 a meeting of party leaders

どうしゅ 同種 同種の犬 dogs of *the same kind* [*sort*]

とうしゅう 踏襲 従来のやり方を踏襲する *follow* the traditional way

とうしょ¹ 当初 当初の目標を達成する reach *one's original* goal / その計画は当初から成功が危ぶまれていた The plan was unlikely to succeed *from the beginning.*

とうしょ² 投書 letter ◯ ‖苦情の投書 *a letter* of complaint / 新聞に投書する *write a letter to* a newspaper
‖投書箱 a suggestion box / 投書欄 a readers' column, a letters-to-the-editor column

とうしょう 凍傷 frostbite ⓤ ; (しもやけ) chilblain ‖左手が凍傷にかかった I *got frostbite* on my left hand. / My left hand *was frostbitten*.

とうじょう¹ 登場 appearance ⓤ◯ ──登場する appear ⓘ, make* an appearance ‖これが彼女のテレビ初登場だ This is her *first appearance* on TV. / この芝居には2組の夫婦が登場する Two couples *appear* in this play. / 毎年続々と新人歌手が登場する Every year new singers *appear* one after another. ◆(脚本のト書きで)ハムレット, 登場 *Enter* Hamlet.
‖登場人物 a character

とうじょう² 搭乗 boarding ⓤ, embarkation ⓤ◯ ──搭乗する《公式的》board ⓘⓘ, go* on board, go aboard, get* on (...) ‖飛行機に搭乗する *go on board* [*go aboard, get on*] a plane ◆彼はその飛行機には搭乗していなかった He wasn't *on board* the plane. / オタワ行きカナダ航空102便にご搭乗いただき, ありがとうございます I would like to welcome you *aboard* Air Canada Flight 102 bound for Ottawa.
‖搭乗員《集合的》the crew ; (1人) a crew member / 搭乗口 a gate / 搭乗券 a boarding pass / 搭乗者名簿 a passenger list / 搭乗手続き boarding procedures

どうじょう¹ 同情 sympathy ⓤ ; compassion ⓤ ; pity ⓤ ──同情する sympathize (with ...); pity ──同情的な sympathetic → コミュニケーションスキル p.1042

> sympathy : 他人の苦しみ・悲しみなどに対する思いやり・理解・共感.
> compassion : 積極的な援助の気持ちを含んだ同情.
> pity : 弱者に対する哀れみ.

同情的な手紙 a *sympathetic* letter / 同情を集める attract *sympathy*

彼はその話で我々の同情を得ようとした He tried to get our *sympathy* by telling the story.

私は彼女に深く同情した I *felt* deep *pity* [*sympathy, compassion*] for her.

友人たちは私の怒りを理解し同情してくれた My friends understood and *sympathized with* my anger.

あんな人には同情できないね I *have no sympathy for* a man like that.

同情なんてしないでください Don't *pity* me.
‖同情票 a sympathy vote

どうじょう² 同上 the same as above, ditto ◯ (❖一覧表などで同上を表すときの記号(〃)

[コミュニケーションスキル] ―同情―

①相手に同情する

(A) I failed the exam.
–Oh, **that's too bad.**
試験に落ちちゃったんだ. ―いや, それはお気の毒に.

(B) My younger sister broke her leg while skiing.
–Oh, **I'm sorry to hear that.**
私の妹がスキーをしていて足の骨を折っちゃったんです. ―まあ, それはお気の毒ですね.

(C) I got food poisoning from some oysters.
–Oh, **that's awful.**
カキにあたっちゃったんですよ. ―おやおや, それは大変ですね.

(D) My parents are getting divorced.
–Oh, **that's tough. I know how you feel.**
両親が離婚しそうなんだ. ―それは大変だね. 君がどんな気持ちか分かるよ.

(E) There was a motorbike accident near here last night. I hear the rider was killed.
–Oh, **that's terrible!** [**How terrible!**]
昨夜この近くでバイクの事故があったんだ. 運転していた人は死んだらしいよ. ―それは恐ろしい!

(F) **I'm sorry to hear** ⌈**that** your father is ill [**about** your father's illness]. I hope he will get well soon.
お父様がご病気だそうで, 大変ですね. 早くよくなられるといいですね.

☞ だれかの不幸や不運な話を耳にして「それはお気の毒に」と同情を示す表現としては, (A) と (B) が最も一般的. (C) の awful は「ひどい」の意味.
☞ (D) の That's tough. は主につらい状況や境遇について同情する場合に用いる表現.
☞ (F) の I'm sorry to hear that [about] … は, (B) の I'm sorry to hear that. より具体的に同情を表す場合に用いる表現.

②相手を気づかう

(A) You look pale. **Are you** ⌈**all right** [**OK**]?
–Just a slight headache. I'm ⌈all right [OK].
顔色がよくないね. 大丈夫かい. ―ちょっと頭が痛いだけさ. 大丈夫だよ.

(B) **How do you feel** this morning?
–(I feel) much better. Thanks.
けさは気分はどうだい. ―ずっといいよ. ありがとう.

(C) **Can I help you with anything?** [**Is there anything I can do for you?**]
–I'm ⌈all right [OK].
何か私にできることはありますか. ―大丈夫です.

(D) You look worried. **What's the matter?**
–My mother has been sick recently.
心配そうな顔をされてどうしたのですか. ―母がこのところぐあいが悪くてね.

☞ (A) はぐあいが悪そうな人を見たり, だれかが転んだりしたときにかける言葉. (B) は特に気分を尋ねる表現. **How are you feeling?** もほぼ同じ意味で用いる.
☞ 困っている人, 困っていそうな人に声をかけるには (C), (D) のようにいう. 積極的に相手を助けたいという気持ちは (C) のほうが強い.

のこと)

どうじょう[3] 同乗 人とタクシーに同乗する *share* a taxi *with* a person / 彼女の車に駅まで同乗させてもらった(→彼女が駅まで車に乗せてくれた) She *gave* me *a lift* [*ride*] to the station.

どうじょう[4] 道場 (練習場) practice hall [C]

どうしようもない あいつはどうしようもない悪がきだ He is such an *impossible* brat. / すみません. どうしようもなかったんです I'm sorry. *I just couldn't help it.* / いよいよどうしようもなくなって(→絶望的になって)彼はサラ金から金を借りた He was so *desperate* that he finally borrowed money from a loan shark.

どうしょくぶつ 動植物 plants and animals(❖日本語の語順と逆になることに注意)

とうじる 投じる ❶【投げる】throw* [他], cast* [他] ‖海中に身を投じる *throw oneself* into the sea
❷【費やす】spend* [他]; (支払う) pay* [他][自] ‖その会社は新しいプロジェクトに巨費を投じた The company *spent* huge sums of money on the new project.
❸【その他】…に賛成[反対]票を投じる *vote for* [*against*] …; *cast a vote for* [*against*] … / 革命運動に身を投じる「*throw oneself into* [*join*] a revolutionary movement
[慣用表現] 一石を投じる ➔ いっせき(一石)

どうじる 動じる 彼は何事にも動じない(→動揺しない) He *is never upset* by anything.

とうしん 答申 report [C] ‖首相に答申を提出する *submit a report* to the prime minister
‖答申案 a draft of a report / 答申書 a report

どうしん 童心 私たちは童心に返って水遊びをした We played in the water *like children*.

どうじん 同人 group [C],《公式的》coterie [kóutəri] [C]; (同人の一員) member [C] ‖同人誌 a little magazine

どうしんえん 同心円〖数学〗concentric circle [C]

とうしんだい 等身大 等身大の像 a *life-size(d)* statue

とうすい 陶酔 彼らは成功の喜びに陶酔していた They *were intoxicated with* [*by*] the joy of success.
‖自己陶酔〖心理〗narcissism

どうすう 同数 その計画については賛成票と同数の反対票があった The plan received *the*

same number of no votes *as* yes votes. / There were *as many* no votes *as* yes votes.

どうせ
どうせ(→いずれにせよ)やらなければいけないのだから早くやってしまおう We have to do it *anyway* [*anyhow, in any case*], so let's do it right away.

どうせ(→きっと)僕が負けるに決まってるよ I'*m sure* [*bound*] *to* lose the game.

どうせ(→仮にも)やるならベストを尽くそう If we try *at all*, let's do our best.

どうせ(→結局)いつかは本当のことを話さなければならなくなるよ You'll have to tell the truth *in the end*.

どうせ(→遅かれ早かれ)怒られるなら今すぐ謝ってしまおう If I must be scolded *sooner or later*, I'll apologize right away.

あいつらにできるのはどうせ(→せいぜい)その程度だ That's *the best* they can do.

💬「あいつまた遅刻してきたよ」「どうせそんなことだろうと思ったよ」"He came late again." "I thought *so* [*as much*]."

💬「君は本当に分からず屋だな」「どうせそうでしょうよ」"You're really stubborn." "*If you say so.*"

とうせい¹ 当世 (現代) the present day; (今日〈こん〉) today Ⓤ / 』当世の若者 today's [*present-day*] young people; (the) young people (*of*) today

◆当世風の建物 an *up-to-date* building

とうせい² 統制 (支配・管理) control Ⓤ (また ~s); (規制) regulation Ⓤ ——統制する control Ⓣ; regulate Ⓣ / 』厳しい[ゆるやかな]統制 strict [*loose*] *control* / 』統制のとれた行進 a *regulated* march / 』統制を敷く[解除する] exert [*lift*] *controls* / 』政府は物価に対する統制を強める[ゆるめる]ことに決めた The government decided to tighten [*loosen*] *controls* over prices. / 』この地域は敵軍の統制下にある This area is *controlled* by [*under the control of*] enemy troops.

』統制経済 a controlled economy / 』思想統制 thought control / 』物価統制 price control

どうせい¹ 同姓 the same surname [family name] / 』彼は私と同姓同名です He has *the same surname and given name* as mine.

どうせい² 同性 the same sex / 』彼女の小説は同性の読者にとても人気がある Her novels are very popular among readers of「*the same* [*her own*] *sex*.

』同性愛 homosexuality; (女性の) lesbianism / 』同性愛者 a homosexual, a gay (❖gayは特に男性同性愛者を指すことがある); (女性同性愛者) a lesbian

どうせい³ 同棲 ——同棲する live together, live with *a person*; (口語的に) shack up (with *a person*) (❖非難の気持ちが含まれる)

どうせい⁴ 動静 (行動) movements; (情勢) situation / 』容疑者の動静を監視する monitor *the movements* of the suspect

とうせき¹ 投石 怒った群衆は警官隊に投石を繰り返した The angry mob *threw stones* repeatedly at the police force.

とうせき² 透析 [医学] dialysis [daiǽləsis] Ⓤ / 』透析を受ける receive [*undergo*] *dialysis* / 』人工透析 artificial dialysis

どうせき 同席 私は彼女のお姉さんと同席した (→同じテーブルに着いた) I *sat at the same table* with her sister. / 』私もその会に同席していました(→出席していた) I *was present* at the meeting, too.

どうせきだい 同世代 同世代の友達 friends of *the same generation* [*age group*]

とうせん¹ 当選 (選挙の) election Ⓤ Ⓒ; (懸賞などの) winning Ⓤ ——当選する (選挙で) be elected, win* an election; (懸賞などで) win a prize

山田氏の知事当選は確実だ Mr. Yamada is sure to *win the* gubernatorial *election*.

彼は当選の見込みはない He has no chance of「*being elected* [*winning the election*].

彼女は国会議員に当選した She「*was elected* to the Diet [*won a seat in Diet*].

彼は懸賞論文に当選した He *won a prize* in the essay contest.

』当選者(選挙の) a successful candidate; (懸賞などの) a prize winner

とうせん² 当籤 ——当せんする win* a prize / 』宝くじで2等に当せんした I *won* (the) second *prize* in the lottery.

』当せん券 a lucky [winning] ticket / 』当せん番号 a lucky [winning] number

とうぜん 当然
of course, naturally ——当然の natural

当然ながら地元住民は新空港計画に強く反対した *Of course* [*Naturally*] the local people strongly opposed the new airport project.

みんながジョンを好きなのは当然だ. 彼は親切で思いやりがあるから *It is natural that* everyone likes John, because he's kind and thoughtful.

◆彼女が彼の頼みを断るのも当然だ(→少しも不思議ではない) *It is no wonder that* she refuses to do what he asked. / 』当然彼はここに来るものと思っていた I *took it for granted that* he would come here. / 』それは彼らには当然の報いだった It *served them right*.

💬「私が彼女に言わなきゃだめなの?」「当然でしょ」"Do I have to say it to her?" "*Of course.*"

💬「助けていただいて本当にありがとうございました」「当然のことをしたまでですよ」"Thank you so much for your help." "Don't mention it. *Anyone would have done the same.*"

どうぜん 同然 彼らは勝ったも同然だ They have *almost* won the game. / 』彼の部屋は掘っ立て小屋同然だ His room is *no better than* a hut. / 』ただ同然の値段でこの本を買った I bought this book for *almost* nothing.

どうぞ
❶【勧誘・要請して】please

どうぞ楽にしてください *Please* make yourself at home.
お先にどうぞ After you, *please*.
お話をどうぞ続けてください *Please* go ahead with your speech.
お茶をどうぞ *Please* have a cup of tea.
◆どうぞよろしくお願いします *How do you do*?

❷【承知して】
🗣「砂糖を取ってください」「はい、どうぞ」 "Pass me the sugar, please." "Yes, *here you are*."
🗣「窓を閉めてもいいですか」「ええどうぞ」 "Do you mind if I close the window?" "*Not at all*."
🗣「辞書を借りてもいいですか」「どうぞ」 "May I use your dictionary?" "*Of course* [*Sure*]."

とうそう¹ 逃走 escape ⓒ; (特に犯罪者の) getaway ⓒ ──逃走する escape ⓘ; (逃げる) run* [get*] away ∥刑務所から囚人が逃走した A prisoner *escaped* from the prison.
◆2人組の泥棒は依然逃走中だ(→逮捕されていない) A pair of thieves are still「*at large* [*on the run*].
∥逃走経路 an escape route

とうそう² 闘争 (戦い) fight ⓒ; (苦闘) struggle ⓒ; (衝突) conflict ⓒ; (ストライキ) strike ⓒ ∥労働組合は会社に対して賃上げ闘争を行っている The labor union is carrying on *a struggle* with the company *for higher wages*.
∥闘争心 fighting spirit / 闘争本能 fighting instinct / 階級闘争 the class struggle / 権力闘争 a power struggle / 武力闘争 armed conflict

どうそう 同窓 私は彼女と同窓です (→同じ学校を卒業した) She and I *graduated from the same school.* / (→同じ学校に通った) She and I *went to the same school.*
∥同窓会(組織) an alumni association; (会合) a class reunion / 同窓生(男性の) an alumnus; (女性の) an alumna; (男女両方) alumni, alumnae

どうぞう 銅像 bronze statue ⓒ

どうぞく 盗賊 (強盗) robber ⓒ; (夜盗・押し込み強盗) burglar ⓒ

どうぞく 同族 (同じ家族) the same family
∥同族会社 a family business / 同族目的語【文法】a cognate object

とうそつ 統率 (指揮権) command ⓤ; (指導) leadership ⓤ ──統率する (命令・指揮する) command ⓘ; (率いる) lead* ⓘ ∥彼はキャプテンとしてチームをよく統率している He *leads* the team well as a captain.
◆新しい監督は統率力のある人だ The new manager is *a good leader.* / The new manager has good *leadership ability*.

とうた 淘汰 selection ⓤ ──淘汰する (選び出す) select ⓘ; (排除する) eliminate ⓘ; (取り除く) weed out ∥企業が淘汰されていくだろう Companies will probably *be weeded out*.
∥自然淘汰 natural selection

とうだい¹ 灯台 lighthouse ⓒ
ことわざ 灯台もと暗し The darkest place is under the candlestick. (→燭台(しょくだい)の下が最も暗い)

とうだい² 当代 the present age ∥彼は当代随一の名優です He is one of the greatest actors in *the present age.* / He is one of *today*'s greatest actors.

どうたい¹ 胴体 (体) body ⓒ; (人・動物の) trunk ⓒ; (頭・手・足を除いた) torso ⓒ (複 ~s); (飛行機などの) fuselage ⓒ ∥胴体着陸 (a) belly landing, (a) crash landing

どうたい² 動態 movement ⓤ ∥人口動態統計 vital statistics

どうたい³ 導体 conductor ⓒ

とうたいかい 党大会 party convention ⓒ

とうたつ 到達 arrival ⓤ ⓒ ──到達する reach ⓘ, arrive at …; (ある点まで来る) come* to …; (目的に) attain ⓘ ∥目標に到達する *attain* a goal / 彼らは結局同じ結論に到達した After all, they「*came to* [*arrived at*, *reached*] the same conclusion. / 私たちは予定より2時間遅れで目的地に到達した We *reached* the destination two hours behind schedule.

とうち¹ 当地 here; (この場所) this place ∥これは当地の名産品です This is the specialty of *this place*.

とうち² 統治 (支配) rule ⓤ; (政治的な) government ⓤ ──統治する (支配する) rule ⓘ; (治める) govern ⓘ ∥人民を統治する *rule one's* people / 当時その国はフランスの統治下にあった The country was *under* French *rule* at that time.

とうち 倒置 【文法】inversion ⓤ ⓒ

とうちゃく 到着 arrival ⓤ ──到着する arrive (at [in] …) (❖その場所を一点と感じている場合は at, 広がりをもっと感じている場合は in を用いる, また, 現場などに到着する場合は on を用いる), get* to …, reach ⓘ
悪天候で東京への到着が遅れた We *arrived in* Tokyo late because of the bad weather. / The bad weather delayed *our arrival* in Tokyo.
列車は3時に名古屋駅に到着した The train *arrived at* Nagoya Station at three.
飛行機は定刻に[定刻より1時間遅れて]到着した The plane *arrived*「*on time* [*one hour behind schedule*].
私たちは目的地に無事到着した We *reached* [*got to*] our destination safely.
神戸には10時に到着予定です We *are due to arrive at* Kobe at 10.
∥到着時刻 arrival time / 到着ホーム an arrival platform / 到着ロビー an arrival lounge [lobby]

どうちゅう 道中 道中ご無事で Have *a nice trip*!

とうちょう¹ 盗聴 (電話の) wiretapping ⓤ; (隠しマイクでの) bugging ⓤ ──盗聴する tap ⓘ, wiretap ⓘ; bug ⓘ
∥盗聴器(電話の) a wiretap; (隠しマイク) a concealed microphone, 《口語的》a bug

とうちょう² 登頂 その女性グループはキリマンジャロの登頂に成功した The women's group made *a* successful *ascent* of Mt. Kilimanjaro.

どうちょう 同調 ──同調する (共感する) sympathize (with ...); (まねをする) follow suit ∥彼女はすぐ人の意見に同調する She always *sympathizes with* other people's opinion. / 彼がその計画に反対したとき私も同調した When he opposed the plan, I *followed suit*.

とうちょく 当直 duty ⓤ ∥今夜は彼が当直だ He *is on duty* tonight.
∥当直医 a night doctor, a doctor on night duty / 当直員 an official on duty

とうてい 到底 今から家を出ても到底間に合わないだろう I can't *possibly* be on time if I leave home now. / この宿題はきょう一日では到底終わらない It is *absolutely* impossible to finish this homework within today. / あのチームには到底かなわない *There is no way* we can beat that team. / 試験の結果は到底満足できるものではなかった The results of the test were「*not at all* [*by no means*] satisfactory.

とうてい 童貞 virginity ⓤ; (人) virgin ⓒ (※「処女」の意味で用いることが多い)

どうでもいい そんなのどうでもいいことだ(→気にしない) I *don't care* about that. / 彼女が来ても来なくても私はどうでもいい(→重要ではない) *It doesn't matter* to me whether she comes or not. / (→関心がない) I'm *indifferent about* whether she comes or not.

どうてん 同点 (試合などの) tie ⓒ; (引き分け) draw ⓒ ∥試合は 3 対 3 の同点に終わった The game ended in *a tie* [*draw*] at 3 to 3. ◆彼のゴールで同点になった His goal *tied the score*. / 伊藤は同点ホームランを打った Ito hit *a game-tying homer*.
∥同点決勝 a playoff

どうてん² 動転 そのときは気が動転していたので彼に何を言ったか覚えていない I *was very upset* at that time, so I don't remember what I said to him.

とうとい 尊い・貴い (貴重な) precious; (価値のある) valuable; (高貴な) noble; (神聖な) holy, sacred ∥命はとても貴いものだ Life is very *precious*. / 貴い経験をしたと思いますI think I had a *valuable* [*precious*] experience.

とうとう¹ 到頭 (ついに) at last; (ようやく・やっと) finally; (最後には) in the end; (結局) after all
彼らはとうとう目的地にたどり着いた They reached their destination *at last*.
とうとう彼の夢が実現する *Finally* his dreams are to be realized.
そのことはとうとう話題にのぼらなかった We didn't discuss it *after all*.
とうとう彼女は怒りだした She got angry *in the end*.

とうとう² 滔々 川の水はとうとうと流れている The river is flowing *swiftly*. / 彼はとうとうと自分の主張を述べた He spoke his opinion *eloquently*.

どうとう 同等 equality ⓤ ──同等の (等しい) equal; (相当の) equivalent ◆大卒または同等の学力のある人 university graduates or *the equivalent* (※この equivalent は「同等のもの」の意味の名詞) / 将来は男女を同等に扱ってくれる会社で働きたい In the future, I want to work for a company that treats men and women *equally*.

どうどう 堂々 選手たちは堂々と競技場に入場した The players entered the field *in a grand manner*. / 彼女は堂々と(→自信をもって)自分の意見を述べた She expressed her views *confidently*. / 彼は負けはしたものの堂々と(→公正に)闘った Though he lost the game, he played *fair*.

どうどうめぐり 堂々巡り 話し合いは堂々めぐりで結論が出なかった The discussion *went around in circles* and we couldn't reach a conclusion.

どうとく 道徳 morals; (道徳性) morality ⓤ ──道徳の・道徳的な moral ∥道徳心を形成する mold *the sense of morality* / 君の行為は道徳的に見て間違っている Your behavior is wrong *from a moral point of view*. / Your behavior is *morally* wrong. ◆それは交通道徳に反する It is against *traffic manners*.
∥道徳観念 (a) moral sense / 道徳教育 moral education / 公衆道徳 public morality / 社会道徳 social morality

とうとつ 唐突 ──唐突な (突然の) sudden, abrupt; (不意の) unexpected ∥そのドラマは唐突な終わり方をした The TV drama came to an *abrupt* end.
◆彼は唐突におなかがすいたと言いだした He *suddenly* said he was hungry.

とうとぶ 尊ぶ・貴ぶ (尊敬する) respect ⑯; (尊重する) value ⑯ ∥努力を尊ぶ *value* effort

とうどり 頭取 bank president ⓒ, the head of a bank
∥副頭取 the vice-president of a bank

とうなん¹ 盗難 (盗む行為) theft ⓤⓒ; (強奪) robbery ⓤⓒ, (押し込み強盗) burglary ⓤⓒ ∥きのう近くの店で盗難があった There was *a theft* at a nearby store yesterday. / 彼は警察に盗難届を出した He reported *the burglary* to the police. ◆彼女は空港で盗難にあった She *was robbed* at the airport.
∥盗難警報装置 a burglar alarm / 盗難事件 a theft, a burglary, a robbery / 盗難車 a stolen car / 盗難品 stolen articles [goods]

とうなん² 東南 the southeast ──東南の southeast, southeastern

とうなんアジア 東南アジア Southeast Asia ──東南アジアの Southeast Asian
∥東南アジア諸国連合 the Association of Southeast Asian Nations(《略語》ASEAN

とうなんとう 東南東 the east-southeast ──東南東の east-southeast

とうに 6 時をとうに(→すでに)過ぎている It is *already* past six. / 彼は 70 をとうに(→かなり)超えている He is *well* over 70.

どうにいる 堂に入る 彼の演技は堂に入っている(→熟達している) He *is quite at home* in his performance. / 彼女のドイツ語は堂に入ったものだ(→自由に使いこなす) She *has a perfect command* of German.

どうにか (何とかして) somehow, someway, in some way; (かろうじて) barely /私たちはどうにか目的地にたどり着いた We *somehow* [*barely*] *got* to our destination. / きっとどうにかなるよ Maybe things will work out *somehow*.
◆彼もアメリカでどうにか暮らしているようだ It seems he *manages* a living in America. / この部屋, どうにかしてくれる? Can you *do something* about this room?

どうにも 彼の失礼な態度にはどうにも我慢できない I *simply* [*really*] *can't stand* his rude attitude. / 私にはどうにもならなかった *There was nothing* I *could do* about it. / 彼女はひどく落ち込んでいてどうにも慰めようがない(→慰める方法がない) She is so depressed that *there is no way* to comfort her.

とうにゅう 投入 ――投入する put* [throw*] ... into ~; (資金を) invest ... in ~ /彼はこの研究に全精力を投入した He *put* [*threw*] all his energy *into* the study. / その会社は新しい工場の建設に多額の資金を投入した The company *invested* a lot of money *in* building new factories.

どうにゅう 導入 introduction ⓤ ――導入する introduce ⑯ /仕事に新しいやり方を導入する *introduce* new methods into *one's* business / コンピュータの導入によって事務処理にかかる時間が短縮された *The introduction* of computers made it possible to reduce the time spent on office work.

とうにょうびょう 糖尿病 〔医学〕diabetes [dàiəbíːtəs] ⓤ ‖糖尿病患者 a diabetic

とうにん 当人 (その人自身) the person himself [herself]; (問題となっている人) the person in question; (当事者) the person concerned /当人からそう聞いたんだ I heard it from *the person concerned*. / 当人はまだそのことを知らない He *himself* [She *herself*] doesn't know it yet.

どうねん 同年 the same year; (同じ年齢) the same age /同年4月に大学に入学した I got into the university in April of *the same year*.

どうねんぱい 同年輩 伊藤さんは私の父親と同年輩だ Mr. Ito is *about* my father's *age*.

どうのこうの 終わってしまったことをどうのこうの言ってもしようがない It's no use saying *this and that* about something that's over.

とうは¹ 党派 (政党) party ⓒ; (派閥) faction ⓒ /党派を組む form *a party*

とうは² 踏破 彼は日本全国を踏破した He *traveled* all over Japan *on foot*.

とうはん 登坂 ⇒とはん

とうばん¹ 当番 (順番) turn ⓒ; (義務) duty ⓤ /今夜は彼が当番だ He is *on duty* tonight. / 今週は私たちが掃除当番だ It's our *turn to clean the room* this week. / それは当番制にしましょう Let's 「*take turns* (at) doing it [do it *by turns*]」.

とうばん² 登板 ――登板する (マウンドに立つ) take* the mound /佐々木はきょうで3試合連続の登板になる Today Sasaki *takes the mound* for the third game in a row.

どうはん 同伴 ――同伴する (いっしょに行く) go* with ...; (ついていく) accompany ⑯ /未成年者は大人の同伴が必要です Minors should *be accompanied* by adults. / 彼は夫人同伴で授賞式に出席した He attended the awards ceremony *accompanied by* [*with*] his wife.
‖同伴者 one's companion

どうはんが 銅板画 copperplate print ⓒ

とうひ¹ 当否 (正しいかどうか) right or wrong; (適切かどうか) fitness ⓤ, propriety ⓤ

とうひ² 逃避 escape ⓤ ⓒ ――逃避する escape ⑯ /彼は厳しい現実から逃避したかった He wanted to *escape* [*run away*] from the hard realities.

とうひょう 投票 (投票すること) voting ⓤ; (票) vote ⓤ ⓒ; (無記名の) ballot ⓤ ⓒ; (投票数) poll ⓒ ――投票する vote ⑯
投票に行く go to *the polls* (❖the polls は「投票所」の意味)
それを投票にかけることにした We decided to put it to *a vote*.
私たちは学級委員を投票で決めた We chose the class committee *by vote*.
投票の結果はもうすぐ明らかになるだろう The result of *the poll* will be known soon.
彼はその法案に賛成[反対]の投票をした He *voted for* [*against*] the bill.
公約を聞いてその候補者に投票することに決めた I decided to 「*vote for* [*cast my vote for*]」 the candidate after hearing his election promises.
◆今回の選挙の投票率は前回を上回った *The voter turnout* of this election was more than the previous one.
‖投票権 the right to vote, voting rights / 投票者 a voter / 投票所 a polling place [station], the polls / 投票(総)数 the (total) number of votes / 投票立会人 an election monitor [observer] / 投票箱 a ballot box / 投票日 an election [a voting] day / 投票用紙 a ballot / 委任投票 a proxy vote / 記名[無記名]投票 an open [a secret] vote / 決戦投票 the final vote [ballot] / 国民投票 a (national) referendum / 信任[不信任]投票 a vote of confidence [nonconfidence] / 不在者投票 an absentee vote [ballot]

とうびょう 闘病 彼は闘病生活を送りながら仕事を続けている He continues to work while *struggling with his disease*.

どうひょう 道標 (道路標識) guidepost ⓒ; (道しるべ) signpost ⓒ

どうびょうあいあわれむ 同病 慣用表現 同病相憐(あ)れむ *Misery loves company*.

とうひん 盗品 stolen article ⓒ; ((集合的))

stolen goods

とうふ 豆腐 🗻 tofu [U], bean curd [U] // 豆腐 1 丁 a cake [block] of *tofu*

‖豆腐屋 a tofu maker [seller]

豆腐は大豆を煮てつぶしたものを固めた食べ物で，もともと中国から伝わりました．低カロリー・高タンパクの健康食品で，今ではアメリカなどでもとても人気があります．
Tofu is made from soybeans that have been boiled, pressed and coagulated. It originated in China, and it is a low-calorie, protein-rich health food. Recently it has become quite popular in America and other countries.

とうぶ[1] 東部 the east, the eastern part; (米国の) the East ―東部の eastern

とうぶ[2] 頭部 the head //彼は頭部をけがして 3 針縫った He was injured in [on] *the head* and a doctor put three stitches in the wound.

どうふう 同封 ―同封する enclose [他] //彼女の手紙には写真が同封されていた Photos *were enclosed* with her letter. / 詳しくは同封のパンフレットをご覧ください For further information, please look at the *enclosed* pamphlet. / 返信用の切手を同封しておきました I *have enclosed* a stamp for return postage.

どうぶつ 動物

animal [C] ―動物の・動物的な animal

動物を飼う keep *an animal* / 動物的本能 an *animal* instinct

この森にはいろいろな動物が生息している A wide variety of *animals* live in this forest.

彼は動物の生態[習性]を調査している He investigates the ⌈life and habits of *animals* [*animal* behavior].

その団体は野生動物の保護に取り組んでいる The organization is engaged in protecting *wild animals*.

彼らは動物実験に反対している They are opposed to *tests* [*experiments*] *on animals*.

‖動物愛護協会 the Society for the Prevention of Cruelty to Animals / 動物学 zoology / 動物学者 a zoologist / 動物性脂肪 animal fat / 動物性タンパク質 animal protein / 動物的本能 an animal instinct / 動物病院 a veterinary hospital / 愛玩(あいがん)動物 a pet / 高等[下等]動物 the higher [lower] animals / 肉食[草食]動物 a carnivorous [herbivorous] animal

どうぶつえん 動物園 zoo [C] //上野動物園 *the* Ueno *Zoo*

とうぶん[1] 当分 for the time being; (今のところ) for the present; (しばらくの間) for some time, for a while //当分これで間に合うだろう This will do *for the present*. / 当分の間家で安静にしていてください Rest quietly at home *for a while*.

とうぶん[2] 等分 ―等分する divide ... equally [into equal parts] //彼女はリンゴを 4 等分した She *divided* the apple *into* four *equal parts*.

とうぶん[3] 糖分 sugar [U] //糖分のとりすぎです You take too much *sugar*. / この食品は糖分を控えてある This food doesn't contain much *sugar*.

とうへき 盗癖 〖医学〗kleptomania [U]
◆その男には盗癖があった The man *was a kleptomaniac*. (❖ kleptomaniac [klèptəméiniæk] は「盗癖のある人」の意味)

とうべん 答弁 answer [C], reply [C]; (弁明) explanation [C] ―答弁する answer [他], reply [自] //首相の答弁はあいまいなものだった The Prime Minister's *explanation* was vague.

とうほう[1] 当方 当方はその件に関しては何の関係もございません *We* have nothing to do with the matter.

とうほう[2] 東方 the east ―東方の east, eastern //日本はアジア大陸の東方に位置している Japan lies *to the east* of the Asian continent.

とうぼう 逃亡 escape [C], flight [C][U] ―逃亡する (逃げる) escape [自], flee* [他]; (逃げ去る) run* away //彼らは逃亡を試みた They attempted to *escape*. / 殺人犯は国外へ逃亡した The murderer *fled* the country.
◆逃亡中である be *on the run*; be *at large*
‖逃亡者 a fugitive, 《口語的》a runaway

どうほう 同胞 (同国民) fellow countryman [C], 《公式的》compatriot [C]

とうほく 東北 the northeast; (地方) the Tohoku district ―東北の northeastern

とうほんせいそう 東奔西走 選挙が近づき，立候補者たちは東奔西走している(→忙しく走り回っている) The candidates *are running around busily* with the election close at hand.

どうまわり 胴回り (ウエスト) waist [C]

どうみても どう見ても その歌手はどう見ても 50 代には見えない *To all appearances*, that singer can't be in his [her] 50s.

どうみゃく 動脈 〖医学〗artery [C] ―動脈の arterial ‖動脈硬化 hardening of the arteries, 〖医学〗arteriosclerosis / 動脈瘤(りゅう) an aneurysm / 大動脈 the main artery

とうみん[1] 冬眠 hibernation [U], winter sleep [U] ―冬眠する hibernate [自] //冬眠に入る go into *hibernation* / 冬眠からさめる awake from *hibernation*
‖冬眠動物 a hibernate animal

とうみん[2] 島民 islander [C] ◆神津島の島民 *the inhabitants* of Kozu Island

とうめい 透明 transparency [U] ―透明な transparent; (澄んだ) clear //無色透明の液体 a *colorless and transparent* liquid / 透明感のある歌声 a *clear* singing voice
◆不透明なガラス *opaque* glass

どうめい[1] 同名 (同じ名前) the same name; (同じ題名) the same title //彼女は私と同姓同名です She and I have *the same family and given name*. / その店と同名の店がうちの近所にあります There is a shop in my neighbor-

どうめい² 同盟 alliance ⓒ 日本は1902年に英国と同盟を結んだ Japan *concluded an alliance* [*allied itself, was allied*] with Great Britain in 1902.
‖同盟国 an ally, an allied power / 軍事同盟 a military alliance / 三国同盟 a triple alliance

どうめいし 動名詞 〖文法〗 gerund ⓒ

> (1)動名詞は, 現在分詞(→げんざいぶんし)と同じ語形だが, 現在分詞と違って, 動詞としての意味を残しながらも名詞の働きをする.
> [主語として] Moderate *jogging* is good for the health. 適度なジョギングは健康によい
> [補語として] One of her bad points is *forgetting* appointments. 彼女の短所の一つは約束を忘れることだ
> [他動詞の目的語として] I remember *singing* that song with my friends. 友達とその歌を歌ったことを覚えている
> [前置詞の目的語として] Thank you for *inviting* me to the party. パーティーに呼んでくれてありがとう
> (2)動詞によっては目的語に動名詞と to 不定詞の両方をとることができるものがあるが, 意味が異なる場合があるので注意が必要 ‖ I will never forget *meeting* you. あなたに会ったことは決して忘れません(❖forget …ing はすでにしたことを忘れる) / Don't forget *to mail* the letter. 手紙を投函(とうかん)するのを忘れないでね(❖forget to … はこれからすることを忘れる)

とうめん 当面 ——当面の (現在の) present; (差し迫った) urgent, pressing, immediate ‖当面の課題 the *urgent* problem / 当面の目標は英単語を1日10個覚えることだ My *present* aim is to learn 10 English words a day. ◆当面はこれで十分だろう This would be enough *for the time being*.

どうも
❶【どうしても】
彼とはどうもうまくいかない *Somehow* I can't get along with him.
どうも集中できない I *just* can't seem to concentrate.
君が話してくれたことはどうも信じられない What you've told us *just* doesn't wash. (❖wash は通用するの意味)
❷【何となく・どういうわけか】somehow
うちの犬はどうもドッグフードが好きじゃないようだ *Somehow* our dog doesn't seem to like dog food.
◆彼にはどうも変わったところがある There's *something* strange about him. / 最近どうも胃の調子が悪い My stomach has been *kind of* bothering me these days. / おかしいと思ったらシャツを後ろ前に着ていた I knew *something* was wrong, and then noticed I had been wearing the shirt backwards.
❸【どうやら】
どうもあの店員が計算間違いをしたようだ *Evidently*, that salesclerk miscalculated.
彼はドイツ人だと思っていたがどうもオランダ人のようだった I thought he was German, but *apparently* he was Dutch.
あいつはどうも涼子が好きみたいだ *It appears* that he likes Ryoko.
どうもあなたの住所を誤って覚えていたようです *I'm afraid* I've mistaken your address.
🅴「あした雨になるのかなあ」「どうもそうみたいだよ」"Will it be rainy tomorrow?" "*I'm afraid* so."
❹【非常に】very; (本当に) really
どうもありがとう Thank you *very much*. / Thanks *a lot*.
手伝ってくれてどうもありがとう It was *very* nice of you to help me.
たいへんご迷惑をおかけしてどうも申しわけありません I'm *really* sorry to have caused you so much trouble.
◆どうもごぶさたしております It's been a long time since last time.
🅴「コーヒーをどうぞ」「あ, どうも」"Here's your coffee." "Oh, *thanks*."

どうもう 獰猛 ——獰猛な (荒々しい) fierce; (凶暴な) vicious, ferocious; (残忍な) savage ‖その家の犬はとても獰猛そうだった The dog at that house looked very *vicious*.

とうもろこし (米) corn ⓤ, (英) maize ⓤ, Indian corn ⓤ

とうやく 投薬 患者に投薬する *give medicine* to a patient

どうやって その猿はどうやっておりから逃げたのですか *How* did the monkey escape from the cage?

どうやら ❶【どうにかこうにか】(何とか) somehow (or other); (かろうじて) barely, with difficulty ‖騒ぎはどうやら収まった *Somehow* the disturbance settled down. / どうやら集合時間に間に合った I was *barely* on time for the meeting.
❷【どうも…らしい】どうやら彼は知らないらしい He *probably* doesn't know that. / 彼女はどうやら元気になったようだ She *seems* to recover from her illness. / どうやらあしたは晴れそうだ It *is likely* to clear up tomorrow.

とうゆ 灯油 (米) kerosene ⓤ, (英) paraffin ⓤ

とうよ 投与 医者は患者に栄養剤を投与した The doctor *gave* the patient a nutrient.

とうよう¹ 東洋 Asia, the East ——東洋の Asian, Eastern ‖東洋医学 Eastern [Asian] medicine / 東洋史 Asian history / 東洋諸国 Asian countries / 東洋人 an Asian / 東洋美術 (an) Asian art / 東洋文明 Asian civilization

とうよう² 盗用 plagiarism ⓤⓒ ——盗用する ⊕ ⓔ; (盗む) steal* ⊕ ‖彼は私の考えたデザインを盗用した He *stole* [*copied*] my design.

とうよう³ 登用 (任用) appointment ⓤⓒ; (昇任) promotion ⓤⓒ ——登用する (任命する) appoint ⊕; (昇格させる) promote ⊕ ‖彼は正社員に登用された He *was promoted* to a 「regular employee [full-time worker].

どうよう[1] 同様 ──同様の（同じ）の同じ（似ている）similar, （等しい）equal ──同様に（同じように）similarly; （…のように）like; （等しく）equally

〖同様〗
同様の話を彼女から聞いた I heard a *similar* story from her.
同じことが日本の学生についてもいえる *The same* (*thing*) can be said of Japanese students.
私も彼らと同様の考えだ My view is *similar* to theirs.

〖同様に〗
2月は1月同様に雪が多かった In February, *like* in January, we had a lot of snow.
◆彼女はお姉さんたちと同様に水泳が得意だ She swims *as well as* her sisters. / その先生には娘同様にかわいがってもらった The teacher loved me *as if I were her own daughter*.

〖その他〗
それはうちの高校においても同様だ It's *the same* with our school.
◆そのスーツは新品同様だった The suit was *as good as new*.

どうよう[2] 動揺 disturbance; (不安) unrest ──動揺する（心の平静を失う）be shaken; (取り乱す) be upset; (心配する) be disturbed /彼女は動揺を隠せない様子だった It seemed she *couldn't hide the disturbance*. / その話を聞いて私はひどく動揺した I *was* very *upset* to hear the story.

どうよう[3] 童謡 (子供向けの歌) children's song; (英米に伝わる) (米)Mother Goose rhyme, (英)nursery rhyme

とうらい 到来 (来ること) coming; (到着) arrival; (重要なものの) the advent ──到来する (来る) come; (到着する) arrive /夏の到来を告げる雷 the thunder that informs us of *the coming* [*arrival*] of summer / スキーシーズンの到来だ The ski season *has come*.
◆チャンス到来だ *Here's* our chance.

とうらく 当落 当落はきょう中に明らかになるだろう *The results of the election* will be known by the end of the day. / その候補者は現在当選線上にいる The candidate's *chances are fifty-fifty* now.

どうらく 道楽 (趣味・気晴らし) hobby, pastime; (放蕩(ほうとう)) dissipation /絵を描くことが父の唯一の道楽だ Painting is my father's only *hobby* [*pastime*]. ◆道楽にふける give *oneself* over to *a dissipated life*
‖道楽息子 a prodigal son

どうらん 動乱 disturbance; (大変動) upheaval; (暴動) riot /彼は動乱の時代を生きた He lived through the period of *disturbance*.

どうり 道理 (理屈) reason; (真理・真実) truth; (思慮分別) sense
彼女がそう考えるのも道理だ She *has good reason* to think so.
彼の意見は道理にかなっている His opinion *stands to reason*. / His opinion *is reasonable*.
彼女の言っていることは道理に反している What she says *is against* [*contrary to*] *reason*. / What she says *is unreasonable*.
◆彼はまだ若いがものの道理をわきまえている He is still young but a *reasonable* [*sensible*] person. / He is still young but he *knows what's what*.
🔊「小さいときから書道を習っているんです」「道理で字がきれいだと思いました(→それが理由を説明する)」"I've been learning calligraphy since I was a child." "*That explains* [*accounts for*] *why* you have good handwriting. / →それで分かった) *Now I know why* you have good handwriting."
🔊「彼, きのう一晩中テレビを見ていたんだって」「道理で眠そうな顔をしていると思ったよ」"He stayed up all last night watching TV." "*No wonder* he looks sleepy."

とうりつ 倒立 handstand ──倒立する do* a handstand, stand* on *one's* hands

とうりゅう 逗留 (滞在) stay ──逗留する stay

とうりゅうもん 登竜門 a gateway to success

どうりょう 同僚 (専門職の) colleague; (仕事仲間) fellow worker, co-worker

どうりょく 動力 (motive) power /この機械は水力を動力としている This machine uses hydraulic *power*.
‖動力炉 a power reactor

とうるい 盗塁 steal, base stealing ──盗塁する steal* a base /石井はきょうだけで2つ盗塁を決めた Today alone Ishii *stole two bases*. ◆二塁に盗塁する *steal* second

どうるい 同類 (同じ種類) the same kind [class] ◆あの人たちと同類には見られたくない I don't want people to think I'm *like* them.

どうれつ 同列 2つの事件を同列に(→同じように)扱うことはできない We can't treat the two incidents *the same way*.

どうろ 道路

road; (街路) street; (幹線道路) highway

4車線の道路 *a four-lane road*
まだ朝早いのに道路は込んでいた There was heavy traffic on *the street* though it was early in the morning.
この道路は駅前で大通りと交差している This *road* crosses the main street in front of the station.
道路を横断するときは気をつけなさい Be careful in crossing *the road*.
エンストしたトラックが道路をふさいでいる A stalled truck is blocking *the road*.
郵便局はこの道路沿いに200メートルほど行ったところにあります The post office is about two hundred meters *along the street*.
彼は道路わきに車を止めた He stopped his car at *the side of a road*.
‖道路工事(修理) road repairing; (建設)

road construction / 道路交通法 the Road Traffic Law / 道路情報 traffic information / 道路地図 a road map / 道路標識 a road sign / 環状道路 《米》a belt highway, 《英》a ring road / 幹線道路 a highway, a main [trunk] road / 高速道路 《米》a speedway, an expressway, a freeway, 《英》a motorway / 主要道路 a main road / 有料道路 a toll road

とうろう 灯籠 (garden) lantern [C] ∥石どうろう *a* stone *lantern*

とうろく 登録 (公的に記録すること) registration [U]; (名簿などへの記入) entry [C][U] ――登録する register [他][自] ∥中国語の初級講座に登録した I *registered for* the introductory course in Chinese. / 私はまだ履修登録をすませていない I *haven't registered for the courses I'm going to take* yet.
∥登録証 a registration card / 登録商標 a registered trademark / (標示などで)登録済み Registered / 登録番号 a registration number / 登録料 a registration fee / 住民登録 resident registration

とうろん 討論 (議論) discussion [C][U]; (公式の場での) debate [U][C] ――討論する discuss [他]; debate [他][自] ➔ [場面・状況別会話] p.1770 ∥活発な討論を行う have *a* lively *discussion* / 時間がなくなってきたので私たちは討論を打ち切った Time was running out, so we closed [ended] *the discussion.* / 委員たちは教育問題に関して討論した The committee members *discussed* educational problems.
∥討論会 a debate, a panel discussion / 討論者 a debater; (シンポジウムなどの) a discussant / 公開討論会 an open forum / テレビ討論会 a TV debate

どうわ 童話 (子供向けの話) children's story [C]; (おとぎ話) fairy tale [story] [C]
∥童話作家 a writer of children's stories

とうわく 当惑 (混乱) confusion [U]; (困惑) puzzlement [U], perplexity [U]; (きまり悪さ) embarrassment [U] ――当惑する be confused; be puzzled, be perplexed; be embarrassed ∥思いがけない質問にすっかり当惑した I *was* quite *puzzled* [*perplexed*] by unexpected questions. / 彼女は当惑した表情で私のほうを見た She looked at me with a *perplexed* [*troubled*] look. / 彼の意見がころころ変わるのには当惑する I *am confused* [*puzzled*] by his frequent changes of opinion.

とえい 都営 ――都営の metropolitan ∥都営住宅 municipal housing / 都営地下鉄 a Tokyo metropolitan subway / 都営バス a Tokyo metropolitan bus

とお 十 ten ➔じゅう(十)

とおあさ 遠浅 遠浅の海 the sea which is *shallow for a good distance from the shore*

とおい 遠い

❶【距離】far, distant
私の学校は駅から遠い My school is *far* [*distant*] from the station.
◆どこか遠いところに行きたい I want to go somewhere *far away.*
💬「郵便局はここから遠いですか」「いえ, そんなに遠くありません」 "Is the post office *far* from here?" "No, it's not so *far.*"

❷【時間】
高校に入ったのが遠い昔のことのように思える I feel as if it was *long ago* that I entered the high school.
彼らの計画が実現するのもそう遠いことではない *It won't be long* before they realize their plan.

❸【関係】
彼は私の遠い親戚(しんせき)です He is a *distant* relative of mine.
彼女の絵は完成というにはほど遠かった Her painting *was far from* being finished.

❹【感覚】
祖母は耳が遠い My grandmother *is hard of hearing.*
電話が遠くて(→接続が悪くて)彼の声がよく聞こえなかった *The connection was so bad* that I couldn't hear his voice well.
あまりの暑さに気が遠くなりそうだった I almost *fainted* in the intense heat.

とおえん 遠縁 distant relative [C] ∥田中さんは私とは遠縁だ Mr. Tanaka is *a distant relative* of mine./ Mr. Tanaka is *distantly related* to me.

とおか 十日 10日間 for *ten days* / 8月10日 August (*the*) *tenth*

とおからず 遠からず (間もなく) before long; (近い将来に) in the near future ∥事の真相は遠からず明らかになるだろう The truth of the matter comes out *in the near future.*
[慣用表現] 当たらずとも遠からず *It is not very far from the truth.*

とおく 遠く

❶【距離が】 ――遠くの distant ――遠くに far, in the distance
彼は遠くの町からこの学校に通っている He comes to this school from a *distant* town.
遠くに山が見える We can see mountains *in the distance.*
あんまり遠くへ行くんじゃないよ Don't go so *far away.*
どこか遠くで波の音がする I hear the sound of the waves somewhere *in the distance.*
その神社は町から遠く離れた所にある The shrine is *far* from the town.
◆ずいぶん遠くまで来てしまった I had gone *a* really *long away.* / わざわざ遠くから来てくれてありがとう Thank you for coming *all this way.* / そのドレスは遠くから見るとピンクの無地に見えるが実際には白の水玉が入っている *From a distance,* that dress looks to be plain pink, but in fact it has white dots on it.

❷【程度が】
私は水泳では彼女には遠く及ばない She is *far* [*much*] better at swimming than I am.

トークばんぐみ トーク番組 《米》talk show

[C],《英》chat show [C]

とおざかる 遠ざかる (離れていく) go* away; (車が) drive* away; (船が) sail away; (音が) die [fade] away; (外部にいる) stay out ‖救急車の音はだんだん遠ざかっていった The siren of an ambulance *was* gradually *fading away*. / 列車は駅から遠ざかっていった The train *went away* from the station. / 彼女は芸能界からしばらく遠ざかっていた She *had stayed away* from the entertainment world for some time.

とおざける 遠ざける keep* *a person* away [at distance] ‖彼らは人を遠ざけて密談した They *kept* other people *away* and talked behind closed doors.

とおし 通し ―通しの through; (連続した) serial; (切れ目のない) consecutive
‖通し切符 a through ticket / 通し番号 serial [consecutive] numbers

-どおし -通し 映画館は込んでいて立ち通しだった The movie theater was crowded and I had to stand *all the way*. / 弟が帰ってくるまで母は心配のし通しだった My mother *had been* worried about my brother until he came back home. / 隣の家は夜通しうるさかった The house next door was noisy *all night*.

とおす 通す

❶【通るようにする】(通過させる) let* ... through, let ... pass; (中に入れる) let in, let ... into ～; (議案などを) pass [他]

この素材は雨や雪を通さずに空気だけを通す This material *lets* air *through*, but not rain or snow.

押し入れの戸をしばらくあけたままにして風を通しなさい Leave the closet door open for a while to *let* air *in*.

彼は門をあけて私たちを通してくれた He opened the gate and *let* us *through*.

政府は今月末までに予算案を通すことを目ざしている The government is trying to *pass* the budget bill by the end of this month.

◆針に糸を通す *thread* a needle; *run thread through* the eye of a needle / 水は電気を通す Water *conducts* electricity. / 豚肉の場合はよく火を通したほうがいい When it comes to pork, you should *cook* it well.

❷【案内する】show* in, show *a person* into ...

お客様をお通ししてもらえますか Would you *show* the guests *in*?

私たちは応接間に通された We *were showed into* the reception room.

❸【最後まで続ける・貫く】(し続ける) keep* (*doing*); (そのままでいる) remain [自]

彼は何を聞かれても沈黙を通した He *kept* silent to all questions.

彼女は生涯独身を通した She *remained* single all through her life.

◆我を通す *have one's* (*own*) *way* / 彼女はいつも自分の意見を通そうとする She always *insists on her own opinion*. / 鶴見先生はどんなときも和服で通している Ms. Tsurumi *is always wearing* a kimono. / 彼はこの夏エアコンなしで通した He *did without* an air conditioner this summer.

❹【目を通す】(ざっと) look over, pass over; (最後まで) look through, read* through; (拾い読みする) browse [自]

書類にサインする前に目を通しなさい You should *look* the document *over* before signing it.

私のレポートに目を通してもらえますか Would you *look over* my paper?

❺【経由する】

テレビを通して世界中から情報が入ってくる We get information from all over the world *through* [*by*] television.

その経験を通して彼は多くのことを学んだ He learned a lot *through* that experience.

彼は実験を通してその仮説が正しいことを確認した He verified the assumption *by* experiments.

トースター toaster [C]
‖オーブントースター a toaster oven

トースト toast [U] (❖数えるときは a piece [slice] of ... とする) ‖朝食にトーストを食べた I had *a piece* [*slice*] *of toast* for breakfast.
◆パンを軽くトーストする *toast* bread lightly

とおせんぼう 通せん坊 男の子は両手を広げて通せん坊をした The boy *blocked* [*stood in*] *my way* with his arms spread.

トータル the total ◆修理費用はトータルで5万円を超えた The expenses for repairs were more than 50,000 yen *in total*.

とおで 遠出 outing [C] ‖久しぶりに遠出をしてとても楽しかった It had been quite some time since I *went on an outing*. I enjoyed it very much.

トーテムポール totem pole [C]

ドーナツ doughnut [C],《米》donut [C]
‖ドーナツ現象 urban sprawl

トーナメント tournament [C] ‖トーナメントに出場する compete in *a tournament*

とおのく 遠のく (音などが) die [fade] away; (危険などが) recede [自] ‖足音はしだいに遠のいていった The footsteps *had died* [*faded*] *away*. ◆いなかにはこのところすっかり足が遠のいている(→行っていない) Recently I *haven't been to* my hometown at all.

ドーバー Dover (❖英国の都市)

ドーピング doping [U] ◆その選手はドーピング検査に引っかかった The player was caught in *a drug test* [*check*].

とおぼえ 遠吠え (遠ぼえの声) howl [hául] [C]
―遠ぼえする howl [自] ‖犬の遠ぼえが聞こえる I hear dogs *howling*.

とおまき 遠巻き 見物人は火事の現場を遠巻きにしていた Spectators *hung back from* the scene of the fire.

とおまわし 遠回し 彼女は彼の態度を遠回しに非難した She criticized his behavior *indirectly* [*in a roundabout way*]. / 彼は遠回しにクラブをやめるかもしれないと言った He *hinted*

と

[suggested] that he might quit the club.

とおまわり 遠回り（回り道）roundabout way ◯;（迂回(うん)路）detour ——遠回りする take* a roundabout way, make* a detour, go* a long way around ‖私たちは遠回りをして家に帰った We went home *by a roundabout way.*

ドーム dome ◯ ‖大阪ドーム the Osaka *Dome* ‖原爆ドーム Genbaku [the Atomic Bomb] *Dome*
◆ドーム球場 a *domed* baseball stadium

とおめ 遠目 その川は遠目にはきれいに見えた The river looked clean *from a distance.* / 彼は遠目がきく He can see *a long distance.*

ドーラン ⚠（油性おしろい）grease paint Ⓤ（✪ 日本語はドイツ語の Dohran から）

とおり 通り
❶【街路】street ◯;（大通り）avenue ◯,《米》boulevard ◯;（車道）road ◯
表［裏］通り *a main* [*back*] *street*
通りは人であふれていた The *street* was filled with people.
通りを歩いていると知らない人にバス停に行く道を聞かれた As I was walking down *the street*, a stranger asked me the way to the bus stop.
彼女はおばあさんの手を引いて通りを渡った She crossed *the street*, leading the old woman by the hand.
銀行はこの通りをずっと行った右側です The bank is on the right side farther down this *street*.
通りで彼女とすれ違ったが彼女は全然気づかなかった I passed her on *the street*, but she didn't recognize me at all.
私たちの学校は通りに面している Our school faces *the street*.
通り沿いに桜の並木が続いている The *street is lined* with cherry trees.
❷【通行】traffic Ⓤ
休みになるとこの道は車の通りが激しい *Traffic* is heavy on this road on holidays.
❸【通ること】
その部屋は風の通りがよくなかった The room was not *airy*.
彼の声は通りがいい His voice *carries well.*
友達の間ではあだ名のほうが通りがいい I'm *better known* by my nickname among my friends.

-とおり -通り ❶【…のように】as;（…に従って）according to … ‖入会の条件は以下のとおりです The entry requirements are *as follows.* / 私の言うとおりにやりなさい You should do *as you are told.*
◆私の言ったとおりでしょう *What did I tell you!* / I told you so! / ほんとに君の言うとおりだよ You're quite *right.*
❷【種類】この問題の解き方には2通りの方法がある There are *two ways* to solve this problem.

-どおり -通り
❶【…のように】as;（…に従って）according to …
いつもどおり8時に学校に着いた I arrived at school at eight *as usual.*
講演会は予定どおり行われた The lecture meeting was held ｢*as scheduled* [*as planned, on schedule*].
予想どおりの結果になった The results turned out *as I had expected.*
彼は約束どおり3時に現れた He came at three *as he had promised.*
◆列車は時間どおり駅に到着した The train arrived at the station *on time.*
❷【…程度】
新しい校舎は九分どおり（→ほぼ）完成した The new school building is *almost* [*nearly*] completed.

とおりあめ 通り雨 (passing) shower ◯
とおりいっぺん 通り一遍 —通りいっぺんの（うわべだけの）superficial;（形式的な）formal;（お決まりの）conventional;（おざなりな）《公式的》perfunctory ‖彼らは通りいっぺんのあいさつを交わした They exchanged *formal* [*conventional*] greetings. / 市当局の通りいっぺんの説明に住民たちは納得できなかった The residents couldn't be satisfied with the *superficial* explanation by the city.

とおりがかり 通り掛かり 彼女は通りがかりの人に駅へ行く道を聞いた She asked *a passer-by* how to get to the station. / 通りがかりに(→途中で)本屋に立ち寄った I dropped by a book store *on the way.*

とおりかかる 通り掛かる（そばを通る）pass by … ‖たまたま事故の現場を通りかかった I happened to *pass by* the scene of the accident.
◆ちょうどそのとき車が通りかかった(→こちらにやってきた) Just then, a car *came along.*

とおりこす 通り越す（通り過ぎる）go* past …;（越えていく）go over … ‖うっかり花屋を通り越してしまった I carelessly *went past* the flower shop.
◆彼の言葉には怒りを通り越してあきれてしまった *Rather than* (being) angered, I was struck dumb by his words.

とおりすがり 通りすがり 彼は通りすがりの人に助けを求めた He asked *a passer-by* for help.

とおりすぎる 通り過ぎる go* past, pass (by) ‖トラックが大きな音を立てて通り過ぎた The truck *went past* with a loud noise. / 彼女は私たちの前を急いで通り過ぎていった She *passed by* hurriedly in front of us.

とおりぬけ 通り抜け 通り抜け禁止《掲示》*No Thoroughfare* / この道は通り抜けできない This road doesn't *go through.*

とおりぬける 通り抜ける go* [pass] through … ‖列車は長いトンネルを通り抜けた The train *went* [*passed*] *through* a long tunnel.

とおりま 通り魔 random killer ◯（✪「無差別殺人者」の意味．「通り魔」にぴったり当てはまる英語はない）

とおりみち 通り道（道筋）way ◯;（通路）

passage ◎ ∥自転車が通り道をふさいでいた A bicycle blocked *the way* [*passage*]. / その店は学校への通り道にある The shop is on *the way* to the school.

とおる 通る

❶【通過する】pass 圓 他; (通り過ぎる) go* by; (通り抜ける) go through …

その船は橋の下を通った The boat *passed under* the bridge.

トラックが通ると家の中の物が揺れた Things in the house shook when a truck *passed by*.

途中で郵便局の前を通るから切手を買ってきてあげるよ I'm *passing by* the post office on the way, so I'll get you some stamps.

新しい法案が国会を通った A new bill *passed* the Diet.

この本は税関を通らないだろう This book *won't pass* (the) customs.

いずれにせよその島へは鹿児島を通っていくことになる In any case, you have to *go through* Kagoshima to get to that island.

◆土砂崩れのため今その道は通れません The road *is closed* because of a landslide. / 群衆は消防士が通れるようわきへ寄った The crowd stepped aside to let the fire fighters *get through*. / 私は彼のことが心配で食事ものどを通らなかった I was so worried about him that I *couldn't eat a thing*. / この部屋は風がよく通る This room *is airy*.

❷【貫通する・達する】

水が砂を通ってしみ出てきた Water filtered *through* the sandy soil.

その道は森の中を通っている The path *runs through* a forest.

壁の穴を通って冷たい空気が流れ込んできた Cold air flowed in *through* a hole in the wall.

その肉は中まで火が通っていなかった The meat *was underdone* in the middle.

❸【合格する】pass 他

彼女は3度目の挑戦で司法試験に通った She *passed* the bar examination on her third try.

ロシア語の試験に何とか通った I managed to *pass* Russian [the certification test for Russian]. (❖前者は授業の試験, 後者は資格試験を指す)

❹【通用する・許される】

彼はピアニストとして通っている He *passes for* [*as*] a pianist. (❖pass for [as] …は,「実際はそうではないが」という意味を表す)

このへんでは彼はボブという名で通っている He *goes by the name of* Bob around here.

彼女は自分の意見が通らず(→拒否され)残念そうだった She appeared to be sorry that her *idea was turned down*.

職場では彼の言うことがそのまま通る At the office, what he says *goes*.

そんな言い訳は通らないよ *That's no excuse*. / We *can't accept such an excuse*.

裁判では原告の主張が通った The plaintiff's *claim was accepted*. / (→裁判所は原告に有利な判決を下した) The court *ruled in favor of* the plaintiff.

❺【その他】

分かりやすく筋の通った文章を書きなさい Write clear and *coherent* sentences.

この文は意味が通らない This sentence *doesn't make any sense*.

彼の声はよく通る His voice *carries* very well.

その問題を避けて通ることはできない We can't *evade* [*duck*] the issue.

彼女のおじは名の通った作家だ Her uncle is a *well-known* writer.

トーン tone ◎ ◆暗いトーンの絵 a *gloomy* picture / 彼女は急に声のトーンを下げた She suddenly *toned* her voice *down*.

-とか 学校が休みの日はよく新宿とか渋谷とかに行きます I often go to Shinjuku, Shibuya *or* places *like that* on days when I don't have school. / 高野さんとかいう人がこれを持ってきたよ *A* Mr. Takano brought this. (❖aは固有名詞とともに用いて「…という人」の意味になる)

とかい 都会 city ◎, town ◎ ──都会の urban ∥いなかと都会, どちらが好きですか Which do you prefer, the country or *the city*? / 彼は都会に働きに出た He went to *a city* to get work. / いずれは都会を離れていなかに住みたい I want to leave *town* and live in the country someday. (❖「都市の中心部, 地域の中心都市」の意味では town は通例無冠詞で用いる) / 彼女は都会育ちだ She *was raised in a city*. / 都会の生活は私の性に合っている *City life* [*Living in the city*] is right for me.

◆私の故郷も都会化が進んでいる My hometown *has been urbanizing*.

∥都会人 a city dweller / 大都会 a big [large] city

どがいし 度外視 ──度外視する (考慮に入れない) leave* … out of consideration, take* no account of …; (無視する) disregard 他, ignore 他 ∥彼らは採算を度外視して計画を進めた They *disregarded* the profit and went ahead with the plan.

とがき ト書き stage direction ◎

とかく 急いでやるととかく失敗しがちだ When we hurry something, we *tend* [*are apt, are liable*] *to* make mistakes. / とかくこの世は住みにくい *Anyway*, this world is a hard place to live.

とかげ 蜥蜴 lizard ◎

とかす¹ 溶かす (固体を熱で) melt 他; (液体の中で) dissolve 他 ∥バターを溶かす *melt* butter / 錠剤を水で溶かす *dissolve* a tablet in water

とかす² 梳かす comb [kóum] 他 ∥彼女は顔を洗って髪をとかした She washed her face and *combed* her hair.

どかす 退かす (動かす) remove 他; (通路から) get* … out of the way; (わきへ) put* aside ∥いすをどかす *remove* a chair / そのか

ばんどかしてくれる？ Can you *put* the bag *aside*?

どかどか 彼らはどかどかと教室に入ってきた They *tramped* into the classroom.

とがめる 咎める ❶【非難する】criticize 🔄;（厳しく非難する）rebuke 🔄;（しかる）reproach 🔄 ∥先生は彼の失敗をとがめなかった The teacher *didn't rebuke* him *for* the failure. / 父に不注意をとがめられた My father *reproached me for* my carelessness.

❷【問いただす】question 🔄 ∥彼は警官にとがめられた He *was questioned* by a policeman.

❸【心が】彼に何も言わずに行くのは気がとがめる I *feel guilty* about going without saying anything to him.

どかゆき どか雪 heavy snowfall 🔲

とがらす 尖らす（先端を）sharpen 🔄;（口を）pout [páut] 🔄 🔄 ∥鉛筆をとがらす *sharpen* a pencil / 父にそのおもちゃを買ってもらえないと聞いてその女の子は口をとがらせた The girl *pouted* when she heard that her father wouldn't buy her the toy. ◆声をとがらせて *in a harsh voice* / 彼らは大統領の警備に神経をとがらせていた They *were on edge about* the security for the President.

とがる 尖る become* sharp ――とがった sharp, pointed ∥つま先のとがった靴 *pointed shoes* / この棒は先がとがっている This stick has a *sharp* point.

どかん¹ bang 🔲,《口語的》wham 🔲 ∥火山がどかんと噴火した The volcano erupted *with a bang*. ◆車が電柱にどかんとぶつかった The car *smashed into* the telephone pole. / 夜空に花火がどかんとあがった Fireworks *banged* [*went bang*] in the night sky.

どかん² 土管 earthen pipe 🔲

とき¹ 時

❶ 時間・時刻	time
❷ 特定の時期・場合	time
❸ …したとき	when; while
❹ 好機	time; chance
❺ 時代・時勢	time

❶【時間・時刻】time 🔲
時はすべてをいやしてくれる *Time* cures everything.
時のたつのは本当に早いものだ *Time* passes [goes by] really quickly.
彼はぶらぶらと時を過ごした He *spent his time* in idleness.
彼らはそのパーティーで楽しい時を過ごした They「*had a good time* [*enjoyed themselves*]」at the party.
その大時計は今も正確な時を告げている Even today the big clock *tells the* right *time*.
時がたつにつれてその事件のことは忘れられていった The event slipped out of their mind「*with the passage of time* [*as time went by*]」.
どちらが正しいかは時がたてば分かることだ *Time will tell* which is right.
テレビを見ていると時のたつのを忘れてしまう（→意識しない）When I watch TV, I *lose track of the time*.

❷【特定の時期・場合】time 🔲 🔲
こんなとき彼がいてくれたらなあ I wish he were [《口語的》was] around *at times like this*.
今はけんかをしているときではない This is no *time* for quarreling.
いい［まずい］ときに彼女が帰ってきた She came home *at the right* [*wrong*] *time*.
私にだってひとりになりたいときがある *There are times when* I want to be alone.
夕食時になると決まって彼が姿を現した He always appeared when it was *time for dinner*.
それは時と場合による That depends on *the time and situation*.
◆時の首相 *the then* Prime Minister / そのとき私はふろに入っていました I was taking a bath *then* [*at that time*]. / ちょうどそのとき雨が降り始めた *Just then*, it started to rain. / どんなときにこれを使ったらいいのか教えてください Please tell me *when* to use this. / 地震のときにはまずガスを止めなさい *In case of an earthquake*, turn off the gas first. / 彼と初めて会ったのは私が17歳のときでした I first met him *when* I was 17. / あるときは支え合い、またあるときはけんかもした *Sometimes* we supported each other *and sometimes* we fought.

🔴「4時に駅で会おうよ」「いいわよ。じゃ、またそのときね」"Let's meet at the station at four." "Sure. See you *then*."

🔴「暇なときは何をしていますか」「たいていは漫画を読んでいます」"What do you do *in your free time*?" "I usually read comic books."

❸【…したとき】when;（…している間）while; as(✦when, while より同時性が強い)
彼が訪ねてきたとき私は庭にいた I was in the yard *when* he visited me.
テレビを見ていたとき外で変な物音がした *As* I was watching TV, I heard a strange sound outside.
彼は疲れているとき以外、決してタクシーを使わない He never takes a taxi *except when* he is tired.
◆この前会ったときから君はちっとも変わってないね You haven't changed at all *since* we last met. / 好きなときに起きて好きなことをしている猫がうらやましい I envy cats, who can get up *whenever they want* and do whatever they want. / 君が今度訪ねてくれるときまでにはこの絵は仕上がっているだろう This painting will have been finished *by the time* you visit me next time. / 彼に初めて出会ったときのことを思い出していた I was thinking about *the time* (*when*) I first met him.

❹【好機】time 🔲;（機会）chance 🔲, opportunity 🔲 🔲
今やまさに行動を起こす時だ Now is *the right*

time to act.

時を見はからって彼女に聞いてみます I'll ask her about it *when the time is right*.

いずれ時が来れば彼にもそれを話すつもりだ I intend to talk to him about it *if I have the chance*.

❺【時代・時勢】time [C]《しばしば複数形 ～s》

ゴルバチョフ書記長のときに in *the time* of Secretary–General Gorbachev

だれも時の流れに逆らうことはできない No one can go against *the current of the times*.

[慣用表現]勝負は時の運だ *Fortune decides* the outcome of a game. / 彼はいちやく時の人になった Overnight he became *the man of the hour* [*moment*]. / 彼らは時を移さず仕事に取りかかった They set about their work *without* (*any*) *loss of time*. / 時を選ばず人の家を訪れる call at a person's house *at all hours*

[ことわざ]時は金なり Time is money.

とき² 朱鷺・鴇〘鳥〙Japanese crested ibis [C]

どき 土器 earthen vessel [C], 《集合的》earthenware [U] //縄文式土器 Jomon *earthenware*

ときあかす 解き明かす solve ⑪, clear up //事件の真相[なぞ]を解き明かす「*clear up* the facts [*solve* the mystery] of the case

ときおり 時折 at times, occasionally

➡ときどき

とぎすます 研ぎ澄ます 刀を研ぎ澄ます *sharpen* a sword / 研ぎ澄まされた感覚の持ち主 a person of *very sharp* sensibility

-ときたら 全くあいつらときたら *Those* guys! / うちの息子ときたら親(→私)の言うことを聞きやしない *That* son of mine doesn't listen to me at all. (❖that, those が人に用いられると軽蔑を表す場合がある)

どきっ 後ろから腕をつかまれてどきっとした I *was startled* [*frightened, scared*] when I was caught by the arm from behind.

どぎつい どぎつい色 a *garish* [*gaudy, loud*] color / どぎつい化粧 *heavy* make–up / そのようなどぎつい表現は避けるべきだ You should avoid using such a *harsh* expression.

ときどき 時々 sometimes; (時たま) occasionally, once in a while, from time to time; (不規則に) (every) now and then

[語法]
> sometimes や occasionally のような頻度を表す副詞は, ふつう一般動詞の前か, 助動詞またはbe 動詞の後に置くが, 文頭や文末に置くこともある // 彼女は時々歩いて学校へ行く She *sometimes* walk to school. / 時々彼は帰りが遅いことがある *Sometimes* he comes home late.

私は空を飛べたらいいのにと時々思う I *sometimes* wish I could fly.

隣の猫が時々遊びにやってくる Our neighbor's cat visits us *occasionally*.

私の両親は時々いっしょに映画を見に行く My parents go to the movies together「*from time to time* [*once in a while*].

寛子は時々私に手紙をくれる Hiroko writes to me (*every*) *now and then*.

晴れ時々曇り Fair, *occasionally* cloudy.

◆彼はその時々で言うことが違う He says different things *at different times*.

どきどき 僕は胸がどきどきするのを感じた I felt my heart「*beating fast* [*thumping, throbbing*]. / 私はどきどきしながら順番を待った I waited for my turn *with my heart pounding* [*thumping*].

ときとして 時として sometimes; (ある場合には) in some cases //真実を告げるのは時として難しい It is *sometimes* difficult to tell the truth.

ときならぬ 時ならぬ (季節はずれの) unseasonable; (不意の) unexpected //時ならぬ訪問 an *unexpected* visit / きのう東京は時ならぬ雪に見舞われた We had *unseasonable* snow in Tokyo yesterday.

ときに 時に (時々) sometimes; (ところで) by the way, incidentally //ちょっとした不注意が時に大きな事故につながることがある Slight carelessness can *sometimes* cause serious accidents. / 時に, ゆうべのサッカーの試合はご覧になりましたか *By the way* [*Incidentally*], did you watch the soccer game last night?

ときには 時には sometimes //時には息抜きすることも必要だ We should *sometimes* take a rest.

ときふせる 説き伏せる persuade ⑪; (説得して思いとどまらせる) dissuade [diswéid] ⑪ //彼女は両親を説き伏せて上京した(→説得して上京させてもらった) She *persuaded* her parents to let her go to Tokyo. / その教師は彼を説き伏せて退学を思いとどまらせた The teacher *dissuaded* him *from* leaving school.

ときほぐす 解きほぐす 釣り糸を解きほぐす *untangle* a fishing line / 難問を解きほぐす *unravel* a difficult problem

どぎまぎ せりふを忘れてどぎまぎする *be embarrassed* to forget *one's* lines / 突然そのことを聞かれてどぎまぎしてしまった I *got confused* [*rattled, flustered*] when I was suddenly asked about it.

ときめき (鼓動) beating [C]; (興奮) excitement [U]

ときめく¹ 彼を見たとたん彼女の胸はときめいた Her heart「*beat fast* [*fluttered*] the moment she saw him.

ときめく² 時めく 彼は今を時めく大スターだ He is a superstar *of today*.

どぎも 度肝 彼らはその船の大きさに度肝を抜かれた The size of the large ship *blew their mind*. / They *were astounded* by the size of the large ship. ➡おどろく

ドキュメンタリー documentary [C] //ドキュメンタリー番組 a documentary program

ドキュメント (文書) document [C]

どきょう¹ 度胸 (勇気) courage [U]; (落ち着き) nerve [U]; (肝っ玉)《口語的》guts //君にそれを言う度胸がありますか Do you have *the*

courage to say that? / あいつは度胸のないやつだ He *has no guts*./ He is *a coward*. / なかなかいい度胸してるね You have a lot of *courage* [*guts*]. / 彼女は度胸を決めて職員室の扉をたたいた She「*worked up* [*gathered*] *her courage* and knocked the door of the teachers' room.
◆三郎は度胸がある Saburo *is brave*.
‖度胸試し a game of chicken

どきょう[2] 読経 sutra recitation [U][C]

ときょうそう 徒競走 footrace [C]

どきり ─どきりとする be startled ⇨どきっ

とぎれとぎれ 途切れ途切れ ─とぎれとぎれの interrupted; (断続的な) intermittent ‖とぎれとぎれの睡眠 an *interrupted* sleep ◆彼女の話はとぎれとぎれにしか(→断片しか)聞き取れなかった I could catch only some *snatches* of what she said.

とぎれる 途切れる そこでしばらく会話がとぎれた Then *there was a lull* in the conversation for a while. / その道をしばらく行くと人家がとぎれた After I walked along the street for a while, the row of houses *ended*. / 橋を渡る車の列がとぎれることなく続いていた The line of cars crossing over the bridge continued *without a break*.

とく[1] 得 (利益) profit [C][U]; (恩恵) benefit [C][U]; (好都合) advantage [C] ─得する gain [他][自], 《公式的》 profit [自], make* a profit; (節約になる) save [他] ─得な profitable; (経済的な) economical
大きい箱のバターを買うほうがお得ですよ Buying a big pack of butter is more *economical*.
今度の取り引きではずいぶん得をした We *made* [*earned*] *a* large *profit* on this deal.
そんなことをしても君には何の得にもならない You *gain nothing* by doing such a thing.
習えるものは何でも習っておいたほうが得ですよ It's to *your advantage* to learn everything you can.
彼らは家賃補助制度のおかげでずいぶん得をした They *saved* a lot of money thanks to the rent subsidy system.
◆彼は何をしても憎まれない得な性格の持ち主だ He has such a *winning* character that he'll be accepted whatever he does.

とく[2] 徳 virtue [U] (❖「徳行」の意味では[C]) ‖彼の徳を慕って多くの若者が集まった Many young people came together, attracted by his *virtue*. ◆知的で徳の高い人物 an intelligent and *virtuous* person

とく[3] 解く
❶【答えを出す】solve [他], work out; (答える) answer [他]; (なぞなどを) clear up
方程式を解く *solve* [*work out*] an equation
その問題を解くのに2時間近くかかった It took me about two hours to *solve* the problem.
そのクロスワードパズルを解くのは簡単だった I found it easy to *solve* [*work out*] that crossword puzzle.
❷【ほどく】undo* [他], untie [他]; (巻いていたものを) unwind* [他], uncoil [他]; (ゆるめる) loosen [他] ⇨ほどく
結び目を解く *undo* [*untie*] a knot
彼女は小包(のひも)を解いた She *undid* the parcel.
❸【取り除く】(取り除く) remove [他]; (解除する) raise [他], lift [他]; (解放する) relieve [他], release [他]
包囲を解く *raise* [*lift*] a siege
彼女は職を解かれた She *was relieved of* her post.
彼はそのシカをわなから解いてやった He *released* the deer from the trap.
◆その誤解はなかなか解けなかった I *couldn't undo* [*clear up*] the misunderstanding easily.

とく[4] 説く (説明する) explain [他]; (教え込む) instill [他]; (説得する) persuade [他]; (提唱する) advocate [他]; (神の教えなどを) preach [他][自] ‖少年の父親は彼に命の尊さを説いた The boy's father *instilled* in him the sense that life is precious. / 彼女は大統領に会って停戦を説いた She met the President and *tried to persuade* him to order a cease-fire. (❖persuade は「説得に成功する」という意味を含むため「…するように説く」はこのように表現する)
◆仏教を説く *teach* Buddhism

とく[5] 梳く comb [kóum] [他] ⇨とかす(梳かす)

とく[6] 溶く melt [他] ⇨とかす(溶かす)

とぐ 研ぐ (鋭くする) sharpen [他]; (研磨する) grind* [他][自]; (米を) wash [他] ‖ナイフを研ぐ *sharpen* a knife / 猫が柱でつめを研いでいた A cat *was sharpening* its claws against a post.

どく[1] 毒
❶【健康や生命を害するもの】poison [C][U]; (蛇・サソリなどの) venom [U]
1服の毒 a dose of *poison* / マムシの毒 *the venom* of a pit viper
女王は毒殺されたといわれている The queen is said to *have been killed by poison*.
◆毒入りチョコレート *poisoned* chocolate / 井戸に毒を入れる *poison* a well / この草には毒がある This plant is *poisonous*. / 彼はフグの毒にあたって死んだ He *was poisoned by eating* the globefish and died.
❷【人を傷つけるもの】harm [U]
飲みすぎは体に毒だ Drinking too much「*does harm to* [*is harmful to, is bad for*] your health.
◆毒のある(→辛辣(しんらつ)な)言葉 *bitter* words
❸【ためにならないもの】
このケーキは目の毒だ This cake is very *tempting*.
‖毒ガス poison gas / 毒キノコ a poisonous mushroom / 毒草 a poisonous plant / 毒蛇 a poisonous [venomous] snake
[ことわざ] 毒を食らわば皿まで One may as well be hanged for a sheep as for a lamb. (→どうせ殺されるなら子羊を盗むよりも親羊を盗んだほうがましだ) / 毒をもって毒を制す Fight evil with evil. (→悪をもって悪と戦う)

と

どく² 退く get* out of the way; (わきへよける) step aside 《そこをどけ *Get out of my [the] way.*／ 車が通れるようにわきへどいた I *stepped aside* to let the car pass by.

とくい¹ 得意
❶【誇らしい】
豊はカレーがとても上手にできたので得意になっている Yutaka *is proud* that he cooked curry and rice very well.
彼女は得意げにその話をした She told the story *proudly* [*with pride*].
その少年は得意になって逆立ちしてみせた The boy *showed off* by standing on his hands.
彼女は絵が展覧会に入選して得意の絶頂にあった She *was very happy and proud* as her painting was accepted for the exhibition.
彼はテストで満点を取って得意顔だった He *looked smug* after he got a perfect score on the test.
❷【上手な】
健はテニスが得意だ Ken is *good at* (playing) tennis.／ Ken is *a good* tennis player.
彼は地理よりも歴史のほうが得意だ He is *better at* history than geography.
得意なスポーツは何ですか What is your *favorite* sport?
彼女はお得意の話題になると身を乗り出した She leaned forward as we started talking about her *pet* subject.
私の得意料理はハンバーグです My *specialty* at cooking is hamburger patties.
彼は平行棒が得意中の得意だ His *very best* event is the parallel bars.
❸【よく店に来る人】(regular) customer ⓒ; (商店・銀行などの) client ⓒ
古くからのお得意様 *an old customer*
上司は朝からお得意先を回っている My boss *has been visiting his regular customers* since this morning.

とくい² 特異 ━━特異な (ふつうでない) unusual; (特有の) peculiar, unique 《この動物には特異な習性がある This animal has an *unusual* habit.
‖特異性 singularity, peculiarity／ 特異体質 《医学》an idiosyncrasy

どくえん 独演 solo (performance) ⓒ ━━独演する perform a solo 《独演会 a one-person [solo] show, 《公式的》a recital

どくがく 独学 self-education ━━独学の self-educated, self-taught 《独学の人 a *self-educated* [*self-taught*] person
◆彼はフランス語を独学で学んだ He *learned* French「*by himself* [*on his own*].

とくぎ 特技 specialty ⓒ 《彼の特技はピアノだ His *specialty* is to play the piano.
◆僕にはこれといった特技がない I have no *special talents* to speak of.

どくさい 独裁 dictatorship ⓒⓤ, autocracy ⓤ, despotism ⓤ 《軍部の独裁 military *dictatorship*
‖独裁者 a dictator／ 独裁政治 despotic government

とくさく 得策 (賢明な策) wise policy ⓒ; (最善の方法) the [one's] best way 《今すぐに出発するのが得策だよ *Your best way* is to start at once.／ It is *best* for you to start at once.

とくさん 特産 和紙は小川町の特産品だ Japanese *washi* paper is *a specialty* [*special product*] of Ogawamachi.

とくし 特使 special envoy ⓒ

どくじ 独自 ━━独自の (ほかにはない) unique; (独立した) independent; (自分自身の) own 《独自の見解を述べる give *one's own* view／ この機種には独自の機能がある This type of machine has a *unique* function.／ 彼らは池の水質について独自の調査を行った They made an *independent* inquiry about the water quality of the pond.／ 生徒はみな, 独自の個性をもっている Every student has an individual character *of his or her own*.
‖独自性(個性) individuality; (独創性) originality

とくしか 篤志家 (慈善家) charitable person ⓒ, philanthropist ⓒ

とくしつ¹ 特質 characteristic ⓒ 《日本文化の特質 *a characteristic* of Japanese culture

とくしつ² 得失 gain and loss; (損得) profit and loss ‖得失点差 goal difference

とくしま 徳島

> 徳島県は, 日本列島四大島の一つである四国島にあります。県庁所在地の徳島市は, 毎年 8 月 12 日から15日にかけて行われる阿波踊りで有名です。阿波踊りは, 数十人または100人以上の人からなる連(れん)が, 三味線・笛・鉦(かね)・太鼓の囃子(ばやし)に乗って町中を踊り歩くカーニバルです。
> Tokushima Prefecture is located on Shikoku Island, one of the four main islands of Japan. The city of Tokushima, the prefectural capital, is famous for *Awaodori*, which is held from August 12 to 15 every year. *Awaodori* is a carnival of dance in which groups of from several dozen to over one hundred dancers dance along the city streets to the accompaniment of *shamisen*, flutes, bells and drums.

とくしゃ 特赦 special pardon ⓒ; (特に政治犯に対する) amnesty ⓤ

どくしゃ 読者 reader ⓒ; (雑誌などの定期購読者) subscriber ⓒ 《一般の読者 *the general reader*／ この小説は若い読者にうけるだろうか Will this novel appeal to young *readers*?
‖読者欄 a readers' column

とくしゅ 特殊 ━━特殊な (特別な) special, peculiar; (比類のない) unique 《彼女は人の心を読むという特殊な能力がある She has the *peculiar* ability to read others' minds.／ 私たちは放射線を防ぐ特殊な眼鏡をかけた We wore a *special* kind of glasses as a shield against the radiation.
‖特殊学級 a special class／ 特殊効果 special

effects

とくしゅう 特集 feature [C] ━特集する feature [他] ∥さて次は特集です Now for *the feature story.* / 『タイム』の今週号は日本についての特集記事を組んでいる This week's *Time features articles* on Japan.
‖特集号 a special issue / 特集番組 a special program

どくしゅう 独習 ピアノを独習する *learn* the piano *by oneself*; *teach oneself* the piano
‖独習書 a teach yourself book

どくしょ 読書 reading [U] ━読書する read* (a book)
読書をするには暗すぎる It is too dark to *read.*
彼は読書好きだ He likes *reading.*
読書しているときはじゃまをしないでくれ Don't interrupt me when I'*m reading.*
宏は読書家だ(→たくさん本を読む) Hiroshi *reads a lot of books.*
‖読書会 a reading circle / 読書感想文 a book report / 読書室 a reading room / 読書週間 Book Week

とくしょう 特賞 grand prize [C]; (最高の賞) the highest prize

とくじょう 特上 ━特上の choicest, superfine

どくしょう 独唱 (vocal) solo [C] (複 ～s) ━独唱する sing* a solo, sing alone
‖独唱会 a (vocal) recital / 独唱者 a soloist

とくしょく 特色 characteristic [C]; (特徴) feature [C] ➾とくちょう(特徴), とくちょう(特長) ∥この辞書の主な特色 *the* main *features* of this dictionary / この学校の特色は何ですか What are *the characteristics* of this school? ◆彼の絵は鮮やかな色使いに特色がある Use of bright colors *is characteristic of* his paintings. (❖この characteristic は「(…に)特有の, (…の)特徴を示す」という意味の形容詞) / His paintings *are characterized* by his use of bright colors.

どくしん 独身 ━独身の single, unmarried ∥独身生活 *single life* / 君のお姉さん, 独身? Is your sister *single*? / 彼は生涯独身だった He remained *single* [*a bachelor*] all his life. (❖bachelor は「独身男性」の意味)
‖独身貴族 a swinging single / 独身者 a single [an unmarried] person

どくする 毒する poison [他] ∥彼ははやりの思想にすっかり毒されている He *is* completely *poisoned* by fashionable thought. ◆青少年を毒する(→悪影響を及ぼす)書物 books which *have a bad influence on* young people

とくせい¹ 特性 characteristic [C], 《公式的》property [C] 《しばしば複数形 properties》 ➾せいしつ ∥鉱物の光学的特性 *the* optical *properties* of a mineral / その生地の熱に強い特性を利用する make use of *the* heatproof *characteristic* of the cloth

とくせい² 特製 特製の品 a *specially made* article / この味の秘訣(ひけつ)はわが家特製のソースにある The secret of this flavor lies in our *specially made* sauce.

どくせい 毒性 toxicity [U][C] ━毒性の toxic, poisonous ➾どく(毒)

とくせつ 特設 特設スタジオ a studio *which is specially set up* / 彼らの祝賀会のために特設会場が設けられた *A hall was specially prepared* for their celebration.

どくぜつ 毒舌 毒舌をふるう(→ひどいことを言う) *use abusive language* / 彼は毒舌家だ He *has a sharp* [*sarcastic*] *tongue.*

とくせん 特選 (特賞) grand prize [C] ━特選の (商品などが) choice
‖特選品 a choice [deluxe] article

どくせん 独占 monopoly [C] ━独占する monopolize [他], have* ... to *oneself* ∥業界全体を独占する *monopolize* an entire industry / 日曜日は父がテレビを独占している On Sundays my father *has* the TV *to himself.* ◆うちのクラスの生徒がレースの上位を独占した Our classmates *filled* the highest places in the race. / 彼女は非常に独占欲の強い人だ She is a very *possessive* person.
‖独占インタビュー an exclusive interview / 独占禁止法 an antimonopoly [antitrust] law / 独占事業 a monopoly

どくぜんてき 独善的 ━独善的な self-righteous

どくそ 毒素 toxin [C]; (有毒物質) poisonous substance [C]

とくそう 特捜 ‖特捜部 a special investigation department

どくそう¹ 独創 ━独創的な original; (創造力のある) creative ∥独創的な作品 an *original* work ◆その小説は非常に独創性に富んでいる The novel shows great *originality.*

どくそう² 独走 ジャイアンツはすでに独走体勢に入った(→他チームを大きく引き離した) The Giants *have* already *left the other teams far behind.*

どくそう³ 独奏 solo [C] (複 ～s) ━独奏する play a solo ∥バイオリン独奏をする *play a* violin *solo*
‖独奏会 a (solo) recital / 独奏者 a soloist

とくそく 督促 (要求) demand [C] ◆税金を納めるよう督促される *be urged* to pay tax
‖督促状(税金などの) a reminder

ドクター (医者・博士) doctor [C] ‖ドクターコース a doctoral program / ドクターストップ a doctor's order to stop fighting (❖「ドクターストップ」は和製英語)

とくだい 特大 ━特大の extra-large, king-size, oversize ‖特大号 a special [an expanded] issue

とくたいせい 特待生 scholarship student [C]

とくだね 特種 scoop [C]; (独占記事) exclusive [C]

どくだん 独断 arbitrary decision [C] ━独断的な arbitrary ━独断で arbitrarily, on *one's* (own) authority ∥独断と偏見に満ちた考え *arbitrary* and prejudiced idea / 彼は独断で予定を変更してしまった He changed the plan *on his own authority.*

どくだんじょう 独壇場 昆虫の話となると彼の

独壇場だ(→だれもかなわない) When it comes to insects, he *is unrivaled* [*unequaled*].

とぐち 戸口 door [C], doorway [C] ∥戸口まで送る see *a person* to *the door* / 彼女は戸口に立っていた She stood in *the doorway*.

とくちゅう 特注 special order [C]

とくちょう[1] 特徴 characteristic [C]; (著しい) feature [C] **―特徴的な** characteristic; (特有の) peculiar; (区別の目安となる) distinctive

新しい素材の特徴 *a characteristic* of a new material / 目立った特徴 *a* prominent *feature*

長い首がキリンの特徴です A long neck *is a characteristic* of the giraffe. / The giraffe *is characterized* by its long neck.

この家の一つの特徴は窓にある One *feature* of this house is its windows.

彼が特徴のある歩き方で近寄って来た He came up to me walking in his *characteristic* way.

彼の顔は特徴がある His face is *distinctive*.

◆彼は背が高く，やせ型で特徴のない顔つきをしている He is a tall, thin man, with *plain* features.

とくちょう[2] 特長 (強み) strong point [C], strength [C][U]; (とりえ) merits ∥素材の特長を生かす make use of *the* 「*strong points* [*merits*] of the material / その先生はそれぞれの生徒の特長を巧みに引き出した The teacher tactfully brought out *the strengths* in each student.

とくてい 特定 **―特定の** (一定の) specific; (具体的な) specified; (ほかならぬ) particular **―特定する** (明確にする) specify [他]; (決定する) determine [他]; (正確な時間・位置などを定める) fix [他] ∥特定の目的で for a *specific* aim [purpose] / 事故の原因を特定する *determine* the cause of the accident / この種が絶滅した正確な時期を特定することはできない We cannot *fix* the exact time when this species died out.

とくてん[1] 得点 (競技一般の) score [C]; (サッカーなどの) goal [C]; (バスケットボール・ラグビーなどの) point [C]; (野球などの) run [C]; (試験の) score [C] **―得点する** score [他][自] ⇒てん(点) ∥今，得点はどうなってる What's *the score* now? / 僕たちのチームは5対0の得点で勝った Our team won with [by] *a score* of 5 to 0. / 絵美の得点は98点だった Emi *scored* 98 points. / 彼女は試験で高得点を取った She got [made] *a high score* on the exam.

◆試合は両チーム無得点のまま後半戦に入った The game reached the last half with both teams *scoreless*.

‖得点掲示板 a scoreboard / 得点圏〖野球〗 scoring position

とくてん[2] 特典 privilege [C][U]; (利益) benefit [C][U] ∥当会の会員になれば次のような特典があります If you become a member of our club, you'll have such *privileges* as follows.

とくと 篤と とくと思案する think *over* [*well, carefully*] / これからみなさんにとくとご覧に入れましょう Now, I'll let you have a *close* [*good*] look.

とくとう 特等 (特別な階級) special class [grade] [C]; (特賞) grand prize [C] ∥くじで特等を当てる win *a grand prize* in the lottery ‖特等席 a special seat

とくとく 得々 得々と語る talk *proudly* [*triumphantly*]

どくとく 独特 **―独特の** (固有の) peculiar, own; (比類のない) unique; (特徴的な) characteristic ∥鷗外独特の文体 Ogai's *characteristic* [*unique*] style / この習慣は日本独特のものです This custom is *peculiar to* Japan. / 各国にはそれぞれ独特の風俗や慣習がある Each country has its *own* manners and customs. / 賢治は彼独特のやり方で問題を解決した Kenji solved the problem in his *own* [*unique*] way.

どくどく 切り口から血がどくどく流れ出た Blood *gushed* out of the cut.

どくどくしい 毒々しい (毒がありそうに見える) poisonous-looking; (どぎつい) garish, gaudy ⇒どぎつい

とくに 特に

(他と比べて) especially; (とりわけ) particularly, in particular; (特別に) specially

京都は特に秋がとても美しい Kyoto is very beautiful, *especially* in fall.

太郎は特に国語が得意だ Taro is *particularly* good at Japanese.

彼女は特に若者のためにその本を書いた She wrote the book *especially* for young people.

買いたい物は特になかった I didn't want to buy anything (*in*) *particular*.

◆彼女は服装には特に注意をした She paid *particular* attention to her clothes. / あすは特に予定がない I have *nothing special* to do tomorrow.

「クラシック音楽は好きですか」「特に好きというわけではありません」 "Do you like classical music?" "Not *especially*."

どくは 読破 彼は学生時代に漱石全集を読破した He *read through* the complete works of Soseki when he was a student.

とくばい 特売 (bargain) sale [C] ⇒バーゲン(セール)，セール ∥このコートは特売で買いました I bought this coat 「*at a sale* [*on sale*].

◆日曜日は米の特売日だ Sunday they *have a special on rice*.

‖特売価格 a bargain price / 特売場 a bargain counter / 特売日 a bargain day / 特売品 a bargain

とくはいん 特派員 (special) correspondent [C] ∥外国特派員 *a* foreign *correspondent*

どくはく 独白〖演劇〗monologue [C][U], soliloquy [C]

とくひつ 特筆 special mention [U] ∥民主主義の確立は人類史上でも特筆に値する出来事である The establishment of democracy *is* 「*worthy of special mention* [*a noteworthy event*]

と

in human history.
とくひょう 得票 (個々の票) vote ©; (得票数) the number of votes polled; (得票総数) a [the] vote ∥大量に得票する get [attract] *a large vote* / だれが最も多く得票するのだろう I wonder who will get *the most votes*.
どくぶつ 毒物 poison ⓤ ∥死んだ男の血液から少量の毒物が検出された Traces of *poison* were found in the dead man's blood.

とくべつ 特別

――特別な (一般とは異なった) special; (特定の) particular; (例外的な) exceptional ――特別に specially, especially; particularly; exceptionally

特別賞を受賞する receive *a special mention* / 特別番組を放送する put on *a special program* / 彼は私にとって特別な人です He's *special* to me.

ミーティングを欠席するのには、何か特別な理由でもあるの Do you have any *special* reason for being absent from the meeting?

このスーツは特別な場合にしか着ない I wear this suit only on *special* occasions.

彼女の誕生日に何か特別なことをするのですか Are you going to do anything *special* for her birthday?

私は美術館の特別の許可でその絵を見ることができた I could see the picture *by special permission* of the museum.

このワインは特別にあなたのために選びました I chose this wine *especially* for you.

今度の日曜日は特別することがない I have nothing *particular* to do next Sunday.

鎌倉は彼らにとって特別思い入れのある (→特別な意味をもつ) 所だった Kamakura had a *special* meaning for them.

今年の夏は特別暑い It's *exceptionally* [*unusually*] hot this summer.

∥特別委員会 a special committee / 特別機 a special plane / 特別号 a special issue / 特別国会 an extraordinary [a special] session of the Diet / 特別席 a special seat / 特別措置 special measures / 特別手当 an extra allowance / 特別料金(割増の) an extra charge; (割引の) a reduced charge / 特別列車 a special train

どくぼう 独房 cell ©
とくめい¹ 匿名 anonymity ⓤ ――匿名の anonymous, nameless ――匿名で anonymously ∥匿名の手紙を受け取る receive an *anonymous* [a *nameless*] letter / 彼は匿名でその書物を翻訳した He translated the book *anonymously*.

◆匿名希望 *Name withheld by request* (✤印刷物で用いる決まった言い方) / *Please do not make my name public.* (✤投書をするときなどに用いる。「名前を公にしないでください」の意味)
とくめい² 特命 special mission ©
∥特命全権大使 an envoy extraordinary
とくやく 特約 special contract © ∥…と特約を結ぶ make *a special contract* with …

∥特約店 a special agency
どくやく 毒薬 poison ©∥毒薬を飲んで自殺する kill *oneself* by taking *poison*
とくゆう 特有 ――特有の peculiar, own; (決まった) specific ⇒どくとく ∥屋久島特有の巨木 giant trees *peculiar to* Yakushima Island / 日本人特有の習慣 a custom *peculiar to* Japanese / ある病気に特有の症状 symptoms *specific to* a disease / どの国民にもそれぞれ特有の性格がある Every nation has its *own* character.

◆この木は熱帯地方に特有のものだ This tree is *characteristic of* the tropics.
とくよう 徳用 ――徳用の(経済的な) economical ∥徳用サイズ an economy size / 徳用品 an economical article
どくりつ 独立 independence ⓤ ――独立の independent ――独立する become* independent

彼は親から独立している He *is independent of* his parents.

彼女は独立心が旺盛(ōうせい)で20歳のときに会社を作った She is so *independent* that she established a company at the age of 20.

その国は独立を宣言した The nation declared *independence*.

インドネシアは1949年にオランダから独立した Indonesia *became independent of* the Netherlands in 1949.

◆彼は経営コンサルタントとして独立した He *set himself up* as a business consultant.

∥独立運動 an independence movement / 独立記念日 Independence Day / 独立国 an independent country / 独立採算制 a self-supporting accounting system / 独立宣言 the Declaration of Independence / 独立戦争 a war of independence
どくりょく 独力 ――独力で by *oneself* ∥彼女は車を買うお金を独力で稼いだ She made money to buy a car *by herself*.
とくれい 特例 special case ©; (例外) exception © ∥今回だけは特例とします I'll make *an exception* just this once.
とぐろ マムシはとぐろを巻いた[巻いていた] The viper「*coiled itself up* [*was lying in a coil*].

[慣用表現] 不良が駅前でとぐろを巻いている Bad boys [girls] *are hanging out* in front of the station.
どくろ 髑髏 skull ©
とげ 刺 thorn ©, prickle ©; (サボテンなどの) spine ©; (木・竹の) splinter © ∥指からとげを抜く pick out *a thorn* from *one's* finger / 指にとげが刺さった I got *a splinter* in my finger. ◆彼女の言葉にはとげがあった Her remark had *a sting*.
とけあう 溶け合う・解け合う blend* (自), merge (自) ∥2つの色は溶け合って紫になる The two colors *blend* into purple.

◆みんなの心が一体となってその壁画は完成した They all *united* to finish the mural.
とけい 時計 (置き時計など) clock ©; (腕時計など携帯用の) watch ©

【時計が・は】
僕の時計は正確だ My *watch* 「*shows the right time* [*keeps good time*].
君の時計は3分進んでいる[遅れている]よ Your *watch* is three minutes fast [slow].
時計が3時を打った[指した] *The clock* struck [showed] three.
この時計は1日に2秒遅れる[進む] This *watch* loses [gains] two seconds a day.
ついに時計がこわれてしまった At last my *watch* broke.
この腕時計はそろそろ電池を交換しなければならない This *watch* will require a new battery before long.
時計が止まっているのに気づいたのはけさになってからだった It was only this morning that I found *the clock* had stopped.
◆あの男の子は3歳でもう時計が読める The three-year-old boy can already *tell the time*.

【時計の】
つまみを回して時計の針を合わせる twist a knob to set *the hands of a watch*
◆時計のバンドをゆるめる loosen *the watchband* [《英》*watchstrap*]

【時計を】
腕時計をはめる put on *a watch* / 時計を1時間進める set *a clock* an hour ahead; move *a clock* forward an hour / 時計を時報に合わせる set *a clock* by the time signal
私は目覚まし時計を5時に合わせた I set *the alarm clock* for five.
私は時計を修理してもらった I had *my watch* repaired.
彼は腕時計をしない主義だ He doesn't wear *a watch* on principle.

【その他】
スイス製の時計 *a clock* of Swiss make; a *clock* made in Switzerland
◆子供たちはいすの周りを時計回りに回った The children went *clockwise* around the chairs.

🅒「あなたの時計では何時ですか」「私の時計では午後3時5分です」 "What time is it by your *watch*?" "My *watch* says 3:05 p.m."
‖時計台 a clock tower / 時計屋(店) a watch [clock] store; (人) a watch [clock] maker / 懐中時計 a pocket watch / クオーツ時計 a quartz watch / 砂時計 a sandglass / 体内時計《生物》 a body [biological] clock / デジタル時計 a digital watch [clock] / ハト時計 a cuckoo clock / 日時計 a sundial / 防水時計 a waterproof watch

とけこむ 溶け込む 彼は新しい学校の雰囲気に溶け込もうと努力した He made efforts to 「*fit into* [*adapt himself to*] the atmosphere of the new school.

どげざ 土下座 彼は土下座して許しを請うた He *fell on his knees* to ask for forgiveness.

とげとげしい とげとげしい言葉 harsh [*stinging, biting*] words / 部屋にはとげとげしい雰囲気が流れていた The room had an *unfriendly* [a *hostile*] atmosphere.

とける¹ 解ける
❶【ゆるむ】(ほどける) come* undone [untied, loose]
靴のひもが解けた My shoelaces *came undone* [*untied, loose*].
◆なかなか彼の誤解は解けなかった His misunderstanding *couldn't be cleared up* easily. / 彼の顔の緊張が解けた All his facial muscles *relaxed*.
❷【解決される】 be solved
6問のうち5問は解けた Five out of the six questions *were solved*.
◆やっとなぞが解けた At last *the mystery was cleared up*.

とける² 溶ける (熱・圧力で) melt ㊥; (水などに) dissolve ㊥; (凍ってたものが) thaw ㊥ /
雪はじきに溶けてなくなるだろう The snow will soon *melt* [*thaw*] *away*. / チョコレートがポケットの中で溶けてしまった The chocolate *has melted* in my pocket. / 塩は水に溶ける Salt *dissolves* in water.

とげる 遂げる (目的を達する) achieve ㊥, accomplish ㊥; (実現する) realize ㊥ ‖思いを遂げる *realize one's* dreams [wishes] / 科学は20世紀にめざましい発達を遂げた Science *has achieved* [*made*] remarkable progress in the 20th century.
◆変貌を遂げる *undergo* a metamorphosis / 非業の死を遂げる *die a* violent *death*

どける 退ける move ㊥, take* away ‖ちょっとわきへかばんをどけてください Will you *move* your bag to the side? / それどけてくれる? *Take* it *away*, will you?

どけん 土建 civil engineering and construction ‖土建会社 a construction company / 土建業者 a contractor

とこ 床 bed 🅒 🅤 ‖床につく go to bed / 床を敷く prepare *the bed* / 母はぐあいが悪くて1週間も床についています My mother has been sick *in bed* for a week.
◆死の床 a deathbed / 床(→ふとん)を上げる put away *the futon* [*bedding*]

どこ

❶【どの場所】where; (どこに・へ・で) where; (どこの) what; (どこから) where ... from
【どこ】
ここはどこですか(→私はどこにいるのか) *Where am I?* (❖ ×Where is here?とはしない)
◆トルコの首都はどこですか *What* is the capital of Turkey? / ❖Where is the capital of Turkey?とすると「トルコの首都はどこにありますか」という意味になる)
【どこに・へ・で】
ジョンはどこにいるの *Where* is John?
あなたはどこに住んでいますか *Where* do you live?
君の学校はどこにありますか *Where* is your school?
案内所がどこにあるかご存知ですか Do you know *where* the information desk is?
まず最初にどこへ行こうか *Where* shall we go first?

とこう

どこへ行けばいいのか分からない I don't know *where* to go.

眼鏡をどこへ置いたか忘れてしまった I've forgotten *where* I put my glasses.

そのコンサートのチケットはどこで手に入りますか *Where* can I get a ticket for the concert?

彼女がどこで生まれたかは私にとって大きな問題だ It matters a lot to me *where* she was born.

◆それは日本全国どこででも手に入る It's available *wherever* [*anywhere*] in Japan.

🎧「やあ, 亮司. どこへ行くの」「ちょっとコンビニへ」 "Hi, Ryoji! *Where* are you going?" "To the convenience store."

🎧「今までどこへ行ってたの」「図書館で宿題してたんだ」 "*Where* have you been?" "I've been to the library to do my homework."

【どこの】

あなたの時計はどこのメーカーですか *What make* is your watch?(❖What make ...? で「どこ製ですか」の意味)

どこの学校へ通っていますか *What school* do you go to?

どこの課の所属ですか *What section* do you belong to?

◆彼がどこの国の出身か知ってますか Do you know *which country* he is from?／あの子たちはどこの子供たち(→だれの子供たち)か知ってるかい Do you know *whose children* they are?／そのかばんどこの店で買ったの At *which store* did you buy the bag?

【どこから】

この手紙はどこから来たのでしょうか *Where* did this letter come *from*?

◆どこからかピアノの音が聞こえてきた There came the sound of a piano *from somewhere*.／どこからともなく黒い服を着た男たちが現れた Men in black appeared *out of nowhere*.

【その他】

◆その猫はどこにもいなかった The cat was *nowhere* to be found.／休みの間どこにも行かなかった I didn't go *anywhere* during the vacation.／どこへでも行ってしまえ, 私はもう関知しない Go *wherever* you like, I'm past caring.／目の前にはどこまでもオリーブ畑が広がっていた The olive groves stretched out *endlessly* before us.／おまえがどこへ行こうかきっと見つけ出してやるぞ *Wherever* you (*may*) *go*, I will find you.／子犬たちは母親の後をどこへでもついていった The puppies followed *wherever* their mother went.／彼女はどこへ行ってもみんなの注目を集める *Wherever* she *goes*, she draws people's attention.／彼は別にどこといって欠点がない He has no *particular* weak points.

❷【どの点】

どこで間違えたんだろう *Where* did I go wrong?

あいつのどこがそんなにいいんだ *What's* so good about him?

彼の話を信用する根拠はどこにもない *There's no* reason to believe his story.

どこから見ても彼は正真正銘の紳士だ *To all appearances*, he is a real gentleman.／ He is a gentleman *in every way*.／ He is *every inch* a gentleman.

彼女はどこまで信用できるか分からない I don't know *how far* I can trust her.

彼とはどこまでいってるの *How far* have you gone with him?

慣用表現 彼女にそのことを伝えたが, まるでどこ吹く風といった様子だった I told her about it, but she was *completely indifferent* to the story.

➔ どこか, どこでも, どこまで, どこまでも, どこも

とこう 渡航 ──渡航する go* abroad, make* a voyage ∥彼はきのう渡航の手続きをすませた He went through the procedures for *going abroad* yesterday.

∥渡航先 a destination／渡航者 a passenger

どごう 怒号 a roar of anger ∥場内には怒号が渦巻いていた The hall was filled with *the roar of anger*.

どこか 何処か somewhere；(疑問文・if の文中で) anywhere

どこかに傘を忘れてきた I've left my umbrella *somewhere*.

彼はまだどこか近くにいるはずだ He must still be *somewhere* about.

彼は仕事でどこかロンドンの近くに行った He went *somewhere* near London on business.

どこかで彼女に会った覚えがある I remember seeing her *somewhere*.

◆どこかいいレストラン知らない Don't you know *any* good restaurants?／このコンピュータはどこかおかしい(→故障している) There's *something* wrong with this computer.／きょう彼はどこかいつもと違っている He looks different *somehow* today.

🎧「この前の日曜日にどこかへ行きましたか」「ええ, 江の島にサーフィンをしに行きました」 "Did you go *anywhere* last Sunday?" "Yes, I went surfing in Enoshima."

とこずれ 床擦れ bedsore ⓒ

どこでも (至る所で[に]) everywhere；(任意の所で[に]) anywhere ∥どこでも好きな所へ行っていいよ You may go *anywhere* you like.

◆美由紀はどこでもよく眠れる Miyuki can sleep well *wherever* she is.

どことなく 彼女は最近どことなく元気がない Lately she doesn't *somehow* look herself.／彼はどことなく賢者の風格があった There was *an air of* a sage about him.／あの2人はどことなく似ている The two resemble each other *in some way*.

とことん thoroughly ∥納得がいくまでとことん話し合う discuss *thoroughly* to *one's* satisfaction／とことんまで戦う fight *to* [*until*] *the bitter end*／今夜はとことんつきあうよ I'll stay with you *to the very end* tonight.

とこなつ 常夏 everlasting summer Ⓤ Ⓒ／

常夏の国 the land of *everlasting summer*

とこのま 床の間

和式住居に見られる一般的な床の間は，ほかより少し高くなっており，後ろの壁には1つから3つの掛け軸(掛け物)がかけられ，床には生けた花が飾られています。
Tokonoma, a kind of decorative alcove in a Japanese-style room, normally has such features as raised flooring, one to three hanging scrolls called *kakejiku* or *kakemono* on the back wall, and a flower arrangement on the floor.

どこまで この道路はどこまで続いているんですか *How far* does this road continue? / この前の授業でどこまで進んだか(→どこで終わったか)教えて Please tell me *where* you left off last time. / 彼女はどこまでお人よしなんだろう *How* good-natured she is! / あいつはどこまで信用していいんだか I wonder「*how far* [*to what extent*]」I can trust him. / どこまでお話ししましたっけ *Where* were we?

どこまでも どこまでもしらを切る pretend not to know *to the* (*very*) *end* / 私たちの頭の上には青空がどこまでも(→果てしなく)広がっていた There was an *endless* blue sky above us.

どこも 彼はどこも(体は)悪くない There's *nothing* the matter with him. / *Nothing* is the matter with him. / パリはどこもかしこも日本人だらけだった Japanese people were seen *everywhere* in Paris.

とこや 床屋 (店)《米》barbershop ⓒ,《英》barber's (shop) ⓒ; (人) barber ⓒ ⇨ 場面・状況別会話 p.1710 / きのう床屋へ行った I *went to the barber* [*barber's*] yesterday. / (→髪を切ってもらった) I *got my hair cut* yesterday.

ところ 所

❶場所	place
❷家・住所	house; address
❸箇所	part

❶【場所】 place ⓒ; (地点) spot ⓒ, point ⓒ

ここは夏合宿をするのによい所だ This is *a good place* to have a summer camp.

私は高い所に上るのが嫌いだ I hate to go up to *a high place*.

このへんに車を止められる所はありませんか Is there *a place* around here to park my car?

私は和歌山県の熊野地方と呼ばれている所で生まれた I was born in *a place* called the Kumano area in Wakayama Prefecture.

この道具箱を元あった所に戻しなさい Put this toolbox back (*in the place*) *where* it was.

その交通事故があった所にお花を供えた I left flowers at *the spot* where the accident had happened.

◆東京は曇り。所によりにわか雨が降るでしょう In Tokyo, it'll be cloudy, *partly* [*scattered*] showers. / 彼はいつも私のいない所で私の悪口を言っている He's always saying bad things about me *when I'm not around*. / 彼女のいる所でその話はしないでくれ Don't talk about it *in her presence*. / 山小屋は満員で，私たちが寝る所(→空き)はなかった The hut was filled to capacity, so there was no *room* for us to sleep. / この机を窓の所に(→近くに)移動してください Move this desk *near* the window. / その公園は私の家から歩いて5分の所にある The park is five minutes' walk from my house. / 子供の手の届かない所に保管してください Keep it *out of the reach of* children.

💬「交番はどこにありますか」「その角(ⓚ)を曲がった所にありますよ」"Where is the police box?" "It's just around the corner."

❷【家・住所】 house ⓒ,《口語的》place ⓒ; (住所) address ⓒ

本田のところに寄ったので帰りが遅くなった I came home late because I dropped in at Honda's *place* [*house*].

終電に乗り遅れたら私のところに泊めてあげるから If you miss the last train, you can come and stay at my *place* [*house*].

弟は友達のところに遊びに行ったきり，帰ってこない My brother has gone to his friend's *house* and hasn't come home yet.

忘れずにおところとお名前をお書きください Don't forget to write your name and *address*. (❖英語では name and address の順になる)

◆次に日本へいらっしゃる折にはぜひ私たちのところへお立ち寄りください Next time you visit Japan, please drop in on *us*.

❸【箇所】 part ⓒ, (特徴) feature ⓒ

この英文のここのところがどうしても分からない I simply can't understand this *part* of this English sentence.

私は居眠りしていてドラマのいちばんいいところを見逃した I slept through *the* best *part* of the drama.

紙の辞書に比べて，CD-ROM の辞書にはすぐれたところがある Compared with a paper dictionary, a CD-ROM dictionary has some good *features*.

◆物好きにもほどがあるよ！ いったい，彼のどんなところが好きなの It's crazy of you! *What* on earth do you like about him? / 弟のそういうところは父にそっくりだ My brother is just like my father in *that way*.

💬「修のやつ，いつも遅刻ばかりしていて，しょうがないやつだ」「まあ，そう言うなよ。あいつにもいいところがあるんだから」"Osamu is always late. He's hopeless!" "Oh, don't be too hard on him. He has *a good side*."

❹【場合・そのとき】

ちょうどいいところへ来た．いす，押さえてて You've come just *at the right time*. Hold the chair.

テレビの野球中継はちょうどいいところで終わってしまった The baseball TV broadcast ended *at the climax*.

きょうのところはこのくらいにしておこう That's

about it *for today*.
もう少しでがけから転落するところだった I *almost* fell over the cliff.
彼はもう少しで泣くところだった He *came close to* crying.
彼女は泣いているところを気づかれたくなかった She didn't want to be noticed *crying*.
🍀「この間買った中古のパソコンどう」「今のところ問題ないよ」 "How is the secondhand PC you bought the other day?" "No problems 「*as yet* [*so far*]."
🍀「ごめん. 待った？」「いや, 僕も今来たところ」 "I'm sorry. Have you waited a long time?" "No, *I've just gotten here*."

❺【範囲】
聞くところによると, 彼女はオリンピックに出場したことがあるらしい *I heard* she took part in the Olympic Games.
その研究機関の発表したところによると, 景気は上向いているらしい *According to* the research institute, the economy is improving.
一見したところ彼らはよくやっているように見える They are doing very well *at first sight*.
彼女はここのところ不運続きだった She took [had] a lot of hard knocks *lately*.
これぐらいのところでがまんしてやる I'll excuse you *for this*.
🍀「太郎が落ち込んでるって聞いたけど」「私が見たところそうでもないみたい(→そうは見えない)」 "I heard Taro has been depressed." "He doesn't *look* like it."

❻【その他】
正直なところ, 私には分かりません *Honestly* [*To be honest*], I don't know.
慣用表現 彼女は所かまわずたばこを吸う She smokes *wherever* she is. / (→回りの状況を考えずに)She smokes *without considering the circumstances*.
ことわざ 所変われば品変わる *So many countries, so many customs*.
⇒ ところせまし と

-どころ　-所　❶【産地】新潟は米どころとして知られている Niigata is famous as *a rice-producing area*.
❷【属する人】その会議には幹部どころ(→幹部たち)が顔をそろえた *The executives* gathered together at the meeting.
❸【…どころではない】この問題はやさしいどころではなかった This problem was 「*anything but* [*far from*] easy. / 教室は騒がしくて勉強どころではなかった The classroom was *too* noisy *to* do any studying.

ところが (しかし) but; (しかしながら) however; (だが一方) while, whereas //我々は事態を楽観していた. ところが現実はそう甘くはなかった We were optimistic about the situation, *but* things were never so easy. / 彼女は犬好きだ. ところが彼女の妹は犬が大の苦手である She likes dogs, *while* her sister hates them.

-どころか ❶【…とは逆に】内気どころか彼女はとても気さくだった *Far from* being shy, she was quite friendly. / 彼の病状はよくなるどころか悪化した His condition got worse *instead of* better. / 彼女はばかではない. それどころか非常に賢い She is not dumb. *Rather* she is very smart.
❷【言うまでもなく】博子は英語どころかフランス語だって話せる Hiroko can speak *not only* English *but* (*also*) French. / Hiroko can speak French, *to say nothing of* English. / 彼女は私には意地悪でないどころか親切ですらあった She was *not* unkind, *but even* generous to me. / 彼は自由に走るどころか歩くことさえままならなかった He couldn't walk *much less* run at will.

ところせましと　所狭しと　棚の上には酒のびんが所狭しと並んでいる Sake bottles *are packed* on the shelf. / その部屋には本が所狭しと(→至る所に)積み上げられていた Books were piled up *throughout the room*.

ところで (さて) well, now; (それはそうと) by the way, incidentally //ところでそろそろお昼にしない？ *Well* [*Now*], how about eating lunch? / ところでお母さんは元気ですか *By the way* [*Incidentally*], how is your mother?

-ところで 心配したところで何にもならない *There is no use* worrying. / いまさらあわてたところでもう手遅れだ *Even if* you get flustered now, it's too late.

ところてん　　tokoroten, a summer snack like transparent noodles made from seaweed called *tengusa*
◆この学校の多くの生徒はところてん式に高校へ進学することができる Many of this school's students can go on to senior high school *automatically*.

ところどころ　所々 in places, here and there //その地図はところどころ破られている The map is torn *in places*. / 今でもその町にはところどころに古いお寺が見られる We can still see old temples *here and there* in the town.

とさか　鶏冠 cockscomb Ⓒ, crest Ⓒ

どさくさ mess Ⓤ (また a ~); (混乱) confusion Ⓤ //彼はどさくさに紛れて(→混乱に乗じて)盗みを働いた He committed a theft taking advantage of *the confusion*.

とざす 閉ざす その家の扉はかたく閉ざされていた The door of the house *was shut* tight. / 彼女は悲しみに口を閉ざした She kept *silent* in grief. / 船が氷に閉ざされて動けなくなっていた A ship *was* 「*locked in the ice* [*icebound*]. / その村は冬になると深い雪に閉ざされる The village *is completely snowbound* in winters.

とさつ 屠殺 slaughter Ⓤ, butchery Ⓤ ── 屠殺する slaughter ⓣ, butcher ⓣ //屠殺場 a slaughterhouse

どさっと　年賀状がどさっと届く *be flooded* with new year's cards / 地面に荷物をどさっと下ろす *dump* the baggage on the ground / 屋根から雪がどさっと音を立てて落ちた Snow fell from the roof *with a thud*.

どさまわり どさ回り barnstorming ◎
どさりと ⇨ どさっと
とざん 登山 (mountain) climbing ◎; (スポーツとしての) mountaineering ◎ ∥彼女は毎週末登山に出かける She goes *climbing* every weekend.
∥登山家 a mountaineer / 登山口 an approach to a mountain / 登山靴 mountaineering boots / 登山者 a mountain climber / 登山隊 a mountaineering party, a party of climbers / 登山鉄道 a mountain railway / 登山道 a mountain trail / 登山用具《集合的》mountaineering equipment

とし¹ 年

❶【時の単位】 year ◎
パソコンブームの年 a boom *year* for PCs
その年にはいろいろなことがあった A lot of things happened *that year*.
その事件は私が高校を卒業した年に起こった The event happened *the year* that I graduated from high school.
年がたつにつれて町はさびれていった The town declined *as years* 「*went by* [*passed*].
どうぞよいお年を (I *wish you a*) *Happy New Year*!
その年の始め[暮れ]に祖母が亡くなった My grandmother died *early* [*late*] *in the year*.
いよいよ年の瀬も押し迫ってきた *The end of the year* is finally approaching.
年が明けるとすぐに試験がある We have a test just *after New Year's*.
彼らは毎年ヨーロッパを旅行する They travel in Europe *every year*.
その村は年ごとに人口が減少している The population of the village is decreasing *year by year*.
ブドウはその年その年で出来不出来がある (→よくできる年もあればそうでない年もある) Grape crops are good *one year and* bad *another*.
🅔「君は何年生まれ」「辰(ﾂ)年だよ」"What *year* of the Chinese zodiac were you born in?" "*The year of the dragon*."

❷【年齢】 age ◎, years
むやみに (→理由もなく) 人の年を聞いてはいけない Don't ask a person's *age* without a reason.
彼女は年をごまかした She lied about *her age*.
彼は年のわりにはふけて見える He looks old *for his age*.
彼女は年相応に見えた She *looked her age* [*years*].
祖父は年のせいで耳がよく聞こえない *Because of his age*, my grandfather doesn't hear well.
いい年をしてそんなばかなことを言うなよ Don't be silly *at your age*. / You *are too old to* be silly.
最近とみに年を感じるようになった Lately I have suddenly begun to *feel my age* [*years*].
君と僕は同じ年だ You and I are *of an* [*one*] *age*. / You are *the same age as* I (am).
15という年の差を越えて二人は結婚した They got married despite *an age difference* of 15 years.
彼女は年に似合わず (→年齢以上に) 色の好みが地味だ She likes quiet colors *beyond her years*.
それはまさに年の功というやつだね It's really what is called *the wisdom of age*!
◆年端もいかぬ少女 a *very young* girl; a girl *of tender years* / 彼女は自動車の運転免許が取れる年だ She is 「*old enough to* get [*over age* for] a driver's license. / 彼は見た目よりも年をとっている He is *older* than he looks. / 田川先生も年をとった Mr. Tagawa *has grown older*. / 父は年をとるにつれて気難しくなる My father is harder to get along with *as he grows older*. / 彼は年老いた両親の世話をしなければならない He has to take care of his *old* parents. / その女優はいつになっても年をとらない The actress is *ageless*. / あなたはまだ年ではありませんよ You are not *old* yet. / 彼は年こそ若いが有能な男だ Though he is young, he is a very capable man. / そんな古い歌を知ってるの? 年がばれるよ You remember such an old song? That *dates him*.
🅔「おじいさん, お年はいくつですか」「86だよ」"*How old are you*, sir?" "I'm 86 years old."

とし² 都市 city ◎; town ◎ (✦行政区分としては city よりも小さい); (大都市) metropolis ◎ ——都市の city, urban; (大都市の) metropolitan ⇨ とかい
大都市圏 *the metropolitan area* / 日本の主要な工業都市 chief *industrial cities* in Japan
その国で2番目に大きい都市はどこですか What is *the* second largest *city* in the country?
大都市は人口が密集している *Big cities* are heavily populated.
◆この地域にも都市化の波が押し寄せている (→都市化されつつある) This area is also *being urbanized*.
∥都市ガス city gas / 都市銀行 a major bank / 都市計画《米》city planning, 《英》town planning / 都市再開発 urban renewal / 都市生活 urban life / 衛星都市 a satellite city / 姉妹都市 a sister city / 商業都市 a commercial city / 百万都市 a city with a population of one million / 臨海都市 a maritime city

どじ (事) stupid mistake ◎, blunder ◎,《主に米・口語的》goof ◎ (複 ~s); (人) stupid fellow ◎, goof ◎ ——どじな stupid, goofy ∥全くどじなやつめ He's quite *a stupid fellow*. / He is quite *stupid*. / どじを踏むな Don't *make a blunder*. / (→やりそこなう) Don't *blow it*.

としあけ 年明け 年明け早々 early in *the New Year* / 年明けまでにはこの仕事を終わらせるつもりだ I'll finish this work by *the begin-*

ning of the next year.

としうえ 年上 ――年上の older, senior ⇨うえ(上) ‖彼は私より3歳年上です He is three years *older than me [my senior]./* He is *older than me [my senior]* by three years. ‖ 4人の中では誠がいちばん年上です Makoto is *the oldest* of the four.

としおとこ[おんな] 年男[女] ‖私は今年年男[女]だ I *was born in a year with the same Chinese zodiac sign as this year*.

としがい 年甲斐 ‖年がいもないことをするな (→年相応にふるまえ) *Act your age.* ‖ その知らせを聞くと彼は年がいもなくはしゃいだ When he heard the news, he became high-spirited *in spite of his age*.

としかっこう 年格好 ‖50くらいの年格好の紳士 a gentleman of *about fifty years of age* ‖母親くらいの年格好の(→同じ年に見える)女性が声をかけてきた A woman who *looked about the same age as* my mother came and talked to me.

としご 年子 ‖あの兄弟は年子だ The brothers *were born within a year of each other*.

としこし 年越し ‖則夫の家は毎年日光で年越しをする (→新年を迎える) Norio's family *greets* every *new year* at Nikko.
‖年越しそば *soba* noodles, which are eaten on New Year's Eve

とじこみ 綴じ込み file Ⓒ

とじこむ 綴じ込む file Ⓤ, keep* ... on file ‖その事件に関する新聞の切り抜きをとじ込む *file* newspaper clippings about the case

とじこめる 閉じ込める shut* (up); (かぎをかけて) lock up ‖鳥をかごに閉じ込める *shut (up)* a bird *into* a cage ‖ 泥棒は牢屋(ろ)に閉じ込められた The thief *was locked up* in the prison. ‖ 私たちは雪で一日中家に閉じ込められた We *were shut up* indoors all day because of the snow.

とじこもる 閉じ籠もる shut* *oneself* (up); (かぎをかけて) lock *oneself* (up) ‖信一は自分の部屋に閉じこもった Shinji *shut himself up* in his room. ◆自分の殻に閉じこもる *retire [go] into one's shell* ‖ いつも自分の世界に閉じこもっているのは健全ではない Always *keeping to oneself* is not healthy. ‖ 冬の間ずっと彼は家に閉じこもっていた Throughout the winter he *stayed at home*.

としごろ 年頃 (だいたいの年齢) age Ⓤ Ⓒ; (結婚適齢期) marriageable age Ⓤ Ⓒ ‖年ごろの娘 a girl of *marriageable age* ‖ 幼稚園に通う年ごろの子 a kid of kindergarten *age* ‖ 彼は多感な年ごろである He is at *an* impressionable *age*. ‖ お母さんはあなたの年ごろであなたを生んだのよ I gave birth to you when I was at your *age*. ◆おまえはもう物事の善悪の分かる年ごろだ You are *old enough to* know right from wrong.

としした 年下 ――年下の younger, junior ‖私は真子子より2歳年下です I am two years *younger* than Makiko./ I am *younger* than Makiko by two years. ‖ 彼女は私より年下だ She is *younger* than me [I].

としつき 年月 years; (時の流れ) time Ⓤ ⇨ねんげつ

-として

❶【立場・資格など】as, for
私はボランティアとして働きたい I'd like to work *as* a volunteer.
彼はピアニストとしての名声を確立した He established his fame *as* a pianist.
キャプテンとしてベストを尽くします I'll do my best *as* captain. (❖ *as* の後の役職名の a, an, the はしばしば省略される)
3月としてはかなり暖かい It is rather warm *for* March.
私個人としてはこれでいいと思う *For my part [Personally]*, I feel this is fine.
◆ 彼らは賠償金として5,000万円を要求した They claimed 50 million yen *in* compensation. ‖ 彼女はピアニストとしては二流だ She is a second-rate pianist.

❷【強調】
弁護士は彼の有罪の証拠はひとつとして(→ひとつも)ないと申し立てた The attorney claimed that there was *no [not a single]* proof of his guilt.
驚いたことにだれひとりとして(→だれも)その問題を解くことはできなかった Surprisingly, *no one [not a single person]* could solve the problem.

-としても (たとえ…としても) even if; (どんなに…としても) however, no matter how ‖事実としても、妙な話だね *Even if* it is true, it seems strange.
◆ 彼は歌手だが、俳優としても有名だ He is a singer, and he is well-known *as* an actor *as well*. ‖ 彼を説得しようとしてもむだだ It is useless trying [to try] to persuade him.

どしどし (ためらわずに) without hesitation; (自由に) freely ‖どしどし質問してください Ask questions *without hesitation*./ *Don't hesitate to* ask questions./ *Please feel free to* ask questions.

としなみ 年波 ‖寄る年波には勝てない You can't resist *the advance of age [growing older]*.

としま 年増 (中年女性) middle-aged woman Ⓒ

とじまり 戸締まり ‖寝る前に家中の戸締まりをした I *locked* the house *up* before I went to bed.

どしゃ 土砂 earth and gravel ‖土砂崩れ a landslide

どしゃぶり 土砂降り heavy rain Ⓒ, downpour Ⓒ ‖彼はどしゃ降りの中を歩いてずぶぬれだった He was wet through after walking in *the heavy rain*.
◆けさはどしゃ降りだった It was *raining heavily [pouring]* this morning.

としょ 図書 books ‖図書閲覧室 a reading room ‖ 図書券 a book coupon [(英)token] ‖ 図書室 a library, a reading room ‖ 図書返却箱 a book drop ‖ 図書目録 a library catalog ‖ 参考図書 a reference book ‖ 推薦図書 recommended books

とじょう 途上 帰宅途上に *on one's way home* / その産業は発展途上にある The industry *is developing*. / 発展途上国の子供たちを援助するために募金が行われている Money is being raised in aid of children in *developing countries*.

どじょう¹ 土壌 soil Ⓤ /やせた土壌 poor [barren] *soil* / その地方の肥沃な土壌は毎年豊作をもたらしてくれる The rich [fertile] *soil* of the region produces good crops each year. ◆ 反戦運動が広がる土壌 *a fertile ground* for the antiwar movement

どじょう² 泥鰌 loach ⓒ ‖ドジョウすくい a loach-scooping dance
[慣用表現] 2匹目のどじょうをねらう(→ 幸運が繰り返すことを期待する) expect *the same good luck to repeat itself*

としょかん 図書館 library ⓒ /図書館から本を借りる borrow books from *the library* / 図書館に本を返却する return books to *the library* / 私は調べものをするために近くの図書館をよく利用します I often go to *a library* nearby to do research.
‖図書館員 a librarian / 図書館長 the chief librarian / 移動図書館 《米》a bookmobile, 《英》a mobile library

としより 年寄り old person [man, woman] Ⓤ, 《婉曲的に》elderly person [man, woman] ⓒ /お年寄りに席を譲る give *one's* seat to *an elderly man* / 彼女は年寄りじみた話し方をする She talks like *an old woman*. ◆ こちらの席はお年寄り専用です These seats are reserved for 「*senior citizens* [*the elderly*].
[慣用表現] うちのじいさんがマラソンに出るなんて年寄りの冷や水だよ(→ 年寄りがマラソンに出るなんて軽率だ) It is *careless of an old man* like my grandad to run a marathon.

とじる¹ 閉じる

close 自他, shut* 自他
傘を閉じる *close* [*fold*] an umbrella / 門を閉じておく *keep* a gate *shut* (※この shut は過去分詞)
本を閉じて黒板を見なさい *Close* your books and look at the blackboard.
彼女は去年店を閉じた She *closed* (*down*) the store last year.
この花は夜になると閉じる This flower *closes* (*up*) in the evening.
目を閉じて浜辺に横たわった I lay down on the beach *with my eyes closed*.
◆ 3日続いた大会は彼のスピーチで幕を閉じた His speech *brought down the curtain* on the three-day convention.

とじる² 綴じる file (away) /プリントをファイルにとじておく *file* (*away*) the handouts
◆ ホッチキスで新聞をとじる *staple together* the newspaper pages / とじていない書類 *loose* papers

どじる どじった！ *I blew it*!

としん 都心 the heart [center] of the city /都心では駐車に苦労する People have trouble parking in *the center of the city*. ◆ 東京の都心に出る(→ 東京の繁華街に出る) go to *downtown* Tokyo(※downtown は「下町」とは一致しない)

どしん 2階でどしんという音がした I heard *a thud* from the second floor. / 彼はどしんとしりもちをついた He fell on his behind *with a thud*. / He flopped down on his behind. / 彼女は段ボール箱をどしんと床に置いた She *slammed down* the cardboard box on the floor.

トス toss ⓒ ◆ アタッカーにボールをトスする *set* the ball to the spiker

どす (短刀) dagger ◆ 男はどすのきいた声で「ドアをあけろ」と言った The man said in a *threatening* voice, "Open the door."

どすう 度数 (目盛りなどの表示) reading ⓒ; (頻度) frequency Ⓤ; (テレホンカードの) unit ⓒ /50度数のテレホンカード a telephone card with 50 *units* on it / 温度計の度数は摂氏40度を示していた The *reading* on the thermometer was 40℃.
‖度数計 a register / 度数料金 (電話の) message rates

どすぐろい どす黒い、dark, blackish ‖事故現場にはどす黒い血の跡が残っていた *Dark* bloodstains remained at the accident site.

どすん 何かがどすんと背中にぶつかった Something *bumped* into my back.

どせい 土星 【天文】Saturn Ⓤ /土星の輪 the rings of *Saturn*

どせきりゅう 土石流 a flood of rocks and earth

とぜつ 途絶 stoppage ⓒ, interruption ⓒ ⇒ とだえる ◆ 大雪のために村との交通は途絶してしまった Access to the village *was blocked* [*interrupted*] by heavy snow.

とそ 屠蘇 *toso*, spiced sake for celebrating the New Year

とそう 塗装 (塗ること) painting Ⓤ; (塗られた塗料) paint Ⓤ ——塗装する paint 他 ‖強い日差しで塗装がはがれてきた The paint is peeling off because of the strong sunlight. / 壁の塗装を仕上げるにはあと2週間必要です We need two more weeks to finish *painting* the wall.
‖塗装工 a painter / 塗装工事 painting

どそう 土葬 burial Ⓤ ⓒ, 《公式的》interment Ⓤ ⓒ

どそく 土足 刑事は土足で部屋に入った The detective went into the room *with his shoes on*. / 土足厳禁 《掲示》*Shoes Off*

どだい 土台 ⓒ (※「建物の基礎」の意味でも、比喩的に「物事の基本」の意味でも用いる) /この家は土台がしっかりしている This house is built on *a secure* [*firm*] *foundation*. / 父は大学時代に事業の土台を築いた My father *laid the foundations of* his business when he was a university student.
◆ この本は彼の10年間のアメリカ生活を土台にしている This book *is based on* his 10 years living in America.

どだい² 宿題を30分ですませるなんてどだい無理だ It is *totally* impossible to finish my homework in half an hour. / うちの親を説得するなんてどだい無理なことだ It would *really* be impossible to persuade my parents.

とだえる 途絶える 9時を過ぎると人通りはすっかり途絶えてしまった The street *was completely deserted* after 9 o'clock. / 雅子からは5年間音信が途絶えている I *haven't heard from* Masako for five years. / 飛行機との無線連絡は1時間前に途絶えた Radio communication with the airplane *was cut off* an hour ago. / その伝統芸能は途絶えることなく今日(誌)まで受け継がれてきた The traditional performing art has been passed on *without a break* even to this very day.

どたキャン 広恵はその旅行をどたキャンした Hiroe *canceled* the trip *at the last minute*.

とだな 戸棚 cabinet ⒞, cupboard ⒞ (❖cabinet はリビング・書斎などに置く(飾り)戸棚を, cupboard は台所に置く食器棚などを指すことが多い)

どたばた (騒々しく) noisily ‖だれかが廊下をどたばた走っている Somebody's running down the hall *noisily*. ◆上の階では子供たちがどたばた騒いでいる Children *are romping about* upstairs. / 突然ドアが開いて、男の子がどたばたと入ってきた Suddenly the door opened and some boys *barged in*. (❖barge in は「押し入る」の意味)
‖どたばた喜劇 a slapstick comedy

トタン ❖galvanized iron sheet ⓤ
‖トタン屋根 a tin roof

とたん 途端 彼女が歌い終えたとたん聴衆から割れんばかりの拍手かっさいが起こった She *had barely* finished singing *when* thunderous applause burst from the audience. / 窓をあけたとたん小鳥が入ってきた I had *just* opened the window *when* a little bird flew in. / 試験が始まったとたん私の頭の中は真っ白になった My mind went blank *as soon as* the exam began. / 広昭を見たとたん彼女の胸はときめいた Her heart fluttered *the moment* she saw Hiroaki.

どたんば 土壇場 the last moment ‖彼はどたんばになってその仕事をキャンセルした He canceled the work *at the last moment*.
◆日本チームはもう1敗もできないというどたんばに追い込まれた The Japanese team *was driven to the「moment of truth [critical point]* where it could no longer afford another loss.

どたんばたん 弟と妹が2階でどたんばたんと暴れている My brother and sister *are romping about and making noise* upstairs.

とち 土地
❶【地面】land ⓤ; (区画) lot ⒞
彼女の一家はいなかに土地をたくさん持っている Her family has a lot of *land* in their hometown.
おじは去年千葉に150 ㎡の土地を買った My uncle bought 150 square meters of *land* in Chiba last year.

東京都心で土地を遊ばしておくのはもったいない It is wasteful to *leave land vacant* in the center of Tokyo.
土地付きの家が売りに出されている A house *with a lot* is for sale.
❷【土壌】soil ⓤ
肥えた土地 fertile [rich] *soil* / 土地を耕す plow [work] *the soil*
このあたりの土地は小麦の栽培に適している The *soil* around here is good for growing wheat.
❸【地方】area ⒞, place ⒞
私はこの土地をよく知りません I *don't know* this *place well*. / I'm a stranger here.
誘拐犯は土地勘のある人間(→土地をよく知っている)にちがいない The kidnapper must *be familiar with the area*.
◆私はその土地の料理になじめなかった I couldn't get used to *the local food*.
‖土地開発業者 a land developer / 土地家屋 real estate / 土地価格 land prices / 土地所有権 landownership / 土地所有者 a landowner / 土地ブローカー a real estate agent

とちぎ 栃木

> 栃木県は本州の中央部に位置しています。この県の一部は日光国立公園に属しており、日本の観光地の一つになっています。徳川家康を祭った日光東照宮を初めとして、見るべき神社があり、中禅寺湖や華厳の滝など風光明媚(%)な所が多くあります。
> Tochigi Prefecture is located in central Honshu. A part of this prefecture belongs to Nikko National Park and is one of Japan's scenic spots. In this area, most visitors are attracted by the Toshogu shrine, dedicated to Tokugawa Ieyasu, and other temples and shrines. There are also many sites of natural beauty, such as Lake Chuzenji and Kegon waterfall.

どちゃく 土着 ──土着の native; (その土地固有の) indigenous ‖土着の文化 the *indigenous* culture
‖土着民 a native

とちゅう 途中
❶【道の】──途中で[に] on the [one's] way, halfway
途中で引き返す turn back *halfway*
途中で先生と偶然いっしょになった I ran across my teacher *on the way*.
学校に行く途中で忘れずにこの手紙を出してくれ Remember to mail this letter *on your way to school*.
帰宅途中にビデオを借りた I rented some videos *on my way home*.
◆優子が途中までいっしょに来てくれた Yuko came *part of the way* with me. / 横浜で途中下車しお昼を食べた I *stopped off* at Yokohama for lunch. / 途中下車前途無効 No *stopovers* are allowed on this ticket. (❖切符の表示)

❷【物事の】
映画の途中で突然明かりがついた *Halfway through* the film the lights were turned on suddenly.

会議の途中で(→会議が終わる前に)抜けるなんて彼女も無責任だ It was irresponsible of her to leave *before the meeting was over*.

弟は宿題を途中でほっぽり出して(→宿題を終わらせずに)テニスをしに行った My brother went out to play tennis leaving his homework *unfinished*.

試験の途中で消しゴムがないことに気がついた I noticed *in the middle of* the exam that I didn't have an eraser.

お話の途中で(→中断させて)申しわけありませんがお電話が入っています *Excuse me for interrupting*, but you are wanted on the phone.

カードが切れて電話が途中で切れてしまった The card ran out and「I *was cut off* [*the phone went dead*].

野球の途中経過をお知らせします Now for *a report of* the baseball games *still in progress*.

とちょう 都庁 (東京都庁) the Tokyo「Metropolitan Government Office [City Hall]

どちら

❶【どこ】 where ⇨ どこ

トイレはどちらですか *Where*'s the bathroom?

この10日間どちらにいらっしゃったのですか *Where* have you been for the last 10 days?

どちらのご出身ですか *Where* are you from?/ *Where* do you come from? (❖国籍を聞くときは*What* is your nationality?という)

「住所はどちらですか *What* [×*Where*] is your address?/ お父さんはどちらの会社にお勤めですか *What* company does your father work for?

❷【いずれの】 which; (どちらか一方) either; (どちらも) both; (どちらも…ない) not either, neither; (どちらの…でも) no matter which, whichever

コーヒーと紅茶ではどちらが好きですか *Which* do you like better, coffee or tea?

君か僕のどちらかが間違っている *Either* you *or* I am wrong. (❖either ... or ～ が主語の場合、動詞は～に一致)

僕のところに2匹の子猫がいるのでどちらか1匹あげるよ I have two kittens; you can have *either* of them.

英語と数学のどちらも得意です I'm good at *both* English *and* math.

彼女は2枚のシャツを試着したがどちらも買わなかった She tried on two shirts but「*didn't* buy *either* [bought *neither*].

どちらの小説もおもしろくなかった *Neither* of the novels was [(口語的)were] interesting.

どちらを選んでも値段は同じです *No matter which* you choose, the price is the same.

どちらでも好きなほうを取っていいですよ You can have *whichever* you like.

◆有紀と聡ではどちらがピアノが上手ですか *Who plays the piano better, Yuki or Satoshi?* (❖whichは用いない) / あなたの猫は雄、雌どちらですか *What sex is your cat?* / 2人のうちどちらかがうそをついている(→1人が) *One of the two is telling a lie.* / 2つの方法のどちらにするか迷っている(→2つの方法の間で迷っている) I*'m caught between* the two alternative methods.

🄮「日本映画は好きですか」「そうですね、どちらとも言えませんね」 "Do you like Japanese movies?" "Well, *it's hard to say*."

❸【だれ】 who ⇨ だれ

🄮「どちら様でしょうか」「坂本(均)です」 "*Who is it, please*?" "This is Sakamoto Hitoshi." / "*May I have your name, please*?" "My name is Sakamoto Hitoshi." (❖前者は電話の会話、後者は受付での会話。どちらの場合も "*Who are you?*" とはいわない。また、英語ではふつう軍人以外などでは名字だけで名乗ることはない)

❹【その他】
彼はどちらかというと他人の意見に左右されやすい He *tends to* be swayed by what other people think.

彼女はどちらかといえばはっきりものを言う She is *rather* outspoken.

私はどちらかといえば父親似だ(→母親よりも父親に似ている) I'm *more* like my father *than* my mother.

彼女は親切ではない。どちらかといえば冷たい She isn't kind. She is, *if anything*, cold.

どちらにしても、彼には電話で伝えておきます *In any case*, I'll tell him about it on the phone.

とちる make* a slip ◆最初の場面でせりふをとってしまった I *blew* [*fluffed*] my lines in the first scene.

とっか 特価 bargain price 🄲 ◆クーラーを特価で買った I bought an air-conditioner *at a special price.*
‖特価品 a bargain item

どっか テレビをつけソファーにどっかと腰を下ろした I turned on the TV and *flopped down on* the couch.

どっかいりょく 読解力 reading comprehension 🄲 ‖生徒の読解力を伸ばす improve students' *reading comprehension*

どっかり ⇨ どっか

とっかんこうじ 突貫工事 競技場の建設は突貫工事で行われた The stadium was built *in a rush*.

とっき 突起 projection 🄲 ‖頭部に突起のある昆虫 an insect with *a projection* on its head

とっきゅう¹ 特急 limited express 🄲 ‖8時30分発富山行きの特急に乗ろう Let's take *the* 8:30 *limited express* for Toyama.
‖特急券 a limited express ticket

とっきゅう² 特級 the highest quality ‖特級のワイン *the highest quality* wine

とっきょ 特許 patent ◻ ∥彼女はその薬の特許を申請した She applied for *a patent* on the medicine. / 中島博士はこの発明で特許を取った Dr. Nakajima obtained *a patent* on this invention. / 新案特許出願中 *Patent Pending* (◆商品名の表示)
∥特許権 a patent (right) / 特許庁 the Patent Office

ドッキング (宇宙船の) docking ◻
◆2つの宇宙船は火星の大気圏外でドッキングした The two spacecraft *docked with* each other above Mars' atmosphere.

とっく 夏休みの宿題はとっくの昔にやってしまった I finished my homework for summer vacation *long ago*. / 11時はとっくに過ぎている It's *well* past 11. / そんなことはとっくの昔に知ってるよ(→新しい情報ではない) That's *no news to* me.

とつぐ 嫁ぐ 姉は鈴木家に嫁いだ My sister *married into* the Suzuki family.

ドック dock ◻◻ ∥船は修理のためにドックに入った The ship *was put into dock* for repairs.

とっくみあい 取っ組み合い grappling ◻, wrestling ◻ ∥通りでは2人の男の子が取っ組み合いのけんかをしていた On the street two boys *were grappling with* each other. / 店主は強盗と数分間取っ組み合いをした The shopkeeper *wrestled with* the robber for several minutes.

とっくり 徳利 sake flask ◻

とっくん 特訓 (特別の訓練) special training ◻; (特別の授業) special lesson ◻ ∥決勝戦を目前に控え,我々は特訓を受けている With the finals just around the corner, we are going through *special [intensive] training*. / アメリカに行く前に浜田先生から英語の特訓を受けるつもりだ I plan to take *special [intensive] lessons* in English from Mr. Hamada before going to America.

とっけ 毒気 みんな彼の毒気にあてられてしまった(→彼はみんなをあぜんとさせた) He *dumbfounded* us all.

とつげき 突撃 charge ◻ ──突撃する charge ◻◻ ∥部隊は敵の要塞(ようさい)めがけて突撃した The troops *charged* the enemy fortress.

とっけん 特権 privilege ◻◻ ∥彼は特権を行使して機密ファイルにアクセスした He exercised *his privilege* to access confidential files. / 会員には種々の特権が与えられている Various *privileges* are given to the members. / 特権を悪用するな Don't abuse *your privileges*.
∥特権階級 the privileged classes

どっこいしょ 父はどっこいしょと(→苦労して)荷物を網棚に載せた My father put the baggage onto the rack *with an effort*.

どっこいどっこい 二人の中間試験の成績はどっこいどっこい(→ほとんど同じ)だった The two got *about the same* grades on the midterm exam. / 彼らの実力はどっこいどっこいだ Their abilities are *almost equal*.

とっこうやく 特効薬 まだ特効薬のない病気がたくさんある There are a lot of diseases for which we have no *specific cure* yet.

とっさ 咄嗟 とっさの出来事で(→急に起こったので)どうすることもできなかった It happened so *suddenly* that we couldn't do anything about it. / 猫が車の前に飛び出してきたので,彼はとっさに(→本能的に)ブレーキを踏んだ A cat ran out in front of his car and he *instinctively* slammed the brake. / 哲也のとっさの(→迅速な)判断で子供は助かった Tetsuya's *quick* judgment saved the child. / その質問にとっさには(→即座には)答えられなかった I couldn't answer the question *immediately*. / とっさに(→はずみでうそをついてしまった I found myself telling a lie *on the spur of the moment*.

どっさり 冷蔵庫には食料がどっさりある We have *a lot of* food in the fridge. / 裕次はバレンタインデーにチョコレートをどっさりもらった Yuji got *a pile of* chocolates on St. Valentine's Day.

ドッジボール ドッジボールをする play *dodge ball*

とっしゅつ 突出 がけの中ほどから岩が突出している There is a piece of rock *sticking out* halfway up the cliff. / 全国的に見ても彼女の記録は突出している Her record *is outstanding* even on a national level.

とつじょ 突如 ⇨ とつぜん

どっしり ──どっしりとした (重い・重そうな) heavy; (建物などが堂々とした) imposing; (態度が威厳のある) dignified ∥窓際にはどっしりとした黒檀(こくたん)の机が置かれていた There was a *heavy* ebony desk near the window. / 薄暗い路地のつきあたりにはどっしりとした石造りの教会が見えた I saw an *imposing* stone church at the end of the dim alley. / 岡教授はいつもどっしりと構えている Professor Oka always *has a dignified air*.
◆君は全力を尽くしたのだからどっしりと構えて(→冷静に)結果を待ちなさい You did your best, so just *stay cool* and wait for the results.

とっしん 突進 ──突進する rush ◻, dash ◻ (◆後者のほうが激しさが強調される) ∥群衆はドアめがけて狂ったように突進した The crowd *rushed* wildly *to* the door. / 彼はゴールに向けて突進した He *dashed for* the goal.

とつぜん 突然 suddenly, all of a sudden (◆後者のほうが強意的); (唐突に) abruptly; (思いがけず) unexpectedly; (全く予想外に) out of the blue
彼は突然後ろを振り返った He *suddenly* turned around.
戸が突然バタンと閉まった The door slammed *abruptly*.
3年間音さたのなかった彼が突然訪ねてきた He called on me *unexpectedly* after three years' silence.
突然母親から来週京都に引っ越すと知らされた *Out of the blue* my mother told me we were moving to Kyoto next week.
◆突然の電話のベルにびくりとさせられた The

sudden ringing of the telephone gave me a start. / 私の真剣な顔を見ると彼は**突然笑いだした** When he looked at my solemn face, he *burst into laughter*.
∥突然死 (a) sudden death / 突然変異 (a) mutation

とったん 突端 岬の突端に灯台がある There is a lighthouse at *the tip* of the cape.

どっち (疑問) which; (どちらか一方) either; (どちらも) both; (どちらも…ない) not either, neither; (どちらの…でも) no matter which, whichever ⇨ どちら

どっちを読むべきだと思う *Which* do you think I should read?

南はどっちですか *Which direction* is south?

どっちがどっちか区別できません I can't tell *which is which*.

どっちの席に座ってもいいよ You may take *either* seat.

私はどっちの写真も好きじゃない I *don't* like *either* photo. / I like *neither* of the photos.

どっちの道を通っても10分もかかりません *Whichever* road you take, it won't take more than 10 minutes.

❷「どっちの自転車が君のなの, これ, それともあれ？」「どっちも僕のだよ」 "*Which* bike is yours, this one or that one?" "*Both* are mine."

❷「お茶とコーヒー, どっちにする」「どっちでもいいよ」 "Tea *or* coffee?" "*Either one's fine*."

慣用表現 どっちもどっちだ *It's six of one and half a dozen of the other.* (→これは6個, あれは半ダースだから, 結局同じだ)

どっちつかず どっちつかずの(→優柔不断な)態度 *one's wishy-washy* behavior / 彼女はいつも僕にどっちつかずの(→あいまいに)返事をする She always *answers* me *ambiguously*. / これはどっちつかずの(→あいまいな)ケースだ This is a *gray area*. / 彼がどっちつかずの(→中立的な)立場をとるのは気に入らない I don't like his taking a *neutral* stance.

どっちみち in any case; (結局) after all; (遅かれ早かれ) sooner or later ∥どっちみちあすは休まなければならない *In any case*, I have to take a day off tomorrow.

とっちめる (口語的)give* *a person* hell, teach* *a person* a lesson ∥今度あいつが弟の悪口を言ったら, とっちめてやる I'll give him *hell* next time he says mean things about my brother.

とっつき 取っ付き この本は初心者でもとっつきやすい This book *is accessible to* beginners. / 彼はとっつきにくい印象を与えるかもしれないが, 本当にいいやつだ He may seem *unapproachable* [*aloof*] but he's actually a good guy. (❖ aloof は「非社交的でよそよそしい」の意味)

とって 取っ手 handle ⓒ; (ノブ) knob [náb] ⓒ ∥スーツケースの取っ手に名札をつけた I tied a name tag onto *the handle* of the suitcase. / 取っ手をゆっくり右に回しなさい Turn *the knob* slowly to the right.

-とって それは我々のテーマにとってはどうでもいいことです That is immaterial *to* our topic. / 小テストは篤志にとってはやさしすぎた The quiz was too easy *for* Atsushi. / 田尾先生のクラスになったのは彼にとって幸運だった It was lucky *for* him to be in Ms. Tao's class.

とっておき 取って置き 彼はとっておきの(→いちばんいい)ジャケットをパーティーに着ていった He wore his *best* jacket to the party. / 父はとっておきの(→最上級の)ウイスキーを客に出した My father served the guests「his *choicest* whiskey [(→特別の機会にとっておいた) the whiskey *kept for special occasions*]. / 本物のスパゲッティが食べたいなら, とっておきの(→ぴったりの)場所があります If you want real spaghetti, I know *just the place*. / とっておきの手(→奥の手)を使おう I'll play *my trump card*.

とっておく 取って置く (保持する) keep* ⓘ; (別にしておく) set* aside; (残しておく) save ∥私が戻るまで私の席をとっておいてくれませんか Would you *keep* my seat until I come back? / 我々の友情のあかしにこれをとっておいてください Please *keep* [*take*] this as a proof of our friendship. / おつりはとっておいてください *Keep* the change. / 彼は彼女の誕生日のプレゼントを買うためにお金をとっておいた He *set aside* some money to buy her a birthday present. / みんなのためにとっておいたせんべいがあります I have some rice crackers *saved* for you.
◆彼は長い冬に備えてまきをとっておいた He *stored* firewood for the long winter.

とってかえす 取って返す 旅先から家へ急いでとって返す *hurry back* home from a trip / 彼は財布を忘れたことに気づき, 家にとって返した He realized he'd forgotten his wallet, so he *went back to* his house.

とってかわる 取って代わる replace ⓘ ∥1960年代にテレビが映画にとって代わった Television *replaced* movies in the 1960s.
◆レコードはCDに完全にとって代わられたわけではない Records *haven't yielded* [*given way*] *to* CDs completely.

とってくる 取って来る fetch ⓘ, go* (and) get* ∥このお皿を1枚取ってきてくれませんか Could you *fetch* me a plate? / ちょっと傘を取ってくるよ I'll *go get* my umbrella.

とってつけたよう 取って付けたよう 取ってつけたような(→わざとらしい)ほほえみ an *artificial* smile / 彼は私の描いた絵を見て, 取ってつけたような(→心にもない)お世辞を言った He paid me some *false* compliments over my painting. / 彼女は私に取ってつけたような(→しかたなくしたような)おじぎをして走っていった She gave me a *forced* bow and ran off.

とっても ⇨とても

どっと この島は夏には観光客がどっと押し寄せる This island *is flooded with* tourists during the summer. / 開店と同時にバーゲン目当ての客がどっとなだれ込んだ As soon as the store opened, bargain hunters *flooded in*. / みなどっと笑いだした Everybody burst 「*into laughter* [*out laughing*]. / 日陰から出ると, どっと汗が出た When I came out of the shade, I *burst into a sweat*. / 先生の冗談にクラス全員がどっと笑った Teacher's joke *set* the entire class *laughing*. / 試験が全部終わると, どっと疲れが出た I *suddenly* began to feel tired when all the exams were over.

とつとつ 訥々 彼女は子供時代のことをとつとつと話した She *fumbled* her *way through* the story of her childhood.

とつとと とつととうせろ *Get lost!* / *Get out of my sight right now*!

とっとり 鳥取

> 鳥取県は本州の西部に位置し, 北側で日本海に面しています。県の特産物としては二十世紀ナシと呼ばれるナシが有名です。また, 鳥取県の主要な観光名所として, 日本では珍しい砂丘, 鳥取砂丘があります。現在, この砂丘には木が植えられたり水が引かれたりしているため, 景色が変わりつつあります。
> Tottori Prefecture is located in western Honshu and faces the Sea of Japan to the north. The prefecture's specialty is a pear called the "nijisseiki nashi," which means 20th century pear. Tottori's sand dunes—sand dunes are rare in Japan—are one of the major tourist attractions. The dunes, however, have been irrigated and planted with trees, so their features are changing.

とつにゅう 突入 警官が建物に突入した The police officers *dashed into* the building. / 両国は戦争に突入した The two countries *plunged into* war.

とっぱ 突破 ――突破する (障害物を) break* through …; (難関を) overcome*⚓; (数値を) exceed⚓ ‖トラックはバリケードを突破した A truck *broke through* the barricade. / 彼らは多くの難関を突破しなければならなかった They had to *overcome* a lot of difficulties. / 市の人口は100万を突破した The population of the city *has exceeded* one million.
◆初戦突破(→初戦に勝つこと)が僕らの目標です It is our goal to *win the first game*. / 優子は入試で競争率20倍の難関を突破した Yuko *got over* the hurdle of the entrance examination, which only one out of twenty applicants could pass. / 彼女の研究は新薬開発の大きな突破口を開いた Her research made *a* major *breakthrough* in the development of a new drug.

とっぱつ 突発 ⓒ ――突発する break* out ――突発的な unexpected ――突発的に unexpectedly ‖きのう国境地帯で銃撃戦が突発した A shoot-out *broke out* near the border yesterday. / 突発的な事故で10人がけがをした Ten people were injured in an *unexpected* accident.

とっぴ 突飛 とっぴな考え a *wacky* idea / とっぴな(→実際的でない)計画 a *harebrained* scheme / とっぴな(→こっけいな)柄のシャツを衝動買いしてしまった I bought on impulse a shirt with a *zany* design on it. / 彼の今度のヘアースタイルはとっぴすぎる(→奇抜すぎる) His new hairstyle is too *eccentric*.

とっぴょうしもない 突拍子もない 彼の突拍子もない発言にその場の一同目が点になってしまった All the people there were confused at his *ridiculous* [(→とっぴな)*off-the-wall*] remark.

トッピング (料理などの) topping ⓒⓊ

トップ the top
彼女は英語の成績がクラスでトップである She is *at the top* of her class in English. / She is *first* in her class in English.
常にトップを守るには大変な努力が必要だ It requires hard work to stay *on top* all the time. (❖*on top* では top は無冠詞)
彼女はライバルからトップの座を奪った She supplanted her rival *at the top*.
◆トップクラスの科学者 a *top-class* [*first-rate*] scientist / パソコンのトップメーカー a *leading manufacturer* of personal computers / トップでゴールインする finish *ahead of the field* / 大統領選がきょうのトップニュースです The presidential election *tops* today's *news*. / レースの現時点でのトップは直美だ The current *leader* in the race is Naomi. / その候補者はトップで再選された The candidate was reelected *at the head of the poll*.
‖トップ会談 a summit conference / トップバッター the leadoff batter

とっぷう 突風 gust ⓒ ‖突風でほこりが舞い上がった A *gust* (*of wind*) stirred up the dust.

とっぷり とっぷりと日が暮れた It became *quite dark*.

どっぷり 温泉に肩までどっぷりとつかった I *soaked myself* up to my shoulders in the hot spring. / 彼女はここのところアーチェリーにどっぷりはまっている She *has been obsessed with* archery recently.

トップレス ――トップレスの topless

とつべん 訥弁 彼は訥弁だ(→話すのが得意でない) He is *not good at speaking*. / He is *a poor speaker*.

とつレンズ 凸レンズ convex lens ⓒ

-とて 今から謝ったとて, どうにもならない It would make no difference *if* you apologize now. / 君とて断るだろう *Even* you would refuse.

どて 土手 bank ⓒ; (人工的な) dike ⓒ; (堤防) embankment ⓒ ‖私たちは川の土手を歩いた We walked along *the bank* of the river. / 豪雨で土手が決壊寸前になった Because of the heavy rain, *the embankment* almost burst.

とてつもない 門をくぐると, そこはとてつもなく(→信じられないほど)広い庭だった When I went through the gate, I found myself in an *incredibly* large garden. / その絵にはとてつもない(→法外な)値段がついていた The price of the painting was *outrageous*.

とても

❶【非常に】very, so (❖形容詞・副詞を修飾する. so は女性や子供がよく用いる); very much (❖動詞を修飾する)

とてもかわいい女の子 a *very* pretty girl

白い男物のシャツを着た彼女はとても魅力的だった She looks *very* attractive in a men's white shirt.

彼女はとても速くタイプを打つ She types *very* quickly.

私はとても映画が好きです I like movies 「*very much* [*a lot*].

正はとても優しいのよ Tadashi is *very* [*so*] kind.

とても寒かったので出かけられなかった It was *so* cold *that* I couldn't go out. (❖この表現は特に男女の区別なく用いられる) / It was *too* cold *to* go out.

◆彼は若いころとてもやせていた He was *really* thin when he was young.

❷【到底…できない】

あの大学に自分が合格するなんてとても想像できない I *can't possibly* see myself passing the entrance examination for that university.

UFOを見たと彼は言っているけど、とても信じられない I *simply can't* believe his claim that he saw a UFO.

とても彼女にはかなわない I *can hardly* match her.

マラソンで早夫に勝つなんてとてもじゃないが無理だよ It would be *just about* impossible to beat Hayao in the marathon.

ととう 徒党 gang ◎ ❖彼らは徒党を組んで旅行者を襲った They formed *a gang* and assaulted tourists.

どとう 怒濤 抗議する人々が大使館に怒濤のように押しかけた People *surged toward* the embassy in protest.

とどうふけん 都道府県 Tokyo and all the prefectures (❖英語では「道」「府」「県」を特に区別せず prefecture という)

とどく 届く

❶【郵便などが】arrive ⊕

もう今ごろは手紙が届いているだろう The letter will *have arrived* by now.

母から小包がけさ届いた The parcel from my mother *arrived* this morning.

◆山本先生からの手紙はきょうの午後私の手元に届いた The letter from Ms. Yamamoto 「*got to* [*reached*] me this afternoon.

❷【手などが】reach ⊕

その棚は高い所にあるので僕には手が届かない The shelf is *too* high for me *to reach*.

彼女は腰まで届く長い髪をしていた She had hair long enough to *reach* her waist.

何度も彼女を呼んだが声が届かなかった I called to her again and again, but 「*my voice didn't reach* her [she *didn't hear me*].

彼の放った矢は的(ﾏﾄ)に届かなかった The arrow he shot *didn't reach* the target.

◆子供の手の届かない所に保管してください Keep it *out of the reach of* children. / 彼はもう少しで成功に手が届く Success is now *within his reach*. / 祖父は80にもうすぐ手が届く My grandfather is *nearly* [*close to*] 80.

❸【その他】

このホテルは行き届いたサービスで知られる This hotel is famous for *its good service*.

このコンピュータは私には高くて手が届かない(→高すぎて買えない) This computer is *too* expensive for me *to buy*.

私たちの祈りが届き、河田さんは1週間で退院することができた Our *prayers were heard* and Mr. Kawada was able to leave the hospital in a week.

とどけ 届け (事前の) notice ◎ ◎; (事後の) report ◎ ∥欠席届は5日以内に提出してください Please hand in *a report of* your *absence* within five days. / 彼女は届けを出さずに学校を休んだ She was absent from school *without notice*.

◆警察に盗難届を出す(→盗難を報告する) *report the theft* to the police / 市役所に婚姻届を出す(→結婚を登録する) *register the marriage* at the city office

∥届け先 (事前の) the receiver's address / 転入[転出]届 a moving-in[-out] notification

とどけで 届け出 交番に朝日公園で財布を拾ったという届け出があった(→だれかが財布を交番に持っていった) Somebody *took* the wallet found in Asahi Park *to* the police box.

とどける 届ける

❶【送る】send* ⊕; (配達する) deliver ⊕

地震で家を失った人々に救援物資が届けられた Relief goods *were sent* [*delivered*] to the people made homeless by the earthquake.

注文品は1週間以内にお届けします We *will deliver* the ordered goods within a week.

◆息子さんは9時までにお宅へ送り届けます I'll get your son *back home* by nine.

❷【通知する】notify ⊕

住所変更を郵便局にまだ届けていない I *haven't notified* the post office of my change of address yet.

◆警察に事故を届け出る *report* the accident to the police

とどこおり 滞り hitch ◎ ∥集会は滞りなく終了した The assembly went off 「*without a hitch* [*smoothly*].

とどこおる 滞る 彼は家賃が3か月滞っている He *is* three months 「*behind with* [*overdue on*] the rent. / (→3か月払っていない) He hasn't paid the rent for three months. / 彼女は1週間の休暇をとったので仕事が滞っている She *is behind with* her work after a week-long vacation.

ととのう¹ 整う 設備の整ったホテル a *well-appointed* hotel / 整った服装 *neat* clothing / 朝食の用意が整いました Breakfast *is ready*. / 出かける準備はすべて整いましたか Have you *got* everything *ready to go*? / 台所は

まだ完全には設備が整っていない The kitchen *is not* fully *equipped* yet. / 彼は整った顔立ちをしている(→顔立ちがよい) He is *good-looking*.

ととのう² 調う 斉藤家と太田家の間で縁談がととのった A match *has been arranged* between the Saito and Ota families.

ととのえる 整える (きちんとする) tidy up; (用意する) get* ... ready

子供たちは写真を撮る前に，身なりを整えた The children *tidied* themselves *up* before being photographed.

オーディションに必要な書類は全部整えてあります I'*ve got* all the papers *ready* for the audition.

◆部屋を整える *straighten up* a room / 彼女は乱れた髪を整えた She *arranged* her messy hair. / チャンピオンは次の試合に向けて体調を整えている The champion is trying to *get in shape* for the next match. / 君が図書館を使えるよう手はずを整えておこう I'll *see* (*to it*) *that* you can use the library.

と

とどまる 止まる・留まる (場所・地位などに残る) remain [自]; (限定される) be limited

現職にとどまる *remain* in *one's* present post

一家は5年間その町にとどまった The family *remained* in the town for five years.

彼の興味は生物学にとどまらない His interests *aren't limited to* biology.

◆彼はその後も日本にとどまって研究を続けた After that, he *stayed in* Japan and continued his research. / 新しい高校の必要性を感じているのは彼女1人にとどまらない(→唯一の人間ではない) She *is not the only person* who recognizes the need for a new high school. / 彼女の論文は問題点の指摘にとどまっている(→彼女が行ったことは問題点の指摘だけだ) *All* she did in her paper was point out problems. / 彼の知識欲はとどまるところを知らない(→飽くことがない) His appetite for knowledge「*is insatiable* [(→限界を知らない) *knows no limits*]. / 彼らのチームの快進撃はとどまるところを知らない(→勝ち続けている) Their team *keeps on winning*.

とどめ 止め・留め 彼は男の胸にナイフを突き刺してとどめを刺した He *finished* the man *off* by thrusting the knife into his chest.

とどめる 止める・留める

彼女は子供のころの面影をとどめている She *retains* her childhood appearance.

彼は戦後の日本の歴史に名をとどめた He *made a mark* on the history of postwar Japan.

事故でその車は原形をとどめないほど大破した The car was smashed *beyond recognition* in the accident.

彼らは戦争の悲惨さを記憶にとどめるために慰霊碑を建てた They raised a memorial to *preserve the memory of* the horrors of war.

彼はその言葉を心にとどめておいた He *kept* those words *close to his heart*.

ミーティングでは新入部員の名前を紹介するにとどめた(→紹介しただけだった) *All* I did at the meeting was (to) announce the names of the new club members.

来月は食費を最小限にとどめる必要がある We have to *keep* the spending on food *at a minimum* next month. / We have to *spend as little as possible on* food next month.

とどろかす 轟かす 頭の上をジェット機が爆音をとどろかして飛んでいった A jet plane flew away over my head *with a roar*.

とどろき 轟き (響き渡る大きな音) roar [C]; (雷などのごろごろいう音) rumble [C] ∥遠くで雷のとどろきが聞こえた I heard *a rumble* of thunder in the distance.

とどろく 轟く roar [自]; (継続的に) rumble [自] ∥突然大砲がとどろいた All of a sudden the gun *roared*.

◆棋士としての彼の名声は天下にとどろいている(→全国的な名声を得ている) He *has won nationwide fame* as a *shogi* player.

ドナー (臓器などの) donor [dóunər] [C]

とない 都内 the Metropolitan [Tokyo] area

となえる 唱える (繰り返す) chant [他]; (提唱する) advance [他]; (公に支持する) advocate [他] ∥呪文(じゅもん)を唱える *chant* an incantation / 念仏を唱える *chant* the name of Amida Buddha / 日本語の起源について新説を唱える *advance* a new theory of the origin of the Japanese language

◆彼女は私たちの決定に異議を唱えた She *raised* an objection to our decision.

トナカイ reindeer [C] (複～)

-となく 彼は夜となく昼となく電話をかけてくる He keeps calling me up *night and day*. / 吉田さんはだれかれとなく自分の車を自慢する Mr. Yoshida brags about his car to *anybody and everybody*.

どなた (受付などで)どなた様ですか *May I have your name, please*? / (電話で) *Who's calling, please*? / どなたかいらっしゃいませんか Is *anyone* there?

[会] (玄関で)「どなたですか」「私です．優子です」 "*Who is it*?" "It's me, Yuko."

どなべ 土鍋 earthen pot [C]

となり 隣

(隣の家) the house next door, the next house; (隣の家の人) *one's* [the] next-door neighbor [《英》neighbour]; (隣の席の人) *one's* [the] neighbor ―隣の (席などが) next; (家が) next-door, neighboring ―隣に next to ..., beside ...; next door

〖隣の〗

隣の猫が時折遊びに来る *Our* (*next-door*) *neighbor's* cat visits us occasionally. (❖文脈上明らかな場合は next-door は省略してもよい)

彼は隣の人に塩を取ってくれるよう頼んだ He asked *his neighbor* to pass him the salt.

お隣の息子さんは今アメリカに留学している The

boy *next door* is now studying in the States.
◆ 2軒おいた隣の家 the house *three houses away*

〖隣に〗

彼はわが家の隣に住んでいる He lives *next door to* us. / (→彼は隣の家の人だ) He is our *next-door* neighbor.

その建物の隣に空き家がある There is a vacant house *next to* the building.

隣に座っていいですか Can I sit 「*next to* [*beside*] you?

隣に越してきた家族にはもう会いましたか Have you met the family who moved in *next door*?

◆ 郵便局は図書館の隣にある The post office is *adjacent to* the library. / 彼は彼女の右隣に座った He sat *on her right*.

〖その他〗

時々隣からのバイオリンの音で目がさめる My *neighbor's* violin playing wakes me up from time to time.

私たちは隣どうしです We *live next to each other*.

‖隣近所 the neighborhood [〖英〗neighbourhood] / 隣部屋 the next room

ことわざ 隣の芝生は青い The grass is always greener on the other side of the fence.

俳句 秋深き隣は何をする人ぞ(松尾芭蕉)
Late in the autumn —
people in the house next door.
I wonder what they do?

となりあう 隣り合う 2つのビルは隣り合っている The two buildings *stand next to each other*. / The two buildings *are adjacent to each other*.

となりあわせ 隣り合わせ デパートと駅は隣り合わせに立っている The department store and the station stand *side by side*. / 映画館で偶然香織と隣り合わせになった I happened to sit *next to* Kaori in the movie theater.

どなりこむ 怒鳴り込む 賢治の所でパーティーをしていると、階下の男がうるさいと言って部屋にどなり込んできた When we had a party at Kenji's place, the man downstairs *stormed into* the room to complain about the noise.

どなりつける 怒鳴りつける 彼女は部下をどなりつけた She *shouted at* her subordinates. / 彼はかっとなって子供たちをどなりつけた He *yelled at* his children in anger.

どなる 怒鳴る 電車の中でそんなにどならないでくれ *Don't shout* like that on the train. / ブドウを取ろうとして、おじいさんにどなられた When I tried to pick the grapes, I *was yelled at* by an old man.

とにかく anyway, at any rate

とにかく始めよう *Anyway*, let's get started.

彼女は大丈夫だと思うけど、とにかく今夜君に電話するよ She'll be fine, but 「*at any rate* [*anyway*]」I'll call you tonight.

◆ とにかく腹ぺこだ I'm *just* starving. / 彼はとにかく力が強い He's *really* strong. / すでに 2 敗しているので、次の試合はとにかく負けるわけにはいかない We've already lost two games, so we *simply* cannot lose the next one. / 今はとにかく少し眠りたい *All I want to do* now *is* get some sleep.

どの

❶ 【疑問】 which, what

どの科目がいちばん好きですか *Which* subject do you like best?

私は妹とどのテレビ番組を見るかでいつも言い争う I always have arguments with my sister about *what* TV program to watch.

❷ 【すべての】 all, each, every; (どの…を〜しても) any; (どの…も〜ない) not 〜 any of …, none of …

どの新聞も今年のノーベル賞受賞者の記事を載せていた *All* the newspapers carried articles on this year's Nobel Prize winners.

どのシングルルームもすべてバス付きです *All of* the single rooms have baths.

どのコップを使ってもいいですよ You can use 「*any* glass [*any of* these glasses].

彼女は展覧会のどの彫刻も気に入らなかった She 「*didn't* like *any of* [liked *none of*]」 the sculptures at the exhibition.

東京は生活費がほかのどの町よりも高い The cost of living is higher in Tokyo than in *any* other city.

◆ その映画は今までに見たどの映画とも違っていた The movie was *unlike anything* I'd seen before.

-どの -殿 青木彩子殿 *Ms.* [*Miss, Mrs.*] Aoki Ayako (❖Missは未婚女性に、Mrs.は既婚女性に、Ms.はいずれにも用いる) / 山田昇殿 *Mr.* Yamada Noboru

どのう 土嚢 sandbag ⓒ

どのくらい

❶ 【時間】 how long

🗨「出発の時間までどのくらいありますか」「20分くらいです」 "*How long* is it until the departure time?" "About twenty minutes."

🗨「日本へ来られてどのくらいになりますか」「もう17年になります」 "*How long* have you been in Japan?" "I've been here (for) 17 years."

🗨「田中はどのくらい前に出発しましたか」「5分前くらいだと思います」 "*How long ago* did Tanaka leave?" "About five minutes ago, I think."

🗨「このノートパソコンの修理にはどのくらい時間がかかりますか」「2、3週間みておいてください」 "*How long* will it take to fix this laptop?" "It should be about two or three weeks."

🗨「どのくらいでこちらに来られますか」「2、3分で行けると思います」 "*How soon* can you get here?" "I can get there in a couple of minutes."

❷ 【長さ・高さ】 (距離) how far; (幅) how wide; (高さ) how high; (身長) how tall

- 「ここから東京タワーまではどのくらいありますか」「だいたい2キロくらいですね」 "*How far* is it from here to Tokyo Tower?" "About two kilometers."
- 「この川幅はどのくらいありますか」「1キロはあると思います」 "*How wide* is this river?" "At least one kilometer, I think."
- 「あの山の高さはどのくらいですか」「2,800メートルくらいですね」 "*How high* is that mountain?" "About twenty-eight hundred meters high."
- 「あのバスケットボール選手の身長はどのくらいかな?」「2メートル以上あるね」 "*How tall* is that basketball player?" "More than two meters, I suppose."

❸【数・回数・量・広さ】 (数) how many; (量) how much; (回数) how often; (広さ) how large, how big

- 「あなたはCDをどのくらい持っていますか」「だいたい300枚くらいかな」 "*How many CDs* do you have?" "Maybe about three hundred."
- 「なべにはどのくらい水を入れればいいのですか」「カップで2,3杯入れてください」 "*How much* water should I put into the pot?" "A few cups of water, please."
- 「1か月にどのくらい図書館を利用しますか」「そうですね.2,3回ですね」 "*How many times* [*How often* in] a month do you use the library?" "Let me see. Two or three times, I think."
- 「この部屋,どのくらいの広さかな」「20畳くらいじゃない」 "*How large* [*big*] is this room?" "About twenty *tatami*."

❹【金額】 how much

- 「君のお父さん,切手を集めてるんだって?」「そうなんだ.父がこれまでに切手にどのくらいお金を使ったか分からないよ」 "I hear your father collects stamps." "That's right. I have no idea *how much* he has spent on his stamps."

❺【程度】

- 「私のどのくらい心配したかあなた分かってるの」「ごめんね,心配させて」 "Do you know *how worried* I was?" "I'm sorry for worrying you."
- 「スキーどのくらいできるの」「まだやっとボーゲンを卒業した程度です」 "*How well* can you ski?" "I've just mastered snow-plowing."

> 【語法】
> 「どのくらい…」はWhat …? を用いて表現する場合もある ∥ 東京の人口はどのくらいですか *What* is the population of Tokyo? / ここから大阪までの距離はどのくらいですか *What* is the distance between here and Osaka? / このピラミッドの高さはどのくらいですか *What* is the height of this pyramid?

とのさま 殿様 feudal lord ⓒ
どのへん どの辺 あなたは東京のどのへんですか In *what part of* Tokyo is your house? / どのへんが痛みますか *Where* does it hurt?
どのみち ⇨ どっちみち
どのような どのような what kind of …
——**どのように** how ⇨ どう¹, どんな ∥ 日本ではどのような映画が人気がありますか *What kinds of* movies are popular in Japan? / 我々はお金をどのように使うか話し合った We discussed *how to* spend the money. / ステーキの焼きかげんはどのようにいたしましょうか *How* would you like your steak?
◆吉田さんはどのような人ですか *What* is Mr. Yoshida *like*?

-**とは** 経験とは過ちの別名である Experience is another name for mistakes. (❖「とは」は「経験」を取り立てて強調しているが,英語には特に訳さない) / 君が謝ったのに無視するとはあなたもひどい人ですね *It is cruel of you to* ignore her apologies. / 君とこんな所で会うとはね! *Fancy* meeting you here! / 駅から僕の家まで歩いて10分とはかかりません It takes *less than* 10 minutes to walk from the station to my house. / 彼は20歳とは思えないほどふけている *Even though* he's 20, he looks much older.

とはいうものの とは言うものの 引退したとはいうものの,彼はまだ大きな影響力をもっている *Although* he has retired, he is still very influential.

とばく 賭博 賭博で一文なしになる lose everything at *gambling*; gamble away all *one's* money / 彼は野球賭博で逮捕された He was arrested for *betting* on baseball games.
∥賭博師 a gambler / 賭博場 a gambling den

とばす 飛ばす
❶【飛ぶようにする】 fly* 他; (吹き飛ばす) blow* off
子供たちが公園でラジコンの飛行機を飛ばしていた Children *were flying* a radio-controlled model plane in the park.
風で帽子を飛ばされそうになった I almost *had* my cap *blown off* by the wind.
❷【急ぐ】 hurry 自他, speed* 自他
空港までタクシーを飛ばした I *hurried* to the airport in a taxi.
彼らは新車で高速道路を飛ばしていた They *were speeding* along the expressway in their brand-new car.
❸【抜かす】 skip 他, leave* out
次の段落を飛ばしてください Please *skip* the next paragraph.
難しい問題を飛ばして,やさしいのを先に解いた I *left out* the difficult questions and solved the easy ones first.
❹【その他】
彼女はそのへまのおかげで地方に飛ばされるところだった She came very close to *being transferred* [《口語的》*packed off*] *to* a local branch due to that blunder.
だれかが悪質なデマを飛ばした Somebody *spread* a malicious rumor.
彼はいつもつまらない冗談を飛ばすので,ひんしゅ

とばっちり 野球部の起こした不祥事のとばっちりを受けてサッカー部まで練習を自粛させられた Even the soccer team had to cancel its practices when the baseball team's scandal *spilled over* onto it.

とはん 登板 ━━登板する climb up the slope ‖登板車線 a (climbing) lane for slower traffic

とび 鳶〖鳥〗(black) kite ◯; (とび職の人) construction worker ◯
慣用表現 とびに油揚げをさらわれる(→全く予想していないときに何かをふいに横から奪われる) *have something snatched away when one least expects it*
ことわざ とびが鷹(たか)を産む Children can surpass their parents.(→子供が親に勝ることがある)

とびあがる 飛び上がる・跳び上がる 驚いてすから跳び上がる *leap* out of the chair in surprise / 正男に電話が通じたので、彼女は跳び上がって喜んだ She *jumped* for joy when she got through to Masao on the phone. / 電車の中で足を踏まれて思わず跳び上がってしまった I *sprang to my feet* in spite of myself when my foot was stepped on in the train.

とびあるく 飛び歩く 彼女はこの数か月、会社設立の資金集めに飛び歩いている She *has been running around* for the last several months to raise money to start a new company. / 彼は毎日友達の家から家を飛び歩いている He *hops* from one friend's house to another every day.

とびいし 飛び石 steppingstone ◯ ‖飛び石伝いに小川を渡った I crossed the stream on *the steppingstones*.
‖飛び石連休 a series of holidays with one or two intervening workdays

とびいた 飛び板 springboard ◯

とびいり 飛び入り コンテストに飛び入りで(→前もって登録なしに)参加したやつが優勝をさらってしまった Somebody took part in the contest *without registering in advance* and ran away with the first prize. / 彼が飛び入りで演奏に参加すると客席が沸いた The audience got excited when he joined the band *spontaneously*.

とびいろ 鳶色 reddish brown ◯; (髪の色が) auburn ◯

とびうお 飛び魚 flying fish ◯ (複~)

とびうつる 飛び移る 彼らは大波が来る前に岩からボートに飛び移った They *jumped* [*leaped*] from the rock onto the boat before a big wave came.

とびおきる 飛び起きる 彼女は目覚まし時計の音でベッドから飛び起きた She *jumped* [*sprang*] out of bed at the sound of the alarm clock.

とびおりじさつ 飛び降り自殺 彼女はそのビルの窓から飛び降り自殺した She *jumped to her death* from a window of the building. / She *committed suicide by jumping* out of a window of the building.

とびおりる 飛び降りる・飛び下りる 燃えさかるビルから人々が飛び降りた People *jumped down* from the burning building. / 男は列車が橋にさしかかる直前に飛び降りた The man *leaped off* the train just before it reached the bridge.

とびかう 飛び交う ジャングルの中では鮮やかな色の鳥が飛び交っていた There *were* brightly colored birds *flitting about* in the jungle. / 様々なうわさや憶測が飛び交っていた There *were* a lot of rumors and speculations *going around*. / 専門用語が飛び交っていて彼らの議論についていけなかった I couldn't keep up with their discussion because it *was full of* technical terms.

とびかかる 飛び掛かる 追いつめられた強盗は警官に飛びかかった Cornered, the robber *flung himself at* the police officer. / 猫がネズミに飛びかかったが逃してしまった The cat *jumped at* the mouse but missed it. / 彼がドアをあけたとたん何者かが彼に飛びかかった The moment he opened the door, someone *jumped* (*on*) *him*. ❖jump at は「…に向かって飛びかかる」の意味で結果的に対象に届かなくてもよい。jump (on) …は飛びかかった結果、相手を組み伏せたり取っ組み合いになったりすることを意味する)

とびきゅう 飛び級 彼は中学2年を飛び級した He *skipped* the eighth grade.

とびきり とびきり上等なワイン a wine of *superb* quality / この店のアップルパイはとびきりおいしい This shop offers *the very best* apple pies.

とびこえる 飛び越える・跳び越える 塀を跳び越える *jump* [*leap*] *over* a fence / 水たまりを跳び越えようとして転んでしまった I fell trying to *jump* [*leap*] *across* the puddle. / 彼女はハードルをすべて跳び越えた She *cleared* all the hurdles.

とびこす 飛び越す・跳び越す シェパードが生け垣を跳び越した A German shepherd *jumped over* the hedge. / 安田さんは課長を飛び越して部長に抜擢(ばってき)された Ms. Yasuda *leapfrogged over* the section chief to become the department head.

とびこみ 飛び込み (競技) diving ◯ ‖飛び込みで3位になる come in third in *diving*
◆彼は美しい飛び込みをした He made *a graceful dive*. / 容疑者は(電車への)飛び込み自殺をはかった The suspect tried to *kill himself by jumping in front of a train*. / 彼らは飛び込みだった(→予約がなかった)が、そのホテルに泊まることができた Although they *didn't have a reservation*, they were able to stay at the hotel.
‖飛び込み台 a diving board, a springboard

とびこむ 飛び込む jump [leap*, plunge] into …; (頭から水中に) dive* into …

風に飛ばされた帽子を取ろうとして川に飛び込んだ I *jumped* [*plunged*, *dived*] *into* the river to get my hat that had been blown off by the wind.

20メートルのがけから海に飛び込むのには大変な勇気がいった It took a great deal of courage to *dive into* the sea from the 20-meter cliff.

◆突然ミステリーが読みたくなったので, 近くの本屋に飛び込んだ I suddenly felt like reading a mystery, so I *rushed into* a nearby bookstore. / 事故の知らせは会議の最中に飛び込んできた The news of the accident *came in* during the middle of the meeting. / バスを降りると旅館の看板が目に飛び込んできた When I got off the bus, the signboard of an inn *caught my eye*.

とびさる 飛び去る チョウは僕がつかまえようとすると一瞬のうちに飛び去った The butterfly *flew away* in an instant when I tried to catch it.

とびだす 飛び出す jump out; (急いで出る) rush out / 茂みからバッタが飛び出した A grasshopper *jumped* [*sprang*] *out of* the bushes. / 彼女は顔も洗わずに家を飛び出した She *rushed out of* the house without even washing her face. / 道路に飛び出してはいけません Don't *rush out into* the street.

◆彼は15のときに家を飛び出した(→家出をした) He *ran away from home* at the age of 15. / 壁からくぎが飛び出していた A nail *was sticking out of* the wall.

‖飛び出す絵本 a pop-up book

とびたつ 飛び立つ (鳥が) fly* away; (飛行機が) take* off / 白鳥は北へ飛び立った The swans *flew away* north. / 飛行機は15分遅れで札幌に飛び立った The plane *took off* for Sapporo 15 minutes behind schedule.

とびち 飛び地 enclave ©

とびちる 飛び散る (液体が) splash ⾃; (破片などが) be scatter / ペンキがズボンに飛び散った The paint *splashed onto* my trousers. / 床にはガラスの破片が飛び散っていた Pieces of broken glass *were scattered* on the floor.

とびつく 飛び付く 犬は侵入者に飛びついた The dog *jumped* [*leaped*] *at* the intruder. / 思ったとおり彼は我々の申し出に飛びついてきた As we expected, he *jumped at* our offer.

トピック topic ©, subject © ⇒ わだい

とびでる 飛び出る 目の玉が飛び出るような(→法外な)値段 an *exorbitant* price

とびとび 飛び飛び とびとびに(→あちこちに)家が建ち始めた They began to build houses *here and there*. / その連載小説はとびとびに(→時々)しか読んでいない I read that serialized novel only *now and then*. / その日の記憶はとびとびだ(→あいまいな記憶しかない) I only have a *vague* memory of that day.

とびぬけて 飛び抜けて 哲也は学校でとび抜けて泳ぐのが速い Tetsuya swims *by far* the fastest in his school. (❖by far は最上級を強調する) / 彼女はとび抜けて英語ができる She is *outstandingly* [*exceptionally*] good at English.

とびぬける 飛び抜ける 彼は宇宙線の研究でとび抜けた業績をあげた He made *outstanding* achievements in the study of cosmic rays.

とびのく 飛び退く バイクがわきを猛スピードで通ったので, 彼は思わず(横に)飛びのいた He *jumped aside* in spite of himself when a motorbike sped past him. (❖「後ろに飛びのく」は jump back)

とびのる 飛び乗る 彼は自転車に飛び乗った He *jumped* [*hopped*] *on* his bicycle. / 彼女は駅に着くとタクシーに飛び乗った She *jumped* [*hopped*] *into* a taxi as soon as she arrived at the station.

とびばこ 跳び箱 (vaulting) horse © ‖跳び箱を跳ぶ vault *a horse*

とびはねる 跳びはねる jump up and down; (はしゃぐ) romp ⾃ / 庭では小犬が跳びはねていた Puppies *were romping* in the garden.

とびひ 飛び火 火事は隣の家に飛び火した The fire leaped to the next house. / 汚職事件はいくつかの政党に飛び火した The corruption case *spread to* some political parties.

とびまわる 飛び回る fly* about; (奔走する) rush around / 夕暮れの空をコウモリが飛び回っていた Bats *were flying about* in the evening sky. / 姉はオーストラリア留学の準備で飛び回っている My sister *is rushing around* getting ready to study in Australia.

どひょう 土俵 (sumo) ring © ‖土俵を割る(→外へ押し出される) be pushed out of the ring

‖土俵入り the ring-entering ceremony of a sumo wrestler

慣用表現 これでようやく我々は同じ土俵に上がったわけだ At last we're on *a level playing field*.

とびら 扉 door ©, (本の) title page ©

どびん 土瓶 earthen teapot ©

とぶ 飛ぶ

❶【空中を移動する】fly* ⾃

私は時々空を飛べたらいいのにと思う I sometimes wish I could *fly*.

彼らは気球に乗って地上100メートルの高さを飛んだ They *flew* in a balloon at a height of 100 meters.

ゴルフボールが私の方に飛んできた A golf ball *came flying* toward me.

煙突から火の粉が飛んだ Sparks *flew* out of the chimney.

彼は社長の命令でロンドンに飛んだ He *flew* to London by order of the president.

語法
英語では飛び方の様態によって異なる動詞を使用する場合がある / チョウが花から花へひらひら飛んでいた Butterflies *fluttered* among the flowers. / カモメが水面すれすれに飛んでいた Seagulls *were skimming* the surface of the water. / 激し

いあらしで彼の家の屋根が吹き飛んだ The roof of his house *blew off* in the heavy storm.

❷【急いでいく】hurry 🈩; (あわてて) rush 🈩
学校が終わると飛んで帰った When school was over, I *hurried home*.
ベルが鳴ると彼女は玄関へ飛んでいった When the doorbell rang, she *hurried to the door*.
刑事は犯行現場に飛んだ The detective *rushed to the scene of the crime*.

❸【その他】
ヒューズが飛んだ The fuse *has blown*.
この本は9ページから16ページまで飛んでいる Pages 9 to 16 *are missing* from this book.
来シーズン彼がチームを抜けるというデマが飛んでいる *There is* a wild rumor *going around* that he will leave the team next season.
政隆は話が飛ぶので，何を言いたいのか分からなかった Masataka *jumped from one topic to another*, so I couldn't understand what he was trying to say.
このプロジェクトが失敗すれば，彼の首が飛ぶことになる If this project fails, he will 「*be fired* [*get the ax*].
父に高校をやめると言ったらいきなりげんこつが飛んできた When I told my father I was going to drop out of high school, he suddenly *struck me with his fist*.

慣用表現 あの歌手は今や飛ぶ鳥を落とす勢いだ (→人気の絶頂にある) That singer *is now at the height of her popularity*. (❖状況に応じて popularity の部分は fame「名声」, power「権力」などとする) / このCDは飛ぶように売れている This CD *is selling like mad* [*hot cakes*]. / 痛いの痛いの飛んでいけ！*Out, out* with the pain!

ことわざ 飛んで火に入る夏の虫 A fool hunts for misfortune. (→愚か者は不運を求める)

とぶ² 跳ぶ

jump 🈩 🈔; (ぴょんぴょんはねる) hop 🈩
走り幅跳びで7メートル跳ぶ *jump* seven meters in the long jump
おりの中でウサギがぴょんぴょん跳んでいた A rabbit *was hopping around* in the cage.
◆その子はソファーの上で跳んだりはねたりした The child *bounced up and down* on the sofa.

どぶ (溝) ditch ⓒ ‖どぶさらいをする *clear a ditch* / 自転車がどぶにはまってしまった My bike got stuck in *the ditch*.
‖どぶ川 a stagnant river

どぶくろ 戸袋 shutter box ⓒ
どぶねずみ brown rat ⓒ, water rat ⓒ
どぶん どぶんと川に飛び込む dive into the river *with a big splash*

とべい 渡米 関田博士は来月渡米して，米国各地の大学で講義を行う予定だ Dr. Sekita will *go to America* [*the United States*] next month and give lectures at universities around the country. (❖動詞は visit も可)

どべい 土塀 earthen wall ⓒ
とほ 徒歩 渋谷まで徒歩でどのくらいですか How long does it take to Shibuya *on foot?* / How long does it take to *walk to Shibuya?* / 映画館は駅から徒歩10分です The movie theater is *a 10-minute walk from the station*. / It takes 10 minutes from the station to the movie theater *on foot*.

とほう 途方 途方もなく (→驚くほど) 高いビル an *amazingly* high building / 火星に都市を建設するという途方もない (→壮大すぎる) 計画 a *grandiose* plan to build a city on Mars / 店主は彼に途方もない (→信じられない) 金額をふっかけてきた The storekeeper charged him an *incredible* amount of money. / 雅美は時々途方もない (→ばかげた) ことを言う Masami says *ridiculous* things from time to time. / 治は新宿のど真ん中で聡を見失い途方にくれてしまった Osamu *was at a loss* after he lost sight of Satoshi in the middle of Shinjuku.

どぼく 土木 私の父は土木関係の会社に勤めています My father works for a *civil engineering* company.
‖土木機械 an earth-moving machine / 土木技師 a civil engineer / 土木工事 construction work / 土木工事 civil engineering (work) / 土木作業員 a construction worker

とぼける とぼけないでよ *Don't play innocent* (with me). / 達也に靖子のことを聞いたんだけど，とぼけられた I asked Tatsuya about Yasuko, but he 「*pretended to be ignorant* [*played dumb*]. / その俳優はとぼけた演技で人気がある The actor is popular for *playing the fool*.

とぼしい 乏しい 乏しい収入 a *meager* [*scanty*] income / 日本は天然資源に乏しい Japan is *poor in natural resources*. / この記事は長いが，内容が乏しい (→あまりない) This article is long but has *little* substance. / 彼はリーダーとしての経験が乏しい He has *little experience as a leader*. / 食料が乏しくなってきた We *are running short of* food. / Food *is getting scarce*.

とぼとぼ その女の子は寂しそうに道をとぼとぼ歩いていた The little girl *was plodding* along the street alone. / 私たちは試合に負けてとぼとぼと (→重い足取りで) 家に帰った We *trudged home* after losing the game.

どぼん ⇨どぶん
どま 土間 earthen floor ⓒ, 《米》dirt floor ⓒ
トマト tomato [təméitou] ⓒ ‖トマトケチャップ tomato ketchup / トマトジュース tomato juice / トマトソース tomato sauce / プチトマト a cherry tomato

とまどい 戸惑い (当惑) puzzlement ⓤ; (混乱) confusion ⓤ ‖彼女はとまどいを隠さなかった She didn't hide *her confusion*.

とまどう 戸惑う (当惑する) be puzzled; (混

とまり 泊まり (滞在) stay ⓒ; (宿泊) lodging ⓤ (またa ~); (当直) night duty ⓤ ——泊まりの overnight ∥泊まりの出張 an *overnight* business trip ◆父は今夜は(→宿直で)泊まりだ My father is *on duty tonight*.
∥泊まり客 an overnight guest / 泊まり賃 a room rate

-どまり -止まり この列車は静岡止まりです This train will *terminate* at Shizuoka. / 彼は課長止まりがいいところだろう He'll be lucky if he makes it *to* section chief. / 彼女が寄付する額は1,000円止まりだろう The amount she'll contribute would be *up to* 1,000 yen.

とまりがけ 泊まり掛け 泊まりがけで友達の家へ遊びに行った I visited a friend to *stay for the night*. / 週末泊まりがけで伊豆へ行く I'm going to Izu *for a weekend*.

とまりぎ 止まり木・留まり木 (鳥の) perch ⓒ; (酒場などの) bar (counter) ⓒ

とまる¹ 止まる

❶【停止する】stop ⓔ; (自然に) come* to a stop; (自動車などが) pull up; (駐車している) be parked
電車が急に止まった The train *stopped* suddenly. / The train *came to a sudden stop*.
このバスは渋谷に止まりますか Does this bus *stop at* Shibuya? (❖運転手・車掌には Do you stop at …?とも聞ける)
時計が止まっている My watch *has stopped*.
とうとうエンジンが止まった The engine *has finally come to a stop*.
1台の車が私の家の前に止まった A car *pulled up* in front of my house.
すごくはでな車がたくさん止まっている A lot of flashy cars *are parked*.
◆(号令で)止まれ! Halt! / (→動くな)Freeze!
/ 渋谷行きのバスが3台も同じバス停に止まっている There are three buses for Shibuya *standing* at the same bus stop. / 米原付近の豪雪のため東海道新幹線が止まった The Tokaido Shinkansen line *was out of service* due to the heavy snow around the Maibara area.

❷【やむ】stop ⓔ; (痛みなどが) go* ⓔ
道路工事の音が止まった The noise from road work *has stopped*.
痛み止めを飲んだので歯の痛みが止まった My toothache *has gone* as I took painkillers.
◆おかしくて笑いが止まらないよ It's so funny. I *can't stop* laughing.

❸【切れる】(水道・電気・ガスなどが) stop ⓔ; be cut off
地震でガス[水道, 電気]が止まった The「gas supply [water supply, electricity] *was cut off* because of the earthquake.

とまる² 留まる
❶【鳥・虫などが】(止まり木などに) perch ⓔ; (降りる) land ⓔ; (じっとしている) settle ⓔ
スズメが3羽電線にとまっている Three sparrows *are perching [sitting]* on the electric wire.
チョウが花にとまった A butterfly *landed* on a flower.
ガが網戸にとまっている A moth *is settling* on the window screen.

❷【その他】
最近太ったのでズボンのボタンが留まらない I *can't button* my pants because I've put on weight recently.
彼の音楽の才能が先生の目にとまった(→興味を引きつけた) His musical talent *attracted* his teacher's *interest*.

とまる³ 泊まる stay ⓔ, put* up; (旅などの途中に短期間滞在する) stop ⓔ
彼女はマイアミではモーテルに泊まった She *stayed [put up]* at a motel in Miami.
またうちに泊まりに来てください Please come and *stay* with us again.
出張で岡山に泊まった I *stopped* at Okayama on a business trip.

どまんなか ど真ん中 ど真ん中のストライク a strike *right over the plate* / その建物は東京のど真ん中にある The building stands *right in the middle* [center, heart] of Tokyo.

とみ 富 (財産) wealth ⓤ, riches; (金) fortune ⓤⓒ ∥富を築く make *a fortune* / 彼の家族は2世代にわたって巨万の富を蓄えた His family accumulated great *wealth* [*riches*] for two generations.

とみに (突然に) suddenly; (急に) quickly ∥ 父は近ごろとみに年をとった My father has gotten old *quickly* recently.

とみん 都民 a citizen of Tokyo, Tokyoite [tóukiouàit] ⓒ

とむ 富む (資源・栄養などが) be rich, 《公式的》abound ⓔ ∥アフリカは天然資源に富んでいる Africa *is rich* [*abounds*] *in* natural resources.
◆富む者と貧しい者 the rich and the poor / 彼は経験に富んだ男だ He is an *experienced* man. / 彼女はユーモアのセンスに富んでいる She has a *good* sense of humor. / その小説は非常に独創性に富んでいる The novel shows *great* originality.

とむらう 弔う (冥福(%)を祈る) pray ⓔ; (葬式をする) hold* a funeral ∥空襲による犠牲者を弔う *pray for* the victims of the air raid ∥弔い合戦 an avenging battle

とめがね 留め金 (かばん・ネックレスなどの) clasp ⓒ; (ドアなどの) catch ⓒ

とめどなく endlessly ∥とめどなく話す talk *endlessly* [(→次から次へと)*on and on*]
◆その映画が終わったとき涙がとめどなく出てきた(→涙を抑えられなかった) When the movie ended, I *couldn't hold back my tears*.

とめる¹ 止める

❶【停止させる】stop 他;（車を）pull up;（駐車する）park 他
そこの角で車を止めてください Please *stop* [*pull up*] the car at that corner.
運転手はホテルの前で車を止めた The driver *pulled up* in front of the hotel.
◆（手を上げて）タクシーを止める *hail* a taxi
💬「どこに車を止めたの」「家の前だけど大丈夫かな」 "Where did you *park* your car?" "In front of the house. Is that OK?"
❷【制止する】stop 他;（せき・痛みなどを）relieve 他;（息を）hold*
けんかを止める *stop* a fight（❖stop fighting は「けんかをやめる」の意味）
この薬はせきを止める This medicine *stops* [*relieves*] coughing.
まず血を止めることが先決だ You need to *stop* the bleeding first.
花子のお父さんは彼女がアメリカへ留学するのを止めた Hanako's father *stopped* her (*from*) studying in America.
アジアの危機が世界の経済成長を止めた The Asian crisis *stopped* the world economic growth.
あまりの悪臭に息を止めた I *held* my breath because of a terrible smell.
◆さびを止める *prevent* rust
❸【消す】turn off;（スイッチを切る）switch off;（エンジンなどを）stop 他
洗濯機を止める *turn* [*switch*] *off* the washing machine
流しの水を止めてください Could you *turn off* the water?
料金未払いでガスを止められた Because I haven't paid the bills, *they have stopped* [*cut off*] the gas.
駐車中はエンジンを止めるべきだ You should *stop* the engine while parked.
❹【禁止する】
父は医者に酒とたばこを止められている The doctor *told* [*ordered*] my father *not to* drink or smoke.

とめる² 留める
❶【固定する】fasten 他;（ピンで）pin 他;（テープで）tape 他;（びょうで）tack 他;（クリップで）clip 他;（ホッチキスで）staple 他
人気歌手のポスターを壁にピンで留める *pin* a pop singer's poster on [to] the wall
❷【注意を】
だれも彼のことを気にとめなかった No one *paid attention* to him.
私はそのことを気にとめていた I *kept* that *in my mind*.
雑誌の小さな記事に目がとまった I *noticed* a small article in the magazine.
❸【ボタンを】
ボタンを留める *do* the buttons / コートのボタンを留める *button* (*up*) the coat

とめる³ 泊める put* *a person* up;（有料で）lodge 他;（収容する）accommodate 他 ∥東京に来たときは我が家に泊めてあげるよ I can *put you up* at my house when you come to Tokyo. / あの民宿は 5 人しか泊めることができない That guesthouse can *accommodate* only five guests.

とも¹ 友 friend ◯ ⇨ともだち ∥心の友 *a bosom friend* / 生涯の友 *a lifelong friend* / 真の友 *a real friend* ◆この犬は彼にとって終生の友(→相棒)だった This dog was his *companion* until the end of his life.
ことわざ 類は友を呼ぶ ⇨るい(類)
短歌 友がみなわれよりえらく見ゆる日は花を買ひ来て妻としたしむ（石川啄木(詩)）
When all of my friends
seem to be doing so much
better than I am,
I go and buy some flowers
and spend some time with my wife.

とも² 供（付き添い人）attendant ◯;（従者）follower ◯ ⇨おとも

-とも¹ ❶【たとえ…でも】何時間かかろうとも彼は彼女が来るまで待つだろう *No matter how* long it will be, he will wait for her until she turns up. / 君が何と言おうとも僕はここに残る *No matter* what [*Whatever*] you say, I will stay here. ⇨おそくとも, すくなくとも
❷【強調】彼は私の忠告を聞こうともしなかった He *wouldn't* listen [*never listened*] to my advice.
💬「今度の週末のパーティーには行きますか」「もちろん行きますとも」 "Are you coming to the party this weekend?" "Yes, of course."
💬「お借りした本, もう2, 3日よろしいですか」「いいですとも」 "Can I borrow your book (for) another few days?" "Certainly."

-とも² -共 ❶【全部】（2つのもの）both;（3つ以上のもの）all;（AとBともに）both A and B;（AもBも…ない）neither A nor B（❖動詞は通例Bに一致するが, 口語では複数で受けることもある）∥両親とも沖縄の出身です *Both* my parents are from Okinawa. / 5人とも同じ学校に通っている *All* five go to the same school. / 彼女は名実ともに日本のトップテニスプレーヤーだ She is a top tennis player *both* in name *and* in fact in Japan. / 兄, 姉ともまだ結婚していない *Neither* my brother *nor* my sister is [are] married.
❷【含めて】including,《公式的》inclusive of… /この周遊券は発売日ともに10日間有効です This excursion ticket is valid for 10 days *including* the date of issue.

-ども 行けども行けども人っ子一人見当たらなかった I went on and on, but I didn't see a soul along the way. ⇨-ても

-ともあろうものが 警官ともあろうものが銀行強盗をするなんて信じられない I just cannot believe that a police officer, *of all people*, robbed a bank.（❖of all people は挿入的に用いられ「人もあろうに, よりによって」の意味）

ともかく ❶【いずれにしても】《口語的》anyway, anyhow（❖文頭・文尾両方に使えるが, 文頭に用いる場合はコンマを後ろに付ける）;（どんな場合でも）in any case ∥ともかくやってみよう *Anyway*, let's do it. / ともかく私は締め切り

までに仕事を終わらせなければならない I must finish my work by the deadline *in any case*.
❷【別として】冗談はともかく *apart from* joking; joking *apart* / 彼女が気に入る入らないはともかく、我々にはそれが必要だ *Whether* she likes it or not, we need it. / ぐあいが悪いならともかく、むやみに早退すべきではない You shouldn't just leave early *unless* you're feeling bad.

ともかせぎ 共稼ぎ ⇨ともばたらき

ともぐい 共食い、（動物の）*cannibalism* Ⓤ
◆えさを入れ忘れたのでコオロギが共食いした The crickets *preyed on each other* because I forgot to feed them. / 共食いを避けるためにその党は各選挙区からの公認候補を1人にしぼった The Party has run a single candidate in each constituency to avoid *mutually harmful competition*.

ともしび 灯火 *light* Ⓒ;（ランプの）*lamplight* Ⓒ;（たいまつの）*torch*

ともす 灯す *light** Ⓣ / 手さげランプをともす *light* a lantern / ろうそくをともす *light [burn]* a candle

ともすると 人間はともすると怠惰になりがちだ People *are apt to* be lazy. / スキューバダイビングはともすると危険を伴う Scuba diving *sometimes* involves risks.

ともだおれ 共倒れ（会社・店などが）*go* under together* / 駅前にあった2つのカメラ屋は共倒れした The two camera shops in front of the station *went under together*.

ともだち 友達

friend Ⓒ;（仲間）*companion* Ⓒ
男[女]友達 a male [female] *friend* / 幼友達 a childhood *friend* / 学校の友達 a school *friend* / 高校からの友達 a *friend* from high school / 親しい友達 a close [good] *friend* / 古くからの友達 an old *friend*

彼女は私の友達です She is *a friend of mine*.（❖a friend of mine は不特定の「友達の一人」の意味，my friend はその友達が前後関係から特定される場合に用いる）

こちらは私のアメリカ人の友達のデイビッド・スミスさんです This is my American *friend*, David Smith.

今年の夏は友達と北海道に行く I'm going to Hokkaido with *a friend*.

あなたはたくさん友達がいますね You have many *friends*.

彼女はどこへ行ってもすぐ友達ができる She makes *friends* easily wherever she goes.

あいつなんかもう友達じゃないよ He's not *a friend* anymore.

彼はいい友達になった I *have become [made] good friends* with him.

近藤さんと友達付き合いをしてもう18年になります I've *been friends* with Mr. Kondo for 18 years now.（❖be [become, make] friends with ... は「…と親しい[親しくなる]」の意味で friends は常に複数形で用いる）

◆彼は小学生のころの遊び友達だ He was *my playmate* when we were in elementary school.

🅔「こんなにしてもらって本当にどうもありがとう」「友達じゃないか」"I deeply thank you for your help." "*That's what friends are for*."

ともども 共々 夫婦ともども *both* a husband *and* a wife / 家族ともども出かけた All the family went out *together*.

ともなう 伴う ❶【いっしょに行く】桜井さんはパーティーに奥さんを伴って来た Mr. Sakurai *brought* his wife *with* him to the party. / スティール氏は秘書と通訳を伴ってきのう来日した Mr. Steel arrived in Japan yesterday *with* his personal assistant and an interpreter.

❷【同時に起こる】*go* hand in hand*;（ついて回る）*involve* Ⓣ /権利には責任が伴う Right *goes hand in hand with* responsibility. / 心臓の手術には常に危険が伴う There are always some risks *involved* in heart operations. ◆わが国では工業化に伴い自然が破壊された *With* industrialization, the natural environment was destroyed in our country.

-**ともなく** 見るともなくテレビを見ていた I was *idly* watching TV. / 彼女はどこからともなく現れた She came *out of nowhere*.

ともに 共に

❶【いっしょに】*together*;（…といっしょに）*(together [along]) with* ...

花子と太郎は共に町を出た Hanako and Taro left the town *together*.

高校に入るには入試の結果とともに内申書も重要な要素だ *Along with* the results of the entrance exam, the school report is crucial in order to receive an offer from a high school.

夕食はいつも家族とともにします I always have dinner *with* my family.

◆祖母は祖父と苦楽を共にしてきた My grandmother *has shared* both sorrows and joys with my grandfather.

❷【両方とも】*both*;（AとBともに）*both A and B*;（AもBも…ない）*neither A nor B*（❖動詞は通例Bに一致するが、口語では複数で受けることもある）

姉が結婚して家を出ることになり父はうれしいとともに寂しくもあるようだ My father looks *both* happy *and* sad as my sister will marry and leave home.

君も彼も共に彼女のことを本当には分かっていない *Neither* you *nor* he really understand(s) her.

❸【…につれて】
彼は年をとるとともに無愛想になっている He gets grumpy「*as* he's grown older [*with age*].

ともばたらき 共働き 共働きの夫婦[家庭] a *double income* couple [family] / うちの親は共働きです My parents *both work*.

ともる 灯る 彼女の部屋の明かりがともっている

A light *is on* in her room. / ろうそくがともっている A candle *is lit*.
どもる 吃る stammer 圓他 ‖彼はどもりながら答えた He *stammered out* an answer.
とやかく とやかく言わずさっさと学校に行きなさい *Stop complaining* [(→ぶつぶつ言う) *quibbling*], and just go to school. / あなたにとやかく言われる覚えはない You have no right to *meddle in my affairs*.
どやどや 生徒が教室にどやどやと入ってきた The students *thundered* [*barged*] *into* the classroom. / 野球部員がバスからどやどやと降りてきた The members of the baseball club *piled out of* the bus.

とやま 富山

富山県は本州日本海側の中央部に位置しています。北は富山湾に面しており、ホタルイカ、ブリ、カニなど海の幸が豊富です。また、日本有数の米どころでもあります。南には北アルプスの山々が連なり、冬には、日本海からの北西の季節風が多くの雪を降らせます。

Toyama Prefecture is located in central Honshu on the Sea of Japan. On the north it faces Toyama Bay, which abounds with firefly squid, yellowtail tuna, crab and other marine products. The prefecture also produces a large amount of rice. The Northern Alps rise to the south. The northwest seasonal winds from the Sea of Japan bring heavy snowfall in the winter.

どよう 土用 (夏の) the dog days (of summer); (盛夏) the hottest season
‖土用波 storm swells during the summer
どようび 土曜日 Saturday Ⓤ Ⓒ ((略語)Sat., S.) ⇨にちようび
どよめき 女性ベストボーカル賞の意外な受賞者に会場にどよめきが起こった The unexpected choice for best female vocal performance caused *a stir* among the audience.
どよめく (鳴り響く) resound [rizáund] 圓 ‖マグワイアが70号本塁打を打つと球場は歓声でどよめいた The stadium *resounded* with cheers when McGwire hit his 70th home run.
とら¹ 虎 tiger Ⓒ; (雌) tigress Ⓒ; (子) (tiger) cub Ⓒ ‖人食いトラ a man-eating *tiger* / トラはネコ科に属する The *tiger* belongs to the cat family.
‖虎刈り unevenly [badly] cropped hair
ことわざ 彼は虎の威を借る狐(きつね)だ He is *a sheep in wolf's clothing*. (❖ a sheep in wolf's clothing は「オオカミの毛皮をかぶった羊」の意味)
とら² 寅 (十二支の第3番目) the Tiger
⇨えと
どら 銅鑼 gong Ⓒ
トライ (ラグビーの) try Ⓒ ‖日本チームはニュージーランドのオールブラックスから初トライをあげた The Japanese national team scored *its* first *try* against the All Blacks from New Zealand.

とらい 渡来 ‖この湖は白鳥の渡来地(→毎年戻ってくる場所)として有名です This lake is famous as *the place where* swans *return to every year*. / ザビエルは1549年に日本に渡来した Xavier *visited* Japan in 1549.
ドライ ⚠ ―ドライな (事務的な) business-like; (割り切った) matter-of-fact; (現実的な) realistic (❖ 英語の dry は人についていうと「ぬれていない」「のどが渇いた」の意味) ‖彼は何事に関してもドライだ He is *matter-of-fact* [*realistic*] about things.
‖ドライアイス dry ice / ドライカレー rice fried with curry powder, vegetables and ground meat / ドライフラワー a dried flower / ドライフルーツ dried fruit
トライアスロン triathlon Ⓤ
トライアングル 〖音楽〗 triangle Ⓒ
ドライクリーニング dry cleaning Ⓤ ◆ そのシャツはドライクリーニングに出したほうがいいよ The shirt should *be dry-cleaned*. / You should take the shirt to *a dry cleaner*.
ドライバー (ねじ回し) screwdriver Ⓒ; (ゴルフクラブ) driver Ⓒ; (運転手) driver Ⓒ ‖プラスのドライバー a Phillips *screwdriver* / マイナスのドライバー *a* common [flathead] *screwdriver*
ドライブ¹ drive Ⓒ ―ドライブする go* for a drive ‖兄は自分の彼女をドライブに連れていった My brother took his girlfriend for *a drive*. / うちの家族は週末によく伊豆へドライブをする My family often *goes for a drive* to Izu on weekends.
ドライブ² 〖コンピュータ〗 (disk) drive Ⓒ
ドライブイン ⚠ (道路沿いのレストラン) road-side restaurant Ⓒ; (車に乗ったまま映画の観覧や食事ができる場所) drive-in Ⓒ
ドライブウエー ⚠ (観光道路) scenic drive Ⓒ (❖ 英語の driveway は通りから自宅の車庫・玄関などへ続く個人の敷地内の道)
ドライブスルー drive-through Ⓒ
ドライヤー (衣類の) (tumble) dryer [drier] Ⓒ; (髪の) hair dryer [drier] Ⓒ
トラウマ 〖心理〗 (心的外傷) trauma Ⓤ Ⓒ
とらえどころ 捕らえどころ ‖彼女は捕らえどころのない人だ She is *hard to figure out*.
とらえる 捕らえる
❶ 【捕まえる】 catch* 他; (動物・捕虜などを) capture 他; (逮捕する) arrest 他
うちの鶏を殺したキツネを捕らえた We *caught* [*captured*] the fox that killed our chickens.
連合軍は100人の捕虜を捕らえた The Allied Forces *captured* 100 prisoners.
警察は殺人容疑者を捕らえた The police *arrested* [*caught*] the murder suspect.
❷ 【気持ち・機会・視野などを】
機会をとらえる *take a chance* [*an opportunity*] / 意味をとらえる *grasp the meaning* / 物事を総体的にとらえる *see things in perspective* / 事件の真相をとらえる *get at the truth of a case*
大統領はそのカリスマ性で国民の心をとらえた The President *won* [*captured*] the

hearts of the nation with his charisma. / この写真は湖の美しさをうまくとらえている This photo *captures* the beauty of the lake.

ドラキュラ Dracula

トラクター tractor

トラスト (企業合同) trust ⓒ

トラック¹ (貨物自動車) 《米》truck ⓒ, 《英》lorry ⓒ / 小型トラック a pickup *truck* (❖単に pickup ともいう) / 大型トラック a large *truck* / トラックの運転手 a *truck* driver / 父は5トントラックを運転する My father drives *a five-ton truck*.

トラック² (競走路) track ⓒ / トラック競技 a *track* event / 全天候型トラック an all-weather *track*

ドラッグ (麻薬) drug ⓒ; (薬品) medicine ⓒ / ドラッグをやる do *drugs*

ドラッグストア 《米》drugstore ⓒ, 《英》chemist('s) ⓒ

ドラッグバント 〔野球〕 drag bunt ⓒ

とらのこ 虎の子 (蓄え) (大切な物) precious thing / 彼は虎の子のお金に手をつけた He has spent *his nest egg*.

とらのまき 虎の巻 (あんちょこ) 《米》pony ⓒ, 《英》study aid ⓒ; (解答集) key ⓒ; (秘伝書) a book of secrets

ドラフト draft ⓒ, selection ⓒ / 山田はドラフトで1位指名された Yamada was picked first in *the draft*. (❖「ドラフト1位」は the top draft pick) / ドラフト会議 a drafting session

トラブル trouble ⓒⓤ, problem ⓒ / エンジントラブル engine *trouble* / トラブルを起こす make *trouble* / 隣近所のトラブルには巻き込まれたくない I don't want to be involved in neighbor's *trouble*. / 最近私のパソコンはトラブル続きだ I've had a lot of *problems* with my computer recently.

トラベラーズチェック traveler's check [《英》cheque] ⓒ / トラベラーズチェックは使えますか Do you accept [take] *traveler's checks*? / トラベラーズチェックをポンドに換えたいのですが I'd like to exchange [cash] *my traveler's check* for pounds.

ドラマ drama ⓒ, play ⓒ / このドラマの舞台は戦後の日本である This *drama* is set in post-war Japan.
◆これはシドニー・シェルダンの小説をテレビドラマ化したものだ This TV show is *a dramatization* of a Sidney Sheldon novel. / 国民体育大会は数々のドラマを生んできた The National Sports Festivals have produced a lot of *dramatic scenes*.
‖ドラマ a TV drama / ホームドラマ a soap opera, a soap / メロドラマ a melodrama / ラジオドラマ a radio drama / 連続ドラマ a serial

ドラマー drummer ⓒ

ドラマチック ―ドラマチックな (劇的な) dramatic / オリンピックでは数々のドラマチックな場面が見られる We can see many *dramatic* scenes in the Olympic Games.

ドラム (太鼓) drum ⓒ / ドラムをたたく beat *a drum* / ロックバンドでドラムを演奏する *play the drums* in a rock band
‖ドラム缶 a drum

どらむすこ どら息子 (甘やかされた) spoiled son ⓒ; (家に帰らない) prodigal son ⓒ

とられる 取られる
❶【盗まれる】(知らないうちに) be stolen; (力ずくで) be robbed
彼はテレビとステレオを留守中に取られた His TV and stereo *were stolen* [He had his TV and stereo *stolen*] while he was out.
彼女は路上でかばんを取られた She *was robbed* of her bag on the street.
❷【要求される】
あのレストランでサンドイッチを1皿頼んだら2,000円とられた That restaurant *charged* 2,000 yen for a plate of sandwiches.
駐車違反で15,000円の罰金をとられた I *was fined* 15,000 yen for illegal parking.
❸【時間を】
1日のうちほとんどの時間を子供たちの世話にとられる Most of my day *is taken up* with looking after my children.
❹【その他】
ハンドルをとられる *lose control of* the wheel
あっけにとられて言葉を失った I *was astonished*, and couldn't say a word.

とらわれる 捕らわれる
❶【つかまる】be caught; (逃亡・抵抗の末) be captured; (捕虜になる) be taken [made] prisoner (❖prisoner は常に無冠詞)
彼はついに捕らわれの身となった He *was taken prisoner* at last.
❷【こだわる】(執着する) stick* 自; (先入観に) be prepossessed
前例にとらわれていたら進歩はない There will be no progress if you *stick to* precedents.
◆彼女は突然恐怖にとらわれた Suddenly she *was seized* with fear. / 他人の意見にとらわれないで(→左右されないで)ください Don't *be swayed* [*influenced*] by the opinions of others.

トランク (かばん) suitcase ⓒ, trunk ⓒ; (車)《米》trunk ⓒ,《英》boot ⓒ

トランクス (男性用下着) boxer shorts; (男性用水泳パンツ) (swimming) trunks (❖ともに数えるときは a pair of ... とする)

トランシーバー walkie-talkie ⓒ, transceiver ⓒ

トランジスター transistor ⓒ / トランジスターラジオ a transistor radio

トランプ ⚠(トランプの札) (playing) card ⓒ; (トランプ遊び) (playing) cards (❖英語の trump は「切り札」の意味) / トランプ一組 a pack [deck] of *cards* / トランプをする *play cards* / トランプを切る shuffle *the cards* / トランプを配る deal *the cards*
‖トランプ占い fortune-telling with cards

トランペット trumpet ⓒ / トランペットを演奏する *play the trumpet* / トランペットを鳴らす blow [sound] *a trumpet*

‖トランペット奏者 a trumpet player, a trumpeter
トランポリン trampoline ⓒ
とり¹ 鳥
❶【動物】bird ⓒ;（鶏）chicken ⓒ;（雄の鶏）cock ⓒ;（雌の鶏）hen ⓒ;（狩猟用・食用の）fowl ⓒ ⓤ（複 ～, ～s）;（家禽(*きん*)類）poultry《複数扱い》
ここでは鳥のさえずりしか聞こえない I can only hear *birds* singing here.
鳥が軒下に巣を作った *The bird* built a nest under the eaves.
一群の鳥が木に舞い降りた A flock of *birds* landed in the tree.
祖父は毎朝庭にやってくる鳥にえさをやる My grandfather feeds *birds* that come to the garden every morning.
朝子は結婚してからかごの中の鳥のような生活をしている Asako lives like *a caged bird* since her marriage.
❷【とり肉】（鶏肉）chicken ⓤ;（鶏肉も含めたアヒル・鴨などすべての食用とり肉）poultry ⓤ
とりのから揚げ fried *chicken*
‖鳥かご a (bird) cage / 鳥小屋 a birdhouse / 水鳥 a waterfowl

とり² 酉（十二支の第10番目）the Cock ➡えと
ドリア ⚠ a chicken [seafood] and rice casserole（❖日本語はフランス語の doria から）
とりあい 取り合い scramble ⓒ ∥前の席の取り合い *a scramble* for the front seat
とりあう 取り合う ❶【互いに取る】その２つの国は手を取り合って協力していくだろう The two nations will cooperate *hand in hand*. / 私たちのチームが勝ったので私たちは手を取り合って喜んだ When our team won, we *grabbed each other's hands* out of joy.
❷【奪い合う】scramble ⓘ ∥姉妹は人形を取り合った The sisters *scrambled* for a doll.
❸【相手にする】消費者は会社まで出かけたが社長はまったく取り合わなかった The consumers went to the office, but the president 「*just ignored [took no notice of]* them. / 父は私の話に取り合わない My father 「*doesn't listen [turns a deaf ear]* to me.
とりあえず 取り敢えず ❶【まず】first (of all), first thing;（ともかく）anyway ∥家に着いたらとりあえず電話をください Please call me *first thing* when you get home. / とりあえず試してみます I will try it *anyway*.
❷【さしあたり】for the time being;（今のところ）for the present [moment], for now ∥とりあえず彼にその仕事を任せてみましょう I'll leave the job to him *for the time being*. / 100ドルあればとりあえず足りるでしょう A hundred dollars will be enough *for the present*. /（レストランの注文などで）とりあえずそれで結構です That'll do (it) *for now*.

とりあげる 取り上げる
❶【手に取る】pick up
姉は電話が鳴るとすぐに受話器を取り上げた As soon as the telephone rang, my sister *picked up* the receiver.
❷【奪う】take* ... away;（力ずくで）seize ⓘ;（財産などを）confiscate ⓘ;（資格を）disqualify ⓘ
父に私の携帯電話を取り上げた My father *took* my cellular phone *away*.
彼は弁護士の資格を取り上げられた He *was disqualified* as a lawyer. / He *had* his license to practice law *canceled*.
❸【採用する】adopt ⓘ;（受け入れる）accept ⓘ;（議題にする）take* up;（論じる）discuss ⓘ, deal* with ...;（報道する）report ⓘ;（特集する）feature ⓘ
私の提案が話し合いで取り上げられた My suggestion *was adopted [accepted]* in the meeting.
その問題については来週取り上げましょう We will 「*take up [discuss]* the issue next week.
そのテレビ番組は騒音公害を取り上げていた The TV program *dealt with* noise pollution.
各紙が首相辞任のうわさを取り上げた All newspapers *reported* the rumor of the Prime Minister's resignation.
その雑誌にスミス氏の悲劇的な死を大々的に取り上げた The magazine *featured* the tragic death of Mr. Smith.
とりあつかい 取り扱い,（物の）handling ⓤ;（人・物の）treatment ⓤ;（客の）service ⓤ ∥ あの店では客の取り扱いが悪い *The service* in that shop is poor.
◆取り扱いがやさしい[難しい] be easy [difficult] to *handle* / この化学薬品の取り扱いには細心の注意が必要だ This chemical must *be handled* with great care. / こわれ物につき取扱い注意 Fragile, *handle with care*（❖小包などの注意書き）
‖取扱い時間 service [business] hours / 取扱説明書 an instruction manual / 取扱店 an agency
とりあつかう 取り扱う（手で物を）handle ⓘ;（人・動物などを）treat ⓘ;（問題などを）deal* with ...;（商品を）deal in ...
彼女は大切なお客様なので丁寧に取り扱ってください Please *treat* her very carefully as she is an important client.
あのコンサルティング会社は主に南米を取り扱っている That consulting company mainly *deals with* South America.
当店では世界各国のワインを取り扱っています Our shop 「*deals in* （→店に置いている）*carries*」wine from all over the world.
◆申しわけありませんが、こちらでは宅配便は取り扱っていません I'm afraid we don't *have* a delivery service.
とりあわせ 取り合わせ（組み合わせ）combination ⓤⓒ;（選んだもの）selection ⓤⓒ ∥彼女の服装は色の取り合わせがいい She dresses in good color *combinations*. / チョコレートと大福をみやげに持ってくるとは彼も妙な取り合わせをしたものだ He made *the* strange *selection* of chocolate and *daifuku* as a present.
◆太郎と花子だって？それはおもしろい取り合わせだね Taro and Hanako? That's *an inter-*

esting *couple*.

とりい 鳥居 a *torii*, a gateway to a Shinto shrine

とりいそぎ 取り急ぎ ファックスをいただきました. 取り急ぎお知らせします I *hasten to inform* you that I have received your fax.

トリートメント hair treatment

とりいる 取り入る (好意を得る) gain [win*] *a person's* favor; (機嫌をとる) curry favor with *a person*; (へつらう)《米口語的》kiss up to …,《口語的》butter up ∥あいつはいつも先生に取り入ろうとしている He's always trying to「kiss up to [butter up] the teachers.

とりいれ 取り入れ harvest ⓊⒸ, harvesting ⇨ しゅうかく (収穫)
◆秋は米の取り入れで忙しい We are busy *harvesting* the rice in fall.

とりいれる 取り入れる
❶ [中に入れる] take* in
洗濯物を取り入れてください Could you *take in* the washing?
❷ (収穫する) (穀物などを) harvest ⓔ; (摘む) pick
彼らは稲を取り入れているところだ They are *harvesting* the rice.
❸ [導入する] (採用する) adopt ⓔ; (導入する) introduce ⓔ; (計画などに組み込む) incorporate ⓔ
新しい技術を取り入れる *adopt* new technology
彼女の提案を来年のカリキュラムに取り入れよう We *will incorporate* her suggestions in next year's curriculum.
奈良時代には多くの中国文化が日本に取り入れられた A lot of Chinese culture *was introduced* into Japan during the Nara period.
◆医学用語には多くのドイツ語が取り入れられている Many medical terms *have been borrowed* from German.

とりえ 取り柄 good point Ⓒ; (価値ある点) merit Ⓒ ∥だれでも何か一つくらいとりえがあるものだ Everyone has at least one *good point*.
◆彼のとりえといえば酒とたばこをやらないことくらいだ His only *strong point* is that he doesn't drink or smoke.

トリオ《音楽》trio [tríːou]

とりおこなう 執り行う (催す) hold* ⓔ ∥卒業式が執り行われた A graduation ceremony「*was held* [*took place*].

とりおさえる 取り押さえる catch* ⓔ; (逮捕する) arrest ⓔ ∥その女の子3人は空き巣をその場で取り押さえた Those three girls *caught* a (cat) burglar on the spot.

とりかえ 取り替え このパーツは取り替えがきかない This part *isn't replaceable*.

とりかえし 取り返し 取り返しのつかない間違いを犯す make a *fatal* mistake

とりかえす 取り返す get* … back ⇨ とりもどす ∥晶子は夕子から彼氏を取り返した Akiko *got* her boyfriend *back* from Yuko.

とりかえる 取り替える change ⓔ, replace ⓔ; (交換する) exchange ⓔ,《口語的》swap ⓔ
電球を取り替える *change* [*replace*] a bulb / 古いマウスを新しいマウスと取り替える *replace* an old mouse with a new one
私は水槽の水を月に1回取り替えます I *change* the water in the fish tank once a month.
セーターをもっと小さいのと取り替えたいのですが I'd like to *exchange* this sweater for a smaller one.
席を取り替えませんか Shall we *exchange* [*swap*] seats?

とりかかる 取り掛かる (始める) start ⓔ, begin* ⓔ; (着手する) set* about …; (専念する) get* down to … ∥東京都は来年にも新しい地下鉄の工事に取りかかるだろう Tokyo metropolitan government will *start* [*set about*] constructing a new subway system next year. / さあ仕事に取りかかりましょう Let's *get down to* work!

とりかこむ 取り囲む surround ⓔ ∥警備員が大統領を取り囲んでいた Security guards *surrounded* the president.

とりかわす 取り交わす exchange ⓔ ∥密約を取り交わす *exchange* a secret agreement

とりきめ 取り決め (協定) agreement Ⓒ; (手はず) arrangement ⒸⓊ ∥取り決めに従う observe *an agreement* ∥ その件に関しては両者の間で取り決めができている *An agreement* has been made about it between the two.

とりきめる 取り決める (手はずをととのえる) arrange ⓔ; (日時を) fix ⓔ; (条約などを) conclude ⓔ ∥和平条約を取り決める *conclude* [*agree on*] a peace treaty ∥ 彼らは試合の日程を取り決めた They *fixed* [*arranged*] the date for the games.

とりくみ 取り組み (試合) match Ⓒ; (相撲などの) bout [báut] Ⓒ, fight Ⓒ ∥その力士は息を切らせて取り組み後のインタビューに答えた The sumo wrestler panted out his words at the *post-fight* interview.
⇨ こうとりくみ

とりくむ 取り組む
(問題などに) work on …; (奮闘する) wrestle [grapple] with …; (解決しようと努力する) tackle ⓔ; (従事する) be engaged in …
難問に取り組む「*wrestle with* [*tackle*] a difficult problem
生徒たちはグループ別にその問題に取り組んでいる The students *are working on* the problem in groups.
政府は核兵器廃絶に真剣に取り組んでいない The government *isn't tackling* the abolition of nuclear weapons seriously.
その漫画家は今, 新作に取り組んでいる The cartoonist *is now engaged in* a new work.

とりけし 取り消し (注文・予約などの) cancellation ⒸⓊ; (撤回) withdrawal Ⓤ ∥発言の取り消しを要求する demand *the withdrawal of a person's* remarks ◆予約の取り消しをする *cancel one's* reservation

とりけす 取り消す （注文・予約などを）cancel 働;（撤回する）take* back, withdraw* 働;（法的に）《公式的》revoke 働
彼は10時の歯医者の予約を取り消した He *canceled* his 10 o'clock dentist's appointment.
その状況では我々は前言を取り消さなければならなかった We had to 「*take back* [*withdraw*] what we had said in that situation.
彼女は医師の資格を取り消された She *had* her medical license *revoked*.

とりこ 虜 あの新しく来た女の子のとりこだ All of the boys in my class *are enthralled* [*captivated*] by the new girl.

とりこしぐろう 取り越し苦労 母は私のことについて取り越し苦労ばかりしている My mother *is* always *overanxious* about me.

とりこみ 取り込み お取り込み中すみません I'm sorry to bother you (*when you're busy*).

とりこむ 取り込む ❶【中に入れる】take* in ∥雨が降りそうなので洗濯物を取り込んだ I *took in* the washing as it looked like rain.
❷【ごたごたする】（忙しい）be busy ∥すみません, 今取り込んでるので後でお電話差し上げます I'm afraid but I'*m busy* now, so I'll call you later.

とりこわし 取り壊し demolition Ⓤ ∥旧館の取りこわし作業 the *demolition* work of the old building

とりこわす 取り壊す demolish 働,《口語的》pull [take*] down ∥市議会は新しいショッピングセンターを作るためにその古いビルを取りこわした The city council *demolished* the old building to build a new shopping center.

とりさげる 取り下げる drop 働,《公式的》withdraw* 働 ∥彼女はその男に対する訴訟を取り下げた She *dropped* the case against the man.

とりざた 取り沙汰 世間では彼女のことをいろいろと取りざたしている There are lots of *rumors* going around about her.

とりざら 取り皿 すみませんが取り皿をもう1つもらえますか Excuse me, but could you bring another *plate*, please?

とりさる 取り去る remove 働,《口語的》get* rid of ... ∥不純物を取り去る *get rid of* impurities

とりしきる 取り仕切る （管理する）manage 働;（責任をもつ）be in charge ∥山田さんが会を取りしきっている（→責任者だ）Mr. Yamada *is in charge of* the organization.

とりしまり 取り締まり （管理）control Ⓤ;（規制）regulation Ⓤ;（法的に厳重な）crackdown Ⓒ ∥犯罪に対する厳しい取り締まり *a* severe *crackdown* on crime
◆警察は麻薬の売人の取り締まりを強化している The police *are cracking* [*clamping*] *down* on drug dealers.

とりしまりやく 取締役 director Ⓒ ∥取締役会 the board of directors / 取締役会長 a chairman [chairperson] of the board / 取締役社長 a president,《英》a managing director / 常務取締役 an executive managing director / 専務取締役 a senior managing director / 代表取締役《米》CEO(❖*Chief Executive Officer* の略語),《英》a managing director

とりしまる 取り締まる （管理する）control 働;（規制する）regulate 働;（法により）crack down ∥生徒を校則で厳しく取り締まる *control* students strictly with school regulations
／ 警察は特に年末年始に飲酒運転を厳重に取り締まる The police strictly *crack* [*clamp*] *down* on drunken drivers especially at the end and beginning of the year.

とりしらべ 取り調べ （警察の捜査）investigation Ⓤ Ⓒ;（尋問）questioning Ⓤ;（徹底した尋問）interrogation Ⓒ Ⓤ ∥その件は現在取り調べ中です The case is now *under investigation*.
◆私は警察の取り調べを受けた I *was questioned* [*interrogated*] by the police.
∥取り調べ室（警察の）an interrogation room

とりしらべる 取り調べる （捜査する）investigate 働;（尋問する）question 働;（徹底的に尋問する）interrogate 働 ∥あの男を取り調べる必要がある We need to *investigate* the man. ／ 私の友人は警察に連行され一晩中取り調べられた A friend of mine was arrested by the police, and *was questioned* [*interrogated*] all night.

とりすます 取り澄ます 彼女はとりすました顔でうそをつく She lies with a *straight* face.

とりそこなう 取り損なう miss 働 ∥ボールを取りそこなう *miss* a ball

とりそろえる 取りそろえる テーブルの上に各種の新聞が取りそろえられていた There were *assorted* newspapers on the table. ／ その店は中古家具を多数取りそろえている The shop *has a wide selection of* second-hand furniture.

とりだす 取り出す （中から）take* (out);（抽出する）extract 働 ∥その子はポケットの中からビスケットを取り出した The child *took* a cookie *out of* [*from*] his pocket. ／ 彼女は宝石箱から指輪を取り出した She *took* a ring *from* the jewelry box.

とりたて 取り立て ❶【徴収】collection Ⓤ ◆年末は借金の取りたてに忙しい I'm busy *collecting* the money I've lent.
❷【新鮮な】祖母から取りたてのリンゴが送られてきた My grandmother sent me *freshly picked* apples. ／ 私は車の免許取りたてだ I *have just got* my driver's license.

とりたてて 取り立てて particularly, especially ∥その作品は取りたてていうほどのものではない The work is not *particularly* good.

とりたてる 取り立てる ❶【徴収する】collect 働 ∥3か月分の家賃を取りたてる *collect* the three-months' rent
❷【よい地位に】（任命する）appoint 働;（昇進させる）promote 働 ∥社長は近藤さんを部長に取りたてた The president *appointed* Mr. Kondo (as) general manager.

とりちがえる 取り違える (…を~として考える) take* ... for ~; (…を~と混同する) confuse ... with ~; (誤解する) misunderstand* ◉ // 私はメアリーをジェーンと取り違えていた I *took* Mary *for* Jane. / 彼はその単語の意味を取り違えた He *misunderstood* the word.

とりちら(か)す 取り散ら(か)す 取り散らかしたものを片づける put away the things *one scattered about*

とりつ 都立 ――都立の metropolitan // 都立高校 a *Tokyo metropolitan* senior high school / 都立病院 a *metropolitan* hospital / 東京都立大学 Tokyo *Metropolitan* University

とりつぎ 取り次ぎ 旅行保険の取り次ぎをする *act as an agent* for travel insurance / 電話の取り次ぎをする *transfer* a phone call

トリック trick © // トリック写真 a *trick* photograph ◆私は彼のトリックに引っかかった I *was tricked* by him.

とりつく 取り付く (妄想などが) obsess ◉; (悪霊などが) possess ◉ // 妄想に取りつかれる *be obsessed* with [by] a delusion / 彼は何かに取りつかれたようにその仕事に打ち込んだ He put his heart and soul into the job *like a possessed man*.
慣用表現 あの男は取りつく島もない That man *wouldn't even give you the time of day*. (→時間を教えてくれることさえしない)

とりつぐ 取り次ぐ 営業部の桜井さんに取り次いでもらえますか Could you *tell* Mr. Sakurai in the sales department that I'm here?

とりつくろう 取り繕う (体裁を) keep* up appearances; (失敗などを) gloss over; (応急的に) patch up // その場を取りつくろう *patch* things *up*; *save* the situation / 彼は自分の失敗を取りつくろおうと四苦八苦していた He was sweating blood to *gloss over* his failure.

とりつけ 取り付け ❶【器具の】 installation © // 取りつけ費用 the *installation* fee
◆この警報装置は取りつけが簡単だ This alarm is easy to *install*.
❷【銀行の】 (預金払い戻し請求) a run © (銀行の) 取り付け騒ぎが発生する start *a run* on a bank

とりつける 取り付ける ❶【備えつける】 (装置などを) install ◉; (備品などを) equip ◉; (固定させる) fix ◉; (ぴったりと) fit* ◉; (付属させる) attach ◉ // 電話を取りつける *install* a telephone / 本棚を壁に取りつける *fit* a bookshelf on the wall / その車にはMDプレーヤーが取りつけられている The car *is equipped with* an MD player.
❷【同意を得る】 get* ◉, obtain ◉ // 彼から合意を取りつけた I *got* agreement from him.

とりで 砦 fort ©; (要塞) fortress ©

とりとめ 取り留め ――取り留めのない rambling // 取り留めのない話 a *rambling* story

とりとめる 取り留める 彼女は一命を取り留めた She *narrowly escaped death*.

とりなおす 取り直す (気を) pull *oneself* together; (相撲を) wrestle the bout again // 気を取り直してもう一度やり直そう Let's *pull ourselves together* and do it over again.

とりなし 執り成し (仲介) mediation ⓤ; (仲介者) mediator © // ジョンのとりなしがなければあの二人は別れていたかもしれない The couple might have been separated without John's *mediation*.

とりなす 執り成す (仲裁をする) mediate ⓘ, intercede ⓘ // 2人をとりなす *mediate between* the two persons / 姉が父に私のことをとりなしてくれた My sister *interceded* for me with my father.

とりに 取りに行く あした写真ができるから取りに行ってきてね The pictures will be ready tomorrow, so *go pick them up*, okay?

とりにがす 取り逃がす (つかまえそこなう) fail to catch; (機会などを) miss ◉ // 警察は泥棒を取り逃がした The police *failed to catch* the thief. / 彼女はまたもチャンスを取り逃がした She *missed* a chance again.

とりのこす 取り残す (残していく) leave* ... behind; (ほうっておく) leave ... alone ◉ // 中世から続くその町は時代の流れに取り残されたかのようだ The medieval town seems to *have been left behind by the times*. / あらしで我々は山小屋に取り残された We *were left alone* in a cottage by the storm.

とりのぞく 取り除く remove ◉, 《口語的》 take* away; (きれいにする) clear ◉; (不快なものを) 《口語的》 get* rid of ... // 歯垢を取り除く *remove* plaque / 人々は歩道から雪を取り除いた People *cleared* the pavement *of* snow [snow *from* the pavement].
◆不安を取り除く *relieve* the anxiety / 痛みを取り除く *kill* [*relieve*] pain

とりはからい 取り計らい arrangements // 彼の取り計らいで彼女に会うことができた I could meet her, thanks to his *arrangements*.

とりはからう 取り計らう (手配する) arrange ◉ // (配慮する) see* (to it) that ... // 秘書があなたに連絡をとるよう取り計らっておきました I've *arranged* for my secretary to get in touch with you. / みんなが満足いくように取り計らうことが私の仕事です That's my job to *see that* everyone is satisfied. ◆仕事が片づくよう取り計らうから心配するな I'll *see* the job *done*. Don't worry. (《see + 名 + done》で「…が~されるように取り計らう」という意味)

とりはずし 取り外し そのCD-ROMドライブは取りはずしができる The CD-ROM drive *is removable* [*detachable*]. / その網戸は取りはずしができない (→固定されている) The window screen *is fixed*.

とりはずす 取り外す remove ◉, 《口語的》 take* away; (一時的に) take out // 壁から絵を取りはずす *remove* a painting from the wall ◆エアコンのカバーを取りはずす *take* the cover *off* of the air conditioner

とりはだ 鳥肌 gooseflesh [U], goose bumps [pimples] //その光景を見て鳥肌が立った The scene *gave* me *gooseflesh*.

とりはらう 取り払う 塀を取り払う *remove* a wall / 建物の周りの足場を取り払う *pull down* scaffolding around the building

とりひき 取り引き (商売) business [U]; (契約) deal [C], dealings; (麻薬などの) traffic [U] ━取り引きする do* business with ..., have* dealings with ..., deal* with ...; (お互いの利益のために) make* a deal

犯人と裏で取り引きをする *make a deal with* a criminal 「*under the table* [*behind the scenes*]

この取り引きで君が損をすることはない You won't lose on this *deal*.

私どもの会社はシンガポールと取り引きしております Our company *is doing business with* Singapore.

わが社はあの会社との取り引きはやめました Our company broke off *the business* with that company.

警察の捜査により麻薬の取り引きが発覚した *The traffic* in drugs was uncovered by the police investigation.

◆銀行との取り引きがある have *an account* with a bank

‖取引先(顧客) a customer; (関係者) a business acquaintance / 現金取引 a cash transaction

トリプル triple ‖トリプルプレー〘野球〙a triple play

ドリブル dribble [C] ━ドリブルする dribble [自] //ドリブルで2人抜く *dribble past* two players

とりぶん 取り分 share [C]《通例単数形》//彼は自分の取り分としてさらに200万円を要求した He demanded another two million yen as his *share*.

とりまき 取り巻き (権力者・金持ちなどの) hanger-on [C] (複 hangers-on); (追従者) follower [C]; (スターなどの) groupie [C]

とりまぎれる 取り紛れる 忙しさに取り紛れて(→あまりに忙しくて)彼女に全然連絡していない I've been *so* busy *that* I've been out of touch with her.

とりまく 取り巻く surround [他] //王女は車を降りるなり報道陣に取り巻かれた As soon as the Princess got out of the car, she *was surrounded* by the reporters.

とりまぜる 取り混ぜる いろいろ取り混ぜたチョコレートの詰め合わせ a box of *assorted* chocolates

とりまとめる 取りまとめる 様々なアイディアを取りまとめる *put* various ideas *together* / ジミー・カーターは中東和平協定を取りまとめた Jimmy Carter *arranged* the Middle East peace accord.

とりみだす 取り乱す (動転する) be upset, 《口語的》go* to pieces; (自制心を失う) lose* *one's* control //彼女は息子が誘拐されたと聞いて取り乱した She *was upset* to hear that her son was kidnapped. ◆母は取り乱すことなく知らせを聞いた My mother *remained calm* and listened to the news.

トリミング (写真の) trimming [U]; (衣服の縁飾り) trimmings

とりめ 鳥目 night blindness [U]

とりもつ 取り持つ (仲介する) mediate [自]; (応対する) entertain [他] //2つのグループの仲を取りもつ *mediate between* the two groups / 彼女は座を取りもつのがうまい She is good at *entertaining guests*. ◆共通の趣味が取りもつ縁で彼らは結婚した The common interest *brought* them to marriage.

とりもどす 取り戻す get* back; (失った物を) recover [他]; (状況・立場を) regain [他]; (意識を) come* to *oneself* //意を決して貸した金を取り戻しに彼の家まで行った I finally decided to go to his house to *get back* the money I had lent him. / 盗まれたお金を取り戻すのは難しい It is difficult to *recover* stolen money. / 彼は急速に健康を取り戻した He rapidly *recovered* [*regained*] *his health*. / 一度失った信用を取り戻すには時間がかかる Once you've lost someone's trust, it takes time to *recover* it.

◆勉強の遅れを取り戻す *catch up on one's* studies / 遅れた時間を取り戻す *make up for* lost time

とりもなおさず 取りも直さず 警察の改革をしなければならない. そしてそれはとりもなおさず国民の信頼を回復するということだ We have to reform our police, *which means* people will be able to trust them again.

とりやめ 取り止め 遠足は取りやめになった The school trip *was canceled*. / あしたのストライキは取りやめになった Tomorrow's strike *has been called off*.

とりやめる 取り止める (予約・予定したことを) cancel [他]; (計画したことを) call off //彼女は病気のため公演を取り止めた She *canceled* [*called off*] her concert due to her illness.

トリュフ ⚠truffle [trʌ́fl] [C] (❖日本語はフランス語の truffe から)

とりょう 塗料 paint [U] //夜光[蛍光]塗料 luminous *paint*

どりょう 度量 彼女は度量の大きい[小さい]人だ She is a *broad-minded* [*narrow-minded*] person.

どりょうこう 度量衡 weights and measures ‖度量衡表 a table of weights and measures

どりょく 努力

effort [U][C]; (大きな努力) endeavor, 《英》endeavour [U][C]; (精を出すこと) hard work [U]; (骨折り) pains ━努力する make* an effort; (やってみる) try [自]; (一生懸命働く) work hard

〘努力が・は〙

努力がついに実を結んだ *My efforts* finally 「paid off [bore fruit].

英語を上達させるにはより一層の努力が必要だ You have to *make a* greater *effort* to improve your English.

彼の努力はすっかりむだになった All his *efforts* came to nothing.

〖努力の〗

努力の賜物(たまもの) the result of *one's efforts*

努力のかいあって彼女は大学に合格した *Thanks to her efforts*, she passed college entrance exams.

〖努力する〗

一生懸命努力すればいつか成功するだろう If you *work hard*, you will succeed some day.

彼らは計画を成しとげようと必死で努力した They *made* desperate *efforts* to carry out the plan.

〖その他〗

彼らは彼女を助けるためには努力を惜しまなかった They spared no *effort* [*pains*] to help her.

◆彼はたいへんな努力家だ He is *a* very *hard worker*.

とりよせる 取り寄せる (手に入れる) get* [他]; (注文する) order [他], send* for ... ∥カタログを取り寄せる *send for* a catalogue / 外国から本を取り寄せる *order* books from foreign countries

ドリル ❶【きり】drill [C] ◆彼はドリルで壁に穴をあけた He *drilled a hole* in the wall./ He *made a hole* in the wall *with a drill*.

❷【練習】drill [C][U] ∥夕食の前に漢字のドリルをやった I did *drills* in Chinese characters before supper.

とりわけ(て) 取り分け(て) (特に) especially; (格別に) particularly; (何にもまして) above all ∥私は日本の歴史, とりわけ平安時代に興味があります I'm interested in Japanese history, *especially* Heian period. / けさの電車はとりわけ込んでいた The train was *particularly* crowded this morning.

とりわける 取り分ける (皿に) dish out ∥彼女はサラダを取り分けた She *dished out* the salad.

ドリンクざい ドリンク剤 health drink [C][U]

とる[1] 取る

❶ 手に持つ	take; get
❷ 得る	get, take
❸ 奪う	take; steal; rob
❹ 取り除く	take off; remove
❺ 注文する	order; subscribe
❻ 徴収する	charge
❼ 食事·休息をとる	eat, have; take

❶【手に持つ·つかむ】(手に取る) take* [他], pick up; (取ってくる) get* [他]; (手や腕を伸ばして) reach [他]

どれでもお手に取ってよくごらんください You can *take* anything *in your hand* and have a close look at it.

彼は彼女の手を取って通りを横切った He *took* her *by the hand* and crossed the street.

どちらでも好きなほうを取っていいですよ You can *take* whichever you like.

彼女は受話器を取って110番を回した She *picked up* the phone and dialed 110.

戸棚からグラスを2つ取ってちょうだい *Get* two glasses from the cupboard for me, will you?

そのひざ掛けを取ってくれない？ Can you *get* [*reach*] me the blanket?

彼は手を伸ばして棚から箱を取った He *reached* a box from the shelf.

ちょっと待って. 傘を取ってくるわ Wait [Just] a minute! I'll「*go* (*and*) *get* [*fetch*] my umbrella.

◆塩を取ってください Please *pass* me the salt. / サラダはどうぞご自由にお取りください Please *help yourself to* the salad.

❷【得る】get* [他], take* [他], 《公式的》obtain [他]; (賞などを) win* [他]; (受け取る) take [他], receive [他]

(成績で)オールAを取る *get* straight A's

私は英語で満点を取った I *got* full marks on English.

今度の試験でいい点を取ったら新しい自転車を買ってくれる？ Will you buy me a new bike if I *get* good grades in the next exam?

僕はきょう車の運転免許を取った I *got* my driver's license today.

パスポートを取るために必要な書類を用意しなければならない I must prepare the requisite papers to *get* a passport.

彼は英語のスピーチコンテストで1等賞を取った He *won* first prize in the English speech contest.

まず学校側の許可を取る必要がある We first need to *obtain* permission from the school administration.

◆彼女は医師の資格を取った She *qualified* as a doctor. / 彼はオックスフォード大学で物理の博士号を取っている He *has* [*holds*] a doctor's degree in physics from Oxford. / ブラジルは前半ですでに3点取っている Brazil *has* already *scored* three goals in the first half.

❸【奪う】take* [他]; (盗む) steal* [他]; (強奪する) rob [他]

だれかが庭の鳥の巣から卵を取った Someone *took* the eggs from the bird's nest in my garden.

私は空港でかばんを取られてしまった I *had* my bag *stolen* in the airport.

◆油断したすきに手に持っていたお菓子を猿に取られてしまった A monkey *snatched* the snacks from my hand while I was off guard. / 老人はその悪徳業者に100万円だまし取られた The old man *was cheated out of* one million yen by the dishonest dealer.

❹【取り除く·取りはずす】take* off; (取り出す) take out; (除去する) remove [他], get* rid of ...

びんのふたを取る *take* the lid *off* a bottle / シャツのしみを取る *remove* a stain from a shirt

私は小学校のときに盲腸を取った I *had* my appendix「*taken out* [*removed*] when I was

男性は室内では帽子を取ることになっている Men are supposed to *take off* their hats indoors.

疲れをとるためにゆっくりおふろにつかりたい I want to soak myself in a hot bath to *get rid of* fatigue.

◆包装紙を取る *undo* the wrapping(s) / 庭の雑草を取る *weed* a garden / プラムの種を取る *pit* a plum

❺【注文して届けさせる】(注文する) order 他, send* out for …; (購読する) subscribe 自, take* 他

地元の新聞をとる *take* a local newspaper

何新聞をとっていますか Which newspaper do you *subscribe to*?

昼食にピザでもとりましょうか Shall we「*send out for* [*order*] (a) pizza or something for lunch?

◆母がお客のためにお寿司(♀)をとった Mother *had* some sushi *delivered* for the guests.

❻【徴収する】(料金を) charge 他自; (罰金を) fine 他

たいていの銀行は週末にお金を引き出すと手数料をとる Most banks *charge* (a) commission for making withdrawals on weekends.

市内であればそのデパートは配達料をとらない That department store *doesn't charge for* delivery within the city limits.

駐車違反で15,000円とられた I *was fined* 15,000 yen for a parking violation.

◆空港から市内で出るのにタクシーだと3,000円はとられる It'll *cost* you at least 3,000 yen to go into the city from the airport by taxi.

❼【食事・休息をとる】(食べる) eat* 他, have* 他, take* 他; (休息をとる) take 他, get* 他

彼は遅い朝食をとった He *ate* [*had*] a late breakfast.

もっと繊維をとりなさい *Take* more fiber.

十分な睡眠をとることはだいじなことだ It is important for you to *get* enough sleep.

医者は彼に十分休養をとるようにと言った The doctor directed him to *take* a good rest.

彼女はまる1週間休暇をとった She *took* the whole week off.

❽【選ぶ・採用する】(選ぶ) choose* 他, take* 他

先生は私にもう1つ語学の授業をとるよう勧めてくれた My teacher encouraged me to *take* another language course.

◆それは結局金を取るか安全を取るかの問題に帰着した It came down to *a choice* between money and safety. / 彼なら冒険するよりも安全性を取るだろう He would *prefer* safety *to* adventure.

❾【数える・測定する・確認する】

脈をとる *take* [*feel*] *a person's* pulse / 出席をとる *call* the roll / レースのタイムをとる *time a* race

彼は洋服の寸法をとってもらっていた He *was being measured* for a suit.

❿【理解する】understand* 他; (解釈する) take* 他

彼の言うことを悪くとる(→誤解する)な Don't *take* [*get*] him *wrong*.

外国人は日本人のあいまいな笑顔を承諾のサインととりがちだ Foreign people *tend to take* the indecisive smile of a Japanese *as* a sign of approval.

◆どうしてもこの英文の意味がとれない I just *can't make out the meaning of* this English sentence.

⓫【予約する】reserve 他

私たちは町の中心にあるホテルに部屋をとった We *reserved* a room at a hotel in the city center.

◆そのコンサートではいい席がとれた I *was able to get* a good seat for the concert.

⓬【確保する】keep* 他; (とっておく) save 他

私が戻るまで私の席をとっておいてくれませんか Will you *keep* [*save*] my seat until I come back?

彼からの手紙は全部とってあります I *have kept* [*saved*] all the letters I got from him.

◆彼らは冬に備えてまきをとっておいた They *stored* firewood for the winter.

⓭【占める】take* up, occupy 他; (時間がかかる) take 他

この小さな車はあまり場所をとらない This small car *doesn't take up* much room.

マニュアルを読むだけでかなり時間をとられてしまった It *took* me a lot of time just to read the manual.

⓮【記録する】take* 他; (書き留める) write* [take, put*] down

学生たちは講義のノートをとった The students *took* [*made*] *notes* at the lecture.

⓯【その他】

積極的な態度をとる *take a* positive *attitude* / 事故の全責任をとる *take* [*accept*, *assume*] full *responsibility* for the accident / 訴訟の手続きをとる *take* [*start*] legal proceedings

賢次は新婚夫婦への乾杯の音頭をとった Kenji *proposed a toast* to the newly married couple.

警察が飲酒運転に対し断固たる措置をとることを切に望む I do hope the police *take* (*a*) strong *action* against drunk driving.

そのウエーターが私たちの注文をとった That waiter *took* our *order*.

人は年をとるにつれて新しい環境に適応しづらくなる As we *get older*, it is difficult to adjust ourselves to a new environment.

高校のときの友人とはまだ連絡をとっていますか Are you still *in touch with* your friends from high school?

彼女は祖父の名をとって自分の子供を亮司と名づけた She named her child Ryoji *after* her grandfather.

彼らはその問題を取るに足りないとはねつけた They dismissed the problem as *trivial*.

受話器を置くと彼女は取るものも取りあえず病院へ急いだ As soon as she hung up, she rushed to the hospital.

→とられる

とる² 捕る catch* ⓣ ‖彼は川で魚をたくさん捕った He *caught* a lot of fish in the river. / 夏休みにはよくセミを捕りに行った I used to go to *catch* cicadas in summer vacation.

とる³ (摘み取る) pick ⓣ; (雇う) employ ⓣ, hire ⓣ; (案などを) adopt ⓣ; (人・手段などを) take* ⓣ ‖山でキノコをとる *pick* mushrooms in the mountains / 私たちはその方法を採った We *adopted* the method. / その会社では新入社員を10人採った The company *employed* [*hired*] 10 new people.

とる⁴ 執る do* ⓣ; (労を) take* ⓣ ‖仲介の労をとる *take* the trouble of mediating / 彼が新しいチームの指揮をとることになった He is to *take* control of the new team. / 彼はその会社で事務をとっている He *does* office work at the company.

とる⁵ 撮る (写真を) take* ⓣ; (映画を) film ⓣ ⇒ 場面·状況別会話 p.1718 ‖彼女はオーストラリアで動物の写真をたくさん撮った She *took* a lot of pictures of animals in Australia. / 湖をバックに写真を撮ってもらった I *had* my picture *taken* with the lake in the background. / 最後のシーンは海岸で撮影された The last scene *was filmed* at the seashore.

とる⁶ 録る record ⓣ; (カセットテープに) tape ⓣ; (ビデオに) videotape ⓣ ‖私はそのドラマをビデオにとった I *recorded* the TV drama *on videotape*. / I *videotaped* the TV drama.

ドル dollar ⓒ (❖記号 $) ‖7ドル30セント seven *dollars* and 30 cents (❖ $7.30 と書く.《米》では seven thirty というのがふつう) / ドルで払う pay *in dollars* / 10ドル札をくずしてもらいますか Could you change [break] *a ten-dollar bill*? / きょうの為替レートは1ドル115円です Today's exchange rate is 115 yen to *the* (U.S.) *dollar*.

‖ドル相場 the dollar exchange rates, the exchange rates for the dollar / ドル高[安] a high [low] dollar rate / ドル箱 a moneymaker, a gold mine

トルコ Turkey (❖公式名 the Republic of Turkey) ── トルコ人 Turk ⓒ ── トルコ語 Turkish Ⓤ ── トルコ(人[語])の Turkish ‖トルコ石 (a) turquoise

トルネード (竜巻) tornado ⓒ

どれ which; (どれでも) whichever, any ‖どれが気に入りましたか *Which* did you like? / 全部似たり寄ったりでどれを買えばいいのか分からない They are all almost the same. I don't know *which* to buy.

どれでも好きなものを注文していいよ You can order *whichever* you like.

🗨「わあ,おいしそうなケーキ」「どれがいい」 "Oh, those cakes look good." "*Which one* do you want to eat?"

🗨「私のかばん取ってくれる?」「いいけど,どれ」 "Can you get me my bag?" "All right, but *which* is it?"

🗨「このクロスワードパズルが解けないんだ」「どれ,貸してごらん」 "I can't solve this crossword puzzle." "*Well*, let me have a try."

どれい 奴隷 slave ⓒ; (奴隷の身分) slavery Ⓤ ‖彼女は流行の奴隷になっている She is *a slave* of [to] fashion.

‖奴隷解放 the emancipation of slaves / 奴隷制度 slavery

トレー tray

トレード trade ⓒ ── トレードする trade ⓣ ‖彼はライオンズにトレードに出された He *was traded* to the Lions.

トレードマーク trademark ⓒ ‖長髪と眼鏡が彼のトレードマークだ Long hair and glasses are his *trademarks*.

トレーナー (シャツ) sweat shirt ⓒ; (訓練する人) trainer

トレーニング training Ⓤ (またa ~) ‖チームは来シーズンに向けたトレーニングを開始した The team went into *training* for the next season. ◆選手たちはトレーニングに励んでいる The players *are training hard*.

‖トレーニングウエア a sweat suit / トレーニングシャツ a sweat shirt / トレーニングパンツ sweat pants

トレーラー trailer ⓒ ‖トレーラーハウス《米》 a trailer,《英》a caravan

どれくらい ここから家までどれくらいかかるんですか *How long* does it take to your house from here? / お金はどれくらい必要なのですか *How much* money do you need? / そのプールの幅はどれくらいですか *How wide* is the swimming pool? / その机の幅はどれくらいですか *What* is the width of the desk? / 靴のサイズはどれくらいですか *What size* shoes do you take?

英作文ノート「どれくらい」に要注意!
インドの人口はどれくらいですか
→×How is the population of India?
→○*What* is the population of India?
★「…の人口はどのくらいですか」は What is the population of …? となる. ただし, How large is the population of India? といういう. この質問に対して「約9億です」と答えるには, It's about nine hundred million. といえばよい.

ドレス dress ⓒ ◆彼女たちはみなドレスアップしていた They *were* all *dressed up*.

とれだか 取れ高 (収穫高) crop ⓒ; (捕獲高) catch ⓒ

どれだけ どれだけ本を持っているの *How many* books do you have? / 彼がどれだけ苦労したか私たちには分かるはずもない We can't understand *how hard* a time he had.

とれたて 取れ立て とれたての野菜 *fresh* vegetables

ドレッシング dressing ⓒⓊ ‖サラダをドレッシングであえる toss a salad *in dressing* / サラダにドレッシングをかけるのは好きじゃないんです I don't like to *put dressing* on my salad.

どれどれ

🗨「この時計かわいいでしょ」「どれどれちょっと見せてよ」 "This watch is cute, isn't it?" "*Oh*, let me see."

トレパン ⚠(トレーニングパンツ) sweat pants

どれほど どれほど彼女に感謝しているか言葉では言い表せない I can't express *how* grateful I am to her. / どれほど英語を覚えてもすぐ忘れてしまう *No matter how much* I memorize English words, I forget them easily.

どれも (すべて) all; (どの…もみな) every, any 《彼の小説はどれもおもしろい *All (of)* his novels are interesting. / いろいろな方法を試してみたがどれもうまくいかなかった I tried various methods, but *every* one of them failed. ◆私は3つの案を出したがどれも採用されなかった I proposed three plans, but *none* was [were] adopted.

とれる¹ 取れる
❶【離れる】(はずれる) come* off; (しみなどが) come out; (除去される) be removed; (痛みなどが) go* 自
シャツのボタンが取れそうなのに気づいた I noticed a button *was coming off* my shirt.
ソースのしみがなかなか取れない The sauce stain will *not come out*.
少し痛みがとれてきた The pain *is going away* a little.
◆ゆっくり休めば疲れはとれるでしょう If you get enough rest, you will *recover from* your fatigue.
❷【解釈される】
この表現は2通りの意味にとれる This expression *can be interpreted* [*taken*] in two ways.
❸【得ることができる】
私たちはそのサッカーの試合で1点も取れなかった We couldn't *score* even one goal in the soccer game.
あしたは忙しくて時間がとれそうにない I'll be so busy tomorrow that I won't be able to *take* the time for it.

とれる² 捕れる きょうは魚がたくさん捕れた I had a big *catch* of fish today.

とれる³ 採れる (生産される) be produced 《この地方では米がたくさんとれる Rice *is produced* in this area in large quantity.
◆今年は桃がよくとれた *There was a good crop* of peaches this year.

とれる⁴ 撮れる 旅行の写真はよく撮れていた The pictures of the trip *have come out* well.

トレンチコート trench coat ⓒ
トレンディー ─**トレンディーな** (流行の先端をいく) fashionable, trendy ⇒ 場面・状況別会話 p.1708
トレンド trend ⓒ
とろ¹ 吐露 彼女は私に真情を吐露した(→心を打ち明けた) She spoke her mind to me.
とろ² (マグロの) fatty tuna ⓤ
どろ 泥 mud, dirt ⓤ
彼女はぼろ切れで靴の泥をふき取った She scraped *the mud* from her shoes with a rag.
トラックに泥をはねられた A truck splashed *mud* on me.
女の子の靴は泥だらけだった The girl's shoes were covered with *mud*.
‖泥水 muddy water / 泥よけ a mud guard [flap]
慣用表現 彼は泥のように眠った He *slept like a log*. (❖sleep like a log で「丸太のように眠る」の意味) / 彼女は私のために泥をかぶって(→責任を負って)くれた She *took the blame* for me. / 親の顔に泥を塗る(→名誉を傷つける)ようなことをするな Don't do things to *disgrace* your parents. / 男はついに泥を吐いた(→罪を白状した) The man finally *confessed (to) his crime*.

とろい (鈍い) dull; (のろい) slow 《あいつは少しとろいけどいいやつなんだ He is a little *dull*, but a nice fellow.

とろう 徒労 彼の努力は徒労に終わった His efforts *have* 「*come to nothing* [*proved fruitless*].

トローチ troche ⓒ (❖あまり一般的ではない); lozenge ⓒ

トロール (底引き網) trawl (net) ⓒ ‖トロール漁業 trawling / トロール船 a trawler

どろくさい 泥臭い (洗練されていない) unrefined; (粗野な) crude 《彼の演技は泥臭い His performance is *crude*.

とろける (溶ける) melt 自; (うっとりする) be fascinated, be charmed 《このチョコレート、口の中で本当にとろけるよ This chocolate really *melts* in your mouth. / 美しいチェロの音色に身も心もとろけるようだった I *was completely fascinated* by the beautiful tones of the cello.

どろじあい 泥仕合 mudslinging ⓤ
◆ 2つの政党は泥仕合を演じている The two political parties *are throwing* [*slinging*] *mud at each other*.

トロッコ ⚠truck ⓒ (❖日本語の「トロッコ」は truck の転じたもの)

どろっとした どろっとしたソース *thick* sauce
ドロップ drop ⓒ
とろとろ とろとろ歩く walk *slowly* / 30分くらいとろとろ煮る *simmer* for about thirty minutes

どろどろ ─**どろどろの** (泥で) muddy; (濃くて) thick; (パルプ状で) pulpy 《どろどろのおかゆ *thick* rice porridge / 雨で道がどろどろになった The road became *muddy* because of the rain.

どろなわ 泥縄 泥縄式の対応策 *last-minute measures*

どろぬま 泥沼 bog ⓒ ◆ 2国間の交渉は泥沼にはまり込んだ The negotiations between the two countries *got bogged down*.

とろび とろ火 (very) low heat ⓤ 《野菜をとろ火で煮る simmer the vegetables over *low heat*

トロフィー trophy [tróufi] ⓒ

どろぼう 泥棒 (こそ泥) thief ⓒ (複 thieves); (強盗) robber ⓒ; (夜盗・押し込み強盗) burglar ⓒ 《昨夜その家に泥棒が入った A *thief* [*burglar*] broke into that house last night. / 彼らは泥棒を追いかけてつかまえた They chased *the thief* and caught him. /

泥棒はその窓から家に侵入したようだ It seemed that *the thief* entered the house through that window. / 泥棒！ *Stop thief!*

どろまみれ 泥まみれ 泥まみれのスニーカー *muddy* sneakers / 彼らは泥まみれになって働いていた They were working *covered with mud.*

とろみ 片栗粉でスープにとろみをつける *thicken* soup with potato starch

とろり とろりとしたスープ *thick and creamy* soup

とろろ grated yam ▫ ‖とろろ芋 a yam

どろん 彼女はねむくてとろんとした目をしていた She was sleepy and had *dull* [*heavy*] eyes.

どろんこ 泥んこ 弟は泥んこになって帰ってきた My brother came home *covered with mud.* / 子供たちは公園で泥んこ遊びをしていた The children *were playing with mud* in the park.

トロント Toronto (❖カナダの都市)

トロンボーン trombone ▫ ‖トロンボーン奏者 a trombonist

とわず 問わず 入会の申し込みは男女を問わず受け付けます We accept membership applications *regardless* [*irrespective*] *of sex.*

どわすれ 度忘れ 店の名前をど忘れしてしまった I *have forgotten* the shop's name *for the moment.* / The shop's name *has slipped my mind.*

どをうしなう 度を失う その質問に彼は度を失った(→取り乱した) He *was upset* by the question.

トン ton ▫; (トン数) tonnage ▫▫ ‖米５トン five *tons* of rice / １万トンの船 a ship of 10,000 *tons* / ３トントラック a three-*ton* truck

ドン ⚠(ボス・リーダー) leader ▫, boss ▫ (❖日本語はスペイン語の don から)

どん 彼は壁をどんとたたいた He *banged on* [*at*] the wall. / よそ見をしていて柱にどんとぶつかった I was looking the other way and *bumped into* the pillar *with a thud.* / 位置について，用意，どん！ On your mark(s), get set, *go!*

どんかく 鈍角 【数学】obtuse angle ▫ ‖鈍角三角形 an obtuse(-angled) triangle

とんカツ 豚カツ (breaded and deep-fried) pork cutlet ▫

どんかん 鈍感 ──鈍感な (感情的に) insensitive; (頭・感覚が) dull; (批判・侮辱などに対して) thick-skinned ‖彼女の気持ちに気がつかなかったなんて鈍感だね How *insensitive* you were not to notice her feelings!

どんき 鈍器 blunt [dull] weapon

どんぐり acorn ▫ ‖どんぐりまなこ *big round eyes* / あの２人はどんぐりの背比べだ The two are *more or less the same.*

どんこう 鈍行 local train ▫

どんじり どん尻 the tail end

とんずら ──とんずらする (逃げる) run* away

どんぞこ どん底 (いちばん深い所) the depths; (底) the bottom ‖彼女は失意のどん底にいる She is in *the depths* of despair. / 彼らはどん底からはい上がってきた They have worked their way up from *the bottom.* / その国は不況のどん底にある The country is at *the bottom* of the depression.

とんだ (ひどい) terrible, awful; (思いがけない) unexpected ‖きょうはとんだ目にあった I had a *terrible* experience today. / とんだところで彼女に会った I came across her in *the most unexpected* place.
◆とんだ災難だったね That's *too bad.*

とんち 頓知・頓智 wit ▫ ‖彼はとんちを働かせた He used *his ready* [*quick*] *wit.*

とんちゃく 頓着 彼は着るものにとんちゃくしない(→注意を払わない) He *doesn't pay attention to* what he wears. / He *is indifferent to* what he wears. / 彼女は人に何を言われてもとんちゃくしない(→気にしない) She *doesn't care* what other people say.

とんちゃんさわぎ どんちゃん騒ぎ その晩はみんなでどんちゃん騒ぎをした We all *whooped it up* that night.

とんちんかん ──とんちんかんな (要点をはずした) off the point; (見当違いの) irrelevant ‖何と答えてよいか分からず，とんちんかんなことを言ってしまった I didn't know what to answer, so I「said something *off the point*」[made *irrelevant* remarks].

どんつう 鈍痛 dull pain [ache] ▫

とんでもない
❶ (思いがけない) unexpected; (ひどい) terrible, awful; (とんだ) outrageous
とんでもない値段 an *outrageous* price
彼はとんでもない間違いを犯した He has made a *terrible* mistake.
きょうはとんでもない目にあった I *had a terrible experience* today.
人の物を勝手に持っていくなんてとんでもないやつだ What an *awful* man to take another's thing without saying anything.
◆それはとんでもない誤解だ It is a *gross* misunderstanding.
❷ (強い否定)
💬「どうもありがとうございました」「とんでもない」 "Thank you very much." "*Not at all.*"
💬「歌が上手なんですね」「いえ，とんでもない」 "You sing well." "No, *far from it.*"
💬「みんな君がやったって言ってたけど」「とんでもない」 "Everyone said you did it." "*Absolutely not!*"

どんてん 曇天 cloudy weather ▫

どんでんがえし どんでん返し (逆転) complete reversal ▫ ◆ドラマの結末はどんでん返しだった(→予想とは全く逆だった) The ending of the TV drama was *quite the opposite of what we had expected.*

とんと (全く) completely; (少しも…ない) not ... at all ‖きのう彼に会う約束をしていたのをとんと忘れていた I *completely* forgot that I had an appointment to meet him yesterday. / それ以来彼女のうわさをとんと聞かない I *haven't* heard about her *at all* since then.
◆とんと見当がつかない I don't have the

slightest idea.

とんとん だれかがドアをとんとんたたく音がする I hear someone *knocking* on the door. / 昨年の収支はとんとんだった We broke even last year. / 彼らの成績はとんとんだ(→ほとんど同じだ) Their grades are *about the same*.

どんどん
❶【音】
太鼓をどんどんたたく beat a drum *loudly*
彼は戸をどんどんたたき続けた He continued to *bang* on the door.

❷【勢いよく】(早く) fast, quickly, rapidly; (着々と) steadily; (ためらわずに) without hesitation; (自由に) freely
彼女は何も言わずにどんどん歩いていった She walked *fast* [*quickly*] without saying anything.
ビルの建設工事はどんどん進んでいる The construction of the building is progressing *steadily*.
世界の人口はどんどん増加している The population of the world has been increasing *rapidly*.
◆事態はどんどん悪化している Things *are getting worse and worse*. / 物価はどんどん上昇している Prices *are getting higher and higher*. / 分からないことはどんどん聞いてください If you have any questions, please 「*feel free* [*don't hesitate*] to ask me.

❸【次から次へと】one after another; (ひっきりなしに) continuously, in succession
彼はどんどん問題を解いていった He solved the problems *one after another*.
映画館から人がどんどん出てきた People streamed *continuously* out of the movie theater.

とんとんびょうし とんとん拍子 とんとん拍子に出世する rise *by leaps and bounds* in the world / 交渉はとんとん拍子に進んだ The negotiation went *smoothly* [*without a hitch*].

どんな
❶【どのような】how
3年間日本を離れるというのはどんな気持ちですか *How* do you feel about leaving Japan for three years?
その物語はどんなふうになるんだっけ(→話はどのように進んだのか) *How* did that story go?
◆お姉さんはどんな(→何の)仕事をしていますか What does your sister do? / どんな(→どんな種類の)商品をお店では扱っていますか What *kind of* goods do you sell in your shop? / それはどんな形ですか What shape is it?
⚫「彼女はどんな人」「とても明るくて優しい人だよ」 "*What* is she *like*?" "She is very cheerful and kind." (❖外見を尋ねるなら What does she look like?)
⚫「どんな味がしますか」「洋ナシのような味がします」 "*How* does it taste?" "It tastes like a pear."

❷【いかなる】any; (すべての) all, every
この規則はどんな場合にも有効です This rule is valid in *any* case.

私はどんな音楽も好きです I like *all* kinds of music.
◆その話を聞いたらどんな人でも驚くだろう *Anybody* would be surprised to hear the story. / 彼らを助けるためならどんなことでもします I'll do *anything* to help them. / どんな人にも欠点はある *Everybody* has their shortcomings. / どんなことがあってもあしたはそこに行きます *No matter what*, I'll go there tomorrow. / どんな反論があろうと自分の意見を貫くべきだ You should stick to your opinion *whatever* objections you meet.

どんなに 私がどんなにショックを受けたか想像もつかないでしょう You can't imagine *how* shocked I was. / どんなにつらいことがあっても彼女は笑顔を絶やさなかった *However* [*No matter how*] hard a time she had, she was always smiling.

トンネル ❶【鉄道などの】tunnel ◯ / 海底トンネル an undersea *tunnel* / 海峡の下にトンネルを掘る cut [dig, bore] *a tunnel* under the channel / 列車は長いトンネルを通り抜けた The train passed through *a long tunnel*.
❷【野球】彼はゴロをトンネルした He *let* a grounder *go* [*pass*] *through his legs*.
‖トンネル会社 a dummy company, a front

とんび 鳶 kite ◯ ⇒とび

どんぴしゃり 彼の予想はどんぴしゃりだった He guessed *just right*.

どんぶり 丼 bowl ◯ / どんぶり1杯のごはん *a bowl* of rice / 卵どんぶり *a bowl* of rice with egg
‖どんぶり勘定 a rough estimate

とんぼ 蜻蛉 dragonfly ◯

とんぼがえり とんぼ返り (宙返り) somersault ◯ / とんぼ返りをする turn *a somersault*
◆彼は出張で大阪に行き,その日のうちに東京へとんぼ返りした(→すぐ引き返した) He went to Osaka on business and *made a quick return* to Tokyo within the same day.

ドンマイ ⚠(気にするな) Don't worry about it. (❖ドンマイ は Don't mind. からだが, この意味ではあまり使わない)

とんや 問屋 (店) wholesale store ◯; (人) wholesaler ◯, wholesale dealer ◯
‖問屋街 a wholesale district
慣用表現 そうは問屋がおろさない(→多くを期待しすぎている) *You are expecting too much*. / *That's expecting too much*.

どんよく 貪欲 greed ◯; (金銭欲) 《公式的》 avarice ◯ ──貪欲な greedy; (金銭欲が強い) 《公式的》 avaricious ──貪欲に greedily ‖彼は名声に貪欲だ He is *greedy* for fame. / 彼女は貪欲に新しい知識を吸収しようとしている She is trying *greedily* to absorb new knowledge.

どんより どんよりした空 a *leaden* [*gray*] sky / ここ数日どんよりした(→陰気な)天気が続いている It has been *gloomy* for the past few days. / 彼女はどんよりした目をしていた She had *dull* eyes.

な

な 名

❶【名前】 name ⓒ ⇒ なまえ

彼の名はヨーロッパ中の芸術家に知られている His *name* is known to artists throughout Europe.

私はコロという名の犬を飼っている I have a dog 「whose *name* is Koro [*named* Koro].

あたりには名も知らぬ花が咲き乱れていた Flowers *whose name* I didn't *know* were in full bloom around there.

彼はこのあたりでは「ひろ」という名で通っている He *goes* [*passes*] *by the name of* Hiro around here.

◆彼女は祖母の名をとって麻里と名づけられた She was named Mari *after* her grandmother. / そのリストには多くの有名人が名を連ねていた There were many famous people [Many famous people *were named*] on the list.

❷【名声】 name ⓒ, fame ⓤ

ジェーンは作家として名をなした Jane *made a name for herself* as a writer.

彼は家族の名をけがした He *disgraced* [*shamed*] *the name* of his family.

彼女はその名に恥じぬ名ピアニストだった She was a great pianist *worthy of the name*.

彼は文学史に名を残した He *left his name behind* in the history of literature.

こんなピッチングでは彼の名が泣く(→名に背(そむ)く) Such pitching *is untrue to* his *name*.

◆名のある人 a person *of note*; a *famous* person / 名もない画家 a *nameless* painter

❸【名目・口実】

名ばかりの会長 the chairperson *in name only*; the *nominal* chairperson

歓迎パーティーとは名ばかりのものだった It was a welcome party *in name only*.

彼は兄の名で金を借りた He borrowed money *in* [*under*] *the name of* his brother.

慣用表現 名を捨てて実(じつ)を取る *More profit and less honor.*

ことわざ 名は体を表す *Names and natures do often agree.* (→名前と性質はしばしば一致する)

-な

❶【禁止】 間違いを恐れるな *Don't* be afraid of making mistakes. / 二度と戻ってくるな *Never* come back. (◆Don't に比べ Never のほうが強い禁止を表す)

❷【確認】 君が僕の本を破ったんだな You ripped my book, *didn't you*? / おまえはここにいろ、いいな You stay here. *OK*?

なあ Hey!; Listen to me. ⇒ ねえ

-なあ

❶【感嘆】 How ...!, What ...! / 暑いなあ *How* hot!/ It's *too* hot. / 難しい問題だなあ *What* a difficult question!

❷【願望】 I wish ...., I hope .... (◆前者は事実に反する願望を表す場合に用い, I wish に続く節中の動詞は仮定法にする. 後者は実現可能な願望を表す) // 英語がぺらぺらだったらなあ I *wish* I *could* speak English fluently. / あしたは晴れるといいなあ I *hope* it will be clear tomorrow. / ◆もう少し背が高かったらなあ *If only* I *were* a little taller! (◆「…でさえあれば」の意味の If only に続く節中の動詞は仮定法)

❸【推測】 あの話は本当なのかなあ I *wonder* if that story is true.

なあに あいつが何と言おうと, なあにかまうものか I don't care *a bit* what he says.

🖋「傷, 痛くない?」「なあに. たいしたことないよ」 "Doesn't your cut hurt?" "*Oh*, it's nothing."

ない・-ない

❶【存在しない】 There is [are] no [not] ...

私たちの町には図書館がない There are *no* libraries in our town.

きょうはいい天気だ. 空には雲ひとつない It's a nice day today. *There is not* a single cloud in the sky.

もう電車がないので, 今夜は泊めてください *There are no* more trains. Please put me up tonight.

きょうは授業がない There is [We have] *no* school today.

◆あれ、ここへ置いておいた自転車がない Oh, no! The bike that I left here *is gone*. / 入試まであと2か月しかない There are only two months left until the entrance exam. / ごめん, このことはなかったことにして(→忘れて) I'm sorry. Please *forget* this.

🖋「お母さん, 何か食べる物ない?」「冷蔵庫にアップルパイがあるわよ」 "Mom, *is there* anything to eat?" "There's some apple pie in the fridge."

🖋「このパソコン, しょっちゅう動かなくなる」「でもないよりはましだろう」 "This PC often freezes up." "But it's *better than nothing*."

🖋「変わりはないかい」「ああ, 特にないよ」 "*What's new*?" "Oh, *nothing* '*in particular* [*special*]'."

❷【所有していない】 do* not have ..., have* no ...

家には車がない We *have no* cars.

1円もお金がなかったので, あせってしまった I *didn't have* any money, so I panicked.

おじには子供がない My uncle *doesn't have* any children.

◆彼には遠慮というものがない He *has a lack of restraint*. / 山の中でガソリンがなくなった(→使い果たしてしまった) We *ran out of* gas in the mountains.

❸【打ち消し】 not, no

語法

[not] be 動詞, 助動詞の場合はその後に置き, 一般動詞の場合は《do [does, did] not

+原形)の形で用いる.
[no]《no＋名詞》の形で，主語や目的語の前に置く.

僕は中学生ではない I'*m not* a junior high school student.
彼女は自転車に乗れない She *can't* ride a bike.
彼は英語の先生ではなく数学の先生だ He *isn't* an English teacher, *but* a math teacher.
田中先生は職員室にいなかった Mr. Tanaka *wasn't* in the teachers' room.
私には兄弟がいない I *don't* have any brothers. / I *have no* brothers.
水は全然残っていない There's *no* water left. / There *isn't* any water left.
父はたばこを吸わない My father *doesn't* smoke.
あわてないで *Don't* hurry.
私は彼のことを知らないし，知りたいとも思わない I *don't* know about him, *nor* do I want to know. (❖nor は not の後で用い，「…もまた~ない」という意味)
いつも食後に歯を磨くわけじゃない I *don't* always brush my teeth after meals.
◆彼女はほとんど泳げない She can hardly swim. (❖hardly は「ほとんど…ない」の意味) / 彼女は朝食を食べないで出かけた She went out *without* having breakfast. / 恥ずかしくないのか Shame on you!

🄮「私のアイスクリーム食べたでしょう？」「僕は絶対食べてない」"You ate my ice cream, didn't you?" "I certainly did *not*."
🄮「ロックは聴かないの？」「いいや，聴くよ」"*Don't* you listen to rock music?" "Yes, I do." (❖英語では疑問文が肯定であるか否定であるかにかかわらず，「する」場合はYes,「しない」場合は No を用いる)
🄮「その歌はあまり好きじゃない」「私もです」"I *don't* like that song very much." "Neither do I. /《口語的》Me, neither."

❹【勧誘】
🄮「うちの部に入らない？」「もうテニス部に入ることに決めてるの」"*Why don't you* join our club?" "I've already decided to join the tennis club."
🄮「ちょっとマクドナルドに寄ってかない？」「いいよ」"*How about* stopping by (the) McDonald's?" "OK."

❺【依頼】
少しの間，手伝ってくれない？ *Can you* help me for a while?
後でもう一度お電話をいただけないでしょうか *Could you* call me again later?

❻【その他】
早くバスが来ないかな I *hope* the bus will come soon.
宝くじで1億円当たらないかな I *wish* I could win 100 million yen in the lottery.
🄮「私に電話なかった？」「なかったわよ」"Did someone call me?" "*No*, I have *no* calls for you."

🄮「知子，ちょっと遅すぎない？」「何があったのかな．彼女，いつも時間に正確なのに」"Tomoko is too late, *isn't* she?" "Something may have happened to her. She's always punctual."
🄮「ごめん．きょう映画に行けなくなった」「え，それはないよ」"I'm sorry, but I *can't* go to the movie with you today." "Really? *That can't be*."
ことわざ ないそでは振れぬ ⇨ そで

-ない -内 領海内で *within* the territorial waters / （美術館などで）館内での写真撮影はかたくお断りします Photography is strictly forbidden *in the museum*. / 時間内にすべての問題に答えることはできなかった I couldn't answer all the questions *within the allotted time*. / 芝生内立入禁止《掲示》*Keep off the grass*.

ナイアガラ ナイアガラの滝 *Niagara* Falls
ナイーブ ⚠ ――ナイーブな（繊細な）delicate [délikət]; (感受性の強い) sensitive; (純真な) innocent (❖英語の naive は「ばか正直な，世間知らずな」といった否定的な意味で用いられることが多い) / 彼はナイーブな人だ He is a *delicate [sensitive]* person.
ないえん 内縁 内縁の妻 a *common-law* wife / 彼らは内縁関係にある They are in a *common-law marriage*.
ないか 内科 (学問) internal medicine Ⓤ; (病院の) the department of internal medicine ‖内科医 a physician
-ないか 君が考えていることを私に話してくれないか *Will you* tell me what you have in mind? / さあ，もう泣くのはよさないか Come on, *don't* cry anymore. / 気分転換に散歩に出ないか *Why don't we* take a walk for a change? / だからやめろと言ったじゃないか I told you not to do that, *didn't I*?
ないかい 内海 inland sea Ⓒ
ないがい 内外 建物の内外 the inside and outside of the building / この映画は国内外で(→国内でも国外でも)絶賛された This film won the highest praise *at home and abroad*. / 今度の旅行の出費は5万円内外(→約5万円)で収めたい I want to keep the cost of this trip under *about* fifty thousand yen.
ないかく¹ 内閣 cabinet Ⓒ《しばしば the Cabinet》 /吉田内閣 the Yoshida *Cabinet* / 内閣は総辞職に追い込まれた The Cabinet was driven to resign en masse. / 内閣の支持率が36パーセントから53パーセントにはね上がった *Support* for the Cabinet leapt from 36 to 53 percent. / また近いうちに内閣改造があるかもしれない There could be another *cabinet reshuffle* in the near future.
‖内閣官房長官 the Chief Cabinet Secretary / 内閣総理大臣 the Prime Minister (《略語》PM) / 内閣不信任案 a motion of no-confidence in the Cabinet / 連立内閣 a coalition government
ないかく² 内角 〘幾何〙interior angle Ⓒ; 〘野球〙inside Ⓤ ‖内角球 an inside pitch
ないかくふ 内閣府 the Cabinet Office

ないがしろ 彼は家族をないがしろにしがちだ He tends to *neglect* [*ignore*] his family. / この問題は決してないがしろにする(→軽視する)ことはできない We can never *make light of* this matter.

ないき 内規 bylaw

ないこうてき 内向的 ──内向的な introverted ∥妹は内向的な性格だ My sister is *introverted*./ My sister is *an introvert*.

ないし 乃至 (あるいは) or; (…から〜まで) from ... to 〜, between ... and 〜 ∥20歳未満の者ないし大学生 people under 20 *or* college students / この仕事は2週間ないし3週間かかります It will take you *from two to three weeks* to do this job.

ないじ 内示 彼は2か月前にオーストラリア転勤の内示を受けた Two months ago, he *was unofficially told* that he would be transferred to Australia.

ないじえん 内耳炎 inflammation of the inner ear; 〔医学〕otitis interna [outáitəs intə́ːrnə]

ないしきょう 内視鏡 〔医学〕endoscope ∥内視鏡検査 an endoscopic examination

ないじつ 内実 会社の内実 the real situation of the company / 彼は内実金に困っていた He was in financial difficulties「*in actual fact* [*in reality*].

ないじゅ 内需 domestic demand ∥内需を拡大する expand *domestic demand*

ないしゅっけつ 内出血 internal bleeding ◆ひざが内出血している My knee *is bleeding internally*.

ないしょ 内緒 ──ないしょの secret ──ないしょに in secret, secretly
このことはほかの人にはないしょだよ Keep this *secret* from everyone else.
彼はだれにもないしょで旅に出た He went on a trip「*in secret* [*secretly*].
◆彼女は親にないしょで(→知らせずに)テレビに出た She appeared on TV *without letting her parents know*./ ないしょの話だけど,次郎は夕子が好きなのよ *Just between you and me,* Jiro likes Yuko.
🅔「ねえ,彼に何をプレゼントするの」「ないしょ」"Say, what will you give him as a present?" "*It's a secret.*"
∥ないしょ話 a private talk

ないじょ 内助 (妻の協力) one's wife's support ∥彼の成功も内助の功あってこそだ He owes his success to *his wife's support*.

ないじょう 内情 敵軍の内情を探る spy into *the internal affairs of* the enemy / 彼女は業界の内情に通じている She knows the business world from *the inside*.

ないしょく 内職 (副業) side job; (家で行う賃労働) piecework at home ∥母は洋裁を内職にしている My mother makes dresses as *piecework at home*.
◆国語の授業中に内職をした(→こっそり別のことをした) I secretly *did something else* during the Japanese class.

ないしん¹ 内心 内心ほっとする be relieved *inside* [*inwardly*] ∥彼は黙ってそれを聞いていたが,内心穏やかではなかった He kept quiet when he heard that, but he wasn't calm *inside* [*inwardly, at heart*].

ないしん² 内申 ∥内申書 a school report; (推薦書) a school recommendation

ナイス ナイスキャッチ! Good [*Nice*] catch!

ないせい 内政 その国の内政問題 the home [*internal, domestic*] *affairs of* the country / 他国の内政に干渉する interfere in *the home* [*internal, domestic*] *affairs of* other countries

ないせん¹ 内戦 civil war

ないせん² 内線 (電話の) extension (《略語》ext., extn.) ∥内線703につないでください Give me *extension* 703, please.
∥内線電話 an extension telephone / 内線番号 an extension (number)

ないそう 内装 interior design [decoration] ◆ホテルのけばけばしい内装 the gaudy *interior* of the hotel
∥内装工事 interior works

ないぞう¹ 内臓 internal organs (❋単数形にすると「(特定の)臓器」の意味になる) ∥内臓を摘出する remove *an internal organ*
◆料理するために魚の内臓を取り除く *clean* fish to cook it
∥内臓疾患 an internal disease

ないぞう² 内蔵 ──内蔵の built-in ∥このカメラはセルフタイマーを内蔵している This camera has a *built-in* self-timer.

ナイター 🅐〔野球〕night game (❋「ナイター」は和製英語) ∥テレビで野球のナイターを見る watch *a night* baseball *game* on TV
∥ナイタースキー night skiing

ないだく 内諾 すでに彼の内諾を得ている I *have* already *obtained* his *consent informally* [*unofficially*].

ないち 内地 (国内) the inside of a country; (内陸部) the interior

ないてい 内定 内定取り消し cancellation of an unofficial job offer / 彼女の昇進が内定した Her promotion *was decided unofficially*. / 彼は銀行に就職が内定している He *has received an unofficial job offer from* a bank.

ないてき 内的 内的要因 an *internal* factor / 人間の内的生活 the *interior* [*spiritual*] life of human beings / その日記には彼の内的葛藤(かっとう)が生々しく描かれていた His *inner* conflicts were described vividly in the diary.

ナイト (称号を与えられた人) knight
ナイトガウン nightgown
ナイトキャップ nightcap
ナイトクラブ nightclub

ないない 内々 ──内々の(秘密の) secret, confidential; (非公式の) informal ∥内々の情報 *private* [*secret*] information ◆内々でお話ししたいことがあります I *have* something to talk about with you *privately* [*in private*]./ 私は3日前にそのことを内々に知らされた I was informed of it *unofficially* three days ago.

ナイフ knife [náif] ⓒ (複 knives [náivz]) (❖食卓用のナイフだけでなく，包丁・小刀なども指す)；(食卓用) table knife ⓒ
ナイフを研ぐ sharpen *a knife* / ナイフを開く[たたむ] open [close] *a knife*
このナイフはよく切れる This *knife* cuts well.
ナイフで鉛筆を削った I sharpened the pencil *with a knife*.
ナイフとフォークで食事をするのは苦手だ I'm not good at eating *with a knife and fork*. (❖knife と fork を対にして用いる場合，fork にはaは付けない)
‖折りたたみナイフ a clasp knife / 果物ナイフ a fruit knife / ジャックナイフ a jackknife / 飛び出しナイフ 《米》a switchblade, 《英》a flick knife / 万能ナイフ a utility knife / ペーパーナイフ 《米》a letter opener, 《英》a paper knife

ないぶ 内部 inside ⓒ, interior ⓒ ——内部の inside, interior, inner ‖体育館の内部はとても広々としていた The gym's *interior* [*The inside* of the gym] was very spacious. / 警察はその事件を内部の者の犯行と断定した The police concluded that the case was *an inside job*. / 彼は会社の内部事情に通じていた He had a lot of *inside information* on [about] the company. / このビルの内部構造は非常に複雑だ *The inner* [*interior*] *structure* of this building is very complex.
◆その政党の内部では大きな変化が起こっている There has been a big change *within* the party.
‖内部監査 an internal audit / 内部工作 inside maneuvering / 内部抗争 an internal struggle / 内部告発 (an) accusation from inside

ないふくやく 内服薬 internal medicine ⓤ

ないふん 内紛 内紛によりその党は2つに分裂した *Internal conflict* [*strife*] split the party in two.

ないぶんぴつ 内分泌 〖医学〗internal secretion ⓤ ‖内分泌腺[医学] an endocrine gland

ないみつ 内密 ——内密に secretly, in secret, privately, in private ‖事件を内密に調査する investigate the case *secretly* / 君と内密に話をしたいのだが I'd like to talk with you *privately*.

ないめん 内面 the inside ——内面の・内面的な inner, internal ‖内面の美しさ[苦しみ] *inner* beauty [*suffering*] / 彼は笑って内面の動揺を隠そうとした He tried to hide his *inner* disturbance with a smile.
◆この小説は鋭い内面描写が特徴的だ This novel is characterized by *its* keen *psychological insight*.

ないものねだり 無い物ねだり 弟はいつもないものねだりをしては親を困らせている My brother is always bothering our parents by *asking for the moon*.

ないや 内野 〖野球〗the infield ‖内野安打[ゴロ] an infield hit [grounder] / 内野手 an infielder / 内野席 the infield stands / 内野フライ a pop fly to the infield

ないよう 内容 (具体的な中身) contents；(意味内容) content ⓤ；(実質)《公式的》substance ⓤ
形式と内容 form and *content* [*substance*] / 内容の薄い講演 a lecture「without meat [lacking in] *substance*
彼の書いた劇は内容がなかった The play he wrote lacked *content* [*substance*].
彼の講義の内容は私たちの興味からは全くかけ離れていた *The contents* of his lectures were remote from any of our interests.
◆…という内容の手紙を書く write a letter *to the effect that …* / 丈二はその講義の内容を書き留めた Joji took notes *of the lecture*. / もっと内容のある議論が聞きたい I want to hear a more *substantial* debate.
🅔「彼の話の内容(→言っていること)が分かりますか」「少しぐらいならね」"Do you understand *what he is saying*?" "Some, I guess."

ないらん 内乱 (内戦) civil war ⓒⓤ；(暴動) rebellion ⓤⓒ ‖その国では内乱が絶えない The country always has *civil wars*.

ないりく 内陸 inland ⓤ ◆関東地方の内陸部 *the inland part* of the Kanto area / 台風は内陸部へ進んだ The typhoon moved *inland*.
‖内陸国 a landlocked country / 内陸性気候 an inland [a continental] climate

ナイルがわ ナイル川 the Nile

ナイロン nylon ⓤ

ナイン 〖野球〗the nine

なう わらで縄をなう *twist* straw *into* a rope

なえ 苗 (種から育てた) seedling ⓒ；(若木一般) young plant ⓒ ‖稲の苗を植える plant *seedlings* of rice / 遅霜のため苗の多くが被害を受けた A late frost injured many of *the seedlings*.
‖苗木 a young plant / 苗床 a seedbed

なえる 萎える その話を聞いたらやる気がなえてしまった(→やる気をなくした) I *lost* my enthusiasm after hearing the story. / 長年の寝たきり生活で彼の足はすっかりなえてしまっていた His legs *were* completely *withered* after he had been bedridden for years.

なお 尚
❶【いっそう】still, even
なお一層の努力が必要です You need to make *still* more effort.
彼女は年齢を重ねてなお美しさを増した She has become *even* more beautiful with age.
うそをつくほうがなお悪い Lying is *even* worse.
フレッシュハーブを使えばなおいっそうおいしくなります Fresh herbs will improve the taste *even more*.
◆それならなおのこと早く彼に相談するべきだ In that case it's *all the more* important to talk with him as soon as possible.
❷【相変わらず】
その問題は今なお討議中だ The problem is *still* under discussion.
事件の真相は今なお(→今日(誇)に至るまで)なぞ

に包まれたままだ The facts of the case are wrapped in mystery *to this day*.
❸【それでも】
彼はひとりになってもなおあきらめなかった He didn't give up *even* after he was left alone.
❹【付言すると】
なお，この価格には消費税は含まれておりません *In addition* [*Furthermore*], this price doesn't include the consumption tax.

なおさら 尚更 all the more; (なおさら…ない) much [still] less / その話を聞いたらなおさら不安になった I felt *all the more* uneasy when I heard the story. / テレビを買う金などないし，車に至ってはなおさらだ I don't have enough money to buy a TV, 「*much less* [*let alone*] a car.
◆彼が手伝ってくれればなおさらありがたい If she helps me, *so much the better.* / 彼女と話せば話すほどなおさら心が引かれていった *The more* I talked with her, *the more* I was charmed by her.

なおざり なおざりな態度 a casual [half-hearted] attitude / 基礎練習をなおざりにしてはいけない You shouldn't *neglect* basic exercises.

なおし 直し repair 回 ; (服などの) mending 回 / CDプレーヤーを直しに出す send a CD player *for repair*
◆ズボンの丈(ﾀｹ)直しをしてもらった I had the length of my pants *adjusted*.

なおす¹ 直す

❶【修理する】repair 働; mend 働;《口語的》fix 働

| repair: 道路・橋・車・機械などを修理する場合に用いることが多い.
| mend: 衣服などを修理する場合に用いることが多い.
| fix: 特に口語で上記のいずれの場合にも用いる.

このボタンが取れそうだ．直してくれない This button is coming off. Will you *fix*?
◆その服のウエストの部分を直してもらわなければならない I have to *have* the dress *adjusted* at the waist. (✜adjustは「調整する」の意味)
🗨「このテレビを直してくれますか」「いいですよ」 "Can you *repair* [*fix*] this TV, please?" "No problem."
❷【訂正する】correct 働
彼女は私の宿題の間違いを直してくれた She *corrected* the errors in my homework.
◆この時計，5分遅れてるから直しておいて Could you *adjust* this clock? It's five minutes slow.
❸【翻訳する】translate 働, put* … into ～
日本語の手紙を英語に直す *translate* [*put*] a Japanese letter *into* English
◆サンスクリット語を漢字に直す(→音写する) *transcribe* Sanskrit *into* Chinese characters
❹【換算する】
円をドルに直す *change* yen *into* dollars
❺【…し直す】
原稿を書き直す *rewrite* a manuscript
もう一度始めからやり直そう Let's *start* all *over* again.
答案を出す前にもう一度見直しなさい You'd better *look* [*read*] your paper *over* again before handing it in.
(電話で) 後でこちらからかけ直します I'll call you *back* later.
❻【その他】
ネクタイを直す *adjust* [(→まっすぐにする) *straighten*] *one's* tie / 化粧を直す *touch up one's* makeup
悪い癖(ｾｷ)を直すのは容易ではない It's not easy to *get rid of* bad habits.
お菓子をあげたら妹は機嫌を直した My sister *got back into a good mood* when I gave her some candy.

なおす² 治す cure 働; (特に外傷を) heal 働
患者[病気]を治す *cure* a patient [disease] / 傷を治す *heal* a wound
彼が母の病気を治してくれた He *has cured* my mother *of* her disease.

なおる¹ 直る be repaired, be mended, be fixed
僕の自転車は簡単に直った My bicycle *was fixed* [*repaired*] easily.
このビデオはもう直らない This VCR 「*can't be repaired* [*isn't repairable*].
◆この単語のつづりがまだ直っていないぞ The spelling of this word has not yet *been corrected.* / 父は食事中に新聞を読む癖(ｾｷ)が直らない My father *can't get rid of* the habit of reading a newspaper at meals. / その老人は孫の顔を見るととたんに機嫌が直った The old man's mood *improved* as soon as he saw his grandchild. / (号令で) 前へならえ！直れ！ Line up! *At ease!*

なおる² 治る get* well, be cured; (外傷などが) be healed; (回復する) recover 働
早く治るといいね I hope you'll *get well* soon.
この病は簡単には治りません This illness *can't be cured* easily.
そのやけどはまだ治っていません The burn *is not yet healed*.
彼女の病気が治るまでに長い時間がかかった It took her a long time to *recover from* her illness.
◆ようやくかぜが治った I finally *got over* my cold. / 頭痛はもう治りましたか *Has* [*Is*] *your headache gone?* / この薬で私の湿疹(ﾋﾁ)は治りますか *Will* this medicine *cure* me *of* eczema?

なか¹ 中

❶【内部】the inside ――中に[で] in, inside ――中へ into
《中に》
森の中に小さな古い社(ﾔｼﾛ)があった There was a small old shrine *in* the woods.
部屋の中に入ってみよう Let's go *into* the room.

ぬれないように中に入りなさい Come *inside* so that you won't get wet.

彼女はパンを袋の中に入れた She put the bread *into* a bag.

洗濯物を家の中に入れてください Please bring *in* the washing.

◆私は地下鉄の中に傘を忘れた I left my umbrella *on* the subway. / この包みの中には非常用の食料や飲料が入っている This pack *contains* food and drinks for emergencies. / 少年はその秘密を心の中にしまっておいた The boy kept the secret *to himself*.

《中が・は》
箱の中が見たい I want to see「*the inside of [inside]* the box.
家の中は涼しい It's cool *inside [in]* the house.
◆家の中が散らかっていてごめんなさい Please excuse *the* messy *house*. / 試験が始まったとたん, 頭の中が真っ白になった My mind went blank as soon as the exam began.

《中を》
2匹の犬が雪の中を走っている Two dogs are running *in* the snow.
私は店の中をのぞいた I looked *into* the store.
その道は森の中を通っている The path lies *through* a forest.

《中から》
そのドアは中からかぎがかかっている The door is locked *from the inside*.
◆栄一はかばんの中から辞書を取り出した Eiichi took a dictionary *out of* his bag. / 茂みの中から(→茂みから)人影が現れた A figure emerged *from* the bushes. / 建物の中から歌声が聞こえた I heard someone singing *from within* the building.

《中で》
◆私は人込みの中で彼を見失った I lost him *among* the crowd. / 電車の中でたばこを吸ってはいけません Don't smoke *on* the train. / この動物は土の中で冬を越す This animal spends winter *under* the ground.

《中の》
トラックが通ると家の中の物が揺れた Things *in* the house shook when a truck passed by.

❷【範囲内で】in (◆団体名などの前で用いる); of (◆数・all などの前で用いる); among (◆3つ以上を表す語の前で用いる)

英雄の中の英雄 a hero *among* heroes
3人の中でだれがいちばんもてるの Who is the most popular *of* the three? (◆「クラスの中で」なら in your class,「クラスメートの中で」なら among your classmates を用いる)
父は家族の中でいちばんの早起きだ My father is the earliest riser *in* our family.
君たちの中で学校からいちばん遠くに住んでいるのはだれですか Which *of* you lives farthest from the school?
この中から1つ選んでください Choose one *out of* these.
◆乗客の中には日本人が15名含まれていた The passengers *included* 15 Japanese. / それらのセーターの中から私は赤いのを選んだ I selected a red one *from* those sweaters. / 彼は私の人生で出会った中で最も正直な人だ He is the most honest man (*that*) I have met in my life.

❸【最中に】
お忙しい中お越しいただいてありがとうございます Thank you very much for coming *in spite of* your busy schedule.
父はすさまじい雨の中, 仕事に出かけた My father went to work *in* a terrible rain.
私たちは日常生活の中で様々なごみを出している We produce all kinds of waste *in* our daily lives.
スミス先生は話の中でいくつかの日本の慣習について触れた *In* her speech, Ms. Smith referred to several Japanese customs.

❹【その他】
心の中を打ち明ける say what's on *one's mind*
その監督の指導は厳しい中にも優しさがあった There was gentleness *even in* the coach's strict leadership.
山田は中4日おいての登板です Yamada is pitching *after a four-day rest*.

なか² 仲 terms; (親戚(%%)・恋愛関係) relationship ◎; (友好関係) friendship ◎◎

仲のいい兄弟 brothers *on good terms with each other*
君と美幸ってどういう仲なの What kind of *relationship* do you have with Miyuki? / What is the *relationship* between you and Miyuki?
彼とは言葉を交わすような仲ではない I'm not on speaking *terms* with him.
けんかして以来, 私たちの仲は冷えきった After the quarrel, our *friendship* [*relationship*] *cooled down*.
◆京子と美加は仲がいい Kyoko and Mika *are good friends*. / 真悟と博は仲が悪い Shingo and Hiroshi *don't get on* [*along*] *well*. (◆get on [along]は「仲よくやる」の意味) / 僕らの仲もこれまでだ It's all over *between* us. / 権力に対する執着が彼らの仲を裂いた Their obsession with power *broke* them *up*. / 彼はその女性と深い仲になった He has become *intimate* with the woman. / そのカップルは仲むつまじく公園の中を散歩していた The couple was taking a walk *closely together* in the park.

[ことわざ]親しき仲にも礼儀あり ➡ したしい

ながあめ 長雨 秋の長雨 *a long* autumn *rain*

ながい¹ 長い

❶【空間的に】long
キリンの首は長い The giraffe has a *long* neck.
あの長い髪の少女はだれですか Who is「*the girl with long hair* [*the long-haired girl*]?
スーザンは母親に長い手紙を書いて送った Susan wrote a *long* letter to her mother.

[e]「世界でいちばん長い川は何ですか」「ナイル川です」 "What is *the longest* river in the world?" "The Nile is."

❷【時間的に】

(きょうは)長い１日だった I've had a *long* day.

長い講義で私たちは疲れてしまった(→長い講義は我々を疲れさせた) The *long* lecture wearied us.

彼がそのショックから立ち直るまで長い時間がかかった It took a *long* time for him to recover from the shock.

長い旅を終えて彼は疲れた様子だった He looked weary after the *long* journey.

彼らはつきあい始めて長い They have *long* been going out.

長いことお待たせしてすみません I'm sorry to have kept you waiting so *long*.

両国は長い間戦争をしていた The two countries were at war *for a long time*.

万里の長城には長い間訪れたいと思っていたのです I have *long* wanted to see the Great Wall of China.

[慣用表現] それはまたずいぶんと気の長い話だね It's a very *long-range* plan. / 長い目で見ればこの投資は損にはなるまい We will profit by this investment *in the long run*.

[ことわざ] 長い物には巻かれろ It's no use taking on superiors. (→目上の者と争ってもむだだ)

ながい² 長居 ―長居する stay (too) long // 思わぬ長居をしてしまいました I *stayed too long* unexpectedly.

◆あちらのお宅であまり長居をするんじゃありませんよ Don't *outstay your welcome* at their house. (❖outstay *one's* welcome は「相手がいやがるほど長居をする」の意味)

ながいき 長生き ―長生きする live long; (…より長生きする) outlive [他] // 一般に女性は男性より長生きする In general, women 「*live longer than* [*outlive*] men.

◆長生きの秘訣(ひけつ)は少食にしてよく体を動かすことだ The secret of *longevity* [*long life*] is to eat less and get a lot of exercise. / 栄子のおじいさんは90歳まで長生きした Eiko's grandfather *lived* to be 90.

ながいす 長椅子 sofa [C], couch [C]

なかがい 仲買 brokerage [U] [C]; (株式仲買) stockbroking [U] // 仲買人 a broker; (株式仲買人) a stockbroker

ながく 長く

❶【空間的に】

彼女は髪を長く伸ばしている She wears her hair *long*.

このズボンをはけば足がもっと長く見えますよ Your legs will look *longer* in this pair of trousers.

❷【時間的に】

彼女はその仕事を長く続けたいと思っている She wants to continue the career (*for*) *long*.

彼は英会話の勉強を始めたが長くは続かなかった He started to learn conversational English, but it didn't last *long*.

日が日増しに長くなっている The days *are getting longer* (*and longer*).

話せば長くなるけれど… It may *take a while* to explain, but ....

その建物が完成するまでそう長くはかからないだろう It won't be *long* before the building will be finished.

長くても１週間あればこの病気は治るでしょう It will take you a week *at the longest* to recover from this disease.

ながぐつ 長靴 boots; (雨靴) rain boots; (ゴム長) rubber boots(❖いずれも数えるときは a pair of ... とする) // 長靴を履く put on *one's rain boots*

なかごろ 中頃 来週の中ごろまでには仕事が終わると思います I think I'll finish my work *by the middle* of next week.

ながさ 長さ length [C] [U] // 適当な長さのスカート a skirt of modest *length* / そのロープの長さはどれくらいですか What is *the length* of that rope? / How *long* is that rope? / このリボンを50センチの長さに切ってください Please cut this ribbon to *a length* of 50 centimeters. / 瀬戸大橋は長さ9.4キロメートルです The Seto Ohashi Bridge is 9.4 kilometers 「*in length* [*long*]. / 彼女はかなりの長さの文章を暗唱した She recited a passage of some *length*.

◆定規で線分の長さを測る *measure* a line with a ruler / そのリボンは５センチだけ長さが足りない That ribbon is just five centimeters *short*.

ながさき 長崎

長崎県は九州の北西部に位置し，主に４つの半島と，対馬や五島列島などの島々から成っています．歴史的に海外との交流が盛んで，江戸時代，日本が鎖国をしている間も，長崎港は，オランダ・中国・朝鮮との貿易を行う海外に対して開かれた唯一の窓口でした．そのため，現代でも異国情緒の色濃い地域です．また，長崎市は，1945年８月，広島に次いで原爆が落とされた所です．
Nagasaki Prefecture is located in northwestern Kyushu. It includes four peninsulas and a number of islands, such as Tsushima and the Goto group. It has a history of contact with foreign countries. In the Edo Period, during Japan's era of seclusion, trade with the Netherlands, China and Korea passed through Nagasaki Port, which was Japan's only window to the world. Therefore many foreign influences can still be found in this area. The city of Nagasaki is also the place where, after the bombing of Hiroshima, the second atomic bomb was dropped in August 1945.

ながし 流し (kitchen) sink [C]

◆流しのタクシー a *cruising* taxi

ながしうち 流し打ち (野球で)清水はきれいに流し打ちを決めた Shimizu *hit* clean *to the opposite field*.

ながしこむ 流し込む 溶かした鉄を鋳型に流し込む *pour* melted iron *into* a mold / 彼はごはんをお茶で流し込んで家を飛び出した He *washed down* his rice *with* tea and ran out of the house.

ながしめ 流し目 彼女は僕に流し目を使ってきた She *made eyes at* me.

なかす 中州 an island in the river; (砂州) sandbank [C], sandbar [C]

ながす 流す

❶【液体を】(水などを勢いよく) flush [他] [自]; (排水する) drain [他]; (血・涙を) shed* [他]

涙を流す *shed* tears

使用後は水を流してください Please *flush* after using.

その工場は長い間排水を川に流していた The factory *has* long *drained* waste water into the river.

警察は一滴も血を流すことなく暴動を鎮圧した The police put down the riot without *shedding* any blood.

◆水を流しっぱなしにしてはいけません Don't *leave* the water *running*. / 自由のために多くの人々の血が流された Many people *bled* for liberty.

❷【液体で物を】

洪水で橋が流された The bridge *was washed* [*carried*] *away* by the flood.

シャワーで汗を全部流したい I'd like to take a shower and *wash off* all this sweat.

少女はササの葉で作った小船を川に流した(→浮かべた) The girl *floated* a little boat made of a bamboo leaf on the river.

気づいたときにはずいぶん沖のほうまで流されていた I *drifted* far *away* from the shore before I noticed.

❸【音・情報などを】

だれがこんなでたらめなうわさを流したのだろう Who *started* [*spread*] such a false rumor?

その喫茶店ではいつもジャズを流している They always *play* jazz at the coffee shop.

❹【その他】

背中を流して(→洗って)くれないか Will you *wash* my back?

我々はよく感情に流される We *are* often *influenced* [*swayed*] by our feelings.

多くのタクシーが大通りを流していた Many taxis *were cruising* the main street.

[慣用表現] お互い今までのことは水に流そうじゃないか Let's *forget* all our bad feelings toward each other.

-なかせ -泣かせ 親泣かせの息子 a son who is *a grief* [*problem*] *to his parents* / この病気は本当に医者泣かせだ This disease is really *a problem for doctors*.

なかせる 泣かせる make* *a person* cry; (感動させる) bring* [move] *a person* to tears ∥僕は妹を泣かせてしまった I *made* my sister *cry*. / 『ガンジー』のそのシーンには本当に泣かされた That scene in *Gandhi* really *brought* [*moved*] *me to tears*.

◆泣かせる話 a *touching* [*moving*] story / あいつはずいぶん多くの女の子を泣かせてきた(→傷心させた)らしい I hear that he *has broken the hearts* of many girls.

ながそで 長袖 長そでのシャツ a shirt *with long sleeves*; a *long-sleeved* shirt

なかたがい 仲違い quarrel [C], 《公式的》discord [U] ━仲たがいする quarrel [自] ∥富雄は彼女と仲たがいした Tomio *quarreled* [*got in a quarrel*] *with* her.

◆彼らは仲たがいしている They *are on bad terms with* each other.

なかだち 仲立ち 交渉の仲立ちを依頼された I was asked to *mediate* [act as *a go-between* in] the negotiations.

ながたらしい 長たらしい long-drawn-out; (長い) lengthy ∥長たらしいあいさつを述べる make a *long-drawn-out* speech

なかだるみ 中弛み (スランプ) slump [C] ∥シーズン中, 彼にも一時中だるみの時期があった He also had *a slump* for a while in the season.

ながちょうば 長丁場 これは長丁場の仕事だから最初からあまりがんばりすぎないほうがいい This job *will take a long time to finish*, so you should pace yourself.

なかつぎ 中継ぎ ∥中継ぎ投手 a middle relief pitcher / 中継ぎ貿易 transit trade

-なかったら 夏休みは宿題さえなかったら思いっきり遊べるのに We could enjoy the summer vacation to the full *if* only we *didn't have* homework. / もし彼女の助けがなかったら私たちは途中で挫折(ざっ)していただろう *If it had not been for* [*Without, But for*] her help, we would have given up halfway. (❖現在の事実と反対の事柄を仮定する場合は, if it were not for ... を用いる. without, but for はいずれの場合にも用いられる)

ながつづき 長続き ━長続きする last long ∥この好天も長続きしないでしょう This good weather *won't last long*.

◆彼は飽きっぽくて何をやっても長続きしない He is so fickle that he *can't stick with* anything *for long*.

なかづり 中吊り ∥中づり広告 (電車の)an advertising poster hanging in the train

なかでも 中でも (とりわけ) above all; (特に) especially ∥彼は果物なら何でも好きだが, 中でも桃には目がない He likes every kind of fruit, but he is crazy about peaches *above all*.

ながでんわ 長電話 陽子はまただれかと長電話をしている Yoko *has been talking* with somebody *for a long time on the phone* again.

なかなおり 仲直り reconciliation [U] 《また a ～》 ━仲直りする make* up with *a person*, be friends again ∥英介とはもう仲直りしたの? *Have* you *made up with* Eisuke yet? / その女の子たちはすぐ仲直りした The girls *were* soon「*friends again* [*reconciled*].

◆どうにかして彼らを仲直りさせたい I want to *get* them *back together* somehow.

なかなか

なかなか

❶ 【かなり】 pretty, quite; (非常に) very

マイケルの新曲はなかなかいい Michael's new song is *pretty* good.

そのインド料理店はなかなかいいけるよ That Indian restaurant is *quite* good.

新しいシャツがなかなか決まってますね You look *very* smart in your new shirt.

▶「映画はどうだった」「なかなかよかったよ」 "How was the movie?" "It was *really* good."

❷ 【簡単には・すぐには】 will not …, not … easily

その戸はなかなかあかなかった The door *wouldn't* open.

恵子はなかなか「うん」と言わなかった Keiko did *not* say yes *easily*.

彼に本を貸したらなかなか返してくれないんだ He borrowed a book from me and *won't* give it back.

◆なかなか治らない(→しつこい)せき a *persistent* cough / 恵理からなかなか(→長い間)連絡がない We haven't heard from Eri *for a long time*. / 民族間の憎しみはなかなか消えない Ethnic hatred *dies hard*. / ゆうべは蒸し暑くてなかなか寝つけなかった(→寝つくのに時間がかかった) It was hot and humid last night, so *it took a while* for me to get to sleep.

ながなが 長々 彼は旅行のことを長々と話した He talked about his trip *at great length*. / 彼はソファーに長々と寝そべった He 「*lay at full length* [*stretched out*]」 on the sofa.

なかには 中には 多くの人々は彼を変人扱いしたが、中には天才とみなす者もいた Many people treated him as an eccentric, but *some* regarded him as a genius.

なかにわ 中庭 courtyard Ⓒ, court Ⓒ; (舗装された敷地) patio Ⓒ (複 ～s)

ながねん 長年 for (many) years; (長い間) for a long time / 父はその会社に長年勤めている My father has served the company *for many years*.

◆ついに長年の夢がかなった My *long-cherished* dream has finally come true. / こういうときは彼の長年の経験がものをいう In this case, his *years of* experience count a lot. / 長年の習慣は振り払うのが大変だ It's hard to shake an *old* habit.

ながの 長野

長野県は内陸県です.3,000メートル以上の山々があり,「日本の屋根」と呼ばれています.県内には,地理的,気候的条件を利用したスキー場やスケートリンクが多くあり,ウインタースポーツが盛んです.1998年には長野県で第18回冬季オリンピックが開催されました.
Nagano Prefecture is a landlocked prefecture. It has mountains higher than 3,000 meters and is called "the Roof of Japan." With its favorable geographical and climate conditions, there are many ski resorts and skating rinks and winter sports are popular. The 18th Winter Olympics were held in Nagano in 1998.

なかば 半ば the middle; (半分) half / 来月の半ばに引っ越すことになりました We're going to move *in the middle of* next month. / 彼は人生の半ばで大きな転機を迎えた He had a turning point *in the middle of* his life. / 選手たちは優勝をなかばあきらめていた The players *half* gave up winning the championship.

◆母は40代半ばです My mother is in her 「*middle* forties [*mid*-forties]」. / 多くのランナーがコース半ばで脱落した Many runners dropped out *halfway* through the course. / 彼は志半ばで(→目的を達することなく)病に倒れた He was struck down by disease *without achieving his goal*.

ながばなし 長話 long talk Ⓒ; (おしゃべり) long chat Ⓒ / ゆうべは彼女と電話で長話をした I had *a long talk* [*chat*] with her on the phone last night.

ながびく 長引く 会議を長引かせる prolong [draw out] a meeting / ジムの日本滞在は長引いた Jim's stay in Japan *was prolonged*. / 今度のかぜは思っていたより長引いた(→治るのに時間がかかった) *It took* me *longer* than expected to get over this cold. / 長引く不況でその会社は倒産に追い込まれた The *long recession* reduced the company to bankruptcy.

なかほど 中程 その池の中ほどに小さな島があった There was a little island *in the middle of* the pond. / 私の家は駅と駅の中ほどにある My house is *halfway* between two stations. / 中ほどまで(→奥の方へ)お詰めください Move *along*, please.

なかま 仲間 (友達) friend Ⓒ, company Ⓤ; (相棒) companion Ⓒ; (同志) comrade Ⓒ; (職場の) colleague Ⓒ; (共通の趣味などで結ばれた集団) circle Ⓒ

僕はふとしたことから彼らの仲間になった I *became friends with* them by chance.

クラブの仲間数人と伊豆へ海水浴に行った I went swimming in Izu with some *friends* from my club.

直美は最近悪い仲間とつきあっているらしい I hear Naomi *has been keeping bad company* recently.

その少女は仲間うちでは評判がよかった The girl had a good reputation *among her friends*. / The girl was well spoken of *by her friends*.

父は飲み仲間と街に繰り出した My father roamed the streets with *his drinking companions*.

姉は仕事仲間とうまくやっているようだ My sister seems to get along well with *her colleagues* [*coworkers*].

彼は文人仲間の間では酒豪として通っていた He was known as a heavy drinker in *his literary circle*.

◆ちょっとした誤解から仲間割れをしてしまった(→２つのグループに分かれた) A small misunderstanding caused us to *split into two groups*. / 成人式も終わりいよいよ彼女も大人の仲間入りだ(→大人の一員だ) Now that the coming-of-age ceremony is over, she is also *a member of* the adult population. / その少年は同級生から仲間はずれにされていたようだ I hear that the boy *was* 「*left out* [*excluded*] *by* his classmates. / 彼らは子供のころ私の遊び仲間だった They were my *playmates* when we were children. / チューリップはユリの仲間だ(→ユリ科に属する) The tulip *belongs to* the lily family. / 彼らは仲間意識が非常に強かった They had *a* very strong *fellow feeling*.

💬「私も仲間に入れてもらえますか」「どうぞ，どうぞ」 "May I *join* you?" "Please do."

なかみ 中身 contents; (実質)《公式的》substance [U] ∥中身のない小説 a novel *with no substance*; a *vacuous* novel
◆中身の詰まったかばん a *stuffed* bag / かばんの中身は何ですか What's *in* the bag? / What are *the contents* of the bag? / 見かけよりも中身が大切だ *What's on the inside* is what counts rather than the appearance.

ながめ[1] 眺め view [C]; (光景) sight [C]; (眺望)《公式的》prospect [C]《通例単数形》 ∥眺めのいい部屋 a room with *a* fine *view* / 屋上からの眺めは最高だったよ We had *a* most wonderful *view* from the roof. / 私たちは山頂から湖のすばらしい眺めを楽しんだ We enjoyed *a* splendid *view* [*prospect*] of the lake from the top of the mountain.

ながめ[2] 長め ―長めの a little long,《口語的》longish ◆前髪は少し長めに切ってください(→短く切りすぎないでください) Don't cut the bangs too short.

ながめる 眺める look [自]; (注意して) watch [他][自]; (じっと見る) stare [自][他], gaze [自]
彼女は遠くの山を眺めている She *is looking at* the mountain in the distance.
私は鬼ごっこしている子供たちを眺めていた I *was watching* the children playing tag.
老婆は子供たちをじろじろと眺めた The old woman *stared at* the children.
そこで眺めていないで手伝ってくれ Don't just stand there *looking* (*on*). Help me.

ながもち 長持ち ―長持ちする last long; (食べ物が) keep* long; (使用に耐える) wear* well; (耐久性がある) be durable ∥この電池は長持ちします This battery *will last long*./ This battery *has a long life*. / この果物は長持ちしません This fruit *won't keep long*. / この靴は長持ちする These shoes *wear well*.

なかやすみ 中休み break [C], rest [U][C] ∥中休みをとる take *a break* [*rest*]

ながゆ 長湯 うちの姉は長湯だ My sister *takes long baths*.

なかゆび 中指 (手の) middle finger [C]; (足の) middle [third] toe [C]

なかよく 仲良く ―仲よくする be friends with *a person*; (うまくやる) get* on [along] well with *a person* ∥私は10年以上高橋さんの家と仲よくしている I *have been friends with* the Takahashis for over 10 years. / 彼はクラスメートと仲よくやってゆけない He *can't get along well with* his classmates.
◆彼らは仲よく幸せに暮らしました They lived happily *together*. / 健太郎はだれとでもすぐに仲よくなれる Kentaro *can make* [*become*] *friends with* anybody easily.

なかよし 仲良し good [close] friend [C] ∥僕らは子供のころから仲よしです We have been *good* [*close*] *friends* since childhood.

-ながら

❶【同時に】 as, while
母は夕食の準備をしながら鼻歌を歌っていた My mother was humming 「*as* she cooked [*while* (she was) cooking] dinner.
◆お茶でも飲みながら話そう Let's talk *over* a cup of tea. / 彼女は目に涙を浮かべながら歌った She sang *with* tears in her eyes. / 犬がしっぽを振りながら私たちの方にやってきた A dog came toward us *wagging* its tail.

❷【…だけれども】 though, although
彼はルーキーながらエースとしての責任を十分に果たした *Though* he was a rookie, he fulfilled his responsibility as ace pitcher.
彼女はそれを知っていながら口にしなかった She didn't say that, *though* she knew it.
◆残念ながらパーティーには出席できません *I'm sorry, but* I can't come to the party. / 微力ながら全力を尽くします I'll do 「*the little* [*what little*] I can. / あれだけの才能がありながら，彼はまだ二軍にいる *With* all that talent, he is still in the minor leagues.

ながらく 長らく long, for a long time ∥たいへん長らくお待たせしました I'm sorry to have kept you waiting so *long*.

ながれ 流れ

❶【水などの】 flow [C]; stream [C]; current [C]
> flow: なめらかで，比較的穏やかな流れを指す.
> stream: 一定した継続的な流れを指す.
> current: 海における海流など，流れの強さや方向を強調する語.

川の流れ *the flow* of a river / 流れを下る go 「down *the stream* [*downstream*]
僕は流れに沿って歩いた I walked *along the stream*.
彼は流れに逆らって泳ごうとした He tried to swim *against the current*.
◆この川は歩いて渡るには流れが速すぎる This river *is too rapid* to walk across.

❷【交通などの】 flow [C], stream [C]
人の流れに逆らって歩く walk *against the flow* [*stream*] of the crowd
この通りは車の流れが絶えることがない *The flow of cars* continues without a break on this street.

❸【血統・流派など】
彼の家は島津家の流れをくむ名門である His family is a noble one which *is descended from* the Shimazu Clan.

正倉院にはヘレニズム美術の流れをくむ(→影響を受けた)宝物がたくさん納められている There are a lot of treasures housed in Shosoin that *were influenced* by Hellenistic art.
❹【その他】
歴史の流れを変える大発見 a great discovery that changes *the course of history* / 時代の流れに従う go with *the flow [stream] of time*
雨で試合はお流れになった The game *was canceled [called off]* because of the rain.
彼の初回のホームランが試合全体の流れを決めた His first-inning home run *set the tone* for the entire game.

ながれおちる 流れ落ちる 涙がその男の子のほおを流れ落ちた Tears *ran down* the boy's cheeks.

ながれこむ 流れ込む その川は東京湾に流れ込んでいる The river *flows [runs] into* Tokyo Bay. / 窓をあけると冷たい空気が部屋に流れ込んできた When I opened the window, cold air *poured into* the room.

ながれさぎょう 流れ作業 assembly line
ながれだす 流れ出す flow out (of ...)
ながれだま 流れ弾 stray bullet ⓒ
ながれぼし 流れ星 shooting star ⓒ
ながれもの 流れ者 drifter ⓒ

ながれる 流れる
❶【水などが】flow ⓐ, run* ⓐ
ナイル川はエジプトを流れている The Nile *flows [runs]* through Egypt.
彼女のほおを涙が流れた Tears *ran down* her cheeks.
◆小川がさらさら流れている The brook *is murmuring.* / 彼の体の中には小説家の血が流れている The blood of a novelist *courses* through his veins. / トイレの水が流れません The toilet won't *flush.*
❷【物が移動する】flow ⓐ
雲が上空をゆっくりと流れていく Clouds *are flowing away* slowly high in the sky.
車は順調に流れている Traffic *is flowing* smoothly.
◆大きな桃が下流へと流れていった A big peach *floated away* downstream.
❸【時が】
またたく間に5年の歳月が流れた Five years *flowed [passed] away* in no time.
❹【その他】
その小説に流れるモチーフ a motif that *runs through* the novel
その電線には電流が流れている Electricity *is flowing* through the wire.
このあたりで妙なうわさが流れているのを知ってるかい Do you know a strange rumor *is circulating* around here?
二人の間に気まずい沈黙が流れた There *was* an awkward silence between the two.
雨で体育祭が流れた Our field day *was 「rained out [called off]* because of the rain].
質に入れた指輪が流れてしまった The ring I had pawned *was forfeited.*

なき¹ 亡き dead, deceased; (故…) late /彼女の亡き夫 her *late* husband

なき² 泣き 慣用表現 今急いていると後で泣きを見る(→ひどい目にあう)ぞ If you are lazy now, *you'll have a hard time later*. / 先生に泣きを入れてレポートの提出期限を先に延ばしてもらった I *begged [pleaded with]* the teacher to put off the deadline for the report.

なぎ 凪 calm ⓤ《また a ～》/朝[夕]なぎ *a morning [an evening] calm*

なきあかす 泣き明かす 一晩泣き明かしたので彼女の目は真っ赤だった Her eyes were red because she *had cried all night.*

なきおとし 泣き落とし 泣き落としにかかる try to 「*persuade a person [win a person over]* with tears」

なきがお 泣き顔 crying face ⓒ; (涙ぐんだ顔) tearful face ⓒ /彼女の泣き顔を見たことがない I have never seen her *crying [tearful]* face.

なきがら 亡骸 (dead) body ⓒ, corpse ⓒ

なきくずれる 泣き崩れる その知らせに彼女は泣き崩れた She *broke down in [dissolved into]* tears at the news.

なきごえ¹ 泣き声 (人の) cry ⓒ; (すすり泣き) sob ⓒ /赤ちゃんの泣き声が聞こえるよ I hear 「*a baby's cry [a baby crying]*」.

なきごえ² 鳴き声 (鳥の) song ⓒ; (犬の) bark ⓒ; (猫の) meow ⓒ; (鳥・虫の) chirp ⓒ /鳥の鳴き声で目がさめた Bird *songs* woke me up.

なきごと 泣き言 whine ⓒ; (不平) complaint ⓒ ⓤ; (ぶつぶつ言う不平) grumble ⓒ
◆彼女は仕事に関して決して泣き言を言わない She never *complains [whines]* about her work.

なぎさ 渚 beach ⓒ; (海岸) shore ⓒ

なきさけぶ 泣き叫ぶ wail ⓐ; (金切り声をあげて) scream ⓐ ⓑ /泣き叫ぶ子供をなだめる quiet (down) a *screaming* child / 彼は痛くて泣き叫んだ He *wailed* with pain.

なきじゃくる 泣きじゃくる blubber ⓐ; (むせび泣く) sob ⓐ

なぎたおす なぎ倒す mow* down; (風が) blow* down; (次々に負かす) beat* ... one after another /きのうの強風で花壇のバラがなぎ倒された The roses in the flower bed *were blown down* by yesterday's strong wind. / 彼は柔道の試合でみいる強豪をなぎ倒した In a judo tournament, he *beat* one strong opponent *after another.*

なきだす 泣き出す 突然彼女は泣きだした Suddenly, she *started crying.*(❖「わっと泣きだす」は burst into tears という)
慣用表現 泣きだしそうな空模様 a *threatening* sky

なきつく 泣き付く 彼女は宿題を手伝ってと兄に泣きついた(→懇願した) She *begged* her brother to help with her homework.

なきっつら 泣きっ面 ことわざ 泣きっ面に蜂 When it rains, it pours.(→降ればどしゃ降り)

なきどころ 泣き所 (弱点) weakness ⓒ,

weak point ◯ ∥泣き所を突かれる be hit in *the weak point* ◆テーブルに弁慶の泣き所(→向こうずね)をぶつけてしまった I hit *my shin* against the table.

なきねいり 泣き寝入り レイプの被害者の多くは泣き寝入りするといわれている Many rape victims are said to *suffer in silence*.

なきはらす 泣き腫らす 泣きはらした顔 *one's* face *swollen from crying*

なきふす 泣き伏す 彼は「彼女が死んだ」と言ってわっと泣き伏した He said, "She died," and *threw himself down in tears*.

なきべそ 泣きべそ その男の子は道に迷って泣きべそをかいていた Having lost his way, the boy *was whimpering [sobbing]*.

なきまね 泣き真似 心配するな。どうせまた泣きまねに決まってるよ Don't worry. She must *be pretending to cry* again.

なきむし 泣き虫 《口語的》crybaby ◯

なきわらい 泣き笑い tearful smile ◯ ― 泣き笑いする smile tearfully

なく¹ 泣く

cry ◉; (涙を流して泣く)《公式的》weep* ◉; (すすり泣く) sob ◉ ◎; (泣き叫ぶ) wail ◉ ◎

cry　weep　sob

もう泣かないで *Don't cry* any more.
その子供はなかなか泣きやまなかった The child *wouldn't stop crying*.
彼は人目も気にせず声をあげて泣いた He *cried out loud*, not caring what people around would think.
もうどうしていいか分からない。泣きたい気分だよ I don't know what to do. I *feel like crying*.
優勝したときはみんなうれしくて泣いてしまった We all *cried [wept] for* joy when we won the championship.
その歌手の告別式で多くのファンが(涙を流して)泣いた Many fans *wept* at the singer's funeral.
夜中に女の人の泣く声が聞こえた Late at night I heard a woman *sobbing*.
「行かないでほしい」と彼は泣きながら言った "Please don't go," he *sobbed*. (◆この sob は「泣きながら言う」の意味)
女の子はそのクマのぬいぐるみを泣いて欲しがった The girl *was crying for* the teddy bear.
◆僕らのチームはその試合でわずか1点の差に泣いた(→負けた) Our team *lost* the game by only one point.
慣用表現 泣いても笑っても試験まであと2日だ *(Whether you) like it or not*, there are only two days left before the examination.

なく² 鳴く (一般に) cry ◉; (鳥がさえずる) sing* ◉; (小鳥・虫が) chirp ◉
耳をすましてごらん。コオロギが鳴いているよ Listen! The crickets *are chirping*.
スズメのちゅんちゅん鳴く声で目がさめた I awoke to 「the sound of the sparrows *singing [the song* of sparrows].

使い分け

動物・虫	動詞
アヒル (duck)	quack
犬 (dog)	(ほえる) bark; (うなる) growl; (遠ぼえする) howl; (くんくん鳴く) whine; (きゃんきゃん鳴く) yelp
馬 (horse)	neigh, whinny
雄牛 (bull)	bellow
おんどり (rooster)	crow
カエル (frog)	croak
ガチョウ (goose)	cackle, honk
カラス (crow)	caw
コオロギ (cricket)	chirp
猿 (monkey)	chatter
スズメ (sparrow)	chirp
猫 (cat, kitten)	meow, miaow, mew
ネズミ (mouse, rat)	squeak
ハト (dove, pigeon)	coo
羊 (sheep)	baa, bleat
ヒバリ (lark)	sing, warble
フクロウ (owl)	hoot
豚 (pig)	grunt, oink
雌牛, 乳牛 (cow)	moo
めんどり (hen)	cackle

なぐ 凪ぐ (海が) calm down, become* calm; (風が) die away [down]

なぐさみ 慰み amusement ◎ ◯, pleasure ◎ ◯; (娯楽) entertainment ◎ ◯; (気晴らし) pastime ◯ ∥彼の唯一の慰みは将棋を指すことだった His only *amusement [pleasure]* was to play *shogi*.

なぐさめ 慰め comfort ◎ ◯, consolation ◎ ◯ ∥人に慰めの言葉をかける speak words of *comfort [consolation]* to a person ∥雄一の言葉は何の慰めにもならなかった What Yuichi said was no *comfort [consolation]* to me.

なぐさめる 慰める (ほっとさせる) comfort ◎; (同情する) console ◎; (元気づける) cheer up ∥遺族を慰める *console* the be-

なくす

reaved family / 僕は落ち込んでいる彼女を何とか慰めようとした I tried to 「*comfort* her [*cheer* her *up*]」 because she was depressed. / 彼女はそういう運命だったのだと自ら慰めた She *consoled herself* by thinking that it had been her fate.
◆故人の霊を慰める *pray for* the dead

なくす¹ 無くす (失う) lose* 他; (規則・制度などを) do* away with ... / いつのまにかばんをなくしたのか思い出せない I can't remember when I *lost* my bag. / 近ごろすっかりサッカーに興味をなくしてしまった Recently I have completely *lost* interest in soccer. / こんな意味のない規則はなくしたほうがいい We should *do away with* such a nonsensical rule.
◆いじめをなくす(→根絶する)ように全力を尽くしましょう Let's do our best to *root out* bullying.

なくす² 亡くす lose* 他 / 私はその事故で[癌(がん)で]友人を亡くした I *lost* my friend 「*in* that accident [*to* cancer]. (❖事故などの場合には in, 病気の場合には to を用いる) / 両親を亡くして初めて親の愛情を知った *Having lost* my parents, I appreciated their love for the first time.

-なくて -無くて お金を使わなくても楽しめることはたくさんある There are a lot of things you can enjoy *without* spending any money. / その植物は水がほとんどなくてもよく育つ The plant can flourish *with little* water. / ほかにすべきことがなくて彼はテレビを見た He watched TV *for lack [want] of* anything better to do. / お金がなくてステレオが買えない I'm *too poor* to buy a stereo. / ボウリングの球は投げるんじゃなくて転がすんだよ You *don't* throw a bowling ball. You roll it. / 空席がなくて車中に立っていなければならなかった There were *no* vacant seats on the train, *so* I had to stand.

なくてはならない 無くてはならない 空気はほとんどの生物になくてはならないものだ Air is *indispensable* [*essential*] to most living creatures.

なくなく 泣く泣く (いやいや) reluctantly, unwillingly / 犬を飼うことを母親に猛反対され,彼女は泣く泣くあきらめた She *reluctantly* gave up the idea of having a dog because her mother strongly objected.

なくなる¹ 無くなる
❶【紛失する】be gone; (見当たらない) be missing; (消える) disappear 自; (なくす) lose* 他
帽子がなくなったんだけど、どこに行ったか知らない？ My cap *is gone* [*missing*]. Did you see where it went?
戻ってみると車がなくなっていた When I came back, my car *was gone* [*had disappeared, was nowhere to be found*].
◆なくなった時計をあちこち捜した I looked everywhere for my *lost* [*missing*] watch.
❷【尽きる】run* out; (不足する) run short
お金がなくなってきた I'm *running out of* money. / My money *is running out*.

燃料がなくなりかけている We're *running short of* fuel. / Fuel *is running short*.
❸【存在しなくなる】
そのときにはもう帰るバスがなくなっていた There were *no* more buses going home then.
その手の音楽には興味がなくなった I've *lost* interest in that kind of music.
その薬を飲んだら痛みがなくなった The pain *was gone* after I took the medicine.
こんな恐ろしい病気はいつかこの世からなくなってほしい I hope someday the world will be 「*rid of* [*free from*]」 these awful diseases.

なくなる² 亡くなる pass away (❖*die* の婉曲的な言い方) / 彼女は 3 年前に亡くなりました She *passed away* three years ago.
◆彼が亡くなって10年になる It is [has been] 10 years since his *death*.

なぐりあい 殴り合い (fist) fight Ⓒ / 会合は殴り合いの場と化した The meeting turned into a *fist fight*. ◆殴り合いを始める begin 「to *fight* [*fighting*]; come to *blows*

なぐりがき 殴り書き scribble Ⓤ (また a ～), scrawl Ⓒ Ⓤ ――なぐり書きする scribble 他, scrawl 他 / 机の上になぐり書きのメモが残されていた There were some *scribbled* notes left on the desk.

なぐりこみ 殴り込み (襲撃) raid / ...に殴り込みをかける make *a raid* on ...
◆海外市場に殴り込みをかける make *one's way* into foreign markets

なぐる 殴る hit* 他 自, strike* 他 自; (続けざまに) beat* 他 自; (強く) knock 他; (こぶしで) punch 他; 人を殴り倒す *knock* a person *down* / 彼は僕の顔を[頭を]殴った He *hit* me 「*in* the face [*on* the head]. (❖He hit my face. とすると殴られた部分が強調される) / 泥棒は警官に殴りかかった The thief *hit* the policeman. / 男は彼をバットで殴った The man *hit* him with a bat. / 私は父にあざができるほど殴られた I was beaten black and blue by my father. / あまりにも腹が立ったので彼を殴りそうになった I got so angry that I *almost punched* him.

なげ 投げ throw Ⓒ / (野球の)上手投げ an overhand *throw*; (相撲の) an outer-arm *throw* / 投げ技 a throwing technique

なげいれる 投げ入れる 紙くずをごみ箱に投げ入れる *throw* the wastepaper *into* a trash can

なげうつ 擲つ 部長の職をなげうつ give up *one's* position as manager / 命をなげうって (→犠牲にして) *at the cost* [*sacrifice*] *of one's* life / 彼は事業のためにすべてをなげうった He *sacrificed* everything for the business.

なげうり 投げ売り 在庫品を投げ売りする sell the stock *at a loss* [*sacrifice*]

なげかける 投げ掛ける cast* 他, throw* 他 / 原発の安全性に疑問を投げかける *cast* [*throw*] doubt on the safety of nuclear power / 問題に新たな光を投げかける *cast* a new light on the matter

なげかわしい 嘆かわしい deplorable; (残念

だ) regrettable ‖最近の若者が社会問題に無関心なのは実に嘆かわしい It *is* really *deplorable* that young people today are indifferent to social problems. ◆嘆かわしいことに会議の出席者はほとんどいなかった *Regrettably*, few people attended the meeting.

なげき 嘆き grief, sorrow ‖彼のギャンブル好きは家族の嘆きの種だ His love of gambling *is the source of* his family's grief [*sorrow*].

なげキッス 投げキッス 彼はスタンドを埋め尽くした観衆に投げキッスを送った He *threw a kiss to* the spectators that filled the stands.

なげく 嘆く （慨嘆する）《公式的》deplore；（悲しむ） grieve；（嘆息する） sigh ‖政治腐敗を嘆く *deplore* political corruption / 自分の身の不運を嘆いている暇はなかった I didn't have time to *grieve for* [*over*] my misfortune.

なげこむ 投げ込む 彼は空きびんをごみ箱に投げ込んだ He *threw* [*pitched*] the empty bottle *into* the trash can.

なげすてる 投げ捨てる throw* away ◆窓から缶を投げ捨てたのはだれだ Who *threw* the can out of the window?

なげだす 投げ出す 足を投げ出す *stretch out one's legs* / ベッドに身を投げ出す *throw oneself* on a bed / 仕事を投げ出す *give up one's job* / 衝突の衝撃で運転手はフロントガラスから投げ出された The impact of the crash *threw* the driver through the windshield. / 彼は自分の命を投げ出して(→犠牲にして)その子を救った He saved the child by *sacrificing* his own life.

なげつける 投げ付ける 弟は私にその本を投げつけた My brother *threw* [*flung, hurled*] the book *at* me.

なげとばす 投げ飛ばす レスラーは相手を場外に投げ飛ばした The wrestler *threw* the opponent out of the ring.

なけなし 無けなし 彼はなけなしの金をはたいてその本を買った He spent *what little* money he *had* on the book.

なげやり¹ 投げ遣り ──投げやりな （ぞんざいな） sloppy, slipshod ‖投げやりに仕事をする do *one's* work *in a slipshod way* [*any which way*] / 彼は仕事がとても投げやりだ He's so *sloppy* [*slipshod*] in his work.
◆彼女の投げやりな(→無責任な)態度にみんな腹を立てた Everyone got angry at her *irresponsible* behavior.

なげやり² 投げ槍 （競技用の） javelin；（武器） spear, lance

なける 泣ける その映画はいつ見ても泣ける The movie always 「*makes me cry* [*moves me to tears*]. / 彼女がわざわざ訪ねてきてくれたのでうれしくて泣けてきた I 「*felt like crying* [*was close to tears*] with joy because she came all the way to see me.

なげる 投げる

❶【放る】 throw*；（ねらいを定めて） pitch；（軽く） toss
塀の向こうにボールを投げる *throw* a ball over the fence / 速球を投げる *throw* [*pitch*] a fastball / 湖に身を投げる *throw oneself* into the lake
窓から缶を投げるな Don't *throw* a can out of the window.
その男の子は空き缶めがけて石を投げた The boy *threw* a stone *at* the empty can. ❖throw ... at ～ は「…を～めがけて投げつける」の意味）
彼は私にタオルを投げてよこした He *threw* a towel *to* me. ❖throw ... to ～ は「…を～に投げ与える」の意味） / He *threw* me a towel.
あまり遠くまでは投げられない I can't *throw* very far.
（野球で）彼は最初の2回を投げた He *pitched* for the first two innings.

❷【あきらめる】 give* up
最初から試合を投げちゃいけないよ Don't *give up* the game from the beginning.

❸【視線・光・疑惑などを】 cast* ⇒ なげかける
人に視線を投げる *cast* a glance at a person

-なければ
もし太陽がなければ生物はみな死んでしまうだろう *Without* the sun [*If it were not for* the sun], every living thing would die.
私の記憶に間違いがなければ彼女はそのとき私たちといっしょにいた *If* my memory *doesn't* fail me [*Unless* my memory fails me], she was with us then.
雨が降っていなければ外出できるのに *If* it *wasn't* raining, we could go out. (❖unlessは仮定法の文では用いられない)
単語のつづりが分からなければ辞書で調べなさい *If* you *can't* spell the word, look it up in the dictionary.
何もなければ伺うつもりです We'll come and see you 「*if nothing* [*unless something*] *prevents us*.
君でなければ(→君以外の人は)彼を説得できない Nobody *but* you can persuade him.
パステル, それがなければ色鉛筆を持ってきなさい Bring pastels, or *failing* that, colored pencils.
おじゃまでなければよいのですが I hope I'm *not* disturbing you.

-なければならない must ⇒ -ならない

なこうど 仲人 a nakodo, a matchmaker；（仲介者） a go-between ‖私の両親がその二人の仲人をした My parents acted as *nakodo* [*matchmakers*] for the couple.

仲人とは男女の間に立って結婚の仲立ちをする人のことです. 本来は男女を引き合わせ, 結婚を見届ける立会人のことでしたが, 最近では結婚式当日にだけ立ち会う形式的な役割がほとんどで, 結婚式で仲人を立てないカップルもいます.
Nakodo are people who make the arrangements for couples to come together to get married. Originally they introduced the bride and groom to each

other and served as witnesses to the marriage, but recently most *nakodo* only play a ceremonial role at weddings, and some couples have weddings without *nakodo*.

なごむ 和む 彼女の絵を見ると心がなごむ My heart *softens* [I *feel at ease*] when I see her paintings. / 彼のスピーチで会場の雰囲気はなごんだ His speech 「*relaxed* the atmosphere [*lightened* the mood] of the place.

なごやか 和やか ━━なごやかな （友好的な） friendly; （平穏な） peaceful 〃話し合いはなごやかな雰囲気で行われた The talks were held in a *friendly* atmosphere.

なごり 名残 ❶【跡】 trace Ⓒ Ⓤ; （遺物） remains, relic Ⓒ 〃その町にはかつての繁栄の名残をどこにもとどめていない The town retains no *traces* of its former prosperity. / その町のあちこちにまだ戦争の名残が見られる *Traces* of war can still be seen all over the town.
❷【別れ】 名残惜しいですがもう行かなければなりません I *hate to say this*, *but* I must go now. / 彼は名残惜しそうに我々に手を振っていた He was waving good-by to us *as if he hated to leave*.

ナサ NASA (❖ *National Aeronautics and Space Administration*（米国航空宇宙局）の略語)

-なさい 好きなようにしなさい *Do* as you like. / 一生懸命練習しなさい，そうすればレギュラーになれるかもしれないよ You *must* practice hard, and then you may be a regular member of the team. / 恥を知りなさい You *should* be ashamed of yourself. / 母は私に行儀よくしなさいと言った My mother *told* me to behave (myself).

なさけ 情け （同情） sympathy Ⓤ, compassion Ⓤ; （親切） kindness Ⓤ; （慈悲） mercy Ⓤ; （哀れみ） pity; （慈善） charity Ⓒ 〃人の情けにすがって生きる live on 「*other people's kindness* [*charity*] / あんなやつに情けをかける必要はない You don't have to show 「*sympathy* for [*kindness* to, *mercy* to] a man like that. / 彼はお情けで私の失敗を見逃してくれた He overlooked my failure *out of pity*. / どうかお情けを Please have *mercy* on me. ◆情け容赦ない攻撃 a *merciless* attack / その強制労働収容所では多くの捕虜が情け容赦なく働かされた Many prisoners were *mercilessly* forced to work at the labor camp. ことわざ 情けは人のためならず One who is kind to others is sure to be rewarded.; Charity is a good investment. (→慈善はよい投資である)

なさけしらず 情け知らず ━━情け知らずの （無慈悲な） merciless; （無情な） pitiless; （冷酷な） heartless; （残酷な） cruel

なさけない 情けない，（哀れな） pitiful; （みじめな） miserable; （恥ずべき） shameful; （嘆かわしい） （公式的） deplorable
そんな情けない言い訳は聞きたくない I don't want to hear such a *pitiful* excuse.

情けない顔して，何かあったの You look so *miserable*. What's up?
君がそんなことをするとは情けない It's *shameful* [*a shame*, *a pity*] that you did such a thing.
◆情けないほど弱い野球チーム a *pitifully* weak baseball team / 自分の能力のなさに我ながら情けなかった I 「*was ashamed of* [*felt humbled by*] my lack of ability. / 情けない話だが私は犬が怖い *I'm ashamed to say this*, *but* I'm afraid of dogs.
❷「疲れちゃった，休憩しない？」「まだ10分しか歩いてないよ．情けないなぁ」 "Why don't we take a rest? I'm tired." "We've walked for only 10 minutes. How *pathetic*!"

なさけぶかい 情け深い，（慈悲深い） charitable, merciful; （哀れみ深い） compassionate; （心の優しい） kindhearted

なざし 名指し 彼らは私を名指しで非難した They accused me *by name*.

なし¹ 梨 Japanese pear Ⓒ; （洋ナシ） pear Ⓒ 慣用表現 それ以来彼からはなしのつぶてだ I've *heard nothing from* him since then.

なし² 無し 何の気なしに *without* any special intentions / 予告なしに *without* notice / 文句なしの演技 a *perfect* performance / 種なしブドウ *seedless* grapes / きょうは仕事の話はなしにしよう *Let's not talk about* business today. / コーヒーはミルク入りにしますか，なしにしますか Do you like your coffee with milk or *without*? / 私は毎朝目覚ましなしで目がさめます I awake *without* using an alarm clock every morning. / 交替なしで5時間働きづめだった I worked for five hours *with no relief*. / このネクタイが気に入らなければ，ネクタイなしですますしかないよ If you don't like this tie, you'll just have to *do without* (one).

なしくずし 済し崩し そのきまりごとはなし崩し的に（→何の議論もなく）無視されるようになった That rule came to be ignored *without formal discussion*.

なしとげる 成し遂げる （達成する） accomplish ⊕, achieve ⊕ ⊕; （やりとげる） carry out [through] 〃偉業を成しとげる *accomplish* [*perform*] a feat / この計画を成しとげるには大変な努力がいるだろう It would take a great deal of effort to *carry out* this project.

なじみ 馴染み ━━なじみの （お気に入りの） favorite; （よく知っている） familiar 〃なじみのレストラン *one's favorite* restaurant / なじみの顔 a *familiar* face / この町にはまだあまりなじみがない I'm not really *familiar with* this town yet. / This town is not really *familiar to* me yet.
◆なじみの客 a *regular* customer

なじむ 馴染む ❶【慣れる】 get* used [accustomed] to ...; （順応する） adapt [adjust] (*oneself*) to ...; （愛着をもつ） become* attached to ... 〃新しい環境になじむ *adapt* [*adjust*] (*oneself*) *to* new surroundings / その土地の料理にはどうもなじめなかった I just *couldn't get used to* the local food.

❷【調和する】新しいグローブを手になじませる *break* a new baseball glove *in* / このシャツは肌になじんできた This shirt *has become comfortable.* / 一晩おけば味がなじむよ(→よくなる) It'*ll taste better* if you let it sit overnight. / このカーテンの色は私の部屋になじまない The color of these curtains *doesn't* 「*match* (*with*) [*go well with, suit*] my room.

ナショナリズム nationalism [U]

[関連語] ナショナリスト a nationalist

なじる 詰る (非難する) blame [他], reproach [他] ∥彼は私の不注意をなじった He *blamed* [*reproached*] me *for* my carelessness.

なす[1] 為す なすすべがない状態 a *hopeless* situation / それは全く予想外のことでなすすべがなかった It was quite unexpected and I *didn't know what to do.* / 父は私のやることなすことに口を出す My father is always meddling in *everything I do.* / 彼らのなすがままにさせてはいけない We should not let them *have it their own way.*

なす[2] 成す 名を成す *make a name* (*for oneself*); *make one's name* / 財を成す *make a fortune* / 君の言うことは意味を成していない What you say *makes no sense.*

なす[3] 茄子 《主に米》 eggplant [C] [U], 《英》 aubergine [C][U]

なすりあい 擦り合い 責任のなすり合いをしている場合ではない This is no time for *blaming* [*putting the blame on*] *each other.*

なすりつける 擦り付ける (こすりつける) rub [他]; (泥・ペンキなどを) daub [他] ∥絵の具をカンバスになすりつける *daub* paint *on* a canvas; *daub* a canvas with paint

◆彼らは他人に罪をなすりつけようとした They tried to 「*put the blame on* [*shift the blame to*] other people.

なする 擦る (こすりつける) rub [他]; (泥・ペンキなどを) daub [他]

なぜ 何故

why; how come, what ... for (❖共にくだけた言い方)

なぜそんなにふさいでいるの *Why* are you so gloomy? / *What makes* you so gloomy?

なぜ英語を習わなければならないか分からない I don't know *why* I have to learn English. (❖×why to learn English は不可)

なぜ宿題をやってないんだ *How come* you haven't done your homework? (❖How come の後ろはふつうの文の語順のまま)

なぜ香港に行くのですか *What* are you going to Hong Kong *for*? (❖What に強勢を置く. for に強勢を置くと目的を強調する)

いったいなぜそんなことをしたんだ *Why ever* [*on earth, in the world*] did you do that?

なぜ彼女はそんなことをしたがるんだろう *Why* should she want to do that? (❖この should は話し手の不可解・いらだちを表す)

なぜ新しいラケットを買うの *Why* buy a new racket? (❖《Why＋動詞の原形》は「なぜ…するのか, …しないほうがよい」の意味)

[会]「先週はなぜ休んだの」「ひどいかぜをひいてしまってね」 "*Why* were you absent last week?" "Because I had a bad cold." (❖理由をいう場合, 答えは because で始める)

[会]「なぜきのう銀座へ行ったの」「映画を見るためさ」 "*Why* did you go to Ginza yesterday?" "To see a movie." (❖目的をいう場合, 答えは不定詞で始めることが多い)

[会]「彼の言うことは信用しないほうがいいよ」「なぜ」 "You'd better not believe what he says." "*Why not?* / *How come?*" (❖否定・禁止などに対して問い返すときは why の後に not を付ける)

[会]「なぜあんなことをしたのかわけを話して」「自分でもなぜなのか分からない」 "Tell me *why* you did a thing like that." "I'm wondering *why* myself."

なぜか 何故か 彼はとても勤勉だがなぜか成功しない He is very hard-working, but *somehow* he never succeeds. / あなたにはなぜかとても親しみを感じるの *I don't know why*, but I feel very close to you. / なぜか知らないけど彼は彼女のことが好きではないようだ *For some reason*, he doesn't seem to like her.

なぜなら 何故なら because; since; 《公式的》 for

> because: 直接の原因・理由を表す.
> since: 話し手・聞き手が互いに承知していることを理由に述べるときに用いる. 通例文頭に置かれる.
> for: 原則として文頭には置かず, 主節の後に通例コンマで区切って補足的な理由を述べるときに用いる.

私は彼女の顔をまともに見られなかった. なぜならうそをついていたから I couldn't look her straight in the eye *because* I had told a lie. / 彼は無罪となるにちがいない. なぜなら確かなアリバイがあるからだ He is certain to be proved innocent, *for* he has a strong alibi.

なぞ 謎 ❶【不思議】 mystery [C][U], riddle [C] ―なぞの mysterious ➔ [場面・状況別会話] p.1722 ∥不可解ななぞ *a* deep *mystery* / なぞを解く手がかり a key [clue] to *a mystery* / なぞの多い人物 a *mysterious* person / 彼の生い立ちはなぞに包まれている His early history is cloaked [shrouded] in *mystery.* / 彼女にはなぞめいたところがある There is something *mysterious* about her.

❷【ほのめかし】 hint [C] ∥彼は彼女になぞをかけてみたが, 通じていないようだった He *was dropping* her *hints*, but she didn't seem to see what he meant.

なぞなぞ 謎々 riddle [C] ∥なぞなぞを解く solve *a riddle* / 人になぞなぞを出す ask a person *a riddle*

なぞらえる 準える 人生はよく航海になぞらえられる Life *is* often *compared* [*likened*] *to* a voyage.

なぞる 手本をなぞって字を練習する practice handwriting by *tracing* a model

なた 鉈 (手おの) hatchet [C]

なだかい 名高い famous, well-known ∥その村は美しい海岸で名高い The village *is famous for* its beautiful beach.

なたね 菜種 rapeseed ©⓪ ∥菜種油 rapeseed oil

なだめる 宥める soothe ⊕; (落ち着かせる) calm ⊕; (怒りなどをやわらげる) appease ⊕; (説得する) coax ∥お菓子で泣く子をなだめる *soothe* [*calm*] a crying child with sweets / 人の怒りをなだめる *soothe* [*calm, appease*] a person's anger / 子供をなだめすかして薬を飲ませる *coax* a child [*into* taking [*to* take] a medicine

なだらか ──なだらかな gentle ∥なだらかな坂 [丘] a *gentle* slope [hill]
◆その道はなだらかな上り坂になっている The road slopes *gently* upward.

なだれ 雪崩 avalanche ©, snowslide © ∥ 雪崩にあう be struck by *an avalanche* ∥表層雪崩 a surface avalanche

なだれこむ 雪崩れ込む バーゲン品目当ての客が店にどっとなだれ込んだ The bargain hunters *rushed* [*surged*] *into* the store.

ナチス the Nazis
[関連語] ナチズム Nazism / ナチ党員 a Nazi

なつ 夏
summer ©⓪

夏の盛りに *at the height of summer* / 夏の初め [終わり] に「*in the beginning* [*at the end*] *of summer*

夏にはたくさんの人が海水浴に行く Many people go swimming in the sea *in* (*the*) *summer*.

山でこの夏を過ごすつもりだ I will spend *this summer* in the mountains.

夏中ずっと雨が降らなかった We had no rain *all through the summer*.

ひと夏に何回ぐらい海に行きますか How many times do you go to the beach *each summer*?

毎年夏にはこの島に日本からたくさんの観光客が訪れる *Every summer* this island gets a lot of visitors from Japan. (❖every, last, next, this などを伴う場合, 前置詞は不要)

夏になると彼のことを思い出す *When summer comes*, I think of him.

∥夏かぜ a summer cold / 夏時間《米》daylight saving time 《略語》DST, 《英》summer time / 夏場所 the Summer Sumo Tournament / 夏日 a day when the highest temperature is above 25℃ / 夏祭り a summer festival / 夏物 summer clothes / 初夏 early summer / 盛夏 midsummer / 晩夏 late summer / 真夏日 a day when the highest temperature is above 30℃ / 冷夏 a cold summer

なついん 捺印 ──捺印する set* [put*] *one's seal on* ... (❖欧米には日本の印鑑に当たるものはない. 公式文書などでは権威をもたせるために蠟にしたろうの上から印を押すこともあるが, 一般には署名(signature)ですませる) ⇒ はん (判)

なつかしい 懐かしい (❖英語にぴったり当てはまる語がないので文脈に応じて意訳する)

故郷をなつかしがる *think fondly of one's* hometown

なつかしい友達(→旧友)から思いがけず電話があった A *dear old friend* called me unexpectedly.

ああ, 日本食がなつかしいなあ (→日本食がなくて寂しい) Oh, I *miss* Japanese food!

私たちがいっしょに過ごしたころをなつかしく思い出します I have *good memories of* our days together.

その写真を見るとなつかしさで胸がいっぱいになる The picture fills me with *nostalgia*.

なつかしむ 懐かしむ 過ぎた日をなつかしむ *look back nostalgically on* the past

なつく 懐く become* [be] attached to ...; (好きになる) take* to ...; (好きである) like ⊕ ∥このクマは飼育係によくなついている This bear *is quite attached to* its keeper. / その男の子はおじいさんによくなついている The boy *likes* his grandfather very much.

ナックルボール [野球] knuckleball

なづけおや 名付け親 godparent ©; (男) godfather ©; (女) godmother © (❖いずれもキリスト教の洗礼時の後見人)
◆その動物園では新しく生まれたカバの名づけ親を募集している The zoo is asking the public to *suggest a name* for the baby hippo.

なづける 名付ける name ⊕ ∥私はその子犬をチッパーと名づけた I *named* the puppy Chipper. / 彼女はおばにちなんで真理子と名づけられた She *was named* Mariko after her aunt.

ナッツ nut ©

なっとう 納豆 🔺

日本の代表的健康食品である納豆は, 蒸した大豆を納豆菌とともに発酵させたものです. 消化がよく, タンパク質・カルシウム・鉄・ビタミン類を多く含んでいます. しかし, 多くの外国人同様, 納豆特有の臭みとねばりが苦手な日本人もいます. 食べ方はいろいろですが, 少量のからし, しょうゆ, 刻んだネギを加え, ごはんにかけて食べるのが最も一般的です.
Natto, a typical Japanese health food, is made of soybeans steamed and then fermented with *natto* bacilli. It is an easily digested food and rich in protein, calcium, iron and vitamins. But its strong smell and stickiness are intolerable for some Japanese as well as for many foreigners. Although there are many ways of eating it, *natto* is most commonly mixed with a little mustard, soy sauce and chopped green onion and eaten as a topping for rice.

なっとく 納得 (満足) satisfaction ⓪; (同意) consent ⓪; (理解する) understand* ⊕©; (満足する) be satisfied

納得のいかないことが多すぎる There're too many things I don't *understand*.

そんな説明では納得できない I'm not *satisfied with* that explanation.

みんなが納得のいくように説明するのは難しい

It's hard to explain *to everyone's satisfaction*.
彼らは双方納得のうえでそうすることに決めた They decided to do so *by mutual consent*.
◆要求に対する納得のいく返答 a *satisfying [satisfactory]* answer to the demand / うまく彼を納得させることができた I had success in *convincing* him. / それで納得がいったよ Now I've got it.

なっぱ 菜っ葉 greens

なつばて 夏ばて このところ夏ばてぎみだ I'm a little *worn out with the summer heat* these days. / 夏ばてしないように十分な睡眠を心がけている I'm trying to sleep well in order not to *be exhausted from the summer heat*.

ナップサック knapsack ⓒ

なつみかん 夏蜜柑 a summer orange with a thick rind

なつメロ 懐メロ old popular song ⓒ,《口語的》oldie

なつやすみ 夏休み《米》summer vacation Ⓤ,《英》summer holidays / 夏休みは 7 月 20 日から 8 月 31 日までです *Summer vacation* is from July 20 to August 31. / 学校は来週から夏休みです Our school closes for (the) *summer vacation* next week. / 夏休みをどうやって過ごそうかと考えているところです I'm wondering how to spend (the [my]) *summer vacation*. / 夏休みの宿題はもう終わったの? Have you finished *your homework for summer vacation* yet?

なつやせ 夏痩せ 私はいつも夏やせする I always *lose some weight in summer*.

なでおろす 撫で下ろす 彼は無事だと聞いて胸をなで下ろした I *was [felt] relieved* to hear that he was safe.

なでがた 撫で肩 sloping shoulders

なでしこ 撫子 pink ⓒ

なでつける 撫で付ける 髪をなでつける(→整える) fix one's hair

なでる 撫でる stroke 他;(動物・子供などを) pet 他 /彼は優しく私のほおをなでた He *stroked* my cheek softly. / 犬はなでられるのが好きだ Dogs like *being petted [stroked]*.
◆夜風が私のほおをなでた The night breeze *touched [caressed]* my cheeks.

など 等
❶【同類】and so on [forth], etc. [et sétrə] (❖英語の and so on に当たるラテン語 et cetera の略語. 商業文・専門書などで用いられる. 文中では通例 and so on [forth]と読む);(例えば…のような) such as ...,《口語的》like
文房具屋で鉛筆や消しゴムなどを買った We bought pencils, erasers, *and 「so on [so forth, the like]* at a stationery shop. (❖前に 2 つ以上の項目を挙げるのがふつう)
私は食べ物, 衣服, 食器などを買った I bought food, clothes, dishes, *etc.* (❖etc.の前にはコンマを打ち, and を付けない. 前が 1 語の場合はコンマは不要)
彼はパリ, ソウルなどたくさんの外国の都市を訪れている He has visited many foreign cities, 「*such as [like]* Paris and Seoul.
❷【打ち消しを強める】
豪華なドレスなどではなく, ごくふつうの物が欲しいんです I just want a casual dress, *nothing* fancy.
彼は決して初心者などではない He *is no* beginner.
彼女には私の気持ちなど決して分からないだろう She will *never* understand my feelings.
❸【謙遜・軽蔑】
私などそんな重要な職務にふさわしくありません Such an important position is not for *the likes of* me.
それが用をなすなら見てくれなどどうでもよい As long as it works, I don't care what it looks like *at all*.

ナトー NATO [néitou] (❖the *N*orth *A*tlantic *T*reaty *O*rganization(北大西洋条約機構) の略語)

ナトリウム ⚠【化学】sodium Ⓤ (❖日本語はドイツ語の Natrium から. 元素記号 Na) ∥塩化ナトリウム *sodium* chloride

なな 七 seven;(7 番目) seventh

ななかいき 七回忌 the sixth anniversary of *a person's* death;(法要) a memorial service held on the sixth anniversary of *a person's* death

ななくさ 七草 春[秋]の七草 *the seven herbs* of spring [fall]

ななころびやおき 七転び八起き 慣用表現 人生は七転び八起きだ *Life is full of ups and downs*. (❖ups and downs は「(人生などの)浮き沈み」の意味)

ななじゅう 七十 seventy;(70 番目) seventieth

ななつ 七つ seven Ⓤ ⓒ ➪ なな ∥七つ道具 a complete set of tools

ななひかり 七光 彼は父親の七光でその地位についた He got the position through *the influence* of his father.

ななふしぎ 七不思議 世界の七不思議 *the Seven Wonders of the World*

ななめ 斜め ――斜めの diagonal, oblique, askew (❖名詞の前では用いない) ――斜めに diagonally, obliquely, askew ∥斜めの線を引く draw a *diagonal [an oblique]* line / 道を斜めに横切る walk *diagonally* across a street / 壁の時計が少し斜めになっている The clock is a bit *askew* on the wall. / 私は彼女の斜め向かい[前, 後ろ]に座った I took a seat *diagonally* opposite [in front of, behind] her. ◆彼はけさはご機嫌ななめだ He *is in a bad mood* this morning.

なに 何

❶【疑問】what
《何が》
何があったんですか *What* happened?
その箱には何が入っているの *What's* in the box? / *What* do you have in the box? / *What* are the contents of the box?
何が原因でそんな大火事になったのですか *What* caused that big fire?

誕生日には何が欲しい？ *What* do you want for your birthday?

自分の金を使って何が悪いのか *What harm is there* in spending my own money?

たとえ何が起きようとも私は決してあきらめない *No matter what* [*Whatever*] *may happen*, I will never give up.

◆何が起こっても大丈夫だ I'm ready for *anything*.

【何を】

そこで何をしているの *What* are you doing there?

何をそんなに怒っているの *What* are you so angry about?

何を根拠にそう言うのですか *What* is the basis for your saying that?

新聞は何をとっていますか *What* newspaper do you take?

君は何をすべきかよく考えなければいけません You must consider *what* you should do.

彼は何をぐずぐずしているんだろう I wonder *what* is keeping him.

◆彼らが何を言おうと私は彼女を信じた *Whatever* [*No matter what*] they *might say*, I believed her.

🅔「きのう新宿で象を見たよ」「何を見たって？」"I saw an elephant in Shinjuku yesterday." "You saw *what*?"

【何に】

あなたは将来何になりたいですか *What* do you want to be in the future?

そんなことをして何になる *What*'s the point [*good*] of doing that?

何について話したらいいのか分かりません I don't know *what*「I should [to] talk about.

🅔「何になさいますか」「紅茶を２つお願いします」"*What* would you like?" "Two teas, please."

【何で】

この机は何でできているのですか *What* is this desk made of?

◆何で(→どうやって)そこへ行ったのですか *How* did you go there?

【何から】

何から始めようか *What* shall we do first?

これは何からできているのか *What* is this made of [from]?

【その他】

ブラジルでは何語が話されていますか *What language* do they speak in Brazil?

この秋は何色が流行していますか *What color* is in fashion this fall?

何言ってるんだ *What are you talking about?* /「ばかなことを言うな」*Don't be silly!*

◆何様のつもりだ *Who do you think you are*!

🅔「ねえ、野原君」「何」"Hey, Nohara." "*Yes*?"

❷《驚き・怒り》what,《主に米》why

何、水がないって *What!* No water?

何だと、おれにけんか売ってるのか *What!* Are you picking a fight with me?

慣用表現 私にはその芝居は何が何だかさっぱり分からなかった I *couldn't understand* the play *at all.* / 彼は自分の専門以外のことは何ひとつ知らない He knows *nothing* outside his field. / 彼は何不自由なく育った He *was born with a silver spoon in his mouth*.

なにか 何か
something; anything

語法
(1) something は肯定文で, anything は否定文, 疑問文, if [whether]節で用いるのが原則. ただし, 疑問文でも肯定的な答えを期待したり, 依頼や勧誘を表す場合, また if [whether]節でも肯定的な予測や期待を含意する場合は something を用いる ∥ 何か飲み物はいかがですか What about *something* to drink? / 何かこげるにおいがしませんか Don't you smell *something* burning?
(2) 形容詞は後ろに置く ∥ 何か新しいこと[もの] *something* new

きょうは何かよいことがありそうな気がした I had a feeling that *something good* would happen today.

きょうの午後, 何か予定はありますか Do you have *anything* to do this afternoon?

妹は買い物か何かに出かけています My sister has gone shopping *or something*.

息子は TRE とか TEF とか何かそんな名前のグループのコンサートに行った My son went to a concert by a group named TRE or TEF, *something like that*.

何か変わったことが起こったら知らせてください Please let me know if *anything* unusual happens.

◆これは何かの間違いです(→何か間違いがあるにちがいない) There must be *some* mistake. / 何か質問はありますか Do you have *any* questions? / テレビで何かおもしろい番組をやってますか Are there *any* interesting shows on TV? / 彼らは何かトランプのゲームをしていた They were playing a card game *of some sort*. / 彼女落ち込んでるみたいだけど, 何かあったの She looks depressed. *What's up*?

なにかしら 何かしら 彼はいつも何かしら悩みを抱えている He's always worrying about *something*. / そのことについて何かしら不安を感じた *Somehow* I felt uneasy about that matter. / この本を読めば何かしら得るところがあるだろう If you read this book, you will learn *something* from it.

なにかと 何かと 今月は何かと忙しかった I've been busy *with one thing or another* this month. / 車の免許を持っていると何かと(→いろいろな点で)便利だ It is convenient *in various ways* to have a driver's license. / 何かとお世話になりました Thank you for *everything*.

なにがなんでも 何が何でも 何が何でもその約束は守らなければならない I have to keep the promise「*at any cost* [*no matter what*].

なにかにつけ 何かにつけ 彼は何かにつけその話題を持ち出す He brings up the subject

whenever there is a chance.

なにからなにまで 何から何まで 彼女には何から何まで世話になった I owe her *everything*. / 彼女は何から何まで他人まかせにして自分では決断を下さない She leaves *everything* to other people and doesn't make any decisions herself.

なにくそ 何糞 なにくそ, 今に見ていろ *Damn it!* Just you wait.

なにくわぬかお 何食わぬ顔 なに食わぬ顔をする put on *an innocent look* / 彼女はなに食わぬ顔でうそをついた She told a lie *with an innocent look*.

なにげない 何気ない casual ——なにげなく casually ‖彼女のなにげないひと言が私の胸にぐさりときた Her *casual* remark struck straight to my heart. / 私はなにげなく窓の外を見た I *casually* looked out of the window.

なにごと 何事 いったい何事だ *What on earth has happened*? / 人は何事にも最善を尽くすべきだ One should try one's best in *everything*. / 何事もなく1年が過ぎた A year passed *peacefully* [*without incident*]. / 親をだますとは何事だ *How shameful of you* to cheat your parents!

なにしろ 何しろ (とにかく) anyway, anyhow, at any rate, in any case; (なぜなら) because; (何といっても) after all ‖なにしろやってみないと分からないよ *Anyway* [*Anyhow, At any rate, In any case*] we won't know until we try it. / 僕の部屋, なにしろ暑くて勉強に集中できないんだ I can't concentrate on studying *because* my room is very warm.

なにとぞ 何卒 please ➪ どうか¹, どうぞ

なにはさておき 何はさておき 何はさておき乾杯しよう *First of all*, let's drink a toast.

なにはともあれ 何はともあれ 何はともあれみんな無事に帰れてよかった *At any rate* [*In any case, Anyway*] I'm glad everyone got home safely.

なにびと 何人 何人も法のもとでは平等である *All people* have equal rights under the law.

なにひとつ 何一つ 彼女はいろいろな習い事をしてきたが何ひとつとしてものになっていない She has taken various lessons but hasn't mastered *anything*.

なにふじゆうなく 何不自由なく 何不自由なく暮らしている live *in ease and comfort* / 彼は何不自由なく育てられた He was brought up *without any cares about money*.

なにぶん 何分 留守中なにぶんとも犬の世話をよろしくお願いします I hope you will kindly take care of my dog during my absence. / なにぶん子供のことなので今回は大目に見ましょう I'll overlook it this time. *After all* he is only a little child.

なにも 何も

❶【ひとつも・少しも】nothing, not ... anything

彼のことは何も知りません I know *nothing* about him. / I do *not* know *anything* about him.

私は罪になるようなことは何もしていない I did *nothing* criminal. / I *didn't* do *anything* criminal. (❖-thing を修飾する語は後ろにくる)

結局何も起こらなかった *Nothing* happened after all. (❖×Anything didn't happen after all.; ×Not anything happened after all. はいずれも不可)

◆彼女は私に何も言わないで帰ってしまった She went home *without saying anything* to me. / 疲れて何もする気が起きない I am too tired to do *anything*. / その計画には何も障害がないように思えた There seemed to be *no* obstacle to the plan. / 何もいい考えが思いつかない I can't think of *any* good idea.

❷【わざわざ】

なにも彼にあんな態度をとることはないだろう *You shouldn't* have acted like that toward him. / (→理由はなかった) *You had no reason* to act like that toward him.

なにもそこまですることはない (→必要はない) There's *no need* to do that much.

なにもかも 何もかも これまでのところ何もかもうまくいっている *Everything* has gone well so far. / 私の努力は何もかもむだになってしまった *All* my efforts came to nothing.

なにもの 何者・何物 ❶【人】あいつは何者だ *Who* is that person? / 私は何者かに跡をつけられているようだ It seems that I am being followed by *someone* [*somebody*].

❷【物】健康は何物にも代えがたい Health is more precious than *anything* else. / 彼の説明は言い訳以外の何物でもない His explanation *is nothing but* an excuse.

なにやかや 何やかや このところ何やかやで忙しい These days I'm busy with *one thing or another*.

なにやら 何やら 彼らは何やらたくらんでいるようだ They seem to be plotting *something*. / オプショナルツアーや何やらで結局旅行費用は20万円を超えた The traveling expenses were more than 200,000 yen with optional tours and *additional charges*.

なにより 何より ご無事で何よりです(→無事でうれしい) *I'm so glad* that you're safe. / こんな寒い日には熱いふろに入るのが何よりだ On such a cold day taking a hot bath is *the best thing of all*. / 彼は甘い物が何より好きだ He likes sweets *better than anything else*. / 何よりもまず君たちは互いに助け合わなければいけない *Above all* [*First of all*], you must help each other. / 何よりだいじなのは人にうそをつかないことだ The *most important* thing is not to tell a lie to others.

ナノ nano- (❖単位を表す名詞と結合して用いられ, 10億分の1を表す;《略記》n) ‖ナノグラム nanogram / ナノテクノロジー nanotechnology

-なのだ それが我々に残された唯一のチャンスなのだ *After all* it is the only chance we have left. (❖強い断定の気持ちを表すには, イントネーションによって表すか, 文脈に応じて適宜意訳する)

- **-なので** because, since, as ⇨ -ので ∥雨なので外出するのはやめにした We chose not to go out「*because* it was raining [*because of* the rain].
- **-なのに** もうすぐ試験なのに全然勉強する気になれない I'll have an exam soon, *but* I don't feel like studying at all. ⇨ -のに
- **なのはな** 菜の花 rape [mustard] blossoms (❖次の俳句の英訳では「レイプ」(rape)や「からし」(mustard)を連想させるこれらの英語を避け, blossoming field「花咲く野辺」を使っている)
  俳句 菜の花や月は東に日は西に (与謝蕪村)
  A blossoming field:
  The moon is off to the East,
  sun to the West.
- **なのり** 名乗り 知事選に名乗りをあげる *announce one's candidacy for* governor / 3つの都市がオリンピックの開催地として名乗りをあげている Three cities *have put themselves forward* to host the Olympic Games.
- **なのりでる** 名乗り出る その仕事をしようと名乗り出る *come forward* [*volunteer*] *to do* the work / この本の持ち主は名乗り出てください Does anyone *claim* this book?(❖claim は「自分の所有物として…を要求する」の意味)
- **なのる** 名乗る 母方の姓を名乗る *use one's* mother's family name / その女性は高田と名乗った The woman *called herself* Takada. / その男は名を名乗らずに電話を切った The man hung up *without giving his name.* / ジャーナリストだと名乗る男が私のところへやってきた A man who *claimed* to be a journalist came to me.
- **なびかせる** その馬はたてがみを風になびかせて駆けていた The horse was running with its mane *streaming* [*waving*] in the wind.
- **なびく** ❶(風や水の流れに) stream ⓥ;(はためく) flutter ⓥ,(翻(⻡)る) wave ⓥ / こいのぼりが風になびいている Koinobori are *streaming* in the wind.
  ❷(屈服する) yield ⓥ ∥彼らは金になびくようなことは決してしない They will never *yield to* money.
- **ナビゲーター** navigator ⓒ
- **ナプキン**(食卓用)(table) napkin ⓒ,《英》serviette ⓒ;(生理用)《米》sanitary napkin [《英》towel] ⓒ / ナプキンをひざにかける put *a napkin* on one's lap / ナプキンで口をふく wipe *one's* mouth with *one's* napkin
  ∥紙ナプキン a paper napkin
- **なふだ** 名札(胸につける) name card ⓒ;(表札) nameplate ⓒ;(荷物につける) (name) tag ⓒ;(座席札) place card ⓒ / 胸に名札をつけている have *a name card* on *one's* chest / スーツケースの取っ手に名札をつける tie *a (name) tag* onto the handle of a suitcase
- **ナフタリン** naphthalene [nǽfθəli:n] ⓤ;(防虫剤) mothballs
- **なぶりごろし** なぶり殺し 人をなぶり殺しにする *torture* a person *to death*
- **なべ** 鍋(片手の平なべ) pan ⓒ;(深い両手なべ) pot ⓒ;(深めでふた付きの片手なべ) saucepan ⓒ;(土なべ) earthen pot ⓒ;(中華なべ) wok ⓒ ∥なべかま類 *pots and pans* / なべを火にかける put *a pot* on the stove / なべで…をいためる fry ... in *a pan*

frying pan
pot
saucepan
earthen pot
wok

∥なべ敷き a pot stand;(3脚の) a trivet / なべつかみ a pot holder, a hot pad / なべもの a dish cooked on the table and served in a pot
- **ナポリタン**(スパゲッティナポリタン) spaghetti napolitana
- **なま** 生 ──生の(熱を通していない) raw, uncooked;(新鮮な) fresh;(生放送・生演奏の) live [láiv]
  ニンジンを生で食べる eat carrots *raw*
  いつかプラシド・ドミンゴを生で聴きたいものだ I want to hear Placido Domingo sing *live* some day.
  箱根駅伝は毎年テレビで生中継される The Hakone Ekiden *is broadcast live* on TV every year.
  ◆この肉まだ生(→生焼け)だよ This meat is only *half-cooked.* / 教師は生徒たちの生の声(→率直な意見)にもっと耳を傾けるべきだ Teachers should pay more attention to *the honest [frank]* opinions of their students.
  ∥生演奏 a live performance / 生クリーム fresh cream / 生魚 raw fish / 生卵 a raw egg / 生テープ a blank tape / 生番組 a live program / 生ビール draft beer / 生水(煮沸していない水) unboiled water;(水道水) tap water / 生野菜 fresh [raw] vegetables
- **なまあくび** 生欠伸 small [slight] yawn ⓒ ∥なまあくびが出る let out *a small yawn* / なまあくびをかみ殺す stifle *a small yawn*
- **なまあたたかい** 生暖かい, なま暖かい風が吹いている An *uncomfortably warm* wind is blowing outside.
- **なまいき** 生意気《口語的》cheek ⓤ;(厚かましさ) impudence ⓤ;(無礼) impertinence ⓤ (❖いずれも具体的な「生意気な言動」を指すとき

は[C]) ――生意気な《口語的》cheeky,《口語的》sassy, saucy; impudent; impertinent; (うぬぼれた) cocky ∥生意気なやつ an *impudent* [a *saucy*] fellow / あいつは本当に生意気だ He's got a lot of *cheek*. / そんなことするなんてあいつも生意気だ It is *impudent* of him to do so./ He is *impudent* to do so. / あいつは生意気にも私のことを笑った He「*had the nerve* [*was impudent enough*] to laugh at me. / 彼の生意気な態度はみんなの反感を買った His *sassy* attitude aroused everyone's hostility. / 私に向かってよくもそんな生意気な口がきけるな How dare [can] you be so *cheeky* to me? / 生意気言うな *None of your cheek*!

なまえ 名前

name[C] ➔ な(名)

[語法]
(1) 英米では, Alan Alexander Milne のように, 名(first name, given name, forename, Christian name)と姓(family name, last name, surname)の間に, 同姓同名の者を区別するためにできたミドルネーム(middle name)が入ることが多い. これは2つ以上つく場合もあり, また頭文字だけで表したりする.
(2) 英米では, 日本とは逆に, 人名を名・姓の順に言う. そのため, 山田五郎という名前は Goro Yamada となるが, 名前は固有のものなので, Yamada Goro と言ってもかまわない. 本辞典では, 日本人の名前は原則として姓・名の順で書かれている.

この動物の名前は何ですか What is *the name* of this animal?/ (→何と呼ぶか) What do you call this animal?

すみません, お名前をもう一度お願いします Sorry, what's *your name* again?

すみません, どうもお名前を思い出せなくて I'm afraid *your name* escapes me.

彼女の名前だけは知っている I *know* her「*only by name* [*by name only*].

私はその名前で呼ばれるのが大嫌いだ I hate it when people call me by that *name*.

あなたのお名前はどう発音するのですか How do you pronounce your *name*?

お名前のスペルを教えていただけますか How do you spell *your name*?

次期社長として彼の名前が挙がっている His *name has been mentioned* as the next president.

◆豊田という名前の男性 a man *named* [*called*] Toyota / 私の名前を出せば彼らは中に入れてくれますよ If you *mention* me, they will let you in. / 女の子なら美智子という名前にするつもりだ If it's a girl, we'll *name* her Michiko. / 私は彼の子供に名前をつけてほしいと頼まれた I was asked to *name* his baby. / 名前は明かせないがある若い男からその話を聞いた I heard the story from a young man *who shall be* [*remain*] *nameless*.

💬「お名前は何とおっしゃいますか」「堀田健一です」"*May I have* [*ask*] *your name*?/ *Could you tell me your name*?" "My *name* is Hotta Kenichi." (❖What's your name? はぶしつけな言い方で, 子供に対する以外は避けたほうがよい)

なまかじり 生噛り ロシア語はなまかじりの(→表面的な)知識しかもっていない I have no more than a *superficial* [(→わずかな) *slight*] knowledge of Russian.

なまがわき 生乾き 生乾きの材木 *green* lumber / このシャツはまだ生乾きだ(→湿っている) This shirt *is*「still *damp* [(→乾いていない) *not quite dry* yet].

なまきず 生傷 プロレスラーは体に生傷が絶えない Pro wrestlers always have *cuts and bruise* on their body.

なまぐさい 生臭い fishy; (血なまぐさい) bloody ◆台所は魚の生臭いにおいがした There was *a smell of raw fish* in the kitchen.

なまけもの 怠け者 lazy person [C],《口語的》lazybones[C] (複～); 〖動物〗sloth[C] ∥この怠け者! 今すぐ宿題をやりなさい You *lazybones*! Do your homework now!
◆怠け者の学生 a *lazy* student

なまける 怠ける be lazy; be idle (❖idle は「仕事のない, 暇な」の意味で必ずしも悪い意味はない); (怠る) neglect [他] ∥怠け癖(ぐせ)がつく get into *the habit of being lazy* / 怠けるな *Don't be lazy*! / 勉強を怠けていたら試験に落ちた I「*was lazy* in [*neglected*] my studies and I've failed the examination. / 怠けている暇はないぞ There's no time to *be idle*.

なまこ 海鼠 sea cucumber[C]

なまごみ 生ごみ (kitchen) garbage[U]

なまじっか なまじっか他人のおせっかいをやかないほうがいいよ You shouldn't meddle in the affairs of others. / 彼はなまじっかの歌手よりも歌がうまい He is able to sing better than those *ordinary* professional singers.

なまず 鯰 catfish[C] (複～)

なまつば 生唾 食卓に並んだごちそうを見て生つばを飲み込んだ *My mouth watered* at the sight of the wonderful food on the table. (❖My mouth watered.は「食欲がそそられて唾液(だえき)が出た」の意味)

なまなましい 生々しい (鮮やかな) fresh; (鮮明な) vivid ∥その経験は今でもまだ生々しく覚えている That experience is still *fresh* [*vivid*] in my mind. ◆事故現場の生々しい映像がテレビで流れた The *terrible* scene of the accident was televised.

なまにえ 生煮え ――生煮えの half-cooked, underdone ∥このニンジンは生煮えだ These carrots are *half-cooked* [*underdone*].

なまぬるい 生温い lukewarm ∥なまぬるいコーヒー *lukewarm* coffee
◆このジュースなまぬるいなあ(→十分冷えていない) This juice is *not cool* [*cold*] *enough*. / そんななまぬるい(→中途半端な)やり方では凶悪犯罪を減らすことはできない Brutal crimes can't be decreased by such *halfway* measures.

な

なまはんか 生半可 ——なまはんかな (浅薄な) superficial; (不熱心な) halfhearted ∥なまはんかな知識 *superficial* knowledge / なまはんかな覚悟ではその仕事はやり通せないだろう With *halfhearted* determination, that job cannot be seen to its end.

なまびょうほう 生兵法 ことわざ 生兵法は大けがの元 A little knowledge is a dangerous thing. (→わずかな学問は危険なもの)

なまへんじ 生返事 (あいまいな返事) vague [noncommittal] answer Ⓒ; (気のない返事) halfhearted answer Ⓒ / 何を聞いても彼女はうわの空で生返事しかしなかった No matter what I asked, she only gave me *vague answers* absentmindedly.

なまほうそう 生放送 live [láiv] broadcast Ⓒ ◆この番組は生放送だ This program *is live*.

なまみ 生身 それは無理な注文だ. 私だって生身の人間だよ You're asking too much. I'm *only human* [*flesh and blood*].

なまめかしい sexy; (女性が) voluptuous

なまもの 生物 (調理していない) uncooked food Ⓤ; (腐りやすい) perishable food Ⓤ; (生魚) raw fish Ⓤ
◆ (表示で)生物につきできるだけお早めにお召し上がりください. *Perishable*. Please consume as soon as possible.

なまやけ 生焼け ——生焼けの underdone; (パン・ケーキなどの) half-baked

なまやさしい 生易しい この計画を成しとげるのはなまやさしいことではない It will 「*not be so easy* [*be no easy thing*]」 to carry this plan through.

なまり¹ 訛 accent Ⓒ; (方言) dialect Ⓒ / 強いなまりがある have *a strong accent* / 日本語なまりのある[ない] 英語を話す speak English with [without] *a Japanese accent* / 彼には少し[強い] 関西なまりがあった He had *a slight* [*strong*] *Kansai accent*.

なまり² 鉛 〖化学〗lead [léd] Ⓤ (✤元素記号 Pb)

なまる¹ 訛る 彼は少しなまった英語を話す He speaks English with *a slight accent*. / 「キャベツ」は英語の"cabbage"がなまったものだ "*Kyabetsu*" is *a corruption* of the English "cabbage."

なまる² 鈍る 運動不足で体がなまってしまった I've got *soft* from the lack of exercise.

なみ¹ 波

❶ 【水面の】 wave Ⓒ; (さざ波) ripple Ⓒ; (打ち寄せる波) surf Ⓤ; (岩などに砕ける波) breaker Ⓒ

きょうは波が高い[荒い] The *waves* are high [rough] today. / The sea is high [rough] today.
波は静まりそうになかった The *waves* [*sea*] didn't seem to have calmed down.
波が海岸に打ち寄せていた The *waves* were 「beating against [washing] the shore.
その船は波に乗って進んだ The boat rode *the waves*.
子供が波にさらわれた A child was washed away by *the waves*.
ボートが波に揺れている[漂っている] A boat is rocking [drifting] on *the waves*.

❷ 【波に似たもの】 wave Ⓒ
不況の波 *a wave* of depression / 景気の波に乗る ride (on) *the waves* of prosperity
◆ 私は人の波を押し分けて進まなければならなかった I had to force my way through *the crowd*. / この村にも時代の波が押し寄せてきている The *trend of the times* has reached even this village. / 彼は成績に波がある His grades *are fluctuating*.

∥波頭 the crest of a wave / 波しぶき sea spray / 波線 a wavy line / 波乗り surfing 短歌 大海の磯もとどろに寄する波われてくだけて裂けて散るかも (源実朝)
On the rocky shore,
with a deep, pounding rumble,
the waves crash and crunch,
split and splatter, boil and break,
and scatter across the strand.

なみ² 並み ——並みの (ふつうの) ordinary, regular; (平均的な) average; (ありふれた) common; (中間の) medium / 並みの人間にはあんなこと考えつかないよ No *ordinary* person would think of such a thing (as that). / 並みの成績じゃあの大学には入れないよ You won't be able to enter that college with *average* grades. / カツ丼の並みを1つください One *regular katsudon*, please.

-なみ -並み 世間並みの(=ふつうの)生活をする lead an *ordinary* life / この夏の暑さは例年並みになりそうだ The temperature this summer will be *average*. / 彼女のピアノはプロ並みだ She can play the piano *as well as a professional*. / Her skills at the piano are *on a professional level*.

なみうちぎわ 波打ち際 beach Ⓒ (✤通例満潮時に水をかぶる所までをいう); (水際) the water's edge

なみうつ 波打つ —— 🅥 wave Ⓔ, roll Ⓔ —— 🅐 wavy / 木々のこずえが風を受けて波打っていた The treetops *were waving* in the wind.

なみかぜ 波風 波風を立てるようなことは言うな Don't say anything to 「*rock the boat* [*make waves*].

なみき 並木 a row [line] of trees
◆ 以前はこの通りに沿ってずっと桜の並木があった There used to be cherry trees all along this street.

∥並木道 a tree-lined street, an avenue

なみだ 涙

tears (✤*a tear* は「ひと粒の涙」の意味)

〖涙～・～涙〗

そら涙 *false* [*artificial*] *tears* / うれし涙[悔し涙]を流す shed 「*tears of joy* [*bitter tears*]」
母は涙もろい My mother *is easily moved* [*reduced*] *to tears*.
彼は涙ながらにその話をした *In tears* [*Tearfully*] he told us the story.
◆ 涙声で *in a tearful voice* / その芝居は典型的なお涙ちょうだいものだった The play was

なやます

a typical *tearjerker* [*sob story*].

《涙が》
父の目に涙が浮かんだ *Tears* came to my father's eyes.
彼女の目には涙があふれそうだった Her eyes were filled with *tears*.
彼の目から涙があふれ出た *Tears* poured from his eyes.
目に涙がこみ上げてきた *Tears* welled up in my eyes.
大粒の涙が彼のほおを伝った Large *tears* rolled down his cheeks.

《涙を》
涙を流す shed *tears* / 涙をぬぐう dry [wipe away] *one's tears* / 目に涙を浮かべて with *tears* in *one's* eyes / 目に涙を浮かべている have *tears* in *one's* eyes
彼女は人前で涙を見せたことがない She has never shed *tears* in public.
私は涙を抑えることができなかった I couldn't hold [keep] back *my tears*. / (→泣かずにはいられなかった) I couldn't help crying.
その事故のニュースは多くの人の涙を誘った The news about the accident moved many people to *tears*.
◆我々のチームは今年もまた決勝戦で涙を飲んだ (→敗れた) Our team *was defeated* in the finals again this year. / 涙を飲んで彼女のことはあきらめた I gave her up *with extreme reluctance*.

《涙に》
涙にうるんだ目 eyes wet with *tears*
彼は飼い犬を亡くしてから何日も涙にくれていた He *had been in tears* for days after he lost his dog.

《涙で》
涙で光る目 eyes glistening with *tears*
私の目は涙でかすんでいた My eyes were dim [misted] with *tears*. / *Tears* blurred my eyes.
彼女の顔は涙でぬれていた Her face was wet with *tears*.

なみたいてい 並大抵 一度失った信頼を取り戻すのは並大抵のことではない It's no easy matter [task] to restore the lost trust of others.

なみだぐましい 涙ぐましい 彼の涙ぐましい努力は結局報われなかった After all his *painful efforts* were not rewarded.

なみだぐむ 涙ぐむ 彼女は涙ぐんでいた Her *eyes were filled [wet] with tears*. / 彼は涙ぐんだ目で私を見つめた He stared at me *with tears in his eyes*.

なみだつ 波立つ 風が強まると海は波立ち始めた The wind became stronger and the 「sea *turned choppy* [*waves began to rise*].

なみなみ 並々 —並々ならぬ (並はずれた) extraordinary; (大きな) great /並々ならぬ関心を示す show *extraordinary* [*no ordinary*] interest / 彼らはその計画を成功させるのに並々ならぬ苦労をした They took *great pains* to make the plan a success.

なみなみと グラスにビールをなみなみと (→縁まで) つぐ fill a glass *to the brim* with beer

なみのり 波乗り ⇨ サーフィン

なみはずれた 並外れた extraordinary, uncommon /並はずれた能力の持ち主 a person of *extraordinary* [*uncommon*] ability
◆父は並はずれて声が大きい My father has an *extraordinarily* [*extremely*] loud voice.

なめくじ slug ⓒ
なめしがわ 鞣し革 leather ⓤ
なめす 鞣す tan ⑯ /鞣皮をなめす *tan* a hide
なめつくす なめ尽くす 火事は町全体をなめ尽くした The fire *swept* [*consumed*] the whole town.

なめらか 滑らか —なめらかな smooth [smúːð] —なめらかに smoothly
なめらかな肌[動き] *smooth* skin [movement]
この生地は肌ざわりがなめらかだ This cloth 「*feels smooth* [*is smooth to the touch*].
なめらかになるまで卵をよくかき混ぜなさい Beat the eggs until they are *smooth*.
◆なめらかに (→流暢(ﾘｭｳﾁｮｳ)に) 英語をしゃべる speak English *fluently* / 木の表面を紙やすりでなめらかにする *smooth* the surface of the wood with sandpaper

なめる 嘗める・舐める
❶【舌で】lick ⑯; (しゃぶる) suck ⑯ ⓘ; (動物がぴちゃぴちゃと) lap ⑯ ⓘ
指についたクリームをなめて取る *lick* cream off *one's* fingers
猫は自分の皿をなめてきれいにした The cat *licked* its plate clean.
子猫がミルクをぴちゃぴちゃなめている A kitten *is lapping* milk.
◆あめ、なめる? Do you *want* a candy?
❷【経験する】experience ⑯, go* through ...
彼女はあらゆる辛酸をなめてきた She *has experienced* [*gone through*] all kinds of hardship.
❸【軽く見る】
おれをなめるなよ (→甘く見るな) Don't *make light of* me. / (→ばかにするな) Don't *make a fool of* me.

なや 納屋 (物置) shed ⓒ; (家畜のえさや作物を蓄えておく) barn ⓒ

なやましい 悩ましい (官能を刺激する) sexy; (誘惑するような) seductive; (頭を悩ませる) worrying /悩ましい問題 a *worrying problem* / 彼女は悩ましい目つきで僕を見た She gave me a *seductive* look.

なやます 悩ます trouble ⑯; worry ⑯; annoy ⑯; bother ⑯

| trouble: 心配や面倒をかけて悩ます.
| worry: 気苦労をかける.
| annoy: いらいらさせ腹を立てさせる.
| bother: じゃまをしていらいらさせる.

少年はたくさん質問して両親を悩ませた The boy *troubled* [*annoyed*] his parents with lots of questions. / 彼は両親をいつも悩ませている He always *worries* his parents. / 彼らは車の騒音に悩まされている They *are annoyed* [*troubled, bothered*] by traffic noise.

なやみ

/ そんなことで僕を悩まさないでくれ You shouldn't *bother* me with such things.
◆彼女はその問題に頭を悩ませた She *puzzled her brains [head] over* the problem. / このところ彼は不眠に悩まされている These days he *is suffering from* insomnia.

なやみ 悩み (心配) worry ⓤⒸ; (苦労) trouble ⓤⒸ; (問題) problem Ⓒ
何か悩みがあるの Do you have any *worries*?
友人は私に悩みを話した My friend told me of [about] *her troubles*.
彼は両親の悩みの種だ He is *a worry* [*trouble*, *problem*] to his parents.
いちばんの悩みはどうやって彼の同意を得るかだ *My major worry* is how to get his consent.

なやむ 悩む worry ⾃, be worried, be troubled; (病気などで) suffer ⾃
彼女は自分の将来のことでとても悩んでいる She is 「*worrying* much [very *worried*] about her future.
何を悩んでいるの What are you *worried about*? / What's your *trouble*? / What's *worrying* you?
彼は自分にも責任があるのではないかと悩んでいる He *is worried* [*worrying*] *that* he's also responsible for it.
そんなつまらないことで悩むのはやめにしたらどう Why don't you stop *worrying about* such trifles?
私が悩んでいるのはどうやって彼にそのことを伝えるかということだ *What worries me is* how I tell him about it.
父は水虫に悩んでいる My father is 「*suffering from* [*troubled by*] athlete's foot.
◆さんざん悩んだ(→ためらった)末に彼はそれを買うことにした *After* so much *hesitation* [(→考えた)*consideration*] he decided to buy it.

なよなよ ──なよなよした (弱々しい) feeble; (女性のような) effeminate

なら 奈良

奈良県は, 大阪への通勤圏内にある北西部の奈良盆地を除いて山地が大部分を占めています. 現在の奈良市は, 8世紀に都が置かれていた所で, 古代日本史にとって政治的, 宗教的中心地でした. また, シルクロードの東の終着点でもあり, そのため, 奈良市内やその周辺には仏教寺院など多くの文化遺産があります.
Most of Nara Prefecture is mountainous, except for the Nara Basin in the northwestern area, which belongs to the commuter belt of Osaka. The city of Nara was Japan's capital in the eighth century and the political and religious center of early Japanese history. It was also the eastern end of the Silk Road. Therefore much heritage remains in this city and the surrounding area, such as Buddhist temples.

-なら ❶【仮定・条件】if; (…という条件で) on condition (that …) ⇒もし / 君が行かないなら僕も行かないよ *If* you don't go, I won't go either. / 私が君ならそんな人絶対に許さないけど I would never forgive a person like that *if* I were you. / 来週中に返してくれるなら貸します I'll lend it *if* [*on condition* (*that*)] you give it back next week.
◆金曜日なら都合がつくよ I'm available on Friday. / この時計が1万円なら安い This watch is cheap at [for] 10,000 yen. / 彼を助けるくらいなら死んだほうがましだ I'd rather die *than* help him.

❷【…に関しては】野球のことなら何でも聞いてください Ask me anything about baseball. / 相撲のことなら彼女は何でも知っている *When it comes to* sumo, she knows everything. / そのことならほかの人に聞いたほうがいいよ *As to* that matter, you'd better ask someone else.

ならい 習い custom ⓤⒸ, habit Ⓒ ◆それが世の習いだ That's *the way of the world*.

ならいごと 習い事 あなたは何か習い事をしていますか Do you take any *lessons*?

ならう¹ 習う (習得する) learn* ⓣ⾃; (学習・研究する) study ⓣ⾃; (レッスンを受ける) take* lessons
車の運転を習う *learn* (how) to drive / 有名なピアニストにピアノを習う *learn*「*the piano* [(*how*) *to play the piano*] *from* a famous pianist
英語を習うのがとても楽しい I really enjoy *learning* English. ✿study English とする と learn にある, 学習の結果が身につく, という含みがなくなり単に勉強する・研究するという意味になる)
きょうは授業で何を習ったの What did you *learn* in class today?
彼は週に2日水泳を習っている He *takes* swimming *lessons* twice a week.
空手を習って5年になる I've been learning karate for five years.
◆だれにその歌を習ったの(→だれが教えたのか) Who *taught* you that song?
慣用表現 習うより慣れよ *Practice makes perfect*. (→練習を積めば完全になる)

ならう² 倣う (従う) follow ⓣ; (まねる) copy ⓣ⾃ /人の例にならう *follow* a person's example / 彼女がその計画から手をひくと残った人たちもそれにならうった She backed out of the project and the others *followed suit*. (✿follow suit は「人のやったとおりにする, 先例にならう」の意味)
◆アメリカにならって作られた制度 a system *modeled on* that in America

ならす¹ 鳴らす
❶【音を】(楽器などを) sound ⓣ⾃; (鐘・鈴などを) ring* ⓣ⾃; (警笛などを) blow* ⓣ⾃
クラクションを鳴らす *sound* [*honk*, *blow*] a horn / 試合開始のゴングを鳴らす *sound* [*strike*] the bell for the start of the match / だれかが玄関のベルを鳴らした Someone *rang*「*the doorbell* [*at the door*].
◆(乾杯して)グラスをかちんと鳴らす *clink* glasses / 音楽に合わせて指を鳴らす *snap one's fingers* in time to the music / 彼は私

をばかにしてふんと鼻を鳴らした He *gave* me *a snort of contempt.* / その猫は飼い主のひざの上でのどを鳴らしていた The cat *was purring* on its owner's lap.

❷【その他】
その問題に関して警鐘を鳴らす *raise* [*sound*] *the alarm* about the problem
彼はかつて名捕手として鳴らした(→有名だった) He *was* once *famous* for being an excellent catcher.

ならす² 慣らす・馴らす accustom ⓗ; (訓練する) train ⓗ; (飼い馴らす) tame ⓗ // 寒さに体を慣らす *accustom* [*habituate*] *oneself to* the cold / 英語に耳を慣らす *accustom one's ears to* English
◆新しい靴を履き慣らす *break in* new shoes

ならす³ 均す (平らにする) level ⓗ; (平均する) average ⓗ ⓗ // 作物を植えるために畑をならす *level* a field to plant crops / 私の睡眠時間は日にならして7時間だ My sleep *averages* seven hours a day. / I *average* seven hours' sleep a day.

ならでは こういった習慣は大阪ならではの(→特有のものだ) These customs are *peculiar to* Osaka.

-ならない

❶【当然・義務・必要】must; have* *to do*, 《口語的》have got to *do*; should; ought to *do*; be to *do*

> must: 話し手の主観に基づく義務・必要を表す.
> have to, have got to: 話し手以外の人の客観的な事情に基づく義務・必要を表す. したがって口語では must よりも穏やかな have to が好んで用いられる.
> should: must, have to より意味が弱く,「…するのはいいことだ」にほぼ等しい.
> ought to: should とほぼ同意だがやや強意的. 客観的・社会的・道徳的な理由に基づく義務・責任を表し, 一般的には should のほうが多く用いられる.
> be to: 掲示・通達など公的・第三者的命令に用いられる.

【語法】must の過去・未来・完了はそれぞれ had to, will [shall] have to, have had to で表す. ただし従属節中では must の過去は must でよい // 私はすぐその場所を立ち去らなければならないと思った I thought I *must* leave the place immediately.

もうおいとましなければなりません I *have to* go now. / I *must* [*should*] *be going now.*
私は今度の土曜は仕事に行かなければならない I'll *have to* go to work next Saturday.
私たちは大雪で引き返さなければならなかった We *had to* turn back because of the heavy snow.
その紛争を解決するために国連が介入しなければならないかもしれない The UN may *have to* step in to settle the dispute. (❖ほかの助動詞とともに用いる場合は have to を用いる)
入院しなければならないほどの病気をしたことがない I have never been so ill that I *had to* be hospitalized. / I have never been so ill as to be hospitalized.
きのうは歯医者に行かなければならなかったのに (行かなかった) I *should* have gone to the dentist yesterday.
今ごろはもう出かけていなければならないはずなのに We *should* be [have been] on our way by now.
◆あなたに言わなければならないことがあります I've got something to tell you. / その傷は3針縫わなければならなかった The cut *needed* three stitches. / あなたに真実を話してもらわなければならない I *need* you to tell me the truth.

💡「すぐにそれをしなければなりませんか」「ええ, そうです[いいえ, その必要はありません]」 "*Must* I do it at once?" "Yes, you must. [No, you don't have to.]" (❖「…する必要がない」という場合には do not have to, do not need to, need not を用いる)

❷【禁止】(…してはいけない) must not; (…するべきではない) should not, ought not to *do*
このことはだれにも話してはならない You *must not* tell anybody about this.
学校の成績だけで人を判断してはならない People *should not* be judged only by their school records.
◆肌をあまり長い間日光にさらしてはならない *Don't* expose your skin to the sun's rays too long.

❸【…せずにはいられない】
彼の安否が気づかれてならない I *can't help* worrying about his safety. / (→とても心配だ) I'm very worried about his safety.
その試合に負けて悔しくてならなかった I *couldn't help* feeling frustrated when I lost the game.

❹【…してはいられない】
私は彼の態度にもう我慢ならなかった I *couldn't* bear his behavior any longer.

ならび 並び (列) line ⓒ, row ⓒ; (側) side ⓒ // 私の家はコンビニの並びにある My house is *on the same side of the street as* a convenience store. ◆歯並びがいい[悪い] have regular [irregular] teeth

ならびに 並びに お名前ならびにご住所をご記入ください Please fill in your name *and* address.

ならぶ 並ぶ

❶【列を作る】line up, 《英》queue ⓗ; (列を作る) form a line [《英》queue]; (…に沿って並ぶ) line ⓗ ⓗ
並んで順番をお待ちください Please「*line up* [*form a line*] and take your turn.
生徒たちは2列に並んだ The students 「*formed two lines* [*lined up two abreast*].
その道の両側には桜の木が並んでいる Cherry trees *line* both sides of the street.
◆人と並んで(→隣に)座る sit down *next to* a person / 人の後ろに並ぶ *get in line after* [*behind*] a person / 子供たちを並ばせる *line*

the children *up* / 彼が彼女と並んで歩いているのを見かけた I saw him walking *side by side with her.* / 何人もの人が店があくのを並んで待っていた A lot of people *were waiting in line* for the store to open. / 私が先に並んでいたのよ I *was in line* ahead of you. / その展覧会を見るために３時間並んだ I *waited in line* for three hours to see the exhibition. / 棚にはわずかな商品しか並んでいなかった *There were only a few items on the shelf.* / テーブルの上に料理が並んでいる *The food has been set out on the table.* / その選手は40キロ地点で先頭に並んだ(→追いついた) The runner *caught up with* the leading runner at the 40-kilometer mark.

❷【匹敵する】equal ⊕, be equal to ..., match ⊕

この分野では彼に並ぶ者はいない No one can *equal* him in this field. / He has no *equal* in this field. (❖後の表現の equal は「匹敵する人」の意味)

◆猫は犬と並んで人気のあるペットだ Cats, *together with* dogs, are popular as pets.

ならべたてる 並べ立てる 不満を並べ立てる *make a series of complaints* / 彼は私の計画の欠点を並べたてた(→列挙した) He *enumerated* the flaws in my plan.

ならべる 並べる
❶【配列する】(整理する) arrange ⊕; (１列に) line up ⊕, put* ⊕; (特定の場所に置く) set* ⊕, place ⊕; (陳列する) display ⊕
アルファベット順に単語を並べる *arrange* words alphabetically / 書かれている内容によって本を並べる *arrange* books according to their contents / 自転車を１列に並べる *line* bicycles *up*; *put* [*set, place*] bicycles *in a row* / いすを丸く並べる *put* [*set, place*] chairs *in a circle* / ショーウインドーに新しい商品を並べる *display* new goods in a show window
食卓にはおいしそうな料理がたくさん並べられていた Delicious-looking dishes *were set* [*spread*] *on the table.* / The table *was set* [*spread*] *with* delicious-looking dishes.

◆机を並べ換える *rearrange* the desks / ２枚の絵を並べて壁にかける hang two paintings *side by side* on the wall / 二人は肩を並べて歩いていた They were walking 「*side by side* [*two abreast*].

❷【言い立てる】
不平を並べる *make a series of complaints*
あれこれ言い訳を並べてないで解決策を考えたらうのう Stop *making* excuses and start looking for solution.

ならわし 習わし (慣習) custom Ⓤ Ⓒ; (伝統) tradition Ⓒ Ⓤ ∥習わしに従う follow *a custom* / その習わしはまだこのあたりに残っている The *custom* is still found around here. / それは古くからの日本の習わしです It is *an old custom* in Japan.

なり¹ (外見) appearance Ⓤ Ⓒ ◆あいつはなりは大きいがまだまだ子供だ Though he's large, he's still a child.

なり² 鳴り 慣用表現 反対派グループはこのところ鳴りを潜(ひそ)めている The opposition group *has been maintaining a low profile* these days.

-なり 道なりに進む go *along* the road / 自分なりにベストを尽くす do *one's best in one's own way* / そのことについては私は自分なりの考えがある I have *my own idea about that.* / CDをかけるなりビデオを見るなり好きなようにしなさい You can play CDs *or* watch videos *or* do whatever you like. / 彼は私を見るなり殴りかかってきた *As soon as* [*The moment*] he saw me he swung at me.

なりあがり 成り上がり upstart Ⓒ

なりきる 成り切る その本を読んでいるうちに私は登場人物の一人になりきっていた As I read the book, I *identified with* one of the characters.

なりきん 成金 nouveau riche [núːvou ríːʃ] Ⓒ; (成り上がり者) upstart Ⓒ ∥成金趣味の家 a house of *nouveau riche taste*
∥土地成金 real estate millionaire

なりすます 成り済ます 彼は関係者になりすましてその建物に潜(もぐ)り込んだ He slipped into the building 「*pretending to be* [*disguising himself as*] someone who belonged there.

なりたち 成り立ち (歴史) history Ⓤ Ⓒ; (起源) origin Ⓒ Ⓤ; (構造) structure Ⓤ Ⓒ ∥文の成り立ち *the structure* of a sentence / 近代社会の成り立ちを追う trace *the history* of modern society

なりたつ 成り立つ ❶【…で構成されている】be made up of ..., consist of ... ∥委員会は５人のメンバーから成り立っている The committee 「*is made up* [*consists*] *of* five members.
❷【ある状態に達する】このあたりではとても商売は成り立たないだろう We'll never be able to *do good business* around here. / こんな安月給じゃ生活が成り立たない I *can't live on* such a small salary. / プロスポーツはスポンサーなしでは成り立たない Professional sports *cannot exist* [*survive*] without commercial sponsors. / この法則はすべての天体について成り立つ This law *holds good* to all the heavenly bodies. / この方程式は $x = 1$ のとき成り立つ This equation *is satisfied* if you substitute 1 for x. / そんな自分勝手な理屈は成り立たないよ Self-serving reasoning like that *doesn't hold water.* (❖hold water は「(説明などが)理にかなっている」の意味で、通例疑問文・否定文で用いる)

なりて 成り手 その芝居は主役のなり手がない(→だれもなりたがらない) Nobody wants to play the leading role in that play.

なりひびく 鳴り響く resound [rizáund] ⊕; (鐘などが) ring* ⊕; (反響する) echo ⊕ ∥救急車のサイレンが通りに鳴り響いた The ambulance siren *resounded* in the street. ◆彼女の名声は外国にまで鳴り響いている Her fame *has spread* even to foreign countries.

なりふり 形振り 彼はなりふりかまわず働いた

He worked *without any regard for how he looks to others*.

なりものいり 鳴り物入り そのピッチャーは鳴り物入りでタイガースに入団した The pitcher joined the Tigers *with a lot of fanfare*.

なりゆき 成り行き (進行) course Ⓤ; (進展) development Ⓤ; (結果) result ⒸⓊ ∥今後の成り行きに注目しなければならない We must keep our eye on *the course [run] of events* from now on. / いまさらじたばたしてもしようがない. 自然の成り行きにまかせよう It's no use making a fuss now. *Let nature take its course*.
◆事の成り行きを見守るほかなかった All I could do was *wait and see* (*how things would turn out*).

なる¹ 成る

❶ ある身分・地位・職業などに	become; be	
❷ ある状態になる	become, get; go	
❸ ほかのものに変わる	turn, change	
❹ …するようになる	come to *do*	
❺ …することになる		
❻ ある結果になる	turn out, prove	

❶【人がある身分・地位・職業などに就く】become* 圊; be 圊

語法
「なりたい」「なるだろう」などのように「これから…になる」という意味では be が多く用いられる ∥私は将来美容師になりたい I want to *be [become]* a beautician in the future. / 弁護士になるのが私の夢です My dream is to *be [become]* a lawyer.

彼女は社長になった She「*became* (the) president [(→社長の地位を得た) *took the post of president*].
彼は20歳で父親になった He *became* a father when he was 20.
モハメド・アリは1964年に初めてヘビー級の世界チャンピオンになった Muhammad Ali first *became* the world heavyweight champion in 1964.
彼は腕のよい職人になるでしょう He will *be [become, make]* a good craftsman. (❖make は「…になる資質がある」の意味で, 後には好ましい意味の形容詞を伴った名詞がくる)
◆どうやって彼女と知り合いになったのですか How did you *get to know* her? / 大人になったら何になりたいの What do you want to be when you *grow up*?

❷【ある状態になる】become* 圊, get* 圊; (変化する) go* 圊 (❖しばしば好ましくない状態になるときに用いる), turn 圊; (しだいに…になる) grow* 圊

語法
いずれも後に形容詞・過去分詞を伴う. ただし become は形容詞・過去分詞に加え名詞を用いていることもできる. 口語では get が become よりよく用いられる ∥その子犬はすぐわが家のお気に入りになった The puppy quickly *became* [×*got*, ×*grew*] the darling of our family. / みんなくたくたになった Everyone *became* [*got, grew*] totally exhausted.

病気になる *get* [*become*] ill
暗くなる前に帰ろう Let's go home before it *gets* [*becomes, grows*] dark.
山頂近くではより肌寒くなる Toward the top of the mountain, it *gets* cooler.
会うたびに彼は背が高くなっている Each time I see him he *has become* [*gotten*] taller.
時間がたつにつれ私は不安になってきた As time went on, I *became* uneasy.
そんなにかたくならないで Don't *get* [*be*] so nervous.
彼の顔は怒りで真っ赤になった His face *turned* [*went*] red with anger.
その牛乳はすぐすっぱくなってしまった The milk soon *turned* [*went*] sour.
木々の葉が赤くなり始めた The leaves of the trees *are turning* [*going*] red.
現代社会はますます複雑になってきた Modern society *has become* more and more complicated.
100年後の地球はどうなるだろう What [*Whatever*] *will become* of the earth in 100 years? / *What will* the earth *be like* in 100 years? (❖become of … は主に what, whatever を主語とし,「…はどうなる」の意味. しばしば不安・懸念を表す)
◆大都市では交通量の多さが大問題となっている Heavy traffic *is* a major problem in big cities. / 今夜は雨になりそうだ It is *likely* to rain tonight. / 私の努力はすべてむだになった All my efforts *came to nothing*. / 彼の夢がとうとう現実になった His dream finally 「*came true* [*became a reality*]. / どうして故郷を出る気になったの(→何がそうする気にさせたのか) What 「*made you* [*led you to*] *leave your hometown*? / タマネギをあめ色になるまでいためてください Fry onions *until* brown. / 今から心配したってしようがないよ. なるようになるさ There's no use (in) worrying about it now. *What will be will be.*

🅒「ゆうべきょうの数学の試験の勉強をしていて寝ちゃったよ」「心配するなよ. なるようになるさ(→いまさらしようがない)」"I fell asleep last night while studying for today's math exam." "Don't worry. *It can't be helped now*."

❸【ほかのものに変わる】turn 圊, change 圊
オタマジャクシがカエルになった The tadpoles *turned* [*changed*] *into* frogs.
水は熱すると水蒸気になる Water *turns* [*changes*] *into* steam when heated.
雨が雪になった The rain *turned* [*changed*] *into* snow.
信号が赤から青になった The (traffic) light *turned* [*changed*] from red *to* green.
◆その戦争で町全体が灰になってしまった The whole town *was burned* [*reduced*] *to ashes* in the war. / 彼女の身にもなってごらん Put

yourself in her *place*. / 赤と青を混ぜ合わせると紫になる (→ 紫が得られる) Mix red and blue together, and you (*will*) get purple.

❹【…するようになる】come* to *do*, get* to *do*; (だんだん) grow* to *do*; (学んで…できるようになる) learn* to *do*; (…し始める) start to *do*, begin* to *do*

彼女の気持ちが分かるようになった I *have come* [*gotten*] *to* understand how she feels.

母は年をとるにつれ早く起きるようになった My mother *has come* [*gotten*] *to* get up early in the morning as she has gotten older.

練習すればだれでも自転車に乗れるようになる With practice anybody can *learn to* ride a bicycle.

いつからここで働くようになったのですか When did you *start* [*begin*] *to* work here?

◆コンピュータは家庭でもふつうに使われるようになってきている Computers *are becoming* more and more commonly used at home.

❺【…することになる】

二人は6月20日に結婚することになっている They *are going to* be married on June 20.

クリスマスパーティーには各自プレゼントを持っていくことになっている Everyone *is supposed to* bring a present to the Christmas party. (❖ be supposed to *do* は「(義務・責任として)…することになっている」の意味)

会議は来月2日になりました The meeting *was set for* the second of next month.

❻【ある結果になる】turn out, prove* ⓐ

その小説が彼の代表作となった The novel *proved* to be his masterpiece.

この先事態がどうなるかは見当もつかない I have no idea how things *will turn out* after this.

◆試験で1番になる come out first [on top] in the test

❼【ある数値・数量に達する】come* [amount] to …

合計で3,000円になります It「*comes to* [*is*] 3,000 yen in all.

◆2に3をかけると6になる Two times three *is* [*makes*] six. / 60秒で1分になる Sixty seconds *make* a minute. / There are sixty seconds in a minute. / 私たちの野球チームは全員で30名になる The members of our baseball team *number* 30 in all. / 近い将来, 老人と若者の比率は3対1になるだろう The proportion of old to young will *become* 3 to 1 in the near future.

❽【ある時点に達する】

5歳になる娘 a daughter *of* five

私は来年17歳になる I'll *be* 17 next year.

彼らは結婚して20年以上になる They've been *married* for over 20 years.

彼が亡くなって10年になる It *is* [*has been*] ten years since he died. / Ten years *have passed* since he died.

日本に来てどのくらいになりますか How long have you been in Japan?

うちの兄も結婚を考える年齢になった My brother *has reached* a marriageable age.

私はそのころ10歳になるかならないかだった I *was scarcely* ten at that time.

秋になると葉が色づき始める The leaves begin to change color *in* (*the*) *fall*.

今となっては後悔してもしかたがない It's no use regretting it *now*.

❷「全部でいくらになりますか」「3,000円になります」"How much *is* it altogether?" "It *comes to* 3,000 yen."

❾【ある役割・機能を果たす】(…として役立つ) serve as [for] … (❖ for は「…の代用として」の意味); (…の役を務める) act as …; (役割を果たす) play ⓐ

クレオパトラ役になる play [act] (*the part of*) Cleopatra

このソファーはベッドになる This sofa *serves as* a bed. / (→ベッドとしても使える) This sofa *can be* also *used as* a bed.

彼は後に続くすべての大統領の模範となった He *served as* a model for every president after him.

彼らの活動は両国間のかけ橋となった Their activities *acted as* a bridge between the two countries.

❿【実現・完成する】

新装なったホテル a *refurbished* hotel / 巨匠の手になる作品 the work *of a* master *hand*

琴光喜の全勝優勝はならなかった Kotomitsuki *was unable to* win the championship without losing a match.

⓫【構成されている】be made up of …, consist of …

二酸化炭素は炭素と酸素から成る Carbon dioxide「*is made up* [*consists*] *of* carbon and oxygen.

◆5章から成る小説 a novel *in* five chapters

⓬【その他】

あいつのわがままには我慢がならない I can't put up with his selfishness.

7時にお越しになるのをお待ちしています I'll expect you at seven.

なる² 鳴る sound ⓐ; (鐘・鈴・電話などが) ring* ⓐ; (警笛などが) blow* ⓐ; (目覚まし・警報などが) go* off

このトランペットはよく鳴らない This trumpet *doesn't sound* well.

私はいつも目覚まし時計が鳴る前に目がさめる I usually wake up before the alarm *rings* [*goes off*].

ベルが鳴ると彼女は玄関へ飛んでいった When the doorbell *rang*, she flew to the door.

きのうは一日電話が鳴りっぱなしだった The telephone *rang* constantly all day yesterday.

試合開始のゴングが鳴った The bell *rang* for the start of the match.

試合終了の笛が鳴った The whistle *blew* for the end of the game.

◆ほら, ベルが鳴ってるよ. 時間だ *There goes the bell*. Time is up. / 空腹でおなかが鳴って

いる My stomach is growling [rumbling] with hunger. / 南の方で雷が鳴っていた It was thundering [There was thunder] in the south.

🗨「電話が鳴ってるよ」「私が出るわ」"The phone is ringing." "I'll get it."

なる[3] 生る (実をつける) bear* [他] [自]; (実る) grow* [自] //庭のイチジクの木に実がなっている The fig tree in the garden is bearing fruit. / Figs are growing on the tree in the garden. / この木には実がなりますか Does this tree bear fruit? / この木は毎年たくさんの実がなる This tree bears a lot (of fruit) every year. ◆実のなる木 a fruit tree

ナルシシスト narcissist [nɑːrsísist] [C]

なるべく (できるかぎり) as ... as possible [one can]; (できれば) if (at all) possible, preferably; (もししなくてすむなら)《口語的》if one can help it //きょうはなるべく早く寝るようにしよう I'm going to bed as early as possible [I can] tonight. / なるべく午前中に来ていただきたいのですが I'd like you to come here before noon, if possible. / お電話いただけますか. なるべくきょう中にお願いしたいのですが I'd like you to call me, preferably today.

なるほど なるほどお金はだいじだが, それがすべてというわけではない It is true that money is important [Money may be important], but it is not everything. / なるほど彼の言うとおりだ He's right, indeed. / (→彼は全く正しい) He's quite right. / 彼の言葉を聞いてなるほどと思った (→彼の言葉に納得した) I was「convinced by [satisfied with] his words.

🗨「こんなふうにしてアメリカの歴史は始まりました」「なるほど」"This is how American history started." "Oh, I see."

🗨「ちょっと用事があるからきょうは早く帰るよ」「なるほどね, 彼女とデートか」"I'm going home early. I've got something to do today." "Well, well, well. [Aha!] So you have a date with your girlfriend."

なれ 慣れ (経験) experience [U]; (実地) practice [U] //この器具をうまく操作するには慣れが必要だ You need experience [practice] to be good with this apparatus.

なれあい 馴れ合い cozy relationship [C]; (示し合わせること) conspiracy [U] [C], 《公式的》collusion [U] //行政と業者とのなれ合い a cozy relationship between the civil service and companies

ナレーション narration [U] [C]

ナレーター narrator [C]

なれそめ 馴れ初め 二人のなれ初めを聞かせてください Please tell me how you first met [got to know] each other?

なれっこ 慣れっこ 隣の部屋の騒音にもう慣れっこになっている I'm completely accustomed [used, hardened] to the noise from the next room.

なれなれしい 馴れ馴れしい overly familiar, too friendly ―なれなれしく overly familiarly, too friendly //彼は先生に対してなれなれしい He is「overly familiar [too friendly] with his teacher. / 彼女はなれなれしく話しかけてきた She talked to me「in an overly familiar manner [overly familiarly]. / 彼になれなれしくするな Don't be「overly familiar [too friendly] with him.

なれのはて 成れの果て あれが天才といわれた男のなれの果てだ (→彼はかつて天才と呼ばれたが今では落ちぶれてしまっている) He was once called a genius but now he has become a wreck [failure].

なれる[1] 慣れる get* [become*] used to ..., get [become] accustomed to ... (❖to の後には名詞・動詞の ~ing 形がくる. 「慣れている」という状態を表すには get [become] の代わりに be を用いる); (新しい環境などに) settle [自]; (順応する) adjust (oneself) to ...

彼女はすぐ新しい学校に慣れた She soon「got used to [got accustomed to, settled into, adjusted (herself) to] the new school.

母は長時間の運転には慣れていない My mother is not used [accustomed] to driving for a long time.

彼は旅慣れた人だ He is used [accustomed] to traveling.

どう, もう (新しい環境・仕事に) 慣れてきた? How are you settling in?

◆履き慣れた靴 broken-in shoes / そのような仕事に慣れていない I'm new [unaccustomed] to such work. / 暗がりに目が慣れてきた My eyes have adjusted to the darkness. / 彼は慣れた手つきでそばを打った He made buckwheat flour noodles「in an experienced way [skillfully]. (❖「慣れない手つきで」は「in an inexperienced way [unskillfully] という)

[慣用表現] 習うより慣れろ ⇨ ならう(習う)

なれる[2] 馴れる become* tame [tamed]; (家畜化される) become domesticated ―なれた tame, tamed, domesticated //よくなれた猫 a tame cat / その馬は人になれない That horse won't be tame [tamed].

◆生徒たちはだんだん新しい先生になれてきた Gradually the students are becoming friendly with the new teacher.

なわ 縄 rope [U] [C]; (細い) cord [C] [U] //わら束を縄で縛る tie [fasten, bind] a bunch of straws with a rope / 荷物の縄を解いた I untied the rope around the load.

‖縄ばしご a rope ladder

なわしろ 苗代 rice nursery [C]

なわとび 縄跳び《米》rope jumping [U], 《英》(rope) skipping [U]; (縄跳びの縄)《米》jump rope [C], 《英》skipping rope [C] ―縄跳びをする《米》jump rope, 《英》skip [自]

なわばり 縄張り (動物・人間の) territory [C] [U]; (親しみのある場所・専門分野) one's turf; (管轄権)《公式的》jurisdiction [U] //人の縄張りを荒らす trespass on a person's turf / ライオンの群れにはそれぞれの縄張りがある Each pride of lions has its own territory.

‖縄張り争い a fight for [to protect] one's territory

なん 難 (困難) difficulty [C]; (不足) shortage ⓒ ⓤ, scarcity ⓤ; (問題) problem ⓒ; (欠点) defect ⓒ; (危険) danger ⓒ; (災難) disaster ⓒ ⓤ ∥ 食糧難 *a shortage [scarcity] of food*／　その会社は財政難に陥っていた The company fell into *financial difficulties*.／　彼は任された仕事を難なくこなした He carried out the task 「*without any difficulty [with ease]*.／　すばらしい案だが, 難を言えば実際にお金がかかりすぎる That is quite a nice plan. But *the only problem [defect] is that* it would cost too much to carry it out.／　彼は見た目はいいが, 性格に難ありだ He is good-looking but *has a defect* in his personality.／　我々は危うく難を逃れた We 「*had a narrow escape from [narrowly escaped] danger*.

◆ここ数年は大変な就職難だ It's been *very hard to get a job* in the last few years.

なん- 何-

❶【(疑) 何】what

● あそこにあるあれは何ですか *What*'s that over there?

● 君は学校では何て呼ばれているの *What* are you called at school?

● 雨だろうと何だろうと行かなければならない I have to go even if it rains *or whatever*.／　何にしてもこの宿題をできるだけ早く片づけてしまわなくては *Anyway*, I have to finish this homework as soon as I can.

💬「あのう, 田中さん」「何ですか」"Uh, Miss Tanaka." "*Yes*?"

💬「夕食はどういうものが食べたいですか」「何だってかまいませんよ」"What kind of food do you want to have for dinner?" "*Anything 「will do [is OK]*."

💬「どうしてそんなことをするの」「何だっていいでしょ」"Why do you do such things?" "*It's none of your business*."

❷【どの・何という】what (❖名詞の前に置いて疑問を表す形容詞句を作る)

● それは何ページに出ていますか *What page* is it on?

● きょうは何曜日ですか *What day (of the week)* is (it) today?

💬「君は何年生ですか」「高校1年生です」"*What grade* are you in?" "I'm in the 10th grade." (❖日本の高校1年生は米国の10年生に当たる)

💬「彼は何月生まれですか」「7月生まれです」"*In which month* was he born?" "In July."

💬「そのレースで彼は何着だったのですか」「2着です」"*Where* did he *finish* in the race?" "He finished second."

❸【いくつ・どれだけ】how many

● 今年何センチ身長が伸びましたか *How many centimeters* have you grown this year?

● 週に英語の授業は何時間ありますか *How many* English classes are there in a week?

● この絵を描き上げるのに彼は何か月かかったのだろうか I wonder *how many months* it took him to paint this picture.

❹【不特定の数】(いくらかの) some, several; (少数の) a few; (多くの) many, a lot of ...

● その子はウサギにニンジンを何本か与えた The child gave *some [a few]* carrots to the rabbits.

● 彼は何百枚もの CD を持っている He has as many as *several hundred* CDs.

● 平均株価がここ何週間かじりじりと上がってきている The average price of stocks has edged up over *the last few weeks*.

● これらの伝統工芸は何世代にもわたって受け継がれてきたものです These traditional arts have been handed down *for many [a lot of] generations*. (❖複数形で数量の多いことを表すこともできるので, 単に for generations としてもよい)

● そこまで何分もかかりませんよ It doesn't take *many minutes* to get there.／　(→ほんの数分で着く) It takes just *a few minutes* to get there.

◆あれから何週間も過ぎた *Weeks* have gone by since then.／　会場には何十人[何百人, 何千人, 何万人]もの人が集まった *Dozens [Hundreds, Thousands, Tens of thousands]* of people gathered in the hall.／　その人は1950何年かの生まれだ The person was born "in *1950 something* [(→1950年代に) in *the 1950s*]."／　その湖へはここから20何キロも歩かなければならない We have to walk "*more than 20* [(口語的) *20-odd*] *kilometers*" from here to get to the lake.

❺【その他】

● 自分で言うのも何ですが (→自慢するつもりはないが), 私は料理の天才だと思うんです *I don't mean to brag, but* I think I'm a genius at cooking.

なんい¹ 南緯 the south latitude ∥ 南緯40度25分の所に at [in] *latitude* 40° 25′ *S* (❖40°25′S は *forty degrees twenty-five minutes south* と読む)

関連語 経度 longitude／　北緯 the north latitude

なんい² 難易　問題の難易度は星印の数で示している *The degrees of difficulty* of the problems are indicated by the number of stars.

なんい³ 何位　そのレースで彼は何位でしたか In *what place* did he finish the race?

なんおう 南欧　Southern Europe

なんか¹ 南下　──南下する go* (down) south, go southward

なんか² 軟化　──軟化する soften [sɔ́ːfən] 🄐 🄱 ∥ 人に対する態度を軟化する *soften one's* attitude toward a person

なんか³ 何か　何か (→どういうわけか) だるいなあ I *somehow* feel sluggish.／　(→少々) I feel *a little* sluggish.／　この電気, 何かだめみたいだよ This light *just* doesn't seem to work.／　何か変なにおいがしないか Don't you smell *something* strange? ⇨ なにか

-なんか　彼は全然紳士なんかじゃない He *is anything but a gentleman*.／　あいつなんかサーフィンができるもんか There's no way he can surf.／　シャツが欲しいならこれなんかどう

If you want a shirt, how about this one? / あなたなんか大嫌い I *hate* you!(❖「なんか」に相当する英語はない. 否定の強意表現など, その場に応じてニュアンスを伝えるようにすればよい)

なんかい¹ 何回 how many times, how often
やめなさいと何回言ったら分かるの *How many times* do I have to tell you to stop it?
この曲は何回聴いても飽きない I never get bored with this song *no matter how*「*many times* [*often*] I listen to it.
◆彼女とは以前に何回か食事をしたことがある I have eaten with her *several* [*a few*] *times* before. / このあたりにはまだ何回か余震があるだろう There will be *some* [*several, a few*] more aftershocks around here. / その映画はもう何回も見た I've seen the movie「*many times* [(→繰り返し) *over and over (again)*]. / (野球で)今, 何回ですか What *inning* is it?
🗨️「イタリアへは何回行ったことがあるの」「3回です」"*How many times* have you been to Italy?" "I've been there three times."
🗨️「年に何回海に行きますか」「1, 2 回かな」"*How many times* a year do you go to beach?" "Once or twice, I think."

> [英作文ノート] **often** と **a, an**
> 週に何回テニスをやっていますか
> →×How *often* a week do you play tennis?
> →○How *many times* a week do you play tennis?
> →○How *often* in a week do you play tennis?
> ★「…につき」の意味の a, an は often とは結びつかない.

なんかい² 難解 ――難解な difficult (to understand) / 彼の詩は難解すぎる His poems are too *difficult* (*to understand*).

なんかん 難関 (困難な点) difficulty ⓒ; (障害) hurdle ⓒ, barrier ⓒ; (難所) a dangerous [difficult] point to pass through / 大学入試の難関を突破する succeed in getting over *the difficulty* [*hurdle*] of the entrance examination for a university / その点が今回の交渉におけるいちばんの難関である That is *the most difficult hurdle* in this negotiation. / That is *the sticking point* in this negotiation. / 登山隊はこのルート中最大の難関である岩場にさしかかった The climbers were approaching the rocky area, which was *the most dangerous point to pass through* on this route.
‖難関校 a school with highly competitive admissions

なんぎ 難儀 (困難) difficulty ⓤ ⓒ; (苦労) trouble ⓤ 《また複数形～s》 ――難儀な hard, difficult; (仕事などが) laborious / 腕を骨折して難儀している I'm having *difficulty* [*troubles*] due to my broken arm. / 難儀な仕事を任された I'm burdened with a *hard* [*difficult, laborious*] task.

なんきゅう 軟球 rubber ball

なんきょく¹ 南極 the South Pole; (南極地方) the Antarctic ――南極の Antarctic ‖南極海 the Antarctic Ocean / 南極観測 Antarctic research / 南極観測基地 an Antarctic base / 南極観測隊 an Antarctic research team / 南極圏 the Antarctic Circle / 南極大陸 Antarctica, the Antarctic Continent / 南極点 the (geographical) South Pole

なんきょく² 難局 (難しい状況) difficult situation ⓒ; (危機) crisis ⓒ (複 crises); (困難・難事) difficulty ⓤ ⓒ /難局に直面する face a「*difficult situation* [*crisis, difficulty*] / 難局を乗りきる get over a「*difficult situation* [*crisis, difficulty*]

なんきん 軟禁 confinement ⓤ; (自宅軟禁) house arrest ⓤ /彼は自宅に軟禁されていた He *was*「*under house arrest* [*confined in his own house*].

なんくせ 難癖 (文句を言う) complain ⓥ; (けちをつける) niggle ⓥ; (非難する) criticize ⓥ; (あら探しをする) find* fault with … /彼は買った物に傷があると店に難癖をつけた He「*complained to* [*niggled at*] the store that the item he had bought had a flaw in it.

なんこ 何個 戸棚の中にコップは何個ありますか *How many glasses* are there in the cupboard? ➡ いくつ

なんこう¹ 軟膏 ointment ⓒ ⓤ, salve [sǽv] ⓒ ⓤ /傷口に軟膏を塗る apply some *ointment* to a cut

なんこう² 難航 ――難航する make* slow progress, proceed slowly /2社間の交渉は難航している The negotiations between the two companies *are*「*making slow progress* [*proceeding slowly*]. / The negotiations between the two companies *aren't proceeding smoothly*.

なんごく 南国 (南の国) southern country ⓒ; (特定の国の南部地方) the south, the southern part of the country /彼は南国生まれの南国育ちだ He was born and raised in *the south* [*southern part of the country*].

なんこつ 軟骨 《解剖》 cartilage ⓒ ⓤ; (食肉の) gristle ⓤ

なんさい 何歳 智美は何歳ですか *How old* is Tomomi?

なんざん 難産 difficult delivery [labor] ⓒ /姉は難産だった My sister had *a difficult delivery* [*labor*].

なんじ 何時 what time; (いつ) when
朝食は何時にとりましたか *What time* [*When*] did you have breakfast? / *What time* was your breakfast?
最終バスは何時に出ますか *What time* [*When*] does the last bus leave?
(電話などで)ひかるさんは何時ごろお帰りですか About *what time* is Hikaru expected?
これは何時までに仕上げればいいのですか *By what time* do I have to finish this?
◆そのレストランは何時までやっていますか How

なんしき 軟式 ‖軟式テニス tennis played with a soft ball / 軟式野球 rubber ball baseball (❖どちらも日本で考案されたもの)

なんじゃく 軟弱 ──軟弱な (弱い) weak, too delicate; (柔らかい・体が虚弱な) soft; (地盤などが) not firm [solid] ‖今の若者は軟弱だとよくいわれる Young people today are often said to be *weak* [*too delicate*]. / その地域の地盤は軟弱だ The ground is「*not firm* [*soft*] around the area.

なんしょ 難所 彼らは今回のマラソンコースの最大の難所にさしかかった They have come to *the* most *difficult part* of this marathon course.

なんしょく 難色 彼らはその案に難色を示した They *expressed reservations* about the proposal.

なんすい 軟水 soft water ⓊⒸ

なんせい 南西 the southwest ──南西の southwest, southwestern

ナンセンス nonsense Ⓤ ‖あいつの言っていることは全くナンセンスだ What he's saying「*is sheer nonsense* [*doesn't make any sense at all*].

なんだ 何だ 何だ, だれかと思ったら良男じゃないか *Oh,* it's you, Yoshio! I didn't notice you. / この程度の熱が何だ I *don't give a damn about* this fever. (❖not ... a damn で「全く…ない」の意味) / 何だ, その口のきき方は What do you mean by talking like that? / 何だと？もう1回言ってみろ *What did you say?* Say that again! / それが何だってんだ *So what?* / 何だ, まだ宿題やってるの？早く終わらせなよ *Hey*, you're still doing your homework? Come on, finish it right away. / 最近は何だかんだ忙しい I've been busy doing *this and that* recently. / 私たちが何だかんだ言っても彼の決心は変わらないだろう He won't change his mind *no matter what* we say.
🔴「きょうはお店はお休みだって」「何だ, がっかり」"They say the store is closed today." "*Oh no*, what a disappointment!"

なんだい 難題 (難問) difficult problem [question] Ⓒ; (無理な注文) unreasonable demand Ⓒ ‖人に難題を吹っかける make *an unreasonable demand* on a person

なんたいどうぶつ 軟体動物 mollusk Ⓒ

なんだか 何だか ❶【何であるのか】それが何かさっぱり分からなかった I didn't have the slightest idea *what* it was. / その映画は何が何だか (→全然) 分からなかった I didn't understand the movie *at all*. / I didn't understand *what* the movie meant *at all*.
❷【何となく】(どういうわけか) somehow, for some reason; (いくらか) 《口語的》a (little) bit, 《口語的》kind of ‖きょうは何だかとても気分がいいな *Somehow*, I feel very fine today. / 何だか眠い I feel「*a bit* [*kind of*] sleepy. / 何だか夢のようだ This is *just like* a dream.

なんだったら 何だったら 何だったら (→お望みならば) 私から彼女に手伝ってくれるよう頼んであげてもいいよ I can ask her to help you out, *if you like*.

なんだって 何だって 何だって彼はあんなことを言ったんだろう *Why* did he say such a thing?
🔴「私, 結婚するの」「何だって」"I'm getting married." "*What?* / *You what?*"
➪なぜ

なんたん 南端 島の南端 the「*southernmost part* [*southern tip*] of the island

なんちゃくりく 軟着陸 soft landing Ⓒ ‖火星に軟着陸する make *a soft landing on* Mars

なんちょう 難聴 祖父は難聴だ My grandfather「*is hard-of-hearing* [*has difficulty hearing*].

なんて 何て 新聞には何て書いてある *What* does the paper say? / なんてすてきな絵なんだ *What* a nice picture! / あなたはなんて人なの *What kind of* person are you? / なんてこった *Holy cow* [*cat, mackerel*]! / なんてったってカレーライスがいちばんさ *Above all*, I like curry and rice best.

-なんて 彼は人の気持ちなんてちっとも考えちゃいない He doesn't think *the least little bit about* how others feel. / ロックなんて聞いたこともありません I have never listened to *what you call* rock. / 宇宙人なんてものは信じない I don't believe in *such things as* extraterrestrials. / 宿題なんてもういやだ I *don't want* to do homework *anymore*. / こんな寒さの中, 泳ぐなんて君はどうかしているよ It is crazy *of you* to swim in this cold weather. / You are crazy *to* swim in this cold weather. / 彼が試験に落ちるなんて！He *has gone and* failed the exam! / 私がしゃべったなんてだれにも言わないでね Don't tell anybody *that* I told you. / 彼女なしで生きるなんて考えられない I *cannot imagine* myself living without her. / 中華料理なんてどう *How about* Chinese food?

なんで 何で why ➪なぜ

なんでも 何でも

❶【どれでも・どんなものでも】anything; (…するものはどんなものでも) whatever; (何もかも) everything

何でも話してね, だれにも言わないから You can

tell me *anything*. My lips are sealed.
言いたいことは何でも言っていいよ You can say *anything* [*whatever*] you want to.
それを手に入れるためなら私は何でもする I would do *anything* to get it.
彼女は何でも自分の思いどおりにしないと気がすまない She must have *everything* her own way.
彼は何でも本気にしてしまう He takes *everything* seriously.
何か荷物を入れる物をください. 何でもいいです Please give me something to carry my things in. *Anything* 「will do [is OK].
赤ん坊は何でもかんでも口に持っていく Babies will put *absolutely anything* into their mouths.
◆彼女はスポーツなら何でも得意だ She is good at *any* kind of sports.
🍀「何飲みたい」「牛乳以外なら何でもいいよ」 "What do you want to drink?" "*Anything* but milk."
❷【どうやら】
何でもあの二人は別れたらしいよ I hear [They say] the two broke up.
‖何でも屋(何でもこなす人) a jack-of-all-trades; (雑貨屋) a general store, a drugstore

なんでもない 何でもない
彼にしてみれば100メートル泳ぐくらい何でもないことだ It's *nothing* (*special*) for him to swim 100 meters. / (→簡単だ) It's *easy* for him to swim 100 meters.
彼らは何でもないことでけんかを始めた They started a quarrel over *nothing*.
彼は友達でも何でもない He isn't my friend or *anything*.
🍀「え？何だって」「何でもない」 "What? What did you say?" "*Nothing*."
🍀「どうして泣いているんだい」「何でもないよ」「何でもないようには見えないけど」 "Why are you crying?" "*Nothing*. / *No reason*." "It doesn't seem to be *nothing*."
なんてん 難点 weak point ◎ ‖その辞書は大きすぎて持ち歩けないのが難点だ Being too large to be portable is *the* 「*weak point* [*weakness*] of the dictionary.

なんと 何と

❶【何・どんなこと・どう】what; (どう) how
英語で「イモリ」を何と言いますか *What* is the English for "imori"? / *How* do you say "imori" in English?
これは何という果物ですか *What* do you call this fruit?
そのとき彼女が何と言ったか覚えていますか Do you remember *what* she said then?
あなたには何とお礼を言っていいか分かりません I don't know *how* to express my thanks to you. / I can't (even) begin to thank you.
何とおっしゃいましたか *What* did you say? / I beg your pardon? / 《口語的》Beg your pardon? / 《口語的》Pardon (me)?

何と言えばいいのか分からず, 彼は彼女を抱きしめた Not knowing *what* to say, he gave her a hug.
他人が何と言おうと, 僕は彼女と結婚するぞ *No matter what* [*Whatever*] *people say*, I'm going to marry her.
◆あの子を厳しくしからないで. 何といってもまだ子供なんだから Don't scold him so severely. *After all*, he's only a child.
🍀「それで, その絵はどんなものでしたか」「何というか, その, 不思議な感じのする絵でした」 "And what did the picture look like?" "Well, *how can I explain it* — it was sort of mysterious."

❷【感嘆】how, what

> **語法** 感嘆文は通例《How＋形容詞[副詞]（＋主語＋動詞）！》か《What＋a [an]）＋形容詞＋名詞（＋主語＋動詞）！》で表す. 一般にはこの形をとらずに It's very big!, Wow, it's big! などの表現をする場合が多い.

なんと大きい雪だるまだろう *How* big this snowman is! / *What* a big snowman (this is)! / This snowman is *very* big!
なんという美しさだ *How* beautiful!
なんという(ひどい)においだ *What* a smell!
◆なんと前の彼氏が私を訪ねてきたのよ Who *should* come to see me but my ex-boyfriend. (◆should は疑問詞とともに用いて驚きの感情を表す) / 彼はなんと100メートルを11秒で走った *Amazingly*, he ran 100 meters in 11 seconds. / くじで何が当たったと思う, なんとパリ旅行よ！ Guess what I won in the lottery — *get this* — a trip to Paris! / なんということだ. こんな悲惨な結果になろうとは *Oh no*! [*Holy cow*!] Who could have imagined a terrible result like this?

なんど[1] 何度

❶【回数】how many times; (どのくらいの頻度で) how often ➡なんかい(何回)

何度言ったら分かるんだ *How many times* do I have to tell you?
このCDは何度聴いても飽きない This CD never makes me bored *no matter how* 「*many times* [*often*] I listen to it.
◆この試験は何度受けてもよい You can take this test *any number of times*. / 子供のころそこへ何度か行きました I went there *several times* when I was a child. / I made *several visits* there when I was a child. / その映画なら以前に何度も見たことがある I've seen that movie *many times* before. / 何度となく君に連絡しようとしたが, 連絡がつかなかった I tried to reach you *many times*, but I couldn't get through. / 階段を駆け下りちゃだめって何度も言ったでしょ I've told you 「*again and again* [*over and over* (*again*)] not to run down the stairs.
🍀「大阪へは何度行ったことがありますか」「3度行きました」 "*How many times* have you been to Osaka?" "I've been there three times."

❷【角度・温度など】

●「角Cは何度になりますか」「50度です」 "*How many degrees* will angle C be?" "It'll be 50°." (❖ 50°は fifty degrees と読む)

●「暑いねえ,何度あるの」「39度だよ」 "Isn't it hot! *What's the temperature?*" "It's 39℃." (❖ 39℃ は thirty-nine degrees centigrade と読む)

●「熱は何度あるの」「38度5分」 "*What* is your *temperature?*" "It's 38.5°C."

●「明石市の経度は何度ですか」「東経135度です」 "*What* is the longitude of Akashi City?" "It's 135° E longitude." (❖ 135° E は one hundred (and) thirty-five degrees east と読む)

なんど² 納戸 storeroom Ⓒ, storage room Ⓒ

なんという 何という ⇒ なんと

なんとう 南東 the southeast ――南東の southeast, southeastern

なんとか 何とか

❶【どうにかして】 somehow (or other), by some means (or means), (in) one way or another / 何とかする manage 自他 (❖ しばしば can や could を伴う)

彼は何とか最終電車に間に合った He caught the last train *somehow*. / He *managed to* catch the last train.

何とかして彼を助けてあげたいのですが I want to help him *somehow* [*by some means, one way or another*].

彼らは何とか暮らしを立てている They make their living *somehow*.

今度の日曜日,何とか都合つけられない? Can't you *manage* the time next Sunday?

ひとりで何とかやれます I *can* [*I'll*] *manage* by myself.

◆それに関しては彼が何とかしてくれるでしょう I hope he'll「*take care of* [*do something about*] the matter. /あのうるさい犬を何とかして (→静かにさせて) ください Would you *do something to silence* the noisy dog? / ラッシュ時の超満員電車,何とかならないものかね (→混雑を減らす方法はないのか) *Isn't there any way to* make rush-hour trains less crowded?

●「調子はどう」「何とかやっているよ」 "How're you doing?" "*Surviving!*"

❷【不確か】

彼は松平とか何とかいう名前だったと思うが,正確には覚えていない His name is *something* (*or other*) Matsudaira, but I can't remember exactly.

確か彼女の名前は中田とか何とかだったと思う I think her name was Nakata *or something*.

さっき何とかさんという男性から電話があったよ Mr. *so-and-so* [*whatshisname*] called you a little while ago. (❖ 女性の場合, Mr. は Ms. [Mrs., Miss], また whatshisname は whatshername となる)

新製品のあの何とかシャンプー,使ってみた? Have you tried that new shampoo, *whatever it's called*?

❸【何か】 something

彼女に何とか言って慰めてやってください Please say *something* to comfort her.

●「あんな人全然興味ないわ」「とか何とか言っちゃって (→そうは言うものの),本当は好きなんでしょ」 "I'm not interested in him at all." "*That's what you say*, but you do like him, don't you?"

なんとしても 何としても somehow or other; (どんなに費用・労力をかけても) whatever the cost; (何があっても) at any cost //何としてもコンサートのチケットを手に入れるぞ I'm going to get a ticket for the concert「*somehow or other* [*whatever the cost, at any cost*].

なんとでも 何とでも そんなはした金,何とでもなるさ I *can manage to get* a small sum like that.

なんとなく 何となく その曲を聞いて何となく (→どういうわけか) 悲しくなった *Somehow* [*For some reason*], I felt sad when I listened to the song. / I don't know why, but I felt sad when I listened to the song. / その2人は何となく (→どことなく) 似ている The two resemble each other *in some way*. / 暇な時間を何となく (→特に目的もなく) 過ごした I spent my free time 「*without any particular purpose* [*aimlessly*]. / その動物は何となくライオンのように見えた The animal looked *something* like a lion.

●「そのとき彼の言ったことを覚えてる?」「うん,何となくだけどね」 "Do you remember what he said at the moment?" "Yes, but 「*not clearly* [*only vaguely*]."

なんとも 何とも

❶【どうとも】(全く…ない) not ... at all

彼のこと,何とも思ってないわ I *don't* care about him *at all*.

彼の冗談はおもしろくも何ともなかった His joke *wasn't* funny *at all*. / His joke was *anything but* funny.

◆それについては何ともしようがない There's *nothing at all* that I can do about it. /彼は人に暴力をふるうのを何とも思っていない He *thinks nothing* of being violent with others. /彼女は階段から落ちたが何ともなかった She fell down the stairs but *was all right*. / (→けがをしなかった) She fell down the stairs but *didn't get hurt*. / 結果がどうなるか,何とも言えないよ I *can't say anything* about what the result will be.

●「彼らはこれからどうなるんだろうね」「何とも言えないね」 "What do you think will happen to them?" "*Who knows?* / *You never can tell*."

❷【全く】 quite; (とても) very; (本当に) really

宝くじが当たったなんて何ともうらやましいな I'm *quite* [*very, really*] envious of your winning the lottery.

それは何とも悲しい物語だった It was 「*quite a* [*a very, a really*] sad story.

何とも申しわけない I'm *quite* [*very, really*] sorry.

なんなく 難なく ➩ なん

なんなら 何なら 何なら私が代わりに部屋の掃除をしますよ I'll clean the room instead of you, 「*if you don't mind* [*if you like, if you wish, if it's OK*].」/ 何ならクラブやめてもいいんだぞ You can quit the club, *if you want to*. / 何なら彼に聞いてみたら？ Why don't you ask him, *then*? / 遊園地が何なら映画でも見に行こう Why don't we go to a movie 「*if the amusement park doesn't suit you* [(→いやなら) *if you don't like the amusement park*]?

なんなり 何なり 私にできることがありましたら何なりとお申し付けください If there is anything I can do for you, please *feel free* to ask.

なんなんせい 南南西 the south-southwest
──南南西の south-southwest

なんなんとう 南南東 the south-southeast
──南南東の south-southeast

なんにち 何日
あれから何日過ぎただろうか How many days have passed since then?
何日かしたらまた来ます I'll be back *in several* [*a few*] *days*.
隣の家はもう何日も留守にしている Nobody's been home in the next house *for (many) days*.
展示会の開催期間は何日から何日までか知っていますか Do you know *between what dates* they will hold the exhibition?
🔴「きょうは何日ですか」「8月19日です」 "*What is the date* today?" / "*What day of the month is it* today?" "It's August 19."
🔴「学校は何日に始まるの」「8日です」 "*What day* [*When*] will school start?" "On the eighth."
🔴「東京には何日間滞在しましたか」「10日間です」 "*How many days* [*How long*] did you stay in Tokyo?" "Ten days."

なんにも 何にも 何にも聞こえないよ I can't hear *anything* at all. / 箱の中には何にもなかった There was *nothing* in the box. / そんなに心配したって何にもならない It's *no use* worrying so much. / It's *useless* worrying so much. / Worrying so much *gets* you *nowhere*. / あれほどの苦労も結局何にもならなかった The great pains I'd taken 「*came to nothing* [*ended in vain*].

なんにん 何人 ご家族は何人ですか How many *people* are there in your family? / How *large* is your family? / このバスには何人の乗客が乗れますか How many *passengers* can this bus accommodate? / 何人かの刑事が行方不明の少年のことを聞き回っている *Some* [*Several, A few*] detectives are asking around about the missing boy. / メンバーのうち何人かはその計画に反対だった *Some* [*Several, A few*] *of* the members were against the plan. / その歌手の周りにはファンが何人も集まっていた *A lot of* fans surrounded the singer. / その試験に受かった人は何人もいなかった (→ほんの少数が受かった) *Only a few* people passed the exam. / (→受かった人はほとんどいなかった) *Few* people passed the exam.

なんねん 何年
眼鏡をかけるようになってからまだ何年もたっていない Not *many years* have passed since I began to wear glasses.
私はもう何年も動物園へ行っていない I haven't been to a zoo *for* [(米) *in*] *years*.
彼らは結婚する何年も前から知り合いだった They had known each other *for years* before they got married.
何年かするうちにこのあたりの景色も変わってしまうことだろう The scenery around here will change *within* 「*a few* [*several*] *years*.
何年かかっても必ずこの作品を完成させるぞ I will finish this work *no matter how many years it takes*.
何年も使っているうちにカーペットはすり切れてしまった *Over the years* the carpet has worn away.
何年前に彼は結婚したの *How many years ago* did he get married?
🔴「イギリスには何年いたの」「4年です」 "*How many years* were you in Britain?" "For four years."
🔴「北海道にいたのは何年から何年までですか」「1990年から1994年までです」 "*What years* [*When*] were you in Hokkaido?" "From 1990 to 1994."
🔴「来年は平成何年でしたっけ」「15年です」 "*What year* of Heisei is next year?" "The 15th year."
🔴「君は今高校の何年なの」「3年です」 "*What grade* [*year*] of high school are you in?" "I'm in the 12th grade [3rd year]." ❖《米》では学年を小学・中学・高校を通して数えるため，grade を用いると高校3年は the 12th grade となる．大学の場合は What year of college are you in？とする．
🔴「何年に中学を卒業しましたか」「1998年です」 "*In what year* [*When*] did you graduate from junior high school?" "In 1998."

なんの 何の
❶ 【疑問】 what
何の映画が上映されているのですか *What* movie is showing?
これは何の刺し身ですか *What kind of sashimi* is this? / *What fish* is this *sashimi* from?
何のためにそれをやっているのですか *What* are you doing it *for*?
それは何の（→何のための）道具ですか *What* is the tool *for*?
こんな夜中に電話してきて，いったい何の用だ *What do you mean* by [*What do you want*,] calling me this late at night?
あしたは何の日 *What*'s special about tomorrow?
🔴「これから彼とデートなんでしょ」「え，何の話」 "You are about to go out with him, aren't you?" "*What are you talking about*?"

❷【少しの】(少しの…もない) not any, no, not ... at all
私の忠告は彼には何の役にも立たなかった My advice「*didn't* do him *any* good [did him *no* good].
今度の日曜は何の予定もありません I *don't* have *any* plans *at all* for next Sunday.
その件に関しては何の問題もありません There's *no* problem about the matter.
◆何の気なしに *without any* particular purpose / 彼はその事件と何の関係もない He has *nothing to do* with the incident.
❸ {その他}
彼, うるさかったのなんって You can't image how noisy he was.

なんのかの 何の彼の 母は何のかのと口うるさい My mother is always nagging at me about *this and that*.

なんぱ¹ 軟派 彼はナンパに失敗した He failed to *pick up a girl*.

なんぱ² 難破 shipwreck ⓊⒸ ——難破する be wrecked / 彼の乗った船はスコットランド沖で難破した His ship *was wrecked* off the coast of Scotland. / He *was shipwrecked* off the coast of Scotland.
‖難破船 a wreck, a shipwreck

ナンバー (番号・曲目) number Ⓒ ((略語)No., no., n.; #の記号を用いることもある); (車の) license [registration] number Ⓒ; (ナンバープレート) 《米》license plate Ⓒ, 《英》numberplate Ⓒ / 70年代のヒットナンバー *a hit number* from the 70's / 品川ナンバーの車 a car with *a Shinagawa license plate* / ロック界のナンバーワンギタリストといえばだれだと思いますか Who do you think is *the number one* guitarist in the rock world?
◆彼はこの学校でナンバーワンの俊足だ He is *the fastest runner* in this school.
‖バックナンバー 《米》a back issue, 《英》a back number

なんばん 何番
彼女の電話番号は何番ですか *What's* her phone *number*?
(間違い電話に対して)何番におかけですか *What number* are you calling?
次の３つのうち, 正しい答えは何番だと思いますか *Which number* do you think is the correct answer in the following three?
佐藤の打順は何番ですか *Where* is Sato *in the batting order*?
英語のテストの成績はクラスで何番でしたか *Where* did you *rank* in the English exam in your class?
埼玉は日本で何番目に大きい県ですか *Where* does Saitama *rank* among Japanese prefectures in terms of area?
●「君の席は前から何番目ですか(→その列で君の机の前にいくつ机がありますか)」「５番目です(→ ４つです)」 "*How many* desks are there *in front of* yours in the line?" "There are four of them."
●「何番目の車両に乗っていますか」「前から５番目です」 "*Which* car are you in [on]?" "The fifth car from the front."
●「クリントンは戦後何番目の大統領ですか」「10番目」 "*How many* postwar presidents were there before Clinton?" "There were nine." (❖「彼は戦後10番目の大統領でした」は He was the 10th postwar president.という)

なんびょう 難病 (容易に治らない) intractable disease Ⓒ; (不治の) incurable disease Ⓒ / 難病を克服する overcome *an intractable disease* / 難病に苦しむ人々 people suffering from *intractable [incurable] diseases*

なんびょうよう 南氷洋 the Antarctic Ocean

なんぶ 南部 the south, the southern part; (米国の) the South ——南部の southern ——この町の南部に in *the southern part* of this city

なんべい 南米 South America ——南米の South American ‖南米諸国 South American countries / 南米大陸 the South American Continent

なんぽう 南方 the south ——南方の south, southern / 小笠原諸島は東京の南方にある The Ogasawara Islands lie to *the south* of Tokyo.

なんぼく 南北 (the) north and (the) south
◆日本は南北に長い国だ Japan is a country which runs *north and south.* / Japan is a country which runs *from north to south.*
‖南北アメリカ North and South America / 南北戦争(米国の) the Civil War / 南北問題 North–South problems

なんみん 難民 refugee Ⓒ, displaced person Ⓒ / 国連は難民のために救済活動を組織した The U.N. organized a relief operation for *the refugees*.
‖難民キャンプ a refugee camp

なんもん 難問 difficult [hard] problem Ⓒ, conundrum Ⓒ / 難問に取り組む wrestle with a「*difficult problem [conundrum]*」/ 難問を抱える have *a difficult [hard] problem* / 彼女の前にはいくつかの難問が立ちふさがっている She has some「*difficult problems [conundrums]*」before her.

なんよう 南洋 the South Seas

なんら 何等 彼がいなくても何ら支障はなかった His absence「*didn't* present *any* problems [presented *no* problems]」to us. / 何ら問題はない There's「*not* a problem [*no* problem]*at all*」/ 彼女はその事件と何ら関係がない She *has nothing to do* with that incident. / それに関しては何らかの対策を講じなければならない We have to take *some* measure *or other* against that.

ニ 〔音楽〕D ⓒⓊ / ニ長調 *D* major
に¹ 荷 (積み荷) load ⓒ; (貨物) freight [fréit] Ⓤ (◆(英)では陸上運送貨物は goods を用いる); (船・飛行機などの) cargo ⓒⓊ (複 ～es, ～s); (重荷) burden ⓒ ◆船に荷を積む[から荷を下ろす] load [*unload*] a ship
慣用表現 これで肩の荷が下りた That *took a load off my mind.* / この仕事は彼には荷が重かったかもしれない This work might *be too much* for him.
に² 二 two; (2番目) second

-に

❶【場所】 at; in; on
❷【方向・目標(点)】 to; toward(s), for
❸【時間】 at; on; in
❹【動作・行為の対象】 to, for
❺【動作主】 by
❻【目的・変化の結果】 to *do*, for
❼【原因・理由】 for, from, with

❶【場所】 at; in; on

語法
[at と in]
(1) at は 1 点と考えられるような比較的狭い範囲の地点を表すのに用いる. in は広い範囲の場所を表す. 通例, 大陸・国・大都市には in を用い, 小さな市・町・村・場所には at を用いる.
(2) 自分の生活・行動している場所など, 「広がりが感じられる場所は小さくても in を用いる」// 私はこの町に 5 年間住んでいる I have lived *in* this town for five years.
(3) 大都市でも, 単に地図上の 1 点, または飛行機などの乗り換え場所を指す場合は at を用いる // 私たちはエジンバラに行く途中ロンドンに寄った We stopped *at* London on our way to Edinburgh.
[on]
(1) on は表面に接触していることを表す // 天井にハエがとまっていた There was a fly *on* the ceiling.
(2) 「…に沿って」「…に面して」「…の側に」の意味でも用いる // 彼は彼女の右側に座った He sat *on* her right.

彼女は受付にいます She is *at* the reception desk.
この電車は豊橋に止まりますか Does this train stop *at* Toyohashi?
この時間はだれも家にいません Nobody will be (*at*) home at this time of the day.
私たちは 9 時前に駅に着いた We arrived *at* the station before nine.
彼らの乗った飛行機は今夜パリに着く予定だ Their plane will arrive *in* Paris tonight.
彼女の弟は今オランダに住んでいる Her brother now lives *in* Holland.
私はホテルの部屋のクローゼットの中に上着を忘れてきた I left my jacket *in* the closet in the hotel room.
僕らの町にドーム球場ができた A domed stadium has been built *in* our city.
壁にかかっている絵をご覧なさい Look at the painting *on* the wall.
父の会社はそのビルの 3 階にある My father's office is *on* the third floor of that building.
その男性は左手の薬指に指輪をしていた That man had a ring *on* his ring finger.
うちの前にパトカーが止まっていた A police car was parked in front *of* my house.
◆旅館の近くに沼があった There was a pond *near* the inn. / 私たちは川に沿って歩いた We walked *along* the stream.
❷【方向・目標(点)】 to; toward, (英)towards, for; into; at

語法
to は「…へ」「…まで」という意味で「到達した[すべき]地点」を表し, 全体の表現はそこへ到着することを前提にする. 一方 for や toward(s) は「…に向かって」という意味で, 単に行く方向を示しており, 到達すべき点に着くかどうかは問わない. into は「…の中に(向かって)」という意味を表す. at はその動作の目的となる対象を表す.

次の角を右に曲がりなさい Turn *to* the right at the next corner.
夏休みに家族で箱根に行った Our family went *to* Hakone during the summer vacation.
洋子は駅の方に向かって歩いていた Yoko was walking *toward* the station.
その男の子の関心は犬に向けられていた The boy's interest was directed *toward* the dog.
このバスは新宿方面に行きますか Is this bus *for* Shinjuku?
彼らは来週南極点に向けて出発する They are setting off *for* the South Pole next week.
彼は洋服も着替えずにベッドに潜(ᵒᵘ)り込んだ He got *into* his bed without changing his clothes.
子供たちはプールに飛び込んだ The children jumped *into* the swimming pool.
その車はガードレールにぶつかった The car ran *into* the guardrail.
猫に石を投げつけるなんて悪い子ね It's nasty of you to throw a stone *at* a cat.
警官は泥棒に飛びかかった The police officer leaped *at* the thief.
❸【時間】 at; on; in

語法
at は「特定の時点・時刻」を指すのに用いる. on

は「特定の日・曜日」に用い, in は「比較的長い期間」を指すのに用る。一般的な「午前・午後」には in を用いるが,「特定の日の午前・午後」には on を用いることに注意。また this week (今週に), next month (来月に), tomorrow morning (あすの朝に) などの句は,前置詞を伴わず副詞的に用いられる場合も多い。

あしたの朝6時に起こしてね Wake me up *at* six tomorrow morning.

正午に教会の鐘が鳴ります The church bells ring *at* noon.

麻子は1985年11月18日に生まれた Asako was born *on* November 18, 1985.

私は月曜と木曜にピアノのレッスンがある I have piano lessons *on* Mondays and Thursdays.

母はいつも朝早くに犬を散歩させる My mother always walks the dog early *in* the morning.

姉が10月にアメリカから帰ってきます My sister is coming back from the United States *in* October.

2050年に地球はどうなっているだろう What will the earth look like *in* 2050?

その事件は5月2日の夜に起きた That incident took place *on* the night of May 2.

土曜の朝に電話します I'll call you Saturday morning.

◆僕は夏休み中に北海道のおじの家を訪ねた I visited my uncle in Hokkaido *during* the summer vacation. / 商品は1週間以内にお手元に届きます The goods will be delivered to your home *within* a week.

❹【動作・行為の対象】to, for (❖動作・行為の対象を示す「…に」は,英語では他動詞の目的語として表される場合も多い)

なぜ試合が延期になったのか僕たちに説明してください Please explain *to* us why the game has been put off.

小麦粉に溶き卵を加えてよく混ぜなさい Add the beaten eggs *to* the flour and mix well.

私は彼にお弁当を作ってあげた I made a picnic lunch *for* him.

喫煙は体によくない Smoking is bad *for* your health.

子供たちはサンタに手紙を書いた The kids wrote a letter *to* Santa. / The kids wrote Santa a letter.

姉は私にTシャツを買ってきてくれた My sister bought a T-shirt *for* me. / My sister bought me a T-shirt.

ドアにかぎをかけるのを忘れてしまった I forgot to lock the door.

◆赤に青を混ぜると紫になる If you mix red *with* blue, you will get purple.

🅰「ふたがどうしてもあかないのよ」「僕に貸してみて」"The lid won't come off." "Give it *to* me."

❺【動作主】by

彼女は友達に「まっぴ」と呼ばれている She is called "Mappi" *by* her friends.

金閣寺は足利義満によって建立されたといわれている Kinkakuji is said to have been built *by* Ashikaga Yoshimitsu.

◆パーティーの司会は相沢さんにやってもらおう We are going to ask Mr. Aizawa to em-cee the party.

❻【目的・変化の結果】to *do*, for

理沙は宇宙工学の勉強にアメリカの大学へ行った Risa went to a university in the United States *to* study space engineering.

彼はやせるために毎朝ジョギングをしている He jogs every morning *to* lose some weight.

私たちは散歩に出かけた We went *for* a walk.

あの家は売りに出ている That house is *for* sale.

◆また近いうちに会いに来てね Come (and) see me again soon. / 大きくなったら何になりたいの What do you want to be when you grow up? / その小説は英語とフランス語に訳されている That novel has been translated *into* English and French.

❼【原因・理由】for, from, with

彼はうそをついたために罰を受けた He was punished *for* telling lies.

世界には飢餓に苦しむたくさんの子供たちがいる There are a lot of children in the world suffering *from* starvation.

私は寒さに震えていた I was shivering *with* cold.

◆彼女はあまりの驚きに声も出なかった (→話せないくらい驚いた) She was so surprised that she couldn't even speak.

❽【比較】

人生はよく航海にたとえられる Life is often compared [likened] *to* a voyage.

数学の点に比べたら英語はまだましなほうだ I'd say my grade in English is rather good compared *to* my grade in math.

❾【割合】

彼は年のわりに若く見える He looks young *for* his age.

ワールドカップは4年に1回開催される The World Cup is held *every* four years.

❿【…として】

祖母の還暦のお祝いに温泉旅行をプレゼントした We gave our grandmother a trip to a spa *as* a present for her 60th birthday.

おばから入試合格のお祝いにお金をもらった I got a gift of money from my aunt *for* passing the entrance exam.

⓫【その他】

その国は天然資源に恵まれている That country is rich *in* natural resources.

にあい 似合い ◇似合いのカップルだ They are a *well-matched* couple. / They make a *fine* pair.

にあう 似合う suit ⓜ, 《公式的》 become* ⓜ, look good [nice] on *a person*; (つり合う) match ⓜ

その髪型がいちばんよく似合うね That hairstyle *suits* you best.

あなたのスーツにはこのスカーフがよく似合います This scarf *matches* your suit well.

にかい

◆彼女は顔に似合わず(→見かけよりも)よく食べる She eats more *than she appears to.* / 祖父は年に似合わず元気です My grandfather is healthy *for his age.*

🄮「このドレス,どう」「とてもよく似合っているよ」"How does this dress look on me?" "It *looks* really *good on you.*"

にあげ 荷揚げ ──荷揚げする unload 🄒 🄓; (特に船から) discharge 🄒 🄓

ニアミス near miss ⓒ /2機の飛行機がニアミスを起こした There was *a near miss* between two airplanes.

にい 二位 (the) second place; (2位の人・団体) runner-up ⓒ (複 runners-up, ~s) /彼女は100メートル走で2位に入った She was *the runner-up* in the 100-meter race. / She ranked [came in] *second* in the 100-meter race.

◆2位に入賞する win (*the*) *second prize*

にいがた 新潟

> 新潟県は,北で日本海に面しています。冬には雪が多く降り,この県の一部では積雪がしばしば4メートル以上になることもあります。県の中央部に広がる新潟平野は,日本で最も長い信濃川が流れており,産出量・品質ともにすぐれた米どころとして有名です。
> Niigata Prefecture faces the Sea of Japan to the north. This prefecture usually receives heavy snow in winter, and in some areas the snow often reaches more than four meters in depth. The Niigata plain stretches across the center of the prefecture and the Shinano, the longest river in Japan, runs through it. This plain is famous as a rice-producing district that is distinguished for both the quantity and quality of its rice.

にいさん 兄さん one's older [elder, big] brother

> 語法
> (1) 英語では,必要なとき以外兄か弟かの区別をせず,「兄さん」も older や big を付けないことが多い。(電話で)お兄さんに代わってもらえますか May I speak to *your brother?*
> (2) 英語では,弟や妹が兄を呼ぶときは,相手の名を指すのがふつう /兄さん,起きてよ Wake up, *Jim.*

ニーズ needs /消費者のニーズにこたえる meet *the needs* of consumers

◆その業界は若い人材のニーズが高い *There's a great demand for* young capable people in that industry.

にいんせいど 二院制度 bicameral [two-chamber] system 🄒

にえきらない 煮え切らない (優柔不断な) indecisive, (公式的) irresolute; (どっちつかずの) noncommittal /彼の煮え切らない態度にいらいらした I was irritated by his *noncommittal* attitude.

にえくりかえる 煮え繰り返る (お湯などが) boil hard /彼の言葉を聞いてはらわたが煮えくりかえった His words *made my blood boil.*

にえたぎる 煮え滾る 煮えたぎったお湯 *boiling* (*hot*) water

にえゆ 煮え湯 boiling water ⓤ
慣用表現 彼は信頼していた友人に煮え湯を飲まされた(→ひどく裏切られた) He *was terribly betrayed* by a friend he had trusted.

にえる 煮える boil, be boiled; (火が通る) cook 🄒, be cooked /野菜が煮えた The vegetables *have been cooked.* / シチューが煮える The stew *is boiling.*

におい 匂い・臭い smell ⓤ ⓒ; (不快な) 《公式的》odor ⓤ ⓒ; (かすかな) scent [sént] ⓤ ⓒ; (芳香) fragrance ⓤ ⓒ; (悪臭) stink ⓒ

このバラはいいにおいがする This rose *has a* sweet *smell* [*scent, fragrance*]. / This rose *smells* sweet.

ごみ置き場はひどいにおいがした The garbage dump *had a bad smell.* / The garbage dump *smelled* bad. / (→ひどく臭かった) The garbage dump *stank.*

部屋は薬のにおいが充満していた The room was filled with *the odor* of medicine.

ああ,いいにおいだ What *a nice smell!*

何,このにおい What is this *smell?*

◆花のにおいをかぐ *smell* flowers / その小屋は木のにおいがした The hut *smelled* of wood. / 何かがこげるにおいがしませんか Can you *smell* something burning? / この香水はせっけんのようなにおいがする This perfume *smells like* soap. / この町は庶民的なにおいがする(→雰囲気がある) There is *a casual atmosphere* in this town.

におう 匂う・臭う smell* 🄒; (悪臭が) stink* 🄒

この魚はにおう This fish [*smells* (*bad*) [*stinks*].

その男はいつも酒がにおう The man always *smells* [*stinks*] *of* liquor.

彼らの関係はにおう(→怪しい) Their relationship *smells fishy.*

◆何かにおわない? *Don't* you *smell* something? (⚠この smell は「…のにおいがする」の意味の他動詞) / その話もにおう(→怪しく聞こえる) The story *sounds fishy.*

におわす 匂わす 彼女は香水をぷんぷんにおわせていた She *gave off a strong odor of* perfume. / その選手は引退をにおわせた The player *hinted at* his resignation. / 彼は犯行をにおわせる発言をした He made a remark which *implied* he committed the crime.

にかい 二階 《米》the second floor, 《英》the first floor ⇨ かい(階) /受付は2階にあります The reception [information] desk is on *the second floor.*

◆2階へ上がる go *upstairs* / 2階建ての家 a *two-storied* [*two-story*] house / 妹は2階でテレビを見ていた My sister was watching TV *upstairs.* / 彼はいすを2階へ運んだ He carried the chair *upstairs.* / 父は2階から(→階下へ)降りてきた My father came *down-*

stairs.
‖2階建てバス a double-decker

にかい² 二回 週に2回水泳を習っている I take swimming lessons *twice* a week. / アメリカに来たのは今回で2回目です This is *the second time* I have been to America.

にがい 苦い
❶【味が】bitter
苦いコーヒー *bitter* coffee
❷【いやな】(つらい) bitter, hard; (不機嫌な) sour
いろいろ苦い経験をした I have had many *bitter* [*hard*] experiences.
その話をすると彼女は苦い顔をした She made a *sour* face when I told her the story.
[ことわざ] 良薬は口に苦し ➔ りょうやく

にがおえ 似顔絵 portrait [C]; (風刺の) caricature [C]; (容疑者の) composite drawing [C] ‖彼女は週刊誌に政治家の似顔絵を描いている She draws *portraits* of politicians for a weekly magazine.

にかこくご 二か国語 two languages ‖彼女は二か国語が自由にしゃべれる She can speak *two languages* fluently. / She is *bilingual.*

にがす 逃がす (自由にする) set* ... free, let* ... go; (取り逃がす) let ... escape ‖トンボを逃がしてやった I *set* the dragonfly *free.* / I *let* the dragonfly *go.* / 彼らは泥棒を逃がしてしまった They *let* the thief *escape* [*get away*]. ◆彼はせっかくのチャンスを逃がした He *missed* a good opportunity.

にがつ 二月 February [U][C] (《略語》Feb.)
➔ いちがつ

にがて 苦手 私は世界史が苦手だ I *am* ｢*weak in* [*poor at*] world history. / I *am not good at* world history. / 私はからい物が苦手です (→好きではない) I *don't care for* spicy food. / 由美は高い所が苦手だ (→怖い) Yumi *is afraid of* heights. / 彼女はカエルが大の苦手だ She *hates* frogs. / 彼はどうも苦手だ (→扱いにくい) Somehow it's *hard* for me *to deal with* him.

にがにがしい 苦々しい 祖父は最近の若者たちの態度を苦々しく思っているようだ It seems my grandfather *is disgusted with* the attitude of young people today.

にがみ 苦み bitterness [U]; (苦い味) bitter taste [C] ‖パセリには苦味がある Parsley has *a bitter taste.* / Parsley tastes *bitter.*

にがむし 苦虫 [慣用表現] 弟は苦虫をかみつぶしたような顔をした My brother made *a sour face* at me.

にかよう 似通う resemble [他] ‖2つの説にはいくつか似通った点がある The two opinions ｢*resemble* each other [*are alike*] in some ways.

にかわ 膠 glue [U] ◆2枚の板をにかわでつける *glue* the two boards *together*

にがわらい 苦笑い 彼は相撲で子供に負けて苦笑いした He *gave an embarrassed smile* when the child beat him at sumo.

にき 二期 two periods, two terms ‖彼は議長を2期務めた He served *two terms* as chairman.

にきび pimple [C], 〔医学〕acne [ǽkni] [U] ‖にきびをつぶす squeeze *a pimple* / 顔ににきびができた *Pimples* came out on my face.
◆兄はにきびだらけの顔をしている My brother has a *pimpled* [*pimply*] face.

にぎやか 賑やか
❶【活気のある】 ―にぎやかな lively; (場所が) busy; (せかせかした) bustling; (込み合った) crowded; (繁盛している) prosperous
バスはにぎやかな通りに出た The bus came to a *busy* [*lively, bustling*] street.
この商店街も以前はにぎやかだった This shopping mall used to be *prosperous.*
◆パーティー会場は花やテープでにぎやかに飾られていた The party room was *gaily* decorated with flowers and streamers.
❷【陽気な】 ―にぎやかな cheerful; (騒がしい) noisy
外がにぎやかだ It is *noisy* outside.
◆彼女はにぎやかな(→よくしゃべる)人だ She is a *talkative* person.

にぎらせる 握らせる 彼に金を握らせる *bribe* him

にぎり 握り grip [C]; (取っ手) handle [C]
◆ひと握りの米 *a handful of* rice / バットの握り方を変えたほうがいい You'd better change *the way you grip* the bat.
‖握り寿司(ずし) (hand-rolled) sushi / 握り飯 a rice ball

にぎりこぶし 握りこぶし (clenched) fist [C] ‖握りこぶしを作る make *a fist*

にぎりしめる 握り締める (ぎゅっと) grasp [他], grip [他]; (しっかりと) hold* ... tightly; (こぶしを) clench [他] ‖こぶしを握りしめる *clench one's* fist / 彼はお守りをぎゅっと握りしめた He *grasped* [*gripped*] the charm firmly. / その男の子は100円玉を握りしめていた The boy *was holding* a 100-yen coin *tightly* in his hand. / 彼女は子供の手を握りしめた She *held* her child's hand *tightly.*

にぎりつぶす 握り潰す (手で) crush ... in *one's* hand; (提案などを) squash [他] ‖空き缶を握りつぶす *crush* an empty can *in one's hand* / 彼の提案は握りつぶされた His proposal *was squashed.*

にぎる 握る
❶【物などを】(しっかりと) grip [他], clasp [他], grasp [他]; (手に持つ) hold* [他], take* hold of ...
ペンを握る *hold* a pen
女の子は母親の手をしっかりと握った The girl *gripped* [*clasped, grasped*] her mother's hand firmly.
クラブをしっかり握って球を打ちなさい *Grip* your club and hit the ball.
◆おにぎりを握る *make* a rice ball / 決勝は手に汗握る熱戦だった The final was an *exciting* [a *gripping*] game.
❷【権力・秘密などを】
彼女に弱みを握られた(→彼女は私にとって不利な何かを知っている) She *had* something *on* me. / (→私の秘密を知っている) She *knows*

my secret.
自民党が現在政権を握っている The Liberal Democratic Party 「*is in power* [*holds power*] now.
わが家は母が財布のひもを握っている My mother *holds* [*controls*] the purse strings in my house.
彼が事件解決のかぎを握っている He *holds* the key to solve the case.

にぎわい 賑わい，(雑踏) bustle ⓤ; (人出) crowd ⓤ 〃休日のディズニーランドは大変なにぎわいを見せる On holidays there is *a great crowd* at Disneyland.

にぎわう 賑わう (人で) be crowded; (活気で) be bustling; (場所が) be alive; (繁栄する) be prosperous 〃土日にはその公園はたくさんの人でにぎわう On Saturdays and Sundays the park *is crowded with* a lot of people. / 商店街はいつもにぎわっている The shopping street *is always prosperous*.

にぎわす 賑わす たくさんの料理が食卓をにぎわしていた A lot of foods *were served* on the table. / ここ数週間, 大統領のスキャンダルが新聞の一面をにぎわしている The President's scandal *has been splashed* across the front pages for the last few weeks.

にく 肉
❶【食用の】meat ⓤ
肉1切れ a piece of *meat* / 肉を焼く roast *meat*
この肉は硬い[柔らかい] This *meat* is tough [tender].
💬「お肉はどのように焼きましょうか」「ミディアムでお願いします」"How would you like *your meat* done?" "Medium, please."
❷【人間・動物の】flesh ⓤ
ライオンはシマウマの肉を食べていた The lions were eating *the flesh* of the zebra.
◆最近肉がついてきた (→体重が増えた) I've gained [put on] *weight* recently. / おなかの肉が落ちた I lost some *weight* around my stomach.
❸【果肉】flesh ⓤ
∥肉牛 beef cattle / 肉切り包丁 a butcher knife / 肉汁 meat juice; (スープ) broth; (肉を焼くときに出る) gravy / 肉団子 a meat ball / 肉離れ ⇨にくばなれ / 肉まん ⇨にくまん / 肉屋 (人) a butcher; (店) a butcher shop / 肉料理 meat dish / 牛肉 beef / 魚肉 fish / とり肉 chicken / ひき肉 ground [minced] meat / 豚肉 pork / 羊肉 mutton

にくい 憎い，憎いことを言う say *nice* things 〃あの男が憎い I *hate* that man.
ことわざ 坊主憎けりゃ袈裟(⑱)まで憎い ⇨ぼうず

-にくい be hard to *do*, be difficult to *do*
彼女の説明は分かりにくかった It was difficult *to* understand her explanation.
彼の字は読みにくい His handwriting *is hard to* read.
◆このペンは書きにくい This pen *doesn't* write *well*. / この紙袋は破れにくい This paper bag *doesn't* tear *easily*.

にくがん 肉眼 the naked eye 〃その島は肉眼でもはっきり見える The island is clearly visible even to *the naked eye*. / We can see the island clearly even with *the naked eye*.

にくきゅう 肉球 pad ⓒ
にくさ 憎さ hatred ⓤ 《また a ～》
にくしみ 憎しみ hatred ⓤ 《また a ～》, hate ⓤ 〃彼に対する憎しみは長い間消えなかった The *hatred* toward him didn't disappear for a long time. / 彼女は両親に対して憎しみをいだいている She has *a hatred* of [for] her parents. ◆彼らは憎しみ合っていた They *hated each other*.

にくしゅ 肉腫 tumor ⓒ, 〔医学〕sarcoma ⓒ
にくしょく 肉食 ——肉食の meat-eating; (肉食性の) carnivorous ∥肉食動物 a meat-eating [carnivorous] animal

にくしん 肉親 blood relation [relative] ⓒ; (家族) family ⓒ 〃彼は事故で肉親を失った He lost *his family* in the accident.

にくせい 肉声 (natural) voice ⓒ (❖機械を通した声と対比するとき以外は, 単に voice という)

にくたい 肉体 body ⓒ, the flesh ——肉体の bodily, physical 〃人の肉体的欠陥をあげつらうのは卑劣だ It's not fair to bring up someone's *physical defects*. / 彼らは肉体関係があった They had *physical relations*.
◆彼女は肉体的にも精神的にも疲れていた She was tired both *physically* and mentally.
∥肉体美 physical beauty / 肉体労働 physical [manual] labor / 肉体労働者 a manual laborer, a blue-collar worker

にくたらしい 憎たらしい，(憎むべき) hateful; (意地の悪い) spiteful, nasty, mean; (生意気な) cheeky, saucy 〃弟は最近憎たらしいことを言うようになった Recently my brother has started saying *cheeky* [*saucy*] things. / なんて憎たらしい女！ What a *nasty* woman!

にくづき 肉付き 彼は肉づきがいい He is *fleshy* [*plump*].

にくづけ 肉付け 脚本に肉づけする *flesh out* a script

にくにくしい 憎々しい hateful; (意地の悪い) spiteful; (悪意のある) malicious; (いまましい) provoking
◆彼は憎々しげに私たちのほうをにらんだ He glared at us *spitefully*.

にくはく 肉薄 敵陣に肉薄する (→近づく) *close in on* the enemy camp / 彼女は前のランナーに肉薄している She is 「*closing in on* [*running close behind*] the runner in front of her.

にくばなれ 肉離れ pulled muscle ⓒ
◆肉離れを起こす *pull a muscle*

にくひつ 肉筆 one's own handwriting
にくぶと 肉太 彼は肉太の字を書く He has a *bold* hand. / He has *bold* handwriting.

にくぼそ 肉細 彼女は字を肉細に書く She writes in a *light* hand.

にくまれぐち 憎まれ口 憎まれ口をたたくのはやめなさい Stop saying *spiteful* [*nasty*] *things*.

にくまれっこ 憎まれっ子 bad boy [child] [C]; (いたずらっ子) naughty boy [child] [C]
[ことわざ] 憎まれっ子世にはばかる Ill weeds grow apace. (→雑草は伸びるのが速い)

にくまれやく 憎まれ役 彼はいつも憎まれ役になる He always plays *the* 「*bad guy* [*villain*].

にくまん 肉饅 meat bun [C]

にくむ 憎む hate [他]; (ひどく嫌う) detest [他]
暴力を憎む *hate* violence
彼女は彼をひどく憎んでいる She *detests* him.
彼らは憎み合っている They *hate each other*.
◆それは憎むべき犯罪だ It is a *hateful* [*detestable*] crime.

にくめない 憎めない 彼は憎めない人だ *It's hard not to like* him. / 彼女は生意気だがどういうわけか憎めない She is cheeky, but somehow I *can't hate* her.

にくらしい 憎らしい hateful; (意地悪な) spiteful; (憎悪すべき) detestable; (しゃくにさわる) provoking ‖本当に憎らしいやつだ He is a really *hateful* man.
◆彼は憎らしいほど頭がいい He is *provokingly* smart.

にぐるま 荷車 cart [C] ‖荷車を引く pull [draw] *a cart*

にぐん 二軍 〔野球〕farm (team) [C] ‖その選手は二軍に落とされた The player *was* 「*sent to the farm team* [*farmed out*].

にげあし 逃げ足 泥棒は逃げ足が速かった The thief made *a* quick *getaway*.

にげおくれる 逃げ遅れる 彼女はその火事で逃げ遅れて大けがをした She *failed to escape from* the fire and she was badly injured.

にげこうじょう 逃げ口上 (口実) excuse [C]; (言い逃れ) evasion [C] ◆彼は逃げ口上がうまい He gives *evasive answers* well.

にげごし 逃げ腰 彼はやる前から逃げ腰になっている (→おじけづいている) He *gets cold feet* before doing it. / 警官が問い詰めると男は逃げ腰になった (→逃げる用意をした) The man *got ready to run away* when he was questioned closely by the policeman.

にげこむ 逃げ込む 猫は茂みに逃げ込んだ The cat *ran* [*fled*] *into* the bush.

にげだす 逃げ出す run* away; (一目散に) take* to *one's* heels ‖男の子は恐怖のあまり逃げ出した The boy *ran away* with terror.

にげば 逃げ場 (逃げ道) escape [C]; (出口) exit [C], way out [C] (複 ways out) ‖2階の住人は逃げ場を失った (→逃げ道を遮断された) The people living on the second floor had *their escape* cut off.

にげまわる 逃げ回る その泥棒は10か月の間あちこち逃げ回ったあげくつかまった The thief was caught after *having been on the run* for 10 months.

にげみち 逃げ道 escape [C], a way of escape ‖四方を追っ手に囲まれ, 男は逃げ道を失った (→遮断された) The man had *his escape* cut off surrounded by pursuers on all sides.

にげる 逃げる run* away; (人・場所などから) get* away; (逮捕などから) escape [自]; (追跡などから) flee* [自] [他]
彼らは地下の駐車場から逃げた They *ran away* from the underground parking garage.
大雨で川の水が増し, 住民は安全な場所に逃げた The river rose with the heavy rains, so the inhabitants *got away* to a safe place.
囚人が刑務所から逃げた The prisoners *have escaped* from jail.
男は国外へ逃げたらしい They say that the man *has fled* overseas.
◆鳥がかごから逃げてしまった The bird *has flown away* out of the cage. / いつまでもこの問題から逃げていてはいけない We shouldn't *avoid* this problem any longer. / 彼は先頭に立つとそのまま逃げ切った Once he took the lead, he *kept the position to the finish*. / 彼女は僕の質問をうまく逃げた She *evaded* [*dodged*] my question.
[ことわざ] 逃げるが勝ち Discretion is the better part of valor. (→慎重さは勇気の大半を占める)

にごす 濁す ❶【気体・液体などを】(水などを) make* ... muddy, make ... cloudy
❷【あいまいにする】私の質問に彼女は言葉を濁した (→あいまいな返事をした) She *gave a vague answer to* my question. / (→あいまいにものを言った) She *spoke vaguely* in response *to* my question.

ニコチン 〔化学〕nicotine [U] ‖ニコチン中毒 nicotine addiction; (人) a nicotine addict

にこにこ 彼は一日中にこにこしていた He *was smiling* [*beaming*] all day. / 彼女はにこにこしながら彼の話を聞いていた She was listening to him *with a smile*.

にこみ 煮込み 野菜の煮込み *a* vegetable *stew*

にこむ 煮込む (よく煮る) cook [boil] ... well; (とろ火で煮る) stew [他], simmer [他] ‖シチューを煮込む *cook* stew *well*

にこやか 彼女はにこやかに出迎えてくれた She welcomed me 「*with a smile* [*smilingly*].

にこり それを聞いて思わずにこりとした I *smiled* involuntarily when I heard it.

にごり 濁り 濁りのない声 a *clear* voice / 濁りのない心 a *pure* heart
‖濁り水 muddy water

にごる 濁る (水などが) become* [get*] muddy, become [get] cloudy; (空気などが) become foul [fául]; (音などが) be voiced ‖大雨が降って川の水が濁った The river water *got muddy* because of the heavy rain. / 部屋の空気は濁っていた The air in the room *was foul*.

にさん 二三 ―二, 三の two or three; (いくらかの) a few, a couple of ... ‖2, 3日もすれば熱は下がるでしょう Your temperature will come down in *a few days*. / 彼女には2, 3回会ったことがある I have met her 「*two or three times* [*a couple of times*].
◆二, 三注意しておきたいことがあります Let me give you *some* advice.

にさんかたんそ 二酸化炭素 carbon dioxide [U]

にし 西

the west ――西の west, western
神戸は大阪の西にある Kobe is to *the west* of Osaka.
◆彼らは西に向かった They went *west* [*westward*]. / そのビルは西向きだ The building *faces west*. / 東京では西も東も分からない(→不案内だ) I'*m a stranger* in Tokyo.
‖西半球 the Western Hemisphere

にじ[1] 二次 ――二次の (2番目の) the second; (二次的な) secondary ‖二次感染 secondary infection / 二次方程式 a quadratic equation / 第二次産業 secondary industry / 第二次世界大戦 World War II (❖IIは twoと読む), the Second World War

にじ[2] 虹 rainbow [C] //空ににじがかかった *A rainbow* appeared [formed] in the sky.

にじかい 二次会 after-party [C] (❖英語には「二次会」に相当する決まった表現がない) //結婚披露宴の二次会でカラオケに行った After the wedding reception, we went to a karaoke place for *the after-party*.

にしかいがん 西海岸 (米国の) the West Coast

にしかぜ 西風 west wind [C]

にしがわ 西側 the west; (西欧圏) the West ‖西側諸国 the West, the Western countries / 西側陣営 the Western bloc

にしき 錦 故郷ににしきを飾る(→大成功とともに故郷へ帰る) *return home with a great success*
‖ニシキゴイ a nishikigoi

にじげん 二次元 two dimensions ――二次元の two-dimensional

-にしては (…のわりには) for; (…を考慮に入れると) considering //この本は小説にしてはかなり短い This book is pretty short *for* a novel. / 高校生にしては彼は大人びている *Considering that* he is a high school student, he looks mature.

-にしても even if, though, granting that //その話が本当であるにしても、私は信じたくない *Even if* the story is true, I don't want to believe it.

にしび 西日 (午後の光) the afternoon sun; (夕日) the setting sun //私の部屋は西日がよくあたる My room gets plenty of *the afternoon sun*.

にじます 虹鱒 rainbow trout [C]

にじみでる 滲み出る (血などが) ooze [自]; (自然に表れる) reveal [他] //彼の額からは汗がにじみ出ていた Sweat *was oozing* from his forehead. / この絵には彼女の人柄がにじみ出ている This painting *reveals* her personality.

にじむ 滲む (ペン・紙などが) blot [自]; (色・インクなどが) run* [自]; (文字などが) be blurred //インクがにじんだ The ink *blotted*. / エプロンを洗ったら色がにじんだ The color *ran* when I washed the apron.
◆彼らは計画を実現させるために血のにじむような努力をした They made a *strenuous* effort to realize the plan.

にしめ 煮染め 🗻 *nishime*, vegetables, meat or fish cooked in soy sauce and other ingredients until most of the liquid is evaporated

にしゃたくいつ 二者択一 彼らは計画を中止するか続行するかの二者択一を迫られている They are forced to *choose between* stopping the project *and* continuing it.

にじゅう[1] 二重 ――二重の (重なった) double; (2つの部分から成る) dual ――二重に double; (2回) twice //彼の言ったことには二重の意味がある What he said has a *double* meaning. / めまいがして物が二重に見えた I felt dizzy and「saw things *double* [had *double* vision]. / プレゼントを二重に包んだ I wrapped the present *double*. / I *double-wrapped* the present. / 電気料金の請求書が二重に送られてきた I received electricity bills *twice*.
‖二重あご a double chin / 二重価格 dual prices / 二重国籍 dual nationality / 二重唱[奏] a duet / 二重人格 (a) dual personality / 二重人格者 a person with (a) dual personality, a Jekyll and Hyde / 二重生活 a double life / 二重否定 a double negative / 二重母音 a diphthong / 二重窓 a double window / 二重丸 a double circle

にじゅう[2] 二十 twenty; (20番目) twentieth //彼はおそらく20代前半[後半]だろう Maybe he is *in his* early [late] *twenties*.

にしょく 二色 two colors ‖2色刷り two-color(ed) printing

-にしろ パーティーに行くにしろ行かないにしろ, 来週までに彼女に返事をしなければならない *Whether* I go to the party *or* not, I must give her an answer by next week.

にしん 鰊 herring [C] (複 ～, ～s)

にしんほう 二進法 binary system [scale] [C]

ニス varnish [U] //彼はいすにニスを塗って仕上げた He finished the chair with *varnish*.

-にすぎない -に過ぎない (単に) only; (…以外の何物でもない) nothing but …; (…以上のものではない) no more than … //それはうわさにすぎない It's *only* a rumor.

にせ 偽

――偽の (模造の) imitation; (本物でない) false; (いんちきの) sham; (偽造した) counterfeit, bogus, fake
偽の免許証 a *false* driver's license
彼は偽医者だった He was *a fake doctor*.
‖偽金 counterfeit money / 偽札 a counterfeit bill [《英》note]

にせい 二世 (日系アメリカ人) nisei [C] 《また Nisei》(複 ～, ～s); (2代目) Junior [C] (《略語》Jr.) //ジョン・スミス2世 John Smith, *Junior* [*Jr.*] ◆エリザベス2世 Elizabeth *II* (❖Elizabeth the second と読む) / 彼はデビュー当時, 中田2世と呼ばれた He was called "*the Second Nakata*" when he made his debut.

にせたいじゅうたく 二世帯住宅 two-family home [C]

にせもの 偽物・偽者 (模造品) imitation [C]; (偽造物) counterfeit [C], fake [C]; (文書・芸術品の) forgery [C]; (人) impostor [C] ∥偽物のルビー an *imitation* ruby / 私が買ったロレックスは偽物だということが明らかになった It turned out that the Rolex I bought was *a counterfeit* [*fake*]. / その刑事は偽者だった The detective was *an impostor*.

-にせよ ➾ -にしろ

にせる 似せる (ならう) model [他]; (まねる) imitate [他]; (正確にまねる) copy [他] ∥字を手本に似せて書く *imitate* [*copy*] the model writing / この公園は有名な庭園に似せて造られた This park *was modeled on* a famous garden.

にそう 尼僧 nun [C]; (カトリックの) sister [C]

にそくさんもん 二束三文 古い家具を二束三文で売った I sold the old furniture *dirt-cheap* [*very cheap, for a song*].

にそくのわらじ 二足の草鞋 [慣用表現] 彼は俳優と画家の二足のわらじを履いている He *wears two hats* as an actor and a painter.

にだい 荷台 (自転車などの) carrier [C]

にだいめ 二代目 the second generation; (息子) Junior

にたき 煮炊き (炊事) cooking [U]

にたつ 煮立つ boil [自], come* to the [a] boil ∥スープが煮立ったら火を止めます Turn off gas when the soup *comes to the boil*.

にたてる 煮立てる 牛乳を煮立てる *boil* (*up*) milk; *bring* milk *to a* [*the*] *boil*

にたにた 彼はにたにたしながら漫画を読んでいた He was reading a comic, *smirking*.

にたもの 似た者 あの二人は似たもの夫婦だ The couple are *two of a kind*.

にたり 彼は私たちを見てにたりと笑った He *grinned* at us.

にたりよったり 似たり寄ったり どれも似たり寄ったり(→ほとんど同じ)なのでいちばん安いのを買った They *are almost the same*, so I bought the cheapest one./ (→ほとんど差はない) There's *not much difference* among them, so I bought the cheapest one.

にだんベッド 二段ベッド bunk beds

-にち -日 day [C] ∥2, 3日したら *in a couple of days* / 私は1日3回歯を磨く I brush my teeth three times *a day*.
◆きょうは何日ですか *What*'s *the date* today? / *What*'s today's *date*? / *What date* is it today? / 体育祭は5月の26日です The sports festival is on May *twenty-sixth*.

にちえい 日英 Japan and Britain ―日英の Japanese-British

にちぎん 日銀 the Bank of Japan ∥日銀総裁 the Governor of the Bank of Japan

にちじ 日時 日時は未定です *The time and date* haven't been fixed yet.

にちじょう 日常 (毎日) every day, daily; (通常) usually; (いつも) always ―日常の everyday, daily; (決まりきった) routine; (いつもの) usual ∥電気は日常生活に欠かせないものだ Electricity is indispensable to *everyday* [*daily*] *life*. / 英語でも日常会話くらいは話せるようになりたい I'd like to speak at least enough English for *everyday conversation*. / 彼が忘れ物をするのは日常茶飯事だ Forgetting things is *an everyday occurrence* for him.

にちどく 日独 Japan and Germany ―日独の Japanese-German

にちふつ 日仏 Japan and France ―日仏の Japanese-French, Franco-Japanese

にちべい 日米 Japan and America ―日米の Japanese-American, Japan-U.S., U.S.-Japan ∥日米安全保障条約 the Japan-U.S. Security Treaty / 日米関係 Japanese-American relations, relations between Japan and the United States

にちぼつ 日没 sunset [U], 《主に米》 sundown [U] ∥彼らは日没まで練習を続けた They went on training until *sunset* [*sundown*].

にちや 日夜 (昼も夜も) night and day, day and night; (常に) always; (絶えず) constantly ∥彼は目標達成のために日夜努力していた He *always* tried hard to achieve his objective.

にちゃく 二着 (第2番目) (the) second place; (2位の人) runner-up [C] (複 runners-up, ～s) ◆そのレースで彼は2着だった He finished *second* in the race.

にちよう 日用 ∥日用雑貨 daily goods / 日用品 daily necessities

にちようがっこう 日曜学校 (キリスト教会の) Sunday school [C][U]

にちようだいく 日曜大工 (仕事) do-it-yourself [U]; (人) do-it-yourselfer [C], Sunday carpenter [C]

にちようび 日曜日

Sunday [U][C] (《略語》Sun.)

日曜日の朝[午後, 夕方]に on *Sunday* morning [afternoon, evening]

日曜日にうちにおいでよ Come over to my house *on Sunday*.

その店は日曜日は休みだ The shop is closed on *Sunday* [*Sundays*].

今度の日曜日はドライブに行こう Let's go for a drive on next *Sunday*.

ある日曜日彼から電話があった He called me on a *Sunday*.

毎週日曜日に部屋の掃除をします I clean my room up every *Sunday*.

にちろ 日露 Japan and Russia ―日露の Japanese-Russian, Russo-Japanese ∥日露戦争 the Russo-Japanese War

-について about, of, on ➾ ついて

にっか 日課 (daily) routine [C][U], daily work [U], daily task [C] ∥朝のジョギングは彼の日課となった Jogging in the morning has become *a routine* in his life.
◆毎朝犬の散歩をすることを日課にしています(→必ず犬の散歩をする) I *make a point of* walking my dog every morning.

につかわしい 似つかわしい suitable; (言動が) becoming ∥その服はきょうのパーティーに似つかわしくない The dress *isn't suitable for*

today's party.
にっかん¹ 日刊 ――日刊の daily
‖日刊紙 a daily (newspaper)
にっかん² 日韓　Japan and South Korea ――日韓の Japanese-South Korean
にっき 日記　diary
彼女は毎日日記をつけている She keeps *a diary* every day.
きょう見た映画のことを日記に書いた I wrote about the movie I had seen today in *my diary*.
‖日記帳 a diary／絵日記 ⇒ えにっき
-につき ―に付き ❶ [⋯ごとに] a, per　‖入場料は1人につき700円です The admission fee is 700 yen *a [per]* person.
❷ [⋯のために] because of ...　‖雨天につき本日の試合は中止させていただきます *Because of* rain, we will call off today's game.
にっきゅう 日給　daily wages
◆日給で働く work *by the day*　‖彼は日給7,000円のアルバイトをしている He works a part-time job for 7,000 yen *a day*.
にっきょうそ 日教組 (日本教職員組合) the Japan Teachers' Union
ニックネーム　nickname ⇒ あだな
にづくり 荷造り　packing ――荷造りする pack　‖旅行の荷造りをする *pack* for the trip
にっけい 日系　日系アメリカ人 a Japanese-American／日系企業 a *Japanese* company／日系2世 a Nisei [*nisei*]
にっけいれん 日経連 (日本経営者団体連盟) the Japan Federation of Employers' Associations
ニッケル 〖化学〗nickel (❖元素記号 Ni)
にっこう 日光 (光) sunlight; (熱と光) sun; (心地よい) sunshine　‖この鉢植えは時々日光にあててください Put this potted plant in *the sun* sometimes.／肌をあまり長い間日光にさらしてはならない Don't expose yourself *to the sun* too long.／子供部屋には日光がよく入る The child's room gets a lot of *sunshine*.／直射日光のあたらないところに保存してください Please keep it out of *direct sunlight*.
◆父は庭で日光浴をしていた My father *was sunbathing* in the garden.
にっこり 女の子はほめられてにっこりした The girl *smiled* [*gave a smile*] when she was praised.
にっし 日誌 (私的な) diary; (公的な) journal　◆学級日誌をつける keep *a daily record of class activities*
にっしゃびょう 日射病　sunstroke　‖日射病にかかる suffer from *sunstroke*; have *sunstroke*
にっしょう 日照　新しいビルが建ち，近くの住民は日照権を奪われた(→新しいビルが近くの住民の太陽の光を奪った) A new building deprived those living nearby of *sunlight*.
‖日照時間 the daylight hours
にっしょうき 日章旗　the Rising Sun Flag
にっしょく 日食　solar eclipse ‖皆既日食 a total eclipse of the sun／部分日食 a partial eclipse of the sun
にっしんげっぽ 日進月歩 (着実な進歩) steady advance; (急速な進歩) rapid progress　‖情報通信の世界は今や日進月歩で発展している The world of information and communication is now making 「*steady advances* [*rapid progress*].
にっすう 日数 (the number of) days　‖修理にはどのくらい日数がかかりますか How many *days* [*How long*] does it take to repair it?
にっちもさっちも　彼は有り金を使い果たしてにっちもさっちもいかなくなった(→窮地に陥っている) He is 「*in a fix* [*driven into a corner*] because he spent all his money.
にっちゅう¹ 日中　日中は暑いですが夜になると涼しくなるでしょう Though it will be hot *in the daytime*, it will be cooler tonight.
にっちゅう² 日中　Japan and China ――日中の Japanese-Chinese ‖日中戦争 the Japanese-Chinese War／日中平和友好条約 the Japan-China Treaty of Peace and Friendship
にっちょく 日直　day duty　‖きょうは彼が日直だ He *is on day duty* today.
にってい 日程　schedule, program; (旅の) itinerary　‖日程を組む plan *a schedule*／今月は日程がだいぶ詰まっている I have *a full [tight] schedule* this month.／旅行の日程は決まりしだいお知らせします We'll let you know *the itinerary* as soon as we make it up.
‖日程表 a program, a schedule
ニット　knitwear ◆ニットのスカート a *knit [knitted]* skirt
‖ニット製品 knit [knitted] goods
にっとう 日当 (1日の手当) daily allowance; (日給) daily wages　◆6,000円の日当を払う *pay* 6,000 yen *a day*
にっぽん 日本　Japan ⇒ にほん
につまる 煮詰まる　boil down, be boiled down ‖シチューが煮詰まって水を足した Because the stew *boiled down*, I added some water to it.／計画はだいぶ煮詰まってきた The plan *has been boiled down* to near completion.
につめる 煮詰める　boil down ‖豆を煮詰める *boil down* the beans ◆もう少しこの企画を煮詰めて(→話し合って)みよう Let's *discuss* this project a little more.
にディーケー 2DK　an apartment with two rooms and a combination kitchen-dining room
にと 二兎　ことわざ 二兎を追う者は一兎をも得ず If you run after two hares, you will catch neither.
にど 二度 (2回) twice, two times; (再度) again; (2度目) the second time
私は週に1，2度その本屋へ行く I go to the bookstore *once or twice* a week.
私は彼女に2度電話した I called her *twice* [*two times*].
祖母は週に2度病院に行く My grandmother

にとう

goes to the hospital *twice* a week.
海外旅行をするのはこれが2度目だ This is *the second time* (that) I have traveled abroad.
ここに来ることは二度とないだろう I'll never come here *again*.
二度とそんなことを言ってはいけません Don't say that *again*.
ことわざ 二度あることは三度ある It never rains but it pours. (→雨が降れば必ずどしゃ降りになる); Misfortunes never come alone. (→不幸は続くものだ)

にとう 二等 (2番目) the second (place); (乗り物の) the second class ━━2等の (2番目の) (the) second; (2級の) second-class ∥2等賞を取る win (*the*) *second prize* ◆彼は50メートル走で2等になった He came in *second* in the 50-meter race. ∥2等車 a *second-class car*

にとうぶん 二等分 私たちはケーキを2等分した We divided [*cut*] the cake *into two equal parts*./ We divided [*cut*] the cake *in half*.

にとうへんさんかくけい 二等辺三角形 isosceles[aisásəliz] triangle

-にとって それは私にとって重要な問題だった It was an important matter *to* me. / このテレビ番組は英語の学習者にとってとても役に立つ This TV program is very useful *for* learners of English.

にどでま 二度手間 弟が食器を洗ったが、結局は母の二度手間になった My brother washed the dishes, but it meant *double work* for our mother.

にどと 二度と 二度とそんなことをしてはいけませんよ Never do that *again*.

ニトログリセリン 【化学】nitroglycerin(e)

になって 担い手 子供たちはこれからの日本のになり手だ(→日本の将来は子供たちにかかっている) Japan's future *rests on* its children.

になう 担う (支える) bear*; (引き受ける) take* ∥彼らは国政をになっている They *bear* the responsibility for governing the country. ◆彼女は周囲の期待をになっている (→しょって立っている) She *carries* the hopes of the people.

ににんさんきゃく 二人三脚 (競技) three-legged race ∥二人三脚をする run *a three-legged race*

ににんしょう 二人称 【文法】the second person

にねんせい 二年生 ❶【学校の】second-year student; (小学校の) second grader; (中学校の) eighth grader; (高校の) eleventh grader; (3年制の高校の) junior; (4年制の高校・大学の) sophomore
❷【植物】二年生植物 *a biennial*

にのあし 二の足 その靴は高いので彼は買うのに二の足を踏んでいる(→ちゅうちょしている) He *hesitates to* buy the shoes because their price is high.

にのく 二の句 慣用表現 彼の答えにはあきれて二の句が継げなかった I *was* 「*struck dumb* [*dumbfounded*] at his reply.

にのつぎ 二の次 結果は二の次だ The result is *of secondary importance*.

にのまい 二の舞 彼女の二の舞を演じてはならない *Don't repeat* her *mistakes*. / *Don't make the same mistakes* she did.

-には

❶【特に取りたてて言う】(✿日本語の「…には」は訳語として前置詞が使える場合と特定の訳語をあてる必要がある場合がある)

この自転車、僕にはサドルが高すぎる The saddle of this bicycle is too high *for* me.
彼は年のわりには若く見える He looks young *for* his age.
フィンランドにはたくさんの湖がある There are a lot of lakes *in* Finland.
母は6時までには帰ってくると思います I think my mother will be home *by* six.
中島さんには私から伝えます I'll tell it *to* Ms. Nakajima.
両親は私には厳しいが妹には甘い My parents are strict *with* me, but soft *on* my little sister.
みんなが何と言おうと僕には僕の考えがある No matter what they say, I have my own idea.
いつもの電車には間に合わなかった I missed my usual train.
彼女にはなぜか人を引きつける魅力がある She has somewhat irresistible charm.
そのワンピースは捨てるには惜しい The dress is too good *to* throw away.

❷【ためには】

9時にそこに着くには家を7時に出なければならない I'll have to leave home at seven *in order to* get there at nine.
大型犬を飼うにはある程度の広さの家が必要だ You'll need a fairly big house *to* keep a big dog.
サッカーをするには人数が足りない There aren't enough people *for* playing soccer.

❸【するにはしたが】

レポートを出すには出したが、点数はあまりよくないと思う I *did hand in* my paper, *but* I don't think it'll get a good grade. (✿did は後ろの動詞を強調する)

にばい 二倍 twice, two times, double ━━2倍の double, twice ∥このひもはそのリボンの2倍の長さがある This string is *twice* [*two times*] as long as that ribbon. / 3の2倍は6だ Two times [*Twice*] three is six. / このかばんはその2倍の大きさだ This bag is *twice* the size of that one. / 物価は20年前の2倍になっている Prices are *double* what they were 20 years ago. / 彼の収入は私の2倍以上だ His income is *over twice as large as* mine.
◆その会社は1年で売り上げを2倍にした The company *doubled* its sales in a year.

にばん 二番 (2着の人) runner-up (複 runners-up, ~s) ━━2番の[に] second ∥期末テストの成績はクラスで2番だった On the finals, I ranked *second* in

my class. / 彼は50メートル走で2番だった He was *second* in the 50-meter dash. / (→2番で入った) He finished *second* in the 50-meter dash. / 私たちは前から2番目の列に座った We sat in the *second* row. / 左から2番目の人が彼のお父さんです The *second* person from the left is his father. / この公園は東京で2番目に広い This is the *second* largest park in Tokyo.
◆彼の新しい映画は前作の二番せんじだ His new movie is *a rehash* of the last one.

ニヒリスト (虚無主義者) nihilist [náiilist] ⓒ
ニヒリズム (虚無主義) nihilism [náiilizm] ⓤ
ニヒル ━ニヒルな (虚無的な) nihilistic [nàiilístik] / (冷淡な) cold

にぶ 二部 two parts; (2冊) two copies; (夜間部) the night school [division] ∥コンサートは2部に分かれている The concert has *two parts*. / その雑誌を2部注文した I ordered *two copies* of the magazine.
∥二部作 a work made up of two parts

にぶい 鈍い dull; (光などが) dim; (動きなどが) slow; (刀などが) blunt
何かが鈍い音を立てて倒れた Something fell with a *dull* sound.
わき腹に鈍い痛みを感じた I felt a *dull* pain in my side.
街灯が鈍い光を放っていた The streetlight was giving off a *dim* light.
彼は動きが鈍い He *is slow* in his movements.

にぶおんぷ 二分音符 《米》half note ⓒ,《英》minim ⓒ

にぶがっしょう 二部合唱 a chorus in two parts

にふだ 荷札 (結びつける) tag ⓒ; (はりつける) label ⓒ ∥スーツケースに荷札をつける put *a label [tag]* on one's suitcase

にぶる 鈍る (刃物・感覚などが) get* [become*] dull; (決心などが) be shaken ∥カッターの切れ味が鈍った The cutter *has gotten dull*. / かぜで味覚が鈍った My sense of taste *became dull* because of a cold. / 彼女のことを考えると決心が鈍った My resolution *was shaken* when I thought of her.
◆料理の腕が鈍った My cooking *skills have become rusty*. / 台風で客の出足が鈍った They *had a poor* customer *turnout* due to the typhoon. (❖turnoutは「人出」の意味)

にぶん 二分 利益を二分する *divide* the profits *in two*; *halve* the profits
∥2分の1 a [one] half

にべもない 彼女にいっしょに来てほしいと頼んだがにべもなく (=きっぱりと) 断られた I asked her to go with me, but she *flatly* refused.

にぼし 煮干し *niboshi*, small dried sardines

にほん 日本

Japan (《略語》Jpn, JPN) ━日本の Japanese, Japan's

語法
Japanese は「日本的な・日本固有の」という意味で用いる. Japan's は「日本(国)としての・日本がもつ・日本に属する」という意味で、特に新聞などで好まれる. 両方を使える場合も多い ∥ 日本文化 *Japanese [Japan's]* culture / 日本の古典 「the *Japanese [Japan's]* classics / 日本の気候 *Japan's* [the *Japanese*] climate / 日本の教育制度 *Japan's* [the *Japanese*] educational system / 日本の外交政策 *Japan's [Japanese]* foreign policy / 日本経済 *Japan's* [the *Japanese*] economy / 日本の将来 *Japan's* future / 日本風の家 a *Japanese-style house*

〖日本が・は〗
日本はこれが初めてですか Is this your first visit to *Japan*?
日本はその国と友好関係を確立した *Japan* established friendly relations with the country.
彼女は日本がだんだん好きになってきた She gradually comes to like *Japan*.

〖日本の〗
日本の国連代表「the *Japanese [Japan's]* delegate to the U.N. / 日本の国際社会への貢献 *Japan's* contributions to the international community
ロシアの飛行機が日本の領空を侵犯した A Russian plane intruded into *Japanese [Japan's]* airspace.
日本の学生は政治にあまり関心がないようだ *Japanese* students don't seem to be very political.
ガリーさんは日本のことにかなり詳しい Mr. Gally knows a lot about *things Japanese*. (❖ things Japanese は「日本の風物」という意味)

〖日本で・に・へ〗
彼は日本で教育を受けた He was educated *in Japan*.
彼は日本における農業の重要性を強調した He emphasized the importance of agriculture *in Japan*.
彼は日本に帰化した He became a naturalized citizen *of Japan*.
ブラジルから日本への直行便はないと思う I don't think there are any direct flights from Brazil *to Japan*.

〖その他〗
日本原産の植物 a plant *native to Japan* / 日本製の時計 a watch *made in Japan*
稲は日本中で育つ Rice grows *all over Japan*.
女王の日本訪問が来年4月に予定されている The Queen's *visit to Japan* is scheduled for next April.
日本円を米ドルに両替してもらえませんか Can you change *Japanese yen* into American dollars?
そのポップグループは日本全土を席捲した The pop group swept *all of Japan*.
彼女はとても日本的な顔立ちをしている She has a *typical Japanese* face. (❖typical は「典型的な」の意味)
◆ベーカー先生は日本びいき[日本嫌い]だ Mr.

Baker is *a Japanophile* [*Japanophobe*]. / 「国籍はどちらですか」「日本です」 "What is your nationality?" "I'm *Japanese*." (※国籍を聞かれた場合, ×It's Japan.とはいわない) ‖日本アルプス the Japan Alps / 日本画 (a) Japanese painting / 日本海 the Sea of Japan / 日本髪 a traditional Japanese hairstyle / 日本銀行 the Bank of Japan / 日本国憲法 the Constitution of Japan / 日本語 ⇨にほんご / 日本国民 the Japanese (people) / 日本史 Japanese [Japan's] history / 日本時間;（日本標準時）Japan Standard Time（《略語》JST）/ 日本車 a Japanese car / 日本酒 sake / 日本食 Japanese food / 日本シリーズ the Japan Series / 日本人 ⇨にほんじん / 日本製品 Japanese products [goods] / 日本政府 「the Japanese [Japan's] government / 日本庭園 a traditional Japanese garden / 日本刀 a Japanese sword / 日本舞踊 Japanese dancing / 日本文学 Japanese literature / 日本間 a Japanese-style room / 日本料理 Japanese cooking / 日本列島 the Japanese Archipelago [Islands] / 東[西]日本 East [West] Japan

にほんいち 日本一 日本一大きい湖を知っていますか Do you know what *the largest lake in Japan* is? / 彼は日本一の(→日本で最も速い)100メートル走者だ He is *the fastest* 100-meter sprinter *in Japan*.

にほんご 日本語 Japanese ⓤ 《略語》Jpn, JPN),the Japanese language;（単語）Japanese word ⓒ ‖エリックは日本語を習っている Eric is learning *Japanese* [*the Japanese language*]. / ジェフはとても流暢(%%)に日本語を話す Jeff speaks 「*Japanese* very fluently [very fluent *Japanese*]. / (→日本語が上手だ) Jeff is good at speaking *Japanese*. / ジミー，君の知っている日本語は？ Jimmy, what *Japanese* do you know? / スティービーの学校には日本語の授業がある Stevie's school has *Japanese* (*language*) classes. (※この場合Japaneseの前にtheはいらない)

🔴 「musicは日本語で何といいますか」「音楽です」"What's *the Japanese* (*word*) for 'music'?" "It's *ongaku*." / "How do you say 'music' in *Japanese*?" "*Ongaku*."

にほんじん 日本人（個人）Japanese ⓒ（複 〜）;（全体）the Japanese《複数扱い》――日本人の Japanese ‖私は日本人です I'm *Japanese*. / そのマラソンには多くの日本人が参加した A lot of *Japanese* took part in the marathon. / 彼は我々日本人の誇りだ *Japanese* (*people*) [*The Japanese*] are proud of him. (※We Japaneseとすると排他的の意味にとられることがあるので避けるのが無難) / それはいかにも日本人的発想だ That's a very *Japanese* idea. / 彼はニューヨークの日本人学校に通っている He is a student at *a Japanese school* in New York.

🔴 「小沢征爾を知っていますか」「ええ, 世界的に有名な日本人の指揮者ですよ」"Do you know who Ozawa Seiji is?" "Yes. He is a world-famous *Japanese* conductor."

にほんだてのえいが 二本立て（演劇・映画などの）double bill ⓒ;（映画の）double feature ⓒ ‖邦画の2本立て a *double feature* of Japanese movies

にまいがい 二枚貝 bivalve ⓒ;（食用の）clam ⓒ

にまいじた 二枚舌 彼女は二枚舌を使う She *is a* "*double-dealing person* [*double-dealer*].

にまいめ 二枚目 good-looking [handsome] man ⓒ ‖彼はなかなかの二枚目だ He is quite *a good-looking man*. / He is quite *good-looking*.

‖二枚目俳優 a good-looking [handsome] actor

-にも 彼は私にもそのことを教えてくれた He told it 「*to me, too* [*also to me*]. / 彼女はそのことは僕にも教えてくれなかった She didn't tell it *to me*, *either*. / このことはだれにも言わないで, 照子にもよ Don't tell it *to* anybody, not *even to* Teruko. / この本はやさしいので子供にも読める This book is easy *even for* children to read. / あす何が起こるかはだれにも分からない *No one* knows what will happen tomorrow. / 私は肉体的にも精神的にも健康だ I'm healthy (*both*) physically *and* mentally. / その少年は家の中にも庭にもいなかった The boy was *neither* in the house *nor* in the yard. / The boy wasn't *either* in the house *or* in the yard. / 都会生活のストレスは子供たちにも及んでいる The stress of urban life affects children *as well*. / 辞書にも(ピンからキリまで)いろいろある There are dictionaries and dictionaries. / There are all kinds of dictionaries, both good and bad. / 彼は親切にも警察署までついてきてくれた He was kind enough to accompany me to the police station. / おばを迎えに行くにも足がない I have no transportation *to* go to meet my aunt. ⇨-も

にもうさく 二毛作 double-cropping ⓤ

にもかかわらず in spite of ..., despite;（であるのに）though, although ⇨かかわらず ‖雨にもかかわらず試合は続いている The game is continuing *in spite of* the rain. / The game is continuing *although* it's raining.

にもつ 荷物
❶《運ぶ物》（旅行の手荷物）baggage ⓤ, luggage ⓤ（※共に荷物全体を表し, 数えるときはa piece of ... とする）;（持ち物）things, belongings;（包み）package ⓒ;（重い荷・積み荷）load ⓒ, 《公式的》burden ⓒ

荷物を網棚に載せよう Let's put *our baggage* [*luggage, things, bags*] on the rack.

荷物がたくさんあるのでタクシーで行きます I have a lot of *baggage* with me, so I'm going by taxi.

荷物をお持ちしましょうか Can I carry *your baggage*?

荷物を預かってもらえませんか May I leave *my luggage* with you?

お荷物はいくつありますか How many pieces of *luggage* do you have?

ごみを捨てて荷物を軽くした I lightened *my baggage* by throwing away some trash.

彼女は荷物をまとめて家を出ていった She packed *her things* and left home.

10分後に出発します。荷物をまとめてください We'll leave in 10 minutes. Get *your belongings* ready.

そのおばあさんは重い荷物をしょっていた The old woman was carrying *a heavy load* on her back.

そんなに化粧品を持っていったって荷物になるだけだよ Taking that much make-up would just be *a burden*.

❷【やっかい者】trouble Ⓤ Ⓒ, 《口語的》drag Ⓒ《通例単数形》

チームのお荷物にならないようにがんばります I'll do my best not to be「*(a) trouble* to [*a drag* on] the team.

‖手荷物預り所《米》a checkroom, a baggage room,《英》a left-luggage office

にもの 煮物 food boiled in broth
◆野菜の煮物 vegetables *boiled in broth*

にゃあ(にゃあ) meow,《英》miaow [miáu] Ⓒ, mew [mjúː] Ⓒ;《meow, miaow よりも弱い声》 ▶子猫が段ボール箱の中でにゃあにゃあ鳴いていた Kittens *were meowing* in the cardboard box.

にやけた (めめしい) effeminate,《口語的》sissy;(気取り屋の)《古風》foppish

にやにや ━にやにやする (意味ありげに微笑する) smile meaningfully;(得意げに) smirk ⓘ;(歯を見せて) grin ⓘ ▶何をそんなににやにやしているんだ Why *are* you *smiling* so *meaningfully*?
◆そのにやにやするのをやめてくれ Wipe that *grin* [*smirk*] off your face.

にやり 男はこちらを見てにやりと笑った The man *grinned at* me.

ニュアンス (含み) overtones;(微妙な違い) nuance Ⓒ Ⓤ, a shade of meaning ‖その2つの表現は微妙にニュアンスが違う The two expressions have slightly different *overtones* from each other./ There is a subtle difference in *nuance* between the two expressions. ◆原文のニュアンスをうまく訳し出すのは困難だ It is difficult to translate *the feeling* of the original.

にゅういん 入院 ━入院する be hospitalized,「go* into [check into, enter] (the) hospital 《❖《米》では通例 the を入れるが,《英》では省く》,(入院している) be in (the) hospital ‖彼女は大けがをして入院した She got injured badly and「*was hospitalized* [*went into the hospital*]./ She got injured badly and *was sent to the hospital*./ 彼は肺炎で入院している He *is in* (the) *hospital* with pneumonia./ 彼は今月で入院3か月目になる(→今月末で3か月入院していたことになる) He will *have been in* (the) *hospital* for three months by the end of this month.
◆生徒たちは入院中の先生を見舞いに行った The students visited their teacher *in* (the) *hospital*./ 彼らは娘を入院させた They had

their daughter *hospitalized*.
‖入院患者 an inpatient

にゅうえき 乳液 emulsion Ⓒ Ⓤ, milky lotion Ⓒ Ⓤ

にゅうえん 入園 ▶妹が保育園に入園した My sister *entered* a nursery school./ 動物園の入園料は500円だった The zoo's *admission fee* was 500 yen./ It *cost* 500 yen *to enter* the zoo.

ニューオーリンズ New Orleans(❖米国の都市)

にゅうか 入荷 ▶新商品が入荷した New products have「*come in* [*arrived*]./ 彼らの新譜はあさって入荷の予定です Their new album is *due* in the day after tomorrow.

にゅうかい 入会 entrance Ⓤ;(入会許可) admission Ⓤ;(加わること) joining Ⓤ ━入会する enter ⓘ;(入会を許される) be admitted to [into] ...; join ⓘ ‖彼は古典研究会に入会した He *joined* [*was admitted to*] the classics study society./ 彼女はその会への入会を断られた She was refused *entrance* [*admission*] to the association.
◆クラブに入会(→クラブの会員になること)を申し込む apply to be [*become*] *a member* of the club
‖入会金 a membership fee

にゅうかく 入閣 ━入閣する become* a member of the Cabinet, join the Cabinet

にゅうがく 入学 (入ること) entrance Ⓤ;(許可されること) admission Ⓤ ━入学する enter ⓘ, get* into ...;(許可される) be admitted to [into] ...

入学おめでとう Congratulations on *your admission to the school*.

姉はこの春大学に入学した My sister「*got into* [*entered*, *was admitted to*] university this spring.

彼は来年大学に入学する予定だ He's going to *enter* [*go to*] university next year.

入学式は月曜日だ *The entrance ceremony* is on Monday.

私は入学願書を書いた I wrote (out) *an application* (*form*) *for admission*.

まだ入学手続きをすませていない I haven't gone through *the entrance procedures* yet.

大学へ裏口入学する人をどう思いますか What do you think about a person who *gets into* a university *through the back door*?
◆きのう行われた本校の一日体験入学に多くの中学生が参加した A lot of junior high students took part in yesterday's *one-day tryout* at our school.

‖入学金 an admission [entrance] fee / 入学資格 entrance requirements / 入学志願者 an applicant / 入学試験 an entrance examination

にゅうがん 乳癌 breast cancer Ⓤ

にゅうぎゅう 乳牛 milk [milch] cow Ⓒ,《集合的》dairy cattle《複数扱い》

にゅうきょ 入居 ▶入居者募集《掲示》*For Rent; To Let* / 彼らはそのマンションに入居し

にゅうきん

た They *moved into* that apartment. / その部屋はいまだにだれも入居していない The room *is not occupied* yet.
‖入居者 a tenant, an occupant

にゅうきん 入金 口座に7万円入金した I "*deposited* 70,000 yen *in* [*paid* 70,000 yen *into*] the bank account. (❖deposit は預金のため, pay は支払いで) / 今月は取引相手から総額800万円の入金があった We *received* a total of eight million yen from our clients this month.

にゅうこう 入港 タンカーが横浜港に入港した An oil tanker *entered* [*came into, put in at*] Yokohama Port.

にゅうこく 入国 (an) entry (to a country); (移住) immigration Ⓤ ──入国する enter ⓗ; immigrate ⓘ / 彼らは無事ノルウェーに入国した They *entered* Norway without any trouble. / They *were granted entry to* Norway without any trouble. / They *were admitted into* Norway without any trouble. / 彼女は入国を拒否された She was refused *entry to the country*. / She was not allowed to *enter the country*. / 入国手続きをすませた I went through *the entry procedures*.
‖入国カード a disembarkation card / 入国管理局 the Immigration Bureau / 入国管理法 the Immigration Control Law / 入国許可書 an entry permit / 入国審査所(空港・港の) immigration / 入国ビザ an entry visa / 不法入国 illegal entry / 不法入国者 an illegal immigrant

にゅうさつ 入札 bid, bidding Ⓤ, tender Ⓒ ──入札する bid* ⓘ, tender ⓘ / 新空港の建設に10社以上が入札している More than 10 companies *are bidding* [*tendering*] *for* the contract to build the new airport.
‖入札価格 a bid / 入札者 a bidder

にゅうさん 乳酸 〖化学〗 lactic acid Ⓤ
‖乳酸飲料 a lactic acid drink / 乳酸菌 lactic acid bacteria

にゅうし¹ 入試 entrance examination [〖口語的〗exam] Ⓒ
東北大学の入試に受かる[落ちる] pass [fail] *the entrance examination* [*exam*] *for* Tohoku University
入試対策は万全だ I'm fully prepared for *the entrance exam*.
‖高校入試 an entrance exam for high school, a high school entrance exam

にゅうし² 乳歯 milk [《主に米》baby] tooth Ⓒ

にゅうじ 乳児 baby Ⓒ, infant Ⓒ
‖乳児食 baby food

ニュージーランド New Zealand ──ニュージーランド人 a New Zealander Ⓒ ──ニュージーランドの New Zealand

にゅうしゃ 入社 ──入社する enter ⓗ, join ⓗ, be hired ❖彼女はシステムエンジニアとして IBM に入社した She *entered* [*joined, was hired by*] IBM as a systems engineer. / 彼は今年で入社3年目になる This is the third year since he *entered* [*joined, was hired by*] *the company*.
‖入社試験 an entrance exam for a company, an employment exam

ニュージャージー New Jersey (❖米国東部の州; 《略称》N.J., 〖郵便〗NJ)

にゅうしゅ 入手 ──入手する get* ⓗ; (努力して) obtain ⓗ ❖そのつぼはどこで入手したのですか Where did you *get* [*obtain*] that vase? / この本の初版は今や入手困難である The first edition of this book *is now difficult to get* [*obtain*].
◆その腕時計は入手不可能だ The watch *isn't available* [*obtainable*]. / The watch *is unavailable* [*unobtainable*].

にゅうしょう 入賞 ──入賞する win* [gain] a prize ❖ダンス競技会で3位に入賞した I *won* third *prize* in the dance competition. / 上位入賞をめざしてがんばります I'm going to do my best to *win a top prize*.
‖入賞作品 a prizewinning work / 入賞者 a prizewinner

にゅうじょう 入場 (入ること) entrance Ⓤ Ⓒ; (入場を許可されること) admission Ⓤ, admittance Ⓤ ──入場する enter ⓗ, be admitted ❖入場禁止(掲示) *No Entrance* / 入場無料(掲示) *Free Admittance* / 入場料1,200円(掲示) *Admission* 1,200 yen / 切符をお持ちでない方の入場お断り(掲示) *No Admittance without a Ticket* / ···への入場を断られる be refused *entrance to* ... / 各国のチームが体育館に入場してきた The teams from all of the countries *are entering* the gymnasium. / 当ホールには18歳未満の方は入場できません Children under 18 *are not admitted to* this hall. / 5歳以下の子供の入場は無料です Children of five and below *are admitted free*. / その美術館の入場料はいくらですか How much is *the admission* [*admission fee, entrance fee*] to the museum?
‖入場券 an admission [entrance] ticket; (駅の) a platform ticket / 入場行進 an entrance march / 入場式 an entrance ceremony / 入場者 a visitor; (観客) a spectator; (出席者全体) the attendance

にゅうしょく 入植 settlement Ⓤ Ⓒ ──入植する settle ⓘ ⓗ (❖ ⓗ の場合はしばしば土地を主語にした受身で用いる); (植民地化する) colonize ⓗ ❖東部出身の多くの人々がカリフォルニアに入植した Many people from the eastern states *settled* in California. / California *was settled* by many people from the eastern states.
‖入植者 a settler, a colonist / 入植地 a settlement

ニュース

news [njúːz] Ⓤ (❖数えるときは a piece [an item] of ..., または a news story, a news item などとする); (番組) the news(単数扱い), 《米》 newscast Ⓒ
〖~(の)ニュース〗
芸能[スポーツ]ニュース entertainment

[sports] *news* / 最新のニュース fresh [the latest] *news* / うれしい[悲しい]ニュース good [bad] *news* / ローカルニュース local *news* / 10大ニュース 10 top *news items* / 国内[海外]のニュース domestic [foreign] *news* / 6時のニュースを見る watch the 6 o'clock *news* [*newscast*]

テレビのニュースによると,その山で雪崩(なだれ)が起こったそうだ According to *the* TV *news*, [*The*] TV *news*] said there was an avalanche on the mountain.

大統領選がきょうのトップニュースです The presidential election *tops* today's *news*.

真美ちゃん,いいニュースがあるんだけど Mami, I have some good *news*.

《ニュースを・に》

そのアナウンサーがニュースを読んだ The announcer read *the news*.

ニュースをお伝えします Now for *the news*.

彼のギターが競売に出されニュースになった The auctioning of his guitar was treated as *news*.

(テレビの) 3時のニュースを見ましたか Did you watch the *3 o'clock news* on TV?

《ニュースは》

その大洪水に関するニュースは世界中に広まった *The news* about the devastating flood was reported throughout the world.

そのニュースはラジオで聞きました I heard *the news* on the radio.

《その他》

彼の引退はけさのニュースで知った I heard about his retirement *on the news* [*newscast*] this morning.

その出来事はニュースバリューが高い The incident *has high news value*./ The incident *is highly newsworthy*.

🖋「何かおもしろいニュースないの」「ううん,あ,そうだ,最近雅夫君と真由美ちゃんがつきあい始めたらしいよ」"Isn't there any interesting *news*?" "Well, um, yeah. I heard Masao and Mayumi have started going out."

‖ニュース解説 a news commentary [analysis] / ニュース解説者 a news commentator [analyst] / ニュースキャスター a newscaster; (総合司会者) an anchorperson, (主に米) an anchor / ニュースソース a news source / ニュース速報 a news flash, a flash

にゅうせいひん 乳製品 milk [dairy] products

にゅうせき 入籍 ――入籍する (結婚を届け出る) register *one's* marriage

にゅうせん 入選 ――入選する (選ばれる) be selected; (入賞する) win* [gain] a prize ‖ 彼女の書が日展に入選した Her calligraphy *was selected for* the Japan Fine Arts Exhibition. / 彼の彫刻が1等に入選した His sculpture *won* (*the*) *first prize*. / He *won* (*the*) *first prize* with his sculpture.

‖入選作品(選ばれた作品) a finalist; (入賞作品) a prizewinning work / 入選者(選ばれた人) a finalist; (入賞者) a prizewinner

にゅうたい 入隊 ――入隊する join ⑯, enlist in ... / 陸軍[海軍, 空軍]に入隊する *join* [*enlist in*] the army [navy, air force]; (→ 徴兵される) *be drafted into* the army [navy, air force]

ニュータウン new town ⓒ

にゅうだん 入団 彼はライオンズに入団した He *joined* the Lions.

ニューデリー New Delhi (❖インドの首都)

にゅうとう 入党 彼女は自民党に入党した She *joined* [(→ 自民党の一員になった) *became a member of*] the Liberal Democratic Party.

にゅうどうぐも 入道雲 thunderhead ⓒ

ニュートラル (ギアの) neutral ⓤ ‖ギアをニュートラルに入れた I shifted (the gears) into *neutral*.

‖ニュートラルコーナー a neutral corner

ニュートリノ 〔物理〕 neutrino ⓒ

にゅうねん 入念 ――入念な (手の込んだ) elaborate; (細心の注意を払う) meticulous; (注意深い) careful; (綿密な) close ――入念に elaborately; meticulously; carefully; closely ‖イベント開催には入念な準備が必要です We have to make *elaborate* [*meticulous*] preparations to put on an event. / 我々は商品の安全性を入念にチェックした We *carefully* [*closely*] examined the safety of the product.

にゅうばい 入梅 the beginning of the rainy season ⇨つゆ(梅雨)

にゅうはくしょく 乳白色 ――乳白色の milk-white, milky

ニューハンプシャー New Hampshire (❖米国北東部の州;〔略語〕N.H.,〔郵便〕NH)

にゅうぶ 入部 私は茶道部に入部した I *joined* [(→ 茶道部の一員になった) *became a member of*] the tea ceremony club.

ニューフェース new face ⓒ, newcomer ⓒ

にゅうまく 入幕 ━━━ ――入幕する enter the top [*Maku(no)uchi*] division of sumo ‖ 新入幕の力士 a new sumo wrestler who *has entered the Maku(no)uchi division for the first time*; a *new Maku(no)uchi wrestler*

ニューメキシコ New Mexico (❖米国南西部の州;〔略語〕N.M., N. Mex.,〔郵便〕NM)

ニューメディア new media (❖単数または複数扱い)

にゅうもん 入門 彼はその落語家のところに入門した (→ 弟子になった) He *became* the comic storyteller's *pupil* [*disciple*]. / パソコンの入門書を買った I bought *a*「*guide to* [*beginner's book on*] personal computers.

‖入門者 a beginner

にゅうよう 入用 あす1万円入用なのですが,都合していただけませんか I *need 10,000 yen for tomorrow*. Could you lend it to me?

にゅうようじ 乳幼児 (幼い子供) small child ⓒ; (総称) babies and small children

ニューヨーク (州) New York (❖米国北東部, 大西洋岸の州;〔略語〕N.Y.,〔郵便〕NY); (市) New York City (〔略語〕N.Y.C., NYC) (❖単に New York ともいう. また, 愛称は the Big Apple)

にゅうよく 入浴 bath ⓒ ——入浴する take* [《主に英》have*] a bath ∥父は今入浴中です My father *is in the bath* now. / きのうの晩は早めに入浴した I *took* [*had*] *a bath* early last night.
∥入浴剤 bath salts

にゅうりょく 入力 input Ⓤ ⓒ (↔output) ——入力する input* ⓔ, 【コンピュータ】enter ⓔ ∥彼女はコンピュータにデータを入力した She *input* [*entered*] the data into a computer. / コードをスピーカーの入力端子につないだ I connected the cord to *the input terminal* on the speaker.

にゅうわ 柔和 ——柔和な (温和な) mild; (優しい) gentle ∥彼はとても柔和な性格だ He has a very *mild* [*gentle*] personality. / 彼女は柔和な顔つきをしている She has a *mild* [*gentle*] face.

にょう 尿 urine Ⓤ ⇨しょうべん ∥尿検査を受けた I underwent *a urine test*.
◆尿意をもよおす feel *a need to urinate*
∥尿素〖化学〗urea / 尿道〖解剖〗a urethra / 排尿 urination / 利尿剤 (a) diuretic

にょうぼう 女房 one's wife ⓔ ∥彼女が文化祭実行委員会の女房役を務めた (→右腕となって仕えた) She served as *the right-hand man* to the head of the executive committee for our school festival. (✿男女にかかわりなく用いられる)

にょきにょき 4月になるとこのあたりにはタケノコがにょきにょきと生えてくる Bamboo shoots *sprout* [*spring*] *up* around here in April. / 駅周辺には高いビルがにょきにょきと建ち始めた Tall buildings *have begun to sprout* [*spring*] *up* around the station.

にょじつ 如実 めちゃくちゃにこわれた車体が衝突の激しさを如実に物語っていた The smashed car body *clearly* showed the intensity of the crash.

にょろにょろ 蛇が道をにょろにょろとはっていった A snake *slithered* [*crawled*] on the road.

にら 韮〖植物〗leek ⓒ
∥レバニラいため liver sautéed with leeks

にらみ 睨み その不良グループには警察がにらみをきかせている (→見張っている) The police *keep watch over* that group of delinquents. / その大会社の社長は政府高官にもにらみがきく (→大変な影響力がある) The president of that big company *has great influence* even *over* high-ranking government officials. / 今の先生は生徒ににらみがきかない (→生徒に対する権威がない) Teachers nowadays *don't have authority over* their students.

にらみあい 睨み合い (膠着(こうちゃく)状態) standoff ⓒ; (争い) 《公式的》 conflict ⓒ Ⓤ; (衝突) confrontation ⓒ Ⓤ ∥賃金の値上げに関して労使間でにらみ合いをしている *There is a standoff* [*conflict, confrontation*] between labor and management over the pay raise. / (→争っている) Labor and management *are at odds with each other* over the pay raise. / 警官隊と武装グループとのにらみ合いが続いている *There has been a long standoff* between the police squad and the armed group.

にらみあう 睨み合う 土俵上の両力士がにらみ合っている The two sumo wrestlers *are glaring at each other* in the ring. / その土地をめぐって2国がにらみ合っている (→相手がどんな動きをとるうかがっている) The two countries *are waiting to see what move the other makes* over the territory. / (→対立している) The two countries *are at odds with each other* over the territory.

にらみつける 睨み付ける 彼は騒がしくしている子供をにらみつけた He *glared* [*glowered*] *at* a noisy child.

にらむ 睨む ❶ 【見る】 (怒って) glare ⓔ, look angrily; (じっと) stare ⓔ ⓕ ∥どうして僕をにらんでいるの Why *are* you *glaring* [*looking angrily*] *at* me? / 母はものすごい目で私をにらんだ My mother *glared* [*stared*] *at* me fiercely.
❷ 【目をつける】 keep* an [*one's*] eye on *a person*, watch ⓔ ∥彼は校則違反ばかりするので先生からにらまれています Teachers *keep an eye on* him because he always breaks school rules.
❸ 【目星をつける】 (疑う) suspect ⓔ; (確信している) be sure ∥彼らは彼女が犯人だとにらんでいる They *suspect that* she is the criminal. / 私は, 彼が必ず姿を現すとにらんでいる I'*m sure that* he will turn up.

にらめっこ 睨めっこ 🖼 *niramekko*, a game in which two people make funny faces at each other, with the one who laughs first being the loser
◆彼はさっきからパソコンの画面とにらめっこしている He *has been staring* at the computer screen for a quite a while.

にりゅう 二流 ——二流の second-class; (あまりよくない) second-rate (✿いずれも通例名詞の前で用いる) ∥二流の野球選手 a *second-class* [*second-rate*] baseball player; a *minor* baseball player / 彼女はピアニストとしては二流だ She is a *second-rate* pianist.

にりんしゃ 二輪車 two-wheeled vehicle [víːɪkl] ⓒ; (自転車) bicycle ⓒ

にる¹ 似る (外見や性格など全体的に) be like ..., be alike, resemble ⓔ; (類似している) be similar to ...; (親など血縁関係がある人に) take* after ...; (外見が) look like ..., look alike (✿いずれも受身・進行形にはできない。また alike は名詞の前では用いない)
彼女は本当にお母さんに似ている She really *resembles* [*looks like*] her mother.
彼女によく似た人に会ったことがある I have seen someone who *looked* a lot *like* her.
その2つは似ても似つかない The two *don't resemble* each other *at all*. / *There is no resemblance between* the two.
その姉妹2人はとてもよく似ている The two sisters *are* [*look*] very much *alike*.
彼らは性格が似ている They *are alike* in their personalities.

あなたのかばんは形が私のと似ている Your bag *is similar to* [*is like, resembles*] mine in shape.
◆ 彼は父親に似てとても背が高い *Like* his father, he is very tall. / 私は親に似ず, 数学が苦手だ *Unlike* my parents, I'm poor at math. / 以前にも似たような症状を経験しましたか Have you experienced *similar* symptoms before?

e 「彼, 絵が上手だよね」「うん, きっとお父さんに似たんだよ. お父さんは絵描きさんだから」 "He is very good at painting, isn't he?" "Yes, he is. I guess he *is like* [*takes after*] his father, who is a painter."

英作文ノート **resemble** に **to** はいらない
彼は母親に似ている
→ ×He *resembles to* his mother.
→ ×He *is resembling* his mother.
→ ○He *resembles* his mother.
★resemble は他動詞なので, to は不要. また進行形にはしない. ほかに take after, look like, is like もほぼ同じ意味で用いられるが, resemble と同じで進行形にはしない.

にる² 煮る boil Ⓗ; (とろ火で) simmer Ⓗ, stew Ⓗ
野菜は20分間煮るんだよ The vegetables should *be boiled* [*simmered, stewed*] for 20 minutes.
肉が柔らかくなるまで煮なさい *Boil* [*Simmer, Stew*] the meat until tender.
慣用表現 あの男は煮ても焼いても食えない(→手に負えない)やつだ That man is *intractable*. / 煮るなり焼くなり好きなようにしてくれ *Do whatever you like*.

にるい 二塁 〖野球〗second (base) Ⓤ ∥二塁を守る play *second* (base)
∥二塁手 a *second baseman* / 二塁打 a *two base hit*, a *double*

にれ 楡 〖植物〗elm Ⓒ (❖「ニレ材」の意味では Ⓤ)

にわ 庭 yard Ⓒ; garden Ⓒ
yard: 《米》では家の周囲の, 草木・芝生などが生えた土地や, 塀などで囲われ通例舗装されている土地をいう. 《英》では後者のみをいう.
garden: 《英》では家の周囲の, 草木・芝生などの生えた庭全体をいう. 《米》では特に庭の中の草木・野菜の育っている部分をいう.

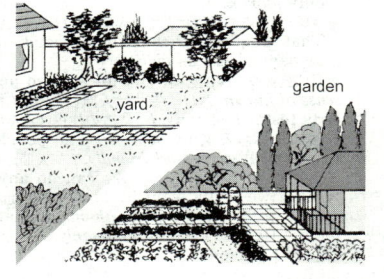

広い庭付きの家 a house *with a* large *yard* [*garden*]
庭の周りに垣根を作った I planted a hedge around *the yard* [*garden*].
庭でトマトを栽培している I grow tomatoes in *the garden*.
犬が庭に放されていた The dog was set loose in *the yard* [*garden*].
彼女は庭にチューリップを植えた She planted *the yard* [*garden*] with tulips.
庭の草むしりをした I weeded *the yard* [*garden*].

∥庭石 a *garden rock* / 庭いじり *gardening* / 庭木 a *yard* [*garden*] *tree* / 庭師 a *gardener* / 裏庭《米》a *backyard*,《英》a *back garden* / 中庭 a *courtyard* / 前庭《米》a *front yard*,《英》a *front garden*

にわか 俄 一天ににわかにかき曇り, 激しい雷雨となった The sky *suddenly* got cloudy, and it began to rain and thunder heavily. / にわか雨に降られた I was caught in a *sudden rain* [*shower*]. / 彼の話はにわかには信じがたい What he says is hard to believe *all at once*. / そんなにわか仕込みの知識では合格は不可能だ You can't pass the exam *with such hastily-acquired* knowledge [*by cramming* like that].

にわとり 鶏 chicken Ⓒ; (おんどり)《主に米》rooster Ⓒ,《主に英》cock Ⓒ; (めんどり) hen Ⓒ; (特に食用) fowl [fául] Ⓒ (複 ～, ～s) ∥庭には2羽鶏がいる There are two *chickens* in the yard. / この鶏は卵を産まない This *hen* won't lay eggs. / 鶏が(→こけこっこうと)鳴いている A *rooster* is crowing (cock-a-doodle-doo). / (→めんどりがこっこっと) A *hen* is clucking. / (どちらとも判断がつかない問題で)鶏が先か卵が先か *Which came first, the chicken or the egg?*
∥鶏小屋 a *henhouse* / 風見鶏 a *weathercock* / 鶏卵 an *egg* / 闘鶏 a *cockfight*, *cockfighting* / 養鶏場 a *chicken ranch*

にん 任 彼が我々の代表者として交渉の任にあたる He *is responsible for* negotiating as our representative.

-にん -人
語法
日本語の「…人」に当たる語は英語にはない. 「…の人」という意味で使うときは数詞＋people [persons], 「…人の何々」という場合は数詞＋「何々」に当たる名詞という形になる. また, 人数のことをいっているのが明らかな場合は数詞だけでもよい.

このホールは700人まで収容できる This hall can accommodate up to *700 people*. / その学校にはおよそ500人の生徒がいる The school has approximately *five hundred students*. / ほとんどの人が島を去り, 今では20人しか残っていない Most people have left the island, so now only *20* remain. / うちは6人家族です We are *a family of six*.

にんい 任意 ――任意の (自由に選択できる) optional; (自発的な) voluntary ――任意に

にんか

optionally; voluntarily ∥お名前のご記入は任意です It's *optional* whether you write your name or not./ 警察は彼女に任意同行を求めた Police asked her to *come to the police station with them voluntarily*.

◆円周上の任意の点 an *arbitrary* point on the circle

∥任意出頭 a voluntary appearance (at the police station)/ 任意団体 a voluntary organization / 任意保険 optional [voluntary] insurance

にんか 認可 authorization ⓤ ⓒ, approval ⓤ ⓒ, clearance ⓤ ⓒ ──認可する authorize ⊕, approve ⊕, clear ⊕ ∥その計画はまだ認可が下りていない The plan *has not been authorized* [*approved, cleared*] yet.

◆ミラー社は日本でビール製造の認可を得ている Miller has *a license* to brew beer in Japan./ (→日本の認可のもとでビールを製造している) Miller brews beer under *license* in Japan.

∥無認可保育園 an unauthorized day-care center

にんき¹ 人気 popularity ⓤ;（支持）favor,《英》favour ⓤ;（流行）fashion ⓒ ⓤ ──人気の popular;（多くに支持されている）favored;（引っぱりだこの）sought-after

〘人気が・は〙

彼[この本]は女性にとても人気がある He [This book] *is* very *popular with* [*among*] women.

そのコメディアンはまるで人気がない The comedian *is not popular* at all.

彼女はその歌で人気が出た She *became popular* with that song.

彼の人気は落ち目だ His *popularity* is fading.

〘人気を〙

その歌手はすっかり人気を失った That singer *has lost popularity* completely.

その商品が今人気を呼んでいる The product *is popular* [*in fashion*].

〘人気の〙

彼女は映画界ではたいへん人気の作曲家だ She is a much *sought-after* composer in the movie world.

◆人気の的 *the center of attraction* / お台場は若者たちに人気のデートスポットだ Odaiba is *a favorite* date spot for young people.

〘その他〙

テレビの人気シリーズ a *popular* TV *series*

彼女は当時人気絶頂だった She was then *at the height of her popularity*.

このデュオは今人気急上昇中だ *The popularity* of this duo *is rising rapidly* now.

◆勝男はクラスの人気者だ Katsuo is *a favorite* of the class.

∥人気歌手 a popular singer / 人気作家 a popular writer / 人気商売 a fad business / 人気投票 a popularity poll [vote] / 人気俳優 a popular actor [actress] / 人気番組 a popular program

にんき² 任期 term ⓒ, a term of office ∥この9月で市長は4年の任期を終えることになる The mayor ends *his* four-year *term* this September./ 前村長の任期満了に伴う村長選挙で中村氏が当選した Mr. Nakamura won election as the village chief when the previous chief's *term expired*.

にんぎょ 人魚 mermaid ⓒ

にんぎょう 人形 doll ⓒ ∥妹は人形で遊んでいる My sister is playing with *dolls*./ 彼女は人形に服を着せていた She was dressing *her doll*.

∥人形劇 a puppet show / 人形つかい a puppeteer / 操り人形 a marionette, a puppet / 着せ替え人形 a dress-up doll / マネキン人形 a mannequin / 指人形 a hand puppet / ろう人形 a waxwork, a wax doll / わら人形 a straw man

にんげん 人間

❶【人類】（個々の）human being ⓒ, human ⓒ, man ⓒ（❖男女平等の観点から man の使用は避ける傾向にある。複数形は men ではなく people を使うのがふつう）;（人類全体）the human race, humanity ⓤ, man ⓤ, mankind ⓤ（❖男女平等の観点から man や mankind の使用は避ける傾向にある）──人間の・人間的な human

〘人間が・は〙

地球上には60億を超える人間がいる There are over six billion「*human beings* [*people*] on the earth.

人間は必ず死ぬものだ All *human beings* are [*Man* is] mortal.

人間はすべての動物の中で最も知性豊かである *Human beings* are [*The human race* is] the most intelligent of all animals.

〘人間の〙

人間の平均寿命 the average *human* life span

それは人間の理解を超えている It's beyond *human* understanding.

〘その他〙

人間としての尊厳 *human* dignity / 人間らしい感情 *human* feelings / 複雑な人間関係 complicated *human* relations

犬の嗅覚(きゅうかく)は人間よりもずっとすぐれている Dogs can smell far better than *humans* [*people*] do.

彼だって間違いをするさ，しょせんは人間なんだから Even he makes mistakes — he's only *human*.

そのピアニストの演奏はとても人間業とは思えない That pianist's performance seems to be beyond *human ability*.

◆私は彼女の人間性を疑った I questioned her *sense of humanity*./ 芸術は人間性をはぐくむ Arts foster *humanity*./ ここの住民はみんな人間味あふれる温かい人たちだ The people here are all *warm and friendly*./ やろうと思えば何でもできる *We* can do anything if we really want to./ 彼は非人間的な扱いを受けた He received *inhumane* treatment./ He was treated *inhumanly*.

❷【人物】person ⓒ

彼は都会派の人間だ He's *a* city *person.*
兄はおしゃれ大好き人間だ My brother is *a fashion person.*
その経験が彼女を強い人間に変えた That experience turned her into *a* strong *person.*
彼女は人間ができている She *is a person of character.*
◆彼は自分ではりっぱな人間だと思っているが実際にはつまらない人間だ He thinks himself to be *somebody* but he's in reality (*a*) *nobody.*
‖人間愛 human love / 人間嫌い《公式的》misanthropy; (人間嫌いの人)《公式的》a misanthrope / 人間工学 human engineering, ergonomics / 人間国宝 a living national treasure / 人間社会 human society / 人間ドック a complete physical check-up [examination]

にんさんぷ 妊産婦 pregnant (women) and nursing mothers

にんしき 認識 recognition [U]《また a ～》, realization [U]《また a ～》; (知識) knowledge [U]《また a ～》; (理解) understanding [U]《また an ～》 ━認識する recognize [他], realize [他]; understand* [他]
彼は事の重大さを認識していない He *doesn't recognize* [*realize, understand*] the importance of the matter.
環境問題についての認識不足を指摘されてしまった They pointed out that I had *inadequate knowledge* [*recognition, understanding*] of environmental problems.
彼女はその作業に対する認識が甘い (→浅い理解しかしていない) She *has only a shallow understanding* of the task. / (→よく理解していない) She *doesn't understand* the task *very well.*
◆その映画を見て宗教に対する認識を新たにした The movie *changed my view* of religion.
‖認識論〔哲学〕epistemology

にんじゃ 忍者 🗻 ninja [C] (複～)

忍者はこれまでに国内外を問わず，多くの映画や物語に登場してきましたが，今ではもう本物の忍者は存在しません．忍者が活躍したのは戦国時代で，一種のスパイとして君主に仕えていました．
Ninja often appear in movies and stories at home and abroad, but real ninja can no longer be seen. They did exist in the Warring States period, serving their lords as spies.

にんしょう[1] 人称〔文法〕person [U][C] ‖一人称で語られる物語 a *first-person* narrative
‖第一[二, 三]人称 the first [second, third] person

にんしょう[2] 認証 certification [C][U] ━認証する certify [他] ‖認証式 an investiture ceremony

にんじょう 人情 human feelings; (優しい心) heart [C][U] ‖それは人情の機微に触れるエピソードを散りばめた本だった The book contains episodes here and there about *the subtleties of human feelings.* / あの人には人情がない That person *doesn't have a heart.* / (→人情の薄い人だ) That person *is cold-hearted.*
◆人情味あふれる東京下町の暮らしが好きだ I like the life in the old areas of Tokyo where everybody *is warm-hearted.* / 祖父はとても人情に厚い人だった My grandfather was a very *warm-hearted* [*kind-hearted, humane*] person. / 無料と言われれば欲しくなってしまうのが人情だ It's only *human nature* to want to get things that are free.

にんしょうだいめいし 人称代名詞〔文法〕personal pronoun [C] (❖英語の人称代名詞は一人称，二人称，三人称に分かれ，数と格に応じて変化する．また，三人称単数形には性による区別がある)

数	人称	主格	所有格	目的格	所有代名詞	再帰代名詞
単数	1	I	my	me	mine	myself
	2	you	your	you	yours	yourself
	3	he	his	him	his	himself
		she	her	her	hers	herself
		it	its	it	—	itself
複数	1	we	our	us	ours	ourselves
	2	you	your	you	yours	yourselves
	3	they	their	them	theirs	themselves

にんじる 任じる (任命する) appoint [他]; (自任する) consider *oneself* (to be)

にんしん 妊娠 pregnancy [U][C] ━妊娠する become* [get*] pregnant; (妊娠している) be pregnant ‖姉は妊娠している My sister *is pregnant.* / My sister *is expecting* (*a baby*). / 彼女は妊娠7か月です She *is seven months pregnant.* / She *is in the seventh month of pregnancy.*
‖妊娠中絶 (an) abortion / 妊娠中毒症 toxemia of pregnancy / 想像妊娠 phantom pregnancy

にんじん 人参 carrot [C] ‖朝鮮ニンジン ginseng

にんずう 人数 the number of people
◆バスの乗客の人数を数える count *the number of passengers* on the bus / 多人数[少人数]の学級 a *large* [*small*] class / 人数がそろったらゲームを始めよう We'll start the game when we have enough *people.* / 君のクラスの人数は何人ですか How many *people* are there in your class?

にんそう 人相 features, looks, 《公式的》lineaments; (人相学での)《公式的》physiognomy [C] ‖その男の人相を教えてもらえませんか Could you describe the man's *features* for me?
◆人相の悪い男がさっきからこちらを見ている An *evil-looking* man has been staring at us.

に

/ きのうバスの中で人相書きに一致する男を見た I saw a man answering *the description* on the bus yesterday.

‖人相見 a physiognomist

にんたい 忍耐 patience [U]; (困難にもかかわらずねばること) perseverance [U]; (長期間の) endurance [U] //外国語を習得するにはかなりの忍耐が必要だ You need a lot of *patience* [*perseverance, endurance*] to master a foreign language. / その作業では彼らの忍耐力が試される Their *patience* [*perseverance, endurance*] will be tested in that job.

◆彼女はとても忍耐強い女性だ She is a very *patient* [*persevering, enduring*] woman.

にんち[1] 認知 (認めること) acknowledgment [U] [C], recognition [U]《また a～》, 《公式的》 cognition [U] ―認知する acknowledge [他], recognize [他] //彼はその子供を認知した He *acknowledged* [*recognized*] the child *as his own*.

‖認知科学 cognitive science / 空間認知 sense of space

にんち[2] 任地 大使は突然任地から呼び戻された The ambassador was suddenly recalled from *his post*.

にんてい 認定 recognition [U]《また a ～》, authorization [U] [C]; (証明・保証) certification [U] ―認定する recognize [他], authorize, 《英》authorise [他]; certify [他]; (資格を与える) qualify [他] //その人は人間国宝に認定された The person *was recognized* [*authorized, certified*] *as* a living national treasure.

‖認定式 a recognition [an authorization, a certification, a qualification] ceremony / 認定証 a certificate, a qualification

にんにく 〔植物〕 garlic [U] //ニンニク1片 a clove of *garlic* / ニンニクで料理を味つけする flavor a dish with *garlic*

にんぷ 妊婦 pregnant woman [C]; (近々母になる人) mother-to-be [C] (複 mothers-to-be) ‖妊婦服 maternity clothes

にんまり 弟はお年玉をたくさんもらってにんまりしている(→満足した笑顔をしている) My brother *has a satisfied smile* because he got a lot of money as New Year's presents.

にんむ 任務 (義務) duty [C] [U]《しばしば複数形 duties》; (課せられた) task [C], assignment [C] [U]; (派遣された人の) mission [C] //彼は重大な任務に就いた He took on important *duties*. / 彼女は看護婦としての任務をりっぱに果たした She 「carried out [did, performed] *the duties* of a nurse well. / 任務をおろそかにしてはならない You shouldn't neglect *your duties* [*tasks, mission*]. / 彼らは実情調査の任務を帯びて来日した They came to Japan on *a* fact-finding *mission*.

にんめい 任命 appointment [U] [C] ―任命する appoint [他], name [他] //総理は彼を外務大臣に任命した The Prime Minister *appointed* [*named*] him (*as*) the Minister of Foreign Affairs. / 彼は私の代理に彼女を任命した He *appointed* [*named*] her to act for me. / 彼女は販売部長に任命された She *has been appointed* [*named*] *to* the post of sales manager. / 議長の任命権は彼にある He has *the power to appoint* the chairperson.

ぬ

ぬいあわせる 縫い合わせる sew* up [together], stitch up 〘傷口を縫い合わせる *sew up* a wound / この衣装は8枚の生地を縫い合わせて作られている This dress is made by *sewing* eight pieces of material *together*.

ぬいいと 縫い糸 (sewing) thread 🔲🔲 〘縫い糸ひと巻き a spool of *thread*

ぬいぐるみ 縫いぐるみ（綿などを詰めたもの）stuffed animal [toy] 🔲,《英》soft toy 🔲; (布で作ったもの) rag doll 🔲; (人が中に入るもの) animal costume 🔲 〘ぬいぐるみの犬 a *stuffed toy dog*
◆彼女はぬいぐるみのクマを両腕に抱きしめた She folded her *teddy bear* in both her arms.

ぬいしろ 縫い代 a margin (to sew up) 〘3センチの縫い代を残す leave *a margin* of three centimeters *to sew up*

ぬいつける 縫い付ける sew* 🔲🔲 〘上着のボタンを縫いつける *sew* buttons *on* a coat

ぬいとり 縫い取り（ししゅう）embroidery 🔲🔲 ◆イニシャルを縫い取りしたハンカチ a handkerchief *embroidered* with *one's* initials

ぬいばり 縫い針 (sewing) needle 🔲

ぬいめ 縫い目 seam 🔲; (1針の) stitch 🔲 〘縫い目をほどく undo *a seam* とうとう縫い目がほころびてしまった The *seam* finally came apart. / この縫い目は粗すぎる These *stitches* are too big. ◆縫い目のないストッキング *seamless* stockings

ぬいもの 縫い物 sewing 🔲; (針仕事・特にししゅう) needlework 🔲 ──縫い物をする sew* 🔲🔲; do* needlework

ぬう 縫う sew* 🔲🔲; (ひと針ひと針を強調して) stitch 🔲
傷口を縫う *sew up* a wound
このゆかたは手で縫われたものですか Is this *yukata sewn* by hand?
◆シャツのほころびを縫う（→つくろう）*mend* a rip in a shirt / 額の傷は3針縫わなければならなかった The cut on my forehead *needed three stitches*. / (オートバイの) ライダーたちは混雑した道路を縫うようにして走った The motorcyclists *weaved in and out of* the heavy traffic.

ぬうっと 霧の中から人影がぬうっと現れた A figure *loomed up* through the mist.

ヌード nude 🔲 ──ヌードの nude 〘モデルはヌードでポーズをとった The model posed *in the nude*.
‖ヌード写真 a nude (photograph) / ヌードモデル a nude model

ヌードル noodles 🔲 ‖カップヌードル《商標名》Cup Noodles

ぬか 糠 rice bran 🔲
ことわざ そんなことをしてもぬかにくぎだ It is like plowing the sand(s). (❖like plowing the sand(s)は「砂地を耕すようなものだ」の意味)

ぬかす¹ 抜かす omit 🔲, leave* out; (省いて飛ばす) skip 🔲🔲 〘誤って文末のピリオドを抜かしてしまった I made a mistake in *omitting* [*leaving out*] the period at the end of the sentence. / 昼食を抜かして時間を浮かせよう Let's *skip* lunch to save time. / 2章抜かして6章に進みましょう Let's *skip over* two chapters to Chapter 6. / どうして僕の番を抜かすんだよ Why did you *skip* me?
慣用表現 彼はインターネットのチャットにうつつを抜かしている He *is infatuated with* the chat on the Internet.

ぬかす² 吐かす 偉そうなことをぬかすな Don't *talk* so big.

ぬがせる 脱がせる undress 🔲 〘私は子供の服を脱がせた I *undressed* my child.
◆彼は私のコートを脱がせてくれた He *helped* me *off with* my coat.

ぬかみそ 糠味噌 🔲 *nukamiso*, salted and fermented rice-bran paste for pickling vegetables
◆ナスのぬかみそ漬け eggplants *seasoned in salted rice-bran paste*

ぬかよろこび 糠喜び（わずかの間の喜び）short-lived joy 🔲; (時期尚早(じきしょうそう)の喜び) premature joy 🔲
◆それはぬか喜びにすぎなかった My joy was only *short-lived*.

ぬかり 抜かり 彼女の仕事はいつも抜かりがない (→完璧(かんぺき)だ) Her work is always *perfect*.

ぬかる¹ 抜かる (しくじる) make* a slip (大失敗する) blunder 🔲
◆抜かるな(→気をつけろ) *Look sharp*!

ぬかる² be muddy; (雪解けで) be slushy 〘きのうの雨で山道はぬかっていた The trail *was muddy* today because of the rain.

ぬかるみ mud 🔲, slough [slúː]; (雪解時) slush 🔲 〘ぬかるみにはまって車輪が動かない The wheels have stuck in *the mud*.

ぬき 抜き 今夜はアルコール抜きで楽しもう Let's try and enjoy ourselves tonight *without* alcohol. / 私はまだやることがあるので私抜きで始めてください I have more things to do. Start *without* me. / 堅苦しいあいさつは抜きにしましょう Let's *skip* the formal greetings. / 彼の5人抜きのドリブルは伝説となっている His dribbling *past* five opponents is legendary.

ぬきあし 抜き足 私は抜き足差し足で部屋に入った I got into the room 「*on tiptoe* [*stealthily*].

ぬきうち 抜き打ち ──抜き打ちの（突然の）surprise 〘抜き打ちテスト a *surprise test* / 抜き打ち検査 a *surprise inspection* / けさ学校で抜き打ちの持ち物検査があった There was a *surprise* inspection of our belongings at school today.

ぬきがき 抜き書き extract 🔲, excerpt 🔲

——抜き書きする extract, excerpt // 彼女はその論文の要点を抜き書きした She *excerpted* the important points from the paper.

ぬきさしならない 抜き差しならない，抜き差しならない状況に陥る land in *a bad fix*; be caught [fixed] in *a dilemma*; get *oneself* in *a difficult jam*

ぬきすてる 脱ぎ捨てる (投げるように) cast* off, throw* off; (靴などをけって) kick off // 彼は服を脱ぎ捨てて池に飛び込んだ He *cast [threw] off* his clothes and jumped into the pond. / 彼女はブーツを脱ぎ捨てた She *kicked off* her boots.

ぬきだす 抜き出す (選ぶ) pick out; (よいものを選ぶ) select; (中から引っぱり出す) pull // 名簿から女性の名前を抜き出す *pick out* women's names from the list / 彼は本棚からその辞書を抜き出した He *pulled (out)* the dictionary from the bookshelf.

ぬきとる 抜き取る pull; (草や羽毛などを) pluck; (盗む) steal* // くぎを抜き取る *pull out* a nail / グラウンドの雑草を抜き取った I *pulled* weeds on the playground. / バッグから財布を抜き取られた The wallet *was stolen* out of my bag. / I *had* my wallet *stolen* from my bag.

‖抜き取り検査 a spot check, a sampling [random] inspection

ぬきんでる 抜きん出る (勝る) excel; (先頭に立つ) lead*; (際立つ) stand* out // 彼女は物理でほかのどの学生よりも抜きん出ている She *excels* over all other students in physics. / 米国はマルチメディアの開発において抜きん出ている The United States *leads* in the development of multimedia. / エイズ予防に関する学術研究の中で彼の仕事は抜きん出ている His work *stands out* in academic research on AIDS prevention.

ぬく 抜く

❶引いて抜く	pull
❷中の気体・液体を抜き出す	let out
❸追い抜く	pass; overtake
❹省く	skip

❶ [引いて抜く] pull, draw* // くぎを抜く *pull out a nail* / 指からとげを抜く *pull a splinter* out of *a person's* finger
庭の雑草を抜きましょう Let's *pull weeds* in the garden. / Let's *weed* the garden.
歯医者で1本虫歯を抜いてもらった I *had a bad tooth pulled (out)* at the dentist's.
警官は犯人に向けて拳銃(けんじゅう)を抜いた The police officer *drew his pistol* and pointed it at the criminal.
◆ 彼はびんの栓を抜いてくれた He *opened* the bottle for me.

❷ [中の気体・液体を抜き出す] let* out; (タイヤ・ボールなどの空気を) deflate; (液体を) drain; (取り除く) remove // 浮き輪の空気を抜く *let the air out of* [*deflate*] a float ring / 田んぼの水を抜く *drain (water)* from) the rice fields
ふろの水を抜いておいてね *Drain* [*Let the water out of*] the bathtub.
シャツのしみを抜いてください Please *remove the stain* from the shirt.

❸ [追い抜く] pass; (追いつき追い越す) overtake*; (…の前に出る) get* ahead of ...
前の車を抜く *pass* [*overtake, get ahead of*] the car in front
ゴール直前で彼を抜いて1位になった I *overtook* him just before the finish line and won first place.
数学では彼女を抜けない I *can't* [*get ahead of* [(→負かす)*beat*] her in math.

❹ [省く] skip
朝食を抜くのは体によくないよ It's not good for your health to *skip* [*go without*] breakfast.

◆ 深呼吸をして肩の力を抜きなさい Take a deep breath and *relax* your shoulders. / この作業は手を抜くわけにはいかない We can't *cut corners* when we do this work. / 最後まで気を抜くな Keep up your concentration to the last.

❺ [その他]
彼女の才能は群を抜いている She *is in a class by herself.* / Her talent *is in a class apart.*
彼は一，二塁間を抜くヒットを放った He hit *a single between first and second.*
その本は黒い表紙にタイトルが白く抜いてある The title of the book is printed *in white against* the black cover.

-ぬく -抜く フルマラソンを走り抜く *complete* a full marathon / 考え抜かれた計画 a *well thought-out* plan / 弾丸は厚い扉を撃ち抜いた The bullet went *through* the thick door.

ぬぐ 脱ぐ (衣服・帽子・靴などを) take* off; (ぱっと脱ぐ) cast* [throw*] off; (衣服を脱ぐ) undress
入り口で靴を脱いでください *Take off* your shoes at the door.
どうぞコートを脱いでゆっくりしてください Please *take off* your coat and make yourself comfortable.
部屋の中では帽子は脱いでください *Take off* your hat [cap] when you are in the room.
彼は急いで服を脱いだ He *undressed himself* quickly.
(比喩的に) とうとう彼は仮面を脱いだ He *threw off his disguise* at last.
慣用表現 彼女のためにひと肌脱ぐとしよう I'll *lend* her *a helping hand*.

ぬぐう 拭う wipe (◆「ぬぐい取る」の意味でしばしばaway, offの副詞を伴う); (水や汗・顔などを) mop // タオルで顔をぬぐう *wipe one's face with* [on] *a towel* / 彼はハンカチで涙をぬぐった He *wiped his tears away* with a handkerchief. / 彼は顔の泥をぬぐった He *wiped* the dirt from [off] his

face.
◆私は疑念をぬぐいきれなかった I couldn't *erase* [*remove*] the doubts from my mind.

ぬくぬく (居心地よく) comfortably; (安心して) snugly; (暖かく) warmly
◆彼は両親のもとでぬくぬくと暮らしている(→ 気楽な生活をしている) He *lives an easy life* as he lives with his parents.

ぬくもり 温もり warmth Ⓤ ∥ベッドにはまだかすかに彼の肌のぬくもりが残っていた There was still *a* slight *warmth* remaining from his body in the bed. / ペットのぬくもりを感じるとリラックスできるような気がする I can relax when I feel *the warmth* of my pets.

ぬけあな 抜け穴 (秘密の通路) secret passage Ⓒ; (地下通路) underground passage Ⓒ; (法律・契約などの) loophole Ⓒ ∥法律の抜け穴を利用した犯罪 a crime which makes use of *a loophole* in the law

ぬけがけ 抜け駆け ——抜け駆けする (…をひそかに出し抜く) steal* a march on …
◆彼はみんなのアイドルなんだからひとりで抜け駆けしちゃだめだよ Everybody has a crush on him, so don't try to *make a pass at* him by yourself.

ぬけがら 抜け殻 (セミなどの) cast-off skin [shell] Ⓒ; (蛇などの) slough [slʌf] Ⓒ
◆セミの抜け殻 *a* cicada *shell* / 恋人を事故でなくしてから彼女は抜け殻のようになってしまった She *has been an empty shell* ever since she lost her boyfriend in an accident.

ぬけげ 抜け毛 fallen hair Ⓤ
◆最近ストレスのために抜け毛がひどい Recently *my hair is falling out* terribly because of a stress.

ぬけだす 抜け出す (場所や状況から) break* out; (人や場所などから) get* away; (そっと場所から) slide* out, slip out ∥決まりきった日常から抜け出す *break out of* a routine / パーティーから抜け出す *get away from* a party / 数人の学生が講義の途中でこっそり抜け出した Some students *slipped out* during the lecture.
◆優勝争いは我々のチームが頭一つ抜け出した Our team *has got a lead* in the race for the championship.

ぬけぬけと (厚かましくも) impudently; (恥知らずに) shamelessly ∥彼は招待された身でありながらぬけぬけと料理に文句をつけた Even though he was a guest, he *impudently* complained about the food.
◆彼はぬけぬけと彼女にうそをついた He told her *a shameless* lie. / よくもまあぬけぬけとそんなことが言えますね *How dare* you say such a thing?

ぬけみち 抜け道 (間道) bypath Ⓒ; (近道) shortcut Ⓒ; (秘密の通路) secret path [passage] Ⓒ; (法律・契約などの) loophole Ⓒ ∥タクシーで急いでいるので、知っていたら抜け道を通ってください I'm in a hurry. So please take *a shortcut* if you know one.

ぬけめ 抜け目 ——抜け目のない shrewd; (鋭い) sharp; (特に金銭的に) canny ——抜け目なく shrewdly; cannily ∥彼は抜け目のない弁護士だ He is a *shrewd* lawyer. / 彼女は抜け目のない取り引きをする She is pretty *sharp* at bargaining.

ぬける 抜ける

❶ 離れて取れる come out
❷ 去る leave
❸ なくなる
❹ 脱落している be missing
❺ 通り抜ける go through …

❶【離れて取れる】(歯・くぎなどが) come* out; (髪・歯などが) fall* out
きのう前歯が1本抜けた One of my front teeth *came out* yesterday.
◆ダンボール箱の底が抜けた The cardboard box *broke at the bottom*. / 床が抜けてしまった The floor *has given way*.

❷【去る】leave* 他 ⾃; (逃げる) escape ⾃
会議の途中で抜けるなんて無責任だ It is irresponsible to *leave* before the meeting was over.
大半の部員がクラブを抜けた Almost all the members *left* [*quit*] the club.

❸【なくなる】
かぜがいまだに抜けない I still *can't get rid of* my cold.
夜ふかしの癖(ｸｾ)がなかなか抜けない I *can't* easily *get rid of* the habit of sitting up late.
タイヤの空気が抜けてしまった The tire *has gone flat*.
この香水はすっかり香りが抜けてしまった This perfume *has* completely *lost its fragrance*.
その話を聞いて全身の力が抜けてしまった All *my strength left me* when I heard the story.
このビールは気が抜けている This beer *tastes flat*.

❹【脱落している】be missing; (省かれている) be left off, be omitted
この本は8ページ抜けている Eight pages *are missing* from this book.
彼の名前が名簿から抜けている His name *has been omitted* from the list.

❺【通り抜ける】go* through …; (…から抜け出る) come* out of …
トンネルを抜ける *come out of* a tunnel
◆公園を抜けて彼らを交番まで案内した I guided them *through* the park to the police station.

❻【その他】
抜けるような青空 a *brilliant* [*clear*] blue sky / 抜けるような肌 a *very fair* complexion
彼はいいやつだけど少し抜けたところがある He's a nice guy, but he's a little *slow*.
すべての中でこの作品がずば抜けてよい This work is *by far* the best of all.

ぬげる 脱げる (はずれて取れる) come* off; (するりと脱げる) slip off ∥この靴は脱げやすい These shoes *come off too easily*.

ぬし 主 (所有者) owner ©; (家主・世帯主)《公式的》householder © (❖男性の場合は the master, 女性の場合は the mistress ともいう)
◆彼はこの寮の主のような存在だ He's *a fixture* of this dormitory.

ぬすみ 盗み theft ©© ∥盗み以外だったら君のために何でもするよ I'll do anything for you short of *theft* [*stealing*]. ◆盗みを働くのはよくない It's not right to *steal*.

ぬすみぎき 盗み聞き eavesdropping ©——盗み聞きする(意識的に) eavesdrop ©; (偶然もれ聞く) overhear* ⊕; (盗聴する) wiretap ⊕, bug ⊕ ∥あなたたちの会話を盗み聞きするつもりは全くありませんでした I never intended to *eavesdrop on* your conversations.

ぬすみぐい 盗み食い パンを盗み食いする *steal* some bread *to eat*

ぬすみみる 盗み見る steal* a glance; (のぞき見る) peek ⊕, peep ⊕ ∥カーテンの間から盗み見る *peep* through the curtains / 彼女は向かいに座った彼の顔をちらと盗み見た She *stole a glance* at him sitting across from her.

ぬすむ 盗む steal* ⊕ ⊕; (強奪する) rob ⊕; (くすねる) snitch ⊕; (万引きする) shoplift ⊕; (持ち逃げする) run* away with ...; (盗用する) plagiarize ⊕; (不法に私物化する) appropriate ⊕
私は空港でかばんを盗まれた I *had* my bag *stolen* at the airport. / I *was robbed of* my bag at the airport. (❖×I was stolen my bag at the airport.とはいわない)
私はきのう財布を盗まれた (→きのうだれかが私の財布を盗んだ) Someone *stole* my wallet yesterday. / My wallet *was stolen* yesterday.
彼らは彼が自転車を盗むところを見た They saw him *steal* a bicycle.
他人のアイディアを盗むのはよくない It's bad to *steal* [*plagiarize*] the ideas of others.
◆私は人目を盗んで(→こっそりと)その家へ入った I entered that house *secretly*. / 先生の目を盗んで(→見ていない間に)お菓子を食べた I ate some sweets *while* the teacher *wasn't looking*.

ぬっと (不意に) unexpectedly; (突然) suddenly, all of a sudden ∥茂みの中からクマがぬっと現れた A bear appeared out of the bushes *unexpectedly*.

ぬの 布 cloth ⊕ (❖布きれの意味で用いるときや種類を表すときは ©) ∥2枚の布 two pieces of *cloth* / 布はひと巻き単位で売られている They sell *cloth* by the roll. / この布は破れにくい This *cloth* doesn't rip easily.
◆彼はひじに当て布をしたジャケットを着ていた He was wearing a jacket with *patches* on the elbows.

ぬま 沼 (湿地) marsh © ©; (湿地) swamp © ©; (湖) lake © (❖日本語の固有名詞で「...沼」という場合, Lake ...と訳したほうが適切なこ とも多い) ∥尾瀬沼 Lake Oze / 底なし沼 *a bottomless swamp*

ぬめぬめ ナメクジのようなぬめぬめした生き物は大嫌いだ I hate *slimy* creatures like slugs.

ぬめり 里芋のぬめりを取る remove *the slime* from taro

ぬらす 濡らす wet ⊕ ∥ぬらしたタオル a *wet* [*damp*] towel / 冷たい水でタオルをぬらしてもらえますか Will you *wet* the towel with cold water?

ぬり 塗り coating © ©, coat ©; (ペンキの) painting ©; (漆の) lacquering ©; (ニスの) varnishing ©; (しっくいの) plastering © ∥ペンキで壁を二度塗りした I gave the wall two *coats of* paint.
◆輪島塗り Wajima *lacquerware*

ぬりえ 塗り絵 a line drawing to be colored in ◆女の子たちは塗り絵をしていた The girls *were coloring pictures*.
∥塗り絵帳 a coloring book

ぬりかえる 塗り替える (塗り直す) repaint ⊕; (記録などを) break* ⊕ ∥台所の壁を塗り替える時期だ It's time to *repaint* the wall of the kitchen. / 彼女は100メートル背泳ぎの世界記録を塗り替えた She *broke* the world record for the 100-meter backstroke.
◆ガレージの色を青色に塗り替えよう Let's *change the color of* the garage and *paint it* blue. / 2度の世界大戦は世界地図を塗り替えた (→書き換えた) Those two world wars *redrew* the world map. / 彼の発見は歴史を塗り替えた His discovery *made history*.

ぬりかためる 塗り固める 壁をしっくいで塗り固める *paint* walls with plaster / うそで塗り固められた決算報告 *window-dressed* accounts

ぬりぐすり 塗り薬 (軟膏) ointment © ©; (液状の) liniment © © ∥私は塗り薬を傷口につけた I applied some *ointment* to the cut. / 医者は彼女の腕に塗り薬をすり込んだ The doctor rubbed *ointment* into her arms.

ぬりたくる 塗りたくる キャンバスに絵の具を塗りたくる *daub* paint on a canvas; *daub* a canvas with paint

ぬりたて 塗り立て ペンキ塗りたて《掲示》 *Wet* [《英》*Fresh*] *Paint* / ペンキ塗りたてのベンチ a *fresh painted* bench / 塗りたてのセメント *wet* cement

ぬりつぶす 塗り潰す (黒く) black out; (ペンキなどで) paint out [over] ∥彼は教科書の挿絵を黒く塗りつぶした He *blacked out* that illustration in his textbook. / 壁の落書きをペンキで塗りつぶした I *painted out* [*over*] the graffiti on the wall.

ぬりもの 塗り物 (漆器) lacquer ware ©
∥塗り物師 a lacquerer, a lacquer-ware artist

ぬる 塗る (ペンキ・絵の具を) paint ⊕; (色を) color ⊕; (薬・化粧品などを) apply ⊕, rub ⊕; (バターなどを) spread* ⊕; (ラッカー・漆などを) lacquer ⊕; (ニスを) varnish ⊕
彼女は箱を黄色に塗った She *painted* [*colored*]

the box yellow.
腕のやけどに軟膏(なんこう)を塗った I *applied* some ointment to the burn on my arm.
背中にオイルを塗ってくれる？ *Rub* some oil on my back, will you?
彼はパンにバターを塗った He *spread* a slice of bread with butter. / He *buttered* a slice of bread.
◆この壁にはしっくいを塗ったほうがいい We should *plaster* this wall. / 何も塗らないトーストは好きですか Do you like *dry* toast?
慣用表現 人の顔に泥を塗る(→人に恥をかかせる) *drag a person's name through the mud*

ぬるい 温い, lukewarm, tepid; (冷めた) cold
ぬるいコーヒーではなく熱いコーヒーが欲しい I want my coffee hot, not *tepid*.
スープが少しぬるかったことを除けばすばらしい夕食だった It was a wonderful dinner except that the soup was a little bit *cold*.
おふろはぬるめのお湯にゆっくりつかるのが好きだ I like taking a long, *lukewarm* bath.
◆手ぬるい警備 *lax security*

ぬるぬる —ぬるぬるした (ねばねばした) slimy; (滑る) slippery /私はぬるぬるした石を踏んで転んだ I tripped on a *slippery* stone.
◆この洗剤で洗うとタッパーのぬるぬるはすぐ取れます This dishwashing liquid quickly removes *the oiliness* from plastic containers.

ぬるまゆ ぬるま湯 lukewarm [tepid] water ⃞ /手ぬぐいをぬるま湯に浸す soak a towel in *lukewarm water*
◆ぬるま湯に入る take *a lukewarm bath* / ぬるま湯につかっているような生活には我慢できない I can't put up with a *monotonous* life.

ぬるむ 温む (温かくなる) become* warmer, warm ⃝; (冷たさが減じる) become less cold /池の水がぬるんできた The water in the pond *is warming*.

ぬれぎぬ 濡れ衣 (不当な罪) false charge [accusation] ⃞; (根拠のない疑い) groundless suspicion ⃞ /このぬれぎぬをきっと晴らしてみせる I will clear myself of this *false charge*.
◆彼らは仲間に窃盗犯のぬれぎぬを着せた They *framed* their comrade for theft. / 私は兄はぬれぎぬを着せられたのだと信じています I believe that my brother *took the rap*. / 彼女はぬれぎぬを着せられたと憤慨している She is indignant that she *was accused unjustly*.
🅔「それは山田君がやったんだってみんな言ってるよ」「ぬれぎぬだ(→うそだ)！僕じゃないよ」 "Everyone says that you did it, Yamada." "It's *a lie*! It wasn't me."

ぬれて 濡れ手 慣用表現 ぬれ手で粟(あわ)の大もうけをする(→容易に大きな利益を得る) *make an easy profit*; *make a fast [quick] buck*

ぬれねずみ 濡れ鼠 突然の大雨でぬれねずみになってしまった I was caught in a sudden downpour and *got soaked to the skin [looked like a drowned rat]*.

ぬれる 濡れる get* wet, wet ⃝; (湿る) moisten ⃝ —ぬれた wet, moist, damp (❖damp は不快感を伴う)
だれも傘を持っていなかったのでみんなぬれてしまった None of us had an umbrella, so we all *got wet*.
私はずぶぬれになった I *got wet [was soaked] to the skin*.
彼女の顔は涙でぬれていた Her face was *wet* with tears.
ぬれた服はすぐ乾くでしょう These *wet* clothes will soon dry.

ね

ね¹ 根
❶ 【植物の】root ©; (球根) bulb ©
木の根 a tree root / 根がつく take root (❖この表現では無冠詞)
その植物は地中深く根を張っている The plant has grown its roots deep in the ground. / The plant is rooted deep in the ground.
ヒヤシンスの球根から根が出てきた Roots have sprouted out from the hyacinth's bulb.

❷ 【根本・根源】root ©
両国間の紛争の根は深い The root of the conflict between the two countries is deep.
◆不正の根を絶つ eradicate [root out] injustice

❸ 【根元・付け根】
歯の根 the root of a tooth

❹ 【本来】
彼女は根が(→生来)素直だ She is *naturally* obedient [obedient by nature].
彼は見かけは怖いが根は優しい男だ Though he looks fierce, he is kind [mild] *at heart*.
慣用表現 彼らは根が生えたようにその場から動かなかった They *were rooted to* the spot [ground]. / 隆は3日前に僕が彼のケーキを食べてしまったことをいまだに根にもっている Takashi still bears 「ill will [a grudge] against me because I ate his cake three days ago. / そのうわさは根も葉もないものだと判明した The rumor proved (to be) *totally groundless*. / その国では本当の意味で民主主義が根を下ろしたことは一度もない Democracy *has* never really *taken root* in that country.

ね² 音
(音) sound ©Ⓤ; (虫の鳴き声) chirp ©; (楽器の音) note ©; (旋律) tune ©; (ゆっくりした鐘の音) toll © //人々は彼の吹く笛の音に合わせて踊りだした People began to dance to *the sound* of his flute. / お寺の鐘の音が聞こえた I heard *the sound* [*tolling*] of the temple bell.
◆窓をあけ,虫の音を楽しみながら読書した I kept the window open and read a book while enjoying *the chirping* of insects. (❖欧米ではこのような習慣はない)
慣用表現 彼は10キロ走れると言っていたのに,たった2キロで音を上げた He *gave up* running at only 2 kilometers from the start though he had said he could run 10 kilometers.

ね³ 値
(価格) price ©Ⓤ; (価値) value Ⓤ ©
➪ねだん //「安[高]値で at a low [high] price /
このレコードは将来値が上がるだろう You will get *a good price* for this record in the future. / 野菜の値が下がった The prices of vegetables have gone down. / Vegetables have fallen in *price*. / 彼のギターはいい値で売れた He sold his guitar [His guitar was sold] at *a high price*.
◆そのバッグはかなり値が張る The bag *is pretty expensive* [*costs a lot*]. / その時計は1万ドルの値がつけられていた The watch *was priced at* 10,000 dollars. / 彼は競売でそのテーブルに50万円の値をつけた He *bid* 500,000 yen for the table at the auction.
∥売り値 a selling price / 卸値 a trade [wholesale] price / 終値 a closing price / 買い値 a cost [buying] price / 底値 a floor, a rock-bottom price

ね⁴ 子 (十二支の第1番目) the Rat ➪えと

ね⁵
💬「ああ,失敗しちゃったよ」「ね,だからやめとけって言ったでしょ」"Oh no, I've failed." "*See*, I told you not to do it, didn't I?"
➪ねえ

-ね
私のこと忘れないでね *Please* don't ever forget me.
お父さん,あの靴買ってよね Buy me the shoes, daddy, *will you*?
だからそうしたんだね So you did it, *right*?
ごめんね I'm sorry.
彼がそう言ったんだね? *Are you sure* he said so?
彼女はもう帰ってしまっただろうね She has left for home, *I think* [*suppose*].
💬「じゃあ,君も彼らといっしょに行くつもりなんだね」「そうだよ」"So you're going with them, *aren't you*?" "Yes, I am." (❖付加疑問文では,相手の同意が疑いない場合は文尾を下げ調子に,疑いのある場合は上げ調子に発音する)
💬「君はスキーをやらないんだったね」「ええ,やりません」"You don't ski, *do you*?" "No, I don't."
💬「喜美子ちゃんって,彼氏がいるんだってね(→彼氏がいるって聞きましたか)」「ええっ,うそでしょう(→まさか! でもそれ本当?)」"*Have you heard* Kimiko has a boyfriend?" "No way! But is it true?"
➪ーねえ

ねあか
彼女はネアカだからいっしょにいてとても楽しい She is (*naturally*) *cheerful* and so anyone can enjoy being with her.

ねあがり 値上がり
a rise [an increase] in price(s), price increase © ──値上がりする go* up (in price), rise* (in price) //その国では物価の値上がりが著しい The rise [*increase*] *in prices* is very remarkable in the country. / 鉄道の運賃がまた値上がりした The train fares *have* 「*gone up* [*risen*] again. / 缶ジュースが10円値上がりした The price of canned juice *has* 「*gone up* [*risen*] by 10 yen.

ねあげ 値上げ
a raise in price(s), price raise © ──値上げする raise [increase,

mark up] (the price of ...) 《その店はせっけんを10円値上げした They *have raised* [*increased, marked up*] *the price of* soap by 10 yen. / 公共料金が大幅に値上げされた Public utility charges *have been* substantially *raised* [*increased*]
◆突然の運賃の値上げは人々の怒りを呼んだ The sudden *raise of* fares aroused the people's indignation.

ねあせ 寝汗 熱があったので昨晩は寝汗がひどかった(→寝ている間にひどく汗をかいた) I *sweated* terribly *in my sleep* last night because I had a fever.

ねいき 寝息 赤ん坊はベッドで静かな寝息を立てていた The baby *was breathing* quietly *while sleeping* in bed.
慣用表現 彼は親の寝息をうかがいながら家を出た He sneaked out of his house *making sure* his parents *were asleep*.

ネイティブ その英会話学校には英語のネイティブ(スピーカー)の先生がたくさんいる There are a lot of *native speakers* of English who teach at the English conversation school. / 私たちはネイティブアメリカンの歴史を勉強した We studied the history of *native Americans*.

ねいりばな 寝入り端 寝入りばなに救急車のサイレンで起こされてしまった I *was awakened* by an ambulance siren *just after I had fallen asleep*.

ねいる 寝入る 彼は床につくとすぐに寝入った He *fell asleep* soon after he went to bed. / そのとき彼はすっかり寝入っていた He *was* fast *asleep* then.

ねいろ 音色 tone ◎ / ピアノの美しい音色 the beautiful *tones* of a piano

ねうち 値打ち value ◎◎, worth ◎(❖value は金銭的な価値, worth は精神的な価値を表す傾向があるが, 多くの場合同様に用いられる) / その土地の値打ちが上がった[下がった] The land went up [down] in *value*. / その発見は我々にとって大変な値打ちがある The discovery *is of great value* to us. / このバイオリンにはたいした値打ちはない[全く値打ちがない] This violin *is of little* [*no*] *value*. / この本は近いうちに値打ちが出るだろう This book will acquire *value* [*worth*] before long. / あなたに彼の値打ちは分からない You can't understand his *value*. / (→彼がどれだけ値打ちがあるか) You can't understand *how valuable* he is.
◆それは1億円の値打ちがある It's *worth* 100 million yen. / その博物館は行ってみるだけの値打ちがあるよ The museum *is worth* 「a visit [visiting]. / It's *worth while* visiting the museum.

ねえ
(呼びかけ) Hey, Say, 《英》I say; (注意を喚起する) Look!, Listen!
語法
(1)「ねえ, 美樹ちゃん」「ねえ, お母さん」などと呼びかける場合, 英語では単に名前をしり上がりに発音するだけでよい / 「ねえ, お父さん」「何だい」 "*Dad?*" "*What?*"
(2) 配偶者・恋人・子供などに対して用いる, 愛情をこめた呼びかけには darling, sweetheart, honey などがある.

ねえ, あなた (*My*) *darling*.
ねえ, 父さん, チェスやろうよ *Hey, Dad. Let's play chess.*
ねえ, これを見て *Hey!* Look at this.
ねえ, この仕事を彼に任せるのどうかと思うんだけど *Listen*, I don't think it's a good idea to let him do this job.

💬「ねえ, reinforce ってどういう意味」「『強化する』って意味だよ」"*Tell me*, what does 'reinforce' mean?" "It means to make something stronger."

💬「ねえ, ジム, 手伝ってくれない」「ごめん, 今手一杯なんだ」"*Oh, Jim, can you give me a hand?*" "Sorry, but I've got my hands full now."

-ねえ
暑いねえ *What* heat!
いい天気だねえ It's a beautiful day, *isn't it?*

💬「あゆみも来るって言ってたよねえ」「そうだっけ? 彼女は来られないと思ってた」"Ayumi is coming, too. *Right?*" "Really? I thought she couldn't come."

💬「彼女, すごく忙しそうだよ」「頼まれたら断れない性格だから**ねえ**」 "She looks really busy." "Because she can't say no to anyone, *you know*."

ねえさん 姉さん *one's* older [elder, big] sister
語法
(1) 英語では, 必要なとき以外姉か妹かの区別をせず,「姉さん」も older や big を付けないことが多い.
(2) 英語では, 弟や妹が姉に呼びかけるときは, 相手の名を用いるのがふつう / (由利) 姉さん, あした暇? *Yuri*, will you be free tomorrow?

僕には姉さんが2人います I have two *older sisters*. / うちの姉さんがそう言っていたよ My *older sister* said so. / お姉さんに代わってもらえますか May I speak to *your older sister*?
◆ (ウエートレスなどに呼びかけて) お姉さん, 水をもらえませんか *Miss*, can I have some water?

ネーブル ⚠ navel orange ◎ (❖navel だけだと「へその意味」)

ネーム name ◎ ⇒なまえ / 父はネーム入りの(→内側に名前をししゅうしてある)コートを着ている My father wears a coat with *his name* embroidered inside.
◆彼には元オリンピック選手としてのネームバリューがある He *has name value* [*recognition*] *as* an ex-Olympic athlete.
‖ネームプレート a nameplate

ねおき 寝起き 弟は寝起きが悪い[よい] My brother *is in a bad* [*good*] *mood when he wakes up*.

ネオン (ネオン灯) neon light ◎; (ネオンサイン) neon sign ◎; (元素) neon ◎ (❖元素記号

Ne) //ネオンがちかちかと点滅していた *A neon sign* flashed on and off. / ネオンの明かりが消えた *The neon lights* went out.

ネガ ⚠negative [C] (↔positive); (現像したフィルム) (developed) film [C]

ねがい 願い

❶【願望】wish [C]; (祈り) prayer [C] ⇒のぞみ

留学したいという君の**願い**をかなえてやろう I'll make your *wish* [(→夢を) *dream*] *to study abroad come true.*

どうか私の**願い**を聞いてください Please hear my *prayer*!

平和は私たちみんなの**願い**です Peace is *the wish* [*prayer*] of all of us.

彼女は流れ星に向かって**願い**事をした She *made a wish* looking up at a shooting star.

◆この記念碑には平和への**願い**がこめられている This monument was made with *the hope for* peace. / 神社で何をお**願い**してきたの What *did you pray for* at the shrine?

❷【要求】request [C]

先生は生徒たちの**願い**を聞き入れた The teacher granted his students' *request*.

人々の**願い**に答えるべく, 彼は力を尽くした He made a great effort to answer people's *requests*.

◆一生のお**願い**だから(→それが欲しくてたまらない), あれ買って *I'm dying to* have that. Please buy it for me. / (→それを買ってくれたらほかの物は求めない) If you buy that for me, *I'll never ask for another thing.* / すみません, お名前をもう一度お**願い**します Sorry, what's your name again, *please*? / あなたにスピーチをお**願い**したいと思います I'*d like* you *to* give a speech. / ちょっとお**願い**したいことがあるのですが *May I ask a favor of you?* / *May I ask you a favor?* / お**願い**だから言い争いはやめて Stop arguing, *for goodness* [*heaven's*] *sake.* / (電話で)望さんをお**願い**します *May I speak to* Nozomi?

💬「何になさいますか」「紅茶を2つお**願い**します」 "What would you like?" "(*We'd like*) two teas, *please*."

💬「もう少しコーヒーをいかがですか」「ええ, お**願い**します」 "Would you like some more coffee?" "Yes, *please*."

❸【願書】application [C]

受講**願い** *an application* for taking the class

◆退職**願い**を提出する hand in *one's resignation*

ねがいさげ 願い下げ 君のような人からの応援なんてこちらから**願い下げ**だ I *would* (*rather*) *refuse* the support of a person like you. / もう学級委員長なんて**願い下げ**だ(→頼まれてももうならない) I *won't be* the class representative again *if asked*.

ねがいでる 願い出る ask (*a person*) for ..., apply (to *a person*) for ...; (提出する) hand in //彼は学生課に学生証の再発行を**願い出た** He *asked* [*applied to*] the student affairs section *for* the reissue of his student ID card.

ねがう 願う

❶【望む】wish [他] [自]; (期待する) hope [他]

彼の成功を**願っています** I *wish* [*hope*] *for* his success.

我々はみな世界平和を**願っている** We all *wish for* world peace.

物事は我々が**願った**とおりに進んだ Things went as well as we *had wished*.

彼はもう一度自分の生まれた土地を訪れたいと**願っていた** He *wished to* visit his birthplace once again.

我々は彼女が試験に通るように**願った** We *hoped that* she might pass the exam.

◆世界中の子供たちの幸せを**願う** *pray for* the happiness of children all over the world / 人々は戦争の終結を心から**願っていた** The people *longed* for the war to end.

💬「彼は来るかなあ」「来ないことを**願う**よ」 "I wonder if he's coming." "I *hope* not."

❷【依頼する】

お**願い**したいことがあるんですが Could I *ask* 「*you a favor* [*a favor of you*]?

核兵器反対の署名にご協力**願え**ますか *Could* you sign the petition against nuclear weapons?

みなさんご静粛に**願い**ます *Will* everyone *please* come to order?

ここではたばこはご遠慮**願え**ませんか *I'd prefer* you not *to* smoke here. / *I would prefer* it if you didn't smoke here.

もっと大きな声でお**願い**します *Please* speak more loudly.

💬「英語を教える代わりに日本語を教えてもらえないか, って彼に言われたんだけど」「**願って**もないチャンスじゃないか」 "He asked me if I could teach him Japanese, and he would teach me English in return." "You *couldn't ask for a better chance than that.*"

[慣用表現] それは**願ったりかなったり**だ(→まさに私が望んでいることだ) That's *exactly what I want*.

ねがえり 寝返り 赤ん坊は時々**寝返り**を打った The baby sometimes 「*rolled over* [*turned over*] in bed. / 彼は眠れずに何度も**寝返り**を打った He *tossed and turned* because he couldn't sleep.

ねがえる 寝返る ❶【寝返りを打つ】roll [turn] over; (何度も) toss and turn

❷【裏切る】go* over to ..., 《口語的》sell* out to ... //彼らは敵対グループに**寝返った** They 「*went over* [*sold out*] *to* the opposite group.

ねがお 寝顔 孫のかわいい**寝顔**に彼の顔がほころんだ He smiled looking at his grandchild's pretty *sleeping face*.

ねかしつける 寝かし付ける lull *a person* to sleep //歌を歌って赤ん坊を**寝かしつける** *lull* a baby *to sleep* by singing to it; sing a baby *to sleep*

ねかす 寝かす ❶【眠らせる】(床につかせる) put* *a person* to bed; (眠らせる) lull *a per-*

son to sleep / 母は弟を8時に寝かせた My mother *put* my brother *to bed* at 8 o'clock. / 彼女は本を読み聞かせて子供を寝かせた She *lulled* her child *to sleep* by reading to him [her]. / She read her child *to sleep.* ◆もうちょっと寝かせて Let me *sleep* a little more.
❷【横にする】lay* 働 /人を床に寝かす *lay* an injured person on the floor ◆その本は立てずに寝かせておいてください Keep the book *on its side* instead of standing it up.
❸【活用せずにおく】駅前の土地を寝かせておくのはもったいない It's unreasonable to *let* the land right in front of the station *lie idle.*
❹【熟成・発酵させる】10年寝かせたワイン wine *aged* for 10 years / それをなべの中で一晩寝かすとおいしくなります *Let it set* overnight in the pot and it will taste better.

ねがったりかなったり 願ったり叶ったり 彼がその仕事を引き受けてくれるのであれば、まさに願ったりかなったりだ If he accepts our offer and takes the work, *we will be satisfied because that's just what we've wanted.*

ねがってもない 願ってもない まさに願ってもないチャンス、これを逃す手はないさ It's really a *heaven-sent* chance. How could I miss it? / その仕事を任されたのは彼にとって願ってもないことだった(→彼が任されたた仕事に彼が欲していたものだった) The task he was entrusted with was *just what* he wanted.

ねぎ 葱 leek 回 (◆leek は日本のネギより太く, 葉も平たい)

ねぎらい 監督は選手たちにねぎらいの言葉をかけた The coach *said some words to* the team *in appreciation of their efforts.*

ねぎらう (感謝する) appreciate 働, thank 働 /彼の労(→がんばり)をねぎらう *appreciate* his efforts; *thank him for* his efforts

ねぎる 値切る beat* [knock] (the price) down; (値段の交渉をする) bargain for a lower price /彼女はその服を8,500円から6,500円に値切った She *beat* [*knocked*] *the price of* the clothes *down* from 8,500 yen to 6,500 yen. / 彼はその新車を値切ろうとした He *tried to bargain for a lower price* on the new car.

ねくずれ 値崩れ 今年はリンゴが大豊作で値崩れを起こしている Apple *prices have fallen* due to the large crop this year.

ねぐせ 寝癖 髪にひどい寝癖がついてしまった(→ぐちゃぐちゃになってしまった) My hair *got messy while I was asleep.* / (→髪型が変になってしまった) My hairstyle *got messed up while I was asleep.* / 彼女は髪をとかして寝癖を直した She brushed and arranged her hair, *which was a mess from sleeping.*

ネクタイ tie 回, (主に米) necktie 回 (◆tie のほうがふつう) /ネクタイをする put on *a tie* / ネクタイをゆるめる loosen *one's tie* / ネクタイをはずす take off *one's tie* / 彼はストライプのネクタイをしている He "has *a striped tie* on [wears *a striped tie*]. / ネクタイが曲がっているよ *Your tie* is not straight.

‖ネクタイピン (クリップ式の) a tie clasp [clip]; (刺して留める) a tiepin, a tie tack / 蝶(ちょう)ネクタイ a bow tie, a bow

ねくび 寝首 人の寝首をかく (→卑怯(ひきょう)な手段を用いて人を陥れる) *snare* a person *by unfair means*

ねくら 彼はネクラだ He *is* (*naturally*) *glum* [*gloomy*].

ねぐら (鳥の) roost 回; (巣) nest 回; (野生動物の) lair 回; (家) home 回回 /カラスがねぐらへ帰っていく Crows are flying back to *their roosts* [*nests*].

ネグリジェ ⚠nightdress 回, nightgown 回 (◆英語の negligee は nightdress などの上に着る部屋着の意味で寝巻きではない)

ねぐるしい 寝苦しい まだ暑くて寝苦しい夜が続いている It's still hot at night, so we *can't sleep well yet.*

ねこ 猫 cat 回, 《小児語》kitty 回 (◆しばしば呼びかけに用いる), 《小児語》pussy(cat) 回

うちの猫がネズミを捕った Our *cat* caught a mouse.
猫がにゃあと鳴いた A *cat* meowed.
猫はのどをごろごろいわせていた The *cat* was purring.
猫が柱でつめを研(と)いでいた A *cat* was sharpening its claws on a post.
猫を飼っていますか Do you have any *cats*?
猫が引っかくかもしれないから気をつけて Be careful! *The cat* may scratch you.
トラはネコ科に属する The tiger belongs to *the cat family.*

‖猫いらず (a) rat poison / 雄猫 a male cat, a tomcat / 飼い猫 a domestic cat / 子猫 a kitten / 野良猫 an alley cat / 招き猫 a figure of a beckoning cat / 雌猫 a female cat

慣用表現 彼女は借りてきた猫のようにおとなしかった She was as meek as *a kitten.* / おじは娘を猫かわいがりしている(→甘やかしている) My uncle *pampers* [(→溺愛(できあい)している) *dotes on*] his daughter. / 通りには猫の子一匹いなかった There was not a soul to be seen on the street. / 年末は猫の手も借りたいくらい忙しい We're so busy and shorthanded at the end of the year that *we would thank anybody who helps us.* / うちの庭は猫の額ほどしかない Our yard is just *a small* [*tiny*] *one.* / その党の政策は猫の目のように変わる The party 「*changes its policy very frequently* [*is fickle about its policy*]. / 猫もしゃくしもそのブランドの商品を欲しがる *Every Tom, Dick, and Harry* wants products with the brand on them. / 彼女は太郎の前では猫をかぶっている She *pretends to be a good quiet girl* in front of Taro.

ことわざ 彼女にそんなプレゼントをしても猫に小判だ Giving her such a present is like *casting pearls before swine.*

-猫のいろいろ-
アビシニアン Abyssinian / アメリカンショートヘア American Shorthair / シャム猫

Siamese / スコティッシュフォールド Scottish Fold / とら猫 tabby / ヒマラヤン Himalayan / ペルシャ猫 Persian / 三毛猫 tortoiseshell / 山猫 lynx / ロシアンブルー Russian blue

ねごこち 寝心地 そのベッドはとても寝心地がよかった The bed *was very comfortable to sleep in*./ It was a *very comfortable* bed *to sleep in*. (❖「寝心地が悪い」は uncomfortable)

ねこじた 猫舌 彼は猫舌だ His *tongue is too sensitive to hot things to eat* [*drink*] *them*.

ねこぜ 猫背 a stoop, a slouch ――猫背の stooped, round-shouldered, hunched //彼女は猫背だ She 「*has a stoop* [*is stooped*].

ねこそぎ 根こそぎ 強風が庭の木を根こそぎにした The strong wind 「*uprooted the tree in the yard* [*pulled out the tree in the yard by the root*]./ 金めの物を泥棒に根こそぎ持っていかれた All of my valuables were stolen by the thief.

ねごと 寝言 彼はよく寝言を言う He *talks a lot in his sleep*./ 何，寝言「→たわごと」言っているんだ What do you mean by talking such nonsense?/ Don't talk nonsense.

ねこなでごえ 猫撫で声 彼女は猫なで声で彼にバッグをねだった She asked him to buy her a bag *in a coaxing* [*coquettish*] *voice*.

ねこばば 猫ばば ――ねこばばする pocket ㊐ //彼は公園で拾った5,000円をねこばばした He *pocketed* 5,000 yen he found in the park.

ねこみ 寝込み 人の寝込みを襲う *launch an attack on a person while he* [*she*] *is sleeping*

ねこむ 寝込む ❶【寝入る】 fall* asleep；(疲労などから)(俗語)conk out //彼はテレビを見ながらソファーの上で寝込んでしまった He 「*fell asleep* [*conked out*] *on the sofa while watching TV*. ◆妹はもうぐっすり寝込んでいる My sister *is already fast* [*sound*] *asleep*. ❷【病気などで】妹は病気で1週間寝込んでいる My sister *has* 「*stayed in bed because of sickness* [*been sick in bed*] *for a week*./ 彼はかぜで寝込んでしまった He *came down with a cold*./ 彼は彼女にふられたショックで寝込んでしまった He was ditched [dumped] by her, and he *took to his bed with shock*.

ねこやなぎ 猫柳【植物】pussy willow ㊐

ねころぶ 寝転ぶ lie* (down) //麗子は畳の上に寝転んでいる Reiko *is lying on the tatami*.

ねさがり 値下がり a fall [drop] in price(s) ――値下がりする 「*go* down [*drop**, *fall**] (*in price*) //株価が値下がりする *a fall* [*drop*] *in stock prices* / 10円値下がりする 「*go down* [*drop, fall*] *in price* *by* 10 *yen* / ガソリンが値下がりした The price of gasoline *has* 「*gone down* [*dropped, fallen*].

ねさげ 値下げ a cut [reduction] in price(s), price cut [reduction] ㊐ ――値下げする cut* [reduce] (the price of ...) //最大40パーセントの値下げ *a price cut* [*reduction*] *by a maximum of* 40 *percent* / 電話料金が値下げされた Telephone charges *were cut* [*reduced*]./ その靴は半額に値下げされた They *cut* [*reduced*] *the price of the shoes by* 「50 *percent* [*in half*].

ねざす 根ざす その国ではまだ民主主義が根ざしていない Democracy *has not yet taken root in that country*./ その紛争は両国間の宗教の違いに根ざしている The conflict 「*is rooted* [*has its root*] *in the difference in religions between the two countries*.

ねざめ 寝覚め けさは寝ざめがよかった[悪かった] I woke up quite refreshed [*uncomfortable*] this morning./ ガラス窓を割ったのを友達のせいにして寝ざめが悪い I *feel guilty and uneasy because I put the blame on my friend for breaking the window*.

ねじ screw ㊐ //ドライバーでねじをしめる[ゆるめる] tighten [loosen] *a screw with a screwdriver* / このねじはゆるんでいる This *screw is loose*. ◆ねじで本棚を壁に留める *screw* a bookshelf *to* a wall / 時計のねじを巻く *wind a watch*

‖ねじ回し a screwdriver

ねじあげる ねじ上げる 彼は男の腕をねじ上げた He *twisted the man's arm*.

ねじける 彼は性格がねじけている His character is *perverse* [*warped*].

ねじこむ ねじ込む (無理やり押し込む) force ㊐；(つっこむ) thrust* ㊐ //すき間にドライバーをねじ込んでふたをはずした I got the lid off by *forcing* [*thrusting*] *a screwdriver into a slight gap*./ 男は私のポケットにお金をねじ込んだ The man *thrust money into my pocket*.

◆体罰を受けた生徒の親たちが教師の謝罪を求めて学校にねじ込んできた(→抗議にやってきた) The parents of the students who received corporal punishment *marched to the school to demand apologies from the teachers*.

ねしずまる 寝静まる 私は家族が寝静まってから勉強を始めた I began to study after everybody in my family *fell fast asleep*.

ねじふせる ねじ伏せる 彼はその男の腕をつかんで地面にねじ伏せた He *held the man down on the ground by twisting his arm*./ 彼女は理屈で彼をねじ伏せた She *subdued* [*defeated*] *him by practicing logic*.

ねじまげる ねじ曲げる (ねじって曲げる) bend* ... by twisting [wrenching]；(歪曲(わいきょく)して伝える) distort ㊐；(曲解する) twist ㊐ //その鉄筋はねじ曲がっていた The reinforcing bar *was bent by twisting*./ 彼らは事実をねじ曲げて伝えた They *distorted the fact*.

ねしょうべん 寝小便 bed-wetting ㊐

◆寝小便をする *wet one's bed*

ねじりとる ねじり取る 彼はねじり取るようにして彼女の手からおもちゃを奪った He *wrenched the toy from her hand*.

ねじりはちまき ねじり鉢巻き 🏔 a *nejiri-hachimaki*, a twisted towel worn around *one's head to indicate one's zeal*

◆姉は受験に備え毎晩ねじりはちまきで勉強している(→勉強に専念している) My sister *sticks*

to studying every night for the entrance exam.

ねじる twist 他 自; (力強く) wrench 他 (❖足首などを「くじいて痛める」の意味でも用いる); (ふたなどを) screw 他, turn ⇒ひねる 《彼はいすに座ったまま体をねじって振り向いた He *twisted* (*his body*) around in his chair. / 足首をねじった I *wrenched* my ankle. / 彼はそのびんのコルクをねじって抜いた He *twisted* [*turned*] the cork *out of* the bottle.

ねじれる get* twisted ⇒まがる 《ひもがねじれている The cord *is twisted*.

ねじろ 根城 home ⓒ, a base (of operations) 《彼らはそのアパートの一室を根城にしている They use the apartment as *their home* [*base of operations*].

ねすごす 寝過ごす oversleep* 自 《2時間寝過ごしてしまった I *overslept* by two hours.

ねずのばん 寝ずの番 《仲間が安心して眠れるよう, 彼はテントの外で寝ずの番をした He kept 「(*an*) all-night watch [(*a*) vigil] outside the tent, so the others could sleep in safety.

ねずみ 鼠 (ドブネズミなど大きい) rat ⓒ; (ハツカネズミなど小さい) mouse ⓒ (複 mice) 《ネズミがちゅうちゅうと鳴いた A *rat* [*mouse*] squeaked.
◆ねずみ算式に増える increase in *geometric progression* / お勝手にネズミ捕りを仕掛けた I set *a mousetrap* [*rattrap*] in the kitchen. / 兄はネズミ捕り(→スピード違反取り締まり)に引っかかったらしい My brother told me he was caught in *a speed* [*radar*] *trap*.
∥ねずみ色 (dark) gray [《英》grey] / ねずみ講 a pyramid scheme / ねずみ花火 a coiled sparkler that spins around on the ground before exploding / ドブネズミ a sewer rat / ハリネズミ a hedgehog
慣用表現 彼は袋のねずみ同然だ He is like *a rat in a trap*.

ねぞう 寝相 《弟は寝相が悪い My brother *is a restless* [*an uneasy*] *sleeper.* / 妹は寝相がよい My sister *is a quiet* [*tranquil*] *sleeper*.

ねそびれる 寝そびれる 《昨夜は遅くまでテレビを見ていて寝そびれてしまった I watched TV until too late last night and so I *couldn't get to sleep*.

ねそべる 寝そべる lie* down [flat]; (手足を伸ばして) stretch 自; (だらしなく手足を投げ出して) sprawl 自 ⇒ねる(寝る), よこたわる 《彼女はソファーに寝そべった She 「*lay down* [*stretched out, sprawled out*] on the sofa.

ねた (小説などの題材) material ⓤ《また複数形~s》; (話題) topic ⓒ; (食材) ingredient ⓒ 《新鮮なねたを使った寿司 sushi made with fresh *ingredients* / 私はエッセイのねたを集めている I'm collecting *materials* for an essay. / もうねた切れで話すことがない I 「*don't have* any more [*have run out of*] *topics* to talk about. ◆ねたは挙がっている. やったと認めたらどうだ We've got *evidence*. You'd better admit you did it.

ねたきり 寝たきり ―寝たきりの bedridden 《寝たきり老人 a *bedridden* old man

[woman, person]; *bedridden* old people
◆彼は事故以来ほとんど寝たきりの生活を続けている He's *been confined to bed* almost all the time since the accident.

ねたばこ 寝煙草 《寝たばこが原因で起こる火事は多い There are a lot of fires caused by *smoking in bed*.

ねたましい 妬ましい (うらやましい) be envious; (嫉妬(とっ)する) be jealous 《彼は彼女がテストで満点を取ったのをねたましく思っている He *is envious* [*jealous*] *of* her getting a perfect score in the exam.

ねたみ 妬み (うらやましく思う気持ち) envy ⓤ ⓒ; (やきもち) jealousy ⓤ 《彼の成功は同僚のねたみを買った His success inspired *envy* [*jealousy*] in his colleagues.
◆あいつはねたみ深いやつだ He is an *envious* [a *jealous*] guy.

ねたむ 妬む (うらやむ) envy 他, be envious; (嫉妬(とっ)する) be jealous (❖envy や be envious より嫌悪感や憤怒など否定的な気持ちが強い) 《彼女は美子の美しさをねたんでいる She *is envious* [*jealous*] *of* Yoshiko's beauty. / She *envies* Yoshiko (*for*) her beauty.

ねだる (懇り)る) ask 他, beg 他; (しつこく) pester 他 《太郎はお母さんにこづかいをねだった Taro *asked* [*pestered*] his mother *for* some pocket money. / Taro *begged* some pocket money from his mother. / 次郎はお父さんに映画に連れていってくれとねだった Jiro *asked* [*pestered*] his father to take him to a movie. / Jiro *begged* his father to take him to a movie. / 三郎はお兄さんにねだって新しい靴を買ってもらった Saburo *pestered* his brother until he bought him new shoes.

ねだん 値段 (料金) price ⓒ; (費用) cost ⓤ ⓒ
高い[安い]値段 a high [low] *price* / 値段を上げる[下げる] raise [reduce] *prices*
ガソリンの値段が上がった[下がった] *The price* of gasoline has gone up [down].
どちらを選んでも値段は同じです Whichever you (may) choose, *the price* is the same.
このカメラの値段はいくらですか What's *the price* of this camera? / How much is this camera? (❖×How much is the price of ...? とはいわない)
革製品が魅力的な値段で売られている Leather goods are sold *at* attractive *prices*.
あまり高い値段にすると売れないだろう If you set too high *a price* on it, it won't sell.
ここのランチ, 値段のわりにはおいしいね The lunch here is *good for its price*.
◆このテーブルは質がよく, 値段もてごろだ This table *is* of good quality, and *priced* reasonably, too. (❖この price は「値段をつける」の意味) / この靴は値段だけの価値はあるだろう These shoes will *give you good value for your money*. / その着物には100万円の値段がついていた The kimono *was priced at* one million yen. / かわいいブラウスだけど, けっこういい値段だなあ This blouse is cute, but

「it *is high-priced* [its *price is too high*]. / この宝石は値段がつけられないほど高価だ This jewel is *priceless*.

ねちがえる 寝違える 首を寝違えてしまった I *got a crick in* my neck *while sleeping*. / I *strained* my neck *while sleeping*.

ねちねち 人にねちねちと小言を言う scold a person *persistently*

ねつ 熱

❶【熱エネルギー】heat ▭ ――熱の thermal 太陽熱 solar *heat*; *the heat of the sun* / 熱を発生させる generate [produce] *heat*
鉄は熱をよく伝える Iron conducts *heat* well.
太陽から光と熱が放射する Light and *heat* radiate from the sun.
◆ほとんどの固体は熱を加えられると膨張する Most solids expand when they *are heated*.

❷【体温】temperature ▭《また a ～》;(病気による) fever ▭▭
平熱 *normal temperature* / 体温計で熱を計る take [see, check] *one's temperature* with a thermometer / 熱を伴うかぜ a cold attended with [by] *fever* / 熱が高い *have a high fever*
彼女は微熱がある She has *a slight fever*.
彼の熱が上がった[下がった] His *fever* went up [down].
赤ちゃんのほおは熱のせいではてっていた The baby's cheeks were burning with *fever*.
彼は熱があるかどうか額にさわってみた He felt his brow to see if *he had a fever*.
彼はきのうの夜高熱を出した He ran [had] a *high fever* last night.
◆きょうは少し熱っぽい I'm a bit *feverish* today.

❸【熱中】(熱狂) enthusiasm ▭ ▭;(熱情) passion ▭;(熱意・興奮) heat ▭, zeal ▭
サッカー熱 *enthusiasm for* soccer
その仕事にはどうも熱が入らないんだ I just *can't work up any enthusiasm* for the job.
◆熱のこもった演説をする make a *passionate* speech / 彼はその転校生に熱を上げている He *is crazy about* the transfer student. / 議論はだんだん熱を帯びてきている The discussion *is getting excited*. / 息子はバイク熱に浮かされている My son *has been bitten by a motor-cycle bug*.
‖熱エネルギー thermal energy / 熱冷まし fever medicine / 気化熱 the heat of vaporization

ねつあい 熱愛 彼は彼女を熱愛している He *loves* her *passionately*. / He *is devoted to* her.

ねつい 熱意 (熱心さ) eagerness ▭;(熱中) enthusiasm ▭ ▭;(仕事・理想などに対する)《公式的》zeal ▭ ‖彼はその仕事に並々ならぬ熱意を示した He showed great *eagerness* [*enthusiasm*, *zeal*] for the work. / あなたの熱意に打たれました I was impressed with your *eagerness*. / I was impressed with how *eager* you are.
◆彼女はその活動に熱意をもっている She *is eager* [*enthusiastic*] about the activities.

ねつえん 熱演 enthusiastic performance ▭ ――熱演する play [perform] ... enthusiastically

ネッカチーフ neckerchief ▭ (複 ～s, neckerchieves)

ねっから 根っから 彼女は根っからの(→生まれついての)正直者です She is「*honest by nature* [*naturally honest*]. / 彼は根っからの(→生まれついての)音楽家だ He is a *born* musician. / 彼女の言うことなんて根っから(→全く)信じていないよ I don't believe what she says *at all*.

ねつき 寝付き 弟は寝つきがよい My brother *falls asleep easily* [*as soon as he gets into bed*]. / 妹は寝つきが悪い My sister *can't fall asleep easily* [*until long after she gets into bed*].

ねっき 熱気 (熱い空気) hot air ▭; (興奮) excitement ▭;(熱狂) enthusiasm ▭ ‖車の中はものすごい熱気がこもっていた The car was filled with terrible *hot air*. / コンサートホールは観客の熱気に包まれていた The concert hall was filled with *the* audience's *excitement* [*enthusiasm*].

ねっききゅう 熱気球 hot-air balloon ▭

ねっきょう 熱狂 ――熱狂する get* excited (at [about] ...), get enthusiastic (about ...), go* wild [《口語的》mad] (about ...) (❖「熱狂している」という状態なら get, go の代わりに be 動詞を用いる) ――熱狂的な enthusiastic, ardent, fervent; (狂信的な) fanatical ‖城がゴールを決めサポーターは熱狂した When Jo scored [made] a goal, the supporters「*got excited* [*went wild*]. / 彼は相撲の熱狂的なファンだ He is an *enthusiastic* [an *ardent*, a *fervent*] sumo fan.
◆そのボクシングの試合は観客を熱狂させた The boxing match *aroused excitement* [*enthusiasm*] *in* the spectators. / The boxing match *drove* the spectators *wild*.

ねつく 寝付く go* to sleep, fall* asleep, get* to sleep (❖get to sleep は通例否定文で用いる) ‖きのうの夜はとても暑くてなかなか寝つけなかった I *couldn't get to sleep* easily because it was very hot last night.

ネック (服のえり) neck ▭; (ギターなどの) neck ▭; (障害) obstruction ▭; (進行を遅らせるもの) bottleneck ▭; (問題) problem ▭ ‖ギターのネック *the neck* of a guitar / その問題がネックになっていて作業が進まない The matter is *the obstruction* [*bottleneck*] in the work. / 我々にとって最大のネックは専用の練習場がないことだ Our biggest *problem* is that we don't have our own place to practice.
◆V[クルー]ネックのTシャツ a V-*neck* [*crew neck*] T-shirt

ねづく 根付く take* root, root 〓 (❖共に比喩的な意味でも用いる) ‖日本にもインターネットビジネスが根づいた Internet businesses *have taken root in* Japan, too.

ネックレス necklace /彼はネックレスをしていた She wore *a necklace*.

ねっけつかん 熱血漢 passionate [hot-blooded] man

ねっこ 根っ子 root; (切り株) stump

ネッシー Nessie, the Loch [lák] Ness monster

ねっしゃびょう 熱射病 heatstroke

ねっしょう 熱唱 彼はその歌を熱唱した He sang the song *passionately*.

ねつじょう 熱情 passion, ardor, (great) enthusiasm ——熱情的な passionate, enthusiastic, vehement
⇨じょうねつ

ねっしん 熱心 ——熱心な eager; (真剣な) earnest; (熱狂的な) enthusiastic, ardent; (献身的な) devoted ——熱心に eagerly, earnestly; enthusiastically, ardently; devotedly; (一生懸命) hard ——熱心さ eagerness; earnestness; enthusiasm

熱心な先生 an *eager* [an *earnest*, a *devoted*] teacher / 勉強熱心な生徒 a student 「*eager in* [*earnest about, devoted to*] his [her] study

彼は部活に熱心だ He is 「*eager in* [*earnest about, enthusiastic about*] his club activities.

彼女はそのバンドの熱心なファンだ She is an *eager* [*enthusiastic*] fan of the band./ She is a *big* fan of the band.

彼はその本を熱心に探し求めている He is looking *eagerly* [*earnestly, enthusiastically, hard*] for the book.

彼女は犬の世話に熱心だ She *is devoted to* caring for her dog.

その問題に取り組む彼の熱心さに感動した I was moved by his 「*eagerness in* [*earnestness about, enthusiasm for*] tackling the problem.

◆私たちは熱心に(→注意深く)先生の話を聞いた We listened *attentively* to our teacher.

ねっする 熱する (熱くする) heat; (熱くなる) get* hot; (熱中する) get enthusiastic /水は熱すると水蒸気になる Water turns into steam when *heated*./ 彼女は何に対しても熱しやすく冷めやすい She *gets enthusiastic but then cools down quickly* about anything./ 油をひいてフライパンを熱してください Oil the pan and *heat* it.

ねっせん 熱戦 (接戦) close [tough] game; (激しい試合) fiery game; (興奮させる試合) exciting game (❖いずれも「戦い」がどんな種類のものかによって game を match, race などに入れ替えて用いる) /江田高校と田中高校が熱戦を繰り広げた Eda High School's team and Tanaka High School's team had *a close* [*a fiery, an exciting*] *game*.

ねつぞう 捏造 fabrication, invention (❖共に「捏造されたもの」の意味では) ——捏造する fabricate, invent /彼がデータを捏造した He *fabricated* [*invented*] the data.

ねったい 熱帯 the tropics, the Torrid Zone (❖後者は気候帯の学問的な名称) ——熱帯の tropical /この木は熱帯に特有のものだ This tree is characteristic of *the tropics*.
‖熱帯雨林 a tropical rain forest / 熱帯魚 a tropical fish / 熱帯植物 a tropical plant / 熱帯性気候 a tropical climate / 熱帯地方 the tropical regions, the tropics / 熱帯低気圧 a tropical depression / 熱帯夜 (最低気温が摂氏25度より下がらない夜) a night with temperature not dropping below 25℃; (蒸し暑い夜) a hot and sultry night, a tropical night (❖tropical night は日本語からの直訳なので"　"を付けて用いるほうがよい)

ねっちゅう 熱中 ——熱中する (没頭している) be absorbed in ...; (熱を入れている) be enthusiastic [wild, (口語的に) crazy] about ...; (興味を持って取り組んでいる) (口語的に) be into ...; (集中している) be concentrated on ... /読書に熱中していて宿題をするのを忘れてしまった I 「*was absorbed in* [*concentrated on*] reading and forgot to do my homework. / 勉は最近ギターに熱中している Tsutomu *is* 「*enthusiastic about* [*into*] the guitar these days./ 彼は何でもすぐに熱中するたちだ He easily *gets* 「*absorbed in* [*into, enthusiastic about*] anything.

ねつっぽい 熱っぽい (熱のある) feverish /けさから熱っぽい I've been feeling *feverish* since this morning.

◆彼はそのことを熱っぽく語った He told us about it *passionately* [*eagerly*].

ネット net (しばしば the ～); (放送網) network; (インターネット) the Net, the Internet ⇨ 場面・状況別会話 p.1700 /その情報をネット上で公開する put the information on display *on the Internet* / 卓球台にネットを張った We put up *a net* on the table-tennis table./ その事件は全国ネットのニュース番組で取り上げられた The incident was treated in the *national network* newscast.

◆ネット裏から野球を観戦したい I want to watch a baseball game from *the seats behind the backstop*.
‖ネットサーフィン Net-surfing / ネット犯罪 (a) Net crime / ネットビジネス a Net business / ネットプレー net play / バックネット the backstop

ねっとう 熱湯 boiling water /容器を熱湯消毒する *sterilize* a container *in boiling water*; *scald* a container

ねっとり ねっとりとしたとろろをごはんにかけて食べた I ate a bowl of rice covered with *thick* grated yam./ このキャンディーの中にはねっとりとしたチョコレートが入っている These candies have *gooey* chocolate inside./ 塩と卵黄をねっとりするまでかき混ぜてください Mix salt and egg yolks until they *become sticky*.

ネットワーク network /コンピュータネットワーク *a* computer *network* ◆このパソコンはネットワークにつながっていない This personal computer *isn't networked*.

ねっぱ 熱波 heat wave

ねつびょう 熱病 fever /多くの人々が熱

ねっぷう　熱風　hot wind

ねつべん　熱弁　impassioned speech／熱弁をふるう make *an impassioned speech*

ねつぼう　熱望――熱望する long for, be eager／彼は作家になることを熱望していた He *longed* [*was eager*] *to* become an author.／人々は戦争の終結を熱望していた The people 「*longed for* [*were eager for*] the end of the war.／The people *longed for* the war *to* end.
◆ファンの熱望(→強い要望)にこたえてそのレコードは再発売された The record was reissued to meet the fans' *strong requests*.

ねづよい　根強い　(根深い) deep-rooted, deep-seated; (長期にわたる) long-lasting／いくつかの国ではまだアジア人に対する根強い偏見がある There is still *deep-rooted* [*deep-seated*] prejudice against Asians in some countries.／そのバンドは本国オーストラリアでは根強い人気がある The band enjoys a *long-lasting* popularity back in their home country Australia.

ねつりょう　熱量　the quantity of heat ⇨ カロリー

ねつれつ　熱烈――熱烈な ardent; (熱狂的な) enthusiastic; (情熱的な) passionate; (心からの) wholehearted――熱烈に ardently; enthusiastically; passionately; wholeheartedly／彼はその歌手の熱烈なファンだ He is an *ardent* [an *enthusiastic*, a *passionate*, a *wholehearted*] fan of the singer.／彼は彼女を熱烈に愛していた He loved her *ardently* [*passionately, wholeheartedly*].

ねどこ　寝床　bed／寝床につく go to *bed*／彼女は寝床で本を読んでいる She is reading a book *in bed*.／彼はけだるそうに寝床から出てきた He languidly got out of *bed*.

ねとねと　レンジ周りが油でねとねとしている The gas stove and the area around it *are sticky* with oil.

ねとまり　寝泊まり　この病室には患者の家族も寝泊まりすることができる The family members of the patients can also *stay the night* in this hospital room.／彼はここ2週間お兄さんのところに寝泊まりしている He's *stayed* 「*at* his brother's house [*with* his brother] for the last two weeks.

ねなしぐさ　根無し草　(1つの住所・仕事などに定着しない人) rolling stone

ネバダ　Nevada (❖米国西部の州; (略語)Nev., 〔郵便〕NV)

ねばつく　粘つく be sticky [glutinous]

-ねばならない　must *do*, have to *do* ⇨ -ならない／お金を得るためには働かねばならない We *must* [*have to*] work to earn money.／きょう中にやらねばならないことがある I have something *to* do today.

ねばねば　ねばねばした sticky, glutinous／納豆はねばねばしていて大嫌いだ I hate *natto* because it is *sticky*.／手を洗ってもなかなかねばねば(→ねばねばした物)が取れない The *sticky* [*glutinous*] *stuff* won't wash off of my hands.

ねばり　粘り　❶【ねばねばすること】stickiness／それらをボールに入れ, ねばりが出てくるまでよく混ぜてください Put them into a bowl and mix them until they *become sticky* [*glutinous*].
❷【根気】(忍耐力) perseverance; (意志の堅さ) tenacity／彼が勝てないのはねばりが足りないからだ The reason he can't win is because he is short of *perseverance* [*tenacity*].

ねばりがち　粘り勝ち　彼女はチャンピオンにねばり勝ちした She *persevered in the game and beat* the champion.

ねばりけ　粘り気　stickiness ⇨ ねばり

ねばりごし　粘り腰　大関はその試合でみごとなねばり腰を見せた In that match, the *ozeki* maintained *a firm stance*.／彼らはねばり腰で商談を成立させた They succeeded in settling the negotiation *through perseverance* [*persistence*].

ねばりづよい　粘り強い, persevering, tenacious／ねばり強い努力 *persevering* [*tenacious*] efforts
◆彼らはねばり強く犯人を追跡した They pursued the criminal *perseveringly* [*tenaciously*].／彼の長所はそのねばり強さだ(→決してあきらめないところだ) His good point is his *perseverance* [*tenacity*].／His good point is that he *never gives up*.

ねばる　粘る　❶【ねばつく】be sticky [glutinous], (くっつく) stick* (to ...)／この納豆はよくねばる This *natto* is very *sticky* [*glutinous*].
❷【根気よく続ける】(忍耐する) persevere; (…し続ける) keep* on *doing*／そのチームはねばって同点に持ち込んだ The team *persevered* and tied up the game.／警察はそこで翌朝までねばったが, ついに犯人は現れなかった The police *kept on waiting* there for the criminal until the next morning, but he didn't turn up.
◆地域住民はその計画の撤廃を要求してねばっている The citizens *are holding out* for the abolition of the plan.／コーヒー1杯でその店に3時間近くねばった I *lingered* at the shop for nearly three hours over a cup of coffee.

ねびえ　寝冷え　きちんとふとんをかけないと寝冷えするよ(→かぜをひく)よ Cover yourself with a futon completely or *your body will get too cool while you sleep* and you'll 「*catch a cold* [(→腹が痛くなる) *get a stomachache*].

ねびき　値引き　discount, reduction ――値引きする discount, reduce [cut*] a price of .../定価から5パーセント値引きでいかがでしょう We'll *give* you a five percent *discount* off list prices.／We'll *discount* list prices five percent.／このバッグ, 値引きしてもらえませんか Could you *discount* [*cut the price of*] this bag for me?
‖値引き競争 a price war

ねびく　値引く　discount

ねぶかい 根深い deep-rooted, deep-seated ∥根深い問題 a *deep-rooted* [*deep-seated*] problem / 両民族間には根深い対立がある There is a *deep-rooted* [*deep-seated*] conflict between the two peoples.
◆彼らの政府に対する不信感は根深い Their distrust toward the government *is deeply rooted*.

ねぶくろ 寝袋 sleeping bag © ∥寝袋で寝る sleep in *a sleeping bag*

ねぶそく 寝不足 (a) lack of sleep ∥寝不足で体中がだるい My body feels heavy and tired because of *a lack of sleep*. / My body feels heavy and tired because I *didn't sleep well*.
◆最近寝不足ぎみだ I'm a little *short of sleep* recently.

ねふだ 値札 （ひもなどでつるした）price tag [ticket] ©; （シールの）price label ©

ねぶみ 値踏み （価格の）valuation © Ⓤ; （評価）evaluation © Ⓤ ──値踏みする value ⓗ; evaluate ⓗ ∥質屋の主人はその宝石を5万円と値踏みした The pawnbroker *valued* the jewelry at 50,000 yen.

ネブラスカ Nebraska（❖米国中部の州;《略語》Neb., Nebr.,〔郵便〕NE）

ねぼう 寝坊 late riser ©　──寝坊する oversleep* ⓘ ∥彼はよく寝坊して学校に遅れる He often *oversleeps* and is late for school.

ねぼけまなこ 寝惚け眼　彼は寝ぼけまなこでテレビを見ていた He was watching TV with *sleepy eyes*.

ねぼける 寝惚ける （半分眠っている）be half asleep; （半分目ざめている）be half awake ∥弟は寝ぼけて階段から落っこちた My brother fell down the stairs while he *was half asleep*. / きのうの夜，君は寝ぼけてわけの分からないことを言っていたよ You said something I couldn't understand at all when you *were half awake* last night.
◆彼は寝ぼけ顔で食卓についた He sat at the breakfast table with *a sleepy look on his face*. / 何を寝ぼけたこと（→ふざけたこと）を言っているんだ What do you mean by talking such *nonsense*?

ねほりはほり 根掘り葉掘り　彼女はそのことについて彼に根掘り葉掘り質問した She *asked* him「*too many detailed questions* about the matter [about the matter *in every detail*]. / 彼は他人のことを根掘り葉掘り聞き出そうとする He *is very inquisitive* about other people.

ねまき 寝巻き・寝間着 nightclothes; （パジャマ）pajamas,《英》pyjamas; （男性用の丈（ɡ）の長い）nightshirt ©; （女性用のゆったりした）nightdress ©, nightgown ©

ねまわし 根回し consensus-building Ⓤ ──根回しする build* consensus (in advance) ∥根回し不足で彼女の案は通らなかった Her plan wasn't passed because she hadn't done enough *consensus-building*. / 彼は企画会議を前に参加者に根回ししておいた He *built consensus among* those present before the decision-making meeting on the project.

ねみみ 寝耳　彼らの結婚は寝耳に水だった Their marriage「*was quite unexpected* [*came as a thunderbolt*, came *out of the blue*].

ねむい 眠い sleepy, dozy, drowsy
僕は疲れていてとても眠い I'm tired and「I'm [I feel] very *sleepy*.
午後の授業は眠い I get *sleepy* in afternoon classes.
彼女ずいぶん眠そうだな She looks very *sleepy*.
彼女の子守り歌を聞いていたら眠くなった Her lullabies made me *sleepy*.（❖以上の用例はすべて dozy, drowsy も可）
彼は眠い目をこすりながら食卓についた He sat at the table rubbing his *sleepy* [*drowsy*] eyes.

ねむけ 眠気 sleepiness Ⓤ, drowsiness Ⓤ ∥眠気ざましに少し体を動かした I exercised for a little while to *shake off my sleepiness* [*drowsiness*].
◆薬を飲んだら眠気をもよおしてきた I've become *sleepy* [*dozy, drowsy*] because of the medicine I took. / 電車の揺れが眠気を誘う The rocking of the train *makes me sleepy* [*dozy, drowsy*].

ねむらせる 眠らせる put* *a person to sleep* ∥犯人は薬を飲ませて彼を眠らせた The criminal made him take a drug that *put him to sleep*.
◆もう眠いよ，そろそろ眠らせてよ I'm sleepy. Please *let me sleep* now. / 彼女は歌を聴かせて赤ん坊を眠らせた She *sang the baby to sleep*.

ねむり 眠り ❶【睡眠】sleep Ⓤ（また a ～）; （仮眠）nap © ∥彼はなかなか眠りにつけなかった He *couldn't get* [*go*] *to sleep* soon. / 彼はその部屋で一眠りした I *had a nap* in the room. / 彼は薬を飲むと深い眠りに落ちた He took the medicine and fell into *a deep sleep*. / 鶏の声で眠りからさめた I woke up from *my sleep* at the crow of a rooster. / 眠りが足りない I lack *sleep*.
◆彼女は眠りが浅い［深い］She is *a light* [*heavy*] *sleeper*.
❷【死去】sleep Ⓤ（❖日本語同様「死」の婉曲表現として用いる）∥彼女はとわの眠りについた She *fell into an eternal sleep*. / She *fell asleep eternally*.
眠り薬 a sleeping pill

ねむりこむ 眠り込む　彼はこたつで眠り込んでしまった He *fell asleep* at the *kotatsu*.

ねむる 眠る
❶【睡眠をとる】sleep* ⓘ, have* a sleep; （眠り始める）fall* asleep, go* to sleep
彼はどこでもよく眠れる He *can sleep* well wherever he is.
赤ん坊が母親のひざの上で眠っている The baby *is sleeping* on its mother's lap.

一晩ぐっすり眠れば気分がよくなるよ Have a good night's *sleep*, and you'll be all right.

私はいつも、ベッドに横になるとすぐ眠ってしまう I always 「*fall asleep* [*go to sleep*] as soon as I lie on my bed.

彼は眠りこけていた He *was sleeping like a log*.

◆私は列車の中でぐっすり眠っていた I was *fast* [*sound*] *asleep* in the train. / 彼女はとても疲れていたが眠れなかった Though (she was) very tired, she *couldn't get to sleep*. (❖get to sleep は「どうにか眠りにつく」の意味。通例否定文で用いる) / 彼女は夜も眠らずに母親の看病をした She *stayed awake* all night, and took care of her sick mother. / あなたを思いながら眠れぬ夜を過ごしました I've spent a *sleepless* night thinking about you. / その大臣は国会の審議中眠っていた The minister *was nodding off* during the session of the Diet. (❖nod off は「こっくりする」の意味)

❶「ゆうべはよく眠れましたか」「ええ、おかげさまで」 "Did you *sleep* well last night?" "Yes, I did. Thank you."

❷「コーヒーはいかがですか」「結構です。眠れなくなるので」 "Would you like some coffee?" "No thanks. Coffee *keeps me awake*."

❷【死ぬ】

祖母はこの墓地に眠っている My grandmother *sleeps* in this cemetery. / My grandmother's body *lies* in this cemetery.

安らかにお眠りください May your soul *rest in peace*.

❸【活用されないでいる】

地下に眠る財宝 treasure *hidden* underground

この土地を眠らせておく(→何もせずにほうっておく)のはもったいない This piece of land is too good to *be left idle*.

その地域には豊富な地下資源が眠っているとされている That area is said to be rich in underground resources.

ねもと 根元 (下部) foot C; (基部) base C / 柱の根元がシロアリにやられてしまっている The foot [*base*] of the wooden pillar was damaged by termites.

◆草を根元(→根)から引っこ抜く *pull* the weed *up by the roots*; *root up* the weed / 彼はユリを根元で折った(→根の近くで折った) He broke the lily *near the roots*.

ねゆき 根雪 remaining snow cover C

◆今回の雪は根雪にはならないだろう This snow 「*won't stay long* [*will soon melt away*]. / このあたりでは12月に根雪になる In this area, we get the *first snow that stays on the ground* in December.

ねらい 狙い

❶【銃などの】 aim U

猟師はウサギにねらいを定めた The hunter *took aim at* a rabbit (with a gun).

彼女のねらいは正確で、的(まと)をはずしたことがない His *aim* is accurate and he has never missed a mark.

彼の撃った弾はねらいがはずれ、シカに当たらなかった His *aim* was off and the bullet missed the deer.

❷【目的】 aim C; purpose C; (意図) intention U C

この本は読者の英語の知識の向上をねらいとしている The *aim* of this book is to extend the readers' knowledge of English.

あのグループのねらいはいったい何だろう I wonder what 「the group's *aim* is [the group *is aiming at*].

実は私の本当のねらいは別のところにあった Actually my true *aim* was somewhere else.

◆そのおもちゃは主に小学生にねらいをしぼって作られた The toy *was designed for* use mainly by schoolchildren. / 彼のねらいどおり、彼の店は若い女性に大いにうけた As he *had expected* [*intended*], his shop become very popular among young women.

ねらいうち 狙い撃ち・狙い打ち 猟師はイノシシをねらい撃ちした The hunter *took aim at* the wild boar *and shot* it. / 彼はシュートをねらい打ちした He *hit* the screwball, *which he'd been expecting*.

ねらいめ 狙い目 家を買うなら今がねらい目だ If you want to buy a house, now's *the chance* [*right time*].

ねらう 狙う

❶【的(まと)などを】 aim 他 自, take* aim

彼はライフルでシカをねらった He *aimed at* a deer with his rifle. / He *aimed* his rifle *at* a deer.

彼は的をよくねらってからボールを投げた He threw the ball after *taking good aim at* the mark.

◆蛇はネズミをねらって飛びかかった The snake jumped *at* a mouse.

❷【手に入れようとする】(目をつけている) have* an [*one's*] eye on ...; (求める)《公式的》seek* 他 ; (他人の物などを) be after ...

猫がテーブルの上の魚をねらっている The cat *has an eye on* the fish on the table.

彼は彼女の職場でのポストをねらっている He *is after* her post at the office.

◆その男は連中に命をねらわれていた The man *had been marked* for death by them. / 男は保険金をねらって彼女を殺害した The man killed her *in order to get* her insurance money.

❸【目ざす】 aim 自

その力士は今場所10勝以上をねらっている The sumo wrestler *is aiming* 「*to* win more than 10 bouts [*for* more than 10 wins] in this tournament.

❹【ターゲットとする】 aim 他 自

そこでは観光客をねらった様々な商売が見られる Various kinds of business which *are aimed at* visitors can be seen there.

◆俗うけをねらった映画 a movie *made to appeal to the popular taste*; a *kitsch* movie

❺【機会を】 watch for ...; (待つ) wait

for ...
そのチームは反撃の機会をねらっていた The team *was watching* [*waiting*] *for* a chance to counterattack.

ねりあげる 練り上げる 彼らは2か月かけて文化祭の計画を練り上げた It took them two months to *work out* a plan for their school festival.

ねりあるく 練り歩く parade 自; (デモ隊などが) march 自 ∥ブラスバンドが町中を練り歩いた The brass band *paraded* through the streets. / デモ隊が市役所周辺を練り歩いた The demonstrators *paraded* [*marched*] around the city office.

ねりなおす 練り直す (考え直す) reconsider 他 ∥計画を練り直す *reconsider* the plan; *work out* the plan *all over again*

ねる¹ 寝る

❶眠る	sleep; go to bed
❷病気で	be sick in bed
❸横になる	lie

❶【眠る】(眠る) sleep* 自, have* [get*] asleep, (床につく) go* [get] to bed, go [get] to sleep

僕はふだん7時間寝る I usually *sleep* for seven hours.

正は今寝ています Tadashi *is sleeping* now.

ひどく疲れていたので私は早く寝た As I was very tired, I *went to bed* early.

寝たのは12時過ぎだった It was past 12 when I *went to bed*.

日曜日は遅くまで寝ていたい I like to *sleep late* [*in*] on Sundays.

彼女はこのところあまり寝ていない She *hasn't got* much *sleep* lately. (❖×many sleeps とはいわない)

寝る前に歯を磨きなさい Brush your teeth *before going to bed*.

いつまで寝てるの，いいかげん起きなさい How long are you going to *sleep*? Get out of bed!

ゆうべは歯が痛くて寝られなかった I *couldn't get to sleep* because of a toothache. (❖ get to sleep は通例否定文で用いる)

本当に留学したいのかどうか一晩寝てよく考えなさい *Sleep on* the question of whether you really want to study abroad.

◆彼女は夫の帰りを寝ずに待った She *waited* [*stayed*] *up for* her husband. / 夕食後彼は寝る時間までゆっくりテレビを見ます After supper he will sit down and watch TV until *bedtime*. / さあ，おまえたち，もう寝る時間だよ Now, children, *time for bed*. / 頭痛はいつも寝て治します I always *sleep* my headache *off*. / 私は寝る暇も惜しんで(→寝る時間を削って)本を読みふけった I read books *by cutting down on my sleep*. / 彼女は寝たふりをしている She *is shamming sleep*. / She *is playing possum*.

❷「いつも何時くらいに寝るの」「だいたい12時くらいかな．君は？」 "What time do you usually *go to bed*?" "Around twelve. How about you?"

❷「疲れてるね．どうしたの」「ゆうべ2時間しか寝てないんだ」 "You look tired. What's the matter?" "I *only slept* for two hours last night."

❷【病気で】be sick in bed
彼女は1か月も病気で寝ている She *has been sick in bed* for a month.

◆かぜひいて寝てるの？彼らしくないね Is he *in bed* with a cold? It's not like him. / 彼はそれ以来寝たきりだ He *has been bedridden* since then.

❸【横になる】lie* 自
あおむけ[横向き，うつぶせ]に寝る *lie* on *one's* back [side, stomach]

彼は川の土手にごろんと寝た He *lay down* on the river bank.

寝て本を読むのは目に悪いですよ It's bad for your eyes to read *lying down*.

❹【セックスする】(口語的／婉曲的) sleep* 自
彼女は彼女と寝た He *slept with* her.
彼女はだれとでも寝る She *sleeps around*.
慣用表現 寝た子を起こすな *Let sleeping dogs lie.* (→眠っている犬はそのままにしておけ) / 彼女は寝ても覚めても彼のことばかり考えている She's only thinking about him, *awake or asleep*. / 寝る子は育つ *A child that sleeps well grows well.*

ねる² 練る ❶【こねる】knead 他 ∥粘土を練る *knead* clay

❷【念入りに作る】(細かい所まで) elaborate 他; (計画を) work out (carefully); (磨きをかける) polish 他 ∥計画を練る *elaborate* a plan; *work out* a plan *carefully* / よく練られたストーリー a *well-elaborated* [an *elaborate*, a *mature*] story / 彼は何日もかけて文章を練った He spent many days *polishing* (*up*) his writing.

❸【その他】あんを練る *cook* bean paste

ねわざ 寝技 grappling technique ⓒⓊ

ねん¹ 年

❶【1年】year ⓒ
年々 *year after* [*by*] *year* / 1年おきに *every other year* / 30数年 *thirty-odd years* / 3年前[後]に *three years ago* [*from now*]; *three years before* [*later*] (❖前者は「今から3年前[後]」，後者は過去のある時点を基準として「その3年前[それから3年後]」の意味)

私は年に1度旅行をする I go on a trip *once a year*.

最後に君に会ってから7年たった *Seven years have passed* since I saw you last.

彼女にはもう何年も会っていない I haven't seen her *for years*.

その学校は3年連続して優勝した The school won the championship *three years in 「a row* [*succession*].

彼は懲役5年の刑に処せられた He was sentenced to *five years' imprisonment*.

❷【年号】year ⓒ

2001年に in (the year) 2001 (❖2001は two thousand (and) one と読む)
1989年はドイツにとって記念すべき年だった The year 1989 was a year to be remembered for Germany. (❖1989は nineteen eighty-nine と読む)
💬「生年月日は?」「1986年9月12日です」 "What is your date of birth?" "(It's) September 12, 1986."
❸【学年】year ⓒ, 《米》grade ⓒ, 《英》form ⓒ ♦がくねん
💬「君は今,高校の何年ですか」「2年です」 "What year of high school are you in now?" "I'm in the second year."

ねん²　念　❶【意識・感じ】(意識) sense ⓤ《また a ~》; (感じ) feeling ⓒ //畏敬(いけい)の念をいだく have a sense [feeling] of awe / 彼には感謝の念が欠けている He has no sense of gratitude. / 彼は彼女を憎悪の念に満ちた目で見た He looked at her with「eyes filled with hateful feelings [hateful eyes].
◆彼はその科学者に尊敬の念をいだいている(→尊敬している) He respects the scientist. / He has respect for the scientist.
❷【注意】急には念を入れて消火の確認をしなさい Make doubly sure that the fire has completely died out. / 彼は本を持ってくるよう彼に何度も念を押した I told [reminded] him repeatedly to bring me that book.
⇨ねんのため

ねんいり　念入り　──念入りな (注意深い) careful; (手の込んだ) elaborate; (綿密な) close ──念入りに carefully; elaborately; closely //念入りに仕上げられた彫刻 a sculpture with a careful [an elaborate] finish; a carefully [an elaborately] finished sculpture / 念入りな調査の結果, その事実が明らかになった On careful [close] examination, the fact was made clear. / 彼女は念入りに部屋の掃除をした She cleaned her room carefully.

ねんえき　粘液　mucus ⓤ

ねんが　年賀　🎴 nenga, New Year's greetings //年賀のあいさつを交わす exchange New Year's greetings
◆年賀状をどうもありがとう Thank you for sending me a New Year's card. / きょうはおじの家に年賀に行くつもりだ I'm going to pay a New Year's visit to my uncle today. ‖年賀はがき a New Year's card [postcard]

> 年賀状を贈る習慣は, 日本で初めて郵便はがきが発行された明治時代に始まりました. それまでは親戚(しんせき)や知人を直接訪問していましたが, はがきでも新年のあいさつをすることができるようになったのです. 最近ではワープロやパソコンを使って年賀状を作る人が増えてきました. また, 絵や文字が印刷された年賀状を買うことも, オリジナルなものを注文することもできます.
> The custom of sending nengajo (New Year's cards) traces back to the Meiji period (1868–1912), when postcards were first issued in Japan. Until then, people visited their relatives and acquaintances to greet them at the New Year, but nengajo enabled people to do so by sending cards. Now with the popularization of word processors and personal computers, more and more people make their own nengajo. At shops you can buy ready-made nengajo with text and pictures printed on them or order original ones.

ねんがく　年額　the annual amount [sum] //会費は年額10万円になります The annual amount [sum] of the membership fee will be 100,000 yen. / You're required to pay 100,000 yen a year for membership.

ねんがっぴ　年月日　the date

ねんがらねんじゅう　年がら年中　(いつも) always; (一年中) all (the) year round [around] //彼は年がら年中同じような服装をしている He always wears clothes of a similar kind.

ねんかん¹　年間　❶【1年の間】年間降雨量[所得] an annual [a yearly] rainfall [income] / 私は年間5万円貯金する目標を立てた I set the goal of saving 50,000 yen a [per] year. / その地域は年間を通して穏やかな気候で, 過ごしやすい The area is good for people to live in because the climate there is mild throughout the year.
❷【…年の間】1年間保証付きのテレビ a television set with a one-year guarantee / 私は英語を6年間勉強しました I studied English for six years. / パソコンはこの10年間で一般に普及してきた Personal computers have become popular among people over [in] the past 10 years. / 今後5年間の日本経済をどう見ますか How do you think the Japanese economy will do over [for, during] the next five years? / 彼らは2年間で(→2年以内に)そのビルを完成させねばならない They have to complete the building in [within] two years.
❸【特定の年代の間】その寺は元禄年間に再建された The temple was rebuilt during the Genroku era.

ねんかん²　年刊　その雑誌は年刊です(→年に1度発行される) That magazine is published annually [yearly].

ねんかん³　年鑑　yearbook ⓒ, 《古風》almanac ⓒ

ねんがん　念願　(望み) one's wish [desire, longing]; (夢) one's dream //念願かなって彼はついにアメリカに留学することとなった His wish [dream] to study in the U.S. has come true at last. ◆おじは長年の念願だった別荘を軽井沢に建てた My uncle built a cottage in Karuizawa after having wanted to do so for a long time.

ねんき　年季　彼は年季の入った(→経験豊富な)コックだ He「has many years of experience as a cook [is an experienced cook]. / ずいぶん年季の入った財布だね(→長年の使用でだいぶ傷ん

でいるね) Your wallet *is well-worn from years of use*, isn't it?

ねんきん 年金 pension [C]; (生涯支払われるもの) annuity [C] ∥年金を受ける receive [draw, collect] *one's pension* / 私の祖父は年金で生活している My grandfather lives on *a pension.*

‖年金受給者 a pensioner, an annuitant / 年金制度 a pension plan [scheme] / 遺族年金 a pension for a bereaved family / 企業年金 a corporate [company] pension / 共済年金 a mutual aid (welfare) pension / 厚生年金 a welfare pension / 公的年金 a public pension / 国民年金 a national pension / 個人年金 a personal pension / 障害年金 a disability pension / 老齢年金 an old-age pension

ねんぐ 年貢 an annual tribute imposed on farmers by landowners

[慣用表現] あの悪党もそろそろ年貢の納め時だ *It all must* soon *be over with* that wicked guy.

ねんげつ 年月 《口語的》years; (時・期間) time [U] [C] ∥その塔の完成には15年という長い年月を要した It took as many as 15 *years* to build the tower. / 2人は30年近い年月を経た後に再会した Nearly 30 *years* had passed before the two met again.

ねんこう 年功 ‖年功序列制度 the seniority system (❖欧米では一般的ではない)

ねんごう 年号 the name of an era

ねんごろ 懇ろ ❶【丁寧】私たちはその猫の死骸(しがい)をねんごろに葬ってやった We buried the cat's body *reverently* [*respectfully*]. / 彼らはねんごろにもてなされた(→心からのもてなしを受けた) They received a *hearty* [*warm*] welcome.

❷【親しい】彼と彼女はねんごろになった The couple *become intimate with* each other. (❖この場合,ふつう He and she ...とはいわない)

ねんざ 捻挫 sprain [C], wrench [C] ──ねんざする sprain [他], wrench [他], twist [他] ∥足首をねんざする *sprain* [*wrench, twist*] *one's* ankle

-ねんさい -年祭 anniversary [C] ∥100年祭 *the 100th anniversary*; *the centennial*; *the centenary* / そのデパートは開店30年祭を行った The department store celebrated *the* 30th *anniversary* of its opening.

ねんさん 年産 annual output [production] [U] 《また an ～》∥その工場は最盛期には年産6,000台のバイクを生産していた The factory had *an annual output* of 6,000 motorcycles at its peak. / Six thousand motorcycles *per year were produced* in the factory at its peak.

ねんし 年始 the beginning of a year

◆両親と年始回りをした My parents and I *paid New Year's visits to several families.*

ねんじ 年次 ──年次の annual, yearly

‖年次休暇 an annual leave / 年次計画 an annual [a yearly] plan / 年次報告(書) an annual [a yearly] report

ねんしき 年式 兄の車は1994年式のスカイラインだ My brother's car is a 1994-*model* Skyline.

ねんしゅう 年収 annual [yearly] income [C], annual [yearly] earnings ∥彼女の年収は900万円だ Her *annual* [*yearly*] *income* is nine million yen./ She *earns* nine million yen *a year*.

ねんじゅう 年中 (いつも) always; (一年中) all (the) year around [round], throughout the year ∥年中無休 《掲示》*Always open*; *Open seven days a week* / 彼は年中母親にしかられている He is *always* scolded by his mother. / 弟は年がら年中テレビゲームをしている My brother is *always* playing video games. / その店は年中無休でやっている The store *is open* 「*all the year around* [*throughout the year*].

ねんしゅつ 捻出 ──捻出する (金を) raise [他], come* up with ... ∥自分のこづかいからそのパーティーの会費を捻出するのは難しい It's hard to *raise* [*come up with*] the expenses for the party from my allowance.

ねんしょ 念書 念書をとる keep *a written record*

ねんしょう[1] 年少 ──年少の young; (より年下の) younger ∥彼女がわがクラブ中最年少のメンバーです She is *the youngest* member in our club.

◆妹は幼稚園の年少の白組だ My sister is in the "white" group in *the junior class* of her kindergarten.

‖年少者 a young [younger] person; (青少年) a juvenile

ねんしょう[2] 燃焼 combustion [U] ──燃焼する[させる] burn* [自] [他] ∥マグネシウムの燃焼の様子を観察する observe how magnesium *burns* / 脂肪を燃焼させる *burn* fat

◆僕らは今度の大会で完全燃焼するつもりだ(→すべての精力を注ぐつもりだ) We're going to *devote all of our energies to* the next competition.

‖完全[不完全]燃焼 complete [incomplete] combustion

ねんしょう[3] 年商 その会社は年商50億円だ *The annual sales* of the company is five billion yen.

ねんじる 念じる (祈る) pray [自] [他]; (願う) wish [自] [他]

ねんすう 年数 その寺は建立から相当の年数を経ている A lot of *years* have passed since the temple was built.

-ねんせい -年生 ❶【学年】その子供は小学1[2]年生です The child is a first-*grader* [second-*grader*]./ The child is in the first [second] *grade*.

[語法]
高校と大学の1年生は a freshman, 2年生はそれぞれ a junior, a sophomore, 3年生は a senior, a junior, 大学4年生は a senior という。

❷「君は何年生ですか」「高校2年生です」"What grade are you in?" "I'm in *the* second *year* of high school./ I'm *a* high school *junior*." (❖grade はふつう小学生に使う. 高校2年生ということは in the second year (of high school) といい, second grade とはいわない)

⇨ がくねん

❷【植物】一年生植物 an annual (plant) (❖二年生は a biennial (plant), 多年生は a perennial (plant) という)

ねんだい 年代 ❶【時代】70年代ファッションの復活 the revival of 70's [70s] fashion (❖70's, 70s は seventies と読む) / このアルバムは1990年代前半 [半ば, 後半] に発表された This album was issued in *the* early [mid, late] 1990's [1990s]. (❖1990's, 1990s は nineteen nineties と読む) / 我々はこれらの化石の年代を特定した We *dated* these fossils. / 仏教の伝来はキリスト教伝来より年代が古い Buddhism was brought into Japan *earlier* than Christianity. / Christianity was brought into Japan *later* than Buddhism. / これらの本は年代順に並べられている These books are arranged *by the date of publication*. / この町にはかなり年代を経た寺社がたくさんある There're many *old* temples and shrines in this town. / この年代物の茶わんはいくらですか How much are you asking for this *antique* cup?

❷【世代】generation ◎ / 祖父の年代の人は大部分戦争を経験している Most people of my grandfather's *generation* have experienced war.

‖年代記 a chronicle / 年代測定法 a dating technique

ねんちゃく 粘着 このテープは粘着力が強い This tape has strong *adhesion* [*stickiness*].

‖粘着テープ (an) adhesive tape

ねんちゅうぎょうじ 年中行事 annual event [function] ◎

ねんちょう 年長 ――年長の older (❖年齢の上下, 特に兄弟・姉妹関係を表すときには〔英〕では elder, eldest を用いるほうがふつう), senior / 年長者を敬いなさい Respect *older* [*senior*] people./ Respect *your* seniors. / 彼女は私より4歳年長だ She is four years *older* than I (am). / 若林君はうちのクラブで最年長のメンバーだ Wakabayashi is *the oldest* member in our club.

◆妹は幼稚園の年長の赤組だ My sister is in the "red" group in *the senior class* of her kindergarten.

ねんど¹ 年度 (一般に) year ◎; (学年度) school [academic] year ◎; (会計年度) fiscal [(英)financial] year ◎ / 年度末 *the end of a* (*school* [*fiscal*]) *year* / 来年度の予算案 *the next year's* budget bill / 2003年会計年度に in the 2003 *fiscal year*; in *fiscal* 2003 / 2001年度卒業の同期生 the class of 2001 (*school year*) / 本年度の当社の総売り上げは良好だ Our gross sales *this year* are good. / 日本では学校の年度は4月から始まる In Japan *the school year* starts in April.

◆2002年度グラミー賞 the 2002 Grammy Awards

ねんど² 粘土 clay ◎ / ひと塊(ﾊﾞ)の粘土 a lump of *clay* / 僕は粘土でペンギンを作った I made a penguin out of *clay*. / 彼は粘土細工が得意だ He is good at「*clay work* [*working with clay*].

‖粘土層 a layer of clay / 紙粘土 papier-mâché [pèiparmaʃéi]

ねんとう¹ 年頭 the beginning of a year, the new year / 県知事が年頭のあいさつをした The prefectural governor made the *new year's* speech.

ねんとう² 念頭 先生の言ったことを念頭においてもう一度やってみなさい Try it again *while keeping* [*bearing*] *in mind* what the teacher said. / 彼女は彼のことなどまるで念頭にない She *doesn't*「*care* at all [*even think* a bit] about him. / 彼は成功することしか念頭にない He *is interested in nothing but* success.

ねんない 年内 彼は冬休みの宿題を年内にすべて片づけるつもりだ He intends to finish all of his winter vacation homework「*before the end of the year* [*within the year*].

ねんね 《小児語》bye-bye ◎◎ ――ねんねする go* bye-bye(s) / さあ, もうねんねしなさい (→ねんねする時間よ) Now, *it's time to go bye-bye(s)*.

◆坊や, さあおねんねよ Hushaby, my boy.

ねんねん 年々 (毎年) every [each] year; (年ごとに) year by year, from year to year / 学齢期の子供の数は年々減っている The number of children old enough for school is decreasing「*every year* [*year by year, from year to year*].

ねんのため 念の為 念のためもう一度数えよう Let's count again *just to make sure*. / 念のため (→万一に備えて) 傘を持ってきた I've brought an umbrella *just in case*. / 念のため申し上げますが, あすは通常より早めの5時で閉店となります *Let me remind you* [*May I remind you*] (*that*) we close at five tomorrow, which is earlier than usual.

ねんぱい 年配・年輩 (年齢) age ◎◎ ――年配の (かなりの年齢の) elderly (❖old の婉曲表現として用いられる) / 年配のご婦人 an *elderly* lady / あの歌手とうちの母とはほぼ同年配だ That singer *is about* my mother's *age*. / That singer *is of almost the same age* as my mother.

◆彼女は僕より3つ年配だ She is three years *older* than I (am).

ねんぴ 燃費 fuel efficiency ◎; (リットル当たりの走行マイル数) mileage ◎◎ / 低燃費車 a car with「*good fuel efficiency* [*high mileage*]; a *fuel-efficient* car / 兄の車は燃費がいい My brother's car「*has good fuel efficiency* [*gets high mileage*]. / そのバイクの燃費はどれくらいですか What is the motorcycle's *fuel efficiency* [*mileage*]?

ねんぴょう 年表 chronological table ◎, chronology ◎ / 日本史の年表 a「*chronologi-*

*cal table [chronology] of Japanese history

ねんぶつ 念仏 念仏を唱える chant *the name of Amida Buddha*
ことわざ 馬の耳に念仏 ⇨ うま(馬)

ねんぽう 年俸 annual salary ⓒ ∥彼の年俸は3億円だ His *annual salary* is 300 million yen./ He *makes* 300 million yen *a year*.
◆プロ野球の選手は年俸制である Professional baseball players *are paid by the year*.

ねんまく 粘膜 〖解剖〗 mucous membrane ⓒⓤ

ねんまつ 年末 the end of the year ─年末の year-end ∥年末に鎌倉を訪れた I visited Kamakura *at the end of the year*./ 年末年始はどの家も忙しい Every family is busy *at the beginning and the end of the year*./ その店では年末大売り出しをしていた The store was having *a year-end sale*.
∥年末ジャンボ宝くじ the year-end jumbo lottery / 年末調整 a year-end tax adjustment

ねんらい 年来 ─年来の (夢・望みなどが) long-cherished; (長年持ち続けられた) long-held ∥その教授の年来の研究テーマ the professor's *long-held* study theme ∥彼女の年来の望みがついにかなえられた Her *long-cherished* wish has come true at last.
◆彼女と私とは10年来の知り合いだ I have known her *for 10 years*./ She and I have known each other *for 10 years*./ この夏は10年来の猛暑だった This summer was the hottest *in (the last) 10 years*.

ねんり 年利 annual interest ⓤ; (利率) annual interest rate ⓒ ∥年利3パーセントで融資する lend money at *the annual interest rate* of three percent

ねんりき 念力 psychokinetic power ⓤ ∥彼は念力で机の上の本を移動させた He moved the book on the desk by using *his psychokinetic power*.

ねんりつ 年率 annual rate ⓒ; (年利) annual interest rate ⓒ ∥年率2パーセントの電力需要の伸びが見込まれている The *annual growth rate* of the demand for electricity is expected to be two percent./ The demand for electricity is expected to grow by two percent *a year*.

ねんりょう 燃料 fuel ⓤ (❖種類を表すときは ⓒ) ∥燃料が切れそうだ *Fuel* is running short./ We're running short of *fuel*./ 車は燃料切れだった The car was *out of fuel*./ 我々は燃料を節約すべきだと彼は力説した He was emphatic that we should save *fuel*./ 自動車はガソリンや軽油などの燃料で走る Cars run on *fuels* such as gasoline and light oil.
◆彼らはその町に立ち寄り車に燃料を補給した They stopped in the town and *refueled* their car.
∥燃料タンク a fuel tank / 燃料費 fuel expenses / 液体燃料 liquid fuel / 核燃料 nuclear fuel / 化石燃料 (a) fossil fuel / 気体燃料 gaseous fuel / 固形燃料 solid fuel

ねんりん 年輪 (the) growth [annual] rings (of a tree)
慣用表現 彼は芸人として年輪を重ねてきた(→長年やってきた) He's *been* an entertainer *for many years*./ (→長年の間にますます熟練してきた) He's *gotten more and more experienced as an entertainer over the years*.

ねんれい 年齢 age ⓤⓒ
(求人広告などで)年齢不問 *All ages accepted*.
彼女は私くらいの年齢だ She is about my *age*.
将棋は年齢，性別に関係なくだれもが楽しめる Anybody can enjoy playing *shogi*, regardless of *age* or sex.
マラソン大会にはあらゆる年齢の人が参加した People *of all ages* took part in the marathon.
彼女は年齢を偽った She gave *a false age*./ She lied about *her age*.
その男の年齢は30歳くらいだ The man's *age* is about thirty./ The man is about thirty *years old*.
その夫婦は20歳の年齢差がある There is *a 20-year difference in age* between the husband and the wife.
その店には10代半ばから20代半ばの年齢層の客が多い Most of the store's customers are in *the* mid-teens to mid-twenties *age group*.
彼に言わせると僕の精神年齢は15だそうだ According to him, my *mental age* is 15.
彼は年齢不詳だ(→だれも知らない) *Nobody knows*「*his age* [*how old* he *really is*]./ (→外見からは分からない) *You cannot tell* his *age from his appearance*.
メンバーの平均年齢は20歳だ The average *age* of the members is 20.
◆彼は年齢(による衰え)を感じさせない He *is well-preserved*.
∥年齢差別(特に老人に対する) ageism / 年齢制限 the age limit / 就学年齢 school age

の 野 field ©; (平原) plain ©《しばしば複数形～s》/ 野に出て働く work in *the* fields
◆野の花 a *wild* flower
‖野菊 a wild chrysanthemum / 野ネズミ a field mouse
慣用表現 後は野となれ山となれ ⇨ あと(後)

-の
❶【所有・所属】 …'s; of

語法
(1) 一般に所有や所属を表す場合, 人・動物には …'s, または代名詞の所有格 (my, your, his, her など)を, 無生物には of を用いる / 私の本 my book; a book *of* mine ✿前者は文脈上明らかな特定の本を, 後者は数ある本の中の不特定の1冊を指す) / 知子の自転車 Tomoko*'s* bicycle / いすの脚 the leg(s) *of* a chair (✿物の場合 the chair legs のように名詞を並べて用いることも多い) / ドイツの首都 the capital *of* Germany
(2) ただし, 新聞用語などでは無生物であっても …'s を用いることが多い. また時間・距離などを表す名詞には通例 …'s を用いる / 日本の経済 Japan*'s* economy / きょうの新聞 today*'s* paper / 歩いて10分の距離 ten minutes' walk

あの人は僕のおばだ She is *my* aunt.
僕の友達がイギリスに留学している A friend *of* mine is studying in Britain.
その俳優の名前がどうしても思い出せない I just can't remember「the actor*'s* name [the name *of* the actor].
容子はバスケ部のキャプテンだ Yoko is the captain *of* the basketball club.
◆私たちは川北高校の生徒です We are students *at* Kawakita High School.
🔴「このかばんはだれのですか」「それは美恵のです」 "*Whose* bag is this?" "It's *Mie's*."

❷【場所・時】
渋谷のデパートで偶然友達に会った I came across a friend of mine at a department store *in* Shibuya.
壁のポスターを見てごらん Look at the poster *on* the wall.
庭のバラは今満開だ The roses *in* our garden are in full bloom now.
そのアナウンサーは7時のニュースを担当している The announcer reads the 7 o'clock news.
私は毎朝7時半の電車に乗ります I take the 7:30 train every morning.
彼は岩手の出身だ He is *from* Iwate Prefecture.

❸【材料・手段】
紙の箱 a paper box; a box *made of* paper / 英語の(→英語で書かれた)絵本 a picture book (*written*) *in* English

❹【分量・数量】
1杯の紅茶 a cup *of* tea / コップ1杯のミルク a glass *of* milk / 1枚の便せん a *piece of* letter paper

❺【同格】
これは妹の美穂です This is my little sister, Miho.
君はお父さんの健一さんにそっくりですね You look just like your father, Kenichi.
パーティーに友達の麻里を連れていってもいい？ Can I bring Mari, a friend of mine, to the party with me?
営業部長の浜田さんにお目にかかりたいのですが I'd like to see the sales manager, Mr. Hamada.

❻【主語・主体を表す】
母親の子供への愛 the love *of* a mother for her child / ゴッホの描いた絵 a painting *by* van Gogh
私たちは日本航空221便の到着を待っていた We were waiting for the arrival *of* JAL Flight 221.
石川さんの作ったケーキはとてもおいしかった The cake Ms. Ishikawa made was very good.

❼【関連・対象】
料理の本 a book *on* cooking / 鯨の研究 research *on* whales / 子供向けの本 a children*'s* book / 成功のかぎ a key *to* success / 行楽のシーズン the season *for* outings / 長い髪の女の子 a girl *with* long hair
これは私のいとこの写真です This is a photo *of* my cousin.
それ以来私は中村さんの消息を聞いていません I haven't heard *of* Mr. Nakamura since then.

❽【…であるもの・こと】
靴がかなりくたびれてきたからそろそろ新しいのを買わなければならない My shoes are getting worn out, so I'll have to buy *new ones* soon.
パプリカの赤いのと黄色いのを1個ずつ買ってきてちょうだい Go (and) get two bell peppers, *one red* and *one yellow*.
許せないのは彼がそれを私に黙っていたことだ *What I can't forgive* is that he didn't tell it to me.
🔴「コートをお探しですか」「ええ. あのグレーのを着てみていいですか」 "Are you looking for a coat?" "Yes. May I try on that *gray one*?"

❾【質問】
顔色が悪いけどどうしたの You look pale. What's the matter (with you)?
春休みはどこかへ行くの Are you planning to go somewhere in the spring vacation?
行くの？ それとも行かないの？ Are you going? Or not going?

❿【命令・断定】
きょうはおとなしく寝てるのよ, いいわね Be a good boy [girl] and stay in bed today. All right?
おまえはそんなこと心配しないで勉強に集中すればいいの You don't have to worry about that. Just concentrate on your studying.
⓫【その他】
彼女は仕事を辞めるの辞めないのと大騒ぎしていた She was making a fuss over quitting her job *or* something like that.

ノイズ (雑音) noise ⓊⒸ
ノイローゼ ⚠ nervous breakdown Ⓒ;〖医学〗(神経症) neurosis Ⓤ (複 neuroses) (※日本語はドイツ語の Neurose から) ‖ノイローゼになる have *a nervous breakdown*; become *neurotic*; suffer from *neurosis*
‖ノイローゼ患者 a neurotic

のう¹ 脳 (器官) brain Ⓒ; (頭脳・知力) brain Ⓒ(通例複数形 ~s) ──脳の〖医学〗cerebral
脳に異常がある have a *brain* disorder / 脳に損傷を受ける suffer *brain* damage
脳の働きはきわめて複雑だ The functions of *the brain* are extraordinarily complex.
◆脳卒中になる have *a stroke*
‖脳溢血 cerebral hemorrhage / 脳炎 encephalitis / 脳外科 brain [cerebral] surgery / 脳外科医 a brain surgeon / 脳血栓 (a) cerebral thrombosis / 脳梗塞(こうそく) (a) cerebral infarction / 脳細胞 a brain cell / 脳死 ⇨のうし / 脳腫瘍(しゅよう) a brain tumor / 脳神経 the cranial [cerebral] nerves / 脳しんとう (a) concussion / 脳性まひ cerebral palsy / 脳卒中 a stroke, (cerebral) apoplexy / 脳波 brain waves / 脳波計 an electroencephalograph / 脳貧血 anemia of the brain, cerebral anemia

のう² 能 (能力・機能) ability ⓊⒸ ⇨ さいのう, のうりょく ◆彼は絵を描くしか能がない All he can do is (to) paint. / His only *ability* [*talent*] is painting. / 一生懸命勉強するばかりが能じゃない Studying hard is *not everything*. / There is *more to life* than (just) studying hard.
ことわざ 能ある鷹(たか)はつめを隠す Still waters run deep. (→静かな川は深く流れる)

のう³ 能 Noh Ⓤ

能は室町時代に観阿弥と世阿弥の親子が大成した舞踏劇で, 武士階級に支持されていました. 能で特徴的なのは役者のつける面ですが, これは能の最も重要な要素です. 役者は面の角度を変えることで微妙な感情の動きを表します. また, 能は非常に簡素化され, 様式化された芸能ですが, これも能の大きな特徴の一つです. 役者は常に決められた型だけで演技をしなければなりません. 能が「動く彫刻」と呼ばれるゆえんです.
Noh is a musical dance drama that was developed fully in the Muromachi period (1338–1573) by Kanami and his son Zeami and supported by the samurai for a long time. Noh is characterized by the masks the actors wear, which have primary importance in the plays. The actors can express very subtle emotions by varying the angle of the mask. Another important feature of Noh is its highly simplified and stylized performances. The actors are allowed to use only certain stylized gestures set by convention. Because of this, Noh is described as moving sculpture.

のうえん 農園 (農場) farm Ⓒ; (綿花・コーヒーなどの大規模農園) plantation Ⓒ ‖農園で働く work on *a farm* [*plantation*]
‖農園主 the owner of a farm [plantation], a farmer, a planter

のうか 農家 (農民) farmer Ⓒ; (家庭) farm [farming] household Ⓒ, farm [farming] family Ⓒ ‖彼の家は農家です His family are *farmers*. / His family *runs* [*operates*] *a farm*. / このあたりの農家は悪天候のためにひどい打撃を受けた *Farmers* in this area were hard hit by the bad weather.
‖兼業[専業]農家 a part-time [full-time] farmer

のうがき (薬の効能書) a list of a medicine's effects ◆父は日本酒のこととなるといつも能書きを垂れる When it comes to sake, my father always *shows off his knowledge* (of it).

のうがく¹ 農学 agriculture Ⓤ ‖農学者 an agronomist / 農学部 the department of agriculture, the agricultural department

のうがく² 能楽 Noh play [dance] Ⓒ ⇨ のう³ ‖能楽堂 a Noh theater

のうかんき 農閑期 the off-season for farmers, the agricultural off-season

のうき 納期 (金銭の) the fixed [due, final] date for payment; (物品の) the agreed [appointed] date of delivery

のうきぐ 農機具 farm implements [tools]; (機械類) farm machines, farm machinery Ⓤ

のうきょう 農協 (農業協同組合) agricultural cooperative (association) Ⓒ

のうぎょう 農業 agriculture Ⓤ, farming Ⓤ ──農業の agricultural, farming
彼は日本における農業の重要性を強調した He emphasized the importance of *agriculture* in Japan.
うちは農業を営んでいます We are engaged in *farming*. / We are *farmers*.
◆おじは会社勤めを辞めて農業を始めた My uncle quit his office work and has become *a farmer*.
‖農業学校[大学] an agricultural school [college] / 農業機械 farm machinery, farm machines / 農業協同組合 an agricultural cooperative (association) / 農業国 an agricultural country / 農業地帯 a farming district

のうぐ 農具 farm [farming] tool Ⓒ

のうこう¹ 濃厚 ──濃厚な（液体が濃い）thick;（密度が）dense;（味・色・香りが）rich;（味が）heavy;（色が）deep ∥濃厚なスープ *thick* soup / 濃厚な味 a *rich* flavor
◆濃厚なラブシーン a *passionate* [*hot*] love scene / この大雨ではコンサートが延期される可能性が濃厚だ With such a heavy rain, 「*there is a strong possibility* [*it is very likely*] that the concert will be postponed.

のうこう² 農耕 agriculture Ⓤ, farming Ⓤ ──農耕の agricultural, farming ∥農耕に適した土地 land suitable for *farming*
∥農耕社会 an agrarian society / 農耕民族 an agricultural people

のうこん 濃紺 navy blue Ⓤ, dark blue Ⓤ
のうさぎ 野兎 hare Ⓒ
のうさぎょう 農作業 farmwork Ⓤ
のうさくぶつ 農作物 crop 《しばしば複数形 ~s》, agricultural [farm] products, agricultural [farm] produce Ⓤ
のうさつ 悩殺 ──悩殺する（魅惑する）bewitch 他;（性的魅力で）knock *a person* out with *one's* sex appeal
のうさんぶつ 農産物 agricultural [farm] products, agricultural [farm] produce Ⓤ
のうし 脳死 brain death Ⓤ ∥あなたは脳死を人の死だとみなしますか Do you think of *brain death* as the true death of a person?
◆その患者は脳死と判定された The patient was judged to be *brain-dead*.
のうしゅく 濃縮（液体の）concentration Ⓤ ──濃縮する concentrate 他 自, condense 他 自 ∥濃縮オレンジジュース *concentrated* orange juice; an orange *concentrate*
◆濃縮ウラン *enriched* uranium
のうじょう 農場 farm Ⓒ;（大規模の）plantation Ⓒ ∥農場で働く work on *a farm* / 農場を経営する run *a farm*
∥農場主 the owner of a farm [plantation], a farmer / 共同農場 a collective farm
のうしんとう 脳震盪 concussion ⒸⓊ ∥彼女は馬から落ちて脳しんとうを起こした She suffered *a concussion* when she fell off a horse.
のうぜい 納税 tax payment Ⓤ, payment of taxes ──納税する pay* *one's* taxes
◆国民は納税の義務を負う The people are liable to *taxation*. / Every citizen has the obligation to *pay taxes*.
∥納税額 the amount of *one's taxes* / 納税期限 the tax deadline / 納税者 a taxpayer
のうそん 農村 farming [agricultural] village Ⓒ;（農村地帯）farming [agricultural] area Ⓒ;（田園地帯）rural area [district] Ⓒ
のうたん 濃淡 light and shade;（陰影）shades
のうち 農地 agricultural [farming] land Ⓤ, farmland Ⓤ
∥農地改革 agrarian reform(s)
のうてんき 脳天気 気が向いたら試験勉強するだなんておまえも脳天気なやつだなぁ It's *too easy* of you to say that you'll study for the exam if you feel like it.

のうど 濃度（密度・比重）density Ⓤ;（液体などの）concentration Ⓤ ∥海水中の塩分の濃度 *the concentration* of salt in sea water
◆高濃度の放射能が大気中から検出された A *high level* of radiation has been detected in the air.
のうどう 能動 ──能動的な active ──能動的に actively
∥能動態〔文法〕the active voice
のうにゅう 納入（金銭の）payment Ⓤ;（物品の）delivery Ⓤ ──納入する（金銭を）pay* 他;（物品を）deliver 他, supply 他
∥納入金（納めた）money paid;（納めるべき）money due / 納入品 school supplies
のうのう のうのうと暮らす live [lead] an easy [a carefree] life
ノウハウ know-how Ⓤ ∥ホテル経営のノウハウを一から学ぶ obtain hotel management *know-how* from the beginning
のうはんき 農繁期 a busy season for farmers
のうひん 納品（納品すること）delivery of goods;（納品された物）delivered goods ──納品する deliver [supply] goods (to ...)
∥納品書 a statement of delivery
のうふ¹ 納付（支払うこと）payment Ⓤ ──納付する pay* 他
のうふ² 農夫（農場主）farmer Ⓒ;（雇用されている人）farmhand Ⓒ, farm worker Ⓒ;（小作農）tenant farmer Ⓒ
のうべん 能弁 ──能弁な eloquent ──能弁に eloquently
のうみそ 脳味噌（器官）brain Ⓒ;（頭脳）brains ∥脳みそをしぼって考える rack [beat] *one's brains*
のうみん 農民 farmer Ⓒ
のうむ 濃霧 dense [thick, heavy] fog ⒸⓊ
∥濃霧注意報 a dense fog warning
のうやく 農薬 agricultural chemicals;（殺虫剤）insecticide Ⓒ;（除草剤）herbicide Ⓒ ∥畑に農薬を散布する spray the field with 「*agricultural chemicals* [*insecticide*]
∥無農薬野菜 chemical-free vegetables
のうり 脳裏 *one's* mind ∥そのときあるアイディアが彼女の脳裏に浮かんだ Then an idea 「*came into* her *mind* [*occurred to* her]. / 過去のことが脳裏をよぎった Images of my past *ran through my mind.* / 戦争の悲惨さはいまだに祖母の脳裏に焼きついている The misery of the war still *haunts* my grandmother's *mind* [*memory*].

のうりつ 能率 efficiency Ⓤ ──能率的な efficient ──能率的に efficiently
能率を上げる raise [increase] *efficiency* / 能率を下げる lower [decrease] *efficiency*
最新の方法を用いたので仕事の能率が上がった Work *efficiency* increased because of up-to-date methods.
パソコンを使えばもっと能率よく作業ができると思う I think we can get it done more *efficiently* by using PCs.
◆あのやり方では能率が悪すぎる That method is *too inefficient*.

のうりょう 納涼 ‖納涼客 people out to enjoy the cool evening breeze [air] / 納涼船 a summer pleasure boat / 納涼大会 a summer evening festival

のうりょく 能力 ability ⓊⒸ; (人間に備わった) faculty ⓊⒸ; (潜在的な・特定分野の) capacity ⓊⒸ; (実際に発揮される) capability ⓊⒸ, power ⓊⒸ, competence ⓊⒸ
能力別にクラスを編成する group students into classes *by ability* / 子供の潜在能力を引き出す bring out children's *latent* [*potential*] *ability*
彼はその仕事をするだけの能力がある He has *the capability for* the job. / He is *capable*「*of* doing [*to* do] the job.
スポーツ選手たちは自分の能力の限界に挑戦し続けている Athletes are testing the limits of their *abilities*.
彼女は自分の能力を生かせる仕事に就きたいと考えている She wants to get a job in which she can show her *ability*.
彼女は実務能力に欠けている She lacks (in) *executive ability*.
言語能力を有することは人間の本質的な特徴の一つである *The power of speech* is one of the essential attributes of human beings.
ナマズに地震の予知能力があるというのは本当ですか Is it true that catfish have *the power* [*ability*] *to foreknow* earthquakes?
‖能力給 merit-based wages / 能力主義 meritocracy / 能力テスト an aptitude test

のうりん 農林 ‖農林水産省 the Ministry of Agriculture, Forestry and Fisheries / 農林水産大臣 the Minister of Agriculture, Forestry and Fisheries

ノー no ⓒⓊ ‖彼は私たちの申し出にノーと言った He said *no* to our offer. ◆ノーと答える answer [reply] *in the negative*

ノーカウント ⚠ 今のはノーカウントだ That *doesn't count*.

ノーカット ⚠ ノーカットの映画 an *uncut* [*uncensored*] movie

ノーゲーム ⚠ 雨で試合はノーゲームになった The game *was rained out* [《英》*off*].

ノーコメント (インタビューなどに対して)ノーコメントです *No comment*. / 彼はその問題についてはノーコメントを通した He「*refused to comment* [*made no comment*] on the matter.

ノースカロライナ North Carolina(❖米国東部の州;《略語》N.C.,〔郵便〕NC)

ノースダコタ North Dakota(❖米国北部の州;《略語》N.D., N.Dak.,〔郵便〕ND)

ノースリーブ ⚠ ──ノースリーブの sleeveless

ノータッチ ⚠ その件には私はノータッチです I「*am not involved in* [*have nothing to do with*] the matter.

ノート (帳面) notebook ⓒ; (メモ・記録) notes
私は彼の言葉をノートに書き留めた I wrote down his words in *my notebook*.
学生たちは講義のノートをとった The students *took* [*made*] *notes* at the lecture.

ノートパソコン ⚠ notebook computer ⓒ

ノーハウ ➡ ノウハウ

ノーヒット 〔野球〕no hit ‖ノーヒットノーランを達成する pitch a *no-hit*, *no-run* game ◆高橋はきょうノーヒットだった Takahashi was [went] *hitless* today.

ノーベルしょう ノーベル賞 Nobel Prize ⓒ ‖ノーベル賞受賞者 a Nobel Prize winner / ノーベル物理学賞 the Nobel Prize for Physics / ノーベル文学賞 the Nobel Prize for Literature / ノーベル平和賞 the Nobel Peace Prize

ノーマル ──ノーマルな (正常な) normal

のがす 逃す (機会などを) miss ⑯ ‖そんないい機会を逃すなんて本当に残念なことをしたね What a pity you *missed* such a good chance [opportunity]!
◆彼は昇進の機会を逃した He *let* the opportunity for a promotion *slip by.* / He *missed out on* a promotion.

のがれる 逃れる (危険・災難などから) escape ⑯; (困難・責任などから) avoid ⑯, evade ⑯ ‖難を逃れる *escape* danger / 彼は親のプレッシャーから逃れたいと思っている He wants to *escape from* his parents' pressure. / 彼は責任を逃れようとしている He is「*trying to avoid* [*running away from*] his responsibilities.

のき 軒 (ひさし) the eaves ‖ツバメがわが家の軒先に巣を作った Swallows made a nest *under the eaves* of our house. / その家の軒下で雨宿りした I took shelter from the rain *under the eaves* of the house. / その通りに古本屋が軒を連ねている Used-book stores stand「*side by side* [*in a row*] on the street.

のきなみ 軒並み 事故のため列車のきなみ遅れた *All* trains were delayed because of the accident.

のく 退く (わきによける) step aside, get* out of *one's* [the] way, make* way ➡ どく(退く)

のけぞる bend* backward

のけもの 除け者 (社会からの) outcast ⓒ
◆彼らは彼女をのけ者にして話の仲間に入れなかった They *left* her *out of* their conversation. / They *did not let* her *join* their conversation. / (→冷たい態度をとって)They *turned a cold shoulder to* her and talked without her.

のける 退ける (わきへ動かす) move aside; (取り除く) take* [put*] away, remove ⑯ ➡ どける ◆そのいすをわきへのけてくれませんか Will you please *move* that chair *aside*?

のこぎり 鋸 saw ⓒ ‖のこぎりの歯 the teeth of *a saw* / のこぎりで木材を切る cut wood with *a saw* ◆木をのこぎりで切って丸太にする *saw* a tree into logs(❖この saw は「のこぎりで切る」という意味の動詞) ‖電動のこぎり a power saw

のこす 残す (後にとどめる) leave* ⑯; (とっておく) set* [put*] ... aside; (しないでおく)

leave ... undone [unfinished]; (食べ物などを余す) leave ... over; (予備に) reserve (他); (節約して) save (他)
彼はあなたにこの伝言を残していきました He *left* 「you this message [this message for you].
父は遺言で私に家を残してくれた My father *left* 「me the house [the house to me] in his will.
この仕事を残したままにはできないので旅行は延期しなければならない I will have to postpone my trip because I can't *leave* this work *unfinished*.
そのお金は全部使わず後のために少し残しておいたほうがいい You shouldn't spend all the money but *save* [*set aside*] some for later.
試験まであと1週間を残すばかりだ There's only one week *left* before the exam.
◆数学の宿題を忘れて放課後残された I had to stay after school because I forgot my math homework. / 彼は妻と2人の子供を残して死んだ He *is survived by* his wife and two children.

のこのこ (平気で) nonchalantly, unconcernedly; (厚かましく) shamelessly, brazenly ‖彼女は1時間も遅れてのこのこやってきた She *nonchalantly* [*shamelessly*] showed up an hour late.
◆わなとも知らず犯人はのこのことその店にやってきた Not realizing that it was a trap set for him, the criminal *carelessly* went to the shop.

のこらず 残らず (すべて) all, everything; (全体) the whole ‖その件について知っていることを残らず話してください Please tell me *everything* [*all*] you know about the matter.
◆委員会は一人残らずその提案に賛成した The committee agreed to the proposal *unanimously*./ The *entire* committee agreed to the proposal.

のこり 残り the rest, the remainder《単数または複数扱い》; (後に残った物) what is left (over), the remains; (食事の残り) leftovers
残りはとっておいてください Keep *the rest* for yourself.
(その日の)残りの時間はビデオを見て過ごした I spent *the rest* of the day watching videos.
◆10から7を引くと残りは3です Seven from ten *leaves* three./ Ten minus seven *leaves* [*equals, is*] three. / きのうの残りのピザが少しある There is some pizza *left over* from yesterday. / 太郎は同意したが残りのメンバーは同意しなかった Taro agreed, but *the others* [*rest*] didn't. / お米が残り少なくなってきている Our stock of rice *is getting low*./ Our rice *is running out*. / ほとんど残り時間がない There is little *time left*. / 今年も残り少なくなった The year *is drawing to a close*.

のこる 残る (残存する) be left over, remain (自); (後にとどまる) stay (自)
コーヒーはたいして残っていない There isn't very much coffee *left*.
依然として問題が1つ残っている There still *remains* a problem.
それでは私がここに残って彼女を待ちましょう Then I'll *stay* here and wait for her.
お寺の門だけが以前のまま残っています Only the gate of the temple *remains* as it was.
◆人の魂はその人の死後も残るといわれている It is said that a person's soul *survives* the death of his body. / 彼女の思い出がいまだに私の心に残っている Memories of her still *linger* (*on*) in my heart. / 中国ではまだ孔子の影響が残っている The Confucian influence *is* still *alive* [*found*] in China. / 彼の名は歴史に残るだろう His name will *go down in history*.

のさばる (いばる・高圧的にする) act important [high-handedly]; (いばり散らす) throw* *one's* weight about [around]; (勝手気ままにする) have* *one's* own way

のざらし 野晒し 自転車が野ざらしになっていた A bike *was left exposed to the weather*.

のし 熨斗 *noshi*, red and white paper folded around a strip of yellow paper (which is) attached to a gift
‖のし袋 a wrapping envelope with an emblematic *noshi* decoration

のしあがる 伸し上がる 彼女は35歳にしてその会社の社長にのし上がった She *worked* [*pushed*] *her way up and became* the president of the company at the age of 35.

のしかかる 伸し掛かる (もたれかかる) lean* on ... ◆きのうのことが彼女の心に重くのしかかっている Yesterday's incident *is weighing* [*lying*] *heavily on* her mind. / この仕事への責任が彼に重くのしかかっている His responsibility for this work *is pressing heavily on* him.

のじゅく 野宿 ―野宿する spend* the night outdoors, sleep* outdoors

ノスタルジア (郷愁) nostalgia [U]

ノズル nozzle [C]

のせる¹ 乗せる (車に) give* *a person* a ride [lift]; (途中で乗車させる) pick up; (乗せて運ぶ) carry (他); (客を車などに) load (他)
車に乗せていただいて本当にありがとうございます It's very kind of you to *give* me *a ride* [*lift*].
彼女は子供を自転車の後ろに乗せていった She *carried* her child *on* the back of her bicycle.
満員の乗客を乗せた観光バスががけから転落した A sightseeing bus that *was loaded to capacity* went over a cliff. (❖be loaded to capacityは「満席」の意味. 立っている人がいる場合は be loaded beyond capacity)
◆彼は幼い娘を馬に乗せた He *lifted* his baby daughter onto the horse. / できるだけ早い時期にビジネスを軌道に乗せたい We would like to *get* our business *going* as soon as

possible. / まんまと乗せられた(→だまされた) I *was* completely *taken in*. / 私もその企画に一口乗せてくれないか Let me 「*in on* [*take part in*] that project, won't you?

のせる² 載せる (上に置く) put 他; (たくさん積む) load 他; (掲載する) carry 他; (広告などを出す) place 他

新聞に広告を載せる *place* [*insert*] an ad *in* the paper

父は私に足をテーブルの上にのせるなと言った Father told me not to *put* [*rest*] my legs *on* the table.

どの新聞も一面にオリンピックの開会式の記事を載せていた Every newspaper *carried* the opening ceremonies of the Olympics on the front page.

のぞき 覗き peep ◎ ‖のぞき穴 a peephole

のぞきこむ 覗き込む 顕微鏡をのぞき込む *peer into* a microscope / 子供たちは窓から暗い部屋の中をのぞき込んだ The children *peeked into* the dark room through the window. / 彼女は私の話が信じられないとでもいうように私の顔をのぞき込んだ She *stared into* my face as if she couldn't believe what I told her.

のぞきみ 覗き見 peep ◎, peek ◎ ──のぞき見する peep 自, peek 自, take* a peep [peek]

のぞく¹ 除く (除去する) remove 他; (不要な物を) get* rid of ...; (除外する) exclude 他

果実から種を除く *remove* seeds from a fruit

◆名前を名簿から除く *cross* [*strike*] *a person's* name *off* the list; *remove a person's* name *from* the list / いくつかの例外を除けば, 今日(ミュニ)ではその病気はほとんど見られない *Except for* a few isolated cases, the disease is not seen these days. / 図書館は月曜日を除く毎日開館しています The library is open every day *except* (*for*) Mondays. / 父はニュースを除くとほとんどテレビを見ない My father hardly watches TV *aside from* the news. / 消費税を除いて(→含めないで)2,000円払った I paid 2,000 yen, *not counting* consumption tax.

のぞく² 覗く (のぞき見る) peep 自, peek 自; (見る) look 自; (立ち寄る) 《口語的》look [drop] in

私は店の中をのぞいた I *looked into* the store.

その子供はかぎ穴からのぞいているのを見つかった The child was caught *peeping through* the keyhole.

カーテンがあいて見慣れた顔がのぞいた The curtains parted and a familiar face *looked out*.

靴の先がスカートの下からのぞいていた The tips of her shoes 「*peeped out* [*showed*] from under her skirt.

帰りにあの新しいお店をのぞいてみない? Why don't we *look in at* that new store on our way home?

◆午後には時々晴れ間がのぞいた A patch of blue sky *was seen* from time to time in the afternoon.

のそのそ (ゆっくりと) slowly; (のろのろと) sluggishly

のぞましい 望ましい desirable; (勧められる) advisable; (好ましい) preferable ‖毎日30分の運動をすることが望ましい It is *advisable* that (you should) get 30 minutes of exercise every day. ◆あの男は私の姉には望ましくない(→ふさわしくない) That man *isn't suitable for* my sister.

のぞみ 望み (期待) hope ◎ ⓤ; (願望) wish ◎; (理想) dream ◎

一縷(ﾙ)の[かすかな]望み *a* slender [slight] *hope*; a ray [gleam] *of hope*

私たちはそのピンチヒッターに望みをかけた We *set our hopes on* the pinch hitter.

彼の唯一の望みも今や絶たれた His single *hope* was now lost.

やっと望みがかなった Finally *my dream* [*wish*] *has come true*.

望みを捨てては何にもならない There's nothing to be gained by giving up *hope*.

彼女に回復の望みはあるだろうか Is there any *hope* [*chance*] of recovery for her?

彼の復帰は望み薄だ There is *little hope* [*chance*] that he will make a comeback.

◆自分の将来に望みをいだいている be *hopeful* about *one's* future / すべては望みどおりにいった Everything turned out *as I had hoped* [*wished*].

のぞむ¹ 望む

❶【希望する】hope 他, wish 他 ⓤ; (欲しい) want 他, desire 他; (期待する) expect 他

お望みならケーキをお持ち帰りください You may take some cake with you *if you wish*.

彼が望んでいたのはつましく穏やかな生活だった All he *wanted* was a simple, quiet life.

【hope＋to do】体重が増えるのを望む力士が多い Many sumo wrestlers *hope to* gain weight.

【hope＋that＋節】君が賞を取ることを望んでいます I *hope that* you'll win the prize.

【want＋名＋to do】父は僕の大学進学を望んでいる My father *wants* me *to* go to college.

天気はそれ以上は望めないほどよかった The weather was *the nicest you could wish for*.

彼に多くは望めない You cannot *expect* much of him.

◆彼女は自分から望んでこの仕事を選んだ She took this job *of her own choice* [*free will*].

❷【見渡す】
私たちの部屋からは富士山のすばらしい景色が望める Our room *commands* a splendid view of Mt. Fuji.

のぞむ² 臨む (面する) face 他, look onto [out on] ...; (見下ろす) overlook 他; (出席する) attend 他 ‖海に臨んだホテル a hotel *overlooking* the sea / 期待をこめて会議に臨む *at-*

tend a meeting with high expectations
◆死に臨んで *on one's deathbed* / 彼は厳しい態度で部下に臨んだ He *took a* tough *attitude* toward his men.

のたうちまわる のた打ち回る 苦痛にのたうち回る *writhe* [*twist about*] in pain

のたれじに 野垂れ死に ━野垂れ死にする die by the roadside; (みじめな死に方をする) die a dog's death

のち 後 ━[前] (時間・順序が) after ━[副] later; (その後) afterward(s)
一瞬の静寂の後, 彼らは拍手した *After* a moment of silence they clapped their hands.
後に彼は大病院の院長となった He became the director of a major hospital *later* [*afterward*].
◆晴, 後曇り Fine [Fair], *to* [*later*] cloudy / 後々のため *for the sake of the future* / 後の世(→来世) the *next* world; (→後の時代) *coming* [*future*] ages

のちほど 後程 また後ほど See you *later.*

ノック knock [C] ━ノックする knock at [《主に米》on] … ‖彼女はドアをノックしたがだれも応答しなかった She *knocked at* [*on*] the door, but nobody answered. / 私たちはドアをノックする音を聞いた We heard *a knock* at the door.

ノックアウト knockout [C] (《略語》 KO, K.O.) ━ノックアウトする knock out ‖ノックアウトで勝つ win by *a knockout*

ノックダウン (ボクシングなどの) knockdown [C] ━ノックダウンする knock down

のっしのっし 象が通りをのっしのっしと歩いていた An elephant *was* 「*walking heavily* [*lumbering*] down the street.

のっそり (ゆっくりと重そうに) slowly and heavily ‖彼はのっそりと起き上がった He sat up *slowly and heavily.*

ノット 〔海事〕knot [C] ‖20ノットを出す do [make] 20 *knots* / 25ノットの船 a ship with a speed of 25 *knots*; a 25-*knot* ship

のっとり 乗っ取り (会社などの) takeover [C]; (飛行機などの) hijacking [C][U]
‖乗っ取り犯(飛行機の) a hijacker

のっとる[1] 乗っ取る (会社などを) take* over; (飛行機などを) hijack [他] ‖彼はその会社を乗っ取ろうと企てた He contrived to *take over* the company. / パリ行きの飛行機が武装した男たちに乗っ取られた An airplane bound for Paris *was hijacked* by armed men.

のっとる[2] 則る 先例にのっとってこの問題を処理しました We dealt with this matter 「*according to* [*following*] (the) precedents. / 我々はスポーツマンシップにのっとり正々堂々と戦うことを誓います We hope for a fair and open competition *in accordance with* the rules of good sportsmanship.

のっぴきならない (避けられない) unavoidable, inevitable ‖彼はのっぴきならない事情のため会議に出席できなかった He couldn't attend the meeting owing to *unavoidable* circumstances.

のっぺらぼう のっぺらぼうの(→のっぺりして表情に乏しい)顔 a *flat, expressionless* face

のっぺり のっぺりした顔 a *smooth* [*sleek*] face

のっぽ 《口語的》beanpole [C], string bean [C] (❖一般に「背が高い人」は a (very) tall person)

-ので ━[接] because; since, as ━[前] for, because of …, due to …

[語法]
because は直接的な理由を表す接続詞で, 明確に理由を述べたい場合に用いる. since, as は聞き手がすでに知っている, または理由を述べることに特に重点をおかない場合に用いる.

バスが遅れたのでいつもの電車に乗れなかった I missed my usual train *because* the bus was late.
友達がノートを貸してくれたので助かった I was relieved *because* my friend lent me her notebook.
彼女には妹がいるので小さな子供の扱いには慣れている She is accustomed to handling little children *since* she has a kid sister.
開演までまだ時間があるのでコーヒーでも飲みませんか *Since* we've got a few minutes before the curtain rises, shall we have a cup of coffee?
夜もふけてきたので私たちはホテルに戻ることにした *As* it was getting late, we decided to come back to the hotel.
母は病気だったので私が代わりに買い物に行った *As* my mother was sick, I went shopping for her.
雨が降ったので体育祭は延期になった Our school's athletic meet was put off *because of* the rain.
◆そのレストランには長い行列ができていたので別の店に入った A lot of people were waiting in a line to get into the restaurant, *so* we went into a different one. / ゆうべはとても疲れていたので夕食を食べずに寝た I was *so* tired last night *that* I went to bed without dinner. / その本はあまりに難しかったので私には理解できなかった The book was *too* difficult for me *to* understand.

のど 喉 throat [C]; (声) voice [C] ‖のどが痛い have *a* sore *throat* / …がのどにつかえる[ひっかかる] get … stuck in *one's throat*
◆のどが渇く *be thirsty*; *feel* [*be*] *dry* / のどをうるおす *relieve* [*quench*] *one's thirst* / 猫が満足そうにのどをごろごろ鳴らしている The cat *is purring* contentedly. / 心配で食事ものどを通りません I am so worried that I 「*have lost my* [*have no*] *appetite.*
‖のどあめ a cough drop / のど自慢大会 an amateur singing contest / のど仏 *one's* Adam's apple
[慣用表現] 彼女はのどがいい She *has a good singing voice.* / あのチケットはのどから手が出るほど欲しい I'*m dying for* one of those tickets. / その言葉がのどまで出かかっていた

The word *was on the (very) tip of my tongue.*
ことわざ のど元過ぎれば熱さを忘れる The danger past and God forgotten. (→危険が過ぎ去ると神は忘れられる)

のどか のどかな (平和な) peaceful; (静かな) quiet; (穏やかな) mild, calm ∥のどかな春の日 a *mild* [*calm, quiet*] spring day / 山々ののどかな農村風景の背景となっている The mountains form a background to the *peaceful* village scene.

-のに

❶【…にもかかわらず】── 園 in spite of ..., despite (❖in spite of よりかたい語) ── 圏 (…だけれども) though, although; (しかし) but
一生懸命勉強したのにテストの成績はよくなかった *Though* I studied very hard, I didn't get a good grade on the exam.
彼はそのレースで優勝確実といわれていたのに結局3位に終わった *Although* he was the favorite to win the race, he ended up third.
ひとりでそこに行くなと言ったのに彼は行くと言い張った I told him not to go there alone, *but* he insisted.
誠はけがをしているのにその試合に出た Makoto played in the game *in spite of* his injury.

❷【…なのに】when; (一方) while
やってみてもいないのにどうしてできないなんて言うの How can you say you can't do something *when* you haven't even tried it?
彼女は社交家なのに彼女の妹はとてもシャイだ She is a sociable person, *while* her sister is very shy.
◆この暑いのにどうしてジャケットなんか着ていられるね How can you keep your jacket on in this heat?
🅔「せっかく沖縄まで行ったのに一度も泳がなかったの?」「天気が最悪だったんだ」"You went all the way to Okinawa, *and* you didn't go swimming at all?" "It's because the weather was terrible."

❸【…するために】
旅行に行くのに軽いスニーカーが欲しい I want a pair of light sneakers *for* the trip.
父は新聞を読むのに眼鏡がいる My father needs glasses *to* read the newspaper.
うちから成田空港まで行くのに2時間以上かかる It takes more than two hours *to* get to Narita Airport from my house.

❹【願望】
うちで猫が飼えたらいいのに *I wish* I could keep a cat at home.
よせばいいのに彼はまだパチンコに燃えている He *should give it up, but* he's still crazy about pachinko.
私にそのことを話してくれればよかったのに You *should have* told me about that.

ののしる 罵る abuse 働, call *a person* names; (悪態をつく) curse 働 働, swear* at ... ∥彼は人前で私をののしった He *called me names* in public.

のばす¹ 伸ばす (長くする) make* ... longer, lengthen 働; (まっすぐにする) stretch 働, straighten 働; (しわなどを) smooth 働; (発達させる) develop 働; (進歩させる) improve 働; (増す) increase 働
ロープを2メートル伸ばす *make* a rope two meters *longer*; *lengthen* a rope two meters / 手足を伸ばす *stretch one's* limbs / テーブルクロスのしわを伸ばす *smooth out* a tablecloth
彼女はロープをつかもうと腕を伸ばした She *stretched out* her arm to catch the rope.
背筋を伸ばしなさい *Straighten* your back.
彼は一生懸命勉強して英語力を伸ばした He studied hard and *improved* his English.
◆髪を長く伸ばしている *wear one's* hair *long* / 需要を伸ばす *boost* demand / 彼女はハンドバッグを取ろうと手を伸ばした She *reached for* her purse. / 圭介はひげを伸ばしている Keisuke *has grown* a beard.

のばす² 延ばす (延長する) extend 働, prolong 働; (延期する) put* off, postpone 働
出発を一日延ばす *put off* the departure by one day
滞在期間をもう少し延ばすことはできますか Can I「*extend* my stay [stay] a little longer?
もうこれ以上決定を先延ばしにはできませんよ You *can't put off* making a decision any longer.
きょうできることをあすに延ばすな Never *put off* till tomorrow what you can do today.

のばなし 野放し 犬を野放しにする (→鎖を解く) *let one's* dog *loose*; (→自由にさせておく) *leave one's* dog *free* / その手の犯罪を野放しにしてはならない (→取り締まらないままではいけない) Such crimes should not *be left uncontrolled* [*unchecked*].

のはら 野原 field Ⓒ

のばら 野薔薇 〖植物〗wild rose Ⓒ

のび 伸び・延び (成長) growth Ⓤ; (進歩・発展) development Ⓤ/生産の伸び率 *a* production *growth rate* / 今年度の経済は着実な伸びを示している The economy has shown steady *growth* [*increase*] this year.
◆雑草は伸びが早い Weeds *grow* fast [rapidly]. / 彼は大きく伸びをした He *had a* good *stretch*.

のびあがる 伸び上がる (腕を伸ばす) reach 働; (つま先で立つ) stand* on tiptoe; (首を伸ばす) crane *one's* neck

のびざかり 伸び盛り ──伸び盛りの (成長過程の) growing ∥伸び盛りの子供 a *growing* child

のびちぢみ 伸び縮み (伸縮性) elasticity Ⓤ ∥この輪ゴムは伸び縮みがきかなくなっている This rubber band has lost *its elasticity*.
◆この生地は伸び縮みする This material「*is elastic* [*stretches*].

のびなやむ 伸び悩む (増加が) increase slowly; (成長が) grow* slowly; (ほとんど進

歩しない) make* little progress ∥今学期は成績が伸び悩んでいる My grades *are making little progress* this term./ (→満足のいくように進歩していない) My grades *are not improving satisfactorily* this term.

◆個人消費はいまだ伸び悩んだままだ Personal consumption *remains sluggish*./ ここ数か月アジアへの輸出が伸び悩んでいる (→予想されたほど伸びなかった) Exports to Asia have *failed to increase as much as expected* [(→着実に伸びなかった) *not increased steadily*] these past few months.

のびのび¹ 伸び伸び のびのびと (→自由に,独立心をもって) 育つ grow up *free and independent*; (→何の心配事もなく) grow up *free from all cares* / のびのびした文章を書く write in a *free and easy* style / 試験がやっと終わって今はのびのびとした気分だ The exam is over finally, and now I *feel relaxed* [*at ease*]./ うちの学校は校則もゆるやかでのびのびしている Our school doesn't have any strict rules and is *pretty relaxed* [*laid back*].

のびのび² 延び延び 会議は延び延びになっている (→繰り返し延期されている) The meeting *has been repeatedly postponed* [*put off*]./ 長期間遅れている) The meeting *has been delayed for a long time*./ 本の返却が延び延びになっている (→返却期限をとっくに過ぎている) This book *has long been overdue*./ 返事が延び延びになって (→返事をもっと早く書かなくて) すみません I'm sorry that I didn't write (to) you earlier.

のびる¹ 伸びる
❶【成長する・長くなる】(成長する) grow* ⾃; (長くなる) get* [become*] longer, lengthen ⾃

彼は3センチ身長が伸びた He *has grown* (by) three centimeters.

その植物の根は相当長く伸びることがある The roots of the plant sometimes *grow* very long.

髪[つめ]が伸びている My hair *has* [My nails *have*] *grown* too long.

◆この生地はよく伸びる This material *stretches* well./ めんが伸びてしまった The noodles *have become soggy* [*too soft*]

❷【能力・数量が増す】(成長する) grow* ⾃; (上達する) improve ⾃, advance ⾃; (増す) increase ⾃; (進歩する) make* progress; (発展する) expand ⾃

彼女の英語力は着実に伸びていった Her English ability steadily *improved*.

この会社はまだまだ伸びる This company *will grow* even more./ (→一層の発展の可能性がある) This company *is capable of* further *growth* [*expansion*].

◆彼はまだまだこれから伸びる (→将来性がある) He *has a future before him*.

❸【身体が参る】
その一撃で伸びてしまった (→たたきのめされてしまった) He *was knocked down* by the blow./ The blow *finished him*.

この暑さで1日働いたらみんな伸びてしまう (→疲れきってしまう) We'll all be ⌈*worn out* [*exhausted*] from working all day in this heat.

のびる² 延びる
❶【延長される】be extended; (期間が) be prolonged

意見が分かれたため会議は1時間も延びた The meeting *was prolonged* [*extended*] for an hour because our opinions were divided.

◆この高速道路は東京から名古屋まで延びている This expressway *extends* from Tokyo to Nagoya./ 日が延びてきた The days *are getting longer*./ 日本人の平均寿命は延び続けている The average life expectancy of the Japanese *has been increasing* [*getting longer*].

❷【延期される】be put off, be postponed
悪天候のため,野外コンサートは1週間延びた The outdoor concert *was postponed* for a week due to the bad weather.

ラグビーの試合が次の日曜日に延びた The rugby game *was postponed* [*put off*] until next Sunday.

❸【広がる】spread* ⾃
このペンキはよく延びる This paint *spreads* well.

ノブ knob Ⓒ ∥ドアノブ a doorknob

のべ 延べ (総数) total Ⓒ ∥この作業はのべ人員5,000人を要した The work required *a total* of 5,000 people.

∥のべ時間 the total number of hours, the total man-hours / のべ日数 the total number of days [workdays, man-days] / のべ床面積 the total floor space

のべつ 彼女はのべつ幕なしにしゃべる She talks ⌈*on and on* [*without ceasing, nonstop*].

のべぼう 延べ棒 (金・銀などの) (metal) bar Ⓒ ∥金ののべ棒 a bar [an ingot] of gold; a gold bar [ingot]

のべる 述べる (表現する) express ⾃; (公式に表明する) state ⾃; (話す) tell* ⾃; (言及する) mention ⾃

自身の考えを述べる *express oneself*; *give one's thoughts* / 意見を述べる *express* [*give, state*] an opinion / 先に述べたとおり as *mentioned* [*stated, described*] above

彼女は討論で自分の意見を明確に述べた She *stated* her views clearly in the discussion.

真実を,そして真実のみを述べなさい *Tell* the truth, and nothing but the truth.

◆祝辞を述べる *make* a congratulatory speech

のほうず 野放図 野放図な (→手に負えない) やつ an *unruly* person / 野放図に (→果てしなく) 金を使う spend money *endlessly*

のぼせあがる のぼせ上がる 彼は成功してのぼせあがっている (→成功が彼をうぬぼれさせている) Success *has gone to* his head./ 彼は彼女に完全にのぼせあがっている (→夢中になっている)

He *is* quite *mad* [*crazy*] *about* her.
のぼせる （めまいがする）be [feel*] dizzy ∥長い時間ふろに入っていてのぼせてしまった I *felt dizzy* from staying in the bath too long.
◆彼は暑さでのぼせている He *is faint from* the *heat*. / (→暑さが彼をぼうっとさせている) The heat *has gone to* his *head*.
のほほん 彼女は大きなミスをしでかしたにもかかわらずのほほんとしている She *seems unconcerned* even though she made a big blunder.
のぼり¹ 上り・登り 上りのエスカレーター an *up* escalator / ここから家までの道はずっと上りになっている The road *ascends* [*goes up*] all the way from here to my house.
∥上り列車 an inbound [up] train
のぼり² 幟（旗）flag ⓒ, banner ⓒ; (吹き流し) streamer ⓒ
のぼりおり 上り下り (道などの) ups and downs ◆階段を上り下りする go up and down the stairs
のぼりぐち 上り口・登り口 (山の) the starting point of the trail [path] to the mountaintop; (階段の) the bottom [foot] of the stairs
のぼりざか 上り坂 uphill road ⓒ, upward slope ⓒ ◆道が上り坂になった The road *went uphill*. / そこからとても急な上り坂になった From there we had *a* very steep *climb*.
のぼりつめる 上り詰める・登り詰める 彼はその組織の頂点に上り詰めた He *reached* [*climbed to, rose to*] the top of the organization. / (→苦労して) He *worked his way up* to the top of the organization.

のぼる　上る・登る・昇る

❶【高い方へ】(山・木に) climb ⓐ ⓑ; (上がっていく) go* up ⓐ; (よじ登る) scale ⓑ
坂を上る *go up* a slope / 丘を登る *climb* (*up*) a hill / がけを登る *scale* [*clamber up*] a cliff
ケーブルカーはゆっくり坂道を上った The cable car slowly *climbed* the slope.
彼は昨年富士山に登った He *climbed* Mt. Fuji last year.
◆サケが川を上り始めた Salmon *have begun swimming upstream*. / 私たちはその古い小舟をこいで川を上った We *rowed* the old boat *up* the river.

❷【上昇する】go* up, rise* ⓐ
エレベーターで昇る *go up* in an elevator
太陽は東から昇る The sun *rises* in the east. (❖通046×rises from the east とはいわない)
煙突から煙が立ち昇っている Smoke *is rising* [*going up*] from the chimney.

❸【ある数量に】go* up; (達する) reach ⓑ; (総計…に) amount to ...
きのうは気温が摂氏30度にのぼった The temperature「*went up* [*rose*] to 30℃ yesterday.
工事費は100万ドルにのぼった The construction costs *amounted to* a million dollars.

❹【その他】

王位に上る *become* king; *ascend to* the throne / 都へ上る *go* (*up*) *to* the capital / 食卓に上る *be served* (*at the table*) / その日の議題にのぼる *be put* on the day's agenda
頭に急に血が上った Blood *rushed to* my head.
彼女の新しい小説がみんなのうわさにのぼっていた Her new novel *was much talked* [*gossiped*] *about*.
慣用表現 天にも昇る心地であった I felt *as if I were*「*walking on air* [*in* (*the*) *seventh heaven*]*.

のませる 飲ませる (与える) give* ⓑ; (動物に水を) water ⓑ ∥患者に薬を飲ませる *give* the medicine to the patient / 馬に水を飲ませる *water* a horse / 水を1杯飲ませてください Could you「*give me* [*let me have*] a glass of water?

のまれる 飲まれる・呑まれる (のみ込まれる) be swallowed; (圧倒される) be overwhelmed [overawed] ∥小さなボートが見る間に波にのまれてしまった The little boat *was swallowed* (*up*) by the waves in no time at all. / 雰囲気にすっかりのまれてしまった I *was* completely *overwhelmed by* the atmosphere.

のみ¹ 蚤 flea ⓒ ∥ノミに食われる be [get*] bitten by a flea / (犬・猫の) ノミ取り用の首輪 a *flea* collar
∥のみの市 a flea market

のみ² 鑿 chisel ⓒ

-のみ (ただ…だけ) only; (それだけ) alone (❖名詞の後で用いる) ➡-だけ ∥神のみが人を裁くことができる *Only* [*None but*] God can judge people.
◆後は彼の返事を待つのみである There's nothing we have to do but [All we have to do now is] wait for his answer.

のみあるく 飲み歩く 彼女はここのところ毎晩飲み歩いている She *has* recently *started to*「*go barhopping* [《英口語的》*go on a pub crawl*] every night.

のみくい 飲み食い eating and drinking (❖語順に注意) ――飲み食いする eat* and drink*

のみぐすり 飲み薬 (a) medicine (for internal use), (a) medicine (to be taken orally)

のみくだす 飲み下す swallow ⓑ; (ぐいっと飲む) gulp down

のみこみ 飲み込み (理解) understanding ⓤ ∥彼は飲み込みが早い[遅い] He *is quick* [*slow*] *at understanding*. (❖彼は飲み込みが早い」は He catches on quickly. ともいう)

のみこむ 飲み込む swallow ⓑ ∥出かかった言葉をぐっと飲み込む *swallow one's words* / その赤ちゃんは10円玉を飲み込んでしまった The baby *swallowed* a 10-yen coin. / 波が船をのみ込んだ The waves「*swallowed up* [*engulfed*] the boat.
◆こつを飲み込む *get* [*learn*] the knack / 5万の観衆をのみ込んだ国立競技場 the National Stadium *packed with* 50,000 spectators

のみち 野道 a track [path] across a field, field path ©

のみならず (AだけではなくBも) not only [merely] A but (also) B; (AはもちろんBも) B as well as A; (そのうえ) besides, moreover ∥彼女は英語のみならずフランス語も話せる She can speak 「not only English but (also) French [French as well as English].

ノミネート ──ノミネートする (候補に挙げる) nominate ∥その映画はアカデミー賞にノミネートされた The movie was nominated for an Academy Award.

のみほうだい 飲み放題 今夜は1,000円で飲み放題です We can drink 「all we want [as much as we like] for 1,000 yen tonight.

のみほす 飲み干す drink* up [off]; (容器を空にする) drain ⑭ ∥グラスの水を一気に飲み干す drink up [off] a glass of water in a gulp ∥彼女はワインを飲み干した She drained [emptied] her wine glass.

のみみず 飲み水 drinking water ⓤ

のみもの 飲み物 ©; (水以外の)(公式的) beverage ©; 温かい飲み物 hot beverages ∥冷たい飲み物でもいかがですか Would you like 「a cold drink [something cold to drink]? ∥お飲み物は何になさいますか What would you like for a drink?

のみや 飲み屋 bar ©, (英)pub ©; (居酒屋) tavern ©

のむ¹ 飲む

drink* ⑭ 国 (❖自動詞の場合，主に「酒を飲む」の意味で用いられる)，have* ⑭; take* ⑭; swallow ⑭; gulp ⑭; sip ⑭; eat* ⑭; smoke ⑭

| drink, have: 飲料を飲む.
| take: 薬を飲む.
| swallow: 飲み込む.
| gulp: ごくごく飲む.
| sip: ちびちび飲む.
| eat: スープを飲む.
| smoke: たばこを吸う.

何か飲むものを持ってきてあげよう I'll go and get you something to drink.

母は毎晩寝る前に牛乳をコップ1杯飲んでいる My mother drinks a glass of milk every night before she goes to bed.

僕のコーラ，全部飲んじゃっただろう? You drank up all my cola, didn't you?

君は何を飲む，紅茶それともコーヒー? Which will you have, tea or coffee?

彼はアルコールはいっさい飲まない He never drinks alcohol.

彼女はお酒が飲めない She can't drink./ She is not a drinker.

父は以前ほど酒を飲まなくなった My father drinks less than he used to.

1日3回食後にこの錠剤を2錠飲んでください Take two tablets after each meal three times a day.

スープを飲むときは音を立てないのがよいマナーです It is good manners not to make noises when you eat soup.

彼はウイスキーのオンザロックをちびちび飲んでいた He was sipping whiskey on the rocks.

◆一杯飲みに行きましょう Let's go out for a drink.

🔴「コーヒーをもう1杯飲みませんか」「はい，お願いします[いいえ，もう結構です]」 "Won't you have another cup of coffee?" "Yes, please. [No, thank you.]"

🔴「相談に乗ってほしいんだ」「いいよ．コーヒーでも飲みながら話そう」 "I need your advice." "OK. Let's talk over a cup of coffee."

のむ² 呑む ❶【受け入れる】accept ⑭, (口語的)swallow ⑭ ∥この条件は絶対にのめない I can never accept these terms.

❷【威圧する】overawe ⑭; (軽視する) underestimate ⑭ ∥相手にのまれてはいけない Don't let yourself be overawed by your opponent. ∥相手チームは最初から我々をのんでかかっていた All along, the other team underestimated us.

❸【抑える】suppress ⑭, hold* back ∥涙をのむ suppress [hold back] one's tears

のめりこむ のめり込む (熱中する・没頭する) get* into ..., be absorbed in ... ∥占いに興味をもつのはいいがあまりのめり込まないようにね It's OK to be interested in fortune-telling, but don't get into it too far. ∥彼は研究にのめり込んでいる He is absorbed in his studies.

のめる¹ (つんのめる) pitch [fall*, tumble] forward

のめる² 飲める ❶【水などが】drinkable ∥この水は飲めますか Is this water drinkable [good to drink]?

❷【酒が】うちの家族はだれも飲めません No one in my family drinks. ⇨のむ(飲む)

のやま 野山 (丘や野原) hills and fields

のらいぬ 野良犬 stray dog ©

のらくら ──のらくらと idly, lazily; (目標なく) aimlessly ◆彼は相変わらずのらくらしている(→何もせずに暮らしている) He is still 「leading an idle life [(→時間を浪費している) idling away his time].

のらしごと 野良仕事 farm work ⓤ

のらねこ 野良猫 stray cat ©

のらりくらり ──のらりくらりと idly, lazily ∥のらりくらりと時間を過ごす spend one's time idly; idle away one's time ◆のらりくらりとした(→はっきりしない)態度 an ambiguous attitude ∥のらりくらりと返事(→やる気のない返事)をする give a noncommittal answer

のり¹ 海苔 🟥 nori, a kind of edible seaweed ∥のり巻き sushi rolled in a sheet of nori ∥味付けのり toasted and seasoned nori ∥焼きのり toasted nori

> のりは海草を乾燥させたもので，昔から一般的な朝の食卓に並んできました．それ以外にも寿司(ɿ)やおにぎりやもちを巻いたり，細かく刻んでいろいろな料理にかけたりします．のりはミネラル豊富な健康食品です．

Nori (laver) is dried seaweed which has long accompanied Japanese-style breakfasts. *Nori* is also often used for wrapping sushi, *onigiri* (rice balls) and *mochi*, and sometimes shredded *nori* is sprinkled on various dishes. It is regarded as a health food, for it contains valuable minerals.

のり² 糊 (でんぷんのり) paste [U]; (接着剤・にかわ) glue [U] (❖いずれも種類をいうときは [C]); (衣類用) starch [U] ‖のりで2枚の紙をくっつける stick two pieces of paper together with *glue*; glue two pieces of paper together / シーツをのりづけする *stiffen* the sheets *with starch*; *starch* the sheets
◆のりのきいたテーブルクロス a *starched* tablecloth / 彼らは壁にのりでポスターをはっていた They *were pasting* posters onto the wall.

のり³ 乗り ❶【調子・感じ】のりのいい音楽 *upbeat* music / 彼ののりにはついていけない I *can't keep pace with* him. / この曲は本当にのりがいいね This song is *catchy*, isn't it?
❷【乗ること】けさは化粧の乗りが悪い *My makeup isn't staying on my skin very well* this morning. / 悪乗りしすぎだ. 今度ばかりは許さないぞ You'*ve gone too far*, and I can't ignore it this time.

-のり -乗り 5人乗りの車 a five-*passenger* car; a five-seater(❖-seaterは「…人乗りの乗り物」の意味) / 2人乗りの自転車 *a tandem* / 自転車の2人乗りをする *ride double* on a bicycle / この飛行機は520人乗りです This plane *can carry* 520 *passengers.* / ここへはジョンが1番乗り(→いちばん最初に着いた人)だった John was *the first* (*person*) to arrive here.

のりあげる 乗り上げる 浅瀬に乗り上げる *run aground* [*ashore*] / 車を歩道に乗り上げてしまった I *ran* my car *onto* (*up*) the sidewalk. / 交渉は暗礁に乗り上げた(→行き詰まった) The negotiations 「*are deadlocked* [*have come to a deadlock*].

のりあわせる 乗り合わせる けさ彼とたまたま同じ電車に乗り合わせた I happened to 「*ride on* [*take*] the same train with him this morning. / 彼女は乗り合わせた客と話し始めた She struck up a conversation with *a fellow passenger*.

のりいれる 乗り入れる 寺の境内に車を乗り入れてはいけない You aren't allowed to *drive* your car *onto* the grounds of the temple. / 間もなくこの地下鉄はJR線に乗り入れる(→JR線に直接つながる) This subway train *will* now *connect directly to* the JR line. / この区間では地下鉄とJRが相互に乗り入れている(→同じ路線を走っている) *Both* the subway and JR trains *run on the same tracks* in this section.

のりうつる 乗り移る 宇宙飛行士が宇宙ステーションに乗り移った The astronaut *went into* the space station. / 彼女に悪霊が乗り移った(→悪霊に取りつかれた) She *was possessed* by an evil spirit.

のりおくれる 乗り遅れる (列車などに) miss [他] ‖けさは1分の差で9時半の電車に乗り遅れた I *missed* [*was too late for*] the 9:30 train by one minute this morning.
◆時流に乗り遅れる *fail to keep up with* the times

のりおり 乗り降り この駅では大勢の人が電車を乗り降りする A lot of people *get on and off* the train at this station.

のりかえ 乗り換え transfer [C] ◆(アナウンスで)上野方面は当駅で乗り換えです *Transfer* [*Change* (*trains*)] here for Ueno. / この駅からなら渋谷まで乗り換えなしで行けます You can go to Shibuya from this station *without changing trains.*
‖乗り換え駅 a transfer station, a station for changing trains; (連絡駅) a junction (station) / 乗り換え切符 a transfer (ticket)

のりかえる 乗り換える (乗り物を) change [自][他], transfer [自] ‖新宿で地下鉄に乗り換える *transfer* [*change* (*trains*)] at Shinjuku *to* the subway / 徳島行きのフェリーに乗り換える *change* [*transfer*] *to* a ferry for Tokushima / 3回も電車を乗り換えるのはめんどうだ It's a nuisance to have to *change* trains three times.

のりかかる 乗り掛かる
[慣用表現] 乗りかかった船だ(→引き返せないほど遠くまで来てしまった) *We have gone* [*come*] *too far to go back.*

のりき 乗り気 彼はその企画にすっかり乗り気になった He *showed* great *enthusiasm for* the plan. / He *took* a lot of *interest in* the plan. / その提案にはあまり乗り気がしない I'*m not interested in* that proposal.

のりきる 乗り切る (あらし・困難などを) ride* out ‖船はあらしを乗りきれず沈没してしまった The ship *couldn't* 「*ride out* [*get through*] the storm, so it sank. / その会社は経済的な困難を何とか乗りきった The company managed to 「*ride out* [(→乗り越えた) *get over*] its economic difficulties.

のりくみいん 乗組員 《集合的》crew [C]; (1人) a member of the crew, crewman [C] ‖全乗組員 *the* whole *crew* / 50名の乗組員 *a crew* of 50 / 乗組員は全員救出された All *the crew* was [were] rescued.

のりくむ 乗り組む (乗り込む) get* [be] on board; (勤務する) serve on board

のりこえる 乗り越える (物の上を) get* [climb] over …; (困難などを) overcome* [他] ‖塀を乗り越える *get* [*climb*] *over* a fence / 苦難を乗り越える *overcome* [*get over*] hardships

のりごこち 乗り心地 この車は乗り心地がいい This is a *comfortable* car to ride in./ This car rides well.

のりこし 乗り越し ‖乗り越し料金 an excess [extra] fare (for the added distance *one* has ridden)

のりこす 乗り越す (電車などで) ride* [go*] past (*one's* stop [destination]); (…まで行く)

の

のりこむ go on to ... / 3駅乗り越す *ride past* three stations / 電車で居眠りして横浜まで乗り越してしまった I fell asleep on the train and *went on to* Yokohama.

のりこむ 乗り込む *get* into* [*onto*] ...（❖タクシーなど小型の乗り物には into，バスなど大型の乗り物には onto を用いる）/ バスに乗り込む *get onto* a bus / タクシーに乗り込む *get into* a taxi / 野球部員がどやどやと乗り込んだ The members of the baseball club *piled into* [*onto*] the bus.

のりすてる 乗り捨てる *leave**,《口語的》*ditch* / 校門の所に自転車が1台乗り捨てられていた A bicycle *was left* [*ditched*] at the school gate.

のりそこねる 乗り損ねる *miss*
⇒ のりおくれる

のりだす 乗り出す（出帆する）*sail*, *set sail*;（始める）*start*, *begin*;（特定の分野で活動を始める）*enter*, *get* into* ...;（身を）*lean* forward*;（窓などから）*lean* [*hang**] *out* / 大海に乗り出す *sail out on* the ocean / 政界に乗り出す *enter* [*go into*] politics / 事業に乗り出す *start* a business / テーブルに乗り出す *lean forward across* a table / 彼女は窓から身を乗り出した She *leaned out of* the window.
◆調停に乗り出す *undertake* mediation / 彼らは危険を冒して荒れた海に乗り出した They *ventured out onto* the stormy sea.

のりつぎ 乗り継ぎ ‖ 乗り継ぎ客 a transit passenger / 乗り継ぎ便 a connecting flight

のりつぐ 乗り継ぐ（連絡する）*make* a connection* /（飛行機）ロンドンでブリュッセル行きに乗り継ぐ *make a* (plane) *connection* at London for Brussels; *catch a connecting flight* to Brussels at London
◆地下鉄からバスに乗り継ぐ *take* a bus *after getting off* the subway

のりと 祝詞 a *norito*, a ritual Shinto prayer / 祝詞をあげる *recite* [*read*] *norito*

のりにげ 乗り逃げ その男はタクシーを乗り逃げした That man *ran away without paying the* taxi *fare*.

のりば 乗り場（バスの）bus stop;（タクシーの）taxi stand [《英》rank];（船の）pier;（プラットホーム）platform

のりまわす 乗り回す（車を）*drive* around*;（馬・自転車を）*ride* around* / 彼は親に買ってもらったフェラーリを乗り回している He *rides around in* a Ferrari that his parents bought for him.

のりもの 乗り物（陸上の）vehicle;（海上の）vessel;（空中の）aircraft;（遊園地の）ride ◆乗り物酔いする *get* [*come down with*] *motion sickness*（❖ふつうは「車」なら *carsick*,「船」なら *seasick*,「飛行機」なら *airsick* などと具体的にいうことが多い）

のる¹ 乗る
❶【乗り物に】（交通手段として）*take**;（乗っていく）*ride**;（乗り込む）*get* on* ..., *get in* [*into*] ...;（飛行機・船などに）*go** [*get*] *on board*;（運転する）*drive** / 超満員のバスに乗った I *got on* an overcrowded bus.
タクシーに乗ってからお金を持っていないことに気がついた After I *got in* [*into*] the taxi, I noticed I had no money.
彼は毎日8時のバスに乗る He *takes* the 8 o'clock bus every day.
エレベーターに乗って5階まで行った I *took* the elevator to the fifth floor.
練習すればだれでも自転車に乗ることができるようになる With practice, anybody can learn to *ride* a bicycle.
私は自転車に乗って彼女の家へ行った I *rode* my bicycle to her house.
修学旅行で阿蘇へ行ったときに馬に乗った I *rode* a horse when I went on a school trip to Aso.
飲んだら乗るな Don't drink and *drive*.
◆始発に乗るために早く起きた I woke up early so that I could *catch* the first train. / 学校へは自転車に乗って行きます I go to school *by* bicycle. / その美術館は駅からバスに乗って30分です The art museum is 30 minutes from the station *by* bus. / 車に乗りませんか Would you like *a ride* [*lift*]?
🔴「バスに乗る，それとも歩く？」「あまり時間がないのでタクシーにしようよ」"Shall we *take* a bus or walk?" "Let's take a taxi. We have almost no time."
❷【物の上に】*get* on* ...;（足をかけて乗る）*step on* ...;（手足を使って登る）*climb up* [*onto*] ...;（馬になど）*mount*
いすに乗らなくてはいちばん上の棚に手が届かない I have to *get* [*stand*] *on* a chair to reach the top shelf.
姉は絶対に家族のいる前では体重計に乗らない My sister never *steps on* the scale in front of anyone in our family.
◆この公園で幼稚園のころブランコに乗って遊んだ I used to *play on* the swing in this park when I was in kindergarten.
❸【応じる・加わる】
その話には一口乗るよ You can *count me in*.
彼だけがこの話に乗ってこなかった Only he *didn't show any interest in* this topic.
彼女は私の相談に乗ってくれた（→アドバイスをしてくれた）She *gave* me some *advice*.
❹【だまされる】*be deceived*,《口語的》*be taken in*
◆あの人はおだてに乗りやすい He *is easily flattered*. / その手には乗らないよ（→効き目がない）That trick *won't work on* me.
❺【その他】
リズムに乗って踊る dance *to the rhythm* / 調子に乗る *get carried away* / 風に乗って運ばれる be carried *on the wind*
きょうは気分が乗らない I'm *not in the mood* today. /《口語的》I *don't feel like it* today.

のる² 載る
❶【置かれる】
君が捜している本は机の上に載っているよ The

book you are looking for *is* (*lying*) *on* the table.

❷【記載される】(新聞などに) appear ⾃; (載っている) be on ...

名簿に載っている be on the list / 地図に載っている be (shown) on the map

彼の写真が地域の新聞に載った His picture *appeared* in the local newspaper.

◆この本には写真がたくさん載っている This book *includes* many pictures. / 彼女[彼女の名前]は電話帳に載っていない She [Her name] *is not listed* in the phone book. / このガイドブックには旅行の計画を立てるのに必要な情報がすべて載っている This guidebook *gives you* [*contains*] all the information you need to plan a trip.

ノルウェー Norway (✤公式名 the Kingdom of Norway) ∥ーーノルウェー人 Norwegian ⓒ ーーノルウェー語 Norwegian ⓤ ーーノルウェー(人[語])の Norwegian

のるかそるか 伸るか反るか のるかそるか (→いちかばちか) やってみよう Let's *take the chance*. / Let's try, 「*win or lose* [*sink or swim*]」.

ノルマ ⚠ (work) quota ⓒ (✤日本語はロシア語の norma から) ∥ノルマを決める fix [set] *a quota* / ノルマを果たす fulfill [meet, assign] *one's quota*; finish *one's assigned work*

のれん 暖簾 🖼 a *noren*, a (divided) short curtain hung over the entrance or under the eaves (of a shop)

[慣用表現] のれんに腕押しだ(→空気[風]を殴るようなものだ) It is (*like*) *beating the air* [*wind*]. / (→労力のむだだ) It's *a waste of effort*. / のれんにかかわる(→店の信用にかかわる) *affect the credit* [*good name*] *of the store* / のれんに傷がつく(→信用をなくす) *lose credit* / のれんを下ろす(→店を閉める) *close the store*

のれんは縦に切れ目が入った短い布で、営業中の食堂、居酒屋、商店などの軒先にかけられます。のれんには店の名前や商品を表すマークが染め抜かれており、店の看板の役割を果たします。のれんは店を象徴するものであることから、徐々に店の信用そのものを表すようになりました。そのため店員に同じ屋号の店をもたせることを「のれん分け」といいます。

Noren, are short curtains with vertical slits hung in front of restaurants, bars, and shops during business hours. The name of the shop or a symbol indicating the products sold there will be dyed into the cloth, so the *noren* also functions as a shop sign. Since a shop's *noren* symbolizes the shop, the term has also come to refer to a business's goodwill. Allowing an employee to set up a shop with the same name is called *noren-wake* (sharing the *noren*).

のろい¹ 鈍い, slow; (頭の働きなどが) dull ∥彼は動作がのろい He is *slow* to move. / 彼は頭の回転がのろい He has a very *slow* mind.

のろい² 呪い, curse ⓒ; (呪文(じゅもん)) spell ⓒ ∥魔女は王子にのろいをかけたThe witch *put a curse on* the prince.

のろう 呪う curse ⓣ ∥のろわれた人 a person (who is) *cursed* [*under a curse*] / 自分の運命をのろう *curse one's* fate

のろける 惚気る 姉は結婚してからだんなさんのことをのろけっぱなしだ(→いつも愛情をこめて話している) Since she got married, my sister always 「*speaks fondly of* [(→自慢げに話している)*talks too proudly about*] her husband.

のろし 狼煙 (合図の火煙) signal fire [flare] ⓒ; (煙による合図) smoke signal ⓒ ∥のろしを上げる light *a signal fire*

◆ (…反対の)のろしを上げる start [*launch into*] *a campaign* (against ...)

のろのろ (ゆっくり) slowly; (ものぐさで動きが遅く) sluggishly

◆のろのろ運転 *slow operation* / のろのろするな！(→急げ) *Hurry up!* / *Be quick!*

のろま slow [dull] person ⓒ (米口語的) slowpoke ⓒ (英口語的) slowcoach ⓒ ーーのろまの stupid, dull(-witted)

のんき 呑気 のんきな (気楽な) easy; (気にかけない) easygoing (気苦労のない) carefree; (楽天的な) optimistic ∥のんきに暮らす live an *easy* [a *carefree*] life; live *in ease and comfort* / のんきに構える take things [it] *easy*

ノンストップ この便は東京からニューヨークまでノンストップで(→止まらずに行く) This flight goes *nonstop* from Tokyo to New York. / (→直行便だ)This is a *nonstop* flight to New York from Tokyo.

のんだくれ 飲んだくれ (酔っ払い) drunk ⓒ; (大酒飲み) drunkard ⓒ

ノンバンク nonbank ⓒ

のんびり ーーのんびりする relax ⓘ, take* it easy, make* *oneself* at home ∥私たちは何もせずにのんびりと1日を過ごした We *took it easy* and did nothing all day. / We spent a *lazy* day doing nothing. / 入試に合格したからといってのんびりばかりはしていられないよ You *can't afford to sit back and relax* just because you passed the entrance exam.

◆こんな大変な仕事を辞めてもっとのんびりした生活を送れたらなあ If only I could quit this tough job and lead a more *leisurely* life.

ノンフィクション nonfiction ⓤ ∥ノンフィクション作家 *a nonfiction writer*

ノンプロ ーーノンプロの nonprofessional ∥ノンプロの選手 a *nonprofessional* (player) ∥ノンプロ野球 nonprofessional baseball

のんべえ 飲兵衛 alcoholic ⓒ, heavy drinker ⓒ, (米俗語的) lush ⓒ, (口語的) boozer ⓒ

のんべんだらり ーーのんべんだらりと (のんびりと) idly; (気乗りのしないまま) halfheartedly, lackadaisically

◆のんべんだらりと過ごす(→だらだらした生活を送る) lead an *idle* life; (→時間を浪費する) *idle* [*dawdle*] *one's* time *away*; (→何もしないで暮らす)live *doing nothing*

は

ハ 〖音楽〗C ⓒⓊ (複 ～s, ～'s) ∥ハ長調[短調]で in (*the key of*) *C major* [*minor*] ∥ハ音記号 a *C clef*

は¹ 歯

❶【人間・動物の】tooth ⓒ (複 teeth)

《歯が・は》
彼は歯がいい[悪い] He has good [bad] *teeth*.
この赤ん坊は, まだ歯が生えていない This baby's *teeth* haven't come in yet.
その子犬は歯が生え始めたばかりだ The puppy has just cutting *teeth*.
前歯が1本抜けた *My front tooth* came out.
その子供は前歯が1本なかった One of the child's *front teeth* was missing.
◆歯が(とても)痛い I have a (terrible) toothache. (❖toothache は「歯痛」の意味)

《歯を》
食事の後は歯を磨きなさい Brush [Clean] *your teeth* after meals.
歯医者で歯を抜いてもらった I had *a tooth* pulled out at the dentist's.
私が近づくと, 犬は歯をむき出した The dog showed *its teeth* as I approached it.

《歯に》
アイスクリームを食べたら歯にしみた One of *my teeth* hurt when I ate ice cream.
何か歯にはさまっている Something is stuck between *my teeth*.

《その他》
上[下]の歯 an upper [a lower] *tooth*

❷【器具の】(くし・のこぎりの) tooth ⓒ (複 teeth); (歯車の) cog ⓒ
のこぎりの歯 the *teeth* of a saw

∥歯医者 ⇒はいしゃ / 歯痛 ⇒はいた / 奥歯 a back tooth

[慣用表現] この本は私には歯が立たない(→難しすぎる) This book *is too difficult* for me. / 歯に衣(ぎぬ)着せぬしぶり *one's outspoken* way of speaking (❖outspoken は「遠慮のない」の意味) / 私の父は歯に衣を着せずに(→非常に率直に)ものを言う My father speaks *very frankly*. / 彼は歯の浮くようなお世辞を並べたてた He made a bunch of *smarmy* compliments. / His string of compliments *set my teeth on edge*. / 寒さで歯の根が合わなかった My teeth *chattered* in the cold. / 少年は歯を食いしばって痛みをこらえた The boy *clenched his teeth* and put up with the pain.

[俳句] 万緑の中や吾子(あこ)の歯生え初むる (中村草田男)
Everything is green.
In the midst of spring my child
starts to grow a tooth.

は² 葉

leaf ⓒ (複 leaves); (細長くて平たい) blade ⓒ; (針葉樹の) needle ⓒ; (1本または複数の草・木全体の) foliage Ⓤ

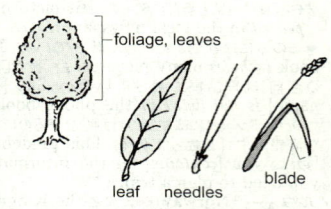

4つ葉のクローバー a *four-leaf* clover / お茶の葉 tea *leaves*
木の葉が色づき始めている The *leaves* of the trees are turning red.
庭の木々に葉が出ている The trees in the garden are now *in leaf*. (❖in leaf は「葉が出て」の意味の成句で, leaf の前は無冠詞)
大部分の木々は秋に葉を落とす Most trees shed *their leaves* in (the) fall.
◆葉の茂った木 a *leafy* tree

は³ 刃

blade ⓒ; (刃のへり) edge ⓒ ∥かみそりの刃 a razor *blade* / この包丁の刃はよく切れる[切れない] (→鋭い[鈍い]刃をしている) This kitchen knife has *a sharp* [*dull*] *edge*. ◆包丁の刃を研(と)ぐ *sharpen* a kitchen knife

は⁴ 派

(集団・グループ) group ⓒ; (学派・流派) school ⓒ; (党派) party ⓒ; (派閥) faction ⓒ; (宗教上の) sect ⓒ ∥反対派 an opposition *group* / ロマン派の詩人 a poet of *the Romantic school*

∥革新派 reformists / 保守派 conservatives

-は

❶【主題】⇒ -が
僕は谷口裕太といいます I'm Taniguchi Yuta.
きょうは暑いねえ Isn't it hot today?
うそをつくのはよくない It's wrong to tell a lie.
キリンは首が長い Giraffes have long necks.

❷【対照】
その提案に君は賛成でも, 私は反対だ Even if you agree with the proposal, I don't. (❖you と I を強く読む)
僕はコーラにするよ. 君は? I'm going to drink a Coke. How about you?

❸【限定・強調】
私, チーズは好きじゃないの I don't like cheese.
彼女がなぜそう言ったのか, 私には全く分からない I don't know why she said so at all.
これ全部は食べられないよ I can't eat all of these.

❹【譲歩】
 "君の飼っているポチってどんな犬なの" "犬は犬でも, ただの犬じゃないよ. とにかくいろんな芸ができるんだ" "What sort of dog is your

Pochi?" "Well, he's no ordinary dog. He can do a whole lot of tricks."

ば 場

❶【場所】place ◎; (特定の場所) spot ◎; (現場) scene ◎; (余地) room ◎; (分野) field ◎
公共の場で in *a* public *place*; in public / 話し合いの場をもつ have *a place* to talk
犯人はその場で取り押さえられた The criminal was caught *on the spot*.
彼女は偶然，その場に居合わせた She happened to be「*on the scene* [*there*].
彼は新しい活動の場を探している He is looking for *a* new *field* of activities.

❷【場合】case ◎; (機会) occasion ◎
彼女の服装はその場に最もふさわしいものだった She was perfectly dressed for *the occasion*.
◆彼が機転をきかせて，何とかその場は治まった His quick wit settled the *situation* somehow. / この場をお借りしてお礼申し上げます I *would like to take this opportunity* to express my gratitude.

❸【劇の】scene ◎
『オセロ』第1幕第2場 *Othello*, Act I, *Scene* ii (❖Act one, scene two と読む)

-ば if ⇨もし¹/それ，欲しければ持っていっていいよ You can take it *if* you want it. / もっと一生懸命勉強していれば，彼は試験に合格していただろう He would have passed the exam *if* he had studied harder.(❖「今から言っても始まらないが…」というニュアンスを含む場合は仮定法を用いる) ◆このカードを入口で見せれば(=を見せることによって)，中に通してもらえる You will be admitted *by* showing this card at the entrance.

はあ (はい) yes; (ええまあ) well; (なるほど) I see. ⇨はい¹
💬「私といっしょに来ていただけますか」「はあ，そう言われるなら」"Will you come with me?" "*Yes*, if you ask me."
💬「日本の学校はどうですか」「はあ，だいぶ慣れました」"How are you getting along at school in Japan?" "*Well*, I'm getting used to it."

バー¹ (酒場) bar ◎ /バーで飲む drink at *a bar* / 彼はそのバーの常連の一人だった He was one of the regulars at the *bar*.

バー² (棒高跳びなどの) bar ◎

パー (ゴルフの) par ◎

ばあい 場合

(事例) case ◎; (状況) circumstances; (時) time ◎; (機会) occasion ◎
たいていの場合は in most *cases* / 場合によっては depending on *the circumstances*
その規則はこの場合には当てはまらない The rule doesn't apply in this *case*.
そのような場合，アメリカではどうするのですか What do you do in such *a case* in the U.S.?
今はもめている場合じゃない This is no *time* for arguing.
緊急の場合に備えて食料を蓄えておかなければならない We must store food *in case of emergency*.
◆それは時と場合による That (*all*) *depends.* / It *all depends.*(❖決まり文句で, depends の後には on the circumstances が省略されている) / 出席できない場合には (=出席できなければ), お知らせください Please let us know *if* [*in case*] you are not able to attend.

パーキング パーキングエリア a parking area / パーキングメーター a parking meter

はあく 把握 ――**把握する** (つかむ) grasp ⓗ; (理解する) understand* ⓗ /状況を把握する *grasp* the situation / 文の意味を正しく把握することが大切だ It is important to *understand* the correct meaning of a sentence.

ハーケン ⚠(登山用の) piton ◎ (❖日本語はドイツ語の Haken から)

バーゲン(セール) (特売) sale ◎ (❖bargain は「掘り出し物，買い得品」の意味) /春のバーゲンセール *a* spring *sale* / このワンピースはバーゲンで買った I bought this dress「*on sale* [*at a sale*].

バーコード bar code ◎

パーコレーター percolator ◎

パーサー (飛行機・船などの) purser ◎

バージニア Virginia(❖米国東岸の州;《略語》Va.,『郵便』VA)

バージョン version ◎ /このCDにはその曲の別バージョンが入っているよ You can enjoy another *version* of the tune on this CD.

バージョンアップ upgrade ◎ (❖「バージョンアップ」は和製英語) ――**バージョンアップする** upgrade ⓗ ⓗ /最新版へのバージョンアップには5,000円かかる *The upgrade* to the latest version costs 5,000 yen. / パソコンのOSをバージョンアップしたばかりだ I've just *upgraded* the operating system of my PC.

バージン (処女) virgin ◎

パース Perth(❖オーストラリアの都市)

バースデー birthday ◎ ⇨たんじょうび /バースデーケーキ a birthday cake / バースデープレゼント a birthday present [gift]

パーセンテージ percentage ◎ ⇨わりあい /日本の人口における高齢者のパーセンテージは年々増え続けている *The percentage* of elderly people in Japan is increasing year by year.

パーセント percent,《主に英》per cent ◎ (複 ~) (❖記号は％); (比率・割合) percentage ◎ /10パーセント引きで商品を売る sell goods at a 10 *percent* discount / 6パーセントの利子で at six *percent* interest / 出席者の70パーセントが女性だった Seventy *percent* of those present were female.(❖... percent of の後の名詞が複数のときは複数扱い，単数のときは単数扱いになる) / 防衛予算は10パーセント削減された The defense budget was slashed by 10 *percent.* / 日本の成人の何パーセントが喫煙していますか What *percentage* of Japanese adults smoke?

パーソナリティー (個性) personality ◎ ⓤ; (番組司会者) host ◎; (パネリスト) panelist,

《英》panellist ◯

ばあたり 場当たり ──場当たり的な haphazard ／それは非常に場当たり的な対策で、長期的には何の解決にもならない They are such *haphazard* measures that they won't be able to settle the matter in the long run.

バーチャル virtual ∥バーチャルリアリティー virtual reality

パーツ（部品）part ◯ ∥パーツを組み立てる put *parts* together

パーティー party ◯ ⇒ 場面・状況別会話 p.1758 ∥パーティーに出席する go to [《文語》attend] *a party* ／来月に パーティーを開く計画があります We plan to hold *a party* next month. ／たくさんの客がパーティーに招かれた A lot of guests were invited to *the party*. ／昨夜のパーティーは楽しかった I enjoyed *the party* last night.
∥ダンスパーティー a dance, a dance party

バーテン(ダー)《米》bartender ◯；(男性)《英》barman ◯；(女性)《英》barmaid ◯

ハート heart ◯ ∥ハートのエース the ace of *hearts* ／ついに彼は彼女のハートを射止めた He won her *heart* at last.
◆ハート形のクッキー a *heart-shaped* cookie

ハード
❶【厳しい】──ハードな hard ∥ハードな仕事 *hard work*
❷【ハードウェア】hardware ◯ (※×hard とはいわない)
∥ハードコンタクトレンズ a hard contact lens

パート ⚠
❶【パートタイム】(仕事) part-time job ◯；(仕事をする人) part-timer ◯, part-time worker ◯ ∥パートの口を探す look for *a part-time job* ◆デパートでパートをする work *part-time* at a department store (※この part-time は「パートで」の意味の副詞)
❷【音部・声部】part ◯ ∥アルトのパートを歌う sing the alto *part*

ハードウエア【コンピュータ】hardware ◯ ∥過去10年間におけるコンピュータのハードウエアの進歩は著しい Computer *hardware* has made remarkable progress over the past 10 years.

バードウォッチング bird-watching ◯, birding ◯
◆僕たちは沼の周りでバードウォッチングをした We *watched wild birds* around the pond.

ハードカバー (硬表紙の本) hardback ◯, hardcover ◯ (※どちらも形容詞として, a hardback [hardcover] book のようにも用いられる)

ハードスケジュール ⚠ tight schedule ◯ (※tight は「時間的余裕がない」の意味)

パートタイマー part-timer ◯

パートタイム (仕事) part-time job ◯

ハードディスク【コンピュータ】hard disk ◯

ハードトレーニング hard training ◯
◆試合に向けてハードトレーニングを行う *train hard* for a game

パートナー partner ◯ ∥ダンスのパートナー a dancing *partner*

◆テニスのダブルスで理佐とパートナーを組んだ I 「*partnered* (*with*) Risa [was Risa's *partner*] in the tennis doubles.

ハードボイルド ──ハードボイルドの hardboiled (※名詞の前に用いる)
∥ハードボイルド小説 hardboiled fiction (※小説のジャンルを表す言い方)

ハードル hurdle ◯; (競技) the hurdles ∥ハードルを飛び越える clear *a hurdle*
◆このソフトは初心者にはハードルが高い (→使うのが難しい) It's *hard* for beginners to use this software.

バーナー burner ◯

はあはあ 子供たちみな、はあはあ言いながら走っていた All the children *were panting heavily* as they ran. ／彼は家からずっと走り通しだったので、はあはあ言っていた (→息が切れていた) He *was out of breath* after running all the way from home.

ハーフ ⚠ 彼女はフランス人とベトナム人のハーフです She is *half* French and *half* Vietnamese. (※この half は副詞で「半分だけ」の意味. 英語では×She is a half. とはいわない)

ハーブ (薬用植物) herb ◯
∥ハーブティー herb tea

ハープ harp ◯ ∥ハープを奏でる play *the harp*
∥ハープ奏者 a harpist

パーフェクトゲーム (完全試合) perfect game ◯ ∥パーフェクトゲームを達成する pitch *a perfect game*

ハープシコード harpsichord ◯

ハーフタイム【スポーツ】half time ◯

ハーフバック【サッカー・アメリカンフットボール】(位置) halfback ◯; (選手) halfback ◯

バーベキュー barbecue ◯ ∥庭でバーベキューをする have *a barbecue* in the garden
◆牛肉をバーベキューにする *barbecue* beef
∥バーベキューソース barbecue sauce ／バーベキューパーティー a barbecue (party)

バーベル barbell ◯ ∥バーベルを持ち上げる lift *a barbell*

パーマ ⚠《公式的》permanent wave ◯,《口語的》perm ◯,《米口語的》permanent ◯
◆髪にパーマをかけてもらう have one's hair *permed*; *get a perm* ／彼女の髪は天然パーマです (→生まれつきカールしている) Her hair is *naturally curly*.
∥パーマ屋 (美容院) a beauty salon

バーミンガム Birmingham (※英国の都市・米国の都市)

ハーモニー harmony ◯ ◯

ハーモニカ harmonica ◯, mouth organ ◯ ∥ハーモニカでフォスターの曲を吹く play a Stephen Foster song *on the harmonica*

バーモント Vermont (※米国北東部の州;《略語》Vt.,《郵便》VT)

パーラー (専門店)《主に米》parlor ◯

パール pearl ◯ ⇒ しんじゅ

はい

❶【質問に対する返事】(肯定の問いや相手の言葉に対して) yes,《口語的》yeah; (否定の問いに対して) no

日本語の「はい」,「いいえ」と違い,英語では問いが肯定か否定かに関係なく,返答の内容が肯定であればyesを,否定であればnoを用いる.

世論調査の対象となった人の70パーセント以上が「はい」と答えた More than 70 percent of the people polled said *yes*.

💬「彼は毎日ここへ来ますか」「はい,来ます」 "Does he come here every day?" "*Yes*, he does."

💬「眠くないのですか」「はい,眠くないです」 "Aren't you sleepy?" "*No*, I'm not." (❖日本語につられて×Yes, I'm not.としない)

💬「クッキーはいかがですか」「はい,いただきます」 "Would you like some cookies?" "*Yes*, please." (❖いらないときは No, thank you. などと答える)

💬「あなたは名古屋にお住まいでしたね」「はい,そうです」 "You live in Nagoya?" "(*Yes*.) That's right." (❖That's right.は相手の言っていることが正しいときに用いる)

💬(電話で)「加藤政夫さんですか」「はい,そうです」 "Is this [《英》that] Mr. Kato Masao?" "*Yes*, this is he. / *Speaking*." (❖女性なら, Yes, this is she. となる)

❷【承諾】yes; (もちろん) certainly, of course, 《主に米・口語的》sure, surely; (いいですよ) 《口語的》all right, OK

💬「塩を取ってくれませんか」「はい,ちょっと待ってくださいね」 "Pass the salt, please." "*Yes*. Just a moment, please."

💬「電話をお借りしてもよろしいですか」「はい,どうぞ」 "May I use the phone?" "*Certainly./ Sure./ Of course*."

❸【出欠・点呼の返事】yes; (出欠の) here, present

💬「川村君」「はい」 "Kawamura." "*Yes*, sir [ma'am]./ *Here*./ *Present*." (❖sirは男性に, ma'amは女性に対して答える場合.点呼ではいずれも省略されることが多い)

❹【注意を促す】
(物を差し出して)はい,どうぞ *Here it is./ Here you are.* (❖前者が物に,後者が相手に重点をおいた言い方)

はい,話をやめて *Now*, be quiet.

英作文ノート「はい」だけど **No**
「ここでたばこを吸ってもいいですか」「はい,どうぞ」
→×"Do you mind if I smoke here?" "*Yes*, go ahead."
→○"Do you mind if I smoke here?" "*No*, go ahead."
★mindは「気にする」の意味だから,吸ってもかまわない場合は,「いいえ,気にしません」の意味で No で答える. "May I smoke here?"と聞かれたときは, "Yes, go ahead."となる.

はい² 灰 ash ◯ (また複数形 ~es) ‖たばこの灰 cigarette *ash*/ その火事で町は焼けて灰になった The fire reduced the town to *ashes*.
◆死の灰 fallout

はい³ 肺 lungs (❖「片方の肺」を指す場合は a lung) ‖彼女は少し肺を患っている She has some trouble with *her lungs*.

-はい¹ 一杯 (湯のみの1杯) cup ◯; (コップの1杯) glass ◯; (ごはん茶わんなどの1杯) bowl ◯ ‖コーヒー1杯 *a cup of* coffee / オレンジジュース2杯 *two glasses of* orange juice / ごはん2杯 *two bowls of* rice

-はい² 一敗 (負け) loss ◯ (↔win), defeat ◯ (↔victory) ‖彼はきのう今季4敗目を喫した He suffered *his* fourth *loss* of the season yesterday.

ばい 倍
❶【2倍】
倍の速さで走る run at *double* [*twice*] the speed (❖×at the double [twice] speed とはいわない)

彼は人の倍働く He works *twice* as hard as others.

3の倍は6である *Twice* [*Two times*] three is six.

本の値段は20年前のほぼ倍だ(→2倍かかる) Books cost almost *double* [*twice*] what they did two decades ago.

この町の人口はここ30年で倍になった The population of this town *has doubled* in the last 30 years.

❷【-倍】
その土地は東京ドームの3倍の広さがある The land is *three times as large as* Tokyo Dome./ The land is *three times* the area *of* Tokyo Dome.

彼は私の2[3]倍の数のCDを持っている He has *twice* [*three times*] *as many* CDs *as* me. (❖数を比較する場合には many を用いる)

彼は私の2[3]倍のお金を持っている He has *twice* [*three times*] *as much* money *as* me. (❖量を比較する場合には much を用いる)

アメリカは日本の何倍の大きさですか *How many times larger* is the U.S. *than* Japan? (❖何倍かを尋ねる場合は比較級を用いるのがふつう)

◆倍率200倍の望遠鏡 a 200-*power* telescope (❖-power は「倍率が…倍の」の意味) / 5倍の増加 a five-*fold* increase

パイ (菓子) pie ◯ ‖まるごと一つのパイは a pie. それを切ったものは a piece of pie になる); 《英》tart ◯ (❖《英》では,果物やクリーム入りで中の見えるものを tart と呼んで pie と区別する) ‖パイを焼く bake *a pie*
‖パイ皮 piecrust / アップルパイ (an) apple pie / ミートパイ (a) meat pie

はいあがる 這い上がる crawl up, creep* up; (よじ登る) climb up ‖私たちは急な斜面をはい上がるように登った We *climbed up* a steep slope.
◆どん底からはい上がる *work one's way up* from the bottom

バイアスロン biathlon ◯

はいあん 廃案 (却下された法案) rejected bill ◯ ◆その法案は結局廃案になった The bill *was rejected* [(→検討を打ち切られた) *dropped*] after all.

はいいろ 灰色 gray, 《英》grey ◯ ――灰色

の gray, 《英》grey ‖灰色のコート a *gray coat* / 彼は灰色の目をしている He has *gray eyes*. ‖灰色の(→憂鬱(ｿﾞﾂ)な)人生 a *dreary* [*gloomy, gray*] *life*
‖灰色高官 a government official under a cloud

はいいん 敗因 the cause of *one's defeat* / 彼の敗因はスタミナ不足だ The *cause of his defeat* was a lack of stamina.

ばいう 梅雨 the rainy season ⇒ つゆ(梅雨)
◆梅雨前線の活動が活発である The *seasonal rain front* is active.

ハイウェー ⚠ (高速道路) 《米》expressway Ⓒ, freeway Ⓒ, 《英》motorway Ⓒ

> 英語の highway と日本語の「ハイウェー」の意味のずれに注意. 英語の highway は国道や県道なども含む「幹線道路」の意味で使われる.

はいえい 背泳 the backstroke ⇒ せおよぎ

はいえき 廃液 waste fluid Ⓤ, liquid waste Ⓤ ‖海に廃液を垂れ流す discharge *liquid waste* into the sea

はいえつ 拝謁 audience Ⓒ ‖国王との拝謁を許される be granted *an audience* with the king

ハイエナ 【動物】hyena Ⓒ

はいえん¹ 肺炎 【医学】pneumonia [njuːmóunia] Ⓤ ‖肺炎にかかる catch [《公式的》contract] *pneumonia*

はいえん² 排煙 smoke extraction Ⓤ (また a ~) ‖排煙装置 a smoke extraction system

ばいえん 煤煙(煙) smoke Ⓤ, (すす) soot Ⓤ ‖この町の人々は長年, 工場からの煤煙に苦しんでいる The people in this city have suffered from *smoke* from factories for many years.

ハイオク ⚠ ――ハイオクの high-octane
‖ハイオクガソリン high-octane gasoline

パイオニア (先駆者) pioneer Ⓒ ‖遺伝子工学のパイオニア *a pioneer* in the field of genetic engineering

バイオリズム biorhythm Ⓤ Ⓒ

バイオ(テクノロジー) biotechnology Ⓤ

バイオリニスト violinist Ⓒ

バイオリン violin Ⓒ, 《口語的》fiddle Ⓒ ‖バイオリンを弾く play *the violin* / 人にバイオリンで1曲弾いて聞かせる play a person a tune *on one's violin*
‖バイオリン奏者 a violinist

はいが 胚芽 【植物】embryo Ⓒ (複 ~s)
‖胚芽米 semi-polished rice

ハイカー hiker Ⓒ

はいかい 徘徊 wandering Ⓤ ――徘徊する (うろつく) wander around; (特に犯罪目的で) prowl around

ばいかい 媒介 ――媒介する (病原菌などを) carry ⓔ, transmit ⓔ ‖マラリアはある種の蚊が媒介する Malaria *is carried* [*transmitted*] by some types of mosquitoes.

はいガス 排ガス exhaust (gas) Ⓤ, exhaust fumes
‖排ガス規制 exhaust restrictions

はいかつりょう 肺活量 vital capacity Ⓤ ‖肺活量計 a spirometer

はいかん¹ 拝観 ――拝観する (見る) see* ⓔ, look at …; (訪れる) visit ⓔ ‖その寺の寺宝を拝観する *see* the treasures of the temple
‖拝観料 an admission fee

はいかん² 配管 (集合的) piping Ⓤ; (1本1本の) pipe Ⓒ; (特に建物の中の) plumbing [plʌ́miŋ] Ⓤ ‖配管工 a plumber [plʌ́mər] / 配管工事 plumbing

はいかん³ 廃刊 discontinuance of publication ――廃刊する discontinue ⓔ

はいがん 肺癌 lung cancer Ⓤ ‖肺癌にかかっている suffer from *lung cancer*

はいき¹ 排気 exhaust Ⓤ ◆排気量3,000ccの車 a car with *a 3,000 cc displacement*
‖排気ガス (gas), exhaust fumes / 排気口 a vent / 排気装置 an exhaust system

はいき² 廃棄 ――廃棄する (不用なものを) scrap ⓔ, dispose of … ⇒ すてる ‖古い洗濯機を廃棄(処分に)する *scrap* an old washing machine ◆その工場は日に2トンの産業廃棄物を出す The factory produces two tons of *industrial wastes* a day.
‖放射性廃棄物 radioactive waste(s)

ばいきゃく 売却 sale Ⓒ ――売却する sell* ⓔ ⇒ うる(売る) ‖土地を売却する *sell one's land* / 売却済み 【揭示】Sold

はいきゅう 配給 (統制による割り当て) rationing Ⓤ; (供給) supply Ⓤ; (配布) distribution Ⓤ ――配給する ration ⓔ; supply ⓔ ‖被災者への食料の配給 *the distribution* [*supply*] of food to the victims / その地域では1週につき卵が3個まで配給される They *are rationed* three eggs a week in that district.
‖配給会社(映画の) a film distributor

はいきょ 廃墟 ruin Ⓒ (しばしば複数形 ~s) ‖大火のため町全体が廃墟と化した After a big fire the whole city *was a ruin*. / The whole city *was reduced to ruins* after a big fire.
◆廃墟と化した宮殿 a *ruined palace*

はいぎょう 廃業 ――廃業する (事業をやめる) give* up *one's business*; (店じまいをする) close down *one's store* [*shop*]; (開業医・弁護士などが) give up *one's practice*; (力士が) retire from the ring

はいきょうしゃ 背教者 apostate Ⓒ; (裏切り者) renegade Ⓒ

ばいきん 黴菌 germ Ⓒ; (細菌) microbe Ⓒ; (ウイルス) virus Ⓒ ◆足の傷からばい菌が入った(→感染した) The wound in my leg *has become infected*.

ハイキング hiking Ⓤ; (1回の) hike Ⓒ ‖きょうは絶好のハイキング日和(ﾋﾞﾖﾘ)だ This is an ideal day for *hiking*. / ハイキングはとても楽しかった We had a lot of fun on *the hike*. / 来週の土曜日高尾山へハイキングに行きませんか How about *going on a hike to* [*on*] Mt. Takao next Saturday?

バイキング ⚠❶ 【海賊】Viking Ⓒ
❷ 【料理】smorgasbord Ⓤ Ⓒ; (立食形式の食事) buffet [bəféi] Ⓤ Ⓒ

はいく 俳句 haiku (複 ～), haiku poem ‖俳句を詠む(→作る) compose [make] *haiku* (*poems*)

> 俳句は5・7・5のわずか17音節で構成され、世界で最も短い詩形と言われています。短歌と異なり、俳句には必ず季語を入れるという約束があります。俳句は海外でも有名で、英語で俳句を詠む人もいます。
> Haiku, composed of three phrases in the pattern of 5-7-5 syllables (the total of which comes to only 17 syllables), is said to be the shortest poetic form in the world. Unlike a *tanka*, there is a rule that a haiku must have a seasonal word in it. Haiku have become popular overseas, and there are some enthusiasts who make haiku in English.

バイク motorcycle ; (小型の)(米) motorbike ; (スクーター) scooter ; ❖英語のbikeはふつう「自転車」の意味で用いる) ‖バイクに乗る ride *a motorcycle* [*motorbike*] ‖マウンテンバイク a mountain bike

はいぐうしゃ 配偶者 (公式的) spouse ; (夫) *one's* husband, (妻) *one's* wife

ハイクラス ――ハイクラスの (高級な) high-class

はいけい¹ 背景

❶ (景色・絵などの) background (↔foreground)
その写真の背景には山並みが写っていた There were mountains *in the background* of the picture.
大きな噴水を背景にして写真を撮ってもらった I had my picture taken *with* a big fountain *in the background*.
◆白い壁を背景にして(→白い壁と対照を成して)その絵は魅力的に見えた The picture looked attractive *against* the white wall.

❷ (舞台の) scenery ; (装置) setting ; (個々の場面) scene
湖の背景を描く paint a picture of *the scenery* at a lake

❸ (背後の事情) background
事件の歴史的[政治的]背景 the historical [political] *background* of an incident
◆今回の出来事の背景には、長年にわたる両国の複雑な関係がからんでいる *Behind* this event is the long, complicated relationship between the two countries.

はいけい² 拝啓

> 英文で手紙を書く場合、日本語の「拝啓」に相当するあいさつの言葉は特にない。個人あての手紙では、書き出しを Dear ... で始め、親しさの度合いに応じて使い分ける。未知の個人に対する正式な手紙では Dear Sir [Madam], 既知であれば Dear Mr. [Miss, Mrs., Ms.] + 姓とする。

拝啓ブラウン様 *Dear* Mr. [Ms.] Brown

はいけっかく 肺結核 〖医学〗(pulmonary) tuberculosis

はいけつしょう 敗血症 〖医学〗blood poisoning , septicemia

はいけん 拝見 ――拝見する (見る) see*, look at ...
❷ (列車で)「切符を拝見いたします」「はい」 "May I *see* your ticket, please?" "Certainly."

はいご¹ 背後 the back, the rear ――背後に[で] behind, at the back of ..., (米口語的) in back ⇨ うしろ ‖敵の背後を攻撃する attack an enemy 「*from the back* [*in the rear*] ‖彼は帰宅途中、背後から襲われた He was attacked *from* 「*the rear* [*behind*] on his way home. ‖我々の背後で奇妙な物音がした There was a strange sound *behind* us. ‖その社長の背後にはある大物政治家がいる There is the support of an important politician *behind* the president. / The president *is backed by* an important politician.
◆警察は事件の背後関係(→背景)を現在調査中である The police are now investigating *the background* of the case.

はいご² 廃語 obsolete word

はいこう 廃校 the closure [closing] of a school ◆その学校は来年3月末で廃校になる The school will *be closed* at the end of March next year.

はいごう 配合 (混ぜ合わせること) compounding ; (組み合わせること) combination ――配合する (混ぜ合わせる) mix, compound ; (添加する) mix, add ‖絵の具を配合する *mix* [*compound*] (some colors of) paint ‖その絵の色の配合 the 「*combination* of colors [color *scheme*] in the painting (❖scheme は「構成、配置」の意味) ‖この飲料にはコラーゲンが配合されている Collagen is 「*mixed* into [*added* to] this beverage.
◆このペットフードには犬に必要な栄養分がバランスよく配合されている This pet food *is blended with* a good balance of the nutrients that dogs need.

はいざら 灰皿 ashtray

はいし 廃止 (法律・制度などの) abolition ; (打ち切ること) discontinuation ; (使わなくなること) disuse ――廃止する abolish, 《口語的》do* away with ...; discontinue ‖死刑制度を廃止する *abolish* the death penalty ‖その鉄道は利用客激減のため廃止された The railway service *was discontinued* because the number of passengers had decreased sharply.

はいしゃ¹ 歯医者 dentist ‖歯医者に行く go to *the dentist* [*dentist's*] ‖歯が痛かったので、歯医者に診(ミ)てもらった I had a toothache, so I 「went to see [consulted] *a dentist*.

はいしゃ² 敗者 loser (↔winner) ‖敗者復活戦 a consolation match

はいしゃ³ 廃車 (廃棄された車) scrapped car ◆車を廃車にする *scrap* a car

はいしゃ⁴ 配車 allocation of cars ――配車する allocate cars

はいしゃく 拝借 ――拝借する borrow ⇨ かりる

💬「ペンを拝借してよろしいですか」「はい，どうぞ」 "May I *borrow* your pen?" "Sure. Here you go."

ばいしゃく 媒酌 matchmaking [U] ━媒酌する （関係を取りもつ） act as (a) go-between; （結婚を世話する） arrange a match between ... ◆私たちは木村夫妻の媒酌で結婚した We were married *through the good offices of* Mr. and Mrs. Kimura.

‖媒酌人(結婚の) a matchmaker

ハイジャック hijacking [U] (❖具体的な事件を指す場合は [C])， hijack [C] ━ハイジャックする hijack [他] ➔のっとる(乗っ取る) ∥XYZ航空の旅客機がハイジャックされたというニュースが入った The news has come in that an XYZ Air Lines airplane *was hijacked*.

‖ハイジャック犯 a hijacker

ハイジャンプ 〔競技〕 the high jump

ばいしゅう 買収 ❶【贈賄】 bribery [U], bribe [C], 《口語的》payoff [C] ━買収する （わいろを贈る）bribe [他], 《口語的》buy* [pay*] off ∥役人を買収する *bribe* [*buy off*] officials (❖前者は味方につけるために，後者は罪を見逃してもらうために買収すること) / 彼は買収の容疑で取り調べを受けた He was questioned on suspicion of *bribery* [*paying bribes*].

❷【購入】 ━買収する buy* [他], 《公式的》purchase [他] ➔かう(買う) ∥工場の建設用地を買収する *buy* [*purchase*] the land for a factory site

はいしゅつ[1] 排出 （気体・液体などの）《公式的》discharge [U][C] ━排出する discharge [他] ∥廃液を海に排出する *discharge* liquid waste into the sea

‖排出口 an outlet

はいしゅつ[2] 輩出 その大学はすぐれた科学者を多数輩出している That university *has produced* a lot of great scientists.

ばいしゅん 売春 prostitution [U] ━売春する prostitute *oneself*

‖売春婦 a prostitute, 《軽蔑的》a whore

はいじょ 排除 （取り除くこと） removal [U]; （締め出すこと） exclusion [U][C] ━排除する remove [他]; exclude [他] ∥デモ隊を広場から排除する *remove* demonstrators from the square

ばいしょう 賠償 compensation [U], 《公式的》reparations (❖reparations は，特に戦争によって敗戦国に生じるものを指す) ━賠償する compensate *a person* for ..., make* reparations for ... ∥工場側の賠償責任を認める判決が出た The court admitted that the factory has an obligation to pay *compensation*. / 遺族は事故に対する賠償(金)として2,000万円を要求した The bereaved family demanded 20 million yen *in compensation for* the accident.

◆遺族は会社に対して損害賠償の訴えを起こした The families of the dead *sued* the company *for damages*.

はいしょく[1] 配色 （色の配合） color scheme [C], a combination of colors

はいしょく[2] 敗色 ジャイアンツの敗色濃厚だ(→状況が不利である) *The odds are against* the Giants.

はいしん 背信 （信頼を裏切ること） a breach of faith; （裏切り） betrayal [U]

◆彼のしたことは会社に対する背信行為として(→彼は会社を裏切ったと)非難された He was accused of *having betrayed* his company.

はいじん 俳人 haiku poet [C]

ばいしん 陪審 jury [C] (❖地域の住民から選ばれた12人ぐらいの陪審員(juror)から構成され，有罪か無罪かの評決(verdict)を下す．特に《英》では，構成員に注目する場合，a jury で複数扱いとなることがある) ‖陪審員 a juror / 陪審制度 the jury system

はいすい[1] 排水 drainage [U]; （下水設備を使った） sewerage [U] ━排水する drain [自][他]; （ポンプでくみ出す） pump out ∥この駅は排水が十分ではない This station *is not well drained*.

‖排水管 a drainpipe / 排水口 a drain / 排水設備 drainage / 排水ポンプ a drain pump / 排水量 displacement

はいすい[2] 廃水 wastewater [U] ∥その川には生活廃水が垂れ流しになっている *Household wastewater* is discharged into the river.

はいすい[3] 配水 water supply [U]

‖配水管 a water pipe

はいすいのじん 背水の陣 [慣用表現] チーム全体はその試合に背水の陣で(→後に引くことを考えずに)臨んだ The whole team took part in the game *with no thought of giving in*.

ばいすう 倍数 〔数学〕 multiple [C] ∥6は3の倍数である Six is *a multiple* of three.

ハイスクール high school [C]

➔こうこう(高校)

はいする[1] 配する （配列する） arrange [他]; （人を配置する） post [他], place [他] ➔はいち ∥危険箇所には警官が配された Policemen *were posted* [*placed*] at the dangerous spots.

はいする[2] 排する （取り除く） clear away

◆万難を排して(→あらゆる困難にもかかわらず) *in spite of all difficulties*

はいせき 排斥 boycott [C] ━排斥する boycott [他] ➔ボイコット ∥その州では日本製品の排斥運動が起こっている There's a movement to *boycott* Japanese products in the state.

はいせつ 排泄 excretion [U] ━排泄する excrete [他][自]

‖排泄物 excreta; （特に大便） excrement

はいぜつ 廃絶 （兵器・制度などの） abolition [U] ━廃絶する abolish [他] ∥全世界の人々が核兵器の廃絶を願っている The whole world hopes for *the abolition* of nuclear weapons.

はいせん[1] 配線 wiring [U] ━配線する wire [他] ∥家に配線工事をする *wire* a house / 配線ミスが原因で火事が起こった A fire broke out because of *faulty wiring*.

‖配線図 a wiring diagram

はいせん[2] 敗戦 defeat [U] ◆日本が敗戦を迎えた年，祖父は15歳だった My grandfather was 15 years old when Japan *was defeated*.

‖敗戦国 a defeated nation / 敗戦投手 a losing pitcher

ばいせん 焙煎 roasting ⓤ
◆焙煎コーヒー *roasted* coffee beans

ハイセンス ⚠ ——ハイセンスな (高級な) elegant; (センスのよい) stylish

はいそ 敗訴 ——敗訴する lose* a suit [case] ∥原告側が敗訴した The plaintiff *lost the suit* [*case*].

はいそう¹ 配送 delivery ⓤ ——配送する deliver ⓗ ➪はいたつ ∥商品の配送には2日かかる It will take two days to *deliver* the goods. / 市内であれば商品の配送は無料だ The goods *are delivered* free within the city limits.

はいそう² 敗走 ——敗走する《公式的》be routed ∥敵は敗走した The enemy *was routed*.

ばいぞう 倍増 ——倍増する double ⓗ ➪ばい ∥この語学学校の生徒数は2年間で倍増した The number of students of this language school *doubled* in two years.

はいぞく 配属 ——配属する (割り当てる) assign ⓗ, (所属させる) attach ⓗ, post ⓗ ∥純は情報システム部に配属された Jun *was assigned to* the Information Systems Division.

ハイソサエティー (上流社会) high society ⓤ

ハイソックス ⚠ long socks (❖数えるときは a pair of ... とする)

はいた 歯痛 toothache ⓒⓤ

はいたい 敗退 ——敗退する be defeated ∥そのチームは初戦で敗退した The team *was defeated* in the first game.

ばいたい 媒体 medium ⓒ (複 ~s, media) (❖通信・情報などでの「媒体」を表すときは、複数形に media を用いる) ➪ メディア
∥印刷媒体 print media / 電子媒体 electronic media / ニュース媒体 news media

はいたつ 配達 delivery ⓒⓤ ——配達する deliver ⓗ
1日2回郵便の配達がある There are two *deliveries* of mail a day. / The mail *is delivered* twice a day.
その手紙はけさ事務所に配達された The letter *was delivered* to our office this morning.
その店は市内は無料で配達してくれる The shop *delivers* free of charge within the city limits.
夕食にピザを配達してもらった We *had* pizzas *delivered* for dinner.
◆新聞配達をする have *a paper route*
∥配達区域 a delivery zone / 配達先 the destination / 配達人 a delivery person / 配達料 a delivery charge

はいたてき 排他的 ——排他的な (他を排除する) exclusive; (閉鎖的な) closed; (不親切な) unfriendly ∥排他的なクラブ an *exclusive* club / 排他的な態度 an *unfriendly* attitude

バイタリティー (活気) vitality ⓤ; (精力) energy ⓤ, vigor ⓤ ∥その新人投手はバイタリティーにあふれている The rookie pitcher is full of *vitality* [*vigor*].

はいち 配置 (配列) arrangement ⓒ; (部署・持ち場) station ⓒ ——配置する (配列する) arrange ⓗ, (決まった場所に) place ⓗ, (部署・持ち場に) post ⓗ, station ⓗ ∥展示品の配置を替える change *the arrangement* of the exhibits / 家具を部屋に配置する *arrange* the furniture in the room / 空港の入口には警官が配置された Police *have been posted* [*stationed*] at the entrance to the airport.
◆先月、従業員の配置転換があった There was *a reshuffle* of employees last month. / The employees *were reshuffled* last month.

ハイツ ⚠ apartment house ⓒ (❖英語の heights は「高台の意味」)

ハイティーン ⚠ ハイティーンの少女 a girl *in her late teens* / 彼女はハイティーンのころ引っ込み思案だった She was shy *in her late teens*.

ハイテク (ハイテクノロジー) high technology ⓤ ——ハイテクの high-tech, hi-tech ∥その事故はハイテク社会の弱点をさらけ出した The accident revealed some weak points in *high-tech* society.
∥ハイテク産業 high-tech industries

はいでる 這い出る crawl [creep*] out ∥子供が穴からはい出てきた A child *crept out of* the hole.

はいてん 配点 allocation of marks ◆この問題の配点は10点だ(→10点が割り当てられている) Ten points *are allotted* to this question.

はいでん 配電 supply of electric power ——配電する supply electricity
∥配電盤 a switchboard

ばいてん 売店 stand ⓒ;《主に英》stall ⓒ; (特に駅・駅前の) kiosk ⓒ ∥駅の売店でチューインガムを買った We bought chewing gum at *the stand* in the station.

バイト¹ ⚠ (アルバイト) part-time job ⓒ ➪ アルバイト, 場面・状況別会話 p.1688 ∥バイトをする do *a part-time job*

バイト² 〖コンピュータ〗(情報量の単位) byte ⓒ
∥ギガバイト a gigabyte / キロバイト a kilobyte / テラバイト a terabyte / メガバイト a megabyte

はいとう 配当 (株式の) dividend ⓒ; (分け前) share ⓒ ∥配当(金)を支払う pay *a dividend*

はいとく 背徳 (不道徳) immorality ⓤ
◆背徳行為 an *immoral* act

ばいどく 梅毒 〖医学〗syphilis ⓤ

パイナップル pineapple ⓒ (❖果肉を指すときは ⓤ) ∥パイナップルの缶詰 canned *pineapple*

はいにち 排日 ——排日の anti-Japanese ∥排日運動 an *anti-Japanese* campaign

はいにん 背任 a breach of trust ∥その会長には背任行為の疑いがある The president is suspected of *a breach of trust*.

ハイネック ⚠ ——ハイネックの high-necked; (タートルネック) turtleneck ∥ハイネックのドレス a *high-necked* dress

はいはい 這い這い ——はいはいする crawl ⓗ ➪ はう ∥赤ちゃんが床の上ははいはいしている The baby *is crawling* across the floor.

バイバイ bye-bye, by-by(❖小児語であるが、大人どうしの会話でも使われる); (後でね) See you. ⇨ さようなら

ばいばい 売買 buying and selling(❖日本語とは「売り」と「買い」の語順が逆であることに注意); (取り引き) trade, transaction ─売買する (取り引きする) deal* in …, trade / 彼は株の売買でひともうけした He made a lot of money「through *stock trading* [by *buying and selling stocks*]. ‖売買契約 a sales contract

バイパス (迂回道路) bypass ‖バイパス手術 a bypass operation

ハイパワー ─ハイパワーの high-powered ‖ハイパワーエンジン a *high-powered* engine

はいばん 廃盤 そのCDは廃盤になっている That CD *is no longer being produced*.

はいび 配備 deployment ─配備する deploy / 国境付近に部隊を配備する *deploy* troops in border areas

ハイヒール high heels, 《公式的》high-heeled shoes ‖ハイヒールを履いた女性 a lady wearing「*high heels* [*high-heeled shoes*]

ハイビジョン ─ハイビジョンの (日本形式の) Hi-Vision; (高解像度の) high-definition ‖ハイビジョンテレビ a high-definition television /《略語》HDTV / ハイビジョン放送 high-definition broadcasting

ハイビスカス 《植物》hibiscus

はいびょう 肺病 (結核) 《古風》consumption (❖現在では tuberculosis を用いる)

はいひん 廃品 waste materials; (廃棄物) waste (また複数形〜s), refuse / 廃品を再利用する recycle *waste materials* ‖ 廃品回収 the collection of waste materials / 廃品回収業者 a junk dealer

はいふ 配布 (手渡す) hand out, give* out, 《公式的》distribute / 彼は駅前で通行人にパンフレットを配布した He「*handed out* [*distributed*] pamphlets to passers-by in front of the station.

パイプ ❶【管】pipe / このパイプは詰まっている *This pipe* is clogged. / パイプから油がもれている Oil is leaking from *the pipe*. / 水が凍ってパイプが破裂した The freezing of the water made *the pipe* crack.
◆両国のパイプ役を務める *serve as a pipeline* between the two countries
❷【たばこの】pipe / パイプに火をつける light *one's pipe* / パイプをふかす smoke *a pipe*
‖パイプオルガン a pipe organ / パイプライン a pipeline

ハイファイ ─ハイファイの (高忠実度の) high-fidelity, 《口語的》hi-fi ‖ハイファイビデオ a *high-fidelity* [*hi-fi*] video

はいふく 拝復 (手紙で) Dear … ⇨ はいけい (拝啓)

はいぶつ 廃物 waste, waste materials ‖廃物利用 recycling of waste materials

ハイブリッド ─ハイブリッドの hybrid ‖ハイブリッドカー a *hybrid* car

バイブル (聖書) the Bible; (権威のある書物) bible / その参考書は受験生のバイブルとされている That study aid is regarded as *the bible* for students preparing for entrance exams.

バイブレーション (振動) vibration

バイブレーター vibrator

ハイブロー (知識人ぶる人) 《軽蔑的》highbrow [háibràu] ─ハイブローの highbrow

ハイフン hyphen ⇨ 巻末付録 (句読法)
◆ハイフンでつながれた単語 a *hyphenated word*

はいぶん 配分 (割り当てること) allocation, allotment; (分配) distribution; (分け前) share ─配分する allocate, allot; (分け合う) share / 利益の配分にあずかる have *a share* in the profits

はいべん 排便 bowel movement ─排便する move [《公式的》evacuate] *one's bowels*

ハイボール (飲み物) 《米》highball, 《英》whisky and soda

はいぼく 敗北 defeat (❖個々の「敗北」を指すときは) ─敗北する be defeated, suffer a defeat / まける 選挙は与党の敗北に終わった The election ended in the ruling party's *defeat*. / 彼は自分の敗北を認めようとしなかった He would not acknowledge having been defeated. / わがチームは敗北を喫した Our team *suffered a defeat*.

ばいめい 売名 (自分を宣伝すること) self-promotion / 彼女のあの発言は売名行為にすぎない She said that only out of *self-promotion*. / Her saying that is just *a way to get publicity*.

はいめん 背面 the back, the rear ⇨ うしろ / 敵の背面を攻撃する attack the enemy *in the rear*

ハイヤー chartered taxi ‖ハイヤーを呼ぶ call *a chartered taxi*

バイヤー (買う人) buyer

はいやく 配役 (役を割り当てること) casting, cast; (役) role ⇨ キャスト

ばいやく¹ 売約 売約済み 《掲示》Sold

ばいやく² 売薬 patent medicine

はいゆう 俳優 actor (❖性別にかかわらず用いられる); (女優) actress / 映画俳優 a film *actor* [*actress*] / 舞台俳優 a stage *actor* [*actress*]

ばいよう 培養 (細菌の) culture ─培養する culture, cultivate / バクテリアを培養する *culture* bacteria
‖培養液 culture fluid / 培養土 compost

ハイライト (最も注目を浴びる部分) highlight / F1レースのハイライト *the highlights* of Formula One races

はいりこむ 入り込む go* [get*] into …; (入ってくる) come* in …, come into … / 台所で料理をしている間に、猫が家に入り込んできた A cat *came into* my house while I was cooking in the kitchen. ◆コインが自動販売機の下に入り込んでしまった A coin *got* under the vending machine.

ばいりつ 倍率 ❶【レンズの】《光学》magnification ◎, power ◎ ∥高倍率のレンズがついたカメラ a camera with a *high-power* lens / 倍率120倍の望遠鏡 a 120-*power* telescope / 望遠鏡の倍率を上げる[下げる] raise [lower] *the magnification* [*power*] of a telescope / この双眼鏡は倍率10倍だ These binoculars have *a magnification* [*power*] of 10.
❷【競争】competition ∥その大学は昨年より倍率が上がった(→より多くの競争があった) There was more *competition* this last year to enter the college. / 黒川大学に合格するためには、高い倍率を突破しなければ(→熾烈(しれつ)な競争に生き残らなければ)ならない You must survive fierce *competition* to pass the entrance examination for Kurokawa University.

はいりょ 配慮 (思いやり) consideration ⓤ, thoughtfulness ⓤ; (気づかい) regard ⓤ, concern ⓤ; (骨折り) trouble ⓤ ――配慮する consider ⓗ, think* about ... ∥彼は年寄りに対する配慮が欠けている He has no *consideration* [*regard*] for the elderly. / この建物は車いす使用者のことを十分に配慮した造りになっている This building has been constructed *with* thorough *consideration for* wheelchair users. / いろいろご配慮いただいてありがとうございます Thank you very much for *your concern* [*trouble*].
◆このホテルの客に対する配慮は申し分ない(→申し分ないサービスをしてくれる) This hotel has quite satisfactory *service*.

バイリンガル bilingual ◎ ――バイリンガルの bilingual

はいる 入る

❶ 中へ	come in; go in
❷ 加入する	enter; join
❸ 着く	arrive
❹ 含まれる	
❺ 収容する	hold; seat

❶【中へ】come* in, come into ... (❖中にいる人から見た場合); go* in, go into ... (❖外にいる人から見た場合); (ある場所へ) enter ⓗ, (歩いて) walk in, walk into ...
私たちは彼女が部屋に入ってきたのに気づかなかった We didn't notice that she *came into* the room.
私たちは案内人の後から洞窟(どうくつ)の中へ入った We *went into* the cave after the guide.
車はトンネルに入った The car *entered* the tunnel.
◆目にごみが入った I *got* something in my eye. / 昨夜、近くの宝石店に泥棒が入った The nearby jeweler's *was broken into* last night. (❖break into ... は「(泥棒などが)…に押し入る」の意味) / 光が十分入るように居間のカーテンをあけておいた I left the curtain open in the living room to *get* enough light *in*.
/ お宅の犬をうちの庭に入れないでください Please *keep* your dog *out of* my garden. (❖keep ... out of ~ で「…を～から遠ざける」の意味) / 私が電話したとき、彼はちょうどふろに入っていた He *was taking* a bath when I phoned.

e「入っていいですか」「どうぞ」 "May I *come in*?" "Sure."

❷【加入する】 enter ⓗ, 《口語的》get* into ...; (加わる) join ⓗ; (入学などを許可される) be admitted to ...; (入学などの手続きをする) enroll in ...
彼は東京大学に入った He *entered* [*was admitted to*] the University of Tokyo.
彼女はテニス部に入った She *joined* the tennis club.
◆彼女は俳句同好会に入っている(→メンバーの一人である) She's *a member of* the haiku society.

❸【着く】arrive ⓘ; (駅や港に) come* in
特急列車が4番ホームに入ってきた The express train *arrived* [*came in*] on track 4.
(店員が)ご注文いただいた本が入りました The book you ordered *has arrived* [*come in*].

❹【含まれる】
ビールにはアルコールが入っている(→ビールはアルコールを含んでいる) Beer *contains* alcohol.
ホテル宿泊費にはサービス料が入っている(→サービス料を含んでいる) The hotel's room rate *includes* a service charge.

❺【収容する】(容器などが) hold* ⓗ; (座席数がある) seat ⓗ, accommodate ⓗ
この箱にはフロッピーが100枚入る This box *can hold* 100 floppy disks.
そのホールには500人入る The hall *can hold* 500 people. / The hall *seats* 500 people.

❻【中にある】
この箱の中に何か入っていますか Is there anything in this box?
バケツには水がいっぱい入っている The bucket *is full of* water.
会員のデータはこのコンピュータに入っている The data on the members *is stored* [*kept, recorded*] *in* this computer.

❼【サイズ・形などが合う】fit* ⓘ
この電球はソケットに入らない This bulb *doesn't fit into* the socket.

❽【ある時期・段階になる】
学校は2学期に入ろうとしていた(→もうすぐ2学期の始まりだった) It *was almost the beginning of* the second term.
今ブドウは最盛期に入っている(→旬(しゅん)である) Grapes *are now in season*.
前置きはこれくらいにして、本題に入りましょう So much for the introduction; now let's *proceed to* the main topic.

> 英作文ノート 「梅雨に入る」の英語は？
> 沖縄はすでに梅雨に入った
> →×They *have* already *entered* the rainy season in Okinawa.
> →○The rainy season *has* already *set*

ハイレグ

in in Okinawa.
★「入る」=enter と単純に考えたことによる間違い. 雨期や台風など通常「不快な天候が始まる」という場合は set in を用いて表現する.

❾ 【利用できる状態になる】
コンピュータの電源は入っている The computer *is plugged in*.
ここはラジオの音がよく入らない(→受信状態がよくない) Radio reception isn't good here.

❿ 【得点が】
彼のタイムリーヒットで2点が入った His timely hit *brought in* two runs.
後半, 日本チームに1点入った The Japanese National Team *scored* one point in the latter half.

ハイレグ ⚠ ──ハイレグの high-cut ‖ハイレグの水着 a *high-cut* swimsuit [bathing suit]

はいれつ 配列 arrangement Ⓤ Ⓒ ──配列する arrange ⓗ ‖(コンピュータで)デスクトップのアイコンの配列を変える change *the arrangement of* the desktop icons / 図書館の本は探しやすいように配列されている The books in the library *are arranged* for easy reference.

ハイレベル ──ハイレベルの high-level

パイロット pilot Ⓒ ‖旅客機[戦闘機]のパイロット *an* airline [*a* fighter] *pilot*
‖パイロットランプ a pilot lamp

パイン (パイナップル) pineapple Ⓒ

バインダー binder Ⓒ ‖書類をバインダーにとじる put papers into *a binder*

はう 這う creep* ⓗ; (腹ばいになって進む) crawl ⓗ ‖その古い建物の壁にはツタがはっていた Ivy *was creeping over* the walls of the old building. / 大きな蛇が地面をはっていた A big snake *was crawling across* the ground. / その子供はフェンスの下の小さなすき間をはって通り抜けた The child *crawled through* a small opening under the fence.

ハウス ⚠ (温室) greenhouse Ⓒ; (大型の温室) hothouse Ⓒ ‖ハウス野菜 *hothouse* vegetables

パウダー powder Ⓤ
‖ベーキングパウダー baking powder / ベビーパウダー baby powder

ハウツー 料理のハウツー本 a *how-to* book on cooking

バウンド ⚠ bounce, bound Ⓒ (❖ボールなどの「バウンド」には bounce を用いるのがふつう)
──バウンドする bounce ⓗ, bound ⓗ
➡ はずむ ‖ワンバウンドでボールをつかむ catch a ball *on the first bounce [bound]* / ボールは二塁手の前でイレギュラーバウンドした The ball *made an erratic bounce* in front of the second baseman.

パウンドケーキ pound cake Ⓒ

はえ 蠅 fly Ⓒ ‖ハエを追い払う drive *the flies away* / ハエをたたく flap [swat] *a fly* / 天井にハエがとまっていた There was *a fly* on the ceiling.
‖ハエたたき a flyswatter / ハエ取り紙 (a) flypaper
俳句 やれ打つな蠅が手を摺(す)り足をする(小林一茶)
Hey, don't *swat* that fly!
Watch how he's rubbing his hands and scraping his feet.

はえかわる 生え変わる 歯が生え変わる(→乳歯が抜けて永久歯が生える) lose one's baby [milk] *teeth and get permanent teeth*

はえぎわ 生え際 hairline ‖彼は生え際が後退している He has *a receding hairline*.

はえなわ 延縄 trawl line Ⓒ
◆魚をはえなわで捕る trawl for fish
‖はえなわ漁業 longline fishing / はえなわ漁船 a longliner

はえぬき 生え抜き ──はえ抜きの(その土地に生まれ育った) native-born ◆彼ははえ抜きの外交官だ He is *a career diplomat*.

はえる¹ 生える (成育する) grow* ⓗ; (芽・葉などが) sprout ⓗ; (歯が) cut* ⓗ ‖この植物は清流のほとりにしか生えない This plant *grows only along crystal(-clear)* streams.
◆若ジカに角(つの)が生えた The young deer *has sprouted* antlers. / 赤ちゃんに歯が生え始めた The baby *is cutting* teeth.

はえる² 映える・栄える (光に照らされて輝く) shine* ⓗ, glow ⓗ; (美しく見える) look nice [beautiful, attractive] ‖紅葉が太陽の光に映えていた The autumn leaves *glowed* in the sun. / 彼女はその赤いドレスを着ると映える She *looks nice* in that red dress.

はおと 羽音 (虫) hum Ⓒ, buzz Ⓒ; (鳥) flap Ⓒ

はおり 羽織 ⚠ a *haori*, a short coat worn over a kimono

はおる 羽織る put* on ➡ きる(着る) ‖コートをはおる *put on* a coat

はか 墓 grave Ⓒ; (大きな) tomb [túːm] Ⓒ; (墓地) cemetery Ⓒ; (教会の墓地) graveyard Ⓒ
墓を掘る dig *a grave* / 墓を建てる build *a tomb* / 墓参りをする visit *one's ancestor's grave* ‖墓石 a gravestone, a tombstone

ばか 馬鹿

(人) fool Ⓒ, idiot Ⓒ; (愚かさ) foolishness Ⓤ, stupidity Ⓤ; (無意味な言動) nonsense Ⓤ ──ばかな foolish; stupid; silly; absurd

| foolish: 判断力・思慮に欠けていること.
| stupid: 知力が劣り判断・理解が遅いこと.
| silly: 他人が笑うような常識のなさ.
| absurd: 常識がなく明らかに誤っていること.

〚ばかだ〛
彼女にあんなことを言うなんてばかだよ You were *silly* [It was *silly* of you] to say such a thing to her.
彼を信じるなんて, なんてばかだったんだろう What *a fool* I was [How *foolish* of me] to believe him!

〚ばかな〛
ばかな間違いをしてしまった I made a *silly* [*stupid*] mistake.
ばかなまねはよせ Stop *that nonsense*!

💬「彼は君が怪しいって言ってるよ」「そんなばかな」 "He says he suspects you." "*How absurd*!"

💬「あの会社, 倒産したよ」「そんなばかな」 "That company went bankrupt." "(→信じられない) *I can't believe it*./ (→冗談だろう) *You're kidding*!"

〖ばかを〗
ばかを言うな *Don't be a fool*./ *Don't talk nonsense*.
彼の言うとおりにしてばかを見た I *felt like a fool* obeying him.

〖ばかにする·なる〗
人をばかにするのもいいかげんにしろ Stop *making a fool of* me now.
◆交通費だってばかにならない (→軽視できない) We *can't make light of* the transportation expenses. / そのねじはばかになっている The screw *has been stripped*. / かぜをひいて鼻がばかになった (→においが分からない) I *can't smell* because of my cold. / 彼の意見もばかにしたもんじゃない His opinion *is not to be sneezed at*. (❖be not to be sneezed at は「軽く扱えない」の意味)

〖その他〗
ばか野郎! *You fool*! (❖この場合, fool の前に冠詞は不要)
彼はそんな話を信じるほどばかじゃない He「*is not such a fool as* [*knows better than*] *to* believe a story like that. (❖know better than to *do* は「…しないだけの分別がある」の意味)

💬「僕の宿題やってくれない?」「ばかも休み休み言え」 "Can you do my homework?" "*None of your nonsense*!"

[慣用表現] ばかとはさみは使いよう (→うまく使えばどんなものでも役に立つ) *Everything is useful if you use it properly*. / ばかにつける薬はない *There is no medicine for curing a fool*. / 彼女はばかの一つ覚えのようにいつも同じ鼻歌を歌っている She is always humming the same song *as if it was the only one she knows*.

ばか- 馬鹿- ばか力 *enormous strength* / ばかでかい船 a *huge* [《米俗語》*humongous*] ship / ばか正直である (→正直すぎる) *be too honest*; *be honest to a fault* / ばか騒ぎをする make *a big fuss* / ばか丁寧な応対をする respond *with excessive politeness*

はかい 破壊 destruction [U] ――破壊する destroy [他] ――破壊的な destructive
環境破壊 environmental *destruction* / 自然環境を破壊から守る protect the environment from *destruction*
港全体がその地震で破壊された The whole of the harbor *was destroyed* by the earthquake.
◆これ以上環境を破壊しないことが重要だ It is important not to *damage* our environment any more. (❖damage は「…に損害を与える」の意味)
‖破壊活動防止法 the Anti-Subversive Activities Act / 破壊力 destructive power

はがいじめ 羽交い締め そのレスラーは相手をはがい締めにした The wrestler *put* his opponent *in a full nelson*.

はがき 葉書 postcard [C], (postal) card [C]
⇒ [巻末付録] (手紙·はがきの書き方)
はがきを受け取る receive *a postcard* / 彼にはがきを出す send him *a postcard*
彼女は両親にはがきを書いた She wrote *a postcard* to her parents.
‖絵はがき a picture postcard / 往復はがき a postcard with a prepaid reply attached (❖英米にはない)

はかく 破格 ――破格の (ふつうでない) extraordinary; (特別な) special; (先例のない) unprecedented; (例外的な) exceptional ‖破格の出世をする get an *exceptional* [*unprecedented*] promotion
◆破格の待遇を受ける be given *exceptionally good treatment* / 破格の値段 (→とても安い値段) で at *a very low price*

ばかげた 馬鹿げた (思慮に欠けた) foolish, stupid; (不合理な) absurd; (こっけいな) ridiculous ⇒ばか ‖それは全くばかげたことだ That's just plain *stupid*.
◆彼はばかげた行動をした He acted *foolishly*.

はがす 剥がす (注意深く) peel off; (破いて) tear* off [away], remove [他] ‖びんからラベルをはがす *peel* the label *off* [*from*] the bottle / 彼は壁からポスターをはがした He *tore* a poster *off* (of) the wall.

ばかす 化かす (魔法をかける) bewitch [他], enchant [他]; (だます) trick [他] ‖彼女はタヌキに化かされた She *was bewitched* by a raccoon dog.

ばかず 場数 彼は場数を踏んでいる (→経験が豊富だ) He *has much* [*wide*] *experience*./ He *is rich in experience*.

はかせ 博士 doctor [C] ◆彼は野球博士だ (→野球に詳しい) He「*is familiar with* [*knows everything about*] *baseball*.

はかどる progress [自], make* progress, get* along [on] with ..., go* well ‖彼の勉強ははかどっている He *is getting along with* his studies. / その道路工事はあまりはかどっていない The road work *is progressing little*. ◆新しいソフトのおかげで仕事がはかどった The new software *speeded up* the work.

はかない (一時的な) transient, temporary; (短命の) short-lived; (むなしい) vain, empty ‖はかない人生 *transient* life / はかない夢 a *vain* [an *empty*] dream / 花の美しさははかない The beauty of flowers is *transient*. / 私たちの幸福ははかなかった Our happiness was *short-lived*.

はかなむ (絶望する) despair [自]; (むなしく思う) feel* empty ◆世をはかなんで (→絶望して) 自殺する kill *oneself in despair*

ばかに 馬鹿に (とても) very; (ひどく) terribly, awfully; (極端に) extremely; (法外に) unreasonably ‖きょうはばかに暑い It is *very* [*extremely*] hot today.

はがね 鋼 steel [U]

はかば 墓場 cemetery [C], graveyard [C]

はかばかしい (満足な) satisfactory; (順調な) smooth ‖彼女の病状ははかばかしくない She is not making a *satisfactory* recovery from her illness. / 作業の進みぐあいがはかばかしい My work isn't 「making *smooth* progress [progressing *smoothly*].

ばかばかしい 馬鹿馬鹿しい、(ばかげた) foolish, stupid; (不合理な) absurd; (こっけいな) ridiculous ⇒ばか ‖そんなばかばかしい申し出は聞いたことがない I've never heard of such a *ridiculous* offer. ◆ばかばかしい！ *Nonsense*!/ *That's rubbish*!

はかま 袴 　　 a *hakama*, a long, pleated, culotte-like Japanese garment

ばかやろう 馬鹿野郎 ⇒ばか

はがゆい 歯痒い、feel* impatient [irritated] ‖彼は息子がぐずぐずしているのが歯がゆかった He *felt impatient* [*irritated*] at his son's delay.

はからい 計らい、(尽力・あっせん・好意) good [kind] offices; (裁量) discretion ⓤ ‖山下さんのはからいでその会社に入れた I got a job in the company *through the good offices of* Mr. Yamashita. / 私たちはその件を彼のはからいに任せた We left the matter to his *discretion*.

はからう 計らう、(…するよう気をつける) see* (to it) that …; (手はずを整える) arrange ⓣ ‖あなたが彼女に会えるようにはからいます I'll see (to it) that you can see her.

ばからしい 馬鹿らしい、(ばかげた) foolish, stupid; (不合理な) absurd; (こっけいな) ridiculous

はからずも 図らずも、(思いがけず) unexpectedly; (偶然に) by chance, by accident, accidentally ‖私たちの計画ははからずも成功した Our plan succeeded *unexpectedly*. / 私ははからずもそこで彼女に会った I saw her there *by chance*. / I *happened* to see her there.

はかり 秤 scale ⓒ《しばしば複数形 ~s》; (天秤(ぴん)) balance ⓒ; (体重計) the (weighing) scales ‖…をはかりにかける weigh …「on *the scales* [in *the balance*]

-ばかり

❶【およそ】about, around, nearly, roughly, … or so
彼は1時間ばかりで戻ります He will be back in 「*about* an hour [an hour *or so*].
私たちの高校は1,000人ばかりの生徒がいます Our high school has *roughly* one thousand students.

❷【…だけ】only, nothing but …, mere; (すべて…そのもの) all
彼は仕事のことばかり考えている He thinks of *nothing but* his work. / His mind is *only* on his work.
君は当てずっぽうばかり言っている You are *only* guessing.
彼は金のことばかり気にしている *All* [*The only* thing] he cares about is money.
この番組は子供ばかりでなく大人にも人気がある This TV program is popular *not only* among children *but* (*also*) adults.

❸【たった今】just, just now; (…から来たばかりの) fresh from …
バスは今出たばかりだ The bus has *just* gone.
彼女は高校を出たばかりだ She is *fresh from* high school.
これらの花は庭から摘んできたばかりだ These flowers are *fresh from* my garden.
◆生まれたばかりの赤ん坊 a *new-born* baby

❹【いつも】(いつも) always; (絶えず) constantly
彼は仕事について不平ばかり言っている He is *always* complaining about his job.
彼女は遅れてばかりだ She is *constantly* coming late.

❺【ほとんど…しそう】be on the verge of …, be ready to *do*, be about to *do*
その少女は今にも泣きださんばかりだった The girl *was on the verge of* tears.
◆彼女が歌い終えたとたん、聴衆から割れんばかりの拍手かっさいが起こった Hardly had she finished singing when *thunderous* applause burst from the audience.

❻【…のために】
私が忙しかったばかりに子供たちの面倒をあまり見てやれなかった I was busy, *so* I could hardly take care of my children.

はかりごと (計画) plan ⓒ; (たくらみ・陰謀) scheme ⓒ《しばしば複数形 ~s》, plot ⓒ; (計略) trick ⓒ ◆政府に対してはかりごとを企てる *plot* against the government

はかりしれない 計り知れない、(計算できない) immeasurable, beyond measure; (想像できない) unimaginable, inconceivable ‖アインシュタインは20世紀の物理学にはかり知れない影響を与えた Einstein had an *immeasurable* effect on 20th century physics.

はかる¹ 計る・測る・量る measure ⓣ; (時間を) time ⓣ; (調査・観察によって) take* ⓣ; (水深を) sound ⓣ; (重さを) weigh ⓣ
気温を計る *take* a temperature reading /
人の身長を測る *measure* [*take*] a person's height / 机の寸法を測る *take* the dimensions of a desk
私のタイムを計ってください *Time* me, please.
看護婦は患者の体温[脈拍]を計った The nurse *took* the patient's temperature [pulse].
彼らは川幅を測った They *measured* the width of the river.
私たちはその池の深さを測った We *sounded* [*measured the depth of*] the pond.
私は毎日体重を量る I *weigh* myself every day.

はかる² 図る・諮る・謀る

❶【企てる】(試みる) attempt ⓣ (◆しばしば果たせずに終わることを含意する), try ⓣ; (陰謀を) plot ⓣ
彼は自殺をはかった He *attempted suicide*. / (→自殺した) He *committed suicide*.
彼らは政府の転覆をはかった They *plotted* to overthrow the government.

❷【便宜を】
人に便宜をはかる *give* a person *facilities*; *accommodate* a person
❸【会議に】bring* up, broach [他], refer [他]; (意見を聞く) ask *a person's* opinion; (相談する) consult [他]
私たちはその問題を会議にはかった We *brought up* the problem at the meeting.
それについては上司にはかってみます I'll *ask* my boss's *opinion* about it.
❹【だます】trick [他], deceive [他], take* in
私は自分がはかられていたことが分かった I realized that I *had been tricked*.

はがれる 剥がれる come* [peel] off ∥ラベルはきれいにはがれた The sticker *peeled off* cleanly. / そのポスターがはがれかかっていた The poster *was coming off*.

バカンス ⚠vacation [C], holidays (❖日本語はフランス語の vacance から)

はき[1] 破棄 (取り消し) cancellation [U]; (法律・契約などの) annulment [U], 《公式的》abrogation [U]; (約束・協定などの) breach [U] ──破棄する cancel [他]; annul [他], 《公式的》abrogate [他]; break* [他] ∥契約を破棄する *cancel* [*annul*] a contract / 彼は彼女との婚約を破棄した He *has broken* (*off*) his engagement to her.
◆高等裁判所は地方裁判所の判決を破棄した The high court *set aside* the district court's decision.

はき[2] 覇気 (意気込み) spirit [U]; (野心・野望) ambition [U] ∥彼は覇気がない He *lacks* [*has no*] *spirit*. / 彼は覇気がある He *is a man of spirit*./ He *is full of ambition*.

はぎ 萩 bush clover [C]

はきけ 吐き気 nausea [C], sickness [C]
◆吐き気がする *feel sick* [*nauseous*] / 彼女はその話を聞いて吐き気がした The story *made* her *sick*.

はきごこち 履き心地 この靴はとても履き心地がよい These shoes *are* very *comfortable*.

はぎしり 歯軋り 彼は睡眠中歯ぎしりをすることがある He sometimes *grinds his teeth* in his sleep. / 彼女は試合に負けたとき, 歯ぎしりして悔しがった She *gnashed her teeth* with vexation when she lost the game. (❖gnash *one's* teeth は「怒り・悔しさなどで歯ぎしりする」の意味)

はきすてる 吐き捨てる 「出ていけ」と彼は私に吐き捨てるように言った "Get away," he *spat* (*out*) at me.

はきだす 吐き出す (つば・血などを) spit* (out); (煙などを) give* out, emit [他] ∥彼女は桃の種を吐き出した She *spat* (*out*) the peach pit.
◆息を吐き出す *breathe out* / 彼女に悩みを全部吐き出してすっきりした I felt refreshed after I *unburdened myself* to her.

はきだめ 掃き溜め garbage heap [C], rubbish heap [C]
[ことわざ] はきだめに鶴(つる) A jewel in a dunghill. (→家畜のふんの山に宝石)

はきちがえる 履き違える ❶【履き物を】(他人の物と) put* on another person's shoes by mistake; (左右を) put *one's* shoes on the wrong feet
❷【誤解する】misunderstand* [他]; (…を～ととり違える) take* [mistake*] ... for ～ ∥彼は個人主義の意味をはき違えている He *misunderstands* what individualism means. / 彼女は自由と無責任とをはき違えている She *mistakes* liberty *for* irresponsibility.

はぎとる 剝ぎ取る (無理に) tear* [他]; (衣服・皮を) strip off ∥彼女はその雑誌から数ページをはぎ取った She *tore* a few pages *from* the magazine. / 彼は壁からポスターをはぎ取った He *tore* a poster *off* the wall.

はきはき(と) (きびきび) briskly; (はっきり) clearly; (活気のある様子で) spiritedly ──はきはきした brisk; clear; spirited; (意見を率直に言う) outspoken ∥彼は先生の質問にはきはきと答えた He answered his teacher's question *briskly* [*clearly*]. / 彼女ははきはきものを言う人だ She is *outspoken* in her remarks.

はきもの 履物 (靴) shoes; (総称) footwear [U], footgear [U]

はきゅう 波及 ──波及する (及ぶ) spread* [自], extend [自]; (影響を与える) affect [他], influence [他] ∥株価暴落の影響は世界中に波及した The influence of the stock prices' sharp fall *spread* throughout the world.
∥波及効果 a ripple effect

バキュームカー ⚠honey truck [C], a tank truck with a vacuum hose for collecting night soil

はきょく 破局 (最後) end [C]; (悲劇的な結末) catastrophe [C]; (崩壊) collapse [C]; (仲違(たが)い) breakup [C] ∥かろうじて破局は避けられた *A catastrophe* was narrowly averted. / 汚職事件が会社を破局に導いた The corruption case *brought catastrophe* to the firm.
◆彼らの結婚生活は破局を迎えた Their married life *ended in failure*.

はぎれ 歯切れ 歯切れの悪い(→あいまいな)答え an *ambiguous* answer / 彼の話し方は歯切れがいい He has a *clear and crisp* way of speaking./ He talks *crisply*.

はく[1] 吐く
❶【吐き出す】(つば・血などを) spit* [他] [自]; (嘔吐(おうと)する) vomit [自] [他]
路上につばを吐く *spit* on the road
彼は食べた物を全部吐いた He *vomited* [《口語的》*threw up*] everything he had eaten.
◆私は吐きそうだ I *feel sick* [*nausea*].
❷【煙・息などを】(煙を) give* out, emit [他]; (息を) breathe out
工場の煙突が煙を吐いていた The factory chimney *was* 「*giving out* [*emitting*] smoke.
ゆっくり息を吐いて *Breathe out* slowly.
❸【言葉・考えなどを】
彼は仕事に関しては決して弱音を吐かなかった He *never complained* about his work.
その容疑者は警官に悪口雑言を吐いた The suspect *cursed* at the policeman.

彼は本音を吐いた(→本心を明かした) He *revealed his real intentions.*

はく[2] 履く (身につける) put* on; (身につけている) wear* [他], have* ... on
靴下を履く *put on one's* socks
背が高く見えるよう彼女はハイヒールを履いていた She *wore* high heels so that she could look taller.
その女の子は赤いスカートをはいていた The girl *had* a red skirt *on.*
◆彼は新しい靴を履いて出かけた He went out *in* [*wearing*] his new shoes.
💬「この靴いいなあ」「履いてみたらどう?」 "These shoes look nice." "Why don't you *try* them *on?*"

はく[3] 掃く sweep* [他][自]; (はけで) brush [他]
ほうきで掃く *sweep* with a broom
彼女は歩道を掃いている She *is sweeping* the path.
◆彼は裏庭の落ち葉を掃き集めた He *raked up* the fallen leaves in the backyard.
[慣用表現] 彼には掃いて捨てるほど(→使い切れないほど)お金がある He has *more* money *than he can spend.* / こんな小説は掃いて捨てるほどある Novels like this one are *a dime a dozen.* (❖a dime a dozen は「ありあまるほどある, ありふれた」の意味)

はく[4] 箔 foil [U], leaf [U] // 金箔 gold *foil* [*leaf*] / アルミ箔 aluminum *foil*
◆彼は学者としてのはくがついた He *has gained prestige* [*a reputation*] as a scholar.

-はく -泊 1泊旅行 an *overnight* trip / 3泊4日の旅行に行く take a *four-day* trip / 我々は友人の家に1泊した We *stopped overnight* at our friend's house. / 1泊いくらですか How much is *an overnight stay?* / このホテルは1泊2食つきで1万5千円だ The charges at this hotel are 15,000 yen *a night with* [*including*] *two meals.*

はぐ 剝ぐ (無理に) tear* [他]; (衣服・皮を) strip [他] // 壁からポスターをはぐ *tear* the poster *off* [*from*] the wall / 木の皮をはぐ *strip* bark *off* wood

バグ 〖コンピュータ〗 bug [C] // バグを見つける find *a bug* / このソフトにはいくつかバグがある This software has some *bugs.*
◆プログラムのバグをとる *debug* a program

はくあ 白亜 白亜の殿堂 a *white* hall ‖白亜紀 the Cretaceous (period)

はくあい 博愛 (人間に対する愛) love of [for] people [humankind], philanthropy [U]; (慈善) charity [U] ‖博愛主義 philanthropism / 博愛主義者 a philanthropist

はくい 白衣 white robe [C]; (医者などの) white coat [apron] [C]
◆白衣の天使 *a nurse* [*an angel*] *in white*

ばくおん 爆音 (爆発音) explosion [C]; (飛行機などの) roar [C] // 遠くで爆音が聞こえた I heard *an explosion* in the distance. / ジャンボジェット機は爆音を立てて飛び立った The jumbo jet took off *with a roar.*

ばくが 麦芽 malt [U]
‖麦芽糖 malt sugar, maltose

はくがい 迫害 persecution [U] ―迫害する persecute [他] // 彼らは信仰を理由にずっと迫害されてきた They *have been persecuted* for their beliefs.
‖迫害者 a persecutor

はくがく 博学 wide [broad] knowledge [U], great [extensive] learning [U] ―博学な learned [lə́ːrnid] // 博学な人 a person *of great* [*extensive*] *learning*

はくがんし 白眼視 ―白眼視する (冷たい目で見る) look at ... coldly, look askance at ...

はぐき 歯茎 gums // 歯を磨くと歯ぐきから血が出ますか Do *your gums* bleed when you brush your teeth?

はぐくむ 育む (子供を育てる) bring* up; (技能・心身を養う) cultivate [他] // 道徳心を育む *cultivate* the moral sense

ばくげき 爆撃 bombing [C] [U], bombardment [C] [U] ―爆撃する bomb [他], bombard [他] // その爆撃で町全体が燃え上がった The *bombing* set the whole town ablaze. / その町は敵の爆撃を受けた The city *was bombed* by the enemy. ‖爆撃機 a bomber

はくさい 白菜 Chinese cabbage [C] [U]

はくし[1] 白紙 (白い紙) white paper [U]; (何も書いていない紙) blank paper [U] ―白紙の blank // 彼女の答案用紙は白紙だった Her answer sheet was *blank.*
◆この計画はいったん白紙に戻して立て直そう We should *wipe the slate clean* for this project and start over. / 夏の合宿を行うかどうかはまだ白紙の状態です Whether we will have a summer training camp or not *hasn't been decided* yet.
‖白紙委任 carte blanche [kɑ́ːrt blɑ́ːnʃ]

はくし[2] 博士 doctor [C] (《略語》Dr.) // スミス博士 *Dr.* Smith / 医学博士 *a Doctor* of Medicine (《略語》MD)
◆生物学の博士号を取る get *a Ph.D.* in biology (❖Ph. D. は Doctor of Philosophy の略語で「博士・博士号」の意味. [píːèitʃdíː] と読む)
‖博士課程 a doctoral course / 博士論文 a doctoral dissertation [thesis]

はくしき 博識 ―博識な learned [lə́ːrnid] // 博識な教授 a *learned* professor

はくしゃ 拍車 spur [C] ◆科学技術の発達は環境破壊に拍車をかけている The development of technology *has quickened* environmental destruction.

はくしゃく 伯爵 (英国の) earl [C]; (英国以外の) count [C] 《しばしば Count》 ◆伯爵夫人 *a countess* (❖英国でもこのようにいう)

はくじゃく 薄弱 ―薄弱な (弱い) weak, feeble; (根拠が) invalid, flimsy // 意志が薄弱である have a *weak* will; be *weak*-willed / 根拠の薄弱な主張 an *invalid* claim

はくしゅ 拍手 clapping [U], clap [C]; (拍手かっさい) applause [U], ovation [C] ―拍手する clap (*one's* hands); applaud [他][自] // 大きな拍手 loud *applause* / 彼を拍手で迎える greet him *with applause* / 我々はその役者に拍手を送った We *applauded* the actor.

は

はくしょ 白書 white paper [book] [C] //経済白書 *an economic white paper*

はくじょう[1] 白状 confession [C] [U] ―白状する confess [他] [自], make* a confession; (認める) admit [他] [自] //彼は罪を洗いざらい白状した He *made a* full *confession* of his crimes. / 彼は私の時計を盗んだことを白状した He *confessed* that he had stolen my watch. ◆白状しろ *Out with it*!/ *Spit it out*!

はくじょう[2] 薄情 ―薄情な (冷淡な) cold, cold-hearted, heartless; (不親切な) unkind, unfriendly //薄情な男 a *cold-hearted* [*heartless*] man; a man *with a cold heart* / 手伝ってくれないなんて彼らも薄情だね It's *heartless* of them not to help us. / そんな薄情なこと言うなよ Don't say such *heartless* things.

ばくしょう 爆笑 a burst [roar] of laughter ―爆笑する burst* into laughter, roar with laughter //私の冗談を聞いて彼らは爆笑した They *burst into laughter* when they heard my joke.

はくしょく 白色 ‖白色光 white light / 白色人種 the white race

はくしょん (くしゃみの音) ahchoo [ɑːtʃúː], achoo [ətʃúː], 《英》atishoo [ətíʃuː]

はくしん 迫真 ―迫真の realistic, vivid //彼女の迫真の演技は観客を大いに感動させた Her *realistic performance* made a deep impression on the audience.

はくじん 白人 white [C], white person [C]; (総称) the white race

ばくしん 驀進 彼女は出世街道をばく進している She *is on the highroad* to promotion. (❖the highroad は「(ある状態へ至る)確実な道」の意味)

ばくしんち 爆心地 the center of the explosion

はくする 博する win* [他], gain [他], earn [他] ➔える //彼女はピアニストとしての世界的な名声を博した She *won* [*gained*] *a* world-wide *reputation* as a pianist. / 彼の新曲は若者の間で人気を博している His new song *has won popularity* among young people.

はくせい 剝製 剝製の鳥 a *stuffed* bird / クマを剝製にする *stuff* a bear

はくせん 白線 white line [C] //白線の内側にお下がりください Please step [stay, keep] behind *the white line*.

ばくぜん 漠然 ―漠然とした (はっきりしない) vague; (ぼんやりとした) dim; (大ざっぱな) general ―漠然と vaguely //漠然とした考え a *vague* idea / 漠然とした言い方をする speak in *general* terms / 私は自分の将来に漠然とした不安を感じている I feel 「*vague* anxiety [*vaguely* anxious] about my future. / 当時のことは漠然とした記憶しかない I have only *vague* [*dim*] memories of those days.

ばくだい 莫大 ―莫大な huge, vast, enormous //莫大な額のお金 a *huge* [an *enormous*] amount of money / 親類から莫大な財産を相続する inherit a *vast* fortune from *one's* relative

はくだつ 剝奪 deprivation [U] ―剝奪する deprive [他] //彼は政治的権利を剝奪された He *was deprived of* his political rights.

ばくだん 爆弾 bomb [bám] [C]
爆弾を投下する drop *a bomb* / 爆弾を爆発させる set off *a bomb*
車に仕掛けられた爆弾が爆発した *The bomb* in the car exploded.
飛行機に時限爆弾が仕掛けられた *A time bomb* was planted in the airplane.
◆会議の席上彼から爆弾発言があった He dropped *his bombshell* at the meeting.
‖原子爆弾 an atomic bomb / 水素爆弾 a hydrogen bomb / 中性子爆弾 a neutron bomb

はくち 白痴 (人) idiot [C]; (状態) idiocy [U] ―白痴の idiotic

ばくち 博打 gambling [U] //彼はばくちで全財産を失った He lost all his fortune by *gambling*. ◆大ばくちを打つ (→大きな危険を冒す) *take* [*run*] *great risk* / おじはばくちを打つ(→賭(か)け事をする)のが好きだ My uncle likes to *gamble*.
‖ばくち打ち a gambler

ばくちく 爆竹 firecracker [C], cracker [C], squib [C] //爆竹を鳴らす explode [set off] *firecrackers*

はくちず 白地図 blank map [C]

はくちゅう[1] 白昼 その犯罪は白昼堂々と行われた The crime was carried out *in broad* [*full*] *daylight*. ‖白昼強盗 daylight robbery / 白昼夢 a daydream

はくちゅう[2] 伯仲 両チームの実力は伯仲している The two teams *are almost* [*nearly*] *equal* in ability.

はくちょう 白鳥 swan [C]; (ひな) cygnet [C] ‖白鳥座〔天文〕the Swan, Cygnus

ぱくっ ➔ぱくり

ぱくつく (がつがつ食べる) devour [他], gobble [他] [自]; (むしゃむしゃ食べる) munch [他] [自] //ハンバーガーをぱくつく *munch* (*on*) a hamburger

バクテリア bacteria (❖bacterium の複数形)

はくないしょう 白内障〔医学〕cataract [C] [U] //白内障の手術をする remove *a cataract* / 彼は左目が白内障になった He got *a cataract* in his left eye.

はくねつ 白熱 ―白熱した heated; (興奮させる) exciting //白熱した議論になる get into a *heated* argument
◆彼らの討論はしだいに白熱してきた Their debate *has become hotter and hotter*.
‖白熱電球 an incandescent lamp

ばくは 爆破 blowing up [U], blast [U] ―爆破する blow* up, blast [他] //彼らはその岩を爆破した They *blasted* the rock.

バグパイプ ⚠bagpipes

ぱくぱく 金魚は口をぱくぱくさせていた The goldfish *was opening and closing its mouth*. / その犬はえさをぱくぱく食べた The dog *munched* (*on*) its food.

はくはつ 白髪 white [gray] hair [U] ―白髪の white-haired //白髪の男性 a man *with*

は

white [gray] hair; a white-haired man

ばくはつ 爆発 explosion C C; (火山の) eruption C C ━━爆発する explode ⓐ; erupt ⓐ ━━爆発的な explosive
▸ガス爆発 a gas explosion / 《略語》核爆発 a nuclear explosion / 火山の爆発 a volcanic eruption / 怒りの爆発 an explosion of anger
▸石油化学工場で大爆発が起こった There was a tremendous explosion at the petrochemical plant.
▸ビルの中で爆弾が爆発した A bomb exploded inside the building.
▸その火山は3年前に爆発した The volcano erupted three years ago.
▸彼の言葉を聞いて彼女は怒りを爆発させた Hearing what he said, she exploded with anger.
‖爆発音 an explosion / 爆発物 an explosive (substance) / 人口爆発 a population explosion

はくひょう¹ 白票 (白紙の票) blank ballot [vote] C; (賛成票) white ballot C ▸白票を投じる cast a blank ballot [vote]

はくひょう² 薄氷 ▸薄氷を踏む思いである be (skating) on thin ice

ばくふ¹ 幕府 the shogunate ‖徳川幕府 the Tokugawa shogunate

ばくふ² 瀑布 waterfall ➡たき(滝)

ばくふう 爆風 a blast (from an explosion) ▸その爆風で5人が軽いけがをした Five people were slightly injured in the blast.

はくぶつがく 博物学 natural history U ‖博物学者 a naturalist, a natural historian

はくぶつかん 博物館 museum C ‖科学博物館 a science museum / 民族博物館 an ethnographic museum / 私たちはきのう大英博物館を見学した We visited the British Museum yesterday.

はくぼ 薄暮 dusk U, twilight U ➡ゆうべ, ゆうぐれ

はくぼく 白墨 chalk U ➡チョーク

はくまい 白米 polished rice

ばくまつ 幕末 (江戸幕府の末期) the last days of the Tokugawa shogunate

ばくやく 爆薬 explosive C C ▸その古いビルを取りこわすのに爆薬が使われた They used explosives to tear down the old building.

はくらい 舶来 ━━舶来の (外国製の) foreign-made; (輸入された) imported ‖舶来品 a foreign-made [an imported] article

はぐらかす dodge ⓔ, sidestep ⓔ ▸彼は私の質問をはぐらかした He dodged [sidestepped] my question. / (→答えるのを避けた) He avoided answering my question.

はくらんかい 博覧会 exhibition C; (大規模な) exposition C (《略語》expo.); (物産展・見本市) fair C ▸国際博覧会が来年当市で開かれる A world [An international] exposition is to be held in this city next year. / 1970年の大阪万国博覧会には77か国が参加した Seventy-seven countries attended the Osaka Exposition in 1970.
‖博覧会場 an exhibition [exposition] ground, a fairground

ばくり ▸犬は肉片にばくりとかみついた The dog snapped at the piece of meat. / 傷口がばくりと口をあけた The wound gaped [split open].

はくりたばい 薄利多売 small profits and quick returns

はくりょく 迫力 power U, 《口語的》punch U ▸彼の演説は迫力に欠けた His speech lacked power [punch]. ◆彼らのライブ演奏は非常に迫力があった Their live performance was very powerful [(→強い印象を与えた) impressive]. / きのうの試合は迫力満点だった Yesterday's game was terribly exciting.

はぐるま 歯車 gear C, cogwheel C ‖歯車がうまくかみ合っている The gears [cogs] mesh well. (❖cog は歯車の「歯」) ◆その事件以来、2人の歯車は狂ってしまった The two of them have not meshed since the incident. / 君は組織の中の一歯車に甘んじるのか Are you content to be a cog in the machine?

はぐれる stray ⓐ; (見失う) lose* sight of ... ▸女の子は人込みの中で母親とはぐれてしまった The little girl 「strayed from [lost sight of]」 her mother in the crowd.
◆はぐれないように手をつないでいてね Hold my hand so that you won't get lost.

ばくろ 暴露 exposure U C, disclosure C ━━暴露する expose ⓔ, disclose ⓔ, reveal ⓔ, bring* ... to light ▸秘密を暴露する expose [disclose] a secret / 市当局の腐敗は新聞に暴露された Corruption in the city hall was exposed by [in] the press. / その本は彼女がスパイだったことを暴露している The book discloses that she was a spy.

はけ 刷毛 brush C ▸彼ははけにペンキをたっぷりつけた He put plenty of paint on his brush. ◆パン生地に卵黄をはけで塗りなさい Brush the dough with yolk.

はげ 禿げ (はげていること) baldness U; (部分) bald spot C; (人) bald(-headed) person C ━━はげた bald ➡はげる(禿げる) ▸彼の後頭部にははげがある He has a bald spot on the back of his head. / 彼ははげを隠すためにいつも帽子をかぶっている He always wears a hat to cover his baldness. / 彼は若はげだ He is prematurely bald.

はげあたま 禿げ頭 bald head C

はけぐち 捌け口 (液体・気体・感情などの) outlet C, vent C ▸水のはけ口 an outlet for water / 感情のはけ口 an outlet for one's feelings [emotions] / 子供たちはエネルギーのはけ口を必要としている The children need outlets for their energy.

はげしい 激しい

(勢いが強い) violent; (厳しい) severe, hard; (はなはだしい) intense, heavy, extreme ━━激しく violently; severely; hard; intensely, heavily
▸激しい雨 a violent [heavy] rain / 激しい風 a violent [strong] wind / 激しい地震 a violent [severe, strong] earthquake / 激しい頭痛 a

コミュニケーションスキル —励ます—
①「がんばって」と言いたいとき

(A) I'm afraid I'm not up to this.
–No! You're doing fine! [You can do it!]
こんなこと, 僕には無理だよ.—何言ってるんだ. 君ならできるさ.

(B) Just another kilometer to the finish line! Stick to it! [《米口語的》Hang in there!]
ゴールまであと1キロだ. がんばれ!

(C) Don't give up! Just keep going! [Keep at it!; 《米口語的》Hang in there!]
あきらめちゃだめだ! がんばれ!

(D) Keep your chin up!
へこたれるな! [がんばれ!]

(E) Good luck!
がんばってね!

☞ 人を「がんばれ」と励ます場合, (A)～(C)のような表現をよく用いる. (A)は「君ならできる」と暗示をかけて, 相手に自信を与える表現. (B), (C)は stick to ...(…をやり通す), keep at ...(ペースなどを守る), hang in there(踏みとどまる)のような「ねばり強さ」を強調した表現である. (E)は「幸運を祈る」が元の意味で, 試験を受ける友達などを励ますときなどによく使われる.

☞ 英米では chin(あご)を「気力」の象徴と考える傾向がある. (D)の keep one's chin up は「あごを上げたままにする」→「へこたれずにがんばる」という発想から生まれた表現.

②相手を安心させたり, 促したりする表現

(A) Don't worry. She'll be back soon.
大丈夫だよ. 彼女はすぐに帰ってくるよ.

(B) There, (there,) you're a good boy [girl].
さあ, いい子ね.

(C) Hey, come on, Jack, you can tell me. What happened to you?
さあ, ジャック, 話してごらん. 何があったの.

(D) (Just) Pull yourself together. It's not like you to be so depressed.
さあ, 元気を出して. そんなに落ち込んだりして, 君らしくないぞ.

☞ (A)の Don't worry. は「心配しないで, 気にするな」の意味で, 頻繁に用いられる表現. この後に Everything will be fine [okay]. (大丈夫, うまくいくよ)などの励ましの言葉を続けていうことが多い.

☞ (B)は, 泣いている子供などを大人がなだめる言葉. 文頭の There, (there)は「よしよし」に相当する.

☞ (C)の come on は, 態度がはっきりしない相手に行動や決断を促す表現で, 親しい者どうしの会話でよく使われる.

☞ (D)の pull *oneself* together は「元気を出す, しっかりする」の意味. 落ち込んでいる相手を励ます決まった言い方.

---

violent [severe] headache
彼女は気性が激しい She has a *violent* [*fiery*] temper.
突然背中に激しい痛みを覚えた Suddenly I felt a *severe* pain in my back.
私の提案は激しい反対にあった My proposal met *intense* [*heavy, keen*] opposition.
昨夜激しい雨が降った It rained *heavily* [*hard*] last night.
その知事は激しく非難された The governor was criticized *intensely*.
◆その道路は交通が激しい That road *is busy with traffic.* / この業界では競争が激しい There is *keen* competition in this business. / 私は彼と激しく優勝を争った I competed *keenly* with him for the championship. / 我々はそのことについて激しく議論した We had a *heated* [*bitter*] argument about the matter.

バケツ bucket ⓒ, 《主に米》pail ⓒ / バケツに水をくむ fill *a bucket* [*pail*] with water / バケツ1杯の水 *a bucket(ful)* [*pail(ful)*] *of* water

慣用表現 バケツをひっくり返したような雨だった The rain came down [It rained] *in buckets*.

ばけのかわ 化けの皮 (正体を隠す仮面) mask ⓒ / あいつの化けの皮をはいでやる I will "rip away his *mask* [unmask him].
◆今にあの偽善者も化けの皮がはがれるさ That hypocrite will *show his true character* [*colors*] before long.

はげまし 励まし encouragement Ⓤⓒ / 励ましの言葉 words of *encouragement* / あなたの励ましがなければとうにあきらめていただろう Without your *encouragement*, I would have given up long ago.

はげます 励ます (元気づける) cheer up; (勇気・希望を与える) encourage ⓣ
⇒ コミュニケーションスキル
医師は患者を励ました The doctor *cheered up* the patient.
私は彼女の言葉に励まされた I *was encouraged* by her words.
私はもう一度やってみるよう彼を励ました I *encouraged* him *to* try again.

はげみ 励み (励ますもの) encouragement Ⓤⓒ; (刺激) incentive Ⓤⓒ / あなたの手紙は私にとって大きな励みになりました Your letter was *a great encouragement* to me. / 彼の大学合格が私の勉強の励みになった His success in the college entrance examination gave me *an incentive* "to study [for studying].

はげむ 励む 仕事に励む work hard / 彼女は車を買うために貯蓄に励んでいる She *is saving money diligently* to buy a car. / 彼は日夜勉学に励んだ He *studied very hard* day and night.

ばけもの 化け物 (怪物) monster ⓒ; (幽霊) ghost ⓒ ⇒ おばけ / 魔女は王女を恐ろしい化け物に変えてしまった The witch changed the princess into *a frightening monster*.

はげやま

はげやま 禿げ山 bare [bald] mountain ⓒ; (木のない山) treeless mountain ⓒ

はける 捌ける (水などが) drain ⓐ; (商品が) sell* out ∥大水はすぐにはけるだろう The flood will soon *drain away*. / 在庫は1日ではけた The stock *sold out* in a day.

はげる¹ 禿げる go* [get*] bald, lose* *one's* hair ∥彼ははげてきた He *is going* [*getting*] *bald*. / 父は頭のてっぺんがはげている My father *is bald* on the top of the head.

はげる² 剥げる (塗料などが落ちる) peel off, come* off; (色があせる) fade ⓐ ∥塀のペンキがはげかけている The paint *is peeling off* (from) the fence.

ばける 化ける (姿を変える) change [turn] *oneself* into ..., take* the shape [form] of ...; (変装する) disguise *oneself* as ... ∥魔女は猫に化けた The witch *changed herself into* a cat.

はけん¹ 派遣 dispatch Ⓤ ――派遣する send* ⓐ, (公式的) dispatch ⓐ ∥紛争地域に特派員を派遣する dispatch a correspondent to the trouble spot / 政府はただちに救助隊を被災地に派遣した The government *sent* a rescue team to the disaster area immediately.
∥派遣社員 a temp / 人材派遣会社 a temporary employment agency, a temp agency

はけん² 覇権 hegemony Ⓤ; (支配権) supremacy Ⓤ, dominance Ⓤ ∥覇権を握る hold *hegemony* [*supremacy*] / 彼らは日本市場での覇権を争っている They are struggling for *supremacy* in the Japanese market.

ばけん 馬券 a betting ticket (on a horse) ∥馬券売場 a betting ticket office; (私設の) a betting shop

はこ 箱

box ⓒ; case ⓒ; chest ⓒ; (米) pack ⓒ, (英) packet ⓒ; carton ⓒ

> box: 四角形の「箱」を表す最も一般的な語. ふつうふた付きの物を指す.
> case: 特定の物を入れるための, いろいろな形の容器.
> chest: 保管用の大型で丈夫な箱.
> pack, packet: たばこの箱など包装用の小型の箱.
> carton: 牛乳などを入れる, 紙またはプラスチック製の箱.

木[紙, 段ボール, プラスチック]の箱 a wooden [paper, cardboard, plastic] *box* / リンゴを箱で買う buy apples *by the case*

彼女は缶詰を箱に詰めた She packed *a box* with canned food. / She packed canned food into *a box*.

その箱のふたがどこかへ行ってしまった The *box* has lost its top.

その箱には何が入っているのですか What's in the *box*? / What does the *box* contain?

1日にたばこを2箱吸うのは吸いすぎだ Smoking two *packs* of cigarettes a day is too much.

◆石油はその国のドル箱(→金を生み出すもの)である Oil is a 「*gold mine* [*moneymaker*] for the country.
∥空き箱 an empty box / 茶箱 a tea chest / 宝石箱 a jewelry box [case]

はごいた 羽子板 a *hagoita*, a (Japanese) battledore (❖battledore はバドミントンの前身の羽根つき遊びで使われたラケットのこと. なお, 羽根つきの羽根は shuttlecock)

はこいりむすめ 箱入り娘 彼女は箱入り娘だ(→過保護に育てられてきた) She *has been brought up too carefully by her parents*. / She *has been overprotected by her parents*.

はごたえ 歯応え この肉は歯ごたえがある[ない] This meat *is tough* [*too tender*].

はこづめ 箱詰め ――箱詰めする pack ... in a box [case] ∥オレンジを箱詰めする *pack* oranges *in a box*; *pack* a box *with* oranges / 箱詰めのリンゴ apples *packed in a box*; *boxed apples*

はこにわ 箱庭 miniature garden ⓒ

はこび 運び その事業は遠からず完成の運びとなる(→完成するだろう) The project will *be completed* before long. / 我々の計画は実現の運びとなった(→実現することになった) We've *decided to realize* our plan. / (→実現した) Our plan *was realized*. / 彼らは試合運びがうまかった[まずかった] They *played* well [badly] *in the game*.

はこびこむ 運び込む 彼らは居間にソファーを運び込んだ They *carried* the sofa *into* the living room.

はこぶ 運ぶ

❶ (移動させる) carry ⓐ, (主に乗り物で) (公式的) convey ⓐ, (輸送する) transport ⓐ

ベッドを部屋の中[外]に運ぶ *carry* the bed *into* [*out of*] the room

彼らは大きな箱を肩にかついで運んでいた They *were carrying* big boxes on their shoulders.

彼らはけがをした女性を車で病院に運んだ They *carried* [*took*] the injured woman to the hospital by car.

そのトラックは下関から大阪まで魚を運んでいる The truck *transports* [*conveys*] fish from Shimonoseki to Osaka.

◆ウェーターが料理をテーブルに運んできた A waiter *brought* the food to the table.

❷ (物事が進行する) go* ⓐ, (❖通例, 進行のしかたを表す副詞を伴う), progress ⓐ

万事うまく運んでいる Everything *is going well* [*all right*].

事は彼の思うようには運ばなかった Things *didn't go as he expected*.

はこぶね 箱舟 ノアの箱舟 Noah's Ark

はこべ(ら) chickweed Ⓤ

はこぼれ 刃毀れ a nick on [in] a blade

バザー bazaar ⓒ ∥バザーを開く give [hold] *a bazaar* / このリースは教会のバザーで買った I bought this wreath at [in] *the church bazaar*. / バザーの利益は小児病院に寄付される The profits from *the bazaar* will be given [donated] to the children's hospital.

||チャリティーバザー a charity bazaar
ハザードランプ hazard lights
はざかいき 端境期 the off-crop season, the months before the harvest time
ばさっと 雑誌がばさっと床に落ちた The magazine fell to the floor *with a thud*.
ばさばさ ばさばさの髪 *stiff and dry* hair / 棚から書類がばさばさと音を立てて落ちてきた The paper *rustled* as it fell from the shelf.
ばさばさ このパンはばさばさしている(→乾いていてまずい) This bread *is dry and tasteless*.
はざま 狭間 雲のはざまから太陽がのぞいている The sun is peeking out from *between* the clouds. / 彼は生死のはざまをさまよっている He is hanging by a thread *between* life and death.
はさまる 挟まる be put in [between] ..., get* caught in [between] ...; (しっかりはさまり込む) get stuck in [between] ... / そのちらしはきょうの新聞にはさまっていた The leaflet *was put in* today's paper. / かばんが電車のドアにはさまった My bag *got* [*was*] *caught in* the train door. / 何かが奥歯の間にはさまっている Something *is stuck in* [*between*] my back teeth.
◆ 1枚の木の葉が本の間にはさまっていた I found a leaf between the pages of the book.
はさみ 鋏 scissors; (つめ切りばさみなど) clippers; (木の剪定(せんてい)などに用いる) shears(◆以上いずれも数えるときは a pair of ... とする); (カニの) claw

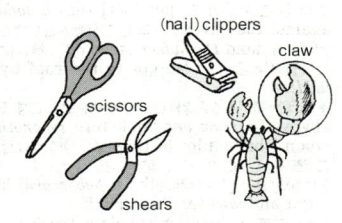

(nail) clippers
claw
scissors
shears

はさみで紙[布]を切る cut paper [cloth] with (a pair of) *scissors* / 袋をあけるのにはさみを使う use *scissors* to open a sack
このはさみはとてもよく切れる These *scissors* cut very well.
◆木をはさみで刈り込む *trim* a tree / 切符にはさみを入れる *punch* a ticket
||断ちばさみ(裁縫用の) sewing scissors / つめ切りばさみ (nail) clippers / 料理用はさみ kitchen scissors
はさみうち 挟み撃ち 敵をはさみ撃ちにする (→両側から攻撃する) *attack* the enemy *from* [*on*] *both sides*
はさみこむ 挟み込む put* ... in 〜, insert ⇒はさむ /書類にメモをはさみ込む *put* a memo *in* the papers

はさむ 挟む

(物と物の間に入れる) put* ... in [between] 〜; (差し込む) insert; (指などを) catch* ... in [between] ~
本にしおりをはさむ *put* a bookmark *between* the pages (of a book); *put* a bookmark *in* a book / 書類をファイルにはさむ *insert* papers *in* a file
ドアに指をはさんでしまった I「*caught* my finger [*had* my finger *caught*] *in* the door.
◆その家は2つの高いビルの間にはさまれている The house *is sandwiched between* two tall buildings. / この町は2本の川にはさまれている The city *is* [*lies*] *between* two rivers. / 銀行は通りをはさんで郵便局と向かい合っている (→通りの向かい側にある) The bank *is across the street from* the post office. / 彼らはテーブルをはさんで向かい合って座った They sat *across* the table *from* each other. / They sat *face to face* at the table. / 彼女は私たちの話に口をはさんだ She「*cut in on* [*interrupted*] our talk.
ばさりと 書類が机からばさりと落ちた The papers fell from the desk *with a thud*.
はさん 破産 bankruptcy ──破産する go* bankrupt; (口語的) go broke ||破産を宣告する declare *bankruptcy* / 彼は破産しかけている He *is going bankrupt*. / (→破産寸前である)He *is on the verge of bankruptcy*.

はし¹ 橋

bridge
瀬戸大橋 the Seto Ohashi *Bridge*(◆橋の名前にはこのように the が付くものと、London Bridge のように the が付かないものがある) / 川に橋をかける build [construct] a *bridge* across a river / 橋を渡る cross *a bridge* / 歩いて[車で]橋を渡る walk [drive] over *a bridge*
その川には市内で3つの橋がかかっている There are three *bridges* over the river in this city.
郵便局は橋を渡ってすぐです The post office is just over *the bridge*.
||橋げた a bridge girder / つり橋 a hanging bridge; (大きな) a suspension bridge / はね橋 a drawbridge

はし² 端

(細長い物の末端・先端) end; (周縁) edge; (側端) side; (隅) corner
⇒さき(先), すみ(隅), ふち(縁), へり
ページの端を折る *turn back the corner of* a page; *dog-ear* a page
ロープの一方の端をもう一方と結びなさい Tie [Join] one *end* of the rope to the other.
彼女はベンチの端に腰かけた She sat *at the end of* the bench.
彼はナプキンの端を破って自分の電話番号を書いた He tore *the edge* off his napkin and wrote down his phone number on it.
テーブルの端に頭をぶつけた I hit my head against *the edge* of the table.
トラックは道の端に止まった The truck pulled

over to *the side* of the road.
この街は端から端まで歩いても30分しかかからない
It'll take only 30 minutes to walk *from end to end* of this city.
◆この通りは端から端まで(→長さが)400メートルある *The length* of this street is 400 meters.

はし³ 箸 chopsticks(❖数えるときは a pair of ... とする) / ごはんをはしで食べる eat rice with *chopsticks*
◆彼は夕食に全くはしをつけなかった He *didn't eat* [*touch*] his dinner at all.
‖はし置き a chopstick rest
慣用表現 あいつははしにも棒にもかからないやつだ He is *a good-for-nothing*. / (→見込みがない)He is just *hopeless*. / 父ははしの上げ下ろしにもうるさい(→どんなことにもいちいち厳しい) My father is always strict about *everything*.

かしこまった席ではしを使うときには, 注意すべき点がいくつかあります. はしをなめる, はし置きを使わずにはしを食器に渡して置く, はしを持ったまま何を取るか迷う, 食べ物を突き刺す, などはすべて嫌われます. また大皿から自分の皿に料理を取り分ける際に, 自分のはしを使わなければならないときは, 反対側に持ちかえる配慮が必要です.
There are several dos and don'ts in using chopsticks on formal occasions. Licking chopsticks, resting them over bowls or plates instead of on a chopstick rest, holding the chopsticks above dishes while choosing what to eat, or stabbing food with chopsticks — these are all taboos. On the other hand, it is considered good manners to use the other end of one's chopsticks when one has to take food from a platter.

はじ 恥
shame ⓊⒸ (❖「恥ずべきこと[人]」の意味では a ~); (屈辱) humiliation ⓊⒸ; (不名誉) disgrace ⓊⒸ
困ったときに助けを求めるのは恥ではない There is no *shame* in asking for help when you are in trouble.
彼に間違いを指摘されて恥をかいた I *was「put to shame* [*humiliated*]」when he pointed out my mistakes.
彼は両親に恥をかかせた He *brought shame* [*disgrace*] *on* his parents.
あいつは恥知らずだ That guy *has no shame*. / That guy *is shameless*.
おまえはうちの恥さらしだ You're *a disgrace* [*shame*] *on* your family.
恥を知れ *Shame* on you!
◆彼は恥も外聞もなく(→世間体をかまわず)道の真ん中で泣きわめいた He wailed in the middle of the street *without caring about how he looked*. / 恥を知りなさい You should *be ashamed of yourself*. / 彼は恥を忍んで(→自尊心を抑えて)彼女に金を貸してくれるよう頼んだ He *swallowed his pride* and asked her to lend him some money.
ことわざ 聞くは一時の恥, 聞かぬは一生の恥 ⇒きく(聞く・聴く)

はしか 麻疹 《単数扱い》 ‖はしかにかかる catch [get] (*the*) *measles*

はしがき 端書き (序文) preface Ⓒ; (特に著者以外の人による) foreword Ⓒ

はじきだす 弾き出す この工程で不良品ははじき出される(→取り除かれる) Defective products *are eliminated* [*gotten rid of*] at this stage. / 我々は建築費を5,000万円とはじき出した(→計算して見積もった) We *calculated* [*estimated*] the construction cost at 50 million yen.

はじく 弾く (指で) flip 他; (水などを) repel 他 ‖上着についた虫をはじき飛ばす *flip* an insect from *one's* jacket / この布は水をはじく This cloth *repels* water. / (→防水加工されている)This cloth *is waterproof*.

はしくれ 端くれ 私だって画家のはしくれです I'm *a bit of* a painter.

はしけ 艀 (はしけ船) lighter Ⓒ; (平底荷船) barge Ⓒ

はじける 弾ける (口が開く) burst* [split*] open; (音を立てて開く) crack open, pop 自 ‖豆のさやがはじけた Pea-pods *have burst* [*split*] *open*. ◆その部屋で子供たちのはじけるような笑い声が上がった A *burst of laughter* rose from children in the room.

はしご 梯子 ladder Ⓒ ‖はしごを上る[降りる]「climb (up) [climb down] *a ladder* / 軒(㊀)にはしごをかける put [set] (up) *a ladder* against the eaves / はしごを動かないように押さえる hold *the ladder* steady / 彼ははしごで屋根に登った He got to the roof by *a ladder*.
◆私は時間があるときはいつも本屋をはしごする I always *go from one* bookstore *to another* when I have a lot of time. / ゆうべははしご酒をしてひどく酔っ払った I *went barhopping* [《英口語的》*on a pub-crawl*] last night and was terribly drunk.
‖はしご車 a (hook and) ladder truck / 縄ばしご a rope ladder / 避難ばしご a fire escape

はしたがね はした金 a small sum [amount] of money, 《俗語》chicken feed, 《米口語的》peanuts

はしたない (慎みのない) 《古風》immodest; (不作法な) improper ◆はしたないふるまいをする behave *improperly*

ばしっ (ばしっという音) whack Ⓒ, thwack Ⓒ ‖彼は馬の背中をむちでばしっと打った He「*gave* the horse *a whack* [*whacked* the horse] on the back with a whip.

ぱしっ (ぱしっという音) crack Ⓒ, snap Ⓒ
◆氷がぱしっと割れた The ice *cracked*.

ばじとうふう 馬耳東風 慣用表現 彼は私の警告を馬耳東風と聞き流した(→聞こうともしなかった) He *turned a deaf ear to* my warning.

はじまり 始まり beginning Ⓒ, start Ⓒ;

(起源) origin ©©; (原因) cause © ➡ はじめ ∥宇宙に始まりがあったかどうかはまだ答えが出ていない Whether the universe had *a beginning* or not is open to question. / 事の始まりは何だったのか What was *the cause*? / What *started* it?

ことわざ うそつきは泥棒の始まり ➡ うそつき

はじまる 始まる

begin*@; start@; open@; originate@

- begin: 一般的な語. 目的をもった行動や期間が始まることを強調する.
- start: begin と同様に使われるが, 単に行為や期間の始まりをいう.
- open: 会, 店などが開くことを表す.
- originate: 起源・原因を表す.

学校は 8 時 40 分に始まる School *begins* [*starts*] at eight forty.

会議は10時に始まった The meeting *started* at 10.

第 2 次世界大戦は1939年に始まった World War II *started* [(→勃発(ぼっぱつ)した) *broke out*] in 1939.

式典は市長のスピーチで始まった The ceremony *opened* with the mayor's speech.

その風習は中国で始まった The custom *originated* in China.

彼がいないと始まらない We *can't begin* if he's not here.

◆その祭りは平安時代初期に始まった (→さかのぼる) The festival *dates back to* the beginning of the Heian period. / 過去のことを悔やんでも始まらない (→利益がない) *There's no percentage* [*point*] in regretting the past. / 彼女の友達の悪口がまた始まった *There* she *goes again*, saying bad things about her friends. / ほらまた始まった *There* you *go again*!

はじめ 初め・始め

beginning ©, start ©; (会などの) opening ©©; (起源) origin ©©

年の初めに *at the beginning* of the year

何事も初めが肝心だ (→よい始まりはよい終わりを作る) *A good beginning* makes a good ending.

初めはクラスになじめなかった I couldn't get used to the class *in the beginning*.

私はその映画を初めから終わりまで見た I saw the movie *from beginning to end*.

私はその考えに初めから反対だった I was against the idea *from the start* [*beginning*].

◆15世紀の初めに (→初期に) *early* in the 15th century; *in the early part* of the 15th century / 初めは彼の話を信じなかった I didn't believe him *at first*. / 初めに彼に電話した I called him *first*. / 初めの 3 日間はとても忙しかった I was very busy during the *first three days*. / 初めから知っていた He knew who stole his bag *all along*. / 父をはじめ家族全員動物が好きだ My father *and* everyone else in my family likes animals.

はじめて 初めて

first, for the first time
——初めての first

生まれて初めて *for the first time* in *one's* life

初めて彼女に会ったのは 3 年前だった I *first* met her three years ago.

私は初めてテニスで彼に勝った I beat him at tennis *for the first time*.

彼の小説を読んだのはこれが初めてだ This is the *first* time I've read his novel.

日本はこれが初めてですか Is this your *first* visit to Japan?

◆きのうになって初めて彼女の結婚のことを知った *It was not until* yesterday *that* I knew of her marriage. / こんな美しい景色を見たのは初めてだ (→今までにない) I've *never* seen such a beautiful sight before.

はじめまして 初めまして

How do you do?, Nice [Glad] to meet you.

話法
How do you do?は改まった場面で用いる言い方で, やや堅苦しい印象を与える. 言われたほうも How do you do? と答える. Nice [Glad] to meet you.は一般的な言い方. それに対する返答は Nice [Glad] to meet you, too.などという. また, 改まった場面でなければ Hi! や Hello! ですますことも多い.

はじめる 始める

begin @, start @; (会・店などを) open @; (取りかかる) set* about ...

新しい事業を始める *start* [*open*] a new business

朝食後, 彼は仕事を始めた He *began* [*started, set about*] his work after breakfast.

彼女は 3 か月前にスペイン語を習い始めた She *began* [*started*] *to* learn Spanish three months ago. / She *began* [*started*] learning Spanish three months ago.

雨が降り始めたよ It's *beginning* [*starting*] *to* rain. (❖「…し始める」の意味で, begin, start が進行形のときは後に to *do* をとる)

10時に会議を始めます We *will open* the meeting at 10.

では始めましょう Now, *let's get started*.

◆何から始めましょうか (→最初に何をしましょうか) *What shall I do first* [*to begin with*]?

はしゃ 覇者 (優勝者) champion ©; (勝者) winner ©

ばしゃ 馬車 carriage ©; (大型の) coach © ∥2頭[4頭]立ての馬車 a *carriage* and 「a *pair* [*four*] ∥荷馬車 a cart / 幌(ほろ)馬車 a covered wagon

はしゃぐ 子供たちがパジャマではしゃぎ回っている (→飛び回っている) The children *are romping about* in pajamas. / 大学の入試に受かったからといって, はしゃぎすぎてはいけない (→浮かれ騒ぎすぎるな) *Don't kick up your heels too much* just because you passed the entrance exam for the university.

ばしゃばしゃ 子供たちはプールで水をばしゃばしゃするのが好きだ Children like to *splash*

in the pool.

パジャマ (上下で1組の) pajamas, 《英》pyjamas (✤数えるときはa pair of ... とする。また上着をtop, ズボンをbottomsという) ∥パジャマのズボン pajama bottoms (✤形容詞的に用いるときは単数形) / 彼女はパジャマのまま昼食をとった She had a lunch *with her pajamas on*. / 彼はパジャマで家を飛び出した He rushed out of the house in (his) *pajamas*.

ばじゅつ 馬術 (乗馬の技術) horsemanship ◯; (馬術競技) equestrian events

はしゅつじょ 派出所 (交番) police box ◯

ばしょ 場所

❶【所・位置】place ◯; (特定の地点) spot ◯; (位置・立地) location ◯; (置かれた場所) position ◯

会議の時間と場所 the time and *place* for the meeting

ここは彼が生まれた場所だ This is *the place* where he was born.

彼は隠れるのに適当な場所を探した He looked for *a* likely *place* to hide.

すべて元の場所に返しなさい Put everything back in *its place*.

場所を替わってくれませんか Can we switch *places*?

ここはフライフィッシングにいい場所だ This is *a* good [nice] *spot* for fly-fishing.

そのホテルはいい場所にある The hotel is in *a* good *location*.

私のいる場所からはその建物が見えない I can't see the building from my *position*.

◆その学校の場所を教えてください Please tell me *where* the school is. / 彼のいる場所を知っていますか (→彼がどこにいるか) Do you know *where* he is?

❷【空間】space ◯; (余地) room ◯

このテーブルは場所を取りすぎる This table takes up too much *space* [*room*].

私が座る場所はなかった There was no *room* for me to sit.

❸【相撲】tournament ◯

春場所ではだれが優勝するだろう Who will win *the spring grand tournament*?

はしょうふう 破傷風〔医学〕tetanus ◯,《口語的》lockjaw ◯

ばしょがら 場所柄 彼らは場所柄をわきまえずに大声でずっと笑っていた They kept on laughing loudly regardless of *where they were*. / 場所柄をわきまえなさい Remember *where you are*.

はしょる (すそを短く上げる) tuck in [up]; (短縮する) cut* [make*] ... short ∥スカートのすそをはしょる *tuck up* one's skirt / はしょって話せば *to make* [*cut*] *a long story short*; *in short*

はしら 柱

❶【垂直の材】pillar ◯; (装飾的な円柱) column ◯; (電柱など) pole ◯, post [póust] ◯

これらの大きな柱が屋根を支えている These big *pillars* support the roof.

彼らは2本の柱を立て、その間にロープを張った They put [set] up two *poles* and then stretched a rope between them.

❷【中心となる人・もの】mainstay ◯, pillar ◯ ∥一家の柱 [大黒柱] the mainstay [sole support, breadwinner] of the family / 彼はチームの柱である He is *the mainstay* of the team.

∥柱時計 a (wall) clock

はじらい 恥じらい (特に女性がつつましいこと) demureness ◯ ∥あの女の子たちには恥じらいというものが全くない Those girls are not *demure* at all. / 彼女は恥じらいを見せて(→恥ずかしそうに)笑った She smiled *shyly*.

はしらす 走らす run* ⦿◯; (車を) drive* ⦿◯ ∥彼は空港に車を走らせていた He *was driving* (his car) to the airport. / 彼は手紙に目を走らせた She *ran* (her eyes) over the letter. ◆彼は突然原稿用紙にペンを走らせた(→書き始めた) He suddenly *started writing* on the manuscript paper.

はしり 走り ❶【走ること】running ◯

◆ひと走りする take *a run*

❷【初物】走りの果物 (an) *early fruit* / 走りのカツオ the *first* bonito *of the season*

❸【先駆者】pioneer ◯, forerunner ◯ ∥彼はこの分野の走りだった He was *a pioneer* in this field.

はしりがき 走り書き hurried note ◯, scribble ◯, jottings ――走り書きする write* hurriedly, scribble ⦿, jot ⦿ ∥走り書きのメモ a *scribbled* note / 私は彼の電話番号を手帳に走り書きした I *scribbled* [*jotted*] his phone number down in the notebook.

はしりたかとび 走り高跳び the high jump ◆走り高跳びの選手 *a high jumper*

はしりづかい 走り使い ⇨つかいはしり

はしりはばとび 走り幅跳び the running long jump,《米》the running broad jump ∥亮司は走り幅跳びで7メートル跳んだ Ryoji jumped seven meters in *the running long jump*. ◆走り幅跳びの選手 *a long* [《米》*broad*] *jumper*

はしりまわる 走り回る run* about [around] ∥犬は広々とした野原を走り回った The dogs *ran around* in the open field.

はしりよみ 走り読み ――走り読みする (急いで読む) read* hurriedly; (目を通す) run* (one's eye(s)) over ... ∥本を走り読みする *read* a book *hurriedly*

はしる 走る

❶【人・動物が】run* ⦿◯; (急いで) dash ⦿, rush ⦿, make* a rush; (ゆっくり) jog ⦿

彼はグラウンドを走っている He *is running* in the playground.

私たちは駅まで走った We *ran* to the station.

学校まで走って5分です It takes five minutes to *run* to school.

彼は全力で走った He *ran* as fast as 「he could [possible].

みんながドアの方へ走った Everyone *rushed* [*made a rush*] for the door.

彼は100メートルを11秒で走れる He *can run*

100 meters in 11 seconds.
犬が私に向かって走ってきた A dog *came running* toward me.
彼はその場から走り去った He *ran「away* from there [*off*].
◆彼は走るのが速い He *is a fast runner*.
❷【乗り物が】run* ⓐ, go* ⓐ, travel ⓐ
地下鉄は5分おきに走っている The subway *runs* every five minutes.
あの車はすごいスピードで走っている That car *is traveling* [*going, moving*] very fast.
この列車は今時速100キロで走っている This train *is* now *going* (at) 100 kilometers an hour.
スポーツカーが何台か走り過ぎていった A few sports cars *ran by* [*past*].
❸【道路・川などが】run* ⓐ
この道路は能登半島の先端まで走っている This road *runs* to the tip of the Noto Peninsula.
鉄道は川と平行に走っている The railroad *runs* parallel to the river.
❹【その他】
極端に走る *go to extremes* / 感情に走る *act on one's emotion*
彼は非行に走った He *became delinquent*.
背筋に寒気が走った Chills *ran up* my spine.
ことわざ 悪事千里を走る ⇒ あくじ

はじる 恥じる be [feel*] ashamed //彼は自分自身のばかなふるまいを恥じた He *was ashamed of* his own silly conduct. / 彼らは己(おのれ)を恥じるべきだ They should *be ashamed of* themselves.
◆生徒会長の名に恥じぬよう一生懸命がんばります I'll do my best *to live up to the title of* student council president.

はしわたし 橋渡し (仲介) mediation ⓤ; (仲介者) mediator ⓒ ◆日本はその2国間の平和の橋渡しをした Japan *mediated* peace *between* the two countries.

はす¹ 斜 ——はすに slantwise, askew, obliquely ⇒ ななめ ◆彼女の家はコンビニのはす向かいにある Her house is *diagonally opposite* [*across from*] the convenience store.

はす² 蓮 lotus ⓒ //ハスの花 a *lotus* flower

-はず -筈

❶【予定】(…することになっている) be supposed [expected] to *do*, be to *do*; (時刻・期日に関して) be due to *do*
彼女は4時に来るはずだ She *is supposed* [*expected*] *to* come at four.
彼は会議に出席するはずだった(がしなかった) He *was to have attended* the meeting.
その船は3時にここに到着するはずだ The ship *is due* (*to* arrive) here at three.
🅴「きょうジムに会ったよ」「それは変だ. 今はロンドンにいるはずなのに」"I saw Jim today." "That's funny. He *is supposed to* be in London now."
❷【当然】(…するはずだ) ought to *do*, should *do*; (…するはずがない) can't *do*
彼はあれだけ勉強してきたんだから試験に合格する

はずだ He *ought to* pass the exam because he's been working so hard.
彼女は今ごろはもう町を後にしているはずだ She *should* have left town by now.
そんなはずはない It *can't be*. / It *can't be true*.
彼がそれに反対するはずがない He *can't* object to it.
彼女が昨夜そこにいたはずがない She *can't* have been there last night.
◆彼は成功するはずだ *I'm certain that* he will succeed. / 彼がうそをついていたはずはない *It's impossible for* him *to* have told a lie. / 絶対に彼がそんなことを言うはずがない He is *the very last man* to say such a thing.

バス¹

bus ⓒ (複 ~es, 《米／まれ》busses); (長距離バス) coach ⓒ
バスで通学する go to school *by* [*on a*] *bus*(❖ by の後では無冠詞. by bus は「バスを使って」, on [in] a bus は「バスに乗って」の意味); (→学校までバスで行く) *take a bus* to school / バスに乗る[から降りる] get on [off] *a bus*
私はバスに乗り遅れた I missed *the bus*.
その競技場はバスで行ける The stadium is accessible *by bus*.
このバスは平和台に行きますか Does this *bus* go to Heiwadai?
次の調布駅行きのバスは何分ですか What time is *the* next *bus* for Chofu Station?
最終バスは何時に出ますか What time does *the last bus* leave?
けさはバスが遅れている *The bus* is late this morning.
バスは定刻どおりに運行しています *Buses* are running on schedule.
私たちは何とか8時のバスに間に合った We somehow managed to catch *the* 8 o'clock *bus*.
‖バス会社 a bus company / バスガイド a (bus) conductor(❖「バスガイド」は和製英語) / バスターミナル a bus terminal [depot] / バス代 a bus fare / バス停留所 a bus stop / バス旅行 a bus tour / バスレーン a bus lane / バス路線 a bus route [line] / 観光バス a sightseeing bus / 深夜バス a late-night bus / スクールバス a school bus / 2階建てバス a double-decker / マイクロバス a microbus, a minibus

バス² (ふろ) bath ⓒ //バストイレ付きの部屋 a room *with a bath* (and toilet)
‖バスタオル a bath towel / バスタブ a bathtub / バスマット a bath mat / バスルーム a bathroom / バスローブ a bathrobe

バス³ 〔音楽〕bass [béis] ⓤⓒ //バスを歌う sing *bass*
‖バス歌手 a bass

パス ❶【券】(無料入場・乗車券) (free) pass ⓒ; (定期券) commuter pass ⓒ, 《英》season (ticket) ⓒ
❷【合格】——パスする pass ⓐ ⇒ ごうかく //

彼は青山大学の入学試験をパスした He *passed* the entrance examination to Aoyama University.

❸ 【スポーツでの】 pass ⓒ ——パスする pass ⓗ ‖彼にボールをパスする *pass* the ball to him / フォワードにロングパスを送る *make a long pass* to the forward

❹ 【トランプなどでの】 ——パスする pass ⓘ ‖ (トランプなどで順番が回ってきて) 僕はパス I *pass.* / (申し出を) 悪いけどきょうはパスするよ I'm sorry, but I'*ll pass* today.

はすう 端数 【数学】 fraction ⓒ ‖端数を切り捨てる omit *fractions*
◆端数のない数字 a *round* number

バスーン 【音楽】 bassoon ⓒ
‖バスーン奏者 a bassoonist

ばすえ 場末 (町はずれ) the outskirts of a town; (裏通り) back alley ⓒ ‖場末の酒場 a drinking place in *a back alley*

はすかい 斜交い ——はすかいに slantwise, askew, obliquely ⇒ななめ

はずかしい 恥ずかしい
(罪悪感を感じる) be ashamed; (ばつが悪い) be embarrassed; (てれくさい) be shy
私は彼女にあんなうそをついたことが恥ずかしい I *am* [*feel*] *ashamed of* having told such a lie to her. / I *am* [*feel*] *ashamed that* I told such a lie to her.

恥ずかしくて自分がミスをしたとは言えなかった I *was* too *ashamed* to say that I had made a mistake.

駅のホームで彼にキスされてとても恥ずかしかった I *was* very *embarrassed* when he kissed me on the platform.

僕は恥ずかしくて彼女にあいさつもできなかった I *was* too *shy* to say hello to her.

◆恥ずかしいことだが, 私は試験でカンニングをしてしまった *Much to my shame*, I cheated on the exam. / 香織は恥ずかしそうに僕の手紙を受け取った Kaori accepted my letter *shyly*. / 私たちは大人として恥ずかしくない (→とるべき) 行動をとるべきだ We should behave as adults *would behave.* / 彼はどこへ出しても恥ずかしくない (→どこでも通用する) 実力のあるラガーマンだ He *can be accepted* everywhere as a competent rugby player.

はずかしがる 恥ずかしがる 恥ずかしがらずにしゃべりなさい *Don't be shy.* Go ahead and speak. / 私の弟は人前で話すことを恥ずかしがる My brother *is bashful* about speaking in front of people. / 彼女は恥ずかしがり屋だ She's *a shy* [*bashful*] *person*.

はずかしめ 辱め humiliation ⓤ ⓒ, insult ⓒ

はずかしめる 辱める disgrace ⓗ, humiliate ⓗ; (女性を犯す) rape ⓗ ‖その教授の事件への関与は大学の名を辱めることとなった The professor's involvement in the case *disgraced* the university's name.

パスカル (圧力の単位) pascal ⓒ; (コンピュータ言語) Pascal ⓤ

ハスキー その歌手はハスキーな声をしている The singer has a *husky* voice.

バスケット basket ⓒ ‖バスケット一杯のオレンジ a *basket*(*ful*) of oranges

バスケットボール basketball ⓤ (❖「バスケットボールのボール」の意味では ⓒ) ‖バスケットボールをする play *basketball*

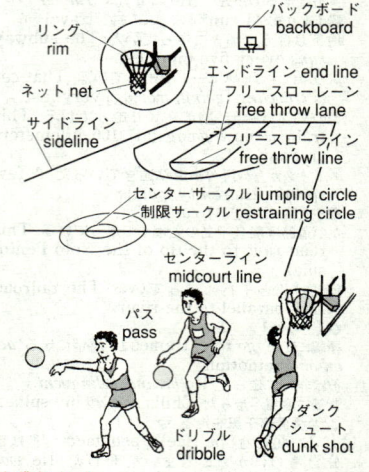

リング rim
ネット net
サイドライン sideline
バックボード backboard
エンドライン end line
フリースローレーン free throw lane
フリースローライン free throw line
センターサークル jumping circle
制限サークル restraining circle
センターライン midcourt line
パス pass
ドリブル dribble
ダンクシュート dunk shot

はずす 外す
❶ 【取る】 (取り去る) remove ⓗ; (身につけている物を) take* off; (ベルトやボタンを) undo* ⓗ
眼鏡をはずす *take off* one's glasses
彼はカバーをはずしてモーターを点検した He *removed* the cover and inspected the motor.

彼女は部屋に入るとすぐコートのボタンをはずした As soon as she entered the room, she 「*undid* the buttons on [*unbuttoned*] her coat.

◆1人で家にいるときはドアのチェーンをはずさないように *Don't unchain* the door when you are alone in your house. / このびんのキャップをはずしてもらえませんか Would you *unscrew* the top on this bottle?

❷ 【含めない】 leave* out, count out
彼はスタメンからはずされた He *was left out of* the starting lineup.
その計画を実行するつもりなら, 僕ははずしてくれ If you intend to carry out the plan, *count* me *out*.

❸ 【離れる】
彼は会議の途中で席をはずした He *left* his seat during the meeting.
田中はただ今席をはずしています (→席にいません) Tanaka *isn't at his* [*her*] *desk* just now.
ちょっと席をはずしてもいいですか Can I be *excused* for a moment?

❹ 【そらす】
彼は矢を射ったがわずかに (→数センチ) 的(まと)をは

ずした He shot an arrow but *missed* the target by a few centimeters.
冗談を飛ばすタイミングをはずしてしまった I *missed* the chance to crack a joke.

パスタ (スパゲッティ・マカロニ類) pasta [U]

パステル pastel [U] [C] ‖パステル画 a pastel / パステルカラー pastel colors, pastels

バスト バストが小さい have *a* small *bust* / 彼女のバストは80センチだ Her *bust measurement* is 80 centimeters.

パスポート passport [C] ∥パスポートを申請する apply for *a passport* / パスポートを交付する issue *a passport* / 私のパスポートは4月に切れる My *passport* will expire in April.

パスボール ⚠〘野球〙 passed ball [C] (❖キャッチャーが投球を後ろにそらすこと. ×pass ball とはいわない) ∥パスボールで逆転する turn the tables on *a passed ball*

はずみ 弾み ❶【勢い】テレビで報道されてキャンペーンにはずみがついた The campaign *gathered* [*gained*] *momentum* after it was reported on TV. / 新しい幹線道路によってその市の発展にはずみがついた The new highway *spurred* the development of the city.
❷【成り行き】もののはずみで軽率なことを言って後悔している I regret that I said careless things *on the spur of the moment*.
❸【瞬間】通行人をよけようとしたはずみに自転車から落ちた I fell off my bike trying to dodge a pedestrian.

はずむ 弾む
❶【はね返る】
このボールはよく弾む This ball *bounces* well.
ボールは弾んで柵(さく)を越えた The ball *bounced* over the fence.
❷【活気づく】
週末のデートのことを思うと心がはずむ My heart *jumps with joy* when I think about our date this weekend.
ニュージーランド旅行について話がはずんだ(→活発な会話をした) We *had a lively conversation* about our trip to New Zealand.
電話の彼女の声がはずんでいた(→興奮した声で話していた) She *was talking in an excited voice* over the phone.
❸【その他】
小さな女の子が息をはずませて僕の所に走ってきた A little girl ran *panting* to me.
おじさんはお年玉をはずんでくれた(→大きい額のお金をお正月のプレゼントとしてくれた) My uncle *gave* me *a generous amount of money* as a New Year's gift.

はすむかい 斜向かい うちのはす向かいには公園がある There's a park *diagonally opposite* [*across from*] my house.

パズル puzzle [C] ∥パズルを解く solve [work out] *a puzzle* / クロスワード[ジグソー]パズルをする do *a* crossword [jigsaw] *puzzle*

はずれ 外れ ❶【当たらない】君の推測はみんなはずれだ All your guesses *are wrong*. / 私の引いたくじははずれだった(→空くじを引いた) I drew *a blank*.
❷【期待に添わない】おいしそうなのでリンゴを買ったんだけど, はずれだった I bought some apples because they looked good, but actually they were *a letdown*. (❖letdown は「期待はずれのもの」の意味) / その車の性能は期待はずれだった The car's performance *was disappointing*.
❸【周辺部】その一家は町はずれで暮らしている The family lives on *the outskirts of* town.

はずれる 外れる
❶【離れる】come* off (...); (ボタンなどが) be undone; (関節が) be put out of joint
取っ手がはずれた The knob *came off*.
引き戸を閉めようとしたら, レールからはずれてしまった The sliding door *came off* its rail when I tried to close it.
彼のシャツはボタンが1つはずれていた A button on his shirt *was undone*.
そのタックルで肩の関節がはずれた My shoulder *was put out of joint* by that tackle.
◆そのレストランは繁華街を少しはずれた所にある The restaurant is a bit *away from* the busy area. / 人工衛星は軌道をはずれた The satellite *strayed out of orbit*. / 受話器がはずれている The phone *is off the hook*. / その2台のレーシングカーはコースからはずれてしまった These two racing cars *went off* [*out of*] the course. / 彼の歌は音程がはずれている He is singing 「*out of tune* [*off key*].
❷【当たらない】(的(まと)を) miss [他]; (予想などが) prove* wrong
矢は的(まと)をはずれた The arrow *missed* the target.
きょうの天気予報ははずれた The weather forecast for today *has proved wrong*.
◆宝くじがはずれた I *didn't win the lottery*. / 誕生日祝いにおじに自転車を買ってもらえると思っていたが, 当てがはずれた I thought my uncle would buy me a bicycle for my birthday but I *guessed wrong*.

パスワード password [C] ∥(自分の)パスワードを入力する enter [type] *one's password* / (自分の)パスワードを変更する change *one's password*

はぜ 沙魚 goby [C]

はせい 派生 (起源) derivation [U] [C]; (進展) development [U] ―派生する derive [自]; develop [自] ∥イタリア語, スペイン語, フランス語はみんなラテン語から派生した Italian, Spanish and French all *derived from* Latin. / 思いがけない事態がその事故から派生した An unexpected situation *developed from* the accident.
‖派生語 a derivative

ばせい 罵声 (ブーという声) boo [C] (複 ～s), hoot [C] ◆デモ参加者は警官に罵声を浴びせた The demonstrators *booed* [(→ののしった) cursed at, swore at] the police officer.

パセリ 〘植物〙 parsley [U]

はせる 馳せる 彼女は故郷に思いをはせた She *thought of* her hometown. / 斉藤氏は物理学者として名をはせた(→名声を得た) Mr. Saito *gained fame* as a physicist.

はせん[1] 波線 波線を引く draw *a wavy line*

はせん² 破線 破線を引く draw *a broken line*
パソコン personal computer ◯ (《略記》PC) (❖「パソコン」は和製略語) ⇒ 場面・状況別会話 p.1698 ‖パソコン通信 online communication (service)

はそん 破損 damage [dǽmidʒ] ⓊC; (割れること) breakage Ⓤ ——破損する be damaged; be broken ‖洪水による家屋の破損は大きかった The flood caused heavy *damage* to the houses. / 衝突事故で船が破損した The boat *was damaged* by the crash. / 皿は輸送中に破損した The dishes *were damaged* [*broken*] in transit.

はた¹ 旗 flag ◯ ‖旗をあげる hoist [raise] *a flag* / 旗を降ろす lower *a flag* / 子供たちは旗を振って市長を歓迎した The children waved *flags* to welcome the mayor. / たくさんの国の旗が風にはためいていた *The flags* of many nations were fluttering in the wind. / 彼は月面に旗を立てた He planted *a flag* on the moon's surface.
‖旗ざお a flagpole / 旗日 a national holiday
慣用表現 彼らは平等の旗のもとで戦った They fought under *the flag* [*banner*] *of equality*. / 兄は一旗あげるために上京した My brother went to Tokyo to *make「his fortune* [*a name for himself*]*.

はた² 機 loom ◯ ‖機を織る weave on *a loom*

はた³ 傍 一輪車に乗るのははたで見るほど難しくはない Riding a unicycle isn't *as difficult as it seems*.

はだ 肌 skin ⓊC ‖彼は肌が白い[黒い] He has (*a*) *fair* [*dark*] *skin*. / 私は冬になると肌が荒れる I get rough *skin* in the winter. / 僕は乾燥肌です I have (*a*) *dry skin*. / 肌の色による差別はあってはならない People should not be judged [discriminated against] by the color of *their skin*.
◆彼らは浜辺で肌を焼いた They *tanned themselves* on the beach. / 大井さんは芸術家肌だ Mr. Oi *has an artistic turn of mind*. / 海外を旅行して英語の重要性を肌で感じた(→じかに感じた) I *realized* the importance of English *firsthand* when I traveled overseas. / 彼女は彼に許そうとしない She *won't give herself to* him. / 外は肌を刺すような寒さだ It *is biting* cold outside.
慣用表現 彼とはどうも肌が合わない(→うまくやっていけない) I *don't get along well with* him.
短歌 やはだのあつき血汐にふれも見でさびしからずや道を説く君(与謝野晶子)
Does it make you sad,
you upright, didactic man,
not to try to touch
the fiery streams of blood
that churn beneath my soft skin?

バター butter Ⓤ ‖パンにバターを塗る spread *butter* on bread; spread bread with *butter* / バターを塗ったパン *bread and butter*
◆朝食はいつもバターを塗ったトーストとコーヒーです I always have *buttered* toast and coffee for breakfast.
‖バター入れ a butter dish / バターナイフ a butter knife / バターロール a butter roll
バター 〔ゴルフ〕 putter ◯

はたあげ 旗揚げ 一座は先週渋谷で旗揚げした(→初めての公演を行った) The troupe *gave its first performance* in Shibuya last week. / 父の会社は去年の4月に旗揚げした(→会社を始めた) My father *started* his company in April last year.

ばたあし ばた足 flutter kick ◯

はだあれ 肌荒れ 彼女は冬になるとひどい肌荒れに悩まされる She suffers from very *rough skin* in the winter.

パターン pattern ◯ ‖ワンパターン ❖彼は大学院でコウモリの行動パターンを研究している At graduate school, he is studying *the* behavior *patterns* of bats. / そのロボットの動きは一定のパターンに従っている The movement of the robot follows *a set pattern*.
◆こういった展開はサスペンスドラマにはよくあるパターンだ This kind of turn in the story *can often be seen* in suspense programs.

はたいろ 旗色 (勝算) odds; (形勢) the tide ‖僕たちのチームは旗色が悪かった[よかった] *The odds* were「*against our team* [*in our team's favor*]. / 我々の旗色が悪くなってくると彼は寝返った When *the tide* began to go against us, he sold out.

はだか 裸 ——裸の naked [néikid]; (主に絵・写真などの) nude; (木などが) bare
裸のモデル a nude model
彼は上半身裸だった He was *naked* [*stripped*] to the waist.
少年は真っ裸で家の中を走り回っていた The boy was running around in the house *stark naked*.
この木は冬には裸になる This tree becomes *bare* in winter.
◆その男の子は裸になって海に飛び込んだ The boy *took off his clothes* and jumped into the sea. / 彼女は裸で眠る She sleeps *with nothing on*.
‖裸電球 a naked [an unshaded] light bulb / 裸電線 a naked wire
慣用表現 彼は裸一貫から巨万の富を築き上げた He made a huge fortune *from scratch*.

はたき duster ◯ ◆家具にはたきをかける *dust* the furniture

はだぎ 肌着 《集合的》underwear Ⓤ, underclothes

はたく 叩く 彼女は落とした帽子を拾ってほこりをはたいた She picked up the hat she dropped and *dusted it* (*off*). / 姉は貯金をはたいて新車を買った(→貯金を全部使った) My sister *spent all her savings on* a new car.

バタくさい バタ臭い 彼はバタくさい(→ヨーロッパ人のような)顔立ちをしている He has *European* features. / その通りにはバタくさい(→西洋風の)建物が並んでいる The street is lined with *Western-style* buildings.

はたけ 畑 field ◯ (❖「専門分野」の意味でも用いられる) ‖小麦畑 *a wheat field* / 畑を耕す

plow *a field* / 私は夏休みに畑仕事を経験した I experienced *working in the fields* during summer vacation. / 畑にトウモロコシをまいた We sowed *the field* with corn./ We sowed corn in *the field*. / 父の専門は社会学なので生物学は畑違いだ My father is a sociologist, so biology *is outside his field*.

◆コーヒー畑 a coffee *plantation* / 茶[花]畑 *a* tea [flower] *garden* / トウモロコシ畑 *a cornfield* / ブドウ畑 *a vineyard*

はだける 彼は胸をはだけた He *exposed* his chest. / 朝起きたら胸がはだけていた When I woke up in the morning, my chest *was bare*.

はださむい 肌寒い 山頂近くは肌寒かった It *was chilly* near the top of the mountain.

はだざわり 肌触り touch [U], the [a] feel // この布は肌ざわりがなめらかだ This cloth is smooth to *the touch*.

◆このセーターは肌ざわりがよい[悪い] This sweater *feels soft* [*rough*].

はだし 裸足 浜辺は熱くてはだしで歩けなかった The beach was so hot that I couldn't walk *barefoot* [*with bare feet*].

-はだし -裸足 彼のピアノの腕は玄人(くろうと)はだしだ(→玄人よりも上手だ) He plays the piano *better than even professionals*.

はたして 果たして はたして(→思ったとおり)試合は延期された *As I thought* [*expected*], the game was put off. / はたして(→本当に)彼がその小説を書いたのだろうか I wonder if he *really* wrote that novel. / はたして(→いったい)だれが優勝するのだろうか Who「*on earth* [*in the world*] will win the first prize?

はたじるし 旗印 彼らは自由の旗印のもとに戦った They fought「*under the banner* [*in the cause*] *of* freedom. (❖banner は比喩的な意味の「旗印」, cause は「大義名分」の意味)

はたす 果たす (義務を) fulfill [他]; (役割を) play [他]; (約束を) keep* [他]; (目的を) achieve [他]; (夢を) realize [他]

山下さんはりっぱに義務を果たした Ms. Yamashita *fulfilled* [*performed*] her obligations well.

自動車産業はこの市の経済にきわめて重要な役割を果たしている The automobile industry *plays* a vital role in the economy of this city.

あなたは約束を果たす義務がある You are under an obligation to *keep* [*fulfill*] your promise.

彼は目的を果たしてアメリカに帰った He *achieved* [*accomplished*] his purpose and returned to America.

彼女は去年カナダ留学の夢を果たすことができた She *realized* her dream of studying in Canada last year.

はたせるかな 果たせるかな はたせるかな(→思ったとおり)彼は次の日学校を休んだ *As I expected*, he was absent from school the next day.

はたち 二十(歳) 日本では二十歳で成人とみなされる In Japan, you are regarded as an adult when you turn *twenty* (*years old*).

ばたっと 彼はばたっと床に倒れた He fell *flat* on the floor.

はたと 彼ははたとひざを打って私を呼び止めた He slapped his knee *suddenly* and called me to stop. / 通りを走る車の音がはたとやんだ The sound of the traffic from the street fell silent *all of a sudden*. / 英語で「羽根つき」を何というか尋ねられて, はたと困った(→答えに困った) Asked what the English word is for "hanetsuki,"I *found myself at a loss for an answer*.

はたはた 星条旗が風にはたはたとはためいていた The Stars and Stripes *was flapping* [*fluttering*] in the wind. (❖flap は「大きくはためく」, flutter は「小刻みにはためく」の意味)

ばたばた 鳥が羽をばたばたさせた A bird *flapped* its wings. / 学生が何人か廊下をばたばた(→騒々しく)走っていった Some students went running along the hall *noisily*. / 兵士がばたばたと(→次々に)倒れた Soldiers fell *one after another*. / 兄はアメリカ留学の準備でばたばたしている(→忙しい) My brother *is busy* preparing to study in America.

ぱたぱた 彼は廊下をぱたぱたと走っていった He went *pattering* down the hall. / 旗が風にぱたぱたとなびいていた The flag *was flapping around* in the wind.

バタフライ 私はバタフライで泳ぐことができない I can't swim *the butterfly* (*stroke*).

はだみ 肌身 彼女は家族の写真を肌身離さず持っている(→持ち歩いている) She *always carries* a photo of her family *about with* her.

はため 傍目 彼女ははた目(→他人がどう思うか)を気にしすぎる She cares too much about *what others think*. / その夫婦ははた目には(→ほかの人たちには)幸せそうだった The couple seemed *to others* to be happy.

はためいわく 傍迷惑 昇はいつもはた迷惑なことばかりしている Noboru is always making *trouble for others*. / 違法駐車は本当にはた迷惑だ Illegal parking is *a* real *nuisance*.

はためく 日の丸が風にはためいていた The Rising Sun Flag *was fluttering* in the wind.

はたらかす 働かす ➔はたらかせる

はたらかせる 働かせる work [他]; (頭・想像力などを) use [他] //監守は多くの捕虜を情け容赦なく働かせた The guard *worked* many prisoners mercilessly. / いいレポートを書くつもりなら頭を働かせなさい If you want to write a good paper, *use* your brains. / 彼女は想像力を自由に働かせてこの小説を書いた She *used* her imagination freely in writing this novel.

はたらき 働き (仕事をすること) work [U]; (機能) function [C]

彼女は新しい製品の開発で重要な働きをした She *did* some important *work* on the development of the new product.

唇は発声器官の働きをする The lips「*perform a function* [*function*] *as* a vocal organ.

は

◆彼は週末に働きに出る He *goes to work* on weekends. / 彼は今働き盛りだ He *is in his prime* now. / 彼は働きが悪い(→収入が少ない) He *does not earn enough money*. / 自然の働きは時として神秘的だ The *workings* of nature are sometimes mysterious. / この薬品は殺菌剤の働きをする This chemical *acts as a* germicide. / 疲れて頭の働きが鈍くなった(→疲労が頭の働きを鈍くした) Fatigue made *my mind dull*.

∥働き口 a job / 働き手(一家の) a worker, the breadwinner / 働きバチ a worker bee; (仕事中毒の人)a workaholic / 働き者 a hard worker

はたらきかけ 働きかけ 地域の人々の働きかけで市役所の近くに新しい駅が造られた *At the urging of* the community, a new train station was built near the city hall.

はたらきかける 働きかける 私たちは駅前に駐輪場を造るように市に働きかけた We *urged* the city to build a bicycle parking lot next to the station.

はたらく 働く

❶【仕事をする】work 圓他

フルタイムで[アルバイトとして]働く *work* full-time [part-time]

彼女は同時通訳として働いている She *works as* a simultaneous interpreter.

彼女は月曜日から金曜日まで働いている She *works* from Monday to [through] Friday.

私の姉は出版社で働いている My sister *works for* [*at, in*] a publishing company.

彼らは8時間交替で働いている They *work* eight-hour shifts.

最近君は働きすぎだ You've been working too much [hard] recently. / You've been overworking recently.

◆私は時間給で働いている I *am paid by the hour*.

❷【機能する】work 圓, function 圓

暑いと頭がよく働かない My head *doesn't work* well when it's hot.

事故はブレーキがうまく働かなかったために起こった The accident happened because the brake *didn't function* properly.

◆科学のこととなると頭が働かなくなる I *have a mental block* about science. / 新たに出てきた証拠は不利に働くだろう The newly-found evidence will *militate against* him.

❸【悪事を行う】commit 他

貧困のつらさから彼は強盗を働いた The hardship of poverty made him *commit* robbery.

◆盗みを働くのはよくない It's not right to *steal*.

ばたりと へとへとに疲れていたのでベッドにばたりと倒れ込んだ I was worn out, so I *flopped onto* the bed.

ぱたりと ついてたがぱたりと倒れた The screen fell *with a plop*. / コオロギの声がぱたりと(→急に)やんだ The crickets fell silent suddenly.

はたん 破綻 彼らの結婚生活は1か月で破綻した Their marriage *failed* [*fell apart*] after a month. / 資金不足のために彼らの計画は破綻をきたした Financial difficulties *caused* their plan *to fall through*.

はだん 破談 縁談は破談になった The engagement *was canceled* [*broken off*].

ばたんきゅう 父はその日は疲れていたので家に帰ってくるなりばたんきゅうだった My dad was so tired that day that he *conked out* the moment he came home.

ばたんと 彼女は怒ってドアをばたんと閉めた She *slammed* the door angrily. / 彼はふたをばたんと閉じた He *banged the lid down*. / 自転車がばたんと倒れた The bicycle fell *with a bang*.

ぱたんと 本をぱたんと閉じる *slam* the book *shut*

はち¹ 蜂 bee ⓒ ∥ハチは巣箱の周りをぶんぶんいいながら忙しく働いていた The *bees* were working busily, humming around the hive. / ハチに腕を刺された I was stung on the arm by *a bee*. / (→ハチが私の腕を刺した)A bee stung my arm.

∥アシナガバチ a long-legged wasp / 女王バチ a queen bee / スズメバチ a wasp / 働きバチ(仕事中毒の人) a worker bee; a workaholic / ミツバチ a honey bee

ことわざ 泣きっ面に蜂 ⇒なきっつら

はち² 八 eight; (8番目) eighth /スケートで8の字に滑る skate *a figure eight*

はち³ 鉢 (どんぶり鉢) bowl ⓒ; (植木鉢) (flower) pot ⓒ / 小鉢で料理を出す serve the food in *a small bowl*

ばち¹ 罰 punishment ⓒⓊ ∥この事故は彼がいつも無謀運転していたばちだよ This accident is *punishment* for his habitual reckless driving. ◆そんなことをしてるとばちがあたるぞ If you do that, you'll *pay for it*. / ばちがあたったんだよ *It serves you right*. (※「ばちがあたった人」に応じて you の部分を him, her などに変える)

ばち² 撥 (太鼓などの) drumstick ⓒ; (三味線(しゃみせん)などの) pick ⓒ

はちあわせ 鉢合わせ 学校をサボって映画館に行ったら兄と鉢合わせしてしまった When I skipped school and went to the movies, I *ran into* my brother.

はちうえ 鉢植え potted plant ⓒ
◆鉢植えのサボテン a *potted* cactus

ばちがい 場違い 大学生の中にいて場違いな気がした I felt *out of place* among the university students. / 何だか場違いな所にいる気がする Somehow I *don't think I belong here*.

はちがつ 八月 August Ⓤⓒ ((略語)) Aug.)
⇒いちがつ

はちきれる はち切れる burst* 圓 /袋はリンゴではち切れそうだった The bag *was bursting* with apples. / 新入生は喜びではち切れんばかりだった The new students *were bursting with* joy.

はちくのいきおい 破竹の勢い そのコンピュー

タ会社は破竹の勢いだ That computer company *is like a steamroller*.(❖steamroller は「地ならし用のローラー」の意味)

ばちくり コンテストで1等賞を取ったと言ったら彼は驚いて目をぱちくりさせた He *blinked (his eyes)* in surprise when I told him that I had won the first prize in the contest.

はちじゅう 八十 eighty; (80番目) eightieth

はちじゅうはちや 八十八夜 *hachijuhachiya*, the 88th day after the start of spring

はちのす 蜂の巣 honeycomb ⓒ; (巣箱) beehive ⓒ
[慣用表現] 女性の悲鳴が聞こえると, 場内は蜂の巣をつついたような騒ぎになった (→悲鳴が場内を大きな混乱に陥れた) A woman's scream *threw the hall into utter confusion*.

ぱちぱち 暖炉でまきがぱちぱち音を立てた The wood *crackled [snapped]* in the fireplace. / 僕がステージに登場すると子供たちはぱちぱち拍手した The children *clapped their hands* as I appeared on the stage. / 彼らはその女優の写真をパチパチと撮った They *snapped shots of the actress one after another*.

はちぶおんぷ 八分音符【音楽】《米》eighth note ⓒ, 《英》quaver ⓒ

はちぶんめ 八分目 腹八分目にするのは健康によい It's good for your health to *leave some space in your stomach after meal*.

はちまき 鉢巻き a *hachimaki*, a headband (❖ふつう髪が垂れるのを防ぐためのもので, 「はちまき」のように気持ちを引き締める意味はない) ◆その塾では生徒は授業中気持ちを引き締めるためにはちまきをする At the cram school pupils *tie towels around their heads to focus their attention in class*.

はちみつ 蜂蜜 honey Ⓤ

はちミリ 八ミリ (8ミリ映画) 8-mm movie ⓒ (❖mm は *millimeter* の略記); (8ミリカメラ) 8-mm camera ⓒ; (8ミリビデオ) 8-mm video recorder ⓒ

はちめんろっぴ 八面六臂 山口さんはそのプロジェクトで八面六臂の活躍をした (→多くの面で才能を発揮した) Mr. Yamaguchi *showed great ability in many aspects* of the project.

ばちゃばちゃ 子供たちはプールでお互いに水をばちゃばちゃかけていた The children *were splashing* water *on* each other in the swimming pool. / 彼らは雨上がりの道をばちゃばちゃ (と水を飛び散らして) 走っていった They ran *splashing* down the road after the rain stopped.

ばちゃんと 彼女は海にばちゃんと飛び込んだ She jumped into the sea *with a splash*.

はちゅうるい 爬虫類 reptile ⓒ

はちょう 波長【物理】wavelength ⓒ / 波長の短い電波 an electric wave with *a short wavelength* / 正樹とは波長が合う Masaki and I *are on the same wavelength*.
◆NHK に波長を合わせる *tune in to* NHK

パチリと 彼はヘリコプターをパチリと写真に収めた He *snapped a photo of* the helicopter.

パチンコ (ゲーム) pachinko Ⓤ; (子供のおもちゃ)《米》slingshot ⓒ, 《英》catapult ⓒ / パチンコをする play *pachinko* / 彼はパチンコでハトをねらった He aimed *his slingshot* at a pigeon.
‖パチンコ屋 a pachinko parlor

パチンコは日本で考案されたゲームで, 英語では日本式ピンボールと説明されることもあります。スロットマシンを組み合わせるなど, 様々な工夫を凝らしたパチンコ台が開発されています。多くの人々が手軽な娯楽としてパチンコを楽しみますが, 中にはパチンコで生計を立てている人もいます。
Pachinko is a game invented in Japan and sometimes described in English as "Japanese pinball." Some new ideas and devices have been added to pachinko machines such as incorporating the function of a slot machine. Most people play pachinko just for fun, but some do it for a living.

ぱちんと 彼女はバッグをぱちんと閉じた The woman *snapped* her bag *shut*. / The woman *closed her bag with a snap*. / 彼女は指をぱちんと鳴らした She *snapped* her fingers. / 彼はライトをぱちんとつけた [消した] He *snapped* a light *on [off]*.

はつ 初 ─初の (初めての) first / 初デートの日にかぜをひくなんて彼女もついてないね It's rough on her, catching cold on her *first* date. / これは彼女の映画初出演だ This is her *first* appearance on the screen. / 日本陸上女子初の金メダルはマラソンだった Japan's *first* gold medal in women's track and field was in the marathon.

-はつ -発 上野発の夜行列車 a night train *from* Ueno / 19時30分発の上り列車 the 19:30 inbound train (❖19:30 は nineteen thirty と読む) / 警官は銃を2発撃った The police officer fired two *shots*. / 彼に1発食らわせた I landed *a punch* on him.

ばつ¹ 罰 punishment ⓒ Ⓤ; (刑罰) penalty ⓒ Ⓤ
先生は彼に軽い [重い] 罰を与えた The teacher gave him *a light [heavy] punishment*.
彼は罰として校庭を20周走らねばならなかった He had to run 20 laps of the school's field as *punishment*.
彼らは当然の罰を受けた They received *a just punishment*.
この法律はその種の犯罪に対し厳しい罰を規定している This law prescribes heavy *penalties* for that kind of crime.

ばつ² 私の解答にはばつがついていた My answer was marked with *an X*./ (→誤答の印がついていた) My answer was marked as *incorrect*.

ばつ³ 彼とデートをしているときに父親に出くわしてばつの悪い思いをした I *felt embarrassed [awkward]* when I ran into my father while I was on a date with my boyfriend.

ばつ

ばつ⁴ 閥 (派閥) faction ⓒ; (排他的集団) clique ⓒ ‖学閥 a school clique

はつあん 発案 (考案) idea ⓤ; (提案) suggestion ⓒ ‖その旅行は酒井さんの発案だった The trip was Ms. Sakai's *idea*. / 彼の発案で去年の夏, 富士山に登った We climbed Mt. Fuji last summer *at his suggestion*.
‖発案権 the initiative / 発案者 a proposer

はついく 発育 growth ⓤ ──発育する grow* ⓘ ‖粗食は子供の自然な発育を妨げることがある A poor diet can arrest *the* natural *growth* of a child. / この地方は今年ジャガイモの発育が悪い Potatoes *are growing* slowly in this area this year. / 姉の子供はみんな発育がよい My sister's children are all *growing quickly*.
‖発育期 the period of growth / 発育不全 incomplete development

ばついち 彼らはばついちどうしのカップルだ Both of them *have been divorced once*.

はつえき 発駅 この列車の発駅は東京です (→東京から出発する) This train *starts from* Tokyo.

はつおん 発音 pronunciation ⓤ ──発音する pronounce ⓘ ‖彼の英語の発音はかなりよくなった His English *pronunciation* showed considerable improvement. / 'island'の's'は発音されない The 's' in 'island' *is not pronounced*. / あなたのお名前はどう発音するのですか How do you *pronounce* your name?
‖発音記号 a phonetic sign [symbol]

はつか 二十日 20日間 for *twenty days* / 6月20日 June (the) *twentieth*

はっか¹ 発火 combustion ⓤ ──発火する ignite ⓘ, catch* fire ‖ガソリンは発火しやすい Gasoline easily *ignites* [*catches fire*].
‖発火点 an ignition point / 自然発火 spontaneous combustion

はっか² 薄荷 peppermint ⓤ

はつが 発芽 germination ⓤ ──発芽する germinate ⓘ, sprout ⓘ ‖豆が発芽した The beans *have germinated*.

ハッカー hacker ⓒ

はつかおあわせ 初顔合わせ 来週, 新入部員の初顔合わせがある (→新入部員が紹介される) The new members of the club *will be introduced* next week. / この試合は両チームの初顔合わせ (→初めての試合) です This is *the first game* between the two teams.

はっかく 発覚 彼女がスパイだったことが発覚した It *was uncovered* [*found out*] that she was a spy.

はっかく (けい) 八角(形) octagon ⓒ

はつかねずみ 二十日鼠 mouse ⓒ (複 mice)

はっかん¹ 発刊 publication ⓤ ──発刊する publish ⓘ ‖彼の新作が間もなく発刊される His new book *will be published* soon.

はっかん² 発汗 perspiration ⓤ, sweating ⓤ (❖perspiration のほうが上品な語)

はつがん 発癌 ──発癌性の cancer-causing, carcinogenic ‖発癌物質 a carcinogen

はっき 発揮 ──発揮する show* ⓘ ‖彼は非凡な音楽の才能を発揮し始めた He began to *show* [*display*] remarkable ability in music. ◆彼は野球となると本領を発揮する He is *in his element* playing baseball.

はつぎ 発議 (提案) proposal ⓤ, suggestion ⓒ ‖彼女の発議で新しい役職が作られた A new post was created *at her suggestion*.

はっきゅう¹ 発給 政府は彼にビザを発給しなかった The government *refused to issue* a visa to him.

はっきゅう² 薄給 small salary ⓒ, low wages ⓒ ‖姉は薄給で働いている My sister works for *a small salary*.

はっきょう 発狂 ──発狂する go* mad [crazy] ‖恐怖で発狂しそうだった I almost *went crazy* with fear.

はっきり

❶【明瞭な】 ──はっきりした clear; (生き生きした) vivid; (明白な) obvious; (まぎれもない) distinct

その点ははっきりさせておこう Let's make that point *clear*.

この絵が偽物だということははっきりしている It is *obvious* that the picture is a fake.

私は祖父のことをはっきりと覚えています (→はっきりとした記憶がある) I have *vivid* memories of my grandfather.

その昆虫は背中にはっきりとした模様がある The insect has a *distinct* pattern on its back.

◆彼の部屋から東京タワーがはっきりと見えた I could see the Tokyo Tower *clearly* from his room. / もっとはっきりしゃべりなさい Speak more *clearly*. / 彼がいつ来るかははっきりとは (→正確には) 知らない I don't know *exactly* [*for certain*] when he will come. / 彼女ははっきりとした (→明確な) 返事をくれなかった She didn't give me a *definite* answer. / 彼ははっきり「ノー」と言った He *definitely* said no. / 彼女の将来の計画ははっきりしていない (→あいまいである) Her plans for the future *are vague*.

❷【遠慮がない】 ──はっきりした outspoken; (率直な) frank; (直接的) direct

彼ははっきりものを言う He *is outspoken*.

はっきり言いすぎてごめんなさい I'm sorry for *being so direct*.

はっきり言って彼の小説は全然理解できない *To be frank* [*Frankly speaking*], I don't understand his novel at all.

◆この際はっきり言わせてもらうけど, 君のそういう態度にはうんざりなんだ *Let me be quite blunt* (*with you*) on this occasion, I'm sick and tired of that attitude of yours.

❸【天気や意識が明確な】

ここ2, 3日はっきりしない (→不安定な) 天気が続いている The weather has been *unsettled* for the last few days.

コーヒーを1杯飲んだら頭がはっきりした (→1杯のコーヒーが頭をすっきりさせてくれた) A cup of coffee *cleared* my head.

彼の体は弱っていたが, 意識ははっきりしていた Though his body was weak, his mind

はっきん¹ 白金 〖化学〗 platinum ▢ (❖元素記号 Pt)

はっきん² 発禁　彼の小説は発禁になった The *publication* of his novel *was banned* [*placed under a ban*].

ばっきん　罰金 fine ▣; (違約金) penalty ▣　∥1万円の罰金を科す impose *a fine* of 10,000 yen ／　クラブの会合に遅れたので500円の罰金を払った I paid *a penalty* of 500 yen for being late for the club meeting.
◆彼はスピード違反で5万円の罰金を科された He *was fined* 50,000 yen *for* speeding.

バッキンガム　∥バッキンガム宮殿 Buckingham Palace

パッキング　packing▢ ⇒にづくり

バック　⚠(背景) background ▣▣; (後援者) supporter ▣; (逆手打ち) backhand (stroke) ▣　━バックする[させる] (後退する) back (up), move back　∥お城をバックに写真を撮ってもらった I had my pictures taken with the castle *in the background*. ／ あの議員には有力なバックがついている That politician has *a powerful supporter*. ／ 彼は車をバックさせて車庫に入れた He *backed* his car (*up*) into the garage. ／ 少しバックしてもらえますか Would you *move back* a little, please?
◆ギアをバックに入れる put the gears into *reverse* ／ オーケストラをバックに歌う sing *with orchestral backing* ／ 彼女はボールをバックハンドで打った She hit the ball *backhand*. ／ 私はバックで泳げない(→背泳ぎができない) I *can't do the backstroke*. ／ 行き止まりに来てしまったので私は車をバックさせた I had come to a dead end, so I *put the car into reverse*. ／ 彼は髪をオールバックにしている He wears his hair *back*.
∥バックギア reverse gear ／ バックシート a back seat ／ バックストレッチ a backstretch ／ バックストローク backstroke ／ バックハンド a backhand (stroke) ／ バックライト a backup light

バッグ　bag▣ ⇒かばん

パック　pack▢　∥サクランボを1パック1,000円で買った I bought *a pack* of cherries for 1,000 yen. ／ 彼女は寝る前に顔にパックをする She applies *a pack* to her face before she goes to bed.
◆真空パックのコーヒー *vacuum-packed* coffee ／ 牛乳2パック two *cartons* of milk

バックアップ　(援助) backing▢; (コンピュータの) backup▢▣　━バックアップする (支援する) support 🌐, back (up)　∥彼は党幹部のバックアップで議長に選ばれた He was elected chairperson with *the backing* of the party leaders. ／ 私たちは彼女の計画をバックアップした We *supported* [*backed* (*up*)] her project. ／ データのバックアップはとってありますか Did you make *a backup* of the data?/ Did you *back up* the data?

バックグラウンド　(背景) the background　∥バックグラウンドミュージック background music

バックス　⚠〖スポーツ〗 the backfield (❖×backs とはいわない)

バックスキン　buckskin▢

バックスクリーン　⚠〖野球〗 the centerfield screen(❖×back screen とはいわない)

はっくつ　発掘 excavation ▢▣　━発掘する excavate 🌐　∥古代都市の発掘が現在進行中だ *The excavation* of an ancient city is now under way. ／ 彼らは隠された財宝の発掘に成功した They succeeded in *excavating* [*unearthing*] hidden treasure.
◆彼女の仕事は有能な人材を発掘することにある Her job is *finding* capable persons.
∥発掘現場 an excavation site ／ 発掘品 an excavated item

パックツアー　⚠ package tour ▣ (❖「パックツアー」は和製英語)　∥正男は去年パックツアーでニューヨークに行った Masao went to New York on *a package tour* last year.

バックナンバー　back issue [number]▣

バックネット　backstop ▣ (❖×back net とはいわない)

バックホーム　⚠ 亮太のみごとなバックホームでそのランナーはアウトになった Because of Ryota's strong *throw to home*, the runner was tagged out. (❖「バックホーム」は和製英語)

バックボーン　the backbone

バックミラー　⚠ rearview mirror ▣ (❖×back mirror とはいわない)

ぱっくり　傷口はぱっくり開いてしまった The wound came *wide* open.

バックル　buckle▣　∥バックルを締める[はずす] fasten [undo] *a buckle* ／ ベルトのバックルを締める[はずす] *buckle* [*unbuckle*] a belt

はづくろい　羽繕い　枝にとまった鳥が羽づくろいをしていた The bird on the branch *was preening its feathers*.

ばつぐん　抜群 ━抜群の (傑出した) outstanding; (驚くべき) remarkable; (無比の) unrivaled　∥彼女は抜群の成績で大学に入学した She was admitted to a university with *outstanding* grades. ／ 彼の記憶力は抜群だ(→抜群の記憶力をもっている) He has a *remarkable* memory. ／ 彼女の英語力は抜群だ She *is unrivaled* in English. ◆彼女は洋服のセンスが抜群だ(→すばらしいセンスをもっている) She has *excellent* taste in clothes.

パッケージツアー　⇒パックツアー

はっけっきゅう　白血球 〖生理〗 white blood cell ▣, leukocyte ▣

はっけつびょう　白血病〖医学〗 leukemia▢

はっけん　発見 discovery ▢▣　━発見する discover 🌐
その発見は歴史の流れを変えた The *discovery* changed the course of history.
日本のアマチュア天文学者が新しい彗星(☆)を発見した An amateur Japanese astronomer *discovered* a new comet.
ラジウムはキュリー夫妻によって発見された Radium *was discovered* by the Curies.
◆その遺体の第1発見者 *the discoverer* of the dead body ／ その癌(☆)は早期に発見された

はつげん 発言 remark ⓒ, statement ⓒ ━━発言する speak* 圓
不用意な発言をする make careless remarks [comments]
その後不用意な発言が彼女にとってマイナスになった That rash remark reflected badly on her.
その政治家の無礼な発言に多くの人が憤慨した Many people were outraged at the politician's offensive statement.
きのうの会議では発言する機会がなかった I didn't have a chance to speak at yesterday's meeting.
◆私に少し発言させてもらえませんか Would you permit me a few words? / 議長は彼女に発言権を与えなかった The chairperson didn't give her the floor. / すべての国民が平等に発言権をもっている Every citizen has an equal voice. / 昨夜の発言(→言ったこと)は撤回します I withdraw what I said last night.
‖発言者 a speaker

はつこい 初恋 one's first love ‖僕の初恋は実らなかった My first love didn't blossom. / 学は私の初恋の人です Manabu was my first love.

はっこう¹ 発行 (本・新聞の) publication Ⓤ; (雑誌・貨幣などの) issue Ⓤ ━━発行する publish 圓; issue 圓 ‖私たちは学級新聞を発行することに決めた We decided to publish a class paper. / 来週記念切手が発行される Commemorative stamps will be issued next week. / この雑誌は毎週発行されている This magazine is issued every week.
◆年2回発行の雑誌 a「twice yearly [biannual] magazine / この雑誌は発行部数が月間50万部である This magazine has a monthly circulation of 500,000.
‖発行所 a publishing house / 発行人 a publisher

はっこう² 発光 emission of light ━━発光する emit light 圓 ‖発光塗料 luminous paint

はっこう³ 発効 この法律は来年発効する This law will come into effect next year.

はっこう⁴ 発酵 fermentation Ⓤ ━━発酵する ferment 圓
◆みそは発酵させた大豆から作られる Miso is made from fermented soybeans.

はつごおり 初氷 きのう湖に初氷が張ったYesterday the lake froze over for the first time this winter.

はっこつ 白骨 (骸骨(がいこつ)) skeleton ⓒ
‖白骨死体 a skeleton

ばっさい 伐採 deforestation Ⓤ ━━伐採する(切り倒す) cut* down, fell 圓 ‖この山の木はすべて伐採された All the trees on this mountain have been「cut down [felled].

はっさく 八朔 grapefruit-like citrus fruit ⓒ

ばっさり 枝をばっさりと(→一撃で)切り落とす cut down a branch with a single stroke / 今年私たちのクラブは予算をばっさり(→大幅に)削られた The budget for our club has been cut drastically this year.

はっさん 発散 (気体などの) emission Ⓤⓒ; (熱・光線などの) radiation Ⓤ ━━発散する emit 圓; radiate 圓 ‖この薬品は強いにおいを発散する This chemical emits [gives off] a strong scent.
◆彼女はやけ食いをして怒りを発散させた She let [worked] off her anger by eating a lot.

ばっし¹ 抜糸 きょう傷の抜糸をしてもらった I had the stitches removed from the wound today.

ばっし² 抜歯 (an) extraction (of a tooth) ━━抜歯する extract [pull out] a tooth ‖1時間前に抜歯してもらったばかりなので食事ができない I can't eat because I had a tooth extracted [pulled out] just an hour ago.

バッジ 彼は帽子にバッジをつけている He wears a badge on his cap.

はつしも 初霜 きのう初霜があった We had the first frost of this winter yesterday.

はっしゃ¹ 発車 departure ━━発車する depart 圓 圓, leave* 圓 圓 ‖次の東京行きの列車は11時に2番線から発車します The next train for Tokyo departs [leaves] (from) platform 2 at 11 o'clock. / バスは毎時0分, 15分, 30分, 45分の発車です The buses leave on the quarter hour.
‖発車時刻 the departure time

はっしゃ² 発射 (ロケットなどを) launch; (銃などを) fire 圓 ‖ミサイルを発射する launch a missile / 警官はその車に向けて銃を発射した The police officer fired his gun at the car.
‖発射台 a launching pad

はっしょう 発祥 このあたりがメソポタミア文明発祥の地といわれている This area is said to be the cradle [birthplace] of Mesopotamian civilization.

はつじょうき 発情期 the mating season

はっしょく 発色 この生地は発色がよい(→よく染まる) This cloth dyes well.
‖発色剤 a coloring agent

はっしん¹ 発信 ━━発信する send* 圓, transmit 圓 ‖そのタンカーは沈没する前にSOSを発信した The tanker sent (out) an SOS before it sank.
◆そのデマの発信源(→情報源)は小松さんだった The source of the false rumor was Mr. Komatsu.
‖発信音(電話の) a dial [(英)dialling] tone / 発信局 a sending office / 発信地 a place of dispatch; (流行などの) a source / 発信人 a sender

はっしん² 発疹 この病気にかかると発疹が出る If you catch this disease, you break [come] out in a rash.

はっしん³ 発進 (動き出すこと) start ⓒ; (離陸) takeoff Ⓤ ━━発進する start 圓; take* off ‖爆撃機は3時間後に発進する The bomber will take off in three hours.

バッシング (強い非難) bashing Ⓤ

ばっすい 抜粋 extract [C], excerpt [C] **——抜粋する** extract [他] ∥これはその新聞記事からの抜粋です This is *an excerpt from* the newspaper article. / その本から必要な内容を数箇所抜粋した I *extracted* some necessary passages *from* the book.

ハッスル **——ハッスルする** hustle [自] ∥彼女が試合の応援に来たので篤志はハッスルした Atsushi *hustled* because his girlfriend came to cheer him in the match.

はっする 発する ❶【出す】(熱・光線などを) give* off, emit [他]; (音声を) give [他]; (警告・声明などを) issue [他] ∥この液体は温めると甘い香りを発する This liquid *gives off* a sweet fragrance when heated. / そのろうそくは柔らかな光を発していた That candle *was emitting* a gentle light. / 机の上に大きなクモがいたので思わず大声を発してしまった I *gave* a cry without thinking because I saw a big spider on my desk. / 津波警報が1時間前に発せられた A tsunami warning *was issued* an hour ago.

◆彼女はショックのあまりひと言も発することができなかった She was so shocked that she *couldn't utter* a single word.

❷【始まる】rise* [自] ∥この川はアルプスに源を発する This river *rises* [*has its source*] *in* the Alps. ◆その暴動は反政府運動の指導者の逮捕に端を発していた The riot 「*started with* [*originated in*] the arrest of the leaders of the antigovernment movement.

ばっする 罰する punish [他] ∥犯罪者を厳しく罰する *punish* a criminal harshly [severely]; *impose a* harsh [severe] *punishment on* a criminal / 危険な運転は法律で厳しく罰せられるべきだ Dangerous driving should *be punished* severely by the law.

はっせい[1] 発生 (疫病・災害などの) outbreak [C]; (事故・事件などの) occurrence [U] [C] **——発生する** break* out; occur [自] ∥科学者はペストの発生を防ぐことができなかった Scientists couldn't prevent *the outbreak of* the plague. / 昨夜学校の近くで火災が発生した A fire *broke out* near our school last night. / この交差点で先週3件の交通事故が発生した Three traffic accidents *occurred* [*happened*] at this crossing last week.

◆今年の秋, イナゴが大量発生した(→繁殖した) Locusts *bred in great numbers* this autumn. / 夜になると霧が発生した A mist *arose* at night. / その山の上空に雨雲が発生した A rain cloud *has formed* over the mountain. / この地区は白血病の発生率が高い *The incidence of* leukemia is high in this area.

はっせい[2] 発声 vocalization [U] ◆その俳優は毎日発声練習をしている The actor does *vocal exercises* every day.

∥発声器官 a vocal organ / 発声法 vocalization

はっそう[1] 発送 dispatch [U] [C], shipment [U] [C] **——発送する** dispatch [他], ship [他], send* out [off] ∥招待状を発送する *dispatch* [*send out*] invitations / 早急の発送をお願いします We are looking forward to *your* early *shipment*. / ご注文の商品は代金が振り込まれしだい発送いたします Your order will *be shipped* as soon as the price is paid into our account.

はっそう[2] 発想 (考え) idea [C] ∥彼の発想はいつも奇抜だ His *ideas* are always novel. / 彼らはその発想をさらに進めて新製品を開発した They carried the *idea* further and came up with a new product.

◆典型的な発想(→考え方) *a* typical *way of thinking* / 君は発想の転換をする(→物事を別の角度から見る)べきだ You'd better *look at things from a different angle*.

はっそく 発足 ➔はっそく

ばっそく 罰則 penal regulations; (スポーツの) penalty [C] ∥その選手には罰則が適用された *A penalty* was applied to the player. / The player *was penalized*.

ばった grasshopper [C]

バッター batter [C], hitter [C] ∥右[左]バッター *a* right-handed [left-handed] *batter* / 佐々木がバッターボックスに入った Sasaki stepped into *the batter's box*. (❖×batter box とはいわない) / 審判はバッターアウトを宣告した The umpire called *the batter out*.

はつたいけん 初体験 *one's* first time ∥カヌーは今回が初体験です This is *my first time* canoeing. ◆(セックスの)初体験はいつですか When did you *first* have sex?

はったつ 発達 development [U]; (成長) growth [U] **——発達する** develop [自]; grow* [自]

ビタミンは身体の発達に不可欠だ Vitamins are indispensable to physical *development* [*growth*].

マスメディアの発達は社会的大変革をもたらした *The development* of the mass media has brought about a social revolution.

東シナ海で台風が発達している A typhoon *is developing* over the East China Sea.

◆ウエートリフティングで筋肉を発達させる *develop one's* muscles by weight lifting / その国では鉄道があまり発達していない Railroads *are not* well *developed* in that country.

∥発達心理学 developmental psychology / 発達段階 a developmental stage

はったり bluff [U] [C] ∥彼はその仕事を3日で仕上げると言っているけど, ただのはったりだよ He says he'll finish the job in three days but 「*it's* only *a bluff* [he *is* only *bluffing*].

◆英語がぺらぺらだという彼女のはったりを正男は信じてしまった She *bluffed* [*fooled*] Masao *into* believing that she was very fluent in English.

ばったり きのう駅で旧友にばったり会った I *ran into* an old friend of mine at the station yesterday. / 彼女はうつぶせにばったり倒れた She *fell flat* on her face. / 10時を過ぎると街の人通りはばったり(→突然)途絶えた After 10 o'clock the streets were *suddenly* deserted.

は

ぱったり ➡ばったり

はっちゃく 発着 arrival and departure (◆語順に注意) ◆このホームからは通常列車は発着しません Usually trains *don't arrive at or depart from* this platform.
‖発着時刻 arrival and departure times / 発着時刻表 a timetable

はっちゅう 発注 彼はデジタルカメラを20台発注した He *ordered* [*placed an order for*] 20 digital cameras.

ばっちり きのうのパーティーでの彼女の(格好)はばっちり決まっていた(→全く完璧(炫)だった) The way she dressed *looked just perfect* at the party yesterday.
❢「英語の試験はどうだった?」「ばっちりだよ」 "How did the English exam go?" "*Great*."

ばっちり 彼女は目はぱっちりしていて、とてもかわいい She is very cute and *has big bright eyes*.

パッチワーク patchwork Ⓤ (◆作品は Ⓒ)

バッティング batting Ⓤ
‖バッティングアベレージ a batting average / バッティングオーダー a batting order / バッティングコーチ a batting coach

ばってき 抜擢 靖子が主役に抜擢された Yasuko *was picked out for* the leading role.

バッテリー battery Ⓒ (◆「蓄電池」、野球の「投手と捕手」の両方の意味で使える) ‖バッテリーが上がっている The battery *is dead*. / 僕は修とバッテリーを組んでいる I *form a battery* with Osamu.

はってん 発展 development Ⓤ; (成長) growth Ⓤ ──発展する develop Ⓘ; grow* Ⓘ
新空港はその地域の経済発展を促すだろう The new airport will help *the economic development* of the area.
東南アジアの経済は急速に発展している The economies of Southeast Asia *are growing* very fast.
その紛争は戦争へと発展した The dispute *developed* into war.
◆3つの政党が発展的解消をして新しい党が結成された(→再編成された) Three political parties *were reorganized* into a new party.
‖発展途上国 a developing country

はつでん 発電 generation of electricity ──発電する generate electricity
‖発電機 a generator, a dynamo / 火力[水力、原子力]発電所 a thermal [hydro, nuclear] power station

はっと ❶[突然意識する様子] 彼女は彼の提案を全く誤解していたことにはっと気づいた It *suddenly* came to her that she had misunderstood his proposal completely. / 気がつくとみんなが私たちを見ていた When we *came to ourselves*, we found that everyone was watching us.
❷[驚く様子] はっとするような真紅のスカーフ a *stunning* scarlet scarf / その絵の美しさにみんなはっと息を飲んだ The beauty of the painting made them all *catch their breaths*. / 電話が突然鳴ったのではっとした I *was startled* by the sudden ringing of the telephone. / The sudden ringing of the telephone *gave me a start*. / 彼はその物音にはっとしていすから立ち上がった He *started* up from the chair at the noise.

バット bat Ⓒ ‖バットを振る swing *a bat* / バットを短く[長く]持つ choke up [down] on *the bat*
‖金属バット a metal bat

パット (ゴルフ) putt Ⓒ

ぱっと 彼女が部屋に入ってくると彼の顔はぱっと(→急に)輝いた His face lit up *suddenly* when she came into the room. / そのスイッチを押すと部屋の明かりがぱっとついた When I pressed the switch, the light in the room *flashed on*. / 彼はぱっとひらめいた A good idea *flashed into my mind*. / そのうわさが町中にぱっと(→すぐに)広まった The rumor spread *quickly* through the town. / おじの商売はこのところぱっとしない(→不振だ) My uncle's business *is slow* these days. / 期末試験はぱっとしない成績(→不満足)だった The results of the term exam were *unsatisfactory*.

パッド pad Ⓒ ‖肩パッド shoulder pads

はつどう 発動 大統領は強権を発動して暴動を鎮圧した The president *invoked* the power of the state to suppress the riot.

はつどうき 発動機 (エンジン) engine Ⓒ; (モーター) motor Ⓒ

はっとうしん 八頭身 8頭身の(→長身で均整のとれた)モデル a model *with a tall, well-proportioned figure*

ハットトリック 彼はハットトリックを達成した He scored *a hat trick*.

はつに 初荷 the first freight [fréit] of the New Year

はつねつ 発熱 an outbreak of fever; (熱) fever Ⓤ Ⓒ ‖かぜで発熱する have [run] *a fever* with a cold

はつのり 初乗り 初乗り運賃は150円です *The base fare* is 150 yen.

はっぱ 発破 blasting Ⓤ ◆彼らはその岩に発破をかけた They *blew up* the rock *with dynamite*. / コーチは選手たちにはっぱをかけた(→激励した) The coach *pepped up* the players. / 山田さんは部下にはっぱをかけてその仕事を3日で終わらせた Mr. Yamada *prodded* his subordinates *into* finishing the work in three days.

はつばい 発売 sale Ⓤ; (CDや本などの) release Ⓤ ──発売する put* ... on sale; release Ⓘ ‖新製品が10月に発売される予定です A new product is to *be released* in October. / そのテレビゲームは発売禁止になった The sale of the video game *was banned* [*prohibited*]. / 新しい辞書はいつ発売されますか When will the new dictionary *be put on sale* [*the market*]? ◆彼女の新しいCDが発売中です Her new CD *is* 「*on sale* [*available*]」 now. / このビデオの発売部数は1万本だ This

video *has sold* 10,000 *copies*.
‖発売元 a sales agency

ぱっぱと 彼は机をぱっぱと片づけた He straightened up his desk *quickly*. / 兄は給料が入るとぱっぱと使ってしまう As soon as my brother gets paid, he just *blows it all*. / 彼女はラーメンにコショウをぱっぱと振りかけた She *sprinkled* pepper on her ramen.

はっぴ 法被 happi (coat) C

江戸時代，武家や商店の奉公人や職人はいつも，着物の上着であるはっぴを着ていましたが，今日(こんにち)はっぴを日常的に着用しているのはとび職，大工など一部の職人になりました．しかし，祭りの日にははっぴを着た人々が街にあふれます．
In the Edo period (1603–1867), servants of the military and merchants as well as workmen used to wear happi coats. Now they are only worn in everyday life by scaffolding builders, carpenters and the like. But many people in happi can be seen around town on festival days.

ハッピーエンド ⚠ happy ending C (❖ × happy end とはいわない) ‖私はハッピーエンドの映画が好きです I like films with *a happy ending*.

はつひので 初日の出 私たちは初日の出を拝みに江ノ島に行った We went to Enoshima to watch *the first sunrise of the year*.

はつびょう 発病 彼は帰国途中の飛行機の中で発病した He「*got sick* [*fell ill*]」on the plane back home.

はっぴょう 発表 announcement U C ——発表する announce ⊕
試験の結果はあす発表されます The results of the exam *will be announced* tomorrow.
大統領は最終決定を記者団に発表した The President *announced* his final decision *to* the press.
その会社はパソコン用の新しいソフトを発表した The company *made an announcement* of new software for personal computers.
◆ピアノの発表会 a piano *recital* / 彼らは彼女が無実であると発表した They *proclaimed that* she was innocent. / あした研究論文を発表することになっている I'm supposed to *read* [*deliver*] my research paper tomorrow. / 私は来週ゼミで発表することになっている I'm going to *give a presentation* in the seminar next week. / 彼の新しい小説はまだ未発表だ(→原稿の段階だ) His new novel *is* still *in manuscript*.

はっぷ 発布 promulgation U ——発布する promulgate ⊕ ‖法令を発布する *promulgate* [*publish*] a law

はつぶたい 初舞台 one's debut [deibjúː] ‖彼女は5歳で初舞台を踏んだ She made *her debut* [*first appearance on stage*] at the age of five.

はっぷん 発奮 私は兄のアメリカ留学の話を聞いて大いに発奮した I *was greatly inspired* by my brother's story of his studying in America.

はっぽう¹ 八方 彼女は八方手を尽くして(→くまなく)盗まれた自転車を捜した She searched *high and low* for her stolen bicycle. / 八方手を尽くした(→あらゆる手段を講じた)が彼女のコンサートチケットを手に入れることはできなかった I「*tried every possible means* [*left no stone unturned*]」but couldn't get a ticket for her concert. / 問題は八方丸く(→みんなを満足させる形で)収まった The problem was solved *in a way which satisfied everyone*. / 純は八方美人だから(→みんなに気に入られようとするから)僕は好きじゃない I don't like Jun because she *tries to please everyone*. / 私たちの計画は八方ふさがりだ Our plan *is up against a wall*. / 連続2試合に負けて彼の態度は八方破れだった Having lost two matches in a row, he assumed a *desperate* attitude.

はっぽう² 発砲 発砲事件 *a shooting* (*incident*) / 強盗は警察に向かって数回発砲した The robber *fired* several *shots at* the police.

はっぽうスチロール 発泡スチロール styrene foam U,《米》(商標名)Styrofoam U

ばっぽんてき 抜本的 ——抜本的な (思い切った) drastic; (根本的な) radical ‖景気を回復させるために抜本的な対策がとられるべきだ Some *drastic* [*radical*] measures should be taken to revitalize the economy.

はつまご 初孫 one's firstborn grandchild

はつみみ 初耳 それは初耳だ That's *news to me*. / I haven't *heard* that *before*.

はつめい 発明 invention U C ——発明する invent ⊕
パソコンは画期的な発明だ The personal computer is *a revolutionary invention*.
テレビの発明は我々の生活を大きく変えた *The invention* of television changed our lives greatly.
エジソンは電球を発明した Edison *invented* the electric light bulb.
‖発明家 an inventor
ことわざ 必要は発明の母 ⇒ ひつよう

はつもうで 初詣で hatsumode, visiting a shrine or a temple at the New Year ◆友人と近くの神社に初もうでに行った I *paid a New Year's visit to* a nearby shrine with my friends.

年が明けて最初に神社や寺にお参りをすることを初もうでといいます．ふつう三が日の間にすませますが，大みそかの夜から元日にかけて出かける人も多く，大都市では終夜運転する公共交通機関もあります．有名な神社や寺は大勢の人でごった返します．
Hatsumode is the year's first visit to shrines or temples usually made during the first three days of the New Year. In some big cities, public transportation services operate all night on New Year's Eve for those who want to observe *hatsumode* as the year turns. Famous shrines and temples get very

はつもの　初物　きょう初物のナシを食べた I ate *the first pears of the season* today.

はつゆき　初雪　the first snow of the year [season]　◆昨夜初雪が降った Last night *it snowed for the first time this winter*.

はつゆめ　初夢　the [one's] first dream of the New Year　//富士山の初夢は縁起がいいとされている It's considered lucky if *your first dream of the New Year* is of Mt. Fuji.

はつらつ　潑剌　はつらつとした青年 a *lively young man* / テニスをしているときの哲也は実にはつらつとしている Tetsuya *is really full of life* when he plays tennis. / 子供たちははつらつとした足取りで歩いていた The children were walking *with a spring in their steps*.

はつれい　発令　(official) announcement ⓊⒸ　——発令する announce 他　//今月の1日付けで辞令が発令され,父はロンドンに単身赴任した Assignments *were (officially) announced* on the first day of this month. My father left for a post in London, leaving us behind.　◆気象庁は乾燥注意報を発令した The Meteorological Agency *issued* a dry-weather warning.

はつろ　発露　その行為は彼らの愛校心の発露(→しるし)だった The act was *a manifestation of their love for their school*.

はて¹　果て　the end　//ここは北海道の北の果てだ This is *the northern end* of Hokkaido. / 斉藤さんは新種のチョウの発見のためなら地の果てまでも行くつもりだ Mr. Saito will go to *the end of the earth* to find a new species of butterfly.　◆果てもなく広がる星空を眺めているとリラックスできる It relaxes me when I look up at *vast expanses of stars*.

はて²　はて,傘をどこに置いたっけ *Let me see*, where did I put my umbrella?

はで　派手　——はでな (軽蔑的)loud; (色の鮮やかな) bright; (人目を引く〈軽蔑的〉)showy; (安っぽくごてごてした) gaudy; (けばけばしい) garish　//はでな広告 a *loud* advertisement / 近藤先生はいつもはでな色の服を着ている Mr. Kondo always wears *bright-colored clothes*.
　◆はでな(→ぜいたくな)生活をする lead a *luxurious life* / 君たちはずいぶんとはでに(→人目立つほどに)けんかしたもんだね You quarreled with each other *conspicuously* [〈口語的〉*in a big way*], didn't you?

ばてい　馬蹄　hoof Ⓒ, (horse)shoe Ⓒ　//馬蹄形磁石 a *horseshoe* magnet

はてしない　果てしない　(終わることのない) endless; (限りなく広い) boundless, limitless; (無限の) infinite　——果てしなく endlessly; boundlessly, limitlessly; infinitely ⇨いつまでも, はて(果て)　//果てしなく広がる砂漠 a *boundless* [*limitless*] *desert* / 意味のない議論が果てしなく続いた The meaningless discussion went on *endlessly* [*without end*]. / 宇宙は果てしない The universe *is boundless* [*infinite*].

はて(な)　はて,どうしたもんだろう What *on earth* shall I do? / はてな,あの男,前にどこかで会ったことがあるような気がする *Let me see*. I think I have seen that man somewhere before.

はてる　果てる　(終わる) end 自; (死ぬ) die 自　//その会議はいつ果てるとも知れなかった It seemed that the meeting *would never end*. / The meeting *seemed to have no end*. (❖後の表現中の end は名詞)
　◆精も魂も尽き果てた I'm *completely done for*. / 彼らは放蕩(ほうとう)息子にほとほと困り果てている Their prodigal son *is their great trouble*. / 彼女の頑固さにはあきれ果てた I *was dumbfounded* at her stubbornness.

ばてる　2晩徹夜続きですっかりばててしまった I *was exhausted* [〈口語的〉*dead tired*, *pooped out*] after staying up two nights in a row. / 暑さで彼らはちょっとばてぎみだ They look a little *tired* with heat.

はてんこう　破天荒　——破天荒の (前例のない) unprecedented; (前代未聞の) unheard-of　//破天荒の事業に着手する start an *unprecedented* [*unheard-of*] project

パテント　patent Ⓒ　⇨とっきょ

はと　鳩　pigeon Ⓒ; dove Ⓒ　(❖pigeon は飼っているハトや都市の公園などにすんでいるハト, dove は野バト)　//ハトがくうくう鳴いている *A pigeon is cooing*. / 手品師は箱の中からハトを取り出した The magician pulled *a pigeon* out of a box. / ハトは平和の象徴として知られている *The dove* is known as a symbol of peace. (❖この意味では pigeon は用いられない)
‖鳩時計 a cuckoo clock / ハト派 a dove / 伝書バト a carrier [homing] pigeon

[慣用表現] 突然そう言われて彼は鳩が豆鉄砲を食らったような顔をしていた When he was suddenly told that, *his eyes popped out*.

はどう　波動　〔物理〕wave ⒸⓊ

ばとう　罵倒　invective Ⓤ [əbjúːs], 〈公式的〉 invective Ⓤ　——罵倒する abuse [əbjúːz] 他, 〈公式的〉inveigh (against ...)　//彼らは互いに相手を罵倒した They *shouted abuse* at each other. / They *called each other names*.

パトカー　⚠　police car Ⓒ, patrol car Ⓒ, 〈米〉squad car Ⓒ

はとこ　second cousin Ⓒ

はとば　波止場 (埠頭(ふとう)) wharf Ⓒ (複 wharves); (桟橋) pier Ⓒ　//船が波止場を離れた The boat left *the wharf*.

バドミントン　〔スポーツ〕badminton Ⓤ　//バドミントンをする play *badminton*

はどめ　歯止め　brake　//増大する軍事費に歯止めをかける *put a brake on* increasing military spending
　◆姉は食べ始めると歯止めがきかなくなる My sister *can't stop* once she starts eating.

パトロール　patrol ⓊⒸ　——パトロールする patrol 他　//警官はパトロール中だ The police officer is *on patrol*. / 夜には何人かのボランティアたちがその地区をパトロールする Some volunteers *patrol* the district at night.

‖パトロールカー a patrol [police] car

パトロン patron [péitrən] [C]; (女性の) patroness [C]

ハトロンし ハトロン紙 brown paper [U]

バトン baton [C] ‖バトンを手渡す hand *the baton* ◆生徒会長の仕事を後輩にバトンタッチする *transfer* [*hand over*] the duties of the student council president to *one's* junior ‖バトンタッチ a baton pass / バトントワラー a baton twirler; (鼓笛隊を率いる) a majorette

はな[1] 鼻

nose [C]; (象の) trunk [C]; (豚などの) snout [C]; (犬などの) muzzle [C] ―鼻の nasal (❖名詞の前で用いる)

〖鼻は・が〗

鼻がむずむずする *My nose* tickles.

鼻が詰まっていてにおいが分からない I can't smell because *my nose* is stuffed [stopped] up.

長い鼻が象の特徴だ Elephants are distinguished by *their* long *trunks*.

花粉症で目と鼻がとてもかゆい *My* eyes and *nose* itch terribly because of hay fever.

犬は鼻がきく A dog *has a good nose*.

〖鼻の〗

鼻の先 the tip of *one's nose*

その馬が鼻の差で優勝した The horse won *by a nose*.

◆鼻の穴 *a nostril*

〖鼻を・に・で〗

彼は僕の鼻を殴った He punched me on [in] *the nose*.

赤ん坊は泣いて鼻にしわを寄せた The baby cried and wrinkled *his nose*.

象が鼻で材木を運んでいた An elephant was carrying wood with *its trunk*.

彼は鼻にかかったような話し方をする He speaks *through his nose*.

彼女はすぐ他人の問題に鼻をつっこむ She always *pokes* [*sticks*] *her nose* into other people's affairs.

その川のあまりの臭さに私は鼻をつまんだ The odor of the river was so strong that I *held my nose*.

鼻をほじるのはやめなさい Stop *picking your nose*.

◆悪臭が鼻をついた I *smelled* a bad odor. / 彼は一日中鼻をぐすぐすいわせていた He kept *sniffing* all day. / 馬は鼻を鳴らしていた Horses *were snorting*.

〖その他〗

鼻水が出てるよ You have *a runny nose*. / Your nose is running.

【鼻が高い】彼も息子が医者になって鼻が高いことだろう He must *be proud* because his son has become a doctor.

【鼻高々】その小さな女の子はきれいな着物を着て鼻高々だった The little girl looked *very pleased with herself* in her pretty kimono.

【鼻であしらう】彼女に交際を申し込んだが鼻であしらわれた(→きっぱり拒絶された) I asked her to go out with me but she *flatly turned me down*.

【鼻にかける】《口語的》be stuck up; (自慢する) boast [自] [他], brag [自] ‖彼女は金持ちであることを鼻にかけたりしない She never *boasts of* being wealthy.

【鼻につく】あのタレントはいい人ぶっているのが鼻につく That TV personality is always trying to show he's a nice person, and that *gets on my nerves*.

【鼻の下が長い】彼は美人に囲まれて鼻の下が長くなっていた He *drooled over* all the beautiful women around him.

【鼻も引っかけない】彼女はクラスの男子には鼻も引っかけない She *turns her nose up at* the boys in her class.

【鼻を明かす】(出し抜く) outwit [他] ‖いつかきっとあいつの鼻を明かしてやる I'm sure I'll *outwit* him some day.

【鼻を鳴らす】ばかにしてふんと鼻を鳴らす *give a snort* of contempt

【鼻をへし折る】あいつの鼻をへし折ってやった I *brought* [*took*] him *down a peg* (*or two*).

> [コロケーション] -nose-
>
> 〖形容詞＋～〗 高い～ a long nose (❖×a high nose とはいわない) / 低い～ a short nose / 大きい～ a large [big] nose / 小さい～ a small nose / ぺちゃんこの～ a flat nose / わし～ an aquiline nose / かぎ～ a hooked nose / しし～ a snub [turned-up] nose / とがった～ a sharp nose / 団子っ～ a bulbous nose

‖鼻声 a nasal voice / 鼻柱 a bridge / 鼻孔 a nostril / 小鼻 a wing of the nose

➾はな(洟)

はな[2] 花・華

❶【植物】flower [C]; (果樹の) blossom [C]; (鑑賞用) bloom [C]

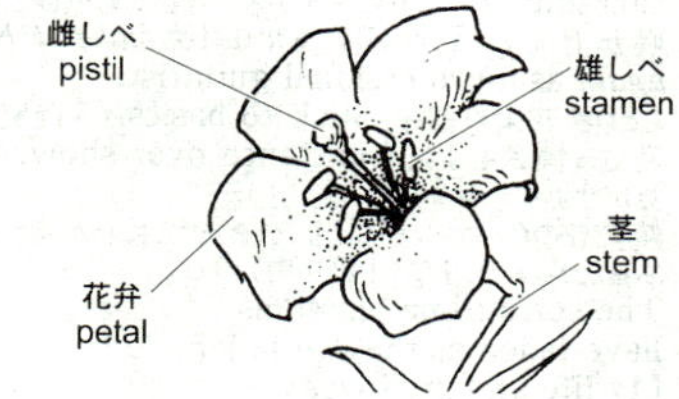
雌しべ
pistil
雄しべ
stamen
茎
stem
花弁
petal

花を植える plant *flowers* / 花に水をやる water *flowers*

それらの花は1年の今ごろ咲く Those *flowers* come out at this time of the year.

その花はまだつぼみだ The *flowers* are still in bud.

桜の花が満開だ *The* cherry *blossoms* are in full bloom.

この花はもうすぐ種ができる This *flower* is about to go to seed.

はな

少女たちは野原で花を摘んだ The girls picked [gathered] *flowers* in the field.

アンが花びんに花をさした Ann put some *flowers* in the vase.

私の母は花を生けるのがとても上手です My mother arranges *flowers* very well.

彼女はその布に花柄模様をプリントした She printed *a flower design* [*pattern*] on the cloth.

チョウが花から花へひらひら飛んでいた Butterflies fluttered 「*among the flowers* [*from flower to flower*]」

ユリの花言葉は純潔だ Lilies signify purity in *the language of flowers*.

◆リンゴの花が咲いている The apple trees *are blooming*. / The apple *blossoms are out*. / このスイセンは初春に花を咲かせる This daffodil *blooms* in the early spring.

❢「女の子に花を贈りたいんですが, 何がいいですか」「バラなんかどう」"I want to give some *flowers* to a girl. What would you recommend?" "How about roses?"

❷ [生け花]
彼女の母親はお花の先生をしている Her mother teaches *flower arrangement*.

❸ [最盛期]
父はよく「学生のころが花だった」とぼやいている "*My best days* were when I was in college," my father often grumbles.

その選手は実力があるだけでなく華もある The player is not only competent but (also) *has star quality*.

‖花屋(店) a flower shop, a florist's; (人) a florist

慣用表現 それは言わぬが花だ *It's better left unsaid*. / 中学の同級生たちとの久しぶりの再会ですっかり話に花が咲いた When I saw my classmates from junior high school after a long time, I *had a really good talk* [*chat*] with them. / 今度だけはおまえに花を持たせてやろう I'll let you *take credit for it* only this time. / プロのギタリストとしてもうひと花咲かせたい I really want to *make it big again* as a professional guitarist.

ことわざ 花より団子 Stick to basics. (→確実な利益に固執せよ); Substance over show. (→見かけよりも中身)

短歌 花の色はうつりにけりないたづらにわが身世にふるながめせしまに (小野小町)
The springtime blossoms
have faded as they've fallen.
My life and my loves
have faded and fallen, too,
like the rain that never ends.

はな³ 洟 (nasal) mucus Ⓤ ◆はなをかむ blow *one's nose* / はなをたらす *have a runny nose* / 彼はきのう一日中はなをすすっていた He *was sniffling* all day yesterday.
‖はなたれ小僧 a snotty boy

はないき 鼻息 慣用表現 私たちの監督は来年も優勝するぞと今から鼻息が荒い Our coach *is already determined to* win the championship again next year. / 彼はいつも上司の鼻息をうかがっている (→機嫌に敏感だ) He is always *sensitive to* his boss's *mood*.

はなうた 鼻歌 hum Ⓒ ◆彼女は鼻歌を歌いながらやってきた She came *humming (a song)* to herself.

はなお 鼻緒 a thong (of geta)

はなかぜ 鼻風邪 head cold Ⓒ ‖はなかぜをひく catch a 「*head cold* [*cold in the nose*]」

はながた 花形 花形産業 *a popular industry* / 彼はそのチームの花形選手だった He was *the star player* of the team.

はながみ 鼻紙 tissue Ⓤ Ⓒ, 《商標名》Kleenex Ⓤ Ⓒ ⇨ちりがみ

はなくそ 鼻糞 dried mucus Ⓤ, 《口語的》snot Ⓤ ◆鼻くそをほじくる pick *one's nose*
ことわざ 目くそ鼻くそを笑う ⇨わらう

はなぐもり 花曇り 花曇りの空 *a slightly cloudy sky in spring*

はなげ 鼻毛 nose hair Ⓤ Ⓒ

はなごえ 鼻声 nasal tone Ⓒ, twang Ⓒ (通例単数形) ‖鼻声で話す speak 「*in a nasal tone* [*through one's nose*]」
◆徹はひどい鼻声をしていた Toru's *voice sounded* awfully *nasal*.

はなざかり 花盛り 花盛りだ The roses *are in full bloom* in the garden now. / インターネット関連産業は今花盛りです Internet-related industry *is prosperous* [*in its heyday*] now.

はなし 話

❶	話すこと	talk; speech; chat
❷	話題・話の内容	topic, subject; story
❸	物語	story
❹	うわさ	rumor
❺	相談・交渉	

❶ [話すこと] talk Ⓒ Ⓤ; (演説) speech Ⓒ; (おしゃべり) chat Ⓒ ‖はなす (話す)

私は小田先生と進路について長いこと話をした I *had a long talk* with Mrs. Oda *about* my future. / I *talked* with Mrs. Oda for quite a while about my future.

靖夫は私たちの話に口をはさんだ Yasuo *cut in on* our *talk*.

生徒たちはその先生の長い話にうんざりしていた The students were bored with the teacher's long *speech*.

先生が教室に入ると私たちは話をやめた We stopped 「*our chats* [*chatting*]」 when the teacher entered the classroom.

◆ちょっとお話があるのですが I *have something to talk about* with you. / Could I *have a word* with you? / 私たちはお茶を飲みながらサッカーの話をした We *talked* soccer over a cup of tea. (◆この talk は「…について議論する」の意味) / どうぞ話を続けてください *Continue talking* [*Carry on*], please. / 英二は話がうまい [下手だ] Eiji *is a good* [*poor*] *talker*. / 彼は私を話に引き込んだ He engaged me in *conversation*. / 他人の話に耳を傾けることは大切です It is important for you to *listen to others.* / ここだけの話だけど, 私クラブをやめるつもりなの *Just between you and me,* I'm planning to quit the club. / 彼らは話に夢中で, 私が部屋に入ったことに気づかなかった They *were so deep in conversation* that they did not notice that I had come into the room.

❷【話題・話の内容】(話題) topic Ⓒ, subject Ⓒ; (話の内容) story Ⓒ

話をそらす change *the subject* [*topic*].
その話はもうやめよう Let's *drop the subject.*
彼の話はあちこちへ飛んだり He kept jumping from one *topic* to another.
彼女の話はとてもおもしろかった Her *story* was very amusing to us.
彼の話にはいくつか疑問点がある I have some doubts about his *story.*
話がだいぶこみ入ってきた *The story* has become very complicated.
だけど, それはまた別の話だ But that's *another story.*
私たちは電車が遅れて遅刻したことになってるから話を合わせてね I said we were late because the train was late. *Keep to that story,* okay?

◆それは話の種になった That gave us *something to talk about.* / 話は違うけれど(→ところで), 最近義明に会った? *By the way,* have you seen Yoshiaki recently? / 久保田君とは話が合う Kubota and I *speak the same language.* / どうやら話が横道にそれてしまったようです I seem to *have wandered off the point.* / ビートルズの話になると彼女は目を輝かせる *When* the Beatles *come up,* her eyes brighten.

❸【物語】story Ⓒ

この話は事実に基づいている This *story* is founded on facts.
おじいさんはよく昔の話をしてくれた My grandfather often told me *stories* about the old days.
妹は小さいころ『白雪姫』の話が好きだった My sister liked *the story* of Snow White when she was a child.

❹【うわさ】rumor Ⓒ

あなたについてはいろいろ話を聞いています I've heard「many *rumors* [a lot] about you.

◆あの学校のバスケットボール部は強いという話だ *They say* [*I hear, It is said*] (*that*) that school has a strong basketball team. / 今や町中が彼女の話でもちきりだ She is now the *talk* of the town. / そんな話, 聞いたことがない I never heard of *such a thing.*

❺【相談・交渉】

アパートの部屋代についてはすぐ話がまとまった We soon *agreed* on the rent for the apartment.
全員同じ額を払うことで話が決まった We *settled* that all of us pay the same amount of money.
話がとんとん拍子で進んだ *The negotiations* went on very smoothly.

慣用表現 そのピアノが買いたかったが, 値段が高すぎてお話にならなかった I wanted to buy the piano, but it was so expensive that buying it *was out of the question.* / そんな話がうますぎて信用できないよ That's *too good a story* to be true. / 君が会に出席しないなんて, それでは話が違うじゃないか You aren't going to attend the meeting? That's *not what you said!* / ニュージーランド旅行について話がはずんだ(→活発な会話をした) We *had a lively conversation* about our trip to New Zealand. / 話によってはお金を貸してあげるよ *Depending on why you need it,* I may lend you money. / 彼のおやじさんは話の分かる人だ His father is an *understanding* person. / あの人の話は話半分に聞いたほうがいい You should take his stories *with a grain of salt.* / 早い話, 僕はその案には反対なんだ *To make a long story short,* I'm against the proposal. / まじめな話, 一滴も飲めないんです *Seriously,* I can't drink at all. / そんなのよくある話さ It's *the same old story.*

-ぱなし -放し talk ずっとしゃべりっぱなしだった He *talked throughout* [*all the time*].
ドアをあけっぱなしにするな Don't *leave* the door *open.*
◆つづける, -れま

はなしあい 話し合い talk Ⓒ, discussion Ⓒ Ⓤ; (交渉) negotiation Ⓒ Ⓤ (しばしば複数形 ~s) /活発な話し合い *an* active *discussion* / 文化祭について話し合いをもった We「*had a talk* [*talked*] about the school festival. / 彼らはその問題を力によってではなく話し合いで解決した They solved the problem not by force but *by discussion.*

はなしあいて 話し相手 someone [somebody] to talk with(❖疑問文・否定文・条件節では通例 anyone [anybody] を用いる) /彼には話し相手がだれもいなかった He didn't have *anyone to talk with* [*to*].

はなしあう 話し合う talk ⓘ, discuss ⓣ /この問題について先生方と話し合う場が必要だ We need to have an opportunity to「*talk* with our teachers *about* this problem [*discuss* this problem with our teachers]. / 校則についてよく話し合いましょう Let's *talk over* the school rules.

はなしか 咄家・噺家 (落語家) comic storyteller Ⓒ

はなしがい 放し飼い, 放し飼いの鶏 free-range chickens(❖free-range は豚や鳥に用いる) / 馬を放し飼いにする(→放牧する) *pasture* [*graze*] *the horses; turn the horses to pasture* / 犬を放し飼いにする(→つながずにおく) *keep* a dog *unchained*

はなしかける 話し掛ける speak* [talk] to *a person* /今は話しかけないで *Don't speak* [*talk*] *to me now.* / 駅で知らない人に話しかけられた I *was spoken to* by a stranger at the station.

はなしごえ 話し声 隣の部屋から話し声が聞こえた I could hear people *talking* from the next room.

はなしことば 話し言葉 spoken language Ⓤ

はなしこむ 話し込む (長時間話す) have* a long talk, talk for a long time; (話に夢中になる) be absorbed [lost] in talking ∥もうこんな時間！すっかり話し込んじゃったね Look what time it is! We've really [*had a long talk* [*been absorbed in talking*], haven't we? ◆私たちはその計画について夜ふけまで話し込んだ We *talked* about the plan *far into the night*.

はなしじょうず 話し上手 (人) good talker ⓒ, conversationalist ⓒ

はなしずき 話し好き ──話し好きな talkative, 《口語的》chatty

はなしちゅう 話し中 彼に電話をかけたが話し中だった I called him up, but *his line was busy* [《英》*engaged*]. / お話し中失礼しますが, ちょっとお尋ねしてもよろしいでしょうか (*I'm*) *sorry to interrupt you*, *but* may I ask you something?

はなして 話して 話し手 speaker ⓒ

はなしぶり 話し振り the way one talks, one's way of talking ∥言葉こそ謙虚だが, 彼の話しぶりには並々ならぬ自信がうかがえる Though his language is modest, [*the way he talks* [*his way of talking*]] suggests that he is very self-confident.

はなしべた 話し下手 poor talker ⓒ

はなしょうぶ 花菖蒲 iris ⓒ

はなす¹ 話す

speak* 自⊕; (おしゃべりをする・話し合う) talk 自⊕; (伝える・述べる) tell* 他⊕ ➡ はなし
英語が話せますか Do you *speak* English? (❖Can you speak English?だと能力を問うことになるので失礼な感じを与える)
4か国語を話せることが彼の自慢です He's proud that he *can speak* four languages.
英語は世界中の多くの人々によって話されている English *is spoken* by many people throughout the world.
もう少しゆっくり話していただけませんか Could you *speak* a little more slowly?
講演者はいじめについて話した The lecturer *spoke about* [*on*] bullying.
何を話しているの What *are* you *talking about*?
彼女は話していて楽しい She is pleasant *to talk with*.
恵美とはさっき電話で話しました I *talked with* Emi *on* [*over*] the telephone a little while ago.
電車の中では大声で話すべきではない You shouldn't *talk* loudly in the train.
彼女に本当のことを話した I *told* her the truth. / I *told* the truth to her.
その事故について詳しく話してください Please *tell* me about the accident in detail.
◆彼はよくあなたのことを話して(→言及して)いました He would often *mention* you to us. / だれかに自分の気持ちを話さずには(→共有せずには)いられなかった I *couldn't help sharing* my feelings with someone. / 祖母は物語を話すのがとても上手だった Grandmother was a very good *storyteller*.

● 「話したいことがあるんだけど」「いいわよ」"I have something to *tell* you." "Go ahead."

● 「ブラジルでは何語が話されていますか」「ポルトガル語です」"What language do they *speak* in Brazil?/ What language *is spoken* in Brazil?" "Portuguese."

● 「何かおもしろいことがありましたか」「いいえ, 話すほどのことは何もありません」"Have you found anything interesting?" "No, *nothing to speak of*."

はなす² 離す part ⊕, separate ⊕ ➡ はなれる, わける
僕たちは2匹の犬を離そうとした We tried to *part* [*separate*] the two dogs.
◆机を離して(→間隔をおいて)並べる put the desks in a row *with some space in between* / 彼は2位を500メートル離してゴールした He reached the finish line 500 meters *ahead of* the second finisher. / 彼はいつもその辞書を手元から離さない He always *keeps* the dictionary *near at hand*. / もう二度と君を離さない I'll never *let* you *go* again. / この子から目を離さないでね Please *keep an eye on* this boy. / *Don't take* your eyes *off* this boy, please. / 今手が離せないから電話に出て！ I *have my hands full* now. You answer the phone!

はなす³ 放す let* ... go, release ⊕; (自由にする) set* ⊕; ... free
「放して」とその女性は叫んだ "*Let* me go," cried the woman.
腕を放せ *Let go* (*of*) my arm.
ハンドルから手を放してらだめだぞ Don't *let go of* the steering wheel.
私はカメを海に放してやった I *released* the turtle into the sea.
女の子はかごから鳥を放してやった The girl *set* the bird *free* from the cage.

はなすじ 鼻筋 the ridge of the nose
◆彼は鼻筋の通った端正な顔をしている He is handsome and *has a shapely nose*.

はなせる 話せる 彼は思ったよりも話せる男だった He was a more *understanding* man than I thought. ➡ はなす(話す)

はなぞの 花園 flower garden ⓒ

はなたば 花束 bouquet ⓒ, a bunch of flowers ∥努は私にバラの花束をくれた Tsutomu gave me *a bouquet* [*bunch*] of roses.

はなぢ 鼻血 nosebleed ⓒ ∥鼻血が出ているよ You have *a nosebleed*. / Your nose is bleeding.

はなつ 放つ (光・においなどを) give* off [out], emit ⊕; (発射する) shoot* ⊕ ∥矢を放つ *shoot* [*release*] an arrow / そのどぶは悪臭を放っていた The ditch *gave off* a bad smell. ◆彼は久しぶりに長打を放った He *hit* a long drive for the first time in a long time. / あれでは虎(ᨈ)を野に放つようなものだと人々はうわさした People said that that was practically the same as *setting a tiger free* *in the wild.*

はなっぱしら 鼻っ柱 the bridge of the nose
慣用表現 彼女は鼻っ柱が強い She *is hard-nosed* [*arrogant, overconfident*].(❖arrogant は「高慢な」、overconfident は「自信過剰な」の意味) / いつかあいつの鼻っ柱をへし折ってやる I'*ll take* [*bring*] him *down a peg* (*or two*) some day.

はなつまみ 鼻摘み (やっかい者) nuisance ⓒ

はなづまり 鼻詰まり 鼻詰まりで息が苦しい *My nose is stuffed* and I can't breathe freely. / この薬は鼻詰まりに効く This medicine is good for *a stuffy nose.*

バナナ banana ⓒ / バナナ1房 a bunch of *bananas* / 熟した[熟していない]バナナ *a ripe* [*green*] *banana*

はなはだ 甚だ very(much) ⇒ とても, ひじょうに 《このようなことをされてははなはだ迷惑だ Being treated like this bothers me *very much.*

はなはだしい 甚だしい はなはだしい誤解 a *gross* misunderstanding / こんなことも知らないとは非常識もはなはだしい(→全く常識に欠けている) If you don't know that, then you *completely* lack common sense. / 彼に文句を言うなんて心得違いもはなはだしい(→完全に間違っている) You are *completely* wrong to complain to him.

はなばなしい 華々しい (みごとな・りっぱな) brilliant; (劇的な) spectacular /彼ははきのうの試合で華々しいデビューを飾った He made a *brilliant* [*spectacular*] debut in yesterday's game. / 彼女の華々しい活躍の陰には血のにじむような努力があった She sweated blood to achieve her *spectacular* success.

はなび 花火 fireworks /今夜, 花火をしようよ Let's do some *fireworks* tonight. / 多摩川で花火が打ち上げられた *Fireworks* were set off on the Tama River. / 私たちはきのう花火見物をした We *enjoyed watching fireworks* yesterday.
‖花火大会 fireworks / 仕掛け花火 set fireworks / 線香花火 a sparkler / ねずみ花火 a coiled sparkler that spins around on the ground before exploding / ロケット花火 a rocket

はなびら 花びら petal ⓒ, leaf ⓒ (複 leaves)

はなふだ 花札 hanafuda, Japanese playing cards

パナマ パナマ Panama ‖ パナマ運河 the Panama Canal / パナマ帽 a Panama hat

はなみ 花見 *hanami*, cherry blossom viewing
◆上野公園に花見に行った We went to Ueno Park to *see* [*enjoy*] *the cherry blossoms.*

花見は昔から行われてきた春の恒例行事です。本来は桜の美しさを鑑賞するためのものですが、近年では実質的に野外の宴会といった様相をとっています。桜の名所では、よい場所を確保するために朝早く、あるいは前日からシートを広げたり綱を張ったりする人もたくさんいます。

Hanami, cherry blossom viewing, has long been a typical event in spring. The original purpose was to appreciate the beauty of cherry blossoms, but nowadays the most significant aspect of *hanami* has changed to the gathering itself, the open-air party. At the places famous for their cherry blossoms, there are a lot of people who put plastic sheets on the ground or rope off an area early in the morning, or even on the day before, to secure a spot with a fine view.

はなみずき 花水木 〖植物〗(flowering) dogwood ⓒ

はなみち 花道 (elevated) aisle [áil] ⓒ; (相撲の) a passageway to the sumo ring
◆力士たちが続々と花道を引き上げてくる Sumo wrestlers are coming back from the ring *through the passageway* one after another.
慣用表現 彼は男の花道を飾った(→男らしい引退をした) He *took a manly retirement*.

はなむけ 餞 farewell gift ⓒ
◆はなむけの言葉 *farewell* words

はなむこ 花婿 bridegroom ⓒ ❖短縮して groom ともいう

はなめがね 鼻眼鏡 pince-nez [pǽnsnèi]《複数扱い》 ◆鼻眼鏡で新聞を読む read a paper *with one's glasses on the tip of one's nose*

はなもちならない 鼻持ちならない, 鼻持ちならない(→耐えがたい)態度 an *intolerable* [*insufferable*] attitude / あいつはきざったらしくて鼻持ちならない(→我慢できない) I *can't bear* [*stand*] his affected attitude.

はなやか 華やか ──華やかな (華々しい) brilliant, spectacular; (豪華な) gorgeous ──華やかに brilliantly, spectacularly; gorgeously ‖華やかに着飾った女性たち women *gorgeously* dressed / 夜の東京ディズニーランドは色とりどりのイルミネーションでとても華やかだった Tokyo Disneyland was very *brilliant* with colorful lights in the evening. / 彼女は華やかなスターの生活にあこがれていた She dreamed of the *spectacular* [*colorful*] lives of stars.

はなやぐ 華やぐ 場内の華やいだ雰囲気 the *cheerful* [*bright*] atmosphere in the hall / 地元チームの優勝で町全体が華やいでいた The whole town *was brightened* because of the victory of the home team.

はなよめ 花嫁 bride ⓒ
‖花嫁衣装 a wedding dress / 花嫁修業 training in housekeeping

はならび 歯並び 彼は歯並びがよい[悪い] He *has regular* [*irregular*] *teeth*.

はなれ 離れ detached room ⓒ; (別館) annex ⓒ

ばなれ 場慣れ 場慣れした司会者 an *experienced* emcee / 彼のスピーチは場慣れがしている He *is experienced at* making speeches.

-ばなれ -離れ 彼女のスタイルは日本人離れして

はなれじま

いる She has an *unusual* figure *for a Japanese person*. / 彼はいまだに親離れができていない(→親に頼っている) He *is* still *dependent on his parents*. / 彼女の歌声は素人離れしている(→プロ並みだ) Her singing voice *is on the professional level*. / 若者の政治離れが進んでいる(→以前よりも無関心になっている) Young people are more *indifferent to political matters* than before.

はなれじま 離れ島 solitary [isolated] island ⓒ

はなればなれ 離れ離れ 私たちは長い間離ればなれだった We *were separated (from each other) for a long time.* / 彼は家族と離ればなれで生活している He lives *apart* [*away*] *from* his family.

はなれる 離れる

❶ [遠ざかる・別れる] leave* 他 自; (分離する) separate 自

持ち場を離れる *leave one's post*
船は港を離れた The ship *left* the harbor.
日本を離れるのはとてもつらい It is painful for me *to leave* Japan.
君とはもう離れられない I *can't 「separate from* [*leave*] *you* now.

◆その子は母親にしがみついて離れなかった The child clung to his mother and wouldn't *let go.* / 離れないでついてきなさい Stay close to me. / 彼の心はとうに彼女から離れてしまっていた He *lost* his love for her a long time ago. / ほんの小さな出来事が彼女の心から長い間離れなかった Little things *stuck in her mind* for a long time. / その美しい風景が心に焼きついて離れない The beautiful landscape *has been imprinted on my mind.* / 震災の際、彼らは利害を離れて(→私心を捨てて)協力し合った After the earthquake, they cooperated with one another *selflessly*. / 子供の手が離れたので、彼女は職場に復帰した Her children *were off her hands*, so she went back to work.

❷ [隔たっている]

僕は両親と離れて暮らしている I live *away* [*apart*] *from* my parents.
その2軒の家はかなり離れて建っている The two houses stand *far apart*.
その寺は都心からずいぶん離れた所にある The temple is situated well *away from* the center of the city.
私の祖母は遠く離れた所に住んでいます My grandmother lives *far away*.
その駅はここから2キロ離れた所にある The station is two kilometers *away from* here.
東京と大阪はどのくらい離れていますか How *far apart* are Tokyo and Osaka?
(バスから)ドアから離れてお立ちください Please stand *clear of* the door.
あの2人はずいぶん年が離れている There is *a large difference in age* between the two.
ここから離れていなさい *Keep out of* here. / *Stay away* from here.

はなれわざ 離れ業 (妙技) stunt ⓒ, feat ⓒ /離れ業を演じる do *a stunt* [*feat*]

はなわ 花輪 wreath [ri:θ] ⓒ; (頭や首につける) garland ⓒ /葬儀の花輪 a funeral *wreath*

はにかみや はにかみ屋 bashful person ⓒ ──はにかみ屋の bashful

はにかむ be shy [bashful] /サムに紹介したとき、彼女はとてもはにかんでいた She *was* very *shy* [*bashful*] when I introduced her to Sam. ◆少女ははにかんでうつむいた The girl looked down *shyly* [*bashfully*].

ばにく 馬肉 horsemeat Ⓤ

パニック panic Ⓤⓒ /金融パニック a financial *panic* / 火事が起こるとデパートにいた人々はパニックに陥った When the fire broke out, the people in the department store 「*went into a panic* [*panicked*].

バニラ vanilla Ⓤ /彼はバニラアイスクリームに目がない He is partial to *vanilla ice cream*.

はにわ 埴輪 a haniwa, an ancient Japanese clay image

はね¹ 羽・羽根

❶ [羽毛] feather ⓒ; (装飾用の大きな) plume ⓒ; (羽毛全体) (集合的) plumage Ⓤ

羽が抜ける lose *feathers* / 鶏の羽をむしる pluck *feathers* from a chicken; *pluck a chicken* / 色鮮やかなクジャクの羽 colorful peacock *feathers*
彼女はその赤ちゃんを羽でくすぐった She tickled the baby with *a feather*.

❷ [翼] wing ⓒ

タカが羽を広げた The eagle spread [stretched] *its wings*. (❖「たたんだ」なら folded its wings とする)
そのチョウは美しい羽をしている Those butterflies have beautiful *wings*.
白鳥たちが湖のほとりで羽を休めている The swans are resting *their wings* by the lake.

❸ [バドミントンのシャトル] shuttlecock ⓒ

慣用表現 たまには休みをとってどこかで羽を伸ばしたい(→くつろぎたい) I want to take vacation and *relax* somewhere once in a while.

はね² 跳ね ペンキのはね *a splash* [*flick*] of paint / オートバイがはねを上げながら通り過ぎた A motorcycle passed by *spattering mud*.

ばね 発条 spring ⓒ /このばねはもう弾力がない This *spring* has already lost its life. / この選手は足腰のばねが非常に強い This player's legs have *a very strong spring*.
‖ばねばかり a spring balance

はねあがる 跳ね上がる jump [leap*] up; (価格が) shoot* up /冷夏による米の不作で米の価格がはね上がった Because of the bad harvest after the cold summer, the price of rice *leaped* [*shot*] *up*.

はねおきる 跳ね起きる 彼女は不審な物音を聞いてベッドからはね起きた She *sprang* [*bounced*] from her bed when she heard a strange noise.

はねかえす 跳ね返す 彼らはその要求をはね返した(→却下した) They *rejected* [*turned* *down*] the request. / 彼女はプレッシャーをはね返して(→克服して)みごとに優勝した She *overcame* pressure and won the championship.

はねかえる 跳ね返る bound ⓐ, bounce ⓐ, rebound ⓐ (❖*rebound* には「つけが回る」という比喩的な意味もある) ‖ボールは塀にぶつかって私の方にはね返ってきた The ball hit the wall and *bounded* [*bounced*] *back* to me. / そのような行いはきっとおまえ自身の身にはね返ってくることになるだろう Such an action is certain to *rebound against* you.
◆はね返ったボール a ball *on the bound* (❖この用法は名詞)

はねかかる 跳ね掛かる (ばしゃっと) splash ⓐ; (ばらばらと) spatter ⓐ ⇨ かかる (掛かる), はねる

はねかける 跳ね掛ける (ばしゃっと) splash ⓗ; (ばらばらと) spatter ⓗ ⇨ かける (掛ける・架ける), はねる

はねつき 羽根突き 〔絵〕 *hanetsuki*, Japanese badminton

はねつける turn down, brush off, reject ⓗ, rebuff ⓗ ‖委員会はダムの建設計画をはねつけた The committee *rejected* [*rebuffed*] a proposal for building a dam. / 彼女は言い寄る男の子をみんなはねつけてしまった She *brushed off* every boy who approached her.

はねとばす はね飛ばす 車にはね飛ばされる *be knocked down* by a car / 気力で眠気をはね飛ばす *shake off* one's drowsiness by force of will

はねのける はね除ける ふとんをはねのける *throw off* a quilt; *push* a quilt *aside* (❖前者は「かなぐり捨てる」、後者は「押しのける」の意味) / 彼女は私の手をはねのけた She *slapped* my hand *away*.

はねぶとん 羽布団 feather quilt ⓒ

はねまわる 跳ね回る jump [romp] around (❖*romp* は「子供たちがはしゃぎ回る」の意味) ‖子供たちは雪野原をはね回った The children *jumped* [*romped*] *around* on the snow-covered field.

ハネムーン honeymoon ⓒ ‖ハネムーンに出かける go on *a honeymoon*

パネラー ⚠ panelist ⓒ (❖「パネラー」は和製英語)

パネリスト panelist ⓒ

はねる 跳ねる
❶【跳び上がる】jump ⓐ, leap* ⓐ; (弾む) bounce ⓐ, bound ⓐ; (水が) splash ⓐ, spatter ⓐ (❖*splash* は「ばしゃっと」、*spatter* は「ばらばら」の意味)
彼女はカエルが道端をはねてゆくのを見ていた She watched a frog *jumping* along the roadside.
その子はソファーの上で跳んだりはねたりしていた The child *bounced* (*up and down*) on the sofa.
泥がスカートにはねた Mud *splashed on* my skirt.
❷【はじきとばす】hit* ⓗ, knock down

私の目の前で少年が車にはねられた A boy *was hit* [*knocked down*] by a car in front of me.
❸【除く・拒否する】(除く) eliminate ⓗ; (拒否する) reject ⓗ
要求をはねる *reject* a demand
最終試験で数名の志願者がはねられた A few candidates *were eliminated* [*rejected*] in the last examination.
❹【興行が終わる】end ⓐ, come* to an end, be over ⇨ おわる
そのロックコンサートは10時にはねました The rock concert *ended* at 10.
❺【その他】
上前をはねる *pocket a kickback* / 人の首をはねる *cut off the head* of a person

パネル panel ⓒ ‖パネルディスカッション a panel discussion / パネルヒーター a panel heater

ハノイ Hanoi (❖ベトナムの首都)

パノラマ panorama ⓒ ‖山頂からの壮大なパノラマ *a* magnificent *panorama* from the mountain top
‖パノラマ写真 a panoramic photograph

はは 母
mother ⓒ
生みの母 one's natural *mother* / 育ての母 one's foster *mother* / 義理の母 one's mother-in-law / 未婚の母 an unmarried [*a* single] *mother* / 子供に対する母の愛 the love of *a mother* for her children / 母なる自然 *Mother Nature* / 母の日 *Mother's Day*
母は今, 外出中です *Mother* [*Mom*] is out now. (❖自分の母親のことをいうとき、myを付けず、大文字で書き始め、固有名詞のように扱うことがある)
彼女は来月2児の母になる She will become *a mother of two* next month.
母鳥がひなたちにえさをやっている *The mother bird* is feeding her baby birds.
‖まま母 a stepmother

はば 幅 width ⓤ ⓒ, breadth ⓤ ⓒ; (変動の) range ⓤ ⓒ
運賃の値上げ幅を抑える limit *the range of the price increase* for the fares
この道の幅はどれくらいですか What is *the width of* this road? / How *wide* is this road?
◆幅の広い選択 *a wide* choice / 幅の広い川 a *wide* river; a river *of great width* / 株価の小幅な値動き *narrow* fluctuations in share prices / このプールは長さ25メートル, 幅8メートルです This pool is 25 meters long and 8 meters *wide*. / 彼も中年になって考え方に幅が出てきた His outlook *has widened* as he reached middle age.
慣用表現 彼はその方面ではかなり幅をきかせている(→影響力をもっている)らしい I hear he *has* considerable *influence* in that field.

パパ dad ⓒ, 〈小児語〉 daddy ⓒ, 〈米口語的〉 〈英/古風〉 papa ⓒ (❖現在では dad, daddy がふつう) ⇨ おとうさん ‖パパ, 帰りは何時ごろ

Dad, when are you going to come home?

パパイヤ〔植物〕papaya

ははおや 母親 mother ◎ ❖ はは, おかあさん ‖彼女はいい母親になりそうだ She promises to be *a good mother*. / 彼は昨日初めて実の母親と対面した Yesterday he met *his real [biological] mother* for the first time. / 彼女はそのかわいそうな少年の母親代わりだった She was (*like*) *a mother to* the poor little boy.

ははかた 母方 彼女は母方のおばです She is my aunt *on my mother's side* [my *maternal* aunt].

はばかる 彼女は人目もはばからずに車内で化粧をしていた She *didn't mind* putting on make-up on the train *with people watching*. / 彼は自分が学校の中でいちばん足が速いと公言してはばからなかった He *didn't hesitate to declare* that he was the fastest runner at his school. / そんな品のない言葉は口にするのもはばかられる I *hesitate* even to say such a vulgar word.

はばたき 羽ばたき flap ◎;（せわしない）a [the] flutter

はばたく 羽ばたく flap [beat*] (*one's wings*);（せわしなく）flutter (*one's wings*) ‖タカは翼を羽ばたかせた The hawk *flapped its wings*.
◆その会社は世界へと羽ばたこう(→進出しよう)としていた The company was about to *expand* (*its business*) *internationally*.

はばつ 派閥 faction ◎;（排他的な）《集合的》clique ◎ ‖その党は2つの派閥に分裂した The party [was] divided into two *factions*.
‖派閥争い factional strife, a factional struggle [dispute] / 党内派閥 an intraparty faction

はばとび 幅跳び〔スポーツ〕《米》the broad jump,《英》the long jump
‖立ち幅跳び the standing broad jump / 走り幅跳び the (running) broad jump

ばばぬき 婆抜き〔トランプ〕old maid

はばひろい 幅広い wide, broad, extensive ‖幅広い階層の人々 *a wide range of* people / 彼女は日本文化に関する幅広い知識をもっています She has *wide* [*broad, extensive*] knowledge of Japanese culture. / 彼女は幅広い読書によって見聞を広めた She enriched her stock of information through *wide* reading.

はばむ 阻む obstruct ⓜ, block ⓜ;（遅らせる）hinder ⓜ ➡ さまたげる, そし ‖敵の前進を阻む *obstruct* [*block, check*] the progress of the enemy / 倒木が我々の行く手を阻んでいた A fallen tree *blocked* [*was in*] our way.
◆武双山は思わぬ伏兵に連勝を阻まれた Musoyama's winning streak *was broken* by an unlikely opponent.

はばよせ 幅寄せ ——幅寄せする pull over

ババロア Bavarian [bavérian] cream ⓤ ❖日本語はフランス語の bavarois から

はびこる be rampant;（植物などが）be overgrown with ...（❖...の部分に「はびこるもの」がくる）;（害虫などが）be infested with ...（❖...の部分に「はびこるもの」がくる）‖畑には雑草がはびこっていた The field *was overgrown with* weeds. / Weeds *grew rampant* in the field. / あの町には暴力がはびこっていた Violence *is rampant* in that city.

パビリオン（展示館）pavilion ◎

パピルス〔植物〕papyrus ⓤ（❖「パピルス紙」の意味にもなる. 「パピルス古文書」の意味では ◎）

パフ（powder）puff ◎

パブ pub ◎

パフェ《米》parfait [pɑːrféi] ⓤ ◎（❖フランス語から）

パフォーマンス performance ◎

はぶく 省く
❶（省略する）omit ⓜ, leave* out;（削除する）eliminate ⓜ
冒頭のあいさつを省く *omit* [*leave out*] an opening address
細かい説明は省きます We'll *omit* [*leave out*] the detailed explanation.
❷（節約する）（手間などを）save ⓜ;（切り詰める）cut* down;（減らす）reduce ⓜ
むだを省く *reduce* unnecessary waste
パソコンのおかげでずいぶん手間が省ける The computer *saves* me a lot of *work*.
彼女は彼にファックスを送って，行く手間を省いた She faxed him and *saved* [*spared*] *herself* the trouble of going.

ハプニング⚠（思いがけない出来事）accident ◎ ⓤ, unexpected incident ◎（❖happening は単に「出来事」の意味）

はブラシ 歯ブラシ toothbrush ◎

はぶり 羽振り〔慣用表現〕彼女は最近とても羽振りがいい(→金回りがいい)ようだ She seems to be very *prosperous* [*well off*] these days. / 彼は金融界では羽振りがきく(→影響力がある) He *has great influence* in financial circles.

パプリカ paprika ⓤ

バブル（バブル経済）the bubble (economy) ‖バブルがはじけて，日本経済はかつてなかった状況に陥った The Japanese economy fell into an unprecedented situation when *the bubble burst*.

はへい 派兵 ——派兵する send* troops

はへん 破片 broken piece ◎;（粉々に割れた）fragment ◎;（木・瀬戸物などの）chip ◎;（薄くとがった）splinter ◎ ➡ かけら ‖割れた鏡の破片 *a fragment* of a broken mirror / 彼はガラスの破片で指を切った He cut his finger on *a [broken piece [splinter]* of glass.

はま 浜 beach ◎ ‖浜風 a breeze [the wind] from the sea ➡ はまべ

はまき 葉巻 cigar ◎ ‖葉巻をゆらす smoke [puff] *a cigar*

はまぐり 蛤 clam ◎

はまち〔魚〕（ブリの幼魚）young yellowtail ◎

はまべ 浜辺 beach ◎;（海岸）the (sea)shore ‖浜辺は人でいっぱいだった The *beach* was jammed [crowded] with people. / 子供たちは浜辺で砂遊びをしていた The children were playing in the sand on *the*

beach.

はまゆう 浜木綿 crinum [kráinəm] ©

はまりやく 嵌まり役 the right person for the job [role] ⇒ てきやく

はまる 嵌まる ❶【ぴったり合う】fit* ⊕ ⊜
⇒ はめる ∥このふたはこのびんにはまらない This cap *doesn't fit* on this bottle.
◆彼の型にはまらない発想が若者の支持を集めている His *unconventional* way of thinking is getting support from young people.(◆「型にはまった」は conventional を用いる)
💬「何してるの」「コートのボタンがなかなかはまらないんだ」 "What are you doing?" "This coat *won't button up*."
❷【役などに】彼は武士の役にはまっている He *is suitable for* the role of a samurai.
❸【わななどに】敵の計略にはまる「*fall into* [*be caught in*] the enemy's trap」∥車がぬかるみにはまってしまった My car *got stuck in* the mud. ⇒ はめる
❹【熱中する】《口語的》be hooked on ... ∥最近，インターネットにはまってるんだ I *am hooked on* the Internet these days.

はみがき 歯磨き (歯を磨くこと) teeth brushing ⓤ; (練り歯みがき) toothpaste ⓤ ∥歯みがき1本 a tube of *toothpaste*
◆私は毎食後歯磨きをする I *brush my teeth* after every meal.

はみだす はみ出す ズボンからシャツのすそがはみ出している(→ぶら下がっている)よ Your shirt tail *is hanging out* of your trousers./ 列からはみ出さないでください Don't *get* [*fall*] *out* of line, please./ サンドイッチの端からジャムがはみ出した(→あふれ出した) Jam *overflowed* from the edges of the sandwich.

ハミング humming ⓤ ──ハミングする hum ⊕ ⊜

ハム¹ (食品) ham ⓤ © ∥ハム1切れ a slice of *ham*
∥ハムエッグ ham and eggs / ハムサンド a ham sandwich

ハム² (無線家) (radio) ham ©

はむかう 歯向かう・刃向かう 権力に歯向かう「*revolt against* [*resist*] the authorities / おまえは親に歯向かうつもりか Do you mean to *disobey* us, your parents? / あいつには歯向かわないほうがいい You *shouldn't fight against* him.

ハムスター 【動物】hamster ©

はめ 羽目 苦しい羽目に陥る be put into *an awkward position* / 結局，その難しい仕事を引き受ける羽目になった I ended up taking that difficult job.
慣用表現 ゆうべは飲みすぎて羽目をはずしてしまった I drank too much and *went wild* last night.

はめいた 羽目板 《米》wood siding ⓤ, panel ©

はめこむ 嵌め込む fit* ⊕; (宝石などを) set* ⊕, mount ⊕ ⇒ はめる ∥ブレスレットに宝石をはめ込む *set* gems *into* a bracelet

はめつ 破滅 ruin ⓤ, destruction ⓤ; (没落)

downfall ©《通例単数形》(◆いずれも「破滅の原因」も意味する) ∥破滅する be ruined, ruin *oneself* ∥その国は破滅への道をたどっていた The country was on the path to *ruin*./ 酒とギャンブルが彼の破滅の原因だった Drinking and gambling were his *ruin*./ (→ 酒とギャンブルが彼の破滅をもたらした) Drinking and gambling brought about his *ruin*.

はめる 嵌める ❶【身につける】put* on; (はめている) wear* ⊕ ∥手袋をはめる *put on one's gloves* / 彼女は指にルビーの指輪をはめていた She *wore* a ruby ring on her finger.
❷【はめ込む】fit* ⊕ ∥窓にガラスをはめた I *fit* a pane of glass into the window. ◆ジャケットのボタンをはめる *button up one's* jacket
❸【だます】cheat ⊕, 《口語的》take* in ∥どうやらあいつにはめられたらしい It seems that I *was taken in* by him.

ばめん 場面 scene ©; (光景) sight © ∥「ロミオとジュリエット」の最後の場面を覚えていますか Do you remember the last *scene of Romeo and Juliet*? / テレビの視聴者はみんなその場面にショックを受けた The entire TV audience was shocked at that *scene*./ 街を歩いていて，とても愉快な場面に出会った I came across *a* very pleasant *sight* when I walked along the street.

はもの 刃物 edged tool ©; (総称) cutlery ⓤ; (ナイフのたぐい) knife © (複 knives) ∥私は突然見知らぬ男に刃物を突きつけられた I was suddenly threatened with *a knife* by a man I didn't know.

はもん¹ 波紋 ripple ©, (water) ring © ∥湖面に波紋が広がった *The ripples* spread across the surface of the lake. ◆教育界に波紋を投げかける *have repercussions* in the educational world / 彼の新作映画は大きな波紋を呼んだ(→物議をかもした) His new film *created* 「*quite a stir* [*a great sensation*]」.

はもん² 破門 (教会からの)【宗教】excommunication ⓤ ©; (追放) expulsion ⓤ © ∥破門する excommunicate ⊕; expel ⊕ ∥彼を異端として破門する *excommunicate him* as a heretic / とうとう彼は師から破門されてしまった He *was* finally 「*expelled* by [*forced to leave*]」 his master.

はやあし 早足 早足で歩く walk fast [*at a brisk pace*]

はやい 早い

early ──早く early; (すぐに) soon; (素早く) quickly, fast

語源
大まかにいって「(時刻などが) 早い」には early や soon，また「(速度などが) 速い」には fast や quick (quickly) などが対応するが，以下の用例にも見るように日本語では「早い」というところを英語では fast や quick (quickly) で表現することもあるので注意を要する ∥ 月日がたつのは早いなあ Time flies so *fast*!

私はいつも朝早く起きる I always get up *early* in the morning./ I am an *early* riser.

今夜は早く帰ってきてね Please come home *early* tonight.
けさはいつもより20分早く家を出た This morning I left home 20 minutes *earlier* than usual.
冬は日の沈むのが早い In winter the sun sets *early*.
工事が始まるのは早くて来年だ The construction will start next year *at the earliest*.
私たちはきのうの夜遅く, というよりけさ早く家に着いた We got home late last night, or rather *very early this morning*.
私たちは予定より1時間早く駅に着いた We arrived at the station *an hour「earlier than [in advance of] the scheduled time*.
できるだけ早くお返事ください Please reply *as soon [quickly] as possible*.
この問題の一日も早い解決を望んでいます I hope that this problem is resolved *as soon [quickly] as possible*.
早く日本の生活に慣れるといいですね I hope you'll get used to the Japanese way of life *soon*.
早くクリスマスが来ないかなあ I wish Christmas would come *sooner*.
早く服を着なさい Get dressed *quickly*.
タクシーに乗ろう. バスで行くよりそのほうが早いよ Let's take a taxi. It's *faster* than going by bus.
◆今すぐここから逃げるんだ. 早く！ Run away from here right now. *Quick*! [*Hurry up*!] / 彼女は結婚するにはまだ早い(→若すぎる) She *is too young* to get married. / 天文学は最も発展し, あらゆる学問の手本となった Astronomy was developed *first* and became a model for all of the other sciences. / 早い話, いずれの場合でも結果は同じということだ *In short*, the rusult will be the same no matter what.
❡「もう何もかもおしまいだ」「あきらめるのはまだ早いよ」"It's all over for [with] me." "It's *too early* to give up."
❡「いつ始めましょうか」「早ければ早いほどいいですね」"When shall we begin?" "*The sooner, the better*."
慣用表現 早い者勝ち *First come, first served*.

はやい² 速い

(速度が) fast; (動作が) quick; (速度・動作が) rapid, speedy, 《格式的》swift ━速く fast; quickly; rapidly, speedily, swiftly ⇒はやい(早い)

僕はあまり足が速くない (→速い走者ではない) I *am not* a very *fast* runner. / (→速く走れない) I *can't* run very *fast*.
彼は歩くのが速くて私はついていけなかった He walked so *fast* that I couldn't keep up with him.
光は音よりも速く進む Light travels *faster* than sound.
ハツカネズミは繁殖が速い Mice breed *fast [quickly]*.
この川の流れはとても速い The current in this river is very *rapid*.
私たちはテンポの速い曲に合わせて踊った We danced to a tune with a *quick* tempo.
彼は計算が速くて正確だ He is *quick [rapid]* and correct in his calculations.
彼は頭の回転が速い He has a *quick* mind. / He is a *rapid* thinker.
彼女はタイプを打つのがとても速い She types very *quickly*.
❡「そんなに速く話さないでください」「分かりました. もっとゆっくり話しましょう」"Don't speak *so fast*." "All right. I'll speak more slowly."

はやうち 早撃ち quick shooting Ⓤ
はやうまれ 早生まれ 🔺 *hayaumare*, to be born between January 1 and April 1, or a person born during this period
はやおき 早起き ━早起きする get* up early ∥彼が早起きすることなどめったにない He hardly ever *gets up early*.
◆父は家族の中でいちばんの早起きだ My father is *the earliest riser* in the family.
ことわざ 早起きは三文の得 The early bird catches the worm. (→早起きの鳥は虫を捕らえる)
はやおくり 早送り fast-forward Ⓤ ━早送りする fast-forward 🔵
はやがてん 早合点 ━早合点する jump to「a (hasty) conclusion [conclusions]」 ∥ベルが鳴ると母は父が帰ってきたものだと早合点した When the doorbell rang, my mother *jumped to the conclusion* that my father had come home.
はやく¹ 早く (時間が) early; (すぐに) soon; (素早く) quickly, fast ⇒はやい(早い)
はやく² 速く (速度が) fast; (動作が) quickly ⇒はやい(速い)
はやく³ 端役 端役を演じる play *a small [bit, minor] part*
はやくち 早口 あの先生は早口だ That teacher *talks [speaks] fast*.
∥早口言葉 a tongue twister
はやくも 早くも 高校を卒業して早くも(→すでに)半年が経過した Half a year has *already* passed by since I graduated from high school. / 日本では早くも10世紀には『伊勢物語』などのすぐれた物語が作られた In Japan, outstanding stories such as *The Tales of Ise* were written *as early as the 10th century*.
はやさ 速さ speedⓊⓊ, 《公式的》velocity Ⓤ; (素早さ) quicknessⓊ ⇒はやい(速い) ∥音の速さを測定する measure *the speed* of sound / 彼女は驚くべき速さで仕事をこなした She did her work *with astonishing speed*.
◆彼は足の速さなら学校のだれにも負けない(→だれよりも速く走ることができる) He *can run faster* than any other student in his school.
はやざき 早咲き 早咲きの桜 an *early-blooming* cherry blossom
はやし¹ 林 wood Ⓒ 《しばしば the 〜s》; (森林) forestⓊⒸ; (果樹林) grove Ⓒ ∥林の中を小川が流れている A stream runs through *the woods*.

はやし² 囃子 *hayashi*, musical accompaniment performed for Noh or kabuki with flutes, drums, *shamisen*, etc.

はやしたてる 囃し立てる (やじる) jeer, scoff /浩二が優子といっしょに教室に入ってくるとクラスメートたちがいっせいにはやしたて た When Koji went into the classroom along with Yuko, all their classmates *jeered* them.

はやじに 早死に early death
◆彼の息子は早死にした His son *died young*.

はやじまい 早仕舞い 店を早じまいにする(→いつもよりも早く閉める) *close* the store *earlier than usual*

ハヤシライス rice with hashed meat

はやす¹ 生やす grow* /口ひげを生やす *grow* a mustache ◆父は庭の雑草を生やしっぱなしにしている My father *lets* the weeds in the garden *grow*. (❖この grow は自動詞) / おじさんはあごひげを生やしている My uncle *wears* [*has*] a beard. (❖「生やしている状態」を表すときは wear や have を用いる)

はやす² 囃す (やじる) jeer, scoff; (ちゃかす) make* fun of ...; (かっさいする) cheer; (拍手かっさいする) applaud /彼が芸を決めるたびに見物人はやんやとはやした Every time he performed a trick perfectly, the onlookers *cheered* [*applauded*] (*for him*).

はやてまわし 早手回し 早手回しに(→早めに)パーティーの会場を予約する reserve a place *early* for a party

はやとちり 早とちり ――早とちりする jump to「a (hasty) conclusion [conclusions] ⇒はやがてん

はやね 早寝 ――早寝する go* to bed early, have* an early night
◆早寝早起きは健康によい *Keeping early hours* is good for the health.

はやばまい 早場米 early rice crop

はやばや(と) 早々(と) /彼女はきょうは早々と(→いつもより早く)帰宅した Today, she went home *earlier than usual*. /彼は早々とトーナメントから姿を消してしまった He was defeated *early* in the tournament.

はやばん 早番 (朝番) the morning shift /あしたは早番だ I'll be on the morning shift tomorrow.

はやびけ 早引け ――早引けする leave* school [work] early ⇒そうたい(早退)

はやぶさ falcon

はやまる¹ 早まる ❶【時間が】コンサートの開演時間が1時間早まった(→繰り上げられた) The starting time for the concert was「*moved up* [*advanced*] one hour.
❷【軽率になる】早まった決定[判断]を下す make a *hasty* decision [judgment] / どうやら結論を出すのを早まったようだ It seems that I drew a conclusion *too hastily*. / 早まるな Don't be hasty!

はやまる² 速まる quicken /私は脈が速まるのを感じた I felt my heart [pulse] *quicken*.

はやみち 早道 shortcut ⇒ちかみち /「早道をする take a shortcut /彼に直接会って話したほうが早道だ(→簡単だ) It *would be easier to* talk with him directly.

はやみみ 早耳 彼の早耳には本当に驚いた I was very surprised that he *hears about things so quickly*.

はやめ 早め ――早めの early ――早めに early, in good time /早めの夕食 an *early* dinner / (約束の時間より)少し早めに来てください Please come a little bit *earlier* (than the appointment).

はやめる¹ 早める hasten; (期日を繰り上げる) advance, bring* [put*] forward, move up /出発を早める *hasten one's* departure / 過労が彼の死期を早めた Overwork *hastened* his death. / 先生は試験の日程を3日早めた Our teacher「*moved up* [*advanced*] the date of the exam by three days.

はやめる² 速める quicken, hasten; (速度を上げる) speed* up /トマトの成長を速める *speed* (*up*) the growth of tomatoes / 私たちは足を速めた We *quickened* our pace.

はやらせる 流行らせる bring* ... into fashion

はやり 流行 (服などの) trend (❖現在では fashion よりも多く用いられる); (一時的な) vogue (また a ～) ――はやりの fashionable; trendy ⇒ 場面・状況別会話 p.1708 /はやりの髪型 a *fashionable* [*trendy*] hairstyle / 今年はやりの色は赤だ The color that's *in fashion* this year is red.
◆最近はショートパンツがはやりだ Short pants *are in* these days.
‖はやり物 goods in fashion

はやりすたり 流行り廃り 服の色にもはやりすたりがある(→時の移り変わりとともにはやったりすたれたりする) The colors of clothes also *go in and out of fashion over time*.

はやる¹ 流行る
❶【音楽や服などが】(流行している) be in fashion; (人気がある) be popular
今年はどんな服がはやっていますか What kind of clothes *are in fashion* this year?
最近この歌が子供たちの間ではやっている This song *is popular* these days among children.
◆お守りを持つのが彼らの間ではやっている It *is fashionable* among them to carry charms.
❷【店が】 do* a good business; (医者や弁護士が) have* a large practice
あのピザ屋はとてもはやっている That pizza shop *is doing a* very *good business*.
❸【病気が】 go* around
今学校でインフルエンザがとてもはやっている The flu is「*really going around* [*prevalent, raging*] in the school. (❖prevalent は「蔓延している」, rage は「猛威をふるう」の意味)

はやる² 逸る はやる気持ちを抑える control *one's eagerness* / 久しぶりに家に帰れるかと思

はやわざ

うと心がはやった When I thought about returning home after a long absence, I *got all excited.* / 血気にはやった若者たちが暴動を起こした *Reckless* young people started a riot.

はやわざ 早業 目にもとまらぬ早業で *like a streak (of lightning)*

はら 腹

❶【腹部】stomach ⓒ; belly ⓒ; abdomen ⓒ
stomach:「腹・腹部」を意味する一般的な語.
belly: 口語でよく用いられるが stomach より下品な言い方とされる.
abdomen:「腹部」を意味する医学用語. 動物・昆虫などにも用いる.

〚腹が〛
◆腹が減ってもう1歩も歩けない I'm so *hungry* that I can't walk anymore. / もう腹がいっぱい I'm *full* now. / けさから腹が痛い I've *had a stomachache* since this morning. / 彼は最近腹が出てきた He *has gotten fat around the middle.* / 《口語的》He's *been getting a spare tire.*

〚腹を〛
彼は食べすぎで腹をこわした He's *got an upset stomach* from eating too much. / (→下痢している) He *has diarrhea* from eating too much.
◆腹をすかせた少年たちはスプーンでテーブルをがんがんたたいた The *hungry* boys hammered the table with their spoons. / 彼の冗談にみんな腹を抱えて笑った Everyone *doubled up with laughter* at his joke. / Everyone *split their sides with laughter* at his joke.

〚腹に〛
揚げ物は腹にもたれがちだ Deep-fried foods tend to *be heavy on the stomach.*

〚その他〛
下腹 *the lower abdomen* / ビール腹 *a beer belly*
すきっ腹でアルコールを飲むのは体によくない It's not good for your health to drink alcohol *on an empty stomach.*
◆太鼓腹 *a potbelly* / 昼食を食べそこなって腹ぺこだ I missed my lunch, so I'm *very hungry [starving].* / 食事は腹八分目にしなさい (→ほどほどに食べなさい) Eat *moderately.* / 左わき腹に痛みを感じる I have a pain *in my left side.*

❷【心中・本心】
彼は腹の中では何を考えているか分からない I can't read his *mind.*
あいつらは腹の中では僕のことを笑っているにちがいない They must be *secretly* laughing at me.

❸【物の中央】
アイシャドウを指の腹でのばしなさい Spread the eye shadow with *the soft part of your finger.*

❹【その他】
【腹が黒い】
あいつは腹が黒い He is an *evil-minded* [*a wicked*] guy.

【腹がすわる】 彼女は腹がすわっている (→何事にも動じない) She *is never upset* [*fazed*] *by anything.*

【腹が立つ・腹を立てる】 get* [become*] angry; (感情を害する) take* offense, be offended / あまりにも腹が立ったので彼を殴りそうになった I *got* so *angry* that I almost hit him. / つまらないことで腹を立てるな Don't *get angry* over trivial matters. / 彼女の不注意な言葉に彼は腹を立てた He *was offended* by her careless words. / Her careless words *offended* him.

【腹が太い・太っ腹な】 私たちの上司は太っ腹な (→気前のよい) 人だ Our boss is a *generous* person.

【腹に収める】 このことは君だけの腹に収めておいてほしい I want you to *keep* this just *to yourself.*

【腹に据(ⁿ)えかねる】 彼の勝手なふるまいは腹に据えかねる I *can't stand* his selfish behavior.

【腹を決める】 彼女は仕事を辞めるかどうか、まだ腹を決めかねている She *hasn't decided* yet whether to quit the job or not.

【腹をくくる】 彼は自分が事故の全責任をとると腹をくくっている He *is determined to* take full responsibility for the accident himself.

【腹を探る】 私は彼女の腹を探ろうとした I tried to *find out* her *real intentions.*

【腹を据える】 腹を据えて仕事にかからないとだめだ You must get to work *with determination.*

【腹を読む】 キャッチャーは常にバッターの腹を読まなければならない A catcher always has to *guess what* a batter *is thinking.*

【腹を割る】 腹を割って (→素直に) 話そう Let's talk *frankly* [*openly*].

慣用表現 痛くもない腹を探られたら (→理由もなく疑われたら) だれでも不愉快になるだろう Anybody will be annoyed if they *are suspected without reason.* / 腹が減っては戦(ᵢ⁵)はできぬ (→空腹では何もできない) You can't do anything on an empty stomach. / 彼は腹に一物ありげな (→何かをたくらんでいるような) 顔をしていた It looked *like he was plotting something.* / 彼は腹の底から笑った He gave a *hearty laugh.* / あいつに仕返しするまでは腹の虫が納まらない I *won't be satisfied* until I get my revenge on him.

ばら¹ 薔薇 rose ⓒ / 野バラ *a wild rose* / バラのとげ *a rose* thorn / バラはまだつぼみだった The roses were still *in bud.*
◆バラ色の未来 *a rosy* future

ばら² ──ばらの *loose* / ばら売りのトマト *loose* tomatoes / 色鉛筆をばらで買う buy colored pencils *loose*
‖ばら銭 *loose change* [*money*]

バラード 《音楽・詩》ballad ⓒ

はらい 払い (支払い) payment ⓤ; (勘定) bill ⓒ / 前[一括, 分割, 現金] 払い *payment in advance* [*full, installments, cash*] / 月5,000円の12回払い *12 monthly payments of 5,000 yen* / もう払いはすんだの？ Have you paid *the bill* yet?

◆その店は私たちが3回払いで払えるようにはからってくれた The store arranged for us to pay *in three installments*.

はらいおとす 払い落とす (振り落とす) shake* off; (ほこりなどを) brush [dust] (off) ➩はらう(払う)

はらいこむ 払い込む (支払う) pay* [他][自] ➩はらう(払う), ふりこむ(振り込む) ∥電気代を銀行の口座に払い込む *have one's* electricity bills automatically *paid* from a bank account

はらいさげる 払い下げる (売る) sell* [他]; (安く売り払う) sell off ∥国有地を払い下げる *sell* (*off*) nationally-owned land

はらいせ 腹癒せ 彼は母親にしかられた腹いせに弟にあたった He was scolded by his mother and *took out his anger* on his little brother.

はらいのける 払い除ける 彼が彼女の肩に手をかけると彼女はその手を払いのけた She *brushed* his hand *aside* [*away*] when he put it on her shoulder. / 彼女は必死にその考えを払いのけようとした She desperately *tried to brush* [*sweep*] the idea *aside*.

はらいもどし 払い戻し refund [C]; (預金の) withdrawal [U] [C]; (割り戻し) rebate [C]; (返すこと) repayment [U] ∥このチケットを払い戻ししてほしいんですけど Can I have *a refund* for this ticket?

‖払い戻し金 a refund

はらいもどす 払い戻す refund [他], pay* back; (預金を) withdraw* [他]; (返す) repay* [他] ∥彼は会に欠席したので会費が払い戻された His fee *was refunded* [*paid back*] (to him) because he was absent from the meeting.

はらう[1] 払う

❶【支払う・費やす】pay* [他][自]; (返す) pay back ➩しはらう

恵が昼食の勘定を払った Megumi *paid* the bill for lunch.

私はあなたに500円払わなければなりません I must *pay* you 500 yen. / I must *pay* 500 yen *to* you.

現金[カード, 小切手]で払えますか *Can I pay* 「in cash [with a credit card, by check]?

私たちには税金を払う義務がある We have a responsibility to *pay* taxes.

彼らは独立のために多大な犠牲を払った They *paid a* high *price* for independence.

◆どんな犠牲を払ってもこの仕事をやりとげなければならない I must accomplish this job *at* 「*any price* [*all costs*].

❷【意識を向ける】

年配の人々に敬意を払う *show respect* for the elderly

彼らは彼女の言葉に注意を払わなかった They *paid no attention* to what she said.

彼らはその花びんを細心の注意を払って運んだ They carried the vase *with the greatest care*.

❸【払いのける】brush [他]; (掃(は)く・ふき取る) sweep* [他][自] (❖「掃くようにさっと動かす」という意味もある)

母は箱の上のほこりを払った My mother 「*brushed* dust *off* [*swept* dust *off*, *dusted*] the top of the box.

彼は突然足を払われてひっくり返った He *was* suddenly *swept off* his legs and fell down.

◆木の枝を払う *lop* [*cut, trim*] some branches *off* the tree

はらう[2] 祓う exorcise [他], drive* away (❖いずれも「悪霊などを追い払う」の意味) ➩やくよけ ∥けがれをはらう *drive away* impurity

バラエティー (多様性) variety [vəráiəti] [U]; (バラエティー番組) variety [U], variety show [C] ◆彼の作る料理はバラエティーに富んでいる The food he cooks *is* [The dishes he cooks *are*] *quite varied.*

パラグライダー paraglider [C]

パラグラフ paragraph [C]

はらぐろい 腹黒い evil-minded, blackhearted, designing

はらげい 腹芸 彼は腹芸(→言葉を使わずに自らの考えを表現すること)にたけている He is good at *expressing himself without using words.*

ばらける たきぎの束がばらけた A bundle of firewood 「*came loose* [*fell apart*]. / 先頭集団がばらけ始めた The leading group started to *spread out*.

はらごしらえ 腹拵え 山登りをする前にしっかり腹ごしらえをした(→十分に食べた) We *ate* enough before we climbed the mountain.

はらごなし 腹ごなし 腹ごなしに散歩する take a walk *for one's digestion*; (→食後に) take a walk *after a meal*

パラシュート parachute [C]

はらす 晴らす 彼は友人の疑いを晴らすためにあらゆることをした He did everything to 「*clear* their doubt about his friend [(→無実を証明する) *prove* his friend (to be) innocent]. / サラリーマンの多くは飲んでうさを晴らす Many office workers *forget* their troubles by drinking. / Many office workers drink their troubles *away*. / 彼女はうっぷん晴らしによくカラオケへ行く She often goes to a karaoke room to *let off steam*. / あいつにうらみを晴らさないと気がすまない I must *settle* a score with him. / その女性は15年かかってやっと自分の無実の罪を晴らした It took the woman about fifteen years to *prove* her innocence.

ばらす (分解する) take* ... apart, 《公式的》 dismantle [他]; (正体・秘密などを) reveal [他]; (秘密を) disclose [他]; (殺す) kill [他] ∥ラジオをばらしたら元に戻せなくなった I *took* my radio *apart*, and now can't put it back together. / 彼は秘密をばらすぞと言って私をおどした He threatened to *reveal* [*disclose*] my secret.

パラソル sunshade [C], parasol [C]

‖ビーチパラソル《米》a beach umbrella

パラダイス paradise [C] (❖「天国」の意味では無

冠詞で Paradise)
はらだたしい 腹立たしい 《神経を逆なでする》irritating; 《我慢できない》annoying; 《侮辱的な》offensive; 《しゃくにさわる》exasperating ∥彼女の態度は本当に腹立たしい Her attitude is so *irritating*. / だれもそのことを私に話してくれなかったことが腹立たしい It's *annoying* that no one told me about that.
はらだち 腹立ち 《怒り》anger ⓤ; 《激怒》rage ⓤ; 《かんしゃく》temper ⓤ ∥彼は腹立ちまぎれにごみ箱をけとばした He kicked a trash can *in a fit of anger* [*rage, temper*].
はらちがい 腹違い, 腹違いの兄弟[姉妹] a brother [sister] *born of a different mother*; a *half* brother [sister] (❖後の表現は父親が違う場合も意味する)
ばらつき このクラスは化学の点数のばらつきが大きい The chemistry test scores *vary widely* in this class. / 参加者の経験にばらつきがあった The participants *varied* in experience. / あの店のハンバーガーは品質にばらつきがある The quality of hamburgers sold at that shop *is uneven*.
バラック 《掘っ立て小屋》shack ⓒ, shanty ⓒ (❖英語の barracks は「兵舎」の意味)
ばらつく ⇒ばらつき
ぱらつく 《雨が》sprinkle ⓘ ∥けさ小雨がぱらついた It *sprinkled* this morning.
はらっぱ 原っぱ field ⓒ
ばらづみ ばら積み 商品をばら積みにする *load goods in bulk*
はらづもり 腹積もり 彼は彼女に責任を押しつけようという腹づもりだ He *intends to* put the blame on her. ⇒つもり
はらどけい 腹時計 僕の腹時計によればもうそろそろ昼だな My stomach is telling me it's almost lunchtime.
パラドックス paradox ⓒⓤ
ばらにく 肋肉 rib ⓒ
パラノイア 〔医学〕paranoia ⓤ
はらばい うつ伏せになりなさい *Lie on your stomach*. / 彼は腹ばいになって垣根の下をくぐった He *crawled* under the fence.

はらはら
❶【散り落ちる様子】
露天ぶろにモミジの葉がはらはらと散っている The maple leaves *are fluttering down* to the open-air bath.
彼女ははらはらと涙を流した (→涙が彼女のほほを流れ落ちた) *The tears trickled down* her cheeks.
❷【気をもむ様子】
はらはらさせるドラマ an *exciting* [a *thrilling*] drama
彼がうっかり口を滑らすのではとはらはらした I *was worried* that he might let it slip.
その映画は観客をはらはらさせ通しだった The movie *kept* audiences *in suspense*.
あの番組はいつもはらはらするところで終わる That program always ends with *a cliff-hanger*.
花子の乱暴な運転には本当にはらはらしたよ I *was really scared* with Hanako's reckless driving.
彼女が包丁を使うのを見ているとあまりの不器用さにはらはらする Watching her using a kitchen knife *makes me nervous*, because she is very clumsy with it.

ばらばら
❶【粒状のものが落ちる様子】
雹(ひょう)が突然ばらばらと降ってきた The hailstones suddenly *pelted down*.
袋が破れて中のあめが床にばらばらこぼれてしまった The packet broke and the candies inside *were scattered down* on the floor.
❷【分散】
弟は修理するためにラジオをばらばらにした My brother *took* the radio *apart* to repair it.
その小さな船は岩にぶつかってばらばらになった The small boat *broke up* on the rocks.
内戦でその家族はばらばらになってしまった The family *was scattered* because of the civil war.
みんなばらばらに食事をした Everyone ate *separately*.
そのけんか以来彼らの気持ちはばらばらになってしまった They *have grown apart* since the quarrel.
同じ商品なのに店によって値段が全くばらばらだ The same item has a completely *different* price at each store.
その書類をばらばらにしないよう気をつけてください Please be careful *not to make a mess of* the documents.
∥ばらばら死体 a dismembered body

ぱらぱら ❶【粒状のものが落ちる様子】雨がぱらぱらと降りだした It started *sprinkling*. / 母は料理の仕上げにごまをぱらぱらと振りかけた My mother *sprinkled* sesame seeds over the dish to finish it.
❷【ページなどをめくる様子】彼女は雑誌をぱらぱらとめくった She *leafed* [*flipped*] *through* the magazine.
❸【まばらな様子】山田教授の講演会にはぱらぱらとしか出席者がいなかった There were only *a few* people *scattered about* for professor Yamada's lecture.
❹【その他】残り物のごはんはぱらぱらだ Leftover rice *is drying up*.
パラフィン paraffin ⓤ; 《パラフィン紙》wax paper ⓤ
パラフレーズ paraphrase ⓒ
はらぺこ 腹ぺこ 腹ぺこだよ I'm *starving*.
パラボラアンテナ ⚠ parabola ⓒ, parabolic antenna ⓒ; 《衛星放送用の》(satellite) dish ⓒ
はらまき 腹巻き 🗾 a *haramaki*, a stomach band to keep *one* warm
ばらまく ❶《まき散らす》scatter ⓘ; 《行き渡らせる》spread* ⓘ ∥赤ん坊は床にポップコーンをばらまいた The baby *scattered* popcorn on the floor. / あの政治家は票集めにかなりの金をばらまいたらしい It's said that the politician *spread around* lots of cash to buy votes.

はらむ 孕む （含む） involve; （子を宿す） become* [get*] pregnant ∥インターネットは非常に便利ではあるが, 個人情報を悪用される危険もはらんでいる It is true that the Internet is very useful, but it also *involves* the danger that someone might abuse your personal information.

はらもち 腹持ち パスタ料理は腹持ちがいい Pasta dishes *are filling*.

ばらり 机から紙がばらりと落ちた A piece of paper *fluttered* from the desk.

パラリンピック the Paralympics

はらわた 腸 guts ∥魚のはらわたを取り除く take *the guts* out of a fish; *gut* a fish
慣用表現 彼の言動にははらわたが煮えくり返る思いだ What he says and does *makes my blood boil*.

はらん 波乱・波瀾 （もめごと） trouble; （騒動） disturbance; （盛衰） ups and downs ∥波乱を呼ぶ cause *a disturbance* / 私の人生は波乱万丈だ My life *is full of ups and downs*. ◆この試合はもうひと波乱ありそうだ It seems the situation of this game *will change again*. / 今場所の大相撲は横綱が初日から3連敗するなど, 波乱含みの展開となっている This sumo tournament has turned out to be a *stormy* one with three successive *yokozuna* losses beginning on the first day.

バランス balance ∥仕事と家庭のバランスをうまくとる keep *the proper balance* between work and home / 彼女はバランスを失って転んだ She lost *her balance* and tumbled.
◆やせるためにはバランスのとれた食事をすることが重要だ It's important to have a *balanced* diet if you want to lose some weight. / 彼は平均台の上で両手を広げてバランスをとった He *balanced* (*himself*) on the balance beam by spreading out his arms.

はり¹ 針 （裁縫・注射・レコードの） needle; （留め針） pin; （釣りの） hook; （時計の） hand; （ホッチキスの） staple; （ハチなどの） sting; （外科手術の） stitch

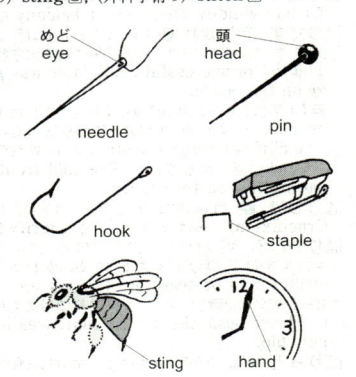

- めど eye
- 頭 head
- needle
- pin
- hook
- staple
- sting
- hand

針の穴［先］ the eye [point] of *a needle* / 針に糸を通す thread *a needle* / 釣り針にえさをつける put bait on *a hook*
針と糸, 持ってる? Do you have *a needle and thread*? / （→裁縫道具）Do you have a *sewing kit*?
針で指を刺した I pricked my finger with *a needle*.
額の傷をふさぐために3針縫わなければならなかった The cut on my forehead needed three *stitches*.
◆時計の針を進める put *the clock* forward / 時計の針は10時5分前を指していた The clock said five to ten. / 連絡板に針でメモを留めた I *pinned* a note on the message board.
∥針刺し a pincushion / 針仕事 needlework
慣用表現 意見を言ったが一笑に付され, その後会議が終わるまで私は針のむしろに座るような心持ちだった They laughed off my opinion, and I felt *like I was sitting on a bed of nails* until the meeting ended.

はり² 鍼 （はり療法） acupuncture

中国に始まり奈良時代に日本へ伝わったはりは, 灸（きゅう）と並び伝統的な東洋医学として定着しており, この2つはしばしば併用されます。体中に点在するつぼ（経穴）に非常に細い針を刺していくと, つぼはそれぞれ決まった器官とつながっているので, 針で与えられた刺激がその器官の不快な症状を緩和します。はりは西洋医学の医師からも高く評価されてきています。

Hari, which is called acupuncture or needle therapy in English, developed in China and was introduced to Japan in the Nara period (710-784). It is widely recognized as a style of Asian traditional medicine in conjunction with *kyu*: the two are often used together. Hair-thin needles are inserted at therapeutic points called *tsubo* or *keiketsu* found all over the body. Because each *tsubo* is directly connected to certain organs, the physical stimulation given by *hari* at the right *tsubo* relieves the irregularity. *Hari* is now highly appreciated even by some doctors who belong to Western medicine.

はり³ 張り 彼は張りのある声をしている His voice is full of *energy* [*life*]. / 彼女は年齢のわりに張りのある肌をしている She has *supple* skin for her age. / 父は退職後生きる張りを失ったようだ My father seems to have lost *his sense of purpose* since his retirement. / 最近, 勉強に張りが出てきた I've begun to *feel motivated* to study harder.

はり⁴ 梁 beam

ばり 罵言 abuse ◆上司は私に罵言雑言を浴びせた My boss *cursed* me *out*.

-ばり -張り 板張りの床 a *wood* floor / ガラス張りの建物 a *glass-covered* building / マイケル・ジョーダン張りのダンクシュート a slam-dunk *reminiscent of* Michael Jordan / 東山魁夷張りの絵 a painting *in the style* [*man-*

パリ **Paris** [pǽris]（❖フランスの首都）‖パリ祭 the Fourteenth of July, Bastille [bæstíːl] Day；パリ市民 a Parisian；(女性) a Parisienne [pərìzién]

バリア 彼女は私たちに対してバリアを張っているみたいだ She seems to have put up *a barrier* against us.

はりあい 張り合い 張り合いのある仕事がしたい I want to do a *challenging* job. ∥ 彼女は生きる張り合いをなくした He lost *interest* in life. ∥ 彼女は張り合いのない生活にいやけがさし，会社を辞めて海外留学した She was sick of her *dull* life and resigned her job to study abroad. ∥ ライバルがいると勉強にも張り合いが出る I can *stay enthusiastic* about studying because I have a rival.

はりあう 張り合う （…と競争する) compete with [against] …；(…をめぐって争う) fight* over … ∥ 彼女はすべてにおいて夕子と張り合っている She *competes with* Yuko in everything. ∥ 彼らは1人の女の子をめぐって長い間張り合っていた They *fought over* a girl for many years.

はりあげる 張り上げる (声を) raise ⊕；(叫ぶ) shout ⊕ ∥ そんなに声を張り上げないでふつうに話してください Don't *raise your voice*, but talk calmly.
◆彼は声を張り上げて（→ありったけの声で）演説をした He made a speech *at the top of his voice*.

バリアフリー ──バリアフリーの barrier-free ∥ 駅のバリアフリー化を進める make train stations *barrier-free*

ハリウッド **Hollywood**（❖米国ロサンゼルス市の一区名）

バリウム 〔化学〕 barium [bέəriəm] ⓤ（❖元素記号 Ba）∥ 胃のレントゲン検査のためバリウムを飲む take *barium* for an examination by stomach X-ray

はりえ 張り絵 collage ⓒ

バリエーション variation ⓒⓊ

はりかえる 張り替える 壁紙を張り替える *repaper* the wall

はりがね 針金 wire ⓒⓊ（❖数えるときは a wire または a piece of … とする）

はりがみ 張り紙 (掲示) notice ⓒ；(ビラ) bill (ポスター) poster ⓒ ∥ 張り紙をはって put up *a notice* ∥ 張り紙お断り《掲示》*Post No Bills*

バリカン ⚠(hair) clippers（❖数えるときは a pair of … とする．日本語はフランスの製作所の名前 Bariquand et Marre から）

ばりき 馬力 ❶【単位】horsepower ⓤ（《略語》hp, HP）∥ 30馬力のエンジン a 30-*horsepower* engine
❷【力】(精力) energy ⓤ；(機械などの) power ⓤ ◆彼は馬力のある男だ He is an *energetic* man. ∥ このモーターは馬力がある This motor is *powerful*.

はりきゅう 鍼灸 ⇒しんきゅう(鍼灸)

はりきる 張り切る (がんばる) work hard；(元気を出す) be in high spirits；(元気である) be vigorous；(熱心な) be enthusiastic；(闘志を燃やす) be all fired up ∥ あの新入社員ははりきってるな The new guy *works hard*. ∥ 子供たちはあしたから夏休みなのではりきっている The children *are in high spirits* as the summer vacation starts from tomorrow. ∥ 選手はみんな優勝を目ざしてはりきっている The players *are all fired up* for the victory.

バリケード barricade ⓒ ∥ バリケードを築く build [set up] *a barricade*

ハリケーン hurricane ⓒ

はりこのとら 張り子の虎 paper tiger ⓒ ∥ 彼は威圧的だが，実際には張り子の虎だ He looks overbearing, but is actually *a paper tiger*.

はりこみ 張り込み stakeout ⓒ ∥ 張り込み中の刑事 a detective on *the stakeout*

はりこむ 張り込む ❶【見張る】(人を) keep* watch for …；(場所を) keep watch over …, stake out；(張り込みを置く) put* up a stakeout ∥ 刑事らしい男が隣の家をここ 2，3日張り込んでいる A man who looks like a detective *has kept watch over* the next-door neighbor's house these past few days.
❷【奮発する】私たちは昨晩張り込んで一流ホテルで食事した We *treated ourselves to* dinner at a first class hotel last night. ∥ 入試合格を期して姉は張り込んで1,000円をさい銭箱に入れた In the hope of passing the entrance exams, my sister made a *generous* offering of 1,000 yen.

はりさける 張り裂ける 私の胸は悲しみで張り裂けそうだった My heart *was* almost *breaking* with sorrow.

はりたおす 張り倒す (殴り倒す) knock *a person down*；(平手打ちで) slap *a person hard* ∥ 彼氏の浮気を知った妹はそいつを張り倒した My sister discovered her boyfriend's affair and *slapped* him *hard*.

はりだし 張り出し (建築) overhang；(出窓) bay window ⓒ；(ベランダ) balcony ⓒ

はりだす 張り出す ❶【掲示する】put* up, post ⊕ ∥ 合格者のリストが掲示板に張り出された The list of successful candidates *was put up* on the board.
❷【上方に】overhang* ⊕；(天気図で) move over … ∥ そのがけは小川の上に張り出している The cliff *overhangs* the stream. ∥ 寒冷前線が東日本に張り出している The cold front *is moving over* eastern Japan.

はりつけ 磔 crucifixion ⓒ；(キリストの) the Crucifixion ──はりつけにする crucify ⊕

はりつける 張り付ける・貼り付ける はがきにシールをはりつけてください *Stick* [*Put*] a sticker on a postcard. ∥ （コンピュータで) コピーした文章を新しいファイルにはりつけてください Please *paste* the copied sentences in a new file.

ぱりっと (身なりが) dashing, smart；(食べ物

はりつめる 張り詰める ❶【気・雰囲気が】(緊張する) be under great tension ━━張りつめた tense, strained 〃張りつめた雰囲気の中、声も出せなかった I couldn't say a word in the *tense* atmosphere. / 張りつめていた気持ちが一気にゆるんで彼はぐったりといすに腰を下ろした *His strained nerves* suddenly relaxed, and he sank into the chair.
❷【氷が】庭の池に氷が張りつめている The pond in the garden *is frozen over*.
バリトン 〖音楽〗baritone ⓊⒸ 〃山田さんはバリトンで歌う Mr. Yamada sings (*in*) *baritone*. 〃バリトン歌手 a baritone
はりねずみ 針鼠 hedgehog Ⓒ
ばりばり ❶【精力的に】あの新人はばりばり働く The newcomer works *like a horse*. / 彼女はもう80歳だが、ばりばりの現役だ She is already 80 years old, but is still *active on the front lines*.
❷【音】彼はセロリをばりばりとかじった He *crunched* celery. / 彼らは壁のベニヤ板をばりばりはがした They *ripped* the plywood down from the wall.
ぱりぱり ❶【新しい様子】ぱりぱりの新調の背広 a *crisp* new suit / ぱりぱりしたせんべい a *crunchy* rice cracker / ぱりぱりしたポテトチップス *crispy* potato chips
❷【音】弟は焼きのりをぱりぱり食べた My brother *crunched* roasted seaweed. / 薄氷がぱりぱりと割れた The thin ice *cracked*.
はりばん 張り番 (警戒) a lookout; (警備員などによる) watch Ⓤ(また a ～); (警備員) guard Ⓒ
はりめぐらす 張り巡らす (網などを) set* up; (囲む) surround ⃝ 〃情報網を張りめぐらす *set up* an information network / 池には金網が張りめぐらされていた The pond *was surrounded* by a wire fence.

はる¹ 春

spring ⓊⒸ
春物のデザイン the *spring* style
春が来た *Spring* has come.
春はもう間近だ *Spring* is just around the corner.
桜のつぼみは春のきざしだ Cherry buds are a signal that *spring* is coming.
今年の春は雨が多い It's rainy this *spring*.
兄はこの春大学を卒業した My brother graduated from college this *spring*.
わが家は春(→次の春)新居に引っ越す予定だ We are going to move into a new house *next spring*.
春先に沖縄に行くつもりだ I'm planning to go to Okinawa in early *spring*.
春になると私はアレルギーが出る I have an allergy *in* (*the*) *spring*.
姉は2000年の春に結婚しました My sister got married in *the spring* of 2000. (❖特定の春の場合には は省略できない)
∥春一番 the first southerly gale in the spring / 春がすみ a spring haze / 春風 a spring breeze / 春休み a spring vacation
短歌 春過ぎて夏来にけらし白妙の衣ほすてふ天の香具山(持統天皇)
Spring has now ended
and summer seems to have come,
for the white garments
hang to dry beneath the sky
on the slopes of Kagu Hill.

はる² 張る

❶【伸ばす・広げる】(引き伸ばす) stretch 🅐 🅑; (一面に広げる) spread* 🅐 🅑; (つるす) string* 🅑
ロープを木の間に張る *stretch* [*string*] a rope between the trees
松が四方に枝を張っている The pine tree *spreads* (*out*) its branches in all directions.
◆ネットを張る *put up* a net / 雑草が深く根を張っている Weeds *are* deeply *rooted*. / 私たちは川のそばにテントを張った We *pitched* a tent by the river. / (インターネットで)このページにはご自由にリンクをお張りください Please feel free to *link* this page.
❷【覆う】
けさ今年初めて氷が張った This morning *it froze* for the first time this year.
天井にクモの巣が張っている *There is* a spider's web on the ceiling. (❖「クモが巣を張っている」なら A spider is weaving a web. とする)
警察庁は逃亡中の容疑者を逮捕するために日本全国に捜査網を張った The National Police Agency *has set up* a dragnet throughout Japan to arrest the suspect at large.
❸【突き出す】
胸を張って歩く walk *with one's head held high*
彼はほお骨が張っている He has *prominent* cheekbones.
私たちは全力を尽くしたと胸を張って(→自信をもって)言うことができる We can say *confidently* that we did our best.
❹【ふくらむ】
産後は乳が張る The breasts *swell* after birth.
腹が張ってもう食べられない I'm so *full* (*up*). I can't eat any more.
❺【その他】
ふろに水を張る *run* a bath
その花びんは値が張る The vase *is very expensive*.
彼女は食い意地がはっている She *is greedy*.
意地をはるのもほどほどにしなさい Don't *be* so *stubborn*.
彼はすぐ見えをはる He's often *pretentious*.

はる³ 貼る put* 🅑; (ぴったりと) stick* 🅑; (のりなどで) paste 🅑; (ビラなどを) post 🅑 〃このはがきに切手をはってから後でポストに入れてもらえますか Could you *put* a stamp on this postcard and mail it later? / 壁にポスター

をはるのは禁止されている You are not allowed to *put up* posters on the wall. / 日本ではふつう履歴書に顔写真をはる In Japan you usually *stick* a head-and-shoulder's photo on a résumé.
◆先週の日曜日はふろ場のタイルをはった I *tiled* the bathroom last Sunday.

-ばる -張る 角張った顔 a *square* face / 形式ばったあいさつ a *formal* speech

はるか 遙か ❶【距離】(ずっと遠くに) far; (距離をおいて) in the distance //天気がよければはるか向こうに富士山が見える If the weather is fine, you can see Mt. Fuji *in the distance*.
❷【時間】(昔) a long time ago; (昔にさかのぼって) far back //彼女に初めて会ったのははるか昔のことだ It was *a long time ago* that [when] I saw her for the first time. / この話ははるか紀元前4000年にさかのぼる This story dates as *far back* as 4000 BC.
❸【程度】much, far (❖いずれも比較を強める) //彼女の演技のほうがはるかにすぐれていた Her performance was *much* [*far*] better. / 彼の知能は平均をはるかに上回っている His intelligence is *far* above average. (❖×much above とはいわない)

バルコニー balcony [C] //バルコニーからすばらしい海の景色が見えた We had a wonderful view of the sea from *the balcony*.

はるさき 春先 in early spring

はるさめ 春雨 spring shower [C]

バルトかい バルト海 the Baltic Sea ―バルト海の Baltic

バルトさんごく バルト三国 the Baltic States (❖旧ソ連の Estonia, Latvia, Lithuania の三国)

はるばしょ 春場所 the Grand Sumo Tournament in the spring, the spring tournament

はるばる all the way //彼女は日本の書道を学びにはるばるケニアからやってきた She came *all the way from* Kenya to learn Japanese calligraphy.

バルブ (弁) valve [C]

パルプ (製紙原料) (wood) pulp [U]

はるまき 春巻き spring roll [C], 《米》 egg roll [C]

はるめく 春めく 雪も解けだし春めいてきた It's *becoming springlike* as the snow started melting.

はれ¹ 晴れ
❶【天候】 ―晴れた (晴天の) fair; (雲のない) clear; (天気のよい) fine
あしたは晴れかな I wonder if it will be *fair* tomorrow.
東京は晴れです It is *fine weather* in Tokyo.
(天気予報などで) 今週いっぱいは晴れのお天気が続くでしょう We can expect *clear* skies throughout the week.
❷【表向き】
私は晴れの舞台で大失敗をしてしまった I made a terrible mistake on 「the *big* day [a *formal* occasion].

はれ² 腫れ swelling [U] //肩のはれは自然にひいた *The swelling* in my shoulder has gone away naturally.

はれあがる¹ 晴れ上がる clear up //あらしが去って空は晴れ上がった The storm has passed and the sky *has* completely *cleared up*.

はれあがる² 腫れ上がる swell* up

バレエ ballet [bæléi] [C] [U] //バレエを踊る dance *ballet*
‖バレエ団 a ballet company / バレエダンサー (男女ともに) a ballet dancer; (女性の) a ballerina / 古典バレエ (a) classical ballet

バレー ➔バレーボール

ハレーション halation [U]

ハレーすいせい ハレー彗星 Halley's Comet

パレード parade [C] ―パレードする parade [他] [自] //優勝パレードに私たちは興奮した *The victory parade* lifted our spirits.

バレーボール (競技) volleyball [U]; (ボール) volleyball [C] //バレーボールをする play *volleyball*

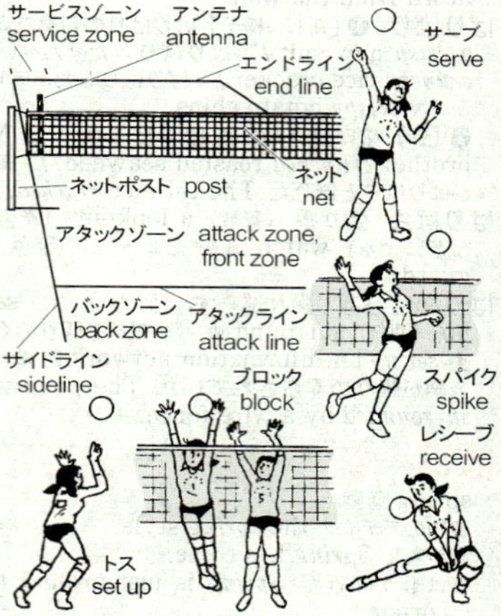
サービスゾーン
service zone
アンテナ
antenna
サーブ
serve
エンドライン
end line
ネット
net
ネットポスト post
アタックゾーン attack zone, front zone
バックゾーン
back zone
アタックライン
attack line
サイドライン
sideline
ブロック
block
スパイク
spike
レシーブ
receive
トス
set up

はれがましい 晴れがましい (公式の) ceremonial; (すばらしい) grand //晴れがましい場で on a *ceremonial* [*grand*] occasion

はれぎ 晴れ着 *one's* Sunday best, *one's* best clothes 《複数扱い》 //姉は晴れ着姿で成人式に出かけた My sister went out *in her best clothes* to the Coming of Age ceremony.

はれすがた 晴れ姿 息子の晴れ姿をビデオに撮った We filmed our son *dressed up*. / 山川夫妻は孫娘の結婚式の晴れ姿を楽しみにしている Mr. and Mrs. Yamakawa look forward to seeing their granddaughter in *her wedding dress*.

パレスチナ Palestine [pǽləstàin] ―パレスチナ人 Palestinian [pæ̀ləstíniən] ―パレス

チナの Palestinian
‖パレスチナ解放機構 the Palestine Liberation Organization (《略語》PLO)

はれつ 破裂 (水道管などの) burst ⓒ; (爆弾などの) explosion ⓒ; (内臓などの) rupture ⓒ ――破裂する[させる] burst* ⓐ ⓗ; explode ⓐ, blow* up; rupture ⓐ ⓗ ‖水道管が凍結して破裂した The water pipe *burst* from freezing. / 試験管が破裂して粉々になった The test tube *burst* into pieces. / 心臓が破裂しそうだった My heart almost *burst*.
‖破裂音 an explosive sound

パレット palette ⓒ
‖パレットナイフ a palette knife

はればれ 晴れ晴れ ――晴れ晴れ(と)した (明るい) bright; (陽気な) cheerful; (爽快な) refreshed ‖彼女は晴れ晴れした顔をしている She looks *cheerful*. / 試験も終わり晴れ晴れした気分だ I feel *refreshed* now that the exam is over.

はれぼったい 腫れぼったい puffy ‖はれぼったい目をしている You have *puffy* eyes.

はれま 晴れ間 梅雨の晴れ間 *a lull* in the rainy season / 午後には晴れ間が見えた *A patch of blue sky* was seen in the afternoon.

はれもの 腫れ物 (はれ) swelling ⓒ; (できもの) boil ⓒ, (腫瘍) tumor, 《英》tumour ⓒ ‖顔にはれものができた I've got *a boil* on my face.
[慣用表現] はれものにさわるように人を扱う treat a person *with kid gloves*

はれやか 晴れやか ――晴れやかな (明るい) bright; (まばゆい) radiant; (陽気な) cheerful ――晴れやかに brightly; radiantly; cheerfully ‖卒業生たちの表情はみな晴れやかだった Every graduate had a *bright* expression. / 明るい色の服を着たら何だか気分が晴れやかになった I felt *cheerful* in bright-colored dress.
◆ 会場内は晴れやかに着飾った人々でいっぱいだった The hall was filled with *well-dressed* people. / 身の潔白を証明できてとても晴れやかな気分です Because I was able to prove my innocence, I *feel* quite *relieved*.

バレリーナ ballerina ⓒ

はれる¹ 晴れる
❶【天気が】(青空が出る) clear up, become* clear; (霧などが) clear away, lift ⓐ
あした晴れたらサッカーやろうよ If *it clears up* tomorrow, let's play soccer.
空が晴れてきましたよ The sky *is becoming clear*.
霧が晴れて運転しやすくなった The fog *has cleared away* and it's safe to drive now.
◆ あしたは晴れるといいのですが I hope *it* [*the weather*] *will be fine* tomorrow.
❷【気分が】(楽しくなる) be cheered up; (一新する) be refreshed
◆ 友達と電話でおしゃべりしたら気が晴れた I was chatting with a friend on the phone, and that *cheered* me *up*. / いい汗かいて気分が晴れた Good exercise *refreshed* me. / 彼女が励ましてくれたにもかかわらず気分は晴れなかった I *felt none the better* for her encouragement.
❸【疑いが】(消える) disappear ⓐ; (潔白が証明される) be cleared; (ぬぐい去る) be dispelled
彼の疑いがすべて晴れてとてもうれしい I'm so glad that he *was cleared* of all suspicion.

はれる² 腫れる (ふくらむ) swell* up; (炎症を起こす) be inflamed ‖彼女は突き指して指がはれた Her finger *swelled up* from the sprain. ◆ 扁桃腺(へんとうせん)がはれたので学校を休んだ I didn't go to school because my tonsils *are swollen*.

バレル (容積の単位) barrel ⓒ ‖100万バレルの石油 one million *barrels* of oil

ばれる (明るみに出る) come* out; (もれる) leak out; (見つかる) be discovered; (正体が) be found out ‖脱税がばれた The tax evasion *was discovered*. / 秘密がばれた The secret「*came out* [*leaked out*].

ハレルヤ hallelujah [hæ̀liluːjə] ⓒ, alleluia [æ̀ləluːjə] ⓒ (❖神を賛美する叫び・祈り)

バレンタインデー ⚠ St. Valentine's Day

はれんち 破廉恥 ――破廉恥な (恥知らずの) shameless(❖名詞の前で用いる); (不名誉な) (公式的) flagrant, infamous ‖破廉恥な行為 a *shameless* behavior [act]
‖破廉恥罪 an infamous crime [offence]

はろう 波浪 wave ⓒ ➾ なみ(波)
‖波浪注意報 a high sea warning

ハロウィーン Halloween

ハロー hello [helóu]

バロック 【建築・美術・音楽】 the baroque ――バロック(様式)の baroque ‖バロック建築[音楽] *baroque* architecture [music]

パロディー parody ⓒ ‖この映画はいくつかの有名な古典映画のパロディーです This movie is *a parody* of some famous classic movies.

バロメーター barometer [bərámitər] ⓒ ‖血圧は健康のバロメーターだ Blood pressure serves as *a barometer* of health.

パワー (力) power ⓒ; (体力・筋力) strength ⓤ; (精力・活力) energy ⓤ; (元気・気力)《口語的》guts ‖彼は4番を打つにはパワーが足りない He lacks *the power* [*strength*] to hit cleanup. / 金メダルを取るためにはもっと足にパワーをつけなければなりません You have to add more *strength* to your legs to win the gold medal. / 今晩全部の宿題をやるだけのパワーが彼女にあるかな Does she have enough *energy* to do all the homework tonight?
◆ パワーアップする *become more powerful* / この車はエンジンのパワーがこれまで私が運転していたものとまるで違う The engine of this car is much more *powerful* than that of the ones I've ridden in before.
‖パワーステアリング power steering
パワーショベル power shovel ⓒ, excavator ⓒ

ハワイ Hawaii(❖ハワイ諸島から成る米国の州;

ハワイアン　《略語》《郵便》HI　——ハワイ人 Hawaiian ◯　——ハワイ語 Hawaiian ◯　——ハワイ(人[語])の Hawaiian
‖ハワイ諸島 the Hawaiian Islands
ハワイアン ⚠ Hawaiian music ◯

はわたり　刃渡り　刃渡り10センチのナイフ a knife with *a blade* 10 centimeters *long*

はん¹ 半 (半分) half ◯ (複 halves) ∥10時半 *half* past ten (❖英口語では past を省略することもある); ten *thirty* / 1時間半 an hour and *a half*; one and *a half* hours / 半マイル *a half* mile; a *half* mile / 卵を半ダース買ってきてちょうだい Go and get *half a dozen* eggs for me, will you? / うちの大学は夏休みが2か月半もある Our university's summer vacation stretches out for as long as *two and a half months*.
◆丁か半か Odd or even?
‖半円 a semicircle / 半休 a half-holiday

はん² 判 ❶[印鑑] seal ◯, stamp ◯ (❖欧米では印鑑を政府や会社の公文書に用い, 個人は署名がふつう) ⇒ はんこ / その書類には会社の判が押してある The document bears *the seal of the corporation*. ◆私は契約書にサインして判を押した I signed and *sealed* the contract. ❷[規格の大きさ] size ◯
‖三文判 a ready-made seal
使用表現 だれに聞いても判で押したような答えしか返ってこなかった Everyone repeated the *stereotyped* answer.

はん³ 版 edition ◯ ∥版を重ねる go through several *editions* / 版を改める publish *a* new *edition*; revise *an edition* / その辞書の第3版は10刷を数えた The third *edition of* the dictionary went through 10 printings [impressions]. ◆ポーのフランス語版 the French *translation* [*version*] *of* Poe / 海賊版 a pirate [bootleg] edition / 改訂版 a revised edition / カラー版(新聞の) a color supplement / 限定版 a limited edition / 豪華版 a deluxe edition / 最新版 the latest edition / 再版 a reprint, a reissue / 縮刷版 an abridged edition / 初版 the first edition; (初版の本) a first edition / 地方版 a local edition / 日曜版 the Sunday edition / ペーパーバック[ハードカバー]版 a paperback [hardback, hardcover] edition / 廉価版 a popular edition

はん⁴ 班 group ◯; (特定の任務にあたる) team ◯, 《集合的》crew ◯; (部隊) squad ◯ ∥カメラ班 a camera *crew* / 救護班 a rescue *squad* / 爆弾処理班 a bomb disposal *squad* / 私たちは6つの班に分かれて方言の調査研究を行った We were divided into six *groups* to do some research on local dialects.
‖班長 a group [section, squad] leader

はん⁵ 藩 feudal clan ◯; (藩の領地) feudal domain ◯ ∥薩摩藩 the Satsuma *Clan*
‖藩主 (封建時代の) a seigneur [seinjə́ːr]

はん-¹ 反- anti-, counter- ∥反作用 (*a*) *counter*action / 反核運動 an antinuclear movement / 反時計回りに[の] counterclockwise, 《英》anticlockwise / 反社会的行為 an *anti-social* act / 反日感情 *anti-Japanese* feeling [sentiment]

はん-² 汎- pan- ∥汎太平洋の *pan*-Pacific ∥汎神論 pantheism

バン van ◯ ∥ライトバン a delivery van, a wagon (❖×light van とはいわない)

ばん¹ 晩
(日没から寝るまでの時間) evening ◯ ◯; (日没から日の出までの時間) night ◯ ◯ ⇒ よる(夜)
毎晩 every *evening*; in *the evenings* / 一晩中 all through *the night*; all *night* (through) / 朝から晩まで from morning till [to] *night* / 晩に in *the evening* / あしたの晩に tomorrow *evening* (❖every, tomorrow, yesterday, this, that, one などが付くときには前置詞は不要)
今晩外食しない? Shall we eat out *this evening*?
会議は晩の7時に開かれた The meeting was held at seven *in the evening*.
土曜日の晩にパーティーを開こう Let's hold a party *on* Saturday *evening*. (❖特定の日の場合には前置詞は on になる)
その親切な農場主は私を1晩泊めてくれた The thoughtful farmer put me up *for the night*.
我々はそのホテルに2晩泊まった We stayed at the hotel (*for*) *two nights*.
‖晩ごはん an evening meal, (a) supper, (a) dinner / 晩秋 late autumn [fall]

ばん² 番
❶[順番] *one's* turn
自分の番を待つ wait for *one's* turn
まだ君の番じゃないよ It's not your *turn* yet.
次は君がスピーチをする番だ It's your *turn* to make a speech.
やっと私の番が来た My *turn* has come at last.
◆彼女は自分の番ではないのに話し始めた She began to speak *out of order* [*turn*]. / 彼は1番にやってきた He was *the first* to come. / 僕は数学ではクラスで1番だ I'm *at the top* of the class in math. / 君は学校で何番ぐらいなんだい What *place* [*number*] are you in your grade at school? / 前列の向かって左から5番目にいるのが私の父です My father is *the fifth* from the left in the front row. / 大阪は日本で2番目に大きな都市だ Osaka is the *second* largest city in Japan.
💬「次はだれの番だい」「私よ」"Whose *turn* is it [next]?" "(It's) mine."
❷[番号] number ◯ (《略語》No.)
モーツァルトの交響曲第40番 Mozart's Symphony *No.* 40
3番のバスに乗りなさい Take 「a *number* 3 bus [a bus *number* 3].
この書類は13番窓口に提出してください You have to hand in this form at window *number* 13.

あの子の電話番号は何番だい *What*'s her telephone [phone] number? / 何番におかけですか *What number* are you calling? / ◆僕の受験番号は163番だった My exam seat number was *163*. / マリーは5番街に住んでいる Mary lives on *Fifth* Street [Avenue]. / 7番ゲートへお進みください Please proceed to Gate *7*, please. / 詳細は6860-0185番にお問い合わせください Call us at *6860-0185* for further information. / 内線123番をお願いします Give me extension *123*.

🅔「東京行きの電車は何番線ですか」「12番線です」 *"Which platform* does the train for Tokyo leave from?" *"Twelve."* / 「缶詰はどこにありますか」「2番通路です」 "Where're the canned foods?" "They're in aisle *two*."

❸【試合】match ⓒ; (格闘技などの) bout ⓒ
5番連続して勝つ win five *bouts* in a row / 3番勝負 a three-game *match*; *a* three-round *bout*

❹【見張り】
店の番をする *mind* [⦅米⦆*tend*] the store / 彼はヤギの番をしている He *is tending* his goat. / 荷物の番をしててね *Keep an eye on* my baggage.

‖番小屋 a box

ばん³ 盤 board ⓒ〖碁[将棋]盤 a go [*shogi*] board

パン

Ⓐ bread Ⓤ(✿種類をいうときはⓒ); roll ⓒ; bun ⓒ(✿日本語はポルトガル語のpãoから)

> bread: パン類の総称だが，ふつう食パンを指す．
> roll: 様々な形の小型のパンのこと．
> bun: ⦅米⦆では主にハンバーガー用のパンを指し，⦅英⦆では甘い菓子パンを指すことが多い．

パン1個[1枚, 1切れ] a roll [slice, piece] of *bread* / パン1斤[2斤]「a loaf [two loaves] of *bread* / スライスされたパン sliced *bread* / (オーブンで)パンを焼く bake *bread* in an oven; (→トーストする) toast *bread* / パンにバターを塗る spread butter on *bread* / 母はいつもお店でパンを薄切りにしてもらう My mother always has *bread* sliced at the bakery. / 焼きたてのパンはおいしい *Bread fresh from the oven* is delicious. / 朝はパン食ですか，それともごはん食ですか Which do you *eat* for breakfast, *bread* or rice?

◆パンの耳 (a) crust

‖パン生地 dough [dóu] / パンくず crumbs / パン粉 breadcrumbs / パン屋(人) a baker; (店) a bakery, a baker's (shop) / あんパン a bean-jam bun / ブドウパン raisin bread / フランスパン French bread / ライ麦パン rye bread / ロールパン a roll (of bread)

はんい 範囲 range Ⓤ⦅またa～⦆; (領域) area ⓒ; (手の届く) reach ⓒ; (限界) limit ⓒ; (活動の) sphere ⓒ; (能力・知識・研究の) scope Ⓤ

彼の政治活動は広い範囲にわたっている His political activities cover *a wide range*. / 光化学スモッグが広範囲に広がった Photochemical smog spread *over a wide area*. / 姉の交際範囲はとても広い My sister maintains *a* wide *range of acquaintances [friends]*. / この理論は私の理解の範囲を超えている This theory is beyond *the reach of* my *understanding*.

◆私の知っている範囲では彼は犯罪を犯すような人には見えなかった *As far as* I know [*To the best of* my knowledge], he didn't look like a person who would commit a crime. / ベクトルは今度の試験の範囲だ Vectors *are on* the next exam. / 出費を予算の範囲内に抑えたい I want to keep the expenses *within* [*under*] the budget. / この公式は応用範囲が広い This formula *has*「*wide application* [*a wide range of applications*]. / その要求は我々の許容範囲を超えている The request is *unbearable* to us. / 私のできる範囲で彼女を助けましょう I'll help her *as much as possible*. / I'll help her *to the best of my ability*.

🅔「今度の英語の試験の範囲はどこまでだい」「レッスン5から7までらしい」 "What does the next English exam *cover*?" "Lessons 5 to 7, I hear."

‖交際範囲 a range [circle] of acquaintances [friends] / 適用範囲 coverage

はんいご 反意語 antonym ⓒ(↔synonym), opposite ⓒ〖「出席」は「欠席」の反意語です "Presence" is *the antonym* of "absence."

はんえい¹ 反映 reflection Ⓤⓒ ――反映する reflect ⦿ⓘ〖映画は世相を反映している Movies *reflect* social conditions. / この記事は我々の意見を反映していない This article doesn't *reflect* our opinion.

はんえい² 繁栄 prosperity Ⓤ ――繁栄する (主に金銭的に) prosper ⓘ; (成長・発展する) thrive* ⓘ〖国家の繁栄 the prosperity of a nation / わが社はここ20年，繁栄を続けている Our company *has been thriving* these 20 years.

はんえいきゅうてき 半永久的 CD-ROMを使えば大切な情報を半永久的に(→ほぼ永久に)保存することができる You can save your important data *almost permanently* by using CD-ROMs.

はんえん 半円 semicircle ⓒ ――半円(形)の semicircular ‖半円アーチ a *semicircular* [*half-round*] arch / 彼らは半円状に座った They sat *in a semicircle*.

はんおん 半音 ⦅音楽⦆half tone ⓒ, ⦅米⦆half step ⓒ, ⦅英⦆semitone ⓒ〖半音上げる[下げる] raise [lower] a note *by a half tone*

◆(ある)音を半音低く[高く]演奏する play a note *flat* [*sharp*]

‖半音階 a chromatic scale

はんが 版画 print ◯, engraving ◯; (木版画) woodcut ◯; (銅版画) etching ◯; (石版画) lithograph ◯
‖版画家 an engraver, a print artist

ばんか¹ 挽歌 (死者を悼む歌) elegy ◯, lament ◯ ‖友への挽歌 an *elegy* for a friend

ばんか² 晩夏 (the) late summer

ハンガー (coat) hanger ◯ ‖コートをハンガーにかける put an overcoat on *a hanger*
‖ハンガーボード a pegboard

バンカー 【ゴルフ】 bunker ◯, (米) sand trap ◯ ‖ボールをバンカーに打ち込む hit a ball into *a bunker*

ハンガーストライキ hunger strike ◯

はんかい 半壊 ——半壊する be partially [partly] destroyed
‖半壊家屋 a partially destroyed house

ばんかい 挽回 (回復) recovery ◯; (修復) restoration ◯ ——挽回する recover ⾃他; restore ⾃他 ‖名誉を挽回する *recover [restore] one's honor* ◆ 2点差なら挽回可能だ If we're only two runs [points, goals] behind, we can still have a comeback.

ばんがい 番外 ——番外の extra ‖番外の特別出演 an *extra* performance
◆あいつは番外だ(→特別だ) He's *special*.

はんかがい 繁華街 downtown ◯◯; (にぎやかな通り) busy street ◯ ——繁華街へ[の] downtown ‖繁華街の店 a *downtown* store / 東京の繁華街で in *downtown* Tokyo / きのう繁華街へ買い物に出かけた I went out shopping *downtown* yesterday.

はんかく 反核 ——反核の antinuclear ‖反核運動 (an) antinuclear movement / 反核集会 an antinuclear rally [meeting] / 反核団体 an antinuclear group / 反核デモ an antinuclear demonstration

はんがく 半額 half (the) price; (乗り物料金) half (the) fare ‖私はそのパソコンを定価の半額で買った I bought the personal computer *at「half (the) price [50 percent discount]*. / 12歳未満のお子様は半額でこの映画をご覧になれます Children under 12 are allowed to see this movie *at half price*.
◆その靴は半額に(→半額分)値下げされた They reduced the price of the shoes *by 50 percent*.
‖半額セール a 50 percent discount sale, a half-off sale

ハンカチ handkerchief ◯(複 ～s, handkerchieves) ‖レースのハンカチ a lace *handkerchief* / ハンカチをひざの上に広げる unfold *a handkerchief* on one's lap

ハンガリー Hungary(✿公式名 the Republic of Hungary) ——ハンガリー人 Hungarian ◯ ——ハンガリー語 Hungarian ◯ ——ハンガリー(人[語])の Hungarian

バンガロー ⚠ cottage ◯; (簡素な造りの) cabin ◯ ‖英語の bungalow は「ベランダのついた平屋建て住居」の意味

はんかん 反感 bad [ill] feeling ◯◯; (敵意) antipathy ◯◯, hostility ◯◯; (嫌悪) dislike ◯ ‖彼女は彼に反感をいだいた She took *a dislike* to him. (✿「反感をいだく」なら take の代わりに have を用いる) / 彼の行動はチームのメンバーの反感を買った His behavior *caused ill feeling* among the members of the team.

はんかんはんみん 半官半民 ——半官半民の semiofficial, semi-governmental

はんき¹ 反旗 彼らは指揮官に反旗を翻(ひるがえ)した They *rebelled [revolted]* against their commander.

はんき² 半期 half term ◯; (1年の半分) half year ◯ ◆上[下]半期の売上目標 a sales target for *the first [second] half year* / 半期に1度のバーゲンセール a *once-a-half-year* sale
‖四半期 a quarter of the year

はんき³ 半旗 a flag at half-mast ‖半旗を掲げる hoist [fly] *a flag at half-mast*

はんぎゃく 反逆 treason ◯; (反乱) revolt ◯ ——反逆する revolt ⾃, rise* ⾃ ‖国王に反逆する *commit treason* against a king
◆彼は反逆者のレッテルをはられた He was labeled (as) *a rebel*.
‖反逆行為 an act of treason / 反逆罪 high treason

はんきゅう 半球 hemisphere ◯ ‖北[南]半球 the northern [southern] hemisphere

はんきょう 反響 ❶【音】 echo [ékou] ◯, resonance ◯ ——反響する echo ⾃他 ‖だれもいない廊下に私たちの足音が反響した Our footsteps *echoed* in the empty corridor.
❷【反応】 response ◯◯; (大評判) sensation ◯ ‖そのテレビ番組への反響は予想以上だった *The response* to the TV program was beyond expectations. / 彼の発言は大きな反響を呼んだ His comment caused *a great sensation*.

はんきょうらん 半狂乱 ——半狂乱の half-crazed ◆彼はその知らせを聞いて半狂乱になった He *went half crazy* at hearing the news.

パンク¹ ⚠(タイヤの破裂) puncture ◯, blowout ◯; (パンクしたタイヤ) flat tire ◯ ——パンクする go* flat, blow* out, puncture ⾃ ‖自転車の後輪がパンクしてしまった The rear wheel of my bicycle *has gone flat*. ◆回線がパンクした The lines *were overloaded*.

パンク² (パンクロック) 【音楽】 punk (rock) ◯

バンクーバー Vancouver(✿カナダの都市)

ハンググライダー hang glider ◯; (飛ぶこと) hang gliding ◯

ばんぐみ 番組 program ◯ ‖スポーツ番組をテレビで見る watch *sports programs* on TV / これは子供たちの間で最も人気のあるテレビ番組の一つです This is one of the most popular *TV programs* among children. / 今夜, 僕がラジオ番組に出るよ I'm going to be on *a radio program* this evening. / この番組はロンドンから衛星生中継でお送りしています We're bringing this *program* to you live by satellite from London.

🅔「何かいい番組ある」「映画があるわ」"Are there any good *programs* on TV?" "There's a movie."
🅔「どんな番組が好きなの」「バラエティー番組かな」"What kind of *TV program* do you like (the) best?" "Well, *variety shows*."
‖クイズ番組 a game [quiz] show / 深夜番組 a late program / 特別番組 a special / ニュース番組 the news, 《米》a newscast

ハングリー ━━ハングリーな hungry
◆彼にはハングリー精神がある He *is extremely ambitious*.

ハングル（ハングル文字）the Hangul [Hankul, Korean] alphabet

ばんくるわせ 番狂わせ upset ◎; (驚きの結果) surprise ◎ / きょうのJリーグは番狂わせが多かった We had a lot of *upsets* in today's J-League matches. / 好美がマラソン大会で優勝するとはまさに番狂わせだ It is *a surprise* that Yoshimi won first place in the marathon.
◆わが校の野球チームは番狂わせで（→思いがけず）優勝候補に勝った Our school's baseball team (*unexpectedly*) *upset* the favorite.

はんけい 半径 radius [réidiəs] ◎ (複 radii [réidiài], ~es)《略語》r. / 半径10センチの円 a circle with *a radius* of 10 centimeters / 半径3マイル以内の距離に within *a three mile radius* / この円の半径はどのくらいですか What is *the radius* of this circle?
‖行動半径 a range of activities

パンケーキ pancake ◎, hot cake ◎;（小型の）《米》flapjack ◎

はんげき 反撃 counterattack ◎ ━━反撃する counterattack ⑩ ⑧, fight* [hit*, strike*] back / 反撃の機をうかがう look for a chance to *fight back* / 試合の後半に日本チームはブラジルに対して反撃に出た The Japan team started to *make a counterattack* on Brazil in the second half of the game.

はんけつ 判決 ruling ◎, judgment,《英》judgement ◎◎; (決定) decision ◎; (刑の宣告) sentence ◎◎ / 厳しい判決 a severe *sentence* / 判決をくつがえす reverse *a ruling* [*decision*] / 判決を破棄する set aside *a ruling* [*decision*] / …に判決を言い渡す pronounce [pass] *sentence* on *a person*
◆…に不利な[有利な]判決を下す decide against [for, in favor of] … / …に終身刑の判決を言い渡す sentence *a person* to life imprisonment / その男に有罪[無罪]判決が下った The man *was found guilty* [*not guilty*]. / その殺人犯は死刑[懲役15年の]判決を受けた The murderer *was sentenced* to death [15 years in prison].

はんげつ 半月 half moon ◎; (半月形) semicircle ◎ ━━半月(形)の semicircular

はんけん 版権 copyright ◎◎ / 版権を取得する secure *a copyright* (on …) / 版権を侵害する infringe *a copyright*
◆版権所有 *All rights reserved*.

はんけん 半券 stub ◎;（預けた荷物の）baggage claim ◎

はんげん 半減 ━━半減する be reduced [cut down on …] by half / 節約したおかげで今月の支出は半減した Due to cost-cutting, our expenses *were reduced* [*cut down on*] *by half* this month.
◆彼女が来ないと聞いてパーティーに対する興味が半減した I've *lost half of my interest* in the party because I heard she's not coming.

ばんけん 番犬 guard dog ◎, watchdog ◎

はんこ 判子 ⇒はん(判)

日本では正式な書類にはサインではなくはんこ(印鑑)が必要です．はんこには名前(名字が一般的)が彫ってあり，素材は木，プラスチックから高級はんこ用の象牙(ぞうげ)や水晶までいろいろです．また，特に重要な取り引きなどには役所で登録してある実印が必要となり，印鑑証明書の提出も要求されます．三文判と呼ばれるできあいのはんこも店で安く買うことができます．
In Japan it is *hanko* or *inkan* (seal) not a signature that is required for formal documents. On *hanko* are engraved names, usually family names, and the materials vary from wood and plastic to ivory and crystal for deluxe ones. And for very important transactions you have to use a made-to-order *jitsuin*, which is registered at a local government office. It may also be necessary to submit a certificate of authenticity. Ready-made and inexpensive *hanko* called *sammonban* are available at local shops.

はんご 反語 (皮肉) irony [áiərəni] ◎◎; (修辞疑問) rhetorical question [áiə]
◆反語的な言い方をする speak *ironically*

はんこう[1] 反抗 resistance ◎◎《また a ~》; (不服従・反発) disobedience ◎, rebellion ◎ ◎; (挑戦・命令の無視) defiance ◎ ━━反抗的な resistant; disobedient, rebellious; defiant ━━反抗する resist ⑩ ⑧, rebel ⑧; defy ⑩

権威に反抗するのは若者の常だ *Resistance* [*Disobedience*] *to* authority is one of the inevitabilities of youth.

その生徒たちは先生に反抗してばかりいる The students always *disobey* their teacher.

彼女はいつも彼に反抗的な態度をとる She always takes *a rebellious* [*defiant*] *attitude* toward him.

うちの娘は今反抗期なんですよ My daughter is at *a rebellious age* [*stage*] now.

兄は最近両親に反抗的だ My brother has recently been「*rebellious against* [*defiant toward*] our parents.

はんこう[2] 犯行 crime ◎◎; (法などに対する違反) offence ◎◎《通例単数形》⇒はんざい ‖計画的犯行 *a premeditated crime* / 犯行を企てる attempt [plot, plan] *a crime* / 犯行を認める[否認する] admit [deny] *a crime* / 犯行はつかまるまで次々と犯行を重ねていた He had committed one *crime* after another before he was caught.

‖犯行現場 the scene of a crime
はんごう 飯盒 mess kit ©

ばんごう 番号
number © (《略語》No., no.)
この部屋のコンピュータにはすべて番号がついている Every computer in this room has its own *number*. / Every computer in this room *is numbered*.
(電話で)番号違いですよ (I'm afraid) you have *the wrong number*.
◆カードを番号順に並べる line up cards *in numerical order* / (号令で)番号! *Count off*! / 《英》*Number off*! / ページの下に番号をつけなさい *Number* the pages at the bottom.
‖番号札 a numbered ticket / 暗証番号 a personal identification number (《略語》PIN) / 学生番号 one's student number / 電話番号 a phone number / 通し番号 a serial number / 当選番号 a winning number / 郵便番号 (a) zip code, 《英》(a) postcode

バンコク Bangkok (※タイの首都)

ばんこく 万国 all nations ─万国の (万人に共通の) universal; (国際的な) international / 公衆トイレの落書きは万国共通のものなのだろうか Is graffiti in public toilets *common to all nations*?
‖万国旗 bunting / 万国博覧会 an international exhibition [exposition], a world fair

はんこつ 反骨 我々のリーダーは反骨精神の塊(鋳)だ Our leader has *a strong rebellious spirit*.

はんごろし 半殺し 人を半殺しにする *beat* a person *nearly to death* / 彼は半殺しの目にあった He was half-killed.

ばんこん 晩婚 late marriage © ◆彼女は晩婚だった She *married late (in life)*.

はんざい 犯罪
crime ⓤ © (※個々の犯罪行為をいう場合には ©); (軽い) offense, 《英》offence ©; (未成年者の) delinquency ⓤ © ─犯罪の criminal
犯罪を犯す commit *a crime* / 犯罪を防止する prevent *crime* / 犯罪を根絶する wipe out *crime*
最近この地域では犯罪が増加[減少]している Recently *crime* in this area has been on the increase [decrease].
彼女はその犯罪に何ら関与していない She didn't take part in the *crime* at all.
万引きはりっぱな犯罪だ Shoplifting is *an obvious criminal offense*.
‖犯罪行為 a criminal offense / 犯罪者 a criminal, an offender; (未決の) a culprit; (既決の) a convict / 犯罪心理学 criminal psychology / 犯罪捜査 criminal detection [investigation] / 犯罪容疑 suspicion of a crime / 完全犯罪 a perfect crime / 凶悪犯罪 a felony, a violent crime / 軽犯罪 a minor crime / 少年犯罪 juvenile delinquency / 性犯罪 a sex crime / 組織犯罪 organized crime

ばんざい 万歳 ❶【行為】banzai © (※英米では日本語の万歳と同じ習慣はない); (歓声) cheer © / 万歳三唱(をする) (give) *three cheers* (※リーダーが Hip! Hip!と言った後に全員で Hurray!と続けるのを3回繰り返す) / 出席した人は全員万歳をした All of those present shouted *banzais*.
❷【掛け声】hurray [həréi], viva [víːvə] / 万歳, ついにやったぞ *Hurray*, we've made it!
◆女王[国王]陛下万歳 *God Save* the Queen [King]!

ばんさく 万策 ついに万策尽きた We *have come to the end of our resources* at last. / *There is nothing more we can do*.

はんざつ 煩雑 ─煩雑な (こみ入って複雑な) complicated; (めんどうな) troublesome ‖煩雑な手続き a *complicated* procedure

ハンサム ─ハンサムな good-looking, handsome (※handsome は「きりっとした, りりしい」という意味で女性にも用いる) ◆彼は背が高くてハンサムな男だ He is a tall and *handsome* man.

はんさよう 反作用 reaction ⓤ ©, counteraction © ‖作用と反作用 action and *reaction* / 反作用を引き起こす cause *reaction* [*counteraction*]

ばんさん 晩餐 dinner ⓤ ‖人を晩餐に招待する invite a person to *a dinner* / 晩餐会 a dinner (party)

はんし 半紙 △ *hanshi*, Japanese paper for calligraphy

はんじ 判事 judge © ‖判事席 the bench / 判事補 an assistant judge / 最高裁判事 a Supreme Court justice / 主席判事 a senior judge

ばんじ 万事 万事うまくいった Everything [All] worked out well. / 彼女に万事心得ているから大丈夫です You can trust her as she *knows her stuff*. / 万事休すだ It's all over with me. / My number has come up.
慣用表現 一事が万事 ⇒ いちじ(一事)

パンジー pansy ©
バンジージャンプ ⚠ bungee jumping ⓤ
◆今度バンジージャンプにチャレンジしてみたい I want to try *bungee-jumping* some time.

はんしゃ 反射
(光·音などの) reflection ⓤ; (運動の) reflex © ─反射する reflect ⊜ ⊜
湖面が月の光を反射している The surface of the lake *is reflecting* the moonlight. / The moonlight *is reflecting off* the surface of the lake.
この壁は音を反射せずに吸収する This wall *doesn't reflect* sound, but absorbs it.
彼は反射神経がいい He has good *reflexes*.
◆背後に足音が近づいてくるのを聞いて彼は反射的に身構えた Hearing footsteps approaching behind his back, he *reflexively* stood ready to fight.
‖反射鏡 a reflector / 反射熱 reflected heat / 反射望遠鏡 a reflecting telescope, a reflector / 条件反射 a conditioned reflex [response] / 乱反射 irregular reflection

はんしゃかいてき 反社会的 ─反社会的な

ばんぜん

anti-social, antisocial ∥彼女の行動は反社会的とみなされた Her behavior was regarded *antisocial*.

ばんしゃく 晩酌 晩酌をする have *a drink with dinner*; *drink while having dinner*

はんしゅう 半周 (半円) semicircle ［C］ ――半周する go* halfway (around ...)
◆私は毎朝公園を半周走る I *run halfway around the park every morning*.

ばんしゅう 晩秋 (the) late fall [autumn]

はんじゅく 半熟 ――半熟の half-boiled, half-done ∥半熟卵 a *half-boiled* [*half-done*] egg ◆卵を半熟にゆでる boil an egg *soft*

はんしゅつ 搬出 商品を倉庫から搬出する *carry* goods *out of the warehouse*

ばんしゅん 晩春 (the) late spring

ばんしょ 板書 ――板書する write* ... on the blackboard ∥彼は板書がうまい He *writes* neatly *on the blackboard*.
◆板書(→黒板に書かれていること)を写しなさい Copy *what is written on the blackboard*.

はんしょう 反証 (反証すること)《公式的》disproof ［U］; (証拠) counter example [evidence] ［C］,《公式的》disproof ［C］(◆〜s) ――反証する disprove ⑭ ∥その理論に対する反証を挙げるのは難しい It's difficult to *disprove* the theory.
◆検察側の主張に対する弁護側の反証には説得力が全くなかった The defense's *evidence against* the statement by the prosecution wasn't convincing at all.
∥反証可能性 refutability

はんじょう 繁盛 prosperity ［U］ ――繁盛する (金銭的に) prosper ⑭; (事業などが成功する) thrive* ⑭
◆彼の店は繁盛している His store *is prosperous* [*thriving, doing well*]. / 彼女の経営のもとでその店は繁盛した Under her management the shop *did well*. / その店は繁盛している That shop *is doing a good business*.

ばんしょう¹ 万障 会合には万障お繰り合わせのうえご出席ください(→出席してくださることを切に願っています) We do hope you will attend the meeting.

ばんしょう² 晩鐘 vesper (bell) ［C］

バンジョー banjo ［C］(複‒(e)s)

はんしょく 繁殖 (動物の) breeding ［U］; (動植物の) multiplication ［U］,《公式的》propagation ［U］ ――繁殖する breed* ⑭; multiply ⑭,《公式的》propagate ⑭ ∥ネズミは繁殖が早い(→すぐに増える) Rats *breed* [*multiply*] quickly. ◆カモノハシは卵で繁殖する Duckbills *reproduce* by laying eggs.
∥繁殖期 the breeding season

はんしん 半身 (上下の) a half of the body; (左右の) one side of the body ∥彼は交通事故で半身不随になった He *was paralyzed in* 「*one side* [*half*] *of his body* in a traffic accident.
∥半身像(彫刻などの) a bust / 上[下]半身 the upper [lower] part of *one's* body / 右[左]半身 the right [left] side of *one's* body

はんしんはんぎ 半信半疑 最初にその話を聞かされたときは半信半疑だった(→全面的には信じられなかった) When I was told the story, I *couldn't quite believe* it at first.

はんすう¹ 半数 (…の半数) half of ... ⇨はんぶん ∥調査した学生の半数は学校に満足していない *Half of* the students surveyed are not satisfied with their schools.
◆半数以上(→過半数)がその案に反対だった The majority were against the proposal.

はんすう² 反芻 ――反すうする ruminate ⑭, chew the cud
◆彼は先生の忠告を反すうした He *thought* [*chewed*] *over* what the teacher told him.
∥反すう動物 a ruminant

ハンスト ⚠ hunger strike ［C］ ∥ハンストをする go on *a hunger strike*

パンスト ⚠ pantyhose《複数扱い》(◆「パンスト」は panty stocking を省略したもの)

はんズボン 半ズボン shorts(◆《米》では「男性用パンツ」の意味もある)

はんする 反する (信条・規則などに背(そむ)く) go* against ...; (…と逆である) be contrary to ... ∥我々の期待に反して, 彼は決勝で負けた *Contrary to* our expectations, he lost in the finals. / 公共のマナーに反する発言は慎むべきだ You should avoid saying anything that *goes against* public manners. / そういう行動は我々の方針に反する It *goes against* our policy to act like that.
◆この報道には事実に反する内容が含まれている This report includes material that *is not true to* the facts.

はんせい¹ 反省 reflection ［U］; (後悔) regret ［U］ ――反省する reflect ⑭; regret ⑭
彼は両親の言ったことが正しかったかもしれないと反省した He *reflected* that his parents might have been right.
私は自分勝手な行動をとったことを反省している I *regret* that I acted in a selfish way.
彼女には反省の色が全く見られなかった She showed no *sign of regret*.
◆昨夜のことについては深く反省しています I'm very *sorry* about last night. / 私たちは部室で試合の反省会をした We had a meeting in our club room *to review* the game.

はんせい² 半生 half *one's* life ◆その芝居は実在する女優の半生を題材にしている The play is based on *the life of* an actual actress.

はんせん¹ 反戦 ――反戦の antiwar(◆名詞の前で用いる) ∥反戦運動[デモ] an *antiwar* movement [demonstration]

はんせん² 帆船 《米》sailboat ［C］,《英》sailing boat ［C］; (大型の) sailing ship ［C］

はんぜん 判然 彼の本当の目的が判然としない His real intention is not *clear*.

-ばんせん -番線 《米》track ［C］,《英》platform ［C］ ∥次の東京行きの列車は2番線から発車します The next train for Tokyo leaves on [from] *Track* 2.

ばんぜん 万全 準備は万全かと尋ねると, 彼はにっくりとうなずいた I asked him if *everything was ready*, and he nodded. / 万全の体調ではなかったが彼女はその試合に勝った Though

はんそう 帆走 sailing ⓤ ―帆走する sail ⓘ /風を受けて[に逆らって]帆走する *sail* with [against to] the wind

ばんそう¹ 伴奏 accompaniment ⓤⓒ ―伴奏する accompany /ギターの伴奏に合わせて歌う sing *to the accompaniment* of a guitar / 彼の友達がピアノで彼の伴奏をした His friend *accompanied* him on [at, with] the piano. ◆彼女はその曲を伴奏なしで歌った She sang the song *unaccompanied*.
‖伴奏者 an accompanist

ばんそう² 伴走 ‖伴走車 an escort vehicle

ばんそうこう 絆創膏 adhesive bandage ⓤ,(英)(adhesive) plaster ⓤⓒ;(救急絆創膏)(米)(商標名)Band-Aid ⓒ /傷口に絆創膏をはる apply *an adhesive bandage* [*a Band-Aid*] to the cut

はんそく 反則 (競技の) foul ⓒ;(規則を破ること) violation of the rules ―反則する foul ⓘ, commit a foul;(規則を破る) violate [break*] the rules ―反則の foul (❖名詞の前で用いる) /彼は前半ですでに2回反則をしている He's already committed two *fouls* in the first half. / その力士は相手のまげをつかんで反則負けになった The sumo wrestler *lost* the match *on a foul* by grabbing his opponent's topknot. / 彼は反則で退場させられた He *fouled* out of the game.
◆桜木は相手のユニフォームをつかんで反則をとられた Sakuragi *was penalized* for grabbing an opponent's uniform.

はんそで 半袖 short sleeves ―半そでの short-sleeved /半そでのシャツ a *short-sleeved* shirt; a shirt *with short sleeves*

はんだ solder ⓤ ‖はんだごて a soldering iron

パンダ (giant) panda ⓒ

ハンター hunter ⓒ

はんたい 反対

❶【逆】the opposite, the contrary ―反対の opposite, reverse;(対立した) contrary;(もう一方の) the other

銀行は反対方向にあります The bank is *in the opposite direction*.

"light"の反対は何ですか What's *the opposite* of "light"?

彼女はとても引っ込み思案だったが,今は全く正反対だ She used to be very shy, but now she's gone to *the opposite* [*other*] *extreme*.

予想とはまるで反対の結果が出た The results were totally *contrary to* what had been expected.

彼にはつい思っていることと反対のことを言ってしまう I can't help telling him *the contrary of* what I really think.

◆都会に行きたがる人もいれば,反対に都会を離れたがる人もいる Some people want to move into cities *while* others want to leave them.

❷【不賛成】opposition ⓤ, objection ⓤⓒ ―反対する oppose ⓘ, object ⓘⓘ

政府は地域の人々の反対を無視している The government ignores *the opposition* of the local people.

地元の人々は新空港の建設に強く反対している The local people strongly *object* to the construction of a new airport.

彼女の両親は彼女が若すぎるといって結婚に反対している Her parents *object* to her marriage because she is too young.

彼らはその計画に猛反対した They *were violently opposed* to the plan.

彼は家族の反対を押し切ってアメリカへ渡った He went to the United States *in spite of* his family's *opposition*.

あいつなら反対するに決まってるさ Of course he would *object*!

◆私の提案に賛成なの,それとも反対なの? Are you for or *against* my proposal? / 核兵器反対! *No* nukes!

‖反対意見 an objection, an opposition / 反対運動 an opposition movement / 反対語 an antonym / 反対者 an opponent / 反対尋問 a cross-examination / 反対派 the opposition

はんたいせい 反体制 ―反体制の antiestablishment, dissident /彼は反体制作家とみなされ投獄された He was imprisoned for being *an antiestablishment writer*.

パンタグラフ pantograph ⓒ

バンダナ bandanna, bandana ⓤⓒ /バンダナを頭に巻く have *a bandanna* around *one's* head

バンタムきゅう バンタム級 the bantamweight division ◆バンタム級の選手 *a bantamweight*

パンタロン pantaloons [pæntəlúːnz]

はんだん 判断

judgment,(英)judgement ⓤⓒ;(決定・決心) decision ⓤⓒ ―判断する judge ⓘⓘ;(決める) decide ⓘⓘ

〖判断は・が〗

ある点から見れば君の判断は正しかった From one point of view, your *judgment* was right.

私はプロのミュージシャンになるという夢をあきらめるべきか否か判断がつかない I *can't decide* whether I should abandon my dream of becoming a professional musician or not.

彼の言うことをどの程度信じていいのか判断が難しい It is difficult to *judge* how far I can trust what he says.

〖判断を〗

判断を誤る make an error of *judgment*; err in *one's judgment* / 的確な判断を下す give *an* accurate [*a* precise] *judgment*

疲れが彼の判断を鈍らせた His fatigue clouded his *judgment*.

〚判断に・で〛
彼らはそれを彼女の判断に任せるのが適当だと考えた They saw fit to leave it up to her *judgment*.
あなたの判断に従います I will follow your *judgment*.
自分の判断で何をするべきかを決めなさい Use your own *judgment* to decide what to do.
〚判断する〛
空模様から判断すると… *judging from* the sky, …; *to judge from* the sky, …
外見で人を判断するな Don't *judge* a person by his or her appearance.
〚その他〛
彼は情熱と冷静な判断力を兼ね備えている He has both passion and good *judgment*.
登山ではちょっとした判断ミスが大きな事故につながりかねない Little *errors of judgment* can cause a major accident in mountaineering.
◆このレースの結果はオリンピック代表選手選考の大きな判断材料になる(→影響を与える) The result of this race *will have a* great *influence on* the selection of the runners for the Olympics.
‖夢判断 interpretation of a dream

ばんたん 万端 準備万端だ *Everything's ready.*

ばんち 番地 (各戸の番号) (house) number [C] (❖実際に「…番地」という場合はふつう数字のみを用いる); (住所) *one's* address ∥北区堀船2丁目17番地 2-17 Horifune, Kita-ku
◆その手紙は番地が違っている The letter *is wrongly addressed.*

パンチ (こぶしで殴ること) punch [C]; (迫力) 《口語的》punch [U]《また a ～》∥鼻にパンチを食らう get *a punch* on the nose / 彼のパンチで対戦相手はよろめいた His *punch* staggered the opponent. / 彼女はパンチのきいた歌を歌う She sings *with punch.*
‖パンチカード a punch card / パンチパーマ a tightly-curled permanent

ばんちゃ 番茶 🗻 *bancha*, (low-grade) coarse green tea

パンチャー puncher [C]

はんちゅう 範疇 category [C] ∥それは倫理学の範疇に属する問題だ The problem belongs to *the category* of ethics.

はんちょう 班長 group leader [C]

パンツ ❶【下着】(男性用の) underpants, 《米》briefs, 《主に米》shorts, 《英》pants (❖pants は女性用にも用いる); (女性・子供用の) panties; (男性用トランクス) boxer shorts, boxers (❖いずれも複数扱いで, 数えるときは a pair of … とする)
❷【ズボン】《主に米》pants, trousers (❖いずれも複数扱いで, 数えるときは a pair of … とする)
‖海水パンツ swimming trunks / トレーニングパンツ sweat pants

はんつき 半月 half a month

ばんづけ 番付 (一覧表) list [C]; (相撲の) ranking list [C]

ハンデ ⚠ handicap [C] ∥神田さんのハンデは5だ Mr. Kanda is a five-*handicap* player. / Mr. Kanda's (*golf*) *handicap* is five.
◆彼は身体的なハンデを背負っている He *is* physically *handicapped.* / 35度を超す暑さは日本選手たちに大きなハンデとなった The heat over 35 degrees was *a* great *obstacle* to the Japanese players.

はんてい 判定 (決定) decision [C]; (判断) judgment, 《英》judgement [C] ──判定する decide [他][自]; judge [他][自] ∥審判の判定に激怒する get furious about the umpire's *decision* (❖umpire は野球・テニス・卓球などの審判. バスケット・ボクシング・フットボールなどは referee) / 挑戦者はチャンピオンに判定で勝った[負けた] The challenger「*won a decision* over [*lost a decision* to] the champion. (❖ボクシングなど得点によるものは win [lose] on points という) ◆審判はそれをファウルボールと判定した The umpire *called* it a foul ball.
‖写真判定 a photo finish

ハンディー handy ∥ハンディー(な)カメラ a *handy* camera

パンティー ⚠panties (❖数えるときは a pair of … とする) ‖パンティーストッキング《米》pantyhose, 《英》tights

ハンディキャップ ⇒ハンデ

はんてん[1] 斑点 spot [C]; (小さな斑点) speckle [C] ∥背中じゅうに赤い斑点が出た I got red *spots* all over my back.

はんてん[2] 反転 ──反転する (ひっくり返る[返す]) turn over; (反対にする) reverse [他]

バント bunt [C] ──バントする bunt [自] ∥石井はバントで一塁走者を二塁に送った Ishii advanced the runner to second *with a bunt.*
‖送りバント a sacrifice bunt / セーフティーバント a drag bunt / プッシュバント a push bunt

バンド[1] (ひも・輪) band [C]; (時計の) strap [C]; (ベルト) belt [C] ‖ゴムバンド a rubber band / ヘアバンド a hair band

バンド[2] band [C] ∥彼はバンドでギターを弾いている He plays (the) guitar in *a band.*
‖バンドマン a bandsman / ブラスバンド a brass band / ロックバンド a rock band

はんドア 半ドア あなたの側のドアが半ドアだ The door on your side *is not completely closed.*

はんとう 半島 peninsula [C] (《略語》pen.) ──半島の peninsular ∥能登半島 *the* Noto *Peninsula*

はんどう 反動 (反応・反作用) reaction [U]《また a ～》∥2週間甘い物を我慢していた反動でケーキを全部食べてしまった I had given up sweets for two weeks, and *as a reaction to* that, I ate a whole cake.
‖反動主義者 a reactionary

ばんとう 番頭 chief [head] clerk [C]

はんどうたい 半導体 semiconductor [C]

はんとうめい 半透明 ──半透明の translucent

バンドエイド 《商標名》Band-Aid [C][U]

はんどく 判読 ──判読する (解読する)

は

はんとし 半年 half a year, six months (◆英語では half a year よりも six months ということが多い) ‖我々は賃貸契約の期限をさらに半年延長した We renewed our lease *for another six months*.

ハンドバッグ handbag ©, (米)purse ©

ハンドブック handbook ©

ハンドボール handball ©

パントマイム pantomime © ©, mime ©‖パントマイムをする perform *a pantomime* [*mime*] ‖パントマイム俳優 a mime

ハンドル ⚠ (自動車などの) steering wheel ©; (自転車・オートバイの) handlebar © (通例複数形〜s); (柄・取っ手) handle ©‖左ハンドルの車 a car *with a left-hand steering wheel*; a *left-hand drive* car‖ハンドルを右に切る turn *the steering wheel* (to the) right‖ハンドルをとられる lose control of *the steering wheel*
◆そのときは兄が(車の)ハンドルを握っていた My brother *was at [behind] the wheel* then.
‖ハンドルさばき driving skill

ばんなん 万難 万難を排して(→どんな犠牲を払っても)この計画を成功させるつもりです I'll make this project a success *at any cost*.

はんにえ 半煮え 半煮えの underdone, half-cooked

はんにち¹ 半日 half a day‖コンピュータを修理しているうちに半日つぶれた I spent *half a day* repairing my computer.

はんにち² 反日 ―反日の anti-Japanese‖そのような発言は彼らの反日感情をあおるだろう Such remarks will reinforce their *anti-Japanese* feelings.

はんにゅう 搬入 工場に新しい機械が搬入された New machines *were carried into* the factory.

はんにん 犯人 (犯罪者) criminal ©, offender ©; (容疑者) culprit © (◆英語では「殺人犯」を murderer,「強盗犯」を robber,「誘拐犯」を kidnapper など, その犯罪に応じて用いるのがふつう)‖犯人を逮捕する arrest *a criminal*‖警察は犯人を現行犯でつかまえた The police caught *the criminal* in the act.‖彼が真犯人であることは間違いない There's not a shred of doubt that he is *the criminal*.

ばんにん¹ 万人 all people, everyone, everybody ‖この映画は万人向きだ(→だれもが楽しめる) *Everybody* can enjoy this movie.
◆万人に愛される歌手 a singer of *universal appeal*

ばんにん² 番人 (見張り) watchman ©; (警備員) guard ©; (管理人) caretaker ©

はんにんまえ 半人前 まだ半人前の仕事しかできません(→未熟ですが), よろしくお願いします I'm *inexperienced* in this job, but I'll do my best.

はんね 半値 half (the) price ‖その店では去年の型のコンピュータを定価の半値で売っていた They sold the last year's model computers *at [for] half* the list *price* at that shop.

ばんねん 晩年 *one's* later years
◆私は彼女の晩年の作品が好きだ I like her *later works*.

はんのう 反応 reaction © ©, response © © ―反応する react ®, respond ®
刺激に対する反応 *a reaction [response]* to a stimulus‖卵のアレルギー反応が出る show *an allergic reaction* to eggs‖連鎖反応を引き起こす set off *a chain reaction*
瞳孔(ぎう)は光に反応する The pupil *reacts to* light.
彼の反応を見てみたい気がする I am interested to see his *reaction*.
市場は首相の発言に敏感に反応した The market *reacted* sensitively to the Prime Minister's remark.
彼はその知らせにどんな反応を示しましたか How did he *react* to the news?
◆患者は移植手術から10時間後に拒絶反応を示した The patient showed *rejection* 10 hours after the transplant operation.
‖化学反応 a chemical reaction‖ツベルクリン反応 a tuberculin reaction

ばんのう 万能 ―万能の (多才な) (米)all-around, (英)all-round (◆名詞の前で用いる); (全能の) all-powerful; (多目的の) all-purpose (◆名詞の前で用いる) ‖万能ナイフ an *all-purpose* knife‖洋子はスポーツ万能だ Yoko is an *all-around* athlete.
‖万能薬 a panacea, a cure-all

はんぱ 半端 ―はんぱな odd (◆名詞の前で用いる) ‖はんぱな布を縫い合わせてクッションカバーを作った I patchworked *odd* pieces of cloth into a cushion cover.
◆はんぱな気持ちでやるのならやらないほうがましだ It's better not to do it rather than do it *halfheartedly*.
‖はんぱ物 (1つ) an odd piece; (集合的に) odds and ends, oddments
⇨ちゅうとはんぱ

バンパー bumper

ハンバーガー hamburger ©

ハンバーグ (ステーキ) ⚠ hamburger (steak) © (◆×hamburg とはいわない)

はんばい 販売 sale © © ―販売する sell* ® ©
現金[信用, カタログ]販売 *a cash [credit, catalog] sale*
販売計画は変更の余地がない *The sales plan* allows of no alteration.
昨年その会社は1,000万個以上の乾電池を販売した Last year the company *sold* more than 10 million dry-cell batteries.
その薬は販売禁止になった *The sale* of the medicine was banned.
◆新製品の販売促進を行う *promote* new products ‖このCDは今では販売されていない This CD is no longer *on the market*.‖その食器棚は通信販売で買った I bought the cupboard *by mail order*.

‖販売員 a salesperson, a salesclerk / 販売価格 an offering price / 販売促進 sales promotion / 委託販売 selling on commission / 自動販売機 a vending machine

はんばく 反駁 ──反駁する (反論する) argue against ...; (反対する) contradict 他

ばんぱく 万博 international exposition C (❖ しばしば expo [ékspou] と略される)

はんぱつ 反発 (嫌悪・不快感) repulsion U; (抵抗) resistance U (また a 〜); (反抗) reaction U ──反発する (はね返す) repel 自 他; (抵抗) resist 他 自; (反抗する) react 自, rebel 自 ‖新しい規則に対する反発 *reaction against* the new rules / 厳しい父親に反発する *rebel against one's* strict father / 消費税率の引き上げに対して国民の反発が強かった People *strongly resisted* against the raise of consumption tax rate.
◆彼の命令的な口調には反発を感じる I *find* his commanding way of speaking *repulsive*. / 円がドルに反発した The yen *rallied against* the dollar.

はんはん 半々 ──半々の half-and-half ──半々に half and half, fifty-fifty ‖ケチャップとマヨネーズを半々に入れてよくかき混ぜなさい Take ketchup and mayonnaise *half and half* and mix well. / 子供たちはそのケーキを半々に分けた The children divided the cake *fifty-fifty*.

ぱんぱん 一日中立ち通しで足がぱんぱんだ (→むくんでいる) My legs *are swollen* from standing all day long. / うちの犬はおなかがぱんぱんになるまで食べる Our dog never stops eating till he *is stuffed*.

はんびょうにん 半病人 sickly person C

はんびらき 半開き ──半開きの half open ‖ドアは半開きになっていた The door was left *half open*.

はんぴれい 反比例 inverse proportion U (↔direct proportion) ──反比例の inverse (❖ 名詞の前で用いる) ‖農作物の価格は収穫量に反比例する Prices of agricultural products are *in inverse proportion to* the crop.

はんぷ 頒布 (配布) distribution U ──頒布する distribute 他

はんぷく 反復 repetition C U ──反復する repeat 他 自 ◆反復練習は英語の学習には不可欠な要素だ *Repeated practice* is an essential factor in learning English.
‖反復記号 〖音楽〗a repeat

パンプス pumps, 《英》court shoes ‖ローヒールのパンプス low-heeled *pumps*

ばんぶつ 万物 (すべての物) all things; (神の創造物) 《公式的》creation U ‖人間は万物の霊長である Man is the lord of *(all) creation*.

パンフレット (小冊子) pamphlet C; (営業・宣伝用の) brochure C; (1 枚刷りのちらし) leaflet C

はんぶん 半分
half C U (複 halves) ──半分の half (❖ 名詞の前で用いる) ──半分に half

リンゴを半分に切る cut an apple 「*in half* [*into halves*].

教授は今回の課題で学生の半分に落第点をつけた The professor failed *half* the students on the assignment.

彼女が利益の半分を受け取るべきだ She should receive *half* (of) the profit.

半分が 2 つで全体になる Two *halves* make a whole.

そのタンクは半分空だった The tank was *half* empty.

彼の推測は半分当たっていた His guess was *half* right.

タクシーに乗ったらいつもの半分の時間で家に帰りついた It took me *half* as long as usual to get home by taxi.

僕の携帯電話はこの携帯電話の約半分の重さだ My cellular phone is about *half* as heavy as this one.

宿題は半分以上終わった I've finished *more than half* of my homework.

その工場で働く人の数は当時の半分にも満たない The number of workers at the factory *is less than half of* what it was in those days.

そのとき彼女は半分やけになっていた She was *half* desperate then.

◆冗談半分に *half-jokingly*; *just for fun* / この機械はその仕事にかかる時間を半分にすることができる This machine can *halve* the time needed for the work. (❖ この halve は「半分にする」という意味の動詞) / その本はまだ半分までしか読んでいない I'm only *halfway* through the book.

はんべい 反米 ──反米の anti-American ‖反米感情 *anti-American* feeling [sentiment]

はんべそ 半べそ その女の子は財布をなくしたことに気づいて半べそになった When the girl noticed that she had lost her purse, she *almost began to* whimper.

はんべつ 判別 distinction U C ──判別する (区別する) distinguish 他 自, tell* ... from 〜 ‖ヒヨコの雌雄を判別するのは難しい It's difficult to *distinguish* the sex of baby chicks.

はんぺん hampen, soft, puffy cake made of fish paste

はんぼいん 半母音 〖音声〗semivowel C

ハンマー hammer C ‖ハンマーでくぎを打つ hit a nail with *a hammer*
‖ハンマー投げ the hammer throw / ハンマー投げ選手 a hammer thrower

はんめい 判明 ──判明する (… と分かる) prove* 自, turn out; (明らかになる) become* clear ‖そのうわさは事実無根だということが判明した The rumor *proved* [*turned out*] (to be) groundless. / その事故の原因はまだ判明していない The cause of the accident *hasn't become clear* yet.
◆被害者の身元が判明した The victim *has been identified*. / 選挙の結果はあすの朝判明します The results of the election *will be*

ばんめし 晩飯 supper, dinner

はんめん¹ 反面 その先生は非常に厳しかったが, 反面, 情にもろいところもあった The teacher was very strict, *but on the other hand* he was also easily moved. / その映画は恐ろしい反面, どこかユーモラスでもある That movie is terrifying, *but at the same time* it's somewhat humorous.
‖反面教師 a bad [negative] example that serves as a good example

はんめん² 半面 (一方の面) one side; (他方の面) the other side ‖君は問題の半面しか見ていない You see only *one side* of the problem.

はんも 繁茂 ──繁茂する grow* thick

はんもく 反目 (敵意) hostility; (長期にわたる確執) feud ──反目する feud
◆彼はそのとき以来, 父親と反目している He's *been at loggerheads with* his father since then. (❖at loggerheads with …は「…と言い争いをして」の意味)

ハンモック hammock

はんもん¹ 反問 ──反問する (問い返す) ask … back

はんもん² 煩悶 (悩み) worry; (苦悩) agony ──煩悶する agonize, be in agony (over …)

ばんゆういんりょく 万有引力 universal gravitation ‖万有引力の法則 the laws of *universal gravitation*

はんよう 汎用 (いろいろな用途に用いる) multipurpose, all-purpose ◆汎用コンピュータ a *general purpose* computer

はんら 半裸 ──半裸の half-naked

はんらん¹ 反乱 rebellion; (短期間で終わる) revolt; (突発的でしばしば失敗に終わる) uprising ‖反乱を鎮圧する crush [put] down *a rebellion* / 反乱を引き起こす provoke *a rebellion* [*revolt*] / 昨夜未明, パキスタンで政府に対する反乱が起こった *A rebellion* against the government broke out late last night in Pakistan.
◆彼らは独裁者に対して反乱を起こした They *revolted against* the dictator. / 首都は反乱軍の手に落ちた The capital was seized by *the rebel army*.

はんらん² 氾濫 (洪水) flood, overflow ──氾濫する[させる] flood, overflow ‖きのうの激しい雨で川が氾濫した Yesterday's heavy rain *flooded* the river. / 川が氾濫して, 町中が水浸しになった The river *flooded* the whole town. / タイやベトナムといった国では日本製のオートバイが氾濫している Japanese motorcycles *have flooded* countries like Thailand and Vietnam.

ばんりのちょうじょう 万里の長城 the Great Wall (of China)

はんりょ 伴侶 (連れ) companion; (相手) partner; (配偶者) 《口語的/戯言的》 one's better [other] half ‖生涯の伴侶 one's life *companion*; *a companion* for life / よき伴侶を見つけることは単に金を稼ぐことよりはるかに大切だ Finding *a good partner* is much more important than just making money.

はんれい¹ 凡例 (本の巻頭にある説明書) explanatory [introductory] notes

はんれい² 判例 (判決の実例)〖法律〗precedent

はんろ 販路 (市場) market; (販売店) outlet ‖販路を開拓する develop *a new market*

はんろん 反論 (異議) objection; (反対意見) (opposing) argument ──反論する object; argue back ‖どんな反論があろうと自分の意見を貫くべきだ You should stick to your opinion whatever *objections* you meet. / 彼女の言うことに反論の余地はない *There's no room for objections* in what she says.

ひ

ひ¹ 日

❶【太陽】the sun; (日光) sun Ⓤ, sunlight Ⓤ, sunshine Ⓤ

語法
> 天体としての「太陽」は定冠詞の付いた the sun で表すが,「日の光」の意味では the を付けず, 不可算名詞として用いられる. sunlight が「日の光」だけを指すのに対して, sunshine は「太陽」の放つ「熱」も含む.

《日が》
日がさんさんと照っている *The sun* is shining brightly.
一行は日が昇る前に出発した The group started before *the sun* rose.
この部屋は日がよく当たる[あまり当たらない] This room「gets a lot of [doesn't get much] *sun* [*sunshine*].
窓から居間いっぱいに日が差し込んでいた *Sunlight* was pouring into the living room through the windows.
《日の》
湖面は日の光を受けてきらきら輝いていた The surface of the lake was shimmering in *the sunshine*.
◆食べ物は日の当たらないところ(→日陰)に置いておきなさい. Keep food *in the shade*.
《日に》
強い夏の日にさらされて庭の植物がしおれている The flowers in the garden are wilting under *the strong summer sunshine*.
◆休暇中に彼はすっかり日に焼けた He got very *suntanned* during his vacation.

❷【日中】day Ⓒ (↔night)
秋になると日がしだいに短くなる *The days* get shorter and shorter in the fall. (❖《get ＋比較級＋and＋比較級》で「しだいに…になる」の意味)
◆日が暮れてきた(→暗くなってきた) *It is getting dark*. ╱ 日が暮れる前に家に着いた I came back home *before dark*.

❸【1日】day Ⓒ; (時間) time Ⓤ
ある風の強い日に on *a* windy *day*
今年の夏は蒸し暑い日が多かった We had many sultry *days* this summer.
私たちの試合の日がだんだん近づいていた *The day* of our match was getting closer.
あなたが目標を達成する日がいつかきっと来るだろう *The day* will come when you achieve your goal. (❖when は day を先行詞とする関係副詞)
日がたつにつれて事件の記憶は少しずつ薄れていった *As time* [(*the*) *days*] *went by*, the incident faded away in our minds.
ある日ひょっこりおばが遊びに来た *One day* my aunt called on me unexpectedly. (❖one day は過去形または未来形とともに用いる)
来る日も来る日も少年は飼い猫が戻ってくるのを待ち続けた *Day after day*, the boy kept waiting for his cat to return.
また日を改めて(→別のときに)伺います I'll come back again *some other time*.
◆彼女が営業課に配属されてまだ日が浅い It's *not long* since she was assigned to the sales department.

❹【日付・期日】the date
私たちはハイキングの日を決めた We fixed *the date* for going on a hike.

ひ² 火

❶【火炎】fire Ⓤ Ⓒ; (炎) flame Ⓒ Ⓤ; (たばこ・ライターなどの) light Ⓒ
《火が・は》
火が勢いよく燃え上がった *The fire* blazed up.
新聞紙に火がついた The newspaper *caught fire*.
バーナーの火が消えた *The flame* on the burner has gone out.
《火に》
火に近づかないように Keep away from *fire*.
車はたちまち火に包まれた The car *was enveloped in flames* in a moment.
《火を》
ちょっと火を貸していただけませんか Will you *give* me *a light*, please?
◆マッチでろうそくに火をつける *light* a candle with a match

❷【炊事用の火・たき火など】fire Ⓒ
火をおこす make [build] *a fire* ╱ 火を消す「put out [《公式的》extinguish] *a fire*╱ やかん[なべ]を火にかける put a kettle [pot] on *a fire* ╱ 火にまきをくべる feed *a fire* with wood; feed wood to *a fire*
子供たちは手を火にかざして暖めた The children warmed their hands over *the fire*.
◆私たちは暖炉の火にあたった We *warmed ourselves* at the fireplace. (❖warm *oneself* で「火のそばで体を暖める」の意味)

❸【火事】fire Ⓒ Ⓤ
火は台所から出た *The fire* started in the kitchen. (❖×started from the kitchen とはいわない)
火は隣のアパートに燃え広がった *The fire* spread to the apartment house next door.
だれかが駐車場のバイクに火をつけた Someone *set* the motorbike *on fire* in the parking lot.
住民たちは消防車が到着する前に火を消し止めた The residents *had put out the fire* before the fire engine arrived.
近ごろ火事が多いから火の用心をしなさい There are so many fires these days, so *beware of fire*.

❹【熱】

このステーキはよく火が通っている[いない] This steak *is well-done* [*not well-done*]. (※ well-done は「よく火が通った」の意味の形容詞)

彼女は前の晩に作ったカレーにもう一度火を通した(→温め直した) She *heated up* the curry she had cooked on the previous night.

慣用表現 顔から火が出るほど恥ずかしかった I *was flushed* with shame. / *My face was burning* with shame. / 赤ん坊が火がついたように(→激しく)泣き始めた The baby began to cry *fiercely*. / 彼の発言は火に油を注ぐようなものだ His statement is *just like throwing fuel on the fire*. / 上空から見ると町全体はまさに火の海だった The whole town looked *a sea of flames* from up in the sky. / 祭りが終わって町は火の消えたように(→墓場のように)寂しくなってしまった The town *became as lonesome as a graveyard* after the festival was over. / わが家は近ごろ火の車だ(→家計が非常に苦しい) We *are very hard up (for money)* these days. / 彼が事業に失敗することは火を見るよりも明らかだ(→非常にはっきりしている) His failure in business is "*quite obvious* [*as clear as day*]." / 机の角(☆)に頭をぶつけて目から火が出た I *saw stars* when I knocked my head against the corner of the desk.

ことわざ 火のない所に煙は立たぬ Where there's smoke, there's fire.

ひ³ 比 ❶[比率] ratio [réiʃou] C /その同好会の男女比は1対3である *The ratio* of men to women in the club is 1:3. (※ 1:3 は one to three と読む)

❷[比較] (張り合う相手) match C; (匹敵する人・物) equal C /フランス語を話すことにかけては,彼は私の比ではない(→私は彼の足元にも及ばない) I'*m no match for* him in speaking French.

ひ⁴ 非 (過ち) mistake C, error C; (欠点) fault C /彼は自分の非を認めた He *admitted his mistake* [*error*]. / 非は私にある It's my *fault*. / *The fault* is mine.

慣用表現 彼の演説には非の打ちどころがなかった(→完璧(☆)だった) His speech *was perfect*.

ひ⁵ 灯 light C ⇨ あかり

ひ⁶ 妃 princess C (※ 英語の princess は広く皇族の男性の妻も指す) /ダイアナ妃 *Princess* Diana

ひ⁷ 碑 (記念碑) monument C /碑を立てる put [set] up *a monument*; (公式的) erect *a monument*

ひ- 非 non-, un- /非言語コミュニケーション *non*verbal communication / 非社交的な *un*sociable

-ひ -費 (経費) expenses; (費用) cost C, expenditure C (また複数形 ~s) /東京での生活費はとても高い *The cost of living* is very high in Tokyo.

‖軍事費 military expenditure / 交通費 transportation expenses / 食費 food expenses

び 美 beauty U /自然の美 natural *beauty* / 日本の美 the *beauty* of Japan

ひあい 悲哀 sorrow U (また複数形 ~s), grief U /彼は人生の悲哀をしみじみと感じた He deeply felt the *sorrows of life*.

ひあがる 干上がる (完全に乾く) dry up /川の水がすっかり干上がってしまった The river *has dried up*.

ピアス ⚠ pierced earring C (通例複数形 ~s) (※ pierced は「…に穴をあける」の意味の動詞 pierce の過去分詞。日本語の「ピアス」はこの部分だけがカタカナ語化したもの) /奈子はピアスをつけている Nanako wears *pierced earrings*. / 彼は耳にピアスの穴をあけてもらった He *had* his ear *pierced*. (※ 両耳の場合は his ears とする)

ひあそび 火遊び 火遊びはやめなさい Don't *play with matches* [*fire*]. (※ play with fire は日本語同様,比喩的に「危ないことをする」の意味でも用いられる)

ひあたり 日当たり 日当たりのよい庭 a *sunny* garden / この部屋はとても日当たりがよい This room *gets a lot of sun*.

ピアニスト pianist

ピアノ piano C
ピアノを弾く play *the piano* / ピアノの練習をする practice *the piano* / ピアノに合わせて歌う sing to *the piano*

妹はピアノを習いたがっている My sister wants to take *piano* lessons.

玲子はピアノが上手だ(→ピアノを上手に弾く) Reiko plays *the piano very well*. / (→ピアノの上手な弾き手である) She *is a good pianist*. (※ 英語の pianist はプロの「ピアニスト」だけでなく「ピアノを弾く人」の意味でも用いられる)

彼は私たちにその流行歌をピアノで弾いてくれた He played the popular song *on the piano* for us.

‖ピアノ協奏曲 a piano concerto / ピアノ曲 a piano piece / ピアノ線 a piano wire / ピアノソナタ a piano sonata / アップライトピアノ an upright piano / グランドピアノ a grand piano

ヒアリング ⚠ (聞き取って理解すること) listening comprehension U; (公聴会) public) hearing C /彼はヒアリングテストで高い得点をマークした He got a high mark in *a listening comprehension test*. (※ 英語の hearing test は「聴力検査」の意味)

ピーアール PR (広報活動) public relations 《単数扱い》《略記》P.R.); (宣伝) publicity U; (広告) advertisement C ―PRする (人々に知ってもらう) make* ... known to the public; (宣伝する) advertise ⊕, publicize ⊕ /新製品をPRする *advertise* [*publicize*] a new product / そのイベントはわが社のいいPRになった Our company *got a lot of publicity* through the event. ◆市長は新しい図書館のPRに努めた The mayor *tried to inform the public* about the new library.

‖PR映画 a public-relations film

ビーカー (実験用の) beaker C

ひいき 晶屓 (愛顧) favor, 《英》favour U ―ひいき(に)する favor ⊕, show* favor to ...; (不当に) be partial to ... ——**ひいき の** お気に入りの favorite /その先生は頭のいい生徒ばかりひいきする That teacher *favors* [*is partial to*] smart students. / (店が得意客に) 毎度ごひいきにあずかりましてありがとうございます We thank you for *your favor* [*patronage*].

◆ハワード氏は日本びいきだ Mr. Howard is *pro-Japanese*. /その作家は生前この店をひいきにしていた(→常連客だった) The writer *used to be a regular customer* of this store during his lifetime.

慣用表現 どうひいき目に見ても(→せいぜい)彼は二流の役者だ He is *at best* a second-rate actor. / ルーキーをこんなにほめては、ひいきの引き倒しだ(→このような過度の賞賛はそのルーキーの才能をだめにする) Such excessive admiration *will ruin that rookie's talent*.

ピーク (頂点) peak ⓒ /帰省ラッシュはこの2日間がピークだ The homecoming rush is *at its peak* during these two days. / 7時から8時の間にこのあたりの交通量はピークに達する The traffic *reaches its peak* between seven and eight around here.

◆仕事で忙しいのは9月がピークだ(→9月がいちばん仕事で忙しい) I'm *busiest* with my work in September.

ピーケー PK penalty kick ⓒ, pk ⓒ ‖PK戦 a penalty kick shoot-out

ピーケーエフ PKF ⚠ ((国連の)平和維持軍) UN peacekeeping force ⓒ (❖PKFという略語は英語ではあまり用いられない)

ピーケーオー PKO ⚠ ((国連の)平和維持活動) UN peacekeeping operation ⓒ (❖PKOという略語は英語ではあまり用いられない)

ビージーエム BGM ⚠ (背景音楽) background music Ⓤ, background Ⓤ (❖BGMという略語は英語では用いられない)

ビーズ bead ⓒ ‖ビーズに糸を通してつなぐ thread *beads* together on a string

ピース (セットを構成する1品) piece ⓒ /6ピース1セットの皿 a six-*piece* set of dishes / 500ピースのジグソーパズル a 500-*piece* jigsaw puzzle; a jigsaw puzzle of 500 *pieces*

ヒーター heater ⓒ ‖ヒーターのスイッチを入れる[切る] turn *the heater* on [off]

ビーだま ビー玉 glass marble ⓒ ‖ビー玉をして遊ぶ play *glass marbles*

ビーチ beach ⓒ ‖ビーチウエア beachwear / ビーチサンダル beach sandals / ビーチパラソル[ボール] a beach umbrella [ball] / ビーチバレー beach volleyball

ピーティーエー PTA (❖*Parent-Teacher Association*の略語) ‖PTAの集まりに出席する attend *a PTA meeting*

ひいては 今回の事件は県警の、ひいては警察庁の威信(→県警だけではなく警察庁全体の威信)にかかわるものである This incident seriously affects *not only* the Prefectural Police *but (also)* the National Police Agency.

ひいでる 秀でる excel ⓘ ——秀でた excellent; (抜きん出た) outstanding /彼は英語に秀でている He *excels* in English.

ビート (拍子) beat ⓒ ‖8ビートの曲 a song *in eight-beat time* / ビートのきいた音楽 music *with a strong beat*
‖ビート板(水泳の) a kickboard

ビーナス 〖ローマ神話〗Venus(❖愛と美の女神)

ピーナツ peanut ⓒ ‖ピーナツバター peanut butter

ビーバー 〖動物〗beaver ⓒ

ひいひい 赤ん坊がひいひい泣いているのが聞こえた I heard a baby *crying* [*wailing*]. (❖wailは「声を上げて泣く」の意味)

ぴいぴい ひな鳥たちはおなかをすかせてぴいぴい鳴いていた The chicks *were peeping* because they were hungry.

慣用表現 彼は金がなくてぴいぴいしている(→困っている) He *is very hard up*.

ピーピーエム ppm, PPM (❖*parts per million*(百万分率)の略語)

ビーフ (牛肉) beef Ⓤ ‖ビーフカレー beef curry / ビーフシチュー beef stew / ビーフステーキ a beef steak / ビーフストロガノフ beef stroganoff [strɔ́ːɡənɔ̀ːf]

ピーマン green pepper ⓒ (❖日本語はフランス語の piment から)

ひいらぎ 柊 〖植物〗holly ⓒ

ヒール (かかと) heel ⓒ (通例複数形 ~s)

ビール beer Ⓤ (❖店で注文する場合や種類をいうときは ⓒ) ‖缶入りの[びん入りの]ビール canned [bottled] *beer* / 生ビール draft [〖英〗draught] *beer* / 黒ビール dark *beer* / ビール1本 a bottle of *beer* / ビールを飲む drink *beer* / 彼は冷えたビールを1杯、ごくごくと飲み干した He gulped down a glass [mug] of cold *beer*. (❖a mug of beerは「ジョッキ1杯のビール」の意味) / ビール2つください Two *beers*, please. / ビールを1杯おごるよ I'll buy you a *beer*. / 私はビールで酔っ払った I got drunk on *beer*.
‖ビール工場 a brewery / ビール腹 a beer belly [gut] / ビールびん a beer bottle

ビールス virus [váirəs] ➡ ウイルス

ヒーロー (英雄) hero ⓒ (❖女性形は heroine) ‖みんなのヒーロー a folk *hero*

ひうちいし 火打ち石 flint ⓒ

ひうん 悲運 misfortune Ⓤ, bad luck Ⓤ ➡ ふうん ‖悲運に遭う have *bad luck*; suffer *a misfortune*

ひえいせい 非衛生 ——非衛生的な unsanitary, insanitary ➡ ふえいせい

ひえいり 非営利 ——非営利の non-profit ‖非営利団体 a nonprofit organization

ひえこむ 冷え込む become* [get*] cold ◆けさは冷え込んだ(→とても寒かった) It was *very cold* this morning.

ひえしょう 冷え性 彼女は冷え性だ(→血行が悪い) She *has poor circulation*.

ひえびえ 冷え冷え その教会の中は冷え冷えとしていた It was *cold* [*chilly*] inside the church.

ひえる 冷える (空気が) become* [get*, grow*] cold [chilly](❖cold は「寒い」ことを表す最も一般的な語. chilly は「肌寒い」の意味); (体が) be chilled; (食べ物などが) cool

ピエロ

(down) (❖比喩的に人間関係などが「冷える」意味でも用いられる)
だいぶ冷えてきた It's *getting cold* [*chilly*].
スープはすっかり冷えていた The soup *had cooled down*.
両国の関係は冷え切ってしまった The relationship between the two countries *has cooled down*.
彼は体の芯(しん)まで冷えてしまった He *was chilled to the bone*.
◆よく冷えたビールが飲みたい I'd like to have a [some] *well-chilled* beer.
🅔「けさは冷えますね」「本当に」 "It's *awfully cold* [*chilly*] this morning, isn't it?" "Yes, it really is."

ピエロ ⚠clown ◯ (❖日本語はフランス語のpierrotから) 踊るピエロ a dancing *clown*

びえん 鼻炎 nasal inflammation ◯, 〔医学〕 rhinitis [ráináitəs] ◯ ∥鼻炎にかかっている have *nasal inflammation*
∥アレルギー性鼻炎 allergic *rhinitis*

ビエンチャン Vientiane (❖ラオスの首都)

ビオラ 〔音楽〕viola ◯

ひか 皮下 このおなかの皮下脂肪をどうにかしなきゃ I've got to do something with this *fat around my middle*.
∥皮下脂肪〔解剖〕subcutaneous [sÀbkjutéiniəs] fat; 皮下注射 a hypodermic [hàipədɔ́ːrmik] injection

びか 美化 ──美化する (きれいにしておく) keep* ... clean; (掃除をする) clean ⓤ; (美しくする) beautify ⓤ; (実際以上によいものと考える) romanticize ⓤ ∥車内美化にご協力ください We'd like to ask for your help (to) *keep* the car *clean*. / 彼は結婚生活を美化している He *is romanticizing* married life.
∥美化運動 a cleaning campaign

ひがい 被害 damage ◯; (損害・損失) loss ◯
暴風雨は東海地方に大きな被害をもたらした The storm caused [did] extensive *damage* to the Tokai district.
被害は最小限に食い止められた The *damage* [*loss*] was kept to a minimum.
その火災による会社の被害は総額数十億円にのぼった The *damage* [*loss*] done to the firm by the fire amounted to several billion yen.
政府は被害状況の把握に努めている The government is making efforts to grasp *how much the damage* [*loss*] *is*.
◆地震による被害が最も大きかった地域はどこですか Which area *suffered* most *from* the earthquake? / 遅霜は苗の多くに被害を与えた A late frost *damaged* many of the seedlings.
∥被害額 the amount of damage / 被害者 (犠牲者) a victim; (死傷者) casualties / 被害地 a disaster area, a damaged area / 被害妄想 a persecution complex

ひかいち びかー 彼は水泳にかけては学校でびかーだ He is *the number one* swimmer in our school. / (→最も水泳がうまい) He is *the best* swimmer in our school. / 子供たちの人気という点では，ライオンズの松坂がぴかーだ (→最も人気がある) The Lions' Matsuzaka is *the most* popular player among children.

ひかえ 控え (写し) copy ◯; (複製) duplicate ◯ ∥領収書の控えをとる make *a copy of* a receipt
∥控え室 (待合室) a waiting room; (次の間) an anteroom / 控え a reserve

ひかえめ 控え目 ──控えめな (節度を保った) moderate; (謙虚な) modest; (慎み深い) reserved; (評価・見積もりなどが) conservative ──控えめに modestly; with reserve ∥彼らの要求は控えめだった Their demands were *moderate*. / 隆は実に控えめな人だ Takashi is really a *modest* man. / 彼女は控えめな話し方をする She speaks in a *reserved* manner. / 損害額は控えめに見積もっても数百万円になるだろう The damages will amount to several million yen *at a conservative estimate*. ◆控えめに言ってもたばこの煙は不快だ Cigarette smoke is unpleasant, *to say the least*.

ひがえり 日帰り (日帰りの旅行) a [one] day trip, a day's trip ∥日帰りで日光へ行った We took *a day trip* to Nikko.
◆京都までなら十分日帰りできる You can *go* as far as Kyoto *and* (*come*) *back in a day*.
∥日帰り客 a day tripper, a day's visitor

ひかえる 控える
❶【抑制する】(量を減らす) cut* down [back] on ...; (適量を守る) be moderate in ...; (酒・たばこなどを) abstain from ...; (保留する) reserve ⓤ; (言動を慎む) refrain from ...
甘い物を控える *cut down* [*back*] *on* sweets
医者は彼にたばこ[酒]を控えるよう忠告した The doctor advised him to *abstain from* smoking [alcohol].
しばらく激しい運動は控えたほうがいいだろう You'd better *refrain from* vigorous exercises for a while.
詳細が明らかになるまで我々はこの件について判断を控えよう Let's *reserve* judgment on this until we get more detailed information.
◆私はかぜぎみなので外出を控えた (→家にいた) I *stayed indoors* because I had a slight cold.
❷【近くにある】
彼女はテニスの試合を1週間後に控えている (→試合に出るのを待っている) She *is waiting* to have a tennis match a week from now.
年末を目前に控えて (→年末が目前に迫っていて) 私たちはとても忙しい We are very busy *with* the end of the year *close at hand*.
彼の背後にある有力な政治家が控えているというもうわさだ People say that he *has* a certain influential politician *behind him*.
❸【書き留める】write* down; (メモをとる) make* a note of ..., jot down
彼のメールアドレスを手帳に控えておいた I「*wrote down* [*made a note of*]」 his e-mail address in my notebook.

ひかく¹ 比較 comparison ◯ ──比較する

compare 働 ――比較的 comparatively;(相対的に) relatively ⇨ くらべる

彼の描いた絵と私の描いた絵では比較にならない There is no comparison between his picture and mine.(❖「彼の描いた絵」のほうがずっとすぐれていることを表す)

2人の作家の文体を比較しなさい Compare the styles of the two writers.

パソコンを組み立てるのは比較的簡単である It is *relatively* easy to assemble a personal computer.

アメリカの学校を日本の学校と比較すると多くの違いに気づくだろう If you *compare* American schools *with* Japanese ones, you'll find many differences.

ニューヨークと比較すると東京は安全だ Tokyo is rather safe 「*in comparison with* [*compared to*]」 New York City.

‖比較研究 a comparative study / 比較言語学 comparative linguistics / 比較文学 comparative literature

ひかく² 非核 ‖非核三原則 the three nonnuclear principles / 非核宣言 a nuclear-free declaration

ひかく³ 皮革 leather ⓤ ‖合成皮革 synthetic leather

びがく 美学 esthetics [esθétiks]

ひかくきゅう 比較級《文法》the comparative degree

> 比較級は,形容詞・副詞の比較変化の一つであり,2つのもの[グループ]の性質・数量・程度などを比較するときに用いられる.
> ⇨ さいじょうきゅう
>
> [規則変化]1音節の語と2音節の語の一部は,原級に-er を付ける.2音節の語の多くと3音節以上の語は,原級に more を付ける / She is *taller* than her husband. 彼女は彼女の夫より背が高い / I get up *earlier* than my father. 私のほうが父よりも早く起きる(❖-er を付ける際, y を i に変える,子音字を重ねるなど,つづりに変化を生じるものもある) / In Japan, baseball is *more popular* than basketball. 日本では野球のほうがバスケットボールより人気がある
>
> [不規則変化]次のように全く違う語に変化するものもある / He is getting *better*. 彼はだんだんよくなっている(❖この better は well の比較級) / I have *more* CDs than Mami. 私は真美よりたくさん CD を持っている(❖この more は many の比較級)

ひかげ 日陰 shade ⓤ《しばしば the ~》‖日陰でひと休みする take a rest *in the shade* / 私たちは日陰でお昼を食べた We had a lunch *in the shade*.

ひがさ 日傘 sunshade ⓒ;(特に女性用の) parasol ⓒ ‖日傘をさす put up *a sunshade* [*parasol*]

ひがし 東

the east ――東の east, eastern

風は東から吹いている The wind is blowing *from the east*.

太陽は東から昇る The sun rises *in the east*.

その町は京都から10キロ東にある The city lies 10 kilometers (*to the*) *east* of Kyoto.

私の部屋は東向きだ My room *faces east*.

島の東側に(→東部に)高い山々がある There are high mountains *in the eastern part of* the island.

東の空が明るくなってきた The *eastern* sky has brightened up.

◆東へ向かう列車 an *eastbound* train(❖-bound は「…行きの」の意味)

‖東アジア East Asia / 東海岸 the east coast / 東シナ海 the East China Sea / 東日本 Eastern Japan / 東半球 the Eastern Hemisphere

ひかぜい 非課税 ――非課税の tax-free,《公式的》tax-exempt ‖非課税品 *tax-free* articles

ひがた 干潟 tideland ⓒ

ぴかっ 稲妻がぴかっと光った Lightning *flashed*. / 暗やみで何かがぴかっと光った Something *glinted* in the dark.

ぴかぴか

> 語法
>
> 「ぴかぴか」「ぴかっと」「きらきら」「ぎらぎら」のような擬態語は,日本語では副詞として用いられるが,英語では glitter「ぴかぴか光る」,flash「ぴかっと光る」,twinkle「きらきら光る」,glare「ぎらぎら輝く」のように動詞を使って表すことが多い.

――ぴかぴかの(真新しい) brand-new ‖ぴかぴかの新車 a *brand-new* car / 彼はそのぴかぴかなコインを私たちに見せた He showed us the *glittering* coin.

◆ぴかぴかの(→よく磨かれた)靴 *well-polished* shoes / 生徒たちは教室の床をぴかぴかに磨き上げた The students made the floor of their classroom *shiny*.

ひがみ 僻み 彼はひがみからあんな無礼な態度をとったのだ(→劣等感が彼に無礼な態度をとらせた) His *inferiority complex* made him behave in such a rude manner. / 彼女はひがみっぽい(→すぐ嫉妬(ᡄど)する) She *easily gets jealous*.

ひがむ 僻む 彼は自分だけキャンプに行けないのでひがんでいる He *is jealous* because he is the only boy that cannot take part in the camp.

ひからす 光らす make* ... shine;(磨く) polish 働 ‖目を光らす(→注意して見張る) *watch carefully*

ひからびる 干からびる (すっかり乾く) dry up, be dried up;(しなびる) shrivel up ‖花びんの花はすっかり干からびてしまっていた The flowers in the vase *had shriveled up*.

ひかり 光

❶【明かり】 light ⓤ ⓒ; ray ⓒ; beam ⓒ; gleam ⓒ; flash ⓒ; sparkle ⓒ

> light:「光」を指す最も一般的な語. sunlight「太陽の光」, candlelight「ろうそくの光」, lamplight「ランプの光」のように複

びかり

合語を多く作る.
ray: 一筋の光.
beam: rayが集まった「光の束」を指す.
gleam: 一瞬のうちに現れて消える弱い光.
flash, sparkle: 目がくらむような強い光.

光は音よりもはるかに速く進む *Light* travels much faster than sound.

明るい日の光が部屋いっぱいにあふれていた Bright *sunlight* was pouring into the room.

まぶしい光に私は目がくらんだ I was blinded by a dazzling *light*.

かすかな光を頼りに私たちは出口を探し当てた We found an exit by following *a dim light*.

ずっと遠くにぼんやりした光が見えた We saw *a gleam* far in the distance.

❷【希望】
かすかな希望の光を見いだす find *a faint gleam [glimmer] of hope*

研究を続けても彼にはいっこうに光が見えてこなかった He couldn't see *a ray of hope* at all in continuing his study.

短歌 久方の光のどけき春の日にしづ心なく花のちるらむ (紀友則)
It's a warm spring day,
a calm, windless, quiet day,
a nice, peaceful day.
Why do the cherry blossoms
fall nervously from the trees?

ぴかり ⇒ぴかっ

ひかりかがやく 光り輝く shine* brightly

ひかりファイバー 光ファイバー optical fiber ◎ ‖光ファイバーケーブル a fiber-optic cable / 光ファイバー通信 fiber-optic communications

ひかる 光る

❶【光を放つ】(輝く) shine* ⓤ; (星などが) twinkle ⓤ; (ぎらぎらと) glare ⓤ; (かすかに) gleam ⓤ; (きらきらと) glitter ⓤ; (ぴかっと) flash, sparkle ⓤ; (ぬれた物が) glisten ⓤ

彼の顔は汗で光っていた His face *was shining* with sweat.

彼はぴかぴかに光るまでその靴を磨き上げた He polished the shoes till they *shone brightly*.

夜空に星がきらきら光っていた Stars *were twinkling [shining]* in the night sky.

トンネルの中で何かがぴかっと光った Something *flashed [sparkled]* in the tunnel.

❷【際立つ】stand* out, shine* out; (ほかよりすぐれている) (公式的) outshine* ⓤ

新人の中では彼が断然光っている He *shines out* among the rookies. / He *outshines* the other rookies.

◆そのゲームでは彼のプレーが光っていた His performance *was outstanding* in the game.

ひかれる 引かれる (心を引かれる) be attracted; (魅了される) be fascinated, be charmed ‖人々は彼の人柄に引かれた People *were attracted* by his personality. / 彼はその絵に心を引かれた He *was fascinated* [*charmed*] by the picture.

ひがわり 日替わり ‖日替わり定食 today's special (lunch [dinner])

ひかん¹ 悲観 ——悲観的な pessimistic (↔optimistic) ‖悲観的な考え方 a *pessimistic* view / 自分の将来を悲観してはいけない Don't *be pessimistic about* your future.

◆彼は事業に失敗して悲観している (→絶望している) He *is in despair* because he is failing in his business.

‖悲観論 pessimism / 悲観論者 a pessimist

ひかん² 避寒 ‖避寒地 a winter resort

ひがん¹ 彼岸 a *higan*, the week of the equinox ‖お彼岸に墓参りに行った We visited our family grave during *the week of equinox*.

‖彼岸会 Buddhist services performed during the equinoctial week / 彼岸桜 cherries blooming around the equinox / 彼岸の入り the beginning of the equinoctial week / 彼岸の中日(春分) the spring [vernal] equinox; (秋分) the autumnal equinox / 彼岸花 a (red) spider lily

ことわざ 暑さ寒さも彼岸まで Neither heat nor cold lasts beyond the equinox.

> 彼岸とは, 仏教と関わりの深い宗教的な期間で, 人々は花や故人の生前好きだった食べ物などをもって墓参りをします. 年に2回春分の日と秋分の日を中日としてもので, それぞれ1週間あります. また, 彼岸にはおはぎを先祖にお供えし, 人々もそれを食べるという習慣があります.
> *Higan* is a religious period based on Buddhism during which people hold memorial services for their ancestors, visiting the family graves with flowers and foods that the deceased liked. There are two *higan* a year around the vernal and autumnal equinoxes, and each of them lasts seven days. People often offer to their ancestors *ohagi* (typical Japanese-style confectionery made by covering glutinous rice with sweet red bean paste) and they also eat it.

ひがん² 悲願 *one's* long-cherished wish (long-cherished は「長い間心にいだいている」の意味) ‖悲願を達成する realize [fulfill] *one's long-cherished wish*

びかん 美観 beauty ⓤ (また複数形 beauties); (美しい光景) beautiful sight ◎ ‖自然の美観 *the beauties* of nature / 高い煙突が町の美観を損ねている The high chimney spoils *the beauty* [(→外観) *appearance*] of the city.

びがんじゅつ 美顔術 beauty culture ⓤ, facial ◎

ひき¹ 引き (愛顧) favor,《英》favour ⓤ; (影響力) influence ⓤ,《口語的》pull ⓤ(また a ~) ‖社長の引きで今の地位に就いた He got his present position *through the influence [pull]* of the president.

ひき² 悲喜 慣用表現 悲喜こもごもといったところ

だ(→喜びと悲しみの混ざった感情をいだいている) I *have a feeling of mixed joy and sorrow.*

-ひき -匹 犬2匹 two dogs / 3匹の小さな魚 three little fish (❖「-匹」に相当する英語はないので《数詞＋可算名詞》の形で表す)

-びき -引(き) 3割引でパソコンを買った I bought a personal computer *at a* 30 percent *discount*.

ひきあい 引き合い 自分の名前が引き合いに出される(→言及される)のは不愉快だ I feel unpleasant about my name *being mentioned* [*referred to*]. / その製品について何件かの引き合い(→問い合わせ)があった There were some *inquiries* about that product.

ひきあう 引き合う (割に合う) pay* [自] ‖こんな安い値段で売ってはとても引き合わない It *will never pay* to sell at such a low price.

ひきあげ 引き上げ・引き揚げ

❶【賃金・価格などの】increase [C], rise [C], raise [C], 《米口語的》hike [C]

[語法]

> 「給料の引き上げ」＝「昇給，賃上げ」を表すには《米》ではraise，《英》では rise を用いる．「物価の引き上げ」という場合は，《米》《英》ともに rise を用いるのがふつう．

物価の引き上げ *a* price *rise* [*increase*] / 従業員は賃金の10パーセント引き上げを要求した The employees demanded *a* 10 percent wage *increase* [《米》*raise*, 《英》*rise*].

❷【引っぱり上げること】pulling up [U]; (沈没船などの) salvage [U] ‖(船の)引き揚げ作業 a *salvage* operation

ひきあげる 引き上げる・引き揚げる ❶【賃金・価格などを】increase [他], raise [他], 《米口語的》hike [他] ‖来年税金が引き上げられそうだ It seems that taxes *will be raised* next year.

❷【引っぱり上げる】pull up; (船を) salvage [他] ‖沈没船を引き揚げる *salvage* [*raise*] a sunken ship / 男の子はおぼれる寸前に川から引き上げられた The boy *was pulled out of* the river just before he would have drowned.

❸【撤退する】pull out; (軍隊などが) withdraw* [自], pull back; (立ち去る) leave* [他] [自]; (本国へ帰る) be repatriated ‖敵の軍隊は前線から引き揚げた The enemy troops *withdrew* [*pulled back*] from the front line. / 取材を終えると記者たちは引き上げた The reporters *left* after collecting news material. / 多くの人々が第二次世界大戦後にシベリアから引き揚げてきた Many people *were repatriated* from Siberia after the Second World War.

ひきあわせる 引き合わせる ❶【紹介する】introduce [他] ‖講演者をスタッフに引き合わせる *introduce* a speaker *to one's* staff

❷【照合する】check [他]

ひきいる 率いる (引き連れる) lead* [他]; (軍隊などを指揮する) command [他]; (楽団を) conduct [他] ‖朝比奈隆率いる大阪フィルハーモニー管弦楽団 the Osaka Philharmonic Orchestra *conducted* by Asahina Takashi / 将軍に率いられた軍隊は隣国に攻め入った An army *commanded by* the general invaded the neighboring country.

ひきうける 引き受ける

❶【仕事・任務などを】take* [他], 《公式的》undertake* [他]; (承諾する) accept [他]

議長の役を引き受ける *take on* the role of a chairperson

彼はその仕事を引き受ける決心をした He decided to *take* [*undertake, accept*] the job.

❷【面倒を見る】take* care of ...

あなたが留守の間，お子さんは私が引き受けましょう I'*ll take care of* your children while you are away.

❸【保証する】guarantee [他], vouch for ...

彼の身元は私が引き受けます I'*ll vouch for* him.

ひきうつし 引き写し (写し) copy [C] ‖君のレポートはこの文庫本の解説の引き写しじゃないか Your report is just *a copy* of the explanation in this pocket book.

ひきうつす 引き写す copy [他] ‖彼はイェーツの詩から引き写したことを認めた He admitted that he *had copied* Yeats' poetry.

ひきおこす 引き起こす (原因となる) cause [他]; (もたらす) bring* about; (ある結果へと導く) lead* to ...; (誘発する) provoke [他] ‖たばこの火の不始末が大火災を引き起こした Failure to put out a cigarette *caused* a big fire. / 急激な人口増加は多くの問題を引き起こした Rapid population growth *has brought about* [*provoked*] many problems.

◆この薬を飲みすぎると心臓発作を引き起こす可能性がある An overdose of this medicine can *induce* heart attack. (❖induce は「誘発する」の意味)

ひきおとす 引き落とす 公共料金は口座から直接引き落とされている(→支払われている) Utilities *are paid* directly from my bank account.

ひきおろす 引き下ろす・引き降ろす pull [draw*] down; (旗などを) haul down

ひきかえ 引き換え・引き替え 品物と引き換えに(→品物の到着時に)代金を支払う pay cash *on delivery* / (商取引で)代金引き換えでお送りいたします We will send it *C.O.D.* (❖C.O.D. はcash *on* delivery の略語) / 男は人質と引き換えに3,000万円を要求してきた The man demanded 30 million yen *in exchange for* the hostages.

‖引換券(品物を預かるときの) a claim ticket [tag]; (景品などの) a coupon

ひきかえす 引き返す (もといた場所へ帰ってくる[行く]) come* [go*] back; (戻る) return [自]; (向きを変えて) turn back ‖途中で引き返す *turn back* halfway / 私たちは傘を取りにホテルへ引き返した We *went back to* the hotel to get our umbrellas. / 旅客機はエンジントラブルのため羽田空港へ引き返した The airliner *turned back to* Haneda Airport because of some engine trouble.

ひきかえる 引き換える・引き替える 姉は美人で優等生だが，それにひきかえ私は何をやってもだ

ひきがえる

student, *while* I always end up in failure.
ひきがえる 【動物】toad ⓒ
ひきがたり 弾き語り ギターで弾き語りをする *sing (and talk) to one's own accompaniment* on the guitar
ひきがね 引き金 trigger ⓒ ∥銃の引き金を引く *pull the trigger*
◆国境をめぐる紛争が両国の戦争の引き金となった A border conflict *triggered* the war between the two countries.
ひきげき 悲喜劇 tragicomedy ⓒ
ひきこみせん 引き込み線 (鉄道の) railway siding ⓒ; (電線の) service wire ⓒ
ひきこむ 引き込む (引っぱり込む) pull in, pull into …; (引きずり込む) drag in, drag into …; (魅了する) attract ⑮, fascinate ⑮ ∥宇宙の神秘についての彼の話に引き込まれた I *was attracted* by his story about the wonder of space.
ひきこもる 引き籠る (家の中に) stay home [indoors]; (閉じこもる) shut* *oneself* in; (病気で寝込む) be laid up ∥彼女は一日中家に引きこもっていた She *stayed home* [*indoors*] for the whole day. / 夕食を終えると彼は自分の部屋に引きこもった He *shut himself in* his room after dinner.
ひきころす 轢き殺す そのダンプカーは猫をひき殺した The dump truck *ran over* a cat *and killed* it.
ひきさがる 引き下がる (退く) withdraw* ⑮; (立ち去る) leave* ⑮; (意見などを引っ込める) back down ∥だれも彼の意見に賛成しなかったので彼は引き下がるしかなかった He couldn't help *backing down* because no one agreed with his opinion.
ひきさく 引き裂く tear* [téər] (apart); (ずたずたに) tear … to [into] pieces, rip up; (人間関係を) separate ⑮ ∥彼女は怒りのあまりその手紙をずたずたに引き裂いた She was so angry that she *tore* the letter *to pieces*. / 彼の心は悲しみに引き裂かれた His heart *was torn* by grief. / その戦争は二人の間を引き裂いた The war *separated* the two from each other.
ひきさげる 引き下げる (価格・水準などを) lower ⑮, bring* down; (賃金・費用を) cut* ⑮, reduce ⑮ ∥時給を100円引き下げる *reduce* [*cut*] *a person's* hourly wage by 100 yen / 日銀は公定歩合を0.5パーセント引き下げた The Bank of Japan *reduced* [*slashed*] its official discount rate by 0.5 percent.
ひきざん 引き算 subtraction Ⓤ ──引き算する subtract ⑮
ひきしお 引き潮 the ebb (tide) ∥今は引き潮だから水位が下がっている The tide is on the ebb now, so the seawater level is low.
ひきしまる 引き締まる ──引き締まった (体つきが) lean, compact; (表情が) firm ∥引き締まった顔つき *firm* features / 彼は引き締まった体をしている He has got a *lean* figure.
[慣用表現] 入学試験を前に身が引き締まる思いだ (→緊張している) I *feel tense* waiting for the entrance examination.
ひきしめる 引き締める (きつくする) tighten ⑮; (気分を) brace *oneself* (up) ∥ここ数か月は家計を引き締めないといけない We will have to *tighten* (*up*) our household budget for several months.
ひぎしゃ 被疑者 suspect ⓒ
ひきずりこむ 引き摺り込む pull in, pull into …; (強引に) drag in, drag into … ∥彼は車の中に引きずり込まれそうになった He was almost *dragged into* the car.
◆多くの子供たちが戦争に引きずり込まれた (→巻き込まれる) Many children *got involved in* the war.
ひきずりだす 引き摺り出す pull out; (強引に) drag out ∥容疑者を車から引きずり出す *pull* [*drag*] the suspect *out of* the car
ひきずりまわす 引き摺り回す pull around [about]; (強引に) drag around [about]; (無理に連れ回す) take* *a person* around [about]
◆これ以上この問題に引きずり回される (→巻き込まれる) のはごめんだ I no longer want to *be involved in* this problem.
ひきずる 引き摺る (足を) drag ⑮; (衣服のすそを) trail ⑮ ∥犬はけがをした足を引きずっていた The dog *was dragging* its wounded leg. / 彼女のドレス (のすそ) が地面を引きずっていた Her dress *was trailing* on the ground.
◆彼は2年前の交通事故の後遺症を引きずっている (→後遺症にずっと悩んでいる) He *has been suffering from* an aftereffect of the car accident two years ago.
ひきだし 引き出し ❶【机などの】drawer ⓒ ∥机のいちばん上の引き出しをあける[閉める] open [shut] *the top drawer* of a desk / 引き出しをあけっぱなしにしておく leave *the drawer* open / 彼女は引き出しの中をかき回してかぎを捜した She raked through *the drawer* looking for the key.
❷【現金の】withdrawal Ⓤ
ひきだす 引き出す (引っぱり出す) pull [draw*] out; (預金などを) withdraw* ⑮, draw out; (結論などを) draw ⑮ ∥討論から最終的結論を引き出す *draw* a final conclusion from a discussion / 私は銀行口座から5万円引き出した I *withdrew* [*drew out*] 50,000 yen from my bank account.
ひきたつ 引き立つ 金のブローチをつけるとこの黒のドレスは引き立つ This black dress *looks nice* with a golden brooch. / 彼女の金髪が濃い青色の服でよく引き立っていた (→対照を作り出していた) Her blonde hair *contrasted well with* her deep blue dress.
ひきたて 引き立て 毎度お引き立て (→ご愛顧) いただきましてありがとうございます Thank you very much *for your patronage*. / 今後ともお引き立てのほど (→ご愛顧をくださるよう) お願い申し上げます We hope that we may receive *further favor* from you. (❖英語はかなり堅苦しく古風な表現)
ひきたてる 引き立てる ❶【魅力的に見せる】

この額はその絵を引き立てる This frame *sets off* the painting.
❷【愛顧する】favor,《英》favour⊕, patronize⊕;(支える)support⊕;(支援する)back up / 彼にはずいぶん引き立ててもらった He *has backed* me *up* very much.
❸【気分を盛り上げる】cheer up;(勇気づける)encourage⊕ / ベテラン選手たちがチームを引き立てた Experienced players *cheered up* the team.

ひきちぎる 引きちぎる tear*⊕ / 男は電話機からコードを引きちぎった The man *tore* the cord from the telephone.

ひきつぎ 引き継ぎ 後任へ仕事の引き継ぎをする a *hand over one's work* to *one's successor*

ひきつぐ 引き継ぐ (仕事などを)take* over;(引き渡す)hand over;(財産などを)inherit⊕ / 前任者から事務を引き継ぐ *take over* official duties from one's predecessor / 彼はおじの農場の仕事を引き継いだ He *inherited* the farming job *from* his uncle.

ひきつけ 引き付け fit◻ / 引きつけを起こす have *a fit*

ひきつける 引き付ける ❶【引き寄せる】(磁石などが物を)attract⊕ / 磁石が鉄を引きつける Magnets *attract* iron.
❷【魅了する】attract⊕, magnetize⊕;(心に訴える)appeal to … / 彼の表情豊かな演技は多くの観客を引きつけた His expressive performance *attracted* [*magnetized*] a large audience. / 彼に会ったとたん私たちは彼の人柄に引きつけられた We *were attracted* [*magnetized*] by his personality as soon as we met him.
❸【けいれんを起こす】have* a fit

ひきつづき 引き続き いくつかの予告編に引き続き本編が上映された *Following* some previews, the film was shown. / この展示会は引き続き大阪で催される This exhibition will be put on *subsequently* in Osaka.

ひきつる 引き攣る (筋肉が)have* [get*] a cramp(✦cramp は「けいれん」の意味);(顔が緊張などで)twitch⊕ / 緊張のため彼の顔は引きつっていた His face *twitched* with tension.

ひきつれる 引き連れる 彼は子供たちを引き連れて博物館へ出かけた He *took* his children to the museum.

ひきて 引き手 handle◻;(ドアの)knob◻

ひきでもの 引き出物 a present given to the guests at a banquet

ひきど 引き戸 sliding door◻

ひきとめる 引き止める・引き留める (とどまらせる)keep*⊕;(行くのを止める)stop⊕ / 彼を引き止めることはだれにもできないだろう No one will be able to *stop* [*keep*] him. / お帰りのところお引き止めしてすみません I'm sorry to *keep* you when you're about to leave.

ひきとる 引き取る (店が返品に応じる)take* back;(面倒を見る)take care of …, look after … / レシートがあればどんな商品もお引き取りいたします We *take back* any goods with a receipt. / 妻のほうが娘を引き取るということで話が決まった They have decided that the wife *will take care of* their daughter.
◆彼は体調がすぐれません、きょうはどうぞお引き取りください He's not feeling well. Please *leave* him *alone* today.

ビキニ bikini [bikíni]◻ / ビキニ姿の若い女性 a young lady *in a bikini*

ひきにく 挽き肉 minced [ground] meat◻
◆豚[牛]ひき肉 *ground pork* [*beef*]

ひきにげ 轢き逃げ (ひき逃げ事故)hit-and-run (accident)◻ / ひき逃げをしたドライバー a *hit-and-run* driver / その男の子はひき逃げにあった(→ひき逃げの犠牲となった) The boy was a victim of *a hit-and-run* (*accident*).

ひきぬき 引き抜き (人材の)head-hunting

ひきぬく 引き抜く ❶【物を】pull out, draw*⊕,《公式的》extract⊕;(木を)uproot⊕ / くぎを引き抜く *pull out* a nail ❷【人材を】headhunt / 彼女はライバル会社に引き抜かれた She *was headhunted* by a rival firm.

ひきのばす¹ 引き伸ばす (写真などを)enlarge⊕,《口語的》blow* up / この写真を引き伸ばしてほしいのです I'd like to have this picture *enlarged* [*blown up*].

ひきのばす² 引き延ばす (延長する)extend⊕;(先送りする)put* off;(遅らせる)delay⊕
◆会議を引き延ばす *prolong* [*draw out*] a meeting / 野党は審議を引き延ばす作戦に出た The opposition parties took a *delaying* move.

ひきはなす 引き離す (競争などで差をつける)outdistance⊕;(離ればなれにする)pull apart, separate⊕ / 彼は他の走者を大きく引き離した He *outdistanced* the other runners by a long way. / レフェリーは2人のレスラーを引き離した The referee *separated* the two wrestlers.

ひきはらう 引き払う 私たちが訪ねたとき彼はすでにアパートを引き払った後だった He *had moved out of* the apartment when we went to visit him.

ひきまわす 引き回す (連れ回す)take* around

ひきもどす 引き戻す pull back;(人を連れ戻す)take* back

ひきやぶる 引き破る (引き裂く)tear* [téər]⊕, rip⊕

ひきょう¹ 卑怯 (臆病(おくびょう)な)cowardly;(不公平な)unfair;(不正な)foul / あいつはなんて卑怯なんだ How *cowardly* of him! / そんな卑怯だ That's *unfair*. / That's *not fair*.
◆卑怯なまねはよせ Don't *play the coward*.(✦play the coward は口語で「卑怯なるまいをする」の意味) / 卑怯者 a coward

ひきょう² 秘境 (未探検の地域)unexplored region◻ / 秘境に足を踏み入れる set foot in *the unexplored regions*

ひきよせる 引き寄せる pull near [closer] / 彼女はそのいすをテーブルへ引き寄せた She *pulled* the chair *near* [*closer*] to the table.

ひきょり 飛距離 (スキージャンプの)leap◻;(ゴルフ)carry◻ / 彼は110メートルの飛距離を出

した His leap was 110 meters.

ひきわけ 引き分け（引き分け試合）tie [tie] game ◎, draw ◎, tie ◎ ∥試合は7対7の引き分けに終わった The game ended in a tie [draw], 7 to 7.
◆北川高校と青木高校のサッカーの試合は引き分けだった Kitagawa High School tied Aoki High School in the soccer match.

ひきわける 引き分ける（相手と）tie ⾃ ◎; （試合を）draw* ⾃ ◎ ∥ドラゴンズはジャイアンツと5対5で引き分けた The Dragons 「tied (with) [drew with] the Giants, 5 to 5.

ひきわたす 引き渡す（品物を）deliver; （犯人などを）hand [turn] over ∥彼らはその泥棒を警察へ引き渡した They handed the thief over to the police.

ひきん 卑近 ──卑近な（身近な）familiar; （日常的な）common, ordinary ∥卑近な例を挙げて give a familiar example

ひきんぞく 非金属 nonmetal ◎ ⓤ ──非金属の nonmetallic ∥非金属元素 a nonmetallic element

ひく¹ 引く

❶ 引っぱる	pull; draw
❷ 導く	lead
❸ 注意・関心を	catch, attract
❹ 辞書を	look up
❺ 引用する	quote
❻ 線を	draw

❶【引っぱる】pull ◎; draw* ◎; drag; tug; haul ◎; tow ◎

  pull: 必要に応じた力を入れて，自分の方へ一度に「引く」こと．
  draw: 一定の力を入れながら，ゆっくりと「引く」こと．
  tug, haul: どちらも力をこめて「ぐいと引く」ことだが，haul は「重いものを苦労しながら引っぱる」という含みをもつ．
  tow: 船や車などを綱やチェーンを使って「引く」場合に用いる．

銃の引き金を引く pull the trigger / 弓を引く draw a bow / カーテンを引く draw a curtain（❖カーテンを「あける」場合と「閉める」場合の両方に用いる）

そのドアは手前に引けばあきます Pull the door and it will open.
男たちはロープを懸命に引き続けた The men went on pulling the rope with all their strength.
もう少しあごを引きなさい Pull [Draw] in your chin a little more.

❷【導く】lead* ◎
彼女は娘の手を引いて通りを渡った She led her daughter by the hand across the road.

❸【注意・関心を】catch* ◎, attract ◎, get* ◎
その子は母親の注意を引こうとスカートを引っぱった The boy pulled at his mother's skirt to get [catch, attract] her attention.
彼女の格好は人目を引いた The way she dressed attracted [drew] people's attention.

❹【辞書を】（語句を）look up; （辞書を調べる）consult ◎
単語を辞書で引く look up a word in a dictionary
彼は分からない単語に出会うといつも辞書を引く He always consults a dictionary when he runs into an unfamiliar word.

❺【引用する】quote
彼は演説で聖書から一節引いた He quoted a phrase from the Bible in his speech.

❻【線を】draw* ◎; （下線を）underline ◎
ペンで直線を引く draw a straight line with a pen
彼は重要な単語に線を引いた He underlined important words.

❼【水道・電気などを】lay* ◎; （取り付ける）install ◎
水道［ガス］を引く（→水道［ガス］管を引く）lay a water [gas] pipe
この山小屋には電話が引いてある A telephone has been installed in this hut.

❽【数字を】（引き算をする）subtract ◎
◆ 7 引く 3 は 4 7 minus 3 is [equals] 4. / Subtract 3 from 7 and you get 4.

❾【金額を】cut* ◎, reduce ◎; （税金として）deduct ◎; （割引する）discount ◎, give* ◎ a discount
給料から1割引く cut 10 percent from a person's pay; reduce a person's pay by 10 percent
表示価格から1割お引きします We'll give a 10 percent discount from the marked price.
所得税としてバイト代から2,000円引かれた Two thousand yen was deducted from the pay for my part-time job as income tax.

❿【引き継ぐ】
彼女は中国人の血を引いている She has a bit of Chinese blood.

⓫【かぜを】catch* ◎
かぜをひく catch (a) cold
◆ 彼は今かぜをひいている He has a cold now.

⓬【下がる・元に戻る】go* down; （静まる）（公式的）subside ⾃; （潮が）ebb ⾃ ◎
けさになってやっと熱が引いた The fever finally 「went down [subsided] this morning.
洪水が引くまではまだ長い時間がかかるだろう It'll be a long time until the floods subside.
潮が引き始めた The tide has begun to ebb. / The tide is now on the ebb.

⓭【その他】
くじを引く draw lots / フライパンに油を引く oil a frying pan
（トランプで）この中から1枚引いて Pick one of these cards.
私はその仕事から手を引いた I backed out of the business.
こうなった以上引くに引けない（→手を引くには遅

すぎる) It's too late to back out now.
[慣用表現] 後には引けない ➾ あと(後)

ひく² 退く (引き下がる) withdraw* 圓; (後退する) retreat 圓; (退職する) retire 圓 ∥前線からひく withdraw from the front ∥ 政界から身をひく retire from the political world

ひく³ 弾く (楽器を) play 他 ∥ピアノを弾く play the piano / ショパンを弾いてください Please *play* me some Chopin. (❖この Chopinは「ショパンの作品」の意味)

ひく⁴ 轢く run* over 他 ∥もう少しで猫をひいてしまうところだった I almost *ran over* a cat. / 彼は車にひかれて死んだ He *was run over by a car* and killed.

ひく⁵ 碾く (すりつぶす) grind* 他 ∥豆をひいて粉にする *grind* beans into powder

ひく⁶ 挽く (のこぎりで) saw* 他

びく 魚籠 fish basket ©, creel ©

ひくい 低い

❶【高さが】 low; (背が) short (↔tall); (鼻が) flat
低い塀 a *low* wall / 低い鼻 a *flat* nose
この部屋は天井が低い This room has a *low* ceiling.
私は健より背が低い I am *shorter* than Ken.
◆このあたりは海面より1メートル低い(→海面より1メートル下にある) This area is one meter *below* sea level.

❷【声の調子などが】 low, low-pitched
彼は記者会見の間中、ずっと低い声で話した He spoke in a *low-pitched* [*deep*] voice throughout the press conference.

❸【身分・地位などが】 low, humble (↔noble)
身分の低い人 a person of *low* standing
彼は社会的地位が低いことを気にしているようだ It seems that he is worrying about his *low* position.

❹【基準・程度が】 low
この国の生活水準は全体的に低い The standard of living is generally *low* in this country.
きのうは全国的に非常に気温が低かった The temperature was extremely *low* all across the country yesterday.
その新製品の価格は低く抑えられた The price of the new product was set *low*.
◆次元の低い話 a *gutter-level* conversation / 彼が成功する確率はとても低い(→小さな可能性しかない) There is only a *small* probability that he will succeed.

ひくつ 卑屈 ──卑屈な (こびへつらう) obsequious; (奴隷のような) servile ∥彼は上役に対していつも卑屈な態度をとる He always takes an *obsequious* attitude to his superior.

びくっ 私は大きな物音にびくっとした I *was startled at* the loud noise. / 彼女はびくっとして振り向いた She turned around *with a start*.

ぴくっ 緊張で彼のほおがぴくっと動いた His cheek *twitched* because of strain.

ひくて 引く手 彼は多くの会社から引く手あまただ He *has been sought after* by a lot of companies.

びくともしない 彼らはその石を持ち上げようとしたがびくともしなかった(→少しも動かなかった) They tried to lift the stone, but it *wouldn't move an inch*.

ピクニック picnic ©

[語法] 日本語の「ピクニック」は「食事を持って(遠くに)出かける」ことだが、英語のpicnicは単に「野外で食事をする」ことを指すため、例えば「自分の家の庭で食事をする」こともpicnicという。

ピクニックの弁当 a *picnic* lunch / 今度の日曜日にピクニックに行こう Let's *go on a picnic* next Sunday. / 私たちは公園でピクニックをした We「*had a picnic* [*picnicked*] in the park. / きょうはピクニックにもってこいの天気だ It's a nice day for *a picnic* today.

ぴくぴく ──ぴくぴくする (顔・手足の筋肉などが) twitch 圓 ➾ ぴくっ

びくびく その子は母親にしかられるのではないかとびくびくしていた The child *was afraid that* his mother would scold him. / 彼はびくびくしながら(→おびえた顔で)その洞窟(影)に入った He went into the cave *with a frightened look*. / びくびくするな(→怖がるな) Don't *be so scared*.

ぴくぴく 彼はほおがぴくぴくするのを感じた He felt his cheek *twitch*.

ひぐま 羆 brown bear ©

ひぐらし 【昆虫】 clear-toned cicada ©

ピクルス pickles [píklz] ◆キュウリのピクルス *pickled* cucumbers

ひぐれ 日暮れ (日没) sunset ⓤ; (たそがれ) dusk ⓤ; (夕方) evening ⓤ ∥夜明けから日暮れまで from dawn till *dusk* [*dark*] / 私たちは日暮れにその村に着いた We arrived at the village *toward*(*s*) *evening*.
◆彼女は子供たちに日暮れまでに(→暗くなる前に)戻るように言った She told her children to come back *before dark*.

ひけ 引け [慣用表現] 彼女は英語にかけてはうちのクラスのだれにも引けを取らない(→だれにも劣らない) As for English, she *is second to none* in my class.

ひげ¹ 髭

❶【人間の】 beard [bíərd] © (❖特にあごひげ、あごからほおにかけてのひげを指す); (口ひげ) 《米》mustache [mʌ́stæʃ] ©, 《英》moustache [məstɑ́ːʃ] ©

beard   mustache

濃い [薄い] ひげ a heavy [light] *beard* / 口ひ

げの男 a man with *a mustache*
うちの祖父はあごひげを生やしている My grandfather has [wears] *a beard*.
◆ひげをそったらすっきりした気分になった I felt refreshed after *shaving*. / 彼は無精ひげを生やしている(→ひげをそっていない) He *is unshaven*.
❷【動物の】(猫などの) whiskers; (魚の) barbel [C]
‖ひげそり(かみそり) a razor; (電気かみそり) a shaver / ひげそり道具 shaving things / ひげ面(づら) a bearded face; (無精ひげの) an unshaven face

ひげ² 卑下 ―卑下する humble *oneself* ‖卑下する必要はない You don't need to *humble yourself*.

ピケ ⚠picket (line) [C] ◆工場の門にピケを張る *picket* the gate of a factory

ひげき 悲劇 tragedy [C] ―悲劇の・悲劇的な tragic ‖ギリシャ悲劇を上演する play *a* Greek *tragedy* / 悲劇の主人公を演じる play a *tragic* hero [heroine] / 悲劇的な事故 a *tragic* accident / 一家を悲劇が襲った The whole family was struck by *a tragedy*. / その実験は悲劇的な結末に終わった The experiment came to a *tragic* end. / そのドライバーはレース中に悲劇的な死を遂げた The driver *died a tragic death* during a race. / だれも愛せないなんて悲劇だ It is *a tragedy* that you cannot love anybody.

ひけつ¹ 秘訣 secret [C]; (最も大切なこと) key [C]; (要領) knack [C] ‖健康の秘訣は十分な睡眠と規則正しい食事だ *The secret* of good health is good sleep and regular meals. / あなたの成功の秘訣は何ですか What's *the secret* of your success?

ひけつ² 否決 rejection [C] ―否決する reject [他]; (投票で) vote down ‖その法案は否決された The bill *was rejected* [*voted down*].

ひけどき 引け時 (終業時刻) closing time [C]

ひけめ 引け目 彼はほかのクラスメートに対してひけ目を感じていた(→劣っていると感じていた) He *felt inferior to* the other classmates. / 友人たちの前で私はいつもひけ目を感じる(→小さく感じる) I always *feel small* in the presence of my friends.

ひけらかす (得意そうに) show* off, flaunt [他], 《口語的》parade [他] ‖彼はことあるごとに自分の知識をひけらかす He uses every opportunity to *show off* his knowledge.

ひげんじつてき 非現実的 (現実とかけ離れた) unrealistic; (実用的でない) impractical ‖非現実的な提案 an *unrealistic* proposal

ひけんしゃ 被験者 (実験などの) subject [C]

ひご¹ 庇護 protection [U] ➔ほご(保護)

ひご² 卑語 (下品な言葉) vulgar word [C]; (下品な表現) vulgarism [U]

ひこう¹ 飛行 (1回の飛行) flight [C]; (飛ぶこと) flying [U] ―飛行する fly* [自], make* a flight ‖その飛行機は飛行中にエンジントラブルに見舞われた The airplane had some trouble with its engine *during the flight*. / 本機は現在3万3千フィート上空を飛行中です Our plane *is* now flying 33,000 feet up. / リンドバーグは大西洋を無着陸で横断飛行した Lindbergh *made a nonstop flight across* the Atlantic.
‖飛行距離 a flight / 飛行禁止区域 a no-fly zone / 飛行士 a flier; (操縦士) a pilot / 飛行場 an airport / 計器飛行 an instrument flight / 試験飛行 a trial flight / 単独飛行 a solo flight / 夜間飛行 a nocturnal flight

ひこう² 非行 《公式的》delinquency [U]; (間違った行為) 《公式的》misdeed [C] ‖青少年の非行 juvenile *delinquency*
◆非行に走る become *delinquent*
‖非行少年[少女] a juvenile delinquent

ひごう 非業 [慣用表現] 彼は非業の死を遂げた He *died an unnatural* [*a violent*] *death*.

びこう¹ 尾行 (行為) shadowing [U], 《俗語》tailing [U] ―尾行する shadow [他], 《俗語》tail [他] ‖彼はこの3日間ずっと警察に尾行されている He *has been shadowed* [*tailed*] by the police for the last three days.
◆尾行をまく shake off *a shadow* / 人に尾行をつける put *a shadow* [*tail*] on a person / 我々はだれかに尾行されているようだ It seems we *have a shadow on our tail*.

びこう² 備考 note [C] ‖備考欄 notes

びこう³ 鼻孔 nostril [C]

ひこうかい 非公開 ―非公開の (秘密の) private; (部外者を閉め出した) closed-door ‖非公開の会議 a *closed-door* conference / この資料は非公開だ This document is *private*.
◆裁判は非公開で行われる予定である The trial will be held *behind closed doors*.

ひこうき 飛行機 plane [C], 《米》airplane [C], 《英》aeroplane [C]; (航空機全般) aircraft [C] (複～) (❖ヘリコプター・グライダー・飛行船など「空を飛ぶ乗り物」全般を指す)
飛行機を操縦する fly *a plane* [*an airplane*] / バンコク行きの飛行機に乗る *board a plane* for Bangkok / 飛行機を降りる get off [out of] *a plane* [*an airplane*]
その飛行機には350人の乗客が乗っていた There were 350 passengers on the *plane*.
我々の乗った飛行機は1時間遅れて出発した Our *plane* left the airport one hour late.
飛行機から下にグランドキャニオンが見えた *From the plane* we could see the Grand Canyon below.
テレビのニュースによるとインドで飛行機墜落事故があったそうだ According to TV news, there was *a plane crash* in India.
◆ハワイまで飛行機でどれくらい時間がかかりますか How long does it take to Hawaii *by air*? / 飛行機で旅行するのは今回が初めてだ This is my first time to *travel by air*. / 彼は東京から大阪まで飛行機で行った He *flew* from Tokyo to Osaka./ (→飛行機に乗った) He *took a plane* from Tokyo to Osaka. / 彼女は飛行機に酔いやすい She *often suffers from airsickness*.
‖飛行機雲 a contrail, a condensation trail / 紙飛行機 a paper plane / 軽飛行機 a light (air)plane / 水上飛行機 a seaplane /

模型飛行機 a model plane

ひこうしき 非公式 unofficial; (略式の) informal; (個人的な) private ──非公式に unofficially; informally; privately ∥非公式の会議 an *unofficial* meeting ／ …を非公式に訪問する pay an *unofficial* visit to … ／ 大統領と非公式に会見する have an *informal* interview with the President ／ 外務大臣はその件について非公式の見解を述べた The Foreign Minister stated his *private* opinion.

ひこうせん 飛行船 airship ◯; (小型の) blimp ◯

ひごうほう 非合法 ──非合法の illegal, unlawful ∥非合法活動 *illegal* [*unlawful*] *activities*

ひこく 被告 defendant ◯; (特に刑事事件の) the accused ∥被告は無罪を主張した The *defendant* maintained his innocence. ／ 証人は被告に不利な証言をした The witness testified against *the accused*.
∥被告席 the dock

ひごと 日毎 日ごとに秋めいてきた It is getting to be more like fall *day by day*.

ひごろ 日頃 (常々) always; (長い間) for a long time ──日ごろの (毎日の) everyday; (日々の) daily ∥彼は日ごろから食事に気をつけている He *always* takes care of his meals. ／ 苦境にあっては日ごろの努力がものをいう Your *everyday* [*daily*] effort counts in hard times. ／ 日ごろのご愛顧に感謝しておりますWe thank you for your *daily* patronage.

ひざ 膝 (ひざ頭) knee [níː] ◯; (座ったときの腰からひざ頭までの部分) lap ◯ (❖単数形の lap で「左右両方のひざ」を指す)

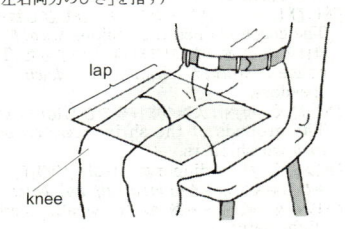

lap

knee

ひざを曲げる bend *one's knee* ／ ひざをすりむく scrape *one's knee* ／ ひざ枕で眠る sleep *with one's head on a person's lap*
彼はテーブルの角(ʰ)にひざをぶつけた He hit his *knee* on the corner of the table.
その猫は飼い主のひざの上に座っていた The cat sat *on its owner's lap*.
◆ひざ丈(飛)のスカート a *knee-length* skirt ／ 彼女はひざまでのブーツを履いていた She wore *knee-high* boots. ／ 彼女はひざをついて祈った She *knelt down* and prayed. ／ 彼らはひざまで水につかりながら助けを待っていた They were waiting for rescue *knee-deep in water*.
∥ひざ当て a kneepad ／ ひざかけ 《米》a lap robe, 《英》a rug ／ ひざ小僧 a knee

慣用表現 山の下りでひざが笑ってしまった My knees *gave way* while I was climbing down the mountain. (❖give way は「崩れる, 屈する」の意味) ／ どうぞひざをくずして(→くつろいで)ください Please *make yourself at home*. ／ 私たちはひざを突き合わせて(→顔を向き合わせて)その件を話し合った We talked about the problem *face to face*. ／ 彼とはいつかひざを交えて(→心と心を通わせて)話をしたいものだ I'd like to have a *heart-to-heart* talk with him some day.

ビザ visa [víːzə] ◯ ∥観光ビザを発給する issue *a tourist visa* ／ オーストラリアへの入国ビザを申請する apply for *an entry visa* to [for] Australia ／ ビザを書き換える必要がある I need to renew *my visa*. ／ 彼はまだビザがおりていない The *visa* has not been issued to him yet.

ピザ pizza [píːtsə] ◯ ◯ (❖「ピザ 1 切れ」は a slice of pizza という) ∥ピザの生地 *pizza dough* ／ ピザを焼く bake *a pizza* ／ ピザを注文する order *a pizza* ／ 昼食にピザを届けてもらった We had *a pizza* delivered for lunch.
∥ピザ専門店 a pizzeria [piːtsəríːə], a pizza house

ひさい 被災 被災地に救援物資を送る send relief goods to *the disaster area* ／ ハリケーンの被災者に食料と水を供給する supply food and water to *the* hurricane *victims* ／ 彼の家族はその地震で被災した His family *suffered from* the earthquake.

びさい 微細 ──微細な (ごく小さい) minute [mainjúːt]; (粒子などが細かい) fine

ひさし 庇 (家の) eaves; (帽子の) visor ◯, peak ◯

慣用表現 あの男にはひさしを貸して母屋(勢)を取られる目にあった *I gave* that man *an inch and he took a mile*.

ひざし 日差し sunlight ◯, sun ◯, sunshine ◯ ∥夏のぎらぎらした日差しの中を歩く walk in *the* glaring summer *sunlight* ／ きょうは日差しが強い The *sun* is strong today. ／ 5 月になるとどんどん日差しが強くなってくる The *sunshine* gets stronger and stronger in May. ／ 私たちは日差しを避けて大きな木の下に座った We sat under a big tree, sheltering *from the sun* [*sunlight*].

ひさしい 久しい 彼女には久しく会っていない I have not seen her *for a long time*. ／ その作家が死んでから久しい(→死んでから長い時間がたっている) *It's been a long time* since the writer died.

ひさしぶり 久し振り after a long time [interval]

語法
日本語の「久しぶりに」は, 久しぶりにどうしたのかによって訳し分けることができる. よく使われる表現としては, 以下のようなものがある.
(1) after a long silence「長い沈黙の後で」: 音信不通だった人から電話や手紙をもらったような場合.
(2) after a long absence「長い不在の後で」: どこかへ出かけていた人が戻ってきたよう

な場合.
(3) after a long separation「長い別離の後で」: 長い間会っていなかった人と再会したような場合.

私は久しぶりに映画を見に行った I went to the movie *after a long interval* [*for the first time in quite some time*].

久しぶりに薫から電話があった Kaoru phoned me *after a long silence*.

彼は久しぶりに日本へ帰ってきた He came back to Japan *after a long absence*.

私は横浜で旧友と久しぶりに会うことになっている I'm going to see one of my old friends at Yokohama *after a long separation*.

◆金沢を訪れるのは本当に久しぶりだ(→前回金沢を訪れてから長い時間がたっている) *It's a long time since* I visited Kanazawa *last*. / (→何年もの間金沢を訪れていなかった) I haven't visited Kanazawa *for many years*. / あしたは久しぶりに(→長い雨続きの後で)晴れそうだ We'll have a beautiful day *after a long spell of rainy weather*.

🅔「お久しぶりですね, いかがお過ごしですか」「ありがとう. 元気でやっていますよ」"*It's a long time since* I saw you *last*. How have you been?" "Thank you. I've been doing all right."

ひざづめ 膝詰め 彼は上司とひざ詰め談判(→直接交渉)をした He *had direct negotiations with* his boss.

ひざまずく kneel* [ní:l] 圁, go* down on *one's knees* ∥彼女は祭壇の前にひざまずいて祈った She *knelt* (*down*) in front of the altar and prayed.

ひさめ 氷雨 (冷たい雨) a cold rain

ひざもと 膝元 彼は親のひざ元を離れ東京で暮らし始めた He *left his parents and began his life in Tokyo*. / その反乱は幕府のおひざ元(→すぐ近く)で起こった The revolt broke out *very near* the headquarters of the shogunate.

ひさん 悲惨 ──悲惨な (みじめな) miserable, wretched; (ひどい) 《口語的》terrible; (無惨な) cruel; (悲劇的な) tragic ∥悲惨な生活を送る live a *miserable* [*wretched*] *life* / 悲惨な死を遂げる die a *tragic death* / 彼の悲惨な状態を見て友人たちはショックを受けた His friends were shocked to see him in such a *miserable* [*terrible*] state.

◆彼女は戦争の悲惨さについて語った She talked about the *cruelty* of war.

ひじ 肘 elbow © ∥ひじに当て布をしたジャケット a jacket with patches on *the elbows* / ひじを曲げるとひどく痛んだ *My elbow* hurt terribly when I bent it. / 食事中にテーブルにひじをつくのはエチケットに反する It is against etiquette to lean *your elbow* on the table during a meal. / このセーターはひじの所がすり切れてきた This sweater has worn out at *the elbows*.

ひじかけいす 肘掛け椅子 armchair ©

ひしがた 菱形 lozenge [lázindʒ] ©; 〘幾何〙 rhombus © ⇨ずけい, 図版

びしっ 中島さんはきょうスーツでびしっと決めている Mr. Nakajima *looks really cool* in his suit today.

びしっ 熱い麦茶を注ぐとそのガラスポットはびしっと音を立てて割れた The glass bottle broke *with a crack* when I poured hot barley tea into it. / 彼は馬にむちをびしっと当てた He *cracked* his whip at the horse.

ひじてつ 肘鉄 彼女をスキーに誘ってみたがひじ鉄を食わされた I invited her to go skiing with me, but she *gave me a brush-off*.

ビジネス business ⓤ © ∥ベンチャービジネス (a) venture *business* / 彼はビジネスで大阪へ行った He went to Osaka *on business*.

◆サイドビジネスで金をもうける derive money from *a second job* / 彼は何よりもビジネス優先だ He *places his work above* everything. / ビジネスライクにいこう Let's settle it *in a businesslike way*. (✤「冷たい・非常に事務的な」の意味で用いる場合は overly などの語を補う)

∥ビジネス英語 business English / ビジネス街 a business district / ビジネスクラス a business class / ビジネススクール a business school / ビジネスホテル an economy hotel, a budget hotel (✤ ×business hotel とはいわない)

ビジネスウーマン (会社員) female office worker ©; (実業家) businesswoman ©

ビジネスマン (会社員) office worker ©; (実業家) businessman ©

ひしひし 彼女の悲しみがひしひしと伝わってきた I *really felt* her grief. / 私は責任の重さをひしひしと感じている I feel *heavily* the weight of responsibility.

びしびし コーチは新人選手たちをびしびし鍛えた The coach trained the rookies *hard*. / 警察はスピード違反をびしびし取り締まった The police *cracked* [*clamped*] *down on* speeders.

ひしめく 境内は大勢の参拝者でひしめいていた The grounds of the shrine *were crowded with* worshippers.

ひしゃく 柄杓 dipper ©, ladle [léidl] ©
◆ひしゃくで水をくむ *ladle* [*dip up*] *water*

びじゃく 微弱 ──微弱な weak, feeble, slight, faint

ひしゃたい 被写体 (写す対象) object © ◆写真家の被写体になる *sit for* a photographer

びしゃり 彼女は戸をびしゃりと閉めて出ていった She went out, *slamming* the door behind her. / 彼は馬にむちをびしゃりと当てた He *cracked his whip at* the horse. / 洋子は彼の顔をびしゃりとたたいた Yoko *slapped* his face. / Yoko *slapped* him in the face. / 彼の妥協案はびしゃりとはねつけられた His compromise proposal *met with a flat refusal*.

ひじゅう 比重 〘物理〙 specific gravity ⓤ; (重要度) weight ⓤ, importance ⓤ ∥私たちの学校では英語に比重をおいている Our school *gives* [*attaches*] *weight to* English. / 演劇部の活動は彼の生活の中で大きな比重を占めている

The activities of the drama club *occupy a great part of* his life.
‖比重計 a gravimeter; (液体比重計) a hydrometer

びじゅつ 美術 art, the fine arts
美術の時間に外へ行って写生をした In *the art class* we went outside to draw pictures.
‖美術家 an artist / 美術界 the art world / 美術学校 an art school / 美術館 an art gallery [museum] / 美術工芸 arts and crafts / 美術史 history of art, art history / 美術商(人) an art dealer; (店) a fine art(s) shop / 美術展 an art exhibition / 美術評論家 an art critic / 美術品 a work [an object] of art; 《集合的》(fine) art / 近代美術 modern art / 現代美術 contemporary art / 工芸美術 industrial arts / 造形美術 plastic arts

ひじゅん 批准 ratification ──批准する ratify, confirm ‖条約を批准する *ratify* a treaty
‖批准書 an instrument of ratification

ひしょ¹ 秘書 secretary, administrative assistant (※役職名としては後者を用いることが多い) ‖彼は山崎氏の秘書だ He is Mr. Yamazaki's *administrative assistant*. / 母は昔秘書をしていた My mother used to be *a secretary*.
‖秘書課 the secretarial section

ひしょ² 避暑 避暑に軽井沢へ行く go to Karuizawa *to escape the summer heat*
‖避暑客 a summer visitor / 避暑地 a summer resort

びじょ 美女 beauty, beautiful woman ‖絶世の美女 *a marvel of beauty*

ひじょう¹ 非常 (非常事態) emergency
非常の場合には *in an emergency*; *in case of (an) emergency* / 非常の場合に備える prepare for *emergencies*
‖非常階段 emergency stairs, an emergency staircase / 非常口 an emergency exit [door], a fire exit / 非常呼集 an emergency call [summons] / 非常コック an emergency handle / 非常手段 emergency measures / 非常食 emergency rations [provisions] / 非常停止ボタン an emergency stop / 非常ブレーキ《米》an emergency cord,《英》a communication cord / 非常ベル an emergency bell; (火災用) a fire alarm; (防犯用) a burglar alarm

ひじょう² 非情 ──非情な (冷酷な) heartless, cold-hearted; (残酷な) cruel

びしょう 微笑 smile ──微笑する smile ‖満足そうな微笑 a contented *smile* / かすかな微笑 a ghost of *a smile*

ひじょうきん 非常勤 ──非常勤の[で] part-time / 非常勤で働く work *part-time*
‖非常勤講師 a part-time teacher / 非常勤職員 a part-time worker, a part-timer

ひじょうしき 非常識 ──非常識な (思慮を欠いた) thoughtless; (愚かな) absurd; (理性的でない・法外な) unreasonable ‖そんなことをするなんて非常識だ It's *thoughtless* of you to do such a thing. ◆彼は非常識だ He *has no common sense*. / He *lacks common sense*.

ひじょうな 非常な (大きな) great, very; (極度の) extreme; (並みはずれた) extraordinary ‖非常な喜び a *great* pleasure / 非常な難問 a *very* difficult problem / 私たちは彼を非常な敬意をもって迎えた We welcomed him with *great* respect.

ひじょうに 非常に

very, very much; (大いに) greatly; (極度に) extremely; (並みはずれて) extraordinarily

語法
(1) very は「非常に」の意味の最も一般的な語で, 原級の形容詞・副詞, 形容詞的に用いられる動詞の現在分詞を修飾する.
(2) 過去分詞は much または very much を用いて修飾するが, 感情・心理状態を表す amused, interested などには, 口語では very が用いられる. また, 純粋に形容詞として扱われるものに関しては very を用いるのがふつうである.
(3) 動詞を修飾するときは very ではなく very much などが用いられる.

非常に高価な腕時計 a *very* expensive watch / 非常に優秀な学生 an *extraordinarily* bright student
彼のスピーチは私たちを非常に感動させた His speech moved us *greatly*.
きのうは非常に暑かった It was *very* [*extremely, awfully*] hot yesterday.
この国の自然破壊は非常に深刻だ The destruction of nature in this country is *very* serious.
彼の期末試験の成績には非常にがっかりさせられた I was (*very*) *much* disappointed by his results on the final examinations.
私はコンピュータグラフィックスに非常に興味がある I am *very* interested in computer graphics.
今回の旅行は非常に楽しかった I enjoyed this trip *very much*.
◆非常に苦労して with *great* difficulty / 彼の足は非常に速くて私たちは追いつくことができなかった He ran *so* fast that we could not catch up with him. / 彼女は非常に親切だ(→親切そのものだ) She is kindness *itself*. / 非常に緊張しました I got *awfully* [*terribly*] nervous.

びしょうねん 美少年 handsome boy

びしょく 美食 gourmet [gúərmei] food; (美食すること) epicurism, gastronomy ‖美食家 a gourmet, an epicure

びしょぬれ びしょ濡れ 私はびしょぬれになった I *got soaked to the skin*. / まあ大変, あなたびしょぬれよ! Oh dear! You*'re all wet*!

びしょびしょ 服がびしょびしょになった My clothes *got soaking wet*.

ビジョン vision ‖ビジョンがある人 a man *of vision* / 長期的ビジョン *a long-range vision*

びじれいく 美辞麗句 flowery words [expressions] ∥美辞麗句を連ねる use *flowery words* [*expressions*]
◆美辞麗句を並べた文章 *purple passages*

びしん 微震 slight [weak] earthquake ⓒ, tremor ⓒ

びじん 美人 beauty ⓒ, beautiful woman [girl] ⓒ ∥すごい美人 She is a *striking beauty* ∥彼女は美人だ She *is beautiful*.
∥美人コンテスト a beauty contest [pageant]

ひすい 翡翠 (宝石) jade Ⓤ ∥ひすい色 jade (green)

ビスケット ⚠ 《米》cookie ⓒ, 《英》biscuit ⓒ (❖biscuitは《米》では小型のパンを指す) ∥ビスケットの入った箱 a packet of *cookies* ∥ビスケットの詰め合わせ assorted *cookies*

ヒステリー hysteria [histíriə] Ⓤ; (発作) hysterics [histériks] ──ヒステリーの hysterical ∥ヒステリーを起こす go into *hysterics*; (→感情的になる) become *hysterical* ∥集団ヒステリー mass *hysteria*

ヒステリック ──ヒステリックな hysterical ──ヒステリックに hysterically ∥ヒステリックに笑う laugh *hysterically*

ピストル pistol ⓒ, handgun ⓒ, gun ⓒ ∥ピストルで撃つ shoot with *a pistol* ∥彼は私にピストルを突きつけた He *pulled* (*out*) *a pistol* on me. ∥その子は箱の中からおもちゃのピストルを取り出した The child fished *a toy gun* out of the box.
◆ピストル自殺する shoot oneself
[俳句] ピストルがプールの硬き面(ɔ)にひびき (山口誓子)
It was a pistol:
echoing off the hard walls
of the swimming pool.

ピストン 〘機械〙 piston ⓒ; (金管楽器の) valve ⓒ ◆バスが駅とホテルの間をピストン輸送している Buses *shuttle* between the station and the hotel.

ひずみ 歪み (反(ɔ)り) warp ⓒ; (画像・音などの) distortion ⓒⓊ ∥ひずみのない澄んだ音 (a) clear sound with no *distortion*
◆経済のひずみ (an) economic *imbalance* ∥床にひずみがある There is *a warped* plane in the floor.

ひずむ 歪む (反(ɔ)る) be warped; (画像・音などが) be distorted ∥この板はひどくひずんでいる This board *is* badly *warped*.

びせい 美声 beautiful [sweet] voice ⓒ

ひせいげんようほう 非制限用法 〘文法〙 non-restrictive use ⓒⓊ

> 非制限用法は, 関係詞節が先行詞に説明・理由などを付け加えるだけで, 先行詞の内容を限定する役割を果たさない関係用法である. 反対に先行詞の内容を限定する関係詞の用法を「制限用法」(restrictive use)という. 書く場合, 非制限用法では先行詞と関係代名詞との間をコンマで区切り, 制限用法では区切らない ∥ He has two sons, *who* are both lawyers. 彼には2人の息子がいて, 2人とも弁護士になっている ∥ He has two sons *who* are both lawyers. 彼には弁護士になった息子が2人いる (❖「ほかにも弁護士でない息子がいる」という可能性がある)

びせいぶつ 微生物 microbe ⓒ, microorganism ⓒ
◆私たちが作っている多くの物質は微生物で分解されません Many of the substances we produce are not *biodegradable*.
∥微生物学 microbiology ∥ 微生物学者 a microbiologist

びせきぶん 微積分 〘数学〙 (differential and integral) calculus Ⓤ

ひせんきょけん 被選挙権 eligibility (for election) ◆被選挙権がある be *eligible*

ひせんきょにん 被選挙人 eligible (person)

ひそ 砒素 〘化学〙 arsenic Ⓤ (❖元素記号 As)

ひそう¹ 悲壮 悲壮な決意をする make *a tragic but brave resolution* ∥ 悲壮な最期を遂げる die *a tragic but brave death*

ひそう² 悲愴 悲愴な話 a *pathetic* [*sorrowful, mournful*] story

ひそう³ 皮相 ──皮相な superficial, shallow ∥皮相な見解 a *superficial* view

ひぞう 秘蔵 ──秘蔵の treasured ⑯ ∥この日本刀は祖父の秘蔵の品だ This Japanese sword is *a treasure* of my grandfather's.
∥秘蔵っ子 (お気に入りの弟子) one's favorite disciple

ひそか 密か ──ひそかな (秘密の) secret; (内々の) private; (人目を忍んだ) stealthy ──ひそかに secretly, in secret; privately, in private; stealthily ∥その女優はひそかに外国へ行った The actress *secretly* went abroad. ∥彼女はひそかに彼に会った She met him *in private*. ∥伸子は私にひそかに合図を送った Nobuko gave a *stealthy* signal to me.

ひぞく 卑俗 ──卑俗な vulgar

ひそひそ 彼らは何やらひそひそ相談していた They were talking over something *in a low voice*.
∥ひそひそ声 a murmur of voices ∥ ひそひそ話 a whispered talk

ひそむ 潜む (隠れる) hide* (*oneself*); (潜在する) lurk ⑯ ∥物陰に潜む *lurk in* the shadow(s) ∥与党の政策には大きな危険が潜んでいる A great danger *lurks* in the ruling party's policy.

ひそめる 潜める ❶【身を】hide* (*oneself*) ∥木立に身を潜める *hide* (*oneself*) among the trees
❷【声を】声を潜める lower one's voice ∥ 声を潜めて話す speak *in a low voice*
[慣用表現] そのバンドはここのところ鳴りを潜めている (=活動していない) The band *has been inactive* these days.

ひだ 襞 fold ⓒ; (衣服や布の) pleat ⓒ ∥スカートのひだ *pleats* on a skirt
∥ひだスカート a pleated skirt

ひたい 額 forehead [fɔ́:rəd] ⓒ, brow [bráu] ⓒ ∥広い[狭い]額 a broad [narrow] *forehead*

／額にしわを寄せる knit *one's brow* ／彼は熱があるかどうか額にさわってみた He felt *his brow* to see if he had a fever. ／彼は額の汗をふいた He wiped the sweat from *his forehead*.

慣用表現 額に汗して働く work *by the sweat of one's brow* ／私たちは額を集めて相談した We *put* [*laid*] *our heads together*.

ひだい 肥大 （組織や臓器の） hypertrophy Ⓒ ──肥大する （組織や臓器が） hypertrophy 働 ◆心臓肥大 *enlargement of the heart*

びたいちもん 微対一文 彼はびた一文持っていなかった He *didn't have a penny*.

ピタゴラスのていり ピタゴラスの定理 the Pythagorean theorem

ひたす 浸す （少し） dip 働; （たっぷり） soak 働; （漬けておく） steep 働 ／パンをミルクに浸す *soak* bread in milk ／豆を１晩水に浸しておく *steep* the beans in water overnight ／私は小川に足を浸した I *dipped* my feet in the stream.

ひたすら （熱心に） earnestly; （心から） from the bottom of *one's* heart; （懸命に） (very) hard; （一心に） intently ／彼女は息子のふるまいをひたすらわびた She *earnestly* apologized for her son's behavior. ／彼は試験に合格しようとひたすら勉強した He studied (*very*) *hard* to pass the examination.

ひたはしる ひた走る （ひたすら走る） run* and run; （走り続ける） keep* running

ひたひた さざ波が岸にひたひたと寄せていた Ripples *were lapping against* the shore.

ひだまり 日溜まり sunny spot [place] Ⓒ

ビタミン vitamin [váitəmin] Ⓒ ／レモンはビタミンＣが豊富だ Lemons are rich in *vitamin C*. ／ビタミン欠乏症 a vitamin deficiency disease, 〔医学〕 avitaminosis ／ビタミン剤 a vitamin pill

ひたむき 直向き ──ひたむきな （熱心な） earnest; （いちずな） single-minded ──ひたむきに earnestly; single-mindedly ／ひたむきに努力する make an *earnest* effort ／彼は仕事にひたむきだ He is *earnest* [*single-minded*] about his work.

ひだり 左

❶【方向】 the left (↔the right) ──左の; left; （左側の・左向きの） left-hand ⇒みぎ

３番目の角(ホネ)を左に曲がる take the third turn to *the left*

浜名湖が左手に見える Lake Hamana is visible *on the left*.

彼は私の左に座った He sat *on my left*.

左から３人目の人が小崎さんです The third person *from the left* is Ms. Kosaki.

（号令で）左向け左！ *Left face!*

◆左回りに（→反時計回りに）意見を述べていってください Could each person give your opinion, going *counterclockwise*?

❷【左翼】（個人） leftist Ⓒ; （集団） the left (wing)

彼は少し左寄りだ He *is* a bit *to the left*.

ぴたり ドアをぴたりと閉める close the door *tightly* ／彼は私の年をぴたりと言い当てた He guessed my age *exactly* [*correctly*]. ／隣の部屋の物音がぴたりとやんだ The sounds from the next room stopped *suddenly*. ／電車は駅の手前でぴたりと止まってしまった The train *came to a dead stop* just before it reached the station. ／その薬を飲んだら痛みはぴたりと治まった I took the medicine and the pain *went away very easily*.

ひだりうちわ 左団扇 左うちわで暮らす *live in comfort* [*ease*]; lead an easy life

ひだりがわ 左側 the left (side), the left-hand side ──左側の left, left-hand ／左側通行《掲示》*Keep to the Left* ／その公園の左側に郵便局がある There is a post office *on* [*to*] *the left of* the park.

ひだりきき 左利き left-handed person Ⓒ, left-hander Ⓒ; (左利きの投手) southpaw Ⓒ ──左利きの left-handed ／彼は左利きだ He *is left-handed*.

ひだりて 左手 the left hand; (左側) the left (side) ／左手に見えるのが雷門です You can see "Kaminari-mon" *on your left*.

◆左手で書く write *left-handed*; write *with one's left hand*

ひだりまえ 左前 着物を左前に着る wear a kimono *with the left side under the right* ／あの会社は左前だ（→経営が苦しい） That company *is in financial difficulties*.

ひたる 浸る ❶【つかる】 soak 働 ／肩まで熱い湯に浸る *soak in* a hot bath up to *one's* shoulders

❷【ふける】 indulge *oneself*, be lost ／思い出に浸る *be lost in one's* memories ／酒に浸る *indulge oneself in* drinking

ひだるま 火達磨 エンジンに引火し、車はあっという間に火だるまになった The engine caught fire and the car *was enveloped in flames* in an instant.

ひたん 悲嘆 grief Ⓒ ／彼女は幼い息子を事故で亡くして悲嘆に暮れていた She *abandoned herself to grief* after her young son was killed in an accident.

びだん 美談 （よい話） beautiful [good] story Ⓒ; （感動的な話） moving story Ⓒ; （賞賛すべき話） admirable story Ⓒ

びだんし 美男子 handsome [good-looking] man Ⓒ

びちく 備蓄 stockpile Ⓒ, supply Ⓒ, stock ⒸⓊ ──備蓄する stockpile 働 ／飲料水の備蓄 *a supply* of drinking water ／石油を備蓄する *stockpile* petroleum ／我々の原油の備蓄は少ない Our *stock* of crude oil is low.

ぴちぴち 池の魚がぴちぴちはねている Fish in the pond are jumping *sprightly*. ／彼女はぴちぴちのジーンズをはいていた She wore *very tight-fitting* jeans.

びちゃびちゃ （道路が） sloppy; （雪が） slushy; （泥で） muddy; （ひどくぬれて） soaking (wet)

びちゃびちゃ 赤い長靴を履いた女の子は水たまりをびちゃびちゃと走り回った The girl in red rain boots ran around *splashing* in pud-

ひつう 悲痛 grief ◎, sorrow ◎ ——悲痛な sad, grievous, sorrowful, heartrending ∥悲痛な面もちを *sad* face [look] / 悲痛な叫び a *heartrending* [*grievous*] cry / 悲痛な光景 a *sorrowful* sight

ひっかかる 引っ掛かる ❶【物に】catch* ⓐ, be caught ∥彼女のブラウスが針金のフェンスに引っかかった Her blouse *caught on* the wire fence. / ハエが1匹クモの巣に引っかかっていた A fly *was caught in* the spider's web. ◆魚の骨がのどに引っかかった A fishbone *stuck in* my throat.

❷【だまされる】fall* for ..., be taken in ∥私は彼の甘い言葉に引っかかった I *"fell for* [*was taken in by*] his sweet talk.

❸【検問などに】関に引っかかる fail to pass censorship; be rejected by censorship / その容疑者は検問に引っかかった The suspect *was caught at* a checkpoint.

ひっかきまわす 引っ掻き回す (物を捜して) rummage ⓐ, ransack ⓑ ∥彼は車のかぎを捜して引き出しの中を引っかき回した He *rummaged* (*about*) in [through] the drawer, looking for the car key. / He *ransacked* the drawer for the car key.
◆彼は余計な発言をして会議を引っかき回した (→混乱させた) His unnecessary statement *put* [*threw*] the meeting *into confusion*.

ひっかく 引っ掻く scratch ⓑ, paw ⓑ ∥猫がドアを引っかいている The cat *is scratching at* the door. / バラのとげでひざを引っかいた I *scratched* my knee on a rose thorn.

ひっかける 引っ掛ける ❶【つるす】hang* ⓑ ∥彼はコートを洋服かけに引っかけた He *hung* his coat on the hook.

❷【くぎなどに】catch* ⓑ ∥そでをくぎに引っかけた I *caught* my sleeve on a nail.

❸【だます】trick ⓑ, cheat ⓑ ∥彼は彼女を引っかけてそれを買わせた He *tricked* her into buying it.

❹【さっと着る】throw* on ∥彼は上着を引っかけて出ていった He *threw on* his jacket and went out.

❺【酒を飲む】drink* ⓑ ∥ビールを一杯引っかける *drink* a glass of beer

❻【異性を】pick up ∥街で女の子を引っかける *pick up* a girl on the street

❼【水・泥などを】splash ⓑ ∥車が私に泥を引っかけた A car *splashed* me with mud.

ひっき 筆記 writing ◎ ——筆記する (書き留める) write* down ∥私たちは先生の言ったことを筆記した We「*wrote down* [*took note on*] what our teacher said. ◆筆記体で書く write in *script* [*cursive letters*]
∥筆記試験 a written examination [test] / 筆記用具 writing materials [implements] / 口述筆記 dictation

ひつぎ 柩 coffin ◎, 《米/婉曲的》casket ◎

ひっきりなし ——ひっきりなしに (継続的に) continually; (絶え間なく) continuously, incessantly; (休みなく) without a break ——ひっきりなしの continuous; incessant ∥彼女はひっきりなしに文句を言っている She is *continually* complaining. / きのうからひっきりなしに雨が降っている It has been raining *continuously* [*without a break*] since yesterday. / 朝からひっきりなしに電話が鳴っている The telephone has been ringing *without a break* since morning.

ビッグ big ∥ビッグニュース a *big* news / ビッグビジネス *big* business

ピックアップ ——ピックアップする (選択する) pick out (❖英語の pick up は「物を拾う」「(人を)車に乗せる」の意味), choose* ⓑ ∥問題点をいくつかピックアップする *pick out* several problems

ビッグバン 〖天文〗the Big Bang ∥ビッグバン理論 the big bang theory / 金融ビッグバン the financial Big Bang

びっくり ——びっくりする be surprised; (非常に) be astonished, be amazed; (ショックを受ける) be shocked; (怖がる) be frightened
私たちはその知らせにびっくりした We *were surprised at* the news.
その人形が動いたときは本当にびっくりした I *was astonished* to see the doll move.
その少女の演奏にはびっくりした I *was amazed* by the girl's performance.
彼女は突然の物音にびっくりした She *was frightened at* the sudden noise.
◆彼にはいつもびっくりさせられる He always *astonishes me*. / びっくりさせないでよ *You scared me*! / 祖母は年のわりにびっくりするほど元気だ My grandmother is *amazingly* lively for her age.
∥びっくり箱 a jack-in-the-box

びっくりかえす 引っ繰り返す (横転させる) overturn ⓐ, upset* ⓑ; (上下を逆にする) turn upside down ∥テーブルをひっくり返す *overturn* a table / 彼女は花びんをひっくり返してしまった She *upset* the vase. / 赤ちゃんがその箱をひっくり返した The baby *turned* the box *upside down*.
◆彼は書類を捜して事務所中をひっくり返した He *ransacked* the office for the papers.

びっくりかえる 引っ繰り返る (横転する) overturn ⓐ, upset* ⓑ; (上下が逆になる) turn upside down; (倒れる) fall* ⓐ; (逆転する) be reversed ∥ボートはあっという間にひっくり返った The boat *overturned* very quickly. / その男の子はつまずいてひっくり返った The little boy stumbled and *fell* (*down*). / 形勢は完全にひっくり返った The situation *was* completely *reversed*.

ひっくるめる 引っ括める include ⓑ ∥費用は税金をひっくるめて総額200万円になる The expenses amount to two million yen *including* tax. ◆全部ひっくるめていくらになりますか How much does it cost *all together*?

ひづけ 日付 date ◎ ∥領収書の日付はいつになっていますか What's *the date* of the receipt? / このカメラは写真に日付を入れられる This

camera can put *a date* on photos.
◆この小切手は6月23日の日付だ This check *is dated* June 23.
∥日付印 a date stamp / 日付変更線 the (International) Date Line

ひっけい 必携 高校生必携の本 a book *indispensable for* high school students / 運転免許証必携のこと *Remember [Don't forget] to carry* your driver's license. / ジャズが好きならこのCDは必携だ This CD is *a must* if you like jazz.

ピッケル ⚠ ice ax(e) ◉ (❖日本語はドイツ語の Pickel から)

ひっこし 引っ越し move, removal ◎ ∥新居への引っ越し *a move* to a new house
◆喜んで引っ越しの手伝いをします I'm perfectly [quite] willing to help you *move*. / 引っ越し先の住所を教えて Give me *your new address*.
∥引っ越し業者 a moving company

ひっこす 引っ越す move ◉, remove ◉ ∥岡山から名古屋に引っ越す *move* from Okayama to Nagoya / 郊外に引っ越す *moved [into]* the suburbs / いつ新居に引っ越すのですか When *are* you *moving to [into]* your new house?

ひっこみ 引っ込み 慣用表現 いまさら引っ込みがつかない I've come *too far to back out*. / 彼女はとても引っ込み思案だ She *is* very *shy*.

ひっこむ 引っ込む ❶【退く】 retire ◉, withdraw* ◉ ∥いなかへ引っ込む *retire [draw back] into* the country / 彼は夕食がすむと部屋に引っ込んだ After dinner, he *withdrew into* his room.
◆おまえは引っ込んでいろ(→おまえには関係ない) *None of your business*. / *Mind your own business*.
❷【奥にある】 彼女の家は通りから引っ込んでいる Her house *stands back from* the street.

ひっこめる 引っ込める ❶【引っ込ませる】 withdraw* ◉, draw* [take*, pull] in ∥首を引っ込める *pull in one's* head / 彼女はなべからすぐに手を引っ込めた She quickly *withdrew* her hand from the pan.
❷【撤回する】 withdraw* ◉ ∥彼らは要求を引っ込めた They *withdrew* their demands.

ピッコロ〔音楽〕piccolo ∥ピッコロを吹く play *the piccolo*

ひっさつ 必殺 必殺のパンチ *a deadly* punch

ひっし¹ 必死 ──必死の desperate ──必死に desperately, in desperation ∥必死に戦う fight *desperately*; fight *tooth and nail* / 彼は成功しようと必死の努力をした He made *desperate* efforts to succeed.

ひっし² 必至 ──必至の(避けることができない) inevitable, unavoidable; (必然的な) sure ∥その2国間の対立は必至だ A conflict between the two nations is *inevitable [unavoidable]*.

ひつじ¹ 羊 sheep ◎ (複~s); (雄の) ram ◎; (雌の) ewe [jú:]◎; (子羊) lamb [lǽm]◎ ∥羊の群れ a flock [herd] of *sheep*
◆羊の毛皮 (a) *sheepskin*

∥羊飼い a shepherd; (女性の) a shepherdess / 羊肉 mutton; (子羊の) lamb

ひつじ² 未 (十二支の第8番目) the Sheep
⇨えと

ひっしゃ 筆者 writer ◎, author ◎

ひっしゅう 必修 ──必修の (米) required, compulsory ∥数学は1年生の必修だ Mathematics is 「*required of [compulsory for]* the first-year students.
∥必修科目 a required [compulsory] subject

ひつじゅひん 必需品 necessity ◎ (❖necessaries よりも必要性が強い), necessaries,《口語的》a must ∥生活必需品 *the necessities* of life

ひっしょう 必勝 僕たちは必勝を期して試合に臨んだ We faced in the game, *firmly expecting to win*.

びっしょり 汗びっしょりのシャツ a shirt *saturated with sweat* / 雨でびっしょりぬれた I *was soaked to the skin* in the rain.

びっしり closely, densely ∥甲子園球場には観客がびっしり入っていた The Koshien Stadium was *closely [densely]* packed with spectators.
◆きょうは予定がびっしり詰まっている I *have a heavy schedule* today. / My schedule *is very tight* today.

ひっす 必須 ──必須の essential, indispensable ∥この仕事には英語の知識が必須だ A knowledge of English is *essential for* this job.
∥必須科目 a required [compulsory] subject / 必須条件 an indispensable [essential] condition, a precondition

ひっせき 筆跡 handwriting ◎ ∥読みやすい[読みにくい]筆跡 readable [unreadable] *handwriting* / これは彼の筆跡ではない This is not his *handwriting*.
∥筆跡鑑定 handwriting analysis [identification]

ひつぜつ 筆舌 その女優の美しさは筆舌に尽くしがたい The actress is beautiful *beyond description [expression]*.

ひつぜん 必然 necessity ◎ ◎, inevitability ◎ ──必然の necessary, inevitable; (論理上) logical ──必然的に necessarily, inevitably; logically ∥必然の結果 *a necessary* consequence / 戦争は必然的に不幸をもたらす War *inevitably* brings misery.

ひっそり その部屋はひっそりしていた The room was *quiet*. / 通りはひっそりしていた The streets were *deserted*. / 老夫婦はひっそりと暮らしている The elderly couple live *quietly* in *obscurity*.

ひったくり (行為) snatch ◎; (人) snatcher ◎

ひったくる snatch ◉ ∥私はかばんをひったくられた I *had* my bag *snatched*. / その男は彼女のハンドバッグをひったくって逃げた The man *snatched* her purse and ran away.

ぴったり
❶【密着して】 tightly, close(ly)
ドアをぴったりと閉じる close the door *tight-*

ly / 彼女の猫は彼女にぴったりくっついた Her cat stuck *close* to her. / 高橋は先頭集団にぴったりついて走っている Takahashi is running *close behind* the leading group. / ◆体にぴったりのドレス a *tight-fitting* dress
❷【正確に】exactly, correctly / 彼の予想はぴったり的中した He guessed *exactly* [*correctly*]. / 彼は7時ぴったりに出かけた He went out *just* [*exactly*] at seven. / He went out at seven o'clock *sharp*.
❸【適当な】/ このワンピースは私にぴったりだ (→サイズが合う) This dress *fits* me *perfectly*. / 彼女は彼にぴったりだ She *is a perfect match for* him.

ひつだん 筆談 ——筆談する communicate in [by] writing

ひっち 筆致 (書画の) touch ⓒ, brushwork ⓤ; (文体) style ⓒ ‖ くだけた筆致 a familiar *style*

ピッチ ⚠
❶【速度・ペース】(速度) speed ⓤ; (ペース) pace ⓒ (◆英語のpitchは「投球」「(声・音などの)調子」などの意味) / 急ピッチで at *a fast pace* [*speed*] / 私たちは仕事のピッチを上げた We *quickened* the *pace* of our work. / We *speeded up* our work.
❷【サッカーの競技場】field ⓒ, 《英》pitch ⓒ

ヒッチハイク hitchhiking ⓤ ——ヒッチハイクする hitchhike ⓘ ‖ 彼は青森までヒッチハイクした He *hitchhiked* to Aomori.

ピッチャー ❶【野球】pitcher ⓒ ‖ 左ピッチャー a left-handed pitcher; 《米》a *southpaw* (*pitcher*) / リリーフピッチャー a relief *pitcher* / 先発ピッチャー a *starting pitcher; a starter*
‖ピッチャー返し a comebacker / ピッチャーゴロ[フライ] a grounder [fly] to the pitcher / ピッチャープレート the pitcher's rubber [plate]
❷【水差し】pitcher ⓒ

ひっちゃく 必着 申込書は6月27日必着のこと Applications *must reach* us by June 27.

ピッチング pitching ⓤ ◆彼はいいピッチングをした He *pitched* a good game.
‖ピッチングマシーン a pitching machine

ピッツバーグ Pittsburgh (◆米国の都市)

ひってき 匹敵 ——匹敵する (同等である) be equal to …; (互角である) be a match for … ‖ 岩手県の面積は四国地方に匹敵する Iwate Prefecture *is equal to* the Shikoku district in area [size].
◆この分野で彼に匹敵する者はいない No one *equals* him in this field. / He *has no equal* in this field.

ヒット ❶【野球】(base) hit ⓒ; (単打) single (hit) ⓒ ——ヒットを打つ get* [make*] a hit, hit* ⓘ ‖ レフト前ヒット a hit to left / 相手チームをヒット4本に抑える limit the opposing team to four *hits*
❷【大当たり】hit ⓒ; (成功) success ⓤ ——ヒットする be a hit, catch* on ‖ その曲は大ヒットした The song was *a big* [*great*] *hit*. / このテーマソングはヒットし始めている This theme song is beginning to *catch on*.
◆ヒットチャートの1位になる top *the charts*
‖ヒット曲 a hit song / タイムリーヒット an RBI ⇨ タイムリー / ポテンヒット a blooper, a dying quail

ビット 《コンピュータ》bit ⓒ ‖ 64ビットのコンピュータ a 64-*bit* computer

ひっとう 筆頭 彼の名前が筆頭に挙がっている His name *is at the top of the list*. / His name *heads the list*.
‖筆頭株主 the largest stockholder

ヒットエンドラン 監督はヒットエンドランのサインを送った The manager gave the signal for *a hit-and-run play*.

ひつどく 必読 この本はSFファンなら必読だ This book *is a must* for a science-fiction fan. / Every science-fiction fan *must read* this book.
‖必読書 a must book

ひっぱく 逼迫 金融市場はひっ迫している The money market *is getting tight*. / その国の財政はひっ迫している The country *is financially depressed*. / The finances of the country *are very tight*.

ひっぱたく slap ⓘ; (罰として) smack ⓘ
◆そいつを思いっきりひっぱたいてやればよかったのに You should *have* [*smacked him hard* [*given him a hard smack*].

ひっぱりこむ 引っ張り込む 君たちの争いに引っぱり込まないでくれ Don't *drag* me *into* your quarrel.

ひっぱりだこ 引っ張り凧 彼は各地の講演に (→講演者として) 引っぱりだこである He is「*in great demand* [*very popular*] in various places as a lecturer.

ひっぱりだす 引っ張り出す 彼女は押し入れからスーツケースを引っぱり出した She *dragged* her suitcase *out of* the closet. / 彼は市長選に引っぱり出された (→説き伏せられて立候補した) He *was persuaded to* run for mayor.

ひっぱる 引っ張る
❶【引く】pull ⓘ; (強く引く) tug ⓘ; (引きずる) drag ⓘ ⇨ ひく (引く)
だれかが私のそでを引っぱった Someone *pulled* at my sleeve.
子供は母親の手を引っぱった The child *pulled* his mother *by* the hand.
私はそのひもを引っぱった I *pulled* [*tugged*] the cord. / I *gave a pull* [*tug*] *on* [*at*] the cord.
◆彼は私を部屋の隅に引っぱっていった He *took* me into the corner of the room. / 修理工場まで車を引っぱっていってもらった I had my car *towed* to the garage.
❷【連行する】
彼はきのう警察に引っぱられた He *was taken* to the police station yesterday.

ヒッピー hippie

ヒップ hips (◆英語のhipはウエストより下の張

り出した部分の片方を指し，日本語の「腰」に当たる)；（しり）buttocks,《口語的》bottom [C] // このスカートはヒップがちょっときつい This skirt is a little tight around *the hips*.

ひづめ 蹄 hoof [C]

ひつめい 筆名 pen name [C]

ひつよう 必要

necessity [U], need [U] ―必要な necessary;（絶対必要な）essential;（不可欠な）indispensable ―必要とする need [他],《公式的》require [他]

[語法]
「…することが必要である」は文意に応じて must, have to, should, ought to, need などの助動詞を用いて表すこともある．助動詞 need は否定文・疑問文・条件文で用いられ，肯定文では《他動詞 need＋不定詞》を用いる // あなたがここに来る必要はない You don't need to come here. / You needn't come here.

[英作文ノート] **necessary の主語は？**
私は老いた両親の面倒を見る必要がある
→×*I'm necessary* to take care of my old parents.
→○*It is necessary* for me to take care of my old parents.
★necessary の主語は「人」ではなく「物事」．I を主語にするならば I have to take care of ... のようにいえばよい．

水はすべての生き物に必要である Water *is* 「*necessary* for [*indispensable* to] all living things.

あなたには休養が必要だ You *need* some rest. / You *are in need of* some rest.

その問題を解くのにあと数分必要だ I *need* a few more minutes to solve the problem.

その仕事には忍耐力が必要だ The job *requires* a lot of patience.

そのピアノは調律が必要だ The piano *needs* tuning. / The piano *needs* to be tuned.（❖need *doing* は need to be *done*「…される必要がある」の意味）

もう一度テストを受ける必要がありますか Is there any *necessity* [*need*] to take another test?

彼がそこに行く必要はない *He* 「*need not* [*doesn't have to*] go there. / *There is no need* for him to go there.

地球の環境問題に取り組むことが絶対必要だ It *is essential* that we (should) address global environmental problems. / It *is essential* for us to address global environmental problems.

彼女は必要以上に物を欲しがる She wants *more than is necessary*.

彼は必要に迫られて土地を手放した He gave up his land *from* [*out of*] *necessity*.

父親たちの多くが子供たちとより多くの時間をいっしょに過ごす必要性を感じている Most fathers *feel the necessity* of spending more time with their children.

急ぐ必要はない *There's no* (*need to*) *hurry*.

◆電池を換える必要がある The battery *should* be changed.

‖必要悪 a necessary evil / 必要経費 necessary expenses / 必要条件 a necessary condition

[ことわざ] 必要は発明の母 Necessity is the mother of invention.

ビデ bidet [bidéi] [C]

ひてい 否定 denial [U][C] ―否定する deny [他] ―否定的な negative

否定的な返答 a *negative* answer

その訴えは否定的な反応を引き起こした The appeal drew a *negative* response.

その女優は離婚のうわさを否定した The actress *denied* the rumor of a divorce.

彼はその前の夜彼女と会ったことを否定した He *denied* that he had met her the previous night.

その事実を否定することはできない *There is no denying* [*You can't deny*] the fact.

◆彼らは状況を否定的に見ている They look *negatively* at the situation.

‖否定語(句)〔文法〕a negative / 否定文 a negative sentence / 二重否定〔文法〕a double negative

びていこつ 尾てい骨〔解剖〕the coccyx [káksiks] [C]（複～es, coccyges)

ビデオ video [U][C];（ビデオテープ）videotape [C][U] //ビデオを再生[ダビング]する *play* [*dub, copy*] *a video*(*tape*) / そのシーンまでビデオを巻き戻す[早送りする] *rewind* [*fast-forward*] *the videotape* to that scene / 映画のビデオを見る *watch a* movie *video* / 番組をビデオに撮る *make* [*record*] *a video* of a program; *record* a program *on video* / その映画はビデオで見たことがある I have *watched* the film *on video*. / その映画はビデオになっていますか Is the film *on video*? / 私はそのコンサートのビデオを借りた I *rented the video* of the concert. ◆運動会の様子をビデオに撮ろうよ Let's *videotape* the sports day.

‖ビデオカセット a videocassette / ビデオカセットレコーダー a videocassette recorder (《略語》VCR) / ビデオカメラ a video camera / ビデオクリップ a video clip / ビデオゲーム a video game / ビデオショップ a video shop;（レンタルの）a video rental shop / ビデオソフト a video / ビデオデッキ a video, a videocassette recorder

びてき 美的 esthetic //美的センス *an esthetic sense*; *a sense of beauty* / この建築は美的価値がある This building has *esthetic* value.

ひでり 日照り dry weather [U]; drought [dráut] [U][C]（❖drought は dry weather が続いた状態をいう）//去年は日照り続きで不作だった Owing to 「*the* long *drought* [the long spell of *dry weather*], the crops failed last year.

ひでん 秘伝 secret [C], special technique [C]

びてん 美点 (長所) merit◎ //慎み深さは彼女の最大の美点だ Modesty is her greatest *merit*.

ひでんか 妃殿下 Highness, Imperial [Royal] Highness //雅子妃殿下 (Her Highness) Princess Masako

ひと 人

❶【人間】 human being ◎, human ◎, man ◎; (人類) mankind ⓤ, the human race;〚生物〛Homo sapiens ——人の human

語法
従来は「人類・人間一般」を指して man または mankind が用いられてきたが、性差別を避けるため people や humans、または human beings を用いることが多くなってきている。

類人猿と人との最大の違いは後者は火を使うことである The greatest difference between apes and *human beings* is that the latter use fire.

人の歴史などまだ浅いものだ *Human history* is still young.

❷【個々の人物】 person ◎; (男性) man ◎ (複 men); (女性) woman ◎ (複 women); (だれか) someone, somebody; (人々) people

彼は正直な人だ He is *an* honest *man* [*person*].

鈴木という人があなたを訪ねてきましたよ *A man called Suzuki* [*A Mr. Suzuki*] came to see you.

彼女は決してうそをつくような人ではない She is *the* last *person* to tell a lie.

彼しかその任務を果たせる人はいない He is *the* only *person* who can accomplish the mission.

その秘密を知っている人がきっといるはずだ There must be *someone* who knows the secret.

中国語が分かる人はいますか Is there *anyone* who understands Chinese? (✦疑問文・否定文・条件節では someone, somebody の代わりに anyone, anybody を用いる)

彼のことを悪く言う人もいる *Some people* speak ill of him.

人は自分が苦しんで初めて他人の苦しみが分かるようになる *People* learn to appreciate the suffering of others only after having suffered themselves.

◆彼は九州の人(→出身)だ He is [comes] *from* Kyushu. / 彼女はこの町の人ではない(→この町には住んでいない) She doesn't live in this town. / (→どこかよそから来た) She came from some other place. / きのう市役所の人(→職員)が祖母を訪ねてきた *A city official* came to see my grandmother yesterday.

❸「あそこにいる人はだれですか」「あの人は私のおばです」 "Who is *that lady* over there?" "*It*'s my aunt."

❸「岡さんってどんな人？」「しっかりしていて頼りになる人だよ」 "What's Ms. Oka like?" "She is *a* steady, reliable *woman*."

❸「今度の土曜日、映画に行かない？」「ごめん、午後に人と会う約束があるの」 "Shall we go to a movie this Saturday?" "Sorry, I've got *an appointment* in the afternoon."

❸【他人】 (ほかの人たち) other people, others; (世間一般の人々) people

彼は人の言うことなど気にしない He doesn't care what *other people* say.

彼女は人の目(→他人が自分をどう思うか)ばかり気にしている She is always anxious about *what other people think* of her.

人に頼ってばかりいないで自分でやりなさい Stop depending on *others* and do it yourself.

人が言うには彼は刑務所に入ったことがあるそうだ *People say that* he was once in prison.

人と比べて自分がかなり楽観的だとは思いませんか Don't you find yourself much more optimistic *than others*?

あいつは人を人とも思わないやつだ That guy *doesn't care a fig about other people's feelings*.

◆私は人に知られずにパーティーを抜け出した I left the party *without being noticed* (*by anyone*).

❹【自分・私】

人を何だと思っているの What do you think *I* am?

人をからかわないでください Stop teasing *me*, please.

❺【人柄】 personality ◎ⓤ, character ◎ⓤ

彼は人がいい He *has a good personality.* / He *is a good-natured person.*

◆彼女はすっかり人が変わってしまった She *has changed* completely. / She *has become a* completely *different person.* / 君は人を見る目がない[ある] You *are no* [*a good*] *judge of others*.

❻【労働力】 worker ◎, hand ◎

我々は人が足りなくて困っている We are suffering from a shortage of *workers*.

◆この仕事に向かいい人(→適任者)を知りませんか Could you think of *someone fit for this job*?

慣用表現 人の気も知らないで勝手なことを言うな Don't just say whatever you want *without considering my feelings.* / 人のふりみてわがふり直せ *Learn wisdom by the follies of others.* / 人は見かけによらないものだ *You shouldn't judge people by their appearance.* / 人を食った(→傲慢(ごうまん)な)態度 an *insolent* [*a haughty*] attitude

ひとあし 一足 彼は私たちより一足先に(→少し前に)帰った He left *a little before* us. / 一足違いでバスに乗り遅れた I missed the bus *by a second.* / I *just* missed the bus.

ひとあじ 一味 このレストランの魚料理はひと味違う *There's something different* about this restaurant's seafood.

ひとあたり 人当たり 長島さんは人当たりのいい人だ Mr. Nagashima is *an affable* [*a friendly*] *person*.

ひとあめ 一雨 ひと雨来そうだ *It looks like rain.* / (→にわか雨がありそうだ) *It is going to*

shower. / 朝のうちにひと雨あった *We had a rainfall* in the morning.

ひとあわ 一泡 やつらにひと泡吹かせてやる(→思いもつかないようなことをしてやる) I'm going to *show* them *something they never expected.*

ひどい 酷い

❶【むごい】(残酷な) cruel, harsh; (卑劣な) mean; (つらい) hard, bitter

彼女が謝っているのに無視するとはあなたもひどい人だ It is *cruel* of you to ignore her apologies.

彼は私にひどい言葉を浴びせた He flung *harsh words* at me.

彼女をだますなんて彼はひどい It is *mean* of him to deceive her.

きのうはひどい目にあった I *had a hard time* yesterday.

◆彼にあんなひどいことをしたのを後悔している I'm sorry for *having treated* him so *badly.* / 僕をばかにするとひどい目にあわせるぞ *I'll teach you* to make a fool of me.

❷【激しい】violent, severe; (はなはだしい) intense, terrible, bad

ひどい雨 a *violent* [*heavy*] rain / ひどい事故 a *terrible* accident

左脚にひどい痛みを感じた I felt a *severe* [an *intense*, an *acute*] pain in my left foot.

ひどいかぜで彼は一日中寝込んでいた He stayed in bed all day because of a *bad* cold.

このひどい騒音にはもう耐えられない I can't bear this *terrible* noise any more.

彼女のけがはひどかった Her injury was very *serious.* / She was *seriously* [*badly*] injured.

❸【悪い】bad, awful; (へたな) poor

彼らの労働条件は劣悪だが我々の場合はもっとひどい Their working conditions are terrible, but ours are *worse*.

彼女のフランス語は本当にひどい(→へただ) Her French is so *poor.* / She speaks French so *poorly.*

◆ひどいにおい a *horrible* [*nasty*] smell / なんてひどい天気だ What *terrible* [*awful, nasty*] weather! / ひどい格好だな,君は You *look like a mess.*

ひといき 一息 (ひと呼吸) a [one] breath; (ひと休み) a rest, a break / 彼はその話をひと息にしゃべった He told the story *in one breath.* / ひと息入れよう Let's *take* [*have*] *a rest* [*break*]. / ビールをひと息に飲み干す *swallow* a glass of beer *in a gulp* / それを聞いてほっとひと息ついた(→安堵(ﾄﾞ)した) I *felt relieved* to hear that. / もうひと息で終わりだ *Just one more start* [*push*] and the work will be done.

ひといきれ 人いきれ 部屋は人いきれでむっとしていた(→込み合って蒸し暑かった) The room was *crowded and stuffy*.

ひといちばい 人一倍 彼は人一倍(→ほかの人よりずっと)よく働く He works *much harder than others.* / 母は人一倍(→非常に)頑固だ My mother is *extremely* stubborn.

びとう 尾灯 (自動車などの) taillight ◯

びどう 微動 ジープはいくら押しても微動だにしなかった The jeep *didn't move* [*budge*] *an inch* no matter how hard we pushed it.

ひとえ 一重 彼女は一重まぶただ She has *single*(*-edged*) *eyelids.* / 天才と狂人は紙一重だ Genius is *only once removed from* insanity.

ひとえに (全く) entirely,《文章》solely; (ひたすらに) earnestly / 私が今あるのはひとえにあなたのおかげです I owe *entirely* to you what I am today.

ひとおし 一押し a [one] push / ドアはひと押しであいた The door opened *with one push.* / 軽くひと押ししてやれば彼女は決意するだろう If you *give* her *a gentle push*, she will be determined.

ひとおもいに 一思いに いっそひと思いに死んでしまいたいと思った I wanted to kill myself *once and for all.*

ひとがき 人垣 私は首を伸ばして人垣の向こうを見た I craned my neck to see over *the crowd.* / 通りには人垣ができていた The street *was lined with people.*

ひとかげ 人影 figure ◯ / 彼女は暗やみの中に人影を見ておびえた She was frightened to see *a figure* in the dark.

◆夜の公園には全く人影がなかった *Not a soul was to be seen* in the park at night. / The park *was* completely *deserted* at night. / 通りには人影もまばらだった There were only *a few people* on the street.

ひとかたならぬ 一方ならぬ ひとかたならぬお世話になりありがとうございました Thank you very much for all your kindness. / 彼にはひとかたならぬ世話になった(→恩を受けている) I'*m greatly indebted to* him.

ひとかど 彼は自分をひとかどの人物(→重要人物)だと思っている He thinks he is *someone* [*somebody, something*].

ひとがら 人柄 personality ◯◯, character ◯◯ / 彼の温かい人柄は人々の心を引きつける His warm *personality* attracts people. / この手紙には彼女の人柄が出ている Her *personality* shows in this letter.

ひとかわ 一皮 夏の間のトレーニングで彼はひと皮むけた感じだ He seems to *have made great improvements* due to his summer training.

ひとぎき 人聞き 人聞きの悪いことを言わないでくれ Don't say such a *scandalous* thing about me.

ひときれ 一切れ a piece; (薄切りの) a slice / 1切れの肉 *a piece of* meat

ひときわ 一際 (目立って) remarkably; (いちだんと) much, still (❖比較級を強める) / その試合で彼のプレーはひときわすばらしかった He played *remarkably* well in the game. / 彼女はそのドレスを着るとひときわ美しく見える She looks *much* [*still*] *more beautiful* in that dress.

ひどく (非常に) very, terribly, extremely,

びとく 美徳 《口語的》badly, 《口語的》awfully; (激しく) hard, severely ∥ひどく疲れた I'm *very [terribly]* tired. / この薬はひどく苦い This medicine tastes *extremely* bitter. / 彼女は携帯電話をひどく欲しがっている She wants a mobile [cellular] phone *badly.* / 雨がひどくなってきた The rain has become *harder.* / 彼は父親にひどくしかられた He was *severely* scolded by his father. ◆かぜがひどくなった My cold has got *worse.*

びとく 美徳 virtue ⓤⓒ ∥人の話を辛抱強く聞いてやるのはすばらしい美徳である Listening to others patiently is *a fine virtue.*

ひとくせ 一癖 ∥彼は一癖も二癖もある人だ He has some *peculiarities* in his character.

ひとくち 一口 ❶【飲食物のひと口】a mouthful; (ひとかじり) a bite; (液体の) a sip ∥少女はアップルパイをひと口食べた The girl took [had] *a bite* of the apple pie. / 満腹でもうひと口も食べられない I'm so full I can't eat another *mouthful.* / このジュースをひと口飲んでみなさい Try *a sip* of this juice. / 犬はその肉をひと口で食べてしまった The dog ate the piece of meat *in a bite.* ◆私がシチューをひと口味見した I had [took] *a taste* of the stew.

🅔「ひと口ちょうだい」「いいよ, ほら」 Can I take *a bite*?" "Sure. Here you are."

❷【ひと言】a word ∥一口に言うと彼は要領がいい *In a word [In short],* he is clever.

◆一口に辞書といってもいろいろある *There are all sorts* of dictionaries.

❸【単位・割り当て】a share ∥我々の計画に一口乗りませんか Won't you *take a share in* our project?

ひとけ 人気 人けのない通り a *deserted* street / 家の中には人けがなかった There were *no signs of life* in the house.

ひどけい 日時計 sundial ⓒ

ひとけた 一桁 1けたの数 *single* figures / 計算を1けた間違える miscalculate *by a digit*

ヒトゲノム human genome

ひとごこち 人心地 ∥コーヒーを1杯飲んで人心地ついた(→気分がよくなった) I *felt refreshed* after a cup of coffee.

ひとこと 一言 a (single) word ∥母は英語はひと言も話せない My mother can't speak 「*a single word* of English [English *at all*]. / このことについてはひと言も触れるな Don't say *a word* about this. / ひと言お礼を言わせてください Let me say *a word* of thanks. / ひと言で言うと彼女は自信過剰なのだ In 「*a word [short],* she is overconfident. / 彼はいつもひと言多い He always *says one word too many.*

◆あなたにひと言言いたいことがある I *have something to say to* you. / この件についてひと言(→意見を)お願いします Let me have *your comments* on this matter. / 彼が結婚したなんてひと言も言わなかったじゃない You didn't mention *anything* about his marriage! / 君が間違っているなんてひと言も言った覚えはない I have never meant that you are wrong.

ひとごと 人事・他人事 ∥彼はまるでひと事のような(→それと無関係であるような)顔をしていた He looked *as if he had nothing to do with it.* / その事故はひと事とは思えなかった I felt *as if the accident were my own affair.* / ひと事ではない(→あなたにも起こるかもしれない) *It may happen to you.*

ひとこま 一齣 (一場面) scene ⓒ; (フィルムの) frame ⓒ ∥このエッセーで彼女は日常生活のひとこまをユーモラスに描いている In this essay, she humorously describes *one scene* of her daily life. / それはまるで映画のひとこまのようだった It was like *a scene from a movie.*

ひとごみ 人込み crowd ⓒ ∥人込みを押し分けて進む push *one's way through the crowd* / 人込みを抜け出す work *one's way out of the crowd* / 人込みを避けるために裏通りを歩いた We walked down the back street to avoid *the crowds.* / その男は人込みに紛れていなくなった The man 「*disappeared into* [*was lost in*] *the crowd.*

ひところ 一頃 (かつて) once; (一時期) at one time; (以前) formerly ∥彼はひところ次期社長といわれていた He 「*was once [used to be*] talked of as the next president.

ひとごろし 人殺し murder ⓤⓒ; (殺人者) murderer ⓒ ∥人殺しをする commit *murder* / 彼女は「人殺し!」と叫んだ She cried "*Murderer!*"

ひとさしゆび 人差し指 one's forefinger, one's index finger

ひとざと 人里 ∥彼は人里離れた所に住んでいる He lives in a place *far [remote] from any town or village.*

ひとさらい 人攫い, kidnapping ⓤⓒ; (誘拐犯) kidnapper ⓒ

ひとさわがせ 人騒がせ 人騒がせな人 *a scaremonger* / 人騒がせなことを言うな Don't *cry wolf.* 🔹cry wolf は「うそを言って人を騒がせる」の意味

ひとしい 等しい (数量・程度・価値などが) equal, equivalent; (同一の) the same ∥1インチは2.54センチに等しい One inch *is equal [equivalent] to* 2.54 centimeters. / 正三角形の3つの辺は長さが等しい The three sides of a regular triangle *are* 「*equal in* length [*the same length*].

◆君のしたことは犯罪に等しい What you did *amounts to a crime.* / 交渉の効果はないに等しかった The negotiations *produced virtually no effect.*

ひとしお (それだけに一っそう) all the more; (特に) especially ∥多くの失敗の後での成功は喜びもひとしおだった The success was 「*all the more* [*especially*] pleasing after so many failures.

ひとしきり (しばらくの間) for a while, for some time ∥彼女は私にひとしきり夫のぐちを言った She complained to me about her husband *for a while.* / (→延々と) She *kept on* complaining to me about her husband.

ひとしく 等しく（平等に）equally;（また）too, also ∥お金は彼らに等しく分配された The money was divided *equally* among them.

ひとじち 人質 hostage ∥人質をとる *take* [*hold*] *a hostage* / 人質を解放する *liberate* [*release*] *a hostage* / 男は支店長を人質にとった The man *took* [*held*] the manager (*as a*) *hostage*.

ひとしれず 人知れず secretly, in secret;（内心）inwardly ∥彼らは人知れずその計画を進めていた They were *secretly* going ahead with the plan.

ひとしれぬ 人知れぬ unknown;（内心の）inward ∥彼は人知れぬ努力を続けてきた He has made constant efforts *unknown to others*.

ひとずき 人好き 人好きのする人 an *attractive* [a *likable*, a *pleasant*] *person*

ひとすじ 一筋 ❶【線】（煙・光などの）a thread;（光線）a ray;（細い流れ）a trickle ∥一筋の煙 *a thread of* smoke / 一筋の陽光が雲の間からさした *A ray of* sunlight pierced through the clouds. / 一筋の血が彼の額を伝った *A trickle of* blood ran down his forehead.
❷【いちず】彼は30年間カメの研究ひとすじだ He *has been devoted to* studying turtles for 30 years. / 父は仕事ひとすじに生きた My father *devoted his life to his work*. /（→仕事のためだけに生きた）My father *lived only for his work*.

ひとすじなわ 一筋縄 彼は一筋縄ではいかない男だ（→扱いにくい）He is *hard to deal with*. /（→手強い）He is *a tough customer*.

ひとそろい 一揃い set ◎, suite ◎ ∥新しい家具ひとそろい *a suite* [*set*] *of* new furniture / 母は食器ひとそろいをプレゼントしてくれた My mother gave me *a set of* tableware.

ひとだかり 人集り a crowd (of people) ∥黒山の人だかり *a large crowd*(*s*) *of people* / 彼の周囲には人だかりができていた There was *a crowd of people* around him.

ひとだすけ 人助け I think it will「*help others* [*be a help to others*]. / 人助けだと思って彼女といっしょに行ってやってくれ（→彼女といっしょに行ってくれれば私は助かる）It will save me *a lot of trouble* if you go with her.

ひとたび 一度 once ⇒いったん（一旦）

ひとたまりもない うちのチームは昨年の優勝チームの前にはひとたまりもなかった（→簡単に負けた）Our team *was easily beaten* by the last year's championship team. /（→相手にならなかった）Our team *was no match for* the last year's championship team. / その小さい家は竜巻にあってひとたまりもなく（→という間に）ばらばらになった The tornado completely destroyed the small house *in a moment*.

ひとちがい 人違い
●「失礼ですが城さんですか」「違います」「すみません、人違いでした」"Excuse me, but are you Mr. Jo?" "No, I'm not." "I'm sorry. *I took you for someone else*."
●「きのう渋谷で京子を見たよ」「人違いだよ（→別の人だったにちがいない）. 彼女は今週札幌だもの」"I saw Kyoko in Shibuya yesterday." "*It must have been a different person*. She is in Sapporo this week."

ひとつ 一つ

❶【1個・1単位】one ──1つの one, a, an;（たった一つの）single, only
彼女は私にリンゴを1つくれた She gave me *an* apple.（❖「1」という数を強調する場合以外は a [an] を用いるのがふつう）
すみません、コーヒー1つください. *One* coffee, please.
彼女は私より1つ（→1歳）年上だ She is *one year* older than me [I].
箱の中にはキャンディーが1つしか残っていなかった There was *only one* candy left in the box.
姉が旅行のおみやげを2つ買ってきてくれた. 1つはおせんべいで、もう1つはキーホルダーだった My sister gave me two presents she bought during her trip. *One* was *sembei* packed in a bag, *the other* was a key ring.
彼はそのレモンの中の一つを取った He took *one of* those lemons.
彼のただ一つの夢は大リーグ選手になることだった His *one and only* dream was to become a major league player.
この本が読者を引きつけるのは、一つにはストーリーの展開が速いからだ This book attracts readers. *For one thing*, the story line evolves rapidly.
◆サンドイッチをもう1つもらえますか Can I have *another* sandwich?
●「このオレンジはいくらですか」「1つ100円です」"How much are these oranges?" "They're 100 yen *each*."
⇒ひとつも

❷【同じ】── 一つの the same
一つ屋根の下に住む live「*under the same roof* [*in the same house*]
◆心を一つにして（→団結して）困難に打ち勝つ *be united as one* to get over difficulties /（→協力して）get over difficulties *through close cooperation*

❸【さえも】even
彼は足し算ひとつまともにできない He can't *even* add properly.
◆彼女はまばたきひとつせず、画面を見つめた She gazed at the screen *without a* blink. / 現場には足跡ひとつ残っていなかった Not *a single* footprint was left at the scene.

❹【ちょっと】
ひとつ私がやってみよう I'll *just* try it. / I'll have a try.
ひとつ彼に頼んでみるか Well [Now], I'll *just* ask him.

ひとつおきに 一つ置きに alternately ── 1つおきの every other, alternate ∥彼らは

ひとつおぼえ

いすに1つおきに腰かけた They sat on *every other* chair.

ひとつおぼえ 一つ覚え 慣用表現 ばかのひとつ覚え ⇒ばか

ひとづかい 人使い 私の上司は人使いが荒い My boss *works his people hard*./ My boss is *a slave driver*.

ひとつかみ 一摑み a handful ‖缶からひとつかみのピーナツを取り出す take *a handful of* peanuts out of the can ◆強盗は札束をひとつかみにして逃げた The robber *grabbed the wad of bills* and ran away.

ひとづきあい 人付き合い 彼は人づきあいがいい[悪い] He is *a sociable* [*an unsociable*] person./ He is *a good* [*bad*] *mixer*./ 彼女はほとんど人づきあいをしない(→ほとんど人に会わない) She meets very few people.

ひとっこひとり 一人っ子一人 通りには人っ子一人いなかった Not a figure [soul] was (to be) seen on the street./ The street was deserted.

ひとつずつ 一つずつ one by one, one at a time ‖彼は質問に1つずつ答えていった He answered the questions「*one by one* [*one at a time*]. ◆子供たちにリンゴを1つずつ与えた I gave the children *an apple each*./ I gave *an apple* to *each child*.

ひとづて 人伝で 彼がアメリカに行ったことを人づてに聞いた I heard it *secondhand* [I heard *the hearsay*] that he left for America./ I heard it *on the grapevine* that he left for America.

ひとっぱしり ⇒ひとはしり

ひとつひとつ 一つ一つ one by one ‖それらを一つ一つ数えた I counted them *one by one*.

◆私共の工場では製品の一つ一つが細心の注意を払って製造されています *Every single* product is made with great care in our factory.

ひとつぶ 一粒 (穀物・砂などの) a grain; (液体の) a drop ‖ひと粒の米もむだにできなかった We couldn't afford to lose even *a single grain* of rice.
‖一粒種 *one's only child*

ひとづま 人妻 (既婚女性) married woman ©

ひとつまみ 一つまみ a pinch ‖スープにひとつまみの塩を加える add *a pinch of* salt to the soup

ひとつも 一つも no, not a (single) (◆ not a ... is no ... よりも強い否定を表す) ‖映画館では空いている席はひとつもなかった There was *no* [*not a*] vacant seat in the movie theater.

ひとで¹ 人手 ❶【働き手】 worker ©; (助力) hand ©; (手助け) help ◎ ‖この計画には人手が必要です We need more *hands* for this project./ 私たちには人手が足りない We are short of *hands* [*help*]./ We are *short-handed*./ 彼は人手を借りずに(→独力で)ガレージを建てた He built the garage *by himself*.
❷【他人の所有】 彼の家は人手に渡った His house *passed into other hands*.

ひとで² 人出 (出席者・観客) turnout ©; (群衆) crowd © ‖そのイベントは人出が多かった[少なかった] There was *a good* [*poor*] *turnout* at the event./ 遊園地はたいへんな人出だった There was *a large crowd of people* in the amusement park./ The amusement park *was crowded with people*.

ひとで³ 海星 starfish © (複 ~s, ~es)

ひとでなし 人でなし (けだもののような人) animal ©, beast ©, brute ©; (冷血漢) cold-hearted fellow [beast] ©

ひととおり 一通り ――通りの (一般的な) general; (全部の) all ‖Eメールについては一通りのことは知っています I know about e-mail *in general*./ あなたがおっしゃっていた名所は一通り回りました I have visited *all* the sites you mentioned.

◆報告書に一通り(→ざっと)目を通す「*look over* [*run through*] the report / 今回の調査の目的について一通り(→簡単に)説明します I'll explain the purpose of this survey *briefly*./ I'll give a *brief* account of the purpose of this survey.

ひとどおり 人通り 人通りの多い通り a *busy* street / このあたりは夜は人通りが少ない *Few people pass* through here at night.

ひととき 一時 午後の静かなひととき a *quiet hour* in the afternoon / 彼はそこで楽しいひとときを過ごした He had a *good time* there.

ひととなり 人となり one's nature [personality] ⇒ひとがら

ひととび 一飛び 飛行機なら東京から沖縄までひと飛びだ It's just *a short flight* from Tokyo to Okinawa.

ひとなつっこい 人懐っこい (友好的な) friendly; (愛想のよい) affable, amiable ‖彼女の飼っている犬はとても人なつっこい The dog she has *is very friendly*./ 男の子は人なつっこい笑顔を見せた The boy gave me a *friendly* [*an amiable*] smile.

ひとなみ 人並み ――人並みの (平均的な) average; (ふつうの) ordinary; (満足できる) decent ‖人並みの暮らしがしたい I want to enjoy an *ordinary* standard of living./ 中学時代は人並みの成績だった My grades were about *average* when I was a junior high school student.

◆人並みにかぜをひいた I've caught a cold *like everyone else*./ 彼は人並み以上に努力した He worked harder *than others*./ 彼女は人並みはずれた才能の持ち主だ She is *extraordinarily* talented.

ひとにぎり 一握り a handful ‖ひと握りの砂 *a handful of* sand / このパーティーに参加できるのはほんのひと握りの人たちだ Only *a handful of* people are able to attend the party.

ひとねむり 一眠り (うたた寝) nap ©; (短い眠り) short sleep © ‖夕ごはんができるまでひと眠りした I took [had] *a nap* until dinner was ready.

ひとはしり 一走り ひと走り行って取ってくる *run* and fetch it / 酒屋までひと走り行ってき

てくれる？ Can you *run* to the the liquor store?

ひとはた 一旗 彼は一旗揚げようと都会に出ていった He went to the city to *make a name for himself*.

ひとはだぬぐ 一肌脱ぐ 彼女のために一肌脱ぐ（→手を貸す）つもりだ I'll *lend* her *a helping hand*.

ひとばん 一晩 night ◯ ∥私たちは彼女の家に1晩泊まった We stayed *overnight* at her house. ∥ 一晩考えさせてください *Let me sleep on it*. ∥ 雨は一晩中降り続いた It continued to rain *all night*.

ひとびと 人々 people ⇒ ひと ∥多くの人々がそのテレビ番組を見た A lot of *people* watched the TV program.

ひとひねり 一捻り 将棋ではあいつなんかひとひねりだ I *can beat* him *easily* at shogi.

ひとまえ 人前 彼は人前で話すのに慣れている He is accustomed to speaking *in public*. ∥ 人前でそんな大声を出すもんじゃない Don't speak so loudly *in front of other people*. ∥ 人前に出るといつもあがってしまう I am always nervous *in company*. ∥ 彼は人前に出たがらない（→社交的ではない）He *is not sociable* [*is unsociable*].

ひとまかせ 人任せ 彼は何でも人まかせだ He leaves everything *to others*.

ひとまず 一先ず (まず第一に) first (of all); (しばらく) for a while, for a [some] time; (差し当たり) for the time being, for the present ∥ひとまずやってみましょう Let's try it *first*. ∥ 彼らはひとまず引き上げることにした They decided to return「*for the time being* [*for the present*].

ひとまとめ 一纏め 荷物をひとまとめにしておいてください Please get your baggage *together*. ∥ 母は古新聞をひとまとめにしてごみ置き場に持っていった My mother carried the old newspapers *in a bundle* to the garbage dump.

ひとまね 人真似 (物まね) mimicry ◯; (模倣) imitation ◯ ◆人まねばかりしていないで自分のやり方を考えなさい Don't *imitate others*. Come up with your own way.

ひとまわり 一回り (一周) round ◯; (大きさ) size ◯; (12年) twelve years ∥これより一回り大きいサイズのはありますか Do you have a skirt *a size larger* than this? ∥ 彼女には一回り年の違うお姉さんがいる She has a sister who is *twelve years* older than she.
◆私は公園を一回りした I *went around* the park. ∥ 彼は一回り大きくなって アメリカから帰ってきた He *had considerably matured* when he returned home from America.

ひとみ 瞳 pupil ◯; (目) eye ◯ ∥つぶらなひとみ lovely round *eyes*
◆私はひとみを凝らして部屋の中をのぞいた I *strained* to look into the room.

ひとみしり 人見知り 彼は人見知りする He *is shy* [*timid*] *with strangers*.

ひとむかし 一昔 (長い間) age ◯; (10年) decade ◯ ∥この歌がはやったのは一昔前のことだ It has been *ages* since this song was popular.

慣用表現 **十年ひと昔** ⇒ じゅうねん

ひとめ¹ 一目 (見ること) look ◯; (ちらりと見ること) glance ◯; (目撃) sight ◯ ∥ひとめ見てすべての状況が分かった I understood the whole situation *at a glance*. ∥ 彼女はひとめでその腕時計が気に入った She liked the watch *at first sight*. ∥ 彼は幹江にひとめぼれした He *fell in love with* Mikie *at first sight*.
◆彼女にひとめ（→少しの間だけでも）会いたい I wish I could see her *even only for a minute*. ∥ 丘からは町をひとめで見渡せる From the hill we can see the *whole* town.

ひとめ² 人目 (public) notice ◯, (public) attention ◯ ∥人目を避ける avoid *attention* [*notice*] ∥ 彼女の赤いワンピースは人目を引いた Her red dress「*attracted attention* [*was eye-catching*].
◆どうしてそんなに人目を気にするの Why do you worry so much about how *other people* see you? ∥ 彼らは人目につかないように裏から会場を出た They left the hall through the back door「*in secret* [*secretly*]. ∥ 彼女は人目をはばからず大泣きした She cried loudly *in public*.

ひとめぐり 一巡り a round ◆私たちは池をひと巡りした We *went around* the pond.

ひとやく 一役 彼はこの新企画に一役買っている He *plays a role* in this new plan.

ひとやすみ 一休み (休憩) a rest; (小休止) a break ∥もう3時だ. ひと休みしよう It's almost three. Let's take a *rest* [*break*].

ひとやま 一山 a pile, a stack; (ひと塊(*かたまり*)) a lot ∥リンゴひと山 *a stack of* apples ∥ このトマトひと山300円です These tomatoes are 300 yen *per lot*. (❖lot は per の後では無冠詞)

慣用表現 **一山当てる** *make a hit*

ひとり 一人・独り

❶【1人】one (person) ━━1人の one, a; (ただ一人の) only

娘が1人いますが息子はいません I have *a* daughter but no sons.

1人の男が順番を無視してタクシーを待つ列に割り込んできた *A* man broke into the taxi queue out of turn.

ピカソは世界で最も有名な画家の一人だ Picasso is *one of* the most famous painters in the world.

彼は彼女のただ一人の友人だ He is her *one and only* friend.

1人っ子一人見えなかった *Not a person* was to be seen.

彼は一人娘[息子]を甘やかした He indulged *his only daughter* [*son*]. (❖*one's* only daughter [*son*] は「娘[息子]が1人だけである」ことを表し、特に「ひとりっ子の娘[息子]」という意味にはならない)
◆あと1人来るだろう There will be *another* to come. ∥ それは私一人の責任です I'm *solely*

ひどり

responsible for it. / 彼女は子供たち一人一人にケーキを1切れずつ与えた She gave a piece of cake to *each of the children*. / ひとりでそこへ行くのは気が進まない I'm reluctant to go there *alone*. / 彼がそれをひとりでやったかどうかは疑わしいと思う I doubt if he did it *by himself*. / 頼むからひとりにしてくれ Just leave me *alone*. / 彼女には親戚(いんせき)がひとりもいない She *doesn't have any relatives*. / 彼女はひとりでいるのが好きではない She doesn't like to *be (all) on her own*. / 私が着いたとき、客は一人残らず帰ってしまっていた By the time I got there, *all* the guests had gone home. / その店での食事には1人あたり2,000円かかった The meal at the restaurant cost 2,000 yen *per person*.

● 「ご家族といっしょにお住まいですか」「いいえ、私はひとり暮らしです」 "Do you live with your family?" "No, I *live alone*."

❷ [独身] ─ひとりの single

● 「お姉さんは結婚しているの?」「いいえ、まだひとりです」 "Is your sister married?" "No, she's still *single*."

‖ひとり芝居 a one-man play / 1人部屋(ホテルなどの) a single room

ひどり 日取り the date / 次の会合の日取りは6月14日に決まった *The date* of the next meeting has been set for June 14.

ひとりあるき 独り歩き いとこの赤ちゃんはひとり歩きできるようになった My cousin's baby is now able to *walk by himself*. / 夜道のひとり歩きは危ないよ It's dangerous to *walk alone* at night. / 数字がひとり歩きをして,たくさんの人々を不安がらせている The figures *have taken on a life of their own* and are making many people worried.

ひとりがち 一人勝ち 昨夜のマージャンは彼のひとり勝ちだった He was *the sole winner* at mah-jong last night.

ひとりがてん 独り合点 彼女は先生の話もよく聞かずにひとり合点している She *is jumping to conclusions [is making a hasty decision]* without listening carefully to the teacher.

ひとりぐらし 一人暮らし・独り暮らし 兄は高校を卒業し,ひとり暮らしを始めた My brother started to *live alone [by himself]* after his graduation from high school.

ひとりごと 独り言 彼は授業中ひとり言を言っていた He *was talking [muttering] to himself* during the class.

ひとりじめ 独り占め ─ひとり占めする have* ... to *oneself*, monopolize / 彼は利益をひとり占めした He *had* the profit *all to himself*.

ひとりだち 独り立ち ─ひとり立ちする be [become]* independent, stand* on *one's* own feet / 子供はみんなひとり立ちした All my children *became independent*.

ひとりっこ 一人っ子 only child

ひとりでに 独りでに (自然に) by itself [themselves]; (自動的に) automatically / ドアがひとりでにあいたのでびっくりした I was surprised that the door opened *by itself*.

ひとりひとり 一人一人 先生は生徒一人一人に(→順に)成績表を渡した The teacher handed a report card to the students *one by one*. / どの生徒も一人一人(→めいめい)部屋を割り当てられた *Each* student was assigned a room.

ひとりぶたい 独り舞台 きのうのカラオケは彼のひとり舞台だった He *attracted most of the admiration and attention* at karaoke yesterday.

ひとりぼっち 一人ぼっち・独りぼっち ─ひとりぼっちの (ひとりで) alone; (孤独で寂しい) lonely; (孤独を好む) solitary / 地震で両親を亡くし、彼女はひとりぼっちになった She was *alone* after her parents were killed in the earthquake.

ひとりむすこ 一人息子 ⇒ひとり

ひとりむすめ 一人娘 ⇒ひとり

ひとりも 一人も 質問に答えられた人はひとりもいなかった *Nobody [No one]* could answer the question.

ひとりよがり 独り善がり ─ひとりよがりの (自己満足の) self-satisfied; (独善的な) self-complacent, self-righteous / ひとりよがりの態度 a *self-satisfied* attitude

ひな 雛 young bird ; (鶏などの) chicken ; (生まれたばかりの) chick / ひなをかえす hatch *chicks*

‖ひな壇 a tiered stand (for dolls) / ひな人形 a *hina* doll / ひな祭り ⇒ひなまつり

ひながた 雛型 (模型) model ; (小型模型) miniature ; (書式) form

ひなぎく 雛菊 〖植物〗daisy

ひなた 日向 the sun; (日のあたっている場所) sunny place / 猫が日なたで気持ちよさそうに眠っていた The cat was sleeping contentedly *in the sun*. / おばあちゃんは庭で日なたぼっこをしている My grandmother *is 'sitting in the sun [sunning herself]'* in the garden.

ひなびた 鄙びた (いなか風の) countrified; (素朴な) rustic / ひなびた寺 a *rustic* temple

ひなまつり 雛祭り

女の子がいる家庭では、3月3日のひな祭りに、ひな人形を飾って娘の成長と健康を祝います。日本古来の宮廷衣装を着たひな人形が5,6段のひな壇に並べられます。しかし、ひな飾りは大変高価でしかも場所をとるので、簡単に男女一対の人形だけを飾ったり、あるいは特に何もしないという家庭も増えています。

On March 3, the day of *hinamatsuri* (the Girls' Festival or the Dolls Festival), families with girls celebrate their growth and good health by displaying *hina* dolls at home. The dolls are arranged on a stand with five or six levels and dressed in ancient court costumes. But because they are very expensive and take up a lot of space in a room, more and more families buy only a pair of male and female dolls or do nothing at all for *hinamatsuri*.

ひなん[1] 非難 (批判) criticism [U] [C]; (とがめること) blame [U]; (穏やかな) reproach [U] [C]; (言葉や文章による) attack [C] ―非難する criticize [他]; blame [他]; reproach [他]; attack [他] //この政策は世間の非難を免れないだろう This policy will not be able to escape *the criticism* [*reproach*] of the public. / 彼の発言は非難の的になった His statement became *the target of criticism.* / マスコミは政府の税制改革案を非難した The media *criticized* [*attacked*] the government's tax reform plan. / 彼は自分勝手だと非難された He *was blamed for* being selfish. / 彼女は彼がうそをついていたと非難した She *criticized* him *for* having told a lie.

◆大臣はわいろを受け取ったことで非難を浴びた The Minister *came under fire* for having taken a bribe.

ひなん[2] 避難 (風雨・危険などからの) shelter [U]; (危険・災難などからの) refuge [U]; (疎開) evacuation [U] ―避難する take* shelter [refuge], shelter [自]; (疎開させる) evacuate [他] //大雨のため彼らは近くの体育館に避難した They *took shelter* [*refuge*] from the heavy rain in the gymnasium nearby. / たくさんの人々がその地区から避難させられた Many people *were evacuated* from the area.

◆きょう学校で避難訓練があった We had *a disaster drill* at school today.

‖避難所 a shelter, a refuge / 避難命令 an evacuation order

ビニール ⚠ vinyl [váinəl] [U], plastic [U] (❖英語の vinyl は化学用語で「ビニール樹脂」の意味. 日本語の「ビニール」に相当する語は plastic)

‖ビニールハウス a plastic greenhouse / ビニール袋 a plastic bag

ひにく 皮肉 irony [U] [C]; (いやみ) sarcasm [U]; (冷笑) cynicism [U] ―皮肉な ironic, ironical; sarcastic; cynical //運命の皮肉 *the irony* of fate / 彼の言葉には多少の皮肉がこめられていた There was a touch of *irony* in what he said. / 「ご親切にどうもありがとう」と彼女は皮肉たっぷりに言った "It's very kind of you," she said *with great irony.* / 彼は私を皮肉った He *made sarcastic* [*cynical*] *remarks* about me.

◆皮肉なことに試合の中止が決まったとたん晴れてきた *Ironically,* it began to clear up as soon as the game was called off.

‖皮肉屋 a cynic, a sarcastic person

ひにくる 皮肉る ➔ひにく

ひにひに 日に日に day by day //日に日に涼しくなっている It is getting cooler *day by day.*

ひにょうき 泌尿器 the urinary organs

‖泌尿器科 urology

ひにん[1] 否認 denial [U] [C] ―否認する deny [他] //男は犯行を全面的に否認した The man completely *denied* the crime.

ひにん[2] 避妊 contraception [U]; (産児制限) birth control [U] ―避妊する prevent conception; practice birth control ‖避妊薬 a contraceptive; (経口避妊薬) an oral contraceptive, the pill

ひねくれもの ひねくれ者 perverse person [C]

ひねくれる ひねくれた人 a *twisted* personality / どうしてそうひねくれた見方しかできない (→物事をまっすぐに見られない)の Why *can't* you *see things straight?*

びねつ 微熱 slight fever [C] //けさから微熱がある I've had *a slight fever* since this morning.

ひねる 捻る

❶【回す】twist [他]; (スイッチなどを) turn [他], switch [他]

蛇口をひねる *turn* a tap / ガス栓をひねる *turn on* [*off*] the gas

彼女は転んで足首をひねった She fell down and *twisted* her ankle.

❷【考えをめぐらす】

頭をひねる *think hard*; *rack one's brains*

みな彼の言うことに首をひねるばかりだった Everyone *was* totally *puzzled* [*confused*] by what he said.

これはずいぶんひねった問題だね This is a very *tricky* question.

❸【その他】

何とか本を買うお金をひねり出した I managed to *squeeze out* enough money to buy a book.

ひのいり 日の入り sunset [U] [C], 《主に米》 sundown [U]

ひのき 檜 Japanese cypress [C] [U]

ひのきぶたい 檜舞台 ひのき舞台を踏む perform on *a big stage* / 彼はオリンピックというひのき舞台で活躍した Participating in the Olympic games put him into *the limelight.*

ひのくるま 火の車 今月は火の車だ We're *on a very tight budget* this month.

ひのけ 火の気 火の気のない場所から出火した A fire broke out at a place where there wasn't any *sign of fire.*

ひのこ 火の粉 sparks //火の粉が舞い上がった *Sparks* fluttered through the air.

ひのて 火の手 (火事) fire [C]; (炎) flame [C] //ビルの3階から火の手が上がった *The fire erupted* on the third floor of the building.

ひので 日の出 sunrise [C] [U] //初日の出 *the first sunrise of the year* / 私たちは日の出前に出発した We started before *sunrise.*

ひのまる 日の丸 the Rising Sun (Flag); (日本の国旗) the Japanese national flag

ひのめ 日の目 彼の作品はついに日の目を見る(→世に出る)ことはなかった His works never *saw the light of day.* / 彼女の本がようやく日の目を見る(→出版される)ことになった Her book will *be published* at last.

ひのもと 火の元 出かける前には火の元を確かめなさい Before going out, make sure that *the gas and the heater are turned off.*

ひばいひん 非売品 an article not for sale

◆非売品《掲示》*Not for Sale*

ひばく 被爆 ―被爆する be bombed; (原爆により) be atom-bombed [A-bombed] //日

本は被爆国です Japan *has been atom-bombed.* ◆彼女は長崎で被爆した She *was a victim of the atomic bombing* at Nagasaki.
‖被爆者 an atomic bomb victim / 被爆地 a bombed area

ひばし 火箸 🗻 *hibashi*, metal chopsticks which are used to pick up charcoal

ひばち 火鉢 🗻 hibachi [C], Japanese charcoal brazier [C]

ひばな 火花 spark [C] ‖火花を出す throw *sparks*
◆２つのチームは火花を散らして(→必死で)戦った The two teams fought *desperately.*

ひばり 雲雀 lark [C], skylark [C]

ひはん 批判 criticism [U] [C] ―批判的な critical ―批判する criticize [他]
批判的態度 a *critical* attitude
彼は冷静に批判を受け入れた He took *the criticism* calmly.
彼女はその提案を批判した She *criticized* [*expressed criticism of*] the proposal.
どの新聞も最近の政府の政策に批判的だ Every newspaper is *critical* of recent government policy.
彼らはその新説を痛烈に批判した They severely [bitterly] *criticized* the new theory.
‖自己批判 self-criticism

ひばん 非番 きょう彼は非番だ He *is off duty* today.

ひひ 狒々 〘動物〙baboon [C]

ひび[1] (割れ目・裂け目) crack [C]; (あかぎれ) chaps ‖カップにひびが入っている There is *a crack* in the cup.
◆ひび割れた唇 *chapped* lips / 壁にひびが入った The wall *cracked.* / そのうわさが元で彼らの友情にひびが入った The rumor *caused a rift* [*split*] in their friendship.

ひび[2] 日々 (毎日) every day; (日ごとに) day by day ―日々の everyday, daily ‖日々努力する make efforts *every day*
◆充実した日々を送る live *a* full *life*

ひひいん 馬がひひいんと鳴いた The horse *neighed.*

ひびき 響き (音響) sound [C] [U]; (反響) echo [C]; (印象) ring [C] ‖鐘の響き *the sound* [*peal*] of a bell / 彼の声には安堵(あんど)の響きが感じられた I caught *a ring* of relief in his voice.

ひびく 響く
❶【周りに伝わる】(音が伝わる) sound [自], ring* [自]; (反響する) echo [自], resound [自]
子供たちの笑い声が部屋中に響いた The children's laughter *rang* [*sounded*] through the room.
静かな通りに叫び声が響き渡った A cry *echoed* through the silent streets.
先生の言葉がずっと耳に響いている The teacher's words still *ring* in my ears.
❷【影響を及ぼす】affect [他], tell* on
公共料金の値上げは家計にひびく A rise in utility bills *affects* [*tells on*] our family budget.
偏った食事は健康にひびく Having an unbalanced diet *affects* your health.

びびたる 微々たる slight; (重要ではない) trifling, insignificant, unimportant
◆私の力など微々たるものです(→私があなたにしたことはたいしたことではない) What I did for you was really *nothing.*

ひひょう 批評 criticism [U] [C]; (書物・演劇などの) review [U] [C]; (論評) comment [U] [C] ―批評する criticize [他]; review [他]; comment [自], make* a comment
小説の批評をする *criticize* a novel
きょうの新聞に新刊本の批評が出ていた *The review* of new books was in today's newspaper.
彼は雑誌にその映画の批評を書いた He wrote *a review* [*critique*] of the movie in a magazine.
‖批評家 a critic

びひん 備品 equipment [U]; (移動できるもの) furniture [U]; (備えつけ家具) furnishings; (取りつけたもの) fixtures; (移動可能な) fittings ‖会社の備品 office *equipment*

ひふ 皮膚 skin [U]
彼女は皮膚が弱い She has delicate *skin.*
その子は皮膚が荒れている The child has chapped *skin.*
‖皮膚炎 dermatitis / 皮膚科 dermatology / 皮膚癌(がん) skin cancer / 皮膚病 a skin disease

びふう 微風 light breeze [C] [U]

ひぶそう 非武装 demilitarization [U] ‖非武装地帯 a demilitarized zone / 非武装中立 unarmed neutrality

ひぶた 火蓋 彼らは反撃の火ぶたを切った They *started* to make a counterattack. / 選挙戦の火ぶたが切って落とされた The election campaign *has just started.*

ビフテキ ⚠steak [U] [C], beefsteak [U] [C]

ひぶん 碑文 inscription [C]; (墓碑銘) epitaph [C]

びぶん 微分 differential calculus [U]

ひへい 疲弊 ―疲弊する (人・国が) be exhausted

ひほう[1] 秘宝 treasure [U] [C]

ひほう[2] 悲報 sad news [U] ‖彼女は旅行先でその悲報を聞いた She received the *sad news* while traveling.

ひぼう 誹謗 (ののしり・悪口) abuse [U]; (中傷) slander [C] [U] ―誹謗する abuse [他]; slander [他]

びぼう 美貌 (顔立ちの美しさ) good looks; (美しさ) beauty [U] ‖彼女はたぐいまれな美貌の持ち主だ She has *a* rare *beauty.*

ひぼし 日干し 魚を日干しにする *dry* fish *in the sun*

ひぼん 非凡 ―非凡な (際立った) uncommon, remarkable; (ふつうでない) unusual ‖彼は幼いころから音楽に非凡な才能を発揮した He showed *uncommon* [*remarkable*] ability in music since childhood.

ひま 暇

❶【自由な時間】free [spare] time [U]; (働いていない時間) leisure [U] ―暇な free

僕はきょう暇だ I'm *free* today.
今度の土曜日は暇？ Are you *free* this Saturday?
彼は暇さえあれば漫画を読んでいる *Whenever he has free time*, he reads comic books. / He spends *all his spare time* in reading comic books.
私は入院中、暇に飽かせてたくさんの小説を読みふけった I read a lot of novels while I was in the hospital, *taking advantage of my abundant free time*.
◆彼女は仕事を辞めてから暇をもてあましている She 「*has too much time to kill* [*is at loose ends*] after quitting her job. / テレビを見て暇をつぶした I watched television to *kill time*.
❷【特定のことをする時間】time Ⓤ
とても忙しくてじっくり考える暇もない I'm so busy that I have no *time* to stop to think.
おしゃべりしてる暇があるんだったらこっちを手伝ってよ If you have so much *time* for chattering, help us out here.
❸【その他】
この商売は夏がいちばん暇だ Summer is *the slackest* season in this business.
彼は3人の従業員に暇を出さざるをえなかった（→解雇した）He had to *let* three employees *go*.
今は仕事が忙しいので9月に暇をもらう（→休暇をとる）つもりだ As we've got so much work to do now, I'll *take my vacation* in September.

ひまご 曾孫 great-grandchild Ⓒ;（男の）great-grandson Ⓒ;（女の）great-granddaughter Ⓒ

ひましに 日増しに（日ごとに）day by day;（毎日）every day / 患者は日増しに回復している The patient is getting better *day by day*.

ひまつぶし 暇潰し 暇つぶしに本屋に寄った I stopped by a book store *to kill time*.

ヒマラヤ ヒマラヤ山脈 the Himalayas; the Himalaya Mountains

ひまわり 向日葵 sunflower Ⓒ
短歌 向日葵は金の油を身にあびてゆらりと高し日のちひささよ（前田夕暮）
Giant sunflowers:
glittering golden oil
covering them all
as they rock on their tall stalks,
behind them the tiny sun

ひまん 肥満 fatness Ⓤ,《公式的》obesity Ⓤ /食べすぎは肥満の元だ Eating too much is a cause of *obesity*.
‖肥満児 a fat [an overweight] child

びみ 美味 ──美味な delicious, tasty

ひみつ 秘密

secret Ⓒ;（秘密にすること）secrecy Ⓤ ──秘密の secret
秘密を守る keep *a secret* / 秘密をばらす disclose [reveal] *a secret*
彼は私たちに秘密を打ち明けてくれた He told [confided] *his secret* to us.
私は他人に秘密をもらしたりしない I don't tell *secrets* to others.
この話は秘密にしておいてください Please keep this story *a secret*.
どこからか秘密がもれてしまった *The secret* leaked out from somewhere.
これは私たちだけの秘密です This is *a secret* among us.
◆その会談は秘密裏に行われた The meeting was held *secretly*.
‖秘密警察 the secret police / 秘密結社 a secret society [organization] / 秘密文書 a secret [confidential] document / 企業秘密 a trade [an industrial] secret

びみょう 微妙（繊細な）delicate;（かすかな）subtle;（微妙に）fine / これは非常に微妙な問題だ This is a very *delicate* problem. / その2つの言葉は微妙に意味が違う There is a *subtle* difference in meaning between the two words.

ひめ 姫 princess Ⓒ

ひめい 悲鳴 scream Ⓒ;（金切り声）shriek Ⓒ / 隣の家から悲鳴が聞こえた I heard *a scream* from the neighbor's house.
◆彼女は驚いて悲鳴をあげた She *screamed* [*shrieked, cried out*] in fright.
慣用表現 商品が予想を上回る人気で、会社はうれしい悲鳴をあげている（→圧倒されつつも大喜びである）The company *is swamped but delighted* at the unexpected popularity of their products.

びめい 美名 彼らは老人福祉という美名に隠れてわいろをもらっていた They accepted a bribe *in the name of* helping old people.

ひめる 秘める（話さないでおく）keep* ... to oneself / 彼は彼女への思いをずっと胸に秘めていた He *kept* his feeling for her *to himself*.
◆彼女は強い意志を内に秘めている She *has* a strong will inside her. / その女の子はピアニストになる可能性を秘めている The girl *has* the potential to be a pianist.

ひめん 罷免 dismissal Ⓤ, discharge Ⓤ ──罷免する dismiss Ⓔ, discharge Ⓔ

ひも 紐（細い）string Ⓤ Ⓒ;（太い）cord Ⓤ Ⓒ
ひもを結ぶ[ほどく] tie [untie] *a string*
彼女は包みにひもをかけた She tied the package with some *cord*.
◆靴ひもがほどけているのに気づかなかった I didn't notice *my shoelace* came loose. / 母は小包のひもをほどいた My mother *untied* the package. / 彼はかがんで靴ひもを結んだ He bent down and *tied his shoes*.
慣用表現 母はわが家の財布のひもを握っている My mother *holds the purse strings* in our family.

ひもじい hungry /ひもじい思いをする feel *hungry*

ひもつき 紐付き ひも付きの金 money *with strings* [*conditions*] *attached*

ひもと 火元 火元は1階の食堂だった（→火事は食堂から始まった）The fire started [origi-

nated] in the cafeteria on the first floor.

ひもとく 古典をひもとく *read* Japanese classics

ひもの 干物 dried fish [C] [U]

ひや 冷や (冷水) cold water [U]; (冷や酒) cold sake [U] ◆すみません, お冷やください Excuse me, *a glass of water*, please.

ひやあせ 冷や汗 cold sweat [C] [U] ‖スピーチをしたときは緊張して冷や汗をかいた I *broke out in a cold sweat* from the strain of giving a speech.

ビヤガーデン beer garden [C]

ひやかし 冷やかし (からかい) teasing [U] ◆ひやかし半分で言う say *teasingly* / 彼女はひやかしで店の中を見て歩いた She *just had a look at the things* in the shop.

ひやかす 冷やかす (からかう) make* fun of ...; (軽くいじめる) tease [他] ‖姉と歩いていたのに, 友達にひやかされた Though I walked with my sister, I *was made fun of* by my friends.

ひやく 飛躍 (跳躍) jump [C], leap* [C]; (論理などの) gap [C] ――飛躍的な (急速な) rapid, fast ――飛躍的に rapidly ――飛躍する jump [自], leap* [自] ‖医学は飛躍的に進歩している Medical science has made *rapid* progress. / この製品の売り上げは飛躍的に伸びている The sales of this product have increased *rapidly*. / 彼の論理には飛躍がある There is *a gap* in his reasoning.

ひゃく 百

a [one] hundred; (100番目) hundredth

100分の7 *seven-hundredths*

145円です It's *one hundred* (*and*) *forty five yen*.

彼は100メートル走で1位だった He won first prize in *the 100-meter dash*.

この道をあと2, 3百メートル行くと大通りに出ます If you go down this street *two or three hundred* meters more, you'll get to a main street.

その地区では数百世帯が台風の被害を受けた *Hundreds of houses* in the area suffered damage from the typhoon.

[慣用表現] そんなことは百も承知だ I *am well aware of* it.

びやく 媚薬 aphrodisiac [C]

ひゃくがい 百害 こういう雑誌は子供には百害あって一利なしだ This kind of magazine *is harmful* to children whatsoever.

ひゃくしょう 百姓 (小作農) peasant [C]; (農場主) farmer [C]

ひゃくてん 百点 (得点) one [a] hundred points; (満点) full marks ‖日本史の試験は100点だった I got *full marks* on the Japanese history test.

ひゃくとおばん 110番 彼はすぐに110番した He「*dialed 110* [*made an emergency call to the police*] at once. (❖一般に《米》では911, 《英》では999)

ひゃくにちぜき 百日咳 whooping cough [U]

ひゃくにちそう 百日草 〔植物〕 zinnia [C]

ひゃくにんいっしゅ 百人一首 🗻 *hyakunin-isshu*, (a card game of) one hundred poems by one hundred poets

ひゃくねんさい 百年祭 centenary [C]

ひゃくパーセント 百パーセント one hundred percent ‖私たちはあなたの意見に100パーセント賛成です We are *one hundred percent* in favor of your opinion.

ひゃくはちじゅうど 百八十度 one hundred and eighty degrees ◆病気が治ってから彼は生活様式を180度変えた He changed his style of living *completely* after his illness.

ひゃくぶん 百聞 [ことわざ] 百聞は一見にしかず Seeing is believing. (→見ることは信じること)

ひゃくぶんりつ 百分率 percentage [U] [C]

ひゃくまん 百万 a [one] million ‖何百万もの人々 *millions of* people / 彼らのアルバムは1か月で200万枚売れた Their album sold *two million copies* in a month.

◆100万分の1 *a millionth*

‖百万長者 a millionaire

> [英作文ノート] 「何百万人もの…」の英語は？
>
> 昨夜は何百万人もの人々がその試合を見た
>
> →×*Million people* watched the game last night.
>
> →○*Millions of people* watched the game last night.
>
> ★「何百万人もの…」は millions of ... と必ず複数で表現する. a million people は「百万人の人」の意味. なお「何万人もの人」は tens of thousands of people という.

びゃくや 白夜 a night with a midnight sun, white night [C]

ひやけ 日焼け (sun)tan [C]; (炎症を起こすほどの) sunburn [U] 《また a ～》 ――日焼けする get* suntanned, get a (sun)tan; get sunburned ‖彼はこんがり日焼けして沖縄から帰ってきた He came back from Okinawa *with a* nice *suntan*. / 暑い中を歩いていたら少し日焼けした I *got a* slight *tan* after walking outside in the hot weather.

◆日焼けした顔 a *suntanned* face / 小麦色に日焼けする *be* [*get*] *tanned* to a golden brown

‖日焼け止めクリーム a (cosmetic) sunscreen

ヒヤシンス 〔植物〕 hyacinth [háiəsinθ] [C]

ひやす 冷やす

cool [他], chill [他]; (氷で) ice [他]

氷で頭を冷やす *cool one's* head with ice

冷蔵庫にジュースを冷やしておいた I *have cooled* [*chilled*] the juice in the refrigerator.

体を冷やさないようにしなさい *Keep* your body *from getting chilled*.

[慣用表現] 頭を冷やしなさい *Cool* [*Calm*] *down*. / 肝を冷やす ➔ きも

ひゃっかじてん 百科事典 encyclopedia [C]

ひゃっかてん 百貨店 department store [C]

ひやっと 冷やっと 階段から足を滑らせそうになってひやっとした I *felt a chill* when I almost slipped on the stairs.

ひゃっぱつひゃくちゅう 百発百中 彼の放った矢は百発百中だった *Every* arrow he shot *hit the target.* / テスト問題の予想は百発百中だった I *guessed right* about what questions would be asked in the test.

ひやとい 日雇い (日雇い労働者) day laborer ⓒ

ひやひや 冷や冷や うそをついたのがばれはしないかとひやひやした I *was afraid* that my lie might be exposed.

ビヤホール beer hall ⓒ

ひやむぎ 冷や麦 *hiyamugi*, noodles chilled by ice and water and served with dipping sauce

ひやめし 冷や飯 彼は会社で長い間冷や飯を食わされた (→冷遇された) He *was given the cold shoulder* at his office for a long time.

ひややか 冷ややか ―冷ややかな (冷淡な) cold, chilly; (そっけない) cool / 冷ややかな視線 *cold* stares / 彼女は私たちに冷ややかな態度をとった She took a *chilly* attitude toward us.

ひやり 冷やり 財布をなくしたかと思って一瞬ひやりとした *A chill came over* me when I thought I had lost my wallet.

ヒヤリング ⇒ ヒアリング

ひゆ 比喩 (言葉のあや) a figure of speech; (隠喩) metaphor ⓒ; (直喩) simile ⓒ ―比喩的な figurative; (隠喩的な) metaphorical ―比喩的に figuratively; metaphorically / 私はその言葉を比喩的な意味で用いた I used the word「*in a figurative sense* [*figuratively*].

ぴゅう 彼は口笛をぴゅうと吹いた He *whistled.* / ホースから水がぴゅうと出た The water *spurted out* from the hose.

ヒューズ fuse ⓒ / ヒューズが飛んだ *The fuse* has blown.

ヒューストン Houston (❋米国の都市)

ひゅうひゅう 北風がひゅうひゅう吹いていた The north wind *was howling* [*whistling*]. / やかんがひゅうひゅう鳴っている The kettle *is whistling.*

びゅうびゅう 台風の接近でその夜は風がびゅうびゅう吹いていた The wind *was howling* that night as the typhoon approached.

ぴゅうぴゅう 弟はぴゅうぴゅう口笛を吹いていた My brother *was whistling.* / 木枯らしがぴゅうぴゅう吹いている The cold winter wind *is whistling* [*wailing*].

ピューマ 〔動物〕puma ⓒ, cougar ⓒ

ヒューマニスト ⚠ (人道主義者) humanitarian ⓒ (❋英語の humanist には「弱者を助ける人」の意味はない)

ヒューマニズム ⚠ (人道主義) humanitarianism ⓊⓊ; (人間味) humanity Ⓤ (❋英語の humanism はこの意味では用いない) / ヒューマニズムにあふれる映画 a film full of *humanity*

ヒューマン human / ヒューマンドキュメント *human* documentary

ピューリタン (清教徒) Puritan ⓒ

ヒュッテ ⚠ (山小屋) mountain hut ⓒ (❋日本語はドイツ語の Hütte から)

ビュッフェ buffet ⓒ (❋フランス語から) / 列車のビュッフェで軽い食事をした I had a light meal at *the buffet* of the train.

びゅん オートバイが車をびゅんと追い抜いていった A motorcycle *zoomed* past a car.

ひょいと 彼女は溝をひょいと飛び越えた She jumped *lightly* over the ditch. / 彼は重いかばんをひょいと持ち上げた He lifted the heavy bag *easily.*

ひょいひょい その子は水たまりをひょいひょい飛び越えていった The child jumped *lightly* [*nimbly*] across the puddles.

ひよう 費用 (出費) expense Ⓤⓒ; (代価) cost Ⓤⓒ
パーティーの費用を見積もる estimate the「*expenses for* [*cost of*] the party
その費用は会社が負担することに決まった It was decided that the company should pay the *expenses.*
当時, 海外旅行はとても費用のかかるものだった Traveling abroad was *a great expense* in those days.
彼らは費用を折半した They shared *the expenses.*
費用を切り詰めなければならない We have to cut down on *the cost.*
◆リフォームの費用はどのくらいかかりましたか How much did it *cost* to remodel your house?

ひょう¹ 表 (目録) list ⓒ; (一覧表) table ⓒ
それちゃんと表に載っている It *is*「*on the list* [*listed*].
私は今月の気温を表にした I *made* the temperatures of this month *into a table.*
◆調査の結果は表に示したとおりです The result of the survey *is as listed.*
‖時刻表 a timetable / 成績表《米》a report card,《英》a report / 予定表 a schedule

ひょう² 票 vote ⓒ / その提案に賛成[反対]票を投じる cast *a vote for* [*against*] the proposal / 議案は39票対6票で可決された The bill was passed by 39 *votes* to 6. / その2人の間で票が割れた *The votes* were split between the two. / 彼らは票を集めるのに必死だ They are desperately gathering *votes.* / 彼女は大量の票を獲得した She received *a large vote.* / 私はその候補者に1票を投じた I cast *my vote* for the candidate.
‖組織票 organized votes / 浮動票 floating votes / 無効票 a spoiled vote

ひょう³ 豹 leopard ⓒ; (クロヒョウ) panther ⓒ; (アメリカヒョウ) jaguar ⓒ

ひょう⁴ 雹 hail Ⓤ; (1粒の) hailstone ⓒ
◆きのう雹が降った It *hailed* yesterday.

ひょう⁵ 評 (批評) criticism Ⓤ; (論評) review Ⓤ

びよう 美容 (美) beauty Ⓤ; (手入れ) cosmetic treatment Ⓤ ⇒ 場面・状況別会話 p.1696 / 十分な睡眠は美容にいい Plenty of sleep is good *for your beauty.* / 豆腐は美容食だ Tofu is *food for beauty.* ◆彼女は美容と健康のためにダンスを習っている She takes lessons in dancing for her health and *figure*. ∥美容院 ⇨ びよういん / 美容師 a beautician / 美容整形 cosmetic surgery / 美容体操 calisthenics

びょう¹ 秒 second ©(《略語》s, sec) ∥彼女は100メートルを15秒で走った She ran 100 meters in 15 *seconds*.

びょう² 鋲 tack ©; (金属板用の) rivet ©; (靴底の) hobnail ©; (画びょう) thumbtack © ◆カレンダーをびょうで留める *tack* a calendar

ひょういもじ 表意文字 ideogram ©, ideograph ©

びよういん 美容院 beauty salon [parlor] ©
⇨ 場面・状況別会話 p.1710

びょういん 病院 hospital ©
⇨ 場面・状況別会話 p.1694
弟を病院に連れていった I took my brother to *the hospital*.
祖父は週に1度病院に通っている My grandfather goes to (*the*) *hospital* once a week.
負傷した男性は救急車で最寄りの病院に運ばれた The injured man was taken to *the nearest hospital* by ambulance.
彼は父を見舞いに病院へ行った He went to *the hospital* to see his father.
◆病院に行ったほうがいいよ(→医者に診(み)てもらったほうがいい) You should *go see the doctor*.
∥救急病院 an emergency hospital / 国立病院 a national hospital / 個人病院 a private hospital / 精神病院 a mental hospital / 総合病院 a general hospital / 大学病院 a university hospital / 動物病院 a veterinary hospital

ひょうおんもじ 表音文字 phonogram ©

ひょうか 評価 evaluation ⓊⒸ; (見積もり) estimation Ⓤ; (真価を認めること)《公式的》appreciation ⓊⒸ; (度合い) rating Ⓒ ―― 評価する evaluate ⓗ; estimate ⓗⓘ; appreciate ⓗ
人の能力を評価する *evaluate* a person's ability
その治療の成果を評価するのは難しい The results of that medical treatment are hard to *evaluate*.
彼女の能力は社内で正当に評価されている Her abilities *are* justly *estimated* in the company.
その監督はファンから高い評価を得ている The manager has been given *a high rating* by the fans.
◆評価基準 *criterion* / 高く評価されているルネサンス絵画 a *highly valued* Renaissance painting / 彼女はピアニストとして国際的な評価を得ている She has gained *an international reputation* as a pianist. / 彼はこれまでマスコミによって様々に評価されてきた He *has been* variously *judged* by the press so far. / その土地の評価額は2億5,000万円だ The land *is valued at* 250 million yen. / その映画については審査員の評価が分かれた The judges' *opinions* were divided about the movie. / 彼は自分の才能を過大[過小]評価している He *overestimates* [*underestimates*] his own ability.

ひょうが 氷河 glacier © ∥氷河期 the ice age, the glacial epoch [period]
慣用表現 就職の氷河期 *a bad time* to look for a job

ひょうかい 氷解 これですっかり疑問が氷解した This *removed* all my doubts.

ひょうき 表記 十進法表記 decimal *notation* / 表記の住所 the address *written on the cover*

ひょうぎ 評議 conference Ⓤ; (討議) discussion Ⓤ ――評議する (討議する) discuss ⓗ ∥評議員 a councilor; (理事) a trustee / 評議(員)会 a council; (学校などの) a board of trustees

びょうき 病気 illness ⓊⒸ; sickness ⓊⒸ; disease ⓊⒸ ――病気の sick; ill
⇨ 場面・状況別会話 p.1694

語法
(1) illness は「病気である状態[期間]」を意味する語. sickness は「病気・吐き気」を意味するが, 特に《英》では通例「吐き気」の意味で用いる. disease は「具体的な病名のつく病気」を指す.
(2) 「病気の」「病気にかかっている」というとき, 《米》では通例 sick を用い, ill はややかたい言い方になる. 《英》では ill を用いるのがふつうで, sick は「吐き気がする」の意味で使う. ただし, 名詞の前で用いる場合は《英》でも通例 sick を用いる.

【病気は・が】
彼の病気はその食べ物が原因だ His *illness* was attributed to the food.
彼の病気はかなり進行していた His *disease* was rather advanced.
◆彼女の病気はすぐによくなるだろう She will *get well* [*get over her illness*] soon.
🗣「お父様のご病気はいかがですか」「おかげさまで, だいぶよくなりました」 "*How's* your father?" "He's getting better, thank you."

【病気で】
病気で苦しむ suffer from (*a*) *disease*
妹は病気で1週間寝込んでいる My sister has been *sick* in bed for a week.
その俳優は去年心臓の病気で亡くなった The actor died of heart *disease* last year.

【病気に】
病気になる *get sick*
その薬は彼の病気に驚くほど効いた The medicine worked remarkably well on his *illness*.
毎日適度の運動をしていると病気になりにくくなる Exercising moderately every day lessens the chance of *getting sick*.

【病気の】
病気の克服 the conquest of *disease* / 病気の娘の看病をする take care of *one's sick daughter*

【病気を】

病気を治す cure (a) disease / 病気を予防する prevent (a) disease
私は入院するほどの病気をしたことがない I have never been so *sick* that I had to be hospitalized.
〖その他〗
病気と闘う fight [struggle with] (an) *illness* / 子供たちを病気から守る protect children from *disease*
彼が病気だとは考えられない It is unlikely that he is *sick*.
私は子供のころ病気がちだった I *frequently got sick* when I was a child.
彼女の猫好きもここまでくるとほとんど病気だ(→度が過ぎている) I know she loves cats, but I think *she's gone way too far* these days.

ひょうきん 剽軽 ——ひょうきんな *funny, comical* ‖ひょうきん者 a *funny* [*comical*] *person*
びょうく 病苦(病気) *illness* ①⓪, *sickness* ①⓪ /病苦と闘う fight [struggle with] *one's illness*
ひょうけいほうもん 表敬訪問 表敬訪問する pay *a courtesy call* [*visit*]
ひょうけつ¹ 氷結 ——氷結する *freeze** 倒, be frozen
ひょうけつ² 票決(投票) *vote* ⓪ ——票決する *vote* 倒, take* a *vote* /法案は票決に付された The bill was put to *the vote*. / 私たちはその提案について票決した We *voted* on the proposal.

ひょうげん¹ 表現

expression ⓪①; (芸術作品などによる) *representation* ① ——表現する *express* 倒; *represent* 倒
表現の自由 freedom of *expression*
これはよく使われる表現です This *expression* is often used.
彼は表現力豊かにピアノを弾く He plays the piano *with great expression*.
自分の考えをうまく表現できなかった I couldn't *express* my ideas well.
この感動は言葉では表現できません I can't *express* how moved I am.

ひょうげん² 氷原 *ice field* ⓪, a *field of ice*
びょうげん 病原 the cause of a disease ‖病原菌 a (disease) germ / 病原体 a pathogen
ひょうご¹ 標語 (スローガン) *slogan* ⓪, *catchword* ⓪; (モットー) *motto* ⓪ /火災予防週間の標語 the *slogan* of Fire Prevention Week
ひょうご² 兵庫

兵庫県は、南で瀬戸内海、北で日本海に面しています。変化に富んだ風土のため、「日本の縮図」といわれることがあります。県庁所在地の神戸市は、港町として発展してきた都市で、神戸港は国際港として阪神工業地帯で重要な役割を果たしています。兵庫は、1995年に起こった阪神淡路大震災によって大きな被害を受けました。

Hyogo Prefecture faces the Seto Inland Sea to the south and the Sea of Japan to the north. It is sometimes called Japan in miniature because of the variety of its geography and climate. The city of Kobe, the capital of the prefecture, has developed as a port city, and Kobe Port plays an important role as an international harbor for the Hanshin Industrial Zone. The earthquake of 1995 caused major damage to the Hyogo area.

びょうご 病後 彼は病後間もない(→病気から回復したばかり)のでまだ体が弱っている He is still weak because he *has just recovered from an illness*.
ひょうこう 標高 altitude ⓪ⓒ, (a) height above sea level ◆標高1,000メートル 1,000 meters *above sea level*
ひょうさつ 表札・標札(名札) nameplate ⓒ; (番地札・名札) doorplate ⓒ
ひょうざん 氷山 iceberg
〖慣用表現〗最近発覚した官庁の汚職は氷山の一角にすぎない The government office's corruption that recently came to light is only *the tip of the iceberg*.
ひょうし¹ 表紙 (本の) *cover* ⓒ ‖表[裏]表紙 a front [back] *cover* / 青い表紙の本 a book with a *blue cover*
ひょうし² 拍子 ❶〖調子〗*time* ⓤ; (リズム) *rhythm* ⓤ ‖8分の6拍子 six-eighths *time* / 彼は音楽を聴きながら足で拍子をとっていた He was beating [keeping] *time* with his feet listening to music.
❷〖はずみ〗立ち上がった拍子に上着のボタンが取れた The button of my jacket came off *when* [*as*] I stood up. / きっと何かの拍子に思い出すよ You must remember it *by some chance*.
〖慣用表現〗テストが思ったより簡単だったので拍子抜けした I *was surprised* because the test was easier than I had expected.
ひょうじ 表示 ——表示する (示す) show* 倒; (指し示す) indicate 倒; (表現する) express 倒 ‖注意書きは箱の裏に表示されている The directions *are shown* [*indicated*] on the back of the box. / 彼らにはっきりと意思表示する必要がある We need to *express our will* clearly to them.
ひょうし 病死 その画家は若くして病死した The painter *died* young *of an illness* [*a disease*].
ひょうしき 標識 sign ⓒ; (目印) mark ⓒ, marker ⓒ; (航空の) beacon ⓒ ‖道路標識 a road *sign* / 交通標識を無視する ignore a traffic *sign* /「一方通行」の標識が出ている There is a "One Way" *sign*./ There is a *sign* saying "One Way."
びょうしつ 病室 sickroom ⓒ; (病棟) ward
ひょうしゃ 評者 reviewer ⓒ, critic ⓒ
びょうしゃ 描写 (言葉による) description ⓤ

びょうじゃく

□; (絵・文章での) portrayal □, depiction □ □ ――描写する portray □, depict □ ∥この小説は庶民の生活を生き生きと描写している This novel vividly *describes* people's lives. / 女子高校生の心理描写にかけてはその小説家の右に出る者はいない The novelist is second to none in her *psychological descriptions* of female high school students. / その作家は主人公の性格を巧みに描写していた The writer effectively *portrayed* the character of the hero.
∥性格描写 character portrayal

びょうじゃく 病弱 ――病弱な (体が弱い) weak; (病気がちの) sickly ∥病弱な母 a *sickly* mother / 彼は生まれつき病弱だ He was born with *a weak disposition*.

ひょうじゅん 標準 (基準) standard □ □; (平均) average □ □ ――標準の standard; average

標準以上[以下]の above [below] *the average* / 標準的な日本の家庭 an *average* Japanese family

その製品の品質は標準に達していない The quality of the product isn't up to *standard*.

彼女は標準的な英語を話す She speaks *standard* English.

∥標準価格 a standard price / 標準語 standard language; (日本の) standard Japanese / 標準時 a standard time; (グリニッジ標準時) Greenwich (mean) time

ひょうしょう 表彰 ――表彰する commend ⊕; (栄誉を与える) honor ⊕; (賞を与える) award ⊕ ∥彼らは燃えている家から人を助け出して警察から表彰された They *were commended* by the police for rescuing people from a burning house. ◆選手たちは表彰台に上がった The players mounted *an honor platform*.
∥表彰式 a commendation ceremony / 表彰状 a testimonial

ひょうじょう 表情 expression □ □; (目つき・顔つき) look □; (顔) face □

コロケーション ―expression―
【形容詞＋～】うれしそうな～ a happy *expression* / 落ち着いた～ a calm *expression* / 驚いた～ a surprised *expression* / 悲しげな～ a sad *expression* / 自信に満ちた～ a confident *expression* / 真剣な～ a serious *expression* / 当惑した～ a puzzled *expression* / びっくりした～ an amazed *expression* / ぼんやりした～ a blank *expression*

私は彼の表情が変わったのを見逃さなかった I didn't fail to notice his change of *expression*.

彼女は心配そうな表情をしていた She had *a worried look*. / She *looked* worried.

その女優は表情が豊かだ The actress has *an expressive face*.

その話を聞いて彼の表情がこわばった His *face* hardened as he heard the story.

びょうしょう 病床 sickbed □ ◆祖父は長いこと病床にふしている My grandfather has *been sick [ill] in bed* for a long time.

びょうじょう 病状 (健康状態) condition □; (病気の程度) condition □ ∥今のところ患者の病状に変化は見られない So far there is no change in *the patient's condition*. ◆おばあさんの病状はいかがですか How is your grandmother?

びょうしん¹ 秒針 second hand □

びょうしん² 病身 病身の母 one's *sickly* mother

ひょうする¹ 表する express ⊕; (示す) show*; (意志を表す) offer ⊕ ∥彼はその決定に遺憾の意を表した He *expressed* his regret at the decision. / 彼女は彼らの援助に深く感謝の意を表した She *showed* deep appreciation for their help.

ひょうする² 評する (批評する) criticize ⊕; (公式に表明する) proclaim ⊕ ∥評論家たちは彼の新しい小説を傑作であると評した The critics *proclaimed* his new novel a masterpiece.

ひょうせつ 剽窃 plagiarism □ □ ――剽窃する plagiarize ⊕⊕

ひょうそ ひょう疽 whitlow □

ひょうそう 表層 (うわべ) surface □; (外側の層) the outer layer

びょうそう 病巣 focus □ ∥病巣を切除する[摘出する] 「cut off [extract] *the focus*

びょうそく 秒速 秒速50メートルで at (*a speed* of) 50 meters *per second*

ひょうだい 表題・標題 title □; (特に挿絵・写真などの) caption □ ◆「秋の空」という表題の本 a book *entitled Autumn Sky*

ひょうたん 瓢箪 gourd □
慣用表現 ひょうたんから駒 (→驚いたことに冗談が現実のものとなった) To my surprise, my joke turned out to be true.

ひょうちゃく 漂着 ――漂着する drift ashore ∥漁船が島に漂着した A fishing boat *drifted ashore* on the island.

ひょうてい 評定 (ランクづけ) rating □; (評価) evaluation □ ――評定する rate ⊕; evaluate ⊕ ∥勤務評定 efficiency rating

ひょうてき 標的 target □, mark □ ∥標的にされる be made *a target*

びょうてき 病的 ――病的な (精神・考えなどが) morbid; (異常な) abnormal ――病的にmorbidly; abnormally ∥病的な思想 a *morbid* idea / その小説の主人公は病的な性格だった The hero of the novel had an *abnormal* character.

ひょうてん¹ 氷点 the freezing point ∥気温が氷点下に下がった The temperature dropped *below* 「*the freezing point* [*zero*]. / けさは気温が氷点下10度だった It was 10 degrees *below* 「*the freezing point* [*zero*] this morning.

ひょうてん² 評点 (試験の点数) mark □; (成績・評価) grade □

ひょうでん 評伝 critical biography □

ひょうでん² 票田 (有権者) voters; (その支持) grass-roots support □

びょうとう 病棟 (hospital) ward □ ∥一般[内科]病棟 a general [medical] ward

びょうどう 平等 equality □ ――平等な

equal ——平等に equally ⇒ あくびょうどう, ふびょうどう
法のもとの平等 equality under the law
人はみな生まれながらにして平等である All men are created equal.
彼の財産は2人の息子の間で平等に分けられた His property was equally divided between his two sons.
彼らは費用を平等に負担した They bore the cost equally [evenly].
この会社では男女が平等に扱われている In this company, men and women are treated equally.
彼は人種間の平等のために闘った He fought for racial equality.
男女平等に向けての動きが高まっている There is a growing movement toward equality between the sexes.
‖平等主義 egalitarianism

びょうにん 病人 sick person ©; (病弱者) invalid ©♣◆(やや差別的なニュアンスをもつ); (患者) patient © ‖病人を看護する tend [take care of] a sick person / その病人は近くの病院にかつぎ込まれた The sick person was carried to the hospital nearby.

ひょうのう 氷嚢 ice pack ©

ひょうはく 漂白 bleaching Ⓤ ——漂白する bleach ⊕ ‖しみのついたブラウスを漂白する bleach the stain out of the blouse
‖漂白剤 bleach

ひょうばん 評判 (評価) reputation Ⓤ 《また a ~》; (人気) popularity Ⓤ ——評判の (有名な) famous; (人気のある) popular
彼は気前がよいとの評判だ He has a reputation for being generous.
彼女は教師としての評判がいい[悪い] She has a good [bad] reputation as a teacher.
彼は男子には評判がいいが, 女子の評判はよくない He is popular among boys but not among girls.
このスキャンダルで彼の評判は地に落ちた This scandal「hurt his reputation seriously [ruined his reputation].
あのレストランはサービスが行き届いていると評判だ That restaurant is famous for good service.
あの映画は評判倒れだった(→評判はどではなかった) That movie didn't live up to its reputation.
◆彼女は近所で評判の美人だ She is known for her beauty in the neighborhood. / これが今評判の(→話題になっている)最新式テレビだ This is the newest TV set in the news. / 彼らはつきあっているのではないかともっぱらの評判だ Rumor has it [People say] (that) they are going together. / 前評判どおり彼はレースで圧倒的な強さを見せた He won an overwhelming victory in the race as everyone expected.

ひょうひ 表皮 〘解剖〙 epidermis Ⓤ ©; (細胞層) cuticle ©

ひょうひょう 飄々 彼はいつもひょうひょうとしている(→世俗から超然としている) He always seems comfortably detached from the world.

びょうぶ 屏風 🏔

びょうぶは, 何枚かのパネルをつなげて作った折りたたみ式の仕切り板です. 絵や文字で装飾され, 芸術的価値の高いものもあります.
A byobu is a folding partition with several panels. Decorated with pictures or calligraphy, some byobu have great artistic value.

ひょうへん 豹変 誘いを断ると彼女の態度は豹変した When I declined her invitation, she changed her tune right away.

ひょうぼう 標榜 ——標榜する advocate ⊕ ‖平和主義を標榜する advocate the cause of pacifism

ひょうほん 標本 specimen ©; (見本) sample © ‖昆虫の標本 specimens of insects

ひょうめい 表明 ——表明する express ⊕; (宣言する) declare ⊕; (公にする) announce ⊕ ‖反対を表明する express one's disapproval / 辞意を表明する express one's intention to resign / 彼は次の大統領選には出馬しないと表明した He declared [announced] (that) he will not run in the next presidential election.

びょうめい 病名 the name of a disease

ひょうめん 表面
❶ 〘外側の面〙 surface ©
地球の表面 the surface of the earth
この紙は表面がざらざらしている This paper has a rough surface.
ついに彼らの意見の違いが表面化した At last their difference of opinion「came to the surface [surfaced].
❷ 〘うわべ〙 the surface
物事の表面だけを見てはいけない Don't look only at the surface of things.
◆表面上の理由 an apparent reason / 彼のコメントはいかにも表面的なものだった His comment was quite superficial.

ひょうめんせき 表面積 surface area Ⓤ ©

ひょうよみ 票読み (票の数の予測) a projection for the number of the vote

びょうよみ 秒読み countdown © ‖ロケット発射の秒読み the countdown to the rocket launch
慣用表現 内閣退陣は秒読み段階に入った The resignation of the Cabinet is in the countdown stage./ (→まさに退陣しようとしている) The Cabinet is about to resign.

ひょうりいったい 表裏一体 親切とおせっかいは表裏一体だ Kindness and meddling are two sides of the same coin.

びょうりがく 病理学 pathology Ⓤ ‖病理学者 a pathologist

ひょうりゅう 漂流 ——漂流する drift ⊕, be adrift ‖船は潮流に乗って漂流した The boat drifted [went adrift] with the current.
‖漂流者 a castaway, a drifter / 漂流物(遭難船の) flotsam

びょうれき 病歴 medical history ◯ //患者の病歴を把握する know *the medical history* of the patient

ひょうろん 評論 criticism ◯ ◯; (本などによる) review ◯ ◯; (意見) comment ◯ ◯ //映画評論 *movie reviews* / 文芸評論 *literary criticism* ◆美術[文説]評論家 *an art* [*a literary*] *critic* / 経済[政治]評論家 *an economic* [*a political*] *analyst* ❖ニュースなどの解説者は critic ではなく analyst

ひよく 肥沃 ──肥沃な rich, fertile, (公式的) fecund //肥沃な土地 *rich* [*fertile*] land

びよく 尾翼 ‖水平[垂直]尾翼 (米) a horizontal [vertical] stabilizer

ひよけ 日除け sunshade ◯, sunblind ◯; (店先などの) awning ◯; (車の日よけ板) sun(visor) ◯

ひよこ 雛 chick ◯; (未熟者)《口語的》greenhorn ◯

ひょこひょこ 彼は週末になるとひょこひょこどこかに出かけていく He goes out somewhere *for a carefree stroll* every weekend.

ぴょこん ぴょこんと (→軽く) おじぎをする make *a slight, quick bow*

ひょっこり (思いがけず) unexpectedly; (偶然) by chance [accident] //街で幼なじみにひょっこり出会った I met a childhood friend on the street *by chance*. / 彼はパーティーも終わろうというころになってひょっこり現れた He 「*came unexpectedly* [*blew in*]」 when the party was coming to an end.

ひょっと ひょっとしたら志保も行くかもしれないよ Shiho may *possibly* go with us. / ひょっとして彼のことをご存じですか Do you know him *by any chance*?

ひよどり 鵯 (鳥) bulbul ◯

ぴよぴよ ヒヨコがぴよぴよ鳴いている Some chicks *are cheeping* [*peeping*].

ひより 日和 (天候) weather ◯ ◆きょうは絶好のハイキング日和だ It is *an ideal day for hiking* today. ‖小春日和 an Indian summer

ひよりみ 日和見 ‖日和見主義 《軽蔑的》opportunism, fencesitting / 日和見主義者 《軽蔑的》an opportunist, a fencesitter

ひょろながい ひょろ長い spindly, (人が) lanky, gangling

ひょろひょろ ひょろひょろしている be *lanky*

ひよわ ひ弱 ──ひ弱な delicate, weak //ひ弱な子供 a *delicate* child

ぴょんと 棒切れでつつくとそのカエルは前にぴょんと跳んだ As I poked the frog with a stick, it *hopped* [*leaped*] forward.

ひょんな ひょんなことから彼と知り合いになった I got acquainted with him 「*through strange circumstances* [(→思いがけなく) *by chance, unexpectedly*].

ぴょんぴょん スズメたちはぴょんぴょん跳ねながらえさをついばんだ Sparrows pecked at seeds, *hopping around*.

ピョンヤン 平壌 Pyongyang (❖北朝鮮の首都)

ひら 平 彼はまだ平社員だ He is still *a rank-and-filer*.

ビラ (はり紙) bill ◯; (ポスター) poster ◯; (手で配る) handbill ◯ //駅前でビラを配る distribute *handbills* in front of the station

ひらあやまり 平謝り 平謝りに謝る make *profuse* apologies; apologize *profusely*

ひらいしん 避雷針 (米) lightning rod ◯, 《英》lightning conductor ◯

ひらおよぎ 平泳ぎ breaststroke ◯《通例 the ～》‖平泳ぎで泳ぐ swim *the breaststroke* / 彼は200メートル平泳ぎの世界記録を破った He broke the world record for *the 200-meter breaststroke*.

ひらがな 平仮名 ━━━ *hiragana*, one of the two Japanese syllabaries, which is used in combination with Chinese characters (❖syllabary [sɪ́ləbèri] は「字音表」の意味)

ひらき 開き ❶【開くこと】両開きの戸 *double doors*
❷【隔たり】年齢の開き age *spread* / 両者の実力には大きな開きがある There is *a great gap* [*difference*] between the two in abilities.
❸【魚の】アジの開き a horse mackerel *spread open and dried*

ひらきなおる 開き直る 彼女は開き直った態度でカンニングを認めた She admitted with a *defiant* air that she had cheated in the exam.

ひらく 開く

❶【あく・あける・広げる】open 自 他; (花が咲く) come* out
包みを開く *open* [*undo, unpack*] a parcel
そのドアは内側に開く The door *opens* inwards.
そのパン屋は9時に開きます The bakery *opens* at nine.
なぜか妹は口を開こうとしなかった For some reason my sister wouldn't 「*open* her mouth [*say a word*].
バラのつぼみが開きかけている The rose buds *are* just *opening*.
教科書の3ページを開きなさい *Open* your textbooks to [at] page three.
◆先頭走者との差が大きく開いてしまった The gap between the leading runner and me greatly *widened*.
❷【開催する】hold* 他, give* 他, have* 他
来月10日に健治の誕生パーティーを開きます We *will give* [*hold, have*] a birthday party for Kenji on the 10th of next month.
オリンピックは4年ごとに開かれる The Olympic Games *are held* every four years.
❸【始める】
銀行に口座を開く *open* an account with a bank
彼女は家の近くに小さな花屋を開いた She *opened* a small flower shop near her house.
徳川家康は江戸に幕府を開いた Tokugawa Ieyasu *established* the shogunate at Edo.
❹【その他】

開かれた皇室 an *open* Imperial Family

スエズ運河を開いたのはだれですか Who *opened* the Suez Canal?

世界へ目を開きなさい *Open* your eyes to the world.

彼が私に心を開いてくれるまでずいぶんと時間がかかった It took him a long time to *open* his heart to me.

彼の研究は動物行動の研究に新たな分野を開いた His work 「*opened up* [*broke*] new ground in the study of animal behavior.

社会人にも門戸を開く大学が増えている An increasing number of colleges *open their doors* to workers.

ひらける 開ける ❶【広がる】open (out); (視界などが) spread* (out) //山頂付近で視界がぱっと開けた The view suddenly *spread* [*opened*] *out* when we neared the top of the mountain. ◆運が開けてきた Fortune *begins to smile on me*.

❷【近代化する】develop ⾃⾃, modernize ⾃⾃ //近ごろはうちのいなかもずいぶん開けてきたようだ It seems that my hometown *has been* greatly *developed* recently.

❸【物分かりがよい・進歩的である】祖母は年のわりに考え方が開けている My grandmother *is open-minded*, her age considered.

ひらたい 平たい flat, even //平たい土地 a *flat* land

[慣用表現]平たく言うとその計画は失敗だった *In plain words*, the project failed.

ひらて 平手 父親に口答えをして平手打ちを食らった I *got a slap* [*smack*] from my father for talking back to him.

ピラニア 〘魚〙piranha

ひらひら イチョウの葉がひらひらと舞い落ちている The ginkgo leaves *are fluttering down*. / チョウが花から花へひらひら飛んでいた Butterflies *were fluttering* among the flowers.

ピラフ pilaf(f) Ⓤ Ⓒ //エビピラフ shrimp *pilaf*(*f*)

ひらべったい 平べったい flat

ピラミッド pyramid Ⓒ (しばしば Pyramid》

ひらめ 平目 flatfish Ⓒ (複 ~, ~es), flounder Ⓒ

ひらめき 閃き flash Ⓒ; (才能などの) spark Ⓒ; (霊感) inspiration Ⓤ //天才のひらめき *a spark* of genius / 直観的なひらめきで with *an intuitive flash* / 天才とは1％のひらめきと99％の汗である (✿エジソンの言葉) Genius is one percent *inspiration* and ninety-nine percent perspiration.

ひらめく 閃く flash ⾃; 《遠くで稲妻がひらめいている Lightning *is flashing* in the distance. / いい考えがひらめいた A good idea *flashed* 「*into* my mind [*on me*]. / I *hit on* a good idea.

ひらや 平屋 a house of one story, a one-story [one-storied] house

ひらりと 馬にひらりとまたがる *spring* on a horse / 彼は敵の一撃をひらりとかわした He dodged the enemy's blow *nimbly*.

びり the last, the bottom //私は駆けっこではいつもびりだった I was always (*the*) *last* in a race. / 彼は今度の試験でクラスのびりから2番目だった He was the second from *the bottom* of his class in this exam.

ピリオド 〘米〙period Ⓒ, 〘英〙full stop Ⓒ ➡ [巻末付録] (句読法) //文末にピリオドを打つ put *a period* at the end of a sentence / その出来事が私と彼との交際にピリオドを打った That event *put a period* [*an end*] *to* my relationship with him.

ひりき 非力 ——非力の powerless, helpless //非力で彼女のために何もできなかったことが残念だ I regret that I was *powerless* to do anything for her.

ひりつ 比率 ratio [réiʃou] Ⓒ (複 ~s), proportion Ⓒ Ⓤ; (パーセンテージ) percentage Ⓒ //4対3の比率で at *a ratio* of 4 to 3 / この地域は外国人居住者の比率が高い This district has a high *percentage* of foreign inhabitants. / 僕たちのクラブの男女の比率は2対1です The *ratio* [*proportion*] of boys to girls in our club is 2 to 1.

ぴりっ ぴりっとした批評 *spicy* [*pungent*] criticism / このドレッシングはぴりっとからい This dressing is *hot* [*spicy*, *pungent*].

ひりひり ——ひりひりする smart ⾃; (刺すように) sting* ⾃; (さわると痛い) be sore //傷口がひりひりする The wound *smarts* [*is sore*]. / 日焼けでいまだに背中がひりひりする My back still *smarts* from the sunburn. / トウガラシのせいで舌がひりひりする My tongue *is stinging* [*burning*] from the red pepper.

びりびり 父は書類をびりびりに破いた My father tore [ripped] the papers *into pieces*. / 静電気で指先がびりびりした My fingers *got a shock* from static electricity. / 家の前をダンプカーが通ると窓ガラスがびりびりと鳴った (→震えた) The windows *trembled* when a dump car passed by my house.

ぴりぴり 入試当日になると、いつもは楽天的な彼もぴりぴりしていた He is always optimistic, but even he seemed to *be* 「*all nerves* [*very tense*] on the day of the entrance exam.

ビリヤード billiards《単数扱い》; (特にポケットビリヤード) pool Ⓤ //ビリヤードをする play [shoot] *billiards* [*pool*]

‖ビリヤード場 a billiard room, a poolroom

びりゅうし 微粒子 minute [mainjúːt] particle Ⓒ, 〘物理・化学〙corpuscle [kɔ́ːrpəsl] Ⓒ

ひりょう 肥料 fertilizer Ⓒ Ⓤ; (有機) manure Ⓤ; (堆肥(たい)) compost Ⓤ //畑に肥料をまく 「*spread fertilizer over* [*fertilize*] a field / 庭から出るごみは腐るとよい肥料になる Rotted garden waste makes fine *compost*.

‖化学肥料 a chemical fertilizer

びりょう 微量 small amount Ⓒ //微量の睡眠薬 a *small* [*minute*] *amount of* sleeping drug

びりょく 微力 微力ながら (→できるだけ) ご協力いたします I'll *do my best to* help you.

ひる¹ 昼

❶【昼間】day, the daytime
兄は夜勉強して、昼は寝ている My brother studies at night and sleeps during *the daytime* [*day*].
工事は昼も夜も休みなく続いている The construction work is going on *day and night*.

❷【正午】noon
日曜日はたいてい昼まで寝ています I usually sleep until *noon* on Sundays.
昼ごろ激しく雨が降りだした *Toward noon*, it began to rain heavily.
◆彼女過ぎに(→午後に)もう一度電話して Call me again *in the afternoon*.

❸【昼食】lunch
お昼をごちそうするよ I'll treat you to *lunch*.

ひる² 蛭 【動物】leech

ビル ⚠building (《略語》bldg.) (◆英語の building は建物一般を指す語で、高層建築物に限らずふつうの家屋などにも用いられる)
5階建てのビル a five-story *building*
彼らは古い家屋をこわして新しいオフィスビルを建てた They pulled down the old houses and built *a new office building*.
‖ビル街 a street lined with large buildings / ビル風 a gust of wind blown around the building / 高層ビル a high-rise building

ピル (経口避妊薬) the pill ‖ピルを服用している be on *the pill*

ひるいない 比類ない (比べるもののない) incomparable, unparalleled

ひるがえす 翻す 彼はマントを翻してそこに立っていた He stood there with his cloak *flying* [*fluttering*]. / 彼女はそう言うとさっと身を翻して立ち去った After saying so, she quickly *turned around* and left. / 君はこの件に関して意見を翻すべきではない You should not *reverse* [*change*] your opinion on this matter.

ひるがえって 翻って 翻って考えると(→一方)、わが国は国土も狭く天然資源にも恵まれていない *However*, our country is small and not rich in natural resources.

ひるがえる 翻る fly* ; (はためく) flutter ; (波打つように) wave ‖校旗がそよ風に翻っている The school flag *is flying* [*fluttering, waving*] in the breeze.

ひるがお 昼顔 【植物】convolvulus

ひるさがり 昼下がり early in the afternoon

ビルディング building (《略語》bldg.) ⇒ビル

ひるね 昼寝 (afternoon) nap ‖昼寝をする have [take] *a nap*

ひるま 昼間 day, the daytime ‖その部屋は昼間でも薄暗かった The room was dim even in *the day*. / 彼は夜働き、昼間睡眠をとる He works at night and sleeps *during the day*.

ビルマ Burma (◆ミャンマーMyanmarの旧称)

ひるむ (恐怖などで) flinch ; (後ずさりする) shrink* ‖敵軍を見てひるむ *flinch* at the sight of the enemy / 彼女は男がひるんだすきに家から逃げ出した She ran away from the house *the moment* the man *flinched*.
◆彼は少しもひるむことなくその大男に立ち向かった He fought against the giant *unflinchingly* [*dauntlessly*].

ひるめし 昼飯 lunch ⇒ちゅうしょく

ひるやすみ 昼休み noon recess ; (昼食時間) lunch break [hour] ‖昼休みにサッカーをしようよ Let's play soccer during the 「*lunch break* [*noon recess*].

ヒレ (ヒレ肉) fillet ‖ヒレステーキ a fillet steak

ひれ 鰭 fin ‖【胸[腹, 尻]びれ the pectoral [*ventral, anal*] *fin*

ひれい 比例 proportion ——比例の proportional ——比例する be proportional (to ...); (相関する) be relative (to ...) ‖距離は時間に比例する Distance *is proportional* [*relative*] *to* time.
‖比例代表制 proportional representation / 正比例 direct proportion / 反比例 inverse proportion

ひれつ 卑劣 ——卑劣な mean, dirty; (下劣な) 《口語的》low-down ; (◆名詞の前で用いる) ‖卑劣なやり方 a *dirty* [*mean*] trick / 陰で人の悪口を言うなんて彼はなんて卑劣なやつなんだ It was very *mean* [*nasty*] of him to speak ill of others behind their backs.

ひれふす 平伏す throw* *oneself* at *a person's feet*

ひれん 悲恋 tragic love ‖悲恋物語 a story of *tragic love*

ひろい 広い

❶【面積などが】large, big; (非常に広い) vast; (広域の) extensive; (部屋などが) spacious, roomy
恵子の家はかなり広い Keiko's house is quite *large* [*big*].
私たちの学校は校庭が広い Our school has a *large* [*big*] playground.
洞窟(どうくつ)の中は思ったよりも広かった The inside of the cave *was roomier* [*more spacious*] than I had expected.
🗣「日本とメキシコではどちらが広いですか」「メキシコです」 "Which is *larger*, Japan or Mexico?" "Mexico is."

❷【幅が】wide, broad
広い門 a *broad* gate
父は肩幅が広い My father has *broad* shoulders. / My father is *broad-shouldered*.
この川はこの地点の川幅が最も広い This river is *the widest* at this point.

❸【範囲や抽象的なものが】
単語を広い意味で理解する take a word *in a wide* [*broad*] *sense*
彼は趣味が広い(→広範囲にわたる趣味をもっている) He has *a wide range of* interests.
この問題は応用範囲が広い This problem is of *wide* application.

彼女は日本古代史に関して広い知識がある She has *extensive* [*wide, broad*] knowledge about the Japanese ancient history.

新井さんは心の広い人です Mr. Arai is *broad-minded* [*generous*].

彼は物事を広い視点でとらえることのできる人だった He was a man who could take *a broad view* of things.

➜ ひろく

ひろいあげる 拾い上げる pick up

ヒロイズム heroism [U]

ひろいぬし 拾い主 finder [C]

ひろいもの 拾い物 (掘り出し物) find [C]
◆拾い物を警察に届ける turn in *the thing one found* to the police

ひろいよみ 拾い読み ―拾い読みする browse through ...; (ざっと読む) skim [他] [自] ‖その本はまだ拾い読みしただけだ I *have* only *browsed through* the book.

ヒロイン heroine [hérouən] [C]

ひろう[1] 拾う

(拾い上げる) pick up; (見つける) find* [他]

ドングリを拾う *pick up* acorns

彼は何かぴかぴか光っているものを拾った He *picked up* something shining.

通りで財布を拾った I *found* [*picked up*] a purse on the street.

この拾った子犬, 飼ってもいいかな Can I keep this little puppy that I *found*?

おれ車で行くから, 途中でおまえを拾ってやるよ I'm going by car, so I'll *pick* you *up* on the way.

◆タクシーを拾う *get* a taxi / 勝ちを拾う *get* a lucky victory / 彼女は近所の公園で小枝を拾い集めた She *gathered* sticks in the park nearby.

ひろう[2] 疲労 tiredness [U], fatigue [U]; (極度の) exhaustion [U]

疲労を感じる feel *fatigue*

彼は疲労が重なって病気になった He got sick *due to an excess of fatigue.*

◆疲労の極に達する (→極度に疲れる) be utterly *tired* / 彼女は心身ともに疲労していた She *was tired* both mentally and physically. / 選手たちは相当に疲労がたまっている The players *have got* considerably [pretty] *tired.* / 彼は疲労の色が濃かった (→疲れきっているようだった) He *looked* 「*tired out* [*exhausted*]. / 私はいくつもの用事が重なり疲労困憊(ぱい)していた I *was exhausted* [*tired out, worn out, dead tired*] because I had to do a lot of things at the same time.

‖眼精疲労 eyestrain / 肉体疲労 physical fatigue

ひろう[3] 披露 announcement [C] [U], introduction [U] [C] ―披露する announce [他], introduce [他] ‖新製品を披露する *announce* a new product ◆結婚披露宴を開く hold [give] *a wedding reception* / 彼は人前で手品を披露した He 「*performed* magic [*gave* a magic show] in public.

ビロード ⚠velvet [U] ‖ビロードの上着 a *velvet* coat / その表面はビロードのようになめらかだった The surface was as smooth as *velvet.*

ひろがり 広がり サハラ砂漠の広大な広がり *the* vast *extent* of the Sahara desert / 消費者運動の広がりに政府が重い腰を上げた *The spread* of consumerism made the government finally take action.

ひろがる 広がる

spread* [自], extend [自]; (及ぶ) stretch [自]; (広くなる) broaden [自], become* wide

変なにおいが教室全体に広がった A strange smell *spread* all over the classroom.

そのニュースはまたたく間に広がった The news *spread* quickly.

見渡すかぎり砂漠が広がっている The desert *spreads* as far as the eye can reach.

その畑は数マイルにわたって広がっている The field *stretches* for miles.

川はその橋の下流で広がっている The river *broadens out* downstream from that bridge.

◆一面に広がる田んぼ *a* wide *spread* of rice fields (❖この spread は名詞) / 両者の差はどんどん広がった The gap between the two *got wider and wider.* / 地震による被害はさらに広がっている (→ひどくなっている) The damage from the earthquake *is worsening.*

ひろく 広く widely ―広くする widen [他] ‖彼の成功談は広く知られている His success story is *widely* known. ◆ベッドを処分したら部屋が広くなった The room *seemed bigger* after I got rid of the bed.

ひろげる 広げる

(開く) open [他]; (周りに) spread* [他] [自]; (面積を) enlarge [他]; (幅を) widen [他], broaden [他]; (たたんだものを) unfold [他]

本を広げる *open* a book / ベランダを広げる *enlarge* a veranda / 机の上に地図を広げる *spread* (*out*) a map on the desk / ハンカチをひざの上に広げる *unfold* a handkerchief on *one's* lap

ツルは翼を広げた The crane *spread* its wings.

その通りは道幅を広げる工事をしている The road is *being widened.*

留学は私の視野を広げてくれた Studying abroad *widened* [*broadened*] my horizons.

その会社はいろいろな方面に手を広げている The company *spreads* [*branches*] *out* into various fields.

◆知識を広げる *broaden one's* knowledge / 彼女の父親は両手を広げて私を歓迎してくれた Her father welcomed me *with open arms.* / 雑誌がテーブルの上に広げてあった A magazine lay *open* on the table.

ひろさ 広さ (面積) area [U] [C]; (幅) width [U] [C] ‖彼女の知識の広さにはみんなが舌を巻いた Everybody was astonished at her *width* [*breadth, extent*] of knowledge.

◆その家は私たち家族には十分な広さだった The house was *large* enough for our family. / アメリカは日本の約26倍の広さである America is about twenty-six times as *large* as Japan. / かろうじて車の向きを変えられるだけの広さしかなかった There was barely enough *room* to turn the car around.

🔑「この部屋はどのくらいの広さですか」「40平方メートルです」"What is *the area* of this room?/ How *large* is this room?" "It's 40 square meters."

ピロシキ piroshki《複数扱い》

ひろしま 広島

広島県は瀬戸内海に面しています。この県の大部分は山がちで、工業が発展した人口が密集した都市は南部の沿岸部に集まっています。これらの沿岸の都市では、自動車産業、鉄鋼産業、機械工業が盛んです。県庁所在地の広島市は、原爆による被害を最初に被った都市として世界的に知られており、平和への願いをこめて保存されている原爆ドームは世界遺産に指定されています。
Hiroshima Prefecture faces the Seto Inland Sea. Most of this prefecture is mountainous; its industrialized and densely populated cities are concentrated along the southern coastal areas. In these coastal cities, the automobile, steel, and machinery industries flourish. The city of Hiroshima, the capital of this prefecture, is known around the world for having been the first city to suffer the explosion and aftermath of an atomic bomb. The A-bomb Dome, which is kept as a symbol of the desire for peace, is a registered World Heritage site.

ひろば 広場 (public) square ◯; (空き地) open space ◯ /何百人もの学生がその広場に集まった Hundreds of students gathered in *the square*./ きょうは市役所の横の広場で盆踊りがある The *Bon* dance festival will be held at *the public square* by the city hall tonight.

ひろびろ 広々 そのドームの内部は広々としていた The interior of the dome *was spacious*. / 犬は広々とした野原を走り回った The dogs ran around in the *open field*.

ひろま 広間 hall ◯; (ホテルなどの) saloon ◯

ひろまる 広まる spread* ⓘ; (流通する) circulate ⓘ; (普及する) become* popular /そのうわさはたちまち学校中に広まった The rumor *spread* [*circulated, got around*] all over the school very quickly. / 鎌倉時代になると仏教は民衆の間に広まっていった Buddhism *became popular* among people during the Kamakura era.

ひろめる 広める spread* ⓗ; (普及させる) make* ... popular /いったいだれがこんなうわさを広めたのだろう Who on earth *has spread* such a rumor? / この会社がファーストフードを広めた This company *made* fast food *popular*.

◆見聞を広める enlarge [enrich] one's experience (❉enlargeは「広くする」, enrichは「豊かにする」の意味)/ 改宗後、彼はイエスの教えを広めるために奔走した After the conversion, he made every effort to *propagate* [*preach*] the doctrine of Jesus. (❉propagateは「(教えなどを)伝える」, preachは「伝導する」の意味)

ひろんりてき 非論理的 ──非論理的な illogical ◆彼の話はいつも非論理的だ He always talks *illogically*.

ひわ 秘話 unknown episode ◯; (歴史・伝説などの) anecdote ◯

びわ¹ 枇杷 loquat ◯

びわ² 琵琶 🎵 a biwa, a Japanese lute

ひわい 卑猥 ──卑わいな obscene, dirty, indecent ◆わいせつ

ひん 品 ❶【品格】(人為的な) elegance Ⓤ; (生まれながらの) grace Ⓤ; (洗練) refinement Ⓤ ◆あの品のよい婦人はどなた? Who is that *elegant* [*graceful*] lady? / 彼の言葉づかいには品がない His language is *vulgar* [*rude*].

❷【品物】article ◯, goods《複数扱い》

びん¹ 瓶 bottle ◯; (広口の) jar ◯; (デカンター) decanter ◯; (ジャグ) jug ◯

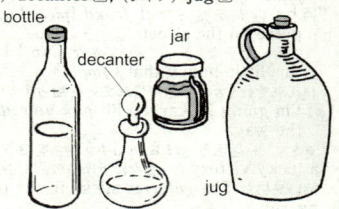

bottle
jar
decanter
jug

びんを空にする[いっぱいにする] empty [fill] *a bottle* / びんにふたをする cap *a bottle*

家族へのおみやげにブルーベリージャムを1びん買った I bought *a jar* of blueberry jam as a present for my family.

∥空きびん an empty bottle / 牛乳びん a milk bottle / ビールびん a beer bottle / ほ乳びん a baby bottle

びん² 便 ❶【交通手段】(飛行機の) flight ◯ /(バス・電車の) service ◯ /パリ行き123便 *Flight* 123 to Paris / 成田からロサンゼルスまでの直行便 *a direct flight* from Narita to Los Angeles / 父は午後3時の便でロンドンへ行きます My father will leave for London on *the* 3 p.m. *flight*.

❷【郵便】(米)mail Ⓤ, (英)post Ⓤ /船便で by sea [surface] mail ◆手紙を航空便で送る send a letter (by) airmail

ピン¹ pin ◯ (❉「留め針」のほか,「ゴルフの旗ざお」「ボウリングのピン」も意味する)

写真を壁にピンで留める fasten a picture with *a pin* [*pin up* a picture] on the wall ∥安全ピン a safety pin / ネクタイピン a tiepin / ヘアピン a hairpin

ピン² 慣用表現 ホテルといってもピンからキリまである There are *all kinds* of hotels.

ひんい 品位（威厳）dignity; （品）elegance, grace ∥品位を落とす lower one's dignity; lower oneself / 厳しい状況にあっても彼女は品位を保っていた She maintained [kept] her dignity despite the tough situation.

ひんかく 品格 dignity ⇒ひんい

びんかん 敏感 ——敏感な sensitive ∥敏感肌 sensitive skin / 犬はにおいに敏感だ A dog is sensitive to odors. / 彼女は杉花粉に敏感です She's sensitive to cedar pollen.
◆若者たちはいつも流行に敏感だ Young people are always fashion-conscious.

ひんきゃく 賓客 a guest (of honor)

ひんきゅう 貧窮《公式的》destitution ⇒ひんこん

ピンク pink ∥ピンク色のリボン a pink ribbon / 彼女はピンクの服を着ていた She was dressed in pink. / 女の子はピンク色のほおをしていた The girl had rosy cheeks.
∥ピンク映画 a porn(ographic) film, a blue movie

ひんけつ 貧血 anemia [əníːmiə] ∥貧血で倒れる faint from anemia

ビンゴ bingo

ひんこう 品行《公式的》conduct; （ふるまい）behavior ∥品行方正な人 a person of good conduct [behavior]; a moral person / 彼は不品行のためにクラブへの出入りを禁じられた He was barred from the club for bad conduct [behavior].

ひんこん 貧困 poverty ——貧困な poor ∥貧困家庭 a poor [miserable] family / 貧困から抜け出す emerge from poverty / 彼の家族は貧困のどん底にあえいでいた The family was in great poverty. / 思想の貧困が叫ばれて久しい They have long clamored the poverty of thought.
◆彼はボキャブラリーが貧困だ He has a limited vocabulary.

ひんし¹ 瀕死 彼女は瀕死の重傷（→致命傷）を負った She was fatally injured. / 彼は瀕死の状態だった He was「near death [at death's door].

ひんし² 品詞〔文法〕a part of speech

ひんしつ 品質 quality ∥品質の向上に努めるtry to make progress in quality / これらの商品は品質がよい[よくない] These goods are of good [poor] quality. / 高価な物が高品質であるとは限らない Expensive goods are not necessarily of high quality.
∥品質管理 quality control

ひんじゃく 貧弱 ——貧弱な poor; （体格などが）lean, thin ∥貧弱な体 a poor [lean, thin] physique / この論文は内容が貧弱だ This thesis is poor in content.
◆その工場の設備は貧弱なものだった The factory was poorly-equipped.

ひんしゅ 品種 variety; （育成品種）breed ⇒しゅるい / 彼は新しい品種の牛 a rare breed of cattle / 彼は新しい品種のバラを育てている He grows a new variety of rose.
∥品種改良 breeding, improvement of breed

ひんしゅく パーティーでの彼の言動はみんなのひんしゅくを買った His words and deeds were frowned on by everyone at the party.

ひんしゅつ 頻出 この種の問題は入試問題に頻出する This kind of problem appears frequently in the entrance exam.

びんしょう 敏捷 agile; （機敏な）alert; （素早い）quick ——敏捷に agilely; alertly; quickly ∥敏捷な動物 an agile [alert] animal / 宮本は敏捷な身のこなしで（→素早く）打球をさばいた Miyamoto handled with the ball quickly [with agility].

びんじょう 便乗 会社まで(彼女の車に)便乗させてもらった I got a lift to the office (in her car). / She gave me a lift to the office (in her car). / その会社は旅行ブームに便乗して（→利用して）大もうけした Taking advantage of a boom in tourism, the company made a great profit. / Jumping on the tourism bandwagon, the company made a great profit.
∥便乗値上げ an opportunistic price hike

ヒンズーきょう ヒンズー教 Hinduism
∥ヒンズー教徒 a Hindu

ひんする 瀕する その王国は滅亡の危機に瀕していた The kingdom was on the verge [brink] of falling. / その鳥は絶滅の危機に瀕している That bird「is threatened with [faces] extinction.

ひんせい 品性 character ∥品性を疑う wonder about a person's character

ピンセット ⚠tweezers（◆日本語はオランダ語の pincet から）

びんせん 便箋 letter paper, notepaper, writing paper（◆教えるときはa sheet of ... とする）; （1冊の）letter pad

ひんそう 貧相 彼女は貧相な身なりをしていた She was shabbily [poorly] dressed.

びんそく 敏速 ——敏速な quick, prompt, swift ——敏速に quickly, promptly, swiftly ∥敏速な行動 quick [prompt, swift] action / 彼は敏速に問題を処理した He dealt with the matter quickly [promptly, swiftly].

びんた 父から往復びんたを食った I was slapped on one cheek and then the other by my father. / あの男にびんたを食らわせてやったわ I「gave him a slap [slapped him] in the face.

ピンチ pinch; （危機）crisis ∥ピンチに陥る get into a pinch / 彼女は何とかピンチを切り抜けた She managed to get out of the pinch.
◆彼は絶体絶命のピンチに追い込まれた He was driven into a corner.
∥ピンチヒッター a pinch hitter / ピンチランナー a pinch runner

びんづめ 瓶詰め ピクルスのびん詰め bottled pickles / オリーブをびん詰めにする bottle olives

ヒント hint; （手がかり）clue ∥問題解決のヒントを得る get a hint [clue] to solve the problem / ヒントをください Please give [drop] me *a hint*.

◆この故事にヒントを得て, 彼は1編のすぐれた短編小説を書いた *Taking a cue* [*hint*] *from this historical event, he wrote a fine short story*.

ひんど 頻度 frequency ⓊⒸ /彼らはその地点で事故が起こる頻度を調べた They investigated「*the frequency* of the accidents [*how often* the accidents occurred]」at the point. ◆これらの英単語は使用頻度が非常に高い(→頻繁に用いられる) These English words *are used very frequently*.

ピント ⚠ focus Ⓒ; (要点) point Ⓒ (❖日本語はオランダ語の brandpunt から) /この写真はピントが合っている[いない] This picture is in [out of] *focus*. / 君の言っていることはピントがはずれているよ What you're saying is beside [off] *the point*. ◆あの女の子にカメラのピントを合わせてくれる? Will you *focus* the camera on that girl?

ぴんと ❶【まっすぐにする】背筋をぴんと伸ばして立つ stand (up) *straight* / 彼は綱をぴんと張った He stretched the rope *tight*. / 物音に犬は耳をぴんと立てた The dog *pointed* its ears at the sound.

❷【張りつめる】ぴんと張りつめた空気の中, 的(まと)を射抜く矢の音が響き渡った The sound of an arrow hitting the target echoed in the *tense* atmosphere.

❸【思い当たる】そのときに寛子という名前を聞いてもぴんとこなかった The name Hiroko didn't「*ring a bell* [*click*]」then. / 現代音楽はどうもぴんとこない(→心に訴えかけない) Modern music *doesn't appeal to me*. / 彼のそのしぐさを見ただけで彼女はぴんときた At the mere sight of his behavior, she *took the hint*. (❖take the hint は「ほのめかしなどの意味を悟る」の意味)

ひんば 牝馬 mare Ⓒ

ひんぱつ 頻発 その通り沿いで似たような事件が頻発した Similar cases *occurred* [*happened*] *frequently* along the street.

ピンはね 彼は売上金の一部をピンはねした He pocketed a kickback from the proceeds.

ひんぱん 頻繁 ――頻繁に (公式的)frequently, often /近ごろ拓也は頻繁に私に電話してくる Takuya *often* calls me up these days. / 彼は取材のためにその地を頻繁に訪れた He *frequently* visited there to collect material.

◆その時間帯はバスは頻繁に来る Buses come *at frequent intervals* during those hours.

ひんぴょうかい 品評会 (農・畜産物などの)(米)fair Ⓒ; (展覧会) exhibition Ⓒ, show Ⓒ

ぴんぴん 病気だと聞いて見舞いに行ったら, 彼はぴんぴんしていた I heard he was sick and went to see him, but he *was「alive and kicking* [*as fit as a fiddle*]」.

ひんぷ 貧富 (貧者と裕福) wealth and poverty; (貧者と富者) (the) rich and (the) poor (❖貧富の順序が日本語とは逆になることに注意) /その国では貧富の差が激しい The gap between (*the*) *rich and* (*the*) *poor* is wide in that country.

ひんぼう 貧乏 poverty Ⓤ ――貧乏な poor 彼は貧乏な家に生まれた He was born into a *poor* family. / He was born *poor*.

彼女は貧乏だが, いつも笑顔を絶やさない She is *poor*, but she is always smiling.

父親が死ぬと私の家はたちまち貧乏になった After my father died, my family *fell into poverty* at once.

◆頼むからその貧乏ゆすりをやめてくれ Please stop *jiggling your legs*, will you? / うちの母は貧乏性だ My mother *doesn't know how to enjoy life*.

慣用表現 彼女はいつも貧乏くじばかり引いている She always *draws the short straw*. / (→いちばんついていない) She is always *most unlucky of all*.

ことわざ 貧乏暇なし The poor has no leisure.

ピンぼけ がっかりしたことに旅行先で撮った写真のほとんどがピンぼけだった To my disappointment, most of the pictures I took while traveling were *out of focus*.

ピンポン (口語的)ping-pong Ⓤ, table tennis Ⓤ /ピンポンをする play *ping-pong* / ピンポン玉ほどの大きさの卵 an egg about the size of *a ping-pong ball*

ひんみん 貧民 poor people 《複数扱い》, the poor《複数扱い》

‖貧民街 a deprived area, a slum area

ひんもく 品目 item Ⓒ; (目録) list of items [articles] /輸入品目 *imported items* / ここにある品目の中から選んでください Please choose among [from] *the items* here.

ひんやり 川の水はひんやりして気持ちがよかった The river water *felt cool* and pleasant. / 地下室の空気は夏でもひんやりとしている The air in the cellar *feels cool* even in (the) summer.

びんらん 便覧 handbook Ⓒ, manual Ⓒ; (履修案内) catalog, (英)catalogue Ⓒ

びんわん 敏腕 ――敏腕の able, capable /敏腕刑事 *an able* [*a capable*] *detective*

◆彼は大臣として大いに敏腕をふるった He really *showed his ability* as a government minister.

ふ

ふ[1] 府 (行政区) prefecture [C]; (中心) center [C], seat [C] ∥大阪府 Osaka *Prefecture* / 学問の府 *a seat* of learning / 立法府 *a* legislative *center*

‖府議会 a prefectural assembly / 府知事 a prefectural governor / 府庁 a prefectural office / 府立高校 a prefectural high school / 府立図書館 a prefectural library

ふ[2] 負 ──負の negative (↔positive), minus (↔plus) ∥負の数 a *negative* number

ふ[3] 歩 (将棋・チェスの) pawn [C]

ふ[4] 腑 彼の言うことはどうも腑に落ちない (→理解できない) I *can't understand* what he says. / (→納得できない) *I'm not satisfied with* what he says.

ふ[5] 譜 (musical) score [C], music [U]

ぶ[1] 部 ❶【部分】part [C] ∥5部から成る小説 a novel in five *parts* / 市の中心部 *the* central *part* of the city

❷【部門】department [C], division [C]; (編集部) desk [C] ∥人事部 *the* personnel *department* [*division*] / 社会部 *the* city *desk*

❸【クラブ】club [C]; (クラブチーム) team [C] ➡ [場面・状況別会話] p.1748 ∥彼はサッカー部に入った He joined *the* soccer *club*. / 彼女はアーチェリー部に入っている She is in [a member of] *the* archery *club*.

> **-部のいろいろ-**
>
> 映画研究部 cinema club / 園芸部 gardening club / 演劇部 drama club / 化学部 chemistry club / 合唱部 chorus club / 華道部 flower arrangement club / 弓道部 Japanese archery club / 剣道部 kendo club / コンピュータ部 computer club / サッカー部 soccer club / 茶道部 tea ceremony club / 写真部 photography club / 柔道部 judo club / 手芸部 handicraft club / 新聞部 school newspaper club / 吹奏楽部 brass band / 相撲部 sumo club / 生物部 biology club / ソフトボール部 softball club / 体操部 gymnastics club / 卓球部 table tennis club / 鉄道研究部 railway study club / テニス部 tennis club / 軟式テニス部 softball tennis club / 軟式野球部 rubber-ball baseball club / バスケットボール部 basketball club / バドミントン部 badminton club / バレーボール部 volleyball club / ハンドボール部 handball club / 美術部 art club / 文芸部 literary club / 放送部 school broadcasting club / 野球部 baseball club / ラグビー部 rugby club / 陸上部 track and field club / ワンダーフォーゲル部 hiking club

❹【書物の】copy [C] ∥私たちはその雑誌を2部注文した We ordered two *copies* of the magazine. ◆この月刊雑誌は発行部数が50万部である This magazine has *a* monthly *circulation* of 500,000.

ぶ[2] 分 (パーセント) percent,《主に英》per cent [C] ∥その社債は年に4分の利子がつく The corporate bond yields [bears] four *percent* interest a year.

◆私たちの方に分がある[ない] *The odds are* 「*in* our *favor* [*against* us]. / 彼が勝つ見込みは五分五分だ It is *even chances* that he will win. / 彼女の熱は37度8分だった Her temperature was 37.8 *degrees*. (❖37.8は thirty seven point eight と読む)

ファ 〘音楽〙 fa [U][C]

ファースト 〘野球〙(一塁) first (base) [U] (❖通例無冠詞); (一塁手) first baseman [C]

‖ファーストクラス first class / ファーストミット a first baseman's glove [mitt]

ファーストフード fast food [U] ∥ファーストフード店 a *fast-food* restaurant

ファーストレディー (大統領夫人) the first lady《しばしば the First Lady》

ファール foul [C] ➡ファウル

ぶあい 歩合 (割合) rate [C]; (百分率) percentage [C]; (手数料) commission [C][U] ∥彼らは売り上げに対して10パーセントの歩合をもらう They get *a* 10 percent *commission* on sales.

‖歩合給 a commission salary / 歩合制 a commission system / 公定歩合 the official discount rate

ぶあいそう 無愛想 ──無愛想な (よそよそしい) unfriendly; (交際嫌いの) unsociable; (ぶっきらぼうな) blunt, bluff; (冷淡な) cold ──無愛想に bluntly, bluffly; coldly ∥無愛想な態度で in an *unfriendly* [*a cold*] manner / 無愛想に返事する answer *bluntly*

ファイト (闘志) fight [U], fighting spirit [U]; (試合) fight [C]

> [語法]
> 落ち込んでいる人を元気づけるときは, Cheer up!, 何かやろうとしている人を激励するなら, Good luck!, 競技中の選手に言うなら, Come on! や Stick it out! などと言う.

彼はファイト満々だ He is full of *fight*. / He has plenty of *fight* in him.

‖ファイトマネー fight money

ファイナル (決勝戦) the final

ファイバー fiber,《英》fibre [C][U] ‖ファイバーグラス fiberglass / ファイバースコープ a fiberscope / 光ファイバー (an) optical fiber

ファイル (書類) file [C]; 〘コンピュータ〙 file [C] ──ファイルする file [他] ∥書類をファイルする *file* papers / その件に関するファイル *a file* on the matter / ファイルを開く[閉じる] open [close] *a file* / ファイルを作成する[削除する] create [delete] *a file* / ファイルをコピーする

ファインダー

[編集する] copy [edit] *a file* / ファイルを保存する[印刷する] save [print] *a file* ‖ファイル名 a file name / システムファイル a system file / テキストファイル a text file / 添付ファイル（電子メールの）an attachment / バイナリファイル a binary file

ファインダー (view)finder ◯ ‖ファインダーをのぞく look through *a viewfinder*

ファインプレー good [fine, spectacular] play ◯ ‖ファインプレーをする make *a good [fine, spectacular] play*

ファウル〘スポーツ〙foul ◯ ──ファウルする foul ◯/ファウルを犯す commit *a foul* ‖ファウルグラウンド foul territory / ファウルチップ a foul tip / ファウルフライ a foul fly / ファウルボール a foul (ball) / ファウルライン a foul line

ファクシミリ facsimile ⇒ ファックス

ファゴット〘音楽〙bassoon ◯（◆日本語はイタリア語の fagotto から）‖ファゴット奏者 a bassoonist

ファジー ──ファジーな fuzzy ‖ファジー工学 fuzzy engineering / ファジー集合 a fuzzy set / ファジーマッチング〘コンピュータ〙fuzzy matching / ファジー理論〘コンピュータ〙fuzzy theory

ファシスト（国粋主義者）fascist ◯

ファシズム（国粋主義）fascism ◯ ──ファシズムの fascist

ファスナー ⚠ zipper ◯,《英》zip ◆スカートのファスナーを上げる[下ろす]「*zip up [unzip]* a skirt / 彼はかばんのファスナーをあけた[閉めた] He *zipped* his bag *open [shut]*.

ぶあつい 分厚い thick, fat ⇒ あつい（厚い）/ 分厚い本 a *thick [fat]* book

ファックス fax ◯◯, (公式的)facsimile ◯◯ ⇒ 巻末付録（ファックスの書き方）◆彼女にファックスを送る send (off) *a fax to her* / ファックスを受け取る receive [get] *a fax* from him / 返事はファックスで送ってください Please send the reply to me *by fax*. / Please *fax* the reply to me. / この電話はファックスにもなる This phone also functions as *a fax*.

ファッショ fascism ◯

ファッション (服装などの) fashion ◯◯ ⇒ 場面・状況別会話 p.1708 ‖今流行のファッション current [prevailing] *fashions* / 最新のファッションを追う follow *the latest fashions* / パリは世界のファッションの中心地だ Paris is the *fashion* capital of the world. ‖ファッション界 the fashion scene / ファッションショー a fashion show / ファッションデザイナー a fashion designer / ファッションモデル a fashion model

ファミコン《商標名》Nintendo ◯; (ビデオゲーム) a video game / ‖ファミコンで遊ぶ play *a video game*

ファミリー family ◯ ‖ファミリーレストラン a family restaurant

ふあん 不安
anxiety ◯◯; (落ち着かないこと) uneasiness ◯; (心配) worry ◯◯; (懸念) fear ◯◯; (社会的) unrest ◯ ──不安な anxious; uneasy; worried
期待と不安 hopes and *fears* / 一抹の不安 a touch of *anxiety [uneasiness]* / 先行きの不安 *uneasiness* about the future / 漠然とした不安感 a vague *sense of fear* / 不安になる become *anxious [uneasy]* / 不安な一日を送る pass an *uneasy* day
彼は自分の将来に不安をいだいている He is *anxious [uneasy]* about his future.
彼の顔には不安が表れていた His face showed *anxiety*.
石油不足が社会不安を引き起こした The oil shortage caused *social unrest*.
彼女のまなざしは不安に満ちていた Her eyes were full of *anxiety*.
◆彼女は不安げにあたりを見回した She looked around *uneasily*.

ファン ❶〖愛好者〗fan ◯; (崇拝者) admirer ◯; (スポーツチームの) supporter ◯ ‖大ファン a big fan / サッカーファン a soccer fan / マイケル・ジャクソンのファン a fan of Michael Jackson / その歌手の熱烈なファン an enthusiastic *admirer* of the singer / 私はその歌手の隠れファンだ I am *a secret admirer* of that singer. ◆その俳優はファンが多い That actor *has a wide following*.
❷〖送風機〗fan ◯
‖ファンクラブ a fan club / ファンレター ⇒ ファンレター

ファンクションキー〘コンピュータ〙function key ◯

ファンシー ‖ファンシーグッズ《米》gift shop items,《英》fancy goods / ファンシーショップ《米》a gift shop,《英》a fancy goods shop

ファンタジー fantasy ◯◯

ふあんてい ──不安定な unstable; (危うい) insecure; (変わりやすい) changeable, unsettled ‖不安定なはしご an *unstable* ladder / 不安定な天気 *changeable [unsettled]* weather / 不安定な職 an *insecure* job / 政情は依然として不安定だ The political situation is still *unstable [fluid]*. / 彼は情緒不安定だ He is *emotionally unstable*.

ファンデーション (化粧品) foundation (cream) ◯; (体型補整用下着) foundation (garment) ◯ ‖ファンデーションを塗る[落とす] apply [remove] *foundation (cream)*

ファンド (基金) fund ◯

ふあんない 不案内 unfamiliar
◆私はこのあたりは不案内です I'm *a stranger* in this neighborhood.

ファンファーレ fanfare [fǽnfeər] ◯ ‖彼らはファンファーレとともに登場した They appeared with *a fanfare*.

ファンブル fumble ◯◯, bobble ◯◯
◆田中の（打った）ゴロをファンブルする *fumble [bobble]* Tanaka's grounder

ファンレター fan letter ◯,《集合的》fan mail ‖ファンレターを書く write *a fan letter*

ふい¹ 不意 ──不意の（突然の）sudden,

abrupt; (思いがけない) unexpected ──不意に suddenly, all of a sudden, abruptly; unexpectedly ∥不意の質問 a *sudden* [an *unexpected*] question / きのうは不意の客があった I had an *unexpected* [a *surprise*] visitor. / バスは不意に止まった The bus stopped *suddenly* [*all of a sudden*]. / The bus made a *sudden* stop.

◆彼のループシュートはゴールキーパーの不意をついた His looping shot *took* the goalkeeper *by surprise*.

ふい² 彼女とデートするチャンスをふいにする *miss* a chance to have a date with her / 私たちの努力がすべてふいになった All our efforts 「*came to nothing* [*were wasted, went for nothing*].

ブイ buoy [búːi] ⓒ ∥救命ブイ a life *buoy*

ブイアイピー VIP ⓒ (✤*v*ery *i*mportant *p*erson の略語)

フィアンセ (男) one's fiancé [fiːɑːnséi] ⓒ; (女) one's fiancée [fiːɑːnséi] ⓒ

フィート foot ⓒ (複 feet) (✤30.48センチメートル; (略語)ft.; 数字の後に′を付けて表す) ∥12インチは1フィートだ Twelve inches make one *foot*. / 彼は身長が6フィート2インチある He is six *feet* [*foot*] two inches tall. / He is 6′ 2″ tall.

フィードバック feedback Ⓤ ──フィードバックする feed* back

フィーリング (感情・感じ) feeling ⓒⓊ

◆彼とはフィーリングが合わない (→仲よくやっていけない) He and I *don't get along well*.

フィールディング 〖野球〗〖守備〗fielding Ⓤ

フィールド field ⓒ ∥フィールド競技 field sports; (種目) a field event / フィールドワーク fieldwork

ふいうち 不意打ち surprise attack ⓒ

◆相手に不意打ちを食わせる *take* [*catch*] an opponent *by surprise*

フィギュア(スケート) figure skating Ⓤ

フィクション fiction ⓒⓊ ∥このドラマはフィクションだ This drama is *fiction*.

ブイサイン Vサイン V sign ⓒ, victory sign ⓒ ∥Vサインをする make a *V sign*

ふいちょう 吹聴 ──吹聴する broadcast* ㊟; (意見などを) air ㊟ ∥自分の意見を吹聴する *air one's* opinion / 彼女は息子の成功を吹聴している She *is broadcasting* her son's success.

ふいっち 不一致 disagreement ⓒⓊ; (不和) (公式的) discord Ⓤ ∥意見の不一致 *disagreement* in opinions ◆彼は言行不一致だった He *said one thing and did another*. / 性格の不一致が原因で二人は離婚した They divorced because of their *incompatibility*.

フィットネスクラブ fitness club ⓒ

ブイティーアール VTR (録画されたもの) video (recording) ⓒ; (機器) VCR ⓒ (✤*v*ideo *c*assette *r*ecorder の略語), VTR ⓒ (✤*v*ideo *t*ape *r*ecorder の略語) ∥この場面をVTRで見てみよう Let's watch *a video* of this scene.

ぶいと 彼女は怒ってぷいと横を向いた She suddenly turned away her face in anger.

フィナーレ 〖音楽・演劇〗finale ⓒ (✤イタリア語から)

フィヨルド fjord [fiɔ́ːrd] ⓒ, fiord ⓒ

ブイヨン bouillon [búljɑn] ⓒ

フィラデルフィア Philadelphia (✤米国の都市)

フィリピン the Philippines (✤公式名 the Republic of the Philippines) ──フィリピン人 (男性) Filipino ⓒ; (女性) Filipina ⓒ ──フィリピン(人)の Filipino ∥フィリピン諸島 the Philippine Islands, the Philippines

フィルター filter ⓒ ∥(たばこの) filter tip ⓒ ∥フィルター付きたばこ a cigarette with *a filter tip*; a *filter* cigarette

フィルハーモニー philharmonic orchestra ⓒ

フィルム film ⓒⓊ ∥フィルム1本 a roll of *film* / カラー[白黒]フィルム color [black-and-white] *film* / 36枚撮りフィルム a 36 exposure roll of *film* / 高感度フィルム (a) fast *film* / フィルムを現像する develop *film* / カメラにフィルムを入れる load a camera with *film*; load *film* in [into] a camera / フィルムを巻き戻す rewind *film* ∥フィルムライブラリー a film library

フィン fin ⓒ

ぶいん 部員 member ⓒ;《集合的》the staff (✤(英)では単数形で複数扱いになることがある) ∥テニス部の部員 *a member* of the tennis club ∥新入部員 a new member

フィンランド Finland (✤公式名 the Republic of Finland) ──フィンランド人 Finn ⓒ,《集合的》the Finns, the Finnish ──フィンランド語 Finnish Ⓤ ──フィンランド(人[語])の Finnish

ふう¹ 風
❶ 〖様子〗look ⓒ, appearance ⓒ, air ⓒ
彼は芸術家風だ He has *the look* [*appearance, air*] of an artist. / He *looks like* an artist.
❷ 〖様式・型式〗style ⓒⓊ, type ⓒ, manner ⓒ
日本風の庭園 a Japanese-*style* garden / ミケランジェロ風の絵 a painting 「in *the manner* of [after] Michelangelo
彼はヘミングウェイ風に書く He writes in *the style* of Hemingway.
❸ 〖方法・ぐあい〗way ⓒ, manner ⓒ
はしはこんなふうに持ちなさい Hold your chopsticks 「(*in*) *this way* [*in this manner*].
そんなふうにふるまってはいけない Don't behave 「(*in*) *that way* [*like that*].
◆どういうふうにこの問題を解決すればよいだろう *How* should we settle the problem?
〖慣用表現〗利いたふうな口をきくな(→何でも知っているようなふりをするな) Don't *talk as if you know everything*.

ふう² 封 seal ⓒ ∥手紙の封を切る *break the seal of* a letter; *open* [*unseal*] a letter
◆手紙の封をする *seal* a letter

ふうあつ 風圧 wind pressure Ⓤⓒ
∥風圧計 a pressure anemometer

ふういん 封印 seal [C] **—封印する** seal [他] ‖封印を破る break *the seal* / 手紙を封印する *seal* (*up*) a letter

ブーイング booing [U] ◆その選手のプレーにブーイングする *boo* the player's play

ふうう 風雨 wind and rain; (暴風雨) (rain)storm [C], the elements ‖その自転車は風雨にさらされてさびてしまった Exposure to 「*wind and rain* [*the elements*] caused the bicycle to rust. / 明け方には風雨が強まるでしょう *The wind and rain* will become stronger at dawn. / 飛行機は風雨のため離陸できなかった The plane was unable to take off because of *the* (*rain*)*storm*.

ふううん 風雲 (風と雲) winds and clouds [慣用表現] 風雲急を告げている *The situation is tense* [*threatening*].

ふううんじ 風雲児 lucky adventurer [C]

ふうか 風化 weathering [U] **—風化する** weather [自]; (記憶などが) fade (away) **—風化した** weathered ‖その地震の記憶は徐々に風化しつつある Memories of the earthquake are gradually *fading*.

ふうかく 風格 (雰囲気) air [C]; (威厳) dignity [U] ‖彼には王者の風格が漂っている He shows *a* kingly [royal] *air*. / 彼にはチャンピオンとしての風格がある He has *the dignity* of a champion.

ふ

ふうがわり 風変わり **—風変わりな** strange; (人・行動・服装などが) eccentric; (奇妙な) odd; (一風変わった) peculiar; (形・意味などが) fantastic ➔ へん(変), きみょう ‖風変わりな服装 *strange* clothes / 風変わりな男 an *eccentric* [an *odd*, a *peculiar*] man / 風変わりな図案 *fantastic* designs

ふうき 風紀 (社会道徳) public morals; (規律) discipline [U] ‖風紀を乱す corrupt *public morals* / 風紀をよくする improve [enforce] *public morals* / 風紀を取り締まる control *public morals* / その高校の風紀は乱れていた *Discipline* was lost at the high school.

ふうきり 封切り release [C][U] **—封切る** release [他] ‖この映画は来月封切られる This film will *be released* next month.
‖封切り映画 a newly released film [movie], a first-run film [movie] / 封切り館 a first-run theater

ふうけい 風景 (特定の場所の) scene [C]; (ある地方全体の) scenery [U]; (眺め) view [C]
街角の風景 street *scenes* / アルプスの山岳風景 *the* mountain *scenery* of the Alps
バルコニーから美しい田園風景が見えた I had *a* beautiful *view* of the countryside from the balcony.
‖風景画 (a) landscape (painting) / 風景画家 a landscape painter

ブーゲンビリア 〔植物〕 bougainvillea [bùːɡənvíliə] [C]

ふうこう 風向 wind direction [C][U] ‖風向計 a weathervane

ふうこうめいび 風光明媚 この地方は風光明媚な(→景色が美しい)所だ *The scenery is beautiful* in this region.

ふうさ 封鎖 blockade [C]; (賃金などの凍結) freezing [C] **—封鎖する** blockade [他]; freeze* [他] ‖経済封鎖 *an* economic *blockade* / 海上の封鎖を解く lift [raise] *the blockade* of a port / 市内の道路がすべて封鎖された All the roads in the city *were blockaded*.

ふうさい 風采 appearance [U][C], presence [U] ‖風采のりっぱな人 a man of great *appearance* [*presence*] / 彼は風采があがらない (→風格がない) He *has an undignified appearance*. / (→印象的でない) He *is not very impressive in appearance*.

ふうさつ 封殺 〔野球〕 force-out [C] **—封殺する** force out ‖ランナーはセカンドで封殺された The runner *was forced out* at second.

ふうし 風刺 satire [C][U] **—風刺の** satiric **—風刺する** satirize [他] ‖この小説は人間社会を風刺したものだ This novel is *a satire* of human society.
‖風刺画 a caricature / 風刺画家 a caricaturist / 風刺作家 a satirist / 風刺小説 a satirical novel / 風刺漫画 a cartoon

ふうじこめる 封じ込める (感情などを) contain [他]; (閉じ込める) shut* in; (反対意見などを) silence [他]

ふうしゃ 風車 windmill [C]
‖風車小屋 a windmill (shed)

ふうしゅう 風習 custom [C], manners; (慣例) practice [C][U] ‖古い風習 *an* old *custom* / 風習を守る observe *a custom* / その風習は今でも日本に残っている That *custom* is still found in Japan.

ふうしょ 封書 (sealed) letter [C]

ふうじる 封じる (阻止する) block [他]; (黙らせる) silence [他] ‖相手の攻撃を封じる *block* an opponent's attack / 彼の口を封じる *silence* him

ふうしん 風疹 〔医学〕 rubella [U], German measles《単数扱い》

ブース booth [C] ‖投票ブース *a* voting [polling] *booth*

ふうすいがい 風水害 storm and flood damage

ブースター (増幅器) booster [C]
‖ブースターケーブル jumper cables

ふうせつ 風雪 (風と雪) wind and snow; (吹雪) snowstorm [C]; (苦難) hardships ‖彼は人生の幾多の風雪に耐えてきた (→苦難を乗り越えてきた) He *has overcome many hardships* in life.
◆その寺は何世紀にもわたって風雪に耐えてきた (→損なわれていない) The temple *has remained intact* over the centuries.

ふうせん 風船 balloon [C] ‖紙[ゴム]風船 *a* paper [rubber] *balloon* / 風船をふくらませる blow up *a balloon* / 風船を飛ばす fly *a balloon* / 風船が破裂した *The balloon* burst.
‖風船ガム bubble gum

ふうぜんのともしび 風前の灯 その子の命は風前の灯だ The child's life *hangs by a thread* [*hair*].

ふうそく 風速 wind speed [velocity] [U] ‖最大瞬間風速 *the* maximum instantaneous *wind speed* [*velocity*]

◆風速10メートルの風が吹いている The wind is blowing at 10 meters per second.

‖風速計 a wind gauge, an anemometer

ふうぞく 風俗 (風習) customs [C], manners; (社会の風紀) public morals; (性風俗産業) the sex trade

現代の風俗 *the manners* of today / 風俗を乱す corrupt *public morals*

‖風俗営業 entertainment and amusement business(es); (性風俗) sex business(es) / 風俗画 a genre picture / 風俗習慣 manners and customs / 風俗小説 a novel of manners / 風俗店 a massage parlor, a brothel

ふうち 風致 (自然の趣) scenic beauty [U], the beauty of the scenery

◆風致を損なう destroy *the scenery*

‖風致地区 a scenic area / 風致林 a forest grown for scenic beauty

ふうちょう 風潮 (傾向) tendency [C], trend [C]; (社会・時代などの) climate [C] [U], current [C]《通例単数形》; (世論などの) tide [C] ‖時代の風潮に従う go [swim] with *the current* [*tide*] of the times / 時代の風潮に逆らう go [swim] against *the current* [*tide*] of the times / オフィスで働かずに自宅で働く風潮が強くなっている There is *a* growing *tendency* for people to work at home instead of in offices.

ブーツ boots ‖1足のブーツ a pair of *boots* / 彼女はブーツを履いた[脱いだ] She ｢put on [took off] her *boots*.

ふうてい 風体 appearance [U] [C], look [C]

◆怪しい風体の男 a *suspicious-looking* man

ふうど 風土 climate [C] ‖彼の作品は熊野の風土と切り離して考えることができない You can't consider his works and *the climate* of Kumano separately. ◆その習慣は風土に深く根ざしている The custom is deeply rooted in *the land and climate*.

‖風土病 an endemic (disease), a local disease

フード[1] (食物) food [U] ‖ドッグフード dog *food* / ジャンクフード junk *food* / ベビーフード baby *food*

フード[2] (ずきん) hood [húd] [C] ‖フードをかぶる wear *a hood* / フード付きのジャケット a jacket *with a hood*; a *hooded* jacket

ふうとう 封筒 envelope [C] ‖封筒に切手をはる stick a stamp on *an envelope* / 返信用封筒 *a* return *envelope* / 封筒をあける[に封をする] open [seal (up)] *an envelope* / 彼女は手紙を折って封筒に入れた She folded the letter and put it in *the envelope*.

プードル 〘動物〙 poodle [C]

ふうにゅう 封入 ——封入する enclose [他] ‖手紙に小切手を封入する *enclose* a check with a letter

ふうび 風靡 ➔いっせい(一世)

ブービー ⚠ 父は今回のゴルフのコンペでブービー(→びりから2番目)だったらしい My father said he *came in second to last* in this golf competition.

‖ブービー賞 a second-to-last prize (❖ a booby prize は｢最下位賞｣の意味)

ふうひょう 風評 rumor [C] [U] ➔うわさ

ふうふ 夫婦 husband and wife (❖無冠詞で用いることもある), (married) couple [C], pair [C]《単数または複数扱い》 ——夫婦の married (❖名詞の前で用いる)

彼らは夫婦だ They are *husband and wife*.

ビルとケイトは申し分のない夫婦だ Bill and Kate are *a* perfect *couple*.

◆夫婦になる *get married* / 石川さん夫婦 *Mr. and Mrs.* Ishikawa; *Mr.* Ishikawa *and his wife* / 父と母はよく夫婦げんか(→口げんか)をする My father and mother often have *quarrels* [*fights*]. / 彼らは夫婦仲がいい The couple *are getting along well* (with each other). / They *are happily married*. / 今度はご夫婦で(→妻[夫]と)おいでください *Please come with your wife* [*husband*] next time.

‖夫婦愛 love between husband and wife / 夫婦関係 marital relations / 夫婦生活 married life / おしどり夫婦 a well-matched couple, 《口語的》lovebirds / 新婚夫婦 a newly wedded couple, newlyweds / 中年夫婦 a middle-aged couple / 老夫婦 an elderly couple / 若夫婦 a young couple

[ことわざ] 夫婦げんかは犬も食わない A fight between a married couple is best ignored by everyone else. (→夫婦げんかはほうっておくに限る)

ふうふう ふうふう息を吹きかけてスープを冷ました I *blew on* my soup to cool it. / 最終電車に間に合うために全速力で走ったので，彼はふうふういっていた He *was breathing hard*, because he ran as fast as he could to catch the last train. / 彼女は仕事が忙しくてふうふういっている(→ひと休みする暇もない) She *is too busy* with her work *to take a rest*.

ぶうぶう (不平を言う) complain [自], grumble [自]; (豚が) grunt [自]; (警笛を鳴らす) blow* on ‖彼女はいつも何かにつけてぶうぶう文句を言っている She *is* always *complaining* [*grumbling*] about something.

ふうぶつ 風物 日本の風物 *things* Japanese (❖形容詞は後に置かれる) / セミは夏の風物詩だ(→夏が来たことを感じさせる) The cicadas *make us feel that summer has come*.

ふうふべっせい 夫婦別姓 separate surnames for married couples

◆彼と結婚しても夫婦別姓(→旧姓のまま)がいいな I want to *keep my maiden name* even if I marry him.

ふうぼう 風貌 look [C], appearance [U] [C], presence [U] ‖彼は気品のある風貌をしている He has *a* noble *look*.

ふうみ 風味 flavor [U] [C]; (味) taste [U] [C] ‖ほのかなココナッツ風味 a hint of coconut *flavor* / そのケーキはチョコレート風味だった The cake had *a* chocolate *flavor*. / ワインを入れるとソースの風味がよくなった Wine imparted good *flavor* to the sauce. / 母はスープにコシ

ブーム

ョウを入れて風味を加えた My mother added some pepper to give the soup more *taste*.

ブーム boom ⓒ ‖戦後のベビーブーム *the post-war baby boom* / パソコンブームの年 a *boom* year for PCs ◆この手の音楽は今大変なブームです This kind of music is 「*all the rage* [*very popular*]」 now. / その年はイタリア料理がブームになった Italian food became *a big fad* that year.

ブーメラン boomerang ‖ブーメラン効果 a boomerang effect

ふうらいぼう 風来坊（放浪者）wanderer ⓒ, vagabond ⓒ;（気まぐれな人）capricious person ⓒ

フーリガン hooligan ⓒ

ふうりゅう 風流 elegance Ⓤ, taste Ⓤ, refinement Ⓤ ——風流な elegant, tasteful, refined / 風流な人 a person of 「(refined) *taste* [*poetic mind*]」

ふうりょく 風力 the force [velocity] of the wind;（動力）wind power ‖風力計 a wind gauge / 風力発電 wind power generation

ふうりん 風鈴 wind bell ⓒ ‖風鈴が鳴っている *The wind bell is tinkling*.

プール ❶［水泳場］(swimming) pool ⓒ / 温水プール a heated (swimming) pool / 屋内［屋外］プール an indoor [outdoor] (swimming) pool / プールに泳ぎに行く go swimming in *a pool* / プールに飛び込む dive into *a pool*
❷［蓄えること］pool ⓒ ——プールする pool Ⓣ ‖資金をプールする *pool* money
‖プールサイド the poolside

ふうん 不運 misfortune ⓒⓊ, hard [bad] luck Ⓤ ——不運な unfortunate, unlucky, ill-fated ⇒ふこう ‖その事故は本当に不運だった The accident was *a real misfortune*. / 彼はここのところ不運続きだ He's had *a run of hard luck* lately.
◆彼は不運にも財産を失った *Unfortunately* [*Unluckily*], he lost everything he owned. / It was unlucky [unfortunate] that he lost everything he owned.

ぶうん ハチが部屋の中でぶうんと音を立てていた A bee *was buzzing* in the room.

ふえ 笛（横笛）flute ⓒ;（縦笛）pipe ⓒ;（ホイッスル）whistle ⓒ ‖笛を吹く play *the flute*; blow *a whistle* / 彼は公園で笛の音を聞いた He heard the sound of *a flute* in the park.

フェア¹ ——フェアな（公正な）fair (↔unfair);〚野球〛fair (↔foul) ‖フェアにやろうよ Let's *play fair*.
‖フェアグラウンド fair territory / フェアプレー fair play

フェア²（展示会）fair ⓒ ‖ブックフェア a book fair

フェアウエー 〚ゴルフ〛fairway ⓒ

ふえいせい 不衛生 poor sanitation ——不衛生な unsanitary ‖不衛生な環境 an *unsanitary* environment

フェイント 〚スポーツ〛feint ⓒ ——フェイントをかける feint Ⓘ

フェードアウト fade-out Ⓤ ——フェードアウトする fade out

フェードイン fade-in Ⓤ ——フェードインする fade in

フェーンげんしょう フェーン現象 foehn [féin] phenomenon ⓒ

フェザーきゅう フェザー級 〚ボクシング〛featherweight class ⓒ ◆フェザー級の選手 a featherweight

フェスティバル festival ⓒ ⇒まつり

ふえて 不得手 ——不得手な poor, bad ⇒へた（下手）‖私は料理が不得手だ I am *poor* [*bad*] at cooking.

フェニックス（不死鳥）phoenix [fíːniks] ⓒ

ブエノスアイレス Buenos Aires（✿アルゼンチンの首都）

フェミニスト ⚠feminist ⓒ（✿男女同権論者，女権拡張論者を指し，「女性に優しい男性」の意味はない）;（女性に優しい男性）chivalrous man ⓒ, a man who is kind to women

フェミニズム（男女同権主義）feminism Ⓤ

フェラチオ fellatio [fəléiʃiòu] Ⓤ

フェリー ferry (boat) ⓒ ‖横浜行きのフェリーに乗る board *a ferry* to Yokohama
‖カーフェリー a car ferry

ふえる 増える・殖える increase Ⓘ (↔decrease);（数・量を増やす）gain Ⓣ (↔lose) ⇒ふやす，ます（増す）

その市の人口は1990年以降5万人増えた The population of the city *has increased* by 50,000 since 1990.

中途退学する生徒の数は年々増えている The number of students who drop out of school *is increasing* every year. / *More and more* students are dropping out of school every year.

私たちの出費は増える一方だ（→着実に増えている）Our expenses *are increasing steadily*.

この冬体重が2キロ増えた I *gained* [*put on*] *two kilograms* this winter.

◆（子供が生まれて）家族が1人増えた We *had an addition to* our family. / 結婚後も仕事を続ける女性がますます増えている *More and more* women continue to work after getting married.

フェルト felt Ⓤ ‖フェルトのスリッパ (a pair of) felt slippers
‖フェルトペン a felt pen / フェルト帽 a felt hat

フェロモン pheromone

フェンシング fencing Ⓤ ‖フェンシングをする do fencing; fence
‖フェンシング選手 a fencer

フェンス fence ⇒さく（柵）, へい（塀）

フェンダー（自動車の泥よけ）fender ⓒ,《英》wing ⓒ

ぶえんりょ 無遠慮 ——無遠慮な（厚かましい）impudent;（不作法な）rude, impolite ——無遠慮に impudently; rudely, impolitely ‖無遠慮なふるまい *rude* behavior / 彼の無遠慮な言葉で彼女は気を悪くした She was offended by his *rude* [*impolite, impudent*]

remarks./ 彼は無遠慮にその女性の年齢を聞いた He *impolitely* asked the woman how old she was

フォアグラ foie gras [fwɑː grɑ́ː]ⓤ(❖フランス語から.太らせたガチョウの肝臓・そのペースト)

フォアボール (野球で) a base on balls, walk ⓒ / ⚠打者にフォアボールを与える give a batter *a base on balls*; (→フォアボールで歩かせる) walk a batter / 彼はフォアボールで一塁に歩いた He *walked* (*to first*)./ He got a *walk*.

フォーカス (焦点) focus ⓒ ◆オートフォーカスのカメラ an *autofocus* camera
‖ソフトフォーカス soft *focus*

フォーク fork ⓒ (❖食事用のフォークと農作業用のフォークの両方を指す) ‖ナイフとフォークで食べる eat with (a) *knife and fork* (❖1つのセットとして考えるので, fork の前に a は不要) / 父はナイフとフォークの使い方が下手だ My father is awkward with his *knife and fork*. / 妹はナイフとフォークを器用に使う My sister handles *a knife and fork* skillfully.

フォークソング folk song
‖フォークソング歌手 a folk *singer*

フォークダンス (レクリエーションの) dance ⓤⓒ; (民族舞踊) folk dance ⓤⓒ ‖フォークダンスをする dance ⓥⓘ; folk-dance ⓥⓘ

フォークボール 〖野球〗forkball ⓒ

フォークリフト fork-lift [forklift] (truck) ⓒ

フォースアウト 〖野球〗force-out ⓒ ◆ランナーをフォースアウトにする force *a runner out*

フォーマット (コンピュータ) (データ形式) format ⓒ; (書式・ひな形) form ⓒ ◆フロッピーディスクをフォーマットする *format* a floppy disk

フォーマル ―フォーマルな (公式的な・格式ばった) formal ◆あすのパーティーはフォーマルな服装でお越しください Please dress *formally* for tomorrow's party.
‖フォーマルドレス[スーツ] a *formal* dress [suit]

フォーミュラ (レーシングカーの規格) formula ⓤ (❖後に数字を伴う)
‖フォーミュラカー a *formula* car

フォーム (スポーツで動作の型) form ⓒ, action ⓒ ‖投球フォームを変える change *one's pitching form* / 彼はすばらしいフォームで泳ぐ He has *an* excellent *swimming form*./ His *swimming form* is excellent. / 彼女は美しいフォームで着地した She landed *in a beautiful action*.

フォーメーション (陣形) formation ⓤⓒ

フォーラム (公開討論会) forum ⓒ ‖捕鯨に関する国際フォーラムがあす京都で開催される An *international forum* on whaling will be held in Kyoto tomorrow.

フォールト 〖テニス〗(サーブの失敗) fault ⓒ ‖ダブルフォールト a double *fault*

フォグランプ fog light [lamp] ⓒ

フォト (写真) photo(graph) ⓒ

ぶおとこ 醜男 ugly(-looking) man

フォロースルー (テニス・野球・ゴルフなどの) follow-through ⓤⓒ

フォワード (球技で) forward ⓤⓒ (❖ポジションを表す場合はⓤ, 選手を表す場合はⓒ; 〘略語〙fwd.); 〖ラグビー〗pack ⓒ ‖フォワードを務める play *forward*
‖センターフォワード (a) center forward

ふおん 不穏 ―不穏な (不安にさせる) disquieting; (険悪な) threatening, ugly ‖不穏な情勢 a *threatening* [an *ugly*] situation / 不穏なうわさが広まっている There are *disquieting* rumors going around.

フォンデュ (料理の) fondue [fɑndjúː]ⓤⓒ

フォント 〖印刷〗font ⓒ (❖同じ書体・サイズの活字のひとそろい)

ふおんとう 不穏当 (不適切な) improper ‖不穏当な発言 *improper* remarks

ふか¹ 不可 (成績の) F ⓤ (複～'s, ～s) (❖failing の略語) ‖2つ不可をとる get two *F*'s / 数学で不可をとった I 「got an *F* in [*failed*] mathematics.
◆彼の発表は可もなく不可もないというところだった His presentation was 「*neither good nor bad* [*only so-so*]. / 写真撮影不可《掲示》 *No Photographs*

ふか² 付加 addition ⓤ ―付加する add ⇒ふかかわる

ふか³ 孵化 hatching ⓤ, incubation ⓤ ―孵化する hatch ⓥⓘⓥⓣ, incubate ⓥⓘⓥⓣ ‖孵卵器の中でひなが3羽孵化した Three chicks (*were*) *hatched* in the incubator.
‖人工孵化 artificial incubation

ふか⁴ 鱶 shark ⓒ ‖フカヒレ a shark's fin / フカヒレスープ shark's fin soup

ぶか 部下 one's people (複数扱い), (米) one's assistant, (英) one's junior; (集合的) one's staff ⓒ (❖ⓤでは単数形で複数扱いになることがある) ‖彼はいつも部下をこき使っている He always makes *his people* work hard. / 彼女には5人の部下がいる She *has* five *assistants* [*juniors*]. / 彼は部下の一人にデータを収集するように命じた He ordered one of *his staff* [*assistants*] to collect data.
◆将校と彼の部下 an officer and *his men* / 私は3年間彼の部下だった I *worked for* him for three years.

ふかい¹ 深い

❶[空間] deep ―深く deep, deeply (❖空間的な意味での「深く」は deep がふつう)
深い池[穴] a *deep* pond [hole] / (奥行きが) 深い森 [洞窟 (ﾄﾞｳｸﾂ), 引き出し] a *deep* forest [cave, drawer] / 額の深いしわ *deep* creases on one's forehead / 雪深い村 a village *covered with deep snow* / 水中深く潜 (ﾓｸﾞ) る dive *deep* into the water; make a *deep* dive into the water / ジャングルに深く分け入る go [push] *deep* into the jungle / 深くおじぎをする bow *deeply* / 深く息を吸う breathe in *deep* [*deeply*]; draw a *deep* breath
バイカル湖は世界一深い湖である Lake Baikal is *the deepest in the world*.

❷[程度] deep; (知識・理解などが) profound ―深く deeply

彼女は深い眠りからさめた She awoke from a *deep* [*sound*] sleep.
彼は深いため息をついた He sighed a *deep* [*heavy*] sigh.
その映画を見て深い感動を覚えた I was *deeply* [*profoundly*] impressed by the movie.
町は深い悲しみに沈んでいる The town is engulfed [sunk] in *deep* grief [*sorrow*].
彼の言葉は深い知識に裏付けられている What he says is based on *deep* [*profound*] knowledge.
スキャンダルを引き起こしたことを深く反省している I *deeply* regret having caused a scandal.
聴衆は彼の演説を聞いて深く感動した The audience was *deeply* moved by his speech.
この問題は深く検討する必要がある We have to study this problem *deeply*. / This problem requires *deep* study.
◆深い(→濃い)霧 *thick* [*dense*] fog / 君は深く考えすぎだ You take things too *seriously*. / この2つの出来事の間には深い(→密接な)関係がある There is a *close* relationship between the two events. / ご親切に深く感謝します Thank you *very much* for your kindness. / I am *deeply* [*heartily, sincerely*] grateful to you for your kindness.

ふかい² 不快 discomfort ⓤ, (不愉快) displeasure ⓤ ──**不快な** unpleasant, offensive, disgusting(❖後になるほど不快さが強くなる); (不快に感じている) displeased, offended ∥たばこの煙は多くの人に不快感を与える Cigarette smoke is *unpleasant* for many people. / 彼の下品な冗談で彼女は不快な気分になった She was *displeased* with [*offended* at] his coarse joke. / His coarse joke displeased [offended] her. / 彼はそのとき不快な顔をした He looked *displeased* then. ◆部屋の中は暑くて不快だった It was so hot in the room that I *felt sick*.
∥不快指数 discomfort index

ぶかい 部会 (個々の部門) section ⓒ; (クラブの会合) club meeting ⓒ

ぶがいしゃ 部外者 outsider ⓒ ∥私は部外者だったので口を出すことはできなかった I was *an outsider*, so I couldn't say anything.
◆部外者立入禁止《掲示》*Private*

ふがいない 腑甲斐ない (意気地がない) cowardly, spineless, 《口語的》gutless; (屈辱的な) humiliating ∥闘わずに降参するとは彼もふがいない It was *cowardly* of him to give in without fight. / 私たちのチームはふがいない負け方をした Our team suffered a *humiliating* defeat. ◆我ながらふがいない(→自分が恥ずかしい) I'm ashamed of myself.

ふかいり 深入り その問題にはあまり深入りしたくない I don't want to「*go too far into* [*get too deeply involved in*] the matter.

ふかかい 不可解 ──**不可解な** mysterious, enigmatic ∥不可解な事件 a *mysterious* incident / 不可解な行動 one's *enigmatic* [*mysterious*] behavior / 彼の話には不可解なところがある There is something mysterious [enigmatic] about what he says.
◆彼女がどうしてそんなことをしたのかどうも不可解だ I *just can't understand* why she did such a thing.

ふかかち 付加価値 added value ⓤ ∥付加価値税 value-added tax(❖英国および欧州諸国の消費税の一つ; 《略語》VAT)

ふかぎもんぶん 付加疑問文〔文法〕 tag question ⓒ

平叙文の後に付加語句(tag)を付けて, 疑問文にする疑問形式のことを付加疑問文という.
[肯定の平叙文＋否定の付加語句] *You know her, don't you?* あなたは彼女を知っていますね / *She's a beautiful bride, isn't she?* 美しい花嫁ですね
[否定の平叙文＋肯定の付加語句] *Your father doesn't smoke, does he?* お父さんはたばこを吸わないのですね / *Taro won't go to the party, will he?* 太郎はパーティーに行かないのですね
例えば You know her, don't you? というとき, 相手がその女性を知っているかどうかはっきり分からない場合は語尾を上げる. 逆に相手がその女性を知っているということがはっきり分かっている場合には語尾を下げる.

ふかく 不覚 不覚をとる(→不注意な失敗をする) make a blunder, (予想外の敗北を喫する) *suffer an unexpected* [*unforeseen*] *defeat* / 彼は不覚にも(→思わず)涙を流してしまった He started crying *despite himself*. / 前後不覚に(→ぐっすり)眠る sleep *soundly* [*a sound sleep*] / 彼は前後不覚に陥る(→意識がなくなる)まで飲んだ He drank himself *unconscious* [*into a stupor*]. / 彼に金を貸したのは私の一生の不覚だった I *made the biggest mistake of my life* in lending money to him.

ふかくじつ 不確実 uncertainty ⓤ ──**不確実な** uncertain; (信頼できない) unreliable ∥不確実な情報 *uncertain* [*unreliable*] information

ふかくてい 不確定 ──**不確定な** indefinite, uncertain ∥不確定な要素 *indefinite* [*uncertain*] factors

ふかけつ 不可欠 ──**不可欠な** indispensable, essential ∥現代生活に電気は不可欠である Electricity *is indispensable for* modern life. / 小説家には想像力が不可欠だ Imagination is *essential to* novelists.

ふかこうりょく 不可抗力 不可抗力の事故 an *inevitable* accident / この水害は本当に不可抗力の災害だったのだろうか Is it true that this flood was「*a natural calamity* [*an act of God*]? / あの事故は不可抗力だった The accident was *inevitable* [*beyond our control*].

ふかさ 深さ depth ⓤⓒ ∥川の深さを測る measure [sound] *the depth of a river* / その船は深さ200メートルの海底で発見された The boat was found *at a depth of 200 meters*. (◆depthのみで「深み, 水底」の意味がある) ◆この井戸は30メートル以上の深さがある This well *is* more than 30 meters *deep* [*in depth*].
🅔「この池の深さはどれくらいありますか」「いち

ばん深いところで約5メートルです" "*How deep is* the pond?" "It is about five meters deep at its deepest."

ふかざけ 深酒 彼は深酒がたたって体をこわした He ruined his health by *drinking heavily* [*too much*].

ふかざら 深皿 dish ◎

ふかさんめいし 不可算名詞〘文法〙uncountable noun ◎ ◆めいし(名詞)

ふかしぎ 不可思議 ━━**不可思議な** mysterious; (超自然的な) supernatural; (奇妙な) strange ◆ふしぎ

ふかしんじょうやく 不可侵条約 nonaggression pact [treaty] ◎

ふかす¹ 吹かす たばこをふかす *puff on* a cigarette / エンジンをふかす (→回転させる) *run* an engine; (→うるさく空ぶかしする) *race* [*rev*] an engine *loudly* [*noisily*]

ふかす² 蒸かす ジャガイモをふかす (→蒸す) *steam* potatoes

ぶかつ 部活 club [extracurricular] activities ⇨ 場面・状況別会話 p.1748 ∥彼は部活に忙しくて家で勉強する暇がない He spends so much time on *club activities* that he has no time to study at home. / 私たちの学校では部活に参加することが義務づけられている We have to take part in *club activities* at our school.

ぶかっこう 不格好 ━━**不格好な** (形の崩れた) shapeless; (動作などがぎこちない) awkward, clumsy ∥不格好な靴 *clumsy* [*shapeless*] shoes / 彼女は不格好な歩き方をする She has a *clumsy* [*an awkward*] way of walking. / She walks in a *clumsy* [*an awkward*] way.

ふかっぱつ 不活発 ━━**不活発な** inactive, dull ∥市場は不活発な状態が続いている The market remains *inactive* [*dull*].

ふかづめ 深爪 深つめをする *cut* [*pare*] *a* nail 「*too short* [*to the quick*]

ふかで 深手 深手 (→重傷) を負う be wounded *seriously*

ふかのう 不可能 impossibility ◎ ◎ (◆「不可能性」を表す場合は ◎, 「不可能なこと」を表す場合は ◎) ━━**不可能な** impossible; (実行不可能な) impracticable
実現不可能な計画 an *impossible* [*impracticable*] plan
努力しないで成功するのは不可能だと分かった I found it *impossible* to succeed without making an effort. / I found that it was *impossible* to succeed without making an effort.
それは不可能に近い It's *almost* [*nearly*] *impossible*.
それをあしたまでに終わらせるのは事実上不可能です It is 「*virtually impossible* [*impracticable*] to finish it by tomorrow.
その発明が不可能を可能にした The invention *made the impossible possible*.

ふかひ 不可避 ━━**不可避の** inevitable, unavoidable ◆さける(避ける) ∥不可避の事故 an *unavoidable* [*inevitable*] accident / 戦争は不可避だと思いますか Do you think that war is *inevitable*?

ふかふか ━━**ふかふかの** (ふわふわ毛羽立った) fluffy; (柔らかい) soft ∥ふかふかのかけぶとん a *fluffy* quilt / ふかふかの (→柔らかくて心地よい) ソファー a *soft and comfortable* sofa

ふかぶか 深々 彼はその婦人に向かって深々と頭を下げた He bowed *deeply* [*very low*] to the lady. / He made *a deep bow* to the lady. / 彼はいすに深々と腰を下ろした He 「*sat back* [*sank*] *into* the chair.

ぶかぶか この靴はぶかぶかだ (→大きすぎる) These shoes are *too large* for me. / その少年はぶかぶかのズボンをはいていた The boy wore *baggy* trousers. (❖baggy はふくらんだ感じのものに用いる)

ぷかぷか 川をぷかぷかと流れていく *float down* a river / プラスチックのアヒルが浴槽にぷかぷかと浮いている A plastic duck *is floating* in the bathtub. / その漫画のキャラクターはいつもパイプをぷかぷかとふかしている That cartoon character *is* always *puffing* on his pipe.

ふかぶん 不可分 ━━**不可分の** inseparable ∥政治と経済は不可分である Politics and the economy are *inseparable* (*from each other*). / The economy is *inseparable from* politics.

ふかまる 深まる 時がたつにつれ, 彼の彼女への愛はますます深まった His love for her *deepened* as time went by. / 新しい証拠が出現して彼への疑いがさらに深まった Suspicion of him *increased* as new evidence appeared. / その本を読んで古代ギリシャ文化に対する理解が深まった By reading the book, I *acquired a deeper understanding of* ancient Greek culture. / 両国の関係がより深まることを期待している We hope that the relationship between the two countries will *become closer*. / 秋も深まってきた It is now well [*deep*] *into* (*the*) *fall*. / The fall is well *advanced*.

ふかみ 深み (深い所) deep place ◎; (深さ, 知性などの深み) depth ◎, profundity ◎ ◎ ∥川の深みにはまる *fall into a deep place* in a river / 彼の書くものには深みがない His writing *lacks depth*.
◆彼はいかがわしい商売の深みにはまって (→深入りしすぎて) しまい, 抜けられなくなった He 「*got too deeply involved in* [*went too far into*] some shady business and couldn't get himself out of it.

ふかめる 深める deepen ⊕ ∥(…との) 友情を深める *deepen* [*improve*] *one's* friendship (*with ...*) / この本はその問題についてのあなたがたの知識を深めるのに役立つだろう This book will help you (to) 「*deepen* your knowledge [*gain better* knowledge] about the problem.
◆両国の相互理解を深める *promote* better understanding between the two countries / その成功で私は自分の能力について自信を深めた The success *gave* me *more* confidence in my ability.

ぶかん 武官 (陸軍の) military officer ©; (海軍の) naval officer ©

ふかんしょう 不干渉 nonintervention ⓤ ‖内政不干渉 nonintervention in internal [domestic] affairs

ふかんしょう² 不感症 frigidity ⓤ ──不感症の frigid

ふかんぜん 不完全 incompleteness ⓤ, imperfection ⓤ ──不完全な incomplete, imperfect; (欠陥がある) defective ‖不完全な計画 an *incomplete* [*imperfect*] plan / その件については不完全な情報しか得ていない We have been given only *imperfect* information about the matter. / 私のその事件に関する記憶は不完全だ My memory about the case is *imperfect* [*not perfect*]. ◆工場の設備は不完全だ The factory is *imperfectly* equipped. ‖不完全燃焼 incomplete combustion

ふき 付記 supplementary [additional] note ©; (書物の補遺) addendum ⓒ (複 addenda) ──付記する add ⓗ

ふき² 蕗 【植物】(Japanese) butterbur ‖ふきのとう a butterbur flower stalk

ぶき 武器 arms (✿複数形で総称的に用いる); weapon ⓒ ‖武器を捨てる (→武器を渡して降伏する)「give up [surrender] *one's arms*; (→地面に置く) lay down *one's arms* / 彼らは武器を取って戦った They took up *arms* and fought. / 警察は彼らから武器を取り上げた The police took *the weapons* away from them. / ペンを武器に社会悪と戦う *write* to fight against social evils ‖武器弾薬 arms and ammunition

ふきあげる 吹き上げる blow* up, spout ⓗ ‖風が土ぼこりを吹き上げた The wind *blew up* the dust. / その鯨は潮を吹き上げた The whale *spouted* water.

ふきあれる 吹き荒れる rage ⓗ, blow* hard ‖一晩中あらしが吹き荒れた The storm *raged* [*blew hard*] all night.

ふきおろす 吹き下ろす (風が) blow* down

ふきかえ 吹き替え (音声の) dubbing ⓤ; (代役) stand-in ⓒ ──吹き替える (音声を) dub ⓗ ‖そのフランス映画は日本語で吹き替えられた The French movie *was dubbed into* Japanese. / その映画を吹き替えではなく字幕で見たい I want to see that movie with subtitles instead of *dubbed*.

ふきかえす 吹き返す 彼は人工呼吸で息を吹き返した He *came around* [*to*] after artificial respiration.

ふきかける 吹き掛ける (息などを) blow* on; (液体を) spray ⓗ; (煙などを) puff ⓗ ‖彼女は指に息を吹きかけて暖めた She *blew on* her fingers to warm them. / 彼は私の顔にたばこの煙を吹きかけた He *puffed* cigarette smoke in my face.

ふきけす 吹き消す blow* out ‖少女はろうそくをひと吹きで吹き消した The little girl *blew out* the candles in one puff.

ふきげん 不機嫌 bad mood [temper, humor] ⓒ, sullenness ⓤ ──不機嫌な bad-tempered, sullen ‖不機嫌な顔をする look sullen; wear a frown / 私が電話したとき, 彼女は不機嫌だった When I called her, she *was in a bad mood* [*temper, humor*]. / ジャイアンツが負けて父は不機嫌になった My father *was sullen* [*grumpy*] because the Giants lost the game.

ふきこぼれる 吹きこぼれる boil over ‖スープが吹きこぼれた The soup *boiled over*.

ふきこむ 吹き込む ❶【風・雨などが】 blow* into ‖冷たい風が部屋の中に吹き込んだ The cold wind *blew into* the room.
❷【息を】 blow* up [into] ‖少年は風船に息を吹き込んだ The boy *blew up* [*into*] a balloon.
❸【思想などを】 put* … into *a person's* head, 《口語的》 feed*ⓗ, breathe ⓗ ‖だれがそのような考えを彼女に吹き込んだのか Who *put* that idea *into her head*? / 彼にそんなうそを吹き込まないで Don't *feed* him such lies. / Don't *feed* such lies to him. / Don't *feed* him with such lies.
❹【録音する】 record ⓗ ‖その歌手は新曲を吹き込んだ The singer *has recorded* a new song.

ふきさらし その自転車は長い間吹きさらしになっている The bicycle *has been exposed to the wind* for a long time.

ふきすさぶ 吹き荒ぶ blow* hard ‖一晩中あらしが吹きすさんだ The storm *blew hard* all night.

ふきそ 不起訴 nonprosecution, nonindictment ◆彼は証拠不十分で不起訴になった He *was not prosecuted* [*indicted*] because of a lack of evidence.

ふきそうじ 拭き掃除 (ふくこと) wiping ⓤ; (磨くこと) scrubbing ⓤ ◆床のふき掃除をする *wipe* [*scrub*] a floor (clean)

ふきそく 不規則 irregularity ⓤ ──不規則な irregular (↔regular) ──不規則に irregularly ‖不規則な生活をする live [lead] an *irregular* life / その明かりは不規則な間隔で点滅していた The light was flashing on and off *at irregular intervals*. / 彼女は夕食の時間が不規則だ She eats dinner *irregularly*.
‖不規則動詞【文法】an irregular verb / 不規則変化【文法】an irregular conjugation

ふきたおす 吹き倒す blow* down ‖強風のために木が何本か吹き倒された (→強風は木を何本か吹き倒した) The gale *blew down* several trees.

ふきだす 吹き出す・噴き出す ❶【勢いよく出る】(液体が) spout (out); (風が) begin* [start] to blow; (煙が) puff ⓗ; (芽が) sprout ⓗ, bud ⓗ; (不満などが) erupt ⓗ ‖水道管から水が吹き出した Water *spouted* [*gushed*] *out* from the water pipe.
◆体からどっと汗が吹き出した I *broke out* in sweat all over.
❷【笑いだす】 burst* out laughing, burst into laughter ‖彼女は彼の冗談でふきだした She *burst out laughing* at his joke.

ふきだまり 吹き溜まり drift ⓒ ‖裏道に雪の

吹きだまりがある There are「snow *drifts* [*snowdrifts*] filling the back streets.

ふきちらす 吹き散らす blow* away [off] // 扇風機が机の上の紙を吹き散らした The electric fan *blew away* the paper off the table.

ふきつ 不吉 ━不吉な (不運な) unlucky; (悪事が起こりそうな) ominous //不吉な黒い雲 an *ominous* dark cloud / 日本では 4 は不吉な数だ Four is an *unlucky* number in Japan. / 不吉な予感がする I have「an *ominous* feeling [a premonition].

ふきつける 吹き付ける ❶【雨・風などが】blow* against ... //昨夜は雨が雨戸に激しく吹きつけていた The rain *was blowing* hard *against* the shutters last night.

❷【塗料・殺虫剤などを】spray [他] //父は壁にスプレー塗料を吹きつけた My father *sprayed* paint on the wall. / My father *sprayed* the wall with paint.

ぶきっちょ clumsy //私はぶきっちょなので日曜大工は苦手だ I'm not good at do-it-yourself projects because I'm *clumsy*.

ふきでもの 吹き出物 (にきび) pimple [C]; (発疹(ほっしん)) rash [C] //顔に吹き出物ができた I've got *pimples* on my face.

ふきとばす 吹き飛ばす ❶【風などが】blow* away [off] //台風20号は多くの家屋を吹き飛ばした Typhoon No.20 *blew* many houses *away*.

❷【払いのける】寒さなんか吹き飛ばして(→無視して)しまいなさい *Ignore* the cold *away*.

ふきとぶ 吹き飛ぶ ❶【風などで】be blown away [off] //激しいあらしにうちの屋根が吹き飛んだ The roof of my house *was blown off* in the heavy storm.

❷【心配などが】ガールフレンドの笑顔で悩みも吹き飛んだ(→ガールフレンドの笑顔が悩みを吹き飛ばした) My girlfriend's smile *drove* my worries *away*.

ふきとる 拭き取る wipe away [off] //汚れをふき取る *wipe away* the dirt

ふきながし 吹き流し streamer [C]

ふきぬけ 吹き抜け (階段の) stairwell [C]; (ホテルなどの) atrium [C] (複 atria, ～s) //そのホテルのロビーは吹き抜けになっている The hotel's lobby is in *an atrium*.

◆ 1 階の居間は吹き抜けになっている The living room on the first floor *is open to* the second floor.

ぶきみ 不気味・無気味 ━不気味な (不思議な) weird [wíərd]; (怖い) eerie [íri]; (幽霊が出そうな)《口語的》spooky //暗やみで何か不気味な気配がした I sensed something *weird* in the darkness. / 何だかこの家は不気味だな This house seems kind of *spooky*.

◆あたりは不気味なほどひっそりと静まり返っていた The area was *spookily* quiet.

ふきや 吹き矢 blowgun [C]

ふきゅう¹ 普及 the spread; (大衆化) popularization [U] ━普及する (一般的になる) become* popular; (広がる・広める) spread* [自] [他]; (大衆化する) popularize [他]

インターネットの普及は我々の生活を変えた *The spread* of the Internet has changed our lives.

途上国において義務教育の普及は重要だ It is vital to *spread* compulsory education in developing countries.

DVD プレーヤーはますます普及するだろう DVD players will *become* increasingly *popular*.

この地域ではケーブルテレビの普及率はそれほど高くない Cable television *has not become so popular* in this area.

ふきゅう² 不朽 ━不朽の (不滅の) immortal; (永久の) everlasting //これは彼の不朽の名作といわれている It's said that this is his *immortal* masterpiece.

ふきょう¹ 不況 (長期に渡る深刻な) depression [C]; (一時的な景気後退) recession [C] [U]; (事業などの不振) slump [C] //不況から回復する recover from *the recession* / 長引く不況のため多くの人が職にあぶれている *The* prolonged *recession* has left many people unemployed. / 石油産業の不況は多くの業界に影響を与えた *The slump* in the oil industry made an impact on a lot of businesses.

ふきょう² 布教 (伝道) mission [C]; (布教活動) missionary work [U] ━布教する spread* [他], 《公式的》propagate [他] //彼女は布教活動に非常に熱心だ She is very much involved in *missionary work*.

ふきょう³ 不興 彼女の両親の不興を買ってしまった I've *offended* [*displeased*] my girlfriend's parents.

ぶきよう 不器用・無器用 ━不器用な (ぎこちない) awkward, clumsy //新井さんは恋愛に不器用だ Mr. Arai is *awkward* in love. / 彼は不器用な手つきでくぎを打っていた He was hammering a nail *in an awkward way*.

◆私は不器用なので折り紙は苦手だ I'm not good at origami because I *am all thumbs*.

ふきょうわおん 不協和音〘音楽〙discord [C], dissonance [C]

[慣用表現] あの 2 人の間には不協和音が生じている There is *a note of discord* between them.

ぶきょく¹ 部局 department [C]

ぶきょく² 舞曲 dance music [U]

ふぎり 不義理 ━不義理な (恩知らずの) ungrateful //あいつは不義理な男だ He is an *ungrateful* man.

◆田中先生のところにはお礼にも伺わず不義理をしています I *have been remiss* to Mr. Tanaka because I haven't gone to thank him.

ぶきりょう 不器量・無器量 ━不器量な (顔立ちがぱっとしない) plain, 《米》homely //彼女は恥ずかしがり屋で不器量な女の子だ She is a shy and *homely* girl.

ふきん¹ 付近 neighborhood, 《英》neighbourhood [U]; (一帯) the vicinity ━付近の neighboring, 《英》neighbouring; (すぐ近くの) nearby

付近の家々 *neighboring* houses

この付近には飲食店がたくさんある There are plenty of restaurants in *the neighbor-*

ふきん

◆この付近には有名人がたくさん住んでいる Many celebrities live *around* [*near*] here. / 付近の住民はパチンコ店進出に反対した The *neighbors* protested against building a pachinko parlor in the area.

ふきん² 布巾 (皿ふき) cloth ⓒ; (皿をふくための) 《米》dish towel ⓒ, 《英》tea towel ⓒ

ふきんこう 不均衡 imbalance ⓤ, a lack of balance (❖unbalance は「精神的不安定」の意味) ━━不均衡な unbalanced // 日本は率先して貿易不均衡を是正するべきだ Japan should take the initiative in rectifying *the trade imbalance*.

ふきしん 不謹慎 (無分別) indiscretion ⓤ; (下品) indecency ⓤ ━━不謹慎な indiscreet; indecent // 彼の不謹慎な態度には我慢できない I cannot stand his *indiscreet* manner. / ここでそんな下品な冗談を言うなんて君は少し不謹慎だ It's *indecent* of you to make such a dirty joke here.

ふく¹ 服

clothes [klóuz] (複数扱い); (帽子・スカーフなども含めて集合的に) clothing ⓤ; (ドレス) dress ⓒ ➡ 場面・状況別会話 p.1726

服を着る[脱ぐ] 「put on [take off] one's *clothes* / おしゃれな[はやりの]服 smart [fashionable] *clothes*

急いで服を着替えなさい Change your *clothes* quickly.

彼は3着しか服を持っていない He has only three suits of *clothes*.

彼女はたくさんの服を持っている She has a lot of *clothes* [*dresses*].

私たちは服の好みが違う Our tastes in *clothes* are different.

彼女はこの服を着るといちばん美しく見える She looks most beautiful in this *dress*.

この服を洗濯機に入れておいてくれない？ Will you put these *clothes* into the washing machine?

◆赤い服を着た女性 a woman *in* red / 彼女はピンクの服を着ていた She *was dressed* in pink./ She *was in* a pink *dress*.

∥子供服 children's wear / 紳士服 men's wear / 婦人服 women's wear

ふく² 吹く

❶ [風が] blow* 🔊

ゆうべは強い風が吹いた It [The wind] *blew* hard last night.

南風が吹いている A wind *is blowing* from the south./ The south wind *is blowing*.

◆涼しくて心地いい風が吹いている *There is* a lovely cool breeze this morning. / きょうは一日中風が吹いていた It *was windy* all day today.

❷ [楽器を] (演奏を) play 🔊; (特にトランペット・ホルンなどを) blow* 🔊

縦笛を吹く *play* the recorder

彼はトランペットを吹き鳴らした He *blew* a trumpet.

❸ [その他]

ろうそくの火を吹き消す *blow out* a candle / スープを吹いて冷ます *blow on* soup to make it cool

彼女は口笛を吹いて犬を呼んだ She *whistled* to call her dog.

あの男はほら吹きだ The guy always *talks big*.

鯨が潮を吹くのを見たことがありますか Have you ever seen a whale *spout water*?

慣用表現 両親がやっている店は吹けば飛ぶような小さな店だ My parents' shop is *small and shaky*.

ふく³ 拭く

(こすって) wipe 🔊; (きれいにする) clean 🔊; (モップで) mop 🔊; (乾かす) dry 🔊

彼は額の汗をふいた He *wiped* the sweat from his forehead.

彼女はふきんでテーブルをふいた She *cleaned* [*wiped*] the table with a cloth.

このハンカチで涙をふきなさい *Wipe* (*away*) [*Dry*] your tears with this handkerchief.

私はタオルで手をふいた I *dried* my hands with a towel.

ふく⁴ 噴く (火が) burst* into flames; (液体が) spout 🔊; (煙が) smoke 🔊; (噴火する) erupt 🔊 // 桜島はここ2，3日煙を噴いている Sakurajima *has been smoking* for a few days.

ふく⁵ 副 (書類などの控え) copy ⓒ, duplicate ⓒ // 書類は正副2通提出してください Please hand in the documents *in duplicate*.

∥副会長 a vice-chairman / 副教材 supplementary material / 副菜 side dish / 副支配人 an assistant manager / 副社長 a vice-president / 副収入 subsidiary income / 副賞 a supplementary prize / 副操縦士 a copilot / 副総理 a deputy prime minister / 副題 a subtitle / 副大統領 a vice-president / 副知事 a deputy governor / 副読本 a supplementary reader / 副領事 a vice-consul

ふく⁶ 福 (幸運) good luck ⓤ
◆福の神 the god of *wealth*

ふく⁷ 葺く わらでふいた家 a *thatched* house

ふぐ 河豚 blowfish ⓒ, globefish ⓒ ∥フグ中毒 blowfish [globefish] poisoning

ふくあん 腹案 idea ⓒ

ふくい 福井

福井県は本州の中央部に位置し、北で日本海に面しています。曇りがちで多湿な日本海側に特有の気候で、特に北部では降水量が、降雪量が多いのが特徴です。昔から麻布や政治の中心であった関西との関係が深く、敦賀は、江戸時代に日本海沿岸の貿易において大きな役割を果たしました。今日（こんにち）、県内にある発電所は、人口の密集した関西方面に電力を供給しています。
Fukui Prefecture is located in central Honshu and faces the Sea of Japan to the north. The climate is typical of the Sea of Japan coast: cloudy and humid. The northern part of the prefecture re-

ceives heavy rainfall and snowfall. Fukui is closely tied to the Kansai area, which for a long time has been a major commercial and political center in Japan. In the Edo period, Tsuruga played a key role in trade along the Sea of Japan coast. Today, power plants in this prefecture provide electricity to the heavily populated Kansai area.

ふくいん 福音 (キリスト教の) the gospel; (よい知らせ) good news Ⓤ
‖福音書 the Gospel

ふぐう 不遇 その画家は不遇のうちに死んだ The painter died *in obscurity*.

ふくえき 服役 (懲役) penal servitude Ⓤ
◆刑務所に2年間服役する *serve* two years in prison; *serve one's* two-year prison *sentence* / 彼女の夫は服役中だ Her husband is *in prison*. / 服役者 a prisoner

ふくおか 福岡

福岡県は九州の北部に位置し, 北は日本海に, 東は瀬戸内海に面しています. この県の沿岸部には, 昔から多くの港町が発達しました. その1つである県庁所在地の福岡市は, 古くから九州における政治, 商業の中心地でしたが, 今日(こんにち)では, アジア, 太平洋地域での国際的な交通の中心地でもあります. また博多では毎年有名な「博多どんたく」という祭りが行われます.
Fukuoka Prefecture is located in northern Kyushu. It faces the Sea of Japan to the north and the Seto Inland Sea to the east. Many port cities have been developed in this prefecture's coastal areas, including Fukuoka City, which is the present capital of the prefecture and has been the political and commercial center of Kyushu for a long time. Today, it is one of the most important centers for international transport in Asia and the Pacific. In addition, the famous festival called Hakata Dontaku is held in Hakata every year.

ふくがく 復学 彼は1年間の入院後大学に復学した He *returned* [*came back*] to university after he was in hospital for one year.

ふくがん 複眼 compound eye Ⓒ

ふくぎょう 副業 sideline Ⓒ; (アルバイト) part-time job Ⓒ /私は副業として翻訳の仕事をやっている I have *a sideline* as a translator.

ふくげん 復元・復原 restoration Ⓤ ─復元する restore ⓗ /絵画の一部が復元された A part of the painting *was restored*.
‖復元図 a diagram of a restored building

ふくごう 複合 ‖複合汚染 compound pollution / 複合企業 a conglomerate / 複合競技 (スキーの) Nordic combined / 複合語 a compound (word) / 複合物 a composite

ふくざつ 複雑
(入り乱れた状態) complication; (構造などがこみ入った状態) complexity Ⓤ ─複雑な complicated; complex; (入り混じった) mixed
問題自体はそれほど複雑ではない The problem itself is not so *complicated*.
彼女には複雑な事情があるようだ She seems to be in a *complicated* situation.
この都市には複雑な地下鉄網が敷かれている There is a *complex* subway network in this city.
私たちはその知らせを聞いて複雑な気持ちだった We had *mixed* feelings when we heard the news.
◆彼はよく考えずに発言するのでいつも問題がますます複雑になる(→問題を複雑にする) He always *confuses* the matter because he speaks without thinking it over. / 君がうそをつけば, 状況はますます複雑になる(→状況を複雑にする)だろう If you tell a lie, you will *complicate* the situation.
‖複雑骨折 a compound fracture

ふくさよう 副作用 side effect Ⓒ 《通例複数形 ~s》 ‖この薬はよく効くが副作用もある This medicine works very well but also has some *side effects*.

ふくさんぶつ 副産物 (製造過程における) by-product Ⓒ; (予期せぬ) spin-off Ⓒ

ふくし¹ 福祉 welfare Ⓤ
社会福祉関係の仕事をしたい I'd like to work in the area of *social welfare*.
何よりも国民の福祉の充実をはかるべきだ Above all things, we should promote *the welfare* of the people.
すべての市民は福祉サービスが受けられる All citizens are eligible to receive *welfare services*.
‖福祉国家 a welfare state / 福祉事業 welfare work / 福祉施設 welfare facilities / 福祉事務所 a welfare office / 医療福祉 medical welfare / 公共福祉 public welfare / 児童福祉 child welfare / 老人福祉 welfare services for the elderly

ふくし² 副詞 〔文法〕 adverb Ⓒ
‖副詞句 an adverbial phrase

(1)副詞は動詞, 形容詞, 名詞, 代名詞, ほかの副詞, 句や節, あるいは文全体を修飾する場合に用いられる.
(2)副詞はふつう文の最後に置かれる. ただし, 「よく」「時々」など, 漠然と頻度を表す場合, 動詞の直前, 助動詞や be 動詞の直後に置かれる ‖ He *always* eats supper at seven. 彼はいつも7時に夕食を食べる / She is *often* busy on weekdays. 彼女は平日忙しい日が多い
(3)文の内容に対する話し手の評価や話し手がどういう態度で話しているかを表す副詞は, 文全体を説明することになる. このような副詞は, ふつう文頭に置く ‖ *Frankly*, I don't believe your story. 率直に言って, あなたの話は信じられない

ふくじ 服地 (clothing) material ⓊⒸ

ふくしきこきゅう 腹式呼吸 abdominal breathing Ⓤ

ふくじてき 副次的 ―副次的な（二次的な）secondary;（重要でない）minor // 副次的な効果 a *secondary* effect

ふくしま 福島

福島県は，本州の北部，東北地方の最南端に位置し，東で太平洋に面しています．福島県は全体的に夏が暑く冬が寒い県です．農業が重要な産業で，県内でとれる農作物はバラエティーに富んでいます．米，キュウリやトマトなどの野菜，桃やナシなどの果物，それにたばこなどが多く栽培されています．
Fukushima Prefecture is located in northern Honshu in the southernmost part of the Tohoku district and faces the Pacific Ocean to the east. It generally has hot summers and cold winters. The prefecture's major industry is agriculture, and a wide variety of crops are produced there. In addition to rice and vegetables and fruit such as cucumbers, tomatoes, peaches and pears, tobacco is also grown in large amounts.

ふくしゃ 複写 copy [C];（コピー機による）photocopy [C];（正確な複写）duplicate [C];（美術品・著作物などの）reproduction [U] [C] ―複写する copy [他]; photocopy [他]; duplicate [他]; reproduce [他] //あなたの写真をTシャツに複写することができます Your photos can *be reproduced* on T-shirts. / 資料の複写は個人的な研究を目的としたものに限ります You can only *copy* [*make copies of*] materials for personal study.
‖複写機 a copy(ing) machine, a copier

ふ

ふくしゃねつ 輻射熱 radiant heat [U]

ふくしゅう[1] 復習 《米》review [U] [C], 《英》revision [U] ―復習する 《米》review [他] [自], 《英》revise [他] [自] //数学の小テストに備えて公式の復習をしなければならない I have to *review* some formulas for a math quiz.
‖復習問題 a review exercise

ふくしゅう[2] 復讐 revenge [U];（報復）retaliation [U] ―復讐する revenge *oneself* on ..., take* *one's* revenge on ...; retaliate against [on] ... //復讐を誓う vow *revenge* / 彼は父を殺した男に復讐をしようとした He tried to *take his revenge on* the man who killed his father. / 彼はそのピッチャーへの復讐に燃えていた He was burning with desire for *revenge* on the pitcher.

ふくじゅう 服従（命令に従うこと）obedience [U];（屈服）submission [U] ―服従する obey [他]; submit [自] //権威に対する服従 *obedience* to authority / 彼らは王に絶対服従を誓った They swore that they would *obey* [*submit to*] the king *absolutely*.

ふくじゅそう 福寿草 〘植物〙 adonis [C]

ふくしょう 復唱 ―復唱する repeat [他] //お名前とご住所を復唱させていただきます Let me *repeat* your name and address.

ふくしょく[1] 服飾 clothing and accessories
‖服飾デザイナー a fashion [dress] designer / 服飾品 accessories

ふくしょく[2] 復職 おばは出産1か月後に復職した My aunt *returned to work* one month after she gave birth.

ふくしょく[3] 副食 dishes served with rice ➔おかず

ふくしん[1] 副審 assistant umpire [judge, referee] [C]

ふくしん[2] 腹心 山田君は私の腹心の部下だ Mr. Yamada is my *right-hand man*.

ふくじん 副腎 〘医学〙 adrenal [ədríːnəl] gland [C] ‖副腎皮質ホルモン an adrenal cortex hormone

ふくじんづけ 副神漬け 🗻 *fukujinzuke*, sliced vegetables pickled in soy sauce

ふくすい 覆水 spilt water [U]
[ことわざ] 覆水盆に返らず What's done is done.（→すんだことはすんだこと）; It is no use crying over spilt milk.（→こぼれたミルクを嘆いてもしかたがない）

ふくすう 複数 plural [U] ―複数の plural //mice は mouse の複数形だ "Mice" is *the plural form* of "mouse."
◆複数の容疑者が警察署に連行された *More than one* suspect was taken to the police station.（❖more than one は意味的には複数だが，文法的には単数扱い）

ふくする 服する（喪に）go* into mourning;（兵役・刑に）serve [他];（命令に）obey [他] //30年の刑に服する *serve* a 30-year sentence / 彼は妻の喪に服している He *has gone into mourning* for his wife.

ふくせい 複製（複製品）reproduction [U] [C];（非常に精巧な複製品）replica [C];（全く同じもの）duplicate [C] ―複製する reproduce [他]; duplicate [他] //ピカソの複製画 *a reproduction* of a painting by Picasso / 不許複製 *Reproduction prohibited* | *All rights reserved*（❖美術品・著作物などにつける）

ふくせん[1] 伏線（手がかり）clue [C];（ほのめかし）hint [C] //第1章にだれが犯人かの伏線が張られている There is *a* 「*clue* to [*hint*] who is the culprit in the first chapter.

ふくせん[2] 複線 double-track [C], two-track line [C] ‖複線工事 double-tracking

ふくそう 服装 dress [U], clothes [klóuz]
服装を正す straighten *one's clothes*
私たちの学校には服装のきまりはない There is no *dress code* in our school.
父は服装にはむとんちゃくだ My father doesn't care about *clothes*.
私は服装を気にしません I don't bother about *my clothes*.
その男性はりっぱな服装をしていた The man was wearing fancy *clothes*.
◆あしたのパーティー，どんな服装で行けば（→何を着て行けば）いいかな *What* should I *wear* to tomorrow's party? / 彼はカジュアルな服装をしている He *is* casually *dressed*. / あなたはもっと服装（→外見）に気をつけたほうがいいよ You should be more careful about your *appearance*. / 彼女はいつも身ぎれいできちんとした服装をしている She *is* always clean and

ふくぞう 腹蔵　腹蔵のない意見 a *candid* opinion
ふぐたいてん 不倶戴天　不倶戴天の敵 a *deadly* [*mortal*] enemy
ふくつ 不屈　彼女は不屈の精神の持ち主だ She has an *indomitable* spirit.
ふくつう 腹痛 stomachache ⓒ,《口語的》bellyache ⓒⓊ ∥腹痛がする have *a stomachache*
ふくどく 服毒 ──服毒する take* poison // 服毒自殺をする kill *oneself* by *taking poison*
ふくとしん 副都心　新宿は東京の副都心だ Shinjuku is one of *commercial and business hubs* of Tokyo.
ふくびき 福引 lottery ⓒ, prize drawing ⓒ ∥福引を引く enter [take part in] *a lottery* [*prize drawing*] / 福引でデジカメ 1 等賞 が当たった I won "a digital camera [the first prize]" in *a lottery*.
∥福引券 a lottery ticket
ふくぶ 腹部〔解剖〕abdomen ⓒ, stomach ⓒ
ぶくぶく　ぶくぶくと口をゆすぐ rinse *one's* mouth *vigorously* / なべの中の水がぶくぶくいいだしたらすぐに火を弱めなさい When the water in the pan starts to *bubble*, reduce the heat immediately. / 彼はとてもスリムだったのに今ではぶくぶく太っている He used to be very slim, but is *so fat* now.
ふくぶくしい 福々しい　彼女は福々しい顔をしている She's got *plump and cheerful* looks.
ふくふくせん 複々線 four-track [quadruple-track] line ⓒ
ふくぶくろ 福袋 🔼 a *fukubukuro*, a grab bag that contains various goods
ふくぶん 複文〔文法〕complex sentence ⓒ
ふくへい 伏兵 ambush ⓒ;（意外な実力の持ち主）dark horse ⓒ
ふくまくえん 腹膜炎〔医 学〕peritonitis [pèrətənáitəs]
ふくみ 含み（言外の）implication ⓒ;（単語の持つ）connotation ⓒ;（隠された意味）overtones ∥彼は皮肉っぽい含みのある発言をした He made a remark with cynical *implications*.
◆彼女は何か含みのある言い方をした She *implied* something by what she said.
∥含み笑い a suppressed [meaningful] smile

ふくむ¹ 含む
❶【含有する】（構成成分として）contain ⓗ;（全体の一部として）include ⓗ
この飲み物にはアルコールが含まれている This drink *contains* alcohol.
料金には10パーセントの手数料が含まれている The price *includes* a commission of 10 percent.
乗客の中に日本人旅行客が15名含まれていた The passengers *included* 15 Japanese tourists.
◆牛乳にはタンパク質が豊富に含まれている Milk *is rich in* protein.
❷【口に】
私は水を口に含み渇きをいやした I *took* some water in my mouth to satisfy my thirst.
❸【心に留める】
この件に関してはよくお含みおきください Please *keep* this matter *in mind*.
❹【暗示する】
彼女はうれいを含んだ瞳で私を見つめた She stared at me with her *sorrowful* eyes.
彼の言葉に重要な意味が含まれていたことに気づかなかった I missed an important message *in* his words.

ふくむ² 服務（公務）service Ⓤ
∥服務規定 service regulations / 服務時間 office hours
ふくめる 含める　消費税を含めると10,512円になる It's 10,512 yen *including* consumption tax. / それは送料を含めたお値段ですか Is that the total price, postage *included*?
ふくめん 覆面 mask ⓒ ∥覆面をかぶる wear [put on] *a mask*
◆覆面をした男 a *masked* man
∥覆面パトカー an unmarked police car
ふくよう 服用　◆薬を服用する take medicine
ふくよかな plump;（特に子供が）chubby;（胸の豊かな）buxom;（豊かな）rich ∥ふくよかな胸の女性 a *buxom* woman / ワインのふくよかな香り a *rich* aroma of wine
ふくらしこ ふくらし粉 baking powder Ⓤ
ふくらはぎ 脹ら脛 calf [kǽf] ⓒ（複 calves [kǽvz]）
ふくらます 膨らます（吹いて）blow* up;（ガス・空気などで）inflate ⓗ;（空気・水などで）swell* ⓗ;（ほおなどを）puff out;（パン・ケーキなどを）raise ⓗ ∥風船をふくらます *blow up* a *balloon* / ボールを空気入れでふくらます *inflate* a ball by an air pump
◆その新入生は希望に胸をふくらませていた The new student *was full of* hope.
ふくらみ 膨らみ（膨張による）swell ⓒ;（出っ張り）bulge ⓒ;（ふわっとした）puff ∥彼女の胸のふくらみが目に焼きついて離れない I can't forget *the bulge* of *her breasts*.
ふくらむ 膨らむ（大きくなる）swell* ⓗ;（伸び広がる）expand ⓗ;（張り出す）bulge ⓗ;（パンなどが）rise* ⓗ
彼は希望に胸がふくらんだ His heart *swelled* with hope.
ここ数日で桜のつぼみがふくらみ始めた The buds on the cherry trees began *swelling* these past several days.
かばんがふくらんでいるけど何が入っているの Your bag *is bulging*. What's in there?
ふくり¹ 福利 welfare Ⓤ
∥福利厚生 a welfare program
ふくり² 複利 compound interest Ⓤ
ふくれあがる 膨れ上がる　新しく20人が入って会員数は90人にふくれ上がった Twenty newcomers joined the club, *swelling* the ranks to ninety.
ふくれっつら 膨れっ面（怒っている）sulky face [look] ⓒ;（むっつりした）sullen face

[look] ◆彼はふくれっ面をしている He looks *sulky* [*sullen*]. / ふくれっ面をするのはやめなさい Stop *pouting*.

ふくれる 膨れる
❶【膨張する】(空気・水などで) *swell** / 水に浸しておいたワカメがふくれた Soaked seaweed has *swelled*. / 観衆は約5万人にふくれた The audience *swelled* to around fifty thousand. / ◆2人分食べたのでおなかがふくれた My stomach *was swollen* because I ate two portions.
❷【機嫌が悪くなる】(何かに怒って) *get* sulky*, sulk; (不満で) *get sullen* / 彼女はすぐふくれる She easily *gets sulky* [*sullen*].

ふくろ 袋
bag; (大型で丈夫な) *sack*; (ポーチなど有袋類動物の) *pouch*; (ミカンなどの) *segment*; (1包み) *pack* / 紙[ビニール, ごみ]袋 a paper [plastic, garbage] *bag* / 買い物袋 (米) a shopping *bag*, (英) a carrier *bag* / 1袋のジャガイモ a sack of potatoes / 袋詰めしたクッキー a pack of cookies / 彼はポテトチップスを1日に3袋も食べる He eats three *bags* of potato chips a day. / (レジで)袋は結構です I don't need a *bag*. / コアラの赤ちゃんはいつもお母さんの袋の中にいる A baby koala is always in a mother's *pouch*. / 🔖「牛乳とお弁当を別々の袋にお入れいたしますか」「同じ袋に入れてくださって結構です」"Shall I put the milk and the box lunch in separate *bags*?" "One *bag* is fine with me."
慣用表現 彼は袋のねずみ同然だ He is like *a rat in a trap*.

ふくろう 梟
owl [ául] / フクロウが鳴いている An *owl* is hooting.

ふくろこうじ 袋小路
dead end, *blind alley*; (私道などの) *cul-de-sac* (◆通例単数形) / 袋小路に入る reach *a dead end*

ふくろだたき 袋叩き
——袋だたきにする *beat* up* / 彼は不良グループに袋だたきにされた He *was beaten up* by the street gang.

ふくわじゅつ 腹話術
ventriloquism [ventríləkwìzm] / 腹話術師 a *ventriloquist*

ふけ dandruff
/ 彼はひどいふけ性だ He's got very bad *dandruff*. ◆ふけ防止用シャンプー — *antidandruff* shampoo

ふけい 父兄
(両親) *parents*; (保護者) *guardian*

ふけい² 婦警
policewoman, (英) *woman constable*

ふけいき 不景気
(時世) *hard* [*bad*] *times*; (長期にわたる不況) *depression*; (一時的な景気後退) *recession*; (事業などの不振) *slump* ——不景気な (閑散とした) *slack*, *slow*; (活気のない) *dull* / 不景気なご時世にぜいたくは言っていられない I cannot be choosy in *hard times*. / 不景気が多くの会社に打撃を与えた The *recession* hit many businesses. / どこもかしこも不景気だ Business is *slack* [*dull*] everywhere. / 建設業界は今不景気だ The building industry *is suffering from a depression* now.
慣用表現 不景気な顔しているな You look *blue* [*gloomy*].

ふけいざい 不経済
——不経済な (経済的に悪い) *uneconomical*; (むだな) *wasteful* / 歩いて行ける所にタクシーで行くのは不経済だ It's *uneconomical* to take a taxi when it's within walking distance.

ふけこむ 老け込む
age / 父は最近めっきり老け込んだ My father *has aged* a lot recently.

ふけつ 不潔
——不潔な *dirty*; (非常に汚い) *filthy*; (不衛生) *unsanitary* / そんな不潔な手で料理にさわらないで Don't touch the dish with such *dirty* [*filthy*] hands. / あいつはごく不潔だ That man is *filthy*.

ふける¹ 老ける
age, *become* old* / 最近母はめっきり老けた Recently my mother *aged* noticeably. / ◆彼は実際の年より10歳くらい老けて見える He looks 10 years or so *older* than his age. / He looks 10 years or so *older* for his age.

ふける² 更ける
夜もふけてきたのでもう寝るよ It's *getting late*. I'm going to bed now. / 夜がふけるまで我々は愛とは何かについて語り合った We talked about what love is *till late at night*.

ふける³ 耽る (おぼれる)
give oneself over* [*up*] *to* ...; (没頭する) *be absorbed in* ...; (気を取られる) *be lost in* ... / 賭(か)け事にふける *give oneself over* [*up*] *to* gambling / いとこたちは昨夜ジグソーパズルにふけっていた My cousins *were absorbed in* working on a jigsaw puzzle last night. / 彼女はさっきから物思いにふけっている She *has been lost in thought* for a while.

ふけんこう 不健康
poor [*ill*] *health* ——不健康な *unhealthy*; (精神的・道徳的に) *unwholesome* / 不健康な遊び *unwholesome* pleasure / 不健康なダイエットで彼女は体をこわした An *unhealthy* diet damaged her health.

ふげんじっこう 不言実行
不言実行 (→言葉より行動のほうがものを言う) *Actions speak louder than words.* / 必要なのは不言実行だ What we need is *not words but deeds*.

ふけんぜん 不健全
——不健全な (道徳的に) *unwholesome*; (精神的に・身体的に) *unhealthy* / 不健全な雑誌 an *unwholesome* magazine / 不健全な考えからは何も生まれない An *unhealthy* idea breeds nothing.

ふこう 不幸
❶【不幸せ】 *unhappiness*; (みじめで悲惨な状態) *misery*; (不運) *bad luck*; (ひどい不運) *misfortune* ——不幸な *unhappy*; *miserable*; *unfortunate* ——不幸にも *unfortunately* / 不幸な生い立ち an *unhappy* childhood / 不幸な一生を送る lead an *unhappy* [*unfortunate*] life / 不幸にも彼女は両親を一度に失った Unfortu-

nately she lost her parents at the same time.

当時私は不幸のどん底にいた I was in the depths of *misery* in those days.

人の不幸につけ込むのはやめろ Don't take advantage of *the misery* of others.

彼女は結婚をして以来不幸の連続だ She has suffered a series of *miseries* since she got married.

幸か不幸かうちには盗まれるようなものは何もない *Fortunately or unfortunately*, we don't have anything worth stealing in our house.

◆不幸の手紙 *a chain letter* (❖a chain letter は「受取人がもらった同内容の手紙を数名の人に出すよう要求される手紙」のことで, 必ずしも「不幸な」内容とは限らない) / あんなひどい事故でだれも死ななかったのは不幸中の幸いだ (→慰めになる) It is *consoling* that no one died in that horrible accident.

❷【死】

お隣で不幸があった There was *a death* in the family next door.

このたびのご不幸に心よりお悔やみ申し上げます I would offer you my deepest sympathy at this time of *bereavement*.

ふごう[1] 符号 (印) mark [C]; (記号) sign [C]; (電信符号) code [C] ‖正の符号 *the* plus [positive] *sign* / 負の符号 *the* minus [negative] *sign*

‖モールス符号 the Morse code

ふごう[2] 符合 ━符合する agree [自] ‖彼の言っていることは事実と符合しない What he says doesn't *agree* with the facts.

ふごう[3] 富豪 very rich [wealthy] person [man, woman] [C], millionaire [C] ➔ かねもち ‖大富豪 a multimillionaire, a billionaire

ふごうかく 不合格 failure [U] ━不合格になる fail [他]; (拒まれる) be rejected ‖姉は運転免許試験に不合格だった My sister *failed* her driving test. / 数名の志願者が不合格にされた Several applicants *were rejected*.

‖不合格者 a failure

ふこうへい 不公平 (公正でないこと) unfairness [U]; (えこひいきすること) partiality [U]; (不当なこと) injustice [U] ━不公平な unfair; partial; unjust ━不公平に unfairly; partially ‖不公平な審判 a *partial* [an *unfair*] referee / 不公平な裁判 an *unfair* [*unjust*] trial / 不公平な扱いを受ける have *unfair* treatment / それは不公平だよ That's *unfair*./ That's *not fair*. / あの先生は生徒を不公平に扱う The teacher treats students *partially*.

ふごうり 不合理 ━不合理な unreasonable, irrational; (非論理的な) illogical ‖それは不合理な要求だ That's an *unreasonable* request.

ふこく 布告 declaration [U] [C], 《公式的》 proclamation [U] [C] ━布告する declare [他] [自], proclaim [他]

‖宣戦布告 a declaration of war

ふこころえ 不心得 ━不心得な (不道徳な) immoral; (無作法な) rude ‖自分の犬のふんの後始末をしない不心得な飼い主もいる There are some *immoral* dog owners who don't pick up droppings of their own dogs.

ぶこつ 無骨・武骨 ━無骨な (洗練されていない) unrefined; (不作法な) rude

ふさ 房 (果実などの) bunch [C]; (花・実などの) cluster [C]; (毛髪・羽根・草などの) tuft [C]; (ふさ飾り) tassel [C], fringe [C] ‖ブドウ1房 *a bunch* [*cluster*] of grapes / バナナ1房 *a bunch* of bananas / サンタクロースの帽子には白いふさ飾りがついている Santa Claus's hat has *a* white *tassel*.

ブザー buzzer [bʌ́zər] [C] ‖ブザーを鳴らす sound *a buzzer* / ブザーが鳴っていますよ There goes *a buzzer*. / 何かご用のときはブザーを押してください Please press *the buzzer* when you need my help.

ふさい[1] 夫妻 スミス夫妻は来月息子さんといっしょに来日する予定です *Mr. and Mrs.* Smith [*Mr.* Smith *and his wife*] plan to visit Japan with their son next month. (❖Mr. and Mrs.を使ったほうが丁寧)

ふさい[2] 負債 debt [dét] [C] [U] ‖その会社の負債は数十億ドルに達する *The debts* of the company run into the billions of dollars. / 彼は多額の負債を抱えている He is heavily in *debt*.

ふざい 不在 absence [U] [C] ━不在である be out, be not in; (家にいない) be not at home; (長期にわたり) be away ‖私の不在中に何かあったらすぐ連絡してください Please contact me immediately if anything happens *in* [*during*] *my absence*. / 母は今不在です My mother 「*is not in* [*is not at home*] at the moment. / 川口さんは不在ですか *Is* Mr. Kawaguchi *out*? / 申しわけありませんが桜井はただ今上海へ出張中で不在です I'm afraid Sakurai *is away* to Shanghai on business.

‖不在者投票 an absentee ballot

ぶさいく 不細工 ━不細工な (物の形が) awkward; (顔が) plain ‖あの娘は不細工だ That girl is *plain*.

ふさがる 塞がる ❶【閉じる】close [自] ‖傷口はふさがった The wound *closed up*.

❷【場所などが】be blocked; (何かが詰まって) be clogged; (特に障害物で) be obstructed ‖道路は事故車でふさがっている The road *is blocked* [*obstructed*] by [with] a wrecked car.

❸【空いていない】(席・部屋などが) be taken, be occupied; (予約で) be reserved, be booked; (時間が) be engaged; (手があいていない) be busy ‖この席はふさがっていますか *Is* this seat *taken*? / あいにくシングルルームはすべてふさがっています I'm afraid all single rooms *are occupied*. / ごめん, あすはちょっとふさがっているんだ Sorry, I'*m busy* tomorrow. / その予約専用電話番号はいつもふさがっている The line for reservations *is* always *busy*.

◆手がふさがっている My hands *are full*. (❖

ふさぎこむ

「物をたくさん持っている」「仕事をたくさん抱えている」の意味)

🔴「今度の金曜日の午後に予約を取りたいのですが」「申しわけありませんが金曜日はすべてふさがっています」 "I'd like to make a reservation for this Friday afternoon." "We're afraid this Friday *is fully booked*."

ふさぎこむ 塞ぎ込む (落ち込む) *get** [*be*] *depressed*; (憂鬱だ) *feel* low* ∥どうしてそんなにふさぎこんでいるの Why *are* you so *depressed*? / 彼は近ごろふさぎこんでいる He's *been feeling low* lately.

ふさく 不作 *bad* [*poor*] *crop* [*harvest*] ⓒ ∥ 今年は米が不作だ We have *a bad crop of rice* this year. ◆今年の音楽界は期待できる新人が不作だった *Few* prospective stars appeared among the newcomers on the music scene this year.

ふさぐ 塞ぐ ❶【閉じる】(栓などで) *plug* ⓣ; (満たす) *fill* ⓣ; (埋める) *stop* ⓣ; (覆う) *cover* ⓣ ∥穴をセメントでふさぐ *fill* a hole with *cement* / そのひどい騒音を聞いたとき我々は耳をふさいだ We *plugged* our ears when we heard the terrible noise.
◆傷口をふさぐ *close* a wound
❷【場所などを】*block* ⓣ; (障害物を置いて) *obstruct* ⓣ; (スペースを占める) *occupy* ⓣ, *take* up* ∥エンストしたトラックが道路をふさいでいる A stalled truck *is blocking* [*obstructing*] the road. / 大きなテーブルがその部屋のかなりの部分をふさいでいる A large table *occupies* [*takes up*] a lot of space in the room.
❸【気分が】*get** [*be*] *depressed*
➡ふさぎこむ

ふざける (冗談を言う) *joke* ⓘ, *make* a joke*; (いたずらをする) *play a trick*; (子供たちが跳びはねる) *romp around* [*about*] ∥ちょっとふざけて言っただけだよ I *was* only *joking*. / 子供たちは家の中でふざけて遊んでいた The children *were romping around* [*about*] in the house.
◆ふざけるな! *Stop this nonsense*!

ぶさた 無沙汰 ごぶさたしています I *haven't seen* you *for a long time.*/ *Long time no see*. / 彼は手持ちぶさたのようだ He seems to be *at loose ends*.

ふさふさ 70歳の祖父はまだ髪の毛がふさふさだ My 70-year-old grandfather still has *thick* hair. / うちの猫はふさふさのしっぽをしている My cat has a *bushy* tail.

ぶさほう 無作法・不作法 (行儀が悪いこと) *bad manners*; (無礼) *rudeness* ⓤ ——無作法な *bad-mannered*; *rude, impolite* ∥人を無作法にじろじろ眺める *give a person a rude stare* / 私は彼の無作法を見て見ぬふりをした I ignored his *bad manners*.

ぶざま 無様・不様 ——ぶざまな (屈辱的な) *humiliating*; (不器用な) *awkward*; (ぎこちない) *clumsy*; (恥ずかしい) *shameful* ∥私たちのチームはぶざまな負け方をした Our team suffered a *humiliating* defeat. ◆彼はぶざまな格好で転んだ He fell down *clumsily*.

ふさわしい 相応しい (適した) *suitable*; (適切な) *proper, appropriate*; (好ましい) *good*; (合っている) *fit*; (価値のある) *worthy*; (ぴったりの) (口語的) *right*
功労にふさわしい報酬 a *fit* reward / 賞賛するにふさわしい映画 a movie *worthy of* praise
この着物は友達の披露宴にふさわしいかしら I wonder if this kimono is *suitable* [*good*] for a friend's wedding reception.
彼はその仕事に応募するにふさわしい経歴の持ち主だ He has the *appropriate* background to apply for the position.
◆その映画はアカデミー賞を受賞するにふさわしい The movie *deserves* an Oscar.

ふさんせい 不賛成 (意見の不一致) *disagreement* ⓤ; (不承知) *disapproval* ⓤ; (反対) *objection* ⓤ
◆彼の意見には不賛成だ I *disagree* [*cannot agree*] with you. / 彼の提案にはみんなが不賛成だ Everyone is *against* the proposal.

ふし 節 ❶【結節】(木・板の) *knot* ⓒ; (竹の) *joint* ⓒ, *node* ⓒ ∥この木の幹は節だらけだ This trunk is full of *knots*.
❷【関節】*joint* ⓒ; (指の付け根の) *knuckle* ⓒ ∥年をとると体の節々が痛む When you get old, your *joints* hurt.
❸【旋律】*melody* ⓒⓤ, *tune* ⓒ ∥彼はおかしな節をつけて歌った He sang to *a strange tune*.
❹【箇所】*point* ⓒ ◆そう言われてみると思い当たる節がある What you said reminds me of *something*.

ふじ¹ 不治 ——不治の *incurable* ∥不治の病 an *incurable* disease [*illness*] / 結核はもう不治の病ではない Tuberculosis is no longer *incurable*.

ふじ² 藤 *wisteria* ⓤⓒ ∥藤色 *pale* [*light*] *purple*, *mauve* / 藤棚 a *wisteria trellis*

ぶし 武士 *samurai* (*warrior*) ⓒ; (戦士) *warrior* ⓒ ∥武士道 *Bushido*, Japanese chivalry, the code of the samurai's loyalty to his master

ぶじ 無事 (安全) *safety* ⓤ; (平穏) *peace* ⓤ ——無事な *safe*; *peaceful*; (大丈夫) *all right* ——無事に *safely*; *peacefully*
無事帰宅する *return home safe*
故障した飛行機は無事着陸した The troubled plane landed *safely*.
彼らは平穏無事に暮らしている They live in *peace* and quiet.
ああよかった、無事だったのね Thank God, you are *safe* [*all right*].
みんな無事にやっているから心配しないで We are doing *all right*, so don't worry.
◆ご無事で(旅に出る人に) *Have a nice trip*!/ *Bon voyage*! / 例の件は無事に解決した That matter was solved *without any problems*. / 今週も無事に終わってよかった It's good to get through another week *without any problems*.

ふしあな 節穴 *knothole* [náthoul] ⓒ ∥節穴からのぞく *peep through a knothole*
[慣用表現] おまえの目は節穴か *Are you blind*?

ふしあわせ 不幸せ *unhappiness* ⓤ ——不

幸せな unhappy ⇒ふこう ∥不幸せな結婚 an *unhappy* marriage

ふしぎ 不思議 wonder ⓒⓤ; (なぞ) mystery ⓒ; (奇跡) miracle ⓒ ――不思議な mysterious; (奇妙な) strange, odd ――不思議に mysteriously; strangely, oddly
世界の七不思議 the Seven *Wonders* of the World / 不思議な光景 a *strange* sight
彼らが全員逮捕されたのは少しも不思議ではない It's no *wonder* that all of them were arrested.
あれは不思議な事件だった That was a *mysterious* event.
だれもそのことに気づかなかったとは不思議だ It's *strange* that no one realized it.
不思議なことに彼女とそこで会わなかった *Oddly* enough, I didn't see her there.
彼の勘は不思議なほどよく当たる *Strangely*, his hunches are often right.
◆この薬は不思議なほどよく効く This medicine is *amazingly* effective.

ふしくれだつ 節くれ立つ ――節くれだった (枝・幹・手などが) gnarled [náːrld] ∥その老人の手は節くれだっていた The old man's [woman's] hands were *gnarled*.

ふしぜん 不自然 ――不自然な unnatural; (ぎこちない) awkward; (人為的な) artificial ∥不自然な作り笑い an *artificial* [a *forced*] smile / 彼の行動は最近少し不自然だと思いませんか Don't you think his behavior has been a bit *unnatural* lately?

ふしだら (不道徳な) immoral; (性的に不道徳な) sexually immoral

ふじちゃく 不時着 (不時着陸) emergency landing ⓒ; (機体損傷覚悟の着陸) crash landing ⓒ ∥不時着を試みる try to make *an emergency landing*

ふしちょう 不死鳥 phoenix [fíːnɪks] ⓒ

ぶしつ 部室 club room ⓒ

ぶしつけ 不躾 (無作法) bad manners; (厚かましさ) impudence ⓤ ――ぶしつけな impudent; (無作法な) impolite (無礼な) rude; (無遠慮な) blunt ∥ぶしつけな態度 *impudent* [*impolite, rude, blunt*] behavior
◆ぶしつけなことをお聞きしますが, ご結婚されていらっしゃるのですか Are you married, *if I may ask*? / *Excuse me for asking*, but are you married?

ふじびたい 富士額 a *fujibitai*, a hairline shaped like Mt. Fuji, which was once considered to be among the requirements for a beauty

ふしぶし 節々 体の節々が痛い have pains in one's joints

ふしまつ 不始末 (へま) blunder ⓒ; (業務上などの) misconduct ⓤ ――不始末な careless ∥火の不始末 *careless handling* of a fire / 私はきのうのパーティーで大変な不始末をしてしまった I made *an* awful *blunder* at yesterday's party.

ふじみ 不死身 ――不死身な (決して死なない) immortal; (タフな) tough ∥あいつは不死身の男だ He is a really *tough* guy.

ふしめ¹ 伏し目 彼女は伏し目がちに話した She talked with *her eyes lowered*.

ふしめ² 節目 私の人生において結婚が一つの節目となった Getting married was *an important turning point* in my life.

ふじゆう 不自由
❶【不便】inconvenience ⓤ ⓒ ――不自由な inconvenient
断水でたいへん不自由した The stoppage of water caused us a lot of *inconvenience*.
近くに店がないのでここでの暮らしは不自由だ It's *inconvenient* to live here because there are no stores nearby.
彼は外国で暮らしていたとき部屋が狭くてひどく不自由な思いをした When he lived abroad, he suffered great *inconvenience* because his room was small.
◆あれだけ話せれば英語には少しも不自由しない You'll *get along* very well in English since you can speak it so fluently.
❷【窮乏】(貧困) poverty ⓤ; (欠乏) shortage ⓒ ――不自由な poor; short of ...
不自由な(→貧しい)生活をする live in *poverty*
私は交通費にさえ不自由している I am even *short of* transportation money.
◆彼らは何不自由なく暮らしている They are *well provided for*. / They live *in comfort*.
❸【身体】――不自由な physically handicapped [challenged], disabled
体の不自由な方に席をお譲りください Please give up the seat to *physically handicapped* [*challenged*] people.
◆目の不自由な女性 a *visually challenged* woman / 彼女は耳が不自由だ She is *hard of hearing*. / 彼は足が不自由だ (→歩行が困難) He has *difficulty* walking. / 私はコンピュータを何不自由なく使いこなせます I can use computers *without major problems*.

ふじゅうぶん 不十分 ――不十分な insufficient, not enough
彼女の英語力は留学するにはまだ不十分だ Her English is 「*not* good *enough* [*insufficient*] to study abroad.
彼は証拠不十分で釈放された He was released *on insufficient evidence*.
その問題を解決するには私の力では不十分でした I was *not* good *enough* to handle the problem.

ふしゅび 不首尾 結局それは不首尾に終わった That was *unsuccessful* in the end.

ふじゅん¹ 不純 ――不純な impure ∥私は不純な動機で彼女に声をかけたわけではない I didn't speak to her from *impure* motives.
∥不純物 impurities

ふじゅん² 不順 ――不順な (不規則な) irregular; (変わりやすい) changeable ∥近ごろ天候が不順だ The weather has been *changeable* recently. ◆最近生理が不順です I've had my period *irregularly* recently.

ふじょ¹ 扶助 (援助) aid ⓤ; (助力) help ⓤ
∥相互扶助 mutual aid

ふじょ² 婦女 woman ⓒ (複 women)
∥婦女暴行 (a) rape

ぶしょ 部署 (任務の場所) one's post; (配置された場所) one's station; (会社などの) section ⓒ, department ⓒ, division ⓒ ∥警備員は各部署についた The security guards took up their posts [stations]. / 我々の部署は新しい仕事に取り組み始めた Our section undertook the new work.

ふしょう¹ 負傷 (事故などによる) injury ⓒⓊ; (刃物・銃などによる) wound ⓒ ――負傷する be injured; be wounded ∥名誉の負傷 honorable wounds / きのうのガス爆発で6名が死亡, 21名が負傷した Six people were killed and twenty one people were injured by yesterday's gas explosion. / その兵士は足を負傷した The soldier was wounded in the leg.
∥負傷者 an injured person, 《集合的》 the injured

ふしょう² 不肖 ∥不肖の息子 an unworthy son / 不肖(→私)未熟ながら精一杯がんばる所存です I'm a beginner but I promise I'll do my best.

ふしょう³ 不詳 ――不詳の (知られていない) unknown; (身元不明の) unidentified; (作者不明の) anonymous ∥彼女の年齢は不詳だ Her age is unknown.

ふじょう¹ 浮上 ――浮上する rise* [come* up] to the surface, surface ⊕ ∥潜水艦が浮上した The submarine surfaced.
◆タイガースが2位に浮上した The Tigers rose to second place.

ふじょう² 不浄 ∥不浄の金 dirty money

ぶしょう 無精・不精 laziness Ⓤ ――無精な lazy ∥父親ゆずりの無精 laziness from one's father / 彼は無精な男だ He is a lazy guy.
◆彼は筆無精だがEメールはよく送ってくる He hardly writes letters, but often sends me e-mails.
∥無精ひげ (短い) stubble; (長く伸びた) a three-day beard / 無精者 a lazy fellow, 《口語的》a slob / 出無精 a stay-at-home

ふしょうじ 不祥事 (スキャンダル) scandal ⓒ; (恥ずべきこと) disgraceful event [affair] ⓒ ∥彼が党首に選ばれた直後に, その不祥事が発覚した The scandal broke right after he was elected leader of the party.

ふしょうじき 不正直 dishonesty Ⓤ ――不正直な dishonest ∥あんな不正直な男とはもうつきあわない I will not see such a dishonest man.

ふしょうぶしょう 不承不承 (いやいやながら) unwillingly; (気の進まないまま) reluctantly ∥私は不承不承その男と会うことに決めた I decided to meet the man unwillingly. / その修正案は不承不承受け入れられた The amendment was reluctantly accepted.

ふしょうふずい 夫唱婦随 ∥昔は夫唱婦随がふつうだった A wife used to follow her husband's lead all the time in the old days.

ふじょうり 不条理 absurdity ⓒⓊ ――不条理な absurd

ふしょく 腐食 corrosion Ⓤ ――腐食する corrode ⊕⊕ ∥ドアのちょうつがいが腐食している The door's hinge is corroded.
∥腐食剤 a corrosive

ぶじょく 侮辱 insult Ⓤⓒ, contempt ⓒ ――侮辱する insult ⊕ ∥それは働く女性に対する侮辱だ It is an insult to working women. / 君を侮辱するつもりはなかったんだ I didn't mean to insult you.
∥法廷侮辱罪 contempt of court

ふしん¹ 不信 distrust Ⓤ (また a～) ――不信の distrustful ∥彼らの政府に対する不信感は根深い Their distrust toward the government is deeply rooted. / 彼女は不信の目で私を見た She looked at me with distrust. / 彼は女性不信に陥っている He has almost become distrustful of all women.
◆彼女は夫に対して不信の念をいだいている She distrusts her husband.

ふしん² 不振 (不調) slump ⓒ ――不振な dull; (成績などが) poor, bad ∥山田選手は今月に入って不振が続いている Yamada has been in a slump since the beginning of this month. / この夏旅行業界は不振だった The travel industry was dull this past summer. / その監督はチームの成績不振を理由に解雇された The manager was fired because his team made a poor showing.
◆ここ数週間食欲不振だ I've had no appetite for a couple of weeks.

ふしん³ 不審 doubt ⓒⓊ; (疑念) suspicion Ⓤⓒ ――不審な doubtful; suspicious; (奇妙な) strange ∥不審な人物 a doubtful [suspicious] character / 不審な点がございましたらどうぞ私共にご連絡ください If you have any doubts, please contact us. / 彼には不審な点が多すぎる He is too suspicious. / 私はその男を不審に思った I was suspicious of the man. / 不審な物音を聞いて彼女はベッドから飛び起きた Hearing a strange noise, she sprang out of bed. ◆警察の不審尋問を受ける be questioned by a police officer
∥不審火 a suspicious fire

ふしん⁴ 普請 building Ⓤ ――普請する build* ⊕ ∥安普請の家 a jerry-built house

ふじん¹ 婦人 woman Ⓒ (複 women); (丁寧な言い方) lady ∥老婦人 an old woman / ご婦人方, テーブルのご用意ができました Ladies, the table is ready.
∥婦人科 gynecology / 婦人科医 a gynecologist / 婦人会 a women's association / 婦人警官 a policewoman / 婦人雑誌 a women's magazine / 婦人参政権 women's suffrage / 婦人病 a women's disease / 婦人服 women's [ladies'] wear [clothes]

ふじん² 夫人 (妻) wife ⓒ (複 wives); (敬称) Mrs. ∥(デビッド・)スミス夫人 Mrs. (David) Smith / 近藤さんはご夫人同伴です Mr. Kondo is accompanied by his wife.

ふしんじん 不信心 impiety [impáiəti] ――不信心な impious [ímpiəs]

ふしんせつ 不親切 unkindness Ⓤ ――不親切な unkind ∥彼は不親切だ He is unkind.
◆あの店は不親切だ That shop gives poor service. / この説明書は専門用語が多すぎて不親

切だ (→理解しにくい) There are so many technical terms in this operating manual that it is difficult to understand.

ふしんにん 不信任 no-confidence ‖内閣不信任案を提出する propose *a vote of no-confidence* in the Cabinet

ふしんばん 不寝番 night watch; (人) night guard

ブス 《米俗語》dog

ふずい¹ 不随 paralysis ‖全身不随 total *paralysis* ◆下半身不随になる *be paralyzed* from the waist down / 彼女は脳卒中で半身不随になった She *was paralyzed* in half of her body after the stroke.

ふずい² 付随 新制度導入人には付随する様々な問題がある There are various problems *incidental to* the introduction of a new system.

ぶすい 無粋・不粋 ——無粋な (鈍感な) insensitive ‖彼女を食事に誘わないなんて君も無粋なやつだな It's *insensitive* of you not to ask her out for dinner.

ぶすう 部数 the number of copies; (新聞・雑誌などの) circulation ‖この新聞は日本でいちばん発行部数の多い英字新聞だ This newspaper has *the largest circulation* among English papers in Japan. / その地域雑誌の発行部数は2,000くらいだ The local magazine has *a circulation* of approximately two thousand.

ぶすっと 兄はぶすっとした顔で帰ってきた My brother came back with a *sullen* face. / いったい何をぶすっとしているんだい What *are you pouting* about? / 彼女は注射針を患者の腕にぶすっと刺した She *poked* the hypodermic needle into the patient's arm.

ぶすぶす たき火はぶすぶすとくすぶっていた The bonfire *was smoldering*. / オーブンに入れる前にジャガイモをフォークでぶすぶすと突き刺した I *stuck* a potato with a fork *several times* before putting it in the oven.

ふすま 襖

ふすまは日本の伝統的な横開き戸のことで、両面に厚手の紙や布が張ってあります。部屋と部屋の間の仕切りとして、または押し入れの戸として使われます。
A *fusuma* is a set of traditional Japanese sliding doors, both sides of which are covered with thick paper or cloth. The main uses of *fusuma* are as room partitions and as doors for *oshiire* (Japanese-style closets).

ぶすり 彼はナイフでぶすりとやられた He *was stabbed* with a knife.

ふする 付する その件は役員会議に付されることになった That issue *has been referred* to the board meeting.

ふせ 布施 offering

ふせい 不正 (不当な行為) injustice; (不正直) dishonesty; (不法) illegality ——不正な unjust; dishonest, wrong; illegal; (不公平な) unfair

不正をあばく expose *an injustice* / 不正を働く commit *an injustice* / 大学に不正入学をする enter a university *by dishonest means* / 不正なもうけ *dishonest [ill-gotten]* gains 彼は不正なことは何もしていないと言い張った He insisted that he did nothing *wrong*.

◆試験で不正行為をする *cheat* on [in] the exam / (電車に) 不正乗車をする (→ただ乗りをする) *steal a ride on a train*; (→運賃をごまかす) *cheat on train fares* / 彼らは不正にその熱帯植物を日本に持ち込んだ They *illegally* brought the tropical plant into Japan.

‖不正行為 a cheat / 不正手段 dishonest [unfair] means

ふせい² 父性 paternity ‖父性愛 paternal love

ふぜい 風情 彼らは風情ある日本庭園をパリに作った They built a *tasteful* Japanese garden in Paris. / この町には風情がある This city *has a charm of its own*. / 金沢は京都の風情をもった (→京都を思い起こさせる) 街だ Kanazawa *reminds* me of Kyoto.

ふせいかく 不正確 ——不正確な (間違っている) incorrect; (正確でない) inaccurate ‖不正確な翻訳 an *inaccurate* translation ◆あの時計は不正確だ That clock is *wrong [not correct]*.

ふせいこう 不成功 (失敗) failure ‖——不成功の unsuccessful ‖実験は不成功に終わった The experiment ended in *failure*. / 作戦は不成功だった The strategy was *unsuccessful*.

ふせいじつ 不誠実 (誠意のないこと) insincerity; (不正直) dishonesty ——不誠実な insincere; dishonest ‖彼がそんな不誠実な人だとは知らなかった I didn't know he was such a *dishonest* person.

ふせいしゅつ 不世出 ——不世出の incomparable ‖彼女は不世出の女流作家だ She is an *incomparable* female writer.

ふせいせき 不成績 今回の大会では私たちのチームは不成績に終わった Our team has an *unsatisfactory* finish in this competition.

ふせいりつ 不成立 failure ‖商談は不成立に終わった The business negotiations ended in *failure*.

◆第一次予算案は不成立となった (→通らなかった) The first budget bill *failed* to pass.

ふせき 布石 strategic move ‖次期選挙へ向けての布石を打つ *make a strategic move* toward the next election

ふせぐ 防ぐ

(守る) protect 働; guard 働; (予防する) prevent 働; (防御する) defend 働

水の事故を防ぐ *prevent* water accidents / 伝染病の蔓延(まんえん)を防ぐ *prevent* an infectious disease from spreading
私は日焼けを防ぐために長そでのシャツを着ています I wear a long-sleeved shirt to *protect* my skin from the sun.
キシリトールは虫歯を防ぐそうだ I've heard that xylitol *prevents [guards against]*

tooth decay.
ミサイル攻撃を防ぐ(→国を守る)ために国は偵察衛星を打ち上げた The government launched a spy satellite to *defend* the country from missile attacks.
◆寒さを防ぐために二重サッシにした We double-glazed the windows to *keep out* the cold. / その国は頭脳の流失を防ぐことができなかった That country could not *stop* its brain drain.

ふせつ 敷設 **―敷設する** (建設する) build* [他], construct [他]; (敷く) lay* [他] ∥パイプラインを敷設する *lay* a pipeline / 鉄道を敷設する *build* [*lay*] a railroad

ふせっせい 不摂生 neglect of *one's* health **―不摂生する** neglect *one's* health ∥父は不摂生がたたり入院する羽目になった My father ended up being hospitalized after *neglecting his health.*
◆不摂生な生活をする lead an *unhealthy* life

ふせる 伏せる
❶【下にする】(身を) lie* down; (表を下にして) put* … face down; (上部を下にして) put … upside down
私は銃声を聞いてとっさに床に身をふせた As soon as I heard the gunshot, I instinctively *lay down* on the floor.
終わった者は回答用紙を机の上にふせなさい When you finish, *put* your exam paper *face down* on your desk.
彼はコップをふせてテーブルの上に置いた He *put* the glass *upside down* on the table.
◆彼女は私を見ると目をふせた She *cast down* her eyes when she saw me.
❷【隠す】keep* … a secret
この件に関しては山本さんにはふせておいてください Please *keep* this *a secret* from Mr. Yamamoto.
❸【病気で】be sick in bed
母は近ごろ床にふせていることが多い My mother *is* often *sick in bed* these days.

ふせん[1] 不戦 不戦勝になる *win by default* / 不戦敗になる *lose by default*

ふせん[2] 付箋 《商標名》Post-it [C], slip [C]

ぶぜん 憮然 彼はぶぜんとして(→がっくりして)そこに立っていた He was standing there *dejectedly.*

ふせんめい 不鮮明 **―不鮮明な** not clear, indistinct ∥この印刷は不鮮明だ This printout is *not clear.*

ぶそう 武装 armament [U]; (装備) armaments **―武装する** arm *oneself* **―武装した** armed ∥銃で武装した男が銀行に立てこもった A man *armed* with a gun holed up in the bank.
‖武装解除 disarmament / 武装警官 an armed police officer / 核武装 nuclear arms / 再武装 rearmament / 非武装地帯 a demilitarized zone

ふそうおう 不相応 **―不相応な** (ふさわしくない) unsuitable; (不適当な) improper ∥BMW なんて彼には身分不相応な車だ A BMW is an *unsuitable* car *for* his *means.*

ふそく[1] 不足
❶【不十分】lack [U]《しばしば a～》; want [U]; shortage [U] [C]; insufficiency [U]《また an～》; deficiency [U] **―不足する** lack [他] [自], be [run*] short of …, be lacking in …
lack: 必要なものが足りないこと.
want: 重要なものが足りないこと.
shortage: 必要量に足りないこと.
insufficiency: 目的のために不十分なこと.
deficiency: 本質的な物の欠如.
水[人手]不足 *a* water [labor] *shortage*
私は睡眠不足に悩まされている I've been suffering from *a lack of sleep.*
私たちは資金不足のためその計画をあきらめた We gave up the plan for *lack of funds.*
政府は米不足に真剣に取り組んでいない The government isn't tackling *the rice shortage problem* seriously.
資金が不足してきた We *are running short of* funds.
食糧が不足している We *are short of* food.
私はまだ経験不足です I'*m lacking in* experience.
◆何不足なく(→快適に)暮らす live *in comfort* / おつりが10円不足している The change is 10 yen *short.* / 私は運動不足だ I do *not* get *enough* exercise.
❷【不満】
いったい何が不足だっていうんだ What more do you want?
彼らなら相手にとって不足はない If they were the opponent, it would be *a perfect match.*

ふそく[2] 不測 **―不測の** (予測できない) unexpected; (偶然の) accidental ∥不測の災害に備える prepare for an *unexpected* disaster / 不測の事態に我々は動転した We were in a panic due to an *unexpected* event.

ふそく[3] 付則 supplementary provision [C]

ふぞく 付属・附属 **―付属の** attached ∥これは大学に付属した研究機関だ This is an institute *attached* to the university.
‖付属高校 a (senior) high school attached to a university / 付属設備 attached equipment / 付属品 an attachment, an accesory

ぶぞく 部族 tribe [C]

ふぞろい 不揃い **―不ぞろいの** irregular; (でこぼこの) uneven ∥このブドウの粒は大きさが不ぞろいだ These grapes are *irregular* in size. / These grapes are *not of the same* size. / 彼の歯は不ぞろいだ He's got *uneven* teeth.

ふそん 不遜 **―不遜な** (傲慢(ごう)な) impudent; (見下した) contemptuous ∥彼の不遜な態度には我慢がならない I cannot bear his *impudent* attitude.

ふた 蓋 (なべなどの) lid [C]; (びんなどの) top [C]; (ペンなどの) cap [C]; (覆い) cover [C] ∥フライパンにふたをする put *a lid* on a frying pan / なべのふたを取る take *a lid* off a pan / ペンのふたをする put *the cap* on the pen
◆缶[箱]のふたをあける[閉める] *open* [*close*]

a can [box] / ビンのふたがあいている[閉まっている] The bottle *is open* [*not open*].
[慣用表現] 結果はふたをあけてみるまで分からない You *can't predict* the results.

ふだ 札 (はりつけた) label [C]; (下げ札) tag [C]; (値段などが記された) ticket [C]; (トランプの) (playing) card [C]; (お守り) talisman [C], charm [C] //トランプの札を切る shuffle *the cards* ◆小包には「こわれもの」の札がはってあった The parcel *was labeled* "FRAGILE".
‖名札 a name tag / 値札 a price tag / 番号札 a number ticket

ぶた 豚 pig [C]; (成長した食用の)《米》hog [C]; (成長した雌の) sow [C]; 《米》《通例集合的》swine [C] //太った豚 *a* fat [gross] *pig* / 彼は豚を飼育している He breeds *pigs*. / 豚のようにがつがつ食べる eat *like a pig* / 豚がぶうぶう鳴いている *Pigs* are grunting.
‖豚小屋《米》a pig,《英》a pigsty / 豚肉 pork / 子豚 a piglet / 焼き豚 roast pork
[ことわざ] 豚に真珠 It's like casting pearls before swine.

ふたい 付帯・附帯 ‖付帯決議 a supplementary resolution / 付帯工事 related work / 付帯条件 an incidental condition

ぶたい[1] 舞台

❶【演劇などの】stage [C]
初舞台を踏む *make one's first appearance on the stage*; *make one's debut*
彼女はあす3年ぶりに舞台に立つ She'll *appear on stage* tomorrow after an interval of three years.
◆彼らはきっとすばらしい舞台(→演技)を見せてくれるだろう They'll surely give *a* wonderful *performance*.

❷【活動の場】stage [C], scene [C]
パリはフランス革命の舞台だった Paris was *the stage* [*scene*] of the French Revolution.
日本は国際舞台で重要な役割を演じています Japan is playing an important role on *the international stage* [*scene*].
その計画を成功させるために舞台裏で多くの人が努力している A lot of people are working hard *behind the scenes* to make a success of the project.
◆野球となると彼のひとり舞台だ(→かなう者がいない) When it comes to baseball, he *is unrivaled* [*unequaled*].

❸【小説・映画などの】scene [C]
その物語の舞台は戦後の日本に設定されている *The scene* of the story is (set) in postwar Japan. / The story is set in postwar Japan.
‖舞台衣装 a theatrical costume / 舞台監督 a stage director / 舞台げいこ a dress rehearsal / 舞台芸術 the performing arts / 舞台効果 stage effects / 舞台照明 stage lighting / 舞台装飾 stage decoration / 舞台装置 stage setting / 舞台道具 a property,《口語的》a prop / 舞台俳優 a stage actor [actress]

ぶたい[2] 部隊 unit [C]; (専門技術をもった) corps [kɔ́ːr] [C] (複 ～ [kɔ́ːrz])

ふたいてん 不退転 その計画を不退転の決意でやりとげる carry the plan out *with immovable resolve*

ふたえ 二重 ‖二重まぶた a double eyelid

ふたく 付託 referral [C] [U] ―付託する refer [他] //議案を委員会に付託する *refer* a bill to a committee

ふたご 双子 twins; (双子の一方) twin [C]
➩ ふたござ //彼らは双子だ They are *twins*. / 健は双子だ Ken is *a twin*. / (→双子のきょうだいがいる)Ken has a *twin* brother [sister].

ふたごころ 二心 二心をいだいている (→忠実でない)*be disloyal* [*insincere*]; (→裏表がある) *have two faces*; *be two-faced* / 二心がない *be honest* [*loyal, sincere*]

ふたござ 双子座〔天文・占星〕Gemini [U] (❖「双子座の人」の意味では [C])

ふたことめには 二言目には 母は二言目には勉強しろと言う My mother *is always telling* me to study hard.

ふたしか 不確か ―不確かな uncertain; (当てにならない) unreliable //不確かな証拠 *uncertain* [*unreliable*] evidence / その日のことは不確かな記憶しかない I have only an *uncertain* [a *dim*, a *vague*] recollection of the day.

ふたたび 再び again
彼は少し間をおいてから再びしゃべり始めた After a pause, he started talking *again*.
再びお目にかかれるのを楽しみにしています I'm looking forward to seeing you *again*.
再びこんなミスを犯さないように Never make such a mistake *again*.
◆再び(→2度目の)チャンスがめぐってきた I got a *second* chance. / 彼は日本を去り,再び戻ることはなかった He left Japan, never to *return* [*come back*].

ふたつ 二つ two [U] [C]; (両方) both ―2つの two; (両方の) both
紙を2つに折る fold a sheet of paper「in *two* [in *half*, *double*]
彼女はクッキーを2つに割った She broke the cookie「in *two* [(→半分に) in *half*, into *halves*].
妹は私よりも学年が2つ下です My sister is *two* grades below me at school.
グラスが2つとも割れていた *Both* of the glasses were broken.
◆机を2つ1組に配置する arrange the desks *in pairs* / 私は2つとも買えない I *can't* buy *either*. / I can buy *neither*. / 原宿は新宿から2つ目の駅です Harajuku is the *second* station from Shinjuku.
[慣用表現] この皿はこの世に二つとない代物(しろもの)だ This plate is *unique*. / さらに努力するかあきらめるか,二つに一つだ You'll either have to try harder or give up. *You can't have it both ways*. / 彼らは二つ返事で(→即座に)その仕事を引き受けた They *promptly* [(→快く) *readily*] took the job.

ふだつき 札付き ―札付きの (悪名高い) notorious, infamous [ínfəməs] //札付きのちんぴら a *notorious* [an *infamous*] lowlife

ふたて 二手 二手に分かれる divide into two groups

ふたとおり 二通り この問題には2通りの解き方がある This problem can be solved in *two* ways.

ぶたばこ 豚箱 (留置場) lockup ⓒ

ブダペスト Budapest (❖ハンガリーの首都)

ふたまた 二股 二またに分かれた道 a *forked* road / 大学受験で二またをかけている (→2校受ける) take the entrance exams of *two* colleges / 彼は二またをかけて女の子とつきあっている He is going with *two* girls. / そこで二またに分かれている The road *forks* [*branches off*] (*in two*) there.
‖二またソケット a *two-way* socket

ふため 二目 それは二目と見られない光景だった It was a *horrible* [*shocking*, *frightful*] scene.

ふたり 二人 two (people); (一組) pair ⓒ, couple ⓒ; (両者) both

2人1組になって踊る dance *in pairs* / 婚約中の二人 *an engaged couple*

その事故で2人が命を失った *Two people* were killed [*Two lives* were lost] in the accident.

私たち2人はその金を分けた We divided the money between *the two* of us. (❖the がないと「3人以上いるうちの2人」の意味)

私の両親は2人とも仕事を持っている *Both* of my parents have jobs. / My parents *both* have jobs.

7時に2人予約したいのですが I'd like to reserve a table for *two* at seven o'clock.

◆自転車に2人乗りする ride a bicycle *double* / 二人は今月結婚することになっている They are to be married this month. / 私たちは2人とも英語が得意ではない *Neither* of us is good at English. / 彼は2人きょうだいだ (→兄弟[姉妹]が1人いる) He *has* a brother [*sister*].

ふたん 負担 burden ⓒ ――負担する (支払う) pay*他; (義務・責任などを負う) bear* 他 / 費用の一部を負担する pay [bear] a portion of the expenses / その仕事がだんだん負担になってきた The work is becoming *a burden* to [on, for] me. / それでは彼女の負担が重すぎる It's too heavy *a burden* for her. / 彼の協力のおかげで私の負担が軽くなった His cooperation lightened [lessened] my *burden*. / バイクのローンによる経済的負担が徐々に私にのしかかってきた The economic *burden* of the loan for my motorcycle is beginning to weigh on me.

◆本の読みすぎは目に負担をかける Too much reading *strains* [*taxes*] your eyes. / 私は自分の問題で他人に負担をかけたくない I wouldn't like to *bother* other people with my own troubles.

ふだん¹ 普段 (ふつう) usually,; (常に) always ――ふだんの usual, everyday
⇨いつも
ふだんの生活 *everyday* [*daily*] life
彼はふだんはコーヒーを飲まない He *usually* doesn't drink coffee. (❖He doesn't usually drink coffee. は「彼はいつもコーヒーを飲むわけではない」の意味)

けさはふだんより早く家を出た I left home earlier than *usual* this morning.

ふだんの力を出せば次の試合は勝てるよ You'll win the next game if you do as well as you *usually* do.

ふだんどおり彼女は11時に床についた *As usual*, she went to bed at 11.

ふだんから食べすぎには注意している I'm *always* trying not to eat too much.

◆きょうの彼女はどこかふだんと違う There's something *unusual* about her today.
‖ふだん着 casual [everyday] clothes

ふだん² 不断 彼女は不断の(→絶え間ない)努力によって司法試験に合格した She has succeeded in passing the bar examination by her *constant* [(→根気強い) *tireless*] effort.

ふち¹ 縁 (端) edge ⓒ; (グラス・わん・帽子などの) brim ⓒ; (丸い物の) rim ⓒ / がけの縁 *the edge* of a cliff / 縁まで牛乳の入ったコップ a glass full to *the brim* with milk / この茶わんは縁が欠けている There is a chip on *the edge* [*brim*, *rim*] of this rice bowl.

◆縁なしの眼鏡 *rimless* glasses / 金縁の眼鏡 *gold-rimmed* glasses / 眼鏡の縁 frames; eyeglass *rims*

ふち² 淵 (よどみ) pool ⓒ; (深み) the depths ‖彼女は悲しみのふちに沈んでいる She is in *the depths* of sorrow.

ふち³ 不治 不治の病 an *incurable* disease

ぶち 斑 spot ⓒ / 茶色いぶちの犬 a dog with brown *spots* ◆ぶちの猫 a *spotted* [*mottled*] cat

ぶちこわし ぶち壊し 彼のせいで雰囲気はぶちこわしになってしまった He *spoiled* [*wrecked*] the atmosphere.

ぶちこわす ぶち壊す (台なしにする) spoil* 他, ruin 他, wreck 他 / 計画をぶちこわす *spoil* [*ruin*, *wreck*] a plan

ふちどり 縁取り border ⓒ, hem ⓒ ――縁取りする border, edge 他 / レースの縁取りのあるテーブルクロス a tablecloth with a lace *border* / 彼女のスカートはレースの縁取りがある Her skirt *is bordered* [*edged*] with lace.

ふちどる 縁取る border 他, edge 他; (飾りをつける) fringe 他 / 花で縁取られた小道 a path *bordered* with flowers / レースで縁取られた枕カバー a pillowcase *fringed* with lace

ぶちぬく ぶち抜く (貫通する) go* through ..., pierce 他 自, penetrate 他 自 / 弾丸は厚い扉をぶち抜いた The bullet *went through* the thick door. ◆仕切りをはずして2部屋をぶち抜いた We removed the partitions to *make* the two rooms *into one*.

ぶちのめす overwhelm 他, knock down
⇨うちのめす

ぶちまける (中身を) dump 他, empty 他; (感情などを) vent 他; (不満などを) air 他; (真

相などを) reveal 他 //かばんの中身をぶちまける *dump* the contents out of a bag / 彼女は夫に怒りをぶちまけた She *vented* her anger on her husband.

ふちゃく 付着 stick* 自, adhere 自 ➪ つく(付く) //海藻がその岩に付着していた Some seaweed *stuck* [*adhered*] *to* the rock.

ふちゅうい 不注意 carelessness ⓤ; (無思慮) thoughtlessness ⓤ; (怠慢) negligence ⓤ ──**不注意な** careless; thoughtless; negligent //その事故の原因は運転手の不注意によるものである The accident is attributable to the driver's *carelessness* [*negligence*]. / 彼の不注意な発言がほかの人たちの感情を害した His *careless* [*thoughtless*] words caused offense to the others. / ドアにかぎをかけなかったのは私の不注意だった It was *careless* of me to leave the door unlocked.

ふちょう¹ 不調 我々のチームはこのところ不調が続いている Our team has been 「*out of form* [*in bad form*]」 recently. / 和平会談は不調に終わった The peace talks ended *in failure*. / 彼はよく体の不調を訴えている He's often complaining about 「*not feeling well* [*his bad condition*]」.

ふちょう² 婦長 head nurse ⓒ

ぶちょう 部長 (会社の) a head of a department, manager ⓒ; (クラブなどの) the president //営業[人事]部長 *the* sales [personnel] *manager* / 社交ダンス部の部長を務める *serve as president* of the social dance club

ふちょうわ 不調和 disharmony ⓤ ──**不調和な** disharmonious //心と体の不調和 *disharmony* between mind and body

ふちん 浮沈 ups and downs ➪ うきしずみ

ぶつ hit* 他 自; (平手で) slap 他 自 ➪ たたく, なぐる ◆一席ぶつ(→演説する) *give a talk*; *make a speech*

ふつう¹ 普通

(いつもは) usually, (一般的に) generally, commonly ──**ふつうの** common; usual; ordinary; general; normal; average

| common: ありふれた, 当たり前の.
| usual: いつもの.
| ordinary: 通常の.
| general: 一般的な.
| normal: 正常な, 通常の.
| average: 平均的な.

ふつうの人 an *ordinary* [*average*] person / ふつうの背丈の男性 a man of *average* height / ふつうの大きさのテーブル a table of *normal* size

私はふつう6時ごろ帰宅する *Usually* [*Generally, As a rule*] I get home about six.

このCDはふつうの店では買えない You can't get this CD at an *ordinary* store.

コンピュータは家庭でもふつうに使われるようになってきている Computers are becoming more and more *commonly* used at home.

アメリカでは10代で自動車の運転免許を取るのはふつうである It is *common* for teenagers in the U.S. to get a driver's license.

この習慣は日本人にはふつうのことです This custom is *common* among Japanese.

ふつうに考えると(→常識的には)そんなことが起こるはずがない *According to common sense*, that can't happen.

あの選手はうまくもないし下手でもない, ふつうだよ That player isn't good or bad. He's just *average*.

◆きょうの彼女はふつうじゃないね She 「*is not* [*doesn't look*]」 *herself* today. / 彼はふつうの男の子に比べると行儀がよかった He was well-behaved, *as* boys *go*.

∥普通科(高校の) a general course (at high school) / 普通教育 general education / 普通選挙 a popular [universal] election / 普通名詞《文法》a common noun / 普通郵便 ordinary mail / 普通預[貯]金 an ordinary account / 普通列車 a local train

ふつう² 不通 その区間の列車は大雪のため不通になっている Train services on that section 「*are suspended* [*have stopped*]」 because of the heavy snow. / その道路は事故のために不通になっている The road *is closed* because of the accident. / その地域の電話はきのうから不通になっている In that area the telephone service *has been suspended* [*cut off*] since yesterday.

ふつか 二日 4月2日に on April *2* [*2nd*] (◆ 2 [2nd]は (the) second と読む) / 2日間学校を休む stay away from school *for two days* / 2日おきに(→3日目ごとに) *every* 「*third day* [*three days*]」 / 彼女には2日後にまた会った I met her again *two days later*.

ぶっか 物価 prices //物価の上昇[下落, 変動] a rise [fall, fluctuation] in *prices* / 物価を安定させる stabilize *prices* / 最近物価が上がり[下がり]始めた *Prices* have begun to go up [down] these days. / このへんの物価は東京の物価よりずっと高い[低い] *The prices* here are much higher [lower] than those in Tokyo. / ここ数年物価は安定している *Prices* have been stable for the past few years.

∥(消費者)物価指数 a (consumer) price index

ふっかける 吹っ掛ける 人にけんかをふっかける *pick a quarrel with* a person / 人に議論をふっかける(→いどむ) *challenge* a person to a debate / 店員はその服に法外な値をふっかけてきた The salesclerk *tried to charge me an outrageous price* for the dress.

ぶっかける ぶっ掛ける (水を浴びせかける) throw* 他; (注ぐ) pour 他

ふっかつ 復活 revival ⓤ, (公式的に) rebirth ⓤ ⓒ ──**復活する** revive 自 (◆他動詞で「復活させる」の意味もある) //70年代ファッションの復活 the *revival* of 70's fashion / 古い伝統を復活させる *revive* [*restore, bring back*] old traditions

∥復活祭 Easter (◆キリストの復活 the Resurrection を祝う記念祭)

ふつかよい 二日酔い hangover ⓒ //二日酔いになる have [get] *a hangover*; *be hung over*

ぶつかる

❶ 衝突する　　　　hit, strike
❷ 遭遇する　　　　meet with ...
❸ 日時がかち合う

❶【衝突する】hit* 働他, strike* 働他;(どんと) bump 働自, knock 他;(車などが) run* into ...;(動いている人・物が) collide 自

ボールが頭にぶつかった A ball hit 「me on the head [my head].

ボールは塀にぶつかって私のほうにはね返ってきた The ball hit (against [on]) the wall and bounded back to me.

道で人とぶつかった I bumped into someone on the street.

彼女はハンドルを切りそこねて電信柱にぶつかった She failed to turn the wheel and ran into a telephone pole.

交差点でバスがトラックとぶつかった A bus collided with a truck at the crossing.

❷【遭遇する】meet* with ..., run* [come*] up against ...;(立ち向かう) face 他

私たちは最後の段階で思いがけない問題にぶつかった We 「met with [faced] an unexpected problem in the final stage.

私たちは1回戦から優勝候補の一角とぶつかった We 「ran up against [(→対戦した) competed with] one of the top favorites in the first match.

◆交通渋滞[ラッシュアワー]にぶつかる(→巻き込まれる) get caught in 「a traffic jam [the rush hour]

❸【日時がかち合う】
彼の出発は私の試験とぶつかったために，見送りに行けなかった His departure clashed with my examination, so I was not able to go to see him off.

今年の勤労感謝の日は日曜日とぶつかる This year's Labor Thanksgiving Day will fall on (a) Sunday.

❹【その他】
正面から問題にぶつかる(→取り組む) tackle a problem head-on

私たちの間で意見がぶつかった There was a conflict of opinions between us.

弟は父とつまらないことでよくぶつかる(→けんかをする) My brother often quarrels with my father about trifles.

ふっかん 復刊 ——復刊する resume publishing [publication];(再版する) reissue 他

ふっき 復帰 return ©U, comeback ©(通例単数形) ——復帰する return 自, come* back, go* back //彼女は半年後職場に復帰した She returned to work six months later. / そのボクサーは3年前にいったん引退したがその後現役に復帰した The boxer retired three years ago but has since made a comeback.
◆社会復帰する resume one's place in society; resume one's former life

ぶつぎ 物議 首相の発言は大いに物議をかもした The Prime Minister's remarks caused quite a dispute.

ふっきゅう 復旧 ——復旧する(再開する) resume 働他;(修復する) restore 他 //その地域の水道は復旧のめどが立っていない There is no prospect of when 「water service will be restored [water supply will be restored]」 in that area. / 中央線は深夜になって復旧した The Chuo Line resumed (normal) service late at night.
|復旧作業 restoration [repair] work

ぶっきょう 仏教 Buddhism Ⓤ ——仏教の Buddhist //仏教僧 a Buddhist priest / 仏教徒 a Buddhist / 仏教美術 Buddhist art

ぶっきらぼう ——ぶっきらぼうな blunt, curt ——ぶっきらぼうに bluntly, curtly // ぶっきらぼうに返事をする answer bluntly [curtly]; make a blunt [curt] answer / 彼の話し方はぶっきらぼうだった His way of speaking was blunt [curt].

ぶつぎり ぶつ切り 魚をぶつ切りにする chop up a fish

ふっきれる 吹っ切れる 彼女の力強い励ましの言葉で迷いが吹っ切れた Her strong encouragement dispelled my anxiety.

ふっきん 腹筋 [解剖] abdominal muscle ©, abdominals,《口語的》abs;(腹筋運動) sit-up © //30回腹筋をする do 30 sit-ups

フック hook ©;(ゴルフ・ボウリングなどの) hook ©;[ボクシング] hook © //コートをフックにかける hang a coat on the hook / 右フックを打つ hit a right hook

ブックエンド bookends

ブックカバー (book [dust]) jacket ©

ふっくら ふっくらとしたほお round [full] cheeks / パンはふっくらと焼き上がった The bread was baked soft and puffy.

ブックレビュー (書評) book review ©

ぶつける hit* 他;(どすんと) bump 他;(ガチンと) crash 他;(投げつける) throw* 他, fling* 他 //彼女はベッドの角(かど)にひざをぶつけた She hit her knee against the corner of the bed. / 彼女は壁に車をぶつけてしまった She crashed [bumped] her car into a wall. / 僕は雪合戦で友達めがけて雪玉をぶつけた I threw a snowball at my friend during a snowball fight.
◆人に質問をぶつける put [pose] a question to a person / 彼に怒りをぶつけてもしかたがない There's no use venting your anger at him.

ふっけん 復権 ——復権する(法律上の資格・権利を) recover legal status;(復位・復職する) be rehabilitated

ぶっけん 物件 (物) thing ©;(物品) article ©;(資産) estate Ⓤ //証拠物件 evidence

ふっこう 復興 (伝統などの) revival Ⓤ©;(回復) recovery Ⓤ(また a ~);(再建) reconstruction Ⓤ ——復興する be reconstructed, be restored //経済の復興 economic recovery [reconstruction, revival] / めざましい復興をとげる make a remarkable recovery / その町の復興は着実に進んでいる The reconstruction of the town is in steady prog-

ress.
‖文芸復興(期)〖歴史〗the Renaissance

ふつごう 不都合 (不便) inconvenience ⓊⒸ; (害) harm Ⓤ; (不適切なこと) impropriety ⓊⒸ ――不都合な inconvenient; (悪い・間違った) wrong ◆彼にその話をしても何も不都合はない *It does no harm* to tell him about it.

ふっこく 復刻・覆刻 ――復刻する reprint ⓉⒾ ‖復刻版 a reprinted edition

ぶっさん 物産 product Ⓒ; (野菜・果物などの)(集合的) produce Ⓤ ‖鹿児島県の物産展 *a display of the products* of Kagoshima Prefecture

ぶっし 物資 (品物) goods Ⓟ; (必需品) supplies; (資源) resources; (原料) (raw) material(s) ‖地震で家を失った人々に救援物資が届けられた *Relief supplies [goods]* were sent to the people who were left homeless by the earthquake.
‖緊急物資 emergency supplies / 生活物資 daily necessities, essential commodities

ぶっしき 仏式 仏式の葬式 a *Buddhist* funeral / 二人の結婚式は仏式で行われた Their wedding ceremony was held *according to Buddhist rites [rituals]*.

ぶっしつ 物質 matter Ⓤ (✿spirit, mind に対する語); (個々の具体的な) substance Ⓒ ――物質の・物質的な material
物質的援助 *material* assistance
モルヒネは医薬品としては有用な物質だ Morphine is *a useful substance* as medicine.
◆私たちは物質的に恵まれた生活をしている We are well off *materially*.
‖物質文明 material civilization / 物質名詞 〖文法〗a concrete [material] noun / 化学物質 a chemical substance / 抗生物質〖生化学〗antibiotics / 合成物質 a compound substance / 放射性物質 radioactive material / 有害物質 a hazardous substance

プッシュホン push-button phone Ⓒ

ぶっしょう 物証 (physical) evidence Ⓤ

ふっしょく 払拭 ――払拭する (一掃する) 〖公式的〗eradicate ⓉⒾ, sweep* away
◆その会社は古くさいイメージを払拭しよう(→改善しよう)としている The company is trying to *improve* its old-fashioned image.

ぶっしょく 物色 ――物色する (探す) look for ..., search ⓉⒾ ‖泥棒は金めの物はないかと室内を物色した The robber *searched* the room for valuables.

ぶっしん 物心 物心両面で人を支える support a person *both materially and spiritually*

ぶつぜん 仏前 仏前に(→位牌(いはい)の前に)花を供える offer flowers *before the tablet of* the dead

フッそ フッ素 〖化学〗fluorine Ⓤ (✿元素記号 F)

ぶっそう 物騒 ――物騒な (危険な) dangerous, unsafe ‖物騒な世の中だ It's a *dangerous* world. / 玄関にかぎをかけないで出かけるなんて物騒だな It's *dangerous* to go out with the door unlocked.
◆最近, 物騒な(→人を不安にさせる)事件が続いている *Disquieting* events have taken place one after another recently.

ぶつぞう 仏像 an image of Buddha, Buddhist image Ⓒ

ぶつだ 仏陀 Buddha

ぶったい 物体 object Ⓒ; (物理学で) body Ⓒ ‖未確認飛行物体 *an* unidentified flying *object* (✿UFO のこと) / 奇妙な物体が空を飛んでいるのが目撃された People saw *a strange object* flying in the air.

ぶつだん 仏壇 [図] a *butsudan*, a Buddhist family altar

ぶっちぎり 彼はぶっちぎりで(→ほかの走者を大きく引き離して)ゴールした He *had a huge lead* when he crossed the finish line.

ぶっちょうづら 仏頂面 仏頂面をしている make *a sullen [sour] face*

ぶっつけほんばん ぶっつけ本番 ぶっつけ本番でスピーチをする make a speech 「*without any preparation [impromptu]* / 時間がない. ぶっつけ本番でやるしかないだろう We have no time left. We'll have to *play it by ear*.

ぶっつづけ ぶっ続け 彼は20時間ぶっ続けで仕事をしている He's been working for 20 hours *straight*.

ふっつり 彼は2年前ふっつり(→突然)姿を消した He *suddenly* disappeared two years ago.

ぶっつり 軽く引いただけでその糸はぶっつりと切れた The thread *snapped* when I only pulled it lightly.

プッツン 彼女のわがままに私はプッツンしそう(→かっとしそう)になった I almost *lost it* at her selfishness.

ふてい 払底 その業界では若く有能な人材が払底している The industry *is short of* young and capable people.

ぶてき 物的 物的証拠はまだ見つかっていない We've not found any *physical [material] evidence* yet.

ふってわく 降って湧く その空港建設計画は我々にとっては全く降ってわいたような(→思いもかけない)話だった The airport construction project 「*was totally unexpected [came out of blue]* for us.

ふってん 沸点 boiling point ⒸⓊ

ぶってん 仏典 (集合的) Buddhist scriptures; (個々の経) sutra Ⓒ

ふっと 彼女の口からふっとため息が(→かすかなため息が)もれた A *slight* sigh escaped her lips. / ふっと(→急に)名案が浮かんだ A good idea *suddenly* occurred to me.

ぶっと ぶっと吹き出す let out *a little* burst of laughter

ふっとう 沸騰 ――沸騰する・させる boil ⓘ ⓉⒾ ‖メタノールは摂氏64.65度で沸騰する Methyl alcohol *boils* at 64.65℃. / やかんの水が沸騰している The (water in the) kettle *is boiling*. ◆そのことについて議論が沸騰した(→白熱した議論になった) We *got into a heated argument* over that matter.

ぶっとおし ぶっ通し 5時間ぶっ通しで(→休

みなく)歩く walk for five hours *without a break* / その祭りは3日間ぶっ通しで行われる The festival continues for three days *on end*.

ぶっとばす ぶっ飛ばす 高速道路を160キロでぶっとばす *tear down* an expressway at 160 kilometers per hour / あいつに歯向かうとぶっとばされるよ If you get into a fight with him, he is sure to *beat* you *up*.

ふっとぶ 吹っ飛ぶ (風で) be blown off; (なくなる) disappear [自] ‖強い風で看板が吹っ飛んだ The signboard *was blown off* by the strong wind. / ゲームセンターで遊んでいたらあっという間に5,000円が吹っ飛んだ When I was playing at the video arcade, 5,000 yen *disappeared* in no time.
◆急用のためにその予定は吹っ飛んでしまった The plan *fell through* because of urgent business.

フットボール football [U] (❖「フットボール用のボール」は[C]. 《米》ではアメリカンフットボールを指し, 《英》などではサッカーまたはラグビーを指す) ‖フットボールをする play *football* / フットボール選手 a *football* player
‖アメリカンフットボール American football

フットライト footlights

フットワーク footwork [U] ‖華麗なフットワークをしている have fancy *footwork*

ぶっぴん 物品 (商品) goods; (品物) article [C] ‖物品税 commodity tax; (国内消費税) excise tax

ぶつぶつ[1] 彼は何かぶつぶつ言いながら歩いていた He was *muttering* something while walking. / 彼女は隣のピアノの音がうるさいとぶつぶつ言っていた She *was muttering* [*grumbling*] about her neighbor's noisy piano playing.

ぶつぶつ[2] rash [C] ‖背中にぶつぶつができた I came [broke] out in *a rash* on my back.

ぶつぶつこうかん 物々交換 barter [U]
◆食べ物を服と物々交換する *barter* food for clothes

ぶつめつ 仏滅 🗻 a *butsumetsu*, a very unlucky day ➔ たいあん

ぶつもん 仏門 仏門に入る *become a Buddhist priest*

ぶつよく 物欲 material desire [C], possessiveness [U][C] ◆物欲の強い人 a *materialistic* person

ぶつり 物理 (物理学) physics 《単数扱い》 ―物理的な physical ‖物理的変化 a *physical* change ◆それは物理的に不可能だ It's *physically* impossible.
‖物理化学 physical chemistry / 物理学者 a physicist

ぷつり 魚がかかったと思ったら糸がぷつりと切れた The line *snapped* the moment I hooked a fish.

ふつりあい 不釣り合い その帽子は服と不つり合いだ The hat *doesn't match* [*go with*] the dress. / その部屋には不つり合いなほど大きなテーブルがあった There was a *disproportionately* large table in the room. / 彼らは不つり合いなカップルだ They are an *ill-matched* couple.

ふで 筆 (毛筆) writing brush [C]; (絵筆) (paint)brush [C]
筆で字を書く write with *a writing brush*
‖筆立て a pen stand / 筆箱 a pencil case
[慣用表現] きょうはちっとも筆が進まない I *can't make any progress with my writing* today. / 彼は筆が立つ He *writes well.* / He *is a good writer*. / 彼女は筆まめ[筆不精]だ She is *a good* [*bad*] *correspondent*. / 私は絵に仕上げの筆を入れた I *added the* finishing *touches* to my painting. / 筆を置く *stop writing* / 先生は私の原稿に筆を加えた(→直した) The teacher *made* some *corrections* to my manuscript. / その作家は突然筆を断った The writer suddenly *gave up writing*. / この映画は監督自らシナリオの筆を執った The director himself *wrote* the screenplay for this film.
[ことわざ] 弘法筆を選ばず ➔ こうぼう / 弘法も筆の誤り ➔ こうぼう

ふてい[1] 不定 ―不定の (不明確な) indefinite; (不安定な) unsettled; (不規則な) irregular; (変わりやすい) variable
◆逮捕されたのは住所不定, 無職の男だった A man with *no* occupation or *fixed address* was arrested.
‖不定冠詞〖文法〗an indefinite article / 不定詞 ➔ ふていし / 不定代名詞 ➔ ふていだいめいし

ふてい[2] 不貞 …に不貞を働く *be unfaithful to …*

ふていき 不定期 ―不定期の (不規則な) irregular ―不定期に irregularly ‖不定期の会合 an *irregular* meeting
‖不定期便 a nonscheduled flight

ふていさい 不体裁 ―不体裁な (見苦しい) unseemly, graceless; (不適当な) improper ➔ ていさい

ふていし 不定詞 〖文法〗 infinitive [C]

不定詞には《to＋動詞の原形》の to 不定詞(to-infinitive)と to が付かない原形不定詞(bare infinitive)がある.
[**to** 不定詞]to 不定詞は, 文中での働きによって以下のように分類することができる.
(1)名詞的用法…主語・補語・目的語になる ‖ *To know* oneself is difficult. (❖主語) 自分を知ることは難しい / My dream is *to become* a baseball player. (❖補語) 私の夢は野球選手になることです / I want *to eat* delicious ramen. (❖目的語) 私はおいしいラーメンが食べたい
(2)形容詞的用法…名詞・代名詞を修飾する ‖ It's time *to go* to bed. (❖名詞を修飾) もう寝る時間です / Can I have something cold *to drink*? (❖代名詞を修飾) 冷たい飲み物をください
(3)副詞的用法…動詞・形容詞を修飾する ‖ I took the first train *to catch* the airplane. (❖動詞を修飾) 飛行機に乗るために始発列車に乗った / I'm glad *to see* you.

(❖形容詞を修飾)あなたに会えてうれしい [原形不定詞]see, hear などの感覚動詞や make, let などの使役動詞といっしょに用いられる // I've *heard* her *sing* that song. (❖感覚動詞と)彼女がその歌を歌うのを聞いたことがある / No one can *make* me *change* my mind. (❖使役動詞と)だれも私の気持ちを変えることはできない

ふていだいめいし 不定代名詞 〖文法〗 indefinite pronoun ▶

不定代名詞は，次の2種類に分類することができる．(1)「あれ」「これ」と指し示すことのできないものを表す言葉で，日本語では「何か」「だれか」などに当たる．anything, somebody など．(2)定まっていない数や量を表す言葉で，日本語では「いくつか」「たくさん」などに当たる．some, many など．

ブティック boutique ⓒ
ふてき 不敵 ──**不敵な** (大胆な) bold;(恐れを知らない) fearless //男は*不敵な*面(%)構えをしていた The man had a *fearless* look on his face. ◆彼は不敵な笑いを浮かべた He grinned *fearlessly*.
ふでき 不出来 ──**不出来な** (下手な・劣った) poor, bad;(不十分な) unsatisfactory //*不出来な*作品 a *poor* work ◆今年のリンゴは不出来だった The apple crop *failed* this year.
ふてきかく 不適格 ──**不適格な** (ふさわしくない) inappropriate, inadequate;(能力のない) incompetent //私はその仕事には*不適格*だと思います I feel *inadequate* for the job.
ふてきせつ 不適切 ──**不適切な** inappropriate, improper //*不適切な*発言 an *improper* [*inappropriate*] remark
ふてきとう 不適当 ──**不適当な** unsuitable;(場所・目的などに) improper, inappropriate;(能力・資格のない) unfit //*不適当な*表現 an *inappropriate* [*improper*] expression / この靴は山登りには*不適当だ* These shoes are「*unsuitable* [*not good*] for mountain climbing.
ふてきにん 不適任 彼は教師には*不適任だ* He is *unfit*「to be [*for*] a teacher.
ふてぎわ 不手際 今後はこのような*不手際*がないように気をつけます We'll try not to make such *a mistake* again. / 旅行業者の*不手際*で私たちは出発を延期せざるをえなくなった We were forced to put off our departure because of the travel agency's *mismanagement*.
ふてくされる ふて腐れる sulk 🖲, get* sulky //妹は*ふてくされて*しばらく部屋から出てこなかった My sister *sulked* [*was sulky*] and didn't come out of her room for a while.
◆*ふてくされた*顔 a *sulky* [*sullen*] look
ふってい 不徹底 ──**不徹底な** (不十分な) insufficient;(一貫していない) inconsistent;(中途半端な) halfway //*不徹底な*処罰 an *insufficient* punishment
◆その事件に関する警察の捜査は*不徹底*だった(→徹底的に捜査しなかった) The police did *not* conduct a *thorough* investigation into the incident. / The police did *not* investigate the incident *thoroughly*.
ふてね 不貞寝 健司は母親にしかられて*ふて寝している* Kenji *is sulking in bed* after being scolded by his mother.
ふてぶてしい (厚かましい) impudent //*ふてぶてしい*態度で in an *impudent* manner
ふと (突然) suddenly;(偶然) by chance, by accident;(何の気なしに) casually;(思いもよらず) unexpectedly ⇨ふとした
彼女に初めて会った日のことを*ふと*思い出した I *suddenly* remembered the day I first met her.
*ふと*窓の外を見ると雨が降っていた I looked out the window *casually* and saw it was raining.
◆*ふと*名案を思いつく *hit on* a good idea / *ふと*立ち寄った店でずっと探していた本を見つけた I *happened to* drop by a bookstore, and there I found a book I had long been searching for. / *ふと*気がつくと12時を回っていた It had turned 12 *before I knew it*.

ふとい 太い

❶【幅・径が】thick, big;(線・文字などが) bold
太い指 *thick* fingers / 太いまゆ *thick* [*bushy*] eyebrows / 太いペン a *thick* [*broad*] pen
その橋は8本の太い柱で支えられている The bridge rests on eight *big* [*thick*] pillars.
あの選手の腕はとても太い That player has very *big* arms.
その言葉は太い字で書かれていた The word was written in a *bold* [*thick*] hand.
❷【声が】deep
彼は声が太い He has a *deep* voice.
❸【図太い】(大胆な) bold;(恥知らずの) shameless;(厚かましい) impudent
◆あいつは本当に太い神経をしているな He's got a lot of *nerve*.

ふとう¹ 不当 injustice Ⓤ Ⓒ ──**不当な** (不正な) unjust;(不公平な) unfair;(不合理な) unreasonable ──**不当に** unjustly; unfairly; unreasonably //*不当な*待遇を受ける receive *unfair* treatment; be treated *unfairly* / *不当な*利益をあげる make an *unfair* profit; profit *unfairly* / 原告団は判決の*不当性*を訴えた The plaintiffs complained about the *injustice* of the court's ruling. / 私たちはみな，彼の*不当な*要求にあきれている We are all disgusted with his *unreasonable* demands. / 弱者に対する不当な差別は私たちの社会にいまだ残っている *Unjust* discrimination against the weak still remains in our society.
ふとう² 埠頭 wharf ⓒ (複 wharves, ~s);(桟橋) pier ⓒ
ふどう¹ 不動 ──**不動の** firm, unshakable //*不動の*信念の持ち主 a person with a *firm* [*an unshakable*] belief / 彼はその映画で名監督として*不動*の地位を獲得した He attained a

ふどう

firm [an *unassailable*] reputation as an excellent movie director with that film.

ふどう² 不同 順不同で[に] *in random order*

ぶとう 舞踏 dance Ⓒ, dancing Ⓤ ‖舞踏会 a dance, a ball (❖後者は公式で規模の大きなもの)

ぶどう¹ 葡萄 （1粒の実）grape Ⓒ; （木）vine Ⓒ, grapevine Ⓒ ‖1房のブドウ a bunch [cluster] of *grapes*
‖ブドウ園 a vineyard / ブドウ酒 wine / ブドウ糖 glucose, grape sugar / 種なしブドウ seedless *grapes* / 干しブドウ a raisin

ぶどう² 武道 🈁 *budo*, the (*Japanese*) *martial arts*

ふとういつ 不統一 (a) lack of unity, disunity Ⓤ; （一貫性のなさ）inconsistency Ⓤ; （不調和）disharmony Ⓤ ‖不統一な議論 an *inconsistent* argument
◆その問題に関しては我々の間に意見の不統一がある (→意見が分かれている) We *are divided in opinion* on that issue.

ふとうこう 不登校 不登校の生徒 a student *who refuses to go to school*
⇒ 場面・状況別会話 p.1744

ふとうごう 不等号〔数学〕a sign of inequality

ふどうさん 不動産 real estate [property] Ⓤ ‖不動産業 real estate business / 不動産業者 （米）a real estate agent,（英）an estate agent

ふとうしき 不等式〔数学〕an (expression of) inequality

ふどうとく 不道徳 immorality Ⓤ ━━不道徳な immoral

ふどうひょう 浮動票 （米）swing [undecided] vote Ⓒ, （英）floating vote Ⓒ ‖浮動票を獲得する attract *swing* [*undecided*] *votes*

ふとうくつ 不撓不屈 不撓不屈の精神 an *unyielding* spirit

ふとうめい 不透明 ━━不透明な opaque ‖不透明な液体 *opaque* liquid
◆景気の先行きは不透明なままだ Economic prospects are still *gray* [*muddy*].

ふとく 不徳 すべて私の不徳の致すところです (→すべて私が悪い) It's *all my fault*.

ふとくい 不得意 ━━不得意な poor, weak ‖私は人前で話すのが不得意だ I *am poor* [*weak*] *at* speaking in public. / (→得意ではない) I'm *not good at* speaking in public.
‖不得意科目 one's *weak subject*

ふとくてい 不特定 ━━不特定の unspecified ‖不特定多数の人々 a large number of *unspecified* people

ふところ 懐 ❶【胸部】（内ポケット）inner [inside] pocket Ⓒ ‖彼はふところから手帳を取り出した He took out a notebook from *his inner pocket*. ◆山のふところにいだかれた村 a village in the *heart of the mountains*

❷【所持金】きょうはふところが暖かいね [寂しいね] I 「*have a lot of* [*am short of*] *money* today.

🅴「あのカメラ買うつもりなの？」「ふところと相談してから決めるよ」 "Are you going to buy that camera?" "I'll decide after consulting my *pocketbook*." (❖*pocketbook* は「ふところぐあい」の意味)

❸【その他】彼はふところが深い (→度量が大きい) He is *very broadminded*.

ふとさ 太さ thickness Ⓤ Ⓒ; （直径）diameter Ⓤ Ⓒ; （幅）width Ⓤ
🔴「この綱の太さはどれくらいですか」「10センチです」"How *thick* is this rope?" "It's 10 centimeters thick." / "What's *the diameter* of this rope?" "It's 10 centimeters in diameter."

ふとじ 太字 thick letter [character] Ⓒ; （印刷）boldface Ⓤ, bold type Ⓤ

ふとした ふとしたことから (→偶然) 新しい仕事が見つかった I got a new job *by chance*. / 彼女のふとした (→なにげない) 言葉が彼の気にさわった Her *casual* words offended him. / 私たちはふとしたことから知り合いになった We became acquainted with each other *by chance*.

ふとっぱら 太っ腹 ━━太っ腹な （気前のいい）generous; （度量の大きい）broad-minded

ふとどき 不届き ━━不届きな （無礼な）rude; （とんでもない）outrageous ‖不届き者 an outrageous person

ふとめ 太目 太めの ━━太めの大根 a *rather thick daikon* / 太めのズボン baggy [*full*] trousers / 彼は少し太めだ He *is on the plump side*. (❖*on the ... side* は「幾分…」の意味)

ふともも 太腿 thigh Ⓒ

ふとる 太る・肥る

get* [grow*, become*] fat (❖*fat* には軽蔑的な含みがある. そのため plump, large, stout などの遠回しな表現を用いることが多い); （体重が増す）gain [put* on] weight
3キロ太る *gain* three kilos / まるまる太った赤ん坊 a *plump* [*chubby*] baby
しばらく見ないうちに彼はだいぶ太った He *has* 「*become* very *stout* [*gained* a lot of *weight*] since I saw him last.
◆少し太りすぎだと医者に言われた I was told by the doctor that I *was* a little *overweight*. / 最近ちょっと太りぎみだ I've been *on the plump side* recently. / 太りやすい食べ物はできるだけ避けるようにしている I'm trying to avoid *fattening* food whenever possible.

🅴「少し太ったんじゃない？」「最近運動してないからね」"You've *gained* a little *weight*, haven't you?" "I haven't exercised recently."

ふとん 布団 🈁 futon Ⓒ, Japanese quilted bedding placed on the floor; （寝具）bedding Ⓤ (❖英語の *futon* はマットレスなどから成るソファーベッドを指す) ‖ふとんを上げる put away *the futon* / ふとんを敷く spread [lay out] *the futon* / ふとんをかける put on *a futon* / ふとんをたたむ fold up *the futon* / ふとんを干す air (out) *the futon*

ふとんは敷きぶとんと掛けぶとんからなる日本の寝具です. 使わないときは押し入れにたたんでし

まうので，あまり広くない畳の部屋も有効に使えます．
Futons are Japanese beds. A set of futons includes a *shikibuton* (mattress) and *kakebuton* (quilt). When not used, the futons are folded up and placed inside a closet called an *oshiire*. Futons allow small Japanese rooms to be used more efficiently.

ふな 鮒 crucian (carp) [C]

ぶな 橅 beech [C]

ふなあそび 船遊び・舟遊び boating [U]; (ヨット遊び) yachting [U], sailing [U]

ふなうた 舟歌 sailor's song [C]

ふなか 不仲 彼らは実は不仲だとささやかれている It is said that they *are* in fact *on bad terms with* each other.

ふながいしゃ 船会社 shipping company [C]

ふなかじ 船火事 a fire on a ship; (海上での火事) a fire at sea

ふなだいく 船大工 shipwright [C]

ふなたび 船旅 voyage [C]; (遊覧) cruise [C] ∥世界一周の船旅をする take *a cruise* around the world

ふなちん 船賃 (乗客の) fare [C], passage [C]; (荷物の) freight [U]

ふなつきば 船着き場 (港) harbor, ((英))harbour [C]; (波止場) wharf [C]

ふなづみ 船積み ━船積みする load [他] [自]; (出荷する) ship [他]

ふなで 船出 sailing [U] ━船出する sail [自], set* sail ∥神戸へ向けて船出する *sail for* Kobe
◆新しい人生に船出する *start* a new life

ふなのり 船乗り sailor [C], seaman [C]

ふなびん 船便 sea mail [U]; (郵便の) surface mail [U] (❖航空便 air mail 以外のもので，陸上の便も含まれる) ∥船便で…を送る send … *by sea mail*

ふなよい 船酔い seasickness [U]
◆船酔いしてさんざんな目にあった I *was* [*got*] *seasick* and had a really miserable time.

ふなれ 不慣れ inexperience [U] ━不慣れな not used [accustomed] to …, ((公式的)) unaccustomed to …; (経験のない) inexperienced; (なじみがない) unfamiliar ∥彼は不慣れな仕事に苦労している He's having trouble with his work because of *his inexperience*.
◆すみません，このあたりは不慣れなもので Sorry, but I'm *a stranger* here. / 弟は不慣れな手つきでリンゴの皮をむいている My brother is peeling an apple *with an awkward hand*.

ぶなん 無難 ━無難な (より安全な) safer; (よりたやすい) easier; (一応満足のいく) acceptable ∥無難な道を選ぶ choose a *safer* [*an easier*] way / 無難な演技を見せる give an *acceptable* performance / しばらくここにとどまったほうが無難だろう It would *be safer* for us to stay here for a while.

ふにあい 不似合い unsuitable; (似つかわしくない) unbecoming ∥彼はおとなしそうな外見に不似合いな乱暴な言葉づかいをする He uses rough language *unbecoming to* his gentle appearance. ◆不似合いなカップル an *ill-matched* couple

ふにゃふにゃ ━ふにゃふにゃの (柔らかい) soft; (ぐにゃぐにゃした) limp; (たるんだ) flabby ◆マシュマロはふにゃふにゃしていてどうも食べる気がしない I don't like to eat marshmallows because they're *too squishy*.

ふにん[1] 赴任 福岡に赴任する「*be transferred to* [*take up a post in*] Fukuoka
‖赴任地 the place of assignment / 単身赴任 a job transfer without *one's* family

ふにん[2] 不妊 infertility [U], sterility [U] ◆不妊症の女性 an *infertile* [*a sterile*] woman
‖不妊手術 sterilization / 不妊治療 fertility treatment

ふにんき 不人気 unpopularity [U] ━不人気な unpopular ∥その俳優は日本ではなぜか不人気だ For some reason, the actor *is unpopular* in Japan.

ふにんじょう 不人情 ━不人情な (不親切な) unkind; (冷淡な) cold, cold-hearted, (残酷な) cruel ∥不人情な仕打ち *unkind* treatment / 家族を見捨てるなんてあいつは不人情なやつだ It's *cold* of him to desert his own family.

ふぬけ 腑抜け (臆病(おくびょう)者) coward [C]; (間抜け) idiot [C] ∥このふぬけめ！ You *idiot*!

ふね 船・舟

ship [C]; boat [C]; ((公式的)) vessel [C]

> ship: 最も一般的な語で大型の船を指すことが多い．代名詞はしばしば she で受ける．
> boat: 通例覆いのない小型の船を指すが，口語では ship とほぼ同義にも用いられる．
> vessel: 大型船．ship, boat よりもかたい語．

上海行きの船 *a ship* (bound [leaving]) for Shanghai / 釣り船 *a fishing boat* / 船を操縦する sail [navigate] *a ship*

その船は午後3時に神戸を出航した The *ship* left Kobe at 3 p.m.

名古屋から船に乗った We got on *the ship* at Nagoya.

横浜で船を降りた We got off *the ship* at Yokohama.

船で神戸まで行った I went to Kobe *by ship* [*boat, sea*].

私たちは舟で川を下った We went down the river *in a boat*.

◆私は船に酔いやすい I *get seasick easily*. / I'*m not a good sailor*.

[慣用表現] 乗りかかった船だ．最後までつきあおう *We have gone too far to go back* now. Let's stick together to the end. / 舟をこぐ (→居眠りする) *doze* [*nod*] *off* / 彼の申し出は渡りに船だった His proposal *was quite timely*.

ふねっしん 不熱心 ━不熱心な (熱意のない) unenthusiastic; (無関心な) indifferent

ふねん(せい) 不燃(性) ━不燃性の nonflammable, incombustible; (耐火性の) fireproof ∥不燃性の材料 *nonflammable* material
‖不燃ごみ incombustible waste / 不燃物 nonflammables

ふ

ふのう 不能 impossibility ⓊＣ; (性的不能) impotence Ｕ ◆そのボクサーは病気で再起不能になった The boxer became *unable to make a comeback* because of illness. / この一節は理解不能だ(→私の理解を超えている) The meaning of this passage *is beyond me* [*my understanding*].

プノンペン Phnom Penh (❖カンボジアの首都)

ふはい 腐敗 decay, rot; (道徳的な) corruption Ｕ ── 腐敗する decay ⓐ, rot ⓐ ◆政治腐敗 political *corruption*; *corruption* in politics
◆腐敗した政権 a *corrupt* regime / その国では政治家のモラルが腐敗している The morals of politicians *have been corrupted* in the country.

ふばい 不買 日本製品に対する不買運動を起こす start *a boycott of* [*boycotting*] Japanese goods

ふはつ 不発 我々のキャンペーンは不発に終わった Our campaign *misfired*.
‖不発弾 an unexploded shell

ふばらい 不払い nonpayment Ｕ

ふび 不備 (不足) lack; (しばしば a ~); (欠陥) defect Ｃ, flaw Ｃ ◆防災施策の不備が被害を大きくした The *defects* in the disaster prevention measures magnified the damage.
◆私の報告書に何か不備がありますか Is there anything *wrong* with my report?

ぶひ 部費 club dues ◆来週末までに部費を1,000円払ってください Please pay 1,000 yen for your *club dues* by the end of next week.

ふひつよう 不必要 ── 不必要な unnecessary; (余計な) superfluous ◆不必要な出費 *unnecessary* expenses ◆不必要に細かい説明 an *unnecessarily* detailed explanation

ふひょう 不評 (不人気) unpopularity Ｕ; (悪評) bad reputation Ｃ ◆新しい先生は厳しすぎると不評だ The new teacher *has a bad reputation for* being too stern.
◆彼の小説は女性の間では不評だ His novels *are unpopular* among women. / その計画は市民の不評を買った The plan *was received unfavorably* by the citizens.

ふびょうどう 不平等 inequality ⓊＣ《しばしば複数形 inequalities》── 不平等な unequal; (不公平な) unfair ◆男女間の不平等 *inequality* between men and women / 社会的不平等を是正する correct social *inequalities* ◆不平等な扱いを受ける be treated *unequally* [*unfairly*]
‖不平等条約 an unequal treaty

ふびん 不憫 ── 不憫な (哀れな) pitiful; (かわいそうな) poor ◆私はその子供たちが不憫でならなかった I couldn't help *feeling pity for* the children.

ふひん 部品 part Ｃ; (構成要素) component Ｃ ◆車の部品 auto *parts* / 予備の部品 spare *parts* / 部品を組み立てる put together *the parts* / 部品を交換する replace a part

ふひんこう 不品行 misbehavior Ｕ, bad conduct [behavior] Ｕ ◆不品行な人 an immoral person; a person *of loose morals*

ふぶき 吹雪 snowstorm Ｃ; (猛吹雪) blizzard Ｃ ◆外は激しい吹雪だった There was a heavy *snowstorm* outside.
‖紙吹雪 confetti

ふふく 不服 (不満) dissatisfaction Ｕ; (不平) complaint ⓊＣ ◆彼は裁決に不服を申し立てた He *made a complaint* [*complained*] *about* the judgment.
◆計画に対して不服を唱える make [raise] *an objection to* a plan / 彼女は我々の提案に不服そうな顔をしていた She looked *dissatisfied* [*discontented*] with our proposal.

ふぶく 吹雪く きのうは一日中ふぶいていた There was *a blizzard* all day yesterday.

ふん 私が店の中へ入ると店員が鼻先でふふんと笑った(→冷笑した) The clerk *sneered at* me as I walked into the store. / ふふん、まあそのうち分かるさ Bah. You'll see someday. (❖bah は軽蔑・いらだち・不信などを表す)

ぶぶん 部分 part Ｃ; (割り当てられた部分) portion Ｃ; (切り取られた部分) section Ｃ
➩いちぶ、だいぶぶん
この話は2つの部分に分かれている This story is divided into two *parts* [*sections*].
飛行機の前方部分に異常がある There is something wrong with *the forward part* of the plane.
その研究は歴史の隠れた部分に光をあてた The research threw a spotlight on *a hidden part* of history.
彼女の説明にはところどころ分かりにくい部分があった Some *parts* of her explanation were hard to understand.
下線の部分を英訳しなさい Translate *the underlined parts* into English.
費用の一部分を負担することになっている I'm supposed to bear *a portion of* the expenses.
◆部分的な合意に達する reach a *partial* agreement / 市庁舎は部分的に完成した The city hall was *partly* finished. / ベッドがその部屋のかなりの部分を占めている The bed occupies much *space* in the room. / この地図の赤い部分が地震で大きな被害を受けた The red *area* on this map suffered a lot of damage from the earthquake.
◉「映画のどの部分がいちばんよかったですか」「最後の部分に感動しました」"What *part* of the movie did you like best?" "*The last part* moved me."
‖部分食《天文》a partial eclipse

ぶぶんひてい 部分否定《文法》partial negation Ｕ

「すべて…するわけではない」「いつも…するわけではない」などのように部分的に否定する言い方を部分否定という ◆ I haven't seen *all* the director's movies. その監督の映画をすべて見ているわけではない / I *don't always* get up early. いつも朝早く起きるわけではない / I *don't really* like classical music. クラシックはあまり好きではない

ふぶんりつ 不文律 unwritten rule [code] ◎

ふへい 不平 complaint Ⓤ Ⓒ
不平を並べる make a series of *complaints*
不平があればはっきり言ってください If you have any *complaints*, tell me honestly.
彼らは不平を言わずに仕事を続けた They kept working without *a complaint*.
彼女はいつも仕事に対して不平たらたらだった She was always full of *complaints* about her job.
姉は決して不平を言うような人ではない My sister is never one to「*make a complaint* [*complain, grumble*]」.
◆父は私のとった態度に不平を言った My father *complained to* me *about* the way I acted. / 彼は忙しすぎるといつも不平を言っている He *is* always *complaining* [*grumbling*] *that* he's too busy.

ぶべつ 侮蔑 contempt Ⓤ ⇨けいべつ

ふへん¹ 不変の（永続的な）eternal, permanent;（変えられない）unchangeable;（一定の）constant //不変の真理 an *eternal truth*
◆会社の基本方針は創立以来不変だ The company's basic policy *has remained unchanged* since its foundation.

ふへん² 普遍（普遍性）universality Ⓤ ――普遍的な universal //普遍的真理 a *universal truth*
◆人間の社会に普遍的に認められる現象 a phenomenon observed *universally* in all human societies

ふべん 不便 inconvenience Ⓤ Ⓒ ――不便な inconvenient
留守番電話がないと不便だ It is *inconvenient* not to have an answering machine. / Not having an answering machine is *an inconvenience*.
これくらいの不便は我慢しなければならない We have to put up with *inconveniences* like this.
ご不便をおかけして申しわけありません I'm sorry for *the inconvenience*.
ここは住むには不便な所だ This is an *inconvenient* place to live.
初めてアメリカに行ったときは英語が下手でひどく不便な思いをした When I「*first visited America*, I「*suffered* great *inconvenience* [*had a lot of trouble*]」because of my poor English.
◆このパソコンは持ち歩くには少々不便だ This PC *is not convenient* [*handy*] *to carry around*.

ふべんきょう 不勉強 不勉強がたたってテストのできはさんざんだった I did very badly on the exam because I *had not studied hard*.

ふぼ 父母 *one's* parents ⇨おや（親）//父母会 a Parent-Teacher Association（《略語》PTA）;（会合）a PTA meeting

ふほう¹ 不法 ――不法な illegal, unlawful // 不法な取り引き an *illegal deal* ◆ごみを不法に投棄する dump garbage *illegally*

//不法行為 an *illegal act* / 不法就労者 an *illegal worker* / 不法所持 illegal *possession* / 不法侵入 trespassing, (a) *trespass* / 不法侵入者 a *trespasser* / 不法占拠 squatting, illegal *occupation* / 不法滞在 an *illegal stay* / 不法滞在者 an *illegal alien* / 不法入国 illegal *entry* / 不法入国者 an *illegal alien*

ふほう² 訃報 訃報に接する hear *the news of a person's death*

ふほんい 不本意 不本意ながら彼らの指示に従った I followed their directions「*against my will* [*reluctantly, unwillingly*]」. / 試験のできは不本意な（→満足のいかない）ものだった My performance in the exams was *unsatisfactory* [（→がっかりさせる）*disappointing*].

ふまえる 踏まえる 事実をふまえた（→に基づいた）議論 an argument *based on* facts

ふまじめ 不真面目 不まじめな態度 a *flippant attitude* / 不まじめな答えをする give a *flippant answer* / あいつは不まじめなやつだ He's *not* a *serious* fellow.

ふまん 不満 discontent Ⓤ, dissatisfaction Ⓤ;（不平）complaint Ⓤ Ⓒ ――不満な discontented, dissatisfied
⇨ コミュニケーションスキル p.1332
多くの人々が増税に不満の意を表した Many people showed *dissatisfaction* with the tax increase.
世の中に対するあなたの不満をこの掲示板に書き込んでください Please write your *complaints* about the world on this bulletin board.
私はチームの今回の成績に不満だ I *am*「*dissatisfied with* [*unhappy about*]」our team's results this time.
◆彼はいつも何か不満を言っている He *is* always *complaining* [*grumbling*] *about* something.
🅔「校則に何か不満がありますか」「ええ. 少し厳しすぎると思います」"Do you have any *complaints* about the school regulations?" "Yes. I think they are too strict."

ふまんぞく 不満足 dissatisfaction Ⓤ, discontent Ⓤ ◆彼らからは不満足な回答しか得られなかった I only received *unsatisfactory* answers from them.

ふみいれる 踏み入れる 彼らは地図に載っていない地域に足を踏み入れた They *set foot in* uncharted territory.

ふみえ 踏み絵 a *fumie*, a plate with a picture of Christ or the Virgin Mary used by the Tokugawa shogunate during the Edo period to identify Christians by making them step on it

ふみきり 踏切・踏み切り（鉄道の）(railroad) crossing Ⓒ;（跳躍などの）takeoff Ⓒ //無人踏切 *an* unattended *crossing* / 踏切を渡る go past [over] *a* (*railroad*) *crossing* / 1回目のジャンプでは踏み切りのタイミングが合わなかった On my first jump, the timing of *my take-off* was wrong.

//踏切板 a springboard / 踏切番 a crossing

[コミュニケーションスキル] ―不満―

(A) **I want to complain about** the fax machine I bought at your store yesterday.
きのうお宅の店で買ったファックスのことで困っているのです.
(B) **I can't understand** your explanation.
あなたの説明では納得できません.
(C) **It's very annoying** that my computer freezes (up) suddenly.
コンピュータが突然フリーズして[動かなくなって]しまうのは全く困ったものだ.
(D) **I'm very annoyed at** the way he treats me.
彼の私の扱い方はどうも気に食わない.
(E) **I can't stand any more of** his complaints.
彼のぐちにはもうこれ以上我慢できない.
(F) **I just can't stand** being treated like a child.
子供扱いされるのはもう我慢できない.
(G) **I'm tired [sick] of** her talking on and on. / **I've had enough of** her stories going on and on.
彼女の長話にはもううんざりです.
(H) **I don't like** her pedantic way of speaking.
彼女の学者ぶったしゃべり方が私は嫌いだ.
(I) **I was very disappointed in** that movie.
あの映画には全く失望しました.

☞ (A) の complain about ... は日本語の「クレームをつける」に相当する表現で, 買った製品や店の対応などに不満をいうときに使う. これは非常に直接的な言い方になる.
☞ annoying(迷惑な)は物を主語にするか, または (C) のように It is annoying that ... の形で用いる. (D) の I'm annoyed at ... は物または事柄を対象にして, 「…に困っている」の意味を表す.
☞ (E), (F) は「…に我慢できない」という気持ちを率直に述べる表現. can't の前に just を入れると, さらに強い不快感を表すことができる.
☞「うんざり」, 「飽き飽き」, 「もうたくさん」という気持ちにぴったりなのが (G). **be fed up with** ... (…にうんざりである[辟易(へきえき)する])という表現もよく使われる.
☞ 英語では特に苦情や不満などはあいまいではなく, 理由をはっきり述べて意思を伝えることが必要である. (H) は好き嫌いをはっきり述べる表現.
☞ (I) の be disappointed in [at / with / about] ... (…にがっかりする)は失望を表す決まった言い方.

keeper
ふみきる 踏み切る 二人は結婚に踏み切った(→心を決めて結婚した) They *made up their minds* and got married. / 準備不足だったが計画の実行に踏み切った We *took the plunge* and put the plan into practice, though we had not been well prepared. (❖ take the plunge は「思いきってやってみる」の意味) / その国はついに軍事行動に踏み切った(→始めた) The country finally *started* military action.
ふみこえる 踏み越える (困難などを) overcome* [他][自]; (限度を) overstep [他]
ふみこたえる 踏み堪える (抵抗する) hold* out ➔ もちこたえる
ふみこむ 踏み込む step into ...; (警察の手入れ) raid [他] // 警察はその一味の事務所に踏み込んだ The police *raided* [*carried out a raid on*] the gang's office.
◆その件についてはもっと踏み込んだ(→詳しく)議論をすべきだ We should discuss the matter *in* more *detail*.
ふみしめる 踏み締める 頂上までの急坂を一歩一歩踏みしめて登った I climbed the steep slope to the top of mountain *firmly step by step*.
ふみだい 踏み台 stool [C]; (脚立(きゃたつ)) stepladder [C]; (出世・成功の) steppingstone [C] // 彼は私を踏み台にして販売部長に出世した He *used* me *as a steppingstone* and got promoted to sales manager.
ふみたおす 踏み倒す 彼は借金を踏み倒した(→払わなかった) He *didn't pay his debt*.
ふみだす 踏み出す (前に出る) step forward; (1歩進む) take* a step; (始める) start [他] // 彼女は夢の実現へ向けて第一歩を踏み出した She *took the first step* toward the realization of her dream.
ふみだん 踏み段 step [C]
ふみつける 踏み付ける stamp [他][自], trample [他][自] // 私はその箱を踏みつけてぺしゃんこにした I *stamped* the box flat.
ふみつぶす 踏み潰す stamp [他][自], trample [他][自] // 花を踏みつぶさないよう注意しなさい Be careful *not to trample* (*down*) the flowers.
ふみとどまる 踏み止まる (残る) remain [自]; (自制する) control *oneself* // 我々のチームはかろうじて優勝圏内に踏みとどまった Our team barely *remained* within range of victory. / 彼に言い返したかったが踏みとどまった I felt like talking back to him, but I *controlled myself*.
ふみならす[1] 踏み均す 地面を踏みならす *stamp* the ground *flat*
ふみならす[2] 踏み鳴らす stamp (*one's* foot) // 聴衆はいらだたしげに床を踏み鳴らした The audience impatiently *stamped* (*their feet*) *on* the floor.
ふみにじる 踏みにじる (権利・感情を) trample [他][自]; (無視する) ignore [他] // 彼の好意を踏みにじるわけにはいかない I *can't trample* (*on*) his kindness.
◆子供たちの夢を踏みにじる(→こわす) *destroy* [*ruin*] the children's dream
ふみば 踏み場 彼の部屋は足の踏み場がないくらい散らかっている His room is in such a mess that *there's hardly a place to step*.
ふみはずす 踏み外す 階段から足を踏みはずし

そうになった I almost *lost my footing* on the stairs. / 人の道を踏みはずしてはならない You must not *stray from the right path*.

ふみん 不眠 彼らは不眠不休で作業を続けた They continued to work *without rest or sleep*.

ふみんしょう 不眠症 insomnia ⓤ /不眠症に悩む人が増えている More and more people are suffering from *insomnia*.

ふむ 踏む
❶【足で】step 圓;（踏みつける）tread* 圓 他;（強く）stamp 圓 他
アクセルを踏む *step on* the accelerator
電車の中でだれかの足を踏んでしまった I *stepped on* someone's foot on the train.
彼は地団駄(だ)を踏んで悔しがった He *stamped his feet* in frustration.
◆彼らは初めてアフリカの土を踏んだ They *set foot on* African soil for the first time. /（→訪れた）They *visited* Africa for the first time.
❷【手続きなどを】
パスポートの取得には所定の手続きを踏まなければならない You must *go through* a specific procedure to get a passport.
❸【見積もる】estimate 他
車の修理代を5万円と踏んだ I *estimated* the cost of repairing my car *at* 50,000 yen.
❹【経験する】
彼女はあす初舞台を踏む(→デビューする) She *will make her debut* tomorrow.
彼は場数を踏んでいるから大きな大会でも実力を発揮できるだろう *With his experience*, he should do well even at a major tournament.

ふむき 不向き ――不向きな（ふさわしくない）unsuitable;（適さない）unfit /その服はきょうのパーティーには不向きだ That dress is *unsuitable for* today's party. / この土地は農業には不向きだ This land *is unfit for* farming. ◆私は教師には不向きだ I'm *not cut out to* be a teacher.

ふめい 不明 ――不明の（はっきりしない）obscure, vague, ambiguous;（分からない）unknown;（未確認の）unidentified
その話には不明な点が多い There are many *obscure* points in the story.
その後の彼の消息は不明だ It *is unknown* [We *do not know*] what became of him after that.
今のところ遺体の身元は不明だ The body *is unidentified* at present.
◆機械の故障の原因は不明だ(→明らかでない) The cause of the machine breaking down *is not clear*. / とうとう警察は行方不明の少女を見つけた At last the police found the *missing* girl. / 犯人の男は何か意味不明のことをわめいていた The criminal was shouting something *incomprehensible*. / 彼は自らの不明を恥じた He was ashamed of his *ignorance*.

ふめいかく 不明確 ――不明確な（はっきりしない）unclear;（漠然とした）indefinite;（あいまいな）vague, ambiguous

ふめいよ 不名誉（不面目）disgrace ⓤⓒ, dishonor ⓤⓒ ――不名誉な disgraceful, dishonorable /このような事件はわが国にとっての不名誉だ This kind of incident is *a disgrace to* our nation.

ふめいりょう 不明瞭 ――不明瞭な unclear, indistinct, obscure;（言葉などが）inarticulate /不明瞭な態度 an *obscure* attitude / テープの音が不明瞭でよく聞こえなかった The sound of the tape was *indistinct* and I couldn't hear it well.

ふめいろう 不明朗 ――不明朗な（不審な）questionable /この会計簿にはいくつか不明朗な点がある There are some *questionable* items in this account book.

ふめつ 不滅 immortality ⓤ ――不滅の immortal /不滅の名声 *immortal* fame / 肉体は滅びても霊魂は不滅だ Even if the body dies, the soul *is immortal*.

ふめん 譜面（楽譜）music ⓤ;（1枚刷りの）sheet music ⓤ ‖譜面台 a music stand

ふもう 不毛 ――不毛の（作物のできない）sterile, barren;（荒れ果てた）waste;（実りのない）unfruitful, fruitless /不毛の土地 *sterile* [*barren*] land / 不毛な議論を続けていてもしかたがない It's no use continuing a *fruitless* argument.

ふもと 麓（山の下の部分）foot ⓒ;（低い部分）bottom ⓒ;（基部）base ⓒ /山のふもとの町 a town at *the foot of* the mountain

ふもん 不問 それは不問に付す(→問題にしないでおく)べきではない We shouldn't *leave it unquestioned*.

ぶもん 部門（部類）class ⓒ;（範疇(ちゅう)）category ⓒ;（会社などの）department ⓒ, section ⓒ;（分野）field ⓒ /営業部門 a sales *department* / 彼の絵は高校生部門で2位に入賞した His painting won second prize in the high school student *category*.

ふやかす ゼラチンを水でふやかす *soften* gelatin in water

ふやける（ふくれる）swell* 圓, become* swollen /ふろから上がるころには指先がふやけていた My fingertips *became swollen* [(→しわだらけになった)*wrinkled*] by the time I came out of the bath.

ふやす 増やす·殖やす increase 他;（さらに加える）add to ...
財産を増やす *add to* one's fortune
その雑誌は発行部数を2万部から2万5千部に増やした The magazine *increased* its circulation from 20,000 copies to 25,000.
彼女は読書で知識を増やした She *increased* her knowledge by reading.
◆彼らは従業員の給料を増やした(→上げた) They *raised* the salary of the employees.

ふゆ 冬

winter ⓤⓒ ――冬の winter
冬を越す pass *the winter*
今年の冬は去年に比べると暖かい It has been milder this *winter* than the last.

冬の間はその植物は室内に入れておいたほうがよい You'd better keep the plant indoors during *the winter*.
母は冬物の服を押し入れにしまった Mother has put *winter* clothes away in the closet.
きょうの日本列島は冬型の気圧配置になっている Today the Japanese Archipelago is experiencing a *winter* pressure pattern.
‖冬景色 a winter scene / 冬山 a mountain in (the) winter
短歌 山里は冬ぞさびしさまさりける人めも草もかれぬとおもへば(源宗于(むねゆき)朝臣)
In a mountain home
wintertime is lonelier
than in the city.
All the people stay away
and all the plants waste away.

ふゆう¹ 浮遊 ──浮遊する (浮かぶ) float ⃝; (漂う) drift ⃝ ‖浮遊物 floating matter; (遭難船の) flotsam

ふゆう² 富裕 ──富裕な affluent ‖富裕階級 the upper class

ぶゆう 武勇 bravery ‖武勇伝 a story of bravery

ふゆかい 不愉快 ──不愉快な (いやな) unpleasant, disagreeable
きょうは彼のせいで不愉快な思いをした I felt *unpleasant* because of him today.
あの店員の態度はとても不愉快だ That clerk's attitude *is* very *unpleasant*.
あいつは本当に不愉快なやつだ He is a really *disagreeable* man.
◆彼女の言うことを聞いていたら不愉快になった (→腹が立った) I *got offended* when I listened to what she said.

ふゆがれ 冬枯れ 冬枯れの山 a *desolate winter* mountain

ふゆきとどき 不行き届き (不注意) carelessness ⃝; (怠慢) negligence ⃝ ‖生徒たちのけがは先生の監督不行き届きによるものだった The students were hurt「because of the teacher's *carelessness* [(→気をつけていなかったせいだ) because the teacher *didn't take care of them*].

ふゆげしょう 冬化粧 旅館の窓から冬化粧した山々が見えた From the window of the inn, I could see mountains *draped with snow*.

ふゆごもり 冬籠り ──冬ごもりする (冬眠する) hibernate ⃝; (冬の間室内で過ごす) keep* indoors in the winter

ふゆしょうぐん 冬将軍 冬将軍がやってきた (*Old*) *Jack Frost* has come. (❖(Old) Jack Frostは冬を擬人化した言い方)

ふゆぞら 冬空 winter sky ⃝

ふゆやすみ 冬休み winter vacation ⃝, 《英》winter holidays ‖冬休みに家族でスキーに行った I went skiing with my family *during winter vacation*.

ふよ¹ 付与 ──付与する (与える) give* ⃝; (権力・性質などを) invest ⃝ ‖権限を付与される be invested with authority

ふよ² 賦与 彼女は生まれつき音楽の才能を賦与されている She *is endowed* [*gifted*] with a talent for music.

ぶよ 蚋〔虫〕 gnat [nǽt] ⃝

ふよう¹ 不用 ──不用の (捨てられた) discarded; (使われていない) disused; (役に立たない) useless ◆この机は不用になった This desk *has fallen out of use*.
‖不用品 discarded articles

ふよう² 不要 ──不要な (不必要な) unnecessary, needless ‖この手続きに印鑑は不要です A seal is *unnecessary* for this procedure.
◆3か月未満の滞在であればビザは不要だ You *don't need* a visa for a stay of less than three months.

ふよう³ 扶養 support ⃝ ──扶養する support ⃝ ‖彼には家族を扶養する義務がある He has a duty to *support* his family.
‖扶養家族 a (family) dependent / 扶養控除 a deduction [tax exemption] for dependents / 扶養者 a supporter / 扶養手当 a family allowance

ふよう⁴ 浮揚 ──浮揚する float ⃝; (水面に) rise* to the surface

ぶよう 舞踊 dance ⃝ ⃝; (踊ること) dancing ⃝ ‖舞踊家 a dancer / 日本舞踊 Japanese dancing / 民族舞踊 (a) folk dance

ぶようい 不用意 ──不用意な (不注意な) careless; (思いやりのない) thoughtless ──不用意に carelessly; thoughtlessly ‖不用意な発言は慎みなさい You should avoid making *careless* [*thoughtless*] remarks.

ふようじょう 不養生 ことわざ 医者の不養生 Doctors often neglect their own health.

ぶようじん 不用心・無用心 ──無用心な (安全でない) unsafe; (不注意な) careless ‖窓をあけたままで寝るのは無用心だ It is *unsafe* to sleep with the window open.

ふようど 腐葉土 leaf mold ⃝

ぶよぶよ 父は太って*ぶよぶよ*している(→たるんでいる) My father *is fat and flabby*.

ブラ bra ⃝

フライ¹ (料理) deep-fried food ⃝
◆魚をフライにする *deep-fry* fish
‖フライ返し a slotted spatula, 《英》a fish slice / エビフライ a deep-fried prawn

フライ² (野球) fly (ball) ⃝ ‖レフトにフライを打ち上げる hit *a fly* to left; *fly* to left ◆彼はライトフライに倒れた He *flied out to right*.
‖犠牲フライ a sacrifice fly

フライきゅう フライ級 the flyweight class ‖フライ級選手 a flyweight

フライト (飛行機の便) flight ⃝ ‖台風のためすべてのフライトは欠航になりました Due to the typhoon, all *flights* have been canceled.
‖フライトレコーダー a flight recorder

プライド pride ⃝ (またa ～) ‖彼の言葉でプライドが傷ついた My *pride* was hurt by his words. / 彼女に謝るのは彼のプライドが許さなかった His *pride* wouldn't let him apologize to her. / He was too *proud* to apologize to her.
◆私は自分の仕事にプライドをもっている I'm *proud of* my work. / 彼らはプライドが高い民族だ They are a *proud* people.

フライドチキン fried chicken [U]
フライドポテト ⚠《主に米》French fries, 《英》chips
プライバシー privacy [U] ∥プライバシーの侵害 an invasion of *privacy*
◆そういう質問は彼のプライバシーにかかわることなので答えられません Those questions relate to his *private affairs*, so I can't answer them.
フライパン frying pan [C], 《米》frypan [C]; (小さな) skillet [C]
プライベート ―プライベートな (私的な) private; (個人的な) personal ∥プライベートなことに口出ししないでください Don't interfere in a *private* matter.
フライング ⚠〔スポーツ〕false start [C] (❖a flying start は「助走スタート」の意味) ∥フライングをする make *a false start*
ブラインド blind [C], 《米》window shade [C] ∥ブラインドを上げる「draw up [raise] *the blinds* / ブラインドを下げる「pull down [lower] *the blinds* / その部屋のブラインドは下ろされていた *The blinds* of the room had been「pulled down [lowered].
ブラインドタッチ ⚠〔コンピュータ〕touch-typing [U] ◆ブラインドタッチができますか Can you *touch-type*?
ブラウス blouse [C]
ブラウンかん ブラウン管 ⚠(picture) tube [C], 〔電気〕cathode-ray tube [C] (《略語》CRT) (❖Braun tube はまれに使われるが cathode-ray tube のほうがふつう)
プラカード placard [C] ∥「核兵器反対」のプラカードを掲げる hold up *a placard* that says "No Nukes"
ぶらく 部落 (村落) village [C]
プラグ plug [C] ∥プラグをコンセントに差し込む put *a plug* into an outlet
◆ドライヤーのプラグを差し込む[抜く]「*plug in* [*unplug*] the dryer
プラザ (広場・市場) plaza [C]
ぶらさがる ぶら下がる hang* [自]; (揺れながら) dangle [自] ∥鉄棒にぶら下がる *hang from* a bar / 女の子は母親の腕にぶら下がっていた The girl *was hanging on to* her mother's arm. ◆子供たちは木の枝にぶら下がって遊んでいた The children were enjoying *swinging* from a branch.
ぶらさげる ぶら下げる hang* [他] ∥首にタオルをぶら下げる *hang* a towel from *one's* neck
◆おじは手におみやげをぶら下げていた My uncle *carried* a present.
ブラシ brush [C] ∥私は上着にブラシをかけた I gave my jacket *a brush.* / I *brushed* my jacket.
◆髪をブラシでとかす *brush one's* hair
‖歯ブラシ a toothbrush / ヘアブラシ a hairbrush / 洋服ブラシ a clothes brush
ブラジャー 《口語的》bra [C], brassiere [C] ∥ブラジャーを着ける[はずす]「put on [take off] *a bra*
ブラジリア Brasilia (❖ブラジルの首都)
ブラジル Brazil (❖公式名 the Federative Republic of Brazil) ―ブラジル人 Brazilian [C] ―ブラジル(人)の Brazilian
ふらす 降らす 関東に雨を降らせた低気圧は東の海上に抜けた The low pressure that *brought* rain to the Kanto district has passed to the eastern sea.
プラス plus [C]; (利益) advantage [U] ―プラスする add [自] ―プラスの plus
4プラス3は7 Four *plus* three is seven.
この合併は両社にとって大きなプラスになるだろう This merger will be *a* great *advantage* to both companies.
きょうの入場者数は500人プラスアルファになると思われる The number of today's visitors will be「500 *plus something extra* [*over* 500]. (❖×plus alpha とはいわない)
◆そんなことをしても君には何のプラスにもならない Doing that *won't get* you *anywhere.* / プラスマイナスゼロになった It was *no gain and no loss* for us.
‖プラス記号 a plus (sign) / プラス極 the positive pole / プラスねじ a Phillips screw
フラスコ flask [C]
プラスチック plastic [U] ―プラスチックの plastic
‖プラスチック製品 plastic products [goods], plastics
フラストレーション frustration [U][C]
◆渋滞の中で運転するのは本当にフラストレーションがたまる I really *get frustrated* when I drive in a traffic jam.
ブラスバンド brass band [C]
プラズマ plasma [U] ‖プラズマディスプレー a plasma display
プラタナス 〔植物〕plane (tree) [C]; (アメリカスズカケノキ) sycamore [C]
フラダンス ⚠hula [C] ∥フラダンスを踊る dance *the hula*; hula
ぶらち 不埒 ―不埒な (無礼な) rude, offensive ∥彼の不埒なふるまいに私は怒りを抑えられなかった I couldn't control my anger at his *offensive* behavior.
プラチナ 〔化学〕platinum [U] (❖元素記号 Pt)
ふらつく 微熱があって頭がふらつく I *feel dizzy* because I have a slight fever. / 父は酔って足元がふらついていた My father was drunk and his steps *were unsteady.* / 今までどこをふらついていたんだ Where *have* you *been wandering around*? / まだ考えがふらついている My mind *is* still *wavering.*
ぶらつく (散歩する) stroll [自]; (あてもなく歩き回る) wander [自] ∥浜辺をぶらついていたら涼しい風が吹いてきた A cool breeze blew while I *was strolling* along the beach. / 彼は繁華街をぶらついた He *wandered around* downtown.
ブラック black ∥コーヒーをブラックで飲む drink *one's* coffee *black*
‖ブラックコーヒー black coffee / ブラックホール a black hole / ブラックボックス a black box / ブラックユーモア black humor
ブラックバス 〔魚〕black bass [C]

ブラックリスト blacklist ◎ ‖その男はブラックリストに載っている The man is *on a blacklist* [*blacklisted*]
フラッシュ (閃光(ﾊ)) flash ⓤ, flashlight ⓤ (❖どちらも装置をいうときは◎); (電球) flashbulb ◎ ‖フラッシュをたく use *a flash* / フラッシュ付きのカメラ a camera *with a built-in flash*
‖フラッシュ撮影 flash photography
フラッシュバック flashback ◎ (❖映画の技法の一つ)
フラット 【音楽】flat ◎ ◆彼女は100メートルを15秒フラット(→きっかり)で走った She ran 100 meters in 15 seconds *flat*.
ふらっと (目的もなく) for no particular purpose; (不意に) unexpectedly ◆彼がふらっと訪ねてきた He visited me *unexpectedly*.
◆急にふらっとして〔→めまいがして〕気分が悪くなった Suddenly I *felt dizzy* and sick.
ぶらっと ⇨ ぶらりと
プラットホーム platform ◎ ‖上り[下り]のプラットホーム an inbound [outbound] *platform*
フラップ (飛行機の下げ翼) flap ◎
プラネタリウム planetarium ◎ (複 ～s, planetaria)
プラハ Prague (❖チェコの首都)
ふらふら ❶【体が】きょうは暑くてふらふらする(→めまいがする) It's hot today and I *feel dizzy*. / 彼はふらふらと部屋を出ていった He left the room *unsteadily*. / 男性が通りをふらふら歩いていた A man *staggered down* the street. / 彼らはおなかがすいてふらふらだった They were *faint* with hunger.
❷【気持ちが】まだ気持ちがふらふらしている(→決心ができない) I *am* still *unable to make a decision*.
ぶらぶら ❶【揺れる】男の子はテーブルの下で足をぶらぶらさせていた The boy *was swinging* his legs under the table.
❷【歩き回る】することがなかったので家の近くをぶらぶらした I had nothing to do, so I *strolled around* near my house. / 約束の時間まで銀座をぶらぶらした I *wandered* about Ginza until the appointed time.
❸【何もしない】退職してから父はぶらぶらしている My father *has been idle* since he retired.
ブラボー Bravo!
フラミンゴ (鳥) flamingo ◎ (複 ～es, ～s)
プラム 【植物】plum ◎
フラメンコ flamenco ⓤ◎ (複 ～s) ‖フラメンコを踊る dance *the flamenco*
プラモデル plastic model ◎ ‖自動車のプラモデルを組み立てる put together *a plastic model* of a car
ふらっと ⇨ ふらっと
ぶらりと 彼らはぶらりと(→行き先を決めず)旅に出た They went travelling *with no particular destinations* in mind. / ブドウが棚からぶらりと垂れ下がっている Bunches of grapes *are dangling* from the trellis.
ふられる 振られる 彼女にふられてしまった My girlfriend *left* [*dumped*] me. / 彼は女の子にふられて落ち込んでいる He is depressed because the girl *turned* him *down*. (❖turn downは「拒絶する、はねつける」の意味)
⇨ ふる (振る)
フラン franc [fræŋk] ◎ ((略語)fr., Fr.) (❖フランス・スイス・ベルギーなどの貨幣単位)
ふらん 腐乱 ‖腐乱死体 a decomposed body
プラン plan ⇨ けいかく
ブランク (空欄) blank ◎; (時間的な空白) gap ◎ ◆彼女はけがで1年間ブランクがあった(→1年間休んだ)とは思えない走りを見せた She ran so well that we couldn't believe she took a year *off* because of her injury.
プランクトン plankton
フランクフルト (ソーセージ) frankfurter ◎
ブランコ swing ◎ ‖ブランコに乗る get on *a swing* ‖空中ブランコ a trapeze
フランス France (❖公式名 the French Republic) ——フランス人 (総称) the French; (男性) Frenchman ——(女性) Frenchwoman ——フランス語 French ⓤ ——フランス(人[語])の French
‖フランス革命 the French Revolution / フランスパン French bread / フランス料理 French food; (料理法) French cuisine
プランター planter ◎
ブランチ brunch ⓤ◎
フランチャイズ (野球の) franchise ◎; (一定地域での販売権) franchise ◎
‖フランチャイズチェーン a franchise chain
ブランデー brandy
‖ブランデーグラス a brandy glass
ブランド brand ◎ ‖うちの姉はとてもブランド志向が強い My sister *is very brand-conscious*. / 彼女が着るとノーブランドの服も高級なものに見える Even *off-brand* clothes look elegant on her.
◆ブランドもののスーツ a *designer* suit
‖ブランド品 a name brand (product)
プラント plant ⓤ◎
‖プラント輸出 plant exports
ふり¹ 不利 disadvantage ◎; (妨げとなるもの) handicap ◎, 《口語的》liability ◎ ——不利な disadvantageous; (好ましくない) unfavorable ——不利に disadvantageously; unfavorably

背が低いことはバレーボール選手にとってかなり不利だ Being short is *a great disadvantage* to a volleyball player.

不利な条件にもかかわらず、彼らは試合に勝った In spite of *their handicaps*, they won the game.

今の状況は私たちには不利だ The present situation is *disadvantageous* for us.

◆証人は被告に不利な証言をした The witness testified *against* the accused.
ふり² 振り ❶【ふるまい】その子は寝たふりをした The child *pretended* to be sleeping. / 彼は彼女のことを知らないふりをした He *affected* [*pretended*] not to know her. / 会社はその事実について見て見ぬふりをしてきた(→無視し

てきた) The company *has ignored* that fact.

❷【振ること】swing ⓤⓒ ◆彼はバットの振りがいい He *swings* the bat well.

慣用表現 人のふり見てわがふり直せ *Learn wisdom from the follies of others*. (→他人の愚行から知恵を学べ)

ふり³ 降り (雨) rain ⓤ; (雪) snow ⓤ ∥降りが激しくなってきた *The rain* has become heavier.

ぶり 鰤 yellowtail ⓒ

-ぶり -振り
❶【様子】
彼女の仕事ぶりはりっぱだ She *works* well.
彼は食べっぷりがいい *The way he eats* is quite impressive.
そのとき現場はものすごい混乱ぶりだった The scene *was* terribly *confused* at that time.

❷【時間の経過】
彼女は1年ぶりに(→1年後)仕事に復帰した She returned to work *after* a year.
浩子と会うのは3年ぶりだ(→3年間会っていない) I *haven't seen* Hiroko *for* three years.
1週間ぶりに(→1週間で初めて)雨が降った We had rain *for the first time* in a week.
彼は2年ぶりに(→2年間の不在の後)故郷に帰った He returned home *after* two years' *absence*.
こんなに楽しい夕食は何年ぶりだろう *How many years ago* did I *last* have such a pleasant dinner?

ふりあげる 振り上げる 父は怒って弟にこぶしを振り上げた My father *raised* his fist at my brother in anger.

フリー —フリーの(自由な) free; (自由契約の) freelance ∥フリーの通訳 a *freelance* interpreter ◆フリーサイズのトレーナー a *one-size-fits-all* sweatshirt / 彼はフリーで働いている He is working *freelance*.
∥フリーキック a free kick / フリースタイル a freestyle / フリースロー a free throw / フリーダイヤル a toll-free number / フリーバッティング batting practice

フリーザー freezer ⓒ

フリージア〖植物〗freesia ⓒ

フリーズ —フリーズする freeze* ⓤ ∥そのアプリ(ケーション), またフリーズしたの? *Has* that application *frozen* again?

フリーター ⚠ とりあえず今はフリーターです I *live by working part-time without having a regular job* for the time being.
⇒ 場面・状況別会話 p.1688

プリーツ pleat ⓒ ∥プリーツスカート a pleated skirt

フリーパス 彼はその美術館はフリーパスだ He *can get into* the museum *free*.

フリーハンド freehand ∥フリーハンドで描く draw *freehand*

ブリーフ briefs (◆数えるときは a pair of ...)

ブリーフケース briefcase ⓒ

フリーマーケット (のみの市) flea market ⓒ

フリーランサー freelance ⓒ, freelancer ⓒ

フリーランス フリーランスのカメラマン a *freelance* photographer

ふりえき 不利益(不利) disadvantage ⓤ; (損) loss ⓒ ⓤ ∥不利益な disadvantageous ∥会社はその事業で不利益をこうむった The company suffered *losses* from the business.

ふりおとす 振り落とす 私は馬に振り落とされた I *was thrown off* the horse.

ふりおろす 振り下ろす おのを振り下ろす *swing* an ax *down*

ふりかえ 振替 (郵便の) (postal) transfer ⓤ ∥振替で送金する send money by *postal transfer*
◆JR線の事故のために地下鉄,バスによる振り替え輸送が行われている Because of an accident on the JR line, *the passengers are given free transportation* by subway trains or buses.
∥振替休日 a substitute holiday / 振替口座 a transfer account

ぶりかえす ぶり返す (暑さなどが) return ⓘ; (病気が) come* back ⓘ ∥今週になって暑さがぶり返してきた The hot weather *has returned* this week. / かぜがぶり返すといけないから早く寝なさい Go to bed early so that your cold won't *come back*.

ふりかえる¹ 振り返る
❶【後ろを向く】(体の向きを変える) turn around; (目の向きを変える) look back
一瞬呼ばれたような気がして振り返った For a moment I had a feeling that someone was calling me, so I *turned around*.
彼女は振り返って私たちの方を見た She *looked back* at us.
❷【回顧する】look back; (反省する) reflect ⓘ
学校生活を振り返る *look back* on *one's* school days

ふりかえる² 振り替える (変更する) change ⓘ ∥予定を振り替える *change* the schedule

ふりかかる 降り掛かる fall* on ...; (身の上に起こる) happen to ... ∥火の粉が降りかかった Sparks *fell on* us. / 彼の家に突然災いが降りかかった Suddenly disaster *happened to* his family.

ふりかけ 振り掛け 🔲 *furikake*, powdered fish or seaweed for sprinkling on rice

ふりかける 振り掛ける sprinkle ⓘ; (粉末を) dust ⓘ ∥魚に塩を振りかける *sprinkle* salt on a fish

ふりかざす 振り翳す (振り上げる) raise ... over *one's* head; (誇示する) show* off ∥権力を振りかざす *show off one's* authority

ふりかた 振り方 今後の身の振り方を考えなくてはならない I have to decide *what I am going to do* after this.

ふりがな 振り仮名 🔲 *furigana, kana* written above or at the side of *kanji* to show the pronunciation

ふりかぶる 振りかぶる (刀などを) raise ...

ブリキ

high; 《ピッチャーが》wind* up 《ピッチャー, 振りかぶって第一球を投げました The pitcher *wound up* and threw the first pitch.
ブリキ ⚠tinplate Ⓤ, tin Ⓤ ❖日本語はオランダ語の blik から》《ブリキのおもちゃ a *tin* toy 《ブリキ缶 a can, 《英》a *tin*
ふりきる 振り切る shake* off 《彼は追っ手を振り切って逃げた He *shook* the pursuer *off* and ran away. 《彼女は両親が止めるのを振り切って(→無視して)単身フランスに渡った She went to France by herself, *ignoring* her parents' objection.
ふりきれる 振り切れる 《スイカをはかりにかけたら針が振り切れた When I put a watermelon on the scale, the pointer *wavered beyond the maximum mark*.
ふりこ 振り子 pendulum Ⓒ 《振り子時計 a pendulum clock
ふりこう 不履行 nonfulfillment Ⓤ 《義務の不履行 *nonfulfillment* of one's duty; *failure to fulfill* one's *duty*
ふりこみ 振り込み 《入会金を銀行振り込みで払った I paid the membership fee *through the bank*. 《給料は銀行振り込みだ My salary *is deposited into* my *bank account*. ‖振込手数料 a transfer fee
ふりこむ¹ 振り込む 《クラブの年会費を銀行に振り込んだ I *paid* [*deposited*] the annual fee *into* the club's *bank account*.
ふりこむ² 降り込む come* into ... 《窓のすき間から雨が降り込んでくる Rain *is coming into* my room through a gap in the window.
ふりこめられる 降り籠められる 《きょうは雪に降りこめられた I *was kept indoors* by the snow today.
ふりしきる 降り頻る 《雨の降りしきる中を出かけなければならなかった I had to go out *in the heavy rain*.
ふりしぼる 振り絞る 《彼は持てる力をふりしぼって走った He ran *with all his strength*. 《彼女は声をふりしぼって叫んだ She shouted *at the top of her voice*.
フリスビー 《商標名》Frisbee [frízbi] Ⓒ Ⓤ 《フリスビーをする play *Frisbee*
ブリスベーン Brisbane (❖オーストラリアの都市)
プリズム prism Ⓒ
ふりそそぐ 降り注ぐ 《落ちてくる》fall* 自; 《日光が》shine* 自; 《雨が》rain 自 《浜辺には太陽の光が降りそそいでいた The sun *was shining* on the beach.
ふりそで 振り袖

振りそでは高級で高価な着物で、長いそでと華やかな模様が特徴です。未婚の若い女性が正月、成人式、または卒業式や結婚式といった特別な機会に着用します。

A *furisode* is a deluxe and expensive kimono with long sleeves and splendid patterns. Unmarried young women wear *furisode* on special occasions such as New Years Day, Coming-of-Age Day, graduations and wedding receptions.

ふりだし 振り出し 《出発点》starting point Ⓒ; 《手形の》drawing Ⓤ 《この問題は振り出しに戻って考える必要がある We have to go back to *the starting point* and reconsider this problem.
◆交渉は振り出し(→始まったところ)に戻った The negotiation went back to *where it had started*.
‖振出人 a drawer
ふりだす 振り出す 《手形・小切手などを》draw* 他 《10万円の小切手を振り出す *draw* a 100,000 yen check
ふりつけ 振り付け・振付 choreography Ⓤ
◆バランシン振付作品 a work *choreographed by* George Balanchine
‖振付師 a choreographer
ぶりっこ ぶりっ子 《その歌手はデビュー当時, ぶりっ子といわれていた That singer was called *a pretentious cutie* when she debuted.
ブリッジ 《トランプのゲーム》bridge Ⓤ; 《橋・船・眼鏡・差歯などの》bridge Ⓒ
ふりつづく 降り続く 《もう3日間も雨が降り続いている It *has been raining* for three days.
ふりつもる 降り積もる 《けさ起きたら外には雪が降り積もっていた When I got up this morning, the snow *had piled up* outside.
ふりはらう 振り払う 《払いのける》shake* off 《彼は上着についていたほこりを振り払った He *shook* the dust *off* his jacket.
◆彼女は彼が差し出した手を振り払った She *brushed off* the hand he held out to her.
ぷりぷり 《ちょっとからかっただけなのに彼女はぷりぷり怒っている I was just kidding, but she *is in a real huff*.
プリペイドカード prepaid card Ⓒ
ふりほどく 振り解く 《縄を振りほどく *shake* a rope *off*
ふりまく 振り撒く 《彼女はだれにでもあいきょうを振りまいている She *turns on the charm* to everybody. 《花嫁は笑顔を振りまいていた The bride *was smiling* at everybody.
プリマドンナ prima donna Ⓒ
ふりまわす 振り回す 《振り動かす》swing* around; 《刀などを》wave 他; 《乱用する》abuse 他; 《誇示する》show* off 《権力を振り回す *abuse* one's *authority* 《女の子は歩きながら傘を振り回していた The girl *was swinging* her umbrella *around* while she walked.
◆彼にはいつもみんな振り回されている Everybody *is always ruled by* him.
ふりみだす 振り乱す dishevel 他 《彼女は髪を振り乱して走っていた She was running *with her hair disheveled*.
ふりむく 振り向く 《体の向きを変える》turn around; 《振り返って見る》look back 《彼女は私のほうを振り向いてにっこりと笑った She *turned around* toward me and smiled. 《大きな音がしたのでみんないっせいに振り向いた Everybody *looked back* at once at the loud

noise.
ふりやむ 降り止む ようやく雪が降りやんだ At last the snow *has stopped*.
ブリュッセル Brussels (❖ベルギーの首都)
ふりょ 不慮 ――不慮の（予期しない）unexpected; (偶然の) accidental ∥不慮の死をとげる die an *accidental* death / 彼らは不慮の事故にあった They met with an *unexpected* accident.
ふりょう¹ 不良 ❶【状態がよくない】――不良の bad; (質の劣った) poor; (欠陥がある) defective ∥今年の米の作柄は不良だった We had a *bad* rice crop this year. / 天候不良でイベントは中止になった The event was canceled because of *the bad weather*. ◆消化不良を起こす get [suffer from] *indigestion*
❷【人】bad boy [girl] Ⓒ; (非行少年・少女) juvenile delinquent Ⓒ; (乱暴者) hooligan Ⓒ ――不良の bad; (非行の) delinquent ∥不良になる go bad; *turn delinquent* / 彼は不良グループとつきあっていた He was mixed up with *a group of hooligans*.
∥不良債権 a bad debt / 不良品 a defective product
ふりょう² 不漁 けさは不漁だった We had a *poor catch of fish* this morning.
ふりょく 浮力 buoyancy Ⓤ
ぶりょく 武力 military force [power] Ⓤ, arms ∥武力に訴える resort to *military force* ◆彼らは武力で紛争を解決しようとしている They are trying to settle the dispute by *force*.
∥武力介入 armed intervention / 武力衝突 an armed clash
フリル frill Ⓒ ◆フリルのついたカーテン *frilled* curtains
ふりわける 振り分ける（分割する）divide ⓔ; (割り当てる) allot ⓔ ∥先生は生徒を6つの班に振り分けた The teacher *divided* the students into six groups.
ふりん 不倫 彼の妻は若い男と不倫している His wife *is having an affair with* a young man. / 彼の不倫が元で彼らは離婚した They divorced because he had *an affair* [*a fling*].
プリン ⚠ caramel custard Ⓤ Ⓒ (❖日本語は英語の pudding がなまったもの)
プリンス prince Ⓒ ◆歌舞伎界のプリンス *a promising young actor* in the kabuki world
プリンセス princess Ⓒ
プリンター printer Ⓒ
プリント (印刷物) handout Ⓒ; (生地) print Ⓤ Ⓒ; (写真) print ――プリントする print ⓔ ∥ネガから写真をプリントする *print* photographs from the negatives / プリントを配るのを手伝ってくれる？ Can you help me give out some *handouts*? / 彼女はプリント地の服を着ていた She wore a *print* dress.
プリントアウト 〚コンピュータ〛printout Ⓒ Ⓤ ――プリントアウトする print out
フル フルスピードで走る run *at full speed* /

辞書をフルに活用する *make full use of* a dictionary / 彼らは試合で実力をフルに発揮した They showed their abilities *to the fullest* in the game. / 注文が殺到し彼らは全員フル回転で働いている A rush of orders came in, so they're all working *at full speed*.

ふる¹ 降る

fall* ⓔ; (雨が) rain ⓔ; (雪が) snow ⓔ
あしたは雨が降るだろうか Will *it rain* tomorrow?
20日ぶりに雨が降った *It rained* for the first time in 20 days.
先月はたくさん雪が降った *It snowed* a lot last month. / We *had* a lot of *snow* last month.
今にも降りだしそうだ It's going to *rain* any moment.
出かけようとしたら雨が降りだした When I was going out, *it began to rain*.
一日中雨が降ったりやんだりしていた *It rained off and on* all day.
◆1日は雨に降られたがとてもよい旅だった We *were caught in the rain* on one day, but it was a very good trip. / それは降ってわいたような（→思いがけない）事件だった It was an *unexpected* incident.
[俳句] 降る雪や明治は遠くなりにけり (中村草田男)
The snow is falling
and all the years of Meiji
are now far away.

ふる² 振る

❶【振り動かす】shake* ⓔ; (1点を軸に大きく動かす) swing* ⓔ; (手・旗などを) wave ⓔ

子供はいやだと言って首を横に振った The child said no and *shook his head*.
この薬はびんをよく振ってから飲んでください *Shake* the bottle well before you take this medicine.
彼女は思いきりバットを振った She *swung* the bat with all her strength.
彼は私に気づいて手を振った He noticed me and *waved his hand*.
観客は旗を振って選手を応援した The spectators *waved* flags and cheered the players.
◆首を縦に振る nod one's head; (→同意して) *nod in agreement* / さいころを振る *throw* [*cast, roll*] *the dice* / 犬は私を見るとしっぽを振った The dog *wagged its tail* when it saw me. / まず肉に塩を振ります First, *sprin-*

ふる

kle salt on the meat.
❷【捨てる・断る】
大臣の地位を振る *give up one's* post as a minister
彼はせっかくのチャンスを棒に振った He *threw away* a rare chance.
あんなやつふっちゃえば？ Why don't you *drop* [*dump*] him?(❖*drop*は口語で「…とつきあうのをやめる」の意味)
❸【割り当てる】
読めない漢字に仮名をふった I *wrote* kana next to the Chinese characters I couldn't read.
私たちはチケットに番号をふった We *numbered* the tickets.

ふる³ 古 このズボンは兄のお古だ These trousers *were handed down* from my brother. ‖古新聞 an old newspaper

-ぶる (見せかける) pretend ⓐ；(…のふりをする) pose as … ‖彼女は上品ぶっているだけだ She only *pretends* to be a graceful lady.
彼はいつも紳士ぶっている He always *poses as a gentleman*.

ふるい¹ 古い

old；(古代の) ancient；(流行遅れの) old-fashioned, out-of-date(❖名詞の後で用いるときは out of date とする)
古い慣習を打ち破る break an *old* custom
ずいぶん古い時計だね That's a very *old* watch.
父は古い友人に会いに行った My father went to see an *old* friend of his.
奈良には古い寺がたくさんある There are a lot of *ancient* temples in Nara.
うちの両親は考え方が古すぎる My parents' way of thinking *is too old-fashioned*.
その歌はもう古いよ The song is *out of date*.
うちの冷蔵庫も古くなってきた Our refrigerator *is getting old*.
◆このパンは古くなっている This bread has gone *stale*.

ふるい² 篩 sieve ⓒ ◆小麦粉を2回ふるいにかける *sift* the flour twice / 応募者たちは書類選考でふるいにかけられた The applicants *were screened* by examining their papers.

ぶるい 部類 (種類) class ⓒ, kind ⓒ；(範疇(はんちゅう)) category ⓒ ‖それはこちらの部類に入る It falls into this *category*.
◆この作品はほかのと比べればましな部類だ This work is good relative to the others.

ふるいおこす 奮い起こす 彼らはもう一度勇気を奮い起こした They *plucked* [*mustered*, *summoned*] *up* their courage again.

ふるいおとす ふるい落とす shake* off, throw* off；(選抜する) screen out；(排除する) eliminate ⓐ ‖木から葉っぱをふるい落とす *shake* the leaves *off* a tree / 筆記試験で多くの人がふるい落とされた Many people *were screened out* through the written examination.

ふるいたつ 奮い立つ 試合を前に選手たちは奮い立った The players *roused themselves* as

the game was about to start.

ふるいわける ふるい分ける 砂と砂利をふるい分ける *sift* the gravel from the sand

ふるう¹ 振るう ❶【振り回す】(振り動かす) shake*ⓐ；(剣などを) brandish ⓐ ‖刀を振るう *brandish one's* sword / 彼は弟にこぶしを振るった He *shook* his fist at his brother.
❷【発揮する・行使する】use ⓐ, exercise ⓐ ‖腹が立っても暴力を振るってはいけない You should not *use* violence even if you get angry.
◆彼女は熱弁をふるった She *made a passionate speech*. / 台風が一晩中猛威をふるった The typhoon *raged* all night. / 彼はそのチームのコーチとして腕をふるった He *showed his ability* as the coach of the team.
❸【勢いがある】テストの成績が振るわない I'm *not doing very well* on tests. / このごろ商売が振るわない Business *is slow* these days.

ふるう² 奮う 彼は勇気をふるってもう一度その場所に近づいた He 「*plucked up* [*summoned*] his courage and approached the place again.

ブルー blue ⓤ ⇨あお

ブルーカラー blue-collar worker ⓒ ——ブルーカラーの blue-collar

ブルース (the) blues [blúːz] ‖ブルース歌手 a blues singer

フルーツ fruit ⓤⓒ ‖フルーツケーキ (a) fruitcake / フルーツサラダ (a) fruit salad / フルーツジュース fruit juice / フルーツパーラー a coffee shop that sells fruit dishes / フルーツポンチ (a) fruit punch

フルート flute ⓒ ‖フルートを吹く play *the flute* ‖フルート奏者 a flutist

ふるえ 震え shake ⓒ；(恐怖・興奮による) tremble ⓒ；(恐怖・嫌悪による) shudder ⓒ；(寒さなどによる) shiver ⓒ
◆寒くて震えが止まらなかった It was so cold that I couldn't stop *shivering*.

ふるえあがる 震え上がる tremble ⓐ；(寒さなどで) shiver ⓐ；(恐怖などで) shudder ⓐ ‖そのニュースを聞いて彼らは震えあがった They *trembled* to hear the news. / 彼女は外に出たとたん寒さで震えあがった She *shivered* with cold as soon as she went outside.

ふるえる 震える shake* ⓐ；(恐怖・寒さで) tremble ⓐ；(寒さ・恐れなどで身震いする) shiver ⓐ；(突然激しく) shudder ⓐ；(かすかに) quiver ⓐ；(声などが) quaver ⓐ
子供たちは恐怖に震えていた The children *were shaking* [*trembling*, *shuddering*] with fear.
彼女は緊張のあまり声が震えている She is so nervous that her voice *is trembling* [*quavering*].
彼は震える手で封筒をあけた He opened the envelope with *trembling* hands.
子猫は寒さで震えていた The kitten *was shivering* with cold.

フルカウント full count ⓒ

ふるがお 古顔 old-timer ⓒ

ふるかぶ 古株 (木の) old stump ⓒ；(古顔)

old-timer ◯
ふるぎ 古着 old clothes; (着古し) used [secondhand] clothing
∥古着屋(店) a secondhand clothes store; (人) an old-clothes dealer
ふるきず 古傷 old wound ◯ (✤比喩的にも用いられる) ∥古傷が痛む My old wound hurts. / 彼女は彼の古傷に触れた She opened his old wounds.
ふるく 古く ここは古くは海だった This was the sea many years ago. / それは古くから知られている It has been known since ancient times.
ふるくさい 古臭い (古い) old; (時代遅れの) old-fashioned, out-of-date; (陳腐な) hackneyed ∥古くさい表現 a hackneyed expression / 私の父は考え方が古くさい My father's way of thinking is old-fashioned.
フルコース (食事) full-course dinner ◯
ふるさと 故郷 one's home; (生まれ育った町) one's hometown / 心のふるさと one's spiritual home / ここは私の第二のふるさとだ This is my second home.
短歌 ふるさとの訛(なまり)なつかし停車場の人ごみの中にそを聴きにいく (石川啄木(たくぼく))
I miss the accent
of the town where I grew up.
Now I walk through crowds
in the city train station,
listening for sounds of home.
ブルジョア upper class person ◯; (全体) the upper class
ふるす 古巣 one's old place ◆彼は古巣のチームに戻った He returned to his old team.
フルスピード その車はフルスピードで走っった The car was running at full speed.
ブルゾン blouson ◯
フルタイム フルタイムで働く work full-time
ふるだぬき 古狸 (経験を積んだずる賢い人) old fox ◯
ふるって 奮って ふるってご参加ください You are cordially invited to join us.
ふるどうぐ 古道具 secondhand article ◯; (家具) used furniture ∪ ∥古道具屋(店) a secondhand store [shop]; (がらくた屋) a junk shop; (人) a junk dealer
ブルドーザー bulldozer ◯
ブルドッグ bulldog ◯
プルトニウム 〖化学〗plutonium ∪ (✤元素記号 Pu)
ふるびる 古びる grow* old ――古びた old; (時代遅れの) old-fashioned ∥古びたコート an old coat
ぶるぶる 外に出ると寒くて体がぶるぶる震えた I shivered with cold when I went outside. / 緊張して手がぶるぶる震えた I was so nervous that my hands shook [trembled]. / 子供たちは怖くてぶるぶる震えていた The children were trembling with fear.
フルベース ⚠ ツーアウトフルベースになった The bases are loaded with two outs.
ブルペン 〖野球〗bull pen, bullpen ◯
ふるぼけた 古ぼけた old; (使い古した) worn-out, timeworn
ふるほん 古本 used [secondhand] book ◯ ∥古本屋(店) a used [secondhand] bookstore; (店・人) a used [secondhand] bookseller
ブルマー bloomers (✤数えるときは a pair of ... とする)
ふるまい 振る舞い, (行動) behavior,《英》behaviour ∪; (道徳的観点から見た) 《公式的》conduct ∪ ∥彼女は彼の自分勝手なふるまいに腹を立てた She got angry at his selfish behavior. / 彼は自分のふるまいを恥じた He was ashamed of his silly conduct.
ふるまう 振る舞う ❶【行動する】behave ⊕, act ⊕ ∥彼は何の心配もないかのようにふるまった He behaved [acted] as if he were free from worry.
❷【もてなす】(ごちそうする) entertain ⊕; (おごる) treat ⊕ ∥彼はみんなに夕食をふるまった He treated everybody to dinner.
ふるめかしい 古めかしい (古い) old; (時代遅れの) old-fashioned ∥古めかしい表現 an old-fashioned expression
ふるわせる 震わせる (振り動かす) shake* ⊕; (激しく身震いする) tremble ⊕; (ぶるぶるする) shiver ⊕; (小刻みに震える) quiver ⊕ ∥彼女は声を震わせて泣いていた Her voice was shaking when she cried. / 彼は怒りで体を震わせていた His body was trembling with anger.
ぶれ (映像の) blur ◯; (カメラが動くこと) camera shake ◯ ◆この写真には少しぶれがある This photo is slightly blurred.
ふれあい 触れ合い, contact ∪ ∥自然との触れ合いを失う lose contact with nature ◆親子の触れ合い a close relationship between parents and children / 多くの現代人が心の触れ合いを求めている Many people today want better communication [interactions].
ふれあう 触れ合う come* in(to) contact, touch ⊕ ∥私たちの手が触れ合った Our hands touched. / その動物園では子供たちに小動物と触れ合う機会を提供している Children are allowed to come in contact with small animals at that zoo.
フレアスカート ⚠ flared skirt ◯
ぶれい 無礼 rudeness ∪, impoliteness ∪ ――無礼な rude, impolite ∥どうか息子の無礼をお許しください Please pardon my son's rudeness. / 彼の無礼な態度[発言]は教師たちを怒らせた His rude manner [remarks] made his teachers angry.
ブレイク 去年はこの手の音楽が大ブレイクした This kind of music suddenly became very popular last year.
ぶれいこう 無礼講 今夜は無礼講でいきましょう Let's enjoy ourselves without formalities tonight. (✤without formalities は「堅苦しいことなしで」の意味)
フレー フレー, フレー！ Hip, hip, hurray [hurrah, hooray]!
プレー play ◯ ――プレーする play ⊕ ⊕ ∥フ

ェア[ファイン, ラフ]プレー a fair [fine, rough] play / 珍プレー好プレー odd plays and fine plays / ゴルフを1ラウンドプレーする play a round of golf

プレーオフ playoff ⓒ, runoff ⓒ //優勝争いはプレーオフにもつれ込んだ They went into *the playoff* for the championship. / 両チームの間でプレーオフが行われた The two teams had *a playoff*.

ブレーカー 〔電気〕(circuit) breaker ⓒ //ブレーカーが下りた[落ちた] The circuit breaker shut off.

プレーガイド ⚠ (ticket) agency ⓒ (❖「プレーガイド」は和製英語)

ブレーキ brake ⓒ (しばしば複数形 ~s) //ブレーキを踏む step on *the brakes* / 彼女の自転車はほとんどブレーキがきかなかった The brakes of her bicycle hardly worked. / 父は急ブレーキをかけた My father *braked* suddenly.
‖ブレーキランプ 《米》a stoplight, 《英》a brake light / エアブレーキ an air brake / サイドブレーキ an emergency brake / ディスクブレーキ disc brakes / ハンドブレーキ a hand brake
慣用表現 彼の不振がブレーキとなった(→チームに影響を及ぼした) His slump *had an effect* on the team.

フレーク flake ⓒ //コーンフレーク cornflakes

フレーズ (章句) phrase ⓒ; (楽句・楽節) phrase ⓒ, passage ⓒ //このフレーズはどこかで耳にしたことがある I have heard this *phrase* somewhere.
‖キャッチフレーズ a catch phrase

プレート (板) plate ⓒ; 〔地質〕plate ⓒ; (ピッチャープレート) rubber ⓒ, plate ⓒ //海洋プレート *an* oceanic *plate*
‖プレートテクトニクス 〔地質〕plate tectonics / ナンバープレート 《米》a license plate, 《英》a number plate / ホームプレート〔野球〕the (home) plate

フレーバー (風味) flavor, 《英》flavour

プレーボーイ ⚠ (女好きの男) ladies' man ⓒ; (女たらし) womanizer ⓒ, 《口語的》Don Juan ⓒ (❖英語の playboy は「金持ちの道楽者」の意味)

プレーボール Play ball!

フレーム (枠組み) frame ⓒ (❖眼鏡・ボウリングのフレームも表す)

プレーヤー (選手・演奏者) player ⓒ; (レコード・CDなどの) player ⓒ //CDプレーヤー *a* CD *player*

プレーリードッグ 〔動物〕prairie dog ⓒ

ブレーン the brains //彼は首相のブレーンだ He is one of *the brains* of the Prime Minister.
‖ブレーンストーミング brainstorming

ふれこみ 触れ込み その車は低燃費という触れ込みだったが、実際はそれほど燃費がよくなかった The car *was advertised* as having good mileage, but in fact it wasn't as fuel-efficient as advertised.

ブレザー (ブレザーコート) blazer ⓒ

プレス (アイロンなどの) press ⓒ ──プレスする press ⓗ //このズボンはよくプレスがかかっている These trousers *are* well *pressed*.

ブレスレット bracelet

プレゼント present ⓒ ──プレゼントする give* ⓗ //私は彼の誕生日のプレゼントに手袋をあげた I gave him a pair of gloves as a birthday *present*. / 気に入ったのならこの絵を君にプレゼントしよう I'll *give* you this picture if you like it. / それをプレゼント用に包んでください Could you *gift-wrap* it?

フレックスタイム flextime Ⓤ //うちの会社はフレックスタイム制を採用している Our company has adopted *flextime*. ◆ 彼の仕事はフレックスタイムだ He works [is on] *flextime*.

プレッシャー pressure Ⓤ ⓒ //プレッシャーのかかる試合 a *high-pressure* game / 君がそんなにプレッシャーを感じる必要はないんだ You needn't feel so much *pressure*. / 彼はプレッシャーに弱い He is easily overwhelmed by *pressure*. / その国の政府は国旗を掲げるよう企業にプレッシャーをかけた The government of the country 「*put pressure on* [*pressured*] companies to display the national flags.

フレッシュ ──フレッシュな fresh //フレッシュな果物 *fresh* fruit
◆ 1位から3位まではすべて本トーナメント初参加の選手、とフレッシュな顔ぶれがそろった The first, second and third place winners were all *newcomers* taking part in this tournament for the first time.

フレッシュマン ⚠ (新入社員) new worker [employee] ⓒ; (大学の新入生) freshman ⓒ (❖女性にも用いる)

プレトリア Pretoria (❖南アフリカ共和国の行政上の首都)

プレハブ prefab(ricated) house ⓒ, 《口語的》prefab ⓒ

ふれまわる 触れ回る spread* (about), broadcast* ⓗ ⇨いいふらす

プレミア ⓗ premium ⓒ ⇨プレミアム

プレミアム premium ⓒ //…をプレミアム付きで売る sell ... *at a premium* / この切手にはプレミアムがついている They set [put] *a premium* on this stamp.

プレリュード 〔音楽〕(前奏曲) prelude ⓒ

ふれる 触れる

❶【軽く触る】touch ⓗ ⓒ; (触ってみる) feel* ⓗ
赤ちゃんのほほにそっと触れる *touch* a baby's cheek lightly
だれかが私の肩に触れた Somebody *touched* me *on* the shoulder. / Somebody *touched* my shoulder.
展示品に触れないでください Please don't *touch* the exhibits.
◆ 泡は軽く触れただけで割れてしまった The bubble burst *at a slight touch*. (❖この touch は名詞) / 刃物は子供の手の触れない(→届かない)所に置かないとだめだよ You must put cutting tools *out of* children's *reach*.
❷【関わる・言及する】(接触する) come* into

contact with ...; (言及する) refer to ..., mention ⊕

アイヌの文化に触れる機会があった I had a chance to *come into contact with* the Ainu culture.

柳先生は話の中で日本の祭りについて触れた In her speech, Ms. Yanagi 「*referred to* [*mentioned*]」 Japanese festivals.

◆これらの新聞は主要な問題に触れていない These papers *don't touch* the central issue. / 母は折りに触れてそのとき起こったことを話してくれた *On occasion* my mother told me about what happened then. / 彼は問題の核心に触れる発言をした He made a statement that *touched on the heart* of the problem.

❸【さしさわる】
彼の発言は人々の怒りに触れた His remark *aroused* people's *anger*. / His remark *made* people *angry*.

法に触れなければ何をしてもいいというものではない、You shouldn't think you can do anything as long as you *aren't breaking the law*.

❹【その他】
人の心の琴線に触れる *touch* a person's heartstrings

コンピュータに触れた(→コンピュータを使った)のはそのときが初めてでした It was the first time that I *used* a computer.

その石碑は通りからはずれた所にあるので人の目に触れることが少ない The stone monument *isn't often noticed*, because it's away from the street.

外気に触れる(→さらされる)と気分がよくなった When I *was exposed to* the air, I felt better.

ぶれる この写真はぶれている This picture *is blurred* [*out of focus*].

フレンチドレッシング French dressing Ⓤ
ブレンド blend Ⓒ ——ブレンドする blend ⊕ //ブレンドコーヒー *blended coffee*

ふろ 風呂

bath Ⓒ

ふろに入る take [(主に英)have] *a bath* / ふろを沸かす prepare [heat] *the bath*; (湯を張る) run *a bath* / ふろ(→銭湯)に行く go to *a public bath*

彼が赤ん坊をふろに入れます He gives the baby *a bath*.

ふろから上がった後，スイカを食べた I ate slices of watermelon after getting out of *the bath*.

まきでふろを炊いたことがありますか Have you ever heated *a bath* by burning wood?

🗨「もう，おふろは沸いてる？」「ああ，沸いてるよ」 "Is *the bath* ready?" "Yes, you can get in."

🗨「ふろの湯かげんはどう」「ちょっとぬるい[ちょっと熱すぎる，ちょうどいい]」 "How is *the bath (water)*?" "It's 「not hot enough [a little (too) hot, just about right]."

‖ふろおけ a bathtub / ふろ場 a bathroom

プロ professional Ⓒ, 《口語的》pro Ⓒ (複 ~s)
——プロの professional //プロチームとサッカーの試合をする play a soccer game against a *professional* team / プロテニス選手 a *professional* tennis player / そのテニス選手は去年プロに転向した The tennis player turned *professional* last year. / 彼のスキーの腕前はプロ級だ(→プロの水準にある) His skiing skills are *of professional level*.

◆彼の行為はプロにあるまじきものだった His conduct was *unprofessional*.

‖プロ意識 professionalism / プロ野球 professional baseball

ふろう 浮浪者 (物ごい) 《公式的》vagrant Ⓒ; (ホームレス) homeless person Ⓒ; (放浪者) tramp Ⓒ

ふろうしょとく 不労所得 unearned income Ⓤ

ふろうふし 不老不死 ——不老不死の ageless; (不死の) immortal

ブロー ▲a blow-dry ——ブローする blow-dry ⊕ //彼女は毎朝30分かけてブローしている She spends as long as 30 minutes *blow-drying* her hair every morning.

ブローカー broker
ブローチ brooch Ⓒ, pin //えり元にブローチをつける wear *a brooch* at *one's* throat
フローチャート (作業工程図) flow chart [diagram] Ⓒ
フロート コーヒーフロート *an iced-coffee float*
ブロードウェー Broadway(❖米国ニューヨーク市の大通り)
フローリング ⚠ フローリングの床 a floor with *wood flooring*
ふろく 付録 (おまけ) extra Ⓒ; (追加記事・別冊) supplement Ⓒ; (巻末の) appendix Ⓒ (複 ~es, appendices) //その雑誌には毎号付録としてポスターがついてくる Every issue of the magazine comes with a poster as *an extra*.

プログラマー 〖コンピュータ〗programmer Ⓒ
プログラミング 〖コンピュータ〗programming Ⓤ //プログラミング言語 (a) programming language

プログラム program Ⓒ; 〖コンピュータ〗program Ⓒ //プログラムを作る (催し物の) arrange *a program*; (→コンピュータの) make *a computer program* / 歓迎会のプログラム *the program* for a reception / プログラムの最初は校長先生のあいさつです The first item on *the program* is the principal's speech.

◆このソフトは故障すると自己修復するようにプログラムされている This software *is programed to* perform self-maintenance in the event of a malfunction.

‖プログラム学習 programmed learning
プロジェクター (映写機) projector Ⓒ
プロジェクト project Ⓒ //当時私はそのプロジェクトに参加していた At that time I took part in the *project*.

‖プロジェクトチーム a project team

ふろしき 風呂敷 a *furoshiki*
‖ふろしき包み a package wrapped in a *furoshiki*

> ふろしきは物を包むのに使うスカーフのような四角い布のことです。ふろしきは江戸時代に銭湯で脱いだ衣服を包むのに使われたのが最初とされています。以前はひんぱんに使われましたが、今ではかばんや手さげ袋などに取って代わられ、贈り物を包むなどの限られた用途以外ではあまり使われなくなりました。
> A *furoshiki* is a square piece of cloth like a scarf which is used for wrapping things. It is said that *furoshiki* were first used to wrap clothes at public baths during the Edo period. They were very popular in the past, but bags and sacks have replaced *furoshiki*. These days most people use them only for limited purposes like wrapping gifts.

プロセス process ⇒ かてい(過程)
‖プロセスチーズ processed cheese

プロダクション (番組などの制作会社) production company ◆芸能プロダクション a theatrical *agency*

フロック (フロックコート) frock coat

ブロック ❶【建築物】(concrete) block ◆その橋は石のブロックで作られている The bridge is made of stone *blocks*.
❷【おもちゃ】《米》block, 《主に英》brick
❸【街区・区域】block (◆4辺を道路で囲まれた区画、またはその1辺の距離を指す) ‖図書館は2ブロック先です The library is two *blocks* away. ◆私たちのチームは関東ブロックの代表になった Our team has been chosen the representative for the Kanto district.
❹【球技の】blocking ──ブロックする block ‖斉藤のスパイクをブロックする *block* Saito's spike
❺【政治・経済上の】bloc
❻【その他】ブロック体で名前を書きなさい Write your name *in print*.
‖ブロック経済 bloc economy / ブロック塀 a concrete block wall

ブロッコリー 〖植物〗broccoli

フロッピーディスク 〖コンピュータ〗(floppy) disk, diskette ‖フロッピーディスクを初期化する format *a (floppy) disk* / フロッピーディスクにデータを保存する save data on [to] *a (floppy) disk*

プロテイン protein
プロテクター protector
プロテスタント 〖キリスト教〗(教徒) Protestant; (教義) Protestantism ──プロテスタントの Protestant
プロデューサー producer
プロトタイプ prototype
プロバイダー (Internet service) provider, ISP
プロパガンダ propaganda
プロパンガス propane (gas)
プロフィール profile [próufail] ‖その雑誌は毎週新人歌手のプロフィールを紹介している The magazine carries *a profile* of a new singer every week.

プロペラ propeller
‖プロペラ機 a propeller-driven plane

プロポーション (体形) figure (◆proportion(s)は「つり合い」「大きさ」の意味) ‖プロポーションのいい女性 a woman with *a* beautiful *figure*; a well-*proportioned* woman

プロポーズ proposal ──プロポーズする propose ‖彼女は彼のプロポーズを受けようか断ろうか迷った She wavered between accepting and refusing his *proposal*.
🅔「喜美子にプロポーズしたんだって」「うん、でも断られたよ」 "I heard you *proposed to* Kimiko." "Yes, I did. But she「refused me [turned me down]."

ブロマイド 人気歌手のブロマイド a picture of a popular singer (◆日本語は bromide paper(印画紙の一種)から)

プロモーション promotion
‖プロモーションビデオ a promotional video

フロリダ Florida (◆米国南東部の州;《略語》Fla., 〖郵便〗FL)

プロレス pro(fessional) wrestling
[関連語] プロレスラー a pro(fessional) wrestler

プロレタリア proletarian ──プロレタリアの proletarian
‖プロレタリア革命 a proletarian revolution / プロレタリア文学 proletarian literature

プロローグ prologue, 《米》prolog

フロンガス chlorofluorocarbon (《略語》CFC) ‖代替フロンガス CFC substitute

ブロンズ bronze ──ブロンズの bronze ‖ブロンズ像 a bronze statue

フロンティア the frontier

フロント 《米》the front desk, 《主に英》the reception desk ‖貴重品はフロントに預けたほうがいいよ You should leave your valuables at *the front desk*.
‖フロント係 a desk clerk

ブロンド ──ブロンドの blond, blonde (◆ blondを男性、blondeを女性に用いる場合もある) ‖ブロンドの髪 *blond(e)* hair / 美しいブロンドの女性 a beautiful *blond(e)* woman; a beautiful *blond(e)* (◆後の表現のblond(e)は名詞で「ブロンドの人」の意味)

フロントガラス 《米》windshield, 《英》windscreen (◆「フロントガラス」は和製英語)

ふわ 不和 《公式的》discord ;(もめごと) trouble (また複数形 ~s);(衝突)《公式的》conflict ‖家庭の不和 a domestic *conflict* / 2人の間が不和になった The two have fallen into discord with each other. / 宝くじに当たったことが彼らの不和のもとになった(→不和を引き起こした) Winning the lottery caused *discord* between them.

ふわたり 不渡り 〖商業〗(手形) dishonored bill [draft]; (小切手) dishonored check ◆不渡りを出す bounce *a check* / その小切手は不渡りになった The check「*was dishonored* [《口語的》*bounced*].

‖不渡り小切手 a dishonored check;《口語的》a rubber check

ふわふわ ❶【柔らかくふくらんだ】——ふわふわの fluffy;〔柔らかい〕soft ∥ふわふわしたベッド a *fluffy* [*soft*] bed / 彼女は卵をふわふわになるまで泡立てた She beat the eggs until (they were) *fluffy*.
❷【軽々と漂う】タンポポの綿毛がふわふわと漂っている The fluff of a dandelion *is floating along*.
❸【心などが落ち着かない】そんなふわふわした気持ちでいては勉強がきちんとできないぞ If you are so *frivolous*, you won't be able to study properly.

ふわらいどう 付和雷同 他人の言うことに付和雷同する(→盲目的に従う) *follow blindly* what others say

ふわり ふわりとした綿あめ *fluffy* cotton candy / パラシュートがふわりと着地した The parachute landed *softly* [*lightly*].

ふん¹ 分

❶【時間】minute Ⓒ
15分 15 *minutes*; *a quarter* (*of an hour*) / 30分 30 *minutes*; *half an hour* / 歩いて5分の道のり a five-*minute* walk
今7時10分過ぎです It's ten *minutes* past seven.
あの時計は5分遅れて[進んで]いる That clock is five *minutes* slow [fast].
次郎は2，3分で戻ります Jiro will be back in a few *minutes*.
◆この列車は11時35分に出ます This train leaves at eleven thirty-five.
🅔「今，何時」「8時5分前よ」"What time is it?" "It's *five* (*minutes*) *to* eight."
❷【角度】
北緯28度17分 28 degrees 17 *minutes* north latitude (✿28° 17′ N. Lat.と略す)
慣用表現 分刻みのスケジュール a *minute-by-minute* schedule

ふん² humph, bah, pah ∥ふん，そんなの知らないよ *Humph*, I don't know anything about that. ◆ばかにしてふんと鼻を鳴らす *give a snort* of contempt

ふん³ 糞 《公式的》excrement Ⓤ;〔鳥・動物の〕droppings;〔牛・馬などの〕dung Ⓤ
◆犬のふんは飼い主が始末してください Please clean up after your dog.

ぶん¹ 分

❶【割り当て】share Ⓒ《通例単数形》
自分の分の勘定を払う pay *one's share* of the bill
彼女は自分の分の仕事をさっさと終わらせた She quickly finished her *share* of the work.
◆今月分の(→今月の)給料はもう銀行に振り込まれているはずだ This month's salary must have already been paid into my bank account. / 私の分のケーキもとっておいてよ Leave some cake *for me*.
❷【分量】
3メートル分のひも three meters *of* line / 2,000円分の花 2,000 yen *worth of* flowers /

アルコール分の多い[少ない]ビール *strong* [*weak*] beer / ビタミンCの足りない分(→不足)を補う supply *a deficiency* in vitamin C
彼は僕より頭1つ分背が高い He is taller than me *by* a head.
私は7人分の食事を用意した I prepared dinner *for* seven.
この牛乳は脂肪分が(→脂肪分)少ない This milk is low *in* fat.
けさ早く起きた分(→早く起きたので)今夜は早く眠くなった As I got up early this morning, I got sleepy early tonight.
余った分の(→残った)お金でお菓子を買ってもいいよ You may buy some candy with the money *left over*.
❸【分数】⇒ ぶんすう
2分の1 *a half* / 5分の3 *three-fifths* / 1万分の1の確率 odds of *ten thousand to one*
ホールの4分の3はもう埋まっている *Three quarters* of the auditorium is full now.
❹【身の程】
分を尽くす do *one's duty* / 分相応[不相応]の暮らしをする live *within* [*beyond*] *one's means*
彼女はよく自分の分をわきまえている She *knows her place* well.
❺【その他】
このCDプレーヤーは見た目はぼろいが聞く分には全然問題ない Although this CD player looks beat-up, there's no trouble *when* you play CDs on it.
この分だと(→空模様から判断すると)あしたは晴れそうだ *From* [*Judging from*] *the look of the sky*, it will be fine tomorrow.
この分では(→このペースでは)当分仕事は終わりそうにない *At this rate* the work won't be finished for a while.
資金は多い分にはいくら多くてもよい *The* more funds, the better.

ぶん² 文 〔文法〕sentence Ⓒ;〔文章〕text Ⓒ Ⓤ
英語の文を作る compose *a sentence* in English
次の文を日本語に直しなさい Translate *the following sentences* [*text*] into Japanese.
◆僕は文を書くのはうまくないんだ I'm not good at *writing*.
‖肯定[否定]文 an affirmative [a negative] sentence / 単[重，複]文 a simple [compound, complex] sentence / 平叙[疑問，命令，感嘆]文 a declarative [an interrogative, an imperative, an exclamatory] sentence

ぶんあん 文案 〔草稿〕draft Ⓒ ∥文案を練る work on *a draft*

ぶんい 文意 the meaning of a text ∥文意をつかむ catch [grasp] *the meaning of a text*

ふんいき 雰囲気 atmosphere Ⓤ Ⓒ ∥家庭的な雰囲気 *a* family [homey] *atmosphere* / 重苦しい[緊張した，なごやかな]雰囲気 *a* heavy [tense, friendly] *atmosphere* / パーティーのいい雰囲気をこわす destroy *the good atmosphere* of the party / その場の雰囲気にのまれ

ふんえん

...be overwhelmed by *the atmosphere* of the place / どうも新しい学校の雰囲気になじめない I somehow can't get used to *the atmosphere* of my new school. / カーテンを取り替えると部屋の雰囲気ががらっと変わった When I replaced the curtain, *the atmosphere* of the room completely changed.

◆彼女は相当落ち込んでいてとても話しかけられる雰囲気ではなかった She was very depressed. It was not the right time at all to talk to her. / 彼のそのひと言で一瞬気まずい雰囲気になった His remark led to *an uncomfortable moment*.

ふんえん 噴煙 the smoke (of a volcano), volcanic smoke Ⓤ ∥火山から噴煙が立ち昇っているのが見えた I saw *the smoke* rising [going up] from the volcano.

ぶんえん 分煙 公共の施設では分煙化が進んでいる More and more public facilities have *separate smoking and nonsmoking areas*.

ふんか 噴火 eruption Ⓤ Ⓒ ――噴火する erupt ⓘ ∥その火山は3年前に噴火した The volcano *erupted* three years ago.
∥噴火口 a crater

ぶんか¹ 文化

culture Ⓤ Ⓒ ――文化の・文化的な cultural ∥文化活動 *cultural activities* / 大衆文化 *mass culture* / 異文化間のコミュニケーション *cross-cultural* communication / 文化交流を推進する promote *cultural exchange* / イギリスとフランスの文化の違い the *culture* gap between Britain and France

このことはその国の高い文化水準を物語っている This shows *the high level of culture* of the country.

文化が異なれば身ぶりも異なるのは当然だ It's natural that gestures are different in different *cultures*.

今日(にち)、日本文化に目をむける西洋人が増えている Nowadays, more and more Western people turn their attention to (*the*) *Japanese culture*.

∥文化遺産 cultural heritage / 文化勲章 the Cultural Medal / 文化功労者 a person of Cultural Merit / 文化財 a cultural asset / 文化人 a cultured person / 文化人類学 cultural anthropology / 文化庁 The Agency for Cultural Affairs / 文化の日 Culture Day / 有形[無形]文化財 a tangible [an intangible] cultural asset

ぶんか² 分科 branch Ⓒ ⇨ ぶもん

ぶんか³ 文科 the humanities [literary] course ――文科の humane, (米)academic (✦名詞の前で用いる) ∥文科系と理科系 the *humanities* and natural sciences

ぶんか⁴ 分化 ――分化する divide ⓘ, be divided; (細胞などが) differentiate ⓘ ∥現代科学は専門が分化してその全貌(ぼう)をとらえるのが難しい Modern science *is divided into* so many special fields that it's hard to grasp its entirety.

ふんがい 憤慨 (不正などに対する) indignation Ⓤ; (個人的理由による) resentment Ⓤ Ⓒ ――憤慨する get* indignant; resent ⓣ ∥その政治家の無責任な発言に多くの人が憤慨した Many people *got indignant at* the politician's irresponsible remark. / 彼女は不公平な待遇にひどく憤慨した She greatly *resented* the unfair treatment.

ぶんかい 分解 (要素・成分への) decomposition Ⓤ, resolution Ⓤ ――分解する decompose ⓘ ⓣ, resolve ⓣ ⓘ; (機械などを) take* ... apart ∥私たちは化学の時間に塩をナトリウムと塩素に分解した We *decomposed* salt into sodium and chlorine in our chemistry class. / この時計を分解して故障を調べてください Please *take* this clock *apart* and see what is wrong with it.
∥分解修理 an overhaul

ぶんがく 文学

literature Ⓤ ――文学の・文学的な literary

私は大学でアメリカ文学を専攻している I am majoring in *American literature* in college.

翻訳では外国文学のよさが十分に分からない We can't fully appreciate *foreign literature* in translation.

こう見えても若いころはけっこう文学青年だったんだ Believe it or not, I was rather *literary* when I was young.

∥文学界 the literary world / 文学作品 a literary work, 《集合的》literature / 文学史 a history of literature / 文学士 a Bachelor of Arts (《略語》B.A.) / 文学者 a literary man / 文学修士 a Master of Arts (《略語》M.A.) / 文学賞 a literary prize / 文学博士 a Doctor of Literature (《略語》Litt.D.) / 文学部 the Department of Literature, the Literature Department / 現代文学 contemporary literature / 古典文学 classical literature, the classics / 自伝文学 autobiography / 児童文学 juvenile literature / 純文学 serious literature / 大衆文学 popular literature

ぶんかさい 文化祭 (学校の) school festival Ⓒ ∥私たちは文化祭の準備に忙しい We are busy preparing for *the school festival*. / 文化祭で私たちはおでんの模擬店をやります We are going to run an *oden* stand during *the school festival*.

ぶんかつ 分割 division Ⓤ Ⓒ ――分割する divide ⓣ ∥部屋を2つに分割する *divide* a room into two parts

◆パソコンを20回の分割払いで買う buy a PC *on a 20-month installment plan* / 車を分割で買った I bought a car *by installments*.
∥分割払い payment by installment(s)

ふんき 奮起 ――奮起する stir *oneself*, rouse *oneself*, be roused ――奮起させる stir ⓣ, rouse ⓣ ∥新社長は社員の奮起を促した The new president *stirred* the employees *up*. / 彼女の言葉が彼を奮起させた Her words *roused* him to action.

ぶんき 分岐 ――分岐する diverge ⓘ, branch ⓘ, split* ⓘ; (二またに) fork ⓘ ∥国

道は2キロ先で分岐している The national road *diverges* [*branches, splits*] two kilometers ahead.
◆ **人生の分岐点に立つ** stand at *the turning point* of *one's* life (❖ 道路などの「分岐点」は fork, 鉄道の「分岐点」は junction という)

ふんきゅう 紛糾 (混乱) confusion ⓤ; (複雑な状態) complication ⓒⓤ ──**紛糾する** get* [become] confused; get [become] complicated ∥**その法案をめぐって国会の審議は紛糾した** Deliberations in the Diet *got confused* over the bill. / **彼女の発言は議論の紛糾を招いた** Her remark caused the discussion to become *confused*.

ぶんきょう 文教 ∥**文教政策** an educational policy / **文教地区** an educational area

ぶんぎょう 分業 (a) division of labor ∥**当時のわが国の手工芸では分業体制が確立していた** *The division of labor* was established in the handicraft industry of our country at that time.
◆ **医薬分業** *separation* between medical and drug treatment

ふんぎり 踏ん切り **彼女は何事に関しても踏ん切りが悪い**(→ためらってばかりいる) She *hesitates* over everything. / **彼は会社を辞めるべきかどうか踏ん切りがつかずにいる**(→決心できない) He *can't make up his mind* whether to leave the company or not.

ぶんけい[1] 文型〖文法〗sentence pattern ⓒ

ぶんけい[2] 文系 ──**文系の** humane, 《米》academic (❖ 名詞の前で用いる)
◆ **文系に進む** major in *the humanities*

ぶんげい 文芸 (学芸) arts and science; (文学) literature ⓤ ∥**文芸作品** a literary work / **文芸雑誌** a literary magazine / **文芸批評** literary criticism / **文芸復興** the Renaissance / **文芸欄** a literary column

ぶんけん[1] 文献 literature ⓤ; (記録) document ⓒ ∥**私はフォークナーに関する文献をあさった** I searched for *literature* on Faulkner.
∥**参考文献** a bibliography, a reference

ぶんけん[2] 分権 (地方分権化) decentralization ⓤ ──**分権化する** decentralize ⓗ

ぶんこ 文庫 (双書・叢書) library ⓒ ∥**岩波文庫の本を集める** collect the books in *the* Iwanami *Library*
∥**文庫本** a pocket book;(文庫版) the pocket version of a book

ぶんご 文語 (書き言葉) written language ⓒ
∥**文語体** literary style

ぶんこう 分校 branch school
ぶんごう 文豪 great writer ⓒ

ふんさい 粉砕 ──**粉砕する** (押しつぶすように) crush ⓗ; (瞬時に) smash ⓗ; (破片を飛び散らせて) shatter ⓗ ∥**我々はその試合で相手チームを粉砕した** We *crushed* [*smashed*] the opposing team in the game.
∥**粉砕機** a crusher

ぶんさい 文才 a talent for writing ∥**彼女には文才がある** She has *a talent for writing*.

ぶんざい 分際 **子供の分際で大きな口をたたくな** Don't talk big as you are *only* a child.

ぶんさん 分散 dispersion ⓤ, breakup ⓒ; (集中したものの) decentralization ⓤ ──**分散する** disperse ⓗⓘ, break* up; decentralize ⓗⓘ ∥**首都機能を分散させる** *decentralize* the functions of the capital / **彼は敵の勢力を巧みに分散させた** He *dispersed* [*broke up, scattered*] the enemy force skillfully.

ぶんし[1] 分子〖物理・化学〗molecule ⓒ;〖数学〗numerator ⓒ; (特定集団内の) element ⓒ《しばしば複数形 〜s》∥**党内の異端分子** rebellious *elements* in the party / **酸素分子は原子を2つもつ** *A molecule* of oxygen has two atoms.
∥**分子構造** molecular structure / **分子式** a molecular formula / **分子生物学** molecular biology / **分子量** molecular weight

ぶんし[2] 分詞〖文法〗participle ⓒ ((略語)p., part.)⇒**かこぶんし, げんざいぶんし**
∥**分詞構文** ⇒ **ぶんしこうぶん** / **現在[過去]分詞** the present [past] participle

ぶんしこうぶん 分詞構文〖文法〗participial construction ⓤ

現在分詞や過去分詞に導かれる句が副詞句として文全体を説明する働きをしている構文を分詞構文という。時(「…するとき」「…すると」), 付帯状況(「…しながら」「…して, そして」), 原因・理由(「…ので」), 仮定(「…ならば」) などの意味を表す ∥ *Walking* [*While walking*] in Roppongi, I saw a famous baseball player. (❖ 文意をはっきりさせるために, 接続詞を添えることもある。ただし理由の接続詞 as, since, because を添えることはできない) **六本木を歩いていたら, 有名な野球選手を見た** / *Not knowing* how to deal with this matter, I asked for her advice. **この問題をどう扱ってよいか分からなかったので, 私は彼女の助言を求めた** / *Having spent* all our money, we had to give up the rest of our plans. **お金をすっかり使ってしまったので, 残りの計画はあきらめなければならなかった** / *Born* in Quebec, he is proficient in French. **ケベックで生まれたので, 彼はフランス語が上手だ** (❖ 受身の分詞構文の場合の being, having been は省略することができる)

ふんしつ 紛失 loss ⓤⓒ, disappearance ⓤⓒ ──**紛失する** lose* ⓗ ∥**彼はその事件に関する重要資料を一部紛失した** He *lost* some important papers relating to the case.
∥**紛失届** a report of the loss of an item / **紛失物** a missing [lost] item

ぶんしつ 分室 branch office
ふんしゃ 噴射 jet ⓒ; (ロケットの) burn ⓒ ──**噴射する** jet ⓗⓘ; burn ⓗⓘ
◆ **ロケットは炎を噴射しながら飛んでいった** The rocket *spewed out flames* as it flew.

ぶんしゅう 文集 a collection of works; (選集) anthology ⓒ
∥**卒業文集** a (school) year-book

ふんしゅつ 噴出 gush ⓤ, spouting ⓤ; (溶岩などの) eruption ⓤⓒ ──**噴出する** gush ⓘ, spout ⓘ; erupt ⓘ ∥**火口から溶岩が噴出しているのが確認された** They observed lava erupting [spouting, gushing] from the crater.

ぶんしょ 文書 (書類) document ⓒ, papers; (書かれたもの) writing ⓤ ∥文書にてご返答ください. Please give us your reply *in writing.*
∥外交文書 a diplomatic document / 偽造文書 a forged document / 機密文書 a secret [classified] document / 公文書 an official document / 私文書 a private document

ぶんしょう 文章 (文) sentence ⓒ; (文章の一節) passage ⓒ; (書いたもの) writing ⓤ, text ⓒⓤ ∥凝った文章 a sophisticated piece of *writing* / 文章を暗記する recite *a passage* / 平易で分かりやすい文章を書きなさい Make your *writing* plain and clear.
◆彼は文章が下手[上手]だ He *writes* badly [well]. / He is *a* bad [good] *writer.*

ぶんじょう 分譲 土地を分譲する *subdivide* property
∥分譲住宅 a house built for sale / 分譲地 land for sale in lots; (1区画) a subdivision / 分譲マンション《米》a condominium,《米口語的》a condo

ふんしょくけっさん 粉飾決算 window-dressing accounts

ふんしん 分針 minute hand ⓒ

ふんじん 粉塵 dust ⓤ
∥粉塵公害 particulate pollution

ぶんしん 分身 alter ego ⓒ

ぶんじん 文人 literary man [woman] ⓒ,《公式的》a man [woman] of letters

ふんすい 噴水 fountain ⓒ ∥池の真ん中で噴水が上がっている *A fountain* is rising at the center of the pond.

ぶんすいれい 分水嶺 divide ⓒ

ぶんすう 分数 《数学》fraction ⓒ ── 分数の fractional

<語法>
(1) 分数は, 分子を基数で先に, 分母を序数で後に読む. 分子が2以上の場合は, 分母にsを付ける. 1/3, 3/5, 2 1/5はそれぞれ one [a] third, three fifths, two and one [a] fifth と読む. ただし分母が2の場合, 1/2, 3/2 などは, one [a] half [×second], three halves [×seconds]となる.
(2) 分子, 分母とも基数で《分子 over 分母》と読むこともできる. 分子と分母が2けた以上の場合はこの読み方で読むことが多い. この読み方では, 13/20, 15/27はそれぞれ thirteen over twenty, fifteen over twenty-seven となる.

∥仮分数 an improper fraction / 真分数 a proper fraction / 帯分数 a mixed fraction

ふんする 扮する (演じる) play ⓓ; (扮装(ｽﾞ)する) make* up ∥彼はハムレットに扮した He *played (the role of)* Hamlet. / He *made himself up* for Hamlet.

ぶんせき¹ 分析 analysis ⓒⓤ ── 分析する analyze, 《英》analyse ⓓ ∥そのデータは現在分析中である The data *is* [*are*] *being analyzed.* / 我々はその問題を詳細に分析した We *analyzed* the problem closely. / We *made a close analysis* of the problem. / 分析の結果, その農作物には微量の放射性物質が含まれていることが分かった *Analysis proved* that the crops contain a small amount of radioactive substances.
∥化学分析 a chemical analysis / 精神分析 psychoanalysis

ぶんせき² 文責 (文章の最後で) 文責新井正光 Arai Masamitsu (✥英語では名前を書くだけでよい)

ふんせん 奮戦 ── 奮戦する fight* hard
◆わが柔道部は奮戦むなしく1回戦で敗退した Our judo club's *brave struggle* came to nothing, and we lost in the first round.

ふんぜん 憤然 憤然たる表情 an *indignant* expression / 彼は憤然として席を立った He left his seat *indignantly* [*in a rage*].

ふんそう¹ 紛争 (主に国家間の) conflict ⓒⓤ; (もめごと) trouble ⓤ (また複数形~s); (騒動) disturbance ⓒ ∥紛争を平和的に解決する settle *a dispute* peacefully
◆その紛争地域で多くの犠牲者が出た Many people lost their lives in *the disputed area.*
∥国際紛争 an international dispute / 地域紛争 a regional conflict / 民族紛争 a racial dispute / 労使紛争 a labor dispute

ふんそう² 扮装 makeup ⓤ; (変装) disguise ⓒⓤ ── 扮装する make* up; disguise ⓓ ∥サンタクロースの扮装をする *make oneself up as* Santa Claus

ふんぞりかえる ふんぞり返る ふんぞり返って(→横柄な態度で)いすに座る sit back in a chair *arrogantly* [*with a swagger*]

ぶんたい 文体 style ⓒⓤ ∥鷗外の文体をまねて書く write *in the style of* Ogai / この本は平易な文体で書かれている This book is written in *a plain style.*

ふんだくる (奪い取る) snatch ⓓ, grab; (法外な値段を要求する)《口語的》rip off ∥男は彼女のハンドバッグをふんだくって逃げた The man *snatched* her handbag and ran away. / その飲み屋ではビール1杯で4,000円もふんだくられた I *was ripped off* 4,000 yen for one glass of beer at the bar.

ふんだりけったり 踏んだり蹴ったり きのうは彼女にふられるわ, 財布は落とすわで踏んだり蹴ったりだった Yesterday my girlfriend dumped me and I lost my wallet. *It was just one thing after another.*

ふんだん 私たちには時間がふんだんに与えられていた We were given *plenty of* time. / この料理には新鮮な海の幸がふんだんに使われています *Plenty of* fresh delicacies from the sea are used in this dish.

ぶんたん 分担 (負担 分) share ⓒ (通例単数形); (課せられたもの) assignment ⓒ ── 分担する share ⓓ; (割り当てる) assign ⓓ ∥費用[責任]を分担する *share* the expenses [responsibilities] / その仕事は彼女に分担させよう We'll *assign* 「the work to her [her (to do) the work]. / 両親は家事を分担している

My parents *share* the housework. / みんな自分の分担の仕事をしなければならない Everyone must do their *share* of the work. / 私たちは大掃除の分担を決めた We decided how to *share* the general cleaning.

ぶんだん[1] 分断 大雨で鉄道が分断された The heavy rain *cut off* the railway *at several points.* / その戦争で祖国が分断された The war *divided* my mother country.

ぶんだん[2] 文壇 the literary world, literary circles ∥彼は文壇で活躍している He moves in「*the literary world* [*literary circles*].

ぶんちょう 文鳥 〘鳥〙 Java sparrow [C]

ぶんちん 文鎮 (paper)weight [C] ∥紙の上に文鎮を置く put *a weight* on a piece of paper

ぶんつう 文通 correspondence [U] [C] ━文通する exchange letters, correspond [自] ∥彼女と文通を始めて3年になる I *have been*「*in correspondence* [*corresponding*] *with* her for three years. / 私と文通してもらえませんか Would you「*exchange letters* [*correspond*] *with* me? / Would you be my *pen pal*?

ふんづける 踏ん付ける stamp [自] [他], step [自] ∥ガムを踏んづける *step on* a wad of chewing gum

ふんとう 奮闘 struggle [C] ━奮闘する struggle [自] ∥強敵を相手に奮闘する *struggle* against a strong enemy / 彼らはコメディアンを目ざして奮闘中だ They *are struggling* to be comedians.

◆奮闘のかいあって(→努力のおかげで)我々はその試合に勝利した *Thanks to our efforts,* we won the game.

ぶんどき 分度器 protractor [C]

ふんどし 褌 🖼 a *fundoshi*, a Japanese loincloth ∥ふんどしを締める wear *a fundoshi*; (→本気で取りかかる) gird *one's* loins

[慣用表現]人のふんどしで相撲をとる *warm oneself by another's fire*(→他人の火で暖まる)

ぶんどる 分捕る capture [他], seize [他]; (奪う) rob [他] ∥敵のジープを分捕る *capture* [*seize*] the enemy's jeep / あいつにかばんを分捕られた I *was robbed of* my bag by him.

ぶんなぐる ぶん殴る hit* *a person* hard, 《口語的》clobber [他], 《口語的》wallop [他]

ぶんのう 分納 授業料を分納する *pay* tuition fees「*in installments* [*by installment*]

ぶんぱい 分配 distribution [U]; (分け前などの) sharing [U]; (分けること) division [U] [C] ━分配する distribute [他]; share [他]; divide [他] ∥利益を分配する *distribute* [*divide*] the profit / 昔, 人々は捕った獲物をみんなで平等に分配していた A long time ago, people *distributed* [*divided*] the game they caught equally.

◆思わぬ利益の分配にあずかった I took *an* unexpected *share* of the profit.

ふんぱつ 奮発 祝儀を奮発する give *a person* a *big* [*generous*] tip / 奮発して新しい服を買うことにした I decided to *treat myself to* a new dress.

ふんばり 踏ん張り (がんばり) effort [U] [C] ∥もうひとふんばりする *make* another *effort*

◆地面がぬかるんでいてふんばりがきかなかった I *couldn't brace myself* because the ground was muddy.

ふんばる 踏ん張る (足を) brace *oneself*; (しっかり立つ) stand* firm ∥リポーターは強風に耐えるように足をふんばっていた The reporter「*braced himself* [*stood firm*] against the strong wind.

ぶんぴつ[1] 分泌 〘生理〙《公式的》secretion [U] ━分泌する secrete [他] ‖分泌腺(せん) a secretory gland / 分泌物 (a) secretion

ぶんぴつ[2] 文筆 (ものを書くこと) writing [U], pen [C]《通例単数形》 ∥文筆で生計を立てる earn *one's* living *by one's pen* ◆文筆活動を再開する restart *one's literary work*

‖文筆家 a writer / 文筆業 the literary profession

ぶんぷ 分布 distribution [U] [C] ━分布する be distributed ∥この花は日本各地に広く分布している This flower「*has a wide distribution* [*is widely distributed*] in Japan. / この種の動物はオーストラリアにしか分布していない Animals of this kind *are distributed* only in Australia.

‖分布図 a distribution map

ぶんぶつ 文物 彼は韓国の文物の紹介に努めた He worked to promote *things* Korean. (❖things の後に形容詞を置くと「…の文物」の意味を表す)

ぶんぶん (ハチ・機械などの) buzz [C], hum [C], whir [C]《通例単数形》 ━ぶんぶんいう buzz [自], hum [自], whir [自] ∥部屋の中でハチがぶんぶん音を立てていた A bee *was buzzing* [*humming*] in the room.

◆中村はバットをぶんぶん(→威勢よく)振り回した Nakamura swung his bat *vigorously*.

ぷんぷん その部屋の中はたばこの臭いがぷんぷんしていた There was a *strong* cigarette [tobacco] odor in the room. / 彼女は香水をぷんぷんさせていた She *reeked* [*stank*] *of* perfume. (❖reek of ..., stink of ... は特に不快感を伴う場合に用いられる) / 彼女はさんざん待たされてぷんぷんしていた She *was fuming* [*very angry*] because she was kept waiting for a long time.

ふんべつ 分別 (慎重さ) discretion [U], prudence [U]; (良識) sense [U]; (判断力) judgment, 《英》judgement [U]; (賢明さ) wisdom [U]; (成熟) maturity [U] ━分別のある discreet, prudent; sensible; wise; mature ⇨むふんべつ ∥分別のある人 a person *of discretion* [*prudence, good sense*] / 彼は彼女の思いやりのない言葉に分別をなくした He *lost his judgment* at her thoughtless remark.

◆分別をわきまえて話す speak *sensibly* [*maturely*] / 彼はもう少し分別のある男だと思っていたんだが I thought he *knew better*.

‖分別盛り mature age [years]

ぶんべつ 分別 ごみを分別する *sort* garbage / 私の町でもびんと缶の分別収集が始まった They have started to *collect* bottles and

cans *separately* in my town, too.
‖分別ごみ sorted garbage

ぶんべん 分娩 delivery [U][C], childbirth [U] ‖分娩室 a delivery room / 自然分娩 natural childbirth / 無痛分娩 painless delivery [childbirth]

ぶんぼ 分母 〔数学〕 denominator [C] ∥分母を払う cancel *the denominator* / 分母をそろえる find *the* common *denominator*
‖公分母 a common denominator

ぶんぽう 文法 grammar [U] ―文法(上)の grammatical ∥英文法 *English grammar*; *the grammar of English* / 文法上の誤りを犯す make a *grammatical* mistake / その表現は文法にかなっているが慣用的でない That expression is *grammatical* but not idiomatic. ◆この文は文法的に間違っている This sentence is *grammatically* incorrect.
‖文法学者 a grammarian / 文法書 a grammar (book)

ぶんぼうぐ 文房具 stationery [U] ‖文房具店 a stationer's, a stationery store

ふんまつ 粉末 powder [U] ∥お茶の葉を粉末状にする *reduce* tea leaves *to powder*
‖粉末ジュース powdered juice

ふんまん 憤懣 彼は憤まんやるかたない(→怒りをどう抑えてよいか分からない)様子だった It seemed that he *didn't know how to repress his indignation*.

ぶんみゃく 文脈 context [U][C] ∥文脈から言葉の意味を推測する guess the meaning of a word from *the context* / 彼の著作は難解で知られるが, 文脈さえたどっていけば必ず理解できる His works are known for their difficulty, but you can certainly understand them as long as you follow their *context*.

ふんむき 噴霧器 spray [C], sprayer [C]

ぶんめい 文明 civilization [U][C]
古代エジプト文明 *the civilization* of ancient Egypt / 古代文明の発祥地 the birthplace of *ancient civilization*
彼らはすでに非常に高度な文明に達していた They had already reached a very high level of *civilization*.
文明が進むにつれて私たちの生活様式も多様化してきた As *civilization* advances, our way of living has diversified.
◆文明の利器 a *modern* convenience
‖文明開化 civilization and enlightenment / 文明国 a civilized country / 文明社会 a civilized society

ぶんめん 文面 手紙の文面から判断すると, 彼の病状は重いらしい According to *the letter*, he seems to be in serious condition.

ぶんや 分野 field [C] (❖*one's* field で「専門分野」の意味にもなる) ∥彼の研究分野は経済学だ His *field of study* is economics. / それは私の専門分野ではありません That's outside *my* (*special*) *field*. / 彼は化学の分野ではよく知られている He is famous in *the field* of chemistry. ◆コンピュータは彼の得意分野だ Computers are his *specialty*.

ぶんらく 文楽 🗻
文楽は江戸時代に発展した伝統的な日本の人形劇です. ふつう3人で1つの人形を操ります. 劇全体は太夫(たゆう)と呼ばれる特別な歌い手と三味線演奏者によって奏でられる伴奏とともに進められます.
Bunraku is the traditional puppet theater developed in the Edo period (1600–1868). Usually three persons cooperate in the operation of one puppet. *Bunraku* is performed to musical accompaniment played by special chanters called *tayu* and by *shamisen* accompanists.

ぶんり 分離 separation [U] ―分離する separate [他][自] ∥酸素を空気から分離する *separate* oxygen from air / 酢と油はすぐに分離してしまう Vinegar and oil *separate* easily.
‖分離課税 separate taxation / 分離主義 separatism / 政教分離 the separation of ｢church and state [religion and politics] / 中央分離帯 《米》a median strip, 《英》a central reserve

ぶんりつ 分立 ‖三権分立 the separation of powers

ぶんりょう 分量 quantity [C]; (総量) amount [C]; (薬などの) dose [C], 《公式的》dosage [C] 《通例単数形》
水の分量を確かめなさい Check *the quantity* of water. / See *how much* water there is.
ここで指示どおりの分量の塩を混ぜてください Now mix salt in *the quantities* called for.
◆まだ相当な分量の(→相当多くの)仕事が残っていた *Quite a lot of* work still remained.

ぶんるい 分類 classification [U][C]; (仕分け) assortment [U] ―分類する classify [他], group [他]; sort [他]
厳密な分類 rigorous *classification* / 文を5つの型に分類する *classify* sentences *into* five types
彼はすべての本を主題別に分類した He *classified* [*grouped*] all the books by subject.
◆これらの症例は大きく分けて2つのタイプに分類される These cases generally *fall into* two types.
‖分類表 a classified list

ぶんれつ 分裂 division [U][C]; (不和による) split [C] ―分裂する divide [自]; split* [自] ∥その党は3つに分裂した The party *split up* into three groups.
‖核分裂〔物理〕 (nuclear) fission / 細胞分裂〔生物〕 cell division / 精神分裂症〔医学〕 schizophrenia

ふんわり ふんわりしたタオル a *soft* towel / ふんわり焼きあがったパン *fluffy* bread fresh from the oven / 夏空に雲がふんわりと浮かんでいる Clouds *are floating* in the summer sky.

へ 〔音楽〕F ⓊⒸ ∥ヘ長調[短調]で in (the key of) F major [minor]
∥ヘ記号〔音楽〕an F clef, a bass clef

へ 《米》gas Ⓤ, 《英》wind Ⓤ, 《卑語》fart Ⓒ
——屁をする pass gas, break* wind, 《卑語》fart ⓘ
[慣用表現] それくらいは屁でもない(→簡単だ) That's *quite easy*./ That's *a piece of cake*./ そんなことは屁とも思わない(→全く気にしない) I *don't give* [*care*] *a damn about* it.

ーへ

❶【動作の方向】to; for; toward, 《主に英》towards

[語法] to は「到着した[すべき]地点」を示し, for は行く方向を示す. for は交通機関の目的地を表すときによく用いられる. toward は方向を強調するときの言い方. ただし, 日本語では「……へ」の表現でも, 英語では前置詞を使わず, 副詞を用いて表現する場合もある ∥ 私は京都へ行った I went *to* Kyoto. (❖実際に京都へ着いたことを意味する)/ I started out *for* Kyoto. (❖京都へ向けて出発したという意味)/ その赤い車は海の方へ行った The red car went *toward* the ocean./ 外国へ行く go *abroad*/ 家へ帰る go [come] *home*/ 次の角を右へ曲がる turn *right* at the next corner

今年は修学旅行で九州へ行った This year we went *to* Kyushu on a school trip.

オーストラリアへは2度行ったことがある I've been *to* Australia twice.

歌舞伎座へ行くにはどこで降りたらいいですか Where am I supposed to get off *for* Kabukiza?

◆このぶんだと頂上へ着くのはお昼過ぎになる At this pace, we'll *reach* the top of the mountain past noon./ 兄はきょうもまた神保町へ古本をあさりに行った Today my brother went hunting for used books *in* Jimbocho again./ 寒いから部屋へ入ろう It's cold. Let's go *into* the room./ この箱にはパソコンが入っているので, そっと床へ置いてください There's a personal computer in this box. Put it down *on* the floor carefully.

💬「これは松本へ行く列車ですか」「いいえ. 松本なら, 隣のホームで『スーパーあずさ』に乗ると行けますよ」"Is this the train *for* Matsumoto?" "No. If you want to go to Matsumoto, you should take the *Super Azusa* on the next platform."

❷【動作の対象】
(贈り物などの上書き)良二さんへ *To* Ryoji
もう遅いから家へ電話をしたほうがいいのでは It's very late. You should call *home*.

💬「これ, あなたへのクリスマスプレゼント」「ありがとう. あけてもいい？」"Here's a Christmas present *for* you." "Thanks. Can I open it?"

❸【その他】
ちょうど夕食のしたくができたところへ母が帰ってきた My mother came home *just when* dinner was ready.

ヘア hair ⓊⒸ; (陰毛) pubic hair ⓊⒸ ➪ [場面・状況別会話] p.1710
◆ロング[ショート]ヘアの女性 a *long-haired* [*short-haired*] woman
∥ヘアアイロン curling irons / ヘアカーラー a hair curler / ヘアクリーム hair cream / ヘアケア hair care / ヘアコンディショナー (a) hair conditioner / ヘアスタイル a hairstyle / ヘアスプレー (a) hairspray / ヘアダイ hair dye / ヘアデザイナー a hair stylist [designer] / ヘアトニック (a) hair tonic / ヘアドライヤー a hair drier [dryer] / ヘアネット a hairnet / ヘアバンド a hair band / ヘアピース a hairpiece / ヘアピン ➪ ヘアピン / ヘアブラシ a hairbrush / ヘアマニキュア hair coloring

ベア ➪ ベースアップ

ペア pair Ⓒ《単数または複数扱い》∥ペアになって踊る dance *in pairs* ◆私はテニスの試合で彼女とペアを組んだ I *was paired* [*partnered*] (*up*) *with* her in the tennis match. / だれとペアを組みたい Who do you want to *pair* (*up*) *with*? / 彼らはペアルックだった They wore *matching clothes*.

ヘアピン hairpin Ⓒ, 《米》bobby pin Ⓒ, 《英》hairgrip Ⓒ
∥ヘアピンカーブ a hairpin (bend [curve])

ベアリング 〔機械〕bearings

へい¹ 塀 (壁) wall Ⓒ; (柵 (?)) fence Ⓒ ∥泥棒は塀を乗り越えて逃げていった The thief climbed over *the wall* and ran away. / 彼らは家の周りに高い塀をめぐらした They built *a high wall* around their house.
∥石塀 a stone wall / 板塀 a wooden [board] fence / ブロック塀 a concrete block wall / れんが塀 a brick wall

へい² 兵 (兵士) soldier Ⓒ; (軍隊) army Ⓒ, troops

ペイ この計画がペイする可能性は十分ある There's a good possibility that this project *will pay* (*off*).

へいあん 平安 (平和) peace Ⓤ; (落ち着き) calmness Ⓤ ——平安な peaceful; calm ∥心の平安を取り戻す restore *peace* of mind
∥平安時代 the Heian period

へいい 平易 ——平易な easy; (平明な) plain; (単純な) simple ∥平易な英語 *plain* [*simple, easy*] English / 専門用語を平易な言葉に言い換える translate technical terms into *plain* [*simple, easy*] language
◆平易に説明する explain *plainly* [*simply*]

へいえき　兵役 military service; ‖兵役を免除される be exempt [exempted] from *military service* ◆兵役につく serve in the army

へいおん　平穏 (平和) peace; (落ち着き) calmness; (静寂) quietness, quiet ──平穏な peaceful; calm; quiet ‖平穏な生活を送る live a *quiet* life / 平穏無事に暮らす live *in peace and quiet*

へいか　陛下 Majesty (❖男性には His, 女性には Her, 両者に対しては Their を付けて用いる. 直接呼びかけるときは Your を付ける. すべて三人称単数扱い) ‖天皇陛下 *His Majesty* the Emperor / 皇后陛下 *Her Majesty* the Empress / 天皇皇后両陛下 *Their Majesties* the Emperor and the Empress

べいか　米価 the price of rice ‖米価審議会 the Rice Price Council / 消費者米価 the consumer rice price / 生産者米価 the producer rice price

へいかい　閉会 ──閉会する close, break* up ‖会は午後5時に閉会予定です The meeting will *close* [*be closed*] at 5 p.m. ◆閉会の辞 a closing address / オリンピック大会の閉会を宣言する *declare* the Olympic Games *closed* / 国会は次の土曜日で閉会する The Diet *will rise* next Saturday. ‖閉会式 a closing ceremony

へいがい　弊害 喫煙は非喫煙者の健康にも弊害をもたらす Smoking has *a bad effect* even on nonsmokers' health.

へいかん　閉館 本日閉館 (掲示)*Closed Today* / 図書館は午後8時に閉館する The library *closes* [*is closed*] at 8 p.m. ‖閉館時 (a) closing time

へいがん　併願 3つの大学を併願する (→3つの大学に入学願書を出す) send in applications for admission to three colleges

へいき¹　平気 ──平気な (冷静な) calm, cool; (無関心な) indifferent, unconcerned 平気なふりをしてたけど, 内心びくびくしてたんだ I pretended to be *calm*, but I was really scared inside.

あんなひどいこと言われてよく平気でいられるね I wonder how you can stay *calm* [*cool*] when you are told such a terrible thing.

彼女が困っているというのに平気じゃいられない I cannot remain [act] *indifferent* when she's in trouble.

◆私は人に何と言われようと平気だ (→気にしない) I *don't care* what people say about me. / 僕は暑さなんか平気だよ (→いやでない) I *don't mind* the heat. / 君の家の前に車止めても平気? Is it *all right* to park my car in front of your house? / あいつは平気で約束を破るから信用できない I can't trust him because he *has no scruples about* breaking his promise. (❖scrupleは「良心のとがめ」の意味) / 私はテレビなんかなくても全然平気だ I *won't miss* television at all. (❖missは「…がなくて困る」の意味) / この水は飲んでも平気(→安全)ですか? Is this water *safe* for drinking? / 彼はみんなをだましておきながら平気な(→何事もなかったよう

な)顔をしていた After he deceived everyone, he carried on *as if nothing had happened.* / 急がなくても平気だよ (→急ぐ必要はない) You *don't have to* hurry.

💬 「大丈夫?」「平気だよ」"Are you [*all right* [OK]?" "Yes, *I'm OK*."

へいき²　兵器 arms, weapon ‖兵器庫 an arsenal, an armory / 兵器工場 a weapons [an arms] factory, an arsenal / 化学兵器 chemical weapons / 核兵器 nuclear weapons / 細菌兵器 bacteriological weapons / 通常兵器 conventional weapons

へいきん　平均

❶【中間値】an [the] average ──平均の average

平均(値)を出す take [strike] *an average* / 10月の平均降雨量[気温] the *average* rainfall [temperature] for October

3と8と10の平均は7だ The *average* of three, eight and ten is seven.

選手の平均身長は180センチを超えている The *average height* of the players is over 180 centimeters.

父は1日平均15本たばこを吸う My father smokes「15 cigarettes a day *on* (*the*) *average* [*an average* of 15 cigarettes a day].

中間試験で平均80点取った I got *an average score of* 80 on the midterm exams.

彼女の英語の点数はクラス平均よりはるかに上[下]だった Her marks in English were well above [below] *the class average*.

自分は平均的な日本人だと思う I think I am an *average* Japanese.

◆利益は週に平均すると50万円だ The profit *averages* 500,000 yen a week. (❖動詞 averageは「平均して…する, 平均して…を得る」の意味)

❷【均衡】balance (また a～)

体の平均を保つ[失う] keep [lose] *one's balance*

‖平均寿命 the average life span / 平均台 【スポーツ】a (balance) beam / 平均点 the average mark [score] / 平均余命 the average life expectancy

へいげん　平原 plain; (北米の) prairie

べいご　米語 American English

へいこう¹　平行 parallelism ──平行の parallel ‖直線Aに対して平行な線を引く draw a line *parallel* to line A; draw a *parallel* (line) to line A / 直線Aと直線Bは平行である Line A *is parallel to* [*with*] line B. / この道路は3キロその川と平行して走っている This road「*runs parallel to* [*parallels to*] the river for three kilometers.

‖平行四辺形 a parallelogram ⇨ずけい 図版 / 平行線 parallel lines / 平行棒 parallel bars

慣用表現 和平交渉は平行線をたどったままだ (→進展がない) The peace negotiations *are getting nowhere.* / (→合意に至っていない) The peace negotiations *haven't been settled yet.*

へいこう[2] 平衡 balance [C], equilibrium [ìːkwilíbriəm] [U] [C] (複 equilibria) ‖平衡を保つ[失う] keep [lose] *one's balance*
‖平衡感覚 a sense of balance [equilibrium]

へいこう[3] 並行 3選手は40キロ地点までは並行して走っていた The three runners were running *abreast* [*side by side*] until the 40 kilometer mark. / 警察はその2つの事件の捜査を並行して(→同時に)進めている The police are investigating the two cases *at the same time*.
‖並行輸入 parallel import; (個人輸入) personal import

へいこう[4] 閉口 この暑さには閉口だ(→耐えられない) I *can't bear* this heat. / 彼女の自慢話にはみんな閉口した(→うんざりした) We all *got sick and tired of* her boastful talks. / 彼のぐちには閉口する(→いらいらする) *I'm annoyed* by his grumbling.

へいごう 併合 (領土などの) annexation [U] [C]; (会社などの) merger [C] [U] ―併合する annex [他]; merge [他] [自]

べいこく 米国 the United States (of America) (《略語》 the U.S., the U.S.A.) ―米国の American ⇒ アメリカ
‖米国人 an American

へいさ 閉鎖 closing [U] [C], closure [U] [C] ―閉鎖する close [他] ―閉鎖的な closed ‖閉鎖的な社会 a *closed* [an *exclusive*] society / 工場の閉鎖は地域にとって大きな痛手だった *The closing* [*closure*] of the factory was a great loss to the community. / その学校は3年前に閉鎖された The school *was closed* three years ago. / その道は1時間前から事故のために閉鎖されている The road *has been closed* for an hour because of an accident. ◆私たちのクラスはインフルエンザのために3日間学級閉鎖になった Our class *was suspended* for three days because of the flu.

べいさく 米作 (栽培) rice growing [U]; (収穫) rice crop [C] ‖天候は米作を大きく左右する The weather greatly influences *the rice crop*.
‖米作地帯 a rice-producing district

へいさつ 併殺 〖野球〗 double play [C]

へいし 兵士 soldier [C]

へいじ 平時 peacetime [U]

へいじつ 平日 weekday [C] ‖平日は午前11時から午後9時まであいています We're open from 11 a.m. to 9 p.m. 「*on weekdays* [*during the week*].

へいしゃ 兵舎 barracks 《単数または複数扱い》

べいじゅ 米寿 *one's* 88th birthday

へいしょ 閉所 enclosed space [C]
‖閉所恐怖症 claustrophobia / 閉所恐怖症者 a claustrophobic

へいじょう 平常 ―平常の (正常な) normal; (いつもの) usual ‖年末も平常どおり営業いたします We'll do business *as usual* at the end of the year. / 今月の売上高は平常より多かった This month's sales were larger *than usual*.
◆平常心(→落ち着き)を保つ[失う] maintain [lose] *one's presence of mind* / 列車の運行はまだ平常に戻っていない The train service has not returned to *normal* yet. (❖この normal は「常態」の意味の名詞) / 平常は午後8時に閉店です We *usually* close at 8 p.m.

へいしんていとう 平身低頭 平身低頭して謝る(→ひたすら謝る) *make profuse apologies*; *apologize profusely*

へいせい[1] 平静 (落ち着き) calmness [U]; (沈着) composure [U], presence of mind; (平和) peace [U] ―平静な calm, quiet; peaceful ‖平静を保つ[失う, 取り戻す] keep [lose, recover] *one's composure* / 私は内心穏やかではなかったが努めて平静を装った Though I felt uneasy inside, I tried to pretend to be *calm* [*cool, composed*]. / 町はようやく平静になった At last the town became *quiet* [*peaceful*].

へいせい[2] 平成 Heisei
◆私は平成14年に中学を卒業した I graduated from junior high school in 2002 [the 14th year of *Heisei*]. (❖年号は日本独自のものなので西暦を用いるほうがよい)

へいぜい 平生 usually ―平生の usual, everyday ◆健康増進には平生の心がけが肝心だ Improving your health requires a *constant* commitment.

へいせつ 併設 本社にはショールームが併設されている A showroom *is attached to* the head office.

へいぜん 平然 彼女はその知らせを聞いても平然としていた She stayed *calm* even when she heard the news.

へいそ 平素 ―平素の usual, everyday ‖平素の行動 *everyday* conduct
◆平素のごぶさたをおわび申し上げます *I'm sorry for my long absence*.

へいそん 併存 coexistence [U] ―併存する coexist [自]

へいたい 兵隊 soldier [C]

へいたん 平坦 ―平坦な (でこぼこのない) flat, even; (水平な) level; (なめらかな) smooth ‖この先数キロは平坦な道が続く A *flat* path continues for a few kilometers from here. / 優勝までの道のりは平坦ではなかった The road to the championship was not *smooth*.

へいち 平地 flat land [U] ‖山を切り崩して平地にする level a hill to make *flat land*

へいてい[1] 平定 pacification [U] ―平定する (平和をもたらす) pacify [他]; (反乱などを鎮圧する) suppress [他]; (支配下に置く) bring* ... under control

へいてい[2] 閉廷 10月20日まで閉廷する *adjourn the court* until October 20

へいてん 閉店 ―閉店する close [他] [自] ‖本日閉店《掲示》*Closed Today* / その店は10時に閉店する The store *closes* [*is closed*] at 10. / あと30分で閉店です We*'re closing* in a half hour. / 売り上げ不振でその店は閉店に追い込まれた They were forced to *close* the store because of the poor sales.
‖閉店時間 the closing time

へいねつ 平熱 normal temperature ©
◆熱が平熱になった My temperature *has* 「*fallen to* [*become*] *normal*. / 体温は平熱より少し高めだった My temperature *was a little above normal*.

へいねん 平年 normal year ©, average year ©; (うるう年でない年) common year ©
◆この夏の降雨量は平年並みだった The rainfall of this summer *was average*. (❖「平年を上回る[下回る]」は above [below] average) / 今年の梅雨入りは平年より多少早かった The rainy season began a little earlier this year than *usual*. / 春一番は平年3月ごろに吹く The first spring gale *usually* blows in around March.
‖平年作 an average crop

へいはつ 併発 彼女はかぜから肺炎を併発した (→かぜが肺炎になった) Her cold *developed into* pneumonia.

へいふく 平服 (普段着) ordinary [everyday] clothes; (私服) plain clothes
◆平服でお越しください. Dress informally. (❖招待状などで用いる)

へいべい 平米 square meter © / 1坪は約3.3 平米だ A *tsubo* is equal to about 3.3 *square meters*.

へいべい (下っぱ) underling ©; (未熟者) greenhorn ©; (初心者) novice ©

へいほう 平方 〖数学〗square © 《略語》sq.) / 5平方メートル five *square* meters / 30センチ平方の紙 a piece of paper 30 centimeters *square* / 1平方メートル当たり10キロの圧力 a pressure of 10 kilograms *to the square meter* / 2の平方は4である *The square* of two is four.
‖平方根〖数学〗a square root

へいぼん 平凡 (ふつうの) ordinary; (ありふれた) common, commonplace; (月並みな) mediocre [míːdióukər]; (波乱のない) uneventful
平凡な家庭 an *ordinary* [a *common*] family / 平凡な生活を送る lead an *uneventful* life
事件の犯人は平凡なサラリーマンだった The criminal in the case was an *ordinary* office worker.
この推理小説は筋立ては平凡だがとてもおもしろい Though the plot *is commonplace*, this mystery is very interesting.

へいまく 閉幕 7時開演, 10時閉幕 The curtain rises at seven and *falls* at ten. / サミットはこれといった成果もないまま閉幕した (→終わった) The summit *came to an end* without producing any special results.

へいめい 平明 彼女の本はどれも平明な文体で書かれている All her books are written in a *clear* style.

へいめん 平面 plane © / 2つの直線は同一平面上にある The two lines are on *the same plane*.
‖平面幾何学〖数学〗plane geometry / 平面図〖建築〗a floor plan / 平面図形 a plane figure

へいや 平野 plain © / 庄内平野 the Shonai *Plain*

へいよう 併用 この薬はほかの薬と決して併用しないでください Please make sure not to *take* this medicine *together with* any other medicine.

へいりょく 兵力 military power [strength] © / 兵力を増強する build up *military power*
◆兵力3万人の軍隊 an army 30,000 *strong*; a 30,000-*strong* army

へいれつ 並列 〖電気〗parallel / 乾電池を並列につなぐ connect dry batteries *in parallel*
‖並列回路 a parallel circuit / 並列処理〖コンピュータ〗parallel processing

へいわ 平和 peace © (また a～) ――平和な peaceful ――平和に peacefully
平和を維持する keep [maintain] *peace* / 紛争を平和的に解決する settle a dispute *peacefully* [*in a peaceful way*]
ようやく戦争が終わり平和が戻ってきた The war is finally over and *peace* has been restored.
核兵器は人類の平和をいまだ脅(おびや)かしている Nuclear weapons are still threatening *the peace* of the human race.
私たちはみな, 強く平和を願っている We all earnestly desire *peace*.
その出来事は町の平和を乱した The event broke [disturbed] *the peace* of the town.
すべての人が平和に暮らす権利をもっている Every person has a right to live *peacefully* [*in peace*].
世界平和のため我々は力を合わせなければならない We must work together for *world peace*.
‖平和維持活動 a peacekeeping operation / 平和維持軍 a peacekeeping force / 平和共存 peaceful coexistence / 平和主義 pacifism / 平和主義者 a pacifist / 平和条約 a peace treaty

へえ oh, gee; (本当に?) really, indeed
🅔「毎朝5時に起きるんだ」「へえ, そうなの」"I get up at 5 o'clock every morning." "*Oh*, do you?"
🅔「彼女3か国語を話すんだ」「へえ, 語学の天才だね」"She is trilingual." "*Gee*, she must be a genius with languages."

ベーカリー (パン屋) bakery ©

ベーコン bacon Ⓤ / ベーコン1切れ a piece [slice, strip] of *bacon*
‖ベーコンエッグ bacon and eggs

ページ page © (❖page は p., pages は pp. と略す)
反対側のページ the opposite [facing] *page* / ページをめくる turn *a page* / ページにしおりをはさむ insert a bookmark between *the pages* / ページの端を折る dog-ear *a page* / 本を20ページ読む read 20 *pages* of a book / 25ページを開きなさい Open your book to [《英》at] *page* 25 [*p*. 25].
詳しくは20ページから35ページをご覧ください For details, see 「*pages* 20 to 35 [*pp*. 20–

35].

38ページから始めましょう Let's begin on [《英》at] *page* 38.

58ページに[から]続く Continued on [from] *p.* 58.

15ページ以下を参照 See *p.* 15 *ff.*(❖ff.は and the following pages の意味)

このレポートは60ページ以上もある This report has more than 60 *pages.*/ This report is over 60 *pages* long.

それは何ページに出ていますか *On what page* does it come?

図は10ページの上[中ごろ，下]に出ている The illustration is「at the top [in the middle, at the bottom] of *page* 10.

この発見は自然科学の歴史に新たな1ページを加えた This discovery *added a new page to* the history of natural science.

ベージュ beige [béiʒ] [U] ━ベージュの beige

ベース (基礎) basis [C] (複 bases), base [C]; (塁)〔野球〕base [C][U]; (楽器) bass [C][U] ‖ベースを踏む step on *the base* / サードベースに達する reach third *base* / 私たちは彼女のアイディアをベースにその計画を立てた We made the plan on *the basis* [*base*] of her idea.
‖ベースギター a bass (guitar) / ベースキャンプ a base camp / ベースライン a baseline / ダブルベース a double bass, a bass violin

ペース pace [U]《また a ～》 ‖速い[一定の，ゆったりした]ペースで at *a* fast [*an* even, *a* slow] *pace* / 仕事のペースを上げる[落とす] quicken [slacken] *the pace* of *one's* work / 急がなくてもいいから自分のペースで続けなさい You don't have to hurry. Just keep on going *at your own pace.* / 突然先頭走者のペースが落ちた[上がった] *The pace* of the leading runner「fell off [picked up] suddenly. / これ以上君のペースについていけない I can no longer *keep pace with* you. / 我々のチームは序盤から試合のペースを握った Our team set *the pace* of the game from the start. / 彼はレースでペース配分を誤った He *didn't control his pace well* in the race.

ベースアップ ⚠(昇給) (pay) raise [《英》rise] [C] (❖「ベースアップ」は和製英語) ‖4パーセントのベースアップを要求する demand *a* four percent *raise*

ペースト paste [U] ━ペーストする〔コンピュータ〕paste [他][自] ‖レバーペースト liver *paste*

ペースメーカー 〔医学〕(脈拍調整装置) pacemaker [C]; (レースなどの) pacemaker [C], pacesetter [C]

ペーソス (哀愁) pathos [U]

ペーハー 〔化学〕(水素イオン濃度指数) pH [píːéitʃ] [U]《また a ～》

ペーパー (紙) paper [U]

[語法]
日本語が「ペーパー…」の複合語でも，英語では paper … とはならないこともあるので注意が必要 ‖ ペーパーテスト a *written* test / (❖英語の paper test は「紙質試験」の意味) / 父はペーパードライバーだ My father *has a driver's license but doesn't drive.*

‖ペーパーカンパニー (実体のない会社)a paper company (❖「製紙会社」の意味でも用いられる); (いんちき会社)a bogus [fake] company / ペーパータオル a paper towel / ペーパーナイフ《米》a letter opener,《英》a paper knife / ペーパーバック a paperback

ベール veil [C] ‖ベールをかぶる wear *a veil* / 彼女の生い立ちはなぞのベールに包まれている Her early life is hidden [under] *a veil* of mystery.

-べからず 他言するべからず *Don't* tell it to anyone. / ごみ捨てるべからず *No* littering. / 芝生に入るべからず Keep off the grass.

-べき (義務・必要) must, have* to *do*, should, ought to *do*

できるだけ早いうちに医者のところに行くべきです You *must* [*should*] visit the doctor as soon as possible.

学生時代にもっと多くの友人を作っておくべきだった I *should have* made more friends when I was a student.

どんな小さな罪も見逃すべきではない Even the smallest sins *should* [*must*] *not* be passed over. (❖don't have to *do* は「…する必要はない」の意味になるので注意)

彼は暴力に訴えるべきではなかった He *shouldn't have* resorted to force.

◆我々はみなやるべきことがある We all have work *to* do. / それは少しも恥ずべきことではない It's nothing *to* be ashamed of. / 彼らに協力すべきかどうか分からない I don't know *whether to* cooperate with them or not.

へきえき 辟易 彼の長話には辟易する I'*m fed up with* his long story.

へきが 壁画 mural [C], wall painting [C]

へきち 僻地 remote place [area] [C], out-of-the-way place [area] [C]

へきめん 壁面 (壁) wall [C]; (表面) the face of a wall

ペキン 北京 Beijing [bèidʒíŋ] (❖中華人民共和国の首都．Peking [pìːkíŋ] ともいう)
‖北京原人 a Peking man

ヘクタール (面積の単位) hectare [C] (《略語》ha) (❖フランス語から)

ヘクトパスカル (気圧の単位) hectopascal [C] (《略語》hPa)

ベクトル 〔数学〕vector [C]

へこたれる (落胆する) be discouraged ‖そんなことでへこたれるな Don't *be discouraged* over such a thing.
◆彼は途中でへこたれる(→あきらめる)ことなく目標を達成した Never *giving up* halfway, he achieved his goal.

ベゴニア 〔植物〕begonia [C]

ぺこぺこ おなかがぺこぺこだ I'*m starving* [*starved*]. / あんなやつにぺこぺこする必要はないよ You don't have to「*bow and scrape to* [(→へつらう)*flatter*] a man like that.

へこます 凹ます なべをへこます「*make a dent in* [*dent*] a pot / 父はおなかをへこますた

めにジョギングを始めた My father began jogging to *flatten* his stomach. / 先生は彼女にへこまされた(→言い負かされた) The teacher *was argued down* by her.

へこみ 凹み hollow ⓒ; (衝撃による) dent ⓒ //へこみをなくす remove *a dent*

へこむ 凹む (衝撃など) dent ⓔ, be dented; (圧力などで) yield ⓔ //追突されたがバンパーがへこんだだけですんだ My car was run into from behind, but only the bumper *got dented*. / この缶は軽く押しただけでへこむ This can *yields* to light pressure.

ぺこり 彼は頭をぺこりと下げてあいさつした He *bobbed* his head and said hello.

へさき 舳先 bow [báu] ⓒ 《しばしば複数形 ～s》

へしおる 圧し折る break* ⓔ
慣用表現 鼻をへし折る ⇒はな(鼻)

ベジタリアン vegetarian ⓒ

ペシミスト pessimist ⓒ (↔optimist)

ペシミズム pessimism ⓤ (↔optimism)

ベスト¹ (最良) (the) best //ベストを尽くす *do one's best*; *do the best one can* / その本は世界的なベストセラーです The book is *a worldwide bestseller*. (❖「ベストセラー作家」は a best-selling writer) / 我々のチームはベストメンバーで試合をした Our team played the game with *its best members*. / 彼女はきのう自己ベストを出した She recorded *her best time* yesterday.
◆彼女はベストフォー[ベストエイト]に残った She became one of *the semifinalists [quarterfinalists]*. / (→準決勝[準々決勝]に進んだ) She advanced to *the semifinals [quarterfinals]*. / 私たちはベストコンディションで試合に臨んだ We took part in the game *in top condition*. / この歌は今週ベストテン入りした[からはずれた] This song has reached [dropped out of] *the top ten* this week. (❖ ×the best ten とはいわない)
‖ベストドレッサー the best dresser

ベスト² (チョッキ) 《米》vest ⓒ, 《英》waistcoat ⓒ

ペスト (the) plague
‖ペスト菌 a plague bacillus

へそ 臍 navel ⓒ, 《口語的》belly button ⓒ
‖へその緒 an umbilical cord
慣用表現 あいつは本当にへそ曲がりだ He's really *a perverse fellow*. / ちょっとからかっただけなのに彼はへそを曲げてしまった I was only kidding, but he *got sullen*.

べそ 迷子になった女の子はべそをかいていた The girl *was sobbing* because she got lost.

へそくり secret savings
◆家計の一部をへそくりする *salt away* part of the family budget

へた¹ 下手 ━下手な poor, bad, not good (❖bad は poor よりも強意的。not good は婉曲的な表現); (ぎこちない) awkward, clumsy; (熟練していない) unskilled
字が下手である have *poor* handwriting / 私はテニスが下手です I'm *a bad* tennis player. / I'm *bad at* playing tennis.

日本語は通じなかったので下手な英語を使わなければならなかった People didn't understand Japanese, so I had to use my *poor* English.
そんな下手な言い訳は聞きたくもない I don't want to hear such a *poor [bad, weak, feeble]* excuse.
父は口下手だ My father is *a poor talker*.
君はうそが下手だね You are *a bad liar*.
◆彼は子供の扱いが下手だ(→扱い方を知らない) He *doesn't know how to* handle children. / しばらく使っていないのでドイツ語がかなり下手になった(→さびついてしまった) I haven't used German for a long time, so my German *has gotten* fairly *rusty*. / 彼女には下手に口出ししないほうがいい You'd better not *interfere with* her.
慣用表現 音楽のことなら彼女は下手な(→並みの)専門家より知識がある She knows more about music than *those ordinary* specialists. (❖those は「そこらの」といったニュアンスを加える) / 下手の横好きです(→下手だけが好きだ) I like painting pictures, though I am poor at it. / 下手をすると(→事がうまく運ばないと)命も危ない *If things don't go well*, you'll be killed. / (→気をつけないと) *If you are not careful*, you'll be killed.
ことわざ 下手な鉄砲も数撃ちゃ当たる He that shoots oft at last shall hit the mark. (→何度も射る者はついには的(ま)を射抜く)

へた² 蔕 (ナスなどの) calyx [kéiliks] ⓒ (複 ～es, calyces); (イチゴの) hull

へだたり 隔たり (時間・空間などの) distance ⓒ ⓤ; (相違) difference ⓒ ⓤ; (意見などの) gap ⓒ //年齢の隔たり the age *difference* [*gap*] / 世代の隔たり the generation *gap* / 心の隔たりを埋める reduce *the* psychological *distance* / 我々の予想と現実の結果にはかなりの隔たりがあった There was *a considerable difference [gap]* between our prediction and the actual result.

へだたる 隔たる ここから3キロほど隔たった所にその村はある The village is about three kilometers *away [distant]* from here. / その事件は発生から20年隔たった今でも多くの人が記憶している Twenty years *have passed* since the event occurred, but a lot of people still remember it.

べたつく 肌が汗でべたついている My skin *is sticky* with sweat.

へだて 隔て (仕切り) partition ⓒ; (区別) distinction ⓒ ⓤ; (差別) discrimination ⓤ
◆隔てなく(→率直に)話す speak *frankly* / 私は子供たち全員に分け隔てなく接するようにしている I try to treat the children all *equally [alike]*.

へだてる 隔てる separate ⓔ, divide ⓔ //このフェンスがうちの庭と隣の庭を隔てている This fence *divides* our yard from our neighbor's. / 日本は他国と海で隔てられている Japan *is separated* from other countries by the sea. / 言語能力を有することが人間をほかの動物と隔てている The power of speech is

what *separates* us human beings from other animals. / ささいな行き違いが2人の仲をすっかり隔ててしまった A little misunderstanding *separated* them entirely.
◆山を1つ隔てた(→越えた所にある)村 a village *beyond* a mountain / 通りを隔てて(→通りの反対側に)人だかりがしていた There was a large crowd of people *across* the street. / 私はテーブルを隔てて(→はさんで)彼女と向かい合った I faced her with a table *between* us. / 私たちは5年の時を隔てて再会した We met again *after* five years.

へたばる get* tired out, get exhausted ∥きつい練習でへたばった I *got exhausted from* hard training.

へたへた その知らせを聞くと彼はその場にへたへたと座り込んだ(→力なく崩れるように座り込んだ) When he heard the news, he *sat down* to the floor *weakly*.

べたべた ❶【べたつく】手のひらが汗でべたべたしている My palm *is sticky* with sweat.
❷【やたらに塗る・はる】べたべた(→厚く)化粧をする paint *one's* face *thickly* / 彼は壁に写真をべたべた(→至る所に)はった He plastered the wall *all over* with photos. / 彼女はパンにバターをべたべたと塗った She spread butter *thick(ly)* on a slice of bread.
❸【まとわりつく】人前でべたべたするカップルを見ても私は気にならない It doesn't bother me to see couples *making out* in public. / べたべたくっつくな Don't *stick* [*cling*] *to* me.

ぺたぺた だれかが廊下をぺたぺた歩く音が聞こえた I heard someone walking *pit-a-pat* along the hallway.

べたぼめ べた褒め 先生は彼女の作品をべたぼめした The teacher *praised* her work *very highly*.

へたりこむ へたり込む あまりのショックに彼はその場にへたり込んだ He was so shocked that he *sank* to the ground.

ペダル pedal Ⓒ ◆自転車のペダルを踏む *pedal one's* bicycle

ぺたん 封筒に切手をぺたんとはる *stick* a stamp on an envelope(✧「ぺたん」は特に訳さない) / 畳にぺたんと座る sit *flat* on tatami

ペチカ ⚠ Russian stove Ⓒ (✧日本語はロシア語の pechka から)

ペチコート petticoat Ⓒ

へちま 糸瓜 loofa(h) Ⓒ

ぺちゃくちゃ 私たちは映画スターについてぺちゃくちゃおしゃべりしていた We *were chatting* about film stars.

ぺちゃぺちゃ 子猫がミルクをぺちゃぺちゃなめている The kitten *is lapping* (*up*) the milk.

ぺちゃんこ 空き缶を踏んでぺちゃんこにした I stepped on the empty can and *flattened* it. / 彼の帽子はぺちゃんこになってしまった His hat *got crushed flat*. / 私の家はその地震でぺちゃんこになってしまった My house *collapsed* in the earthquake. / The earthquake *flattened* my house. / 車はぺちゃんこになったが運転手は一命を取り留めた The car was *a complete write-off*, but the driver narrowly escaped death.

べつ 別
❶【ほか】(ほかのもの) another ——別の(もう一つの) another; (他の) other; (異なった) different
別の大きな問題が持ち上がった *Another* big problem reared its head.
別の話題に変えようよ Shall we switch the talk to *another* subject?
このセーターは少し大きすぎます。別のを見せてください This sweater is a little too big. Show me *another*.
別の約束がなければあなたといっしょに行くのですが I would go with you, only (that) I have *another* appointment.
おもしろい考えですが, それはまた別の話です It's an interesting idea, but that's *another* story.
知っていることと教えることは全く別のことだ To know is one thing, to teach is quite *another* (*thing*).
それはまたいつか別のときに話そう Let's talk about it some *other* time.
行き詰まったときには, 別の観点から問題を見るとよい You should look at a problem from a *different* viewpoint if you reach a deadlock.
◆みんな, スパゲッティにするの? それなら私は別の物にする Are you all going to order spaghetti? Then I'll have something *else*. / 私は間違って別の番号をダイヤルしてしまった I dialed a *wrong* number by mistake.
🅔「太田さん, お願いします」「申しわけありませんが, ただ今別の電話に出ています」"May I speak to Ms. Ota?" "I'm sorry, but she's on *another* line now."

❷【区別】
表示価格とは別に(→に加えて)消費税を払わなければならない You must pay the consumption tax *in addition to* the marked price.
このマラソン大会は男女の別なく参加できる Anybody can take part in this marathon race *regardless of* their sex.
このチョコレートだけ別に包んでもらえますか Would you please wrap this chocolate *separately*?
うちでは家族がそれぞれ別の(→自分の)メールアドレスを持っている All of my family have our *own* e-mail addresses.
私たちはグループ別にその問題に取り組んでいる We are working on the problem *in groups*.
彼はすべての本をテーマ別に(→テーマに従って)分類した He divided all the books *by subject*.
このペンションでは朝食は別料金だ You have to pay *extra* for breakfast at this lodge.

❸【特別】
あすは別に何もすることがありません I have nothing *particular* to do tomorrow.
別にあなたを批判しようとしたわけではない I

didn't intend *any* criticism (of you).
- 「何か悩みでもあるの」「いや，別に」 "Are you worried about anything?" "No, *not particularly*."
- 「どうかしたの」「別に」 "Is something wrong?" "*Nothing* (*in particular*)."

❹【除外】
郵便屋さんは別にして，午前中はだれも家に来なかった *Apart* [*Aside*] *from* a mail carrier, nobody came to the house in the morning.
冗談は別にして，あなたは本当に落語家になりたいの？ *Joking aside* [*apart*], do you really want to be a *rakugoka*?
ときどき遅刻する点を別にすれば，健太はいい友達だ Kenta is a good friend *except* that he is sometimes late.

べつうり 別売 アダプターは別売になります The adapter *is sold separately*.

べっかく 別格 ──別格の (特別な) special; (例外的な) exceptional ‖別格の待遇を受ける be given *special* [*exceptional*] treatment
◆このレストランは別格だ This restaurant *is in a class of its own*.

べっかん 別館 annex ◎ ‖市役所別館 *an annex* to the city hall

べっきょ 別居 separation ◎
◆その夫婦は結局別居することにした The couple decided to *separate* [*live separately*] in the end. / 彼は家族と別居して北海道で働いている He's working in Hokkaido, *living apart from* his family.

べっけんたいほ 別件逮捕 (an) arrest on a different charge ◆別件逮捕する *arrest a person on a different charge*

べっこう¹ 別項 応募に必要な条件は別項にまとめられています The requirements for application are blocked as *a separate paragraph*.

べっこう² 鼈甲 tortoiseshell ◎ ‖べっ甲細工 tortoiseshell work

べっさつ 別冊 separate volume ◎; (雑誌などの) extra number [issue] ◎ ◆雑誌の別冊付録 *a supplement* to a magazine

べっし¹ 別紙 attached sheet [paper] ◎ ‖詳細は別紙を参照 See *attached sheet* for details.

べっし² 蔑視 ──蔑視する despise ⊕, (口語的に) look down on *a person* ⇒けいべつ

べっしつ 別室 (もう一つの部屋) another room; (分かれた部屋) separate room ◎

べっしゅ 別種 別種の問題 a problem *of another* [*different*] *kind*

べつじょう 別状・別条 彼女は病院に運ばれたが，命に別状はないようだ She was taken to the hospital, but seems to *be in no danger* of losing her life.

べつじん 別人 彼は昔の彼とはすっかり別人だ He looks quite *different* from what he used to be. (◆主に外見の変化をいう場合．内面も含むなら He has changed a lot. などという) / その事件の首謀者は逮捕された男とは別人だった The instigator of the case was another [*a different*] *person* from the man who had been arrested. / 彼が研究をしているときは別人だ He is *a different man* when he is doing research.

べっせい 別姓 その国では夫婦別姓が認められている In that country married couples are allowed *separate surnames*.

べっせかい 別世界 海に潜(%)るとそこは全くの別世界だった I was in *a quite different world* once I dived into the sea.

べっそう 別荘 (小さな) cottage ◎; (大きな) villa ◎ ‖週末は別荘でのんびり過ごした I spent a quiet weekend at *my cottage*.
‖貸し別荘 a rental cottage

べったり 彼のTシャツには絵の具がべったり(→一面に)ついていた His T-shirt was stained *all over* with paint. / そのポスターは塀にべったりはりついていて，はがれなかった The poster stuck so *fast* to the wall that I couldn't tear it off. / その子供はどこへ行っても母親にべったりくっついている The child *sticks* [*clings*] *to* his mother wherever he goes.

べつだん 別段 別段異状は認められない Nothing is wrong *in particular*.

へっちゃら このくらいのけがはへっちゃらだ An injury like this *is nothing to me*.

べってんち 別天地 different world ◎, another world ◎ ⇒べっせかい

ヘッド (ゴルフクラブの) head ◎; (テープレコーダーの) (magnetic) head ◎
‖ヘッドギア headgear / ヘッドコーチ a head coach / ヘッドスライディング a head-first sliding / ヘッドハンティング head-hunting / ヘッドレスト a headrest

べっと 別途 このサービスは別途(→追加の)料金がかかります This service is an *additional charge*. / 消費税は別途(→別に)申し受けます You'll be charged consumption tax *separately*.

ベッド bed ◎ ◎
ベッドで寝る sleep in *a bed* / ベッドに入る[から出る] get into [out of] *bed* / ベッドを整える make a [*one's*] *bed*
彼女は赤ん坊をベッドに寝かせた She laid her baby on the bed.
目覚ましが鳴ると彼女はベッドから飛び起きた When the alarm went off, she sprang out of *bed*.
‖ベッドカバー a bedspread / ベッドシーン a bedroom scene / ベッドタウン a bedroom town [suburb] / ベッドルーム a bedroom / ウオーターベッド a waterbed / シングルベッド a single bed / ソファーベッド a sofa-bed / ダブルベッド a double bed / ツインベッド a twin bed / 二段ベッド a bunk bed

ペット pet ◎ ⇒ 場面・状況別会話 p.1720 ‖ペットに犬を飼う have [keep] a dog as *a pet* / ペットお断り (掲示) *No Pets Allowed*
- 「何かペットを飼ってますか」「はい，猫を2匹飼ってます」 "Do you have any *pets*?" "Yes, I have two cats."
‖ペットショップ a pet shop / ペットフード

pet food
ペットボトル plastic [PET] bottle [C]
ヘッドホン headphones ‖ヘッドホンで音楽を聴く listen to music on *headphones*
ヘッドライト headlight [C] 《しばしば複数形 ~s》
べっとり 彼のシャツにはペンキがべっとりついていた His shirt *was smeared with* paint.
べつに 別に 別に買いたい物はありません I don't want to buy anything *in particular*. ⇒べつ
べっぴょう 別表 attached table [C]
へっぴりごし へっぴり腰 彼女はへっぴり腰でスキーをしていた She was skiing *with her rear stuck out*.
べつびん 別便 請求書は別便で送ります I'll send the bill *in a separate envelope*.
べつべつ 別々 ──別々の separate; (異なる) different; (おのおのの) respective ──別々に separately; (離れて) apart ‖卒業後彼らは別々の道に進んだ They went their *separate* [*respective*] ways after graduation. / その双子は別々の学校に通っている The twins go to *different* schools. / 兄は私たちとは別々に暮らしている My brother lives *apart from* us. / 別々に包んでもらえますか Would you wrap them *separately*? / 勘定は別々でお願いします *Separate* checks, please.
べつめい 別名 another name; (特に犯罪者の) alias [C] ‖黒姫山には「信濃富士」という別名がある Mt. Kurohime has *another name*, "Shinano-Fuji."
べつもんだい 別問題 確かに猿は人の言葉をしゃべらないが, 何も考えていないかどうかは別問題だ It is true that monkeys don't speak human language, but it is *another question* whether they think or not.
へつらい flattery [U]
へつらう flatter [他] [自], 《口語的》 play [make*] up to *a person* ‖上司にへつらう *flatter* [*play up to*] *one's* boss
べつり 別離 parting [U] [C] ‖恋人との別離を嘆く grieve over *parting with one's* lover
ヘディング ⚠〖サッカー〗 header [C] ──ヘディングする head [他] ‖ボールをヘディングする *head* a ball / 中山はヘディングシュートを決めた Nakayama *scored with a header*. / 彼のヘディングは惜しくもバーの上を越えた Unfortunately his *header* went over the bar.
ベテラン ⚠(熟練者) expert [C]; (老練家) veteran [C] (❖veteran は《米》ではしばしば「退役軍人」の意味で使われるので注意が必要) ──ベテランの expert; (経験を積んだ) experienced ‖ベテランパイロット an *expert* [an *experienced*, a *veteran*] pilot / 彼女はその道のベテランだ She is *an expert* [*a veteran*] in the field.
ぺてん swindle [C], trick [C] ◆私はぺてんにかかって100万円も取られた I *was swindled* [*cheated*] out of no less than a million yen. / 母はぺてんにかかって偽物のダイヤモンドを買わされた My mother *was tricked* [*cheated*] into buying a false diamond.
‖ぺてん師 a swindler, a con artist
へど 反吐 vomit [U] ──へどを吐く vomit [自] [他], 《口語的》 throw* up ◆あいつの名前を聞いただけでへどが出そうだ The mere mention of his name 「*is disgusting* [*makes me sick*].
べとつく ヘアワックスで手がべとついている My hands *are sticky* with hair wax.
ベトナム Vietnam (❖公式名 the Socialist Republic of Vietnam) ──ベトナム人 Vietnamese [C] (複~) ──ベトナム語 Vietnamese [U] ──ベトナム(人[語])の Vietnamese ‖ベトナム戦争 the Vietnam War
へとへと 新居への引っ越しでへとへとだ I'm 「*tired out* [*exhausted*] from moving to my new house.
べとべと 手がのりでべとべとだ My hands are *sticky* with glue. / 緊張して手が汗でべとべとだった I got nervous and my hands were *sticky* with sweat.
へどろ sludge [U], slime [U] ‖湖の底は厚いへどろで覆われていた The bottom of the lake was covered with thick *sludge*.
へなへな その知らせを聞いて彼女はへなへなと座り込んでしまった She *sank down* to the floor when she heard the news. / こんなへなへなの板では棚は作れないよ You can't make a shelf with these *thin, soft* sheets of wood.
ペナルティー penalty [C] ‖違反者に罰金10万円のペナルティーを科す impose *a penalty* of 100,000 yen on an offender
‖ペナルティーエリア a penalty area / ペナルティーキック a penalty kick
ペナント pennant [C] ‖ペナントを争う compete for *the pennant*
‖ペナントレース a pennant race
べに 紅 紅をさす(→口紅を塗る) put on *lipstick*
‖紅色 crimson / ベニザケ (a) sockeye salmon / 紅ショウガ red pickled ginger / 薄紅色 light crimson
ペニー penny [C] (複 pence, pennies)

[語法]
英国の通貨単位で100分の1ポンド(pound)を指す. 略語は p. 金額の複数形は pence, 硬貨そのものの複数形には pennies を用いる. また, 米国やカナダでは1セント貨(cent)を指して用いる.

ペニシリン penicillin [U]
ベニス Venice (❖イタリアの都市)
ペニス penis [C]
ベニヤいた ベニヤ板 ⚠plywood [U] (❖英語の veneer は, 合板の表面の「化粧板」の意味)
ベネルックス Benelux (❖ベルギー (Belgium), オランダ (the Netherlands), ルクセンブルク (Luxembourg) の3国の総称)
ペパーミント 〖植物〗 peppermint [U] ‖ペパーミント味のガム chewing gum with a *peppermint* flavor
へばりつく stick* to ..., cling* to ..., become* attached to ... ‖トカゲが岩にへばりついていた A lizard *was sticking* [*clinging, at-*

へ

へばる

tached] to a rock. / 彼女はへばりつくようにしてショーウインドウをのぞいていた She was clinging to the show window and looking into it.

へばる get* 「tired out [worn out]」 / うちの犬はこの暑さでへばっている My dog is worn out by the heat.

へび 蛇 snake ⓒ, 《文語》serpent ⓒ ◆snakeより大型で威厳があるものノ / 大きな蛇が地面をはっていた A big snake was crawling on the ground. / その蛇はとぐろを巻いた The snake coiled (up).

∥蛇皮 snakeskin / 蛇使い a snake charmer / ウミヘビ a sea snake / ガラガラヘビ a rattlesnake / 毒蛇 a poisonous [venomous] snake / ニシキヘビ a python

慣用表現 彼は先生の前では蛇ににらまれた蛙(がえる)のようにびくりとも動かなかった He didn't move a bit in front of the teacher like a frog in front of a snake.

関連語 アオダイショウ a common blue-green snake / アナコンダ an anaconda / コブラ a cobra / ハブ a habu, a pit viper / ボア a boa / マムシ an adder / ヤマカガシ a grass snake

ヘビー それはかなりヘビーな仕事だ It is quite a heavy task. / 彼が私に話した悩みはヘビーな内容だった The problems that he told me about were serious.

∥ヘビー級 the heavyweight division (◆ヘビー級の選手は a heavyweight) / ヘビースモーカー a heavy [chain] smoker / ヘビーメタル《音楽》heavy metal

ベビー baby ⓒ ∥ベビーカー（箱型の）《米》a baby carriage [buggy], 《英》a pram; (いす型の)《米》a stroller, 《英》a pushchair / ベビーサークル《米》a playpen (◆×baby circle とはいわない) / ベビーシッター a baby-sitter / ベビーパウダー baby powder / ベビーフード baby food / ベビーブーム a baby boom / ベビー服 babies' wear / ベビーベッド《米》a crib, 《英》a cot (◆×baby bed とはいわない) / ベビー用品 baby goods / 試験管ベビー a test-tube baby

ヘビメタ（ヘビーメタル）heavy metal Ⓤ

ヘブライご ヘブライ語 Hebrew Ⓤ

へべれけ その男性はへべれけに酔っ払っていた The man was helplessly [terribly, dead] drunk.

へぼ あんなへぼ役者のどこがいいんだ How come you like such a clumsy [an awkward, a shabby] actor?

ヘボンしき ヘボン式 ヘボン式ローマ字つづりでは,「し」は si でなく shi とつづる In the Hepburn system of Romanization, the Japanese letter "し" is spelled "shi," not "si."

へま blunder ⓒ / あいつはひどいへまをやらかした He made an awful blunder.

ヘモグロビン《生化学》hemoglobin Ⓤ

へや 部屋

❶ 〖住居・ホテルの〗 room ⓒ; (アパートなどの貸間)《米》apartment ⓒ, 《英》flat ⓒ

⇒ 場面・状況別会話 p.1724

〖～の(部屋)〗
広い[狭い]部屋 a large [small] room / 片づいた[散らかった]部屋 an orderly [a messy] room / 奥の部屋 an inner room / 階上の部屋 the room above / 5メートル四方の部屋 a room five meters square

僕は畳の部屋にじゅうたんを敷くつもりだ I'll lay a carpet in my tatami room.

〖部屋を・に〗
部屋に入る[を出る] enter [go out of] a room
ホテルに部屋を予約した I have reserved a room at a hotel.
私は鹿島さんに部屋を借りている I rent a room [an apartment] from Mr. Kashima.

〖部屋が・は〗
僕の部屋は北向きだ My room faces north.
その部屋はがらんとしていた The room was empty.
彼の部屋は10階にある His room [apartment] is (located) on the 10th floor.

〖部屋の〗
彼女は部屋の明かりをつけた She turned on the light in her room.
自分の部屋の掃除をしなさい Clean your room.

〖その他〗
ホテルの部屋割りをどうしようか考えています I'm thinking of how to assign rooms at the hotel.
薬のにおいが部屋中に満ちていた The room was filled with the odor of medicine.
私たちは高い[安い]部屋代を払っている We pay a high [low] rent for our room.

❷ 〖相撲〗 stable
時津風部屋 the Tokitsukaze stable

∥部屋着（化粧着）a dressing gown; (くつろぎ着）comfortable clothes / 空き部屋 a vacant room / 子供部屋 a children's room / (育児室) a nursery / 勉強部屋(自室) one's (bed)room; (書斎) a study / 屋根裏部屋 an attic

へら 箆 (料理・絵の具などの) spatula ⓒ; (裁縫の) sewing spatula ⓒ / 竹べら a bamboo spatula / 靴べら a shoehorn

へらす 減らす reduce ⓗ, lessen ⓗ; (消費量などを) cut* down (on ...); (徐々に) decrease ⓗ; (体重を) lose* ⓗ

電気の消費量を15パーセント減らす reduce [cut down (on)] electricity consumption by 15 percent
そのバンドはコンサートで演奏する曲数を減らした The band reduced the (number of) tunes they would play at the concert.
警察は犯罪を減らすよう努力している The police are trying to reduce [lessen, decrease] crime.
その料理に入れる肉を200グラムから150グラムに減らした I reduced the meat in the dish from 200 to 150 grams.
塩分を減らすことで病気になる危険性を減らすことができる Reducing [Cutting down (on)] salt can reduce [lessen] the risk of developing diseases.

彼は毎日ジョギングをして体重を減らした He *has lost* weight by jogging every day.

へらずぐち 減らず口 減らず口をたたくな (→憎まれ口をきくな) *Stop saying spiteful [nasty] things.*／ (→口答えするな) *Stop talking back to me.*

へらぶな 箆鮒〔魚〕 deep-bodied crucian carp ⓒ

へらへら 質問されても彼はへらへら笑っているだけだった Asked questions, he did nothing but *smile stupidly*.

ぺらぺら 先生が教室に入ってきても生徒たちはまだぺらぺらおしゃべりをしていた Students didn't stop *chattering* even when their teacher came into the classroom.／ 彼女は秘密にしておいてほしいことでもぺらぺら(→軽はずみに)しゃべってしまう She *thoughtlessly lets out to anybody* what you want her to keep secret.

ぺらぺら ❶【話す様子】(流暢(りゅうちょう)に) fluently ∥ ジャックは日本語がぺらぺらだ Jack speaks Japanese *fluently*.／ Jack is a *fluent* speaker of Japanese.
◆セールスマンはぺらぺらとまくしたて、彼女にそれを買わせた The salesman *gave her a spiel [sales pitch]* and made her buy it.
❷【薄い】──ぺらぺらの thin ∥ ぺらぺらの板 a *thin* sheet of board
❸【ページをくる様子】 辞書をぺらぺらめくる *leaf through* a dictionary

べらぼう──べらぼうな (値段が法外な) unreasonable；(ものすごい) terrible, awful──べらぼうに unreasonably; terribly, awfully ∥ べらぼうな値段 an *unreasonable* [a *terribly high*] price ∥ その力士はべらぼうに強い。The sumo wrestler is *terribly [awfully]* strong.

ベランダ ⚠(2階以上にある) balcony ⓒ；(建物1階の側面にある) veranda(h) ⓒ,《米》 porch ⇨ えんがわ 図版

へり 縁 (道・家具などの) edge ⓒ；(グラス・わんなどの) brim ⓒ；(ある平面の) border ⓒ；(布・衣服の) hem ⓒ ∥ このたんすはへりを丸くしてある This chest of drawers has round *edges*.／ This chest of drawers is round-*edged*.／ コップはへりが欠けていた There was a chip on the *brim* of the glass.

ヘリウム〔化学〕 helium ⓤ (✦元素記号 He)

ペリカン pelican ⓒ

へりくだる abase [humble] *oneself*, be modest [humble] ◆へりくだった言葉づかいをする use *modest [humble]* language

へりくつ 屁理屈(筋の通らない理屈) sham logic ⓒ, sophistry ⓤ；(逃げ口上・難癖(なんくせ)) quibble ⓒ ∥ あいつはいつも屁理屈をこねて自分の失敗を言い逃れようとする He always tries to explain his faults away by using「*sham logic [sophistries, quibbles]*.
◆あいつは屁理屈ばかりで自分では何もしようとしない He *quibbles* a lot, but wouldn't do anything by himself.

ヘリコプター helicopter ⓒ,《口語的》copter ⓒ,《口語的》chopper ⓒ ∥ ヘリコプターが1機私の頭上で旋回した *A helicopter* wheeled in the air above me.

ヘリポート heliport ⓒ

へる¹ 減る
❶【数量などが】 decrease ⓘ (↔increase)；(徐々に) dwindle ⓘ, decline ⓘ；(急激に) fall* ⓘ；(体重が) lose* ⓘ (↔gain)；(すり減る) wear* ⓘ
その種の事件は数の上では減ってきている Cases of that kind *have been decreasing* in number.／ Cases of that kind *have been getting fewer*.
その魚の水揚げは年々減り続けている The catch [haul] of the fish *keeps decreasing* year by year.
村の人口は2,000人に減った The population of the village *decreased [dwindled, declined]* to 2,000.
そのおもちゃの需要は急激に減ってしまった The demand for the toy *has fallen [declined]* sharply.
彼女はこの2か月で5キロ体重が減った She *has lost* five kilograms in the last two months.
彼はかかとの減った靴を履いている He wears shoes with their heels *worn* (out).
◆あっ、私のシャンプーが減っている Oh, my shampoo *is disappearing*!／ ねえ、ちょっと見せてくれたっていいじゃない。減るもんじゃなし (→自分のことばかり考えないで) Come on, let me have a look. Don't be selfish!
❷【腹が】
おなかが減って死にそうだ I'm dying of *hunger*.／ I'm *starved* to death.
慣用表現 私が小さいころよく母親は「口の減らない子だね」(→いつも口答えする)と言って困った顔をした When I was a little child, my mother often said embarrassedly to me "*You are always talking back to me*."

へる² 経る ❶【時・年月】 pass ⓘ, go* by ∥ 事件から30年を経てついに真相が明かされた The truth about the incident was made clear at last after 30 years *had passed [gone by]*.／ 時を経るに従い、人々はそのことを忘れていった People gradually forgot it as time *passed [went by]*.
◆町には年代を経た(→古い)寺社がたくさんある There're many *old [ancient]* temples and shrines in the town.
❷【過程】 go* through ...; (経験する) experience ⓘ ∥ こみ入った手続きを経る *go through* a complicated procedure ∥ 彼は様々な困難を経て、ついにその論文を書き上げた He has finished up the thesis by「*going through [experiencing]*」various difficulties.
❸【場所】 札幌を出た車は帯広を経て釧路にたどり着いた The car, which had started from Sapporo, reached Kushiro「*passing through [via, by way of]*」Obihiro.

ベル bell ⓒ；(玄関などの) doorbell ⓒ ∥ 私はベルを鳴らした I rang *the bell [doorbell]*.／ 終了時間になればベルが鳴ります A bell will ring

when the time is up. / ベルが鳴ると彼女は玄関へ飛んでいった When *the doorbell* rang, she flew to the door.
‖カウベル a cowbell / 非常ベル an emergency [alarm] bell / ポケットベル a beeper, a pager, 《英》a bleeper(❖「ポケットベル」は和製英語)

ベルギー Belgium(❖公式名 the Kingdom of Belgium) ‖ベルギー人 Belgian ◯ ──ベルギー(人)の Belgian

ベルサイユ Versailles(❖フランスの都市) ‖ベルサイユ宮殿 the Palace of Versailles

ヘルシー ヘルシーな(健康によい) healthy, healthful
‖ヘルシーフード healthy food

ペルシャ Persia(❖イランの旧称) ──ペルシャ語 Persian ⓤ ──ペルシャ(語)の Persian ‖ペルシャじゅうたん a Persian carpet / ペルシャネコ a Persian cat / ペルシャ湾 the Persian Gulf

ヘルシンキ Helsinki(❖フィンランドの首都)

ヘルス (健康) health ⓤ
‖ヘルスケア health care

ヘルスセンター ⚠ recreation center ◯(❖英語の health center は「診療所・保健所」の意味)

ヘルスメーター ⚠ (bathroom) scale《しばしば複数形 ~s》(❖「ヘルスメーター」は和製英語)

ヘルツ (振動数・周波数の単位) hertz ◯ 《複 ~》《略語》Hz) ‖キロヘルツ a kilohertz(❖1,000ヘルツ;《略語》kHz) / メガヘルツ a megahertz(❖100万ヘルツ;《略語》MHz)

ベルト belt ◯; (シートベルト) seat belt ◯ ‖ベルトをする[はずす] "put on [take off] *a belt*" / 彼はズボンのベルトをきつくした[ゆるめた] He tightened [loosened] *his belt*. / 座席のベルトをお締めください Please fasten *your seat belts*.
‖ベルト穴 a punch hole / ベル通し a belt loop / ガーターベルト 《米》a garter belt, 《英》a suspender belt / チャンピオンベルト a champion belt

ベルトコンベヤー ⚠ conveyor (belt) ◯

ヘルニア 〖医学〗hernia ◯ⓤ, 〖医学〗rupture ◯ⓤ ‖椎間板(ついかんばん)ヘルニア 〖医学〗a slipped disc

ヘルパー (助力者・お手伝いさん) helper ◯; (ホームヘルパー)《米》in-home aide ◯, 《英》home help ◯

ベルファスト Belfast(❖英国の都市)

ヘルペス 〖医学〗herpes ⓤ

ベルベット velvet ⓤ

ベルボーイ bellperson ◯, bellboy ◯, 《米》bellhop ◯, 《英》page ◯

ベルボトム bell-bottoms
◆ベルボトムのジーンズ bell-bottom jeans

ヘルメット helmet ◯; (レース用の) crash helmet ◯; (工事用の) hard hat ◯

ベルリン Berlin(❖ドイツの首都) ‖ベルリンの壁 the *Berlin* Wall

ベルン Bern(❖スイスの首都)

ベレー beret [bəréɪ] ◯(❖フランス語から)
‖グリーンベレー a Green Beret

ヘロイン heroin ⓤ

ぺろぺろ 犬は僕の顔をぺろぺろなめた My dog *licked* my face *sloppily*. / 父はぺろぺろに酔っ払っていた My father was *dead* [*blind*] drunk.

ぺろぺろ トカゲは舌をぺろぺろさせていた The lizard *repeatedly stuck out* its tongue. / 彼女はアイスのふたの裏側をぺろぺろなめた She *licked* the inner side of the lid of the ice cream cup.

ぺろり 少年はソフトクリームをぺろりとなめた The boy *took a big lick of* his soft ice cream. / 彼女は失敗してぺろりと舌を出した She *stuck out her tongue in embarrassment* when she failed. / 彼は3人前の寿司(し)をぺろりと平らげた He *ate up* sushi for three people 「*very easily* [*in an instant*].

へん¹ 変

❶【ふつうでない】──変な strange; odd; funny; peculiar; eccentric; (怪しい) suspicious; (調子が悪い) wrong(❖名詞の前では用いない) ──変に strangely, in a strange way

> strange: なじみのない物事, 不自然な物事, 理解・説明の困難な物事などをいう一般的な語.
> odd: 標準・慣習からずれていることをいう.
> funny: 疑わしさ, 困惑を伴う場合に用いる. また「おかしな, こっけいな」の意味もある.
> peculiar: ほかと共有しない性質を示していることをいう. 特に不快感を伴う場合に用いる.
> eccentric: 常軌を逸して風変わりなことをいう.

彼は本当に変なやつだ He's really a *strange* [an *odd*, a *funny*, a *peculiar*, an *eccentric*] person.(❖funny は「こっけいな」の意味にもとれる)

牛乳の味が変だ The milk tastes *strange* [*funny*].

私には変な癖(くせ)がある I have a *strange* [an *odd*, a *funny*, a *peculiar*] habit.

彼の報告には何か変なところがある There is something *strange* [*odd*, *funny*, *suspicious*] in his report.

彼がこんなに早く来るなんて変だな It's *strange* [*funny*] that he should come so early.

変な男が家の周りをうろついている A *strange* [*suspicious*] man is walking around outside my house.

だれかが変なうわさを広めているようだ Somebody seems to be spreading a *strange* rumor.

彼はゆうべちょっと様子が変だった He was acting a bit *strange* last night.

そのひどい服を着ていた私は変な目で見られた People gave me a *suspicious* look when I wore that loud dress.

CDプレーヤーが変なんだ. ちょっと見てもらえないかな Something *is wrong* with my CD player. Can you check it?

きょうの彼は変に明るい He is *strangely* cheer-

ful today.
◆あいつ, 頭が変なんじゃない? He must *be crazy*./ 強烈なにおいに鼻が変になりそうだった I *almost lost my sense of smell* because of the stench./ 君がそんな弱音を吐くなんて変だよ(→君らしくない) It's *unlike* you to whine like this./ 何も悪いことをしていないのに怒られたなんて, そんなの変だよ(→道理に合わない) It *was unreasonable* that you were scolded when you had done nothing wrong.

💬「きょう亜由美ちゃんに会ったよ」「それは変だ. 今はロンドンにいるはずなのに」"I saw Ayumi today." "That's *strange* [*funny*]. She is supposed to be in London now."

💬「この髪型どう」「あはは, 変なの」"How do you like this hairstyle?" "Ha-ha. *Crazy* [*Funny*]!"

❷【事件】
桜田門外の変 *the incident* (which took place) in front of the Sakurada Gate of Edo Castle

❸【音楽の】
変ロ長調の曲 a tune in B *flat* major
‖変音記号【音楽】a flat

へん² 辺 ❶【多角形の】side ⓒ ‖正方形は4つの同じ長さの辺をもつ A square has four equal *sides*.

❷【場所】このへんにコンビニはありませんか Is there any convenience store「*around here* [*near here, in this neighborhood*]/ その店はどこらへんにあったの Where「was the store [did you find the store]?/ 橋のへんで彼らに追いつくだろう We'll catch up with them *near* the bridge.

💬「ねえ, 僕のペンどこにあるか知らない」「そのへんにあったと思うけど」"Hey, do you know where my pen is?" "Guess I've seen it *around* [*over*] *there*."

❸【漠然と示す事柄】そのへんのことはよく分からないので I don't know *about* it well.

❹【程度】テレビゲームはこのへんでやめておこう I'm going to stop playing the video game *now* [*here*]./ きょうはこのへんで終わりにしましょう Let's call it a day./ *So much for today*.(❖前者は仕事などに関して用いる. 後者は先生が授業の終わりを告げて用いる)

へん³ 偏 the left-hand radical of a *kanji*

へん⁴(不満や疑いを表して) humph [hʌ́mf];(軽蔑・いらだち・不信などを表して) bah

-へん¹ -編 高橋教授編の論文集 a collection of papers *edited* [*compiled*] *by* Professor Takahashi/ この本は彼の詩5編を収録している This book has "five of his poems [five *pieces* of his poetry]" in it./ その物語は3編に分かれている The story is divided into three *parts*./ このマニュアルは入門編と応用編に分かれている This manual is in two *parts*, *introductory* and *advanced*.

-へん² -遍 time ⓒ(❖3回以降は三度のようにいうが, 1回は once, 2回は twice というのがふつう) ➡かい(回), ど

べん¹ 便 ❶【便利なこと】convenience ⓤ;(バスなどの) service ⓒⓤ ‖その図書館は利用者の便にかなえて閉館時刻を遅くした They kept the library open later for its users' *convenience*./ うちの近辺はバスの便がよい[悪い] Bus *service* is good [poor] around my house.

◆私の学校は駅に近くて交通の便がよい My school *is convenient* to the station./ その博物館は交通の便がよい(→多くの交通機関がある) The museum *is served by many forms of transportation*./ The museum *is accessible via many transportation services*.

❷【便通】《公式的》excrement ⓤ, feces,《医学》stools ‖ここ数日便が柔らかい[硬い] I've had soft [hard] *stools* for the last several days./ けさ便に血が混じっていた I had「blood in *my stools* [a bloody *stool*] this morning.
‖血便 bloody stools/ 軟便 soft [loose] stools

べん² 弁 ❶【話すこと】田中校長就任の弁 *the* inaugural *address* by Principal Tanaka/ 彼女は弁が立つ She *is a fluent* [*an eloquent*] *speaker*./ 彼は弁を弄(㌼)して事故の責任は自分にはないと主張した(→言い逃れようとした) He tried to *talk his way out of responsibility* for the accident.

❷【その地方の言葉】(なまり) accent ⓒ;(方言) dialect ⓒⓤ ‖彼は名古屋弁で話す He speaks「with *the* Nagoya *accent* [in *the* Nagoya *dialect*].

❸【液体・気体の流れを調節するもの】valve ⓒ ‖安全弁 a safety *valve*

❹【花びら】petal ⓒ

ペン pen ⓒ
太い[細い]ペン a broad [fine] *pen*/ 油性[水性]ペン a *pen* with oil-based [water-based] ink
名前をペンで書いてください Please write your name *with a pen*.
そのペンは書きやすかった The *pen* wrote well./ The *pen* was easy to write with.
‖ペン画 a pen-and-ink drawing/ ペン先 a nib, a pen point/ ペン習字 penmanship/ ペンだこ a callus on a finger made by much writing/ ペンネーム a pen name, a pseudonym/ ペンフレンド a pen pal,《英》a pen-friend/ ペンライト a penlight/ 蛍光ペン a highlighter/ サインペン a felt-tip(ped) pen/ 羽ペン a quill/ ボールペン a ballpoint pen

[慣用表現] ペンは剣よりも強し *The pen is mightier than the sword.*/ その作家はペンを折る(→執筆活動を終える)決心を固めた The writer decided to *put an end to his writing career*./ 彼はその事件を世に知らしめるためにペンをとった He *put* [*set*] *pen to paper* in order to inform people of the incident./ アイディアが浮かぶと彼女はものすごい勢いで原稿用紙にペンを走らせた When she came up with an idea, she started *writing* energetically *on* the manuscript paper.

へんあい 偏愛 favoritism ⓤ, favor,《英》favour, partiality 《また a ～》 ──偏愛する favor, 《英》 favour

へんあつ 変圧
∥変圧器 【電気】 a transformer

へんい 変異 【生物】 variation
∥変異体 (動植物の) a variation, a variant, a sport / 突然変異 (a) mutation / 突然変異体 a mutant

べんい 便意 便意をもよおす *feel the need to* 「*move one's bowels* [*answer the call of nature*]

へんおんどうぶつ 変温動物 【動物】 poikilotherm

へんか 変化

change; (一様・単調でなくなること) variation; (多様性) variety 《また a ～》; (構造などが完全に変わること) transformation ──変化する change; vary (❖ change, vary は「変化させる」の意味の他動詞としても用いられる); become* transformed

天候の変化 *a change* in the weather / 心境の変化 *a change* of heart / 周囲の変化 *changes* around *a person* / 生活に変化をもたらす bring about *a change* [*variation*] in *one's* life / 仕事に変化をつける add variety to [*vary*] *one's* work

私たちはここ20年間で非常に多くの変化を目にしてきた We have seen a great many *changes* in the past 20 years.

彼女は私の態度の変化に気づいていた She perceived *a change* in my manner.

その植物は環境の変化に弱い The plant is easily damaged by environmental *changes*.

水は温度の変化に伴い形態を変化させる Water *varies* its form as the temperature *changes*.

状況は徐々に変化しつつある The situation *is* gradually *changing*.

その林はわずか数年ですっかり住宅地へと変化を遂げた The woods *have been transformed* completely into a residential area in only a few years.

◆変化に富んだ景色 *a varied* landscape / 私の仕事は変化に乏しい My work *is monotonous.* / 日本は四季の変化に富んでいる Japan has four *very distinct* seasons.

🖝「あれからどうなった」「変化なし」 "What's happened since then?" "*Nothing's changed*."

コロケーション –change–
【形容詞＋～】 大きな～ a great [big] change / 激しい～ a violent change / 際立った～ a striking change / それと分かる～ a noticeable change / わずかな～ a subtle change / 急激な～ a drastic change / 突然の～ a sudden change / 絶え間ない～ continual changes / めまぐるしい～ kaleidoscopic changes / ゆっくりとした～ a slow change / ゆるやかな～ gradual changes

---

∥変化球 a breaking ball / 化学変化 (a) chemical change / 規則変化 regular conjugation / 不規則変化 【文法】 irregular conjugation

べんかい 弁解; (正当化) justification; (釈明) explanation ──弁解する make* an excuse, excuse (*oneself*); justify; explain away /彼女は待ち合わせに遅れたことをいろいろ弁解した She *made* many *excuses for* being late for the appointment. / 彼がしたことに弁解の余地はない There's no excuse [*justification*] for what he did. / What he did *was inexcusable.* / 彼がいくら弁解してもその警官は聞き入れてくれなかった The police officer wouldn't accept his *excuses* [*explanations*] no matter how much he insisted on them. / 彼らは今回の事故について弁解してこのように述べた They said this 「*as an excuse for* [*in explanation of, in justification of*] the accident this time. / 僕はこの件に関してあえて弁解はしないよ I won't try to 「*excuse myself for* [*justify, explain away*] the matter. / 弁解がましいことを言うな Don't try to excuse [*justify*] yourself.

へんかく 変革 (変えること) change; (変換) transformation; (改革) reform; (大きな) revolution ──変革する change; transform; reform; revolutionize /東欧は歴史的な変革を遂げた Eastern Europe underwent massive *changes* [*transformations*]. / 通信技術の発達は社会的大変革をもたらした The development of telecommunications technology has brought about *a social revolution.* / 制度の変革が必要だ We need to *change* [*transform, reform*] the system.

べんがく 勉学 study ──勉学する study /勉学にいそしむ *study hard*

へんかん¹ 返還 return, restoration, (公式の)reversion ──返還する return, restore /彼らは領土の返還を要求した They demanded *the return* [*restoration, reversion*] of the land. / 沖縄は1972年に日本に返還された Okinawa *was returned* [*restored*] *to* Japan in 1972.

へんかん² 変換 change; (目的に適するよう変えること) conversion ──変換する change; convert /マイクは振動を電気信号に変換する Microphones *change* [*convert*] vibrations *into* electric signals. / このキーを押せばひらがなを漢字に変換できます Press this key and you can *change* [*convert*] *hiragana* into Chinese characters.

べんき 便器 toilet; (男子用小便器) urinal; (差し込み便器) bedpan

べんぎ 便宜 convenience; (得) advantage /彼はわいろを受け取り, 代わりにその会社に便宜をはかってやった He received the bribe and, in return, *gave* the company *an advantage.* / 便宜上, それらを１から10までの数字で呼ぶことにする For convenience [*For convenience'(s) sake*], we call them by the

numbers from one to ten respectively.
◆その処置は便宜的な(→当座の)ものだ That is a *temporary* treatment.

ペンキ （house) paint ◎（❖日本語はオランダ語の pek から) ‖ペンキ塗りたて《掲示》*Wet* [《英》*Fresh*] *Paint* / このペンキは乾いていますか Is this (*house*) *paint* dry? / 塀のペンキがはげかかっている The (*house*) *paint* is coming off the fence.
◆犬小屋をペンキでねずみ色に塗った I *painted* the kennel gray. / 彼はペンキ塗りが得意だ He is good at (*house*) *painting*.
‖ペンキ屋(店) a (house) paint store; (塗装工) a (house) paint painter

へんきゃく 返却 return ◎ ──返却する return ⊕ ‖返却期日は来週の月曜です The due date for the *return* will be next Monday. / 食器はこちらへ返却してください *You are expected to return* the dishes here. / 自動販売機の返却口に100円玉が忘れられていた A 100-yen coin was left in *the coin return* of the vending machine.
◆図書館で借りたこの本はとうに返却期限を過ぎている This book, which I borrowed from the library, *is long overdue*.

へんきょう¹ 辺境 （人里離れた地域) remote region ◎; (国境地域) border region ◎
◆その辺境の村に着くまで車で2日かかった It took two days' drive to get to the *remote* [*border*] village.

へんきょう² 偏狭 ──偏狭な (人が) narrow-minded; (心などが) narrow; (土地が) small

べんきょう 勉強

❶【学ぶこと】study ◎◎ （❖「特定分野の研究」の意味では, しばしば複数形 studies), work ◎; (学校の勉強) schoolwork ◎ ──勉強する study ⊕⊜; (習う・習得する) learn ⊕⊜; (努力する) work ⊜

  study: 身につけるための意識的な努力を含意する.
  learn: 授業などで受動的に学ぶこと, また学習の結果が身についたことも含意する.
  work: 学業に限らず何かに熱心に取り組むことを指す.

勉強は順調に進んでいますか Are your *studies* going well?
進は勉強ができる Susumu is good at 「*his studies* [*studying*].
剛はもっぱら英語の勉強に力を入れている(→時間を使う) Tsuyoshi devotes his time to 「*the study* of English [*studying* English].
いちばん上の兄は時々私の勉強を見てくれます My oldest brother sometimes helps me with my *studies*.
その教室では中国語の勉強会が行われていた A *study session* for the Chinese language was being held in the classroom.
知子はよく勉強する Tomoko *studies* [*works*] *hard*. / (→勉強家だ) Tomoko *is a hard worker*.
期末試験に向けてみんな一生懸命勉強している All *are studying* [*working*] hard for the final exams.
僕はもっと英語の勉強をしないといけない I *must study* English harder.
君たちは若いうちにたくさん勉強したほうがよい *It is better* for you *to learn* a lot while you are young.
カナダで勉強させてほしいと両親に頼み込んだ I implored my parents to let me *study* in Canada.
大学では何を勉強するつもりですか What are you going to *study* at university? / (→専攻する) What are you going to *major in* at university?
彼女はひどい勉強嫌いだ She *hates studying* very much.
とんだへまをやってしまったが, いい勉強になった(→その経験から多くを学んだ) I made a terrible blunder. But *I learned a lot from the experience*.
◆俊子はテストに向けて詰め込み勉強をしている Toshiko *is cramming* for the exam.
❷「どの時代の歴史を勉強してるの」「ルネサンス時代だよ」"Which period of history *are you studying*?" "The Renaissance."
❷【安く売る】
消費税分は勉強させていただきます *We're glad to discount* the consumption tax (on it).
さあ, いらっしゃい. 勉強しますよ Come on, step right up! *I'll give you a discount*. (❖英語には特に決まった表現はない)
‖勉強時間 one's study hours / 勉強机 a (study) desk / 勉強道具 school supplies / 勉強部屋 (書斎) a study; (自分の部屋) one's (bed)room

へんきょく 編曲 arrangement ◎ ──編曲する arrange ⊕ ‖その曲はオーケストラ用に編曲された The piece *was arranged for* orchestra.
‖編曲者 an arranger

へんきん 返金 (払い戻し) refund ◎; (返済) repayment ◎◎ ──返金する refund ⊕; repay* ⊕ ‖レシートをお持ちでないとご返金できません *We can't refund you your money* if you don't have a receipt.

ペンギン penguin ◎ ‖イワトビペンギン a rockhopper (penguin) / オウサマペンギン a king penguin / コウテイペンギン an emperor penguin / フェアリーペンギン a fairy penguin / フンボルトペンギン a Humboldt penguin

へんくつ 偏屈 ──偏屈な bigoted; (偏狭な) narrow-minded; (つむじ曲がりの) perverse; (頑固な) obstinate ‖あの老人は相当な偏屈者だ That old man is quite *a bigoted* [*a narrow-minded, a perverse, an obstinate*] *one*.

へんけい 変形 (ゆがむこと・ゆがめること) deformation ◎; (完全に変形) transformation ◎ ◎ ──変形する change in shape; (ゆがむ) become* deformed; (完全に) become transformed ‖熱でゴムのボール

へんけん

が変形した The rubber ball *was deformed* by heat.
◆僕の眼鏡のつるが彼に踏まれて変形してしまった(→曲がった) The arms of my glasses *were bent* because he stepped on them.
‖変形生成文法〖言語・文法〗transformational-generative grammar

へんけん 偏見 (いわれのない嫌悪) prejudice ◯◯; (好みの偏り) bias ◯◯ ‖人種的偏見 racial *prejudice* / 差別や偏見のない社会の実現を目ざす try to create a society without any discrimination or *prejudice* / いくつかの国ではまだ女性に対する根強い偏見がある There is still deep-rooted *prejudice* [*bias*] against women in some countries.
◆エイズ患者に対して偏見をもつ人がいる Some people *are prejudiced* [*biased*] *against* the sufferers of AIDS.

べんご 弁護 defense, 《英》defence ◯ ◯; (正当化) justification ◯◯ ――弁護する defend ⓗ ⓘ, stand* up for ..., speak* up for ...,〖法律〗plead* ⓗ ⓘ (❖受身にはできない); (正当化する) justify ⓗ ‖自己弁護する *defend* [*justify*] oneself / 僕が答えに窮すると杉山君が僕を弁護してくれた Sugiyama *defended* [*stood up for, spoke up for*] me when I didn't know how to answer. / その有名な弁護士が彼を弁護した That famous lawyer *defended* [*pleaded for*] him. / (→彼の事件を) That famous lawyer *pleaded* his case.
‖弁護団(被告側[原告側]) counsel (for the defense [plaintiff]) / 弁護人 a counsel / 弁護料 a lawyer's fee

へんこう¹ 変更 change ◯◯; (部分的に変えること) alteration ◯◯; (目的に合うよう手直しすること) modification ◯◯; (再調整) rearrangement ◯◯ ――変更する change ⓗ; alter ⓗ; modify ⓗ; rearrange ⓗ

リストに少し変更があります There are some *changes* [*alterations, modifications, rearrangements*] in the list.

計画には変更の余地がない The plan allows of no *change* [*alteration, modification, rearrangement*].

彼らは政策にいくつか変更を加えた They *changed* [*altered, modified*] their policy in a few respects.

彼らは突然行く先を変更した They suddenly *changed* their destination.

会議は1時から3時に変更になった The meeting *has been changed* from 1 o'clock to 3.
◆テレビ局は予定を変更して(→予定されていた番組の代わりに)地震のニュースを伝えた The TV station broadcast news about the earthquake *instead of* the scheduled program.
‖日付変更線 the (International) Date Line

へんこう² 偏向 (偏り) bias ◯◯; (逸脱) deviation ◯◯ ――偏向した (偏った) biased
‖偏向教育 (a) politically biased education

へんこう³ 偏光 ‖偏光レンズ〖写真〗a polarized lens

べんごし 弁護士 lawyer ◯,《米》attorney ◯; (法廷弁護士) 《米》counselor ◯,《英》barrister ◯ ‖弁護士に相談する consult *a lawyer* / 弁護士を頼む engage [employ] *a lawyer* / 田中弁護士 *the lawyer* Tanaka
◆弁護士を開業する practice *law* / 弁護士の資格を得る be admitted to *the bar*
‖弁護士会 a bar association / 弁護士事務所 a lawyer's office / 顧問弁護士 a legal adviser; (会社の) a corporation lawyer,《米》a general counsel

へんさ 偏差 〖統計〗deviation ◯
◆彼女は英語の偏差値が高い She has *a high percentile ranking* on English exams.
‖偏差値教育 (an) education which emphasizes students' deviation values in exams / 標準偏差〖統計〗a standard deviation

べんざ 便座 toilet seat ◯
‖便座カバー a toilet seat cover

へんさい 返済 repayment ◯◯ ――返済する pay* back, repay* ⓗ ‖借金を返済する "*pay back* [*repay*] one's debt / 彼は彼女に貸した金の返済を迫った He pressed her for *the repayment of* the money he had lent her. / 返済期限が迫っている The deadline for *repayment* is drawing near. / おじは家のローンの返済に追われている My uncle is having a tough time earning money to *repay* his housing loan. ◆彼はついに借金を全額返済し終えた He *paid off* all of his debt at last.

へんさん 編纂 (資料を集めて編集すること) compilation ◯; (編集) editing ◯ ――編纂する compile ⓗ; edit ⓗ ‖百科事典を編纂する *compile* an encyclopedia
‖編纂者 a compiler, an editor

へんし 変死 (不自然な死) unnatural death ◯ ‖変死体 a body found in suspicious circumstances

へんじ 返事

answer ◯, reply ◯, response ◯◯ ――返事する answer ⓗ ⓘ, reply ⓘ ⓗ, respond ⓘ

知子から手紙の返事が来た I've got *an answer* [*a reply, a response*] to my letter from Tomoko.

ドアをノックしてみたが、中からは返事がなかった I knocked on the door, but there was no *answer* [*reply, response*] from inside.

私のあいさつに哲二は何の返事もしなかった Tetsuji *didn't answer* [*reply, respond*] to my greeting.

私は彼女の手紙にすぐに返事を出した I *answered* her letter immediately.

返事が遅れたことをお許しください Please forgive my delay in *answering*.

名前を呼ばれたら大きな声で返事してください *Answer* [*Reply, Respond*] in a loud voice when your name is called.

彼女は「すぐ行きます」と返事をした She *answered* [*replied, responded*] "I'm coming."

彼女に「つきあって」と言われて返事に困ってしまっ

た I didn't know what to *answer* when she asked me to go out with her.
あいつは返事ばかりで何もしない(→頼めば「はい」と答えるが実際は何もしない) He *is ready to answer "yes" when you ask him to do something, but in reality he doesn't do anything*.

◆返事ぐらいしろよ *Talk to me!* / きょうは健二に返事を書こう *I'll write back to Kenji today*. / 彼は二つ返事で(→快く)その仕事を引き受けた He *readily [willingly, gladly] took on the task*. / (手紙の結びで)返事を楽しみに待っています I'm looking forward to「*your letter [hearing from you]*」.

> **コロケーション** -answer-
> 〘形容詞+〜〙 あいまいな〜 an ambiguous answer / いいかげんな〜 a casual answer / 色よい〜 a favorable answer / きっぱりとした〜 an emphatic answer / 気乗りのしない〜 a reluctant answer / 断りの〜 a negative answer / そっけない〜 a curt [terse] answer / 冷たい〜 a cold answer / 短い〜 a brief answer

べんし 弁士 (演説者)《公式的》orator ⓒ
へんしつ 変質 (質的な変化) qualitative change; (劣化) deterioration Ⓤ ――**変質する** change in quality, change qualitatively; (劣化する) deteriorate ⓘ / この薬は変質しやすいので高温多湿な場所を避けて保管してください Please don't store this medicine where the temperature and humidity are high, because it *easily deteriorates*.
‖変質者 a pervert
へんしゃ 編者 editor ⓒ, compiler ⓒ
へんしゅ 変種 〘生物〙variation ⓒ, variety ⓒ; (突然変異体)〘生物〙mutant ⓒ
へんしゅう 編集 editing Ⓤ (✤映画などの編集もいう); (資料を集めてまとめること) compilation Ⓤ ――**編集する** edit ⓣ; compile ⓣ ――**編集の** editorial / 彼は編集の仕事に携わっている He is engaged in *editing [compilation]*. / 私がその学校新聞を編集した I *edited* the school paper. / そのフィルムは編集され短くまとめられた The film *was edited* and made shorter. / 彼はお気に入りの曲を集めてオリジナルのMDを編集した He *compiled* his favorite tunes *into* his original MD.
‖編集会議 an editorial meeting / 編集局長 a managing editor / 編集室 an editorial office / 編集者 an editor, a compiler / 編集長 an editor in chief, a chief editor / 編集部 an editorial department / 編集部員(全体) an editorial staff; (個人) a member of an editorial staff / 編集プロダクション a company engaged in editing for a publisher / 編集方針 an editorial policy / 編集ライター an editorial writer
べんじょ 便所 (家庭用の)《主に米/婉曲的》bathroom ⓒ,《主に英》toilet ⓒ; (公共の場の)《米》restroom ⓒ,《英》toilets (✤男性用は《米》a men's room,《英》the gents (単数扱い), 女性用は《米》a women's [ladies'] room,《英》the ladies ((単数扱い)); (特に飛行機内などの)《公式的》lavatory ⓒ ⇨ **トイレ**
勉君、便所はどこだい Tsutomu, where is *the bathroom*?
ちょっと便所に行ってくるから待っててよ Wait here, because I'm going to *the bathroom*.
お便所貸してもらえます? Can I use *the bathroom*?
便所が空いていない *The bathroom* is occupied.
‖公衆便所 a public restroom,《米/婉曲的》a comfort station,《英公式的》a (public) convenience / 水洗便所 a flush toilet / 洋式便所 (a room with) a commode style toilet / 和式便所 (a room with) a squatting style toilet
へんじょう 返上 汚名を返上する *clear one's name* / 彼は日曜を返上してレポートを書き上げた He *gave up* his Sunday to finish the report.
べんしょう 弁償 compensation (for a damage *one* has done) ――**弁償する** compensate ⓣ,《公式的》recompense ⓣ; (支払う) pay ⓣ / 彼は店の商品をこわしてしまい, 弁償させられた He *was persuaded to compensate [pay]* the store *for* the goods he had broken. / 私の傘をもしなくしたりしたら弁償してもらうからね If you lose my umbrella, you're going to have to *pay me back*.
‖弁償金 a compensation,《公式的》(a) recompense
べんしょうほう 弁証法 〘哲学〙dialectic Ⓤ
へんしょく¹ 変色 (a) change in color; (汚く) discoloration Ⓤ ――**変色する[させる]** change (...) in color; (汚く) discolor ⓘⓣ; (色あせる) fade ⓘ / その液体をたらしたリトマス試験紙が変色した The litmus paper *changed in color* when we dripped the liquid on it. / *The color of the litmus paper changed* when we dripped the liquid on it. / 3日前に買ったバナナはかなり変色してしまった The bananas I bought three days ago *have become* quite *discolored*.
へんしょく² 偏食 偏食を続けていると体をこわすよ You will become sick if you keep on「*eating an unbalanced diet [eating only what you want to]*」.
ペンション resort lodge ⓒ, resort inn ⓒ (✤英語のpensionは通例「年金」の意味で用いる)
ペンシルバニア Pennsylvania (✤米国北東部の州;《略語》Pa., Penn.,《郵便》PA)
へんしん¹ 返信 reply ⓒ, answer ⓒ /返信はがき a reply card / きょう彼からの返信が届いた I received his *reply [answer]* (to my letter) today. / 友達にメールを返信した I *sent an e-mail in reply [answer]* to my friend.
◆返信用封筒を同封する enclose *a "return envelope* [(→あて名を書き, 切手をはった)*self-addressed stamped envelope*](✤後者は《英》でa stamped addressed envelope ともいう;《略

へんしん

語》s.a.s.e., 《英》s.a.e.)

へんしん² 変身 transformation Ⓤ Ⓒ ――変身する（自身を変える）transform [change, turn] oneself ∥彼はウルトラマンに変身した He transformed [changed, turned] himself into the Ultraman. / いつもはおとなしい和郎が, サッカーの試合が始まるとスーパープレーヤーに変身した Kazuro, who is usually a quiet boy, transformed [changed, turned] himself into a super player when the soccer game started.

◆ヒギンズはただの花売り娘を貴婦人に変身させた Higgins *molded* an ordinary flower girl *into* an elegant lady.(✤mold は「成長を促して変える」の意味)

へんじん 変人 eccentric (person) Ⓒ,《口語的》freak Ⓒ,《口語的》weirdo Ⓒ (複 ～s)

ベンジン《化学》benzine Ⓤ

ペンス pence (✤penny の複数形;《略記》p)

へんすう 変数《数学・物理》variable Ⓒ

へんずつう 偏頭痛 migraine Ⓒ

へんせい 編成（組織化）organization Ⓤ;（形成）formation Ⓤ;（配列）arrangement Ⓤ;（番組・配列などの配列）line-up Ⓒ ――編成する（組織する）organize Ⓤ;（形成する）form ⓗ;（構成する）make* up (of …);（案などを編成する）draw* up;（配列する）arrange ⓗ ∥チームを編成するにはあと2人選手が必要です Two more players are needed to *organize* [*form, make up*] a team. / 電車は3両編成だった The train *was made up of* three cars. / 彼らは来年度予算の編成作業を終えた They've finished *drawing up* the next year's budget bill. / そのテレビ局は番組編成を変えた The TV station changed *their* programming *arrangement* [*line-up*].

◆4人編成のバンド a four-*piece* band / その曲は小編成のオーケストラで演奏できるように編曲されていた The piece was arranged for a *small* orchestra.

へんせいき 変声期 うちの弟はちょうど今変声期だ My brother's *voice is changing* now.

へんせいふう 偏西風 the prevailing westerlies in the middle latitudes

べんぜつ 弁舌（話しぶり）speech Ⓤ ∥彼女は弁舌さわやかだ Her *speech* is fluent. / She is a fluent speaker. / She speaks fluently.

◆彼はその問題に関して長々と弁舌をふるった（→長い演説を行った）He *made* a long *speech* on the matter.

へんせん 変遷 change Ⓒ Ⓤ,《公式的》transition Ⓒ Ⓤ ∥わが町の変遷を調べた We investigated *the changes* [*transitions*] our town had gone through. / （→歴史を調べた）We investigated *the history* of our town.

ベンゼン《化学》benzene Ⓤ

へんそう¹ 変装 disguise Ⓒ Ⓤ ――変装する disguise *oneself* ∥変装した男 a man *in disguise* / 変装用の口ひげをつける wear a mustache *as a disguise* / 男は老人に変装し警察の目を逃れた He evaded the police「*by disguising himself* [*disguised*] *as* an old man.

へんそう² 返送 ――返送する（送り返す）

send* back;（返す）return ⓗ ◆（通信販売などの）返送料はお客様のご負担になります Customers are responsible for paying *the shipping charges for returns*.

へんぞう 変造 変造硬貨 an *illegally altered* coin

へんそうきょく 変奏曲《音楽》variation Ⓒ

へんそく¹ 変則 ――変則的な（規則どおりでない）irregular;（異例の）《公式的》anomalous;（典型的でない）atypical ∥あしたは2時間だけの変則的な時間割になります Tomorrow we have only two classes in all, which is an *irregular* [*anomalous*] schedule.

へんそく² 変速 21段変速の自転車 a 21-*speed* bicycle

∥変速機（自動車・バイクなどの）a transmission, a gearbox;（自転車の）a derailleur / 変速レバー《米》a gearshift,《英》a gear lever

へんたい¹ 変態（昆虫などの）metamorphosis Ⓒ Ⓤ（複 metamorphoses）;（性的倒錯者）(sexual) pervert Ⓒ, sexually abnormal person Ⓒ;（性的倒錯）sexual perversion Ⓤ Ⓒ ∥変態性欲 (a) perverted sexual desire / 完全変態《生物》complete metamorphosis / 不完全変態《生物》incomplete metamorphosis

へんたい² 編隊 formation Ⓒ Ⓤ ∥航空ショーで飛行機が編隊を組んで飛んだ The planes flew *in formation* in the air show.

∥編隊飛行 (a) formation flight

ペンタゴン the Pentagon (✤米国国防総省の俗称)

ペンダント pendant Ⓒ ∥ペンダントをつける put on *a pendant*

ベンチ bench Ⓒ;（スポーツの選手席）bench Ⓒ;（ダッグアウト）dugout Ⓒ ∥そのピッチャーはベンチで控えている The pitcher is sitting on *the bench*. / The pitcher is in *the dugout*. / その選手に対しベンチ（→監督）から指示が出された *The coach* gave the player some signs *from the bench*.

∥ベンチウォーマー a benchwarmer

ペンチ ⚠combination pliers《複数扱い》(✤数えるときは a pair of … とする。英語の pinc(h)ers は「やっとこ・くぎ抜き」の意味)

∥ラジオペンチ needle-nose(d) [long nose] pliers

関連語 ニッパー diagonal cutting pliers [nippers], wire cutters / プライヤー (slip joint) pliers

ベンチャー ∥ベンチャー企業 a venture company / ベンチャーキャピタル (a) venture capital / ベンチャービジネス (a) venture business

へんちょう¹ 偏重 ――偏重する make* [think*] too much of …, put* too much value on …

∥学歴偏重社会 a society which puts too much value on *a person's* academic background / 学歴偏重主義 diplomaism

へんちょう² 変調 強い精神的なショックで体に変調をきたす（→体調を悪くする）場合もある Severe mental shock may「*bend one out of*

shape [*put one in poor health*].

べんつう 便通 (bowel) movement [C] (❖婉曲的に BM という) ∥便通がある have *a bowel movement* / 僕は便通がよい[悪い] I have regular [irregular] *bowel movements*.

ペンディング この件はペンディングにしておこう Let's leave this matter *pending*, shall we?

へんてつ 変哲 彼が誇らしげに見せてくれたのは何の変哲もないただの石だった What he showed me proudly was *just an ordinary* stone.

へんてん 変転 change [C], 《公式的》 vicissitudes ―変転する change [自] ∥変転極まりない人生 life full of *changes* [*vicissitudes*]

へんでんしょ 変電所 substation [C]

へんとう 返答 answer [C], reply [C], response [U][C] ―返答する answer [他][自], reply [自][他], respond [自][他] ➜へんじ

へんどう 変動 change [C][U]; (物価・気温などの) fluctuation [U][C]; (価格・世論などの) swing [C] ―変動する change [自]; (物価などが) fluctuate [自] ∥株価の変動 *changes* [*fluctuations, swings*] *in* stock prices / ここ数日気温の変動が激しい We've been having sharp temperature *changes* [*fluctuations*] for the last few days./ (→激しく変動している) The temperature *has been changing* [*fluctuating*] sharply for the last few days.
‖変動為替相場制 the floating exchange rate system

べんとう 弁当 lunch [U][C]; (弁当箱に詰めた) 《米》 box lunch [C], 《英》 packed lunch [C]
彼は自分で弁当を作った He *boxed* [*packed*] *his lunch* by himself.
僕らは公園で弁当を食べた We had *lunch* in the park.
きょうは弁当を持ってきた I have *a box* [*packed*] *lunch* with me today.
夕飯はコンビニの弁当ですませよう I'm going to eat *a box* [*packed*] *lunch* sold at a convenience store for supper.
‖弁当代 lunch money / 弁当箱 a lunch box / 愛妻弁当 a box lunch made by *one's* wife (❖「妻が作った弁当」の意味) / のり弁当 a box lunch with sheets of *nori* on cooked rice / 幕の内弁当 a box lunch of various kinds of food with rice

へんとうせん 扁桃腺 〔解剖〕 tonsils ∥彼は扁桃腺がはれていた His *tonsils* were swollen.
‖扁桃腺炎 〔医学〕 tonsillitis

へんにゅう 編入 (学校などを移ること) transfer [U][C]; (入ることの許可) admission [U]; (組み入れること) incorporation [U] ―編入する (移す・移る) transfer [他][自]; (入ることを許可する) admit [他] (❖通例受身で); (組み入れる) 《公式的》 incorporate [他] ∥彼は私たちの学校の２年に編入した He *was admitted to* the second year class of our school. / 彼女は英文科から仏文科への編入試験を受けた She took *the examination for admission of her transfer* from the English literature department to the French literature department. / その市は隣接するいくつかの村を編入した The city *incorporated* some neighboring villages.

ペンネーム pen name [C], pseudonym [sjúːdənìm] [C], nom de plume [nɑ̀m də plúːm] [C] (複 noms de plume) ∥サミュエル・クレメンスはマーク・トウェーンというペンネームで小説を書いた Samuel Clemens wrote novels under *the pen name* "Mark Twain."

ペンパル pen pal [C], 《英》 pen-friend [C] ∥ペンパル募集 *Pen pals* wanted.

へんぴ 辺鄙 ―へんぴな (人里離れた) remote, out-of-the-way; (中心地から離れた) outlying (❖名詞の前で用いる) ∥彼の家はへんぴな場所にあった His house was in a *remote* [an *out-of-the-way*, an *outlying*] place.

べんぴ 便秘 constipation [U] ―便秘する become* [get*] constipated (❖「便秘している」状態なら be constipated) ∥3日間便秘している I'*ve been constipated* for three days. / 私は便秘がちだ I *often become* [*get*] *constipated*.
‖便秘薬 (a) medicine for constipation

へんぴん 返品 returned goods ―返品する return [他], take* [turn] back; (送り返す) send* back ∥倉庫には返品の山ができていた There were heaps of *returned goods* in the warehouse. / セール品は返品がきかない You *can't return* [*take back, send back*] sale items.

ペンフレンド pen pal [C], 《英》 pen-friend [C]

へんぺいそく 扁平足 flat feet ―偏平足の flat-footed

べんべつ 弁別 distinction [U][C], discrimination [U] ―弁別する distinguish [他][自], discriminate [自][他], tell* … (apart)

へんぼう 変貌 (成長による) metamorphosis [C][U] (複 metamorphoses); (よい方への) transformation [U][C]; (変化) change [C][U] ―変貌する 《公式的》 metamorphose (into …); (よい方へ) become* transformed (into …); (変わる) change (into …) ∥小さないなか町が大きなベッドタウンへと変貌を遂げた A small rural town *has* 「*undergone a metamorphosis* [*metamorphosed*] *into* a large suburb.

べんまく 弁膜 〔解剖〕 valve [C]

へんめい 変名 false name [C]

べんめい 弁明 (説明) account [C], explanation [C][U]; (言い逃れ) excuse [C][U]; (正当化) justification [C][U] ―弁明する (説明する) account for …, explain [他][自]; (言い逃れをする) excuse *oneself* (for …); (正当化する) justify [他] ∥学校祭の延期について，我々は校長先生に弁明を求めた We demanded our principal to *account for* the delay of the school festival. / 君のしたことは全く弁明の余地なしだね You *can't excuse* [*justify*] *yourself* for what you did in any way./ You can't *justify* what you did in any way.

べんらん 便覧 handbook [C], manual [C]; (履修案内) catalog, 《英》 catalogue [C]

へ

べんり 便利 (都合がよいこと) convenience ⓊU; (使いやすさ) handiness Ⓤ; (有用性) usefulness Ⓤ ——**便利な** (都合がよい・手っとり早い) convenient (↔inconvenient); (使いやすい・扱いやすい) handy (✣ convenient, handy とも口語では「場所が(…に)近くて便利がよい」の意味もある); (役に立つ) useful (↔useless) ——**便利に** conveniently; handily; usefully

便利な道具 a *useful* [*handy*] tool / 待ち合わせに便利な場所 a *convenient* place to meet

そこへはバスで行くのが便利だ It's *convenient* to take a bus to go there.

コンビニエンスストアは本当に便利だ Convenience stores *are* really *convenient* [*handy, useful*].

そのスーパーはうちに近くて便利だ The supermarket *is convenient* [*handy*] *for* us. / The supermarket *is conveniently* [*handily*] *placed for* us.

この裁縫セットは携帯に便利だ This sewing kit *is convenient* [*handy*] *to* carry.

この町にも地下鉄の駅ができて、だいぶ便利になった This town has become a lot more *convenient* now that it has a subway station.

インターネットは様々な情報を引き出せて何かと便利だ The Internet *is* quite *convenient* [*useful*] because you can pick up various kinds of information there.

彼は何でも修理してくれるのでとても便利な人だ He is a very *useful* person, because he kindly fixes anything for me.

彼は都会暮らしの便利さに慣れすぎている He is too accustomed to *the convenience* of urban life.

‖便利屋 a handyman; (雇われて雑用をする人) an odd-job man

べんりし 弁理士 patent agent [attorney] Ⓒ

へんりん 片鱗 そのライブで少年は天才ギタリストの片鱗をうかがわせた The boy *gave us glimpses* of genius on the guitar at that concert.

へんれい 返礼 return Ⓒ Ⓤ, 《公式的》reciprocation Ⓤ /彼は返礼として商品券を彼女に贈った He gave her gift certificates *in return.*

へんれき 遍歴 彼は諸国[様々な職]を遍歴してきた He's *drifted from* one country [job] *to another.* / 週刊誌はこぞってその女優の男性遍歴を書きたてた All the weekly magazines printed stories of the actress's *past love affairs.*

へんろ 遍路 henro, a pilgrimage to Buddhist temples (which Kobo Daishi visited)

べんろん 弁論 (発表・演説) (public) speaking Ⓤ, speech Ⓒ; (討論) debate Ⓤ Ⓒ; (法廷での) pleading Ⓤ Ⓒ; (弁護士の) argument Ⓤ /孝子は県の英語弁論大会で2位になった Takako came in second in *the* prefectural English *speech contest.*

‖弁論部 a debating club / 口頭弁論 oral proceedings / 最終弁論 closing argument

ほ

ホ 〖音楽〗E ⓤⓒ ∥ホ長調[短調] E major [minor] / 変ホ長調 E-flat major

ほ¹ 帆 sail ⓒ ∥帆を上げる[下ろす] hoist [lower] *the sails* / 帆を張る unfurl *a sail*

ほ² 穂 ear ⓒ, spike ⓒ ∥穂を出す form *ears*; come into *ear*

ほ³ 歩 step ⓒ ⇨ いっぽ ∥歩を速める quicken *one's steps* / 彼は2歩前に進んだ[後ろに下がった] He took two *steps* forward [backward].

-ほ -補 (補助の) assistant (❖名詞の前で用いる) ∥書記補 an *assistant* clerk
◆警部補 (米) *a lieutenant*; (英) *an inspector*

ほあん 保安 (平和と安全を保つこと) preservation of peace and security
◆町の保安に努める make efforts to *maintain peace* in a town
∥保安官 a sheriff / 保安林 a forest preserve

ほい 補遺 (本などの付録) supplement ⓒ; (追加されたもの) addendum ⓒ (複 addenda) ∥辞書の補遺 *a supplement* to a dictionary

ぽい 彼はその空のびんをごみ箱にぽいと捨てた He *chucked* the empty bottle *into* the garbage can.

-ぽい

> 語法 日本語の「-ぽい」という言葉は, 英語では語尾が-ishまたは-yという形の形容詞で表す場合が多い.

子供っぽいふるまい *childish* behavior / 黒っぽいコートを着た男 a man in a *blackish* coat / 色っぽい女 a *sexy* woman / 彼は最近どうも忘れっぽい He has become *forgetful* these days. / 彼女は大人っぽいしゃべり方をする (→大人のように話す) She talks *like a grown-up*.

ほいく 保育 child care ⓤ ◆彼女は子供を保育所に預けてから会社に行く She goes to work after leaving her child at the ⌈day-care center [day nursery].
∥保育器 an incubator

ほいくし 保育士 (保育園の) nursery school teacher ⓒ; (幼稚園の) kindergarten teacher ⓒ

ボイコット boycott ⓒ ──ボイコットする boycott ⓗ ∥授業をボイコットする *boycott* a class / 消費者はその会社の製品をボイコットした Consumers *boycotted* the company's products.

ボイスレコーダー voice recorder

ホイッスル whistle ⓒ ∥ホイッスルを鳴らす blow *a whistle*; *whistle* / ホイッスルが鳴った A *whistle* ⌈was blown [blew].

ホイップ (泡立てること) whipping ⓤ ──ホイップする whip ⓗ ∥生クリームを手早くホイップする *whip* cream quickly

∥ホイップクリーム whipped cream

ほいほい 彼は娘の欲しがる物なら何でもほいほい買ってやる He *goes ahead* and buys anything his daughter wants.

ボイラー boiler ⓒ ∥ボイラー室 a boiler room

ホイル foil ⓤ (❖数えるときはa piece [sheet] of ..., a roll of ...) ∥ホイルでサケを包む wrap salmon in *aluminum foil*
∥アルミホイル aluminum foil, tin foil

ボイル ──ボイルする (ゆでる) boil ⓗ

ぼいん¹ 母音 vowel [váuəl] ⓒ ∥短母音 a short vowel / 長母音 a long vowel / 二重母音 a diphthong / 半母音 a semivowel

ぼいん² 拇印 thumbprint ⓒ ∥書類に拇印を押す put *one's thumbprint* on a document

ポインセチア 〖植物〗poinsettia

ポイント ❶【得点】point ⓒ ⇨ てん(点) ∥ポイントをあげる gain [score] *a point* / マッチポイントを迎える reach *a match point* / 私たちは3ポイント差で勝った We won by three *points*. / 100ポイントで景品と交換ができる You can get a free gift in exchange for 100 *points*. ◆彼はわがチームのポイントゲッターだ He is *the main scorer* of our team.
❷【要点】the point ⇨ ようてん ∥ポイントをつかむ[はずす] catch [miss] *the point* / ポイントだけ話してください Please keep to *the point*. (❖keep to the pointは「ポイントからはずれない」の意味) / 彼の発言はポイントをついている His remark *is to the point*.
❸【小数点】(decimal) point ⓒ
❹【活字の大きさ】point ⓒ ∥この本は10ポイントの活字で印刷されている This book is printed in 10-*point* type.
❺【鉄道の】(米)switch ⓒ, (英)points

ほう¹ 方

❶【方向】direction ⓒ; (…への道) way ⓒ
反対の方から from *the opposite direction*
その子はどっちの方へ行きましたか Which *way* did the child go?
奈々子は駅の方へ歩いていった Nanako walked ⌈*in the direction of* [*toward*] the station.
◆その犬は私の方へ近づいてきた The dog came up *to* me. / 左の方に郵便局があります (→左側に) There is a post office *to* the left.
❷【立場・側】
私たちのほうは, その条件で不満はありません There is nothing to complain about the conditions *on our part*. / (→私たちに関するかぎり) *As far as we are concerned*, we have nothing to complain about the conditions.
悪いのは彼のほうだ *It is* he *that* was wrong. (❖It isの後のheを強調する言い方で, この場

合 he を強く読む)
彼女には私のほうから(→私が)伝えておきます *I'll* tell her about it.
❸【分野・部類】
勉強のほうでは彼がクラスで1番だ He's number one in his class in studying.
お体のほうはいかがですか How do you feel?
彼女は怒りっぽいほうだ She's an angry person.
❹【比較】
[語法]
2つのものを比較して「…より〜である」という場合, 英語では《形容詞[副詞]の比較級＋than …》の形で表す.

真紀のほうが(→真紀は)私より背が高い Maki is taller than I [me]. (❖me は口語的な言い方)
私のほうがおじより早く駅に着いた I arrived at the station earlier than my uncle.
2つの中ではこちらのほうが古い This is the older of the two. (❖2つの限定されたものの間で比較を行うときは《the＋比較級》を用いる)
犬より猫のほうが好きです I *prefer* cats *to* dogs. (❖prefer の後には than ではなく to がくる)
甘い物は好きなほうです(→どちらかといえば好きである) I'm *rather* fond of sweets.
どちらでも好きなほうを取りなさい You can take *whichever* you like. (❖whichever は「どちらの…でも」の意味)
❺【…ほうがいい】(…すべきだ) should *do*, ought to *do*, had better *do* (❖挙げた順に強制・命令の感じが強くなる. had better *do* は目上の人には用いないほうがよい); (むしろ…したい) would rather *do*
できるだけ早く医者に診(み)てもらったほうがいい You *should* [*ought to, had better*] see a doctor as soon as possible.
そのことは彼には言わないほうがいい You *shouldn't* tell him that. (❖had better *do* を用いる場合は had better not tell … の語順になる)
ジェットコースターに乗るくらいならここでひとりで待っているほうがいい I *would rather* wait here alone *than* ride the roller coaster. / I *would just as well* wait here alone *as* ride the roller coaster.

ほう² 法 ❶【法律】(個々の法律) law [C]; (法律全体) law [U]《通例 the 〜》➜ほうりつ ∥法の精神 the spirit of *the law* / 法を守る obey [observe] *the law* / 法を破る violate [break] *the law* / 彼の行為は法に反する What he did is against *the law*. / 法のもとではだれもが平等である Everyone is equal under *the law*.
❷【方法】method [C], way [C] ➜ほうほう ∥英単語増強法 *a method* for building *one's* English vocabulary
◆インターネットの活用法が知りたい I want to know *how to use* the Internet.
❸【文法】mood [C] (❖表現内容に対する話し手の心理的な態度を表す動詞の語形変化. 英語では, 直説法(indicative mood), 命令法(imperative mood), 仮定法(subjunctive mood)がある)

ほう³ 報 (報告) report [C]; (知らせ) news [U] ∥私たちは彼の急死の報に接し言葉を失った When we heard *the news* of his sudden death, we were at a loss for words.

ほう⁴ Oh, why, well ∥ほう, そうなんですか *Oh*, is that so? / ほう, あなたは大阪出身なんですか *Well*, are you from Osaka?

ぼう 棒 (棒切れ) stick [C]; (円柱状の) pole [C]; (横木) bar [C]; (さお) rod [C]; (オーケストラの指揮棒) baton [C] ∥棒でたたく strike with *a stick* / 棒を振り回す swing *a stick* around ∥棒切れ a stick / 棒グラフ a bar graph
[慣用表現] 刑事たちは連日足を棒にして(→足が動かなくなるまで)聞き込みを続けた The detectives continued making inquiries *until their legs were stiff*. (❖stiff は「こわばって動かない」の意味) / 彼はコンピュータの故障で1日を棒に振った(→むだにした) He *wasted* the whole day because of some problem with his computer. / 彼は汚職事件で一生を棒に振った(→台なしにした) A corruption scandal *ruined* his life.

ぼう¹- 某- (ある…) a certain … (❖名前や日付などを具体的に出すのを避けるときに用いる言い方) ∥都内の某所で会合をもつ have a meeting at *a certain place* in Tokyo / 昨年の8月某日に on *a certain date* in August last year (❖「某日」は「ある特定の日」を表すので, 前置詞には on を用いる) / 私たちは某氏から, この件に関する最新の情報を得た *A certain person* updated us on this case.

ぼう²- 亡- (亡くなった) late ∥亡父[夫] *one's late* father [husband]

ほうあん 法案 bill [C] ∥銃規制法案 *a* gun control *bill* / 法案を提出する present [introduce, submit] *a bill* / その法案は圧倒的多数で可決された The *bill* passed by an overwhelming majority.

ぼうあんき 棒暗記 ―棒暗記する《軽蔑的》learn* … by rote ➜あんき

ほうい¹ 方位 (方角) direction [C]; (方位計による方向) bearing [C]《しばしば複数形 〜s》∥羅針盤で方位を確かめる get *one's bearings* with a compass

ほうい² 包囲 (取り囲まれた状態) siege [C] [U] ―包囲する (取り囲む) surround [他]; (敵などを) besiege [他] ∥包囲を解く lift *a siege* (of …) / 敵の包囲を突破する break through *an* enemy *siege* / 城は敵に包囲された The castle *was under siege* by the enemy.
∥包囲網 a tight siege; (捜査の) a dragnet

ほういがく 法医学 forensic medicine [U]

ぼういんぼうしょく 暴飲暴食 暴飲暴食(→食べすぎと飲みすぎ)に気をつけなさい Be careful not to *eat and drink too much*. (❖「飲む」と「食べる」の順序が日本語と逆になることに注意)

ほうえい 放映 televising [U], broadcasting [U] ―放映する broadcast* … on television, televise [他] ∥地震の被災地の映像はテレビで世界中に放映された The images of the

earthquake-hit area *were「broadcast on television [televised]* all over the world.
∥放映権 a broadcasting right

ぼうえい 防衛 defense,《英》defence Ⓤ ——防衛する defend ⊕ ∥国家を防衛する *defend* a nation / チャンピオンはタイトルの防衛に成功した The champion succeeded in *defending* his title.
◆コンピュータウイルスに対する防衛策を講じる take *defensive measures* against computer viruses
∥防衛大学校 the Defense Academy / 防衛庁 the Defense Agency / 防衛庁長官 Director General of the Defense Agency / 防衛費 defense spending [costs] / 防衛予算 the defense budget / 防衛力 defense capability / 自己防衛 self-defense / 正当防衛 legitimate (self-)defense

ぼうえき¹ 貿易 trade Ⓤ;(外国との) foreign trade Ⓤ;(通商) commerce Ⓤ ——貿易する trade (with ...)
日中間の貿易 *trade* between Japan and China / 貿易の自由化をはかる liberalize *trade* / 日米貿易 Japan-U.S. *trade* / 日米貿易摩擦 *trade friction* between Japan and the United States
その会社は中東の国々と石油の貿易を行っている The company *trades in* oil *with* Middle Eastern countries.
米国はアジア諸国との貿易を拡大している The U.S. is expanding [increasing] *trade* with Asian countries.
その国の貿易黒字は増加しつつある The country's *trade surplus* is on the increase.
増大する貿易赤字が経済に大きな負担をかけている *The* expanding *trade deficit* is putting an enormous strain on the economy.
∥貿易会社 a trading company / 貿易協定 a trade agreement / 貿易収支 the balance of trade / 貿易風 a trade wind / 貿易不均衡 a trade imbalance / 自由[保護]貿易 free [protective] trade

ぼうえき² 防疫 prevention of epidemics
◆防疫対策を行う take *preventive measures* (against ...)

ぼうえんきょう 望遠鏡 telescope Ⓒ ∥望遠鏡で星を見る look at stars through *a telescope*
∥天体望遠鏡 an astronomical telescope

ぼうえんレンズ 望遠レンズ telephoto lens

ほうおう 法王 (ローマ法王) pope Ⓒ《通例 the ~》——法王の papal ∥法王ヨハネ・パウロ 2世 *Pope* John Paul II《❖IIは the second と読む》∥法王庁 the Vatican

ぼうおん 防音 soundproofing Ⓤ ——防音の soundproof ∥彼女の部屋にはピアノの練習のための防音設備が施されている Her room *is soundproofed* so that she can practice the piano.
∥防音室 a soundproof room / 防音装置 soundproofing / 防音壁 a soundproof wall

ほうか¹ 放火 arson Ⓤ ——放火する set* fire to ..., set ... on fire《❖いずれも「燃やしてはならないものに火をつける」の意味》∥空き家に放火する *set fire to* an empty house; *set* an empty house *on fire* / 彼は放火の罪に問われた He was accused of *arson*. / 警察はそのアパートの火災の原因を放火(→何者かが放火した)と断定した The police concluded that someone *set fire to* the apartment house. / きのうこの近くで,連続して4件の放火事件があった Yesterday there were four *arson cases* one after another in the neighborhood.
∥放火犯 an arsonist

ほうか² 法科 law school [department] Ⓒ
◆法科の学生 a *law* student

ほうか³ 砲火 (発砲) gunfire Ⓤ;(砲撃) (artillery) fire Ⓤ ∥砲火を浴びている be under *fire* / 敵に砲火を浴びせる direct *gunfire* at the enemy

ほうが 萌芽 (芽を出すこと) germination Ⓤ;(芽) bud Ⓒ, sprout Ⓒ ∥悪の萌芽を断つ *nip* a vice *in the bud*

ぼうか 防火 fire prevention Ⓤ ∥この建物は防火設備が十分整っている This building has enough *fire prevention equipment*.
∥防火シャッター a fireproof shutter / 防火壁 a firewall / 防火用水 firefighting water

ほうかい 崩壊 fall Ⓒ, collapse Ⓤ ——崩壊する fall* [break*] down,《公式的》collapse ⊕ ∥古い橋が昨夜地震で崩壊した The old bridge「*fell down [collapsed]* last night due to the earthquake. / その国の軍事政権が崩壊した The country's military regime *collapsed*. ◆家庭の崩壊 family *disruption* / バブルが崩壊した The bubble *burst*.
∥学級崩壊 classroom collapse

ほうがい 法外 ——法外な (常軌を逸した) outrageous;(不当で) unreasonable, criminal ∥法外な要求をする make an *unreasonable [excessive]* demand / 業者はその薬を法外な値段で売っていた The dealer was selling the medicine at an *outrageous [unreasonable]* price.
◆請求額は法外なものだった(→法外に高い額を請求された) They charged me *outrageously [unreasonably]* high prices.

ぼうがい 妨害 disturbance Ⓒ Ⓤ, obstruction Ⓒ Ⓤ;(中断) interruption Ⓒ Ⓤ;(干渉) interference Ⓤ ——妨害する disturb ⊕, obstruct ⊕; interrupt ⊕ ⊕; interfere (with [in] ...) ⇒ じゃま
安眠を妨害する *disturb* a person's sleep / 演説を妨害する *interrupt* a person's speech
反対派は議事の進行を妨害しようとした The opposition group tried to *obstruct* the proceedings.
彼の選挙運動は数回にわたって妨害にあった His election campaign *met with interference* several times.
店の前でそのようなちらしを配ると営業妨害になる Distributing such handbills in front of the store is regarded as *obstructing its business*.

彼は公務執行妨害で逮捕された He was arrested on a charge of *obstructing official business*.

‖守備妨害 interfering with fielding / 電波妨害 jamming / 列車妨害 railway sabotage

-ほうがいい ➔ほう(方), いい

ほうがく[1] 方角 (方向) direction [C]; (…への道) way [C] ➔ほう(方), ほうこう(方向)

来た方角が分からなくなった I couldn't find *the way* I had come from.

警察署はどちらの方角ですか Which *direction* [*way*] is the police station?

その病院は反対の方角にある The hospital is *the other way*.

ほうがく[2] 法学 law [U]; (法律学) jurisprudence [U] ‖法学士(学位) Bachelor of Laws; (人) a bachelor of laws / 法学博士(学位) Doctor of Laws; (人) a doctor of laws / 法学部 the college of law

ほうがく[3] 邦楽 Japanese music [U]

ほうかご 放課後 放課後にクラブ活動がある We have club activities *after school*.

ほうかつ 包括 ━包括する《公式的》comprehend [他]; (含む) include [他] ━包括的な comprehensive

ほうがん 砲丸 shot [C] //砲丸を投げる put *the shot*

‖砲丸投げ the shot put

ぼうかん[1] 防寒 防寒のためにマフラーをする put on a scarf *as protection against the cold*

‖防寒服 clothes for cold weather

ぼうかん[2] 傍観 ━傍観する look on ◆彼はその騒ぎを傍観していた He *just stood by and watched* the disturbance.

‖傍観者 an onlooker, a bystander

ぼうかん[3] 暴漢 thug [C] //その国会議員は帰宅途中暴漢に襲われた The Diet member was attacked on his way home by *a thug*.

ほうがんし 方眼紙 graph paper [U], 《英》section paper [U]

ほうき[1] 放棄 abandonment [U]; (権利などの)《公式的》renunciation [U] ━放棄する (あきらめる) give* up; (やむをえず) abandon [他]; (権利などを)《公式的》renounce [他] ➔あきらめる //戦争を放棄する *renounce* war / 遺産の相続権を放棄する「*give up* [*renounce*] *one's* right to inherit property / 試合を途中で放棄する *give up* a match halfway (through) / 彼らはその計画を放棄するしかなかった They were forced to *give up* the plan.

◆従業員たちは職場を放棄する手段に出た The employees resorted to「*walking off their jobs* [*a walkout*].

ほうき[2] 法規 (法律と規則) laws and regulations ◆交通法規を守る obey [《公式的》observe] *traffic regulations* / 法規上の手続きを行う go through *legal* formalities

ほうき[3] 蜂起 (反乱) revolt [C]; (反逆) rebellion [C]; (暴動) uprising [C] ━蜂起する rise* in revolt [rebellion]; (武器を手に) rise in arms; (決起する) rise (against …) // 農民たちは地主に反発して蜂起した The peasants *rose against* their landowner. / 民衆は全国各地で蜂起した The people *rose in rebellion* [*arms*] in all parts of the country.

ほうき[4] 箒 broom [C] //ほうきで床をきれいに掃(は)きなさい Sweep the floor clean with *a broom*. ‖ほうき星 a comet

ぼうぎ 謀議 (陰謀をはかること) conspiracy [C]; (たくらみ) plot [C] ━謀議する conspire (together); plot (together)

ぼうきゃく 忘却 《公式的》oblivion [U] ◆名前を聞くまで彼のことは忘却のかなたにあった I *had forgotten* him *for a long time* until I heard his name.

ぼうぎゃく 暴虐 tyranny [C][U], atrocity [C][U] //ネロは暴虐の限りを尽くした Nero committed all sorts of *atrocities*.

ほうきゅう 俸給 (給与) pay [U]; (月給) salary [C][U]

ぼうきょ 暴挙 (向こう見ずな企て) reckless attempt [C] ◆暴挙に出る resort to *violence*

ぼうぎょ 防御 defense, 《英》defence [U]; (保護) protection [U]; (相手の攻撃からの) guard [U] ━防御する defend [他]; protect [他]; guard [他] //防御態勢をとる *be on the defense*

‖防御率〔野球〕an earned run average

[慣用表現] 攻撃は最大の防御である ➔こうげき

ぼうきょう 望郷 両親からの手紙を読んで, 私は望郷の念にかられた I *felt homesick* after reading the letter from my parents.

ぼうぐ 防具 protective gear [U]

ぼうくう 防空 ‖防空壕(ごう) an air-raid shelter

ぼうくん 暴君 tyrant [C]; (専制君主) despot [C]

ぼうけい 傍系 ━傍系の《公式的》subsidiary; (重要でない) minor

ほうげき 砲撃 fire [U], shelling [U] ━砲撃する fire [他][自], shell [他][自] //砲撃を開始する[やめる] open [cease] *fire* / 敵は我々の攻撃に対抗して激しい砲撃を加えてきた The enemy replied to our attack with fierce *shelling*.

ほうけん 封建 ━封建的な feudalistic; (封建制の) feudal

◆彼の父親はとても封建的だ(→考え方が古い) His father *is very old-fashioned*.

‖封建時代 the feudal era / 封建社会 feudal society / 封建主義 feudalism / 封建制度 feudalism, the feudal system

ほうげん[1] 方言 dialect [C] //九州の方言で話す speak (in) *the* Kyusyu *dialect*

ほうげん[2] 放言 (不注意な発言) careless comment [remark] [C]; (思慮を欠いた発言) improper comment [remark] [C]

➔しつげん(失言)

ぼうけん 冒険 adventure [C][U]; (危険) risk [C][U]; (賭(か)け) gamble [C] ━冒険的な adventurous //冒険をする have *an adventure* / 彼はアフリカ奥地への冒険に出かけた He went on *an adventure* to the inner part of Africa. / この種の事業に多少の冒険は付き物だ There is always some *risk* in this kind of business. / こんな時期に会社を設立するのは冒

険だ Starting a company at a time like this is *a risk* [*gamble*]. / 彼は冒険談を聞かせてくれた He talked about *his adventures*.
‖冒険家 an adventurer / 冒険心 adventurous spirit

ぼうげん　暴言　violent [abusive] language ⓤ (❖violent は「乱暴な」, abusive は「口汚い」の意味) /その選手は審判に暴言を吐いたとして, 退場処分を受けた The player was ordered off the field because he *used abusive language* toward the umpire.

ほうこ　宝庫　treasure house ⓒ, treasury ⓒ, storehouse ⓒ /百科事典は知識の宝庫です Encyclopedias are「*treasure houses* [*storehouses*] of information.

ほうこう¹　方向
(方向) direction ⓤ; (…への道) way ⓒ; (進路) course ⓒⓤ ➡ ほう (方)
将来の方向を決める decide *the course* of one's life
彼はどっちの方向へ行きましたか Which *way* did he go?
銀行は反対の方向です The bank is *in the opposite direction*.
彼は方向が分からなくなった (→方向感覚を失った) He *has lost his sense of direction*.
私は方向音痴だ (→方向感覚がない) I *have no sense of direction*.
図書館に行くんですか. 私も同じ方向に行くところです Are you going to the library? I am going *the same way*.
◆彼女は駅の方向へ歩いていった She walked *toward* [*in the direction of*] the station. /
車は方向転換をして (→向きを変えて) 走り去った The car *turned around* and drove away. /
政府は経済政策の方向転換をはかっている The government *is trying to do an about-face in* its economic policy. (❖do an about-face は「(方針などを)180度転換する」の意味) /
事態はよい方向へ向かっている (→よくなってきている) The situation *is* 「*getting better* [*taking a turn for the better*]. / その計画を見直す方向で話がまとまった We have agreed to *aim at* reviewing the plan.
‖方向指示器 a direction indicator, 《米》a blinker, 《英》a winker

ほうこう²　芳香　fragrance ⓒⓤ; (特に花などの) perfume ⓤ (またa ～) /ランの花が甘い芳香を放っている The orchids give off *a sweet fragrance*.
‖芳香剤 an air freshener

ほうこう³　奉公　service ⓤⓒ; (徒弟の) apprenticeship ⓤⓒ /これが会社への最後のご奉公だ This is *my last service* to my company.

ほうこう⁴　放校　(学校からの追放) expulsion from school ⓤⓒ ◆その学生は無免許運転で交通事故を起こして放校処分になった The student *was expelled* from the school for causing a traffic accident without a driver's license.

ほうごう　縫合　suture ⓤⓒ ◆傷口を縫合する stitch up a wound

ぼうこう¹　暴行　(暴力行為) violence ⓤ, assault ⓒ; (婦女暴行) rape ⓤⓒ, 【法律】assault and battery ──暴行する use violence, assault ⓗⓘ; rape ⓗ /婦女暴行罪で逮捕される be arrested *on a charge of rape* [*sexual assault*] / その記者は取材中に暴行を加えられた The reporter *was assaulted* while gathering information.

ぼうこう²　膀胱　bladder ⓒ ‖膀胱炎 cystitis [sistáitis], bladder infection

ほうこく　報告　report ⓤ; (事情の説明) account ⓒ ──報告する report ⓗⓘ, make* a report (on [of] …) (❖「詳細な報告」の場合は前置詞に on を用いる)
実験結果について報告する *make a report on* the results of an experiment
この件は上司に報告しておいたほうがいい You should *report* this matter to your boss.
その事故については彼女から何も報告を受けていない I haven't received any *report* from her about the accident.
現地からの報告がファックスで届いた We've just received *an on-the-spot report* by fax.
彼はその調査についての報告書を作成した He wrote [drew up] *a report* on the investigation.
‖中間報告 an interim report

ぼうさい　防災　disaster prevention ⓤ
◆防災の日 *Disaster Drill Day* / 防災訓練に参加する take part in *a disaster drill* / その工場の防災対策は十分ではない The factory has not taken enough *measures against disasters*.

ほうさく¹　豊作　(特定の作物の) good [bumper] crop ⓒ; (作物全体の) rich [good] harvest ⓤ /今年はリンゴが豊作だった We have had *a good crop* of apples this year. / この地域はここ数年, 豊作続きだ This area has had *a succession of good harvests*.

ほうさく²　方策　(対策) measure ⓒ (しばしば複数形～s); (手段) step ⓒ; (計画) plan ⓒ /事故防止の方策を講じる take *measures* [*steps*] to prevent accidents

ぼうさつ　忙殺　彼はここ数週間, 仕事に忙殺されている He *has been frightfully busy with* his job for several weeks.

ほうさん　硼酸　【化学】boric acid ⓤ
‖ホウ酸水 boric acid solution

ほうし¹　奉仕　service ⓤ ──奉仕する serve ⓗⓘ /社会に奉仕する *serve* the community ◆地域の奉仕活動に専念する devote *oneself to volunteer work* in the community
‖奉仕価格 a bargain price / 奉仕品 a bargain

ほうし²　胞子　spore ⓒ

ほうじ　法事　a (Buddhist) memorial service (for the dead) ‖法事を営む hold *a (Buddhist) memorial service for the dead*

ぼうし¹　帽子
(縁のある) hat ⓒ; (縁のない) cap ⓒ

ぼうし

英語では「縁」の有無でhatとcapを使い分けることに注意。例えば、「麦わら帽子」は縁があるのでstraw hatとなる。一方、「野球帽」は縁がないので、baseball capである。

帽子をかぶる put on *one's* hat [*cap*] / **帽子を脱ぐ** take off *one's* hat
◆彼女は赤い帽子をかぶっていた She was wearing *a* red *hat*./ She had *a* red *hat* on. (⟵後の表現中のonは「身につけて」の意味)

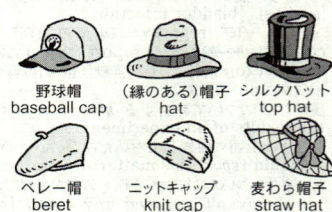

- 野球帽 baseball cap
- (縁のある)帽子 hat
- シルクハット top hat
- ベレー帽 beret
- ニットキャップ knit cap
- 麦わら帽子 straw hat

‖**帽子屋(人)** a hatter; **(店)** a hat shop; **(婦人用帽子の店)** a milliner
関連語 カウボーイハット a cowboy hat / シルクハット a silk [top] hat / 水泳帽 a swimming cap / 制帽 a school cap / ハンチング a hunting cap / 山高帽 《米》 a derby 《英》 a bowler

ぼうし² 防止 prevention ⓤ; **(抑制)** check ⓒ ──**防止する** prevent ⓗ; check ⓗ / **犯罪を防止する** *prevent* crime / **事故を未然に防止する** *prevent* accidents from happening (⟵preventに「未然の意味が含まれる」) / **病気の蔓延(まんえん)を防止する** *prevent* [*check*] the spread of disease / **学校でのいじめの防止策をすぐ講じなければならない** We must take *measures* at once *to prevent* bullying (*from occurring*) in schools.

ほうしき 方式 (形式) form ⓒ; **(方法)** method ⓒ; **(体系)** system ⓒ / **所定の方式に従う** follow *the* standard *form* / **VHSはホームビデオで最も広く使われている録画方式である** VHS is the most widely used recording *system* for home video.
◆**試合はトーナメント方式で行われた** The games were played in *a tournament*.

ほうじちゃ 焙じ茶 roasted tea ⓤ

ほうしゃ 放射 (特に光・熱などの) radiation ⓤ; **(外へ放つこと)** emission ⓤ ──**放射する** radiate ⓗ; emit ⓗ / **熱[光]を放射する** *radiate* heat [*light*] / **放射冷却のためあしたの朝は冷え込みが厳しいだろう** It will be very cold tomorrow morning because *the heat will radiate away during the night.* / **凱旋(がいせん)門を中心に街路が放射状に伸びている** The streets *radiate* from the Arc de Triomphe.
‖**放射熱** radiant heat

ぼうじゃくぶじん 傍若無人 ──傍若無人な (無礼な) insolent; **(ずうずうしい)** impudent / **彼女は傍若無人にふるまった** She behaved 「*in an insolent way* [*with no regard to the feelings of others*].

ほうしゃせい 放射性 ──放射性の radioactive ‖**放射性元素** a radioactive element / **放射性降下物** radioactive fallout / **放射性同位元素** a radioisotope / **放射性廃棄物** radioactive waste / **放射性物質** a radioactive substance

ほうしゃせん 放射線 radiation ⓤ, radioactive ray ⓒ **(しばしば複数形 ~s)** / **その事故で40人以上の人々が放射線を浴びた** More than 40 people were exposed to *radiation* in the accident.
‖**放射線技師** a radiologist / **放射線療法[治療]** radiotherapy

ほうしゃのう 放射能 radioactivity ⓤ, radiation ⓤ / **放射能を浴びる** be exposed to *radiation* / **高レベルの放射能を検出する** detect a high level of *radiation* / **その地域の土壌は放射能で汚染されている** The soil in that area has been contaminated by *radioactivity*.
‖**放射能汚染** radioactive contamination / **放射能もれ** a radiation leak

ぼうじゅ 傍受 ──傍受する (通信などを意図的に) monitor ⓗ; **(偶然受信する)** pick up / **ラジオで暗号無線を傍受した** We *monitored* a coded message on the radio.

ほうしゅう 報酬 (給料) 《口語的》 pay ⓤ, salary ⓒⓤ, **《公式的》** remuneration ⓤ, **(専門職への)** fee ⓒ; **(報い)** reward ⓒⓤ / **…の報酬として** in *reward* for … / **1,000ドルの報酬** *a fee* of 1,000 dollars / **その私立探偵は高額の報酬を要求した[受け取った]** The private detective demanded [received] *a high fee*.

ほうじゅう 放縦 ──放縦な (わがままな) self-indulgent; **(だらしない)** loose / **放縦な生活を送る** lead a *loose* life

ぼうしゅう 防臭 deodorization ⓤ
‖**防臭剤** (a) deodorant

ほうしゅつ 放出 (光・熱・においなどの) emission ⓤⓒ; **(大量の)** spout ⓒ; **(排出)** discharge ⓒⓤ; **(解放)** release ⓤ ──**放出する** emit ⓗ; spout ⓗ; discharge ⓗ; release ⓗ / **その爆発で大量の有毒ガスが空気中に放出された** A huge amount of toxic gas *was released* [*emitted, spouted*] into the air by the explosion.

ほうじゅん 芳醇 ──芳醇な mellow / **芳醇なワイン** *mellow* wine

ほうしょう¹ 褒賞 (ほうび) prize ⓒ; **(報い)** reward ⓒ

ほうしょう² 法相 (法務大臣) the Minister of Justice

ほうしょう 傍証 《法律》 supporting [collaborating] evidence ⓤ

ほうしょうきん 報奨金 reward ⓒ / **その犯人に関する情報提供に対して1,000ドルの報奨金が与えられる** *A reward* of 1,000 dollars is offered for information on the criminal.

ほうしょく 飽食 satiation ⓤ ──**飽食する** satiate *oneself* (with …)

ほうじる 報じる report ⓗ; **(書かれている) 《口語的》** say* ⓗ / **インドで鉄道事故があったとき, きょうの新聞が報じている** Today's newspaper

ほうしん¹ 方針 (主義・信条) principle ⓒⓊ; (政策) policy ⓒⓊ; (行動の) course ⓒ; (党などの) line ⓒ
方針を立てる set [establish] *a policy* / 方針に従う follow *a principle* / 方針を誤る follow [take] *a wrong course* [*policy*] / 方針を180度転換する do an about-face [《英》about-turn] in *one's policy*
そういう行動は我々の方針に反する It's against our *policy* to act like that.
その計画は党の方針に沿って作成された The plan was drawn up along *the lines* set by the party.
‖営業方針 a business policy / 外交方針 a foreign policy / 教育方針 an educational policy

ほうしん² 放心 救助されたとき, その少女は放心状態だった(→ぼう然としていた) The girl *appeared completely dazed* when she was rescued.

ほうじん¹ 邦人(日本人)Japanese ⓒ (複~); (日本人全体) the Japanese ‖在留邦人 *Japanese residents*

ほうじん² 法人(会社)corporation ⓒ ‖法人税 corporation tax / 法人組織 a corporate organization / 学校法人 an educational foundation / 宗教法人 a religious corporation

ぼうず 坊主(Buddhist) priest ⓒ, bonze ⓒ
◆ 坊主刈りにする have one's hair cropped close
‖坊主頭 a close-cropped head
ことわざ 坊主憎けりゃ袈裟(ゖさ)まで憎い If you hate a bonze, you also hate his clothes.; If you hate someone, you hate everything about him [her].

ほうすい 放水 ――放水する (水をかける) hose [hóuz] ⓗ⑤; (水を流す) drain ⓗ⑤ ‖デモ隊に向けて放水する turn water hoses on demonstrators / 消防士たちは燃えているアパートに放水した The fire fighters *aimed their hoses at* the burning apartment house. / 上流のダムが放水を開始した The upstream dam began to *release its water*.
‖放水路 a drain, a drainage canal

ぼうすい 防水 ――防水の (水がしみない) waterproof; (水が入らない) watertight ‖防水加工の繊維 a *waterproof* fabric / この時計は防水(加工)してある This watch *is waterproof*.
‖防水シート a tarpaulin / 防水時計 a waterproof watch

ほうせい 砲声 the roar of artillery
ぼうせい 暴政 tyranny Ⓤ ⇒ あっせい

ほうせき 宝石(研磨した)jewel ⓒ, gem ⓒ, (宝石類)《集合的》jewelry,《英》jewellery Ⓤ; (原石) precious stone ⓒ ‖宝石をはめ込んだブレスレット a bracelet set with *jewels*; a *jeweled* bracelet (❖*jeweled* は形容詞で「宝石で飾られた」の意味) / 彼女の母親はたくさんの宝石を身につけていた Her mother was wearing a lot of *jewels*.
‖宝石商 a jeweler / 宝石店 a jeweler's,《英》a jewelry store / 宝石箱 a jewel case [box]

ぼうせき 紡績 spinning Ⓤ ‖紡績会社 a spinning company / 紡績業 the spinning industry / 紡績工場 a spinning factory [mill]

ぼうせん¹ 防戦 defensive fight ⓒ ――防戦する defend ⓗ⑤ ‖我々のサッカーチームは後半, 防戦一方だった Our soccer team *did nothing but defend ourselves* in the second half.

ぼうせん² 傍線 sideline ⓒ (❖英文では横書きが基本なので underline「下線」がふつう) ‖傍線を引く draw *a sideline*
‖傍線部 a sidelined part

ぼうぜん 呆然 彼女はその知らせを聞いてぼう然となった She *was stunned* by the news. / 選手たちはグラウンドにぼう然と立ち尽くしていた The players stood on the field *in a daze*.

ほうせんか 鳳仙花 balsam ⓒ, touch-me-not Ⓤ

ほうそ 硼素 《化学》 boron Ⓤ (❖元素記号 B)

ほうそう¹ 放送

broadcasting Ⓤ; (1回分の放送) broadcast ⓒ; (放送される番組) program ⓒ ――放送する broadcast* ⓗ⑤; (テレビで) televise ⓗ, telecast* ⓗ
その試合はあすの午後テレビ[4チャンネル]で放送される The game *will be broadcast* on TV [Channel 4] tomorrow afternoon.
首相の演説はラジオで全国放送された The Prime Minister's speech *was broadcast nationwide* on the radio.
◆放送中《掲示》 On (the) Air / この番組の放送時間は午後9時から11時までです *The air time* of this program is from 9 to 11 p.m. / そのテレビ番組は再放送された The TV program *was rebroadcast*.
‖放送衛星 a broadcasting [telecommunications] satellite / 放送局 a broadcasting station, a TV [radio] station / 放送室 a studio / 放送大学 the University of the Air / 放送網 a TV [radio] network / AM [FM]放送 an AM [FM] broadcast / 衛星放送 a satellite broadcast / 校内放送(放送システム) the (school) PA system; (放送の内容) a (school) PA announcement (❖PA は *p*ublic-*a*ddress の略語) / 深夜放送 a late-night program / 生放送 a live broadcast / 2か国語放送 a bilingual broadcast

ほうそう² 包装(包むこと) wrapping Ⓤ; (梱包(ぶ)) packing Ⓤ ――包装する wrap ⓗ; pack ⓗ ‖包装紙 wrapping paper

ぼうそう 暴走(自動車などの) reckless driving Ⓤ ――暴走する drive* recklessly
◆会議で暴走する *make reckless remarks* in a meeting / トラックが暴走して(→制御不能にな

って)通行人をはねた A truck *went out of control* and hit some passersby.
‖暴走族 a motorcycle gang

ほうそうかい 法曹界 legal circles

ほうそく 法則 (自然科学などの) law [C] //万有引力の法則 *the law* of gravitation / 自然の法則 *the laws* of nature

ほうたい 包帯 bandage [C] //足の包帯を取る remove *a bandage* from a leg / 包帯を替える change *bandages* / 看護婦は足首に包帯を巻いてくれた The nurse *wound the bandage* around my ankle. ◆彼は腕に包帯をしていた He *had* his arm *bandaged*.

ほうだい 砲台 (gun) battery [C]

-ほうだい -放題 このレストランではピザが食べ放題だ(→好きなだけ食べることができる) You *can eat as much* pizza *as you like* at this restaurant. / その子はわがままのし放題だ(→何でもしたいことをする) The child *willfully does whatever he likes* [*wants*]. / 彼は討論会で言いたい放題だった(→遠慮なくしゃべった) He *spoke without hesitation* in the debate. / 庭は雑草で荒れ放題だった(→雑草がひどく生い茂っていた) The garden *had become badly overgrown with* weeds.

ぼうだい 膨大 ──膨大な (非常に大きい) very big, huge, enormous //膨大な量のデータを分析する analyze a *huge* [*an enormous*] amount of data / 彼は膨大な切手のコレクションを所蔵している He has a 「*very big* [*huge*] collection of stamps.

ぼうたかとび 棒高跳び (the) pole vault

ぼうだち 棒立ち 彼は驚いて棒立ちになった He *stood petrified* with surprise.

ほうだん[1] 砲弾 shell [C]

ほうだん[2] 放談 (遠慮なくしゃべること) free [frank] talk [C]

ぼうだん 防弾 ──防弾の bulletproof ‖防弾ガラス bulletproof glass / 防弾チョッキ a bulletproof vest

ほうち 放置 ──放置する (置いておく) leave* [他]; (そのままにしておく) leave [let*] ... alone; (無視する) neglect [他] //駅の近くにはたくさんの自転車が放置されていた There *were* a lot of bikes *left* near the station. / 事態は放置できない We *can't leave* the situation as it is.

ほうちこく 法治国 constitutional [law-governed] state [C]

ぼうちゅう 忙中 [慣用表現] 忙中閑あり *You're never too busy to take a break.* (→どんなに忙しくとも休憩をとることはできる)

ぼうちゅうざい 防虫剤 (虫よけ) (insect) repellent [C]; (特に衣類の) mothball [C] 《しばしば複数形 ~s》

ほうちょう 包丁・庖丁 kitchen knife [C]; (肉を切り分ける) carving knife [C]; (大型の肉切り包丁) cleaver [C] //彼女の包丁さばきはみごとだ(→包丁を非常に巧みに操る) She *handles kitchen knives* very deftly.

ぼうちょう[1] 膨張 expansion [U]; (ふくれ上がること) swelling [U] ──膨張する expand [自] [他]; swell* [自] [他] //気体は熱を加えられると膨張する Gases *expand* when they are heated.
‖膨張率 the expansion rate, the rate of expansion

ぼうちょう[2] 傍聴 ──傍聴する hear* [他], listen to ... //その裁判を傍聴するために何百人もの人々が列を作った Hundreds of people lined up to *hear* the trial.
◆その会議は傍聴ができる[できない](→一般の人々に開かれている[いない]) The meeting *is open* [*closed*] *to the public.*
‖傍聴券 an admission ticket / 傍聴席 the visitors' gallery

ほうっておく 放って置く (そのままにしておく) leave* ... alone; (無視する) neglect [他] //ほうっておいてくれ *Leave* me *alone.* / 彼のことをほうっておけない I can't *leave* him *alone.* / この病気はほうっておくとやっかいなことになる This disease will give you more trouble if you *neglect* it.

ぼうっと ❶【はっきりしない様子】(ぼんやりと) dimly; (かすかに) faintly; (漠然と) vaguely; (はっきりとではなく) indistinctly //遠くに白い建物がぼうっと見えた I saw a white building *dimly* in the distance.
◆涙で視界がぼうっとなった(→涙が視界をぼんやりとさせた) Tears *blurred* my vision.
❷【放心した様子で】vacantly, absent-mindedly //彼はぼうっと空を眺めていた She was looking *vacantly* at the sky. / ぼうっとしていて名前を呼ばれたことに気づかなかった I *was* so *absent-minded* that I didn't notice my name was called.
◆彼は起きたばかりでまだ頭がぼうっとしている He just got up, so he's still *half asleep.*

ぽうっと 彼は恥ずかしくて顔がぽうっと赤くなった He *blushed* with shame. / 彼は彼女の美しさにぽうっとなった He *was stunned* [*carried away*] by her beauty.

ほうてい[1] 法廷 court [U] [C], 《公式的》court of law //現在, 法廷が開かれている *The court* is now in session. / その件は法廷の場に持ち込まれた The case *was brought to court for trial.* / 私は法廷へ出頭するよう命じられた I was summoned to *appear in court.*

ほうてい[2] 法定 ──法定の legal ‖法定金利 the legal interest (rate) / 法定相続人 a legal heir / 法定代理人 a legal representative / 法定伝染病 a legal epidemic

ほうていしき 方程式 〔数学〕equation [C] //方程式を解く solve [work out] *an equation*
‖一次方程式 a linear equation / 二次方程式 a quadratic equation / 三次方程式 a cubic equation / 連立方程式 simultaneous equations

ほうてき 法的 ──法的な legal ──法的に legally //法的措置をとる take *legal action* / 財産に対して法的権利をもつ have *legal claim* to the property / 弁護士は私たちに法的手続きについて説明してくれた The lawyer explained *the legal procedure* to us.

ほうでん 放電 (electric) discharge [U] ──放電する discharge (electricity)
‖真空放電 a vacuum discharge

ほ

ぼうと 暴徒 《集合的》mob ⓒ, rioters ‖暴徒を鎮圧する get the mob [rioters] under control

ぼうとう 放蕩 (快楽などにおぼれること) dissipation Ⓤ; (浪費) prodigality Ⓤ ──放蕩する live licentiously ‖放蕩にふける indulge in licentiousness [dissipation]
‖放蕩息子 a prodigal son / 放蕩者 a prodigal

ほうどう 報道
report Ⓤ; (ニュース) news Ⓤ; (ニュース放送) newscast ⓒ ──報道する report ⑯; (取材する) cover ⑯
新聞の報道によると… according to a newspaper report, …
新聞各紙はそのテロ事件について詳しく報道した Every paper reported [covered] the terrorist attack in detail.
旅客機の乗客は全員無事だと報道されている It has been reported that all the passengers on the plane are safe.
多くの新聞がその誘拐事件の報道を差し控えていた Many newspapers refrained from reporting the kidnapping case.
基地内では徹底した報道管制が敷かれていた There was a complete news blackout on the base.
◆その事件は朝刊で大きく報道された(→大きな見出しで載った) The case made the headlines in the morning paper. / 報道の自由が脅(おびや)かされていると感じている人もいる Some people think that freedom of the press is threatened.
‖報道カメラマン a press photographer / 報道関係者《集合的》the press / 報道機関 the news media / 報道写真 a news photograph / 報道陣 the press, reporters / 報道番組 a news program

ぼうとう 冒頭 beginning ⓒ, opening ⓒ ‖演説の冒頭で at the opening [beginning] of one's speech ◆会議では冒頭から活発な議論が繰り広げられた The meeting opened with animated discussion.
‖冒頭陳述 an opening statement

ぼうとう² 暴投 wild pitch [throw] ⓒ ──暴投する throw* a wild pitch ‖野村の暴投で走者は二塁へ進んだ The runner got to second on Nomura's wild pitch.

ぼうとう³ 暴騰 sharp [sudden] rise ⓒ ──暴騰する rise* sharply [suddenly], go* up sharply [suddenly], 《口語的》skyrocket ⑯ ‖昨年は地価が暴騰した Land prices「rose sharply [skyrocketed] last year.

ぼうどう 暴動 riot ⓒ; (反乱) uprising ⓒ; (混乱) disturbance ⓒ ⇨ はんらん(反乱) ‖その町の中心部で暴動が起きた A riot broke out in the center of the city. (❖break out は「(戦争・反乱などが)起こる, 勃発(ぼっぱつ)する」の意味) / 警察はその暴動を鎮圧するために警官隊が出動した The police force was sent to suppress the riot.
◆彼らはその新しい法案に反対して暴動を起こした They rioted against the new bill.

ぼうとく 冒瀆 blasphemy Ⓤ, profanity Ⓤ (❖個々の「冒瀆行為」を指す場合はどちらも ⓒ) ──冒瀆する blaspheme ⑯, profane ⑯ (❖blaspheme は特に言葉によって「冒瀆する」ことをいう) ‖彼の言葉は芸術に対する冒瀆だ His words are a blasphemy to art.

ぼうどくマスク 防毒マスク gas mask ⓒ ‖防毒マスクを着用する wear a gas mask

ほうにち 訪日 a visit to Japan ──訪日する visit Japan ◆訪日中の米大統領がテレビに出演した The American president, now in Japan, appeared on TV.

ほうにん 放任 子供を放任する leave one's children alone
‖放任主義 permissive parenting

ほうねん 豊年 (豊作の年) fruitful [bumper, rich] year ⓒ

ぼうねんかい 忘年会 〔六〕 a bonenkai, a year-end party ‖彼は忘年会で幹事を務めた He arranged the year-end party.

> 忘年会とは文字どおりには, 過ぎゆく年を忘れるための会です. 12月には会社の同僚や親しい友人たちと開くのが一般的です. 人々は1年を楽しい気分で締めくくるため, 飲んで, 食べて, 時には歌ったり踊ったりもします.
> A bonenkai literally is a party to forget the passing year. They are usually held among coworkers and close friends in December. They always involve eating, drinking and sometimes singing and dancing, all done to wind up the year with happy feelings.

ほうのう 奉納 ──奉納する 《公式的》dedicate ⑯; (神前に) offer ⑯ ‖神社に絵馬を奉納する dedicate [offer] an ema to a shrine

ぼうはつ 暴発 ──暴発する「go* off [discharge] accidentally ‖拳銃(けんじゅう)が暴発した The gun「went off [discharged, fired] accidentally.

ぼうはてい 防波堤 breakwater ⓒ ‖大きな波が防波堤に打ちつけた The huge waves crashed against the breakwater.

ぼうはん 防犯 crime prevention Ⓤ, prevention of crime ‖防犯カメラ a security camera / 防犯ベル a burglar alarm

ほうび 褒美 reward ⓒ (また a ~); (賞) prize ⓒ ‖一生懸命勉強したごほうびに, その子はサッカーボールを買ってもらった The child got a soccer ball as a reward for working hard. ◆いい子にしていたら, ごほうびにケーキを焼いてあげる I'll bake a cake for you if you are good.

ぼうび 防備 defense, 《英》defence Ⓤ; (保護) protection Ⓤ ──防備する defend ⑯; (攻撃から身を守る) guard ⑯ ‖敵の攻撃に備えて防備を固める strengthen the defense against an attack by the enemy

ぼうびき 棒引き 借金を棒引きにする(→帳消しにする)「write off [cancel] a person's debts

ほうふ¹ 豊富 richness Ⓤ, (多量) abundance Ⓤ ──豊富な rich; (たくさんある) plenty of …; (ありあまるほどの) abundant,

ほうふ

ほうふ ──豊富に richly; abundantly 天然資源が豊富な a country *rich* [*abundant*] *in* natural resources
食糧は豊富にある We have *plenty of* food.
卵はタンパク質が豊富だ Eggs *are rich in* protein.
◆語彙(ぃ)を豊富にするのに最もよい方法は何ですか What is the best way to *enrich* my vocabulary? / この店は品ぞろえが豊富だ(→多くの種類の品物を置いている) There *is a wide variety of* goods at this shop. / 彼は人生経験が豊富だ He has had *broad* experience in life. / 彼はアメリカ文化について豊富な知識をもっている He knows *a lot* about American culture.

ほうふ² 抱負 (野望) ambition ⓒ; (計画) plan ⓒ ∥その選手は来期の抱負を語った The player told us about *his ambitions* [*plans*] for the next season.

ほうふう 暴風 storm ⓒ; (強風) windstorm ⓒ ∥この3日間, 暴風が吹き荒れている A *storm* [*windstorm*] has been raging for the past three days.
∥暴風域 a storm zone [area] / 暴風警報 a storm warning

ほうふうう 暴風雨 storm ⓒ, rainstorm ⓒ ∥暴風雨に巻き込まれる be caught in *a storm* [*rainstorm*] / 暴風雨は地域に大きな被害をもたらした *The storm* [*rainstorm*] caused extensive damage to the district.

ほうふうりん 防風林 windbreak ⓒ

ほうふく 報復 (復讐(ふく)) revenge Ⓤ; (仕返し) retaliation Ⓤ; (国家間の) reprisal Ⓤ ⓒ ──報復する revenge ⓔ, take* *revenge* on …; retaliate ⓐ; make* a reprisal ∥彼らは武装ゲリラによる報復を恐れている They fear that the armed guerrillas *will take revenge on* them.
◆アメリカ政府はその国に何らかの報復措置をとることを検討している The U.S. government is now considering taking some *retaliatory measures* against the country.

ほうふくぜっとう 抱腹絶倒 私たちは彼の物まねに抱腹絶倒した(→おなかの皮が裂けるほど笑った) We *nearly split our sides laughing at* his mimicry. / We *laughed our heads off at* his mimicry.

ほうふざい 防腐剤 (殺菌用) antiseptic ⓒ; (腐敗防止の) preservative ⓒ

ほうふつ 彷彿 彼女は亡くなった彼女のおばさんをほうふつとさせる(→思い出させる) She *reminds* me *of* her late aunt. / (→たいへんよく似ている) She *closely resembles* her late aunt. / この壁画は当時の人々の暮らしぶりをほうふつとさせる This wall painting *shows clearly* how people lived in those days.

ほうぶつせん 放物線 parabola ⓒ ∥ 放物線を描く describe *a parabola*

ほうぶら mosquito larva ⓒ, wriggler ⓒ ∥ 水たまりにほうぶらがわいた *Mosquito larvae* hatched in the pool. (✿larvae は larva の複数形)

ほうへい 砲兵 (集合的)artillery ⓒ; (一人の) artilleryman ⓒ ∥砲兵隊 the artillery

ほうべん 方便 (手段) means ⓒ (複 〜); (得策) expedient ⓒ
ことわざ うそも方便 ⇨ うそ

ほうほう 方法

way ⓒ; (論理的な) method ⓒ; (手段) means ⓒ (複 〜)
英単語をたくさん覚えられる方法はないだろうか Is there *a way* to be able to memorize many English words?
私もそれと同じ方法を試したが, うまくいかなかった I tried it in *the same way* [*manner*], but I couldn't do it.
それがみんなを納得させるいちばんよい方法だ It's *the best way to* convince everyone.
彼らは生産コストを削減する方法について話し合った They discussed *the way to* [*how to*] reduce the cost of production.
これまではそこに行くにはバスを利用するしか方法がなかった Using the bus had been *the only way to* go there until now.
マニュアルに書いてある方法でやれば簡単にできる If you use *the method* written in the manual, you can do it easily.
私たちはその子供の命を救うためにありとあらゆる方法を試した We tried every [all] possible *means* to save the child's life.
◆彼はそのソフトをインストールする方法を同僚に説明した He explained to his colleague *the procedure* for installing the software.

ほうぼう 方々 (至る所に) everywhere; (あちこちに) here and there ∥方々捜したが, かぎは結局見つからなかった I looked for the key *everywhere*, but I couldn't find it.
◆方々に電話して, やっと兄の居場所が分かった I telephoned *around* and finally found out where my brother was. / 彼らは方々から東京に集まった They gathered at Tokyo *from all directions*. / ニューヨークに着いた翌日, 私たちは市内の名所を方々(→たくさん)訪ねた The day after we arrived in New York, we visited *a lot of* famous places in the city.

ほうぼう その庭は草ぼうぼうだった(→雑草がひどく生い茂っていた) The garden *was overgrown* [(公式的に)*rank*] *with weeds*. / 彼の髪の毛はぼうぼうに伸びていた His hair *was left to grow wild*. / ビルの中で火がぼうぼう燃えている A fire *is raging* in the building.

ほうほうのてい ほうほうの体 泥棒はほうほうの体で(→大あわてで)逃げ出した The burglar ran away *in a great hurry*.

ほうぼく 放牧 grazing Ⓤ ──放牧する put* … to pasture [grass] ∥羊を放牧する *put* sheep *out to pasture*
∥放牧地 a pasture

ほうまん¹ 放漫 ──放漫な (だらしのない) loose [lúːs] ⓒ; (手ぬるい) lax ∥放漫経営がたたって, その会社は倒産に追い込まれた The company went bankrupt because of *lax management*.

ほうまん² 豊満 ──豊満な voluptuous,

plump; (女性が) buxom
◆豊満なバスト an *ample* bosom

ほうむ 法務 ‖法務省 the Ministry of Justice / 法務大臣 the Minister of Justice

ほうむる 葬る (墓に埋める) bury [他]; (議案などを棚上げする) shelve [他] ‖彼女は生まれ故郷に葬られた She *was buried* in her hometown. ◆その事件の真相は永久にやみに葬り去られた(→隠ぺいされた) The real facts of the case *were hushed* [*covered*] *up* forever. / その不祥事が原因で彼は政界から葬り去られた He *was excluded from* politics because of the scandal.

ぼうめい 亡命 exile [U]; (政治亡命) political asylum [U]; (敵国などへの亡命) defection [U] ―亡命する go* into exile; seek* political asylum; defect (to ...) ‖そのチェロ奏者はアメリカに亡命した The cellist 「*went into exile* [*sought political asylum*] in the United States.
‖亡命者(政治亡命者) a political refugee; (敵側の国に亡命した人) a defector / 亡命政権[政府] a government in exile

ほうめん[1] 方面 ❶【方向・地域】(方向) direction [C]; (地域) area [C]; (地区) district [C] ‖松本方面への電車は現在不通である Trains going *in the direction of* Matsumoto are now suspended. / 台風は九州方面に大きな被害をもたらした The typhoon caused a lot of damage to *the* Kyushu *area*.
❷【分野】(研究・活動などの) field [C]; (角度) angle [C]; (面) aspect [C] ‖その会議には各方面の第一人者が出席した Authorities from various *fields* were present at the conference. / この問題は様々な方面から検討を加える必要がある We should examine this problem from various *angles* [*aspects*].

ほうめん[2] 放免 release [U]; (容疑からの) acquittal [U] [C] ―放免する release [他], set* ... free; acquit [他] ‖彼は無罪放免になった He *was acquitted of the charge*.

ほうもつ 宝物 treasure [U] (❖個々の宝物は [C]) ‖宝物殿 a treasury

ほうもん 訪問 visit [C]; (短い) call [C] ―訪問する visit [他], pay* a visit to ...; (人を) call on ...; (家を) call at ...
会社訪問をする *visit a company for an interview* / 表敬訪問する *pay a courtesy call*
先週東京の北野氏を訪問した I *visited* [*called on*] Mr. Kitano in Tokyo last week.
きょう家庭訪問がある *The teacher will call at my house* today.
それは私にとって初めてのパリ訪問だった That was my first *visit to* Paris.
アメリカの大統領は韓国を訪問中である The U.S. president *is* now 「*on a visit to* [*visiting*] South Korea.
首相は中国を公式訪問した The prime minister *paid an official visit to* China.
‖訪問着 a semi-formal kimono / 訪問客 a visitor, a caller / 訪問販売 door-to-door sales

ぼうや 坊や (男の子) boy [C]; (子供) child [C]; (息子) son [C] ‖さっきお宅の坊やを公園で見かけましたよ I saw your *son* in the park a few minutes ago. / 坊や, お母さんはどこかい Where is your mother (, *little boy*)? (❖little boy, boy, child, son などの呼びかけの語は, 特に言わない場合も多い)

ほうやく 邦訳 Japanese translation [U] (❖「翻訳したもの」を個々に指す場合は [C]) ‖スタインベックの小説のほとんどは邦訳で読むことができる Almost all of Steinbeck's novels are available in *Japanese translation*. / その小説の邦訳は出ていない *A Japanese translation* of the novel isn't available.

ほうよう[1] 抱擁 hug [C], embrace [C] ―抱擁する hug [他], embrace [他]

ほうよう[2] 法要 Buddhist service [C] ‖法要を営む hold *a Buddhist service*

ほうようりょく 包容力 彼は包容力がある He *is broad-minded* [*tolerant*].

ぼうよみ 棒読み 彼のスピーチはまさしく原稿の棒読みだった He gave a speech just by *reading* his manuscript *in a monotonous tone*.

ぼうらく 暴落 sudden [sharp] fall [C]; (株価などの) slump [C]; (大暴落) crash [C] ―暴落する fall* sharply [suddenly]; (株価などが) slump [自]; (大暴落する) crash [自] ‖ニューヨーク株式市場で株価が暴落した Stocks *fell* [*crashed*] on the New York stock market. / *There was a crash* on the New York stock market.

ぼうり 暴利 excessive profit [C] ‖暴利をむさぼる make *excessive profits*

ほうりあげる 放り上げる throw* up; (ひょいと乱暴に) toss up ‖ボールを放り上げる *throw up* a ball

ほうりこむ 放り込む throw* in, throw ... into ～ ‖彼女はチョコレートを口に放り込んだ She *threw* [*popped*] a piece of chocolate *into* her mouth.

ほうりだす 放り出す (物を外へ) throw* out; (放棄する) give* up; (未完成のままにする) leave* ... unfinished ‖酔っ払いを通りに放り出す *throw out* a drunken man *into* the street / 仕事を途中で放り出すなんて君らしくない It isn't like you to *leave* your work *unfinished*.

ほうりつ 法律 (個々の) law [C]; (全体) law [U]《通例 the ～》; (法学) law (❖学問としての law には冠詞を付けない) ―法律の (法律にかなった) lawful; (法律の上での) legal
法律を守る obey [《公式的》observe] *the law* / 法律を破る break [violate] *the law* / 法律を施行する enforce *a law*
彼は大学で法律を学んだ He studied *law* in college.
その法律を制定するにはまだ時間がかかるだろう It will take much more time to enact the *law*.
わいろを受け取ることは法律で禁止されている Accepting a bribe is prohibited *by law*. (❖by law の law には冠詞を付けない) / *The law* prohibits accepting a bribe.

その警察官の行為は法律に照らして厳しく罰せられるべきだ The policeman's behavior should be punished severely *according to the law*.
それは法律違反だ That's *against the law*.
◆私は法律に触れるようなことは何もしていない I didn't do anything *unlawful* [*against the law*].
‖法律家 a lawyer / 法律事務所 a law office / 法律用語 a legal [law] term

ほうりなげる 放り投げる throw* [他] //私はソファーの上にコートを放り投げた I *threw* my coat onto the sofa.

ぼうりゃく 謀略 (たくらみ) plot [C]; (わな) trap [C] //謀略をめぐらす form *a plot* / 敵の謀略にはまる fall into *a trap* set by the enemy

ほうりゅう 放流 ─放流する (水を) discharge [他]; (魚などを) stock [他] //ダムの水を放流する *discharge* water from a dam / 川に魚を放流する *stock* a river with fish

ほうりょう 豊漁 good [big] catch [C]

ぼうりょく 暴力 violence [U]; (力ずく) force [U] //暴力はやめろ Don't use *violence*! / その男子生徒はクラスメートによく暴力を振るう The boy student often uses *violence* against his classmates./ The boy is often *violent* to his classmates. / 彼女は夫の暴力が許せなかった She couldn't tolerate her husband's *violence*. / 私は暴力に訴えることには絶対反対だ I'm strongly opposed to *resorting to violence*. / この映画は暴力シーンが多すぎると思う I think there's too much *violence* in this movie.
‖暴力行為 an act of violence / 暴力団(組織) a gang; (組員) a gangster / 家庭内暴力 domestic violence / 校内暴力 school violence

ボウリング bowling [U] ◆ボウリングをしに行く go *bowling*
‖ボウリング場 a bowling alley

ほうる 放る (投げる) throw* [他]; (無造作に) toss [他] //私はその犬にパンを1切れ放ってやった I *threw* a piece of bread to the dog.

ボウル (容器) bowl [C] //サラダボウル *a* salad *bowl*

ほうれい 法令 (法律) law [C]; (成文法) statute [C]; (条例)《公式的》ordinance [C]
‖法令集 a statute book, a book of statutes

ぼうれい 亡霊 (幽霊) ghost [C] //ある晩父の亡霊が彼のまくら元に現れた One night *the ghost* of his father appeared near the head of his bed.

ほうれつ 放列・砲列 battery [C] //その会社の正面玄関前にはカメラの放列が敷かれていた *A battery* of cameras was set up in front of the company's front entrance.

ほうれんそう spinach [spínitʃ] [U] //ホウレンソウ1把 a bunch of *spinach*

ほうろう[1] 放浪 ─放浪する (さまよう) wander (about); (ぶらぶらする) roam (about) // 彼はひとり放浪の旅に出た He set out *wandering* alone. ◆放浪生活を送る lead *a wandering* [*vagabond*] *life*
‖放浪癖(へき) wanderlust

ほうろう[2] 琺瑯 enamel [U] ◆ほうろうの鍋 an *enameled* pot

ぼうろん 暴論 (ばかげた主張・意見) absurd comment [C] //暴論を吐く make *an absurd comment* / それは暴論だ That's really *an absurd comment*.

ほうわ[1] 飽和 saturation [U] //飽和状態に達する reach *the saturation point* ◆駅前の駐車場はすでに飽和状態だ The parking lot in front of the station *is* already *filled to capacity*.
‖飽和液 a saturated solution

ほうわ[2] 法話 sermon [C] //法話をする preach *a sermon*

ほえごえ 吠え声 (犬の) bark [C]; (猛獣の) roar [C]; (オオカミなどの遠ぼえ) howl [C] //犬のほえ声で目をさました I woke up at *the bark* of a dog.

ほえる 吠える (犬が) bark [自]; (猛獣が) roar [自]; (オオカミなどが遠ぼえをする) howl [自] //犬は私に向かって激しくほえ始めた The dog *began to bark* loudly *at* me.
[慣用表現] ほえる犬はめったにかまない *Barking dogs seldom bite*.

ほお 頬 cheek [C] (❖左右両方の「ほお」を指すときはcheeksと複数形で用いる)
彼のほおを涙が伝って流れた Streaks of tears ran down *his cheeks*.
彼はほおがこけていた He had hollow *cheeks*./ His *cheeks* were sunken.
彼は彼女のほおにキスした He kissed her on *the cheek*.
[慣用表現] 私の言葉を聞いて彼女はほおを染めた (→赤くなった) She *blushed* at my words. / 先生がしかると, 彼女はほおをふくらませた She *puffed her cheeks out* when the teacher scolded her.

ボーイ ⚠(レストランの) waiter [C]; (ホテルなどの) bellboy [C],《米》bellhop [C]; (客船などの) steward [C] //ボーイさんがメニューを持ってきた *A waiter* brought a menu.

ボーイスカウト (団体) the Boy Scouts; (団員) boy scout [C] //私の弟はボーイスカウトに入っている My younger brother belongs to *the Boy Scouts*.

ボーイッシュ その少女はいつもボーイッシュな服装をしている The girl always wears *boyish* clothes.

ボーイフレンド ⚠boyfriend [C] (❖日本語の「ボーイフレンド」に比べて, 恋人として関係の深い相手を指す. 特に性別を示す必要がなければfriend of mineとすればよい)

ポーカー (トランプの) poker [U] //ポーカーをする play *poker*

ポーカーフェース ─ポーカーフェースの poker-faced ◆ポーカーフェースを装う assume *a poker face*

ほおかぶり 頬被り 彼らの不正な行為にほおかぶりをする(→無視する)わけにはいかない We cannot *ignore* their unlawful act.

ボーカル vocal [C]《しばしばthe ～s》// 女性ボーカル female *vocals*

ほ

◆彼はそのロックバンドのボーカルだ He is *the vocalist* of the rock band.

ボーク 〘野球〙 balk [C] ━ボークをする balk [自] ‖ボークをとられる be called for *a balk* / ボークで一塁走者は二塁へ進んだ The first-base runner advanced to second *on a balk*.

ポーク pork [U]
‖ポークカツ a pork cutlet / ポークソテー sautéed pork

ほおじろ 頰白 (Japanese) bunting [C]

ホース hose [hóuz] [C] ‖ゴムホース *a rubber hose* / 消火用のホース *a* fire *hose* / ホースで庭に水をまく water a garden with *a hose*

ポーズ[1] (姿勢) pose [C] ‖私の話に彼が関心を示したのは, 単なるポーズだった His interest in my story was *a* mere *pose*. ◆(カメラの前で)ポーズをとる *pose* for a photo

ポーズ[2] (休止) pause [C] ‖少しポーズをおいてから彼女はまた話し始めた After *a pause*, she started talking again.

ほおずき 〘植物〙 ground cherry [C]
‖ほおずき市 a ground cherry fair

ほおずり 頰ずり 赤ん坊にほおずりをする *press one's cheek against* a baby

ボーダーライン (境界線) borderline [C] ‖彼女は合否のボーダーライン上にいた She was on *the borderline* between passing and failing.

ポータブル ━ポータブルの portable
‖ポータブルテレビ a portable television

ポーチ[1] (車寄せ) porch [C]

ポーチ[2] (小物入れ) pouch [C]

ほおづえ 頰杖 ほおづえをつく *rest one's chin on* [*in*] *one's hand*(*s*)

ボート 《米》rowboat [C], 《英》rowing boat [C], boat [C] (❖boatは汽船・客船も含む) ‖池でボートをこぐ row *a boat* on a pond
‖ボートピープル boat people / ボートレース a boat race / 貸しボート a boat for hire [rent] / 救命ボート a lifeboat / ゴムボート a rubber raft

ポートレート portrait [C]

ボーナス bonus [C] ‖あなたの会社ではボーナスはいつ出ますか When do you get *your bonus* at your company?

ホーバークラフト ➔ ホバークラフト

ほおばる 頰張る その子はクッキーをほおばった The child *stuffed* [*filled*] *his mouth with* cookies. / 彼は食べ物をほおばったまま(→口の中をいっぱいにして)話した He spoke *with his mouth full*.

ほおひげ 頰髯 sideburns

ホープ hope [C] ‖彼はうちのチームのホープだ He is *the hope* of our team.

ほおべに 頰紅 (cheek) rouge [U]
◆ほお紅をつける *rouge one's cheeks*

ほおぼね 頰骨 cheekbone [C] ‖彼女はほお骨が出ている She has high *cheekbones*.

ホーマー homer [C], home run [C] ➔ ホームラン ‖彼は60号ホーマーを放った He slammed *his* 60th *home run* (of the season).

ホーム[1] ⚠(プラットホーム) platform [C] ‖彼はホームから私に手を振った He waved at me from *the platform*. / 大阪行きの列車は5番ホームから出ます The train for Osaka will start from *Platform* No. 5.

ホーム[2] ⚠(家庭) home [C] (❖「家庭」の意味で用いる「ホーム」のついた日本語は, 和製英語が多いので注意が必要); (施設) home [C]; (本塁) home plate [U], home [U]
‖ホームグラウンド *one's* home (grounds) / ホームゲーム a home game / ホームドクター a family doctor / ホームドラマ a family drama / 老人ホーム a retirement community [home]; (看護付きの) a nursing home

ホームイン ⚠ 古田の二塁打で一塁ランナーがホームインした The runner on first base *reached home* on Furuta's two-base hit. (❖「ホームイン」は和製英語)

ホームシック homesickness [U] ━ホームシックの homesick ‖ホームシックになる feel [get, be] *homesick*

ホームスチール ⚠ a steal of home (❖「ホームスチール」は和製英語) ◆鈴木は鮮やかにホームスチールを決めた Suzuki *stole home* excellently.

ホームステイ homestay [C]
➔ [場面・状況別会話] p.1752
◆この夏オーストラリアでホームステイをするつもりだ I'm going to「*stay with an* Australian *family* [*do a homestay* in Australia] this summer.

ホームストレッチ the homestretch

ホームプレート 〘野球〙 home plate [C], home [C], home base [C], the plate

ホームページ 〘コンピュータ〙 (トップページ) home page, homepage [C]; (ウェブサイト) website, Web site, web site [C] ➔ [場面・状況別会話] p. 1700 ‖東京書籍のホームページにアクセスする access *the* Tokyo Shoseki *home page*
💬「自分のホームページを作ったよ」「すごい. アドレス教えて」 "I made my own *Web site*." "Great! Tell me the address."

ホームベース ➔ ホームプレート

ホームヘルパー ⚠(障害者・高齢者などの介護を行う人) 《米》in-home aide [C], 《英》home help [C] (❖「ホームヘルパー」は和製英語) ‖祖母にはホームヘルパーが必要だ My grandmother needs *an in-home aide*.

ホームラン 〘野球〙 home run [C], homer [C] ‖彼は今季ホームランを45本打った He hit [slammed] 45 *home runs* this season.
‖ホームラン王 the home-run king [leader] / ホームランダービー a home-run derby / ホームランバッター a home-run hitter [slugger, producer]

ホームルーム homeroom [C][U] ‖ホームルームでいじめについて話し合った We discussed bullying in *homeroom*.

ホームレス 《集合的》the homeless; (個人) homeless person [C] ━ホームレスの homeless

ポーランド Poland (❖公式名 the Republic of Poland) ━ポーランド人 Pole [C] ━

ほ

ポーランド語 Polish ⃝ ──ポーランド(人[語])の Polish
ボーリング ⇨ ボウリング
ボーリング² (穴をあけること) boring ⃝ ──ボーリングする bore 他自
‖ボーリングマシーン a boring machine
ホール¹ (建物・大広間) hall ⃝ ‖コンサート[ダンス]ホール a concert [dance] hall / このホールは1,000人を収容できる広さがある This hall is large enough to hold 1,000 people.
ホール² 〖ゴルフ〗hole ⃝ ‖ホールインワンをする get a hole-in-one
ボール¹
❶【球】ball ⃝
テニス[ゴルフ]ボール a tennis [golf] ball / ボールを投げる[打つ] throw [hit] a ball
◆キャッチボールをする play catch
❷【野球の悪球】ball ⃝
ツーストライクスリーボール three balls and two strikes; three and two (❖日本語と語順が逆になることに注意) / ボール球に手を出す swing at a ball
‖ボールカウント the count
ボール² ⇨ ボウル
ボールがみ ボール紙 cardboard ⃝, pasteboard ⃝, paperboard ⃝
ホールディング (バレーボール・サッカーなどの反則) holding ⃝
ボールばこ ボール箱 carton ⃝, cardboard box ⃝
ボールペン ⚠ ballpoint (pen) ⃝, ball-point (pen) ⃝, 《英》biro (❖×ball pen とはいわない)
ほおん 保温 ──保温する keep* ... warm [hot] ◆このスキーウエアは保温性にすぐれている This ski suit retains heat very well.
ぼおん 寺の鐘がぼおんと鳴るのが聞こえた I heard the bong [dong] of the temple bell.

ほか 外・他

❶【別の】──another other, else (❖疑問詞や something, someone などの不定代名詞の後に置く);(もう1つ別の) another
私たちは寺院やそのほかの場所を観光してきた We went sightseeing at the temples and other places.
彼女はクラスのほかのだれよりも絵がうまい She paints better than any other student in her class.
ほかの人はみんな賛成した Everyone else agreed.
どこかほかの所に傘を忘れたにちがいない I must have left my umbrella somewhere else.
それはだれかほかの人の車だ That's somebody else's car.
このシャツは私には大きすぎます。ほかの物を見せてください This shirt is too big for me. Show me another one, please.
◆ほかに質問はありますか Do you have any more [further] questions? / Any other questions? / 彼は経験があったのでほかの人たちより有利だった The experience gave him an advantage over the others. / ジムはカナダ人でほかの人たちはイギリス人です Jim is Canadian, and the rest of them are British. (❖rest は「残りの人」の意味)
❷【…以外】except (for) ..., but (❖通例 all, anywhere, everybody, nothing などの語とともに用いる)
マイクのほかは、みんなポピュラー音楽が好きだ All but Mike like pop music.
図書館は月曜日のほかは毎日開いている The library is open every day except Monday.
雨が少し降ったほかは楽しい遠足だった We enjoyed our school outing except for a little rain.
君のほかにこの役を演じられる人はいない Nobody but you could play this part.
彼が来るのを待つほかはなかった I had no choice but to wait for him to come.
❸【…に加えて】
彼は言語学のほかに心理学の博士号も持っている He has a doctor's degree in psychology besides one in linguistics.
民子は英語のほかにフランス語も話せる Tamiko can speak not only English but (also) French.
彼女は女優業のほかに画家としても活躍している She is active as an artist as well as an actress.
その事件でその会社の社長ほか3名が辞職した The president and three others at the company resigned because of the incident.

ぼか blunder ⃝ ‖またぼかをやってしまった I made [committed] a blunder again.
ほかく 捕獲 capture ⃝ ──捕獲する capture 他, catch* 他 ‖捕獲高 a catch
ぼかす 暈す (色を) shade 他, gradate 他; (あいまいにする) obscure 他 ‖問題の焦点をぼかす obscure the point of an issue
◆答えをぼかす(→あいまいな答えをする) give a vague answer
ほかならない 彼の頼みは命令にほかならない His request is nothing「less than [but, short of] an order. / それは社長にほかならなかった It was none other than the president. / あなたの言ったことはセクハラにほかなりません What you said is nothing「less than [but, short of] sexual harassment.
ほかならぬ ほかならぬ君の頼みだから、できるだけのことはしよう Since the request comes from you and no one else, I will do my best.
ほかほか ほかほかのパン fresh-baked bread; bread fresh [hot] from the oven / ほかほかのごはん steaming hot rice
ぼかぼか 彼は私をぼかぼか殴った He rained blows on me.
ぽかぽか きょうはぽかぽかしている It is nice and warm today. / 走ったら体がぽかぽかしてきた I got warmer after running.
ほがらか 朗らか ──朗らかな cheerful, bright, merry ──朗らかに cheerfully, brightly, merrily ‖朗らかに笑う laugh

cheerfully [*merrily*] / 彼は朗らかな人だ He is *a cheerful* person.

ぼかり(と) 彼は私の頭をぼかりと殴った He gave me *a whack on* the head.

ほかん 保管 keeping ⦿, safekeeping ⦿, custody ⦿, storage ⦿ ――保管する keep* ⊕, hold* ⊕ /彼の財産は安全に保管されている His fortune *is in* safe *keeping*. / この薬は子供の手の届かない所に保管してください Keep this medicine out of the reach of children.

ぼかんと 少年はぼかんと口をあけて立っていた The boy was standing *with his mouth wide open*. / 彼女はぼかんとした顔をしていた She had *a vacant* look on her face. / 彼はドアの所でぼかんとつっ立っていた He stood *absent-mindedly* at the door.

ぼき 簿記 bookkeeping ⦿
‖簿記係 a bookkeeper / 商業簿記 commercial bookkeeping

ボギー 〖ゴルフ〗bogey ⦿ /(ダブル)ボギーをたたく make *a* (double) *bogey*

ぼきっ 倒れたときに腕の骨がぼきっと折れた When I fell, my arm broke *with a snap*.

ぼきぼき 子供たちは小枝をぼきぼき折った The children *snapped off* twigs. / 彼は指をぼきぼき鳴らした He *cracked* his knuckles.

ボキャブラリー vocabulary ⦿⦿ /彼女はボキャブラリーが豊富だ She has *a large vocabulary*.

ほきゅう 補給 supply ⦿, 《公式的》replenishment ⦿ ――補給する supply ⊕, replenish ⊕ /人に食料を補給する *supply* food *for* [*to*] a person; *supply* a person *with* food / 燃料を補給する *replenish* fuel
‖補給基地 a supply base [depot] / 補給路 a supply route

ほきょう 補強 reinforcement ⦿⦿ ――補強する reinforce ⊕ /取っ手を針金で補強する *reinforce* a handle with steel wire / この古い橋は補強が必要だ This old bridge needs 「some *reinforcement* [more *support*].

◆その球団は投手陣を補強した(→増やした) The baseball team *increased* the number of the pitching staff.
‖補強工事 reinforcement work

ぼきん 募金 fund raising ⦿; (教会などでの) collection ⦿ ――募金する raise funds, collect contributions /募金額は200万円に達した *The sum of the collection* reached two million yen.

◆新しい図書館建設のため募金を始める start *a campaign to raise money* for the new library / 世界の恵まれない人々のために募金をお願いします Please *donate* some *money* for the poor around the world.
‖ 募金活動 a fund-raising campaign [drive] / 募金箱 a donation [collection] box / 共同募金 the community chest

ぼきん ぼきんと音を立てて *with a snap* / 棒をぼきんと折る *snap off* a stick

ほきんしゃ 保菌者 carrier ⦿ /コレラの保菌者 *a* cholera *carrier*

ぼく 僕 Ⅰ(⦿日本語では自分を表す言い方は「僕」「私」「おれ」などいろいろあるが、英語ではⅠのみ) ⇨わたし(私) /ねえ、僕、この近くに公園はあるかな Is there a park near here, *little boy*?

ほくい 北緯 north latitude (《略語》N.L.) /北緯40度25分の所に at [in] *latitude* 40° 25′ *N* (⦿40° 25′ N は forty degrees twenty-five minutes north と読む)

ほくおう 北欧 (ヨーロッパ北部) Northern Europe; (スカンジナビア) Scandinavia ――北欧の Northern European; Scandinavian ‖北欧人 a Northern European; a Scandinavian / 北欧神話 Norse mythology

ほくげん 北限 the northernmost point; (生物の) the northern limit /この動物の北限は青森県だ Aomori Prefecture is *the northern limit* of this animal.

ボクサー boxer ⦿ (⦿犬にもいう); (プロの) prizefighter

ぼくし 牧師 minister ⦿ (⦿《米》では新教,《英》では長老派・非国教会派の聖職者を指す); clergyman ⦿ (⦿《米》では一般に聖職者, 《英》では bishop 以下の英国国教会の聖職者を指す); pastor ⦿ (⦿通例カトリック・英国国教会以外の牧師を指す) /牧師になる become *a minister*; enter *the ministry*; enter [go into] *the Church* ◆キング牧師 (*the*) *Reverend* King (⦿Reverend は「…師」に当たる尊称)

ぼくじゅう 墨汁 India ink

ほくじょう 北上 ――北上する go* [move] north /台風は現在四国を北上している The typhoon *is going* [*moving*] *north* over Shikoku Island now.

ぼくじょう 牧場 stock farm ⦿, ranch ⦿ (放牧場) pasture ⦿⦿ /牧場を経営する run *a* 「*stock farm* [*ranch*] / 牧場で働く work on *a* 「*stock farm* [*ranch*] / 牛が牧場で草を食べていた Cows were grazing in *the pasture*.
‖牧場主 a rancher

ボクシング boxing ⦿ ‖ボクシングの試合 *a boxing* match

ほぐす (もつれを) disentangle ⊕, unravel ⊕; (緊張を) relax ⊕, ease ⊕ /もつれた糸をほぐす *disentangle* [*unravel*] the twisted string / 緊張をほぐす *relax* [*ease*] *the tension*; take the strain off ◆肩の凝りをほぐす give [do] *a* shoulder *massage*

ほくせい 北西 the northwest ――北西の northwest, northwestern

ぼくそう 牧草 grass ⦿, pasture ⦿ ‖牧草地 a meadow, (a) pasture

ほくそえむ ほくそ笑む chuckle to *oneself*, gloat ⊕ /彼はライバルの失敗にほくそえんだ He *chuckled to himself* [*gloated*] over his rival's failure.

ほくたん 北端 the northernmost part [point], the northern end

ぼくちく 牧畜 livestock farming ⦿, (牛を育てること) cattle breeding ⦿

ほくとう 北東 the northeast ――北東の northeast, northeastern

ぼくとう 木刀 wooden sword ⦿

ぼくどう 牧童 herdboy ⦿; (羊の) shep-

ほくとしちせい 北斗七星 the (Big) Dipper, the Plough

ぼくとつ 朴訥 ――朴訥な unaffected [simple] and honest ∥朴訥な性格 an *unaffected* [a *simple*] *and honest* personality

ほくぶ 北部 the north, the northern part ――北部の northern, north, upper ∥フランス北部 *the north of* France / マンハッタン北部 *upper* Manhattan

ほくべい 北米 North America ――北米の North American ∥北米大陸 the *North American* Continent

ほくほく 彼は給料が出てほくほく顔だった He *was pleased to* get his salary.

ほくほくせい 北北西 the north-northwest ――北北西の north-northwest

ほくほくとう 北北東 the north-northeast ――北北東の north-northeast

ぼくめつ 撲滅 《公式的》 eradication Ⓤ, extermination Ⓤ ――撲滅する 《公式的》 eradicate Ⓗ, exterminate Ⓗ ∥コレラの撲滅 the *eradication* of cholera / 犯罪を撲滅する *eradicate* crime
∥撲滅運動 a crusade

ほくよう 北洋 the north(ern) sea ∥北洋漁業 north-sea fisheries

ほぐれる (ほどける) get* [come*] loose, disentangle Ⓗ; (緊張が) relax Ⓘ ∥もつれた毛糸がほぐれた The tangled yarn *got* [*came*] *loose*. / 彼の言葉で緊張がほぐれた His words helped me to *relax* my tension.

ほくろ 黒子 mole Ⓒ, 《英》 spot Ⓒ ∥付けぼくろ a beauty *spot* / 目元のほくろ a *mole* under the eye / 彼女は右のほおにほくろがある She has *a mole* on her right cheek.

ぼけ 惚け senility ◆ぼけが始まる begin to go *senile* / まだ休みぼけなんだね *Your head is still on vacation*, isn't it?
∥ぼけ老人 a senile old person / 時差ぼけ jet lag

ほげい 捕鯨 whaling Ⓤ, whale fishing Ⓤ
∥捕鯨船 a whale ship, a whaler, a whaling vessel

ぼけい 母系 the maternal line, *one's* mother's side ――母系の maternal (◆名詞の前で用いる) ∥母系家族 a maternal family

ほけつ 補欠 substitute Ⓒ, spare Ⓒ, 《米》 alternate ◆ ◆彼はこの大学に補欠で入学した (→空きを埋めるために) He was admitted to this university *to fill a vacancy*.
∥補欠選挙 a by-election / 補欠選手 a substitute player, a reserve; (野球の) a benchwarmer

ぼけつ 墓穴 grave Ⓒ ∥余計なことを言ってかえって墓穴を掘った I said more than is necessary and *dug my own grave*.

ぼけっ(と) 彼は窓の外をぼけっと眺めていた He was looking out of the window *absent-mindedly*.

ポケット pocket Ⓒ
胸のポケット a breast *pocket* / ポケット版の英和辞典 a *pocket-size(d)* English-Japanese dictionary / ポケットに手をつっ込む stick *one's* hands in [into] *one's* pockets
彼は上着のポケットに切符を入れた He put the ticket in *his* coat *pocket*.
彼女はポケットから財布を取り出した She took her wallet out of *her* pocket.
かぎを出そうとポケットを探った I searched *my* pockets for the key.
∥ポケットカメラ a pocket camera / ポケットベル a pager, a beeper, a bleeper (◆「ポケットベル」は和製英語) / ポケットマネー pocket money / 内ポケット an inside [inner] pocket

ポケベル ⚠pager Ⓒ, beeper Ⓒ, bleeper Ⓒ

ぼける (もうろくする) become* [go*] senile; (ピントが) be out of focus ∥祖父はぼけてきた My grandfather *is becoming* [*going*] *senile*. / この写真はぼけている This picture *is* ⌜*out of focus* [*blurred*]⌝.

ほけん 保険 insurance Ⓤ, 《英》 assurance Ⓤ

保険に入る buy *insurance* / 保険に入っている carry [have] *insurance* / 保険に勧誘する sell *insurance*

◆5,000万円の生命保険をかける *insure oneself* [*one's life*] for 50 million yen / 私は事故に備えてABC生命の自動車保険をかけた I *insured* my car against accidents with ABC Life Insurance Company. / I *bought* accident *insurance* for my car with ABC Life Insurance Company. / 私の家には3,000万円の火災保険がかけてある I *have insured* my house *against fire* for 30 million yen.
∥保険会社 an insurance company / 保険勧誘員 an insurance salesperson / 保険期間 the term [period, duration] of insurance / 保険業 the insurance business / 保険金 insurance (money) / 保険金受取人 a beneficiary / 保険金詐欺 life insurance fraud / 保険金殺人 a murder for insurance / 保険契約 an insurance contract / 保険契約者 a policyholder / 保険証書 an insurance policy / 保険代理店 an insurance agency / 保険料 a premium / 健康保険証 a health insurance card

---
-保険のいろいろ-

介護保険 long-term care insurance / 海上保険 marine insurance / 火災保険 fire insurance / 簡易保険 postal life insurance / がん保険 cancer insurance / 強制保険 compulsory insurance / 健康保険 health insurance / 災害保険 casualty insurance / 失業保険 unemployment [jobless] insurance / 自動車保険 《米》 automobile insurance, 《英》 motor insurance / 社会保険 social insurance / 終身保険 whole life insurance / 傷害保険 accident insurance / 生命保険 life insurance / 損害保険 accident insurance / 団体保険 group insurance / 任意保険 voluntary insurance / 養老保険 endowment insurance

ほけん² 保健 (健康の維持) preservation of good health, keeping good health ⓤ; (衛生) sanitation ⓤ ‖保健室 a clinic; (特に学校の) the nurse's office / 保健所 a (public) health center / 保健体育 health and physical education / 保健婦 [士] a (public) health nurse / 世界保健機構 the World Health Organization ((略語)WHO)

ほご¹ 保護

(守ること) protection ⓤ; (維持・保存) preservation ⓤ, conservation ⓤ ──保護する protect ⓗ; preserve ⓗ, conserve ⓗ
森林保護 forest *conservation* / 自然環境の保護 *protection* of the natural environment / 警察に保護を求める ask the police for *protection* / 紫外線から肌を保護する *protect* one's skin from ultraviolet rays / 後世のために美術品を保護する *preserve* art works for posterity

熱帯雨林を保護しなければならない We need to *preserve* rain forests.

政府は環境保護に多額の金をあてた The government *appropriated* a large sum of money for *environmental protection*.

◆生活保護を受けて暮らす live on *welfare* [*relief*] / その少年は保護観察下にある The boy is *on probation*.

‖保護預かり safe deposit / 保護関税 a protective tariff / 保護区 a sanctuary / 保護者 a guardian; (芸術家などの) a patron; (両親) parents / 保護者会 a PTA meeting / 保護色 protective coloring / 保護処分 probation / 保護鳥 a protected bird / 保護貿易 protective trade / 保護林 a forest preserve / 環境保護団体 an ecological [environmental] group

ほご² 反故・反古 (いらない紙) waste paper ⓤ
◆約束をほごにする (→破る) break one's promise

ほご³ 補語 〖文法〗complement ⓒ

> 5文型の要素の一つ. 不完全自動詞を補って主語を説明する主格補語 (subjective complement) と不完全他動詞を補って目的語を説明する目的格補語 (objective complement) がある ⮕ ごぶんけい

ぼご 母語 (幼児期に最初に習得した言語) one's mother [native] tongue, one's native [first] language

ほこう¹ 歩行 walking ⓤ ──歩行する walk ⓘ ‖彼は障害のために歩行が困難だ He has trouble [difficulty] *walking* because of a handicap.

◆歩行者専用 《掲示》*Pedestrians Only*
‖歩行器 a walker / 歩行訓練 walking exercises / 歩行者 a walker, a pedestrian / 歩行者天国 a pedestrian-only street

ほこう² 補講 supplementary lesson [class] ⓒ

ぼこう¹ 母校 one's old school, one's alma mater [ǽlmə mɑ́ːtər] ◆私の母校は埼玉県立川越高校です I *graduated from* Saitama Prefectural Kawagoe High School.

ぼこう² 母港 home port ⓒ

ぼこく 母国 one's (home [mother]) country, one's homeland ‖母国語 one's mother [native] tongue, one's native language

ほこさき 矛先 彼は私たちの非難の矛先をかわした He *evaded* [*dodged*] our criticism. / 住民は抗議の矛先を市長に向けた The residents *directed* their protest *against* the mayor.

ぼこぼこ そのうちぼこぼこにしてやるぞ I'll *beat* you *to pulp*.

ほこらしい 誇らしい proud ──誇らしげに proudly, with pride ‖彼女は息子を誇らしく思っている She *is proud of* her son. / 彼は自分のワインコレクションを誇らしげに自慢した He *proudly* boasted of his wine collection.

ほこり¹ 埃 dust ⓤ ──ほこりっぽい dusty

ほこりっぽい道 a *dusty* road / 本をかぶった本 a book *covered with dust* / ほこりを立てる *raise dust*

棚にほこりがたまっていた *Dust* had collected on the shelves.

彼の部屋はほこりだらけだった His room was covered with *dust*.

◆彼女は家具のほこりを払った She *dusted* the furniture. (✿この dust は「ほこりを払う」という意味の動詞)

ほこり² 誇り pride ⓤ; (自尊心) self-respect ⓤ ──誇りにする be proud of ..., take* pride in ...

誇りを傷つける hurt [wound] *a person's pride*
彼はわが国の誇りだ He is *the pride* of our country.

私は日本人であることに誇りをもっている I *take pride in* being Japanese.

彼らは息子の成功を誇りにしている They *are proud of* their son's success.

◆助けを求めることは彼女の誇りが許さなかった (→誇りが高すぎて助けを求めることができなかった) She was too *proud* to ask for help. / 彼らは誇り高い民族だ They are a *proud* people.

ほこる 誇る be proud of ..., take* pride in ..., pride *oneself* on ...; (自慢する) boast (about [of] ...) ⮕ じまん ‖彼は自分の母校を誇っている He *is proud* of his alma mater. / 安藤忠雄は日本の誇る建築家の一人だ Ando Tadao is one of the architects the Japanese *are proud of.* / この図書館は国内一の蔵書数を誇っている This library *boasts* the largest collection in the country.

ほころばせる 彼は顔をほころばせた He *broke into* a smile.

ほころび 綻び rip ⓒ, tear ⓒ ‖シャツのほころびをつくろう mend *a rip* in a shirt

ほころびる 綻びる (縫い目が) come* apart; (花が咲く) open ⓘ, bloom ⓘ ‖コートの縫い目がほころびてしまった The seam of my coat *has come apart.* / 梅の花がほころび始めた The plum blossoms began to *open*

ほさ
[bloom].
ほさ 補佐 ─補佐する assist 他⑥, help 他⑥ ‖社長付き補佐 an assistant to the president ‖大統領補佐官 a presidential aide
ほざく 讒言く (→黙れ)! Shut up!
ぼさつ 菩薩 〖仏教〗 Bodhisattva [bòudʌɪvə] ⓒ, Buddhist saint
ぼさっと ぼさっとつっ立ってないでこっちを手伝ってよ Don't *just stand there*. Come here and help us out.
ぼさぼさ ぼさぼさの髪の毛 *ragged* hair; *a mop of* hair / 彼は髪をぼさぼさに伸ばしている He has long *disheveled* [*unkempt*] hair.
ぼさん 墓参 彼は10年ぶりに両親の墓参をした He *visited* his parents' *graves* for the first time in 10 years.

ほし 星

❶ 〖天体〗 star ⓒ
きらきら輝く星 bright *stars* / 星を観察する observe *the stars*
空には星がきらめいていた The sky was blazing with *stars*.
星がたくさん出ている Many *stars* have come out.
空にはひとつの星も見えなかった We couldn't see any *stars* in the sky.
彼女は日本水泳界の星です She is *the star* [*hope*] of Japan's swimming world.
◆ 星の出ている夜 a *starlit* [*starry*] night / 星の出ていない夜 a *starless* night
🅒「恵子にふられちゃったよ」「落ち込むなよ。女の子は星の数ほどいるんだから」 "Keiko broke up with me." "Don't feel bad. *There are other fish in the sea*." (❖There are other fish in the sea. は「いい人はほかにもいる」の意味の慣用表現)
❷ 〖運勢〗 star ⓒ
彼は幸運[不運]な星のもとに生まれた He was born under *a lucky* [*an unlucky*] *star*.
❸ 〖星印・星の形をしたもの〗 (＊印) asterisk ⓒ; (☆, ★などの印) star ⓒ
この花は星のような形をしている This flower is shaped like *a star*.
その単語には星印がつけられている The word is marked with *an asterisk*.
❹ 〖犯人〗 culprit ⓒ
ほしを挙げる (→つかまえる) arrest [catch] *a culprit*
‖星明かり starlight / 星くず stardust / 星空 a starry sky / 流れ星 a falling [shooting] star / ほうき星 a comet
ほじ 保持 maintenance ⓤ ─保持する keep* 他⑥, maintain 他; (記録・タイトルなどを) hold* 他⑥, retain 他 ‖あのボクサーは世界ヘビー級のタイトルを3年間保持した The boxer *held* [*retained*] the world's heavyweight title for three years.
◆ 彼女はマラソンの世界記録保持者だ She *is the world-record holder* for [in] the marathon. / (→世界記録を保持している) She *holds the world record* for [in] the marathon.

‖タイトル[選手権]保持者 a titleholder
ぼし 母子 mother and child [baby] ‖母子家庭 a fatherless family, a family consisting of a mother and her child [children] / 母子手帳 a maternity (health) record book
ポジ 〖写真〗 (photographic) positive ⓒ

ほしい 欲しい

❶ 〖手に入れたい〗 want 他, would like (❖want より控えめで丁寧な表現)
どんなスーツが欲しいのですか What suit *would* you *like*?
何か冷たい飲み物が欲しい I *want* something cold to drink.
欲しいだけあげよう You may have *as many* [*much*] *as you want*.
ちょうどこれが欲しかったんだ This is just what I *have wanted*.
◆ 今は安らぎと静けさが欲しい (→必要だ) I *need* some peace and quiet now. / 彼は確かに成績優秀だが、もっと積極性が欲しい (→積極性が足りない) It's true he's an excellent student, but he lacks assertiveness. / 6月にも1日くらいは祝日が欲しい I'd *love to have* at least one holiday in June.
🅒「誕生日のプレゼントには何が欲しい」「何か身につけるものがいい」 "What do you *want* for your birthday?" "I'd like something to wear."
❷ 〖…してもらいたい〗 want 他, would like (❖want よりも丁寧な表現), wish 他⑥
【want＋名＋to do】子供たちには希望をもって生きてほしい I *want* my children *to* live in hope. / 私の個人的な問題に口出ししてほしくない I *don't want* you *to* stick your nose in my personal affairs.
【would like＋名＋to do】この手紙を投函(銭)してほしいのですが I *would like* you *to* mail this letter.
加藤さんがすぐに来てほしいとのことです Mr. Kato *wishes* (*for*) you to come over immediately.
◆ 彼女は今のままの彼女でいてほしい I *hope* she'll stay the way she is now.
🅒「今度の週末に東京を案内してほしいんだけど」「どういう所に行きたいの」 "I'd *like* you *to* take me around in Tokyo next weekend." "What kind of places do you want to see?"
ほしいまま 欲しいまま 権力をほしいままにする exercise *one's power* [*authority*] *at will* / ほしいままにふるまう *have one's own way* / 彼女はその映画で大女優としての名声をほしいままにした She *enjoyed a reputation* as a great actress because of that movie.
ほしうらない 星占い、(占星術) astrology ⓤ; (個々の占い) horoscope ⓒ ‖その雑誌の星占いはよく当たる That magazine's *horoscopes* often prove right.

─星座のいろいろ─
おひつじ座 Aries / おうし座 Taurus / ふた

ご座 Gemini / かに座 Cancer / しし座 Leo / おとめ座 Virgo / てんびん座 Libra / さそり座 Scorpio / いて座 Sagittarius / やぎ座 Capricorn / みずがめ座 Aquarius / うお座 Pisces

ポシェット pochette ©（❖フランス語から）
ほしがる 欲しがる want ⊕ ⇒ほしい ∥彼女は必要以上に物を欲しがる She *wants* more than is necessary.
◆その子はそのおもちゃを欲しがって泣いた The child *cried for* the toy.
ほしくさ 干し草 hay © ∥干し草を作る make hay ∥干し草の山 a haystack
ほじくる ❶【地面を】dig* ⊕ ∥地面をほじくる *dig* (*in*) the ground
❷【鼻・歯などを】鼻[歯]をほじくる *pick one's* nose [teeth]
❸【詮索(せんさく)する】pry into … ∥人の過去をほじくる *pry into* a person's past
ポジション position © ∥スコアリングポジション《野球》scoring position
ほしぶどう 干し葡萄 raisin ©; (種なしの) currant ©
ほしもの 干し物（洗濯物）washing ©, wash ©; (干物) dried fish ©© ∥干し物をする hang *the washing* out to dry
ほしゃく 保釈 bail © ∥保釈する let* *a person* out on bail, release *a person* on bail ∥彼は保釈中である He is out *on bail*.
◆彼は500万円払って保釈になった He paid five million yen to *be bailed out*./ He *was released on bail* of five million yen.
∥保釈金 bail (money)
ポシャる その計画は経済的な問題のためにポシャった The plan *fizzled out* because of financial problems.
ほしゅ¹ 保守 ❶【古い習慣・制度などを守ること】——保守的な conservative ∥保守的な見解 a *conservative* view ∥イギリス人は保守的だ The English are *conservative*.
❷【機械などの維持】maintenance © ——保守する maintain ⊕
∥保守主義 conservatism / 保守主義者 a conservative / 保守政権 a conservative government / 保守党 a conservative party, 《英》the Conservative Party, the Tories / 保守党員 a member of a conservative party, 《英》a Conservative, a Tory / 保守派 the conservatives
ほしゅ² 捕手 《野球》catcher ©
ほしゅう¹ 補習 supplementary lesson [class]©, extra lesson [class]© ∥英語の補習を受ける take [attend] *a supplementary lesson* in English
ほしゅう² 補修 repair ©, mending © ——補修する repair ⊕, mend ⊕, fix ⊕ ∥そのビルは現在補修中だ The building is now *under repair*./ この道路は補修する必要がある This road needs *repairing*.
∥補修工事 repair work / 補修材料 repair [mending] materials
ほじゅう 補充（追加）supplement ©; (取り替えること) replacement ©©; (元の状態に戻す) replenishment ©——補充する fill ⊕, supplement ⊕; replace ⊕; replenish ⊕ ∥食料を補充する *replenish* [*resupply*] food / 欠員を補充する *fill* a vacant position

ほしゅう 募集 (人の) recruitment ©; (寄付金などの) collection ©——募集する recruit ⊕, look for *a person*, seek* ⊕; raise ⊕, collect ⊕; (集める) gather ⊕
アイデアを募集する *gather* ideas
私たちの会社はプログラマーを数人募集している Our company *is* 「*recruiting* [*looking for, seeking*] several programmers.
◆アルバイト[店員]募集中《掲示》Part-timers [Clerks] *Wanted* / 生徒募集中《掲示》New Students *Invited* / 彼は販売員募集の広告を出した He *advertised for* a salesclerk.
∥募集広告 a want ad / 募集人員 the number to be accepted [admitted] / 募集要項 an application booklet [brochure]
ほじょ 補助 help ©, aid ©, support ©, assistance ©——補助する help ⊕, aid ⊕, support ⊕, assist ⊕ ∥私たちは彼の仕事を補助した We *helped* him *with* his work./ 彼は妹の学費を補助している He *helps* his sister *with* her school expenses./ その産業は国の経済的補助を受けている The industry receives financial *aid* [*support*] from the government.
∥補助いす a spare [an extra] chair; (バスなどの) a jump seat / 補助員 an assistant / 補助教材 teaching aids / 補助金 a subsidy, a grant / 補助食品 a dietary supplement

ほしょう¹ 保証

guarantee ©; (請け合い) assurance ©——保証する guarantee ⊕; (請け合い) assure ⊕, warrant ⊕
1年間保証付きのテレビ a television with *a* one-year *guarantee*
それが真実であると保証します I *assure* you that it is true.
彼が失敗しないという保証はない *There is no guarantee* that he will not fail.
それはまだ保証期間中ですか Is it still *under guarantee* [*warranty*]?
彼女はその真珠が本物であると保証した She *guaranteed* 「*that the pearl is* [*the pearl to be*] *genuine*.
このカメラは3年間の保証付きです This camera *is guaranteed* for three years.
◆精一杯やってみるが何も保証はできない（→約束できない）I'll do my best, but I *can't promise* anything./ 彼の人柄は私が保証します I *vouch for* his personality./ おじにローンの保証人になってもらった I asked my uncle to be *the guarantor* for my loan.
∥保証期間 the period of guarantee / 保証金 security [guaranty] money, a deposit / 保証書 a warranty, a written guarantee
ほしょう² 保障 security ©, guarantee ©——保障する secure ⊕, guarantee ⊕ ∥国家

ほしょう

の安全保障 national *security* / 社会保障(制度) social *security* / 国連安全保障理事会 the U.N. *Security* Council / 日米安全保障条約 the U.S.-Japan *Security* Treaty / 言論の自由を保障する *secure* [*guarantee*] freedom of speech / 私たちの会社では労働者の権利が十分に保障されている Workers' rights *are* fully *secured* at our company.

ほしょう³ 補償 compensation ⓤ,《公式的》reparation ⓤ ──補償する compensate ⊕ //彼女は彼に損害に対しての補償をした She *compensated* him *for* the loss.
◆1,000万円の補償を要求する *claim* 10 million yen (in) *damages*
‖補償金 compensation

ほしょう⁴ 歩哨 sentry ⓒ, guard ⓒ //歩哨に立つ stand *sentry* [*guard*]

ほしょうにん 保証人〔法律〕guarantor ⓒ

ほしょく 補色 complementary color ⓒ

ほじる ⇒ほじくる

ほす 干す・乾す dry ⊕, hang* [put*] … (out) to dry; (風・熱で) air ⊕
服を日なたで干す *dry* clothes in the sun / 洗濯物を(外に)干す *hang* [*put*] the washing (*out*) *to dry* / ふとんを干す *air* a futon
[慣用表現]その俳優はこのところ仕事を干されている The actor *has been deprived of any work* lately.

ボス boss ⓒ, head ⓒ ◆不良グループのボス a gang *leader*

ポスター poster ⓒ //ポスターをはる put up *a poster* / 彼は壁からポスターをはぎ取った He tore *a poster* off the wall.
‖ポスターカラー (a) poster paint

ホステス (客を接待する女性) hostess ⓒ; (バーなどの) bar hostess ⓒ

> 英語のhostessは「パーティーなどで客をもてなす役の女性」という意味で,日本語のホステス(バーやナイトクラブで客の接待をする女性)とはかなり意味が異なる.また女性客を接待する「ホスト」も欧米では一般的ではない.

ホスト (客を接待する男性) host [hóust] ⓒ; (女性向けバーの) host ⓒ, male attendant ⓒ
‖ホストクラブ a club for women customers with male attendants / ホストコンピュータ a host computer

ポスト ⚠
❶【郵便ポスト】《米》mailbox ⓒ,《英》postbox ⓒ //手紙をポストに入れる《米》*mail* [《英》*post*] a letter
❷【地位】post [póust] ⓒ, position ⓒ //責任のあるポストにある hold *a* responsible *post*
‖ポストカード a postcard

ホストファミリー host family ⓒ

ポストモダン ──ポストモダンの postmodern

ボストン Boston (❖米国の都市)

ボストンバッグ ⚠(traveling) bag ⓒ

ホスピス hospice ⓒ //祖父はホスピスに入院した My grandfather went into *a hospice*.

ほする 補する (補佐する) assist ⊕; (任命する) appoint ⊕ //社長は彼を営業部長に補した The president *appointed* him *as* sales manager.

ほせい 補正 revision ⓤ, correction ⓤ ──補正する revise ⊕, correct ⊕
‖補正予算 a revised budget

ぼせい 母性 motherhood ⓤ, maternity ⓤ ──母性の motherly, maternal //母性的な女性 a *motherly* woman / 母性本能をくすぐる appeal to *a person's maternal instincts*
‖母性愛 maternal love

ほぜん 保全 conservation ⓤ, preservation ⓤ //環境保全 environmental *conservation*; *preservation* of the environment
◆領土を保全する *preserve* the territorial integrity

ほそい 細い

❶【物・線などが】(太さが) thin; (幅が狭い) narrow; (繊細に細い・鋭い) fine; (ほっそりした) slender, slim
細い線 a *thin* [*fine*] line / 先の細いペン a pen *with a fine point*
その枝はブランコを下げるには細すぎる The branch is *too thin* to hang a swing from.
彼女は足が細い She has *slender* [*slim*] legs. (❖体型に関してthinを用いるとしばしば「やせすぎ」といった否定的な意味にとられやすい)
私は細い路地をたどって彼の家に着いた I followed a *narrow* path to his door.

❷【その他】
細い(→小さい)声 a *small* [*weak*] voice
そんなに神経が細いと彼らとやっていけないよ You are too *sensitive* to get along with them.
彼は食が細い(→あまり食べない) He *doesn't eat much*.

ほそう 舗装 pavement ⓤⓒ ──舗装する pave ⊕ //その道路はアスファルトで舗装されている The road *is paved with* asphalt.
◆舗装工事 *paving work* / 舗装された道路 a *paved* road / 舗装されていない道路 an *unpaved* road

ほそうで 細腕 彼女は女の細腕一つで(→独力で)老舗(しにせ)の旅館を切り盛りしてきた She has managed the old hotel *all by herself*.

ほそおもて 細面 slender [narrow] face ⓒ //細面の美人 a beautiful woman *with a slender face*

ほそく 補足 ──補足する supplement ⊕; (補って完全にする) complement ⊕; (付け加える) add ⊕ //私は彼の説明にいくつか関連事項を補足した I *supplemented* his explanation with some related information.
◆補足説明をする give *a supplementary explanation*

ぼそっと 「ごめん」と彼はぼそっと言った "I'm sorry," he "*said in a low voice* [*mumbled*].

ほそながい 細長い (長い) long; (幅の狭い) narrow; (細い) thin; (ほっそりした) slender //細長い影 a *long* shadow / 細長い布切れ a (*long*) *strip* of cloth (❖stripは「細長い1片」の意味) / あの細長い箱には何が入っているの

What is in that *long* box? / その花びんは細長い形をしている The vase has a *slender* shape.

ぼそぼそ 彼はぼそぼそと何か言ったがよく聞こえなかった He *mumbled* [*murmured*] something but I couldn't hear him very well.

ほそぼそと 細々と 彼は妻と地方の町で細々と暮らしている He and his wife「*make a meager living* [*earn a bare living*]」in a country town.

ほそみ 細身 細身の刀 a *narrow* sword / 彼女はいつも細身のパンツをはいている She always wears *rather tight* pants.

ほそめ 細目 細目をあける *open one's eyes a little* / 窓を細めにあけておく keep the window *slightly* open

ほそめる 細める 彼女は明るい太陽の光に目を細めた She *squinted* at the bright sunshine. / 彼は道路標識を読もうとして目を細めた He *squinted* to read the sign. / 老婦人は子供たちから絵をプレゼントされて目を細めた The old woman's *eyes wrinkled with pleasure* when the children gave their pictures to her. (❖narrow *one's eyes* は疑惑・怒りの表現なので、日本語の「目を細める」には当てはまらない)

ほそる 細る 食が細る *lose one's appetite* / 恥ずかしくて身の細る思いがした I *shrank* in embarrassment.

ほぞん 保存 preservation ⓤ ――保存する (とっておく) keep* ⓗ ⓘ; (腐敗などから守る) preserve ⓗ / 食料をびんに入れて保存する *preserve* food in jars / その壁画は保存状態がよい The mural is「*well preserved* [*in a good state of preservation*]」.
◆ファイルをハードディスクに保存する *save* a file on a hard disk

💬「このドレッシングはどのくらい保存がききますか」「冷蔵庫で2週間です」"How long *can* this dressing *be kept* [*preserved*]?/ How long *does* this dressing *keep*?" "For two weeks in the refrigerator."
‖保存液(コンタクトレンズの) a wetting solution ⓤ / 保存食 preserved food / 保存料 a preservative

ポタージュ pot(t)age ⓤ (❖フランス語から), cream soup ⓤ, thick soup ⓤ

ぼたい 母体 ❶【母親の体】mother's body / ダイオキシンは母体だけでなく胎児にも蓄積する Dioxin accumulates not only in *the mother's body* but also in the embryo.
❷【元になるもの】(政治家などの) 支持母体 a *power base* / いくつかの市民グループがその運動の母体(→核)になっている Several citizens' groups form *the nucleus* of the movement.

ぼだい 菩提 菩提を弔う (→死者のために祈る) *pray for the dead*
‖菩提寺 a temple where *one's* family graves are located

ぼだいじゅ 菩提樹 linden [lime] (tree) ⓒ

ほだされる 情にほだされて (→同情の念に動かされて) 彼はその男に金を貸した *Moved with* sympathy, he lent money to the man.

ほたてがい 帆立貝 scallop ⓒ

ぼたぼた 黄色のペンキが彼のはけからぼたぼた床に落ちた *Drips* of yellow paint fell down from his paintbrush onto the floor.

ぽたぽた 水滴が洞窟の天井からぽたぽた落ちている Drops of water *are dripping* from the roof of the cave.

ぼたもち ぼた餅 🔲 a *botamochi*, a (Japanese) rice cake covered with bean paste
慣用表現 棚からぼたもち (→予想外の授かり物を得る) *get a windfall*; (→予想外の利益を得る) *get a windfall profit* (❖windfall はもともと「風で落ちた果実」の意味) ➡ たなぼた

ほたる 蛍 firefly ⓒ, 《米》lightning bug ⓒ
‖ホタルイカ a firefly squid

ボタン button ⓒ / 3つボタンのジャケット a *three-button* jacket / コートのボタンをかける [はずす]「*do up* [*undo*] the buttons of *one's* coat;「*button* (*up*) [*unbutton*] *one's* coat」/ コートにボタンをつける sew *a button* on a coat / ボタンが1つはずれているよ One of your *buttons* is undone. / シャツのいちばん上のボタンがとれてしまった The top *button* of my shirt has come off. / このボタンを押せば機械が始動します Push [Press] this *button* to start the machine.
‖ボタンダウンシャツ a button-down shirt / ボタン穴 a buttonhole / 飾りボタン a fancy button / カフスボタン cuff links

ぼたん 牡丹 (Japanese tree) peony ⓒ
‖ぼたん雪 large snowflakes
俳句 牡丹散りて打ちかさなりぬ二三片 (与謝蕪村) Peonies shedding
one on top of the other:
two or three petals

ぼち 墓地 (寺などの) graveyard ⓒ; (教会の) churchyard ⓒ; (共同の) (public) cemetery ⓒ / J.F.ケネディーはアーリントン国立墓地に埋葬されている J.F. Kennedy is buried in Arlington National *Cemetery*.

ホチキス ➡ ホッチキス

ぼちぼち ぼちぼち (→そろそろ) 行こうか Well, let's get going *now*.

💬「商売はどうですか」「ぼちぼちといったところです」"How's your business?" "Well, just *so-so*."

ぽちゃぽちゃ その赤ん坊は手足がぽちゃぽちゃしていた The baby had *plump* [*chubby*] arms and legs.

ぽちゃん ぽちゃんと水中に落ちる fall into the water *with a plop*; plop into the water

ほちょう 歩調 (歩く速度) pace ⓤ; (歩き方) step ⓤⓒ / ほかの人たちと歩調を合わせる *keep pace with* others / 行列はゆっくりとした歩調で進んでいった The procession moved on *at a slow pace*. / 次の角で彼は歩調を速めた [ゆるめた] He quickened [slowed down] *his pace* at the next corner. / 彼女は老婦人たちと歩調を合わせて歩いた She walked *in step with* the old ladies. / 彼はいつも歩調を乱す He always *falls out of step*. (❖比喩的な意味でも用いる)

ほちょうき 補聴器 hearing aid ⓒ / ‖補聴器を

使う use [wear] *a hearing aid*

ぼつ 没 1985年没 *Died* in 1985.（❖事典などでは d. 1985 と略す）/ 私の原稿は没になった My manuscript *was rejected* [*not accepted*].

ほっかい 北海 the North Sea

ほっかいどう 北海道

> 北海道は，日本の都道府県内で最大の面積を誇ります．本州に次いで2番目に大きな島，北海道島とその他，いくつかの島から成っています．北海道は南フランスとほぼ同緯度にありますが，日本最北端に位置し，冬は寒く，夏の短い地方です．食べ物が豊富で，サケやカニなどの魚介類，ジャガイモをはじめとする農産物，ほかに乳製品などが有名です．また北海道には日本の先住民族であるアイヌ民族が住んでいます．
> Hokkaido is the largest prefecture in Japan. It includes Hokkaido Island, the second largest in Japan after Honshu, and a number of other islands. Hokkaido is at about the same latitude as southern France, but, located at the northernmost end of Japan, it is cold in the winter and the summers are short. You can enjoy there a variety of foods. It is famous for its fish and shellfish such as salmon and crab, potatoes and other farm products, and dairy products. The Ainu people, who are indigenous residents of Japan, live in Hokkaido.

ぼっかてき 牧歌的 ―牧歌的な pastoral // 牧歌的な風景 a *pastoral* landscape

ぽっかり 空には白い雲がぽっかり浮かんでいた A white cloud *was floating* in the sky. / 私たちの足元には深いクレバスがぽっかり口をあけていた A deep crevasse *yawned* beneath our feet. / 彼がいなくなって私の心にぽっかりと穴があいたようだ His leaving *left* [*created*] *a vacuum* in my heart.

ほっき 発起（提案）proposal [C]；（事業を始めること）promotion [C]
[慣用表現] 彼女は一念発起して毎朝のジョギングを始めた She *made up her mind* and started to jog every morning.

ぼっき 勃起 erection [C]，《口語的》hard-on [C] ―勃起する have* [get*] an erection // アダルトビデオを見ているうちに勃起した I *got an erection* [*a hard-on*] watching a porn video.
‖勃起不全 impotence

ほっきにん 発起人（提案者）proposer [C]；（会社設立などの）promoter [C]；（組織・運動などの）initiator [C] ◆コンテストの発起人になる *sponsor* a contest

ほっきょく 北極 the North Pole ―北極の Arctic // 北極地方に生息する動物たち animals living in *the Arctic* (*region*)
‖北極海 the Arctic Ocean / 北極グマ a polar bear / 北極圏 the Arctic Circle / 北極星 the North Star, the Polestar / 北極探検(隊) an Arctic expedition / 北極点 the geographical north pole, the North Pole

ぽっきり 雪の重みで木の枝がぽっきり折れてしまった The weight of snow caused the tree branch to *snap*. / この店のランチは1,000円ぽっきりで食べ放題だ This restaurant offers an all-you-can-eat lunch *for only 1,000 yen*.

ホック（凹凸2つの金具から成るもの）《米》snap (fastener) [C]，《英》press stud [C]；（かぎ状の金具と受けから成る）hook [C]，hook and eye（❖単数形は a hook and eye，複数形は hooks and eyes となる）// 彼女は息子が学生服のホックを留めるのを手伝った She helped her son fasten *the snaps* on his school uniform.
◆ワンピースのホックを留める[はずす]「*hook up* [*unhook*] *one's* dress / わきにホックのついたスカート a skirt *hooked* on the side

ボックス box [C] ‖ボックス席 a box seat, a booth / 電話ボックス《米》a phone booth,《英》a phone box / ワンボックス車 a van

ぽっくり ぽっくり死ぬ die *suddenly*;《口語的》pop off

ホッケー《米》field hockey [U]，《英》hockey [U]（❖《米》で hockey というとアイスホッケーを指す場合が多い）‖アイスホッケー ice hockey

ぼつご 没後 after *one's* death
◆モーツァルト没後200周年を記念する commemorate *the 200th anniversary of* Mozart*'s death*

ぼっこう 勃興 オスマン・トルコの勃興 *the sudden rise* of the Ottoman Empire

ぼっこうしょう 没交渉 彼は世間と没交渉である He *lives isolated from* the world.

ほっさ 発作 attack [C]；（比較的軽い）fit [C] // 心臓発作 *a* heart *attack* / 喘息(ぜんそく)[せき]の発作に襲われる have *an* asthmatic *attack* [*a* coughing *fit*] / 発作は間もなく治まった *The attack* [*fit*] passed soon.
◆その女性は発作的に電車に飛び込んだ The woman threw herself in front of a train *on a sudden impulse*.

ぼっしゅう 没収 confiscation [U]，forfeiture [U] ―没収する confiscate [他] // 彼は収集品を政府に没収された He *had* his collection *confiscated* by the government.
‖没収試合 a forfeited game

ほっしん 発疹 rash [C] ➔はっしん(発疹)

ほっする 欲する want [他]，《公式的》wish [他][自]，《公式的》desire [他] // 彼は己(おのれ)の欲するままに行動する He acts *as he*「*wants to* [*wishes*].

ぼっする 没する（沈む）sink* [自]，set* [自]；（死ぬ）die [自]，pass away

ほっそく 発足（始まり）start [C]；（設立）establishment [U] ―発足する be established, be set up ◆演劇部を発足させる *establish* [*set up, found, start*] a drama club

ほっそり ほっそりした少女 a *slender* [*slim*] girl; a girl *of slender* [*slim*] *build* / 彼女は指[足]がほっそりしている She *has slender fingers* [*legs*].

ぼったくり 彼はその店でぼったくりの被害にあったそうだ I heard that he *got ripped off* at that store.

ほ

ほったてごや 掘っ建て小屋 hut ⓒ, shanty ⓒ, shack ⓒ

ほったらかす 子供をほったらかす neglect one's child / 仕事をほったらかす leave one's work undone [unfinished]; neglect one's work / 仕事をほったらかしたまま帰るわけにはいかない(→仕事が終わるまでは帰れない) I can't go home until I finish my work. / その家は長年ほったらかしにされてすっかり傷んでいた The house had decayed during the years of neglect.

ほったん 発端 origin ⓒ, beginning ⓒ /事の発端は何だったのか What was the origin of the affair? / (→どのように始まったのか) How did it start [begin]? / 事件の発端は彼女からかかってきた1本の電話だった The incident had its beginning in a telephone call to her. / The incident started [began] with a telephone call to her.

-ぽっち これっぽっちの金ではほとんど助けにならない Such a small amount of money would be of little help. / 冷蔵庫にはこれっぽっちの食料もなかった There was not a scrap of food in the refrigerator.

ホッチキス ⚠stapler ⓒ(❖「ホッチキス」は考案者の名前から) ◆紙をホッチキスでとじる staple sheets of paper together / ホッチキスの針 a staple

ぽっちゃり ぽっちゃりした男の子 a chubby [plump] boy

ぼっちゃん 坊ちゃん (他人の息子) a person's son; (呼びかけ) boy(❖英語では名前が分かるときは名前で呼ぶのがふつう) /お宅の坊ちゃんはおいくつですか How old is your son? ◆彼は坊ちゃん育ち(→良家で甘やかされた息子)で世間知らずだ He is the pampered son of a good family and doesn't know anything about the world.

ほっつきあるく ほっつき歩く wander around [about], walk about ◆こんな時間までどこをほっつき歩いていたんだ(→どこにいたんだ) Where have you been until this late?

ぼってり ─ぼってりした (太った) fat; (ふっくらした) plump, full

ホット ─ホットな hot(❖hotには「熱い」のほか「新しい, 人気のある, 熱烈な, からい」などの意味があり, 日本語の「ホット」とは意味はほぼ重なる) /ホットコーヒー2つお願いします Two (hot) coffees, please. / これが今いちばんホットな品だ This is the hottest number now. ‖ホットニュース hot news

ほっと ほっと安堵(ﾄﾞ)のため息をつく give a sigh of relief / その知らせを聞いてほっとした I felt [was] relieved at the news. / 試験が全部終わってほっとした It's a relief for me to finish all the exams. / ああ, ほっとした What a relief (it is)!

ポット ⚠(魔法びん)! thermos (bottle) ⓒ(❖英語のpotは, 丸くて深さのある容器(なべやつぼなど)を指し,「魔法びん」の意味はない)

ぽっと 彼女はぽっとほおを赤らめた Her cheeks blushed.

ぼっとう 没頭 ─没頭する be absorbed in ..., devote oneself to ...; (集中する) concentrate on ... /彼は研究に没頭している He is「absorbed in [devoted to] his research.

ほっとく ほっといてよ! Leave me alone! / あいつのことなんかほっとけよ Leave him alone. / そんなけがなんかほっといてもすぐ治るよ Such an injury will heal soon without doing anything.

ホットケーキ pancake ⓒ, (米) hot cake ⓒ /ホットケーキを焼く make [cook] pancakes

ホットコーヒー (hot) coffee ⓤ ⓒ

ホットドッグ hot dog ⓒ

ホットプレート hot plate ⓒ

ホットライン (首脳間の直通電話) hot line (❖種々の電話相談サービスも指す) /両首脳はホットラインでその問題を協議した The two leaders discussed the problem on a hot line.

ぼつにゅう 没入 ─没入する be absorbed in ... ⇨ぼっとう

ぼっぱつ 勃発 outbreak ⓒ ─勃発する break* out / 2国間で戦争が勃発した A war has broken out between the two countries. / 小さな事件が重なってついには戦争の勃発につながった A series of small incidents led up to the outbreak of war.

ほっぴょうよう 北氷洋 the Arctic Ocean

ホップ ❶【植物】hop ⓒ(❖ビール製造に使われる乾燥した雌花は通例複数形～sで用いる)
❷【跳び方】hop ⓒ(❖the hop, step, and jumpは三段跳び(the triple jump)の口語的表現)

ポップアート pop art ⓒ

ポップコーン popcorn ⓤ / 1袋のポップコーン a bag of popcorn / ポップコーンがなべの中ではじけ始めた The popcorn began to pop in the saucepan.

ポップシンガー pop singer ⓒ

ポップス (ポピュラー音楽) pop music ⓤ, pop ⓤ, (歌謡曲) pop song ⓒ ⓒ ⇨場面・状況別会話 p.1702 /彼女はフレンチポップスが好きだ She likes French pop music.

ほっぺ(た) 頬っぺ(た) one's cheek ⇨ほお

ほっぽう 北方 the north ─北方の north, northern ‖北方領土 the Northern Territories(❖通じない場合は four islands in the Kuril chain disputed between Japan and Russia などと説明する)

ぼつぼつ 校庭には子供たちがぼつぼつ集まってきている Children are coming onto the school grounds in twos and threes. / このへんはぼつぼつ家が建ち始めた New houses are being built「one by one [one after another] in this neighborhood. / ぼつぼつみんなが来るころだ They will come soon [before long]. / じゃ, ぼつぼつ(→そろそろ)出かけようか Well, let's get going now.

ぽつぽつ 雨がぽつぽつ降ってきた It began to rain lightly.

ぽっぽと そのからいカレーを食べたら体がぽっぽとほてってきた I felt hot after I ate the spicy curry.

ぼつらく 没落 fall ◯, downfall ◯; (破滅) ruin ◯ ──没落する suffer a fall [downfall] ∥清朝の没落の原因は何だったのか What caused *the fall* [*downfall*] of the Qing Dynasty? / ローマ帝国は没落に近づきつつあった The Roman Empire was approaching *its fall* [*downfall*].

ぽつ 彼女は「そうじゃない」とぽつり言った "It's not that," she said *in a low voice*.

ぽつりぽつり 雨がぽつりぽつり落ちてきた *Drops* of rain began to fall. / 彼はぽつりぽつりと(→少しずつ)身の上話を始めた He began to talk about himself *little by little*.

ほつれる (衣服・ロープなどが) become* frayed ∥セーターのそで口がほつれてしまった My sweater *has become frayed* at the wrist. ◆ほつれ髪 one's loose [stray] hairs

ぽつんと ぽつんと離れた村 an *isolated* village / 首筋に水滴がぽつんと落ちてきた *A drop* of water fell on my neck. / 野原に木が1本ぽつんと立っていた There stood a *solitary* tree in a field. / 女の子は公園のベンチにぽつんと(→ひとりで)座っていた The girl sat *alone* on a bench in the park.

ボディー (体) one's body ◯, (車体・機体などの) body ◯ ◆ ボディーコンシャスな服 a tight(-)fitting dress / 彼女はボディーラインを保つよう努力している She is trying to keep *her figure*.
∥ボディースーツ(女性用下着) a bodysuit, a body briefer / ボディーブロー《ボクシング》 a body blow / ボディーペイント body paint / ボディーランゲージ body language ⇒ 場面・状況別会話 p.1762

ボディーガード bodyguard ◯∥彼の周りにはいつも数人のボディーガードがついている He always has several *bodyguards* around him.

ボディーチェック ⚠body search ◯; (荷物検査を含む) security check ◯ (❖英語のbody checkはアイスホッケーで、体当たりで相手の動きを阻止することをいう) ∥ボディーチェックを受ける *undergo a security check*; 《口語的》*be frisked*

ボディービル ⚠body-building ◯

ボディーボード (スポーツ) body boarding ◯; (板) body board ◯

ポテト potato ◯ ∥ポテトサラダ potato salad / ポテトチップス 《米》(potato) chips, 《英》(potato) crisps / フライドポテト 《主に米》French fries, 《英》chips / マッシュポテト mashed potato(es)

ぼてぼて ぼてぼての ゴロを打つ hit a *slow grounder*

ほてり 火照り (紅潮) flush ◯ (通例単数形), a glow ⇒ ほてる

ホテル hotel ◯; (小さな) inn ◯ ∥一流[高級]ホテル *a first-class* [*deluxe*] *hotel* / ホテルを予約する reserve a room at *a hotel* / そのホテルにチェックインする check in at *the hotel* / ホテルをチェックアウトする check out of *a hotel* / ホテルに3泊する stay three nights at *a hotel*
∥ビジネスホテル a budget hotel / リゾートホテル a resort hotel

ほてる 火照る (紅潮する) flush ◯, glow ◯; (熱くなる) burn* ◯ ∥恥ずかしさで彼女の顔はほてった Her face *flushed* [*was flushed*] with embarrassment. / 赤ちゃんのほおは熱のせいでほてっていた The baby's cheeks *were burning* with fever.

ほてん 補塡 ──補塡する (埋め合わせる) cover ◯, make* up for ... ∥赤字を補塡する *cover* [*make up for*] the red ink

ほど 程

❶【程度】
相手の力の程は(→どのくらい強いか)分からない I don't know *how strong* the opponent is.
その試合は期待したほどおもしろくなかった The game was not *as* [*so*] *exciting as* I (had) expected. ❖not as ... as のほうが not so ... as よりも口語的.
僕は口もきけないほど疲れていた I was *too tired to speak*. / I was *so tired that* I *couldn't speak*.
彼は一生かけても使いきれないほどのお金を手に入れた He got *more money than* he could spend in his lifetime.
彼女はそんな話を真に受けるほどお人よしじゃないよ She isn't simple *enough to* take such a story seriously.
入院しなければならないほどの病気はしたことがない I have never been *so ill as to* be hospitalized. / I have never been *so ill that* I had to be hospitalized.
きょうの水泳の練習で死ぬほど疲れたよ I'm *dead tired* from today's swimming practice.
その問題は驚くほどやさしかった The problem was *surprisingly* easy.
彼女はどこへ行っても必ずと言っていいほど問題を起こす She is *nearly always* a problem wherever she goes.
その景色は言葉にできないほど美しかった The landscape was beautiful *beyond expression*.
彼女は数えきれないほどの切手を集めた She collected *countless* stamps.
そのニュースはテレビで報道するほどのものではなかった(→報道に値しなかった) The news "wasn't *worth* [didn't *rate*] a mention on TV.
💬 「何かおもしろいことがありましたか」「いいえ、お話しするほどのことは(→話すべきことは)何もありません」 "Have you found anything interesting?" "No, nothing *to speak of*."
💬 「寒いですか」「いいえ、それほどでもありません」 "Do you feel cold?" "No, *not so much*."

❷【比較】
時間ほど大切なものはない Nothing is *more precious than* time. / Nothing is *so precious as* time.
木村君ほど一生懸命勉強する生徒はいない No other student studies 「*as hard as* [*harder than*] Kimura.
父は以前ほど酒を飲まなくなった My father

drinks *less than* he used to.
私は母ほど料理がうまくない I can't cook *as* [*so*] well *as* my mother.
❸【限度】
冗談にも程があるぞ(→行きすぎだ) You are carrying your [the] joke *too far*.
何事にも程というものがある Everything has *its limits*.
❹【およそ】about, some
私は毎日1時間ほど散歩をする I take a walk for *about* an hour every day.
30分ほどで宿題が終わります I'll finish my homework in「*about* half an hour [half an hour *or so*].
私は毎年30枚ほど年賀状をもらう I get *about* thirty New Year's cards every year.
このセーターは8,000円ほどした This sweater cost *some* eight thousand yen.
❺【…すればするほど】
相手が強ければ強いほどやる気がわいてくる *The stronger* my opponent, *the more* motivated I get.
話せば話すほど彼女に引かれていった *The more* I talked with her, *the more* I was charmed by her.
❻【ころ】
後ほどお電話ください Please call me *later*.
❼【様子・ぐあい】
真偽の程は定かではないが, 彼女は来年留学するそうだ *For what it's worth*, they say she'll go abroad to study next year.
ご都合の程(→いつが都合がよいか)をお知らせください Please tell me *when it is convenient for you*.

ほどう¹ 歩道 《米》sidewalk ⓒ,《英》pavement ⓤ; (遊歩道) promenade ⓒ ∥歩道を歩きなさい Keep to the *sidewalk*.
◆動く歩道 a moving walkway
∥歩道橋 a pedestrian overpass ∣ 横断歩道 a crosswalk

ほどう² 補導 その少年たちは警察に補導された The boys *were caught and admonished* by the police.

ほどく 解く (結び目などを) undo* ⓣ, untie ⓣ; (からまっている物を) disentangle ⓣ ∥結び目をほどく *undo* [*untie*] a knot ∣ 小包をほどく *undo* a parcel ∣ コードがからまってほどくのにひと苦労した Cords got entangled and I found it very hard to *disentangle* them.
◆靴ひもをほどく *unlace one's* shoes ∣ 彼女は小さくなった子供のセーターをほどいた She *unknitted* the sweater that got too tight for her child.

ほとけ 仏 (仏陀 (ﾀﾞ)) Buddha ⓒ; (仏像) Buddhist image ⓒ; (死者) dead person ⓒ; (死体) body ⓒ
仏の慈悲にすがる throw *oneself* on the mercy of *Buddha*
祖母は毎朝仏様を拝む My grandmother prays to *a Buddhist image* every morning. ∣ (→先祖を供養する) My grandmother offers a prayer to *her ancestors* every morning.
◆そのとき彼はふと仏心を起こした Then, he suddenly had *mercy*. ∣ 佐藤先生は「仏の佐藤」と呼ばれていた They called Mr. Sato "Sato *the Kind*." ∣ そんな判決では仏が浮かばれない Given a ruling like that, *the soul of the dead* can't rest in peace.

ことわざ 知らぬが仏 ⇨する(知る) ∣ 仏の顔も三度 Even Buddha gets angry if you behave rudely toward him three times.; It's enough to try the patience of a saint.(→聖人の忍耐力を試すにはそれで十分だ)

ほどける 解ける come* undone, come untied; (ゆるむ) come loose ∥靴のひもがほどけた The shoestring *has come undone*.

ほどこす 施す ❶【与える】give* ⓣ ∥金銭を施す *give a person* some money
◆人の施しを受けるつもりはない I'll never *take anything* from others.
❷【装飾などを加える】ハンカチにししゅうを施す *embroider* a handkerchief ∣ そのジープは迷彩が施されていた The jeep *was camouflaged*.
❸【手段などを講じる】けが人に手当てを施す *give* medical care to an injured person ∣ 火は燃え広がってすでに手の施しようがなかった The fire had already spread and *there was no way to stop it*.

ほどとおい 程遠い その小説は傑作というにはほど遠いものだった The novel was *far from* being a masterpiece. ∣ 医療機関の現状は理想とはほど遠い The present situation of medical institutions is「*far from* [*a long way from*] ideal.

ほととぎす little cuckoo ⓒ

ほどなく 程なく (間もなく) soon, before long ∥その建物はほどなく完成する予定だ The building is to be completed *soon* [*before long*].

ほとばしる gush ⓘ, spout ⓘ ∥鮮血が傷口からほとばしった Crimson blood *gushed out* of the wound. ◆彼女はほとばしるような情熱の持ち主だった She had *a gush of* emotion. (❖この gush は名詞)

ポトフ pot-au-feu [pɑ̀ːtoufǎ] ⓤ (❖フランス語から)

ほとほと (全く) quite, completely; (本当に) really ∥彼女の長電話にはほとほと閉口した I was *completely* annoyed at her for talking so long on the phone. ∣ 彼のわがままにはみんなほとほと困り果ててていた His selfishness was *really* a great trouble to everyone. ∣ 反抗期の娘にはほとほと手を焼いている I'm *quite* at a loss how to deal with my daughter at this rebellious age.

ほどほど 程々 この手の器(ｳﾂﾜ)ならほどほどの値段で手に入る This kind of vessel is available at a *moderate* [*reasonable*] price. ∣ いたずら [冗談] もほどほどにしろ Don't carry your mischief [joke] too far.

ぽとぽと 油がフィルターを通ってぽとぽとと落ちている Oil *is dripping* through the filter.

ほとぼり 彼は事件のほとぼりが冷めるまで(→混乱が収まるまで) 身を隠した He hid himself until the excitement over the affair 「*cooled down* [*settled*]」.

ほどよい 程よい (適度の) moderate, proper; (妥当な) reasonable ——ほどよく moderately, properly; reasonably ∥ほどよい湯かげんのふろ a *moderately* hot bath / ジョギングにはほどよい陽気だった The weather was *reasonable* [*okay*] for jogging. / この袋は大きさがほどよい This bag has a *reasonable* size.

ほとり そのホテルは湖のほとりにある The hotel is *on* the lake. / 川のほとりにきれいな花が咲いている Some pretty flowers are blooming *by* the river.

ぽとり 彼女の両目から大粒の涙がぽとりと落ちた A large tear *dropped* from each of her eyes.

ボトル bottle ⓒ ⇒ びん(瓶)

ほとんど

❶【肯定文で】 almost, nearly; (実質的に) practically, virtually ——ほとんどの most, almost all; practical

> 語法
> [**almost と nearly**] (1) 具体的に比較・計測できるものには両方使えるが, そうでない場合は nearly は使えない.
> (2) いずれも数詞や all, every, everyone, everything, always などとともに用いられる.
>
> [**most と almost all**] 全体のうち大半を占める場合に most を用い, ほぼ全体に近い場合は almost all を用いる.

宿題はほとんど終わった I have *almost* [*nearly*] finished my homework.

そのびんはほとんど空だよ That bottle is *almost* [*nearly*] empty.

私はほとんど毎日ピアノを弾く I play the piano *almost* every day.

町のほとんどすべての人がそこにいた *Practically* all the people in the town were there.

◆英語はほとんど世界の共通語になった English has *for the most part* become the world's common language.

> [英作文ノート] **almost** は形容詞ではない
> ほとんどの学生がアルバイトをしている
> →×*Almost* students have part-time jobs.
> →○*Almost* all (of) the students have part-time jobs.
> ★almost は副詞なので名詞の前に付けて用いることはできない. most は「たいてい(の), 大部分(の)」の意味で, 形容詞としても代名詞としても用いる. *Most* (of the) students have part-time jobs. (大部分の学生がアルバイトをしている)

❷【否定文で】 ——ほとんど…ない hardly, scarcely, barely; (めったにない) seldom; (量・程度が) little; (数が) few

彼らはほとんど食べ物を持っていなかった They had *hardly* [*scarcely*] any food. / They had *almost no* food.

彼は朝食はほとんど食べることがない He *hardly ever* [*almost never*] eats breakfast.

彼女の声は騒音の中でほとんど聞き取れなかった Her voice could *hardly* be heard above [over] the noise.

祖父が出かけることはほとんどない My grandfather *seldom* goes out.

去年の夏は雨がほとんど降らなかった We had *little* rain last summer.

その女優の私生活はほとんど知られていない *Very little* is known about the actress's private life.

その当時はアメリカでもまだ自動車はほとんどなかった There were *few* cars at that time, even in the United States.

多くの人がレースに参加したが, ゴールまでたどり着けた人はほとんどいなかった Many people took part in the race, but *few* were able to finish.

ポニーテール ponytail ⓒ ∥髪をポニーテールにする have *a ponytail*; wear *one's* hair in *a ponytail*

ほにゅう 哺乳 ∥ほにゅうびん a baby bottle / ほ乳類 mammals

ぼにゅう 母乳 mother's milk Ⓤ, breast milk Ⓤ ∥彼らはみな, 母乳で育てられた All of them *were fed on breast milk*. / All of them *were breast-fed*.

ほね 骨

❶【体の骨】 bone ⓒ

> 語法
> 「足の骨を折る」「腕の骨を折る」などは break a bone in *one's* leg, break a bone in *one's* arm などともいえるが, ふつうは bone を用いず以下のようにいう ∥ 腕の骨を折る *break one's arm* / 首の骨を折る *break one's neck* / あごの骨を折る *break one's jaw* / 私はスキーをしていて足の骨を折ってしまった I *broke my leg* while skiing.

魚の骨がのどに引っかかった A fish *bone* got stuck in my throat.

この魚は小骨が多い This fish is full of *fine* [*small*] *bones*.

カルシウムが足りないと骨がもろくなる Lack of calcium makes *your bones* fragile.

彼はやせているが骨太だ He is thin, but he has *large bones*.

父はイワシを骨ごと食べた My father ate sardine, *bones and all*.

彼女は彼のために魚の骨を取り除いてやった She removed *the bones* from the fish for him.

◆骨(→遺骨)を拾う *gather a person's ashes* / 彼女は骨になって(→灰になって)日本へ帰ってきた She came back to Japan *in ashes*. / 彼らはその恐竜の骨(→骨格)を復元した They restored *the skeleton* of the dinosaur.

❷【物の骨】(傘・扇子(苎)などの) rib ⓒ; (骨組み) frame ⓒ

風で傘の骨が折れてしまった The wind broke

my umbrella's *rib*. / 何本かの障子の骨が折れている Some *frames* of the *shoji* are broken.

❸【困難・尽力】
彼を説得するのは骨だ It is *hard* to persuade him.
彼女はボランティアとして骨を惜しまず働いた As a volunteer, she *spared no effort* in her work.
山下先生は私の就職に際して骨を折ってくれた Mr. Yamashita *went to a lot of trouble* to find a job for me.

❹【気骨】backbone Ⓤ
祖父は骨のある人だった My grandfather was a person *with backbone*.

‖あご骨 a jawbone / あばら骨 a rib / 肩甲骨 a shoulder blade / 腰骨 a hipbone / 鎖骨 a collarbone / 頭蓋骨 a skull / 背骨 a backbone, a spine / 大腿骨(だいたい) a thighbone / ほお骨 a cheekbone

慣用表現 これは骨が折れる仕事だ This is *hard work*. / 父にパソコンの使い方を教えるのは骨が折れそうだ It seems to be *difficult* to teach my father how to use a personal computer. / アフリカの骨と皮ばかりの人々の写真を見て胸が痛んだ When I saw pictures of Africans who were *all skin and bones*, I felt deep sorrow. / 彼は骨の髄まで教師だ He is a teacher *to the bone*. / 彼は日本に骨を埋(う)める(→残りの人生を日本で過ごす)つもりだ He intends *to stay in Japan for the rest of his life*. / お父さん、温泉にでもつかってゆっくり骨を休めてきたら？ Dad, how about going to a hot spring to *take a (good) rest*?

ほねおしみ 骨惜しみ 彼は骨惜しみせずによく働く He works hard and *spares no effort*.

ほねおり 骨折り pains; (努力) effort Ⓤ Ⓒ /お骨折りいただきありがとうございました Thank you very much for *taking great pains* for me.

慣用表現 わざわざ市場に出かけたが骨折り損だった(→むだだった) I took the trouble to go to the market, but it *was useless* [*in vain*].

ことわざ 骨折り損のくたびれもうけ Great pains but all in vain.(→大変な苦労もすべてむだ)

ほねおる 骨折る take* *great pains* (to do) /教え子の就職に骨折る *take great pains to* find a job for *one's* pupil

ほねぐみ 骨組み ❶【骨格】frame Ⓤ Ⓒ /がっしりした骨組み a sturdy *frame*
❷【構造】framework Ⓒ, skeleton Ⓒ /計画の骨組みを変更する change *the framework* [*skeleton*] of the plan / ビルの骨組みはすでに完成した *The framework* [*skeleton*] *of the building has already been completed*.

ほねぬき 骨抜き その法案は審議を重ねるうちにすっかり骨抜きにされてしまった The bill *was completely gutted* [*watered down*] after several discussions.

ほねばった 骨張った bony, raw-boned / 骨ばった手 a *bony* hand

ほねぶと 骨太 ——骨太の big-boned

◆彼は骨太な(→気骨のある)若者だ He is a young man of *backbone*.

ほねみ 骨身 骨身を惜しまずに働く work *without sparing of pains* / 骨身を削って仕事をする do *one's job very hard* / 寒さが私たちの骨身にしみた The cold *pierced us to the bone*. / 彼女の厳しい言葉が骨身にこたえた Her stern words *hit home* [*came home to me*].

ほねやすめ 骨休め (休養) rest Ⓤ Ⓒ; (息抜き) relaxation Ⓤ Ⓒ /彼女は骨休めに温泉に出かけた She went to a hot spring to *take a (good) rest*.

ほのお 炎 flame Ⓒ; (激しい) blaze Ⓒ 《通例 a ~》/情熱[怒り]の炎 a *flame* of passion [rage] / まきは炎を上げて燃えた The firewood burst into *flame(s)*. / 私たちはキャンプファイアの燃えさかる炎をじっと眺めていた We were staring at *the blaze* of the campfire. / その家はあっという間に炎に包まれた The house *was engulfed in flames* in an instant. ◆彼女は恵美に対して嫉妬(しっと)の炎を燃やしていた She *was burning with jealousy* toward Emi.

ほのか 仄か ——ほのかな faint, slight; (色・においなどが) delicate; (ほの暗い) dim /ほのかな梅の香り a *faint* [*slight, delicate*] fragrance of Japanese plum blossoms / ほのかな月明かりが道を照らしていた *Faint* [*Dim*] moonlight lit the way. / 少女はその男性にほのかな思いを寄せていた The girl had a *slight* love [affection] for the man.

ほのぐらい 仄暗い dim, dusky /ほの暗い森の小道 a *dim* [*dusky*] path in the wood

ほのぼの 仄々 ほのぼのと夜が明ける Day is dawning. / その歌のほのぼのとした雰囲気が人々にうけたらしい It seemed that the *heart-warming* atmosphere of the song appealed to the people.

ほのめかす 仄めかす (それとなく言う) hint ⓗ; (暗に示す) suggest ⓗ, imply ⓗ /彼は両親に高校中退をそれとなくほのめかした He *hinted* [*suggested*] to his parents that he might quit high school.

◆彼女は犯行をほのめかし始めた She began to *give* [*drop*] *a hint* of her crime.(❖この hint は名詞)

ホバークラフト hovercraft Ⓒ
ほばしら 帆柱 《海事》mast Ⓒ
ほはば 歩幅 step Ⓒ, stride Ⓒ /歩幅が広い walk with long *steps* [*strides*]
ぼひ 墓碑 headstone Ⓒ, gravestone Ⓒ, tombstone Ⓒ /墓碑銘 an epitaph
ポピー 【植物】poppy Ⓒ
ポピュラー ——ポピュラーな popular ⇒にんき(人気) ‖ポピュラー音楽 pop(ular) music / ポピュラー歌手 a pop(ular) singer / ポピュラーソング a pop(ular) song
ほふ 保父 ⇒ほいくし
ボブスレー (競技用そり)【スポーツ】bobsled Ⓒ, bobsleigh Ⓒ; (競技) bobsledding Ⓤ
ポプラ poplar Ⓒ /ポプラ並木の道 a road *lined with poplars*
ポプリ potpourri Ⓤ (❖フランス語から)

ほへい 歩兵 foot soldier ©, infantryman © ‖歩兵隊 infantry

ボヘミア Bohemia (❖チェコ共和国の西部地方) ‖ボヘミアガラス Bohemian glass

ボヘミアン Bohemian © 《しばしば bohemian》

ほほ 頬 cheek © ➪ ほお

ほぼ¹ (ほとんど) almost, nearly; (およそ) about; (実質上) practically ‖ホールはほぼ満員だった The hall was *nearly* [*practically*] full. / その建物はほぼ完成していた The building was *almost* [*just about*] completed. / 山頂に達するのにほぼ3時間を要した It took me *about* [*almost*] three hours to reach the top of the mountain. / どちらを買うにしても値段はほぼ同じです Whichever you buy, the prices are *almost* the same.

ほぼ² 保母 ➪ ほいくし

ほほえましい 微笑ましい (心温まる) heart-warming; (気持ちのよい) pleasant ‖ほほえましい光景に見とれる gaze at a *heart-warming* scene / 小さな女の子が赤ちゃんの弟をあやしているのはほほえましかった It was *heart-warming* to see a little girl taking care of her baby brother.

ほほえみ 微笑み smile © ‖with *a smile* / その子は楽しげなほほえみを浮かべていた The child wore *a* pleasant *smile*.

ほほえむ 微笑む smile ⊕ ‖彼女はうれしそうにほほえんだ She *smiled* happily. / 晶子にほほえみかけられて僕は胸がどきどきした My heart started beating wildly when Akiko *smiled* at me. / 勝利の女神が私にほほえんだ Victory *smiled* on me.
◆彼は私に気づいてほほえんだ He acknowledged me with *a smile*. (❖この smile は名詞)

ポマード pomade ©

ほまれ 誉れ an honor [《英》honour], credit ©《通例単数形》‖彼女は本校の誉れである She is *an honor* [*a credit*] to our school.
◆テンポイントは名馬の誉れが高かった(→名高い競走馬だった) Ten Point was a *renowned* race horse.

ホメオスタシス 《生物》(恒常性) homeostasis ©

ほめたたえる 褒め称える praise ... highly; (公の場で) celebrate ⊕ ‖人々は彼の勇気をほめたたえた People *praised* him *highly* for his courage.

ほめちぎる 褒めちぎる だれもが彼の演技をほめちぎった Everyone *spoke highly of* his performance. / マスコミは彼女の音楽の才能をほめちぎった The mass media *praised* her *very highly* for her musical talents.

ほめる 褒める praise ⊕, compliment ⊕ (❖compliment には「お世辞を言う」という意味もある); (よく言う) speak* well of *a person*; (賞賛する) admire
➪ コミュニケーションスキル p.1399
先生は僕の努力をほめてくれた The teacher *praised* my efforts.
みんな君のことをほめているよ Everybody *speaks well of* you.
その少年は正直なのでほめられた The boy *was praised* for his honesty.
伸子は私のワンピースをほめてくれた Nobuko *complimented* me *on* my dress.
◆監督はめったにほめ言葉を口にしない The manager seldom gives *compliments*. / それはほめすぎだ That's *excessive praise*.
慣用表現 そのような行為は決してほめられたものではない Such an act will never「*do you credit* [*be a credit to you*]」.

ホモ homosexual ©, 《口語的》gay © (❖homosexual は「同性愛者」の意味で, 男女ともに用いられる. gay は特に男性に用いられる. いずれの語にも軽蔑的な含みはない); (同性愛) homosexuality © ――ホモの homosexual, gay

ホモサピエンス Homo sapiens

ぼや small fire © ‖近所の家がぼやを出した *A small fire* broke out in my neighborhood.

ぼやく complain ⊕, 《口語的》gripe ⊕; (ぶつぶつ言う) grumble ⊕ ‖彼はいつも部下のことでぼやいている He *is* always *complaining* [*griping, grumbling*] about his staff.

ぼやける be [become*] blurred; become fuzzy ‖子供のころの記憶はぼやけてしまっている My memories of childhood *are blurred*.
◆ぼやけた写真 *blurred* [*fuzzy*] photograph / 彼女の発言で議論の焦点がぼやけてしまった Because of her remark, the point of the discussion *became vague*.

ぼやっと はらはら, ぼやっとしてたらみんなに置いていかれちゃうよ Hey, if you *keep staring off into space*, everyone's going to leave you behind.

ほやほや できたてほやほやのパン bread *hot* [*fresh*] *from the oven* / 彼らは新婚ほやほやだ(→結婚したばかりだ) They *have just got married*.

ぼやぼや ぼやぼやして電車を乗り過ごしてしまった I was so *careless* [*absent-minded*] that I missed my stop. / ぼやぼやしてると(→気をつけろ, そうしないと)車にひかれるぞ Look out, or you'll be run over by a car.

ほゆう 保有 holding ©, possession © ――保有する hold* ⊕, possess ⊕; (失わずにいる) retain ⊕ ‖権利を保有する *retain one's right* / その会社の株を保有する *hold* shares of the company
‖核保有国 a nuclear power

ほよう 保養 (休養) rest ©©, (骨休め) relaxation ©; (病後の) recuperation © ――保養する take* [have*] a rest; relax ⊕ ⊕; recuperate ⊕ ⊕ ‖保養に出かける go away for *a rest*
◆北アルプスの美しい自然は目の保養になった The beautiful natural scenery in the Northern Alps was *a feast for the eyes*. / 彼は夏休みを湖の近くの保養地で過ごす He spends his [the] summer vacation at *a* (*health*) *resort* near the lake.
‖保養所 a sanitarium, a convalescent hospital

コミュニケーションスキル —ほめる—

① 服装などをほめる

(A) **How do you like my dress?**
 –Oh, **it looks great [gorgeous]!**
 このドレス,どう.—いやあ,すごくすてきだよ.
(B) **I really like [love] your hairdo.**
 –Thanks.
 君の髪型,すごくすてきだね.—ありがとう.
(C) **You look 「just great [terrific] in that red dress.**
 –Oh, thank you.
 赤いドレスがとても似合うよ.—まあ,ありがとう.
(D) **Nice sweater!**
 –Thank you. It's hand-knitted.
 すてきなセーターね.—ありがとう.これ手編みなの.
(E) **What a beautiful garden!**
 –I like it, too.
 なんてきれいな庭なんだろう.—私も気に入っているんです.
(F) I met your daughter yesterday. **She is so cute!**
 きのうあなたの娘さんに会いましたよ.とてもかわいらしい娘さんですね.
(G) Oh, is this the puppy you told me about? **How adorable!**
 あら,これがあなたが話していた子犬ね.なんてかわいいんでしょう.
(H) Sara, you must try this chocolate cake. **It's delicious!**
 サラ,このケーキを食べてごらん.すごくおいしいよ.

☞ 人の服装をほめる場合,物(dress や tie など)そのものを主語にするより,相手の人自身を主語にしたほうが,ほめる気持ちがずっと伝わりやすい.服装を選んだり,化粧したりする,その人のセンスを含めてほめるほうが,英米では好まれる.

☞ ほめられたときは,Thanks. のようにいって,相手の賞賛を素直に受け入れるのがふつう.日本式に「いいえ,それほどでもありません」などの謙遜(けんそん)した言い方をしても,かえって不自然に思われてしまう.

☞ (F), (G) の cute, adorable は赤ん坊や子供,ペットをほめるときによく使われる語.

② 相手の行動などをほめる

(A) **You did a good job,** Mike! / **Well done,** Mike!
 マイク,よくやったぞ.
(B) **Great! / That's great! / Fantastic! / Super! / Terrific!**
 すばらしい!
(C) I passed the exam.
 –**You made it! / You did it! / Good for you! / Terrific!**
 試験に受かったんだ.—やったね!
(D) **Congratulations!**
 –Thanks a lot.
 おめでとう!—どうもありがとう.
(E) You're really **on the ball** today!
 きょうは本当にさえてるね.

☞ 先生が生徒をほめたり,上司が部下の仕事をほめたりするときは,(A) のようにいうのが最も一般的.(B) のように感嘆文として great, fantastic, super などの単語 1 語で気持ちを表す場合も多い.

☞ (C) は試合に勝ったり,試験に合格したときに使われる表現.make it = be successful(うまくいく,成功する)の意味で口語でよく使われる.代わりに (B) の表現を使ってもよい.

☞ (D) の Congratulations! は何かを努力して達成した人に向かって用い,誕生日やクリスマスなどのあいさつには用いない.必ず複数形で使うことに注意.**Congratulations on winning the championship!**(優勝おめでとう!)のように,祝福の対象となる物事を続けていう場合もある.

☞ (E) の on the ball は「頭の働きがよい」ことをいう成句で,日本語の「さえている」に相当する.

ほら¹ (見てごらん) Look!; (聞いてごらん) Listen!; (分かっただろう) See?; (物を差し出して) Here it is., Here you are. ∥ほら,富士山が見えるよ *Look*! We can see Mt. Fuji. ◆ ほら,僕らの乗るバスが来たよ! *There* comes our bus! / ほらね,だから言わないこっちゃない *There*, I told you so.
ほら² 法螺 (うそ) tall tale [story] ⓒ; (大言壮語) big talk ⓒ ◆ ほらを吹くな Don't *talk* *big*.
 ∥ほら貝 a conch, (a) trumpet shell / ほら吹き a big talker, a braggart
ボラ 〘魚〙 mullet ⓒ
ホラー ∥ホラー映画 a horror movie [film]
ほらあな 洞穴 cave ⓒ; (大きな) cavern ⓒ
ポラロイド 〘商標名〙 Polaroid ⓒ (❖カメラ (Polaroid camera) および撮った写真を表す)
ボランティア (人) volunteer ⓒ
→ 場面・状況別会話 p.1750
 ボランティアの仕事をする do *volunteer* work
 彼女はボランティアで公園の清掃をしている She cleans up the park *as a volunteer*.
 私たちの学校ではボランティア活動が奨励されている Our school is encouraging us to do *volunteer* activities.
 ∥ボランティアグループ[組織] a volunteer group [organization]
ほり¹ 堀 moat ⓒ ∥敵の侵入を防ぐために城に堀をめぐらす build *moats* around the castle to prevent an invasion by an enemy
ほり² 彫り 彼は彫りの深い(→ 目鼻立ちのはっきりとした)顔をしている He has *finely chiseled* features.
ほりあてる 掘り当てる strike* ⓗ ∥石油[金]を掘り当てる *strike* oil [gold]
ポリープ 〘医学〙 polyp ⓒ ◆ その歌手ののどにポリープができたらしい It seems the singer has got *a small tumor* in his [her] throat.
ポリウレタン 〘化学〙 polyurethane ⓤⓒ
ポリエステル 〘化学〙 polyester ⓤ
ポリエチレン 〘化学〙 〘米〙 polyethylene ⓤ, 〘英〙 polythene ⓤ
ポリオ 〘医学〙 poliomyelitis ⓤ, polio ⓤ
 ∥ポリオワクチン polio vaccine

ほりおこす

コミュニケーションスキル —意見・判断の保留—

(A) Well, I'll (have to) think about it [I'll think it over].
まあ、考えておきましょう。
(B) Well, let me 「think about it [think it over.]
ううん、少し考えさせてください。
(C) Ask me again later. I'll give it some thought.
後でまた聞いてくれ。少し考えてみるよ。
(D) I'm not sure yet.
まだ分かりません。
(E) I suppose [think] that it all depends on the result of the next election.
次期選挙の結果しだいだと思いますよ。
(F) I haven't decided yet whether to agree or disagree with it.
そのことに賛成するかしないかまだ決めていません。
(G) I'm not in a position [I'm in no position] to make any comments on that issue.
私はその問題について何もコメントできる立場
ありません。
(H) I'll see if there's anything I can do.
ご希望に添えるかどうか、考えてみます。

☞ 相手の質問などにすぐに答えず、またセールスの勧誘にあったときなど、一時態度や意見を保留にする場合、(A), (B) が最も一般的な言い方。
☞ (A), (B) で、I'll think it over. や Let me think it over. というと、think about よりも「じっくり考える」の意味が強い。
☞ (E) の I suppose ... は I think ... の場合よりもやや根拠が弱い感じがする。
☞ (F), (G) は意識的に意見を述べるのを控える表現で、態度をあいまいにするのとは違うことに注意。答えたくない問題、または慎重に対処する必要がある問題については、このような表現を使ってよい。(F) はかなり明確な判断の保留を表しているが、もう少し態度をぼやかして、**I'd rather wait before saying anything about it.** ということもある。
☞ 相手の希望や願望などをかなえてあげられるかどうか自信がないときは、(H) のような慎重な表現を選ぶとよい。

ほりおこす 掘り起こす dig* up, turn up; (切り株などを) grub ㊥ ‖荒れ地を掘り起こす *dig up* the wasteland
◆彼は日本各地に埋もれた伝統工芸品を掘り起こす (→見つける) 仕事に生涯をささげた He devoted his life to *finding* traditional hand-crafted objects hidden all over Japan.
ほりかえす 掘り返す dig* up, turn up ‖水道管の修理のために道路が掘り返されていた The road *was being dug up* to repair the water main.
ほりさげる 掘り下げる dig* down
◆問題を掘り下げて (→深く) 考える consider a problem *deeply* [*to the root*]
ポリシー one's policy ‖そんなことをするのは私のポリシーに反する It's against *my policy* to do such a thing.
ほりだしもの 掘り出し物 find ㊌; (買い得品) bargain ㊌ ‖その古いおもちゃは思わぬ掘り出し物だった The old toy was *a real find*.
ほりだす 掘り出す dig* up ㊥ ㊠; (採掘する) mine ㊥ ㊠ ‖芋を掘り出す *dig* (*up*) potatoes ‖鉱石を掘り出す *mine* (*for*) ore
ポリタンク plastic canteen ㊌
ポリバケツ plastic bucket ㊌
ポリぶくろ ポリ袋 plastic bag ㊌
ぼりぼり たくあんをぼりぼり食べる *crunch* [*munch*] *takuan* ‖ 背中をぼりぼりかく *scratch one's* back *hard*
ほりもの 彫り物 (彫刻品) carving ㊌; (入れ墨) tattoo ㊌ ‖彫り物師 a tattooist
ほりゅう 保留 (一時的) suspension ㊤ ㊌; (延期) 《公式的》deferment ㊤ ㊌ ——保留する suspend ㊥ 《公式的》 defer ㊥
コミュニケーションスキル ‖回答を保留する *suspend* response ‖ 態度を保留して様子を見る *suspend* to make *one's* position clear

◆この問題は保留にして(→未解決のままにして)次に進もう Let's leave this problem *open* [*unresolved*] and go on to the next one.
ボリューム ❶【音量】volume ㊤ ‖ラジオのボリュームを下げて Turn down (*the volume* on) the radio.
❷【分量】ボリュームのある朝食 a *big* breakfast ‖ その店の定食はかなりボリュームがある The set meals at that restaurant *are very filling.* ‖ パーマをかけると髪にボリュームが出る Getting a permanent *gives* your hair *more body.*
ほりょ 捕虜 a prisoner (of war) 《略語》POW) ‖捕虜になる be taken prisoner ‖捕虜収容所 a prison camp
ほる¹ 掘る dig* ㊥ ㊠; (発掘する) excavate ㊥ ㊠; (採掘する) mine ㊥ ㊠
井戸を掘る *dig* a well ‖ 石炭を掘る *mine* (*for*) coal ‖ 地面に深さ2メートルの穴を掘る *dig* a hole two meters deep in the ground ‖ 海底トンネルを掘る *dig* [*drive, bore*] an undersea tunnel
さあ、ジャガイモを掘ろう Now let's *dig for* potatoes.
ほる² 彫る carve ㊥; (刻む) engrave ㊥
石碑に文字を彫る *engrave* letters *on* the stone monument
彼は木を彫って仏像を作った He *carved* the wood *into* a Buddhist image. / He *carved* a Buddhist image *out of* wood.
私たちは木の板に自分の名前を彫った We *carved* our names *in* the wooden board.
ぼる ゆうべ飲み屋でぼられた I was 「*ripped off* [*overcharged*]」 at the bar last night.
ポルカ polka
ボルシチ borscht ㊥ (❖ロシア語から)
ホルスタイン 〔動物〕《米》Holstein ㊌, 《英》

Friesian [C]
ホルダー holder [C] ‖キーホルダー a key ring / タイトルホルダー a title holder
ボルテージ 話しているうちに彼のボルテージは上がってきた As he spoke, he *got more and more excited.*
ボルト[1] (ねじ) bolt [C] ‖ボルトでしめる fasten with *a bolt*
ボルト[2] 〔電気〕 volt [C] (《略語》v, V); (ボルト数) voltage [C][U]
ポルトガル Portugal (❖公式名 the Portuguese Republic) ―ポルトガル人 Portuguese [C] (複～) ―ポルトガル語 Portuguese [U] ―ポルトガル(人[語])の Portuguese
ポルノ pornography [U], 《口語的》porn [U] ―ポルノの pornographic; (成人向きの) adult ‖ポルノ映画 a porn(o) [an adult] movie / ポルノ作家 a pornographer / ポルノ雑誌 a porn(o) magazine / ポルノショップ a porn(o) shop / ポルノ女優 a porn(o) queen [star]
ホルマリン 〔化学〕 formalin [U]
ホルモン 〔生化学〕 hormone [C]
‖ホルモン剤 a hormone drug / ホルモン療法 hormone therapy / 女性ホルモン a female hormone / 成長ホルモン a growth hormone / 男性ホルモン a male hormone
ホルン 〔音楽〕 horn [C] ‖ホルンを吹く play *the horn*
‖ホルン奏者 a hornist
ボレー 〔テニス・サッカー〕 volley [C]
ほれこむ 惚れ込む 星野監督はその投手の気の強さにほれ込んだ Mr. Hoshino *fell for* the pitcher's stubbornness.
ほれぼれ 惚れ惚れ ―ほれぼれする be charmed; (引きつけられる) be attracted; (うっとりする) be fascinated ‖その城の天守閣の姿はいつ見てもほれぼれする I *am* always *charmed* [*fascinated*] by the shape of the castle's tower.
◆ほれぼれするような歌声 a *charming* [*an attractive*, a *fascinating*] singing voice
ほれる 惚れる (好きになる) love [他], fall* in love with ...; (魅せられる) be charmed by ..., be attracted to ... ‖「あの子にほれちまったらしい」と彼は言った "I think I *have fallen in love with* her," he said. / 社長はすっかり彼の心意気にほれた The president *was* completely「*charmed by* [*attracted to*] his spirit.
ボレロ (服) bolero [C]; (舞踊) bolero [C]
ほろ 幌 (車・馬車の) 《米》top [C], 《英》hood [C]; (ベビーカーの) hood [C]
‖幌馬車 《米》a covered wagon
ぼろ (布) rag [C]; (服) rags ‖ぼろをまとった老婆 an old woman dressed in *rags*; a *ragged* old woman ◆ぼろ靴 *worn-out shoes* / ぼろ家 *a shabby house*
[慣用表現] 彼女はしゃべりすぎてぼろを出した(→欠点[無知]を露呈した) She talked too much and *exposed her faults* [*ignorance*].
ぼろ- ぼろ勝ち *an easy victory* / 12対2で僕らはぼろ負けだった We *were clobbered* 12 to 2.
ぼろい ぼろいのでよかったら僕の自転車, 使っていいよ You can use my *crummy old* bike if you like. / その仕事はぼろいもうけになった I *got easy money* from the job.
ぼろくそ 彼の新作は多くの批評家からぼろくそにけなされた His new work *was trashed* by many critics.
ホロコースト (ナチスのユダヤ人大虐殺) the Holocaust
ポロシャツ polo shirt [C]
ほろにがい ほろ苦い (少し苦い) slightly bitter; (楽しくも苦しくもある) bittersweet ‖ほろ苦い思い出 a *bittersweet* memory
ポロネーズ polonaise [C] (❖ポーランドの舞踏(曲))
ほろびる 滅びる die out, 《公式的》perish [自]; (国などが) fall* [自]; (滅ぼされる) be destroyed; (絶滅する) become* extinct
生ある物はすべていつかは滅びる All that live must *die out* some day.
インカ帝国は1533年に滅びた The Inca Empire *fell* [*was destroyed*] in 1533.
恐竜は白亜紀末に滅びた Dinosaurs *became extinct* at the end of the Cretaceous.
◆滅びゆく自然 nature *coming to ruin*
ほろぼす 滅ぼす (破壊する) destroy [他]; (没落させる) ruin [他]; (転覆させる) overthrow* [他] ‖1867年ついに徳川幕府は滅ぼされた At last the Tokugawa shogunate *was destroyed* [*overthrown*] in 1867. / 自分の不注意で彼は身を滅ぼした He *ruined himself* through his carelessness./ His carelessness led to *his ruin*.
ぼろぼろ ―ぼろぼろの (破れたりすり切れたりして) ragged; (糸が見えるほどにすり切れて) threadbare; (使い古して・疲れて) worn-out; (もろくなって) crumbly, friable ‖ぼろぼろのジーンズ *ragged* jeans / ぼろぼろの壁 a *crumbly* [*friable*] wall / そのぼろぼろの靴は捨てたら? Why don't you throw out those *worn-out* shoes? / 彼女は心身ともにぼろぼろだった She was *worn-out* mentally and physically.
◆彼のほおを涙がぼろぼろこぼれた Tears *streamed down* his cheeks. / そのパンは食べるとぼろぼろくずれる The bread *crumbles* when you eat it. / その機械には欠陥がぼろぼろ(→次から次へと)見つかった Defects were found in the machine *one after another*.
ぽろぽろ 大粒の涙がぽろぽろと彼女のほおを流れ落ちた Large drops of tears *trickled* down her cheeks. / このクッキーはぽろぽろして食べにくい These cookies are *crumbly* and not easy to eat. / その子はごはんを床にぽろぽろこぼした The child *kept dropping* rice on the floor.
ぼろもうけ ぼろ儲け 彼女はそれらの発明品でぼろもうけした She「*made a killing* [*hit it big*] on her inventions.
ほろよい ほろ酔い ―ほろ酔いの slightly drunk, 《口語的》tipsy, 《口語的》mellow ‖ほろ酔い機嫌になる get *slightly drunk*

ほろり(と)

ほろり(と) ほろりとさせる話 a *touching* [*moving*] story / 彼の話に,聞く人はみなほろりとなった His story *moved* everyone who heard it *to tears*.

ぽろり(と) 本音がぽろりと(→思わず)口をついて出た I let out what I really thought *in spite of myself*. / 彼のグラブから球がぽろりとこぼれた The ball *slipped out* of his glove.

ホワイトカラー ⚠ white-collar worker ◯

ホワイトデー ⚠ "White Day (March 14)," the day when men give gifts, such as candy, to women in return for Valentine's Day gifts (◆「ホワイトデー」は和製英語)

ホワイトハウス the White House

ホン phon ◯ /その地点での騒音は90ホンに達した The noise at the point reached 90 *phons* [*decibels*].

ほん 本

book ◯

難しい[やさしい]本 a difficult [*an easy*] *book* / 童話の本 a children's *book* / 本を出す(→出版する) publish a *book* / いくつかのエッセーを1冊の本にまとめる compile several essays into a *book* [*volume*]

その本はとてもおもしろかった The *book* was very interesting. / I found the *book* very interesting.

近ごろ本を読む暇がない I have no time to read (*books*) these days.

若いうちにできるだけたくさん本を読みなさい Read as many *books* as you can when you are young.

エンデの本,何か持ってない? Don't you have any *books* by Ende?

図書館から本を何冊か借りた I borrowed some *books* from the library.

その本を3冊注文した I ordered *three copies of that book* at a bookstore.

木星について書いてある本(→木星に関する本)を探しているんだ I'm looking for *a book* about [on] Jupiter.

彼女は子供たちに本を読んで聞かせた She read *the book* to her children.

彼は部屋に本を1,000冊も持っている He has no fewer than 1,000 *books* in his room.

本(→本のページ)の間から昔の手紙が出てきた I found an old letter *between the pages of the book*.

◆ 5巻ものの本 a work in five volumes

🗨 「僕は本を読むのが好きなんだ」「どんな本を読むの」 "I like reading *books*." "What kind of *books* do you read?"

‖絵本 a picture book / 古本 a secondhand book / 漫画本 a comic book

慣用表現 彼は小さいころ本の虫だった He was *a bookworm* in his childhood.

関連語 ハードカバー (a) hardback / ペーパーバック (a) paperback

ほん- 本-(本物の) genuine; (主な) main, head; (この) this, present /本革 genuine leather / 本通りの main street / 本館 the main building / 本書は4章から成る This book consists of four chapters.

◆本(→正式の)契約 a *formal* contract

-ほん -本

語法 英語で「…本」に当たる決まった言い方はなく,数えられる名詞の場合は単に数をいえばよい. ただし不可算名詞を数えるときは,piece, bottle などを適宜用いる.

傘1本 *an* umbrella / 鉛筆3本 *three* pencils / ビール5本 *five bottles of* beer / 1本[2本]のチョーク *a piece* [*two pieces*] *of* chalk / 彼は今季ホームランを45本打った He hit *45* home runs this season. / 私は虫歯が2本あります I have *two* decayed [*bad*] teeth.

ぼん¹ 盆 tray ◯

ことわざ 覆水盆に返らず It is no use crying over spilt milk. (→こぼれたミルクを嘆いてもしかたがない)

ぼん² 盆 ⚠ *Bon*, the Buddhist souls festival ‖盆踊り the *Bon* dance

盆は先祖を供養するための仏教行事で,7月や8月の真夏に行われます.盆の間,先祖の魂が戻ってくるとされており,ごちそうや飲み物,あるいは踊りなども披露しながらご先祖様をもてなします.盆は多くの会社が休みになり,故郷を離れて暮らしている人々も里帰りして家族と盆を過ごすことができますで,帰省ラッシュで交通機関がごった返す時期でもあります.

Bon is the Buddhist souls festival at midsummer in July or August to pay homage to the spirits of ancestors that are believed to return during that time. People entertain the spirits with offerings of food, drinks and sometimes dance. In the *Bon* period, many offices are closed so that those living away from their hometowns can share the festival with their families. During *Bon*, public transport and roads get jammed with people going home.

ぽん シャンパンのコルクがぽんと音を立てた The champagne cork *popped*. / 彼女は定夫の背中をぽんとたたいた She *patted* [*clapped, slapped*] Sadao on the back. / 彼は新聞をテーブルの上にぽんと放り投げた He *tossed* the newspaper onto the table. / その老人は孤児院に大金をぽんと(→気前よく)寄付した The old man *generously* made a donation of a lot of money to the orphanage.

ほんい¹ 本位 実力本位の社会 a *meritocratic* society / 彼は興味本位で(→単なる好奇心から)その会に参加した He took part in the meeting *merely out of curiosity*. / 自分本位の考え方を捨てなさい Give up your *selfish* way of thinking. / 私は品質本位で物を選ぶ I *give priority to quality* when choosing things. / 利益本位のやり方が(→利益ばかりを追求したために)その会社をすっかりだめにしてしまった The company was completely ruined because it *pursued profit exclusively*.

‖金本位制 the gold standard
ほんい² 本意 *one's* real intention
⇒ ふは921;本 / それは彼の本意ではなかった That wasn't his *real* intention.
ほんか 本科 regular course ⓒ
ほんかいぎ 本会議 plenary session ⓒ
ほんかく 本格 事故の本格的な調査が始まった They started a *full-scale* investigation into the accident. / それは日本初の本格的な(→大規模な)美術館だった It was the first *large-scale* museum in Japan. / ついに本格的な冬が到来した *Real* winter has finally arrived. / 雪が本格的に降りだした The snow began to fall *in earnest*. / その国では地球温暖化に対する取り組みがずいぶん前から本格化している(→本格的に取り組んでいる) The country has long grappled *in earnest* with the problem of global warming.
ほんかん¹ 本管 (ガス・水道などの) main ⓒ 給水本管 *a* water *main* / ガスの本管が止められている The gas is turned off at *the main*.
ほんかん² 本館 the main building
ほんき 本気 seriousness Ⓤ, earnestness Ⓤ ━━本気の serious, earnest ━━本気で[に] seriously, earnestly, in earnest /彼が本気になったのは達也一人だった Tatsuya was the only one she was *serious about*. / 彼は何でも本気にしてしまう He *takes* everything *seriously*. / 政府は貧困の問題に本気で取り組み始めた The government began to wrestle with the problem of poverty *in earnest*. / 宇宙人がいるなんて君は本気で信じているのかい Do you believe *seriously* that extraterrestrials exist?
◆本気で新しい事業を始めるつもりですか Do you *really* mean to start a new business? / 彼が本気を出せば私など到底かなわない If he *puts his heart into it*, there's no way I can beat him. / プロのボクサーに本気で殴られたら絶対にけがをするよ If a professional boxer hits you *for real*, you are sure to get injured.
🔴「大学をやめてお笑い芸人になるよ」「本気なの？」"I'm going to quit college and become a comedian." "*Are you serious?*"
ほんぎまり 本決まり 海外赴任が本決まりになった It *was decided formally* [*definitely*] that I would go abroad to work.
ほんきょ 本拠 (根拠地) base ⓒ, home ⓒ; (本部) headquarters 《単数または複数扱い》
◆大阪を本拠とする会社 an Osaka-*based* company / その会社は東京に本拠を置いている The company *is based* in Tokyo.
ほんぎょう 本業 *one's* main occupation / 彼は本業のかたわら小説を書いている Besides *his main occupation*, he writes novels.
ぼんくれ 盆暮れ 盆暮れの付け届け *midyear and year-end* presents
ほんけ 本家 (宗家) the head [main] family; (元祖) originator ⓒ
ほんこう 本校 (分校に対する) the main campus [school]; (わが校) this [our] school
ほんごく 本国 *one's* own country, *one's*

home /彼らは本国に飛行機で送還された They were flown back to *their home* (*country*).
ほんごし 本腰 本腰を入れて仕事にかかろう Let's *settle* [*buckle*] *down* to work. / 彼らはその計画に本腰を入れて取り組んだ(→集中した) They *gave* [*set*] *their minds* to the project.
ぽんこつ (がらくた) junk
◆ぽんこつ車《俗語》*a junker*;《口語的》*a jalopy*;(→廃車) *a junked car*
ホンコン 香港 Hong Kong
ぼんさい 盆栽 bonsai ⓒⓊ (複 ～), dwarf tree ⓒ / 盆栽を楽しむ appreciate *a bonsai* / 今では欧米でも盆栽が静かなブームになっている Now *bonsai* enjoys quiet but steady popularity in Europe and America.
ぼんさい 凡才 (平凡な才能) ordinary [common, mediocre] ability Ⓤⓒ; (凡人) ordinary [common, mediocre] person ⓒ
ほんざん 本山 the head temple (of a sect)
ほんしき 本式 私はまだ本式の(→本物の)フランス料理を食べたことがない I have never eaten the *authentic* [*real*] French cuisine. / 彼女は本式に華道を習い始めた(→正式なレッスンを始めた) She began to take *formal* [*regular*] lessons in flower arrangement.
ほんしけん 本試験 (主要な試験) the main examination
ほんしつ 本質 《公式的》essence Ⓤ; (実質) 《公式的》substance Ⓤ; (性質) nature Ⓤⓒ ━━本質的な essential; substantive /言語の本質 *the essence* [*nature*] of human language / 理論の本質的な部分 an *essential* part of the theory / 彼には物事の本質を直観的に見抜く力があった He was able to see through to *the essence* of things intuitively. / 両者の本質的な相違を見落としてはならない You shouldn't miss the *essential* difference between the two.
◆彼の指摘は問題の本質(→核心)を突いていた It was *the heart* [*core*] of the problem that he pointed out.
ほんじつ 本日 today /本日休業《掲示》*Closed Today* / この券は本日限り有効です This ticket is good *only* (*for*) *today*.
ほんしゃ 本社 the main [head] office
ほんしゅう 本州 Honshu; (島) Honshu Island
ほんしょ 本署 (警察などの) headquarters《単数または複数扱い》((略語))HQ
ほんしょう 本性 true character [nature] /金の話になると彼女は本性を現した When it came to money, she *showed her true character* [*nature*].
ほんしょく 本職 ❶【本業】*one's* (main) occupation, *one's* job /彼は作曲家として有名だが, 本職は銀行員だ He is well known as a composer, but *he* is a bank clerk by *occupation* [*his main occupation* is as a bank clerk].
❷【プロ】professional ⓒ ━━本職の professional /本職の大工 a *professional* carpenter / 彼女のピアノは本職はだしだ(→プロ並みだ)

Her piano skill *is on the level of a professional*.

ほんしん 本心 私は彼の本心を突き止めようとした I tried to get at his *true intentions*. / 僕には直美の本心が分からない I don't know what Naomi *is really thinking* [*feeling*]. / 本心からそうしたいと思っているわけじゃない I don't *really* want to do it.

ほんじん 凡人 ordinary [common] person ⓒ; (凡才) mediocre person ⓒ

ポンず ポン酢 soy sauce with citrus juice

ほんすう 本数 夜はバスの本数が少ない *The number* of buses is small at night. / あなたが1日に吸うたばこの本数はどのくらいですか *How many* cigarettes do you smoke a day?

ほんすじ 本筋 彼の話はしばしば本筋からそれた He often strayed from *the subject* [*point*] of his speech. / まず彼女に謝るのが本筋(→当然)だろう It would be *proper* to apologize to her first.

ほんせき 本籍 (本籍地) one's permanent legal address ∥ 本籍を東京に移す transfer *one's legal address* [*domicile*] to Tokyo

ほんせん 本線 the main [trunk] line ∥ 山陽本線 the Sanyo *main* [*trunk*] *line*

ほんそう 奔走 計画の実現のために奔走する *make every effort* to realize the plan / おじの奔走で(→尽力で) 就職することができた I got a job *by the good offices of* my uncle.

ほんぞん 本尊 the central Buddhist image (in a temple)

ぼんだ 凡打 わがチームの打線は凡打の山を築いた The batters of my team hit a pile of *easy flies and grounders*.

ほんたい 本体 the (main) body ∥ その車の本体には様々な部品が取りつけられている Various custom parts are fixed to *the body* of the car. ◆ パソコンの本体 the *main unit* of a personal computer ∥本体価格 a net price

ほんだい 本題 the main subject ∥それでは本題に入りましょう Let's get down to「*the main subject* [《口語的》*brass tacks*].

ぼんたい 凡退 三者凡退に打ち取る *get three batters out easily* / 彼はきょうここまで2打席凡退している He *has been easily put out* in two at bats so far today.

ほんたて 本立て bookends

ほんだな 本棚 bookshelf ⓒ (❖本箱の棚の1枚を指す); (本箱) bookcase ⓒ ∥作りつけの本棚 a built-in *bookcase*

ぼんち 盆地 basin ⓒ ∥奈良盆地 the Nara *Basin*

ほんちょうし 本調子 (正常な状態) the [*one's*] normal condition; (好調) good condition ⓒ 《また a ～》 (❖condition は「健康状態」も表す) ∥本調子を取り戻す recover *good condition* / 彼女はまだ本調子にはほど遠い She is far from *her normal condition* yet. ◆ 彼はやっと本調子になってきたようだ It seems that he *has hit his stride* at last.

ほんてん 本店 (店舗) the main [head] store; (営業所) the main [head] office ∥日本橋三越本店 *the main store* of Mitsukoshi at Nihombashi

ほんでん 本殿 the main shrine

ほんど 本土 the mainland ∥ギリシャ本土 *the mainland of* Greece / その島は橋によって本土とつながった The island was joined to *the mainland* by a bridge. ◆ 日本本土 Japan *proper*; *the main islands* of Japan

ボンド ⚠ (接着剤) adhesive ⓒ Ⓤ, glue Ⓤ (❖Bondは日本の商標名)

ポンド (通貨単位) pound ⓒ (《略語》L, £); (重さの単位) pound ⓒ (《略語》lb.) ∥8ポンド20ペンス £8.20; eight *pounds* [*quid*] (and) 20 (pence)

ほんとう 本当
❶【真実】 ——本当の true; real; actual ——本当に truly; really; actually
> true: うそではない、また現実や事実に即しているという意味。
> real: まがい物、あるいは想像上の物ではないという意味。
> actual: 現実に存在するという意味。

これは本当の話です This is a *true* story.
彼の言ったことは本当だと決めてかかっていた I assumed his statement was *true*.
結婚したって本当ですか Is it *true* that you got married?
本当の理由は何なの What is the *real* reason?
ゆうべ本当に幽霊を見たんだ I tell you I *really* saw a ghost last night.
彼は若く見えるが、本当は50歳を過ぎている He looks young, but *actually* he is over 50.
彼女には本当の意味での友達はひとりもいなかった She didn't have any friends *in a true sense*.
◆ 彼女に本当のことを言う勇気がない I dare not tell her *the truth*. / 本当のことを言うと寝坊して遅れたのです *To tell the truth*, I am late because I overslept. / 僕は関係ないよ、本当だよ I'm not involved, *I'm sure*. / 本当の(→本物の)イタリア料理というものを教えてやろう I'll show you what *genuine* Italian cooking is like.
🅔 「試験に合格したよ」「本当?」 "I passed the exams." "*Really*? / *You did*?"
🅔 「この映画、つまらないね」「本当だね」 "This movie is dull, isn't it?" "*Absolutely*."

❷【非常に】
本当にすばらしい試合だった It was a *truly* [*really*] wonderful game.
君は本当に絵がうまいなあ You *really* draw well, don't you?
子供は本当に成長するのが早い Children grow *very* rapidly.
彼女は本当にチョコレートが好きだ She *does* like chocolate. (❖この do(es) は動詞を強調する)
お待たせして本当に申しわけありません I'm *very* [*truly*, 《口語的》*terribly*] sorry to have kept you waiting.
本当にありがとうございました Thank you *very*

much.
ほんどう¹ 本堂 the main building of a Buddhist temple
ほんどう² 本道 彼は学者としての本道を歩んできた(→正統的な経歴をもっている) He has *an orthodox career* as a scholar.
ほんどおり 本通り《米》the main street, 《英》the high street
ほんにん 本人 a person himself [herself]; (当の本人) the person in question ∥私は大統領夫人本人にお会いしました I met the First Lady *herself*. / パスポートは本人が受け取らなければならない You have to pick up your passport *yourself* [*in person*]. (❖*in person* は「代理人ではなく本人が」の意味)/ うわさをしているところに当の本人が現れた *The person in question* appeared when we were talking about him. / 本人から聞いたんだから間違いない It's certain because I heard it from the *person in question*.
ほんね 本音 one's real [actual] intention ⇒たてまえ ∥本音を吐く reveal *one's real intention* / 誠は彼女の本音を巧みに引き出した Makoto craftily dragged *the real intention* out of her.
ボンネット ⚠(車の)《米》hood [húd] Ⓒ, 《英》bonnet Ⓒ
ほんの only, just, merely ∥彼はまだほんの子供 He is *only* [*just, merely*] a child. / ほんのかすり傷 It's *only* [*just*] a scratch. / 彼女はそのときほんの12歳だった She was *only* 12 years old then. / 私はほんの少しだけ英語が話せます I can speak English *only* a little. / 山のほんのてっぺんだけが雲の上に見えた *Only* the top of the mountain showed above the cloud.
◆これはほんのお礼のしるしです This is a *slight* token of my gratitude.
ほんのう 本能 instinct Ⓒ Ⓤ ──本能的な instinctive ──本能的に instinctively, by instinct ∥雅史は本能的に危険を感じた Masashi *instinctively* felt the danger. / 人間のいかなる知性的な行動も本能に根ざしている Every intelligent activity of a human being is rooted in *instinct*.
◆彼女のひと言は彼らの闘争本能をかきたてた Her words stirred their *fighting spirit*.
∥帰巣本能 (a) homing instinct / 防衛本能 the instinct of self-preservation / 母性本能 (a) maternal instinct
ぼんのう 煩悩 (earthly) passion Ⓤ Ⓒ; (欲望) (earthly) desire Ⓒ Ⓤ
ほんのり (かすかに) faintly; (わずかに) slightly ∥1杯のビールで彼女のほおはほんのり赤くなった A glass of beer made her cheeks *slightly* flushed.
◆ほんのり桜の香りがする There is a *faint* smell of cherry blossoms.
ほんば 本場 home Ⓒ; (発祥地) birthplace Ⓒ(通例単数形) ∥信州はそばの本場です The Shinshu area is *the home* of soba [buckwheat noodles]. / アメリカは言わずと知れた野球の本場だ As everyone knows, America is *the home* [*birthplace*] of baseball. / 先月韓国に行って本場物のキムチを食べてきた I went to Korea last month and ate kimchi *at its home*. / 彼のロシア語は本場仕込みだ His Russian *was learned in Russia*.
ほんばこ 本箱 bookcase Ⓒ
ほんばしょ 本場所 (相撲の興行) regular sumo tournament Ⓒ
ほんばん 本番 the real thing ∥(テレビなどの収録で) 本番です This is 「*the real thing* [*a take*]. ◆彼は本番になるとふだん以上の力を発揮した He shows more ability than usual *when it really counts*. / もうすぐ夏も本番だ(→本格的な夏だ) *Real* summer will come soon.
⇒ぶっつけほんばん
ぽんびき ぽん引き pimp Ⓒ
ほんぶ 本部 the head [main] office; (司令部) headquarters《単数または複数扱い》; (中心) center Ⓒ ∥捜査本部を設置する set up *the investigation headquarters* / 国連本部はニューヨークにある *The United Nations Headquarters* are [is] in New York.
◆参謀本部 *the General Staff Office*
◆ポンプ pump Ⓒ ∥給油ポンプ *a petrol pump*
◆ポンプで水をくみ上げる *pump up* water
ほんぶり 本降り ∥雪が本降りになってきた It began to *snow hard* [*in earnest*].
ほんぶん¹ 本文 (注釈・序文などに対して) text Ⓒ; (本論) body Ⓒ ∥本文に脚注をつける add footnotes to *the text*
ほんぶん² 本分 one's duty ∥学生としての本分を尽くす do *one's duty* as a student
ボンベ ⚠cylinder Ⓒ (❖日本語はドイツ語の Bombe から) ∥ガス[酸素]ボンベ *a gas* [*an oxygen*] *cylinder*
ほんぽう¹ 奔放 ──奔放な (自由な) free, uninhibited; (気ままな) unrestrained ∥自由奔放な生き方 a *free* [*an uninhibited*] way of living / 彼女は奔放に育てられた She was raised up to be *unrestrained*.
ほんぽう² 本邦 our [this] country
◆本邦(→日本)初公開の映画 a film that is released for the first time in *Japan*
ポンポン pompon Ⓒ
ぽんぽん 名案がぽんぽん(→次から次へと)浮かんだ Good ideas occurred to me *one after another*. / 彼女は思いついたことをぽんぽん(→ためらわずに)口に出す She says what pops into her mind *without hesitation*. / 後ろから肩をぽんぽんとたたかれた Someone *clapped* me *on* the shoulder from behind.
ほんまつてんとう 本末転倒 それでは本末転倒だ It's like *putting* [*setting*] *the cart before the horse*.
ほんみょう 本名 one's real name
ほんむ 本務 one's duty ∥本務を果たす do [perform] *one's duty*
ほんめい 本命 the favorite ∥本命に賭(か)ける bet on *the favorite*
◆選挙の本命候補 *the probable winner* of the election / 彼の本命は純だ The girl he's *really after* is Jun.

ほんもう 本望　本望を遂げる realize *one's long-cherished wish* / ここまで善戦できれば本望(=満足)だ I *am satisfied* as I have played well so far.

ほんもの 本物　the real thing, 《口語的》the real McCoy　——本物の real, genuine; (真正な) authentic; (天然の) natural /この料理サンプルは本物そっくりだ This wax food looks like *the real thing*. / お母さん、これ本物のダイヤ？ Mom, is this a *real* [*genuine*] diamond? / 本物のSLを見たのはそのときが初めてだった It was the first time that I saw a *real* steam locomotive. / このピカソの絵は本物であることが証明されている This painting of Picasso has been certified to be *genuine*.

◆本物のサイン a *true* [an *authentic*] autograph / 彼のこの企画に対する熱意は本物だ(→本気で取り組んでいる) He wrestles with this project *in earnest*.

ほんもん 本文　text ⇨ ほんぶん(本文)

ほんや 本屋　(店舗)《主に米》bookstore ⓒ,《主に英》bookshop ⓒ; (人) bookseller ⓒ

ほんやく 翻訳　translation ⓒⓊ　——翻訳する translate ⓗⓥ / 原文に忠実な翻訳 *the translation* close to the original / 英語を日本語に翻訳する *translate* English *into* Japanese / カフカの作品を翻訳で読む read Kafka *in translation* / その翻訳は間違っていた The *translation* was incorrect. / 彼の作品の多くがフランス語から日本語に翻訳された Many of his works *were translated* from French *into* Japanese. / 彼女は研究所で翻訳の仕事をしている She *translates* for a research institute. / この詩を翻訳するのはほとんど不可能に近い It's virtually impossible to *translate* this poem.

‖翻訳権 the right of translation / 翻訳者[家] a translator / 翻訳書 a translation / 機械翻訳 machine translation

ぼんやり

❶【はっきりしない】　——ぼんやりした dim, vague　——ぼんやりと dimly, vaguely

事件のことはぼんやりと覚えている I have a *dim* [*vague*] memory of the incident.

部屋の片隅には明かりがぼんやりとともっていた A *dim* light was on in the corner of the room.

霧の中にぼんやりと家の輪郭が見えた I saw a *vague* outline of the house in the fog.

◆きのうは一日中、二日酔いで頭がぼんやりしていた(→はっきりものが考えられなかった) Yesterday I *couldn't think clearly* all day because of my hangover.

❷【放心した】　——ぼんやりした (うわの空の) absent-minded, vague; (不注意な) careless　——ぼんやりと absent-mindedly, vaguely; carelessly

ぼんやりしていて違う電車に乗ってしまった I was so *careless* that I took the wrong train.

彼女はぼんやりと窓の外を眺めていた She looked out of the window *absent-mindedly*.

◆彼女はぼんやりと(→何もせずに)休日を過ごした She spent the holiday *idly*. / (バスなどで)ぼんやりしてると(→気をつけていないと)乗り過ごしてしまうよ If you don't *pay attention*, you'll miss your stop.

ぼんよう 凡庸　mediocrity Ⓤ　——凡庸な mediocre ‖凡庸な作品 a *mediocre* work

ほんらい 本来

❶【もともと】　(元来) originally; (生まれつき) naturally, in nature; (本質的に) essentially　——本来の original; natural; essential

彼女は本来陽気な人たちです She is「*naturally cheerful* [*cheerful in nature*].

あなたはこの言葉の本来の意味を知っていますか Do you know the *original* meaning of this word?

オリンピックの本来の目的は友好と親善にある The *original* purpose of the Olympic Games is the promotion of friendship and goodwill.

◆彼はカウンセリングを受けて本来の自分を取り戻した After he underwent counseling, he *came to himself*.

❷【当然のこと】

この仕事は本来なら彼女自身がやるべきものだ *By rights*, she herself should do this job.

ほんりゅう 本流　the mainstream ‖西欧絵画の本流 *the mainstream* of Western paintings / 私たちの船は支流から本流へと出た Our boat came from the branch to *the mainstream*.

ほんりゅう² 奔流　(急流) rapid stream ⓒ; (激流) torrent ⓒ

ほんりょう 本領　*one's* (own) ability, the [*one's*] (true) stuff; (特質) characteristic ⓒ ‖ここ一番というときに秋山は本領を発揮した Akiyama「*showed his true stuff* [《口語的》*did his stuff*] in the very important case.

ほんるい 本塁　〖野球〗home plate Ⓤ 《しばしば the home plate》

‖本塁打 a home run, a homer

ほんろう 翻弄　運命に翻弄される *be played* by fate / 船は荒波に翻弄された The ship *was*「*tossed* by [*at the mercy* of] the rough waves.

ほんろん 本論　the main subject [theme]; (主な問題点) the main issue / では本論に入りましょう Now let's proceed to *the main subject* [*theme*].

ほんわか 彼は新婚生活のほんわかしたムードに酔っている He's feeling *mellow* in his newly married life.

ま

ま¹ 間

❶【時間】time Ⓤ Ⓒ; (合い間) interval Ⓒ; (休止) pause Ⓒ ⇨ あいだ, ひま
- コンサートが始まるまでにまだ少し間がある There is a little more *time* before the concert begins.
- 新聞を読む間もないほど忙しい I'm so busy that I don't even have *time* to read a newspaper.
- アナウンサーは少し間をおいてから次のニュースを読み上げた After *a* short *pause* [*interval*], the announcer read another piece of news.
- 俳優のせりふの間の取り方で芝居全体の印象が決まる The overall impression made by a play depends on how well the actors 「put *pauses* [*pause*] between their lines.
◆彼は休む間もなく(→休憩なしに)絵を描き続けた He continued drawing the picture *without rest*. / 彼は日本に来てからまだ間がない(→長いこと日本にいない) He *has* not *been* in Japan *long*. / あっという間に(→それに気がつく前に)20年が過ぎてしまった Twenty years had passed *before I knew it*. / あっという間に(→一瞬のうちに)家全体が炎に包まれた The whole house was enveloped in flames *in an instant*.

❷【間隔】interval Ⓒ ⇨ あいだ
- 道路の両わきには一定の間をおいて街灯が立てられている Street lamps were put up along both sides of the road at regular *intervals*.

❸【部屋】room Ⓒ
- 2間の家 a two-*room* house / 日本間 a Japanese-style *room*
- 6畳2間の家に家族3人が暮らしていた The family of three lived in a house with two six-mat *rooms*.

慣用表現 今ごろになってそんなことを言うなんて、彼は間が抜けている(→ばかげている) It is *stupid* of him to say that now. / 初めて彼と会ったので間がもたなかった(→話題がなかった) Since I was meeting him for the first time, we *had nothing to talk about*. / 間が悪い(→不運な)ことに, 駅へ向かう途中で車がパンクした It was *quite unlucky* of me to have a flat tire on the way to the station. / 元彼女と通りで会って間が悪い思いをした(→気まずかった) I felt awkward [*embarrassed*] when I ran into my ex-girlfriend on the street. / 全く間の抜けた(→愚かしい)話だ It is quite an *absurd* story.

ま² 魔

——魔の (危険な) dangerous; (不吉な) unlucky //魔の金曜日 an *unlucky* Friday / ここは過去数年間, 事故が多発している魔の交差点だ This is a *dangerous* intersection where a lot of accidents have occurred over the past several years.

慣用表現 部費を着服するなんて, 彼は魔がさした(→悪魔に取りつかれた)にちがいない To pocket the club dues, he must *have been possessed by an evil spirit*.

ま³ 真

彼は私の言葉を真に受けた(→深刻に受け止めた)らしい It seems he *took* me *at my word*. / It seems he *took* me *seriously*. / 彼はすぐに私の冗談を真に受ける He always *takes* my jokes *seriously*.

ま- 真-

その公園は駅のほぼ真北にある The park is almost *due north*.

-ま -魔

freak Ⓒ //電話魔 a telephone *freak*
◆放火魔 an arsonist / 通り魔 a random attacker [*killer*]

まあ

❶【驚きを表す】Oh!, Well!, Oh well!, Wow!(❖最も一般的な語); Oh, dear!, Oh, my!, Dear me!, My!(❖いずれもやや女性的な表現. 前二者は Oh の後にコンマ(,)を付けることに注意); Good heavens!, (My) goodness! (❖ひどく驚いたような場合に用いる)

語法
「おやまあ」とひどく驚いた場合, 英語では Oh (my) God! または My God! のように言うことが多い. ただし, これらの表現はいずれも God「神」という言葉を含むため, 人前で使うと下品とされる場合がある. Good heavens! や (My) goodness! はいずれも, これらの代わりに用いられる婉曲表現. ⇨ ああ¹

- まあ, なんてかわいいお子さんでしょう *Oh*, what a lovely child!
- まあ大変, あなたびしょぬれよ *Oh dear*! You're all wet!
- まあ, なんという散らかし方なの *Wow*! What a mess!
◆まあよかった. 電車に間に合ったわ Thank God [*goodness*]! We're just in time for the train.
💬「これ, 君の分のチケットなんだけど」「まあ, うれしい. ありがとう」"Here is a ticket for you." "*Oh*, how nice [kind] of you. Thank you so much."
💬「数学の試験で満点を取ったんだ」「まあ, 本当なの? すごいじゃない」"I got a perfect score in mathematics." "*Oh*, really? That's great!"
💬「かぜひいちゃってね」「まあ, それはお気の毒に」"I've caught (a) cold." "*Oh*, that's too bad."

❷【控えめな気持ちを表す】(かなり) fairly, rather(❖fairly が肯定的な気持ちを表すのに対し, rather は否定的な気持ちを表すことが多い); (たぶん) perhaps; (何とか) somehow; (例えば) say, I [we] should say ⇨ まあまあ

- 彼としては, まあよくできたほうだろう We can say he did it *fairly* well.
- クラシック音楽はまあ好きなほうです I *rather*

like classical music.
彼のことだから、まあ大丈夫だろう Perhaps [Probably] he will be all right.
まあ彼女ならこの件をうまくまとめてくれるだろう She will settle this case somehow.
彼ならまあ2日でそれを仕上げるだろう He'll finish it in, say [I suppose], two days.
◆まあとにかくお入りください Anyway, please come in. / まあそんなところだ That's about it.(◆話を切り上げるときの表現) / (→そのようなものだ) It's something like that.
💬「来月結婚するんだって？」「まあね」"You are going to get married next month, aren't you?" "Well, yes."
💬「アメリカに留学したいんだろう？」「うん、まあね」"You want to study in America, don't you?" "Yes, sort [kind] of."
❸【ちょっと】just
まあ聞きなさい Just listen!
まあ、やってみるけど期待しないでね I'll just try it. Don't count on me.

まあい 間合い 彼は1歩下がって相手との間合いをとった He took a step back and made a space between him and his opponent.

マーカー marker

マーガリン margarine [mάːrdʒərən] Ⓤ ‖植物性マーガリン vegetable margarine

マーガレット【植物】marguerite Ⓒ

マーク ❶【印】(目印) mark Ⓒ; (記号) sign Ⓒ; (図柄) picture Ⓒ; (商標) trademark Ⓒ ——マークする (印をつける) mark ⊕, put* a mark on ... ➡しるし、シンボル ‖彼はその書類に赤いマークをつけて、重要であることが分かるようにした He put a red mark on the document [He marked the document in red] to show that it was important. / 彼女のかばんには子猫のマークがついていた Her bag had a picture of a kitten on it. / この会社の製品はイルカのマークが目印だ(→イルカを登録商標に使っている) The company uses a dolphin as its trademark.
❷【監視】 ——マークする (特別な注意を払う) keep* an [one's] eye on ...; (ブラックリストに載せる) put* ... on a blacklist, blacklist ⊕; 【スポーツ】cover ⊕ ‖やつを徹底的にマークしろ Keep your eye on the guy. / 警察はどうやらその男をマークしているようだ It seems that the police have「put the man on their blacklist [blacklisted the man]. / (スポーツで)君は10番をマークしてくれ I want you to cover 〔⑧〕mark〕 No. 10.
❸【記録の樹立】 ——マークする set* [establish, make*] a record ‖彼はスピードスケートで世界記録をマークした He set [established, made] a world record in speed skating.

マークシート ⚠(用紙) answer sheet Ⓒ (◆「マークシート」は和製英語) ——マークシート(方式)の (コンピュータ化された) computerized ‖マークシート(方式)のテスト a computerized test

マーケット market Ⓒ ‖家に帰る途中、近くのマーケット(→市場(いちば))で野菜を買った On my way home, I bought some vegetables at the nearby market. / 新しいマーケット(→市場(しじょう))を開拓することは、我々にとって緊急の課題である It is an urgent challenge for us to develop [cultivate, open up] new markets.

マーケティング marketing Ⓤ ◆市場調査・宣伝などの企業活動全般のこと ‖マーケティングリサーチ marketing research

マージャン 麻雀 mah-jong(g) [mὰːʒɔ́ŋ] Ⓤ (◆中国語から) ‖マージャンをする play mah-jong / マージャンのパイ a (mah-jong) tile ‖マージャン屋 a mah-jong parlor

マージン (利ざや) (profit) margin Ⓒ; (余白) margin Ⓒ ‖(文書の編集で)マージンを設定する set the margins / 我々の仕事はマージンがけっこう多い[ごく少ない] In our business the (profit) margin is「fairly large [very small].

まあたらしい 真新しい brand-new ‖真新しい車 a brand-new car

マーチ (行進曲) march Ⓒ ‖マーチを演奏する play a march
‖ウエディングマーチ a wedding march

まあまあ ❶【程度】(けっこうよい[よく]) fairly good [well]; (それほど悪くない) not so bad, (よくも悪くもない) neither good nor bad, 《口語的》 so-so ‖ 1学期はまあまあの成績だった I got fairly good grades in the first term. / スピーチコンテストでの彼のできばえはまあまあだった He did fairly well in the speech contest. ◆彼は初心者にしてはまあまあうまくスキーを滑った He skied well enough for a beginner.
💬「映画はどうだった」「まあまあだったよ」"What did you think of the movie?" "It was all right."
💬「最近勉強のほうはどうだい」「まあまあってとこかな」"How are your studies going?" "So-so, I guess."
❷【人をなだめる表現】Now [Come], now.; 《英》Come, come. ‖まあまあ、そう言わずに試してごらんよ Now, now, just try it.

マーマレード marmalade [mάːrməlèid] Ⓤ

まい- 毎-
❶【…ごとに】(どの…も) every; (各…) each 語法
every は一つ一つを個別的に意識しつつ、同時に全体を表す表現。each は一つ一つの個別性を強調する語。いずれも、後には単数名詞がくるのがふつう。

毎水曜日彼女は絵の教室に行く She goes to a drawing class every [each] Wednesday. / She goes to a drawing class on Wednesdays.
彼は毎食後に歯を磨く He brushes his teeth after every [each] meal.
この雑誌は毎号 CD-ROM の付録がついている Every [Each] issue of this magazine has a CD-ROM supplement.
彼は毎月1度釣りを楽しむ He enjoys fishing「every month [once a month]. (◆once a ...で「…につき1回」の意味)

❷【…につき】 a [an], per
台風は毎時40キロの速さで日本に接近している The typhoon is approaching Japan at a speed of 40 kilometers *an* [*per*] hour.

-まい¹ -枚 (一定の大きさ・型をもつ紙などの) a sheet of …; (大きさ・型が定まっていない紙など) a piece of …; (パンなどの) a slice of …; (窓ガラスの) a pane of …

【語法】
英語の paper や bread は不可算名詞として扱われる。したがって、不定冠詞を付けて×a paper としたり、×two papers のように数詞を付けることはできない。「一枚」と数える場合は、その形状を表す piece や sheet を使って、a piece of paper「紙 1 枚」、two pieces of paper「紙 2 枚」のようにいう。一方、「切符」や「切手」など、紙でできた商品は可算名詞として扱うので、two stamps「切手 2 枚」のように名詞の複数形に数詞を付ける。

紙 3 枚 three *sheets* [*pieces*] *of* paper / 新聞紙 1 枚 a *piece of* newspaper / 食パン 2 枚 two *slices of* bread / ガラス 3 枚 three *panes* [*sheets*] *of* glass
◆切符 2 枚 two *tickets* / 80円切手 3 枚 three 80-yen *stamps* / 36枚撮りのフィルム 1 本 a roll of film with 36 *exposures*(❖exposure はフィルムの 1 コマのこと) / 私たちはピザを 2 枚注文した We ordered two *pizzas*.(❖「ピザ 1 切れ」は a slice of pizza という)

-まい² 彼女はそのような申し出は受けまい She *will not* accept such an offer. / 彼はもう二度と我々の前には姿を見せまい He *will never* appear before us again. / あの相手では彼は到底かなうまい He *can't possibly* beat his opponent. (❖can't possibly は「とても…できない」という強い否定の意味) / だれがそんなことをしたのか、だれにも分かるまい *No one can* guess who did it. (❖主語の No one は「だれも…ない」という強い否定の意味) / もう何も言うまい I *won't* say any more. / 子供じゃあるまいし、自分で判断しなさい *Since you're no longer a child*, you should decide it by yourself. / 結婚しようとしまいと私の勝手でしょ It has nothing to do with you *whether I get married or not*.

❓「敵が我々の動きを察知したということはありえるだろうか」「いや、そんなことはあるまい」 "Is it possible that the enemy became aware of our activities?" "*No, I don't think so*."

まいあがる 舞い上がる (上へ向かって飛ぶ) fly* up; (空高く上昇する) soar ⦿; (風に飛ばされる) be blown up; (ほこりなどが) be stirred up; (渦を巻きながら) be whirled up ‖ジェット機は空高く舞い上がった The jet plane *flew* [*soared*] *up* into the sky. / 車が通るたびにほこりが舞い上がった The dust *was stirred* [*whirled*] *up* every time a car passed. / 彼は優勝してすっかり舞い上がってしまった(→うれしくて我を忘れた) He *was beside himself* with joy when he won the championship.

まいあさ 毎朝 every morning ‖父は毎朝散歩をする My father goes for a walk *every morning*.

マイアミ Miami (❖米国の都市)

まいおりる 舞い降りる (飛んできたものが) fly* down ‖1 羽のツルが湿原に舞い降りた A crane *flew down* onto the marsh.

マイカー ⚠(個人所有の車) one's own car, private car ⦿; (家族用の車) family car ⦿ ‖兄は毎日会社までマイカーで通勤している My brother *goes* to his office *in his own car* every day. / (→会社まで車を運転する) My brother *drives* to his office every day.
‖マイカー族 an owner-driver

まいかい 毎回 every [each] time ──毎回の every (❖後にはふつう名詞の単数形がくる) ‖彼女はそのコンテストに毎回出場している She enters the contest *every* [*each*] *time*. / 彼は毎回司法試験に落ちている He fails (in) *every bar exam*. / 不祥事が明るみに出るたびに、社長は毎回頭を下げた The president apologized *every time* a scandal was revealed. (❖この every time は接続詞で「…するたびに」の意味)
◆毎回同じ注意をさせるな I'm fed up with giving you the same advice *again and again*.

まいきょ 枚挙 この種の事件は枚挙にいとまがない Cases like this *are too many to count*.

マイク microphone ⦿, 《口語的》mike ⦿ ‖マイクのスイッチを入れる[切る] turn *a mike* on [off] / マイクに向かって話す speak into *a microphone* / 彼はマイクで全校生徒に演説をしている間、ずっと緊張しているように見えた He seemed tense the whole time he spoke through *the microphone* to all the students. / マイクが入っていない *The mike* isn't working. / レポーターたちはいっせいに彼にマイクを向けた The reporters pointed *their microphones* toward him.

マイクロ micro- ‖マイクロコンピュータ a microcomputer / マイクロチップ a microchip / マイクロバス a minibus, a microbus / マイクロフィッシュ microfiche (❖マイクロフィルムをシート状にした物) / マイクロフィルム microfilm

マイクロホン ➡マイク

まいげつ 毎月 ➡まいつき

まいご 迷子 lost child ⦿ ──迷子になる get* lost ‖その男の子は遊園地で迷子になった The boy *got lost* in the amusement park.
◆迷子の猫 a *stray* cat.

まいこむ 舞い込む 1 羽のカナリアが私たちの家に舞い込んできた(→迷い込んできた) A canary *strayed* [*wandered*] *into* our house. / ある古い友人からの手紙が舞い込んだ(→手紙を受け取った) One day I *got* [*received*] a letter from an old friend of mine.

マイコン ⚠ microcomputer ⦿, 《口語的》micro ⦿ (複 ~s) (❖「マイコン」は和製略語)

まいじ 毎時 (1時間につき) an [per] hour ‖電車は毎時30分に来ます The train comes *every hour* on the half (hour). / 台風は毎時40キロで北東に向かって進んでいる

The typhoon is heading northeast at (a speed of) 40 kilometers *an* [*per*] *hour*. (❖ 40 k.p.h.と略して書くこともある)

まいしゅう 毎週 (1週間ごとに) every week, weekly; (1週につき) a [per] week ——毎週の weekly ‖この雑誌は毎週発行されている This magazine is issued *every week.* / 毎週の会合を月曜の午後に決めた We have chosen Monday afternoons for our *weekly* meetings.

◆彼女は毎週水曜日にピアノのレッスンを受けている She has a piano lesson「*every* Wednesday [on Wednesdays].

まいしん 邁進 ——まい進する (大いに努力する) make* great efforts; (精を出す) push forward ‖仕事にまい進する *push forward with one's* work

まいすう 枚数 the number of ...

<語法> 何かの「枚数」を数える場合, それが可算名詞 (ticket「切符」など) なら名詞の前に数詞を付けて, three tickets「切符3枚」のようにいう. ただし glass「ガラス」などの不可算名詞では, two sheets of glass「ガラス2枚」のように, その形状を表す名詞を使って「-枚」を表す. ⇒まい(-枚)

はがきの枚数を数える count *the number of* postcards

◆この1週間で売れた切符の枚数(→切符が何枚売れたか)を教えてください Please tell me *how many tickets* were sold this week.

まいそう 埋葬 burial [bériəl] ⓊⒸ ——埋葬する bury [béri] ‖彼の遺体は共同墓地に埋葬された His body *was buried* in a cemetery. ‖埋葬式 a burial service

まいぞう 埋蔵 ——埋蔵する bury [béri] ... underground ‖このあたりには貴重な宝が埋蔵されているといわれている It is said that a valuable treasure *is buried underground* somewhere around here.

◆石油の埋蔵量 oil *reserves*

まいもんじ 真一文字 ‖彼は口を真一文字に結んでいた His lips were closed *in a thin, tight line.*

まいつき 毎月 (1か月ごとに) every [each] month, monthly; (1か月につき) a [per] month ——毎月の monthly ‖私たちは毎月20日に給料をもらう We receive our salary on the 20th of *every month.* / この雑誌は毎月発行される This magazine is published *monthly.* / その会議は毎月1度開かれる The meeting is held once *a month.*

まいど 毎度 every [each] time ‖毎度同じ失敗を繰り返すんじゃない Don't keep making the same mistake *every time.*

◆彼が会議中に居眠りをするのは毎度のことだ(→いつも居眠りをする) He *always* dozes off during meetings. / (お店で)毎度ありがとうございます Thank you for coming again. / 毎度(→しばしば)お手数をおかけしてすみません I'm sorry to trouble you *so often.*

まいとし 毎年 (1年ごとに) every [each] year, annually, yearly; (1年につき) a [per] year ——毎年の annual, yearly ‖毎年行われる行事 an *annual* [a *yearly*] event ‖その国の人口は毎年0.5パーセントの割合で増加している The population of that country is increasing by 0.5 percent *every year.* / このコンテストは毎年1回開かれる The contest is held once *a year.*

◆毎年夏になると, この島には日本からたくさんの観光客がやってくる *Every* summer a large number of tourists from Japan visit this island. / 毎年毎年私たちは山に木を植え続けた We planted trees on the mountain *year after year.* / 毎年今ごろは沖縄で休暇を過ごす I spend my holidays in Okinawa *about this time of (the) year.*

マイナー ——マイナーな minor ‖彼はマイナーなサッカー選手だ He is a *minor* soccer player.

‖マイナー指向 nonconformist tastes / マイナーチェンジ a minor change / マイナーリーグ a minor league; (集合的)the minor leagues, the minors

マイナス

❶【数学で】minus Ⓒ ——マイナスの minus; (負の) negative
2 マイナス10はマイナス8 Two *minus* ten equals [is] *minus* [*negative*] eight.
きのうの最低気温はマイナス5度だった Yesterday's minimum temperature was「*minus* five degrees [five degrees *below zero*].

◆家計は今月は2万円のマイナス(→赤字)だ Our household budget is 20,000 yen *in the red* this month. / そのイベントの収支はプラスマイナスゼロだった(→損得なしだった) We *just broke even* on the event. / (→何の利益もなかった)The event *was no gain* for us.

❷ [不利] disadvantage Ⓒ ——マイナスの minus, negative

融通のきかないところが彼にとってマイナスになった His inflexibility worked as *a disadvantage* against him.

科学技術にはマイナスの面とプラスの面がある Technology has both *negative* and positive aspects.

◆彼の不用意な発言はわが党全体にとってマイナスイメージとなる(→悪い影響を及ぼす)だろう His careless remark will *reflect badly on* our whole party.

‖マイナス記号 a minus (sign), a negative sign / マイナス極 the negative pole / マイナス成長 negative economic growth / マイナス要因 a negative factor

まいにち 毎日 every day; (来る日も来る日も) day after day; (日ごとに) day by day; (日々) from day to day; (1日につき) a [per] day ——毎日の everyday, daily

娘は毎日ピアノの練習をしている My daughter practices the piano *every day.*

毎日最低3回はメールをチェックします I check my e-mail at least three times *a day.*

彼女は毎日毎日家族のために必死に働いた She

worked hard for her family *day after day.*
運動は私にとって毎日の習慣になっている Exercise has become a *daily* habit for me.
彼女は毎日のように(→ほとんど毎日)友人と電話で話す She talks with her friends on the phone *almost every day.*

まいねん 毎年 ⇨ まいとし

まいばん 毎晩 every evening [night] ━ 毎晩の nightly ∥毎晩のニュース番組 a *nightly* news program / 私は毎晩ふろに入る I take a bath *every night.*

マイペース ⚠ ━マイペースで(自分に合ったスピードで) at *one's* own pace; (自分のやり方で) in *one's* own way ∥彼はゴールまでマイペースで走り続けた He kept running *at his own pace* to the goal. / 彼はマイペースで仕事をこなしている He is doing his work「*at his own pace* [*in his own way*].
◆マイペースでやるさ I'll go my own way.(❖ go *one's* own way で「自分の好きなようにやる」の意味)

マイホーム ⚠ *one's* own house ∥彼はこの春, 念願かなってマイホームを手に入れた His dream of getting *his own house* came true this spring.
∥マイホーム主義 a family-[home-]oriented way of life / マイホーム主義者 a family-[home-]oriented person

まいぼつ 埋没 ━埋没する be buried [bérid] ∥がけが崩れて3軒の家が土砂に埋没した Three houses *were buried* under the landslide.

まいもどる 舞い戻る その知らせを聞いて, 彼は大阪から舞い戻ってきた(→大急ぎで戻ってきた) Hearing the news, he *came back* from Osaka *in a great hurry.*

まいよ 毎夜 ⇨ まいばん

マイル mile ◎ (❖ 1 マイルは約1.6キロ) ∥時速10マイルで走る run at (a speed of) 10 *miles* an [per] hour / 駅は約半マイル離れた所にある The station is about half *a mile* away.

まいる 参る ❶【行く・来る】go* ⓐ; come* ⓐ

[語法] 相手の方へ話者が移動する場合, go ではなく come を用いることに注意. なお, 日本語の「参る」に相当する謙譲表現は英語には特にない.

それでは参りましょうか Shall we *go* now? / (そろってある場所へ「移動する」意味なので, この場合 come は使えない) / ただ今(そちらへ)参ります I'm *coming.* / I'll be right there.
◆課長はあと30分ほどで戻って参ります The chief *will be back* in half an hour. / お忙しいようなら, 会合には私が代わりに参ります(→出席する) I'll *attend* the meeting instead if you are busy.

❷【参詣(けい)する】(寺[神社]に) visit a temple [shrine]; (寺[神社]へ拝みに行く) go* to worship at a temple [shrine]

❸【負ける】(勝負事で) be defeated; (屈服する) surrender ⓐ; (あきらめる) give* up; (耐えられない) can't stand [bear] ∥どうだ, 参ったか So *do you give up?* / So *are you ready to surrender?* / 参った. 僕の負けだよ I *give up!* [I'm *defeated.*] You win! / この暑さには参った I *can't stand* [*bear*] this heat.
◆君が参ったと言う(→敗北を認める)まで放さないよ I won't let you go until you *admit defeat.*

🗨 「参ったか」「まだまだ」 "*Do you give up?*" "No. Let's continue."

❹【困る】be [feel*] embarrassed, (口語的) be in a fix; (疲れ果てる) be tired [worn] out, be exhausted; (途方にくれる) be at a loss ∥彼のいびきには全く参ったよ I *was* really *embarrassed* [(→悩まされた) *bothered*] by his snores. / あの事件以来, 彼女はすっかり参っている She *has been* really *tired* [*worn*] *out* since that incident.
◆携帯電話がバッテリー切れだ. 参ったなあ(→どうしたらいいだろう) The battery on my cellular phone is dead. *What shall I do?* / 参ったなあ(→何ということだ). バスに傘を忘れちゃったよ *Oh, no!* I left my umbrella on the bus.

❺【心が奪われる】彼女はあの男に参っている She *is crazy about* that man.

マイルド マイルドな(→刺激の少ない)せっけん *mild* soap / マイルドな(→まろやかな)味 a *mild* taste

まう 舞う (舞いを) dance ⓐ; (ひらひらと) flutter ⓐ; (回転しながら) whirl ⓐ; (物が) fly* ⓐ ∥外では雪が舞っている The snow *is fluttering* outside. / たこが空中でくるくる舞っていた A kite *was whirling about* in the sky. / レーシングカーはガードレールに激突した後, 宙を舞った(→空中に飛ばされた) The racing car *was flown into the air* after it crashed into the guardrail.

まうえ 真上 ━真上に right [just] over …, right [just] above …; (頭上に) overhead ⇨ うえ(上) ∥私たちの真上を1羽のカラスがかすめるようにして飛んでいった A crow flew past us *overhead.* / 太陽は今私たちの真上にある The sun is now *right* [*just*] *above* [*over*] us. / 真上から突然コンクリートの塊(かたまり)が落ちてきた Suddenly a block of concrete fell *from overhead.*

ましろ 真後ろ ━真後ろに right [just, directly] behind …, (口語的) right at the back of …, right in back of … ⇨ うしろ ∥私たちの車の真後ろをパトカーが走っていた A police car was running *just behind* our car. / いつの間にか男は私の真後ろに立っていた Before I knew it, the man was standing *right in back of* me.

マウス (動物・コンピュータの) mouse ◎ (複 mice) (❖ 複数形はコンピュータのマウスの意味では mouses も可) ∥ (口) mouth ◎ ∥マウスをパッドの上で動かす move *a mouse* on a pad / マウスのボタンをクリックする click the button of *a mouse* / マウスをドラッグする drag *a mouse*
∥マウスパッド a mouse pad / マウスピース a mouthpiece / マウスポインタ a mouse

pointer
マウンテンバイク mountain bike

マウンド〖野球〗(pitcher's) mound ‖先発の野茂は中5日のマウンドだった(→5日間おいてマウンドに立った) Nomo, the starting pitcher, *took the mound* after a five-day rest. ◆5回に先発ピッチャーをマウンドから引きずり下ろす(→ノックアウトする) *knock out the starting pitcher in the fifth inning* ‖ピッチャーマウンド the pitcher's mound

まえ　前

❶【場所】 ── 图 front《通例 the ～》── 形 front(❖名詞の前で用いる) ── 前 (正面に) in front of ..., before (↔behind); (前部に) in the front of ...; (前方に) ahead of ...; (人前で) in the presence of ... ── 副 ahead, in front; forward(❖動きを伴う場合のみ用いる)

in front of the restaurant

in the front of the car

《～の前に》
パトカーが近所の家の前に止まっていた A police car was parked *in front of* my neighbor's house.
広大な農場が私たちの前に広がっていた A vast farm lay *before* us.

《～の前で》
その少女は大勢の人々の前でピアノを弾いた The girl played the piano *before* a lot of people.
その自動車事故は私たちすぐ目の前で起きた The car accident took place right *in front of* our eyes.
生徒たちの前で私は恥をかかされた I was embarrassed *in the presence of* students.

《～の前を》
家の前をダンプカーがひっきりなしに通る Dump trucks pass *in front of* our house one after another.
私たちの前を高校生たちの一団が歩いていた A group of high school students were walking *ahead of* us.
前をよく見なさい Look *ahead*. /(→進む方向を)Look *where you're going*.

《～の前へ》
1歩前へ足を踏み出す take [make] a step *forward*(s)
トラックが突然前へ動き出した The truck suddenly started to move *forward*.

《～の前の方》
私たちは教室の前の方に座った We sat *in the front of* the classroom.

私はホームの前の方で電車を待っていた I was waiting for the train *at the front end of* the platform.
もう少し前の方へ行こうか Let's go up *front*.

〖その他〗
前の席に座ってください Please sit *in front*.
彼女は前から3列目に座った She sat in the third row *from the front*.
前の車との車間距離をもっととりなさい Leave more space between you and the car *ahead*.
駅前の喫茶店で会いましょう How about meeting at the coffee shop *in front of the station*?
◆それは前のページにあるよ That is on the *previous* page. /　白線より前に出ないでください(→白線の後ろにいてください) Please stay *behind* the white line.

❷【時間】 ── 前に before; (現在より…前に) ago ── 前の previous; (この前の) last(❖共に名詞の前で用いる)

《…前に》
食事の前にこの薬を飲みなさい Take this medicine *before* meals.
彼女は4時少し前に学校を出ました She left school a little *before* 4 o'clock.
私たちは列車が発車する20分前に駅に着いた We (had) arrived at the station 20 minutes *before* the train started.(❖出来事が起こった順番が明らかな場合は, 過去完了形の代わりに過去形を使うことが多い)
彼は3年前に東京へ引っ越した He moved to Tokyo three years *ago*.
バスはどのくらい前に出ましたか How long *ago* did the bus leave?
姉はいつも寝る前にストレッチをする My sister always does some stretching *before*「she goes to bed [going to bed].
少し前に彼女から電話があった *A little while ago*, I got a call from her.

《前の》
この前の日曜日, 車で伊豆まで出かけた I drove to Izu *last* Sunday.
彼女はこの前の選挙に落選した She lost the *last* election.
前の晩に彼女を駅前の本屋で見かけたと彼は言っていた He said that he had seen her at the book shop in front of the station「the night *before* [the *previous* night].
私の祖父母は戦争終結の前の年に結婚した My grandparents got married *the year before* the war ended.
60年前のきょう, 戦争が始まった The war broke out 60 *years ago today*.

《…前から》
医者が注射を打つ前から子供はもう泣きだしていた The child had already begun crying *before* the doctor gave him an injection. (❖「…する前にすでに」という意味は過去完了で表す)
◆その女の子は5日前から(→5日間) 行方不明になっている The girl has been missing *for* five days. /　あなたとはもう何年も前から(→何

年間も)知り合いのような気がする It seems as if I have known you *for years*.

🅔「今何時ですか」「5時15分前です」 "What time is it?" "It's (a) quarter *to* [《米》*of*] five."

❸【以前】 ——前に before; (かつて) once; (もともとは) formerly ——前の former (※名詞の前で用いる); (古い) old

その会社の前の社長 the 「*former* president [*ex*-president] of the company

前のコンピュータはどうしたのですか What did you do with your *old* [*former*] computer?

彼と前のようにまた仲よくできればいいのだが I wish I could be friends with him *as before*.

その映画は前に見たことがある I have seen that movie *before*.

前に言ったとおり、これはとても難しい仕事だ This is a very difficult task, as I told you *before*.

スリランカは前はセイロンと呼ばれていた Sri Lanka was *formerly* called Ceylon.

◆クリントンの前の大統領 the President *prior to* Clinton / 彼女は前(→この前会ったとき)よりも元気そうだった She looked better than *last time*. / 彼とはずっと前からの(→長いこと)知り合いです I've known him *for a long time*. / 前はこの通りに沿ってずっと桜の並木があった There *used to be* cherry trees all along this street. (※used + to 不定詞で「以前は…した」の意味) / もっと前にあなたは英語の勉強を始めるべきだった You should have begun studying English *earlier*.

❹【年齢】(…より下で) under

その賞を受賞したとき、彼女はまだ二十歳(はたち)前だった She was *under* 20 when she was awarded the prize.

❺【…人前】(…人分の) for

私は毎日5人前の食事の用意をする I prepare dinner *for* five every day.

◆私たちはチャーハンを3人前注文した We ordered three *plates* of fried rice.

まえあし 前足・前脚 (動物の) forefoot Ⓒ (複 forefeet); (足首から上の部分) foreleg Ⓒ; (一般に動物の足) paw Ⓒ

まえうしろ 前後ろ ⇨ うしろまえ

まえうり 前売り (切符などの) advance sale Ⓤ ——前売りする sell* … in advance ‖前売券 an advance ticket

まえおき 前置き (導入部) introduction Ⓒ, introductory remarks; (準備のための) preliminary remarks ‖前置きはこれくらいにして、そろそろ本論に入りましょう So much for *the introduction*; now let's proceed to the main topic. / 彼はいつも話の前置きが長い His *introductory remarks* are always lengthy.

まえかがみ 前屈み 前かがみで歩く walk *with a stoop*

まえがき 前書き preface [préfəs] Ⓒ; (序文) foreword Ⓒ

まえかけ 前掛け apron [éiprən] Ⓒ ⇨ エプロン

まえがみ 前髪 forelock Ⓒ ◆彼女は前髪を下ろしている She *has* [*wears*] bangs. (※bang は「切り下げた前髪」の意味)

まえがり 前借り 給料から2万円前借りした I *borrowed* 20,000 yen *in advance* on my salary. / 来月のおこづかいを前借りできる? May I *have an advance on* next month's allowance?

まえきん 前金 (前もって支払われる金) money paid in advance ◆賃貸契約の前金として10万円支払った I paid 100,000 yen *in advance* for the lease contract. / 前金は不要です(→前払いする必要はありません) You don't have to *pay* any *money in advance*.

マエストロ (巨匠) maestro [máistrou] (複 ～s, maestri)

まえだおし 前倒し front-loading Ⓤ ——前倒しする front-load ⑭ ‖公共事業の予算を前倒しする *front-load* the budget for public works

まえのめり 前のめり 危うく前のめりに倒れるところだった I almost *fell forward*.

まえば 前歯 front tooth ‖前歯にすき間がある have a gap between *one's front teeth* / 転んだ拍子に前歯が1本折れてしまった I lost one of *my front teeth* when I fell down.

まえばらい 前払い advance payment Ⓤ Ⓒ ——前払いする pay* … in advance ‖税金[家賃]を前払いする pay the tax [rent] *in advance*

まえひょうばん 前評判 この映画は前評判がいい This movie has good *advance reviews*.

まえぶれ 前触れ (予告) notice Ⓤ Ⓒ; (前兆) sign Ⓒ; (警告) warning Ⓒ Ⓤ ‖あらしの前触れ *a sign* [*warning*] of a storm / 何の前触れもなく賃金がカットされた The wages were cut without any (*prior*) *notice*.

まえまえから 前々から 前々から(→長いこと) オランダを訪ねてみたいと思っていた I have *long* wanted to visit the Netherlands. / I have wanted to visit the Netherlands *for a long time*. / たばこをやめるように君には前々から(→いつも)注意していたはずだ I think I've *always* advised you to give up smoking.

まえむき 前向き ——前向きの (積極的な) positive; (建設的な) constructive ‖前向きの姿勢で問題に取り組むべきだ We should take a *positive* approach toward problems. ◆前向きに検討します I'll consider it *positively*.

まえもって 前もって (あらかじめ) beforehand, in advance ‖30分ばかり遅れることを彼には前もって電話で連絡しておいた I called him *beforehand* [*in advance, ahead of time*] and told him that I would be late for about thirty minutes.

◆前もって決めておいた(→約束した)時間に3人はそのバーで落ち合った The three people met at the bar at the *appointed* time.

まがいもの 紛い物 (模造品) imitation Ⓒ; (いんちきな品物) fake Ⓒ; (偽物) counterfeit Ⓒ ‖まがい物のダイヤモンドをつかまされた I was deceived by *an imitation* [*a fake*] diamond.

まがお 真顔 私の質問に彼は真顔で答えた He answered my question *with a serious expression*. / 彼は一瞬真顔になってその話は事実だと言った He *became serious* for a moment and said that the story was true.

マガジン (雑誌) magazine ⓒ; (フィルム巻き取り用の) magazine
‖マガジンラック a magazine rack

まかす 負かす (打ち負かす) beat* ⓗ; (敗北させる) defeat ⓗ; (議論などで相手を)《口語的》get* the better of ... /チェスではだれも彼を負かすことができない No one can *beat* him at chess. / 私たちのチームは僅差で相手のチームを負かした Our team narrowly *defeated* our opponent. / きょうのグループディスカッションで私は彼女を負かした I *got the better of* [*beat*] her in today's group discussion.

まかせる 任せる
❶ 【責任などをゆだねる】 leave* ... to ~; (信頼してゆだねる) trust [entrust] ... with ~
パソコンのトラブルなら彼に任せなさい *Leave* the troubleshooting of your PC *to* him. / You can *trust* [*entrust*] him *with* the troubleshooting of your PC.
まあ、僕を信用して任せておけよ Just trust me and *leave* it *to* me.
私たちはすべて彼の判断に任せることに決めた We decided to *leave* everything *to* his judgment.
(後は)ご想像にお任せします I *leave it to your imagination*.
こうなったらすべてを運に任せるしかない Now all we can do is to *leave* everything *to chance*.
彼にはこの仕事を任せられない We *can't trust* [*entrust*] him *with* this job. / He *can't be trusted with* this job.
◆この仕事を彼に任せては(→やらせてみては)どうだろう How about *letting* him *do* this job? / 皿洗いは弟に任されている My brother *is in charge of* doing the dishes. / 私はレジを任されている I'm *responsible for* being the cashier.

❷ 【放任する】
感情に身をまかせる *give oneself up to* one's emotions
このことは自然の成り行きにまかせるしかないな We can do nothing but *let* this matter take its own course.
彼は庭を荒れるにまかせた He *let* his garden grow wild.
慣用表現 彼女は金にまかせて(→費用のことは気にせずに)高価な宝石を次々と買い求めた She bought one expensive jewel after another *regardless of the cost*. / 彼は力にまかせて(→全力を出して)その男を殴りつけた He hit the man *with all his strength*.

まがった 曲がった ❶ 【まっすぐでない】 (腰・木の枝などが) bent; (湾曲した) curved; (ゆがんだ) crooked [krúkid]; (道路の) a *curved* [*crooked*] road / 腰の曲がった老婆とすれ違った I passed an old lady *with a bent back*.

❷ 【正しくない】(心がひねくれた) crooked [krúkid]; (不誠実な) dishonest; (不正な) unfair /心の曲がった人 a *dishonest* [*crooked*] person / 彼は曲がったことをするのが嫌いだ He hates to do things that are *unfair*.

まかない 賄い (食事) board ⓤ /賄い付きの下宿 *a rooming house with board*; *a boardinghouse*

まかなう 賄う (寮や下宿で食事を出す) board ⓗ; (家計などをやりくりする) cover ⓗ /彼は30万円で毎月の家計をまかなっている He 「*covers* the household expenses [*manages* the household, *runs* the house] on 300,000 yen a month.

まがり¹ 曲がり (曲がった部分) bend ⓒ, turn ⓒ; (湾曲した部分) curve ⓒ ◆針金の曲がりを直す(→まっすぐにする) *straighten* a wire

まがり² 間借り ——間借りする rent a room /彼はおじの家に間借りしている He *rents a room* from his uncle. / He *lives in a rented room* at his uncle's.
‖間借り人《米》a roomer,《英》a lodger

まがりかど 曲がり角 (街角) (street) corner ⓒ; (道路の) turn ⓒ, bend ⓒ; (転換点) turning point ⓒ /彼女はその通りの曲がり角で彼を見失ってしまった She lost sight of him at *a turn* of the street. / 車は急な曲がり角を曲がりきれずに、ガードレールに激突した The car crashed into the guardrail after it failed to turn *the sharp corner*. / 今、日本の福祉政策は曲がり角にきている Japanese welfare policy *has* now *reached a turning point*.

まがりくねる 曲がりくねる (川・道路などが) wind* [wáind] ⓗ /その道路は谷間を曲がりくねりながら走っている The road *winds* through the valley. ◆バスは曲がりくねった坂道を登っていった The bus went up the *winding* [*meandering*] slope.

まかりとおる 罷り通る (正当化される) be justified /君は本当にそんな理屈がまかり通ると思っているのか Do you really think that such an argument *can be justified*?
◆警察による不正さえまかり通る(→罰せられずにすむ)世の中だ Now we live in an age when even injustices committed by the police *go unpunished*.

まがりなりにも 曲がりなりにも (何とか) somehow or other /彼は曲がりなりにもその論文を書き終えた *Somehow or other* he finished writing the paper. / He *managed to* finish writing the paper. (❖ manage to do は「何とか...する」の意味) / (→不完全ながらも) *Though it was imperfect*, he finished writing the paper. / 曲がりなりにも彼女は大学生である She is a college student, *anyway*.

まかりまちがう 罷り間違う まかり間違っても(→どんなことが起きても)彼にこのことを話してはいけない *Whatever happens*, don't tell him about this. / まかり間違えば(→最悪の場合は)その地区全体が火の海になるだろう *If* (*the*) *worst comes* to (*the*) *worst*, the whole area will become a sea of flames.

まがる 曲がる (力が加わって) bend* ⓗ, be

bent; (曲線を描いて) curve 亀; (向きが変わる) turn 亀; (川・道路などが) wind* [wáind] 亀; (ねじれる) twist 亀 ⇨ まがった
針金は簡単に曲がった The wire *bent* easily.
その道はこの先で右に曲がっている The road *curves* round to the right ahead.
次の角を左に曲がってください *Turn* left at the next corner.
彼は年で腰が曲がっている He *is bent* with (old) age.
◆背中が曲がっているよ．まっすぐ座りなさい You're *slouching*. Sit up straight. / 壁の絵が曲がっている The picture on the wall *is tilted*. / あいつは根性が曲がっている He *has a twisted mind*. / 彼は心が曲がっている He *is crooked at heart*. / 警察署は角を曲がった所にある The police station *is just around the corner*. / ネクタイが曲がっていますよ Your tie *is crooked*.

マカロニ macaroni [mækəróuni] Ⓤ

まき¹ 薪 (fire)wood Ⓤ /初めてまき割りをした I *chopped wood* for the first time.

まき² 巻 (本の) volume Ⓒ ⇨ -かん (-巻)

まきあげる 巻き上げる (カーテンなどを) roll ... up; (ほこりなどを) raise 亀, whirl ... up; (奪う) rob *a person* (of ...); (だまし取る) cheat *a person* (of ...), swindle *a person* (out of ...) /ダンプカーがほこりを巻き上げながら通っていった The dump truck passed, *raising* a cloud of dust. / 男は彼女をだまして金を巻き上げようとした The man tried to *cheat her* (*out*) *of* her money.

まきおこす 巻き起こす (発生させる) cause 亀, create 亀; (生み出す) produce 亀 ⇨ ひきおこす /その映画は若者の間に一大センセーションを巻き起こした The movie *caused* [*created*] a great sensation among young people.

まきかえし 巻き返し comeback Ⓒ /巻き返し作戦[政策] a *comeback* operation [policy] / その歌手は1年のブランクの後，新曲で巻き返しをはかっている The singer is trying to *make a comeback* with a new song after staying away from show business for a year. ◆野党は勢力の巻き返しをはかっている(→勢力を回復しようとしている) The opposition parties *are trying to regain their strength*. / 敵は兵力を増強して巻き返しに転じた(→勢力を回復した) The enemy *regained their strength* after strengthening their forces.

まきかえす 巻き返す (勢力を回復する) regain *one's* strength

まきげ 巻き毛 curl Ⓒ; (長めの) ringlet Ⓒ ⇨ カール /美しい金色の巻き毛の少女 a girl with beautiful golden *curls*

まきこむ 巻き込む 陰謀に巻き込まれる *be drawn into* a plot / 君たちのけんかに彼女を巻き込むな *Don't involve her in* your quarrel. / その船はあらしに巻き込まれた The ship *was caught in* a storm. / その少女が何らかの事件に巻き込まれた可能性がある It is possible that the girl *got involved in* some incident. / 彼は指を機械に巻き込まれた He *got* his finger *caught in* a machine.

まきじた 巻き舌 巻き舌で話す speak *with a trill*; roll [trill] *one's* r's❖舌を震わせて r の音を発音するこという

まきじゃく 巻き尺 tape measure Ⓒ

まきぞえ 巻き添え けんかの巻き添えを食う *get involved* [*mixed up*] *in* a quarrel / 彼は交通事故の巻き添えになった He *got involved in* a traffic accident.

まきた 真北 ─真北に due north ⇨ きた，ま-

まきちらす 撒き散らす (ばらまく) scatter 亀 /金をまき散らす *scatter one's money around* / 風が庭に木の葉をまき散らした The wind *scattered* 「*leaves on* the garden [the garden *with* leaves].
◆そのカラオケボックスは深夜まで騒音をまき散らしている(→騒音を発生させている) The karaoke place *makes* a lot of noise until late at night.

まきつく 巻き付く wind* [wáind] 亀; (ツルなどが) twine 亀; (蛇などが) coil 亀 /ツルが松の木に巻きついた Vines *wound* [*twined*] around a pine tree. / その蛇は木に巻きついた The snake *coiled* around the tree.

まきつける 巻き付ける wind* [wáind] 亀; (しっかりと) tie 亀; (ぐるぐると) coil 亀 /マストにロープを巻きつける *wind* a rope around [to] a mast

まきとる 巻き取る wind* [wáind] 亀 /糸を糸巻きに巻き取る *wind* thread on a spool

まきば 牧場 (放牧地) pasture Ⓒ; (牧草地) meadow Ⓒ

まきもどし 巻き戻し rewinding Ⓤ

まきもどす 巻き戻す rewind* [ri:wáind] 亀 /ビデオテープを巻き戻す *rewind* a videotape

まきもの 巻物 scroll Ⓒ /巻物を広げる unroll *a scroll*

まぎらす 紛らす 推理小説を読んで気を紛らした I *diverted myself* by reading a detective novel. / 彼は悲しみを酒で紛らした He *drowned his sorrows*.

まぎらわしい 紛らわしい (誤解を招く) misleading; (混乱する) confusing; (はっきりしない) vague /私のクラスには田中という名前の人が3人もいるのでまぎらわしい There are three Tanakas in my class, so it *is confusing*. / そういうまぎらわしい言い方はよせ Don't speak in such *vague* terms.

まぎれこむ 紛れ込む 男は人込みの中に紛れ込んだ The man *disappeared into* the crowd. / 君の捜していた書類が私のファイルに紛れ込んでいた The papers you've been looking for *were mixed with* papers in my file.

-まぎれに -紛れに 彼女は腹立ちまぎれに(→一時的に腹を立てて)，その写真をびりびりに破った She tore the photo into pieces *in a fit of anger* [*passion*]. / 苦しまぎれに(→窮地に追い込まれて)彼は息子にうそを言った *Driven into a corner*, he lied to his son.

まぎれもない 紛れもない (間違えようのない) unmistakable; (明らかな) obvious ──まぎれもなく (疑いもなく) undoubtedly /それは

まぎれる

まぎれもない事実だ It is an *unmistakable* [*obvious*] fact. / この筆跡はまぎれもなく彼のものだ This is *undoubtedly* his handwriting.

まぎれる 紛れる (気が) be diverted; (時間が) be beguiled; (見えなくなる) disappear into...; (混ざり合う) slip into... / ‖ゲームをしているうちに気が紛れた I *was diverted by playing a game*. / その少年は人込みに紛れて見えなくなってしまった The boy *slipped into the crowd* and the next moment was nowhere to be seen. / The boy *disappeared into the crowd*.

◆忙しさに紛れて連絡が遅くなりました I've been *so busy that* I couldn't contact you sooner.

まぎわ 間際 ——間際に just before ... —— 間際で be about to *do*, be on the point of *doing* / ‖その女性が店に入ってきたのは閉店間際だった It was *just before* closing time when the lady came into the shop. / 出かける間際になって私は財布がないことに気がついた I was「*about to leave*[*on the point of leaving*]」when I found that my wallet was missing.

まく¹ 巻く (ねじなどを) wind* [wáind] ⊕; (マフラーなどを) wrap ⊕; (包帯などを) bandage ⊕; (ぐるぐると) coil ⊕; (丸く) roll ⊕ / ‖時計のねじを巻く *wind* a clock / *wind* yarn / じゅうたんを巻く *roll up* a rug / 看護婦は足首に包帯を巻いてくれた The nurse「*bandaged* my ankle [*wrapped* my ankle *with a bandage*]」.

◆スカーフを首に巻く *wear* a scarf around *one's* neck / 彼はバンダナを首に巻いていた He *had* a bandanna around his neck. / 彼は煙に巻かれて死んだ He *was suffocated* [*choked to death*] *by smoke*. / 私は彼女の英語のうまさに舌を巻いた I *was really impressed by how well she speaks English*.

まく² 幕 (カーテン) curtain ©; (劇の) act © / ‖6 幕ものの劇 a six-*act* play; a play in six *acts* / 『オセロ』第1幕第2場 *Othello*, *Act* I, Scene ii / 幕がゆっくりと上がった The curtain rose [was raised] slowly. / 幕が下りた The curtain fell [came down].

慣用表現 ここは君の出る幕ではない (→君のやるべきことではない) *It's none of your business*. / (→自分のやるべきことだけしていろ) *Mind your own business*. (❖ business は「本分, 務め」の意味) / プロ野球ペナントレースの幕が切って落とされた The professional baseball pennant race *started* [*began*]. / マルチメディアの時代が幕をあけた The age of multimedia *has dawned*. / 50年にわたる王政が幕を閉じた The 50-year monarchy *came to an end*.

まく³ 蒔く (種などを) plant ⊕, sow* ⊕ (❖ sow は一度に大量の種をまく場合に用いることが多い) / ‖庭にコスモスの種をまく *plant cosmos seeds in the garden* / 農夫は畑にレタスの種をまいた The farmer *planted* [*sowed*] lettuce seeds in the field.

慣用表現 いまさら何言ってんだ. 自分でまいた種だろう What are you talking about? *You asked for it*.

ことわざ まかぬ種は生えぬ ⇒たね / 自分でまいた種は刈らねばならない As you sow, so shall you reap.

まく⁴ 撒く

❶【まき散らす】(ばらまく) scatter ⊕; (肥料などを) spread* ⊕; (水・砂などを振りかける) sprinkle ⊕; (ちらしなどを配る) hand out / ‖畑に肥料をまく *spread* fertilizer *over a field* / 校庭に水をまく *sprinkle* water *on the playground* / 凍った道路に砂をまく *sprinkle* sand *on* an icy road; *sprinkle* an icy road *with* sand / 広告ビラをまく *hand out* advertising fliers / その老人はハトにえさをまいた The old man *scattered* some food for the pigeons.

❷【はぐらかす】
彼はまんまと尾行をまいた He *shook off his shadow* [*tail*] *successfully*. / 《口語的》He *gave his shadow* [*tail*] *the slip*.

まく⁵ 膜 (薄い皮膜) a film; (液状の表面にできる) skin ©; (粘膜) membrane © ⊕ / ‖油の薄い膜 a thin *film* of oil / ホットミルクの表面に膜が張った A *film* formed on the surface of the hot milk.

まくあい 幕間 《米》intermission ©, 《英》interval [íntərvəl] © / ‖幕間にトイレに行く go to the rest room *during the intermission*

まくあけ 幕開け (芝居の) the opening; (時代などの始まり) the beginning / ‖芝居の幕あけ *the opening of* the play / 冷戦の終結は新時代の幕あけとなった The end of the Cold War *marked the beginning* of a new era.

まくうち 幕内 【相撲】(階級) the *makuuchi*, the senior grade division; (力士) a sumo wrestler of the senior grade division

まくぎれ 幕切れ (結末) end © / ‖その熱い試合はあっけない幕切れとなった The exciting game *came to a sudden end*.

まくした 幕下 【相撲】(階級) the *makushita*, the junior grade division; (力士) a sumo wrestler of the junior grade division

まくしたてる まくし立てる jabber ⊕, gabble ⊕, talk on and on (❖いずれも「わけの分からないことを早口でしゃべる」の意味) / ‖彼女は電話越しに英語でまくしたてていた She *was jabbering* [*gabbling*] *away* in English over the phone.

まぐち 間口 (建物の正面) frontage ©; (幅) width ©© / ‖間口が10メートルの建物 a building with *a frontage* [*width*] of 10 meters

マクドナルド McDonald's [məkdánldz] (❖米国生まれのハンバーガーチェーン)

マグニチュード (地震の規模を示す単位) magnitude © (❖個々の地震についていう場合は ©) / ‖マグニチュード7.2の地震 an earthquake with *a magnitude* of 7.2 / チリの地震はマグニチュード6.8を記録した The earthquake in Chile registered *a magnitude* of 6.8 on the Richter scale. (❖ the Richter [ríktər] scale(リヒタースケール)は地震の強さを表す等級で, ふつう a magnitude of ... の後にくる)

マグネシウム 〘化学〙 magnesium [mægníːziəm] Ⓤ (❖元素記号 Mg)

マグネット (磁石) magnet Ⓒ

まくのうち 幕の内 ‖幕の内弁当 a box lunch containing rice and various kinds of food

まくひき 幕引き 紛争の幕引きをする(→終結させる) put an end to a disturbance

マグマ 〘地質〙 magma Ⓤ

まくら 枕 pillow Ⓒ / 彼は頭をまくらに当てた He laid his head on *the pillow*. ◆ 彼は本をまくらにして(→本の上に頭をのせて)眠っていた He was sleeping with his head on the book. ‖まくらカバー a pillowcase(❖×pillow cover とはいわない) / まくら木 《米》a tie,《英》a sleeper

慣用表現 これでまくらを高くして眠る(→心配なく眠る)ことができる Now I can *sleep without worries*.

まくらもと 枕元 まくら元に(→ベッドのわきに)呼ぶ call *a person to one's bedside* / 懐中電灯をまくら元に置いて寝た I slept with a flashlight *at* [*by*] *my bedside*. / 目をさますと姉が私のまくら元に(→ベッドの頭の所に)立っていた I woke up to find my sister standing *at the head of my bed*.

まくる 捲る (まくり上げる) roll up, tuck up; (折り返して) turn up /ズボンのすそをまくる *turn up* the bottom of *one's trousers* / 彼はワイシャツのそでをまくった He *rolled* [*tucked*] *up* his shirt sleeves.

-まくる しゃべりまくる talk and talk; *talk on and on* / 彼女はカラオケで歌いまくった She *sang and sang* karaoke. / ゆうべはポーカーでつきまくった I *was on a roll* at the poker game last night. (❖ be on a roll は「(ギャンブルで)勝ちが続いている」という意味の口語的表現)

まぐれ 紛れ (思いがけない幸運) fluke Ⓒ (❖スポーツやテスト, くじなどに広く使うことができる); (まぐれ当たり) chance [lucky] hit Ⓒ / ただのまぐれだ I was just *a fluke*. / (→幸運だっただけだ) I was just *lucky*. ◆ まぐれで100点を取る get a score of 100 *by chance*

まくれる 捲れる (服 などが) get* rolled up / 突然前を歩いている女性のスカートが風でまくれた Suddenly, the skirt of the woman walking ahead of me *got rolled* [*blown*] *up* by the wind.

マクロ (接頭辞) macro-; 〘コンピュータ〙 macro Ⓒ (複 ~s) ‖マクロウイルス a macro virus (❖コンピュータウイルスの一種) / マクロ経済学 macroeconomics / マクロ言語 a macro language

まぐろ 鮪 tuna ⒸⓊ (複 ~, ~s) ‖マグロの刺身 slices of raw *tuna*

まけ 負け (敗北) defeat Ⓤ; (試合などの) loss Ⓒ / 彼女は自分の負けを認めようとしなかった She was unwilling to admit *the defeat*. / あのチームは最近負けが込んできた(→負ける数のほうが勝つ数より多い) That team *has had more losses than wins* recently.
◆ 私の負けだ(→あなたの勝ちだ) You win! (❖現在形を使うことに注意) / 先に声を出したほうが負けだよ If you make a sound first, you'll be *the loser*.

‖負け戦(いくさ)(負けた戦い) a lost battle; (敗色の濃い戦い) a losing battle / 負け犬(敗北者) a loser / 負け試合(負けた試合) a lost game; (負けそうな試合) a losing game / 負け投手 a losing pitcher

まけおしみ 負け惜しみ そんなの彼の負け惜しみだよ I think he's just crying *sour grapes*. (❖sour grapes は「すっぱいブドウ」が原義.『イソップ物語』から) / 彼はいつも負け惜しみばかり言っている He *is* always *a bad loser*. (❖ bad loser は「負け惜しみを言う人」, また good loser は「負け惜しみを言わずに潔く負けを認める人」の意味)

まけこす 負け越す そのチームは他球団すべてに負け越した(→負けた数のほうが勝った数より多くなった) The team *suffered more losses than wins* [*had a losing record*] against all of the other teams.

まけずおとらず 負けず劣らず 彼は父親に負けず劣らず意志が強い He is *no less* strong-willed *than* his father. / 兄弟は2人とも負けず劣らず(→等しく)スポーツが得意だ Both of the brothers are *equally* good athletes.

まけずぎらい 負けず嫌い ――負けず嫌いな (屈服しない) unyielding; (競争心の強い) competitive

まけっぷり 負けっぷり 負けっぷりのよい[悪い]人 a good [bad] *loser*

まける 負ける

❶ 【敗北する】 (負かされる) be beaten, be defeated; (勝利を逃す) lose* 🔊 🔊 (↔win)

試合に負ける *lose* a game / 戦い[議論]に負ける *lose* a battle [an argument] / 賭(か)け[けんか]に負ける *lose* a bet [fight] / トランプで負ける *lose* at cards

ジャイアンツはスワローズに3対2で負けた The Giants 「*were beaten* by [*lost the game to*] the Swallows by (a score of) 3 to 2.

我々のチームは5点差で負けた Our team *lost the game* [*was beaten*] by five points. (❖野球でなら five runs, サッカーでなら five goals となる)

彼は前回の選挙で対立候補に負けた He *was beaten* [*defeated*] by the other candidate in the last election.

◆ タイガースはベイスターズに2点負けている(→後れをとっている) The Tigers *are* two runs *behind* the BayStars. / 彼の作る料理はプロのシェフの作るものに負けないくらいおいしい The food he cooks is *as* delicious *as* food cooked by a professional chef. / 気持だけは若い者には負けない I'm *as young* in spirit *as those young people*. / ポーカーでは彼女はだれにも負けない *Nobody can beat* her in poker.

❷ 【降参する】 yield 🔊, give* in, give way to ...; (圧倒される) be overcome

悲しみに負ける *be overcome with* grief

彼は誘惑に負けてそのオートバイを買ってしまった He *gave in [yielded] to* temptation and bought the motorbike.

君の熱意には負けたよ．このプロジェクトは君に任せよう I *give in to* your eagerness. I'll put you in charge of this project.

◆病気なんかに負けてはだめだ(→病気に心を圧倒させるな) Don't let your illness *dominate* your mind.

❸【値引きする】(割引する) *give* a discount, discount*

現金でお買い上げの品物はすべて20パーセントまけておきます We'll *give you a* 20 percent *discount* on all cash purchases.

◆2,000円[2,000円]にまける *cut the price by [to]* 2,000 *yen* / あの八百屋はよくまけてくれる That vegetable store often *has good bargains*. (➡good bargain は「安い買い物」の意味)

🎤「このお刺身，少しまけてくれない？」「いいよ，2 パック700円でどう」"Could you *give me a discount* on this *sashimi*?" "OK. I'll make it 700 yen for two packs."

ことわざ 負けるが勝ち *Find victory in defeat.*

まげる 曲げる
❶【物を】(力を加えて) *bend**; (曲線を描くように) *curve* ⊕; (ねじる) *twist*

腕[足，ひざ]を曲げる *bend one's* arms [legs, knees]

彼はその針金をペンチで曲げた He *bent* the wire with pliers.

◆腰を曲げるととても痛い It hurts very much when I *bend down*.

❷【ゆがめる】(規則などを) *deviate [depart] from …*; (言葉などを曲解する) *distort* ⊕, *twist* ⊕

事実を曲げる *twist the truth*

私たちはやむなく規則を曲げることになった We could not help but *deviate [depart] from* the rules.

どうして君はいつも私の言葉を曲げてほかの人に伝えるのか Why do you always *distort* my words when you quote me to other people?

◆彼は最後まで信念を曲げなかった(→守り通した) He *stuck to* his convictions.

まけんき 負けん気 彼は子供のころから負けん気が強かった He *was very unyielding [competitive]* ever since he was a child.

まご 孫 *grandchild* ⓒ (複 grandchildren); (孫息子) *grandson* ⓒ; (孫娘) *granddaughter* ⓒ ∥お孫さんはいらっしゃいますか Do you have any *grandchildren*?

∥孫の手 a *back scratcher* / 初孫 *one's first grandchild*

まごころ 真心 (誠実さ) *sincerity* Ⓤ, *cordiality* Ⓤ ∥彼は真心をこめて中国からの客をもてなした He treated the guest from China *with warm cordiality [all their heart]*.

◆息子から真心のこもった贈り物が届いた I received a *warmhearted* present from my son.

まごつく (困惑する) *be [get*] confused, be [feel*] bewildered*; (途方にくれる) *be at a loss* ∥その種の仕事に慣れていなかったので新しい仕事にすっかりまごついてしまった I completely *got confused* by the new job because I wasn't used to that kind of work. / 駅で見知らぬ人から話しかけられてまごついた I *was [felt] bewildered* when a stranger spoke to me at the station. / 試験当日になってまごつかないように，私は大学までの道順をあらかじめ確認しておいた I checked the route to the university beforehand so that I *would not get confused* on the examination day.

まこと 誠 (真実) *truth* Ⓤ Ⓒ ──まことの *true* ∥それがうそかまことか私には判断できない I can't judge whether it is *true* or false.

まことしやか ──まことしやかな (もっともらしい) *plausible*; (見た目とうらはらの) *specious* ∥まことしやかなうそをつく *tell a plausible lie* / まことしやかな口実を並べて，彼はその責任から逃れた He avoided responsibility by making *plausible* excuses.

まことに 誠に (非常に) *very, very much*; (本当に) *truly, really*; (心から) *sincerely* ∥長いことお待たせしまして，まことに申しわけありません I'm *very [sincerely]* sorry to have kept you waiting so long. / 本日はご来店いただき，まことにありがとうございます Thank you *very much* for visiting our store today. / 彼はまことに優秀な人材です He is *truly [really]* a capable person.

まごびき 孫引き 孫引きせず，元の本にあたりなさい Refer to the original book yourself instead of *using other people's quotes from it.*

まごまご ──まごまごする (途方にくれる) *be at a loss (what to do)*; (困惑する) *be bewildered [confused]* ∥彼は友人との待ち合わせ場所が分からなくてまごまごした He *was at a loss* because he couldn't find the place where he was supposed to meet his friend. / 彼女はまごまごしていてバスに乗り遅れた She *was so confused that* she missed the bus.

◆まごまごしていると(→注意していないと)彼に先を越されるぞ He'll *get ahead of you unless you're careful.* / まごまごしている時間はない There is no time *to lose*.

まさか
❶【相づち】

語法 「まさか」に相当する英語の相づちの表現には，以下のようなものがある．多くは語尾を下げて発音し，「とんでもない」あるいは「信じられない」という驚きや疑いの気持ちを表す．

🎤「あの二人，来年の春結婚するんですって」「え，まさか」 "I hear they're going to get married next spring." "*Not really*!" / (→冗談でしょう)*No [You're] kidding*!"

🎤「きょうの野球の試合は中止だって」「ええ，まさか」 "Today's baseball game has been called off." "*Oh, no*! / *No way*!"

● 「幹夫が青森の学校へ転校するってうわさだよ」「まさか」 "It is rumored that Mikio is going to transfer to a school in Aomori." *"You don't say!"* (❖You don't say!は「そんなことは言わないでしょうね」が元の意味)

● 「おれ, 司法試験に受かっちゃったよ」「まさか(→信じられない)」 "I passed the bar examination." *"I don't believe it!"*

● 「そのグループは解散するらしいよ」「まさか(→それは本当であるはずはない)」 "I hear the band is going to break up." *"No! That can't be true!"*

❷ 【驚き・疑い】(まさか…ではないでしょうね) Don't tell me ..., surely ... not

まさか本当に彼の言葉を信じていたんじゃないでしょうね *Don't tell me* you believed what he said.

まさか彼に電話するのを忘れたんじゃないだろうね You *surely haven't* forgotten to call him?

◆まさか彼が離婚するとは思わなかった(→夢にも思わなかった) I *never dreamed that* he would divorce his wife. / まさか彼女がそんなことを言うはずがない She *can't have* said such a thing. / まさか彼女がそんな下品な言葉を使うとはね(→彼女がそんな下品な言葉を使うなんて驚きだ) *Fancy* her using such bad language! / まさか彼女がこんな手紙を送ってよこすことはしないだろう She is *the last person to* send me such a letter. (❖the last person to *do* で「…する最後の人」,「最も…しそうにない人」の意味) / まさかと思うでしょうが(→信じられないかもしれませんが)彼は25歳です *Believe it or not*, he is 25 years old.

❸ 【緊急】
まさかのときは(→緊急の場合は)自宅に電話してください Please call me at home *in case of emergency*.

まさかのときに備えて(→最悪の場合に備えるために)食糧を買い込んでおいた I stocked up on [with] food *to prepare for the worst*.

慣用表現 まさかのときの友こそ真の友 *A friend in need is a friend indeed.*

マザコン ⚠ an abnormal attachment to *one's* mother(❖「マザコン」「マザーコンプレックス」は和製英語) / マザコンの少年 a *mother's* [*mommy's*] boy / 彼はマザコンだ(→何か決めるときは母親にいつも頼る) He *always depends on his mother to make decisions for him.*

まさしく 正しく (確かに) certainly, surely; (疑いもなく) undoubtedly, no doubt; (本当に) really; (ちょうど) just; (正確に) precisely, exactly ⇨まさに

マサチューセッツ Massachusetts(❖米国北東部の州;《略語》Mass., 《郵便》MA)

まさつ 摩擦 ❶ 【こすること】 friction Ⓤ / 2枚の紙の摩擦 the *friction* between two sheets of paper

❷ 【衝突・不和】 conflict Ⓤ Ⓒ, friction Ⓤ Ⓒ; (もめごと) trouble Ⓤ / 摩擦を生じる create [produce] *friction* / 日米間の貿易[経済]摩擦 trade [economic] *friction* between Japan and the United States
‖摩擦熱 frictional heat

まさに 正に ❶ 【ちょうど】 just; (正確に) precisely, exactly / それこそまさに私の言いたいとです That's *just* [*exactly, precisely*] what I mean. / それこそまさに私が強調したかった点です It is *just* [*exactly*] the point (that) I wanted to emphasize. / (→まさにその点を私は強調したかった) It is *the very* point (that) I wanted to emphasize. (❖名詞の前に置いて, 通例 the very, this [that] very, *one's* very の形で用いる) / ライオンは今まさにハンターに襲いかかろうとしていた The lion *was just about to* attack the hunter.

◆彼女は私が空港で見かけた, まさにその人でした(→彼女は私が空港で見かけた女性以外のだれでもなかった) She *was none other than* the woman I saw in the airport.

● 「では君はこの失敗の責任は彼女にあると思っているわけですね」「まさにそのとおりです」 "So you think she is responsible for this failure." *"Exactly./ Absolutely."*

❷ 【本当に】 really; (まことに) truly; (確かに) certainly, surely; (疑いもなく) undoubtedly, no doubt / ニューヨークはまさに人種のるつぼである New York is *really* a melting pot. / 彼はまさにアメリカの英雄です He's *truly* an American hero. / その写真に写っている女性はまさに私の妹だった The woman in the picture was *undoubtedly* my sister.

まざまざと (はっきりと) clearly; (鮮明に) vividly / その事故現場の記憶がまざまざとよみがえる I can recall the scene of the accident *vividly* [*clearly*]. / I have a *vivid* [*clear*] recollection of the scene of the accident.

まさゆめ 正夢 (予言的な夢) prophetic dream Ⓒ / きのう見た夢は正夢だった(→まさにきのう夢で見たとおりになった) Things happened *just as I dreamed* last night.

まさる 勝る (質・価値がよりよい) be better than …, be superior to …; (量や程度が) surpass ⓖ; (相手より上回る) exceed ⓖ

この辞書は使いやすさではかの辞書よりずっと勝っている This dictionary is *much better than* the others in its ease of use.

スタミナに関して韓国チームは日本チームより勝っている The Korean team *is superior to* the Japanese team in terms of stamina.

日本美術に対する造詣(ぞうけい)の深さという点で, あの学者に勝る者はいない *No other* scholar *surpasses* him in deep knowledge of Japanese art.

◆彼は聞きしに勝る(→私が聞いた話よりもずっと努力家だった) He *was more* hard-working *than I had heard*. / わが家に勝るものはない *There is no place like* home.

慣用表現 英語を勉強する熱意において加奈子は徹に勝るとも劣らない(→加奈子は徹と同じくらい熱意がある) Kanako is *as* anxious to study English *as* Toru. / (→加奈子は徹に劣らず熱意がある) Kanako is *no less* anxious to study English *than* Toru.

まざる 混ざる・交ざる mix (with …) ⇨まじ

まし る，まぜる ∥油と水は混ざらない Oil and water *don't* mix./ Oil *doesn't mix with* water.

まし (…より よい) be better than …; (むしろ) would rather, might (just) as well ——ましな better ∥このいすのほうがそれより少しはましだ This chair *is* a little *better than* that one./ 彼の言うことを聞くくらいなら死んだほうがましだ I *would rather* die *than* obey him./ I *might* (*just*) *as well* die *as* obey him./ 渋滞がひどくて歩いたほうがましなくらいだった The traffic was so heavy that we *might as well* have walked./ もっとましな言い訳は思いつかないの？ Can't you invent a *better* excuse?/ 遅くてもしないよりはまし *Better* late *than* never.

-まし -増し (増加) increase ◻ ◆彼の給料は昨年の1割増しだった His salary *has increased* by 10 percent over last year./ あのレストランは午後10時以降2割増しの料金になる The restaurant charges an *extra* 20 percent after 10 p.m.

まじ あいつまじで怒ってるぞ He is *really* angry.
⏺「来週パリに行くんだ」「まじ？」"I'm going to Paris next week." "*For real?*"

まじえる 交える 敵軍と砲火を交える *exchange* fire *with* the enemy / 彼女は冗談を交えながら話した (= 冗談で話に味つけをした) She *spiced* her conversation *with* jokes.

ましかく 真四角 (正方形) square ◻ ——真四角の square

ました 真下 ——真下に right [just] under …; (…よりも低い位置に) right [just] below … ⇨した(下) ∥私たちの乗った遊覧船はベイブリッジの真下を通過した Our pleasure boat passed *right under* the Bay Bridge. (❖この場合, 橋の「下方」をくぐることをいうので, below は使えない) / 今その鯨は今この船の真下を泳いでいる The whale is now swimming *just* [*right*] *below* our ship.

マジック (魔法・手品) magic ◻ ∥マジックインキ (マーカーなどの太いペン) a felt-tip marker (❖「マジックインキ」は日本の商標名) / マジックテープ (衣服を留めるのに用いる特殊テープ) (商標名) Velcro (❖「マジックテープ」は日本の商標名) / マジックナンバー 【野球】 the magic number / マジックペン (サインペンなどの細いペン) a felt-tip pen / マジックミラー a one-way mirror (❖「マジックミラー」は和製英語)

まして (否定文の後で) let alone, much less; (肯定文の後で) much [even, still] more; (言うまでもなく) not to mention, not to speak of …, to say nothing of … ∥テレビを買う金など私にはないし，まして車はなおさらだ I don't even have enough money to buy a TV, *much less* [*not to speak of*, *to say nothing of*] a car./ 彼女は現在でも十分魅力的だし，まして若いころはさぞ美しかったにちがいない She is very attractive even now, so she must have been *even more* beautiful when she was young.

まじない 呪い (呪文) spell ◻, charm ◻; (迷信的で意味不明の呪文)《口語的／軽蔑的》mumbo jumbo ◻; (魔力) spell ∥まじないを解く break *a spell* / 悪霊よけのまじないを唱える recite *a spell* against evil spirits / まじないをかける cast [put] *a spell* on *a person*

まじまじ 私の言葉が信じられないといった表情で, 彼女は私の顔をまじまじと見つめた She *stared* (*at*) me in the face as if she could not believe what I said.

まじめ 真面目 ——まじめな (本気の) serious; (真剣な) earnest; (正直な) honest [ánəst] ——まじめに seriously; earnestly, in earnest; honestly [ánəstli]

彼女はまじめな顔をして何かを考え込んでいた She was thinking over something with a *serious* look.

彼はまじめな男だ He is an *earnest* man.

まじめな話(→まじめに言って), お酒は全然飲めないんです *Seriously* (*speaking*), I can't drink at all.

その学生は私の質問にまじめに答えようとしなかった The student wouldn't answer my question *seriously*.

彼は私の冗談をいつもまじめに受け取る He always takes my jokes *seriously*.

◆君は数学をもっとまじめに(→一生懸命)勉強しないとだめだ You should study mathematics much *harder*.

⏺「ずっと私のことを愛していたなんて冗談でしょ」「いや, 僕はまじめだ」"You've been in love with me for a long time? You must be joking." "No. I'm *serious*."

まじめくさる 真面目くさる まじめくさった顔で冗談を言う make a joke *with a straight face*

まじゅつ 魔術 (魔法) magic ◻
∥魔術師 a magician / 黒魔術 black magic

マシュマロ marshmallow [máːrʃmèlou] ◻ ◻

まじょ 魔女 witch ◻
∥魔女狩り a witch hunt

ましょうじき 真正直 彼は私の話を真正直に (→言葉どおりに) 受け取ったらしい It seems that he took me *at my word*.

ましょうめん 真正面 ——真正面に (向かい側に) just [right] opposite (to) …; (真ん前に) just [right] in front of … ∥私の家は市役所の真正面にある My house is *just* [*right*] *opposite* (*to*) the city office./ 真正面の大きな建物は美術館だ The large building *just* [*right*] *in front of* us is a museum.

◆私たちは生命倫理の問題に真正面から取り組むべきだ We should tackle the problem of bioethics *head-on*.

まじりけ 混じり気・交じり気 混じり気のない (→純粋な) 国産のはちみつ *pure* honey made in Japan

まじる 混じる・交じる (紛れ込む) mingle (with …); (混じり合う) mix (with …)

群衆に交じる *mingle with* the crowd

雨に雪が混じり始めている Snow has become *mingled with* the rain.

◆彼は現地スタッフに交じって(→現地スタッフの中で)働いた He worked *among* the local

office staff. / 父の頭には白いものが交じっていた(→白髪が点々と生えていた) My father's head *was sprinkled* [*streaked*] *with gray*. / 彼女にはイタリア人の血が混じっている She *has* Italian *blood*.

まじわり 交わり (交際) association ⓤ

まじわる 交わる ❶【交差する】cross ⓗ ⓐ, 《公式的》intersect ⓗ ⓐ / 2直線は点Cで直角に交わっている The two lines *cross* [*intersect*] at right angles at A. / この道路はこの先で国道と交わっている This road *crosses* [*intersects*] (*with*) a national highway ahead.
❷【つきあう】悪い友達と交わる *keep* bad *company*

ます¹ 増す (数量が[を]) increase ⓐ ⓗ; (力・重さなどが[を]) gain ⓐ ⓗ; (加わる[加える]) add (to ...); (水面が上昇する) rise* ⓐ
英会話教室に行き始めてから彼女の英会話力は増した She *has increased* her English conversation ability since she started to go to the English conversation class.
列車は丘を下るにつれ速度を増した The train *gained* [*increased*] speed as it went down the hill.
インターネットはここ数年ますます重要性を増してきた The Internet *has gained* more and more importance over the past several years. / The Internet *has become more and more* important over the past several years.
百科事典は私たちが知識を増すのに役立つ Encyclopedias help us *add to* our knowledge.
あらしの後、川は3メートル水かさを増した The river *rose* three meters after the storm.
◆彼女は以前にも増して美人になった She is *more beautiful than before*. / 新しい地位に就いて彼の責任は増すだろう(→新しい地位がより大きな責任をもたらすだろう) The new position will give him *more* responsibility.

ます² 升 (計量器具) measure ⓒ / 升売りする sell by *the measure*
‖升席 a box seat

ます³ 鱒 〖魚〗 trout ⓒ (複 ~, ~s) (❖マスの肉をいうときは ⓤ)

まず 先ず ❶【最初に】first, first of all; (列挙したものの中で) in the first place; (理由などを挙げて) to begin [start] with
まずあなたのお名前を教えてください *First of all*, can I have your name, please?
私はまずスーパーへ行き、次に本屋へ行った I went to the supermarket *first* and then to the bookstore.
まず私がやってみましょう I'll try it *first*.
彼女をその仕事に推薦するのに2つの理由があります。まず彼女の英語力は抜群であること、そしてこのあたりの地理にとても詳しいということです There are two good reasons why I recommend her for the job. *To begin with* [*In the first place*], her English is perfect and second [in the second place], she's very familiar with this area.

◆私は朝起きるとまず体操をする(→朝最初にすることは体操だ) *The first thing* I do in the morning *is* do some exercises. / この仕事にはまず何よりも(→ほかの何よりも)根気が必要だ This work needs patience *more than anything else*.

❷【たぶん】(おそらく) probably; (ほとんど) almost
彼女はまず試験に合格するだろう *Probably* she will pass the exam.
彼が犯人であることはまず間違いない I'm *almost* sure that he is the criminal.
◆彼女はまず私たちの言うことを信じないだろうな I *suppose* she won't believe us. (❖I suppose ... は、かなりの自信をもって"…だと思う"と推定する表現) / かなり目立つ看板だから見逃すことはまずないよ(→見逃すはずはない) The signboard is very noticeable. You just *can't* miss it. / 彼が私たちの提案を受け入れることはまずないだろう(→受け入れる可能性はゼロに等しい) *There is no possibility that* he will accept our proposal. / まずそんなところでしょう That's about right.

🅔 「あすまでにこの仕事を終えられますか」「まず無理でしょうね」"Do you think you can finish this work by tomorrow?" "*Not a chance*." (❖not a [an] ... で「ただの一つも…ない」の意味)

❸【とにかく】anyway
かぎが見つかってまずはよかった *Anyway*, you're lucky you found the key.

ますい 麻酔 anesthesia ⓤ; (麻酔薬) anesthetic ⓒ / 局部[全身]麻酔をかける *give a person a* local [*general*] *anesthetic* / 麻酔からさめる recover from *anesthesia* / 1時間もすると麻酔が切れてきた The effect of *the anesthetic* began to wear off in an hour.
‖麻酔科医 an anesthesiologist / 麻酔銃 a tranquilizer gun

まずい

❶【味が悪い】not good, do not taste good

〖語法〗
「まずい」は形容詞の bad ではなく, not good 「おいしくない」を使って遠回しに表現するのがふつう。また, bad には「(食べ物が)腐っている」の意味もあり, 例えば This egg is bad. は, ふつう「この卵はおいしくない」ではなく「この卵は腐っている」の意味になる。

この肉はまずい This meat *doesn't taste good*.
このレストランでカレーを食べたら、まずかった I ate curry and rice at this restaurant, and it *was not good*.

❷【下手な】(技術などが劣っている) poor, bad; (ぎこちない) clumsy ⓗ ヘた(下手)
まずい言い訳をして、彼はガールフレンドを余計に怒らせてしまった He made his girlfriend even more angry by making a *poor* [*clumsy*] excuse.
彼のまずい歌でせっかくのパーティーが台なしになった His *bad* singing spoiled the party.

❸【都合が悪い】bad;（状況・時期などが）awkward;（好ましくない）unfavorable
我々の状況は非常にまずいことになっている Our situation is very *bad*.
今そのことを公表するのはまずい（→公表するにはふさわしくない時である）This is a *bad* [an *awkward*] time to make it public.
そのことが上司の耳に入るとまずいことになる It would be *awkward* if my boss heard about it.
彼はまずいときに私の事務所を訪ねてきた He visited my office at an *awkward* time.
◆彼をそこにひとりで行かせるのはまずい（→よい考えとは思わない）I *don't think it is a good idea* to let him go there alone.

マスカット〘植物〙muscat (grape) [C]

マスカラ mascara [mæskǽrə] [U] ∥彼女はグリーンのマスカラをつけていた She wore green *mascara*.

マスク（仮面・面）mask [C];（流感予防用の）flu mask [C];（キャッチャーなどがかぶる）face mask [C] ∥彼は（流感予防の）マスクをしていた He wore *a flu mask*.
◆彼は甘いマスクをしている He *is good-looking*./ He *has good looks*.
∥ガスマスク a gas mask / 酸素マスク an oxygen mask / デスマスク a death mask

マスクメロン〘植物〙muskmelon [C]

マスゲーム ⚠（集団で行う競技）mass games（❖×mass game とはいわない）

マスコット mascot [C]（❖幸運のシンボルとして選ばれた動物・人・物のこと）∥その会社はイルカをマスコットとして採用した The company has adopted a dolphin as *its mascot*.
∥マスコットガール a mascot（❖× mascot girl とはいわない）

マスコミ（ユニケーション） ⚠（情報の伝達機関）the (mass) media [míːdiə]（❖media「媒体」は, medium の複数形だが, 単数扱いであることが多い）

[語法]
日本語の「マスコミ（ュニケーション）」は mass communication「（情報の）大量伝達」がカタカナ語化したものだが, 実際には新聞・テレビ・ラジオなどの「伝達機関」を指すことが多い. この意味では, 英語は the (mass) media が当たる.

そのスキャンダルはマスコミで大きく取り上げられた The scandal got a lot of attention from *the media*.

まずしい 貧しい
❶【貧乏な】poor;（暮らしが）be badly-off
彼は生活が貧しい He *is poor* [*badly-off*].
彼女は貧しい家に生まれた She was born to a *poor* family.
貧しい人々に食糧が配給された Some food was supplied for [to] *the poor*.
❷【貧弱な】poor;（乏しい）scanty;（十分でない）insufficient
私の経済学の知識は非常に貧しい I have very *poor* knowledge of economics.
彼は表現力がとても貧しい His powers of expression are so *poor*.

マスター[1] ⚠（店などの所有者）owner [C];（店などの経営者）manager [mǽnidʒər] [C];（バーの主人）《米》barkeeper [C],《英》landlord [C];（修士）master [C]（❖店の主人の意味では master はふつうは用いない. また「マスター」と呼びかけるときは Mr. ..., もしくは親しい間柄であればファーストネームを用いる）
∥マスターキー a master key

マスター[2] **─マスターする**（習得する）master [他] ∥英語をマスターする *master* English

マスタード mustard [U] ∥マスタードを塗ったホットドッグ a hot dog with *mustard* / このサンドイッチはマスタードがきいている This sandwich is spiced with *mustard*.
∥マスタードガス mustard gas（❖皮膚がただれる毒ガス）

マスト（帆柱）mast [C] ◆2本マストの船 a two-*masted* ship

マスプロ（ダクション）（大量生産）mass production [U] ∥マスプロ教育 education on a mass-production basis / マスプロ大学《米口語的》a diploma mill（❖「卒業証書製造工場」という意味の軽蔑的表現）

ますます 益々（しだいに多く）more and more;（しだいに少なく）less and less;（しだいに増えて）increasingly;（それだけますます）all the more
ここ数年ますます多くの観光客がその島を訪れている *More and more* tourists have visited the island over the past several years.
行方不明者の捜索はますます困難になってきている It is becoming [getting] *more and more* difficult to search for the missing.
彼女はますます来そうになくなってきた It's becoming *less and less* probable that she will come.
彼氏ができて彼女はますますきれいになった She became *all the more* beautiful after she got a boyfriend.
◆事態はますます悪くなった Things got *worse and worse*. / 騒音はますます大きくなった The noise became *ever* louder.（❖ever は比較級の louder を強める）/ ますます困ったことに, 雨が降りだした *To make matters worse* [*What was worse*], it began to rain. / 年をとるにつれて彼女はますます母親に似てきた *The older* she grew, *the more* she resembled her mother.

まずまず 先ず先ず（かなりよい）fairly good;（それほど悪くない）not so bad
⇒まあまあ ∥まずまずの天気 *fairly good* weather / その映画はまずまずだった The movie was「*fairly good* [*not so bad*].
[e]「エンジンを修理した後, 車の調子はどうだい」「まずまずだよ」"How's your car been since you repaired the engine?" "It's been *so-so*."

ますめ 枡目（原稿用紙などの）square [C] ∥チェス盤のます目 *the squares* of a chessboard

マスメディア the mass media [míːdiə]《単数または複数扱い》⇒マスコミ（ュニケーション）

まずもって 先ずもって (第一に) first, first of all ⇒まず

まぜあわせる 混ぜ合わせる mix 他 《このボールの中で小麦粉と水を混ぜ合わせてください *Mix* flour and water in this bowl.

まぜかえす 混ぜ返す 彼はいつも私たちの話を混ぜ返す(→話に口をはさんだりからかったりする) He always *cuts in on and makes fun of our conversation.*

まぜこぜ 彼の机の引き出しにはあらゆる書類がまぜこぜに入っていた All kinds of documents *were jumbled* [*mixed*] *up* in his desk drawer.

まぜもの 混ぜ物 (添加物) additive ⓒ; (混合物) mixture ⓒ; (不純物) adulterant ⓒ

ませる —ませた (年齢に似合わず大人びている) too mature (for *one's* age); (早熟な) precocious 《君の弟は中学生のくせにずいぶんませているじゃないか Your brother *is* much *too mature* for a junior high school student, isn't he? / あの女の子はずいぶんませている That girl *is* very *precocious*.
◆彼女はませた口をきく(→大人のような話し方をする) She *talks like a grown-up.*

まぜる 混ぜる・交ぜる mix 他, blend 他(◆mixのほうがふつう)
青の絵の具を白の絵の具と混ぜる *mix* [*blend*] blue paint *with* white
牛乳と小麦粉と卵を混ぜなさい *Mix* [*Blend*] the milk, flour, and eggs.
酢に油を加えてよく混ぜる Add some oil to vinegar and *mix* them *up* well.

マゾヒスト masochist [mǽsəkist] ⓒ

また¹ 又

❶【再び】again; (後で) later; (いつか) some day
彼はまた遅刻した He was late *again*.
またお会いできるといいですね I hope I can see you *again*.
それじゃ, また(後で)ね See you (*later*)! (◆すぐには再会できないような相手には See you again. という)
いずれまた伺います I'll come and see you *some day*.
ああ, またやっちゃった Oops! I did it *again*.
😠「目覚まし時計, こわれちゃった」「また？」 "The alarm clock broke." "*Not again*! / *Again*?"
😠「今度こそたばこをやめるぞ」「また始まった」 "I'm going to quit smoking this time." "*There* you *go again*!"

❷【同様に】(…もまた) too, also, as well (◆tooが最も口語的); (否定文で) not ... either ⇒-も
彼もまた野球ファンだ He is a baseball fan, *too*. / He is *also* a baseball fan.
彼女もまたそのことを知らなかった She *didn't* know about that, *either*.
◆私はこの絵が気に入っているし, 彼女もまた気に入っている I like that picture, and 「*so does* she [she likes that picture, *too*].

❸【その上】and; (さらに) and besides [moreover, what is more] ⇒そのうえ
彼は科学者であり, また小説家でもある He is a scientist *and* (a) novelist. / (→科学者であると同時に小説家でもある) He is a novelist *as well as* a scientist.
この車は乗り心地がとてもよいし, また燃費もいい This car is very comfortable, *and besides* [*moreover*] it is economical.
◆その子は字が読めないし, また書くこともできない The boy ca*n't* read *or* [×and] write. / He can *neither* read *nor* write. / 一人また一人と(→次々と)その部屋から出ていった They left the room *one after another*.

❹【別の】 —またの another, some other
この問題はまたの機会に議論することにした We decided to discuss the matter on *another* [*some other*] occasion.
ナイチンゲールはまたの名を「ランプを手にした婦人」といった *Another* name for Nightingale was "the Lady with the Lamp."

❺【強調】
何でまた(→いったいなぜ)彼女にそんなこと言ったんだよ Why 「*on earth* [*in the world*] did you say such a thing to her?

また² 股 (人体・ズボンの) crotch ⓒ; (もも) thigh ⓒ; (木の枝の) fork ⓒ
◆また(→足)を広げる stretch [spread] *one's legs* apart
慣用表現 彼は世界をまたにかけて(→世界中で)商売をしている He does business *all over the world*.

まだ

❶【まだ…ない】not ... yet; (これまでのところ) so far
彼女はまだホテルに到着していない She *hasn't* arrived at the hotel *yet*.
その本を私はまだ読んでいない I *haven't* read that book *yet*.
私たちはまだその事故に関する連絡は受けていない We *haven't* been contacted about the accident *so far*.
◆私はまだアメリカへ行ったことがない I *have never* been to America. (◆〈have never + 過去分詞〉で「一度も…したことがない」という経験を表す) / 何時間もこの問題と取り組んでいるのだが, まだ解決することができない I have been wrestling with the problem for hours, but I *still* can't solve it. (◆否定文の中のstillは「終わるべきものがまだ終わらない」ことを表す)
😠「彼女にはもう電話したの」「いや, まだだよ」 "Have you called her *yet*?" "No, *not yet*."
😠「準備はできた？」「まだだよ」 "Are you ready?" "*Not yet*."

❷【今でもなお】still (◆〈be 動詞＋現在分詞〉や継続の意味を含む動詞とともに用いる)
外はまだ雨が降っている It is *still* raining outside.
座席にはまだ十分の空きがあります There are *still* plenty of seats available.
彼に初めて会った日のことをまだ覚えています I *still* remember the day (when) I first

met him.

❸【さらに】still;（もっと）more
出発まであと2時間あります We *still* have two hours before departure.
まだやらねばならないことがたくさんある There are a lot *more* things to do. / I *still* have a lot *more* things to do.

❹【やっと】(…にすぎない) only
中国語を勉強し始めて、まだ1年にしかならない It has been *only* a year since I began to study Chinese.
彼女はまだ子供だ She is *only* a child.
眠いのですか、まだ9時ですよ Are you sleepy? It's *only* 9 o'clock.

❺【どちらかと言えば】
こんな荒れ模様では、外出するより家の中にいるほうがまだましだ（→外出するより家の中にいるほうがいいだろう）It *would* be better to stay at home *rather than* going outside in such a rough weather.

またいとこ 又従兄弟・又従姉妹　second cousin ⓒ

またがし 又貸し（家や土地の）sublease ⓒ
——また貸しする sublease ⓗ, sublet* ⓗ ∥部屋をまた貸しする *sublease* [*sublet*] a room
◆図書館の本をまた貸しするのはいけない You are not allowed to *lend to another person* books borrowed from the library.

またがる 跨がる ❶【人が馬などに】sit* astride, straddle ⓗ;（飛び乗る）jump on … ∥馬にまたがる *straddle* a horse; *sit astride* a horse

❷【広がる】extend ⓗ ∥その平野は2県にまたがる The plain *extends* over two prefectures.
◆その事件の捜査は全国4県にまたがる（→全国4県で行われている）大規模なものだ The investigation of the case is so extensive that it is being conducted in *four prefectures nationwide*.

またぎき また聞き　second-hand information ⓤ ——また聞きする（間接的に聞く）hear* … secondhand ∥これはまた聞きだけど、彼は来年アメリカへ留学するらしい This is just *second-hand information*, but it seems that he is going to study in America next year.

またぐ 跨ぐ（足で踏み越える）step over [across] …;（横断する）cross ⓗ ∥敷居をまたぐ *step across* [*cross*] the threshold
慣用表現 二度とこの家の敷居をまたぐな *Never darken my door again.*

またした 股下（また下丈 ⑮）inseam ⓒ ∥また下78センチのジーンズを探しているのですが I'm looking for a pair of jeans with *an inseam* of 78 centimeters.

まだしも 暑いだけならまだしも（→何とかできるけれど）この湿気には耐えられない I *can manage* this heat *somehow*, but I can't stand the humidity.

またせる 待たせる（ずっと待たせておく）keep* *a person* waiting ∥彼女は私を2時間も待たせた She *kept* me *waiting* for as long as two hours.
◆私が戻ってくるまで彼を待たせておいて（→待つように頼んで）ください Please *ask* him *to wait* till I come back. / タクシーを待たせてあります I *have* a taxi *waiting* now.
🔊「お待たせして申しわけありません」「いや、いいんですよ」"I'm sorry to *have kept* you *waiting*." "That's all right."

またたき 瞬き（光の）wink ⓒ;（星の）twinkle ⓒ

またたく 瞬く（光などが点滅する）wink ⓗ, blink ⓗ;（星などが）twinkle ⓗ ∥夜空に星がまたたいているのが見えた We could see the stars *twinkling* [*winking*] in the night sky.
慣用表現 またたく間に家全体が炎に包まれた The whole house was enveloped in flames *in an instant*. / そのうわさはまたたく間に学校中に広まった The rumor *ran through* the entire school.

またとない これは一生にまたとない（→一生に一度の）機会だ This is the chance *of a lifetime*. / これはまたとない一品だ This is a *unique* [*one-of-a-kind*] item.

マタニティ ∥マタニティドレス a maternity dress / マタニティ用品 maternity goods

またの ⇒また(又)

または or (✿選択すべき対等の語と語、句と句、節と節を結ぶ);（2つのうちどちらか）either … or ~ ∥デザートにはアイスクリームまたはケーキが選べる You can choose ice cream *or* cake for dessert. / そこへはバスまたは電車で行けます You can go there [*either* by bus *or* by train] [by *either* bus *or* train].

まだまだ（今でもなお）still;（なおいっそう）still, much, far, even (✿後には比較級がくる);（まだ…ない）not … yet ⇒まだ ∥彼はまだまだ未熟だ He is *still* inexperienced. / 10月になってもまだまだ暑い It's *still* hot even in October. / 彼女の英語力はまだまだ上達するだろう She will make *still* [*even*] more progress in her English. / 私はまだまだあきらめてはいない I *haven't* given up *yet*.
◆春はまだまだ先だ（→遠い）Spring is a *long* way off [*away*].
🔊「いい仕事をしましたね」「いえ、まだまだ勉強不足で（→ありがとうございます、でもまだ学ぶことがたくさんあります）」"You did a good job." "Thank you, but I *still* have a lot more to learn."

マダム（夫人）madam ⓒ, matron ⓒ;（女性）woman ⓒ (複 women) ∥有閑マダム a woman who has a lot of money and leisure time

まだら 斑（斑点 ⑮）spot ⓒ;（小さな斑点）speckle ⓒ;——まだら（模様）の spotted; speckled;（不規則な）mottled ∥白と茶色のまだらの犬（→茶色いぶちの白い犬）a white dog with brown *spots*;（→茶色と白の犬）a *brown and white* dog

まだるっこい（動作が緩慢な）slow;（表現が回りくどい）roundabout ∥まだるっこい言い方は

やめろ Stop「talking in a *roundabout* way [beating around the bush].

まち 町・街

(都市) town ⓒ; (市) city ⓒ; (通り) street ⓒ (❖town は village「村」よりは大きく, city より小さい行政区分をいう)

町をぶらぶら歩き回る walk around *the town*

私の（住んでいる）町は高い山に囲まれている My *town* is surrounded by some high mountains.

町中が観光客でにぎわっていた The whole town was alive with tourists.

高田馬場は学生の町だ Takadanobaba is *a student town*.

先日街で順子に会った I met Junko *on* [《英》*in*] *the street* the other day.

私たちは金沢の街を手をつないで歩いた We walked along *the streets* of Kanazawa hand in hand.

◆午後は街へ〔→繁華街へ〕買い物に行くつもりだ I'm going to go *downtown* to do some shopping this afternoon.

‖町医者(一般開業医) a general practitioner (《略語》GP); 町役場 a town [《米》city] office; (建物) a town [《米》city] hall

まちあいしつ 待合室 (病院・駅などの) waiting room ⓒ; (ホテル・空港などの) lounge ⓒ

まちあわせる 待ち合わせる (人と会う) meet* ⑩; (ある場所で人を待つ) wait for ... ∥ 私は彼女と1時に美術館の入口で待ち合わせることにした I *have arranged to meet* her at the entrance to the museum at 1 o'clock. (❖arrange to *do* は「…するよう手はずを整える」の意味) / 今友達と待ち合わせしているんです I*'m* just *waiting for* a friend of mine.

◆待ち合わせ場所 a *meeting place* / 彼は待ち合わせた(→約束した)時間についに現れなかった He didn't appear at the *appointed* time after all.

まちうける 待ち受ける (待つ) wait for ...; (運命などが) 《文語》await ⑩ (❖抽象的な物事を待つ場合に多く用いられる); (期待して待つ) look forward to ... ∥ 我々は彼からの電話をじりじりしながら待ち受けた We impatiently *waited for* a call from him. / 彼は新しいパソコンの到着を今や遅しと待ち受けた He eagerly *looked forward to* the arrival of his new computer. / 悲惨な結末が彼らを待ち受けていた A tragic ending *awaited* them.

◆男は待ち受けていた(→警戒中の)警察官に逮捕された The man was arrested by police officers who *had been on the alert*.

まぢか 間近 中間試験が間近に迫っている The midterm examination is getting *near* [*close at hand*]. / その温泉地では野生の猿を間近で目にすることができる We can see wild monkeys up *close* at the hot spring resort. / そのゲームソフトは完売間近だ The game software *is about to* sell out.

まちがい 間違い

❶【誤り】 mistake ⓒ; error ⓒ; blunder ⓒ; slip ⓒ; fault ⓒ

[語法] error の方が mistake より改まった語で, 失敗を非難する気持ちが含まれる. blunder は, 日本語の「へま, どじ」に近い言葉で, しばしば「ばかげた間違い」を指すのに用いられる語. slip は不注意から生じる「ちょっとしたミス」の意味. また, fault は「間違い」そのものより「失敗の責任」を問題にする語で, It's my fault.「私が悪いのです」のように用いる.

彼はよく計算間違いをやらかす He often makes *mistakes* [*errors*] in his calculations.

私は何度も同じ間違いを犯した I made *the* same *mistake* over and over.

彼女の英作文にはつづりの間違いが多かった Her English composition has many「spelling *errors* [*misspellings*].

彼らは同僚が犯した間違いを隠そうとした They tried to cover up *the mistakes* made by their colleagues.

彼がそんなことをするはずがない. これはきっと何かの間違いだ He cannot have done such a thing. There must be some *mistake*.

だれかが助けてくれると思ったら大間違いだ You're making *a big mistake* if you think someone will help you.

私は間違い電話をかけてしまった I called a *wrong number by mistake*.

それはただの言い間違いだった It was just *a slip of the tongue*.

この計画の実行にはささいな間違いも許されない You mustn't make even *the* tiniest *slip* when carrying out this plan.

◆彼の答えのうち3つが間違いだった(→間違っていた) Three of his answers were *wrong*. / 彼女にその仕事を任せたのがそもそも間違いだった It was *wrong* of us [We were *wrong*] to leave the job to her to begin with. / 私の記憶に間違いがなければ(→記憶が正しければ), 彼女のお父さんは若いころオリンピック選手だった *If I remember correctly*, her father was an Olympic athlete when he was young.

🅔「すみません. これは私の間違いでした」「いいんだよ. だれにだって間違いをすることはあるんだから」"I'm sorry. It was my *mistake* [*fault*]." "It's all right. Everyone *makes mistakes* sometimes."

🅔「電話だれからだったの」「間違い電話だった」"Who was on the phone?" "It was *a wrong number*."

❷【事故】

旅行中に彼女に何か間違いでもあったのかと我々は心配していた We were afraid that *something* had happened to her during her trip.

彼らは2日ほど連絡がない. 何も間違いがなければよいが We've been out of contact with him for two days. I hope *nothing has happened to* him.

まぢかい 間近い 今年も暮れが間近い The end of the year *is*「*close at hand* [*just around the corner*].

まちがいない 間違いない （確かな） certain
——間違いなく certainly, surely; （必ず） without fail, for sure ∥彼がその試験に合格することは間違いない It is certain that he will pass the exam. / He will surely pass the exam. / He is sure to pass the exam. / ご注文の本は1週間以内に間違いなくお届けします The books you ordered will surely [certainly] arrive within a week. / このことは彼に間違いなく伝えておきます I'll let him know about that *without fail [for sure].*/ I'll be sure to let him know about that.
◆彼女なら間違いない（→信頼できる）She *can be trusted.* / She is a *reliable* person.

まちがう 間違う make* a mistake ——間違って by mistake ⇨まちがえる
またしても同じところで間違ってしまった I *made the same mistake* again!
どんなベテランでも間違うことはある Any expert may *make a mistake.*
間違って隣の家のドアをノックしてしまった I knocked on the door of the house next door *by mistake.* / （→うっかり）I *carelessly* knocked on the door of the house next door.
◆私の妹は小さいころよく男の子と間違われた My sister *was* often *taken for a boy* when she was very young. / その建物はとても変わった形をしているから間違うことはないよ You can't *mistake* the building as it has a very strange shape. / これは絶対に彼の前では口にするな *Whatever happens,* you mustn't talk about this matter in his presence. / （→決して）*Never* talk about this matter in his presence. / ひとつ間違えば私たちはその山で遭難するところだった *If a single thing had gone wrong,* we would have had an accident on the mountain.

まちがえる 間違える
❶【間違いを犯す】make* a mistake, mistake* ◎, make [commit] an error
途中で計算を間違えた I *made a mistake* in the calculations in the middle.
彼はよくつづりを間違える He often *makes* spelling *mistakes* [*errors*].

> 語法
> 英語で「…を間違える」という場合，形容詞のwrong「間違った」を使って，《動詞＋a [an, the]＋wrong＋名詞》の形で表現することが多い ∥ 彼は答えを間違えた He *gave a wrong answer.* / 君はあの交差点で道を間違えたのだと思うよ（→間違った方向に曲がった）I think you *took a wrong turn* at that intersection. / もう少しで部屋を間違えるところだった（→間違った部屋に入りそうになった） I almost *went into the wrong room.* / 電話で番号をお間違えのようですが I'm afraid that you *have the wrong number.*

❷【取り違える】（…を～と取り違える）mistake* [take*] ... for ～; （…を～と混同する） confuse ... with ～
私はよく姉と間違えられる I'm often *mistaken [taken] for* my sister.
彼のお母さんはとても若く見えたので，私はお姉さんと間違えてしまった His mother looked so young that I *mistook [took]* her *for* his sister.
私はかぜ薬を胃腸薬と間違えてしまった I *confused* the cold pills *with* the stomach pills.
◆だれかに傘を間違えられた（→だれかが私の傘を間違って持っていった）らしい It looks like someone took my umbrella *by mistake.*

まちがった 間違った wrong （↔right）; （不正確な）incorrect （↔correct）（❖ wrongは「道徳的に間違っている」という意味でも用いられる）⇨まちがえる ∥間違った判断を下す make a *wrong* judgment / あわてていたので，間違ったバスに乗ってしまった I was so upset that I took the *wrong* bus. / 彼女のその考え方は間違っている That way of thinking of hers is *wrong* [*incorrect*].

まちかど 街角・町角 （通りの角） (street) corner; （通り） street ◎ ∥街角の風景 *street scenes* / 街角の小さな本屋で本を1冊買った I bought a book at the small bookstore *on the corner.* / 街角で担任の先生とばったり会った I ran into my homeroom teacher *on the street.*

まちかねる 待ち兼ねる ∥ほら，お待ちかねのものが届いたよ *What you've been waiting for* has arrived. / 姉は今からスキーシーズンの到来を待ちかねている My sister is already *waiting impatiently* [*eagerly*] *for* the ski season to come.

まちかまえる 待ち構える ∥報道陣が首相の到着を待ちかまえていた The press *was eagerly waiting for* the arrival of the prime minister.

まちくたびれる 待ちくたびれる ∥彼女は順番が来るのを待ちくたびれて眠ってしまった She *got* so *tired of waiting for* her turn that she fell asleep.

まちこがれる 待ち焦がれる （期待して待つ） look forward to …; （…したくてたまらない） be dying「for … [to do] ∥うちの子供たちはその映画の公開を待ちこがれている My children *are looking forward to* the release of the film. / 彼は恋人との再会を待ちこがれている He *is dying to* see his girlfriend again.

まちじかん 待ち時間 waiting time ◎ ∥その映画の待ち時間は今1時間ほどだ The *waiting time* to see the film is about an hour. / （→1時間待たねばならない）You *will have to wait* an hour to see the film.

まちどおしい 待ち遠しい （楽しみに待つ） look forward to …; （今か今かと待つ） wait eagerly for … ∥私は毎日お弁当の時間が待ち遠しかった I *looked forward to* eating my box lunch every day. / 来週のクリスマスパーティーが待ち遠しい I've been *waiting eagerly for* the Christmas party next week.

まちなか 町中 （街路） the street; （商業地区）

the downtown area ―町中の[に] down-town /町中に住む live *downtown*
まちなみ 町並み この写真を見ると金沢の美しい町並みを思い出す This photo reminds me of *the beautiful streets and houses* of Kanazawa.
まちのぞむ 待ち望む (期待して待つ) look forward to ...; (熱望する) long for ... /その国の人々はみな戦争の終結を切から待ち望んでいる All the people in that country *are longing for* the end of the war.
まちはずれ 町外れ the outskirts of a town /町はずれに小さな工場がある There is a small factory on *the outskirts of the town*.
まちぶせ 待ち伏せ ambush Ⓤ Ⓒ ―待ち伏せする ambush ⓗ /兵士たちは川岸の茂みで敵を待ち伏せした The soldiers *ambushed* the enemy in the shrubbery along the riverside. / (→ 隠れて待った) The soldiers *hid themselves* in the shrubbery along the riverside *and waited for* the enemy.
まちぼうけ 待ち惚け 私はきのう彼女に待ちぼうけを食わされた I *waited for* her yesterday, but she *never showed up.* / (《口語的》) She *stood* me *up* yesterday.(❖後の表現は特にデートの相手に待ちぼうけを食わせる場合に用いる)
まちまち ―まちまちな (様々な) various; (異なった) different /その問題について彼らの意見はまちまちだった They had *different opinions* [Their opinions *varied*] about the matter.
◆ひと口にワインといっても高級な物から料理用までまちまちだ When someone says wine, it could be *anything from* expensive wine *to* cooking wine.
まちわびる 待ち侘びる 子供たちは母親の帰りを待ちわびていた The children *were waiting impatiently* [*eagerly*] *for* their mother to come home.

まつ¹ 待つ

❶【待ち受ける】wait ⓘ ⓗ;《公式的》await ⓗ (❖抽象的な物事を待つ場合に多く用いられる); (楽しみに待つ) look forward to ...; (期待する) expect ⓗ (❖好ましくないことにも用いる)
彼は彼女(が来るの)を待っていた He *was waiting for* her (to come).
信号が青になるまで待ちなさい *Wait* until the signal turns green.
その電車に乗り遅れたので、次の電車を待たなければならなかった I missed the train and had to *wait for* the next.
救助隊の到着を待っている余裕などなかった We had no time to *wait for* the rescue party's arrival.
彼女はとてもせっかちでレストランの順番を待つのが苦手だ She is very impatient and hates *waiting* in line to enter restaurants.
私たちは雨があがるのを待って出発した We *waited for* the rain to stop before we left.
ゆうべあなたから電話がかかってくるのを待ってたのに I *was expecting* your call last night.
またあなたにお会いできるのを楽しみに待っています I'm *looking forward to* seeing you. ❖この to の後には名詞・動名詞がくる。×I'm looking forward to see you.とはしない)
お待ちしておりました。こちらへどうぞ *I've been looking forward to seeing you.* Please follow me.
スペースマウンテンは今2時間待ちだ We have to *wait* (for) two hours to ride Space Mountain now.
兄は夏が来るのを待ちきれず沖縄にダイビングをしに行った My brother *couldn't wait for* summer to come, so he went to Okinawa to go diving.
大学を卒業すると、待ってましたとばかりに保険の勧誘員が次から次へとやってきた When I graduated from college, insurance salespersons came one after another *as if they had been waiting for a long time.*
犯行動機の解明は今後の捜査が待たれる We *expect* that the investigation will discover the motive for the crime.
待てど暮らせど注文したはずの品は届かなかった I *waited and waited*, but my order didn't arrive.
◆ (電話で) 切らずにそのままお待ちください *Hold the line*, please. / 千秋楽を待たずに武双山の優勝が決まった Musoyama's victory was decided *even before* the last day of the sumo tournament. / 待ちに待った手紙がきょう届いた The *long-awaited* letter arrived today.
💬「ちょっと待っててくれる？ 傘を取ってくるから」「いいよ」 *"Just a minute.* I'll go get my umbrella." "All right."
❷【頼る】(信頼する) rely on ...; (依存する) depend on ...
この計画が成功するかどうかは、彼の実行力に待つところが大きい This project *depends a great deal on* his ability to carry it out.
◆教育制度の見直しが必要であることは論を待たない (→ 言うまでもない) *It goes without saying that* [*Needless to say,*] the educational system needs to be reviewed.
ことわざ 歳月人を待たず ⇨ さいげつ / 待てば海路の日和(ひより)あり ⇨ かいろ (海路)

まつ² 松 pine (tree) Ⓒ /松食い虫 a (Japanese) pine sawyer / 松葉 a pine needle / 松林 a pine grove / 松ぼっくり a pine cone / 松やに (pine) resin

まっか 真っ赤 ―真っ赤な (deep) red; (深紅色の) crimson; (緋(ひ)色の) scarlet /西の空が真っ赤だった(→ 真っ赤に燃えていた) The western sky glowed *crimson*. /彼女はそれを聞くと、恥ずかしさで真っ赤になった She *turned* [*flushed*] *red* with shame when she heard it. / 彼は目を真っ赤にして泣いていた His eyes were *red* from crying.
慣用表現 彼の証言は真っ赤なうそだった His testimony was *a downright lie.*

まっき 末期 (最後) end; (病気などの) terminal stage ——末期の terminal /末期患者 a *terminal* patient / 彼は肝臓の末期癌ということだ I hear he has *terminal cancer* of the liver. / この寺は平安時代の末期に建てられた This temple was built at *the end* of the Heian period.

慣用表現 支持率も急落し,現政権は末期的症状を呈してきた The approval rating of the present government dropped down drastically, and the government *came to the verge of collapse*.

マッキンリー Mount McKinley (⚠米国アラスカ州の山)

まっくら 真っ暗 complete [utter] darkness ——真っ暗な completely dark, pitch-dark /外は真っ暗だった It was *pitch-dark* outside./ There was complete [utter] *darkness* outside. / 突然停電になって,部屋が真っ暗になった Suddenly the light went out and the room became *completely dark*.

慣用表現 お先真っ暗だ My future looks [appears] *completely dark* [*black*]. / その知らせを聞いたとき,目の前が真っ暗になった When I heard the news, 「*everything went black before me* [(→絶望的な気持ちになった)] *I was plunged into despair*」.

まっくろ 真っ黒 ——真っ黒な pitch-black, jet-black, inky /真っ黒な髪 *jet-black* hair / その男の子の手は真っ黒に汚れていた The boy's hands were *pitch-black*. / 真っ黒な雲が出てきた *Inky* clouds are gathering.

◆彼女は真っ黒に日焼けした She *got tanned almost black*. / トーストが真っ黒にこげてしまった The toast burned *black*.

まつげ 睫 eyelash, lash /つけまつ毛をする wear *false eyelashes*

まっこう 真っ向 私の両親は私の計画に真っ向から反対した My parents were opposed *directly* to my plan. / その新人投手は松井に対して真っ向勝負をいどんだ The rookie pitcher confronted Matsui *fair and square*.

まつごのみず 末期の水 私は母の末期の水を取った(→母の臨終に立ち会った) I was 「*with my mother when she died* [*present at my mother's death*]」.

マッサージ massage [məsáːʒ] ——マッサージする massage, give* a massage /腰をマッサージしてもらった I had a back *massage*./ I had my back *massaged*.
‖マッサージ師(男性) a masseur; (女性) a masseuse / マッサージ店 a massage parlor

まっさいちゅう 真っ最中 私たちの夕食の真っ最中に彼女はやってきた She visited us *in the middle of* our dinner. / そのビルは今工事の真っ最中である The construction of the building is *in full progress*.

まっさお 真っ青 ——真っ青な (deep) blue, azure; (顔色が) (deadly) pale /真っ青な空 the *deep* [*clear*] *blue* sky / 彼女は恐怖で真っ青になった She turned 「*deadly pale* [*white (as a sheet)*]」 with fear. / 彼は今にも倒れそうなほど真っ青な顔色をしていた He was so *pale* that he was about to faint.

まっさかさま 真っ逆様 彼は木から真っ逆さまに落ちた He fell *headlong* [*head over heels*] from the tree.

まっさかり 真っ盛り 夏の真っ盛りに *in the height of* (the) summer / 桜は今が真っ盛りだ The cherry blossoms are 「*in full bloom* [*at their best*]」 now.

まっさき 真っ先 私は東京に戻ると真っ先に彼女のもとを訪れた When I came back to Tokyo, I visited her *first of all*. / 彼は真っ先に(→だれよりも先に)手を挙げた He raised his hand *before anyone else*.

まっさつ 抹殺 (無視する) ignore; (殺害する) kill /少数意見を抹殺する *ignore* a minority opinion / 彼女は社会的に抹殺された She *was ignored completely* by society. / 彼らは反対派に抹殺された They *were killed* by their opponents.

まっさら 真っ新 彼はまっさらなユニホームにそでを通した He put on his *brand-new* uniform.

まっしぐら 牛は闘牛士めがけてまっしぐらに突進していった The bull made a *headlong* rush at the bullfighter. / 彼は出世街道まっしぐらだ(→出世街道の王道を進んでいる) He *is marching along on the royal road to success*.

マッシュポテト ⚠mashed potatoes
マッシュルーム mushroom

まっしょう 抹消 ——抹消する cross off, erase /彼らは名簿から彼の名前を抹消した They *crossed* his name *off* the list.

まっしょうめん 真っ正面 ➡ましょうめん

まっしろ 真っ白 ——真っ白な completely white, snow-white /真っ白なワイシャツ a *completely white* shirt / 真っ白な雲 a *snow-white* cloud

慣用表現 試験が始まったとたん,頭の中が真っ白になった My mind *went blank* as soon as the exam began.

まっすぐ 真っ直ぐ
❶【曲っていない】 ——まっすぐな straight; (直立した) upright, erect ——まっすぐ(に) straight; upright
まっすぐな線[道] a *straight* line [road] / まっすぐに伸びた枝 a branch growing *straight*
彼女の髪はまっすぐだ She has *straight* hair.
背筋をまっすぐにして立ちなさい Stand up with your back *straight*.
この道をまっすぐに行くと郵便局があります Go *straight* along this street, and you'll find the post office.
◆私のネクタイをまっすぐにしてください Please *straighten* my tie.
❷【正直な】 ——まっすぐな honest ——まっすぐに honestly
彼はまっすぐな人だ He is an *honest* man. / He is *honest*.
彼は何事においてもまっすぐだ He is *honest* [*straight*] in everything.
❸【寄り道しない】 ——まっすぐ(に) direct,

直に

彼はまっすぐにロンドンへ行った He went *directly* to London.
◆学校が終わったらまっすぐ家に帰ってきなさい Come *straight* [*right*] home after school.

まっせき 末席 the bottom (of the table), the lowest seat ∥テーブルの末席に座る sit at *the bottom of the table*
慣用表現 私は委員会の末席をけがしている I *have the honor of being a member of* the committee. (❖have the honor of *doing* で「…する光栄に浴する」の意味)

まった 待った ちょっと待った *Wait* [*Just*] *a moment*. ／ 私たちの計画に先生の待ったがかかった Our teacher *ordered the suspension of* our plan. ／ 地球温暖化に対する対策は待ったなしの時期に来ている Measures against global warming *can't wait any longer*.

マッターホルン the Matterhorn

まったく 全く
❶【完全に】quite, completely;（絶対に）absolutely ──全くの complete; absolute
彼らは性格が全く違う They are *quite* unlike in character.
彼女はウェディングドレスを着ると全く別人のように見えた She looked *completely* [*quite*] different in her wedding dress.
知っているということと教えるということは全く別だ To know is one thing, to teach is *quite* another.
◆君の言うことは全く正しい You are *perfectly* [*quite, absolutely*] right.

❷【全く…ない】not [no] … at all, no
彼の話には全く興味がもてなかった I *didn't* get interested in his story *at all*.
彼は母親の忠告を全く気にとめなかった He took *no* notice of his mother's advice.
テニスでは彼女に全く歯が立たなかった I was *no* match for her in tennis.
◆私はその事件とは全く関係ありません I *have nothing* [I *don't have anything*] to do with the case.
🗨「おなかすいた？」「いいえ．全く」"Are you hungry?" "No, *not at all*."

❸【本当に】really ──全くの real
彼女の勤勉さには全く感心してしまう I am *really* impressed by her diligence.
あの騒音は全く迷惑だ That noise is a *real* annoyance.
あいつは全くどうしようもないやつだ That guy is *really* a lot of trouble.
🗨「彼は本当に勇気のある人ですね」「全くです」"He is a real man of courage." "Yes, *exactly*."
🗨「彼女とってもきれいね」「全くだ」"She is very beautiful." "*Quite* (so)."

まつたけ 松茸 a *matsutake*, a fragrant and very expensive mushroom that grows chiefly in red-pine forests ∥松茸の吸い物 *matsutake* soup ／ 松茸ごはん rice cooked with *matsutake*

まっただなか 真っ只中 彼女は青春の真っただ中にいる She is *in the midst of* her youth.

まったん 末端 end ⓒ;（先端）tip ⓒ
◆組織の末端 *the bottom of* an organization
∥末端価格 the end [retail] price;（麻薬などの）the street price [value] ／ 末端消費者 an end user

マッチ¹ match ⓒ ∥マッチ1箱 a box [pack] of *matches* ／ マッチをする strike [light] *a match* ／ 火のついたマッチ a lighted *match* ／ マッチの燃えかす a burned-out *match* ／ マッチをお持ちですか Do you have *a match*? ／ このマッチは火がつかない This *match* won't light. ／ 彼はマッチでろうそくに火をつけた He lit the candle with *a match*.
∥マッチ箱 a matchbox ／ マッチ棒 a match(stick) ／ 紙マッチ a paper match
短歌 マッチ擦るつかのま海に霧ふかし身捨つるほどの祖国はありや（寺山修司）
As I strike a match ―
at that very moment ― fog
rolls in from the sea.
Do I have a native land
that I would care to die for?

マッチ² ──マッチする match ⓐ, go* well ⇒あう（合う）／そのカーテンはこの部屋にマッチしている The curtains *match* [*go well with*] this room.

マッチ³（試合）match ⓒ ∥タイトルマッチ a title *match* ／ リターンマッチ a return *match*
∥マッチプレー【ゴルフ】match play ／ マッチポイント (a) match point

まっちゃ 抹茶 powdered [ground] (green) tea ⓤ

マット mat ⓒ ∥マットを編む weave *a mat* ／ 床にマットを敷く stretch *a mat* out on the floor ／ 中に入る前にマットで靴の泥を落としなさい Scrape your shoes on *the mat* before entering.
∥マット運動 mat exercises ／ ドアマット a door [welcome] mat, a doormat ／ バスマット a bath mat

まっとう 真っ当 ⇒まとも

まっとうする 全うする 職務をまっとうする *fulfill one's* duty ／ 祖母は天寿をまっとうした My grandmother *died of old age*.

マットレス mattress ⓒ

マッハ Mach [mάːk] (number) ⓒ ∥そのジェット機はマッハ2で飛ぶ The jet flies at *Mach 2*.

まつばづえ 松葉杖 crutch ⓒ ∥彼は松葉づえをついて歩いていた He was walking on *crutches*.

まつび 末尾 the end, the close, the tail ∥手紙の末尾に *at the end of* a letter
◆宝くじの末尾の数字 the *final* number of a lottery ticket

まっぴら 真っ平 その会議に出席するなんてまっぴらごめんだ（→決して出席したくない）I will *never* attend the meeting. ／ こんな事件はもうまっぴらだ We've had enough of incidents like this.

まっぴるま 真っ昼間 彼らは真っ昼間から酒盛りをしている They have been on a binge

まっぷたつ 真っ二つ スイカを真っ二つに割った I cut a watermelon *right in half* [*two*]. / その問題をめぐって党は真っ二つに割れた The party split *in two* over the question.

まつむし 松虫 pine cricket ◯

まつり 祭り festival ◯ ⇒ あとのまつり, おまつりきぶん, おまつりさわぎ
夏祭り *a summer festival*
近くの神社でお祭りがあった There was *a festival* at the shrine nearby.
神田の古本祭りは毎年秋に行われる *The secondhand book festival* in Kanda is held every fall.
立ち並ぶ屋台と祭りばやしがお祭り気分を盛り上げていた The rows of stalls and *the festival music* livened up *the festive mood*.

まつりあげる 祭り上げる *set* a person up* ‖彼は委員会の議長に祭り上げられた He *was set up* as chairman of the committee.

まつる 祭る (神として) deify [déiifài] ⓐ; (神社を建てて) dedicate ⓐ; (崇拝する) worship ⓐ ‖先祖を祭る *worship one's* ancestors / その神社は戦争の犠牲者を祭っている The shrine ⌈*is dedicated to* [*enshrines*]⌉ the victims of the war.

まつろ 末路 (終わり) end ◯; (最後の日々) last days; (運命) fate ◯Ｕ ‖彼女は不幸な末路をたどった Her life had *an* unhappy *end*.

まつわりつく 纏わり付く (つきまとう) follow around [about], cling* to … ‖その子は一日中母親にまつわりついている The child *follows* her mother *around* [*about*] all day long.

まつわる 纏わる その事件にまつわる話 a story *about* the incident / この地方にまつわる伝説 legends *concerning* [*related to*] this region

まで 迄

❶ [時間] until, till, to, up to …; (までに) by, by the time (❖until, till がその時点まで行為状態が継続していることを表すのに対し, by はその時点までに行為・状態が終了していることを表す)
3時まで休憩にしよう Let's take a rest *until* [*till*] three.
最後まであきらめるな Never give up *until* the end.
雨はけさまで降り続いた It continued to rain *until* this morning.
彼は2, 3日前まで病気で寝ていた He had been ill in bed *up to* a few days ago.
あいつが来るまで待とうよ Let's wait *until* [*till*] he shows up. (❖時を表す副詞節の中では, 未来のことであっても現在形で表す)
祖母は98歳まで生きた My grandmother lived *until* [*till*] she was 98. / My grandmother lived *to* the age of 98.
この事実はいままでだれにも知られていなかった No one knew this fact *until* [*till, up to*] now.
こんなに遅くまで何をやっていたの What have you been doing *until* [*till*] this late?
彼らは朝から晩まで働いた They worked from morning *till* night.
そのときまでにはこの仕事を終わらせておきます I will have finished this work *by* then.
学生たちは今月末までにレポートを提出しなければならない The students must hand in their papers *by* the end of this month.
あなたが帰ってくるころまでには夕食の準備をしておきましょう Dinner will be ready *by the time* you get home.
君が次に来てくれるときまでにはこの絵を描き上げているだろう I'll have finished this painting *by the time* you visit me next time.
◆今までのところ彼からから返事を受け取っていない *So far* I haven't got an answer from him. / その映画はこれまでに見たどの映画とも違っていた The movie was unlike anything I'd seen *before*. / 彼女はこれまで(→生まれてこのかた)何ひとつ不自由したことがない She has never wanted for anything *in her life*. / これはいつまでに提出すればいいのですか(→締め切りはいつですか) What is the deadline for turning this in?

🔴「この店は何時まであいているんですか」「11時までです」 "*How late* are you open?" "We are open *until* [*till*] 11."

❷ [場所] to, up to …, as far as … ❖to は方向と到着点「…へ」を表し, up to … は到着点「…に至るまで」を強調する. as far as … は限度「(ある場所)までは」を表すことが多い
彼は新宿までバスで行った He went *to* [*as far as*] Shinjuku by bus. (❖この場合, to なら新宿が目的地であり, as far as ならさらにその先に行ったことを含意する)
彼女の犬は彼女のところまで走ってきた Her dog ran *up to* her.
父は会社までバスと電車を利用する My father takes a bus and a train *to* his office.
3階までエレベーターに乗った We took the elevator *to* the third floor.
このスカートはくるぶしまでくる This skirt comes *to* my ankles.
ここから博物館まではどのくらいありますか How far is it from here *to* the museum?
彼女は頭のてっぺんからつま先までびしょぬれになった She got wet from head *to* toe.
◆プールを端から端まで3回泳いだ I swam three *lengths* of the pool.

🔴「どちらまで行かれますか」「静岡までです」 "*How far* are you going?" "(I'm going *as far as*) Shizuoka."

❸ [程度・範囲] to, up to …
最初から最後まで from beginning *to* end; from first *to* last / 1から10まで数える count (up) from one *to* ten / ある[かなりの]程度まで *to* some [a large] extent
この劇場は2,000人まで入れます This theater can hold *up to* 2,000 people.
◆彼はそのビデオをすり切れるまで何度も見た He played the video again and again *until* it was worn out. / きょうはここまで *So much* for today. / *That's all* for today. / 彼をど

こまで信じていいか分からない I don't know *how far* I can trust him. / 本は一度に3冊まで(→最大で3冊)借りられます You can borrow *a maximum of* three books at a time. / 彼女は私のことをうそつきとまで言った She went *so [as] far as to say* I was a liar. (❖go so [as] far as to *do* で「…しさえする」の意味)

❹【強調】(…でさえも) even; (ただ単に) only, just, merely

君までそんなひどいことを言うのか *Even* you say such a cruel thing?

参考までに,それにいくら払ったの *Just* out of interest, how much did you pay for it?

私は当然のことをしたまでです I *just [only]* did what I should do.

◆そこまで言うのならもう止めはしないよ I won't try to stop you any longer, as you are insisting *so*.

❺【必要がない】

それは説明するまでもない You *don't need to explain* that.

言うまでもなく彼は優秀だ *Needless to say*, he is excellent. / *It goes without saying* that he is excellent.

まてんろう 摩天楼 skyscraper © //ニューヨークには摩天楼がそびえている *The skyscrapers* tower over New York.

まと 的

❶【標的】target ©, mark ©

的に当たる hit *a target* / 的をはずれる[はずす] miss *a target* / 的をめがけて矢を射る shoot (off) an arrow at *a target*

矢は的から大きくそれてしまった The arrow went wide of *the target*.

❷【要点】

的を射た発言 an *apt* remark / 的はずれな質問 an *irrelevant* question

彼の意見は的はずれだ His opinion *is beside the point*.

彼女のスピーチは簡潔で的を射ていた Her speech *was* short and *to the point*.

我々はこの点に議論の的をしぼる(→議論をこの点に集中させる)べきだ We should *focus* our arguments on this point.

❸【対象】target ©, object ©; (焦点) focus ©, center ©

注目[興味]の的 the *center* of attention [interest] / 批判の的 a *target* of criticism

◆議論の的となっている問題 a *controversial issue* / 彼の新しい小説は注目の的になった His new novel was *in the spotlight*. / 彼は嘲笑(ଚょぅ)の的となった He *was held up to ridicule*. / その車は男の子みんなのあこがれの的だった The car was *the envy* of all the boys.

まど 窓 window ©

窓をあける open *a window* / 窓を閉める close [shut] *a window* / 窓から外を眺める look out of *a window* / がたがたする窓 *a loose window*

その窓から泥棒が侵入した A thief got in through that *window*.

この窓からの眺めはすばらしい The scenery from this *window* is wonderful.

彼は窓からこちらに向かって手を振っていた He was waving to me from *the window*.

窓から身を乗り出してはいけない Don't hang out of *the window*.

窓に指をはさんだ I pinched my finger in *the window*.

その窓はあけた[閉めた]ままにしておいてください Leave that *window* open [closed], please.

彼女は窓のカーテンを引いた She drew the curtains over *the window*.

◆社会の窓があいているよ *Your fly* is open.

‖窓ガラス a windowpane / 窓枠 a window frame / 出窓 a bay window / 天窓 a skylight / 二重窓 a double window

まといつく 纏い付く ➔ まつわりつく

まとう 纏う wear* ⓜ ➔ きる(着る)

◆民族衣装を身にまとった人々 people *dressed* in their folk costume

まどぎわ 窓際 窓際の席 a *window* seat / 窓際に座る sit *by [at] a window*

‖窓際族 office workers who are not given work and have nothing to do

まどぐち 窓口 window © /切手は5番窓口です You can buy stamps at *window* No.5.

まとはずれ 的外れ ➔ まと

まどべ 窓辺 窓辺に座る sit *by [near] the window*

まとまった 纏まった ❶【多くの】large //まとまった額のお金 a *large* sum of money / その政治家はまとまった票を集めた The politician got a *large* vote.

❷【定まった】definite //その問題に関してはまとまった考えをもっていない I have no *definite* idea about the problem.

❸【団結した】よくまとまった家族 a *tight-knit* family / よくまとまったチーム a *highly organized* team

まとまり 纏まり まとまりのあるクラス a *tight-knit* class / まとまりのない論文 an *incoherent* paper; a paper that *lacks coherence [unity]*

まとまる 纏まる

❶【一つになる・集まる】(意見が) agree ⓜ ⓜ; (集められる) be collected

それについて彼らの意見がまとまった They *agreed* on that point.

その料理番組で紹介されたレシピが1冊の本にまとまった The recipes shown in that cooking program *were collected* into a book.

◆まとまって(→一団となって)行動する act *in a body* / その問題に関して私たちの意見はまとまらなかった Our opinions *were divided* on the matter. / その日以来,私たちのクラスは一つにまとまった Our class *got united* after that day.

❷【成立する】be concluded, be settled

交渉は首尾よくまとまった The negotiations *were concluded* successfully.

これで話はまとまったな It's all *settled* then.

◆両国間の和平交渉はまとまらなかった(→失敗に終わった) The peace negotiations between the two countries *ended in failure*. / その縁談はまとまった The match *has been arranged*.

❸【整う】
考えがうまくまとまらない My ideas *aren't well organized*.
君の報告書はよくまとまっている Your report *is well organized*.

まとめ 纏め（要約）summary, digest ⓒ; （結論）conclusion ⓒ

まとめやく 纏め役（調停者）mediator ⓒ; （平和のため）peacemaker ⓒ; （調整者）coordinator ⓒ; （紛争の）troubleshooter ⓒ

まとめる 纏める
❶【一つにする・集める】collect ⓤ, put* together; （統合する）integrate ⓤ ——まとめて all together; （支払いなどを一括して）in a [one] lump
提案をまとめる *put together* a proposal
彼は論文を一冊の本にまとめた He *collected* his essays into one volume.
私はすべての情報を1つの報告書にまとめなければならない I must *integrate* all the information into a single report.
家賃を3か月分まとめて払った I paid three months' rent *in a lump*.
◆荷物をまとめる *pack one's bags* / 私は週に1度食料品をまとめて買う I *buy all* my groceries once a week. / 彼は人をまとめる力がある He is able to *bring* people *together*.

❷【決着させる】settle ⓤ, conclude ⓤ
交渉をまとめる *conclude* negotiations / 労使間の紛争をまとめる *settle* a dispute between employers and employees
◆商談をまとめる *close* [*strike*] *a bargain*; *put through* a business deal

❸【整える】
縁談をまとめる *arrange* a marriage
仕事にかかる前に考えをまとめなさい *Collect your thoughts* before you begin your work.
彼は話の内容を2, 3の要点にまとめた He *condensed* the contents of his speech into a few major points.
委員は長い討論を通して意見をまとめた The committee members *formed* an opinion through lengthy discussions.

まとも
❶【きちんとした】——まともな（世間並みの）decent ——まともに（適切な）proper ——まともに（真剣に）seriously
彼はまともな人間だ He is a *decent* person.
もっとまともな暮らしがしたい I want to lead a「more *decent* [*better*] life.
私は何週間もまともな食事をとっていない I haven't had a *proper* meal for weeks.
彼はだれからもまともに相手にしてもらえない He isn't taken *seriously* by anybody.
◆あんなことはまともな人間のすることではない（→正気の人間ならしないだろう）No *sane* person would do a thing like that.

❷【正面】——まともに square, fair; （まっすぐ）right, straight

石が私の頭にまともに当たった The stone hit me *square* [*fair*, *right*] in the head.
私は彼女の目をまともに見ることができなかった I couldn't look her *right* [*straight*] in the eye.
◆父の会社は円高の影響をまともに（→激しく）受けた My father's company was hit *hard* by the rising value of the yen. / 彼は私の冗談をまともにとった He took my joke *seriously*. / まともに闘ったら私は絶対に彼に勝てないだろう I'll never be able to beat him if I fight him *head-on*.

まどり 間取り the plan [layout] of a house, the house plan ◆彼の家は間取りがいい[悪い] His house *is well* [*badly*] *planned*.

マドリード Madrid（❖スペインの首都）

まどろっこしい ⇨まだるっこい

まどろむ doze ⓘ, take* a nap ‖木立さの静けさに彼女はまどろみ始めた The quiet of the grove lulled him into *a doze*.

まどわす 惑わす（だます）delude ⓤ, deceive ⓤ; （誘惑する）tempt ⓤ ‖女性を甘い言葉で惑わす *tempt* a woman with honeyed words / くだらないうわさに惑わされてはいけない You shouldn't *be deluded* by an absurd rumor.
◆彼女の美貌(ぼう)に惑わされない男はいない Her beauty never fails to *blind* men.

まとわりつく ⇨まつわりつく

マトン（羊肉）mutton ⓤ

マドンナ（聖母）the Madonna; （あこがれの女性）one's idol ‖彼女は私のマドンナだ She is my *idol*.

マナー ⚠manners ‖テーブルマナー table manners / 彼女はマナーがいい[悪い] She has good [no] manners. / She *is well-mannered* [*bad-mannered*].

まないた 俎 cutting [chopping] board ⓒ
慣用表現 彼はまないたの鯉(こい)同然だ（→彼らのなすがままだ）He *is at their mercy*. / （→全く無力だ）He *is completely helpless*.

まなこ 眼 eye ⓒ ‖彼女は寝ぼけまなこで私を見た She looked at me with *sleepy eyes*.

まなざし 眼差し look ⓒ ‖愛情のこもったまなざし *a loving look* / 彼は私を冷たいまなざしでじっと見た He fixed me with *a cold look*.

まなつ 真夏 midsummer ⓤ, high [full] summer ⓤ ‖真夏の恋 *a midsummer romance*
◆きのうの東京は真夏日になった（→気温が摂氏30度を超えた）*The temperature climbed above 30°C in Tokyo yesterday*.

まなでし 愛弟子 one's favorite pupil

まなぶ 学ぶ
（身につける）learn* ⓤ ⓘ; （勉強・研究する）study ⓤ ⓘ
彼は大学で物理学を学んでいる He *studies* physics at a university.
私は松田教授のもとでフランス文学を学んだ I *studied* French literature under Professor Matsuda.
その経験を通して私は多くのことを学んだ I *learn-*

ed a lot through that experience.
環境保護に関して日本はヨーロッパの国々に学ぶべきことがたくさんある Japan has many things to *learn* from European countries about environmental protection.
[ことわざ] よく学びよく遊べ All work and no play makes Jack a dull boy.（→勉強ばかりで全く遊ばないと子供はだめになる）

マニア ⚠ maniac [méiniæ̀k] [C], enthusiast [C],《口語的》freak [C]（❖英語の mania は「異常なまでの執心」の意味）∥兄はカーマニアだ My brother is *a* car *maniac* [*enthusiast*]./ My brother has *a mania* for cars. / その雑誌はコンピュータマニア向けだ The magazine is meant for computer *maniacs*.

まにあう 間に合う
❶【時間に】be in time,《口語的》make* it; (乗り物に) catch* [他] (↔miss)
かろうじて終バスに間に合った I barely *caught* [*made it to*] the last bus./ I *was* barely *in time for* the last bus.
今出ればまだ間に合うよ We can still *make it* if we leave now.
◆ちょっとの差でいつもの電車に間に合わなかった I just barely *missed* my usual train. / 道が込んでいてコンサートの開演に間に合わなかった The street was jammed and I「*was late for* [*missed*] the opening of the concert. / 今ごろ試験勉強を始めてももう間に合わないよ(→遅すぎる) *It's too late* now to start studying for the exam. / 早く応募はがきを出さないと締め切りに間に合わないよ Send your application postcard quickly, or you *won't meet* the deadline.
❷【役に立つ・用が足りる】do* [他] [自]
この箱で間に合いますか Will this box *do*?
彼に会いに行く必要はない. 電話で間に合うだろう You don't have to go out to see him. A telephone call will *do*.
◆2,000円あれば間に合う(→十分)だろう Two thousand yen will *be enough* [*sufficient*]. / 野菜は間に合っています(→必要ない) We *don't need* any vegetables.

まにあわせ 間に合わせ makeshift [C], stopgap [C] ―間に合わせの makeshift, stopgap; (仮の) temporary ∥間に合わせの案 a *makeshift* plan / 間に合わせの手段をとる adopt *temporary* [*stopgap*] measures / バッグを家に忘れてきてしまったので間に合わせに紙袋を買った Since I left my bag home, I bought a paper bag as *a makeshift*.

まにあわせる 間に合わせる (期日に) meet* [他]; (…ですます) do* with ..., make* do with ... ∥昼食はサンドイッチで間に合わせた I *made do with* sandwiches for lunch. / 何とかこの品を納期に間に合わせなければならない We must manage to *meet* the deadline for delivery of these goods.

まにうける 真に受ける 彼の言うことを真に受けるな Don't *take* him「*at his word* [*seriously*].

マニキュア ⚠(マニキュア液)《米》nail polish [U][C],《英》nail varnish [U][C]（❖英語の manicure [mǽnikjùər] は「手とつめの手入れ」の意味）∥彼女は銀色のマニキュアをしていた She was wearing silver *nail polish*. / マニキュアを落とすのがめんどうくさい It's a pain to remove *the* (*nail*) *polish* from my nails.
◆つめにマニキュアをする *polish* [*paint*] *one's* nails

まにし 真西 ―真西に due west
➩にし, ま-

マニュアル (手引き書・説明書) manual [C]
∥マニュアル車 a car with a manual transmission

マニラ Manila [mənílə]（❖フィリピンの首都）

まぬがれる 免れる ❶【逃れる】escape [他]; (救われる) be saved from ... ∥逮捕[処罰]を免れる *escape* capture [punishment] / 彼女はかろうじて死を免れた She just *escaped* death. / いつもより遅く家を出たので運よく事故を免れた I left home later than usual, so I fortunately *escaped* [*was saved from*, *missed*] getting caught in the accident.
◆いくつかの建物は焼失を免れた Some buildings *survived* the fire. / 人間はみな死を免れない All human beings *are mortal*.
❷【回避する】avoid [他], evade [他] ∥彼は責任を免れようとした He tried to *avoid* [*evade*] responsibility.
◆彼は兵役を免れた(→免除された) He *was exempted from* military service.

まぬけ 間抜け fool [C], idiot [C] ―間抜けな foolish, stupid ➩ばか ∥この間抜け You *fool*! / 私はなんて間抜けだったんだろう What *an idiot* I have been!

まね 真似
❶【模倣】imitation [C][U], mimicry [U] ―まねする imitate [他], mimic [他] ➩まねる
彼はみごとにその男優のまねをした He *did* [*gave*] *a* good *imitation* of the actor.
九官鳥には人の言葉をまねする能力がある Mynas have the power to *imitate* [*mimic*] human words.
彼はマイケル・ジャクソンのまねがうまい He is good at *mimicking* Michael Jackson.
彼女は姉のまねをして化粧をした She made herself up *in imitation of* her sister.
❷【ふり】
彼女は泣くまねをした She *pretended* to cry.
❸【ふるまい】
ばかなまねをする play [act] *the fool* / 見苦しいまねをする *behave* in an improper manner
子供みたいなまねをするのはやめなさい Stop *acting like a child*./ Stop *being so childish*.
ばかなまねはよせ Stop that *nonsense*!

マネージャー (支配人) manager [mǽnidʒər] [C]; (代理人) agent [C] ◆野球部のマネージャー(→世話役) *a caretaker* of a baseball club

まねき 招き invitation [U][C] ➩しょうたい(招待) ∥招きに応じる accept *an invitation* / 招きを断る refuse [decline] *an invitation* / 彼らは日本政府の招きで来日した They came to Japan *at* [*on*] *the invitation of* Japanese

マネキン mannequin, dummy

まねく 招く
❶【招待する】invite, ask
我々は田中夫妻をパーティーに招いた We *invited* the Tanakas to the party.
彼女は歓迎会に招かれた She *was「got*] *invited* to the reception.
◆お招きくださりありがとうございます Thank you very much for your *invitation*. / It is very kind of you to *invite* me.
❷【頼んで来てもらう】call in, invite; (雇う) employ
私は彼らの顧問として招かれた I was「*called in [employed*] as their adviser.
❸【引き起こす】cause, incur
この汚職事件は大衆の政治不信を招いた This corruption scandal *caused* [*generated*] public distrust in politics.
彼の演説は厳しい批判を招いた His speech *incurred* severe criticism.
❹【手招きする】beckon
彼女はそばに来るよう私を手で招いた She *beckoned* me to her side.

まねごと 真似事 せめて結婚式のまねごとだけでもしよう Let's at least do *something that looks like* a marriage ceremony.

まねる 真似る imitate, mimic, copy /彼はいつも兄の行動をまねる He always *imitates* [*copies*] his brother. / 子供たちは先生の声をまねた The children *mimicked* the teacher's voice.
◆ディズニーをまねた映画 a film *imitative of* Disney / この町はパリをまねて作られた This town was *modeled on* [*after*] Paris.

まのあたり 目の当たり 私はその事故を目の当たりにした (→目の前で起きた) The accident happened *in front of* my eyes.

まのび 間延び 間延びした話し方 a *lazy* way of talking / 彼らは間延びした顔をしていた They had *stupid-looking* faces.

まばたき 瞬き blink ——まばたきする blink /彼はまばたきひとつせずにその光景をじっと見つめていた He was staring at the sight without *blinking* [*a blink*].

まばゆい 目映い・眩い まばゆいばかりのダイヤモンド *dazzling* diamonds ⇒まぶしい

まばら 疎ら ——まばらな sparse, thin ——まばらに sparsely, thinly /父の髪はまばらになってきた My father's hair is getting *thin*. / 出席者はまばらだった The attendance was *sparse* [*thin*].
◆車を走らせるにつれて人家はまばらになっていった The farther I drove, *the fewer* [*sparser*] the houses got. / 通りは人影がまばらだった (→人が少なかった) There were *few* people on the street.

まひ 麻痺 paralysis ——まひする be paralyzed; (感覚がなくなる) become* numb [nÁm] /寒さで指がまひした My fingers *became numb* [*dead*] from the cold. / 大雪のために東京の鉄道機能がまひした Train services in Tokyo *were paralyzed* by the heavy snow.
◆彼は心臓まひで死んだ He died of「*heart failure* [*a heart attack*]. / その病気で彼は左半身[下半身]がまひした The disease *paralyzed* him「*on his left side* [*below the waist*]. / 彼は金銭感覚がまひしている He *has no sense* for money. / He *is insensitive* to the value of money.

まひがし 真東 ——真東に due east ⇒ひがし、ま-

まびきうんてん 間引き運転 (列車[バス]の)間引き運転をする (→本数を減らす) reduce the number of train [bus] *runs*

まびく 間引く thin out /新芽を間引く *thin out* the sprouts

まひる 真昼 (正午) (high) noon, midday; (日中) broad [full] daylight /真昼の太陽のもとで彼は庭の草取りをしていた He was weeding the garden in the *midday* [*noon*] sun.

マフィア the Mafia

マフィン muffin

まぶか 目深 彼女は帽子を目深にかぶった She pulled her hat *over her eyes*.

まぶしい 眩しい dazzling, glaring, bright /太陽のまぶしい光 the *glaring* [*bright*] light of the sun / 自動車のまぶしいライトで目がくらんだ I was dazzled by the *bright* lights of the car.
◆太陽がまぶしかった The sunlight *dazzled* my eyes. / The sunlight *was dazzling*.

まぶす (振りかける) dust; (覆う) coat /ケーキに砂糖をまぶす *dust* a cake with sugar; *dust* sugar on a cake

まぶた 眼瞼 eyelid, lid /上[下]まぶた *the* upper [lower] *eyelid* / 彼女は一重[二重]まぶただ She has single [double] *eyelids*.
◆時々以前つきあっていた彼女の笑顔がまぶたに浮かぶ (→思い出す) I sometimes *remember* [*recall*] my ex-girlfriend's smiling face.

まふゆ 真冬 midwinter, the middle [dead, depths] of winter /私は真冬にドイツを旅行したことがある I have traveled through Germany *in midwinter* [*the middle of winter*].

マフラー ❶【えり巻き】scarf (複 ～s, scarves),《古風》muffler (❖ scarf を用いるほうが一般的) /彼女は首にマフラーを巻いていた She wore *a scarf* around her neck.
❷【消音器】《米》muffler,《英》silencer

まほう 魔法 magic; (呪文) spell ——魔法の magic /魔法を使う (practice, work) *magic* / 魔法を解く break *a spell* / 魔法のつえ a *magic* wand / 魔法のじゅうたん a *magic* carpet / 魔女は彼に魔法をかけた The witch cast [put] *a spell* on him. / カボチャは魔法で馬車に変えられた The pumpkin was turned into a carriage *by magic*.
‖魔法使い a magician; (男) a wizard; (女) a witch / 魔法びん a thermos (bottle), a vacuum bottle

マホガニー mahogany /マホガニーの家具 *mahogany* furniture

まぼろし 幻 vision ◯, illusion ◯; (幻影) phantom ◯ ∥死んだ祖母の幻を見た I saw my dead grandmother in *a vision*.
◆幻の名画 a *visionary* masterpiece

ママ mother ◯, 《米口語的》mom ◯, 《米口語的》mam ◯, 《米口語的》mommy ◯, 《英口語的》mum ◯, 《英口語的》mummy ◯ ∥彼女は教育ママだ She is *an education-minded mother*./ She is enthusiastic about her children's education.

まま 間々 田中先生だってうっかりミスをすることはままあるさ Even Mr. Tanaka *sometimes* makes careless mistakes.

-まま -儘
❶【そのまま】
その窓をあけたままにしておいてください Leave [Keep] that window open, please.
彼はしばらくの間黙ったままだった He *remained* [*kept*] silent for some time.
その事件は未解決のままだ The case *remains* unsolved [to be solved].
コートを着たまま眠ってしまった I fell asleep *with* my coat *on*. (❖(with+名詞+形容詞(句)[副詞(句)])で「…を～した状態で」の意味)
口をいっぱいにしたまましゃべるな Don't speak *with your mouth full*.
兄は彼女と遊びに出かけたままです My brother *has gone out* with his girlfriend.
その寺は修復のため閉まったままだ The temple *is* closed for restoration.
この町は昔のままだ This town is *the same as before*.

❷【…に従って】
本能のままに行動する act *on* instinct
彼はいつも上司に言われるままだ He always does [acts] *as* his boss tells him.
彼女は彼のなすがままだった She was *at his mercy*.
彼は医者の忠告のままにたばこをやめた He gave up smoking *on* his doctor's advice./ He *followed* his doctor's advice and gave up smoking.
彼女の思うままにやらせておきなさい Let her do *as* she *pleases* [*likes*, *wishes*]./ Let her have her *own way*.

ままこ 継子 stepchild ◯; (男) stepson ◯; (女) stepdaughter ◯ ◆人をまま子扱いする *leave* a person *out*; *neglect* a person

ままごと ままごとをする play *house*

ままちち 継父 stepfather ◯

ままならぬ 人生はままならぬ Life *doesn't go as we want*./ Life goes against us./ 最近は忙しくて新聞を読むことさえままならない These days I'm so busy that I *can't even find* time to read the newspaper.

ままはは 継母 stepmother ◯

まみず 真水 fresh water ◯

まみなみ 真南 ──真南に due south
⇨ま-, みなみ

-まみれ 彼の衣服は血まみれだった His clothes were *bloody*./ 彼の部屋は暗くてほこりまみれだった The room was dark and *dusty*./ 子供たちは全身泥まみれだった The children *were covered with mud all over*./ The children *were muddy all over*.

まみれる 売れ残ったかばんがほこりにまみれている The unsold bags *are covered with dust*.

まむかい 真向かい 彼女の家は図書館の真向かいにある Her house is [stands] *right opposite* the library./ 彼はテーブルをはさんで私の真向かいに座った He sat *just across* the table *from* me./ He sat *face to face with* me *across* the table.

まむし 蝮 a *mamushi*, a pit viper

まめ¹ 豆 bean ◯; (エンドウマメ) pea ◯; (大豆) soybean ◯ ∥豆をひいて粉にする grind *beans* into powder/ 豆を一晩水に浸しておく steep *the beans* in water overnight/ 畑に豆をまく sow *beans* [*soybeans*] in a field/ 豆の缶詰 canned *beans*/ 豆のさやをむく shell *peas*/ 豆の木 a *pea* plant/ コーヒー豆をひいて、コーヒーをいれた I ground some *coffee beans* to make coffee.
∥豆台風 a baby typhoon/ 豆鉄砲 a peashooter, a popgun/ 豆電球 a miniature bulb, a midget lamp/ 豆本 a miniature book

まめ² (水ぶくれ) blister ◯; (たこ・魚の目) corn ◯ ∥まめをつぶす burst *a blister*/ まめがつぶれた *The blister* has burst [broken]./ 足の裏にまめができている[できた] I have [got] *blisters* on the sole of my foot.

まめ³ 彼女はまめに働く She works *hard* [*diligently*]./ 彼は筆まめだ He is *a good correspondent*.

まめつ 摩滅 ──摩滅した worn-out, worn-down ──摩滅する be worn out [down] ∥摩滅したタイヤ a *worn-out* old tire

まめつぶ 豆粒 屋上から見下ろすと下の人たちは豆粒のように見えた When I looked down from the rooftop, the people down below looked like *little specks*. (❖speck は「小さなしみ」の意味)

まめまき 豆まき bean-scattering ceremony ◯ ⇨せつぶん

まめまめしい ──まめまめしく (忠実に) faithfully; (勤勉に) diligently ∥彼女はまめまめしく働く She works *diligently* [*hard*]./ 彼はまめまめしく仕えてくれる He serves me *faithfully*.

まもなく 間も無く
山下さんは間もなくここに来るだろう Mr. Yamashita will be here *soon* [*presently, shortly, before long, in a short time, in a little while*].
間もなく雨が降り始めた *Before long* it began raining.
彼女は間もなく戻ってきた It was not long *before* she returned.
その後間もなく彼は病気になった He got ill *shortly* after that.
間もなく11時だ It's *almost* 11 o'clock.
間もなくクリスマスシーズンがやってくる Christmas time is *just around the corner*.

まもの 魔物 (悪魔) demon ◯, devil ◯; (悪霊) evil spirit ◯

まもり 守り defense, protection /
彼らは敵の攻撃に備えて海岸の守りを固めた They strengthened their coastal *defense* against enemy attack. / 相手チームは守りが堅い Our opponent has *a* tight *defense*.

◆私たちのチームは守りについた Our team *took the field*.

‖守り神 a guardian deity [angel]

まもる 守る

❶【保護する】(攻撃などから) defend; (危険や敵から) protect; (警護する) guard
危険から自分の身を守る *defend oneself* from danger

彼らは敵から国を守った They *defended* their country against their enemies.

我々が自然環境を汚染や破壊から守るのは当然のことだ It is right that we should *protect* the environment from [against] pollution and destruction.

このせっけんはあなたの手を様々な雑菌から守ります This soap *protects* your hands from [against] various kinds of germs.

シークレットサービスは大統領を危険から守っている The Secret Service *guards* the president against danger.

◆彼はふだんレフトを守っている He usually *plays left.* / 将人がゴールを守っている(→ゴールキーパーだ) Masato is the goalkeeper.

❷【履行する・従う】(約束などを) keep*; (規則・法律などを) obey, observe, follow

法律を守る *keep* [*obey, observe*] the law / スケジュールを守る *keep* [*stick*] *to one's schedule* / 規則を守る *obey* [*follow*] *the rule(s); go by* the rulebook / スピード制限を守る *observe* the speed limit

彼は約束を守る人だ He *keeps* his promise [*word*]. / He is a man of his word.

秘密を守ると約束してくれるかい Will you give your word to *keep* the secret?

◆彼は約束を守らなかった He *broke* [*was false to*] his promise [*word*]. / 順番を守ってよ(→自分の番を待て) *Wait* your turn. / 彼女はいつも約束の時間をきちんと守る She *is* always *punctual* for appointments.

❸【維持する】keep*, maintain
治安を守る *keep* the peace

彼女は沈黙を守った She「*maintained* her silence [*kept* her silence, *kept silent*].

その村の人々は日本古来の伝統芸能を守っている The villagers *maintain* traditional Japanese performing arts.

◆常にトップの座を守る(→トップでいる)には大変な努力が必要だ It requires hard work to *stay* on top all the time.

まやかし (いんちき) fake, counterfeit ―まやかしの false, fake / そんなまやかしの数字にだまされるな Don't be tricked by such *false* figures.

まやく 麻薬 drug, 《口語的》dope, 《主に米》narcotics ‖麻薬をやる take [use, 《俗語》do] *drugs* / 彼は麻薬をやっている He is on *drugs*. / 麻薬の運び屋 a *drug* runner

‖麻薬常用者 a drug user [addict] / 麻薬中毒 drug [narcotic] addiction / 麻薬取締官 a narcotics agent / 麻薬取締法 the Narcotic Control Act [Law] / 麻薬密売人 a drug [dope] dealer / 麻薬乱用 drug abuse

関連語 覚醒(かくせい)剤 a stimulant (drug),《口語的》speed / コカイン cocaine / 大麻 hemp; (マリファナ) marijuana / ヘロイン heroin

まゆ¹ 眉 eyebrow, brow / まゆを描く pencil *one's eyebrows* / 彼はまゆが濃い[薄い] He has thick [thin] *eyebrows*.

‖まゆ墨 an eyebrow pencil

慣用表現 彼はその知らせを聞いてもまゆひとつ動かさなかった(→平然としていた) He *remained calm* even when he heard the news. / 彼女は彼の返事にまゆをつり上げた(→非常に怒った) She *got very angry* at his answer. / 母はそれを見てまゆをひそめた My mother *frowned* [*knitted her (eye)brows*] when she saw it.

まゆ² 繭 cocoon / 繭から糸を取る reel silk off *cocoons*

まゆげ 眉毛 eyebrow ⇒ まゆ(眉)

まゆつば 眉唾 彼の話はまゆつばものだ(→信用できない)His story *is not believable.*/ (→割り引いて考える)His story *must be taken with a grain* [*pinch*] *of salt*.

まよい 迷い (ためらい) hesitation; (妄想) delusion / 彼女の言葉で迷いからさめた I woke up from a delusion because of her words. / I was disillusioned by her words. / 彼と結婚すべきかどうかいくらか迷いがある I still have some *hesitation* about marrying him.

まよう 迷う

❶【道に迷う】lose* *one's* way, get* [be] lost; (はぐれる) stray
私は森の奥深く入っていって道に迷った I walked deep into the woods and *got lost*.

小鳥がうちの台所に迷い込んできた A little bird *strayed* into our kitchen.

❷【当惑する】be doubtful, be in doubt, be at a loss; (ためらう) hesitate, waver
彼女はテストのために何をしたらいいか迷っている She *is doubtful* (*about*) what she should do for the test.

迷ったときは担当の人に聞きなさい When you *are in doubt*, ask the person in charge.

彼の思いがけない質問に驚いて言葉に迷った Surprised by his unexpected question, I *was at a loss* for words.

彼は大学か就職かで迷った He *wavered* between college and a job.

彼女は彼のプロポーズを受けようか断ろうか迷った She *wavered* between accepting and refusing his proposal.

◆彼女は次に何をすべきか迷った(→分からなかった) She *didn't know* what to do next.

❸【魅せられる・誘惑される】
彼は彼女の美しさに迷った He *was fascinated*

[*charmed*] by her beauty.

まよけ 魔除け (お守り) talisman [C], charm [C], amulet [C]
◆彼はいつも魔よけにそのお守りを持ち歩いている He always carries the charm with him *to protect himself from harm*.

まよこ 真横 真横から見た像 a statue *viewed directly from the side*

まよなか 真夜中 the middle of the night; (午前0時) midnight [U] ➾ よる(夜) [図版] ∥渋滞を予想して彼らは真夜中に出発した Expecting heavy traffic, they started *in the middle of the night*. / 彼女の赤ちゃんは真夜中過ぎに生まれた Her baby arrived just *after midnight*.

マヨネーズ mayonnaise [méiənèiz] [U] ∥レタスにマヨネーズをかける use [put] *mayonnaise* on lettuce

まよわす 迷わす ❶【当惑させる】 puzzle [他]
◆彼はよく人を迷わす珍説を吐く He often comes out with *puzzling* odd theories.
❷【誤らせる】 mislead* [他] ∥競馬では欲に心を迷わすと損をする You will lose money on horse racing if you *are misled* by your desire for money.

マラソン ⚠ marathon (race) [C] (❖英語の marathon は 42.195 km のマラソン競技にしか使わない. 学校のマラソン大会のような場合は a long-distance race (長距離レース) などという) ∥マラソンに出る run *a marathon*; take part in *a marathon*
‖マラソン走者 a marathon runner

マラリア malaria [məléəriə] [U] ∥マラリアにかかる contract [be infected with] *malaria*
‖マラリア患者 a malarial patient

まり 毬 ball [C] ∥まりを投げる[つく] throw [bounce] *a ball*

マリア 〖キリスト教〗(聖母マリア) the Virgin Mary, the Blessed [blésid] Virgin (Mary)

マリネ ⚠marinade [C][U] (❖日本語はフランス語の mariné から)
◆マスのマリネ *marinated* trout

マリファナ marijuana, marihuana [mæ̀riwɑ́ːnə] [U] ∥マリファナを吸う smoke *marijuana*

まりも 毬藻 a *marimo*, spherical moss

まりょく 魔力 magic [U]; (魅力) charm [C]

マリンスポーツ ⚠ (水上スポーツ) water sports, watersports (❖英語の marine sports はあまり一般的ではない)

マリンバ marimba [C]

まる 丸 circle [C] ∥丸を描く draw *a circle* / 二重丸 a double *circle* / 三重丸 *a* triple *circle* / 正しい答えの番号を丸で囲みなさい Enclose the number of the correct answer with *a circle*. / *Circle* the number of the correct answer.

まる- 丸- full ∥彼らは箱根でまる2日過ごした They spent *a full two days* in Hakone. (❖形容詞が付くと two days をひとまとまりのものと考えて a を付けるのがふつう. two full days ともいう) / 観光にまる1日かけるのはもったいない It's not worthwhile to spend a *full* [*whole*] day sightseeing.

まるあらい 丸洗い このセーターは丸洗いできる This sweater *is washable*.

まるあんき 丸暗記 rote memorization [U]
—丸暗記する learn* ... by heart [rote] ∥私はこれらの文を丸暗記した I *learned* these sentences *by heart*.

まるい 丸い・円い round; (円形の) circular; (球形の) spherical, globular —丸く (輪になって) in a circle; (円満に) peacefully, smoothly
丸いテーブル a *round* table
彼は丸い顔をしている He has a *round* face.
私たちは机を丸く並べた We arranged the desks *in a circle* [*ring*].
彼女は二人のけんかを丸く収めた She settled the quarrel between the two *peacefully*.
◆先が丸くなった鉛筆 a *blunt* pencil / 背中を丸くする *hunch up one's* back / 猫が縁側で丸くなっている The cat is lying *curled up* on the porch. / 彼は年齢とともに性格が丸くなった He *mellowed* with age. / He *developed a gentler personality* with age. / 彼はその光景を目を丸くして(→目を大きく開いて)見た He stared at the sight *with his eyes wide open*.

まるうつし 丸写し copy [C] —丸写しする copy [他] ∥彼は試験中に隣の生徒の答えを丸写しした He *copied* the answers from the student next to him during the exam.

まるがお 丸顔 round face [C] —丸顔の round-faced ∥彼は丸顔だ He has *a round face*.

まるがかえ 丸抱え そのパーティーの費用は会社の丸抱えだった(→会社がすべて支払った) The company *paid all* the party expenses.

まるがり 丸刈り 頭を丸刈りにしてもらった I *had* my hair *cropped closely*. / 彼は頭を丸刈りにしている He *has close-cropped* hair.

まるき 丸木 log [C] ‖丸木橋 a log bridge / 丸木舟 a canoe, a dugout

マルキシズム Marxism [U]

マルク mark [C], Deutschmark [C] (❖ドイツの貨幣単位; 《略語》DM)

まるくび 丸首 丸首のセーター a *round-necked* [*crew-neck*] sweater

まるごし 丸腰 —丸腰の (武装していない) unarmed

まるごと 丸ごと 魚をまるごと(→骨ごと)食べる eat a fish, *bones and all* / リンゴをまるごと(→皮をむかずに)食べる eat an apple *without peeling* it / その子はケーキをまるごと食べた The child ate the cake *whole*.

まるぞん 丸損 —丸損する suffer a total loss

まるた 丸太 log [C] ∥木をのこぎりで切って丸太にする saw a tree into *logs*
‖丸太小屋 a log cabin [house]

まるだし 丸出し その男はなまりを丸出しにして話した The man spoke *with* [*in*] *a broad provincial accent*. / 彼女は背中丸出しの服を着ていた She wore a dress *with her back exposed* [*bare*]. / 彼は私に対して敵意丸出しだった He *showed open hostility* to me. / He *was openly hostile* to me.

マルチ ‖マルチ商法 multilevel marketing [merchandising], pyramid selling / マルチ人間 a versatile person

マルチメディア multimedia ‖マルチメディアパソコン a *multimedia* personal computer / マルチメディアの時代が幕をあけた The age of *multimedia* has dawned.

まるっきり 丸っ切り（少しも…ない）not ... at all;（完全に）completely, entirely ‖彼はドイツ語をまるっきり話せない He *can't* speak German *at all*. / 私の考えはあなたのとはまるっきり違う My opinion is *completely* [*entirely*] different from yours.

まるっこい 丸っこい 丸っこい字 a *roundish* character

まるつぶれ 丸潰れ パーティーの準備で1日丸つぶれになった（→まる1日かかった）Preparations for the party *took up a whole day*. / 私の面目は丸つぶれになった I *lost face completely*.

まるで
❶【全く】（少しも…ない）not ... at all;（完全に）completely, entirely

あなたの言うことがまるで分からない I *can't* understand what you say *at all*.

私の見解は君のとはまるで違う My ideas are *completely* [*entirely*] different from yours.

◆彼は次に何をすべきかまるで見当がつかなかった He *didn't have the least* [*slightest*] *idea* of what to do next.

❷【あたかも】as if [though], (just) like ... (❖as if [though]の後ろには仮定法がくることが多いが, 実現の可能性が高い場合は直接法がくる)

彼はまるで何でも知っているような口ぶりだ He talks *as if* he knew everything.

私はまるで何もかもをスローモーションで見ているような気がした I felt *as if* I was seeing it in slow motion.

彼はまるで老人のような話し方をする He talks *as if* he were [was] an old man.

それはまるでオレンジのような味がする It tastes *like* an orange.

スピーチコンテストで1位になるなんてまるで夢のようです Winning first place in the speech contest is *just like* a dream.

彼女はまるで天使のようだ She is *just like* an angel.

それはまるで本物のように見えた That looked *just like* the real thing.

まるのみ 丸飲み・丸呑み 蛇は卵を丸飲みした The snake *swallowed* the egg *whole*. / 彼らは彼女の話を丸飲みした He *believed everything* she said.

まるはだか 丸裸 ──丸裸の［で］stark naked ‖子供たちは丸裸でプールで遊んでいた The children were playing in the swimming pool *stark naked*. ◆彼はギャンブルで丸裸になった（→全財産を失った）He *lost all his fortune* by gambling.

まるばつしき ○×式 ○×式テスト a *true-false* test;（→多肢選択式の）a *multiple-*

choice test

マルひ マル秘 マル秘書類 *confidential* papers

まるぼうず 丸坊主 ──丸坊主の close-cropped ‖丸坊主の頭 a *close-cropped* head / 彼は頭を丸坊主にしている He has *close-cropped* hair. ◆頭を丸坊主にしてもらった I *had* my hair *cropped closely*.

まるまる¹ 丸まる curl [roll] up ‖彼女は丸まって眠った She *curled up* and fell asleep.

まるまる² 丸々 ❶【よく太った】丸々太った赤ん坊 a *plump* [*chubby*] baby / 彼は丸々とした顔をしている He has a *round* face.
❷【全部】whole;（完全な）complete ‖まるまる1年彼と会っていない I haven't seen him for a *whole* year. / 彼らはその取り引きでまる損をした They suffered a *complete* [*total*] loss on the deal.

まるみ 丸み・円み roundness ◆丸みのある葉 a *roundish* leaf / やすりで板の端に丸みをつける *round off* the edge of a board with a file / 彼は年とともに人柄に丸みがでてきた（→円熟してきた）He *has mellowed* with age.

まるみえ 丸見え この部屋は通りから中が丸見えだ People *can see everything* in this room from the street. / The interior of this room *is fully exposed to view* from the street.

まるめこむ 丸め込む wheedle ‖母を丸め込んでパソコンを買ってもらった I *wheedled* [*cajoled, coaxed*] my mother into buying me a personal computer.

まるめる 丸める round;（体を）curl (oneself) up;（巻く）roll;（くしゃくしゃにする）crumple ‖卒業証書を丸める *roll up* one's diploma / 彼はその手紙をくしゃくしゃに丸めた He *crumpled* the letter *up* (*into a ball*). / 彼は唇を丸めて口笛を吹いた He *rounded* his lips and whistled. / 猫はソファーの上で体を丸めた The cat *curled up* on the sofa. / 彼は背中を丸めて歩く癖（き）がある He has a habit of walking 「*with his shoulders rounded* [*with a stoop*].
◆頭を丸める（→そる）*shave* one's *head*

マルメロ 【植物】quince

まるもうけ 丸儲け clear profit ‖株で40万円丸もうけした I *made a clear profit* of 400,000 yen on stocks.

まるやき 丸焼き 豚の丸焼き a *barbecued* [*roasted*] pig; a pig *roasted whole* / 子羊を丸焼きにする *roast* a lamb *whole*; *barbecue* a lamb

まるやけ 丸焼け 昨夜の火事で彼の家は丸焼けになった His house *burned down* in the fire last night. / His house *was completely* [*totally*] *destroyed* by last night's fire.

まれ 稀・希 ──まれな rare;（めったにない）uncommon;（ふつうでない）unusual ──まれに rarely, seldom; uncommonly ‖彼女はまれにみる美人だ She is an *uncommonly* beautiful woman. / She is a woman of *rare* [*uncommon, singular*] beauty. / 彼女

がスカートをはくのはまれだ It is *rare* for her to wear a skirt. / 彼はまれにみる天才だ He is *uncommonly* [*exceptionally*] bright. / 彼が遅刻するのはまれだ He is *rarely* [*seldom*] late for school.

マレーシア Malaysia —マレーシア人 Malaysian ⓒ —マレーシア語 Malay ⓤ —マレーシア(人[語])の Malaysian

マロニエ 〖植物〗horse chestnut (tree)ⓒ

まろやか —まろやかな mild (↔strong), smooth, mellow ∥まろやかなチーズ a *mild* [*mellow*] cheese / このワインはとてもまろやかだ This wine is very *mellow*.

まわしもの 回し者 spy ⓒ

まわしよみ 回し読み 私たちはその本を回し読みした We *took turns reading* the book.

まわす 回す

❶【回転させる】turn ⓗ; (速く) spin* ⓗ ∥かぎ[ノブ]を回す *turn* a key [knob] / こまを回す *spin* a top

取っ手を左に回しなさい *Turn* the handle to the left.

🅔「こちらの方向に回すんですか」「いいえ, その逆です」"Do you *turn* it this way?" "No, the other way."

❷【順に送る】pass ⓗ; (手渡す) hand ⓗ

このパンフレットをほかのみんなに回してください Please *pass* [*hand*] this pamphlet *on* to everybody else.

お金を集めるのに帽子が回された A hat *was passed around* to collect money.

◆この仕事は後に回そう Let's *put* that work *off until later*.

🅔「塩を回してくださいませんか」「はいはい, どうぞ」"*Will* you *pass* (me) the salt, please?" "Of course, here you are."

❸【移動させる】send* ⓗ; (転任させる) transfer ⓗ

とても忙しいので5人ほど回して We're very busy. *Send* (*around*) about five people.

車をホテルに回して社長を乗せてください Please *send* a car (*around*) to the hotel to pick up the president.

彼女は経理部に回された She *was transferred* to the accounting department.

しばらくお待ちください. 担当の者に電話をお回しします Wait a minute. I'll *transfer* this call to the person in charge.

❹【その他】

旅行を取りやめてその金をパソコン購入の費用に回した I canceled my trip and *put* the money *aside for* buying a personal computer.

彼は彼女の腰に手を回した He *put* his arm *around* her *waist*. / He *took* her *around the waist*.

あいつを敵に回すとやっかいだ It would be tough to *be* his *enemy*.

まわた 真綿 floss (silk) ⓤ ◆彼らは真綿で首をしめるように(→遠回しにじわじわと)私を責めた They attacked me *indirectly bit by bit*.

まわり¹ 周り (外周) circumference ⓒ ⓤ; (周辺) surroundings; (環境) environment ⓒ ⓤ; (付近) neighborhood ⓒ ➡しゅうい

その島の周りは約20キロある The island is about twenty kilometers in *circumference*.

その建物は周りにうまく溶け込んでいる The building blends in well with *its surroundings*.

弟は周りに影響されやすい My brother is easily influenced by *his environment*.

私の家の周りには本屋がない There are no bookstores in my *neighborhood*.

◆彼女は首の周りにウールのスカーフを巻いていた She was wearing a woolen scarf *around* her neck. / 地球は太陽の周りを回る The earth moves *around* the sun. / 私たちは周りの人々とうまくやっていかなければいけない We have to relate to *other people around us*.

まわり² 回り

私たちは公園をひと回り散歩した We took *a short turn* in the park. / We walked *once around* the park.

強風のため火の回りが速かった(→火はすぐに広がった) *The fire spread quickly* because of the strong wind.

おじのところへ年始回りに行った I went to my uncle's on *my round of New Year's calls*. / I paid *a New Year's visit* to my uncle's.

彼はフランクフルト回りでパリへ行った He went to Paris *via* [*by way of*] Frankfurt.

この酒は回りが速い This liquor *works fast*.

私は姉とひと回り(→12歳)違う I'm *12 years younger than* my sister.

まわりくどい 回りくどい, circular 回りくどい説明 a *roundabout* [*circular*] explanation / 彼女は回りくどい言い方をした She talked in a *roundabout* [*circular*] way.

まわりまわって 回り回って 回り回ってようやくホテルに着いた *After many detours*, I finally reached the hotel. / 回り回って結局その仕事は彼のところに持ち込まれた The job eventually found its way to him *after going through everyone else*.

まわりみち 回り道 detour ⓒ, roundabout way [route] ⓒ ∥彼は回り道をして私を車で送ってくれた He made *a detour* to drive me home. / 私たちは回り道をしてここに来た We came here by *a roundabout way*. / We took *a roundabout way* to come here.

まわりもち 回り持ち ➡もちまわり

まわる 回る

❶【回転する】turn ⓗ; revolve ⓗ, rotate ⓗ; spin* ⓗ

> turn:「回る」を表す最も一般的な語. 1回転未満から複数回の回転まで用いられる.
> revolve, rotate: 本来 revolve はほかの物の周りを, rotate は自分を中心として回転することを意味するが, 区別されないことも多い.
> spin: 高速で回転すること.

月は地球の周りを回る The moon *turns* [*re-*

volves, moves, goes] around the Earth.
地球は地軸を中心に回る The Earth *rotates* on its axis.
そのバレリーナはつま先でくるくると回った The ballerina *spun around* on her toe.
世界は自分を中心に回っていると彼は思っている He thinks the world *revolves around* him.
◆物がみんな回って見えた Everything *swam* before my eyes. / 土井は一塁を回って二塁へ向かっています Doi *has rounded* first and now is heading for second. / 何千もの人工衛星が地球の周りを回っている Thousands of satellites *are orbiting* the Earth.

❷【巡回する】make* a round; (訪ねて回る) make the rounds; (周遊する) make a tour; (見て回る) look around
訪問して回る make *a round* of visits
彼は得意先を回った He *made the rounds* of his customers.
我々は2週間でヨーロッパを回った We *made a tour* of Europe in two weeks.
彼女は新しい家を探して街を見て回った She *looked around* the city for a new house.
◆何人かの刑事が行方不明の少年のことを聞き回っている Some detectives *are asking around* about the missing boy. / 彼は車のセールスに一軒一軒回った He *went from door to door* trying to sell cars.

❸【回り道をする】go* around; (立ち寄る) drop by, drop in
銀行に回ってから帰宅した I 「*went around* to [*dropped in* at] the bank on my way home.
◆彼はパリからロンドンを回って帰ってきた He returned home from Paris *via* [*by way of*] London.

❹【移る】
裏口に回ってください Please *come around to* the back door.
私は裏口に回った I *went around to* the back door.
私たちは敵の背後に回った We *moved around to* the enemy's rear.
彼の順番が回ってきた His turn *came (around)*.
私は彼の補佐役に回る(→補佐役になる)つもりだ I'm going *to be* a helper for him.
つきが回ってきた My luck *has turned*.

❺【行き届く】take* effect
ウイスキーが回ってきた The whiskey has begun to *take effect.* / I'm getting drunk on the whiskey.
毒が回った The poison *has taken effect*.
◆そこまで気が回らなかったよ I couldn't think *of* that. / グラスは(全員に)回りましたか Does everyone *have* a glass?

❻【時刻が】
3時半を回ったばかりだ It *has* just *turned* half past three.
もう夜中の12時を回っているよ It's already *past* midnight.
ことわざ 急がば回れ ⇨いそぐ

まわれみぎ 回れ右 《米》 about-face ⓒ, 《英》 about-turn ⓒ // 回れ右をする do *an about-face* [*about-turn*]
◆(号令で)回れ, 右! *About face* [*turn*]!

まん¹ 万 ten thousand(✦英語には「万」に当たる単語はないので「10×1,000」と考える)
1万を超える人の署名が集まった More than *ten thousand* people signed the petition.
◆5万5千 *fifty-five thousand* / 100万 *a [one] million* / 50万 *half a million* / 何万もの[数十万もの]人々 *tens [hundreds] of thousands* of people / 1万分の1 *a ten-thousandth*
慣用表現 彼が生きて戻る可能性は万に一つもなかった *There was not the slightest possibility* that he would come back alive.

まん² 満 息子は満10歳だ My son is *10 years old*.(✦英米では常に満年齢で数えるため特別な表現はない) / 彼らが結婚してから満5年になる It has been *a full* [*whole*] *five years* since they got married.
慣用表現 満を持す (→時が熟すのを待つ) *wait until the time is ripe*; (→十分準備する) *prepare fully*

まんいち 万一 万一の場合は (→緊急の場合)*in case of an emergency*; (→最悪の事態になったら)*if worst comes to the worst* / 万一の可能性 an *outside* chance / 万一に備えて複数のクレジットカードを持っていったほうがいい You had better take more than one credit card *(just) in case.* / 母は万一に備えていつもいくらかのお金を貯金している My mother always has some money put away *for a rainy day.* / 万一ぐあいの悪いことが起こったらこのボタンを押しなさい *If* anything should go wrong, just press this button.

まんいん 満員 —満員の full, crowded // そのホールは満員だった The hall was *full.* / The hall was *filled* [*packed*] *to capacity*.(✦capacityは「収容能力, 定員」の意味)
◆満員の観客 a *capacity* audience / 列車は通勤客で満員だった The train *was jammed* with commuters. / 展覧会場は訪れた人たちで超満員だった The exhibition hall was *jam-packed* [*overcrowded*] with visitors.
‖満員電車 a jammed [packed] train

まんえつ 満悦 その女の子はおなかいっぱいケーキを食べてすっかりご満悦の様子だった The girl looked *deeply satisfied* because she ate cake until she was full.

まんえん 蔓延 spread ⓤ, prevalence ⓤ —蔓延する spread* ⓘ, be prevalent // エイズの蔓延を防ぐ prevent [check] *the spread* of AIDS / インフルエンザがクラス中に蔓延した Influenza *has spread* throughout the class. / この病気は中央アフリカで蔓延していた This disease *was prevalent* in Central Africa. ◆政府内には汚職が蔓延している The government *is rife* with corruption.

まんが 漫画 (本) comic (book) ⓒ; (続き漫画) comic strip ⓒ; (政治漫画) cartoon ⓒ (✦「アニメーション」の意味もある); (風刺漫画)

caricature ⇨ 場面・状況別会話 p.1706
1コマ漫画 *a single-frame cartoon* / 4コマ漫画 *a four-frame comic strip* / 漫画を描く draw *a cartoon* [*comic strip*] / テレビで漫画を見る watch *a cartoon* on TV / 子供は漫画(本)を読むのが好きだ Children like reading *comics* [*comic books*].

‖漫画映画 an animated film, a cartoon film, a (movie) cartoon / 漫画家 a cartoonist, a comic artist;(風刺の)a caricaturist / 漫画雑誌 a comic magazine / 漫画欄 the comic section

漫画は若者から大人まで日本で広く読まれています。通勤電車の中で漫画本に熱中しているスーツ姿の人を見かけることがよくあります。多くの漫画がアニメ化されており、海外に輸出されているものもあります。また、なるべく多くの人々に簡単に理解してもらおうと歴史や経済を分かりやすく説明した漫画本もあります。
Comic books called *manga* are very popular in Japan not only among young people but also among adults. You can often see people in business suits absorbed in reading comics on the train. Many comics have been made into animated films, and some of them are exported to other countries. There are also comic books in which history or economics is explained in an easy style so that many people can understand the topics more easily.

まんかい 満開 満開になる come into *full bloom* / バラの花が満開だ The roses are *in full bloom*. / The roses are *at their best*.
まんがいち 万が一 ⇨ まんいち
まんき 満期 その債券は2008年で満期になる The bond *matures* in 2008. / この定期預金は10年満期だ This time deposit *matures* in 10 years.
‖満期日 the due date, the date of maturity
まんきつ 満喫 私たちはフランス料理を満喫した We *enjoyed* French food *to the full*. / アルプスの美しい風景を満喫した I *enjoyed* the beautiful scenery of the Alps *fully*.
まんげきょう 万華鏡 kaleidoscope [kəláidəskòup]
まんげつ 満月 full moon ◯ ‖満月の夜 a night with *a full moon*
◆今夜は満月だ The moon *is full* tonight.
マンゴー 〖植物〗 mango ◯ (複〜(e)s)
まんさい 満載 その船は救援物資を満載していた The ship *was fully loaded with* relief supplies. / この辞書は挿絵を満載している This dictionary *is full of* illustrations.
まんざい 漫才 *manzai*, a comic dialogue by two or more comedians
‖漫才師(2人組の)a comic duo;(1人の)a cross-talk comedian

漫才は、ふつう2人の漫才師によるかけ合い演芸の一種です。冗談やしゃれをテンポよく飛ばして客を笑わせます。
Manzai is a kind of performing art of comic dialogues usually carried out by two comedians. They toss rapid-fire jokes and puns back and forth to make the audience laugh.

まんざら 満更 彼の計画もまんざら悪くはない His plan *isn't altogether* bad. / そのうわさはまんざらうそでもない The rumor *is not completely* false. / 彼女は雅人にデートに誘われてまんざらでもなさそうだった She *didn't look altogether unwilling* when she was asked to go out on a date by Masato.
まんしつ 満室 そのホテルは満室だった There were *no vacancies* at the hotel. / The hotel was *full up*. / 満室《掲示》*No Vacancy* [*Vacancies*]
まんしゃ 満車 駐車場は満車だった The parking lot was *full* [*packed*]. / 満車《掲示》*Full*
まんじゅう 饅頭 a *manju*, a steamed bun with a bean-paste filling

まんじゅうは和菓子の一種で、ふつう、中に甘い小豆あんの入った蒸し菓子です。皮には小麦粉や米が使われ、また中に詰めるあんにもいろいろな豆を用います。
A *manju*, a kind of Japanese-style confectionery, is a steamed bun usually stuffed with sweet red-bean paste. Flour or rice is used to make the crust and a variety of beans are used for the filling.

まんじょう 満場 満場の観客が立ち上がってその歌手に拍手をした The whole audience stood up and clapped for the singer. / 委員たちは満場一致で彼の提案を可決した The committee members decided *unanimously* to approve the proposal. / The committee members were *unanimous* in approving the proposal.
マンション ⚠ (分譲マンション)《米》condominium ◯,《米口語の》condo ◯, flat ◯;(賃貸マンション) apartment (house) ◯,《英》flat ◯ ❖英語のmansionは大邸宅の意味。ただし《英》では「…マンション」の意味で固有名詞に付けて … Mansionsの形で使われる)‖ワンルームマンション《米》*a studio apartment*;《英》*a studio flat* / 彼はマンションに住んでいる He lives in *a condominium* [*an apartment*].
まんじり 昨夜はまんじりともできなかった(→一睡もできなかった)I *didn't「get a wink of sleep* [*sleep a wink*] last night.
まんしん¹ 満身 満身の力をこめて with *all one's strength* / 彼は満身創痍(ｿｳｲ)だった He *was covered with injuries*. / He *was injured all over*.
まんしん² 慢心 conceit ◯, pride ◯
◆彼は自らの成功に慢心している He *is conceited* about his success.
まんせい 慢性 ──慢性の chronic ‖彼は慢性の気管支炎だ He is suffering from *chronic bronchitis*. / その会社は慢性的な赤字に苦しん

まんせき

でいた The company suffered from *chronic* deficits. / 不況が慢性化している The recession *has become chronic*.
∥慢性病 a chronic disease / 慢性病患者 a chronic invalid

まんせき 満席 満席《掲示》House Full; Full House / そのホールは満席だった The hall was *full*. / The hall was *filled [packed] to capacity*.

まんぜんと 漫然と (当てもなく) aimlessly;(ぼんやりと) vacantly ∥彼は漫然と時を過ごした He spent his time *aimlessly*. / He *idled (away) his time*. / 彼女は漫然と海を見ていた She was looking *vacantly* at the sea.

まんぞく 満足
❶【満ち足りていること】satisfaction Ⓤ, contentment Ⓤ ――満足な satisfactory ――満足する be satisfied, be content(ed), be happy, be gratified
私は自分の人生に満足している I *am satisfied [content, contented] with* my life.
彼は試験の結果に満足だった He *was happy about [with]* his exam results.
新しい秘書は仕事に満足している様子です The new secretary seems to *be happy with* her job.
彼は息子の成功にとても満足した He *was most gratified at [by, with]* his son's success.
彼女は満足した顔つきでほほえんだ She smiled with a *satisfied [contented]* look.
警察は我々に満足のいく説明をしなかった The police didn't give us a *satisfactory* explanation.
すべてご満足いただけておりますか Is everything *satisfactory* to you?
彼女はボランティア活動で大きな満足を得ている She gets great *satisfaction* from her volunteer activities.
私共はすべてのお客様に十分ご満足いただけるように努力しております We're trying our best to give full *satisfaction* to all our customers.
僕らは満足のいく結論に達した We came to a *satisfactory* conclusion.
❷【十分なこと・適切なこと】――満足な (十分な) enough, sufficient;(きちんとした) decent ――満足に enough, well, sufficiently;(適切に) properly
きのうから満足な食事をしていない (→十分食べていない) I haven't eaten *enough* since yesterday.
彼は満足な服を一着も持っていない He doesn't have any *decent* clothes.
昨夜は満足に眠れなかった I didn't sleep *well [enough]* last night.
その子は字も満足に書けなかった The child couldn't even write *properly*.
◆彼女は五体満足な(→健康で正常な)子を産んだ She had a *healthy and normal* baby.
∥満足感 a feeling of satisfaction [contentment]

まんタン 満タン 満タンにしてください *Fill it [her] up*, please. / 満タンです The tank is *full*.

まんだん 漫談 (大衆演芸) comic monologue Ⓒ;(とりとめのない話) idle [small] talk Ⓤ ∥漫談家 a comic storyteller

マンチェスター Manchester(❖英国の都市)

まんちょう 満潮 high [full] tide Ⓤ ∥満潮時に at *high [full] tide* / 満潮は午後3時だ *High tide* is at 3 p.m. / *The tide is high* at 3 p.m.

マンツーマン ――マンツーマンの one-to-one;(スポーツ) man-to-man ∥マンツーマンのディフェンス a *man-to-man* defense / マンツーマンで英語を教える teach English on a *one-to-one* basis

まんてん¹ 満点 ❶【最高点】full marks ∥彼は英語で満点を取った He got 「*full marks [a perfect score]* in English.
◆私は150点満点で100点取った I got 100 points out of 150.
❷【申し分のないこと】――満点の perfect, excellent ∥彼の演技は満点だった His performance was *perfect [excellent]*. / あの店はサービス満点だ The service is *perfect [excellent]* at that store. / They give *perfect [excellent]* service at that store.
◆チーズは栄養満点だ Cheese is 「*full of [rich in] nourishment*.

まんてん² 満天 満天の星の下で私たちはキャンプをした We camped beneath *a sky full of stars*.

マント ⚠cloak Ⓒ(❖日本語はフランス語のmanteauから)

マンドリン mandolin [mǽndəlìn] Ⓒ ∥マンドリンを弾く play *the mandolin*
∥マンドリン奏者 a mandolinist

マントルピース mantelpiece Ⓒ

まんなか 真ん中 the middle, the center, the heart ――真ん中の middle
(兄弟の中で)真ん中の子 the *middle* child
川の真ん中に小さな島が2つある There are two small islands in *the middle* of the river.
彼女は髪を真ん中で分けている She parts her hair in *the middle*.
50円玉は真ん中に穴があいている Fifty yen coins have a hole in *the center*.
彼は京都の真ん中に住んでいる He lives in *the center [heart]* of Kyoto.
◆学校は私の家と彼の家のちょうど真ん中あたりにある Our school is *halfway [midway]* between my house and hers.

マンネリ ⚠stereotype Ⓒ(❖「マンネリ」の語源である英語の mannerism は「(言葉・動作などの)癖(ᕽ)」,「(芸術などの)型にはまった技法」の意味)
――マンネリの (型にはまった) stereotyped;(お決まりの) routine ∥その式典はマンネリ化してしまっている The ceremony *has become routine*.
◆マンネリを抜け出す get out of *a rut*(❖rutは「マンネリに陥った状態」を指す)

まんねんどこ 万年床 彼は万年床だ(→ふとんを上げない) He *never puts away his futon*.

まんねんひつ 万年筆 fountain pen Ⓒ ∥万年

筆で書く write with *a fountain pen* / 万年筆にインクを入れる fill [refill] *a fountain pen*

まんねんゆき 万年雪 perpetual snow ⓤ

マンハッタン Manhattan(❖米国ニューヨーク市の中心地区)

まんびき 万引き (行為) shoplifting ⓤ; (人) shoplifter ⓒ ──**万引きする** shoplift ⓘ / 万引きの常習犯 *a habitual shoplifter* / その子は万引きでつかまった The child got caught for *shoplifting*.

まんびょう 万病 かぜは万病の元 Colds may develop into *all kinds of illness*.

まんぴょう 満票 the votes of all present / 彼は満票を獲得した He received *the votes of all present*.
◆彼は満票で(→全員一致で)当選した He was elected *unanimously*.

まんぷく 満腹 full stomach ⓒ ──**満腹の** full / 満腹時に激しい運動をしないほうがいい You shouldn't do hard exercise *on a full stomach*. / 満腹だ I'm *full*.
∥満腹感 a feeling of fullness

まんべんなく 満遍なく (均等に) equally; (全体に) all over / 試験に合格するには全教科をまんべんなく勉強しなければならない You must study every subject *equally* to pass the examination. / テーブルにペンキをまんべんなく塗った I painted the table *all over*.

マンボ mambo ⓤⓒ / マンボを踊る dance *the mambo*

マンホール manhole ⓒ / マンホールのふた a *manhole* cover

まんぽけい 万歩計 pedometer ⓒ

まんまえ 真ん前 その車は私の家の真ん前に止まった The car stopped *right* [*just*] *in front of* my house. / 駅の真ん前に大きなビルが建った A big building was built *right* [*just*] *across from* the railroad station. (❖

right [*just*] *across from* …は「道路をはさんで…の前に」の意味)

まんまと べてん師にまんまと(→すっかり)だまされた I was *nicely* [*completely*] taken in by the swindler. / 泥棒はまんまと(→首尾よく)逃走した The thief got away *successfully*.

まんまる 真ん丸 perfect circle ⓒ

まんまるい 真ん丸い perfectly round
◆真ん丸い月 a *full* moon

まんまん 満々 彼は自信満々だった He was *full of self-confidence*. / 彼女はやる気満々だ She is *full of drive* [*pep*]. / 彼は野心満々だ He is a person *of great ambition*.

まんめん 満面 彼女は喜色満面だ She *is all smiles*. / 彼は満面の笑みを浮かべて私たちを出迎えた He greeted us with *a big* [*broad*] *smile*.

マンモス mammoth ⓒ ∥ マンモス企業 a mammoth enterprise / マンモス大学 a mammoth university / マンモスタンカー a mammoth tanker / マンモス都市 a megalopolis

まんゆう 漫遊 tour ⓒ, pleasure trip ⓒ ──**漫遊する** tour ⓣ, make* a tour / ヨーロッパを漫遊する *tour* Europe
∥漫遊記 travel sketches

まんりき 万力 vise ⓒ

まんりょう 満了 expiration ⓤ, 《公式的》 termination ⓒⓤ ──**満了する** expire ⓘ / 大統領の任期は来月で満了になる The president's term (of office) *expires* next month. / 彼は任期満了により会長職から退いた He retired from the chairmanship at [on] *the expiration* of his term of office.

まんるい 満塁 満塁ホームラン *a grand slam*; *a bases-loaded home run* / ノーアウト満塁だ The bases are loaded [*full*] with no outs. (❖満塁のことを「フルベース」というのは和製英語)

ミ 【音楽】mi [míː] ⓤ ⓒ

み¹ 身

❶【身体】body ⓒ; (自分の体) oneself
身のこなしが軽い carry *oneself* easily / ベッドに身を投げ出す throw *oneself* on the bed 彼は木の陰に身を隠した He hid *himself* behind a tree.
彼女は社会事業に身も心もささげた She *devoted herself to* social work.
◆最新の流行に身を包んだ女性 a woman *dressed in* the latest fashion / 彼はいつもジーンズとTシャツを身につけている He always *wears* jeans and a T-shirt. / 窓から身を乗り出してはいけない Don't *hang* [*lean*] *out of* the window. / 彼女は彼に話しかけられると身を硬くした She *stiffened* as he spoke to her. / 私たちは1つの傘に身を寄せ合った We *huddled together* under one umbrella.

❷【自分】
身の潔白を証明する show [prove] *one's* innocence / 非難に身をさらす lay *oneself* open to criticism / 危険から身を守る defend *oneself* from danger
彼は酒とギャンブルで身を滅ぼした He ruined *himself* with alcohol and gambling.
言われたとおりにしたほうが身のためだぞ You'd better do as you are told *for your own sake*.

❸【立場・身分】place ⓒ
身の程を知る know *one's* place
彼女の身にもなってごらん Put yourself in her *place* [*shoes*].
◆晴れて自由の身となった I *was* formally *set free*.

❹【肉】meat ⓤ (❖通例, 食用の獣肉や果物などの果肉を指す); (皮・骨に対する) flesh ⓤ
赤身 lean *meat* / 脂身 fatty *meat* / カニ[クルミ]の身 crab [walnut] *meat; meat* of a crab [walnut] / 白身の魚 white *meat* fish /
身を骨から切り取る cut *the meat* off a bone
◆身の締まった魚 *firm* fish

❺【その他】
【身が入る】こううるさくちゃ勉強に身が入らないよ I can't study *hard* with all this noise. / 話に身が入る(→熱中する)につれて彼の声は大きくなった As he *got absorbed in* the talk, his voice grew louder.
【身がもたない】そんな無理を続けていたら身がもたない(→体をこわす)よ You'*ll ruin your health* if you keep working so hard.
【身に余る】おほめにあずかり身に余る光栄です To receive such praise is *more honor than* I deserve.
【身にしみる】(感謝する) be grateful; (感銘を受ける) be touched; (痛感する) keenly [fully] realize / 人の親切がつくづく身にしみた I *was* deeply *touched by* other people's kindness. / 健康のありがたさが身にしみて分かった I *keenly realized* the value of good health.
◆寒さが身にしみる The cold *pierces* me *to the bone*.

【身につく・つける】(習得する) acquire ⓔ, master ⓔ / 外国語の正しい発音を身につけるのは難しい It is hard to *acquire* [*master*] the right pronunciation of a foreign language. ◆身についた習慣はなかなか抜けない A *fixed* habit is not easily broken.

【身につまされる】彼女の家が地震の被害を受けたと聞いて身につまされた I *felt very sympathetic* [*My heart went out to* her] when I heard her house was damaged by the earthquake.

【身を入れる】(…に打ち込む) put* *one's* heart into …; (腰をすえる) settle down 「to … [to do] / 身を入れて働く「*put one's heart into* [*settle down to*] work / きょうは身を入れて授業を受けることができなかった I couldn't *settle down to* classes today.

【身を起こす】彼は一介(かい)のサラリーマンから身を起こし億万長者になった He *rose* from being an ordinary office worker to become a millionaire.

【身を固める】彼女はそろそろ身を固めても(→結婚して落ち着いても)いい年だ He's old enough to *get married and settle down*.

【身をこがす】彼女は彼への愛に身をこがしている She *is consumed with* love for him.

【身を立てる】彼女は作曲家として身を立てた She *established herself as* a composer.

【身を投げる】彼はがけから身を投げた He *killed himself by jumping* off a cliff. / He *jumped to his death* from a cliff.

【身を引く】(辞職する) resign ⓘ ⓔ; (引退する) retire ⓘ; (…から手を引く) back out of … / 彼は社長の職から身を引く覚悟だ He's determined to *resign* (his post) as president.

【身をもって】それは身をもって(→自分で)経験しなければ分からないだろう You won't be able to understand it unless you experience it *personally*. / 彼は人間の可能性を身をもって我々に示してくれた He showed us the potential of human beings *by personal example*.

【身を寄せる】当時私はおじの所に身を寄せていた I *stayed with* my uncle then.

慣用表現 今さら謝っても遅いよ, 身から出たさびだ(→自業自得だ) It's too late to apologize. *You asked for it*. / それは身に覚えがない(→何も知らない) I *don't know anything about* it. / それは身に覚えがある I *have nothing to do with* it. / 恥ずかしくて身の置き所がなかった I was so ashamed that I didn't know what to do with myself. / 今後の身の振り方(→何をするか)はまだ決めていません I've not decided yet *what I'm going to do* after this. / そう言ってしまっては身もふたもない(→それはあまり

に遠慮のない言い方だ) That's *too outspoken* a way of saying it. / 外では身を切るような風が吹いていた A *cutting* [*biting*] wind was blowing outside. / 彼は家族を養うために身を粉(こ)にして働いた He worked his 「*fingers to the bone* [《口語的》*butt off*] to support his family.

ことわざ 悪銭身につかず ⇒ あくせん / 芸は身を助ける ⇒ げい

み² 実
❶【果実】fruit ⓊⒸ (❖果物の総称としてはⓊ、種類を表す場合はⒸ); (木の実・堅果) nut Ⓒ; (イチゴの類の) berry Ⓒ
木の実を割る crack *a nut*
この桃の木は去年はよく実がなった This peach tree bore a lot of *fruit* last year.
庭のカキの木に実がなっている The persimmon tree in the garden is bearing [in] *fruit*.
実がなり始めた *The fruit* is coming on.
❷【中身】substance Ⓤ
実のない講演 a lecture with no *substance*
◆実のある議論 a *substantial* debate
慣用表現 彼女の長年の努力がとうとう実を結んだ At last her years of effort *bore fruit*.

み³ 巳 (十二支の第6番目) the Serpent, the Snake ⇒ えと

-み -味 赤みを帯びた黄色 yellow with *a tinge of red* / これは少し苦味がある This has *a slightly bitter taste*. / 彼の話には真実味があった His story had *the ring* of truth.

みあい 見合い 🖼 a *miai* / 彼はおばの紹介で見合いをした He had a *miai* [*a formal meeting with a prospective partner*] through his aunt. ◆兄は見合い結婚です My brother had *an arranged marriage*.

見合いは結婚相手を探している男女が初めて正式に顔を合わせることです. 日取りや場所は仲介者が決めます. 見合いを終えた男女は相手の印象を仲介者を通して間接的に伝えます. 見合いが縁となった結婚を見合い結婚といいます.
Miai is the first formal meeting of a man and a woman who are seeking marriage partners. A go-between arranges the *miai* and fixes the date and place. The man and woman later report their impressions of the other indirectly through that person. A marriage arranged through *miai* is called *miai-kekkon*.

みあう 見合う 収入に見合った暮らしをする live *within one's* income / 仕事に見合った給料を得る get *adequate* pay for *one's* work / この罰にはその犯罪に見合わない. This punishment just doesn't *fit* the crime.

みあきる 見飽きる このドラマはもう見飽きた I'm *tired of watching* this drama. / あいつの顔はもう見飽きたよ I've *had enough of* him.

みあげる 見上げる ❶【上を見る】look up / 空を見上げると飛行機が飛んでいた When we *looked up* at the sky, an airplane was flying past [by, over(head)]. ◆見上げるような大男 a man of *towering* height

❷【感心する】(賞賛する) admire ⓉⒾ /君の勇気は見上げたものだ I *admire* you *for* your courage. / I *admire* your courage.

みあたらない 見当たらない 財布が見当たらない I *can't find* my wallet. / My wallet *is missing*. / そのあたりでは店は一軒も見当たらなかった There weren't *any* shops around there.

みあやまる 見誤る mistake* ... for ~; (誤解する) misunderstand* ⓉⒾ; (判断を誤る) misjudge ⓉⒾ /味方を敵と見誤る *mistake one's friend for one's* enemy / 我々は問題の本質を見誤っていた We had *misunderstood* [*misjudged*] the nature of the problem.

みあわせる 見合わせる 互いの顔を見合わせる look *at each other* / 計画を見合わせる(→断念する) *give up* a plan / 判断を下すのを見合わせる(→留保する) *suspend* judgment / 祖母の病気のため母親は旅行を見合わせた(→中止した) My mother *called off* her trip because of my grandmother's illness.

みいだす 見出す find* ⓉⒾ; (未知のものを) discover ⓉⒾ /彼は家族と暮らすことに幸福を見いだした He *found* happiness in living with his family. / その女優は有名なプロデューサーに見いだされた The actress *was discovered* by a famous producer.

ミーティング meeting Ⓒ /ミーティングをする hold *a meeting*

ミート¹ (肉) meat Ⓤ ∥ミートソース meat sauce / ミートパイ a meat pie / ミートボール a meatball / ミートローフ (a) meat loaf

ミート² 彼はミートのうまい選手だ He is a *contact* hitter. / 私はボールをしっかりたたいてミートすることを心がけている I tried to hit the ball and *make good contact*.

ミーハー (軽薄な人) airhead Ⓒ; (流行を追いかける人) fashion slave Ⓒ
💬「彼女, 松田聖子が結婚式をした教会で結婚するんだって」「ミーハーだよね」 "She says she's going to get married at the same church where Matsuda Seiko had her wedding." "She's *so silly*."

ミイラ ⚠ mummy Ⓒ (❖日本語はポルトガル語の mirra から)
◆ミイラ化した遺体 a *mummified* body
ことわざ ミイラ取りがミイラになる Many go for wool and come home shorn. (→羊毛を求めて行ったのに逆に毛を刈られて帰ってくる)

みいられる 魅入られる (魅了される) be fascinated [enchanted] (by [with] ...)
◆悪霊に魅入られた(→取りつかれた)男 a man *possessed by* an evil spirit

みいり 実入り (収入) income ⓊⒸ, earnings /実入りのいい仕事 a *profitable* job

みいる 見入る 彼は彼女の横顔に見入っていた He *fixed his eyes on* her profile.

みうける 見受ける あの方はかなりの年配とお見受けしました(→年配に見えた) He *seemed* a very old man. / 同様の間違いがあなたのレポートにも見受けられる We *have noticed* some mistakes of the same kind in your paper.

みうごき 身動き 電車は満員で乗客は身動き一つできなかった The train was so crowded that the passengers *could not move an inch.* / みんなは身動き一つしないで彼女の話を聞いた Everybody listened to her story *without moving.* / 彼は借金で身動きがとれなくなっていた He *was up to his neck in* a debt.

みうしなう 見失う lose* sight of ...; (所在・動向を) lose track of ... 《その通りの曲がり角で彼を見失ってしまった I *lost sight of* him at a bend in the street. / 警察は脱獄者の行方を完全に見失った The police *lost all track of* the escaped convict.
◆彼は入試にすべて落ちて自分自身を見失った He *fell apart* after he failed all the entrance examinations.

みうち 身内 (家族) family ⓒ; (親戚(しんせき)) relative ⓒ 《あいつは身内の恥だ He's a disgrace to *our family.* / この事実は彼女の身内の者にしか知らされていなかった Only her *close relatives* were informed of this fact.

みうり 身売り その会社は去年サッカーチームを身売りした The company *sold off* its soccer team last year.

みえ¹ 見栄 (誇示) show ⓤ (また a ～); (虚栄心) vanity ⓤ ──見えをはる (よく見せる) show* off; (本裁をつくろう) keep* up appearances 《私は見えをはっていちばん高い料理を注文した I ordered the most expensive dish 「*for show* [*out of vanity*]. / あいつは見えをはっているだけだ He's just *showing off.*
慣用表現 2年で弁護士になると彼は見えを切った (→自信満々で宣言した) He *declared in a confident manner* that he would become a lawyer in two years.

みえ² 三重

三重県は近畿地方の東部に位置しており、奈良、京都に近く、名古屋、大阪からも交通の便のいいところにあります。気候は温暖で、海と山の景観に富んでおり、観光地もいろいろあります。なかでも伊勢神宮は、神道の聖地として古来からよく知られています。名物には伊勢エビや松阪牛があります。

Mie Prefecture is located in the eastern part of the Kinki district. It is close to Nara and Kyoto, and it's easily accessible from Nagoya and Osaka. It is blessed with a mild climate and spectacular mountains, sea and sightseeing spots. The Ise Shrine has been especially well known as a sacred Shinto site since ancient times. Among the prefecture's specialties are spiny lobsters and Matsuzaka beef.

みえかくれ 見え隠れ 月が雲の間に見え隠れしている The moon *is seen off and on* among the clouds.

みえすいた 見え透いた (明白な) obvious; (透明な) transparent 《見えすいたうそ an *obvious* [*a transparent*] lie / そんな見えすいたお世辞, 彼には通用しないよ Such *obvious* flattery will not influence him at all. / 君の本心は見えすいている Your real intentions *are obvious.*

みえっぱり 見栄っ張り show-off ⓒ 《彼女は本当に見えっぱりだ She's really *a show-off.*

みえみえ 見え見え あいつが何かたくらんでいるのは見え見えだ It's *obvious* that he's up to something.

みえる 見える

❶【目に映る】see* 他 圁 (◆進行形にはできない。しばしば can, could とともに用いる); (現れる) show* 圁

晴れた日にはここから大島が見えます You *can see* Oshima from here on a clear day.

私は注意して見たが何も見えなかった I looked carefully but *saw* nothing.

彼が演壇に上がるのが見えた We *saw* him appear on the podium.

彼女の顔には心配の色が見えた The worry *showed* on her face.

下着が見えてますよ Your underwear *is showing.*

◆霧の中からすばらしい城が見えてきた A grand castle *came into sight* [*view*] out of the fog. / その男の子は飛行機が見えなくなるまで手を振り続けた The boy kept on waving till the plane *went out of sight.* / その星は肉眼でもはっきり見える The star *is clearly visible* even to the naked eye. / 放射能は目に見えない Radioactivity *is invisible.* / 彼はキーボードを扱うのが目に見えてうまくなった He made *noticeable* progress in operating the keyboard. / そろそろ結果が見えてきた The result is beginning to *take shape.* (◆take shape は「形になる」の意味)

❷【思われる】look 圁; (主観的に) seem 圁, appear 圁 (◆seem よりも形式ばった語)

あのカメラは高そうに見える That camera 「*looks* expensive [*has an expensive look*].

君が彼が正直な男だと言うが, 僕にはそんなふうには見えない You say he is an honest man, but he doesn't *seem* that way to me.

その動物はライオンのように見えた The animal *looked like* a lion.

この写真だと彼は実際よりずっと若く見える This photo makes him *look* much younger than he really is.

よっぽど気に入ったと見えて彼は毎日その店に通っている *It seems that* he likes the store very much, because he goes there every day.

❸【視力がある】

猫は暗がりでも目が見える Cats *can see* even in the dark.

私は眼鏡なしではよく見えない I *don't* [*can't*] *see* well without my glasses.

私は片方の目が見えない I *am blind* in one eye.

彼女はその事故で目が見えなくなった(→失明した) She *lost her eyesight* in the accident.

彼はその手術で目が見えるようになった His *eyesight was restored* by the operation.
❹【察知される・推測できる】
彼には全く反省の色が見えなかった He *showed* no signs of regret.
このレースでだれが勝つかはちょっと見えないね You *can't judge* who will win this race.
❺【来る】come* ⓐ; (到着する) arrive ⓐ
先生がお見えになりました The teacher *has arrived*.
◆渡辺さん、お客様がお見えです You *have a visitor*, Mr. Watanabe.

みおくり 見送り 《口語的》send-off ⓒ ∥私たちは空港で盛大な見送りを受けた We *were given a big send-off* at the airport.
◆友人を見送りに空港まで行ってきたところです I've been to the airport *to see* my friend *off*. ∥ その件に関する決定は再び見送りとなった (→先延ばしになった) The decision on that matter *was*「*put off* [(→棚上げになった) *shelved*] again. ∥ 原は見送りの三振だった Hara *struck out looking*.

みおくる 見送る
❶【出発を】see* off
駅で彼を見送った I *saw* him *off* at the station.
❷【先延ばしにする】(延期する) postpone ⓣ, put* off; (中止する) cancel ⓣ, call off; (棚上げにする) shelve ⓣ
行事の開催を見送る *call off* an event
その件に関する議論はきょうは見送られた The argument over that matter *was shelved* today.
◆電車を1本見送る (→次の電車を待つ) *wait for the next train* ∥ 彼は昇進を見送られた He *was passed over* for promotion. ∥ 今回はその大会に参加するのを見送ることにした (→参加しないことにした) I *decided not to* enter the contest this time.
❸【その他】
私は遠ざかる車を見送った I *looked after* the car as it drove away.
バッターは初球を見送った The batter *let* the first pitch *go by*.

みおさめ 見納め この景色もきょうで見納めだ Today *is the last chance to see* this scenery.

みおとし 見落とし oversight ⓒⓊ ∥見落としがないか書類を何度も見直した I *looked over* the document again and again to avoid *oversights*.

みおとす 見落とす miss ⓣ, overlook ⓣ ∥私はいくつかのスペルミスを見落とした I *missed* [*overlooked*] some errors in spelling. ∥ 一つ重要なことを見落としていますね You *have missed* one important thing.

みおとり 見劣り ほかの人たちの作品は彼女のものに比べて見劣りがする The works of other people *pale in comparison with* hers. ∥ この車は新しいものと比べて少しも見劣りしない This car *doesn't look inferior to* the new ones at all.

みおぼえ 見覚え その犬には見覚えがあった I remembered seeing the dog. ∥ The dog *looked familiar to* me. ∥ このかばんに見覚えはありますか Do you *recognize* this bag?

みおろす 見下ろす look down; (一望する) overlook ⓣ ∥私たちは山頂から町を見下ろした We *looked down on* the town from the top of the mountain. ∥ そのタワーからは海が見下ろせる The tower *overlooks* [*commands*] the sea.

みかい 未開 ──未開の (原始的な) primitive; (文明化されていない) uncivilized; (開発されていない) undeveloped ∥未開の地 an *undeveloped* land
∥未開社会 a primitive [an uncivilized] society∥未開人 a barbarian

みかいけつ 未解決 未解決の問題 an *unsolved* [*unsettled*] problem ∥ その殺人事件は未解決である The murder case *remains unsolved* [*to be solved*].

みかいたく 未開拓 未開拓の土地 *uncultivated* [*undeveloped*] land ∥ 日本はその産業の未開拓 (→発展の可能性がある) 市場だ Japan is a *potential* market for that industry. ∥ 自然科学には未開拓の (→研究されていない) 分野がまだ数多く残っている There still remain lots of *unexplored* fields in natural science.

みかいはつ 未開発 ──未開発の undeveloped; (発展中の) developing ∥未開発の developing countries ∥ 東京近郊に未開発の土地はほとんどない There's little land left *undeveloped* in the suburbs of Tokyo.

みかえす 見返す 答案を見返す時間はなかった I had no time to *look over* my exam paper *again*. ∥ 彼は鋭い目つきで私を見返してきた He *stared back at* me with a piercing look. ∥ いつかあいつを見返してやる I'*ll get even with* him someday.

みかえり 見返り 大臣は多額の献金の見返りにその企業に対して様々な便宜をはかっていた The minister gave the company every advantage「*in return* [*as a reward*] *for* a heavy contribution. ∥ 私は何らかの見返りを期待して彼らに協力したわけではない I didn't help them because I expected any *rewards*.

みがき 磨き 磨きのかかった靴 *well-polished* shoes ∥ 渡米する前に英語に磨きをかけなければならない I have to *polish up* my English before I go to America. ∥ 彼女の演技は年とともにますます磨きがかかってきた Her performance *has* increasingly *improved* as she gets older.
∥磨き粉 polishing powder

みかぎる 見限る (見捨てる) abandon ⓣ; (見切りをつける) give* up on …; (背を向ける) turn *one's* back on … ∥両親まで彼を見限った Even his parents *gave up on* him.

みかく 味覚 (the sense of) taste ∥この食べ物は日本人の味覚に合わない This food doesn't suit *the* Japanese *taste*. ∥ かぜで味覚が鈍った A cold dulled *my sense of taste*.

みがく 磨く
❶【きれいにする】(つやを出す) polish ⓣ; (光らせる) shine ⓣ; (ごしごしこする) scrub ⓣⓐ;

みかくにん

(ブラシなどで) brush 他; (レンズなどを研磨する) grind* 他; (やすりをかける) file 他; (砂で) sand 他

靴を磨く *polish* [*shine*] one's shoes; give one's shoes *a polish* [*shine*] / 床を磨き上げる *polish* [*clean*] *up* the floor

食後には歯を磨きなさい *Brush* [*Clean*] your teeth after meals.

流しをクレンザーででかぴかに磨いた I *scrubbed* the sink clean with cleanser.

❷【向上させる】improve 他, polish 他

彼は毎日レッスンを受けてピアノの腕を磨いた He 「*polished* (*up*) [*improved*] his piano playing by taking daily lessons.

みかくにん 未確認 ──未確認の unconfirmed 《未確認の情報 *unconfirmed* information

‖未確認飛行物体 an unidentified flying object (《略語》UFO)

みかけ 見掛け (外見) appearance ⓤⓒ, look ⓒ; (見せかけ) show ⓤ 《また a ~》 人を見かけだけで判断してはいけない Don't judge people only by *their appearances* [*looks*]. /

見かけによらず彼はすごくデリケートだ He's quite delicate *despite his appearance*.

◆彼は実は見かけほど年をとっていない He isn't really *as old as he looks*. / 彼は見かけどおり気難しい人だ He is *as hard to please as he looks*. / プロレスラーはたいてい見かけ倒しだ(→見かけほど強くない) Most pro wrestlers *are not as strong as they look*. / 彼は見かけはまじめそうだが実はそうでない He *looks* serious but really he's not.

ことわざ 人は見かけによらぬもの Appearances can be deceiving [deceptive]. (→見かけは当てにならない)

みかげいし 御影石 granite [grǽnit] ⓤ

みかける 見掛ける see* 他, catch* [get*, have*] sight of ... 《彼を見かけたらすぐ私に電話してください If you ever *see* [*catch sight of*] him, call me at once. / 彼女が家の前を通るのをよく見かける I often *see* her passing in front of my house. / この俳優は映画ではほとんど見かけない We rarely *see* this actor in movies. ◆それはこのあたりではよく見かける光景だ It is a *common* [*familiar*] sight around here.

みかた¹ 味方 friend ⓒ; (一方の側) side ⓒ; (同盟国〔者〕) ally ⓒ ──味方する take* *a person's side*, take sides with ..., side with ...; (支援する) stand* by ..., support 他

正義の味方 *a friend* [*champion*] of justice

君は彼の味方をするつもりか Are you *taking* 「*his side* [*sides with* him]?

運が私に味方した Luck *was on my side*.

ようやく彼らを味方につけることができた We managed to *get* them *over to our side*.

内戦のために彼らは敵味方に分かれなければならなかった The civil war separated them into *two opposing sides*.

❢「おまえはだれの味方なんだ」「僕はいつもあなたの味方ですよ」"Whose *side* are you on?" "I'm always on your *side*."

みかた² 見方 view ⓒ; (観点) a point of view, viewpoint ⓒ; (態度・姿勢) attitude ⓒ 《その問題に関する彼の見方は私のとは違う His *view* of the problem is different from mine. / 彼はこの本を読んで宗教に対する見方を変えた The book changed *my view* of religion. / 物価は上昇するとの見方が一般的だ *The common view* is that prices will go up. / 見方を変えれば彼の言うことにも一理ある There's a certain logic in what he says, if it is seen *from another point of view*. / 彼女は結婚に対して進歩的な見方をしている She has *a liberal attitude* toward marriage.

◆彼は他人と違ったものの見方をする He *sees things differently from others*. / このグラフの見方を教えてください Please tell me *how to read* this graph.

みかづき 三日月 crescent (moon) ⓒ; (新月) new moon ◆三日月形のクッキー a *crescent* cookie

‖三日月湖 an oxbow lake

みがって 身勝手 selfishness ⓤ ──身勝手な selfish 《そんな身勝手は決して許されない Such *selfishness* is never permitted. / あいつはなんて身勝手なんだ How *selfish* of him!

みかねる 見兼ねる 彼の横暴な態度を見かねて注意した I *couldn't put up with* his tyrannical attitude and gave him warning. / 困っている彼を見るに見かねて手を貸した(→手伝わずにはいられなかった) Knowing he was in trouble, I *couldn't but* help him.

みがまえる 身構える (姿勢をとる) take* [assume] a posture, stand* ready 《自分の身を守ろうと身構える *take a* defensive *posture* / 泥棒は警官に飛びかかろうと身構えた The thief *stood ready* to spring at the policeman.

みがら 身柄 警察は容疑者の身柄を拘束した The police took the suspect into custody. (❢特に「身柄」に当たる英語はない)

みがる 身軽 ──身軽な light; (敏捷(びんしょう)な) agile, nimble ──身軽に lightly; nimbly 《彼女は身軽な服装でやってきた She came in *light* clothes. / 彼は身軽に塀を乗り越えた He *lightly* [*nimbly*] climbed over the wall.

◆君は身軽でうらやましいよ I wish I could be *footloose* like you. (❣*footloose* は「家庭・仕事などの束縛がない」の意味)

みがわり 身代わり substitute ⓒ; (他人の罪・責任の) scapegoat ⓒ 《警察官が人質たちの身代わりになった A policeman acted as *a substitute for* the hostages.

◆父は私の身代わりになって死んだ My father died *for* [*in place of*] me.

みかん¹ 未完 ──未完の (仕上がっていない) unfinished; (不完全な) incomplete 《未完の作品 an *unfinished* [*incomplete*] work

◆その野球選手は未完の大器(→将来有望)といわれながら、結局芽が出なかった The baseball player had been said to be *promising*, but after all was not able to succeed.

みかん² 蜜柑 a *mikan*, a Japanese orange,

a mandarin orange; (温州(うんしゅう)ミカン) satsuma (orange) ◎
短歌 街をゆき子供の傍(そば)を通る時蜜柑の香せり冬がまた来る(木下利玄)
I walk around town,
and when I pass some children playing in the street
I catch a whiff of oranges.
Winter is coming again.

みかんせい 未完成 ──未完成の(仕上がっていない) unfinished; (不完全な) incomplete
◆体育館はまだ未完成だ The gymnasium *is not* yet *finished* [*complete*].

みき 幹 trunk ◎

みぎ 右

❶【方向】the right (↔the left) ──右の right; (右側の・右向きの) right-hand
〖右(の)〜〗
右足を机にぶつけた I knocked *my right leg* against the desk.
彼は彼女の右隣に座った He sat on her *right*.
紙の右の余白に書いてください Please write in the *right* margin of the paper.
そこを左に曲がると,右手に郵便局があります Turn left at that corner, and you'll find the post office *on the right*.
それは棚の右上[右下]にあります It's on the *upper* [*lower*] *right* shelf.
◆彼は左投げ右打ちだ He throws left and *hits right*.
〖右に・へ〗
ハンドルを右に切る turn the steering wheel (*to the*) *right* (❖right は副詞としても用いられる)
あの角を右に曲がれば,すぐにその店が見つかりますよ Turn (*to the*) *right* at the corner, and you will soon find the shop.
道は右へ折れている The road turns *to the right*.
そのポスターは右に傾いている The poster leans *to the right*.
彼はこの写真の最前列の右にいます In this picture, he is in the front row *on the right*.
◆ねじを右に(→時計回りに)回す turn a screw *clockwise*
〖その他〗
父はこの写真の最前列の右から2番目にいます In this picture, my father is the second *from the right* in the front row.
この手袋は左と右が違う These two gloves *don't match*.

❷【右翼】(集合的) the right (wing); (個人) rightist ◎
その政党は少し右寄りだ The political party is a bit *to the right*.
◆その作家は一般には右寄りだと考えられている The writer is generally regarded as *right-wing*.

❸【前に述べたこと】
(縦書きの書類などで)右のとおり相違ありません I affirm *the above* to be true in every particular. (❖英語では横書きなので「上のとおり」になる)
慣用表現 彼は金づかいが荒くて給料も右から左だ He's extravagant and his salary just *slips through his fingers*. / ギターの腕前にかけては彼の右に出る者はいない(→匹敵する者はいない) He *has no equal* [*Nobody can equal* him] in playing the guitar. / 彼の話はすべて右の耳から左の耳へ抜けていった Everything he said to me *went in one ear and out the other*. / 彼女がその招待を断るとほかの人たちも右へならえした She declined the invitation and the others *followed suit*. (❖follow suit は「人のやったとおりにする,先例にならう」の意味) / 先週引っ越してきたばかりなのでまだ右も左も分からない I'm still *a complete stranger* here because I just moved last week.

みぎうで 右腕 *one's* right arm
慣用表現 彼女は社長の右腕だ She's the president's *right hand*.

みぎがわ 右側 the right (side), the right-hand side ──右側の right, right-hand ∥ 右側通行《掲示》*Keep* (*to the*) *Right* / その角を右に曲がれば右手に郵便局があります Turn left at the corner, and you'll see the post office *on your right-hand side*.

みぎき 見聞き 彼はそこで見聞きしたことを私たちに話そうとはしなかった He would never tell us about what he *saw and heard* there.

みぎきき 右利き(人) right-handed person ◎, right-hander ◎ ──右利きの right-handed ∥ 右利き用のグローブ a *right-handed* glove / 私は右利きだ I'm *right-handed*.

ミキサー ⚠(野菜・果実などを砕く)《米》blender ◎, 《英》liquidizer ◎, (攪拌(かくはん)機) (food) mixer ◎; (音声調整装置[係]) mixer ◎ ∥ 野菜をミキサーにかける mix vegetables in *the blender*
∥コンクリートミキサー(車) a concrete [cement] mixer / ハンドミキサー a hand mixer

みぎて 右手 *one's* right hand; (方向) the right ∥ 答えが分かったら右手を上げなさい Hold up *your right hand* if you know the answer. / この道をまっすぐ行くと右手に高いビルが見えてきます If you go straight down this street, you'll find a tall building on *the* [*your*] *right*.
◆右手の親指 *one's* right thumb

みきり 見切り 監督はその選手に見切りをつけ,スタメンからはずした The manager *gave up on* the player and left him out of the starting lineup. / 私たちはその計画を見切り発車した(→詳細を議論しないうちに実行した) We *put* the project *into execution before we discussed the details of it*.
∥見切り品 clearance goods

みきわめる 見極める 事の成り行きを見きわめる(→最後まで見守る) *watch* the course of events *to the end* / 事件の真相を見きわめる(→究明する) *investigate* [*inquire into*] the fact of the case / 彼らの真意を見きわめる(→確かめる)のは難しい It is difficult to *make sure of* their true intention.

みくだす 見下す look down on [upon] *a person*, despise [他] ∥理由はどうあれ人を見下してはいけない Don't *look down on* people whatever the reason. ◆彼女の人を見下した(→傲慢(ごうまん)な)態度には抵抗を感じる Her *arrogant* attitude puts me off.

みくびる 見縊る (過小評価する) underestimate [他][自]; (軽んじる) make* light of *a person* ∥相手を見くびってはいけない You should never *underestimate* your opponent.

みくらべる 見比べる 本物のダイヤと偽物を見比べる *compare* a genuine diamond *with* a fake / 彼女は私と彼の顔を見比べた(→交互に見た) She *looked alternately* between my face and his.

みぐるしい 見苦しい (醜い・不格好な) ugly; (品のない) 《公式的》unseemly; (恥ずべき) shameful ∥見苦しい服装 *ugly* clothes / そんな言い訳をするなんて見苦しいぞ It's *unseemly* to make such an excuse.
◆人前に出るときくらいは見苦しくない格好をしなさい Dress *decently* at least when you appear in public.

みぐるみ 身ぐるみ その旅行者はロサンゼルスの路上で身ぐるみはがれた(→すべて奪われた) The tourist *was robbed of everything he had* on the street in Los Angeles.

ミクロ ⚠ ミクロの世界 the *microscopic* world (❖microscopic は「顕微鏡でしか見えない, 非常に小さな」の意味)
∥ミクロ経済学 microeconomics / ミクロコスモス a microcosm

ミクロン micron [máikrɑn] [C] (複 ～s, micra) (❖100万分の1メートル. 記号は μ)

みけいけん 未経験 ━未経験の inexperienced, 《口語的》green ∥この仕事は未経験です I ｢*am inexperienced* [*have no experience*] *in* this work. / その野球チームのメンバーは未経験者ばかりだった The baseball team was made up of only *inexperienced people*.
◆未経験者可(→経験不問) *No experience necessary*.

みけつ 未決 ━未決の (懸案の) pending; (解決していない) unsettled ∥未決事項 a *pending* matter; a matter *unsettled* / 未決書類 *pending* documents
∥未決囚 an unconvicted prisoner, a prisoner awaiting trial

みけねこ 三毛猫 tortoiseshell (cat) [C]

みけん 眉間 the middle of the forehead
◆彼女は眉間にしわを寄せた(→まゆをひそめた) She *knitted her brows*.

みこ 巫女 🖼 Shinto priestess [C]; (霊媒) medium [C]; (預言者) oracle [C]

みこし 神輿 🖼 a *mikoshi*, a portable shrine ∥みこしをかつぐ carry *a mikoshi*
⇒おみこし

みこす 見越す 渋滞を見越して早めに出発した *In anticipation* [*expectation*] *of* a traffic jam, we started earlier. / 10年先を見越した経営方針を立てる必要がある We need to prepare a business plan that *looks* 10 years ahead.

みごたえ 見応え 彼の映画はどれも見ごたえがある(→見る価値がある) All his movies *are worth seeing*.

みごと 見事 ━見事な (すばらしい) wonderful, fine; (すぐれた) excellent; (美しい) beautiful; (壮大な) magnificent, splendid; (最上の) superb; (賞賛に値する) admirable
公園にみごとなバラが咲いている *Beautiful* roses are in bloom in the park.
私たちはみごとな眺めに圧倒された We felt overwhelmed by the *magnificent* view.
彼女のスピーチは実にみごとだった Her speech *was* truly *excellent*.
おみごと！ *Excellent*!/ *Wonderful*!/ *Superb*! / *Bravo*!/ (→よくやった) *Well done*!
◆彼はみごとに(→首尾よく)大役を果たした He carried out an important task *successfully*. / 彼らはみごとに(→完全に)私の計略にはまった They *completely* fell into my trap. / この絵は戦争の悲惨さをみごとに(→完璧(かんぺき)に)描写している This painting *perfectly* catches the horror of war.

みこみ 見込み
❶【可能性・望み】chance [U][C]; (可能性) possibility [U] 《また a ～》, likelihood [U] 《また a ～》; (見通し) prospect [U][C]; (望み) hope [U][C]
彼女が成功する見込みは十分ある She has *a* good *chance* of success. / There's *a* good *chance* that she will succeed.
うちのチームが勝つ見込みはほとんどない There's little *hope* [*chance*] that our team will win. / Our team has little *hope* [*chance*] of winning.
彼が受賞する見込みはありますか Is there any *chance* of his winning the prize?
雨のために試合は中止になる見込みだ *There is a possibility* [*likelihood*] that the game will be canceled because of rain. / The game *is likely to* be canceled because of rain.
その仕事を終えられる見込みが立って私はほっとした *The prospect* of finishing the work relieved me.
◆このピッチャーはなかなか見込みがある This pitcher *is* very *promising* [*hopeful*].
❷【予想】
台風は今夜, 九州地方に上陸する見込みだ The typhoon *is expected to* hit the Kyushu area tonight.
予報によると今年の夏は例年より涼しい見込みだ The weather forecast says this summer *will* be cooler than usual.
彼らはきっと協力してくれると思っていたのだが, 私の見込み違い(→誤算)だった I thought they would surely help us, but it was *a miscalculation* (on my part).

みこむ 見込む ❶【予想する】(期待する) expect [他]; (見積もる) estimate [他]; (…を考慮に

入れる) take* ... into consideration, allow for ... ∥今後私たちは彼女の協力を見込めない We can't *expect* her to help us from this time on. / 今年の経済成長はゼロと見込まれている The economic growth for this year *is「expected to be [estimated at]* zero.
◆引っ越しの準備に 1 週間を見込んでおく *allow a week* to prepare for a move (❖*allow* は「(時間・費用などに)余裕を見ておく」の意味) / 彼は昇給を見込んで車を購入した He bought a car *in anticipation of* a pay raise.
❷【信頼する】君を見込んで(→君が信頼できることを知っているので)頼みがある *I know you to be reliable [trustworthy]*, so I'd like to ask you a favor. / 彼は監督に見込まれて(→監督の信頼を得て)レギュラーになった He *won the confidence* of the manager and became a regular member.

みごもる 身ごもる 洋一の子をみごもる *be pregnant* by Yoichi / *be pregnant* with Yoichi's child

みごろ 見頃 上野公園の桜は今が見ごろだ(→盛りだ) The cherry blossoms in Ueno park are *「at their best*[(→満開だ)*in full bloom]* now.

みごろし 見殺し 彼女を見殺しにするわけにはいかない I can't *leave* her *in the lurch*. (❖*leave a person* in the lurch で「(困っている人を)見捨てる」の意味)

みこん 未婚 ——未婚の single, unmarried ∥未婚者 a *single* [an *unmarried*] person / 未婚の母 an *unmarried* mother

ミサ ⚠【キリスト教】Mass, mass ⓒⓊ (❖日本語はラテン語の missa から) ∥ミサに出席する attend [go to] *Mass* / ミサを行う hold *Mass* / ミサをささげる say [read] *Mass*
∥ミサ曲 a mass

ミサイル missile ⓒ ∥ミサイルを配備する position *a missile* / ミサイルを発射する launch [fire] *a missile* / …にミサイルを向ける target *a missile* on ...
∥ミサイル基地 a missile base [site, installation] / ミサイル兵器 a missile force / 核ミサイル a nuclear missile / 迎撃ミサイル an interceptor missile / 巡航ミサイル a cruise missile / 戦略ミサイル a strategic missile / 弾道ミサイル a ballistic missile / 誘導ミサイル a guided missile

みさかい 見境 最近彼はパソコンに凝っていて,関係する本を見境なく買っている These days he's crazy about computers and *indiscriminately* buys books related to them. / あまりに腹が立って前後の見境がつかなくなった I got so angry that I *lost my reason [head]*.

みさき 岬 cape ⓒ, point ⓒ (❖いずれも主に地名を表す固有名詞とともに用いる); promontory ⓒ ∥納沙布岬 *Cape* Nosappu

みさだめる 見定める 目標を見定める *make sure of* one's goal / まずは状況を見定めるべきだ We should 「*make sure of [size up]* the situation first. (❖*size up* は「(人・状況などを)評価・判断する」の意味)

みじかい 短い

short; (つかの間の・簡潔な) brief
短い距離 a *short* distance / 短い旅行 a *short [brief]* trip / 髪を短くしてもらう wear one's hair *short* / 髪を短くしてもらう have one's hair cut *short*
短い休憩をとった We had a *short [brief]* break.
彼は短い間にめざましい進歩を遂げた He has made a noticeable advance in a *short [brief]* period.
彼女とは短い会話しか交わしたことがない I've only had *short [brief]* conversations with her.
彼女は先日,15 年という短い生涯を閉じた She ended her *short* life of 15 years the other day.
彼は要所要所で短い説明を入れた He gave a *short [brief]* explanation at every key point.
夏至を過ぎて日がだんだん短くなってきている The days are 「*getting shorter [shortening]* after the summer solstice.
時間がないので,短めにお願いします We have little time. Please be *brief*.
このズボンは私には短かすぎる These trousers *are too short* for me.
◆ 私はむだな箇所を省略して話を短くした I *shortened* the story by cutting out the waste. / 治しても最悪 3 周間かかりますが,たぶんもっとずっと短くてすむでしょう At the worst, it will take three weeks to recover, but probably *much less*. / うちの母は気が短い My mother is *short-tempered*. / うちの犬は先が短い(→何年も生きることはないと)獣医に言われた The vet told me that my dog *didn't have many years to live*.

ミシガン Michigan (❖米国中北部の州;《略語》Mich., 〖郵便〗MI)

ミシシッピ Mississippi (❖米国南部の州;《略語》Miss., 〖郵便〗MS)

みじたく 身支度 彼女は急いで身じたくをした She 「*dressed (herself) [got dressed]* in a hurry.

みしみし この階段はみしみしいう These stairs *creak*.

みじめ 惨め ——みじめな miserable, wretched
みじめな生活をする lead a *miserable* life; live *in misery*
みじめな顔して,何かあったの You look *miserable*. What's up?
私はこれ以上ないというほどみじめな思いをした I couldn't have felt more *miserable*.
◆あなたのすてきな服と比べるとみじめになるわ Your nice clothes *put me [mine] to shame*. (❖*put ... to shame* で「…に劣等感をいだかせる」の意味)

みじゅく 未熟 ——未熟な (成熟していない) immature; (経験の浅い) inexperienced, green; (熟練していない) unskilled; (下手な) poor ∥未熟な運転によって引き起こされた事故

みしらぬ

an accident caused by *poor* driving / 彼は頭はいいがまだまだ未熟だ Though he is bright, he's still *immature*.
∥未熟児 a *premature* baby / 未熟者 an *inexperienced person, a greenhorn*

みしらぬ 見知らぬ *strange*;（なじみのない）*unfamiliar* ∥見知らぬ土地での車の運転に地図は欠かせない A map is indispensable for driving in a *strange* land.
◆見知らぬ人が私に近寄ってきた A *stranger* approached me.

みじろぎ 身じろぎ 彼女は身じろぎもせず座っていた She was sitting *motionless*.

ミシン ⚠sewing machine ⓒ ∥…をミシンで縫う sew ... on *a sewing machine*
∥ミシン糸 sewing machine thread / ミシン針 a sewing machine needle / ミシン目(切手など) *perforations*

みじん 微塵 (小片) piece ⓒ, bit ⓒ,《口語的》*smithereens* ∥コップはみじんに砕けた The glass was broken into *pieces* [*bits, smithereens*].
◆タマネギをみじん切りにする *chop* an onion *finely* / 彼を困らせるつもりはみじんもなかった I *didn't* have the *slightest* intention of troubling him.

ミス¹ ⚠mistake ⓒ, error ⓒ ⓤ ─ミスする make* a mistake [an error]（◆「誤り」の意味の「ミス」に近い英語は, miss ではなく, mistake や error）/ 大きな［ささいな, 単純な, 致命的な, よくある］ミス a big [little, simple, fatal, common] *mistake* / 事故は人為的なミスによって起きた The accident was caused by human *error*. / この手紙はスペルミスだらけだ This letter is full of *spelling mistakes*.

ミス² 2002年のミス日本 *Miss* Japan of 2002; the 2002 *Miss* Japan

ミズ Ms., Ms [míz]（◆既婚か未婚か分からない, あるいはそれを問題にしたくない場合に Miss, Mrs. の代わりに用いる）

みず 水

water ⓤ（◆温度に関係なく湯にも用いる）；（湯に対して）cold water ⓤ

〖水が・は〗
水は摂氏0度で凍る *Water* freezes at zero degrees Celsius.
この水は飲めますか Is this *water* safe for drinking?
蛇口から水が出なかった *Water* didn't come out of the tap.
どこからか水がもれているようだ It looks like *water* is leaking from somewhere.
(洪水の)水が引くまでにはだいぶ時間がかかるだろう It'll be a long time until「*the water* subsides [*the floods* subside].
◆ふろの水があふれている The bath *is overflowing*.

〖水を〗
(水道の)水を出して［止めて］ください Please *turn on* [*off*] *the water*.
水を1杯ください Can I have a glass of *water*, please?

水を出しっぱなしにしないで Don't leave *the water* running.
ふろの水を抜いておいて Let *the water* out of the bathtub. / Drain the bathtub.
旅行先では水道の水をそのまま飲まないほうがいい You should not drink *tap water* while traveling.
◆トイレの水を流す *flush* the toilet / この地域は利根川から水を引いている This area *is watered by* the Tone River. / この花には水をやりすぎないようにしなさい Don't *water* this flower too much.

〖水に〗
氷は水に浮く Ice floats *on water*.
この薬はお湯には溶けるが水には溶けない This medicine dissolves *in hot water*, but not *in cold water*.
◆水に落ちにくいマスカラ *waterproof* mascara / 家が大雨で床上まで水につかった My house *was flooded* above the floor level by heavy rain.

〖水で〗
タオルを水でぬらす wet a towel *with water* / 水で薬を飲んだ I took the medicine *with water*.
◆スープは少し水で薄めたような味がした The soup tasted as if it *had been watered down* a little.

〖慣用表現〗あの兄弟は水と油だ Those brothers are like *oil and water*.（◆日本語と語順が逆であることに注意）/ 過ぎたことは水に流そう *Let bygones be bygones*. / 国会周辺は水も漏らさぬ(→厳重な)警戒ぶりだ *Tight* security is in force around the Diet building. / 英語では彼女にだいぶ水をあけられている(→遅れをとっている) I *fall* far *behind* her in English. / 会場は水を打ったようにしんとしていた(→ピンの落ちる音さえ聞こえそうなほどだった) *You could have heard a pin drop* in the hall. / 彼はサッカーをしているときは水を得た魚のようだ(→生き生きしている) He *looks lively* when he is playing soccer. / 彼が努力しているのに水を差すんじゃない Don't *throw a wet blanket on* [*over*] his efforts.（◆a wet blanket は「熱意を失わせる人［物］」の意味）/ 彼らの仲に水を差すつもりは全くなかった I never meant to *ruin* [*destroy*] their relationship.
⇒みずのあわ

みずあげ 水揚げ (漁獲高) catch ⓒ; (売り上げ) takings, take ⓒ 〖通例単数形〗∥1日の水揚げを計算する count the day's *takings* [*take*] / イワシの水揚げは年々増えている［減っている］*The* sardine *catches* are getting larger [smaller] year by year.
◆港に水揚げする *unload a ship* at a port

みずあそび 水遊び ─水遊びをする play with [in the] water

みずあび 水浴び bathing ⓤ; (泳ぐこと) swimming ⓤ ─水浴びする take* a bath; swim* ⓐ, 《主に英》bathe [béið] ⓐ

みずあらい 水洗い ─水洗いする wash ... with [in the] water

みすい 未遂 ─未遂の *attempted*（◆名詞の

前で用いる), abortive ‖自殺[殺人]未遂 an *attempted* suicide [murder] / その暗殺は未遂に終わった The assassination attempt「*was abortive* [*ended in failure*].

みずいらず 水入らず 久しぶりに家族水入らずで(→自分たちだけで)食事をした My family had dinner *all by ourselves* for the first time in quite some time.

みずいろ 水色 light [pale] blue [U]

みずうみ 湖 lake [C] ‖湖でボートに乗る enjoy boating on *a lake*

[短歌] みづうみの氷は解けてなほ寒し三日月の影波にうつろふ(島木赤彦)

The ice on the lake
has melted into water,
but still the night's cold.
The light of the crescent moon
is shimmering on the waves.

ミズーリ Missouri (❖米国中部の州; 《略語》 Mo., 〔郵便〕 MO)

みすえる 見据える 我々は将来を見据えて行動すべきだ We must act *with our eyes fixed on* the future.

みずかき 水掻き (水鳥などの) web [C]

◆カモノハシには水かきがある A platypus *is web-footed*.

みずかけろん 水掛け論 (実りのない議論) fruitless argument [C]; (きりのない議論) endless argument [C] ‖その議論は結局水かけ論になってしまった The dispute was reduced to *a fruitless argument*.

みずかさ 水嵩 あらしの後, 川は3メートル水かさを増した The river *rose* three meters after the storm. (❖「水かさが減る」は fall)

みすかす 見透かす see* through … ‖私たちの作戦は初めから見透かされていた Our tactics *was seen through* from the start.

みずがめざ 水瓶座 〖天文・占星〗 Aquarius [U] (❖「水瓶座の人」の意味では [C])

みずから 自ら *oneself*; (独力で) for *oneself*; (じきじきに) personally, in person ‖彼は最後の手段として自らそこへ行った He *himself* went there as a last resort.

◆自らの運命を切り開く work out *one's own* destiny

みずぎ 水着 swimsuit [C], swimwear [U], 《主に米》 bathing suit [C], 《英》 swimming costume [C]; (海水パンツ) (swimming) trunks

ミスキャスト あの女優がクレオパトラなんてミスキャストだ That actress *is miscast* as Cleopatra.

みずきり 水切り (台所の水切り台) draining board [C]; (水切りボウル) colander [C]; (水切り遊び) ducks and drakes

みずぎわ 水際 the water's edge; (岸) shore [C][U] ◆密輸を水際で食い止める prevent smuggling *at ports of entry*

‖水際作戦 shoreline operations

みずくさ 水草 water plant [C], waterweed [C]

みずくさい 水臭い どうしてもっと早く言ってくれなかったんだ. 水くさいじゃないか(→友達じゃないか) Why didn't you tell me about it earlier? *We are friends, aren't we?*

みずけ 水気 water [U]; (湿り気) moisture [U]; (汁) juice [U][C] ‖タオルで水気を吸い取る soak up *water* with a towel

◆水気の多い果物 *juicy* fruit / 洗った後野菜の水気を切ってください Please *drain* the vegetables after washing them.

みずけむり 水煙 ジェットボートは水煙を立てて水上を走っていた The jetboat was running on the water, raising *a cloud of spray*.

みすごす 見過ごす overlook [他]; (見落とす) miss [他] ‖今回は君の失敗を見過ごすわけにはいかない I can't *overlook* your mistake this time. / 私はその掲示を見過ごしていた I've *missed* [*overlooked*] the notice.

みずさきあんない 水先案内 ―水先案内をする pilot [他] ‖水先案内人 a pilot

みずさし 水差し 《米》 pitcher [C], 《英》 jug [C]

みずしぶき 水しぶき (水煙) spray [U][C] ‖波は防波堤に打ち寄せて水しぶきを立てた The waves whipped up *spray* on the breakwater.

◆水しぶきを上げて川に飛び込む jump into the river with *a splash* (❖splash は「バシャッという音」の意味) / 水しぶきを立てて車が通り過ぎた A car *splashed* past.

みずしょうばい 水商売 (飲食業) the restaurant and bar business; (不安定な商売) chancy [risky] business [C]

みずしらずの 見ず知らずの 見ず知らずの人が私を訪ねてきた *A total* [*complete*] *stranger* visited me.

みずすまし 水澄まし whirligig beetle [C]

ミスター Mr., Mr ‖ミスタープロ野球 *Mr.* Professional Baseball

みずたま 水玉 (水玉模様) polka dots ◆水玉模様のネクタイ a *polka-dot* [*polka-dotted*] tie

みずたまり 水溜まり puddle [C], pool [C] ‖雨がやむと校庭には水たまりがいくつかできていた There were some *puddles* in the schoolyard after the rain.

みずっぽい 水っぽい watery; (こくのない) thin ‖水っぽいスープ a *watery* [*thin*] soup

みずでっぽう 水鉄砲 water pistol [C], 《米》 squirt gun [C]

ミステリー (不思議) mystery [C][U]; (小説・映画などの) mystery [C]

➩ [場面・状況別会話] p.1722

‖ミステリーサークル a crop [corn] circle / ミステリー作家 a mystery writer

みすてる 見捨てる desert [他], abandon [他]; (残して去る) leave* [他] ‖彼らは私を見捨てて逃げてしまった They ran away *leaving* me *behind*. / 彼女が彼を最も必要としているときに彼は彼女を見捨てた He *deserted* [*abandoned*] her when she needed him most.

みずとり 水鳥 water bird [C], waterfowl [C] (複 ~s, ~)

みずのあわ 水の泡 我々の長年の努力は一瞬にして水の泡になってしまった Our years of effort「*came to nothing* [*went down the drain*] in an instant.

み

みずのみば 水飲み場 a place for drinking water(❖英語では drinking fountain「噴水式水飲み器」, (water) faucet「蛇口」などと具体的にいうのがふつう); (動物の) watering place [C]

みずはけ 水捌け この野球場は水はけがよい[悪い] This baseball field *drains well* [*badly*]. / This baseball field *has good* [*bad*] *drainage*.

みずばしら 水柱 沖合いで水柱が上がった There rose *a column of water* offshore.

みずひき 水引き a *mizuhiki*, a ceremonial paper cord used to tie the wrapper of a gift

みずびたし 水浸し 雨漏りで床が水びたしだ The floor *was flooded* (*with water*) because of the leaky roof.

みずぶくれ 水脹れ blister [C] ‖水ぶくれをつぶす burst *a blister* / 足に水ぶくれができた I got *a blister* on my foot.

ミスプリント "night"はたぶん"knight"のミスプリントだろう "Night" is probably *a misprint for* "knight."

みずべ 水辺 the waterside ‖水辺の植物 *waterside* plants

みずぼうそう 水疱瘡 chicken pox [U]

みすぼらしい 見すぼらしい shabby ‖みすぼらしい家 a *shabby* house

◆彼はいつもみすぼらしい身なりをしている He's always *shabbily* [*poorly*] *dressed*.

みずまき 水撒き watering [U] ◆庭の水まきをする *water* [*sprinkle water on*] the garden

みずまくら 水枕 water pillow [C]

みずまし 水増し 水増し入学させる *admit more students than the fixed number* / 彼は経費を100万円も水増ししていた He *padded* the expense account by no less than a million yen. / 先生が点数を水増ししてくれたおかげで進級できた Because the teacher *jacked up* my score, I was able to move up to the next grade.

みすみす 私はみすみす(→分かっていながら)好機を逸した I let slip a good chance, *though I knew I could have taken it*.

みずみずしい 瑞々しい みずみずしい果物 *fresh and juicy* fruit / みずみずしい肌をしている have「*fresh and youthful* [*dewy*] skin

みずむし 水虫 athlete's foot [U] ‖水虫になる get *athlete's foot*

みずもの 水物 勝負は水物だ(→運に支配されている) Games *are ruled by chance*.

みずもれ 水漏れ この容器は水漏れする This container *leaks*. / このひびから水漏れしている *Water is leaking* from this crack.

みずわり 水割り ウイスキーの水割り whiskey *and water* / ウイスキーを水割りにする *dilute* [*mix*] whiskey *with water*

みせ 店

《主に米》store [C], 《英》shop [C]

[語法]

> (1)《米》では「花屋」a flower shop,「理髪店」a barbershop,「肉屋」a butcher shop のように専門店・サービス業の店・制作[加工]する店に shop を用いる傾向がある.
> (2) store は《英》では主に「大型店・デパート」を指す.

〘店は〙

その店は朝9時にあきます The *store* opens at 9 a.m.

あの店は平日は午後9時に閉まる[まであいている] That *store*「closes at [is open until] 9 p.m. on weekdays.

この店はとても安い[高い] This *store* is very cheap [expensive]. / Prices at this *store* are very low [high].

〘店を〙

店を出す open *a store* / 店をたたむ close (down) *a store*

ほかの店をあたってみます I'll look at [in] another *store*.

きのうはおじの店を手伝った I helped out in my uncle's *store* yesterday.

〘店に・で(は)〙

お店に行って牛乳を買ってきてくれない? Can you go *to the store* and buy some milk?

この店に入ってみようよ Why don't we go *in* this *store*?

彼は父親が経営する店で働いている He works *at* [*in*] *a store* managed by his father.

私はその店でセーターを買った I bought a sweater *at* the *shop*.

その輸入雑貨の店では様々な外国製品を扱っている They deal in various foreign products *at* the import *shop*.

みせいねん 未成年 〘法律〙(未成年者) minor [C]; (未成年期) minority [U] (❖《米》では通例21歳未満, 一部の州では18歳未満.《英》では18歳未満) ‖彼はまだ未成年だ He's still *a minor*. / 未成年者の喫煙は法律で禁じられている *Minors* are prohibited by law from smoking. / 未成年者お断り《掲示》*No Minors* (*Allowed*); *Adults Only*

みせかけ 見せ掛け pretense [U]《また a ～》, show [U]《また a ～》; (偽物) sham [U]《また a ～》 ―見せかけの pretended, sham, false ‖彼の同情は見せかけだけだ His sympathy is only *a pretense* [*show, sham*].

◆見せかけの(→表面的な)美しさに目をくらまされていた I was blinded by *superficial* beauty.

みせかける 見せ掛ける (ふりをする) pretend [他] [自], make* [put* on] a show of ... ‖彼は困っているように見せかけてみんなの同情を引こうとした He tried to get everyone's sympathy by *pretending* to be in trouble.

◆交通事故に見せかけて人を殺す kill a person *making it appear* to be a traffic accident

みせじまい 店仕舞い その本屋はいつもより早めに店じまいした The book store *closed* earlier than usual. / 長引く不況のために彼らは店じまいせざるをえなかった They were forced to「*close* (*down*) [*shut* (*up*)] *the store* because of the prolonged depression.

みせしめ 見せしめ (警告) warning [C] [U];

(戒め) example ◎; (教訓) lesson ◎ //先生は生徒たちへの見せしめに遅刻した生徒を怒った The teacher told off the pupil who was late as *an example* to the other pupils.

ミセス (敬称) Mrs., Mrs; (既婚女性) married woman ◎; (主婦) homemaker ◎ //ヤングミセス *a young married woman*

みせつける 見せ付ける そのカップルは仲のよいところを見せつけた The couple *made a show [display] of* their affection. / 我々はその地震で自然の力を見せつけられた(→思い知った) We *realized* [*became very aware of*] the power of nature after the earthquake.

みせどころ 見せ所 ここが私たちの腕の見せどころだ This is *a chance to show* [*where we can show*] our skill.

みぜに 身銭 彼らは身銭を切ってその組織を運営している They *pay the expenses out of their own pockets* to manage the organization.

みせば 見せ場 highlight ◎, high point ◎; (最高潮の場面) climax ◎ //その芝居にはこれといった見せ場はないのにとてもおもしろい The play doesn't have any notable *highlights*, but is very interesting.

みせばん 店番 ちょっと店番してくれる？ Will you *mind the store* for a minute?

みせびらかす 見せびらかす show* off, parade ⓘ //彼は友達に新車を見せびらかした He *showed off* his new car to his friends. / 彼は友達に新車を見せびらかした He *paraded* his new car in front of his friends.

みせびらき 店開き 家の近くに新しい花屋が店開きした A new flower shop *opened* near my house.

みせもの 見世物 show ◎; (華やかな) spectacle ◎ //あっちへ行け、見せ物じゃないんだ Get lost! This is not *a show*.
//見せ物小屋 a show tent

みせられる 魅せられる 私はその絵にすっかり魅せられた I *was* absolutely *charmed* [*fascinated, enchanted*] *with* the painting.

みせる 見せる

❶【示す】show* ⓘ
ほかのかばんを見せてください Please *show* me another bag.
彼はパスポートを見せて身元を証明した He proved his identity by *showing* his passport.
妹は決して人に弱みを見せない My sister never *shows* her weakness to other people.
彼女はコンピュータに慣れているところを見せた She *showed* proficiency in operating a computer. / She *showed* that she was proficient in operating a computer.
こんな大金を見せられたらだれだって目がくらむよ Anyone who *is shown* so much money will be blinded by it.
◆あの本買ったんだって？ 見せてよ I hear you've bought that book. *Let me see it!* / メニューを見せていただけますか *Could I see* the menu? / 彼は驚いた表情を見せた He *gave* me *a surprised look*.

❷【思わせる】
父は自分を若く見せようと必死だ My father is trying hard *to「look* young [*make* himself *look* young].
このスーツはそのアクセサリーをいっそう美しく見せる This suit *shows off* the accessory even more beautifully. (✧ show off は「(ほかのものを)引き立てる」の意味)

❸【姿を】
彼は約束の時間を過ぎても姿を見せなかった He didn't *appear* [*show up*] even though it was past the appointed time.

❹【診察を受ける】
子供を医者に見せる(→連れていく) *take* a child *to a doctor*
手遅れになる前に医者に見せたほうがいいよ You'd better *go see a doctor* before it's too late.

❺【…してみせる】
このぬれぎぬは必ず晴らしてみせる I *will* certainly [*surely*] clear myself of this false charge.
まず先生がそれをやってみせた First the teacher *showed* us how to do it.
実際にやってみせてほしい(→やるところを見たい) I'd like to see you actually do it.

みぜん 未然 私たちは事故を未然に防ぐための対策を立てた We planned some measures to *prevent* accidents. (✧prevent に「未然に」の意味が含まれる)

みそ 味噌 miso, soybean paste
//みそ汁 *miso* soup / みそ漬け fish [vegetables] preserved in *miso*
慣用表現 そこがみそ(→要点)だ That's *the point.* / みそもくそもいっしょにする *mix good things with bad*

みそは原料である大豆を蒸したものをひきつぶし、こうじと塩を混ぜ発酵させたものです。みそを使った料理としてみそ汁が有名ですが、そのほかにもみそとよく合う料理はたくさんあります。同じ大豆を使った豆腐同様、みそも健康的な食品として高く評価されています。
Miso is made of soybeans that are steamed, ground, mixed with salt and malted rice and fermented. *Miso* soup is one popular dish in which *miso* is used, and there are many more dishes that go well with it. Like tofu, which is also made of soybeans, *miso* is highly appreciated as a health food.

みそ 溝 ditch ◎; (道路の排水溝) gutter ◎; (敷居・レコードなどの) groove ◎; (気持ち・関係の) gap ◎, gulf ◎ //溝を掘る dig *a ditch* / 引き戸を溝にはめる fit a sliding door into *a groove* / 車が溝にはまってしまった My car fell into *a ditch*. / 両者の間の溝は広がった[狭(セマ)まった] *The gap* between the two has widened [narrowed]. / 私たちは彼らとの間にある溝を埋められなかった We failed to fill *the gap* between us and them.

みぞう 未曾有 未曾有の(→先例のない)事件 an *unprecedented* case

みぞおち 鳩尾 the pit of the stomach, the solar plexus

みそぎ 禊 purification ◆再選されたことで汚職事件のみそぎはすんだ(→許された)と思っている国会議員もいる Some Diet members think they *have been excused for* their corruption by being reelected.

みそこなう 見損なう ❶[見逃す] miss //部活が長引いたのでテレビの連続ドラマを見そこなった I *missed (seeing)* a serial TV drama because the club activity dragged on.
❷[評価を誤る] misjudge; (過大評価する) overrate //彼が約束を破ることなんて絶対ないと思っていたのに、見そこなったよ I thought he would never break promises but I *have overrated [misjudged]* him. (※ misjudge は実際に評価よりよかった場合にも使える)

みそっ歯 味噌っ歯 decayed baby [milk] tooth

みそめる 見初める 父親は職場で母を見初めた(→ひとめぼれした) My father *fell in love with* my mother *at first sight* in his office.

みぞれ 霙 sleet ◆みぞれ混じりの雨 *sleety rain* / みぞれが降っている *It's sleeting.*

-みたい ❶[類似] あの雲はパンみたいだ That cloud *looks like* a piece of bread. / 彼はひどく落ち込んでいるみたいだけどどうしたの How is it that he *seems* so depressed? / 広昭はまるでアメリカ人みたいに英語を話す Hiroaki speaks English 「*just like* [*as if he were*] an American. / 君みたいな学生なら半年でドイツ語をマスターできるだろう A student *like* you will be able to master German in half a year. / 子供みたいなまねをするのはやめなさい Stop *acting like* a child.
❷[…してみたい] 金銭的に余裕があればギリシャに行ってみたい I'*d like to* visit Greece if my financial condition permits. →-たい

みだし 見出し (新聞などの) headline; (辞書などの) headword, entry //見出しには「神戸の教訓」とある The *headline* says "Lessons of Kobe." / その事故は大見出しで掲載された The accident 「*made big headlines* [*hit the headlines*].
‖見出し語 a headword, an entry

みだしなみ 身嗜み one's appearance //兄は身だしなみが悪いのでよく先生に注意される My brother *is* often reproved by his teacher because he *is careless of his appearance.*
◆和也はいつも身だしなみがいい Kazuya always *keeps himself neat.*

みたす 満たす (満足させる) satisfy; (いっぱいにする) fill //コップに水を満たす *fill a glass with water* / 私たちが満たさなければならない条件は何ですか What are the conditions we have to *satisfy* [*meet*]? / 夕食の残り物を食べて空腹を満たした I *satisfied my hunger* by eating the leftovers from dinner. ◆その車は私の要求を満たしていない The car is not *satisfactory for* my needs.

みだす 乱す (平和・秩序などを) disturb; (交通などを) disrupt; (心を) confuse, upset* //大雪が列車のダイヤを大幅に乱した Heavy snow *disrupted* the train schedule considerably. / 核実験は地域の平和を乱した The nuclear test *disturbed* the peace of the region. / その知らせは彼女の心を乱した The news *confused* her.
◆列を乱してはいけない Don't *get out of line.*

みたて 見立て (診断) diagnosis (複 diagnoses); (選択) choice //坂井先生の見立てでは胃潰瘍だ Dr. Sakai's *diagnosis* is a stomach ulcer. / このネクタイはガールフレンドの見立てです This tie is my girlfriend's *choice.*

みたてる 見立てる (選ぶ) choose*; (なぞらえる) liken //このスーツはおじが見立ててくれた My uncle *chose* this suit for me.

みたない 満たない、基準に満たない fall short of (the) standard / その講演の出席者は20人にも満たなかった There were fewer than 20 people attending the lecture. / そのツアーは定員に満たなかったため中止になった The tour was canceled because *it didn't get the minimum number of people.*

みため 見た目 appearance //晴子は自分の見た目ばかり気にしている Haruko only cares about her *appearance.*
◆その問題は見た目はやさしそうだが実は難しい The problem *seems easy on the surface*, but in fact it is difficult. / 山田先生は見た目よりも年をとっている Mr. Yamada is older *than he looks*. / 見た目には分からないだろうが彼はかつらをしている You *can't tell by looking at him*, but he's wearing a hairpiece.

みだら 淫ら ─みだらな (わいせつな) obscene, dirty; (ふしだらな) promiscuous //みだらな写真 *obscene pictures* / 彼のみだらなジョークはいつもひんしゅくを買っている His *dirty* jokes always draw frowns.

みだりに 妄りに みだりに(→理由なしに)机を動かさないでください Don't move the desks *without a reason.* / みだりに(→許可なしに)この部屋から本を持ち出してはいけません You can't take books out of this room *without permission.*

みだれ 乱れ 世の乱れ social disorder / 祖父はいつも日本語の乱れを嘆いている My grandfather always deplores *the corruption of the Japanese language.* / 誠は職員室に入る前に服装の乱れを直した Makoto *tidied* his clothes before entering the teachers' room. / 髪の乱れを直しなさい Straighten (up) *your ruffled hair.* / ダイヤの乱れは10時ごろまで続いた(→10時ごろに復旧した) *The disruption in the train schedule* was relieved at about 10 o'clock.

みだれる 乱れる
踏み切り事故のためダイヤが大幅に乱れた The train schedule was greatly *disrupted* because of an accident at a crossing.
最近この町は風紀が乱れている This town *is morally corrupt* nowadays. / This town *has no discipline* nowadays.
彼は20代には乱れた生活を送っていた He led *a loose life* in his twenties.

コミュニケーションスキル —道を尋ねる—
①道や場所を尋ねる

(A) **Can [Could] you tell me the way to** Sendagaya Station?
 -Sure. **Go straight along** this street **for two more blocks.**
千駄ヶ谷駅までの道を教えていただけますか. ―いいですとも. この通りをまっすぐ2ブロックほど行ってください.

(B) **Can [Could] you tell me how to get to** the Medical Center?
 -Of course. **Turn right at the next corner and you'll see** a big white building on the left. That's it.
医療センターへはどう行けばいいのか教えていただけますか. ―いいですよ. 次の角を右に曲がると, 左手に白い大きな建物が見えます. その建物がそうです.

(C) **Can [Could] you tell me the way to** the nearest post office?
 -Oh, I'm sorry. **I'm a stranger here myself.** Please ask somebody else.
ここからいちばん近い郵便局までの道を教えていただけますか. ―すみません. あいにく私もこのあたりは不案内なもので. だれか別の人に聞いてください.

(D) **Is there** a convenience store **around [near] here**?
 -Oh, there's one near the police station. **I'm going (in) that direction, so I'll take you there.**
この近くにコンビニはありますか. ―ああ, コンビニなら警察署の近くにありますよ. 私も方角が同じですから, 連れていってあげましょう.

(E) **Can [Could] you tell me where the ladies' room is?**
 -**It's on the left side of** the elevator.
婦人用のお手洗いはどちらでしょうか. ―エレベーターの左手になります.

(F) **Can [Could] you tell me where I can find the toy department?**
 -Certainly. **It's on** the seventh floor.
おもちゃ売り場はどこか教えていただけますか. ―はい. 7階にございます.

☞(A)〜(D)は道を尋ねる場合, (E)や(F)は建物の中での位置を尋ねる場合の一般的な表現. いずれも Excuse me. で始めるとより丁寧な言い方となる. 日本語の「…を教えていただけますか」に動詞の teach ではなく, tell を用いることに注意.

☞ 道順を人に説明する場合, 交差点や目印となる店や建物などを示しながら, 要領よく説明する. 1つの道路から次の道路までの建物(の集まり)が a block (1ブロック)となるので, ブロックの数や曲がる角をはっきり伝える.

☞ その土地に詳しくない場合は, (C)のように説明する.

②交通機関を尋ねる

(A) **Does this bus go to** Central Park?
 -No, it doesn't. **Take the number 7 bus.**
このバスは中央公園に行きますか. ―いいえ, 行きません. 7番のバスに乗ってください.

(B) **How do I get to** Yotsuya?
 -**Take this train. Change trains [Transfer] at** the next station and **take the train on Track 1.**
四ツ谷へはどう行ったらいいのですか. ―この電車に乗って次の駅で1番線の電車に乗り換えてください.

☞(A)のように聞かれた場合は,「行くのか行かないのか」を Yes/No ではっきりと答えた後で, (A)のように「何番のバス」と教えるのが親切.

☞「(電車など)を乗り換える」は change trains のように複数形になることに注意. 1語では transfer ということもできる.

③所要時間を尋ねる

(A) **How long will it take to** the airport by taxi?
 -**It will take** about half an hour from the hotel.
空港へはタクシーでどれくらいかかるでしょうか. ―ホテルからは30分ほどですね.

(B) **How far is it to** the National Museum **from here?**
 -**It's about a fifteen-minute walk.**
ここから国立博物館まではどれくらいありますか. ―歩いて15分ほどです.

☞ 目的地までの所要時間を尋ねるには, (A)のように How long will it take to …? の形を用いる. by 〜 で交通手段を表す場合, 冠詞を付けないことに注意.

☞(B)は「歩いて…分」という決まった言い方.「車で15分ほど」なら **It's about a fifteen-minute ride.** (自分が車を運転する場合は **a fifteen-minute drive**)となる.

風で髪が乱れた The wind *messed up* my hair.
いなかに残してきたボーイフレンドのことを思うと洋子の心は乱れた Thoughts of the boyfriend Yoko left behind in her hometown *upset* her.

みち¹ 道

❶【道路】(車道・公道) road ©; (街路) street ©; (小道) path ©; (道筋) way ©
➔ コミュニケーションスキル
アスファルトで舗装された道 *a road* paved with asphalt / 道を間違える go *the* wrong *way*
道は急カーブしている *The road* bends sharply.
2つの道はここで交わっている *The two roads* meet here.

この道を5分ほど行ってください Go along this *street* about five minutes.
探検隊はジャングルを切り開いて道をつけた The expedition cleared *a path* through the jungle.
新宿駅への道を教えていただけませんか Could you tell me *the way to* Shinjuku Station?
◆私たちは山で道に迷った We *got lost* in the mountains. / 我々は先を急ぐ救急車に道をあけた We *made way for* the speeding ambulance.

❷【距離】
京都まで道は長い It's *a long way* to Kyoto.
30キロの道を歩いたのでへとへとだ I'm exhausted after walking *30 kilometers*.

❸【進路】
卒業後私たちはそれぞれの道を歩んだ After graduation, we went *our separate ways*.
そのスキャンダルで彼は出世の道を断たれた The scandal *precluded* him *from* getting a promotion.
彼は辞任して後進に道を譲った He resigned his post to *make way for* his junior.
悪友のために彼は道を誤った He *was misled* by bad companions.

❹【道徳・教え】
人の道に反する残虐行為 an outrage *against humanity*
人の道を踏みはずすようなことはしたくない I don't want to *go astray from* the moral *principles*.
彼女は15年間アメリカで仏の道を説いてきた She has been preaching *the teachings of Buddhism* in America for 15 years.

❺【分野】field ⓒ, subject ⓒ
その道の大家 an authority on *the subject*
◆教師の道を選ぶ(→教師になる) *become* a teacher

❻【手段】way ⓒ
学校に行かなくてもフランス語を学ぶ道はいろいろある There are a lot of *ways* to learn French without going to school.
ロープを下ろすしか、その子供を救う道はなかった *The* only *way* to rescue the child was to drop a rope.
‖でこぼこ道 a rough [bumpy] road / 山道 a mountain path / わき道 a side road
慣用表現 すべての道はローマに通ず *All roads lead to Rome*.

みち² 未知 ——未知の unknown ‖未知の国 an *unknown* country ◆宇宙からの未知の生命体 *strange* beings from outer space

みちあんない 道案内 駅に行くんだったら僕が道案内をしましょう If you are going to the station, I'll "*show you the way* [*guide you*]. / 父親が運転し姉が道案内をした My father drove and my sister *navigated*.

みちか 身近 ——身近な(人が) close; (物・事が) familiar ‖彼女はその問題を身近な友人に相談した She talked the matter over with *close* friends. / 何か身近な例を挙げてくれませんか Would you please cite some *familiar* examples?
◆僕はこの辞書をいつも身近に置いている I always "*have this dictionary at hand* [*keep this dictionary by my side*].

みちがえる 見違える 理恵はアメリカで見違えるほど変わった(→彼女だと分からなかった) Rie has changed so much in America that I *could not recognize* her. / ペンキを塗ったら壁は見違えるようにきれいになった Painting this wall *made it look much nicer*.

みちくさ 道草 道草を食っていたらバスに遅れてしまった I *wasted my time on the way* and I missed the bus. / きょうは道草を食わずに帰ろう *I'll go straight home* today.

みちしお 満ち潮 a flood tide

みちじゅん 道順 the way ‖図書館への道順を教えてくれませんか Would you tell me *the way to* the library? / 道順を間違えた I took *the* wrong *way*.

みちしるべ 道しるべ signpost ⓒ ‖道しるべに従っていけば隣村に出ます Follow *the signposts* [*guideposts*] and you'll come to the next village.

みちすう 未知数 unknown quantity ⓒ (❀ 日本語同様比喩的にも用いる) ‖彼の役者としての才能はまだ未知数だ His ability as an actor is still *an unknown quantity*.

みちすじ 道筋 route ⓒ ‖駅に行く道筋にはコンビニが何軒もある There are a lot of convenience stores standing along *the route* to the station.

みちたりる 満ち足りる be satisfied ‖その村では人々は満ち足りた生活をしている In the village, people *are satisfied with* their lives. / その老人は満ち足りた顔つきでベンチに座っていた The old man was sitting on the bench with a *satisfied* [*contented*] look.

みちづれ 道連れ traveling companion ⓒ ‖京都に行く途中、1人の男性と道連れになった A man became *my traveling companion* on my way to Kyoto.
◆彼女は2人の娘を道連れに心中した(→2人の娘を殺し自殺した) She *killed* her two daughters *and committed suicide*.

みちなり 道なり 郵便局までこの通りを道なりに進んでください *Keep following* this street until you come to the post office.

みちのり 道程 distance ⓒ ‖この駅から競技場までは10キロの道のりだ It's *a distance* of 10 kilometers from this station to the stadium.
◆歩いて5分の道のり *a five-minute walk* / 名古屋まではまだ長い道のりだ It's still a *long way* to Nagoya. / 土地改革は長く困難な道のりになるだろう Land reform will be *a long and difficult process*.

みちばた 道端 the roadside ‖男はうめきながら道端に横たわっていた The man was lying groaning "*by the roadside* [*beside the road*].

みちはば 道幅 the width of a road
◆この道路は道幅が20メートルある This road is 20 meters *wide*. / その路地は道幅が狭いのでトラックは通れない The alley *is too narrow*

for a truck to go through.

みちひ 満ち干 潮の満ち干 *the ebb and flow* of the tide / このあたりは潮の満ち干が激しい *The tide varies greatly* near here.

みちびく 導く (先導する) lead* [他]; (案内する) guide [他] //新監督はチームを優勝に導いた The new manager *led* the team *to* the championship. / 田中博士は記者を研究室に導いた Dr. Tanaka *guided* the reporters *to* the laboratory.

◆答えを導く (→見つける) *find* an answer

みちる 満ちる (満ちている) be full of ... //独創的な考えに満ちた小論 an essay *full of* original thoughts / 人生は試練に満ちている Life *is full of* trials. / 彼は冒険心に満ちあふれていた He *was full of* adventure.

◆自信に満ちた態度 a *confident* manner / 彼女は幸せに満ちあふれていた She *was bubbling over with* happiness. / 潮が満ちてきた The tide *is coming in.*

みつ[1] 蜜 (はちみつ) honey [U]; (花の) nectar [U]; (シロップ) syrup [U] //花のみつを集める gather *nectar* from the flowers

みつ[2] 密 人口が密な地域 a *densely* populated area / 日本経済はアジア近隣諸国の経済と密に結びつくようになるだろう Japan's economy will be *tightly* [*closely*] tied to those of its Asian neighbors.

みつあみ 三つ編み《米》braids,《英》plaits // 敬子は髪を三つ編みにしている Keiko *wears* her hair *in braids.*

みっか 三日 3日間 for *three days* / 11月3日 November (*the*) *third*

◆博は何事にも三日坊主だ (→長続きしない) Hiroshi *can't stick to* anything *for long.* / 先月日記をつけ始めたが, 三日坊主に終わった (→すぐにやめた) I began to keep a diary last month but *gave it up soon.*

みっかい 密会 secret meeting [C]

◆首相がその会社の社長と密会したことが週刊誌に報道された It was reported in a weekly magazine that the Prime Minister *met* the president of the company *secretly.*

みつかる 見付かる be found; (発見される) be discovered; (悪いことをしているところを) be caught

この欠員を埋める人は見つからなかった No one *was found* to fill this vacant post.

この化石は富山で見つかった This fossil *was discovered* in Toyama.

こっそり部屋を抜け出そうとしているところを見つかった I *was caught* sneaking out of the room.

◆その店はあの角を右に曲がればすぐに見つかりますよ Turn right at that corner, and you *will* soon *find* the shop. / あちこち捜したがまだかぎは見つからない I've looked everywhere but I still *can't find* the key.

みつぐ 貢ぐ 彼は給料をすべて多恵子に貢いだ He *spent* his entire salary *on* Taeko.

ミックス ―ミックスする mix [他] //2種類のフルーツジュースをミックスする *mix* two kinds of fruit juice

◆これは牛乳とはちみつをミックスしたものです This is *a mixture* of milk and honey.

‖ミックスジュース mixed juice / ミックスダブルス mixed doubles / ケーキミックス (a) cake mix

みつくろう 見繕う パーティーに適当なCDを見つくろって (→何でも好きなCDを) 持ってきてください Please bring *whatever* CD's *you like* to the party.

みつける 見付ける find* [他]; (発見する) discover [他]; (悪いことをしているところを) catch* [他]

偶然その本を見つけた I *found* the book by accident.

とうとう彼らは行方不明の少女を見つけた At last they *found* the missing girl.

彼が図書館で勉強しているのを見つけた I *found* him studying in the library.

近くにいいレストランを見つけた I *discovered* a nice restaurant nearby.

母は泥棒が家に忍び込むところを見つけた My mother *caught* a thief stealing into the house.

◆解決方法を見つける *work out* a solution / 私はすぐに人込みの中から彼女を見つけることができた I easily *spotted* her in the crowd.

みつご 三つ子 (三つ子の一人) triplet [C]; (3歳児) three-year-old [C] //先日姉が三つ子を産んだ My sister gave birth to *triplets* the other day.

[ことわざ] 三つ子の魂百まで The child is father of the man. (→子供は大人の父である)

みっこう 密航 ―密航する stow away //貨物船でアメリカに密航する *stow away* on a cargo boat for America

‖密航者 a stowaway

みっこく 密告 彼が社長を警察に密告した He *informed on* [*against*] the president *to* the police.

‖密告者 an informer

みっしつ 密室 密室殺人事件 a case of murder in *a locked* [*sealed*] *room*

‖密室会議 a closed-door session

みっしゅう 密集 その地区は人口が密集している The district *is densely* [*heavily*] *populated.* / 僕の家の周りは民家が密集している Houses stand *close together* in my neighborhood. / その山のふもとには松が密集して生えている Pine trees grow *thickly* at the foot of the mountain.

ミッションスクール (キリスト教の学校) Christian school [C]; (布教のための学校) mission school [C]

みっせい 密生 空き地にはクローバーが密生している Clovers *grow thickly* in the vacant lot. / The vacant lot *is densely covered with* clovers.

みっせつ 密接 ―密接な close ―密接に closely //彼はその委員会と密接な関係がある He has *close* links with the committee. / 肺癌(はいがん)は喫煙と密接に関連しているという They say lung cancer is *closely* linked with smoking.

みつぞう 密造 ワインを密造する *produce* wine *illegally*; *bootleg* wine
‖密造者 a bootlegger / 密造酒 an illicit liquor, 《主に米口語的》moonshine

みつぞろい 三つ揃い three-piece suit [C]

みつだん 密談 confidential meeting [C] ∥2人はよくこの部屋で密談している The two often *have confidential meetings* in this room./ The two often *talk secretly* in this room.

みっちゃく 密着 この下着は肌に密着する This underwear *fits skin-tight*. / その小説家はいつも生活に密着した題材を取り上げる The novelist always takes up subjects *closely related to* daily life. / そのレポーターは芸能人の密着取材が専門だ The reporter is a specialist in *up-close coverage* of entertainers.

みっちり 兄はイギリスに行く前にみっちり英語を勉強した My brother studied English *hard* before going to Britain. / 山田さんに空手をみっちりと仕込まれた Mr. Yamada gave me *severe* training in karate. / カンニングがばれて石黒先生にみっちりしぼられた Mr. Ishiguro gave me *a good* telling-off [scolding] for cheating in the exam.

みっつ 三つ three [U][C] ➜ さん(三)

ミット 〖野球〗mitt [C] ∥キャッチャーミット *a* catcher's *mitt*

みつど 密度 density [U][C] ◆密度の濃い議論 a *meaty* discussion / その町は人口密度が高い[低い] The town *is densely* [*sparsely*] *populated*.

💬「この国の人口密度はどのくらいですか」「1平方キロメートル当たり300人です」 "What is *the population density* of this country?" "It's 300 people per square kilometer."

みつどもえ 三つ巴 今度の県知事選は田中，鈴木，山本の三つどもえの戦いになるだろう The coming election for prefectural governor will be *a three-way contest between* Tanaka, Suzuki and Yamamoto.

みっともない (恥ずべき) shameful; (不名誉な) disgraceful; (不格好な) clumsy-looking
駅前でナンパなんてみっともないまねはできないよ I can't pick up girls in front of a station. It's so *shameful*.
あのチームに負けるなんてみっともない It's *disgraceful* to lose to that team.
そんなみっともないシャツを着るのはいやだ I don't want to wear such a *clumsy-looking* shirt.
◆みっともない(→恥を知れ) *Shame on you*! / そんな口のきき方はみっともない(→無作法)ですよ It's *bad manners* to speak that way.

みつにゅうこく 密入国 smuggling [U], illegal immigration [U] ◆その男は3年前にアメリカに密入国した The man *smuggled himself into* America three years ago.
‖密入国者 an illegal alien

みつばい 密売 illicit sale [C] ◆その暴力団は覚醒(かくせい)剤の密売をしていた The gang *was dealing illegally* [*trafficking*] *in* stimulant drugs.
‖密売人 an illicit seller

みつばち 蜜蜂 honeybee [C], bee [C] ∥ミツバチの群れ a swarm of *bees*
◆ミツバチの巣 *a honeycomb*

みっぷう 密封 ──密封する seal [他] ∥封筒を密封する *seal* (*up*) an envelope

みっぺい 密閉 びんを密閉する *seal* (*up*) a jar / 彼女は砂糖を密閉容器に入れた She put the sugar in *an airtight container*.

みつぼうえき 密貿易 illicit trading [U], smuggling [U]

みつまた 三つ股 道はこの先で三つまたに分かれている The road splits *in three directions* up ahead.

みつまめ 蜜豆 🗻

> みつ豆はゆでた豆，寒天，ミカンやナシ，あるいは桃といったフルーツにみつをかけて食べるデザートの一種です。
> *Mitsumame* is a kind of dessert consisting of boiled beans, *kanten* (small cubes of cooked gelatin) and pieces of fruit such as *mikan* (Japanese orange), Japanese pear or peach. People eat *mitsumame* with syrup poured over it.

みつめる 見詰める gaze [自]; (特に意識して) stare [自] (❖人に対して用いると「じろじろ見る」といったニュアンスになり失礼とされることがある)
その少女に見つめられて彼は赤面した He blushed when the girl *gazed at* him.
私は彼の顔をじっと見つめた I *gazed into* his face.
2人はしばし見つめ合った The two *gazed at each other* for a while.
彼女は顔を上げて私をじっと見つめた She looked up and *stared at* me.
その少年は私の目をじっと見つめた The boy *stared into* my eyes.
彼は机の一点を見つめて考え事をしていた He was thinking about something as he *gazed* [*stared*] *at* a point on the desk.
◆自分のことをもっと客観的に見つめるべきだ You should *be* more *objective about* yourself.

みつもり 見積もり estimate [C] ∥およその見積もり *a* round *estimate* / 佐藤さんが絵画の修復費の見積もりをした Ms. Sato *made an estimate of* the repair of the picture.
◆ビルの建設費用の見積もり *a quotation for* the construction of the building
‖見積書 a written estimate

みつもる 見積もる estimate [他], make* an estimate of … ∥彼はわが家の塗装費用を30万円に見積もった He *estimated* the cost of painting my house *at* 300,000 yen.
◆地震による損害額は少なく見積もっても10兆円にのぼる The damage by the earthquake is 10 trillion yen *at a conservative* [*moderate*] *estimate*.

みつやく 密約 secret agreement [C] ∥吉田は斉藤と密約を結んだ Yoshida *made a secret agreement with* Saito.

みつゆ 密輸 smuggling ⓤ ——密輸する smuggle ⓥ ∥彼は銃を日本に密輸した He *smuggled* guns *into* Japan.
∥密輸業者 a smuggler / 密輸品 smuggled goods

みつゆしゅつ 密輸出 コカインを密輸出する *smuggle out* cocaine

みつゆにゅう 密輸入 象牙(ぞうげ)を密輸入する *smuggle in* ivory

みつりょう 密猟・密漁 poaching ⓤ
◆象を密猟する *poach* elephants
∥密猟[密漁]者 a poacher / 密漁船 a poaching boat

みつりん 密林 thick forest ⓒ, jungle ⓒ

みてい 未定 ・未定の unfixed, undecided ∥姉の結婚式の日取りはまだ未定です The date of my sister's wedding 「*is* still *unfixed* [*hasn't been set* yet].

みてくれ 見てくれ appearance ⓒ ∥彼は人を見てくれで判断する He judges people by *appearances*. ◆このリンゴは見てくれは悪いがとてもおいしい This apple *doesn't look nice* but it tastes great.

みてとる 見て取る realize ⓥ ∥彼が退屈しているのが見て取れた I *could realize* that he was bored. ◆彼女は彼の表情のかすかな変化を見て取った She *observed* a slight change in his expression.

みてみぬふり 見て見ぬ振り いじめを見て見ぬふりをするのはいじめに加わっているのと同じだ *Pretending not to see* [*Ignoring*] bullying is the same as being a bully yourself. / 私は彼の無作法を見て見ぬふりをした I *turned a blind eye to* his bad manners. / 彼は私の失敗を見て見ぬふりをしてくれた He *passed over* my mistake.

みてもらう 診てもらう すぐに医者に診てもらったほうがいいよ You'd better *see a doctor* at once.

みとう 未到・未踏 人跡未踏の地 an *untrodden* land / 前人未踏の分野 an *unexplored* field

みとおし 見通し (視界) visibility ⓤ; (見込み) prospects, outlook ⓒ; (洞察) insight ⓤⓒ
今夜は霧のために見通しが悪い *Visibility is poor* tonight due to the fog.
将来の見通しは明るい[暗い] *The prospects* are looking bright [gloomy] for the future.
次の10年間は明るい見通しだ We have *a* bright *outlook for* the next decade.
◆見通しの悪い道ではスピードを落としなさい Slow down when you *can't see far ahead* on the road. / 丸山先生は君の考えなんかお見通しだよ Mr. Maruyama *can see what* you'*re thinking*.

みとおす 見通す 山頂からは遠くまで見通せる You *can see* far into the distance from the mountaintop. / 50年後の日本を見通すのは極めて困難だ It is extremely difficult to *foresee* what Japan will be like 50 years from now.

みどころ 見所 ❶【見せ場】highlight ⓒ ∥その映画の見所ははでなアクションです The *highlight* of the film is its vivid action scenes.
❷【将来性】彼女ははなかなか見所のある若者だ She is a *promising* young woman.

みとどける 見届ける 靖子が電車に乗ったのを見届けてから(→確かめてから)駅を出た I left the station after *making sure* that Yasuko got on the train. / 寛子は父の最期を見届けた(→自分の目で見た) Hiroko *saw* her father die *with her own eyes*.

みとめいん 認め印 書類に認め印を押す stamp the paper with *a personal seal*

みとめる　認める

❶【承認する】(適切性を) accept ⓥ; (隠された真実を) acknowledge ⓥ; (自分に不利なものをしぶしぶ) admit ⓥ; (正当なものとしてしぶしぶ) concede ⓥ (公式的に) concede ⓥ
彼女は僕の言い訳を認めてくれなかった She *didn't accept* my excuses.
彼は収賄事件への関与を認めた He *acknowledged* his involvement in the bribery scandal.
彼は絶対に自分の罪を認めないだろう I'm afraid he *would never admit* his guilt.
少年は花びんを割ってしまったことを認めた The boy *admitted* having broken the vase.
俊二は敗北を認めようとしなかった Shunji *wouldn't concede* defeat.
彼らは私の解答が正しいと認めた They *conceded that* my answer was correct.

❷【高く評価する】appreciate ⓥ, recognize ⓥ
彼の小説は彼の死後に認められた His novels *were appreciated* after his death.
彼は犯罪心理学の専門家として認められている He *is recognized as* an expert on criminal psychology.

❸【許可する】(許可する) permit ⓥ; (容認する) allow ⓥ; (よいと認める) approve ⓥ
先生は試験で辞書の使用を認めた The teacher *permitted* [*allowed*] us *to* use dictionaries in the exam.
父は私が父の本を読むのを認めている My father *allows* me *to* read his books.
彼らは公共の場での喫煙を認めなかった They *didn't approve of* smoking in public places.

❹【判断する】(みなす) consider ⓥ
みんなが彼をハンサムだと認めている Everybody *considers* him handsome.

❺【確認する】
通りに人影は認められなかった There was not a soul *to be seen* in the street.
検査の結果、片方の肺に異常が認められた The results of the examination *showed* something is wrong with a lung.

みどり 緑 (色) green ⓤ (◆種類を指す場合はⓒ); (草木) greenery ⓤ ——緑の green
牧場は緑に覆われていた The pasture was covered with *green*.
その町には緑が点在している The city is dotted with *greenery*.

‖緑の週間 Arbor Week / みどりの日 Greenery Day

みとりず 見取り図 sketch ⓒ

ミドルきゅう ミドル級 the middleweight class ◆ミドル級の選手 *a middleweight*

みとれる 見とれる 彼女の美しさに見とれてしまった I *was fascinated by* her beauty. / I *feasted my eyes on* her beauty. / 私はその山々の美しさに見とれた I *was lost in admiration of* the beauty of the mountains.

ミトン ⚠mittens (❖数えるときはa pair of ... とする) / ミトンをはめる put on mittens

みな 皆 ➡みんな

みなおし 見直し この計画は見直しが必要です This plan needs to *be reviewed [reexamined]*.

みなおす 見直す (もう一度見る) look over again; (再検討する) review ⓤ, reexamine ⓤ; (再評価する) re-evaluate ⓤ, have* a better opinion of ... / 答案を見直す時間がなかった I didn't have time to *look over* answers *again*. / その計画は細部を見直す必要がある It is necessary to *review [reexamine]* the details of the plan. / 最近日本で彼の小説が見直されてきた His novels *have been reevaluated* recently in Japan.
◆昔ながらの日本家屋が見直されてきている People *have begun to take another look at* traditional Japanese houses. / 彼って案外料理が上手なの、見直しちゃった He's a surprisingly good cook. I *look at* him *differently* now.

みなぎる 漲る be full of ... / そのボクサーは闘志がみなぎっていた The boxer *was full of* fight.
◆それを聞いて全身に力がみなぎってくるような気がした When I heard that, my whole body *felt energized [invigorated]*.

みなげ 身投げ 彼は湖に身投げした He *threw himself into* the lake. / He *drowned himself in* the lake. (❖前者は身投げの結果死ななかった可能性もある)

みなごろし 皆殺し (大量虐殺) massacre ⓒ
◆銀行強盗は人質を皆殺しにした The bank robbers *massacred [killed]* all the hostages.

みなさん 皆さん everyone, everybody; (演説などでの呼びかけ) ladies and gentlemen (❖男性のみの場合はgentlemen, 女性のみの場合はladiesという)
みなさん、周りに集まってください Gather round, *everybody*.
みなさん、井上教授に乾杯をお願いします *Ladies and gentlemen*, I give you Professor Inoue!
家族のみなさんはいかがお過ごしですか How is *everybody in your family* getting along?
◆みなさん、ご静粛に願います Will *all of you* please come to order? / (生徒たちに) みなさん、教科書を開いてください Open your textbooks, *class*.

みなしご 孤児 orphan ⓒ

みなす 見做す regard ⓤ, consider ⓤ / 多くの人が日本を世界の経済大国とみなしている Many people *regard* Japan *as* a world economic power. / 彼はアメリカの最も偉大な作曲家の一人とみなされている He is「*considered to be* [*regarded as*] one of the greatest composers in America.

みなと 港 harbor ⓒ; (商港) port ⓒ / 多くの船が港に停泊していた Many ships were riding at anchor in the harbor.
‖港町 a port town

みなまたびょう 水俣病 Minamata disease

みなみ 南
the south ― 南の south, southern
風向きが南に変わった The wind turned to *the south*.
その町が国境の南にある The town lies *to the south of* the border.
その美術館はここから南へ約１キロの所にある The museum is about one kilometer *to the south of* here.
私の大学は東京の南の方 (→南の地域) にある My college is on *the south side* of Tokyo.
南口で待ち合わせしよう Let's meet at *the south exit*.
◆南へ針路をとる take a *southward* course / 車で南へ走る drive *southward* [*to the south*] / 私の家は南向きだ My house *faces south*. (❖この southは副詞で「南へ, 南に」の意味)
南の地方にはもう春が来ている It's already spring *down south*.

みなみアフリカ 南アフリカ South Africa (❖公式名は the Republic of South Africa) ──南アフリカ人 South African ⓒ ──南アフリカ (人) の South African

みなみアメリカ 南アメリカ South America ──南アメリカ人 South American

みなみかいきせん 南回帰線 the Tropic of Capricorn

みなみかぜ 南風 south wind ⓒ
◆あすは南風が吹くだろう The wind will blow *from the south* tomorrow.

みなみじゅうじせい 南十字星 the Southern Cross

みなみたいへいよう 南太平洋 the South Pacific

みなみはんきゅう 南半球 the southern hemisphere

みなもと 源 the source; (起源) the origin
◆四万十川はこの山に源を発している The Shimanto River *rises [has its source] in* this mountain.

みならい 見習い (徒弟) apprentice ⓒ; (実習生) trainee ⓒ / 見習いの大工 an *apprentice* carpenter / まだ見習い中です I'm still「*a trainee* [*in training*]」.
‖見習い期間 a probationary period

みならう 見習う follow *a person's* example / お兄さんを見習ってもっと勉強しなさい *Follow* your brother's *example* and study harder.

みなり 身なり one's appearance / 彼女は身

なりにむとんちゃくだ She is careless [casual] about *her appearance*.
◆彼はいつもきちんとした身なりをしている He's always *neatly dressed*. / 彼女はドアをノックする前に身なりを整えた She "*tidied herself up* [*straightened her clothes*]" before knocking on the door.

みなれる 見慣れる 見慣れた[見慣れない]顔 a *familiar* [an *unfamiliar*] face / 彼の髪型は最初は変だと思ったが最近では見慣れてしまった At first I thought his hairstyle was strange, but recently I've *become accustomed* [*used*] *to seeing* it. / 見慣れない人が父を訪ねてきた A *stranger* came to see my father.

ミニ mini- ‖ミニコミ誌 a magazine with a very small circulation / ミニコンポ a miniature stereo system / ミニサイクル a compact bicycle / ミニスカート a mini-skirt, a mini / ミニバイク a minibike; (原付自転車) a moped

ミニカー ⚠(模型自動車) miniature [model] car ◯ (❖minicarは「小型自動車」の意味)

みにくい 醜い (容貌(ぼう)などが) ugly (❖人については婉曲表現としてplain, homelyを用いることが多い); (恥ずべき) shameful
男の背中には醜い傷跡があった The man had an *ugly* [*unsightly*] scar on his back.
彼らはその土地をめぐる醜い争いをした They had a *shameful* [*disgraceful*] dispute over the land.
◆彼は醜い心の持ち主だと誤解されている They are wrong to think that he is a *bad* person.

みにくい² 見難い ここからは黒板が見にくい It *is difficult to see* the blackboard from here. / 山口先生の字はとても見にくい Ms. Yamaguchi's handwriting *is* very *hard to read*.

ミニチュア miniature ◯ ‖ミニチュアカー *a miniature of a car*

みぬく 見抜く see* through ... /彼にはうそを見抜く洞察力がある He has the insight to *see through* a lie. / 靖子は彼のたくらみを見抜いた Yasuko *saw through* his tricks.
◆彼らは彼の真意を見抜いた They *guessed* his true intention.

みね 峰 (山頂) peak ◯; (尾根) ridge ◯ /ここから雪に覆われた峰々がよく見える We can see snow-covered *peaks* clearly from here.

ミネアポリス Minneapolis(❖米国の都市)

ミネソタ Minnesota(❖米国中西部の州; (略語) Minn., 〔郵便〕MN)

ミネラル mineral ◯
‖ミネラルウオーター mineral water

みのう 未納 未納の税金 *unpaid* taxes / 先月の電気料金が未納だ I *haven't paid* my electricity bill for last month *yet*.
‖未納金 arrears

みのうえ 身の上 気の毒な身の上 *unfortunate circumstances* / バスの中で私は彼の身の上話を聞かされた He made me listen to *the story of* his *life* on the bus.
‖身の上相談欄 a personal advice column, 《英口語的》an agony column

みのがし 見逃し 彼は見逃しの三振に倒れた He *was called out on strikes*.

みのがす 見逃す (見そこなう) miss ⓗ; (大目に見る) overlook ⓗ
寝てしまい, そのドラマを見逃してしまった I fell asleep and *missed* the TV drama.
彼はとても背が高いので人込みの中でも見逃すことはないですよ He is very tall, so you can't *miss* him even in a crowd.
先生は僕の誤りを見逃してくれた The teacher *overlooked* my mistakes.
今回だけは見逃してあげよう I'll "*overlook it* [*let it pass*]" just this once.
◆どんな小さな罪も見逃すべきではない Even the smallest sins shouldn't *be passed over*. / 彼は絶好の機会を見逃した He *let a golden chance go by*.

みのけ 身の毛 身の毛のよだつ話 a *hair-raising* story / その光景を見て身の毛がよだった The scene *made my hair stand on end*.

みのしろきん 身代金 ransom ◯ ‖彼は1,000万円の身代金を要求した He demanded *a ransom* of 10 million yen.
‖身代金誘拐 kidnapping for ransom

みのほど 身の程 身の程 彼女をデートに誘うなんて君は身の程知らずだね You *don't know your place* asking her out. / 次郎に身の程を思い知らせてやろう I'll *put* Jiro *in his place*.

みのまわり 身の回り 身の回りの物を整頓(とん)しなさい Put *your things* in order. / 姉が父親の身の回りの世話をしています My sister "*takes care of* [*looks after*]" my father.

みのむし 蓑虫 bagworm ◯

みのり 実り crop ◯, harvest ◯ ‖実りの秋 autumn, the *harvest season* / 今年はミカンの実りがよかった[悪かった] We *had a good* [*poor*] *crop of* satsumas this year.
◆実りのある討論 a *fruitful* discussion / 会議は実り多いものであった The meeting was *productive*.

みのる 実る (実がなる) bear* fruit(❖比喩的な意味でも用いる); (成果が上がる) produce good [fruitful] results
ビワは初夏に実る Loquats *bear fruit* in early summer.
彼女の10年にわたる研究がようやく実った Her 10 years of research "*produced good results* [*bore fruit*]" at last.

みばえ 見栄え 見栄えのしない絵 a *boring* painting / この花は花びんに生けると見栄えがよくなるでしょう Arranged in a vase, these flowers will *look more attractive*. / 彼女は背が高いのでそのドレスを着ると見栄えがする She's tall, so she'll *look good* in that dress.

みはからう 見計らう 姉は父親がいないころを見計らって家に戻ってきた My sister *waited till* our father was out before she came home. / ころ合いを見計らって由美に電話した I *chose the right time* and phoned Yumi.

みはったつ 未発達 日本のインターネットは様々な点でまだまだ未発達(→発達不十分)といえる We can say that the Internet in Japan *is* still *underdeveloped* in many respects.

みはっぴょう 未発表 未発表の論文 a *previously unpublished* paper / 応募作品は未発表のものに限ります Contributions are limited to *unpublished* works. / 彼の新しい小説はまだ未発表だ(→原稿のままだ) His new novel *is* still *in manuscript*.

みはなす 見放す give* up on *a person*, abandon [他] ∥医者はその患者を見放した The doctor *gave up on* the patient. / 彼は友人から見放された He *was abandoned* [*deserted*] by his friends.

みはらい 未払い 未払いの給料 (an) *unpaid* salary

みはらし 見晴らし view [C] ∥見晴らしのいい窓 a window *with a fine view* / このデパートの屋上は見晴らしがいい The rooftop of this department store *commands a great view*.

みはらす 見晴らす ベランダからは富士山が見晴らせる You *can get a view of* Mt. Fuji from the balcony. / The balcony *has a view of* Mt. Fuji.

みはり 見張り guard [C] ∥見張りに立つ *stand guard* / 銀行強盗は入り口に見張りを置いた The bank robbers *put a guard* at the entrance. ◆彼らは2時間交代で見張りをする They *keep watch* in two-hour shifts.

みはる 見張る

❶【監視する】(人などを) watch [他]; (場所に張り込む)《口語的》stake out

刑事が3人で容疑者を見張っている Three detectives *are watching* the suspect.

刑事たちはその家を見張った The detectives *staked out* the house.

◆2人の男が門の所で見張っていた Two men *were standing guard* at the gate. / ガードマンが金庫を見張っている Security guards *are keeping watch on* the safe. / その店では私服の警備員が万引きを見張っている Plain-clothes guards *are watching for* shoplifters at the store. (❖watch for ... は「…を待ちかまえる」の意味)

❷【目を】

今日(こんにち)コンピュータがこなす仕事には目を見張るものがある *It's amazing* what computers can do today.

みびいき 身贔屓 (えこひいき) favoritism [U]; (縁者びいき) nepotism [U] ∥身びいきする *practice favoritism*

みひらき 見開き 見開きの広告 *a double-page spread of* an advertisement

みぶり 身振り gesture [C]

彼女はいつもおおげさな身ぶりで話す She always talks with grandiose *gestures*.

私たちは身ぶり手ぶりで意志の疎通をはかった We communicated「*with a lot of* [*by making full use of*] *gestures*.

◆先生は身ぶりで彼らに立つように合図した The teacher「*motioned* them [*gave* them *a sign*] to stand up.

みぶるい 身震い (恐怖・興奮などによる小刻みの) trembling [U]; (寒さ・ショックなどによる小刻みの) shiver [C]; (寒さ・恐怖・嫌悪などによる一瞬の) shudder [C] ―身震いする tremble [自]; shiver [自]; shudder [自] ∥恐怖で身震いする *tremble* with fear / 彼は事故の光景に身震いした He *shuddered at* the scene of the accident.

みぶん 身分 (社会的地位) (social) position [U] [C], (social) standing [U] [C]; (身元) identity [U]

身分の高い人 a person *of high position*

その当時身分の違う人たちは結婚を許されなかった In those days, people of different *social standings* [*positions, classes*] were not allowed to marry.

◆彼女は身分不相応な暮らしをしている She *lives beyond her means*. / 1か月も夏休みをとれるなんて斉藤さんは結構な身分だ Mr. Saito *is comfortably off* if he is able to take a month-long summer vacation. / 男は身分を明かさなかった The man *didn't identify himself*. / 身分を証明するものを持っていなかったので中へ入れてもらえなかった In the absence of *identification*, I was not allowed to enter.

∥身分証明書 an identity [ID] card

みぼうじん 未亡人 widow [C] ∥鈴木さんの未亡人 Mr. Suzuki's *widow* / 彼女は5年前に未亡人になった She became *a widow* five years ago.

みほん 見本 (商品の) sample [C]; (実例) example [C]

カーテン生地の見本を見せてください Let me see some *samples* of curtain materials.

彼女の失敗は「弘法も筆の誤り」のよい見本だ Her failure is *a good example* of the proverb "Even Homer sometimes nods."

◆田尾先生はすぐれた英語教師の見本だ Ms. Tao is *a role model* of a good English teacher. / Ms. Tao is a *model* English teacher.

∥見本市 a trade fair

みまい 見舞い

芳恵は彼に見舞いを言った Yoshie *expressed sympathy* [*her concern*] for him.

心からお見舞い申し上げます *Allow me to express my sincere sympathy*.

入院中の彼女にお見舞いの手紙を送った I sent *a get-well letter* to her in the hospital.

山田先生に暑中見舞いを出した I sent Mr. Yamada *a summer greeting card*. (❖暑中見舞いの習慣は英米にはない)

哲也が僕の彼女にちょっかいを出したので一発お見舞いしてやった I *punched* Tetsuya because he made a pass at my girlfriend.

∥見舞客 a visitor (to a sick person) / 見舞金 a gift of money / 見舞い状 a letter of sympathy; (病人を見舞う) a get-well letter / 見舞い品 a present (to a sick person)

みまう 見舞う

❶【病人などを】(訪問する) visit [他]

優子は入院中の祖母を見舞った Yuko *visited*

her grandmother in the hospital. / Yuko *went* to the hospital *to see* her grandmother.

❷【襲う】

高知県地方は先週台風に見舞われた Kochi Prefecture *was hit* [*struck*] *by* a typhoon last week.

この地域はこれまで数多くの自然災害に見舞われている This district *has had its share of* natural disasters.

みまちがえる 見間違える 駅名を見間違えてしまった I *misread* the station's name.

みまもる 見守る watch ⊕, keep* an eye on … ∥事の成り行きを見守る *watch* the course [run] of events / 僕たちは小鳥がえさを食べるのを見守った We *watched* the birds feed.

◆その画家は家族に見守られて息を引き取った The painter passed away *with* all his family *at his bedside.*

みまわす 見回す 会場内を見回す *look around* the hall / 私は友達を探してあたりを見回した I *looked around* trying to find my friend.

みまわり 見回り (巡視) patrol ⓤⓒ; (点検) inspection ⓤⓒ ∥彼は今見回りに出ている He *is on patrol* now.

◆西川さんと中原さんがその地区の見回りをする Mr. Nishikawa and Mr. Nakahara *patrol* the district.

みまわる 見回る 夜警が２時間おきにこの工場を見回っている A night watchman *patrols* [*makes the rounds of*] this factory every two hours.

みまん 未満 100円未満の端数を切り捨てる omit [ignore] fractions of *less than* 100 yen / 18歳未満の方は入場できません Children *under* 18 are not admitted.

みみ 耳

❶【身体部位】ear ⓒ

手で耳をふさぐ cover *one's ears* with *one's* hands

ウサギは長い耳が特徴だ A rabbit is characterized by *its* long *ears*.

彼は彼女の耳に何かささやいた He whispered something into her *ear*.

きのうから耳鳴りがしている My *ears have been ringing* since yesterday.

◆耳の穴 an *earhole* / 彼女は耳にピアスをしている She wears pierced earrings.

❷【聴覚】hearing ⓤ, ear ⓒ

彼の耳はまだしっかりしている His *hearing* is still good.

彼は子供のころ耳が聞こえなくなった He lost *his hearing* in his childhood.

君は耳がいいね You *have good hearing* [*ears*].

彼は耳が遠い He *is hard of hearing.* / His *hearing is poor.*

歌手にはよい耳が必要だ A singer needs *a good ear.*

直樹は音楽を聞く耳がある Naoki has *a good ear for* music.

◆彼らの音楽は耳に心地よい Their music *is nice to listen to.*

❸【物のへり】edge ⓒ; (パンの) crust ⓒ

彼は本を読みながらおもしろいページの耳を折る癖(くせ)がある He has a habit of turning down *the edges* of interesting pages when reading a book.

彼はサンドイッチを作るためにパンの耳を切り落とした He cut *the crusts* [*edges*] off the bread to make sandwiches.

❹【慣用表現】

【耳が痛い】その話をされると耳が痛いよ(→その話は痛いところをつく) That story *hits a sore spot*.

【耳が肥えている】斉藤さんはクラシック音楽に対する耳が肥えている Ms. Saito *has an ear for* classical music.

【耳が早い】彼女は近所のうわさに関しては耳が早い She *has quick ears* for neighborhood gossip.

【耳に入れる】君の耳に入れて(→知らせて)おきたいことがあるんだ I have something to *tell* you.

【耳にする】彼女が町を出るとのうわさを耳にした I *heard* a rumor she was leaving the town.

【耳にたこができる】そのことなら耳にたこができるほど聞いたよ(→そのことを聞くのはうんざりだ) I'm sick and tired of hearing that.

【耳につく】赤ん坊の泣き声が耳について(→原因で)眠れない I can't get to sleep because of the crying baby.

【耳に残る】その交通事故の音がまだ耳に残っている The sound of the traffic accident *is still ringing in my ears.*

【耳に入る】雅彦に関する変なうわさが耳に入った(→偶然聞こえてきた) I *happened to hear* a strange rumor about Masahiko.

【耳を疑う】彼女が離婚したと聞いたとき、私は耳を疑った(→信じられなかった) I *couldn't believe my ears* when I heard she got divorced.

【耳を貸す】ちょっと耳を貸してください *A word in your ear.* / (→知らせておきたいことがあります) *I have something to tell you.* / 先生は僕の言い訳に耳を貸そうとしなかった The teacher *turned a deaf ear to* my excuses.

【耳を傾ける】聴衆は彼女の講演に熱心に耳を傾けた The audience *listened to* her lecture eagerly.

【耳をすます】耳をすますと遠くで雷が鳴っていた When I *strained my ears* I could hear thunder in the distance.

【耳をそばだてる】彼は隣のテーブルの会話を耳をそばだてて聞いた(→耳を立てていた) He 「*pricked up his ears at* [(→注意して聞いていた) *listened attentively to*] the conversation at the next table.

【耳をそろえる】今すぐ耳をそろえて(→まとめて)借金を返してくれ Pay back your debt to me *in a lump sum* right now.

∥耳あか earwax / 耳かき an ear pick / 耳栓 earplugs / 耳掃除 ear cleaning

みみあたらしい 耳新しい それは僕には耳新し

みみうち 耳打ち 母は耳打ちをしようと私をわきの方へ連れていった Mother took me aside to *whisper* something *in my ear*. / 彼は私に家に帰るよう耳打ちした He *whispered to* me to go down.

みみがくもん 耳学問 彼は耳学問でたくさんのことを学んだ He *learned* [*picked up*] a lot of things *by ear* [*listening to other people*].

みみざわり 耳障り 場内アナウンスは耳ざわりだ The announcements over the PA system「*offend my ear* [*grate on my ears, are irritating*]. / この自転車のブレーキの音は本当に耳ざわりだ This bicycle's brakes make a really *grating* sound.

みみず earthworm ◆ミミズがはったような(→汚い)字 *bad* [*poor*] *handwriting* / むちで打たれ、その囚人の背中にはみみずばれができた The whipping raised *welts* on the prisoner's back.

みみずく 木菟 〘鳥〙horned owl ⓒ
みみたぶ 耳朶 earlobe ⓒ, lobe ⓒ
みみっちい (心が狭い) mean; (けちな) stingy
みみもと 耳元 彼女は私の耳元でささやいた She *whispered in* my *ear*.
みみより 耳寄り 君に耳よりな話があるよ I have some *good* [*welcome*] news for you.

みむき 見向き 彼はそのポスターに見向きもしなかった He「*paid no attention to* [*didn't even look at*] the poster. / 彼女は年下の男には見向きもしない(→全く興味がない) She *has absolutely no interest* in younger men.

みめい 未明 けさ未明、上野で火事があった There was a fire in Ueno「*at early dawn* [*before daybreak*] this morning.

みもち 身持ち 身持ちが悪い男 a man *of loose morals* / 彼女は身持ちがよい[悪い] She *leads a straight* [*dissipated*] *life*.

みもと 身元 (正体) one's identity; (生い立ち) one's background
彼らはその男の身元を調査した They checked up on the man's *background*.
◆身元の確かな人 a person *with good* [*clear*] *references* / 死体は指紋で身元が確認された The dead body *was identified* by its fingerprints.
∥身元照会先[人] a reference / 身元引受人 a guarantor, a surety

みもの 見物 その芝居はなかなかの見ものだった The play *was well worth seeing*. / その日の見ものは彼の手品だった *The highlight of the day* was his magic. / 彼らがどこに行くか見ものだ I'm *curious to see* where they are going.

みや 宮 (神社) (Shinto) shrine ⓒ; (皇族) prince ⓒ, princess ⓒ (✿前者は男性、後者は女性を指す); (皇居) the Imperial Palace

みやぎ 宮城

宮城県は本州北部に位置しており、東で太平洋に面しています。漁業が主要産業の一つで、イワシやマグロ、サバの水揚げが多いことで有名です。西部には、スキー場や温泉などの行楽地があり、なかでも蔵王や鳴子が有名です。県庁所在地である仙台市の七夕祭りは、毎年夏に行われます。
Miyagi Prefecture is located in northern Honshu and faces the Pacific Ocean to the east. Fishing is one of its main activities, and it is famous for producing large amounts of sardines, tuna and mackerel. In the western part of the prefecture, there are several leisure spots, including ski slopes and hot springs, with Zao and Naruko among the most famous. The Tanabata Festival in Sendai City, the capital of the prefecture, is held yearly in summer.

みゃく 脈 pulse ⓒ
患者の脈は72だった The patient's *pulse* was 72.
看護婦はその男の脈をとった The nurse *felt* [*took*] the man's *pulse*.
私は脈が速くなるのを感じた I felt *my pulse* quicken.
◆理沙がノーと言わなかったのは脈がある証拠だ(→希望がある) Risa didn't say no and it means *there is still some hope* for her.
∥不整脈 an irregular pulse

みゃくはく 脈拍 pulse ⓒ ⇒みゃく

みゃくみゃく 脈々 仏教の精神は脈々と受け継がれる(→ずっと残る)だろう The spirit of Buddhism will *live on*. / その伝統は日本人の中に脈々と生き続けてきた The tradition *has been in the blood* of the Japanese *throughout generations*.

みゃくらく 脈絡 彼のエッセーには脈絡がない(→一貫性がない) His essay *is incoherent*. / 由美子はそれまでの話とは脈絡のない(→関係がない)ことをしゃべりだした Yumiko began to talk about something which *had no connection with* what she had been saying.

みやげ 土産 (自分のための記念品) souvenir ⓒ; (他人への贈り物) gift ⓒ, present ⓒ / バリ旅行のみやげにスカーフを買った I bought a scarf as *a souvenir of* my trip to Bali. / このコースターは哲也のオーストラリアみやげです This coaster is *a present* Tetsuya brought back from Australia.
◆みんな彼女のニューヨーク旅行のみやげ話を聞きたがった Everybody wanted to hear *the story* of her trip to New York.
∥みやげ物店 a souvenir [gift] shop

みやこ 都 (都市) city ⓒ; (首都) the capital / 花の都パリ Paris, *the beautiful city*
◆彼はそのプロジェクトで大きな損失を出して都落ちとなった(→地方支店に転勤になった) He caused the project a big loss and *was transferred to a provincial branch*.
[ことわざ] 住めば都 Any place can be home once you get used to it.; There's no place like home.(→わが家に勝る所はない)

みやざき 宮崎
宮崎県は九州の南東部に位置しており、東で太

平洋に面しています．暖かい気候を利用して野菜や果物の促成・抑制栽培が盛んに行われています．観光地としては，南国的な雰囲気のリゾート地，日南海岸国定公園が有名です．また，宮崎県は，多くの神話伝説の舞台としても知られています．
Miyazaki Prefecture is located in southeastern Kyushu and faces the Pacific Ocean to the east. The warm climate allows the cultivation of early and late crops of fruits and vegetables. As a sightseeing spot the Nichinan Seacoast National Park, a resort with a tropical atmosphere, is famous. This prefecture is also well known as the place of origin of many myths and legends.

みやすい 見易い 彼女の字は見やすい(→読みやすい) Her handwriting *is easy to read.* / この席からは舞台が見やすい This is a *good* seat *to watch* the stage from. / 見やすい所にこのポスターをはってください Please put up this poster where it *can be easily seen.*

みやびやか 雅びやか **—みやびやかな** elegant ∥みやびやかな着物 an *elegant* kimono

みやぶる 見破る see* through ..., detect [他] ∥彼女は裕二のたくらみを見破った She *saw through* Yuji's plot. ◆彼はすぐに私の正体を見破った He soon *found* me *out.*

ミャンマー Myanmar (❖公式名 the Union of Myanmar) **—ミャンマー人** Myanmarese [C] **—ミャンマー(人)の** Myanmarese (❖英語では旧称の Burma, Burmese を用いることが多い)

ミュージカル musical [C] ∥このミュージカルは1975年に初めて上演された This *musical* was first staged in 1975. / そのミュージカルは3年間上演された The *musical* ran for three years.

みよう 見様 見ようによれば彼は非常に大胆だ *In a sense,* he is very bold. / 彼女は見よう見まねで簿記を覚えた She learned bookkeeping *by following the examples of others.*

みょう 妙 ❶【不思議】 **—妙な** (奇妙な) strange; (好奇心をそそる) curious; (ふつうでない) odd **—妙に** strangely; oddly; (異常に) unusually ∥玄関で妙な音がした I heard a *strange* sound from the entrance hall. / 彼の話し方には妙な癖(くせ)がある He has an *odd* mannerism in his speech. / この部屋にはだれもいないはずなのに妙なことに中からかぎがかかっている There can't be anybody in this room, but 「*strange to say* [*curiously*], the door is locked from the inside. / きょうは妙に疲れてるみたいだけど，どうしたの You look *unusually* tired today. What happened? ◆冬は妙に(→どういうわけか)人恋しくなる I get lonesome *for some reason* during the winter.

❷【巧みさ】 彼は説得の妙(→こつ)を得ている He has *a knack for* persuading people. / 言い得て妙だ *That's aptly put* [*expressed*].

みょう- 明- 明12月3日に *tomorrow,* on December 3

みょうあん 妙案 great idea [C], happy thought [C] ∥妙案が浮かんだ I got *a great* [*bright*] *idea.*

みょうぎ 妙技 (すばらしい技術) amazing skill [U]; (曲芸) feat [C] ∥妙技を披露する display *amazing* [*wonderful*] *skill*

みょうごにち 明後日 the day after tomorrow ◆明後日の朝 *the morning after next*

みょうじ 名字 family name [C], surname [C] ◆結婚前の名字 *one's name before marriage*

みょうじょう 明星 (金星) Venus ‖明けの明星 the morning star / 宵(よい)の明星 the evening star

みょうちょう 明朝 tomorrow morning [U]

みょうにち 明日 tomorrow [U] ➔ あす

みょうばん 明晩 tomorrow night [U]

みょうやく 妙薬 恋の病に効く妙薬(→奇跡のような薬)はない There is no *miracle drug* for people who are lovesick.

みょうり 冥利 こんな大役をもらって役者冥利に尽きる I'*m as happy as* an actor *can be* to be cast in such a major role.

みより 身寄り その老女には身寄りがなかった The old woman had no *relatives* [*family*].

ミラーボール mirror ball [C]

みらい 未来

the future **—未来の** future

未来を予測するのは難しい It is hard to predict *the future.*

未来には人類は月に住むようになるかもしれない *In the future,* humans may live on the moon.

大統領は国民にバラ色の未来を約束した The President promised the people *a* rosy *future.* (❖形容詞で修飾される場合は a ... future)

彼は小説家として洋々たる未来がある He *has a* bright *future* as a novelist. / He is a *promising* novelist.

こちらが私の未来の妻[夫]です This is my *future* wife [husband].

◆その家は未来的な外観をしていた The house had a *futuristic* exterior.

‖未来完了形〔文法〕 the future perfect / 未来時制〔文法〕 the future tense / 未来進行形〔文法〕 the future progressive form / 未来都市 a futuristic city / 近未来 the near future

ミリ milli- ‖ミリグラム a milligram (《略語》mg) / ミリバール a millibar (《略語》mb) / ミリメートル a millimeter (《略語》mm) / ミリリットル a milliliter (《略語》ml)

ミリオンセラー million seller [C]; (本の) million-selling book [C] ∥彼女のデビューアルバムはミリオンセラーになった Her debut album became *a million seller.*

みりょう 魅了 **—魅了する** fascinate [他] ∥彼は彼女の美しさに魅了された He *was fascinated* by her beauty.

◆観客は彼の演技に魅了された The audience *was gripped* [*captivated*] by his performance.

みりょく 魅力 (人を引きつける力) attraction ⓊⒸ; (人を魅了する力) charm ⓊⒸ, fascination ⓊⒸ; (人の心に訴える力) appeal ⓊⒸ
——**魅力的な** attractive; charming, fascinating; appealing

僕は彼女の笑顔に魅力を感じた I *felt an attraction to* her smile. / I *was attracted to* her smile.

革製品が魅力的な値段で売られている Leather goods are sold at *attractive* prices.

東京は若者にとって非常に魅力がある Tokyo *has* great *charm* for young people.

星占いには魅力的な男性が現れるって書いてあるわ The horoscope says a *charming* man may come my way.

彼女は都会生活に魅力を感じていた She *felt the fascination for* urban life.

クラシック音楽は私には魅力がない Classical music「*has no appeal* [*doesn't appeal*]to me.

◆みんな鈴木さんの温かい人柄に魅力を感じた Everyone *was fascinated* [*charmed*] by Ms. Suzuki's warm personality.

みりん 味醂 和 *mirin*, sweet sake for cooking

みる¹ 見る

❶【目で見る】(目に入る・見物する) see* ⓗ; (目を向ける) look ⓐ; (主に動くものをじっと見る) watch ⓗⓐ; (観察する) observe ⓗ

UFO を見たと彼は言っている He says he *saw* a UFO.

その映画は前に見たことがある I *have seen* that movie before.

暗やみの中で彼女は男性の人影が近づいてくるのを見た In the dark she *saw* a male figure approaching.

東京には見るべき所がたくさんある There are a lot of places to *see* in Tokyo.

先週は京都を見て回った I *looked around* Kyoto last week. / I *saw the sights of* Kyoto last week.

彼らは車を止めて地図を見た They stopped the car and *looked at* the map.

彼女は鏡を見た(→鏡の中の自分自身を見た) She *looked at* herself in the mirror.

窓から外を見たら雪が降っていた We *looked out* the window and found that it was snowing.

彼は左右を見て通りを渡った He *looked* right and left, then crossed the street.

さあ, 注意して見てください Now *watch* carefully.

きのうは10時からテレビを見た Yesterday, I *watched* TV from 10 o'clock.

テレビで野球のナイターを見た I *watched* a night baseball game on TV.

申しわけありませんが荷物を見ていてくださいますか I'm sorry to trouble you, but could you *watch* [*keep an eye on*] my luggage?

どうやって様々なパーツが組み立てられるかよく見ていてください *Observe* carefully how the various parts are put together.

◆その写真を見てもいいですか Can I *have a look at* those photos? / 私は時計をちらっと見た I *took a quick look at* my watch. / 彼は彼女の方をちらっと見た He *cast a glance at* her. / 人の顔をそんなふうにじろじろ見るものじゃない Don't *stare at* people's faces like that.

❷【判断する・推測する】 judge ⓗ

そこに到着するのに約3時間かかるだろうと見ています I *judge* it will take about three hours to get there.

◆多くの人は彼が次期首相になると見ている Many people *see* [*regard*] him *as* the next prime minister. / 私は円高がさらに進むと見ています I *think* the yen will go up higher. / 経済的な観点から見るとその計画は欠点だらけだ *From an economic viewpoint* the plan is full of demerits. / この指紋は犯人のものと見られます *It is presumed that* the fingerprint belongs to the suspect. / どう見ても君に勝ち目はないよ *In every way* you have no chance at all to win.

❸【調べる】 check ⓗ

予定表を見てみます I'll *check* my schedule.

きのうは掲示板を見なかった I *didn't check* the bulletin board yesterday.

◆中村先生が僕のレポートを見てくれた Ms. Nakamura *looked over* my report for me. / おふろが沸いてるか見てきてちょうだい Go and *see if* the bath is ready. / 郵便物が来たかどうか見てきましょう I'll *find out whether* the mail has come in.

❹【…してみる】

サイズを確かめたいのでこれを着てみてもいいですか May I *try* this *on* for size?

考えてみるとずいぶんおかしな話だ *Thinking it over*, it's quite a strange story.

このコーヒーを飲んでみてください Please *try* this coffee.

❺【その他】

私たちはここ20年間で非常に多くの変化を見てきた We *have seen* a great many changes in the past 20 years.

彼は英語ができなかったのでアメリカで痛い目を見た He *had a terrible experience* in the U.S. because he couldn't speak English.

おじとおばが祖父の面倒を見ている My uncle and aunt *are*「*taking care of* [*looking after*] my grandfather.

兄が英語の宿題を見てくれた(→手伝ってくれた) My brother *helped* me *with* my English homework.

慣用表現 今に見てろ *You'll be sorry for this*! / それ見たことか *I told you so*. / 見たところこの問題はやさしそうだ This question *seems* easy. / 見てのとおりまだ部屋の掃除をしていません *As you can see*, I haven't cleaned up my room yet. / 見も知らぬ人が親しげに私に話しかけてきた *A stranger* spoke to me in a friendly manner. / 彼は見る影もなくやつれてしまった He was worn *to a shadow*. / 見ると聞くとでは大違いだ There's a big difference between *what you see and what you hear*. / 動物たちがあんなに残酷に扱われている様子は見るに耐えなかった I *couldn't bear to see* the animals treated so cruelly. / 私の包丁使いを見るに見かねて母が自分でその魚をさばいた *Unable to stand idly by watching* me use the cutting knife, my mother cut up the fish herself. / あの男は見るのもいやだ I *can't stand the sight of* that man. / 見れば見るほど彼は中田に似ている *The more you look at* him, *the more* he looks like Nakata.

みる² 診る 田中先生は1日に5人の患者を診る Dr. Tanaka *sees* five patients a day. / 傷を医者に診てもらった I *had* the wound *examined* by a doctor. / すぐ医者に診てもらったほうがいい You'd *better see a doctor* at once.

ミルウォーキー Milwaukee (❖米国の都市)

みるからに 見るからに 伊藤博士は見るからに大学教授だ *Just one glance tells you* [*You can tell at a glance that*] Dr. Ito is a university professor. / 見るからに岡本さんは芸術家だ *Obviously* Mr. Okamoto is an artist.

ミルク milk ⓤ; (コーヒー用の) cream ⓤ / 私の紅茶にもう少しミルクを足していただけますか Could you add some more *milk* to my tea? / コーヒーにミルクをお願いします I'd like *cream* in my coffee.
◆ ミルク入りのコーヒー *white coffee* / 彼女は赤ん坊に1日8回ミルクをやる She *feeds* her baby eight times a day.
‖ミルクセーキ a milk shake / ミルクティー tea with milk / 粉ミルク powdered [dried] milk / コンデンスミルク condensed milk / スキムミルク skimmed [skim] milk

みるまに 見る間に 火の手は見る間に隣家に広がった The fire spread to the house next door *in an instant*.

みるみる 見る見る 成績がみるみる上がった My grades improved *very quickly*. / 煙がみるみる部屋中に広がった Smoke spread throughout the room *in an instant*.

みるめ 見る目 彼女は絵を見る目がある She has *an eye for* paintings. / 彼は人を見る目がある[ない] He *is a good* [*poor*] *judge of* people.

みれん 未練 僕はまだ典子に未練がある I「*am still attracted to* [*still think about*] Noriko. / 私は彼にもう未練はない I*'ve gotten over* him. / 彼はその家を売るのに未練はない He *has no regrets* about selling the house. / 未練がましいことを言うな *Don't harp on what was done*.

みわく 魅惑 fascination ⓤ ──魅惑する fascinate ⓗ ──魅惑的な fascinating / 彼はその絵の美しさに魅惑された He *was fascinated* by the beauty of the painting. / 彼女の声は魅惑的だ She has a *fascinating* voice.

みわけ 見分け 彼らはあまりに似ているので私には見分けがつかない They are so similar that I *can't* 「*tell* them *apart* [*distinguish between* them]. / どっちがどっちか見分けがつかない I *can't tell* which is which.

みわける 見分ける 羊とヤギを見分けることができますか Can you *distinguish* [*tell*] a sheep *from* a goat? / 毒キノコと食用キノコの見分け方を教えてください Please tell me *how to distinguish* a poisonous mushroom *from* an edible one.

みわたす 見渡す (見晴らす) look out over …, look around … 〘我々は塔のてっぺんから町を見渡した We *looked out over* the city from the top of the tower. / 彼は会場を見渡した He *looked around* the hall.
◆ 見渡すかぎり雪で白一色だった *As far as the eye could see*, it was all white with snow.

みんい 民意 この法案は民意を反映していない The bill does not reflect *the will of the public opinion*. / 今度の選挙で民意が問われることになる The coming election will ask *the will of the people*.

みんえい 民営 private ownership ⓤ
◆ 民営の鉄道会社 a *private* railroad company / その公団は去年民営化された The corporation *was privatized* last year. / その国はすべての産業を民営化しつつある The country *is converting* all of its industry *to private enterprise*.
‖民営化 privatization

みんか 民家 (private) house ⓒ

みんかん 民間 ──民間の (公でない) private; (軍に対して) civilian 〘民間からの出資 investments from *the private sector*
◆ その宗教はすぐ民間に広まった The religion spread *among the people* quickly. / 審査員は民間から選ばれる Judges will be chosen *from among the public*.
‖民間機 a civilian aircraft / 民間企業 a private enterprise / 民間人 a private citizen / 民間伝承 folklore / 民間療法 a folk remedy

ミンク 〘動物〙 mink ⓒ (複 ～, ～s) / ミンクのコート a *mink* coat

みんげい 民芸 folk art ⓤ, folkcraft ⓤ
◆ 民芸調のデザイン a *folksy* design
‖民芸品 a folkcraft, a folk handicraft / 民芸品店 a folkcraft shop

みんじ 民事 civil affairs
◆ 民事事件 *a civil case* / 民事訴訟を起こす bring *a civil action* [*suit*]
‖民事裁判 a civil trial / 民事訴訟法 the Code of Civil Procedure

みんしゅ 民主 ──民主的な democratic 〘民主的な社会 a *democratic* society / その方針決定の方法は民主的ではない The way of deciding the policy is not *democratic*.
‖民主化 democratization / 民主国家 a democratic country, a democracy / 民主主義 democracy / 民主主義者 a democrat / 民主政治 democratic government / 民主党(米国の) the Democratic Party / 民主

党員 a Democrat
みんしゅう 民衆 the people ∥彼の演説はテロ行為に対する民衆の怒りをかきたてた His speech drove *the people* into a rage against terrorism.
◆民衆の蜂起(ほうき) a *popular* uprising
みんしゅく 民宿 tourist home ⓒ,《英》guesthouse ⓒ
みんせい 民政 civil government Ⓤ
みんぞく¹ 民族 people ⓒ, nation ⓒ; ethnic group ⓒ (❖言語・文化が共通していることを強調した表現)
ドイツ民族 *the* German *people*
モンゴル人は誇り高い民族だ The Mongolians are *a* proud *people*.
日本人は最も勤勉な民族の一つだといわれている The Japanese are said to be one of the most industrious *peoples*.
◆インドは多民族国家だ India is *a multiethnic country*. / アイヌは日本の少数民族だ The Ainu are *an ethnic minority* of Japan.
∥民族意識 ethnic consciousness / 民族衣装 a folk costume / 民族音楽 ethnic music / 民族学 ethnology / 民族学者 an ethnologist / 民族自決 ethnic self-determination / 民族主義 nationalism / 民族性 ethnicity / 民族舞踊 a folk dance / 民族紛争 an ethnic conflict / 民族料理 ethnic food
みんぞく² 民俗 folk customs
∥民俗音楽 folk music / 民俗学 folklore / 民俗学者 a folklorist
ミンチ ⚠《米》ground meat Ⓤ,《英》mince

みんな 皆

❶【すべての人】everyone, everybody (❖後者の方がくだけた言い方. 共に単数扱い); (全員) all

彼のぐちにはみんなうんざりだ *Everyone* is sick and tired of his complaints.
みんな自分の分担の仕事をしなければいけない *Everyone* must do their share of the work.
私たちはみんな期末試験に向けて一生懸命勉強している We are *all* working hard for the term exams.
何人かの外国人に会ったが,彼らはみんな教師だった I met several foreigners. *All* of them were teachers.
私にはあなたがたみんなが必要だ I need you *all*.
◆みんなフランス語ができなかった *Nobody* [*None of us*] could speak French. (❖Everyone couldn't speak French.は「みんながフランス語ができたわけではない」の意味) / 私たちはみんなその俳優と握手をした *Each of us* shook hands with the actor. / 近所の人たちみんながパーティーにやってきた The *whole* neighborhood came over to the party.
❷【すべて】everything, all
ポケットに入っている物をみんな出しなさい Take *everything* out of your pockets.
あの本みんな捨てちゃったの? Did you throw away *all* of those books?
みんぺい 民兵 (組織) militia ⓒ;(個人) militiaman ⓒ
みんぽう¹ 民法 civil law Ⓤ
みんぽう² 民放 commercial broadcasting Ⓤ;(局) commercial broadcasting station ⓒ
みんよう 民謡 (traditional) folk song ⓒ
∥民謡歌手 a folk singer
みんわ 民話 folk tale ⓒ;(民間伝承) folklore ⓒ ∥この小説は古い民話に基づいている This novel is based on *an old folk tale*.

む

む 無 nothing ⓤ; (ゼロ) zero ⓤ ∥彼は彼女の好意を無にした He *treated* her kindness *as if it were nothing.* / 無から有は生じない Nothing comes from *nothing.* / 彼らの努力はすべて無になった All their efforts *have come to nothing.*

むい 無為 idleness ⓤ ――無為の idle ――無為に idly, in idleness ∥彼女は若いころ無為に時を過ごしていた She *led* [*lived*] *an idle life* when she was young.
◆政府は災害対策に無為無策だった The government *had no measures* for dealing with disasters.

むいか 六日 1月6日 January *sixth* / 6日間 *six days*

むいしき 無意識 unconsciousness ⓤ ――無意識の unconscious; (知らず知らずの) involuntary ――無意識に unconsciously; involuntarily ∥私は無意識に髪に手をやっていた I touched my hair *unconsciously.*
◆街で先生を見かけて無意識に(→本能的に)店に隠れた When I saw my teacher in town, I *instinctively* hid in a shop.

むいそん 無医村 a village without a doctor

むいちもん 無一文 ――無一文の penniless, (口語的) broke (❖名詞の前では用いない) ∥今月は無一文だ I'm *broke* this month. / 自分で事業を興そうとして無一文になった I *went broke* trying to start my own business.

むいみ 無意味 nonsense ⓤ ――無意味な (意味のない) meaningless, senseless; (むだな) useless ∥無意味な言い争いはやめよう Let's stop this *meaningless* argument. / そんな物買ってもどうせ使いこなせないのだから無意味だ You won't be able to use that, so it's *useless* to buy it.

ムース mousse ⓤ

ムード ⚠(雰囲気) atmosphere ⓤⓒ; (気分) mood ⓒ; (人に与える印象) air ⓒ
語法
ふつう英語のmoodは人の気分を表すので,その場の雰囲気という意味の「ムード」を表すにはatmosphereを用いる.

そのレストランはムードのある店だった The restaurant had (*a nice*) *atmosphere.* (❖niceがなくても「いい雰囲気」という意味で使われる) / 町中にお祭りムードが漂っていた There was *a festive mood* throughout the town.
◆武司と絵里はなかなかいいムードだ Takeshi and Eri *are romantically involved.* / 彼には独特のムードがある He has *a unique aura.*
∥ムード音楽 mood music

ムールがい ムール貝 mussel ⓒ

むえき 無益 ――無益な useless ∥無益な言い争いはやめろ Stop that *useless* quarrel.
◆その本は有害無益だ That book *does more harm than good.*

むえん 無縁 その件は宗教とは全くの無縁だ That incident *has* absolutely *nothing to do with* religion. / 彼は女とは無縁だ He *has nothing to do with* women.

むが 無我 selflessness ⓤ ――無我の selfless ∥多くの若い僧侶(*ガ)が無我の境地に達するための修行に励んでいる Many young monks practice ascetic discipline to attain *a state of selflessness.*
⊃ むが(むちゅう)

むかい 向かい 郵便局は市役所の向かい側です The post office is *opposite* the city hall. / 彼女はお向かいさんです She is *my neighbor across the street.*

むがい 無害 ――無害な harmless, innocuous ∥この薬は人体には無害だ This medicine *is harmless* to people.

むかいあう 向かい合う (人が) face each other; (建物が) be opposite each other / 2人は電車の中で向かい合って座った The two sat *facing each other* on the train. / 2軒の花屋は向かい合っている The two flower shops *are opposite each other.*
◆朝子は五郎と向かい合って話した Asako talked *face to face* with Goro.

むかいあわせ 向かい合わせ 向かい合わせの席を予約する reserve *facing seats* / 列車で由美と向かい合わせに座った I sat *face to face* with Yumi on the train.

むかいかぜ 向かい風 headwind ⓒⓤ ∥強い向かい風のため私の歩くスピードはだんだん遅くなっていった Because of *the intense headwind*, my pace became slower and slower. ◆私たちは向かい風を受けて海辺を走った We ran *against the wind* along the beach.

むかう 向かう

❶【面する】
向かって右から2人目が桜井さんの奥さんです *The second person from the right* is Mr. Sakurai's wife. (❖このような場合, 特に「向かって」を訳す必要はない)
彼は珍しく机に向かっている He's *sitting at his desk* for once.

❷【対する】
その犬は私に向かってほえた The dog barked *at* me.
強盗は店員に向かって銃を突きつけた The robber pointed the gun *at* a shop clerk.
風に向かって自転車をこいだ I pedaled my bike *against* the wind.
あいつは面と向かってよくそんなことを君に言えたものだ How could he say such a thing *to* you?

❸【目ざす】
彼は東京を去って故郷へ向かった He *left* Tokyo *for* home.

彼らはコンゴの奥地へ向かった They *traveled into* the Congo.

私は駅へ向かう途中にペンダントをなくした I lost my pendant *on the way to* the station.

仕事の後，彼はまっすぐ家へ向かった He *headed* straight home after work.

今そちらへ向かっています I'm *on my way*.

❹【ある状態になっていく】

彼女の健康状態は快方に向かった Her condition *took a turn* for the better.

経済は回復の方向へ向かっているようだ It seems that the economy *is heading* toward recovery.

むかえ 迎え 駅にだれか迎えをよこしてください Please send someone to *meet* me at the station. / 空港まであなたを迎えに行きます I'll come to the airport to *pick* you *up*. / 毎朝幼稚園のバスが娘を迎えに来る The school bus from the kindergarten comes to「*pick up* [*collect*] my daughter every morning.

‖迎え酒 a [the] hair of the dog (that bit *one*)

むかえうつ 迎え撃つ F-16機は敵機を迎え撃った F-16 fighters *intercepted* the enemy planes. / あす私たちのチームはホームグラウンドで相手チームを迎え撃つ Our team *will take on* the opposing team on our home field tomorrow.

むかえる 迎える

❶【人を】(会う) meet* [他]; (迎えに行く) pick up, collect [他]; (歓迎する) welcome [他]; (言葉・動作で歓迎する) greet [他]; (正式に歓迎する) receive [他]; (招待する) invite [他]

おじが私たちを駅で迎えてくれた We *were met* at the station by our uncle.

カナダのホストファミリーは私を温かく迎えてくれた My host family in Canada *welcomed* me warmly./ I *received a* warm *welcome* from my host family in Canada.

彼は握手で私を迎えた He *greeted* me by shaking hands.

ヒギンズ教授をオックスフォード大学からお迎えした We *invited* Professor Higgins from Oxford University.

> [英作文ノート] サンドイッチ語順
> 5時に家の前まで車で迎えに行くよ
> →×I'll *pick up* you at five in front of your house.
> →○I'll *pick* you *up* at five in front of your house.
> ★代名詞が目的語のときは，「動詞＋代名詞＋前置詞」と‘サンドイッチ語順’にする．そのほかは pick up the phone でも pick the phone up でも可．

❷【時期・状態を】(入る) enter [他]; (達する) reach [他]; (めぐってくる) come* around; (喜んで) greet [他], welcome [他]

今や宇宙旅行の時代を迎えようとしている We *are* now *entering* the era of space travel.

祖母は古稀(こき)を迎えた My grandmother *has reached* the age of 70.

私はいなかで新年を迎えた I *greeted* the New Year back home.

戦争の終結は喜びをもって迎えられた The end of the war *was greeted* with joy.

◆よいお年をお迎えください *I wish you a Happy New Year.*

むがく 無学 ―無学な (無知な) ignorant; (教育のない) uneducated ‖無学を恥じることはない *Being uneducated* is nothing to be ashamed of.

むかし 昔

the old days; (大昔) ancient times; (過去) the past ―昔の (古い) old; (大昔の) ancient; (以前の) former; (過去の) past

昔なじみ *an old friend*

母校に来ると昔に戻ったような気がする When I visit my old school, it reminds me of *my old days*.

だれも昔には戻れない No one can go back to *the past*.

祖母は昔をなつかしみながらよく若いころの話をする My grandmother misses *the old days* and often talks about them.

きのう昔の恋人に会った I met my *old girlfriend* [*boyfriend*] *yesterday*.

大昔の人は太陽を崇拝した People *in ancient times* worshiped the sun.

近藤君は昔からの友達だ Kondo is an *old* friend of mine.

◆昔からのやり方 the *conventional* method / 昔ながらの生き方 *old-fashioned* ways of life / 昔かたぎの大工 an *old-fashioned* carpenter / 昔このあたりに大きな木があった *Once* there was a big tree around here. / 昔はよく山歩きをしたものだ I *used to* go hiking in the mountains. / 彼は昔の彼とはすっかり別人になっている He is totally different from *what he used to be*. / 恐竜は大昔に地球上から姿を消した Dinosaurs vanished from the face of the earth *a long time ago*. / その銅像は昔からここにある The statue has *always* been here. / 昔々ある村におじいさんとおばあさんが住んでいました *Long, long ago* [*Once upon a time*], there lived an old man and woman in a village.

[慣用表現] 昔とった杵柄(きねづか)で写真展に応募した *I used to be pretty good at* photography, so I entered the photo contest.

むかしばなし 昔話 old story [tale] [C] ‖子供たちに昔話を聞かせる tell *an old story* to children ◆高校のクラス会では昔話に花が咲いた We *had a really good talk about our* high *school days* at the class reunion.

むかつく ❶【吐き気がする】feel* sick ‖胃がむかつく I *feel sick* in my stomach.

❷【腹が立つ】(怒る) get* angry ‖夜中にいたずら電話がかかってきてすごくむかついた I *got* really *angry* when I received a prank call at midnight.

◆あの男には本当にむかつく That man really *makes me sick*.

むかっぱら むかっ腹　わけもなくむかっ腹が立った I *flew into a temper* for no reason.

むかで 百足　centipede ⓒ

むかむか　食べ過ぎてむかむかする I *feel sick* because I ate too much. / 彼の態度にはむかむかする His attitude「*is irritating* [*irritates* me].

むがむちゅう 無我夢中　私は無我夢中で(→死にものぐるいで)泳いで岸にたどり着いた I swam *for my life* and reached the shore. / 彼女と同じ大学に入りたくて無我夢中で(→狂ったように)勉強した I studied *like mad* because I wanted to enter the same college as my girlfriend.

むかん 無冠　無冠の帝王 an *uncrowned* king

むかんかく 無感覚　━━無感覚な (刺激に対して) insensitive; (まひした) numb [nʌm] ∥寒さで指が無感覚になった My fingers have become *numb* with the cold.

むかんけい 無関係　━━無関係な irrelevant, unrelated ∥その質問はこの議題とは無関係だ That question *is irrelevant* to this topic.
◆私はそのいじめ事件とは無関係だ I *have nothing to do with* the bullying case.

むかんしん 無関心　(気にかけない) indifference ⓤ; (心配しない) unconcern ⓤ ━━無関心な indifferent; unconcerned ∥彼は他人のことにはいつも無関心である He is always *indifferent* to others. / 彼女は自分の将来に無関心だ She *is unconcerned* about her future.
◆私は芸能界には無関心だ I *have no interest in* show business.

むかんどう 無感動　━━無感動な unmoved; (表情が) impassive ∥彼は何に対しても無感動だ He *is unmoved* by anything.

むき¹ 向き
❶【方向】 way ⓒ, direction ⓒ
風の向き *the direction* of the wind; *the* wind *direction*
テレビの向きを変えた I changed *the direction* of the TV.
◆僕の部屋は北向きだ My room *faces north*. / 風向きが南に変わった The wind shifted *to* the south. / ヨットは右に向きを変えた The yacht *turned to* the right.
❷【適合】
この絵本は3歳以下の子供向きだ This picture book *is suitable for* children under three years old.
人には向き不向きというものがある Some people may *be suitable for* that while others may *not*.
この新しい家の造りは高齢者向きだ This new house is designed *for* the elderly.
❸【傾向】
学生は入試科目以外の教科を軽視する向きがある Students *tend* not *to* study seriously the subjects that don't come up on entrance exams.

むき² 彼女はすぐむきになる She is quick to *get serious and angry*.
🅔「そんなばかなことは絶対ない」「分かったよ、そんなにむきになるなよ」"That's total garbage!" "OK, OK. Don't *get so excited*."

むき³ 無期　━━無期の indefinite　━━無期に indefinitely ∥その計画は無期延期となった The plan was postponed *indefinitely*. / 友達が無期停学になった A friend of mine was suspended from school *indefinitely*.
∥無期懲役(終身刑) life imprisonment

むき⁴ 無機　━━無機の inorganic ∥無機化学 inorganic chemistry / 無機質[物] inorganic matter

むぎ 麦　(大麦) barley ⓤ; (小麦) wheat ⓤ, 《主に英》corn ⓤ ∥麦茶 barley tea / 麦畑 a barley [wheat] field / 麦飯 boiled rice and barley

むきあう 向き合う　face each other ∥私たちは互いに向き合って座っていた We sat *facing each other*.
◆今は問題に正面から向き合うことが大切だ What you have to do now is *face* the problem *directly*.

むきげん 無期限　━━無期限の indefinite ━━無期限に indefinitely ∥その航空会社のマイレージプログラムは無期限に使用できる That airline's mileage program is valid for *an indefinite period*.

むきず 無傷　━━無傷の (けがをしていない) uninjured, unhurt; (完璧(な)な) perfect ∥その兵士は無傷で帰還した The soldier came back *uninjured*. / 幸いなことにその事故では無傷でした Fortunately I *was unhurt* in the accident. / 彼は借りた物を無傷で返したためしがない He has never returned the things he borrowed *in perfect condition*.

むきだし 剥き出し　むき出しの足を投げ出す stretch out *one's bare* legs / 感情をむき出しにする *show one's* feelings *openly*

むきだす 剥き出す　その犬は歯をむき出して不審者にほえた The dog *showed its teeth* and barked at the stranger.

むきどう 無軌道　━━無軌道な (向こう見ずな) reckless, unruly; (だらしのない) loose ∥無軌道な若者たち reckless young people / 彼の無軌道な生活ぶりには全くあきれるよ I'm stunned by his *loose* [*unruly, reckless*] life.

むきなおる 向き直る　turn around [about] ∥彼女は向き直ると軽く会釈した She *turned around* and made a slight bow.

むきめい 無記名　━━無記名の (無署名の) unsigned; (匿名の) anonymous
◆このアンケートは無記名で答えてください Please answer this questionnaire *anonymously*. / 議長は無記名投票で選ばれた The chairperson was elected by (*secret*) *ballot*.

むきゅう¹ 無休　年中無休 (掲示) Open All Year / 父はここ数か月無休だ My father has had *no days off* for several months. / 当店は今月は無休で営業します We're open every day this month.

むきゅう² 無給　━━無給の (給料のない) unpaid; (名誉職の) honorary ∥無給のボランティア活動 *unpaid* volunteer work
◆私はこの夏おじのペンションで無給で働いた I worked at my uncle's resort lodge *with-*

むきょういく 無教育 ――**無教育な** uneducated

むきょうよう 無教養 ――**無教養な** uncultured ∥あいつは大卒だが無教養だ He is a college graduate, but he's *uncultured*.

むきょか 無許可 彼らは無許可でたこ焼きの露店を出していた They operated a *takoyaki* street stand *without「a permit [permission]*.

むきりょく 無気力 無気力な若者たち *lethargic* young people ∕ 彼はこのごろ何だか無気力だ He *is lethargic* [(→関心がない)*apathetic*] these days.

むぎわら 麦藁 straw Ⓤ ∥麦わら帽子 a *straw hat*

むきん 無菌(状態) asepsis Ⓤ ――**無菌の**(包帯・器具などが) aseptic; (消毒済みの) sterilized
∥無菌室 an aseptic [a sterilized] room ∕ 無菌状態 aseptic [sterile] conditions

むく¹ 向く

❶ 【**向きを変える**】 turn ⾃; (見る) look ⾃
上[下]を向く *look up* [*down*]
彼女はカメラの方を向いた (→体を向けた) She *turned to* the camera. ∕ (→見た) She *looked at* the camera.
後ろを向くと友人が立っていた When I *looked back*, I saw a friend standing there.
こっちを向きなさい *Look* this way.

❷ 【**面する**】 face ⾃他
私の部屋は東に向いた窓から朝日がさし込む My room gets the morning sun through the window *facing* east.

❸ 【**適する**】 be suitable [suited]
この仕事は君には向かない This job *is not suitable* [*suited*] for you. ∕ You're *not suited* to this job.
ここの土地は稲作に向いている This land *is suited* for growing rice.

❹ 【**気持ちが動く**】
妹は気が向いたときだけ母の手伝いをする My sister helps our mother only when she's *in the mood*.
🍏「庭の草取りしない？」「きょうは何となく気が向かないな」"How about weeding the garden?" "*I don't feel like it today*."

むく² 剝く peel ⾃他; (ナイフで) pare ⾃他 ∥リンゴ[タマネギ]の皮をむく *peel* [*pare*] an apple [onion] ∕ バナナの皮をむく *peel* a banana

むく³ 無垢 ――**無垢な** (純真な) innocent; (色などが) pure ∥白無垢の花嫁 a bride in *a pure white dress* ∕ 彼女は無垢な女の子だ She is an *innocent* girl.

むくい 報い (善行に対する) reward ⒞Ⓤ; (悪事に対する) punishment Ⓤ Ⓒ ∥何か報いがないとこの仕事はやっていられない I cannot do this work without some sort of *reward*. ∕ 彼女は罪に対する報いを受けた She「*received punishment* [*was punished*] for her sin.
◆(悪いことをしたのだから) 彼は報いを受けて当然だ He *deserves all he gets*. (❖この表現はよい意味でも使われる) ∕ きっとその報いを受けるぞ You'll *pay for* that!

むくいる 報いる (報酬などで) reward ⾃他; (行為で) repay ⾃他, return ⾃他 ∥彼女の長年にわたる研究はノーベル賞という形で報いられた Her many years of research *were rewarded* with a Nobel Prize. ∕ みなさんから受けた恩に報いるようがんばります I'll try my best to *repay* the favor I received from all of you.

むくち 無口 ――**無口な**(おとなしい) quiet; (寡黙(かもく)な) reticent ∥彼は無口な男だ He is a *quiet* man. ∕ He is a man of *few words*.

むくどり 椋鳥 starling

むくみ swelling Ⓤ ∥顔のむくみがとれた The *swelling* on my face is gone.

むくむ be swollen ∥彼女は長時間立っていたので足がむくんだ Her legs *were swollen* because she had been standing for a long time.

むくむく 入道雲が空にむくむくと沸き上がってきた A huge mass of thunderheads *is rising up* into the sky.

むくれる あの男の子はすぐむくれる The boy gets *bad-tempered and sulky* easily. ∕ 彼女はパーティーでむくれた顔をしていた She *looked sullen* at the party.

むくわれる be rewarded [repaid] ∥いつかあなたの努力が報われるときが来る One day your efforts will *be rewarded*.
◆報われない恋 *unrequited* love

-むけ -向け 幼児向けテレビ番組 a TV program *for* children ∕ 成人向けの映画 an *adult* [*X-rated*] movie ∕ この工場ではアメリカ向けの車を生産している At this factory, we produce cars *for* the United States.

むけい 無形 有形無形の援助をする offer *moral and material* support
∥無形文化財 an intangible cultural asset

むけいかく 無計画 ――**無計画な** unplanned; (統御されていない) uncontrolled ∥無計画な土地開発によって森の自然は破壊された The nature in the forest was destroyed by *uncontrolled* land development.
◆弟は無計画に (→考えずに) 金を使う My brother spends money *without thinking*.

むけつかくめい 無血革命 bloodless revolution Ⓒ

むけっせき 無欠席 私は高校3年間無遅刻無欠席だった I was *never late or absent* during all three years of high school.

むげに 無下に (きっぱりと) flatly; (即座に) out of hand ∥親友の頼みをむげに断るわけにはいかない I cannot refuse my best friend's request *flatly*.

むける¹ 向ける (体・顔などを) turn ⾃他; (視線・注意・努力などを) direct ⾃他; (銃などを) point ⾃他, aim ⾃他; (目的地に) head ⾃他
彼は突然警官に背を向けて逃げ出した He suddenly *turned his back to* the police officer and ran away.
強盗が銃を向けたとき私は恐怖で震えた When the robber *pointed* the gun at me, I

記者はその政治家にマイクを向けた The reporter *pointed* the microphone *at* the politician.

彼の批判は日本政府に向けられたものだった His criticisms *were aimed at* the Japanese government.

彼らは船をその島へ向けた They *headed* the ship for the island.

◆その船は香港に向けて出港した The ship sailed *for* Hong Kong. / 私たちは文化祭に向けて準備を進めている We are preparing *for* the school festival. / 使いの者をそちらに向けます I'll *send* a messenger to you.

むける² 剝ける peel 圓 ‖この桃はよく熟しているので簡単に皮がむける This peach is very ripe, so it *peels* easily. / 日に焼けて皮がむけだした I got sunburned and my skin started *peeling*.

むげん 無限 infinity ◎;(永遠) eternity ◎ ──無限の (はかり知れない) infinite;(永遠の) eternal;(限度のない) limitless;(尽きない) inexhaustible ‖宇宙は無限なのか,有限なのか Is the universe *infinite* or finite? / 子供たちは無限の可能性を秘めている Children have *infinite* possibilities. / 水資源は無限ではない Water resources are not *inexhaustible*.

むこ 婿 (娘の夫) son-in-law (複 sons-in-law);(花婿) (bride)groom ◎

◆兄は婿養子になった My brother *married into* his *wife's family*. / 彼らは娘に婿をとった They took *a husband* for their daughter.

むごい 惨い・酷い (恐ろしい) horrible, terrible;(残酷な) cruel;(無慈悲な) merciless;(残忍な) brutal ‖むごい仕打ち *cruel* treatment / むごい死に方をする die a *horrible* death / あの独裁者はむごいことをする人間だ That dictator is a *cruel* [*brutal*] man.

◆彼はその戦争でむごい殺され方をした He was killed in the war *cruelly* [*mercilessly*].

むこう¹ 向こう

❶【反対側】the opposite side;(もう一方側) the other side

私の家は公園の向こうにある My house is on *the other side* of the park.

塀の向こうにはだれがいるのですか Who is on *the other side* of the fence?

◆向こう三軒両隣 *one's nearest neighbors* / あの山の向こうには湖がある *Beyond* the mountain is a lake. / 彼女は道の向こうから私に声をかけた She called to me *from across* the street. / 着替えるから向こうを向いてて I'm going to change, so look *the other way*.

❷【相手】
向こうの言い分にも一理ある *They* also have a point.

💬「どうして太郎君とけんかしたの」「向こうが最初に手を出したんだよ」"Why did you fight with Taro?" "*He* started it first."

❸【今後】
あなたは向こう1週間安静にしている必要がある You need to stay in bed for the *next* week.

❹【あちら側】
(我々は)向こうへはいつ着きますか When are we arriving *there*?

向こうではのんびりとした生活をしていました I led a relaxed life *over there*.

慣用表現 その店はライバル店の向こうを張って (→対抗して) 全品を値下げした *In competition with* a rival, the store marked down all its goods.

むこう² 無効 invalidity ◎ ──無効な invalid;(契約などが法的に) void ‖無効な契約 a *void* contract / この券は無効だ This ticket is *invalid*.

‖無効票 an invalid vote

むこういき 向こう意気 奈穂は向こう意気が強い Naho *doesn't yield to others easily*.

むこうがい 無公害
‖無公害車 a pollution-free car

むこうぎし 向こう岸 向こう岸まで泳いで渡ることができる? Can you swim *across* [*to the other side of*] *the river*?

むこうずね 向こう脛 shin ◎ ‖向こうずねを柱にぶつけた I banged *my shin* on the post.

むこうみず 向こう見ず ──向こう見ずな (無謀な) reckless;(軽率な) rash ‖彼女は少し向こう見ずなところがある She is a bit *reckless* [*rash*].

むこくせき 無国籍 ──無国籍の stateless
‖無国籍者 a stateless person / 無国籍料理 cosmopolitan food

むごたらしい 惨たらしい (残忍な) cruel;(恐ろしい) horrible ‖テレビでその戦争のむごたらしい場面を見た I saw a *horrible* scene from the war on TV.

むごん 無言 無言の (→暗黙の) 約束 a *tacit* agreement / 彼は無言で部屋から出ていった He left the room *without saying a word*. / 彼は会議の間無言だった He *was silent* during the meeting. / 時々家に無言電話がかかってくる We sometimes get *silent phone calls*.

むざい 無罪 innocence ◎ ──無罪の innocent;(裁判などで) not guilty ‖被告人は無罪を主張した The defendant maintained his *innocence*. / 裁判所は彼が無罪であると判決を下した The court judged him (to be) *not guilty*.

むさく 無策 自治体の災害に対する無策ぶりにはあきれるばかりだ We are very disappointed about our local government's *lack of policy* on disasters.

むさくい 無作為 ──無作為の random ──無作為に at random ‖陪審員は無作為に選ばれる The members of a jury are selected *at random*.

‖無作為抽出 random sampling

むさくるしい (不潔な) messy;(乱雑な) untidy ‖むさくるしい格好をしているな You look *messy*.

◆むさくるしいところですが今度遊びにいらしてください *Our house is a mess*, but please come and visit us sometime.

むささび flying squirrel ◎

むさべつ 無差別 indiscrimination Ⓤ ━━無差別の indiscriminate ━━無差別に indiscriminately 《その都市で無差別殺人事件が起こった》 *An act of indiscriminate murder occurred in the city.*
∥無差別級《柔道》the open-weight (division) / 無差別攻撃 an indiscriminate attack

むさぼりよむ むさぼり読む devour ⓗ / 《里美は学生時代本をむさぼり読んだ》 Satomi *devoured* books when she was a student.

むさぼる 貪る (がつがつ食べる) devour ⓗ (❖比喩的にも用いる); (利益などを) profiteer ⓘ / 《男は出された食べ物をむさぼり食った》 The man *devoured* the food provided. / 《父はアメリカ出張から戻ると日本語の新聞をむさぼるように読んだ》 My father *devoured* Japanese newspapers when he came back from his business trip to America. / 《あの会社は開発の名のもとに暴利をむさぼった》 The company *profiteered* under the name of development.

むざむざと (たやすく) easily; (惜しげもなく) freely / 《むざむざと引き下がるわけにはいかない》 I cannot give up so *easily*. / 《これをむざむざと彼の手に渡すようなことはしない》 I won't give this up to him *freely*.

むざん 無残・無惨 (恐ろしい) horrible; (悲惨な) tragic; (残酷な) cruel; (痛ましい) pitiful / 《列車の衝突事故現場は見るも無残な光景だった》 The scene of the train crash was a *horrible* sight. / 《我々の試みは無残な結果に終わった》 Our attempt met a *tragic* end. ◆ 《彼の希望は無残にも打ち砕かれた》 His hopes were destroyed *miserably*.

むし¹ 虫

(昆虫の) insect ⓒ; (特に人に不快感を与える虫) bug ⓒ (❖昆虫一般を指す意味でも使う); (害虫)《公式的》vermin Ⓤ; (コオロギ・鈴虫など) cricket ⓒ; (ミミズ・ウジなど) worm ⓒ / 《日本には古くから虫の音を楽しむ習慣がある》 Japan has long enjoyed the custom of listening to *crickets* chirp.
《腕を虫に刺された》 I was bitten on my arm by *a bug*.
◆ 《お気に入りのコートを虫に食われた》 My favorite coat was *moth-eaten*. / 《このリンゴは虫に食われている》 This apple *is wormy*.
∥虫かご an insect cage / 虫捕り網 a butterfly net / 虫よけ ➡ むしよけ
慣用表現 《彼は仕事の虫だ》 He's *a workaholic*. / 《腹の虫がまだ納まらない》 I'm still *angry*. / 《彼女は本の虫だ》 She is *a bookworm*. / 《何となく彼は虫が好かない》 He is *a disagreeable* man. / 《君は虫がよすぎるよ》 You're asking too much. / 《あの人はもう虫の息だ》 That man is *at death's door [on his death bed]*. / 《彼女は虫の居所が悪いようだ》 She seems to *be in a bad mood*. / 《あれは虫の知らせというものだ》 That was *a premonition*. / 《彼女は虫も殺さぬ顔をしているけれど、陰では人の悪口ばかり言っている》 She looks as if she *wouldn't harm a fly*, but actually she always speaks ill of others behind their backs. / 《父は私に悪い虫がつかないかといつも心配している》 My father is always worried that I might *have a bad boyfriend*.
ことわざ 一寸の虫にも五分の魂 ➡ いっすん / 《たで食う虫も好き好き》 ➡ たで

むし² 無視 ━━無視する ignore ⓗ; (軽視する) disregard ⓗ; (怠る) neglect ⓗ; (注意を払わない) pay* no attention (to …) / 《あの赤い車は信号を無視した》 That red car *ignored* the traffic lights. / 《桂子は太郎のことを無視している》 Keiko *ignores* Taro. / 《会議で私の提案は無視された》 My proposal *was disregarded* at the meeting. / 《彼女は医者の警告を無視した》 She *neglected* the doctor's warning.

むし³ 無私 ━━無私の (利己的でない) selfless; (利害関係のない) disinterested / 《野球の審判は公平無私であるべきだ》 A baseball umpire should *be fair and disinterested*.

むじ 無地 ━━無地の plain / 《無地の壁紙》 *plain* wallpaper

むしあつい 蒸し暑い hot and humid, sticky, sultry, 《口語的》muggy / 《日本の夏は蒸し暑い》 The summer in Japan *is hot and humid*. / 《きょうは蒸し暑いね》 Today is a *muggy* day.

むしかえす 蒸し返す (繰り返す) repeat ⓗ; (問題などを) bring* up again / 《彼はいつも私の昔の過ちを蒸し返す》 He always *brings up* my past faults *again*.

むしかく 無資格 ━━無資格の unqualified; (免許のない) unlicensed / 《その医師は無資格だったことが分かった》 The doctor was found to be *unqualified [unlicensed]*.

むしき 蒸し器 steamer ⓒ

むしくい 虫食い ━━虫食いの (木材・果物などが) worm-eaten; (衣類が) moth-eaten / 《虫食いのビワ》a *worm-eaten* loquat / 《虫食いのスーツ》a *moth-eaten* suit

むしくだし 虫下し vermifuge ⓒⓊ

むしけら 虫けら worm ⓒ

むしけん 無試験 / 《中央中学から中央高校へは無試験で入れる》 You can go from Chuo Junior High School to Chuo High School *without taking an exam*.

むじこ 無事故 (機械の) 無事故運転 trouble-free operation / 《祖父は50年間無事故運転だ》 My grandfather has driven *with no accidents* for 50 years. / 《彼女は20年間無事故無違反だ》 She's had *a perfect driving record* for 20 years.

むしさされ 虫刺され insect bite ⓒ

むしず 虫酸 / 《あいつの声を聞くだけで虫酸が走る》 Just hearing his voice *disgusts* me.

むじつ 無実 innocence Ⓤ ━━無実の innocent / 《彼女は自分の無実を主張した》 She asserted her *innocence*. / 《She asserted that she was *innocent*.》
◆ 無実の罪 *a false* charge

むしば 虫歯 (虫歯の穴) cavity ⓒ; (悪くなった歯) decayed [bad] tooth ⓒ; (歯が悪くなること) tooth decay Ⓤ / 《虫歯になる》 get *a cavity*

/ 虫歯に詰め物をする fill *a cavity* / 私は虫歯が 2 本ある I have two *cavities* [*decayed teeth*]. / 虫歯予防には歯みがきが大切だ It is important to brush your teeth to prevent *tooth decay*.

むしばむ 蝕む destroy ... gradually, undermine [他] //白血病が彼女の体をむしばんでいた Leukemia *was destroying* her *gradually*. ◆喫煙は本人のみではなく周りの者の健康をもむしばむ(→影響を及ぼす) Smoking *affects* not only smokers but also the health of people around them.

むじひ 無慈悲 ―無慈悲な merciless; (薄情な) heartless; (残酷な) cruel //無慈悲な扱いをする[受ける] give [have] *merciless* treatment

むしぶろ 蒸し風呂 steam bath [C]

むしぼし 虫干し airing [C] ―虫干しする air [他] //母は私たちの冬服を虫干しした My mother *aired* our winter clothes.

むしまんるい 無死満塁 無死満塁だ The bases are *full* [*loaded*] *with no outs*.

むしむし きょうはすごくむしむしする It's very *muggy* today. ➾むしあつい

むしめがね 虫眼鏡 magnifying glass [C], magnifier [C] //虫眼鏡でアリを観察する observe ants through *a magnifying glass*

むしゃ 武者 warrior [C], soldier [C] ◆武者震いする *shake with excitement* / 彼はアメリカに英語の武者修業に出かけた He went to America *in order to brush up his English*.

むしやき 蒸し焼き (オーブンで)鶏を蒸し焼きにする *roast* chicken / 魚をアルミホイルで包んで蒸し焼きにする *bake* a fish *wrapped in aluminum foil*

むじゃき 無邪気 innocence [U] ―無邪気な (純真な) innocent; (子供らしい) childlike (❖childish は「子供っぽい」という好ましくない意味) //子供たちの無邪気な笑顔 *innocent* smiles of children

むしゃくしゃ きょうはむしゃくしゃする I *feel irritated* today.

むしゃむしゃ あの大男は出されたものすべてをむしゃむしゃ食べていた That big fellow *was munching* everything served.

むしゅう 無臭 ―無臭の odorless
◆この液体は無色無臭だ This liquid *has no color or odor*.

むしゅうきょう 無宗教 わが家は無宗教だ Our family *doesn't have any particular religion*.

むしゅうにゅう 無収入 先月から無収入になった I *have had no income* since last month.

むじゅうりょく 無重力 zero gravity [U] ‖無重力飛行 a zero-gravity [weightless] flight

むしゅみ 無趣味 彼女は無趣味だ She *has no hobbies*.

むじゅん 矛盾 (相反すること) contradiction [U][C]; (首尾一貫していないこと) inconsistency [U][C] ―矛盾する contradict [他] //社会の矛盾 *the contradictions* of society / 彼の議論は矛盾だらけだ His argument is a mass of *contradictions*. / その会社の貸借対照表と損益計算書は矛盾している The company's balance sheet *contradicts* its income statement.
◆この論文の結論は内容に矛盾している The conclusion of this essay *is inconsistent* with the body.

むしょう 無償 無償で貧しい人たちに治療をする treat poor people *for nothing*
‖無償配布 free distribution

むじょう[1] 無常 (一時的であること) transience [U]; (空虚) emptiness [U] //無常観にさいなまれる suffer *a sense of emptiness*

むじょう[2] 無情 ―無情な (薄情な) heartless; (無慈悲な) merciless //無情な仕打ち *heartless* [*merciless*] treatment

むじょう[3] 無上 生徒会長に選ばれたことは私にとって無上の喜びです It's *the greatest pleasure* to be elected president of the student council.

むじょうけん 無条件 ―無条件の unconditional ―無条件に unconditionally //無条件であなたを金銭的に援助するつもりはない I'm not going to give you financial help *unconditionally*.
‖無条件降伏 unconditional surrender

むしょうに 無性に 私は恵子の態度にむしょうに腹が立った I got *very* angry at Keiko's attitude. / 何だかアイスクリームがむしょうに食べたい I'*m dying for* some ice cream.

むしょく[1] 無職 ―無職の (失業した) jobless, unemployed //彼女は無職だ (→失業中だ) She *is jobless* [*unemployed*]. / (→働いていない) She *does not work*.

むしょく[2] 無色 ―無色の colorless //無色透明の液体 a *colorless, transparent* liquid

むしよけ 虫除け insect repellent [C][U]

むしょぞく 無所属 無所属で立候補する run for election as *an independent*
‖無所属議員 an independent / 無所属候補 an independent candidate

むしる 毟る (鳥の羽などを) pull [他], pluck [他]; (調理した魚などを) pick [他]; (草を) weed [他] //鶏の羽をむしる *pull* the feathers off [*pluck*] a chicken / この前の日曜日は庭の草をむしった I *weeded* the garden last Sunday.

むしろ[1] rather (than ...)
彼の言うことは意見というよりむしろ不満だ What he says is a complaint *rather than* an opinion.
私は出かけるよりむしろ家にいるほうがいい I'*d rather* stay home *than* go out. / I *prefer* staying home *to* going out. / I *prefer to* stay home *rather than* go out.
むしろ君には学級委員をやってもらいたい I'*d rather that* you were the class representative.
彼は犬を散歩に連れていきたいというよりもむしろたばこを吸いたいだけだ He wants to walk the dog, *or rather* he wants to smoke.
◆きょうはむしろ昼間のほうが寒かった *If anything*, it was colder during the day today.

むしろ[2] 筵 straw mat [C]

む

むしん 無心

❶【無邪気】innocence ― 無心な innocent ― 無心に innocently ／ 子供たちが公園で無心に遊んでいる Children are playing *innocently* in the park.

❷【ねだる】― 無心する beg ／ おじは私の両親によくお金を無心する My uncle often *begs* my parents for money.

むじん 無人

‖ 無人宇宙船 an unmanned spaceship ／ 無人駅 an unmanned station ／ 無人スタンド（新聞などの）a self-service stand ／ 無人島 a desert [an uninhabited] island ／ 無人踏切 an unmanned crossing ／ 無人ロケット an unmanned rocket

むしんけい 無神経

insensitivity ― 無神経な（思いやりのない）insensitive，（非難などに対して鈍感な）thick-skinned ／ そんなことを彼女に言うなんて君も無神経だね It was *insensitive* of you to say that to her. ／ 彼は無神経なので他人の批判など屁（^）とも思わない He is so *thick-skinned* that he doesn't give a damn about others' criticism.

むじんぞう 無尽蔵

‖ 無尽蔵な inexhaustible ／ 地球上の天然資源は無尽蔵ではない The earth's natural resources are not *inexhaustible* [*unlimited*].

むしんろん 無神論

atheism [éiθiìzm] ‖ 無神論者 an atheist [éiθiist]

むす 蒸す

❶【ふかす】steam ／ ジャガイモを蒸す *steam* potatoes

❷【蒸し暑い】きょうは蒸すね It's *muggy* today.

むすう 無数

― 無数の countless, innumerable；（非常に多くの）《口語的》zillions [millions] of ... ／ 空の無数の星 *countless* stars in the sky ／ インターネット上には無数のウェブサイトがある There are *zillions of* websites on the Internet.

むずかしい 難しい

❶【難解な・困難な】difficult, hard；（深刻な）serious；（骨の折れる）tough

この大学の入試の英語は難しいことで知られている This university's English entrance exam is known for being *difficult* [*hard, tough*].

私は難しい立場に置かれている I'm in a *difficult* situation.

両国の関係は今難しい状況だ The relations between the two countries are *in a serious situation* at the moment.

◆そんなに難しく考えないでいいですよ Don't take it so *seriously*.

❷【気難しい】（人が扱いにくい）difficult；（不機嫌な）sullen

うちの祖父は難しい人だ My grandfather is a *difficult* person. ／（→なかなか喜ばない）My grandfather is *hard to please.*

そんな難しいことは言わないで Don't say such a *difficult* thing.

難しい顔をしてどうしたんだい You look *sullen*. What's wrong with you?

むずがゆい

背中がむずがゆい My back *itches* [*is itchy*].

むずかる

（赤ん坊が）fret, be fretful

むすこ 息子

son，《口語的》boy（❖成人した男性にも用いる）

うちの末の息子 our youngest *son*

メープル夫人には息子が4人いる Mrs. Maple has four *sons* [*boys*].

彼は一人息子に財産を譲渡した He handed over the property to *his only son*.

むすばれる 結ばれる

幾多の紆余(ǔ)曲折の末，二人は晴れて結ばれた（→結婚した）After many twists and turns, they *were* formally *married*.

むすび 結び

（結末）end；（結論）conclusion ― 結びの（最後の）last, final；（結論の）concluding；（締めの）closing ／（相撲の）結びの一番 *the last* [*final*] *bout* ／ 演説では結びの言葉が大切だ *The conclusion* is an important part of a speech.

◆ひもの結びが甘い The cord *is tied loosely*.

むすびつき 結び付き

（つながり）connection；（きずな）ties ／ 両国は軍事的な結びつきが強い The two nations have "a close military *connection* [close military *ties*] with each other.

むすびつく 結び付く

be connected ／ あの警官は暴力団と結びついているとのうわさがある It's rumored that the police officer *is connected* with a group of gangsters. ／ あの少年の学校でのまじめな姿と家庭内暴力はどうしても結びつかない It's hard to *connect* that boy's serious demeanor at school with domestic violence.

むすびつける 結び付ける

（結わえつける）tie；（しっかり固定する）fasten；（関係づける）connect ／ 彼女はバンダナを枝に結びつけた She *tied* a bandanna to the branch. ／ 警察は2つの事件を結びつけて考えることにした The police decided to *connect* the two events.

むすびめ 結び目

knot ／ ゆるい[固い]結び目 *a loose* [*tight*] *knot* ／ 結び目を作る make [tie] *a knot* ／ 結び目を解く undo [untie] *a knot*

むすぶ 結ぶ

❶【つなぎ合わせる】（結わえる）tie；（結び目を作る）knot；（縛る）bind*

帽子にリボンを結ぶ *tie* a ribbon around a hat

その小さい女の子はまだ自分で靴のひもを結べない The little girl can't *tie* [*do*] her shoelaces by herself yet.

私は小包をひもでしっかり結んだ I *tied* [*bound*] the parcel tightly with a string.

❷【2点をつないで】connect；（密接に連結する）link

点AとBを線で結ぶ *connect* points A and B with a line；*draw* a line between points A and B

本州と北海道は青函トンネルで結ばれている The Seikan Tunnel *links* Honshu and Hokkaido.

❸【関係などを】form；（条約などを締結する）

conclude ⑭;（連合する）**ally** *oneself* **with** ...;（手を）**join hands with** ...
日本は中国と平和条約を結んだ Japan *concluded* a peace treaty with China.
2社は手を結ぶことにした The two companies decided to *join hands with each other*.
◆彼はそのチームと選手契約を結んだ He *signed* a contract to play with the team.
❹【締めくくる】**end** ⑭, **conclude** ⑭
彼は感謝の言葉で演説を結んだ He *ended* [*concluded*] his speech by expressing his thanks.
❺【実を結ぶ】**bear* fruit**
彼女の努力が実を結び始めた Her efforts started *to bear fruit*.
❻【固く閉じる】
口を固く結ぶ *shut* [*close*] *one's* lips tight

むずむず 背中がむずむずする（→かゆい）My back *is itching* [*itchy*]. / 鼻がむずむずする（→くすぐったい）My nose *is tickling*. / その秘密を今彼女に言いたくてむずむずしている I *have an itch* to tell her the secret now.

むすめ 娘
❶【親から見た】**daughter** ⓒ,《口語的》**girl**
彼は一人娘を甘やかした He pampered *his only daughter*.
❷【若い女性】（若い未婚の女性）**girl** ⓒ;（成人した女性）**young woman** ⓒ;（特に呼びかけなどに使う）**young lady** ⓒ
その娘がとてもかわいそうだと思った I felt really sorry for *the girl*.
娘さん，すみませんが網棚の袋を取ってもらえますか Excuse me, *young lady*. Could you get the bag from the rack for me?
◆うちの犬は人間でいえば20歳くらいの娘盛りだ If our dog were human, she would be about twenty years old and *in the bloom of youth*.
‖娘時代 *one's* girlhood

むせい 夢精 wet dream ⓒ;《生理》**nocturnal emission** ⓒⓤ ‖夢精をする **have *a wet dream***

むぜい 無税 ——無税の tax-free;（関税が）**duty-free** ‖無税で買い物をする do *tax-free* shopping

むせいげん 無制限 ——無制限の（限りのない）**unlimited**;（条件をつけない）**unrestricted** ‖この一日券で無制限にこの遊園地の乗り物に乗れる This one-day pass allows *unlimited* use of all rides at this amusement park.

むせいふしゅぎ 無政府主義 anarchism [ǽnərkizm] ⓤ ‖無政府主義者 an anarchist

むせいふじょうたい 無政府状態 anarchy [ǽnərki]

むせきつい 無脊椎 ——無脊椎の invertebrate ‖無脊椎動物 an invertebrate

むせきにん 無責任 irresponsibility ⓤ ——**無責任な irresponsible** ‖この重要な会議の途中で抜けるなんて彼女も無責任だ It was *irresponsible* of her to leave before this important meeting was over.

むせっそう 無節操 ——無節操な（道義心のない）**unprincipled**;（移り気な）**fickle** ‖彼女は無節操なところがある She is sometimes *unprincipled*.

むせびなく むせび泣く その女性は悲しみにむせび泣いた The woman was sad and *choked* with tears.

むせぶ 涙にむせぶ *be choked* with tears

むせる（息が詰まる）**choke** ⑭, **be choked** ‖私は煙にむせた I *choked* on the smoke. / 私はたばこの煙にむせた I *was choked* by the smoke.

むせん¹ 無線 radio ⓤ ‖彼らは無線で連絡をとり合った They contacted each other *by radio*.
‖無線技師 a radio operator / 無線局 a radio station / 無線操縦 radio control / 無線タクシー a radio dispatched taxi / 無線電話 (a) radiotelephone

むせん² 無銭 彼は無銭飲食でつかまった He was caught for *not paying the bill at the restaurant*. / 父は若いころよく無銭旅行をしたそうだ My father told me that he used to *travel without money* when he was young.

むそう 夢想 dream ⓒⓤ;（空想）**fancy** ⓒⓤ;（白昼夢）**daydream** ⓒ ——**夢想する dream*** ⑭;**daydream*** ⑭ ‖私はこんなこと夢想だにしなかった I *never dreamed* of such a thing.
‖夢想家 a dreamer, a daydreamer

むぞうさ 無造作 ——無造作に（さりげなく）**casually**;（深く考えずに）**carelessly**;（たやすく）**easily** ‖純子は無造作に髪を後ろで束ねている Junko has her hair tied *casually* in the back. / 彼は無造作に財布をテーブルの上に置いた He put his wallet on the table *carelessly*. / 彼女は無造作にそれをやってのけた She pulled it off *easily*.

むだ 無駄
❶【浪費】**waste** ⓤ《また a ~》——**むだな wasteful**
時間のむだだ It's *a waste* of time.
◆お金をむだにする *waste one's money* / 電気をむだに使ってはいけません You shouldn't *waste* electricity. / あなたは時間のむだを省くことが必要だ You need to *stop wasting time*. / 一流の料理人の動きにはむだがない Top cooks *make no wasted* motions.
❷【無益】**no good** ⓤ ——**むだな useless**
彼を説得しようとしてもむだだ It's *useless* trying [to try] to persuade him.
今となっては彼女に何を言ってもむだだ It's *no good* [*use*] telling her anything now.
◆止めてもむだです You *can't stop* me. / こんな話し合いをしてもむだだ This discussion will *get us nowhere*. / 流した涙はむだではなかった The tears I cried weren't shed *in vain*.

むだあし 無駄足 むだ足を踏まないよう，あらかじめ電話してから彼女の家へ行った Since I didn't want to *waste my time*, I called her in advance and visited her house. / 彼女に会いに行ったがむだ足だった I went to see her *only to find that she was out*.

むだぐち 無駄口 むだ口をたたくのはやめろ

Stop *talking nonsense*.
むだげ 無駄毛 むだ毛をそる shave off *unwanted hair*
むだづかい 無駄遣い 大変なお金のむだづかいだ It's *a terrible waste* of money. / 修学旅行でむだづかいをしないように Don't *waste your money* during the school trip.
むだばなし 無駄話 むだ話をする *talk idly*
むだぼね 無駄骨 とんだむだ骨を折った I *wasted my time and effort*.
むだん 無断 無断欠勤する be absent from work *without notice* / 私は彼女の辞書を無断借用した I used [borrowed] her dictionary *without permission* [*asking*]. / 彼はよく無断で学校を休む He often stays away from school *without permission*./ He often *plays hooky*. / 弟は無断で私のCDを持ち出した My brother took my CD *without asking*.
◆このページの画像の無断複製を禁止します *Unauthorized reproduction* of the graphics on this page is prohibited.
むたんぽ 無担保 彼は無担保で融資を受けた He received the loan *without collateral*.
むち¹ 無知 ignorance ⓤ; (知識の欠如) lack of knowledge ——無知な ignorant / 無知を装う pretend *ignorance* [*to be ignorant*] / 政治に無知な若者もいる Some young people are *ignorant* of politics.
むち² 鞭 whip ⓒ; (乗馬用の) riding crop ⓒ
◆馬をむちで打つ *whip* a horse / あめとむち carrot and *stick* / 彼はむち打ち刑になった He was sentenced to *flogging*.
むちうちしょう 鞭打ち症 whiplash ⓤ ∥むち打ち症になる suffer from *whiplash*
むちうつ 鞭打つ whip ⓒ, lash ⓒ; (罰として) flog ⓒ ∥その調教師は馬をむち打った The trainer *whipped* [*lashed*] the horse.
慣用表現 久保田氏は老骨にむちを打って働いた Mr. Kubota *pushed himself to work in spite of his old age*.
むちつじょ 無秩序 disorder ⓤ; (大混乱) chaos [kéiɑs] ⓤ ——無秩序な disordered; chaotic ∥終戦直後のこの地は無秩序状態だった This place was「in *chaos* [*chaotic*] just after the war.
むちゃ 無茶 (理屈に合わない) unreasonable; (無謀な) reckless; (常識に合わない) absurd; (ばかげた) ridiculous ∥君の計画はむちゃだよ Your plan is *unreasonable*. / なんてむちゃな運転だ! What a *reckless* driving! / そんなむちゃを言わないで Don't be *ridiculous*!
むちゃくちゃ 無茶苦茶 ——むちゃくちゃな (ひどい) awful; (非現実的な) unrealistic; (理屈に合わない) unreasonable ∥その値段はいくら何でもむちゃくちゃだ That price *is just unreasonable*.

● 「この前の数学のテストどうだった」「むちゃくちゃ悪かった. もう死にたいくらい」 "How did you do on the last math test?" "*Awful*. I could just die."
むちゃくりく 無着陸 無着陸飛行をする make *a nonstop flight*
むちゅう 夢中 僕は彼女に夢中だ I'm *mad* [*crazy*] *about* her. 彼は今インターネットに夢中だ He *is crazy about* the Internet now.
入社したばかりの兄は今仕事に夢中だ My brother was just hired by a company and now *is absorbed in* his work.
彼は夢中で漫画雑誌を読んでいた He was reading a comic magazine *madly*.
男は警官から夢中で逃げた The man ran *for his life*.
彼らは話に夢中になっていたので, 私が部屋に入ったことに気づかなかった They *were so deep in* conversation that they didn't notice when I came into the room.
むちんじょうしゃ 無賃乗車 ——無賃乗車する steal* a ride
むつ 鯥 〔魚〕 Japanese bluefish ⓒ
むつう 無痛 ——無痛の painless ∥無痛分娩(ʙ) painless childbirth
むっくり クマがむっくりと起き上がった The bear got up *heavily*.
むっちり 彼女はむっちりとした体つきの女性だ She is a *plump* woman.
むっつ 六つ six ⓒⓤ ⇨ろく
むっつり あいつ, きょうはいやにむっつりしているね He *looks* very *sullen* today, doesn't he? / あの老人はむっつりしている That old man is *taciturn*. / 中年のむっつりすけべっていやね I hate middle-aged *lechers* who don't talk much.
むっと 彼女の言葉にむっとした I 「*was offended by* [*got angry at*] her remarks. / 部屋の中はむっとしていた The room *was stuffy*. / むっとするにおいに思わず手で鼻を覆った I instinctively covered my nose with my hand at the *nasty* smell.
むつまじい 睦まじい harmonious; (幸せな) happy ∥うちの祖父母は仲むつまじい My grandparents are a *harmonious* [*happy*] couple.
むていけん 無定見 彼は無定見だ (→信条がない) He *has no principles*.
むていこう 無抵抗 nonresistance ⓤ ——無抵抗の nonresistant; (逆らわない) passive ∥マハトマ・ガンジーの無抵抗主義 Mahatma Gandhi's *policies of passive resistance* / 彼らは無抵抗の人々を殺した They killed *nonresistant* people.
むてき¹ 無敵 ——無敵の invincible; (匹敵するもののない) unrivaled ∥無敵艦隊 the *Invincible Armada*(❖ 16世紀後半世界最強を誇ったスペインの艦隊) / 我々は無敵のサッカーチームだ We are an *unrivaled* soccer team.
むてき² 霧笛 foghorn ⓒ ∥霧笛を鳴らす sound *a foghorn*
むてっぽう 無鉄砲 ——無鉄砲な reckless; (無分別な) rash ∥ひとりであの雪山に登ろうなんて無鉄砲な男だ He's *reckless* to climb that snowy mountain alone.
むでん 無電 radio ⓤ ⇨むせん(無線)
むてんか 無添加 ——無添加の additive-free ∥無添加食品 additive-free food
むとうはそう 無党派層 independent [un-

affiliated] voters

むとくてん 無得点 ――無得点の scoreless // 無得点に終わる end *scoreless*

むとどけ 無届け 彼は学校に無届けでバイク通学している He goes to school by motorbike *without permission* from the school.

むとんちゃく 無頓着 ――むとんちゃくの (無関心の) indifferent; (気にかけない) unconcerned //兄は服装にはむとんちゃくだ My brother *is indifferent to* what he wears. / 彼は周りのことにむとんちゃくだ He *is unconcerned about* what is happening around him.

むないた 胸板 breast ⓒ, chest //彼は胸板が厚い He has a thick *chest*.

むなくそ 胸糞 そのことを考えただけで胸くそが悪くなる The mere thought of it *makes* me *sick*.

むなぐら 胸倉 彼は上司の胸ぐらをつかんで(→シャツをつかんで)壁に押しつけた He seized [grabbed] his boss *by the shirt* and pressed him against the wall.

むなぐるしい 胸苦しい feel* tight [pressure] in the chest

むなげ 胸毛 chest hair Ⓤⓒ //彼は胸毛がある He has *chest hair*./ He has a *hairy* chest.

むなさわぎ 胸騒ぎ 何だか胸騒ぎがする For some reason I *feel uneasy*.

むなざんよう 胸算用 私はこの商売で100万円はもうかると胸算用した I *counted on* earning one million yen in this business.

むなしい 空しい・虚しい (空虚な) empty; (役に立たない) useless; (実を結ばない) fruitless

むなしい努力 a *useless [fruitless]* effort

夏も終わりに近づき何となくむなしい気になる The summer is almost over, and I feel *empty*.

◆わが校のチームは善戦むなしく(→よく戦ったが)敗れてしまった Our school's team *put up a good fight* but was beaten.

むなしさ 空しさ・虚しさ (空虚) emptiness Ⓤ; (価値のなさ) vanity Ⓤ //名声のむなしさに気づく discover the *vanity* of fame

むなもと 胸元 chest ⓒ; (特に女性の) breasts //その銀行強盗は彼の胸元に銃を突きつけた The bank robber pointed a gun at his *chest*./ 彼は胸元をはだけていた He was exposing *his chest*.

むに 無二 僕らは無二の親友だ We are *best friends*.

ムニエル ――ムニエルの meunière [mənjéər] (❖フランス語から) //シタビラメのムニエル sole *meunière*

むにゃむにゃ 彼は何かむにゃむにゃつぶやいていたが聞きとれなかった He *was mumbling*, but I couldn't make it out.

むね¹ 胸

❶(胸部) chest ⓒ; (特に胸の上部) breast ⓒ; (女性の両乳房) breasts; (特に女性の胸回りの寸法) bust ⓒ

胸のレントゲン a *chest* X-ray / 大きな胸(→男性)a broad [large] *chest*; (→女性) large *breasts* / 胸ポケット a *breast* pocket / 胸に聴診器を当てる put the stethoscope to *a person's chest*

かぜをひいて胸が痛い I've caught a cold and have *chest* pains.

その母親は娘を胸に抱きしめた The mother held her daughter to her *breast*.

◆彼女は胸がない[豊かだ] She *is flat-chested [full-breasted]*./ 胸いっぱいに空気を吸った I took a *deep* breath.

❷[心臓] heart ⓒ

彼女を見ると僕は胸がどきどきする My *heart beats fast* when I see her.

[慣用表現] そのニュースに胸が痛む I *feel sorry about* the news./ The news is *heartrending*./ 幸せで胸がいっぱいだ My heart is 「*full of [filled with]* happiness./ 胸がすっとした I *felt relieved*. / あの事故を思い出すたびに胸が張り裂ける思いがする My heart *almost bursts* every time I remember the accident./ 彼のひと言が胸にこたえた His remark 「*came home to me [hit home]*./ 彼女の話は胸に迫るものがある Her story *touches me*./ 自分の胸に聞きなさい *Ask yourself*./ 胸に手を置いて考えると私にも落ち度があった *Thinking it over again*, I realized that I was to blame, too./ このことは一生胸に秘めておきます I *will keep* it *to myself* for the rest of my life./ あなたにすべてを話して胸のつかえがとれた *All my anxieties* disappeared after I told you everything./ 両親は弟のことで胸を痛めている My parents *are deeply worried* about my brother./ その映画に胸を打たれた I *was deeply moved* by the movie./ 彼女は1年先輩の男の子に胸をこがしている She *is burning with love* for a boy who's a year ahead of her in school./ 検査の結果が陰性で胸をなで下ろした I *felt relieved* to learn that the results of the medical test were negative./ 胸を張って生きなさい *Keep your chin up and live with confidence*./ 私は期待に胸をふくらませた I *was full of* hope.

むね² 旨 その旨お母様によろしくお伝えください Please tell your mother *about that*./ 宅配便が届いた旨の電話をもらった I got a phone call *that* the parcel had arrived.

むね³ 棟 (屋根の) the ridge; (家) house ⓒ //5棟が浸水した Five *houses* were flooded.

むねあげ 棟上げ ――棟上げする set* up the framework of a house

むねやけ 胸焼け heartburn Ⓤ //胸焼けがする I have *heartburn*.

むねん 無念 (残念) regret Ⓤⓒ; (悔しさ) frustration Ⓤⓒ //無念の涙 tears of *regret* / 無念にも頂上に到達できなかった *To my regret [Regrettably]*, I could not reach the top of the mountain.

◆無念無想の境地に達する achieve *freedom from worldly thoughts*

むのう 無能 incompetence Ⓤ, lack of abil-

むのうやくさいばい

むのう 無能 ——無能な incompetent; (できない) incapable ‖無能な経営者 an incompetent manager / 彼は研究者としてはすぐれているが教育者としては無能He is an excellent researcher but *is incapable* as an educator.

むのうやくさいばい 無農薬栽培 これらはすべて無農薬栽培の野菜です These are all *organic* [*organically grown*] vegetables.

むはい 無敗 彼は過去12年間レスリングで無敗である He *has been undefeated* at wrestling for the past 12 years.

むひ 無比 ——無比の (唯一の) unique; (対抗するものがない) unrivaled ◆ 正確無比な計算 *perfectly accurate* calculations

むひょうじょう 無表情 ——無表情な expressionless; (ぽかんとした) blank ‖彼女はいつも無表情(→表情のない顔)だ She always *has an expressionless face*.

むふう 無風 ——無風の windless; (穏やかな) calm ‖その日は無風だった The day was *windless*.
◆政局はこの半年ほど無風状態だ The political situation *has been stable* for the past six months.

むふんべつ 無分別 ——無分別な thoughtless; (軽率な) indiscreet ‖あなたがそんなに無分別な人だとは思わなかった I didn't think you were so *thoughtless*.

むほう 無法 ——無法な (法を無視した) lawless ‖社会の無法分子 *lawless elements* in society / ここは無法地帯と化した This area has become *a lawless zone*.
‖無法者 an outlaw

むぼう 無謀 ——無謀な (むちゃな) reckless; (あさはかな) thoughtless ‖無謀運転 *reckless* driving / 君の計画は無謀だ Your plan *is thoughtless* [*reckless*].

むほうしゅう 無報酬 無報酬で働く work *without payment* / これは無報酬の仕事だ This is *unpaid* work.

むぼうび 無防備 ——無防備な defenseless; (防御を固めていない) unfortified ‖その国境地帯は隣国に対して無防備だ The border region *is defenseless* against the neighboring country.

むほん 謀反 (国家・君主などに対する) treason Ⓤ; (反乱) rebellion Ⓤ Ⓒ ‖彼は主君に対して謀反を企てた He *plotted treason* [*a rebellion*] against his lord.

むみ 無味 この薬品は無味無臭だ This chemical *has no taste or odor*. / 彼女の話は無味乾燥だ(→退屈だ) Her stories *are dull*.

むめい 無名 ——無名の unknown; (人目につかない) obscure; (名前の知れない) nameless ‖彼女の無名歌手時代のサイン an autograph signed when she was *an unknown singer* / 無名戦士の墓 the Tomb of *the Unknown Soldier*

むめんきょ 無免許 彼女は無免許の歯科医だった She was *an unlicensed dentist*. / 兄は無免許運転でつかまった My brother was caught for *driving without a license*.

むやみ 無闇 ——むやみに (過度に) excessively; (区別なく) indiscriminately; (不当に) unreasonably, without a good [fair] reason ‖彼はバイクを運転するときむやみにスピードを出す He rides his motorbike *excessively fast*. / むやみやたらに(→理由もなく)人を疑うべきではない You shouldn't doubt others *without a good reason*.

むゆうびょう 夢遊病 sleepwalking Ⓤ
‖夢遊病者 a sleepwalker

むよう 無用 ——無用の (役に立たない) useless, of no use; (不要の) unnecessary ‖それは無用の長物だ It's *useless* [*a white elephant*]. / 旅行に無用な物は持っていかないほうがよい You shouldn't pack *unnecessary* stuff when traveling.
◆通り抜け無用《掲示》*No Trespassing* / 問答無用 *No more discussion*. / 他言無用 *Don't tell* this *to anyone*. / 心配は無用です You *don't need to* worry.

むよく 無欲 ——無欲な (利己的でない) unselfish; (無関心な) indifferent ‖彼は出世に無欲だ He *is indifferent* to promotion.

むら¹ 村 village Ⓒ ‖私の家は村のはずれにある My house is on the edge of *a village*. / 隣村には鉄道が通るらしい We hear that they will build a railroad in *the* neighboring *village*.
‖村人 a villager / 村役場 a village office / キャンプ村 a campground / 芸術家村 an artists' colony

慣用表現 男は村八分になった The man was *cold-shouldered* [《公式的》*ostracized*].

むら² ——むらのある (一様でない) uneven; (形が不ぞろいな) irregular; (行動・感情が) erratic ‖彼女は気持ちにむらがある She *is erratic*. / 彼の仕事にはむらがある He is an *erratic* [*uneven*] worker.
◆壁に塗られたペンキにはむらがある The wall was painted *unevenly*.

むらおこし 村興し 私たちは村おこしのためにインターネットの利用を考えている We have a plan to use the Internet to *stimulate the economy of our village*.

むらがる 群がる (集まる) gather 圓 他; (込み合う) crowd 圓 他; (押し合いへし合いしながら) throng 圓 他; (人・動物が) flock 圓; (虫などが) swarm 圓 他 ‖はだしの子供たちは観光客の周りに群がった Barefooted children *gathered* around the tourists. / 人々が事故現場に群がった People *crowded* the scene of the accident. / あめの周りにアリがたくさん群がった A lot of ants *swarmed* [*gathered*] around the candy.

むらき 斑気 ——むら気な moody ‖彼女はむら気な子だ She is a *moody* girl.

むらさき 紫 (赤みがかった) purple Ⓤ; (青みがかった) violet Ⓤ ‖そのワインは濃い[薄い]紫色をしている The wine is deep [light] *purple*.
◆唇が紫色(→真っ青)だよ Your lips are *blue*.

むらむらと 彼の話を聞いてむらむらと怒りがこみ上げた *Anger surged up within me* after I heard his story. / ポルノ雑誌を見て少年はむらむらしてきた A pornographic magazine *turned* the boy *on*.

むり 無理

❶【不合理】 ——無理な unreasonable; (不当な) unjustifiable; (不自然な) unnatural
無理な要求 an *unreasonable* [*unjustifiable*; (→不可能な)*impossible*] demand
彼女は無理な注文ばかりする She always makes *unreasonable* requests.
◆無理のないスウィング a *natural* swing / 彼がクラブをやめたのも無理はない *It's natural that he quit the club.* / He *had a good reason* to quit the club. / これは無理なお願いでしょうか Am I asking you *too much*?
🔴「このCD, ちょうだい」「無理を言わないでよ. このCD, もう手に入らないんだから」"Give me this CD." "*Don't be unreasonable.* It's no longer available."

❷【不可能・困難】 ——無理な impossible
1週間でこの本を全部読めって？ そんなの無理だよ Do I have to read all these books in a week? That's *impossible*.
◆無理を承知でお願いしたいのですが、一晩泊めていただけませんか *I know I'm asking too much*, but could you please put me up for the night? / あまり無理しないでください Don't *work too hard*. / 年をとると無理がきかなくなる When you get older, you *can't push yourself hard* anymore.
🔴「田中先生に女子高生の役頼んでみる？」「ちょっとそれは無理があるんじゃないかな」"Shall we ask Mrs. Tanaka to play the role of the high school girl?" "Oh, I don't think we should …"

❸【強制】
無理にドアをあける *force* a door open
私に無理じいしないでください Don't *force* me.
私は満腹だったが無理に食べた Although I was full, I *forced* myself to eat.
両親は私に無理にその学校を受けさせた My parents *made* [*forced*] me *to* apply to the school.
彼女は無理に結婚させられた She *was forced to* get married.

むりかい 無理解 うちの親は私のボランティア活動に対して無理解だ My parents *are unsympathetic* to my volunteer work. / 大衆の難民に対する無理解をどう思いますか What do you think about the public's *lack of understanding* of refugees?

むりし 無利子 無利子で金を借りる borrow money *at no interest*; get a *no-interest* loan

むりじい 無理強い、子供に勉強の無理じいはいけない You shouldn't *force* your child to study.

むりやり 無理やり 母親は幼い息子に無理やり英語のアルファベットを覚えさせた The mother *forced* her young son to learn the English alphabet. / 私は彼らに無理やりパーティーに連れてこられた I *was forced* to come to the party by them.

むりょう 無料 ——無料の free (of charge) (❖名詞の前では常に free) ‖無料駐車場《掲示》 *Free* Parking / 無料の券 a *free* ticket / 本日に限り入場は無料です Admission is *free of charge* today only.
◆当ホテルご利用のお客様はそのレストランで無料でお食事ができます Our hotel guests can eat *free* in that restaurant.
‖無料奉仕 unpaid work

むりょく 無力 powerlessness Ⓤ; (病人・幼児または軍隊などの) helplessness Ⓤ; (無能) impotence Ⓤ ——無力な powerless; helpless; impotent ‖無力感 feelings of *powerlessness* / 現代科学も往々にして自然の前では無力だ Modern science *is* often *powerless* against nature.

むるい 無類 ——無類の unparalleled; (かなう者のない) unrivaled ‖あいつは無類の女好きだ He is an *unparalleled* womanizer.

むれ 群れ (集団) group Ⓒ; (群衆) crowd Ⓒ; (牛・馬・シカなどの) herd Ⓒ; (羊・鳥などの) flock Ⓒ; (虫の) swarm Ⓒ; (魚の) school Ⓒ; (オオカミの) pack Ⓒ; (ライオンの) pride Ⓒ
1頭の牛が群れからはぐれた A cow strayed from *the herd*.
渡り鳥の群れが冬の訪れを告げる *The flocks* of migratory birds tell us that winter is coming.
オオカミはふつう群れで獲物を狩る Wolves usually hunt *in packs*.
◆群れを作らない動物 animals *of solitary habit*

むれる 蒸れる ごはんが十分蒸れるまでもう少し待ってね Wait a minute until the rice *is* well *steamed*. / 足がよく蒸れる My feet often *get sweaty*.

むろん 無論 of course, naturally ‖むろん君が正しいよ *Of course*, you are right.

むんむん コンサートホールは若者の熱気でむんむんしていた The concert hall *was filled with* the enthusiasm of young people. / 暑さでその部屋はむんむんしていた The room *was stuffy* because of the heat.

め¹ 目

❶ 体の器官	eye
❷ 視力	eyesight
❸ 目つき・視線	eye; look
❹ 見方・観点	eye; *one's* point of view
❺ 眼力・判断力	eye
❻ 経験	experience

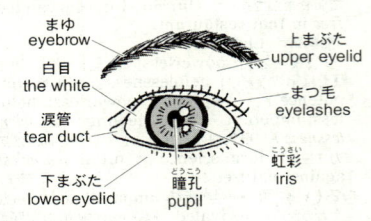

❶【体の器官】eye ◯

- まゆ eyebrow
- 白目 the white
- 涙管 tear duct
- 下まぶた lower eyelid
- 上まぶた upper eyelid
- まつ毛 eyelashes
- 虹彩 iris
- 瞳孔 pupil

【〜目】
涙ぐんだ目 watery *eyes* / つぶらな目 small round *eyes* / 澄んだ目 clear *eyes* / 細い目 narrow *eyes*

【目が・は】
彼女は目が大きい She has large *eyes*.
長時間コンピュータの画面を見ていると目が疲れる *My eyes* get sore when I keep watching the computer screen for a long time.
目がごろごろ[しょぼしょぼ]する *My eyes* feel gritty [bleary].
泣いていたのか, 彼女は目が赤かった (→充血していた) *Her eyes* were bloodshot maybe because she had been crying.
朝起きたら目が少しはれていた When I woke up in the morning, *my eyes* were a little swollen.
しばらくすると徐々に目が暗さに慣れてきた After a while, *my eyes* gradually got used to the darkness.
🗣「目はかゆいし鼻水は止まらないし, もうさんざんだよ」「そうだね. 花粉症の人にはつらい季節だよね」"*My eyes* feel itchy and my nose is runny. I'm really having a hard time." "I know. This is such a tough season for people with hay fever."

【目を】
彼女は黒い[青い, 茶色の]目をしている She has dark [blue, brown] *eyes*. (❖日本人のような「黒い目」は dark eyes という. a black eye は「殴られてあざのできた目」を指すので注意)
目を閉じて10数えてごらん Close *your eyes* and count to 10.
もう目をあけていいよ You can open *your eyes* now.
あまりに眠くて目をあけていられない I'm so sleepy (that) I can hardly keep *my eyes* open.
彼は彼女の話を聞いて目をうるませた While he listened to the story, *his eyes* became moist (with tears).
人と話すときはその人の目を見なさい When you talk to someone, you should look him or her *in the eye*.
彼は夢を見ているのではと何度も目をこすった He rubbed *his eyes* again and again as he thought he might have been dreaming.
彼女は急な質問にびっくりして目をぱちくりさせた She blinked *her eyes* in surprise at the abrupt question.

【目に】
目にごみが入った I got a speck of dust in *my eye*.
野外での料理は煙が目にしみるのが難点だ The trouble with outdoor cooking is that smoke stings *your eyes*.
その子は目にいっぱい涙を浮かべて口をぎゅっと結んでいた The child shut his lips tight with *his eyes* full of tears.
彼女の目に喜びの色が浮かんだ (→彼女の目が喜びで輝いた) *Her eyes* gleamed with pleasure.

【その他】
彼女の夫は彼女の目の前で車にはねられた Her husband was run over by a car *in front of her eyes*.
自分の目で確かめてみたらどうだい Why don't you check it *with your own eyes*?
彼女は目の下にくまができていた She had shadows *under her eyes*.
彼女の目からみるみる涙があふれ出た Tears welled up from her *eyes*.
🗣「金井さんってどんな人だっけ」「ほら, あの目のぱっちりした美人だよ」"What does Miss Kanai look like?" "You know, that pretty woman with big bright *eyes*."

❷【視力】eyesight ◯, **sight** ◯, **vision** ◯
私は目がいい[悪い] I have good [poor] *eyesight*.
この仕事を始めてからだんだん目が悪くなったようだ *My sight* seems to have been getting worse since I started this job.
暗い所で本を読んでいると目を悪くするとよく親に言われた I was often told by my parents that it would damage *my eyesight* if I read books in dim light.
祖父は左の目が見えない My grandfather is blind in *his left eye*.
その事故で彼は目が見えなくなった He lost his *sight* in the accident.
涙で目がかすんだ Tears blurred *my vision*.
◆そのミュージシャンは生まれつき目が見えない

The musician was born *blind*. / 猫は暗やみでも目が見える Cats *can see* in the dark.
❸【目つき・視線】eye ⓒ; (顔つき) look ⓒ《通例単数形》

テレビゲームの話をしているとき, 彼の目は輝いていた His *eyes lit up* when we talked about video games.

獰猛(どうもう)そうな犬と目が合ってしまった *My eyes met* a fierce-looking dog's.

彼はふと棚の上の古い写真に目をやった *His eyes fell on* an old photo on the shelf.

彼女の目はその絵にじっと注がれていた *Her eyes were fixed on* the painting.

その話題に及ぶと彼女は目をふせた When they brought up the topic, she *lowered her eyes*.

言葉にはならなかったが父の目がすべてを語っていた Father didn't speak but his *eyes* said everything.

彼の目は憎しみでいっぱいだった His *eyes* were filled with hatred.

私は走り去っていく子供たちを目で追った I *followed* the children *with my eyes* as they ran away.

◆このゲームは笑ったり相手から目をそらしたりしたら負けです In this game you lose if you laugh or *look away* from your opponent. / 警察は彼を疑いの目で見ていた The police regarded him *with suspicion*. / 村の人々は彼を好奇の目でじろじろ見た People in the village stared at him *curiously*. / 彼女のドレスはあまりにも露出度が高く目のやり場に困った Her dress was so scanty that I *didn't know where to look*. / 道端でいびきをかいて寝ている酔っ払いを通行人は白い目で見ていた Passersby *were looking coldly at* a drunk snoring on the street. / 恵美は私に話を合わせるように目で合図した Emi *gave me a wink* to make me go along with her story.

❹【見方・観点】eye ⓒ; (観点) *one's* point of view

公平な目で見れば *with an impartial eye*

プロの目から見たら私の作品など何の価値もないだろう My work must be nothing *in the eyes of a professional*.

私の目から見ればどちらの言い分にも一理ある *From my point of view*, I find truth in what both say.

彼女はあらゆるものを画家の目で見ている She views everything *with the eyes of a painter*.

◆彼の失敗はだれの目にも明らかだった His failure was apparent *to everyone*. / 長い目で見れば今回の失敗もいい経験になるさ Your mistake this time will be a good experience *in the long run*.

❺【眼力・判断力】eye ⓒ《通例単数形》

彼女は骨董(こっとう)品を見る目がある She *has an eye for* antiques.

(だましそうって)おれの目はごまかされないぞ You *can't pull the wool over my eyes*! (❖ pull the wool over *a person's* eyes は「(人の)目をごまかす」という意味の慣用的表現)

◆彼には人を見る目がない(→人の性格を正しく判断できる人ではない) He's *a poor judge* of character.

❻【経験】experience ⓒ ⓤ

ハワイではさんざんな目にあった I *had some terrible experiences* in Hawaii.

◆彼女はどんなにつらい目にあっても明るさを失わなかった She never lost her cheerfulness *no matter how hard a time she had*. / あいつは一度痛い目にあわないと(→困ったことにならないと)分からないよ He'll never learn until *he gets into real trouble*. / 家族を危険な目にあわせたくない I don't want to put my family *at risk*.

❼【目に似たもの】eye ⓒ

針の目 *the eye of* a needle; *a* needle's *eye* / 台風の目 *the eye of* a typhoon

◆さいころの目 *a pip*; *a spot* / (さいころ遊びで)いい目が出たぞ I've got *a lucky roll* [*spot*]!

❽【間隔・仕切り】(やすり・のこぎりの) tooth ⓒ《通例複数形 teeth》; (織物の) texture ⓤ; (縫い目) stitch ⓒ; (網の目) mesh ⓒ; (木目) grain ⓤ; (碁盤の) cross ⓒ

◆目の細かい[粗い]ざる a *fine-meshed* [*coarse-meshed*] colander / この上着は目のつんだ生地でできているからとても暖かい This jacket is very warm because it's made of *tightly woven* fabric. / 野菜はすべてさいの目に切りなさい *Dice* all the vegetables. / *Cut* all the vegetables *into small cubes*.

❾【その他】

君だったらあいつなんて目じゃないよ(→彼は君の相手にはなれない) He's *no match for* you.

❿【慣用表現】

【お目にかかる】初めてお目にかかります It's a great pleasure to *meet* you. / 鈴木さんにお目にかかりたいのですが I'd like to *see* Ms. Suzuki. / お目にかかれてうれしく思います I'm glad to *meet* you.

【お目にかける】おもしろい写真をお目にかけましょう I'll *show* you an interesting picture.

【目がきく】have* an eye ∥ 姉は商売柄, 宝石には目がきく My sister *has a keen [sharp] eye for* gems since she deals in them.

【目がくらむ】(光などで) be blinded [dazzled]; (めまいがする) feel* dizzy ∥ 対向車のヘッドライトに一瞬目がくらんだ I *was blinded* a moment by the oncoming car's headlights. / その役人は欲に目がくらんでわいろを受け取った The official *was blinded* by greed and accepted a bribe. (❖日本語と同様, 比喩的にも用いる) / がけの上から下を見下ろすと目もくらむほどの高さだった When I looked down from the top of the cliff, it was so high that I *felt dizzy*. ◆目のくらむような光 a *blinding* [*dazzling*] flash

【目が肥えている】画家の息子らしく彼は絵に関しては目が肥えている Being a son of a painter, he *has a critical eye for* paintings.

【目がさえる】ゆうべは目がさえてなかなか寝つけなかった I was *wide awake* last night and it was a long time before I could get to sleep.

【目がさめる】wake*⑧, be awakened ∥ けさは目覚ましが鳴る前に目がさめた I *woke* (*up*) *before the alarm rang this morning*. ◆彼女は目のさめるようなブルーの衣装を着ていた She *was dressed in a bright blue costume*.

🔴「洋子があの彼と別れたんだって」「ほんと？ やっと目が覚めたってわけね」"Did you hear that Yoko broke up with that guy?" "Really? So she'*s come to her senses* at last."

【目がすわる】彼は酔っ払って目がすわっていた He *was drunk and his eyes were glazed over*.

【目が高い】そのコートをお選びになるとはお目が高い You *are a good judge of quality* to pick that coat.

【目が点になる】その絵の値段を聞いて目が点になった(→目が飛び出しそうになった) *My eyes almost popped out* when I heard the price of the painting.

【目が届く】生徒が40人もいると全員に先生の目が届かなくても無理はない No wonder a teacher *can't take care of* all the students if there are as many as 40 of them.

【目がない】香織はアイスクリームに目がない Kaori *loves ice cream*./ Kaori *has a weakness for* ice cream.

【目が離せない】歩き始めたばかりの赤ちゃんからは目が離せない You *can't take your eyes off* toddlers.

【目が回る】feel* dizzy ∥ 連続して前転をしたら目が回った The succession of forward rolls made me *feel dizzy*. ◆一日中目が回るような忙しさだった It *was terribly busy all day*.

【目からうろこが落ちる】彼女のアドバイスで目からうろこが落ちた(→はっと真理に目ざめた) I *was suddenly awakened to the truth* by her advice.

【目から鼻へ抜ける】美香は目から鼻へ抜けるような人だ(→頭の回転が速い) Mika is *very quick and smart*.

【目から火が出る】頭を天井にぶつけたときは目から火が出た I *saw stars* when I hit my head against the ceiling.

【目と鼻の先】その博物館は私の学校からほんの目と鼻の先にある The museum is *very close to my school*. / The museum is only *a stone's throw* (*away*) *from my school*.

【目に余る】今の若者言葉は目に余る(→我慢できない) I *can't stand* the young people's language nowadays.

【目に入れても痛くない】彼は娘を目に入れても痛くないほどかわいがっている His daughter is *the apple of his eye*. (◆*the apple of a person's* eye は「(目の)ひとみ」のことで大切な物・人を指す)

【目に浮かぶ】その知らせを聞いたときの彼女のうれしそうな顔が目に浮かぶ I *can imagine how happy she will be when she hears the news*.

【目に狂いはない】その選手を選んだスカウトの目に狂いはなかった The scout *was right* in his choice of the player.

【目につく】最近その会社の広告がよく目につく(→どこでも見られる) Recently the company's advertisements *can be seen everywhere*. / ベストセラーはどの本屋でも目につくところに置いてある Best-sellers are placed where they *can be easily found* at any bookshop.

【目にとまる】新聞のある小さな記事が彼の目にとまった A small article in the newspaper *caught his eye*. / 彼は有名な映画監督の目にとまって映画出演を果たした He *came to* a famous film director's *attention* and appeared in a movie.

【目に入る】麻子が何かに熱中しているときはほかのことは全く目に入らない When Asako is into something, she really *can't think of anything else*.

【目には目を】目には目を, 歯には歯を *An eye for an eye*, a tooth for a tooth.

【目に見える】彼のギターの腕は目に見えて上達した He made *remarkable* progress in playing the guitar. / 近いうちにその店がつぶれるのは目に見えている(→簡単に分かる) You *can easily see* that the shop will soon go out of business. / 地域住民は目に見えない放射能汚染の恐怖におののいていた Local people shuddered with fear of the *invisible* radioactive contamination.

【目にもとまらぬ】その鳥は目にもとまらぬほどの速さで急降下した The bird swooped down *faster than the eye could follow*.

【目の色が変わる】勝った人には賞品が出ると聞いて彼の目の色が変わった When he knew there was a prize for the winner, he *got into it*.

【目の色を変える】妹は急に目の色を変えて勉強しだした My sister suddenly began to study *like mad*. / 大道芸人になるといったら父は目の色を変えて怒った My father *blew up* when I told him I wanted to become a street performer.

【目の上のこぶ】あいつは昔から目の上のこぶだ(→やっかい者だ) He has always been *a pain in the neck*.

【目のかたきにする】どうして彼女を目のかたきにするの Why do you *treat her like an enemy*?

【目の黒いうち】
🔴「彼と結婚するわ。止めてもむだよ, パパ」「私の目の黒いうちは(→私が生きているかぎり)絶対許さんぞ」"I will marry him! You can't stop me, Dad." "I won't let you *as long as I live*! / *Over my dead body*!" (◆後の表現は「(どうしてもというなら)私を殺してからにしろ」という意味から)

【目のつけどころ】彼の企画は目のつけどころがいい(→いいところをついた) His plan *hit the nail on the head*.

【目の毒】ダイエット中の私にはその番組は目の毒だ Since I'm on a diet, that TV program is *too much of a temptation*.

【目の保養】彼女は宝石展に行って目の保養をした She *feasted her eyes* on the jewelry exhibition.

【目の前が暗くなる】パスポートをなくしたことに気づいたときは一瞬目の前が暗くなった The world turned black for a moment when I noticed I had lost my passport.

【目もあてられない】試験の結果は目もあてられないものだった The results of the exam were too awful to look at.

【目もくれない】彼女は同じクラスの男の子たちには目もくれない She *couldn't care less* about the boys in her class.

【目を疑う】その写真を見たとき私は目を疑った When I saw the picture, I *couldn't believe my eyes*.

【目を奪う】僕は彼女の美しさに目を奪われた Her beauty *swept me off my feet*.

【目を覆う】彼はその痛ましい光景に目を覆った He *turned his eyes* from the terrible sight. (❖cover *one's* eyesとすると「まぶしくて手をかざす」の意味になる)

【目をかける】(世話をする) look after ..., take* care of ...; (ひいきする) favor ⓐ 〃大輔は監督に目をかけられている(→ひいきされている) Daisuke *is favored* by the coach.

【目をくらます】犯人は変装して警察の目をくらまそうとした The criminal disguised himself, *trying to deceive the eyes of* the police.

【目を凝らす】strain *one's* eyes 〃彼は薄暗い明かりの中でその絵を見ようと目を凝らした He *strained his eyes* to see the painting in the dim light.

【目をさます】けさはどしゃ降りの雨で目をさました The sound of pouring rain *woke me up* this morning. / 音楽にばかりうつつを抜かしてないでいいかげん目をさましたらどうだ Why don't you *wake up* to reality and stop being hooked on music?

【目を皿のようにする】子供たちはあやつり人形を目を皿のようにして見ていた The children *were all eyes* watching the puppets.

【目を白黒させる】そのきれいな女の人が実は男だと言うと、父は目を白黒させていた My father *was very surprised* when I told him the beautiful woman was really a man.

【目をそむける】現実から目をそむけてはいけない You shouldn't *look away* from reality.

【目をつける】have* *one's* eye 〃このワンピース、前から目をつけてるんだけどどう思う I've had my eye on this dress. What do you think? ◆その役人は収賄の容疑で警察に目をつけられている The official *is being watched* by the police on suspicion of taking bribes.

【目をつぶる】close [shut*] *one's* eyes (to ...); (見て見ないふりをする) turn a blind eye (to ...); (見逃す) overlook ⓐ 〃今回だけは君のミスに目をつぶってやろう I'll *overlook* your mistake this time only.

【目を通す】look through [over]; (ざっと見る) skim ⓐ 〃この報告書に目を通していただけますか Would you *look through* this report?

【目をとめる】彼女はテーブルの雑誌に目をとめた She *noticed* a magazine on the table.

【目を盗む】彼は時々親の目を盗んで酒を飲んでいる He sometimes drinks *behind his parents' back*.

【目を離す】ちょっと目を離したすきに魚が黒こげになってしまった The fish got burned *when I turned my eyes away* for a moment. / 赤ちゃんから目を離さないようにしなさい Keep an *eye on* the baby.

【目を光らせる】先生は生徒のカンニングに目を光らせていた The teacher *kept a watchful eye on* students' cheating.

【目を引く】attract *a person's* attention, catch* *a person's* eye 〃彼女の真っ赤なコートが目を引いた Her red coat *caught my eye*.

【目を細める】彼女は遠くの標識を読もうと目を細めた She *squinted her eyes* trying to read a faraway sign. / 彼はわが子の写っているビデオを目を細めて見ていた His eyes were smiling while watching a video of his child. (❖「目を細める」を直訳して narrow *one's* eyes とすると疑いや怒りを表すしぐさになるので注意)

【目を丸くする】子供たちはみんなそのケーキの巨大さに目を丸くした All the children *looked* at the huge cake *in amazement*.

【目を回す】(気絶する) faint ⓐ ◆彼はチャンピオンの一撃で目を回した He *was knocked out* by one blow from the champion.

【目をみはる】私はその町の変貌(ぼう)ぶりに目をみはった I *was amazed by* the tremendous change in the city.

ことわざ 目は口ほどにものをいう The eyes are as eloquent as the tongue. (→目は舌と同じくらい雄弁だ)

め² 芽 sprout Ⓒ, shoot Ⓒ; (つぼみ) bud Ⓒ

庭にまいた種から芽が出た The seeds I had planted in the garden 「*put up shoots* [*sprouted*].

いじめの芽は早いうちに摘んでおくべきだ Bullying should be nipped in *the bud*.

◆桜の木はじきに芽を出すだろう The cherry tree(s) will soon begin to *bud*. / 彼は役者としては芽が出ないままに終わった He ended his career as an actor *without success*.

-め -目

❶【順序】
1時間目 *the first period*
3番目の角を右に曲がりなさい Turn right at *the third* corner.
第1段落の2行目から読んでください Read from *the second line* of the first paragraph.
2番目の息子さんはどうしているのですか How is your *second* son doing?
ここに来たのは今回で2回目です This is *the second time* I came here.
花屋はここから5軒目です The flower shop is *five doors away* from here.
家を買って2年目に彼らに子供が生まれた They had a child *the second year* after they bought the house.

❷「山手線で行くと、渋谷は新宿からいくつ目ですか(→渋谷と新宿の間にいくつ駅がありますか)」

「3つ目(→2つ)です」 "How many stations are there between Shibuya and Shinjuku on the Yamanote Line?" "There are *two*."
❷【程度】
彼はいつもより遅めに家を出た He left home *later* than usual.
この服は少し小さめだ This dress is a bit *on the small side*.
お支払いはお早めにお願いします Please pay *as soon as possible*.
【その他】
私は子供のころ,季節の変わり目にはいつも喘息(ぜん)の発作に苦しんだ When I was a child, I always came down with asthma *when the seasons changed*.
めあたらしい 目新しい (新しい) new; (新奇な) novel; (独創的な) original ‖目新しいものに飛びつく jump at something *novel* / その店には特に目新しいものは売っていなかった The store didn't carry anything *new*.
めあて 目当て (目的) aim, purpose ⓒ; (目印) guide ⓒ, landmark ⓒ ‖いったい何が目当てなの What on earth is *your aim [purpose]*?
◆彼は金目当てに彼女に近づいた He approached her *for her money*. / あの高い塔を目当てに歩きなさい Walk along *keeping* that tall tower *in sight*.
💬「きょうのクラブ活動はつまらなかったな」「お目当ての彼女が休みだったからだろ」 "Today's club activity was boring." "That's because the girl you *have an eye on* was absent, isn't it?"
めい 姪 niece ⓒ
めい-¹ 名- (すぐれた) excellent; (偉大な) great; (有名な) famous, well-known ‖名ピアニスト a *great* pianist / 彼女は往年の名女優だ She was once a *famous* actress.
めい-² 迷- 迷答 a *confused* answer / 迷探偵 a *bumbling* detective
-めい -名 20名の生徒がキャンプに参加した *Twenty* students took part in the camp.
(◆数字だけで「…名」を表すことができる)
めいあん¹ 名案 good idea ⓒ ‖それは名案だ That's *a good idea*. / 突然名案が浮かんだ A *good* idea suddenly came [occurred] to me./ Suddenly I hit on *a good idea*.
めいあん² 明暗 light and shade ◆人生の明暗 the *bright and dark sides* of life / その1球が試合の明暗を分けた That one pitch *decided the outcome* of the game.
めいい 名医 skilled physician [doctor] ⓒ
めいうん 命運 この試合にわがチームの命運がかかっている This game will decide *the fate* of our team.
めいえん 名演 excellent performance ⓒ
めいおうせい 冥王星 【天文】 Pluto
めいが 名画 (絵) (傑作) masterpiece ⓒ; (有名な絵) famous picture ⓒ; (映画) excellent film ⓒ; (古典的な) film classic ⓒ
めいかい 明快 ─明快な clear ─明快に clearly ‖先生の説明は明快だった The teacher's explanation was *clear*. / 彼はすべての質問に明快に答えた He gave *clear* answers to all the questions.
めいかく 明確 ─明確な (はっきりした) clear; (違いが明らかな) distinct; (確実な) definite ─明確に clearly; distinctly; definitely ‖この問題について立場を明確にしておく必要がある We have to make our position *clear* about this problem. / 2つの説の間には明確な違いがある There is a *distinct* difference between the two theories.
めいがら 銘柄 brand ⓒ; (株式の) issue ⓒ, stock ⓒ ‖銘柄品 brand goods
めいき¹ 明記 ─明記する write* ... clearly; (明確に書く) specify ⊕ ‖必ず氏名を明記してください Please make sure to *write* your name *clearly*. / それは契約書に明記されているはずだ It should *be specified* in the contract.
めいき² 銘記 今の先生の言葉を心に銘記しておこう I'll bear [*keep*] what the teacher said just now *in mind*.
めいぎ 名義 one's name ‖人に名義を貸す lend *one's name* to a person / この家は母の名義になっている This house is *in my mother's name*.
◆口座を息子の名義に書き換えた I *transferred* the bank account to my son.
めいきゅう 迷宮 labyrinth ⓒ, maze ⓒ
◆事件は迷宮入りした[迷宮入りになっている] The case *went unsolved [is still unsolved]*.
めいきょく 名曲 (有名な曲) a famous piece of music; (傑作) (musical) masterpiece ⓒ
メイク makeup ⓤ ⊕ →メーク
めいげつ 名月 bright moon ⓒ; (満月) full moon ◆中秋の名月 *the harvest moon*
[俳句] 名月を取つてくれろと泣く子かな(小林一茶) There's the harvest moon.
"I want it! Get it for me!"
the little child cries.
めいげん¹ 名言 (気のきいた言葉) witty remark ⓒ; (格言) maxim ⓒ; (言い習わし) wise saying ⓒ
◆それは名言だ That's *well said*.
めいげん² 明言 definite statement ⓒ ─明言する (はっきりと言う) say* definitely; (宣言する) declare ⊕
◆市長はその問題については明言を避けた The mayor avoided *making any definite comment* about the matter.
めいさい¹ 明細 details ‖明細書 (勘定などの) a detailed statement; (仕様書) specifications
めいさい² 迷彩 【軍事】camouflage ⓤ ⓒ
◆戦車に迷彩を施す *camouflage* a tank ‖迷彩服 camouflage [jungle] fatigues
めいさく 名作 (すぐれた作品) great [fine] work ⓒ; (傑作) masterpiece ⓒ ‖この小説は日本文学の名作の一つだ This novel is one of *the greatest works* of Japanese literature.
めいさん 名産 special [well-known] product ⓒ; (特産品) specialty ⓒ ‖ミカンはこの地方の名産です Mandarin oranges are *a spe-*

めいし¹ 名刺 business card ◎
◆名刺を交換する exchange *cards* / 彼は私に名刺を差し出した He gave *his card* to me.
∥名刺入れ a card case

> 日本ではほとんどのビジネスに名刺が欠かせません。仕事で人に会うとまず名刺交換をし、それから本題に入るというのが一般的です。最近ではプライベートなつきあいにも名刺を使う人がいますが、ビジネス用に比べ堅苦しくないものが好まれるようです。
> *Meishi* (business cards) are indispensable for almost all kinds of business in Japan. Normally when meeting for the first time on business people start by exchanging their *meishi* and then move on to the main subject. Nowadays some use *meishi* for their private affairs; personal cards are more informal than those for business use.

めいし² 名士 （有名人） celebrity ◎, distinguished [noted] person ◎ ∥パーティーには文壇の名士がたくさん招かれた Many literary *celebrities* were invited to the party.

めいし³ 名詞〔文法〕 noun ◎（（略語）n.） ∥名詞句 a noun phrase / 可算名詞 a countable noun / 固有名詞 a proper noun / 集合名詞 a collective noun / 抽象名詞 an abstract noun / 不可算名詞 an uncountable noun / 普通名詞 a common noun / 物質名詞 a material noun

> 英語の名詞には、日本語の名詞と違って複数形がある。日本語では「1冊の本」「2冊の本」のように単数でも複数でも「本」は同じだが、英語では単数形 book、複数形 books のように単数と複数でしばしば名詞の形が異なる。1つ、2つ、1冊、2冊のように数えて、単数の場合は単数形を、複数の場合は複数形を用いる名詞のことを「可算名詞」または「数えられる名詞」という。また、ふつうは1つ、2つ、1冊、2冊のように数えない名詞のことを「不可算名詞」または「数えられない名詞」という。「可算名詞」「不可算名詞」はそれぞれ以下のような種類の名詞からなる。
>
> ［可算名詞］
> (a)普通名詞：一定の形をもった具体的な物を示す名詞(book「本」、house「家」など)
> (b)集合名詞：同じ種類や性質のものの集合を示す名詞(audience「聴衆」、family「家族」など)⇒しゅうごうめいし
>
> ［不可算名詞］
> (a)物質名詞：一定の形をもたない物質を示す名詞(air「空気」、water「水」など)
> (b)抽象名詞：抽象的なものやことを示す名詞(happiness「幸福」、health「健康」など)
> (c)固有名詞：そのものだけを示す名詞で大文字で始まる(Japan「日本」、Tom「トム」など)⇒こゆうめいし

めいじ¹ 明示 ──明示する （はっきりと言う） express clearly; （はっきりと示す） indicate [show*] clearly ∥方針を明示する show the policy *clearly*

めいじ² 明治 Meiji ◆明治37年、日露戦争が始まった The Russo-Japanese war began in 1904 [the 37th year of *the Meiji era*].(❖年号は日本独自のものなので西暦を用いるほうがよい)
∥明治維新 the Meiji Restoration / 明治時代 the Meiji era [period]

めいじつ 名実 彼は名実ともに僕たちのチームの中心人物だ He is the central figure of our team *both in name and in fact*.

めいしゃ 目医者 eye doctor ◎; （眼科医） ophthalmologist ◎

めいしゅ 名手 expert ◎ ◆彼はギターの名手だ He is *an expert guitar player*.(❖このexpertは「熟達した」の意味の形容詞)

めいしょ 名所 a place of interest, noted place ◎; （観光地） the sights ∥ニューヨークの名所を見物する see *the sights* of New York ◆京都は紅葉の名所だ Kyoto *is famous for* its autumn colors.
∥名所旧跡 places of scenic and historical interest / 観光名所 a tourist attraction

めいしょう¹ 名称 name ◎ ∥名称を改める change *the name*
∥正式名称 the [*one's*] official name

めいしょう² 名勝 a place of scenic beauty

めいじる¹ 命じる （命令する） order ⊕, command ⊕, tell* ⊕; （任命する） appoint ⊕ めいれい ∥先生は彼に教室から出るよう命じた The teacher *ordered* him to go out of the classroom. / 医者は彼にしばらく静養するよう命じた The doctor *told* him to take a rest for a while. / いとこは札幌支店への転勤を命じられた My cousin *was told* that he would be transferred to the Sapporo branch. / 彼は課長を命じられた He *was appointed* to the post of section chief.

めいじる² 銘じる 彼の言葉を肝に銘じておきます I'll *keep* his words *in mind*.

めいしん 迷信 superstition ◎◎ ──迷信的な superstitious ∥迷信を信じる believe in *superstitions* / 夜、つめを切ると親の死に目に会えないというのは迷信だ It is said that if you cut your nails at night, you won't be able to be at your parents' bedside when they die. But it's *a superstition*.
∥迷信家 a superstitious person

めいじん 名人 ❶【熟練した人】expert ◎; （大家） master ◎ ∥書道の名人 *a master* of calligraphy / 彼女はケーキ作りの名人だ She is *an expert* at [in] making cakes./ She *is extremely good* at making cakes.
❷【将棋・碁の】*Meijin*, the highest title for *shogi* [*go*] players
∥名人芸 a masterly performance

めいせい 名声 fame ◎; （評判） reputation ◎（またa 〜） ∥名声に傷をつける *damage one's reputation* / 彼は富と名声を追い求めている He seeks *fame* and fortune. / 彼女は歌手として世界的な名声を得た She gained *world fame* as a singer.
◆彼はデザイナーとして名声が高い He *is famous* as a designer.

めいせき 明晰 ―明晰な clear ◆頭脳明晰である be *clear-headed* [*intelligent*]

めいそう¹ 迷走 ―迷走する stray ⑬, wander ⑬

めいそう² 瞑想 meditation Ⓤ ―瞑想する meditate ⑬ ∥兄は瞑想にふけっていた My brother was lost in *meditation*.

めいだい 命題 〖論理〗proposition Ⓒ

めいちゅう 命中 ―命中する hit* ⑬ ∥彼の放った矢は的(まと)に命中した The arrow he shot *hit* the target.

めいちょ 名著 (偉大な本) great book Ⓒ; (有名な本) famous book Ⓒ; (傑作) masterpiece Ⓒ

めいっぱい 目一杯 この前の週末は海に行って目一杯楽しんできた I went to the beach and enjoyed it *to the full* last weekend.

めいてんがい 名店街 a street of famous stores

メイド ⇒メード

めいど 冥土 the next [other] world ∥冥土のみやげに私の秘密を教えてやろう I'll tell you one of my secrets so you can *take it to the next [other] world*.

めいとう¹ 名答 (正しい答え) the right answer ◆ご名答！ *You're right*!

めいとう² 名刀 (すぐれた刀) excellent sword Ⓒ; (有名な刀) famous sword Ⓒ

めいにち 命日 あしたは父の命日だ Tomorrow is *the anniversary of* my father's *death*.

めいはく 明白 ―明白な (はっきりした) clear; (一見して分かる) obvious; (単純明快な) plain; (周囲の状況などから明らかな) evident ―明白に clearly; obviously; plainly; evidently ∥明白な事実 an *obvious* fact / 彼らの意図は明白だ Their intention *is clear*. / 彼女が無実であることは明白だった It *was evident* that she was innocent.

めいふく 冥福 死者の冥福を祈る pray for *the peaceful repose of the dead* / お母様のご冥福をお祈りいたします May your mother's *soul rest in peace*!

めいぶつ 名物 (名産品) special [noted] product Ⓒ, specialty Ⓒ; (呼び物) feature Ⓒ, attraction Ⓒ ∥ウナギは浜名湖の名物だ Eel is a 「*special product* [*specialty*] of Lake Hamana.
◆彼は野球部の名物男だ He is *a popular figure* in our baseball club.

めいぶん¹ 名文 (すぐれた作品) excellent composition Ⓒ; (美しい一節) beautiful passage Ⓒ ∥名文家 a great writer

めいぶん² 明文 provision Ⓒ
◆それは法律に明文化されている It *is* 「*provided for* [*stipulated*] in the law.

めいぼ 名簿 list Ⓒ; (住所も記した) directory Ⓒ; (登録簿) register Ⓒ; (出席簿) roll Ⓒ ∥会員名簿を作成する make [draw up] *a membership list* [*directory*] / 私の名前は名簿から削除された My name was removed from *the list*. / 彼女の名前は乗客名簿に載っている Her name is on *the passenger* [*boarding*] *list*.
∥学生名簿 a student directory / 職員名簿 a staff list / 選挙人名簿 a pollbook / 同窓会名簿 an alumni directory

めいめい¹ 銘々 each ―めいめいの each; (個々の) individual; (自分自身の) one's own; (各自の) respective ∥私たちはめいめい辞書を持ってきた We *each* [*Each* of us] brought a dictionary. / 先生は生徒めいめいにプリントを配った The teacher distributed handouts to 「*each* student [*each* of the students]. / これに関してはめいめいで調べてきなさい *Each of you* should examine this by yourself. / 生徒たちは修学旅行についてめいめいの感想を述べた The students gave *their own* impressions of the school trip.

めいめい² 命名 ―命名する (名前をつける) name ⑬; (呼ぶ) call ⑬; (人・船などを) christen ⑬ ∥その宇宙船はエンデバー号と命名された The spaceship *was named* [*christened*] the Endeavor.

めいめつ 明滅 ―明滅する blink ⑬; (揺らめく) flicker ⑬

めいもく 名目 name Ⓒ; (口実) pretext Ⓒ ∥彼らは謝礼という名目でその役人にわいろを贈った They offered a bribe to the official *under the pretext of a reward*.
◆彼は名目だけの党首だ He is the *nominal leader of the party*.

めいもん 名門 distinguished [famous] family Ⓒ ∥その俳優は名門の出だ The actor comes from *a distinguished family*.
◆その高校は野球の名門校だ The high school is *famous* [*well known*] for its baseball club's outstanding record.
∥名門校 (一流校) a prestigious [prestige] school

めいもんく 名文句 clever expression Ⓒ; (有名な) famous expression Ⓒ

めいやく 名訳 excellent translation Ⓒ

めいゆう¹ 名優 great actor [actress] Ⓒ; (すぐれた) excellent actor [actress] Ⓒ

めいゆう² 盟友 (固い約束を結んだ友) sworn friend Ⓒ

めいよ 名誉

honor [ǽnər], 《英》honour Ⓤ; (信望・評判) credit Ⓤ; (評判) reputation Ⓤ; (恩恵) privilege Ⓤ (❖いずれも具体的な事柄は Ⓒ)
〖名誉を〗
名誉を挽回(ばんかい)する redeem [retrieve] *one's reputation*; clear *one's name*
祖父は名誉を重んじる人だ My grandfather makes much of *honor*.
彼らは彼女の名誉を傷つけた They hurt her *reputation*.
◆彼らの行為は学校の名誉をけがした Their deeds *brought disgrace* on the school.
〖名誉に〗
それは彼の名誉にかかわる問題だ It will affect his *honor*.
私の名誉にかけてこの仕事をやり通してみせます *On my honor*, I will carry out this task.
〖その他〗

コミュニケーションスキル —命令—

①～しなさい
Be quiet.
静かにしなさい.
Sit at the table.
テーブルに着いて.
Leash all pets.
ペットはすべてひもでつなぐこと.
Take your purse with you.
財布は携帯しなさい.
Handle with care.
取扱いに注意(しなさい).
Please stay in your seat.
着席したままでいてください.

☞ 基本的な命令文は主語(You)がなくて動詞の原形で文が始まる.
☞ please を付けると丁寧な響きになる.

②～しないでください

a) No ～
No Smoking 禁煙
No Swimming 遊泳禁止
No Photographing Allowed 撮影禁止

b) Do not ～.
Don't be late. 遅れるなよ.
Do not use elevators in case of fire. 火事のときはエレベーターを使うな.
Please don't do that again. もうしないでください.

☞ No ～ は掲示によく使われる.
☞ 禁止を表すには次のように no や don't を用いない表現もある.
Keep Off 立入禁止
Off Limits 立入禁止区域
Swim at your own risk. 泳ぐな(泳ぐなら自分の責任で)

③上記以外の命令文

Adults only. 未成年者お断り.
Shirt and shoes required. シャツと靴を着用すること.
All passengers are required by law **to** wear seat belts. 法律により乗客はみなシートベルトの着用が義務づけられています.
You must take your seat when the bell rings. チャイムが鳴ったら席に着くこと.
You better go and see her right now. 今すぐ彼女に会いに行ったほうがいいよ.

☞ You better ... は You'd better [had better] ... の省略形. どちらも目上の人や知らない人に対しては失礼な表現になるので使わない.

この賞をいただいたことは大変な名誉です It is *a great honor* for me to win this prize.
金メダルを取ることは選手にとっても国にとっても名誉なことだ To win a gold medal is *an honor* [*a credit*] to both the athletes and their country.
◆名誉ある地位 an *honorable* position / その俳優はある雑誌を名誉毀損(きそん)で訴えた The actor sued a magazine for *libel*.
∥名誉会員 an honorary member / 名誉会長 an honorary president / 名誉革命 the Glorious [Bloodless] Revolution / 名誉毀損(文書による) libel;(口頭による) slander / 名誉教授 a professor emeritus / 名誉市民 an honorary citizen / 名誉職 an honorary post

めいりょう 明瞭 ——明瞭な (はっきりした) clear;(単純明快な) plain;(鮮明な) distinct;(証拠などから明らかな) evident;(発音などが) articulate ∥明瞭な発音 clear [*articulate*] pronunciation / 自分の意見を明瞭にする make *one's* opinion *clear* / 彼は私たちの質問に簡単明瞭に答えた He gave a *plain* answer to our question.

めいる 滅入る feel* gloomy [depressed,《口語的》blue](❖feel の代わりに get も用いられる) ∥天気が悪くて気がめいる Bad weather makes me *feel gloomy*. / 期末試験のことを考えると気がめいる I *get depressed* when I think of the final exam.

めいれい 命令

order ⓒ《しばしば複数形 ～s》;(権力・権限のある人の) command ⓒ;(指示) directions;(指図) instructions ——命令する order ⓗ; command ⓗ; direct ⓗ; instruct ⓗ
⇨ コミュニケーションスキル
彼女は黙って命令に従った She silently obeyed [followed] *the orders*.
彼らは隊長の命令に背(そむ)いた They disobeyed their leader's *order* [*command*].
将軍は大声で命令を下した The general gave *an order* with a loud voice.
彼は社長の命令でロンドンに飛んだ He flew to London *on the order* of the president.
【order＋名(人)＋to do】コーチは選手にすぐ練習を始めるよう命令した The coach *ordered* the players *to* start practice at once. / 彼は今月中に帰国するよう命令された He *was ordered to* return home within this month. / 住民に避難命令が出された The residents *were ordered to* evacuate.
◆彼は命令口調でそう言った He said so *in a commanding tone*. / 財務再建が会社の至上命令だ It's *vital* [*essential*] for the company to get its finances in order.
∥命令形《文法》an imperative form / 命令文《文法》an imperative sentence

めいろ 迷路 maze ⓒ, labyrinth ⓒ ∥迷路のような細い道 *a maze* of narrow paths

めいろう 明朗 ——明朗な (明るい) bright;(陽気な) cheerful;(明らかな) clear;(公正な) honest, clean ∥明朗快活な生徒 a *cheerful and energetic* student / 会計を明朗にしなければならない We must make the accounting *clear*.

めいわく 迷惑

(面倒) trouble ⓤ;(うるさいもの) annoyance ⓤ;(やっかいな人[もの]) nuisance ⓒ;(不便)

メイン

inconvenience ⓤ ──迷惑な (面倒な) troublesome; (いらだたせるような) annoying; (不都合な) inconvenient
人に迷惑をかける cause a person *trouble* / 迷惑そうな顔をする make *a look of annoyance* / 迷惑行為 *annoying behavior*
夜遅くにピアノを弾くのは近所迷惑だ Playing the piano late at night is *a nuisance to the neighbors*.
人の迷惑にならないようにしなさい Don't make *a nuisance of yourself*.
ご迷惑でなければご一緒したいのですが If it's no *trouble* [If it *isn't inconvenient*], I'd like to go with you.
◆ご迷惑をおかけしてすみません I'm sorry to *trouble* [*bother*] *you*. / I'm sorry to *have troubled* [*bothered*] *you*.(❖前者はこれから迷惑をかけするとき、後者はすでに迷惑をかけたとき) / 彼女の長電話には迷惑している I'm annoyed with her for talking too long on the phone. / 車内での携帯電話のご使用はほかのお客様の迷惑となりますので、電源をお切りくださいますようお願い申し上げます The use of cell phones on the train *disturbs* the other passengers, so please turn off your phones.
⇨ありがためいわく

メイン ──メインの main ⇨メーン¹
めうえ 目上 (地位などが上の人) one's superior; (年長者) one's senior / 目上の人を敬う respect [be respectful to] one's seniors
めうし 雌牛 cow ⓒ
めうつり 目移り いろいろなケーキに目移りしてどれを買うか決められない So many cakes *catch my eye* and I can't decide which one to buy.
メーカー maker ⓒ (❖しばしば複合語を作る); (製造業者) manufacturer
◆世界最大の自動車メーカー the world's largest *automaker* / その時計はどこのメーカーですか What *make* is your watch?
‖メーカー品 a name-brand item
メーキャップ makeup ⓤ ──メーキャップする make* up, put* on *one's* makeup / 彼女は女王役のメーキャップをしている She *is making herself up* for the role of the queen.
メーク ⚠makeup ⓤ ──メークする make* up, put* on makeup / メークを落とす take off *one's* makeup
メーター (長さの単位) meter ⓒ; (計器) meter ⓒ / ガスのメーター *a gas meter* / メーターを調べる read *the meter*
‖タクシーメーター a taximeter
メーデー May Day
メード maid ⓒ; (家政婦) housemaid ⓒ
メートル meter ⓒ / 400メートルリレー a 400-*meter* relay / このひもの長さは３メートルある This string is three *meters* long.
‖メートル法 the metric system
メーリングリスト〔コンピュータ〕 mailing list ⓒ
メール (電子メール) e-mail, email, E-mail ⓒⓤ (❖mailはⓤだが, e-mailはⓒとしても用いられる); (郵便) mail ⓤ, 《英》 post ⓤ ❖前後見返し / メールを太郎に送った I sent (an) *e-mail* to Taro. / I *e-mailed* Taro. / 寛子からメールを受け取った I got [received] (an) *e-mail from Hiroko*. / そのメーリングリストに入ったら毎日50通以上のメールが来るようになった After I subscribed to that mailing list I started getting more than 50 *e-mails* every day. / メール友達が欲しい I want some *e-mail friends*.
🔎「あしたの集合場所、真理子に知らせた？」「うん、メールを送っといたよ(→メールで知らせた)」 "Did you tell Mariko where we're going to meet tomorrow?" "Yes. I let her know by *e-mail*."
‖メールオーダー mail order / メールボックス a mailbox / エアメール air mail / ダイレクトメール direct mail

メーン¹ ──メーンの main ◆彼は歌手としてデビューしたが、最近では俳優としての活動がメーンになっているようだ Although he started as a singer, he seems to be active *mainly* as an actor recently.
‖メーンイベント the main event / メーンスタンド the grandstand / メーンストリート the main street / メーンディッシュ the main dish / メーンテーブル the main table
メーン² Maine(❖米国北東部の州;《略語》Me.,〔郵便〕ME)
メカ (機械類) machines, machinery ⓤ / 父はメカに強い My father knows a lot about *machinery*.
メガ- mega- / メガトン a megaton / メガバイト〔コンピュータ〕 a megabyte (《略語》Mb, MB) / メガヘルツ〔電気〕 a megahertz (《略語》MHz)
めかくし 目隠し (目を覆う物) blindfold ⓒ; (視界などをさえぎる物) screen ⓒ / 人に目隠しをする put *a blindfold* over a person's eyes; *blindfold* a person
めがける 目掛ける 彼は的(♗)をめがけて球を投げた He *aimed* the ball *at* the target.
◆彼らは出口めがけて一目散に走った They ran *toward* the exit for their lives.
めがしら 目頭 その光景に目頭が熱くなった I *was moved to tears* at the sight. / 彼女はそっと目頭を押さえた She *wiped away her tears* secretly.
めかす (盛装する) dress up / きょうの彼女はずいぶんめかしこんでいる She *is all dressed up* today.
めかた 目方 weight ⓤ / 目方が増えた[減った] I have gained [lost] *weight*.
◆荷物の目方を量る *weigh* the baggage
メカニズム mechanism ⓒⓤ
めがね 眼鏡
❶〔眼鏡〕(eye) glasses, 《公式的》spectacles (❖共に数えるときはa pair of ... とする)
銀縁の眼鏡 silver-rimmed *glasses* / 度の強い眼鏡 strong [thick] *glasses*
彼は眼鏡をかけた[はずした] He「put on [took off] *his glasses*.

あの眼鏡をかけた人が私の兄です The man with *glasses* on is my brother.

彼女は授業中は眼鏡をかけている She wears *glasses* during class.

姉は眼鏡をやめてコンタクトにした My sister switched from *glasses* to contact lenses.

眼鏡がないと黒板の字が見えない I can't read the letters on the blackboard without *my glasses*.

外から部屋に入ると眼鏡が曇った *My glasses* were misted over when I entered the room from outside.

最近眼鏡の度が合わなくなってきた(→この眼鏡ではよく見えない) I can't see well with these *glasses* recently. (❖My glasses don't fit recently.だと「眼鏡が顔に合わない」の意味になる)

祖父は眼鏡越しに私を見た My grandfather looked at me *over his glasses*.

❷【判断力】judgment,《英》judgement [U] (❖「判断」「審査」の意味では [U][C])

◆彼女は先生のめがねにかなった(→気に入られた)らしい She seems to *have found favor with* the teacher. / 私は彼を助手に選んだがとんだめがね違いだった I chose him as my assistant, but it was *a* terrible *misjudgment*.

‖眼鏡入れ a glasses case / 眼鏡屋(店) an optical shop; (人) an optician / 遠近両用眼鏡 bifocals / 水中眼鏡(水泳用) swimming goggles; (潜水用) a face mask / 縁なし眼鏡 rimless glasses

メガホン megaphone [C]

めがみ 女神 goddess [C]

メガロポリス megalopolis [C]

めきき 目利き (鑑定人) judge [C],《米》appraiser [C]; (美術品などの) connoisseur [C] ∥彼は美術品の目利きだ He is *a good judge* of works of art.

◆骨董(こっとう)品の目利きをする *judge* antiques

メキシコ Mexico(❖公式名 the United Mexican States) ─メキシコ人 Mexican [C] ─メキシコ(人)の Mexican

メキシコシティ Mexico City(❖メキシコの首都)

めきめき (著しく) remarkably; (速く) rapidly, quickly ◆彼女のテニスはめきめき上達している She has been making *remarkable* [*rapid*] progress in tennis.

めキャベツ 芽キャベツ Brussels sprouts

-めく 日に日に春めいてきた It is getting to *be more like spring* every day. / 彼の言葉には批判めいたところがあった There was *a touch of criticism* in what he said.

めくじら 目くじら ささいなことに目くじらを立てる(→腹を立てる) *get angry about* trivial matters / 彼女は人の言うことにすぐ目くじらを立てる(→あらを探す) She always *finds fault with* what other people say.

めぐすり 目薬 (点眼液) eyedrops ∥目薬をさす put *eyedrops* in *one's* eyes

めくばせ 目配せ (ウインク) wink [C]

◆兄は私にドアを閉めるようにと目くばせした My brother「*signaled* me [*gave* me *a signal*] *with his eyes* to shut the door.

めくばり 目配り ─目配りする keep* (a) watch, be watchful, be observant ∥遠足の間中, 先生は生徒に目配りしていた The teacher *was keeping a watch on* her students during the excursion.

めぐまれる 恵まれる be blessed with ...; (才能などに) be gifted [endowed] with ...; (資源などに) be rich in ... ∥ニュージーランドは温暖な気候に恵まれている New Zealand *is blessed with* a mild climate. / 彼女は芸術的才能に恵まれている She *is gifted with* artistic talent. / この国は鉱物資源に恵まれている This country *is rich in* mineral resources.

◆恵まれた生活を送る lead a *comfortable* life / わが家はみな健康に恵まれている Everyone in my family *enjoys* good health. / 彼は恵まれた家庭に育った He was brought up in a *happy* home environment. / そのテレビ局は恵まれない人々のためにチャリティーショーを催した The TV network put on a charity show for *underprivileged* people.

めぐみ 恵み (賜物(たまもの)) blessing [C]; (施し) charity [U] ∥自然の恵み nature's *blessings* / 神の恵み God's *blessings*; *the grace* of God

◆恵みの雨 a *welcome* [*lucky*] rain

めぐむ 恵む 彼はその子供たちに金を恵んだ He *gave* money to the children.

めぐらす 巡らす ❶【囲む】surround [他], enclose [他] ∥王は城に城壁をめぐらした The king *surrounded* the castle with walls.

❷【思い・策などを】(考える) think* [他]; (回顧する) look back on ...; (工夫する) devise [他]; (たくらむ) plot [他] ∥策をめぐらす *devise* a scheme / それをどうやろうかと彼は思いをめぐらした He *thought about* how to do it. / 彼女は自分の子供時代に思いをめぐらした She *looked back on* her childhood.

めぐり 巡り (遍歴) tour [C]; (循環) circulation [U] ∥血の巡りが悪い have poor blood *circulation* / (→頭が悪い) be slow on *the uptake* / パリで美術館巡りをした I made *a tour* of art museums in Paris.

めぐりあう 巡り会う meet* ... by chance, come* across ... ∥彼女は旅行中に夫となる男性に巡り会った She *met* her future husband *by chance* during her trip.

めぐりあわせ 巡り合わせ (運) fortune [U]; (運命) fate [U] ∥不思議な巡り合わせで私はまた彼といっしょに働くことになった By *a* strange *stroke of fate*, I was to work with him again.

めくる 捲る (ページなどを) turn (over); (ぱらぱらと) leaf through ...; (カードなどを) turn up ∥トランプをめくる *turn* a card *up* / 生徒たちは教科書のページをめくった The students *turned over* the page of the textbook. / 彼女は雑誌を手に取ってページをぱらぱらとめくった She took the magazine in her hand and *leafed through* it.

◆彼らがふとんをめくると, もぬけの殻だった

めぐる

They *pulled up* the futon only to find nobody there.

めぐる 巡る　春がめぐってきた Spring *has come [arrived]*. / 彼は日本各地のお寺を巡る旅に出かけた He went on a trip to *visit temples* all over Japan. / その問題をめぐり私たちの意見は分かれた We were divided *over* the issue.

めくれる 捲れる　上着のすそがめくれているよ The hem of your jacket *is turned up*.

めげる（がっかりする）be discouraged [disappointed];（めいる）be depressed　//そんなにめげないで *Don't be so disappointed [depressed]*.

◆困難にもめげず，彼女は最後までがんばった *Undaunted* by difficulties, she did her best to the very end.

めこぼし 目溢し　どうかお目こぼし願います Please *overlook* it.

めさき 目先　彼はいつも目先のことばかり考えている He thinks only about *the present*. / 目先の変わった(→新しいタイプの)番組が見たい I want to watch a *new [novel]* type of TV program. / 目先の利益にとらわれるばかりではいけません Don't think only about the *short-term* benefits.

慣用表現 目先がきかない(→先見の明がない) *have no foresight* / 目先がきく(→先見の明がある) *have foresight*

めざし 目刺し　*mezashi*, salted and dried sardines

めざす 目指す・目差す (ねらう) aim at …, aim to *do*

彼らは新しい制度の実現を目ざしている They *are aiming at* realization of the new system.

彼女はデザイナーを目ざしている She *aims* 「*to become [at becoming]* a designer.

◆彼らはゴール地点を目ざし必死にボートをこいだ They rowed the boat hard *toward* the finish line.

めざとい 目敏い　sharp-eyed

◆弟は私のかばんの中のあめを目ざとく見つけた My brother *quickly* found the candies in my bag. / 彼女は漢字の間違いを目ざとく見つける She *has a sharp eye for* the wrong *kanji*.

めざまし 目覚まし (目覚まし時計) alarm (clock) Ⓒ　//目覚ましを止める stop [turn off, shut off] *the alarm* / 目覚ましを7時に合わせた I set *the alarm clock* for 7 o'clock. / 目覚ましが鳴る前に目がさめた I woke up before *the alarm* went off.

◆目覚ましに冷たい水を1杯飲む drink a glass of cold water as *an eye-opener*

めざましい 目覚ましい（著しい）remarkable　—メザマしく remarkably　//医学はめざましく進歩している Medical science has been making *remarkable* progress. / その国はめざましい発展を遂げた The country has undergone *remarkable* development.

◆きょうの試合で彼はめざましい活躍を見せた He *distinguished himself* in today's game.

めざめ 目覚め　自我の目ざめ *the awakening of one's* self / けさはとても目ざめがよかった I *woke up pleasantly* this morning.

めざめる 目覚める（起きる）wake* (up), awake* 卣, (気づく) wake (up), awake 卣　//長い眠りから目ざめる *wake up* from a long sleep / 彼は英語を学ぶおもしろさに目ざめた He 「*woke (up) [awoke] to* the pleasure of studying English.

◆性に目ざめる *be awakened* sexually / 彼女は現実に目ざめた She *opened her eyes to* the reality.

めざわり 目障り　eyesore Ⓒ　//あの高いビルが目ざわりだ That high building is *an eyesore*. / あいつは目ざわりなやつだ(→見ていて不愉快だ) He presents an *unpleasant* sight.

めし 飯 ❶【ごはん】(boiled [cooked]) rice Ⓤ　/飯をたく boil *the rice*

❷【食事】meal Ⓒ (❖時間によって breakfast, lunch, dinner, supper と具体的に呼ぶことが多い); (食物) food Ⓤ　//飯のしたくをする prepare *a meal* / さあ，飯にしよう Now, let's have *dinner [breakfast, lunch, supper]*.

◆兄は三度の飯よりか(→ほかの何よりも)映画が好きだ My brother likes movies *more than anything else*.

❸【生計】He *makes a living* as a writer. / 飯の種だからこの仕事をやめるわけにいかない I can't quit this job because it's *my bread and butter*. / そんなことをしたら飯の食い上げだ(→仕事を失ってしまう) If I do that, I will *lose my job*.

メシア the Messiah

めしあがる 召し上がる　何を召し上がりますか What would you like to *have*? / クッキーをどうぞ召し上がれ Help *yourself to* the cookies.

めした 目下 (地位などが下の人) one's subordinate; (年少者) one's junior

めしつかい 召使　servant Ⓒ; (女性の) maid Ⓒ　/召使を置く keep *a servant*

めしべ 雌蕊　pistil Ⓒ

メジャー ❶【巻き尺】tape measure Ⓒ

❷【主要な・有名な】—メジャーな (主要な) major; (有名な) famous

❸【長調】【音楽】major　//メジャーリーグ the major leagues

めじり 目尻　the corner of the eye

◆目じりのしわ *crow's-feet* / 目じりの上がった人 a person *with upturned eyes* / 彼はかわいい女の子を見るとすぐ目じりを下げる He *is always fascinated* by cute girls.

めじるし 目印　mark Ⓒ; (標識) sign Ⓒ; (建物など) landmark Ⓒ　//地図に目印をつけておいた I've put *a mark* on the map. / うちに来るには小学校が目印になると思います The elementary school may be *a landmark* to find my home.

◆彼は目印にそのページにしおりをはさんだ He put a bookmark between the pages *to mark his place*.

めじろ 目白　white-eye Ⓒ

◆楽しいイベントが目白押しです There's a

メス ⚠️(手術・解剖用の) scalpel C (❖日本語はオランダ語の mes から)
◆彼らはその汚職事件に捜査のメスを入れた(→徹底的な捜査を開始した) They *began to probe into* the payoff scandal.

めす¹ 雌 female C,《口語的》she C ——雌の female, she-(❖she-は複合語を作って用いられる) //雌猫 a *female* cat; a *she*-cat / その犬は雄ですか、雌ですか Is the dog 「a male or *a female* [a he or *a she*]?

めす² 召す お年を召した方 an *elderly* person / お気に召しましたか Did you *like* it? / このドレスをお召しになってみませんか Why don't you *try* this dress *on*?

めずらしい 珍しい

❶【まれな】 rare; (ふつうでない) unusual; (並はずれた) uncommon; (風変わりな) unique

水族館で珍しい魚をたくさん見た I saw a lot of *rare* fish at the aquarium.

彼女が計算間違いをするなんて珍しい It is *unusual* [*rare*] for her to make a mistake in calculation.

彼が遅刻するのは珍しいことではない It is not *unusual* for him to be late.

珍しい地名ですね It is an *uncommon* place name, isn't it?

◆彼女は珍しく(→いつもの彼女と違って)元気がない *Unlike her normal self*, she looks depressed. / まあ珍しい、あなたにお会いするのは何年ぶりかしら Oh, *what a surprise*! I haven't seen you for ages. / ここでお会いするとは珍しい *Fancy* meeting you here!

❷【目新しい】

きょうは珍しい客があった I had an *unexpected* visitor today.

女の子はその花を珍しそうに見ていた The girl looked at the flower *curiously*.

その国から来た子供たちには日本で見るもの聞くもののすべてが珍しかった Everything the children from that country saw or heard in Japan *was new* to them.

メゾソプラノ 〔音楽〕mezzo-soprano U C (複 ~s)

メソポタミア Mesopotamia

めそめそ 弟は母に怒られて自分の部屋でめそめそ泣いていた My brother was scolded by my mother and *was sobbing* in his room. / めそめそしないで *Stop sobbing*./ (→元気を出して)*Cheer up*!

めだか (Japanese) killifish C

めだつ 目立つ —— 動 stand* out —— 形 noticeable, conspicuous; (傑出した) remarkable, outstanding

彼女は赤いドレスを着ていたので目立った She 「*stood out* [*was conspicuous*] because she wore a red dress.

時間割を教室の目立つところにはった I put up the class timetable in a *noticeable* part of the classroom.

彼はチームでもひときわ目立つ存在だ He is *outstanding* among our team.

彼は目立ちたがり屋だ(→目立とうとする)He *likes to make himself conspicuous*./ (→注目の的(まと)になりたがる)He *likes to be the center of attention*.

◆彼女はクラスでは目立たない存在だった She was an *inconspicuous* student in the class. / このカーテンは汚れが目立たない This curtain *doesn't show* dirt. / 彼は最近白髪が目立ってきた His hair *has been turning* gray recently. / 定職に就かない若者の数が目立って増えてきている The number of young people without steady jobs has been *noticeably* increasing.

メタノール ➡ メチルアルコール

メタファー (隠喩(いんゆ)) metaphor C U

めだま 目玉 eyeball C (呼び物) feature C //彼のピアノソロがそのコンサートのいちばんの目玉だった His piano solo was *the* chief [*major*] *feature* of the concert.

◆その指輪は目玉が飛び出るような値段がついていた The ring 「had an *eye-poppingly high price* [was *tremendously expensive*].

‖目玉商品(客寄せのための特価品) a loss leader; (客の目を引くもの) an eye-catcher

めだまやき 目玉焼き fried egg C ◆卵は目玉焼きにしてください I want my eggs *sunny-side up*.

メダリスト medalist C //金[銀, 銅]メダリスト a gold [silver, bronze] *medalist*

メタル metal U ◆メタルフレームの眼鏡 *wire-rimmed* [*wire-framed*] glasses
‖メタルウッド a metal wood / メタルテープ a metal tape

メダル medal C //日本は今回のオリンピックで7個の金メダルを獲得した Japan won seven *gold medals* at this Olympic games.

メタンガス methane (gas) U

めちゃくちゃ ——めちゃくちゃな (乱雑な) messy; (理屈に合わない) unreasonable, (無謀な) reckless /君の言っていることはめちゃくちゃだ What you are saying is *quite unreasonable*.

◆子供部屋はめちゃくちゃに散らかっていた The child's room was *in a terrible mess*. / 彼のせいで計画がめちゃくちゃになった He *messed up* our plan. / きのうはめちゃくちゃ暑かった It was hot 「*as hell* [*like anything*] yesterday.

めちゃめちゃ トラックは事故でめちゃめちゃになった The truck *was wrecked* [*smashed up*] in the accident. / つぼが床に落ちてめちゃめちゃにこわれた The pot fell on the floor and *shattered into pieces*. / 赤ん坊が僕の部屋をめちゃめちゃにした The baby *messed up* my room.

メチルアルコール 〔化学〕methyl alcohol U

メッカ (イスラム教の聖地) Mecca; (あこがれの地・中心地) mecca C //長野はスキーのメッカだ Nagano is *a mecca* for skiers. (❖×for skiing とはしない)

めつき 目付き look C //意味ありげな目つきで with *a meaningful look* / 目つきが悪い

have *a* sinister *look* / 彼は鋭い目つきで私を見た He gave me *a* sharp *look*.

めっき 鍍金 plating ⓤ; (金の) gilding ⓤ
◆銀めっきの皿 a *silver-plated* dish / このスプーンには金めっきがしてある This spoon *is* 「*plated with gold* [*gilded*]」

慣用表現 彼女は着飾って上品ぶっているけど、めっきがはげる(→本性を現す)のも時間の問題だ She is dressed up and pretending to be elegant, but soon she will *reveal her true nature*.

めっきり (かなり) considerably; (著しく) remarkably; (目立って) noticeably ∥近ごろめっきり冷え込んできた It has become *considerably* colder recently. / この町の人口はめっきり少なくなった The population of this town has declined *remarkably*.

めっけもの めっけ物 (掘り出し物) (lucky) find ⓒ ◆パスポートが見つかっただけでもめっけものだ(→幸運だ) You are *lucky* just to have found your passport.

めつけやく 目付け役 (監督役) overseer ⓒ, supervisor ⓒ

メッシュ ❶【網目状のもの】mesh ⓤ ∥メッシュの靴下 *mesh* stockings
❷【毛染め】髪に赤のメッシュを入れる *streak one's* hair red

メッセ (会議や見本市などを開催する建物) convention center ⓒ (❖日本語はドイツ語のMesse から)

メッセージ (伝言) message ⓒ; (声明) statement ⓒ ∥メッセージを受け取る receive *a message* / 電報でメッセージを送る send *a message* by telegraph / ピーという発信音の後にメッセージをお入れください Please leave *a message* after the beep.
∥メッセージソング a *message song*

メッセンジャー messenger ⓒ ∥メッセンジャーボーイ a *messenger boy*

めったうち めった打ち その投手は相手チームにめった打ちされた The pitcher *was hit hard* by the other team.

めったな 彼はめったなことでは(→簡単には)驚かない He isn't *easily* surprised. / 彼女は口が軽いからめったなことは言えない(→秘密を打ち明けられない) She has a loose tongue, so I can't confide in her.

めったに (めったに…ない) rarely, seldom, hardly ever(❖いずれも「否定」の意味を含むので not は不要)
この地方では雪はめったに降らない It *rarely* [*seldom, hardly ever*] snows in this region.
彼はめったに学校を休まない He is *rarely* [*seldom, hardly ever*] absent from school.
◆彼女が怒ることはめったにない It is *rare* for her to get angry. / こんなチャンスはめったにない Chances like this are *few and far between*.

めつぼう 滅亡 (没落) fall ⓒ, downfall ⓒ; (崩壊) ruin ⓤ —滅亡する (町などが) fall* ⓘ; (死滅する) die out ⇨ほろびる ∥インカ帝国の滅亡 *the fall* of the Inca Empire
◆核戦争が起きたら人類は滅亡するかもしれない Nuclear war may lead to *the destruction* of mankind.

めっぽう 滅法 きょうはめっぽう暑い It is *terribly* [*awfully*] hot today. / 彼はけんかにめっぽう強い He is a *devastating* fighter.

めづまり 目詰まり 網戸が目詰まりしてきた The window screen has become *clogged with dust*.

メディア medium ⓒ (複 media) ∥テレビや新聞などのメディアは日常生活に欠かせない *Media* such as TV and newspapers are indispensable to our daily life.
∥マスメディア mass media / マルチメディア multimedia

めでたい (喜ばしい) happy, joyful; (さい先のよい) auspicious ——めでたく happily; (首尾よく) successfully

おめでたい a *happy* occasion
めでたい知らせにみな大喜びした Everyone was very glad to hear the *happy* news.
彼らは去年の秋にめでたくゴールインした *Happily*, they got married in the autumn of last year.
物語はめでたしめでたしで終わった(→幸せな結末だった) The story had *a happy ending*.
❢「彼、試験に合格したんだって」「それはめでたい」"I hear he passed the exam." "*I'm happy to hear that.*/ *That's good news.*/ *That's great.*"
⇒ おめでたい

めど 目処 ようやく新しい橋の完成のめどがついた The completion of the new bridge *is in sight* at last. / 山手線の復旧のめどはまだ立っていない There is still no *indication* of when the Yamanote Line will resume normal service. / 8月末をめどにこの仕事を終えるつもりです I'll finish this work *around* the end of August.

メドレー medley ⓒ ∥彼らはジャズの名曲をメドレーで演奏した They played *a medley* of famous jazz pieces.
∥メドレーリレー a medley relay / 個人メドレー the individual medley race

メトロノーム 【音楽】metronome ⓒ

メトロポリス metropolis ⓒ

メニュー (献立表) menu ⓒ ∥メニューを見せていただけますか Could I see *the menu*, please? / 今晩のメニューは何ですか(→何がメニューに載っていますか) What's on *the menu* this evening? / (→夕食は何ですか) What is today's *dinner*? / この店はメニューが多い[少ない] This restaurant has *a large* [*limited*] *menu*.
◆練習メニュー a practice *schedule*

メヌエット 【音楽】minuet ⓒ

めぬきどおり 目抜き通り main street ⓒ

めのう 瑪瑙 agate ⓤⓒ

めのたま 目の玉 eyeball ⓒ ⇨ め(目), めだま
◆その値札を見て目の玉が飛び出るほど驚いた When I looked at the price tag, I was so surprised that *my eyes popped out*.

めのまえ 目の前 その店では主人が客の目の前でてんぷらを揚げてくれる The chef fries

tempura *before the customers' very eyes* at that restaurant. / 文化祭はもう目の前だ The school festival *is「close at hand [just around the corner]*.

めばえ 芽生え (芽生えること) sprouting ⓤ; (新芽) sprout ⓒ; (きざし) awakening ⓤ

めばえる 芽生える (芽が出る) sprout ⓥ, bud ⓥ; (育ち始める) begin* to grow //草木が芽生える季節 the season when the trees and grasses *sprout* / 二人の間に愛が芽生えた Love *began to grow [bloom]* between the two.

めはな 目鼻 彼女の新しい小説もやっと目鼻がついてきた Her new novel *began to take shape*. / 彼は目鼻立ちがはっきりしている He *has a distinctive face*. / その女の子は目鼻立ちが整っている The girl *is good-looking*.

めばな 雌花 female flower ⓒ

めばり 目張り 窓に目張りをする *seal up* a window

めぶく 芽吹く (つぼみをつける) bud ⓥ; (芽を出す) sprout ⓥ //桜の木が芽吹き始めた Cherry trees are beginning to *bud*.

めぶんりょう 目分量 目分量でしょうゆを量る measure the soy sauce *by eye* [*sight*]

めべり 目減り 物価の上昇で貯金が目減りした *The value* of personal savings *has dropped* because of the price increase.

めぼし 目星 警察はもう犯人の目星をつけているようだ It seems the police *have* already *spotted* the criminal.

めぼしい めぼしい(→価値のある)ものはほとんど盗まれていた Almost all *the valuables* had been stolen. / その映画にはめぼしい(→すぐれた)役者はあまり出ていなかった Few *outstanding* actors appeared in the movie.

めまい 眩暈 dizziness ⓤ, giddiness ⓤ
◆めまいがするような高さのビル a building with a *dizzy* [*giddy*] height / 朝からめまいがする I've been feeling dizzy [giddy] since this morning.

めまぐるしい 目まぐるしい (速い) quick; (目が回るような) dizzying ──めまぐるしく quickly //世の中はめまぐるしく変化している The world is changing *quickly*.

めめしい 女々しい (男らしくない) unmanly; (女のような) womanish; (弱虫の) sissy
◆めめしいことを言うな *Don't be a sissy.* (❖この sissy は「意気地なしの男の子」の意味の名詞)

メモ ⚠ (簡潔な記録) note ⓒ; (連絡票) memo ⓒ ──メモをする take* [make*] a note, write* [jot] down

| 日本語の「メモ」に最も近い英語は note で, memo は会社などでの事務連絡票の意味で用いられることが多い. |

彼はメモをとりながら先生の話を聞いた He listened to what the teacher said while taking [making] *notes*.
彼女はメモを見ながら話した She spoke from *notes*.
帰りのバスの時刻を手帳にメモした I *wrote* [*jotted*] *down* the time of the return bus in my notebook.
‖メモ帳 a memo [scratch] pad / メモ用紙 memo [note] paper

めもと 目元・目許 彼女は目元がぱっちりしている She has bright and clear *eyes*.

めもり 目盛り scale ⓒ, graduation ⓒ //温度計の目盛りを読む read *the scale* [*graduation*] of a thermometer / この物差しにはインチの目盛りがついている This ruler has *a scale* in inches.

メモリー 〖コンピュータ〗(記憶装置) memory ⓤ; (思い出・記憶) memory ⓒ //私は自分でパソコンのメモリーを64メガバイトから128メガバイトに増設した I increased my PC's *memory* from 64 to 128 megabytes by myself.

めやす 目安 翻訳の完成は来月を一応の目安(→仮の締め切り)にしている I made next month *the tentative deadline* for the completion of the translation. / パソコンを買うとき,何を目安にすればいいですか By what *standard* should I choose a PC to buy?

めやに 目脂 eye mucus ⓤ; (口語的) sleep ⓤ //目やにを取る rub *the sleep* out of *one's* eyes

メラニン 〖生物〗melanin ⓤ

めらめら その枯れ木はめらめらと燃え上がった The dead tree *blazed up*.

メリーゴーラウンド merry-go-round ⓒ

メリーランド Maryland (❖米国東部の州;《略語》Md.,《郵便》MD)

めりこむ めり込む sink* in ...; (はまり込む) stick* in ... //自転車がぬかるみにめり込んだ The bicycle *sank* [*stuck*] *in* the muddy ground.

メリット ⚠advantage ⓒ (❖英語の merit は「長所・美点」という意味で,日本語の「メリット」はむしろ「利点」を表す advantage に近い) ➡ デメリット //この方法にはほとんどメリットがない There are few *advantages* in doing this way.
◆そんなばかなことをして何のメリットがあるのですか What's *the point* of doing a stupid thing like that?

めりはり 彼の歌い方はめりはりがきいている His singing style *is well-modulated*.

めりめり 雷が落ち,木はめりめりと音を立てて倒れた The lightning hit the tree, making it fall with *a「cracking sound* [*crack*]*.

メリヤス ⚠knit [knitted] goods, knitwear ⓤ (❖日本語はスペイン語の medias から)

メルトダウン (炉心溶融) meltdown ⓤ

メルヘン ⚠fairy tale ⓒ (❖ドイツ語の Märchen から)

メルボルン Melbourne (❖オーストラリアの都市)

メロディー melody ⓒ, tune ⓒ

メロドラマ melodrama ⓒ; (テレビ・ラジオの連続ドラマ) soap opera ⓒ

メロン melon ⓒ ⓤ ‖マスクメロン a muskmelon

めん¹ 面
❶【仮面】mask ⓒ; (剣道の) face guard ⓒ //面をつける put on *a mask* [*face guard*]

子供たちは動物のお面をかぶって踊った The children danced wearing animal *masks*.
❷【顔】face ⓒ
面と向かって話す talk *face to face*
彼女は面と向かって彼に注意した She warned him *to his face*.
❸【表面】(側) side ⓒ；(表面) surface ⓒ；(多面体の) face ⓒ
紙の白い面を上にしてください Please set the paper with *the* white *side* facing up.
❹【局面】side ⓒ, aspect ⓒ；(点) respect ⓒ
彼にいい面もある He has a good *side*, too.
原子力発電にはマイナスの面とプラスの面がある Nuclear power generation has both negative and positive *aspects*.
◆この計画はあらゆる面から見直すべきだ This plan needs to be reconsidered from every *angle*. / 彼らは金銭面でその活動を支援している They support the activity *financially*.
❺【新聞の】page ⓒ
社会面 the human interest *page*
その記事は新聞の1面に載っていた The article was on *the* front *page* of the newspaper.

めん² 綿 cotton ⓤ /綿100パーセントの靴下 a pair of pure-*cotton* [all-*cotton*] socks
‖綿織物 cotton fabrics / 綿花 raw cotton / 綿製品 cotton goods

めん³ 麺 (めん類) noodles

めんえき 免疫 immunity ⓤ ―免疫の immune (❖「免疫がある」の意味でも用いる) /その病人は細菌に対する免疫力が低下している The patient's *immunity* to [against] bacteria has been weakened. / 水ぼうそうには免疫がある I *am immune* to chickenpox. / 父のお説教には免疫ができている I *am immune* to my father's sermonizing. (❖日本語と同様, 比喩的にも用いる)
‖免疫学 immunology

めんかい 面会 (会う) see* ⓥ；(約束して) meet* ⓥ /面会の方がお見えです There is someone to *see* you.
◆面会謝絶 (掲示)*No Visitors* / 面会時間は3時から6時までです *The visiting hours* are from three to six. / 彼らは知事に面会を求めた They asked for *an interview* with the governor.
‖面会人 a visitor / 面会日 a visiting day

めんきょ 免許 license,《英》licence ⓒ；(証明書) certificate ⓒ /彼は調理師の免許を持っている He has a chef's *license*. / 先週運転免許を取った I got *my driver's license* last week. / 彼女は免許証を更新した She renewed *her driver's license*. / その高校生は無免許運転でつかまった The high school student was caught *driving without a license*.
‖教員免許状 a teacher's certificate, a certificate to teach

めんくい 面食い 兄は面食いだ My brother *goes for good-looking women*. / My brother *has a weakness for good-looking women*.

めんくらう 面食らう (まごつく) be embarrassed；(困惑する) be confused；(不意の事態に驚く) be taken aback /彼の思いも寄らない申し出に面食らった I *was embarrassed* [*confused*] by his unexpected offer.

めんざい 免罪 acquittal ⓤⓒ；(宗教上の) remission of sin ◆男は免罪になった The man *was acquitted of a crime*.
‖免罪符 an indulgence

めんしき 面識 acquaintance ⓤ 《また an ～》 /彼の名前は知っているが面識はない I know his name, but「I *have no acquaintance with him* [I'm not personally *acquainted with him*].
◆私は中島さんと面識があります I'm *acquainted with* Mr. Nakajima.

めんじょ 免除 (義務などの) exemption ⓒⓤ；(負債・刑などの) remission ⓤ ―免除する (義務・責任などを) exempt ... from ～；(解除する) excuse ... from ～；(負債・刑を) remit ⓥ /彼は学費を免除されている He *is exempted from* school fees. / 彼女は1次試験を免除された She *was excused from* the primary examination.

めんじょう 免状 (証明書) certificate ⓒ；(許可証) license, 《英》licence ⓒ；(卒業証書) diploma ⓒ /彼女は華道の先生の免状を持っている She has *a license* to teach flower arrangement.

めんしょく 免職 dismissal ⓒⓤ；(解雇) discharge ⓤ ―免職する dismiss [discharge] *a person* from office
◆その国会議員は収賄で免職になった The member of the Diet *was dismissed* [*discharged*] *from his post* for taking bribes.

めんじる 免じる 今回は彼女に免じて許してやろう I'll forgive you *for her sake* this time.

めんしん 免震
‖免震構造 seismically isolated structure

メンス ⚠ menstruation ⓤ, the menses, period ⓒ ⇒せいり(生理)

めんする 面する face ⓥ, look out on ... /危機に面する *face* a crisis / そのビルは大通りに面している The building *faces* [*looks out on*] the main street.

めんぜい 免税 tax exemption ⓤ ―免税の [で] tax-free, free of tax；(関税が) duty-free /空港では香水が免税で買える We can buy perfume *duty-free* at the airport.
‖免税店 a duty-free shop / 免税品 a duty-free article

めんせき¹ 面積 area ⓤⓒ；(床面積) floor space ⓤⓒ /この台形の面積を求めなさい Find *the area* of this trapezoid. / この花壇の面積は40平方メートルだ This flower bed is 40 square meters in *area*. / *The area* of this flower bed is 40 square meters. / This flower bed has *an area* of 40 square meters.

めんせき² 免責 exemption from responsibility
‖免責条項 an escape [exemption] clause

めんせつ 面接 interview ⓒ；(口頭試験) oral examination ⓒ ―面接する inter-

view ㊥ ‖私はあしたその会社の**面接**試験を受ける I will have *an interview* at the company tomorrow. / I'm going to *be interviewed* at the company tomorrow.
‖面接官 an interviewer / 個人面接 an individual interview

めんぜん 面前 公衆の面前で *in public* / 彼女はみんなの面前で彼を非難した She blamed him「*in front of* [*in the presence of*] other people.

メンタルテスト (知能検査) mental test ㊄

めんだん 面談 (面接) interview ㊄; (個人面談) face-to-face talk ㊄
◆三者面談 *a three-party conference* / (広告などで) 委細面談 Particulars to be arranged personally.

メンチ ‖メンチカツ a deep-fried minced meat cutlet / メンチボール a fried meatball

メンツ 面子 (面目) face ㊄; (名誉) honor ㊂ ‖彼女の面子はまるつぶれだった She lost *face* completely. / 彼はその試合に勝って面子を保った He won the game and saved *face*. / 彼は面子にこだわる He puts a high priority on *his personal honor*. / それでは私の面子にかかわる That will affect my *honor*.

めんてい 免停 彼はスピード違反で免停を食らった He *had his driver's license suspended* for speeding.

メンテナンス maintenance [méintənəns] ㊂
◆その車はメンテナンスにお金がかかる It costs a lot to *maintain* that car.

めんどう 面積
❶【手数・やっかい】 trouble ㊂, bother ㊂ ―面倒な troublesome, bothersome
手紙を書くのは面倒だなあ Writing letters is too much *trouble* for me.
親にはさんざん面倒をかけた I caused my parents a lot of *trouble*.
ご面倒でなければあしたもう一度来てもらえませんか Could you come again tomorrow *if it isn't too much trouble*?
彼は面倒な仕事を引き受けてしまった He took a *troublesome* task.
面倒がらずに掃除をしなさい Do the cleaning *without acting like it's so much trouble*.
◆部屋の掃除をするのはとても面倒 *It's a big nuisance* to clean my room. / ご面倒をおかけしました *I'm sorry to have troubled* [*bothered*] *you*.
❷【トラブル】 trouble ㊂ 《また複数形 ～s》
また彼が面倒を起こした He got into *trouble* again.
面倒なことになる前にこの問題を解決しなければならない We must solve this problem before we get into (any) *trouble*.
❸【世話】 care ㊂
おばが買い物に行っている間, 私が赤ちゃんの面倒を見た I「*took care of* [*looked after*] the baby while my aunt went shopping.

◆もう彼の面倒は見きれない (→しりぬぐいできない) I can't *pay for* his *blunder* any longer.

めんどうくさい 面倒臭い   troublesome, bothersome
◆それはすごくこみ入っているので説明するのがめんどうくさい It's *a bother* to explain it because it's very complicated. / 妹は髪を乾かすのをめんどうくさがって寝てしまった My sister was *too lazy* to dry her hair and just went to bed.

めんどうみ 面倒見 彼女は弟の面倒見がいい She *takes good care of* her brother.

めんどり 雌鳥 hen ㊄

メンバー member ㊄; (試合の出場選手) line-up ㊄
彼は昔そのバンドのメンバーだった He used to be *a member* of the band.
両チームの先発メンバーが発表された *The starting lineups* of both teams were announced.
◆姉はテニスクラブのメンバーだ (→所属している) My sister *belongs to* a tennis club. / 野球のメンバー (→人数) がやっとそろった Finally we gathered enough *people* to play baseball. / 我々はベストメンバーで試合に臨んだ We took part in the game with *our team's best players*.

めんぼう 綿棒 《米》cotton swab ㊄, 《商標名》Q-tip ㊄; 《英》cotton bud ㊄

めんぼく 面目 (名誉) honor ㊂; (面子(ﾂﾞ)) face ㊂; (信用) credit ㊂; (名声) reputation ㊂ ‖それは私の面目にかかわることだ That would affect my *honor*. / 一連のスキャンダルでその女優は面目を失った The actress lost *face* because of a series of scandals. / 彼女は5位入賞でなんとか面目を保った She won fifth prize and somehow「*saved face* [*did herself credit*].
◆こんなひどい間違いをして面目ない I'm really *ashamed of* making such a terrible mistake. / チャンピオンの面目躍如たる (→期待された) 勝利だった The champion won *as expected*.

めんみつ 綿密 ―綿密な minute [mainjúːt]; (詳細な) detailed; (精密な) close; (注意深い) careful; (細心の) scrupulous ―綿密に minutely; closely; in detail; carefully ‖装置を綿密に検査する examine a device *minutely* [*closely*] / 彼らは綿密な計画を立てた They made a *detailed* plan. / 警察は事件を綿密に調査した The police「*made a careful* investigation into the case [*investigated the case carefully*].

めんめん¹ 面々 野球部の面々「*each member* [*the members*] of the baseball club

めんめん² 綿々 彼女はノートに自分の思いを綿々とつづった She wrote her feelings down in her notebook *in a continuous stream*.

めんもく 面目 ⇒めんぼく

めんるい 麺類 noodles

も

も¹ 喪 mourning ▢ // 喪に服する go into *mourning* / 喪が明ける come out of *mourning* / 私は父の喪に服している I'm in *mourning* for my father.

も² 藻 algae [ǽldʒi:]《複数扱い》; (海草) seaweed ▢; (水草) waterweed ▢

-も

❶ …もまた	too, also, as well
❷ …も~も	both A and B; not only A but (also) B
❸ …さえ	even
❹ …ほども	as ~ as …, no less than …
❺ どちらでも	
❻ たとえ…でも	even if [though] …; in spite of …

❶【…もまた】 too, also, as well; (否定文で) not … either, neither

【語法】
(1) 一般に too, as well は文尾, also は一般動詞の前, 助動詞・be 動詞の後に置くことが多い // 彼女はギターも弾く She plays the guitar, *too*. / She *also* plays the guitar. / She plays the guitar *as well*.
(2) too はふつう文尾に置くが, 修飾する語を明確にしたり強調したい場合はその語の直後に置く // 玲子もまたクラス委員に選ばれた Reiko *too* was elected class representative.
(3) also は too や as well より形式ばった語で, 書き言葉で用いられることが多い.
(4) 否定文では not … either, neither を用いる // 彼は結局どちらの家も買わなかった He *didn't* buy *either* house after all. / He bought *neither* house after all.

私も旅行がしたい I want to go traveling, *too*.
彼は作家だが映画の監督もする He is a writer and *also* directs films.
彼女を招待するの？ じゃあ彼女の妹も呼んであげて Are you inviting her? Then, invite her sister *as well*.
牛乳とパンを買ってきて. あと卵も Will you go (and) get some milk and bread? — And eggs, *too*.
僕は運転免許を持っていないし, 兄も持っていない I don't have a driver's license, and "*neither* does my brother [my brother *doesn't*, *either*]*.
◆ 予報ではあしたも雨らしい The weather forecast says it will rain *again* tomorrow.

🍵「カプチーノ, お願いします」「私も」"I'll have a Cappuccino, please." "*Me*, *too*." (❀くだけた言い方)
🍵「ミュージカルが大好きなんです」「私もです」"I love musicals." "*So do I*."
🍵「実はトマトが苦手なんだ」「僕もさ」"As a matter of fact, I don't like tomatoes." "*Me*, *neither*."
🍵「その歌はあまり好きじゃない」「私もです」"I don't like the song very much." "*Neither do I*."

❷【…も~も】(AもBも) both A and B; (Aばかりでなく Bも) not only A but (also) B; (Aはもちろん Bも) B as well as A; (AもBも…ない) neither A nor B

彼女は歌も踊りも得意だ She is good at *both* singing *and* dancing.
子供ばかりでなく大人もそのアニメに夢中になった *Not only* children *but* (*also*) adults were fascinated by the animated film.
彼は英語だけでなくフランス語も堪能(カムノウ)だ He is fluent in French *as well as* in English.
父は酒もたばこもやりません My father *neither* drinks *nor* smokes.
◆ 祖父も祖母も健在です My grandparents are *both* well. / そこへは JR でも地下鉄でも行ける You can get there *either* by JR *or* by subway. / 私は2枚のワンピースを試着したがどちらも買わなかった I tried on two dresses, but *didn't* buy *either* of them.

❸【…さえ】 even

そんなことは子供でも知っている *Even* a child knows such a thing.
彼女は目玉焼きも作れない She can't make *even* a sunny-side up egg.
きょうはとても忙しくてお昼を食べる時間もなかった I was so busy today that I didn't *even* have time for lunch.
食べてもしないで嫌いだなんてどうして言えるの How can you say you don't like something when you haven't *even* tried it?

❹【…ほども】 as ~ as …, no less than …

その事故で18人もの人が犠牲になった *As many as* 18 people were killed in the accident.
彼は僕の倍も稼いでいる He earns twice *as much as* I do.
その本を読むのに2週間もかかった It took me *as long as* two weeks to read the book.
彼女は20万円もするかばんを持っている She has a bag which costs *no less than* 200,000 yen.
◆ 5分もしないうちに彼からメールの返事が来た He sent me a reply e-mail *within* five minutes. / 中古のノートパソコンなら10万円もしないで買える You can get a secondhand notebook PC for *less than* 100,000 yen. / 半日もあればその町を観光して回れる(→観光するのに十分だ) Half a day will be *enough* to do sightseeing in the town.

❺【どちらでも】

そのミーティングは出ても出なくてもいい You can *either* attend the meeting *or not*.
彼が成功してもしなくても私は彼の味方だ I'll be on his side *whether or not* he succeeds.
❻【たとえ…でも】even if [though] …; (…にもかかわらず) in spite of …, despite
タクシーで行ったとしても間に合わないよ *Even if* you take a taxi, you won't make it.
成功する見込みがほとんどなくても我々はそれをやらなければならない *Even though* we might have little chance of success, we must do it.
彼女は富と名声はあってもあまり幸せな人生ではなかった She led an unhappy life *in spite of* her wealth and fame.
❼【その他】
もうだれも信じられない I *can't* trust *anyone* any more.
だれもひと言も口をきかなかった *Nobody* spoke a word.
そんな偽物を売るほうも売るほうだけど、買うほうも買うほうだよ It's true that selling such a fake is shameless, but at the same time buying it is shameful.

もう¹

❶【すでに】already; yet

> ふつう already は肯定文に、yet は否定文・疑問文に用いられるが、already を疑問文に用いて驚きや意外な気持ちを表すことがある。また、これらの言葉を使わなくても完了時制を用いただけで「もう…してしまった」「もうずっと…している」というニュアンスを表せる場合もある。

外はもう暗い It's *already* dark outside.
もう11時だ It's *already* 11 o'clock.
学校に着いたときにはもう授業が始まっていた The class had *already* started when I got to school.
郵便はもう届きましたか Has the mail arrived *yet*?
えっ，もう宿題をすませたの？ Have you finished your homework *already*?
彼はもう10年近くランニングをしている He *has been* running for almost 10 years.
私はもう何年も故郷に帰っていない I *haven't been* home for [《米》in] years.
◆健太はもう（→今ごろ）家に着いているはずだ Kenta must have reached his home *by now*. / 事故はもう２週間前のことになる The accident is *now* two weeks past. / もう寝る時間だよ It's time「(that) you went to bed [for you to go to bed]. (◆It is time that …は「もうとっくに…していい時間だ」の意味で、後ろに続く節は仮定法になる、また通例省略する) / もう大学生なんだからひとり暮らしをしなさい *Now that* you are a college student, you should live alone.
🄔「もう夕食はすませたの？」「いいえ、まだです」 "Have you eaten dinner *yet*?" "No, not yet."

❷【さらに】more; (もう１つ[１人]の) another
もう５分待とう I'll wait「five *more* [*another* five] minutes.
私はピクニックに靴をもう１足持っていった I took *another* pair of shoes to the picnic.
コーヒーをもう１杯いかがですか Would you like *another* cup of coffee?
ワインをもう少し召し上がりませんか Won't you have *some more* wine?
子供がもう１人押し入れに隠れていた *One more* child was hiding in the closet.
◆もう一度やってごらん Try it *once again*. /（相手の言うことが聞き取れず）もう一度言ってください I beg your pardon? / Would you say that *again*?
🄔「仕事は終わった？」「いやまだです。もう２，３時間かかりそうです」 "Have you finished your work?" "No, not yet. I need a few *more* hours."

❸【もはや…ない】no longer, not … any longer, no more
もう我慢できない I *can't* stand it *any longer*.
彼らはもうここには住んでいない They *no longer* live here.
もう子供じゃないわ I'm *no longer* a child.
もう戦争はごめんだ *No more* war.
冗談はもうやめろよ *No more* of your jokes.
さあ，もう泣かないで Here, *don't* cry *any more*.
もうこれ以上迷惑はかけないよ I will bother you *no more*. / I *won't* bother you *any more*.
◆彼のぐちはもうたくさんだ I'*m fed up with* his complaints. / 今からじゃもう遅すぎるよ It's *too late* now.

❹【強調】
場内はもう大変な騒ぎだった There was a *really* great noise in the hall.
またこわしたの？ 全くもう！ *Oh, no*! You broke it again?
いいかげんにしてよ，もう！ Stop it *for goodness [heaven's] sake*!

❺【間もなく】⇨ もうすぐ
もう行かなくては I have to go *now*.

❻【もう少し】⇨ もうすこし

もう²（牛の鳴き声）moo [múː] ⓒ ◆牛がいっせいにもうもう鳴き始めた The cows started *mooing* all together.

もう- 猛 - 敵の猛攻撃にあう be attacked fiercely by the enemy / 試験を来月に控えて彼は猛勉強している He's *studying very hard* for the exam next month. / 彼らはその計画に猛反対した They *were violently opposed* to the plan. / 車は猛スピードで私たちの前を通り過ぎた The car passed by us *at great [full] speed*.

⇨ もうれんしゅう

もうい 猛威 rage Ⓤⓒ, fury Ⓤ ∥あらしの猛威 *the rage [fury]* of a storm
◆当時ペストがヨーロッパ中で猛威をふるった Pestilence *raged* throughout Europe in

those days.
もうがっこう 盲学校 a school for the blind
もうかる 儲かる (利益を得る) make* money, make a profit; (採算がとれる) pay* 自
▶いくらもうかったの How much *money* did you *make*?
▶その取り引きで10万円もうかった I *made a profit of* 100,000 yen from the trade.
▶そんな商売で本当にもうかるのかい Does that business really *pay*?
▶この仕事はあまりもうからない This work *doesn't pay* very well.
◆もうかる商売 a *profitable* [*lucrative*] business
もうかん 毛管 capillary tube ©
∥毛管現象〖物理〗capillary action
もうきん 猛禽 a bird of prey
もうけ 儲け profit ©©, gain © ∥不正なもうけ dishonest *gains* / その仕事でかなりのもうけをあげた I made *a* good *profit* from the business.
◆彼は競馬で大もうけした He *won a lot of money* at the horse races. / その商売はまるでもうけにならなかった The business *didn't* 「*yield any profit* [(→採算がとれない) *pay at all*]. / このテレビは拾い物なんだから映っただけでももうけ物だ I'm *lucky*, because at least this TV that I found works.
もうける¹ 設ける ❶【施設などを】set* up ∥その事故を調査するための特別委員会が設けられた The special committee *was* 「*set up* [*formed, organized*] to investigate the accident. / この駅のプラットホームには喫煙場所が設けてある A smoking area *is provided* on the platform at this station.
❷【規則などを】…に制限を設ける put [place, impose] restrictions on … / その町ではごみの不法投棄に対して厳しい罰則が設けられている Rigid penal regulations *are* 「*laid down* [*set up*] against unlawful dumping in the town.
❸【その他】酒の席をもうける give [hold] a drinking party / 彼は適当な口実をもうけて旅行の誘いを断った He turned down the invitation to trip *on some pretext or other*. / その夫婦は1男2女をもうけた The couple *had* a son and two daughters.
もうける² 儲ける make* money, make a profit, gain ∥彼女は株でずいぶんもうけた She 「*made a good profit* [*made much money*] on the stock market. / 努力をしないで金をもうけようなんて虫がよすぎないか Do you want to *make money* without effort? You are asking too much!
もうけん 猛犬 fierce dog ©
◆猛犬注意《掲示》Beware of (the) *Dog*
もうこはん 蒙古斑 Mongolian spot ©
もうこん 毛根 (hair) root ©, the root of a hair
もうさいけっかん 毛細血管〖解剖〗capillary ©
もうしあげる 申し上げる 何も申し上げることはございません I have nothing to *tell* you.
▶入試合格のお祝いを申し上げます I *offer* you my congratulations on (your) passing the entrance examination.
▶お父様のご逝去を深くお悔やみ申し上げます *Let me express* my deep regret over your father's death.
▶電車が遅れてご迷惑をおかけしたことをおわび申し上げます We *apologize* for any inconvenience caused by the delay of trains.
もうしあわせ 申し合わせ 各社の申し合わせにより, その展示会の開催は中止された The fair was called off *by agreement* of the companies. / かねてからの申し合わせどおり, 彼らは新党を結成した They organized a new political party *as they had agreed* [*arranged*].
∥申し合わせ事項 an agreed item
もうしあわせる 申し合わせる その二人はきのう申し合わせたかのように学校を休んだ The two were absent from school yesterday, *as if they had prearranged it*. / 彼らは政府に早急な対策を要請することを申し合わせた They *agreed* to make a request to the government for prompt measures.
もうしいれ 申し入れ (申し出) offer ©; (提案) proposal ©©; (要求) request © ∥彼らは彼のこの申し入れを断った They denied this *offer* [*proposal*] of his.
◆資金援助の申し入れを行う(→申し出る) *offer one's* financial help
もうしいれる 申し入れる 話し合いを申し入れる *ask* to have a talk / 彼らは文書で要求を申し入れた They *made* a request in writing.
もうしおくる 申し送る (譲り渡す) hand over ∥重要事項を後任者に申し送る *hand* important matters *over* to a successor
もうしかねる 申し兼ねる 私からは申しかねます I'm *not in the position to tell* you.
もうしご 申し子 彼は時代の申し子だった He was *the child of the age*.
もうしこみ 申し込み (応募) application ©©; (提案) proposal © ∥テニス部に入部の申し込みをする *make an application* to the tennis club for membership / 申し込みの締め切りはいつですか When is the deadline for *the application*? / お申し込みはお早めにお願いします Make early *application*, please. / キャンプの申し込みはあすまで受け付けます Camp *applications* [*Applications* for the camp] will be accepted up until tomorrow. / 彼は彼女に結婚の申し込みをした He made *a* 「*proposal* of marriage [*marriage proposal*] to her. / 申込書は事務所で手に入ります *Application forms* are available at the office.
∥申込者 an applicant
もうしこむ 申し込む
❶【応募する】apply 自; (頼む) ask 他; (参加を) enter 自他
▶コンテストに参加を申し込む *enter* a contest
▶入会を申し込むときに必要なものは何ですか What do I need when *applying for* mem-

bership?
ここで公民館の部屋の使用を申し込むことができますか Can we *ask* to use a room in the town hall here?
◆ファンクラブに入会を申し込んだ I *signed up for* membership in the fan club.
❷【挑戦する】challenge 他
僕は彼に卓球の試合を申し込んだ I *challenged* him *to* a game of table tennis.
❸【求婚する】propose 他 自
今夜彼女に結婚を申し込むつもりです I'm going to 「*propose (marriage)* [*make a (marriage) proposal*] *to* her tonight./ I'm going to *ask* her *to marry* me tonight.

もうしたて 申し立て（陳述）statement 回;《法律》plea 回 ‖虚偽の申し立てをする make *a false statement* / 無罪の申し立てを行う put in *a plea* of not guilty

もうしたてる 申し立てる（述べる）state 他; 《法律》plead* 他 自 ‖(法廷で被告が)無罪を申し立てる *plead not guilty* / 弁護士は彼の有罪の証拠はひとつとしてないと申し立てた The attorney *stated* that there was no proof of his guilt.
◆…に異議を申し立てる make [raise] an objection to [against] … / その決定に不服を申し立てる make *a complaint about* the decision; *appeal against* the decision / 彼は監督官庁に苦情を申し立てた He *complained to* the qualified governing authorities.

もうしで 申し出 offer 回; (提案) proposal 回 回 ‖援助の申し出をする make *an offer of* help / 私は喜んで彼の申し出を受けた I gladly *accepted his offer*./ ご好意はありがたく存じますが，お申し出をお受けすることはできません While we appreciate your good intentions, *your proposal* is impossible for us to accept.

もうしでる 申し出る offer 他 自; (自発的に) volunteer 他 自 ‖彼は私の援助を申し出た He *offered to* help me./ 彼らは私たちの土地を1,000万円で買おうと申し出た They *offered* us 10 million yen *for* our land.
◆パンフレット希望者はお申し出ください Those who want brochures, please *let* us [me] *know*.

もうしひらき 申し開き みんなの前で申し開きをする *justify* [*defend*] *oneself* in public / もはや申し開きが立つまい(→言い訳できないだろう) You *have no* more *excuses*, do you?

もうしぶん 申し分 ──申し分ない (完璧(%)な) perfect; (理想的な) ideal; (満足な) satisfactory ‖申し分のない成績 *satisfactory grades* / 釣りには申し分ない天気だった It was a *perfect* [an *ideal*] day for fishing./ この家は立地は申し分ない This house is in a *perfect* location./ 彼は仕事のパートナーとしては申し分のない男だった He was a *perfect* [an *ideal*] man as a work partner.

もうじゃ 亡者 あいつは金の亡者だ He *is money-mad* [(→金にとりつかれている) *obsessed with money*].

もうじゅう¹ 猛獣 fierce animal 回; (野獣)

wild animal 回 ‖猛獣狩り big game hunting / 猛獣使い a wild animal trainer

もうじゅう² 盲従 blind obedience 回
◆権威に盲従する *obey* authority *blindly* [*unquestioningly*]

もうしょ 猛暑 intense [fierce, scorching] heat 回; (熱波) heat wave 回
◆ここ数日東京は猛暑に見舞われている In Tokyo we have had *terribly hot weather* these past few days.

もうしわけ 申し訳（言い訳）excuse 回 回
──すみません
これではチームを応援してくれているファンに申しわけが立たない We'll *have no excuse* for this to the fan who cheers (for) our team.
ランチセットには申しわけ程度の(→わずかな)サラダがついてきた The set lunch came with *a tiny excuse of* a salad.
◆彼には本当に申しわけないことをした(→悪いことをした) I've done 「*him great wrong* [*great wrong to him*]./ どうやらこれで申しわけが立ちそうだ It seems I can now *justify myself* somehow./ ご面倒をかけて申しわけありませんが，荷物を見ていてくださいますか *I'm sorry* to trouble you, but could you watch my luggage? / 遅くなって申しわけありません *Please excuse me* for being late./ Please *excuse* my being late./ *I'm sorry* (that) I'm late.

もうしわたす 申し渡す tell* 他; (判決を) sentence 他 ‖岡先生は彼に停学処分を申し渡した Mr. Oka *told* him that he was suspended from school.

もうしん 盲信 blind faith 回 ──盲信する believe blindly

もうじん 盲人 blind person 回,《集合的》the blind

もうす 申す (言う) say* 他 自 (❖日本語の敬語「申す」を直接表す言い方は英語にはない) ‖母がそう申しておりました My mother *said* so.
◆はじめまして，私は田中と申します How do you do? *My name is* Tanaka.

もうすぐ soon ‖もうすぐクリスマスがやってくる Christmas is coming *soon*.
◆夏休みはもうすぐだ Summer vacation is *just around the corner*./ 祖父はもうすぐ90歳だ(→90歳に近づきつつある) My grandfather *is approaching* 90./ みんながんばれ！（そこまで）もうすぐだぞ Cheer up, everyone! We're *almost* there.

もうすこし もう少し（量・程度）a little more；(数) a few more ──もう少しで（ほとんど）almost, nearly；(今にも…しそうになる) come* near [close] to *doing*
もう少し塩を足してください Add *a little more* salt, please.
もう少し日数が必要だ I need *a few more* days.
もう少しゆっくり話していただけませんか Would you speak *a little more* slowly?
治はもう少しで車にひかれるところだった Osamu was *almost* run over by a car.

彼女はもう少しでおぼれるところだった She came near to drowning. (❖口語では to は省略可能だが、その場合 near は前置詞とみなされる)
◆お茶をもう少しもらってもいいですか Can I have *some more* tea? / もう少し背が高かったらなあ If only I were *a little* taller!

もうぜん 猛然 ──猛然と (荒々しく・激しく) fiercely; (決然と) resolutely; (果敢に) bravely ∥彼はゴールに猛然とダッシュした He dashed for the goal *fiercely*. / ジョンはその判定に猛然と抗議した John protested against the judgement *fiercely* [*resolutely*].
◆それを機に彼女は猛然と(→狂ったように)勉強を始めた After that, she began to study *like mad*.

もうそう 妄想 〔医学〕delusion ©; (強迫観念) obsession ∥彼は他人がいつも彼を欺いているという妄想に取りつかれていた He was haunted by *the delusion* that others were always deceiving him.
◆被害妄想にかられる be *paranoid*; suffer from *paranoia*
∥誇大妄想 *delusions of grandeur*

もうだ 猛打 6回表ベイスターズ打線の猛打が爆発した The BayStars' batters *went on the offensive* in the top half of the sixth inning.

もうちょう 盲腸 〔解剖〕appendix ©; (虫垂炎) appendicitis Ⓤ ∥盲腸で入院するを be hospitalized with *appendicitis* / 彼は去年盲腸の手術をした He had an operation for *appendicitis* last year. / (→盲腸を取った) He had his appendix「taken out [removed] last year.
∥急性盲腸炎 acute appendicitis

もうでる 詣でる ⇨さんばい

もうてん 盲点 〔解剖〕blind spot © (❖「自分で気づかない弱点」という比喩的な意味もある); (法などの抜け道) loophole © ∥相手の盲点をつく hit the enemy from their *blind spot* / 法の盲点をつく take advantage of *a loophole* in the law

もうとう 毛頭 彼を招待する気など毛頭ない I don't have the slightest [least] intention of inviting him.

もうどうけん 盲導犬 guide dog ©, seeing eye dog ©

もうどく 猛毒 deadly poison © ──猛毒の highly poisonous

もうはつ 毛髪 (集合的) hair Ⓤ ⇨かみ(髪)

もうひつ 毛筆 (writing) brush

もうひとつ もう一つ リンゴをもう1つもらってもいいですか Can I have *another* [*one more*] apple? / 彼の意図がもうひとつはっきりとつかめない I can't *really* understand what he thinks. / そのコンサートはもうひとつ(→やや)盛り上がりに欠けた The concert lacked *a little* in excitement.
❷「あそこのカレーはどう」「ううん、もうひとつだね」"How is the curry at that restaurant?" "Well, *it needs a little something*."

もうふ 毛布 blanket © ∥広樹に毛布をかけてあげてくれる? Will you put *the blanket* over Hiroki?

もうまく 網膜 〔解剖〕retina [rétənə] © ∥網膜剝離 retinal detachment

もうもう もうもうと立ち昇る砂ぼこり *a cloud of dust* / その焼き鳥屋の店先からは煙がもうもうと上がっていた Smoke was rising *thickly* [*densely*] from the yakitori store.

もうもく 盲目 blindness Ⓤ ──盲目の・盲目的な blind ──盲目的に blindly ∥盲目的な愛情 *blind* affection / 彼らはリーダーに盲目的に従っているだけだ They are just *blindly* following the leader.
慣用表現 恋は盲目 *Love is blind.*

もうら 網羅 ──網羅する (含む) contain ⓔ; (一部として含む) include ⓔ; (範囲が…に及ぶ) cover ⓔ ∥この双書には彼の代表作がすべて網羅されている This series *covers* [*contains, includes*] all his masterpieces.
◆網羅的なリスト an *exhaustive* list

もうれつ 猛烈 ──猛烈な (激しい) violent, hard; (強烈な) intense; (すさまじい) fierce ──猛烈に violently, hard; intensely; fiercely ∥夏の猛烈な暑さ the *intense* [*fierce, terrible*] heat of summer / 彼は試験前になると猛烈に勉強する He studies「*very hard* [*intensely*]」before examinations. / 針にかかった魚は猛烈に抵抗した The hooked fish struggled *violently* [*fiercely*]. / 登山に行くといったら両親の猛烈な反対にあった When I said I would go mountain climbing, my parents opposed it *fiercely*.
◆猛烈な競争 *keen* [*fierce*] competition
∥猛烈社員(仕事中毒の人) a workaholic

もうれんしゅう 猛練習 オーケストラは今度のコンサートに向けて猛練習している The orchestra *is practicing hard* [*intensely*] for the coming concert.

もうろう 朦朧 暑さで頭がもうろうとしていた I *wasn't clear* in the head because of the heat. / その事故については記憶がもうろうとしている(→あいまいな記憶しかない) I only have a *vague* memory of that accident.

もうろく 耄碌 senility Ⓤ, dotage Ⓤ ──もうろくする become* senile [síːnail] ∥祖父はすっかりもうろくして物忘れがひどい My grandfather has「*become senile* [*fallen into his dotage*]」and terribly forgetful.

もえあがる 燃え上がる burn* up, blaze up; (炎を上げて) flame up; (ぱっと) flare up ∥その建物はみるみるうちに燃え上がった The building *burned* [*blazed*] *up* in a moment. ◆機体は一気に燃え上がった The body of the airplane *burst into flames*.

もえうつる 燃え移る 火は隣の家に燃え移った The fire *spread to* the next house.

もえがら 燃え殻 (まき・石炭などの) cinder ©; (灰) ashes

もえさし 燃えさし (まき・石炭などの) embers

もえつきる 燃え尽きる burn* out ∥ろうそくが燃え尽きた The candle *burned out*. / 彼女は2度のオリンピック出場で燃え尽きてしまった

She *burned herself out* by participating in the Olympic Games twice.

もえひろがる 燃え広がる　火事は町中に燃え広がった The fire *spread* through the town.

もえる 燃える

burn* 自; (炎を上げて) blaze 自; (炎・煙を出さずに) glow 自

小屋が燃えている The hut *is burning*./ The hut *is on fire*.

枯れ草は燃えやすい Dead grass *burns* [*catches fire*] *easily*.

彼は怒りに燃えていた He *was burning* [*glowing, blazing*] with anger.

嵐山は燃えるような紅葉がみごとだった Arashiyama was *glowing* with beautiful autumn colors.

燃えさしが暖炉で赤々と燃えていた Embers *were glowing* in the fireplace.

◆燃えるような夕焼け *the glow* of sunset; the *fiery* sunset / 何かが燃えているようなにおいがする I can smell something *burning*./ 彼らは燃えている家から脱出した They escaped from [out of] the *burning* house. / この地域は燃えるごみは月・水に、燃えないごみは木曜に収集されます *Combustibles* are collected on Monday and Wednesday and *incombustibles* on Thursday in this area. / 彼女は今ダンスの練習に燃えている She is *enthusiastically* practicing dancing now.

モーグル 〖スポーツ〗moguls《単数扱い》

モーション motion C
◆モーションを起こす(→動きだす) start to *move*《ただし野球の「投手が振りかぶる」は start to wind up という》/ 彼は花子にモーションをかけた(→言い寄った) He 「*made advances to* [*made a pass at*] Hanako.

モーセ Moses [móuziz]
◆モーセの十戒 the Ten Commandments

モーター motor C; (エンジン) engine C
‖モーターショー an auto [《英》a motor] show / モーターバイク(オートバイ) a motorcycle; (原付自転車)《米》a motorbike / モータープール(駐車場) a parking lot, 《英》a car park(❖英語の motor pool は「官庁や会社で待機する自動車群」の意味) / モーターボート a motorboat; (競艇などの) a speedboat

モーテル motel [moutél] C (❖《米》では自動車で旅行する人のための宿泊施設のこと)

モード mode C, fashion C U ‖パリ発の最新モード *the latest mode* [*fashion*] from Paris / 周りのみんなは受験モードに入っている Everyone around me is now in exam *mode*.

モーニング ⚠(男子用礼服の上着) morning coat C; (礼服一式) morning dress U

モーニングコート morning coat C

モーニングコール ⚠ wake-up call C (❖「モーニングコール」は和製英語)

モーニングサービス a light set menu for breakfast(❖英米ではあまり一般的でない。英語の morning service は「朝の礼拝」の意味)

モール ⚠(衣類の縁どりなどの) braid U (❖日本語はポルトガル語の mogol から); (商店街)《米》(shopping) mall C ‖金モールで縁どりされている be trimmed with gold *braid*

モールス ‖モールス信号 Morse code

モカ mocha U (❖コーヒーの種類)

もがく struggle 自; (苦しみなどで身をよじる) writhe 自 ‖子ギツネがわなから逃れようともがいていた A young fox *was struggling* to escape from the trap. / 彼はあまりの痛さにもがき苦しんだ He *writhed* with pain.

もぎ 模擬 ‖模擬試験 a trial [mock, practice] examination / 模擬店 a (refreshment) booth [stand] (at a fair)

もぎたて 捥ぎたて　もぎたてのナシ a *freshly picked* pear

もぎとる 捥ぎ取る　(ねじり取る) wrench 他 ‖彼は彼女の手から金をもぎ取った He *wrenched* the money from her hand.
◆カキの実をもぎ取る *pluck* a persimmon

もく 目 〖生物〗order C

もぐ 捥ぐ pick 他, pluck 他 ‖彼は木からリンゴをもいでいる He *is picking* apples from the trees.

もくぎょ 木魚　a *mokugyo*, a wooden gong used for Buddhist rites

もくげき 目撃 ——目撃する witness 他 ‖銀行強盗を目撃する *witness* a bank robbery
◆目撃者はその公園ではだれにも会わなかったと証言した The (eye)*witness* testified that he had met nobody in the park. / 私は彼が本屋で万引きしているのを目撃した I *saw* him shoplifting at the bookstore.

もぐさ 艾 moxa [máksə] U

もくざい 木材 wood U C,《米》lumber U,《主に英》timber U ➡ ざいもく

もくさつ 黙殺 ——黙殺する (deliberately) ignore 他 ‖その訴えは黙殺された The complaint *was ignored*.

もくさん 目算 rough estimate C; (予測) expectation U C ——目算する estimate roughly / 費用を目算する *estimate* the expense *roughly* / 目算がはずれる fall short of *one's expectation*

もくし 黙示 implication C U
◆ヨハネの黙示録 (the book of) Revelations; the Apocalypse

もくじ 目次 a table of contents(❖本の目次の見出しは通例 Contents と書く)

もくする 目する　(予想する) expect 他; (みなす) consider 他 ‖彼は次の大統領選挙の最有力候補と目されている He *is considered* to be the prospective winner of the next presidential election.

もくせい¹ 木星 〖天文〗Jupiter

もくせい² 木製 ——木製の wooden ‖木製バット a *wooden* bat

もくせい³ 木犀 fragrant olive [álɪv]

もくぜん 目前 ❶〖目の前〗私の目前で車が壁にぶつかった A car crashed into the wall *right before* my eyes. / 悪天候のために、彼らは頂上を目前にして引き返さなければならなかった Because of bad weather, they had to turn back when they *were very close to*

もくぞう　木造　——木造の wooden, built of wood ‖彼の家は木造だ His house is *built of wood.* / 木造家屋は住み心地がいい *Wooden houses* are comfortable to live in. / この寺は世界最古の木造建築物だといわれている It is said that this temple is *the* oldest *wooden structure* in the world.

もくそく　目測　そのイチョウの高さは目測で20メートルはある The ginkgo tree is 20 meters tall *by (my) eye.* / 彼女は池までの目測を誤った She *misjudged* the distance to the pond.

もくたん　木炭 charcoal ◎（※数えるときは a stick of ... とする）
‖木炭画 a charcoal drawing

もくてき　目的

purpose ◎◎；(ねらい) aim ◎；(目標) objective ◎；(努力などの) goal ◎

人生の究極の目的 ultimate *goals* in life

僕は必ず目的を果たしてみせる I will achieve [accomplish] *my goal.*

旅行の楽しみ方はその目的によって様々だ The pleasure of travel varies according to the *purpose.*

目的にかなった本が見つからなかった I couldn't find a book that served *my purpose* [*aim*].

彼女はいつも明確な目的意識をもって行動している She always acts with *a clear sense of purpose.*

◆目的達成のための手段 a means to *an end* / 研究の目的で（→研究するために）渡米する go to America (*in order*) *to* study / 彼らは何の目的でここへやってきたんだ What did they come here *for*? / Why did they come here? / 渋谷には目的もなく街をぶらついている多くの若者がいる There are many young people who wander about *aimlessly* in Shibuya.

💬「どういう目的で韓国へ行くのですか」「観光です」"What's *the purpose* of going to Korea?" "Sightseeing."

‖目的格【文法】the objective case / 目的論【哲学】teleology

もくてきご　目的語【文法】object ◎ ‖間接目的語 an indirect object / 直接目的語 a direct object

---
目的語は5文型の要素の一つ．I'll give her this flower. 「この花を彼女にあげよう」のこの flower（この花を）を「直接目的語」，her（彼女に）を「間接目的語」という．動詞だけではなく，前置詞と一部の形容詞も目的語をとる
⇒ ごぶんけい

もくてきち　目的地 destination ◎ ‖一行はようやく目的地に着いた The party finally arrived at *its destination.*

もくとう　黙禱 silent prayer [préər] ◎ ——黙禱する pray silently / 事故の犠牲者に黙禱をささげる *offer silent prayer* for the victims of the accident

もくどく　黙読 silent reading ◎ ——黙読する read* silently, read to *oneself*

もくにん　黙認《公式的》tacit permission ◎ ——黙認する permit tacitly；（大目に見る）overlook ◎ ‖この手の違法行為はこれまで黙認されてきたというのが実状だ Actually this kind of illegality *has been permitted tacitly* so far.

もくば　木馬 wooden horse ◎；（揺り木馬）rocking horse ◎

もくはん　木版（板） woodcut ◎, wood block ◎；（木版画）woodcut ◎, woodblock print ◎（※後者は「木版刷り」の意味にもなる）

もくひ　黙秘 容疑者は黙秘を続けている The suspect is remaining [keeping] *silent.* / あなたには黙秘権があります You have *the right to remain silent.*（※《米》では合衆国憲法第5条で黙秘権を認めていることから「黙秘権を行使する」を take [invoke] the Fifth ということもある）

もくひょう　目標（努力などの）goal ◎；（到達目標）target ◎；（ねらい）aim ◎

今月の売上目標 *the sales targets* for this month / 目標を高く設定する set *one's goal* [*aim*] high

私は年間50万円貯金する目標を立てた I set *the goal* [*target*] of saving 500,000 yen a year.

私たちはついに当初の目標を達成した We finally achieved [reached, attained] *our original goal.*

◆彼女は決勝戦に進むことを目標にしていた She *was aiming* to reach the final. / 近くに何か目標（→目印）になるものはありますか Is there anything useful as *a landmark* near there?

もくへん　木片 a block of wood；（小さな）a chip [piece] of wood

もくめ　木目 grain ◎（しばしば the ～）‖木目の粗い木材 wood of coarse *grain*；coarse-*grained* wood / そのたんすは木目がとても美しい *The grain* of the chest of drawers is very beautiful.

もくもく¹ もくもくと沸き上がる入道雲 thunderheads rising *massively* / 工場の煙突からは黒い煙がもくもくと立ち昇っている *Billows of* black smoke are rising from the factory chimneys.

もくもく²　黙々 ——黙々と silently, in silence ‖彼女は文句を言わず黙々と働いた She 「*worked hard in silence* [*was absorbed in her work*]」 without complaining.

もぐもぐ ——もぐもぐする（口ごもる）mumble ◎◎；（食べる）munch ◎◎ ‖もぐもぐパンを食べる *munch* bread / 彼は返事に困って口をもぐもぐさせた He *mumbled,* not knowing what to say.

もくようび　木曜日 Thursday ◎ ◎（《略語》Thu., Thur., Thurs.）⇒ にちようび

もぐら mole [C] ‖モグラ塚 a molehill

もぐり 潜り ❶【潜水】diving [U] ◆彼は潜りが得意だ He's good at *swimming underwater*. ❷【無免許】もぐりの医者 an *unqualified* [*unlicensed*] doctor / その店はもぐりで酒を売っている The store sells liquor *without a license*. / この界わいで彼の名を知らないような人間はもぐりだ A person who doesn't know his name must be *a stranger* around here.

もぐりこむ 潜り込む ベッドに潜り込む *get* [*crawl*] *into* bed / 彼らは観光客を装ってその国に潜り込んだ They disguised themselves as tourists to 「*get into* [*infiltrate*] the country.

もぐる 潜る (水中に) go* [stay] underwater, dive* [自] (❖go underwater, dive は潜る動作を, stay は潜っている状態を表す)

明は1分以上水に潜っていられる Akira *can stay underwater* for more than a minute.

彼はプールに潜って私のゴーグルを拾ってくれた He *dived under* the pool and found my goggles.

◆(活動家などが)地下に潜る *go underground* / 僕はグアムで毎日海に潜った I *went diving* every day in Guam. / この種のエビは敵から身を守るために砂に潜る This kind of shrimp *gets into* the sand to protect itself from its enemies. / その子は雷が怖くてふとんに潜った The child *got* [*crawled*] *into bed* because he was afraid of the thunder.

もくれい[1] 目礼 人に目礼する *greet* a person *with one's eyes* / 互いに目礼を交わす exchange *nods* with each other

もくれい[2] 黙礼 bow [C] ―黙礼する bow (silently) [自] [他] ‖私は先生に黙礼した I *bowed to* my teacher.

もくれん 木蓮 magnolia [C]

もくろく 目録 (表) list [C]; (カタログ) catalog, 《英》catalogue [C]; (商業用の) inventory [C] ‖…の目録を作る make *a list* of ...

‖在庫目録 a store inventory / 図書目録 a book catalog

もくろみ (計画) plan [C], project [C]; (意図) intention [U][C] ‖もくろみがはずれた *The plan* ended in failure.

◆事は我々のもくろみどおりには運ばなかった Things didn't go *as we had planned*.

もくろむ (悪事を) plot [他]; (計画する) plan [他] [自] ‖彼らは現金輸送車から現金を強奪しようともくろんでいた They *were plotting* [*planning*] to steal the money from a security van.

もけい 模型 model [C]; (特に小型の) miniature [C] ―模型の model; miniature (❖共に名詞の前で用いる) ‖模型自動車 a *model* car / 実物大模型 *a* full-size *model*, *a mock-up* / 飛行機の模型を作る make a *model* plane; make *a model* of a plane

もげる 捥げる come* off ‖なべの取っ手がもげた The handle of the pan *came off*.

もさ 猛者 tough guy [C]

モザイク (模様) mosaic [mouzéiik] [C] ‖画像の一部にモザイクをかける obscure part of the picture with *mosaic pattern*

‖モザイク画 a mosaic picture

もさく 模索 ―模索する (探し求める) grope [自] ‖マルチメディアの新しい可能性を模索する *grope for* new possibilities of multimedia

もし[1]

❶【条件を示して】if; (…の場合は) in case

もし天気がよかったらパーティーは庭でやろう *If* the weather is good, let's have the party in the garden.

もしだれかから電話があったらこちらからかけ直すと伝えてね *If* someone calls, tell them that I'll call them back.

もし味が薄かったらこのソースをもう少しかけてください *If* it tastes weak, please add some more of this sauce.

もし私が遅れたら(私を置いて)先に行ってて. すぐ追いかけるから *In case* I'm late, go ahead without me. I'll catch up soon.

もし忘れていたら言ってください *In case* I forget, please remind me.

◆もし君がいっしょに来てくれないなら僕はそこへは行かないよ I won't go there *unless* you come with me. / I won't go there *if* you *don't* come with me.

❷【仮定して】if; (…と仮定して) suppose

[語法]

> (1)［未来のことに関する仮定］if 節の動詞は現在形を用いる ‖あしたもし雨だったら何をしようか What shall we do if it *rains* tomorrow?
> (2)［現在の事実に反する仮定］if 節の動詞は過去形を用いる ‖もしお金を持っていたら絶対買うのだが If I *had* money with me, I would surely buy it.
> (3)［過去の事実に反する仮定］if 節の動詞は過去完了を用いる ‖もしあのとき彼と出会っていなければ今とは全く違った人生を送っていただろう If I *hadn't met* him then, I would have led a totally different life.

もし彼女の電話番号をご存知でしたら教えてもらえませんか *If* you know her phone number, could you give it to me?

もし僕が君だったら彼女に謝ると思う *If* I were you, I would apologize to her.

もしあと500円あればこの本が買えるのに *If* I had 500 yen more, I could buy this book.

もしあの日いつもの電車に乗っていたら私もその事故に巻き込まれていたところだった *If* I had taken the usual train that day, I would have been involved in the accident.

もし世界があしたで終わるとしたら何をしますか *Suppose* the world is going to end tomorrow, what would you do?

❸【勧誘・提案して】

もしよかったら君も来ていいよ You can come *if you like*.

もしご希望でしたら, オプションでエーゲ海クルーズがつけられます *If* you are interested,

we could offer you an Aegean cruise as an option.

もし² 模試 trial [mock, practice] exam ⓒ

もじ 文字 (表音文字) letter ⓒ; (表意文字) character ⓒ; (仮名などの音節文字) syllabary ⓒ // 大[小]文字で書く write in capital [small] *letters* / この文字が読めますか Can you read this *character*? / 英語のアルファベットは26文字ある The English alphabet has 26 *letters*.

◆彼は文字どおり一文無しだった He was *literally* penniless. / 私は彼女の言葉を文字どおりに受け取った I took her words *literally*. / 文字面(ホッ)にとらわれると肝心のことが理解できなくなる If you are influenced by the *surface*, you won't be able to understand the important thing.

∥文字多重放送 teletext / 文字盤 a dial; (時計の) a face

もしかしたら possibly; perhaps; maybe (❖ possibly より話者の確信度が高い) ➡たぶん / もしかしたら君の言うとおりかもしれない *Perhaps* [*Maybe*] you're right. / もしかしたら今週末お宅に伺うかもしれません *Perhaps* I'll call on you this weekend. / もしかしたら電車は出たばかりなのかもしれない The train *may perhaps* have just left. (❖may とともに確実度がより低いことを表す)

もしかして もしかしてあなたが中村さんですか Are you Mr. Nakamura *by any chance*? / もしかして私たち今テレビに映ってるの We're not on TV now, are we?

もしかすると ➡もしかしたら

もしくは ➡または

もしも もしものときのこと(→最悪の場合)も考えておかなくては We have to consider *the worst possible case*. / もしものことがあったら(→緊急の場合に)連絡します I'll call you *in case of emergency*. / そのけがでスキーに行くなんて、もしものことがあったらどうするの If you go skiing with that injury, what will you do *if something goes wrong*?

もしもし (電話で) hello; (呼びかけ) excuse me / もしもし、浩正君はいますか *Hello*, may I speak to Hiromasa? / もしもし、その傘は私のですが *Excuse me*, but that umbrella is mine.

もじもじ 彼女は初対面の人の前ではいつももじもじしてしまう She always *feels a little shy* [*uneasy*] when she meets a stranger. / さあ、もじもじしていないでみんなの前に出なさい Now, *don't hesitate* to stand in front of everybody.

もしや もしやと思って行ってみると案の定彼はそこで昼寝をしていた I thought he *might* be there, and sure enough I found him taking a nap there. / ➡もしかして

もしゃ 模写 copy ⓒ; (複製) reproduction Ⓤ (❖「複製品」の意味では ⓒ) ──模写する copy ⓔ; reproduce ⓔ // ピカソを模写する *copy* a Picasso

もじゃもじゃ ──もじゃもじゃの shaggy, bushy; (とかしていない) unkempt // 雅人はもじゃもじゃの髪をしていた Masato had *shaggy* [*bushy, unkempt*] hair.

もしゅ 喪主 the chief mourner // 喪主を務める act as *the chief mourner*

もしょう 喪章 (腕章) mourning band ⓒ; (リボン) mourning ribbon ⓒ // 腕に喪章をつける put *a mourning band* on one's sleeve

もじる (パロディを作る) parody ⓔ, make* a parody of ...

もす 燃す burn* ⓔ ➡もやす

もず 百舌 shrike ⓒ, butcher bird ⓒ

モスク (イスラム教寺院) mosque ⓒ

モスグリーン moss green ⓒⓊ

モスクワ Moscow [máskau] (❖ロシアの首都)

もぞう 模造 imitation Ⓤ (❖「模造品」の意味では ⓒ) ──模造の imitation; (偽の) fake // 模造真珠 an *imitation* [*artificial*] pearl / 模造品に大金を払ってしまった I paid good money for *imitations*.

∥模造紙 Japanese vellum paper

もぞもぞ ポチはふとんの中でもぞもぞし始めた Pochi began to 「*move restlessly* [*fidget*] in the futon. / 背中がもぞもぞする I feel something *creeping* [*crawling*] on my back.

もだえる 悶える 恋にもだえる suffer an agony of love / その兵士はベッドに横たわってもだえ苦しんでいた The soldier lay 「*in agony* [*writhing*] on the bed.

もたげる 蛇がかま首をもたげた The snake *raised* its head. / ふと彼に対する疑念が頭をもたげ始めた Suddenly I *began to doubt* him. / Suddenly I *was seized* by suspicion against him.

もたせかける もたせ掛ける lean* ⓔ, rest ⓔ // 体を壁にもたせかける lean [rest] (oneself) against the wall (❖lean, rest いずれも自動詞で「もたれかかる」の意味がある)

もたせる 持たせる 人に期待をもたせる get [build] a person's hopes *up* / 話に真実味をもたせる *give* the story reality / 子供に手紙を持たせる (→持っていかせる) *have* one's child carry a letter; send one's child along with a letter / 彼女はいつも勘定を連れの男にもたせている (→払わせる) She always *makes* the man with her *pay* the bill. / 私たちは何とか目的地までガソリンをもたせた We managed to *make* the gasoline *last* until our destination.

もたつく 警察は犯人の特定にもたついた It *took* the police *a lot of time* to identify the criminal. / 外野手が球の処理をもたつく間にランナーは三塁に達した As the outfielder *was slow* in handling the ball, the runner reached the third base.

モダニスト modernist

モダニズム modernism Ⓤ

もたもた もたもたするな！ *Don't be slow!* / (→早くしろ)*Hurry up!* / もたもたしてると彼女をほかの男に取られちゃうよ Some other guy will take her away if you *keep dillydallying*. (❖dillydally は「(決心がつかずに)ぐずぐずする」の意味)

もたらす (持ってくる) bring* ⓔ; (引き起こす)

bring about, **cause** ㊥ (❖ bring about は因果関係が漠然として間接的な場合, cause は明瞭(㍾)で直接的な場合に用いる) / その台風は大雨をもたらした The typhoon *brought* with it a lot of rain. / 彼らは本国に吉報をもたらした They *brought* good news to their country. / 彼が放ったホームランはチームに勝利をもたらした His home run *brought* a victory to the team. / 暴風雨はその地域に大きな被害をもたらした The storm *caused* extensive damage to the district. / コンピュータは私たちの生活に多大な変化をもたらした Computers *have brought about* profound changes in our lives.

もたれかかる もたれ掛かる 壁にもたれかかる **lean** *against* a wall / 親にもたれかかった生活 life *dependent on one's* parents

もたれる (壁などに) **lean*** ㊥; (食べ物が) **sit*** heavily on *one's* stomach / 彼女はもたれてその絵を眺めていた She was looking at the picture *leaning against* the wall. / 昼に食べたてんぷらがまだ胃にもたれている The tempura I had for lunch still *sits heavily on my stomach*.
◆もたれる食事 a *heavy* meal

モダン ──モダンな **modern**; (現代風の) **up to date** ‖モダンアート **modern art** / モダンジャズ **modern jazz** / モダンバレエ (a) **modern ballet**

もち¹ 持ち ❶【耐久性】この果物はもちが悪い (→すぐに悪くなる) This fruit *spoils easily*. / 水切りをすると花のもちがよくなる A flower 「*lasts longer* [*keeps better*]」 if you cut it in the water.
❷【負担】費用は各人もちです (→各人が払わなければならない) Everyone *must pay* the expenses. / このパーティの費用は会社もちです Our company *is footing* the bill for this party.

もち² 餅 **mochi**, **rice cake** ‖もちをつく make *mochi* / もちを焼く toast some *mochi* / 近所の地域センターでもちつき大会があった Our local community center held *a mochi making and eating party*.
|慣用表現| もちはもち屋 *Better leave it to an expert*. (→それは専門家に任せておくほうがよい)

> もちは祝い事, 特に正月には欠かせない食べ物です. 蒸したもち米をうすに入れ, きねでついて作ります. 今日(㏉)ではスーパーや食料品店で購入することができます.
> *Mochi*, rice cake, is an essential food for happy occasions, especially New Year. It's made by putting steamed glutinous rice into an *usu* (a special kind of mortar) and then pounding with a *kine* (a mallet). Nowadays you can buy *mochi* at supermarkets and other grocery stores.

もちあがる 持ち上がる この機械はどうしても持ち上がらない This machine *won't lift*. / 別の大きな問題が持ち上がった Another big problem 「*came up* [*reared its head*]」. / 来年私たちのクラスは池田先生が持ち上がる(→担任を続ける)らしい I hear Ms. Ikeda will *continue to be in charge of* our class next year.

もちあげる 持ち上げる ❶【上に上げる】**lift** ㊥; (重いものを) **heave** ㊥ ‖この机を持ち上げられる? Can you *lift* this desk? / タクシーの運転手は私の重い荷物を持ち上げてトランクの中に入れた The taxi driver *heaved* my heavy baggage into the trunk.
◆頭を持ち上げる **raise** *one's* **head**
❷【おだてる】**flatter** ㊥ ‖彼はみんなから持ち上げられてすっかり得意になっていた He was *flattered* by everyone and felt very happy.

もちあじ 持ち味 俳優の持ち味(→才能)を生かした劇 a play which makes most of *the talent* of the actor / そのシェフは材料の持ち味を上手に引き出した The chef brought out *the (natural) flavor* of the ingredients well. / 少々のことではへこたれないのが彼女の持ち味(→長所)だ Her *strong point* is that she is not discouraged easily.

もちあるく 持ち歩く **carry** ㊥ ‖海外旅行をするときはたくさんの現金を持ち歩かないようにしている I *don't carry* too much cash (*with* me) when I travel abroad.

もちあわせ 持ち合わせ あいにく現金の持ち合わせがありません I'm sorry I don't *have enough money with* [*on*] *me*.

もちあわせる 持ち合わせる 私はそのときペンを持ち合わせていなかった I *didn't have* any pens *with* [*on*] *me*.

もちいえ 持ち家 *one's* own house

モチーフ **motif** ▢ ‖その小説に流れるモチーフ *a motif* that runs through the novel

もちいる 用いる
❶【使う】**use** ㊥; (手段などを)《公式的》**employ** ㊥
1語を2つの意味で用いる *use* a word in two senses
次に挙げる語を用いて文を作りなさい Make a sentence *using* the following words.
この素材は広く用いられている This material *is* widely *used*.
彼らは目的を達成するためにあらゆる手段を用いた They *employed* every available means to achieve their goal.
❷【採用・登用する】
ついに彼女の提案が用いられた At last her proposal *was adopted*.
彼はその重要な任務にベテランを用いた(→ベテランに任せた) He *entrusted* the important task *to* an experienced person.

もちうた 持ち歌 *one's* **repertoire** [répərtwàːr], *one's* **repertory**

もちかえり 持ち帰り (持ち帰り用料理)《米》**takeout** ▢,《英》**takeaway** ▢
☞「チーズバーガー2つとコーラのMを2つ」「こちらでお召し上がりですか, それともお持ち帰りですか」"Two cheeseburgers and two medium colas, please." "For here or *to go*?"

もちかえる¹ 持ち帰る **take*** ㊥, **bring*** ㊥;

もちかえる

(飲食物を店から)《米》take out, 《英》take away ∥彼はヨーロッパから珍しい帽子を持ち帰った He *brought back* a unique hat from Europe. / 父は仕事を家に持ち帰ってきた My father *brought* his work *home*. / ごみは持ち帰るようお願いします Please *take* your trash *with you*.

もちかえる² 持ち替える 彼女はかばんをもう一方の手に持ち替えた She *shifted* her bag from one hand to the other.

もちかける 持ち掛ける …に話(→提案)を持ちかける approach *a person with* a proposal / その件に関して彼から相談を持ちかけられた I *was consulted* by him about the matter.

もちかぶ 持ち株 ∥持ち株会社 a holding company

もちきり 持ち切り 今や学校中が彼女の話でもちきりだ(→彼女は話の種になっている) She is now *the talk* of the whole school. / 新聞はその事件のことでもちきりだ The newspapers *are full of* that incident.

もちぐされ 持ち腐れ 慣用表現 君がそんな仕事をしているなんて宝の持ち腐れだ(→才能のむだづかいだ) It's *a waste of* your talent to do such a job.

もちくずす 持ち崩す 酒で身を持ち崩す *ruin oneself* by drinking

もちこす 持ち越す 結論を持ち越す(→延期する) *postpone* [*put off*] the decision / この議論は次の会議に持ち越すことにしましょう Let's *carry* this discussion *over* to our next meeting. / スワローズの優勝はあすに持ち越された The Swallows *will have to wait* until tomorrow for their chance to win the pennant.

もちこたえる 持ちこたえる (重みなどに)hold*, bear*; (病人が) pull through ∥これ以上の本を載せても棚はもちこたえられるだろうか Will the shelf *hold* if we put any more books on it? / その患者は一時危篤状態にあったが何とかもちこたえた The patient was in critical condition for a while, but somehow he *pulled through*.
◆その食料で5日はもちこたえられるだろう We'll *last* [*hold out*] for five days with the food. / The food will *last* us (for) five days.

もちこみ 持ち込み その試験はノートの持ち込みが認められていた We were allowed to *take* [*bring*] our notebooks *to* the examination. / 危険物持ち込み禁止 《掲示》Dangerous Articles Prohibited
∥持ち込み料 corkage

もちこむ 持ち込む take*, bring* ∥事件を裁判に持ち込む *take* [*bring*] a case *to* court / そのような荷物は飛行機に持ち込めません You *can't bring* [*take*] such baggage *onto* the airplane.
◆公の場に私的な感情を持ち込まないでほしい I want you *not to carry* your private feelings *over* into public occasion. / 最近このような苦情が持ち込まれることが多くなった This kind of complaint *has often been filed* recently. / そのサッカーの試合は延長戦に持ち込まれた The soccer game *was sent* [*put*] *into* the extra time.

もちごめ 糯米 glutinous rice Ⓤ

もちさる 持ち去る carry [take*] away ∥美術館から数点の絵画が何者かによって持ち去られた Some paintings *were carried* [*taken*] *away* from the museum by someone.
◆私のペンを持ち去ったのはだれですか Who *walked off with* my pen?

もちじかん 持ち時間 持ち時間は1人2分です *The time allowed* for each person is two minutes.

もちだし 持ち出し その国では通貨の持ち出しに申告が必要だ You must declare to *take* currency *out of* the country. / 費用の不足分は持ち出しになった(→自分で払わなければならなかった) We *had to pay* the shortfall on the expenses *out of our own pockets*.

もちだす 持ち出す (運び出す) take* [carry] out; (問題・話題などを) bring* up ∥新しい話題を持ち出す *bring up* a new subject / これらの参考図書はこの部屋から持ち出すことはできません You can't *take* [*carry*] *out* these reference books from this room. / 国外に通貨をひそかに持ち出す *smuggle out* currency

もちつもたれつ 持ちつ持たれつ その2つの業界は持ちつ持たれつの関係にある The two industries have a *give-and-take* relationship.

もちなおす 持ち直す かばんを左手に持ち直した I *shifted* the bag *to* my left hand. / 患者は何とかもち直した The patient managed to *rally* [*pick up*]. / いまだに景気がもち直すきざしは見られない There are still no indications that business *will rally* [*pick up*, *improve*]. / 天気がもち直した The weather *got better again*.

もちにげ 持ち逃げ 彼は店の売上金を持ち逃げした He *made* [*ran*] *off with* the proceeds of the store.

もちぬし 持ち主 owner Ⓒ, 《公式的》the possessor ∥あの車の持ち主はだれですか Who is *the owner* of that car? / Who owns that car?
◆冷静な頭脳の持ち主 *a person with* a cool head / 彼は現実的な考えの持ち主だ(→持っている) He *has* a practical mind. / この建物はここ数年のうちに何度も持ち主が変わった This building *has changed hands* many times in a few years.

もちば 持ち場 post Ⓒ ∥持ち場を離れる leave *one's post* / 持ち場を守る keep [stand by] *one's post*
◆できるだけ早く自分の持ち場(→仕事)に戻りなさい Return to your *duty* as soon as possible.

もちはこび 持ち運び 持ち運びのできるCDプレーヤー a *portable* CD player / この小型テレビは持ち運びに便利だ This small television is easy to carry.

もちはこぶ 持ち運ぶ carry ∥この辞書は大きくて持ち運べない This dictionary is too large to *carry*.

もちぶん 持ち分 （分担） *one's* share

もちまえ 持ち前 **—持ち前の** （生まれもった） natural; （特有の） characteristic ∥持ち前の行動力を発揮する show *one's natural* ability to act / 彼女は持ち前の明るさで多くの困難を乗り越えた She overcame many difficulties with her *characteristic* cheerfulness.

もちまわり 持ち回り 会の幹事は持ち回りで務めている We *take turns* being in charge of arrangements for the meeting.

もちもの 持ち物 （所持品） things, belongings,《口語的》stuff [U] ➡ てにもつ ∥個人の持ち物 personal *belongings* / 警官は彼の持ち物を調べた The police officer inspected his *things.* / 三村先生がホームルームの時間に持ち物検査をした Ms. Mimura *checked our belongings* during homeroom.

もちゅう 喪中 **喪中につき**新年のごあいさつを失礼させていただきます I *am in mourning*, so I will not be able to send New Year's greetings to you this year.（❖英米では喪中のためクリスマスカードなどを出さないという習慣はない）

もちよる 持ち寄る 私たちは作品を**持ち寄って**展示会を開いた Each of us *brought* his [her] works and we held an exhibition *together.* / 来週の週末うちで**持ち寄りパーティー**をしない？ How about having *a potluck party* at my house next weekend?

もちろん 勿論

of course（❖口語では単に course ともいう）, certainly ,《米口語的》sure(ly), by all means（❖by all means はほかよりも丁寧な表現）; （AだけでなくBも） B as well as A, not only A but also B; （言うまでもなく） not to mention, not to speak of ..., to say nothing of ..., needless to say（❖needless to say は通例文頭に置き，文全体を修飾する）

1等賞は**もちろん**彼が取るだろう He will win the first prize, *of course.*

結婚式には出席します．**もちろん**披露宴にも出ます よ I will attend the wedding ceremony and *of course* the reception.

あのこと，彼女には**もちろん**言ってないだろうね *Of course* you didn't tell her about it, did you?

彼はロック**はもちろん**インド音楽や日本の民謡にも詳しい He knows a lot about 「Indian music and Japanese traditional folk songs *as well as* rock [*not only* rock *but also* Indian music and Japanese traditional folk songs].

正直が最良の策であるの**はもちろんのことだ** *Needless to say*, honesty is the best policy.

父はギャンブル**はもちろんのこと**酒もたばこもやらない My father doesn't drink or smoke, 「*not to mention* [*not to speak of, to say nothing of*] gamble.

◆彼は本は**もちろん**鉛筆1本買う金さえ持っていなかった He didn't even have money to buy just one pencil, 「*much less* [*let alone*] a book.

💬「お茶をもう1杯いただけますか」「**もちろん**いいですよ」"Can I have another cup of tea?" "*Of course.*/ *Sure.*/ *Certainly.*/ *By all means.*/ *No problem.*/ *With pleasure.*"

💬「いっしょにパーティーに行かない？」「**もちろん**行くよ」"Are you going to the party with me?" "*Of course* I am. / I'm *glad* to."

💬「試験に落ちたんじゃないだろうね」「**もちろん**（落ちませんでした）」"You didn't fail the exam, did you?" "*Of course* [*Certainly*] *not.*"

💬「彼女はきょう来ますか」「**もちろん**」"Is she coming today?" "*Definitely.*"

もつ[1] 持つ

❶手に持つ・携える	have; hold; carry
❷所有する	have, have got; own, possess
❸心にいだく	have, hold, bear
❹ある属性を備えている	have
❺ある状態のままで続く	last, hold; keep
❻負担する	pay
❼受け持つ	

❶**【手に持つ・携える】** have* [他]; （しっかりと） hold* [他]; （持ち歩く） carry [他]

彼は右手にラケットのような物を**持っていた** He *had* something like a racket in his right hand.

私はその留学生にはしの**持ち方**を教えてあげた I showed the exchange student *how to hold* chopsticks.

コートを着る間かばんを**持っててもらえる？** Will you *hold* my bag while I put on my coat?

私は電車に乗るときはいつも文庫本を**持っている** I always *carry* a pocket-sized book when taking a train.

そんなに大きなスーツケースを**持って歩く**のは大変だ It's a lot of work to *carry* such a big suitcase *around.*

💬「おばあちゃんへのプレゼントは**持った**？」「あっ，忘れてた」"You'*ve got* the present for Grandma, don't you?" "Oh, I forgot."

💬「何か書く物，**持ってる**？」「ちょっと待って．確かペン**持ってた**と思う」"Do you *have* something to write with?" "Just a second ..., I think I *have* a pen with me."

💬「このCD欲しいけどきょうお金あんまり**持ってない**んだ」「いくらか貸してあげられるよ」"I want this CD, but I *haven't got* much money today." "I could lend you some."

❷**【所有する】** （持っている） have* [他],《口語的》have got; （所有する） own [他], possess [他]; （経営する） run* [他]

私は携帯電話を**持っていない** I *don't have* a cellular phone.

この寮の学生は各自個室を**持っていますか** Does

each student in this dorm *have* a separate room?
中居君は自分専用の電話番号を持っている Nakai's *got* his own phone number.
彼の父親は車を2台持っている His father *owns* two cars.
おばは青山にブティックを持っている My aunt *runs* a boutique in Aoyama.
◆彼女は走り幅跳びの世界記録を持っている(→保持している) She *holds* the world record in the long jump.

❸【心にいだく】have*㊥, hold*㊥, bear*㊥

私は彼に対して好感をもっている I *have* a good impression of him.
彼女は子育てに関して確固たる考えをもっている She *holds* strong views about how children should be raised.
警察は被害者にうらみをもつ者の犯行と見ている The police suspect the culprit *had* [*bore*] a grudge against the victim.
◆もっと自分に自信をもちなさい You should *be* more *confident* in yourself. / 彼女はこの古い家に深い愛着をもっている She *is* deeply *attached to* this old house.

❹【ある属性を備えている】have*㊥

正方形は4つの同じ長さの辺をもつ A square *has* four equal sides.
イルカは高度な知能をもつといわれている Dolphins are said to *have* a high degree of intelligence.
彼女はとても美しい声をもっている She *has* a very beautiful voice.

❺【ある状態のままで続く】last ㊤㊥, hold*㊥㊤; (食品などが) keep*㊤

この金で1か月はもつだろう This money will *last* for one month.
そのカキはあすまでもつまい Those oysters won't *keep* [*stay good*] overnight.
この好天があしたまでもってくれればいいが I hope this good weather will *last* [*hold*] till tomorrow.
医者にうちの猫は来月までもたないかもしれないと言われた The vet told us our cat *might not live* until next month.
◆週末まで働いていたら身がもたない(→健康を損なう)よ You'*ll ruin your health* if you keep working even on weekends.

❻【負担する】pay*㊥㊤

ここは私がもちます *Let me pay the bill.* / (口語的) *This is on me.*
交通費は自分もちだが宿泊は無料だ You'*ll have to pay* the transportation expenses, but you won't be charged for the accommodation.

❼【受け持つ】

姉はその小学校で2年生のクラスをもっている My sister teaches a second grade class at the elementary school.

❽【その他】

うちのチームはほとんど彼ひとりでもっているようなものだ(→彼の能力に頼っている) Our team *depends* almost solely *on* his ability.

もつ² (内臓) entrails, guts; (鳥の) giblets
もっか 目下 now, at present, presently / 事故の原因については目下調査中です We are *now* investigating the cause of the accident. ◆目下の課題 the *present* problem / 目下の仕事 the job *in* [*at*] *hand*
もっかんがっき 木管楽器 (個々の) woodwind instrument ㊒; (全体) woodwind ㊒ ㊤; (オーケストラの木管部) woodwinds, the woodwind section
もっきん 木琴 xylophone [záiləfòun] ㊒ ‖木琴奏者 a xylophonist
もっけのさいわい もっけの幸い そこに彼女が通りかかったのはもっけの幸いだった It was *a stroke of good luck* that she happened to pass by there.
もっこう 木工 《米》woodworking ㊤, 《英》woodwork ㊤ ‖木工所 a sawmill / 木工職人 a woodworker / 木工品 woodwork
もったいない それを捨てるのはもったいないよ It's "*a waste* [《口語的》*a shame, wasteful*] to throw it away. / お金がもったいないので僕はそれを買わなかった I didn't buy it because I thought it would be *a waste* of money. / それ,捨てちゃうの? なんてもったいない You're going to throw it away? *What a waste*! / 観光にまる1日かけるのはもったいない It's *not worthwhile* to spend a whole day sightseeing. / この万年筆は僕にはもったいない This fountain pen is *too good for* me. / 彼はアマチュアミュージシャンにしておくにはもったいないくらいの才能をもっている He's an amateur musician, but he has *much more* talent *than* that.
もったいぶる 彼は非常にもったいぶった話し方をする(→重々しい様子で話す) He talks *with too much dignity*. / 何があったの? もったいぶらずに(→じらさないで)教えてよ What's happened? *Don't keep me hanging* [*in suspense*]. Tell me about it.

もって

❶【…によって】

当選者の発表は景品の発送をもって代えさせていただきます The winners will be notified *by* sending them their prizes.
彼の器用さをもってすれば犬小屋くらい簡単にできてしまうだろう *With* his dexterity, he could easily make a kennel.
戦争の終結は喜びをもって迎えられた The end of the war was greeted *with* joy.

❷【…を最終に】

午後7時をもって閉店いたします We'll close *at* seven in the evening.
9月10日をもって締め切りとさせていただきます The closing date is September 10.
5月1日をもって店の名前が変わります The name of our store will change *on* [*as of*] May 1. (❖as of ... は「…以後」の意味)

❸【強調】

彼は全くもって無知である He is *completely* [*absolutely*] ignorant.

もっていく 持って行く take*㊥, (持ち運ぶ) carry ㊥; (聞き手などの所へ) bring*㊥

旅行に行くときには地図を持っていきなさい *Take* [*Carry*] a map *with you* when you travel.

この箱を部屋まで持っていってくれない？ Will you *take* [*carry*] these boxes *to* the room?

入院中の彼女に本でも持っていってあげたら？ Why don't you *take* some books to her in the hospital?

◆だれか私の傘を持っていった(→盗んで持ち去った) Somebody *made off with* my umbrella. / 彼はいつも話を自分の得意な分野へ持っていく He always *leads* the topic of conversation *to* his favorite field.

💬「何か音楽が聞きたいね」「うん，じゃあ，CD を何枚か持っていくよ」"We need some music, don't we?" "Yes, well, I'*ll bring* some CDs."

もってうまれた 持って生まれた **持って生まれた**音楽的才能 an *innate* [an *inborn*, a *natural*] talent for music / 彼女のせっかちな性格は**持って生まれた**ものだ She *was born with* an impatient personality.

もってかえる 持って帰る (持ち去る) take* [他]; (持ってくる) bring* [他] //それを勝手に**持って帰っちゃ**だめだよ *Don't* you *take* it *home with you* without permission. / この本はちゃんと**持って帰ってきて**ね Don't forget to *bring* this book *back* (*here*).

もってくる 持って来る bring* [他]; (取って戻ってくる) get* [他]; (行って持ってくる) go* (and) get, fetch [他] (❖《米》では fetch よりも bring, go (and) get などを使うほうがふつう)

あしたその CD を**持ってきて**よ *Bring* the CD tomorrow.

彼は彼女にバラの花を**持ってきた** He *brought* her some roses. / He *brought* some roses to [for] her. (❖to を用いると対象の人や場所が強調され，for を用いると「(人)のために」ということが強調される)

そこの本，ちょっと**持ってきて** *Bring* [*Get*] me the book there.

もっとお金を**持ってくれば**よかったなあ I *should have brought* more money *with me*.

僕の部屋からギターを**持ってきて**くれない？ Will you *go* (*and*) *get* the guitar from my room?

もってこい 持って来い ―**もってこいの** (最もよい) (the) best; (理想的な) ideal; (申し分のない) right //ここは本を読むには**もってこいの**場所だ This is 「*the best* [an *ideal*] place *for* reading. / 彼は学級委員長には**もってこいの**人だ He is the *right* person *to be* our class representative.

もってのほか もっての外 部長が部活をサボるとは**もってのほか**だ It is 「*out of the question* [*unallowable, inexcusable*] for the club leader to skip the club activities.

もってまわった 持って回った **もってまわった**言い方はよしてくれ Stop *talking in a roundabout way*./ Stop *beating around the bush*. (❖beat around the bush は「遠回しに言う」の意味)

もっと

(より多く) more (❖通例形容詞・副詞の比較級を用いて表す)

[語法]

> more は 2 音節以上の形容詞・副詞の前に置いて比較級を作る．1 音節の語と 2 音節の語の一部は，原級に -er を付ける．

このクッションのほうがそれより**もっと**座り心地いいよ This cushion is *more* comfortable than that one.

もっとはっきりしゃべりなさい Speak *more* clearly.

この作業には**もっと**人員が必要だ We need *more* people to do this task. (❖この more は形容詞 many の比較級)

もっと繊維質をとりなさい Take *more* fiber. (❖この more は形容詞 much の比較級)

これより**もっとかわいい**人形が欲しいな I want a *prettier* doll than this.

このセーターを**もっと**小さいのと取り替えたいのですが I'd like to change this sweater for a *smaller* one.

もっとましな言い訳は思いつかないの？ Can't you come up with a *better* excuse?

もっとそばにおいでよ Come *closer* to me.

彼は**もっとずっと速く**走れるはずだ He should be able to run *much faster*.

それは確かにいい考えですが，私には**もっといい**考えがあります That sure is a good idea, but I have a still [an even] *better* one. (❖much, still, even は比較級を強調する)

もっとちょうだいよ Give me some *more*! (❖この more は「もっとたくさん」の意味の代名詞)

あなたの家族について**もっと**教えてください Please let me know *more* about your family.

もっともっと多くの人に私の絵を見てもらいたい I'd like *many* [*a lot*] *more* people to see my paintings. (❖more は many, a lot, much などの後で「さらに多くの，より以上の」の意味)

もっともっと雨が必要だ We need *much* [*a lot*] *more* rain.

◆**もっとほかに** CD は持ってないの？ Don't you have *any other* CDs? / **もっと安い**靴はありませんか Do you have any *less expensive* shoes?

モットー motto [C] (複 ～es, ～s) //「何にでも一生懸命取り組む」というのが私の**モットー**だ My *motto* is "Work hard at everything you do."

もっとも[1] 最も

(❖通例，形容詞・副詞の最上級を用いて表す)

日本で**最も長い**川は信濃川です *The longest* river in Japan is the Shinano river.

これは私がこれまで見た中で**最も**おもしろい映画だ This is *the most* interesting movie that I've ever seen.

そこへ行くのに**最もよい**方法は列車を使うことだ *The best* way to get there is to take the train.

それは最も偉大な発明の一つだ It is one of *the greatest inventions*.

今世界で最も速く走れる人がだれか知ってる? Do you know who can run (*the*) *fastest* in the world?

彼は我々のクラスで最も流暢(りゅうちょう)に英語を話す He speaks English (*the*) *most* fluently in our class.

彼女は今最も彼を必要としている She needs him *most* now.

だれが最も多く得票するか私には分からない I have no idea who will get *the most* votes.

もっとも²

❶【当然】——もっともな natural; (理屈に合った) reasonable; (正当な) justified

もっともな要求 a *reasonable* demand / もっともな理由 a *justified* reason

彼が落ち込むのももっともだ It's *natural* that he gets depressed. / He *may well* get depressed.

君の言うことはもっともだが, 僕は同意できない What you say sounds *reasonable*, but I can't agree.

◆ごもっともです *You're quite right.* / 彼女がそれを断ったのにはもっともな理由があった She *had a good reason* for turning it down. / それはもっともですが, 1つ重要なことを見落としていますね That's *fair enough*, but you have missed one important thing. (❖fair enough は会話で相手の言葉や行為に対してほぼ同意するときに用いる)

❷【ただし】though, although

我々はきのうパーティーに行った. もっとも本当は行きたくなかったのだけど We went to the party yesterday, *though* [*although*] we really didn't want to. / We went to the party yesterday. We really didn't want to, *though*. (❖although は文末には置かない)

もっともらしい (まことしやかな) plausible; (まじめくさった) solemn ‖彼女はもっともらしい言い訳をした She made a *plausible* excuse. / 彼らはその商品にもっともらしい名前をつけて売り出した They gave the product a *solemn* name and then put it on the market. ◆もっともらしい顔で人をだましてはいけない Don't lie to people with a *straight face*.

もっぱら 専ら 彼女は休みの日にはもっぱら映画を見て過ごす She spends most of her time watching movies when she's off. / その俳優が近々この町にやってくるというもっぱらのうわさだよ *It is widely rumored* [*People all around say*] that the actor will visit this town soon.

モップ mop ◯ ◆床にモップをかける *mop* the floor

もつれ 縺れ (もつれた部分) tangle ◯; (もつれた状態) entanglement ◯ ◯ ‖チェーンのもつれを解く *undo the tangle* in the chain; *untangle* the chain / 感情のもつれ an emotional *entanglement* / 恋愛のもつれから殺人事件が起こった A love *tangle* [*entanglement*] caused a murder.

もつれこむ 縺れ込む 試合は延長戦にもつれ込んだ(→入った) The game *went into* the overtime. (❖野球の場合は The game went into extra innings. とする)

もつれる 縺れる (糸などが) tangle ⓐ, get* tangled [entangled] ‖コードがもつれた The cord *has tangled* [*got tangled*]. / 話し合いがもつれてけんか別れになってしまった The negotiation *got tangled* [*complicated*] and we left angry at each other.

◆もつれた関係 (a) *tangled* relationship / その早口言葉は舌がもつれてしまってうまく言えない I can't say the tongue twister because my tongue really *gets twisted*. / その走者は足がもつれて転んだ The runner *tripped over his own feet* (*and fell*).

もてあそぶ 弄ぶ (物を) play (about [around]) with ..., toy with ... ‖彼は授業中ずっとペンをもてあそんでいた He *played* [*toyed*] *with* a pen throughout the class. / あいつは彼女の心をもてあそんだのだ He *played* [*toyed*, *trifled*] *with* her heart.

もてあます 持て余す 先生はそのわがままな生徒をもてあましていた(→どうしていいのか分からなかった) The teacher *didn't know what to do with* the selfish student. / 私は時間をもてあましている I *have too much time on my hands*. / *Time hangs* [*lies*] *heavy on my hands*. / 彼はその難解な本をもてあましていた(→彼には難しすぎて読めなかった) The book *was too difficult for him to read*.

もてなし (歓待) hospitality ◯, welcome ◯; (受け入れ) reception ◯ ◯ (通例単数形) ‖おもてなしいただき, ありがとうございました Thank you for *your hospitality*. / 私は厚いもてなしを受けた I「*was given* [*received*] *a warm welcome*. / 私はそのパーティーで特別な客としてのもてなしを受けた I accepted *their hospitality* as a special guest at the party.

もてなす (接待する) entertain ⓐ; (ふるまう) treat ⓐ ‖彼らはフランス料理でもてなされた They *were entertained* with French food.

◆彼女は手作りのケーキでもてなしてくれた She *served* me her homemade cake.

もてはやす 持て囃す (高く評価する) regard highly; (重んじる) make* much of ...; (賞賛する) praise ⓐ ‖言語学者の間ではその理論がもてはやされている The theory *is highly regarded* among linguists.

◆厚底の靴が女の子にもてはやされていた(→人気があった) Platform shoes *were very popular among* young girls.

モデム 〖コンピュータ〗 modem [móudem] ◯

モデラート 〖音楽〗 moderato

もてる¹ (女に) もてる (→人気がある) 男 a man *popular with* women / 彼女は男の子にもてる She *is popular with* boys. / She *is a favorite of* boys.

もてる² 持てる 持てる者と持たざる者 *the haves* and the have-nots / 彼女は持てる力すべてを社会福祉にささげた She spent *all her*

energy on social welfare.

モデル

❶【絵・写真・文学作品などの】model ©

男性モデル *a male model* / 写真のモデル *a photographic model* / ファッションモデル *a fashion model*

彼女はファッション誌のモデルをしている She works as *a model* for a fashion magazine.

その劇の主人公は実在の人物をモデルとしている They used an actual person as *a model* for the main character of the play.

◆その写真家は彼女にモデルになってくれるよう頼んだ The photographer asked her to *model* for him.

❷【手本・見本】model ©

天文学は最も早く発展し、あらゆる科学のモデルとなった Astronomy was developed first and became *a model* for all other sciences.

◆その条例はS県のものをモデルとして作られた The regulation *was modeled on* the one of S prefecture.

❸【型】model ©

その車のニューモデル *the new model* of the car

会社はバイクのモデルチェンジを行った The company 「*had a model changeover* [*changed the model*] of their motorcycle.

‖モデルガン a model gun / モデルケース a model case / モデルハウス a model house / モデルルーム a model apartment (❖ × model room とはいわない)

もと¹ 元・本・基

❶ 起こり・出所		the origin; the source
❷ 原因		cause
❸ 基礎		base
❹ 原材料		
❺ 元手		
❻ 以前		former

❶【起こり・出所】(起源) the origin; (根源) the root; (出所) the source; (始まり) the beginning

日本人とイヌイットの人々は元は同じ種族だと推測されている The Japanese and the Inuit are thought to have *the same origin*.

そのうわさの元は小さな新聞記事だった *The source* of the rumor was a small newspaper article.

英語の soy という語の元は日本語の「しょうゆ」だという説がある One theory says that *the origin* of the English word 'soy' is the Japanese word '*shoyu*.'

かぜは万病の元 A cold can be *the root* of all sicknesses. / (→かぜはあらゆる病気をもたらす) A cold can *lead to* all sicknesses.

元から彼の考えには反対だった I was against his idea from *the beginning*.

◆火の元に注意 Beware of *fire*. / 柔道は元は日本で生まれたものだが今では世界中に知られている Judo *originated* in Japan, but now it's known all over the world. / 話を元に戻そう Let's go back to the point *where we started*.

🄮「画面を元に戻すのはどうすればいいの」「undo のキーを押すんだよ」 "How can I *restore* the screen?" "Press the 'undo'."

❷【原因】cause ©

けんかの元は何だったの What was *the cause* of the quarrel?

◆過労が元で死ぬ die 「*due to* [*from, because of*] overwork / スピードの出しすぎは事故の元だ Speeding *causes* accidents. / 彼はその小さな傷が元で足を切断せざるをえなくなった The little wound *led to* the amputation of his leg.

❸【基礎】base ©, basis © (複 bases); (土台) foundation ©

これらが有名な『ゲルニカ』の元になったデッサンです These drawings were *the basis* for the famous painting *Guernica*.

◆この小説は彼の子供のころの体験が元になっている This novel *is based on* his childhood experiences. / みんなの意見を元に(→集めて)企画をまとめてみた I *gathered* everyone's ideas to make a plan.

❹【原材料】

スープの元 *soup stock*

その酒は米を元にして作られる The liquor *is made from* rice.

❺【元手】

彼は宝くじで当たった10万円を元に株を買った He bought some stock *with* the 100,000 yen he won in a lottery.

設備投資に金をたくさんつぎ込んだので元を取るのに2，3年はかかるだろう We've invested a lot of money in equipment, so it'll take a couple of years before we *recover the investment*.

このブーツは高かったからいっぱい履いて元を取らなきゃ(→できるだけ利用しなきゃ) I've got to wear these boots a lot 「*to make the most of* them [(→払った金をむだにしないために) to get my money's worth out of them] because they were expensive.

❻【以前】——元の former, ex-(❖「前…」の意味の場合にも用いられることがある)——元は formerly; (かつて) once

カーター元大統領 *former* president Carter; *ex*-president Carter

その俳優はディアスの元恋人だ The actor is Diaz's *former boyfriend*.

彼女は元の地位に復帰した She was restored to her *former* position.

彼は元は高校の数学教師をしていた He *once* taught math at a high school.

◆すべて元の場所に返しなさい *Put* everything *back in its place*. / もと来た道を戻ったほうがいい We should go back *the way we came*.

🄮「これ、だれのタオル」「ああ、それ、元からそこにあったのよ」 "Whose is this towel?" "Oh, it's been there for a while."

もと

慣用表現 彼らは大げんかをしたが結局元のさやに収まった(→また仲のよい友達になれた) They had a big fight, but after all they *became good friends again*. / 元はといえば(→突き詰めれば)これは彼が言いだした計画だ *When you get right down to it*, he brought up this plan. / 客が10人しか来ないんじゃ元も子もない(→完全な損失になる) If we can get only 10 customers, *it'll be a total loss* for us. / もし今彼女を怒らせたら元も子もなくなるよ(→今までの努力がむだになる) If you make her angry now, *all your effort will have come to nothing*.

ことわざ 口は災いのもと ➡くち

もと[2] 下 /私は亀井教授のもとで研究している I'm studying *under* Prof. Kamei. / すべての人は法のもとに平等である All people are equal *under the law*. / その空爆は正義の名のもとに行われた The air strike was made *in the name of* justice. / 悪天候のもとで運動会が開かれた The sports festival was held *in bad weather*. / 彼はいまだに親のもとを離れない(→親と暮らしている) He is still living *with* his parents.

もどかしい 彼にうまく気持ちを伝えられなくてもどかしかった I *felt impatient* [*irritated*] because I couldn't get my feelings across to him well. / そのプレゼントの包みをあけるのももどかしかった I *could hardly wait to* open the present.

モトクロス motocross ⓊⓊ

もとじめ 元締め (ボス)《口語的》boss Ⓒ; (金銭の) chief treasurer Ⓒ /彼がグループの総元締めだ He is *the boss of* the whole group.

もどす 戻す
❶【元に】(元の状態へ返す) restore ⓗ; (元の場所へ返す) return ⓗ,《口語的》put* back; (時計を) turn [put, set*] back

使ったら元の所に戻しておいてね *Put* it *back* [*Return* it] where it was after you use it.
時計を3分戻した I *turned* [*put, set*] *back* the watch by three minutes.
寺の外観は建立当時の姿に戻された The exterior of the temple *was restored to* its original design.
◆話を元に戻そう Let's *return* [*go back*] *to* the point where we started. / ビデオを彼が出てくる場面に戻して *Rewind* the video *to* the scene in which he appeared.
❷【吐く】《口語的》throw* up, vomit ⓔⓗ
その子は食べた物を全部もどしてしまった That kid *vomited* [*threw up*] everything he had eaten.
◆その光景を見てもどしそうになった I *felt sick* when I saw the scene.

もとせん 元栓 the main cock ◆ガスの元栓をしめる turn off the gas at *the main*

もとづく 基づく be based on ...; (由来する) come* from ... /彼の新しい小説は古い民話に基づいている His new novel *is based on* an old folk tale. / それは偏見に基づいた考え方だ That is a view *based on* prejudice.

◆…という信念に基づいて *under* [*in*] the conviction that ... / 税金は所得に基づいて課される Taxes are imposed *on the basis of* income.

もとで 元手 (seed) capital Ⓤ; (事業資金) seed money Ⓤ /商売を始めるにはかなりの元手がかかる You need a lot of money as (*seed*) *capital* if you want to start business. / 彼は300万円の資金を元手に事業を興した He started a business with three million yen as *capital* [*seed money*].

もとどおり 元通り /彼は割れたつぼを元どおりに直した He restored the broken vase to *the way it was before*. / 彼の視力は手術ですっかり元どおりになった His eyesight *was completely restored* by the operation. / 本は読み終わったら元どおりにしておいてね(→元の場所へ戻して) *Put* the books *back where they were* after you read them. / よく洗濯したらシャツは元どおり(→以前のように)きれいになった I washed the shirt well and it became *as clean as before*.

もとね 元値 cost price Ⓤ, cost ⓊⒸ

もとのもくあみ 元の木阿弥 せっかくダイエットしたのにパーティー続きで元の木阿弥になった Although I succeeded in losing some weight, all these parties *sent me straight back to where I started*.

もとめ 求め (要望) request ⓊⒸ; (要求) demand Ⓒ /彼の求めに応じる answer his *request* [*demand*] /彼は客の求めに応じて品を作る He makes articles *by* customers' *requests*.
◆どういったかばんをお求めでしょうか What type of bag *would you like*? / その時計はどちらでお求めになられましたか Where did you *buy* your watch?

もとめる 求める

❶【頼む・要求する】ask ⓗ, request ⓗ(◆後者のほうがかたい言い方),《公式的》call on *a person*; (強く要求する) demand ⓗ
市長は住民に意見を求めた The mayor *asked* citizens *for* opinions. / The mayor *asked* (*for*) citizens' opinions.
彼女に討論会へ参加するよう求めた We *asked* her to take part in the discussion.
私たちは入口で学生証の提示を求められた We *were requested to* show our student ID cards at the entrance.
彼女はその件で弁明を求められた She *was called on to* account for the matter.
労働者は(会社側に対し)賃上げを求めた The workers *demanded* higher wages (*from* [*of*]) the company).
◆その火事の現場では人々が助けを求めて叫んでいた People were shouting *for help* at the fire. / 私に何を求めているのですか What do you *expect of* me?

❷【探す】look for ...,《公式的》seek* ⓔⓗ; (見つける) find* ⓗ
最近職を求めて多くの人が日本にやってくる Nowadays a lot of people come to Ja-

pan *looking for* jobs.
yの値を求めなさい *Find the value of* y.
彼は(高い)地位も名声も求めなかった He *didn't seek* either high position or fame.
◆彼らは沈没船の宝を求めて潜水した They dove *for* the sunken ship's treasure. / マルコ・ポーロは冒険を求めてイタリアを後にした Marco Polo left Italy *in quest* [*search*] *of* adventure. / 求むラガーマン《掲示》*Wanted*: Rugby Players
❸【買う】buy* 他 ⇨ かう(買う)

もともと 元々 (初めから) from the beginning [start, (very) first]; (本来は) originally; (生まれつき) by nature; (今までずっと) always (❖通例完了形とともに用いる)
もともとそんなことやりたいとは思っていなかったのだ I haven't been interested in doing it *from the beginning* [*first*].
『蛍の光』はもともとは Auld Lang Syne というスコットランドの民謡だ "Hotaru no Hikari" is *originally* a Scottish folk song called "Auld Lang Syne."
私はもともと体が弱い I'm physically weak *by nature*.
💬「彼って前より優しくなったと思わない?」「えっ、もともと優しいよ」"Don't you think he has become kinder than before?" "Well, he's *always* been kind."
💬「彼女をデートに誘うの? ふられない自信あるの?」「いいや、だめでもともとだよ」"Are you going to ask her for a date? Are you confident?" "No, but *I've got nothing to lose*."

もとより 彼女はピアノはもとより(→言うまでもなく)ギターやバイオリンも弾ける She can play the guitar and the violin, *not to mention* the piano. / 断られることはもとより(→初めから)承知していた I knew *from the beginning* that I would be turned down.

もとる 人情にもとる(→反する)行い a behavior that *goes against* the human heart / それは道理にもとる(→筋が通らない) That is *unreasonable*.

もどる 戻る
❶【元の場所へ】return 自,《口語的》get* back; (戻っていく) go* back; (戻ってくる) come* back (❖相手の所へ「戻っていく」という意味で用いることも可能); (引き返す) turn back
私が戻ってみると彼は仕事をほとんど終えていた When I *returned* [*got back*], he had almost finished his work.
さて最初の話題へ戻りましょう Now then, *let's return* [*get back, go back*] *to* the original subject.
彼は急いで家に戻った He *returned* [*went back*] home hurriedly.
彼はまだ学校から戻らない He's *not returned* [*come home*] from school yet.
北海道にはいつ戻るの When will you *go back to* Hokkaido? / When will you *come back to* Hokkaido?
自分の席に戻りなさい *Go back to* your seat.
(コンピュータなどの表示で)1つ前の画面に戻ってください *Go back to* the previous screen.
ちょっと買い物に出るけどすぐに戻るからね I'm going shopping now, but I'll *come* [*be*] *back* soon.
◆10時ごろ電話をしたが彼はまだ家に戻っていなかった I called him at around 10, but he *wasn't* (*back*) home yet. / 盗まれた自転車は私のところに戻ってきた(→返された) My stolen bike *was restored* [*returned*] *to* me.
❷【元の状態に】return 自,《口語的》get* back; (回復する) recover 自 他; (取り戻す) regain 他
仕事に戻ってください *Get back to* your job.
祭りも終わり村に静けさが戻った The festival was over and silence *has returned to* the village.
二人の関係はもう元には戻らないだろう The relationship between the two *won't recover*.
やっと体調が戻った I've *recovered* [*regained*] my health at last.
◆ふつうの生活に戻る *go back to* normal life

もなか 最中 a *monaka*, a wafer cake with bean paste inside
モナリザ the "Mona Lisa", "La Gioconda"
モニター ⚠❶【監視装置】monitor C ——モニターする (モニターで監視する) monitor 他
❷【試して意見を言う人】(商品の) test user C; (新聞などの) test reader C; (テレビの) test viewer C; (ラジオの) test listener C (❖英語の monitor にはこの意味はない)
∥モニターカメラ a monitoring camera / モニタースピーカー a monitor speaker / モニターテレビ a monitor screen / 消費者モニター a consumer tester

もぬけのから もぬけの殻 彼がドアをあけるとその部屋はすでにもぬけの殻だった He opened the door and found the room was already *empty*.

もの¹ 物
❶【物体・物品】thing C,《口語的》stuff U; (何か) something (❖否定文・疑問文では通例 anything); (何も…ない) nothing; (何でも) everything

語法
something, anything, everything, nothing を修飾する語はこれらの後ろに置く / 背中に何か白い物がついてるよ You've got *something white* on your back. / 書く物が何もない I don't have *anything to write with*.

私は甘い物が大好きだ I love sweet *things*.
日本は物が高い *Things* are expensive in Japan.
彼女はあまり物に執着しない She doesn't get obsessed with *things*.
彼は油っこい物を控えている He tries to avoid *anything greasy*.
姉は欲しい物はすべて手に入れる My sister gets *everything* [*whatever*] *she wants*.
突然私たちの目の前にコンクリートの塊(かたまり)のよう

もの

な物が落ちてきた Suddenly *something like a block of concrete fell down in front of us.*

◆彼は最近頭に白い物が目立ち始めた *The white in his hair has become noticeable recently.*／ここにあるイヤリングは少し大きすぎるので, もう少し小ぶりの物はありませんか *These earrings here are a bit too big. Do you have any smaller ones?*（❖不定称の物の代名詞は one を用いる）

🔊「ああ, おなかすいた. 何か食べる物ない」「バナナならあるよ」 "*I'm starving. Is there anything to eat?*" "*I've got some bananas.*"

🔊「ちょっと休んで冷たい物でも飲みませんか」「いですね. じゃ, ここに入りましょう」 "*Why don't we stop and have something cold?*" "*Sounds good. Shall we go in here then?*"

❷【所有物】*one's things, one's belongings,*《口語的》*one's stuff*

身の回りの物を整頓(だん)しなさい *Put your things in order.*
自分の物は自分で管理すること *Take care of your own belongings.*
私の物を勝手に使わないでよ *Don't use my stuff without asking me!*

◆ここにある本はすべて恭子の物です *All the books here belong to Kyoko.*／妹は他人の持っている物を欲しがる *My sister wants to have whatever other people have.*／彼は私の物よ *He is mine.*

❸【品質】
このコートはものがいいから何年も着られる *This coat is of such good quality that you can wear it for many years.*
これは安いけどものは確かだ *This is not expensive, but it's of excellent quality.*
彼のギターはそこいらのギターとはものが違う *His guitar is not an ordinary one.*／*His guitar is in a different class.*

❹【不特定の物事】
ものには限度がある *There's a limit to everything.*
彼女は僕らとものの考え方が全然違う *Her way of thinking is totally different from ours.*
彼はものに動じない（→簡単には動揺しない）人だ *He doesn't get upset easily.*
この新人は粗削りだがいいものをもっている（→素質がある） *This newcomer has got talent, even though it hasn't been fully developed yet.*
彼女は特に美人ではないがどこか人を引きつけるものがある *She is not especially beautiful, but there's something attractive about her.*

❺【言葉】word ⓒ
◆彼はものの言い方を知らない *He doesn't know how to put things.*／その国では最近になるまで自由にものが言えなかった *In that country there had been no freedom of speech until recently.*

🔊「先月の電話代, 5 万円超えちゃった」「5 万？

あきれてものが言えないよ」 "*The last month's telephone bill was over 50,000 yen.*" "*Fifty thousand? I'm dumbfounded.*"

❻【道理】sense ⓤ
◆彼はものの分かった[分からない]人だ *He is a sensible [an unreasonable] man.*

❼【その他】
【ものともしない】彼はけがをものともせず（→けがにもかかわらず）試合に出場した *He played in the game in spite of his injury.*

【ものにする】（習得する）learn* ⓗ；（習熟する）master ⓗ；（得る）get* ⓗ∥彼女は 2 年間のアメリカ生活で英語をものにした *She mastered English during the two years in America.*／あいつ, どうやってあんな美人をものにしたんだろう *I wonder how he could get such a beautiful woman.*

【ものになる】彼は野球選手としてはものにならなかった（→成功しなかった） *He didn't succeed as a baseball player.*

【ものの数】その程度の損失は彼にとってはものの数ではない *That amount of loss is nothing to him.*

【もののはずみ】私はもののはずみで（→なぜだか分からないが）その仕事を引き受けてしまった *I don't know why but I undertook that job.*

【もののみごとに】彼の矢はもののみごとに的(まと)に命中した *His arrow successfully hit the center of the target.*

【ものは考えよう】ものは考えようだ *It all depends on how you look at it.*

【ものは試し】ものは試しで（→どうなるのか）やってみよう *Let's give it a try and see what will happen.*

【ものを言う】金がものを言う *Money talks.*／プロスポーツは実力がものを言う世界だ *Your ability is what counts in professional sports.*／*You can depend only on your ability in professional sports.*

【ものを言わせる】その会社は金にものを言わせて有能な人材をライバル会社から引き抜いた *The company lured talented people from its rival with the power of money.*

もの² 者

私は田中という者です *I'm Tanaka.*
物理の知識では彼にかなう者はいない *No one equals him in knowledge of physics.*
マラソンに参加したい者は金曜日までに申込書を提出すること *Anybody who wants to take part in the marathon, hand in the application by Friday.*
家の者に取りに行かせます *I'll send one of my family members there to take it.*
彼は年下の者の面倒をよく見る *He looks after ⌈his juniors [younger people] well.*
許可証のない者入場お断り *No admittance without a pass.*
彼は嫌われ者だ *He is disliked by everybody.*
その試験に合格した者もいれば不合格の者もいた *Some people passed the exam, while others didn't.*

🔊（ノックなどを聞いて）「どなたですか」「隣の者で

す」"Who is it [there]?" "It's *your neighbor*."

-もの

語法
「-もの」に当たる部分が英語としてはっきりと表現されない場合も多い。日本語の意味を考えて、そのニュアンスが英語の文章全体から伝わるようにすればよい。

❶[回想・希望・感動]
昔は子供たちがこの公園で遊び回っていたものだ Children *used to* play around in this park.
あのころは彼女とよくこの喫茶店に来たものだ In those days I *would often* come to this coffee shop with her.
彼女とデートしてみたいものだ I'*d really like to* go on a date with her.
彼もりっぱになったものだ *What* a great man he has grown into!

❷[傾向]
だれだって失敗はするものさ Everyone fails *sometimes*.
中高年の再就職には依然厳しいものがある *It's still very difficult* for middle-aged and elderly people to find new jobs.
人生はそんなものさ *That's life*.

❸[断定]
親の言うことは聞くものだ You *should* obey your parents.

❹[理由]
全部食べちゃった. すごくおなかすいてたんだもの I ate it all *because* I was so hungry.
遅れてすみません. 雪でダイヤが乱れていたもので I'm sorry for being late. The train schedule was disrupted *because* of the snow.

ものいい 物言い, 失礼な[ストレートな]物言い *a rude [frank] way of speaking* / (相撲で)その一番は物言いがついて取り直しとなった *The referee's decision* in the match *was contested*, so the wrestlers had a rematch.

ものいり 物入り この時期は何かと物入りだ We have a lot of *expenses* for this and that at this time of the year.

ものいれ 物入れ (容器) container ◯, case ◯; (納戸) storeroom ◯

ものうい 物憂い, (人が) listless; (人・日などが) lazy, languid; (憂鬱(うつ)な) melancholy ∥物憂い昼下がり *a lazy [languid] early afternoon* / 彼女は物憂げな目つきで彼を見た She looked at him with *listless* eyes.
◆物憂げに話す talk *languidly*

ものうり 物売り (屋台などの人) vendor ◯, (行商人) 《米》peddler ◯, 《英》pedlar ◯; (訪問販売員) door-to-door salesperson ◯

ものおき 物置 (建物の中の) storeroom ◯, 《主に米》closet ◯, 《主に英》lumber room ◯; (物置小屋) shed ◯; (納屋) barn ◯

ものおじ 物怖じ 彼女はひとりで舞台に立つことでも全く物おじしない She *isn't timid [shy, bashful]* at all even when she has to stand alone on the stage.

ものおしみ 物惜しみ 彼は物惜しみしない(→気前のよい)人だ He is a *generous* person. / 物惜しみして, どんなものでも捨てようとしない My mother's *a pack rat* and never throws anything away. (❖pack rat は口語的な表現で「何でもため込む人」の意味)

ものおと 物音 sound ◯◯; (不快な) noise ◯◯ ∥物音ひとつしなかった Not *a sound* was heard.

ものおぼえ 物覚え 物覚えが遅い[速い] *learn slowly [quickly, fast]* / 物覚え(→記憶力)がよい[悪い] have *a good [bad] memory* / 祖父は物覚えが悪くなってきたと言っていた My grandfather said that 「*his memory* had been failing. [(→忘れっぽくなった) he had become forgetful].

ものおもい 物思い 彼は窓の外を眺めて物思いにふけっていた He *was deep [lost] in thought* looking out the window.

-ものか あんな所, 二度と行くものか I will *never* go there again! / そんなたいじなことをだれがおまえなんかに頼るものか *No one would* ask you to do such an important thing.

ものかげ¹ 物陰 僕の猫は知らない人が近づくといつも物陰に隠れる My cat always *hides* when a stranger is around. / 突然物陰から男の人が飛び出してきたのでびっくりした I was surprised because a man suddenly appeared from *behind something*.

ものかげ² 物影 (姿) form ◯◯; (人影) figure ◯ ∥木々の間で物影が動くのが見えた I saw *a form* move among the trees.

ものがたり 物語 story ◯, tale ◯; (寓話(ぐうわ)) fable ◯; (空想・伝奇・恋愛物語) romance ◯ ∥長い[短い]物語 *a long [short] story* / 『平家物語』*The Tale of Heike* / 『イソップ物語』*Aesop's Fables* / 『アーサー王物語』*The romances of King Arthur* / 桃太郎の物語 *the story [tale] of Momotaro* / 子供のころはよく母が物語を聞かせてくれた My mother used to tell me *stories* when I was a child.
∥物語作家 a storyteller / 恋愛物語 a love story / 冒険物語 an adventure story, a story of adventure

ものがたる 物語る (語る) tell* ◯◯; (示す) show* ◯◯; (表情などが示す) say* ◯◯ ∥町の無残な姿が戦争の激しさを物語っている *The terrible condition of the town* tells *much about the violence of war*. / 言葉にはならなくとも父の目がすべてを物語っていた Father couldn't speak but the expression in his eyes *said everything*.
◆その証拠は彼の無実を物語っている The evidence *proves* that he is innocent.

ものがなしい 物悲しい sad, plaintive ∥そのピアノはどこことなく物悲しい音色がする The tone of the piano sounds somehow *sad [plaintive]*.

ものぐさ (ものぐさな人) lazy [idle] person ◯, 《口語的》lazybones ◯ (複~) ――ものぐさな lazy, idle

モノクロ(-ム) ――モノクロ(-ム)の monochrome, black-and-white ∥モノクロ映画 a *monochrome* [*black-and-white*] movie

ものごい 物乞い (行為) begging [U],《米口語的》panhandling [U]; (人) beggar [C],《米口語的》panhandler [C] ―物ごいする beg [他][自]; (路上で)《米口語的》panhandle [自][他] ∥その子供は通行人に物ごいしていた The kid *was begging from* passersby.

ものごころ 物心 物心ついて以来(→記憶しているころから)ずっとピアノを弾いている I've been playing the piano *ever since I can remember.* / 物心がついたころにはすでに東京から沖縄に越していました Our family had moved from Tokyo to Okinawa before I *reached the age of reason.* (❖the age of reason で「道理の分かる年ごろ」の意味)

ものごし 物腰 manner [U]《また a ～》,《文語》bearing [U]《また a ～》 ∥穏やかな[上品な, 落ち着いた]物腰 *a* gentle [fine, calm] *manner* / 彼は物腰が柔らかい He has a very mild *manner.*/ He is mild-*mannered.*

ものごと 物事 things; (すべて) everything ∥彼は物事を深く考えるたちではない He's not inclined to think deeply about *things.* / 物事にはすべて初めと終わりがある There is a beginning and an end to *everything.*

◆彼は物事の道理が分かっていない He doesn't know *what's what.* / おまえはもう物事の善悪の分かる年ごろだ You are big enough to know *right* from *wrong.*

ものさし 物差し (定規) ruler [C]; (判断の尺度・基準) gauge [C], yardstick [C] ∥物差しでこのひもの長さを測ろう Let's measure this string with *a ruler.* / 株価は経済の活況を計る物差しである Stock prices are *a gauge* of economic activity.

◆自分の物差しだけで物事を判断しては危険だ It's dangerous to measure things with your own *reckoning.*

ものさびしい 物寂しい lonely ⇒ さびしい

ものしずか 物静か ―物静かな quiet; (穏やかな) gentle; (落ち着いた) calm ―物静かに quietly; gently; calmly ∥物静かな女性 a *quiet* woman

ものしり 物知り 姉は物知りだ My sister is「*a knowledgeable person* [*knowledgeable*]. / (→何でも知っている) My sister *knows everything.* / 彼はいつも物知り顔で話す He always talks *knowingly.* / 文化人とやらが物知り顔で(→何でも知っているかのように)テレビでコメントしていた A so-called "cultured person" made comments on a TV program *as if he knew everything.*

ものずき 物好き ―物好きな (変な) strange,《口語的》crazy,《口語的》weird; (好奇心の強い) curious ∥あんな危険な場所にひとりで行ったの? あなたって物好きね Did you go to that dangerous place by yourself? You're really *crazy.*

ものすごい 物凄い (はなはだしい)《口語的》terrible,《口語的》awful (❖名詞の前で用いる); (恐ろしい) horrible; (荒々しい) fierce ―ものすごく《口語的》terribly,《口語的》terrifically,《口語的》awfully; (大いに) extremely

昨夜はものすごい雷だった We had *terrible* [*awful*] thunder last night.

事故現場はものすごい光景だった The scene of the accident was *terrible* [*horrible*].

彼は怒ってものすごい形相をしていた His face was *fierce* with anger. / He had a face *like thunder.*

そのテレビ番組はものすごく人気がある The TV program is *awfully* [*extremely*] popular.

ものたりない 物足りない (人が満足していない) be not satisfied with …; (物・事が満足のいくものでない) be not satisfactory; (十分でない) be not enough; (何かを欠いている) lack something ∥この食事は僕には物足りない I'*m not satisfied with* this meal. / This meal *is not satisfactory to* me. / あの映画はどこか物足りない感じがした I felt the movie *was lacking something.*

-ものなら コンクールで賞が取れるものなら取ってみろ *If* you think you can win a prize at the contest, show me you can do it. / 許されるものならそうしてみたい I'd do it *if* it was permitted. / 無断外泊なんかしようものなら二度と家に入れてもらえなくなる *If* I should stay out all night without my parents' permission, I would never be admitted into the house.

ものの 物の こんな仕事はものの1分で片づけてやるさ(→たった1分で十分だ) *Only* [*Just*] one minute is enough for me to finish this task. / ものの3分としないうちに彼はふろから上がってきた He finished taking a bath *in less than* three minutes.

-ものの though, although (❖although は though よりやや形式ばった語) ∥パーティーに参加するとは言ったものの, 彼に場所を聞くのを忘れていた *Though* I said I would take part in the party, I've found I forgot to ask him the place.

もののけ 物の怪 evil spirit [C]

もののみごとに 物の見事に 彼女はもののみごとにそれを成しとげた She carried that off *splendidly.* / そのボクサーはもののみごとに相手をノックアウトした The boxer knocked the opponent out *cleanly* [*successfully*].

ものほし 物干し (洗濯物を干す設備) equipment for drying the wash; (物干し綱) clothesline [C], washing line [C] (❖英米ではさおより綱が一般的) ∥彼女は洗濯物を物干しにかけた She hung out the washing on *the clothesline.*

∥物干しざお a bar for drying the wash, a clothes-drying bar / 物干し台(物干しざおをかけるもの) a set of poles for supporting clothes-drying bars / 物干し場 a balcony for drying the wash

ものほしそうな 物欲しそうな 妹はアイスを食べる私をもの欲しそうな顔で見ていた My sister looked at me「*with a wistful look* [*wistfully*] when I was eating ice cream.

も

ものまね 物真似 mimicry ⓤ, imitation (有名人の) impression ⓒ ——物まねする mimic ⑯, imitate ⑯ ∥謙一はよくタレントの物まねをする Kenichi often *mimics* [*imitates*] TV entertainers. / 良男は物まねがうまい Yoshio is good at *mimicry*. / Yoshio is a good *mimic*. / 彼はみごとに有名男優の物まねをした He *did a good imitation* [*impression*] *of* the famous actor.
∥物まね芸人 a mimic, an impressionist

ものみ 物見 事故現場周辺は物見高い人々であふれかえっていた There was a crowd of *curious* people around the scene of the accident. / そこには多くの人が物見遊山(ゆさん)に訪れた A lot of people visited the place for *sightseeing*.
∥物見やぐら a watchtower

ものめずらしい 物珍しい 物珍しい光景 an *unusual* [*a strange*] scene / 子供たちは物珍しそうにそのカメを見た The children looked at the turtle「*quite curiously* [*with curious eyes*].

ものもち 物持ち 姉は物持ちがいい My sister *takes good care of her things so that they last long*.

ものものしい 物々しい 通りには警官が立ち並び物々しい雰囲気だった There was a line of policemen on the street and the atmosphere was *heavy*. / 大統領を護衛が物々しく取り囲んでいた The president was *heavily surrounded by guards*.

ものもらい 物貰い (目にできる) sty(e) [stái] ⓒ; (物ごい) beggar ⓒ,《米口語的》panhandler ⓒ ∥右目に物もらいができた I had a *sty(e)* in my right eye.

ものやわらか 物柔らか ——物柔らかな gentle, mild; (優しい) soft ——物柔らかに gently, mildly; softly ∥私は彼の物柔らかな話し方が好きです I like his *gentle* way of speaking.

モノラル ——モノラルの monaural, monophonic, mono ∥モノラル放送 monaural [monophonic, mono] broadcasting / モノラル録音 monaural [monophonic, mono] recording

モノレール (交通機関) monorail ⓒ; (車両) monorail car ⓒ; (列車) monorail train ⓒ ∥モノレールで by *monorail*(❖交通手段を表す場合, by の後の名詞は無冠詞)

モノローグ monologue ⓒ

ものわかり 物分かり 彼のお父さんは物分かりがよくてうらやましい I envy him because of his *understanding* father. / あいつは物分かりがいい(→素早く要点を理解する) He *catches on quickly*. / (→分別がある) He *is sensible*. / うちの弟は物分かりが悪い My brother *is slow to understand*.

ものわかれ 物別れ 2社間の話し合いは物別れに終わった The talks between the two companies *broke down*. / The two companies *failed to reach an agreement* in the talks.

ものわすれ 物忘れ 祖母はこのごろ物忘れが激しい My grandmother is very *forgetful* these days.

ものわらい 物笑い 人を物笑い(の種)にする *make a fool of* a person; *laugh at* a person / そんなことをすれば学校中の物笑い(の種)になってしまう I will be「*laughed at by* [*the laughingstock of*] the whole school if I do a thing like that.

モバイル ——モバイルの mobile [móubəl]
∥モバイルコンピュータ a mobile computer / モバイルコンピューティング mobile computing / モバイル通信 mobile communications

もはや (今では) now;(もはや…ない) no longer, not ... any longer; (すでに) already ∥もはや手遅れだ It's too late *now*. / その規則はもはや有効ではない The rule「*no longer* stands [*doesn't stand any longer*].

もはん 模範 (role) model ⓒ, (good) example ⓒ, pattern ⓒ《通例単数形》——模範的な model (❖名詞の前で用いる) ∥模範的な生徒 a *model* student / 彼は後に続くすべての大統領にとっての模範となった He served as *a role model* for every president after him. / 私たちは下級生に模範を示すべきだ We should set a「*good example* [*pattern*] for the youngsters.
∥模範演技 a demonstration / 模範解答 a model answer

モビール 《美術》mobile [móubəl] ⓒ

もふく 喪服 mourning ⓤ, mourning clothes, black ⓤ ∥母は喪服姿だった My mother *wore mourning* [*black*].

モヘア mohair ⓤ ⓒ ∥モヘアのセーター a *mohair* sweater

もほう 模倣 imitation ⓤ ⓒ ——模倣する imitate ⑯, copy ⑯ ∥他人の模倣ばかりではいけない You shouldn't always *imitate* what others do. / この彫刻は彼の作品の模倣だ(→模倣して作られた) This sculpture was made *in imitation of* his. / (→模造品だ) This sculpture is *an imitation* [*a copy*] *of* his.

もまれる 揉まれる 船は波にもまれて激しく揺れた The boat *was tossed* wildly by the waves. / 人波にもまれているうちに友達とはぐれてしまった I lost sight of my friends while *being jostled* in the crowd. / 彼は世間の荒波にもまれて鍛えられた He's been strengthened by *having experienced* [*gone through*] the hardships of life.

もみ¹ 籾 (もみ米) paddy ⓤ, rice in the husk, rough rice ⓤ;(もみがら) husk ⓒ, chaff ⓤ(❖後者は脱穀して取られた殻)

もみ² 樅【植物】fir (tree) ⓒ

もみあう 揉み合う (押し合う) jostle ⑯ ⑳;(取っ組み合う) struggle ⑳ ∥議員たちは議長を取り囲んでもみ合った Members of the assembly *jostled against each other* around the chairperson.

もみあげ 揉み上げ sideburns, 《英》sideboards

もみくちゃ 揉みくちゃ 彼は満員電車でもみくちゃにされた He *was jostled* [*pushed and*

もみけす 揉み消す (たばこの火を) stub out; (隠す) cover [hush] up, suppress 働 ∥たばこをもみ消す *stub out* a cigarette / 不祥事をもみ消す *cover* [*hush*] *up* a scandal

もみじ 紅葉 (カエデ) maple 回; (紅葉(読み)) autumn leaves [colors], fall foliage回 ∥家族で山へ紅葉狩りに(→紅葉を楽しみに)行った Our family went to the mountains to *enjoy the autumn leaves* [*colors*].

短歌 奥山に紅葉ふみわけ鳴く鹿の声きく時ぞ秋は悲しき (猿丸大夫)
Deep in the mountains,
the rustle of fallen leaves,
the cry of a stag.
I hear it and then I know:
Autumn is the sad season.

もみで 揉み手 もみ手をする *rub one's hands* (❖英米ではわびたり頼み事をするときのしぐさではない) / 彼は私に１万円貸してくれとらもみ手をして(→下手(したて)に出て)頼んできた He came asking me to lend him 10,000 yen *with a humble attitude*.

もみほぐす 揉みほぐす 肩のこりをもみほぐす *massage a person's* shoulders *to relieve stiffness*

もむ 揉む ❶ (体・物などを) (マッサージする) massage 働; (食べ物を) rub 働 ∥私は毎日祖父の肩をもんであげます I *massage* my grandfather's shoulders every day. / 肉をしょうゆでもんで下味をつけておいた I *rubbed* pieces of meat with soy sauce as preparation.
❷ (鍛える) 一丁もんでやる。かかってこい I'll *give* you a workout. Come on!
❸ (気を) つまらないことで気をもむな *Don't worry* over trifles. / 電車に乗り遅れたろうようと気をもんだ I *was worried* that I should miss the train.

もめごと 揉め事 trouble 回(また複数形 〜s) ∥家庭内のもめごと domestic *troubles* / 彼はもめごとを起こしてばかりいる He is always making [causing] *trouble*. / 連中ともめごとになるのは避けたい I want to avoid having [getting into] *trouble* with them.

もめる 揉める ❶ [争う] have* trouble(s); (口論する) quarrel 働, (論争する) dispute 働, argue 働 ∥その夫婦は子供の教育のことでもめている They *are quarrelling with each other* about their children's education.
◆その会議は大もめにもめた They *had a big argument* at the meeting.
❷ [落ち着かない] 試験に通っているかどうか気がもめる I *feel uneasy about* whether I have passed the exam or not.

もめん 木綿 cotton 回; (布) cotton cloth 回 ∥木綿100パーセントのシャツ an all-*cotton* [a 100 percent *cotton*] shirt
∥木綿糸 cotton (thread) / 木綿豆腐 tofu which has cotton cloth impressions on its surface

もも¹ 腿・股 thigh [θái] 回 ∥もも肉 (鶏などの) dark meat; (豚の) a ham; (牛の) a round

もも² 桃 (実) peach 回; (木) peach (tree) 回 ∥桃の缶詰 canned *peaches* / 桃の花 peach blossoms
◆桃色の帽子 a *pink* cap / 桃の節句 the Dolls' [Girls'] Festival

もや 靄 haze 回回, mist 回回 (❖haze より濃い) ∥その湖はもやに包まれていた The lake was covered in a veil of *haze* [*mist*]. / 東京上空にはきょうもやがかかっている There is a haze hanging over Tokyo today. / The sky above Tokyo *is hazy* today.

もやし bean sprouts
∥もやしっ子 a scrawny [weedy] child

もやす 燃やす burn* ∥新聞紙を燃やす *burn* a newspaper
◆彼はその商品の宣伝に情熱を燃やしている He 「*is enthusiastic about* [*devotes all of his energies into*] advertising the product.

もやもや きょうは何だか気分がもやもやする I *don't feel comfortable* [*well*] somehow today. / 彼女に相談して気持ちのもやもやが晴れた I could get rid of *worries* by talking to her.

もよう 模様
❶ [柄・図案] design 回, pattern 回; (動物・乗り物などの) marking 回 (通例複数形 〜s)
縞(しま)模様 a striped pattern; stripes / 水玉模様 a polka-dot pattern; polka dots / ペイズリー模様 a paisley pattern; paisley / 幾何学模様 a geometric pattern / 花柄模様のティーカップ a teacup with 「a flower *design* [a *design* of flowers]
このガの羽には目玉のような模様がある This moth has eye-like *markings* on its wings.
❷ [様子・状態] look 回 (通例単数形); (状況) situation 回
この空模様ではあしたは雨だろう From *the looks of the sky*, it will rain tomorrow.
◆あすの空模様(→見込み) *the weather outlook* for tomorrow / コンサートは中止になる模様だ It 「*seems that* [*looks like*] the concert will be canceled. / アナウンサーがレースの模様を伝えている The announcer is reporting *how* the race *is going*.
⇒あれもよう

もようがえ 模様替え (配置替え) rearrangement 回回; (改装) redecoration 回回 ——模様替えする rearrange 働; redecorate 働 ∥妹は部屋の模様替えをした My sister *decorated* [*rearranged*] her room.

もよおし 催し (行事) event 回; (余興) entertainment 回; (祭典) ceremony 回 ∥当ホールの今月の催し物 this hall's *events* for this month / 王の即位10周年を祝う催しが開かれた An event [A ceremony] was held to celebrate the king's 10th anniversary.

もよおす 催す ❶ [開催する・行う] hold* 働, give* 働, have* 働 ∥彼らは退職する教授のために会を催した They *held* [*gave*, *had*] a party for a professor who was retiring. / その展示会は大阪で催される The exhibition *will be held* [*given*] in Osaka.

❷【気分・感じなどを】feel* 🔁 🔄 //眠気をもよおす *feel* [*become*] sleepy / 腐った食べ物のにおいに吐き気をもよおした I *felt* sick at the smell of the rotten food. / 彼は尿意をもよおしてトイレに駆け込んだ He *felt* a need to urinate and dashed into the bathroom.

もより 最寄り ──最寄りの the nearest // 最寄り駅 *the nearest* station / 負傷した男性は救急車で最寄りの病院へ運ばれた The injured man was taken by ambulance to *the nearest* hospital.

もらいて 貰い手 だれか子猫のもらい手になってくれる人はいないだろうか Isn't there anybody who will *take* our kittens?

もらいなき 貰い泣き 彼が涙を浮かべて話すのを見て思わずもらい泣きしてしまった Seeing him weep as he spoke, I involuntarily *wept along with him*.

もらいもの 貰い物 present 🔁, gift 🔁 《❖*present* よりも儀礼的な感じを伴う》//お隣からのもらい物 *a present* from the next-door neighbor

もらう 貰う

❶【受け取る】receive 🔄, have* 🔄; (手に入れる) get* 🔄; (与えられる) be given

高い給料をもらう *get* [*draw*] a high salary / コンテストで1等賞をもらう *get* [*win*, *take*] the first prize in a contest

オーストラリアの友達から手紙をもらった I *received* [*got*] a letter from a friend in Australia.

私は彼女から誕生日にプレゼントをもらった I *got* a present from her for my birthday.

やっとのことで犬を飼う許しをもらった I barely *got* [*had*] permission to keep a dog.

水を1杯もらえますか Can I *have* a glass of water?

けさ則夫から電話をもらった I *had* a phone call from Norio this morning.

◆一郎は彼女を嫁にもらった(→結婚した) Ichiro *got married to* her. / この勝負はもらった This game is *mine*. / 弟が学校でひどいかぜをもらってきた My brother *caught* a bad cold at school. / あなたから便りをもらえてとても光栄です It is a great joy to *hear from* you. / (店で)このTシャツもらいます I'll *take* this T-shirt.

❷「このカタログをもらってもいいですか」「ええ,どうぞ」"Can I *have* this catalogue?" "Sure you can."

❷【…してもらう】

【語法】
「(人)に…してもらう」は《have＋人＋*do*》あるいは《get＋人＋to *do*》で表し,「(物)を…してもらう」は《have＋物＋*done*》あるいは《get＋物＋*done*》で表す.いずれも get を用いるほうが口語的.「人に…してもらいたい」という場合は《want＋人＋to *do*》,《would like＋人＋to *do*》で表す.後者のほうが丁寧な言い方.また「…してもらえませんか」という場合は Can you …?あるいは Could [Would] you…?を用いる.後者のほうが丁寧な言い方.

姉に宿題を手伝ってもらった I *had* my sister help me with my homework. / I *got* my sister *to* help me with my homework.

先週髪を切ってもらった I *had* my hair cut last week. / I *had* a haircut last week. (❖I cut my hair とすると「自分で髪を切った」という意味になる)

カメラを直してもらった I *had* [*got*] my camera repaired.

君に仕事を手伝ってもらいたい I *want* you *to* help me *with* my job.

コショウを取ってもらえますか Can [Could] you give [pass, get] me the pepper?

◆先生にお昼をおごってもらった My teacher *treated* me to lunch. / 熱があったので医者に行って診(み)てもらった I had a fever, so I went to *see* [*consult*] a doctor. / あなたには本当のことを話してもらわなければならない I *need* you *to* tell me the truth.

もらす 漏らす ❶【水などを】leak 🔄

◆その子はおしっこをもらした The child *wet himself* [*his pants*].

❷【秘密などを】(意図的に) leak 🔄; (うっかり) let* out, 《口語的》let on about …; (言う) tell* 🔄 // 健治がうっかり秘密をもらしてしまった Kenji *has let* the secret *out*.

◆彼はクラブをやめたいともらした He *confided* that he wanted to quit the club. / 彼はそのことで不満をもらした He *complained* about the matter.

❸【逃す】miss 🔄; (…しそこなう) fail to *do* // 集合時間を聞きもらしてしまった I *missed* [*didn't catch*] the time we should be there.

◆彼は原稿を一字一句もらさずチェックした He checked *every single word* of the manuscript.

モラトリアム (支払猶予(ゆうよ)・猶予期間) moratorium 🔁 //モラトリアム人間 an immature (young) adult

モラリスト (道徳家) moralist 🔁

モラル morals, morality 🔁 //モラルのない人 a person with no *morals* [*sense of morality*] / あの男性はモラルを欠いている That man lacks *morals* [*morality*]. / インターネット上のやり取りでは利用者のモラルが問われる *Morals* [*Morality*] must be required when communicating on the Internet. / そんなことをするのは公共のモラルに反する It's against public *morals* [*morality*] to do such a thing.

もり¹ 森 《しばしば複数形 the ～s》; forest 🔁 🔁; 《文語》grove 🔁

> wood(s): 人の手が入った人里近くの森.
> forest: woods よりも大きく,人の手が入っていない森林.
> grove: woods よりも小さく,通例下生えのない木立ち.

うっそうとした森 *a dense woods*(❖woods は

もり 《米》ではしばしば単数扱い) / 沼は森の奥深くにある The pond is deep in *the forest*. / 私は森の中をさまよった I wandered through *the woods*.

もり² 盛り (食べ物のひと盛り) serving ⓒ, helping ⓒ, portion ⓒ ‖あのそば屋は盛りが大きい The soba shop gives you *a good portion*. / 盛り皿 a dish

もり³ 銛 spear ⓒ; (捕鯨用の) harpoon ⓒ
◆魚をもりで突く *spear* a fish

もりあがり 盛り上がり 市民運動の盛り上がり *the groundswell* of a citizen's movement / 祭りは大変な盛り上がりを見せた (→成功だった) The festival *was really successful*. / その曲は盛り上がりに欠ける The song *lacks a climax*.

もりあがる 盛り上がる
❶【物が】(上がる) rise*ⓘ; (ふくらむ) swell*ⓘ
あそこの地面が盛り上がっている所に宝が埋まっているにちがいない The treasure must have been buried over there where the ground *rises*.
◆彼が腕を曲げると筋肉が盛り上がった The muscle *bulged* when he bent his arm.
❷【会・運動などが】
コンサートはだんだん盛り上がってきた The concert *is livening* [*picking*] *up*.
ごみ処理場建設に対する反対運動が盛り上がっている People are *enthusiastic about* the movement opposing the building of a refuse incineration plant.

もりあげる 盛り上げる (活気を与える) liven up, 《口語的》pep up ‖彼は手品を披露して会を盛り上げた He *livened* [*pepped*] *up* the party by performing magic.
◆みんなで協力して文化祭を大いに盛り上げよう Let's pull together and *make* our school festival *a big success*.

もりあわせ 盛り合わせ 旬(½*)の野菜の盛り合わせ *a smorgasbord* [*an assortment*] of vegetables in season

もりかえす 盛り返す (勢い・市場などが) rally ⓘ; (回復する) recover ⓘ; (力を取り戻す) regain *one's* strength [power] ‖レースの終盤で彼は勢いを盛り返した He *rallied* toward the end of the race. / そのことで一時的に景気は盛り返した(→立ち直らせた) It made the economy *rally* [*recover*] for a short time.

もりこむ 盛り込む (含める) include ⓘ; (組み入れる) 《公式的》incorporate ⓘ; (書き込む) write* ... into ~ ‖彼らはその雑誌に様々な記事を盛り込んだ They *included* [*incorporated*] various articles *in* the magazine. / 新たな協定に新たな条項が盛り込まれた A new clause *was written into* the agreement.

もりだくさん 盛り沢山 きょうのイベントは楽しい企画が盛りだくさんだった Today's event *was* [*full of various* [*with a variety of*]] entertainments.

もりたてる 守り立てる support ⓘ, give* [offer] support, back ⓘ ‖彼らは一丸となってその候補[活動]をもり立てた They all sup-ported the candidate [activities].

もりつける 盛り付ける 野菜を皿に盛りつける *dish up* vegetables / 大皿に刺身が美しく盛りつけてあった Sashimi was beautifully *arranged* on a platter.

もりもり もりもり食べて大きくなれ Eat *a lot* and grow big. / きょうはもりもり働くぞ I'll work *hard* today. / 僕は元気もりもりだ I'm *full of energy*. / 彼は筋肉もりもりだ He has *a very muscular body*.

もる¹ 盛る (積み上げる) heap ⓘ, pile ⓘ; (いっぱいにする) fill ⓘ; (料理を皿に) dish up; (毒を) poison ⓘ ‖そこに土を盛ってマウンドにした We made a mound *by heaping* [*piling*] *up* some earth there. / 茶わんにごはんを盛った I *filled* my bowl *with* rice. / その男は王に毒を盛った The man *poisoned* the king.

もる² 漏る leak ⓘ ‖この容器は(水が)もるから気をつけて Be careful because this container *leaks*.

モルタル (壁などに塗る) stucco ⓤ; (れんがなどを接合する) mortar ⓤ
◆それは木造モルタル塗りの家だった It was a *stuccoed* wooden house.

モルト (麦芽) malt ⓤ
‖モルトウイスキー (a) malt whisky

モルヒネ morphine [mɔ́ːrfiːn] ⓤ
‖モルヒネ中毒 morphine addiction / モルヒネ中毒患者 a morphine addict

モルモット ⚠ guinea [gíni] pig ⓒ (❖「実験台」という意味で比喩的にも用いる。英語のmarmotは「マーモット」という別の動物) ‖彼らは新薬開発のためのモルモットにされた They were used as *guinea pigs* for development of a new medicine.

モルモンきょう モルモン教 Mormismⓤ

もれ 漏れ (水・ガスなどの) leak ⓒ, leakage ⓤⓒ; (脱落) omission ⓒ ‖放射能[水]もれ *a radiation* [*water*] *leak* / 彼の申込書にはたくさんの記入もれがあった There are a lot of *omissions* on his application.
‖ガスもれ感知器 a gas leakage detector

もれきく 漏れ聞く (人づてに聞く) know* secondhand [by hearsay], hear* ⓘ; (偶然耳にする) overhear* ⓘ ‖もれ聞くところによると彼は野球部をやめるそうだ I *know secondhand* [*hear*] *that* he will quit the baseball club.

もれなく 漏れなく 当店でお買い上げのお客様にはもれなく割引券を差し上げます Everyone who buys at our store, *without any exception*, will receive a coupon.

もれる 漏れる
❶【液体などが】leak ⓘ, escape ⓘ
タイヤから空気がもれている Air *is leaking* out of the tire.
ドアの下から明かりがもれていた Light *was escaping* from under the door.
このバケツ,もれるから気をつけて Be careful. This bucket *leaks*.
◆おしっこがもれそうだ I'm going to wet my pants. / 《口語的》I'm bursting. / I can't keep it in any longer. / その力士が負けると会場から

もろい – もんく

ため息がもれた Spectators *sighed* [*gave sighs*] when the sumo wrestler was defeated.

❷【秘密などが】leak ⊜

彼はその事実がもれるのを何とかして防ごうとした He tried everything he could to keep the fact from *leaking out*.

❸【抜け落ちる】

リストから彼の名前がもれていた His name *was* 「*omitted* from [*left off of*] the list.

彼の俳句は俳句コンテストの選にもれた His haiku *was not chosen* [*accepted*] for the haiku contest.

もろい 脆い (こわれやすい) fragile, frail; (弱い) weak; (折れやすい) brittle

その土器は非常にもろく，触れたら簡単にこわれてしまった The ancient earthen pot was so *fragile* [*frail*] that it broke easily when I touched it.

彼の理論はその点をつかれると案外もろい His theory is *weaker* than you may think when attacked at that point.

骨粗鬆(しょう)症は骨がもろくなる病気だ Osteoporosis is a disease that makes the bones *brittle*.

◆ もろい土壌 *crumbly* soil / 母は情にもろい My mother is *very sentimental* [*easily moved*]. / 彼女は涙もろい She *cries easily*.

もろくも (容易に) (too) easily; (あまりに早く) all too soon ‖そのチームはもろくも初戦で敗退した The team lost「*too easily* [*all too soon*] in the first round.

もろて 諸手 彼の考えにもろ手を挙げて(→無条件に)賛成した I am *absolutely* for his ideas.

もろとも 諸共 (いっしょに) (together) with ... ‖彫像は土台もろとも崩れてしまった The statue collapsed *together with* its base [pedestal]. / 彼は洪水で車もろとも流された He was washed away *with* his car in the flood.

もろに 諸に (まっすぐに) full, straight,《口語的》slap; (真っ向から) squarely; (はっきりと) obviously, clearly; (完全に) fully, completely ‖ボールはもろに彼の顔に当たった The ball hit him *full* [*straight, slap*] on his face. / 彼はその件で周囲からもろに批判を浴びた He's been criticized *squarely* by people around for the matter. / 彼のギター演奏にはクラプトンの影響がもろに出ている His guitar playing *obviously* [*clearly*] shows influences from Clapton.

もろは 諸刃 慣用表現 原子力発電はもろ刃の剣だ Nuclear power generation is *a double-edged sword*.

もろもろ 諸々 ——もろもろの (様々な) various

もん¹ 門 ❶【家などの】gate ◎ (◈両開きの場合は門が1つでも複数形 gates になる) ‖門は閉まっていた The *gate* was closed. / 私たちは門の所でしばらく待った We waited for a while at *the gate*. / 彼は門をあけて私たちを通してくれた He opened *the gate* and let us through.

❷【分類上の】〖生物〗phylum ◎, 〖植物〗division ◎

‖裏門 a back gate / 表門 a front gate / 城門 a castle gate / 正門 the main gate

慣用表現 その大学は競争率20倍の狭き門となった *It was hard to pass the entrance examination* for the university since there were 20 times as many applicants as places. /

彼はその芸人の門をたたいた(→弟子にしてくれるよう頼んだ) He *asked* the entertainer *to let him be* his apprentice.

もん² 紋 ❶【家・団体などの印】crest ◎; (盾形の，盾などが描き込まれた) a coat of arms (複 coats of arms)

❷【模様】design ◎, pattern ◎

‖家紋 a family crest

もんえい 門衛 gatekeeper ◎

もんか 門下 …の門下に入る be admitted into *a person's school*

‖門下生 a pupil, a disciple

もんがいかん 門外漢 layperson ◎ (複 〜s, laypeople) (◆男女の区別なく layman ともいう．特に女性ということを表したい場合には laywoman); (部外者) outsider ◎ ‖クラシックについては私は全くの門外漢です I'm just a *layman* where classical music is concerned.

もんがいふしゅつ 門外不出 これは門外不出のつぼです This vase *is not to be taken out of here*.

もんがまえ 門構え 重厚な門構えの館(やかた) a house *with an impressive gate*

もんきりがた 紋切り型 ——紋切り型の (型にはまった) stereotyped; (使い古された) hackneyed ‖紋切り型の表現 a *stereotyped* [*hackneyed*] expression

もんく 文句

❶【不平】complaint ◎ ©; (ぐち) grumble ©; (非難) criticism ◎ ©; (異議) objection ◎ © ——文句を言う complain ⊜ ⊕; (ぶつぶつと) grumble ⊜; criticize ⊕; object ⊜ ⊕

何か文句があるならはっきり言ってください If you have any *complaints*, go ahead and tell me.

いまさら文句を言っても始まらない It is no use *complaining* now.

彼はウエーターにコーヒーがぬるいと文句を言った He *complained to* the waiter *that* the coffee was not hot.

彼は彼女の話し方に文句をつけてばかりいる He *is always*「*complaining about* [*criticizing*] the way she talks.

すばらしい．この絵には文句のつけようがない(→いかに非難できようか) Wonderful. How could I *criticize* this painting?

彼はそんな所へ行きたくないと文句を言った He *objected that* he didn't want to go to such a place.

◆このアルバムは文句なしに彼の最高傑作だ *Nobody can deny that* this album is the best of all his albums. / This album is *without any doubt* the best of all his albums.

❷【語句】words; (表現) expression ◎; (句) phrase ◎

歌の文句 the words of a song; (→歌詞) the lyrics of a song∥決まり文句 a fixed expression; a set phrase; (→陳腐な)a cliché∥くどき(→人を説得する)文句 persuasive words; (→異性をくどく)flirtatious words∥うたい文句 a catch phrase; a slogan∥名文句 a clever expression∥殺し文句 a telling expression
その広告に書かれた文句はしゃれていておもしろかった The phrases on the advertising bill were witty and humorous.

もんげん 門限 curfew ⓒ∥彼女は門限を守った[破った] She observed [broke] her curfew.∥門限に遅れるとお父さんに怒られてしまう I'd be scolded by my father if I should be late for the curfew.
🅔「祐子ちゃんって門限あるの?」「うん,9時なんだ」 "Yuko, do you have curfew?" "Yes, I have to be back home by nine."

もんこ 門戸 …への門戸を閉ざす close [shut] the door on [to]…∥その会社はやっと女性にも門戸を開いた The company opened the door to woman employees at last.

もんし 門歯 〖解剖〗incisor ⓒ

もんじゅ 文殊(文殊菩薩(ぼさつ)) Manjusri [mándʒuʃriː]
ことわざ 三人寄れば文殊の知恵 ➔ さんにん

もんしょう 紋章 a coat of arms, crest ⓒ∥紋章学 heraldry

もんしろちょう 紋白蝶 cabbage butterfly ⓒ

もんしん 問診 医者はまず私の病歴について質問した The doctor first asked me about my medical history.

モンスーン the monsoon

モンスター monster ⓒ∥これは世界中で1,000万枚以上売れたモンスターアルバムだ This is a monster [《米》megahit] album which sold more than 10 million all over the world.

もんぜん 門前 彼はそのクラブの見学を希望したが門前払いを食わされた He wanted to see the activities of the club but「they shut [slammed] the door in his face [(→追い返された)he was turned away at the door].
ことわざ 門前の小僧習わぬ経を読む Learning by osmosis. (❖ learn by osmosis は「環境によって自然と身につける」の意味)

モンタージュ ∥モンタージュ写真 a montage, 《米》a composite [《英》an identikit] (photograph)

もんだい 問題

❶【質問·問い】question ⓒ, problem ⓒ
今度のテストはどんな問題が出るんですか What questions will be on the next exam?
次の問題に答えなさい Answer the following question.
私はこの問題を解くのにおよそ2時間かかった It took me about two hours to solve the problem.
私たちのだれもその数学の問題を解けなかった None of us could solve the math problem.
◆ 先生が生徒に問題用紙を配り始めた The teacher began distributing the test papers to the students.

❷【解決されるべき事柄】problem ⓒ; question ⓒ; issue ⓒ; subject ⓒ; matter ⓒ

> problem: 解決すべき問題.
> question: 特に長い間懸案となっている政治的な問題.
> issue: 多くの人に影響を与える社会的・政治的問題.
> subject: マスコミなどで広く取り上げられている問題.
> matter: かかわりのある事柄.

彼らはすぐに大きな問題に直面した They soon faced a major problem.
まだ未解決の問題が山積している There are still a pile of unsolved [outstanding] problems.
急激な人口増加は多くの問題を引き起こしている Rapid population growth is creating many problems.
これらの論評は肝心の問題に触れていない These comments don't touch on the central issue.
どちらかといえばそれはささいな問題だ Relatively (speaking), it's a trivial matter.
彼の考え方には問題がある There are some problems with his way of thinking.
依然として問題が1つ残っている There still remains a problem.
問題は彼らをいかにして説得するかだ The question [point] is how we should persuade them.
この都市でも交通量の多さは切実な問題となっている Heavy traffic is an urgent problem in this city, too.
その問題は何度となく論じられてきた The issue has been remarked on many times.
この問題をめぐって専門家の間で意見が分かれている The opinions of the experts are divided on this subject [issue].
彼は社会問題に無関心だ He is indifferent to social problems.
世界的に環境問題が深刻化している Environmental problems are getting worse all over the world.

❸【関係する事柄·関心事】matter ⓒ, question ⓒ
好みの問題 a matter of preference [taste]
それは私の個人的な問題だ That's my personal matter [affair].
それは全く別問題だ That's quite another matter.
それは常識[良心, 程度]の問題だ It's a matter of 「common sense [conscience, degree].
彼女が成功するのは時間の問題だ Her success is just a matter [question] of time.
彼が昇進するなんて全く問題外だ His promotion is completely out of the question.
◆ 彼は中東問題の権威だ He is the authority on Middle East affairs.∥彼女がどこで生まれたかは私にとっては問題ではない It doesn't matter to me where she was born.∥この程度

のミスはほとんど**問題にならない** A mistake like this *is not important*. / 私たちはその問題を日本だけでなくアジア全体の**問題**としてとらえるべきだ We should take up *the problem* not only in Japan but also in Asia as a whole. / その国の人々は概して社会福祉に関する**問題意識が高い**(→強い関心をもっている) In general, the people in the country *have much interest* in social welfare. (❖「問題意識をもつ」などという場合は critical mind (批判的な精神)を用いる)

❹【面倒】trouble [U], problem [C]

土地開発とそれに伴う**諸問題** land development and its attendant *problems*

彼女はやっかいな**問題**に巻き込まれた She got into *trouble* [*a tigh spot*].

その少年たちは事あるごとに**問題を起こした** The boys「*caused trouble* [*made waves*] whenever there was a chance.

法律上は何の**問題**もない There is no *problem* in the eyes of the law.

◆あの車は安すぎるからきっと何か**問題**があるんだ That car is very cheap. There must be *a catch* somewhere. (❖a catch は「隠された問題点」の意味の口語的な表現) / 私たちは彼女の行動を**問題視している** We *are concerned about* her behavior.

💬「彼は何か**問題**を抱えていると思うよ」「かもね」 "I think he has *a problem*." "Could be."

❺【注目を集めている事柄】 **—問題の** in question

そのとき**問題の**男が姿を現した The man *in question* appeared then.

◆この映画は**問題作**として話題を集めた This film was much talked about as *a controversial work*.

‖**問題児** a problem child / **問題集** a workbook / **外交[国内]問題** external [internal] affairs / **時事問題** current topics, topics of the day / **食糧問題** the food problem / **人種問題** the race problem / **引っかけ問題** a trick question

モンタナ Montana (❖米国北西部の州; 《略語》Mont., 〔郵便〕MT)

もんちゃく 悶着 (トラブル) trouble [U] 《また複数形 ～s》; (口論) quarrel [C] ‖グループ内でひと**もんちゃく**ありそうだ There's going to be *trouble* [*a quarrel*] in the group.

もんちゅう 門柱 gatepost [C]

もんつき 紋付き 🗻 a *montsuki*, a kimono with *one's* family crest on it ‖彼は**紋付き**はかま姿で現れた He turned up *in montsuki and hakama*.

もんと 門徒 (門弟) follower [C]; (信者) believer [C]

もんとう 門灯 gate lamp [C]

もんどう 問答 (質問と答え) a question and an answer; (議論) argument [C]; (対話) dialogue [U] [C] **—問答する** exchange questions and answers; argue [他] [自] ‖この本は団体の活動内容を**問答**形式で説明している This book explains the group's activities in「*a question and an answer style* [*a Q&A format*]. / **問答無用**. 今すぐにすべて片づけなさい *There's no use arguing*. Remove everything right now.

モントリオール Montreal (❖カナダの都市)

もんなし 文無し **—文無しの** penniless, 《口語的》broke (❖名詞の前では用いない) ‖私は全くの**文無し**だ I'm「totally *penniless* [flat *broke*]. / 彼女は仕事に失敗し**文無し**になった She failed in her business and「became *penniless* [went *broke*].

もんばん 門番 gatekeeper [C]

もんぶかがくしょう 文部科学省 the Ministry of Education, Culture, Sports, Science and Technology

もんぶしょう 文部省 the Ministry of Education, Science, Sports and Culture (❖2001年文部科学省に統合) ➩もんぶかがくしょう

モンブラン Mont Blanc [mɔːn bláːŋ] (❖アルプスの最高峰); (ケーキ) cake topped with chestnut paste and whipped cream

もんもう 文盲 illiteracy [U] **—文盲の** illiterate, 《公式的》unlettered

もんもん 悶々 当時彼は様々なことに挫折(ざせつ)し**悶々**とした日々を過ごしていた At that time, he had failed in various things and so was living *in worry*.

もんよう 文様・紋様 pattern [C]

も

や

や¹ 矢 arrow ◻; (投げ矢) dart ◻ ∥矢を弓につがえる fix *an arrow* to a bow / 的(ホホ)をめがけ矢を放つ shoot *an arrow* at a target / 矢は的に当たった *The arrow* hit the target.
[慣用表現] 主役として彼に白羽の矢が立った He *was chosen [selected]* for the leading role. / 彼らから金を返せと矢の催促を受けている He *has been pressing me hard* to return the money. / 彼女はその部屋から出たくて矢も盾もたまらなかった She *was dying to* leave the room.
[ことわざ] 光陰矢のごとし ⇨ こういん(光陰)

-や¹ (そして) and; (または) or ∥赤やピンクの花が咲いていた Red *and* pink flowers were blooming. / 新聞や雑誌ではそれについては何も触れていなかった Nothing was written about that in the newspapers *or* magazines.

-や² -屋 ❶【店】花屋 a flower *shop* / パン屋 a bakery
❷【店の人】本屋 a book*seller* / 床屋 a bar*ber*
❸【ある性格をもった人】気取り屋 an affected *person* / 恥ずかしがり屋 a shy *person*

やあ hey, hi ∥やあ, 隆, 元気かい *Hey [Hi]*, Takashi, how are you?

ヤード yard ◻ ((略語))yd (✦約91.4cm に相当。1 ヤードは 3 フィート)

-やいなや -や否や as soon as …, the moment … ∥彼は授業が終わるやいなや教室を飛び出した *As soon as* school was over, he ran out of the classroom.

やいのやいの 母に夏休みの宿題をやれとやいのやいの言われている My mother *is nagging* me to do my summer vacation homework.

やえ 八重 ∥八重桜(花) double cherry blossoms; (木) a double-flowered cherry tree / 八重歯 ⇨ やえば

やえい 野営 camp ◻◻ ∥彼らは湖畔で野営した They「*made a camp [camped]*」by the lake.

やえば 八重歯 double tooth ◻

やおちょう 八百長 fix ◻ ∥あの取り組みはきっと八百長だ That bout must have been「*a fix [fixed, rigged]*」.

やおもて 矢面 社長は激しい非難の矢面に立たされた The president *became the target of severe criticism*.

やおや 八百屋 (店) ((米))grocery (store) ◻ (✦穀物や缶詰なども売っている), ((英))greengrocer's (shop) ◻; (人) ((米))grocer ◻, ((英))greengrocer ◻

やおら 彼はやおら(→ゆっくり)席を立った He got up from his seat *slowly*.

やかい 夜会 ∥夜会服 ((集合的)) evening dress; (女性用の) an evening dress

やがい 野外 ――野外の open-air, outdoor ◆私たちは野外でお昼を食べた We had lunch *outdoors*.
∥野外活動 outdoor activities / 野外劇場 an open-air theater / 野外コンサート an open-air concert

やがく 夜学 night [evening] school ◻ ∥夜学に通う go to *a night [an evening] school*

やかた 館 (大邸宅) mansion ◻, palace ◻

やかたぶね 屋形船 〜 a *yakatabune*, a pleasure boat

やがて (間もなく) soon, before long, shortly; (しばらくして) after a while; (そのうちに) in time, in course of time; (いつかは) someday, eventually; (かれこれ) almost, nearly
やがて新学期が始まる A new school term will start *soon [before long, shortly]*.
やがて彼女が戻ってきた She came back *after a while*.
彼らはやがて解決法を見つけるだろう *Eventually* they will find a solution.
中国語を習い始めてからやがて 3 か月になる It's *almost [nearly]* three months since I started learning Chinese.

やかましい 喧しい
❶【騒々しい】(雑音などでうるさい) noisy; (音や声が大きい) loud
彼らの話し声がやかましい Their voices *are noisy [loud]*.
やかましい! *Don't be so noisy!* / (→静かにしろ)*Be quiet!*
テレビの音がやかましくて本が読めない The sound of the TV *is so noisy that* I can't read my book.
❷【厳しい】strict
うちの高校は規則がやかましい My high school's rules *are strict*.
◆彼女は食べる物にはやかましい She *is particular about* food.
❸【しつこく言う】
母に傘をなくさないようにやかましく言われた My mother told me *again and again* not to lose my umbrella.

やから 族・輩 (連中) ((口語的))bunch ◻, lot ◻; (やつ) fellow ◻

やかん¹ 夜間 night ◻◻ ∥その店は夜間も営業している The shop is open *at night*, too.
∥夜間飛行 a night flight / 夜間部 a night school

やかん² 薬缶 kettle ◻ ∥やかんでお湯を沸かす boil water in *a kettle* / 母はやかんを火にかけた My mother put *the kettle* over the fire.

やき 焼き このステーキは焼きが足りない This steak *is not done [cooked enough]* yet.
[慣用表現] 焼きが回る(→頭の働きが鈍くなる) *become dull* / 焼きを入れる(→訓戒する) *give a person a lesson*

やぎ 山羊 goat ◻; (子ヤギ) kid ◻ ⇨ やぎざ ∥ヤギ皮 goatskin

やきあみ 焼き網 grill ⓒ, gridiron ⓒ
やきいも 焼き芋 a *yakiimo*, a baked [roasted] sweet potato ‖焼き芋屋 a baked sweet potato vendor / 石焼き芋 a sweet potato baked among heated stones
やきいん 焼き印 (印) brand ⓒ; (器具) brand(ing) iron
やぎざ 山羊座 【天文・占星】Capricorn ⓤ (❖「山羊座の人」の意味では ⓒ)
やきざかな 焼き魚 《主に米》broiled [《英》grilled] fish ⓤ
やきすてる 焼き捨てる burn* up [away]; (火にくべる) throw* ... into the fire ‖彼女は別れた彼にもらった手紙を全部焼き捨てた She *burned up* all the letters she got from her ex-boyfriend.
やきそば 焼きそば *yakisoba*, noodles fried with vegetables
やきたて 焼き立て 焼きたてのクロワッサン croissants *hot* [*fresh*] *from the oven*
やきつく 焼き付く その美しい風景が心に焼きついて離れない The beautiful landscape *has been imprinted on* my mind.
やきつくす 焼き尽くす 火はその地域全体を焼き尽くした The fire *burned down* the whole area.
やきつけ 焼き付け (写真の) printing ⓤ; (陶器の) baking ⓤ 《プリント
やきつける 焼き付ける (写真を) print ⓣ; (陶器を) bake ⓣ ‖ネガから写真を焼きつける *print* photographs from a negative
やきとり 焼き鳥 *yakitori*, grilled chicken on skewers
やきなおし 焼き直し (作品などの) rehash ⓒ ‖彼の新しい映画は前作の焼き直しだ His new movie is *a rehash* of the last one.
やきなおす 焼き直す (食べ物を) bake [roast, broil] ... again; (著作を) rehash ⓣ
やきにく 焼き肉 grilled [broiled] meat ⓤ, barbecue ⓤ
やきはた 焼き畑 ‖焼畑農業 slash-and-burn agriculture
やきはらう 焼き払う burn* up [down]; (灰にする) reduce ... to ashes; (田畑などを) burn off ‖敵の軍隊によって町中が焼き払われた The whole town *was burned down* by the enemy's army.
やきぶた 焼き豚 roast pork
やきまし 焼き増し この写真を焼き増ししてほしいのですが I'd like to *have* this photograph *reprinted*.
やきめ 焼き目 sear ⓒ
やきめし 焼き飯 fried rice ⓤ
やきもき 私たちはやきもきしながら彼が来るのを待った We waited for him *impatiently*. / 兄の就職が決まるまで母はやきもきしていた (→心配していた) My mother *worried* until my brother got a job.
やきもち 焼き餅 jealousy ⓤ
◆やきもちやきの人 a *jealous* person / たぶん彼女はあなたにやきもちをやいているのよ Probably she *is jealous of* you.
やきもの 焼き物 (陶器) pottery ⓤ; (磁器) porcelain ⓤ, chinaware ⓤ; (陶磁器) ceramics

やきゅう 野球 baseball ⓤ ➡ 野球 p.1530
野球の試合を見に行く go to see a *baseball* game
きのう友達と野球をした I played *baseball* with my friends yesterday.
父はテレビで野球の試合を見ている My father is watching a *baseball* game on TV.
‖野球界 the world of baseball / 野球場 (グラウンド) a baseball field; (球場全体) a baseball stadium, a ball park / 野球選手 a baseball player / 野球チーム a baseball team / 野球部 a baseball club / 野球ファン a baseball fan / 野球帽 a baseball cap / 草野球 amateur baseball / 高校野球 high school baseball / プロ野球 professional baseball / プロ野球選手 a professional baseball player

やぎゅう 野牛 【動物】bison ⓒ (複 ~, ~s), buffalo ⓒ (複 ~, ~(e)s)
やきん¹ 夜勤 night duty ⓤ; (交替制の) night shift ⓤ ‖彼女はきょうは夜勤だ She is *on night duty* today. / She is working (*on*) *the night shift* today.
‖夜勤手当 a night-work [night-shift] allowance
やきん² 冶金 metallurgy ⓤ

やく¹ 焼く

❶[燃やす] burn* ⓣ
庭で落ち葉を焼いた I *burned* fallen leaves in the garden.
◆火事で家を焼いた (→家が焼けた) My house *burned down* in a fire.
❷[食べ物に火を通す] (直火で) 《主に米》broil ⓣ, 《英》grill ⓣ; (大きな肉を網で) roast ⓣ; (パンなどをオーブンで) bake ⓣ; (肉などを蒸し焼きにして) barbecue ⓣ
夕食に魚を焼いた I *broiled* fish for dinner.
休日にはよくパイを焼きます I often *bake* a pie on holidays.
🗨「ステーキの焼き方はいかがいたしましょうか」「ミディアムでお願いします」"*How would you like your steak?*" "Medium, please."
❸[肌を] get* a tan [suntan], tan ⓣ ⓘ
彼らは浜辺で肌を焼いた They *got a tan* on the beach.
❹[その他]
かまどれんがで[つぼを]焼く *bake* bricks [a pot] in a kiln / ネガを1枚焼く *print* a copy from the negative

やく² 役

❶[役割] part ⓒ, role ⓒ; (仕事) job ⓒ; (職務) duty ⓤ ⓒ
彼はその計画の実現に重要な役を果たした He played *an important part* [*role*] in carrying out the plan.
彼女は司会役を引き受けた She took *the role* of the chairperson.
食器を洗うのは私の役だ It is *my job* [*duty*] to wash the dishes.

テーマ別表現集

●野球

❶投手に関する表現

1. きょうの先発投手はだれだと思いますか.
   Who do you think is the 「starting pitcher [starter] today?
2. 投手は変化球［カーブ, フォーク, スライダー］を投げました.
   The pitcher threw a 「breaking ball [curve, forkball, slider].
3. 投手は内角低めの球を投げました.
   The pitcher threw his pitch 「down and in [low and inside].
4. 投手は外角高めの球を投げました.
   The pitcher threw his pitch 「up and away [high and outside].
5. 投手は打者に（敬遠の）フォアボールを与えました.
   The pitcher walked the hitter (intentionally).
6. 投手は岡野に一［二, 三］塁打を許してしまいました.
   The pitcher gave up a single [double, triple] to Okano.
7. 新人投手の鈴木は時速150キロくらいの速球をよく投げます.
   The rookie pitcher Suzuki often throws fastballs at around 95 mph.
8. コントロールのよくない田中に代わって高橋がマウンドに立ちました.
   Tanaka, who had poor control, was replaced on the mound by Takahashi.

❷打者に関する表現（「打者」は hitter, batter のどちらも可）

1. 中野が打席に入りました.
   Nakano stepped to the plate.
2. 打者は（空振りの, 見逃しの）三振をしました.
   The hitter struck out (swinging, looking).
3. 打者はツーストライク・スリーボールから三振をしました.
   The hitter struck out on a 3-2 pitch.
4. 打者はデッドボールを受け一塁に進みました.
   The hitter was hit by a pitch and given first base.
5. 打者はホームラン［満塁ホームラン, さよならホームラン］を打ちました.
   The hitter hit 「a home run [a grand slam (home run), a game-winning home run].
6. 打者はサードゴロを打ちました.
   The hitter hit a grounder to the third baseman.
7. 打者はセンターにヒットを打ちました.
   The hitter singled to center.
8. 4番打者は二塁打を打ちました.
   The cleanup batter hit a double.
9. 打者は平凡なフライを打ち上げました.
   The hitter hit a routine fly.
10. 打者は犠牲バントで走者を進塁させました.
    The hitter laid down a sacrifice bunt to advance the runner.
11. 彼は強打者ですが守備が下手です.
    He is a power hitter, but his fielding is poor.
12. 彼の打率はチームで最高です.
    His batting average is the highest on the team.

❸守備に関する表現

1. ライトのエラーで, タイガースは2点を許してしまいました.
   The Tigers gave up two runs because of the right fielder's error.
2. ショートは平凡なゴロをトンネルしてしまいました.
   The shortstop allowed a routine grounder to go through his legs.
3. ドラゴンズはダブルプレーでピンチを脱しました.
   The Dragons made a double play and got out of a jam.
4. 三塁手は走者をタッチアウトにしました.
   The third baseman tagged out the runner.

❹その他

1. 今, どちらのチームが勝っていますか.
   Which team is leading now? / Who is winning now?
2. 3対1でライオンズが勝っています.
   The Lions are on top, 3 to 1.
3. 2.5ゲーム差でスワローズがベイスターズをリードしています.
   The Swallows are two and a half games ahead of the BayStars.
4. ジャイアンツは7回表［裏］に3点入れました.
   The Giants got three runs in the top [bottom] of the seventh inning.
5. ノーアウト満塁です.
   The bases are loaded [full] with nobody out.
6. 一塁走者が二塁に盗塁しました.
   The runner on first stole second base.

日本語の「ツーストライク・スリーボール」, 略して「ツースリー」は英語では three balls and two strikes と語順が逆になり, on a 3-2 count （ツースリーのカウントで）などとして用いられる. また,「内角低め」も英語では down and in または low and inside といずれも日本語と逆になる.

◆彼は30年間支配人の役を務めた He served as manager for 30 years.
❷【芝居の】role ⓒ, part ⓒ
彼は医者の役でデビューした He made his debut in *the role* of a doctor.
彼女はそのミュージカルでドロシー役を演じた She played (*the part of*) *Dorothy* in the musical.
その俳優は難しい役をうまくこなしていた The actor played *a* difficult *part* well.
彼は一人二役を演じた He played 「*a double role* [*two roles*].
ハムレットは彼のはまり役だ He is *perfect for the role* of Hamlet.
◆彼女は妖精(ようせい)の役をもらった She *was cast as* a fairy.
❸【地位】post ⓒ, (社会的に重要な) position ⓒ; (官職) (公式的の) office ⓤ
社長は病気で役を退いた The president resigned from *his post* because of illness.
祖父は会社で重要な役に就いていた My grandfather held *an* important *position* in the company.
❹【「役に立つ」の形で】(有用な) useful, of use; (助けになる) helpful, of help
この雑誌には役に立つ情報がたくさん出ている There is a lot of *useful* information in this magazine.
これが何か役に立つかもしれない This may be *of some use*.
そんなことを考えても何の役にも立たない It's (*of*) *no use* to think about it.
少しでもお役に立てたのならうれしいです I'm glad if I've *been of some help*.
◆あまりお役に立てず申しわけありませんでした I'm sorry *I couldn't be of more assistance*.／こんなことを覚えて何の役に立つのだろう What is *the use* of memorizing such a thing?／彼のアドバイスがとても役に立った His advice *helped* me a lot.

やく³ 約 about;《口語的》around; some; approximately; ... or so; nearly; almost

about: 数・量・時間などについて広く用いられる.
around: 口語的な言い方で, about と同じように用いられる.
some: 数詞の前でのみ用いられる.
approximately: about より格式ばった言い方.
... or so: 「…かそこら」という意味で口語的に用いられる.
nearly: この語の後に示す数にもう少しで一致することを表す. 差がわずかなことを強調する.
almost: この語の後に示す数に近いがそれに達するには不足している, という状態を表す.

東京ドームは約5万人収容できる The Tokyo Dome holds *about* [*around, some, approximately*] fifty thousand people.
学校まで電車で約40分です It is *about* [*around*] forty minutes to school by train.
この川の幅は約50メートルあります This river is *nearly* [*almost*] fifty meters wide.

やく⁴ 訳 translation ⓤⓒ／うまい訳 *a good translation* ◆その英文に訳をつける *translate* the English sentence
‖訳者 ➡ やくしゃ(訳者)／意訳 a free translation／現代語訳 a modern translation／誤訳 a mistranslation／逐語訳 a word-for-word translation／直訳 a literal [word-for-word] translation／日本語訳 a Japanese translation [version]

やく⁵ 厄 (災難) misfortune ⓒ; (悪霊) evil spirit ⓒ ➡ やくどし／厄払いする「*drive away* [*exorcise*] *evil spirits*

やく⁶ 妬く (嫉妬(しっと)する) be jealous; (うらやむ) be envious ➡うらやむ, やきもち

やく⁷ 薬 (麻薬) drug ⓒ, (口語的)dope ⓤ

やぐ 夜具 (寝具) bedding ⓤ

やくいん 役員 (会社・団体などの) officer ⓒ, official ⓒ; (企業の) director ⓒ, executive ⓒ ◆おじは市民体育祭の役員(→実行委員会のメンバー)を務めた My uncle served as *a member of the executive committee* of the city sports festival.
‖役員会 a meeting of officers; (取締役会) a board of directors／役員室 a boardroom

やくがい 薬害 (一般の薬による) harmful effect of medicine; (農薬による) damage by agricultural chemicals ‖薬害エイズ HIV infection caused by the use of tainted blood products／薬害訴訟 a lawsuit over the harmful effects of medicines

やくがく 薬学 (調剤学) pharmacy ⓤ; (薬理学) pharmacology ⓤ ──薬学の pharmaceutical ‖薬学者 a pharmacologist／薬学部 a pharmaceutical department

やくがら 役柄 (役) part ⓒ, role ⓒ, position ⓒ, office ⓒ; (役の性質) the nature of *one's position* [*office*]／彼は自分の役柄をわきまえている He knows *his role*.

やくご 訳語 (単語) word ⓒ; (用語) term ⓒ; (相当語) equivalent ⓒ／この日本語に当たる英語の訳語が見つからない There is no English *equivalent* for this Japanese term.

やくざ a *yakuza*; (一員) gangster ⓒ; (暴力団) gang ⓒ, (集合的)the mob; (ごろつき)《口語的》hoodlum ⓒ
‖やくざ映画 a gang(ster) movie

やくざい 薬剤 medicine ⓤⓒ
‖薬剤師 a pharmacist,《米》a druggist,《英》a chemist

やくじほう 薬事法 the Pharmaceutical Affairs Law

やくしゃ¹ 役者 (男優・女優) actor ⓒ; (女優) actress ⓒ／役者になる become *an actor*; go on the stage
慣用表現 彼のほうが役者が一枚上だった He *was a cut above* me.／役者がそろったところで, 本題に入ろうか Now that we *have all the people who are supposed to be here*, let's get started on the main subject.
‖歌舞伎(かぶき)役者 a kabuki actor／大根役者 a poor actor [actress]／花形役者 a star actor [actress]／舞台役者 a stage actor [ac-

tress]

やくしゃ² 訳者 translator [C]

やくしゅつ 訳出 この小説は訳出するのにとても苦労した I had a lot of trouble *translating* this novel.

やくしょ 役所 public [government] office [C] ◆役所に勤める work for *the government* ‖お役所仕事 red tape / 区役所 a ward office / 市役所《米》a city hall,《英》a town hall

やくじょ 躍如 ⇒めんぼく

やくしょく 役職 (管理職) managerial post [position] [C] ◆彼は委員会の中で重要な役職に就いている He takes *an* important *position* [*post*] in the committee. ‖役職手当 an executive allowance

やくしん 躍進 rapid [remarkable] progress [U] ─躍進する (急激に発展する) advance rapidly [remarkably] ‖その会社はここ数年でめざましい躍進を遂げた The company has made *rapid* [*remarkable*] *progress* for the past few years.

やくす 訳す translate [他], put* ... into ～ ‖次の英語を日本語に訳しなさい *Put* the following English *into* Japanese. / この表現はうまく英語に訳せない I *can't translate* this expression *into* English well.

やくすう 約数 divisor [C]

やくそう 薬草 (medical) herb [C]

やくそく 約束

promise [C];(日時・場所を明確にした)《公式的》appointment [C];(拘束力の強い重要な)《公式的》engagement [C];(規則) rule [C] ─約束する promise [他][自], make* a promise

〚約束が・は〛

約束は守りなさい Keep *your promise*.

彼女と約束がある I have *an appointment* with her.

今になって行かないなんて，それじゃ約束が違うよ Now you say you aren't coming with us? *That's not what you promised*.

◆(受付で)お約束(→予約)はありますか Do you have *a reservation*?

〚約束を・に〛

君が約束を守らなかったと彼が怒っていたよ He was angry that you didn't keep *your promise*.

彼は約束を破るような人ではない He is not the kind of man to break *his promise*.

いつか必ず約束を果たすつもりです I will certainly「carry out [fulfill] *my promise* to you someday.

彼女とあしたの7時に会う約束をした I *made an appointment* to meet her at seven tomorrow.

彼女は珍しく約束に遅れた She was late for *the appointment*, which is unusual for her.

〚約束の〛

約束の物を持ってきたよ I brought what I *promised* to you.

◆すぐ行かないと約束の時間に着かない If I don't go at once, I won't get there at the *appointed* time.

〚約束で〛

来週中に返すという約束で彼に本を借りた I borrowed the book from him *on the promise* I would return it within the next week.

〚約束する〛

父は僕に新しい自転車を買ってくれると約束した My father *promised*「to buy me a new bicycle [that he would buy me a new bicycle].

それはあしたやるよ，約束する I'll do it tomorrow, I *promise*.

約束したとおり彼はそのCDを持ってきてくれた He brought me the CD *as promised*.

◆彼にはサッカー日本代表の座が約束されている (→だれも反対しないだろう) *Nobody would disagree* about his being elected a member of the all-Japan soccer team. / 彼女は将来を約束されたエリートだ She is an elite person whose future *is guaranteed*.

〚その他〛

社会にはだれもが守るべき約束事というものがある In the world, there are *rules* which everyone should observe.

(受付で)何時のお約束ですか What time is *your appointment*?

‖約束手形 a promissory note / 口約束 a verbal promise

やくたたず 役立たず (人) good-for-nothing [C];(物) garbage [U] ‖あいつは本当に役立たずだ He's really「*a good-for-nothing* [《口語的》*useless*].

やくだつ 役立つ (有益な) be useful;(助けになる) be helpful ‖この参考書は英作文をするのに役立った This study-aid book *was useful* for writing English compositions.

やくだてる 役立てる put* ... to good use;(うまく利用する) make* use of ... ‖お金を恵まれない子供たちのために役立てる *put* the money *to good use* to help underprivileged children

やくちゅう 訳注 (翻訳と注釈) translation and annotation [notes];(訳者のつけた注) annotation by the translator

やくどう 躍動 ─躍動的な (活発な) lively;(精力的な) energetic ◆オーケストラの演奏は躍動感にあふれていた The orchestra's performance *was full of energy*.

やくとく 役得 fringe benefits, perquisites, perks ‖役得を得る get *fringe benefits*

やくどし 厄年 🗻

厄年とは，災難が降りかかりやすいので注意を要するとされる年齢をいいます．一般的に，男性は数えで25，42，60歳，女性は同じく19，33歳が厄年とされています．

Yakudoshi are ages when it is said that unlucky events are likely to happen to you and so you should be careful. It is generally said that *yakudoshi* are the 25th, 42nd and 60th calendar years for

やくにん 役人 government official; (公務員) public [civil] servant ◎
◆外務省の役人 an official in the Ministry of Foreign Affairs
‖役人根性 officialism

やくば 役場 ‖町役場 a town office [hall] / 村役場 a village office [hall]

やくび 厄日 unlucky [bad] day ◎

やくひん 薬品 (医薬品) drug ◎; (特に内服薬) medicine ◎; (化学薬品) chemical ◎

やくぶそく 役不足 彼女にはこの仕事は役不足だった(→やさしすぎた)かもしれない This task may have been too easy for her.

やくぶつ 薬物 drug ◎; (特に内服薬) medicine ◎ ◎; ⋯に薬物を混入する mix a drug into ⋯ / その池の水から薬物が検出された Drugs were detected in the pond.
‖薬物アレルギー a drug allergy / 薬物中毒 chemical poisoning / 薬物乱用 drug abuse / 薬物療法 medication

やくぶん¹ 約分 reduction ◎
◆10分の5を約分すると2分の1になる Five tenths reduce to one half.

やくぶん² 訳文 translated sentence ◎

やくほん 訳本 translation ◎

やくまわり 役回り 彼にいやな役回りを押しつけられた He forced me to play [take on] a disagreeable role.

やくみ 薬味 spice ◎ ◎

やくめ 役目 (仕事) job ◎《通例単数形》; (任務) duty ◎ ◎; (役割) role ◎, part ◎; (責任) responsibility ◎; (機能) function ◎
役目(→任務)を果たす fulfill one's duty
彼女は案内係としての役目をりっぱに果たした She did a satisfactory job as a guide.
彼は議長の役目を引き受けた He took on the role of chairperson.
カタツムリの殻は外敵から身を守る避難所のような役目をする The shell of a snail 「has a function [functions] as a shelter from outside enemies.
◆ヨーグルトは整腸剤の役目も果たす Yogurt also functions as medicine for intestinal disorders. / 彼は役目柄部下にいやな仕事もさせなければならない His position sometimes requires him to make his subordinates do unpleasant jobs.

やくよう 薬用 ‖薬用植物 a medicinal plant [herb] / 薬用せっけん medicated soap

やくよけ 厄除け 厄よけのお守り a talisman; an amulet / これは厄よけになる This wards off bad luck.

やぐら 櫓 (大きな建物の上の) turret ◎; (塔) tower ◎ ‖火の見やぐら a fire tower

やくわり 役割 role ◎, part ◎ ‖日本は国際舞台で重要な役割を演じている Japan plays an important role [part] on the international scene. ◆この置物は貯金箱の役割も果たす(→貯金箱としても使える) This ornament can also be used as a coin bank.

やけ desperation ◎ ‖やけ酒を飲む drink out of desperation
◆兄は仕事で大失敗をしてやけになった My brother got desperate because he made a big mistake in his job. / 彼女はやけになってその手紙を破いた She tore up the letter in despair.

やけあと 焼け跡 焼け跡から老夫婦の遺体が発見された An old couple was found dead in the ruins of the fire.

やけい¹ 夜景 night view [scene] ◎

やけい² 夜警 (仕事) night watch ◎ ◎; (人) night watchman ◎ ‖夜警をする keep night watch

やけいし 焼け石 慣用表現 借金を返すのにこのくらいの金では焼け石に水だ This much money is only a drop in the bucket [ocean] to pay back my debt.

やけおちる 焼け落ちる be burned down ‖その火災で寺の本堂が焼け落ちた The main hall of the temple was burned down in the fire.

やけくそ 彼は試験に失敗してやけくそになった He failed the examination and became desperate.

やけこげ 焼け焦げ burn ◎ ◆たばこでじゅうたんに焼け焦げができた The cigarette burned [scorched] the carpet.

やけしぬ 焼け死ぬ be burned to death

やけだされる 焼け出される be burned out (in [by] a fire); (住むところをなくす) lose* one's home in a fire ‖そのマンションの火事で5世帯が焼け出された Five families were burned out of their homes in that apartment house fire.

やけつく 焼け付く 焼けつくように暑い日 a blazing [scorching] hot day

やけど 火傷 burn ◎; (熱湯・蒸気による) scald ◎ ‖彼はその火事で軽い[ひどい]やけどを負った He received a slight [deep] burn in the fire.
◆やかんにさわって指にやけどをした I burned my fingers on the kettle. / 熱いシチューで舌をやけどした I burned [scalded] my tongue on the hot stew.
慣用表現 やけどをしないうちにその事業から手を引いたほうがいい You should back out of the business before you get burned.

やけに この部屋はやけに冷える It's terribly [awfully] cold in this room. / きょうの彼女はやけにおとなしい She is rather quiet today.

やけのこる 焼け残る escape the fire ‖幸運にもその寺は焼け残った Fortunately the temple escaped [survived] the fire.

やけのはら 焼け野原 burned field ◎

やける¹ 焼ける
❶ 【燃える】 burn* ◎, be burned
その建物は火事ですっかり焼けた The building was completely burned down by the fire.
◆その火事で多くの家が焼けた(→焼失した)

やける

Many houses *were destroyed* in the fire.
❷【食物が】(直火(ぢ^か)で)《主に米》be broiled, 《英》be grilled; (オーブン・直火で) roast 他; (パンなどが) bake 他
お肉が焼けてきた The meat *is roasting*.
パンはまだ焼けていない The bread *has not finished baking* yet.
◆これはよく焼けていない[焼けすぎだ] This *is underdone* [*overdone, burnt*].
❸【日に】get* a tan [suntan], be [get] tanned; (ひどく) be [get] sunburned
彼はよく日に焼けている He *has a good tan* [*suntan*]./ He *is well tanned*.
❹【変色する】(色が悪くなる) discolor 自; (あせる) fade 自
本の表紙が日に焼けた The cover of the book *has discolored* [*faded*] in the sunlight.
❺【その他】
つぼが焼けた The vase *has been fired*.
きょうは焼けるように暑い It's *sizzling* hot today.
弟たちは本当に世話が焼ける My brothers *give me a lot of trouble*.

やける² 妬ける あいつが彼女とデートだなんてやけるなあ I'm *jealous* [*I could just die*] because he got a date with her.
やご 蜻蛉(やご) dragonfly larva 回
やこう¹ 夜光 ‖夜光塗料 luminous paint
やこう² 夜行 夜行性の動物 a *nocturnal* animal / 夜行列車 a *night train*

やさい 野菜 vegetable 回; (青物) greens
彼は菜園でいろいろな野菜を作っている He grows many kinds of *vegetables* in his garden.
私は野菜嫌いだ I hate [don't like] *vegetables*.
‖野菜いため stir-fried vegetables / 野菜サラダ vegetable salad / 野菜ジュース vegetable juice / 野菜スープ vegetable soup / 野菜畑(家庭の) a vegetable garden; (市場向けの)《米》a truck farm, 《英》a market garden / 生野菜 raw vegetables / 有機野菜 organic vegetables / 緑黄色野菜 brightly colored vegetables

やさき 矢先 出かけようとした矢先に雨が降りだした I *was just about to* go out *when* it started to rain.

やさしい¹ 優しい

(親切な) kind, good, nice; (温和な) gentle, mild; (思いやりのある) tender, kindhearted, tenderhearted ――優しく kindly; gently; tenderly
祖母は私にとても優しい My grandmother is very *kind* [*good, nice*] to me.
優しいお心づかいをありがとうございます Thank you for your *kind* consideration.
手伝ってくれるなんてあなたって本当に優しいのね How *kind* [*sweet*] of you to help me!
馬はとても優しい目をしている Horses have very *gentle* eyes.
真美は気立ての優しい子だ Mami is a *tender-hearted* girl.
彼女は子供たちに優しく話しかけた She talked to the children *gently* [in a *gentle* voice].
この薬は胃にやさしい This medicine is *gentle* on [to] your stomach.
◆ 初心者にやさしいパソコン a *beginner-friendly* PC / この車は環境にやさしい This car is *friendly* to the environment.

やさしい² 易しい
(容易な) easy; (簡単な) simple; (分かりやすい) plain
その物語はやさしい英語で書かれている The story is written in *plain* [*simple*] English.
テストは決してやさしくはなかった The test was by no means *easy*.
その問題は彼にはやさしかった It *was easy for* him to solve the question. / The question *was easy for* him to solve.

やし 椰子 (ヤシ科の植物の総称) palm [pá:m] (tree) 回; (ココヤシの木) coconut palm 回; (ココヤシの実) coconut 回
やじ 野次 (演説での) heckling 回; (声) boos, hoots; (あざけりの言葉) jeers; (口笛) catcalls ◆ 聴衆は彼にやじを飛ばした The audience *heckled* [*hooted at, booed*] him.
やじうま 野次馬 (curious) onlooker 回, rubbernecker 回 ‖事故現場にはすぐにやじ馬が集まった *Curious onlookers* [*Rubberneckers*] soon gathered at the scene of the accident.
‖やじ馬根性 (a sense of) curiosity
やしき 屋敷 (邸宅) mansion 回, 《公式的》residence 回; (家屋敷) premises

やしなう 養う
❶【扶養する】support 他; (食べさせる) feed* 他; (養育する) bring* up; (育てる) raise 他
家族を養う *support one's family*
私はおじに養ってもらった I *was「brought up* [*raised*] by my uncle.
❷【養成する】(培う) cultivate 他; (発達させる) develop 他; (形成する) form 他; (増進させる) build* up; (向上させる) improve 他
運動して体力を養う *build up one's* strength *by exercising*
書道は集中力を養ってくれる Practicing calligraphy *develops* your ability to concentrate.
彼はのみの市に足しげく通って古美術を見る目を養った By going to flea markets frequently, he *developed* an eye for antiques.

やしゅ 野手 《野球》fielder 回
やしゅう 夜襲 night attack 回
やじゅう 野獣 wild animal [beast] 回
やしょく 夜食 midnight [late-night] snack 回
やじり 矢尻・鏃 arrowhead 回
やじる 野次る heckle 他; (ブーイングする) boo 自 他; (はやしたてる) hoot 自 他; (あざける) jeer 自 他 ‖彼らは候補者をやじった They *heckled* the candidate.
やじるし 矢印 arrow 回 ‖彼女は矢印に沿って進んだ She followed *the arrows*.

やしろ 社 (Shinto) shrine ©
やしん 野心 (大望) ambition ©©; (抱負) aspiration ©© ──野心的な ambitious ©
彼にはいつか政権を握りたいという野心があった He had *an ambition* to come into power someday. / 兄は野心満々だ My brother is 「*full of ambition* [*very ambitious*]*.
∥野心家 an ambitious person, a person of ambition / 野心作 an ambitious work
やす (魚などを刺す道具) gig ©
-やす -安 円安 the *weak* yen / その株は前日比12円安だった The stock was 12 yen *lower* than the previous day.
やすあがり 安上がり ──安上がりな (安い) cheap; (経済的な) economical; (てごろな値段の) inexpensive ∥4人だったら電車よりタクシーで行ったほうが安上がりだ With four people, it's *cheaper* to go by taxi than by train.

やすい¹ 安い

cheap; inexpensive; low-priced; low ── 安く cheap, cheaply; inexpensively

> cheap: 値段も安いが品物もよくないといった含みがある.
> inexpensive: 品質のわりに値段が安いというニュアンスが含まれる.
> low-priced: 客観的に価格が低いことを表す.
> low: 価格・給料など, 金額が低いことを表す.

このシャツは安い This shirt is *cheap* [*inexpensive, low-priced*].
あのスーパーは安い That supermarket is *cheap*. / They sell everything *cheaply* [*cheap*] at that supermarket.
この時計が1万円なら安い This watch is *cheap* [*a bargain*] at 10,000 yen.
彼の給料は安い His salary is *low*.
このあたりは都心に比べて物価が安い Prices are *lower* around here than in the center of the city.
彼はとても安い値段でコンピュータを買った He bought a computer at a very *low* price.
もう少し安いのはありますか Do you have anything a little *cheaper*?
私はその車を安く買った I bought the car *cheap* [*cheaply, inexpensively*].
バスを使ったほうが安くつくと思います It would be *cheaper* if we took a bus.
◆野菜の値段が安くなった (→下がった) The price of vegetables 「*came down* [*fell*].
❢「この中古ビデオを2万円です」「少し安くしてもらえませんか」 "This secondhand VCR is 20,000 yen." "Could you make it a little *cheaper*?"

やすい² 易い
❢「この荷物を部屋まで運んでもらえますか」「おやすいご用です」 "Would you take this baggage to the room?" "*Certainly.* / *No trouble at all.* / *Of course.* / *With pleasure.*"
ことわざ 言うは易(ギ)く行うは難(ガ)し という

-やすい -易い
❶ 【容易な】 be easy to *do*
このはさみは使いやすい These scissors *are easy to* use.
◆暮らしやすい (→快適な) 環境 a *comfortable* environment to live in
❷ 【傾向がある】 tend to *do*, be prone to *do*; be apt to *do* (✿通例悪い意味で用いる); (病気になりやすい・影響を受けやすい) be susceptible to …
私は車に酔いやすい I *am prone to* get carsick.
彼は人の言うことを信じやすい He *is apt to* believe what other people say.
冬の間はかぜをひきやすい People *are more susceptible to* colds in the winter.
◆彼は感情が出やすい He shows his feelings *easily*. / 雨で道路が滑りやすくなっていた The rain made the road *slippery*.
やすうけあい 安請け合い 安請け合いをしたが, とても大変な仕事だった I *readily agreed to* do it, but it was very hard work.
やすうり 安売り sale © ∥その店ではバッグの安売りをしている The shop is having *a sale* on handbags. / 安売りでテレビを買った I bought a TV at *a sale*.
∥安売り店 a discount store [shop] / 安売り日 a bargain day
やすげっきゅう 安月給 low [small] salary ©
やすっぽい 安っぽい cheap ∥安っぽいアパート a *cheap* apartment house / そういう言葉づかいをすると人間が安っぽく見えるよ Such language will make you look *cheap*.
やすね 安値 low price © ∥家具を安値で売った I sold the furniture *at a low price*.
やすぶしん 安普請 安普請の家 a *jerry-built* house
やすませる 休ませる きょうは息子に体育の授業を休ませたいのですが I'd like to *excuse* my son from gym class today.
やすまる 休まる (体を) be [feel*] rested; (心が) feel at ease, be [feel] relieved, be [feel] relaxed ∥紅茶を飲むと心が休まる I *feel at ease* when I drink tea.
◆きょうは忙しくて体の休まる暇もない I am too busy to *rest myself* today.

やすみ 休み

❶ 【休息】 (休憩) rest ©; (仕事などの休憩) break ©; (休み時間) recess ©©
ひと休みしませんか Let's take *a break* [*rest*], shall we? (✿take は have でも可)
次の授業までに15分の休みがある There is *a 15-minute break* [*recess*] before the next class.
彼らは休みなく働いた They worked *without a rest* [*break*].
休み時間に先生に質問をしに行った I went to ask my teacher some questions during *recess*.
◆雨が休みなく降り続いている It has been raining 「*on and on* [*non-stop*].
❷ 【休日】 holiday ©; (休暇) vacation ©
お盆休み *the Bon vacation* / 正月休み *the*

やすみやすみ

New Year's vacation
10日間の休みがとれた I was able to take *a 10-day vacation.*
休みの日はいつも何をしていますか What do you usually do *on holidays*?
父は休みの日はよく釣りに行く My father often goes fishing *on holidays.*
夏休みはどこに行きますか Where are you going during *the summer vacation*?
◆毎週月曜日は休みだ I have Monday(s) *off.* / I'm *off* on Monday(s). / 今度の水曜日にお休みをしたいのですが I'd like to take *a day off* next Wednesday. / きょうは学校が休みだ We have *no* school today. / その店は日曜日が休みだ(→休業している) The shop *is closed* on Sunday(s).
❸〖欠席・欠勤〗absence Ⓤ
◆彼女はきょうはお休みです She *is absent* today. / 最近休みの人が多い Many people have been *absent* recently.

やすみやすみ 休み休み 登山者たちは途中休み休み頂上を目ざした The mountain climbers went up toward the top *taking a rest every few steps.* / ばかも休み休み言いなさい *None of your nonsense*!

やすむ 休む
❶〖休息する〗rest Ⓑ, take* [have*] a rest; (くつろぐ) relax Ⓑ
少し休もう Let's *take a rest* [*break*].
選手たちは10分休んだ後トレーニングを再開した The players started training again after「they *had a 10-minute rest* [they *rested* for 10 minutes].
祖父は散歩の後ソファーで休んでいた My grandfather *rested* [*took a rest*] on the sofa after his walk.
今週は休む暇がない I have no time *to rest* this week.
日曜日は家でゆっくり休んだ I *relaxed* at home on Sunday.
◆彼らは2時間休まずに芝居の練習を続けた They continued to rehearse the play for two hours *without a break.* / 当店は祝日も休まず営業します We *are open* even on national holidays.
❷〖欠席・欠勤〗(欠席する) be absent, stay away from ...; (休暇をとる) take* [have*] a day off (...), be off (...)
彼は病気で学校を休んでいる He *is absent from* school because of illness.
あしたは休みます I'll「*take a day off* [*be off*]」tomorrow.
彼女はかぜで仕事を2日休んだ She caught a cold and *took two days off* work.
◆この1年間学校を休まなかった I *didn't miss* any school this year. / ぐあいが悪かったので学校を休んだ I felt ill and *didn't go to* school.
❸〖眠る〗sleep* Ⓑ; (床につく) go* to bed
よく休めましたか Did you *sleep* well?
きのうは早く休んだ I *went to bed* early yesterday.

◆お休みなさい *Good night.* / 母はまだベッドで休んでいる My mother *is* still *in bed.*
❹〖その他〗
(号令で) 気をつけ！ 休め！ Attention! *At ease!*

やすめる 休める (休息させる) rest Ⓑ, give* ... a rest; (心を安心させる) set* one's mind at rest [ease] ∥頭を休める *rest one's brain* / コンピュータを使った後しばらく目を休めた I *rested my eyes* for a while after using the computer.
◆体を休めたほうがいいですよ You should have [take] *a rest.* / 彼は仕事の手を休めた He *stopped working.*

やすもの 安物 cheap article [thing] Ⓒ; (総称) cheap goods ◆このかばんは安物だが丈夫だ This bag is *cheap* but strong.
ことわざ 安物買いの銭失い If you buy cheap things, you will lose your money in the end.; Buy cheap, get cheap. (→安く買うと安っぽいものしか手に入らない); You can't afford to buy cheap things. (→安物を買うほど金銭的な余裕はない)

やすやすと (簡単に) easily, with ease; (難なく) without difficulty ∥彼はやすやすと重たい箱を持ち上げた He lifted up the heavy box *easily.*

やすやど 安宿 cheap hotel [inn] Ⓒ
やすらか 安らか ――安らかな peaceful ――安らかに peacefully, in peace ∥赤ちゃんの安らかな寝顔 a baby's *peacefully* sleeping face / 安らかに眠れ Rest *in peace.* (❖墓石に刻む文句) (略語) R.I.P.)

やすらぎ 安らぎ peace of mind ∥人々は彼の歌に心の安らぎを求めている People seek *peace of mind* through his songs.

やすらぐ 安らぐ その詩集を読むと心が安らいだ I felt *at ease* when I read the collection of poems.

やすり 鑢 file Ⓒ; (紙やすり) sandpaper Ⓤ
◆つめにやすりをかける *file one's* fingernails

やせい¹ 野生 ――野生の wild ∥野生のバラ *wild* roses
∥野生植物 a wild plant / 野生生物 wildlife / 野生動物 a wild animal

やせい² 野性 wild nature Ⓤ ――野性的な wild; (粗野な) rough ∥動物園のトラは野性味を失っている Tigers in the zoo have lost *their wild nature.* ◆野性に返る return to *the wild* / その俳優には野性的な魅力がある The actor has *unpolished* charm.

やせおとろえる 痩せ衰える become* thin and feeble, become emaciated; (骨と皮ばかりになる) be reduced to skin and bones ∥長患いで祖父はやせ衰えた My grandfather *became thin and feeble* because of a long illness.

やせがた 痩せ型 やせ型の女性 a *slim* [*slender*] woman

やせがまん 痩せ我慢 本当はそれが食べたいのに彼女はやせ我慢している (→そうでないふりをしている) Actually she wants to eat it, but「she *pretends* she doesn't [(→それを認めるの

はプライドが許さない)she *is too proud to admit it*. / やせ我慢するな *Don't be a martyr.*
◆martyr 「má:rtər」は「犠牲者ぶる人」の意味.
やせこける 痩せこける ──やせこけた emaciated ◆やせこけたほお *hollow cheeks* / 大病を患い, 彼はすっかりやせこけてしまった *After his serious illness, he was nothing but skin and bones.*
やせち 痩せ地 (やせた土地) poor land Ⓤ; (不毛の土地) sterile [barren] land Ⓤ
やせっぽち 痩せっぽち skinny person Ⓒ
やせほそる 痩せ細る become* thin; (体重が減る) lose* weight ──やせ細った (やせた) thin; (やせ衰えた) emaciated /やせ細った足 *thin [emaciated] legs* / 愛犬に死なれたショックで彼女はやせ細ってしまった *She became thin over the shock of losing her dog.*

やせる 痩せる

❶【人が】get* [become*] thin; (体重が減る) lose* weight ──やせた (❖「やせすぎ」というニュアンスがある); (すらっとした) slender; (ほっそりした) slim; (締まった) lean
彼は最近急激にやせた *He has* rapidly *「lost weight [gotten thinner]* lately.*
彼女のお姉さんはとてもやせている *Her sister is very thin [slender, slim].*
◆ 3か月で2キロやせた *I lost two kilos in three months.* / 母はやせようと努力している *My mother is trying to slim down.*
❷【土地が】──やせた poor; (不毛の) barren, sterile
この畑はやせていて作物はできない *This field is too poor to grow any crops.*

慣用表現 やせても枯れても(→落ちぶれても), 人の助けは受けない *Even if my fortunes decline, I'll never need other people's help.*

やせん 野戦 field battle
‖野戦病院 a field hospital
やそう 野草 wild grass Ⓤ Ⓒ
やそうきょく 夜想曲 nocturne Ⓒ
やたい 屋台 stand Ⓒ, stall Ⓒ /ゆうべ屋台のラーメン屋でラーメンを食べた *I ate ramen at a ramen stand [stall]* last night. / 神社の縁日にはたくさんの屋台が出る *There are many stands [stalls] at the shrine on festival days.*
やたいぼね 屋台骨 その部門はこの会社を支える屋台骨となっている *The department is the mainstay of this company.* / 政界の汚職事件は現政権の屋台骨を揺るがした *The political scandal shook the foundation of the present government.*
やたら ──やたらに (無差別に) indiscriminately; (過度に) too; (ひどく) terribly /やたらに人を疑うのはよくない *You shouldn't doubt others indiscriminately.* / あの店は何でもやたらに高い *Everything is too expensive at that shop.* / きょうはやたらに込んでいる *It's terribly crowded today.*
やちょう 野鳥 wild bird Ⓒ; (総称) wild fowl Ⓤ ‖野鳥観察 bird-watching / 野鳥の会 a bird-watching society / 野鳥保護区 a wild-bird sanctuary

やちん 家賃 (house) rent Ⓤ Ⓒ ‖家賃を払う *pay the rent* / このアパートの家賃はいくらですか *How much is the rent for this apartment?* / 彼らは3か月分の家賃を滞納していた *They owed three months rent.*
やつ 奴 ❶【人】guy Ⓒ, fellow Ⓒ, 《英》chap Ⓒ ‖あいつはいいやつだ *He is a nice guy [fellow].* / 彼はたいしたやつだ *He is really quite a guy.*
❷【物】
⬤「そこにある私のかばん取って」「どっちが君の?」「赤いやつ」"Could you get my bag there for me?" "Which (one) is yours?" "*The red one.*"
やつあたり 八つ当たり 妹は私に八つ当たりした *My sister took it out on me.*

やっかい 厄介

❶【面倒】trouble Ⓤ; (負担) burden Ⓒ
やっかいな troublesome; (困難な) difficult
ごやっかいをおかけして申しわけありませんでした (迷惑をかけたとき) I'm sorry to *have given you trouble.*; I'm sorry to *have troubled you.* / (何かをしてもらったとき) Thank you for *your help.*
やっかいな仕事を引き受けてしまった *I have taken on a troublesome* job.
この問題を解くのはなかなかやっかいそうだ *It seems very difficult to solve this problem.*
私をやっかい者扱いするなんてひどいよ *It's cruel of you to treat me as a burden.*
◆やっかいなことになってきた *The situation has become complicated.*
❷【世話】care Ⓤ ──やっかいになる (頼る) depend on ...; (世話になる) live off ...; (泊まる) stay ⾃
彼女は大学卒業後も親のやっかいになっている *She depends on [lives off] her parents even after having graduated from university.*
昨夜は友達の家にやっかいになった *I stayed at my friend's house last night.*
◆あの男は幾度となく警察のやっかいになっている *The man has been in trouble with the police many times.*
やっかだいがく 薬科大学 a college of pharmacy [pharmaceutical science]
やっかむ get* jealous
◆彼はやっかんで彼女に意地悪をした *He acted nasty to her out of jealousy.*
やっき 躍起 彼女は躍起になって(→必死になって)そのことを弁解した *She desperately made excuses for it.* / その候補者は支持者を増やそうと躍起になっている(→できるかぎりの努力をしている) *The candidate is going all out to support his supporters.*
やつぎばや 矢継ぎ早 矢つぎばやの質問 *a hail of questions* / 記者たちは矢つぎばやに彼に質問を浴びせた *Reporters showered him with questions.*
やっきょう 薬莢 cartridge (case) Ⓒ
やっきょく 薬局 pharmacy Ⓒ, 《米》drug-

store [C],《英》chemist's [C];（病院などの）dispensary [C]

ヤッケ ⚠anorak [C], parka [C], windbreaker [C]（❖日本語はドイツ語の Jacke から）

やった やった！ ついに市原君に将棋で勝ったぞ *I did it*! I beat Ichihara at *shogi* at last.

💬「中央高校受かったよ」「やったね」"I got an offer from Chuo High School." "*Well done*!"

💬「誕生日に好きなゲームソフトを買ってやるよ」「やった！ お父さんありがとう」"I'll buy you any game software you want on your birthday." "*Great*! Thanks, Dad!"

やっつ 八つ eight [U][C] ➔ はち(八)

やっつけしごと やっつけ仕事 rough and hasty job [C];（雑な）sloppy [slipshod] job [C]

やっつける beat* [他],《口語的》let* *a person* have it ∥我々のチームはそのチームをこてんぱんにやっつけた Our team *beat the pants off* the other team. / 彼女は議論でその男をやっつけた She *let* the man *have it* with her argument.

やっていく やって行く（人とうまくやっていく）get* along [on] with *a person*;（暮らしていく）get along (on);（何とかする）manage [自][他] ∥私はだれとでもうまくやっていくことができる I can *get along with* anyone. / 君がいないと僕はやっていけない I *can't manage* without you.

◆大学生の兄は親からの月10万円の仕送りでやっていかなければならない My brother at college has to *get by on* a monthly allowance of 100,000 yen from my parents.

やってくる やって来る come* [自];（近寄ってくる）come up;（遠方から）come over;（定期的にめぐってくる）come around;（ひょっこり現れる）turn up ∥彼女はためらうことなく私の方へやってきた She *came up* to me without hesitation. / ジュリアは茶道を学ぶためにニューヨークからはるばる日本にやってきた Julia *came* all the way to Japan from New York to study the Japanese tea ceremony.

◆野球のシーズンがもうすぐやってくる The baseball season *will be here* soon.

やってのける accomplish [他],《口語的》pull off ∥彼女は全勝優勝をやってのけた She *pulled off* a clean sweep victory. ◆彼はその交渉をとてもスマートにやってのけた He *handled* the negotiations with much grace.

やってみる try [自][他], have* a try;（いちかばちか）take* a chance ∥やってみるだけの価値はあると思うよ I think it's worth *trying*. / 私はもう一度やってみることにした I decided to「*have* another [*give it* one more] *try*.

💬「ほとんどの人が失敗しているよ」「分かってる。でもいちかばちかやってみるよ」"Almost everyone has failed it." "I know. But I'*ll take a chance*."

やっと

❶【ついに】（とうとう）at last,《公式的》at length;（最後に）finally

やっと暑い夏が終わった The hot summer came to an end *at last*.

太郎に電話をかけ続けてけさやっと連絡がとれた I kept calling Taro, and I *finally* caught him this morning.

💬「君のお姉さん、会計士の試験に受かったんだって？」「うん，やっとね」"I heard your sister passed the exam to be a professional accountant." "Yes, *finally*."

❷【かろうじて】barely, only,《口語的》just (only)

その授業はついていくのがやっとだ I can *barely* keep up with that class.

この本は1日に5，6ページ読むのがやっとだ I can *only* read five or six pages of this book a day.

◆彼はやっとのことで冷静さを取り戻した He recovered his composure *with great difficulty*. / やっとの思いで目的地に着いた We *finally* reached our destination.

やっとこ pincers（❖数えるときは a pair of ... とする）

やっぱり 矢っ張り ➔ やはり

ヤッホー yoo-hoo [júːhùː] ∥私は山頂でヤッホーと叫んだ I「shouted *yoo-hoo* [*yoo-hooed*] on the top of the mountain.

やつれた thin;（心配などで）haggard;（病気などで）gaunt ∥やつれた顔[人] a *haggard* face [person] / 長い入院生活で彼はやつれていた He「*was gaunt* [*looked drawn*] because he'd been in the hospital for a long time.

やつれる become* thin;（心配などで）become haggard;（病気などで）become gaunt ∥彼は奥さんに先立たれやつれてしまった He *has become thin* since his wife died.

◆彼女は見る影もないほどにやつれている She *is worn* to a shadow.

やど 宿 lodging [U];（ホテル）hotel [C];（いなかの小さな）inn [C] ∥日も暮れてきたのでどこかに宿をとろう It's getting dark. Let's find「*a hotel* somewhere [somewhere to *stay*].

‖宿帳 a hotel register / 宿賃 a room charge, hotel charges [rate]

やとい 雇い（雇うこと）employment [U];（雇われた人）employee [C]

‖日雇い(人) a day laborer / 臨時雇い(人) a temporary employee

やといいれる 雇い入れる ➔ やとう(雇う)

やといにん 雇い人 employee [C]

やといぬし 雇い主 employer [C]

やとう¹ 雇う employ [他]; hire [他]（❖《英》では hire は一時的に人を雇うときに用いる）

タクシー[ガイド]を雇う *hire* a taxi [tour guide]

父の会社は10人ほど人を雇っている My father *employs* about ten people in his company.

私はおじの経営するレストランに雇ってもらった I *was hired* by the restaurant my uncle manages.

◆彼は自分の家の設計に有名な建築家を雇った He *engaged* a famous architect to design his house.

やとう² 野党 opposition party ◯; (野党全体) the Opposition ∥野党議員全員がその法案に反対した All members of the *Opposition* were opposed to the bill. / その党が野党第一党になった The party became *the leading opposition party*.
やどかり 宿借り hermit crab ◯
やどなし 宿無し homeless man [woman] ◯;《集合的》the homeless《複数扱い》; (浮浪者) tramp ◯
やどや 宿屋 inn ◯; (旅館) Japanese-style inn ◯ ∥箱根の宿屋に2日間滞在した I stayed at *an inn* in Hakone for two days.
やどりぎ 宿り木 mistletoe [mísltòu] ◯
やどる 宿る 健全な精神は健全な肉体に宿る (→健康な体は健康な心を作る) A healthy body *makes* a healthy mind. / 私のおなかには新しい生命が宿っている *There is* new life in my body.
やなぎ 柳 willow ◯; (シダレヤナギ) weeping willow ◯; (コリヤナギ) osier ◯
∥柳腰 a woman's slim waist
慣用表現 柳の下にいつもどじょうはいない *Good luck doesn't repeat itself*. (→幸運は繰り返しては起こらない)
やなみ 家並み a row of houses
やに 脂 (樹脂) resin ◯◯; (たばこの) tar ◯
∥松やに pine resin
やにわに suddenly ∥父はやにわに表へ飛び出した My father *suddenly* went outside.
やぬし 家主 (男性の大家) landlord ◯; (女性の大家) landlady ◯; (家の持ち主) the owner of the house

やね 屋根 roof ◯
かわらで屋根をふく cover *a roof* with tiles; *roof* a house with tiles
その丘の上には赤い屋根の家が建っている There is *a house with a red roof* [a red-*roofed* house] on the hill.
ヒマラヤ山脈は世界の屋根だ The Himalayas are *the roof* of the world.
∥屋根板 a shingle / 屋根裏部屋 an attic (❖しばしば物置として使う), 《主に英》a loft; (狭くて暗い) a garret / 瓦屋根 a (roof) tile / かわら屋根 a tiled roof / トタン屋根 a tin roof / わらぶき屋根 a thatched roof
慣用表現 彼は親と一つ屋根の下に住んでいて親に食べさせてもらっている He and his parents *live under the same roof* and he is supported by them.

やばい やばい, 逃げろ *Damn*! Let's get out of here! / 今度のテストは30点以上取らないと本当にやばいよ If I don't get a score of at least 30 in the next exam, I'll really *be in trouble*.

やはり
❶【同様に】also, too
彼女は美人だが, お母さんもやはりきれいな人だ She is beautiful, and her mother is 「*also* beautiful [beautiful, *too*]. / She is beautiful, and *so* is her mother.
❷【たとえそうでも】even so
彼はみんなに好かれているけれど, やはり私は彼とはうまく行かない Everyone likes him, but *even so* I can't get along with him.
❸【依然として】still; (また) again
やはり彼女に会うつもりですか Are you *still* going to see her?
やはりきょうも彼女は遅刻してきた She came late today *again*.
❹【思ったとおり】as *one* thought; (予測どおり) as *one* expected
やはり私の思ったとおりだった It was just *as I thought* [*expected*].
❺【結局】after all
やはり島田高校へ行くことにした I decided to go to Shimada High School *after all*.
やはり自分の生まれた故郷がいちばんだ *After all* your home town is best.
◆デジカメを買おうと思ったが, やはり(→考え直した結果)やめることにした I thought of buying a digital camera, but *on second thought* I decided not to buy one.

やはん 夜半 midnight ◯ ∥台風20号は夜半過ぎに紀伊半島に上陸した Typhoon No. 20 made a landfall on the Kii Peninsula after *midnight*.
やばん 野蛮 ——野蛮な (残虐な) savage; (原始的な) barbarous ∥野蛮な行為 one's savage [*barbarous*] acts
∥野蛮人 a barbarian
やひ 野卑 ——野卑な (下品な) vulgar; (いやしい) mean ∥野卑な言葉を吐く say *vulgar* words
やぶ 藪 thicket ◯; (草むら) the grass; (低木の茂み) bush ◯ ∥竹やぶ a bamboo *thicket* [*grove*] / ウサギはやぶの中に逃げ込んだ The rabbit ran into *the thicket*.
慣用表現 昨夜夕食中に兄は家を出ることにしたとやぶから棒に言いだした During dinner last night, my brother said *out of the blue* that he was going to leave home. / 真相は依然としてやぶの中だ The truth remains *a mystery*.
やぶいしゃ 藪医者 quack (doctor) ◯
やぶか 藪蚊 (Aedes) mosquito ◯
やぶく 破く (薄い物を) tear* [téər] ⊕ ⇒やぶる ∥紙をびりびりに破く *tear* paper into pieces
やぶける 破ける (薄い物が) tear* [téər] ⊖ ⇒やぶれる (破れる)
やぶさか 吝か あなたに協力するにやぶさかでない I'*m willing to* help you.
やぶさめ 流鏑馬 *yabusame*, Japanese archery on horseback
やぶへび 藪蛇 それはやぶへびだ It's like *waking a sleeping dog*. (❖「眠っている犬を起こすようなものだ」の意味)

やぶる 破る

❶【引き裂く】tear* [téər] ⊕; (乱暴に) rip ⊕
封筒を破ってあける *tear* an envelope open
彼女は彼からの手紙をすべて破ってしまった She *tore* [*ripped*] *up* all his letters.
ズボンをくぎに引っかけて破ってしまった I *tore* my pants on a nail.

やぶれ

弟とちゃんばらをしていて障子を破ってしまった I was playing at sword figting with my brother and *tore* a *shoji*.

❷[こわす] **break**;
金庫を破る *break* [*crack*] a safe
警官はドアを破り建物の中に入った The police *broke down* the door and entered the building.
けたたましい叫び声が夜の静寂を破った A shrill cry *broke* the silence of the night.

❸[反する] **break**; (違反する) violate; (伝統などを) ignore
約束を破る *break* a promise
彼は校則をことごとく破った He *broke* [*violated*] every single school regulation.

❹[記録などを] **break**
彼女はその世界記録を5年ぶりに破った She *broke* the world record that had stood for five years.

❺[負かす] **beat**, defeat
イタリアはフランスを2対1で破った Italy *beat* [*defeated*] France by 2 goals to 1.

やぶれ 破れ tear [téər], rip
ズボンのひざの破れをつくろう mend *a tear* at the knee of the trousers

やぶれかぶれ 破れかぶれ
その社長は会社が倒産して破れかぶれになっていた The company went bankrupt and the president was *desperate*. / 彼は破れかぶれの気持ちでその馬に持ち金全部をかけた *Not caring what happened next*, he bet all his money on the horse.

やぶれる¹ 破れる
❶[裂ける] **tear** [téər], **get** torn; (勢いよく) rip
この紙は破れにくい This paper doesn't *tear* [*rip*] easily.
毛糸の帽子がくぎに引っかかって破れた My woolen cap *got torn* on a nail.
◆紙袋がぬれて破れた(→穴があいた) The paper bag got wet and *broke*.

❷[成功しない]
彼女は恋に破れた She *has lost* in love.
彼のプロ野球選手になる夢はけがのために破れた His dream of becoming a professional baseball player *was shattered* because of the injury.

やぶれる² 敗れる (試合に) **lose**; (負かされる) be beaten [defeated]
日本は決勝でロシアに敗れた Japan *lost* the final *to* Russia. / Japan *was beaten by* Russia in the final.
我々は4対1で西高チームに敗れた We *lost* the game *to* the Nishi High School team 4 to 1. / We *were defeated* 4 to 1 *by* the Nishi High School team.

やぶん 夜分 night
夜分遅くにお電話してすみません I'm sorry to call you「at this time of [so late at] *night*.

やぼ 野暮 ——野暮な (愚かな) stupid; (人の気持ち気づかない) insensitive; (のみ込みが遅い) dense
そんなこと聞くなんて君も野暮なやつだな It'd be *stupid* of you to ask a question like that.
💬「あの2人もこっちのテーブルに誘わない?」「野暮なこと言うなよ。2人きりにしておいてあげようよ」 "Why don't we ask them to join our table?" "Don't be so *stupid*. Just leave them alone."
‖野暮用 odds and ends, bits and pieces

やぼう 野望 ambition (◆具体的な望みは ⓒ)
彼の政治家としての野望は大統領になることだ His *ambition* as a politician is to become President.

やぼったい 野暮ったい (センスのない) unfashionable; (あか抜けない) unrefined, unsophisticated
彼女、いつも高い服着ているけど野暮ったいのよね She always wears expensive clothes, but her taste is *unrefined*.

やま 山

❶[山岳] **mountain** ⓒ; (小山) hill ⓒ; (固有名詞に付ける) Mount, Mt. [máunt]

> (1) 固有名詞の前では mountain ではなく, Mount またはその略語の Mt. を用いる ∥ 雲取山 Mount [Mt.] Kumotori
> (2) mountain はふつう高くそびえる山, 周囲の地形から突出している山を指すので, 5, 6 百メートルに満たない山は, hill と呼んだほうが誤解が少ない場合が多い.

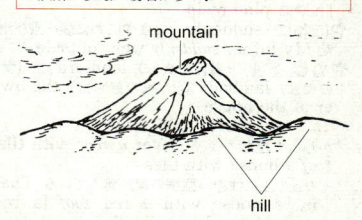

高い[低い]山 *a high* [*low*] *mountain* / はげ山 *a bare mountain* / 山に登る「go up [climb, ascend] *a mountain* / 山を降りる「go down [descend] *a mountain*
私は山でこの夏を過ごすつもりだ I will spend this summer in *the mountains*.
山の空気はすがすがしい The air in *the mountains* is fresh and clean.
その村は浅間山のふもとにある The village is at the foot of *Mt. Asama*.
◆日本は山が多い Japan is a *mountainous* country.

❷[積み重ねた物] pile ⓒ; (整然とした) stack ⓒ; (雑然とした) heap ⓒ

heap, pile   stack, pile
洗濯物の山 *a heap* of laundry

その店ではナスビが1山150円だ Eggplants are sold at 150 yen *a pile* at that store.
流しには皿の山ができていた There was *a stack [pile] of* dishes in the sink.
❸【たくさん】⇒やまほど
聖子は宿題の山と格闘している最中だった Seiko was in the midst of grappling with 「*a ton [loads] of* assignments.
その歌手は毎日山のような手紙をもらうらしい I hear the singer gets 「*a ton [loads, heaps] of* letters every day.
話したいことが山のようにある I have *tons [lots and lots] of* things I want to tell you.
❹【推測】(推測) guess ⓒ
こうやってはあすの試験は山をかけるしかない All I can do now is make *an educated guess* about what will be on tomorrow's exam.
◆山が当たった(→正しく推測した) I *guessed* right.
❺【山場】climax ⓒ; (危機) crisis ⓒ (複 crises)
その章がこの小説の山だ That chapter is *the climax* of this novel.
彼の病気は山を越したようだ *The crisis* in his illness appears to be over.
俳句 分け行つても分け行つても青い山
(種田山頭火)
No matter how far I go,
no matter how deep I go:
only green mountains

やまあい 山間 mountain valley ⓒ; (深く切り立った峡谷) ravine ⓒ
やまあらし 山荒 〖動物〗porcupine ⓒ
やまあるき 山歩き 私たちはこの前の日曜日に山歩きを楽しんだ We enjoyed *hiking* last Sunday.
やまい 病 illness Ⓤ; (病名の分かっている) disease ⓒⓤ /不治の病 *an* incurable *disease* / 病に倒れる be struck down by *a disease*
◆彼は病に臥(ふ)している He is *ill* in bed.
ことわざ 病は気から The mind rules the body.(→心が体を支配する)
やまいも 山芋 yam ⓒ
やまおく 山奥 私の祖父母は山奥に住んでいる My grandparents live *deep in the mountains*.
やまおとこ 山男 (登山する人) mountain climber ⓒ; (本格的な登山家) alpinist ⓒ, mountaineer ⓒ
やまかげ 山陰 月が山陰に隠れた The moon is *behind the mountain*.
やまかじ 山火事 forest fire ⓒ /その山火事で多くの動物が死んだ Many animals were killed by the *forest fire*.
やまがた 山形

山形県は本州の北部に位置していて、西で日本海に面しています。この県の土地の大部分は山がちですが、県下最大の川である最上川の河口付近は平野になっています。農業と林業が主要産業で、特にサクランボの生産は日本一として知られています。一方温泉やスキーのためのリゾート地も数多く、中でも宮城県との境界に位置する蔵王山は温泉地としても スキー場としても有名です。
Yamagata Prefecture is located in northern Honshu and faces the Sea of Japan on the west. Most of its terrain is mountainous, though the mouth of the prefecture's major river, the Mogami, forms a plain. Agriculture and forestry are among the major industries in this prefecture, and its cherry production is known as the largest in Japan. Yamagata also has many hot spring and ski resorts. Among them Zao, which lies on the border with Miyagi Prefecture, is particularly well known for both its hot spring and ski resorts.

やまがり 山狩り 警察は殺人容疑者を追って犬を放ち山狩りをした The police released the dogs and *combed the forests [hills]* for the murder suspect.
やまかん 山勘 (wild) guess ⓒ /私は山勘で答えた I answered with *a wild guess.*/ 彼女の山勘はよく当たる Her *guess* is often right./ She often *guesses* right.
やまくずれ 山崩れ landslide ⓒ
やまぐち 山口

山口県は本州最西端の県で、関門海峡をはさんでトンネルと橋で九州と結ばれています。瀬戸内海沿岸の都市は古くから西日本の交通の要衝の地として発達し、現在では、重工業・化学工業が盛んです。また、山口県は三方を海に囲まれて多くの漁港があり、漁業も盛んです。中でも、フグの水揚げは日本一で、山口のフグはとても有名です。
Yamaguchi Prefecture is the westernmost part of Honshu and is linked to Kyushu across the Kammon Strait by tunnel and bridge. The cities along the Seto Inland Sea have long been keys in the transportation network in western Japan. Today heavy and chemical industries flourish. This prefecture faces the sea on three sides and has many fishing ports. Its fisheries thrive, and it is Japan's major port for the unloading of globefish. Yamaguchi Prefecture's globefish are well known all over Japan.

やまぐに 山国 (国) mountainous country ⓒ; (地域) mountainous region ⓒ
やまごや 山小屋 mountain hut ⓒ; (登山・避暑・スキーなどのための) lodge ⓒ /山小屋で1泊する stay one night at *a mountain hut*
やまざくら 山桜 (花) wild cherry blossoms; (木) wild cherry tree ⓒ
やまざと 山里 mountain village ⓒ
やまし 山師 (投機家) speculator ⓒ; (詐欺師) swindler ⓒ
やましい feel* guilty, have* a guilty conscience /何かやましいことでもあるの *Are you*

やまづみ 山積み 山積みの本 *a pile of* books / 流しには汚れた皿が山積みになっていた Dirty dishes *were piled* [*heaped*] *up* in the sink. / 問題が山積みされている There are *many* problems *left*.

やまでら 山寺 mountain temple ◎

やまと 大和 *Yamato*, an ancient name of Japan
‖大和言葉 a native Japanese word / 大和魂 the Japanese spirit / 大和なでしこ (日本女性) a graceful Japanese woman / 大和民族 the Japanese ethnic group

やまどり 山鳥 mountain bird ◎; (キジ科の鳥) copper pheasant ◎

やまなし 山梨

山梨県は本州のほぼ中央部に位置する内陸県で東京都の西に位置します．県庁所在地の甲府市がある甲府盆地では果実の栽培が盛んです．中でもブドウと桃の栽培が有名で，ワインも大量に生産されています．また富士山や富士五湖，八ヶ岳や南アルプスの山々など美しい自然を楽しめる観光地も数多くあります．
Yamanashi Prefecture, a landlocked prefecture, is located to the west of Tokyo in central Honshu. The growing of fruit flourishes in the Kofu Basin, in which lies the city of Kofu, the prefectural capital. The production of grapes and peaches is famous and wine is produced abundantly in this prefecture. Yamanashi has many tourist attractions such as Mt. Fuji and Fujigoko (five lakes around Mt. Fuji), the Yatsugatake mountains and the Southern Japan Alps, where you can enjoy beautiful natural scenery.

やまねこ 山猫 wildcat ◎

やまのて 山の手 (高台の住宅地の) a residential district in a hilly area
‖山手線 the Yamanote (Loop) Line

やまのは 山の端 the edge of a mountain

やまのぼり 山登り mountain climbing ⓤ; (本格的な登山) mountaineering ⓤ / 私は週末よく山登りをする I often go *mountain climbing* on weekends. / 山登りは台風の接近のため中止となった The climb [*hike*] was canceled because of the approaching typhoon. (❖ 1 回の山登りは climb, hike などという. climb は本格的な登山 (＝山歩き))

やまば 山場 climax ◎; (危機) crisis ◎ (複 crises), critical moment ◎; (転機) turning point ◎ / テレビドラマがちょうど山場のときに電話が鳴った Just when the drama on TV reached *its climax*, the phone rang.

やまはだ 山肌 the surface of a mountain

やまばと 山鳩 (キジバト) turtledove ◎

やまびこ 山彦 echo ◎ / ヤッホーと叫ぶと山びことなって帰ってきた I shouted yoo-hoo, and *the echoes* came back.

やまびらき 山開き the beginning of the mountaineering season

やまぶき 山吹 (花) Japanese rose ◎ ‖山吹色 bright yellow

やまほど 山ほど まだ夏休みの宿題が山ほど残っている I have 「*a ton* [*loads*] *of* summer vacation homework left. / やるべきことが山ほどある I've got *stacks of* things to do.

やまみち 山道 mountain path [track, trail] ◎; (車これる) mountain road

やまもり 山盛り a heap of ...; (スプーンに) a heaping spoonful of ...; (茶碗に) a bowlful of ... / コーヒーにスプーン山盛り 2 杯の砂糖を入れる put two *heaping spoonfuls of* sugar in coffee / 彼は茶わんに山盛りのごはんをあっという間に食べてしまった He ate up *a bowlful of* rice in no time.

やまやき 山焼き burning the dead grass off a mountain [hill]

やまやま 山々 ❶【本当は】キャンプにご一緒したいのはやまやまなのですが，日曜日には模試がありまして I'*d really like to* go camping with you, *but* I have a trial exam this Sunday. ❷【多くの山】mountains / うちのベランダからは遠くに秩父の山々が見える We can see *the mountains* of Chichibu in the distance from our balcony.

やまゆり 山百合 golden-rayed lily ◎

やまわけ 山分け ——山分けする (等分する) split* [divide] ... equally; (2 人で等分する) go* fifty-fifty [half-and-half] / 宝くじが当たったらみんなで山分けしよう If we win the lottery, we'll *split* [*divide*] the money *equally* among us. / 彼らはもうけを 2 人で山分けした They *went fifty-fifty* [*halves*] with each other on the profit.

やみ 闇 darkness ⓤ; (暗い所) the dark / 心のやみ *darkness* [*the dark*] in *one*'*s* soul / やみの中で何かが動いた Something moved in *the dark*. / 彼らはやみに紛れてその車に近づいた They approached the car *under cover of darkness*. / 夜になるとあたり一帯はやみに包まれた When night came, the area was enveloped in *darkness*.
◆黒ずくめの男は夜のやみに消えた The man in black disappeared into *the night*.
慣用表現 一寸先はやみだ *Who can predict the future?* (→いったいだれが先を予測できるだろうか) / 真実はやみに葬られた (→覆い隠された) The truth *was covered up*.
‖やみ献金 a secret contribution / やみ取引 black-marketing / やみルート illegal channels

やみあがり 病み上がり 彼女は病み上がりで体がまだ弱っている She is still weak because she *has just recovered from her illness*.

やみうち 闇討ち (不意の) surprise attack ◎; (暗い中での) an attack under (the) cover of darkness

やみくも 闇雲 男はやみくもに銃を乱射した The man fired the gun *at random*. / やみくもに反対してもむだだ Don't just object to it *thoughtlessly*. It leads nowhere.

やみつき 病み付き インターネットにやみつきになってこのごろ睡眠不足だ I'm not getting enough sleep these days because I'm 「*addicted to* [*hooked on*] the Internet. / 弟はコンピュータゲームにやみつきだ My brother *abandons himself to* computer games.

やみよ 闇夜 dark night ◯; (月の出ていない) moonless night ◯

やむ¹ 止む (雨・雪などが) stop 他自; (風などが) die down; (音などが徐々に) die away 雪がやんだ The snow *has stopped*. / It *has stopped* snowing.
子供は泣きやんだ The child *stopped crying*.
どうやら風はやんだようだ It seems the wind *has died down*.
◆雨が降ったりやんだりする日がここ数日続いている It has rained on and *off* all day for the last few days. / ご成功を願ってやみません I wish you success *from the bottom of my heart*.

やむ² 病む 肺を病む suffer from a lung *disease* / 病んだ社会 a *diseased* society / 私は彼のことで気を病んでいる I *worry* about him.

やむなく 止む無く (いやいや) reluctantly; (しぶしぶ) unwillingly //忙しかったけれどやむなく彼女を手伝った I was busy, but I helped her *reluctantly* [*unwillingly*].

やむにやまれず 止むに止まれず 彼は貧困からやむにやまれず盗みを働いた He *had no choice* but to steal because of poverty.

やむをえず 止むを得ず どしゃ降りになったのでやむをえずソフトボール大会を中止した We *had to* cancel the softball games because it began to rain heavily. / その道は通行止めになっておりやむをえず引き返した I *had no choice but* to go back because the road was closed to traffic.

やむをえない 止むを得ない (避けられない) unavoidable, inevitable; (必要な) necessary //やむをえない事情で予定をキャンセルした I canceled the appointment due to an *unavoidable* problem.
◆それはやむをえない It *can't be helped*.

やめる¹ 止める

❶【中止する】stop 他, 《口語的》quit* 他自; (一時的に) suspend 他; (取りやめる) cancel 他

> 語法
> 「…することをやめる」といいたいときは stop *doing* の形を用いる. stop to *do* は「…するために立ち止まる」の意味になる // 私たちは話すのをやめた We *stopped talking*. / 私たちは話すために立ち止まった We *stopped to talk*.

(子供などに)やめなさい Stop it! / Cut it out!
みなさん、おしゃべりをやめてください Everyone, please *stop* talking.
私たちは旅行に行くのをやめた We *canceled* our trip.
私は2人の言い争いをやめさせた I *stopped* the two (*from*) arguing.
◆それだけはやめて(→しないで)ください Please *don't do* that.

❷【断念する】give* up
父が酒とたばこをやめて1年たつ It's been a year since my father *gave up* drinking and smoking.
彼らは夢を追い求めることをやめた They *gave up* pursuing their dream.
◆妹と私は父に賭(か)け事をやめさせた My sister and I *persuaded* our father *to quit* gambling. (❖persuade … to *do* は「…を説得して〜させる」の意味)

やめる² 辞める (辞職する) resign 他自, 《口語的》quit* 他; (去る) leave* 他; (定年退職する) retire 自
彼女は来月で仕事を辞める She *will* 「*resign (from)* [*quit*] her job next month.
彼は定年で会社を辞めるまでにできるだけたくさんの貯金をするつもりでいる He intends to save as much money as he can before he *retires (from his company)*.
あのときクラブをやめなくてよかった It's a good thing I didn't *leave* [*quit*] the club then.
その少年は入学してわずか3か月で学校をやめた The boy *left* [*quit*] school only three months after he entered it.
父は家業を継がせるために私に会社を辞めさせた My father *made* my brother *leave* the company to have him take over the family business.
◆彼は学校をやめさせられた He *was expelled from* school. / 社長は一度に5人辞めさせた (→解雇した) The president *dismissed* [*fired*] five people at once.

やもめ (女) widow ◯; (男) widower ◯

やもり gecko ◯ (複 〜(e)s)

やや (少し) a little, 《口語的》a bit; (わずかに) slightly; (多少) somewhat //こちらの生地はやや高めです This material is *slightly* [*a little*] more expensive. / ここ2, 3か月景気はややもち直してきた Business has been improving *somewhat* these past few months.

ややこしい (複雑な) complicated; (混乱する) confusing //ややこしい人間関係 a *complicated* relationship / 話がややこしくなってきた The story is getting *confusing*.

ややもすれば 我々はややもすれば責任を人に押しつけがちだ We *are apt* [*liable*] *to* leave responsibility to others.

やゆ 揶揄 その記事は政治家たちをやゆしていた The article *made fun of* politicians.

-やら 姉はいつになったら結婚するのやら I *wonder* when my sister will get married. / あれやらこれやらすることがたくさんあって忙しい I'm very busy doing *this and that*. / 家事やら子育てやらパートやらで母はいつも駆けずり回っている *Between* housekeeping, childcare *and* a part-time job, my mother is always busy. / 悪天候やら交通渋滞やらで私たちの旅は最悪だった *What with* the bad weather *and* the heavy traffic, our trip was terrible.

やらい 夜来 夜来の雨でグラウンドには水たまりができている There are some puddles on the ground due to *the rain having fallen through the night*.

やらかす 今度はいったい何をやらかしたんだ What on earth *have* you *done* this time? / とんだ大失敗をやらかしてしまった I really *messed up*.

やらせ あのドキュメンタリー番組はやらせだ That documentary program is *staged*.

やらせる (無理に) make* *a person do*; (自由に) let* *a person do* ‖彼はいやなことはいつも私にやらせる He always *makes me do* things he doesn't want to do. / 彼女の好きにやらせておきなさい *Let her do* as she pleases.

やられる 太郎は次郎にこてんぱんにやられた Taro *was beaten to a pulp* by Jiro. / 私もとうとうインフルエンザにやられた I finally *came down with* the flu. / しまった，すりにやられた Oh, no! I *had* my pocket *picked*. / 台風で作物がやられてしまった The crops *were ruined* by the typhoon.

やり 槍 spear ⓒ; (やり投げ用の) javelin ⓒ ◆敵をやりで突く *spear* an enemy ‖やり投げ the javelin (throw)

やりあう やり合う (口論する) argue ⓔ; (口げんかする) quarrel ⓔ
💬「あれ，きょうは純子といっしょじゃないの？」「うん，実はきのう彼女とちょっとやり合っちゃってね」"Oh, aren't you with Junko today?" "No, I *had a quarrel* with her yesterday."

やりがい やり甲斐 これはやりがいのある仕事だ This is a「job *worth doing* [*rewarding* job, *challenging* job].

やりかえす やり返す 彼女にはいつも言われっぱなしでやり返すチャンスがない She's always picking on me, and I never have a chance to *get back at* her. / 彼にひっぱたかれたので私も彼にやり返した He slapped my face, so I *got back at* him. / やられたらやり返せ(→殴られたら殴り返せ) If someone hits you, then *hit back*.

やりかけ やり掛け やりかけの仕事 *unfinished* [*half-done*] work / 妹は宿題をやりかけのまま遊びに行ってしまった My sister went out leaving her homework *unfinished*.

やりかた やり方 昔からのやり方に従ってやる do by *the conventional method* / ライバルを次々と買収していくその会社のやり方にはうんざりだ It's disgusting *the way* the company keeps acquiring its rivals. / 彼女は大体のやり方を教えてくれた She showed me「*how to* [*the way to*] *do it*. / 彼らは会社のやり方を苦々しく思っていた They were bitter about the company's *policy*.

やりきれない ❶【完了しない】徹夜しても宿題をやりきれないよ I *will not be able to finish* my homework even if I stay up all night. / この仕事は彼一人ではやりきれない It *is impossible* for him *to do* this work by himself.
❷【耐えられない】事故で親を亡くしたその幼い兄弟のことを考えるとやりきれなくなる I *can't bear* to think about the young brothers who lost their parents in the accident. / 彼のぐちを聞かされるのはやりきれない I *can't stand* [*bear*] his grumbling.

やりくち やり口 あいつのやり口は汚い *The way* he does things is sleazy.

やりくり やり繰り ──やりくりする (うまく調整する) manage ⓔⓣ; (時間などを) juggle ⓣ ‖何とか時間をやりくりする *juggle one's time somehow* / 彼は安い給料で何とかやりくりしている He *manages* [*gets by*] on his small income somehow.
◆母はやりくり上手だ My mother is *a good household manager*.

やりこなす 私にはこの難役をやりこなす自信がない I'm not sure if I can *fill* [*do*] this difficult role.

やりこめる やり込める (言い負かす) talk [argue] *a person down* ‖彼女は弁護士をやり込めた She *argued* the lawyer *down*.

やりすぎ やり過ぎ テレビゲームのやりすぎは目によくない If you play video games *too much*, it's going to damage your eyesight.
💬「彼のこと訴えようと思っているんだけど」「それはちょっとやりすぎじゃないの？」"I'm thinking of suing him." "*Isn't* that *going a bit too far*?"
💬「あの人たちは自分たちが金持ちだということを見せびらかしたくてベルサイユ宮殿のような家を建てたらしいよ」「やりすぎだよね」"I heard they built a house like the Versailles Palace to show off how rich they are." "That's *overdoing it*."

やりすぎる やり過ぎる あまり仕事をやりすぎないようにね Don't work *too hard*.

やりすごす やり過ごす 込んだバスを1台やり過ごした I *let* a packed bus *go past*.

やりそこなう やり損なう (失敗する) fail ⓔ; (チャンスを逃す) miss ⓣ ‖今度やりそこなったらもうだれも助けてくれない If I *fail* next time, no one will help me any more. / この前は時間がなくてそれをやりそこなった I *missed* it last time because I didn't have enough time.

やりだま 槍玉 彼は今回の不祥事でやり玉に挙げられた He *was singled out for criticism* in this scandal.

やりつける これはやりつけているので心配はご無用です *I'm used to* this, so please don't worry.

やりっぱなし やりっ放し 彼女は何をやってもやりっぱなしが多い(→物を出しっぱなしにする) Whatever she does, she usually「*leaves things lying around* [(→途中でやめてしまう) *leaves it unfinished*].

やりて やり手 (有能な人) real achiever ⓒ; (敏腕家) go-getter ⓒ; (商売などで) wheeler-dealer ⓒ(◆軽蔑的な意味が含まれることもある) ‖新しい店長はやり手らしい I hear the new shop manager is *a go-getter*. / 彼はかなりのやり手だから気をつけたほうがいいよ He's quite *a wheeler-dealer*, so you'd better be careful with him.

やりとげる やり遂げる (完成する) complete [他]; (達成する) accomplish [他]; (実行する) carry out [through] //何が起ころうと我々はこの仕事をやりとげるつもりです We intend to *complete* this job, come what may. / 私はこの計画をやりとげる自信がある I'm confident I can「*carry out* [*accomplish*] this plan.

やりとり やり取り exchange [C] ――やり取りする exchange [他] //喜美子とは2,3回手紙のやり取りをしたことがある I *have exchanged* letters with Kimiko a few times.

やりなおし やり直し それはやり直しがきかないから注意してね Be careful.「It *can't be redone*. [You *can't do* it *over again*.]

やりなおす やり直す (再びやる) do* ... over again; (最初からやり直す) start [begin*] all over again; (繰り返す) repeat [他]; (勉強し直す) study ... again

この問題の答えは違っている. もう一度やり直しなさい Your answer to this problem is wrong. *Do it over again*.

けんかのことは忘れてもう一度やり直そうか What do you say about forgetting our quarrel and *starting all over again*?

こんな漢字も読めないの? 小学校からやり直したほうがいいよ Can't you read this *kanji*? You should *repeat* elementary school.

姉は英語をやり直すために語学学校へ通うつもりだ My sister plans to go to a language school to *study* English *again*.

◆彼は人生をやり直す決心をした He made up his mind to *make a new* [*fresh*] *start* in life.

やりにくい やり難い 外がうるさくて宿題をやりにくかった *It was hard* for me *to do* my homework because it was noisy outside. / 太郎の雄弁なスピーチの後ではやりにくいな Taro's eloquent speech is a *difficult* act to follow.

やりぬく やり抜く carry out [through] //何が何でも最後までやり抜くつもりだ I'll *carry* it *out* [*through*] to the end at any cost.

やりば やり場 彼の話を聞き私はやり場のない怒りを感じた I *didn't know how to give vent to* my anger after I heard his story.

💬「あの2人, 電車の中でキスしてたね」「ああ. 全く目のやり場に困ったよ」"Those two were kissing on the train, weren't they?" "Yes. I *didn't know where to turn my eyes*."

やる

❶【する】(❖状況に応じた動詞を用いる)

私がやります I'*ll do* that.

どなたかこれを私が戻ってくるまでにやっておいてくれますか Could someone *finish* this before I come back?

来年はスペイン語をやるつもりです I plan to *study* Spanish next year.

弟もサッカーをやりたがっている My brother also wants to *play* soccer.

よくやった *Well done*!/ *Great*!

とにかくやってみなよ Anyway,「*try* it [*give* it *a try*].

やるだけのことはやった(→ベストを尽くした) *I did my best*./(→できることはすべてやった) *I tried everything I could*.

💬「やりましたね」「ええ, やりました」"You *made* [*did*] *it*!" "Yes, I *made* [*did*] *it*."

❷【与える】give* [他]; (えさを) feed* [他]; (水を) water [他]

その本, 君にやるよ I'*ll give* you that book.

私が2週間留守にする間, 犬にえさをやるのと花に水をやるのを忘れないでね Don't forget to *feed* the dog and *water* the flowers while I'm away for two weeks.

❸【行かせる】send* [他]

彼は一生懸命働いて子供をみんな大学へやった He worked hard and *sent* all his children *to* college.

徹を駅まで迎えにやるよ I'*ll send* Toru to meet you at the station.

❹【移す】

朝刊, どこへやった Where did you *put* the morning paper?

ここにあったかぎ, どこにやったの Where did you *put* the key that was here?

そのいも虫, どこかへやって *Get* the caterpillar *away* from here.

敬子は次郎にちらっと目をやった Keiko *glanced* at Jiro.

❺【その他】

一杯やる *have* a drink

おばは原宿で美容院をやっている My aunt *runs* a beauty salon in Harajuku.

あの後, 彼女とやった(→セックスした)のか? Did you *do it* with her after that?

いつか仕返ししてやる I'*ll* get back at you some day.

💬「元気でやってる? お給料足りてるの?」「何とかやってるよ」"*Are you doing okay*? Are you making enough money?" "I'*m getting by*."

💬「映画でも見に行かない?」「今何をやっているんだろう」"How about going to see a movie?" "What'*s showing* now?"

💬「アイスクリーム落としちゃった」「泣かないで. また買ってやるから」"I dropped the ice cream." "Don't cry. I'*ll get* you another one."

💬(店などで)「すみません. まだやってますか」「はい, 8時までやってます」"Excuse me. *Are* you still *open*?" "Yes, we *stay open* until 8 o'clock."

やるき やる気 (意欲) drive [U]; (動機づけ) motivation [U]

きょうの彼はやる気満々だ He is full of *drive* [*enthusiasm*] today.

彼女はやる気がない She has no *drive*.

彼女はもうやる気を失ったようだ She seems to have lost *her motivation*.

◆きょうは何もやる気がしない I *don't feel like*

やるせない

doing anything today. / 彼の言葉が私にやる気を起こさせた His remark *motivated* me. / やる気出せよ Show more *enthusiasm*.

やるせない (みじめな) miserable; (無力な) helpless /何だかやるせない気持ちになった I felt *miserable* [*helpless*] somehow.

やれ やれクラブ活動だのやれ塾だのと弟はほとんどうちにいない *What with* school club activities *and* the cram school, my brother is hardly ever at home.

やれやれ やれやれ期末試験もこれで終わりだ *Thank God*! The term exams are over now. / やれやれやっとひと息つける *Whew*! Now I can relax. / やれやれやっと到着だよ *Well*, here we are at last.

やろう 野郎 あんな野郎はうっておけ Don't take *him* seriously. / この野郎 *Damn you*! / 野郎どもばっかりじゃないか,女の子たちはどうした Only *men* are here. Where are the girls?

やわらかい 柔[軟]らかい

❶【硬くない・柔軟な】 soft; (肉などが) tender
芯(しん)の柔らかい鉛筆 a *soft* pencil / 柔らかいソファー a *soft* sofa / 柔らかい肉 *tender* meat
彼女は柔らかい髪をしている She has *soft* hair.
赤ちゃんの肌は柔らかい Babies' skin is *tender* [*delicate*].
◆体柔らかいね You are really *supple* [*flexible*].

❷【穏やかな】(性格などが) mild, gentle; (光・色彩などが) soft
柔らかい色 *soft* color
彼は物腰が非常に柔らかい He has the *mildest* manners.
大きな窓からは柔らかな光が降り注いでいた Soft [*Mild*] sunshine was pouring through the big window.

❸【融通のきく】
彼は頭が柔らかい His way of thinking is *flexible*.

やわらぐ 和らぐ (声・態度などが) soften [sɔ́ːfən] 自; (痛み・気持ちなどが) ease 自; (風などが) die down //彼の声がやわらいだ His voice *softened*. / 薬が効き始め,痛みがやわらいだ The pain *eased* as the medicine began to work.
◆寒さがやわらいだ The cold *got less severe*.

やわらげる 和らげる (声・態度などを) soften [sɔ́ːfən] 他; (痛みなどを) ease 他; (怒りなどを) calm 他 //苦痛をやわらげる *ease* [*alleviate*] suffering / 彼女は急に態度をやわらげた She suddenly *softened* her attitude. / このシートは衝突時の衝撃をやわらげます This seat *softens* the impact during collisions.
◆おいしい料理は彼の怒りをやわらげた The delicious food *blunted* his anger.

ヤンキー ⚠(不良少年・少女) a (young) punk 🔲; (暴走族) motorcycle gang 🔲, a gang of hot-rodders(❖前者は「バイクの暴走族」,後者は「車の暴走族」の意味)

ヤング (若者たち) young people,《集合的》 the young //ここはヤング向けの店だ This is a shop for *young people*.

ヤンゴン Yangon(❖ミャンマーの首都。ただし英語では旧称のRangoonを用いることが多い)

やんちゃ ——やんちゃな naughty /弟は小さいころはやんちゃ坊主だった When my brother was little, he was a *naughty* boy.

やんや やんや,やんやのかっさい *loud* applause

やんわり (穏やかに) gently; (遠回しに) indirectly //彼は申し出をやんわり断った He turned down the offer *indirectly*.

ゆ

ゆ 湯 (hot) water ◎ (❖英語では「湯」も「水」も water といい、特に区別する必要がある場合だけ hot water とする); (ふろ) bath ◎, bathwater ◎
　ぬるま湯 *lukewarm* [*tepid*] *water* / 湯につかる soak in *a bath* / 浴槽に湯を張る run *a bath*; run *hot water* into a bathtub
　お湯が沸いている *The water* is boiling.
　彼女はお茶をいれるためにお湯を沸かした She boiled *water* to make some tea.
　みそ汁がからかったのでお湯をさした The *miso* soup was too salty, so I poured some *hot water* into it.
　いいお湯でした I very much enjoyed *the bath*.
　父は湯上がりにビールを飲む My father drinks beer *after his bath*.
　🔴「湯かげんはどう」「ちょうどいいよ」 "*How's the bathwater*?" "It's just right."
　‖湯あか scale / 湯冷まし cool boiled water

ゆあつ 油圧 oil [hydraulic] pressure ◎
　‖油圧計 an oil pressure gauge / 油圧ブレーキ oil [hydraulic] brakes

ゆいいつ 唯一 ──唯一の only, sole (❖いずれも名詞の前で用いる), one and only (❖only を強調した言い方) /町で唯一の病院 the *only* hospital in the town / 甘い物を食べることが私の唯一の楽しみだ Eating sweets is my *only* indulgence. / 彼女はそのコンテストで入賞した唯一の日本人だ She was the *sole* Japanese prizewinner in that contest.

ゆいごん 遺言 (遺言状) will ◎; (死に際の願い) *one's* dying wish / 遺言を書く make [draw up] *one's will* / 父は遺言で私に家を残してくれた My father left me the house *in his will*. / My father willed "me the house [the house *to* me]. (❖動詞 will は「…を遺言で残す」の意味) / 遺言に従って私たちは彼を生まれ故郷に埋葬した We buried him in his hometown *in accordance with his will*.

ゆいしょ 由緒 由緒ある家柄 a family *of good lineage* / 由緒ある(→長い歴史のある)建物 a building *with a long history*; (→歴史的に重要な)a *historic* building

ゆいしんろん 唯心論 〔哲学〕spiritualism ◎, idealism ◎
　‖唯心論者 a spiritualist, an idealist

ゆいのう 結納 *yuino*, (a ceremonial exchange of) engagement gifts / 結納を交わす exchange *engagement gifts*
　‖結納金 engagement money

ゆいぶつしかん 唯物史観 historical materialism ◎

ゆいぶつろん 唯物論 〔哲学〕materialism ◎
　‖唯物論者 a materialist

ゆう¹ 優 A ◎ (複 ~'s, ~s) /英語で優を取る get *an A* in English / 全科目優を取る get straight *A's* [*As*]

> 米国の成績評価では日本の「優」に相当するのが A (Excellent), 「良」が B (Good), 「可」が C (Average) か D (Below Average), 「不可」が F (Failure) である.

ゆう² 結う 日本髪に髪を結う do *one's* hair in traditional Japanese style

ゆう³ 言う ⇨いう

ゆうあい 友愛 friendship ◎◎

ゆうい 優位 (有利) advantage ◎◎; (優越) superiority ◎ /ハイテク分野ではその国は他の国の優位に立っている The country 「has *superiority over* [*is superior to*] other countries in the area of high technology. / チャンピオンは挑戦者よりも心理的優位に立った The champion gained *a* psychological *advantage over* his opponent.
◆男性優位の社会 a *male-dominated* society

ゆういぎ 有意義 ──有意義な (意味のある) meaningful; (意味深い) significant; (有益な) useful /きょうは有意義な討論ができた We had a *meaningful* discussion today.
　夏休みを有意義に過ごす spend the summer vacation *meaningfully*; (→うまく使う) *make good use of* the summer vacation / 値は張ったが有意義なお金の使い方だった It cost me a lot, but it was money *well spent*.

ゆういん 誘因 (原因) cause ◎; (刺激) incentive ◎◎ /喫煙は肺癌(がん)の大きな誘因となる Smoking is a major *cause* of lung cancer.

ゆううつ 憂鬱 (意気消沈) depression ◎; (陰気) gloom ◎ (また a ~); (物悲しいこと) melancholy ◎. ──憂鬱な depressed; gloomy /テストのことを考えただけで憂鬱になる (→テストのことが私を憂鬱にさせる) The very thought of the exam makes me *feel depressed* [*blue*]. / 彼は憂鬱そうな顔をしていた He looked *depressed* [*gloomy*].
　毎年この時期は憂鬱な天気が続く The *depressing* [*gloomy*] weather lasts a long time at this time of year. (❖depressing は「憂鬱にさせる」の意味)

ゆうえい 遊泳 swimming / 遊泳禁止《掲示》*No Swimming*
　‖宇宙遊泳 a space walk

ゆうえき 有益 ──有益な (役に立つ) useful; (教訓的な) instructive; (助けになる) helpful; (利益をもたらす) beneficial; (金銭的価値が高い) valuable /この本は初心者には特に有益だ This book *is useful*, especially for beginners. / 先生は有益な忠告をしてくれた The teacher gave me some *useful* advice. / その旅はとても有益だった That trip *was* very *instructive* for me. / 彼らの提案は私たちにとっても有益だった Their offer *was* also *beneficial* for us. / その発明が人類にとって有益かどうかは疑わしい It is doubtful whether the invention would be *beneficial* [*profit-*

able] to humankind.
◆限られた予算を有益に使わなければならない We must *spend* the limited budget *usefully*. / We must *make good use of* the limited budget. / 夏休みを有益に使うべきだ You should *make the most of* your summer vacation.

ゆうえつ 優越 彼はクラブのほかのメンバーに対して優越感をいだいていた He 「*felt superior to* [*had a superiority complex over*] the other members in the club.

ユーエッチエフ UHF, uhf (◆*ultra*high frequency (極超短波)の略語)

ゆうえんち 遊園地 amusement park ©

ゆうが 優雅 ——優雅な (動作などが) elegant; graceful ——優雅に elegantly; gracefully ∥バレリーナの優雅な跳躍 the ballerina's *graceful* leaps
◆優雅な (→気楽な) 生活を送る lead an *easy* [(→ぜいたくな) a *luxurious*] life

ゆうかい 誘拐 kidnapping ⓤ ©, abduction ⓤ © ——誘拐する kidnap ⊕, abduct ⊕ ∥先月誘拐され、その安否が気づかわれていた少年がきょう無事解放された The boy (whom) people had been worried about since he *was kidnapped* last month was released safely today.
∥誘拐犯 a kidnapper, an abductor

ゆうがい 有害 ——有害な harmful, 《公式的》injurious, evil; (悪い) bad ∥健康に有害な食品添加物 a food additive *harmful to* health / テレビ番組の中には子供に有害とみなされているものがある Some TV programs are perceived as being 「*harmful to* [*bad for*] children.
◆このような制度は有害無益だ Such a system *does more harm than good*.
∥有害物質 a hazardous substance

ゆうがお 夕顔 bottle gourd ©; (夜顔) moonflower ©

ゆうしょうけん 有価証券 securities

ゆうかぜ 夕風 evening breeze ©

ゆうがた 夕方 evening © ⓤ (◆通例日没から寝る時間までを指す。night は日没から日の出までをいう) ⇒よる(夜) 図版
5月2日の夕方に on *the evening* of May 2 / 日曜日の夕方に on Sunday *evening* (◆ある決まった日の「夕方に」というときは on を用いる)
夕方になると涼しくなる It gets cool in *the evening*.
彼は毎日夕方に散歩をする He takes a walk every *evening*. (◆evening の前に every, yesterday, tomorrow などを付けるときは前置詞は不要)
その店は夕方6時まであいています The store is open till six in *the evening*.
夕方までには帰ってきなさい Come home *by evening*.
天気は夕方にかけて崩れるでしょう The weather will change for the worse *toward evening*.

ゆうがとう 誘蛾灯 light trap ©

ユーカラ (アイヌの叙事詩) yukar ©, Ainu epic ©

ユーカリ 【植物】 eucalyptus © ⓤ (複 ~es, eucalypti)

ゆうかん¹ 勇敢 ——勇敢な brave, courageous ——勇敢に bravely, courageously ∥私たちは彼の勇敢な行為にとても感動した We were greatly touched by his *brave* [*courageous*] act. / 彼は勇敢にもひとりで政府と戦った He was *brave* to fight against the government by himself.

ゆうかん² 夕刊 (朝刊に対して) evening edition ©; (夕刊紙) evening paper ©

ゆうかん³ 有閑 ∥有閑階級 the leisure class / 有閑マダム a woman of leisure

ゆうかんじしん 有感地震 an earthquake strong enough to be felt

ゆうき¹ 勇気 courage ⓤ; (勇敢さ) bravery ⓤ (◆courage は精神的な勇気, bravery は行動に表れた勇気をいう)
いやなことはきっぱり断る勇気が必要だ You need *the courage* to refuse flatly what you don't want to do.
とてもそんなことをする勇気はない I don't have enough *courage* to do something like that.
私は勇気を出してやってみた I gathered [summoned up] all *my courage* and tried.
どたんばになって彼は勇気をなくした At the last moment he lost *his courage*.
◆勇気ある行動 *courageous* conduct / 彼に反対するなんて勇気があるね You *are courageous* [*It is courageous of* you] *to* oppose him. / 彼は味方がたくさんいると知って勇気がわいた (→勇気づけられた) He was *encouraged* to learn that many people were on his side.

ゆうき² 有機 ——有機の・有機的な organic (↔inorganic) ——有機的に organically ∥有機化学 organic chemistry / 有機化合物 an organic compound / 有機体 an organism / 有機農法 organic farming / 有機肥料 (an) organic fertilizer / 有機物 organic matter / 有機野菜 organic vegetables

ゆうぎ¹ 遊戯 play ⓤ; (ゲーム) game ©
◆お遊戯をする *play and dance*
∥遊戯室 a playroom / 遊戯場 a playground

ゆうぎ² 遊技 (娯楽) amusement ©; (パチンコ・ビリヤードなど) game ©
∥遊技施設 recreation facilities / 遊技場 a place of amusement

ゆうきゅう¹ 有給 (有給休暇) paid vacation © ⓤ ∥彼女は有給休暇中だ She's on *a paid vacation*. ◆有給休暇を5日とる take five *days off with pay*

ゆうきゅう² 遊休 ∥遊休施設 idle [unused] facilities / 遊休地 idle [unused] land

ゆうきょう 遊興 (楽しみ) pleasure [pléʒər] ⓤ; (娯楽) amusement ©
∥遊興費 entertainment expenses

ゆうぐう 優遇 経験者優遇 *higher salaries for experienced workers* / 少数の人だけが優遇されている Only a few people *are given preferential treatment*. / その会社は資格を

もつ従業員を優遇している(→いい給与を払っている) The company *pays* qualified employees *a good salary*.

ユークリッド Euclid [júːklid]
‖ユークリッド幾何学 Euclidean geometry

ゆうぐれ 夕暮れ (夕方) evening ⓒⓤ (*通例日没から寝る時間までをいう*) ➔ よる (夜) 図版; (たそがれ) twilight ⓤ, dusk ⓤ (*twilightが暗くなったとき*) ‖夕暮れ時に *in the evening*; *at dusk*

短歌 寂しさに宿を立出でてながむればいづこもおなじ秋の夕暮 (良選(りょうぜん)法師)
I'm feeling lonely
so I step out of my hut
and I look around.
But still wherever I look
it's the same autumn twilight.

ゆうけい 有形 私は彼らから有形無形の援助を受けた I received *both moral and material* aid from them.
‖有形財産 tangible property / 有形文化財 tangible cultural properties

ゆうげきしゅ 遊撃手 〖野球〗 short(stop) ⓒ

ゆうげん 有限 limited, finite ‖地球の地下資源は有限である The earth's underground resources *are limited*.
‖有限会社 a limited liability company (*会社名では Corp. や Inc. などの略語を用いる*); (小さな会社) a small company

ゆうけんしゃ 有権者 (投票者) voter ⓒ; (選挙人) elector ⓒ, (集合的) electorate ⓒ (*単数または複数扱い*) ‖多くの有権者が増税に不満の意を表した Many *voters* showed dissatisfaction with the tax increases.
‖有権者名簿 electoral rolls

ゆうこう¹ 有効 ——有効な (効果的な) effective; (効力のある) valid, good
最近その病気に対する有効な治療法が見つかった An *effective* remedy against the disease was found recently.
この規則は来月から有効になる This rule 「*becomes effective* [*comes into effect*] next month.
この券は20日間有効です This ticket *is valid* [*good*] for 20 days.
◆私たちは限りある資源を有効に使わなければならない。We must *make good use of* limited resources. / 応募は10月31日の消印まで有効です Entries *must be postmarked not later than* October 31. / 私のパスポートは来月で有効期限が切れる My passport *expires* next month.

ゆうこう² 友好 friendship ⓤⓒ ——友好的な friendly ‖この会合により我々の友好は深まるだろう This meeting will allow us to deepen our *friendship*. / 両国間の友好を促進するための会議が開かれた A conference was held to promote *friendship between* the two countries. / 日本はその国と友好関係を確立した Japan established *friendly relations with* the country. / 会談は友好的なムードの中行われた They had talks in a *friendly* atmosphere.
‖友好国 a friendly nation / 友好条約 a treaty of friendship [amity]

ゆうごう 融合 fusion ⓤⓒ; (統合) integration ⓤ ——融合する fuse ⓐⓥ ‖2つの文化が融合して新しい文化が生まれた The two cultures *fused* to produce a new one.
‖核融合 nuclear fusion

ゆうこく¹ 夕刻 evening ⓒⓤ ‖夕刻に *in the evening*

ゆうこく² 憂国 (愛国心) patriotism [péitriətizm] ⓤ ◆憂国の士 *a patriot*

ユーザー (利用者) user ⓒ; (顧客) customer ⓒ ‖メーカーはユーザーのニーズを先取りしなければならない Manufacturers must anticipate what *users* will need. ◆ユーザーにやさしいパソコン a *user-friendly* PC
‖ユーザーインターフェース〘コンピュータ〙 a user interface / エンドユーザー an end user

ゆうざい 有罪 guilt ⓤ ——有罪の guilty ‖その男に殺人罪の有罪判決が下った The man *was found guilty of* murder. / 彼が有罪だという証拠は全くない There is no evidence that he *is guilty*.

ゆうさんかいきゅう 有産階級 the propertied classes

ゆうし¹ 融資 (資金を融通すること) financing ⓤ; (貸付金) loan ⓒ ——融資する finance ⓥ; (資金を供給する) provide funds ‖大規模な事業に融資する *finance* a large business operation / 銀行から5,000万円の融資を受ける *get a loan* of 50 million yen from a bank; (→借りる) *borrow* 50 million yen from a bank / その計画のための融資がようやく得られた We managed to get [obtain] *financing* for the project. / 銀行はその会社への融資の打ち切りを決定した The bank decided to *cut off its financing* to the company.
‖融資会社 a finance company / 不正融資 an improper loan

ゆうし² 有志 (関心をもつ人) interested person ⓒ; (志願者) volunteer ⓒ ‖このクラブは去年数人の有志によって作られた This club was established by several *interested people* last year. / 私たちに協力してくれる有志を募っています We are accepting *volunteers* to help us.
◆有志の寄付を募る collect *voluntary* donations

ゆうし³ 有史 有史以来の (→歴史上の) 出来事 events *in history* / 有史以前の遺跡 *prehistoric* ruins
‖有史時代 historic times

ゆうし⁴ 勇士 (勇敢な人) brave person ⓒ; (勇敢な兵士) brave soldier [sóuldʒər] ⓒ

ゆうし⁵ 雄姿 霧の中から富士山の雄姿が見えてきた The *magnificent figure* of Mt. Fuji came into sight out of the fog.

ゆうじ 有事 (緊急事態) emergency ⓒⓤ ‖有事に備える provide for [against] *emergencies* / 有事の際には *in an emergency*; in case of *emergency*

ゆうしかく 有資格
‖有資格者 a qualified [an eligible] person

ゆうしきしゃ 有識者 knowledgeable [well-informed] person ⓒ; (専門家) expert ⓒ /有識者に意見を求める ask *well-informed people* for advice

ゆうしてっせん 有刺鉄線 barbed wire Ⓤ

ゆうしゃ 勇者 brave person ⓒ

ゆうしゅう¹ 優秀 ──優秀な excellent; (他を上回る) superior; (抜きん出た) outstanding ──優秀さ excellence Ⓤ; superiority Ⓤ

その大学には全国から優秀な学生が集まってくる The university attracts many *excellent* [(→頭のよい) *brilliant*] students from all over the country.

彼は音楽コンクールで優秀な成績を収めた He achieved *excellent* results in the music contest.

その会社の製品は実に優秀だ That company's products *are* truly *excellent*.

◆彼女は学校の成績は優秀, おまけにどんなスポーツも万能だ She not only *does well* in school but also excels at all kinds of sports. /彼はサッカーチームの最優秀選手に選ばれた He was voted *MVP* of the soccer team. (❖MVPは the *m*ost *v*aluable *p*layer の略語)
∥最優秀賞 top prize

ゆうしゅう² 有終 彼らはシーズン最後の試合に勝利し有終の美を飾った They capped [ended] the season *with a flourish* by winning the last game.

ゆうしゅう³ 憂愁 (悲しみ) sorrow Ⓤ; (憂鬱(ﾕｳｳﾂ)) gloom Ⓤ(また a ~), melancholy Ⓤ

ゆうじゅうふだん 優柔不断 ──優柔不断な indecisive, 《公式的》irresolute /彼はよく言えば思いやりがあるが, 悪く言えば優柔不断だ To put it nicely, he is considerate of others; more bluntly, though, he *is indecisive*.
◆彼の優柔不断にはいらいらする His *indecisiveness* irritates me.

ゆうしゅつ 湧出 ──湧出する (わき出る) well (up); (噴出する) gush (out)

ゆうしょう¹ 優勝 victory ⓒⓊ; (選手権) championship ⓒ ──優勝する win* ⓐⓑ; (1位になる) win [get*] first prize

私たちのチームがそのサッカー大会で優勝した Our team *won* the soccer tournament.

我々は彼のチームと優勝を争った We competed with his team「*to win first prize* [*for the championship*].

ドジャースは早くも優勝争いから脱落した The Dodgers have already dropped out of *the race for the championship*.

優勝パレードに私たちは興奮した *The victory parade* lifted our spirits.

◆ワールドカップの優勝候補はオランダだ The Netherlands are *the favorite* to win the World Cup.
∥優勝旗 a championship flag / 優勝決定戦 a playoff / 優勝者 a champion, a winner / 優勝チーム a championship team, a winning team / 優勝杯 a championship cup; (優勝記念品)a trophy

ゆうしょう² 有償 2回目以降の修理・交換は有償です *There is a charge for* repair or replacement the second time or later.

ゆうじょう 友情 friendship Ⓤⓒ

> **コロケーション** –friendship–
> 《形容詞+~》浅い~ a shallow friendship / 温かい~ a warm friendship / 美しい~ a beautiful friendship / 固い~ a firm [solid, strong] friendship / 変わらぬ~ a lasting friendship / 真の~ a true [genuine] friendship / 親密な~ a close friendship / 長年の~ a long-time friendship

友情をはぐくむ develop *a friendship*

彼らの間に新たな友情が生まれた A new *friendship* grew up between them.

友情のあかしにこれをとっておいてください Keep this as proof of *our friendship*.

私たちは強い友情のきずなで結ばれている We are bonded together by great *friendship*.

その誤解が元で彼らの友情にひびが入った The misunderstanding caused a rift in their *friendship*.

◆彼女は友情に厚い人だ She is a *very friendly* person.

ゆうしょく 夕食 supper Ⓤ; dinner ⓒ (❖いずれも種類や1人分の食事の意味では ⓒ)

> supper: 1日の最後にとる食事.
> dinner: 1日3食のうちで主な食事. 夕食と重なることが多いが, 休日などは昼食が dinner になることもある. また, レストランで dinner といえばコース料理を指す.

遅い[早めの, 軽い]夕食をとる have *a* late [*an* early, *a* light] *supper*

母は台所で夕食のしたくをしている My mother is cooking *dinner* in the kitchen.

💬「夕食ができましたよ」「行きます」"*Dinner* is ready." "Coming!"

💬「夕食は何がいい」「中華がいいな」"What do you want to eat for *dinner*?" "Chinese would be nice."

💬「今晩夕食をいっしょにどう」「喜んで」"Would you like to have *dinner* together tonight?" "Yes, I'd love to."

ゆうしょくじんしゅ 有色人種 colored race ⓒ, people of color

ゆうじん¹ 友人 friend ⓒ ⇨ともだち 《彼の結婚披露宴で私は友人代表としてスピーチをした I made a speech *on behalf of his friends* at his wedding reception.

ゆうじん² 有人 ──有人の manned
∥有人宇宙船 a manned spacecraft / 有人宇宙飛行 (a) manned space flight

ゆうしんろん 有神論 theism Ⓤ (↔atheism)
∥有神論者 a theist

ゆうすう 有数 有数の (主要な) leading, major; (すぐれた) distinguished, eminent 《クウェートは世界有数の産油国の一つだ Kuwait is one of the world's *leading* oil-producing countries.

◆彼は世界でも有数のゴルファーだとだれもが認めています We all know that he is *one of the best* golfers in the world.

ゆうずう 融通 ❶【柔軟性】flexibility ⓤ, elasticity ⓤ; (順応性) adaptability ⓤ.
◆今週はスケジュールの融通がききます My schedule *is flexible* [*elastic*] this week. / もう少し融通をきかせて考えたらどう Can't you *be a little more flexible* [*elastic*] in your thinking? / あいつは融通のきかないやつだ He is an *inflexible* [*obstinate*] guy.
❷【貸借】──融通する accommodate ⓗ; (貸す) lend* ⓗ ⓐ /５万円ほど融通してもらえませんか Could you *lend* me 50,000 yen? / 両親が彼に新商売の資金を融通した His parents *accommodated* him *with* funds for his new business.
◆彼らは1台のパソコンを融通し合って仕事をしている They work *sharing* one personal computer.

ゆうすずみ 夕涼み 川の土手で夕涼みをした I enjoyed 「*the cool of the evening* [*the evening cool*] on the river bank.

ユースホステル (youth) hostel ⓒ

ゆうせい 優勢 ──優勢な superior, predominant //敵の軍隊は数の上では我々より優勢であった The enemy forces *were superior to* us in numbers.
◆この分野では女性が優勢である Women *predominate* in this field. / 今のところ日本代表が優勢に試合を進めている(→リードしている) The all-Japan team *is leading* so far.
‖優勢勝ち a win by a decision

ゆうせい² 郵政 postal administration
‖郵政省 the Ministry of Posts and Telecommunications(✦2001年総務省に統合)
⇨そうむしょう

ゆうせい³ 優性 dominance ⓤ ──優性の dominant (↔recessive) /優性の法則 the law of *dominance*
‖優性遺伝 dominant inheritance / 優性形質 a dominant (character)

ゆうぜい 遊説 ──遊説する stump ⓗ ⓐ, barnstorm ⓗ ⓐ; (投票を頼んで回る) canvass ⓗ ⓐ /その政治家は全国を遊説して回った The politician *stumped* throughout the whole country.

ゆうせいおん 有声音〖音声〗voiced sound ⓒ(↔voiceless sound)

ゆうせいらん 有精卵 fertilized (chicken) egg ⓒ

ゆうせん¹ 優先 priority ⓤ(✦「優先事項」の意味では ⓒ)
この車線はバスが優先だ Buses have [are given] *priority* in this lane.
その国では経済的問題がすべてに優先している In that country, economic considerations take [have, get] *priority over* everything else.
秩序と安全の維持が我々の最優先事項だ The maintenance of good order and safety is our *first* [*top*] *priority*.
警察は人質の安全を最優先した The police gave highest [*top*] *priority to* the safety of the hostage.
計画を立てるにあたって何を優先するかを決めなくてはならない In making plans, we have to *decide our priorities*.
この件は優先順位が高い[低い] This matter *is high* [*low*] *in priority*.
◆彼はいつも仕事よりも家族を優先している He always *places* his family *above* his job.
‖優先順位 the order of priority / 優先席 a priority seat, priority seating

ゆうせん² 有線
‖有線テレビ cable television (《略語》CATV), closed-circuit television / 有線放送 cable [closed-circuit] broadcasting

ゆうぜん 悠然 みんながそわそわする中、彼女は悠然と構えていた She *remained calm* while everybody else was nervous.

ゆうそう¹ 郵送 ──郵送する《米》mail ⓗ,《英》post ⓗ, send* ... by mail [《英》post] /現金は郵送しないでください Please *don't send* cash *by mail*. / 不審な小荷物が私のところに郵送されてきた A suspicious parcel *was mailed to* me.
◆郵送料はいくらですか What is *the postage*?

ゆうそう² 勇壮 ──勇壮な (興奮させる) stirring; (雄々しい) heroic //勇壮な祭り a *stirring* festival

ユーターン U-turn ⓒ ──Uターンする make* a U-turn / 〖Uターン禁止《掲示》〗*No U-turn*
◆故郷にUターンする *return to one's* hometown / 彼は大学卒業後、Uターン就職した After graduation from college he *found a job in his hometown*.

ゆうたい 勇退 彼は後進のために勇退を決めた He decided to *retire voluntarily* in favor of a younger person.

ゆうだい 雄大 ロッキー山脈の雄大な眺め the grand [*magnificent*] spectacle of the Rockies / 自然の雄大さに打たれる be touched by *the grandeur* of nature

ゆうたいけん 優待券 (招待券) complimentary ticket ⓒ; (割引券) discount coupon

ゆうたいるい 有袋類 (有袋動物) marsupial ⓒ

ゆうだち 夕立 (にわか雨) shower ⓒ /夕立にあう be caught in *a shower* / 夕立がありそうだ It looks like *a shower*.

ゆうだん 勇断 勇断をふるう(→思いきった決断をする) make *a bold decision*

ゆうだんしゃ 有段者 🀄 a *yudansha*, a rank holder; (黒帯) a black belt

ゆうち 誘致 invitation ⓤ ──誘致する invite ⓗ; (引きつける) attract ⓗ /いくつかの町がその企業のプラント誘致に名乗りをあげている Several cities have come forward to *invite* the company *to* build a plant there. / その村はあの手この手を使って観光客を誘致しようとしている The village is trying to *attract* tourists by various means.

ゆうちょう 悠長 悠長な(→のんびりした)性格 an *easygoing* character / 悠長に構えているわけにはいかない We can't afford to 「*take things easy* [*sit back and relax*]. / もうそんな悠長なことは言っていられない(→そんなことを

ゆうづき 夕月 evening moon ⓒ ‖夕月夜 a moonlight [moonlit] evening

ユーティリティー ‖ユーティリティープレーヤー《野球》a utility player / ユーティリティールーム a utility room

ゆうてん 融点〘物理〙the melting point

ゆうとう 優等 honors ‖彼は大学を優等で卒業した He graduated *with honors* from college. ◆優等生的な(→当たりさわりのない)答え *a safe answer*
‖優等賞 an honor (prize) / 優等生 an honor student

ゆうどう 誘導 (案内) guidance Ⓤ; (指示) instructions; (電気の) induction Ⓤ ──誘導する guide ⓒ; (導く) lead* ⓒ; (制御する) control ⓒ ‖先生は生徒たちを安全な場所に誘導した The teacher led [guided] the students *to* a safer place. / 私たちは係員の誘導でその工場を見学した We toured the factory 「*under the guidance of* [*guided by*] the person in charge. / パイロットは管制塔の誘導に従った The pilot followed *the instructions* from the control tower.
◆誘導尋問をする ask *a leading question*
‖誘導ミサイル a guided missile / 誘導路(飛行場の) a taxiway

ゆうどく 有毒 ──有毒な poisonous, toxic ‖有毒ガス poisonous [toxic] gas / 有毒廃棄物 (a) poisonous [toxic] waste / 有毒物質 a poisonous [toxic] substance

ユートピア utopia ⓒⓊ(また Utopia)

ゆうに 優に ‖この絵は優に1億円以上の価値がある This painting is worth *well* over 100 million yen. / 都心までは優に2時間以上かかる It takes *a good* two hours to get to the center of the city.

ゆうのう 有能 ──有能な able; capable; competent

> able: 一定の水準を超えて能力・技能がすぐれていること.
> capable: able よりも実際的で, 特定の仕事に対する有能さを指す.
> competent: ある仕事をするだけの十分な能力があること, 積極的に評価されないこともある.

有能な弁護士 a *competent* lawyer / 彼は有能な実業家だ He's an *able* [a *capable*] businessman. / どんなに有能な人でもひとりでできることには限界がある No matter how *capable* a person is, there is a limit to what he or she can do alone.

ゆうばえ 夕映え the evening glow
◆夕映えの雲 clouds *glowing* [*shining*] *in the setting sun*

ゆうはつ 誘発 ──誘発する (引き起こす) cause ⓒ, 《公式的》induce ⓒ; (至る) lead* to ... ‖急激なダイエットが様々な病気を誘発した The crash diet *caused* many illnesses.

ゆうはん 夕飯 (1日の最後にとる食事) supper ⓒⓊ; (1日のうちで主な食事) dinner ⓒⓊ
⇒ゆうしょく

ゆうひ 夕日 (夕方の太陽) the evening sun; (入り日) the setting sun ‖山々は夕日に染まっていた The mountains were dyed red by *the setting sun*.

ゆうび 優美 grace Ⓤ; (上品) elegance Ⓤ; (繊細) delicacy Ⓤ ──優美な graceful; elegant; delicate ‖優美な踊り a *graceful dance* / 優美なデザイン *elegant* design

ゆうびん 郵便 (郵便制度)《米》mail Ⓤ,《英》post Ⓤ; (郵便物)《集合的》《米》mail Ⓤ,《英》post Ⓤ; (電子メールに対して) snail mail Ⓤ(◆数えるときは a piece of ...にするか, a letter(手紙), a parcel(小包)のように具体的な名詞を使う)
〖郵便が/は〗
郵便は1日2回配達される The mail is delivered twice a day. / There are two deliveries of *mail* a day.
郵便が来たかどうか見てきましょう I'll find out whether *the mail* has come [arrived].
きょうはあなたあての郵便は来ませんでしたよ There wasn't any *mail* for you today.
〖郵便を〗
たくさんの郵便を受け取る receive a lot of *mail* / 郵便を配る deliver *the mail*
◆忘れずにこの郵便を出してください Remember to mail this *letter*.
〖郵便で〗
カタログは郵便で送ります I'll send the catalog *by mail*. / I'll mail the catalog.
そのパンフレットは郵便で送られてきた The brochure came 「*by mail* [*in the mail*].
‖郵便受け《米》a mailbox,《英》a letter box / 郵便為替《米》a money order,《英》a postal order / 郵便切手 a postage stamp / 郵便業務 postal service / 郵便局 a post office / 郵便局員 a post office worker / 郵便局長 (男) a postmaster; (女) a postmistress / 郵便小包 a postal parcel,《集合的》parcel post / 郵便制度 a postal system / 郵便貯金 postal savings / 郵便配達 postal delivery / 郵便配達人 a mail carrier / 郵便はがき a postcard / 郵便箱(郵便受け)《米》a mailbox,《英》a letter box; (郵便ポスト)《米》a mailbox,《英》a postbox, a pillar box / 郵便番号《米》a zip code,《英》a postcode, a postal code / 郵便物《米》mail,《英》post / 郵便振替 a postal transfer / 郵便ポスト《米》a mailbox,《英》a postbox, a pillar box / 郵便料金 postage, postal charges / 外国郵便 foreign mail / 国内郵便 domestic mail

ユーフォー UFO [júːèfóu] ⓒ (複 ~s) 《☆an unidentified flying object(未確認飛行物体)の略語》⇨ 場面・状況別会話 p.1722

ゆうふく 裕福 ──裕福な rich, wealthy ‖彼女は裕福な家庭の出だ She is from a *rich* [*wealthy*] family.
◆裕福に暮らす live *well*; be *well-off*

ゆうべ[1] 夕べ evening ⓒⓊ ‖ある8月の夕べ *an* August *evening* / 親睦(ﾎﾞ<)[音楽]の夕べを催す have *a* social [musical] *evening*

ゆうべ[2] 昨夜 last night, yesterday evening ⇒ さくや

ゆうへい 幽閉 confinement Ⓤ ——幽閉する confine 他; imprison 他

ゆうべん 雄弁 eloquence Ⓤ ——雄弁な eloquent ‖雄弁な演説 an *eloquent* speech / その話になると彼女は急に雄弁になった She suddenly became *eloquent* when it came to talking about it. / 彼のけがの大きさが事故の激しさを雄弁に物語っている The extent of his injury *is eloquent of* the violence of the accident.

◆雄弁をふるう *speak eloquently*
‖雄弁家 an eloquent speaker

ゆうぼう 有望 ——有望な promising, hopeful ‖そのチームには有望な若手選手がそろっている There are a lot of *promising* young players on that team. / 彼はわが社一の有望株だ He is the most *promising* of all the young men at our company.

◆その会社は将来有望だと思う I think the company *has a bright future*.

ゆうぼく 遊牧 ‖遊牧生活 a nomadic life / 遊牧民 a nomad / 遊牧民族 a nomadic tribe [people]

ゆうほどう 遊歩道 promenade Ⓒ

ゆうめい 有名 ——有名な famous; well-known; famed; celebrated; eminent, distinguished; notorious

| famous: 最も一般的な語. よい意味で有名な.
| well-known: よい意味でも悪い意味でもよく知られた.
| famed: 新聞・雑誌で好まれる語.
| celebrated: 際立った才能・特徴などで有名な.
| eminent, distinguished: 専門分野などで有名な.
| notorious: 悪名高く有名な.

【有名な】
シェークスピアの最も有名な劇の一つ one of the *best-known* plays by Shakespeare
私たちは古代の遺跡で有名な町を見物した We visited a city *famous for* its ancient monuments.
彼女は世界的に有名な映画俳優である She is a *world-famous* movie star.

【有名だ】
和歌山はミカンの産地として有名だ Wakayama *is famous* [*well known*] *as* an *mikan*-producing district. (✦well-known は述語的に用いられる場合ハイフンなしで書くのがふつう)
その公園は桜で有名だ The park *is famous* [*well known*] *for* its cherry blossoms.
東京は住宅事情の悪さで有名だ Tokyo *is notorious for* its terrible housing situation.
彼がかつて百万長者だったということは有名だ *It is well known that* he used to be a millionaire. / *Everybody knows that* he used to be a millionaire.

【有名に】
彼女はオリンピックで金メダルを取りいちやく有名になった She *suddenly became famous* [*leaped into fame*] after she won a gold medal at the Olympics.

【その他】
去年は有名校ばかり受験した I applied only to *famous* [*prestigious*] *schools* last year.
このあたりには有名人がたくさん住んでいる A lot of「*famous people* [*celebrities*] live around here.

ゆうめいむじつ 有名無実 ‖有名無実な契約 a *nominal* contract; a contract *in name only*

ユーモア humor, (英) humour Ⓤ; (冗談) joke Ⓒ
彼にはユーモアのセンスがある[ない] He has「a good [no] sense of *humor*.
彼女のスピーチはさりげないユーモアにあふれていた Her speech was full of dry *humor*.
この種のユーモアは日本人には理解されにくい This kind of *humor* doesn't come across very well to Japanese.
‖ブラックユーモア black humor

ゆうもう 勇猛 ——勇猛な brave, daring
◆勇猛果敢に敵に立ち向かう confront an enemy *bravely* [*daringly*]

ユーモラス ——ユーモラスな humorous; (楽しい) amusing; (こっけいな) funny ‖この話は悲劇的でありながら, どこかユーモラスでもある This story is tragic, but at the same time it's somewhat *humorous*.
◆このエッセーで, 彼は日常のありふれた出来事をユーモラスに描いている In this essay he describes everyday events *humorously*.

ゆうやけ 夕焼け sunset Ⓒ Ⓤ, evening glow Ⓤ ‖静かな川の流れが燃えるような夕焼けを映し出していた The calm stream reflected *the* fiery *sunset*.
‖夕焼け雲 sunset clouds / 夕焼け空 the sky at sunset

ゆうやみ 夕闇 dusk Ⓤ ‖夕やみが迫るにつれ, あたりは静けさを増した As (the) *dusk* gathered, the area became quieter.

ゆうゆう 悠々 彼はゆうゆうとパイプをふかしていた He was smoking a pipe *in a leisurely manner*. / 彼女ならゆうゆう試験に合格するだろう She will be able to pass the exam *easily* [*with ease*]. / 私たちのチームは決勝までゆうゆうと勝ち進んだ Our team got through to the finals *without difficulty*. / 急がなくてもゆうゆう間に合うよ There's no hurry. You'll *be in plenty of time* [*well in time*]
慣用表現 父は去年退職して悠々自適の生活を送っている Having retired last year, my father *is*「*living in ease and comfort* [*leading a leisurely life*].

ゆうよ 猶予 (遅延) delay Ⓒ Ⓤ; (仕事や支払いの) grace Ⓤ ‖もはや一刻の猶予も許されない状況だ Now the situation doesn't permit any *delay*. / 支払いはきょうだが彼は私に1週間の猶予をくれた Though payment is due today, he gave me a week's *grace*.
◆被告は懲役1年執行猶予3年の判決を受けた The accused was sentenced to one year in prison with *a three-year suspended sentence*.

ゆうよう 有用 ——有用な (有益な) useful; (助けになる) helpful ‖有用な人材 a *useful*

person / モルヒネは医薬品としては有用な物質だ Morphine is a *useful* substance as medicine.
ユーラシア Eurasia ‖ユーラシア大陸 the Eurasian Continent / ユーラシアプレート the Eurasian Plate
ゆうらん 遊覧 sightseeing Ⓤ ‖遊覧船 a pleasure boat [craft] / 遊覧バス a sightseeing bus / 遊覧飛行 a sightseeing flight

ゆうり[1] 有利 advantage Ⓒ Ⓤ ――有利な (好都合な) advantageous, favorable; (利益になる) profitable, beneficial
何か資格があると有利だ Any qualification is *an advantage*.
彼女は経験があったのでほかの人たちより有利だった Her experience *gave* her *an advantage over* the others. / She *has an advantage over* the others because of her experience.
契約条件は彼らに有利なものだった The conditions of the contract「*were advantageous to* [*favored*] them.
転職したのは彼女にとってとても有利だった Changing jobs *was* a very *profitable* move for her.
彼の得点で我々のチームは一気に有利になった His goal suddenly *gave* our team *the advantage*.
いくつかの要因が彼に有利に働いた Several factors worked「to his *advantage* [in his *favor*].
◆証人は被告に有利な証言をした The witness testified *in favor of* the accused. / 形勢は我々に有利に傾いた The tide *turned*「*in our favor* [*our way*].

ゆうり[2] 遊離 彼らの議論は現実から遊離している Their argument *is out of touch with* reality.

ゆうり[3] 有理 ‖有理数〔数学〕a rational number

ゆうりょ 憂慮 両国間の関係は憂慮すべき(→深刻な)状況にある The relations between the two countries are in a *serious* situation. / だれもが事態の成り行きを憂慮している Everyone *is worried* [*concerned*] *about* how things will turn out. / 我々はもう少し事態を憂慮する(→深刻に受け止める)べきだ We should *take* it a bit more *seriously*.

ゆうりょう[1] 有料 修理・交換は有料です *There is a charge for* repair or replacement. / 東名高速は有料です(→通行料を払わなければならない) We *have to pay a toll* to drive on the Tomei Expressway.
‖有料駐車場 a toll parking lot / 有料テレビ pay TV / 有料トイレ a pay toilet / 有料道路 a toll road

ゆうりょう[2] 優良 excellent, superior ◆子供のころは健康優良児だった(→とても健康だった) I *was in excellent health* when I was a child. ◆品質の優良な商品 goods of *high* [*good*] quality
‖優良株〔経済〕a blue-chip stock / 優良企業 a blue-chip company

ゆうりょく 有力 ――有力な (強力な) strong, powerful; (影響力をもった) influential; (主要な) leading
我々には彼が無実だという有力な証拠がある We have *strong* [*convincing*] evidence that he is innocent.
その会社は有力な議員たちに次々とわいろを贈った That company bribed *influential* [*powerful*] legislators one after another.
彼女が次期生徒会長選の最有力候補です She is *the strongest* [*most likely*] candidate for president of the student council in the next election.
◆私たちは問題解決のための有力な手がかりを得た We got an *important* clue for solving the problem. / そのピッチャーはタイガース入りが有力視されている People consider it likely that the pitcher will join the Tigers.
‖有力紙 a leading newspaper / 有力チーム a strong [powerful] team

ゆうりょくしゃ 有力者 influential man [woman]; (指導者) leader Ⓒ; (大立て者) big man [woman]
◆彼は政界の有力者だ(→政界に強い影響力をもっている) He *exerts a strong influence on* the political world.

ゆうれい 幽霊 ghost Ⓒ, 《口語的》spook Ⓒ, phantom Ⓒ; (霊的存在) spirit Ⓤ
⇨ 場面・状況別会話 p.1722 ‖そのホテルには幽霊が出るらしい It is said that *a ghost* sometimes *appears* at the hotel. / The hotel is said to *be haunted*.
◆何だかこの家は幽霊が出そうだな This house is kind of *spooky*.
‖幽霊会社 a bogus [ghost] company / 幽霊船 a phantom ship / 幽霊屋敷 a haunted mansion

ゆうれつ 優劣 2つのアイディアの優劣を論じる discuss *the relative merits* of the two ideas / 選手たちの能力には優劣(→差)がほとんどない There is little *difference in* ability among the players. / そんなことで優劣を競ってもしかたがない There's no point in *competing for superiority* in a matter like that. / どの案も一長一短で優劣はつけがたい Every plan has both advantages and disadvantages, so *it's hard to decide which one is better than the others*.

ユーロ (通貨単位) euro Ⓒ (複 〜, 〜s)

ゆうわ 融和 (調和) harmony Ⓤ Ⓒ; (統合) integration Ⓤ ◆近隣諸国との融和をはかる *try to establish harmonious* [*friendly*] *relations with* neighboring countries

ゆうわ[2] 宥和 appeasement Ⓒ Ⓤ ――宥和する appease 〔動〕
‖宥和政策 an appeasement policy

ゆうわく 誘惑 temptation Ⓤ Ⓒ, enticement Ⓤ Ⓒ; (たぶらかすこと) seduction Ⓤ Ⓒ ――誘惑する tempt 〔動〕, entice 〔動〕; seduce 〔動〕 ‖私は一時の誘惑に負けてしまった I gave way [yielded] to *a momentary temptation*. / 彼女は誘惑に勝てずその箱をあけてしまった(→箱をあけたいという誘惑に勝てなかった)

She couldn't overcome [resist] *the temptation to* open the box. / 都会は誘惑が多い Big cities are full of *temptations.* / 彼らは非常に高額の給与で私を誘惑した They *tempted* me with a very large salary.

ゆえ 故 reason [C] [U] ➔ じじょう(事情), りゆう, わけ ∥彼はゆえあって学校をやめた He left school *for a certain reason.*

ゆえに 故に therefore ∥我思う. ゆえに我あり I think, *therefore* I am. (❖デカルトの言葉)

ゆえん[1] 所以 彼女がみんなに尊敬されているゆえんはそこにある That is (*the reason*) *why* she is respected by everyone.

ゆえん[2] 油煙 lampblack [U]; (すす) soot [U]

ゆか 床 floor [C] ∥板張りの床 *a* wood [wooden] *floor* / 床に座る sit on *the floor* / 床が抜けてしまった *The floor* has given way. / コップが床に落ちて粉々になった The glass fell onto *the floor* and shattered. / 床に赤いじゅうたんを敷いた We spread a red carpet over *the floor*. ◆私の家の床面積は100平方メートルです My house is 100 square meters in *area* [*floor space*].

‖床板 a floorboard / 床運動 floor exercises / 床暖房 floor heating

ゆかい 愉快 ━愉快な pleasant, delightful; (陽気な) cheerful; (物事・経験などが) enjoyable

それは実に愉快な体験だった It was a very *pleasant* [*enjoyable*] experience for me.

君のお父さんは愉快な人だね Your father *is* very *pleasant* [*cheerful*], isn't he?

私たちは思い出話をしながら愉快な夜を過ごした We spent a *pleasant* [an *enjoyable*] evening talking about our memories.

◆きょうぐらいは愉快にやりましょう Let's「*enjoy ourselves* [*have fun*] for today at least. / 彼女は愉快そうにその話をしていた She was talking about it *cheerfully.* / あいつの鼻をあかすことができてとても愉快だ I'*m* very *pleased* that I could outwit him. (❖pleasant が「他者を喜ばせる」のに対して pleased は「本人[主語]が喜んでいる」の意味)

‖愉快犯 a criminal who commits a crime just for the pleasure of watching other people's reactions

ゆかうえ 床上 私の家は大雨で床上浸水した My house *was flooded above the floor level* by heavy rain.

ゆがく 湯掻く blanch [他], parboil [他]

ゆかげん 湯加減 ちょっと, 湯かげん見てくれる? Hey, can you see *how hot the water is*? / 湯かげんはどうですか *How is the bath*(*water*)?

ゆかしい 床しい 古式ゆかしい習慣 a *time-honored* custom

ゆかした 床下 このあたり一帯の家が大雨で床下浸水した All the houses in this neighborhood *were flooded below* [*up to*] *the floor level* by heavy rain.

ゆかた 浴衣 🖼 a *yukata*, a light cotton kimono worn in summer or after a bath

ゆがみ 歪み (反(そ)り) warp [C] 《通例単数形》; (心の) a warp; (物・画像・音などの) distortion [U] [C]; (ねじれ) twist [C] ∥性格のゆがみ *a warp* in *one's* character ◆その家は年月がたち柱にゆがみが生じた The pillars of the house *were warped* with age.

ゆがむ 歪む be warped, be twisted, be distorted ∥この扉は少しゆがんでいる This door *is* a little *warped.* / 彼の顔は苦痛にゆがんだ His face *was twisted* [*distorted*] with pain. ◆ゆがんだ社会 a *warped* [*twisted, distorted*] society / 彼女は何であんなに性格がゆがんでしまった(→何が彼女の性格をゆがめた)のだろう I wonder what *warped* her personality like that.

ゆがめる 歪める distort [他], twist [他], warp [他] ∥事実をゆがめる *distort* [*twist, warp*] a fact / その事件に関する報道はかなりゆがめられていた The report on the affair *was* highly *distorted.* ◆彼の名前を聞いただけで彼女は顔をゆがめた(→彼女の顔はゆがんだ) Her face *became distorted* [*twisted*] at the mere mention of his name.

ゆかり 縁 (関係) relation [C] [U]; (結びつき) connection [C] ◆縁もゆかりもない人 a complete stranger / ここは夏目漱石ゆかりの地です(→夏目漱石との連想で知られる) This place *is known for its associations with* Natsume Soseki. / 縁もゆかりもない土地に引っ越した I moved to an area *quite new to me.*

ゆき[1] 雪

snow [U] (❖1回の降雪を表すときや雪の状態を表す形容詞を伴う場合は [C]); (降雪) snowfall [C]; (雪片) snowflake [C]

〚雪が・は〛

去年はたくさん雪が降った We *had* a lot of *snow* last year. / *It snowed* a lot last year.

2月は1月同様に雪が多かった In February, as in January, we had a lot of *snow.*

雪が20センチ積もった *The snow* was [lay] 20 centimeters deep.

雪が解け始めてだんだん暖かくなってきた *The snow* has begun to melt [thaw] and it is getting warmer.

◆家を出るとすぐに雪が降りだした I had scarcely left home when it started to *snow.* / 雪はすぐやむだろう It should stop *snowing* soon.

〚雪の〛

父は雪の中, 帰ってきた My father came home *in* [*through*] *the snow.*

大雪のために東京の鉄道機能がまひした Train services in Tokyo were paralyzed by *the heavy snow.*

◆北陸は雪の多い所だ(→雪がたくさん降る) *It snows a lot* in the Hokuriku district.

〚雪に〛

雨が雪に変わった The rain turned *into* [*to*] *snow.*

村は深い雪にすっぽりと覆われていた The village was covered *in* deep *snow.*

◆天気予報では今夜は雪になる The weather

ゆ

report says that *it will snow* tonight. / 1時間ほど雪に閉じ込められた We *were snowed in* for about an hour.

〖雪で〗

大雪で電車が遅れた The trains were delayed *due to a heavy snow*.

〖その他〗

雪をいただいた山 a mountain *crowned [capped] with snow*

喜美子は雪のように白い肌をしていた Kimiko's skin was 「*as white as snow [snow-white]*」.

屋根の雪下ろしはひと仕事だった It was quite a job to *clear the roof of snow*.

私たちは歩道の雪かきをした We *cleared the pavement of snow*. / We *cleared snow from* the pavement.

富士山はうっすらと雪化粧していた(→わずかに雪で覆われていた) Mt. Fuji *was* slightly *covered with snow*.

このゲレンデの雪質(→雪)はすばらしい *The snow* on this ski slope is excellent.

雪不足の影響でスキー客が減った There were fewer skiers because of *the lack of snow*.

◆雪道にはタイヤチェーンが必要だ Chains are needed on *snowy roads*.

‖雪明かり snow light / 雪男 an abominable snowman, a yeti / 雪女 a snow witch / 雪囲い a snow fence / 雪国(国) a snowy country; (地域) a snowy area [region] / 雪景色 a snowscape / 雪だまり a snowdrift / 雪祭り a snow festival / 雪山 a snow mountain / 淡雪 light snow / 粉雪 powdery [powder] snow / 小雪 a light snow(fall) / 処女雪 virgin snow / 初雪 the first snow of the season / ぼたん雪 snow in large flakes / 万年雪 perpetual snow

短歌 田子の浦に打ち出でてみれば白妙の富士の高嶺(たかね)に雪はふりつつ (山部赤人)
At the Tago shore
I step out and look around.
Rising tall and white,
it's the peak of Mount Fuji
receiving the falling snow.

ゆき² 行き ⇒いき(行き)
ゆきあう 行き会う ⇒いきあう
ゆきあたりばったり 行き当たりばったり ⇒いきあたりばったり
ゆきおろし 雪下ろし ⇒ゆき(雪)
ゆきかう 行き交う ⇒いきかう
ゆきかえり 行き帰り ⇒いきかえり
ゆきがかり 行き掛かり ⇒いきがかり
ゆきがけ 行き掛け ⇒いきがけ
ゆきかた 行き方 ⇒いきかた(行き方)
ゆきがっせん 雪合戦 snowball fight ⓒ /雪合戦しようよ Let's have *a snowball fight*.
ゆきき 行き来 ⇒いきき
ゆきさき 行き先 ⇒いきさき
ゆきすぎ 行き過ぎ ⇒いきすぎ
ゆきすぎる 行き過ぎる ⇒いきすぎる
ゆきずり 行きずり 行きずりの恋 a casual romance / 行きずりの人(→通りすがりの人)に助けを求めた I asked *a passerby* for help.
ゆきだおれ 行き倒れ ⇒いきだおれ
ゆきだるま 雪だるま snowman ⓒ /雪だるまを作る make [build] *a snowman*
慣用表現 負債はあっという間に雪だるま式に大きくなった The debt *snowballed* in no time.
ゆきちがい 行き違い ⇒いきちがい
ゆきつけ 行き付け ⇒いきつけ
ゆきづまり 行き詰まり (交渉などの) deadlock ⓒⓤ, impasse ⓤ (また an～); (物事の) dead end ⓤ /行き詰まりを打開する break *the deadlock*
ゆきづまる 行き詰まる deadlock ⓔ; (袋小路に入る) reach an impasse; (完全に停止する) come* to a full stop /仕事に行き詰まったら信頼できる上司に相談するとよい If you feel you've *reached an impasse* at work, just go to a boss you trust and talk.
◆その計画は資金繰りに行き詰まっている The project *has gotten stuck* for lack of funds. / 交渉は完全に行き詰まっている The negotiations *are at a complete standstill*.
ゆきどけ 雪解け thaw ⓒ /両国間の関係は徐々に雪解けが進んでいる There has been *a gradual thaw* in relations between the two countries.
◆そろそろ雪解けが始まるだろう The snow will begin to *thaw [melt]* soon. / It will begin to *thaw* soon.
‖雪解け水 snowmelt / 雪解け道 a slushy road
ゆきとどく 行き届く ⇒いきとどく
ゆきどまり 行き止まり ⇒いきどまり
ゆきやけ 雪焼け 彼女は雪焼けしないように日焼け止めを顔に塗った She applied sunscreen to her face in order not to *get tanned from the snow*.
ゆきわたる 行き渡る ⇒いきわたる
ゆく 行く ⇒いく(行く)
ゆくえ 行方 whereabouts 《単数または複数扱い》
その子供の行方はまだ分からない The *whereabouts* of the child are [is] still unknown.
ようやく彼の行方を突き止めることができた We finally managed to「determine his *whereabouts* [*locate* him].
◆警察は脱走者の行方を追っている The police *are searching for* the escaped prisoner. / 男は事件の当日に行方をくらました The man *disappeared* on the very day of the incident. / その議論の行方は多くの人に注目されている *The progress* of the debate is being watched by a lot of people. / とうとう彼らは行方不明の少女を見つけた At last they found the *missing* girl. / 死者と行方不明者の合計は現在のところ200人を超える The total of the dead and *the missing* is, at present, over 200.
ゆくさき 行く先 ⇒いきさき
ゆくすえ 行く末 the [one's] future /彼らは子供の行く末を案じている They are anxious

for their child's *future*.

ゆくて 行く手 行く手にぼんやりと明かりが見えた I saw a dim light *ahead of* me. / 警察が私の行く手をさえぎった A policeman *stood in* my *way*. / 倒木が我々の行く手を阻んでいた A fallen tree 「*blocked* our *way* [*was in our way*].

ゆくゆく 行く行く ゆくゆくは彼と結婚するつもりだ I'm going to marry him 「*in the future* [*someday*].

ゆげ 湯気 steam Ⓤ /なべから湯気が立っていた Steam *was rising* from the pot. / 湯気で眼鏡が曇った My glasses (got) *fogged up* with *steam*.

◆湯気の立っているスープ a bowl of *steaming* soup

ゆけつ 輸血 (blood) transfusion ⒸⓊ /人に輸血をする give a person *a blood transfusion* / 輸血を受ける get [receive, be given] *a blood transfusion* ◆父に私の血を輸血した I *gave blood* to my father.

ゆけむり 湯煙 steam Ⓤ

ゆさぶり 揺さぶり 相手に心理的な揺さぶりをかける give one's opponent *a psychological jolt*

ゆさぶる 揺さぶる shake* ⓗ; (激しく) jolt ⓗ /強風が絶え間なく船を揺さぶった A strong wind *jolted* the boat continuously. / 社会を揺さぶる事件が立て続けに起こった Events that *shook* [*jolted*] our society occurred one after another.

ゆざめ 湯冷め ――湯冷めする be chilled after a bath ◆湯冷めしないように暖かくしなさい Dress warmly so you don't *get chilled*.

ゆさゆさ 木の枝がゆさゆさ揺れている The branches *are swaying around*.

ゆし 油脂 oils and fats

ゆしゅつ 輸出 export Ⓤ (↔import) (※「輸出ム輸出額[高]」の意味ではⒸで，複数形で用いることが多い) ――輸出する export ⓗ ⓘ

この製品は日本への輸出が禁じられている The *export* of this product to Japan is banned.

半導体が当社の輸出の6割を占める Semiconductors account for 60 percent of our company's *exports*.

ここ数か月，対米輸出が伸び悩んでいる *Exports* to the United States have been sluggish for the past few months.

日本は多くの国に車を輸出している Japan *exports* cars to many countries.

輸出産業は急激な円高に大打撃を受けた *Export industries* were hit hard by the sharp rise in the yen.

米はタイの主要な輸出品の一つだ Rice is one of Thailand's main *exports* [*exported goods*].

‖輸出業者 an exporter / 輸出国 an exporting country, an exporter / 輸出超過 (an) excess of exports (over imports)

ゆず 柚〘植物〙 a *yuzu*, a kind of citrus fruit

ゆすぐ 口をゆすぐ *rinse* one's *mouth* / 洗濯物をゆすぐ *rinse out* the wash

ゆすぶる 揺すぶる shake* ⓗ ⇒ゆさぶる

ゆすり 強請 (恐喝) blackmail ⓗ; (強要) extortion ⓗ /ゆすりを働く commit [practice] *blackmail* ◆ゆすりにあう be *blackmailed*

-ゆずり -譲り 彼女の積極性は父親譲りだ She *inherited* her aggressiveness *from* her father.

ゆずりあい 譲り合い give-and-take Ⓤ; (譲歩) mutual concessions /譲り合いの精神 a spirit of *give-and-take*

ゆずりあう 譲り合う 道を譲り合う 「*make way for* [*give way to*] *each other*」 / 席を譲り合う *offer a seat to each other* / 合意に達するためには互いに譲り合う必要がある To reach an agreement, we must *compromise with each other*.

ゆずりうける 譲り受ける (相続する) inherit ⓗ; (商売などを引き継ぐ) take* over; (買う) buy* ⓗ /彼女は父親から譲り受けた会社を発展させた She developed the company she *took over* from her father. / 友人からCDプレーヤーを格安で譲り受けた I *bought* a CD player at a bargain price from my friend.

ゆずりわたす 譲り渡す hand over, transfer ⓗ /彼は一人娘に全財産を譲り渡した He *handed* all his property *over* to his only daughter.

ゆする¹ 揺する (上下左右に強く) shake* ⓗ; (前後左右に規則的に) rock ⓗ /揺りかごを揺する *rock* a cradle / 彼らは木を揺すって木の実を落とそうとした They tried to *shake* the nuts from the tree. / 私は彼女の体を揺すって「話を聞け」とどなった I *shook* her and yelled, "Listen to me!"

ゆする² 強請る (恐喝する) blackmail ⓗ; (ゆすり取る) extort ⓗ /人から金をゆすり取る *extort* money from a person / その秘密をねたに彼は私をゆすった He *blackmailed* me about the secret.

ゆずる 譲る

❶【渡す・与える】 hand over, transfer ⓗ; (与える) give* ⓗ; (権利・立場などを) yield ⓗ

彼はその家を娘に譲った He 「*handed over* [*transferred*] the house *to* his daughter.

電車でお年寄りに席を譲った I *gave (up)* my *seat to* an elderly person on the train.

彼女は余ったチケットをただで譲ってくれた She *gave* me a spare ticket for free.

◆救急車に道を譲るために車を路肩に寄せた I pulled my car over to the side to 「*make way for* [*give way to, yield to*] the ambulance. / 彼は辞任して後進に道を譲った He resigned his post to *make way for* a younger person. / そう簡単に相手に勝ちを譲るわけにはいかない I won't *let* my opponent *win* so easily.

❷【譲歩する】 concede ⓗ ⓘ, make* a concession

これ以上譲ることはできません I can't *make* any more *concessions* to you.

彼は議論の中で1点だけ私に譲った He *conceded* only one point to me in the argument.

◆その協議では双方とも一歩も譲ろうとしなかった Neither side *would give* [*budge*] *an inch* in the discussion.
❸ [売る] sell* ⊕
友達に3,000円でテレビを譲った I *sold* my friend a TV for 3,000 yen.
❹ [先に延ばす]
その件についての検討は後日に譲ることにした We decided to *postpone* [*put off*] consideration of that matter.

ゆせい¹ 油性 ——油性の oily, oil-based // 油性塗料 *oil-based* [*oil*] paint
◆油性のマジックペン a *permanent* marker (*permanent* は「永続的な」の意味)

ゆせい² 油井 oil well ⓒ

ゆそう¹ 輸送 transportation ⓤ ——輸送する transport ⊕, carry ⊕
皿は輸送中に破損した The dishes were damaged「*during transportation* [*in transit*].
その国では象も重要な輸送手段だ In that country elephants are *an important means of transportation*.
◆香港から神戸に輸送中の品物 goods *in transit* from Hong Kong to Kobe
// 輸送船[船] a transport / 輸送費 the cost of transportation / 輸送ルート a transportation route / 海上輸送 marine [ocean] transportation / 公共輸送 public transportation / 航空輸送 air transportation / 水上輸送 water transportation / 鉄道輸送 railroad transportation / 陸上輸送 ground [land] transportation

ゆそう² 油槽 oil tank ⓒ
// 油槽船 an oil tanker

ユタ Utah (❋米国西部の州;《略語》Ut., 〖郵便〗UT)

ゆたか 豊か ——豊かな rich, wealthy, affluent; (裕福な) well-off; (ありあまるほどの) abundant
豊かな家庭に生まれる be born into a *rich* [*wealthy*] family
彼女の家は父親の代にはとても豊かな暮らしをしていた Her family *was* quite *well-off* in her father's time.
その国は豊かな土地に恵まれている The country is blessed with *rich* [*fertile*] land.
その医師はまだ若いが経験は豊かだ The doctor is still young but *is rich in* experience.
シベリアには豊かな鉱物資源がある (→鉱物資源が豊富だ) Siberia *is rich in* minerals.
ちょっとしたことでも私たちの生活を豊かにしてくれることがある Even the littlest thing can「*make* our life *rich* [*enrich* our life].
◆想像力豊かな人 a *quite imaginative* person / このチームは才能豊かな選手がそろっている This team is staffed with players *full of* talent. / 人間はすべての動物の中で最も知性豊かであるといわれている It is said that humans *are* the most *intelligent* of all animals. / 彼女の歌声は実に表情豊かだ Her singing *is highly expressive*. / このクラスの生徒たちはみな個性豊かだ Every student in this class *is quite individual*. / 色彩の豊かさが彼の絵の特徴の一つだ The richness [wealth] of color is one of the characteristic features of his paintings.

ゆだねる 委ねる leave* ⊕ // 彼は弁護士に財産の管理をゆだねた He *left* his property in the hands of his lawyer. / 最終的な結論はあなたの判断にゆだねます We *leave* the ultimate conclusion to your judgment.
◆彼は運命に身をゆだねた He *resigned himself to* fate.

ユダヤ ——ユダヤ(人)の Jewish
// ユダヤ教 Judaism / ユダヤ人 a Jew

ゆだん 油断 carelessness ⓤ ——油断する be careless, be off (*one's*) guard
この交通事故は運転手の一瞬の油断から起こった This traffic accident resulted from the driver's momentary *carelessness*.
油断したすきに相手に得点されてしまった The opposing team scored a goal *when we were off guard*.
◆油断しろな! *Be alert!*/ *Be on your guard*! / 油断して秘密をもらしてしまった I *carelessly* let the secret slip. / 愛想はとてもいいが彼は油断のならない人だ (→信用できない) Though he's very friendly, *you can't trust* him. / いくら慣れた仕事とはいえ油断は禁物だ Even though you're accustomed to that work, you *must be careful* [*on your guard*].
〖慣用表現〗油断大敵 *Security* [*Complacency*] *is our greatest enemy*. / 最近は手の込んだ詐欺が増えているので油断も隙(✐)もあったものではない These days elaborate swindles are on the rise, so we *can't be too careful*.

ゆたんぽ 湯湯婆 hot-water bottle ⓒ (❋英米の物はふつうゴム製)

ゆちゃく 癒着 adhesion ⓤⓒ ◆政界とその業界の癒着(→なれ合いの関係)は社会問題になっている *Collusive relationships* between the political world and that industry have become a social issue.

ゆっくり
❶ [速さが] slowly; (徐々に) gradually
もう少しゆっくり話していただけませんか Would you speak a little more *slowly*?
物価はゆっくりだが着実に上昇している Prices are rising *slowly* [*gradually*] but steadily.
深く息を吸って!はい、ゆっくり吐いて Take a deep breath! Now let it out *slowly*.
順番を待つ間、時間がたつのがゆっくり感じられた Time seemed to pass *slowly* when I was waiting for my turn.
❷ [余裕・ゆとりをもって]
ゆっくり(→十分)休んで疲れをとったほうがいい You'd better get *a good* rest to recover from your fatigue.
電車の時間にはゆっくり間に合った I was *well* in time for the train.
この部屋なら15人はゆっくり入れる (→十分な広さがある) This room is large *enough* for 15 people.
その件についてはゆっくり (→時間をかけて) 話し合いましょう Let's *take our time* discussing

the matter.

日曜日はゆっくり(→遅くまで)寝ていたい I'd like to sleep *late* on Sundays.

ゆっくり(→のんびり)旅行でもしたら，お母さん Why don't you travel *leisurely*, Mom?

久しぶりに家でゆっくりすることができた I *relaxed* [*took it easy*] at home for the first time in a long while.

ゆっくりしていって(→好きなだけ長くいて)ください *Please stay as long as you like.*

💬「お食事いっしょにいかがですか」「すいません，きょうはゆっくりしていられない(→長居できない)んです」"Would you like to have dinner with us?" "I'm sorry. I *can't stay long* today."

💬「ちょっと待ってください．すぐ行きますから」「ごゆっくりどうぞ」"Wait a minute. I'll be right there." "Please *take your time*."

ゆったり ゆったりした上着 a *loose* [an *easy*] coat / ゆったりしたキッチン a *spacious* [*roomy*] kitchen / そでのゆったりしたシャツ a shirt *loose* [*easy*] at the sleeves / 私たちはゆったりしたペースで仕事を続けた We kept working at an *easy* pace. / 空を眺めているうちにゆったりした気分になった I felt *relaxed* as I looked at the sky. / 空には雲がゆったりと流れていた Clouds floated *lazily* across the sky. / きのうは何もせずにゆったりと過ごした I *took it easy* and did nothing yesterday. / もうゆったり構えてはいられないよ We can't afford to *sit back and relax* any longer.

ゆでたまご 茹で卵 boiled egg [C] (❖硬ゆで卵は hard-boiled egg，半熟卵は soft-boiled eggという)

ゆでる 茹でる boil [他] //ジャガイモをゆでる *boil* potatoes

ゆでん 油田 oil field [C]

ゆどうふ 湯豆腐 🗻 *yudofu*, tofu boiled in *kombu* stock

ゆとり (空間の) space [U], room [U]; (時間の) time (to spare) ➜よち(余地)，よゆう

この部屋にはそんな物を置くゆとりはない There is no *space* to put a thing like that in this room.

◆ゆとりのある教育 education *free of pressure* / ゆとりをもって(→少し早めに)出発しましょう Let's start *a little early*. / そのころの私には人の心配をするゆとりがなかった At that time I *couldn't afford to* worry about other people. / 私たちは生活にゆとりがない[ある] We 「*barely make ends meet* [*live comfortably*].

ユニーク ―ユニークな (唯一の・独特の) unique (❖英語の unique には日本語の「ユニーク」にある「おかしな」「変わった」という意味はふつうない)；(おかしな) funny; (珍しい) unusual //ユニークな才能の持ち主 a person of *unique* ability / この製品にはユニークな機能が搭載されている This product has a *unique* function.

ユニオンジャック (英国国旗) the Union Jack

ユニセックス ユニセックスな服が若者に人気だ *Unisex* clothing is popular among young people.

ユニセフ UNICEF (❖*U*nited *N*ations *I*nternational *C*hildren's *E*mergency *F*und (国連児童基金)の略語. 1953年に United Nations Children's Fund と改称されたが，略称はそのまま用いられている)

ユニット unit [C], module [C] //彼は新しいユニットを組んでアルバムを製作した He formed *a* new *unit* and made an album.

‖ユニット家具 modular furniture / ユニットキッチン a sectional kitchen / ユニットバス a bathroom unit

ユニバーシアード the Universiade (❖ the World University Games (国際学生競技大会)の通称)

ユニホーム uniform [C] //ユニホーム姿の選手と写真を撮ってもらった I had my picture taken with the player *in uniform*. (❖in uniform では冠詞は不要. 複数の場合は in uniform(s))

ゆにゅう 輸入 import [U] (↔export) (❖「輸入品，輸入額[高]」の意味では [C] で，複数形で用いることが多い) ―輸入する import [他]

日本は世界中からたくさんの食料を輸入している Japan *imports* large amounts of food from all over the world.

農家の人たちは食料の輸入に強硬に反対している Farmers are protesting strongly against *the import* of food.

安価な輸入品が国産メーカーの大きな脅威になりつつある Cheap *imports* are becoming a serious threat to domestic manufacturers.

輸入ものの家具が今売り出し中です *Imported* furniture is now on sale.

政府は外国車の輸入拡大を決議した The government resolved that *imports* of foreign cars *should be expanded*.

農産物の輸入自由化が急速に進んでいる *The liberalization of* agricultural *imports* is progressing very fast.

彼らは日本に輸入制限を撤廃するよう強く迫っている They insist that Japan (should) abolish *import restrictions*.

‖輸入業者 an importer / 輸入国 an importing country, an importer / 輸入超過 (an) excess of imports (over exports) / 逆輸入 reimport / 並行輸入 parallel import; (個人輸入) personal import

ユネスコ UNESCO (❖*U*nited *N*ations *E*ducational, *S*cientific, and *C*ultural *O*rganization (国連教育科学文化機関)の略語)

ゆのみ 湯飲み (tea)cup [C]

ゆび 指

(手の) finger [C]; (足の) toe [C]

(1)日本語の「指」と異なり，英語の finger は手の指だけをいう．ただし，手の親指は thumb といい，ふつうは finger に含めない // 親指 *the thumb* / 人差し指 *the index finger*; *the*

ゆ

ゆびおり

forefinger / 中指 *the middle finger* / 薬指 *the ring finger* / 小指 *the little finger*; *the pinkie*

(2)上記以外に手の親指以外の指を親指側から数えて,「人差し指」the first finger,「中指」the second finger,「薬指」the third finger,「小指」the fourth finger と呼ぶこともあるが,親指を最初の指と考えて,「人差し指」the second finger,「中指」the third finger,「薬指」the fourth finger,「小指」the fifth finger と呼ぶこともあるので, (1)で挙げた英語を使うほうが誤解が生じない.

(3)足の「親指」は the big [great] toe といい, ほかの指は, 親指側から the second toe, the third [middle] toe, the fourth toe, the fifth [little] toe という.

【指を】
両手の指を組み合わせる interlace *one's fingers*

割れたガラスで指を切った I cut *my fingers* on the broken glass.

窓に指をはさんだ I pinched *my finger* in the window.

父は指をぱちんと鳴らしてウェーターを呼んだ My father snapped *his fingers* to call the waiter.

彼は細い[太い]指をしている He has slender [thick] *fingers*.

指をしゃぶるのをやめなさい Don't *suck your thumb*.

◆指をぽきぽき鳴らす crack *one's knuckles* (❖ knuckles は「指の関節」の意味)

【指で】
その子は指で10まで数えられるようになった The child learned to count to 10 *on his fingers*.

彼は右手の親指でボタンを押した He pushed the button *with his right thumb*.

彼女はいらだたしそうに指で机をたたいていた She was impatiently tapping *her fingers* on the desk.

【指に】
彼女は指に大きなダイヤの指輪をはめている She wears a big diamond ring *on her finger*.

指に息を吹きかけて暖めた I blew *on my fingers* to warm them.

∥指サック a fingerstall / 指人形 a hand [glove] puppet / 指ぬき a thimble

[慣用表現] 彼は日本で5本の指に入る映画監督だ He is *among the five best* film directors in Japan. / うちの娘には指一本触れさせないぞ I'll never let you *lay a finger on* my daughter. / 私たちは彼女の華々しい活躍を指をくわえて (→うらやましげに) 見ていた We watched her spectacular success *enviously*.

ゆびおり 指折り 彼女は間違いなく世界でも指折りのピアニストだ She is surely *one of the greatest* pianists in the world. / 彼と会える日を指折り数えて待っている (→彼に会うことをとても楽しみにしている) I'm looking forward eagerly to seeing him.

ゆびきり 指切り 🔰 *yubikiri*, a pledge to keep a promise by linking each other's little fingers

◆ 指切りして約束する make a promise *by linking each other's little fingers*

ゆびさき 指先 fingertip ©
◆ 母は指先が器用だ My mother *is clever with her fingers* [*hands*]. / 私は緊張で指先が思うように動かなかった I was so nervous that I *was all thumbs*.

ゆびさす 指差す point 圓 ⑯ 〘人を指さすのはあまり行儀のいいことではない It's not very polite to *point at* a person. / 彼は沖の船を指さした He *pointed to* a ship out at sea. (❖ at は対象そのものを, to は方向や離れてある物を指す場合に用いる)

ゆびずもう 指相撲 thumb wrestling Ⓤ
◆ 子供たちは指相撲をしていた The children *were thumb-wrestling*.

ゆびわ 指輪 ring © 〘ダイヤ[金]の指輪 a diamond [gold] *ring* / 指輪をはめる[はずす]「put on [take off] *a ring* / 彼は中指に指輪をはめている He wears [has] *a ring* on his middle finger.

∥結婚指輪 a wedding ring / 婚約指輪 an engagement ring

ゆぶね 湯船 bathtub © (❖単に bath, tub ともいう) 〘湯ぶねにつかる[から出る]「soak in [get out of] *a bathtub*

ゆみ 弓 bow [bóu] ©; (弓術) archery Ⓤ 〘弓を引く draw [bend] *a bow* / 弓で矢を射る shoot an arrow from *a bow* / 弓に矢をつがえる put [fix] an arrow to *a bow* / バイオリンは弓で弾く A violin is played with *a bow*.

ゆみず 湯水 金を湯水のように使う spend money *like water*

ゆみなり 弓なり 彼はいすに座ったまま両手を挙げて体を弓なりに反(ｿ)らせた He raised his arms up and *arched his back* while seated.

ゆみや 弓矢 a bow and arrow(s)

ゆめ 夢

❶【睡眠中に見る】dream ©
ゆうべいい[悪い]夢を見た I *had* a good [bad] *dream* last night. (❖「夢を見る」は ×see a dream, ×watch a dream とはいわない)

故郷の夢を見た I *had a dream of* [*about*] my hometown. / I *dreamed of* [*about*] my hometown. (❖動詞 dream の過去・過去分詞形は,《米》では dreamed,《英》では dreamt を好む)

イノシシに追いかけられる夢を見た I「*had a dream* [*dreamed*]」that I was run after by a wild boar.

夢からさめると汗でびっしょりだった I was soaked with sweat when I *woke up from a dream*.

けさは恐ろしい夢で目がさめた An awful *dream* woke me up this morning.

借金取りは夢にまで出てきた The debt collector even *appeared in my dream*.

こんなごちそうを食べられるなんて夢のようだ It's *like a dream* to be able to eat such wonderful dishes.

きのう夢の中で昔の友達に会った Last night, I saw an old friend in *a dream*.
彼は夢にまで見た新車を買った He bought the new car *of his dreams*.
私の初夢は正夢になった My *first dream of the New Year* came true.
◆ほおをつねって夢を見ているのではないことを確かめた I pinched my cheek to make sure I *wasn't dreaming* [*in a dream*]. / 優勝するなんて夢にも思わなかった I *never dreamed* of winning the tournament.
❷ [望み・理想] dream ⓒ; (野心) ambition ⓒ
《夢が・は》
私には大きな夢がある I have *a big dream*.
彼女の夢はデザイナーとして成功することだ Her *dream* is to make it as a designer.
君の夢はいつか必ず実現するだろう Your *dream* will surely come true someday.
我々の夢は粉々に打ち砕かれた Our *dreams* were shattered into pieces.
彼には全く夢がない (→現実的すぎて夢がもてない) He *is too realistic to have dreams*.
《夢を》
将来の夢を教えてください Could you tell me *your dreams* for the future?
そんなに簡単に夢をあきらめるなんて君らしくない It is unlike you to give up *your dream* so easily.
夢を追い続けるのも楽じゃない It isn't easy to keep pursuing [chasing] *a dream*.
彼女は宇宙飛行士になるという長年いだいていた夢をかなえた She realized *her long-held dream* of becoming an astronaut.
子供たちの夢をこわすようなことは言うな Don't say anything that would destroy [ruin] the children's *dreams*.
◆まだ若いんだからもっと夢をもてよ You're still young and should *be more ambitious*.
《その他》
今シーズン, 彼のチームは優勝も夢ではない Winning the championship *is not altogether a dream* for his team this season.
◆長い間温めてきた計画が夢と消えた The plan I had been nursing for a long time *ended in smoke*. / あの大学に合格するなんて私には夢のまた夢だ I *can't even dream* of passing the entrance exam for that college.
俳句 旅に病んで夢は枯野をかけ廻る (松尾芭蕉)
Ill from my journey,
in my dreams I romp around
the dry winter fields.

ゆめうつつ 夢現 私は彼の話を夢うつつで聞いていた I was listening to him *half dreaming*.

ゆめごこち 夢心地 私たちは夢心地で (→夢を見ているかのように) その美しい景色を眺めた We gazed at the beautiful scenery *as if we were dreaming* [*in a dream*].

ゆめみ 夢見 夢見心地で *as if in a dream* / このごろ夢見が悪い (→悪い夢を見る) I've had bad dreams recently.

ゆめみる 夢見る dream* ⓐ ⓗ /子供のころ私は科学者になることを夢見ていた In my child-hood, I *dreamed of* becoming a scientist.
◆夢見るような目つき [表情] a *dreamy* look [expression] / 夢見がちな少年 a *dreamy* [*romantic*] boy

ゆめものがたり 夢物語 あんなぜいたくな暮らしは私にとって全くの夢物語だ To lead such a luxurious life is quite *an impossible dream* for me.

ゆゆしい 由々しい ゆゆしい事態 a *serious* [*grave*] situation / それはゆゆしい問題だ It is a *serious* [*grave*] problem.

ゆらい 由来 (起源) origin ⓒ ⓤ; (歴史) history ⓒ / 月の名前の由来を知っていますか Do you know *the origins* [*histories*] of the names of the months? / その神社の由来は江戸時代にさかのぼる The shrine traces *its origin* back to the Edo period.
◆学校の名前は創立者の名に由来する The name of the school *comes from* its founder. / (→創立者にちなんで名づけられている) The school *was named after* its founder.

ゆらぐ 揺らぐ (揺れる) shake* ⓐ; (心が) waver ⓘ, be shaken; (組織・制度などが) totter ⓘ /いざというときになって彼の決心は揺らいだ His decision *wavered* [*was shaken*] at the last moment.

ゆらす 揺らす rock ⓗ, sway ⓗ ⓘ /母親はゆっくりと揺りかごを揺らした The mother *rocked* the cradle slowly. / 風が木の葉を揺らした The wind *swayed* the leaves. / 彼らは音楽に合わせて体を揺らした They *swayed* (*their bodies*) to the music.

ゆらめく 揺らめく flicker ⓘ, waver ⓘ /ろうそくの明かりが揺らめいた The candlelight *flickered* [*wavered*].

ゆらゆら ケーブルカーのゴンドラは風を受けてゆらゆら揺れた The cable car gondola *swayed* [*swung*] in the wind. / たばこからゆらゆら煙が立ち昇っていた The smoke *wavered* as it rose from the cigarette. / クラゲが水中をゆらゆら漂っていた Jellyfish *were floating* in the water.

ゆらり ろうそくの火がゆらりと揺れた The candle flame *swayed* [*flickered*].

ゆり 百合 lily ⓒ

ゆりいす 揺り椅子 rocking chair ⓒ, rocker ⓒ

ゆりうごかす 揺り動かす sway ⓗ /彼女の演説に多くの人が心を揺り動かされた A lot of people *were swayed* by her speech.

ゆりおこす 揺り起こす shake* *a person awake* [*out of sleep*] /授業中に居眠りをして先生に揺り起こされた I dozed off in class and *was shaken awake* by the teacher.

ゆりかえし 揺り返し (余震) aftershock ⓒ

ゆりかご 揺り籠 cradle ⓒ /揺りかごから墓場まで *from the cradle to the grave* / 母親はゆっくりと揺りかごを揺らした The mother rocked *the cradle* slowly.

ゆりもどし 揺り戻し (余震) aftershock ⓒ

ゆるい 緩い (締まりが) loose; (仮などが) gentle; (遅い) slow; (柔らかい) soft; (規律・警備などが) lax

ゆるい結び目 a *loose* knot / ゆるい坂 a *gentle* [*gradual*] slope / ゆるい球を投げる throw a *slow* ball

この靴は少しゆるい These shoes are a little *loose*.

ダイエットをしたらベルトがゆるくなった My belt got *looser* after I went on a diet.

頂上に近づくにつれて傾斜はゆるくなった The slope got *gentler* as we got near to the top.

この川は流れがゆるいから泳いで渡れる This river runs *slow*, so you can swim across it.

このところ便がゆるい I've had *soft* stools recently.

この周辺は地盤がゆるい The ground is *soft* around here.

その国では銃の所持に対する規制がかなりゆるい In that country the regulations on the possession of firearms are fairly *lax*.

◆ゆるくウェーブした髪 *gently* waving hair / 道は左にゆるくカーブしていた The road curved *gently* to the left. / 2本のひもをゆるく結んだ I tied the two strings *loosely*.

ゆるがす 揺るがす shake* ⊕ //飛行機の爆音が大地を揺るがした The roar of the plane *shook* the earth. / その体験は私の信念を大きく揺るがした Those experiences greatly *shook* my beliefs.

◆世界を揺るがすニュース *earthshaking* [*earthshattering*] news

ゆるぎない 揺るぎない firm, solid //彼女は歌手として揺るぎない地位を築いた She has established a *firm* [*solid*] position as a singer. / 彼らは揺るぎない友情のきずなで結ばれている They are tied to each other by *firm* [*solid*] friendship.

ゆるし 許し (許可) permission Ⓤ, (公式的) leave Ⓤ; (容赦・勘弁) forgiveness Ⓤ, (公式的) pardon Ⓤ //両親から新しいテレビゲームを買う許しを得た I got *permission* [*leave*] from my parents to buy a new video game. / 彼は博物館からの許しを得ずにその絵の写真を撮った He took a picture of the painting without the museum's *permission* [*leave*]. / 私は彼女に、窓ガラスを割ってしまったことの許しを請うた I begged 「her for *forgiveness* [her *pardon*] for my breaking the windowpane.

ゆるす 許す

❶【許可する・させておく】allow ⊕; (公式的) permit ⊕; let* ⊕

> allow: 「許可する」のほかに「させておく」「するのを妨げない」という意味で用いる.
> permit: 権限に基づいて許可する場合などに用いられ, 形式ばったニュアンスがある.
> let: 日常語で, allow と permit の両方の意味で用いる.

父は僕がひとりで旅行するのを許してくれた My father *allowed* [*permitted*] me to travel alone. / My father gave me *permission* to travel alone.

私服(→制服以外の服)で登校することは許されていない We *are not allowed* [*permitted*] *to* come to school in clothes other than the school uniform.

未成年者の飲酒は許されていない Drinking by minors *is not allowed* [*permitted*]. / (→禁止されている) Drinking by minors *is prohibited*.

その施設にテレビカメラが入ることが許された The facilities *allowed* [*let*, *admitted*] TV cameras in.

2等の銀メダルを受け取ることは彼女のプライドが許さなかった Her pride *wouldn't let* her accept the silver medal for second place. / She was *too proud to* accept the silver medal for second place.

一刻の猶予(ﾕｳﾖ)も許されない状況だ The situation *doesn't permit* any delay.

時間の許すかぎりごゆっくりお楽しみください Please enjoy yourself *as long as time permits*.

天候が許せばあしたここを出発したい I want to leave here tomorrow *if the weather permits*.

◆法律の許す範囲で *within* the law / そんな話し方は許しません I *won't stand* you [your] talking that way. / I *won't stand for* you *to* talk that way. / 5名しか入部を許されなかった(→5名だけが許された) Only five students *were admitted to* the club.

🅔「今から友達のうちに行ってもいいでしょ?」「何時だと思ってるの. お母さんは許しませんからね」"It's okay for me to go to my friend's house now, isn't it?" "What time do you think it is? No, I *won't let* you (go)." (❖文脈から判断できる場合, 原形不定詞を省く場合がある)

❷【容赦する】forgive* ⊕; excuse ⊕; (公式的) pardon ⊕ (❖進行形にはできない); overlook ⊕

> forgive: 人・罪を許すこと.
> excuse: 通例小さな過ちや失礼を許すこと.
> pardon: forgive よりもかたい語で, やや大げさな響きがある.
> overlook: 誤り・過失などを大目に見ること.

もう二度としませんから許してください Please *forgive* me. I'll never do it again.

今度またやったら決して許さないぞ If you do that again, I'll never *forgive* you.

息子の無礼をお許しください Please *forgive* [*pardon*] my son's rudeness.

彼の裏切りは決して許されまい His treacheries *will never be forgiven*.

彼はその子が窓ガラスを割ったのを許してやった He *forgave* [*excused*, *pardoned*] the child *for* breaking the window.

今回の失敗は許してやろう I'll *overlook* your error this time.

◆失敗は許されない Failure *is unforgivable* [*inexcusable*, *unpardonable*]. / 彼のしたことは許しがたいことだ What he did was *unforgivable* [*inexcusable*, *unpardonable*].

❸【認める】

彼女は自他ともに許す(→広く一般に認められている)ファッションデザイン界の大御所だ She *is generally regarded as* the leading figure in the fashion design world.

❹【その他】

この病は気を許すとすぐに再発する This disease will easily return if you *lower your guard.*

あいつに心を許したら、きっとひどい目にあうぞ If you *trust* him, you'll pay for it.

そのキーパーは試合前半で相手チームに4点を許してしまった The goalkeeper *allowed* the opponent four points in the first half of the game.

ゆるみ 緩み 運転手の一瞬の気のゆるみが大事故を引き起こした The driver's momentary *carelessness* caused a grave accident.

ゆるむ 緩む get* [become*, come*] loose, loosen ㊥ ∥靴ひもがゆるんでるよ Your shoelace *has gotten loose.* / このねじはすぐにゆるんでしまう This screw *gets loose* easily.

◆寒さは徐々にゆるんできている The cold *is gradually becoming less severe.* / 大雨で地盤がゆるんでいる The ground *has gotten soft* because of the heavy rain. / 強敵に勝ったことで気がゆるんで次の試合では思わぬ負けを喫してしまった Having defeated a strong opponent, we *slacked off* — and that's the reason we lost the next game unexpectedly. / 彼女の緊張した顔が一気にゆるんだ Her tense expression suddenly *relaxed into a smile.*

ゆるめる 緩める

❶【締めつけ・張りを】loosen ㊥; (力を) relax ㊥; (たるませる) slacken ㊥

ねじ[ネクタイ]をゆるめる loosen「a screw [one's tie] / ギターの弦をゆるめる loosen [slacken] the guitar strings

彼はロープを握っている手をゆるめた He *loosened* [*relaxed*] his grip on the rope.

❷【厳しさを】relax ㊥, ease ㊥; (規則・制限などを) loosen ㊥

校則をゆるめる *relax* school regulations

警戒をゆるめるのはまだ早すぎる It's still too early to *relax* our guard.

この機械を動かすときは決して気をゆるめることができない When I operate this machine, I can never *relax*.

❸【遅くする】slow down [up]

交差点でスピードをゆるめた I *slowed down* at the intersection.

私は歩調をゆるめて息を整えた I *slowed down* my pace and got my breath back.

ゆるやか 緩やか ━━**ゆるやかな** gentle; (ゆっくりした) slow; (刑罰などが) lenient ∥ゆるやかな坂 a *gentle* [*gradual*] slope / 彼らに対する処置はかなりゆるやかなものだった The punishment they received was rather *lenient.*

◆ゆるやかな校則 *mild* school regulations / 道はここからゆるやかに下っている The road

goes down *gently* from here.

ゆるゆる ━━**ゆるゆるの** (ゆるい) loose; (だぶだぶの) baggy ∥このズボンはウエストはゆるゆるだ These trousers *are loose* around the waist.

ゆれ 揺れ ボートの揺れ *the rock* [*roll, pitch*] of the boat / がくんとひと揺れして列車は動きだした The train began to move *with a jolt.* / 明け方に大きな揺れ(→地震)を感じた I felt *a* big *earthquake* at dawn.

ゆれうごく 揺れ動く 枝が風に揺れ動いている The branches *are swaying* in the wind. / 多額の報酬を提示されて彼の気持ちは揺れ動いた When he was offered a large reward, he *wavered* [*fluctuated*] between accepting and refusing the offer.

ゆれる 揺れる shake* ㊥; swing* ㊥; sway ㊥; rock ㊥; jolt ㊥; flicker ㊥; roll ㊥

shake: 振動する.
swing: 振り子のように揺れる.
sway: ぐらりと・ゆっくりと揺れる.
rock: 規則的に揺れる、あるいは激しく揺れる.
jolt: がたん・がくんと激しく揺れる.
flicker: 炎などが揺らめく.
roll: 船などが横に揺れる.

地震で家が激しく揺れた The house *shook* [*rocked, rattled*] violently in the earthquake. (❖rattleは「がたがた音を立てる」の意味)

木の枝にかかったハンモックがかすかに揺れていた The hammock hanging from the branches *was swinging* slightly.

コスモスが秋風に揺れている The cosmoses *are swaying* in the autumn wind.

強風のために船は激しく横に揺れた[縦に揺れた] Because of the strong wind, the ship *rolled* [*pitched*] heavily.

突然機体ががくんと大きく揺れた Suddenly the airplane *jolted* heavily.

彼はろうそくの揺れる炎を見つめていた He was gazing at the *flickering* flame of the candle.

◆彼に本当のことを話すべきかどうか彼女の心は揺れた She *wavered* (about) whether to tell him the truth or not. / カーテンがそよ風に揺れていた The curtains *were waving* in the breeze. (❖waveは「波打つ(ように揺れる)」の意味) / 町長逮捕のニュースに町全体が揺れている The news that the mayor was arrested *has shaken* [*rocked*] the whole town. (❖このshake, rockは「揺らす」という意味の他動詞) / つり橋がちょっと揺れただけで彼女は大声をあげた She screamed after *a* slight *sway* of the hanging bridge. (❖このswayは名詞)

ゆわえる 結わえる tie ㊥, bind* ㊥ ➡しばる、むすぶ ∥靴ひもを結わえる *tie one's* shoelace / ひもで新聞紙の束を結わえる *bind* a pile of newspapers with string

ゆわかし 湯沸かし kettle Ⓒ ∥湯沸かしを火にかける put on *a* kettle

∥湯沸かし器 a water heater

よ

よ¹ 世

❶【世の中】world ⓒ《しばしば the ～》
➡よのなか

世に出る(→出世する) go [come] up in *the world*; rise *in the world*
彼の絵は彼の死後世に認められるようになった His paintings were appreciated by *the world* after he died.
ビートルズは当時まだ世に知られていなかった The Beatles weren't known well by *the world* yet at that time.
成功した人がねたまれるというのは世の常だ A successful person is envied. That's *the way of the world*.
世はまさに情報化の時代だ *The world today* is in the information age.
将来は世のため人のために働きたい I want to work *for people and the world* in the future.
◆世の親たちは子供の幸福を切に願っている Parents (*in general*) are anxious for the welfare of their children. / 彼女は世に言う無党派層だ She is「*what is called* [*what they call*]」an independent voter. / 彼女の最初の小説が世に出た(→出版された)のは,彼女が35歳のときだった It was when she was 35 years old that her first novel *was published*. / 彼は少し世の荒波にもまれたほうがいい He had better experience *the difficulties of life*.

❷【現世】
あなたにとってこの世でいちばん大切なものは何ですか What is the most valuable thing *in this world* for you?
その島はこの世の楽園だった The island was heaven *on earth*.
信長は49歳で世を去った Nobunaga「*left this world* [*died*]」when he was 49.
彼は世をはかなんで自らの命を絶った He *felt life was meaningless* and killed himself.

❸【時代】
武家の世 *the age* of military ascendancy
世が世なら(→違う時代に生きていれば)彼は一国の王だった He would be a king of a country *if he lived in different times*.
そんな不正がまかり通るようじゃ世も末だ If such an injustice is committed with impunity, *there's no justice left in the world*.

❹【その他】
彼の家は世にも(→非常に)不思議な形をしている His house has an *extremely* strange shape.

‖あの世 the other [next] world, the world to come

よ² 夜 night ⓒⓤ ➡よる(夜) ‖友達とおしゃべりして夜を明かした I *stayed up all night* talking with my friends. / 夜がふけると急に冷えてきた It got chilly suddenly *late at night*. / 彼は夜を徹して仕事をした He worked *all night*. / 近ごろ夜な夜なタヌキが出没しては畑を荒らしてゆく Recently raccoon dogs appear and do damage to the field *night after night*. ◆もうすぐ夜が明ける *The day will break* soon.
[慣用表現] 彼は孫娘がいないと夜も日も明けない(→生きてゆけない)ありさまだった He *couldn't live* without his granddaughter.

よ³ 余 百余名の参加者があった A hundred-*odd* people took part in it. (❖ odd は端数のない数の後に用いて「…と少し」の意味)

-よ 一生懸命勉強しないと入試に失敗するよ(→だろう) Study hard, or *you'll* fail the entrance examination. / 彼は自分でそれをやってみるべきだよ(→と思う) I *think* he should try it himself. / 定雄は後で来ると思うよ(→推測する) I *suppose* Sadao will come later. / あなたはきっと試験に合格しますよ You're *sure* to pass the exam. / *I'm sure that* you will pass the exam. / 全く彼は変わった男だよ He is *really* a strange man. / ねえ,もう行こうよ Come on, let's go.

よあけ 夜明け dawn ⓤⓒ ➡ よる(夜) 図版, daybreak ⓤ;(事の始まり) the dawn ‖新時代の夜明け *the dawn* of a new era / 夜明け前に目がさめた I woke up before *dawn*. / 夜明けに出発しよう Let's start *at dawn [daybreak]*.

よあそび 夜遊び ―夜遊びする go* (out) on the town at night

よい¹ 良い・好い・善い

❶【良好な】good, fine, nice;(健康な・満足のいく) well

よい知らせ *good* news / 古きよき時代 the *good old days*
食べすぎは健康によくない Eating too much「*isn't good* [*is bad*]」for the health.
この辞書のほうがそれよりよい This dictionary is *better* than that one.
このパソコンがいちばんよい This personal computer is *the best*.
きょうは気分がよくない I *don't feel well* today.
よい天気ですね It's a *nice* day, isn't it?
きのう見た映画はかなりよかった The movie I saw yesterday was fairly *good*.
天気は午後にはよくなるでしょう The weather will「*be better* [*improve*]」this afternoon.
その患者は日ごとによくなってきている The patient *is getting better* day by day.
◆彼女の提案は委員会にうけがよかった Her proposals were *well* received by the committee. / そのコンサートは客の入りがよかった The concert was *well* attended. (❖ この well は副詞) / 彼のけがはすぐによくなった(→回復した) He *recovered from* the wound

rapidly. / 運動すると血行がよくなる(→血行を刺激する) Exercise *stimulates* the circulation of blood. / その夫婦は私が若いころずいぶんよく(→親切に)してくれた The couple *was* very *kind to me* when I was young. / お行儀よくしなさい *Behave yourself*!

💬「よいクリスマスを」「ありがとう．あなたもね」 "Have a *good* Christmas!" "Thank you. Same to you!"

❷【うれしい】

君に会えてよかった *I'm glad to* have met you.

ああよかった，無事だったのね *Thank God*, you are safe!

💬「レギュラーに選ばれたんだ」「それはよかったね」 "I was chosen as a regular player." "*That's good.*"

💬「こんなにおいしいステーキ，食べたことがありません」「ありがとう．お気に召してよかったわ」 "This is the best steak I've ever had." "Thank you. *I'm glad* you like it."

❸【さしつかえない】

よかったら身の上話を聞かせてくれませんか *Would you mind* telling me your life story?

よかったら，車で迎えに行くよ *If you want* [*like*], I'll pick you up.

今夜働かなくてもよかったらなあ If only I *didn't have to* work tonight!

❹【正しい・適切な】(正しい) right, correct; (適した) good, suitable

渋谷へ行くにはこの地下鉄でよいのですか Is this the *right* subway line to Shibuya?

ここはたこあげにちょうどよい場所だ This is a *good* [*suitable*] place for flying a kite.

◆人にうそをつくのはよくないことだ It is *bad* to tell a lie to others.

❺【…すべき】should (❖後に完了形の動詞を用いると「…すればよかったのに(…しなかった)」と，行為が実現されなかったことを示す); had better (❖had better には命令的な響きがあり，ふつう目下の人に用いられる) ➡ほう(方)

もう席についたほうがよい You *should* take your seat now.

せめて電話くらいくれてもよかったのに You *should* at least *have called* me.

◆あんなこと言わなきゃよかった I *wish* I hadn't said that. (❖wish の後ろの節中は仮定法になる)

[慣用表現] 終わりよければすべてよし ➡おわり ➡いい

よい² 宵 early evening [U] //まだ宵の口だ It's still *early evening*. / The night is still *young*.

よい³ 酔い ❶【酒による】drunkenness [U]

◆酔いが回る *get drunk* / 彼は夜風にあたって酔いをさまそうとした He tried to *sober himself up* with the night breeze.

❷【乗り物による】motion sickness [U]

◆船酔い[車酔い]してしまった I'm *seasick* [*carsick*].

よいごし 宵越し 彼は宵越しの金は持たない(→気前よく金を使う)主義だ He is *generous with his money*.

よいしょ (掛け声) yo-ho [jouhóu] ―よいしょする (おだてる) flatter [他], butter up //あいつはいつも上司をよいしょしている He's always *buttering up* his boss.

よいしれる 酔いしれる 彼らは勝利に酔いしれていた They *were drunk with* victory.

よいっぱり 宵っ張り night person [C], 《口語的》night owl [C]

◆彼女は宵っ張りの朝寝坊だ She *stays up late* and gets up late.

よいつぶれる 酔い潰れる get* dead [blind] drunk, get plastered

よいどめ 酔い止め motion sickness pill [drug] [C]

よいのくち 宵の口 宵の口から雨が降りだした It began to rain *early in the evening*.

よいのみょうじょう 宵の明星 the evening star; (金星) Venus

よいまちぐさ 宵待ち草〘植物〙evening primrose [C]

よいん 余韻 (音の響き) lingering sound [C]; (反響音)《公式的》reverberation [U] [C]《通例複数形～s》; (楽しかったことの) afterglow [U] //選手たちがグラウンドを去った後もサポーターたちは熱戦の余韻に浸っていた After the players left the field, the supporters *stayed basking in the afterglow* of the exciting game.

よう¹ 用

❶【用事】something (to do), business [U]

何か用ですか Do you want me for *something*?

何か急ぎの用でもあるのですか Do you have any urgent *business*?

ごめん，今晩は用があるんだ I'm sorry, but I have 「*something to do* [*some business*] this evening.

◆(客に)どういうご用ですか *May I help you*? / (客に)ご用は承っておりますでしょうか *Are you being served* [*attended to*]? / 用がすんだらそれを私に返してください Give it back to me *when you are through*. / 彼の態度はもう私には用はないと言わんばかりだった He behaved as if to say he *no longer needed* me. / 用もないのに(→理由もなく)人の部屋に入らないで Don't just walk into my room *for* 「*no reason* [*nothing*]. / その国では英語で何とか用を足すことができた In that country I *managed to make myself understood* in English. (❖make *oneself* understood で「自分の言うことを理解してもらう」の意味)

❷【働き】

男子用更衣室 a *men's* locker room; a locker room *for men* / 家庭用ミシン a sewing machine *for home* [*family*] *use*

差し当たってはこのペンで用が足ります This pen *will do* me for the present.

たいていの買い物はこのスーパーで用が足りる We *can do* most of the shopping at this supermarket.

縮尺が間違っていたのでは地図としての用をなさない It *doesn't serve* as a map as it has a

よ

wrong scale.
このはさみは料理用です These scissors are *for* kitchen *use*.
私は自分用にネクタイを買った I bought a tie *for* myself.
その会社はパソコン用の新しいソフトを発表した The company made an announcement of new software *for* personal computers.
❸【用便】
ちょっと用を足してきます Excuse me. I'd like to *go to the rest room*.

よう² 要 彼の発表は簡潔で要を得ていた His presentation *was* simple and *to the point*. / 要は彼がそれを認めるかどうかだ *The point is* whether he will admit it or not.

よう³ 洋 ❶【海洋】the ocean //太平[大西, インド]洋 *the* Pacific [Atlantic, Indian] *Ocean*(❖Oceanは省略できる)

❷【東洋と西洋】この遊びは洋の東西を問わず(→東洋でも西洋でも)古くから親しまれてきた This play has been familiar for a long time *both in the East and in the West*.

よう⁴ 酔う (酒に) get* drunk; (乗り物に) get sick //父は酔うと必ず私たちに説教を始めるのだった Whenever my father *got drunk*, he used to begin preaching to us. / 彼はひどく酔っていた He *was dead drunk*. / 私は船に乗ると必ず酔う I *get sick* [*seasick*] every time I get on「a ship [board]. (❖「車[飛行機]に酔う」なら get carsick [airsick]とする)

◆酔ったうえでのけんか *a drunken* fight / 彼は酔った勢いで友人に暴言を吐いた He used abusive language toward his friend *out of a drunken impulse*. / 彼らは祭りの華やいだ雰囲気に酔っていた They *were intoxicated with* the bright atmosphere of the festival.

よう⁵ (呼びかけ) Hi!, Hey! //よう, 元気か *Hi*! What's up?

-よう¹ -様

❶ 様子	seem; look; appear
❷ 類似	like
❸ 例示	suck as …, like
❹ しかた	as, like
❺ 目的・命令	to *do*

❶【様子】seem ⓐ; look ⓐ; appear ⓐ
 seem: 主観的に「…のように思われる」という意味を表す.
 look: 客観的に「…のように思われる」という意味を表す.
 appear: seem よりも形式的で, 視覚的に「…のように思われる」という意味を表す.

彼は少し疲れているようだ He *seems* [*looks, appears*] (*to be*) a little tired.
うちのテレビはこわれているようだ Our TV set *seems to be* out of order.
だれかが私の傘を持っていってしまったようだ It *seems* someone took my umbrella.
彼は犬が好きではないようだ He *doesn't seem to* like dogs.
だれかが私の後をつけているようだった There *seemed to* be someone following me.

◆彼は私の言うことを理解していないようだ *I'm afraid* he doesn't understand me. (❖*I'm afraid* …で「(残念ながら)…のようだ」という意味を表す) / この前電話で話したときは彼女は元気なようだった She *sounded fine* last time I talked with her over the phone. / あしたは雨のようだ It's *likely* to rain tomorrow.

❷【類似】like
アリのように働く work *like* an ant
それは毛皮のような手ざわりがする It feels *like* fur.
彼女は私にとって姉のような存在だ She is *like* a sister to me.
きみのような変わった少年は見たことがない I've never seen 「a strange boy *like* you [*such* a strange boy *as* you].
髪を短くしたら彼女は男の子のようだ She *looks like* a boy with her hair cut short.

◆彼はまるで老人のような話し方をする He talks *as if* he were [was] an old man. (❖*as if* 節中では仮定法が用いられる) / その鳥は雪のように白かった That bird was *as* white *as* snow. / 私たちは机を輪のように並べた We moved the desks *in a circle*.

❸【例示】such as …, like
彼女はニンジンやブロッコリーのような野菜を食べない She doesn't eat vegetables, *such as* carrots and broccoli.
彼はホーキング博士のような科学者になりたいと思っている He wants to be a scientist *like* Dr. Hawking.

◆日本のスポーツの中には, 例えば柔道のように世界中で人気のあるものがある Some Japanese sports, judo *for instance*, are very popular all over the world. / だれもあなたのように優しくはなかった Nobody was *as* kind *as* you. / もし気が変わるようなことがあったら呼んでください If you *should* change your mind, call me. (❖仮定を表す条件節中でshouldを用いると改まった調子になる)

❹【しかた】as, like
君の好きなようにしろよ Do *as* you like.
このように手を伸ばしてください Straighten your arms *like this*.
彼女はいつものように歩いて登校した She walked to school *as usual*.

◆ナイフとフォークはこのように使いなさい Use your knife and fork *in this way* [*manner*]. / あなたの国ではどのようにクリスマスを祝いますか *How* do you celebrate Christmas in your country?

❺【目的・命令】to *do*(❖最もふつうの言い方), in order to *do*, so as to *do*, so that … can [will](❖口語では that が省略される)
伸男は試験に受かるように一生懸命勉強した Nobuo studied hard *to* [*in order to*] pass the exam.
いじめをなくすように全力を尽くしましょう Let's do our best *to* stop bullying.
私は会議の報告をするように求められた I was re-

quired *to* make a report on the meeting.

先生は私たちに静かにするように言った The teacher told us *to* be quiet.

私は彼に2時間したら起こしてくれるように頼んだ I asked him *to* wake me up two hours later.

間違いをしないように心がけなさい Try *not to* make a mistake.

彼は電車に遅れないように駅まで走った He ran all the way to the station *so as* ｢*to* catch [*not to* miss] the train.

人が通れるように自転車を何台かわきに寄せた I moved some bicycles aside *so* (*that*) people *could* pass.

だれにも聞かれないように小声で話をした We whispered *so that* no one *would* hear our conversation.

◆私は医者に診(み)てもらうよう彼に勧めた I suggested that he (*should*) go to see a doctor. / 彼は最近酒を飲まないようにしている He ｢*keeps off* [*refrains from*] drinking in these days.

❻【…するようになる】come* [grow*] to *do*

彼は正義の重要性を理解するようになった He *came* [*grew*] *to* understand the importance of justice.

◆とうとうバイクに乗れるようになった I finally *learned to* ride a motorcycle. / CD技術のおかげですばらしい音質を楽しめるようになった CD technology *has enabled* us *to* enjoy better sound quality. / 今日(こんにち)ではますます多くの若者が海外旅行をするようになっている Today more and more young people travel abroad.

❼【祈願】

神のお恵みがありますように！ (*May*) God bless you!/ Bless you!

写真がうまく撮れていますように *I hope* the pictures will come out nicely.

-よう² ❶【勧誘】急行に乗り換えよう *Let's* change to an express train. / 会う場所を決めよう *Let's* fix the place for the meeting.
❷【意志】私が彼らに代わって答えよう I*'ll* answer for them. / その後何が起こったか話してあげよう I*'ll* tell you what happened after that. / 欲しいだけあげよう(→君は好きなだけ取っていい) You *may* have as many as you want. / 彼に電話しようとしていたところにちょうど彼から電話がかかってきた I *was just about to* call him when he gave me a call.
➾-しよう

ようい¹ 用意

preparation [U]《また ～s》; (手はず) arrangement [C]《通例複数形 ～s》 ―用意する prepare [他][自], get* ready (for .../to *do*); arrange [他][自]

彼女は僕たちのために夕食の用意をしてくれた She *prepared* us supper./ She *prepared* supper *for* us.

そろそろ出かける用意をしたほうがいいよ You'd better *get ready to* go now.

君は本当に用意がいいね You are really *well-prepared*.

あしたまでに1,000万円用意しろ *Get* 10 million yen *ready* [*Get together* 10 million yen] by tomorrow.

◆用意はできた？ *Are you ready*? / あしたの用意は全部できた Everything *is* now *ready* [*arranged*] *for* tomorrow. / 知美，食卓の用意をしてくれない？ Would you *set the table*, Tomomi? / 社長は彼女によい地位を用意した(→与えた) The president *offered* ｢her a good position [a good position *to* her]. / 彼は万事に用意周到だ He *is very careful* about everything. / 位置について，用意，ドン On your mark, *get set* [《英》*steady*], go! (❖レースの合図)

💬｢晶子，夕食の用意ができたわよ｣｢はい，今行きます｣ "Akiko, dinner *is ready*." "OK. I'm coming."

ようい² 容易 easiness [U] ―容易な easy ―容易に easily, with ease ➾かんたん(簡単), やさしい(易しい) ‖先頭に追いつくのは容易なことではない *It is not easy to* catch up with the leader. / このソフトを導入したことでデータの検索が容易になった The introduction of this software made it *easy* to retrieve data. / 彼女ががっかりしていることは容易に察しがついた I can *easily* [*It was easy to*] guess her disappointment.
◆この事件は容易に解決しそうにもない(→解決するのは難しい) This case seems to be *difficult* to solve.

よういく 養育 ―養育する bring* up, raise [他]; (里親として) foster [他] ‖養育費 the expense of bringing up children

よういん¹ 要因 factor [C]; (原因) cause [C] ‖プラス[マイナス]要因 *a* plus [minus] *factor* / いくつかの要因が彼に有利[不利]に働いた Several *factors* worked ｢to his advantage [against him].

よういん² 要員 代替要員を待機させる make *substitutes* stand by / 彼は打撃不振で代打要員に回された He got a batting slump and was demoted to *a pinch hitter*.

ようえき 溶液 solution [U][C]

ようえん 妖艶 ―妖艶な glamorous

ようか 八日 8日間 for *eight days* / 5月8日 May (*the*) *eighth*

ようが 洋画 (絵) Western [European] painting [C]; (外国映画) foreign movie [film] [C] ‖私は圧倒的に邦画より洋画を見ることが多い I see *foreign movies* much more often than Japanese ones.

ようかい¹ 妖怪 (怪物) monster [C]; (幽霊) ghost [C], 《文語》specter [C]

ようかい² 溶解 〘化学〙dissolution [U] ―溶解する (液体中に) dissolve [dizálv] [他][自]; (熱などで) melt [自][他] ‖溶解液 solution

ようがく 洋楽 Western [European] music [U]

ようがし 洋菓子 (Western-style) confectionery [U], (Western-style) sweet [C] ‖洋菓子店 a confectionery

よ

ようかん 羊羹

ようかんの主な材料は砂糖とともに練った小豆のあんで、もともとは茶道のための茶菓子として定着した和菓子です。今日(誌)でもようかんは代表的な和菓子として多くの人に愛されており、作り方や中に入れる材料を変えることによっていろいろな種類のようかんを楽しむことができます。
Yokan, usually made of adzuki beans mashed with sugar, developed as confection for the tea ceremony. It is a typical Japanese sweet that is loved by many people. You can enjoy a variety of *yokan* made in different ways and with a variety of ingredients.

ようがん 溶岩 〖地学〗lava ⓤ ∥噴火口から溶岩が流出した *Lava* flowed from the crater. ∥溶岩ドーム a lava dome / 溶岩流 a lava flow

ようき¹ 陽気 ❶〖天候〗weather ⓤ ∥きょうはいい陽気ですね Nice [Lovely] *weather* we're having today. / 暖かい陽気に誘われてハイキングに出かけた The warm *weather* made us want to go on a hike.
❷〖快活〗──陽気な cheerful, merry / 陽気に cheerfully, merrily / 陽気な性格 a *cheerful* [*merry*] character / 彼女は努めて陽気にふるまった She tried to behave *cheerfully* [*merrily*].
◆彼の陽気さにはいつも救われる His *cheerfulness* always gives me hope.

ようき² 容器 container ⓒ ⇨いれもの

ようぎ 容疑 suspicion ⓤⓒ ∥彼は窃盗の容疑で逮捕された He was arrested *on suspicion* [*a charge*] *of* theft. / 男は容疑を認めて[否認して]いる模様だ It is said that the man admits [denies] *the suspicion*.
◆殺人の容疑がかかる[晴れる] be suspected [cleared] *of* murder / 容疑者は警察署に連行された The *suspect* was taken to the police station.

ようきゅう¹ 要求

demand ⓒ; (当然の権利としての) claim ⓒ; (要望) request ⓒ ──要求する demand ⓣ; claim ⓣ;《公式的》request ⓣ; (法律・規則などによって) require ⓣ (❖通例受身で用いられる)

もっともな要求 a reasonable *demand* / 法外な要求 *an* excessive [exorbitant] *demand* / 不当な要求 *an* unreasonable *demand* / 賃上げ要求 *a demand for* higher wages / 要求を受け入れる[退ける] accept [reject] *one's demand*

彼は彼女のねばり強い要求に屈した He yielded to her persistent *demand*.

彼らは賠償金として5,000万円を要求した They *claimed* 50 million yen in compensation.

黒人たちは公民権を要求して立ち上がった Black people arose to *demand* their civil rights.

学生たちは現代文学に関するレポートを書くことを要求された Students *were required to* write a paper on contemporary literature.

【demand+名+(from [of] 名)】労働者は会社に賃上げを要求した The workers *demanded* higher wages *from* the company. / 彼はその出版社に謝罪を要求した He *demanded* an apology *from* [*of*] the publishing company.

【demand+to *do*】彼らは直接社長と会って話をすることを要求した They *demanded to* see the president directly and speak to him.

【demand+that 節】警察は家宅捜索を要求した The police *demanded that* the house (should) be searched.

◆それをやりとげるためには人一倍強い精神力が要求される(→必要だ) You *need* greater mental strength than other people in order to accomplish it.

ようきゅう² 洋弓 (Western) archery ⓤ

ようぎょ 幼魚 young fish ⓒ; (稚魚) fry《複数扱い》

ようぎょう 窯業 ceramics《単数扱い》, the ceramic industry

ようきょく¹ 陽極 〖電気〗positive pole ⓒ

ようきょく² 謡曲 a *yokyoku*, a Noh chant

ようぎょじょう 養魚場 fish farm ⓒ

ようぐ 用具 (小さな道具) tool ⓒ; (特に農耕具など) implement ⓒ; (精巧な器具) instrument ⓒ; (特定の目的の用具一式) gear ⓤ, outfit ⓒ
∥園芸用具 gardening implements / 洗面用具 toiletries / 体操用具 gymnastic gear / 調理用具(一式) a cooking outfit / 釣り[ゴルフ]用具(一式) fishing [golf] gear / 筆記用具 writing instruments [materials]

ようけい 養鶏 poultry farming ⓤ
∥養鶏場 a poultry farm [ranch]

ようけん¹ 用件 business ⓤ ∥用件に取りかかる get down to *business* ◆どんなご用件ですか What can I do for you?

ようけん² 要件 (→必要な条件)を満たす fulfill [meet] *the necessary conditions* / 要件(→重要な事柄)のみを伝える tell *important matters* only

ようご¹ 用語 term ⓒ; (業界用語) jargon ⓤ; (特定分野の専門用語)《集合的》terminology ⓒⓤ∥用語集 a glossary / 医学用語 a medical term / コンピュータ用語 computer terminology / 専門用語 a technical term / 法律用語 a legal term

ようご² 擁護 (防衛) defense,《英》defence ⓤⓒ; (保護) protection ⓤ; (支持) support ⓤ ──擁護する defend ⓣ; protect ⓣ; support ⓣ *defend one's* rights [ideas] / 民主主義の基本原理を擁護する *support* fundamental principles of democracy / この法律は人権の擁護を目的として制定された This law was established in order to *protect* human rights.

ようご³ 養護 (世話) care ⓤ; (介護) nursing

‖養護学校 a school for physically and mentally disabled children / 養護教員(保健の先生) a school nurse / 児童養護施設 a foster care facility

ようこう¹ 要項 (重要項目) important [essential] points ◆私は東北大学の募集要項を取り寄せた I sent away for *the application guidebook* for Tohoku University.

ようこう² 要綱 (大要) outline ◎; (概論) summary ◎

ようこうろ 溶鉱炉 blast furnace ◎

ようこそ 私たちの学校へようこそ Welcome to our school. / (来客などに)ようこそいらっしゃいました I'm glad to see you. / (I'm) glad you could come.

ようさい¹ 洋裁 dressmaking ⓤ
‖洋裁学校 a dressmaking school

ようさい² 要塞 fortress ◎, fort ◎, stronghold ◎

ようさん 養蚕 sericulture ⓤ, silkworm-breeding ⓤ

ようし¹ 用紙 paper ⓤ; (書式の印刷された) form ◎ /この用紙に記入してください Please fill in [out] this *form*. / 申込用紙は受付で手に入ります Application *forms* are available at the reception desk.
‖グラフ用紙 graph paper / 試験用紙 an examination paper / 答案用紙 (米)an answer sheet / 投票用紙 a ballot (paper) / メモ用紙 notepaper / 問題用紙 a question paper [sheet] / レポート用紙 a notepad

ようし² 要旨 (要点) the gist ◎; (大要) outline ◎ /話の要旨がはっきりしない I'm not clear about *the gist* of the story.
◆論文の要旨をまとめる *summarize* [*sum up*] the thesis / 彼の話の要旨をつかめなかった I couldn't grasp *the point* of his speech.

ようし³ 容姿 (姿) figure ◎; (顔立ち) features, looks; (風采(ふうさい)) one's personal appearance ◆彼女は容姿端麗で仕事もできる She is *good-looking* and capable.

ようし⁴ 養子 adopted child ◎
◆彼はその家の養子になった He was *adopted* by [into] the family. / 夫婦はその男の子を養子にする決心をした The couple decided to *adopt* the boy.
‖養子縁組 (an) adoption

ようし⁵ 陽子 〖物理〗proton ◎

ようじ¹ 用事 something (to do), business ⓤ; (使いの) errand ◎; (約束) 《公式的》engagement ◎
◇やらねばならない用事があります I have some *business* to do.
今夜は用事が入っている I have a *business engagement* tonight.
父は用事で外出しています My father is out on some *business*.
◆ふとだいじな用事を思い出した Suddenly I remembered *an* important *thing to do*. / あしたは特に用事はない I have *nothing to do* in particular tomorrow. / 用事を頼まれてくれないか Can I ask a favor of you?

ようじ² 幼児 young child ◎; (よちよち歩きの) toddler ◎ ‖幼児期 (an) early childhood / 幼児虐待 child abuse [əbjúst] / 幼児教育 preschool education

ようじ³ 幼時 (early) childhood ⓤ◎ /その写真を見て幼時の記憶がよみがえった The picture recalled (early) childhood memories.
‖幼時体験 the experiences of childhood

ようじ⁴ 楊枝 (つまようじ) toothpick ◎; (糸ようじ) dental floss ⓤ

ようしき¹ 様式 style ⓤ◎; (しかた) way ◎; (型) pattern ◎; (独特の) 《公式的》mode ◎ /ゴシック[ルネサンス]様式 the Gothic [Renaissance] *style* / 近代的な建築様式 a modern *style of architecture* / 生活様式をがらりと変える change one's *style* [*way*] *of life* completely; change one's *lifestyle* completely

ようしき² 洋式 ——洋式の Western-style ‖洋式のトイレ a *Western-style* toilet

ようしゃ 容赦 forgiveness ⓤ, 《公式的》pardon ⓤ ——容赦する forgive* 他, 《公式的》pardon 他; (大目に見る) overlook 他 /今度こんなまねをしたら容赦しないからな I won't *forgive* you if you do such a thing again. / 品切れの節はご容赦ください Please *forgive* us if the items you ask for are out of stock.
◆マスコミは情け容赦なく政府の税制改革案を非難した The media attacked the government's tax reform plan *mercilessly* [*without mercy*]. / レポート提出の締め切りは容赦なく迫ってくる The deadline for the paper is getting *inexorably* closer.

ようしゅ 洋酒 Western [foreign] liquor ⓤ (❖種類をいうときは◎)

ようしょ¹ 要所 important [key] point ◎; (軍事上の) strategic point ◎ /この町はスイスからイタリアへと行く交通の要所だ This town is *an important point for the traffic* from Switzerland to Italy. / コースの要所要所に道しるべが立っているので道に迷う心配はない You need not worry about losing your way because signposts stand *at every key point* of the course.
◆彼は10安打を許したが要所を締めてジャイアンツを1失点に抑えた He allowed 10 hits, but *got some big* [*key*] *outs* and held the Giants to one run.

ようしょ² 洋書 Western [foreign] book ◎

ようじょ 養女 adopted daughter
⇨ようし(養子)

ようしょう¹ 幼少 幼少のころの楽しい思い出 happy recollections of *one's childhood*

ようしょう² 要衝 交通の要衝 a transportation hub / 軍事上の要衝 a strategic point

ようじょう 養生 ——養生する (体をいたわる) take* good care of *oneself*; (病気から回復する) recuperate 他自 /温泉にでもつかって養生しなさい *Recuperate* by soaking in a hot spring.

ようしょく¹ 洋食 Western food ⓤ /ふだん朝は洋食ですか, 和食ですか Which do you usually have for breakfast, *Western food* or Japanese?

ようしょく² 要職 要職に就く hold *an impor-*

tant post [position] / 彼は当時その組織の要職にあった He served in an important position in the organization then.

ようしょく³ 養殖 culture ⓤ, farming ⓤ / その地方ではカキの養殖が盛んだ Oyster farming [culture] is flourishing in the area.

◆養殖のウナギ a farm-raised eel / 養殖の真珠 a cultured pearl / ハマチを養殖する raise [breed] young yellowtails

‖養殖漁業 aquiculture / 養殖場 a farm

ようじん¹ 用心

(注意) care ⓤ; (警戒) precaution ⓒ ──用心する take* care, be careful, watch out

かぜ をひかないように用心する be careful not to catch cold

火の元には特に用心しよう Let's take special care to prevent fires.

人込みではすりに用心したほうがいい We should 「be careful of [watch out for, be on our guard against]」 pickpockets in the crowd.

彼女は用心のために傘を持って出かけた She took an umbrella with her 「as a precaution [to be on the safe side]」. / She took the precaution of taking an umbrella with her.

◆火の用心 《掲示》Beware of Fire / 足元に用心してください Watch your step, please. / 彼はとても用心深い He is very cautious.

‖用心棒 a bodyguard; (ナイトクラブなどの) a bouncer

ようじん² 要人 very important person ⓒ, (口語的) VIP [víːaipíː] ⓒ (◆very important personの略語) /政府の要人 a government VIP / 要人の警護にあたる guard a VIP

ようす 様子

❶【ありさま・状況】

コロの様子がおかしい There's something wrong with Koro.

新しいクラスはどんな様子ですか What is your new class like?

子供たちはヒマワリが大きくなってゆく様子(→どのように成長するか)を観察した The children observed how the sunflowers grew.

この分では仕事はしばらく終わりそうにない At this rate we can't finish our work for a while.

私たちはしばらく様子を見ることにした We decided to 「see how it went [wait and see]」 for a while.

🅔「彼の様子はどう?」「相変わらずだよ」 "How does he look?" "Same as always."

❷【そぶり・態度】(外観・表情) look ⓒ(通例単数形), appearance ⓤⓒ; (雰囲気) air ⓒ(通例 an ~), (容貌(ぼう)) looks

彼女は驚いた様子で私を見た She glanced at me with a surprised look.

あの男の様子からすると, 彼は疲れているにちがいない By [From] his look(s), he must be tired.

◆その少女は彼のサインをもらってご満悦の様子だった The girl looked delighted to get his autograph. / 彼はその事件について何も知らない様子だった He looked as if he knew nothing about the incident. / 彼女はその知らせを聞いても特にがっかりした様子はなかった She showed no signs of disappointment when she heard the news. / その男の様子を話してください Please describe the man to me.

❸【気配】

この分だと台風は九州に上陸しそうな様子だ Judging from things so far, it seems that the typhoon will hit Kyushu.

昼になってもいっこうに気温の上がる様子がない Though it's already noon, the temperature doesn't seem to be rising at all.

ようすい 用水 ‖用水池 a reservoir / 用水路 an irrigation channel [canal, ditch] / 灌漑(がい)用水 irrigation water / 工業用水 water for industrial use / 防火用水 fire fighting water

ようすこう 揚子江 the Yangtze [jǽŋtsi] (River)

ようずみ 用済み 彼女は用済みの(→不要になった)ファイルをすべて消去した She deleted all the files which became unnecessary. / 彼はもう用済みだ I don't need him anymore. / I will have nothing more to do with him.

ようする¹ 要する need ⊕, 《公式的》require ⊕;(進行形にはできない); (時間・費用を) take* ⊕ /この仕事は忍耐を要する This task requires [needs, demands] patience. / You need patience to do this task. / この化学薬品の取扱いには細心の注意を要する Handling this chemical needs great care. / コンピュータのプログラムを組むのはかなりの時間と労力を要する Making a computer program takes [costs] much time and effort.

◆急を要する問題 an urgent [a pressing] issue / 技術を要する仕事 a skilled job

ようする² 擁する 大軍を擁する lead a big army / 東京は人口1,200万を擁する大都市である Tokyo is a big city which has population of 12 million. / その高校は3人のエースを擁して甲子園に臨んだ The high school attended the Koshien Baseball Tournament with three ace pitchers.

ようするに 要するに in short, in brief, in a word ⇨つまり /要するに見込みはないってことだ In short [In brief, In a word], we have no hope. / 要するに何が言いたいのか What do you mean 「in short [in brief, in a word]」?

ようせい¹ 要請 request ⓒ; (要求) demand ⓒ ──要請する 《公式的》request ⊕; demand ⊕ ‖もとめ, もとめる ‖正式の[非公式の]要請 an informal [a formal] request / その国は日本に財政援助を要請した The country made requests to Japan for financial assistance. / The country requested financial assistance from Japan. / 党首脳部は彼に選挙戦への出馬を要請した The leading members of the party requested that he (should) run for the election. / 彼は監督就任の要請を受けた[断った] He accepted [refused] the request that he (should) take the post of manager. / 市は住民の要請を受け, 湖の水質調査を始めた At the request of citizens, the city started to analyze the water of the lake.

ようせい 養成 training ⓤ 《また a ～》 ━━養成する train ⓗ 《優秀な技術者の養成 training of excellent technicians / この学校は看護婦を養成して看護師にしている This school trains students to be nurses.
‖養成課程 a training program / 養成所 a training school

ようせい³ 陽性 ━━陽性の (性格が) cheerful; (抗体反応が) positive 《ツベルクリンの陽性反応 a positive tuberculin response [reaction] / 彼女はエイズ検査で陽性と出た She tested HIV positive.

ようせい 妖精 fairy ⓒ; (小妖精) elf ⓒ (複 elves)

ようせき 容積 (容量) capacity ⓤ 《また a ～》; (体積) volume ⓒ; (かさ) bulk ⓤ 《タンクの容積 the capacity [volume] of a tank

ようせつ¹ 溶接 welding ⓤ ━━溶接する weld ⓗⓣ 《溶接工 a welder

ようせつ² 夭折 (若くして死ぬこと) early [premature] death ⓤ ━━夭折する die young [prematurely]

ようそ¹ 要素 (成分) element ⓒ; (要因) factor ⓒ 《合金の構成要素 component elements of an alloy / 外国語の学習に反復練習は不可欠な要素だ Repetition is an essential factor in learning foreign languages. / 彼の作った曲には多分に日本的な要素が含まれている The music he composed contains a lot of elements of Japanese culture.

ヨウそ² ヨウ素 〔化学〕 iodine [áiədàin] ⓤ 《❖元素記号 I》

ようそう¹ 洋装 (洋服) Western clothes [klóuz] 《複数扱い》 《その演歌歌手は珍しく洋装で現れた (→ 洋装で現れたが, それは彼女には珍しいことだった) The enka singer appeared in Western clothes, which was unusual for her.

ようそう² 様相 (局面) aspect ⓒ; (段階) phase ⓒ; (外見) appearance ⓤⓒ 《奇怪な様相 monstrous appearance / その地震による被害で街の様相は一変した Because of the earthquake damage, the appearance of the town changed completely.
◆紛争は長期化の様相を呈してきた It began to appear that the dispute would be prolonged.

ようだい 容態・容体 condition ⓤ 《また a ～》 《患者の容態は今は安定している The patient's condition is stable now. / 祖父の容態が悪化した The condition of my grandfather became worse.

ようたし 用足し (用事) business ⓤ 《ちょっと用足しに出かけてきます I'll go out on business.

ようだてる 用立てる このお金は何かに用立てて(→必要なときに使って)ください Please use this money when you need it. / お金を少々用立てて(→貸して)いただけないでしょうか Would you lend me some money?

ようち¹ 幼稚 ━━幼稚な (軽蔑的)childish, infantile; (未熟な) immature 《そんな幼稚な考えは捨てなさい Put away such childish ideas.

ようち² 用地 site ⓒ; (土地) land ⓤ 《彼らがビル建設のための用地買収にあたった They took charge of buying the land for the building.
‖建築用地 a building site / 農業用地 farmland

ようちえん 幼稚園 kindergarten ⓒⓤ 《❖アメリカではふつう 5 歳のときに 1 年間だけ通う》; nursery (school) ⓒ 《❖通例 2, 3 歳から 4 歳まで》 《弟は幼稚園に通っている My brother goes to kindergarten.
‖幼稚園児 a kindergarten [nursery school] child

ようちゅう 幼虫 larva ⓒ (複 larvae); (いも虫) caterpillar ⓒ; (カブトムシの) grub ⓒ 《チョウの幼虫 the larva of a butterfly

ようちゅうい 要注意 その国で夜間に外出するときは要注意だ You need to be cautious when you go out at night in the country. / 彼は要注意人物として警察から目をつけられている The police have an eye on him as a marked man.

ようつう 腰痛 lumbago [lʌmbéigou] ⓤ, lower back pain ⓤⓒ 《彼女は腰痛もちだ(→慢性的に腰痛に悩まされている) She is suffering from chronic lumbago [lower back pain, backache].

ようてん 要点 point ⓒ 《早く要点を言ってください Get to the point quickly. / 彼の話は冗長で要点をつかむのに苦労する His speech is so lengthy that it's hard to grasp its points. / 彼女は論文の内容を二, 三の要点にまとめた She condensed the contents of her thesis into a few (major) points.

ようと 用途 use [jú:s] ⓒ, purpose ⓒ 《この機械の用途は非常に限られている The uses for this machine are very limited. / プラスチックは用途が広い Plastic has many uses.

ようとん 養豚 pig [hog] raising ⓤ 《❖hog は 54 キロ以上の食用豚》
‖養豚場 a pig farm, (英) a piggery

-ような -様な ➪ よう(-様)
ようなし 洋梨 pear [péər] ⓒ
-ように -様に ➪ よう(-様)

ようにん 容認 (受け入れ) acceptance ⓤⓒ; (是認) approval ⓤ ━━容認する accept ⓗ; approve ⓗⓣ 《私たちはそのような行動を容認するわけにはいかない We cannot accept [approve (of)] such behavior.

ようねん 幼年 幼年期の経験 the experiences of childhood / 幼年時代を思い出すと彼の表情はやわらいだ His childhood memories softened his face.

ようは 要は ➪ よう(-要)

ようび 曜日 the day of the week

[語法]

Sunday「日曜日」, Monday「月曜日」,

Tuesday「火曜日」, Wednesday「水曜日」, Thursday「木曜日」, Friday「金曜日」, Saturday「土曜日」の用法は次のとおり.
(1) しばしば無冠詞で用いる ∥ きょうは12月7日，木曜日です Today is *Thursday*, December 7. / この店は月曜日から金曜日まであいている This store is open from *Monday* to *Friday*.
(2)「…曜日に」というときは，前置詞は on を用いるが，特に《米》と《英口語的》では on が省略されることがある ∥ 日曜日に渋谷で会わない？ How about meeting in Shibuya (*on*) *Sunday*?
(3) last, next などとともに副詞的に用いる ∥ この前[先週]の火曜日，学校を休んだ I was absent from school last *Tuesday*.
(4) 形容詞的にも用いる ∥ 彼女は水曜日の朝，大阪を発(た)ちました She left Osaka on *Wednesday* morning. (❖前置詞が in にならないことに注意)

その店は第1水曜日が休みです The store is closed on *the first Wednesday of the month*.
🖝「きょうは何曜日」「木曜日だよ」 *"What day (of the week) is it today?" "It's Thursday."*

ようひし 羊皮紙 parchment Ⓤ
ようひん¹ 用品 (必要な品) supplies, necessities ∥学用品 school supplies / 家庭用品 household goods / 事務用品 office supplies / スポーツ用品 sporting goods / 台所用品 kitchen utensils / 日用品 daily necessities
ようひん² 洋品 ∥洋品店 a clothing store; (ブティック) a boutique [buːtíːk] / 紳士用品《米》haberdashery
ようふ 養父 adoptive father Ⓒ; (里親) foster father Ⓒ
ようふう 洋風 ──洋風の Western-style
ようふく 洋服 (服) clothes [klóuz]《複数扱い》(❖数えるときは a suit of ... とする); (和服に対して) Western clothes; (婦人服) dress Ⓒ ⇨ ふく(服) ∥洋服を着る[脱ぐ]「put on [take off] *one's clothes* / 新しい洋服が欲しいな I want *a new dress*. / 彼女は洋服にかなりのお金を使う She spends a fair amount of money on *clothes*.
∥洋服かけ a clothes hanger / 洋服だんす a wardrobe / 洋服屋(人) a tailor, a dressmaker (❖主に tailor は紳士服, dressmaker は婦人服を作る人); (店) a tailor's (shop), a dressmaker's (shop)
ようふぼ 養父母 adoptive parents; (里親) foster parents
ようぶん 養分 nourishment Ⓤ; (栄養素)《公式的》nutrient Ⓒ ⇨ えいよう ∥この植物は葉に養分を蓄える This plant saves *nourishment* [*nutrients*] in its leaves.
ようぼ 養母 adoptive mother Ⓒ; (里親) foster mother
ようほう¹ 用法 (使い方) how to use; (言葉の) usage ⒰Ⓒ; (使用説明) directions ∥薬の用法に従う follow *directions* of the medicine / この言葉の用法を教えてください Tell me *the usage of* this word. / Tell me *how to use* this word.
ようほう² 養蜂 beekeeping Ⓤ, bee culture Ⓤ ∥養蜂家 a beekeeper
ようぼう¹ 要望 request Ⓒ Ⓤ ∥顧客の要望にこたえる meet *the request of* customers / 視聴者からはその番組の再開を求める多くの要望が寄せられた Viewers made a lot of *requests* that the program (should) be restarted. / 市は市民の要望にこたえて施設を一般に開放している The city opens the facility to the public *at* [*in response to*] popular *request*.
ようぼう² 容貌 looks, features ∥容貌の美しい女性 a woman of good *looks*
ようま 洋間 Western-style room Ⓒ
ようみゃく 葉脈《植物》vein
ようむいん 用務員 (主に米) janitor Ⓒ, 《英》caretaker Ⓒ
ようむき 用向き business Ⓤ Ⓒ ⇨ ようけん (用件), ようじ (用事)
ようめい 用命 (注文) order Ⓒ
　◆洋書のご用命承ります Please *order* foreign books from us. ❖この order は「注文する」という意味の動詞)
ようもう 羊毛 wool [wúl] Ⓤ; (1頭分の) fleece Ⓒ ──毛の woolen /羊毛製品 woolen goods / 彼は羊毛アレルギーだ He has an allergy to *wool*.
ようもうざい 養毛剤 hair growth tonic Ⓒ Ⓤ
ようやく¹ at last, finally; (かろうじて) (only) just, barely; (徐々に) gradually ⇨ やっと
　強風がようやくおさまった The strong wind has fallen *at last*.
　私たちはようやく目的地にたどり着いた *Finally* we reached our destination.
　ようやく学校に間に合った I was「(*only*) *just* [*barely*]」in time for school.
ようやく² 要約 (要約すること) summing-up Ⓒ (複 summings-up); (要約したもの) summary Ⓒ; (あらまし) outline Ⓒ ──要約する summarize ⊕⊕, sum up ∥論文の要約を書く write *the summary of* a thesis / 次の文章を250語程度に要約しなさい *Summarize* the following text in about 250 words.
ようよう 洋々 彼は前途洋々たる医者だ He is *a promising* doctor. / コンピュータ産業は前途洋々だ(→明るい未来がある) The computer industry *has a bright future*.
ようらん¹ 要覧 (手引き) handbook Ⓒ, catalog,《英》catalogue Ⓒ ∥学校要覧 a school *catalog*
ようらん² 洋蘭 tropical orchid Ⓒ
ようりつ 擁立 3党は連合して候補者に関氏を擁立した The three parties formed a coalition to「*back* Mr. Seki *up* [*support* Mr. Seki] as a candidate.
ようりょう¹ 要領 ❶ 【やり方】 the way; (こつ) the [a] knack [nǽk] ∥要領さえ覚えてしまえば操作は簡単です Once you get *the knack*

[hang] of it, it's easy to operate.
◆私は何事においても要領が悪い I'm *clumsy* about everything. / 弟は要領がいい My brother is *a clever fellow*. / 進は要領よく(=効率的に)仕事を片づけた Susumu *efficiently* finished the work.
❷【要点】the point //彼の説明は要領を得た[得ない]ものだった His explanation was *to* [*off*] *the point*.

ようりょう² 容量（容積）capacity Ⓤ《また〜》//ハードディスクの記憶容量 the storage *capacity* of a hard disk drive / この入れ物は3リットルの容量がある This container has a *capacity* of three liters.

ようりょくそ 葉緑素〔生化学〕chlorophyll [klɔ́ːrəfil]

ようれい 用例（典型的な例）example Ⓒ；（例文）example sentence Ⓒ；（例証）illustration Ⓒ //用例を挙げる give *an example*

ようろういん 養老院（老人ホーム）nursing home Ⓒ, old people's home Ⓒ

ヨーグルト yog(h)urt [jóugərt] Ⓤ

ヨーデル yodel Ⓤ Ⓒ

ヨード ⚠〔化学〕iodine [áiədàin] Ⓤ（❖日本語はドイツ語の Jod から）
‖ヨードチンキ tincture of iodine

ヨーヨー yo-yo Ⓒ //ヨーヨーをする play with *a yo-yo*

ヨーロッパ Europe [júərəp] ——ヨーロッパ人 European [jùərəpíːən] Ⓒ ——ヨーロッパの European ‖ヨーロッパ大陸 the European Continent / ヨーロッパ連合 the European Union((略語))EU)

よか¹ 余暇 leisure [líːʒər] Ⓤ, leisure time Ⓤ；（余った時間）spare time Ⓤ；（自由な時間）free time Ⓤ //余暇を活用する make good use of *one's leisure time* / 余暇に音楽を聴く listen to music in *one's spare* [*free*] *time* / 私は読書をして余暇を過ごした I spent *my spare* [*free*] *time* (in) reading a book.

よか² 予価 expected price Ⓒ

ヨガ yoga [jóugə] Ⓤ //ヨガをする practice *yoga*

よかぜ 夜風 night breeze Ⓒ

よかったら よかったらクッキー食べてね Help yourself to the cookies *if you like*. / よかったら(→迷惑でなければ)迎えに行くよ *If you don't mind*, I'll call for you. / よかったらこの本貸してもらえる？ *Could* [*Would*] *you* lend me the book?

よかれあしかれ 善かれ悪しかれ for better or worse, right or wrong //よかれあしかれこのやり方でいくしかない *For better or worse*, we have to do it this way.

よかん 予感 hunch Ⓒ, feeling Ⓒ；（よくない）premonition Ⓒ, presentiment Ⓒ //不吉な予感 *an ominous presentiment* / きょうの試験はうまくいきそうな予感がする I have *a hunch* [*feeling*] that today's test may go well. / 地震が来そうな予感がした I had *a premonition* of an earthquake.

よき 予期 expectation Ⓤ Ⓒ《しばしば複数形〜s), anticipation Ⓤ ——予期する expect ⒽⓉ, anticipate ⒽⓉ //予期に反してその商品はよく売れている Contrary *to expectations*, the goods are selling well. / 予期していたとおりの結果になった The results turned out as I *had expected*.
◆予期せぬ出来事が起こった An *unexpected* thing happened.

よぎ 余技（趣味）hobby Ⓒ；（気晴らし）pastime Ⓒ //彼は余技でバイオリンを弾く He plays the violin as *a hobby*.

よぎない 余儀ない 彼らは村を離れることを余儀なくされた They *had to* leave the village. / 余儀ない事情で計画は中止された The plan was suspended due to *unavoidable* circumstances.

よきょう 余興 entertainment Ⓤ Ⓒ //彼は余興に芸能人のものまねをした He mimicked entertainers by way of *entertainment*.

よぎり 夜霧 night fog Ⓒ

よぎる 両親のことが一瞬脳裏をよぎった Thoughts of my parents *flitted* [*flashed*] *through* my mind.

よきん 預金（預けること）deposit Ⓤ Ⓒ；（銀行口座）bank account Ⓒ ——預金する deposit ⒽⓉ //彼女は（銀行に）預金が100万円ある She has one million yen in *her bank account*. / She has *a deposit* of one million yen in the bank. / 彼は(銀行から)預金を1万円引き出した He withdrew 10,000 yen from *his bank account*. / 銀行に5万円預金した I *deposited* 50,000 yen in a bank.
‖預金口座 *one's* bank account / 預金者 a depositor / 預金通帳 a bankbook / 定期預金 a fixed [time] deposit / 当座預金（米）a checking account,（英）a current account / 普通預金 an ordinary deposit

よく¹ 良く・好く

❶ 十分に	well, fully
❷ 上手に	well; skillfully
❸ しばしば	often, frequently
❹ 感嘆	
❺ 良好に	well

❶【十分に】well, fully；（全く）quite；（完全に）completely, perfectly；（徹底的に）thoroughly；（注意深く）carefully；（一生懸命）hard
その俳優は歌手としてもよく知られている The actor is also *well* known as a singer.
子供たちはよく眠っている The children are sleeping *well*.
この肉はよく焼けていない This meat is not cooked *well*.
質問の意味がよく分かりません I don't *quite* understand the meaning of the question.
この問題についてよく調べる必要がある We have to investigate this matter *thoroughly*.
この図をよく見てください Look at this chart *carefully*. / Have a *good* look at this chart.

よく

聡美はよく勉強する Satomi studies *hard*.
◆分かるまでよく考えてごらんなさい Think it *over* until you understand. / 彼はやせているのによく(→たくさん)食べる Though he is thin, he eats *a lot*. / それはもう昔のことでよく覚えていません(→ほとんど思い出せない) I can *hardly* remember it as it happened long ago. / 彼女は私と行動パターンがよく似ている Her behavior patterns are *very* similar to mine.

❶「この話の結末はどうなるの」「私もよく知りません」 "How does this story end?" "*I'm not sure* myself."

❷【上手に】well; (巧みに) skillfully
この絵はとてもよく描けています This picture is painted very *well*.
よくやった！ *Well done! / Good for you*!
◆彼女は私にとてもよく(→親切に)してくれた She was very *kind* to me.

❸【しばしば】often, frequently
彼は先生によく怒られる He is *often* scolded by the teacher.
私はよく計算間違いをする I *often* make mistakes in calculation. / (→たくさん)I make *a lot of* calculation mistakes.
◆よくある間違い a *common* mistake / 先週はよく雨が降った We had *a lot of* rain last week. / あなたのうわさはよく聞いています I've heard *a lot* about you. / 妹はよく(→すぐに)笑う My sister laughs *easily*. / 子供のころよく公園で野球をした I *used to* play baseball in the park when I was a child. / そんなのよくあることさ That *happens all the time*. / 彼女にはよくあることだがきょうも遅刻した As *is often the case* with her, she was late for school today.

❹【感嘆】
遠いところをよくおいでくださいました *It's nice [good] of you* to come all the way here.
こんな分厚い本をよく1日で読めたね(→不思議だ) *I wonder how* you could read this thick book in one day.
そんな昔のことをよく覚えていますね(→驚きだ) *It's a wonder* you remember an old story like that.
よくそんなことが言えるね *How can* you say such a thing?
私がここにいることよく分かりましたね(→ここにいることがどうして分かったのか) *How did you know* I was here?

❺「全く, 君は忘れ物が多いんだから」「よく言うよ(→君も同じじゃないか)」 "You often forget your things." "*Look who's talking*."
❺「小学校のころは女の子にもてたんだ」「よく言うよ(→うそだろう)」 "I was popular with girls when I was in elementary school." "*Don't give me that*."

❺【良好に】(元気に) well ⇨ よい(良い・好い・善い)
お父さん, 早くよくなるといいね I hope your father *gets well* soon.
◆午後になると天気がよくなった The weather *improved* in the afternoon. / 数学の成績がずいぶんよくなった My grades quite *improved* in math. / 参加者はよくて10人くらいだろう There will be 10 participants *at most [best]*.

ことわざ よく学びよく遊べ ⇨ まなぶ

よく² 欲

(欲望) desire Ⓤ Ⓒ; (貪欲(どんよく)) greed Ⓤ; (悪いことへの強い欲望) lust Ⓤ; (強い金銭欲)(公式的) avarice Ⓤ; (野心) ambition Ⓤ

【欲が】
彼は金銭[権力, 名誉]欲が強い He has *a strong desire for* money [power, fame].
兄は欲がない My brother *is free of desire.* / (→金もうけに関心がない)My brother *isn't interested in making money*. / (→野心がない)My brother *has no ambition*.
◆学生は知識欲が旺盛(おうせい)だ Students have *a great appetite for knowledge*. / 彼女はとても欲が深い She is very *greedy*. / 彼女は初めは試合に出るだけで満足していたが, 1つ勝つと欲が出てきた At first she was content to take part in the game, but when she won once, she *got ambitious*.

【欲に・の】
彼女は欲に目がくらんでいる She *is blinded by greed [avarice]*.
あいつは欲の塊(かたまり)だ He *is full of greed.* / He is *greediness itself*.

【欲を】
欲を出したばかりに彼女は株で大損した *Her greed got the best of her*, and she lost a lot of money on stocks.
◆彼は成績はいいが欲を言えばもう少し積極的になってもらいたい He has good grades but I *wish* he were a little more aggressive. / 欲を言えばきりがない *The more one has, the more one wants*.

よく- 翌- (次の・今度の) next; (次に続く) following ‖11月8日には, 彼らは目的地に着いた *The next day*, November 8, they arrived at their destination.
よくあさ 翌朝 the next [following] morning
よくあつ 抑圧 (弾圧) suppression Ⓤ; (政治的な) oppression Ⓤ Ⓒ ──抑圧する suppress 他; oppress 他 ‖報道の自由を抑圧する *suppress* freedom of the press / 人々は支配者に抑圧されていた The people *were oppressed* by the ruler.
よくいえば よく言えば 彼はよく言えば慎重だが悪く言えば臆病(おくびょう)なだけだ *To be nice, you can say* he is cautious. To be mean, you can say he's a coward.
よくげつ 翌月 the next [following] month
よくし 抑止 deterrence Ⓤ
 ‖核抑止力 a nuclear deterrent
よくしつ 浴室 bathroom Ⓒ
よくじつ 翌日 the next [following] day
よくしゅう 翌週 the next [following] week
よくじょう¹ 浴場 ‖公衆浴場 a public bath
よくじょう² 欲情 sexual desire Ⓤ

よくする¹ 浴する 私たちは自然の恩恵に浴している We *enjoy the blessings* of nature. / We *benefit* from nature. / 彼はノーベル賞受賞の光栄に浴した He *had the honor of receiving* a Nobel prize.

よくする² 良くする 彼らは日本の社会をよくするために立ち上がった They rose up to *improve* Japanese society. / おじはいつも私にとてもよくしてくれる My uncle *is* always very *kind to* me.

よくせい 抑制 control Ⓤ; (感情などの) restraint Ⓤ Ⓒ ──抑制する control ⓗ; restrain ⓗ ∥インフレを抑制する control [check] inflation / 彼は自分[感情]を抑制できなかった He couldn't *control* himself [his emotions].

よくぞ よくぞいらっしゃいました It's *very* nice of you to come.
✎「このケーキすごくおいしい, どこで買ったの」「よくぞ聞いてくれました (→その質問を待っていた). 実は私が焼いたんだ」"This cake is really delicious. Where did you buy it?" "Thanks, I *was waiting for* that question. Actually, I baked it myself!"

よくそう 浴槽 bathtub Ⓒ

よくて 良くて 私の数学の成績はよくてCだ My grade in math will be a C *at best*.

よくとくずく 欲得ずく ──欲得ずくの (利己的な) selfish, self-interested; (金目当ての) mercenary ∥彼は欲得ずくでその仕事を引き受けた He took the job *out of mercenary motives*.

よくなる 良くなる ⇒ よく(良く・好く)

よくねん 翌年 the next [following] year

よくばり 欲張り (食欲(釣)さ) greediness Ⓤ; (人) greedy person Ⓒ (けち・守銭奴) miser Ⓒ ──欲張りな greedy

よくばる 欲張る be greedy ∥あまり欲張るな Don't *be so greedy*. ◆欲張ってあれもこれも食べてしまった I ate everything *greedily*.

よくぶかい 欲深い greedy; (金銭欲・物欲が強い) avaricious; (けちけちした) 《口語的》stingy

よくぼう 欲望 desire Ⓤ Ⓒ; (強い欲) lust Ⓒ; (野望) ambition Ⓤ Ⓒ ∥欲望を満たす[抑える] satisfy [suppress] *one's desires* / 彼は富と権力に対して強い欲望をいだいている He has *a* strong *desire* for wealth and power.

よくめ 目め (偏見) prejudice Ⓤ Ⓒ; (えこひいき) partiality Ⓤ ◆親の欲目かもしれないがうちの娘は頭がいい I may *be prejudiced in favor of* my daughter, but she is clever.

よくも よくもそんなことが言えるね How can [*dare*] you say such a thing? / よくもこんなひどい目にあわせてくれたな You *did* give me such a hard time.

よくよう 抑揚 intonation Ⓤ Ⓒ ∥抑揚をつけて詩を読む read a poem with *intonation* ◆抑揚のない話し方 a *monotonous* way of speaking

よくよう² 浴用 ∥浴用せっけん bath soap / 浴用タオル a bath towel

よくよく よくよく考えてみると私が悪かった After thinking it over *carefully*, I knew I was to blame. / 犯人はよくよく金に困っていたようだ The culprit seemed to be *very hard up for money*. / 彼女が泣くなんてよくよくのこと She must have had *a good reason* for crying. / 彼が大学進学をあきらめるなんてよくよくのことだ (→やむにやまれぬ理由があったにちがいない) *There must have been unavoidable reasons* for him to give up going on to college.

よくよく 翌々─ 試験の結果は翌々週に発表される The results of the test will be announced *two weeks later*. / その翌々日彼から手紙が来た I received a letter from him *two days after that*.

よくりゅう 抑留 internment Ⓤ Ⓒ; (拘留) detention Ⓤ ──抑留する intern ⓗ; detain ⓗ ∥兵士たちはそこに4年間抑留されていた The soldiers *were interned* [*detained*] there for four years.
∥抑留者 an internee; (主に政治的な理由による) a detainee / 抑留所 a detention camp

よけい 余計 ──余計な (余分な) extra; (不必要な) unnecessary; (多すぎる) too many [much] ──余計に extra; unnecessarily; too many [much]

50円余計に払った I paid 50 yen *extra* [*too much*].

資料は1部余計に作っておいてください Please prepare one *extra* handout.

部屋の掃除をして余計なものを捨てた I cleaned up the room and threw *unnecessary* things away.

余計なことをしないで Don't do *unnecessary* things.

余計な心配はするな Don't worry *too much* about it.

これ以上余計な心配はさせないで Don't make me worry *too much* anymore.

君はひと言余計だ You *say one word too many*.

◆余計なことを言うんじゃない Don't say *more than necessary*. / 余計なお世話だ Mind your *own business*! / *None of your business*. / 彼は人より余計に努力する He works *harder* than others. / 薬を飲んでよけい気分が悪くなった I felt *worse* after taking the medicine. / 来るなと言われるとよけい行きたくなる When we are told not to come, we are *all the more* tempted to go. / 欠点があるからこそ余計に娘がかわいいのです I love my daughter *all the more because* she has faults.

よける 避ける avoid ⓗ; (身をかわさす) dodge ⓗ ⓘ ∥子供たちは水たまりをよけて歩いた The children walked *avoiding* the puddles. / ボールをよけそこねて頭にぶつけた I *failed to dodge* the ball and it hit my head.
◆車が来たので急いでよけた A car was coming so I *stepped aside* quickly.

よけん 予見 (予知) foresight Ⓤ ──予見する foresee* ⓗ

よげん 予言（予測）prediction ⓤⓒ; (宗教上の) prophecy [práfəsi] ⓤⓒ ――予言する predict ⑯, foretell* ⑯; prophesy [práfəsài] ⑯ⓘ ‖彼女の予言は的中した[はずれた] Her prophecy「came true [failed]. ／ 彼が予言したことが実際に起こった What he predicted [foretold] has really happened. ／ 占い師は洪水被害が起こると予言した The fortune-teller prophesied a flood disaster.
‖予言者 (男の) a prophet; (女の) a prophetess

よこ 横

❶【左右の長さ・方向】（短い幅）width ⓤⓒ, breadth ⓤ; （長い幅）length ⓤ

> 日本語では縦は上下の長さ，横は左右の長さを表すが，英語では長さの長いほうを length [long], 短いほうを width [wide]で表す. 例えば，縦4センチメートル，横6センチメートルの長方形は a rectangle six centimeters "in length [long] and four centimeters "in width [wide]" となる. 正方形の場合は 4 辺の長さが等しいので, 通例 length [long], width [wide]を使わず, a square three centimeters on each side (1辺が3センチメートルの正方形)などという.

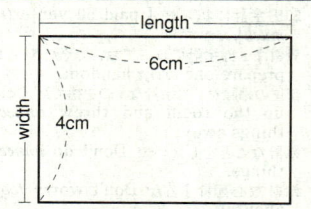

（図：length 6cm, width 4cm の長方形）

ドアは縦2メートル横1メートルある The door is two meters「in length [long] and one meter in width [wide]. ／ The door is two by one meters.

駅前に縦(→高さ)3メートル横6メートルの看板が立っている A billboard three meters "in height [high] and six meters "in width [wide]" stands in front of the station. (❖垂直に立っている物は縦を「in height [high]」を用いて表せば横は「in width [wide]」で示される)

◆紙に横線を引いた I drew a horizontal line on the paper. ／ 私たちはその狭い道を横向きになって通った We passed through the narrow alley sideways. ／ 彼は帽子を横にかぶっていた He wore his cap askew. ／ 彼らは絵を横にして運んだ They carried the picture on its side. ／ 彼女は首を横に振った She shook her head. ／ 少し横になったほうがいいよ You should lie down for a little while.

❷【そば・わき】side ⓒ ――横の side

おばあさんが私の横に座った An old woman sat by my side.

ポストの横に郵便物の収集時刻が書かれている The mail collection schedule is written on the side of the mailbox.

私たちは横のドアから外に出た We went outside by the side door.

彼は髪を横で分けている He parts his hair on the side.

◆電話の横に花びんが置いてある There is a vase of flowers beside [next to] the telephone. ／ 彼女は怖くなって横を向いた She got frightened and looked away. ／ 自転車が来たので彼は横に寄った A bicycle came, so he stepped aside. ／ 子供たちは横に広がって歩いていた The children were walking spread out.

❸「銀行はどこですか」「郵便局の横を曲がった所です」 "Could you tell me where the bank is?" "Turn the corner at the post office, and you'll find it."

慣用表現 この選挙戦では現在有力3候補が横一線に並んでいる Three strong candidates (are) now equal in this election campaign. (❖equal は are があるときは形容詞, ないときは動詞) ／ 横から口をはさまないで Don't interfere [meddle] in my affairs. ／ 我々の部署は横のつながりが強い Our department has strong ties between coworkers. ／ 彼は横のものを縦にもしない(→無精者だ) He is a really lazy fellow.

よこいと 横糸 (織物の) the weft, the woof

よこうえんしゅう 予行演習 rehearsal ⓤⓒ
◆卒業式の予行演習をする rehearse a graduation (ceremony)

よこがお 横顔 profile [próufail] ⓒⓤ ‖人の横顔を描く draw a person in profile ／ 新聞に新しい首相の横顔が紹介されていた There was a profile of the new Prime Minister in the newspaper.

よこがき 横書き ――横書きする write* horizontally; （左から右に書く）write from left to right

よこぎる 横切る cross ⑯ⓘ, go* across ‖私たちは公園を横切って通りに出た We crossed [went across] the park to the street.
◆猫が目の前を横切った A cat cut across in front of me. ／ その子供は道を走って横切った The child ran across the road.

よこく 予告 (通知) notice ⓤ; (公の) preliminary announcement ⓤ; (警告) warning ⓤ ――予告する give* notice ‖出演者は予告なしに変わることがあります Casts are subject to change without (prior) notice.
◆組合は経営者側にストの予告をした The labor union warned the management of a strike. ／ 先生の予告どおり、英語の時間に小テストが行われた We had a quiz during English class as the teacher had announced in advance. ／ いくつかの予告編に続いて本編が上映された Following some previews the film was shown.
‖次号予告 the announcement of the next issue

よこぐるま 横車 横車を押す(→道理に逆らって自分の思うとおりにする) have one's own way against all reason

よこじく 横軸 (グラフの) horizontal axis [C]
よこしま 邪 ―よこしまな (邪悪な) wicked, evil; (不正な) wrong ∥よこしまな心 a *wicked* heart
よこじま 横縞 horizontal stripes
よこす 寄越す (送る) send* [他]; (手渡す) hand over; (与える) give* [他] ∥担当者をよこしてください *Send* the person in charge. / それを全部よこせ *Give* me all of them.
◆彼女はあまり手紙をよこさない She *doesn't* often *write to* me.
よごす 汚す make* [get*] ... dirty, dirty [他]; (しみなどをつける) stain [他]; (汚染する) pollute [他] ∥服を汚さないでね *Don't make* your clothes *dirty.*/ *Don't dirty* your clothes. / ソースでスカートを汚した I *stained* my skirt with sauce. / 工場の煙は空気を汚す The smoke from factories *pollutes* the air.
[慣用表現] 彼らは自分の手を汚さずに荒稼ぎした They made a bundle of money *without soiling their own hands.*
よこすべり 横滑り skid [C], sideslip [C] ―横滑りする (車が) skid [自], sideslip [自]; (地位を) shift [自] ∥凍った路面で車が横滑りした The car *skidded* [*went into a skid*] on the icy road. / 営業部長は人事部長に横滑りした The sales manager *shifted to* the post of the personal manager.
よこたえる 横たえる lay* [他] ∥彼はソファーに体を横たえた He「*laid himself* [*lay*] down on the sofa. (❖laid は lay の過去形, lay は「横たわる」の意味の自動詞 lie の過去形)
よこだおし 横倒し 強風で自転車が横倒しになった The bicycle *fell on its side* because of the strong wind.
よこたわる 横たわる lie* [自] ∥ソファーに横たわってテレビを見た I *lay* [*laid myself*] down on the sofa and watched television. (❖lay は lie の過去形, laid は「…を横たえる」の意味の他動詞 lay の過去形) / 彼は芝生の上に大の字になって横たわった He *lay* at full length on the grass./ He stretched himself out on the grass. / 私たちの前途には多くの困難が横たわっている A lot of difficulties *lie* ahead of us.
よこちょう 横町 side street [C]; (路地) alley [C]
よこづけ 横付け 彼は家の前に車を横づけした (→持ってきた) He *brought* his car in front of his house. / 学校の前に1台の車が横づけになった (→止まった) A car *pulled up* in front of the school.
よこっつら 横っ面 (ほお) cheek [C] ∥彼は男の横っ面を張った He「gave the man a slap [slapped the man] on *the cheek.*
よこづな 横綱 🖼 a *yokozuna*, a grand champion sumo wrestler ∥横綱になる be promoted to *yokozuna*
∥横綱審議委員会 the Yokozuna Promotion Council
よこっぱら 横っ腹 横っ腹が痛い I have a pain in *my side.*
よごと 夜毎 every night ∥その猫は夜ごとわが家の庭に現れるようになった The cat started to appear in our garden「*every night* [*night after night*].
よこどり 横取り ―横取りする (ひったくる) snatch away; (盗む) steal* [他]; (奪う) rob [他] ∥弟が私のあめを横取りした My brother *snatched away* my candy. / おじは私の財産を横取りした My uncle *robbed* me *of* my property.
よこなが 横長 ―横長の oblong
よこながし 横流し 救援物資を横流しする *sell* relief supplies *through illegal channels*
よこなぐり 横殴り 横なぐりの雨 a *driving* [*slanting*] rain / 雨が横なぐりに降っていた It was raining *slantingly.*
よこなみ 横波 side wave [C]
よこならび 横並び 日本は横並びの社会だ (→周りと同じレベルに合わせようとする) Japan is a society where *people try to be on the same level as other people.*
よこばい 横這い 物価は横ばいの状態を続けている Prices *have remained at the same level.*
よこはば 横幅 (幅) width [U] [C], breadth [U] [C] ⇒よこ
よこぶえ 横笛 flute [C]; (軍楽隊の) fife [C]
よこみち 横道 side road [C]; (誤った方向) wrong way [C]
◆話が横道にそれてしまったようです It seems that I've *wandered from* the subject.
よこむき 横向き 横向きの写真 a photograph *in profile* / 横向きに寝る lie *on one's side* / モデルはいすに横向きに座った The model sat in the chair *sideways.*
よこめ 横目 sideways [sidelong] glance [C] ∥彼女は私のバッグを横目で見た She cast *a sideways* [*sidelong*] *glance* at my bag./ She looked *sideways* at my bag.
よこもじ 横文字 (ヨーロッパの言語) Western [European] language [C]; (ローマ字) the Roman alphabet ∥横文字は苦手だ I know little of *Western* [*European*] *languages.*
よこやり 横槍 彼女は私たちの話に横やりを入れた She *butted* [*poked her nose*] into our conversation.
よこゆれ 横揺れ (船などの) rolling [U]; (地震の) lateral vibration [U] [C] ―横揺れする roll [自] ∥しけで船は大きく横揺れした The ship *rolled* heavily in the storm.
よごれ 汚れ dirt [U]; (しみ) stain [C] [U]; (点々とついた) spot [C] ∥手の汚れを洗い落とす wash *the dirt* off *one's* hands / このカーテンは汚れが目立たない This curtain doesn't show *dirt.*/ *Dirt* doesn't stand out on this curtain. / この洗剤は汚れがよく落ちる This detergent removes *dirt* well. / ズボンの汚れがなかなか落ちない *The stain* on these trousers won't come off easily. ◆このシャツは汚れがひどい This shirt is very *dirty.*
∥汚れ物 dirty clothes
よごれやく 汚れ役 the part of a socially undesirable character
よごれる 汚れる (汚くなる) get* [become*]

よ

よさ

よごれる dirty; (しみがつく) be stained; (泥などで) be soiled; (汚染される) be polluted ——汚れた dirty
- 上着が汚れてきたのでクリーニングに出した My coat *was getting dirty* so I sent it to the laundry.
- 白いシャツはすぐ汚れる A white shirt *is easily stained* [*soiled*].
- 彼女の指はインクで汚れていた Her fingers *were stained* with ink.
- 工場の周辺は空気が汚れている The air *is polluted* around the factories.
- 汚れた手でさわらないでね Don't touch with *dirty* hands.
- 汚れた金は受け取れないよ I can't accept *dirty* money.
- ◆壁は血で汚れていた The wall *was smeared with blood*. (◆smearは「(べたべたする物で)…を汚す」の意味)

よさ 良さ・善さ (よい点) good point ⓒ; (長所) merit ⓒ, virtue ⓒ; (質の良さ) good quality ⓤⓒ ∥そのうち彼女のよさが分かるよ You'll see her *good points* soon.
- ◆この小説のよさは私には分からない I can't see what's *good* about this novel.

よざい 余罪 other [additional] crimes ∥警察は彼にいくつか余罪があるものと見て追及している The police suspect he has committed some *other crimes* and are questioning him about them.

よざくら 夜桜 きのうの晩友達と夜桜見物に出かけた I went out to *see the cherry blossoms* with my friends *last night*.

よさん 予算 budget ⓒ; (見積もり) estimate
〖予算が・は〗
- 予算が衆議院を通過した The budget has passed the Lower House.
- 教育予算は削減された The education budget was cut down.
- ◆ご予算はどのくらいですか How much would you like to *spend*?/ (→値段の範囲は) *What price range* are you thinking of?/
- その車を買うには予算が足りない I *don't have enough money* to buy the car.

〖予算を〗
- 予算を超える exceed [go over] *a budget*
- 旅行の予算を立てた I made *a budget* for traveling.
- 政府は予算を作成した The government drew up *a budget*.

〖その他〗
- 巨額の[低]予算 *a huge* [*small*] *budget* / 予算案を提出する submit *a budget*
- 彼は50万円の予算で部屋を改装してもらうつもりだ He is going to have his room repaired *on a budget of* 500,000 yen.
- 支出は予算内に収まった The expenses remained *within the budget*.

∥予算案 a budget / 予算委員 a member of the budget committee / 予算委員会 the budget committee / 予算編成 compilation of a budget / 国家予算 a national budget / 暫定(ざん)予算 a provisional budget / 追加予算 a supplementary budget / 年間予算 an annual budget / 補正予算 a revised budget

よし¹ (よろしい) good; (分かった) all right, OK; (さて) well ∥よし, 僕がやろう All right, I'll do it. / よし, 始めよう Well, let's begin. ◆よしよし, 泣かないで There, there, don't cry.

よし² 由 彼がそんなに苦労していたなんて知る由もなかった I had no *way* of knowing he had had such a very hard time. / お元気の由, 何よりです I'm glad *to learn* you are well.

よしあし 善し悪し (善悪) good and [or] bad; (正誤) right and [or] wrong ∥事のよしあしが分かる *know right from wrong* / 都会に住むのもよしあしだ (→長所と短所がある) Living in a city *has both* 「*merits and demerits* [*advantages and disadvantages*].

よじげん 四次元 four dimensions ——四次元の four-dimensional ∥四次元の空間 *four-dimensional* space
- ◆四次元の世界 *the fourth dimensional*

よじのぼる よじ登る climb ⓗ; (苦労して) clamber ⓗ ∥屋根によじ登る *climb up* to a roof / 彼は柵(さく)をよじ登った He *clambered up* the fence.

よしみ 彼は友達のよしみで僕に忠告してくれた He warned me *for friendship's sake*. / 彼女とは同郷のよしみで(→故郷が同じなので)親しくなった I became friends with her *because* she and I came from the same town.

よしゅう 予習 preparation ⓤ ◆予習をしてから夕ごはんを食べた I ate dinner after I finished *preparing for my lessons*.

よじょう 余剰 surplus ⓤⓒ; (超過) excess ⓤ (またan ~) ——余剰の surplus; excess ∥余剰人員を整理する dismiss *excess* [*surplus*] *workers*
∥余剰金 a surplus / 余剰農産物 a farm surplus / 余剰米 surplus rice

よじょうはん 四畳半 四畳半の部屋 a *four-and-a-half-tatami* room

よじる 苦痛に身をよじる *writhe* in pain / 彼女は身をよじって人込みから抜け出た She *twisted* out from the crowd.

よじれる ベルトがよじれているよ Your belt *is twisted*.
〖慣用表現〗その漫画を読んで腹の皮がよじれるほど笑った I read the comic and laughed *till my sides split*.

よしん 余震 aftershock ⓒ ∥まだ何回か余震があるだろう There will be some more *aftershocks*.

よす 止す (やめる) stop ⓗ, quit* ⓗ; (断念する) give* up ⇒やめる(止める) ∥大声を出すのはよせ *Stop* speaking loudly. / 冗談はよせよ *Stop* your joking.
- ◆そんな遠くにひとりで行くのはよしなさい *Don't* go so far alone. / まだ微熱があるからきょう学校に行くのはよしなさい You'd *better forget about* going to school today because you still have a slight fever.

よそう

よせ 寄席 a *yose*, a theater where *rakugo*, *kodan* and other entertainments are performed; (演芸場) 《米》vaudeville theater ⓒ, 《英》music hall ⓒ
‖寄席芸人 a vaudevillian

よせあう 寄せ合う　鳥たちは枝の上で体を寄せ合っていた The birds *huddled together* on the branch.

よせあつめ 寄せ集め　(ごちゃ混ぜ) jumble ⓒ　‖寄せ集めの布でバッグを作った I made a bag from *a jumble* of pieces of cloth.
◆寄せ集めのチーム a *pickup* [*scratch*] team

よせあつめる 寄せ集める　(集める) gather ⓣ; (収集する) collect ⓣ　‖割れたコップの破片を寄せ集める *gather up* fragments of a broken glass

よせい¹ 余生　the rest of *one's* life　‖父は退職したらのんびりと余生を送りたいと思っている My father wants to spend *the rest of his life* peacefully in the country when he retires.

よせい² 余勢　私たちのチームは地方予選優勝の余勢を駆って全国大会で準決勝まで進んだ *Encouraged by* the victory in the district preliminary, our team got to the semifinal in the national tournament.

よせがき 寄せ書き　私たちは色紙に寄せ書きをして彼に贈った We *wrote our messages and names* on a card and presented it to him.

よせぎざいく 寄せ木細工　wooden mosaic work ⓤ; (床の) parquetry ⓤ

よせつける 寄せ付ける　この洗剤はカビを寄せつけない This detergent *prevents* mold *from* growing. / その山には人を寄せつけない雰囲気があった The mountain had an atmosphere that *kept people at a distance.* / 彼は他を寄せつけない強さでそのレースを制した He was *by far* the winner of the race.

よせなべ 寄せ鍋　*yosenabe*, a Japanese-style stew with fish, vegetables, and so on cooked at the table

よせる 寄せる
❶【近づける】move ⓣ, bring*...close; (引き寄せる) pull [draw*]...close; (わきへ置く) put*...aside

机を右に寄せてください *Move* the desk *to the right.*
自転車を塀に寄せた I *brought* the bicycle *close to* the wall.
彼はいすを本棚の近くに寄せた He *pulled* the chair *close to* the bookshelf.
そのかばんをわきに寄せてください *Put* the bag *aside.*
◆波が浜辺に寄せては返している The waves *are surging against* the beach.

❷【身・心などを】
彼らは親戚(メミ)の家に身を寄せた They *went to live with* their relatives.
人々は地震で親を亡くした子供たちに同情を寄せた People *felt sympathy* for the children who lost their parents in the earthquake.
賢司は隣のクラスの女の子に思いを寄せている Kenji *is in love with* a girl in the next class.
社長は彼に信頼を寄せている The president *puts his confidence in* him.

❸【送る】send* ⓣ; (寄稿する) contribute ⓣ
番組に対するご意見，ご希望をお寄せください Please *send* us your opinion or requests about this program.
彼はその雑誌に手記を寄せた He *contributed* his memoirs *to* the magazine.

よせん 予選　preliminary (trial [heat]) ⓒ; (レースなどの) (trial [qualifying]) heat ⓒ; (サッカーなどの) qualifying round ⓒ　‖彼は100メートル走の予選を通過した He 「got through [passed] *the 100-meter preliminaries.* / 彼女は予選落ちした She *was eliminated in the preliminary.*
‖予選通過者 a qualifier / 1次予選 the first round of the preliminary / 最終予選 the final round of the preliminary

よそ (ほかの場所) some other [another] place ―よその other, another ―よそに somewhere else, elsewhere

彼は先月よそに移った He moved to *another place* last month.
よそで野球をしよう Let's play baseball 「*somewhere else* [*elsewhere*].
◆妹はよその家ではおとなしくしている My sister is quiet at *someone else's* house. / よその人についていってはいけません Don't follow 「*strange people* [*strangers*]. / 晶子は親の心配をよそにひとり暮らしを始めた Akiko started to live alone, *ignoring* her parents' anxiety.

よそいき ⇒よそゆき

よそう¹ 予想　(予期) expectation ⓤⓒ《しばしば複数形～s》; (期待) anticipation ⓤ; (推測) guess ⓤ; (憶測) supposition ⓤⓒ; (見積もり) estimation ⓤ ――予想する expect ⓣ; anticipate ⓣ; guess ⓣ; suppose ⓣ; estimate ⓣ

【予想が】
彼女の予想が当たった[はずれた] Her *guess* proved right [wrong].
◆このレースでだれが勝つかはちょっと予想がつかない I *can't judge* who will win in this race.
【予想に・を】
予想に反して彼が敗れた *Contrary to expectations*, he was defeated.
店の売り上げは予想を上回った The sales of the store exceeded *our expectations.*
【予想する】
渋滞を予想して彼らは明け方に出発した *In expectation* [*anticipation*] of heavy traffic, they started in the early morning.
彼女がそれほど悩むとはだれも予想していなかった Nobody *expected* that she would worry so seriously.
私たちは頂上までもう3時間かかるだろうと予想した We *estimated* it would take three more hours to the top of the mountain.

地球の温暖化は農業をはじめ，様々な方面に影響を与えると予想されている *It is expected that* the global warming will affect various fields, such as agriculture.

〘その他〙

予想どおり彼が当選した He was elected *as we had expected.*

私の予想では久美は来ないと思う *I guess that* Kumi won't come.

そのテレビ番組への反響は予想以上に大きかった The TV program created a great sensation *beyond our expectations.*

◆彼女の反対は予想外だった Her objection *was unexpected.*

‖予想屋 a tout, a tipster

よそう² 装う (皿に盛る) dish up, serve [他]; (食べ物を取り分ける) help *a person* to ...; (自分で) help *oneself* to ... //弟にごはんをよそってやった I *helped* my brother *to* rice.

よそおい 装い 静香はもう夏の装いだった Shizuka *had* already *worn her* summer *dress.* / そのデパートは装いも新たに開店する The department store will reopen *after remodeling* [*a complete face-lift*].

よそおう 装う ❶【着飾る】(着る) dress *oneself* in ...; (着ている) wear* [他], be dressed //はでに[地味に]装う *be* gaily [plainly] *dressed* / パーティーに来た人々は華やかに装っていた The people who attended the party *were dressed* gorgeously.

❷【ふりをする】pretend [他]; (態度をとる) assume [他] [他] //彼女は内心動揺していたが平静を装った She was shaken in her mind but *pretended* to be calm. / 私はかかわり合いにならないように無関心を装った I *assumed* indifference so as not to get involved.

よそく 予測 (事実などに基づく) prediction [U] [C]; (予報) forecast [C] ――予測する predict [他]; forecast* [他]; (予知する) foresee* [他] //試合結果を予測する *predict* the result of the game / 科学者の予測がすべて当たるとは限らない Not all the scientists' *predictions* will come true. / 彼が何と言うか私には予測がつかない I can't *foresee* what he is going to say.

よそごと よそ事 (関心のないこと) a matter of no concern

◆その事件はよそ事とは思えなかった(→大いに関心があった) The incident *was of great concern to* me. / 彼女はまるでよそ事のように言った(→自分には関係のないこと) She talked as if it had been *none of her concern.*

よそみ よそ見 授業中よそ見をして先生にしかられた I was scolded by the teacher for *looking the other way* during the class. / 事故は運転手のよそ見が原因のようだ It seems that the accident happened because the driver *wasn't keeping his eyes on the road.*

よそもの よそ者 stranger [C]; (部外者) outsider [C] //初めのうちはよそ者扱いされた I *was treated as an outsider* at first.

よそゆき 余所行き (晴れ着) *one's* best clothes, Sunday best [U] //恵子はよそゆきの服を着てパーティーに出かけた Keiko went to the party in *her best clothes.* ◆彼は先生の前ではよそゆきの言葉づかいをする He uses *formal* language in front of teachers.

よそよそしい (冷淡な) cold; (態度に隔たりのある) distant; (形式ばった) formal; (不親切な) unfriendly //最近彼がよそよそしい He is「*cold and distant* [*stand-offish*] toward us these days. / 私が学級委員に選ばれてから彼女の態度がよそよそしくなった After I was elected class representative, she had「an *unfriendly and formal* [a *stand-offish*] attitude to me.

よぞら 夜空 the night sky //夜空に無数の星が輝いている Countless stars are shining in *the night sky.*

よたよた 酔っ払いが通りをよたよた歩いていた A drunken man *was staggering* along the street. / 彼は重いかばんを持ってよたよた歩いていた He *was tottering* with a heavy bag.

よだれ 涎 slobber [U]; (唾液(だえき)) saliva [U]

◆赤ちゃんがよだれをたらしている The baby *is slobbering* [*drooling*]. / テーブルに並んだごちそうを見てよだれが出た The feast on the table *made* my mouth *water.* / 彼女はそのバッグをよだれが出るほど欲しがっている She wants that purse so much *it makes her mouth water.* ‖よだれかけ a bib

よだん¹ 予断 preconception [C]; (予言・予測) prediction [U] [C] ➾ よそく

◆景気の動向は予断を許さない(→予測できない)状況が続いている The business trends have been *unpredictable.*

よだん² 余談 《公式的》digression [C] //余談はさておき，話を本題に戻しましょう So much for *the digression.* Let's go back to the main subject.

◆余談になりますが，つまようじの効用を日本で初めて説いたのは道元です *This may be beside the point,* but it was Dogen who first explained the usefulness of toothpicks in Japan.

よち¹ 余地 room [U]; (空所) space [U] //政府の経済政策には改善の余地がある There is *room* for improvement in the government's economic policy. / 彼の話には疑いの余地がない There is no *room* for doubt in his story. ◆彼がしたことに弁解の余地はない *There's no excuse* for what he did. / What he did *is inexcusable.*

よち² 予知 《公式的》foreknowledge [U], foresight [U]; (予言) prediction [U] [C]; (予測) forecast [C] ――予知する 《公式的》foreknow* [他], foresee* [他]; predict [他]; forecast* [他] //地震の発生を予知する *predict* [*forecast*] the occurrence of earthquakes / 彼の発言はあたかも彼がこの事故を予知していたかのようであった His remark was as if he *had foreknown* the accident.

‖予知能力 the power to foreknow [foresee] the future / 予知夢 a dream that tells the future

よちよち 彼の子供はよちよち歩きを始めた(→よちよち歩きができるまでになった) His baby grew big enough to *toddle*. (❖*toddle* は「よちよち歩きをする」という意味の自動詞)

よつあし 四つ足 四つ足の動物 *a quadruped*

よっか 四日 4日間 for *four days* / 9月4日 September (*the*) *fourth*

よつかど 四つ角 crossing ⓒ, crossroads (単数または複数扱い) / 次の四つ角を右に曲がってください Please turn to the right at the next *crossing* [*crossroads*].

よっきゅう 欲求 (強い願望) desire ⓒⓊ; (必要・不足を満たそうとする) wants ⇒ **よく**(欲) / 欲求を満たす[抑える] satisfy [suppress, repress] *one's desires* / 現代人の情報に対する欲求はとどまるところを知らない Modern people's *desire for* information has no limits. / 人間には本来, ものを知りたいという知的欲求がある Human beings naturally have *the intellectual desire to* know things.
◆仕事が思うようにいかず, 彼女は欲求不満がたまっていた As the job didn't go as she wanted, she was「*filled with frustration* [*frustrated*].

よつぎり 四つ切り 紙を四つ切りにする *cut* a sheet of paper *into quarters* [*four pieces*]

よつご 四つ子 (四つ子の1人) quadruplet [kwɑdrúːplət] ⓒ,《口語的》quad ⓒ; (全員) quadruplets

よっつ 四つ four Ⓤⓒ ⇒ **よん**

よって 因って このソフトは旧版です。よってご自分の責任でお使いください This software is the old version. *Therefore* use it at your own risk.

よってたかって 寄ってたかって みんな寄ってたかって僕をいじめる Everyone *gangs up on* me. (❖gang up on *a person* で「(人を)集団で攻撃する」の意味)

ヨット ⚠yacht [ját] ⓒ; (小型帆船)《米》sailboat,《英》sailing boat ⓒ (❖英語の yacht は主に宿泊設備を備えた大型のレース用・遊戯用の船を指す. ふつう日本語でいう「ヨット」は《米》sailboat,《英》sailing boat という) / ヨットは風に逆らって進んだ *The yacht* sailed against the wind. ◆ヨットに乗りに行く go *sailing*
‖ヨットパーカ a parka / ヨットハーバー a yacht harbor [basin] / ヨットレース a yacht race(ing)

よっぱらい 酔っ払い drunk [drunken] person ⓒ, drunk ⓒ ――酔っ払いの drunk, drunken / 通りで酔っ払いの男にからまれた A *drunk* [*drunken*] man picked a fight with me on the street.
‖酔っ払い運転 drunken driving,《米》drunk driving

よっぱらう 酔っ払う get* drunk; (酔っ払っている) be drunk ⇒ **よう**(酔う) /よっぱらった男 a *drunk* [*drunken*] man / 私たちはビールですっかり酔っ払った We *got* quite *drunk* on beer. / 父はウィスキーを飲んでひどく酔っ払っていた My father *was* dead *drunk* on whiskey. / 彼はほとんど歩けないほど酔っ払っていた He *was* so *drunk* that he could hardly walk.

よつゆ 夜露 night [evening] dew Ⓤ

よつんばい 四つん這い 彼女は四つんばいになってコンタクトレンズを捜した She searched for her contact lens「*on her hands and knees*「*on all fours*].

よてい 予定

(計画) plan ⓒ (通例複数形~s); (日程) schedule ⓒ ――予定する plan ⓣⓘ; schedule ⓣ (❖通例受身で用いる)

あなたのあすの予定はどうなっていますか What is your *plan* [*schedule, program*] for tomorrow?

今夜は何も予定はありません I *don't have* any *plans for* tonight / (→何もすることはない)I *have nothing to do* tonight.

きょうは予定がぎっしり詰まっている I have *a tight* [*full, heavy*] *schedule* today.

仕事が忙しくていまだに夏休みの予定が立たない I'm so busy with my job that I still *can't make plans for* my summer vacation.

我々は自分たちで修学旅行の予定を組んだ We *made a plan* [*schedule*] *for* our school trip by ourselves.

来月に予定されていたレースは中止です The race *planned for* next month is now off.

朝, 突然友人がやってきたので一日の予定が狂ってしまった The sudden visit of my friend in the morning *threw* me *off my schedule* for the day.

智子の誕生会, 5月27日にしたから予定に入れておいてね We have set May 27 for Tomoko's birthday party, so please *put* it *on your schedule*.

会議は予定より1時間早く始まった The meeting began an hour「*ahead of schedule* [*early*].

飛行機は予定より20分遅れて着いた The plane arrived 20 minutes *late* [*behind schedule*].

大統領夫人は予定どおりその国に到着した The First Lady arrived in the country *on schedule*.

運動会はきのう予定どおり行われた The athletic meet was held yesterday *as scheduled*.

【plan+to *do*/on do*ing*】彼女は来月イギリスに行く予定だ She *is* planning「*to go* [*on going*] to England next month.

【be scheduled+for 名/to *do*】女王の日本訪問が来年4月に予定されている The Queen's visit to Japan *is scheduled for* next April. / 彼は来週母校で講演を行う予定だ He *is scheduled to* make a speech at his old school next week.

◆新しい病院の建設予定地 *the (projected) site for a new hospital* / 当地にはどのくらい滞在する予定ですか How long *are* you *going to* stay here?(❖be going to *do* は近い未来の予定・計画・意図を表す) / 彼女が到着する予定の時刻はとっくに過ぎていた The time she *was to* arrive passed a long time ago. / その船は午後3時にここに到着予定です The ship *is due* (*to arrive*) here at 3 p.m. / お子さんはいつ生まれる予定ですか When *is* your baby *due*?(❖*due* は単独で到着・出産の予定を表す) / 妻は今月出産の予定です My wife is 「*expecting* (*a baby*) [*having a baby*] this month. / 今週のご予定は？ *What's on your calendar* this week? / 旅先で予定外の出費がかさんだ I had *unexpected* expenses while traveling.

🌀「夏休みは何か予定があるの」「1週間北海道へ行く予定なんだ」"Do you have any *plans* for the summer vacation?" "Yes, I'm *planning to* go to Hokkaido for a week."

‖予定表 a schedule / 行事予定 a schedule of events

よとう 与党 ruling party ◯ (↔opposition party), Government party ◯ ‖与党に票を投じる vote for *the ruling party*

‖与党議員 a member of the ruling party

よどおし 夜通し all night (long), overnight, throughout the night ——夜通しの overnight(❖名詞の前で用いる) ‖彼女たちは夜通しカラオケボックスで歌った They sang songs *all night* in the karaoke-box.

よどみなく 淀みなく 彼は次々と投げかけられる質問によどみなく(→一流暢(りゅうちょう)に)答えた He *fluently* [*freely*] answered the questions posed one after another. / (→ためらいなく) He answered the questions posed one after another *without hesitation*.

よどむ 淀む stagnate ⓥ ——よどんだ(水などが) stagnant; (空気が) stale ‖部屋の中のよどんだ空気 the *stale* air in the room

◆よどんだ目 *dull* eyes / 川の流れのよどんだ所にたくさんの空き缶が浮いていた A lot of empty cans were floating *where the water was still*.

よなか 夜中 ——夜中に (夜に) at night; (真夜中に) in the middle of the night; (夜遅くに) late at night ‖夜中に間違い電話で起こされた *In the middle of the night* the telephone woke me, but it was the wrong number. ◆夜中まで勉強する study *till the small* [*wee*] *hours*(❖*the small* [*wee*] *hours* は0時から2時，3時ごろまでをいう)

よなが 夜長 秋の夜長 the *long* autumn *night*

よなき 夜泣き 姉の子供はひどく夜泣きをする My sister's baby *cries* hard *at night*.

よなべ 夜なべ 母が夜なべ仕事で手袋を編んでくれた My mother *spent a few nights* knitting me a pair of gloves.

よなれた 世慣れた (世才のある) worldly-wise; (あか抜けた) sophisticated ‖彼は世慣れている He is *worldly-wise*. / 彼は *a man of the world*.

よにげ 夜逃げ ——夜逃げする skip off [out] at night, run* away under (the) cover of the night

よねつ 余熱 residual heat ◯ ‖この温水プールにはごみ焼却炉の余熱が利用されている This heated pool uses *residual heat* from a garbage-burning incinerator.

よねん 余念 コンサートをあすに控え，彼らは最後の打ち合わせに余念がない They 「*are absorbed in* [*devote themselves to*] the last arrangements for the concert coming up tomorrow.

よのなか 世の中 world ◯ (しばしば the ～) ⇨せけん

世の中にはいろいろな人がいる *The world* consists of many kinds of people. / There are many kinds of people *in the world*.

君は世の中が分かっていない You know nothing about *the world*.

世の中なんてこんなものさ Such is *the world*.

世の中そう捨てたもんじゃない *The world* is not completely hopeless.

世の中は狭い It's *a* small *world*.

◆世の中(→人生)がつくづくいやになった I am completely sick of *life*. / 今の世の中，携帯電話なしではやっていけない We can't do without cell phones *these days*.

よは 余波 (事件などの) aftereffect ◯《通例複数形 ～s》; (災害の) aftermath ◯ ‖台風の余波 the *aftereffects* [*aftermath*] of the typhoon / 不況の余波はこんななかの村にまで及んだ *The aftereffects* of the depression reached even this remote village.

よはく 余白 (blank) space ◯, blank ◯; (欄外の) margin ◯ ‖余白をあける leave *space* [*a margin*] / 名前は紙の右余白に書いてください Please write your name in *the right margin* of the paper.

よばれる 呼ばれる ❶【声をかけられる】be called ‖名前を呼ばれたら答案用紙を取りに来てください Come and pick up your answer sheet when your name *is called*.

❷【称される】be called ‖ライオンは百獣の王と呼ばれている The lion *is called* the king of beasts.

🌀「あなたはふだん何で呼ばれてるの」「短くカズと呼ばれています」"What *are* you usually *called*?" "I'm *called* Kazu for short." (❖「あだ名をカズと呼ばれている」という場合は I'm nicknamed Kazu. となる)

❸【招かれる】be invited ‖今度の土曜日，パーティーに呼ばれているんだ I *am invited* to a party next Saturday.

❹【呼び出される】be called ‖証人は法廷に呼ばれた The witness *was called* [*brought*,《公式的》*summoned*] to court.

-よばわり -呼ばわり 私をうそつき呼ばわりするな(→うそつきと呼ぶな) *Don't call* me a liar! / 彼は泥棒呼ばわりされた(→泥棒であるかのように言われた) He *was talked of as if* he were a thief.

よび 予備 (スペア) spare ◯; (蓄え) reserve ◯ (しばしば複数形 ～s) ——予備の spare; in reserve; (事前の) preliminary; (準備の) preparatory (❖名詞の前で用いる) ‖予備のかぎ [タイヤ] a *spare* key [tire] / 予備交渉 *preparatory* talks / 私には予備の資金がいくらかある I have some funds *kept* [*held*] in re-

コミュニケーションスキル —呼びかける—

①知らない人に呼びかける

Excuse me. / Pardon me.
《女性に対して》Ma'am. / Madam. / Miss.
《男性に対して》Sir. / Mister.

☞ 人に何か尋ねたりするときに「すみません，ちょっとお聞きしたいのですが」などの「すみません」は Excuse me. で，I'm sorry. とはいわない．miss (lady) や mister はあまりよい呼びかけではない．

②家族の中で呼びかける

Dad. / Daddy. お父さん．
Mom. / Mummy. お母さん．
Grandpa. おじいちゃん．
Grandma. おばあちゃん．
Uncle .... (❖ ....にはおじさんの first name がくる) ...おじさん．
Aunt .... (❖ ....にはおばさんの first name がくる) ...おばさん．

☞ 兄弟，姉妹，夫婦で呼び合うときは first name. 夫婦間では dear, honey, darling, sweetheart も使われる．

③友達，親しい人に呼びかける

Hi. / Hey. / Say. ねえ．，ちょっと．
Hey, Sherry. Wait for a second. シェリー，ちょっと待って！
Look. ちょっと見てよ．
Listen. ちょっと聞いてよ．

☞ 米国では少し親しくなると，ファーストネームで呼び合うのがふつう．Hey, ...! は，よほど親しい友達でもないかぎり使わないほうが無難．失礼だと受け取られることもある．

④その人の職種名で呼びかける

《学校の先生》Mr. .... / Miss .... / Mrs. .... / Ms. .... (❖「マクニール先生」を "Teacher McNeil." などとはいわない)
《大学教授》Professor.
《医者》Doctor.
《看護婦》Nurse.
《運転手》Driver.
《ウエートレス・ウエーター》Waitress. / Waiter.
《船[機]長》Captain.
《交換手》Operator.
《警官（お巡（まわ）りさん）》Officer.

☞ レストランなどでウェートレスやウエーターを呼ぶときは Waitress [Waiter]! と声をかけて軽く手を上げるか目で合図する．また，航空機に乗っている際に機内乗務員を呼ぶときは Excuse me! というのがふつう．

☞「警官」に対しては policeman とか police とはいわない．

⑤大人数に呼びかける

《先生がクラスに呼びかける》Class. / Boys and girls. / Students. / Everyone. / Everybody. (❖ boys and girls は主として小・中学生の場合)
《演説会場など大人の集まっている改まった場所での「みなさん」》Ladies and gentlemen.
《「みなさん，ちょっとよろしいですか」》May I have your attention, please?
《「みなさん」》People. / Folks. /（女性だけのとき）Ladies. /（男性だけのとき）Gentlemen.

---

serve. ◆予備の(→余分の)机を用意する prepare the *extra* desks / 糖尿病の予備軍 *candidates for* diabetes / 彼は何の予備知識もなくその展覧会を見に行った He went to the exhibition *without「knowing anything about it beforehand [any prior knowledge about it]*.
‖ 予備選挙 a preliminary election / 予備調査 a preliminary [pilot] survey / 予備費 a reserve fund

よびあつめる 呼び集める call ... together, rally ⊕ ‖ 監督は選手たちを呼び集めた The manager *called* the players *together*. / The manager *rallied* the players around him.

よびおこす 呼び起こす その香水の香りは彼の古い記憶を呼び起こした The scent of the perfume *awakened* [*brought back*] old memories in him.

よびかけ 呼び掛け call ⓒ; (訴え) appeal ⓤ ⓒ ‖ 彼の支援の呼びかけに多くの友人が応じた Many friends answered his *call* [*appeal*] for support.

よびかける 呼び掛ける call ⊕; (訴える) appeal ⊕ ➡ コミュニケーションスキル ‖ 援助を呼びかける *appeal for* help / 私は知らない人に呼びかけられた A stranger *called out to* me. / 彼は多くの専門家たちに会合への参加を呼びかけた He *appealed to* many specialists *for* participation in the meeting.

よびこう 予備校 ▨ a *yobiko*, a school for helping students pass college entrance examinations ‖ 予備校に通う go to *a yobiko* [*college preparation school*]
‖ 予備校生 a *yobiko* student

よびごえ 呼び声 call ⓒ; (叫び声) cry ⓒ
慣用表現 佐藤氏は次期総裁の呼び声が高い Mr. Sato *is very much talked about* as the best candidate to be the next party leader.

よびこみ 呼び込み (サーカスなどの) 《口語的》barker ⓒ

よびこむ 呼び込む 客を呼び込む *call in* customers *by barking* / 彼のシュートはチームに勝利を呼び込んだ(→もたらした) His shot *brought about* victory for the team.

よびすて 呼び捨て 人を呼び捨てにする(→一つけんどんに呼ぶ) *address* a person *brusquely* [（→敬称をつけずに）*without using the proper form of address*]

よびだし 呼び出し call ⓒ; (召喚) summons ⓒ ➡ よびだす ‖ 警察の呼び出しに応じる[応じない] answer [ignore] *a summons* from the police ◆その生徒たちは個別に学校に呼び出しを受けた(→呼び出された) Those students *were called* to school one by one. / お呼び出し申し上げます，伊藤弘美様，フロントまでお越しください *Paging* Ms. Ito Hiromi. Please come

よびだす 呼び出す call 〔召喚する〕《公式的》summon 〔アナウンスなどで〕page ∥ 職員室に呼び出される be called to the teacher's room / 秘書は上司に呼び出された The secretary *was summoned* by her boss. / 真夜中に友人に電話で呼び出された A friend of mine *called* me *out* by phone at midnight. / 必要なデータを呼び出すにはどうしたらよいのですか Please tell me how to *call up* the necessary data.

よびたてる 呼び立てる お忙しいところお呼びたてして申しわけありません I'm sorry to have *called* you *here* when you were busy.

よびつける 呼び付ける call *a person* ∥ 彼は部下たちを自分の部屋に呼びつけた He *called* his men *to* his room.

よびとめる 呼び止める call to *a person* to stop;〔タクシーを〕hail, flag down ∥ 通りを歩いていたら見知らぬ人に呼び止められた A stranger *called to* me *to stop* when I was walking along the street.

よびな 呼び名 name ©;〔別名〕alias ©;〔愛称〕nickname © ∥ この魚にはいくつかの呼び名がある This fish has several *names*.

よびみず 呼び水 この制度は景気回復の呼び水になる(→導く)ことが期待されている It is expected that this system *will lead* the recovery in the economy.

よびもどす 呼び戻す call back;〔召喚する〕recall ∥〔家に〕call home ∥ 人を故郷に呼び戻す *call back* a person to his [her] hometown / 私たちは急な用事で家に呼び戻された We *were called home* because of urgent business. / 大使は突然任地から呼び戻された The ambassador *was* suddenly *recalled* from his post. / クラクションの音で彼は現実の世界に呼び戻された The sound of a horn *recalled* him to the real world.

よびもの 呼び物 〔催し物などの〕feature ©;〔人を引きつける物〕attraction © ∥ この祭りの最大の呼び物は最後に打ち上げられる花火だ The main *feature* [*attraction*] of this festival is the fireworks which are set off last.

よびょう 余病〔医学〕complication © 〔通例複数形 ~s〕∥ 糖尿病は様々な余病を併発するといわれている It is said that diabetes causes other *complications*.

よびよせる 呼び寄せる call *a person* ∥ その老人は子供たちをまくら元に呼び寄せた The old man *called* his children (*over*) *to* his bedside.

よびりん 呼び鈴 bell ©;〔入り口の〕doorbell © ∥ 呼び鈴を鳴らす ring [sound] *a doorbell*

よぶ 呼ぶ
❶【声をかける】call ㊷ ㊿
ほら！だれかが君を呼んでいるよ Look! Someone *is calling* you.
ナンシーは大声で助けを呼んだ Nancy *called out* for help.
彼はドアの後ろから私を呼んだ He *called* me from behind the door.
先生は彼らの名前をアルファベット順に呼んだ The teacher *called* their names in alphabetical order.

❷【来てもらう】call ㊷;〔呼びにやる〕send* for ...
警察を呼ぶ *call* the police
母はウエーターを呼んでコーヒーを３つ注文した My mother *called* a waiter and ordered three cups of coffee.
すぐに救急車を呼んでくれ *Call* an ambulance right away!
医者を呼んでください Please「*send for* [*call*] a doctor.
助けを呼びにやりましょうか Shall I *send for* help?
◆タクシーを電話で呼ぶ *ring for* a taxi / 均，お母さんが呼んでるよ Hitoshi, Mom *wants* you.

❸【名づける】call ㊷
友達は僕をカツと呼んでいる My friends *call* me Katsu.
「お名前は何といいますか」「僕の名前は鈴木健太です．ケンと呼んでください」"May I have your name, please?" "My name is Suzuki Kenta. Please *call* me Ken."

❹【招く】invite ㊷
哲也もパーティーに呼ぼうよ Let's *invite* Tetsuro to the party, too.
何度か会が開かれたが，彼らにはお呼びがかからなかった The meetings were held several times, but they *were not invited*.

❺【引き起こす】
最近また昔なつかしい駄菓子が人気を呼んでいる Simple, old-style sweets *are popular* [〔口語的〕*catching on*] again these days.
この実験は今後議論を呼びそうだ This experiment is likely to *create controversy*.
そのニュースは日本中に大きな反響を呼んだ The news *created* [*caused*] *a great sensation* all over Japan.
⇨ よばれる

よふかし 夜更かし ── 夜ふかしする stay [sit*] up (till) late;〔習慣的に〕keep* late hours ∥ 彼女は夜ふかしの習慣が抜けない She can't get rid of the habit of *keeping late hours*.

よふけ 夜更け ── 夜ふけに late at night ∥ 夜ふけに家の近くで大きな物音がした There was a loud noise near my house *late at night*.

よぶん 余分 extra ©;〔剰余〕surplus Ⓤ© ── 余分な extra; surplus;〔予備の〕spare ── 余分に extra ∥ 余分なお金は持ってこないように Don't bring *extra* money with you. / 店員さんに余分の取り皿をもらってちょうだい Ask the waiter for some *extra* plates. / 彼女はシチューを少し余分に作った She made stew a little *extra*.
◆余分な物は捨てなさい Throw away things *you don't need*. / 余分なお金はありません I don't have any money *to spare*.

よほう 予報 forecast © ⇨ てんき(天気) ∥ 天

気予報が当たった[はずれた] The weather forecast proved right [wrong]. / 天気予報によるとあしたは雨だ The weather forecast [report] says it will rain tomorrow.

‖気象予報士 a weatherperson, a weather forecaster / 長期予報(天気の) a long-range weather forecast

よぼう 予防 (防止) prevention ⓤ; (予防策) precaution ⓒ ──予防する prevent ⓗ
エイズ予防対策 AIDS *prevention* [*preventive*] *measures* / 虫歯の予防 the *prevention* of tooth decay / 火災の予防策を講じる take *precautions* against fire

うがいはかぜの予防に有効です Gargling is effective for the *prevention* of colds.

この食品には癌(煎)を予防する効果のあることが分かった This food proved to have an effect that *prevents* the cancer.

‖予防医学 preventive medicine / 火災予防 fire prevention

慣用表現 監督は「まだシーズンは始まったばかりですから」と予防線を張った(→慎重に答えた) "The season has just begun," the manager *made a precautious reply*.

よぼうせっしゅ 予防接種 (ワクチンによる) 〔医学〕 vaccination ⓒⓤ; (病原菌による) inoculation ⓒⓤ // ポリオの予防接種を受ける have *a vaccination against* polio

◆人にインフルエンザの予防接種をする *inoculate* a person *against* influenza

よほど 余程 ❶【相当に】僕などより君のほうがよほど歌がうまい You sing *much* better than I. / 彼女, よほど犬が好きなんだろうね She must like dogs *very much*. / 彼女はよほど気に入った食器でないと買わなかった She didn't buy dishes unless she liked them *very much*. / 彼が声を荒げるなんてよほど腹が立っていたにちがいない He must have been *really* angry to speak so roughly. / よほどのことがないかぎり彼女が無断で学校を休むはずがない She wouldn't be absent from school without notice *unless something serious has come up*.

❷【ほとんど】彼女はよほど会社を辞めてしまおうかと思った She *had a good mind to* leave her office. (◆have *a good mind to do* で「とても…したいと思う」の意味)

よぼよぼ よぼよぼの老人 a *doddering* [*doddery, shaky*] old man

よみ 読み (読むこと) reading ⓤ; (判断) judgment ⓒⓤ; (洞察) insight ⓒⓤ; (解釈) interpretation ⓤⓒ // 読みを誤る make errors *of judgment* / 彼女は読みが深い[浅い] She has *a deep* [*shallow*] *insight*.

◆少女はその漢字の読み(→読み方)が分からなかった The girl didn't know *how to read* the Chinese character. / 彼の読みは当たった[はずれた] He *guessed* right [wrong].

よみあげる 読み上げる (声をあげて) read* ⓗ; (名前などを) call out // 声明文を読み上げる *read out* a statement; *read* a statement *aloud* / 彼はリストにある名前を読み上げた He *called out* the names on the list.

よみあやまる 読み誤る misread* ⓗ; (判断を誤る) misjudge ⓗ

よみあわせ 読み合わせ (照合) collation ⓤ
◆台本の読み合わせをする *read through* the script *together*

よみおわる 読み終わる finish reading, read* through [over] // あの本もう読み終わったの? Have you *finished* [*Are you done*] *reading* that book yet?

◆私は第2章まで読み終わりました I've read as far as the second chapter.

よみかえす 読み返す read* again [over], reread* ⓗ // 手紙を何度も読み返す *read* a letter over and over *again* / 久しぶりにその本を読み返した I *read* the book *again* after a long time.

よみがえる 蘇る・甦る イエス・キリストは死からよみがえった Jesus Christ *rose* from the dead. / その古い駅舎は美術館としてよみがえった(→修復された) The old station building *was refurbished* [*restored*] as an art museum. / その歌を聞いていると幸せな思い出がよみがえってくる That song *brings back* happy memories. / Listening to the song, happy memories *come back to* me.

よみかき 読み書き reading and writing // 読み書きを習う learn *reading and writing*
◆母は眼鏡をかけないと読み書きができません My mother can't *read or write* without her glasses. / その時代には読み書きのできない人はたくさんいた There were many *"illiterate people* [*illiterates*] in the period.

‖読み書きそろばん the three R's (◆reading, writing, arithmetic を指す)

よみかた 読み方 reading ⓤ; (発音) pronunciation [prənʌ́nsiéiʃən] ⓤ // この英語の読み方を教えてくれませんか Will you tell me 「*the reading of* [*how to read*] this English?

◆この小説はいろいろな読み方ができる This novel *can be read* in several ways.

よみきり 読み切り 読み切りの小説 a *complete* [*non-serial*] novel

よみごたえ 読み応え 彼のエッセーはなかなか読みごたえがあった(→内容が濃かった) His essays were 「*of much substance* [(→読む価値が十分あった) *well worth reading*].

よみこなす 読みこなす ヘーゲルを読みこなすのは容易なことではない It's not easy to *read and digest* Hegel('s books).

よみさし 読みさし ──読みさしの half-read [hǽfréd] // 読みさしにした本がたくさんある I've *left* a lot of books *half-read* [*unfinished*].

よみすて 読み捨て 今日(ミミネ)ほとんどの雑誌は読み捨てにされる Nowadays, most magazines are *to be read and thrown away*.

よみせ 夜店 a stall at a night fair

よみち 夜道 ひとりで夜道を歩く *walk* alone *at night*

よみで 読みで この歴史小説はずいぶん読みでがありそうだ(→読み通すのに時間がかかる) This historical novel seems to *take me a long time to read through*.

よみとおす 読み通す read* through [over], read ... from beginning to end / 彼女はその大冊を一気に読み通してしまった She *has read* the thick book *through* [*over*] at a sitting.
よみとる 読み取る read* 他 / 郵便番号を読み取る *read* the postal code / 本文から筆者の意図を読み取る *read* [*infer*] the writer's intention from the text / 表情から人の気持ちを読み取る *read* a person's mind from his [her] expression
よみなおす 読み直す read* over [again], reread* 他 ⇨ よみかえす
よみびと 詠み人 (作家) writer 🄲; (詩などの作者) composer 🄲
◆詠み人知らず *Anonymous*
よみふける 読み耽る 彼はさっきから雑誌に読みふけっている He *was absorbed* [*lost*] *in* (*reading*) a magazine for some time.
よみもの 読み物 (集合的) reading 🄌; (本) book 🄲; (記事) reading matter 🄌 ∥軽い読み物 light *reading*

よむ¹ 読む

❶ [本などを] read* 他 自 (❖黙読, 音読いずれの意味もある)
地図[楽譜]を読む *read* "a map [music]
彼女は自分の部屋で本を読んでいる She's *reading* a book in her room.
その本は前に読んだことがある I *have read* the book before.
その子供はまだ字が読めない That child *can't read* yet.
この詩を声を出して読んでください Please *read* this poem aloud.
私は漫画を読んで1時間つぶした I killed an hour *reading* comics.
彼は手軽に読める本を探している He is looking for books that *can be read* easily.
彼の文字は読みにくい His handwriting is 「*hard to read* [*illegible*].
以下が休み中に読むべき本のリストです The following is the list of books *to be read* during the vacation.
本を読む時間がほとんどない I get little time 「*to read* [*for reading*].
私はその記事を最後まで読んだ I *read* the article *through*.
何か読む物を持ってきたほうがいいよ You should bring something *to read*.
あんなに厚い本をもう読み終わったの? Have you 「*read through* [*finished reading*] that thick book already?
【read+名+to 名(人)】≒【read+名(人)+名】彼は私にその詩を読んでくれた He *read* the poem to me. / He *read* me the poem. / 彼女は子供たちに絵本を読んで聞かせた She *read* the picture book *to* her children. / She *read* her children the picture book. (❖the picture book がなければ漠然と「本を読んで聞かせた」という意味になる)
【read+about 名】その事件のことなら新聞で読みました I 「*read about* [*saw*] that event in the paper. (❖*read about* ... は「…について読んで知っている」という意味)
【read+that 節】その病気に対する治療法が発見されたと新聞で読んだ I *read* in the paper *that* a cure for that disease had been found.

◆新聞を2, 3分でさっと読む *skim through* the paper in a few minutes / 彼女は本を読むのがとても速い[遅い] She is *a* very fast [slow] *reader*. / 第8章は飛ばして読んだほうがいいよ You should *skip* Chapter 8. / 彼は高校生のころ芥川の小説をむさぼり読んだ He *devoured* stories by Akutagawa when he was a high school student. / この単語は何と読みますか(→発音しますか) How do you *pronounce* this word?

❷ [把握する]
景気の動向を読む(→予測する) *foresee* [*forecast*] how business will go
プロ棋士は数十手先まで読むといわれている It is said that professional *shogi* players *look* dozens of moves ahead.
こちらの手のうちはすっかり読まれている(→見抜かれている)ようだった My tactics seemed to *be seen through* completely.
彼女には人の心を読むという特殊な能力がある She has the peculiar ability to *read* others' minds.

よむ² 詠む 短歌を詠む *write* [*compose*] a *tanka* / 春の情景を俳句に詠む *describe* a spring scene in a haiku

よめ 嫁 (妻) one's wife (複 wives); (息子の妻) one's daughter-in-law (複 daughters-in-law); (花嫁) bride 🄲 ∥彼の家では嫁を大切にしている His family are kind to *his wife*. / 嫁さんは元気かい How is *your wife*? / これうちの嫁です This is my *daughter-in-law*.
◆姉はこの春お嫁に行った(→結婚した) My sister *got married* this past spring. / 芳子の両親は彼女を医者のところに嫁にやりたい(→医者と結婚させたい)と思っている Yoshiko's parents *want* her *to marry* a doctor.

よめい 余命 one's remaining days ◆彼は余命いくばくもない His *days are numbered*.
∥平均余命 (a) life expectancy

よめいり 嫁入り 新井家に嫁入りする *marry into* the Arai family / あすは姉の嫁入りの日だ My sister's *getting married* tomorrow. / 彼には嫁入り前の娘がいる He has an *unmarried* daughter. / (→結婚適齢期) He has a daughter *of marriageable age*.
∥嫁入りじたく preparation for *one's* marriage / 嫁入り道具 a bride's outfit, (古風) a trousseau

よもぎ 蓬 mugwort 🄲 🄌

よもや よもや戦争の悲惨さを忘れたわけではないだろうね *Surely*, you haven't forgotten the tragedy of the war? ⇨ まさか

よもやまばなし 四方山話 よもやま話をする *talk about all sorts of things*

よやく 予約

❶ [切符・部屋などの] reservation 🄲, (主に

(英)booking ⓒⓊ　——予約する reserve ⑯,
(英)book ⑯⑧, make* a reservation
予約を変更する change *a reservation* / ホテル
の予約をキャンセルする cancel *a hotel reservation*
予約をお願いしたいんですが I'd like to *make a reservation*, please.
前列で予約できますか Can I *reserve* a front row seat?
電話で予約できます You *can make a reservation* by phone.
(レストランなどへ) 7時に2人予約したいのですが I'd like to *reserve* a table for two at 7 o'clock.
コンサートの切符を2枚予約した I *reserved* two tickets for the concert.
私はセントラルホテルにシングルの部屋を予約した I *reserved* [*made a reservation for*] a single room at the Central Hotel.
飛行機の座席はもう予約したの? Have you *reserved* seats on an airplane yet?
すべての席は予約でいっぱいです All seats *are fully reserved*.
❷【診察・面会などの】appointment Ⓒ　——予約する make* an appointment
歯医者に予約をする *make an appointment with* the dentist
彼は10時に歯医者の予約をした He *made a dental appointment* for 10:00. (✪「予約を取り消す」なら make の代わりに cancel にする)
🖋「予約がおありですか」「はい, 2時に予約しています」"Do you have *an appointment*?" "Yes, I have *an appointment* at [for] two."
❸【その他】
映画をビデオで録画予約する *set* a videocassette recorder *to record* a film
私はその雑誌を1年間予約購読している I *have a year's subscription to* the magazine.
∥予約席 a reserved seat

よゆう 余裕

❶【時間・空間の】(余地) room Ⓤ; (時間の) time (to spare)
テントにはもう1人分の余裕がある There is *room for* one more person in the tent.
忙しくて運動をする余裕がない I'm so busy that I don't have *time* to exercise.
余裕をもって空港に着いた I got to the airport *with time to spare*.
◆彼らは余裕をもって(→少し早めに)家を出た They left their house *a little early*.
❷【経済的な】
新車を買う余裕などない I *cannot afford* (*to buy*) a new car. (✪afford は「(経済的に)…の余裕がある」の意味で, 通例 can, could, be able to などとともに用いる)
彼らには息子を留学させるだけの余裕がなかった They *couldn't afford* the expense of letting their son go abroad to study.
この高価な機械を遊ばせておく余裕は我々にはない We *can't afford to* have this expensive machine lying idle.
❸【精神的な】
彼は記者たちを笑わせる余裕を見せた(→笑わせるほど落ち着いていた) He *was calm enough to* make reporters laugh.
まだその走者の表情には余裕が感じられた(→十分エネルギーがあるようだった) The runner still *seemed to have enough energy*.

より 縒り 慣用表現 彼は腕によりをかけて作った(→最善を尽くして料理した)郷土料理をふるまってくれた He served me a regional dish he *did his best to cook*. / 彼らはよりを戻したそうだ I hear (that) they *got back together*.

-より¹

❶【比較】than
弟は私よりもずっと賢い My little brother is much cleverer *than* I (am) [me]. (✪口語では通例 than me を用いる)
彼は私より5センチ背が高い He is taller *than* I [me] by five centimeters. / He is five centimeters taller *than* I [me].
彼女はクラスのだれよりも上手にピアノを弾ける She can play the piano better *than* any other student in her class.
彼は守備よりも打撃がうまい He is better at batting *than* at fielding.
父はいつもより帰ってくるのが遅かった My father came home later *than usual*.
私は以前より2キロやせた I am two kilos lighter *than* I used to be.
東京の人口は大阪より多い The population of Tokyo is larger *than* that of Osaka.
旭川は札幌より北にある Asahikawa is located further north *than* Sapporo.
彼は歌手というよりむしろ俳優だ He is *more* an actor *than* a singer.
◆私は外出するよりも家にいるほうがいい I *prefer* being at home *to* going out. / I'd *rather* stay home *than* go out. / 彼は魚より肉のほうが好きです He *prefers* meat *to* fish. / He has a preference for meat *rather than* fish. / 湿気が多いよりは暑いほうがましです Heat *is preferable to* humidity.
🖋「英語の試験で何点取ったの」「平均点よりは上だったよ」"What did you get on the English exam?" "My score was *above* average."

英作文ノート 「…より」必ずしも **than** ならず
絵画では私より彼女のほうがすぐれている
→×She is superior *than* me in painting.
→○She is superior *to* me in painting.
★比較表現には,「…より」が than ではなく to で表されるものがある. 優劣: superior / inferior, 老若: senior / junior などラテン語からきた形容詞に多い.

❷【…以外】other than … ➡-いがい(-以外)
これよりほかにテープはないの? Don't you have any tapes *other than* these?
◆我々は待つよりしかたなかった We could do nothing *but* wait.
❸【起点】from; (…以来) since ➡-から
本日より新法が施行される The new law

takes effect *from* today (*on*).
ヤシの実が遠い島より流れ着いた A palm fruit was drifted here *from* a distant island.
◆このコースは4月より(→4月に)開講します This course will start *in* April.
❹〔その他〕
その委員会は20人のメンバーより成る The committee *consists of* 20 members.
この企画は政府の協力により(→協力のおかげで)実現した *Thanks to* the cooperation of the government, the plan was realized.
法により未成年者の喫煙は禁止されている Minors are forbidden from smoking *by* law.

-より² -寄り 南[北]寄りの風 a *southerly* [*northerly*] wind / 渋谷よりのホームで *on the Shibuya end of the platform* / 彼の思想は少し右寄りだ His ideas *are* [*lean*] *a little to the right*. ⇨がわ

よりあい 寄り合い (会合) meeting © (❖「集まった人々」の意味では the meeting)
慣用表現 うちのチームは寄り合い所帯だ(→あわてて寄せ集められた) Our team *was thrown together at the last minute*.

よりあつまる 寄り集まる gather ㊙, get* together ⇨あつまる

よりいっそう より一層 より一層の努力を期待したい I hope you will make a *better effort*. ⇨いっそう(一層)

よりかかる 寄り掛かる lean* on [against] …; (依存する) depend on … /木[壁, 机]に寄りかかる *lean against* a tree [wall, desk] ◆親に寄りかかって生活する *live off one's parent*(*s*)

よりごのみ 選り好み 彼は人のより好みが激しい He *is particular* [*fussy*, (口語的)*choosy*, (口語的)*picky*] about people. ⇨えりごのみ

よりそう 寄り添う その小さな少女は母親にぴったりと寄り添った The little girl *nestled* [*snuggled*] *up to* her mother. / そのカップルは寄り添うようにして歩いていた The couple were walking *cuddling*.

よりつく 寄り付く 私の娘はうちにまるで寄りつかない My daughter *never gets near* [*keeps away from*] our house.

よりどころ 拠り所 (根拠) foundation Ⓤ; (典拠) authority ©; (支え) support Ⓤ /故郷は彼の心のよりどころだった His hometown was his spiritual *support*. / 彼はこの実験データをよりどころに新たな理論を展開した He developed his new theory *on the foundation* [*authority*] *of* this data of experiment.

よりどり 選り取り ここのパンツはよりどり3枚で980円だ You can *take any* three pairs of underpants here for 980 yen. / この店はゲームソフトならよりどりみどりだ(→自由に選べる) You *have your pick* [*choice*] of any game software in this store.(❖このpickは「選択権」の意味); (→何でもそろっている) They have *any* game software *you want* in this store.

よりによって 選りに選って よりによってなぜ彼なんかを選んだのだろう Why on earth did they elect him, *of all people*? (❖ on earth は疑問文を強める表現)

よりぬき 選り抜き ──より抜きの (公式的) select (❖名詞の前で用いる); (最高の) (厳選した) choice ◆そこには全国からより抜きの作品が集められていた There were *select* [*the very best, choice*] works gathered from all over the country there.

よりみち 寄り道 ──寄り道する (口語的) drop in「*on a person* [*at* …] *on the way*, (口語的) drop [stop] by … *on the way* /学校帰りにおばの家に寄り道していこう I'm going to *drop in*「*on my aunt* [*at my aunt's house*] *on the way home* from school. / 彼女はどこにも寄り道せずまっすぐ家に帰った She went straight home *without dropping* [*stopping*] by any place *on her way*.
◆札幌へ向かう途中仙台に2日間寄り道した We「*stopped over* [*made a stopover*] *at* Sendai for two days on our way to Sapporo. (❖ stop over at …は「旅行の途中で…に泊まる」の意味)

よりめ 寄り目 寄り目の(→内斜視の)男 a *cross-eyed* man / 彼は寄り目をしてみせた He showed me how he could *turn both his eyes inward toward his nose*.

よりよい より良い better ⇨よい(良い・好い・善い) /よりよい生活を送る lead a *better* life

よりょく 余力 余力があるかぎりこの連載を続けていきます As long as I have *the energy left* [*to spare*], I will continue this serial. / あのランナーはもうほとんど余力が残っていないようだ The runner seems to have little *energy left* [*to spare*].

よりわける 選り分ける (仕分ける) sort ㊙; (分ける) separate ㊙; (選び出す) choose* ㊙ /ヒナの雄と雌をより分ける *sort* chicks *into* males *and* females; *separate* male chicks *from* female ones ◆不燃物をより分ける *set aside* nonflammable trash

よる¹ 夜 (日没から日の出までの暗い時間帯) night ©Ⓤ; (日没から寝る時間まで) evening ©Ⓤ

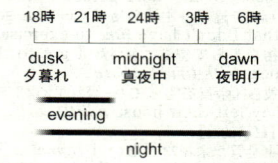

	18時	21時	24時	3時	6時
	dusk 夕暮れ		midnight 真夜中		dawn 夜明け
		evening			
		night			

〖~(の)夜〗
涼しい夜 a cool *night* [*evening*] / あしたの夜 tomorrow *night* [*evening*] / きのうの夜 last *night*; yesterday *evening* / ロンドンの夜 *night* in London
彼は夜働き, 昼間睡眠をとる He works *at night* and sleeps during the day.
我々はその夜川のほとりでキャンプした We camped by a river *for the night*.

あなたを思いながら眠れぬ夜を過ごしました I've spent *a sleepless night* thinking about you.

〖夜の〗
夜の9時 9 o'clock 「*at night* [*in the evening*]」 夜の早い時間に early 「*at night* [*in the evening*]」
夜の公園には人影が全くなかった Not a soul could be seen in the park *at night*.
私は父に夜の外出を禁じられている My father forbids me to go out *at night*.
夜までに5センチの雪が積もった Five centimeters of snow fell 「*during the night* [*overnight*]」.

〖夜が・は〗
夏至には1年でいちばん夜が短くなる We have *the* shortest *night* of the year at the summer solstice.
夜はこのあたりは静かです It's quiet around here *at night*.
◆夜が明けた *The day broke./ It dawned.*

〖夜に〗
最近夜に何度も目がさめる I often wake up *at night* these days.
父は20日[日曜]の夜に帰ってくる My father will come back (*on*) 「*the night* of the 20th [*Sunday night*]」.(❖「1月14日の夜に」などの特定の日の夜を指すときは前置詞に on を用いる)
夜になると近くでフクロウが鳴くのが聞こえる I hear an owl hoot *at night* in the neighborhood.
我々はそこで夜になるのを待った We waited there until *the night fell*./(→暗くなるのを)We waited there until *it got dark*.

〖その他〗
彼は夜遅くまでかかって宿題を仕上げた It took him *until late at night* to finish his homework.
彼女はよく夜遅く私に電話してくる She often calls me *late at night*.
きのうの夜遅くに近所で火事があった There was a fire near my house *late last night*.
話し合いは夜遅くまで続いた The meeting went on *till late at night*.
彼女は朝型人間だが彼女の夫は夜型人間だ She is a day person, but her husband is *a night person*.
🔴「その夜あなたはどこで何をしていましたか」「家で本を読んでいました」 "Where were you and what were you doing *that night* [*evening*]?" "I was reading a book at home."

よる² 因る・拠る

❶【手段】by, by means of ... ➪ -で
言葉による暴力 violence *by means of* language; verbal abuse
この病気は薬によって治すことが可能だ This disease can be cured 「*by taking medicine* [*with medicine*].

❷【行為者】by
住民による環境保護運動 an environmental protection movement *led by* the residents
このつぼは久保さんの手によるものだ This pot *was made by* Mr. Kubo.
◆多数派による支配 *majority* rule / 10代の若者による喫煙はますます深刻な社会問題になってきている *Teenage* smoking is an increasingly serious social problem.

❸【原因】be caused by ..., be due to ...
地震による被害 damage 「*caused by* [*due to*]」 an earthquake
その列車事故は人為的ミスによるものだった The train accident *was* 「*caused by* [*due to*]」 human error.
◆癌(㋑)による死亡者 a cancer death; a death *from* cancer / 大雪により電車が大幅に遅れている The trains are delayed quite a while 「*because of* [*owing to, due to*]」 the heavy snowfall.

❹【…しだいである】depend on [upon] ...(❖進行形・受身にはできない) ➪ したい(次第)
僕たちが勝てるかどうかは君のスパイクのできによる Our victory *depends on* your spiking.
駅まで歩いて行くか自転車で行くかはその日の気分による *It depends on* how I feel each day whether I walk or ride a bicycle to the station.
値段によっては君にこの本を買ってやってもいいよ I will buy you this book, *depending on* the price.
◆ことによると彼もあしたのパーティーに来るかもしれない *Maybe*, he will come to tomorrow's party. / あすは所により雨になるでしょう It will rain in *some places* tomorrow.
🔴「虫歯の治療にはお金がかかるのでしょうか」「うーん、それは場合によりますね」 "Will it cost much to treat a decayed tooth?" "Well, *it depends* (*on time and difficulty*)."

❺【基づく】be based on ..., by ➪ もとづく
双方の合意による決定 a decision 「*based on* [*by*]」 mutual consensus
綿密な調査によってその事実が明らかになった The fact was made clear *by* close examination.
◆国連の名による武力の行使 the employment of force *in the name of* the UN / テレビのニュースによるとインドで飛行機の墜落事故があったそうだ *According to* the TV news, there was a plane crash in India. / The TV news *said* there was a plane crash in India.

よる³ 寄る

❶【移動する・近づく】(動く) move 自; (近づいてくる) come*close, come near; (「近づいていく」なら come の代わりに go を用いる); (わきへ) step aside ➪ ちかづく
彼は私が座ろうとするとベンチの端へ寄った He *moved* (*over*) to the side of the bench when I was about to sit down on it. (❖ move over は「席などを詰める」の意味)

もっとこっちに(→近くに)寄って *Come closer* [*nearer*].

見知らぬ女が私の方に寄ってきた A strange woman *came*「*close to* [*near* (*to*)] me.

彼はその絵のそばに寄って画家のサインを見た He *went*「*close to* [*near* (*to*)] the picture and looked at the signature of the painter.

群衆は消防士が通れるようわきへ寄った The crowd *stepped aside* to let the fire fighters get through.

❷【立ち寄る】(訪ねる) visit [他]; (不意に訪ねる)《口語的》drop in「on *a person* [at ...], 《口語的》drop by; (途中でちょっと)《口語的》stop by [in] ⇒ たずねる(訪ねる), たちよる

帰りに絵梨香の家に寄った I *dropped in at* Erika's house on my way home.

ほんの2, 3分寄っていこうよ Let's *stop by* [*in*] for a few minutes.

◆長野へ行く途中, 高崎に寄ってお昼を食べた We *stopped off at* Takasaki for lunch on our way to Nagano. (❖ stop off (at [in] ...)は「旅の途中で立ち寄る」「途中下車する」という意味の口語的表現) / ちょっとうちに寄っていきなよ Just *come on in* [*into my house*] *and stay* for a while.

❸【集まる】

彼が公園に姿を現すと子供たちが寄ってきた When he appeared in the park, children *gathered* around him.

バッグの中で斜めになって弁当の中身が寄ってしまった The lunchbox [*bento*] was placed at an angle in the bag and so its contents *were pressed to one side.*

彼の顔は年をとってしわが寄っていた His face *was wrinkled* with age.

寄ってたかって彼一人を責めるのはよくない It's wrong to blame only him *among you.*

彼らは寄るとさわると彼の悪口ばかり言っている *Whenever they get together*, they speak ill of him.

落ちているあめにアリが何匹も寄ってきている A lot of ants *are swarming around* some candy on the ground.

[ことわざ] 寄らば大樹の陰 ⇒ かげ(陰)

よる[4] 縒る twist [他] (❖しばしば together を伴う) //わらをよって縄を作る *twist* straws *together* into a rope

よるべ 寄る辺 彼は寄る辺のない身であった(→頼れる人がいなかった) He *had nobody to depend upon.*

よれよれ ―よれよれの worn-out, shabby //よれよれのシャツ a *worn-out* [*shabby*] shirt

よろい 鎧 (よろいかぶと) armor [U] //よろいかぶと(→よろいかぶと一式)を身につける put on *a suit of armor*

よろく 余禄 extra profit [C][U]

よろける (ふらつく) stagger [自], reel [自]; (つまずいて) stumble [自] (❖「よろめきながら歩く」の意味もある), trip [自] //その体操選手は着地したときによろけてしまった The gymnast *staggered* [*stumbled*] when he landed on the floor. / 木の根につまずいてよろけた I *stumbled* [*tripped*] *on* a root of a tree (*and almost fell*).

よろこばしい 喜ばしい (出来事がめでたい) glad, happy; (よい) good; (人がうれしい) glad, happy; (好ましい) welcome; (望ましい) desirable //喜ばしい傾向 a *desirable* trend / 彼らが結婚するのは非常に喜ばしいことだ Their marriage is very *glad* [*happy, joyful*] news. / We're very *glad* [*happy*] that they will get married.

よろこばせる 喜ばせる please [他] (❖進行形にはできない); (幸せにする) make* *a person* happy; (大いに) delight [他] //彼は彼女を喜ばそうとペンダントを作った He made a pendant by himself to *please* her. / 彼は神秘的な手品で観衆を大いに喜ばせた He *delighted* the audience with his mysterious magic.

よろこび 喜び pleasure [U][C]; delight [U][C]; joy [U][C]; (幸せ) happiness [U]; (満足) satisfaction [U][C]

> pleasure: 喜びを表す最も一般的な語.
> delight: 大喜びを表し, pleasure よりも短期間のもの.
> joy: pleasure, delight よりもさらに強い喜びを表す.

〚喜びを・に〛

彼は喜びに満ちた表情をしていた His face was filled with *pleasure* [*delight, joy*].

彼は部活動に喜びを見いだしている He gets *satisfaction* from the club activities.

◆新年のお喜びを申し上げます *I wish you a happy New Year.*

〚~の喜び〛

勝利の喜びを味わいたい I want to experience *the pleasure* [*joy*] of victory.

その老人は人生の喜びも悲しみも経験してきた That old man has known *the joy*(*s*) and sorrow(s) of life.

〚その他〛

◆妹はサンタクロースにプレゼントをもらったと大喜びしている My sister *is very pleased*, saying that she received a present from Santa Claus. / 彼がおいしいものをごちそうしてくれるというので喜びいさんで(→大いに期待して)出かけた I went out *with great expectations* of the delicious meal he said he would treat me to.

よろこぶ 喜ぶ be pleased; (強い喜びを感じる) be delighted; (うれしく思う) be glad; (満足して幸せである) be happy (❖以上の訳語はすべて, about, at などの前置詞のほか, to *do*, that 節を続けることができる)

彼は妹の勝利を喜んだ He *was*「*pleased with* [*delighted at, glad about, happy about*] his sister's victory.

エイミーはげたの贈り物をとても喜んでくれた Amy *was delighted* [*very pleased*] *with* the *geta* I gave her.

人々は平和が戻ってきたことを喜んだ People *were pleased that* peace returned.

君が復帰するって聞いたらみんな喜ぶぞ All of us will *be pleased to* hear you are coming back.

言ってくれればいつでも喜んでお手伝いします If you ask me, I'll *be pleased to* help you.
◆プレゼントはこれにしよう. 彼女の喜ぶ顔が目に浮かぶようだ This is going to be her present. I can imagine her *happy* face. / みんな小躍りして喜んだ Everybody *jumped [danced] for joy*. / 私たちはその提案を喜んで受け入れた We *welcomed* the suggestion.

🔊「僕と踊ってくれませんか」「ええ, 喜んで」 "Will you dance with me?" "Yes, *with pleasure*. / *I'd be pleased* [*delighted, glad, happy*] *to*."

🔊「わあ, きれいなスカーフ. ありがとう」「どういたしまして. よかった, 喜んでもらえて(→気に入ってもらえて)」"Wow, what a beautiful scarf! Thank you." "You're welcome. I'm glad you *liked* it."

よろしい 宜しい

❶【適切である】(正しい) right; (申し分ない) all right; (大丈夫だ) (《口語的》) OK, O.K.; (望ましい) good ➾ よい (良い・好い・善い)

申込書の書き方はこれでよろしいでしょうか Is this the *right* way to fill in the application?

◆準備はよろしいでしょうか Are you ready [*prepared*]? / 6時間ならいつでもよろしいですよ Any time before six will be *fine*.

🔊「今夜電話くださいね」「ええ, 何時ごろがよろしいですか」"Please call me tonight." "Yes I will, but about what time is *good for you*?"

🔊「うどんとそばと, どちらがよろしいですか」「うどんにしてください」"Which would you *like*, *udon* or *soba*?" "*Udon*, please."

❷【よい】 good
田中君の答えはたいへんよろしい Tanaka's answer is very *good*.

❸【…してよい・さしつかえない】 can, may

語法
(1)許可を求める場合, 家族・親しい友人間などでは can を用いる. 丁寧な言い方としては could, may を使用する. ただしその返答のしかたには以下のような注意が必要.
(2)Can I …?に対し Yes, you can.のように答えるのは可能だが, Could I …?に対し Yes, you could.とは答えない. この場合 Yes, you can.となる // 「カメラをお借りしてもよろしいですか」「はい, どうぞ」"*Can* [*Could*] I borrow your camera?" "Yes, you can. [×Yes, you could.]"
(3) Yes, you may. や You may ….という表現は「自分が許可してやる」感じに聞こえるので用いる際には注意が必要 // 「カメラをお借りしてもよろしいですか」「はい, どうぞ」"*May* I borrow your camera?" "Sure. / Go ahead. / Certainly."(🔊ここで Yes, you may.と言うと「よろしい」といった感じになり, 失礼な言い方ととられる場合がある)
(4) 「いいえ」と答える場合には, No, you can't. / No you may not.も可能だが, I'm sorry [afraid] you can't.と答えるほうが丁寧でふつう.

君はもう(用はないから)行ってよろしい You *may* [*can*] go now.
◆よろしければこちらにお名前をお書きください I'd like you to write your name here, 「*if it would be all right* [*if you don't mind*]. / 言いたくなければ言わなくてよろしい If you don't want to say it, you *don't have to*.

🔊「ここに座ってもよろしいですか」「ええ, どうぞ」"*Do you mind* if I sit here?" "Certainly not. / No, not at all. / No, go ahead."(🔊問いの文を Would you mind if I sat here?とするとさらに丁寧な言い方になる. 「ご遠慮ください」は Well, I'd rather you didn't. / Would you please not?など. Yes, I do.はきっぱりと拒絶する場合の表現)

🔊「2, 3分お時間をよろしいでしょうか(→話をしてもいいですか)」「今忙しいので, ちょっと」"*Would it be all right* if I talked to you for a few minutes?" "Well, I'm afraid it wouldn't. I'm busy now."

❹【了解】 all right, OK, O.K.
コンピュータの動かし方が分からないって? よろしい. 私が教えてあげましょう You don't know how to start the computer? *All right* [*OK*], I'll teach you.

🔊「作業終了しました」「よろしい. ではこれから点検に行こう」"We've finished our task." "*Good*. I'm going there to check it."

よろしく 宜しく

❶【あいさつで】(🔊英語にはこれに対応する決まった表現がないので, 以下のようにその場その場に応じた表現を用いる必要がある)
はじめまして, 倉田明雄です. どうぞよろしく(→お会いできてうれしいです) How do you do? I'm Kurata Akio. *Glad* [*Nice*] *to meet you*.
不慣れなものでご迷惑をおかけするかもしれませんが, なにとぞよろしくお願いいたします(→みなさんのお力を借りて一生懸命やります) I'm not accustomed to this job, but with your help I'll do my best.
今後ともよろしくお願いします I look forward to your continued cooperation in the future.
明けましておめでとうございます. 今年もよろしくお願いします(→私たちみんなにとってよい年となるといいですね) (A) Happy New Year. I hope it's going to be a good one for all of us. (🔊I hope 以下はなくてもよい. 英米では年賀状ではなくクリスマスカードに新年のあいさつに相当する言葉を書くことが多いが, その場合は I wish you a Merry Christmas and a Happy New Year.などと書く)

❷【伝言を頼んで】
浩君によろしく *Please say hello to* Hiroshi. (🔊親しい間柄で用いられるくだけた言い方)
両親からもよろしくとのことです My parents *give you their best regards*.
(手紙で)お元気で, ご家族にもよろしく *Best wishes to* you and yours.
ご両親によろしくお伝えください Please 「*give my best* (*regards*) [*remember me*] *to* your

parents.

❸【人に物事を任せて】(✤英語にはこれに当たる表現がないので,「何を」「どう」したいのかなどはっきり表現する必要がある)

留守中,クロのことよろしくお願いします(→面倒を見てくれるように) I hope you will kindly *take care of* Kuro while I'm away.

私はもう寝ます.後のことはよろしく(→後は任せる) I'm going to bed now. I *leave the rest to you.*

僕が片づけをするから,料理は君,よろしく頼むよ(→料理をしてもらいたい) I'll clear away and do the dishes. And so I'*d like you to* cook, please.

それでは準備のほう,よろしくお願いします(→準備をしてください) *Would you please get ready now?*

(放送で)館内は禁煙となっております.ご協力のほどよろしくお願いいたします Smoking is prohibited in this building. *Thank you for your cooperation.*

❢「この作業は私が代わりにやっておきましょう」「どうかよろしくお願いします(→ありがとうございます)」"I'll do this work for you." "*Thank you very much.*"

よろめく stagger ⓐ, reel ⓐ; (つまずく) stumble ⓐ (✤「よろめきながら歩く」という意味もある) ∥彼のパンチで対戦相手はよろめいた The opponent *staggered* when punched by him. / (→彼のパンチがよろめかせた) His punch *staggered* the opponent. / 田川君はよろめきながら立ち上がった Tagawa *staggered to his feet.*

よろよろ その老人は通りをよろよろ歩いていた The old man *was* ⌈*walking unsteadily* [*staggering, reeling*]⌋ along the street.

よろん 世論・輿論 public opinion Ⓤ ∥世論の動向を探る take soundings of *public opinion* / 世論に訴える appeal to *public opinion* / 世論調査をする take [conduct] *a public opinion poll*(✤an opinion poll, a poll ともいう) / 世論の反対にもかかわらずその計画は実行された The project was carried out though *public opinion* was opposed to it. / その法案に関し世論は真っ二つに分かれた *The public opinion* was clearly divided concerning the bill.

◆景気の早期建て直しを求める世論が高まった *Public demands* for the quick restoration of the economy became louder. / 彼らは国際世論の流れに逆らうように核実験を行った They had a nuclear bomb test as if to go against the current of *international opinion.*

よわい 弱い

weak; feeble; delicate; faint; mild; light
──弱くする weaken ⓥ, make* ... weak(er) ──弱くなる weaken ⓥ, become* [get*] weak

> weak:「弱い」を表す最も一般的な語.
> feeble: 体力が衰えている状態や性格の弱さなどを表す語.
> delicate: 体がひ弱なことを表す語.
> faint: 光などかすかなことを表す語.
> mild: 飲み物などがまろやかで,苦(にが)みの少ないことを表す語.
> light: 程度が小さいことを表す語.

《弱い~》
弱いチーム a *weak* team / 弱い心 a *weak* [*feeble*] mind / 弱い風 a *light* [*gentle*] wind / 弱い光 a *faint* [*weak*] light / 体の弱い子供 a *delicate* child / 弱いビール *weak* [*mild*] beer

◆弱い地震 a *slight* [*light*] earthquake

《…が弱い》
私は意志が弱くてダイエットが続かない I have such ⌈*a weak will* [*weak* willpower]⌋ that I can't keep on a diet.

美由紀は理数系が弱い Miyuki is ⌈*weak in* [*poor at*]⌋ science and mathematics.

理恵は胃腸が弱い Rie has a *weak* stomach. / (→消化力が弱い) Rie has *poor* [*weak*] digestion.

心臓が弱い人はこの映画を見ないほうがいい Those who have *weak* hearts shouldn't watch this movie.

◆隆治は視力が弱い Ryuji *has poor* [*weak*] *sight.* / 彼はかぜに対する抵抗力が弱い He *has little resistance* to colds. / He's *vulnerable* to colds. / 昔は体が弱かった(→病気になりやすかった)が水泳のおかげで健康になった I used to *get sick easily*, but swimming has made me healthy. / 彼女は弱々しそうに見えるが実はとてもしんが強い She looks *timid*, but actually she's very strong-minded.

《…には(は)弱い》
◆彼は酒に弱い(→すぐに酔う) He *gets drunk easily.* / He *has a low tolerance for alcohol.* / 私はチョコレートの誘惑に弱い I *can't resist the temptation of chocolate.* / 男は女の涙に弱いというのが定説だ It's widely accepted that men *have a weakness for* women's tears. / 彼は北海道出身なので暑さに弱い He's *sensitive to* heat because he's from Hokkaido. / 父はいちばん下の妹には弱い My father *has a soft spot for* my youngest sister.(✤have a soft spot for ...は「…が大好きだ」の意味) / 歯のエナメル質は酸に弱い The enamel of teeth *is easily affected by* acid. / うちの家は古いので災害に弱いだろう I think my house is *vulnerable* to disasters because it is old.

《弱くなる・弱くする》
彼の足は年々弱くなっていくようだ His legs seem to *weaken* year by year.

うちの犬は歯が弱くなって硬い物は食べられない Our dog's teeth *have become weak*, so he can't eat anything hard.

彼女は病気ですっかり体を弱くしてしまった Illness *has* totally *weakened* her body.

◆ちょっと火を弱くしてちょうだい Will you *lower* [*turn down*] *the heat* a little bit?

よわいものいじめ 弱い者いじめ 弱い者いじめをするな Don't *bully the weak.* / Don't *play the bully.*

よわき 弱気 ——弱気な（弱腰の）《口語的》weak-kneed, spineless;（臆病な）timid;（悲観的な）pessimistic ∥そんな弱気じゃ勝てないぞ You can't win if you're as *weak-kneed* [*timid*] as you are now. / そう弱気になるなよ．きっと合格してるよ Don't be so *pessimistic*. I'm sure you have passed the exam.

よわごし 弱腰 ——弱腰の《口語的》weak-kneed;（臆病な）timid

よわさ 弱さ weakness ∥体の弱さ physical *weakness* [*frailty*] / 意志の弱さ *one's weakness* of determination

よわせる 酔わせる（魅了する）attract, fascinate ∥彼女のピアノは観客を酔わせた Her piano playing *attracted* [*fascinated*] the audience.
◆結婚披露宴で，おじたちは兄に酒を飲ませて酔わせた At the wedding reception, my uncles *got* [*made*] my brother *drunk*.

よわたり 世渡り 彼は世渡り上手だ（→処世術を心得ている）He *knows how to get along in the world*. / （→世知にたけている）He *is worldwise*.

よわね 弱音 彼は何をやってもすぐに弱音を吐く（→泣き言を言い始める）He is prone to *whine* about whatever he does. / 弱音を吐くな《会話》*Never say die!*

よわび 弱火 low flame;（低い熱）low heat ∥野菜を弱火で20分煮た I boiled the vegetables for 20 minutes over「*a low flame* [*low heat*].
◆ガスレンジを弱火にして *Lower the flame* [*heat*] of the gas stove.

よわまる 弱まる weaken;（徐々に）die down ∥雨足が弱まって霧雨になった The rain *weakened* to a drizzle. / その政治家の影響力は弱まった The politician's influence *has weakened*.

よわみ 弱み weakness, weak point ⇒じゃくてん ∥他人の弱みにつけ込む take advantage of another person's *weakness* / 私は直美の弱みを握っている I know Naomi's *weak point*. / I have *something* on Naomi.

よわむし 弱虫（意気地なし）coward,《俗語》chicken, wimp;（泣き虫）《口語的》crybaby

よわめる 弱める weaken;（下げる）lower;（火力などを）turn down ∥彼は学会への影響力を弱めた His influence on the learned society *was weakened*. / エアコンをもう少し弱めて *Turn down* the air conditioner a little bit.

よわよわしい 弱々しい（弱い）weak;（非常に弱い）feeble;（かすかな）faint;（弱く見える）weak-looking, feeble-looking ——弱々しく weakly; feebly; faintly ∥やせていて弱々しい男性 a thin and *weak-looking* [*feeble-looking*] man ∥ 彼は弱々しい声をしている His voice is *weak* [*feeble*]. / He speaks in a *weak* [*feeble*] voice.

よわりめ 弱り目 ことわざ 弱り目にたたり目 Misfortunes never come singly [alone].（→災難は単独では起こらない）; When it rains, it pours.（→降ればどしゃ降り）

よわる 弱る
❶【弱くなる】grow* weak, weaken ∥
彼はすっかり弱ってしまって歩くこともできない He *has grown* [*become*] too *weak* to walk.
病人は徐々に弱ってきている The patient *is* gradually「*growing weaker* [*weakening*].
❷【困る】
ああ，弱ったなあ（→どうしよう）．宿題をし忘れちゃったよ Oh, *what shall I do*? I forgot to do my homework.
事故で電車が止まってしまって本当に弱りましたよ I *was* really *troubled* when the train went out of service because of an accident.
急に意見を求められ弱ってしまった（→何と言うべきか分からなかった）I *didn't know what to say* when I was suddenly asked for an opinion.

よん 四 four;（4番目）fourth ∥4分の1 a fourth, a quarter

よんこままんが 四こま漫画 four-frame comic strip

よんじゅう 四十 forty;（40番目）fortieth

よんどころない よんどころない事情により for an *unavoidable* reason ⇒やむをえない

よんりん 四輪 ∥4輪駆動車 a four-wheel-drive (car)(《略語》4WD)

ら

ラ 〔音楽〕la [lɑ́ː] [U][C]

-ら （❖名詞・代名詞の複数形で表す）➔ -たち ‖子供ら[彼ら]はテレビゲームをしている *Children* [*They*] are playing with a video game. / 岡田氏ら一行は釣りに出かけた *Mr. Okada and his party* went fishing.

ラード （料理用の豚の脂肪）lard [U]

ラーメン ramen, Chinese noodles
‖インスタントラーメン instant ramen / カップラーメン《商標名》Cup Noodles, instant ramen (in a cup)

ラーユ 辣油 sesame oil with red peppers

らい- 来- （次の）next; （来たるべき）coming （❖名詞の前で用いる）‖来学期に in the *next* [*coming*] term / 私たちは来春卒業します We'll graduate *next* [*in the coming*] *spring*.

-らい -来 景子とは10年来の(→10年間ずっと)友達です I'*ve been* friends with Keiko *for* 10 years. / 東京は20年来の(→ここ20年で最大の)大雪に見舞われた Tokyo was struck by the heaviest snow 「*in* 20 years [*of the last* 20 years].

らいい 来意 私は管理人に来意を告げた I told the superintendent *the purpose of my visit*.

らいう 雷雨 thundershower [C]; （激しい）thunderstorm [C] ‖夜半には雷雨になるでしょう There'll be *a thunderstorm* around midnight.

らいうん 雷雲 thundercloud [C]

ライオン lion [C]; （雌）lioness [C]; （子）(lion) cub [C] ‖ライオンは百獣の王といわれている *The lion* is called the king of the beasts.

ライオンズクラブ Lions Club; （正式名）The International Association of Lions Clubs

らいきゃく 来客 （訪問客）visitor [C]; （招待客）guest [C]; （集合的に）company [U] （❖1人でも複数の場合でも用いる） ‖あすは来客がある I'm expecting [having] *guests* [*company*] tomorrow. / 申しわけありませんが，佐藤はただ今来客中です I'm sorry, but Sato *has a visitor* right now.

らいげつ 来月 next month
来月友達とカナダへスキーをしに行きます I'll go skiing in Canada with my friends *next month*.
この店は来月10日に開店する This shop will open on the 10th of *next month*.
‖来月号 next month's issue; (次号) the next issue

らいこう[1] 来校 来月教育委員会の人たちが来校の予定です The members of the board of education will *visit our school* next month.

らいこう[2] 来航 1853年のペリーの来航によって日本は外国に門戸を開いた *Perry's arrival* [*The Perry Expedition*] in 1853 made Japan open up its doors to other countries.

らいさん 礼賛 （賞賛）praise [U]; （崇拝）worship [U] ——礼賛する praise [他]; worship [他] ‖先人の業績を礼賛する *praise* the achievements of predecessors

らいしゃ 来社 月曜日の3時にご来社ください *Please come to my office* at three on Monday.

らいしゅう[1] **来週** next week
来週香港へ行くんだ I'm going to Hong Kong *next week*.
来週の木曜日に宿題を提出しなくてはいけない We have to turn in the assignment 「*next Thursday* [*on Thursday of next week*].
来週中に連絡をください Please call me *within* [*in*] *the next week*.
◆来週のきょう(→きょうから1週間後) *a week from* today

らいしゅう[2] 来襲 attack [C] ——来襲する attack [他] ‖敵の来襲 *an enemy attack*

らいしゅん 来春 next spring, the coming spring ‖その会社は来春50人採用する The company is going to employ 50 people *next* [*in the coming*] *spring*.

らいじょう 来場 車でのご来場はご遠慮ください Please refrain from *coming* by car. / ご来場の皆様にお知らせします Attention, please! / May I have your attention, please?
‖来場者(出席者) (an) attendance

ライス （ごはん）rice [U]

ライスカレー ➔ カレー

らいせ 来世 afterlife [C]《通例単数形》; （次の世）the world to come, the next world; （死後の世界）life after death

ライセンス license, 《英》licence [C][U]
➔ めんきょ

ライター[1] （作家）writer [C] ‖ゴーストライター a ghostwriter / コピーライター a copywriter / シナリオライター a scriptwriter, a scenario writer, a screenwriter / シンガーソングライター a singer-songwriter / フリーライター a freelance writer （❖ ×free writer とはいわない）

ライター[2] （たばこ用の）(cigarette) lighter [C] ‖ライターでたばこに火をつける light a cigarette with *a lighter*
‖ガスライター a gas lighter / 使い捨てライター a disposable lighter
[関連語] 石(ライターの) a flint

ライダー ⚠（オートバイの）motorcyclist [C] （❖英語の rider は単に「乗る人」の意味であり，乗る物はオートバイに限らない）

らいちょう 雷鳥 grouse [C] （複〜），ptarmigan [tɑ́ːrmigən] [C]

らいてん 来店 本日はご来店ありがとうございます Thank you for *coming to our store* today. / またのご来店をお待ちしております Please *come* again (*to our store*). / We are expecting you again.

ライト¹ (照明) light◎ /ちょっと, ライトがついて[消えて]いるよ Hey, *the lights* are on [off].
◆彼は車のヘッドライトをつけた[消した] He turned on [off] *the headlights* of the car.
‖サーチライト a searchlight / スポットライト a spotlight / フットライト footlights

ライト² (野球の右翼) right field ◎; (右翼手) right fielder ◎ /彼はライトを守っている He plays *right field*. / He's *a right fielder*. / そのルーキーはライトスタンドに大きなホームランを放った The rookie hit a big home run to *the right field stands*.

ライトアップ ——ライトアップする light* (up), (イルミネーションを施す) illuminate ⑩; (投光照明で照らす) floodlight* ⑩ (◆通例受身で) /その船は色とりどりの電球でライトアップされていた The boat *was* 「*lit up* [*illuminated*] by colorful bulbs.

ライトきゅう ライト級 lightweight class ◎ ◆ライト級の選手 *a lightweight*

ライトバン (荷物を積める大型乗用車)《米》station wagon ◎,《英》estate car ◎; (配達用の車)《米》delivery truck [《英》van] ◎ (◆「ライトバン」は和製英語)

ライトブルー (薄い青色) light blue ◎

ライトヘビーきゅう ライトヘビー級 light heavyweight class ◎
◆ライトヘビー級の選手 *a light heavyweight*

ライナー〔野球〕liner ◎, line drive ◎; (大洋航路の定期船) liner ◎ /彼は左中間へライナー性の当たりを放った He hit *a liner* [*line drive*] to left center.

らいにち 来日 キアヌ・リーブスが新作映画のプロモーションのため来日した Keanu Reeves 「*came to* [*visited*] *Japan* to promote his new film. / 大統領の来日は延期になった The president's *visit to Japan* was postponed. / その歌手は今チャリティーコンサートのため来日中です The singer *is* now *in Japan* for a charity concert.

らいねん 来年 next year
私たちは来年高校を卒業する We'll finish high school *next year*.
来年の目標は何ですか What is your goal for *next year*?
田中さんは来年の7月に結婚します Mr. Tanaka will get married 「*in July of next year* [*next July*]. (◆next July は現在が7月以降の場合に用いる)
来年の今ごろはドイツ語の勉強のためにドイツにいます I'll be in Germany to study German *about this time next year*.
来年早々引っ越します I'm moving *early next year*.
ことわざ 来年のことを言うと鬼が笑う There's no telling what will happen in the future. (→未来に何が起こるかは知る由(よし)もない)

らいはい 礼拝 worship ◎ ⇒れいはい

ライバル rival ◎, competitor ◎ (◆rival は個人的・感情的意味合いが強い) ——ライバルのrival / ライバル校[チーム] a *rival* school [team] / 彼女は私の最大のライバルだ She is my greatest *rival*. / 私たちはチーム内のいいライバルどうしだ We are 「*good competitors* [*a good match*] for each other on the team. ◆彼らは互いにライバル意識をもっている There's *rivalry* between them.
🅔「彼氏にするんだったら達郎がいいな」「たぶんライバルが多いわよ」"I would choose Tatsuro for my boyfriend." "I guess a lot of girls are after him."

らいひん 来賓 guest ◎, visitor ◎ ‖来賓室(応接室) a reception room / 来賓席 the guests' [visitors'] seats;《掲示》For Guests

ライフ (生命・生活) life ◎◎ (複 lives); (人の一生) life ‖ライフサイクル a life cycle / ライフジャケット a life jacket / ライフスタイル a lifestyle, *one's* way of living / ライフボート a lifeboat / ライフワーク *one's* life-work

ライブ ⚠(生演奏) live performance ◎,《口語的》gig ◎; (生中継・実況放送) live broadcast ◎ (◆英語の live は「生(なま)の」の意味) ——ライブの live /エアロスミスのライブ(コンサート)があすある Aerosmith are giving *a live concert* tomorrow.
‖ライブショー a live music show / ライブハウス a place with live music [performances] (◆「ライブハウス」は和製英語)

ライフル rifle ◎

らいほう 来訪 visit ◎ ——来訪する visit ⑩
◆あすのご来訪をお待ちしています *I'm expecting you* tomorrow.
‖来訪者 a visitor

ライむぎ ライ麦 rye ◎ ‖ライ麦粉 rye flour / ライ麦パン rye bread

らいめい 雷鳴 thunder ◎ (◆a clap [crack, roll] of thunderなどともいう) /激しい雷鳴で赤ちゃんが泣きだした The baby started to cry because of *a violent clap of thunder*. / はるか遠くの方で雷鳴がとどろいた *Thunder* roared [sounded, rumbled] far away.

ライラック〖植物〗(木) lilac ◎; (花) lilac ◎

ライン line ◎ /ボールはラインの上に落ちた The ball dropped *on the line*. ◆僕の成績は青山大の合格ライン(→合格点)に達していない My score hasn't reached *the passing score* [*standard*] of Aoyama University.
‖ラインダンス a chorus line dancing / ゴールライン(陸上競技の) the finishing line; (サッカーなどの) the goal line / スタートライン the starting line

ラインアップ (試合の) the lineup ‖コーチはあしたの試合のラインアップを発表した The coach announced *the lineup* for tomorrow's game.

ラインがわ ライン川 the Rhine [ráin] (◆スイスに発して北海に注ぐ川)

ラインズマン〖スポーツ〗linesman ◎

ラウンジ (ホテル・空港などの) lounge ◎
‖カクテルラウンジ a cocktail lounge

ラウンド (ボクシングなどの回) round ◎; (ゴル

ラオス

フの1試合) round ◯ //現チャンピオンは最終ラウンドでノックアウトされた The reigning champion was knocked out *in the final round.* / 我々はきのうゴルフを1ラウンドプレーした We played *a round* of golf yesterday.

ラオス Laos (❖公式名 Lao People's Democratic Republic) ――ラオス人 Laotian ◯ ――ラオス語 Laotian ◯ ――ラオス(人[語])の Laotian

ラガー ❶【ラグビー】rugby ◯ (❖英語の rugger は選手ではなくラグビーそのものを指す)⇒ラグビー
❷【ビール】lager (beer) ◯
‖ラガーマン a rugby [rugger] player

らがん 裸眼 the naked eye ――私の視力は両方とも裸眼で1.0です I have 20/20 *uncorrected vision* in both eyes. (❖uncorrected は「矯正されていない」の意味) ⇒しりょく(視力)

らく 楽

❶【安楽】(快適さ) comfort ◯; (気楽さ) ease ◯ ――楽な comfortable; easy ――楽に comfortably; at ease
早く仕事に就いて両親に楽をさせたい(→快適な生活を送らせたい) I want to get a job as soon as possible and *let my parents live a comfortable [an easy] life.*
どうぞ楽にしてください Please *make yourself comfortable [at home].*
仕事をしないで楽に暮らすことができたらいいのに I wish I could live *comfortably [at ease]* without working.
君の言葉で気が楽になったよ.ありがとう Your words *have set my mind at ease.* Thanks.
◆楽な(→カジュアルな)服装で in *casual clothes,* (→動きやすい) in clothes *easy to move in* / ソファーでしばらく横になれば楽になるよ If you lie (down) on the sofa for a while, you *will feel better.* / この薬で少しは頭痛が楽になるだろう This medicine *will give you some relief from* your headache. / 前より暮らしは楽になっている I *am better off* than before.
❷【容易】――楽な(たやすい) easy; (単純な) simple; (仕事などが) light ――楽に easily, with ease; (苦もなく) without (any) difficulty, without effort
楽な仕事を世話してもらえませんか Can't you find「an *easy* job [some *light* work] for me?
様々な電気家電製品のおかげで家事労働はぐっと楽になった Various electric home appliances have made housework much *easier.*
そこへ行くのにいちばん楽な行き方を教えてよ Tell me the *easiest* way to get there.
ホテルを経営するのは楽じゃない Managing a hotel *is not simple.*
この程度の問題なら楽に解ける I can *easily* solve the problems at this level. / The problems at this level are *easy* for me to solve.

5キロくらいなら楽に走れるよ I can run five kilometers *without effort.*
◆このソファーは3人楽に座れる This sofa *has enough room* for three people.

らくいん 烙印 brand ◯
◆彼は臆病(ホミッォッ)者の烙印を押された He *was branded (as)* a coward.

らくえん 楽園 paradise ◯ //地上の楽園 *an earthly paradise*; *a paradise* on earth

らくがき 落書き (なぐり書き) scribble ◯; (壁・公衆トイレなどの) graffiti 【複数扱い】 ――落書きする scribble ⑨ //落書き禁止(掲示) *No Scribbling*; *No Graffiti* / 今すぐ壁の落書きを消しなさい Rub off [Erase] that *graffiti* on the wall right now. / 教科書に落書きをしてはいけません You do not *scribble* on the textbooks. / You do not *make scribbles* on the textbooks.

らくご¹ 落語 🎭 *rakugo,* comic storytelling [monologue]
‖落語家 a *rakugoka,* a comic storyteller

> 落語は16世紀の終わりにその起源をもつ話芸です.2人以上で行う漫才と異なり,1人の落語家が客に笑い話を聞かせます.落語家は巧みに声を変え,また話に合わせて次々に表情を変えます.そして最後に落ちをつけて話を結びます.ふつう手ぬぐいと扇子(ポ)を持ちますが,その使い方もだいじな芸の一つです.
> *Rakugo* is a performing art of comic monologue that originated at the end of the 16th century. Unlike *manzai,* which is performed by two or more comedians, in *rakugo* only one *rakugoka* (storyteller) tells a humorous story through sophisticated facial expressions and dexterous use of his voice. He finishes the story with an *ochi* (punch line). Usually *rakugoka* use nothing but a hand towel and a fan on the stage, but their skillful way of using them is also an important part of performance.

らくご² 落伍 ――落伍する drop out; (隊列などから) straggle ⑨ ❖だつらく //30人の参加者がそのレースから落伍した Thirty entrants *dropped out of* the race.
‖落伍者 (社会からの) a dropout; (人生の) a loser; (隊列などからの) a straggler

らくさ 落差 (高度の差) a drop; (高さ) height ◯◯; (隔たり) gap ◯; (違い) difference ◯◯ //この滝はおよそ50メートルの落差がある This waterfall has *a drop* of about fifty meters. / 彼女は理想と現実の落差に悩んでいた She was worrying about *the gap* between the ideal and reality.

らくさつ 落札 successful bid ◯ ――落札する make* a successful bid
◆その絵画は有名な日本人デザイナーに300万円で落札された(→競り落とされた) The painting *was knocked down to* the famous Japanese designer for three million yen.
‖落札者 a successful bidder / 落札値(契約

値) a contract price; (最高の入札値) the highest bid price

らくじつ 落日 the setting sun

らくしょう 楽勝 easy victory [win]◎, 《口語的》walkover◎ ──**楽勝する** win* easily ∥あしたの試合は楽勝だ Tomorrow's game will be *an easy victory*. / We can *win* tomorrow's game *easily*.
◆数学のテストは楽勝だった The math test was *a breeze* [*piece of cake*].

らくせい 落成 (完成) completion◎ ∥先日新しい図書館の落成式が行われた *The completion ceremony* [*The inauguration*] of the new library was held the other day.
◆そのビルは先月落成した The building *was completed* last month.

らくせき 落石 落石注意 (掲示)*Watch for Falling Rock(s)* / その道は落石でふさがっていた The road was blocked by *the fallen rocks*. / その山で落石事故があり3人がけがをした There was *a rockslide* and three were injured on the mountain.

らくせん 落選 (選挙での) defeat◎◎; (出品作などの) rejection◎◎ ──**落選する** be defeated; be rejected ∥彼はこの前の選挙で落選した He *was defeated* in the last election. / He *was not elected* in the last election. / He *lost* the last election. / 残念ながら彼女の絵はコンテストで落選した Unfortunately, her painting *was rejected* in the contest.
∥落選者 a defeated [an unsuccessful] candidate

らくだ 駱駝 camel◎ ∥ラクダのこぶ *a camel's* hump
∥ヒトコブラクダ an Arabian camel, a dromedary / フタコブラクダ a Bactrian camel

らくだい 落第 ──**落第する** (試験に落ちる) fail◎◎, 《主に米・口語的》flunk◎◎ ∥彼は化学の試験に落第した He *failed* [*flunked*] the chemistry test. / 教授はテストで彼女に落第点をつけた(→彼女を落第させた) The professor *failed* her in the exam.
◆一生懸命勉強しないと落第するぞ(→留年することになる) If you don't study hard, you'*ll have to repeat the same grade*. / 英語で落第点を取ってしまった I got *a failing grade* [*mark*] in English. / 彼は研究者としてはすぐれているが教育者としては落第だ He is an excellent researcher but *a failure* as an educator. / そんな態度では社会人として落第ですよ If you behave like that, you *aren't qualified* to be a working adult.
∥落第生(再履修生) 《米》a repeater

らくたん 落胆 ──**落胆する** (やる気をなくす) be discouraged; (気落ちする) be depressed; (がっかりする) be disappointed ∥わが校のチームが負けたという知らせにみな落胆した We all *were discouraged* [*depressed*, *disappointed*] at the news that our school's team had lost the game.

らくちゃく 落着 これで一件落着だ Now the affair *is settled and done with*.

らくちょう 落丁 missing page◎ ∥この本は何ページか落丁がある There are some *missing pages* in this book. / 落丁・乱丁はお取り替えします We will exchange [replace] a book that has *missing pages* and/or is incorrectly [imperfectly] collated.

らくてん 楽天 ──**楽天的な** optimistic ──**楽天的に** optimistically ⇨らっかん ∥彼は楽天的な性格だ He has an *optimistic* character. / He is *optimistic*.
∥楽天家 an optimist / 楽天主義 optimism

らくに 楽に easily ⇨らく

らくのう 酪農 (酪農業) dairy [déəri] farming◎ ∥酪農家 a dairy farmer / 酪農場 a dairy farm / 酪農製品 dairy products

らくば 落馬 彼はもう少しで落馬するところだった He almost *fell off the horse*.

らくばん 落盤 cave-in◎ ∥そのトンネルで落盤事故があった There was *a cave-in* in the tunnel.

ラグビー rugby◎, rugby football◎, 《英口語的》rugger◎ ∥ラグビーをする play *rugby* / 今度の日曜日にラグビーの試合がある We'll have *a rugby match* next Sunday.
∥ラグビー場 a rugby field [pitch] / ラグビー選手 a rugby player / ラグビーボール a rugby ball
短歌 ラグビーの頬(ほ)傷は野で癒(い)ゆるべし自由をすでに怖(お)じぬわれらに (寺山修司)
I should let that scratch
on my face from the rugby
just heal as we play.
We're free now, and we don't fear
our freedom any longer.

らくよう 落葉 (葉が落ちること) the fall of leaves; (落ちた葉) fallen leaves
◆これらの木々は秋には落葉する These trees *shed* [*lose*] *their leaves* in fall.
∥落葉樹 a deciduous tree

らくらい 落雷 thunderbolt ◆そのサッカーの試合中何人かの選手が落雷にあった Some players *were struck by a lightning* during the soccer game.

らくらく 楽々 ──**楽々と** (容易に) easily; (心地よく) comfortably ∥彼はその重い荷物を楽々と持ち上げた He lifted the heavy baggage *easily*. / その生徒は問題を楽々と解いた The student solved the problem *easily*. / もしこれだけのお金があれば残りの人生楽々暮らせるだろう If we have this much money, we can live *comfortably* the rest of our lives.
◆これだけ大きなかばんなら着替えや洗面道具なども 楽々入る A large bag like this has *enough* room for a change of clothes and toilet articles and other things.
⇨らく

ラグラン ∥ラグランそで raglan sleeves

ラケット (テニス・バドミントンなどの) racket◎; (卓球の) bat◎, 《米》paddle◎ ∥テニスのラケット *a tennis racket*

ラジアルタイヤ radial tire [《英》tyre]◎

-らしい
❶ 【…のようである】 seem ◎; look (like …); appear ◎; say* ◎; I [we] hear*

ラジウム

語法
推量を表す「…らしい」に当たる最も一般的な表現は，seem「…のように思われる」，look (like ...), appear「…のように見える」である．say はふつう The weather forecast says ...「天気予報によると…」のような用い方をする．不特定の they を用いて，They say ... という形でいうこともできるが，この場合は，情報源をあいまいにした言い方になり，I hear ... と同じように「うわさでは…だそうだ」という意味を表す．

彼はまじめな人らしい He *seems* [*appears*] (*to be*) a serious man. / *It seems* [*appears*] *that* he's a serious man.

彼女は豊のことを知らなかったらしい She didn't *seem* [*appear*] *to* know Yutaka. / She *seemed* [*appeared*] not to know Yutaka.

圭子は浩が好きらしいが彼は彼女に興味がない Keiko *appears to* like Hiroshi, but he doesn't have any interest in her.

天気予報によるときょうの午後は雨らしい The weather forecast *says* it will rain this afternoon.

今度の数学の先生はかなり厳しい人らしい *They say* [*I hear, It is said*] (*that*) our next math teacher is a very strict person. / Our next math teacher is *said to be* a very strict person.

学校からの帰り道，刑事らしい人が話しかけてきた A man who *looked like* a detective spoke to me on my way home from school.

◆僕が間違っていたらしい（→たぶん僕が間違っていた） *Maybe* I was wrong.

💬「彼らは離婚するらしいよ」「まさか．うそでしょう」"*I hear* (*that*) they are getting divorced." "No! That can't be true!"

💬「新聞に何て書いてある」「強い台風が来るらしいよ」"What does the paper say?" "*It says that* a strong typhoon is coming."

❷[…にふさわしい]（特徴を示している）be like ...; （値する）be worthy of ...

そんなに簡単に夢をあきらめるなんて君らしくない It *is* 「*not like* [*unlike*]」 you to give up your dream so easily.

慈善事業に寄付するなんていかにも彼女らしいね It is just *like* her to make a contribution to charity.

最近は学生らしい（→その名に値する）学生が少ない There *are* few students *worthy of the name* lately.

◆自分らしく（→自分流に）生きる live my life *in my own way*; （→周りに振り回されずに行動する）behave *without being influenced too much by others* / 彼女がそんな女らしい服を着るのは珍しい It is unusual for her to wear such *feminine* [*womanly*] clothes. / 彼は本当にハンサムで男らしい人だった He was really good-looking and *manly*. / 一見，彼はミュージシャンらしくない At a glance he *doesn't appear* (*to be*) a musician.

ラジウム 〖化学〗radium ⓤ（❖元素記号 Ra）
∥ラジウム温泉 a radium hot spring

ラジエーター radiator ⓒ

ラジオ （放送）the radio [réidiou]; （受信機）radio (set) ⓒ
《ラジオを・に》
ラジオをつけて[消して]くれませんか Would you turn on [off] *the radio*?
一晩中ラジオを聞いていた I was listening to *the radio* all night.
彼はラジオをつけたまま本を読んでいた He was reading a book with *the radio* on.
彼女は J-WAVE にラジオを合わせた She tuned *the radio* to J-WAVE.
君の好きなアーティストが今ラジオに出ているよ Your favorite artist is *on the radio* now.
《ラジオの》
ラジオの音を小さく[大きく]してください Please turn down [up] *the radio*.
《ラジオで》
そのニュースはラジオで聞きました I heard the news *on* [*over*] *the radio*.
美香のリクエストはがきがラジオで読まれた Mika's (letter of) request was read *on the radio*.
《その他》
ラジオ英語講座 a *radio* English program [course]
一晩中ラジオがつけっぱなしだったよ *The radio* was on all night.
ここはラジオがよく入らない *Radio reception* is not good here.
私のラジオではすべての局が聞ける I can get [pick up] every station on my *radio*.
∥ラジオ体操 radio calisthenics / ラジオドラマ a radio drama / ラジオ番組 a radio program [show] / ラジオ放送 radio broadcasting / ラジオ放送局 a radio station / トランジスターラジオ a transistor radio

ラジカセ ⚠ radio cassette recorder ⓒ, a cassette recorder with a radio

ラジカル ラジカルな思想 *radical* ideas

ラジコン ⚠ （無線操縦）radio control ⓤ ∥ラジコンカー a radio-controlled model car

らしんばん 羅針盤 compass ⓒ

ラスト the last ◆これでラストだ（→これが最後の1つだ）This is *the last one*. / その映画のラストシーンはとても感動的だった *The last scene* of the film was really moving. / その走者はラストスパートをかけた The runner 「*put on* [*made*] *a last spurt*. / レポートを仕上げるのにラストスパートをかけた I made *the last push* to finish my paper.

ラスベガス Las Vegas（❖米国の都市）

ラズベリー raspberry ⓒ

らせん 螺旋 spiral ⓒ ——らせん（状）の spiral ∥らせん階段 a spiral staircase

らたい 裸体 naked body ⓒ; （絵画・写真などの）nude (body) ⓒ ——裸体の nude ∥裸体画 a nude (picture)

らち 埒 このまま言い争うばかりではらちがあかない（→どうにもならない）If we keep arguing with each other, we 「*will get nowhere*

[*won't get anywhere*].
らち² 拉致 abduction ⓊⒸ, kidnapping Ⓤ ――拉致する abduct 他, kidnap 他 / その男の子は学校からの帰り道何者かに拉致された The boy *was abducted* on his way home from school by somebody.
らっか 落下 drop Ⓒ, fall Ⓒ ――落下する fall* 自 ⇒ おちる
ラッカー lacquer Ⓤ / 食器棚にラッカーを塗った I *coated* the cabinet *with lacquer*./ I *lacquered* the cabinet.
らっかさん 落下傘 parachute Ⓒ
らっかせい peanut Ⓒ
らっかん 楽観 ――楽観的な optimistic (↔pessimistic) / この試合はまだ楽観を許さない We *can't be optimistic about* this game yet. / This game still *doesn't allow for much optimism*. / 真由美はいつでも物事に対して楽観的だ Mayumi *is* always *optimistic about* things. / Mayumi always *takes an optimistic view of* things.
‖楽観主義 optimism / 楽観主義者 an optimist
ラッキー 約束なしで彼に会えてラッキーだった I was *lucky* to see him without an appointment.
‖ラッキーセブン (野球の)the seventh inning (❖単に「7回」の意味で×lucky seven, ×the lucky seventh のようにはいわない)
らっきょう shallot Ⓒ; (漬物の) pickled shallot Ⓒ
ラック rack Ⓒ ‖マガジンラック a magazine rack
ラッコ sea otter Ⓒ
ラッシュ ラッシュアワーの電車に乗るのは避けたい I want to avoid taking a train at [during] *rush hour*. / この駅の通勤ラッシュのピークは朝 8 時 30 分ごろです *The morning rush of commuters* at this station reaches its peak at about eight thirty.
‖ゴールドラッシュ a gold rush
ラッセルしゃ ラッセル車 snowplow, (英)snowplough Ⓒ (❖日本語は英国の発明者 Russell から)
らっぱ (軍隊の) bugle Ⓒ; (トランペット) trumpet Ⓒ / ラッパを吹く blow [sound, play] *a trumpet*
◆彼はジュースをラッパ飲みした(→びんから直接飲んだ) He *drank* juice *straight from the bottle*.
ラッピング これをプレゼント用にラッピングしてほしいんですが I'd like this *wrapped* as a present.
ラップ¹ ⚠(食品包装用) plastic wrap Ⓤ, (主に英)clingfilm Ⓤ / 冷蔵庫に入れる前にラップをしなさい Be sure to「*cover* it *in plastic wrap* [*wrap* it *in plastic*] before you put it in the fridge.
ラップ² (競技用トラックの 1 周) lap Ⓒ
‖ラップタイム (a) lap time
ラップ³ 〖音楽〗rap (music) Ⓤ
‖ラップ歌手 a rapper
らつわん 辣腕 ――辣腕な sharp; (そつがない)

shrewd ‖辣腕家 a shrewd person
◆彼は劇場の経営に辣腕をふるった He *managed* the theater *with great ability*.
ラテン ――ラテンの Latin
‖ラテンアメリカ Latin America / ラテン音楽 Latin music / ラテン語 Latin / ラテン民族 the Latin peoples
らば 騾馬 〖動物〗mule Ⓒ
ラバー (ゴム) rubber Ⓤ ‖ラバーソール(ゴム底の靴) rubber-soled shoes
ラフ (ゴルフの) the rough ――ラフな (大まかな) rough; (カジュアルな) casual / パーティーにはラフな服装で来てください Please come to the party in *casual* [*informal*] clothes. (❖×rough clothes とはいわない) / 家のラフスケッチをした I made [drew] *a rough sketch* of my house.
‖ラフプレー a rough play
らふ 裸婦 nude woman Ⓒ, a woman in the nude
ラブ (愛情・恋愛) love Ⓤ; 〖テニス〗(無得点) love Ⓤ / フォーティーラブでセレシがリード Seles leads forty *love*. / 浩と奈穂はラブラブだ(→お互い深く愛し合っている) Hiroshi and Naho *are madly in love with each other*.
‖ラブゲーム a love game (❖一方が無得点で終わったゲーム) / ラブシーン a love scene / ラブソング a love song / ラブホテル a hotel for lovemaking / ラブレター a love letter / プラトニックラブ platonic love
ラベル label Ⓒ / 私はその箱に「取扱い注意」のラベルをはった I *put* [*placed*] *a* "Fragile" *label* on the box. / I *labeled* the box "Fragile."
ラベンダー 〖植物〗lavender [lǽvəndər] ⓊⒸ; (色) lavender Ⓤ
ラマーズほう ラマーズ法 the Lamaze method
ラマきょう ラマ教 Lamaism Ⓤ
‖ラマ教徒 a Lamaist
ラム (子羊の肉) lamb Ⓤ
ラムしゅ ラム酒 rum ⓒⓊ
ラムネ ⚠a bottled soda pop (with a marble in the neck)(❖「ラムネ」は「レモネード」の転であるが英語の lemonade とはやや異なる)
ラリー (テニスなどの) rally Ⓒ; (自動車の) rally Ⓒ / 長いラリーの末, 彼女が得点した After *a long rally*, she got a point.
られつ 羅列 (列挙) enumeration ⓊⒸ ――羅列する《公式的》enumerate 他 / 実験結果をただ羅列するのでなく, それをまとめて自分の見解を示しなさい Don't just *enumerate* the results of the experiments. Show your interpretation of them as well.
◆彼の話は抽象的すぎて私には単なる言葉の羅列にすぎない What he says is so abstract that it's just *a collection of words* to me.
-られる ⇒ れる
ラワン (木) lauan Ⓒ; (木材) lauan Ⓤ
らん¹ 欄 (新聞・雑誌などの) column Ⓒ, section Ⓒ; (広告のための) column Ⓒ / 新聞のスポーツ欄 *the sports section* [*page*, *column*] of a newspaper / 指定された欄に名前, 住所, 電

話番号を記入してください Please write your name, address and phone number in *the allotted space*.

∥解答欄 an answer column / 家庭欄 a family page / 広告欄 an advertising column / テレビ欄 the TV listing / 投書欄 a letters-to-the-editor column

らん[2] 蘭 orchid ⓒ

らんおう 卵黄 yolk ⓒ ⓤ, the yellow (of an egg)

らんがい 欄外 margin ⓒ ——欄外の marginal(✦名詞の前で用いる)∥欄外にメモを書き留めた I took notes *in the margin*. / 先を読む前に132ページの欄外の注を参照してください Please see the *marginal* notes on page 132 before you read ahead.

らんかいはつ 乱開発 この国では天然資源の乱開発(→見境のない営利目的の開発)が進んでいる In this country, *the indiscriminate exploitation* of natural resources is in progress.

らんかく 乱獲 indiscriminate [excessive] hunting [fishing] ⓤ (✦fishing は漁の場合) ——乱獲する hunt [fish] indiscriminately [excessively] ∥我々は野生動物の乱獲を防ぐ必要がある We need to prevent the wild animals from *being hunted indiscriminately* [*excessively*].

ランカスター Lancaster(✦英国の都市)

らんかん 欄干 (橋・ベランダなどの) parapet ⓒ; (階段などの) (hand)rail ⓒ, balustrade ⓒ ∥彼女は橋の欄干から下を流れる川をのぞき込んだ She looked down at the river below from over *the parapet* of the bridge.

らんきりゅう 乱気流 turbulence ⓒ ∥その飛行機は乱気流に巻き込まれて乗客に負傷者が出た Some passengers were injured when the plane was caught in *turbulence*.

ランキング ranking ⓒ ∥世界ランキング第1位の座を得る gain first place in *the world rankings*

ランク rank ⓒ ⓤ ——ランクする rank ⓣ ⓘ ∥学校を偏差値でランクづけする *rank* schools according to the percentile scores of their students / 現在あのボクシングの選手は世界ランキング第1位にランクされている That boxer *is* currently *ranked* first in the world.

◆この曲は先週から3ランクアップしてチャートのトップテン入りを果たした The song has gone up three *notches* since last week and entered the top 10 on the charts.

らんざつ 乱雑 (混乱) disorder ⓤ; (散らかった状態) clutter ⓤ, mess ⓤ (また a ~) ——乱雑な disorderly; messy, untidy ∥乱雑に in disorder, in confusion ∥その机の上はいつも乱雑になっている The top of the desk is always in *disorder* [*a mess*].

◆床にはたくさんの雑誌が乱雑に置かれていた There were a lot of magazines lying *scattered* on the floor.

らんし[1] 乱視 〖医学〗astigmatism ⓤ ——乱視の astigmatic ∥私は両目とも乱視です I have *astigmatism* in both (my) eyes.

らんし[2] 卵子 〖生物〗ovum [óuvəm] ⓒ (複 ova), 〖生物〗egg ⓒ

ランジェリー (女性用下着) lingerie ⓤ (✦フランス語から)

らんしゃ 乱射 random [wild] shots ——乱射する shoot* wildly ∥その強盗は銃を乱射して逃げた The burglar *shot wildly* and ran away.

◆アメリカの小学校で銃乱射事件が起きた There was *an indiscriminate shooting* in an elementary school in America.

らんじゅく 爛熟 ゴシック建築の爛熟期 *the mature stage* of Gothic architecture

らんせい[1] 乱世 (動乱の時代) turbulent times; (内乱期) a period of civil strife

らんせい[2] 卵生の 〖生物〗oviparous ∥卵生動物 an oviparous animals

らんせん 乱戦 (混乱した戦い) confused fight ⓒ ∥その野球の試合は大乱戦だった That baseball game was *a slugfest* [*barnburner*].

らんそう 卵巣 〖解剖〗ovary ⓒ ——卵巣の 〖解剖〗ovarian

∥卵巣ホルモン ovarian hormones

らんぞう 乱造・濫造 (過剰生産) overproduction ⓤ ——乱造する (粗悪な物を) churn out; overproduce ⓣ ⓘ ∥その工場は粗悪な商品を乱造している The factory 「*churns out* [*overproduces*] goods of poor quality. / The factory *produces* poor quality goods *excessively*.

∥粗製乱造 excessive production of poor quality goods

らんだ 乱打 ∥乱打戦 〖野球〗a slugfest

ランダム ——ランダムの (無作為の) random ——ランダムに at random ∥挑戦者をランダムに選びます We're going to select the challenger 「*at random* [*randomly*].

∥ランダムアクセス 〖コンピュータ〗random access / ランダムサンプリング random sampling

ランタン (手さげランプ) lantern ⓒ

ランチ (昼食) lunch; (日本の食堂の昼の定食) a set lunch ∥ランチは何を食べたの What did you have for *lunch*?

∥ランチタイム lunchtime / お子様ランチ a special lunch [dish] for children

らんちきさわぎ 乱痴気騒ぎ (大騒ぎ) 《口語的》racket ⓤ (また a ~); (酒盛り) (drinking) spree ⓒ ∥乱痴気騒ぎをする make *a racket*; have *a* (*drinking*) *spree*

らんちょう 乱丁 incorrect [imperfect] collating ⓤ ◆落丁・乱丁はお取り替えします We will exchange [replace] a book that has missing pages and/or *is incorrectly* [*imperfectly*] *collated*.

ランデブー rendezvous [rάndeivù:] ⓒ (複 ~ [rάndeivù:z]) (✦フランス語から) ——ランデブーする (人が) make* a rendezvous; (宇宙船が) have* a rendezvous ⇒ デート

らんとう 乱闘 confused fight ⓒ, free-for-all ⓒ; (取っ組み合い) scuffle ⓒ

◆もう少しで彼のチームと乱闘になるところだった

We almost *scuffled with* the his team.
‖場外乱闘 a free-for-all outside the ring

らんどく 乱読 (むさぼり読むこと) omnivorous reading ▢ ──乱読する (手当たり次第に読む) read* at random
‖乱読家 an omnivorous reader

ランドセル ⚠ school backpack ▢, schoolbag ▢ (❖日本語はオランダ語の ransel から. また英米には英語でいうランドセルはなく,各自好みのかばんを使用する)

ランドリー laundry ▢

ランナー (野球・陸上競技の) runner ▢
⇨ そうしゃ(走者) ‖ 短距離ランナー a sprinter / 長距離ランナー a long-distance runner

らんにゅう 乱入 《公式的》irruption ▢
◆きのうその宝石店に金属バットを持った男が乱入した A man with a metal bat *burst* [*broke*] *into* the jeweler's shop.

ランニング running ▢; (ゆっくり走ること) jogging ▢ ──ランニングする run* ⊜; jog ⊜ ‖ランニングシャツ(肌着)《米》a sleeveless undershirt, 《英》a vest; (競技用) an athletic shirt (❖「ランニングシャツ」は和製英語) ‖ランニングシューズ running shoes / ランニングホームラン an inside-the-park home run (❖「ランニングホームラン」は和製英語)

らんぱく 卵白 albumen ▢, the white (of an egg)

らんばつ 乱伐 indiscriminate deforestation ▢ ──乱伐する deforest indiscriminately ‖熱帯雨林の乱伐は地球温暖化の大きな原因の一つである *Indiscriminate deforestation* of the tropical rain forests is one of the major causes of the greenhouse effect.

らんぱつ 乱発 (債券・紙幣などの) overissue ▢ ──乱発する overissue ⊜, issue excessively [recklessly]

らんはんしゃ 乱反射 diffused reflection ▢ ──乱反射する reflect diffusely [irregularly]

らんぴ 乱費 (むだづかい) waste ▢《また a 〜》; (ぜいたくな) extravagance ▢ ──乱費する waste ⊜ ⇨ ろうひ

らんぴつ 乱筆 (なぐり書き) hasty writing ▢, scribble ▢《また a 〜》, scrawl ▢▢
◆乱筆乱文にて失礼します (=雑な書き方をお許しください) Please excuse *my poor writing*.

らんぶ 乱舞 選手たちは勝利を狂喜乱舞した All the players *danced* [*jumped*] *for joy* at the victory.

ランプ¹ (明かり) lamp ▢ ‖ランプをつける[消す] light [put out] *a lamp* / ランプのほや[芯(しん)] a *lamp* chimney [wick]
◆ランプのかさ *a lampshade*
‖アルコールランプ a spirit lamp / 石油ランプ an oil lamp

ランプ² (高速道路の) 《米》ramp ▢, 《英》slip road ▢

らんぼう 乱暴 (暴力) violence ▢ ──乱暴な (暴力的な) violent; (向こう見ずな) reckless; (荒っぽい) rough; (不合理な) unreasonable; (手に負えない) wild ──乱暴に violently; recklessly; roughly; wildly
彼は弟に乱暴を働いた He *did* violence *to* his little brother. / He *treated* his little brother *violently*.
多くの場合事故は乱暴な運転が原因で起こる Many accidents are caused by *reckless* [(→不注意な)*careless*] driving.
君の理屈はずいぶん乱暴なんじゃないか What you say is quite *unreasonable*, isn't it?
これらの楽器を乱暴に扱ってはいけません Don't handle these musical instruments *roughly*.
彼はいつも乱暴な言葉づかいをする He always *speaks roughly*. / He always *uses bad language*.
◆女性に乱暴する (*sexually*) *assault* a woman / そのメモは乱暴な(→ひどい)字で書かれたので全く読めなかった The note was written in *bad* handwriting which I couldn't read at all. / 彼女はドアを乱暴に閉めて(→ばたんと閉めて)出ていった She went out, *slamming* the door behind her.
‖乱暴者 a wild man, 《軽蔑的》a rowdy

らんま 欄間 (ドアや窓の上の明かり取り窓)《米》transom ▢,《英》fanlight ▢

らんまん 爛漫 その公園は桜が咲き乱れてまさに春爛漫といった感じだった Cherry blossoms were blooming in the park, and it looked just as if *spring was in full swing*.

らんみゃく disorder ▢▢; (混乱) confusion ▢; (無秩序) chaos [kéiɑs] ▢ ──乱脈な disorderly; (雑な) careless ‖国の予算の使い方は乱脈を極めている (→大混乱に陥っている) The way of using the national budget *is in complete disorder* [*chaos*]. / その会社は乱脈経営が原因で破綻(はたん)した The company failed because of *their disorderly* [*careless*] *management*.

らんよう 乱用 abuse [əbjúːs] ▢ ▢; (誤用・悪用) misuse ▢▢; (使いすぎ) overuse ▢ ──乱用する abuse [əbjúːz] ⊜; misuse ⊜; overuse ⊜ ‖薬物の乱用 drug *abuse* [《英》*misuse*] / その警察官は職権の乱用で逮捕された The police officer was arrested for *abusing* [*misusing*] his official authority.

らんらん 爛々 茂みの中にヒョウの目がらんらんと光っていた Leopard's eyes *were shining* [*glaring*] in the bush. / コーヒーのせいで目がらんらんとさえて寝つけなかった Coffee kept me *wide awake*, and I couldn't get to sleep.

らんりつ 乱立 新宿にはオフィスビルが乱立している (→やたらにある) *There're too many* office buildings in Shinjuku. / 県議会議員選挙には候補者が乱立している *There is* a horde of candidates *running* for the prefectural assembly.

り

り²　利（有利）advantage ©; (利益) profit ©, gain ©©; (利子) interest © ∥私たちはホームグラウンドという地の利があったにもかかわらず試合に負けた Though we had *the* home field *advantage*, we lost the game. / 彼は実に利にさとい He really *has a quick eye for* 「*a profit* [*gain*].

り²　理（道理）reason © ◆彼女の意見は理にかなっている Her opinion *is reasonable*. / そのことで君のお父さんが怒るのは理の当然だ *It is natural* 「*that* your father gets angry [*for* your father *to* get angry] about it.

リアクション（反応）reaction ©©
◆彼女はそれに対してリアクションが速かった She *reacted* promptly to it.

リアリスト（現実主義者）realist ©
リアリズム（現実主義）realism ©
リアル ――**リアルな**（真に迫った）real; (写実的な) realistic ∥彼女の話は私には実にリアルだった Her story sounded quite *real* to me. / ラジオは開票速報をリアルタイムで伝えた The radio broadcast the election returns *in real time*.
◆その映画は殺人シーンのリアルな描写で話題になっている The *graphic* portrayal of the murder scene in the movie has been much talked about. / 父はアポロ11号の月面着陸をリアルタイムで(→生で)見ていたそうだ I heard that my father watched the lunar landing of Apollo 11 *live*.

リーグ league © ∥リーグ戦(リーグ内の個々の試合) a league game [match]; (リーグ内の全試合) the league series / セントラルリーグ the Central League / パシフィックリーグ the Pacific League / マイナーリーグ(米国の) the minor leagues / メジャーリーグ(米国の) the major leagues

リース¹（賃貸借契約）lease © ――**リースする** lease ® (◆「借りる」の意味もある) ∥その会社は彼らにこのビルをリースしている The company *leases* this building to them. / 機械はすべてその会社からのリースだ We *lease* all our machines from the company.
∥リース会社 a leasing company / リース業 leasing services

リース²（花輪）wreath [ríːθ] ©

リーダー¹（指導者）leader © ∥有史はわがチームのリーダーだ Yuji is *the leader* of our team. ◆キャンプの間中, 彼女はすぐれたリーダーシップを発揮した She exercised excellent *leadership* during the camp.

リーダー²（読本）reader © ∥英語のリーダー an English *reader*

リーディングヒッター〔野球〕the leading hitter

リード ❶【先導すること】lead ©《通例単数形》――**リードする** lead* ® ∥彼女がリードしてくれたおかげで何とか踊れた Thanks to her *lead*, I managed to dance. / 彼はラグビー部員をとてもうまくリードしている He *leads* the members of the rugby team very well.
◆その会社は電化製品において常に時代をリードしている The company *is always ahead of the times* in electrical appliances.

❷【優勢であること】(先頭) the lead; (リードしている差) a lead ――**リードする**(スポーツで) lead* ®; (先頭に立っている) be ahead ∥我々はついにリードを奪われた[奪った] We finally lost [gained] *the lead*. / 彼は第2位の走者を大きく[わずかに]リードしている He *has a* big [narrow] *lead over* the second runner. / うちのチームが5点リードしている Our team *is leading* our opponent by five points. / Our team *has a lead* of five points *over* our opponent.
🅔「今, 試合, どうなってる」「8回終わってうちがリードしてるよ」"How's the game going now?" "The eighth inning is over, and we *are in the lead*."
∥リードボーカル the lead vocal

リール reel ©

りえき　利益
❶【もうけ】 profit ©©, gain ©©《しばしば複数形 ~s》
彼はその取り引きで約500万円の利益をあげた He made [earned] *a profit* of about five million yen on [from] the deal.
彼女は株で莫大(ばくだい)な利益を得た She made *a* large *profit* on the stock market.
私たちは利益を公平に分配した We allotted [shared] *the profits* fairly.
その商売は短期間に相当な利益を生み出した That business returned [yielded] *a* handsome *profit* in a short time.
支出を切り詰めることができれば利益率が上がるだろう If we can cut expenses, *our profit margin* will be greater.
◆利益になる商売 a *profitable* business

❷【役に立つこと】(得) interest ©《通例複数形 ~s》; (恩恵) benefit ©©; (利点) advantage ©, good ©
私たちは公共の利益のために何かするべきだ We should do something for *the* public *benefit* [*interest, good*].
そんなことが何の利益になるんだ What *good* [*use*] is it? / What is *the good* [*use*] of it?
自分の利益のためだけに友人を利用するな Don't use your friends just for your own *benefit*.
彼女は目先の利益にとらわれている She's been thinking about *her* immediate *interests* only.
留学は君の利益になると思う It will be 「*to your advantage* [*good* for you]) to go abroad to study.
∥利益団体 an interest group / 純利益 net

profit / 総利益 gross profit / 不正利益 ill-gotten gains

りえん ⇨りこん

りか 理科 (教科) science ⓤ; (自然科学) natural sciences; (大学での部門) science course ⓒ ‖理科の先生 a *science* teacher / 大学は理科系に進みたいと思っています I'm thinking of majoring in *science* in college.
‖理科室 a *science* room

りかい 理解

(理解力) understanding ⓤ (また an 〜), 《公式的》comprehension ⓤ; (正しい認識・評価) appreciation ⓒⓤ ──**理解する** understand* ⓣⓘ, 《公式的》comprehend ⓣⓘ; appreciate ⓣ
▸この理論は私の理解の範囲を超えている This theory is beyond the reach of my *understanding* [*comprehension*].
▸彼女が言っていることが理解できますか Do you *understand* her [what she says]?
▸山本先生の説明は理解しやすい[しにくい] Mr. Yamamoto's explanation *is easy* [*difficult*] *to understand*.
▸彼女は物事の理解が速い[遅い] She *is quick* [*slow*] *to understand* things.
▸トニーは日本の文化を深く理解している Tony profoundly *appreciates* Japanese culture. / Tony has *a* profound *appreciation of* Japanese culture.
▸彼がなぜそんなことをしたのか理解に苦しむ I *can hardly understand* why he did such a thing.
▸国家間には相互理解が必要だ *Mutual understanding* is essential between nations.
◆私の母は若者のファッションにとても理解がある My mother *is very understanding* about young people's fashion. / 彼女はいつでも私のよき理解者だ She is always *a good friend* to me.

りがい 利害 (利害関係) interest ⓒ ‖私たちと生産者の利害は一致している(→利害を共有している) We *share common interests with* the producers. / その警察官は容疑者と利害関係があることが明らかになった It became clear that the policeman *had shared interests* with the suspect.
‖利害関係者 an *interested party*

りがく 理学 science ⓤ ‖理学士 a Bachelor of Science (《略語》BS, B.Sc.) / 理学博士 a Doctor of Science (《略語》D.Sc.) / 理学部 the department [《米》college] of science / 理学療法 (a) physical therapy / 理学療法士 a physical therapist

りき 利器 convenience ⓒ ‖アーミッシュの人たちは電気や自動車といった文明の利器を使わない The Amish do not use *modern conveniences* such as electricity and automobiles.

りきえい 力泳 ──**力泳する** (全力で泳ぐ) swim* with all *one's* strength; (力強いストロークで泳ぐ) swim with strong strokes

りきがく 力学 〔物理〕 dynamics 《単数扱い》
‖ニュートン力学 Newtonian mechanics / 熱力学 thermodynamics / 流体力学 hydrodynamics / 量子力学 quantum mechanics

りきさく 力作 (傑作) masterpiece ⓒ, tour de force [túər də fɔ́ːrs] ⓒ (複 tours de force) 《通例単数形》; (労作) effort ⓒ

りきし 力士 🔲 sumo wrestler ⓒ

りきせつ 力説 (強調する) emphasize ⓣⓘ, stress ⓣⓘ; (強く言い張る) insist ⓘⓣ ‖彼は日本における農業の重要性を力説した He *emphasized* the importance of agriculture in Japan.

りきそう 力走 ──**力走する** run* as hard [fast] as *one* can

リキッド (液体) liquid ⓒⓤ
‖ヘアリキッド(液状整髪料) hair liquid

りきてん 力点 (強調) emphasis ⓒ ⓤ (複 emphases), stress ⓒⓤ; (てこの支点) fulcrum ⓒ (複 〜s, fulcra) ‖先生は英文法に力点をおいた The teacher *put* [*placed*, *laid*] *an emphasis on* English grammar.

りきとう 力投 ──**力投する** (全力で投げる) pitch with all *one's* strength

りきむ 力む (全力を振り絞る) exert all *one's* strength ‖彼はその重い箱をどかそうと力んだ He *exerted all his strength* to move aside the heavy box. ◆そんなに力むなよ(→気楽にやれ) *Take it easy*.

りきゅう 離宮 (分離した宮殿) detached palace ⓒ ‖桂離宮 the Katsura *Detached Palace*

リキュール liqueur ⓤ

りきりょう 力量 (能力) ability ⓤⓒ; (潜在的な) capacity ⓤⓒ; (適性) competence ⓤ ‖彼女にはその仕事をする力量がある She has *the ability to* do the job. / 彼には教師としての力量が欠けている He lacks *competence* as a teacher.

りく 陸 (陸地) land ⓤ; (岸) shore ⓒⓤ ‖私たちのカヌーはようやく陸にたどり着いた Finally our canoe *came* to [*touched*, *reached*] *land*. / その船はゆっくりと陸を離れた The ship left [moved off] *the shore* slowly.
[慣用表現] 土砂崩れで国道が不通となり,その村は陸の孤島となっている The national highway is blocked because of a landslide, and the village *is left isolated*.

りくあげ 陸揚げ unloading ⓤ, landing ⓒⓤ ──**陸揚げする** unload ⓣⓘ, land ⓣ ‖積み荷を陸揚げする *unload* a ship

りくうん 陸運 (over)land transportation ⓤ, transportation by land
‖陸運会社 an overland [a land] transportation company / 陸運業 (over)land transportation services / 陸運局 Regional Land Transportation Bureau

リクエスト request ⓒ ──**リクエストする** request ⓣ ‖リクエストに応じる answer [respond to] *requests* / 彼女はいちばん好きな歌をリクエストした She *requested* her favorite song. / She *made a request for* her favorite song.
‖リクエスト曲 a request, a requested song

/ リクエスト番組 a request program

りくぐん 陸軍 the army 《単数または複数扱い》 《彼の祖父は陸軍に入隊していた His grandfather had joined the army.
‖陸軍軍人 a soldier / 陸軍士官 an army [a military] officer / 陸軍士官学校 a military academy

りくじょう 陸上 (陸) land ⓤ; (海・川に対する) shore ⓒⓤ 《両生類は水中でも陸上でも生活できる Amphibians are able to live both in water and *on land*.
◆母は学生時代, 陸上をやっていた (→陸上の選手だった) My mother *was a track and field athlete* when she was in school.
‖陸上競技 《主に米》track and field, 《英》athletics, (種目) track and field events / 陸上競技会 a track meet / 陸上競技場 an athletic field / 陸上自衛隊 the Ground Self-Defense Force / 陸上部 a track(-and-field) club / 陸上輸送 (over)land transportation

―陸上競技のいろいろ―
円盤投げ discus throw / 三段跳び triple jump / ハードル hurdles / 走り高跳び high jump / 走り幅跳び long [broad] jump / ハンマー投げ hammer throw / 砲丸投げ shot put / 棒高跳び pole vault / マラソン marathon / やり投げ javelin (throw)

りくせいどうぶつ 陸生動物 land [terrestrial] animal ⓒ
りくち 陸地 land ⓤ ➡りく
りくつ 理屈
❶ [道理] reason ⓤ; (論理) logic ⓤ 《また a～》; (理論) theory ⓤ
つくづく物事は理屈どおりにいかないものだと思った I realized that things don't always go according to *theory*.
君の言っていることは理屈では (→理論的には) 分かるが賛成できない I can understand what you are saying *in theory*, but I cannot agree with you.
平田君の主張は理屈に合っている (→筋が通っている) *There is reason [logic]* in what Hirata claims./ Hirata's claim *is reasonable [logical]*.
彼女はいつも理屈に合わないことばかり言っている She always says things that *have no reason [logic]*./ She always says *unreasonable [illogical]* things.
◆その映画は理屈抜きで (→疑いの余地なく) おもしろいから見たほうがいいよ You('d) better see that movie because it's *unquestionably* funny./ 彼らは理屈の分かった (→思慮分別のある) 人たちだ They are *sensible* people.
❷ [無理にこじつけた論理]【議論】(議論) argument ⓒ; (言い訳) excuse ⓒ
そんな理屈は通らない (→認められない) Such *an excuse* won't be accepted.
彼は何かと理屈をつけて部活をサボる He often skips the club activities *on one excuse or another*.

◆理屈をこねてばかりいないで仕事をしなさい Just stop *quibbling* and get down to work./ 彼女は理屈っぽい (→議論好きな) 人だ She's an *argumentative* person.

りくつづき 陸続き 《かつて日本列島はユーラシア大陸と陸続きだった The Japanese archipelago used *be connected to* the Eurasian Continent.

リクライニングシート reclining seat ⓒ
リクルーター recruiter ⓒ
リクルート ⚠ (新人の募集) recruitment ⓤ (❖英語の recruit は「新人」「新人を募集する」の意味) ‖リクルートカット (就職の面接にふさわしい髪型) a haircut suitable for job interviews / リクルートスーツ a suit appropriate for job interviews

りくろ 陸路 (over)land route ⓒ ――陸路で by land, overland 《彼らは陸路ヨーロッパに向かった They went *overland* to Europe./ They went to Europe *by land*./ They took *the overland route* to Europe.

りけい 理系 science ⓤ 《由紀は大学は理系に進む (→理科を専攻する) らしい I heard that Yuki *will major in science* in college./ 私の彼氏は理系の大学に通っている My boyfriend goes to a *science* college.

りけん 利権 (主に政府から許可された) concession ⓒ; (権益) interest ⓒ; (権利) right ⓤ 《しばしば複数形 ~s》 《アジアにおける米国の利権 American *interests* in Asia / その国は鉱山の採掘の利権を獲得した That country acquired *a mining concession*.

りこ 利己 ――利己的な selfish, egotistic, self-centered ――利己的に selfishly 《利己的な行為 *self-centered* behavior / あなたがそんな利己的な人だったなんて知らなかった I never knew you were so *selfish*.
‖利己主義 egotism / 利己主義者 an egotist / 利己心 selfishness

りこう¹ 利口 ――利口な intelligent; smart; clever; bright; brilliant; wise

> intelligent: 知能が高い, 理解力があるという意味.
> smart:《主に米》で頭がよくて賢い, また抜け目のないという意味も含む.
> clever: 頭の回転が速く器用である, またずる賢い, 抜け目のないという意味も含む.
> bright: 頭のいいという意味で特に子供などに用いる.
> brilliant: 並みはずれて頭がよいという意味.
> wise: 賢明な判断力があるという意味.

彼女はとても利口で物覚えが速い She is very *bright [intelligent, smart, clever]* and learns quickly.
イルカは利口な動物である The dolphin is an *intelligent* [a *clever*] animal.
彼女が彼の申し出を受けなかったのは利口だった *It was wise of* her [She *was wise*] not to accept his proposal.
◆彼女は利口に立ち回る (→抜け目なく行動する) ことのできる人だ She's a woman who can *act cleverly [tactfully]*./ 病院ではお利口さんにする (→いい子でいる) のよ *Be a good boy*

[girl] at the hospital./ (→行儀よくする)*Behave yourself* at the hospital./ お利口さんだね *That's a good boy [girl]*.

りこう² 履行 fulfillment ⓤ ⓒ ──履行する fulfill ⓣ, carry out, perform ⓣ ‖彼は私たちに契約の履行を迫った He pressed us for *the fulfillment of* the contract./ 彼は忠実に約束を履行した He faithfully *fulfilled [carried out]* the promise.

りこうがくぶ 理工学部 the department [《米》college] of science and engineering

りこうけい 理工系 science and engineering

リコーダー (縦笛) recorder ⓒ

リコール 《米》recall ⓤ ──リコールする recall ⓣ ‖その知事をリコールするために私たちは街頭で署名運動を始めた We started a signature-gathering campaign on the street to *recall* the governor.
‖リコール運動 a recall campaign

りこん 離婚 divorce ⓤ ⓒ ──離婚する divorce ⓣ ⓘ, get* a divorce, be [get] divorced ‖彼女は夫と離婚した She *divorced* her husband./ She *got a divorce from* her husband./ She *was [got] divorced from* her husband./ 彼の両親は離婚した His parents *got divorced.*/ 彼女は離婚訴訟を起こした She *filed* [*sued*] *for divorce.*/ 彼には離婚歴がある He *has been divorced.*/ 欧米は離婚率が高い In the West *the divorce rate* is high.
‖離婚者(男性) a divorced man, a divorcé;(女性) a divorcée／ 離婚訴訟 a divorce suit／ 離婚調停 a divorce settlement／ 離婚手続き a divorce procedure／ 離婚届 a divorce notice／ 協議離婚 a divorce by agreement [mutual consent]

リサーチ research ⓤ ‖その件に関してどれくらいリサーチがされていますか How much *research* is carried out on the matter?

リザーブ ⇨よやく

りさい 罹災 ──罹災する suffer ⓣ ‖私たちは地震で罹災した人たちに救援物資を送った We sent relief goods to the people who *suffered from* the earthquake.
‖罹災者 a sufferer;(犠牲者) a victim／ 罹災地 a disaster(-stricken) area

リサイクル recycling ⓤ ──リサイクルする recycle ⓣ 場面・状況別会話 p.1736 ‖ドイツではリサイクルのシステムが進んでいる The system for *recycling* is very advanced in Germany.
‖リサイクル運動 a recycling campaign／ リサイクルショップ(中古品売買の店) a second-hand shop(❖「リサイクルショップ」は和製英語)

リサイタル recital ⓒ ‖彼は来月このホールでピアノのリサイタルを開く He will give *a* piano *recital* at this hall next month.

りざや 利鞘 profit margin ⓒ ‖父は株で利ざやを稼ごうとしている My father is trying to increase *his profit margin* on the stock market.

りさん 離散 (肉親・友人などが離れること) sepa-

ration ⓤ ⓒ;(関係の崩壊) breakup ⓒ ──離散する separate ⓘ; break* up ‖戦争のため彼女の一家は離散してしまった Her family *had broken up* because of the war.

りし 利子 interest ⓤ ‖利子は月5パーセントです *The interest* is five percent a month./ 彼は6パーセントの利子でお金を借りている He has been borrowing money at six percent *interest.*/ 貯金の利子はいくらですか What is *the interest on* savings?／ この債権は7パーセントの利子がつきます This bond yields [bears] seven percent *interest.*/ お金は指定された日までに利子をつけてお返しします I will pay you back the money *with interest* by the appointed time./ 無利子でお金は借りられない You can't get a loan 「*at no interest* [*without interest*].

りじ 理事 director ⓒ;(学校などの) trustee ⓒ ‖理事会 a board of directors／ 理事長 the chairperson of the board of directors, the chief director

りしゅう 履修 ──履修する (勉強する) study ⓣ;(科目を取る) take* ⓣ;(修了する) complete ⓣ ‖必修科目をすべて履修しないと進級できません You must *complete* all required subjects to pass on to the next grade./ 来年は基礎フランス語コースを履修するつもりです I'm going to *take* a basic French course next year.
‖履修単位《主に米》a credit,《主に英》a module／ 履修届 registration for courses

りじゅん 利潤 profit ⓤ ⓒ ‖彼はその取り引きで莫大(ばく)な利潤をあげた He *made* [*earned*] *a* huge *profit* on the deal./ この国の輸出産業は相当な利潤をあげている The export industry of this country *yields a* good *profit.*(❖事業などが主語の場合 yield を用いる)／ これからの企業は利潤を追求するとともに環境問題を考慮するべきだ As the companies of the future *seek profits*, they will have to consider environmental problems.

りしょく¹ 利殖 (金もうけ) moneymaking ⓤ ‖彼は利殖のことしか頭にないみたいだ He seems to think of nothing but *moneymaking*.

りしょく² 離職 あの会社は離職率が高い That company has high *turnover*.

りす 栗鼠 squirrel ⓒ(複 ～s, ～)
‖シマリス a chipmunk

りすう 理数 私は理数系が苦手です I'm very weak in *science and mathematics*.

リスク risk ⓤ ⓒ ⇨ きけん(危険) ‖この企画には大きなリスクが伴うだろう This project will carry a lot of *risk.*/ 先物取引はハイリスクハイリターンです Futures trading entails both *high risk* and high returns.

リスト¹ (一覧表) list ⓒ ‖合宿に必要な物をリストアップした(→リストを作った) I 「*made a list of* [*listed*] what we need at the training camp.(❖list up とはいわない)
◆彼の名前はブラックリストに載っていた His name was on *a blacklist*.

リスト² (手首) wrist ⓒ ‖リストバンド a

wristband

リストラ(クチャリング) (企業再構築) restructuring ⓤⓒ《通例 a ～》 /その会社はリストラの一環として従業員600人を解雇した The company laid off 600 workers as part of *a restructuring*.

リスボン Lisbon(❖ポルトガルの首都)

リズミカル ──リズミカルな rhythmic(al) **──リズミカルに** rhythmically /その人形は音楽に合わせてリズミカルに動く The doll moves *rhythmically* to [with] music.

リズム rhythm ⓤⓒ;(ビート) beat ⓒ /その曲のリズムはとても単純だが印象的だ The *rhythm* of the song is very simple but impressive. / 子供たちは音楽のリズムに合わせて手をたたいた Children clapped their hands *to the rhythm* of the music. / 私たちはタンゴのリズムに乗って踊った We danced *in the rhythm* of the tango [tango *rhythm*]. / 彼らはみなリズム感がいい They all *have「good rhythm* [*a* (*good*) *sense of rhythm*]. / 私には全くリズム感がない I *have no sense of rhythm* at all. / 彼はジャズを聴きながら足でリズムをとっている He *keeps rhythm* with his foot as he listens to jazz. / 最近生活のリズムが乱れてきた Recently my life *has taken on a strange rhythm*.

‖リズムアンドブルース《音楽》 rhythm and blues《略語》R & B, R and B

りせい 理性 reason ⓤ **──理性的な** rational, reasonable **──理性的に** rationally /人間には理性がある A human being「*has reason* [*is rational*]. / だれもが理性に従って行動することができるわけではない Not everyone can act「*according to reason* [*rationally*]. / 災害が起こると私たちは理性を失うものだ When we meet with disaster, we lose「*our reason* [*control of ourselves*]. / 私は彼の理性に訴えようとした I tried to appeal to his *reason*.

りそう 理想 ideal ⓒ《しばしば複数形 ～s》 **──理想的な** ideal

私の姉は理想が高い My sister has high *ideals*.

彼女は理想を実現するために努力を怠らない She is never too lazy to realize *her ideals*.

私の理想の男性は誠実な人です My *ideal* man is an honest person.

彼は君にとって理想的な夫だ He is the *ideal* husband for you.

レストランを建てるのにこの場所は理想的だ This is the *ideal* [*perfect*] place for a restaurant.

◆君は彼女を理想化しすぎている You *idealize* her *too much*. / 理想的には、もう一度初めからやり直すべきだ *Ideally*, we should start all over again. / 多くの若者は自分の将来について明確な理想像をもっていない Many young people have no clear *vision* of their future.

‖理想化 idealization / 理想郷 a utopia, an ideal society [world] / 理想主義 idealism / 理想主義者 an idealist / 理想像 an ideal image, a vision

リゾート (行楽地) resort ⓒ ‖リゾート開発 resort development / リゾート地(海辺の) a seaside resort;(山の) a mountain resort / リゾートホテル a resort hotel,《米》a resort / リゾートマンション a resort condominium

りそく 利息 interest ⓤ /そのローンの利息を毎月支払っています I pay *interest on* the loan monthly.

リターンマッチ return match ⓒ, rematch ⓒ

リタイア シューマッハは第1コーナーでスピンしてリタイアした Schumacher spun off at the first curve and *retired*.

りだつ 離脱 彼は先月その政党から離脱した He *defected* [*seceded*] *from* the political party last month. / He *left* the political party last month.

りち 理知(知性) intellect ⓤⓒ;(知能) intelligence ⓤ **──理知的な** intellectual /彼は理知的な顔をしている He has an *intellectual* face. / He looks *intellectual*. / 彼女は理知的な人だ She is an *intellectual* (*person*).

りちぎ 律儀・律義 **──律儀な** (忠実な) faithful;(正直な) honest;(義務を果たす) dutiful **──律儀に** faithfully; honestly; dutifully /恵子はとても律儀な人でみんなに好かれている Keiko is an *honest* [a *faithful*, a *dutiful*] person and everybody likes her. / 鎌田氏は彼女の言うことに律儀に従った Mr. Kamata obeyed her *faithfully* [*honestly, dutifully*].

りちゃくりく 離着陸 takeoff and landing /ジャンボジェット機が次々と離着陸している The jumbo jets *are taking off and landing* one after another.

りつ 率 (比率) rate ⓒ;(割合) proportion ⓤ;(百分率) percentage ⓒ /わが国の失業率は年々増加している The unemployment *rate* in our country is increasing every year. / その大学の文学部の競争率は非常に高い[低い] The admission *rate* for the literature department at that university is low [high].(❖the admission rate は「入学を許可される率」の意味なので、日本語の高低と英語のhigh, low が逆になることに注意)

◆率のいい(→給料のいい)仕事を見つけるのは大変だ It is hard to find a *well-paying* job.

‖死亡率 the death rate / 出生率 the birth rate

りつあん 立案 planning ⓤ;(企画) plan ⓒ **──立案する** plan ⓗ ⓐ /私たちはこの営業方針を立案しました We *planned* [*drew up, worked out*] this business policy.

‖立案者 a planner

りっか 立夏 *rikka*, the first day of summer, the beginning of summer

りっきゃく 立脚 彼の結論は彼自身の体験に立脚している(→基づいている) His conclusion *is based* [*founded*] *on* his own experience. / 彼らは確固とした立脚点(→地盤)をニューヨーク市場に確立した They established *a* firm *foothold* [*footing*] in the New York market.

りっきょう 陸橋 (高架横断道路)《米》overpass ⓒ,《英》flyover ⓒ

りっけん 立憲 ——立憲制の constitutional ‖立憲君主 a constitutional monarch / 立憲君主国 a constitutional monarchy / 立憲政治 constitutional government

りっこうほ 立候補 candidacy / ——立候補する (選挙に)《主に米》run*, 《英》stand* ‖立候補を表明[断念]する announce [give up] one's candidacy / 山本君は生徒会長に立候補した Yamamoto *ran for* student council president. / 彼女はABC党から市長選に立候補します She's going to *run in* the mayoral election from the ABC Party.
‖立候補者 a candidate

りっしでん 立志伝 (出世物語) success story ; (自力で出世した人の) a story of a self-made man [woman]
◆彼は立志伝中の人として演説をした He gave a speech describing himself as *a self-made man*.

りっしゅう 立秋 *risshu*, the first day of fall [autumn], the beginning of fall [autumn]

りっしゅん 立春 *risshun*, the first day of spring, the beginning of spring

りっしょう 立証 (証明) proof / ——立証する prove* ‖因果関係の立証 *proof* of the relation between cause and effect / 彼女は彼の有罪を立証した She *proved* his guilt. / She *proved* him (*to be*) guilty. / She *proved that* he was guilty.

りっしょく 立食 stand-up meal; (ビュッフェ形式の) buffet
‖立食パーティー a buffet party

りっしんしゅっせ 立身出世 (a) success in life ——立身出世する succeed in life ‖彼は立身出世するために日夜努力をしている He works hard day and night to *succeed in life*.

りっすい 立錐 そのホールは立錐の余地もなかった (→収容能力いっぱいだった) The hall *was filled* [*packed*] *to capacity*.

りっする 律する 自分自身を律する control oneself / 彼はいつも自分の基準で人を律する He always *judges* [*measures*] other people by his own standard.

りつぜん 慄然 私たちはその予言に慄然とした We *were horrified* [*terrified*] *at* [*by*] the prophecy. / The prophecy *gave us the shudders*.

りつぞう 立像 statue

リッター liter, 《英》litre (《略語》l., lit.) この車はリッターあたり33キロメートル走ります This car gets 33 kilometers *to the liter*.

りったい 立体 (数学で) solid ——立体的な solid ; (画像などが) three-dimensional, three-D, 3-D ; (音響が) stereo ‖立体的な映像 a *three-dimensional* image / この写真には立体感がある This photo appears *three-dimensional*.
‖立体幾何学 solid geometry / 立体交差 an overhead crossing, a two-level [multilevel] crossing / 立体駐車場 a multistory parking garage

リッチ リッチな (→高価な) 夕食 an *expensive* dinner / リッチな (→ぜいたくな) 生活をする lead a *luxurious* life

りっち 立地 このホテルは立地条件がよい[悪い] This hotel *has a good* [*bad*] *location*. / This hotel *is conveniently* [*inconveniently*] *located*.

りっとう 立冬 *ritto*, the first day of winter, the beginning of winter

リットル liter, 《英》litre (《略語》l., lit.)

りっぱ 立派
❶【すぐれた】——りっぱな excellent ; (すばらしい) wonderful ; (みごとな) fine ; (偉大な) great ; (傑出した) outstanding ; (賞賛に値する) admirable
君のオフィーリアの演技はりっぱだった Your performance as Ophelia was *excellent* [*wonderful*].
彼女ならりっぱな弁護士になれるだろう She can be an *excellent* [a *great*] lawyer.
彼はりっぱな青年に成長した He has grown to be a *fine* young man.
彼はりっぱな成績で高校を卒業した He graduated from high school with *excellent* [*outstanding*] grades.
彼女の態度はりっぱだった Her attitude was *admirable*.
その政治家は言うことはいつもりっぱだが, それを実行したためしがない What the politician says is always *admirable*, but he never puts it into action.
あの人は本当にりっぱな上司ですよ. いつも私に責任をなすりつけるのですから What a *fine* boss he is! He always shifts the responsibility to me. (❖皮肉の表現)
◆彼女の部屋にはりっぱな装飾が施された洋服だんすが置いてあった There was a *wonderfully* carved wardrobe in her room. / 彼女はいつもりっぱな身なりをしていた She *was* always *nicely* [*well*] *dressed*.
❷【堂々とした】——りっぱな grand ; (威厳のある) dignified, stately ; (巨大な) great
彼はあそこのりっぱな大邸宅に住んでいる He lives in the *grand* mansion over there.
◆彼はりっぱな体格をしている He has a *massive* [*strong*] build.
❸【十分な】
授業に遅れたのにはりっぱな (→正当な) 理由がある I have a *good* reason why I was late for the class.
万引きはりっぱな (→明らかに) 犯罪だ It is *obviously* a crime to shoplift.
彼はもうりっぱな (→十分成長した) 大人だ He is a *full-grown* man now.
彼女はその仕事をりっぱに (→申し分なく) やりとげた She accomplished the task「*very well* [*satisfactorily*].

リップ その政治家はリップサービスが得意だ The politician pays *lip service* very well.
‖リップクリーム (a) lip balm [salve]

りっぷく 立腹 ——立腹する (怒る) get* angry ‖ご立腹はもっともです You have good reason to *get* [*be*] *angry*.

りっぽう¹ 立方 (3乗)〖数学〗cube ― 立方(体)の cubic ▮その入れ物の容積は800立方センチメートルです The volume of the container is 800 *cubic* centimeters.
‖立方根〖数学〗the cube root / 立方体 a cube

りっぽう² 立法 legislation, lawmaking ― 立法(上)の《公式的》legislative (※名詞の前で用いる)
‖立法機関 a legislative [lawmaking] body [organ] / 立法権 the power of legislation, legislative power / 立法府《公式的》the legislature

りづめ 理詰め 理詰めで人を説得する persuade a person by *logical argument*

りてきこうい 利敵行為 それは利敵行為以外の何物でもない It is nothing but *an act that profits [helps] the enemy*.

りてん 利点 advantage;（長所）good point ▮新製品の利点は何ですか What are the「*good points*［*advantages*］of the new product? / この辞書は新語をたくさん収録しているという利点がある This dictionary has *the advantage* of containing a lot of new words. / 彼の新しい計画には前のものより多くの利点がある His new project has many *advantages* over the last one.

りとう¹ 離党 defection;（脱退）《公式的》secession ― 離党する defect;《公式的》secede ▮彼はその党を離党した He *defected from [left]* the party.
‖離党者 a defector

りとう² 離島（孤立した島）isolated island ◆離島する（→島を去る）若者が年々増えている The number of young people *leaving the island* has been increasing every year.

リトグラフ（石版画）lithograph;（石版印刷）lithography

リトマス〖化学〗litmus
‖リトマス試験〖化学〗a litmus test / リトマス試験紙〖化学〗litmus paper

リニアモーター linear motor
‖リニアモーターカー a linear motor car

りにち 離日 アメリカ大統領は今月14日に離日する予定だ The U.S. president will *leave Japan* on the 14th of this month.

りにゅう 離乳 彼女はそろそろ赤ん坊を離乳させると言っていた She said that she would *wean her baby* soon.
‖離乳期 the weaning period / 離乳食 baby food

りにん 離任 resignation ― 離任する resign ▮彼は突然局長の職を離任した He suddenly *resigned (from)* the post of director.

りねん 理念（考え）idea;（主義）philosophy;（イデオロギー）ideology ▮我々はそれぞれの教育理念について議論した We discussed our *educational philosophies*.

リノリウム linoleum;（英口語的）lino

リハーサル rehearsal
◆私たちは何度もその劇のリハーサルをした We *rehearsed* the play many times.

リバーシブル ― リバーシブルの reversible ▮このコートはリバーシブルです This coat is *reversible*.

リバイバル revival ― リバイバルする revive ▮その映画は最近リバイバルされて注目を集めている That movie *has been revived* lately and it's drawing people's attention.

りはつ¹ 理髪 haircutting, hairdressing
‖理髪師 a barber, a hairdresser / 理髪店《米》a barbershop,《英》a barber's (shop)

りはつ² 利発 bright ▮利発そうな子供 a child who looks *bright*

リハビリ(テーション) rehabilitation (※犯罪者や薬物中毒者の社会復帰訓練も含む) ▮彼女は数か月のリハビリを経て歩けるようになった She was able to walk again after several months' *rehabilitation*. / 医者は私にリハビリを施すだけでなく精神的にも支えてくれた The doctor *rehabilitated* me and gave me moral support as well.
‖リハビリ(テーション)センター a rehabilitation center

リバプール Liverpool (※英国の都市)

りはん 離反 alienation ▮その不祥事が政府からの人心の離反を招いた（→政府は市民の信頼を失った）The government *lost the citizens' trust* because of the scandal.

リビングルーム living room
⇨いま(居間) 図版

リフォーム 自分の古いドレスをリフォームしてクッションカバーにした（→クッションカバーに作り変えた）I *made* my old dress (*over*) *into* a cushion cover. / 母はキッチンをリフォームしたがっている My mother wants to *remodel* the kitchen. / My mother wants to *make some alterations to* the kitchen. (※英語の reform は「(社会制度などの)改善」の意味)

りふじん 理不尽 ― 理不尽な（道理に合わない）unreasonable;（不正な）unfair ▮なぜこのような理不尽な要求がまかり通るのか分からない I can't understand why these *unreasonable* demands have been accepted.

リフト（スキー場の）ski lift, chair lift ▮私はスキー場のリフトに乗るのが苦手です I hate riding *ski lifts*.

リプリント（再販本）reprint ― リプリントする reprint ▮本書はオリジナル版をリプリントしたものだ This book is *a reprint* of the original.

リフレッシュ 少し散歩でもしたらリフレッシュすることができるよ You will *be refreshed* by a little walk. / 熱いシャワーでも浴びてリフレッシュしたらどうですか Why don't you take a nice, hot shower to *refresh yourself*?
‖リフレッシュ休暇 a sabbatical leave

リベート（払い戻し）rebate;（手数料）commission (※悪い意味は含まない);（わいろ）bribe,《口語的》kickback ▮彼は美術商からリベートを受け取っていた疑いで逮捕された He was arrested on suspicion of taking *kickbacks* from the art dealer.

りべつ 離別 parting, separation

——離別する be parted, be separated
⇨ りこん ‖彼は子供のころ両親と離別した He was parted [separated] from his parents when he was a child.

リベラリスト liberal ◯, liberalist ◯

リベラル ——リベラルな liberal ‖彼女はリベラルな考え方の持ち主だ She has liberal views.

リベンジ 私たちは昨年決勝で敗れた西高校へのリベンジに燃えている We're eager to take revenge on Nishi High School, which beat us last year in the finals.

リポート report ◯ ⇨ レポート

リボン ribbon ◯; (帽子などの) band ◯; (プリンターなどの) ribbon ◯ ‖彼女は髪にピンクのリボンをつけている She has [wears] a pink ribbon in her hair. / この箱に黄色のリボンをかけてください Could you tie this box with a yellow ribbon?

りまわり 利回り yield ◯ 《しばしば複数形 ~s》, return ◯◯ 《しばしば複数形 ~s》, (利子) interest ◯◯ ‖債券の利回り the yield on a bond / この債券は利回りがいい[悪い] This bond yields a good [poor] return. (※この yield は「利益などをもたらす」の意)

リミックス その曲のリミックスバージョン the remixed version of the song

リミット limit ◯; (締め切り) deadline ◯ ‖彼はその議論に２時間のタイムリミットを設けた He set a time limit of two hours for the discussion. / 申込書提出のタイムリミットは次の金曜日です The deadline for submission of applications is next Friday.

リムジン (大型の高級乗用車) limousine ◯, 《口語的》limo ◯; (空港送迎バス) airport shuttle ◯, airport [limousine] bus ◯

リメーク その映画をリメークする remake the movie / ジーンズからリメークしたスカートを買った I bought a skirt remade from a pair of jeans.

りめん 裏面 (裏) the back, the reverse (side), the other side ⇨ うら ‖小切手の裏面にサインしてください Please sign on the back of the check.

◆人生の裏面を見る look on the dark [seamy] side of life / 裏面に続く Please turn over. (《略語》P.T.O., p.t.o.) / 《米》Over. / 彼女は一流企業に就職するために裏面工作をしたらしい I heard that she maneuvered behind the scenes to be hired by a leading company.

リモコン ⚠ (リモートコントローラー) remote control ◯; (家電の) handset ◯; (テレビの) 《米口語的》zapper ◯ ——リモコン式の remote-controlled ‖リモコンでテレビのチャンネルを変える change channels with a remote control / このエアコンはリモコン付きですか(→リモコンで操作できますか) Can this air-conditioner be operated by a remote control? / (→リモコン式のエアコンですか) Is this a remote-controlled air-conditioner?

リヤカー ⚠ a two-wheeled cart that is pulled by a bicycle or a person (※「リヤカー」は和製英語)

りゃく 略 (省略) omission ◯◯; (短縮) abbreviation ◯◯ ⇨ しょうりゃく, りゃくす

りゃくご 略語 abbreviation ◯, abbreviated form [word] ◯ (※ふつう略語にはピリオドを付けるが, 《英》では Dr, Mr のように語頭と語尾から成る略語にはつけないことが多い ‖U.N. is United Nations の略語です "U.N." is an abbreviation for [of] the "United Nations." / "U.N." stands for "the United Nations."

りゃくじ 略字 an abbreviation of a 「Chinese character [kanji], a simplified [abbreviated] form of a 「Chinese character [kanji]

りゃくしき 略式 ——略式の informal (↔formal); (カジュアルな) casual ‖パーティーには略式の服装でお越しください Please come to our party in informal [casual] dress [clothes]. / 私は結婚式を略式に挙げたい I want to have an informal wedding.

‖略式起訴(状)《法律》an information / 略式裁判 a summary trial / 略式処分 summary disposition / 略式手続き informal proceedings / 略式命令 a summary order

りゃくしょう 略称 「東大」は「東京大学」の略称です "Todai" is an abbreviation for [of] "Tokyo Daigaku."

りゃくす 略す (省く) omit ⓣ; (短縮する) shorten ⓣ, (しばしば) abbreviate ⓣ ‖この手続きは略してもよい You can omit [leave out] this procedure. / 彼らは補足的なところをカットして話を略した They shortened the story by cutting out the subplot. / October は Oct. と略される "October" is abbreviated to "Oct."

◆木村拓哉は略してキムタクと呼ばれている Kimura Takuya is called Kimutaku for short. / 氏名は略さずに(→全部)書いてください Please write your name in full.

りゃくず 略図 rough map [sketch] ◯ ‖その駅への略図を描いてください Please draw a rough map to the station.

りゃくだつ 略奪 plunder ◯, loot ◯ ——略奪する plunder ⓣⓘ, loot ⓣⓘ ‖軍はその村を略奪した The troops plundered the village.

‖略奪者 a looter / 略奪品 spoils, plunder, 《口語的》loot

りゃくれき 略歴 one's brief personal history [record]

りゆう 理由

reason ◯◯, cause ◯◯; (言い訳) excuse ◯◯; (口実) pretext ◯

〖理由を・に〗

どうしてこんなに遅刻したのか理由を言いなさい Tell me (the reason) why you were so late. (※口語ではしばしば the reason が省略される)

彼女はいつも何かと理由をつけて体育の授業を休む She is always absent from her PE class for one excuse or another.

彼女は仕事を理由に彼とのデートを断った She turned down a date with him under

[on] *the pretext of* having to work.
目覚まし時計が鳴らなかったからなんて遅刻の理由にならない Your alarm not going off *is no excuse for* being late.
◆彼らは信仰を理由にずっと迫害されてきた They have been persecuted *for* their beliefs. / 彼女は病気を理由に学校を休んだ She didn't come to school *because* [*on the grounds that*] she was ill.
〖理由が·は〗
私たちには授業をボイコットするだけのもっともな理由がある We have *a* good *reason* to boycott the classes.
理由はどうであれ人を見下してはいけない Don't look down on people whatever *the reason.*
彼とのけんかの理由は何だったのですか What were *your reasons for* fighting with him? / (→なぜ彼とけんかしたのですか) *Why* did you fight with him?
彼が遅刻した本当の理由は寝坊したからだ *The* real *reason* (*why*) he was late was that [《口語的》because] he overslept.
〖理由で〗
彼はある理由でそこへ行かなければならなかった(→そこへ行かねばならない理由があった) He had *a* certain *reason* for going there.
どういう理由であんなふるまいをしたんだ What's *the reason for* such behavior?
◆彼はただ単に自分がそうしたいからという理由でそうしたのだった He did it simply *because* he wanted to do it. / 彼女は金銭的な理由で英会話学校をやめた She left the English language school 「*because of* money [*for* money *reasons*].
〖その他〗
私はこれといった理由もなく文学部に進んだ I entered the school of literature 「*for no particular reason* [*for nothing*].
ちゃんとした理由もないのにそんなことを言うな Don't say such things *without good cause.*

[り]

りゅう 竜 dragon [C]
-りゅう -流 ❶【やり方】way [C], fashion [U] 《また a ～》; (方法) manner [C]; (様式) style [U][C] ∥何でも自己流でやるのがいつも正しいとは限らない Doing everything *in one's own way* [*fashion, manner, style*] is not always right. / アメリカ流のあいさつではまず握手をする *The American style* of greeting is to shake hands first.
❷【流派】school [C] ∥私のお茶は遠州流です I belong to *the* Enshu *school* of tea ceremony.
りゅうい 留意 ──留意する note [他], pay* [give*] attention to ... ∥この点に留意してください Please *note* [*pay attention to*] this point.
りゅういき 流域 basin [C]; (大河の) valley [C] ∥古代エジプト文明はナイル川流域に栄えた The ancient Egyptian civilization thrived in *the* Nile *valley*.
りゅういん 溜飲 彼を言い負かしたので溜飲が下がった(→満足した) I *am* [*feel*] *satisfied* because I argued him down.
りゅうかい 流会 出席者不足のため会議は流会となった(→中止された) The meeting *was canceled* [*called off*] for want of attendance.
りゅうがく 留学 ──留学する (外国で勉強する) study abroad; (勉強のために外国へ行く) go* abroad for [to] study
➾ [場面·状況別会話] p.1754, p.1756
彼女は18歳のとき留学していた She *studied abroad* when she was 18.
彼女は奨学金をもらって[自費で]留学しています She *is studying abroad* 「on a scholarship [at her own expense].
◆米文学を勉強するため米国に留学するつもりです I plan to *study* American literature *in* the United States. / I plan to *go to* the United States *to study* American literature. / 兄は4年間イェール大学に留学していた(→イェール大学で学んだ) My brother *studied at* Yale University for four years. / 私はこの夏ロンドンに短期留学した I *went to* London *on a short study program* this summer. / 私たちの学校は3人のアメリカ人を交換留学生として受け入れた Our school accepted three Americans as *exchange students*. / 彼はドイツからの留学生です He's *a student from* Germany. / たくさんの外国人留学生が日本で勉強している Many *overseas students* study in Japan.
∥留学生 a student studying abroad, an international student; (海外から来ている学生) a student from overseas, an overseas student(❖a foreign student はやや冷たい印象を与える表現)
りゅうかん 流感 influenza [U], 《口語的》flu [U] ∥流感にかかる catch [get] *the flu* / 去年は流感がクラス中に蔓延(まんえん)した *Influenza* spread throughout the class last year. / 彼女の子供たちは流感にかかっている Her children *have the flu*.
りゅうき 隆起 (土地の) upheaval [U][C] ──隆起する upheave [自], rise* (suddenly) ∥火山活動で土地が隆起した The ground *rose* [*upheaved*] due to the volcanic activity.
りゅうぎ 流儀 (やり方) way [C]; (方法) manner [C]; (様式) style [U][C]; (流派) school [C] ∥私は私の流儀でやらせてください Please allow me to do it *in my own way*. / 彼らは昔ながらの流儀を堅く守ってこれらの人形を作っている They firmly follow *the traditional way* in making these dolls.
りゅうけつ 流血 bloodshed [U] ∥その民族紛争は流血の惨事に至った The ethnic conflict 「develop into [led to] *bloodshed*.
∥流血事件 a bloody affair, a case of bloodshed
りゅうげんひご 流言飛語 流言飛語(→根拠のないうわさ)に惑わされないでください Please don't be confused by *groundless rumors*.
りゅうこう 流行
❶【服装·行動様式などの】fashion [C][U]; (傾向)

trend [C]; (流行の型) style [C] [U], 《公式的》 the mode; (一時的な) vogue [U] 《また a ～》; (一時的な大流行) fad [C], craze [C] ――流行の fashionable; (最新の) trendy; (人気のある) popular ――流行する come* into fashion, become* fashionable; (流行している) be in fashion, be fashionable; be in vogue; be popular ➩ [場面・状況別会話] p.1708

婦人服の流行はめまぐるしく変化する *Fashions* in women's clothing change very quickly.

若者は流行に敏感だ Young people are sensitive to *trends*.

流行にとらわれすぎるな (→流行の奴隷になるな) Don't be a slave of [to] *fashion*.

彼は流行のコートを着ていた He was wearing a *fashionable* [*trendy, popular*] coat.

かかとの高いブーツが流行している High-heeled boots *are* 「*in fashion* [*popular*].

次の夏はショートパンツが流行するだろう Short pants will 「*come into fashion* [*be in fashion*] next summer.

その女性がクラシックなスタイルを流行させた That woman *set a trend toward* classic design.

彼女は流行に遅れないよう常に最新の雑誌をチェックしている She always checks the latest magazines to *keep up with fashions*.

彼女は常に最新の流行を追っている She always *follows the* latest [newest] *fashions*.

最近では女子高校生が流行の先端を行っている High school girls *are the* recent *trend-setters* [*fashion leaders*].

彼女は最新流行の服に身を包んでいた She was dressed in *the latest mode* [*style*].

そのタイプのシャツはもう流行遅れだ That type of shirt *is* already 「*out of fashion* [*old-fashioned*].

そのゲームは去年，大流行した The game was *the craze* last year.

❷【病気などの】epidemic [C] ――流行する (急速に蔓延(まんえん)する) spread* quickly ――流行性の epidemic

その当時たくさんの人々がコレラの流行に苦しんでいた At that time, many people were suffering from *an epidemic* of cholera.

去年は悪質なかぜが全国で流行した Bad colds 「*spread quickly* [(→猛威をふるった) *raged*] throughout the country last year.

‖流行歌 a popular song / 流行歌手 a popular [pop] singer / 流行語 a vogue word, a word in vogue, an in word / 流行作家 a popular writer / 流行性感冒 influenza, 《口語的》 flu

りゅうさん 硫酸 〖化学〗sulfuric acid [U]
‖硫酸アンモニウム ammonium sulfate / 硫酸塩 sulfate / 硫酸銅 copper sulfate

りゅうざん 流産 miscarriage [U][C] ∥その女性は妊娠4か月で流産した The woman 「*had a miscarriage* [*miscarried*] in the fourth month of pregnancy.

りゅうし 粒子 particle [C]

りゅうしつ 流失 たくさんの家屋が洪水で流失した (→押し流された) Many houses *were washed away* by the flood.

りゅうしゅつ 流出 outflow [C]; (財産などの) drain [U] 《また a ～》 ――流出する flow [run*] out ∥金の国外流出 *the outflow* [*drain*] of gold *from the country* / 貴重な美術品が国外へ流出しているようだ It seems that valuable works of fine art *are flowing out of* the country. / まだ噴火口から溶岩が流出している The lava *is* still *flowing out of* the crater.
‖流出物 effluent; (大量の) (an) outpouring / 流出量 a flow, the volume of effluent / 頭脳流出 a brain drain

りゅうせい[1] 流星 shooting [falling] star [C], meteor [C]
‖流星群 a meteor shower [stream]

りゅうせい[2] 隆盛 prosperity [U] ∥隆盛に向かう head for [toward] *prosperity*
◆その手の商売は当時隆盛を極めた (→たいへん繁盛した) That kind of business *flourished* [*prospered, thrived*] *very much* then.

りゅうせんけい 流線型 streamline [C] ――流線型の streamlined ∥流線型の車は空気抵抗を受けにくい A *streamlined* car has little wind resistance.

りゅうち 留置 detention [U], custody [U] ――留置する detain [他] ∥その容疑者は警察署に留置されている The suspect *has been detained* at the police station.
‖留置場 a detention cell, a lockup

りゅうちょう 流暢 ――流暢な fluent ――流暢に fluently ∥彼女はドイツ語を流暢に話す She speaks German *fluently*./ She speaks *fluent* German./ She is *fluent* in German.

りゅうつう 流通 (貨幣の) circulation [U], currency [U]; (商品の) distribution [U]; (空気の) ventilation [U], circulation [U] ――流通する circulate [自] ∥この部屋は空気の流通が悪い This room has bad *ventilation*. / 新しいお札が流通し始めた The new bills 「*went into circulation* [*began to circulate*].
‖流通革命 a distribution revolution / 流通貨幣 current [circulating] money / 流通機構 a distribution system / 流通産業 the distribution industry / 流通センター a distribution center

リュート 〖音楽〗lute [C]

りゅうどう 流動 ――流動的な (流動性の) fluid; (動的な) mobile; (不安定な) unstable ∥経済情勢は流動的だ The economic situation is *fluid* [*unstable*].
‖流動資産 liquid assets / 流動社会 a mobile society / 流動食 liquid food / 流動性 fluidity; (社会階級などの) mobility; (企業の) 〖経済〗liquidity / 流動体 (a) fluid; (液体) (a) liquid / 流動物 a fluid substance

りゅうとうだび 竜頭蛇尾 [慣用表現] その長編映画の製作は竜頭蛇尾に終わった (→いいスタートを切ったが失敗に終わった) The production of that long film *made a good start, but it finished in failure*.

り

りゅうにゅう　流入 inflow; (一度に大量の)influx ―**流入する** (流れ込む) flow in; (入ってくる) come* in ∥市民は外国製品[外資]の流入に強く反対した The citizens strongly objected to *the inflow* of「products from abroad [foreign capital]. / その国への難民の大量流入は様々な問題を引き起こしている *The influx* of refugees into the country is causing various problems.

りゅうにん　留任 首相は彼を委員会の議長に留任させた The Prime Minister *kept* him *in office* as the chairman of the committee. / 彼は委員会の議長に留任するだろう He will *remain [stay] in office* as the chairman of the committee.

りゅうねん　留年 ―**留年する** (同じ学年にとどまる) remain in the same year [grade], be held back a year; (同じ学年を繰り返す) repeat the same year [grade](❖ grade は高校までの学年のことで,《英》では form という) ∥彼女は大学で1年留年した She *repeated the same year* once at the university.

りゅうは　流派 school ∥あなたの生け花の流派はどちらですか Which *school* of flower arrangement do you belong to?

りゅうび　柳眉 彼女は彼の言葉に柳眉を逆立てた(→まゆをつり上げて怒った) She *got angry at* his words *and it showed in her raised eyebrows*.

りゅうひょう　流氷 drift ice, floating ice; (浮氷塊) (ice) floe ∥流氷が船の進行を阻(はば)んだ *Drift [Floating] ice* stopped the ship from progressing.

りゅうほ　留保 reservation ―**留保する** (差し控える) reserve ⇨ほりゅう ∥彼らはその調査が終わるまで決定を留保すると言った They said that they *will reserve* their decision until the end of the investigation.

りゅうぼく　流木 driftwood

リューマチ rheumatism,《口語的》rheumatics ∥私のおばは手首にリューマチを患っている My aunt *suffers from rheumatism* in her wrists.
∥リューマチ患者 a rheumatic / リューマチ熱 rheumatic fever

りゅうよう　流用 appropriation; (横領) misappropriation ―**流用する** (転用する) divert; misappropriate ∥多くの政府高官が何年も公金を流用していた Many government officials *had misappropriated* public money for years.

りゅうりゅう　隆々 彼は筋骨隆々の身体をしている He has a *muscular* body.

りゅうれい　流麗 ―**流麗な** flowing; (優美な) elegant ∥彼女の手紙は流麗な文体で書かれていた Her letter was written in *flowing [elegant]* style.

リュック(サック) rucksack,《米》backpack; (ナップサック) knapsack ∥彼は大きなリュック(サック)を背負っていた He was carrying a *big rucksack* on his back.

りよう¹　利用 (使うこと) use; (また a ~) (❖「使い道・用途」の意味で use) (活用) utilization ―**利用する** (使う) use; (公式的)utilize, make* use of ...; (機会などをうまく生かす) take* advantage of ...; (自然の力などを) harness

その研究所は原子力の平和的利用について研究している That laboratory looks for *peaceful uses* of nuclear energy.

この機械の利用法は非常に限られている *The uses for* this machine are very limited.

彼はインターネットの上手な利用法を教えてくれた He showed me *how to use* the Internet skillfully.

私は試験勉強のためによく学校の図書館を利用する I often *use* the school library to study for exams.

父はこの箱をいすとして利用するつもりだ My father will *use* this box as a chair.

当時プロパガンダを広める手段としてラジオが利用された At that time radio *was used* as a medium for spreading propaganda.

彼は欲しいものを手に入れるために自分の地位を利用した He *used* his rank to get what he wanted.

自分の利益のためだけに友人を利用するな Don't *use [take advantage of]* your friends just for your own benefit.

君は彼に利用されているだけなのが分からないのか Don't you understand that you *were just used* by him?

私たちは太陽をエネルギー源として利用していかねばならない We have to *utilize [harness]* the sun as an energy source.

彼女は自分の経験を最大限に利用した She *made the best use of* her experience. / She *made the most of* her experience.

海外旅行をうまく利用して英会話の上達をはかるつもりだ I plan to「*make good use of [take advantage of]* overseas travel to improve my conversational English.

彼らは休暇を利用してサイパン旅行へ出かけた They *took advantage of* the vacation and went on a trip to Saipan. / (休暇中に)They went on a trip to Saipan *during* the vacation.

◆駅からあなたの学校までバスを利用できますか Is there any bus service *available* from the station to your school? / 私たちはパーティーに利用できるレストランを探していた We were looking for an *available* restaurant for the party. / そこへ行くなら地下鉄を利用する(→地下鉄に乗った)ほうがいいよ You better *take* the subway to get there. / その情報は君にとって大いに利用価値がある(→役に立つ) The information *is* very *useful for* you. / (実用性がある)The information *has great utility for* you. (❖「利用価値がない」は be useless, have no utility という)
∥利用者 a user / 廃物利用 the recycling [utilization] of waste

りよう²　理容 haircutting, hairdressing ∥理容学校 a barber school / 理容師 a barber, a hairdresser / 理容室《米》a barbershop,《英》a barber's (shop)

りょう[1] 量 (数に対する) amount [C] (❖ただし「総量」の意味では the amount); (質に対する) quantity [U][C]; (総量・数量) volume [U][C]
塩の量を少し減らしたほうがいい You should decrease *the amount* of salt a little.
男の子は食事の質より量を気にすることが多い Boys are often more concerned with *the quantity* of food than the quality.
膨大な量の情報がインターネット上を行き来している *An enormous* [*A massive*] *amount of* information circulates on the Internet.
彼女はかなりの量の仕事をひとりでこなした She did *a considerable amount of* work by herself.
その台風は多量の雨をもたらした The typhoon brought us「*a large amount of* [*large quantities of, a lot of*] rain.
彼女は声量がある Her *voice* has plenty of *volume.*
このあたりは交通量が多い There's「*a heavy volume of traffic* [heavy *traffic*] around here.
◆酒の量を過ごす(→飲みすぎる) drink *too much*

りょう[2] 猟 hunting [U]; (銃猟)《英》shooting [U] (❖《英》では hunting は馬に乗りながら犬を使ってキツネなどを追いかけることを指し, 銃を使用しての狩りには shooting を用いる.《米》ではいずれの場合にも hunting を用いることができる)
◆イノシシ猟をする *hunt* [《英》*shoot*] wild boars / 彼らは山へ猟に行った They *went hunting* in the mountains.
‖猟期 a hunting [shooting] season, an open season / 猟犬 a hunting dog, a hound / 猟場 a hunting [shooting] ground

りょう[3] 漁 fishing [U]; (漁業) fishery [U][C]; (漁獲高) catch [C], take [C] ∥きょうはサケが大漁だった We had *a good* [*large*] *catch* of salmon today. ◆彼は海へマグロ漁に出ている He *has gone fishing for* tuna in the sea.
‖漁期 a fishing season

りょう[4] 寮《米》dormitory [C],《口語的》dorm [C],《英》a hall of residence
◆彼らは息子を全寮制の学校へやった They sent their son to *a boarding school.*
‖寮生 a boarder, a dormitory student / 寮長 a dormitory superintendent / 寮費 room and board charges / 寮母 a housemother / 学生寮 a student dormitory / 独身寮 an apartment house for bachelors

りょう[5] 良 (成績) B [C] ➔ゆう(優) ∥私は英語で良を取った I got *a B* in [for] English.

りょう[6] 両 (列車の車両)《米》car [C],《英》carriage [C],《英》coach [C] ∥10両編成の電車 a 10-*car* train / 新栃木行きの電車は10両編成です The train for Shintochigi is *made up of* 10 *cars.* / 前から2両目にいるからね I'll be in *the* second *car* from the front.

りょう[7] 涼 夕方, 涼を求めて庭に出た I went out into the garden in the evening *to cool off.*

りょう- 両- この川が両国の国境になる This river forms the boundary between *the two countries.* / 道の両側に店がたくさん並んでいた There were many shops on *both sides* of the street.

-りょう[1] -料 (サービスなどの料金) charge [C][U]; (弁護士・医者など専門職への謝礼金・授業料・入場料など) fee [C] (❖a toll (通行料), a premium (保険料)など個別の単語があるものも少なくない) ➔りょうきん ∥駐車料 a parking *charge* / 弁護料 a lawyer's *fee*

-りょう[2] -領 (領土) territory [C][U] ➔りょうど ∥かつてインドはイギリス領だった India used to be British *territory.*

りょういき 領域 (学問などの) domain [C], field [C], territory [C]; (活動などの) area [C]; (領土) territory [C][U] ∥科学の領域 *the domain* [*field, territory*] of science / 日本の領域 Japan's *territory* / そのテーマは私の研究領域外だ That topic is *outside* my *field* [*domain, territory*].

りょういん 両院 both [the two] Houses ∥その法案は両院を通過した The bill passed *both Houses.*
‖両院協議会 a joint conference of the two Houses

りょうえん 良縁 またとない良縁(→結婚相手)を逃してしまった I lost *the match* of a lifetime.

りょうか 良貨 [慣用表現] 悪貨は良貨を駆逐する ➔あっか(悪貨)

りょうが 凌駕 ──凌駕する transcend [他], surpass [他] ➔しのぐ

りょうかい[1] 了解 (理解) understanding [U] 《また an ～》; (同意) consent [U], agreement [U] (❖「協定」の意味では [C]) ──了解する understand* [他][自]; consent [自], agree [自][他] ∥私は両親の了解を得てアメリカ旅行へ出かけた I went on a trip to the U.S. with my parents' *consent.* / 最初にこの件について彼女の了解を求める[得る]べきだ We should「ask for [get] her *consent* to the matter first. / 家賃のことで大家と了解がついた I reached *an agreement* with the landlord about the rent. / 彼とはそのことを黙っておくという暗黙の了解があった I have *a tacit agreement* [*understanding*] with him about keeping the fact a secret. ◆了解 *OK!*/ *All right!*/ (→無線通信で) *Roger!*
‖了解事項 an agreed(-upon) item

りょうかい[2] 領海 territorial waters ∥その船は日本の領海内で漁をしていた The ship caught fish *within the bounds of* Japan's *territorial waters.*
‖領海侵犯 the violation of territorial waters

りょうがえ 両替 exchange [U] ──両替する exchange [他], change [他]; (くずす) break* [他] ∥日本円を米ドルに両替する *exchange* Japanese yen *for* American dollars; *change* Japanese yen *into* [*for*] American dollars / 1,000円札を100円玉に両替できますか Can

り

りょうがわ

you *change* [*break*] a 1,000-yen bill *into* 100-yen coins?
∥両替機 a change machine / 両替所 a money exchange / 両替料 an exchange commission

りょうがわ 両側 both sides ∥その街路の両側には桜の木が並んでいる Cherry trees line 「*both sides* [*either side*] of the street.

りょうかん 量感 この彫刻は量感に富んでいる This sculpture *takes up a lot of volume.* / This is a *massive* sculpture.

りょうがん 両岸 both banks ∥その川の両岸にはコスモスがたくさん咲いていた A lot of cosmoses were blossoming on 「*both banks* [*either bank*] of the river.

りょうきょく 両極 (南北の両極) the two poles, the north and south poles; (陰陽の両極) the positive and negative poles (◆語順に注意); (両極端) the extremes

りょうきょくたん 両極端 彼らの意見は両極端に分かれていた Their opinions *were poles apart.*

りょうきん 料金 charge ⓒⓊ; rate ⓒ; fare ⓒ; fee ⓒ; toll ⓒ

> charge: (公共の)サービス料金・使用料など.
> rate: 郵便料金・ガス料金など一定の規定に基づいた料金.
> fare: 主として乗り物の料金・運賃.
> fee: 弁護士・医者などの専門職の人に支払われる謝礼金や入場料・授業料など.
> toll: 道路・船橋などの使用料.

私たちはそのサービスに対する法外な料金に驚いた We were surprised at *the excessive charges* for the services.
市内であれば配達の料金は無料だ There is no *charge* for delivery within the city limits.
ひと部屋1泊の料金はいくらですか How much [What] is *the charge for* a room per night? / How much do you *charge for* a room per night?
鹿児島までの料金はいくらですか How much [What] is *the fare* to Kagoshima?
電話料金が来月から値下がりする *The telephone rate* will be lowered starting next month.
そのレストランは24時間営業だが，深夜料金を払わなければならない The restaurant is open 24 hours, but you have to pay *late-night charges.*
クラブの会員なら割引料金で海外旅行に行ける If you are a member of the club, you can travel abroad *at reduced fares.*
ここでは朝食は別料金です You have to pay *an extra charge for* breakfast here.
駐車料金は車の大きさによって異なります *The parking charge* varies depending on the size of the car.
◆彼は私の時計を修理するのに4,000円の料金を請求してきた He *charged* me 4,000 yen to repair my watch.
∥料金所(有料道路などの) a tollgate, a tollbooth / 料金精算 fare adjustment / 料金箱 (バスなどの) a fare box / 料金表 (品物の) a price list; (乗り物の) a list [schedule] of fares; (サービスの) a list of charges / 基本料金 a basic charge / 公共料金 public utility charges, utilities / サービス料金 a service charge / 追加料金 an extra (charge) / 特急料金 an express fare / レンタル料金 a rental fee / 割り増し料金 an additional charge; (乗り物の) an extra fare

りょうくう 領空 territorial airspace Ⓤ ∥その飛行機が日本の領空を侵犯した That plane violated *the territorial airspace* of Japan.

りょうけ 良家 good family ⓒⓊ ∥あの女の人は良家の娘らしいよ I heard that the lady is a daughter of *good family.*

りょうけん 了見 (考え) idea ⓒ; (意図) intention ⓒⓒ; (判断) judgment ⓒⓊ ∥そういう了見だと何もかもうまくいかないよ If you have *ideas* like that, nothing will work out for you. / 悪い[けちな]了見を起こすな(→考えをいだくな) Don't *conceive* evil [petty] *ideas.* / 彼女のせいだというのは君の了見違いだよ Your *judgment is wrong* in saying that she is to blame.
◆彼は了見が狭い He *is small-minded* [*narrow-minded*]. / He *has a small* [*narrow*] *mind.*

りょうけん² 猟犬 hunting dog ⓒ, hound ⓒ

りょうこう 良好 ── 良好な (よい) good; (すぐれた) excellent; (満足のいく) satisfactory ∥良好な成績 *excellent* grades / 本年度の当社の総売り上げは良好です Our gross sales this year are *good.*
◆患者の経過は良好です(→順調に回復している) The patient is improving [progressing, doing] *well.*

りょうさいけんぼ 良妻賢母 彼女は良妻賢母だ(→よい妻であり，よい母でもある) She is *a good wife and also a good mother.*

りょうさん 量産 mass production Ⓤ ── 量産する mass-produce ⓗ ∥わが社は来年4月からその製品の量産を開始する Our company will start to *mass-produce* our products in April of next year.

りょうし¹ 猟師 hunter ⓒ

りょうし² 漁師 fisherman ⓒ

りょうし³ 量子 〖物理〗 quantum ⓒ ∥量子物理学 quantum physics / 量子力学 quantum mechanics / 量子論 quantum theory

りょうじ 領事 consul ⓒ ∥彼は日本駐在スイス領事だ He is *the* Swiss *consul* in Japan.
∥領事館 a consulate / 領事館員(個人) a consular official; (集合的に) the staff of a consulate / 総領事 a consul general / 副領事 a vice-consul

りょうしき 良識 (常識) common sense Ⓤ ∥彼は良識がある He *has common sense.* / 彼は良識がない He *has no common sense.* / He *lacks common sense.*
◆もっと良識をわきまえるべきだ You should *be more sensible.* / 我々は大人として良識ある行動をとるべきだ As grown-ups we should

act sensibly.

りょうしつ 良質 good [fine, high] quality Ⓤ /この地域の土地は良質の米ができる The soil of this area produces「rice *of good quality* [*good-quality*] rice].

りょうしゃ 両者 料理の腕前において両者は互角だ *Both of them* [*The two of them*] are equally matched in their skill at cooking. / 両者の言い分を聞いてからその問題に答えます I'll reply to the question after I hear *both sides*. ⇒ りょうほう(両方)

りょうしゅ 領主 lord Ⓒ

りょうしゅう 領収 ——領収する receive ⓗ /２万円確かに領収しました I certainly *received* 20,000 yen. / 領収済み *Received*/ (→支払い済み) *Paid*
◆これの領収書をください Can I have *a receipt* for this?/ (→書いてください) Please make out *a receipt* for this.

りょうじゅう 猟銃 sporting [hunting] gun Ⓒ; (ライフル銃) sporting [hunting] rifle Ⓒ; (散弾銃) (hunting) shotgun Ⓒ

りょうしょう 了承 (承認) approval Ⓤ; (同意) consent Ⓤ; (理解) understanding 《また an ～》 ——了承する approve ⓗ ⓘ; consent ⓘ; understand* ⓗ ⓘ /会社の了承を求める ask for the company's *approval* [*consent*]/ その件についてはすでに彼の了承を得ています I've already got his「*approval of* [*consent to*] the matter./ 委員会はその新計画を了承した The committee *approved* [*consented to*] the new plan./ 当日の天候によってはイベントが中止になる場合があります。あらかじめご了承ください The event may be canceled depending on the (day's) weather. *Thank you for your understanding*. (❖「あらかじめ」は特に訳出する必要はない)

りょうしん¹ 両親 *one's* parents; (父母) *one's* mother and father
ご両親によろしくお伝えください Please give my regards to *your parents*.

りょうしん² 良心 conscience Ⓤ Ⓒ ——良心的な conscientious ——良心的に conscientiously
《良心が》
彼には全く良心がない He has absolutely no *conscience*.
テストでカンニングをすることは私の良心が許さない My *conscience* would not let me cheat on a test.
うそをつくと良心がとがめる I *have a bad* [*guilty*] *conscience* when I lie.
《良心の》
親友を裏切ったことについて良心の呵責(かしゃく)を感じている (→良心の痛みを感じている) I *feel a prick* [*sting*] *of conscience* about having betrayed my best friend./ (→良心が私を悩ませる) *My Conscience bothers me* about having betrayed my best friend./ (→罪の意識を感じている) I *feel guilty* about having betrayed my best friend.
《良心に》
彼は良心に恥じるところはないときっぱり言った He said flatly that he has *a clear* [*good*] *conscience*./ He said flatly that *his conscience* is clear [good].
良心に反することはできない I cannot go against *my conscience*.
人は常に自分自身の良心に従うべきだと思う I think that a person should always follow his own *conscience*.
良心に誓って私はうそを言っていない I cannot, *in good conscience*, tell a lie. (❖cannot, could not とともに用いる)
《良心的な》
彼らは良心的な仕事をする(→仕事に対して良心的だ) They are *conscientious about* their work./ (→良心的に仕事をする) They do their job *conscientiously*.
◆あの店(の人たち)はとても良心的だ(→信頼できる) They're very *trustworthy* [(→正直だ) *honest*] at that store./ この店は革製品を良心的な(→てごろな)値段で売っている This store sells leather goods at *reasonable* [(→公正な) *fair*] prices.

りょうせい¹ 良性 ——良性の(腫瘍(しゅよう)・病気が) 〔医学〕benign (↔malignant) /腫瘍が良性だと判明してほっとした He felt relieved that the tumor turned out to be *benign*.

りょうせい² 両性 both sexes /婚姻は両性の合意のみに基づいて成立する Marriage shall be based only on the mutual consent of *both sexes*.
‖両性具有 a hermaphrodite / 両性生殖〔生物〕gamogenesis, sexual reproduction

りょうせいばい 両成敗 [ことわざ] けんか両成敗 ⇒ けんか(喧嘩)

りょうせいるい 両生類 amphibian Ⓒ; (両生動物) amphibious animal Ⓒ

りょうせん 稜線 mountain ridge Ⓒ

りょうたん 両端 both ends, either end

りょうち 領地 territory Ⓒ Ⓤ ⇒ りょうど

りょうて 両手 both hands; (両腕) both arms /彼女は両手をこすり合わせた She rubbed *both hands* together./ 彼は両手でロープをしっかりと握った He grasped the rope firmly *with both hands*.
◆彼女は両手を広げて私を歓迎してくれた She welcomed me *with open arms*./ 彼は私の誕生日に両手にいっぱいの花をくれた He gave me *an armful of* flowers for my birthday./ 妹は両手で抱えきれないほど大きなクマのぬいぐるみを持っている My sister has a teddy bear that's so big she *can hardly hold* it *in her arms*.
🅒「僕はあした文子と優子とで映画に行くんだ」「うわあっ、両手に花だな(→美人の間にいられるな)」"I'm going to the movie with Fumiko and Yuko tomorrow." "Wow! You'*ll be between two beauties*!"

りょうてい 料亭 (高級な日本料理店) high-class Japanese restaurant

りょうてんびん 両天秤 美穂は徹と圭介を両天秤にかけていた(→つきあっていた)が、そのうち２人とも去っていった Miho *was going out with* Toru and Keisuke, but both of them soon dropped her. / 両天秤にかけられない(→両方同時に得られない)のは分かっている I understand that I *cannot have it both ways.*

りょうど 領土 territory [C][U]; (他国の支配下にある) possession [C] //これらの島々はその国の領土だ These islands are the country's *territories.* / (→その国に属している) These islands *belong to* the country. / その国は戦争に勝ち領土を拡張した That country won the war and extended *its territory.*

‖領土権 territorial rights / 領土保全 the preservation of territorial integrity / 領土問題 a territorial issue / 北方領土 the Northern Territories

りょうどなり 両隣 両隣の家に相次いで赤ちゃんが生まれた Babies were born to the people who live on *both sides of my house* one after the other.

りょうば 両刃 ―両刃の double-edged, two-edged

[慣用表現] 彼の議論は両刃の剣だ His argument is *a double-edged sword.*

りょうひ 良否 (質) quality [U] //品物の良否を見分ける distinguish *the quality* of goods

りょうびらき 両開き 両開きのドア a *double* door

りょうふう 涼風 cool breeze [C]

りょうぶん 領分 territory [C][U]; (分野) domain [C]; (範囲) sphere [C] //この問題は私の領分ではありません This problem is outside of my *sphere* [*domain*]. / それは子供の領分を侵すことになる That's going to encroach on the children's *territory.*

りょうほう[1] 両方

both

[語法]
(1) 形容詞 both は数えられる名詞の複数形に付ける. the, these, his などがあればその前に置くが, the はしばしば省略される // その本は両方ともおもしろい *Both* (the) books are interesting.
(2) 代名詞 both はしばしば both of ... の形で用いられ, of の後には代名詞または the, these, his などで限定された複数名詞がくる // その衝突事故で車は両方とも大破した *Both of* the cars [×Both of cars] were badly damaged in the collision.
(3) both of の後に代名詞がくる場合, of は省略できない // そのいすは両方とも木製です *Both* (*of*) the chairs are made of wood. / 私は中国語とロシア語を習ったことがあるが両方とも忘れてしまった I once studied Chinese and Russian, but I forget 「*both of* them [×both them].
(4) not ... both はふつう「両方とも…というわけではない」という部分否定を表す. 全否定「両方…ではない」は not ... either や neither を用いる // 両方は買えません I *can't* buy *both.* / 両方とも買えません I *can't* buy *either.* / I can buy *neither.*
(5) both が主語の位置にある場合, both ... not で「両方…ではない」を表すことはふつうしない. その場合は neither を用いる // 答えは両方とも正しくない *Neither* answer is correct.
(6) both を主語の名詞・代名詞と同格に用いる場合はふつう, 助動詞・be 動詞の後, 一般動詞の前に置く // その CD は両方とも私の物です The CDs are *both* mine. / The CDs *both* belong to me.

デザートは何がいいかしら. アップルパイかアイスクリーム? 両方でもいいですよ What would you like for dessert, apple pie or ice cream? Or you can have *both.*

彼は情熱と冷静な判断力の両方を兼ね備えている He has *both* passion *and* good judgment.

母も私も両方とも喜んでいます *Both* my mother *and* I are pleased. (❖×Both of my mother and I ... とはいわない)

💬「何か飼っていますか」「ええ, 猫を2匹飼っていて両方とも雪のように真っ白です」 "Do you have any pets?" "Yes, I have two cats, and *both* are white as snow."

りょうほう[2] 療法 (治療法) treatment [C][U], remedy [C]; (薬や手術によらない) therapy [U][C] ➔ちりょう //それはかぜの民間療法の一つです That's one of *the folk remedies for* colds. ◆彼女は今食餌(しょくじ)療法をしている She is on *a diet* now.

‖温泉療法 a hot spring cure / 化学療法 chemotherapy / 集団療法 group therapy / ショック療法 shock therapy / 物理療法 physiotherapy / 放射線療法 radiotherapy

りょうめん 両面 both sides //紙の両面にコピーしてください Please use *both sides* of the paper when making copies. / 私たちは常に物事の両面を見なければならない We always have to see *both sides* [*each side*] of issues.

‖両面テープ double-sided [double-faced] adhesive tape

りょうやく 良薬 good medicine [U][C]

[ことわざ] 良薬は口に苦(にが)し A good medicine tastes bitter.

りょうゆう 領有 (所有) possession [U] ―領有する possess [他] (❖進行形にはできない) //イギリスはかつて多くの植民地を領有していた Britain used to *possess* a lot of colonies. ◆彼らは土地の領有権を得るために戦っていた They were fighting for *territorial rights.*

りょうよう[1] 療養 (病後の回復) 《公式的》 recuperation [U]; (治療) medical treatment [U] ―療養する recuperate [自]; receive medical treatment //彼女は先月から療養生活を送っている She *has been in recuperation* since last month.

◆彼は自宅療養をしている He *is receiving* [*under*] *home treatment.* / He *is recuperating at home.* / 祖父母は箱根へ転地療養に行った My grandparents *went to* Hakone *for a change of air.*

‖療養所(サナトリウム) a sanatorium; (老人などの) a rest home / 療養費 medical expenses

りょうよう² 両用 ‖遠近両用眼鏡 bifocals, bifocal glasses / 水陸両用車 an amphibious vehicle

りょうり 料理

(調理) cooking Ⓤ; (特有の調理法で作られたもの) cuisine Ⓤ Ⓒ; (作られたもの) dish Ⓒ; (食べ物一般) food Ⓤ ──料理する (火を使って) cook 他 自; (作る) make* 他; (食事のしたくをする) prepare 他, 《主に米口語的》fix 他
⇨ 場面・状況別会話 p.1716

肉[野菜]料理 a meat [vegetable] *dish* / 料理の材料 *cooking* materials [ingredients] / コショウで料理に風味づけをする season *a dish* with pepper

この料理は少ししつこい This *dish* is a little heavy.

フランス料理もイタリア料理も大好きです I like both French and Italian *food* very much.

このレストランの料理はおいしい This restaurant offers [serves] delicious *food.*

私の自慢の料理を作ってあげる I'll cook you my *favorite dish.* (❖favorite は「大好きな」という意味にもなる)

母は台所で夕食を料理している My mother *is cooking* [*making*] dinner in the kitchen.

私は魚を料理するにおいが好きだ I like the smell of fish *being cooked.*

治子は料理が上手だ Haruko *is good at cooking* [*cookery*]. / Haruko *cooks* well. / Haruko *is a good cook.*

この魚の料理のしかたを知ってる? Do you know *how to cook* this fish?

◆ 5品料理 *a dinner of five courses; a five-course dinner* / 中華料理店 a Chinese *restaurant* / (レストランで)きょうのおすすめ料理は何ですか What is today's *special*?

🅔「料理はしますか」「食事はあまり作らないけどケーキはよく作ります」 "Do you *cook*?" "Well, I don't prepare meals but often make cakes."

‖料理学校 a cookery [cooking] school / 料理教室 a cooking class / 料理酒 sake for cooking / 料理人 a cook / 料理番組 a TV cooking program [show] / 料理法 cookery; (個々の料理の) a recipe / 料理の本 a cook [cookery, recipe] book / 料理屋 a restaurant / 家庭料理 home cooking / 郷土料理 a local [regional] dish / 民族料理 ethnic food

りょうりつ 両立 ほとんどの場合, 仕事と楽しみは両立しない Business and pleasure *do not go together* in most cases. / 彼女は勉強とクラブ活動を両立させている She *is doing well both in* her studies *and in* club activities.

りょうりん 両輪 編集部と営業部が車の両輪となって会社の経営を支えた The editorial department and the sales department *worked in cooperation* to manage the company.

りょうわき 両脇 (両方のわき腹) both sides [flanks] ◆彼は大きな箱を両わき(→両腕の下)に抱えて私のところにやってきた He came to me *carrying* big boxes *under his arms.*

りょかく 旅客 (旅行者) traveler Ⓒ; (乗客) passenger Ⓒ
‖旅客運賃 passenger fares / 旅客機 a passenger plane / (大型の定期旅客機) an airliner / 旅客名簿 a passenger list; (乗客名簿) a boarding list / 旅客列車 a passenger train / ジェット旅客機 a jetliner

りょかん 旅館 📛 a *ryokan,* a Japanese-style inn [hotel] ‖旅館を経営する keep [run, manage] *a Japanese-style inn* [*hotel*] ◆その夜私たちは塩原の大和屋旅館に1泊した We stayed at *the Yamatoya Inn* [*Hotel*] in Shiobara for the night.

りょくおうしょくやさい 緑黄色野菜 green and yellow vegetables

りょくち 緑地 a green tract of land ‖緑地帯(都市周辺の) a green belt

りょくちゃ 緑茶 green tea Ⓤ

りょくないしょう 緑内障 〔医学〕glaucoma Ⓤ ‖彼は左目が緑内障になった He developed *glaucoma* in his left eye.

りょけん 旅券 passport Ⓒ ⇨ パスポート

りょこう 旅行

travel Ⓤ (また複数形 ~s); trip Ⓒ; tour Ⓒ; journey Ⓒ; voyage Ⓒ; excursion Ⓒ ──旅行する travel 自, take* [make*] a trip (❖観光の旅行は take を, 仕事上の旅行は make を用いることが多い); (旅行に出かける) go* on a trip ⇨ 場面・状況別会話 p.1686

> travel: 周遊・観光旅行, また《英》では特に遠距離や海外旅行を指し, 冠詞を付けずに単数形で用いる. 複数形は長期の旅行や海外旅行を指す. またほかの語に比べて移動に重点がある.
> trip: 《米》では旅行を表す最も一般的な語で目的や期間がはっきりしている. 《英》では特に短期の旅行を指す.
> tour: 人数に関係なく観光・視察のために各地を回る旅行を意味し, 日本語の団体旅行としての「ツアー」とは多少意味がずれる.
> journey: 陸路による長い旅.
> voyage: 海路または空路による長い旅.
> excursion: 短期間の団体観光旅行, 遠足.

《~旅行》
小旅行 *a short trip* / 日帰り旅行 *a day trip* / 2週間のハワイ旅行 *a two-week tour of Hawaii*

彼女は海外旅行が好きです She likes *traveling* overseas.(❖名詞の travel は修飾語を伴うのがふつう)

いつか私は世界一周旅行をするつもりです I plan to *travel* [*take a trip*] around the world someday.

《旅行を・に》
楽しいご旅行を Have a nice *trip*! / *Bon voyage*! (❖後の表現はフランス語で発音は [bɒ̃vwɑːʒ])

私たちは旅行を2週間延期しなければならなかった We had to delay *our trip* for two

weeks.
今姉は旅行に出かけています My older sister *is* (*away*) *on a trip* now.
両親は箱根の温泉地へ2泊3日の旅行に行った My parents *went on a* 3-day *trip* to a hot spring resort in Hakone.
〖旅行は〗
旅行は楽しかったですか Did you have *a* good *trip*?
今回の旅行は買い物がメインだ A main part of this *trip* is shopping.
💬「京都への旅行はどうでしたか」「とても楽しかったです」"How was *your trip* to Kyoto?" "I enjoyed it very much."
〖旅行の〗
私の旅行の目的は自分自身をリフレッシュすることだ The purpose of my *trip* is to refresh myself.
旅行の準備はもうすっかりできているよ I've already gotten [made] ready for *the trip*.
彼と九州への旅行の計画を立てた I made a plan for *a trip* to Kyushu with him.
〖その他〗
彼女は飛行機で旅行するのが大嫌いだ She can't bear to *travel* by plane [air].
旅行中はレンタカーを借りるつもりだ I will rent a car *during my trip*.
旅行から戻ってみると，植物がいくつか枯れていた *On my return from my trip*, I found some of my plants had withered away.
‖旅行案内 a guide(book), a tourists' guide / 旅行案内所 a tourist information office, a travel bureau / 旅行かばん a traveling bag; (スーツケース) a suitcase; (トランク) a trunk / 旅行記 a traveler's account / 旅行業者 a travel agent / 旅行先(目的地) a destination / 旅行者(観光客) a tourist; (旅人) a traveler, 《英》a traveller / 旅行代理店 a travel agency, 《英》a tour operator / 宇宙旅行 space travel / 観光旅行 a sightseeing tour / 講演旅行 a lecture tour / 自転車旅行 a bicycle trip, a cycling tour / 社員旅行 a company outing / 修学旅行 a school trip / 新婚旅行 a honeymoon / 団体旅行 a group tour; (添乗員付きの旅行) a conducted [guided] tour / 月旅行 a voyage to the moon / 鉄道旅行 rail travel / パック旅行 a package tour

りょしゅう 旅愁 私は湖畔にたたずみ旅愁に浸っていた(→旅の寂しさを感じていた) As I stood at the side of the lake, I felt *the loneliness of my journey*.

りょじょう 旅情 そのポスターは旅情(→旅行をしたいという気持ち)をかきたてた The poster filled me with *wanderlust*.

りょっか 緑化 greening [U], tree planting [U] ━緑化する plant trees, green [他] ‖この町を緑化するために多くの案が出ている There are many suggestions to 「*plant* more *trees* in this town [*add more greenery* this town].
‖緑化運動 a tree-planting campaign

りょてい 旅程 (道のり) distance [C] [U]; (日程) itinerary [C]

りょひ 旅費 traveling expenses; (運賃) fare [C] ‖あなたの旅費は会社が負担します The company will pay your *traveling expenses*.
◆エジプトまでの旅費はいくらかかりますか How much does it *cost to travel* [*go*] to Egypt?

リラ (イタリアの貨幣単位) lira [C] (複 lire, ～s) (《略語》L); 〖植物〗(ライラックの木) lilac [C] [U]

リラックス ━リラックスする relax [自] ‖さあ，リラックスして Now, *relax*. / 早く熱いおふろに入ってリラックスしたい I really want to *relax* in a hot bath. / 彼は私をリラックスさせようとおもしろい話をしてくれた He told me a funny story to *make* me *relax* [*feel relaxed*].
◆この花の香りをかぐと気分がリラックスする(→花の香りが私をリラックスさせる) The scent of this flower *relaxes* me. / 彼女はリラックスした気分でピアノを演奏した She played the piano in a *relaxed* mood.

リリース ジャミロクワイの新曲が来月リリースされる Jamiroquai's new song *will be released* next month.

リリーフ 6回に五十嵐が斉藤をリリーフした Igarashi *relieved* Saito in the sixth inning.
‖リリーフ投手 a relief pitcher

りりく 離陸 takeoff [C] [U] ━離陸する take* off ‖私たちの乗った飛行機は定刻どおり5時に成田を離陸した Our plane *took off* on time from Narita at five. / 離陸直後にその飛行機は墜落した The plane crashed *immediately after* 「*its takeoff* [*it took off*].

りりしい 凛々しい 彼の制服姿はとてもりりしかった(→勇ましかった) He *looked* very *brave* in his school uniform. / その青年は常にりりしい(→勇敢な)態度を示していた The young man always showed a *courageous* attitude.

りりつ 利率 interest rate [C] ‖利率を上げる[下げる] raise [lower] *the interest rate* / 定期預金の利率は年1.3パーセントです *The interest rate* on a fixed deposit is 1.3 percent per year.

リレー (競技) relay (race) [C] ‖彼女は次の400メートルリレーに出る She will compete in *the* next 400-meter *relay race*. / 彼はオリンピックの聖火リレーで走る He will run in *the* Olympic *torch relay*.
◆私たちはバケツリレーで火を消した We put out a fire 「*with a bucket brigade* [*by passing buckets of water from one person to another*].

りれき 履歴 *one's* personal history; (職歴) *one's* career; (素性・経歴) *one's* background ‖彼は手短に履歴を述べた He gave a brief account of *his personal history*. / 彼女はずっと私たちに履歴を偽っていた She had lied to us about *her background*.
‖履歴書 a personal history, 《公式的》a curriculum vitae (《略語》c.v., CV), 《米》a résumé ➾ [巻末付録] (履歴書の書き方)

りろせいぜん 理路整然 ━理路整然とした

り

(論理的な) logical ──理路整然と logically ∥彼の申し立ては理路整然としていた His statement was logical.

りろん 理論 theory Ⓤ (◆個々の理論の意味では Ⓒ) ──理論(上)の・理論的な theoretical ──理論的に theoretically, in theory

私の理論は事実に基づいている My *theory* is grounded on facts.

彼はその機械がどのように作動するのか理論的に説明した He「gave a *theoretical* explanation [explained *the theory*] of how the machine worked.

君の考えが理論的に可能なのは分かるが, 実行するのは難しいと思う I know that your idea is 「possible *in theory* [*theoretically* possible], but I believe it'll be difficult to put it into practice.

アインシュタインは相対性理論を確立した人物だ Einstein is the person who formulated *the theory of relativity*.

∥理論家 a theorist, a theoretician / 理論物理学 theoretical physics

りん¹ 燐 〖化学〗phosphorus Ⓤ (◆元素記号 P)

りん² 厘 彼の打率は2割9分9厘です He has a .299 batting average. (◆.299は two ninety-nine と読む)

りんか 隣家 the house next door

りんかい¹ 臨海 ──臨海の (沿岸の) coastal; (海辺の) seaside

∥臨海学校 a seaside summer school / 臨海工業地帯 a coastal industrial area [region] / 臨海都市 a maritime city

りんかい² 臨界 ──臨界の 〖数学・物理〗critical ∥臨界に達する go *critical*; (→ 臨界点に) reach *the critical point*; (→ 臨界状態に) reach *the critical state*

∥臨界温度 critical temperature / 臨界事故 a criticality accident / 臨界質量 critical mass

りんかく 輪郭 ❶【外形】outline Ⓒ ∥霧の中にぼんやりと富士山の輪郭が見えた I saw *a* vague *outline* of Mt. Fuji through a mist. ❷【概略】outline Ⓒ; (大まかな考え) rough [general] idea Ⓒ ∥このレポートには私たちの計画の輪郭が述べてある This paper gives *a* rough [*general*] *idea* of our plan. / その女性の証言は事件の輪郭を浮き彫りにした The woman's testimony clearly brought out *the outline* of the case.

りんがく 林学 forestry Ⓤ

りんかん 林間 ∥林間学校 an open-air (summer) school

りんぎ 稟議 ∥稟議書(回状) a round robin

りんきおうへん 臨機応変 彼はどんな状況でも臨機応変の処置をとれる人だ He「*can be flexible* [*is equal to the occasion, rises to the occasion*] in any situation. / 私たちは物事に臨機応変に (→ 状況に応じて) 対処するべきだ We should handle things [*as the occasion arises*].

りんぎょう 林業 forestry Ⓤ

リンク (スケートリンク) (skating) rink Ⓒ

リング (輪・指輪) ring Ⓒ; (ボクシングなどの) ring Ⓒ ∥そのレスラーは, はでなアクションでリングに上がった The wrestler entered *the ring* in grand fashion [style].

∥リングサイド(座席) the ringside, a ringside seat / エンゲージリング an engagement ring

りんげつ 臨月 姉は臨月だ My sister *is in her last month of pregnancy.*

りんけん 臨検 (立ち入り検査) inspection Ⓤ Ⓒ; (船の) visitation Ⓒ, search Ⓒ ──臨検する inspect ㊙; visit ㊙, search ㊙

りんご 林檎 (果実) apple Ⓒ; (木) apple (tree) Ⓒ ∥リンゴの花 *apple* blossoms / 彼は私にリンゴの皮をむいてくれた He peeled *an apple* for me.

◆その少女はリンゴのような (→ バラ色の) ほおをしていた The little girl had *rosy* cheeks.

∥リンゴ園 an apple orchard / リンゴジャム apple jelly / リンゴ酒《米》hard cider, 《英》cider / 焼きリンゴ a baked apple

りんごく 隣国 neighboring country, neighbor Ⓒ

りんさく 輪作 crop rotation Ⓤ ──輪作する rotate ㊙ ∥作物を輪作する *rotate* crops

りんじ 臨時 ──臨時の (一時的な) temporary; (暫定(だ)的な) provisionary; (余分の) extra; (特別の) special, extraordinary; (偶発の) incidental

お金が足りないので臨時の仕事を探さなければならない I have to find a *temporary* job because I don't have enough money.

その店は臨時の人を雇うらしい I heard that the shop will hire some *temporary* workers.

臨時の出費がかさんだので新しい時計が買えなかった I couldn't buy a new watch because I had a lot of *incidental* expenses.

◆大型台風の直撃でその地域のほとんどの学校が臨時休校になった Most of the schools in the area *were temporarily closed* due to a direct hit by a large-scale typhoon.

∥臨時閣議 an extraordinary cabinet meeting / 臨時休業 a special [an extra] holiday / 臨時国会 an extraordinary session of the Diet / 臨時試験 a special examination / 臨時収入 extra [incidental] income; (思いがけない収入) unexpected money / 臨時政府 a provisional government / 臨時総会 an extraordinary general meeting / 臨時増刊号 an extra [a special] (edition) (◆edition の代わりに issue も可) / 臨時ニュース a special newscast, a news bulletin; (ニュース速報) a news flash / 臨時雇い temporary employment; (人) a temporary worker, 《口語的》a temp / 臨時予算 a provisional budget / 臨時列車 a special [an extra] train

りんしたいけん 臨死体験 near-death experience Ⓒ (《略記》NDE)

りんしつ 隣室 the next room

りんじゅう 臨終 *one's* end, *one's* death; (最後の時) *one's* last moments; (死の床)

one's deathbed ―臨終の（死に際の）dying;（最後の）last ∥私は彼の臨終に間に合わなかった I could not be with him in his *last moments.* / 母の臨終の言葉は絶対に忘れない I'll never forget my mother's *last* [*dying*] words. / 彼女は臨終の際何か言っていた She said something *on her deathbed.*

◆残念ですが，ご臨終です I'm sorry, but he [she]「*didn't make it* [*has passed away*].

りんしょう[1] 輪唱〔音楽〕round [C] ―輪唱する troll [他][自] ∥私たちは『カエルの歌』を輪唱した We *trolled* "Kaerunouta." / We *sang a round* of "Kaerunouta."

りんしょう[2] 臨床 ―臨床の clinical ∥臨床医 a clinician / 臨床医学 clinical medicine / 臨床実験 a clinical trial [test]

りんじょうかん 臨場感 ステレオにサラウンドスピーカーをつけたら前よりも臨場感あふれるサウンドになった The sound got more *lifelike* than before due to the surrounding speakers connected to the stereo.

りんじん 隣人 neighbor [C]（❖「すぐ隣に住んでいる人」であることを強調する場合は a next-door neighbor という）;《集合的》the neighbors, the neighborhood ∥私たちはよい隣人に恵まれている We are blessed with good *neighbors.*

∥隣人愛 the love of *one's* neighbor

リンス rinse [U][C] ∥髪をシャンプーした後はリンスをした（→リンスを使った）ほうがいいよ You should *use rinse* after you shampoo your hair.（❖rinse *one's* hair は単に「髪をゆすぐ」の意味）

りんせき[1] 隣席 彼は私の隣席に座った He took *the seat next* to mine. /（→私の隣に座った）He sat down *next* to me.

りんせき[2] 臨席 attendance [U][C], presence [U] ∥その式典は大統領の臨席のもと盛大に執(と)り行われた The ceremony was held on a large scale with the President *in attendance.* / 私共の記念祝典にご臨席いただけると光栄に存じます We request the honor of *your attendance* [*presence*] at our commemoration.

りんせつ 隣接 ―隣接する adjoin [他][自] ―隣接した adjacent, neighboring ∥郵便局は図書館に隣接している The post office *adjoins* [*is adjacent to, is next to*] the library. / 兵庫県と鳥取県は隣接している Hyogo and Tottori are *adjacent* [*neighboring*] prefectures.

リンチ ⚠ 彼らは新入生にリンチを加えた They *inflicted violence on* the new student. /（→いじめた）They *gave* the new student *a hard time.* /（→たたきのめした）They *beat up* the new student. / 彼はずっとクラスメートからリンチを受けていた He *was punished* by his classmates for a long time.（❖英語の lynch は「裁判抜きで絞首刑に処する」という意味）

りんてんき 輪転機 rotary press [C]

りんどう[1] 林道 a path through a forest;（材木運搬用の）logging road [C]

りんどう[2] 竜胆〔植物〕gentian [C]

りんどく 輪読 私たちはその本を輪読した（→順番に読んだ）We *read* from the book *in* [*by*] *turns.*

∥輪読会（サークル）a reading group;（会合）a meeting of the reading group

りんね 輪廻（魂の）transmigration [U], metempsychosis [U][C]（複 metempsychoses）

∥輪廻説 the doctrine of transmigration

リンネル（リネン）linen [U]

∥リンネル製品 linens

リンパ（リンパ液）lymph [U];（リンパ節）lymph node [C] ∥リンパ腺(せん)がはれた I have swollen *lymph glands.*

りんばん 輪番 rotation [U][C] ―輪番で（順番に）in rotation;（次々に）in turn;（交替で）by turns ∥その会議の議長は輪番制だ The chairmanship of the conference *is taken by turns.*

りんびょう 淋病〔医学〕gonorrhea [U],《俗語／婉曲的》clap [U]《通例 the ～》

りんり 倫理（個人・職業などの道義）ethics;（道徳）morals ―倫理的な ethical; moral ―倫理的に ethically; morally ∥わいろを受け取るのは政治倫理に反している It *is against political ethics* to take bribes. /（→政治家として倫理的ではない）It *is*「*not ethical* [*unethical*] *for a politician* to take bribes. / それは倫理上の問題として扱うべきだ It should be handled as *an ethical problem* [*a matter of ethics*]. / 彼の判断は倫理的に間違っていると思う I think his judgment is *morally* [*ethically*] wrong.

∥倫理学 ethics, moral philosophy / 倫理学者 an ethicist, a moral philosopher / 倫理観 a sense of ethics

りんりつ 林立 新宿は高層ビルが林立している Shinjuku *bristles with* tall buildings. /（→高層ビルでいっぱいだ）Shinjuku *is crowded with* tall buildings. / その道を行くと林立する煙突が見えてきた As I went down the street, *a forest of* chimneys came into sight.

りんりん 家に帰ると電話がリンリン鳴っていた When I came home, the phone *was ringing.* / その子供は鈴をりんりん鳴らした The child *jingled* [*tinkled*] the bell.

る

ルアー (疑似餌(え)[針]) lure [C]
‖ルアーフィッシング lure fishing

るい[1] 類 (種類) kind [C], sort [C]; (部類) class [C]; (分類上の属) 〘生物〙genus [C] (複genera, ～es) ∥ビタミン類は肌荒れにいい All *kinds* of vitamins are good for your skin troubles.
◆それは世界に類を見ないほど(→比べるものがないほど)残酷な犯罪だった That was a brutal crime *without parallel* in the world. / この国の伝統的な織物製法はほかに類を見ない(→独特な)ものだ This country's traditional method of weaving is *unique*.
[ことわざ] 類は友を呼ぶ Birds of a feather flock together. (→同じ羽をした鳥は集まる)

るい[2] 塁 (ベース) 〘野球〙base [C] [U] ∥塁に出る get on *base*; (→一塁に) 「get to [make, reach] *first base* / 塁に出ている be on *base* / 塁を離れる be off *base*
‖一[二, 三]塁 first [second, third] base (❖theは付けない) / 本塁 (the) home (plate)

るい[3] 累 彼の行為は周囲の人々に累を及ぼす(→迷惑をかける)だろう His act will 「*cause trouble for* [*spill over onto*] those close to him.

るいぎご 類義語 synonym [C] (↔antonym) ∥gladはhappyの類義語だ "Glad" is *a synonym* for "happy." / "Glad" and "happy" are *synonyms*.

るいけい[1] 累計 the total ◆月ごとの出費を累計する *total up* each month's expenses / 台風による死者と負傷者の数は累計で300人になる The number of the dead and injured by the typhoon *amounts to* 300.

るいけい[2] 類型 (型) type [C] ∥文化をいくつかの類型に分ける divide cultures into some *types* ◆類型的な(→型にはまった)推理小説 a *stereotypical* mystery novel

るいご 類語 synonym [C] ⇒るいぎご

るいじ 類似 similarity [U]; (特に外観の) resemblance [U], likeness [U] (❖いずれも「類似点」という意味では[C]) ━類似の similar ━類似する be similar (to ...); resemble [他], be alike ⇒にる(似る)
我々はその2つの犯罪にいくつかの類似点を発見した We have found some *similarities* between the two crimes.
A社とX社の製品は形が類似している The products of A company and those of X company *are alike* [*similar*] in shape.
◆類似品(→偽物)にご注意ください Beware of *imitations*.

ルイジアナ Louisiana (❖米国南部の州; 《略語》La., 〘郵便〙LA)

るいしょ 類書 similar books ∥英文法に関する類書は多い There are lots of *similar books* on English grammar.

るいしょう 類焼 類焼を免れる escape *the fire* / レストランからの出火で3軒の店が類焼した Three shops *burned down in the fire that spread* from the restaurant.

るいしん 塁審 base [field] umpire [C] ∥三塁塁審 *the* third *base umpire*

るいじんえん 類人猿 anthropoid (ape) [C], ape [C]

るいしんかぜい 累進課税 graduated [progressive] taxation [U]

るいすい 類推 analogy [U] ━類推する reason by analogy; (推論する) infer [他]; (推測する) guess [他]; (判断する) judge [他] [自] ∥過去の事例から類推すると, 今回の事件も解決までにはかなり時間を要するのではないだろうか *Judging* from similar cases in the past, this case will also need a lot of time to solve.

るいする 類する be similar to ... ∥これに類する植物は日本にしか見られない Plants that *are similar to* this can be found only in Japan.

るいせき 累積 accumulation [C] [U] ━累積する accumulate [他] [自] ‖累積赤字 a cumulative [an accumulated] deficit

るいせん 涙腺 〘医学〙lachrymal glands
◆話を聞いているうちに涙腺がゆるんできた(→涙があふれてきた) *Tears welled up in my eyes* while I listened to the story.

るいれい 類例 similar example [instance] [C]; (事例) similar case [C] ∥類例を挙げて説明する explain by giving *a similar example* [*case*] ◆このような事件は世界に類例がない(→比べるものがない) Such an incident *is unparalleled* in the world.

ルー (カレーの) roux [rúː] [U] [C] (複 ～ [rúːz])

ルーキー (新人) 《米口語的》rookie [C]

ルージュ ⚠(口紅) lipstick [U] [C] (❖日本語はフランス語のrougeからで, 英語のrougeは「ほお紅」の意味)

ルーズ ⚠ ━ルーズな (いいかげんな) sloppy; (不注意な) careless (❖英語のloose [lúːs]にも日本語の「ルーズな」と同じ意味があるが, 古風な表現で, 「(特に女性が)道徳的にふしだらな」という意味にとられることがあるので注意が必要) ∥彼女はお金にルーズだから貸さないほうがいい Because she is *careless* with money, you shouldn't lend her any. ◆経営のルーズな店 a *sloppily*-run shop / 宇野は時間にルーズで, いつも30分は遅れてくる Uno is *not punctual* and is always at least 30 minutes late.
‖ルーズソックス baggy socks

ルーズリーフ ⚠(ノート) loose-leaf [lúːslíːf] notebook [C]; (紙) loose-leaf paper [U] (❖数えるときはa piece of ... とする)

ルーツ (祖先) roots; (起源) origin [C] ∥彼は自分のルーツを探るために故郷の長崎へ行った He went to Nagasaki, his hometown, to search for his *roots*. ◆サッカーのルーツはイギリスにある Soccer *originated in* Britain.

ルート[1] (道) route [C] 《通例the～》, way

る

ルート

□; (情報伝達の) channel □《しばしば複数形 ~s》; (方法) way □; (コース) course □ ∥外交ルート diplomatic *channels* ∕ 電車で渋谷まで行く最短ルートを教えてください Could you tell me *the* shortest *route [way]* to Shibuya by train? ∕ 警察は麻薬の密輸ルートを突き止めた The police found out *the illegal channel [route]* for the drugs. ∕ このブランド物のバッグは正規のルートを通して手に入れました I got this brand-name bag in the regular *way*.

ルート² ⚠ (平方根)〘数学〙square root □ ∥ルート25は5である *The square root of* 25 *is* 5.

ルーフ roof □ ∥ルーフバルコニー a rooftop balcony ∕ サンルーフ a sunroof

ループ (輪) loop □ ∥ループアンテナ a loop antenna ∥ループシュート a looping shot

ルーブル (ロシアの貨幣単位) ruble, rouble □; (ルーブル美術館) the Louvre

ルーペ ⚠ (拡大鏡) magnifying glass □ (✽日本語はドイツ語のLupeから)

ルーム room □ ∥ルームクーラー an air conditioner ∕ ルームミラー a rearview mirror ∕ ルームメイト a roommate

ルームサービス ルームサービスで朝食を頼んだ I ordered breakfast *from room service*.

ルール rule □ ⇒きそく
  ルールに従う obey [follow] *the rule(s)* ∕ ルールを破る break *a rule*
  ルールを守ってください Please observe *the rules*.
  おい, ルール違反だぞ Hey! That's *against the rules*!
  ∥ルールブック a rulebook ∕ 交通ルール a traffic rule

ルーレット (賭博) roulette □; (用具) roulette wheel □ ∥ルーレットをする play *roulette*

ルクス (照度の単位) lux [lʌks] □ (複 ~, luces, ~es) (《略記》lx)

るけい 流刑 (国家命令などによる) exile □; (追放) banishment □ ◆男はこの島に流刑になった The man *was exiled* to the island.

るす 留守

❶【不在】──留守にする be not (at) home; (外出している) be out; (家を離れている) be away
  父はゴルフに行っていて留守です My father *is out* golfing.
  兄は1週間留守にしている My big brother *has been away* for a week. (✽比較的長い不在のときはoutでなくawayを用いる)
  いつ電話しても彼女は留守だった Every time I called her up, she *was not at home*.
  留守の間に良二から電話があったよ *While you were out*, there was a phone call for you from Ryoji.
  両親に留守番をするように言われた My parents told me to *look after things at home while they were away*.
  ◆私の留守中にだれか来ましたか Did anyone come *during* [*in*] *my absence*? ∕ 留守電にセ

ットしてから家を出ること Set *the answering machine* before you go out. ∕ ただ今留守にしております (→電話に出られません), 発信音の後にメッセージをお願いします I can't come to the phone right now. Please leave a message after the beep [tone].

❷【注意が向いていないこと】
  母に勉強がお留守になっている (→怠けている) としかられた My mom scolded me because I *had been neglecting* my studies.

ルックス (容貌) looks ∥有香の彼氏はルックスがいい Yuka's boyfriend has good *looks*. ∕ ユウカの彼氏はかっこいい Yuka's boyfriend is good-*looking*.

るつぼ 坩堝 (耐熱性の容器) crucible □; (多様な人種・文化などの) melting pot □ ∥ニューヨークはまさに人種のるつぼである New York is *a real melting pot*. ◆アンディ・フグがリングに上がると同時に場内は興奮のるつぼと化した The inside of the hall *entered a state of feverish excitement* as soon as Andy Hug stepped into the ring.

るてん 流転 constant change □, flux □; (人生の浮き沈み) (《公式的》) vicissitudes ∥万物は流転する Everything *is in a state of flux*. ∕ Everything *changes constantly*.

ルネサンス the Renaissance [rènəsɑ́ːns] (✽Renaissanceは形容詞的にも使われる) ∥ルネサンス期の画家 [絵画] *Renaissance* painters [pictures]
  ∥ルネサンス様式 the Renaissance style

ルビ ルビ (→ふり仮名) をふる put *kana* beside [above] *kanji* to show how to read them (✽besideは仮名を横に, aboveは上にふるときに用いる) ⇒ふりがな

ルビー ruby □

るふ 流布 circulation □ ──流布する spread*⊜, circulate⊜ ⇒ひろまる ∥その伝説はこの島に広く流布している The legend *has spread* [*circulated*] in this island.

ルポライター ⚠ reporter □ (✽日本語はルポ (ルタージュ) とライターの合成語)

ルポ (ルタージュ) (現地報告)《公式的》reportage [ripɔ́ːrtɪdʒ] □ (✽フランス語から); (報告・報道記事) report □; (記録作品) documentary □ ∥秋葉原のそのルポはとても印象的だった The *report* on Akihabara made a deep impression on me.

るり 瑠璃〘鉱物〙lapis lazuli □□
  ∥瑠璃色 lapis lazuli, azure (blue)

るる (と) 縷々 (と) るる (→詳細に) 事情を説明した I explained the reason *in detail*.

ろう 流浪 wanderings ──流浪する wander⊜⊖ ∥その男は日本全国を流浪した The man *wandered* all over Japan. ∕ その俳人は流浪の旅の道中にたくさんの句を詠んだ The haiku poet wrote many haiku during *his wanderings*. ◆流浪の民 *wanderers*

ルンバ rumba [rʌ́mbə] □□ (✽スペイン語から)

ルンペン ⚠ (浮浪者) tramp □ (✽日本語はドイツ語のLumpenから)

るんるん 臨時収入があったので一日中るんるん気分だった I *was in a happy mood* all day because I got some extra money.

れ

レ 〘音楽〙 re [réi] ⓊⒸ

レア ━レアの (生焼きの) rare ∥ステーキはレアでお願いします I'd like my steak *rare*, please.

レイ (首にかける花輪) lei Ⓒ

れい¹ 例

❶【手本・見本】example Ⓒ; (図表など) illustration Ⓒ

教科書の例にならって色を塗った I painted according to *the illustration* in the textbook.

この例にならって作図してください *Follow* this *example* when you draw.

❷【事例・先例】case Ⓒ; (代表的な) example Ⓒ; (特定の) instance Ⓒ; (先例) precedent Ⓒ

君のような例は珍しい Your *case* is unusual.

同様の例を私はたくさん知っている I know many similar *cases*.

例をいくつか見てみましょう Let's look at some *examples*.

例を挙げてくれますか Can you give me *an example*?

芸術家が若くして世を去った例は多い There are many *instances* of artists dying young.

そのような例は今まで例がない There is no *precedent* for the case.

◆こんな大型の台風が上陸した例はない A direct hit by such a huge typhoon is *unprecedented*.

❸【その他】

例の裁判どうなった What happened with *that* trial?

例の場所で会おう Let's meet at the *usual* place.

例のごとく彼女は忙しそうだ *As usual* [*always*] she looks busy.

例によって彼は遅れてきた *Typically*, he came in late.

れい² 礼

❶【感謝】(言葉) thanks; (態度) gratitude Ⓤ

ぜひひと言お礼を言わせてください Just let me say a word of *thanks*.

佐藤さんにお礼を言っておいてください Please give *my thanks* to Mrs. Sato.

これは親切にしていただいたほんのお礼のしるしです It's just a token of *my gratitude* for your kindness.

◆私たちはホストの温かいもてなしに礼を述べた We *thanked* the host *for* his warm hospitality. ∕ おばさんに贈り物のお礼の電話をしたほうがいいよ You'd better call your aunt to *thank* her *for* the gift. ∕ 礼には及びません There is no need to *thank* me. ∕ 彼女にお礼の手紙を書いた I wrote to her a *thank-you* letter.

❷【礼儀】courtesy Ⓤ

彼らは礼を尽くして社長夫人をもてなした They treated the wife of the president *with the utmost courtesy*.

◆彼の発言は礼を失している His remark 「*is impolite* [*goes against etiquette*].

❸【謝礼】reward Ⓒ; (弁護士などに対する) fee Ⓒ

なくした指輪を見つけたらお礼に5,000円くれると母は言っている My mother is offering me *a reward* of 5,000 yen if I find her missing ring.

❹【会釈】(おじぎ) bow [báu] Ⓒ

私は田中さんに軽く礼をした I「*made* a slight *bow* [*slightly bowed*] to Mr. Tanaka.

◆起立, 礼, 着席 Stand up. *Bow*. Sit down. (❖英米にはこのような号令の慣習はない)

れい³ 零 zero [zí(ː)rou] Ⓒ Ⓤ (複 ～(e)s), nothing Ⓤ, 《英》nought Ⓒ ∥私は0.15秒差で負けた I lost the race by (*zero*) point one five seconds. (❖zeroは省略されることが多い) ∕ うちの電話番号は03-8210-5403です My phone number is *zero*-three eight-two-one-*zero* five-four-*zero*-three. (❖zeroを [óu] と読むこともある) ∕ 我々は1対0で試合に勝った We won the game one to *zero* [*nothing*].

れい⁴ 霊 spirit Ⓒ; (霊魂) soul Ⓒ (❖宗教的意味合いが強い) ∥霊を祭る honor *the spirits* ∕ 霊に取りつかれる be possessed by *a spirit*

◆戦死者の霊を慰める pray for the war dead ∥地縛霊 a soul bound to and haunting a specific place ∕ 聖霊 the Holy Spirit ∕ 背後霊 a guardian spirit (at *a person's back*)

レイアウト layout Ⓒ ━レイアウトする lay* out ∥花子がこのページのレイアウトをした Hanako「*did the layout of* [*laid out*] this page.

れいあんしつ 霊安室 mortuary Ⓒ

れいえん 霊園 cemetery Ⓒ

レイオフ layoff Ⓒ ━レイオフする lay* off ∥200人の労働者がレイオフされた Two hundred workers *were laid off*.

れいか¹ 零下 below zero ∥きょうの最低気温は零下10度だった The lowest temperature today was 10 degrees *below zero* [*the freezing point*].

れいか² 冷夏 cool summer Ⓒ ∥冷夏なので今年はプールに行く気がしない Due to *the cool summer*, I don't feel like going to the swimming pool this year.

れいかい 例会 regular meeting Ⓒ ∥毎月第3木曜日に例会が開かれる *The regular meeting* is held on the third Thursday of each month.

∥月例会 a monthly meeting

れいがい¹ 例外 exception Ⓒ Ⓤ ━例外の exceptional; (通常ではない) unusual ∥校則の例外規定 *an exception* to school rules ∕ 例外は認められません We allow no *excep-*

tions. / 次の人たちは例外として認める We'*ll make an exception* for the following people. / あなたの場合は例外的なケースです Your case is *exceptional.* / 例外のない規則はない There is no rule without *exception.* / Every rule has *an exception.*

れいがい[2] 冷害 冷害のため米の値段が上がった *The damage to the crops from cold weather* caused the price of rice to rise.

れいかん 霊感 inspiration [U] ‖自然から霊感を得る *derive inspiration* from nature; *be inspired* by nature / 霊感がひらめいた I got *inspiration.*

◆彼女は霊感が強い She *is sensitive to the supernatural.*

‖霊感商法 fraudulent sales of religious charms

れいき 冷気 the chill ‖早朝の冷気 *the chill* [*cool air*] in the early morning

れいぎ 礼儀 (相手への思いやり) courtesy [U]; (丁寧さ) politeness [U]; (作法) manners; (エチケット) etiquette [U]

祖父は礼儀にうるさい My grandfather is fussy about *manners* [*etiquette*].

日本では先生と話をしているときに足を組むのは礼儀に反するとされている In Japan it's considered bad *manners* to cross your legs when talking to a teacher.

あいつは礼儀知らずだ He *has no manners.* / He *is rude* [*impolite*].

◆私は礼儀正しい人が好きだ I like *polite* people. / その子供は私たちに礼儀正しくおじぎをしてあいさつした That kid greeted us *politely* with a bow. / 礼儀をわきまえろ *Don't be rude*!

[ことわざ] 親しき仲にも礼儀あり ➩ したしい

れいきゃく 冷却 cooling [U]; (食品などの) refrigeration [U] ──冷却する cool down; refrigerate [他] ◆二人は冷却期間をおいてから話し合ったほうがよい After *a cooling-off period* they should talk each other.

‖冷却器 a cooler / 冷却水 (a) coolant / 冷却装置 a cooling device

レイキャビク Reykjavik (❖アイスランドの首都)

れいきゅうしゃ 霊柩車 hearse [hɔ́ːrs] [C]

れいきん 礼金 (報酬) reward [C]; (弁護士などに払う) fee [C]; (賃貸の保証金など) key money [U]; (大家に払う) thank-you money [U] (❖英米では部屋や家を借りるときに大家に謝礼を払う習慣はない)

れいぐう 冷遇 (冷たい扱い) cold treatment [U]; (来客に対する) cold reception [U] ──冷遇する treat ... unfavorably ‖彼は会社で冷遇されている He *is treated unfavorably* [*coldly*] at the company.

れいけつ 冷血 ──冷血な cold-blooded; (冷淡な) cold-hearted ‖あいつは冷血な男だ He is a *cold-blooded* [*cold-hearted*] man.

‖冷血漢 a cold-blooded [cold-hearted] fellow / 冷血動物 a cold-blooded animal

れいこう 励行 私は帰宅したときに, うがいと手洗いを励行している I *make a habit* of gargling and washing my hands when I get home.

れいこく 冷酷 ──冷酷な (残酷な) cruel; (血も涙もない) cold-blooded; (冷淡な) cold-hearted; (無情な) heartless ‖冷酷な殺人者 a *cruel* murderer / そんなひどいことを彼に言うなんて君は冷酷な女性だ You're a *cold-hearted* woman to say such a bad thing to him.

れいこん 霊魂 (精神) the spirit; (宗教的な意味での) the soul ‖私は霊魂の不滅を信じる I believe in the immortality of *the soul.*

れいさい[1] 零細 ──零細な (小規模の) small-scale ‖多くの零細企業がこの不況で苦しんでいる Many *small-scale* businesses are suffering from this recession. / 零細農家のため彼は冬の間東京へ出稼ぎに行かなければならない Because he is a *small-scale* farmer, he needs to go to Tokyo to find work during the winter.

れいさい[2] 零歳 彼女の赤ちゃんは0歳です Her baby is *less than* 「*one year old* [*12 months old*].

れいじ[1] 例示 (説明の助けとなる例) illustration [C]; (典型例) example [C] ──例示する illustrate [他]; 《公式的》exemplify [他] ‖このソフトのマニュアルは様々なケースを例示しているので分かりやすい This software manual is easy to follow because it *uses illustrations* of various situations.

れいじ[2] 零時 (午前零時) twelve o'clock midnight [U], twelve midnight [U]; (正午) noon [U]

れいしょう[1] 冷笑 cold smile [C]; (あざ笑い) sneer [C] ──冷笑する sneer [自] ‖出席者は彼の発言を冷笑した The attendants *sneered at* his remark.

れいしょう[2] 例証 (図・絵・実例などの説明) illustration [U] (❖具体的な「例」は [C]); (実例) example [C] ──例証する illustrate [他], 《公式的》exemplify [他] ‖マッカーサー教授は今までの研究結果をもとに彼の新理論を例証した Professor MacArthur *illustrated* his new theory based on the results of his research.

れいじょう[1] 礼状 a letter of thanks, 《口語的》thank-you letter [C] ‖礼状を出す send *a thank-you letter*

れいじょう[2] 令状 warrant [C] ‖殺人容疑で彼に逮捕令状が出された *A warrant* was issued for his arrest on suspicion of murder.

‖家宅捜査令状 a search warrant

れいじょう[3] 令嬢 daughter [C] ‖社長令嬢 *a daughter* of a president / 彼は徳川家の令嬢と婚約している He is engaged to *a daughter* of the Tokugawa family.

れいすい 冷水 cold water [U] ◆毎朝冷水摩擦をする *rub oneself with a cold, wet towel* every morning / 健康増進のために冷水浴をする *take* [*have*] *a cold bath* for an improvement in health

れいせい 冷静 (穏やかさ) calmness [U]; (動じないこと) coolness [U] ──冷静な calm; cool

冷静さを失う lose *one's calmness* [*coolness*] / 冷静な態度 a *calm* attitude / 冷静な判断 a *cool* judgment
君はこの状況でよくそう冷静でいられるな How can you keep so *cool* in this situation?
◆冷静に状況を判断する judge the situation *calmly* / 沈着冷静に行動する behave *calmly*
🔊「あ,地震だ！」「冷静に！落ちついて」"Oh, an earthquake!" "*Calm down*! [*Pull yourself together*!] Don't panic."

れいせつ 礼節 manners, 《公式的》the proprieties ◎ / 礼節を守る observe *the proprieties* / 礼節をわきまえなさい You should know *the manners*.
ことわざ 衣食足りて礼節を知る ⇨いしょく(衣食)

れいせん 冷戦 cold war ◎◎ (◆第二次大戦後の米ソに代表される東西間の冷戦は the Cold War) / 正光と治子は今冷戦状態にある Masamitsu and Haruko are in *a state of cold war*.

れいぜん 霊前 私は亡くなった祖母の霊前に花と果物をささげた I offered flowers and fruits to *the spirit* of my late grandmother.

れいそう 礼装 formal wear [dress] ◎ / 祖父母は友の結婚に礼装で出かけた My grandparents went to the party in *formal wear*.
◆礼装用の靴 *dress* shoes / 礼装用ネクタイ a *dress* tie

れいぞう 冷蔵 cold storage ◎ ——冷蔵する refrigerate ⓗ / 要冷蔵《掲示》*Keep Refrigerated*! / 野菜を冷蔵する *keep* vegetables *in cold storage*; *refrigerate* vegetables / 開封後は冷蔵してください *Refrigerate* after opening.
‖冷蔵庫 a refrigerator, 《口語的》a fridge

れいぞく 隷属 subordination ◎

れいだい 例題 exercise ◎ / 例題1から5をやりなさい Do *exercises* one through five.

れいたん 冷淡 coldness ◎ ——冷淡な (薄情な) cold; (冷たい心の) cold-hearted; (無関心な) indifferent
喜美子はこのごろ僕に冷淡だ Kimiko has been *cold* to me lately.
彼女は美人で頭もいいが冷淡な人だ She is beautiful and smart but *cold-hearted*.
彼は他人の問題に関しては冷淡だ He is *indifferent* to other people's problems.
◆人を冷淡に扱う treat a person *coldly* / 私は彼のところに行ったとき冷淡な扱いを受けた I got a *cool* reception when I visited him.

れいだんぼう 冷暖房 air conditioning and heating; (装置) air conditioning and heating equipment / 当ビルは冷暖房完備です This building is equipped with *air conditioning and heating*.

れいちょうるい 霊長類 (総称的) the primates; (個別) primate ◎

れいてつ 冷徹 ——冷徹な cool and realistic / 冷徹な視点 a *cool and realistic* view

れいてん 零点 zero ◎ ◎, 《英》nought ◎, 《米口語的》goose egg ◎ / もしかしたら昨日の試験は0点かもしれない I might have gotten *a zero* in the yesterday's exam.

れいど 零度 zero (degrees); (氷点) the freezing point / この地方では最高気温が0度以下のことはめったにない It's unusual for the high temperature to be below *zero* in this region.
‖絶対零度 absolute zero

れいとう 冷凍 freezing ◎ ——冷凍する freeze* ⓗ / この料理は冷凍保存しておくことができる You can *keep* this dish *frozen*.
◆魚を急速冷凍する *quick-freeze* fish / 冷凍魚[肉, 野菜] *frozen* fish [meat, vegetables]
‖冷凍庫[室] a freezer / 冷凍車 a refrigerator truck [car] / 冷凍食品 frozen food / 冷凍冷蔵庫 a refrigerator with a freezer

れいねん 例年 例年の行事 an *annual* event / 正月の明治神宮は例年どおり込んでいた Meiji Shrine on New Year's Day was crowded *as usual*. / この冬は例年になく寒い It's *unusually* cold this winter. / その大学の志願者数は例年並みだ The number of applicants to the college is *average*. / 例年今ごろ初雪が降る Snow falls for the first time about this time of *every year*.

れいはい 礼拝 worship ◎; (教会の) (church) service ◎ ——礼拝する worship ⓗ / この聖堂では多くの観光客が礼拝に参加する Many tourists attend *services* in this cathedral. / 私たちは毎日曜日礼拝に行きます We *go to church* every Sunday.
‖礼拝者 a worshipper / 礼拝堂 a chapel

れいばい 霊媒 (spiritualistic [psychic]) medium ◎

れいびょう 霊廟 mausoleum [mɔ̀ːsəlíːəm] ◎ (複 ~s, mausolea)

レイプ rape ◎ ——レイプする rape ⓗ / レイプの被害者 a *rape* victim / 内乱の中多くの女性が兵士にレイプされたといわれている It's said that many women *were raped* by soldiers during the civil war.
‖レイプ犯 a rapist

れいふく 礼服 formal wear ◎ / 礼服を着用する wear *formal wear*; dress *formally*
‖略式礼服 semiformal wear

れいぶん 例文 example (sentence) ◎; (説明用の) illustrative sentence ◎ / 例文を作る give *example sentences* / 和英辞書を引くときは訳語だけではなく例文にも目を通しなさい When you consult a Japanese-English dictionary, you should look at not only the translated words but also *the illustrative sentences*.

れいほう 礼砲 salute ◎ / 礼砲を放つ fire *a salute*

れいぼう 冷房 air conditioning ◎ / 冷房のきかせすぎは体によくない It's not good for your health to be exposed to strong *air conditioning*. / ◆冷房のきいた部屋 an *air-conditioned* room
‖冷房車 an air-conditioned car / 冷房装置 an air conditioner

れいらく 零落 その家は零落して今では見る影もない The family *has come to ruin* and is only a shadow of its former glory now.

れいれいしい 麗々しい ostentatious ― 麗々しく ostentatiously ∥彼女は麗々しい服装をしている She dresses *ostentatiously*.

レインコート raincoat ∥この雨と風ではレインコートを着たほうがいい It's better to wear *a raincoat* in this rain and wind.

レインシューズ ⚠ rain boots(❖数えるときは a pair of ... とする)

レーサー racing driver ⓒ, (car) racer ⓒ ∥F1レーサー a Formula One racer

レーザー laser ⓒ ∥レーザー光線 a laser beam / レーザーディスク a laser disk [disc] / レーザープリンター a laser printer

レーシングカー racing car ⓒ

レース¹ (競走) race ⓒ ∥レースに勝つ[負ける] win [lose] *a race* / 彼はそのレースで3着だった He came in third in the *race*./ He took third (place) in the *race*.

∥自動車レース an auto race / ペナントレース a pennant race

レース² (飾り) lace ⓤ;(レース細工) lacework ⓤ ∥レースのカーテン a lace curtain / 私のお気に入りのハンカチはレースの縁どりがある My favorite handkerchief is trimmed with *lace*.

∥レース編み lacework

レーズン raisin ⓒ ∥レーズンパン *raisin* bread

レーダー radar ⓤⓒ ∥レーダーで気象を観測する make meteorological observations by *radar* / 未確認の航空機がレーダーで探知された An unidentified aircraft was detected on *the radar* (*screen*).

∥レーダー網 a radar network

レート rate ⓒ ∥日本円の米ドルに対してのレートは近ごろ安定している The yen exchange *rate* against the U.S. dollar has been stable these days.

∥外国為替レート the foreign exchange rate

レーヨン rayon ⓤ

レール (鉄道の) rail ⓒ(通例複数形 ~s);(カーテンの) curtain rail ⓒ ∥レールを敷く lay *rails* ◆他人が決めたレールの上を歩く follow *the course of life* which is fixed by other people

レーン (道路・ボウリングの) lane ⓒ

レオタード leotard [líːətɑ̀ːrd]

レガート ―レガートの[で]《音楽》(なめらかな) legato

レガッタ regatta ⓒ, boat race ⓒ

-れき -歴 父は運転歴30年のベテランのタクシードライバーだ My father is an excellent taxi driver who *has been driving* for 30 years. / 田中先生は教職歴5年だ Miss Tanaka is a teacher with five years' *experience*. / 実は私には2度の離婚歴があります To tell the truth, I have「*had two divorces* [*been divorced twice*].

れきがん 礫岩 conglomerate ⓒ

れきし¹ 歴史

history ⓤ(❖過去の特定の重要な出来事を示すときは ⓒ) ―歴史の(歴史に関する) historical(❖通例名詞の前で用いる);(歴史的に重要な) historic ―歴史的に historically / 歴史的な遺産 a *historical* inheritance / 歴史的な発見 a *historic* discovery / 日本の歴史 *the history* of Japan; Japanese *history* / 歴史のクラス[先生] a *history* class [teacher]
わが校はまだ5年の歴史しかない Our school has *a history* of only five years.
私は大学でコンピュータサイエンスの歴史を勉強したい I want to study *the history* of computer science at college.
その国は歴史が浅い That nation doesn't have *a long history*.
彼の演説は歴史に残るだろう His speech will「*go down* [*be remembered*] *in history*.
紫式部は歴史上の人物だ Murasaki Shikibu is a *historical* figure [personage].
私の町は歴史的に有名な所だ My town is a *historically* famous place.

∥歴史家 a historian / 歴史学 history / 歴史小説 a historical novel(❖historic novel は「歴史的に重要な小説」の意味) / 歴史年表 a history chart

慣用表現 歴史は繰り返す *History repeats itself*.

れきし² 轢死 その少年は線路を歩いていて轢死した Walking on the tracks, the boy *was run over and killed by a train*.

れきぜん 歴然 両者に大きな差があるということは歴然としている It is *clear* [*evident, obvious*] that there is a big difference between the two. / 彼が黒幕だということは歴然たる事実である It is an *obvious* fact that he is pulling the strings.

れきだい 歴代 ―歴代の past ∥歴代の首相の写真 photographs of the *past* prime ministers ◆彼の走り高跳びの記録は歴代3位だ His record for the high jump ranks third *in history*.

れきにん 歴任 新任大使は自国で要職を歴任してきた The newly appointed ambassador *has held* various important positions in his country.

れきほう 歴訪 皇太子ご夫婦はアフリカ3か国を歴訪された The Crown Prince and Princess *made official visits* to three African nations.

レギュラー (正規の選手) regular [starting] player ⓒ, regular ⓒ ―レギュラーの regular ∥(テレビ・ラジオの)レギュラー出演者 a *regular* guest / 弟は学校のバスケ部のレギュラーを目ざして毎日練習している My brother practices basketball every day to become *a regular* [*starting*] *player* on the school team. / 彼はテレビのレギュラー番組を週に5本もっている(→毎週5つの番組に出ている) He appears on five *regular* TV programs a week.

∥レギュラーガソリン regular gasoline

レクイエム (鎮魂曲) requiem ⓒ

レクチャー lecture ⓒ

レクリエーション recreation ⓤⓒ ∥勉強ばかりしていないでたまにはレクリエーションも必要だ

よ Don't work too hard. You sometimes need some *recreation*.
∥レクリエーション活動 recreational activity / レクリエーション施設 recreational facilities

レゲエ〘音楽〙reggae [régei] Ⓤ

レコーダー recorder
∥タイムレコーダー a time recorder / テープレコーダー a tape recorder

レコーディング recording Ⓒ ∥僕らの夢はロンドンのアビーロードスタジオで自分たちの曲をレコーディングすることだ Our dream is to「*make a recording of* [*record*] our music at Abbey Road Studios in London.
∥レコーディングスタジオ a recording studio

レコード ❶〘音盤〙record Ⓒ, disk Ⓒ ∥最近あまりレコードをかけることがない I rarely play *records* these days.
❷【記録】record Ⓒ ∥彼女は女子マラソンで世界レコードを作った[破った] She set [broke] *the* world *record* in the women's marathon.
∥レコード音楽 record music / レコード会社 a record company / レコードプレーヤー a record player / レコードホルダー(記録保持者) a record holder / レコード屋 a record store [shop]

レザー ❶【皮革】leather Ⓤ ∥この冬はレザーがはやっている *Leather* is in fashion this winter.
❷【かみそり】razor [réizər] Ⓒ
∥レザーカット a razor (hair) cut / レザージャケット a leather jacket

レジ ⚠(金銭登録機) (cash) register Ⓒ; (レジ係) cashier Ⓒ; (勘定台) checkout counter Ⓒ ∥レジが込んでいる There is a long line at *a checkout counter*. / 私はコンビニでレジのアルバイトをしている I work part-time as *a cashier* at a convenience store.
💬「すみません、お勘定はどこで払えばいいですか」「こちらのレジでお願いします」"Excuse me. Where do you pay?" "At this *register* please. / Please pay this *cashier*."

レシート receipt [risíːt] Ⓒ ∥レシートもらえますか May I have *a receipt*?

レシーバー (受話器など) receiver Ⓒ; (スポーツの) receiver Ⓒ

レシーブ ボールをレシーブする *receive* a ball

レジスタンス resistance Ⓤ; (第二次世界大戦時のフランスのナチに対する) the Resistance ∥軍事政府に対してレジスタンス活動をする put up *resistance* against the military government

レシピ recipe [résəpi] Ⓒ ∥フルーツケーキのレシピ *a recipe* for fruitcake

レジャー ⚠(余暇) leisure [líːʒər] Ⓤ (❖英語の leisure は「仕事を離れた時間」の意味で、日本語の「遊び」の意味はない); (気晴らし) recreation Ⓒ
日本人はレジャーの楽しみ方を知らないとよくいわれる It's often said that Japanese don't know how to spend *leisure time*.
わが家は毎週末レジャーに出かける Our family goes out for *recreation* every weekend.
∥レジャー産業 the leisure industry / レジャー施設 leisure facilities / レジャーセンター a recreation center (❖×leisure center とはいわない) / レジャー用品 recreational equipment

レジュメ (要約) résumé [rézəmèi] Ⓒ (❖フランス語から), summary Ⓒ

レスキュー (レスキュー隊) rescue party

レストラン restaurant Ⓒ ➡ 場面・状況別会話 p.1684 ∥安[高級]レストラン *a cheap* [*fancy*] *restaurant* / 2つ星レストラン *a two-star restaurant* / シドニーには日本食レストランがたくさんある There are many Japanese *restaurants* in Sydney.

レズビアン (女性の同性愛) lesbianism Ⓤ; (女性の同性愛者) lesbian Ⓒ, gay Ⓒ (❖gay はもともと男性の同性愛者を指す言葉だが、最近では女性にも使われる)

レスラー wrestler Ⓒ ∥プロレスラー a pro wrestler

レスリング wrestling Ⓤ ∥きのう兄とレスリングの試合を見に行った I went to a *wrestling* match with my brother yesterday.
◆彼とレスリングをして負けた I *wrestled with* him and lost.

レセプション (正式な歓迎会) reception Ⓒ ∥外国人留学生のためにレセプションが開かれた A *reception* was held for students from overseas.

レター letter Ⓒ ∥レターセット writing paper and envelopes (❖×letter set とはいわない)

レタス lettuce Ⓒ Ⓤ (❖日本でふつうに見られるレタスは iceberg lettuce. また数えるときは a head of ... ともする) ∥レタスの葉1枚 a leaf of *lettuce*

レタリング lettering Ⓤ

れつ 列

(横に並んだ) row Ⓒ; (縦に並んだ) line Ⓒ; (順番待ちの) line Ⓒ, (米)line Ⓒ, (英)queue [kjúː] Ⓒ; (兵士などの横列) rank Ⓒ (❖縦列は file)

私の座席は前から5列目です My seat is in *the* fifth *row* from the front.

ナタリーさんは後列にいる金髪の女性 Natalie is the lady with blond hair in *the* back *row*.

彼女はいすを2列に並べた She arranged the chairs in two *rows* [*lines*].

そのコンサートのチケットを手に入れるために長い列ができていた There was *a long line* for tickets to the concert.

子供たちが(縦)1列にまっすぐ並んでいた The children were standing in *a straight line*.

あの男は列に割り込んだ (米)The man cut [broke] into *the line*. / (英)The man jumped *the queue*.

バス停には10人くらいの人が列を作っている About ten people *are* 「*forming a line* [*lining up*]」 at the bus stop.

列を乱さないようにしてください Please don't *get out of line*.

れつあく

ミッキーマウスが見えるように私たちは最前列に座った We sat *in the front row* to see Mickey Mouse.
警察官の列が待機していた *Ranks* of policemen were standing by.

れつあく 劣悪 —劣悪な terrible; (劣等の) inferior; (質の悪い) poor, bad ∥劣悪な環境に暮らす live under *poor* conditions / 彼らの労働条件は劣悪だ Their working conditions are *terrible*.

れっか 烈火 彼は自分の間違いを指摘されると烈火のごとく怒った He *flew into a rage* when his mistake was pointed out to him.

レッカーしゃ レッカー車 《米》wrecker ⓒ, 《英》breakdown truck ⓒ
◆彼女は警察にレッカー車で車を持っていかれた She *had her car towed away* by the police.

れっき 列記する list ⓗ, make* a list of … ∥参加者の名前をすべて列記する *make a list of* all the names of the attendees

れっきとした 歴とした (明白な) obvious; (反駁(ばく)することのできない) irrefutable; (世間的にきちんとした) very [highly] respectable ∥君が何と言おうとそれはれっきとした事実だ Whatever you say, it is an *obvious* fact. / 彼女にはれっきとしたアリバイがある She has an *irrefutable* alibi. / あの人はみすぼらしい家に住んでいるけどれっきとした家柄の人らしい That man lives in a shabby house, but it's said that he is from a *highly respectable* family.

れっきょ 列挙 enumeration ⓤ —列挙する enumerate ⓗ ∥この英文手紙のスペルミスを列挙したら数えきれないほどあった There were too many misspellings in this English letter to *enumerate*.

れっきょう 列強 great powers ∥その小国は列強に囲まれている That small nation is surrounded by *great powers*.

れっこく 列国 the countries [nations] (of the world) ◆国王の葬儀に列国の元首が参列した The heads of *nations around the world* attended the King's funeral.

れっしゃ 列車 train ⓗ
列車に乗り込む get on *a train* / 列車を降りる get off *a train* / 列車に乗り遅れる miss *a train* / 列車を乗り換える change *trains* / 列車で福岡まで行く go to Fukuoka *by train*
列車が6番線ホームに入ってくる *The train is* approaching platform [track] No.6.
ロンドン行き最終列車は2番線の出発です *The last train* for London leaves from platform [track] No.2.
私は列車の旅が好きだ I like *train* journeys.
この列車は10両編成だ This *train* has 10 cars.
私は松本行きの11時の列車に乗った I took *the 11 o'clock train* for Matsumoto.
大雨のため列車は大幅に遅れている *Trains* have been delayed considerably due to heavy rain.
∥列車事故 a rail accident / 列車時刻表 a train timetable / 貨物列車 a freight [fréit] train, 《英》a goods train / 急行列車 an express (train) / 直通列車 a through train / 特急列車 a limited express / 普通列車 a local train / 夜行列車 a night train / 臨時列車 a special train

れっしょう 裂傷 【医学】laceration ⓒ, cut ⓒ ∥腕に裂傷を負う have *a laceration* on *one's* arm

レッスン lesson ⓒ ∥私は週2回バイオリンのレッスンを受けている I have [take] violin *lessons* twice a week. / 母は子供たちにピアノのレッスンをしている My mother gives piano *lessons* to children.
◆私は毎晩2時間フルートのレッスンをする I *practice* the flute for two hours every evening.

れっせい¹ 劣勢 (不利) disadvantage ⓒ ⓤ; (劣っていること) inferiority ⓒ —劣勢の disadvantageous; inferior ∥日本のバレーボールチームは身長の上でキューバに対して劣勢だ The Japanese volleyball team is *inferior* to the Cuban team in height.
◆きのうの試合でジャイアンツはスワローズに対して初めから劣勢だった In yesterday's game, the Giants *fought a losing battle* against the Swallows from the beginning.

れっせい² 劣性 —劣性の recessive ∥劣性遺伝 *recessive* heredity

れっせき 列席 attendance ⓤ —列席する attend ⓗ, be present at … ∥市議会議員が2, 3人卒業式に列席していた A few members of a municipal assembly *attended* [*were present at*] the graduation ceremony. ◆多くの[少ない]列席者 a large [small] *attendance* (❖ attendance は集合的で常に a [an] を伴って用いる)

レッテル ⚠ (ラベル) label [léibəl] ⓒ (❖日本語はオランダ語の letter から)
慣用表現 彼は女たらしのレッテルをはられた He*'s been labeled* [*branded*] as a womanizer.

れっとう¹ 劣等 inferiority [infiríːrəti] ⓤ
◆私は時々他人に劣等感をいだくことがある I sometimes *feel inferior* to other people. / I sometimes *have a sense of inferiority towards* other people.
∥劣等生 a poor student

れっとう² 列島 【地理】archipelago [àːrkəpéləgòu] ⓒ (複 ~s, ~es), (a chain of) islands ∥日本列島 the Japanese *Archipelago* / アリューシャン列島 the Aleutian *Islands*

れっぷう 烈風 gale ⓒ, a violent wind ∥烈風が一晩中吹き荒れた The gale blew all night.

レディー lady ⓒ ∥レディーの前で失礼ですよ Don't be rude to the *ladies*. / レディーファーストです *Ladies first*.
∥セールスレディー a saleswoman

レディーメード レディーメードの ready-made; (特に洋服が) ready-to-wear ∥レディーメードの背広 a *ready-made* [*ready-to-wear*] suit

レトルト ⚠（レトルト食品）vacuum-packed food ◎（❖retortは専門用語で一般的ではない）

レバー¹（取っ手）lever ◎；（車の変則レバー）《米》gearshift ◎，《英》gear lever ◎ ∥レバーを引く pull *a lever*

レバー²（食品としての肝臓）liver [lívər] ⓤ（❖器官としての肝臓は◎）∥鶏のレバー chicken *liver* / レバーペースト *liver paste*

レパートリー repertoire [répərtwɑːr] ◎（通例単数形），repertory ◎ ∥私のカラオケのレパートリーは広い I have *a large repertoire* for karaoke.

レビュー（論評）review ◎；（歌と踊りのショー）revue ◎

レフェリー referee ◎ ∥サッカーのレフェリーをする *act as a referee for* a soccer match; *referee* a soccer match

レフト（野球の左翼）left field ⓤ；（左翼手）left fielder ◎ ∥太郎はレフトを守っている Taro plays *left field*.

レベル level ◎

彼の料理の腕はプロのレベルだ His cooking is on *a professional level*.

あの中学生は大学レベルの数学を勉強している That junior high school student studies university *level* mathematics.

あの学校はレベルが高い［低い］That school *has a high* [*low*] *academic level*.

草の根レベルでの交流が大切だ Communication on *the* grass-roots *level* is important.

彼の英語のレベルはかなり高い *The level* of his English ability is fairly high.

彼女たちはレベルの低い話題で騒いでいた The girls were fussing about a low-*level* topic.

あの高校は来年レベルダウンが予想される *The academic level* required to enter that high school is expected to *be lower* next year.

◆彼女はさらにレベルアップしてテニスの試合に臨んだ She took part in a tennis tournament after her tennis *had improved*. / 花子は上級レベルの学習者に英語を教えている Hanako teaches English to *advanced* learners.

語法 通例英語のlevel up, level downはそれぞれ平らな面を高くする，低くするという意味で日本語の「レベルアップ」「レベルダウン」とは異なる．「レベルアップする」「レベルダウンする」などといいたいときには，improve（上達する，上達させる），get worse, deteriorate（どちらも「悪くなる」の意味）などを用いる．

レポーター reporter ◎；（報道記者）correspondent ◎ ∥レポーターの山田さんに被災地の人々の活動の様子を伝えてもらいます We'll ask *our correspondent*, Yamada, how the local people are coping with the disaster.

レポート（学生の書く）paper ◎；（公式の報告書）report ◎ ∥現代文学に関するレポートを書く write *a paper* on contemporary literature / 彼は歴史のレポートに熱心に取り組んでいる He is hard at work on *his* history *paper*. / 政府はODAに関するレポートをまとめた The government published *a report* on ODA.

レム（放射線の単位）rem ◎

レムすいみん レム睡眠 REM sleep ⓤ（❖REMはRapid Eye Movement（急速眼球運動）の略語）

レモネード《米》lemonade ⓤ，《英》lemon squash ⓤ（❖《英》ではlemonadeは「レモンスカッシュ」の意味）

レモン lemon ◎ⓤ ∥レモン1切れ a slice of *lemon*

∥レモン色 lemon yellow / レモンしぼり器 a lemon squeezer / レモンスカッシュ《米》lemon soda,《英》lemonade / レモンティー(a) tea with lemon（❖英語のlemon teaは「人工的にレモン風味を加えた粉末の紅茶」の意味）

レリーフ relief ⓤ（❖作品は◎）

-れる

❶【受身】

友人が車にはねられた A friend of mine *was hit* by a car.

なぜみんなに笑われたのか分からない I have no idea why everyone *laughed at me*.

空が雲に覆われていた The sky *was overcast*.

駅に行く途中雨に降られた I *was caught* in a shower on the way to the station.

満員電車で財布をすられた I *had* my wallet *picked* on the jam-packed train.（❖《have＋目的語＋過去分詞》で「…を〜される」の意味になる．×I was picked my wallet. とはいわない）

❷【可能】

あした6時に起きられるかなあ I wonder if I *can get up* at six tomorrow morning.

この実は食べられる This fruit is *edible*.

❸【尊敬】

毎日英字新聞を読まれるのですか Do you *read* an English-language newspaper every day?（❖この場合のように，日本語の敬語表現に当たる英語がないことが多い）

❹【自発】

この絵はがきを見ると去年の夏のことが思い出される This postcard *reminds* me of last summer.

彼はだれかをかばっているように思われる *It seems* that he is covering up for someone.

れんあい 恋愛 love ⓤ；（ロマンス）romance ◎ ⇨ 場面・状況別会話 p.1692

亮子は俊二と恋愛中だ Ryoko and Shunji *are in love*.

彼女はいくつかの恋愛を経験してきたが，今回は本気だ She's had some casual *romances*, but she's really serious this time.

私も彼女のようにかっこいい男の子と恋愛をしたい I want to *have a romance with* a cool guy like she does.

∥恋愛結婚 love marriage / 恋愛事件 a romance；（情事）a love affair / 恋愛小説 a love story

れんか 廉価 **―廉価な** (安価な) inexpensive; (安っぽい) cheap; (大衆的な) popular //こちらは廉価なオーディオシステムです This is an *inexpensive* sound system set.
||廉価版(本の) a popular [cheap] edition

れんが 煉瓦 brick [C][U] //かまでれんがを焼く bake *bricks* in a kiln / れんがを積む lay *bricks* / 赤れんが造りの学校 a school built of red *brick(s)*
||れんが職人 a bricklayer / れんが塀 a brick wall

れんき 連記 (投票の) plural entry [U] //連記無記名投票 a secret vote with *plural entry*

れんきゅう 連休 consecutive holidays
◆今度の3連休を利用して箱根に行きます We are going to Hakone during *the* three-day *holiday.* / 今週末は連休だ This weekend is *a long* [(→3連休) *three-day*; (→4連休) *four-day*] *weekend.*

れんぎょう 連翹 〖植物〗 forsythia [C]

れんきんじゅつ 錬金術 alchemy [U]
||錬金術師 an alchemist

れんげ 蓮華 (ハスの花) lotus flower [C]; (中華用スプーン) Chinese soup spoon [C]

れんけい[1] 連携 cooperation [U] **―連携する** cooperate [自] //青少年非行防止には学校と地域の連携が必要だ The school and the local community should 「*cooperate with each other* [*work in close cooperation*] to prevent juvenile delinquency.

れんけい[2] 連係 combination [U][C]; (チームワーク) teamwork [U] //山田と田中はみごとな連係プレーで(テニスの)第1ゲームを勝ち取った Yamada and Tanaka took [won] the first game by *their* good *teamwork.*

れんげそう 蓮華草 Chinese milk vetch [C]

れんけつ 連結 connection [C], coupling [U] **―連結する** connect [他], couple [他] //次の駅で江ノ島からの列車3両が当列車に連結されます A three-car train from Enoshima *will be connected to* this train at the next stop.
◆16両連結の列車 a 16-*car* train
||連結器 a coupling

れんこ 連呼 候補者の名前を連呼する *call* a candidate's name *repeatedly*

れんご 連語 (語の結びつき) collocation [U]; (複合語) compound word [C]

れんこう 連行 男は窃盗容疑で警察に連行された The man *was taken to* the police station for stealing.

れんごう 連合 (共通の利益をもった) union [C][U]; (国家間などの) alliance [C][U]; (政治上の) coalition [kòuəlíʃən] [C][U] **―連合する** unite [自][他]; ally [他] //小さな商店は連合して大型スーパーに対抗した The small shops *united* against the big supermarket.
||連合軍 allied forces / 連合国 allied powers; (第一次・第二次世界大戦における) the Allies / 連合政権 a coalition government

れんこん 蓮根 lotus root [C]

れんさ 連鎖 連鎖反応を起こす set off *a chain reaction* / 犯罪が連鎖的に起こった There were *a chain* [*series*] of crimes.

れんざ 連座 **―連座する** be involved //その贈賄事件には次期社長の呼び声が高い真田氏も連座していた Mr. Sanada, widely talked of as the next president, *was* also *involved* in the bribery case.

れんさい 連載 serial [C], series [C] (複～) **―連載の** serial **―連載する** serialize [他] //その連載は急に打ち切りになった The *series* was suddenly brought to an end. / 彼はその雑誌に記事を連載している His articles *are serialized* in the magazine.
||連載小説 a serial novel / 連載漫画 serial comics

れんさく 連作 この土地は連作に向いていない This soil is too poor for *long-term cultivation of crops.*

れんざん 連山 mountain range [C], mountains

レンジ ⚠《米》stove [C], 《英》cooker [C]; (ガスの) 《米》gas stove [C], 《英》gas cooker [C]; (電気の) 《米》electric stove [C], 《英》electric cooker [C] (❖英語の range は「料理用加熱器具」の意味だが, これは古い言葉で,「かまど」のようなニュアンスがあるため現在はほとんど使われない)
||電子レンジ a microwave (oven)

れんじつ 連日 (毎日) every day; (来る日も来る日も) day after day //この夏は連日摂氏30度を超す日が続いた This summer the temperature was over 30℃ *every day.*
||連日連夜 night and day, day and night

レンジャー (特殊攻撃部隊) commando [C] (複～(e)s); (森林警備隊員) (forest) ranger [C]

れんしゅう 練習

practice [U][C]; exercise [C]; training [U] 《また a ～》; drill [C][U]; rehearsal [U][C] **―練習する** 《米》practice, 《英》practise [他][自]; exercise [自]; train [他]; drill [他]; rehearse [他][自]

> practice: 最も一般的な語.
> exercise: 体や頭を使って能力を発展させる訓練.
> training: プログラムに従って運動や技術を習得する訓練.
> drill: 指導者のもとに行う反復訓練.
> rehearsal: 芝居や演奏などの予行演習.

猛練習する *do* hard *practice* [*training*]

英語の授業にはいつも発音練習がある We always do *a* pronunciation *practice* in English class.

うちのチームが試合に負けたのは練習不足が原因だ The reason our team lost the game was our lack of *practice.*

きのう近所の中学生が我々のサッカーの練習を見に来た The local junior high school students came to see our soccer *training* yesterday.

多くの者が練習についていけずクラブをやめた Many quit the club because *the training* was too hard for them.

私は毎日ピアノの練習をする I *practice* the piano every day.

アーノルド先生は英語のイントネーションの練習をよくする Mr. Arnold often *drills* us in

English intonation.
私たちは初日に備えて猛練習した We *rehearsed intensively* for the premiere.
‖練習曲 an etude, a practice piece / 練習試合 a practice game [match] / 練習所（訓練所）a training school / 練習帳 an exercise book / 練習問題 an exercise

れんしょ 連署 核兵器反対の請願書に連署する *sign* a petition against nuclear weapons *jointly*

れんしょう 連勝 successive [a series of] victories, straight wins;（連勝中の期間）winning streak [C] ‖我々は6連勝した We had six *straight wins.*/ We *won* six *games in a row.* / タイガースの連勝は4ゲームでストップした The Tigers' *winning streak* stopped [ended] after four games.

レンズ lens [C] ‖高倍率レンズ付きカメラ a camera with *a lens* of high power
‖レンズシャッター a lens shutter / レンズフード a lens hood / 拡大レンズ a magnifying lens / 魚眼レンズ a fish-eye lens / 広角レンズ a wide-angle lens / 凸[凹]レンズ a convex [concave] lens / 望遠レンズ a telephoto lens

れんせん 連戦 わがチームはこのところ連戦連勝[連敗]だ Our team has had *a series of* wins [defeats] recently. / あしたからドラゴンズはジャイアンツとの3連戦を控えている The Dragons will have *a* three-*game series* against the Giants starting tomorrow.

れんそう 連想 association [U] [C] ―連想する associate [他];（思い出させる）remind [他] ‖私はダ・ビンチと聞くと「モナリザ」を連想する I *associate* the name da Vinci *with* the "Mona Lisa."/ The name da Vinci *reminds* me *of* the "Mona Lisa."
◆「戦争」という言葉は何を連想させますか What *comes to your mind* when you hear the word "war"?
‖連想ゲーム an association game

れんぞく 連続 succession [C] [U];（同種のもの）series [C]（複 ～） ―連続の（次々と続く）successive;（とぎれることない）continuous;（間をおかずに続く）consecutive;（通しの）serial
連続強盗事件 *serial* [*successive*] robberies / 連続優勝 *successive* [*consecutive*] victories / 5回連続のテレビドラマ *a series* of five TV dramas
その地域では3か月の間に連続して大地震に見舞われた *A series* of big earthquakes hit the area over three months.
山田氏は2期連続当選した Mr. Yamada has been elected to his second *consecutive* [*straight*] term.
◆きょうで4日連続の雨だ(→降り続いている) It *has been raining* for four days.
‖連続小説 a serial novel / 連続性 continuity / 連続ドラマ a serial drama

れんだ 連打（野球の）consecutive hits;（ボクシングなどの）continuous punches [blows];（ドラムの）drumroll [C]
◆5連打 five *continuous hits*; five *hits in a row* / 彼はチャンピオンに連打を浴びせられた He *was repeatedly hit* by the champion.

れんたい[1] 連帯（結束）solidarity [U];（仲間意識）togetherness [U] ―連帯する unite [自][他] ―連帯の（共同の）joint ‖経営陣との交渉には組合員の強い連帯が必要だ Firm *solidarity* is vital for the union members to negotiate with management.
‖連帯感 a sense of solidarity / 連帯責任 joint [collective] responsibility / 連帯保証 joint liability on guarantee / 連帯保証人 a joint guarantor

れんたい[2] 連隊 regiment [C]
‖連隊長 a regimental commander

レンタカー rent-a-car [C], rental car [C]
◆オーストラリアを旅行するにはレンタカー(→車を借りるの)が便利だ The best way to travel around Australia is to *rent a car.* / 空港でレンタカーを借りられる You *can rent a car* at the airport.

レンタル（賃貸し）rental [C] [U];（レンタル料金）rental (fee) [C] ―レンタルの rental
[会]「『タイタニック』見に行った？」「レンタル(ビデオ)で見た」"Did you go to see *Titanic*?" "I saw it *on a rental video.*"
‖レンタルビデオ店 a video rental shop

れんだん 連弾 four-hand performance [C] ―連弾する play a piano duet
‖連弾曲 a piano duet

れんちゅう 連中（やつら）guys;（仲間）company [U];（男性どうしの仲間）《口語的》pals ‖あんな連中とつきあうな Don't go out with those *guys.* / 気の合う連中とカラオケによく行く I often go to karaoke with *my pals.*

れんとう 連投 彼は3連投した He *threw in* three *successive games.*

れんどう 連動 この熱センサーはスプリンクラーに連動している This heat sensor *is connected to* sprinklers.

レントゲン ⚠（X線）X-rays;（X線写真）X-ray [C]（❖日本語はドイツのX線発見者Roentgenから） ‖胸部のレントゲンを撮った I *had a* chest *X-ray* (*taken*). / I *had* my chest *X-rayed.* / レントゲンの結果は何も異常がなかった *The X-ray* showed nothing wrong.
‖レントゲン技師 a radiographer / レントゲン検査 an X-ray examination

れんぱ[1] 連覇 ―連覇する win* consecutive championships ‖国体で3連覇を成しとげる *win* three *consecutive championships* in the National Sports Festival

れんぱ[2] 連破 私たちのチームはライバルチームを3連破した Out team *won* three *successive victories* against our rival.

れんぱい 連敗 successive [a series of, straight] defeats [losses];（負け続けている期間）losing streak [C] ‖ドラゴンズはスワローズを破り対スワローズ戦の連敗を2で食い止めた The Dragons broke *a* two-game *losing streak* against the Swallows. ◆ジャイアンツはきょうで4連敗だ The Giants *have lost* four *straight games* to date.

れんぱつ 連発 銃を連発する *fire* shots *in succession* / テレビレポーターたちは彼女に質問を連発した TV reporters *fired* questions *at* her *in succession.* / 彼は下手なしゃれを連発した He *kept on making* bad puns.

れんぽう[1] 連邦 federation [C] ―連邦の federal ‖連邦国家 a federation / 連邦最高裁判所《米》the Supreme Court of the United States / 連邦制度 a federal system / 連邦政府 the federal government / 連邦捜査局《米》the Federal Bureau of Investigation (《略語》FBI) / 連邦取引委員会《米》the Federal Trade Commission (《略語》FTC) / 連邦保安官《米》a marshal / 英連邦 the Commonwealth (of Nations) / ロシア連邦 the Russian Federation

れんぽう[2] 連峰 mountain range [C]; (峰) the peaks ‖秩父連峰 *the peaks* of Chichibu

れんめい[1] 連盟 league [C] ‖高校野球連盟 *the* Senior High School Baseball *League*

れんめい[2] 連名 joint signature [C]
◆ 3人の連名で礼状を出した We sent a thank-you letter *signed by three people.*

れんや 連夜 (毎晩) every night; (幾晩も幾晩も) night after night ‖彼は連夜の酒がたたり体をこわした He ruined his health by drinking *night after night.*

れんらく 連絡

❶【人・物とのつながり】contact [U] ―連絡する contact [他], 《口語的》get* in touch

彼女とはもう連絡をとっていない I've lost *contact* [*touch*] with her.

大西洋沖でその飛行機との連絡が途絶えもう1時間になる It's been one hour since we lost *contact* with the plane over the Atlantic.

その件について何か分かったら連絡してください Please *contact* me if you get any information on that.

太郎と連絡がつかない I *can't contact* [*get in touch with*] Taro.

◆警察に連絡する *report to* the police / 連絡先を教えてね Can you tell me *where I can reach you*? / マイクから長い間連絡がない I *haven't heard from* Mike for a long time. / 熱があるので学校を休みますと担任の先生に電話で連絡した I *called* my teacher *and told* him I would be absent from school because I had a fever. / (手紙・Eメールの本文末などで) 連絡待っています《口語的》*Write* soon./ 《口語的》Keep in *touch.*/ 《公式的》I look forward to *hearing* from you. (❖英語には特に決まった敬語表現がないので, 第3文でも友人などに使えばカジュアルな感じになる) / あす行けないときは連絡します I'*ll let you know* if I can't come tomorrow.

[e]「また会えて本当によかったです」「連絡とり合いましょうね」"It was really great to see you again." "*Keep in touch*!"

❷【交通機関の接続】connection [C] ―連絡する connect [自]

あの駅は列車の連絡がいい[悪い] Train *connections* are good [bad] at that station.

そのバスは列車と連絡している The bus service *connects to* the train service.

この電車は次の駅で釧路行きに連絡している This train *connects to* [*with*] the train for Kushiro at the next station.

‖連絡駅 a junction, a connecting station / 連絡係 a messenger / 連絡切符 a transfer ticket / 連絡先 a contact address; (電話番号) a contact number / 連絡船 a ferryboat / 連絡網 a net

れんりつ 連立 ‖連立政権 a coalition government [cabinet] / 連立内閣 a coalition cabinet / 連立方程式 a simultaneous equation

ろ

ろ 〖音楽〗B□ ／ロ長調[短調]で in (the key of) B major [minor]

ろ¹ 炉 furnace □; (暖炉) fireplace □; (炉端) the fireside, hearth □ ／炉にまきをくべる feed *the furnace* with wood; feed wood into *the furnace* ‖原子炉 a nuclear reactor ／ ごみ焼却炉 an incinerator ／ 溶鉱炉 a blast furnace

ろ² 櫓 oar □, scull □ ／櫓をこぐ pull *an oar*; scull *a boat*

ロイヤル ‖ロイヤルボックス (劇場などの貴賓席) a royal box

ろう¹ 労 (めんどう) trouble □; (骨折り) pains《複数扱い》; (骨の折れるつらい仕事) labor, 《英》labour □; (努力) effort □□ ／その紛争では国連が仲裁の労をとった The UN *took the trouble to* mediate in the conflict. ／ 彼らは計画実現のためには労を惜しまなかった They *spared no pains* in realizing the project. ／ 私たちは彼の労に報いるべきだ We need to *reward him for his labor*.

ろう² 蝋 wax □ ‖ろう紙 wax [waxed] paper ／ ろう細工 a waxwork ／ ろう人形 a wax doll [figure]; (特に等身大の) a waxwork ／ ろう人形館 a wax museum, waxworks

ろう³ 牢 prison □□, jail □□

ろう- 老- 老夫婦 an *elderly* couple ／ 老木 an *old* tree

ろうあ 聾唖 ‖聾唖学校 a school for the deaf and mute ／ 聾唖者 a deaf-mute (person)

ろうえい 漏洩 leak □, leakage □□ ／国家機密の漏洩 *the leakage* of a national secret

ろうえき 労役 (hard) labor □ ‖労役に服する do hard work

ろうか¹ 廊下 (ビル・学校の) corridor □, 《米》hall(way) □ (❖ hall(way)は通例玄関の広間を指すが、一般的に廊下の意味でも使われる); (通路) passage(way) □ / 214号室はこの廊下のつきあたり、右側です Room 214 is at the end of this *corridor* on the right side. ／ 廊下を走ってはいけません Don't run in *the hallways*. ／ 小学生のころ先生に怒られてよく廊下に立たされた I was often scolded by my teacher and made to stand in *the hallway* when I was in elementary school.

ろうか² 老化 ag(e)ing □; (もうろく) senility □ ━━老化する age 圓 ／頭の老化を防ぐのによい方法は何ですか What is a good way to prevent the mind from *aging*? ／ 記憶力の衰えは老化現象の一つだ A failing memory is one of *the symptoms of senility*.

ろうかい 老獪 ━━老獪な (ずる賢い) cunning; (政略に富んだ) crafty

ろうかく 楼閣 tower □, high-rise [lofty] building □
◆彼らの案は砂上の楼閣 (→実現しそうもない空想) だ Their idea is *a castle in the sky*.

ろうがっこう 聾学校 a school for the deaf

ろうがん 老眼 presbyopia [prèzbióupiə] □; (老化による遠視) farsightedness caused by aging ◆老眼で新聞の字が読めづらい I'm *farsighted with age* and I can't read the words in the newspaper. ‖老眼鏡 a pair of spectacles [glasses] for the aged; (読書用の眼鏡) a pair of reading glasses

ろうきゅう 老朽 老朽化したビル a *timeworn* building ／ 校舎は老朽化が進んでいる The school building is getting *timeworn* [*too old*].

ろうきょう 老境 advanced [old] age □ ／老境に入る be [reach] *advanced age*

ろうく 労苦 (骨折り) pains《複数扱い》; (労力) labor □; (困難) trouble □; (努力) effort □□ ➡くろう

ろうご 老後 *one's* old age ‖彼女は老後に備えて貯金をしている She is saving money to provide for *her old age*. ／ 老後は沖縄でのんびり過ごしたい In *my old age* I want to lead a leisurely life in Okinawa.

ろうごく 牢獄 prison □□, jail □□

ろうこつ 老骨 父は老骨にむち打って (→老齢にもかかわらず) 働いた My father worked hard *in spite of his old [advanced] age*.

ろうさい 労災 workers' accidents ‖労災保険 workers' accident compensation insurance ／ 労災補償 compensation for workers' accidents

ろうさく 労作 (苦心して作った作品) laborious [painstaking] work □; (努力の成果) (good) effort □ ➡りきさく ／彼女の研究論文は労作だ Her research paper is *a good effort*.

ろうし 労使 labor and management ‖労使紛争を解決する settle *a dispute between labor and management* ‖労使関係 industrial relations, labor relations ／ 労使協調 cooperation between labor and management ／ 労使交渉 negotiations between labor and management

ろうじゃく 老若 《集合的》young and old (❖ 語順に注意)

ろうじょ 老女 old woman □

ろうじょう 籠城 彼らは籠城して (→敵から城を守り) 援軍を待った They *defended the castle against their enemies* and waited for reinforcements. ／ 強盗は人質をとって建物に籠城した (→立てこもった) The robber *shut himself up in* the building with a hostage.

ろうじん 老人 (男性) old [elderly] man □; (女性) old [elderly] woman [lady] (❖ elderly, lady のほうが丁寧な表現); (集合的に) old [elderly] people, the old [elderly]

(❖しばしばelderlyはoldの婉曲表現として用いる); (高齢者) the aged, (婉曲的の)senior citizens, seniors ⇒ 高齢化と介護 p.522
老人に席を譲る give *one's* seat to *an elderly man* [*woman*] / 老人をいたわる respect *old people*
‖老人クラブ a club for senior citizens / 老人差別《米》ageism, agism《英》ageism, agism / 老人性痴呆(ほう)症〖医学〗senile dementia / 老人病 diseases of old age / 老人福祉 welfare services for the elderly / 老人ホーム a retirement community [home]; (看護付きの) a nursing home / 寝たきり老人 a bedridden old man [woman]

ろうすい¹ 老衰 senility ⓤ ◆祖父は老衰のため91歳で亡くなった My grandfather died of *old age* when he was 91.

ろうすい² 漏水 (水もれ) water leak [leakage] ⓤⓒ /天井からの漏水にご注意ください Watch *a water leak* from the ceiling.
◆このパイプから漏水しているようだ It appears *water is leaking* from this pipe.

ろうする¹ 労する スワローズは労せずして3点を取った The Swallows scored three runs *without any trouble* [*effort*].

ろうする² 弄する 詭弁(きべん)を弄する *use* sophistry / 彼は策を弄してその計画を実現させた He pulled off the project *by using a dirty trick*.

ろうせい 老成 彼はまだ若いのに老成している (→円熟している) Though he's still young, he *is mature*. / He's *mature* beyond his years.

ろうぜき 狼藉 狼藉を働く (→暴力を加える) do *violence*

ろうそ 労組 (労働組合)《米》labor union, 《英》trade(s) union

ろうそく 蠟燭 candle ⓒ /ろうそくをつける[消す] light [put out] *a candle* / 妹はバースデーケーキのろうそくをひと吹きで吹き消した My sister blew out *the candles* on her birthday cake in one puff.
‖ろうそく立て a candlestick

ろうたい 老体 祖父は老体にむち打って (→高齢にもかかわらず)一生懸命働いている *Though my grandfather is aged*, he works very hard.

ろうたいか 老大家 日本画の老大家 *an old master* of Japanese painting

ろうでん 漏電 electric(al) leak(age) ⓒ, (a) leakage of electricity; (ショート) 〖電気〗 short (circuit) ⓒ /その機械からの漏電が原因で火事が起きた *The electric leak* in the machine caused the fire.

ろうどう 労働

work ⓤ, labor,《英》labour ⓤ(❖laborは特に骨の折れるつらい仕事を指す)──労働する work ⓘ, labor, 《英》labour ──(❖workのほうが一般的)
彼らは1日に8時間労働を強要されている They are forced to do eight hours' *labor*. / (→1日に8時間働かなければいけない) They have to *work* eight hours a day.
そのニュースは彼の労働意欲をわかせた The news stimulated his *will to work*.
我々は何とかして労働力不足を解消しなければならない We have to solve *labor shortages* somehow.
農作業は重労働だ Farming is *hard labor* [*work*].
◆労働時間の短縮はこの国の重要課題の一つです Shortening *working hours* is one of the major problems of this country. / この会社では1日の労働時間は7時間です This company's *workday* [*working day*] is seven hours. / This company has *a seven-hour workday* [*working day*].
‖労働運動 a labor movement / 労働基準法 the Labor Standards Law / 労働協約 a labor agreement [contract] / 労働組合《米》a labor union,《英》a trade(s) union / 労働災害 workers' accidents / 労働市場〖経済〗the labor market / 労働者 a worker; (肉体労働者) a laborer, (資本家に対する) labor / 労働者階級 the working class / 労働省 the Ministry of Labo(u)r (❖2001年厚生労働省に統合)⇒ こうせいろうどうしょう / 労働条件 working conditions / 労働人口 the labor force, the workforce, the working population / 労働生産性 labor productivity / 労働争議 labor disputes [troubles], industrial disputes; (ストライキ) a strike / 労働党(英国の) the Labour Party / 労働法 the labor law / 労働問題 a labor problem / 労働力 labor, the labor force, the workforce / 強制労働 forced labor / 時間外労働 overtime (work) / 深夜労働 late-night work / 頭脳労働 a mental labor, brainwork / 肉体労働 manual [physical] labor / 日雇い労働 a day labor

ろうどく 朗読 reading ⓒ; (詩の) recital ⓒ (❖どちらも「朗読会」の意味も含む) ──朗読する read* ⓘⓣ; recite ⓣ ◆彼はみんなの前で詩を朗読した He 「*read* the poem *aloud* [*recited* the poem] in front of everybody. / He *read* [*recited*] the poem *to* everybody. / 来週の金曜日に図書室で詩の朗読会を開きます We'll have *a poetry reading* [*recital*] next Friday in the library.

ろうにゃくなんにょ 老若男女 老若男女が年に一度のお祭りを楽しんだ *Men and women of all ages* [*Young and old, men and women*] enjoyed the annual festival.

ろうにん 浪人 (主人のいない武士) a *ronin*, a masterless samurai; (浪人生) a high school graduate who failed college entrance exams and is now studying for the next exam
◆兄は1年浪人して大学に入った My brother got into the university *after failing the entrance exams and studying for a year to prepare for the next year's exams*.

浪人とは元来、封建時代に仕える主人をもたない武士のことを指しました。今日(こんにち)では、大学受験に失敗し、翌年の受験のために勉強する人のこ

とをいいます. また, 高校浪人や就職浪人という言葉もあります.
Ronin, which originally meant a masterless samurai of feudal times, is now the word used for a high school graduate who is preparing for the next year's entrance examination to a college. There are also *ronin* junior high school graduates waiting for another chance to enter high school and *ronin* college graduates seeking jobs.

ろうねん 老年 old [advanced] age Ⓤ ∥老年期に入ると体力が衰えてくる You'll become weak when you reach *old [advanced] age*.

ろうば 老婆 old woman Ⓒ

ろうばい 狼狽 (当惑) confusion Ⓤ; (動揺) upset Ⓤ Ⓒ, dismay; (恐慌状態) panic Ⓒ ——狼狽する be confused; get* upset, feel* dismay; get into a panic ∥彼の思いがけない質問に私は狼狽した I 「*was confused by* [*got upset about, got into a panic about*] his unexpected question. / 彼女は狼狽の色を隠そうとした She tried not to show *her confusion*.

ろうはいぶつ 老廃物 waste Ⓤ (また複数形 ~s), waste matter Ⓤ

ろうばしん 老婆心 老婆心ながら (→ 余計なお世話ですが)ひと言付け加えておきます *Even though it's none of my business*, but I'd like to say one more thing.

ろうひ 浪費 waste Ⓤ (また a ~); (ぜいたく) extravagance Ⓤ ——浪費する waste Ⓤ; (考えなしに) squander 〘文〙; (投げ捨てて) throw* away ∥そんなことをするのは時間の浪費だ It is *a waste* of time to do such a thing. / テレビのつけっぱなしは電気の浪費だ Leaving the television on *wastes* electricity. / 彼女はいつもつまらない物にお金を浪費する She always *wastes* [*squanders, throws away*] her money *on* worthless things.
∥浪費家 a waster; (金づかいの激しい人) a spendthrift; 浪費癖 wasteful habits

ろうほう 朗報 good [happy] news ∥朗報を受け取る receive *good* [*happy*] *news*

ろうむ 労務 labor Ⓤ, work Ⓤ ∥労務課 the labor section / 労務管理 labor management; (人事管理) personnel management / 労務者(肉体労働者) a laborer; (頭脳労働者を含む) a worker; (日雇いの) a day laborer

ろうや 牢屋 prison Ⓤ, jail Ⓤ
➪けいむしょ

ろうりょく 労力 (労働) labor Ⓤ; (努力) effort Ⓤ; (骨折り) pains〘複数扱い〙; (めんどう) trouble Ⓤ; (尽力)〘公式的〙service Ⓒ ∥それをするには大変な労力を要するだろう We will need a lot of *effort* to do this. / 彼女はその仕事にすべての労力を費やした She spent all *her effort* on the job. / 彼の計画を支援するためなら労力は惜しみません I'll spare no *trouble* to support his plan.

ろうれい 老齢 old [advanced] age Ⓤ (❖通例65歳以上を指す) ——老齢の old, elderly (❖しばしば elderly は old の婉曲表現として用いられる); (高齢の) aged ∥そのとき彼は90の老齢に達していた He had reached *the old age* of 90 at that time. / 老齢にもかかわらず, 祖父は僕たちといっしょに山に登った Despite *his advanced age*, my grandfather climbed the mountain with us.
∥老齢(化)社会 an aging society / 老齢人口 the aging population / 老齢年金 an old-age pension / 老齢年金受給者 an old age pensioner(《略語》OAP)

ろうれん 老練 ——老練な (経験豊富な) veteran, experienced; (熟練した) skilled; (専門家の) expert ∥老練な職人 a *veteran* [*an experienced, a skilled*] craftsman

ろうろう 朗々 朗々と(→ 響き渡るように)詩を読む read a poem *resonantly*

ローカル ⚠ ——ローカルな local(❖日本語の「ローカル」には, 都会に対して「いなか」という意味合いがあるが, 英語の local にはそのような意味は含まれず, むしろ「ある特定の地域の, 地元の」という意味で用いられる) ∥彼らはローカルな話をしていた They were talking about a *local* subject. / その行事はローカルカラーにあふれていた That event was full of *local color*.
∥ローカル線(鉄道の支線) a branch line(❖英語の local line は「短い区間を走る路線」の意味) / ローカルニュース local news / ローカル放送 a local broadcast

ローション lotion Ⓤ Ⓒ ∥アフターシェーブローション after-shave lotion, aftershave / スキンローション skin lotion

ロージンバッグ (球技や競技で使う滑り止め) rosin bag Ⓒ

ロース ⚠ (牛肉の) sirloin Ⓒ Ⓤ; (豚肉の) pork loin Ⓤ (❖「ロース」は roast がなまったもの) ∥ロースハム roast ham

ロースト (直火(じかび)・オーブンなどで焼いた[あぶった]肉) roast Ⓒ ∥ローストチキン roast chicken / ローストビーフ roast beef

ローター (機械の回転部分) rotor Ⓒ

ロータリー (円形の交差点)《米》rotary Ⓒ, traffic circle Ⓒ,《英》roundabout Ⓒ ∥ロータリーエンジン a rotary engine / ロータリークラブ the Rotary Club

ローティーン ⚠ ローティーンの少女向けの雑誌 a magazine for girls *in their early teens* (❖「ローティーン」は和製英語)

ローテーション rotation Ⓤ Ⓒ ∥監督は4人の投手のローテーションを組んだ The manager organized [formed] the four pitchers into *a four-man rotation*. / その投手はローテーションからはずされた The pitcher was excluded from *the rotation*.

ロードアイランド Rhode Island (❖米国北東部の州;《略語》R.I.,《郵便》RI)

ロードゲーム road game Ⓒ, away game Ⓒ (↔home game)

ロードショー road show Ⓒ; (最初の特別公開) special first run Ⓒ

ロードレース (1回の) road race Ⓒ; (総称) road racing Ⓤ

ローヒール ローヒールのパンプス *low-heeled*

ロープ

pumps
ロープ rope ⓤⓒ ⇨つな, なわ
ロープウエー ⚠ cable car ⓒ, ropeway ⓒ
(❖ropewayは主に貨物を運ぶ空中索道をいう)
ローマ Rome(❖イタリアの首都) ─ローマ人 Roman ∥ ─ローマ(人)の Roman ∥ ローマカトリック教会《キリスト教》the Roman Catholic Church / ローマカトリック教徒 a Roman Catholic / ローマ神話 the Roman myths / ローマ数字 Roman numerals / ローマ帝国 the Roman Empire / ローマ法王 the Pope / ローマ法王庁 the Vatican
慣用表現 すべての道はローマに通ず *All roads lead to Rome.* / ローマは一日にして成らず *Rome was not built in a day.*
ローマじ ローマ字 Roman letters, the Roman alphabet ∥あなたの名前をローマ字で書いてください Write your name in「*Roman letters* [*the Roman alphabet*]」
ローヤルゼリー royal jelly ⓤ
ローラー (地ならしなどの) roller ⓒ ∥グラウンドにローラーをかける smooth the ground with *a roller*; *roll* a ground
∥ローラー作戦 a house-to-house search
ローラーコースター (ジェットコースター) roller coaster ⓒ, 《英》switchback ⓒ
ローラースケート ⚠ (滑ること) roller-skating ⓤ; (靴) roller skates(❖数えるときは a pair of ... とする)
◆車道でローラースケートをしてはいけません Don't *roller-skate* in the road.
ローラーブレード roller blades
ローリング (船などの横揺れ) rolling ⓤ, roll ⓤ ─ローリングする roll ⓔ
ロールキャベツ ⚠ (meat-)stuffed cabbage ⓤ (❖×roll(ed) cabbageとはいわない)
ロールシャッハテスト Rorschach test
ロールパン (bread) roll ⓒ, 《米》bun ⓒ (❖×roll breadとはいわない)
ローン (貸付金) loan ⓒ; (抵当によって借りた) mortgage [mɔ́ːrɡɪdʒ] ⓒ ─ローンを返済する repay *a loan* / 父は家を買うために2,000万円の住宅ローンを組んだ My father took out *a mortgage* [*housing loan, home loan*] of 20 million yen to buy a house.
∥銀行ローン a bank loan
ろか 濾過 filtration ⓤ ─ろ過する filter ⓔ ∥布で泥水をろ過する *filter* muddy water through a cloth
∥ろ過器 a filter
ろかた 路肩 the shoulder (of a road) ∥路肩注意《掲示》*Soft Shoulders* / 路肩に車を寄せる pull over to *the shoulder*
ロカビリー rockabilly ⓤ
ろく 六 six; (6番目) the sixth
ろくおん 録音 recording ⓤⓒ ─録音する record ⓔ; (テープに) tape(-record) ⓔ ∥テープにラジオ番組を録音した I *recorded* a radio program on a tape. / I *taped* [*tape-recorded*] a radio program.
∥録音機 a (tape) recorder / 録音技師 a recording engineer / 録音室 a recording room; (レコーディングスタジオ) a studio / 録音テープ a recording tape, an audiotape; (何も録音されていない) a blank tape [cassette]
ろくが 録画 videotape recording ⓤ ─録画する record ... on videotape, videotape ⓔ ∥その映画を忘れずに録画しておいてね Don't forget to「*record* the movie *on videotape* [*videotape* the movie]」

ろくがつ 六月 June ⓤⓒ (《略語》Jun.) ⇨いちがつ
ろくさんせい 六三制 ▨▨▨ the 6-3 school education system, the Japanese school education system of six years of elementary and three years of junior high school
ろくじゅう 六十 sixty; (60番目) the sixtieth
ろくしょう 緑青 verdigris ⓤ, copper rust ⓤ ∥そのブロンズ像には緑青が出ている *Verdigris* [*Copper rust*] *has formed* on the surface of the bronze statue.
ろくすっぽ 彼はその本をろくすっぽ読みもしないで批評していた He criticized the book without reading it *well*.
ろくでなし (役に立たない人) good-for-nothing ⓒ; (価値のない人) worthless person ⓒ ∥このろくでなしめ You *good-for-nothing*!
ろくでもない (価値のない) worthless; (役に立たない) good-for-nothing, useless; (愚かな) silly ∥あんなろくでもない男のどこがいいの Why do you like that *worthless* man? / ろくでもないことを言うな Don't be *silly*.
ろくな 彼らといるとろくな(→まともな)人にならないよ You won't be *a decent* person if you hang around with them. / ろくな(→納得のいく)説明もないのに分かるわけがない How can we understand without a *satisfactory* explanation? / この店はろくな物を置いていない(→価値のない物しかない) This shop has nothing but *worthless* stuff. / きょうは朝からろくなことがない(→すべてうまくいかない) From this morning, *everything has gone wrong* for me.
ろくに 彼女はろくに(→ちゃんと)あいさつもできない She can't even say hello *properly*. / とても忙しくてろくに(→ほとんど)休む暇もない Since we're so busy, we *hardly* have time to take a break. / 犬が一晩中ほえていたのでろくに(→十分に)眠れなかった I couldn't get *enough* sleep because dogs were barking all night. / 彼のことをろくに知りもしないのに(→よく知る前に)悪口を言わないで Don't speak ill of him *before you've gotten to know* him *well*.
ログハウス log house ⓒ
ろくまく 肋膜 the pleura
∥肋膜炎《医学》pleurisy
ろくろ 轆轤 (製陶用) potter's wheel ⓒ
ろくろく 時間がなくて彼女とろくろく話もできなかった I didn't have time, so I *hardly* talked with her.
ロケ(ーション) location ⓒⓤ ∥ロケに行く go on *location* / このドラマはほとんどサイパン

でロケが行われた Most of this drama was shot on *location* in Saipan. / そのレストランは花火を見るのに絶好のロケーションだ That restaurant is in perfect *location* for watching the fireworks.

ロケット¹ rocket ◯ /ロケットを打ち上げる launch [fire] *a rocket*
‖ロケットエンジン a rocket engine / ロケット工学 rocketry / ロケット弾 a rocket (bomb) / ロケット発射台 a launch [launching] pad / 3[多]段式ロケット a three-stage [multistage] rocket / 月ロケット a moon rocket

ロケット² (装身具) locket ◯

ろけん 露見 (見破られること) detection ⓤ; (暴露) exposure ⓤ◯, disclosure ⓤ◯ ── 露見する be detected; be exposed, be disclosed; (正体などを見破られる) be found out /その役人は不正が露見してから数日後に辞表を提出した The official handed in his resignation a few days after his illegal acts *were disclosed*.

ロゴ (社名・商標などの) logo ◯ (複 ~s)

ロココしき ロココ式 ──ロココ式の rococo (❖名詞の前で用いる)

ろこつ 露骨 ──露骨な (率直な) frank, open, plain; (遠慮のない) outspoken, blunt; (冗談などが) broad [brɔːd]; (描写などが) explicit ──露骨に frankly, openly, plainly; bluntly /露骨な表現 (an) *open* expression / 彼は露骨に不快感を表した He showed his displeasure *openly*. / 彼女は露骨に政府の政策を非難した She spoke *frankly* in her attack on the government's policy. / そんなに露骨に人の悪口を言うべきではない You shouldn't *bluntly* say bad things about the others like that.

ロザリオ (数珠(ｼﾞｭｽﾞ)) rosary ◯; (ロザリオの祈り) 《キリスト教》 the rosary

ロサンゼルス Los Angeles (❖米国の都市; (略語)L.A.)

ろし 濾紙 filter paper ⓤ

ろじ 路地 (裏通り) alley(way) ◯; (家などの間の) lane ◯ /その店は路地を少し入った所にある The shop is a little way up *the alley*.
‖路地裏 a back alley

ロシア Russia [rʌ́ʃə] (❖公式名 the Russian Federation) ──ロシア人 a Russian ◯; (集合的)the Russians ──ロシア語 Russian ──ロシア(人[語])の Russian
‖ロシア皇帝 a czar [tsar, tzar](❖いずれも発音は [zɑ́ːr]) / ロシア正教会 the Russian (Orthodox) Church

ろじさいばい 露地栽培 露地栽培の野菜 vegetables *grown outdoors*

ろしゅつ 露出 (写真の) exposure ⓤ◯; (地層・鉱脈などの) outcrop ◯ ──露出する (肌を) expose ⊕; (鉱床などが) crop out /露出時間を50分の1秒にする set *the exposure* to one-fiftieth of a second / 彼女は肌を大胆に露出したドレスを着ていた She wore a dress which *exposed* much of her body. ◆露出した岩肌 the *naked* surface of the rock / 写真はどれも露出オーバー[不足]だった All the photos *were overexposed [underexposed]*.
‖露出狂 an exhibitionist / 露出計《写真》a light meter

ろじょう 路上 路上駐車禁止 *Parking on the street* is prohibited. / 路上で遊んではいけません Don't play *in [on] the road*.
‖路上試験(運転免許の) 《米》a road test

ろしん 炉心 (原子炉の) 《物理》reactor core ◯ /炉心溶融 (a) meltdown

ロス¹ (損失) loss ⓤ◯; (浪費) waste ◯ⓤ /いつまでもこんなことをしているのは時間のロスだ Continuing this will only result in *a loss [waste]* of time.
‖ロスタイム(サッカー・ラグビーの) injury time (❖「ロスタイム」は和製英語)

ロス² ⚠ Los Angeles(❖「ロス」は和製略語) ➡ ロサンゼルス

ロゼ (薄赤色のワイン) rosé [rouzéi] ⓤ

ろせん 路線 (交通機関の) line ◯; (決められた道筋) route ◯; (活動方針) line ◯ /その党は路線を変更した The party changed *its lines*. / これらの赤字路線は廃止するべきだ These *routes [lines]* operating in the red should be discontinued. / 警察はホームレスに対する強硬路線をとった The police *took a hard line* on the homeless.
‖路線図 a route map / 路線バス a route bus

ロッカー locker ◯ ‖ロッカールーム a locker room / コインロッカー a coin-operated locker

ろっかく 六角 ──六角の hexagonal ‖六角形 a hexagon

ろっかん 六感 ‖第六感 the sixth sense

ロッキーさんみゃく ロッキー山脈 the Rocky Mountains, the Rockies

ロッキングチェア rocking chair /

ロック¹ (音楽) rock (music) ⓤ ‖ロック歌手 a rock singer / ロックバンド a rock band / ハードロック hard rock

ロック² (錠) lock ◯ ──ロックする lock ⊕ ‖ドアをロックする *lock* the door

ロックアウト lockout ◯ ──ロックアウトする lock out

ロッククライミング rock-climbing ⓤ

ロックンロール rock'n'roll ⓤ (❖rock-and-roll の略)

ろっこつ 肋骨《解剖》rib ◯; (全体) the ribs /彼はその事故で肋骨を3本折った He broke three *ribs* in the accident.

ロッジ lodge ◯ ‖スキーロッジ a ski lodge

ロッド (釣りざお) (fishing) rod ◯ ‖ロッドアンテナ a rod antenna

ろっぽうぜんしょ 六法全書 the Compendium of Laws

ろてい 露呈 ──露呈する (暴露する) expose ⊕; (明らかにする) reveal ⊕, come* out /今回の海外旅行で乏しい英語力が露呈してしまった My poor English *was revealed* during this overseas trip.

ロデオ rodeo ◯ (複 ~s)

ろてん¹ 露店 (street) stand ◯, 《主に英》

(street) stall

ろてん² 露天 the open air, the outdoors ―露天の open-air, outdoor (❖共に名詞の前で用いる)
‖露天商 a street vendor, a stall keeper / 露天ぶろ an open-air [outdoor] bath

ろとう 路頭 会社を首になって路頭に迷っている(→生活に困った) I got fired and I'm hardly able to get by.

ろば 驢馬 donkey ⓒ, ass ⓒ (❖donkey のほうが日常語として用いられる)

ろばた 炉端 the fireside

ロビー (ホテル・劇場などの) lobby ⓒ; (空港などの) lounge ⓒ ‖ホテルのロビー a hotel *lobby* / ロビーは禁煙です You're not allowed to smoke in *the lobby*.
‖出発ロビー (空港の) the departure lounge

ロビイスト lobbyist ⓒ (❖議員に圧力をかけて議案の可否に影響を与える専門家)

ロブ 〖テニス〗(高く打ち上げられた打球) lob ⓒ

ロフト (屋根裏部屋) loft ⓒ ‖ロフト付きの部屋 a room with *a loft*

ロボット robot ⓒ ‖ロボット工学 robotics / 産業用ロボット an industrial robot

ロマン ⚠ 彼はいつもロマン(→理想)を追い求めている He is always pursuing *his ideal.* / その話は男のロマン(→夢)をかきたてる The story arouses men's *dreams*.

ロマンしゅぎ ロマン主義 romanticism Ⓤ
‖ロマン主義者 a romanticist

ロマンス (小説のような恋愛) romance ⓒ; (情事) (love) affair ⓒ; (恋愛の話) love story ⓒ ‖彼女はずっとすてきな男性とのロマンスにあこがれている She has always dreamed of having *a romance* with a handsome man.
◆ロマンスグレーの紳士 a gentleman with *silver hair* / 二人の間にロマンスが芽生えた(→お互いに恋した) They *fell in love with* each other.
‖ロマンスシート(２人がけのソファー) a love seat (×romance seat とはいわない)

ロマンチシズム romanticism Ⓤ
⇒ロマンしゅぎ

ロマンチスト (夢想家) romantic ⓒ (❖英語の romanticist は「ロマン派の芸術家」の意味)

ロマンチック ―ロマンチックな romantic ‖そのレストランはとてもロマンチックなムードだった The mood of this restaurant was quite *romantic*.

ロマンは ロマン派 the romantic [Romantic] school
◆ロマン派の絵画 *Romantic* paintings

ロム 〖コンピュータ〗ROM ⓒ (❖ *read-only memory*(読み出し専用メモリ)の略)

ろめん 路面 road surface ⓒ ◆路面凍結〈掲示〉Icy [Slippery] Road / 凍った路面で車が滑った The car slipped on *the icy road*.
‖路面改修工事 resurfacing [road] work / 路面電車 (米) a street car, (英) a tram

ロリコン Lolita complex ⓒ

ろれつ 呂律 彼はお酒をたくさん飲んでいたのでろれつが回らなかった He drank so much that he *slurred his words*.

ろん 論

❶【議論】argument ⓒ; (討論) discussion ⓒ; (論争) dispute ⓒⓊ
◆この問題が我々にとって非常に重要であるということは論をまたない(→言うまでもない) *Needless to say*, this problem is very important to us. / *It goes without saying that* this problem is very important to us.

❷【評論】criticism Ⓤⓒ; (小論) essay ⓒ; (意見) comment ⓒ, opinion ⓒⓊ; (理論) theory ⓒⓊ
その問題に関して専門家たちの論が分かれている *Opinions* of the specialists are divided on the issue.
その作家の人生論にとても興味を引かれる I'm very interested in the writer's *essay* [*theory*] *on his life.*
‖進化論 the theory of evolution / 抽象論 an abstract argument / 文学論 literary criticism

ことわざ 論より証拠 Example is better than precept.(→実例は教訓に勝る); The proof of the pudding is in the eating. (→プディングの味は食べてみて初めて分かる)

ろんがい 論外な値段[要求] an *outrageous* price [demand] / こんな物に３万円も払うなんて全く論外だよ It's completely *out of the question* to pay 30,000 yen for such a thing.

ろんぎ 論議 (話し合い) discussion ⓒⓊ; (考えを主張すること) argument ⓒ ⇒ぎろん ‖彼らとその問題について激しい論議となった I had [held] *a heated discussion on* the issue with them.
◆その法案は国民の間で大きな論議を呼んだ The bill *aroused* much *controversy* among the citizens.

ろんきゃく 論客 controversialist ⓒ

ろんきゅう 論及 総理は最近の雇用対策に論及した The Prime Minister *referred to* the recent employment measures.

ろんきょ 論拠 (根拠) ground Ⓤⓒ (しばしば複数形～s); (基礎) basis ⓒ (複 bases) ‖どんな論拠があってそう言うのですか What is *the basis of* [*for*] *your saying that*?

ロングシュート ⚠long shot

ロングショット long shot ⓒ

ロングスカート long skirt ⓒ

ロングセラー ⚠long-time seller ⓒ (❖× long seller とはいわない)

ロングヘア long hair Ⓤ

ロングラン ロングランの映画 a *long-running movie* [*film*] / その演劇はロングランが続いている That play has had *a long run*.

ろんご 論語 the Analects of Confucius

ろんこく 論告 the prosecutor's concluding [closing, final] speech

ろんし 論旨 (要点) the point; (要旨) the gist; (趣旨) the drift ‖論旨をつかむ get *the point* [*gist, drift*] / 君のスピーチは論旨が不明確で分かりづらい *The point* [*gist, drift*] of your speech is not clear and not understandable. / その記事の論旨を1,000字[語]以内

にまとめること Write *the main point* of the article within 1,000 characters [words].
(◆英語の場合は字数ではなく語数で指定する)

ろんじゅつ 論述 statement ⓒ ──論述する state ⓗ ‖論述テスト an essay test [exam, examination]

ろんしょう 論証 proof Ⓤⓒ ──論証する prove ⓗ ‖政治学の理論を論証する *prove* a political theory

ろんじる 論じる (主張する) argue ⓗ; (意見を出し合う) discuss ⓗ; (問題を取り上げる) treat ⓗ, deal* with ... ‖私たちは科学技術について論じ合った We *argued with* them about [over] science and technology. / We *discussed* science and technology with them. / この記事は核実験を論じている This article *treats* [*deals with, discusses*] nuclear testing.

ろんじん 論陣 ‖私たちは戦争反対の論陣を張った (→強硬な主張をした) We *made a strong argument* against war.

ろんせつ 論説 (論評) comment [kάment] ⓒⓊ; (小論) essay ⓒ; (新聞・雑誌などの) article ⓒ, (社説) editorial ⓒ, 《英》leader ⓒ, 《英》leading article ⓒ
‖論説委員 an editorial writer, 《英》a leader writer

ろんせん 論戦 (論争) dispute Ⓤⓒ; (討論) debate Ⓤⓒ; (議論) argument ⓒ ‖環境汚染に関して彼らは激しい論戦を繰り広げていた They had *a heated dispute* [*debate, argument*] over environmental pollution.

ろんそう 論争 (感情的な) dispute Ⓤⓒ; (公的で長期の) controversy Ⓤⓒ; (討論) debate Ⓤⓒ; (自分の主張を通す) argument ⓒ ──論争する dispute ⓗ; have* a controversy; debate ⓗⓘ, argue ⓘ
そのニュースは国民の間に大きな論争を引き起こした The news aroused much *controversy* among the citizens.
環境ホルモンについての問題はいまだ論争中だ The issue of the endocrine disrupting chemicals *is* still *in* [*under*] *dispute* [*controversy*].
我々はこの政策について彼らと論争した We *disputed* [*argued, debated*] *with* them *about* [*over*] the policy. / We *had an argument* [*a controversy, a dispute, a debate*] *with* them *about* [*over*] the policy.

ろんだい 論題 a topic [subject, theme] (of discussion)

ろんだん 論壇 (言論界) the world of criticism, the critical circles

ろんちょう 論調 a tone (of argument) ‖新聞各紙はその収賄事件を激しい論調で報道した Each newspaper reported the bribery scandal *in a severe* [*bitter*] *tone*. / 新しい法案について新聞の論調はやや批判的だ The *tone* of the editorial is slightly critical of the new bill.

ろんてき 論敵 an opponent in an argument

ろんてん 論点 (中心点) the main point; (問題点) a point [question] at issue
◆彼の意見は論点がずれている His opinion is besides *the point*.

ロンド 〖音楽〗rondo ⓒ (複 ～s)

ロンドン London [lΛ́ndən](❖英国の首都)
‖ロンドン市民 a Londoner / ロンドン塔 the Tower (of London)

ろんぱ 論破 refutation Ⓤⓒ ──論破する (言い負かす) 《主に米》argue down; (誤りを証明する) refute ⓗ ‖彼は彼女を論破しようと試みたがだめだった He attempted to *argue* her *down* but he failed.

ロンパース (上下がつながった子供服) rompers

ろんばく 論駁 refutation Ⓤⓒ, confutation Ⓤⓒ ──論駁する refute ⓗ, confute ⓗ ‖彼女はその学者の持論を論駁した She *refuted* the scholar's theories.

ろんぴょう 論評 (コメント・意見) comment [kάment] ⓒⓊ; (主に芸術作品の批評) criticism Ⓤⓒ; (演劇・書物などの) review ⓗⓒ ──論評する comment ⓗ; criticize ⓗ; review ⓗ ‖その劇は雑誌で好意的な論評を得た The play got favorable [good] *reviews* in the magazine. / 彼は最近の選挙での新政党の大勝利について論評した He「*commented upon* [*made a comment on*]」the landslide victory of the new party in the recent election.

ろんぶん 論文 (一般的に) paper ⓒ (❖政府機関などの報告書、主に米国ではレポートの意味も含む); (学位請求論文) thesis ⓒ (複 theses), dissertation ⓒ; (学術論文) treatise ⓒ; (小論文) essay ⓒ
言語学に関する論文を書く write *a paper* on linguistics / 博士号を取るために論文を大学に提出する present [submit] *a dissertation* to the university for a Ph.D. [doctorate]
彼は癌(ｶﾞﾝ)に関する論文を発表した He read [delivered] *a treatise* on cancer.
‖研究論文 a research paper / 修士論文 a master's thesis [dissertation] / 卒業論文 a graduation thesis / 博士論文 a doctoral dissertation [thesis]

ろんぽう 論法 (議論の進め方) reasoning Ⓤ; (論理) logic Ⓤ; (議論・主張) argument Ⓤ ‖彼の論法についていけましたか Were you able to follow his *logic*? / 君の論法はおかしい Your *argument* is not reasonable [logical].
‖三段論法〖論理〗a syllogism

ろんり 論理 logic Ⓤ ──論理的な logical (↔illogical) ──論理的に logically (↔illogically) ‖彼の記事には論理の飛躍がある His article has a gap in *its logic*. / 君の考え方は論理的ではない The way you're thinking *is not logical* [*illogical*]. / 彼女はとても論理的な人だ She has a very *logical* mind. / 我々はこの事態をもっと論理的に考えるべきだ We have to think about this situation more *logically*.
‖論理学 logic / 論理学者 a logician

わ

わ[1] 輪 ring [C]; (円) circle [C]; (鎖の) link [C]; (糸などの) loop [C]; (車輪) wheel [C] ∥土星の輪 *the rings* of Saturn; Saturn's *rings* / 鎖の輪 *a link* in the chain / 輪になって座る sit *in a circle* [*ring*] / ロープで輪を作る make *a loop* with a rope
[慣用表現] 彼女は母親に輪をかけてきちょうめんだ She is *more* methodical than her mother.

わ[2] 和 ❶【協調】harmony [U] [C]; (まとまり) unity [U] ∥人の和を重んじる value *harmony* among people / 彼はクラスの和を乱した He disturbed *the harmony* of the class.
❷【合計】the sum, the total ∥5と4の和は9である *The sum* of five and four is nine. / Five plus four equals nine.

-わ[1] -羽 1羽の鳥 *one* [*a*] bird / 電線に数羽の鳥がとまっていた *Several birds* were sitting on the electric wire.

-わ[2] -把 bundle [C]; (野菜などの) bunch [C] ∥市場でホウレンソウを3わ買った I bought three *bunches* of spinach at the market.

わあ (歓声) hurrah, hurray; (驚きの声) oh, wow, 《米》gee, 《米》boy
💬「あの二人, ハワイで結婚式を挙げるんだって」「わあ, すてき」"I heard they will hold their wedding ceremony in Hawaii." "*Oh*, how wonderful! / *Wow*! That's great!"

ワーカホリック (仕事中毒の人) workaholic [C]

ワークショップ (研究会・講習会) workshop [C]

ワークステーション 〖コンピュータ〗workstation [C]

ワークブック (練習帳) workbook [C]

ワースト worst ∥彼は結婚したくないタレントのワーストテンに入っている He is one of *the ten worst* entertainers women don't want to marry.
∥ワースト記録 the worst record / ワーストテン the worst ten (❖ただし, ワーストテン選手 the ten worst players のように, 名詞が後に置かれると語順が変わる)

ワープ warp [C] ◆異次元へワープする *warp to* another dimension

ワープロ ⚠word processor [C] (《略語》WP) ∥ワープロ専用機 *a* dedicated *word processor* / 日本語ワープロ *a* Japanese-language *word processor* / ワープロで手紙を書く write [type] a letter *on* [*with*] *a word processor*

ワールドカップ 〖スポーツ〗the World Cup ∥サッカーのワールドカップは4年に1度開催される *The World Cup* Soccer *tournament* is held every four years.

ワールドシリーズ 〖野球〗the World Series ∥今年のワールドシリーズはどのチームが優勝するだろう Which team will win *the World Series* this year?

わあわあ わあわあ泣く cry *loudly* / 子供たちがわあわあ騒ぐので映画に集中できなかった I couldn't concentrate on the movie because the children *made* so *much noise*.

ワイエムシーエー the YMCA (❖ *Y*oung *M*en's *C*hristian *A*ssociation (キリスト教青年会)の略語)

ワイオミング Wyoming (❖米国北西部の州; 《略語》Wy., Wyo., 〔郵便〕WY)

わいきょく 歪曲 distortion [U] [C] ——歪曲する distort [他] ∥一部のマスコミはしばしば事実を歪曲する Some of the media often *distort* facts.

ワイシャツ ⚠shirt [C], dress shirt [C] (❖通常は shirt でよいが, 特にほかのシャツと区別する場合は dress shirt という.「ワイシャツ」は和製英語) ◆ワイシャツ姿で働く work *in* (*one's*) *shirtsleeves*

ワイじろ Y字路 forked road [C]; (Y字の交差点) Y-junction [C]

わいせつ 猥褻 obscenity [U]; (下品なこと) indecency [U] (❖いずれも言葉や行為を指すときは [C]) ——わいせつな obscene; indecent; (下品な・みだらな) 《口語的》dirty ∥わいせつな冗談 a *dirty* joke
∥わいせつ行為 indecent behavior [conduct] / わいせつ罪 public indecency / わいせつ本 an obscene book, a pornographic book / 強制わいせつ罪 indecent assault / 公然わいせつ罪 indecent exposure

ワイダブリューシーエー the YWCA (❖ *Y*oung *W*omen's *C*hristian *A*ssociation (キリスト教女子青年会)の略語)

わいだん 猥談 dirty [indecent] talk [C], dirty [indecent] story [C] ∥わい談をする tell *dirty stories*

ワイド ∥ワイドショー a daytime TV variety program / ワイドスクリーン a wide screen / ワイド番組(長時間番組) a long program

ワイパー (自動車の) (《米》windshield [《英》windscreen]) wiper [C] ∥ワイパーを動かす turn on *the wipers*

ワイヤー wire [U] [C]
∥ワイヤーロープ a wire rope

ワイヤレス (無線の) wireless
∥ワイヤレスマイク a wireless microphone

ワイルドピッチ 〖野球〗wild pitch [C]

わいろ 賄賂 bribe [C], 《口語的》payoff [C]; (贈収賄) bribery [U] ∥わいろを贈る offer [give] *a bribe* / わいろを要求する solicit *a bribe* / その会社から彼がわいろを受け取ったことは疑う余地がない It is beyond question that he received [accepted] *bribes* from that company. / 彼はいくつかの会社にわいろを強要していた He had extorted *a bribe* from several companies.
◆彼はその証人にわいろを使ってうその証言をさ

せた He *bribed* the witness 「*to give* [*into giving*] *false testimony*.

わいわい 隣の部屋からわいわい騒ぐ声が聞こえてきた There was *a lot of noise* coming from the next room. / 最終的な結論が出てしまったのだからいまさらわいわい言ってもしかたがない It's no use *making such a fuss* about it now that the final decision has been made.

ワイン wine ⓊⒸ ‖甘口[辛口]ワイン sweet [dry] *wine* / 1 びん[グラス 1 杯]の赤[白, ロゼ]ワイン a bottle [glass] of red [white, rosé] *wine* / こくのあるワイン a *wine* with plenty of body
‖ワインカラー wine color / ワイングラス a wineglass / ワインリスト a wine list

ワインドアップ 〖野球〗windup Ⓒ ◆ワインドアップして投げる *wind up* and throw

わえいじてん 和英辞典 Japanese-English dictionary Ⓒ

わおん 和音 〔音楽〕chord Ⓒ

わか 和歌 🖼

和歌は 5 音節と 7 音節の句を組み合わせて作る日本の古典的な詩歌です。昔, 和歌にはいくつかの形式がありましたが, その中の主流であった 5・7・5・7・7 という組み合わせの短歌を残し, ほかの形式は廃(た)れていきました。そして今では和歌といえば短歌を指すようになったのです。
Waka is classical Japanese poetry composed in combinations of five- and seven-syllabled lines. There were several different forms of *waka* in ancient times, but most styles gradually disappeared except for *tanka*, the dominant style of *waka* composed in 5-7-5-7-7 syllabled lines. Now *tanka* is virtually equivalent to *waka*.

わが- 我が- (私の) my; (私たちの) our; (自分の) one's ‖わが町 *my* [*our*] city / 親はだれだってわが子がかわいいものだ All parents love *their* children.

わかい¹ 若い

❶【年齢が】young (↔old); (若々しい) youthful
この若い選手たちがチームの中心となるだろう These *young* players will form the nucleus of the team.
この小説は若い読者に受けるでしょうか Will this novel appeal to *young* readers?
そのレストランは若い女性でいっぱいだった The restaurant was crowded with *young* women.
彼女は彼よりずっと[3 歳]若い She *is* much [three years] *younger than* him.
4 人の中でだれがいちばん若いのですか Who is *the youngest* of the four?
若いうちにたくさん本を読んでおいたほうがよい It's better for you to read a lot *while you are young*.
私の祖母は気が若い My grandmother *is young at heart*.
その作家は若くして亡くなった The writer died *young*.
父は年のわりには若く見える My father looks *young* for his age.
もし私が10歳若ければそのレースに参加するのだが If I *were* 10 years *younger*, I'd take part in the race.
◆彼の祖父は若いころペルーへ移住した His grandfather emigrated to Peru 「*early in his life* [*in his youth*].
💬「彼女のお母さんてまるでお姉さんみたいじゃない?」「ほんとに若いよね」"Her mother looks as if she were her sister, doesn't she?" "I know. She's really *youthful*."

❷【未熟な】immature,《口語的》green
彼の話を信じるとは君もまだ若いね You *are* still *immature* [*green*] if you believe his story.

❸【数字が】low, small
若い数字 a *low* [*small*] number
◆ここにある本を番号の若い順に並べてください Please arrange the books here *in numerical order*.

わかい² 和解 reconciliation Ⓤ《また a ~》; (解決) settlement Ⓤ Ⓒ; (妥協) compromise Ⓤ Ⓒ ━━和解する be reconciled; make* [reach] a settlement ‖和解に応じる accept *a compromise* / 家庭裁判所は二人に和解を勧告した The family court recommended *reconciliation* to the couple.
◆その話し合いで彼は妻と和解した Those discussions *reconciled him with* his wife. / 兄弟二人は長年口をきかなかったが, 母親が病気になってからついに和解した The two brothers had not spoken for years but they *made peace with each other* at last when their mother became sick.

わかい 我が意 わが意を得たりだ(→全く賛成だ) *I quite agree with you*. / (→たいへん満足だ) *I am very satisfied*.

わかがえり 若返り rejuvenation Ⓤ
◆経営陣の若返りをはかる *replace* the managerial staff *with a younger group*; *infuse new blood into* the management

わかがえる 若返る 彼女は離婚してから若返ったようだ She looks *younger* since her divorce. / 流行の服を着ると若返ったような気がする Wearing fashionable clothes *makes me feel young again*.

わかぎ 若木 young tree Ⓒ; (苗木) sapling Ⓒ

わかくさ 若草 young [fresh] grass Ⓤ

わかくさいろ 若草色 bright green Ⓒ Ⓤ

わがくに 我が国 (私の国) my country; (我々の国) our country (❖自国内にいるなら this country でよい)

わかげ 若気 父にあんなことを言ったのは若気の至りだった It was *out of youthful arrogance* that I said that to my father.

わがこと 我が事 祖母は私の大学合格をわがことのように(→自分自身のことであるかのように)喜んでくれた My grandmother was delighted with my success in the college entrance examination *as if it were her own*.

わかさ 若さ (若々しさ) youthfulness ⓤ; (若いこと) youth ⓤ ‖**若さの秘訣** the secret of *one's youthfulness* / 若さを保つ keep *one's youth*; stay *young* / 彼は息子の若さや体力をうらやましいと思った He envied his son for his *youth* and strength.
◆彼女があの若さであれだけの業績をあげたというのはすごいことだ It's amazing she's accomplished that much *at such an early age*. / 彼は18歳の若さで死んだ He died at *the early age* of 18.

わかさぎ 公魚 〖魚〗 (pond) smelt ⓒ

わがし 和菓子 Japanese sweets, (traditional) Japanese(-style) confectionery ⓤ

わかじに 若死に ──**若死にする** die an early [a premature] death; (若くして死ぬ) die young ‖彼は若死にする運命だったのだ He was fated to *die young*.

わかしらが 若白髪 prematurely gray hair ⓤ ‖山本さんは若白髪がある Mr. Yamamoto 「*has prematurely gray hair* [is *prematurely gray*].

わかす 沸かす (沸騰させる) boil ⓗ; (ふろなどを) heat ⓗ; (熱狂させる) excite ⓗ
彼女はお茶をいれるためにお湯を沸かした She *boiled* the water to make tea.
うちでは毎日ふろを沸かします We *heat* the bath every day at my home.
彼はファインプレーで観客を沸かせた He *excited* the spectators with his spectacular play.

わかぞう 若造 (若者) youngster ⓒ, boy ⓒ

わかだんな 若旦那 young master ⓒ; (裕福な家・家柄のいい家の若者) young gentleman ⓒ

わかちあう 分かち合う share ⓗⓘ ‖新婚の二人は生涯苦楽を分かち合って生きていくことを誓った The newlyweds vowed to *share* both joy and sorrow for the rest of their lives.

わかづくり 若作り 彼女はいつも若作りだ(→服装が) She always *dresses herself up to look young*. / (→化粧が) She always *makes herself up to look young*.

わかて 若手 young person ⓒ, young member ⓒ ──**若手の** young ‖彼女は日本の若手科学者の中で卓越した人物だ She is a preeminent figure among *young* Japanese scientists. ◆その試合では若手の選手が活躍した The *younger* players did a good job in the game.

わかどり 若鳥 baby bird ⓒ; (鶏の) spring [young] chicken ⓒ

わかば 若葉 young [fresh] leaves; (新緑) fresh greenery ⓤ

わかはげ 若禿げ 彼は若はげなので，実年齢よりも年をとって見える He looks older than he actually is because he's *prematurely bald*.

わかふうふ 若夫婦 young couple

わがまま 我が儘 selfishness ⓤ, self-centeredness ⓤ ──**わがままな** selfish, self-centered; (甘やかされた) spoiled

わがままな子 a *spoiled* child
彼女は夫のわがままに寛容すぎる She is too tolerant of her husband's *selfishness*.
◆**わがままを通す** have [get] *one's own way* /
わがままを言うな(→自分のことだけを考えるな) Don't think only of yourself. / Don't be selfish.

わがみ 我が身 (自分自身) oneself ‖**わが身を省みる** reflect on *oneself* / わが身かわいさのあまりに彼女は何も言わなかった She didn't say anything *for fear of putting herself in danger*.
🔴「彼は首になったそうだ」「あすはわが身ですよ」"I hear he got fired." "We'll probably be next."

わかみどり 若緑 fresh green ⓤ

わかめ¹ 若布 (soft) seaweed ⓤ

わかめ² 若芽 sprout ⓒ; (新芽) shoot ⓒ; (つぼみ) bud ⓒ

わかもの 若者 (男) young man ⓒ; (女) young woman ⓒ; (全体) young people; (総称) the young(複数扱い) ‖彼の音楽はだんだん若者に人気が出てきた His music is gradually finding favor with *young people*.
‖**若者文化** youth culture

わがものがお 我が物顔 彼女はどんなときでもわが物顔にふるまっている She always 「*behaves as if* [*acts like*] she *owns the place*. / She always *does everything* 「*just as she likes* [*her own way*].

わがや 我が家 (家庭・家屋) my [our, *one's*] home; (家屋) my [our, *one's*] house; (家族) my [our, *one's*] family ‖火事の被災者たちは焼けたわが家を見て泣いた The victims of the fire wept at the sight of *their* destroyed *homes*. / わが家には寝室が3つある There are three bedrooms in *our house*. / その子犬はすぐわが家のお気に入りになった The puppy quickly became the darling of *our family*.

わかやま 和歌山

和歌山県は紀伊半島の南西に位置しています。県庁所在地の和歌山市がある和歌山平野を除けば，ほとんどが山または山の地形で，かつては「木の国」と呼ばれるほど林業の盛んな地域でした。和歌山県は宗教的にも重要な役割を果たしてきましたが，中でも真言宗総本山の金剛峰寺の高野山，熊野三山と呼ばれる3つの神社が有名です。特産物としては，ミカンや梅がよく知られています。
Wakayama Prefecture is located on the southwestern part of the Kii Peninsula. The terrain is almost entirely mountainous except for the Wakayama Plain, where the city of Wakayama, the prefectural capital, is located. In the past, forestry flourished here, and the area was called "Kinokuni," which means "Tree Land." Wakayama Prefecture has played an important role in religion as well. Kongobuji, the head temple of the Shingon sect on Mt. Koya, and the

three Shinto shrines known as Kumano Sanzan are especially famous. Among the prefecture's products, mandarin oranges and plums are well known.

わからずや 分からず屋 (頑固者) obstinate person [fellow] ⓒ; (ばか) 《口語的》 blockhead ⓒ ∥ こんなに言っても分からないのか, 分からず屋め！ You still don't understand after I've told you so many times. You *blockhead*!

わかり 分かり 彼女は分かりが早い[遅い] She *is a quick* [*slow*] *learner*.

わかりきった 分かり切った (明白な) obvious, clear, plain ∥ 分かりきったことを聞くな Don't ask me about something so *obvious*. ∥ その提案が受け入れられないというのは, 最初から分かりきったことだった It was quite *clear* from the beginning that the proposal would be rejected.

わかりにくい 分かり難い 彼の説明はいつも分かりにくい His explanations *are* always *difficult to understand*. ∥ 彼女の字は分かりにくい(→読みにくい) Her handwriting *is illegible*.

わかりやすい 分かり易い この文は分かりやすい This sentence *is easy to understand*. ∥ 分かりやすい言葉で説明してください Please explain in *plain* [*simple*] language. ∥ 分かりやすく筋の通った文章を書きなさい Write *clear* and coherent sentences.

わかる 分かる

❶ 理解する	understand, get; see
❷ 知る	find; know
❸ 判明する	turn out, prove
❹ よさが分かる	appreciate
❺ 理解がある	

❶【理解する】understand* ⓗ ⓘ, 《口語的》 get* ⓗ; (要点などを) see* ⓗ ⓘ

この一節の意味が分かりません I *don't understand* the meaning of this passage.

彼女には私の気持ちなど決して分からないだろう She'll never *understand* how I feel.

姉は英語が全く分からない My sister *doesn't understand* English at all.

その男の子はなぜ自分がしかられているのか分からなかった The boy *didn't understand* why he was scolded.

あなたのおっしゃることがよく分からないのですが I *don't understand* [*get*] what you mean.

私は彼の冗談が分からなかった I *didn't get* his joke.

彼女がなぜその申し出を断ったのか分からない I *don't see* why she didn't accept the offer.

亜紀が何を考えているかは顔を見ればすぐ分かる You *can see* clearly what Aki is thinking (about) from the expression on her face.

私は彼女の話の主旨が分からなかった I *didn't see* her point.

◆古文は僕にはさっぱり分からない Japanese classics *don't make any sense to* me. ∥ その男はわけの分からないことをずっとつぶやいていた The man kept mumbling *nonsense*. ∥ 私の言ってること, 分かる？ *Do you understand what I'm saying?*

💬 「こういうふうにやるのよ. 分かった？」「うん, 大丈夫だと思う」"You do like this. *Got it?*" "Yeah, I think so."

💬 「許せないのは彼女がそれを僕に隠してたってことだ」「君の言いたいことは分かるよ」"What I can't forgive is that she kept it secret from me." "I *know* what you mean."

💬 「彼は本当にすごい選手なんだろうか」「今に分かるさ」"I wonder if he's really a great player." "We'll *see*."

❷【知る】(気づく) find* ⓗ, discover ⓗ; (知っている) know* ⓗ ⓘ, (区別する) tell* ⓗ ⓘ; (それと分かる) recognize ⓗ; (認識する・悟る) realize ⓗ

彼の絵を見れば彼が天才だということが分かるだろう If you see his paintings, you'll 「*find him* [*realize he's*] a genius.

彼女を説得するのは不可能だと分かった I *found* it impossible to persuade her.

これらの症状の原因はまだ分かっていない The cause of these symptoms *hasn't been discovered* yet.

何と言えばいいのか分からず, 彼は彼女を抱きしめた *Not knowing* what to say, he gave her a hug.

喫煙が体に悪いのは分かっているがやめられないんだ I *know* smoking is bad for my health, but I can't quit.

答えが分かったら手を挙げなさい Raise your hand if you *know* the answer.

とぼけるな. おまえがやったのは分かっているんだ Don't put on that innocent look. We *know* you did it.

この写真の少女がだれだか分かりますか Do you *recognize* the girl in this picture?

声の調子から彼女がとても怒っていることが分かった I *could tell* by her voice (*that*) she was very angry.

彼らは星の位置から方角が分かる They *can tell* the direction by the position of the stars.

何が本当に大切なのか僕はだんだん分かってきた I have come to *realize* what is really important.

◆彼女が美人だってことは言われなくても分かっているよ You don't have to remind me how beautiful she is. ∥ あなたは彼を傷つけたということが分かっているの？ *Are* you *aware* that you've hurt his feelings? ∥ 私がどんなに心配したかあなたには分からないでしょう You *have no idea* how worried I was. ∥ あんなにうまくいっているように見えた二人が離婚するなんて, 分からないものだね It's *hard to figure out* why two people who seem to get along so well would get divorced. ∥ 彼がなぜこの町を出ていったのか全く分からない It's

a mystery (to me) why he left this town.
- 「あれ,真希じゃない。久しぶり。元気?」「優子なの? だれだか全然分からなかった」"Hi, Maki! Haven't seen you for a long time. How are you doing?" "Yuko? I *didn't recognize* you."
- 「このプリントをみんなに配ってくれ」「分かりました」"Pass out these handouts to everyone." "*Yes, sir [ma'am]*."
- 「あいつはすぐクラブをやめるつもりだよ」「そんなこと,どうして分かるの」"He'll quit the club soon." "How do you *know*?"

❸【判明する】turn out, prove* ⓐ; (身元が) be identified
そのうわさは根も葉もないものだと分かった The rumor *turned out* to be groundless.
その死体の身元はまだ分かっていない The body *hasn't been identified* yet.
◆試験の結果はいつ分かる(→発表される)の When *will* the results of the exam *be announced*? / 地震の犠牲者の正確な数はまだ分かっていません The exact number of earthquake victims *is not* yet *known*.

❹【よさが分かる】appreciate ⓐ
翻訳では外国文学のよさが十分に分からない We *can't* fully *appreciate* foreign literature in translation.
あんな薄っぺらな人間に僕の絵のよさが分かるものか Such a superficial man will never *appreciate* my paintings.

❺【理解がある】
君のお父さんは話が分かる人だからうらやましいな I envy you because you have an *understanding* father.
そのことについては何度も言っただろう。分からない人(→ばかな人)だな I've told you about it over and over again. You *blockhead*!

わかれ 別れ (別離) parting ⓒⓊ, separation ⓒⓊ; (別れの言葉) goodbye, good-by ⓒⓊ, farewell ⓒⓊ
別れのあいさつ a *farewell* speech / お別れ会 a *farewell* party
愛する人との別れはつらい *Parting* [*Separating*] from someone you love is sad. / It is sad *to part* [*separate*] from someone you love.
彼女に別れを告げるのは彼にとってつらかった It pained him to say *goodbye* to her.
もうお別れしなければなりません I must say *goodbye* now.
お別れにあたってひと言申し上げます Please let me say a few「words *on parting* [*parting* words].

わかれぎわ 別れ際 彼女は別れ際に彼のほおにキスした She kissed him on the cheek *when* [*as*] *they parted*.

わかればなし 別れ話 彼女のほうが別れ話を切り出したらしいよ I hear that she's the one who first started to *talk about breaking up*.

わかれみち 分かれ道 (二また道) forked road ⓒ; (枝道) branch road ⓒ; (十字路) crossroads / 人生の分かれ道 the crossroads of (*one's*) *life*

わかれめ 分かれ目 人生の分かれ目に直面する face *the turning point* in (*one's*) *life* / ここが勝負の分かれ目だ Victory *depends on* this point.

わかれる¹ 別れる
part ⓐ; (去る) leave* ⓐ; (別れを告げる) say* goodbye; (縁を切る) break* [split*] up; (離婚する) divorce ⓐ
私は駅で彼らと別れた I *parted from* them at the station.
彼は去年奥さんと別れた He *divorced* [*got a divorce from*] his wife last year.
◆彼女は親と別れて暮らしている She lives *apart* [*away*] *from* her parents.
- 「正好と千秋,別れたらしいよ」「え,もう別れたの? この間つきあい始めたばかりなのに」"I heard Masayoshi and Chiaki *broke up*." "Really? *Have* they *split up* already? They just started going out with each other."

わかれる² 分かれる (枝分かれする) branch off; (分岐する) fork ⓐ; (分裂する) split* ⓐ; (分割する) divide ⓐ
川はこの地点で分かれる The river「*branches off* [*divides*] at this point.
その問題をめぐり我々の意見ははっきりと分かれた We *were* sharply *divided* over the issue.

わかれわかれ 別れ別れ 私の仕事の都合で夫とは別れ別れに暮らすことになった I had to live *separately* [*apart*] from my husband because of my work. / リーダーがやめてからは,バンドのメンバーもしだいに別れ別れになった After the leader quit, the band gradually「*broke up* [*fell apart*, *went their separate ways*].

わかわかしい 若々しい (若い) young; (はつらつとした) youthful / 私の祖父は年のわりにはとても若々しい My grandfather *is* very *young* for his age. / 彼女の若々しい声を聞くのは心地がよい It is pleasant to hear her *youthful* voice.

わき 脇 ❶【わき腹】side ⓒ / わきを締める keep *one's* arms close to *one's sides*
◆本をわきに抱える have [carry] a book *under one's arm*

❷【そばに・近くに】彼は道路わきに車を止めた He stopped his car *on* [*at*] *the side of* the road. / 家のすぐわきに学校がある There is a school right *near* my house. / わきから口を出すな Don't *interrupt* [*butt in*]!

❸【よそ】わきへ寄る move *aside* [*to the side*] / テーブルをふきますので少しの間皿をわきへよけてください Put the dish *aside* for a second so I can wipe off the table.

わきあいあい 和気藹々 山下高校野球部との合コンは和気あいあいとした雰囲気で行われた The party with the baseball club of Yamashita High School was held *in a friendly atmosphere*.

わきおこる 沸き起こる (生じる) arise* ⓐ / 観客の間に自然に笑いがわき起こった Spontane-

ous laughter *arose* from the audience.
わきが 腋臭 underarm odor ◎; (体臭) body odor◎ (略語)B.O. ∥彼はわきがが強い He has strong *underarm odor*.
わきかえる 沸き返る (熱狂する) be excited; (大騒ぎする) be in an uproar ∥地元の野球チームの優勝で町中が沸き返っていた The whole town *was excited about* the local baseball team winning the championship.
わきげ 腋毛 underarm hair◎
◆わき毛をそる *shave under one's arms*
わきたつ 沸き立つ (湯が) boil furiously; (人々が) be [get*] excited
わきでる 湧き出る gush out [forth] ∥おじの田んぼから温泉がわき出た A hot spring *gushed out* from my uncle's rice field.
わきのした 腋の下 armpit◎
◆わきの下に汗をかいている I'm sweating *under my arms*.
わきばら 脇腹 one's side◎; (特に動物の) flank◎ ∥左わき腹に痛みを感じる I have a pain in *my left side*.
◆彼女は夫のわき腹をつっついた She *poked her husband in the ribs*.
わきまえる 弁える (心得る) know* ⊕ ⓔ; (理解している) understand* ⊕ ⓔ; (心に留めておく) bear* in mind ∥善悪をわきまえる *know* right *from* wrong ∥ 立場[身の程]をわきまえる *know one's place* ∥ 限度をわきまえている *know where* [*when*] *to stop*
◆場所をわきまえなさい You *must not forget where you are*. ∥ 彼は礼儀をわきまえている He *has good manners*.
わきみ 脇見 わき見運転をしてはいけない You must not「*take your eyes off the road* [*look aside*] *while driving*./ Keep your eyes on the road.
わきみず 湧き水 spring water◎
わきみち 脇道 side road◎; (間道) bypath◎, byway◎ ∥私たちはわき道へ入っていった We 「*turned into* [*followed*] *a*「*side road* [*bypath, byroad*]*./*
◆どうやら話がわき道にそれてしまったようです I seem to *have*「*wandered off* [*strayed* (*away*)] *from*] the subject.
わきめ 脇目 わき目もふらずに走る run *eagerly* [*for one's* (*dear*) *life*] ∥彼女はわき目もふらずに仕事をした She *devoted herself to* her work.
わきやく 脇役 (人) supporting player◎; (役) supporting part [role]◎ ∥わき役を務める play *a supporting role*; (→重要でない地位につく) take *a back seat*
わぎり 輪切り タマネギの輪切り *a round slice* of (an) onion ∥ オレンジを輪切りにする *cut oranges into round slices*
わく¹ 枠
❶【縁】(窓・眼鏡などの) frame◎; (囲み) box◎
窓の枠 *a window frame*
左下の四角い枠の中に名前を書いてください Please put your name in *the box* on the lower left side.
❷【制限】limit◎, framework◎
予算の枠内でやりくりする manage *within the limits* [*framework*] *of the budget* ∥ 毎月20万円の枠内で生活する live *within the limits of 200,000 yen a month*
◆常識の枠からはずれる fall outside of *the bounds of common sense* ∥ 枠にはまった考え方 a *stereotyped* [*stereotypical*] *way of thinking*

わく² 沸く
❶【沸騰する】boil ⓔ
お湯が沸いてる The water *is boiling*.
◆おふろが沸いているか(→入れるようになっているか)見てきてちょうだい Go and see if [whether] the bath *is ready*.
❷【興奮する】be [get*] excited
彼女のスーパーショットに観客が沸いた The spectators *got excited* over her super shot.
◆彼のおどけた答えにクラス中が沸いた(→大笑いした) The entire class *roared with laughter* at his comical reply. ∥ 戦争が終わった日, 町は喜びに沸いた On the day the war ended, the city *resounded with joy*.

わく³ 湧く
❶【水・感情などが】(湧き出る) spring* ⓔ, gush ⓔ, well ⓔ; (流れ出る) flow ⓔ
泉から澄んだ水がわいていた Clear water *was gushing out* from the spring.
彼の言葉を聞いて,彼女の目に涙がわいてきた When she heard his words, tears *welled up* in her eyes.
❷【発生する】
犬にシラミがわいた The dog *became infested with* lice.
❸【生じる】spring* ⓔ
彼の不審な行動にますます多くの疑問がわいてきた When I saw his strange behavior, more and more suspicions *sprang to* my mind.
◆そのかわいそうな犬を見て彼女の心に哀れみの情がわいた Pity *stirred in her heart* when she saw the poor dog.
わくぐみ 枠組み (枠) frame ◎; (概略) framework◎, outline◎; (構造) structure◎ ∥組織の枠組みを作る construct *the framework* of an organization
わくせい 惑星【天文】planet◎

―惑星のいろいろ―
水星 Mercury / 金星 Venus / 地球 Earth / 火星 Mars / 木星 Jupiter / 土星 Saturn / 天王星 Uranus / 海王星 Neptune / 冥王星 Pluto

ワクチン 〔医学〕vaccine [vǽksíːn]◎◎
◆インフルエンザのワクチン注射を受けた I *was vaccinated against* the flu./ I *got a* flu *vaccination*.
わくわく ―わくわくする be [get*] excited ∥私たちはみな夏休みの計画にわくわくしていた We *were* all *excited* about our plans for the summer vacation.

◆子供たちはヒーローの登場をわくわくしながら待っていた The children were waiting for the hero to appear *with much expectation [anticipation]*. / 私は胸をわくわくさせてショーが始まるのを待った I waited for the performance to begin *with my heart beating fast with excitement*.

わけ 訳

❶【事情・理由】reason ⓒⓊ

父はわけもなく怒りだすことがある My father sometimes gets angry for no *reason*.

彼がそんなことを言うのには何かわけがあるにちがいない There must be some *reason* why [that] he says that.

なぜこんなことになったのかわけが知りたい I want to know (*the reason*) *why* this happened. (❖口語ではふつう the reason を省略する)

そういうわけで彼は来なかったのです That's (*the reason*) *why* he didn't come.

兄が結婚しないのにはそれなりのわけがあるんだ My brother has good *reason* not to get married.

どういうわけか彼女はその雰囲気になじめなかった She couldn't get used to the atmosphere *for one reason or another*.

◆その光景を見ているうちにわけもなく涙がこみ上げてきた Tears *somehow* rose in my eyes when I saw the scene. / 彼の言葉はどういうわけか私をほっとさせた His words *somehow* relaxed me. / そういうわけなら喜んでお手伝いしましょう *If that is the case*, I'm ready to help you. / それとこれとではわけが違う This and that *are completely different*.

🄔「なぜあんなことをしたのかわけを話して」「これには深いわけがあるんだ」"Tell me *why* you did that." "There is *a deep reason*."

❷【内容・意味】sense ⓒⓊ, meaning Ⓤⓒ

彼女の言っていることはわけが分からない What she says *doesn't make sense*. (❖ make sense で「意味をなす」の意味) / I can't *understand* what she says.

◆君は本当にわけの分からないやつだな You're really *strange* [*weird*]. / (→行動が理解できない) I *can't understand* your behavior. / 酔っ払いがわけの分からないことを叫んでいる A drunken man is shouting「*meaningless things* [*nonsense*]. / 小説の筋が込み入って、すっかりわけが分からなくなってしまった The plot of the novel was so complicated that I was completely *confused*.

❸【意図・つもり】

私がうそをついているとおっしゃりたいわけですか *Are you suggesting* (*that*) I'm lying?

自慢するわけじゃないが、絵画展に入選したことがあるんだ I *don't mean to brag, but* I have had a picture selected for an art exhibition.

❹【当然・はず】

どうりで彼女が怒るわけだ(→怒るのも当然だ) *It is natural* that she (should) get angry. / She *may well* get angry.

彼がそれに反対するわけがない He *can't* object to that. (❖can't は「ありえない」の意味)

そんなこと、彼に私の口から言えるわけないでしょう *How could* I say a thing like that to him?

彼ひとりでこの問題を解けるわけがない *There is no way* (that) he can solve this problem by himself. (❖there is no way は口語で「…の可能性はない」の意味)

❺【…わけにはいかない】

やってみないでそれをあきらめるわけにはいかない I *can't* give up without trying it.

これ以上みんなに心配をかけるわけにはいかない I *can't* make you all worry any longer.

❻【わけではない】

だれもが幸せになれるわけではない *Not everyone* can be happy.

私はその計画についてすべてを知っているわけではない I *don't* know everything about the plan.

彼女をすっかり許しているわけじゃない I *haven't wholly* forgiven her.

私は彼の提案に反対だが、だからといってその提案が気に入らないというわけではない I'm against his proposal, but *it is not that* I don't like it.

🄔「クラシック音楽はお好きですか」「特に好きというわけではありません」"Do you like classical music?" "*Not especially*."

慣用表現 わけあって1週間ほど友人のところに居候(いそうろう)している *For a certain reason* I have lived off a friend of mine for about a week. / もう泣くな、二度と会えないわけじゃあるまいし Don't cry anymore. *It isn't as if* we will never meet again. / 彼はわけ知り顔で説明してくれた He explained it to me *as if he were an expert*.

わけあう 分け合う share ⓜ; (分配する) divide ⓜ ∥私たちは食べ物を分け合って飢えをしのいだ We *shared* food and starved off our hunger.

わけない 訳ない (やさしい) easy, simple ∥ハードディスクの増設なんてわけないよ It's *easy* to install a new hard disk.

わけへだて 分け隔て (差別) discrimination Ⓤ; (えこひいき) partiality Ⓤ ∥彼女は子供たち全員に分け隔てなく接した She treated the children「*without discrimination* [*impartially, all alike*].

わけまえ 分け前 (取り分) share ⓒ; (割り当て) portion ⓒ, (口語的) cut ⓒ ∥利益の分け前をもらう receive *one's share* of the profits

わけめ 分け目 (髪の) (米) part ⓒ, (英) parting ⓒ; (境界線) dividing line ⓒ ◆天下分け目の戦い a *decisive* [*fatal, crucial*] battle

わける 分ける

❶【分割する】divide ⓜ; (髪を) part ⓜ ∥多人数のグループを2つに分ける *divide* a large group into two / ケーキを6つに分ける *divide* [*cut*] a cake into six pieces / 髪を真ん中で「横で」分ける *part* one's hair「*in the middle* [*on the side*]

❷【分配する】divide ⓜ, distribute ⓜ; (分け

合う）share 他
我々は2人でその金を分けた We *divided* the money *between* the two of us.
彼らは利益を公平に分けた They *shared* the profits equally among themselves.
◆お米をちょっと分けてくれませんか Could you *spare* me some rice?
❸【区別する】divide 他; (分類する) classify 他
人の性格を3つのタイプに分ける *divide* personalities *into* three types / 本を項目別に分ける *classify* the books according to subject
❹【分離する】separate 他
(卵の)黄身と白身を分ける *separate* the yolk from the white
❺【その他】
人込みを分けて進む *push one's way* through the crowd
すてきな絵をお描きになるのですね。1枚分けて(→売って)いただけませんか What beautiful pictures you paint! Do you suppose you could *sell* me one (of them)?
わこうど 若人 young people ⇨ わかもの
ワゴム 輪ゴム rubber [《英》elastic] band ⓒ
ワゴン (食車運搬用の) (tea) wagon [《英》trolley] ⓒ; (手押し車) cart ⓒ; (スーパーで使う)《米》shopping cart ⓒ,《英》supermarket trolley ⓒ ‖ワゴン車《米》a station wagon,《英》an estate car
わざ¹ 技 skill ⓒ, technique ⓒ, art ⓒ /技を磨く polish [improve] *one's skill*
◆投げ技をかける *try to throw a person* / (柔道で)技あり！ *Waza-ari*!
わざ² 業 (仕業) act ⓒ; (仕事) work ⓤ ⓒ, task ⓒ; (離れ業) feat ⓒ /それは至難の業だ That is *a most difficult task.*
◆あれはほとんど人間業とは思えない It *seems almost to be beyond human power.*
わさい 和裁 Japanese dressmaking ⓤ, kimono making ⓤ
わざと on purpose, deliberately, intentionally /彼女はわざと難しい質問をした She asked a difficult question *on purpose.* / She *deliberately* asked a difficult question. / 僕はゲームで弟にわざと負けた I *intentionally* lost to my brother in the game.
わざとらしい (不自然な) artificial, unnatural; (無理やりの) forced, affected /わざとらしい笑顔を浮かべる wear [have] a *forced* [an *artificial*] smile
わさび 山葵 (Japanese) horseradish ⓒ ⓤ
(❖作物またはその根の全体を指すときはⓒ,すりおろしたものはⓤ)
わざわい 災い (不運) misfortune ⓤ ⓒ; (災難) disaster ⓒ ⓤ; (ちょっとした不幸な出来事) mishap ⓒ ⓤ /彼の家族に災いが突然降りかかった *Disaster* overtook his family.
◆天候が災いしてお客がほとんどいなかった *Because of* the *bad* weather, there were few visitors.
ことわざ 口は災いのもと ⇨ くち / あきらめちゃいけない。災い転じて福となす,だよ Don't give up. We can turn misfortune into a blessing.

わざわざ
彼女はその展覧会を見にわざわざニューヨークまで飛んだ She flew to New York *especially* to see the exhibit.
わざわざ私のために食事を用意してくださらなくてもいいですよ You don't have to *take the trouble to* prepare dinner just for me.
遠方からわざわざ会いに来てくださってありがとう Thank you for coming *all the way* to see me.
彼はわざわざ空港まで私を迎えに来てくれた He *went out of his way* to pick me up at the airport.
わし¹ 鷲 eagle ⓒ
‖わし座 the Eagle, Aquila / わし鼻 an aquiline [hooked] nose
わし² 和紙 *washi*, (traditional) Japanese paper
わしき 和式 ──和式の Japanese-style ‖和式トイレ a *Japanese-style* toilet
わしつ 和室 Japanese-style room
◆4畳半の和室 *a four-and-a-half mat Japanese room*
わしづかみ 鷲摑み 札束をわしづかみにする *grab* wads of bills
わじゅつ 話術 the art of conversation; (雄弁術) elocution ⓤ
◆彼は話術にたけている(→雄弁である) He *is an eloquent speaker.* / (→座談が上手である) He *is a good conversationalist.*
わしょく 和食 Japanese food [cuisine] ⓤ; (個々の料理) Japanese dish ⓒ
ワシントン (州) Washington (❖米国北西部の州;(略語) Wash.,(郵便で) WA); (首都) Washington, D.C. (❖D.C.は *D*istrict of *C*olumbia (コロンビア特別区)の略語)
わずか 僅か ──わずかな (数) a few; (量) a little; (程度・量) slight; (ほんの) mere
わずかに a little, slightly; (たった) only
わずかな可能性 a *slight* [*poor, slim*] chance
今年の夏休みも残りわずかとなった I have *only a few* days left before the end of this summer vacation.
ごくわずかのお金しか残っていなかった I had *only a little* money left.
二人は結婚してわずか1か月で別れた The couple got divorced after *only* one month of marriage.
わずか1年の間に彼の身長は8センチ伸びた He grew eight centimeters in *only* one year.
私はわずかの間だがニューヨークに住んでいた I lived in New York, although *only for a short time.*
飛行機はわずかに左へ傾いた The airplane swayed *slightly* to the left.
◆今年も我" 残りわずかだ This year *is coming to an end.* / 私たちのチームはわずかの差で優勝を逃した Our team was unable to win the championship *by a small margin.* / 私は故郷のことをほんのわずかしか覚えていない(→ほとんど覚えていない) I remember *little* of my

hometown.

わずらい¹ 煩い (心配) worry Ⓤ, anxiety Ⓤ; (苦労) trouble Ⓤ

わずらい² 患い (病気) illness Ⓤ, sickness Ⓤ, disease Ⓤ

わずらう¹ 煩う (悩む) be worried [anxious], worry ⓐ ∥何も思いわずらうことはない There's nothing to *be* [*get*] *worried* about.

わずらう² 患う (病気である)《米》be sick,《英》be ill; (苦しむ) suffer ⓐ ∥彼は重い病気を患っている He *is suffering from* a serious illness. / He *is* seriously *sick*.

◆彼女は少し肺を患っている She *has* some *trouble with* her lungs.

わずらわしい 煩わしい (めんどうな) bothersome, troublesome (複雑な) complicated ∥最近は何をするのもわずらわしく思えてしまう I find everything *troublesome* [*tiresome*] these days. ∥その手続きはわずらわしすぎるので簡略化したほうがいい The procedure is too *complicated*. You should simplify it.

◆わずらわしい近所づきあいはもううんざりだ I'm fed up with *annoying* relationships with my neighbors.

わずらわす 煩わす (手数をかける) trouble ⓐ; (迷惑をかける) bother ⓐ ∥お手をわずらわせてすみません I'm sorry for *troubling* [*bothering*] you. / I'm sorry to *have troubled* [*bothered*] you.

わすれがたい 忘れ難い (忘れられない) unforgettable; (記憶に残る) memorable

わすれがたみ 忘れ形見 (思い出になるもの) memento Ⓒ (複 ～s, ～es), keepsake Ⓒ ◆この子が彼の忘れ形見です This is *the child* he *left behind*.

わすれっぽい 忘れっぽい forgetful ∥最近父は忘れっぽくなった My father has become *forgetful* lately.

わすれなぐさ 忘れな草・勿忘草〔植物〕forget-me-not Ⓒ

わすれもの 忘れ物 thing left behind Ⓒ; (遺失物) lost article Ⓒ, lost property Ⓤ

◆学校に忘れ物を取りに行ってくる I'm going to go to school to fetch *something I left behind.* ∥忘れ物のないように気をつけてください Please be careful *not to* ⌈*leave anything behind* [*forget anything*]⌉.

∥忘れ物取扱所 the Lost and Found,《英》a lost property office

わすれる 忘れる

❶【思い出せない】forget* ⓐ ⓑ
その店の名前を忘れた I *forgot* the name of the shop. / (→思い出せない) I *can't remember* the name of the shop.
アメリカでの楽しかった日々を決して忘れません I'*ll never forget* the good time I had in America.
彼のことが今でも忘れられない I still *can't forget* him. / I still *can't get* him *out of my mind*.
すんだことは忘れよう It's done and *let's forget* (*about*) it.

忘れないうちに必要な物を全部書き留めておきなさい Write down everything you need *before you forget*.
その子は母親のことを忘れかけている The child *is beginning to forget* his mother.

【forget＋to do】(❖forget to do は「…し忘れる」の意味) 朝食後に薬を飲むのを忘れた I *forgot to do* take my medicine after breakfast. / かぎをかけるのをあと少しで忘れるところだった I *nearly forgot to* lock the door. / この手紙を出すのをすっかり忘れていた I completely *forgot to* post this letter. / あすの朝、ごみを出すのを忘れないでね *Don't forget to* take out the garbage tomorrow morning. / 忘れずに辞書を持ってきてください *Don't forget to* bring a dictionary. / *Don't forget about* bringing a dictionary. / *Remember to* bring a dictionary.

【forget＋doing】(❖forget doing は「…したことを忘れる」の意味) 今回の英語のスピーチコンテストで１位になったことは決して忘れません I'*ll never forget* winning first place in this English speech contest.

【forget＋that 節 /wh- 節〔句〕】6時に歯医者の予約を入れていたのを忘れていた I *forgot that* I had an appointment with the dentist at six. / 眼鏡をどこへ置いたか忘れてしまった I'*ve forgotten where* I put my glasses.

◆彼がほんの子供だということを忘れないでください *Keep in mind* that he's only a child.

❷【置き忘れる】leave* ⓐ
教科書を家に忘れてきた I *left* the textbook at home.

◆傘を忘れて雨でずぶぬれになってしまった I *forgot* my umbrella and got soaked in the rain. (❖忘れた場所を明示しないときは forget が使える) / 財布を忘れるところだった I *was forgetting* my wallet.

❸【その他】
彼女は怒りのあまり我を忘れた She *was beside herself* with fury.
私は夢中でテレビを見ていて時間のたつのを忘れた I was absorbed in watching TV and I *lost track of the time*.

わすれんぼう 忘れん坊 forgetful person Ⓒ

わせ 早稲・早生 (稲) early rice Ⓤ
◆わせのリンゴ *early* apples

わせい¹ 和製 made in Japan, Japanese-made, of Japanese make ◆和製ジェームズ・ディーン a *Japanese* James Dean
∥和製英語(日本で英語らしく作った語) an English-like word coined in Japan; (日本語的英語) Japanese English

わせい² 和声〔音楽〕harmony Ⓤ

わた 綿 cotton Ⓤ; (詰め綿) (cotton) wadding Ⓤ ∥綿入れ a wadded kimono ∥綿菓子 cotton candy ∥綿毛 fluff; (羽毛) down

わだい 話題 (話の主題) a topic [theme, subject] (of conversation); (話の種) talk Ⓒ ∥町中の話題 *the talk* of the town / 話題を変えましょう Let's change *the subject*. / 我々

の話題は政治から宗教に移った Our *topic* veered from politics to religion. / それでは次の話題に移ります Now I'll move on to *the* next *subject*. / 彼女は話題が豊富だ She can talk on a large variety of topics.
◆話題の人 a person *in the news* / 話題の製品 a *much-talked-about* product / 最近よくいじめが話題になる These days school bullying *is* often 「*talked about* [*a topic of conversation*].

わだかまり 蟠り (悪感情) hard [bad] feelings; (うらみ) grudge ⓒ; (よそよそしさ) reserve ⓤ //以前よく衝突したが, 今は彼女に対して何のわだかまりも持っていません We used to disagree quite often in the past but I have no 「*hard feelings* [*grudge*] against [toward] her any more.
◆二人の間のわだかまりが解けて, 私たちみんなもほっとした All of us were relieved that the two finally *came to an understanding*. / あなたの今の言葉のおかげで心のわだかまりが解けました Your words just *took a load off my mind*.

わだかまる 蟠る 二人の間にわだかまっている確執を取り除くのは難しいだろう It would be difficult to resolve the *deep-seated* [*long-standing*] discord between the two.

わたくし 私 ⇨ わたし(私)

わたくしごと 私事 *one's* private affairs
◆私事で恐縮ですが, 結婚することになりました *Excuse me for bringing up a personal subject*, but I'm getting married.

わたくしりつ 私立 ⇨ しりつ(私立)

わたし¹ 私

(私は・私が) I; (私の) my; (私に・私を) me; (私のもの) mine; (私自身) myself

【私が・は】
私はそのころほんの小さな子供だった *I* was only a child at that time.
私は石井と申します *I* am Ishii. / *My name* is Ishii.
あなたと彼[栄次]と私が交代でその仕事をします You, he [Eiji], and *I* take turns doing the work. (✧Iをほかの人称(代)名詞とともに用いる場合は, ふつう二人称, 三人称, 一人称の順に並べる)
私が自分でやりました *I* did it *myself*.
📞「ご注文はお決まりですか」「私はコーヒーをお願いします。あなたは?」"May I take your order?" "Coffee for *me*, please. And you?"

【私の】
私の血液型はA型だ *My* blood type is A.
私の友人もそれを知っていた A friend *of mine* [One of *my* friends] also knew it.
彼女は私の(部屋の)すぐ下の部屋に住んでいる She lives in the room immediately below *mine*.
この手袋は私のじゃありません。私のは青いんです These gloves are not *mine*. *Mine* are blue. (✧mineの指すものが単数なら単数扱い, 複数なら複数扱い)

📞「このCD, だれの」「私のです」"Whose CD is this?" "It's *mine*."

語法
(1) a friend of mine という場合は複数いる友人の中の1人を指す。それに対して my friend という場合は文脈上明らかになっているか, または話し手と聞き手の間で分かっている特定の友達を指す。
(2)所有形容詞 my は a, an, the などの冠詞, this, that, these, those などの指示形容詞, any, some などの数量詞とは併置できないため, a friend of mine (私の友人の1人) [✕a my friend], this camera of mine (私のこのカメラ)[✕my this camera]のように mine を用いて表現する。

【私に】
父は私に時計を買ってくれた My father bought *me* a watch. / My father bought a watch *for me*.
正直なところ, 私には分かりません Honestly, *I* don't know.

【私を】
兄はいつも私を子供扱いする My brother always treats *me* like a child.

【その他】
私としてはあなたの意見に賛成です *As for me*, I agree with your opinion.
📞「そこにいるのはだれ」「私です」"Who's there?" "*It's me*." (✧It's I.は格式ばった表現でふつう使わない)
📞「洋子さんをお願いしたいのですが」「私です」"May I talk to Yoko?" "*This is she*. / *Speaking*." (✧電話の応答では「私です」が上の例のようになる。男性ならば she ではなく he を用いる)
📞「その歌は大好きなんです」「私も」"I like that song very much." "*So do I*. / 《口語的》*Me, too*."

わたし² 渡し ‖渡し場 a ferry / 渡し船 a ferry, a ferry boat / 渡し守 a ferryman

わたしたち 私たち (私たちは・私たちが) we; (私たちの) our; (私たちに・私たちを) us; (私たちのもの) ours; (私たち自身) ourselves

わたす 渡す

❶【手渡す・引き渡す】(与える) give* ⓗ; (手渡す) hand ⓗ, pass ⓗ; (配達する) deliver ⓗ
彼女は彼にその手紙を渡すとすぐにその場を立ち去った She *gave* him the letter and with that she left.
それをこっちに渡しなさい *Hand* it *over* to me.
ご注文の品は土曜日にお渡しします We *will deliver* your order on Saturday.
◆私は彼女にテーブルの下からメモをそっと渡した I *slipped* 「her a note [a note *to* her] under the table.

❷【譲る】give* up; (権利などを) hand over, transfer ⓗ
この主役の座はだれにも渡さない I'll never *give up* this leading part *to* anybody.

❸【その他】

2枚の板の間にロープを渡す *stretch a rope* between two planks / 橋を渡す *build a bridge*
彼は二人を川向こうに船で渡した He *ferried* the couple across the river.

わだち 轍 (車輪の跡) rut [C], wheel track [C]

わたり 渡り 彼女の提案は全く渡りに船だった Her proposal *was* quite *timely.* / 彼はその申し出に渡りに船と飛びついた He *jumped at* the offer.

わたりあう 渡り合う 彼らはその問題について激しく渡り合った They *had a* heated *argument* over the issue. / 私は彼の不当な要求に関して彼と渡り合った I *tackled* him on the question of his unreasonable demands. / 彼はチャンピオンと互角に渡り合った He *was a good match* for the champion.

わたりあるく 渡り歩く 彼女はいくつもの勤め先を渡り歩いてきた She *has often changed from one job to another.* / 彼は新しい生活を求めてあちこち渡り歩いた He *wandered from place to place* in search of a new life.

わたりどり 渡り鳥 migratory [migrant] bird [C]

わたりろうか 渡り廊下 a passage connecting two buildings

わたる[1] 渡る

❶【横断する】cross [他] [自], go* over (❖「…を歩いて渡る」は walk across ..., 「…を走って渡る」は run across ..., 「…を泳いで渡る」は swim across ..., 「…を船で渡る」は sail across ... などという)
ここは渡っちゃいけない. 横断歩道を渡る(→使う)ように You shouldn't *cross* the street here. *Use* the crosswalk.
この橋を渡るな Don't *cross* this bridge.
その島へは飛行機で渡った We *went over* to the island *by plane.*/ We *flew over* to the island.
山田さんは家族といっしょにアメリカに渡った Mr. Yamada *went over* to America with his family.
彼はドーバー海峡を泳いで渡った He *swam across* the Straits of Dover.
◆この川は歩いて渡るには流れが速すぎる This river is too rapid to *wade across.*

❷【やってくる】(渡り鳥が) migrate [自]; (導入される) be introduced, be brought over
今年は例年より早く白鳥たちが渡ってきた This year the swans *have migrated* here earlier than usual.

❸【他人の物になる】pass [自], fall* [自]
結局あの家は人手に渡ってしまった In the end, the house *passed into other hands.*
秘密情報が敵の手に渡った Some secret information *fell into* enemy *hands.*

❹【暮らしていく】get* along
母は私がひとりで世の中を渡っていけるか心配らしい My mother appears to be worrying about whether I *will be able to get along in the world* by myself.
[ことわざ] 渡る世間に鬼はない There is kindness to be found everywhere. (→親切はどこにでも見つかる)

わたる[2] 亘る (及ぶ) extend [自]; (広がる) stretch [自]; (覆う) cover [他]; (持続する) continue [自], last [自] //試験は1週間にわたる The examinations *extend* over a week. / その畑は数マイルにわたって広がっている The field *stretches* for several miles. / 火山灰がその土地を広範囲にわたって覆っていた The volcanic ashes *covered* a large part of the land. / その議論は長時間にわたった The discussion *lasted* [*continued*] for long hours.
◆長年にわたる研究の結果, 彼らは新しいワクチンの発見に成功した They succeeded in discovering a new vaccine after *many years of* research.

わっ ugh [ʌ́g, ú:] (❖嫌悪・恐怖などを表す)

ワックス wax [U] ◆床にワックスをかける *wax* the floor

わっしょい *wasshoi*, heave-ho (❖heave-ho は重い物を持ち上げたり, 引いたりするときの掛け声)

ワット (電力の単位) watt [C] (《略語》W, w) // 100ワットの電球 a 100-*watt* (light) bulb

わっと 人がわっと(→いっせいに)押し寄せてきた *All at once*, people came crowding in on us. / 彼らはわっと笑いだした They *burst* [*broke* (*out*)] *into laughter.* / 智子はわっと泣きだした Tomoko *burst into tears.*

ワッフル waffle [C]

ワッペン ⚠(記章・紋章) emblem [C]; (ステッカー) sticker [C] (❖日本語はドイツ語の Wappen から)

わな 罠 trap [C]; (特に輪を用いる) snare [C] // わなを仕掛ける set *a trap* / ウサギがわなにかかった A rabbit was caught in *the trap.* / その泥棒は警察のわなにはまった The thief was caught in *the* police *trap.*

わなげ 輪投げ quoits《単数扱い》 //輪投げをする play *quoits*

わななく (震える) tremble [自], shake* [自] ➔ ふるえる //恐怖にわななく *tremble* with fear

わなわな 彼女は死体を前にして恐怖でわなわなと震えていた She「*trembled violently* [*shook all over*] with fear in front of the dead body.

わに 鰐 (アフリカ・南アジア産の) crocodile [C]; (米国・中国産の) alligator [C] //ワニ皮のハンドバッグ a *crocodile* [*an alligator*] handbag

わび[1] 詫び apology [C] [U] //おわびの手紙 a letter of *apology* / おわびのしるしにあなたに何か贈り物をしたいのですが I want to give you something *as a token of apology.* / まず最初におわびを言わねばなりません We have to begin with *an apology.*
◆電車が遅れてご迷惑をおかけしたことをおわび申し上げます We *apologize for* any inconvenience caused by the delay of the trains.

わび[2] 侘び 🗻
わびは心の静けさや閑寂な趣を美とするもので, 中世の隠者の生活や思想から発展してきたとされ

わ

ています. わびは, さびと並んで和歌や俳句あるいは茶道の世界において本質的な部分を成しています.
Wabi is an esthetic principle originating in the lifestyle and thoughts of hermits in medieval times. It emphasizes mental serenity and austere beauty. The concept plays a substantial role in *waka*, haiku and the tea ceremony in conjunction with *sabi* (another moral and esthetic principle).

わびしい 侘びしい (みじめな) miserable; (寂しい) lonely, desolate; (みすぼらしい) shabby ∥わびしいひとり暮らしをする lead a *miserable and lonely* existence / わびしい住まい a *shabby* house

わびる 詫びる apologize ⾃ ∥遅れたことを彼女にわびた I *apologized* to her for being late.

わふう 和風 Japanese style ◯Ⓤ ――和風の Japanese, Japanese-style ∥和風建築 *Japanese-style* architecture / 和風庭園 a *Japanese* garden / 和風ドレッシング a *Japanese-style* (salad) dressing

わふく 和服 kimono ◯, Japanese clothes

わぶん 和文 (日本語) Japanese Ⓤ; (日本語で書かれたもの) Japanese writing Ⓤ
∥和文英訳 translation from Japanese into English, Japanese-English translation

わへい 和平 peace Ⓤ ∥和平条約に調印する sign *a peace treaty* / 両国は和平交渉を行った Both countries negotiated for *peace*.
∥和平会談 a peace conference / 和平工作 a peace initiative / 和平交渉 peace negotiations [talks]

わほう 話法 〖文法〗 narration Ⓤ, speech Ⓤ
∥間接話法 indirect narration / 直接話法 direct narration

英語には, ある人が言ったことを別のある人に伝える場合, 発言を引用符 (" ") に入れてそのままの形で伝える「直接話法」と, 自分の言葉に直して伝える「間接話法」とがある. 直接話法と間接話法では, 同内容であっても, 伝達内容を表す部分の「動詞の時制」「代名詞の人称」「時や場所を表す副詞語句」が異なる場合が多いので注意する必要がある ∥ (直接話法) She said, "I'm busy now." (間接話法) She said that she was busy then. /「私は今は忙しい」と彼女は言った / (直接話法) He said to me, "I can't come with you." (間接話法) He told me that he couldn't come with me. (❖直接話法の文の say to … は, 間接話法の文では文脈に応じて tell …, ask … などとなる)「あなたといっしょに行けない」と彼は私に言った

わぼく 和睦 (和解) reconciliation Ⓤ; (講和) peace Ⓤ ∥隣国と和睦する *make peace with* a neighboring country

わめく 喚く (大声をあげる) shout ⾃, cry ⾃; (大声で叫ぶ) yell ⾃; (子供が) bawl ⾃ ∥彼女は激怒して大声でわめいた In a blaze of fury, she *cried out*.

わやく 和訳 (和訳されたもの) Japanese translation ◯; (和訳すること) translation into Japanese Ⓤ
◆次の英文を和訳しなさい *Translate* the following English *into Japanese.*
∥英文和訳 translation from English into Japanese, English-Japanese translation

わようせっちゅう 和洋折衷 a combination of Japanese and Western [European] styles

わら 藁 straw Ⓤ Ⓒ ∥わらにもすがりたい気持ちだった I felt like I *was clutching at straws.*
∥わら細工 straw work / わら人形 a straw doll [figure]
ことわざ おぼれる者はわらをもつかむ ➡ おぼれる

わらい 笑い (general) laugh ◯, laughter Ⓤ; (微笑) smile ◯; (くすくす笑い) chuckle ◯; (歯を見せて笑うこと) grin ◯; (嘲笑) sneer ◯
笑いをこらえる suppress [repress] *a laugh*; stifle *one's laughter*
彼は大笑いした He *laughed a loud* [*hearty*] *laugh.*
私たちは彼女のジョークに大笑いした We *had a good laugh* over her joke.
彼はもうかって笑いが止まらない He is making so much money that he can't stop *chuckling.*
∥笑い声 laughter, a laughing voice / 笑い上戸 (よく笑う人) a person who laughs a lot; (酒を飲んで笑う人) a happy drinker / 笑い話 a joke; (おもしろい話) a funny story

わらいがお 笑い顔 smiling face ◯ ∥彼女は笑い顔がすてきだ Her *smiling face* is charming. / She smiles charmingly.

わらいごと 笑い事 それは笑い事じゃないよ It's no *laughing matter.* / It's no *joke.*

わらいころげる 笑い転げる 彼の冗談のあまりのおかしさに私たちは笑い転げた His joke was so funny that we「*laughed our heads off* [*were rolling on the floor*].

わらいとばす 笑い飛ばす そのことを笑いとばせる日が来るでしょう The time will come when we *can laugh* it *off.*

わらいもの 笑い物 laughingstock ◯ ∥ズボンのファスナーがあいていて, クラスメートの笑い物になった My fly was open, and I was *the laughingstock* of my classmates.

わらう 笑う

❶【楽しくて・おかしくて】laugh ⾃; chuckle ⾃; giggle ⾃; titter ⾃; cackle ⾃;《主に米》snicker ⾃;《英》snigger ⾃; smile ⾃; grin ⾃; smirk ⾃; sneer ⾃

laugh: 声を出して笑うことを表す最も一般的な語.
chuckle: 本を読んだり, おかしな事を考えたりして小さい声で笑う.
giggle: 子供のように, ひっきりなしにくすくす笑う.
titter: 恥ずかしがって, あるいは多少あざけっ

わらじ

- cackle: かん高く, 不快な声で大笑いする.
- snicker, snigger: ばかにしてくすくす笑う.
- smile: ほほえむことを表す最も一般的な語.
- grin: 歯を見せてにっこりする.
- smirk: 得意げににやにや・にんまりする.
- sneer: ばかにして笑いを浮かべる.

laugh　smile

大声で笑う *laugh* loudly; *give a* loud *laugh* / 豪快に笑う *laugh* heartily; *give a* hearty *laugh* / ジョークに笑う *laugh at* a joke / カメラに向かって笑う *smile at* [for] the camera

彼の歌に思わず笑ってしまった I *laughed* despite myself *at* his song.

聴衆はどっと笑いだした The audience *burst out laughing*.

僕らは彼のおかしなダンスに腹を抱えて笑った We *split our sides laughing at* his funny dance.

彼は手紙を読みながらひとりでくすくす笑っていた He *was chuckling* to himself while reading a letter.

彼らは先生のぼさぼさ頭を見て授業中ずっと笑っていた They kept on *giggling at* the teacher's uncombed hair all through the class.

彼はおかしくもないことに大声で笑った He *cackled at* something which was not funny at all.

女の子は鏡に向かってかわいく笑った The little girl *smiled* prettily into the mirror.

君の笑った顔が好きだ I like your *smiling face*. / I like your *smile*.

彼が失敗したのを見て彼女は意地悪そうに笑った She「*grinned nastily* [*sneered*] *at* his failure.

◆ 自分の間違いを笑ってごまかそうったってそうはいかないぞ I won't let you *laugh* your mistake *off*. / 私たちの要求を彼は笑って取り合ってくれなかった He *laughed* our requests *off*. / 君のしたことは笑ってはすまされないぞ What you did *is no laughing matter*. / 「変な格好だね」と彼は笑いながら言った "You look so funny," he *laughed*.

🦔「なぜ笑ってるの」「だってセーターを裏返しに着ているんだもの」"Why *are* you *laughing*?" "Because you're wearing your sweater inside out."

❷【あざ笑う】laugh 自, ridicule 他, mock 他自

人の失敗を笑ってはいけない Don't「*laugh at* [*ridicule, mock* (*at*)] another's failure.

そんな格好をしているとみんなに笑われてしまうよ Everybody will *laugh at* you [You will *be laughed at* by everybody] if you wear those clothes.

笑いたいなら笑えよ. 僕は映画スターを目ざすぞ *You can laugh at me if you want to*. But I'm determined to be a movie star.

◆「私は知りません」だって. 全く笑っちゃうよね. 知らないはずないじゃないか He said "I don't know." *It's*「*a laugh* [*laughable*], *isn't it*? There's no way he didn't know it. / 彼女にジョークを言ったら, 鼻で笑われてしまった She *snorted at* my joke.

❸【その他】
発表会ではひざが笑ってピアノのペダルがうまく踏めなかった At the recital, *my knees knocked with nervousness*, and I couldn't press the piano pedals well.

ことわざ 目くそ鼻くそを笑うだ That's the pot calling the kettle black. (→なべがやかんを黒いというのと同じだ) / 来年のことを言うと鬼が笑う らいねん / 笑う門(かど)には福来たる Laughter is the best medicine. (→笑いがいちばんの薬だ)

わらじ 草鞋 (a pair of) straw sandals
慣用表現 二足のわらじを履く ➪ にそくのわらじ

わらび 蕨 bracken 🇺, brake 🇺

わらぶき 藁葺き わらぶきの屋根 a (straw-)thatched roof

わらべうた 童歌 (童謡) nursery rhyme ©, traditional children's song ©

わらわせる 笑わせる　　make* a person laugh; (おもしろがらせる) amuse 他 / 彼は聴衆を笑わせるこつをつかんでいる He's got the trick of *making the audience laugh*.

◆ 彼女は始終私たちを笑わせた She *had us laughing* all the time. / ふん, 笑わせるんじゃないよ Hah, *don't make me laugh*.

わり　割

❶【10分の1】
私たちの学校では6割の生徒の家にパソコンがある *Sixty percent* of the students at our school have computers at home.

4割の手数料は高すぎるよ A service charge of *40 percent* is too high.

その選手は打率が3割7分5厘でリーディングヒッターです The player's batting average is .375. He's the leading hitter. (✦ .375は three seventy five と読む)

きょうの集まりでは会員の何割が欠席していましたか What *percentage* of the members were absent from today's meeting?

❷【割合】rate ©; (比率) ratio © ➪ わりあい
私は月に1度の割でおばの見舞いに行っている I visit my aunt in the hospital *at the rate of* once a month.

❸【比較の程度】
この仕事は割に合わないよ This job「*does not pay* [*isn't worth it*].

割のいいアルバイト, 知らない？ Do you know any *profitable* part-time jobs? (✦「割の悪い」は unprofitable)

新井さんは年のわりには若く見える Mr. Arai looks young *for his age.* / Mr. Arai looks young *considering his age.*

❹【割り当て】allotment Ⓤ, assignment Ⓤ

‖時間割り a schedule, a timetable / 部屋割り room assignment

わりあい 割合

❶【比率】rate Ⓒ;(率) ratio Ⓒ Ⓤ, proportion Ⓒ;(百分率) percentage Ⓒ

ミルク対コーヒーの割合は1対2だ *The ratio* of milk to coffee is 1 to 2.

この村では人口における子供の割合が年々小さくなっている *The proportion* of children in this village's population is getting smaller every year.

あなたは自分の生活費に占める食費の割合はどれくらいか知っていますか Do you know what *percentage* food accounts for in your total living expenses?

◆私たちのクラスでは3人に1人の割合でインターネットを利用している *One out of three* students in our class uses the Internet.

❷【比較的】

このノートパソコンはわりあい使いやすい This notebook computer is *comparatively* easy to use.

最近わりあい忙しい I've been *rather* busy lately.

試験はわりあいよくできた I did *better* on the exams *than I had expected.*

わりあて 割り当て (仕事などの) assignment Ⓒ, allotment Ⓤ Ⓒ;(割り当て量) quota Ⓒ ‖ 割り当ての分は終わりましたか Have you finished *your assignment*?

わりあてる 割り当てる (仕事などを) assign ㊀;(金・時間などを) allot ㊀;(ある目的のために) allocate ㊀ ‖先生は各生徒に1問ずつ割り当てた The teacher *assigned* a problem to each student. / 私は受付の仕事を割り当てられた I *was* 「*assigned* to be a receptionist [*allotted* the job of receptionist]. / 私たちは準備に1時間割り当てた We *allotted* an hour for preparations.

わりいん 割り印 a stamp over two pages ◆割り印を押す *place a stamp so that it overlaps* [*adjoins*] *two pages*

わりかん 割り勘 支払いは割り勘にしない? How about *splitting the bill* [*check*] *equally*?

わりきる 割り切る そのことについてはもっと割り切って考えるべきだ You should *be more practical* [*businesslike*] about the matter. / 生活のためと割り切って肉体労働をしている I do manual labor *simply* [*just*] to make a living.

わりきれる 割り切れる ❶【数が】12は4でも3でも割り切れる Twelve *can be divided by* both four and three (*without a remainder*).

❷【気持ちが】理屈では割り切れない(→説明できない)こともある Some things just *can't be explained* by reason. / いまだに割り切れない気持ちだ(→不満がある) I'*m not quite satisfied* yet. / (→疑いがある)I'*m* still *doubtful.* / つまらない仕事かもしれないけど仕事と割り切ってがんばろうよ The job might be boring, but *after all* it's a job so let's do our best.

わりこみ 割り込み 割り込み乗車はいけません One shouldn't *cut into line when boarding.*

わりこむ 割り込む (列に) break* into [in] ...;(人の話に) interrupt ㊀, cut* in, 《口語的》butt in ‖1人の男が順番を無視してタクシーを待つ列に割り込んできた A man *broke into* the taxi line out of turn. / 彼はいつも人の話に割り込む He always *cuts in* 「when other people are talking [other people's conversations].

わりざん 割り算 〖数学〗 division Ⓤ ──割り算する divide ㊀

わりだか 割高 東京に比べてこの町では,同じものでも割高だ Everything in this city *is relatively expensive* compared to Tokyo. / ばらで買うと割高になる It *will cost more* if you buy them separately.

わりだす 割り出す (算出する) calculate ㊀;(推定する) deduce ㊀, figure out ‖1日あたりの総費用を割り出した I *calculated* the total cost per day. / 残された手がかりから犯人を割り出すことができますか Can you *deduce* [*figure out*] the identity of the criminal from the clues that were left behind?

わりつけ 割り付け (紙面の) layout Ⓒ ‖割り付けをする make *a layout*

わりと 割と このフライドポテトわりとうまいね These French fries are *pretty* good, aren't they?

わりに 割に (けっこう) rather, fairly, 《口語的》pretty;(比較的) comparatively, relatively ⇨わりあい ‖きょうはわりに寒い It's *rather* cold today. / わりにいいコンサートでしたね It was a *fairly* good concert, wasn't it?

わりばし 割り箸 *waribashi*, disposable chopsticks

わりびき 割引 discount Ⓒ, reduction Ⓒ ──割引する discount ㊀, give* [make*] a discount, reduce ㊀

全品を3割引にする make a「*discount of 30 percent* [*30 percent discount*] on all merchandise

その店ではテレビを3割引で売っている They sell televisions *at*「*a 30 percent discount* [*30 percent off*] at that store.

私はこのかばんを5割引で買った I bought this bag *at a 50 percent discount.*

きょうならデジカメを割引料金でお求めになれます You can buy digital cameras *at a discount* (*price*) today.

この時計は2割引です We'll *discount* [*reduce*] the price of this watch *by 20 percent.*

◆4割引《掲示》40% *Off*

‖割引券 a discount ticket [coupon] / 割引率 a discount rate / 学生割引 a student discount / 団体割引 a group reduction [discount], a discount on a party ticket

わりびく 割り引く discount ㊀, reduce

わりふる

㊙ //定価から10％割り引く discount [reduce] the price by 10 percent
◆彼女の話は割り引いて聞いたほうがいい You should take her story with a grain [pinch] of salt. (❖take ... with a grain [pinch] of saltは「…を話半分に聞く」の意味の決まった表現)

わりふる 割り振る ➡ わりあてる

わりまし 割り増し ──割り増しの extra //日曜日と祝日にそこのテニスコートを利用すると10％の割り増し料金を払わなければならない You have to pay *a* 10 percent *extra charge* if you use the tennis courts on Sundays or holidays. / 夜11時以降にタクシーに乗ると割り増し料金になるよ If you take a taxi after 11 p.m., you have to pay *an extra fare*.

わりもどし 割り戻し (払いすぎの) rebate ⓒ; (払戻金) refund ⓒ

わりやす 割安 割安な(→経済的な)モデル an *economical* model / それらはまとめて買うと割安に(→安く)なる They are *cheaper* [You can get them *cheaper*] if you buy them in bulk.

わる¹ 割る

❶【こわす】 break* ㊙; (粉々に砕く) smash ㊙; (ひびを入れる) crack ㊙
窓ガラスを割る *break* a window / 卵を割る *break* [*crack*] an egg
コップを洗っていて2つ割ってしまった While washing some glasses, I *broke* two.
◆花びんを床に落として割ってしまった(→割れてしまった) I dropped a vase on the floor and it *broke* [*smashed*].

❷【分ける】 divide ㊙; (切って) cut* ㊙; (費用などを) split* ㊙
ケーキを8つに割る *cut* the cake into eight pieces
15 割る 5 は 3 Fifteen *divided* by five is [gives, equals] three.
夕食の勘定を3人で割った We *split* the dinner bill three ways.
◆教室で取っ組み合いのけんかをしている2人の生徒の間に先生が割って入った A teacher *broke up* the two students fighting in the classroom.

❸【裂く】 split* ㊙; (たたき切る) chop ㊙
おので丸太を割る *split* logs with an ax / まきを割る *chop* wood
彼は空手チョップで板を2つに割った He *split* the board in two with a karate chop.

❹【水などを加える】
ウイスキーを水で割る mix [dilute] whiskey with water / ソーダで割ったウイスキー (a) whiskey and soda

❺【ある数量以下になる】
過半数を割る *lose* a majority
1ドルは100円を割った The dollar *fell* [*dropped*] below 100 yen.

[慣用表現] 私たちは腹を割って(→率直に)話し合った We talked *frankly* with each other.

わる² 悪 彼は中学時代相当なワルだった He was quite *a bad kid* while in junior high school.

わるあがき 悪足掻き 悪あがきをする put up *a needless struggle* / 悪あがきはやめろ Don't make *useless efforts*.

わるい 悪い

❶ 道徳に反する	bad, evil; wicked; wrong
❷ 姿勢・行儀などが	bad
❸ 間違っている	wrong; be to blame
❹ 申しわけない	
❺ 悪意をもった	
❻ うれしくない・不吉な	bad; ill
❼ 質・形などが	bad; poor; ugly
❽ 天気が	bad, foul

❶【道徳に反する】 bad (↔good), evil; wicked; wrong (↔right)

> bad, evil: 道徳に反していて、非難されるべきであることを表す。
> wicked: 道徳に反することを意図的にやっていることを含意する。bad, evil よりもさらに強く道徳的な悪さを表す。
> wrong: 道徳的に間違っていることを表す。

悪い行い *bad* [*evil, wicked, wrong*] doings
悪い人間にだまされないよう気をつけよう Be careful not to be deceived by *bad* [*evil, wicked*] people.
うそをつくのは悪いことだ It's *wrong* to tell a lie.
猫に石を投げるなんて悪い子ね It's *bad* of you to throw stones at a cat!

🔴「そんな悪い子はうちに入れません」「ごめんなさい。もう悪いことはしないから入れてよ」"We won't let a *bad* [*naughty*] boy like you into our house." "I'm sorry. I won't do such a *bad* thing again. So let me in."(❖naughtyはいたずらをした子供などに対して用いる語)

🔴「彼女ふってやったよ」「悪いやつだな。あんなにおまえのこと好いてくれてたのに」"I turned her down." "How *bad* [*evil, wicked, nasty*] you are! You knew how much she liked you."

🔴「土曜日に学校サボってゲーセンで遊んでたら、先生に見つかっちゃった」「悪いことはできないねえ」"When I cut school on Saturday, my teacher caught me at the video arcade." "*You can't get away with anything*, can you?"

❷【姿勢・行儀などが】 bad
姿勢が悪い have *bad* posture
彼は言葉づかいが悪い He uses *bad* language.
食事中に音を立てるのは行儀が悪い It is *bad* manners to make a noise at the table.

❸【間違っている】 wrong (↔right); (責任がある) be to blame
君が悪いんだぞ。ちゃんと我々に謝ってくれよ You are「*to blame* [*wrong*]. We want you to apologize to us.
彼に赤ちゃんの世話を任せたあなたが悪い It was *wrong* of you [You were *wrong*] to leave your baby in his care.

わるい

❹【申しわけない】

悪いけれどパーティーには行けない *I'm sorry, but* I can't go to the party.

手伝わせちゃって悪いね *I'm sorry* to have troubled you for help. / (→感謝しているよ) *I really thank you* for helping me.

彼にうそをついて悪かったと思っている I *feel guilty* [*bad*] about telling him a lie.

そんなことやめなさい。英子に悪い(→困らせることになる)よ You should stop doing that. It's going to *trouble* Eiko.

言っちゃ悪いけど君には彼女は似合わないよ *I probably shouldn't say this, but* she isn't your type.

🅔 「おい、遅刻だぞ」「悪い悪い、電車が遅れたもんで」 "Hey, you're late." "*Sorry*, the train was delayed."

🅔 「その CD を買っておいてあげようか」「悪いからいいよ。後で自分で買うよ」 "Shall I buy the CD for you?" "*No, but thank you. I'll buy it later.*"

❺【悪意をもった】

彼女のことを悪く言うな Don't *say bad things about* her.

彼は私が言うことをいつも悪くとる He always *takes* what I say *badly* [*ill*].

彼は口は悪いが、根は優しい He is kind at heart though he「*has a bitter tongue* [*is foul-mouthed*].

君は連れていけないけど、悪く思わないでくれよ We can't take you with us. But please *don't think badly of us*.

❻【うれしくない・不吉な】 bad;(不吉な)《公式的》ill(❖名詞の前で用いる)

悪い知らせ *bad* news / 悪い前兆 a *bad* [an *ill*] omen

彼は悪い病気にかかってしまった He's got a *bad* disease.

最近悪い夢ばかり見る I've had *bad* dreams lately.

彼女は運が悪い She *has bad luck*. / She is *unlucky*.

新しい先生は評判が悪い The new teacher has a bad reputation.

彼は今機嫌が悪い He *is in a bad mood* now.

あんなふうにほめられれば、だれだって悪い気はしないよ You *can't feel bad* when you are praised like that.

彼はあなたにつきあってほしいんだって。OK すれば？ 悪い話じゃないと思うんだけどな Why don't you do it? *It wouldn't be so bad.*

車が途中で故障して、さらに悪いことには雨が降り始めた My car broke down on the way, and *what was worse*, it began to rain.

◆運悪く彼女は事故に巻き込まれてしまった *Unfortunately* [*As luck would have it*], she was involved in an accident.

🅔 「彼は来るのかな。このまま来ないんじゃないの？」「ううん、悪い予感がするなあ。来ないかもね」 "I wonder if he is coming. By the way things look, he isn't, is he?" "Well, I've got a bad feeling that he isn't."

❼【質・形などが】 bad;(粗悪な)poor;(醜い)ugly

このカメラは安いが品質は悪くない This camera is cheap, but the quality isn't *bad*.

このつぼ、形が悪くない？ This pot has a *bad* shape, doesn't it?

このバナナは見た目は悪いけどかなりおいしいよ This banana looks *bad* [*ugly*] but tastes quite good.

◆生物(㌿)は早く食べないとすぐに悪くなってしまう Raw food should be eaten soon because it easily *goes bad* [*rotten*]. (❖go bad [rotten] は「腐る」の意味)

🅔 「このドレスどう」「うん、悪くないんじゃない」 "What do you say about this dress?" "Well, *it's not bad.*"

❽【天気が】 bad, foul

天気が悪いときは海で泳がないほうがよい You shouldn't swim in the sea in *bad* [*foul*] weather.

天気はしだいに悪くなるだろう The weather will gradually get *worse*.

❾【成績・能力などが】 bad, poor;(弱い)weak

彼は試験で悪い点を取った He got *bad* [*poor*] grades on the exams.

私は記憶力が悪い I have a *poor* memory.

私は目が悪い I have *weak* eyes.

濃い霧のために見通しが悪い Visibility is *poor* because of the dense fog.

◆彼はそんな失敗をするほど頭の悪い男じゃないよ He is not so *stupid* as to make such a mistake. / その芝居は客の入りが悪かった The play was *poorly* attended.

❿【適当でない】 bad, wrong;(都合が悪い)inconvenient

家を出たタイミングが悪く、駅で20分も電車を待つことになった My timing was *bad* when I left home, so I had to wait for the train for 20 minutes at the station.

きょうは都合が悪いんだ。あす電話するよ It's *inconvenient* for me today. I'll call you tomorrow.

◆今は時機が悪い。もう少し待とう This is *not* the *right* time yet. [The time is *not ripe* yet.] Let's wait for a while.

🅔 「あ、向こうから来るの昭夫君じゃない？」「本当だ、悪いやつに会っちゃったなあ。君と僕がいっしょにいたってことを触れ回るぜ、きっと」 "Look, isn't that Akio walking toward us?" "It is. We've come across the *wrong* person. He will surely spread it around that you and I were walking together."

⓫【有害である】 bad, harmful, 《公式的》detrimental

たばこは体に悪い Smoking is「*bad for* [*harmful to, detrimental to*]」your health.

彼は圭介に悪い影響を与えている He is a *bad* influence on Keisuke.

🅔 「彼があんなまじめなことを言うなんて珍しいね」

「うん, 何か悪い物でも食べたんじゃないの(→ぐあいが悪いんじゃないの)」"It's unusual for him to talk so seriously, isn't it?" "Yes. He *must not be feeling well*." (❖この英語も日本語と同じように冗談めいた意味合いをもつ)

❷【ぐあい・調子が】wrong; (体調が) sick, bad

このカメラは何か調子が悪い Something is *wrong* with this camera.

母はぐあいが悪くて寝ている My mother *is sick in bed*. (❖be sick in bed は慣用的な表現)

バスに乗ったら気分が悪くなった After I got on the bus, I *felt sick*.

きのうは体調が悪かった I was 「*in bad shape [out of condition]* yesterday.

きのうよりきょうのほうがぐあいが悪い My health *is worse* today than yesterday.

◆このテレビは映りが悪い This television *doesn't have a clear picture.* / このスピーカーは低音の出が悪い These speakers *don't work well* for low sounds. / 顔色が悪いけど, 大丈夫ですか You *look pale.* Are you OK? / 彼は胃が悪い He *has trouble with* his stomach.

🍏「真っ青な顔して, どこか悪いんじゃない?」「いや, どこも悪くないさ」"You look so pale. There must be something *wrong* with you." "No, nothing is *wrong* (with me)."

慣用表現 悪いことは言わないから(→私の助言に従って損はない), それはやめておきなさい。 *You lose nothing by following my advice.* Just don't do it. / 私にすべて任せておきなさい。悪いようにはしない(→後悔させない)から Leave it all to me. *You won't be sorry.* / 悪くするとこの仕事はきょう中には終わらないかもしれない (→うまくいかなかった場合) *If things don't go smoothly*, this work won't be finished today. / (→最悪の事態になった場合) *If worst comes to worst*, this work won't be finished today.

わるがしこい 悪賢い, (狡猾(こうかつ)な) cunning; (ずるい) sly; (策略にたけた) crafty, wily

わるぎ 悪気 悪気はなかったんだ I meant no *harm* [*offense*].

わるくち 悪口 彼は陰で君の悪口を言ってるよ He *says bad things about* you behind your back.

わるさ 悪さ (いたずら) mischief ⓤ; (悪ふざけ) prank ⓒ ∥あの子はいつも何か悪さをしている That child *is always up to some mischief or other.*

ワルシャワ Warsaw (❖ポーランドの首都)

わるだくみ 悪だくみ あいつ, ちょっと悪ずれしている He *is somewhat too wise in the ways of the world.*

わるだくみ 悪巧み (たくらみ) trick ⓒ; (悪計) evil [wicked] design ⓒ; (陰謀) plot ⓒ

わるぢえ 悪知恵 cunning ⓤ, craft ⓤ ∥悪知恵を働かせる use *cunning* [*craft*]

◆悪知恵のある人 a *cunning* [*sly, crafty*] person / 悪知恵をつける teach *craftiness*

ワルツ waltz ⓒ ∥ワルツを踊る dance *a waltz*; waltz

わるのり 悪乗り あいつ, 悪乗りして2回も同じジョークを飛ばした He *got carried away* and cracked the same joke twice.

わるびれる 悪びれる 彼は悪びれずに過ちを認めた He admitted his mistakes *with good grace.* / その少年には悪びれた様子はなかった The boy *didn't look ashamed.*

わるふざけ 悪ふざけ practical joke ⓒ, prank ⓒ ──悪ふざけする play 「*a practical joke* [*pranks*] ◆悪ふざけがすぎるよ You carry *your jokes* too far.

わるもの 悪者 bad person ⓒ; (ならず者), scoundrel ⓒ, 《口語的》crook ⓒ; (劇中の悪者など) villain

◆私一人を悪者にしないで Don't *put all the blame on* me. / Don't *make a scapegoat of* me.

わるよい 悪酔い 彼は飲みすぎて悪酔いしてしまった He *felt sick from* too much *drinking.* / この酒はあまり悪酔いしない This liquor *doesn't have* any *nasty aftereffects.*

われ 我 私たちは我を忘れて先生の所へ駆け寄った We *forgot ourselves* and rushed to our teacher. / 母の呼ぶ声で急に我に返った I suddenly *came to myself* as I heard my mother calling me. / 我と思う者(→自信のある者)はぜひ挑戦してみるといい. *Those of you who are confident* (*in yourselves*) should give it a try. / 怒りで我を忘れてしまった I *got carried away* in anger. / 若者たちは我も我もと先を争ってその CD を買った Young people *scrambled to be the first* to buy the CD.

われがちに 我勝ちに 我勝ちに列車に乗る *push one's way* onto the train / 彼らは我勝ちに外へ出ようとした (→1番に出ようと争った) They *scrambled to get out first.* / (→同時にどっと出口に押し寄せた) They all *made a rush* for the exit at the same time.

われかんせず 我関せず 彼女は全く我関せずというふうだった She *looked* very much *as if she had nothing to do with it*.

われさきに 我先に 乗客は我先に列車から降りようとした The passengers *scrambled to get off the train.*

われしらず 我知らず 我知らず叫び声をあげる let out a cry *in spite of oneself*; let out an *involuntary* cry

われながら 我ながら 我ながらよい考えだと思う It's a good idea, *if I do say so myself.* / 我ながら恥ずかしい I am ashamed of *myself.*

われめ 割れ目 (ひび) crack ⓒ; (裂け目) split ⓒ; (岩などの) crevice ⓒ; (地面の深い) chasm ⓒ ∥壁に割れ目がある There is *a crack* [*split*] in the wall. / その地震で玄関のアプローチに割れ目が入った Our front walk got *a crack* from the earthquake.

われもの 割れ物 fragile article ⓒ, breakables ◆割れ物, 取り扱い注意《掲示》*Fragile*, Handle with Care

われる 割れる

❶【こわれる】break* ㉭, be broken;（粉々になる）smash ㉭, be smashed;（ひびが入る）crack ㉭

ワイングラスは粉々に割れた The wine glass *was* 「*broken* in [*smashed* to] pieces.

コップに熱湯を注ぐとコップが割れた The glass *cracked* when I poured hot water in it.

この皿はすぐに割れそうだ This plate looks 「*easily broken* [*fragile*].

卵は割れやすい Eggs *break easily*.

❷【分かれる】

この問題で私たちの意見が割れた We *were divided* in our opinions on this issue. / Our opinions *were divided* on this issue.

グループの意見が3つに割れた The group's opinion *was split* three ways.

票が割れた The vote *was split*.

❸【その他】

225は15で割れる Two hundred and twenty-five *can be divided* by fifteen.

ついに犯人の身元が割れた (→警察は犯人を特定した) The police *have* finally *identified* the criminal.

彼女が話し終えると割れるような拍手が起こった When she finished her speech, *a thunder of applause* arose.

頭が割れるように痛い I *have a splitting headache*.

このマイクは音が割れる Sound *is distorted* by this microphone.

われわれ 我々 (我々は・我々が) we; (我々の) our; (我々に・我々を) us; (我々のもの) ours; (我々自身) ourselves ∥我々日本人はもっと日本について学ぶべきだ We [*Japanese*] should learn more about Japan.

わん¹ 湾 (小さい湾) bay ⓒ; (大きな湾) gulf ⓒ ∥東京湾 Tokyo *Bay* / ペルシア湾 the Persian *Gulf*

わん² 椀・碗 bowl ⓒ

わんがん 湾岸 ∥湾岸道路 a bay highway

わんきょく 湾曲 curve ⓒ, bend ⓒ ──湾曲する curve ㉭, bend* ㉭

わんさ 展覧会には人がわんさと押しかけた People *thronged* to see the exhibit. / 子供がわんさと寄ってきた Children *came swarming round*. / 彼はお金をわんさと持っている He has *loads* of money.

わんしょう 腕章 armband ⓒ ∥腕章をつける wear [put on] *an armband*

ワンダーフォーゲル ⚠ (徒歩旅行) hike ⓒ (❖日本語はドイツ語の Wandervogel から)
◆ワンダーフォーゲル部 a *hiking* [*backpacking*] club

ワンタッチ ワンタッチ操作 a *one-touch* operation / この扉はワンタッチで開く This door opens *at a single touch*.

ワンタン won ton ⓒ; (スープ) wonton soup ⓤ

ワンナウト one out ∥ワンナウト三塁 It's *one out* with a runner on third.

わんぱく 腕白 ──わんぱくな naughty, mischievous ∥彼はわんぱく坊主だ He's *a naughty boy*.

ワンパターン ⚠ ──ワンパターンの one-track; (紋切り型の) stereotyped; (融通がきかない) not flexible (❖英語の one pattern は「1つの型[様式]」の意味) ∥彼女の考え方はワンパターンだ She has a *one-track* mind.
◆あなたの言い訳はいつもワンパターンだね Your excuses always *follow the same old pattern*. / Your excuses *are* always *all the same*. / 彼は服装がいつもワンパターンだ He always wears *the same kind* of clothes.

ワンピース ⚠ dress ⓒ ◆ワンピースの水着 a *one-piece* swimsuit (❖英語の one-piece は形容詞で「(水着などが)上下ひと続きの」の意味)

ワンマン (独裁者) autocrat ⓒ, dictator ⓒ (❖英語の one-man は「単独の, ひとりで行う」の意味) ∥ワンマン社長 a dictatorial [an autocratic] president / ワンマンショー a one-man [one-woman] show, a solo performance [act] / ワンマンバス a bus without a conductor

わんりょく 腕力 (肉体の力) physical [muscular] strength ⓤ; (暴力) force ⓤ, violence ⓤ ∥腕力では彼にかなう者はいない Nobody can match him when it comes to *physical strength*. / 彼はすぐ腕力に訴える He is quick to resort to *violence*.
◆彼は腕力は十分あるが頭は空っぽだ He has plenty of *muscle* but no brains.

ワンルーム ∥ワンルームマンション a one-room apartment, a studio apartment [《英》flat]

わんわん (犬の鳴き声) bow-wow, arf arf; (犬)(小児語) doggie, doggy ⓒ, bow-wow ⓒ ◆その子はわんわん泣いていた The child *was bawling*.

を

-を

語法
日本語の「…をする」を英語で表現する場合，次のような表現を用いることが多い．
(1) 《他動詞＋名詞》 ∥ テレビを見る watch television
(2) 《自動詞＋前置詞＋名詞》 ∥ 銀行を探す look *for* a bank / 海岸を歩く walk *along* the seashore

❶【動作・作用の及ぶ対象】
彼女は部屋で雑誌を読んでいた She was reading a magazine in her room.
台所の電気を消しておいてね Turn off the kitchen light.
眠れないのでラジオを聞いた I couldn't sleep, so I listened *to* the radio.
子供は母親の腕をつかんだ The child held its mother *by* the arm.

❷【場所を示す】
彼は毎朝公園を散歩する He takes a walk *in* the park every morning.
次の角(ｶﾄﾞ)を右に曲がってください Turn right *at* the next corner.
飛行機が空を飛んでいるのが見えた I saw a plane flying *in* the sky.

❸【動作の起点・経過点を示す】
彼は6時に家を出た He left his house at six.
4時を回ったころ彼女から電話があった There was a call from her *after* four.
車は湖のそばを通り過ぎた The car passed *by* the lake.

ん

ん しりとりゲームでは最後に「ん」のついた言葉を言ったら負けです If you say a word ending with *the "n" sound*, you will lose in the *shiritori* game. / ん, 分かった *OK*. I got it.
🍏「ん, 何か言った？」「別に」 "*Eh? [Huh?]* Did you say something?" "No, not at all."

んん (言葉に詰まって) um [ʌm], uh [ʌ]; (打ち消して) uh-uh [ʌ́ʌ̀]
🍏「そのパーティーに何着ていく」「んん, 分からない」 "What are you going to wear to the party?" "*Um [Uh]*, I don't know."
🍏「守のこと, 好き？」「んん」 "Do you like Mamoru?" "*Uh-uh*."

付録目次

世界の人名 ……………………… 1660
世界の国名 ……………………… 1674
世界の都市名 …………………… 1678
場面・状況別会話 ……………… 1681
電話の英会話 …………………… 1777
手紙・はがきの書き方 ………… 1781
ファックスの書き方 …………… 1785
履歴書の書き方 ………………… 1786
句読法 …………………………… 1788
数と数式 ………………………… 1796
度量衡換算表 …………………… 1801
通貨一覧 ………………………… 1802
主な不規則動詞変化表 ………… 1803

世界の人名

*2000年現在，生存中の人物は生年のみ記載．

ア

アービング，ジョン John Irving（米）作家（1942〜）
アープ，ワイアット Wyatt Earp（米）保安官（1848〜1929）
アームストロング，ニール Neil Armstrong（米）宇宙飛行士（1930〜）
アームストロング，ルイ Louis Armstrong（米）ジャズミュージシャン（1900頃〜1971）
アーロン，ハンク Hank Aaron（米）野球選手（1934〜）
アイアコッカ，リー Lee Iacocca（米）実業家（1924〜）
アイゼンハワー，ドワイト・デービット Dwight David Eisenhower（米）米国第34代大統領（1953〜1961）（1890〜1969）
アイボリー，ジェームズ James Ivory（米）映画監督（1928〜）
アインシュタイン，アルバート Albert Einstein（独・米）物理学者（1879〜1955）
アガシ，アンドレ Andre Agassi（米）テニス選手（1970〜）
アシモフ，アイザック Isaac Asimov（米）作家・化学者（1920〜1992）
アシュケナージ，ウラジーミル Vladimir Ashkenazy（ロシア）ピアニスト・指揮者（1937〜）
アッテンボロー，リチャード Richard Attenborough（英）映画監督（1923〜）
アッバード，クラウディオ Claudio Abbado（伊）指揮者（1933〜）
アップダイク，ジョン John Updike（米）作家（1932〜）
アトキンソン，ローワン Rowan Atkinson（英）コメディアン（1955〜）
アブドゥル・ジャバー，カリーム Kareem Abdul-Jabbar（米）バスケットボール選手（1947〜）
アボガドロ，アメデオ Amedeo Avogadro（伊）化学者（1776〜1856）
アボット，ジム Jim Abbott（米）野球選手（1967〜）
アムンゼン，ロアルド Roald Amundsen（ノルウェー）探検家（1872〜1928）
アラファト，ヤシール Yasser Arafat PLO議長（1929〜）
アリ，ムハマド Muhammad Ali（米）ボクサー（1942〜）
アリストテレス Aristotle 古代ギリシャの哲学者（前384〜前322）
アルキメデス Archimedes 古代ギリシャの数学者・物理学者（前287頃〜前212）
アルトマン，ロバート Robert Altman（米）映画監督（1925〜）
アルマーニ，ジョルジオ Giorgio Armani（伊）デザイナー（1934頃〜）
アレクサンダー大王 Alexander the Great マケドニアの王（前336〜前323）
アレン，ウッディ Woody Allen（米）映画監督・俳優（1935〜）
アロヨ，グロリア・マカパガル Gloria Macapagal-Arroyo（フィリピン）大統領（2001〜）（1947〜）
アングル，ジャン・オーギュスト・ドミニク Jean Auguste Dominique Ingres（仏）画家（1780〜1867）
アンデルセン，ハンス Hans Christian Andersen（デンマーク）童話作家（1805〜1875）
アントニオーニ，ミケランジェロ Michelangelo Antonioni（伊）映画監督（1912〜）

イ・ウ

イーグルス the Eagles（米）ロックグループ
イーストウッド，クリント Clint Eastwood（米）俳優・映画監督（1930〜）
イェーツ，W. B. W(illiam) B(utler) Yeats（アイルランド）詩人（1865〜1939）
イエス・キリスト Jesus Christ キリスト教の祖（前4頃〜後29頃）
イソップ Aesop（ギリシャ）寓話(ぐうわ)作家（前6世紀頃）
イプセン，ヘンリック Henrik Ibsen（ノルウェー）劇作家・詩人（1828〜1906）
ウィーバー，シガニー Sigourney Weaver（米）女優（1949〜）
ウィトゲンシュタイン，ルートビヒ Ludwig Wittgenstein（オーストリア）哲学者（1889〜1951）
ウィリアムズ，ウィリアム・カルロス William Carlos Williams（米）詩人（1883〜1963）
ウィリアムズ，ジョン John Williams（米）映画音楽作曲家（1932〜）
ウィリアムズ，セリーナ Serena Williams（米）テニス選手（1981〜）
ウィリアムズ，テッド Ted Williams（米）野球選手（1918〜）
ウィリアムズ，テネシー Tennessee Williams（米）劇作家（1911〜1983）
ウィリアムズ，ハンク Hank Williams（米）カントリー歌手（1923〜1953）
ウィリアムズ，ビーナス Venus Williams（米）テニス選手（1980〜）
ウィリアムズ，ロビン Robin Williams（米）俳

優 (1952~)
ウィリス, ブルース Bruce Willis (米) 俳優 (1955~)
ウェイン, ジョン John Wayne (米) 俳優 (1907~1979)
ウェブスター, ノア Noah Webster (米) 辞書編集者 (1758~1843)
ウェルズ, オーソン Orson Welles (米) 映画監督・俳優 (1915~1985)
ウェルズ, H. G. H(erbert) G(eorge) Wells (英) 作家 (1866~1946)
ウォーホル, アンディ Andy Warhol (米) 画家 (1928~1987)
ウッズ, タイガー Tiger Woods (米) プロゴルファー (1975~)

エ・オ

エアロスミス Aerosmith (米) ロックグループ
エイゼンシュテイン, セルゲイ Sergei Mikhailovich Eisenstein (ソ連) 映画監督 (1898~1948)
エジソン, トーマス・アルバ Thomas Alva Edison (米) 発明家 (1847~1931)
エバート, クリス Chris Evert (米) テニス選手 (1954~)
エラスムス, デシデリウス Desiderius Erasmus (オランダ) 人文主義者 (1466頃~1536)
エラリー・クイーン Ellery Queen (米) 作家；Frederic Dannay (1905~1982) と Manfred B. Lee (1905~1971) の共同筆名
エリオット, T. S. T(homas) S(tearns) Eliot (英) 詩人・批評家 (1888~1965)
エリザベス1世 Elizabeth I (英) 女王 (1558~1603) (1533~1603)
エリザベス2世 Elizabeth II (英) 現女王 (1952~) (1926~)
エリツィン, ボリス Boris Nikolaevich Yeltsin (ロシア) 政治家・元大統領 (1991~1999) (1931~)
エリントン, デューク Duke Ellington (米) ジャズミュージシャン (1899~1974)
エルウェイ, ジョン John Elway (米) フットボール選手 (1960~)
エル・グレコ El Greco (スペイン) 画家 (1541~1614)
エンゲルス, フリードリヒ Friedrich Engels (独) 社会主義者 (1820~1895)
エンデ, ミヒャエル Michael Ende (独) 作家 (1929~1995)
エンヤ Enya (アイルランド) ポップ歌手 (1962~)
オアシス Oasis (英) ロックグループ
オーウェル, ジョージ George Orwell (英) 小説家 (1903~1950)
オーエンス, ジェシー Jesse Owens (米) 陸上選手 (1903~1980)
オースティン, ジェーン Jane Austen (英) 作家 (1775~1817)
オー・ヘンリー O. Henry (米) 作家；本名 William Sydney Porter (1862~1910)
オーム, ゲオルク Georg Simon Ohm (独) 物理学者 (1789~1854)
オトゥール, ピーター Peter O'Toole (英) 俳優 (1932~)
オニール, シャキール Shaquille O'Neal (米) バスケットボール選手 (1972~)
オリビエ, ローレンス Laurence Olivier (英) 俳優 (1907~1989)
オルコット, ルイーザ・メイ Louisa May Alcott (米) 作家 (1832~1888)

カ

ガーシュウィン, ジョージ George Gershwin (米) 作曲家 (1898~1937)
カーター, ジミー Jimmy Carter 米国第39代大統領 (1977~1981) (1924~)
カーネギー, アンドルー Andrew Carnegie (米) 鉄鋼業者・慈善家 (1835~1919)
ガーファンクル, アート Art Garfunkel (米) ポップ歌手 (1942~)
カーペンターズ the Carpenters (米) ポップグループ
ガウディ, アントニオ Antonio Gaudí (スペイン) 建築家 (1852~1926)
ガガーリン, ユーリー Yuri Alekseevich Gagarin (ソ連) 宇宙飛行士 (1934~1968)
カザノーバ, ジャコモ (Giovanni Jacopo) Casanova (伊) 冒険家・作家 (1725~1798)
カサベテス, ジョン John Cassavetes (米) 映画監督 (1929~1989)
カザルス, パブロ Pablo Casals (スペイン) チェリスト (1876~1973)
カザン, エリア Elia Kazan (米) 映画監督 (1909~)
カストロ, フィデル Fidel Castro (キューバ) 首相 (1959~1976)・国家評議会議長 (1976~) (1927~)
カッブ, タイ Ty Cobb (米) 野球選手 (1886~1961)
カフカ, フランツ Franz Kafka (チェコ・オーストリア) 作家 (1883~1924)
カポーティ, トルーマン Truman Capote (米) 作家 (1924~1984)
カポネ, アル Al Capone (米) ギャングの首領 (1899~1947)
カミュ, アルベール Albert Camus (仏) 作家 (1913~1960)
カラス, マリア Maria Callas (米) ソプラノ歌手 (1923~1977)
カラヤン, ヘルベルト・フォン Herbert von Karajan (オーストリア) 指揮者 (1908~1989)
ガリレイ, ガリレオ Galileo Galilei (伊) 天文物理学者 (1564~1642)
ガルシア・マルケス, ガブリエル Gabriel García Márquez (コロンビア) 作家 (1928~)
カルダン, ピエール Pierre Cardin (仏) デザイナー (1922~)
カルバン, ジョン John Calvin (仏) 宗教改革者 (1509~1564)
ガルボ, グレタ Greta Garbo (スウェーデン) 女優 (1905~1990)
カレーラス, ホセ José Carreras (スペイン) テノール歌手 (1946~)
ガンジー, マハトマ Mahatma Gandhi (インド) インド独立運動の指導者 (1869~1948)

カンディンスキー, ワシリー Wassily Kandinsky (ロシア) 画家 (1866～1944)
カント, イマヌエル Immanuel Kant (独) 哲学者 (1724～1804)

キ

ギア, リチャード Richard Gere (米) 俳優 (1949～)
キーツ, ジョン John Keats (英) 詩人 (1795～1821)
キートン, バスター Buster Keaton (米) 映画監督・俳優 (1895～1966)
ギエム, シルビー Sylvie Guillem (フランス) バレエダンサー (1965～)
キケロ (Marcus Tullius) Cicero ローマの政治家・哲学者 (前106～前43)
ギブソン, メル Mel Gibson (米) 俳優 (1956～)
キム・イル・ソン (金日成) Kim Il Sung (北朝鮮) 国家主席 (1972～1994) (1912～1994)
キム・ジョン・イル (金正日) Kim Jong Il (北朝鮮) 朝鮮労働党総書記 (1997～) (1942～)
キム・デジュン (金大中) Kim Dae Jung (韓国) 大統領 (1998～) (1925～)
キャパ, ロバート Robert Capa (米) 写真家 (1913～1954)
キャリー, ジム Jim Carrey (米) 俳優 (1962～)
キャリー, マライア Mariah Carey (米) ポップ歌手 (1970～)
キャロル, ルイス Lewis Carroll (英) 作家；本名 Charles Lutwidge Dodgson (1832～1898)
キューブリック, スタンリー Stanley Kubrick (米) 映画監督 (1928～1999)
キュリー, マリー Marie Curie (ポーランド) 物理学者・化学者 (1867～1934)
ギリアム, テリー Terry Gilliam (英) 映画監督 (1940～)
キング, キャロル Carole King (米) ポップ歌手 (1942～)
キング, スティーブン Stephen King (米) 作家 (1947～)
キング, B. B. B. B. King (米) ギター奏者・ブルース歌手 (1925～)
キング, マーティン・ルーサー Martin Luther King, Jr. (米) 牧師・黒人市民権運動の指導者 (1929～1968)
キンスキー, ナスターシャ Nastassja Kinski (独) 女優 (1960～)
ギンズバーグ, アレン Allen Ginsberg (米) 詩人 (1926～1997)

ク

クイーン Queen (英) ロックグループ
グーテンベルク, ヨハネス Johannes Gutenberg (独) 活版印刷術の発明者とされる (1400頃～1468)
クーパー, ゲーリー Gary Cooper (米) 俳優 (1901～1961)
クーベルタン, ピエール・ド Baron Pierre de Coubertin (仏) 国際オリンピック競技の創設者 (1863～1937)
グールド, グレン Glenn Gould (カナダ) ピアニスト (1932～1982)
クールベ, ギュスターブ Gustave Courbet (仏) 画家 (1819～1877)
クック, ジェームズ James Cook (英) 軍人・探検家；通称Captain Cook (1728～1779)
グッドマン, ベニー Benny Goodman (米) ジャズミュージシャン (1909～1986)
クライスラー, フリッツ Fritz Kreisler (米) バイオリニスト (1875～1962)
クライトン, マイケル Michael Crichton (米) 作家 (1942～)
クライフ, ヨハン Johan Cruyff (オランダ) サッカー選手・監督 (1947～)
クライン, カルバン Calvin Klein (米) デザイナー (1942～)
グラス, ギュンター Günter Grass (独) 作家 (1927～)
グラフ, シュテフィ Steffi Graf (独) テニス選手 (1969～)
クラプトン, エリック Eric Clapton (英) ロックミュージシャン (1945～)
グリーグ, エドバルド Edvard Grieg (ノルウェー) 作曲家 (1843～1907)
グリーナウェー, ピーター Peter Greenaway (英) 映画監督 (1942～)
グリーン, グレアム Graham Greene (英) 作家 (1904～1991)
クリスティー, アガサ Agatha Christie (英) 作家 (1890～1976)
グリフィー, ケン Ken Griffey, Jr. (米) 野球選手 (1969～)
グリフィス, デビッド D(avid) W(ark) Griffith (米) 映画監督 (1875～1948)
グリム, ウイルヘルム Wilhelm Grimm (独) 言語学者・民俗学者；グリム兄弟の弟 (1786～1859)
グリム, ヤコブ Jacob Grimm (独) 言語学者・民俗学者；グリム兄弟の兄 (1785～1863)
クリムト, グスタフ Gustav Klimt (オーストリア) 画家 (1862～1918)
クリントン, ヒラリー Hillary Rodham Clinton (米) 政治家；ビル・クリントン夫人 (1947～)
クリントン, ビル Bill Clinton 米国第42代大統領 (1993～2001) (1946～)
クルーズ, トム Tom Cruise (米) 俳優 (1962～)
クレイマー, スタンリー Stanley Kramer (米) 映画監督 (1913～)
クレー, パウル Paul Klee (スイス) 画家 (1879～1940)
グレーシー, ヒクソン Rickson Gracie (ブラジル) 柔術家 (1959～)
クレール, ルネ René Clair (仏) 映画監督 (1898～1981)
クレオパトラ Cleopatra 古代エジプトの女王 (前69～前30)
グレツキー, ウェイン Wayne Gretzky (カナダ) アイスホッケー選手 (1961～)
クレメンス, ロジャー Roger Clemens (米) 野球選手 (1962～)

クローネンバーグ，デビッド David Cronenberg（カナダ）映画監督（1943～）
クロケット，デービー Davy Crockett（米）政治家（1786～1836）
クロスビー，ビング Bing Crosby（米）歌手・俳優（1904～1977）
クロムウェル，オリバー Oliver Cromwell（英）政治家（1599～1658）

ケ・コ

ケイジ，ニコラス Nicolas Cage（米）俳優（1964～）
ゲイツ，ビル Bill Gates（米）実業家（Microsoft）（1955～）
ケインズ，ジョン・メナード John Maynard Keynes（英）経済学者（1883～1946）
ゲーテ，ヨハン・ウォルフガング・フォン Johann Wolfgang von Goethe（独）詩人・作家（1749～1832）
ゲーデル，クルト Kurt Gödel（オーストリア・米）数学者・論理学者（1906～1978）
ゲーブル，クラーク Clark Gable（米）俳優（1901～1960）
ゲーリッグ，ルー Lou Gehrig（米）野球選手（1903～1941）
ケネディ，ジョン・フィッツジェラルド John Fitzgerald Kennedy 米国第35代大統領（1961～1963）（1917～1963）
ケプラー，ヨハネス Johannes Kepler（独）天文学者（1571～1630）
ケラー，ヘレン Helen Keller（米）社会福祉事業家（1880～1968）
ケルアック，ジャック Jack Kerouac（米）作家（1922～1969）
玄宗（げんそう）Xuanzong, Hsuan-tsung（中）唐の皇帝（685～762）
ゴア，アルバート Albert Gore（米）政治家（1948～）
孔子（こうし）Confucius, K'ung-tzu（中）思想家（前551～前479）
江沢民（こうたくみん）Jiang Zemin（中）国家主席（1993～）（1926～）
ゴーギャン，ポール Paul Gauguin（仏）画家（1848～1903）
ゴーゴリ，ニコライ Nikolai Vasilevich Gogol（ロシア）作家（1809～1852）
ゴーリキー，マクシム Maksim Gorky（ロシア）作家（1868～1936）
コール，ナット・キング Nat King Cole（米）ジャズミュージシャン（1917～1965）
ゴールディング，ウィリアム William Golding（英）作家（1911～1993）
コクトー，ジャン Jean Cocteau（仏）詩人・作家・映画監督（1889～1963）
コスナー，ケビン Kevin Costner（米）俳優（1955～）
コスビー，ビル Bill Cosby（米）俳優（1937～）
ゴダール，ジャン・リュック Jean-Luc Godard（仏）映画監督（1930～）
ゴッホ，ビンセント・バン Vincent van Gogh（オランダ）画家（1853～1890）
コッポラ，フランシス・フォード Francis Ford Coppola（米）映画監督（1939～）
コナーズ，ジミー Jimmy Connors（米）テニス選手（1952～）
コネリー，ショーン Sean Connery（英）俳優（1930～）
コバーン，ジェームズ James Coburn（米）俳優（1928～）
コペルニクス，ニコラウス Nicholaus Copernicus（ポーランド）天文学者（1473～1543）
ゴヤ，フランシスコ Francisco José Goya y Lucientes（スペイン）画家（1746～1828）
コリンズ，フィル Phil Collins（英）ロック歌手（1951～）
コルテス，ホアキン Joaquín Cortés（スペイン）フラメンコダンサー（1969～）
コルトレーン，ジョン John Coltrane（米）ジャズミュージシャン（1926～1967）
ゴルバチョフ，ミハイル Mikhail Sergeevich Gorbachev ソ連の大統領（1990～1991）（1931～）
コロンブス，クリストファー Christopher Columbus（伊）航海者（1451頃～1506）
コンスタブル，ジョン John Constable（英）画家（1776～1837）

サ

サイモン，ニール Neil Simon（米）劇作家（1927～）
サイモン，ポール Paul Simon（米）ポップ歌手（1941～）
サガン，フランソワーズ Françoise Sagan（仏）作家（1935～）
サザーランド，ドナルド Donald Sutherland（米）俳優（1934～）
サッチャー，マーガレット Margaret Thatcher（英）首相（1979～1990）（1925～）
サティ，エリック Erik Satie（仏）作曲家（1866～1925）
サド，マルキ・ド Marquis de Sade（仏）作家（1740～1814）
ザビエル，聖フランシスコ Saint Francis Xavier（スペイン）イエズス会宣教師（1506～1552）
ザ・フー the Who（英）ロックグループ
ザメンホフ Lazarus Ludwig Zamenhof（ポーランド）言語学者（1859～1917）
サリンジャー，ジェローム・デビッド J(erome) D(avid) Salinger（米）作家（1919～）
サルトル，ジャン・ポール Jean-Paul Sartre（仏）哲学者・作家（1905～1980）
サローヤン，ウィリアム William Saroyan（米）作家（1908～1981）
サンサーンス，シャルル・カミーユ Charles Camille Saint-Saens（仏）作曲家（1835～1921）
サンダース，カーネル Colonel Sanders（米）実業家（1890～1980）
サンタナ Santana（メキシコ）ロックグループ
サンテグジュペリ，アントワーヌ・ド Antoine de Saint-Exupéry（仏）作家（1900～1944）
サンプラス，ピート Pete Sampras（米）テニス選手（1971～）

シ

サンローラン, イブ Yves Saint-Laurent (仏) デザイナー (1936〜)

シーザー Julius Caesar 古代ローマの武将・政治家 (前100頃〜前44)

シートン, アーネスト Ernest Thompson Seton (米) 博物学者・作家 (1860〜1946)

シーボルト, フィリップ・フランツ・フォン Philipp Franz von Siebold (独) 医学者 (1796〜1866)

シールズ, ブルック Brooke Shields (米) 女優 (1965〜)

シーレ, エゴン Egon Schiele (オーストリア) 画家 (1890〜1918)

シーン, チャーリー Charlie Sheen (米) 俳優 (1965〜)

シェークスピア, ウィリアム William Shakespeare (英) 劇作家・詩人 (1564〜1616)

ジェームズ, ウィリアム William James (米) 哲学者・心理学者 (1842〜1910)

ジェームズ, ヘンリー Henry James (米・英) 作家 (1843〜1916)

シェール Cher (米) ポップ歌手・女優 (1946〜)

シェーンベルク, アルノルト Arnold Schönberg (オーストリア) 作曲家 (1874〜1951)

ジェネシス Genesis (英) ロックグループ

ジェファソン, トーマス Thomas Jefferson 米国第3代大統領 (1801〜1809) (1743〜1826)

シェリー, パーシー・ビッシュ Percy Bysshe Shelley (英) 詩人 (1792〜1822)

ジェロニモ Geronimo (米) 北米先住民のアパッチ族の族長 (1829〜1909)

シカゴ Chicago (米) ロックグループ

始皇帝 (しこうてい) Shi Huangdi, Shih Huangti (中) 皇帝 (前259〜前210)

ジッド, アンドレ André Gide (仏) 作家 (1869〜1951)

シナトラ, フランク Frank Sinatra (米) 歌手・俳優 (1915〜1998)

ジバンシー, ユベール・ド Hubert de Givenchy (仏) デザイナー (1927〜)

シベリウス, ジャン Jean Sibelius (フィンランド) 作曲家 (1865〜1957)

ジャームッシュ, ジム Jim Jarmusch (米) 映画監督 (1953〜)

シャーン, ベン Ben Shahn (米) 画家 (1898〜1969)

釈迦 (しゃか) ➡仏陀 (ぶっだ・ぶつだ)

ジャガー, ミック Mick Jagger (英) ロック歌手 (1943〜)

シャガール, マルク Marc Chagall (仏) 画家 (1887〜1985)

ジャクソン, ジャネット Janet Jackson (米) ポップ歌手 (1966〜)

ジャクソン, マイケル Michael Jackson (米) ポップ歌手 (1958〜)

ジャクソン, レジー Reggie Jackson (米) 野球選手 (1946〜)

シャネル, ガブリエル Gabrielle Chanel (仏) デザイナー (1883〜1971)

ジャミロクワイ Jamiroquai (英) ポップグループ

ジャレット, キース Keith Jarrett (米) ジャズミュージシャン (1945〜)

ジャンヌ・ダルク Joan of Arc (仏) 百年戦争の際, フランスの危機を救った少女 (1412〜1431)

シューベルト, フランツ Franz Schubert (オーストリア) 作曲家 (1797〜1828)

シューマッハ, ミヒャエル Michael Schumacher (独) F1レーサー (1969〜)

シューマン, ローベルト Robert Schumann (独) 作曲家 (1810〜1856)

シュトラウス, ヨハン Johann Strauss (オーストリア) 作曲家・指揮者, 「ワルツ王」 (1825〜1899)

シュトラウス, リヒャルト Richard Strauss (独) 作曲家 (1864〜1949)

シュバイツァー, アルベール Albert Schweitzer (仏) 医者・音楽家 (1875〜1965)

シュリーマン, ハインリヒ Heinrich Schliemann (独) 考古学者 (1822〜1890)

シュルツ, チャールズ Charles Schultz (米) 漫画家 (1922〜2000)

シュワルツェネッガー, アーノルド Arnold Schwarzenegger (米) 俳優 (1947〜)

ジョイス, ジェームズ James Joyce (アイルランド) 作家 (1882〜1941)

ジョイナー・カーシー, ジャッキー Jackie Joyner-Kersee (米) 陸上選手 (1962〜)

ジョイナー, フローレンス・グリフィス Florence Griffith Joyner (米) 陸上選手 (1959〜1998)

ジョエル, ビリー Billy Joel (米) ロック歌手 (1949〜)

ショー, ジョージ・バーナード George Bernard Shaw (アイルランド) 劇作家 (1856〜1950)

ジョーダン, マイケル Michael Jordan (米) バスケットボール選手 (1963〜)

ジョーンズ, クインシー Quincy Jones (米) 音楽プロデューサー (1933〜)

ジョーンズ, ジャスパー Jasper Johns (米) 画家 (1930〜)

ショスタコービチ, ドミートリー Dmitri Shostakovich (ソ連) 作曲家 (1906〜1975)

ショパン, フレデリック Frédéric François Chopin (ポーランド) 作曲家・ピアニスト (1810〜1849)

ジョブズ, スティーブ Steve(n Paul) Jobs (米) Apple Computer 設立者の1人 (1955〜)

ジョプリン, ジャニス Janis Joplin (米) ロック歌手 (1943〜1970)

ジョン, エルトン Elton John (英) ロック歌手 (1947〜)

ジョンソン, アービン・マジック Earvin Magic Johnson (米) バスケットボール選手 (1959〜)

ジョンソン, サミュエル Samuel Johnson (英) 辞書編集者 (1709〜1784)

ジョンソン, マイケル Michael Johnson (米) 陸上選手 (1967〜)

ジョンソン, ランディー Randy Johnson (米) 野球選手 (1963〜)

シラー, ヨハン・クリストフ・フリードリヒ・フォン Johann Christoph Friedrich von Schiller (独) 劇作家・詩人 (1759〜1805)

シリトー, アラン　Alan Sillitoe　(英)　作家 (1928〜)
シンガー, アイザック　Isaac Bashevis Singer　(米)　作家 (1904〜1991)
ジンギス・カン　➪チンギス・ハン
シンプソン, O. J.　O(renthal) J(ames) Simpson　(米)　フットボール選手 (1947〜)

ス

スウィフト, ジョナサン　Jonathan Swift　(英)　作家 (1667〜1745)
スーラ, ジョルジュ　Georges Pierre Seurat　(仏)　画家 (1859〜1891)
スコット, ウォルター　Sir Walter Scott　(英)　詩人・作家 (1771〜1832)
スコット, リドリー　Ridley Scott　(英)　映画監督 (1939〜)
スコット, ロバート・ファルコン　Robert Falcon Scott　(英)　探検家 (1868〜1912)
スター, リンゴ　Ringo Starr　(英)　元ビートルズのメンバー (1940〜)
スタージェス, ジョン　John Sturges　(米)　映画監督 (1914〜1992)
スターリン, ヨシフ　Joseph Stalin　(ソ連)　共産党書記長 (1922〜1953)・首相 (1941〜1953) (1879〜1953)
スタインベック, ジョン　John Steinbeck　(米)　作家 (1902〜1968)
スタローン, シルベスター　Sylvester Stallone　(米)　俳優 (1946〜)
スタンダール　Stendhal　(仏)　作家 (1783〜1842)
スチュアート, ロッド　Rod Stewart　(英)　ロック歌手 (1945〜)
スティーブンソン, ロバート・ルイス　Robert Louis Stevenson　(英)　作家 (1850〜1894)
スティング　Sting　(英)　ロック歌手 (1951〜)
ステラ, フランク　Frank Stella　(米)　画家 (1935〜)
ストー, ハリエット　Harriet Beecher Stowe　(米)　作家 (1811〜1896)
ストーン, オリバー　Oliver Stone　(米)　映画監督 (1946〜)
ストライサンド, バーブラ　Barbra Streisand　(米)　歌手・女優 (1942〜)
ストラビンスキー, イーゴリ　Igor Stravinsky　(ロシア・米)　作曲家 (1882〜1971)
ストリープ, メリル　Meryl Streep　(米)　女優 (1949〜)
スパイス・ガールズ　the Spice Girls　(英)　ポップグループ
スハルト　Suharto　(インドネシア)　政治家 (1921〜)
スピルバーグ, スティーブン　Steven Spielberg　(米)　映画監督 (1947〜)
スプリングスティーン, ブルース　Bruce Springsteen　(米)　ロック歌手 (1949〜)
スミス, アダム　Adam Smith　(英)　経済学者 (1723〜1790)

セ・ソ

聖トマス　Saint Thomas　〔聖書〕キリストの十二使徒の1人
聖パウロ　Saint Paul　初期キリスト教の伝道者；新約聖書の著者の1人 (?〜67頃)
聖フランチェスコ　Saint Francis　(伊)　フランシスコ修道会の創始者 (1182頃〜1226)
聖ペテロ　Saint Peter　〔聖書〕キリストの十二使徒の1人
聖母マリア　(the Virgin) Mary　イエス・キリストの母；生没年不詳
聖マタイ　Saint Matthew　〔聖書〕キリストの十二使徒の1人
聖マルコ　Saint Mark　〔聖書〕キリストの弟子の1人
聖ヨハネ　Saint John　〔聖書〕キリストの十二使徒の1人
セザンヌ, ポール　Paul Cézanne　(仏)　画家 (1839〜1906)
セナ, アイルトン　Ayrton Senna　(ブラジル)　F1レーサー (1960〜1994)
セルバンテス, ミゲール・デ　Miguel de Cervantes　(スペイン)　作家 (1547〜1616)
セレス, モニカ　Monica Seles　(米)　テニス選手 (1973〜)
荘子(そうし)　Zhuangzi, Chuang-tzu　(中)　思想家；生没年不詳
ソーサ, サミー　Sammy Sosa　(米)　野球選手 (1968〜)
ソープ, イアン　Ian Thorpe　(オーストラリア)　水泳選手 (1982〜)
ソクラテス　Socrates　古代ギリシャの哲学者 (前470〜前399)
ソシュール, フェルディナン・ド　Ferdinand de Saussure　(スイス)　言語学者 (1857〜1913)
ゾラ, エミール　Émile Zola　(仏)　作家 (1840〜1902)
ソルジェニーツィン, アレキサンドル　Aleksandr Isayevich Solzhenitsyn　(ロシア)　作家 (1918〜)
ソロー, ヘンリー・デビッド　Henry David Thoreau　(米)　作家 (1817〜1862)
孫文(そんぶん)　Sun Yat-sen, Sun Wen, Sun Wên　(中)　政治家 (1866〜1925)

タ

ダーウィン, チャールズ・ロバート　Charles Robert Darwin　(英)　博物学者・進化論の提唱者 (1809〜1882)
ターナー, キャスリーン　Kathleen Turner　(米)　女優 (1954〜)
ターナー, ジョーゼフ・マロード・ウィリアム　J(oseph) M(allord) W(illiam) Turner　(英)　画家 (1775〜1851)
ターナー, ティナ　Tina Turner　(米)　ソウル歌手 (1938〜)
ターナー, テッド　Ted Turner　(米)　実業家 (CNN) (1938〜)
ダール, ロアルド　Roald Dahl　(英)　作家 (1916〜1990)
ダイアナ妃　Princess Diana　(英)　チャールズ皇太子の元皇太子妃 (1981〜1996) (1961〜1997)
タイソン, マイク　Mike Tyson　(米)　ボクサー (1966〜)

ダグラス，マイケル Michael Douglas (米) 俳優 (1944〜)
タゴール，ラビーンドラナート Rabindranath Tagore (インド) 詩人 (1861〜1941)
ダナウェイ，フェイ Faye Dunaway (米) 女優 (1941〜)
ダ・ビンチ ⇨レオナルド・ダ・ビンチ
ダベンポート，リンゼイ Lindsey Davenport (米) テニス選手 (1976〜)
ダライ・ラマ the Dalai Lama (チベット) ラマ教の教主 (1935〜)
タランティーノ，クェンティン Quentin Tarantino (米) 映画監督 (1963〜)
ダリ，サルバドール Salvador Dali (スペイン) 画家 (1904〜1989)
タルコフスキー，アンドレイ Andrei Arsenevich Tarkovsky (ソ連) 映画監督 (1932〜1986)
ダンカン，イザドラ Isadora Duncan (米) ダンサー (1878〜1927)
ダンテ Dante Alighieri (伊) 詩人 (1265〜1321)

チ・ツ

チェーホフ，アントン Anton Pavlovich Chekhov (ロシア) 作家 (1860〜1904)
チェスタートン，ギルバート・キース G(ilbert) K(eith) Chesterton (英) 作家 (1874〜1936)
チェン，ジャッキー Jackie Chan (香港) 俳優 (1954〜)
チェンバレン，ウィルト Wilt Chamberlain (米) バスケットボール選手 (1936〜1999)
チャーチル，ウィンストン Winston Churchill (英) 首相 (1940〜1945, 1951〜1955) (1874〜1965)
チャールズ，レイ Ray Charles (米) ソウル歌手 (1930〜)
チャールズ皇太子 Prince Charles 現英国皇太子 (1948〜)
チャールトン，ボビー Bobby Charlton (英) サッカー選手 (1937〜)
チャイコフスキー，ピョートル Pyotr Ilich Tchaikovsky (ロシア) 作曲家 (1840〜1893)
チャップリン，チャーリー Charlie Chaplin (英) 映画俳優・監督・脚本家・作曲家；本名 Charles Spencer Chaplin (1889〜1977)
チャペック，カレル Karel Capek (チェコ) 作家 (1890〜1938)
チャンドラー，レイモンド Raymond Chandler (米) 作家 (1888〜1959)
チョーサー，ジェフリー Geoffrey Chaucer (英) 詩人 (1340頃〜1400)
チョムスキー，ノーム Noam Chomsky (米) 言語学者・批評家 (1928〜)
チンギス・ハン Genghis Khan (モンゴル) モンゴル帝国の始祖 (1162頃〜1227)
ツタンカーメン Tutankhamen, King Tut 古代エジプト第18王朝の王 (前14世紀)
ツツ，デズモンド Desmond (Mpilo) Tutu (南アフリカ) 反アパルトヘイト運動指導者 (1931〜)
ツルゲーネフ，イワン Ivan Sergeevich Turgenev (ロシア) 作家 (1818〜1883)

テ・ト

デ・シーカ，ビットリオ Vittorio De Sica (伊) 映画監督 (1901〜1974)
デ・ニーロ，ロバート Robert De Niro (米) 俳優 (1943〜)
デ・パルマ，ブライアン Brian De Palma (米) 映画監督 (1941〜)
デ・ラ・レンタ，オスカー Oscar de la Renta (米) デザイナー (1934頃〜)
ディーン，ジェームズ James Dean (米) 映画俳優 (1931〜1955)
ディオン，セリーヌ Celine Dion (カナダ) ポップ歌手 (1968〜)
ディカプリオ，レオナルド Leonardo DiCaprio (米) 俳優 (1974〜)
ディキンソン，エミリー Emily Dickinson (米) 詩人 (1830〜1886)
ディケンズ，チャールズ Charles Dickens (英) 作家 (1812〜1870)
ディズニー，ウォルト Walt Disney (米) アニメ映画製作者 (1901〜1966)
ティツィアーノ Titian (伊) 画家 (1490頃〜1576)
ディマジオ，ジョー Joe DiMaggio (米) 野球選手 (1914〜1999)
テイラー，エリザベス Elizabeth Taylor (米) 女優 (1932〜)
ディラン，ボブ Bob Dylan (米) フォーク・ロック歌手 (1941〜)
デービス，サミー Sammy Davis, Jr. (米) 歌手・俳優 (1925〜1990)
デービス，マイルス Miles Davis (米) ジャズミュージシャン (1926〜1991)
デカルト，ルネ René Descartes (仏) 哲学者・数学者 (1596〜1650)
デフォー，ダニエル Daniel Defoe (英) 作家・ジャーナリスト (1660頃〜1731)
デリダ，ジャック Jacques Derrida (仏) 哲学者 (1930〜)
デンバー，ジョン John Denver (米) ポップ歌手 (1943〜1997)
ドイル，アーサー・コナン Sir Arthur Conan Doyle (英) 作家 (1859〜1930)
トインビー，アーノルド Arnold J. Toynbee (英) 歴史家 (1889〜1975)
トウェーン，マーク Mark Twain (米) 作家；本名 Samuel Langhorne Clemens (1835〜1910)
鄧小平 (とうしょうへい) Deng Xiaoping, Teng Hsiaoping (中) 政治家 (1904〜1997)
トールキン，ジョン J(ohn) R. R. Tolkien (英) ファンタジー作家 (1892〜1973)
ドガ，エドガー Edgar Degas (仏) 画家 (1834〜1917)
トスカニーニ，アルトゥーロ Arturo Toscanini (伊) 指揮者 (1867〜1957)
ドストエフスキー，フョードル Fyodor Mikhailovich Dostoevsky (ロシア) 作家 (1821〜1881)
ドビュッシー，クロード・アシル Claude Achille Debussy (仏) 作曲家 (1862〜1918)

杜甫(とほ) Du Fu, Tu Fu (中) 詩人 (712～770)
ドボルザーク, アントニーン Antonín Dvořák (チェコ) 作曲家 (1841～1904)
ドミンゴ, プラシド Placido Domingo (スペイン) テノール歌手 (1941～)
ドラクロア, ウジェーヌ Ferdinand Victor Eugéne Delacroix (仏) 画家 (1798～1863)
トラボルタ, ジョン John Travolta (米) 俳優 (1954～)
トリュフォー, フランソワ François Truffaut (仏) 映画監督 (1932～1984)
トルーマン, ハリー Harry S. Truman 米国第33代大統領 (1945～1953) (1884～1972)
トルストイ, レフ Count Lev Nikolaevich Tolstoy (ロシア) 作家 (1828～1910)
ドルトン, ジョン John Dalton (英) 化学・物理学者 (1766～1844)
トルバールズ, リーナス Linus Torvalds (フィンランド) プログラマー (Linux) (1969～)
ドルフィー, エリック Eric (Allan) Dolphy (米) ジャズミュージシャン (1928～1964)
トレビノ, リー・バック Lee Buck Trevino (米) プロゴルファー (1939～)
ドロン, アラン Alain Delon (仏) 俳優 (1935～)

ナ・ニ・ヌ・ネ・ノ

ナイチンゲール, フローレンス Florence Nightingale (英) 看護婦 (1820～1910)
ナブラチロワ, マルティナ Martina Navratilova (米) テニス選手 (1956～)
ナボコフ, ウラジーミル Vladimir Nabokov (ロシア・米) 作家 (1899～1977)
ナポレオン・ボナパルト Napoleon Bonaparte (仏) 皇帝 (1804～1815) (1769～1821)
ナンセン, フリチョフ Fridtjof Nansen (ノルウェー) 探検家 (1861～1930)
ニーチェ, フリードリヒ Friedrich Wilhelm Nietzsche (独) 哲学者 (1844～1900)
ニクソン, リチャード Richard Nixon 米国第37代大統領 (1969～1974) (1913～1994)
ニクラウス, ジャック Jack Nicklaus (米) プロゴルファー (1940～)
ニコルソン, ジャック Jack Nicholson (米) 俳優 (1937～)
ニジンスキー, ワスラフ Vaslav Fomich Nijinsky (ロシア) バレエダンサー (1890～1950)
ニュートン, アイザック Sir Isaac Newton (英) 物理学者・数学者 (1642～1727)
ニュートンジョン, オリビア Olivia Newton-John (英) ポップ歌手 (1948～)
ニューマン, ポール Paul Newman (米) 俳優 (1925～)
ヌレエフ, ルドルフ Rudolf Hamertovich Nureyev (ソ連・英) バレエダンサー (1938～1993)
ネール, ジャワーハルラール Jawaharlal Nehru (インド) 政治家 (1889～1964)
ネルソン, ホレーショー Horatio Nelson (英) 提督 (1758～1805)
ネロ Nero 古代ローマ皇帝 (54～68) ; キリスト教徒を迫害したことで有名 (37～68)
ノーベル, アルフレッド Alfred Nobel (スウェーデン) 化学技術者・ダイナマイトの発明者 (1833～1896)
ノーマン, グレッグ Greg Norman (オーストラリア) プロゴルファー (1955～)
ノーマン, ジェシー Jessye Norman (米) ソプラノ歌手 (1945～)
ノストラダムス Nostradamus (仏) 予言者 (1503～1566)

ハ

パーカー, チャーリー Charlie Parker (米) ジャズミュージシャン (1920～1955)
バーグマン, イングリッド Ingrid Bergman (米) 女優 (1915～1982)
ハーディー, トーマス Thomas Hardy (英) 作家・詩人 (1840～1928)
バード, ラリー Larry Bird (米) バスケットボール選手 (1956～)
バートン, リチャード Richard Burton (英) 俳優 (1925～1984)
バーネット, フランセス・イライザ Frances Eliza Burnett (米) 作家 (1849～1924)
パーマー, アーノルド Arnold Palmer (米) プロゴルファー (1929～)
パールジャム Pearl Jam (米) ロックグループ
ハーン, ラフカディオ Lafcadio Hearn (ギリシャ) 作家; 日本名「小泉八雲」(1850～1904)
バーン・ジョーンズ, エドワード・コリー Edward Coley Burne-Jones (英) 画家 (1833～1898)
バーンスタイン, レナード Leonard Bernstein (米) 指揮者・作曲家 (1918～1990)
ハイデッガー, マルティン Martin Heidegger (独) 哲学者 (1889～1976)
ハイドン, フランツ Franz Joseph Haydn (オーストリア) 作曲家 (1732～1809)
ハイネ, ハインリヒ Heinrich Heine (独) 詩人・批評家 (1797～1856)
ハイフェッツ, ヤッシャ Jascha Heifetz (米) バイオリニスト (1901～1987)
バイロン, ジョージ・ゴードン George Gordon Byron (英) 詩人 (1788～1824)
パウンド, エズラ Ezra Pound (米) 詩人 (1885～1972)
バエズ, ジョーン Joan Baez (米) フォーク歌手 (1941～)
パスカル, ブレーズ Blaise Pascal (仏) 哲学者・数学者 (1623～1662)
バスコ・ダ・ガマ Vasco da Gama (ポルトガル) 航海者 (1469頃～1524)
パステルナーク, ボリス Boris Leonidovich Pasternak (ソ連) 作家 (1890～1960)
パゾリーニ, ピエル・パオロ Pier Paolo Pasolini (伊) 映画監督 (1922～1975)
パチーノ, アル Al Pacino (米) 俳優 (1940～)
ハッキネン, ミカ Mika Hakkinen (フィンランド) F1レーサー (1968～)
バック, パール Pearl Buck (米) 作家 (1892～1973)
ハックマン, ジーン Gene Hackman (米) 俳優 (1930～)

バッジオ, ロベルト Roberto Baggio (伊) サッカー選手 (1967～)

バッハ, ヨハン・セバスチャン Johann Sebastian Bach (独) 作曲家 (1685～1750)

パバロッティ, ルチアーノ Luciano Pavarotti (伊) テノール歌手 (1935～)

ハメット, ダシール Dashiell Hammett (米) 作家 (1894～1961)

バリシニコフ, ミハイル Mikhail Baryshnikov (米) バレエダンサー (1948～)

ハリソン, ジョージ George Harrison (英) 元ビートルズのメンバー (1943～)

バルザック, オノレ・ド Honoré de Balzac (仏) 作家 (1799～1850)

バルドー, ブリジット Brigitte Bardot (仏) 女優 (1934～)

バルトーク, ベーラ Béla Bartók (ハンガリー) 作曲家 (1881～1945)

ハレー, エドマンド Edmund Halley (英) 天文学者 (1656～1742)

バレステロス, セベリアーノ Severiano Ballesteros (スペイン) プロゴルファー (1957～)

バレンボイム, ダニエル Daniel Barenboim (アルゼンチン) ピアニスト・指揮者 (1942～)

バロウズ, ウィリアム William Burroughs (米) 作家 (1914～1997)

ハンクス, トム Tom Hanks (米) 俳優 (1956～)

ハンコック, ハービー Herbie Hancock (米) ジャズミュージシャン (1940～)

ヒ

ピアザ, マイク Mike Piazza (米) 野球選手 (1968～)

ビアズリー, オーブリー・ビンセント Aubrey Vincent Beardsley (英) 画家 (1872～1898)

ビージーズ the Bee Gees (米) ロックグループ

ビーティー, ウォーレン Warren Beatty (米) 俳優・映画監督 (1937～)

ビートルズ the Beatles (英) ロックグループ

ピカソ, パブロ Pablo Picasso (スペイン) 画家 (1881～1973)

ビクトリア女王 Queen Victoria (英) 女王 (1837～1901) (1819～1901)

ビスコンティ, ルキノ Luchino Visconti (伊) 映画監督 (1906～1976)

ビゼー, ジョルジュ Georges Bizet (仏) 作曲家 (1838～1875)

ピタゴラス Pythagoras (ギリシャ) 哲学者・数学者 (前570頃)

ヒッチコック, アルフレッド Alfred Hitchcock (英) 映画監督 (1899～1980)

ピット, ブラッド Brad Pitt (米) 俳優 (1963～)

ヒトラー, アドルフ Adolf Hitler (独) ナチスの党首・総統 (1889～1945)

ビバルディ, アントニオ Antonio Vivaldi (伊) 作曲家 (1678～1741)

ヒューストン, ジョン John Huston (米) 映画監督 (1906～1987)

ヒューストン, ホイットニー Whitney Houston (米) ポップ歌手 (1963～)

ビョーク Björk (アイスランド) 歌手・女優 (1965～)

ビリー・ザ・キッド Billy the Kid (米) アメリカ西部開拓時代の無法者 (1859～1881)

ヒンギス, マルティナ Martina Hingis (スイス) テニス選手 (1980～)

ピンクフロイド Pink Floyd (英) ロックグループ

フ

ファーブル, アンリ Jean Henri Fabre (仏) 昆虫学者 (1823～1915)

ファラデー, マイケル Michael Faraday (英) 化学者 (1791～1867)

ファロー, ミア Mia Farrow (米) 女優 (1945～)

フィッツジェラルド, F・スコット F. Scott Fitzgerald (米) 作家 (1896～1940)

フィッツジェラルド, エラ Ella Fitzgerald (米) ジャズ歌手 (1918～1996)

プーシキン, アレクサンドル Aleksandr Sergeevich Pushkin (ロシア) 作家 (1799～1837)

プーチン, ウラジーミル Vladimir Putin (ロシア) 大統領 (2000～) (1952～)

ブーニン, スタニスラフ Stanislav Bunin (ロシア) ピアニスト (1966～)

フェリーニ, フェデリコ Federico Fellini (伊) 映画監督 (1920～1993)

フェルメール, ヤン Jan Vermeer (オランダ) 画家 (1632～1675)

フォアマン, ジョージ George Foreman (米) ボクサー (1949～)

フォーク, ピーター Peter Falk (米) 俳優 (1927～)

フォークナー, ウィリアム William Faulkner (米) 作家 (1897～1962)

フォーサイス, フレデリック Frederick Forsyth (英) 作家 (1938～)

フォード, ジェラルド・ルドルフ Gerald R. Ford 米国第38代大統領 (1974～1977) (1913～)

フォード, ジョン John Ford (米) 映画監督 (1895～1973)

フォード, ハリソン Harrison Ford (米) 俳優 (1942～)

フォード, ヘンリー Henry Ford (米) 実業家 (1863～1947)

フォーレ, ガブリエル Gabriel-Urbain Fauré (仏) 作曲家 (1845～1924)

フォスター, ジョディ Jodie Foster (米) 女優 (1962～)

フォスター, スティーブン Stephen Foster (米) 作詞家・作曲家 (1826～1864)

フォックス, マイケル・J Michael J. Fox (米) 俳優 (1961～)

フォンダ, ジェーン Jane Fonda (米) 女優 (1937～)

フォンダ, ピーター Peter Fonda (米) 俳優 (1939～)

フォンダ, ヘンリー Henry Fonda (米) 俳優 (1905～1982)

フォンテーン, マーゴ Dame Margot Fonteyn (英) バレエダンサー (1919～1991)

フック, ロバート Robert Hooke (英) 科学者・発明家 (1635〜1703)

ブッシュ, ジョージ George H(erbert) W(alker) Bush 米国第41代大統領 (1989〜1993) (1924〜)

ブッシュ, ジョージ George W. Bush 米国第43代大統領 (2001〜) (1946〜)

仏陀(ぶっだ・ぶつだ) Buddha (インド) (釈迦(しゃか)) 仏教の開祖 (前463頃〜前383頃)

プッチーニ, ジャコモ Giacomo Puccini (伊) オペラ作曲家 (1858〜1924)

ブニュエル, ルイス Luis Buñuel (スペイン) 映画監督 (1900〜1983)

ブブカ, セルゲイ Sergei Bubka (ウクライナ) 棒高跳び選手 (1963〜)

ブラー Blur (英) ロックグループ

ブラームス, ヨハネス Johannes Brahms (独) 作曲家 (1833〜1897)

フラ・アンジェリコ, Fra Angelico (伊) 画家・修道士 (1387〜1455)

ブラウニング, ロバート Robert Browning (英) 詩人 (1812〜1889)

ブラウン, ジェームズ James Brown (米) ソウル歌手 (1933〜)

フラック, ロバータ Roberta Flack (米) ポップ歌手 (1939〜)

ブラッドベリー, レイ Ray Bradbury (米) SF作家 (1920〜)

プラトン Plato (ギリシャ) 哲学者 (前427〜前347)

フランク, アンネ Anne Frank (独)『アンネの日記』の作者 (1929〜1945)

フランクリン, ベンジャミン Benjamin Franklin (米) 政治家・科学者 (1706〜1790)

フランシス, サム Sam Francis (米) 画家 (1923〜)

ブランド, マーロン Marlon Brando (米) 俳優 (1924〜)

ブリテン, ベンジャミン Benjamin Britten (英) 作曲家 (1913〜1976)

ブリューゲル, ピーテル Pieter Bruegel (フランドル) 画家 (1525頃〜1569)

プリンス Prince (米) ロック歌手 (1958〜)

プルースト, マルセル Marcel Proust (仏) 作家 (1871〜1922)

ブルータス Marcus Junius Brutus 古代ローマの政治家；シーザー暗殺の首謀者 (前85〜前42)

ブルーナ, ディック Dick Bruna (オランダ) 絵本作家 (1927〜)

ブレア, トニー Tony Blair 英国の首相 (1997〜) (1953〜)

ブレーク, ウィリアム William Blake (英) 詩人・画家 (1757〜1827)

プレスリー, エルビス Elvis Presley (米) ロック歌手 (1935〜1977)

ブレッソン, ロベール Robert Bresson (仏) 映画監督 (1907〜)

フロイト, ジークムント Sigmund Freud (オーストリア) 精神分析学者 (1856〜1939)

フローベール, ギュスターブ Gustave Flaubert (仏) 作家 (1821〜1880)

プロコフィエフ, セルゲイ Sergei Sergeevich Prokofiev (ソ連) 作曲家 (1891〜1953)

プロスト, アラン Alain Prost (仏) F1レーサー (1955〜)

ブロンソン, チャールズ Charles Bronson (米) 俳優 (1921〜)

ブロンテ, エミリー Emily Brontë (英) 作家 (1818〜1848)

ブロンテ, シャーロット Charlotte Brontë (英) 作家 (1816〜1855)

ヘ

ベイカー, ジョセフィン Josephine Baker (仏) ダンサー (1906〜1975)

ペイジ, サチェル Satchel Paige (米) 野球選手 (1906〜1982)

ベイシー, カウント Count Basie (米) ジャズミュージシャン (1904〜1984)

ヘーゲル, ゲオルク Georg Wilhelm Friedrich Hegel (独) 哲学者 (1770〜1831)

ベーコン, フランシス Francis Bacon (英) 哲学者・政治家 (1561〜1626)；(アイルランド・英) 画家 (1909〜1992)

ベートーベン, ルートビヒ・ファン Ludwig van Beethoven (独) 作曲家 (1770〜1827)

ベケット, サミュエル Samuel Beckett (アイルランド・仏) 作家 (1906〜1989)

ヘストン, チャールトン Charlton Heston (米) 俳優 (1923〜)

ベスプッチ, アメリゴ Amerigo Vespucci (伊) 航海者 (1454〜1512)

ベッカー, ボリス Boris Becker (独) テニス選手 (1967〜)

ベッカム, デビッド David Beckham (英) サッカー選手 (1975〜)

ベック Beck (米) ロック歌手 (1970〜)

ペック, グレゴリー Gregory Peck (米) 俳優 (1916〜)

ベッケンバウアー, フランツ Franz Beckenbauer (独) サッカー選手・監督 (1945〜)

ヘッセ, ヘルマン Hermann Hesse (独) 作家 (1877〜1962)

ヘディン, スウェン Sven Anders Hedin (スウェーデン) 探検家 (1865〜1952)

ベネックス, ジャン・ジャック Jean-Jacques Beineix (仏) 映画監督 (1946〜)

ベネット, トニー Tony Bennett (米) ジャズ歌手 (1926〜)

ヘプバーン, オードリー Audrey Hepburn (ベルギー) 女優 (1929〜1993)

ヘプバーン, キャサリン Katharine Hepburn (米) 女優 (1909〜)

ヘミングウェー, アーネスト Ernest Hemingway (米) 作家 (1899〜1961)

ベラスケス, ディエゴ Diego Rodríguez de Silva y Velázquez (スペイン) 画家 (1599〜1660)

ペリー, マシュー Commodore Matthew Perry (米) 提督 (1794〜1858)

ベル, アレキサンダー・グラハム Alexander Graham Bell (英・米) 電話の発明者 (1847〜1922)

ベルイマン, イングマール Ingmar Bergman (スウェーデン) 映画監督 (1918〜)

ベルクソン, アンリ Henri Bergson (仏) 哲学者 (1859〜1941)
ベルディ, ジュゼッペ Giuseppe Fortunino Francesco Verdi (伊) 作曲家 (1813〜1901)
ベルトルッチ, ベルナルド Bernardo Bertolucci (伊) 映画監督 (1940〜)
ベルヌ, ジュール Jules Verne (仏) 作家 (1828〜1905)
ベルモンド, ジャン・ポール Jean-Paul Belmondo (仏) 俳優 (1933〜)
ベルリオーズ, エクトール Hector Berlioz (仏) 作曲家 (1803〜1869)
ベルレーヌ, ポール Paul Verlaine (仏) 詩人 (1844〜1896)
ペレ Pelé (ブラジル) サッカー選手 (1940〜)
ベロー, ソール Saul Bellow (米) 作家 (1915〜)
ペロー, シャルル Charles Perrault (仏) 詩人・作家 (1628〜1703)
ヘロドトス Herodotus (ギリシャ) 歴史家;「歴史の父」と呼ばれる (前484頃〜前425頃)
ベンダース, ビム Wim Wenders (独) 映画監督 (1945〜)
ベンチ, ジョニー Johnny Bench (米) 野球選手 (1947〜)
ヘンデル, ゲオルゲ・フレデリック George Frederick Handel (独) 作曲家 (1685〜1759)
ヘンドリックス, ジミ Jimi Hendrix (米) ロックミュージシャン (1942〜1970)

ホ

ボイス, ヨーゼフ Joseph Beuys (独) 芸術家 (1921〜1986)
ホイットマン, ウォルト Walt Whitman (米) 詩人 (1819〜1892)
ボイル, ロバート Robert Boyle (英) 物理・化学者 (1627〜1691)
ボウイ, デビッド David Bowie (英) ロック歌手 (1947〜)
ポー, エドガー・アラン Edgar Allan Poe (米) 作家・詩人 (1809〜1849)
ホーキング, スティーブン Stephen Hawking (英) 物理学者 (1942〜)
ホークス, ハワード Howard Hawks (米) 映画監督 (1896〜1977)
ホーソーン, ナサニエル Nathaniel Hawthorne (米) 作家 (1804〜1864)
ホー・チ・ミン Ho Chi Minh (ベトナム) 政治家 (1890〜1969)
ボードレール, シャルル Charles Baudelaire (仏) 詩人 (1821〜1867)
ホープ, ボブ Bob Hope (米) 俳優 (1903〜)
ボーボワール, シモーヌ・ド Simone de Beauvoir (仏) 作家 (1908〜1986)
ボーン, サラ Sarah Vaughan (米) ジャズ歌手 (1924〜1990)
ホガース, ウィリアム William Hogarth (英) 画家 (1697〜1764)
ボガート, ハンフリー Humphrey Bogart (米) 俳優 (1899〜1957)
ボス, ヒエロニムス Hieronymus Bosch (オランダ) 画家 (1450頃〜1516)
ボッカチオ, ジョバンニ Giovanni Boccaccio (伊) 作家 (1313〜1375)
ポッター, ベアトリクス Beatrix Potter (英) 絵本作家 (1866〜1943)
ボッティチェリ, サンドロ Sandro Botticelli (伊) 画家 (1445〜1510)
ホッパー, エドワード Edward Hopper (米) 画家 (1882〜1967)
ホッパー, デニス Dennis Hopper (米) 俳優・映画監督 (1936〜)
ホッブズ, トーマス Thomas Hobbes (英) 哲学者・政治思想家 (1588〜1679)
ホフマン, ダスティン Dustin Hoffman (米) 俳優 (1937〜)
ホメロス Homer 古代ギリシャの叙事詩人;生没年不詳
ホラティウス, Horace 古代ローマの詩人 (前65〜前8)
ポランスキー, ロマン Roman Polanski (ポーランド・米) 映画監督 (1933〜)
ポリーニ, マウリツィオ Maurizio Pollini (伊) ピアニスト (1942〜)
ポリス the Police (英) ロックグループ
ホリデー, ビリー Billie Holiday (米) ジャズ歌手 (1915〜1959)
ホリフィールド, イベンダー Evander Holyfield (米) ボクサー (1962〜)
ボルグ, ビヨルン Björn Borg (スウェーデン) テニス選手 (1956〜)
ボルヘス, ホルヘ・ルイス Jorge Luis Borges (アルゼンチン) 作家 (1899〜1986)
ポロック, ジャクソン Jackson Pollock (米) 画家 (1912〜1956)
ポワティエ, シドニー Sidney Poitier (米) 俳優 (1924〜)
ボン・ジョビ Bon Jovi (米) ロックグループ
ボンズ, バリー Barry Bonds (米) 野球選手 (1964〜)

マ

マーティン, リッキー Ricky Martin (プエルトリコ) ポップ歌手 (1971〜)
マードック, アイリス Iris Murdoch (英) 作家 (1919〜1999)
マーフィー, エディ Eddie Murphy (米) 俳優 (1961〜)
マーラー, グスタフ Gustav Mahler (オーストリア) 作曲家 (1860〜1911)
マーリー, ボブ Bob Marley (ジャマイカ) レゲエ歌手 (1945〜1981)
マイケル, ジョージ George Michael (英) ロック歌手 (1963〜)
マキアベリ, ニッコロ Niccolò Machiavelli (伊) 政治学者・歴史家 (1469〜1527)
マキナニー, ジェイ Jay McInerney (米) 作家 (1955〜)
マクレーン, シャーリー Shirley MacLaine (米) 女優 (1934〜)
マグワイア, マーク Mark McGwire (米) 野球選手 (1963〜)
マザーテレサ Mother Teresa (インド) 修道女 (1910〜1997)

マストロヤンニ, マルチェロ Marcello Mastroianni (伊) 俳優 (1924～1996)
マゼール, ロリン Lorin Mazzel (米) 指揮者 (1930～)
マゼラン, フェルディナンド Ferdinand Magellan (ポルトガル) 航海者 (1480頃～1521)
マダックス, グレッグ Greg Maddux (米) 野球選手 (1966～)
マダム・タッソー Madame Tussaud (スイス) ろう細工師・ろう人形館 (Madame Tussaud's) の創立者 (1760～1850)
マッカーサー, ダグラス Douglas MacArthur (米) 陸軍元帥 (1880～1964)
マッカートニー, ポール Paul McCartney (英) 元ビートルズのメンバー (1942～)
マックィーン, スティーブ Steve McQueen (米) 俳優 (1930～1980)
マッケンロー, ジョン John McEnroe (米) テニス選手 (1959～)
マティス, アンリ Henri Matisse (仏) 画家 (1869～1954)
マドンナ Madonna (米) ポップ歌手 (1958～)
マネ, エドワール Édouard Manet (仏) 画家 (1832～1883)
マホメット Mohammed イスラム教の開祖 (571頃～632)
マラドーナ, ディエゴ Diego Maradona (アルゼンチン) サッカー選手 (1960～)
マラマッド, バーナード Bernard Malamud (米) 作家 (1914～1986)
マリー・アントワネット Marie Antoinette (仏) ルイ16世の王妃 (1755～1793)
マリス, ロジャー Roger Maris (米) 野球選手 (1934～1985)
マルクス, カール Karl Marx (独) 哲学者・経済学者 (1818～1883)
マルコ・ポーロ Marco Polo (伊) 商人・旅行家 (1254～1324)
マルソー, マルセル Marcel Marceau (仏) パントマイム俳優 (1923～)
マン, トーマス Thomas Mann (独) 作家 (1875～1955)
マンシーニ, ヘンリー Henry Mancini (米) 映画音楽作曲家 (1924～1994)
マンデラ, ネルソン Nelson Mandela (南アフリカ) 反アパルトヘイト運動指導者・人種隔離政策撤廃後の初代大統領 (1994～1999) (1918～)
マントバーニ Mantovani (英) 指揮者 (1905～1980)
マントル, ミッキー Mickey Mantle (米) 野球選手 (1931～1995)

ミ・ム・メ・モ

ミケランジェロ Michelangelo (伊) 彫刻家・画家・建築家 (1475～1564)
ミッチェル, マーガレット Margaret Mitchell (米) 作家 (1900～1949)
ミネリ, ライザ Liza Minnelli (米) 歌手・女優 (1946～)
ミラー, アーサー Arthur Miller (米) 劇作家 (1915～)
ミラー, ヘンリー Henry Miller (米) 作家 (1891～1980)
ミル, ジョン・スチュアート John Stuart Mill (英) 哲学者・経済学者 (1806～1873)
ミルトン, ジョン John Milton (英) 詩人 (1608～1674)
ミルン, アラン・アレキサンダー A(lan) A(lexander) Milne (英) 詩人 (1882～1956)
ミレー, ジャン・フランソワ Jean François Millet (仏) 画家 (1814～1875)
ミレー, ジョン・エバレット John Everett Millais (英) 画家 (1829～1896)
ミロ, ホアン Joan Miró (スペイン) 画家 (1893～1983)
ムーア, デミ Demi Moore (米) 女優 (1962～)
ムーア, ヘンリー Henry Moore (英) 彫刻家 (1898～1986)
ムーア, ロジャー Roger Moore (英) 俳優 (1927～)
ムソルグスキー, モデスト Modest Petrovich Mussorgsky (ロシア) 作曲家 (1839～1881)
ムッソリーニ, ベニート Benito Mussolini (伊) ファシスト政治家 (1883～1945)
ムンク, エドワルド Edvard Munch (ノルウェー) 画家 (1863～1944)
メイズ, ウィリー Willie Mays (米) 野球選手 (1931～)
メータ, ズービン Zubin Mehta (インド・米) 指揮者 (1936～)
メーテルリンク, モーリス Maurice Maeterlink (ベルギー) 作家 (1862～1949)
メタリカ Metallica (米) ロックグループ
メルビル, ハーマン Herman Melville (米) 作家 (1819～1891)
メルロポンティ, モーリス Maurice Merleau-Ponty (仏) 哲学者 (1908～1961)
メンデル, グレゴール Gregor Johann Mendel (オーストリア) 植物学者 (1822～1884)
メンデルスゾーン, フェーリクス Felix Mendelssohn (独) 作曲家 (1809～1847)
モア, トーマス Sir Thomas More (英) 政治家 (1478～1535)
孟子(もうし) Mencius, Meng-tzu (中) 思想家 (前372～前289)
毛沢東(もうたくとう) Mao Zedong, Mao Tse-tung (中) 政治家; 中華人民共和国の初代国家主席 (1949～1959) (1893～1976)
モーセ, モーゼ Moses 古代イスラエル民族の指導者・予言者; 生没年不詳
モーツァルト, ウォルフガング・アマデウス Wolfgang Amadeus Mozart (オーストリア) 作曲家 (1756～1791)
モーパッサン, ギイ・ド Guy de Maupassant (仏) 作家 (1850～1893)
モーム, サマセット (William) Somerset Maugham (英) 作家 (1874～1965)
モディリアーニ, アメデオ Amedeo Modigliani (伊) 画家 (1884～1920)
モネ, クロード Claude Monet (仏) 画家 (1840～1926)
モンタナ, ジョー Joe Montana (米) フットボール選手 (1956～)
モンタン, イブ Yves Montand (仏) シャンソン歌手・俳優 (1921～1991)

モンロー, マリリン Marilyn Monroe (米) 女優 (1926〜1962)

ヤ・ユ・ヨ

ヤング, サイ Cy Young (米) 野球選手 (1867〜1955)
ヤング, ニール Neil Young (カナダ) ロック歌手 (1945〜)
ユークリッド Euclid 古代ギリシャの数学者 (前300頃)
ユーゴー, ビクトル Victor Hugo (仏) 詩人・作家 (1802〜1885)
U2 U2 (アイルランド) ロックグループ
ユダ Judas (Iscariot) キリストの十二使徒の1人
ユトリロ, モーリス Maurice Utrillo (仏) 画家 (1883〜1955)
ユング, カール Carl Gustav Jung (スイス) 心理学者 (1875〜1961)
楊貴妃 (ようきひ) Yang Guifei, Yang Kuifei (中) 玄宗の妃 (719〜756)
ヨー・ヨー・マ Yo-Yo Ma (米) チェリスト (1955〜)
ヨハネ・パウロ2世 John Paul II ローマ法王 (1978〜)(1920〜)

ラ

ライアン, ノーラン Nolan Ryan (米) 野球選手 (1947〜)
ライアン, メグ Meg Ryan (米) 女優 (1961〜)
ライト, ウィルバー Wilbur Wright (米) 飛行機開発家の兄弟の兄 (1867〜1912)
ライト, オービル Orville Wright (米) 飛行機開発家の兄弟の弟 (1871〜1948)
ライト, フランク・ロイド Frank Lloyd Wright (米) 建築家 (1867〜1959)
ラウシェンバーグ, ロバート Robert Rauschenberg (米) 画家 (1925〜)
ラッセル, ケン Ken Russell (英) 映画監督 (1927〜)
ラッセル, バートランド Bertrand Russell (英) 数学者・哲学者・平和運動家 (1872〜1970)
ラファエロ Raphael (伊) 画家・建築家 (1483〜1520)
ラブクラフト, ハワード H(oward) P(hillips) Lovecraft (米) SF・ホラー作家 (1890〜1937)
ラフマニノフ, セルゲイ Sergei Vasilevich Rachmaninoff (ロシア) 作曲家 (1873〜1943)
ラベル, モーリス Maurice Ravel (仏) 作曲家 (1875〜1937)
ラボアジエ, アントワーヌ Antoine Laurent Lavoisier (仏) 化学者 (1743〜1794)
ラング, フリッツ Fritz Lang (独) 映画監督 (1890〜1976)
ランボー, アルチュール Arthur Rimbaud (仏) 詩人 (1854〜1891)

リ

リー, スパイク Spike Lee (米) 映画監督 (1957〜)
リー, ビビアン Vivien Leigh (英) 女優 (1913〜1967)
リー, ブルース Bruce Lee (香港) 俳優 (1941〜1973)
リード, キャロル Carol Reed (英) 映画監督 (1906〜1976)
リーブス, キアヌ Keanu Reeves (米) 俳優 (1964〜)
リーン, デビッド David Lean (英) 映画監督 (1908〜1991)
リキテンシュタイン, ロイ Roy Lichtenstein (米) 画家 (1923〜1997)
リスト, フランツ Franz Liszt (ハンガリー) 作曲家・ピアニスト (1811〜1886)
リネカー, ガリー Gary Lineker (英) サッカー選手 (1960〜)
李白 (りはく) Li Po, Li Bo (中) 詩人 (701〜762)
リヒテル, スビャトスラフ Sviatoslav Richter (ロシア) ピアニスト (1915〜1997)
リプケン, カル Cal Ripken, Jr. (米) 野球選手 (1960〜)
リルケ, ライナー・マリア Rainer Maria Rilke (独) 詩人 (1875〜1926)
リンカーン, エイブラハム Abraham Lincoln 米国第16代大統領 (1861〜1865) (1809〜1865)
リンチ, デビッド David Lynch (米) 映画監督 (1946〜)
リンドバーグ, チャールズ Charles A(ugustus) Lindbergh (米) 飛行家 (1902〜1974)

ル

ルイス, カール Carl Lewis (米) 陸上選手 (1961〜)
ルーカス, ジョージ George Lucas (米) 映画監督 (1944〜)
ルース, ベーブ Babe Ruth (米) 野球選手 (1895〜1948)
ルーズベルト, セオドア Theodore Roosevelt 米国第26代大統領 (1901〜1909) (1858〜1919)
ルーズベルト, フランクリン Franklin D(elano) Roosevelt 米国第32代大統領 (1933〜1945) (1882〜1945)
ルービンスタイン, アーサー Art(h)ur Rubinstein (米) ピアニスト (1887〜1982)
ルーベンス, ペーテル Peter Paul Rubens (フランドル) 画家 (1577〜1640)
ルオー, ジョルジュ Georges Rouault (仏) 画家 (1871〜1958)
ル・カレ, ジョン John Le Carré (英) 作家 (1931〜)
ルソー, ジャン・ジャック Jean-Jacques Rousseau (フランス) 哲学者・思想家 (1712〜1778)
ルター, マルティン Martin Luther (独) 宗教改革者 (1483〜1546)
ルドン, オディロン Odilon Redon (仏) 画家・版画家 (1840〜1916)
ルノワール, ジャン Jean Renoir (仏) 映画監督 (1894〜1979)
ルノワール, ピエール・オーギュスト Pierre-Auguste Renoir (仏) 画家 (1841〜1919)
ルメット, シドニー Sidney Lumet (米) 映画監督 (1924〜)

レ

- レイ，マン Man Ray (米) 写真家・画家 (1890〜1976)
- レーガン，ロナルド Ronald Reagan 米国第40代大統領 (1981〜1989) (1911〜)
- レーニン，ウラジーミル Vladimir Ilich Lenin (ロシア) ロシア革命の指導者 (1870〜1924)
- レオナルド・ダ・ビンチ Leonardo da Vinci (伊) 芸術家・科学者 (1452〜1519)
- レッド・ツェッペリン Led Zeppelin (英) ロックグループ
- レッドフォード，ロバート Robert Redford (米) 俳優 (1936〜)
- レッド・ホット・チリ・ペッパーズ Red Hot Chili Peppers (米) ロックグループ
- レディング，オーティス Otis Redding (米) ソウル歌手 (1941〜1967)
- レノン，ジョン John Lennon (英) 元ビートルズのメンバー (1940〜1980)
- レバイン，ジェームズ James Levine (米) 指揮者 (1943〜)
- レマルク，エーリヒ・マリア Erich Maria Remarque (米) 作家 (1898〜1970)
- レモン，ジャック Jack Lemmon (米) 俳優 (1925〜)
- レントゲン，ウィルヘルム・コンラート Wilhelm Conrad Roentgen (独) 物理学者 (1845〜1923)
- レンブラント Rembrandt (van Rijn) (オランダ) 画家 (1606〜1669)

ロ

- ロイド，ハロルド Harold Lloyd (米) 俳優 (1893〜1971)
- ロイド・ウェバー，アンドルー Andrew Lloyd Webber (英) ミュージカル作曲家 (1948〜)
- 老子(ろうし) Laoze, Lao-tzu (中) 思想家・道教 (Taoism) の祖；生没年不詳
- ローズ，ピート Pete Rose (米) 野球選手 (1941〜)
- ロートレック，トゥールーズ Henri de Toulouse Lautrec (仏) 画家 (1864〜1901)
- ローパー，シンディ Cyndi Lauper (米) ポップ歌手 (1953〜)
- ローランサン，マリー Marie Laurencin (仏) 画家 (1883〜1956)
- ローリング・ストーンズ the Rolling Stones (英) ロックグループ
- ローレン，ソフィア Sophia Loren (伊) 女優 (1934〜)
- ローレン，ラルフ Ralph Lauren (米) デザイナー (1939〜)
- ローレンス，D. H. D(avid) H(erbert) Lawrence (英) 作家・詩人 (1885〜1930)
- ローレンツ，コンラート Konrad Lorenz (オーストリア) 動物学者 (1903〜1989)
- ロジャーズ，リチャード Richard Rodgers (米) ミュージカル作曲家 (1902〜1979)
- ロス，ダイアナ Diana Ross (米) ポップ歌手 (1944〜)
- ロス，フィリップ Philip (Milton) Roth (米) 作家 (1933〜)
- ロストロポービチ，ムスティスラフ Mstislav Rostropovich (ロシア) チェリスト (1927〜)
- ロセッティ，ダンテ・ゲイブリエル Dante Gabriel Rossetti (英) 画家・詩人 (1828〜1882)
- ロダン，オーギュスト Auguste Rodin (仏) 彫刻家 (1840〜1917)
- ロック，ジョン John Locke (英) 哲学者 (1632〜1704)
- ロックフェラー，ジョン・デービソン John D(avison) Rockefeller (米) 実業家 (1839〜1937)
- ロッシーニ，ジョアキーノ Gioacchino Rossini (伊) オペラ作曲家 (1792〜1868)
- ロッセリーニ，ロベルト Roberto Rossellini (伊) 映画監督 (1906〜1977)
- ロナウド Ronaldo (ブラジル) サッカー選手 (1976〜)
- ロバーツ，ジュリア Julia Roberts (米) 女優 (1967〜)
- ロビンソン，ジャッキー Jackie Robinson (米) 野球選手 (1919〜1972)
- ロメール，エリック Éric Rohmer (仏) 映画監督 (1920〜)
- ロラン，ロマン Romain Rolland (仏) 作家 (1866〜1944)
- ロリンズ，ソニー Sonny Rollins (米) ジャズミュージシャン (1930〜)
- ロンドン，ジャック Jack London (米) 作家 (1876〜1916)

ワ

- ワーウィック，ディオンヌ Dionne Warwick (米) ポップ歌手 (1941〜)
- ワーグナー，リヒャルト Richard Wagner (独) 作曲家 (1813〜1883)
- ワーズワース，ウィリアム William Wordsworth (英) 詩人 (1770〜1850)
- ワイエス，アンドルー Andrew Wyeth (米) 画家 (1917〜)
- ワイダ，アンジェイ Andrzej Wajda (ポーランド) 映画監督 (1926〜)
- ワイラー，ウィリアム William Wyler (米) 映画監督 (1902〜1981)
- ワイルダー，ビリー Billy Wilder (米) 映画監督 (1906〜)
- ワイルダー，ローラ・インガルス Laura Ingalls Wilder (米) 児童文学作家 (1867〜1957)
- ワイルド，オスカー Oscar Wilde (アイルランド) 作家 (1854〜1900)
- ワシントン，ジョージ George Washington 軍人・米国初代大統領 (1789〜1797) (1732〜1799)
- ワット，ジェームズ James Watt (英) 技師；蒸気機関車を発明 (1736〜1819)
- ワトソン，トム Tom Watson (米) プロゴルファー (1949〜)
- ワルター，ブルーノ Bruno Walter (米) 指揮者 (1876〜1962)
- ワンダー，スティービー Stevie Wonder (米) 歌手 (1950〜)

世界の国名

＊一部日本が承認していない国の国名も含む．

ア行

アイスランド Iceland（公式名 the Republic of Iceland アイスランド共和国）
アイルランド Ireland
アゼルバイジャン Azerbaijan（公式名 the Azerbaijan Republic アゼルバイジャン共和国）
アフガニスタン Afghanistan（公式名 the Islamic State of Afghanistan アフガニスタン・イスラム国）
アメリカ合衆国（米国）the United States（公式名 the United States of America アメリカ合衆国）
アラブ首長国連邦 the United Arab Emirates
アルジェリア Algeria（公式名 the Democratic People's Republic of Algeria アルジェリア民主人民共和国）
アルゼンチン Argentina（公式名 the Argentine Republic アルゼンチン共和国）
アルバニア Albania（公式名 the Republic of Albania アルバニア共和国）
アルメニア Armenia（公式名 the Republic of Armenia アルメニア共和国）
アンゴラ Angola（公式名 the Republic of Angola アンゴラ共和国）
アンティグア・バーブーダ Antigua and Barbuda
アンドラ Andorra（公式名 the Principality of Andorra アンドラ公国）
イエメン Yemen（公式名 the Republic of Yemen イエメン共和国）
イギリス（英国）the United Kingdom（公式名 the United Kingdom of Great Britain and Northern Ireland グレートブリテンおよび北部アイルランド連合王国）
イスラエル Israel（公式名 the State of Israel イスラエル国）
イタリア Italy（公式名 the Republic of Italy イタリア共和国）
イラク Iraq（公式名 the Republic of Iraq イラク共和国）
イラン Iran（公式名 the Islamic Republic of Iran イラン・イスラム共和国）
インド India
インドネシア Indonesia（公式名 the Republic of Indonesia インドネシア共和国）
ウガンダ Uganda（公式名 the Republic of Uganda ウガンダ共和国）
ウクライナ Ukraine
ウズベキスタン Uzbekistan（公式名 the Republic of Uzbekistan ウズベキスタン共和国）
ウルグアイ Uruguay（公式名 the Oriental Republic of Uruguay ウルグアイ東方共和国）
エクアドル Ecuador（公式名 the Republic of Ecuador エクアドル共和国）
エジプト Egypt（公式名 the Arab Republic of Egypt エジプト・アラブ共和国）
エストニア Estonia（公式名 the Republic of Estonia エストニア共和国）
エチオピア Ethiopia（公式名 the Federal Democratic Republic of Ethiopia エチオピア連邦民主共和国）
エリトリア Eritrea（公式名 the State of Eritrea エリトリア国）
エルサルバドル El Salvador（公式名 the Republic of El Salvador エルサルバドル共和国）
オーストラリア Australia（公式名 the Commonwealth of Australia オーストラリア連邦）
オーストリア Austria（公式名 the Republic of Austria オーストリア共和国）
オマーン Oman（公式名 the Sultanate of Oman オマーン国）
オランダ the Netherlands（公式名 the Kingdom of the Netherlands オランダ王国）

カ行

ガーナ Ghana（公式名 the Republic of Ghana ガーナ共和国）
カーボベルデ Cape Verde（公式名 the Republic of Cape Verde カーボベルデ共和国）
ガイアナ Guyana（公式名 the Co-operative Republic of Guyana ガイアナ協同共和国）
カザフスタン Kazakhstan（公式名 the Republic of Kazakhstan カザフスタン共和国）
カタール Qatar（公式名 the State of Qatar カタール国）
カナダ Canada
ガボン Gabon（公式名 the Gabonese Republic ガボン共和国）
カメルーン Cameroon（公式名 the Republic of Cameroon カメルーン共和国）
韓国 South Korea（公式名 the Republic of Korea 大韓民国）
ガンビア (The) Gambia（公式名 the Republic of The Gambia ガンビア共和国）
カンボジア Cambodia（公式名 the Kingdom of Cambodia カンボジア王国）
北朝鮮 North Korea（公式名 the Democratic People's Republic of Korea 朝鮮民主主義人民共和国）
ギニア Guinea（公式名 the Republic of Guinea ギニア共和国）
ギニアビサウ Guinea-Bissau（公式名 the Re-

public of Guinea-Bissau ギニアビサウ共和国)
キプロス Cyprus (公式名 the Republic of Cyprus キプロス共和国)
キューバ Cuba (公式名 the Republic of Cuba キューバ共和国)
ギリシャ Greece (公式名 the Hellenic Republic ギリシャ共和国)
キリバス Kiribati (公式名 the Republic of Kiribati キリバス共和国)
キルギス Kyrgyzstan (公式名 the Kyrgyz Republic キルギス共和国)
グアテマラ Guatemala (公式名 the Republic of Guatemala グアテマラ共和国)
クウェート Kuwait (公式名 the State of Kuwait クウェート国)
グルジア Georgia
グレナダ Grenada
クロアチア Croatia (公式名 the Republic of Croatia クロアチア共和国)
ケニア Kenya (公式名 the Republic of Kenya ケニア共和国)
コートジボワール Côte d'Ivoire (公式名 the Republic of Côte d'Ivoire コートジボワール共和国)
コスタリカ Costa Rica (公式名 the Republic of Costa Rica コスタリカ共和国)
コモロ the Comoros (公式名 the Federal Islamic Republic of the Comoros コモロ・イスラム連邦共和国)
コロンビア Colombia (公式名 the Republic of Colombia コロンビア共和国)
コンゴ the Congo (公式名 the Republic of the Congo コンゴ共和国)
コンゴ民主共和国 the Democratic Republic of the Congo

サ行

サウジアラビア Saudi Arabia (公式名 the Kingdom of Saudi Arabia サウジアラビア王国)
サモア Samoa (公式名 the Independent State of Samoa サモア独立国)
サントメ・プリンシペ São Tomé and Príncipe (公式名 the Democratic Republic of São Tomé and Príncipe サントメ・プリンシペ民主共和国)
ザンビア Zambia (公式名 the Republic of Zambia ザンビア共和国)
サンマリノ San Marino (公式名 the Republic of San Marino サンマリノ共和国)
シエラレオネ Sierra Leone (公式名 the Republic of Sierra Leone シエラレオネ共和国)
ジブチ Djibouti (公式名 the Republic of Djibouti ジブチ共和国)
ジャマイカ Jamaica
シリア Syria (公式名 the Syrian Arab Republic シリア・アラブ共和国)
シンガポール Singapore (公式名 the Republic of Singapore シンガポール共和国)
ジンバブエ Zimbabwe (公式名 the Republic of Zimbabwe ジンバブエ共和国)
スイス Switzerland (公式名 the Swiss Confederation スイス連邦)
スウェーデン Sweden (公式名 the Kingdom of Sweden スウェーデン王国)
スーダン the Sudan (公式名 the Republic of the Sudan スーダン共和国)
スペイン Spain
スリナム Suriname (公式名 the Republic of Suriname スリナム共和国)
スリランカ Sri Lanka (公式名 the Democratic Socialist Republic of Sri Lanka スリランカ民主社会主義共和国)
スロバキア Slovakia (公式名 the Slovak Republic スロバキア共和国)
スロベニア Slovenia (公式名 the Republic of Slovenia スロベニア共和国)
スワジランド Swaziland (公式名 the Kingdom of Swaziland スワジランド王国)
セイシェル Seychelles (公式名 the Republic of Seychelles セイシェル共和国)
赤道ギニア Equatorial Guinea (公式名 the Republic of Equatorial Guinea 赤道ギニア共和国)
セネガル Senegal (公式名 the Republic of Senegal セネガル共和国)
セントクリストファー・ネイビス Saint Christopher and Nevis (または Saint Kitts and Nevis セントキッツ・ネイビス)
セントビンセント・グレナディーン諸島 Saint Vincent and the Grenadines
セントルシア Saint Lucia
ソマリア Somalia (公式名 the Somali Democratic Republic ソマリア民主共和国)
ソロモン諸島 Solomon Islands

タ行

タイ Thailand (公式名 the Kingdom of Thailand タイ王国)
タイワン (台湾) Taiwan (公式名 the Republic of China 中華民国)
タジキスタン Tajikistan (公式名 the Republic of Tajikistan タジキスタン共和国)
タンザニア Tanzania (公式名 the United Republic of Tanzania タンザニア連合共和国)
チェコ共和国 the Czech Republic
チャド Chad (公式名 the Republic of Chad チャド共和国)
中央アフリカ共和国 the Central African Republic
中国 China (公式名 the People's Republic of China 中華人民共和国)
チュニジア Tunisia (公式名 the Republic of Tunisia チュニジア共和国)
チリ Chile (公式名 the Republic of Chile チリ共和国)
ツバル Tuvalu
デンマーク Denmark (公式名 the Kingdom of Denmark デンマーク王国)
ドイツ Germany (公式名 the Federal Republic of Germany ドイツ連邦共和国)
トーゴ Togo (公式名 the Republic of Togo トーゴ共和国)
ドミニカ共和国 the Dominican Republic

ドミニカ国 Dominica (公式名 the Commonwealth of Dominica ドミニカ国)
トリニダード・トバゴ Trinidad and Tobago (公式名 the Republic of Trinidad and Tobago トリニダード・トバゴ共和国)
トルクメニスタン Turkmenistan
トルコ Turkey (公式名 the Republic of Turkey トルコ共和国)
トンガ Tonga (公式名 the Kingdom of Tonga トンガ王国)

ナ行

ナイジェリア Nigeria (公式名 the Federal Republic of Nigeria ナイジェリア連邦共和国)
ナウル Nauru (公式名 the Republic of Nauru ナウル共和国)
ナミビア Namibia (公式名 the Republic of Namibia ナミビア共和国)
ニカラグア Nicaragua (公式名 the Republic of Nicaragua ニカラグア共和国)
ニジェール Niger (公式名 the Republic of Niger ニジェール共和国)
日本 Japan
ニュージーランド New Zealand
ネパール Nepal (公式名 the Kingdom of Nepal ネパール王国)
ノルウェー Norway (公式名 the Kingdom of Norway ノルウェー王国)

ハ行

バーレーン Bahrain (公式名 the State of Bahrain バーレーン国)
ハイチ Haiti (公式名 the Republic of Haiti ハイチ共和国)
パキスタン Pakistan (公式名 the Islamic Republic of Pakistan パキスタン・イスラム共和国)
バチカン市国 Vatican City
パナマ Panama (公式名 the Republic of Panama パナマ共和国)
バヌアツ Vanuatu (公式名 the Republic of Vanuatu バヌアツ共和国)
バハマ the Bahamas (公式名 the Commonwealth of the Bahamas バハマ国)
パプアニューギニア Papua New Guinea
パラオ Palau (公式名 the Republic of Palau パラオ共和国；別名ベラウ Belau)
パラグアイ Paraguay (公式名 the Republic of Paraguay パラグアイ共和国)
バルバドス Barbados
ハンガリー Hungary (公式名 the Republic of Hungary ハンガリー共和国)
バングラデシュ Bangladesh (公式名 the People's Republic of Bangladesh バングラデシュ人民共和国)
フィジー Fiji (公式名 the Republic of Fiji フィジー共和国)
フィリピン the Philippines (公式名 the Republic of the Philippines フィリピン共和国)
フィンランド Finland (公式名 the Republic of Finland フィンランド共和国)
ブータン Bhutan (公式名 the Kingdom of Bhutan ブータン王国)
ブラジル Brazil (公式名 the Federative Republic of Brazil ブラジル連邦共和国)
フランス France (公式名 the French Republic フランス共和国)
ブルガリア Bulgaria (公式名 the Republic of Bulgaria ブルガリア共和国)
ブルキナファソ Burkina Faso
ブルネイ Brunei (公式名 Negara Brunei Darussalam ブルネイ・ダルサラーム国)
ブルンジ Burundi (公式名 the Republic of Burundi ブルンジ共和国)
ベトナム Vietnam (公式名 the Socialist Republic of Vietnam ベトナム社会主義共和国)
ベナン Benin (公式名 the Republic of Benin ベナン共和国)
ベネズエラ Venezuela (公式名 the Bolivarian Republic of Venezuela ベネズエラ・ボリバル共和国)
ベラルーシ Belarus (公式名 the Republic of Belarus ベラルーシ共和国)
ベリーズ Belize
ペルー Peru (公式名 the Republic of Peru ペルー共和国)
ベルギー Belgium (公式名 the Kingdom of Belgium ベルギー王国)
ポーランド Poland (公式名 the Republic of Poland ポーランド共和国)
ボスニア・ヘルツェゴビナ Bosnia and Herzegovina
ボツワナ Botswana (公式名 the Republic of Botswana ボツワナ共和国)
ボリビア Bolivia (公式名 the Republic of Bolivia ボリビア共和国)
ポルトガル Portugal (公式名 the Portuguese Republic ポルトガル共和国)
ホンジュラス Honduras (公式名 the Republic of Honduras ホンジュラス共和国)

マ行

マーシャル諸島 Marshall Islands (公式名 the Republic of the Marshall Islands マーシャル諸島共和国)
マケドニア Macedonia (公式名 the (Former Yugoslav) Republic of Macedonia マケドニア（旧ユーゴスラビア）共和国)
マダガスカル Madagascar (公式名 the Republic of Madagascar マダガスカル共和国)
マラウイ Malawi (公式名 the Republic of Malawi マラウイ共和国)
マリ Mali (公式名 the Republic of Mali マリ共和国)
マルタ Malta (公式名 the Republic of Malta マルタ共和国)
マレーシア Malaysia
ミクロネシア連邦 Micronesia (公式名 the Federated States of Micronesia ミクロネシア連邦)
南アフリカ South Africa (公式名 the Republic of South Africa 南アフリカ共和国)
ミャンマー Myanmar (公式名 the Union of

Myanmar ミャンマー連邦)
メキシコ Mexico (公式名 the United Mexican States メキシコ合衆国)
モーリシャス Mauritius (公式名 the Republic of Mauritius モーリシャス共和国)
モーリタニア Mauritania (公式名 the Islamic Republic of Mauritania モーリタニア・イスラム共和国)
モザンビーク Mozambique (公式名 the Republic of Mozambique モザンビーク共和国)
モナコ Monaco (公式名 the Principality of Monaco モナコ公国)
モルディブ the Maldives (公式名 the Republic of Maldives モルディブ共和国)
モルドバ Moldova (公式名 the Republic of Moldova モルドバ共和国)
モロッコ Morocco (公式名 the Kingdom of Morocco モロッコ王国)
モンゴル Mongolia

ヤ行・ラ行

ユーゴスラビア Yugoslavia (公式名 the Federal Republic of Yugoslavia ユーゴスラビア連邦共和国)
ヨルダン Jordan (公式名 the Hashemite Kingdom of Jordan ヨルダン・ハシミテ王国)
ラオス Laos (公式名 the Lao People's Democratic Republic ラオス人民民主共和国)
ラトビア Latvia (公式名 the Republic of Latvia ラトビア共和国)
リトアニア Lithuania (公式名 the Republic of Lithuania リトアニア共和国)
リビア Libya (公式名 the Socialist People's Libyan Arab Jamahiriya 社会主義人民リビア・アラブ国)
リヒテンシュタイン Liechtenstein (公式名 the Principality of Liechtenstein リヒテンシュタイン公国)
リベリア Liberia (公式名 the Republic of Liberia リベリア共和国)
ルーマニア Romania
ルクセンブルク Luxembourg (公式名 the Grand Duchy of Luxembourg ルクセンブルク大公国)
ルワンダ Rwanda (公式名 the Republic of Rwanda ルワンダ共和国)
レソト Lesotho (公式名 the Kingdom of Lesotho レソト王国)
レバノン Lebanon (公式名 the Republic of Lebanon レバノン共和国)
ロシア Russia (公式名 the Russian Federation ロシア連邦)

世界の都市名

ア行

アクラ Accra ガーナの首都
アシガバード Ashgabad トルクメニスタンの首都
アジスアベバ Addis Ababa エチオピアの首都
アスタナ Astana カザフスタンの首都
アスマラ Asmara エリトリアの首都
アスンシオン Asunción パラグアイの首都
アテネ Athens ギリシャの首都
アデレード Adelaide オーストラリアの都市
アピア Apia サモアの首都
アブジャ Abuja ナイジェリアの首都
アブダビ Abu Dhabi アラブ首長国連邦の首都
アムステルダム Amsterdam オランダの首都
アルジェ Algiers アルジェリアの首都
アンカラ Ankara トルコの首都
アンカレッジ Anchorage 米国の都市
アンタナナリボ Antananarivo マダガスカルの首都
アンドララベラ Andorra la Vella アンドラの首都
アンマン Amman ヨルダンの首都
イスラマバード Islamabad パキスタンの首都
インスブルック Innsbruck オーストリアの都市
ウィーン Vienna オーストリアの首都
ウィントフック Windhoek ナミビアの首都
ウェリントン Wellington ニュージーランドの首都
ウランバートル Ulan Bator モンゴルの首都
エジンバラ Edinburgh 英国の都市
エルサレム Jerusalem イスラエルの首都(国際的には未承認)
エレバン Yerevan アルメニアの首都
オークランド[1] Auckland ニュージーランドの都市
オークランド[2] Oakland 米国の都市
オークリッジ Oak Ridge 米国の都市
オスロ Oslo ノルウェーの首都
オタワ Ottawa カナダの首都
オックスフォード Oxford 英国の都市

カ行

カーディフ Cardiff 英国の都市
カイロ Cairo エジプトの首都
カオシュン (高雄) Kaohsiung 台湾の都市
カストリーズ Castries セントルシアの首都
カトマンズ Kathmandu ネパールの首都
カブール Kabul アフガニスタンの首都
カラカス Caracas ベネズエラの首都
カルガリー Calgary カナダの都市
カンタベリー Canterbury 英国の都市
カンパラ Kampala ウガンダの首都
キーウエスト Key West 米国の都市
キエフ Kiev ウクライナの首都
キガリ Kigali ルワンダの首都
キシニョフ Kishinev モルドバの首都
キト Quito エクアドルの首都
キャンベラ Canberra オーストラリアの首都
キングスタウン Kingstown セントビンセント・グレナディーン諸島の首都
キングストン Kingston ジャマイカの首都
キンシャサ Kinshasa コンゴ民主共和国の首都
グアテマラシティ Guatemala City グアテマラの首都
クアラルンプール Kuala Lumpur マレーシアの首都
クウェート Kuwait (City) クウェートの首都
グラスゴー Glasgow 英国の都市
クリーブランド Cleveland 米国の都市
ゲティスバーグ Gettysburg 米国の都市
ケルン Cologne ドイツの都市
ケンブリッジ Cambridge 英国の都市;米国の都市
コナクリ Conakry ギニアの首都
コペンハーゲン Copenhagen デンマークの首都
コロール Koror パラオの首都
コロラドスプリングズ Colorado Springs 米国の都市
コンコード Concord 米国の都市

サ行

サウサンプトン Southampton 英国の都市
ザグレブ Zagreb クロアチアの首都
サナア Sana'a イエメンの首都
サラエボ Sarajevo ボスニア・ヘルツェゴビナの首都
ザルツブルグ Salzburg オーストリアの都市
サンクトペテルブルク St. Petersburg ロシアの都市
サンサルバドル San Salvador エルサルバドルの首都
サンタバーバラ Santa Barbara 米国の都市
サンタフェデボゴタ Santa Fé de Bogotá コロンビアの首都
サンティアゴ Santiago チリの首都
サンディエゴ San Diego 米国の都市
サントドミンゴ Santo Domingo ドミニカ共和国の首都
サントメ São Tomé サントメ・プリンシペの首都
サンパウロ São Paulo ブラジルの都市
サンファン San Juan プエルトリコの中心都市
サンフランシスコ San Francisco 米国の都市
サンホセ San José コスタリカの首都
サンマリノ San Marino サンマリノの首都

シアトル Seattle 米国の都市
シェフィールド Sheffield 英国の都市
シカゴ Chicago 米国の都市
シドニー Sydney オーストラリアの都市
ジブチ Djibouti ジブチの首都
ジャカルタ Jakarta インドネシアの首都
シャンハイ (上海) Shanghai 中国の都市
ジュネーブ Geneva スイスの都市
ジョージタウン Georgetown ガイアナの首都
シンガポール Singapore (City) シンガポールの首都
シンシナチ Cincinnati 米国の都市
スコピエ Skopje マケドニアの首都
ストックホルム Stockholm スウェーデンの首都
ストラトフォードアポンエーボン Stratford-upon-Avon 英国の都市
スバ Suva フィジーの首都
スリジャヤワルダナプラコッテ Sri Jayewardenepura Kotte スリランカの首都
セントアンドルーズ St. Andrews 英国の都市
セントジョージズ St. George's グレナダの首都
セントジョンズ St. John's アンティグア・バーブーダの首都；カナダの都市
セントルイス St. Louis 米国の都市
ソウル Seoul 韓国の首都
ソフィア Sofia ブルガリアの首都

タ行

ダーウィン Darwin オーストラリアの都市
タイペイ (台北) Taipei 台湾の首都
ダカール Dakar セネガルの首都
タコマ Tacoma 米国の都市
タシケント Tashkent ウズベキスタンの首都
ダッカ Dhaka バングラデシュの首都
ダブリン Dublin アイルランドの首都
ダマスカス Damascus シリアの首都
ダラス Dallas 米国の都市
タラワ Tarawa キリバスの首都
タリン Tallinn エストニアの首都
ダルエスサラーム Dar es Salaam タンザニアの首都
チュニス Tunis チュニジアの首都
ティラナ Tirana アルバニアの首都
ティンプー Thimphu ブータンの首都
テグシガルパ Tegucigalpa ホンジュラスの首都
デトロイト Detroit 米国の都市
テヘラン Tehran イランの首都
東京 Tokyo 日本の首都
ドゥシャンベ Dushanbe タジキスタンの首都
ドーハ Doha カタールの首都
ドーバー Dover 英国の都市；米国の都市
トビリシ Tbilisi グルジアの首都
トリノ Turin イタリアの都市
トリポリ Tripoli リビアの首都；レバノンの都市
トロント Toronto カナダの都市

ナ行

ナイロビ Nairobi ケニアの首都
ナッソー Nassau バハマの首都
ニアメ Niamey ニジェールの首都
ニコシア Nicosia キプロスの首都
ニューオーリンズ New Orleans 米国の都市
ニューカッスル Newcastle 英国の都市；オーストラリアの都市
ニューデリー New Delhi インドの首都
ニューヨーク New York 米国の都市
ヌアクショット Nouakchott モーリタニアの首都
ヌクアロファ Nuku'alofa トンガの首都
ノッチンガム Nottingham 英国の都市

ハ行

ハーグ The Hague オランダの都市
バークレー Berkeley 米国の都市
パース Perth オーストラリアの都市
バーミンガム Birmingham 英国の都市；米国の都市
バクー Baku アゼルバイジャンの首都
バグダッド Baghdad イラクの首都
パサディナ Pasadena 米国の都市
バセテール Basseterre セントクリストファー・ネイビスの首都
バッファロー Buffalo 米国の都市
パナマ Panama (City) パナマの首都
ハノイ Hanoi ベトナムの首都
ハバナ Havana キューバの首都
ハボローネ Gaborone ボツワナの首都
バマコ Bamako マリの首都
ハラーレ Harare ジンバブエの首都
パラマリボ Paramaribo スリナムの首都
パリ Paris フランスの首都
パリキール Palikir ミクロネシア連邦の首都
バルセロナ Barcelona スペインの都市
ハルツーム Khartoum スーダンの首都
バレッタ Valletta マルタの首都
バンギ Bangui 中央アフリカ共和国の首都
バンクーバー Vancouver カナダの都市
バンコク Bangkok タイの首都
バンジュル Banjul ガンビアの首都
バンダルスリブガワン Bandar Seri Begawan ブルネイの首都
ハンブルク Hamburg ドイツの都市
ビエンチャン Vientiane ラオスの首都
ビクトリア Victoria セイシェルの首都；カナダの都市
ビサウ Bissau ギニアビサウの首都
ビシュケク Bishkek キルギスの首都
ピッツバーグ Pittsburgh 米国の都市
ヒューストン Houston 米国の都市
ピョンヤン (平壌) Pyongyang 北朝鮮の首都
ビリニュス Vilnius リトアニアの首都
ファドゥーツ Vaduz リヒテンシュタインの首都
フィラデルフィア Philadelphia 米国の都市
ブエノスアイレス Buenos Aires アルゼンチンの首都
ブカレスト Bucharest ルーマニアの首都
プサン (釜山) Pusan 韓国の都市
ブジュンブラ Bujumbura ブルンジの首都
ブダペスト Budapest ハンガリーの首都
フナフチ Funafuti ツバルの首都
プノンペン Phnom Penh カンボジアの首都
プライア Praia カーボベルデの首都
ブラザビル Brazzaville コンゴの首都
ブラジリア Brasilia ブラジルの首都

ブラチスラバ Bratislava スロバキアの首都
プラハ Prague チェコ共和国の首都
フランクフルト(アムマイン) Frankfurt (am Main) ドイツの都市
フリータウン Freetown シエラレオネの首都
ブリストル Bristol 英国の都市
ブリスベーン Brisbane オーストラリアの都市
ブリッジタウン Bridgetown バルバドスの首都
プリマス Plymouth 英国の都市
ブリュッセル Brussels ベルギーの首都
プリンストン Princeton 米国の都市
プレトリア Pretoria 南アフリカの首都
ベイルート Beirut レバノンの首都
ベオグラード Belgrade ユーゴスラビアの首都
ペキン (北京) Beijing, Peking 中国の首都
ベニス Venice イタリアの都市
ヘルシンキ Helsinki フィンランドの首都
ベルファスト Belfast 英国の都市
ベルモパン Belmopan ベリーズの首都
ベルリン Berlin ドイツの首都
ベルン Bern スイスの首都
ホーチミン Ho Chi Minh City ベトナムの都市
ポーツマス Portsmouth 英国の都市
ポートオブスペイン Port of Spain トリニダード・トバゴの首都
ポートビラ Port Vila バヌアツの首都
ポートモレスビー Port Moresby パプアニューギニアの首都
ポートルイス Port Louis モーリシャスの首都
ボストン Boston 米国の都市
ホニアラ Honiara ソロモン諸島の首都
ボルチモア Baltimore 米国の都市
ポルトープランス Port-au-Prince ハイチの首都
ポルトノボ Porto-Novo ベナンの首都
ホンコン (香港) Hong Kong 中国の特別行政区

マ行

マイアミ Miami 米国の都市
マカオ Macao 中国の特別行政区
マジュロ Majuro マーシャル諸島の首都
マスカット Muscat オマーンの首都
マセル Maseru レソトの首都
マドリード Madrid スペインの首都
マナーマ Manama バーレーンの首都
マナグア Managua ニカラグアの首都
マニラ Manila フィリピンの首都
マプート Maputo モザンビークの首都
マラボ Malabo 赤道ギニアの首都
マレ Male モルディブの首都
マンチェスター Manchester 英国の都市
ミネアポリス Minneapolis 米国の都市
ミュンヘン Munich ドイツの都市
ミラノ Milan イタリアの都市
ミルウォーキー Milwaukee 米国の都市
ミンスク Minsk ベラルーシの首都
ムババネ Mbabane スワジランドの首都
メキシコシティ Mexico City メキシコの首都
メルボルン Melbourne オーストラリアの都市
モガディシュ Mogadishu ソマリアの首都
モスクワ Moscow ロシアの首都
モナコ Monaco モナコの首都
モロニ Moroni コモロの首都
モンテビデオ Montevideo ウルグアイの首都
モントリオール Montreal カナダの都市
モンロビア Monrovia リベリアの首都

ヤ行

ヤウンデ Yaoundé カメルーンの首都
ヤムスクロ Yamoussoukro コートジボワールの首都
ヤレン Yalen ナウルの首都
ヤンゴン Yangon ミャンマーの首都

ラ行

ラスベガス Las Vegas 米国の都市
ラパス La Paz ボリビアの首都 (法律上の首都はスクレ Sucre)
ラバト Rabat モロッコの首都
ランカスター Lancaster 英国の都市
リーズ Leeds 英国の都市
リーブルビル Libreville ガボンの首都
リオデジャネイロ Rio de Janeiro ブラジルの都市
リガ Riga ラトビアの首都
リスボン Lisbon ポルトガルの首都
リバプール Liverpool 英国の都市
リマ Lima ペルーの首都
リヤド Riyadh サウジアラビアの首都
リュブリャナ Ljubljana スロベニアの首都
リロングウェ Lilongwe マラウイの首都
ルアンダ Luanda アンゴラの首都
ルクセンブルク Luxembourg ルクセンブルクの首都
ルサカ Lusaka ザンビアの首都
レイキャビク Reykjavik アイスランドの首都
ローマ Rome イタリアの首都
ロサンゼルス Los Angeles 米国の都市
ロソー Roseau ドミニカ国の首都
ロッテルダム Rotterdam オランダの都市
ロメ Lomé トーゴの首都
ロングビーチ Long Beach 米国の都市
ロンドン London 英国の首都
ロンドンデリー Londonderry 英国の都市

ワ・ン

ワガドゥーグー Ouagadougou ブルキナファソの首都
ワシントン D.C. Washington, D.C. 米国の首都
ワルシャワ Warsaw ポーランドの首都
ンジャメナ N'Djamena チャドの首都

場面・状況別会話目次

CD収録 各トピックの番号は付属の CD のトラックナンバーと一致しています

● 生活一般に関するトピック

1. 買い物 …………………………………… 1682
2. 寿司（ず）とそば ……………………… 1684
3. 旅行 ……………………………………… 1686
4. アルバイト ……………………………… 1688
5. 携帯電話 ………………………………… 1690
6. 恋愛 ……………………………………… 1692
7. 病気とけが ……………………………… 1694
8. 健康と美容 ……………………………… 1696
9. コンピュータ …………………………… 1698
10. インターネット ………………………… 1700

● 趣味・娯楽に関するトピック

11. ポップス ………………………………… 1702
12. 映画 ……………………………………… 1704
13. 漫画とアニメ …………………………… 1706
14. ファッション …………………………… 1708
15. ヘアスタイル …………………………… 1710
16. カラオケ ………………………………… 1712
17. 占い ……………………………………… 1714
18. 料理 ……………………………………… 1716
19. 写真 ……………………………………… 1718
20. ペット …………………………………… 1720
21. ミステリー ……………………………… 1722

● 自分の意見を述べたり説明したりするトピック

22. 日本の家と部屋 ………………………… 1724
23. 衣服 ……………………………………… 1726
24. 性格 ……………………………………… 1728
25. 就職と仕事 ……………………………… 1730
26. 天候 ……………………………………… 1732
27. 地震（自然災害） ……………………… 1734
28. ごみとリサイクル ……………………… 1736
29. 環境問題 ………………………………… 1738
30. 核問題 …………………………………… 1740

● 学校［留学］生活やコミュニケーションに関するトピック

31. 試験と成績 ……………………………… 1742
32. いじめ・不登校 ………………………… 1744
33. ALT (Assistant Language Teacher) …… 1746
34. クラブ活動 ……………………………… 1748
35. ボランティア活動 ……………………… 1750
36. ホームステイ …………………………… 1752
37. 留学（1）〈留学前〉 …………………… 1754
38. 留学（2）〈留学先〉 …………………… 1756
39. パーティー ……………………………… 1758
40. 自己紹介 ………………………………… 1760
41. ボディーランゲージ …………………… 1762
42. 掲示 ……………………………………… 1764
43. ディスカッション ……………………… 1766
44. ディベート ……………………………… 1770
45. スピーチ ………………………………… 1774

場面・状況別会話 ❶

●買い物

> Do they sell things cheaply?

> Oh, yeah. They often have sales.

Ann : Osamu, I just moved here, so I don't know where I can go shopping.
アン : 修，ここに引っ越してきたばかりなので，どこに買い物に行ったらよいのか分からないんだけど．
Osamu : Well, you can get daily necessities at the convenience store right in front of the 2-chome bus stop.
修 : そうだね．日用品は2丁目のバス停のちょうど前にあるコンビニで買えるよ．
Ann : OK. That's really nice. But how about clothes and furniture?
アン : そう．それは本当にいいわねえ．だけど，衣服や家具はどうなの？
Osamu : There are some department stores around the station. If you want to save money, you can go to the discount stores on the main street. I always shop at Irohaya.
修 : 駅の周りにデパートがいくつかあるよ．お金を節約したければ，大通りのディスカウントストアに行けばいいよ．僕はいつもいろは屋で買い物をするんだ．
Ann : What kinds of sections do they have?
アン : その店にはどんな売り場があるの？
Osamu : They have a food section on the first floor. On the second floor you can find clothes, furniture and electrical appliances.
修 : 1階は食料品売り場があるよ．2階には衣類，家具，そして電気製品があるんだ．
Ann : Do they sell things cheaply?
アン : 安く売っているの？
Osamu : Oh, yeah. They often have sales. I got this pair of sneakers very cheap.
修 : うん．よくセールをやるんだ．僕はこのスニーカーをとても安く買ったよ．

★ミニ知識★

様々なセール

欧米でも人々は安い物を求めてセールやバーゲンに集まります．日本にもあるクリスマスセール（Christmas sale），開店セール（opening sale），在庫一掃セール（clearance sale）などのほかに，感謝祭セール（Thanksgiving sale），復活祭セール（Easter sale）や，新学期に学用品などを安く売る新学期セール（back-to-school sale）などがあります．ただし，お中元セールやお歳暮セールといったものはありません．セールやバーゲンの情報は，Sunday paperと呼ばれる新聞の日曜版に広告としてよく掲載されています．また，25¢ OFF（25セント引き）などと書かれたcouponとよばれる割引券が商品の広告についていることも多く，それを切り取って財布の中に入れておく人もいます．

表現集

❶買い物に関する一般的な表現

1. それは本当にいい買い物だったね.	That was really a good buy. / That was a real bargain.
2. 眼鏡はどこで買うことを勧めますか.	Where do you recommend I buy a pair of glasses?
3. テレビはどこでいちばん安く買えますか.	Where can I get the cheapest TV set?
4. (高い買い物をして) だまされました.	I got ripped off.
5. 友達と新宿にウインドーショッピングに行きました.	I went window shopping in Shinjuku with my friends.
6. このスカーフはセール [バーゲン] で買ったんです. 30パーセント引きでした.	I got this scarf on sale. It was 30 percent off.
7. その店ではこの金曜日から在庫一掃セールをやります.	The store has a clearance sale starting this Friday.
8. よく衝動買いをしてしまいます.	I often buy things on impulse.

❷日本での買い物に関する表現

1. 日本では物を買うときに消費税を払わなければなりません.	In Japan you must pay consumption tax when you buy things.
2. 日本中のコンビニでお弁当を買うことができます.	You can get 「precooked meals [packed lunches] at convenience stores all over Japan.
3. 通信販売で買い物をする人たちの数が増えつつあります.	The number of people who buy things by mail order is increasing.
4. きょうは肉売り場で10パーセントの割引セールをしています.	Today they have a 10 percent off sale in the meat section.

❸店員との会話で使う表現

1. 見てるだけです.	I'm just looking [browsing].
2. 文具売り場は何階ですか.	What [Which] floor is the stationery section on?
3. この品の在庫はありますか.	Is this item in stock?
4. ショーケースの中の時計を見せてもらえますか.	Can I take a look at the watches in the showcase?
5. これの色違い [Sサイズ] はありますか.	Do you have this 「in another color [in (a) small]?
6. これは割引してもらえますか.	Can you give me a 「special price [discount] on this?
7. これを贈り物用に包んでいただけますか.	Would you gift-wrap this?
8. この時計をください.	I'll take this watch.
9. これを取っておいていただけますか.	Could you keep this for me?
10. (買うかどうかを) 考えます.	I'll 「think it over [give it some thought].
11. ごめんなさい. またにします (→きょうは決められません).	I'm sorry. I can't make up my mind today.
12. (レジで) 全部でおいくらですか.	How much do I owe you altogether?
13. クレジットカードは使えますか.	Do you accept credit cards?
14. 分割払いにできますか.	Can I pay on the installment plan?
15. おつりの額は正しいですか.	Is the amount of change correct?

場面・状況別会話 ❷

●寿司(ずし)とそば

> How do we order sushi?

> You can pick up any dish passing by on the conveyor.

(Sharon is trying *kaitenzushi* with her friend Hideki.)
(シャロンは友達の秀樹といっしょに回転寿司に挑戦しています)

Hideki: First, put a tea bag in the teacup, the *yunomi*, and fill it with hot water. You just hold the *yunomi* and push the lever for hot water like this.

秀　樹：まず、湯のみにティーバッグを入れて、お湯を注ぐんだ。湯のみを持ってこういうふうにお湯のレバーを押すんだ。

Sharon: I see. And how do we order sushi?

シャロン：なるほど。それでお寿司の注文はどうするの？

Hideki: You can pick up any dish passing by on the conveyor. What are you going to start with?

秀　樹：コンベヤーにのって回っているお皿はどれでも取っていいよ。何から始める？

Sharon: I'll try tuna. Why are the dishes different colors?

シャロン：マグロを食べてみるわ。どうしてお皿の色が違うの？

Hideki: The color of the dish will tell you how much it costs. Here in this restaurant, sushi on a white dish costs 120 yen, a patterned dish costs 240 yen, and a red dish costs 300 yen.

秀　樹：お皿の色で値段が分かるんだ。この店では白い皿の寿司は120円、模様の入った皿が240円、赤い皿が300円だよ。

Sharon: You mean they're going to charge us by the color and number of dishes we took?

シャロン：つまり取ったお皿の色と数で勘定が決まるってこと？

Hideki: That's right. Also, you can order any other dish you like if you cannot find one on the conveyor.

秀　樹：そのとおり。それから、自分の好きな寿司がコンベヤーになかったら、何でも注文できるよ。

★ミニ知識★

回転寿司を楽しむ

　最近は欧米でも sushi bar が見られ、握り寿司を楽しむ人々も珍しくありません。欧米人の中にも、光り物はだめ、タコはだめ、ウニはだめ…と好き嫌いの激しい人から何でも大丈夫という寿司通まで、様々な人がいます。寿司屋はあっても回転寿司の店はアジアの一部を除くとあまり見かけないので、日本を訪れた欧米人を案内すると喜ばれるかもしれません。よく出るねたの英語名をあらかじめ勉強しておくとよいでしょう。珍しいねたもあるので説明してあげると喜ばれますが、相手があまり気の進まない物を無理にすすめないようにしましょう。

表現集

❶ (回転)寿司に関する表現

1. 寿司のねたは何が好きですか. — What do you like on your sushi?
2. 何でも好きな物を取ってください. — You can pick any dish you like.
3. ふつう1回の注文で2つ寿司が出てきます./ふつう1皿には2つ寿司がのっています. — Usually one order means two pieces of sushi. / Usually one plate has two pieces of sushi.
4. ワサビ抜きを頼むこともできます. — You can order sushi without *wasabi* [horseradish].
5. しょうゆを少しつけてから食べます. — Dip it a little in soy sauce before eating it.
6. 寿司通の人の中にははしを使わないで, 手で寿司を食べる人もいます. — Some sushi gourmets eat sushi by hand without using chopsticks.
7. 皿を取りそこなっても, あわてないでまた回ってくるのを待ちましょう. — If you miss picking up a dish, don't be upset — just wait for it to come around again.
8. 食べた皿をコンベヤーに戻してはいけません. — Don't return the empty plates to the conveyer.
9. 食べた皿はテーブルの上に重ねておいてください. — Stack the used plates on the table.
10. 食べ終わったら店員さんが皿を数えていくらか教えてくれます. — When you finish eating, the shop person will count the plates and tell you the price.
11. 卵焼きやレタス巻きのような魚でない物もあります. — There are non-fish pieces like baked egg or lettuce roll.
12. このイカはとても柔らかいですよ. よければ食べてみてください. — This squid is very tender. Try it if you like.
13. しょうがは好きなだけ取ってください. — Take as much ginger as you like.
14. 手巻きにして作ってもらえます. — You can ask them to make it into a roll.
15. お好みで持ち帰り用に作ってもらえます. — You can ask them to make sushi to order for takeout.
16. お茶を「あがり」, しょうゆを「むらさき」というように, 寿司屋で使われる特別な呼び方があります. — There are special terms used in sushi bars like *agari* for tea and *murasaki* for soy sauce.

❷ そばに関する表現

1. 熱いそばと冷たいそばのどちらですか. — Which would you like, hot *soba* or cold *soba*?
2. そばをゆでたお湯を「そば湯」と言います. 食後に飲むと体が温まってかぜを治すのにいいです. — The hot water in which *soba* is boiled is called *sobayu*. It is drunk after the meal and is good for curing colds because it warms the body.
3. 日本ではそばをすすって食べるのは正しいマナーと考えられています. — It is considered correct manners in Japan to slurp your *soba*.
4. 早く食べないと伸びてしまいます. — If you don't eat it soon, it'll get soggy.
5. ほとんどの駅や商店街には小さな立ち食いそば屋があります. — There are small noodle stands at most stations and shopping malls where you eat standing up.
6. 日本では大みそかに「年越しそば」を食べる習慣があります. — In Japan there is a custom to eat *toshikoshi-soba* on New Year's Eve.
7. そばは1本1本がとても長いので長寿のシンボルです. — *Soba* is a symbol of long life because each noodle is so long.

場面・状況別会話 ③

●旅　行

> Well, how about Hokkaido?

Alec : Keiko, I want to get away from the city this summer. Do you have any idea where I should go?
アレック：桂子，この夏は都会から逃げたいと思っているんだけど，どこへ行ったらいいと思う？
Keiko : Well, how about Hokkaido? You've never been there, have you?
桂　子：そうねえ，北海道はどうかしら？行ったことないでしょう？
Alec : No. But I know it's the northernmost island of Japan.
アレック：ないよ．でも，日本のいちばん北にある島だってことは知ってるよ．
Keiko : Right. It snows a lot in the winter, but in the summer it's cool and some people go there to avoid the summer heat.
桂　子：そのとおり．冬は雪がたくさん降るけど，夏は涼しいから避暑のためにそこに行く人もいるわ．
Alec : Great! What is it famous for?
アレック：いいねえ．何が有名なの？
Keiko : Well, it's famous for its beautiful and spacious landscape. You can rent a car and drive around.
桂　子：そうねえ，きれいで広大な景色で有名だわ．レンタカーを借りてドライブするといいわよ．
Alec : Good idea! What are the special products up there?
アレック：いい考えだね．そこの特産物は何なの？
Keiko : Potatoes, milk, cheese, crabs, and you can try ramen.
桂　子：ジャガイモ，牛乳，チーズ，カニ，そしてラーメンを食べてみてもいいわね．
Alec : I wonder if there are any hot springs in Hokkaido.
アレック：それから，北海道に温泉はあるのかなあ．
Keiko : There're lots of them. Why don't you visit the Hokkaido government's home page?
桂　子：たくさんあるわ．北海道庁のホームページを見てみたらどうかしら．

★ミニ知識★

経済的で楽しいバックパッキング

　欧米でよくある旅のスタイルに，リュックサックを背負って安いホテルなどに泊まりながら旅をするバックパッキング（backpacking）というものがあります．バックパッキングをする人たちはバックパッカー（backpackers）と呼ばれ，若者を中心に年配の人にまで及んでいます．バックパッキングが人気なのは，できるだけお金を使わないで安く旅を楽しめるという経済的な理由のほかに，ユースホステルなどの共同宿泊施設で旅行者同士が触れ合う機会が多くもてるという魅力があります．また，ヨーロッパの多くの国々ではビザがなくても働けるので，旅先でアルバイトなどをして，資金を調達しながら旅を続けることができるという社会的背景があります．

表現集

❶旅行に関して質問するときの表現

1. 一人旅と団体旅行とどちらの方が好きですか. — Which do you prefer, traveling alone or in a group?
2. 外国に行ったことはありますか. — Have you ever been to a foreign country?
3. どんな国に行ったことがありますか. — What countries have you visited?
4. カナダ旅行はどうでしたか. — How was your trip to Canada?
5. 今まで行った場所でどこがいちばんよかったですか. — What's the nicest place you've ever been to?
6. 最も印象に残っている所はどこですか. — Which place impressed you the most?
7. 新婚旅行はどこに行きたいですか. — Where would you like to go on your honeymoon?
8. ここ日本へは観光ですか. — Are you sightseeing here in Japan?
9. おすすめの観光地はどこですか. — Which tourist spots do you recommend?

❷旅行に関して提案するときの表現

1. 京都に行くことをおすすめします. — I recommend (that) you visit Kyoto.
2. 観光バスに乗って街を回るといいと思います. — I suggest (that) you take a sightseeing bus around the city.
3. その街には訪ねるといい名所旧跡がたくさんあります. — There are many good historic places to visit in the city.
4. 旅行のお土産(みやげ)話を楽しみにしています. — I'm looking forward to hearing about your travels.
5. 旅先から絵葉書を送ってください. — Send me picture postcards from the places you visit.
6. 韓国に行ったらぜひ本場のキムチを食べてみてください. — You must try real kimchi [Korean pickles] when you go to Korea.
7. この週末に一泊[日帰り, スキー]旅行を計画しませんか. — Why don't we plan an overnight [a day, a ski] trip for this weekend?
8. 現地の観光案内所でおすすめの場所を聞いてみませんか. — Why don't we ask the local tourist information center for good places to visit?
9. パック旅行だとガイドさんがすべて通訳をしてくれるので便利です. — A package tour is convenient because a guide will translate everything for you.
10. 海外旅行よりも国内旅行のほうが割高になることもあります. — There are cases where domestic tours cost more than overseas tours.

❸旅行の経験に関する表現

1. 家族旅行で温泉に行ってきました. — I went on a family trip to a hot spring.
2. ブドウ[イチゴ, ナシ]狩りに行ってきました. — I went grape [strawberry, pear] picking.
3. 修学旅行は5泊6日で北九州を回りました. — We went on a six-day school trip around northern Kyushu.
4. 卒業旅行で友達と台湾に行ってきました. — I went on a graduation trip to Taiwan with my friends.
5. 旅行中に友人にばったり出くわしました. — I bumped [ran] into a friend ⌈during my travels [while traveling]⌋.

場面・状況別会話 ❹

● アルバイト

> Meg, have you ever worked part-time?
>
> Yes, I once worked at a fast-food restaurant.

Fumio : Meg, have you ever worked part-time?
文　雄：メグ，アルバイトしたことある？
Meg 　: Yes, I once worked at a fast-food restaurant in my hometown.
メ　グ：ええ，故郷のファーストフード店で昔働いたわ．
Fumio : In some Japanese high schools part-time jobs are prohibited. Maybe this is because some students work too much and can't keep up with their studies.
文　雄：日本の高校ではアルバイトは禁止されているところもあるんだ．たぶん働きすぎて勉強についていけない生徒がいるからなんだよ．
Meg 　: In my country many students work part-time. But their main priority is school. Some students work to pay for their tuition.
メ　グ：私の国ではアルバイトをする生徒がたくさんいるわ．でも学校がいちばん優先なの．授業料を払うために働く生徒もいるわ．
Fumio : Well, in Japan most of the money we earn from part-time jobs goes for food, clothing and entertainment.
文　雄：日本ではアルバイトで稼いだお金のほとんどが食べ物代や洋服代，そして娯楽代になるんだ．
Meg 　: I think working part-time is good experience. It teaches us the value of money.
メ　グ：アルバイトはいい経験だと思うわ．お金の価値を教えてくれるもの．
Fumio : That's good as long as it doesn't harm our studies.
文　雄：勉強の害にならないかぎりいいと思うな．

★ミニ知識★

アルバイトより学業優先

　欧米の高校生や大学生もアルバイトをすることがよくありますが，アルバイトで疲れて遅刻や欠席をしたり，授業中に居眠りをするようなことはあまりありません．あくまでも学業を第一に考えるので，ふつう勉強を犠牲にしてまでアルバイトをしようとはしません．また，日本ではアルバイトで稼いだお金は趣味やレジャーなどに使う人が多いようですが，欧米では学費にあてる人もたくさんいます．レストランのウエーター／ウエートレス，ピザの配達，車の洗車，芝刈りなど，時給は高くなくてもチップをもらえるので好む人もいます．ベビーシッターやレポート・論文のワープロ入力などのアルバイトも学校の掲示板によくはり出されています．アルバイトをして学費や生活費を稼ごうと思う留学生もいますが，実際には授業の予習・復習や宿題などで忙しく，なかなか思うように働けないのが現状です．

表現集

❶アルバイトの種類に関する表現

1. どんなアルバイトをしていますか［したいですか］.
 What kind of part-time job do you have [want]?
2. 今までにどんなアルバイトをしましたか.
 What kind of part-time jobs have you had?
3. 何か割のいいアルバイトを知りませんか.
 Do you know of a part-time job that pays well?
4. 今年の夏はコンビニでアルバイトをします.
 I'm going to work part-time at a convenience store this summer.
5. 週に2回,家庭教師で中学生に数学を教えています.
 I tutor a junior high school student in math twice a week.
6. 肉体労働よりもデスクワーク［オフィスワーク］のほうが好きです.
 I prefer 「a desk job [office work] to manual labor.
7. 原則として,この高校ではアルバイトをすることは禁止されています.
 As a general rule, having a part-time job is prohibited at this high school.

❷アルバイトの条件に関する表現

1. その仕事の時給はいくらですか.
 What does the job pay an hour?
2. 勤務時間はどうなっていますか.
 What are the working hours?
3. 出来高制で支払われます.
 They pay me on a per job basis.
4. 最初の給料は時給800円ですが,数か月働いた後に昇給があります.
 The starting pay is 800 yen per hour, but after working several months they will give you a raise.
5. 場所がいいし,交通費も出ます.
 The location is good, and they pay transportation expenses, too.
6. 給料よりも労働条件をまず考えたいです.
 I'd like to think about the working conditions first rather than the pay.
7. 給料はそれほどよくないですが,食事が含まれているんです.
 The pay isn't so good, but meals are included.
8. 肉体労働はとてもお金になるそうです.
 I hear manual labor pays a lot.
9. 仕事がとても厳しかったので辞めました.
 The job was so demanding that I quit.

❸その他の表現

1. なぜアルバイトをしたいのですか.
 Why do you want to work part-time?
2. 旅行をするためにお金を稼ぎたいです.
 I want to make money so I can travel around.
3. アルバイトで稼いだお金をどのように使いたいのですか.
 How do you want to spend the money you earned from your part-time job?
4. 稼いだお金をすべて趣味のコンピュータにつぎ込んでしまいました.
 I spent all my earnings on my hobby, computers.
5. アルバイトをすることは社会で生きることを学ぶのに役に立ちます.
 Working part-time is useful for learning how to live in society.
6. アルバイトをすることは,卒業後にどんな仕事をしたいのか決める手助けになるいい経験だと思います.
 I think working part-time is good experience in helping me decide what job I want to get after graduation.
7. アルバイトをしすぎて,本業の勉強をおろそかにするのはいいとは思いません.
 I don't think it is good to work part-time too much and neglect your regular studies.

場面・状況別会話 ❺

●携帯電話

> I've got to get on a train right now. I'll call you back.
>
> Oh, OK.

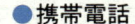

Fred : ... so, what do you think?
フレッド：…で，どう思う？

Noriko : Listen, Fred. I've got to get on a train right now. I'll call you back in about twenty minutes. OK?
典　子：ねえ，フレッド．もう電車に乗らなきゃならないの．20分くらいしたらこちらからかけ直すわね．いい？

Fred : Oh, OK. But I just have to step out for a while. I'll keep my cell phone on. If you can't reach me for some reason, a bad connection or something, leave a message. I'll call you back right away.
フレッド：うん，いいよ．でもこれからちょっと出かけなきゃならないんだ．携帯電話の電源を入れたままにしておくよ．電波の状態やなんかでうまくつながらなかったら，メッセージを残しておいてよ．折り返しすぐ電話するから．

Noriko : When will you come back?
典　子：いつ戻るの？

Fred : In forty or fifty minutes.
フレッド：40分か50分で．

Noriko : Well, suppose I call you again at home about an hour from now.
典　子：じゃあ，1時間後くらいにもう一度家に電話しようか．

Fred : OK. That's fine. Talk to you later.
フレッド：うん，いいよ．じゃあ，また後で．

★ミニ知識★

携帯電話と電話用語

「携帯電話」のことは英語で cellular phone（口語ではしばしば cell phone），mobile phone，portable phone などといいます．cellular はもともとは「細胞状の」「ハチの巣状の」という意味で，通話ゾーンがハチの巣状に広がっていることに由来しています．また，mobile「移動性の」は自動車電話がはやっていた頃によく使われた言葉ですが，携帯電話が主流になった今でも使われることがあります．電話番号をかけるときに使う dial という動詞も，もともとは回転ダイヤル式の電話機で電話をかけるときに用いられた言葉ですが，プッシュホンや携帯電話に代わった今では I pushed 123-4567. などともいうようになっています．また，「電話を切る」の hang up も「受話器をかける」とところから生まれた表現ですが，最近では ring off, turn off, switch off などを使うようにもなっています．電話機の発達によって言葉も変わりつつあります．

表現集

❶かけ直し・メッセージに関する表現

1. 悪いけど,後でかけ直してくれる? — I'm sorry, but will you call me back later?
2. 今,電車の中なので,10分後にこちらからかけます. — I'm on a train right now, so I'll 「call you back [get back to you]」 in 10 minutes.
3. 電波の状態が悪いので,途中で切れるかもしれません. — We have a bad connection. We might be disconnected at any moment.
4. 電波の状態がとても悪いので,もっとよい場所からかけ直します. — This is a really bad connection. I'll try calling you again on a better line.
5. ごめんなさい.今,別の電話に出ているので,後でこちらからかけ直します. — Sorry. I'm on another line right now. I'll call you back later.
6. もし通じなければ,メッセージを残しておいてください. — If you can't reach me, please leave a message.
7. 留守電のメッセージを聞いてくれましたか. — Did you get my message on your answering machine?

❷待ち合わせのときの表現

1. お互いに見つからなかったら,携帯電話で連絡し合いましょう. — If we can't find each other, let's try to get in contact by cellular phone.
2. 駅で私が見つからなかったら,携帯電話にかけてください. — If I'm not at the station, call my cell phone.
3. 遅れるようだったら,あなたの携帯電話にかけます. — If I'm late, I'll call your cell phone.

❸その他の表現

1. ほかの電話が入りました.ちょっと待ってください. — I've got someone on the other line. Hold on a moment.
2. 授業中は携帯電話の電源を切っておくのを忘れないでください. — Don't forget to turn off your portable phones during class.
3. キャッチホンが入りました.じゃあ,また. — I've got a call waiting. I'll see you.
4. 転送電話にセットしておきました. — I set the call forwarding.
5. 私の電話はナンバーディスプレイなので,そちらの番号は分かります. — My phone has a number display function, so I can get your phone number.
6. あなたの電話番号を携帯電話の短縮ダイヤルに登録しておきましょう. — Let me put your number in the speed dial memory of my cell phone.
7. 携帯電話でメール交換しましょう. — Let's keep in touch by e-mail on our cellular phones.
8. 携帯電話を使ってEメールをよく送ります. — I often send e-mail using my cell phone.
9. この携帯電話はスケジュール帳になるほか,占いもでき,計算機能もついています. — This cell phone not only works as a scheduler but also can tell fortunes and has calculator functions.
10. 最近,かわいい着メロ(着信メロディー)をパソコンで作りました. — Recently I created a cute ring tone on my computer.

場面・状況別会話 ❻

●恋愛

> I've got a crush on her.
>
> Oh, have you spoken to her?

Ted : Yumi, do you know Naoko? She sits in the front row.
テッド：由美，直子って知ってる？ 前列に座ってるんだけど．
Yumi : Yes, I do.
由　美：ええ，知ってるわ．
Ted : I've got a crush on her.
テッド：僕，彼女に夢中になっちゃったんだ．
Yumi : Oh, have you spoken to her?
由　美：まあ，彼女に話しかけたことある？
Ted : Just a few times. I don't know what she thinks of me, but I'm just wondering how I should ask her out.
テッド：数回ね．僕のことどう思っているか分からないけど，どうやってデートに誘おうかと思ってるんだ．
Yumi : Ted, I think it would make her nervous if you ask her out. The first thing you should do is to get to know her better.
由　美：テッド，デートに誘うと彼女緊張しちゃうと思うわ．初めにすべきことは彼女をもっとよく知ることだわ．
Ted : How am I supposed to talk to her? My heart starts beating fast whenever I see her.
テッド：どうやって彼女に話しかけたらいい？ 彼女に会うといつも心臓がどきどきしちゃうんだ．
Yumi : Let's see.... Why don't we have lunch together in the cafeteria? I'll invite her to sit with us.
由　美：そうねえ．カフェテリアでいっしょに昼食というのはどうかしら．私たちといっしょに座るように彼女を誘ってみるわ．
Ted : That sounds great.
テッド：それはいいねえ．

★ミニ知識★

様々なデート

　恋人とのデートは2人だけとは限らず，様々な形式があります．まだつきあいの浅い時期などはdouble dateといって2組のカップルがいっしょにデートをしたり（3組ならばtriple date），グループでどこかに遊びに行くgroup dateをしたりします．第三者が面識のない2人を合わせるblind date（ブラインドデート）もよくある形式です．おとなしくて恋愛が苦手な人のために周りの友人がblind dateを計画することもあります．また，デートといっても遊ぶだけとは限らず，図書館などでいっしょに勉強をするstudy date（スタディデート）もあります．最近はインターネットで恋人を見つけることもあるようですが，いいかげんなものも多いので注意が必要です．

表現集

❶恋人とのつきあいに関する表現

1. 彼氏［彼女］がいます． — I have a boyfriend [girlfriend].
2. 彼は私の「お気に入りの人」です． — He is my "Mr. Right."
3. だれか好きな人はいますか． — Is there anyone special [you like]?
4. 健はリサとステディな関係です． — Ken is going steady with Lisa.
5. 彼らは2年間つきあっています． — They have been dating for two years.
6. 彼らは最初のデートですぐに気が合いました． — They「clicked right away [hit it off] on the first date.
7. どんなタイプの男性［女性］が好きですか． — What kind of man [woman] is your type?
8. 彼［彼女］にひとめぼれしました． — I fell in love with him [her] at first sight.
9. 見合い［恋愛］結婚はいい考えだと思いますか． — Do you think arranged [love] marriages are a good idea?
10. 恋愛と結婚は別だと思いますか． — Do you think love and marriage are different?
11. 彼［彼女］のことが頭から離れません． — I can't stop thinking about him [her].
12. インターネットで彼［彼女］に会いました． — I met him [her] through the Internet.
13. 結婚情報サービスを利用する人が増えています． — More and more people use marriage information services.

❷デートに関する表現

1. 食事［お茶，映画］に行きませんか． — Would you like to go out for dinner [a cup of coffee, a movie]?
2. 彼がデートに誘って［食事に連れていって］くれたらなあ． — I wish he would「ask me out [take me out to dinner].
3. デートで彼女をどこに連れていきましたか． — Where did you take her out?
4. デートしてくれない？ — Will you be my date?
5. 放課後，ジムと図書館でスタディデートをします． — I have a study date with Jim in the library after school.
6. サムのためにブラインドデートを計画しない？ — Why don't we plan a blind date for Sam?
7. ダブルデートをしましょう． — Let's go on a double date.
8. 恋人と遠距離恋愛をしています． — I have a long-distance relationship with my boyfriend [girlfriend].

❸トラブルに関する表現

1. リックと私は別れました． — Rick and I broke up.
2. 彼はほかの女の子たちと遊び回っていたことが分かりました． — I found (that) he had been fooling around with other girls.
3. 彼は浮気者です． — He cheats on his girlfriend.
4. 彼は彼女と浮気をしました． — He carried on a flirtation with her.
5. 私をもてあそぶのはやめてください． — Stop playing games with me.
6. 彼はいつも女の子をナンパしようとしています． — He's always trying to pick up girls.

場面・状況別会話 ❼

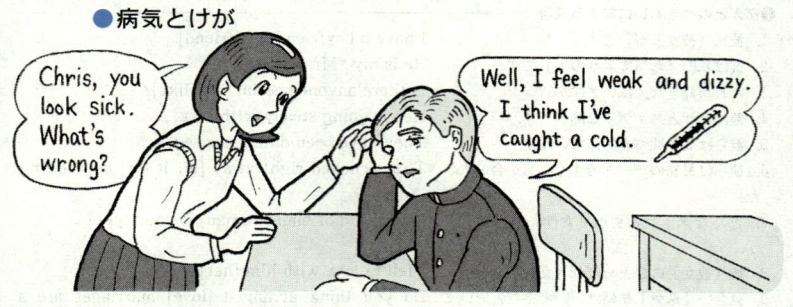

●病気とけが

> Chris, you look sick. What's wrong?

> Well, I feel weak and dizzy. I think I've caught a cold.

Rena : Chris, you look sick. What's wrong?
玲　奈：クリス，ぐあいが悪いみたいだけど，どうしたの？
Chris : Well, I feel weak and dizzy. I think I've caught a cold.
クリス：うーん，力が抜けてめまいがするんだ．かぜをひいてしまったみたい．
Rena : Do you have a fever?
玲　奈：熱はあるの？
Chris : Yeah, I feel a bit feverish. Last night I was wearing light clothes after taking a bath.
クリス：うん，少し熱っぽいかな．きのうの夜，ふろに入ったあと薄着だったんだ．
Rena : That's too bad. I think you should get some rest. Do you want to go to the nurse's office?
玲　奈：それはいけないわ．少し休んだほうがいいと思うわ．保健室に行く？
Chris : Well, I'd rather leave school early. I have to get over my cold completely before the exams next week.
クリス：いや，むしろ早退しようかな．来週の試験までに完全にかぜを治しておかないといけないからね．
Rena : You're right. Don't worry about the classes. I'll show you my notebook later.
玲　奈：そうね．授業のことは心配しないで．あとで私のノートを見せてあげるわ．
Chris : Thanks. I appreciate it.
クリス：ありがとう．感謝するよ．

★ミニ知識★

マスクは医者がするもの

　欧米ではマスクは主に医者が手術の時にするもので，一般の人がかぜをひいてもマスクをする習慣はありません．英語で mask といえば仮面舞踏会などでつける仮面のことを連想する人が多くいます．熱を測るときに体温計（thermometer）はわきの下にはさむほかに，口の中に入れて測ることもあります．華氏（Fahrenheit）なので98.6度以上が高熱になりますが，わきの下よりも舌で測るほうが標準値はわずかに高いとされています．また主に英語圏では，だれかがくしゃみをすると，周りにいる人が God bless you! とささやきます．くしゃみといっしょにその人の魂が体から逃げてしまうという迷信によるもので，魂を失ったかわいそうな人に神の恵みがありますように，という意味で口にされます．

表現集

❶ 病気の症状に関する表現

1. かぜぎみです. — I have「a slight cold [a bit of a cold].
2. インフルエンザにかかったようです. — I think I'm coming down with the flu.
3. (かぜが)ぶり返してしまいました. — I've had a relapse.
4. 寒気がします. — I have the chills. / I feel chilly.
5. めまいがします. — I feel dizzy.
6. 体がふらふらします. — I feel run-down.
7. 吐き気がします. — I feel like I'm going to throw up. / I'm nauseated. / I'm nauseous.
8. 頭[胃,腰]が痛いです. — I have a headache [stomachache, backache].
9. のどが痛いです. — I have a sore throat.
10. 扁桃腺(へんとう)がはれています. — My tonsils are swollen.
11. 鼻が詰まっています. — I have a stuffy nose. / My nose is stuffy. / My nose is stuffed up.
12. 鼻水が出ます. — I have a runny nose.
13. 下痢をしています. — My stomach is upset. / I have diarrhea. / I have loose bowels.
14. 便秘をしています. — I'm constipated.
15. 花粉症です. — I have hay fever.
16. 左耳が耳鳴りしています. — My left ear is ringing.
17. 貧血症でよく倒れそうになります. — I'm anemic and I often feel faint.
18. 左下の奥歯の一つが痛みます. — I have a toothache in one of my lower left molars.

❷ けがの症状に関する表現

1. 足が筋肉痛です. — The muscles in my legs are sore.
2. 足に血まめができてしまいました. — I've got a blood blister on my foot.
3. 右手をやけどしてしまいました. — I burned my right hand.
4. 足を骨折してしまいました. — I broke my leg.
5. ひざを打撲してしまいました. — I bruised my knee.
6. ひじをすりむいてしまいました. — I skinned [scratched] my elbow.
7. 足首をねんざしてしまいました. — I sprained [twisted] my ankle.
8. 親指がはれてしまいました. — My thumb is swollen.
9. 痛みはなくなりました. — The pain is [has] gone.

❸ その他の表現

1. インフルエンザが日本中ではやっています. — There is a lot of flu going around Japan.
2. 彼のかぜがうつったみたいです. — It seems that he has given me his cold.
3. かぜが治りました. — I've gotten rid of my cold. / I've gotten over my cold. / I've beaten my cold.
4. 鼻声ですね. — You sound stuffed up.
5. 車[船]酔いしたようです. — I'm afraid I'm carsick [seasick].
6. 医者に診(み)てもらったほうがいいと思います. — I think you should see a doctor.
7. この薬はとてもよく効きます. — This medicine works pretty well.

場面・状況別会話 ⑧

●健康と美容

> Do you do anything to keep yourself in shape, Sam?

> Well, I try to walk around my neighborhood.

Rumi : Some students skip breakfast to lose weight. I don't think it's a good idea, though.
留 美：やせるために朝食を抜きにする生徒がいるわね。でも，いい考えだとは思わないわ。

Sam : You're right. We should eat regularly to stay healthy.
サ ム：そうだね。健康でいるためには規則的に食事をとらなければいけないよ。

Rumi : I try not to eat too much fatty food. Instead, I try to eat more vegetables.
留 美：私は油っこいものを食べすぎないようにしているわ。その代わり，もっと野菜を食べるようにしているの。

Sam : The important thing is that we should have a balanced diet.
サ ム：大事なことはバランスのとれた食事をすることだよ。

Rumi : Right. Do you do anything to keep yourself in shape, Sam?
留 美：そうね。サム，あなたは何か健康を保つことをしているの？

Sam : Well, I try to walk around my neighborhood. Walking is good exercise.
サ ム：そうだな，家の近所を歩くようにしているんだ。歩くことはいい運動だよ。

Rumi : My dad goes to a fitness club on the weekends, but I worry about him.
留 美：私の父は週末はフィットネスクラブに行ってるんだけど，心配なの。

Sam : Why?
サ ム：どうして？

Rumi : Because he sometimes exercises too much.
留 美：時々運動をしすぎるんですもの。

Sam : Yes, moderate exercise is best.
サ ム：そう，適度な運動がいちばんいいんだ。

★ミニ知識★

フィットネスクラブの流行

肥満（obesity）が大きな問題となっているアメリカでは，多くの人が日ごろから健康管理に強い関心を示し，糖分，塩分，脂肪分などのとりすぎに気をつけています。かつて健康食やダイエットがブームになった時期がありましたが，偽物の健康食品が出回ったり，急激なダイエットが原因でかえって体を悪くする人が増えたため，現在では運動による健康管理へと人々の関心が移りつつあります。だれにでもできる最も簡単な運動はwalkingやjoggingで，特に朝夕に運動をする人の姿が目につきます。エアロビクスやジャズダンスをする施設や，free weights（ダンベルやバーベル類を持ち上げて体を鍛える器具），stationary bicycle（固定式自転車），treadmill（ベルトコンベアー式ランニング器具）などを備えた近代的なフィットネスクラブの設立も相次いでいます。しかし，ヘッドフォンをつけてジョギング中に事故にあったり，無理な運動をして心臓発作を起こすなどの事故も増えています。

表現集

❶健康法に関する表現

1. 健康を保つために何をやっていますか. — What do you do to「keep fit [stay in shape]?
2. 何か運動をしていますか. — Do you do any exercise?
3. 血圧は健康を測るバロメーターです. — Blood pressure is a barometer to one's health.
4. 最近, 健康器具がよく売れています. — Health equipment sells well these days.
5. 酒の飲みすぎや喫煙は健康によくありません[悪いです]. — It's「not good for [harmful to] your health to drink too much or smoke.
6. 健康には十分な睡眠をとることが必要不可欠です. — Getting enough sleep is essential for your health.
7. 水泳は私の健康維持に役立っています. — Swimming has kept me in good shape.

❷食べ物と肥満に関する表現

1. ダイエット中なんです. — I'm on a diet. / I'm dieting.
2. 急激なダイエットは様々な健康上の問題を引き起こします. — Crash dieting will cause us a lot of health problems.
3. 最近, 運動不足で太りました. — I've「put on [gained] some weight through lack of exercise recently.
4. 私は(標準体重より)2キロオーバーです. — I'm two kilograms overweight.
5. 太らないように注意しなければなりません. — I must watch my weight.
6. 食事を作るときにカロリー計算をします. — I count calories when preparing meals.
7. ポテトチップはカロリーが高いです. — Potato chips are high in calories.
8. インスタント食品はあまり栄養価が高くありません. — Instant food is not very nutritious.
9. 油っこい食べ物を控えるようにしています. — I'm trying to cut down on fatty foods.
10. 糖分のとりすぎに注意しています. — I'm careful not to eat too much sugar.
11. 添加物の入っていない食品を買い, 天然水を飲むようにしています. — I try to buy additive-free foods and drink spring water.

❸美容に関する表現

1. 最近, エステに通う女性が増えています. — These days more and more women go to beauty-treatment clinics.
2. ビタミンCはしみやそばかすの除去に効くと言われています. — It is said that vitamin C is effective in removing blotches and freckles.
3. 日焼けのしすぎは皮膚癌(がん)の原因になることがあります. — Getting too much sun can cause skin cancer.
4. 彼女はつやつやした肌をしているので若々しく見えます. — Her lustrous skin makes her look young.
5. 便秘は肌のトラブルの原因となります. — Constipation causes skin problems.
6. にきびを治す何かよい方法はありますか. — Is there any good way to get rid of pimples?
7. 早起きをすると健康によく, 美しさを保てます. — Getting up early is good for your health and keeps you looking beautiful.
8. 私はジョギングをしてシェイプアップをはかっています. — I'm trying to improve my figure by jogging.

場面・状況別会話 ⑨

●コンピュータ

> How can I change this bar graph into a line graph?

> Click on "line graph."

Melissa : Koji. What are you doing?
メリッサ : 浩二．何してるの？

Koji : I'm making a graph on the computer. It's an assignment for my computer class.
浩 二 : コンピュータでグラフを作ってるんだ．コンピュータクラスの宿題なんだよ．

Melissa : Good luck!
メリッサ : がんばってね．

Koji : Thanks. Oh, will you tell me something? How can I change this bar graph into a line graph?
浩 二 : ありがとう．あっ，ちょっと教えてくれないかな．この棒グラフを折れ線グラフに変えるにはどうしたらいいの？

Melissa : That's pretty simple. Click here to open the dialog box, then click on "line graph." That's it.
メリッサ : とても簡単よ．ここをクリックしてダイアログボックスを開いて，「折れ線グラフ」の所をクリックするだけよ．

Koji : Great! Thanks. Actually, when I was making a chart the other day, the computer crashed and I lost an important chart I had worked really hard on.
浩 二 : さすが！ありがとう．実を言うと，この前表を作ってたんだけど，コンピュータが故障しちゃって，とてもがんばって作った大事な表が消えちゃったんだ．

Melissa : That happens. You should save your data often just to be safe.
メリッサ : それってよくあるのよね．安全のために文書はたびたびセーブするようにしておいたほうがいいわよ．

Koji : I will.
浩 二 : そうするよ．

★ミニ知識★

コンピュータは生活の一部

　欧米の大学ではコンピュータは毎日の学業や生活に欠かせないものになっています．例えば，レポート（papers）は手書きのものはほとんど受け付けてもらえません．また，インターネットで調べものをしたり，Eメールを使って先生や友人と連絡をとったりと，コンピュータに向き合わない日はないといっても過言ではありません．各大学にはふつうコンピュータ室（computer lab）があり，学生に解放されています．コンピュータに詳しい学生が補助員のアルバイトをしていることもあり，操作方法を教えてくれたり，トラブルを解決してくれたりします．

表現集

❶パソコンの機能に関する表現

1. このパソコンは（処理スピードが）本当に速いです．
   This computer is really fast.
2. パソコンで画像［動画］を編集できますか．
   Can you edit pictures [videos] on the computer?
3. このパソコンでＤＶＤは再生できますか．
   Can this computer play back DVDs?
4. スキャナーで画像を読み込めます．
   You can upload graphics with a scanner.
5. キーボードではなく，音声で入力できるパソコンがあります．
   There are computers that accept voice input instead of keyboard input.
6. パソコンがフリーズしてしまいました．
   The computer froze.
7. 大切なフロッピーがコンピュータウイルスに感染してしまいました．
   An important floppy disk was infected with a virus.
8. このソフトは私のコンピュータと互換性がありません．
   This software isn't compatible with my computer.
9. ブラインドタッチ（→キーボードを見ない）でタイプすることができますか．
   Can you type without looking at the keyboard?
10. そこの部分を切り取って［コピーして］，この文の後にはりつけてください．
    Cut out [Copy] that section and paste it after this sentence.
11. ファイルが開きません．
    I can't open the file.
12. ここにカーソルを合わせて，2度クリックしてください．
    Put the cursor here and click twice.
13. そのアイコンをドラッグアンドドロップしてごみ箱に捨ててください．
    Drag and drop that icon into the trash.
14. 空欄の中にキーワードを打って［入れて］ください．
    Type [Enter] the key words in the box.
15. スペースキーを押してスクロールしてください．
    Press [Hit] the space bar to scroll up or down.
16. 間違って重要な文書を消してしまったときのために，テキストファイルで保存しておいたほうがいいです．
    You should save important documents as text files in case you erase them by accident.

❷パソコンを話題にした表現

1. 今はパソコンができて当たり前の時代です．
   These days we are expected to be able to use a computer.
2. デスクトップ型より持ち運びが簡単なノート型パソコンのほうが好きです．
   I prefer notebook computers, which are easier to carry around, to desktop models.
3. おじは今，パソコン教室に通っています．
   My uncle is taking a computer class now.
4. 母はパソコンを使って家計簿をつけています．
   My mother uses a computer to do the family accounts.
5. 彼はパソコンで絵を描きたがっています．
   He wants to use a computer to draw pictures.
6. 良夫はよくコンピュータと将棋の対戦をします．
   Yoshio often plays *shogi* against his computer.
7. デジタルカメラで撮った写真を使い，パソコンで年賀状を作りました．
   I made my New Year's cards with a computer using a photo I took with a digital camera.
8. 長時間コンピュータに向かっていたので，目が疲れました．
   My eyes are tired because I had to work at the computer for a long time.

場面・状況別会話 ⑩

●インターネット

> I use the Internet for online shopping.

> That's great.

Erika : I got an e-mail from my host sister.
絵里香：ホストシスター（ホームステイ先の姉妹）からEメールをもらったの．
Bob : Really? What did she say?
ボ ブ：本当？何だって？
Erika : "Happy Birthday!" She remembered my birthday.
絵里香：「お誕生日おめでとう」って．私の誕生日を覚えていてくれたの．
Bob : That's nice. Do you send e-mail very often?
ボ ブ：よかったね．絵里香はEメールをとてもよく使うの？
Erika : Sometimes. I often use the Internet. Last week I was investigating recycling on the web for a paper I have to write. I found a lot of web sites concerning recycling.
絵里香：ときどきね．インターネットはよく使うわ．先週，レポートを書かなければならなくて，リサイクルのことをインターネットで調べていたの．リサイクルについてのホームページがたくさんあったわ．
Bob : The Internet is really helpful for research. Also, I use the Internet for online shopping. For example, you can order books 24 hours a day.
ボ ブ：インターネットは調べ物をするときには本当に役に立つよね．僕はインターネットをオンラインショッピングにも使うんだ．例えば，本を24時間いつでも注文できるんだ．
Erika : That's great. I think online banking is really quick and easy, too.
絵里香：それはいいわよね．オンラインバンキングも本当に簡単で速いと思うわ．

★ミニ知識★

授業の情報はインターネットで

アメリカの大学では学生向けのホームページがあり，生活，ファッションから，レポートの書き方，テスト対策，就職活動のための履歴書の書き方，障害をもった学生向けの就職口まで，様々な情報を手に入れることができます．教授がクラスのホームページを作り，授業の予定表（syllabus）を掲示したり，学生の模範的なレポートを公開したりすることもあります．学生の個人成績をホームページ上で発表する教授もいますが，その場合は学生一人一人が暗証番号を持ち，本人でないと閲覧できないようになっています．また，インターネットのチャット機能を使って学生にオンライン・ディスカッションをさせる教授などもいて，インターネットの存在によってアメリカの大学は大きく変貌（ぼう）しつつあります．

表現集

❶インターネットの機能に関する表現

1. よくインターネットでチャットをします． — I often chat on the Internet.
2. 兄はよくインターネットからゲームソフトをダウンロードしています． — My brother often downloads game software from the Internet.
3. 直美は自分のホームページに最近撮った写真をアップロードしました． — Naomi uploaded onto her web site some photographs that she took recently.
4. 私のホームページからあなたのホームページへリンクを張れますか． — Can I put a link to your web site on my (web) site?
5. キーワードを入力して，関連するホームページを検索してください． — Input a keyword and search related web sites.
6. 気に入ったホームページ（の中の個々のページ画像）はブックマークをつけて，アドレスを保存することができます． — You can bookmark your favorite web sites and save their addresses.
7. アメリカで日本からの電子メールを受け取ったら，文字化けしてしまいました． — When I received an e-mail from Japan in the U.S., I got garbled symbols [characters].
8. このモデムはインターネットをするには通信速度が遅すぎます［十分な速さです］． — This modem is 「too slow [fast enough]」 for accessing the Internet.
9. 相手の承諾なしにデータの大きなファイルを添付して電子メールを送ることはネチケットに違反します． — It's bad netiquette to send e-mail with large file attachments without permission.

❷インターネットを話題にした表現

1. 最近のパソコンはインターネットに簡単に接続できます． — Computers these days are easy to connect to the Internet.
2. 最近，インターネットを始めました． — I recently started using the Internet.
3. 自分のホームページを開きました．ぜひ見てください． — I've put up my own home page. Please be sure to visit it.
4. 携帯電話でインターネットを楽しんでいます． — I enjoy using the Internet on my cellular phone.
5. おばは最近，オンラインショッピングにはまっています． — My aunt is 「obsessed with [into]」 online shopping now.
6. インターネットの掲示板でメール友達を見つけました． — I found an e-mail friend on an Internet bulletin board.
7. インターネットを始める前に，プロバイダーと契約する必要があります． — Before you can access the Internet, you need to sign a contract with a provider.
8. コンピュータハッカーはインターネットを使ってほかのコンピュータに入り込みます． — Computer hackers use the Internet to tap into other computers.
9. このテレビにはインターネット機能が組み込まれています． — Internet functions are built into this television.
10. インターネット上のギャンブルやポルノが大きな問題になってきています． — Internet gambling and pornography have become a big problem.
11. 父はインターネットで新聞を読んだりオンライン辞書を使ったりしています． — My father reads newspapers on the Internet and uses online dictionaries.

場面・状況別会話 ⑪

●ポップス

> Their songs are all big hits.

> I love the lyrics as well as the melody.

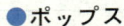

Mika : David, have you heard the new song by the Favorite Girls?
美　香：デイビッド，フェイバリットガールズの新曲聴いた？
David : No, not yet. What's the title?
デイビッド：いや，まだ聴いてないけど．何ていう曲？
Mika : It's called "Be My Love." It appeared on the hit charts last week. Maybe it'll be in the top ten soon.
美　香：「ビーマイラブ」っていうの．先週ヒットチャートに出てきたのよ．たぶんもうすぐベストテンに入るわ．
David : That's right. Their songs are all big hits.
デイビッド：そうだね．彼女たちの歌はみんなすごくヒットしているものね．
Mika : I love the lyrics as well as the melody.
美　香：曲だけでなくて歌詞もいいわ．
David : I'm a big fan of Hitomi. She's really cute.
デイビッド：僕はひとみの大ファンなんだ．すごくかわいいもの．
Mika : You judge by appearance rather than by musical talent, do you?
美　香：あなたって，音楽的才能よりもルックスで決めるのね．
David : Maybe you're right.
デイビッド：そうかも．
Mika : Then why don't we go to one of their concerts?
美　香：じゃあ今度，彼女たちのコンサートにいっしょに行かない？
David : That sounds great.
デイビッド：それはいいねえ．

★ミニ知識★

歌詞は名言の宝庫

　英米ではラジオ局が非常に充実していて，ポップス，ロック，クラシック，ジャズ，イージーリスニングなどといったジャンル別に音楽を流す局がたくさんあります．一般に若者はこうしたラジオやケーブルテレビの音楽専門番組によって最新のヒット曲などを知ります．気に入った曲があるとCDなどを買いにレコード店に行きますが，日本と違って歌詞カードがついていないことが多いので，本格的に歌詞を覚えたいという人は，そのたびに書店で最新曲の楽譜や歌詞の載った音楽雑誌を買い求めます．耳で聴いた歌詞をなにげなく口ずさんでいた人でも，文字になった歌詞を見て初めて勘違いに気づいたり深い意味が分かったりすることもよくあります．恋愛，別れ，人生の機微などを記した歌詞は口語表現も多く，名言の宝庫といえるでしょう．美しい曲を楽しみながら英語の勉強もできるのですから，一石二鳥というわけです．

表現集

❶楽曲・歌などに関する表現

1. 好きな歌手はだれ [グループは何] ですか. — Who is your favorite singer? [What's your favorite group?]
2. ロックよりもポップスのほうが好きです. — I prefer pop music to rock music.
3. スローなバラードが好きです. — I like slow ballads.
4. 今流れているこの曲名は何ですか. — What is the title of this song playing now? / What is this song playing now called?
5. 今人気の最新シングルは何ですか. — What is the hot new single now?
6. 彼の曲はいつも乗りがいいです. — His songs always have good rhythm.
7. この曲を聴いていると踊りたく [感傷的に] なります. — This song makes me feel 「like dancing [sentimental].
8. 作詞者はだれですか. — Who wrote the lyrics [words]?
9. 作曲者はだれですか. — Who wrote the melody [music]?
10. 彼女の曲はテレビドラマの主題歌になってはやりました. — Her song became popular because it was the theme song of a TV drama.
11. この曲は車のコマーシャルに使われています. — This tune is used in a car commercial.
12. 彼女の声量のある [ハスキーな, 伸びのある] 声が大好きです. — I love her powerful [husky, resonant] voice.
13. 彼らの踊りはとてもかっこいいです. — Their dancing is pretty cool.

❷ランキング・コンサートに関する表現

1. 「アイ ミス ユー」は3週連続1位です. — "I Miss You" has been 「at the top [the number one song] for three weeks in a row.
2. 「スイート ラブ」は今週2位から6位に落ちてしまいました. — "Sweet Love" dropped from second to six this week.
3. ビーグルスの「イノセント」はチャート初登場の20位です. — "Innocent" by the Beagles is debuting at number 20 on charts.
4. 彼の曲がベストテンの上位5位までに3曲もランクインしています. — Three of his songs are in the top five.
5. ビジュアル系のバンドがヒットチャートの上位を占めています. — Visual-based bands are sweeping the charts.
6. フェイバリット・ガールズは8月3日に毎年恒例の野外コンサートを開きます. — The Favorite Girls are going to give their annual open-air concert on August 3.
7. フェイバリット・ボーイズはこの夏に全国ツアーを予定しています. — The Favorite Boys are planning to go on a nation-wide tour this summer.
8. 彼らのライブを見に行きましょう. — Let's go see them perform.

❸CD・MDなどに関する表現

1. 彼の新しいCDが来月発売されます. — His new CD is coming out next month.
2. 彼らのセカンドアルバムは250万枚を超す売り上げになりました. — Their second album has sold over 2,500,000 copies.
3. 私は彼の曲をMDに編集しました. — I edited his songs on to an MD.
4. このCDをMDにダビングしてくれますか. — Will you copy this CD to an MD?

場面・状況別会話 ⑫

●映画

> Have you seen any good movies lately, Mieko?

> Yes, I saw "Love Romance." It was just released last week.

Dennis : Have you seen any good movies lately, Mieko?
テニス : 美恵子さん，最近何かいい映画見た？
Mieko : Yes, I saw *Love Romance*. It was just released last week.
美恵子 : ええ，『ラブロマンス』を見たわ．先週公開されたばかりなの．
Dennis : What kind of movie is that?
テニス : どんな映画？
Mieko : It's a romantic comedy. But it's also a mystery and full of action.
美恵子 : 恋愛コメディーよ．ミステリーも入ってるわ．アクションもたくさん出てくるし．
Dennis : Who played the lead?
テニス : だれが主役なの？
Mieko : Nick Johnson. He's so cool. I've become a big fan of his since seeing the movie.
美恵子 : ニック・ジョンソンよ．すごくかっこいいわ．映画を見てから彼の大ファンになっちゃった．
Dennis : Maybe I'll watch it when it's released in the video stores.
テニス : レンタル・ビデオ店に出たら僕も見ようかな．
Mieko : You should go to the theater to appreciate the real power of wide-screen movies.
美恵子 : 映画館で大画面の迫力を味わわなきゃだめよ．
Dennis : Yes, you're right. But still I prefer watching movies lying on a couch at home.
テニス : うん，そうだね．だけど，やっぱり僕は家でソファーに横になって見るほうがいいな．

★ミニ知識★

入れ替え制が原則

　日本に比べると欧米の映画館は入場料が1,000円以下と安いのが特徴です．都会は別として，多くの映画館はウイークデーの昼間は閉まっていて，夜の6時以降に2回上映されます（ウイークエンドはこのほかに昼に1～2回追加されます）．ふつうは上映途中から入場することができないので，上映時間を新聞で調べたり電話で問い合わせたりしてから行かなければなりません．また，入れ替え制なので，1回の上映が終わったら全員が劇場から出なければなりません．日本ではロードショーなどで人気のある映画は立ち見になることもありますが，欧米では席の数以上は入場券を売らないので，立ち見ということはふつうありません．また，日本と違って多くの劇場では食べ物の持ち込みもできません．

表現集

❶映画の上映に関する表現

1. 今，どんな映画をやっていますか． — What movies are on [showing, playing] now?
2. 次はどんな映画が来ますか． — What movies are coming up next?
3. それはアルファ映画館でやっています． — It's showing [playing] at the Alpha Theater.
4. 『タイタニック』の上映時間がどれくらいか分かりますか． — Do you know how long *Titanic* is?
5. 『タイタニック』が始まる時間を調べていただけますか． — Could you check the starting times for *Titanic*?
6. 次の［最初の，最後の］上映は何時に始まりますか． — What time does the next [first, last] show start? / What time is the next [first, last] showing?
7. 2本立てですか． — Do they have a double feature?
8. その映画はいつ封切られますか． — When will the movie be released?
9. プレイガイドで前売券が安く買えます． — You can get an advanced ticket cheaper at a ticket agency.

❷映画の内容に関する表現

1. あの映画は見る価値があります． — That movie is worth seeing.
2. その映画はどうでした． — What do you like about the movie? / How do you like the movie?
3. あまり私の好みの映画ではありません． — That's not my type of movie.
4. その映画にはだれが出ていますか． — Who starred in the film?
5. 監督はだれですか． — Who directed the film?
6. どんな話ですか． — What's the story about?
7. 感動しました［すばらしかったです，まあまあでした，よくなかったです，退屈でした，ひどかったです］． — I found it impressive [excellent, average, poor, boring, awful].
8. ラストシーン［クライマックス］が感動的でした． — I was impressed by the last [climactic] scene. / The last [climactic] scene was impressive.
9. 現地ロケで撮影されたんでしょう． — I think it was filmed on location.
10. ロングラン［流行］の映画になるでしょう． — It'll be 「a long-running film [a popular movie].
11. 日本語の字幕がなくても俳優のせりふが全部分かればいいのになあ． — I hope I can understand every line of the actors and actresses without Japanese subtitles.
12. ステレオ音声の大画面で映画を見るのは本当に感動的です． — It's really impressive to see a movie on a wide screen with stereo sound.

❸俳優の演技に関する表現

1. 彼女の演技は最高です［すばらしいです，とても感動的です，真に迫っています，自然です，硬くないです，わざとらしいです］． — Her acting is superb [excellent, very moving, realistic, natural, not stiff, artificial].
2. 彼女の演技は少し大げさすぎます． — Her performance is a bit exaggerated.
3. 彼女は先生役がうまいです． — She makes a good teacher in the film. / She's just the right actress to portray a teacher.
4. 彼はせりふに説得力がありません． — He doesn't say his lines convincingly.
5. 彼は主演男優賞でオスカーを取るでしょう． — He'll win the Oscar [Academy Award] for best actor.

場面・状況別会話 ⑬

●漫画とアニメ

> I'm always surprised to see adults reading comics on the trains.

> Well, in Japan comics are not only for kids.

Amanda : Takuya, I'm always surprised to see adults reading comics on the trains.

アマンダ：拓也，電車の中で大人が漫画を読んでいるのを見ていつも驚くわ．

Takuya : Well, in Japan comics are not only for kids. The format is the same, but the content is different for children and adults.

拓　　也：日本では漫画は子供だけのものじゃないんだ．体裁(説)は同じだけど，内容が子供向きと大人向きでは違うんだ．

Amanda : Well, I think comics are comics.

アマンダ：でも，漫画は漫画だと思うわ．

Takuya : Not really. Comics for grownups have stories about the lives of business people, politicians and even samurai.

拓　　也：そうでもないよ．大人向けの漫画にはビジネスマンや政治家や侍の人生についてのストーリーさえもあるんだ．

Amanda : Really? That sounds interesting. I didn't realize that Japanese comics had such a wide variety of stories.

アマンダ：本当？　おもしろそうね．日本の漫画にそんなにいろいろなストーリーがあるなんて気がつかなかったわ．

Takuya : Yes. I'd say that comics are an important part of the media in Japan. There are even academic books written in comic form.

拓　　也：そうなんだ．日本では漫画はメディアの重要な一部であると思うよ．漫画の形式で描かれた専門書さえあるんだ．

Amanda : Well, then they might help me with my study of Japanese.

アマンダ：それなら，私の日本語の勉強にも役に立つかもしれないわね．

★ミニ知識★

電車の中で漫画雑誌は読まない

　日本を訪れた多くの外国人が驚くことの一つとして，大人が電車の中で漫画雑誌を読むことが挙げられます．例えば，アメリカやカナダでも大人が漫画を読むこともありますが，一般的には新聞や雑誌に連載される comic strips と呼ばれるこま割り漫画や政治を風刺した漫画などが主で，ストーリーものの漫画を夢中になって読む大人は日本ほど多くはありません．また，子供たちにとって最も身近な漫画はテレビアニメです．特に土曜日の午前中は多くのチャンネルでアニメが放映され，子供たちは朝食のシリアルを食べながらテレビにくぎづけになって親にしかられることがあります．Mickey Mouse, Snoopy, Popeye など，漫画から世界的に有名なキャラクターが生まれることもあります．

表現集

❶漫画に関する表現

1. 漫画を描くのが趣味です. — My hobby is drawing cartoons.
2. 私の似顔絵を描いてくれませんか. — Can you draw a caricature of me?
3. 漫画本はくだらないという人がいます. — Some people say that comics are trashy.
4. 漫画の功罪について論議があります. — There is a controversy about the good points and bad points of comics.
5. 子供に漫画本は有害だとは限りません. — Comics are not always harmful to young kids.
6. 大人が週刊漫画雑誌を電車やバスの中で読むことについてどう思いますか. — What do you think about grownups reading weekly comic magazines on the trains or buses?
7. 人生について学ぶことのできる漫画もたくさんあります. — There are many comics that teach us about life.
8. 歴史や文学といった難しいテーマもやさしく描かれた漫画本を読んで学べます. — We can learn difficult subjects like history or literature by reading easily written comics.
9. 経済学のような難しい話題がやさしく漫画の形式になっていて，よく売れています. — Difficult subjects like economics are simplified in comic form and sell well.
10. 彼の政治を風刺した（1こま）漫画は，もう20年以上その新聞に連載されています. — His political cartoons have been appearing regularly in the newspaper for more than 20 years.
11. その漫画はテレビドラマ化［映画化］されました. — That comic was made into 「a TV drama [a movie].
12. ドラえもんは日本を代表する漫画のキャラクターです. — Doraemon is a well-known Japanese cartoon character.
13. ミッキーマウスやドラえもんのように，様々なキャラクター商品が漫画から生まれています. — Many kinds of character goods are derived from cartoon characters such as Mickey Mouse and Doraemon.
14. 「サザエさん」はもともとは新聞に連載された4こま漫画でした. — "Sazae-san" was originally a four-frame comic strip which was published serially in a newspaper.
15. 日本には漫画喫茶があります. — In Japan there are coffee shops which have comic book libraries.
16. 漫画に出てくるセックスや暴力的な描写が批判されています. — Depictions of sex and violence in cartoons are criticized.

❷アニメに関する表現

1. そのアニメは子供から大人まで幅広いファンがいます. — That animated cartoon has a wide range of fans from children to adults.
2. 日本でもディズニーアニメはとても人気があります. — Disney animated cartoons are very popular in Japan, too.
3. 将来アニメの声優になりたいと思っています. — I want to become a voice artist for animated cartoons in the future.
4. アニメのセル画を集めている人がたくさんいます. — There are many people who collect cell drawings of animated cartoons.
5. 人気のあるアニメの下絵は高い値段で売られています. — Original drafts of popular animated cartoons sell at high prices.

場面・状況別会話 ⑭

●ファッション

> What's the most popular color this year?

> As far as clothing is concerned, it's black.

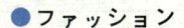

Pat : I love your watch. Is it brand-new?
パット : その時計いいわね．新品なの？
Makoto : Yes. I just bought it yesterday.
誠 : うん．きのう買ったばかりなんだ．
Pat : It seems to have a lot of functions.
パット : いろいろな機能がついてるみたいだけど．
Makoto : Right. It has a stopwatch, of course, a thermometer, a barometer, and an altimeter, too.
誠 : うん．ストップウオッチはもちろん，温度計，気圧計，高度計までついてるんだ．
Pat : Wow. It's perfect for outdoors. Cool!
パット : へぇ．アウトドア用に最適ね．かっこいいわ．
Makoto : I like it because it looks tough. It's waterproof, too, so I'm going to wear it when I go diving.
誠 : 丈夫そうなのが気に入ってるんだ．防水にもなっているからダイビングするときにつけていくつもりなんだ．
Pat : What's the most popular color this year?
パット : 今年はどんな色がいちばん人気があるの？
Makoto : As far as clothing is concerned, it's black.
誠 : 身につけるものだと黒だよ．
Pat : Do you usually buy brand-name stuff?
パット : いつもブランド物を買うの？
Makoto : Well, not always.
誠 : そういうわけでもないよ．

★ミニ知識★

アメリカの若者ファッション

アメリカの若者のファッションは，ビジネスの場合などを除けばふつう機能性重視型です．例えば，日本では学生も学校におしゃれなバッグを持っていきますが，アメリカの学生はリュックサック（backpack）などを好みます．一般に防犯に注意の必要なアメリカでは，車で移動するとき以外はなるべく手荷物を減らすのが常識です．靴に関しても，日常的に車を運転する必要があるので，機能性の高いスニーカーなどが好まれます．積雪地帯も多いので，日本でよく見かけるハイヒールや極端に底を厚くした靴やブーツを履く若者はむしろ少数派です．また，学生はふつう化粧にあまり時間をかけません．彼らの興味はどちらかというと化粧よりもダイエットやフィットネスのほうにあります．

表現集

❶流行に関する一般的な表現

1. 今年の流行色は何ですか. — What color is popular [fashionable, in fashion, in] this year? / What's the fashionable color this year?
2. その格好は今はやっています. — That style is popular [fashionable, in fashion, in] now.
3. 彼が履いているあの靴はもう流行遅れです. — Those shoes he's wearing are old-fashioned now.
4. 来年もブーツの流行は続くでしょう. — Boots will be in fashion next year, too.
5. パリの最新のファッションは何ですか. — What's the latest Paris fashion?
6. 今, 流行の服は何ですか. — What kinds of dresses are in fashion now?
7. またフラノがはやりそうですね. — Flannel seems to be back in fashion.
8. ショルダーバッグを持つのが今はやっています. — It's fashionable now to carry a shoulder bag.
9. 最近流行のファッションは軽くて着心地のいい服です. — The recent trends in fashion favor light, comfortable clothes.
10. このスタイルの流行は長く続かないと思います. — The popularity of this style won't last「for a long time [for long]」.
11. 最新の流行についていくのは大変です. — It's tough to keep up with the latest fashions.
12. 一時的な流行にすぎないと思います. — I think it's just a temporary fad.

❷個人的な趣味に関する表現

1. 彼はファッションセンスが全くありません. — He has no「sense of fashion [fashion sense]」.
2. 彼女はファッションセンスが抜群です. — She has an excellent「sense of fashion [fashion sense]」.
3. 彼は流行に敏感です. — He is fashion-conscious [sensitive to fashion].
4. 彼は最新の流行を追うのが好きです. — He likes to follow the latest fashions. / He's a dedicated follower of the latest fashions.
5. 彼女は流行にうといです. — She doesn't know much about fashion.
6. 彼女は光り物を身につけるのが好きです. — She likes wearing metallic [glossy] stuff.
7. ファッション雑誌で流行を研究しています. — I'm studying what's in fashion in fashion magazines.

❸服装のセンスをほめるときの表現

1. (服装が) すてきですね. — You look nice.
2. きょうはずいぶん (服装が) おしゃれですね. — You look all dressed up today.
3. 彼女はおしゃれですね. — She's a nice dresser. / She's elegant [sharp, cool].
4. ネクタイのセンスがいいですね. — I love your taste in ties.
5. あなたの新しい上着は今とてもはやっていますね. — Your new jacket is very trendy now.
6. 彼のファッションはいつも新しい [現代風] です. — He always wears up-to-date fashions. / He's always up-to-date in fashion.

場面・状況別会話 ⑮

●ヘアスタイル

> How would you like your hair cut?

> I'd like it short above the ears.

Takashi: Hi. I'd like a haircut, a shampoo and a shave.
隆　　　：こんにちは．カットとシャンプー，それとひげそりもお願いします．
Barber: Yes, sir. How would you like your hair cut?
理容師：はい．かしこまりました．カットはどのようになさいますか．
Takashi: I'd like it short above the ears. And just trim it in the front. Please don't make it too short in the back. Take half an inch off my sideburns.
隆　　　：短く，耳が出るくらいでお願いします．前はそろえるだけでいいです．後ろは短くしすぎないでください．もみあげは半インチ（約1.3センチ）くらいそってください．
Barber: Do you want to part your hair?
理容師：髪は分けますか．
Takashi: Yes, in the middle, please.
隆　　　：はい．真ん中でお願いします．
　　　　　(after the cut)　（散髪後）
Barber: How do you like it?
理容師：いかがですか．
Takashi: Can you make the sideburns a little bit shorter?
隆　　　：もみあげをもう少し短くできますか．
Barber: Sure ... How's that?
理容師：はい．…これでどうですか．
Takashi: Perfect. Could you put on some mousse?
隆　　　：ばっちりです．ムースをつけていただけますか．

★ミニ知識★

サービスの指示と料金

　アメリカで理髪店（barbershop）や美容室（beauty salon）に行くときには，電話で事前に予約をとるのがふつうです．最近ではフリーダイヤル（toll-free number）を設けているだけでなく，インターネット上に広告を出したり，Eメールで予約を受け付けている店もあります．散髪（haircut），シャンプー（shampoo），ひげそり（shave）などが別々になっていて，料金も例えば「散髪10ドル」「シャンプー8ドル」というように個々に設定されています．したがって，最初に何を希望するのかをはっきりと伝えておく必要があります．支払うときにはふつう15パーセントくらいのチップを置きます．おもしろいことに客は鏡を背にして座ることもあり，理容師（barber）は間近ではかえって分かりづらい仕上がりぐあいを，少し離れて確認することができます．

表現集

❶ 長さの指示に関する表現

1. 短めにお願いします.	I'd like it short.
2. 耳の上が少し隠れるくらいに, 中くらいの長さでお願いします.	I'd like it to be medium length so it covers the top of my ears.
3. 耳が隠れるくらいに, えりの位置でお願いします.	I'd like it to be collar length with my ears covered.
4. 前髪を半インチくらい切ってください.	Please cut about half an inch off my bangs.
5. トップを短めにしていただけますか.	Would you cut the top short?
6. もみあげは耳の高さでカットしていただけますか.	Would you cut the sideburns at ear level?
7. (ワンレングスのボブで) あごの線までの長さで毛先をそろえるようにお願いします.	I'd like it to be the same length below chin level.

❷ 髪型の指示に関する表現

1. 前髪はそろえるだけにしてください.	Just trim my bangs, please.
2. ムースをつけて髪をセットしていただけますか.	Would you put on some mousse to style it?
3. 後ろを刈り上げていただけますか.	Could you taper it short on the back?
4. サイドを後ろに流してください.	Please style it so that it goes backward on the sides.
5. もう少し軽い感じに見えるようにお願いします.	I'd like it to look a little thinner.
6. ふわっとした感じになるようにお願いします.	I'd like it to be fluffy.
7. 全体的にレイヤーを入れていただけますか.	Would you layer it all around?
8. 毛先にパーマをかけて巻き上げていただけますか.	Would you have the ends permed so they'll flip up?
9. ストレートパーマでお願いします.	I'd like it straightened.
10. メグ・ライアンのような髪型にしたいです.	I want it like Meg Ryan's.

❸ その他の表現

1. 髪を染めたのですか.	Did you dye your hair?
2. 天然パーマなんです.	I have naturally curly hair.
3. ふだん整髪料は使いません.	I usually don't use styling products.
4. 枝毛に悩んでいます.	I'm bothered by split ends.
5. どのように髪をスタイリングしていますか.	How do you style your hair?
6. ヘアアイロンを使って後ろの髪を巻き上げています.	I use a curling iron to flip my hair in back.
7. ブラシで髪をブローして, ボリュームをつけています.	I blow-dry my hair with a brush to make it look fuller.
8. ヘアカーラーで髪をセットしています.	I set my hair with rollers.

場面・状況別会話 ⑯

●カラオケ

> "Love Me Tender." It's my favorite.

> What's the song number?

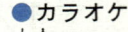

Aya: Dan, what are you going to sing?
綾: ダン, 何を歌う?
Dan: Let me see the booklet. Oh, this is good. "Love Me Tender." It's my favorite.
ダン: 本を見せて. ああ, これ,「ラブミーテンダー」がいいや. 大好きな歌なんだ.
Aya: What's the song number?
綾: 何番?
Dan: It's B-48.
ダン: Bの48番.
Aya: OK. I'll put the number into the machine.
綾: はい. 番号を機械に入れるわね.
(Dan starts singing.)
(ダンが歌い始める)
Dan: Oh, the key is too high. Can you make it lower?
ダン: ああ, キーが高すぎるよ. もっと低くできる?
Aya: Yes. My dad loves this song, too. Once he gets his hands on a microphone, he never lets go. We can put some echo in the voice. That will make your voice sound more professional.
綾: うん, 父もこの歌が大好きなの. マイクを握ったら, 絶対離さないんだから. 声にエコーをかけることもできるわ. プロの歌手みたいに聞こえるわよ.
Dan: Wow, we can have applause, too. Aya, can you teach me how to sing Japanese *enka*?
ダン: わあ, 拍手の音も出せるんだね! 綾, 僕に日本の演歌の歌い方を教えてくれない?

★ミニ知識★

「カラオケ」は世界の共通語

　日本で始まった「カラオケ」も今では欧米やアジア諸国などにも輸出され, karaoke という名称そのままで多くの人々に楽しまれています. もちろん, 各国の人々が使えるように, おのおのの国の歌をおのおのの国の言葉で収録したソフトが作られています. 韓国では日本並みに人気があるほか, アメリカでもカラオケのコンテストが開かれたり, パーティー用にカラオケ機器をレンタルする会社もあります. しかし, 自国の飲食店などでカラオケを経験したことがある人でも, 日本にある大規模なカラオケボックスには行ったことがない場合もあるので, 案内して日本の歌などを教えてあげると喜ばれるかもしれません.

表現集

❶カラオケの利用に関する表現

1. カラオケにいっしょに行きませんか. — Do you want to go to karaoke with me [us]?
2. ここは1時間1,000円です. — The charges here are 1,000 yen an hour.
3. 部屋の使用時間を延長しませんか. — Shall we extend the time for using the room?
4. 何か飲み物を注文しましょうか. — Shall we order something to drink?
5. カラオケはストレス解消にいいです. — Karaoke is good for getting rid of stress.

❷曲・歌に関する表現

1. マイクの[伴奏の]ボリュームをもっと大きく[小さく]してもらえますか. — Will you turn up [down] the volume of the microphone [music]?
2. 歌にエコーをかけたいです. — I want to put an echo in the song.
3. この曲は前奏がちょっと長いですね. — The introductory part of this song is a bit long, isn't it?
4. 次の曲を選びましたか. — Have you chosen your next song?
5. デュエットを歌いましょう. ／いっしょにデュエットを歌っていただけますか. — Let's sing a duet. / Would you join me in a duet?
6. 男性のパートを歌っていただけますか. 私は女性のパートを歌います. — Would you sing the male part? I'll sing the female part.
7. 今度はあなたが歌う番です. — It's your turn to sing.
8. こんなに歌がうまいとは知りませんでした. — I didn't know you were such a good singer.
9. 彼女はレパートリーが豊富です. — She knows a lot of songs.
10. 人前で歌うのは苦手なんです. — I'm not good at singing in front of people.
11. 音痴だからあまり歌いたくないです. — I'm tone-deaf, so I don't want to sing.
12. 歌いすぎて声がかれてしまっています. — I sang too much, so I'm hoarse.
13. 音程がはずれています. — You're out of tune.
14. 伴奏より早くなっています[伴奏に遅れています]. — You're singing「ahead of [behind] the music.
15. 曲が速すぎて, 歌詞を追っていくのが難しいです. — The song is too fast, so it's difficult to keep up with the lyrics.
16. この歌の節は覚えやすいです. — The melody of this song is catchy [easy to remember].
17. ここはリズムをとるのが難しいです. — The rhythm here is difficult to keep up with.
18. 歌が上手ではなくても, 楽しければいいんです. — Even if you're not a good singer, it's worthwhile as long as you enjoy it.
19. 日本的なメロディーは歌いやすいですか. — Is it easy for you to sing Japanese melodies?

❸設備・装置に関する表現

1. このマイクは電源が入っていません. — This microphone is not on.
2. 歌うときはそのモニターを見るといいよ. — You can watch the monitor as you sing.
3. カラオケボックスは防音なので, いくら大きな声を出してもかまいません. — Since karaoke studios are soundproof, you can sing as loud as you like.
4. カラオケの機械をレンタルしようよ. — Let's rent some karaoke equipment.
5. 彼女の家にはカラオケセットがあります. — She has a karaoke set at her home.

場面・状況別会話 ⑰

●占い

> Well, you have a very long lifeline here. That means you'll live a long time.

> Great! How about my love life?

Yasuko : Kenny, do you want me to read your fortune?
靖　子：ケニー，運勢を占ってもらいたい？
Kenny : Are your predictions reliable?
ケニー：本当に当たるのかい？
Yasuko : Trust me. Let me read your palm…. Well, you have a very long lifeline here. That means you'll live a long time.
靖　子：信じてよ．手のひらを見せて．…えっと，ここにすごく長い生命線があるわね．長生きするってことだわ．
Kenny : Great! How about my love life? Will I meet an attractive girl?
ケニー：すごい．恋愛運はどう？すてきな女の子に会えるかなあ？
Yasuko : Well, your marriage line says you'll have a happy marriage and a nice family. By the way, what's your sign?
靖　子：結婚線には幸せな結婚をして，すてきな家庭を持てるとでてるわよ．ところで，星座は何？
Kenny : I'm a Libra.
ケニー：天秤(てん)座だけど．
Yasuko : Then a Gemini girl would be your best partner. This year's cycle favors romance for you. Don't be afraid to take chances.
靖　子：じゃあ，双子座の女性と相性がいいわよ．今年は恋愛運がいい周期に入っているわ．冒険を恐れてはだめよ．

★ミニ知識★

海外の占い

　占い師が道端に小さなテーブルを出して座っている光景は，欧米ではふつう見ることはありません．例えばアメリカでは，店の中で占いを仕事としたり（テレビや新聞に広告を出すこともある），インターネットによる占いはあっても，占い師が通りに座って客を取ることは法律で禁じている州もあります．欧米の占いで最も一般的なのは占星術 (astrology) に基づく星占い (horoscope)，次いで手相占い，タロット (Tarot cards) と続きます．日本で人気のある血液型による性格判断は海外ではあまりはやっていません．日本の生活に慣れていない外国人にいきなり "What's your blood type?" などと聞くと，医者でもないのにどうしてと変に思われることがあります．また，海外の中国料理店では fortune cookie と呼ばれる，運勢や教訓が書かれた紙が中に入っているクッキーがもらえる所もあります．

表現集

❶一般的な表現

1. 占いをしてもらったことがありますか. — Have you ever had your fortune told?
2. 占いを信じますか. — Do you believe in fortune-telling?
3. 占いに行きましょう. — Let's go have our fortunes told [read].
4. あの占い師はよく当たるという評判です. — That fortune-teller is said to be trustworthy. / That fortune-teller has a really good reputation.
5. 占いは当たりましたか. — Did the prediction come true?
6. あの占いはいんちきくさいです. — There is something fishy [tricky] about his [her] fortune-telling.
7. おみくじを引いてみましょう. — Let's try an *omikuji*.

❷占ってもらう人の表現

1. 金銭［結婚, 仕事, 健康］運を占ってもらいたいんです. — I'd like to have my money [marriage, business, health] fortune read [told], please.
2. 全体運はどうですか. — What is my fortune in general?
3. 結婚［運命, 知能, 感情］線はどう出ていますか. — What does my marriage [fate, head, heart] line show [say]?
4. それはよい［悪い］前兆なのですか. — Is it a good [bad] omen [sign]?
5. 占い師は水晶玉を使って将来を占っていました. — The fortune-teller looked into the future using a crystal ball.
6. 私の星座は乙女座です. — I'm a Virgo.
7. おみくじで大吉［吉, 小吉, 凶］が出ました. — My *omikuji* says I'll have「great good [good, fair, bad] luck.

❸占う人の表現

1. あなたの運勢を占ってあげましょう. — Let me tell [read] your fortune.
2. 生年月日からあなたの運勢が分かります. — I can tell your fortune from your birthdate.
3. きょうは金運はいいですが, 恋愛運は最悪です. — Today you have good fortune in money matters, but terrible luck in your love life.
4. 来月, あなたの運気は上昇［下降］します. — Your fortune next month is going to get better [worse]. / Your fortune next month is going to improve [worsen].
5. 今週は波乱含みです. — You will have ups and downs this week.
6. 今週は努力が報われるでしょう. — Your efforts will be well rewarded this week.
7. よい周期に入っているので, 新しい出会いがあるでしょう. — You're on a good cycle during which you'll have a new encounter.
8. あなたのきょうの幸運のお守りは黄色いハンカチです. — Your lucky charm for today is a yellow handkerchief.
9. あなたの今週のラッキーカラーは青です. — Your lucky color for this week is blue.
10. 東南に旅行をするとよいことがあります. — You will have good luck if you travel toward the southeast.
11. 運勢はよい行いを心がければしだいによくなります. — Your fortune always changes for the better if you try to behave properly.

場面・状況別会話 ⓲

●料理

> Now fan the rice to cool it.

> I'll help you with the fan.

Kazuo : First, you put hot rice in the wooden bowl and pour sushi vinegar over the rice.

— 男：まず温かいごはんを飯台に移して，寿司(¿)酢をかけるんだ．

Suzy : Is that regular vinegar?

スージー：ふつうのお酢なの？

Kazuo : Well, it's vinegar with some sugar and salt. Now fan the rice to cool it.

— 男：お酢に砂糖と塩が入ってるんだ．さて，ごはんをうちわであおいで冷まします．

Suzy : I'll help you with the fan.

スージー：私があおぎましょう．

Kazuo : Thanks. Now the sushi rice is ready, so I'm going to make the sushi rolls. You put *nori*, or dried seaweed, on the bamboo rolling mat and spread the rice evenly on the *nori*.

— 男：ありがとう．寿司飯ができたから，寿司を巻くほうに移ろう．のりを巻きすの上に置いて，その上にごはんを均等に広げるんだ．

Suzy : Doesn't the rice stick to your hands?

スージー：ごはんが手につかない？

Kazuo : Well, sometimes. Just dip your hands in vinegar and the rice won't stick. Now let's lay tuna fillet on the rice and roll it up like this. Then you cut the roll into several portions. There you go.

— 男：うん．つくときもあるよ．手を酢に浸せばごはんがつかなくなるよ．さて，マグロの切り身をごはんの上にのせてこうして巻くんだ．いくつかに切り分けて，できあがり．

Suzy : Now I'll try making an avocado roll.

スージー：じゃあ私はアボカド巻きを作ってみるわ．

★ミニ知識★

単位の違いに注意

料理にはレシピ (recipe) がつきものですが，日本と英米では計量の単位が違うので注意が必要ですし，略語も読めるようにしておかなければなりません．1 inch ≒ 2.5 centimeters（長さ），1 ounce ≒ 28 grams, 1 pound ≒ 453 grams（重量），といったぐあいです．ounce は oz という略語を使うので，例えば 100 grams は約 3 1/2oz になります（pound の略語は lb）．容量を量る「小さじ」「大さじ」はそれぞれ teaspoon, tablespoon の略語を使い，2 tsp soy sauce, 2 tbsp water のように表します．また，日本の 1cup は 200 ml ですが米国では約 240 ml なので注意が必要です．レシピに書く「サツマイモ 300 グラム」は 10 1/2 oz sweet potatoes のように量を材料の前に置きます．

表現集

❶材料・用具に関する表現

1. このクッキーを作る材料を教えていただけませんか. — Would you tell me the ingredients for making these cookies?
2. この材料は3人分です. — These ingredients are for three servings [people].
3. 4人分のみそ汁を作るには約60グラムのみそが必要です. — We need about two ounces of *miso* to make four bowls of *miso* soup.
4. ジャガイモは皮をむいて,冷水に浸しておきます. — Peel the potatoes and soak them in cold water.
5. どんな調味料が必要ですか. — What kinds of seasonings are needed?
6. 包丁とまな板を貸してもらえますか. — Can I use a knife and a cutting board?
7. 計量カップはありますか. — Do you have measuring cups?
8. ボールを2つ用意していただけますか. — Would you prepare two mixing bowls?

❷材料の切り方に関する表現

1. ニンジンは斜め切りにします. — Slice the carrots diagonally.
2. 豆腐は1センチ角に切ります. — Dice the tofu into three-eighth-inch cubes.
3. キュウリは薄切りにします. — Cut the cucumbers into thin slices.
4. タマネギはみじん切りにします. — Chop the onion finely.
5. 昆布を5センチの長さに切ります. — Cut the *kombu* into two-inch strips.
6. キャベツは千切りにします. — Shred the cabbage.
7. ニンジンは短冊切りにします. — Cut the carrot into rectangular pieces.

❸煮込みと味つけに関する表現

1. 弱火[中火,強火]で煮ます. — Boil it over low [medium, high] heat.
2. 油を175度に熱しておきます. — Preheat the oil to 350 degrees Fahrenheit.
3. からっと[きつね色に]なるまで揚げます. — Deep-fry it until crispy [golden brown].
4. なべに油を熱し,野菜をいためます. — Heat the oil in a skillet, and stir-fry [sauté] the vegetables.
5. ステーキ用牛肉を1切れ焼きます. — Grill a steak.
6. 弱火でぐつぐつ煮込みます. — Simmer it over low heat.
7. ニンジンを熱湯でゆでます. — Boil the carrots in hot water.
8. 火を弱めて,上のあくをすくいます. — Lower the heat and skim the foam [scum, froth] from the top.
9. 調味料を加え,中火で20分煮ます. — Add seasoning, and cook over medium heat for 20 minutes.
10. しょうゆと砂糖で味つけをします. — Season with soy sauce and sugar. / Add soy sauce and sugar to season.
11. 塩小さじ2分の1杯としょうゆ大さじ1杯をスープに入れます. — Add half a teaspoon of salt and one tablespoon of soy sauce to the soup.
12. 味見をして甘さ[からさ]を調節します. — Taste it to adjust the sweetness [hotness].
13. 刻んだパセリ[のり]を振りかけます. — Sprinkle with cut parsley [*nori*].
14. 皿に盛って,レモンスライスを添えます. — Arrange them on plates, and serve with a slice of lemon.

場面・状況別会話 ⑲

●写真

(Miho and her friend are traveling around.)
(美穂と友達は旅行中です)

Miho : **Excuse me, would you take our picture?**
美　　穂：すみませんが，私たちの写真を撮っていただけますか．
A Passerby : **Sure.**
通　行　人：いいですよ．
Miho : **We'll stand right in front of the gate. We'd like to have that statue in the background.**
美　　穂：門の正面に立ちますね．あの銅像をバックに入れてほしいんですが．
A Passerby : **OK. Is this automatic?**
通　行　人：分かりました．これはオートですか．
Miho : **Yes, you just press the button on the right. The flash will automatically pop up if it's too dark.**
美　　穂：はい，右のシャッターを押すだけです．暗ければ，自動的にフラッシュが出ます．
A Passerby : **All right. Smile!** (pressing the shutter)
通　行　人：はい．笑って！（シャッターを押す）
Miho : **Sorry. I blinked. Would you take one more shot?**
美　　穂：ごめんなさい，まばたきしてしまいました．もう1枚撮ってもらえますか．
A Passerby : **OK. Ready? Say cheese!**
通　行　人：ええ．いいですか．チーズ！

◆ポーズをとっている人にかける言葉
じっとして．Hold it (right there).／まばたきしないで．Don't blink.／あごを引いて．Tuck in your chin.／カメラ［レンズ］を見て．Look at the camera [lens].／顔を少し左に傾けて．Tilt your head a bit to the left.／笑って！Smile (for me)! / Give me your best smile! / Say cheese! / Say money! / Let me see your pearly whites [teeth].／もう1枚撮るから動かないで．One more shot. Please stay still.／もうちょっと木に近づいて．Move a bit closer to the tree.

★ミニ知識★

写真は家族の宝

アメリカの家庭では居間の棚などに家族の写真を飾っておき，訪問客が来たときに見せて説明をすることがよくあります．ふだんはあまり写真を撮らなくても，入学式や卒業式，結婚式など，人生の節目に当たるときの写真は専門のカメラマン（photographer）に撮ってもらう人が多くいます．また，日本では恋人や家族の写真などを職場の机の上に置くことはあまりありませんが，アメリカではふつうです．年に一度のクリスマスカードにも家族や子供の写真を同封して健康でいることを知らせることがあります．写真はアルバムにしまっておくだけのものではないのです．

表現集

❶画像の注文に関する表現

1. 山を背景にして撮っていただけますか. — Would you take a picture of me with the mountains in the background?
2. 全身［上半身］の写真にしてください. — I'd like「a full-length portrait [a portrait from the waist up].
3. 顔のアップの写真にしてください. — I'd like a facial close-up.
4. （グループ写真などでカメラマンに向かって）みんなちゃんと入ってますか. — Is everybody in the picture?
5. 横長ではなく，縦長に撮ってください. — Please take it vertically, not horizontally.
6. パノラマで撮ってもらいたいです. — I'd like this picture to be a panoramic shot.
7. ツーショット写真を撮ってもらえますか. — Would you take a picture of the two of us?

❷人に撮影を依頼するときの表現

1. 自動焦点カメラなので，右にあるシャッターを押すだけです. — The camera focuses automatically. All you have to do is press the button on the right.
2. シャッターを押す前にフィルムを巻いてください. — Would you wind the film before releasing the shutter?
3. シャッタースピードが遅いです. ぶれると写真がぼけるので気をつけて. — The shutter speed is slow. Be careful not to move or you'll get a blurry [blurred] photo.
4. ポラロイドなのですぐに現像できます. — It's a Polaroid camera, so「the developed prints are ready in a minute [the prints are developed immediately].
5. 36枚撮りなので，あと2，3枚は撮れると思います. — It has 36 exposures, so you can take a few more shots.

❸その他の表現

1. あなたといっしょの写真を撮りたいです. — I'd like to have my picture taken with you.
2. いっしょに写真に入っていただけますか. — Would you join me in the picture? / Would you pose with me?
3. 逆光なので，反対側から撮りましょう. — I'm shooting into the light. Let me try taking it「from the opposite side [from the other way].
4. タイマーを使いましょう. — Let's set [use] the self-timer.
5. うまく撮れているといいのですが. — I hope it turns out well [OK].
6. ピンぼけ［露出オーバー，露出不足］でないといいのですが. — I hope it isn't「out of focus [overexposed, underexposed].
7. 彼は写真写りがよい［悪い］です. — He photographs well [badly].
8. いろいろな種類の使い捨てカメラが手に入ります. 自動販売機でも買えます. — Many types of disposable cameras are available. You can buy them even from vending machines.
9. APSフィルムは小さくてカメラに簡単に装着できますが，現像や焼き増しにお金がかかります. — APS film is small and easy to load into the camera, but it's expensive to develop the pictures and have them reprinted.
10. デジカメはフィルムが不要で，パソコンで画像を編集できるのがいいです. — Digital cameras are nice because they don't need film and you can edit the images on a personal computer.

| 場面・状況別会話 ⑳

● ペット

> His name is Lucky.

> Hi, Lucky! Can you shake hands? Oh, he did it. Good dog!

(Yoshio is walking his dog.)
(良夫は犬を散歩させています)

Cathy : Hi, Yoshio. Is this your dog?
キャシー：こんにちは，良夫．これ，あなたの犬？
Yoshio : Yeah.
良　夫：うん．
Cathy : I didn't know you had a dog. What kind of dog is it?
キャシー：犬を飼ってるなんて知らなかったわ．何ていう種類の犬？
Yoshio : It's a Shibainu.
良　夫：柴犬さ．
Cathy : It's so cute. Is it a he or a she?
キャシー：とてもかわいいわね．オス，それともメス？
Yoshio : It's a he. His name is Lucky. He's about 8 years old, which means he's almost 50 years old in human years.
良　夫：オスだよ．名前は「ラッキー」っていうんだ．8歳くらいなんだけど，人間の年齢でいうと50歳ぐらいだね．
Cathy : He has a fine coat of hair. Hi, Lucky! Can you shake hands? Oh, he did it. Good dog!
キャシー：毛並みがいいわねえ．ラッキー，お手できる？あら，やったわ．お利口さんね．
Yoshio : He's good at fetching a ball, too.
良　夫：ボール拾いも得意なんだ．
Cathy : Is he? Do you take him for a walk every day?
キャシー：本当？毎日散歩に連れていってるの？
Yoshio : Yeah. That's good for my health, too.
良　夫：うん．僕の健康のためにもいいからね．

★ミニ知識★

pet-sittingって？

　日本では飼い主が旅行などで家をあける場合，ペットを動物病院やペットホテルに預かってもらうのが一般的ですが，欧米ではそのような施設を利用するほかに pet-sitting service を頼むことができます．（動詞の sit には「世話をする」という意味があります．）これは，飼い主が留守の間にペットにえさや水をやったり，犬なら散歩に連れていったり，遊んでくれたりする人を派遣するサービスです．友達や知り合いに pet-sitting を頼むこともあるようです．pet を具体的な動物名に置き換えて dog-sitting や cat-sitting のようにいうこともできます．

表現集

❶ペットの世話などに関する表現（💠動物の代名詞はふつうitだが，オスかメスか分かっている場合，親密な感情を表すためにheやsheを用いることもある）

1. 金魚に1日2度えさをあげてください． — Please feed the goldfish twice a day.
2. えさは何をあげているのですか． — What do you feed it?
3. このペットは人になれて育てやすいです． — This pet is tame [friendly] and easy to raise.
4. 犬をひもでつながなければいけません． — You need to have your dog on a leash.
5. ふんはきれいに処理しなければいけません． — We must clean up the mess it made.
6. ペットの飼い主はペットに対して責任をもたなければなりません． — Pet owners should be responsible for their pets.
7. ペットシッティングを頼んだらどうですか． — Why don't you use a pet-sitting service?
8. このアパートでペットを飼うことは禁止されています． — You are not allowed to have pets in this apartment.

❷ペットのしつけと芸に関する表現

1. この犬はよくしつけができていますね． — This dog is ⌈trained well [well trained].
2. ペットは子供のうちに厳しくしつけておくべきです． — We should train our pets strictly when they are young.
3. うちの犬は屋内ではおしっこをしません． — My dog never pees inside the house.
4. うちの犬は家の外で排便するようにしつけられています． — My dog is housebroken.
5. この犬は主人に忠実です． — This dog is obedient to its master [mistress].
6. この犬はまだ完全にはなれていません． — This dog isn't completely domesticated yet.
7. 何か芸ができますか．／何か芸を見せてください． — Can it do any tricks? / Please show me some tricks.
8. この犬はお座り［お手，ちんちん］ができます． — This dog can sit [shake hands, stand up on its hind legs].
9. （犬に）「動くな」「転がれ」「ふせ」「後に」「取ってこい」「ほえろ」］を教えているところです． — I'm teaching it to stay [roll over, lie down, heel, fetch, speak].
10. （犬に）いい子だ［よくできた］． — Good dog!

❸ペットの健康に関する表現

1. うちのインコはきのう元気がないようだったので，動物病院に連れていきました． — My parakeet looked sick yesterday, so I took it to the vet.
2. うちのハムスターは最近食欲がないです． — My hamster doesn't have an appetite these days.
3. うちの犬は毎年狂犬病の予防接種を受けています． — My dog gets vaccinated against rabies every year.
4. 犬のノミを取る何かいい方法を知っていますか． — Do you know any good ways to ⌈get rid of fleas on a dog [rid a dog of fleas]?
5. 十分に運動をさせないと犬もストレスがたまります． — Dogs get stressed if they don't get enough exercise.
6. この猫は不妊手術をしてあります． — This cat has been spayed [fixed].
7. シャワーと毛の手入れをお願いします． — I'd like to have her [him] washed and groomed.

場面・状況別会話 ㉑

●ミステリー

A UFO was flying just above the mountains.

You must have seen an airplane or something.

Toshio : Kate, listen.
俊　雄：ケイト，聞いてよ．
Kate　 : What's up?
ケイト：どうしたの？
Toshio : You may not believe me, but I just saw a UFO.
俊　雄：僕の言うこと信じないかもしれないけど，さっきＵＦＯを見たんだよ．
Kate　 : A what?
ケイト：何をですって？
Toshio : A UFO. It was flying just above the mountains.
俊　雄：ＵＦＯだよ．山のすぐ上を飛んでいたんだ．
Kate　 : You must have seen an airplane or something.
ケイト：飛行機か何かを見たんでしょう．
Toshio : I can swear that it was a UFO.
俊　雄：絶対にＵＦＯだよ．
Kate　 : How can you be so sure? How can you tell that it wasn't an airplane or a blimp?
ケイト：どうしてそんなに確信できるの？飛行機や飛行船じゃないってどうして分かるのよ？
Toshio : It was shining in a very odd way. Oh, I should've taken a picture.
俊　雄：とても変な光り方をしていたんだ．ああ，写真を撮っておけばよかったなあ．
Kate　 : All right, all right. Let's get back to work.
ケイト：分かった，分かった．戻って勉強しましょう．
Toshio : You don't believe me, do you?
俊　雄：信じてないんだろう？
Kate　 : No. Not until I see one myself.
ケイト：ええ．この目で見るまではね．

★ミニ知識★

世界の伝説上の生き物

　世界には生存が確認できない生き物がたくさんいます．ヒマラヤ山中の雪男（Abominable Snowman），米国北西部やカナダにすむ大足人間（Bigfoot），ヨーロッパで生まれた吸血鬼（vampire）や狼(おおかみ)人間（werewolf）など，多種多様な生き物が目撃されたとされていますが，本当に存在するのかどうかは明らかではありません．中にはイギリスのネス湖にすむといわれていたネッシー（Nessie）についての証言や写真のように，でっちあげであったと判明するケースもあります．最も身近な話題とされ，写真やビデオも残っているUFO (unidentified flying object) や宇宙人（aliens, extraterrestrials）の存在でさえ，真偽のほどはまだ正式に確認されていません．

表現集

❶UFO・宇宙人に関する表現

1. 丸くて光る物体が空中をジグザグに飛行しているのを見ました. — I saw a round shining object flying zigzag in the air.
2. UFOを目撃したと証言する人はたくさんいます. — There are many people who claim to have seen [sighted, spotted, identified] UFOs.
3. 宇宙人の存在を信じますか. — Do you believe in the existence of aliens [extraterrestrials]?
4. UFOは人間を誘拐するために地球に降りてくるという人がいます. — Some people say UFOs land on earth to kidnap [abduct] human beings.
5. 宇宙人は人間よりもはるかに進んでいるといわれています. — It is said that the aliens are far more advanced than human beings.

❷幽霊・お化け等に関する表現

1. 気味が悪いです. — It's spooky.
2. 3階の女子トイレにはお化けが出るといううわさがあります. — There is a rumor that「the women's restroom on the third floor is haunted [a ghost appears in the women's restroom on the third floor].
3. 亡くなった家族の霊が家の中をさまよっているのが見えました. — The spirits of the dead family were seen wandering in the house.
4. 暗やみに火の玉が浮かんでいるのを見たと彼女は言いました. — She said she saw a ball of fire hovering in the darkness.
5. 心霊写真を見たことがありますか. — Have you ever seen spirit photos?
6. そのホテルで不可思議な出来事にたくさんあいました. — I saw many supernatural events at the hotel.
7. 彼はたたられていると強く思い込んでいます. — The idea that he is cursed has taken a strong hold of him.
8. 寝ていて金縛りにあい, 全く動けませんでした. — While I was sleeping I felt like I was bound hand and foot and couldn't move at all.
9. ここで猫がひかれてからこの道路で自動車事故が多発しています. — Many car accidents have happened on this road since a cat was run over here.
10. 吸血鬼は不死身ですが, 日光やニンニクや十字架に耐えられません. — Vampires are immortal, but they cannot stand sunlight, garlic or crosses.

❸超能力・超常現象等に関する表現

1. 多くの出来事は科学で説明できません. — Many events cannot be explained by science.
2. 何らかの未知の力がその出来事に関係していると思われます. — Some unknown force seems to be related to the incident.
3. 彼はスプーンを曲げる超能力をもっています. — He has the telekinetic power to bend spoons.
4. 彼女は壁を透視できます. — She can see through walls.
5. その泉の水を飲んで病気が治った人がたくさんいます. — Many people recovered from illnesses by drinking the water of the spring.
6. 不思議なことに, その銅像の目から涙が出ているのが見えました. — Strangely, tears were seen coming from the eyes of the statue.

場面・状況別会話 ㉒

●日本の家と部屋

> I went into the house with my shoes on.

> Well, that sometimes happens.

Nicolas: Satoko invited me over the other day. It was funny.
ニコラス：この前，聡子の家に招待されたんだけど，おかしかったよ．

Hiroko: What happened?
弘　子：どうしたの？

Nicolas: It was the first time I was asked to a Japanese house, and I went into the house with my shoes on.
ニコラス：日本人の家に招かれたのは初めてだったから，靴を履いたまま家に上がってしまったんだ．

Hiroko: Well, that sometimes happens. Japanese people draw a clear line between inside and outside a house.
弘　子：ああ，それ時々ある話だわ．日本人は家の中と外をはっきり区別するの．

Nicolas: What is worse, I was shown into a Japanese room with *tatami* mats, and I walked on them with slippers on.
ニコラス：もっと悪いことに，畳の敷いてある和室に案内されたんだけど，スリッパを履いて畳の上を歩いちゃったんだ．

Hiroko: Oh, no. We don't wear slippers on *tatami*. What's more, usually we have special slippers for the bathroom or even for the verandah.
弘　子：まあ．私たちは畳の上ではスリッパを履かないわね．それと，ふつうトイレ用やベランダ用にさえ特別のスリッパがあるのよ．

Nicolas: Then I should be careful not to leave the bathroom with the bathroom slippers on.
ニコラス：それじゃあ，トイレ用のスリッパを履いてトイレから出ていかないように気をつけなきゃいけないね．

Hiroko: Well, even Japanese sometimes make that kind of mistake.
弘　子：日本人でさえ時々そういう失敗をすることもあるわ．

★ミニ知識★

家中を案内

　欧米人の家庭を訪問すると，彼らが家中の部屋を見せてくれるので驚くことがあります．居間やバスルームはもちろんのこと，ダイニングルーム，キッチン，子供部屋，そして夫婦の寝室まで案内してくれることもあります．彼らが自分の家を客に見せて回るのには主に2つの理由があります．一つはトイレの場所などを客に知ってもらい，自由に使えるようにという配慮から，もう一つはインテリアに凝るなど自分の家に誇りをもっている人たちが少なくなく，それを客に見せたがるという文化的背景があるからです．日本ではあまりこういう習慣がありませんが，外国人を自分の家に招待したら装飾品や家具について説明してあげて話題を広げていきましょう．

表現集

❶ 日本の家・部屋と習慣に関する表現

1. 靴を脱いでスリッパを履いてください.
   Please take off your shoes and put on slippers.
2. ベランダに出るときはスリッパを履き替えなければなりません.
   You should change slippers when you go out on the verandah.
3. 日本では使っていないときはトイレや風呂のドアを閉めておきます.
   In Japan, doors to bathrooms should be shut when they're not being used.
4. 私たちはふつう浴槽の外で体を洗ったりシャワーを浴びたりします. 浴槽はお湯につかって温まるために使います.
   We usually wash or take a shower outside the bathtub. We use the bathtub to soak in the hot water and warm up.
5. ふとんの上を歩くのは悪いマナーです.
   It's bad manners to walk on futons.
6. 日本人は天気のよい日にふとんを外に干します.
   Japanese people air out futons when the weather is good.
7. 日本では同じ部屋を食堂や居間や寝室として使う家もあります.
   In some Japanese homes, people use the same room as a dining room, living room and bedroom.
8. 一般的に,日本ではトイレと風呂は別々の部屋になっていますが,最近はいっしょの部屋になっている家もあります.
   Generally, in Japan toilets and bathtubs are in separate rooms, but these days some homes have them in the same room.
9. この家は2世帯住宅です. 私たちが2階で祖父母が1階に住んでいます.
   This house is for two generations. We live upstairs and our grandparents live downstairs.
10. アパートを借りるときには,ふつう敷金と礼金を払わなければなりません.
    When renting an apartment, we must usually pay a deposit and a "thank you" fee.
11. ふつう日本のアパートは家具付きではありません.
    Usually apartments in Japan are unfurnished.

❷ 日本の家屋を説明するための表現

1. 日本の家は狭いので「うさぎ小屋」にたとえる人もいます.
   Japanese houses are small, so some people liken them to "rabbit hutches."
2. 今では洋式の家が一般的ですが,それでもたいてい1室は和室になっています.
   Today, Western-style houses are common, but still they usually have at least one Japanese room.
3. 最近は外国からの木材や建築様式を取り入れている家もあります.
   Recently some houses use wood and building styles imported from abroad.
4. 日本語の「マンション」は大きい豪邸ではなく,鉄筋コンクリートでできたアパートのことです.
   "Mansion" in Japanese doesn't mean a large luxurious house, but a reinforced concrete apartment building.
5. 首都圏では3階建ての家が多くあります.
   There are many three-story houses in metropolitan areas.
6. ふつう日本の家には地下室がありません.
   Usually Japanese houses have no basements.
7. ふつう日本の家と家の間にはコンクリートの壁や柵(さく)があります.
   Usually there are concrete walls or fences between houses in Japan.
8. 日本では部屋の大きさを畳の数で表します.
   In Japan, we measure the size of Japanese rooms by the number of *tatami* mats.
9. 最近はフローリングがとても人気があります.
   Wooden floors are very popular nowadays.

場面・状況別会話 ㉓

●衣服

Daniel: Look, Naoko. There are some girls wearing kimono.
ダニエル：見て直子．着物を着ている女の子がいるね．

Naoko: Yes. That's because it's Coming-of-Age Day today.
直　子：そうね．きょうは成人の日だからよ．

Daniel: Wow, they're beautiful. Before I came to Japan, I thought all Japanese wear kimono every day.
ダニエル：わあ，きれいだなあ．僕は日本に来る前は，日本人はみんな毎日着物を着ていると思っていたんだ．

Naoko: Kimono used to be everyday clothes for Japanese people, but nowadays we wear Western clothes. We wear formal kimono only on special occasions.
直　子：昔は日本人にとって着物はふだん着だったんだけど，今ではみんな洋服を着ているわ．特別な機会にだけフォーマルな着物を着るの．

Daniel: Like what?
ダニエル：例えば？

Naoko: During the New Year, on Coming-of-Age Day, and at commencements and so on. We also have *yukata*, which are informal cotton kimono for summer. Some Japanese people wear them when they go to summer festivals or go to see fireworks.
直　子：お正月や成人の日，大学の卒業式とか．それから「ゆかた」という綿でできた夏用のカジュアルな着物もあるの．夏祭りや花火を見に行くときに着る人がいるわ．

Daniel: Really. Maybe I'll get one as a souvenir to take back to America.
ダニエル：本当．アメリカへ持って帰るおみやげに僕も1枚買おうかなあ．

Naoko: That's a great idea! I think men look really dashing and manly in *yukata*.
直　子：それはいい考えだわ！男の人がゆかたを着るととてもりりしくて男らしく見えるわ．

★ミニ知識★

実用性重視の衣服

一般にアメリカのデパートやディスカウントショップでは衣類売り場の占める面積が広く，カジュアルな日常の衣服ならば，種類，サイズ，数などに事欠くことはあまりありません．アメリカではほとんどの服は洗濯機で洗って乾燥機で乾かす（wash and dry）ので，高温にも耐えられる実用性の高い丈夫な素材が好まれます．衣服のカタログ販売も盛んで，店舗を持たずカタログ販売だけを専門にしている会社も多くあります．見かけよりも実用性や合理性を重んじ，少しくらいサイズが合わなくても気にしないというアメリカの消費者の寛大さが，カタログ販売を盛んにしている一つの理由です．古着の売買もガレージセール（自宅の庭先やガレージで不用品を売ること）などで頻繁に行われます．また，服装に関しては，フォーマルとインフォーマルの区別に気を使います．

表現集

❶服の色・柄に関する表現

1. あなたはピンク（の服）が似合います. — Pink suits you. / You look good in pink.
2. あなたは花柄が似合います. — Floral patterns [prints] suit you. / You look good in floral patterns [prints].
3. あなたのような白い肌の人は明るい色（の服）が似合います. — Since you have fair skin, pastel colors suit you.
4. その服を着るとやせて見えます. — That dress makes you look thin.
5. 赤のスカートに合うものを見つけるのは難しいです. — It's difficult to find anything that matches red skirts.

❷着こなし・コーディネートに関する表現

1. この服は似合いますか. — How does this dress look?
2. このジャケットはいろんなタイプの服に合います. — This jacket goes well with various types of clothes.
3. このスカートの上には何を着たらいいでしょう? — What would be a good top for this skirt?
4. あしたのデートに何を着ていったらいいと思いますか. — Which dress do you think I should wear on my date tomorrow?
5. 彼女の服装はいつもはで［けばけばしい］です. — She always wears something bright [loud].
6. 彼女の服装の趣味は地味すぎます. — Her taste in clothes is too quiet [conservative].
7. 彼女はいつも大人っぽい格好をしています. — She always wears conservative clothes. / She always looks mature in her quiet clothes.
8. 彼はいつも着こなしがいいです. — He always dresses stylishly.
9. 彼はTシャツとジーンズがよく似合います. — He looks great in a T-shirt and jeans.
10. 彼はいつもガールフレンドと服装を合わせています. — He always coordinates his clothes with those of his girlfriend.
11. このジャンパースカートは姉のお下がりです. — This jumper is a hand-me-down from my sister.

❸服のトラブルに関する表現

1. このワイシャツのしみを抜くにはどうしたらいいですか. — How can I remove this stain from my shirt?
2. このスカートはしわがついているので, アイロンがけが必要です. — This skirt is wrinkled. It needs to be pressed.
3. シルクのブラウスに洗濯機は使えません. — Silk blouses are not machine-washable.
4. これは手洗いか, ドライクリーニングでなくてはだめです. — This needs to be either hand-washed or dry-cleaned.
5. 洗濯したらセーターが縮んでしまいました. — My sweater shrunk after washing.
6. シャツのボタンが取れそうです. — The button on my shirt is loose [coming off].
7. ストッキングが伝線してしまいました. — I have a run [《英》ladder] in my pantyhose.
8. ショールのあちこちに毛玉ができてしまいました. — My shawl has fuzz balls all over.
9. シャツから糸が出ています. — There's a thread hanging out of your shirt.

場面・状況別会話 ㉔

●性格

> He looks quiet, but really he's sociable and outgoing.

> That's good. But I think he's a bit impatient.

Nelly : Sometimes my first impression about people turns out to be wrong.
ネリー：人について私の第一印象が間違っていると分かることがあるわ．
Masao : Who are you talking about?
正　男：だれのこと言ってるの？
Nelly : Well, for example, I thought Kiyoshi was quiet and shy, but yesterday at the party I found him rather talkative.
ネリー：例えば，清はおとなしくて恥ずかしがり屋だと思っていたんだけど，きのうのパーティーでけっこう話し好きだと分かったの．
Masao : Yes, he looks quiet, but really he's sociable and outgoing.
正　男：そうだよ，彼はおとなしく見えるけど，本当は社交的で人づきあいもいいんだ．
Nelly : That's good. But I think he's a bit impatient.
ネリー：それはいいわ．でも少し気が短いと思うんだけど．
Masao : What makes you say so?
正　男：どうしてそう思うの？
Nelly : Well, he becomes irritable if some people are late for club meetings.
ネリー：クラブのミーティングに遅れてくる人がいるといらいらしてくるの．
Masao : That's because he's punctual, not because he's short-tempered.
正　男：それは短気だからじゃなくて時間にきちょうめんだからだよ．
Nelly : I see. I also think he's optimistic.
ネリー：なるほど．彼って楽観的でもあるわね．
Masao : That's true. He always tries to look on the bright side of things.
正　男：そのとおり．いつも物事の明るい面を見ようとしているね．

★ミニ知識★

ユーモアのセンス

日本人の性格を表すのによく使われる quiet（おとなしい）や shy（恥ずかしがり屋の）という言葉は，「はにかみ屋でかわいい」というよい意味を表すとは限らず，「自己主張がなく煮え切らない」という悪い意味としてとらえられる場合があります．一般的に欧米で人に好かれるのは cheerful（明るい）で assertive（自己主張のある）な性格の持ち主です．また，a sense of humor（ユーモアのセンス）をもっているかどうかも重要視されます．新聞や雑誌に載っている恋人探しの広告には，男女ともに相手に望む性格として，humorous や witty という形容詞が並んでいることがよくあります．ユーモアがあっておもしろい人がもてるのは世界共通のようです．

表現集

1. 彼女はどんな性格ですか. — What is her personality like?
2. 彼女は生まれつき陽気な性格です. — She has a cheerful personality by nature.
3. 彼は性格上の問題があります. — He has some personality flaws.
4. 彼は性格が変わりました. — His personality has changed.
5. 自分の性格を変えることはできません. — We can't change our personalities.
6. 彼のだらしない性格は直らないです. — His laziness cannot be changed.
7. 彼女の寛大な性格は母親譲りです. — She gets her generosity from her mother.
8. 人は十人十色です. — Different strokes for different folks. / To each his own.
9. 彼は弟と正反対の性格をしています. — His personality is the opposite of his brother's.
10. 彼女の本当の性格は見かけと違います. — Her real personality is different from what it appears to be.
11. 彼はいやな性格をしています. — He has an obnoxious personality.
12. 日本ではおとなしいことはよいことと思われることもあります. — In Japan, a quiet personality is sometimes thought to be good.
13. 心理テストで性格を当てることができます. — I can tell your personality through a psychological test.
14. 私たちは性格の不一致で別れました. — We broke up because we are incompatible.
15. 彼と私は性格が合います[合いません]. — He and I are compatible [incompatible].

● 性格を表す形容詞

よい意味	優しい, 親切な, 思いやりのある	affectionate, genial, gentle, kind, warm-hearted
	心が広い, 寛大な	broad-minded, generous, tolerant
	明るい, 陽気な	cheerful, optimistic, vivacious (❖vivacious は女性に関して用いられることが多い)
	愛想がいい, 友好的な	affable, amiable, companionable, friendly, hospitable
	社交的な, 外向的な	extroverted, outgoing, sociable
	信頼できる, 頼りになる	dependable, reliable, trustworthy
	まじめな, 勤勉な	diligent, hardworking, industrious
	しっかりした, 自己主張のある	assertive, determined, self-confident, strong-willed
	恥ずかしがり屋の, 控えめの, おとなしい, 内向的な, 引っ込み思案の	humble, introverted, modest, quiet, reclusive, reserved, shy, submissive, withdrawn
悪い意味	融通のきかない, 頑固な, かたい	inflexible, obstinate, stubborn
	短気な, 気が短い	impatient, short-tempered
	傲慢(ごうまん)な, 生意気な, 高飛車な	arrogant, haughty
	自分勝手な, 利己的な, わがままな	egocentric, egoistic, egotistical, self-centered, selfish
	冷淡な, うちとけない, 非社交的な	anti-social, callous, unfriendly
	はきはきしない, 優柔不断な	ambivalent, indecisive, wavering
	粗野な, 下品な, 低俗な	coarse, disgusting, indecent, rude, vulgar
	世間知らずの, 狭量な	inexperienced, naive, narrow-minded

場面・状況別会話 ㉕

●就職と仕事

> American companies usually employ workers on an annual contract basis.

> It's just like baseball players.

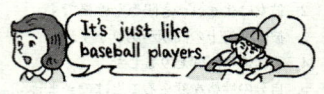

Michael: I heard that Japanese people are rather unwilling to change their jobs. Is it true?

マイケル：日本人はあまり転職したがらないって聞いたけど，本当なの？

Maiko: Basically, yes. Japanese companies in general have a "lifetime employment system" or "seniority system." Once hired, many employees try to stay until they reach the retirement age.

麻衣子：基本的にはそうね．一般的に日本の会社は「終身雇用制度」や「年功序列制度」をとってるの．一度就職したら定年まで同じ会社に勤めようとする人が多いわね．

Michael: Really! American companies usually employ workers on an annual contract basis.

マイケル：本当に！アメリカの会社では年次契約で雇用するのがふつうだよ．

Maiko: It's just like baseball players.

麻衣子：野球の選手みたいね．

Michael: You're right. Also, promotions and raises are mostly based on merit.

マイケル：そうだね．昇進や昇給もだいたい実力主義だしね．

Maiko: But Japanese companies are changing in order to survive competition. A growing number of companies have introduced a merit system. And the lifetime employment system and seniority system are breaking down.

麻衣子：でも，日本の会社も競争に勝ち残るために変わりつつあるわ．実力主義を導入する会社が増えているし，「終身雇用制度」や「年功序列制度」も崩れつつあるわ．

Michael: I guess Japanese companies will become tougher competitors for American companies.

マイケル：日本の会社はアメリカの会社にとってますます手強いライバルになりそうだな．

★ミニ知識★

履歴書の中身で勝負

アメリカには日本のような特定の就職活動の時期というものは存在しません．各々の学生が好きなときに就職を希望する企業に履歴書を提出し，面接や試験を受けます．日本では就職が主に面接で決まるのに対して，アメリカでは面接のほかに履歴書の中身（学業成績，クラブ活動などへの積極的な参加度，そして即戦力を約束する職歴など）が非常に重要視されます．アメリカの学生にとってクラブ活動は自分の個性や能力をアピールする上での重要な「経歴」で，クラブの部長や組織の委員をいくつも兼任している学生も珍しくありません．また，ふつうアメリカの企業には，日本の企業のように新卒の学生を一から教育するという考え方がないので，採用に際しては学生であっても即戦力としての実務経験や専門知識が求められます．そこでアメリカの学生は，在学中に「インターンシップ」(internship) という制度を利用して実務経験を積みます．「インターンシップ」とは，大学生が実際の会社で給料をもらいながら実務訓練を積む企業研修制度のことで，「インターンシップ」の申し込みは実質的に就職活動そのものといえます．（→「履歴書の書き方」p.1786）

表現集

❶ 就職活動に関する表現

1. 就職はもう決まりましたか. — Have you got [found] a job yet?
2. いくつか会社をあたっているけど, まだいい返事がありません. — I have applied to several companies, but I haven't got any favorable answers yet.
3. 商社に就職が決まりました. — I got a job at a trading company. / I was hired by a trading company.
4. 今, 私は就職活動の真っ最中です. — I'm in the midst of job-hunting now.
5. 何かコネはないのですか. — Do you have any connections?
6. 彼は父親のコネで就職しました. — He got a job through his father's connections.
7. だれか就職を世話してくれないかなあ. — I hope someone will help me find a job.
8. 私は外資系企業に就職を希望しています. — I'd like to work for a foreign-affiliated company.
9. いい就職口が見つからなくて困っています. — I'm having trouble finding a good job.
10. インテック社の会社説明会に参加しました. — I attended the「company information [job recruitment] meeting for Intech Inc.
11. 北商事で就職面接を受けました. — I had a job interview with the Kita Corporation.
12. 就職試験は, 小論文, 職業適性検査, 常識問題の3つです. — The employment test has three parts: an essay, a vocational aptitude test, and a common knowledge test.
13. もう10社も会社訪問し, 就職情報を集めました. — I've already visited as many as 10 companies to collect information about employment.
14. 私の志望業種はメーカーで, 事務の仕事がしたいです. — I'm looking for a position in the manufacturing industry. I'd like to do office work.
15. しっかりした育児休暇制度のある企業に就職を希望しています. — I'd like to get a job with a company which has a good child-care leave system.
16. 有給休暇は自由にとれますか. — Can I take a paid vacation whenever I like?
17. 私はこの仕事をするのに十分な能力があると思います. — I think I have sufficient ability to do this job.
18. 私は責任感, 協調性, 統率力があります. — I'm responsible, work well with others, and have leadership ability.
19. 貴社の社訓に引かれました. — I was attracted by your company slogan.
20. ここ数年, 就職難が続いています. — It has been hard to get a job for the last few years.

❷ 雇用に関する表現

1. 去年より, 今年は求人数が減少[増加]しました. — The number of new employees being sought this year has dropped [risen] from last year.
2. 学歴よりも仕事の能力を重視する企業が増えています. — More and more companies place importance on job ability rather than on academic background.
3. この会社の雇用条件に満足しています. — I'm satisfied with the employment conditions of this company.
4. これ以上会社の業績が悪くなったら, リストラで解雇されるかもしれません. — If our company's performance gets any worse, I might be fired due to restructuring.
5. 9月に失業率が4パーセントに上昇しました. — The jobless [unemployment] rate climbed to four percent in September.

場面・状況別会話 ㉖

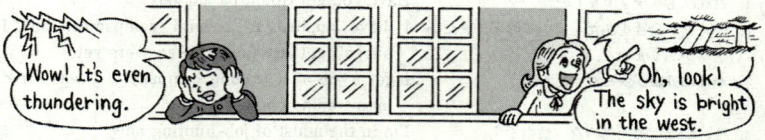

●天候

> Wow! It's even thundering.

> Oh, look! The sky is bright in the west.

Mamoru: Hey! Suddenly it's started raining. Until a moment ago, it was light outside.
守　　：うわあ！急に雨が降りだしてきたよ．さっきまで外は明るかったのに．
Michelle: Yeah, it's pouring. Spring weather really changes quickly.
ミシェル：そうね．どしゃ降りだわ．春の天気は本当に変わりやすいのね．
Mamoru: Oh, no. Now the snow on the ski slopes is going to melt.
守　　：ああ，これじゃあゲレンデの雪が解けちゃうな．
Michelle: But the weather forecast said it would snow in Nagano.
ミシェル：でも天気予報では長野は雪が降るって言ってたわ．
Mamoru: Really? The temperature is still low in the mountains, so maybe it'll be OK. But I hope the weather will clear up this weekend.
守　　：本当？　山沿いじゃあまだ気温が低いから大丈夫かな．でも今度の週末は晴れてほしいな．
Michelle: You're going snowboarding, right? I'd hope for cloudy weather, if I were you.
ミシェル：スノーボードをしに行くんだったわね．私だったら曇ってほしいわ．
Mamoru: Are you worried about getting sunburned? It's true that ultraviolet rays are stronger at high altitudes.
守　　：日焼けを心配しているの？　確かに高いところは紫外線が強いからね．
Michelle: Yes. And besides that, ski clothes are so hot when it's sunny.
ミシェル：そうなの．それにスキーウエアは晴れるとすごく暑いわ．
　　　　　(Thunder and lightning.)
　　　　　（ピカッ，ゴロゴロ）
Mamoru: Wow! It's even thundering. I hope the rain stops by the time school is over.
守　　：ひゃあ！雷まで鳴ってるよ．学校が終わるまでに雨がやむといいな．
Michelle: Oh, look! The sky is bright in the west. I bet it'll clear up by evening.
ミシェル：ほら，見て！西の空が明るいわ．きっと夕方までには晴れるわね．

★ミニ知識★

雨のいろいろ

　新聞やテレビなどの天気予報で使われる雨の表現にはいろいろなものがあります．「大雨」は heavy rain，「小雨」は light rain，「にわか雨」は shower，「こぬか雨」は drizzle，「霧雨」は misty rain といいます．その他，「どしゃ降り」は pouring rain，「雷雨」は thunder shower，「豪雨」は torrential rain，「天気雨」は sun shower，「春雨」は spring shower です．また，「所により雨」は scattered rain，「時々雨」は occasional rain，「断続的な雨」は intermittent rain です．英語で天気予報を読んだり聞いたりして，様々な天候・気象に関する表現を楽しみながら覚えましょう．

表現集

❶日常の天気に関する表現

1. いい［ひどい］天気ですね． — It's nice [terrible] weather, isn't it?
2. 曇ってきました．すぐに雨になりそうです． — It's getting cloudy [overcast]. It looks like it'll rain soon.
3. 風が強いので，きょうは（いつもより）肌寒く感じるかもしれません． — It's windy, so we may feel chillier today.
4. あしたはいい天気でしょうか． — Will it be nice tomorrow?
5. 来週の天気は変わりやすいでしょう． — The weather next week will be changeable.
6. あしたの天気はどうですか． — What will the weather be like tomorrow?
7. そちらの天気はどうですか． — What is the weather like over there?
8. あしたは天気がよくなるでしょう． — The weather will be better tomorrow.
9. 天気予報によると午後は雨になるでしょう． — The weather forecast says (that) it'll rain in the afternoon.
10. 悪天候のため，遠足は中止になりました． — Because of the bad weather, the excursion was cancelled.
11. 天気が許せば，私たちはこの次の日曜日に遊園地に行きます． — Weather permitting, we'll go to the amusement park next Sunday.
12. 最近めっきり寒くなってきました． — It's getting colder these days.
13. 最近は天気予報がよくはずれます［当たります］． — The weather forecast is often wrong [accurate] these days.
14. 彼は雲の動きを見て，翌日の天気を当てられます． — He can tell the next day's weather by looking at the movement of the clouds.
15. 私は穏やかな気候の所に住みたいです． — I want to live where the climate is mild.

❷日本の四季に関する表現

1. 春はもうそこまでやってきています． — Spring is just around the corner.
2. 「春一番」とは2月か3月に吹くその年で最初の南風のことです． — *Haruichiban* means the first southerly wind of the year in February or March.
3. 6月の中旬から北海道を除いて梅雨の季節が始まり，およそ40日間続きます． — The rainy season starts in the middle of June except in Hokkaido, and it lasts about 40 days.
4. 日本の夏は蒸し暑くて，最高気温は摂氏30度以上に上がります． — The summer in Japan is hot and humid, and the highest temperature goes up to more than 30 degrees Celsius.
5. いよいよ本格的な夏になりました． — Summer is really here.
6. 台風は主に8月と9月に日本を襲い，ふつう多くの被害があります． — Typhoons hit Japan mostly in August and September, and there is usually a lot of damage.
7. 秋は涼しくてしのぎやすく，木々の葉が紅葉します． — In autumn it's cool and pleasant, and the leaves of the trees turn yellow or red.
8. 「小春日和(びより)」とは初冬の暖かい日のことです．アメリカで「インディアン・サマー」と呼ばれている日と似ています． — *Koharubiyori* means the warm days at the beginning of winter. It's like the days called "Indian Summer" in America.
9. 冬は日本海側では雪がよく降り，太平洋側では晴れて乾燥します． — In winter, it snows a lot on the Japan Sea coast, while it's fair and dry on the Pacific coast.
10. 地球温暖化に影響されて，日本中で暖冬傾向になっています． — Due to global warming, it tends to be warm in winter all over Japan.

場面・状況別会話 27

●地震（自然災害）

> Did you feel the earthquake last night?
>
> Sure I did. It was big, wasn't it?

Miki : Did you feel the earthquake last night?

美　紀：きのうの夜，地震感じた？

Andy : Sure I did. It was big, wasn't it?

アンディ：もちろん．大きかったよね．

Miki : Yes, it was pretty frightening. The news said it measured four on the Japanese scale.

美　紀：ええ，すごく怖かったわ．ニュースによると震度4だったそうよ．

Andy : Thank God it wasn't any larger.

アンディ：あれ以上大きくなくてよかったよね．

Miki : I know. Incidentally, Andy, didn't you say you were in L.A. when the big quake hit the city?

美　紀：本当．そういえばアンディ，ロスで大きな地震があったときにそこにいたって言ってなかった？

Andy : Oh, yes. It was pretty bad. My apartment didn't collapse, so I was lucky. But my friend's house was destroyed, so he had to rebuild the whole thing.

アンディ：そうそう．あれは本当にひどかったんだ．僕のアパートはこわれなくて幸運だったよ．でも，友達の家が崩壊しちゃって，全部建て直さなければならなかったんだ．

Miki : Boy, that must have been rough.

美　紀：まあ，それは大変だったでしょうね．

Andy : Yes. But the good thing was that he had earthquake insurance, so that helped him a lot.

アンディ：うん．でも，さいわい地震保険に入っていたから，ずいぶん助かったみたい．

★ミニ知識★

震度とマグニチュード

　日本では一般的に「震度」で地震の揺れの程度を表します．例えば，「その地震は震度3を記録しました」は，英語にすると The earthquake registered three on the Japanese scale. となります．これに対し，欧米では地震そのものの大きさを表す「マグニチュード」がふつう用いられるため，There was an earthquake with a magnitude of five (on the Richter scale).「マグニチュード5の地震がありました」のように表すのが一般的です．"the Richter scale" は，この指標の考案者であるアメリカの地震学者 C. Richter に由来しています．震度階級は1996年度から震度5と6に強弱が付け加えられ10階級となりましたが，マグニチュードには原理的に上限も下限もありません．

表現集

❶ 地震に関する表現

1. 揺れてる？
   Do you feel that shaking? / Do you feel a tremor?

2. 落ち着きなさい．ガスの栓を閉めてテーブルの下に潜(%)りなさい．
   Remain calm. Turn off the gas and get under the table.

3. テーブルが激しくがたがたと揺れて，壁から時計が落ちました．
   The table rattled violently and the clock fell off the wall.

4. けさ方の地震の震源地はどこか知っていますか．
   Do you know where the epicenter of the quake this morning was?

5. 震源地は釧路沖で，震源の深さは約90キロでした．
   The epicenter was off the Kushiro coast(line), and the depth was about ninety kilometers.

6. 本震の後，多くの余震が続いています．
   They [We] are having many aftershocks after the main quake.

7. 津波警報が出ています．
   A tsunami [tidal wave] warning has been issued.

8. 地震の後，ほぼ100万戸の家屋で電気の供給が止まりました．
   Electric power was cut to almost one million households after the quake.

9. 多くの電話回線が不通になりました．
   Many telephone lines weren't working.

10. 損害の修復には時間がかかるでしょう．
    The rebuilding will take a lot of time.

11. 日本中の人々が地震の被災者に食料や衣料を送りました．
    People all over Japan sent food and clothes to the victims of the earthquake.

❷ 台風・ハリケーン・竜巻に関する表現

1. 今度の台風は東京を直撃するでしょう．
   This typhoon will hit Tokyo directly.

2. 今度の台風はどういう進路をとるでしょうか．
   What route [path, course] will this typhoon take?

3. 台風が近づいているときは，常に気象情報を聞くようにしましょう．
   We should keep track of the weather reports when a typhoon is coming.

4. 天気予報は，住民にハリケーンに備えるように警報を出しました．
   The weather forecast alerted the residents to prepare for the hurricane.

5. 住民の多くは竜巻を避けて地下室に避難しました．
   Many of the residents took refuge from the tornado in the basements.

6. その竜巻は車や屋根を空中に巻き上げました．
   The tornado sent cars and roofs spinning up into the air.

❸ 大雨・洪水に関する表現

1. 豪雨の後，その地域のほとんどの家が床上浸水しました．
   Most of the houses in the area were flooded above floor level after the heavy rain.

2. 村全体が鉄砲水で流されました．
   The whole village was washed away by flash floods.

3. 記録的な雨で，多量の作物が害を受けました．
   Due to record rains, tons of crops were damaged.

4. 集中豪雨のためにがけ崩れが起きました．
   Landslides occurred due to torrential rain.

場面・状況別会話 ㉘

●ごみとリサイクル

> People should take recycling more seriously.

> At the same time we should try to reduce the amount of waste we produce.

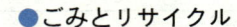

Ellen : These days, people are used to separating combustible waste from non-combustible waste.

エレン：最近、みんな燃えるごみと燃えないごみを分けるのに慣れてきたわね。

Yukio : Yes, but unfortunately there are still some people who throw out plastic food containers or PET bottles with combustible waste.

幸　夫：うん、でも残念なことに、プラスチックの食べ物の容器やペットボトルを燃えるごみといっしょに捨てる人もまだいるんだ。

Ellen : What a shame! People should take recycling more seriously.

エレン：それはひどいわね。もっと真剣にリサイクルのことを考えるべきだわ。

Yukio : I know recycling is effective, but at the same time we should try to reduce the amount of waste we produce.

幸　夫：リサイクルは効果的だと分かっているけど、同時に出すごみの量を減らす努力もすべきだよ。

Ellen : I think companies should also make more of an effort not to use unnecessary containers.

エレン：企業も不必要な容器を使わないようにもっと努力すべきだと思うわ。

Yukio : And consumers should try not to use plastic spoons or forks, and they should bring their own bags to stores and avoid excessive packaging.

幸　夫：そして消費者もプラスチックのスプーンやフォークを使わないようにしたり、店に自分のバッグを持っていったり、過剰包装を避けたりすべきだよ。

★ミニ知識★

リサイクルの王国

　先進国の中でもドイツ、スイス、スウェーデン、オランダ、デンマークなどでは、分別収集 (sorted garbage collecting) やリサイクルの徹底を国を挙げて行っています。例えばドイツやオランダでは、酒類を除く食品に用いられるびんやペットボトルにはあらかじめ保証金 (deposit) が含まれていて、店に返却するとその金額を払い戻してもらえます。また、デンマークではこうしたリターナブルびん (returnable bottles) 以外のびんは国内での使用はもちろん、輸入も禁止されています。また、紙コップやプラスチックの使い捨て商品には高い課税がなされています。このため、びんなどの容器の返却率は約9割という好成績を実現しています。

表現集

❶ごみの収集に関する表現

1. 燃えるごみは火曜日と金曜日,燃えないごみは水曜日に収集されます.
   Combustible [Burnable] trash is collected on Tuesdays and Fridays, and noncombustible [nonburnable] trash on Wednesdays.

2. 資源ごみはびん,アルミ缶,新聞紙,ダンボール紙などを含みます.
   Shigen gomi, recyclable trash, includes bottles, aluminum cans, newspapers and cardboard.

3. びんと缶は別々の箱に入れなければいけません.
   Bottles and cans should be put into separate boxes.

4. ごみは収集日に出してください.
   Take out the garbage on the day it is to be collected.

5. この地域ではごみは名前を書いた半透明のビニール袋に入れることになっています.
   In this area, garbage should be in semitransparent plastic bags with your name on them.

6. 古くなった器具や家具といった粗大ごみを処分するには,市の事務所に電話をして持っていってくれるように頼まなければなりません.また,収集の料金がかかります.
   To dispose of large items like old appliances and furniture, you must call the city office and request that they be picked up. There is also a collection fee (charged).

❷ごみ問題に関する表現

1. ごみ処理はほとんどの先進国で深刻な問題です.
   Disposal of garbage is a serious problem in most developed countries.

2. 近い将来すべてのごみの埋め立て地がいっぱいになるそうです.
   It is said that all garbage landfills will be full in the near future.

3. 私たちはごみをたくさん出さないように努力すべきです.
   We should try not to produce so much waste.

4. ごみの投げ捨ては法律でもっと厳しく罰せられるべきです.
   Littering [Throwing away trash] should be punished more strictly by law.

5. 住民たちはそのごみ処理施設が近くに建設されるのに反対しています.
   The residents oppose the construction of garbage disposal facilities in their neighborhood.

6. ごみの燃焼から生まれた熱は温水プールに[プールを温めるのに]利用されています.
   The heat produced by burning garbage is used to heat the swimming pool.

❸リサイクルに関する表現

1. 使い捨ての物を使わないで,物をリサイクルしたり,再利用することが大切です.
   It is important not to use disposable things but to recycle or reuse things.

2. どんな物がリサイクルできますか.
   What kind of things can be recycled?

3. 新聞紙や牛乳パックからできた再生紙は本やティッシュペーパーを作るのに使われています.
   Recycled paper from newspapers and milk cartons is used in making books and tissues.

4. ペットボトルをリサイクルしてシャツやズボン用の生地が作られます.
   PET bottles can be recycled into cloth for shirts or pants.

5. リサイクルにかかる費用が新しく製品を作るよりも高くなるのは問題です.
   The probrem is that the cost of recycling is higher than producing new products.

場面・状況別会話 ㉙

●環境問題

> I'm trying to buy environmentally safe products.

> That's great.

Cindy : Is the environmental protection movement active here in Japan?

シンディ：ここ日本では環境保護運動は盛んなの？

Keita : Well, unfortunately it's not so active as in some other countries. But these days people are more concerned about using environmentally friendly products.

啓　太：うーん，残念ながらほかの国ほどは盛んじゃないね．でも最近では環境にやさしい製品を使うことにみんな関心をもつようになってきているね．

Cindy : Like what?

シンディ：例えば？

Keita : Well, my ballpoint pens are made of biodegradable plastics.

啓　太：僕のボールペンは微生物によって分解できるプラスチックでできているんだ．

Cindy : But I heard that it costs a lot to make ecofriendly products and they are expensive to buy.

シンディ：でも環境にやさしい製品は作るのにとてもお金がかかるから，買うには高いって聞いたけど．

Keita : Well, I'm trying to buy environmentally safe products, even if the prices are slightly higher than those of conventional ones.

啓　太：僕はこれまでの製品より少し値段が高くても，環境にやさしい製品を買うようにしているんだ．

Cindy : That's great. I think if the number of green consumers increases, the costs will go down.

シンディ：いいことだわ．環境保護を訴える消費者の数が増えれば，原価は下がっていくと思うわ．

Keita : Right. There needs to be cooperation between manufacturers and consumers to promote the use of environmentally safe products.

啓　太：そうなんだ．環境にやさしい製品の利用を広めるためには，生産者と消費者の間の協力が必要なんだよ．

★ミニ知識★

環境保護のための旅

　自然環境保護運動の高まりから，エコツーリズム（ecotourism）という観光事業が最近盛んになっています．アマゾンの熱帯雨林観察からホエールウォッチングまで様々なツアーがあり参加者は訪れた場所の生態系などの自然環境や原住民の生活，文化を損なわずして，楽しみながら自然環境の保護について理解を深めることができます．また，こうした観光事業は同時にその地域の経済発展にも役立っていて，第三世界の大規模開発に伴う環境破壊の解決策としても注目されています．1960年代に北欧で始まったエコツーリズムはその後欧米に伝わり，近年日本でも本格的に普及してきました．eco とはもともと ecology（生態学）の意味ですが，エコツアー（ecotour）のように，最近では環境，自然の意味でも広く使われるようになっています．

表現集

❶環境問題一般に関する表現

1. 私たちは地球規模の環境問題［破壊］にもっと注意を払うべきです．
   We should pay more attention to global environmental issues [destruction].
2. 生産者はより環境にやさしい製品を作るように努めています．
   Manufacturers are making efforts to produce more「ecologically sound [ecofriendly] products.
3. 環境汚染が地球の生態系を破壊しています．
   Environmental pollution disrupts the global ecosystem.
4. 環境の変化が種の絶滅の主な原因になっているようです．
   Changes in the environment seem to be the major cause of species extinction.
5. プラスチック容器のあるものは，電子レンジで調理すると，中の食品を環境ホルモンで汚染するといわれています．
   Some plastic containers are said to contaminate the food inside with endocrine disrupting chemicals when cooked in a microwave oven.

❷地球温暖化・オゾン層に関する表現

1. 地球温暖化は主に大気中の二酸化炭素によって引き起こされます．
   Global warming is caused mainly carbon dioxide in the atmosphere.
2. オゾン層は紫外線から地球上のすべての生命を守ってくれます．
   The ozone layer protects all life on earth from ultraviolet rays.
3. オゾン層の破壊により，皮膚癌(がん)にかかる危険性が高くなるといわれています．
   It is said that the destruction of the ozone layer increases the risk of skin cancer.

❸森林伐採・砂漠化に関する表現

1. 森林は二酸化炭素を酸素に変えます．
   Forests change carbon dioxide into oxygen.
2. 森林伐採によって動植物が絶滅してしまいます．
   Deforestation will bring about the extinction of animals and plants.
3. 生態系のバランスを取り戻すために，再植林の新しい技術が開発されつつあります．
   In order to bring back the balance of the ecosystem, new techniques in reforestation are being developed.
4. 砂漠化によって各地でききんが生じています．
   Desertification has brought about famine in many places.

❹公害・酸性雨に関する表現

1. 大気汚染の原因の一つは車の排気ガスです．
   One cause of air pollution is automobile exhaust.
2. 工場や車は二酸化炭素を多量に排出しています．
   Factories and cars emit a large amount of carbon dioxide.
3. 住民は騒音公害と水質［大気，土壌］汚染に悩まされています．
   The residents are annoyed by noise pollution and worried about water [air, soil] pollution.
4. 最近，多くのバスが赤信号で止まっているときにエンジンを止めています．
   These days many buses stop their engines when standing at red lights.
5. 酸性雨は川の魚を殺すだけでなく，森林にある木や植物を破壊します．
   Acid rain not only kills fish in rivers but also destroys trees and plants in the forests.
6. 政府は公害対策にもっと予算を使うべきです．
   The government should spend more money on antipollution measures.

場面・状況別会話 ㉚

●核問題

Ron : There are still some countries in the world trying to carry out nuclear tests. What do you think about that?

ロ ン：世界にはまだ核実験を行おうとしている国があるけど，どう思う？

Mina : Well, as a person who lives in the only country where atomic bombs were dropped in the past, I strongly object to all nuclear tests.

美 奈：過去に被爆した唯一の国に住む人間として，私はすべての核実験に強く反対するわ．

Ron : Some countries claim that they should possess nuclear weapons for defense purposes.

ロ ン：防衛のために核兵器を保有すべきだという国もあるけど．

Mina : Well, I think that's a selfish excuse. If nuclear war breaks out, everyone everywhere will suffer.

美 奈：それは利己的な言い訳だと思うわ．もし核戦争が起これば，あらゆる所であらゆる人が苦しむのよ．

Ron : That's right. When I visited Hiroshima, I learned so much about the disaster caused by the atomic bomb and how much agony the victims had to go through.

ロ ン：そうだね．広島を訪ねてみて，僕は原爆による災害や被災者たちがどれほどの苦痛を味わわなければならなかったかよく分かったよ．

Mina : I think more and more people should go visit the Peace Memorial Park.

美 奈：もっと多くの人たちが平和記念公園に行くべきだと思うわ．

Ron : I agree. I think people all over the world should work to eliminate nuclear weapons.

ロ ン：同感だよ．世界中の人たちが核兵器をなくすように働きかけるべきだと思うな．

★ミニ知識★

原爆と被爆

　原子爆弾（原爆）は英語では atomic [atom] bomb または A-bomb といいます．bomb という語は「爆弾」という意味の名詞のほかに，「爆弾を投下する」という動詞として使うこともできます．同様に，A-bomb も動詞として使えるので，例えば，「アメリカは長崎に原爆を落としました」は "The U.S. A-bombed Nagasaki." ということができます．また，「彼女は広島で被爆しました」は "She was A-bombed in Hiroshima." となります．原爆や核問題を話題にするときには，唯一の被爆国の一員として自分の意見をしっかりと述べることが必要ですが，同時に感情的になったり個人攻撃になったりしないように気をつけなければなりません．どこの国の人であれ一人一人考え方が違うので，「あなたがた…の国の人は」とか「私たち日本人は」というような一般化した主語を使って意見を述べることも好ましくありません．

表現集

❶核実験に関する表現

1. その国は来月核実験を行うと伝えられています．
   It has been announced that the country will 「carry out [conduct] a nuclear test next month.
2. わが国はその核実験に抗議しました．
   Our country protested against the nuclear test.
3. 核実験を実施する国々は国際社会の信用を失うことになるでしょう．
   Countries which conduct nuclear tests will lose respect in the international community.
4. 包括的核実験禁止条約は核兵器の爆発実験を禁止しています．
   The Comprehensive Nuclear Test-Ban Treaty prohibits nuclear weapon test explosions.

❷核兵器に関する表現

1. 多くの人々がすべての核兵器を廃絶すべきだと考えています．
   Many people think that all nuclear weapons should be eliminated [abolished].
2. 世界中の多くの人々が核兵器がない世の中を望んでいるはずです．
   Many people around the world must be hoping for a world free from nuclear weapons.
3. ＮＡＴＯ諸国の大多数は核軍縮を求めています．
   The majority of NATO members call for nuclear disarmament.
4. 反核運動が世界中で広まっています．
   The antinuclear movement is spreading all over the world.
5. 核兵器の拡散を規制しようとする動きが強まっています．
   Control over the proliferation of nuclear weapons is increasing.
6. 核不拡散条約は核兵器保有国の増加防止を目的としています．
   The Nuclear Non-Proliferation Treaty (NPT) aims at preventing the increase in the number of countries which possess nuclear weapons.
7. 核兵器を所有することは戦争抑止力になると信じている人もいます．
   Some people believe (that) having nuclear weapons can function as a deterrent.
8. その国は他国による核査察を受け入れないでしょう．
   That country will not accept the inspection of its nuclear complex by other countries.

❸原爆に関する表現

1. 世界初の原爆は1945年に広島に投下されました．
   The world's first atomic bomb was dropped on Hiroshima in 1945.
2. 爆心地から１マイル以内にいた人々は焼け死にました．
   People within a mile of the center of the explosion were burned to death.
3. 原爆は大量の放射能を放出しました．
   The atomic bomb emitted a significant amount of radiation.
4. 放射能汚染が原因で髪の毛が抜けてしまった人もいました．
   Some people lost their hair due to radiation poisoning.
5. 放射能を浴びたのが原因で数年以内に亡くなる人がたくさんいました．
   Many people died within a few years because of exposure to radiation.
6. 被爆者たちはその経験を後世に伝えようとしています．
   Atomic-bomb victims are trying to pass on their experiences to future generations.
7. 原爆ドームは私たちに核兵器の恐ろしさを思い起こさせます．
   Genbaku [The Atomic Bomb] Dome reminds us of the terror of nuclear weapons.

場面・状況別会話 ㉛

●試験と成績

> I have to cram overnight.

> I'll try to get a good mark on the multiple-choice questions.

Taeko: Nick, have you prepared for the history exam ?
妙　子：ニック，歴史の試験の準備できた？

Nick: No, I haven't even looked at a page. I'm regretting I fooled around last week.
ニック：いや，まだ1ページも見てないんだ．先週遊んじゃったのを後悔してるよ．

Taeko: The exam covers about fifty pages. That's too much.
妙　子：試験範囲は50ページくらいあるのよ．多すぎるわよね．

Nick: Maybe I'll make a lucky guess at some of the questions.
ニック：たぶん僕は何問かに山をかけるよ．

Taeko: I don't think that'll work. Sometimes Mr. Sato gives us tricky questions.
妙　子：うまくいかないと思うけど，佐藤先生って時々ひねった問題を出すんですもの．

Nick: That's right. But still I have to cram overnight.
ニック：そうだよね．でもどのみち僕は一夜漬けしなきゃいけないな．

Taeko: I'm not good at essay questions, so I'll try to get a good mark on the multiple-choice questions.
妙　子：私は記述式問題は得意じゃないから，選択式で点を取るわ．

Nick: Let's cross our fingers.
ニック：お互いにうまくいきますように．

Taeko: Yes, let's.
妙　子：そうね．

★ミニ知識★

持ち帰ってする試験

日本では試験というと学校で試験時間中にするものと考えられますが，アメリカではこうした in-class exam のほかに take-home exam というものがあります．試験問題を家に持ち帰り，数時間から1週間くらいの決められた期間内にやって提出する試験のことで，もちろん参考書を見ても友人に相談してもかまいません．一見やさしそうに思われますが，じっくりと考えさせる問題や時間のかかる問題であることが多く，かえって in-class exam のほうがいいという人もいます．大学では，特に記述式試験のときに blue book と呼ばれる青い表紙の答案用紙ノートを使うことも多く，書籍部で購入して試験の教室に持っていきます．honor code という一種の紳士協定を理由に，先生は問題用紙を配ると試験監督をせずに教室から出ていってしまうこともあります．

表現集

❶試験に関する表現

1. 中間［期末］試験はうまくいきましたか． — Did you do well on your midterms [finals]?
2. 試験の準備はできていますか． — Are you prepared [ready] for the exam?
3. 「試験範囲を教えてもらえますか」「4課から6課までです」 — "Would you tell me what the exam covers?" "It covers Lesson four through Lesson six."
4. 5から8ページの中から問題が出ると山をかけています． — I'm guessing that the questions will be from page five to page eight.
5. 山がはずれてしまいました． — I failed to make a good [lucky] guess.
6. 恐怖の試験期間が終わったら，映画に行きましょう． — Let's go to a movie when "hell week" is over.
7. 一夜漬けをしました． — I crammed overnight. / I stayed up all night studying. / I pulled an all-nighter.
8. 問題を見て，もうあきらめました． — When I saw the questions, I 「gave up [threw in the towel].
9. 試験になるとあがってしまって，本当の実力が出せません． — I get nervous in exams and cannot show my real ability.
10. 物理の点が悪かったので，追試（再試）を受けなければなりません． — I got a bad grade in physics, so I have to take a make-up exam.
11. 彼はカンニングが見つかってしまいました． — He was caught cheating on the exam.
12. 楽勝でした． — It was a snap.
13. 試験，がんばってください！ — Good luck on the exam(s)!

❷成績に関する表現

1. 英語は何点でしたか． — What was your test score in English?
2. 英語は90点でした． — I got 90 points on the English test. / I got a mark of 90 on the English test.
3. 数学は思ったより成績がよかったです． — I got a better grade in math than I (had) expected.
4. 今学期は科学の成績があまりよくなかったです． — I got rather a bad [poor] grade in science this term [semester].
5. 成績が上［下］がりました． — My grades improved [dropped, went down, fell].
6. 学業平均値が0.5点上がり［下がり］ました． — My grade point average (GPA) improved [dropped] by half a point.
7. 80点以上がAになります． — A grade above 80 corresponds to an A. / An A is 80 points and [or] above.
8. 彼はクラスでトップの［中くらいの，下位の］成績です． — He ranks 「at the top [in the middle, at the bottom] of his class.
9. 成績のことで先生に交渉するつもりです． — I'm going to make an appeal to the teacher about my grade.
10. 試験の結果をあまり気にしないほうがいいです． — You shouldn't worry too much about the results of the test.
11. よい成績を取るには授業への参加が必ず必要です． — Class participation is a must to get a good grade.

場面・状況別会話 ㉜

●いじめ・不登校

> I haven't seen Fumio lately.

> Well, he was bullied by some students.

Rick : I haven't seen Fumio lately. Is he sick or something?
リック：このところ文雄を見てないなあ．病気か何かなの？
Kana : I heard he refuses to come to school.
香　奈：不登校だそうよ．
Rick : You mean he doesn't want to come? Why not?
リック：それって学校に来たくないってこと？　でもどうして？
Kana : Well, I heard he was bullied by some students. But I don't know if that's the only reason.
香　奈：何人かの生徒にいじめられたらしいわ．それだけが原因かどうかは分からないけど．
Rick : Are there many students in Japan who refuse to go to school?
リック：日本では不登校の生徒って多いの？
Kana : I'm not sure, but the number seems to be increasing year by year.
香　奈：確かじゃないけど，年々増えているらしいの．
Rick : Really? It's becoming serious, huh?
リック：本当？　深刻になってきているんだね．
Kana : Yes. And once I saw a TV program saying that some students have no particular reason for not going. They just don't feel like going.
香　奈：そうなの．それに前にテレビで見たんだけど，特別な理由もなく学校に行かない生徒もいるんだって．ただ何となく行きたくないっていうの．
Rick : Maybe they don't like being in groups of people.
リック：たぶん集団の中にいるのがいやなんじゃない．
Kana : That's too bad. I think we need more guidance counselors to help them.
香　奈：それはよくないわね．彼らを助けるカウンセラーがもっと必要だと思うわ．

★ミニ知識★

ピア・サポート

　英米でもいじめや不登校がないわけではありません．個人的な理由のほかに，人種の違いによるいじめも多くあります．また，そうしたいじめが麻薬や銃を伴った事件や犯罪に発展してしまうこともあります．しかし，勉強から友達づきあい，恋愛，家族関係など悩みがあればいつでも相談できるように，学校ではふつうカウンセラー室があり専門のカウンセラーが待機しています．また，カナダ，アメリカ，イギリス，オーストラリアなどでは，「ピア・サポート」(peer support) といって生徒が生徒の悩みを聞くシステムを取り入れている学校もあり，そのための研修授業なども盛んになってきています．大人よりも生徒同士のほうが共感を得やすい，ということのほかに，相談を受けた生徒も教育的に成長するという効果が期待されています．

表現集

❶いじめ・不登校に関する表現

1. いじめの原因は何だと思いますか. — What do you think are the causes of bullying?
2. いじめられて傷つく生徒がたくさんいます. — There are many students who are harmed by bullies.
3. いじめを受けたら周りの人に助けを求めましょう. ひとりで悩んではいけません. — If you are bullied, ask the people around you for help. Don't suffer alone.
4. いじめが行われていることに先生が気づかない場合がしばしばあります. — Teachers often don't notice that bullying is going on.
5. 先生は学校でどのくらいいじめが起きているのか調べるべきです. — Teachers should find out how much bullying is going on in school.
6. 彼はクラスメートに無視されたり仲間はずれにされたと言っています. — He says he was ignored and left out by his classmates.
7. いじめっ子たちは彼ら自身問題を抱えているようです. — Bullies seem to have their own problems.
8. 彼女はいじめを受けて自殺しました. — She killed herself after being bullied.
9. いじめから逃げるために学校を休んでしまう生徒もいます. — Some students skip school to get away from bullying.
10. いじめの対象になる生徒はそのような扱いを受けて当然だという意見もあります. — According to one view, students who are the target of bullies often deserve such treatment.
11. 学校に行きたがらない生徒はカウンセリングを受けて原因を究明することが必要です. — Students who refuse to go to school should get counseling to find out the cause.

❷学校生活に関するその他の問題

1. 小学校ですでに学級崩壊が見られます. — Out-of-control classrooms are already seen in elementary schools.
2. 授業中に言うことを聞かない生徒が増えています. — The number of students who are rebellious in class is increasing.
3. 先生に怒られてキレる生徒がいます. — Some students blow up when scolded by a teacher.
4. 日本の子供たちにとって受験勉強はストレスになることがあります. — Studying for entrance exams can be stressful for children in Japan.
5. 塾や予備校に通っていて自分の時間がほとんどもてない生徒がたくさんいます. — There are many students who go to cram schools or prep schools and so have little time of their own.
6. 校内暴力の原因は学校と家庭のどちらにあると思いますか. — Where do you think the cause of in-school violence originates, the school or the home?
7. 学校における諸問題の一つの原因は大人社会にあると思います. — I think one of the causes of the problems in school lies in adult society.
8. 子供の非行を防ぐには先生と親が密接になって協力すべきです. — Teachers and parents should work closely together to prevent juvenile delinquency.
9. 先生と生徒がお互いに信頼を取り戻すことが必要です. — It is necessary to reestablish mutual confidence between teachers and students.
10. 最近の子供はパソコンばかりやっているので, 親密な人間関係をもちづらくなっています. — These days children spend their time with personal computers, so they find it difficult to form close personal relationships.

場面・状況別会話 33

●ALT (Assistant Language Teacher)

Why are you here so early?

I leave early to avoid the rush hour.

Hiroshi	: Good morning, Ms. Douglas.
浩	: おはようございます,ダグラス先生.
Ms. Douglas	: Good morning, Hiroshi. How come you come to school so early?
ダグラス先生	: おはよう,浩君. どうしてこんなに早く学校に来るの?
Hiroshi	: I have basketball practice at 7:30. How about you, Ms. Douglas? Why are you here so early?
浩	: バスケの練習が7時半からあるんです. ダグラス先生はどうしてこんなに早いんですか.
Ms. Douglas	: I leave early to avoid the rush hour. I can't stand the crowded trains.
ダグラス先生	: ラッシュアワーを避けるために家を早く出るの. 込んでいる電車は耐えられないから.
Hiroshi	: Oh, I understand. It's pretty bad, isn't it?
浩	: ああ,分かります. けっこうひどいですよね.
Ms. Douglas	: Yes. It's hard to believe that people have to stand so close to each other.
ダグラス先生	: そう. 人があんなに近づいて立っていなければならないなんて信じられないわ.
Hiroshi	: How did you commute to school when you were in high school?
浩	: 先生が高校生の時はどうやって学校に通ってたんですか.
Ms. Douglas	: My mom drove me to school. We don't have trains or subways in our town, so people usually use cars for commuting.
ダグラス先生	: 母が車で学校まで送ってくれたのよ. 私の住んでいた町には電車や地下鉄はないから,みんなたいてい車で通うの.
Hiroshi	: So commuting by train must be a new experience for you.
浩	: じゃあ,電車通勤は先生にとっては新しい経験ですね.

★ミニ知識★ 外国人の先生に聞いてはいけないことは?

ALT(外国語指導助手の先生)には授業以外でも気楽に話しかけて,言葉や文化の違いなどを積極的に学ぶ姿勢をもつことが大切です. しかし,文化的違いが原因で意外なことで相手を傷つけたり,相手にいやな思いをさせたりすることもあるので,話題の選択には気をつけなければなりません. 例えば,「足が長いですね」や「鼻が高いですね」といった身体的特徴についてのコメントは避けるべきです. また,「アメリカは危険な所ですね」や「外国人は日本語が下手ですね」といった文化的・社会的偏見や誤解を含むような発言は,相手を不愉快にさせます. さらに,「どうしてまだ結婚しないのですか」や「どんな日本の男性[女性]が好きですか」といったプライベートな質問も,相手に対して失礼に当たります. プライベートな質問としてではなく,「最近結婚しない人が多くいることについてどう思いますか」や「結婚しても子供を作らない人がいますが,どう思いますか」というように,一般的な問題として質問するとよいでしょう.

表現集

❶伝記的背景，趣味，文化の相違などを聞く表現

1. 先生の故郷はどこですか．どんなところですか． — Where's your hometown? What's it like?
2. 先生のご家族はどちらにお住まいですか． — Where does your family live?
3. ご兄弟はいらっしゃいますか． — Do you have any brothers or sisters?
4. 先生の高校時代はどうでしたか．勉強は好きでしたか． — What were your high school days like? Did you like studying?
5. 高校では先生の好きな科目は何でしたか． — What was your favorite subject in high school?
6. 先生は数学が得意でしたか． — Were you good at mathematics?
7. 暇な時は何をしますか． — What do you do in your free [spare] time?
8. 先生の好きな映画俳優はだれですか． — Who is your favorite film star?
9. 先生は何かスポーツをやりますか． — Do you do any sports?
10. 私は今，コンピュータゲームに夢中なんですが，先生は何かなさったことはありますか． — I'm crazy about computer games now. Do you ever play any?
11. 先生は若いころ，どんな本を読むことに興味がありましたか． — What kinds of books were you interested in reading when you were young?
12. だれかとても尊敬している人はいますか． — Is there someone you really admire?
13. 私は家で犬を2匹飼っているのですが，先生は動物が好きですか． — I have two dogs in my house. Do you like animals?
14. 先生の国でも携帯電話がはやっていますか． — Are cellular phones popular in your country, too?

❷日本での生活について聞く表現

1. 日本の生活に慣れましたか． — Have you gotten used to life in Japan?
2. 日本で英語を教えるのは楽しいですか． — Are you enjoying teaching English in Japan?
3. 日本のテレビ番組をどう思いますか． — What do you think about Japanese TV programs?
4. ここ日本の習慣でおもしろいものがありますか． — Are there any customs you are interested in here in Japan?
5. 日本に住んでいて何か困ることはありますか． — Are you having any problems living in Japan?
6. 「プリクラ」ってご存じですか． — Do you know what a *Purikura* is?

❸勉強などのアドバイスを求める表現

1. 将来，海外に留学したいと思っているのですが，どのような準備をしたらよいのか教えていただけますか［何かアドバイスはありますか］． — I'm planning to study abroad in the future. Can you make some suggestions on how to prepare? [Is there any advice you can give me?]
2. 英語をもっと効果的に学ぶ方法を教えていただけますか． — Would you tell me how to study English more effectively?
3. 英語で手紙を書いてみたいのですが，後で英語をチェックしていただけますか． — I'd like to write a letter in English. Would you check my English later?
4. この夏にカナダに行くのですが，行ったほうがよい所を紹介していただけますか． — I'm going to Canada this summer. Would you recommend some nice places to visit?

●クラブ活動

> Students are active in clubs at this school, aren't they?

> Yes. I'm in the brass band myself.

Jessica : Satoshi, students are active in clubs at this school, aren't they?
ジェシカ : 聡, この学校はクラブ活動が盛んなのね.
Satoshi : Yes. I'm in the brass band myself.
聡 : うん. 僕自身もブラスバンド部に入ってるんだ.
Jessica : That's cool. What instrument do you play?
ジェシカ : すごいじゃない. 何の楽器を演奏しているの?
Satoshi : I play the clarinet. We're going to enter a prefectural competition next month.
聡 : クラリネットをやってるんだ. 来月は県大会に出場する予定なんだ.
Jessica : That's great! Good luck!
ジェシカ : すごい! がんばってね!
Satoshi : Thanks. Our brass band is really good. Two years ago, we won fourth place in a national competition.
聡 : ありがとう. うちのブラスバンド部は本当に優秀なんだ. 2年前には全国大会で4位になったくらいだから.
Jessica : I bet you practice really hard. You practice every day, don't you?
ジェシカ : 練習がとても大変そうね. 毎日練習しているんでしょう?
Satoshi : Oh, yes. Strength is the key to playing wind instruments. So we run around the school yard and do sit-ups everyday.
聡 : もちろん. 吹奏楽器を演奏するには体力が命だから, 毎日校庭のランニングと腹筋運動をやるんだ.
Jessica : Wow, it's just like an athletic team.
ジェシカ : へえ, まるで運動部みたいね.

★ミニ知識★

「クラブ」と「チーム」

日本のクラブ活動は文化系もスポーツ系も同様に「クラブ」と呼びますが, 英語ではスポーツ系クラブをclubのほかにteamと呼ぶこともあります. 例えばtennis clubというと学校の中だけで楽しんでいるというニュアンスがあるのに対して, tennis teamというと校外で他校を相手に試合をするというニュアンスがあります. 「私は…クラブに所属している」というときも前置詞が異なり, clubの場合はI'm in the photography club. なのに対して, teamの場合はI'm on the baseball team. となります. また, 合唱部やブラスバンド部など音楽系のクラブ活動は日本では課外活動 (extracurricular activities) ですが, アメリカなどでは授業科目の一つになっていることがあります. つまり, アメリカで「ブラスバンドに所属している」(I'm in the brass band.) といえば, 「ブラスバンドのクラスを選択している」という意味になる場合もあるわけです.

表現集

❶入部・退部に関する表現

1. 私たちのクラブに入りたければ,長谷川先生に連絡をとってください. — If you want to join our club, please contact Mr. Hasegawa.
2. 新入部員の勧誘は来週から始まります. — Students are going to be invited to join clubs starting next week.
3. どのクラブに入ろうか迷っています. — I wonder [can't decide] which club to join.
4. ダンス部に入部希望者が殺到しています. — Applicants are rushing into the dance club.
5. 今年は新入部員が25人も入ってきました. — We've got as many as 25 new members this year.
6. 退部届を提出しました. — I gave notice that I was leaving the club [team].
7. 武は先月退部してしまいました. — Takeshi left our club last month.

❷部活動に関する表現(文化系)

1. 私たちパソコン部の顧問は中谷先生です. — The advisor to our personal computer club is Ms. Nakatani.
2. 英語スピーチ部の部長[副部長]はだれですか. — Who is the president [vice-president] of the English speech club?
3. 放送部は週に3回活動しています. — The broadcasting club meets three times a week.
4. 華道部は毎年市民ホールで華道展を開いています. — The flower arranging club holds an exhibition at the civic hall every year.
5. 軽音楽部のコンサートはいつも文化祭の花です. — The light music club concert is always the main attraction of our school festival.
6. 茶道部は文化祭で模擬店を出す予定です. — The tea ceremony club is planning to open a booth at our school festival.

❸部活動に関する表現(運動系)

1. ハンドボール部は部員が18人います. — The handball team has 18 members.
2. 私たち卓球部のキャプテンは3年生の高野真理子さんです. — The captain of our table tennis club is Mariko Takano, who is in the third year.
3. 相撲部はうちの学校でいちばん伝統のある部です. — The sumo team has the longest history of all the clubs at our school.
4. 毎日7時から8時まで朝練をします. — We have training from seven to eight every morning.
5. 1年生は(テニスの)球拾いをさせられます(→しなければなりません). — First-year students must serve as ball boys [girls].
6. 柔道部はクラブの中でいちばん練習がきついです. — The judo team practices the hardest of all the clubs.
7. 剣道部は毎年夏に合宿を行います. — The kendo team has a training camp every summer.
8. うちのテニス部は県大会でベスト8に残りました. — Our tennis team became one of the eight finalists in the prefectural tournament.
9. うちの空手部は団体戦で全国優勝しました. — Our karate team won the team competition in a national tournament.
10. うちの学校の野球部は甲子園での全国高校野球大会に出場できるように,一生懸命練習に励んでいます. — Our school's baseball team is practicing hard to 「be in [enter] the national high school baseball tournament at Koshien.

場面・状況別会話 ㉟

●ボランティア活動

What are your main activities?

We make regular visits to nursing homes for the elderly.

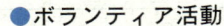

Jim : You said you were a member of a volunteer group. What are your main activities?

ジ ム：ボランティアグループのメンバーだって言ってたけど,主にどんな活動をするの.

Yuri : We make regular visits to nursing homes for the elderly. We also help out with collecting money for charity and with blood drives.

由 里：定期的に老人ホームを訪問したり,慈善募金や献血運動も手伝ったりするわ.

Jim : That's great. Oh, by the way, this morning there were some volunteers collecting money in front of the station, and I donated some money.

ジ ム：それはいいことだね.そういえば,けさ,駅前で募金をしている人がいたから,お金を寄付してきたよ.

Yuri : And you got this red feather, right?

由 里：それでこの赤い羽根をもらったんでしょう?

Jim : Right. Do you know where the money goes?

ジ ム：うん.あのお金は何に使われるか知ってる?

Yuri : Well, most of it is used in caring for poor and elderly people and the disabled.

由 里：ほとんどは貧しい人たちやお年寄り,そして障害をもっている人たちを助けるために使われるのよ.

Jim : Oh, I see. But I wonder if they can raise enough money.

ジ ム：なるほど.でも,十分なお金を集められるのかなあ?

Yuri : Probably not. That's why Japanese should be more interested in volunteer activities.

由 里：たぶん集まらないと思うわ.だからこそ日本人はもっとボランティア活動に関心をもつべきなのよ.

★ミニ知識★

欧米はボランティア活動の先進国

　日本でも最近はボランティア活動が盛んになってきていますが,欧米と比べるとまだ特別なものという印象が抜けないのが現状でしょう.欧米では,キリスト教に基づく平等観や隣人愛の精神の影響から他人どうしが助け合うことが重視されているので,ボランティア活動の歴史も日本よりも古く,また人々の生活により密着したものになっています.例えば,アメリカの大学ではボランティア活動の経験があると入学に際して有利になるなど,若いうちからボランティア活動に携わることが奨励されています.また,歌手がコンサートの売上金を災害援助や障害者援助などのために寄付することも頻繁にあるほか,一般の人々でも定年退職した後に様々な形でボランティア活動に参加することが多いようです.

表現集

❶ボランティア活動一般に関する表現

1. ボランティア活動をしたことがありますか. — Have you ever worked as a volunteer?
2. ボランティア活動をしたいと思っています. — I'd like to work as a volunteer. / I'd like to do some volunteer work.
3. どんなボランティア活動がありますか. — What types of volunteer jobs are there?
4. 私にはどんなボランティア活動ができる[適している]と思いますか. — What kinds of volunteer jobs do you think「I can do [I'm suitable for]?
5. 人の役に立つことをするのはとても楽しいです. — It's a lot of fun to do something useful for other people.
6. 営利を目的としてボランティア活動をしているのではありません. — I [We] don't work as「a volunteer [volunteers] to make a profit.
7. 私はボランティアで留学生に日本語を教えています. — I'm teaching Japanese to some students from abroad「as a volunteer [on a voluntary basis].
8. 災害の知らせを聞いて多くのボランティアが集まりました. — Many people volunteered on hearing of the disaster.
9. 震災でＮＰＯ活動の重要性が認識されました. — The earthquake made us realize the importance of the activities of nonprofit organizations.

❷募金・慈善運動などに関する表現

1. そのテレビ局は地震の被災者のための募金運動を始めました. — The TV station started a fundraising campaign for the victims of the earthquake.
2. この募金運動は交通遺児のためのものです. — This fundraising drive is for the orphans of traffic accident victims.
3. そのミュージシャンはエイズの子供たちのためにチャリティーコンサートを催しました. — The musician gave a charity concert for children with AIDS.
4. 私たちは本を集める運動を計画し, 集まった本を発展途上国の図書館に送りました. — We organized a book drive and sent the collected books to libraries in developing countries.

❸高齢者・障害者の介護に関する表現

1. 私の友人は老人介護のボランティアをしています. — A friend of mine works as a volunteer caring for the elderly.
2. ボランティアたちは車いすの操作のしかたや老人介護のしかたを習いました. — The volunteers learned how to operate wheelchairs and how to take care of the elderly.
3. 私たちは定期的に老人ホームを訪れ, 歌や踊りを披露しています. — We make regular visits to senior citizens' homes where we perform songs and dances.
4. 私の兄は精神障害の子供たちのためのリハビリを手伝っています. — My brother helps in rehabilitation exercises for children with「intellectual disabilities [mental retardation].
5. 私たちは視覚障害者のために点字の本を作っています. — We prepare books in Braille for visually disabled people.
6. 彼女はその会議で手話通訳のボランティアをしました. — She volunteered to work as a sign-language translator at the conference.

場面・状況別会話 36

●ホームステイ

> How late can I take a shower?

> You can take a shower anytime before 11:00 p.m.

Yukio: What time do you have dinner, Mrs. Glenn?
由 紀 夫: グレンさん, 夕食は何時ですか.
Mrs. Glenn: Usually around seven. If you're going to be late, be sure to call.
グレン夫人: ふつう7時ごろよ. 遅れるようだったら, 必ず電話をくださいね.
Yukio: I will. Can I fix my own lunch on weekends?
由 紀 夫: そうします. 週末には自分で昼食を作ってもいいですか.
Mrs. Glenn: Sure. Just help yourself to anything in the fridge.
グレン夫人: ええ. 冷蔵庫の中の物は何でも自由に食べていいわよ.
Yukio: Thank you. How late can I take a shower?
由 紀 夫: ありがとうございます. シャワーは何時まで使っていいですか.
Mrs. Glenn: You can take a shower anytime before 11:00 p.m. And please leave the door open when you finish. That means nobody is using the bathroom.
グレン夫人: 夜11時前ならいつでもいいわ. 終わったらドアをあけたままにしておいてね. だれも使ってないということが分かるから.
Yukio: I see. And how about my laundry?
由 紀 夫: 分かりました. それから洗濯はどうしたらいいんですか.
Mrs. Glenn: There are a washer and a dryer in the basement. I'll show you how to use them later.
グレン夫人: 地下室に洗濯機と乾燥機があるの. 後で使い方を教えてあげますよ.

★ミニ知識★

家族の一員

アメリカでは, ホームステイ先の家族 (host family) は私たちを「お客様」としてではなく,「家族の一員」として迎えます. したがって, ステイ中に特別豪華な食事が続いたり, ベッドメーキングや部屋の掃除をしてくれるわけではありません. いつもと変わらないふつうの生活に私たちが参加し溶け込んでくれることを期待しているので, 日本と違う生活習慣や規則に早く慣れることが必要です. 例えば, 自分の部屋のドアは勉強するときや寝るときには閉めますが, リラックスしているときや学校に行くときにはあけたままにしておくように言われることもあります. また, ふつうは冷蔵庫の中の物を自由に食べたりすることもできます. しかし, 自分の身の回りのことだけではなく, 積極的に食器洗いやバスルームの掃除, そのほか家事の手伝いをすることも期待されています. 週末など, 買い物をしたりどこかに連れていってもらいたいときは, 遠慮しないでお願いするとよいでしょう. 自分から積極的に家族の一員となろうとすることが, 楽しく思い出の多いホームステイを実現させるかぎです.

表現集

❶生活規則に関する表現

1. 守らなければならない規則はありますか. — Are there any rules I should follow?
2. あなたの家に門限はありますか. ／あなたの家の門限は何時ですか. — Do you have a curfew in your family? / What time is the curfew in your family?
3. 門限までに帰れなければ電話を入れます. — I'll give you a call if I can't be home before the curfew.
4. 夕食がいらない場合はお知らせします. — I'll let you know if I'm going to miss dinner.
5. 今夜は遅くなるので夕食はいりません. — I'll be late tonight, so I won't need dinner.
6. 何かお手伝いできますか. — Is there anything I can help you with?
7. 皿洗いを手伝いましょうか. — Shall I help you do the dishes?
8. 今度買い物に行くときにいっしょに行ってもいいですか. 買いたい物があるんです. — Next time you go shopping, can I come along? I have something to get.
9. オーバーをクリーニングに出しておいてもらいたいのですが. — I want to have my overcoat sent to the cleaner's.
10. 自分で軽い食事を作ってもいいですか. — Can I make [fix] myself a snack?
11. 友達を何人か連れてきてもいいですか. — Is it OK to invite some of my friends?
12. こんなことはもうしないと約束します. — I promise this will never happen again.
13. 長電話をしないように気をつけます. — I'll be careful not to speak on the phone for a long time.

❷器具・設備などに関する表現

1. 掃除機を貸してもらえますか. — Can I borrow the vacuum cleaner?
2. 電気スタンドの電球が切れてしまいました. 新しい電球はありますか. — The light bulb on my desk lamp has burned out. Can I have a new one?
3. 冷蔵庫に食べ物を入れておいてもいいですか. — Is it OK to keep some food in the fridge?
4. どのように部屋の温度を調節するんですか. ちょっと暑すぎ［寒すぎ］ます. — How can I adjust the temperature in my room? It's a bit too hot [cold].
5. レンジの使い方を教えていただけますか. — Could you show me how to use the stove?
6. 針と糸をもらえますか. シャツのボタンが取れてしまったんです. — May I have a needle and thread? A button on my shirt came off.
7. 浴槽の水［排水管］が詰まってしまいました. — The bathtub is clogged. / The drain in the tub is clogged.
8. ハンガーをもう少しもらえますか. — May I have some extra hangers?
9. ごみはどうすればいいですか. — How can I dispose of my trash?

❸ホストがよく使う表現

1. 遠慮しないで何でも聞いてください. — Don't hesitate to ask any questions.
2. どうぞ自由に冷蔵庫を使ってください. — Please feel free to use the fridge.
3. 長距離電話をしたいときには教えてください. — Just let me know when you want to make a long-distance call.
4. 安全を確かめないで玄関のドアをあけないように注意してください. — Let me remind you that you should not open the front door without making sure it's safe.
5. 外出のときは玄関のドアのかぎを必ず閉めてください. — Make sure you lock the front door when you go out.

| 場面・状況別会話 ㊲

●留学（1）〈留学前〉

> I want to study English abroad.

> Where do you want to study?

Yasushi : I want to study English abroad when I become a college student.
泰　　　：大学生になったら英語留学をしたいと思ってるんだ．
Lisa　 : That's a good idea. Where do you want to study?
リ　サ：いい考えだわ．どこで勉強したいの．
Yasushi : Well, there are a lot of English-speaking countries, aren't there? Lisa, you are from Australia, right?
泰　　　：そうだなあ．英語を話す国はたくさんあるんでしょう？　リサ，君はオーストラリアの出身だったね？
Lisa　 : Yes. Australia is usually safe and has a lot of natural beauty. The schools are pretty good.
リ　サ：そうよ．オーストラリアはふつうは安全で，自然の美しさにも恵まれているわ．学校はとてもいいわよ．
Yasushi : Is it expensive to live there?
泰　　　：生活するのにお金がとてもかかるの？
Lisa　 : It depends where you live. I mean, do you want to live in a dormitory, an apartment, or do you want to take part in a homestay program?
リ　サ：どこに住むかによるわね．つまり寮とかアパートに住みたいの，それともホームステイをしたいの？
Yasushi : I haven't decided yet. It would be nice if I could work.
泰　　　：まだ決めてないんだ．働くことができればいいんだけど．
Lisa　 : Well, you may have lots of assignments at school, so it might be difficult to both work and study.
リ　サ：そうね．学校では宿題がたくさんあるだろうから，仕事と勉強を両立させるのは難しいかもしれないわ．

★ミニ知識★

楽しい留学は友達から

　留学生は世界中の国々からその学校に集まってきます．現地の国の学生だけではなく，こうした他の国からの留学生どうしがお互いの文化を知り合って友情の輪を広げていくことも留学の貴重な経験になります．英語が母語ではないからといって，英語圏以外の国からの留学生を無視したり，彼らとの接触を避けたりするのはよくありません．留学を楽しいものにするには，勉強を助けてもらったり，悩みを打ち明けたり，いっしょに遊びに出かけたりできる友達をたくさん作ることです．日本よりもかなり宿題やテストが多いので，学生は図書館に行ったり，クラブ活動やアルバイトで放課後や週末も忙しい生活を送っています．相手から声をかけてもらうのを待っているだけでは，友達を作るチャンスはほとんどありません．こちらから積極的に話しかけて一人でも多くの友達を作るように心がけましょう．

表現集

❶留学に関して質問するときの表現

1. 1年間アメリカに留学するのにいくらかかるのだろう.
   I'm wondering how much it will cost to study in the U.S. for one year.
2. 航空運賃, 授業料, 生活費で合計いくらになりますか.
   What will the total amount be for air fares, tuition (fees) and living expenses?
3. 留学についてあまりよく知らないのですが, 国と学校をどのように選んだらよいのですか.
   I don't know much about studying abroad. How can I choose a country and a school?
4. 留学の場所を選ぶのにどんな要素を考えるべきですか.
   What factors should I consider in choosing a place to study abroad?
5. その学校にはよい英語のプログラムがありますか [よい英語の先生がいますか].
   Does the institution have 「a good English program [good English teachers]?
6. プログラムが終わったら正式な修了証書がもらえますか.
   Will I receive an official certificate upon completion of the program?
7. 寮と民間のアパートとどちらに住むほうがよいと思いますか.
   Which do you think is better, to live in a dormitory or in a private apartment house?
8. 外国でホームシックにかかったことはありますか.
   Have you ever gotten homesick in a foreign country?
9. その大学に入るのにどのくらいの英語能力が必要ですか.
   How much English ability is required to enter the college?
10. 留学の準備のために今何をすべきですか.
    What should I do now to prepare to study abroad?

❷留学経験に関する表現

1. 交換留学生として [交換留学制度で] アイルランドに留学しました.
   I've been to Ireland to study 「as an exchange student [on an exchange program]」.
2. 留学して価値観が大きく変わりました.
   Studying abroad changed my values very much.
3. 留学して視野が広がりました.
   Studying abroad 「widened my perspective [broadened my horizons]」.
4. 留学して克服しなければならない最初の障害はリスニングでした.
   When I studied abroad, the first barrier I had to get over was listening comprehension.
5. カナダにいて, 自分が日本についていかに無知か分かりました.
   In Canada, I realized how ignorant I was about Japan.
6. 相互理解が最も重要なことです.
   Mutual understanding is the most important thing.
7. 外国生活ではいつもよいことが起きるとは限りません. 時には誤解, 失望, 病気, そして犯罪さえあります. こういうことすべてが経験なのです.
   Good things don't always happen when living in a foreign country. Sometimes there are misunderstandings, disappointments, illness and even crimes. All these are experiences.
8. 留学の目的を明確にしておくべきです. 学校ではどんな科目を学びたいのか, その国の何を見たいのか, そして将来その経験をどう役立てたいのかということです.
   You should be clear about the purpose of studying abroad: what subject do you want to study in school, what do you want to see in the country, and how do you want to make use of the experience in the future?

場面・状況別会話 ㊳

●留学（2）〈留学先〉

> Could you help me with my course registration?

> Certainly. Let me take a look at your file.

Yutaka	: Dr. Barnes? I'm Kamiya Yutaka from Japan. Could you help me with my course registration?
豊	: バーンズ教授ですか．日本から来た神谷豊と申します．授業の登録について相談に乗っていただけますでしょうか．
Dr. Barnes	: Certainly. Let me take a look at your file.... You're a sociology major?
バーンズ教授	: もちろんです．あなたのファイルを見せてもらえますか．…社会学専攻ですね．
Yutaka	: Yes. I'm especially interested in cross-cultural communication. I'm just wondering how many courses I should take the first semester, because my listening and speaking ability is still poor.
豊	: はい．特に異文化間コミュニケーションに興味があります．リスニングとスピーキングの力がまだ不十分なので，最初の学期に何科目とったらよいか迷っているんです．
Dr. Barnes	: Well, the classes in this country are based on discussion, so you should improve your linguistic ability first. I recommend you take some English courses for international students. As for your major courses, I think you better take only two required courses this semester.
バーンズ教授	: この国の授業はディスカッションが主なので，まず言語能力を伸ばすべきでしょう．留学生のための英語コースをとることをすすめます．専門コースは今学期は必修科目を2つだけにしたほうがよいと思います．
Yutaka	: I see. I'll come back to talk to you after sitting in on some of the classes.
豊	: 分かりました．いくつか授業を聴講してみてから，また相談に伺います．

★ミニ知識★

アメリカのキャンパスライフ

一般的にアメリカの大学のキャンパスは広々としていて，校舎間の移動には自転車が欠かせないところもあります．キャンパスはふつう芝生で覆われ，読書をしたり昼食をとりながらくつろいでいる学生の姿がよく見られます．施設も充実していて，図書館が24時間あいていることも珍しくありません．学生について日本との大きな違いは，その多様性にあります．日本の大学生は18歳から20歳代半ばがほとんどですが，アメリカの大学では一度社会に出てからキャリアアップのために戻ってきた人，学生結婚をして家族寮に住みながら勉強している夫婦，シングルマザーで働きながら勉強を続けている女性など，多様な背景をもった人々がおのおのの目的をもって勉学に励んでいます．アメリカでは大学は人生の通過点ではなく，必要に応じていつでも戻ってくることのできる生涯学習の場なのです．

表現集

❶ 授業の登録に関する表現

1. いくつか授業を受けてみてから，とる科目を決めます． — I'll check a few classes before I decide which courses I should take.
2. 専門の必要条件を満たすために300レベルの歴史の科目を2つとらなければなりません． — I have to take two 300-level history courses to meet the requirements for my major.
3. 経済学は必修科目なのでとらなければなりません． — Economics is a required course, so I have to sign up for it.
4. 選択科目から9単位履修できます． — We can register for nine hours of electives.
5. この科目は数学345の先行必修科目です． — This course is a prerequisite for Mathematics 345.
6. （科目登録の）追加・削除の締め切りはいつですか． — When is the add-drop deadline?
7. 担任教授の署名をもらう必要があります． — I have to get my faculty advisor's signature.

❷ 授業の内容に関する表現

1. 週に何回授業がありますか． — How many times a week do we meet?
2. リー教授［リー教授の授業］は厳しいですか． — Is 「Prof. Lee [Prof. Lee's class] demanding?
3. トーフルの点数は520なのですが，このクラスは難しすぎますか． — My TOEFL score is 520. Do you think this course is too difficult for me?
4. この科目の試験はどんな感じですか． — What are the exams like in this course?
5. ワトソン教授のクラスはレポートが3つ，試験が2回，そして少なくとも1回の発表が課せられます． — In Prof. Watson's class three papers, two exams, and at least one presentation are required.

❸ 実際の授業で使う表現

1. この国で初めての授業です． — This is my first class in this country.
2. きょうの講義の内容がよく分かりませんでした．この授業で役に立つ参考書を教えていただけますか． — I had trouble understanding your lecture today. Could you recommend some texts for outside reading that would help me in this class?
3. リスニング力がまだそれほどないので，講義を録音してもいいですか． — My listening ability is still not that good. Do you mind if I tape your lecture?
4. この前の授業を休んでしまいました．ノートをコピーさせてもらえますか． — I missed the last class. Can I copy [make copies of] your notes?
5. 授業についていくのが大変なので，試験が心配です． — I have some difficulty keeping up with the class. I'm worried about the exam.
6. ゼミで発表しなければならないんです． — I have to make a presentation in the seminar.
7. ジム先生の授業は予習が大変です． — Dr. Jim's class needs a lot of preparation.
8. 授業をたくさんとりすぎました．たぶん1科目やめます［落とします］． — I 「overloaded myself [took too many classes]. Probably I'll drop one course.
9. クラスでの討論に積極的に参加するために予習をしてくることが求められます． — We are expected to come to class prepared so that we can actively participate in class discussions.
10. 授業予定はシラバス（授業計画表）に書いてあります． — The course schedule is in the syllabus.

場面・状況別会話 ㊴

●パーティー

> Can I introduce you to her? She's right there.
> Oh, yes. Let's go talk to her.

Hidehiko : Hi, can I get you something to drink?
英　　彦 : こんにちは. 何か飲み物を取ってきましょうか.

Samantha : Yes, I'd like a Coke. Thank you.
サマンサ : はい. コーラをいただきます. ありがとう.

　　　　　(Hidehiko gives Samantha a glass of Coke.)
　　　　　(英彦はサマンサにグラスに入れたコーラを渡す)

Hidehiko : My name is Hidehiko. Nice to meet you.
英　　彦 : 僕は英彦といいます. はじめまして.

Samantha : Nice to meet you, too. I'm Samantha. Where are you from?
サマンサ : はじめまして. 私はサマンサです. 出身はどちらですか.

Hidehiko : I'm from Japan. I'm here to study English.
英　　彦 : 日本です. 英語を勉強しにこちらに来ました.

Samantha : Good. Is Japanese very different from English?
サマンサ : いいですね. 日本語は英語とだいぶ違うんですか.

Hidehiko : Yes, quite a lot, because the grammar is totally different.
英　　彦 : はい, だいぶ違います. というのは文法が全く違うんです.

Samantha : Sounds difficult. This semester I'm taking French.
サマンサ : 難しそうですね. 今学期は私はフランス語をとっているんです.

Hidehiko : Oh, my friend, Yukiko, is also learning French. Can I introduce you to her? She's right there.
英　　彦 : えっ, 僕の友達の由紀子もフランス語を習っているんだ. 彼女にあなたを紹介してもいいですか. すぐそこにいますから.

Samantha : Oh, yes. Let's go talk to her.
サマンサ : ええ, いいですよ. 行ってお話ししましょう.

★ミニ知識★

積極的な会話を！

　一般に食事や催し物の伴うパーティーでは, 主催者は事前に人数を把握する必要があるので, 招待を受けたら行けるかどうかの返事を必ずするのがエチケットです. 「行けたら行く」などというあいまいな返事はよくありません. 英米のパーティーは立食のバイキング形式であることが多いので, 家に行くときには必ずしも指定された時間ぴったりに行く必要はなく, 帰るときもみなばらばらです. 日本でのように全員がいっせいに帰るということはあまりありません. パーティーの目的は料理を味わうだけではなく会話を楽しむことでもあるので, 知らない人にも積極的に話しかけることが大切です. ふだんからの友達だけが集まったり, 男女に別れてグループができたりするのはむしろ不自然です.

表現集

❶ パーティーでのあいさつの表現

1. 呼んでくれてどうもありがとう. — Thank you for 「inviting me [the invitation].
2. もうみんな来ていますか. — Is everybody here yet?
3. 私の友達を紹介していいですか. — Can I introduce a friend of mine?
4. こちらが私の友達のヘンリーです. — This is my friend, Henry.
5. 彼に私を紹介していただけますか. — Would you introduce me to him?
6. もう帰らなくてはなりません. — I must be going now.
7. とても楽しかったです. — I had a very good time.
8. 本当に食事がおいしかったです. — I really enjoyed dinner.
9. すてきな夜をありがとうございました. — Thank you for the wonderful evening.

❷ 初対面の人と会話するきっかけをつかむときの表現

1. 何か飲み物を取ってきましょうか. — Can I get you something to drink?
2. はじめまして. リナといいます. — Nice to meet you. I'm Rina.
3. あなたをご存じ上げていないと思いますが. ／前にお会いしたことはないと思いますが. — I don't think I know you. / I don't think we've met before.
4. 以前にどこかでお会いしましたか. — Have we met somewhere before?
5. （主人公のジュディーについて）ジュディーとはどのようなお知り合いですか. — How do you know Judy?
6. こんにちは. いいパーティーですね. — Hi. Nice party!
7. こんにちは, あなたのセーターいいですね. — Hi. I love your sweater.
8. 仲間に入ってもいいですか. — Can I join you?
9. ここに座ってもいいですか. — Do you mind if I sit here?
10. 何年生ですか. ／専攻は何ですか. — What year are you in? / What's your major?
11. 学校では何を勉強していますか. — What are you studying at school?

❸ パーティーに招待するときの表現

1. 今度の日曜日に私の誕生パーティーに来ていただけますか. — Would you like to come to my birthday party this coming Sunday?
2. 手ぶらで来てください. — Just bring yourself.
3. 友達を連れてきてください. — Please bring your friends.
4. 来られない場合には連絡してください. — Please let me know if you can't come.
5. 剛のためのサプライズ・パーティーです. — It's a surprise (party) for Tsuyoshi.

--- パーティーの招待状 ---

パーティーをします！

We're Having a Party!

村田恵美さんの誕生パーティーに謹んでご招待いたします. 10月19日午後6時から私の家にて.

10月16日までにご返事ください.

小田典子
北区堀船1-2-3
電話：03-1234-5678

You are cordially invited to a birthday party for Murata Emi at my house at 6:00 p.m. on the 19th of October.

R.S.V.P. by Oct. 16.

Oda Noriko
1-2-3 Horifune, Kita-ku
Phone: 03-1234-5678

場面・状況別会話 ㊵

●自己紹介

❶ 日本の授業でALTまたは留学生を迎えて

My name is Nakamura Tomoko. Everyone calls me Tomo. I am very happy to have an ALT [a friend from abroad] in this class. I have never talked with native speakers of English, so this will give me a great chance to listen to and talk in English. My dream is to study abroad in the future. So I hope it will be all right if I ask you many questions about your country. If you have any questions about Japan, I will be glad to answer them. I hope sometimes we can have lunch together. Thank you.

名前は中村友子です．みんなはトモと呼んでいます．このクラスにＡＬＴ［海外からの友達］を迎えてとてもうれしく思います．英語のネイティブスピーカーと話したことがないので，今回は英語で聞いたり話したりするよい機会を私に与えてくれるでしょう．私の夢は将来留学することです．だから，あなたの国についてたくさん質問させていただきたいと思っています．もし日本について何か質問があれば，喜んでお答えします．ときどき昼食をご一緒できたらと思います．以上です．

❷ 日本のパーティーなどで友達に紹介されて

Hi, my name is Shibata Ryoichi. Takehiro told me a lot about you. He said you were interested in karate. I have been practicing karate since I was little. If you have time some day, why don't you stop by my karate gym? The people there are very friendly and I'm sure you will like them.

こんにちは．柴田良一といいます．武浩からあなたのことはよく聞いています．彼の話では空手に興味があるそうですね．僕は小さいときから空手をやっています．もしいつか時間があれば，僕の空手道場に寄ってください．みんなとても親しみやすいので，彼らのことをきっと気に入るでしょう．

★ミニ知識★

消極的な発言はマイナス

言葉が違う外国で自己紹介 (self-introduction) をするときに，「まだ英語がよく分からないので，よろしくお願いします」と言葉の劣等感を理由に，特別な扱いを求めようとするのはよくありません．また，「おとなしくて，人と話をするのがあまり得意ではありません」などとマイナス面を挙げても，同情を期待することはできません．たとえ言葉はたどたどしくても，明るく自信をもって自分のプラス面をはきはきと言える人ほど，みんなに好かれます．いかにその国の言葉や習慣に溶け込もうとしているか，いかに周りの人と友達になりたいと思っているかなど，積極的な姿勢が感じ取れるようなスピーチをするように心がけることが大切です．

❸ 海外で (1)

My name is Ishibashi Mie. In Japanese "mi" means "beauty" and "e" means "be endowed." So I am endowed with beauty as you see now. Just joking! I am very happy to be here and want to use this chance to make many friends and practice my English. I will be happy to teach you some Japanese, too, while I am here. I want to understand Canada better and hope to help you understand Japan. I believe international understanding is the best way to a peaceful world.

石橋美恵といいます．日本語で「美」は「美しさ」，「恵」は「恵まれる」という意味です．だから，私は今ごらんのとおり美貌(びぼう)に恵まれているのです．ほんの冗談です！ここに来られたことはとても幸せで，この機会を利用してたくさん友達を作り，英語の練習をしたいと思っています．また，私がここにいる間にみなさんに日本語を教えられればうれしいです．カナダのことをもっとよく理解して，そして，みなさんが日本を理解する手助けができればと思います．国際理解が平和な世界への最善の道だと信じています．

❹ 海外で (2)

Hi, I'm Harada Isamu. I'm very excited to have this chance to meet all of you, and I hope that we can become better acquainted. I'm very interested in sports and play soccer and tennis. I hope to be able to play tennis while I'm here. My father is a professional golfer. You may know that it costs a great deal of money to play a round of golf in Japan. I'm amazed at how reasonable the fees are to play golf here and how uncrowded the tennis courts are! I also love movies. I like comedies best. My favorite actor is Robin Williams. I think he is one of the funniest people on the planet. If you are also interested in movies, let me know, and we can go see a film together.

こんにちは．原田勇です．みなさんにお会いできる機会がもてたことをとてもうれしく思い，よりよく知り合えるようになれたらと思います．僕はスポーツにとても興味があって，サッカーとテニスをします．ここにいる間にテニスができればと思います．父はプロゴルファーです．知っているかもしれませんが日本ではゴルフを1ラウンド回るのにとてもお金がかかります．ここではゴルフがとてもでごろな料金でできるし，テニスコートも全く込んでいないので驚きました．それから映画も大好きです．コメディーがいちばん好きです．私の大好きな俳優はロビン・ウイリアムスです．彼は地球上で最もおもしろい人の一人だと思います．もし映画に興味がある人がいたら，教えてください．いっしょに映画を見に行きましょう．

❺ 海外で (3)

I'm Ono Ken. I'm a Libra. Librans are very sensitive and artistic. I practice the guitar every day. Does anyone play the guitar? I want to have a band of my own some day. If any of you are interested in forming a band, please let me know. Also, I'm kind of a computer freak. After school, maybe you see me sitting in front of a computer in the lab. I was very happy to learn that computers are widely used in this country. I have an e-mail address, so if you want to keep in touch with me by e-mail, please tell me your address.

小野謙です．僕は天秤(てんびん)座です．天秤座の人はとても感受性が豊かで芸術家的なんです．僕は毎日ギターの練習をしています．ギターを弾く人はいますか．いつか自分のバンドを持ちたいと思っています．バンドを組むのに興味がある人がいたら，教えてください．それから，僕はかなりのコンピュータマニアです．放課後僕がコンピュータ室のコンピュータの前に座っているのを見かけるかもしれません．コンピュータがこの国では広く使われているということを知りとてもうれしく思います．電子メールのアドレスを持っているので，メールで私と連絡をとり合いたい人がいたら，アドレスを教えてください．

場面・状況別会話 ㊶

ボディーランゲージ（英語圏で通用するもの）

●肩をすくめる

分かりません．
参った．
I don't know.
I give up.

●胸に手をあてる
（人指し指で胸を指す場合もある）

私？
Me?

●手を揺り動かす

まあまあ．
So so.

●親指を上に向ける

いいねえ．
Good!
I agree.

●親指を下に向ける

ひどいねえ．
Bad!
No good.

●頭の横で指を揺り動かす

あっかんべえ！
Naah!

●両手の指を2本立てて曲げる

つまり，いわゆる．
Quote.

●追い払う

もういいよ．
Forget it!

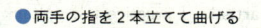

●手招きする
（手の平を上に向けて）

こっちに来て．
Come here.

● こめかみのところで指を回す ● おなかの上で手を回す ● 指を3回振る

ばかじゃない！
Stupid!
Crazy!

おなかすいた．
I'm hungry.

だめ，だめ，だめ．
No, no, no!

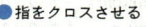

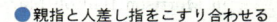

● 祈るように手を合わせる ● 指をクロスさせる ● 親指と人差し指をこすり合わせる

お願い！
Please!
I hope.

幸運をお祈りします．
願わくば…でありますように．
Good luck!
I wish ….

お金．
Money.

● 首を縦［横］に振る（否定疑問文の場合）
コーヒーは好きじゃないの？
Don't you like coffee?

いや．好きだよ．
Yes. I like it.

うん．好きじゃない．
No. I don't like it.

● 数の数え方（**counting**）

指で数を数えるときに，日本では手を開いた状態で親指から順に1，2，3…と折っていきますが，欧米では逆に手を閉じた状態で人差し指や親指などから順に開いていくのがふつうです．

場面・状況別会話 ㊷

掲示

●LOST!!　紛失物!!

LOST!!

A silver bracelet left in the ladies' room in Morrison Hall on Mar. 8. Not valuable but has much sentimental value. Small reward offered to finder. Call Aya at 123-4567 or e-mail me at aya@favje.com.

紛失物!!

銀のブレスレットを3月8日にモリソンホールの女性用トイレに置き忘れました。高価な物ではありませんが、とても思い出がある品です。見つけた人にはささやかなお礼を差し上げます。綾あてに電話 (123-4567) またはメール (aya@favje.com) をください。

●Roommate Wanted　ルームメイト募集

Roommate Wanted

Male Japanese student seeks roommate.
* Share the rent of $500/month plus utilities
* Large studio apt.
* Fireplace
* Close to campus
* Quiet neighborhood
* No pets
* No smoking

Contact Masa at 567-8901

ルームメイト募集

日本人の男子学生がルームメイトを探しています。
*月500ドルの家賃と公共料金をシェアする
*広い（台所、ふろ付きの）1部屋のアパート
*暖炉あり
*キャンパスに近し
*閑静な環境
*ペット禁止
*禁煙

連絡は567-8901マサまで。

★ミニ知識★

トラブルのないように細心の注意を

　物品の売買、アルバイトの求人、ルームメイトの募集、紛失物の案内などのために、欧米では個人的な掲示を出すことが多くあります。簡単で便利ですが、トラブルが起こることもあるので、細かな注意が必要です。例えば、名前や電話を悪用されるおそれがあるので、連絡先には正式なフルネームではなくニックネームを用いるのが常識です。また、物品の売買や契約金の支払いなどに関しては、サインの入った領収書（受取書）や念書を書くとかもらうようにすべきです。金銭のやりとりは小切手を使うのが一般的ですが、受け取るほうは念のため運転免許証やクレジットカードの番号を控えさせてもらうなど、二重三重のチェックを怠らないようにしましょう。

●FOR SALE　売り出し

```
            FOR SALE

Used Bicycle       $120.00
    '98 Schwinn Tourmaster
    * Men's bike
    * Blue
    * New tires
    * Good condition
    * Tire pump included
            Contact Takashi at 456-7890
```

'98 Schwinn Tourmaster Takashi at 456-7890 [repeated tear-off tabs]

　　　　　　売り出し

中古自転車　　　　　　120ドル
　　98年製シュイン・ツアマスター
　＊男性用自転車
　＊ブルー
　＊新品タイヤ
　＊状態良好
　＊空気入れ付き
　　　　　　　連絡は456－7890孝まで．

※掲示の紙の下部にはたいてい連絡先などが記されており，掲示内容に興味をもった人がちぎって持っていけるように切り込みが入っていることが多い．

●GUITARIST WANTED　ギタリスト募集

```
        GUITARIST WANTED

"The Horifune Faves" is looking for a gui-
tarist to join our classic rock cover band.
Vocal ability a plus. We have a few gigs
lined up at school dances, and we will
book more once the position is filled.
        Call Miki at 234-5678 after 7 p.m.
```

　　　　　ギタリスト募集

クラシックロックのコピーバンド「ホリフネフェイブズ」では，ギタリストを募集中．ボーカルができればなお可．スクールダンスパーティーに数回出演することが決まっていますが，ギタリストが決定ししだい出演回数を増やす予定です．

　　午後7時以降に234-5678の美紀まで
　　　　電話をください．

●Want to Learn Japanese?　日本語を学びたいですか

```
    Want to Learn Japanese?

Japanese student will teach you at a place
and time convenient to you.
$8.00 per hour
Let's speak Japanese!
        Phone & Fax: 345-6789 (Masaru)
```

　　　　日本語を学びたいですか

日本人の学生があなたの都合のよい場所と時間に教えます．
1時間8ドル
日本語を話しましょう！
　　　電話・ファックス：345-6789（勝）

場面・状況別会話 ㊸

●ディスカッション

《ディスカッションとは》

ディスカッションでは，ある話題についてお互いに個人的意見を交換し，他人の考えを知ったり問題を解決したりします．ディベートと違って，参加者の一人一人がいつでも自由な意見を自由に述べることができるので，特に質問や反対意見などがあったら，ためらわずにどんどん発言しましょう．ただし，だれかが話している最中に割り込むのは失礼になります．発言する際は手を挙げて司会者の許可を得ることが必要です．人間は一人一人がみな違う意見をもっているはずです．例えば，同じ賛成の意見でも理由は人によって違うはずです．他人の関心を引くには周りの人の意見に同調するのではなくて，オリジナルな意見をもつことが大切です．「分かりません」，「どちらでもよいです」，「それでもよいです」といった意見や自信のない態度を表すことはよくありません．ディスカッションではふつうディベートのような勝敗はありませんが，自分の意見を周りの人に理解してもらうために，論理的な話し方や説得力が必要とされる点はディベートの場合と同じです．

《ディスカッションの注意点》
*積極的に発言する．
*ほかの参加者の意見をよく聞く．
*質問や疑問などがあったらためらわずに尋ねる．
*他人の発言中に割り込まずに，手を挙げて待つ．
*他人の意見を批判するだけでなく独自の意見を述べる．
*議長は参加者全員に平等な発言の機会を与える．
*議長は話の流れを整理し，スムーズな進行を目ざす．

* * * * *

Moderator : Today we are going to talk about life in the city. More and more people today are moving to the city to get jobs, to go to college, or just to enjoy city life. However, there are both advantages and disadvantages in living in the city. What do you think about life in the city? Please feel free to speak out.

議　　長：きょうは都会の生活について話し合います．最近では就職，大学入学，あるいは単に都会生活を楽しむために，都会に移る人が増えています．しかし，都会で生活することにはよい点も悪い点もあります．都会での生活についてみなさんはどう思いますか．どうぞ自由に発言してください．

Hideki : I think I'll live in the city in the future, because there are many kinds of stores in the city and I can get almost anything.

秀　　樹：僕は将来都会で暮らすと思います．都会にはいろいろな店があって，ほとんど何でも手に入れられるからです．

Moderator : Hitomi, would you like to say something?

議　　長：仁美さん，何か意見はありますか．

Hitomi	: Yes, the transportation systems in the city are fast and convenient, so we can go anywhere without much trouble.
仁　美	：はい，都会では交通が速くて便利だから，あまり苦労しないでどこへでも行けるわね．
Moderator	: Naoko?
議　長	：直子さんは？
Naoko	: Well, I agree that it is convenient to live in the city. But what about the pollution and noise problems? My brother moved to Tokyo last year and sent me a letter saying he couldn't sleep well at night because of the traffic noise.
直　子	：都会の生活が便利だということには同意するわ．でも，汚染や騒音の問題についてはどうでしょうか．私の兄は去年東京に越して手紙をくれたけど，交通の騒音で夜はよく眠れないって書いてあったわ．
Akio	: That's true. I can't stand the air pollution and the noise in the city. In addition, the rent for apartments is high, even though the rooms are small.
昭　夫	：そうなんだ．僕は都会の大気汚染と騒音には耐えられないよ．そのうえ，部屋が狭いのにアパートの家賃が高いんだ．
Moderator	: What do you think about the people in the city, Takuya?
議　長	：都会の人たちについてはどう思いますか，卓也君．
Takuya	: Well, I think people are indifferent to the lives of others. Some people living in condominiums don't even know who their neighbors are. I prefer people in the country because they are more friendly.
卓　也	：みんな他人の生活に無関心だと思います．マンションに住んでいる人たちの中には隣近所に住んでいる人がだれなのかさえ知らない人もいます．僕はいなかの人たちのほうが親しみやすいので好きだな．
Moderator	: Yes, Hideki.
議　長	：はい，秀樹君．
Hideki	: For me, city life is ideal because I don't want to be bothered by my neighbors.
秀　樹	：僕は隣近所の人たちにじゃまされたくないから都会生活は理想的だけとな．
Akio	: Excuse me, but that sounds very selfish. We are social animals and nobody can live alone. In fact, many of the crimes in the city are caused by the lack of communication among people.
昭　夫	：すみません．でもそれはとても利己的に聞こえるなあ．僕たちは社会的動物だから，だれもひとりでは生きていけないんだよ．実際，都会の犯罪の多くは人間間のコミュニケーションの欠如によって起こっているんだ．
	‥‥‥ ‥‥‥ ‥‥‥
Moderator	: Now time is up. There is no definite conclusion to this topic. I think all of us have realized the many advantages and disadvantages of living in the city through this discussion. Let's keep these different opinions in mind and think them over at home.
議　長	：では時間が来ました．この話題にはこれといった結論はありません．このディスカッションを通して，みなさんは都会で生活することのよい点と悪い点に気づかれたことと思います．これらの違った意見を頭において，家でよく考えてみてください．

表現集

❶議長の使う表現

1. ディスカッションを始めましょう. きょうの話題は都会での人々の生活についてです. — Let's start our discussion. Today's topic is people's lives in the city.
2. きょうは都会での人々の生活について話し合います. — Today we're going to talk about people's lives in the city.
3. それについての一般的な意見を話すことから始めるのがいちばんよいと思います. — I think it would be best to start off by making some general comments on that.
4. 由美から話を始めてもらいましょうか. — Perhaps we can start the discussion with Yumi.
5. これについてだれか意見はありますか. — Does anyone want to comment on this?
6. 典雄, 何か意見はありますか. — Do you want to say something, Norio?
7. 何か質問や意見はありますか. — (Are there) any questions or comments?
8. 俊夫に何か質問はありますか. — (Are there) any questions for Toshio?
9. 私から一つ質問してもよろしいですか. — Could I just ask a question myself?
10. 聡美がいくつか興味深い指摘をしてくれたのですが, ほかの人はそれについてどう思うか伺いたいと思います. — Satomi has made some interesting points. I'd like to hear what the rest of the participants think about them.
11. 時間がなくなってきたので, 簡潔に意見を述べてください. — Since time is running out, please make your comments brief.
12. 話し合う時間はたっぷりあるので, 遠慮なく発言してください. — We have enough time for discussion, so please don't hesitate to speak out.
13. 文恵, どうぞ(話してください). — Go ahead, Fumie. / Fumie?
14. 本題から(議論が)はずれているように思われます. 議論をきょうの主題の方向に戻していいですか. — We seem to be getting off the main point. Can I bring the discussion back in the direction of today's theme?
15. 都会生活の悪い点に焦点を当てましょう. — Let's focus on the disadvantages of city life.
16. その話題はそれまでにしましょう. — Let's drop the subject.
17. 騒音問題はわきへおいておきましょう. — Let's leave the noise problems aside.
18. 最初の問題に戻りましょう. — Let's return [get back] to the first question.
19. 次の問題に移りましょう. — Let's move on to the next question.
20. 別の話題に変えましょう. — Let's turn to another subject.
21. あと2, 3分だけ残っています. — We have only a few minutes left.
22. 時間がなくなりました. — (Our [The]) time is up. / (Our [The]) time has run out. / We are out of time.
23. 参加者全員にお礼を述べて, この討論を終わりたいと思います. — I'd like to conclude this discussion by thanking all the participants.

❷自分の意見を述べるときの表現

1. 都会に住むほうが便利だと確信しています[強く信じています]. — I'm sure [I strongly believe] that living in the city is more convenient.
2. 大都会にひとりで暮らすのは危険だという感じがします. — I feel it's dangerous to live alone in a big city.
3. いなかのほうが健康でいられるように思われます. — It seems to me that we can stay healthier in the country.
4. 私の意見では, 都会に住むのは楽しいです. — In my opinion, it's exciting to live in the city.

5. 私の見方からすると，便利さだけがすべてではないと思います．	From my point of view, convenience isn't everything.
6. 自分としては都会に住むほうが好きです．	Personally, I prefer living in the city.
7. （私なら）いなかの生活は退屈なのではないかと思います．	I would say that country life is boring.
8. それについて2つ意見を述べたいです．	I'd like to「make two comments on that [say two things about that].
9. すみません．最後まで言わせてください．	Sorry. Could I just finish?

❸相手の発言に対して不同意・反対を述べるときの表現

1. あなたの議論は説得力がありません．	Your argument is unconvincing.
2. それについてあなたには同意できません．	I can't really agree with you on that. / I disagree with you on that.
3. それについてあなたには同意しかねます．	I have trouble agreeing with you on that.
4. 都会生活は危険だという考えは受け入れられません．	I can't accept the idea that city life is dangerous.
5. そのことについては私は健と少し違う意見です．	I have a slight disagreement with Takeshi on the matter.
6. 私の意見は広子と違います．	My opinion differs from Hiroko's.
7. それは疑問ですね．	I doubt it. / That's questionable.
8. それは本題をはずれています［それは重要な点ではありません］．	That's not the point.
9. あなたは拡大解釈をしています．	You are stretching the point.
10. それは私には納得できません．	That doesn't make sense to me.
11. あなたの説明は不十分です．	Your explanation「is insufficient [doesn't cover everything].
12. 必ずしもそういうことにはなりません．	That's not necessarily the case.
13. おっしゃることは分かりますが，あなたは少し楽観的すぎるように思います．	I see what you mean, but I think you are a little too optimistic.
14. そうかもしれませんが，どうしても都会の生活が悪いとは思えないのです．	That may be true, but I just can't believe (that) city life is bad.
15. あなたの言うことは正しいかもしれませんが，私は少し違った見方をしています．	You may be right, but I see it a little differently.
16. でも，前にあなたは都会は生活しやすいと言いましたね？	But you said earlier that it's comfortable to live in the city?
17. ちょっと（発言しても）いいですか．	May I interrupt you? / May I say something?

❹繰り返しや補足説明を求める表現

1. それを証明できますか．	Can you prove that?
2. もう一度言っていただけますか．	Would [Could] you say that again?
3. もう少し詳しく説明していただけますか．	Would [Could] you elaborate [expand] on that? / Would [Could] you explain that in more [further] detail?
4. 何か例を挙げていただけますか．	Would [Could] you give us some examples?
5. この点を明確にしていただけますか．	Would [Could] you clarify this point?

場面・状況別会話 ㊹

●ディベート

《ディベートとは》
　ディベートは，論理や表現力を使って相手を説得する能力を養うためのコミュニケーションゲームの一つです．ある論題に対して肯定側と否定側の2チームに分かれ，なぜ自分たちが論題に対して賛成または反対なのか，そして自分たちの主張が相手チームと比較していかに正当性があるかということについて聴衆や審査員を説得しようとします．ディスカッションと違う点は，1. 賛成側・反対側のどちらかにはっきり分かれること（自分の本当の意見と違う側に分けられることもある）2. いつでも発言できるわけではなく，基本的に賛成側と反対側が交互に意見を述べ合うこと　3. 1回の発言時間が制限されること　4. あらかじめ論題について資料を調べたり，チーム内で相談する時間を与えられたりする場合もあること，などです．

　ディベートのコンテストなどでは論題は直前に知らされるので，短い時間に発言内容や戦略を考えなければなりません．また，相手の出方によって話の方向や反論のしかたを変える必要があるので，相手の主張をよく聞くことも大切です．

《説得力とは》
　ディベートでは，人を説得する上で重要な「論理的思考能力」と「表現力」の両方が必要とされます．「論理的思考能力」とは，単なる主観的・感情的な感想ではなく，きちんとした理由づけ（reasoning）を伴った意見を組み立てる能力のことです．例えば，「高校生のアルバイトは認められるべきです．なぜなら私は今アルバイトをしているから」という意見の述べ方では客観性に欠け，相手を説得したり納得させることはできません．例えば，「対人関係における礼儀を学べるから」や「金銭感覚を養えるから」といった具体的な理由や，客観的事実，統計的データ，専門家の証言や証拠（evidence）などを挙げるように心がけるべきです．また「表現力」とは，声の大きさや明瞭（めいりょう）さ，声の調子，話すスピードなどのほかに，アイコンタクトやジェスチャーなどによる自然な感情表現の能力も含まれています．積極的にコミュニケーションをはかろうとしているという姿勢を示すことが大切です．

《ディベートの進行方法の例》

①肯定側立論（affirmative constructive speech）　　……　約3分
　なぜ論題を支持するのか具体例を挙げながら理由を述べる．

②否定側立論（negative constructive speech）　　……　約3分
　なぜ論題を否定するのか具体例を挙げながら理由を述べる．

　　（作戦タイム）　＊各立論の後に反対尋問（cross-examination）が入る場合もある．

③肯定側反駁（はんばく）（affirmative rebuttal）　　……　約2分
　否定側に対して反論したり，その論理を攻撃する．

④否定側反駁（negative rebuttal）　　……　約2分
　肯定側に対して反論したり，その論理を攻撃する．

｝3回繰り返す

　　（作戦タイム）

⑤否定側まとめ（negative summary speech）　　……　約2分
　否定側の論旨を短くまとめ，自分たちの主張の正当性をアピールする．

⑥肯定側まとめ（affirmative summary speech）　　……　約2分
　肯定側の論旨を短くまとめ，自分たちの主張の正当性をアピールする．

《審査のポイント》

＊論旨が明確で分かりやすく，ルールを守っているか．

＊主張に論理的一貫性があって，データや証拠に裏付けされているか．

＊相手の意見をしっかり聞いて理解し，反論しているか．

*発表態度に積極性が感じられるか.
[注意] 審査員の, 論題に対する個人的な賛否は評価の基準とはならない.

*****

《Proposition》 Students should wear uniforms.
《論題》 生徒は制服を着るべきである.

Chairperson: Now, we will start the debate on the proposition that students should wear uniforms. First, we will have the affirmative constructive speech.
議長：では，生徒は制服を着るべきであるという論題でディベートを始めます．まず，肯定側の立論からお願いします．

《Affirmative Constructive Speech》 We think that students should wear uniforms because uniforms have certain advantages. First of all, it's very economical to wear uniforms. Parents don't have to spend much money on clothing. Also, because all students wear the same uniforms, there will be no jealousy or competition among students about clothing. In addition, uniforms will prevent students from misbehaving. For example, if students in uniforms try to smoke or drink, it is more likely that adults will warn them.
《肯定側立論》制服は利点もあるので生徒は着るべきだと思います．第一に，制服を着ればたいへん経済的です．親は衣服にあまりお金を使う必要がなくなります．また，全生徒が同じ制服を着ているので，学生の間で服装についての嫉妬(しっと)や競争がなくなります．さらに，制服は生徒の不品行なふるまいを防げます．例えば，もし制服を着ている生徒がたばこを吸ったり酒を飲んだりしようとすれば，おそらく大人が彼らを注意することでしょう．

Chairperson: Thank you. Now we will hear the negative constructive speech.
議長：ありがとうございました．では，否定側の立論をお願いします．

《Negative Constructive Speech》 We believe that deciding what to wear reflects the student's personality and judgment. However, in Japan some high schools force their students to wear uniforms and give them no chance to develop their own personalities. Uniforms are usually only worn in the army. School is not the army. Besides, most uniforms are black, which is a depressing color to wear every day. Also, they are hot and uncomfortable.
《否定側立論》どんな服装を選ぶかということに生徒の個性や判断力が表れるものと思います．しかし日本には，生徒に制服着用を強制し，生徒が個性を伸ばす機会を与えない高校があります．制服はふつう軍隊だけで着用されます．学校は軍隊ではありません．そのうえ，ほとんどの制服は黒で，毎日着るには憂鬱(ゆううつ)な色です．また，暑苦しくて着心地もよくありません．

Chairperson: OK. Now we will have a rebuttal and refutation starting with the affirmative side.
議長：では，反論と論駁(ばく)を肯定側からお願いします．

《Affirmative Rebuttal》 The negative side said that uniforms should not be forced on students, but we think that education is more or less a forced act. If the students are allowed too much freedom, they sometimes will wear inappropriate clothing like T-shirts or jeans.

They also said that black uniforms are uncomfortable. But these days blazer type uniforms in cheerful colors are in fashion, and they are not as uncomfortable.

《肯定側反駁》否定側は制服は生徒に強制されるべきではないと言いましたが,教育というものは多かれ少なかれ押しつけられるものだと私たちは思います.もし生徒にあまりにも自由が許されれば,時としてTシャツやジーパンのような不適切な服を着てしまうでしょう.否定側はまた,黒い制服は着心地がよくないと言いました.しかし,最近では明るい色のブレザータイプの制服がはやっていて,それほど着心地が悪いということはありません.

《Negative Rebuttal》 The affirmative side said that abolishing uniforms would make students more likely to misbehave. We think that is incorrect. The affirmative side doesn't trust students. That is not how education should be. Even though more students may misbehave because they don't wear uniforms, it's a necessary transition process. They need to discover how to behave by trial and error. We think, in the long run, students will be able to develop their own judgment as to what is right or wrong.

《否定側反駁》肯定側は,制服を廃止することによって,生徒が不品行なふるまいをするようになりやすいと言いました.私たちはそれは違うと思います.肯定側は生徒を信用していません.それは教育のあるべき姿ではありません.制服を着ないために不品行なふるまいをする生徒が増えたとしても,それは必然的な成長過程なのです.生徒は自分のふるまい方を試行錯誤して見つけることが必要なのです.長い目で見れば,生徒は何が正しく何が間違っているかということについて,自分自身の判断力を育てることができると思います.

Chairperson: Thank you. Now we will hear a summary speech starting with the negative side.
議長:ありがとうございました.では,否定側からまとめのスピーチを聞くことにしましょう.

《Negative Summary Speech》 The affirmative side doesn't trust students at all. They believe that uniforms will control students' behavior. We believe that students should be allowed the freedom to make decisions about their private life. Therefore, students should not be forced to wear uniforms.

《否定側まとめ》肯定側は生徒を全く信用していません.彼らは制服が生徒のふるまいを抑制すると信じています.私たちは生徒は自分の私的な生活について判断をする自由が許されるべきだと信じます.したがって,生徒は制服の着用を強制されるべきではありません.

《Affirmative Summary Speech》 Uniforms are easy and inexpensive to wear and maintain. If all students in a school wear the same type of clothing, there will be little jealousy or competition about clothes. Most importantly, they will be less likely to smoke or drink while in uniform.

《肯定側まとめ》制服は着るのも維持するのも簡単でお金がかかりません.もし学校の全生徒が同じタイプの衣服を着れば,服装についての嫉妬や競争はほとんどなくなるでしょう.いちばん重要なことは,制服を着ていれば生徒はたばこを吸ったり酒を飲んだりする可能性が少なくなるだろうということです.

Chairperson: I'd like to thank all the participants. Now we have a 15-minute break during which the judges will decide in a separate room the winner of the debate.
議長:参加者のみなさん全員に,お礼を申し上げたいと思います.では,15分間の休憩をとります.その間に審査員の方々が別室でディベートの勝者を決定します.

表現集

*ディベートはチーム対抗なので，I, my などの代わりに we, our などを使ってもよい．また，I, my などを使った表現は，多くの場合ディスカッションやスピーチにも適用できる．

❶主題やポイントを明確に示すための表現

1. きょう，私たちは制服について話します． — Today we're going to talk about uniforms.
2. 私の議論の主題は校則の害についてです． — The subject of my argument is the harm caused by school rules.
3. 私が焦点を当てたいのは，制服は着心地が悪いということです． — The point I'd like to concentrate on is that uniforms are uncomfortable.

❷論点を整理するための表現

1. 私がここで議論したい点は2つあります． — I have two points I want to discuss here.
2. 第一の論点は生徒が自分たちで考える必要があるということです． — The first argument is that students need to think for themselves.
3. 例［理由］をいくつか挙げさせてください． — Let me give you some examples [reasons].
4. 最初に，校内暴力の増加について考えたいと思います． — First, I'd like to consider the increase in school violence.
5. 次に［そして］，制服の問題に移りたいと思います． — Next, [Then] I'd like to move on to the question of uniforms.
6. 最後に，この問題を解決するための考えをいくつか提示したいと思います． — Finally [In conclusion], I'd like to present some ideas to solve this problem.
7. 校則の問題に戻りたいと思います． — I'd like to return [get back] to the question of school rules.
8. まとめると，制服はマイナスの効果よりもプラスの効果のほうが多いといえます［結論づけることができます］． — To conclude, we can say [We can therefore conclude] that uniforms have more positive effects than negative ones.

❸反論・反駁(ばく)で使う表現

1. あなたの主張が間違いなのは明らかです． — It's clear (that) your assertion is wrong.
2. 校則は強制されるべきものではないというあなたの意見は間違っています． — You are wrong in saying that school rules should not be forced.
3. あなたの主張は否定側の第1スピーカーの言ったことと矛盾すると思います． — I think your assertion contradicts what the first speaker from the negative side said.
4. 制服は強制されるべきではないと思うなら，校則はどうなるんですか． — If you think (that) uniforms shouldn't be compulsory, what about school rules?
5. 別の見方もあると思います． — I think there is another way of looking at it.
6. ジーパンをはくのがなぜ悪いのですか． — What's wrong with wearing jeans?
7. しかし，個性がだいじだとは思いませんか． — But don't you think (that) individuality is important?
8. そのとおりですが，制服を着るのを気に入っている生徒がいるということも真実です． — That's true, but it's also true that some students love wearing uniforms.
9. あなたのおっしゃることは分かりますが，正しいかどうか私は確信できません． — I'm not sure you are right, though I see what you mean.
10. どのような根拠でそう言うのですか． — On what do you base your opinion?

場面・状況別会話 ㊺

●スピーチ

《スピーチの目的》

　スピーチとは，聴衆を相手にして発表の形をとった大切なコミュニケーション活動の一種です．目的と条件に応じて，意見を述べる，情報を伝える，経験談を話すなど様々な場合があり，かたく論才的なものからユーモアや笑いを含んだ軽いものまで形式もいろいろあります．基本的にスピーチの目的は　1．聞き手に情報を与える　2．聞き手を説得する　3．聞き手を楽しませる　4．聞き手に方法を実演するの4つに分けることができます．

《スピーチの構成》

　いずれの場合についても，話の趣旨がはっきりしていて分かりやすく，最後まで一貫性があることが必要です．一般的には，Ⅰ．導入部 (Introduction)　Ⅱ．本論 (Body)　Ⅲ．結論 (Conclusion) の3つの部分を意識して話を組み立てると，論旨がはっきりした分かりやすいスピーチにすることができます．

Ⅰ．導入部 (Introduction)
　＜目的＞・聞き手の注意を引きつける．
　　　　　・本論に導く．
　＜方法＞・中心となる主題，論点，自分の意見などを述べる．
　　　　　・聞き手に問題を問いかける．

Ⅱ．本論 (Body)
　サポート (Support) 1　　＜目的＞・具体例を挙げて主題や意見をサポートする．
　サポート (Support) 2　　＜方法＞・事物や用語を定義する．
　サポート (Support) 3　　　　　　・分類する．
　　　　　　　　　　　　　　　　　・比較する．
　　　　　　　　　　　　　　　　　・対照する．
　　　　　　　　　　　　　　　　　・因果関係を述べる．
　　　　　　　　　　　　　　　　　・事実を列挙する．

Ⅲ．結論 (Conclusion)
　＜目的＞・主題についての自分の考えを再度強調する．
　＜方法＞・主題をなるべく異なる表現で要約する．聞き手によい印象や余韻を残す．

《スピーチの注意点》

1．導入部でははっきりと主題と自分の意見や立場を明らかにする．言い訳や余計な前置きなどはしない．
2．本論では導入部で述べた趣旨をサポートする具体例をいくつか挙げる．話の内容が趣旨からはずれたり，細部にわたりすぎたりしないように気をつける．
3．一般的に，結論の内容は導入部で述べた意見と矛盾しないようにする．
4．リラックスし，早口にならないように，また自信をもって大きな声で話す．文と文の間やパラグラフの初めなどには十分なポーズを入れる．
5．単調にならないように，抑揚，声の大小，話すスピードなどに変化をつける．特に強調語やトピック・センテンス（パラグラフでいちばん重要な内容を含んだ文）は強くアピールするように話す．
6．視線を聴衆の方に向け，大げさにならない程度にジェスチャーを入れる．

Traveling Alone

I like traveling very much. Some people like traveling alone and others like traveling in a group. Personally there are three reasons I prefer traveling alone.

First, I enjoy making plans about where I want to visit. In group tours planned by a travel agency, I have no choice about where I can visit and what I can see. I want to visit rural areas where tourists don't go and to see things other people haven't seen. Second, for me, one of the purposes of traveling is to improve my English in English-speaking countries. I don't think it's good to depend on others to communicate or to translate English into Japanese. I believe that by talking to the natives directly, I can learn more about the country and about myself. Third, traveling alone allows me to have more free time. If I am on a tour, I have to hurry along to keep up with the other members of the group; when I travel alone, however, I can go at my own pace. Therefore, traveling alone allows me more freedom.

In conclusion, traveling alone allows me to have a lot of fun making plans and arranging everything; it allows me to meet people on a one-to-one basis and to practice my English; and I can have greater freedom and more time to myself. For these reasons, I believe traveling alone is better than traveling in a tour group.

一人旅

私は旅行をするのがとても好きです．ひとりで旅行をするのが好きな人もいれば，団体で旅行をするのが好きな人もいます．私個人としては3つの理由でひとりで旅行をするほうが好きです．

第一に，訪れたい場所について予定を立てるのが楽しいからです．旅行業者が計画した団体旅行では，訪れる場所や見るものについて選択の余地がありません．私は観光客が行かないいなかの地域を訪ね，ほかの人が見たことがないものを見たいのです．第二に，私にとって旅行の目的の一つは，英語を話す国々で自分の英語を磨くことなのです．ほかの人にコミュニケーションを頼ったり英語を日本語に訳してもらったりするのはよくないと思います．直接現地の人たちに話しかけることによって，その国や自分自身についてもっとよく知ることができると私は思うのです．第三に，ひとりで旅をすればより自由な時間をもてます．団体旅行だと，団体のほかの人たちについていくために急がなくてはなりません．しかし，一人旅をすれば，自分のペースで動くことができます．したがって，一人旅はずっと自由になれるのです．

結論として，一人旅は計画を立てたりすべての手はずを整えたりする楽しみを多く与えてくれます．一対一で人々と会うことができ，英語を練習することができます．そして，より大きな自由と自分だけの時間をもつことができます．こうした理由で，私は団体ツアーよりも一人旅のほうがよいと信じています．

★ミニ知識★

原稿作成は初めから英語で

即興のスピーチは別として，ふつうスピーチの準備はまず原稿を書くことから始まります．初めに日本語で原稿を書いて，それを英訳しようとする人がいますが，これはあまりよい方法ではありません．たとえ文法的に正しくても，日本語を直訳すると本来の英語がもつ自然さが損なわれてしまうからです．また，そもそも英語と日本語では発想法が異なるので，スピーチの内容や構成も変わってきてしまいます．例えば，日本語でスピーチをするときによく言う「ただ今ご紹介にあずかりました鈴木と申します」や「初めにお断わりしておきますが，私はあまり英語は得意ではないので…」といった前置きは，英語で話す場合は全く必要ありません．英語のスピーチでは導入部からいきなり自分がいちばん言いたいことを前面に出します．よいスピーチができるかどうかは，いかに頭の中で思考を英語式に整理できるかによります．英語はずばりと自分の意見を述べるのに適した言葉です．初めから英語で原稿を書く習慣をつけましょう．

表現集

❶ 導入部で使う表現

1. 最近，人々は携帯電話を使いすぎます． — People these days overuse cellular phones.
2. セクハラについてのニュースを聞いたことがありますか． — Have you heard news about sexual harassment?
3. ファーストフードは若者の間で人気があるというのは事実です． — It's a fact that fast food is popular among young people.
4. 10年後に日本がどのようになっているか推測できますか． — Can you guess what Japan will be like in 10 years?
5. きょうは喫煙という悪習についてお話ししたいと思います． — Today I'd like to talk about the bad habit of smoking.
6. 私のスピーチの目的は教育制度に関して日本とアメリカを比較することです． — The purpose of my speech is to compare Japan and America in terms of their educational systems.
7. 私が旅行が嫌いな理由は主に3つあります． — There are three main reasons why I hate traveling.

❷ 本論で使う表現

1. 第一に［第二に，第三に，最後に］一人旅はよりお金がかかります． — First [Second, Third, Finally], traveling alone costs more.
2. そのうえ［さらに，加えて］安全性の問題があります． — Moreover [Furthermore, In addition], there is the problem of safety.
3. いくつか例を挙げさせてください． — Let me give you some examples.
4. さて，質問に対していくつか解答を示したいと思います． — Now I'm going to suggest some answers [solutions] to the question [problem].
5. 例えば，ふつう観光ガイドがすべてを説明してくれます． — For example [instance], a tour guide usually explains everything.
6. 具体的には，厚化粧をして髪を染めている女子生徒がいます． — To illustrate, some school girls wear heavy make-up and dye their hair.
7. 二，三の解決策［例］を次に述べます． — The following are a few solutions [illustrations].
8. 3種類のテレビ番組があります． — There are three kinds [types] of TV programs.
9. その問題を解決するには3つのやり方があります［それには3つの理由があります］． — There are「three ways to solve the problem [three reasons for that].

❸ 結論で使う表現

1. 結論として，私はサッカーよりも野球のほうがおもしろいと信じます． — In conclusion [summary], I believe baseball is more interesting than soccer.
2. これでお分かりのとおり，テレビは子供に悪影響をもたらします． — As you can see now, TV has a bad influence on children.
3. 映画についての私のスピーチを要約いたしましょう． — Let me give you a summary of my speech on movies.
4. コンピュータについておもしろいことを知っていただけたことと思います． — I hope you learned something interesting about computers.
5. 英語を勉強することが大切だということを今回実感されたことと確信します． — I'm sure you now realize that studying English is important.

電話の英会話

1 国際電話のかけ方

❶日本からロンドンの0171-123-4567にかける場合

☎ 001（電話会社の識別番号）＋ 44（英国の国番号）＋ 171-123-4567（相手先の番号）

＊電話会社の識別番号001番を使って国際電話をかけた場合です．電話会社によって識別番号は異なります．0171の先頭の0は省略します．電話会社選択サービスや電話会社固定サービスなどを利用した場合はかけ方が異なります．

❷米国から東京の03-5432-6789にかける場合

☎ 011（米国の国際電話識別番号）＋ 81（日本の国番号）＋ 3-5432-6789（相手先の番号）

＊米国・英国・オーストラリアなど海外から日本に国際電話をかける場合は，最初にその国の国際電話識別番号と日本の国番号を付けます．03の先頭の0は省略します．

直通電話以外にも，話したい相手を電話口まで呼び出してもらえる指名通話（person-to-person call），相手が料金を負担するコレクトコール（collect call）などがあります．

2 時差

国際電話をかける際に気をつけたいのは時差です．自分に都合のよい時間帯が相手先によっては真夜中だったり早朝だったりします．日本時間より14時間マイナスするところを間違えてプラスにしてしまうということがよくあります．オペレーターに聞いたり，時差表などでよく確認してからかけるようにしましょう．また多くの国が標準時（《米》standard time;《英》Greenwich Mean Time,《略語》GMT）と夏の間に使う夏時間（《米》daylight saving time,《英》summer time）を採用しています．時差表の時差は標準時を基準にしています．夏時間は標準時よりも1時間早くなります．つまり1月1日東京とロンドンの時差は9時間ですが，8月1日は8時間です．いつ時間が変わるかは国により微妙に違いますが，目安として春分に近い日曜日頃に標準時から夏時間に変わり，秋分に近い日曜日頃に夏時間から標準時に変わると覚えておくといいでしょう．ただし南半球ではこれと逆になります．また米国やカナダ，オーストラリアなどのように国土の広い国では国の中でも時差があります．ニューヨークが午前10時のときロサンゼルスは同日の午前7時です．このあたりのことも注意しましょう．

3 主な国の国番号

米国（1）・カナダ（1）・英国（44）・アイルランド（353）・オーストラリア（61）
ニュージーランド（64）・韓国（82）・中国（86）・台湾（886）・香港（852）・シンガポール（65）

4 電話での表現

❶相手を呼び出す／確認する

(1)ナタリーさんをお願いします．
　Can I talk to Natalie, please?

(2)営業部のジョン・ブラウンさんをお願いします．
　May I speak to Mr. John Brown in the Sales Department?

(3)デイビッドさんはいますか．
　Is David there, please?

(4)内線の179番をお願いします．

Can you give me extension one-seven-nine, please?

(5) ホワイトさんのお宅ですか.

Is this the White residence?

(6) メグさんですか.

Is this Meg?

❷ 自分を名乗る／自分にかかってきたとき

(1) もしもし, 田中です.

Hello, this is Tanaka speaking.

(2) 次郎ですが.

This is Jiro speaking.

(3) あさ子です.

This is Asako.

(4) はい, 私です.

Speaking.

❸ 自分以外にかかってきたとき／当人が不在のとき

(1) ちょっとお待ちください.

Hold on [Just a minute], please.

(2) どちら様ですか.

Who's calling, please?

(3) いるかどうかちょっと見てみます.

I'll check if he [she] is in.

(4) すみませんが今留守にしています.

I'm afraid he [she] is out at the moment.

(5) 今出かけています.

He [She] has gone out.

(6) 今学校［仕事］に行っています.

He [She] has gone to school [work].

(7) 今ちょっと電話に出られないのですが.

I'm afraid he [she] is not available at the moment.

(8) 7時ごろ戻ってきます.

He [She] will be back at about 7 o'clock.

(9) 30分くらいしたら戻ってくると思います.

I think he [she] is coming back in half an hour or so.

(10) あと10分くらいしたらかけ直してもらえますか.

Would you mind calling back in about ten minutes?

(11) 何か伝えておくことはありますか.

Would you like to leave a message?

(12) 伝言を受けましょうか.

Can I take a message?

(13) 戻ってきたらこちらからお電話させましょうか.

Shall I ask him [her] to call you back when he [she] gets back?

❹ 間違い電話

(1) 番号をおかけ間違えですよ.

You have the wrong number.

(2)こちらにはケンという者はおりませんが．
　There isn't anyone named Ken here.
(3)そちらは5432-6789ですか．
　Is this 5432-6789?
(4)すみません．間違えました．
　I'm sorry. I have (got) the wrong number.

❺ 聞き取れない／分からないとき
(1)電話が遠いのですが．
　I can't hear you.
(2)もう少し大きな声で話してもらえますか．
　Could you speak up a bit, please?
(3)もう一度言ってください．
　Pardon?
(4)もう一度繰り返してもらえますか．
　Could you repeat it again?

❻ 不在の相手にメッセージを残すとき
(1)斎藤はな子から電話があったと伝えていただけますか．
　Could you tell him [her] that Saito Hanako phoned?
(2)あしたまたかけると伝えてください．
　Please tell him [her] that I'll call him [her] again tomorrow.
(3)お戻りになったら電話をもらえるよう伝えていただけますか．
　Could you please ask him [her] to give me a call when he [she] gets back?

❼ 留守電にメッセージを残す／留守電用のメッセージを作る
(1)こんにちは次郎です．今土曜日の午後6時です．また後で電話します．
　Hello, it's Jiro here. It's 6:00 p.m. on Saturday. I'll call you back later.
(2)贈り物のお礼を言いたかっただけです．電話はくれなくて結構です．では．
　I just wanted to say thank you for the present. You don't need to call me back. Bye.
(3)これから出かけるので携帯の方へ連絡ください．
　I'm going out now. Please call me on my cell phone.
(4)はい山田実です．ただ今電話に出られません．メッセージを残される方は発信音の後にお話しください．
　Hello, this is Yamada Minoru. I'm not available at the moment. If you'd like to leave a message, please speak after the tone.

⑤ 電話会話例
❶ ホームステイ先で
Jim's mother: Hello.
ジムのお母さん：もしもし．
Hanako: Hello. Is Jim there, please?
はな子：もしもし．ジムさんはいらっしゃいますか．（❖ふつうまず用件を述べ，自ら名を名乗ることはしない）
Jim's mother: I'm afraid he's not in at the moment. Who is calling, please?
ジムのお母さん：あいにくジムは今出かけています．どちら様ですか．
Hanako: This is Hanako from Jim's school. Do you know when he's coming back?
はな子：同じ学校のはな子といいます．何時に帰られるでしょうか．

Jim's mother: I think he's coming back about five. Would you like to leave a message for him?

ジムのお母さん：5時ごろだと思います．何か伝えておきましょうか．

Hanako: Yes, please. Could you tell him I phoned about Lucy's birthday party and I'll call him back later this evening?

はな子：はい，お願いします．はな子からルーシーの誕生パーティーのことについて電話があったと伝えてください．また今晩電話します．

Jim's mother: Certainly. And your name is Hana?

ジムのお母さん：はい分かりました．ハナさんですね．

Hanako: It's Hanako. I'll spell it for you. It's H-A-N-A-K-O, Hanako.

はな子：はな子です．つづりを言います．H-A-N-A-K-O，はな子です．

Jim's mother: Oh, Hanako. OK, I'll tell Jim when he gets back.

ジムのお母さん：ああ，はな子さんですね．ではジムが戻ってきたら伝えておきます．

Hanako: Thank you very much. Bye.

はな子：ありがとうございます．さようなら．

Jim's mother: Bye.

ジムのお母さん：さようなら．

❷ペンフレンドからの電話

Natalie: Hello. Can I speak to Taro?

ナタリー：もしもし．太郎さんお願いします．

Taro: Speaking.

太郎：はい僕ですが．

Natalie: Hello, Taro! This is your pen pal, Natalie.

ナタリー：もしもし，太郎さん！ペンフレンドのナタリーです．

Taro: Natalie! What a surprise! Where are you calling from?

太郎：ナタリー！驚いた！どこからかけているのですか．

Natalie: From America. How are you?

ナタリー：アメリカからです．お元気ですか．

Taro: I'm very well, thank you. How are you?

太郎：ありがとう．とても元気ですよ．あなたは？

Natalie: I'm very well, too.

ナタリー：私もすごく元気です．

Taro: It's so nice to hear your voice.

太郎：声が聞けてとてもうれしいです．

Natalie: Thank you. I've always wanted to hear your voice, too. You sound just like I imagined, Taro.

ナタリー：ありがとう．私もずっとあなたの声を聞いてみたいと思っていたの．想像していたとおりだわ，太郎．

Taro: Pardon? Could you speak a little more slowly? I'm not used to using English in conversation.

太郎：え，何ですか．もう少しゆっくり話してもらえますか．英会話は慣れていないので．

Natalie: I'm sorry. I know it's especially difficult to understand a foreign language on the phone.

ナタリー：ごめんなさい．そうですね．特に電話で外国語を理解するのは難しいですよね．

手紙・はがきの書き方

手紙には会社などにあてるフォーマルなものをはじめ様々な形がありますが，ここでは知り合いや友達などに出す例を挙げます．用紙は日本で出すのと同じように相手にふさわしいものを選びましょう．日本とは違い無地の便せんを使うことが多いですが，カジュアルな内容ならば罫線（けい）の入ったものでもかまいません．航空便用の軽い便せんもありますし，歌舞伎（かぶき）など日本的な絵の入ったものなどは海外で喜ばれるでしょう．手書きの場合は相手に読みやすいように書きましょう．最近ではコンピュータを使って書くことも一般的です．海外郵便の料金は地域，重さなどにより細かく設定されているので郵便局で確認しましょう．

● 便せん

①1-2-3 Harajuku
Shibuya-ku, Tokyo 150-0001
Japan

②March 20, 2002

③Mr. David Smith
100 Maple Avenue
Minneapolis, MN 55300-1234
USA

④Dear Mr. Smith,

⑤　How are you? I'm doing fine. I miss your English class, which I enjoyed very much. I have good news to tell you today. I have been accepted by the University of Iroha. I'm looking forward to studying more English there. I hope I will see you again in Japan.

⑥Sincerely yours,

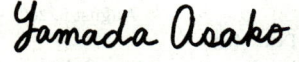

Yamada Asako

⑦Yamada Asako

⑧P.S. My friend Yuko will also go to the same university with me to study French.

①差出人住所：名前は書きません．
②日付
③相手の名前と住所：親しい人あて，簡単な内容ならば通常省略します．
④敬辞：Dear + Mr. [Mrs., Miss, Ms.] + 姓の形式で書きます．Mr. David Smith のようなフルネームは通常使いません．友達など親しい間柄の人には Dear + 名前とします．

⑤ **本文**：書き出しに相手の安否を問うことはありますが，日本のように「桜の便りも聞かれるきょうこのごろです」などの季節のあいさつを述べることはふつうしません．
(訳：お元気ですか．私は元気にやっています．先生の英語の授業がなつかしいです．私の大好きなクラスでした．きょうはよいお知らせがあります．いろは大学に合格しました．大学で英語をもっと勉強することを楽しみにしています．日本でまたお会いできることを祈っています)

⑥ **結辞**：一般的には《米》Sincerely yours，《英》Yours sincerely を使います．親しい相手には Yours, Your friend, Love（特に親戚(しんせき)や親しい相手に対して）などのほか，友達などには全く使わないこともあります．

⑦ **署名**：タイプの場合も必ず自筆の署名を添える．その場合，結辞とタイプしている署名の間に，自筆サインのために2～3行あけます．

⑧ **追伸**：書き忘れたこと，特に相手の注意を引きたい内容は P.S.（postscript の略語）の後に書く．
(訳：友達のゆう子も同じ大学でフランス語を勉強します)

●封筒

```
①Yamada Asako

  1-2-3 Harajuku
  Shibuya-ku, Tokyo 150-0001
  Japan

                                    ②Mr. David Smith
                                      100 Maple Avenue
                                      Minneapolis, MN 55300-1234
                                      USA
③AIR MAIL
```
                                                                     [切手]

① 差出人名前と住所
② 相手の名前と住所：親しい相手には Mr., Mrs., Miss, Ms. を省略し姓名だけを書くことも可能．
③ 航空便の封筒表示：航空便専用の封筒を使わない場合は AIR MAIL と書くか郵便局でくれるラベルをはる．その他の封筒表示：「書留」Registered／「速達」《米》Special Delivery, 《英》Express／「印刷物」Printed Matter／「親展」Private

●はがき

```
        ①August 5, 2001        ⑥Meg Roberts       [切手]
②Dear Meg,                       55 North Street
③Hi! I'm now visiting Okinawa    Los Angeles, CA 90012-5678
  with some friends. We're       USA
  having a great time here.
        ④Take care,            ⑦AIR MAIL
        ⑤Taro
```

① 日付 ② 敬辞 ③ 本文 (訳：こんにちは．今友達と沖縄に来ています．ここですごく楽しんでいます)
④ 結辞 ⑤ 署名 ⑥ 相手の名前と住所 ⑦ 航空便の表示

[文例]

1 ペンフレンドへ
❶初めての手紙

Dear Natalie,

　How do you do? My name is Taro. I got your name and address from your sister who is studying in Japan. I'm writing this in the hope that you will be my pen pal. I'm 17 years old and in my second year of high school. If you're interested, I will tell you more about me. I hope to hear from you.

Sincerely yours,
Yamada Taro

ナタリー様

　はじめまして．僕の名前は太郎といいます．日本で勉強しているナタリーさんのお姉さんに名前と住所を教えてもらいました．ナタリーさんがペンフレンドになってくれたらと思いながらこの手紙を書いています．僕は17歳で高校2年生です．興味を持っていただけたならば自分のことをもっとお話しします．お返事お待ちしています．

敬具
山田太郎

❷2回目以降の手紙

Dear Natalie,

　Thanks for your letter, which I received this morning. It's great to know that you are interested in Japan. Maybe that's your sister's influence.

　I'm enclosing a picture of my family taken in front of our house. My father is on the extreme right. He is a 45-year-old engineer. Next to him is my mother. I won't tell you how old she is because she will not like it. She works part-time as a counselor at a college. The little girl is my sister Naoko, who is a 6th grader. I am standing on the far left.

　Next time I will write you about my hobby.

Your friend,
Taro

ナタリー様

　けさ手紙が届きました．ありがとうございます．ナタリーさんが日本に興味をもっているのを知ってとてもよかったです．お姉さんの影響かもしれませんね．

　家の前で撮った家族の写真を同封します．右端は父です．45歳でエンジニアです．父の隣が母です．母がいやがるので，母の年齢は言いません．母は大学で非常勤のカウンセラーをしています．小さな女の子は妹の直子で，6年生です．僕は左端に立っています．

　次回の手紙では僕の趣味について書きます．

あなたの友達
太郎

2 ホームステイ先へ
❶出発前

Dear Mr. & Mrs. Brown,

　My name is Saito Hanako from Yamakawa High School in Japan. I am happy to hear that you are going to let me stay with you this summer. As you know, it is part of the exchange program with River High School in your town. If you have something you'd like me to bring from Japan, please tell me. I'm looking forward to seeing you soon.

            Sincerely yours,
            Saito Hanako

ブラウン夫妻様

 私は日本の山川高校の斎藤はな子と申します．この夏お宅で私を受け入れてくださることを知りうれしく思います．ご存じのようにそちらの町のリバー高校との交換プログラムの一環です．何か日本からお持ちしたほうがいいものがあれば遠慮なさらずに言ってください．間もなくお会いできることを楽しみにしています．

            敬具
            斎藤はな子

❷ 帰国後

Dear John & Mary,

 Thank you very much for your hospitality while I was staying with you. I spent the most wonderful four weeks. My English improved so much, too. I now feel you are really my parents in America. I hope I can visit you again next summer. And please come to Japan sometime.

            Lots of love,
            Hanako

ジョン，メアリー

 滞在中は温かいもてなしをどうもありがとうございました．とてもすばらしい4週間を過ごしました．私の英語もだいぶ上達しました．今ではお二人のことをアメリカにいる本当の両親のように思います．来年の夏また遊びに行ければと思います．お二人もいつか日本へいらしてください．

            愛をこめて
            はな子

❸ 海外の語学学校への資料請求

Admissions Office

 I will graduate from high school in Japan this spring, and I am interested in studying English in California. Please send a brochure about your school to the following address: Tanaka Hiroshi, 1-20 Minato, Minato-ku, Tokyo 100-1234, Japan. I look forward to hearing from you.

            Sincerely yours,
            Tanaka Hiroshi

入学課殿

 私はこの春に日本の高校を卒業します．カリフォルニアで英語を勉強することに興味があります．そちらの学校の資料をこの住所までご送付ください．〒100-1234 東京都港区港1-20 田中博．ご返事をお待ちしております．

            敬具
            田中博

ファックスの書き方

ファックスは至急にそして確実に海外へ連絡したいときにたいへん便利です．特に決まった形式はありませんが以下のようなカバーページをつけると親切でしょう．内容は手紙よりも簡潔でだれに読まれてもかまわないように書くことが重要です．また一般家庭に送信するときは電話と同じように時差に気をつけましょう．深夜にファックスで相手を起こすのはたいへん失礼です．ファックスの送り方については「国際電話のかけ方」(p.1777)を参照してください．

FAX MESSAGE

①To: Mr. James Roberts
②Fax number: +1-310-123-4567
③Phone number: +1-310-765-4321

④From: Sato Jiro
⑤Fax number: +81-3-1234-5678
⑥Phone number: +81-3-5432-6789
⑦Address: 2-17-1 Horifune, Kita-ku, Tokyo 114-8524, Japan

⑧Date: Friday, July 27
⑨Pages (including this page): 1
⑩Re: My Arrival

----

⑪Dear Mr. Roberts,
My plane will arrive at Los Angeles International Airport at 2:50 p.m. on Sunday, July 29. The flight number is JL064. I'm looking forward to seeing you there.
                                                                                    Jiro

---

①受信者氏名
②受信者のファックス番号
③受信者の電話番号
④送信者の氏名
⑤送信者のファックス番号
⑥送信者の電話番号
⑦送信者の住所：これはなくてもかまわない．
⑧送信日
⑨送信枚数（including this page は「このページを含む」の意味）
⑩件名（訳：到着の件に関して）
⑪本文（訳：ロバーツ様へ　私の乗る飛行機は7月29日の日曜日午後2時50分にロサンゼルス国際空港に到着します．便名はJL064です．空港でお会いできることを楽しみにしています．次郎）

履歴書の書き方

英文履歴書には《米》の résumé と《英》の curriculum vitae があります。ここでは日本でより一般的な英文履歴書である résumé を取り上げます。résumé は白の A4 上質紙にタイプします。なるべく1枚に収まるようにし、2枚を超えることがないようにしましょう。内容はできるだけ短く簡潔に、写真、生年月日、署名、捺印(㊞)は基本的には不要です。性別も基本的には必要ありませんが、混乱を避けるために氏名の後に (Mr.), (Ms.) などと記すこともあります。また応募の動機などを詳しく説明した正式な cover letter（添え状）を添えます。以下はごく基本的な内容を載せた résumé と cover letter のサンプルです。résumé には決まった内容、フォーマットがありません。ささいなことでも仕事に関連していれば積極的にアピールし、最も効果的に自分を売り込めるように工夫をしましょう。

---

①   Sato Jiro (Mr.)
②   2-7-11 Horifune, Kita-ku,
         Tokyo 114-8524, Japan
         Tel/Fax (03) 1234-5678
         E-mail: satoj@xyz.ac.jp

③ OBJECTIVE:
    To utilize programming skills in the computer industry

④ WORK EXPERIENCE:
    Summers 2000 and 2001   ABC-Soft Co., Ltd. (Tokyo)
                                   Programmer in Engineering Department

⑤ EDUCATION:
    XYZ University (Yokohama) B.E. in Computer Engineering expected March 2002

⑥ SKILLS:
    Programming: C, C++, Perl, Java, others
    English: TOEIC 700 (Nov. 2000)

⑦ REFERENCES:
    Available on request

---

①氏名：どちらが姓か明確にするために姓をすべて大文字で書くこともある。
②住所
③志望動機（訳：プログラミングの技術をコンピュータ業界で生かすため）
④職務経験：学生の場合はアルバイトの内容を書くことになるが、なるべく希望職種に合った内容だけを新しいものから順に選ぶ。（訳：2000年、2001年夏 ABC－ソフト株式会社エンジニア部（東京）にてプログラマーとして勤務）
⑤学歴：基本的には高校または大学以上の最終学歴のみを記すが、特に仕事に有利と思われる学歴があればそれも加えるとよい。B.E. は Bachelor of Engineering の略。（訳：2002年3月 XYZ 大学（横浜）でコンピュータ工学における工学士を取得予定）
⑥特技
⑦信用照会先：特に指定がないかぎり連絡先は不要。（訳：請求ありしだい提供可）

2-7-11 Horifune, Kita-ku,
Tokyo 114-8524, Japan
Tel/Fax (03) 1234-5678
E-mail: satoj@xyz.ac.jp

February 20, 2002

Mr. Michael J. Thompson
Human Resources Manager
Nile Dot Com, Ltd.
3-2-1 Nishi Shibuya
Shibuya-ku, Tokyo 150-9876

Dear Mr. Thompson:

 I am interested in the position of computer programmer which you posted on your Web site.

 As shown in my résumé, I will graduate from XYZ University next month with a bachelor of engineering degree in computer engineering. I have programmed extensively in several computer languages. For my senior project, I wrote an application in C++ to allow online retailers to monitor inventory changes. During the past two summers, I worked at ABC-Soft, where I participated in several software development projects.

 I admire Nile Dot Com's many innovations, and I am confident that my skills will allow me to contribute to your continued success. I would be grateful for an opportunity for an interview at your earliest convenience.

Sincerely yours,

Sato Jiro

Sato Jiro

貴社のウェブサイトに掲載されたコンピュータ・プログラマーの仕事に関心があります．

 同封の履歴書に記しましたように，私はコンピュータ工学の工学士として，来月 XYZ 大学を卒業予定です．私は複数のコンピュータ言語により幅広くプログラムを書いた経験があります．専門課程では，オンライン小売業者が在庫の変化を監視できるアプリケーションを C++ で書きました．この2年間は夏に ABC ソフト社で仕事をし，いくつかのソフトウェア開発プロジェクトに参加しました．

 私は，貴社 Nile Dot Com の多くの技術革新に感嘆しておりますとともに，私のスキルが貴社の今後のさらなる発展に大きく貢献できるものであると確信しております．できるだけ早くご都合の良い時期に面接の機会を持っていただけましたら，ありがたく存じます．

句読法

①. period (ピリオド, 終止符)

❶平叙文・命令文の終わりを表します.

We named the dog Minna. (私たちはその犬をミンナと名づけた)
The smile never left her. (彼女は笑顔を絶やさなかった)
Mind your teacher's words. (先生の言うことをよく聞きなさい)

❷略語を表します.

Mr. (=Mister) Tanaka (田中氏)
No. (=number) 3 (第3番)
Sun. (=Sunday) (日曜日)
A.D. (=Anno Domini) … (西暦…)

★ 文末に略語がくるときは, ピリオドを重ねません.

There are 50 states in the U.S.A. (アメリカには州が50ある)

★ 頭字語(複合語の各語の頭文字を組み合わせて作った語で1語として発音する語)の場合は, ピリオドを用いません.

UNICEF [júːnisèf] (=United Nations International Children's Emergency Fund) (ユニセフ)
AIDS [éidz] (=Acquired Immunodeficiency [Immune Deficiency] Syndrome) (エイズ)

❸小数点を表します.

0.15 (=point one five)
1.23 (=one point two three)
12.04 (=twelve point zero four)
$1.52 (=one dollar and fifty-two cents)

②, comma (コンマ)

❶接続詞を用いて2つ以上の文を同列に並べる場合, ふつう接続詞の前に入れます.

I'd like to travel abroad, but I have no money. (海外旅行をしたいが, お金がない)
Hurry up, or you'll be late. (急がないと遅れるよ)

❷3つ以上の語[句, 節]をA, B, ..., and [or] C などの形で同列に並べるときの区切りとして用います. and [or] の前のコンマは省略することができます.

She speaks Japanese, English(,) and Chinese. (彼女は日本語と英語と中国語を話す)
He is young, ambitious(,) and full of confidence. (彼は若くて野心的で自信にあふれている)
Would you like coffee, black tea(,) or green tea? (コーヒーになさいますか紅茶になさいますかそれとも緑茶になさいますか)

★形容詞が限定用法で用いられる場合は，2つのときでもコンマで並べます．

a young, ambitious man (若くて野心的な男)

❸挿入・語句の切れ目などを表すときに用います．

I believe, of course, that I'm right. (私はもちろん自分が正しいと信じている)
Even Satoshi, the smartest student in our class, could not solve the problem.
(クラスでいちばん頭のいい聡でもその問題は解けなかった)

Good morning, Akio. (おはよう，明夫)
Yes, I can. (はい，できます)
Well, I think it's wrong. (そうですね，私はそれは間違いだと思います)
Needless to say, health is important. (言うまでもなく，健康は大切です)

❹直接話法で，引用符（""）でくくられた部分とそれ以外の部分の区切りとして用います．

Our teacher said, "Don't forget to do your assignment."
(「宿題をやるのを忘れないように」と先生が言った)
"Good-bye," said Sachiko. (「さようなら」と幸子が言った)
＊コンマを引用符の中に入れます．

❺付加疑問では，付加語句の前に付けます．

You are going, aren't you? (君，行くよね)
You didn't call her, did you? (彼女に電話をしなかったのね)

❻文の最初の副詞節の後に付けます．

Since you're no longer a child, you have to look after yourself.
(もう子供じゃないんだから自分のことは自分でしなさい)
If you have trouble, please let me know by e-mail.
(困ったことがあったら，メールで知らせてください)

❼対照

This is his umbrella, not mine. (これは彼の傘で，私のではない)

❽数字

数字の区切りを表します．英語では thousand（千）から上は，million（100万），billion（10億）のように3けたずつ表現があるため，数字で書くときも3けたごとにコンマを打つ習慣があります．千の場

合はコンマを入れずに書くこともあります.

1(,)000 = one thousand （1千）
10,000 = ten thousand （1万）
2,540,000 = two million five hundred (and) forty thousand （254万）
3,000,000,000 = three billion （30億）

③ ? question mark （疑問符, クエスチョンマーク）

❶直接疑問文・付加疑問文の最後に書きます.

Do you change your password every month? （あなたはパスワードを毎月変えていますか）
What kind of music do you like? （どんな音楽が好きですか）
You did it, didn't you? （君のしわざだろう？）

❷平叙文や語句の最後に書いて疑問の気持ちを表すために用います.

This is your dictionary? （これはあなたの辞書ですか）
"I've won a trip to Hong Kong." —— "Really?" （「香港旅行に当選したよ」——「ほんと？」）

④ ! exclamation mark ［《米》point］ （感嘆符, エクスクラメーションマーク）

❶強い感情を表すために感嘆文などで用います.

What a wonderful present! （なんてすてきなプレゼントなんだろう！）
It's really huge! （本当にでっかいなあ！）

❷命令文や平叙文で文意を強調するために用います.

Hey, come here! （おい, こっちに来てみろよ！）
Look at the sunset! （ほら夕焼けを見てごらんよ！）
Your ideas are wonderful! （あなたのアイディアはすばらしい！）

❸音を表す言葉などの後に書き強調します.

Plop! A frog jumped into the pond. （ポチャン, カエルが池に飛び込んだ）
Ahchoo! My sneezing won't stop. （ハクション, くしゃみが止まらない）
Phew! The cap finally came off. （ふう, やっとふたが取れた）

⑤ : colon （コロン）

❶具体的な例を示します.

The participants in this soccer tournament are as follows: Japan, Mexico, South Korea(,) and Thailand. （今回のサッカートーナメントの参加国は, 日本, メキシコ, 韓国, タイだ）

❷前の語・句・文を補足する語・句・文を付け加えます.

He's interested in only one thing: money. (彼は1つのことしか関心がない. お金だ)
Warning: smoking causes cancer. (警告. 喫煙は癌(がん)の原因になります)

❸時刻を表すときに用います.

3:00 = three (o'clock) (3時)
10:20 a.m. = ten twenty a.m. (午前10時20分)

⑥ ; semicolon (セミコロン)

❶関連する2つの文を接続詞を用いずにつなぎます.

The door was closed; nobody seemed to be in the room.
(ドアは閉まっていた. 部屋にはだれもいないようだった)

❷コンマを含む文で, 節・句を区別するために用います. この場合, 接続詞の前に用いることもできます.

Our guests are John Gomez, from the United States; Mary Philips, from New Zealand; and Kevin Wong, from Singapore. (我々のお客さんは, 米国のジョン・ゴメズとニュージーランドのメアリー・フィリップスとシンガポールのケビン・ワンです)

❸that is, namely, i.e., e.g. などで説明する場合, これらの語句の前に書くことができます.

This dish makes good use of natural materials; that is, soybeans, burdock root(,) and *daikon* radish. (この料理は自然の素材, すなわち大豆, ゴボウ, 大根をうまく使っている)

⑦ " ", ' ' quotation marks (引用符, クオーテーションマーク)

" " を double quotation marks (ダブルクオーテーションマーク) といい, ' ' を single quotation marks (シングルクオーテーションマーク) といいます. ふつう " " が使われますが, 《英》の印刷物では ' ' がよく使われます.

❶直接話法で発言の部分を表します.

"How about taking a trip with me?" she said. (「いっしょに旅行をしない?」と彼女は言った)
He asked me, "Are you free tomorrow?" (「あした暇?」と彼は私に聞いた)
He said, "I heard someone scream 'Help!'" (「『助けて!』っていう悲鳴が聞こえたんだ」と彼は言った)
＊" " の中にさらに引用符を用いるときは, ' ' を使います. 《英》では逆になることがあります.

❷引用・作品名などを表します.

She describes the movie as "the most exciting movie that I have ever seen." (彼女はその映画を「私がこれまで見た映画の中で最もエキサイティングな映画」と評している)
I watched "Tokyo Story" on video. (僕はビデオで『東京物語』を見た)

＊作品名はしばしばイタリック体でも表します．例：*Gone with the Wind*（『風と共に去りぬ』）
My nickname is "Min."（「ミン」が私の愛称です）

❸強調したり，ふつうとは違うニュアンスで用いていることを表します．

He cooked for me "spaghetti bolognese."（彼は私に「ボローニャ風スパゲッティ」を作ってくれた）
＊語り手がそうした料理を知らないことを表します．

That was their "democratic" style.（それが彼らの「民主的な」やり方だった）
＊語り手が民主的だとは思っていないことを表します．

To walk "pigeon-toed" means to walk with your toes pointed in.（「内また」で歩くというのは，つま先を内側に向けて歩くということです）

★ 引用符とほかの句読点との関係

(1)ピリオド，コンマは，《米》では引用符の中に書きます．《英》では直接話法の場合を除き，引用符の外に書きます．

She read the article "This Week in Travel."（彼女は「今週の旅行」という記事を読んだ）
"I'm busy," he said.（「忙しい」と彼は言った）

(2)疑問符，感嘆符は，引用箇所に関係する場合は，引用符の中に書き，文全体に関係する場合は，引用符の外に書きます．

He said, "Who am I?"（彼は「私はだれ」と言った）
Did you see the words "I love Japan"?（「私は日本が好きです」という言葉を見ましたか）
Did you say, "How stupid you are!"?（「おまえはなんてばかなんだ！」と言ったのか？）

⑧ ' apostrophe （アポストロフィ）

❶短縮形を表します．

I'm (＝I am) busy.（私は忙しい）
She won't (＝will not) object to this plan.（彼女はこの計画に反対しないだろう）
How's (＝How is) it going?（調子はどう）
rock 'n' roll (＝rock-and-roll)（ロックンロール）

❷名詞に 's を付けて所有格を作ります．

Tomoko's bicycle （知子の自転車）　　　　a month's vacation （1か月の休み）
Satomi and Junji's house （里美と純二の家）　　Chris's bicycle （クリスの自転車）

★ s で終わる名詞の複数形では，ふつう 's とせずアポストロフィだけを付けます．

a boys' school （男子校）

❸アルファベット・数字の複数形を作ります.

two s's（sが2つ）　three 7's（7が3つ）　in the 1980's（1980年代に）
＊アラビア数字の場合は省略されることがよくあります.（in the 1980s）

[9] — dash（ダッシュ）

❶語・句・文を挿入したり，付け加えたりするときに用います.

All my family—including our dog Tetsu—got into the car.
（家族全員—愛犬テツも含めて—車に乗り込んだ）
There is a handbag on the table—is it yours?（テーブルの上にバッグがあるけど，君の？）

❷発言が途中でさえぎられたことを表すために用います.

“I don't know exactly,” she began tentatively. “But maybe—” “Maybe what?” he interrupted.（「正確には知りませんが」と彼女がためらいがちに話し始めた.「でもたぶん…」「たぶんどうしたって？」彼が話をさえぎった）

❸以下のようにいくつかの要素を代名詞で受ける場合に用います.

Hitoshi, Shunji, Sunao, Tatsuo, Tomikazu, Yuko—all met Mr. Yamamoto at the class reunion for the first time in 20 years.（均，俊二，淳，達夫，富和，ゆう子，全員が同窓会で20年ぶりに山本先生に再会した）

＊ダッシュには2種類あり，上記❶～❸で用いられているダッシュを「emダッシュ」，それよりも短いダッシュを「enダッシュ」と呼びます.「enダッシュ」は，2000–2005（2000年～2005年），pp. 302–305（302～305ページ）のように数の範囲を表すために使います. 英語では～は使いません. また，タイプライターや電子メールなどでは，emダッシュやenダッシュを使えない場合があります. 特に電子メールの場合，日本語フォントのダッシュを使うと，日本語に対応していないコンピュータでは文字化けを起こします. そのため，emダッシュを2つのハイフン(--)で，enダッシュを1つのハイフン(-)で書きます.

[10] - hyphen（ハイフン）

❶複数の単語をつなげて複合語を作るときに用います.

a self-service gas station（セルフサービスのガソリンスタンド）
She's left-handed.（彼女は左利きだ）

❷数字を書くときに用います.

a hundred and thirty-five (135)

❸接頭辞の後に書きます.

I happened to meet my ex-boyfriend.（私は偶然，以前のボーイフレンドに会った）

❹1つの単語が2行にわたるとき，最初の部分の終わりに付けて1語であることを示します．原則として音節の区切りに付けます．

I think bonsai dupli-
cates nature.（盆栽は自然を写し出していると思う）

11 ( ) parentheses, round brackets（丸かっこ）

❶数字などを加えるときに用います．

Mt. Fuji (3,776 m) is the highest mountain in Japan.
（富士山（3776メートル）は日本でいちばん高い山です）

❷分類するときにアルファベットや数字といっしょに用います．

You can quit this application by (a) clicking the "close" icon, (b) selecting "quit" on the menu bar, or (c) pushing the control key and the "z" key at the same time.（(a)「close」アイコンをクリックする，(b)メニューバーの「quit」を選択する，(c)コントロールキーと「z」キーを同時に押す，これらのいずれかの方法でこのアプリケーションを終了させることができます）

❸補足的な説明を加えるときに用います．

You can use a frying pan (sometimes called a "skillet") in this case.
（この場合，フライパン（「スキレット」とも呼ばれる）を用いることができます）

I already explained about this (see p. 50).
（この点についてはすでに説明しました（50ページ参照））

12 [ ] (square) brackets（角かっこ）

引用文中に引用者のコメントや情報を加えるときに用います．

The picture-book writer added, "I love my hometown [Utrecht]."
（「私は故郷［ユトレヒト］を愛しています」とその絵本作家は言い添えた）

13 ... ellipsis dots（省略記号）

引用文などが省略されていることを表すときに用います．

付録

"Fair is foul, and foul is fair...," as Shakespeare wrote in *Macbeth*.
（シェークスピアが『マクベス』で書いたように，「正しいは正しくない，正しくないは正しい…」）

14 / slash（スラッシュ）

❶or の意味で用います．

If a student works part-time, he/she (=he or she) has to report it to the school.
(学生がアルバイトをする場合は，学校に届け出なければならない)

❷ perの意味で用います．

The price of this cheese is ¥200/100 g (=200 yen per 100 grams).
(このチーズの価格は100グラム200円です)

❸ 日付を表すときに用いることができます．

4/15/2000, 4/15/00 (=15 April, 2000) (2000年4月15日)
＊英国用法では 15/4/2000, 15/4/00 と書きます．

❹ 本来改行して書くべき詩などを追い込んだ場合，改行位置を示すために用います．

The white bird is sad./Beneath the blue of heaven,/above
the blue waves,/she floats alone, always white:/never
blue like sea and sky.
(白鳥(はくちょう)は哀(かな)しからずや空の青海のあをにも染まずただよふ)

⑮ **italics** (イタリック体)

❶ 書名・作品名などを示すためにイタリック体を用います．

He reads the column in *Weekly Student Times* every week.
(彼は『週刊スチューデントタイムズ』のそのコラムを毎週読んでいる)
I like *Early Summer* best of Ozu Yasujiro's movies.
(私は小津安二郎の映画では『麦秋』が最も好きだ)

❷ 語句を強調するために用います．

I've seen *beautiful* flowers, but I've never seen the *beauty* of flowers.
(私は美しい花を見たことはあるが，花の美しさを見たことはない)

⑯ **capital letters** (大文字)

❶ 文・引用文の最初の文字は大文字で書きます．

My mother said, "Come home before dark."
(母は「暗くならないうちに帰ってきなさい」と言った)

❷ 固有名詞・固有な事物の最初の字・一人称のIなどはふつう大文字で書きます．

Japan (日本)
the Netherlands (オランダ) ＊theはふつう大文字にしません．
Christmas (クリスマス)
May I come in? (入ってもよろしいですか)

数と数式

1 基数詞と序数詞

1	one	**first**
2	two	**second**
3	three	**third**
4	four	fourth
5	five	**fifth**
6	six	sixth
7	seven	seventh
8	eight	**eighth**
9	nine	**ninth**
10	ten	tenth
11	eleven	eleventh
12	twelve	**twelfth**
13	thirteen	thirteenth
14	fourteen	fourteenth
15	fifteen	fifteenth
16	sixteen	sixteenth
17	seventeen	seventeenth
18	eighteen	eighteenth
19	nineteen	nineteenth
20	twenty	**twentieth**
21	twenty-one	twenty-first
22	twenty-two	twenty-second
23	twenty-three	twenty-third
24	twenty-four	twenty-fourth
30	thirty	**thirtieth**
40	forty	**fortieth**
50	fifty	**fiftieth**
60	sixty	**sixtieth**
70	seventy	**seventieth**
80	eighty	**eightieth**
90	ninety	**ninetieth**
100	a [one] hundred	(one) hundredth
101	a [one] hundred (and) one	(one) hundred (and) first
102	a [one] hundred (and) two	(one) hundred (and) second
200	two hundred	two hundredth
1000	a [one] thousand	(one) thousandth
1100	a [one] thousand (and) one hundred / eleven hundred	(one) thousand (and) one hundredth / eleven hundredth
1101	a [one] thousand (and) one hundred (and) one / eleven hundred and one	(one) thousand (and) one hundred (and) first / eleven hundred (and) first

* 序数詞は，1，2，3を除いて，基数詞に -th を付けて作ります．ただし，つづりが少し変化する語があります．太字の語には特に注意しましょう．

② 大きな数

❶以下のような単位を表す語を用いて，大きな数を表します．

hundred（百）/ thousand（千）/ million（百万）/ billion（十億）/ trillion（兆）

❷通例 thousand から上は 3 けたずつ区切られています．そのため数字を書くときは 3 けたごとにコンマを打つ習慣があるので，それを目安に読むと読みやすくなります．

```
10,000    ten thousand（1万）
23,000    twenty-three thousand（2万3千）
100,000   a [one] hundred thousand（10万）
670,000   six hundred (and) seventy thousand（67万）
5,000,000 five million（500万）
49,000,000 forty-nine million（4,900万）
815,000,000 eight hundred (and) fifteen million（8億1,500万）
```

❸hundred, thousand, million, billion などの単位を表す語には，ふつう複数形の -s は付けません．

two hundred（200）/ three thousand（3,000）

❹不特定の数は，hundreds of ...（何百もの…），thousands of ...（何千もの…），tens of thousands of ..., many thousands of ...（何万もの…）のように複数形を用いて表します．

Tens of [Many] thousands of people accessed the web site.
（そのウェブサイトには何万もの人々がアクセスした）

③ 時刻

❶以下のように表すのが最もふつうです．

5:00（five と読む）/ 2:35（two thirty-five と読む）/ 10:40（ten forty と読む）

❷「2時」「3時」のようなきりのいい時刻を表す場合は，two o'clock, three o'clock のように o'clock を付けることがあります．「正午」は noon，「午前0時」は midnight を用いて表すこともできます．

I take the *eight o'clock* train every morning.（私は毎朝8時の電車に乗る）
The chime sounds *at noon* every day.（毎日正午にチャイムが鳴る）

❸「午前」「午後」などの表し方

午前10時 → 10:00 a.m. / ten in the morning

午後5時 → 5:00 p.m. / five in the afternoon
夕方6時 → six in the evening

❹「…時〜分過ぎ」,「…時〜分前」の表し方

3時5分過ぎ → five *past* [*after*] three
2時半 → half *past* two / two thirty
6時20分前 → twenty *to* [*before*] six
4時15分前 → a quarter *to* [*before*] four

❺「…時ごろ」の表し方

She'll be back *about* [*around*] seven thirty. (彼女は7時半ごろ戻ります)

④ 日付

❶ 書き方

4月3日 → April 3 / 10月20日 → October 20

＊ややフォーマルな書き方では the third of April, the twentieth of October のようになります．

❷ 読み方

April 3 → April (the) third / October 20 → October (the) twentieth

＊「…日」の部分は序数として読みます．

⑤ 年号

❶ 3けたまでの年号の読み方．ふつうの数の読み方と同じです．

375年 → three hundred and seventy-five
794年 → seven hundred and ninety-four
The capital moved to Nara in 710 [seven hundred and ten].
(710年に都が奈良に移された)

❷ 4けたの年号の読み方．

1900年 → nineteen hundred
1901年 → nineteen o one ＊o は [óu] と読みます．
1991年 → nineteen ninety-one
2000年 → two thousand
2002年 → two thousand two
2010年 → two thousand ten, twenty ten
The *gengo* changed from "Showa" to "Heisei" in 1989 [nineteen eighty-nine]. (1989年に元号が「昭和」から「平成」に変わった)

＊紀元前か紀元後かをはっきりさせたい場合，300 A.D.（西暦300年），400 B.C.（紀元前400年）のように表します．

❸「…年代」の表し方

1990年代 → the 1990's [1990s] (nineteen nineties) / the 90's [90s] (nineties)

6 電話番号

電話番号やパスポートの番号などを読むときは，ふつう数字を1つずつ読みます．

03-5390-7709 → zero three, five three nine zero, seven seven zero nine

＊0は[zí:rou]だけでなく[óu]とも読みます．
＊7709は double seven zero nine とも読みます．

7 小数・分数

3.54 → three point five four
12.07 → twelve point zero seven
1/3 → one third ＊分子を先に読みます．分母は序数詞になります．
2/3 → two thirds ＊分子が2以上のときは分母が複数形になります．
1/2 → a half / one half
1/4 → a quarter / one fourth
3/4 → three quarters / three fourths
2 3/5 → two and three fifths

★分数を形容詞的に使う場合は分母を単数形にします．

2 3/5リットル → two and three fifth liters

8 数式

❶足し算・引き算

5+4=9 → Five plus four is [equals] nine. / Five and four are nine.
9-6=3 → Nine minus six is [equals] three.
2-2.6=-0.6 → Two minus two point six is [equals] minus [negative] zero point six.

❷掛け算・割り算

8×7=56 → Eight times seven is [equals] fifty-six.
30÷5=6 → Thirty divided by five is [equals] six.
20÷6=3…2 → Twenty divided by six is [equals] three with a remainder of two.

❸その他

$y = x^2$ → *y* equals *x* squared.
$y = 2x^3 + 1$ → *y* equals two *x* cubed plus one.
$y = 5^4$ → *y* equals five to the fourth power.
$y = x^{-1}$ → *y* equals *x* to the minus first power.
$y = 2\sqrt{5}$ → *y* equals two times the square root of five.
$y = f(x)$ → *y* is a function of *x* . / *y* equals *f* of *x* .

[9] 金額

300円 → three hundred yen ＊yenは単複同形なので，-sは付けません.
1,980円 → a thousand nine hundred eighty yen / nineteen hundred (and) eighty yen

1ドル → a dollar / one dollar ($1)
7ドル → seven dollars ($7)
10セント → ten cents (10¢)
5ドル50セント → five dollars and fifty cents / five fifty ($5.50)

12ポンド → twelve pounds (£12)
1ペニー → a penny / one penny (1p)
6ペンス → six pence (6p) ＊penceはpennyの複数形です.
15ポンド40ペンス → fifteen (pounds) forty (pence) (£15.40)

★米国の硬貨には以下のような固有の呼び名があります.

1セント硬貨　a penny / 5セント硬貨　a nickel / 10セント硬貨　a dime / 25セント硬貨　a quarter / 50セント硬貨　a half dollar

[10] 温度

摂氏18度　eighteen degrees Celsius [centigrade] (18℃)
華氏68度　sixty-eight degrees Fahrenheit (68°F)
零下摂氏2度　two degrees below zero Celsius [centigrade] (−2℃)

＊英米では華氏を用いるのがふつうです. ➔「度量衡換算表」p.1801

付録

度量衡換算表

● 長さ
- センチメートル (centimeter; cm)　　1 cm = 0.01 m = 0.3937 in.
- メートル (meter; m)　　1 m = 39.3701 in.
- キロメートル (kilometer; km)　　1 km = 1000 m = 0.6214 mi.
- インチ (inch; in.)　　1 in. = 2.54 cm
- フィート (foot; ft.)　　1 ft. = 12 in. = 30.48 cm
- ヤード (yard; yd.)　　1 yd. = 3 ft. = 91.44 cm
- マイル (mile; mi., m.)　　1 mi. = 1760 yd. = 1.6093 km

● 面積
- 平方センチメートル (square centimeter; cm²)　　1 cm² = 0.1550 sq. in.
- 平方メートル (square meter; m²)　　1 m² = 10.7639 sq. ft.
- アール (are; a)　　1 are = 100 m² = 119.6 sq. yd.
- ヘクタール (hectare; ha)　　1 ha = 100 ares = 2.471 acres
- 平方キロメートル (square kilometer; km²)　　1 km² = 100 ha = 247.1 acres
- 平方インチ (square inch; sq. in.)　　1 sq. in. = 6.4516 cm²
- 平方フィート (square foot; sq. ft.)　　1 sq. ft. = 144 sq. in. = 0.0929 m²
- 平方ヤード (square yard; sq. yd.)　　1 sq. yd. = 9 sq. ft. = 0.8361 m²
- エーカー (acre; a.)　　1 acre = 4840 sq. yd. = 40.47 ares
- 平方マイル (square mile; sq. mi.)　　1 sq. mi. = 640 acres = 2.590 km²

● 重さ
- グラム (gram; g)　　1 g = 0.035274 oz.
- キログラム (kilogram; kg)　　1 kg = 1000 g = 2.2046 lb.
- トン (メートルトン) (ton, tonne, metric ton; t., m.t.)　　1 m.t. = 1000 kg = 《米》1.1023 t. = 《英》0.9842 t.
- オンス (ounce; oz.)　　1 oz. = 28.3495 g
- ポンド (pound; lb.)　　1 lb. = 16 oz. = 453.5924 g
- 米トン (ショートトン) (ton, short ton; t., s.t.)　　1 s.t. = 2000 lb. = 907.18 kg
- 英トン (ロングトン) (ton, long ton; t., l.t.)　　1 l.t. = 2240 lb. = 1016.05 kg

● 体積
- 立方センチメートル (cubic centimeter; cm³)　　1 cm³ = 0.0610 cu. ft.
- 立方メートル (cubic meter; m³)　　1 m³ = 1.308 cu. yd.
- 立方インチ (cubic inch; cu. in.)　　1 cu. in. = 16.387 cm³
- 立方フィート (cubic foot; cu. ft.)　　1 cu. ft. = 0.0283 m³
- 立方ヤード (cubic yard; cu. yd.)　　1 cu. yd. = 0.7646 m³

● 容積
- リットル (liter; l, lit.)　　1 l = 《米》0.2641 gal. = 《英》0.2200 gal.
- パイント (pint; pt.)　　1 pt. = 《米》0.4732 l = 《英》0.5683 l
- クオート (quart; qt.)　　1 qt. = 2 pt. = 《米》0.9464 l = 《英》1.137 l
- ガロン (gallon; gal.)　　1 gal. = 8 pt. = 《米》3.785 l = 《英》4.546 l

● 温度
- 摂氏 (Celsius, centigrade; C)　　0℃ = 32°F ／ 20℃ = 68°F ／ 100℃ = 212°F
- 華氏 (Fahrenheit; F)　　0°F = 約−17.8℃ ／ 100°F = 約37.8℃
- ☆華氏 = 摂氏 × 9/5 + 32°　　☆摂氏 = (華氏 − 32°) × 5/9

＊黒字はメートル法，赤字はヤードポンド法の単位

通貨一覧

国名・地域名	通貨単位	略語	参考
アイルランド	アイリッシュ・ポンド* (pound)	£Ir	=100 pence
アメリカ合衆国(米国)	米ドル (dollar)	US$	=100 cents
イギリス (英国)	英ポンド (pound sterling)	£	=100 pence
イタリア	リラ* (lira)	Lit	=100 centesimi
イラク	イラク・ディナール (dinar)	ID	=1,000 fils
イラン	リアル (rial)	Rls	=100 dinars
インド	ルピー (rupee)	Rs	=100 paise
インドネシア	ルピア (rupiah)	Rp	=100 sen
エジプト	エジプト・ポンド (pound)	£E	=100 piastres
欧州連合 (EU)	ユーロ** (euro)	€	=100 cent
オーストラリア	オーストラリア・ドル (dollar)	$A	=100 cents
オーストリア	シリング* (schilling)	S	=100 groschen
オランダ	ギルダー* (guilder)	f.	=100 cents
カナダ	カナダ・ドル (dollar)	Can$	=100 cents
韓国	ウォン (won)	W	=100 chon
ギリシャ	ドラクマ* (drachma)	Dr	=100 lepta
クウェート	クウェート・ディナール (dinar)	KD	=1,000 fils
ケニア	ケニア・シリング (shilling)	KSh	=100 cents
サウジアラビア	サウジ・リアル (riyal)	SRls	=100 halala
シンガポール	シンガポール・ドル (dollar)	S$	=100 cents
スイス	スイス・フラン (franc)	SwF	=100 centimes
スウェーデン	スウェーデン・クローナ (krona)	SKr	=100 öre
スペイン	ペセタ* (peseta)	Pta	=100 centimos
タイ	バーツ (baht)	B	=100 satangs
台湾	新タイワン・ドル (dollar)	NT$	=100 cents
中国	元 (yuan)	Y	=10 角 (jiao), 100 分 (fen)
デンマーク	デンマーク・クローネ (krone)	DKr	=100 øre
ドイツ	ドイツ・マルク* (mark)	DM	=100 pfennigs
トルコ	トルコ・リラ (lira)	LT	=100 kurus
日本	円 (yen)	¥	=100 銭 (sen)
ニュージーランド	ニュージーランド・ドル (dollar)	$NZ	=100 cents
ノルウェー	ノルウェー・クローネ (krone)	NKr	=100 øre
パキスタン	パキスタン・ルピー (rupee)	PRs	=100 paisa
フィジー	フィジー・ドル (dollar)	F$	=100 cents
フィリピン	ペソ (peso)	P	=100 centavos
フィンランド	マルカ* (markka)	Fmk	=100 pennia
ブラジル	レアル (real)	R$	=100 centavos
フランス	フランス・フラン* (franc)	F	=100 centimes
ベトナム	ドン (dong)	D	=100 hao
ベルギー	ベルギー・フラン* (franc)	BF	=100 centimes
ポルトガル	エスクード* (escudo)	Esc	=100 centavos
香港	ホンコン・ドル (dollar)	HK$	=100 cents
マレーシア	リンギ (ringgit)	RM	=100 sen
南アフリカ	ラント (rand)	R	=100 cents
ミャンマー	チャット (kyat)	K	=100 pyas
メキシコ	ヌエボ・ペソ (peso)	Mex$	=100 centavos
ラオス	キープ (kip)	KN	=100 ats
ロシア	ルーブル (ruble)	Rub	=100 kopecks

＊欧州連合の通貨統合により，2002年2月末までに流通が停止．
＊＊2002年1月1日に流通開始．

主な不規則動詞変化表

原　形	過去形	過去分詞
abide （我慢する，とどまる）	abided, abode	abided, abode
alight （止まる）	alighted, alit	alighted, alit
arise （起こる）	arose	arisen
awake （目ざめる）	awoke, awaked	awoken, awaked, awoke
baby-sit （子守をする）	baby-sat	baby-sat
backslide （逆戻りする）	backslid	backslid, backslidden
be [am, is, are] （…である）	was, were	been
bear （運ぶ，実を結ぶ）	bore	borne, born
beat （打つ）	beat	beaten, beat
become （…になる）	became	become
befall （降りかかる）	befell	befallen
beget （子供をもうける）	begot	begotten, begot
begin （始まる）	began	begun
behold （見る）	beheld	beheld
bend （曲げる，体を曲げる）	bent	bent
beseech （嘆願する）	besought, beseeched	besought, beseeched
beset （包囲する）	beset	beset
bespeak （示す）	bespoke	bespoken
bestride （またがる）	bestrode	bestridden
bet （賭ける）	bet, betted	bet, betted
betake （行く）	betook	betaken
bid （値をつける）	bid	bid
（命じる）	bid, bade	bid, bidden
bide （待つ）	bided, bode	bided
bind （縛る）	bound	bound
bite （かむ）	bit	bitten
bleed （出血する）	bled	bled
bless （祝福する）	blessed, blest	blessed, blest
blow （吹く）	blew	blown
break （こわす）	broke	broken
breed （育てる，子を産む）	bred	bred
bring （持ってくる）	brought	brought
broadcast （放送する）	broadcast, broadcasted	broadcast, broadcasted
browbeat （威圧する）	browbeat	browbeaten
build （建てる）	built	built
burn （燃える，燃やす）	burned, burnt	burned, burnt
burst （破裂する）	burst	burst
buy （買う）	bought	bought
cast （投げる）	cast	cast
catch （つかまえる，引っかかる）	caught	caught
chide （しかる）	chided, chid	chided, chid, chidden
choose （選ぶ）	chose	chosen
cleave （裂く）	cleaved, cleft, clove	cleaved, cleft, cloven
（付着する）	cleaved, 《古語》clave	cleaved
cling （くっつく）	clung	clung
come （来る）	came	come
cost （費用がかかる，見積もる）	cost, costed	cost, costed
creep （はう）	crept	crept
cut （切る）	cut	cut
deal （分配する，カードを配る）	dealt	dealt
dig （掘る）	dug	dug

原　形	過去形	過去分詞
dive（飛び込む）	dived,《米》dove	dived
do [does]（する）	did	done
draw（描く，引く）	drew	drawn
dream（夢を見る）	dreamed, dreamt	dreamed, dreamt
drink（飲む）	drank	drunk
drive（運転する，かりたてる）	drove	driven
dwell（住む）	dwelt, dwelled	dwelt, dwelled
eat（食べる）	ate	eaten
fall（落ちる）	fell	fallen
feed（食べ物を与える）	fed	fed
feel（さわる，感じる）	felt	felt
fight（戦う）	fought	fought
find（見つける）	found	found
fit（ぴったり合う）	fitted,《米》fit	fitted,《米》fit
flee（逃げる）	fled	fled
fling（投げつける）	flung	flung
fly（飛ぶ，フライを打つ）	flew, flied	flown, flied
forbear（差し控える）	forbore	forborne
forbid（禁ずる）	forbade, forbad	forbidden
forecast（予報する）	forecast, forecasted	forecast, forecasted
foresee（予知する）	foresaw	foreseen
foretell（予告する）	foretold	foretold
forget（忘れる）	forgot	forgotten, forgot
forgive（許す）	forgave	forgiven
forgo（控える）	forwent	forgone
forsake（見捨てる）	forsook	forsaken
forswear（…をやめると誓う）	forswore	forsworn
freeze（凍る，凍らせる）	froze	frozen
gainsay（否定する）	gainsaid	gainsaid
get（得る）	got	got,《米》gotten
gird（締める）	girded, girt	girded, girt
give（与える）	gave	given
go（行く）	went	gone
grind（穀物などをひく）	ground	ground
grow（成長する）	grew	grown
hang（掛ける，絞首刑にする）	hung, hanged	hung, hanged
have [has]（持っている）	had	had
hear（聞こえる）	heard	heard
heave（船が動く）	hove	hove
hew（おの・剣などで切る）	hewed	hewed, hewn
hide（隠す）	hid	hid, hidden
hit（打つ）	hit	hit
hold（持つ，続く）	held	held
hurt（けがをさせる）	hurt	hurt
inset（挿入する）	insetted, inset	insetted, inset
interbreed（交配させる）	interbred	interbred
keep（保つ，…の状態にある）	kept	kept
kneel（ひざまずく）	knelt, kneeled	knelt, kneeled
knit（編む，編み物をする）	knit, knitted	knit, knitted
know（知っている）	knew	known
lay（横たえる，卵を産む）	laid	laid
lead（導く，案内する）	led	led
lean（傾く，立てかける）	leaned,《主に英》leant	leaned,《主に英》leant

原形	過去形	過去分詞
leap（跳ぶ）	leaped,《主に英》leapt	leaped,《主に英》leapt
learn（学ぶ）	learned,《主に英》learnt	learned,《主に英》learnt
leave（去る）	left	left
lend（貸す, 金を貸す）	lent	lent
let（…させる）	let	let
lie（横たわる）	lay	lain
light（火をつける, 点火する）	lighted, lit	lighted, lit
lose（失う, 負ける）	lost	lost
make（作る）	made	made
mean（意味する）	meant	meant
meet（会う）	met	met
miscast（不適当な役につける）	miscast	miscast
mislay（置き忘れる）	mislaid	mislaid
mislead（誤解を与える）	misled	misled
misread（判断を誤る）	misread	misread
misspell（つづりを間違える）	misspelled, misspelt	misspelled, misspelt
misspend（浪費する）	misspent	misspent
mistake（間違える）	mistook	mistaken
misunderstand（誤解する）	misunderstood	misunderstood
mow（刈る）	mowed	mowed, mown
offset（相殺する）	offset	offset
outbid（…より高い値をつける）	outbid	outbid, outbidden
outdo（勝る）	outdid	outdone
outgrow（…より大きくなる）	outgrew	outgrown
outride（…より速く乗る）	outrode	outridden
outrun（…より速く走る）	outran	outrun
outsell（…より多く売る）	outsold	outsold
outshine（…より明るく輝く）	outshone	outshone
overbid（高すぎる値をつける）	overbid	overbid
overcome（打ち勝つ）	overcame	overcome
overdo（やりすぎる）	overdid	overdone
overeat（食べすぎる）	overate	overeaten
overhang（上に張り出す）	overhung	overhung
overhear（偶然耳にする）	overheard	overheard
overlay（薄く覆う）	overlaid	overlaid
overpay（高すぎる賃金を払う）	overpaid	overpaid
override（無視する）	overrode	overridden
overrun（はびこる）	overran	overrun
oversee（監督する）	oversaw	overseen
overshoot（行き過ぎる）	overshot	overshot
oversleep（寝過ごす）	overslept	overslept
overtake（追いつく）	overtook	overtaken
overthrow（打倒する）	overthrew	overthrown
partake（食べる）	partook	partaken
pay（払う, 支払う）	paid	paid
plead（嘆願する, 弁護する）	pleaded, pled	pleaded, pled
proofread（校正する）	proofread	proofread
prove（証明する, …と分かる）	proved	proved,《米》proven
put（置く）	put	put
quit（やめる）	quit,《主に英》quitted	quit,《主に英》quitted
read（読む）	read	read
rebuild（再建する）	rebuilt	rebuilt
redo（やり直す）	redid	redone

原　形	過去形	過去分詞
relay (敷き直す)	relaid	relaid
remake (作り直す)	remade	remade
rend (引き裂く)	rent	rent
repay (返す)	repaid	repaid
rerun (再放送する)	reran	rerun
reset (合わせ直す)	reset	reset
retake (取り戻す)	retook	retaken
retell (再び語る)	retold	retold
rethink (再考する)	rethought	rethought
rewrite (書き直す)	rewrote	rewritten
rid (取り除く)	rid, ridded	rid, ridded
ride (乗る)	rode	ridden
ring (鳴る, 鳴らす)	rang	rung
rise (上がる)	rose	risen
run (走る)	ran	run
saw (のこぎりで切る)	sawed	sawed, 《英》sawn
say (言う)	said	said
see (見える)	saw	seen
seek (捜す)	sought	sought
sell (売る)	sold	sold
send (送る)	sent	sent
set (置く, 太陽などが沈む)	set	set
sew (縫う)	sewed	sewn, sewed
shake (振る, 揺れる)	shook	shaken
shave (ひげをそる, そる)	shaved	shaved, shaven
shear (毛を刈る)	sheared	sheared, shorn
shed (落とす)	shed	shed
shine (輝く, 磨く)	shone, shined	shone, shined
shoe (靴を履かせる)	shod, shoed	shod, shoed
shoot (撃つ)	shot	shot
show (見せる, 見える)	showed	shown, showed
shrink (縮む, 縮ませる)	shrank, 《米》shrunk	shrunk, 《米》shrunken
shut (閉める, 閉まる)	shut	shut
sing (歌う)	sang	sung
sink (沈む, 沈める)	sank, sunk	sunk, 《まれ》sunken
sit (座る, 座らせる)	sat	sat
slay (殺害する)	slew	slain
sleep (眠る)	slept	slept
slide (なめらかに滑る, 滑らせる)	slid	slid
sling (ゆったりと掛ける)	slung	slung
slink (こそこそする)	slunk	slunk
slit (切れ目を入れる)	slit	slit
smell (におう, においをかぐ)	smelled, 《主に英》smelt	smelled, 《主に英》smelt
smite (強打する)	smote	smitten
sow (種をまく)	sowed	sown, sowed
speak (話す)	spoke	spoken
speed (速く行く, 急がせる)	sped, speeded	sped, speeded
spell (つづる, 文字をつづる)	spelled, 《主に英》spelt	spelled, 《主に英》spelt
spend (金を使う)	spent	spent
spill (こぼす, こぼれる)	spilled, 《主に英》spilt	spilled, 《主に英》spilt
spin (回す, 回る)	spun	spun
spit (つばを吐く)	spat, spit	spat, spit
split (割る, 裂ける)	split	split

原　形	過去形	過去分詞
spoil（台なしにする［なる］）	spoiled, spoilt	spoiled, spoilt
spread（広げる，広がっている）	spread	spread
spring（跳びはねる）	sprang	sprung
stand（立つ［っている］，立てる）	stood	stood
stave（めり込ませる，めり込む）	staved, stove	staved, stove
steal（盗む）	stole	stolen
stick（突き刺す，突き刺さる）	stuck	stuck
sting（刺す）	stung	stung
stink（悪臭を放つ）	stank, stunk	stunk
strew（まき散らす）	strewed	strewed, strewn
stride（大またで歩く）	strode	stridden
strike（打つ，ストライキをする）	struck	struck,《古語》stricken
string（ひもを通す）	strung	strung
strive（懸命に努力する）	strove	striven
sublet（また貸しする）	sublet	sublet
swear（ののしる，宣誓する）	swore	sworn
sweat（汗を流す）	sweated, sweat	sweated, sweat
sweep（掃(は)く）	swept	swept
swell（ふくれる，ふくらませる）	swelled	swollen, swelled
swim（泳ぐ）	swam	swum
swing（揺れる，揺らす）	swung	swung
take（持っていく）	took	taken
teach（教える）	taught	taught
tear（裂く，裂ける）	tore	torn
tell（話す）	told	told
think（考える，思う）	thought	thought
thrive（栄える）	thrived, throve	thrived, thriven
throw（投げる）	threw	thrown
thrust（強く押す）	thrust	thrust
tread（踏む）	trod	trodden, trod
undercut（値段を安くする）	undercut	undercut
undergo（経験する）	underwent	undergone
underlie（根底にある）	underlay	underlain
underpay（十分に支払わない）	underpaid	underpaid
undersell（安く売る）	undersold	undersold
understand（理解する）	understood	understood
undertake（引き受ける）	undertook	undertaken
undo（ほどく）	undid	undone
uphold（支持する）	upheld	upheld
upset（心を乱す，ひっくり返す）	upset	upset
wake（目をさます［さまさせる］）	woke, waked	woken, waked, woke
waylay（呼び止める）	waylaid	waylaid
wear（着ている，すり切れる）	wore	worn
weave（織る，縫うように進む）	wove, weaved	woven, weaved
weep（泣く）	wept	wept
wet（ぬらす，ぬれる）	wet, wetted	wet, wetted
win（勝つ）	won	won
wind（曲がる，巻きつける）	wound	wound
withdraw（引っ込める，退く）	withdrew	withdrawn
withhold（与えずにおく）	withheld	withheld
withstand（耐え抜く）	withstood	withstood
wring（しぼる）	wrung	wrung
write（書く）	wrote	written

付録

Copyright©2001 by Tokyo Shoseki Co., Ltd., Tokyo
All rights reserved.
Printed in Japan

FAVORITE
JAPANESE-ENGLISH
DICTIONARY
フェイバリット和英辞典 CD付 2色刷

2001年11月1日　初版第1刷発行
2002年2月15日　初版第2刷発行

編集委員　代表　浅野　博

発行者　河内義勝

発行所　東京書籍株式会社

〒114-8524　東京都北区堀船2-17-1

電話　販売　03(5390)7544
　　　編集　03(5390)7516

組版・印刷・製本　図書印刷株式会社

落丁本・乱丁本はお取り替えいたします。
許可なしに転載、複製することを禁じます。
ISBN4-487-39521-6 C7582

Eメール文例集

友達あて ― 頼み事のEメール

Helen,

Hi, I have a favor to ask you. I wrote an English letter to a friend of mine in New Zealand. Would you proofread the letter for me? Attached is my original draft. Please reply by e-mail.

Thank you in advance for your help.

Yours,
Keiko

P.S. I'll call you at home tonight.

ヘレンへ

こんにちは，お願いしたいことがあります．ニュージーランドの友達に英語の手紙を書きました．その手紙を校正してもらえませんか．元の原稿を添付してあります．メールで返事をください．

ご協力に感謝します．よろしく．

ではまた
啓子

追伸．今夜自宅に電話します．

多人数あて ― パーティーの招待状

Friends,

We're going to have a Japanese dinner party at Tanaka Jiro's home on Saturday, Oct. 15. We hope to see you there, and please feel free to bring your friends. R.S.V.P. by Oct. 12.

Time: 7:00 p.m., Saturday, October 15
Place: Tanaka Jiro's home, 2-17-1 Horifune, Kita-ku
Phone: 03-1234-5678
Nearest station: Oji Station, Keihin-Tohoku Line.

Thanks.

みなさん

10月15日土曜日に田中次郎君の家で日本食パーティーをします．お越しいただければと思います．自由に友達を連れてきてください．10月12日までにお返事をお願いします．

日時：10月15日，土曜日，午後7時
場所：田中次郎君の家，北区堀船2-17-1
電話：03-1234-5678
最寄り駅：京浜東北線王子駅

以上